THE INTERNATIONAL BIBLE COMMENTARY

THE INTERNATIONAL BIBLE COMMENTARY

with the
New International Version

General Editor (revised edition): F. F. BRUCE

Originally Edited by
F. F. BRUCE
H. L. ELLISON
G. C. D. HOWLEY

Marshall Pickering/Zondervan

First published 1979. Based on RSV version of the Bible.
Copyright © Pickering & Inglis Ltd. 1979.

New edition 1986. Based on the New International Version of the Bible.
Copyright © Marshall Morgan and Scott Publications Ltd. 1986
3 Beggarwood Lane, Basingstoke, Hants. RG23 7LP England
and Zondervan Publishing House, Grand Rapids, Michigan, U.S.A.

This new edition published in 1986 by
Marshall Morgan & Scott Publications Ltd.
Part of the Marshall Pickering Holdings Group
A subsidiary of the Zondervan Corporation

British Library Cataloguing in Publication Data
International Bible commentary.—N.I.V. ed.
Bible—Concordances, English—New
International—Commentaries
220.5'2 BS195.1572
ISBN 0-551-01291-9

Published in the United States by
Zondervan Publishing House
1415 Lake Drive S.E., Grand Rapids, Michigan 49506
Library of Congress Cataloging-in-Publication Data
Main entry under title: The International Bible commentary with the
New International Version.
Rev. ed. of: A Bible commentary for today / general editor G. C. D. Howley,
consulting editors F. F. Bruce, H. L. Ellison. 1979.
Includes bibliographies.
1. Bible—Commentaries. I. Bruce, F. F. (Frederick
Fyvie), 1910- . II. Bible. English.
New International. III. New layman's Bible commentary
in one volume.
BS491.2.I53 1986   220.7'7   86-234
ISBN 0-310-22020-3 (U.S.)

Typeset in Bembo by
Rowland Phototypesetting Ltd, Bury St Edmunds, Suffolk, England

Printed in the United States of America

88 89 90 91 92 93 94 / DH / 11 10 9 8 7 6 5 4

PREFACE TO FIRST EDITION

THIS volume is a development arising from the publication of *A New Testament Commentary* in 1969. Evangelical Christians on all sides gave a warm welcome to the former work and many requests were received for a book that would cover the whole Bible.

It became possible to enlarge our original team, and the present work is the result. We were encouraged by the response received from those who have so willingly made up the body of contributors. One special joy I have derived is that almost every member of the team of authors is linked with me by ties of personal friendship.

Since the earlier volume appeared I have been through a severe illness which has left its mark, and I could not have undertaken the General Editorship were it not for the constant help and counsel of Professor F. F. Bruce. In the New Testament volume Mr. H. L. Ellison served as Consulting Editor, and in the Old Testament section he has also given valuable help over several matters, and perhaps particularly in his editorial work on the book of Numbers, in addition to his article on the Theology of the Old Testament, and his commentary on Genesis 1–11.

Biblical studies can never remain static, for the passage of time brings fresh light to bear upon the text, whether in historical and other factual data as a result of new discoveries, or through the insights of scholars and others who apply themselves to pondering the Word of God. The present climate of theological thought is one in which widely different currents are discernible, both liberal and conservative. The purpose of this commentary is to provide a basis for the exegesis of Scriptures which endeavours to be up-to-date. The nature of the work precludes the placing of emphasis on devotional or hortatory elements; it is rather concerned with a close examination of the text as it stands. While the viewpoint is conservative, it will not (we hope) appear to be obscurantist. We desire to place in the hands of Christians of all types and denominations a volume that takes its stand upon the historical and orthodox belief in the authority of Holy Scripture.

We have tried to avoid being merely academic; our aim is to appeal to the non-expert in theology as well as those with a fuller training and insight in that field of study. While we have tried to be up-to-date throughout, it is well understood that in some matters finality may, perhaps, never be reached owing to the new factors that come to light from time to time. The articles that precede each section of the commentary cover a wide range of subjects, and we hope they will prove as valuable an addition to the work as did the original articles included in *A New Testament Commentary*.

The contributors are drawn from different elements in the Christian Church and are not limited to members of any one group or denomination. They maintain an objective and positive attitude in their work, each man being free to express his own mind on the matters he deals with, and no attempt has been made to press their contributions into a uniform mould.

The Revised Standard Version of the Bible has been used as the basic text, and we express our thanks to the National Council of the Churches of Christ in the U.S.A. for permission to use this text. As in the earlier volume, we send this work forth, seeking the blessing of God upon it and upon all who consult its pages or ponder its contents for the upbuilding and strengthening of their spiritual lives.

G. C. D. HOWLEY

PREFACE TO SECOND EDITION

THE distinguishing feature of this new edition of *Bible Commentary for Today* is the replacement of the Revised Standard Version by the New International Version as the basic text. The opportunity has been taken to introduce some minor corrections and updatings, especially in the bibliographies.

In addition to the late Mr. Andrew Gray, whose work in adapting the Commentary to the N.I.V. is acknowledged below, Dr. Robert P. Gordon and Mr. David G. Deboys have given much valued help in the preparation of this edition.

Since the first edition was published in 1979, two members of the editorial team have been taken from us by death—Mr. G. C. D. Howley and Mr. H. L. Ellison. Both men put much hard work of the highest quality into the *Commentary*, especially Mr. Howley, the editor-in-chief, to whom it stands as a worthy and enduring monument.

F.F.B.

DEDICATED TO THE LATE MR. ANDREW GRAY D.S.C., M.A.
WHO DEVOTED MANY HOURS TO THE
PREPARATION OF THIS NEW EDITION

CONTENTS

Contents

PART THREE: GENERAL ARTICLES—THE NEW TESTAMENT

PART FOUR: THE NEW TESTAMENT

MAPS

KEY

RELIEF
except on map of Ai

- Above 900 metres
- " 600 "
- " 300 "
- " Sea Level
- Below Sea Level
- " −300 metres

Additional contours

~800~

LOCATIONS

- • Town certainly or probably identified
- o Suggested
- o– – –o Alternatives — name Debir at preferred location
- + Other site
- ⌾ lo Levitical town
- ⊙ ⊙ City of refuge } Jos.
- ✳ Canaanite city

NAMES

Gedor — in text
Isdud — modern

Acknowledgement is due to Dr. G. I. Davies of Cambridge University for permission to use his unpublished dissertation on 'The Wilderness Itineraries in the OT', in preparing Map 3. The cartographer remains responsible for all identifications and comments.

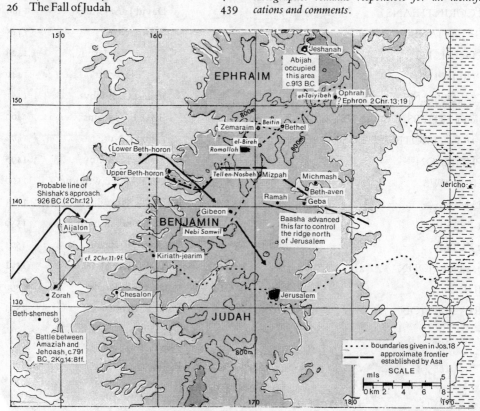

Map 1—The Israel–Judah frontier (1 Kg. 15; 2 Chr. 13–16)

x

LIST OF CONTRIBUTORS

LESLIE C. ALLEN, M.A., Ph.D., Professor of Old Testament, Fuller Theological Seminary, Pasadena, California, U.S.A. *Psalms, Romans.*

CARL EDWIN ARMERDING, B.D., Ph.D., Principal and Professor of Old Testament, Regent College, Vancouver, B.C., Canada. *Judges.*

ERNEST G. ASHBY, B.A., B.D., M.A., A.K.C., formerly Head of Religious Education, Tottenham Grammar School (then The Somerset School). *Colossians, Philemon.*

JOHN W. BAIGENT, B.D., A.R.C.O., Bible Teacher, Pastor, and Convention Speaker, formerly Senior Lecturer and Head of Religious Studies, West London Institute of Higher Education. *Psalms.*

JOHN T. BENDOR-SAMUEL, M.A., Ph.D., Executive Vice-President of Wycliffe Bible Translators and Summer Institute of Linguistics. *Esther.*

The late E. M. BLAIKLOCK, O.B.E., M.A., Litt.D., Emeritus Professor of Classics, Auckland University, New Zealand. *Nahum.*

F. F. BRUCE, M.A., D.D., F.B.A., Emeritus Professor of Biblical Criticism and Exegesis, University of Manchester. *Ezekiel, Revelation, The Old Testament and the Christian, Introduction to the Poetical/Wisdom Literature, Chronology of the Old Testament, The Fourfold Gospel, The General Letters.*

T. CARSON, M.A., Dip.Ed., Editor of *Australian Missionary Tidings. Numbers, James.*

DAVID J. CLARK, M.A., B.D., Ph.D., A.L.B.C., Translation Consultant, United Bible Societies, Port Moresby, Papua New Guinea. *Micah.*

DAVID J. A. CLINES, M.A., Professor of Biblical Studies, University of Sheffield. *Job, 2 Corinthians, Introduction to the Pentateuch, The Language of the New Testament.*

F. ROY COAD, F.C.A., Author, and formerly Editor of *The Harvester. Haggai, Galatians, The Apostolic Church.*

PETER E. COUSINS, M.A., B.D., Editorial Director, The Paternoster Press, Exeter, formerly Principal Lecturer in Religious Studies, Gipsy Hill College, Kingston-upon-Thames. *Deuteronomy, 1 and 2 Thessalonians.*

DAVID J. ELLIS, B.D., M.Th., Minister of the American Community Church, Cobham, Surrey, England, formerly Principal Lecturer and Head of Religious Studies, Trent Park College, Cockfosters. *Zechariah, The Gospel of John, The New Testament Use of the Old Testament.*

The late H. L. ELLISON, B.A., B.D., Author, formerly Missionary and Bible College Lecturer. *Genesis, The Gospel of Matthew, The Theology of the Old Testament, The Religious Background of the New Testament (Jewish).*

L. O'B. DAVID FEATHERSTONE, M.A., Head of Department of Religious Studies, Godolphin and Latymer School, London. *Introduction to the Historical Books of the Old Testament.*

DONALD C. FLEMING, L.Th., Author, Bible Teacher in Australia, Missionary to Thailand. *Ecclesiastes.*

W. WARD GASQUE, B.A., B.D., M.Th., Ph.D., Vice Principal and Professor of New Testament Studies, Regent College, Vancouver, B.C., Canada. *Obadiah, Malachi.*

ROBERT P. GORDON, M.A., Ph.D., Lecturer in Divinity, University of Cambridge. *Exodus, Leviticus, The Ancient Versions.*

MICHAEL C. GRIFFITHS, M.A., D.D., Author, Missionary to Japan, General Director of Overseas Missionary Fellowship and now Principal, London Bible College. *Jonah.*

GEORGE E. HARPUR, Bible Teacher and Convention Speaker. *Ephesians.*

GERALD F. HAWTHORNE, B.A., M.A., B.Th., Ph.D., Professor of Greek, Wheaton College, Wheaton, Illinois, U.S.A. *Canon and Apocrypha, Hebrews.*

The late H. C. HEWLETT, Bible Teacher and Convention Speaker in New Zealand. *Philippians.*

J. M. HOUSTON, M.A., B.Sc., D.Phil., formerly Chancellor of Regent College, Vancouver, B.C., Canada. *The Environmental Background to the Old Testament, An Environmental Background to the New Testament.*

J. KEIR HOWARD, M.D., B.D., M.Th., M.C.C.M.(N.Z.), M.F.O.M., D.I.H., Baptist Minister. Formerly Senior Lecturer in Occupational Medicine, University of Otago, New Zealand. Bible Teacher. *1 and 2 Chronicles, Amos.*

The late G. C. D. HOWLEY, Bible Teacher, Convention Speaker, former Editor of *The Witness. Introduction to the Prophetical Books, The Authority of the New Testament, The Letters of Paul.*

PAUL E. LEONARD, B.Sc., M.Th., Ph.D., formerly Adjunct Professor of New Testament, Trinity Evangelical Divinity School, Deerfield, Illinois, U.S.A. *Joel.*

WALTER L. LIEFELD, Th.B., M.A., Ph.D., Professor of New Testament, Trinity Evangelical Divinity School, Deerfield, Illinois, U.S.A. *The Development of Doctrine in the New Testament.*

JOHN P. U. LILLEY, M.A., F.C.A., A.T.I.I., Chartered Accountant. *Joshua.*

PAUL W. MARSH, B.D., Bible Consultant, Scripture Union, London. *1 Corinthians.*

CHARLES G. MARTIN, B.Sc., B.D., Principal, Bilborough College, Nottingham. *1 and 2 Kings, Proverbs.*

ALAN R. MILLARD, M.A., M.Phil., F.S.A., Rankin Reader in Hebrew and Ancient Semitic Languages, University of Liverpool. *Daniel, The Text of the Old Testament, Archaeological Discoveries and the New Testament.*

ALAN G. NUTE, Bible Teacher and Convention Speaker. *Habakkuk, 1 and 2 Timothy, Titus.*

R. W. ORR, Ph.C., D.B.A., Missionary and Bible Teacher. *The Song of Solomon, 1, 2 and 3 John.*

W. OSBORNE, M.A., M.Phil., Lecturer in Old Testament, The Bible College of New Zealand, Auckland. *Lamentations.*

CHARLES A. OXLEY, M.A., A.C.P., Principal of Tower College, Rainhill; Scarisbrick Hall School, Hamilton College, and Liverpool Bible College. *Ruth.*

DAVID F. PAYNE, B.A., M.A., Registrar, London Bible College. *Genesis, Isaiah, 2 Peter, Jude, The Text and Canon of the New Testament.*

G. J. POLKINGHORNE, Dip.Th., retired Civil Servant, Associate Editor of *Harvester*, and Bible Teacher. *Hosea, 1 Peter.*

The late LAURENCE E. PORTER, B.A., Schoolmaster and Bible College Lecturer. *1 and 2 Samuel, The Gospel of Luke.*

VICTOR A. S. REID, B.D., A.L.B.C., Principal, Belfast Bible College. *Zephaniah.*

HAROLD H. ROWDON, B.A., Ph.D., Senior Lecturer in Church History and Senior Resident Tutor, London Bible College. *The Interpretation of the Old Testament, The Historical and Political Background of the New Testament, The Religious Background of the New Testament (Pagan).*

STEPHEN S. SHORT, M.B., Ch.B., M.R.C.S., L.R.C.P., B.D., A.L.B.C., Bible Teacher and Convention Speaker. *Ezra, Nehemiah, The Gospel of Mark.*

The late ERNEST H. TRENCHARD, B.A., A.C.P., formerly Director of *Literatura Biblica*, Madrid, Missionary and Author. *The Acts of the Apostles.*

D. J. WISEMAN, O.B.E., M.A., D.Lit., A.K.C., F.B.A., F.K.C., F.S.A., Emeritus Professor of Assyriology in the University of London. *Jeremiah, Archaeology and the Old Testament.*

ABBREVIATIONS

OLD TESTAMENT, NEW TESTAMENT AND APOCRYPHA

OT		NT		Apoc.	
Gen.	Genesis	Mt.	Matthew	1 Esd.	1 Esdras
Exod.	Exodus	Mk	Mark	2 Esd.	2 Esdras
Lev.	Leviticus	Lk.	Luke	Tob.	Tobit
Num.	Numbers	Jn	John	Jdt.	Judith
Dt.	Deuteronomy	Ac.	Acts	Ad. Est.	Additions to
Jos.	Joshua	Rom.	Romans		Esther
Jg.	Judges	1 C.	1 Corinthians	Wis.	The Wisdom of
Ru.	Ruth	2 C.	2 Corinthians		Solomon
1 Sam.	1 Samuel	Gal.	Galatians	Sir.	Ecclesiasticus
2 Sam.	2 Samuel	Eph.	Ephesians	Bar.	Baruch
1 Kg.	1 Kings	Phil.	Philippians	S 3 Ch.	Song of the Three
2 Kg.	2 Kings	Col.	Colossians		Holy Children
1 Chr.	1 Chronicles	1 Th.	1 Thessalonians	Sus.	Susanna
2 Chr.	2 Chronicles	2 Th.	2 Thessalonians	Bel	Bel and the
Ezr.	Ezra.	1 Tim.	1 Timothy		Dragon
Neh.	Nehemiah	2 Tim.	2 Timothy	Man.	The Prayer of
Est.	Esther	Tit.	Titus		Manasseh
Job	Job	Phm.	Philemon	1 Mac.	1 Maccabees
Ps.	Psalms	Heb.	Hebrews	2 Mac.	2 Maccabees
Prov.	Proverbs	Jas	James		
Ec.	Ecclesiastes	1 Pet.	1 Peter		
Ca.	Song of Songs	2 Pet.	2 Peter		
Isa.	Isaiah	1 Jn	1 John		
Jer.	Jeremiah	2 Jn	2 John		
Lam.	Lamentations	3 Jn	3 John		
Ezek.	Ezekiel	Jude	Jude		
Dan.	Daniel	Rev.	Revelation		
Hos.	Hosea				
Jl	Joel				
Am.	Amos				
Ob.	Obadiah				
Jon.	Jonah				
Mic.	Micah				
Nah.	Nahum				
Hab.	Habakkuk				
Zeph.	Zephaniah				
Hag.	Haggai				
Zech.	Zechariah				
Mal.	Malachi				

BOOKS AND JOURNALS

ALUOS	Annual of the Leeds University Oriental Society	JPOS	Journal of the Palestine Oriental Society
ANEP	Pritchard, Ancient Near East in Pictures	JSS	Journal of Semitic Studies
ANET	Pritchard, Ancient Near Eastern Texts	JTS	Journal of Theological Studies
		JTVI	Journal of the Transactions of the Victoria Institute
Ant.	Josephus, Antiquities of the Jews	LOB	Aharoni, The Land of the Bible
AOOT	K. A. Kitchen, Ancient Orient and Old Testament, 1966	MBA	Macmillan Bible Atlas
		NBC	New Bible Commentary, 1953
BA	Biblical Archaeologist	NBC³	New Bible Commentary Revised, 1970
BASOR	Bulletin of the American Schools of Oriental Research	NBCR	New Bible Commentary Revised, 1970
BDB	Brown, Driver, Briggs, Hebrew Lexicon	NBD	New Bible Dictionary
BJRL	Bulletin of the John Rylands Library	NCB	New Clarendon Bible
BKAT	Biblischer Kommentar zum Alten Testament	NCentB	New Century Bible
		NICNT	New International Commentary on the New Testament
BZAW	Beiheft zur Zeitschrift für die alttestamentliche Wissenschaft	NICOT	New International Commentary on the Old Testament
CB	The Cambridge Bible	NLC	New London Commentary
CBC	Cambridge Bible Commentary	NTC	G. C. D. Howley (ed.), A New Testament Commentary, 1969
CBQ	Catholic Biblical Quarterly		
CBSC	Cambridge Bible for Schools and Colleges	OTL	Old Testament Library
CD	(Book of) Covenant of Damascus	PCB	Peake's Commentary on the Bible, revised edn., 1962
CHB	The Cambridge History of the Bible		
DBT	Leon-Dufour (ed.), Dictionary of Biblical Theology, 1973	PEQ	Palestine Exploration Quarterly
		RB	Revue Biblique
DOTT	D. W. Thomas (ed.), Documents from Old Testament Times	SBT	Studies in Biblical Theology
		SJT	Scottish Journal of Theology
EAEHL	Avi-Yonah (ed.), Encyclopaedia of Archaeological Excavations in the Holy Land, 1976	SVT	Supplements to Vetus Testamentum
		TB	Tyndale Bulletin
		TB	Babylonian Talmud
EB	Expositor's Bible	TC	Torch Commentary
EBT	J. B. Bauer (ed.), Encyclopaedia of Biblical Theology, 1970	TDNT	Kittel, Theological Dictionary of the New Testament
EQ	Evangelical Quarterly	TDOT	Botterweck and Ringgren, Theological Dictionary of the Old Testament
HC	Code of Hammurabi		
HDB	J. Hastings (ed.), Dictionary of the Bible	Th.Rv.	Theologische Revue
IB	The Interpreter's Bible	TOTC	Tyndale Old Testament Commentary
ICC	International Critical Commentary	Tyn.B.	Tyndale Bulletin
IDB	The Interpreter's Dictionary of the Bible	UT	Gordon, Ugaritic Textbook
		VT	Vetus Testamentum
IEJ	Israel Exploration Journal	WC	Westminster Commentaries
ISBE	The International Standard Bible Encyclopedia	WBC	Wycliffe Bible Commentary
		WTJ	Westminster Theological Journal
JBL	Journal of Biblical Literature	ZAW	Zeitschrift für die alttestamentliche Wissenschaft
JBR	Journal of Bible and Religion		
JJS	Journal of Jewish Studies	ZPEB	The Zondervan Pictorial Encyclopedia of the Bible
JNES	Journal of Near Eastern Studies		

GENERAL ABBREVIATIONS

AB	Anchor Bible	*infra*	below
ad loc.	at the place	*in loc.*	in the place cited
Aq.	Aquila's Greek translation of the Old Testament	JB	Jerusalem Bible
		Lat.	Latin
Aram.	Aramaic	lit.	literally
art.	article	*loc. cit.*	in the passage already quoted
art. cit.	in the article quoted above	LXX	Septuagint
AV	Authorized Version	mg	margin
c.	about (of time)	MS(S)	manuscript(s)
cent.	century	*MT*	Massoretic Text
cf.	compare	NEB	New English Bible
ch(s).	chapter(s)	n.	note
cn.	correction	NASB	New American Standard Bible
cntd.	continued	NAB	The New American Bible
Comm.	commentary	NIV	The New International Version
comp.	compare	*op. cit.*	in the work cited above
contra	in contrast to	p(p).	page(s)
ct.	contrast	pl.	plural
d.	died	*q.v.*	which see
ed.	editor (or edited)	RSV	Revised Standard Version
edn.	edition	RV	Revised Version
e.g.	for example	Sam.	Samaritan
Egypt.	Egyptian	*scil.*	that is to say
esp.	especially	*seq.*	what follows
E.T.	English Translation	SP	Samaritan Pentateuch
EVV	English Versions	*s.v.*	under the word
f(f).	following	Sym.	Symmachus
fn.	footnote	Syr.	Syriac
Gk.	Greek	Targ.	Targum
GNB	Good News Bible (Today's English Version)	tr.	(or trans.) translated or translation
		v(v).	verse(s)
Heb.	Hebrew	*viz.*	namely
ibid.	in the same book (or passage)	Vulg.	Vulgate

GENERAL ABBREVIATIONS

AB	Anchor Bible	
ad loc.	at the place	
Aq.	Aquila's Greek translation of the Old Testament	
Aram.	Aramaic	
art.	article	
art. cit.	in the article quoted above	
AV	Authorized Version	
c.	about (of time)	
cent.	century	
cf.	compare	
chaps.	chapter(s)	
col.	correction	
contd.	continued	
Comm.	commentary	
comp.	compare	
contr.	in contrast to	
	contrast	
	died	
ed.	editor (or edited)	
edn.	edition	
e.g.	for example	
Egypt.	Egyptian	
esp.	especially	
ET	English Translation	
EV	English Versions	
f.(f).	following	
fn.	footnote	
Gk.	Greek	
GNB	Good News Bible (Today's English Version)	
Heb.	Hebrew	
ibid.	in the same book (or passage)	
infra	below	
in loc.	in the place cited	
JB	Jerusalem Bible	
Lat.	Latin	
lit.	literally	
loc. cit.	in the passage already quoted	
LXX	Septuagint	
mg.	margin	
mss.	manuscript(s)	
MT	Massoreted text	
NEB	New English Bible	
n.	note	
NASB	New American Standard Bible	
NAB	The New American Bible	
NIV	The New International Version	
op. cit.	in the work cited above	
p.(p).	page(s)	
pl.	plural	
q.v.	which see	
RSV	Revised Standard Version	
RV	Revised Version	
Sam.	Samaritan	
scil.	that is to say	
seq.	what follows	
SP	Samaritan Pentateuch	
s.v.	under the word	
Symm.	Symmachus	
Syr.	Syriac	
Tg.	Targum	
tr.	or trans.; translated, translation	
v.(vv).	verse(s)	
viz.	namely	
Vulg.	Vulgate	

PART ONE

GENERAL ARTICLES–OLD TESTAMENT

THE OLD TESTAMENT AND THE CHRISTIAN

F. F. BRUCE

THE OT IN THE CHURCH

Quite apart from its status as sacred scripture, the OT is a most interesting and valuable body of literature in its own right, a worthy object of intensive and continued study. Placed in its historical perspective and rightly interpreted, it constitutes indispensable source material for an important phase of the history—especially the religious history—of the ancient Near East. Some of its contents have a literary distinction of the highest order, and much of it still creates a response of spiritual appreciation in the reader and provides him with a means of expressing the deepest aspirations of his own soul. All this is as valid for Christian readers as for others, but Christian readers have to reckon with its status as part of the sacred scriptures of the Christian church.

The OT bears special authority as sacred scripture for Jews and Muslims as well as for Christians. In Jewish orthodoxy the Hebrew Bible, comprising the Law, the Prophets and the Writings, is the complete Word of God. Its interpretation is regulated by tradition, and for polemic or apologetic purposes the tradition has at times been given a status equal to that of the text, but in principle, as in fact, the written text is prior and normative. In Islam the *tawrat* (the Jewish scriptures), along with the *injīl* (the Christian scriptures), records the revelation of God given through earlier prophets, to be re-affirmed finally in the revelation given through Muhammad and written down in the Qur'ān.

As for the Christian church, the OT is traditionally recognized as recording the earlier stages of that on-going process of divine revelation and human response which found its fulfilment in Christ, the NT being the record of that fulfilment. If what God spoke to our forefathers through the prophets at many times and in various ways is preserved in the OT, the NT in its turn tells what 'in these last days he has spoken to us by his Son' (Heb. 1: 1 f.). But if we put it thus, we may overlook the fact that for the first few generations of its existence the church had no Bible but the OT, and got on very well with the OT alone. When our Lord affirms of the scriptures, 'it is they that bear witness to me' (Jn 5: 39), it is the OT scriptures that are meant. When Timothy is told that 'all scripture is inspired by God', the reference is to those 'sacred writings' with which he had been acquainted from childhood —that is, the OT writings (in the LXX version, incidentally). These are the writings which, he is reminded, 'are able to instruct you for salvation through faith in Christ Jesus' and provide such all-round training 'that the man of God may be thoroughly equipped for every good work' (2 Tim. 3: 15–17). It was from the OT that the early Christian preachers, following their Master's example, drew their texts, formally and expressly when they addressed Jewish audiences, implicitly in their approach to Gentiles. As Jesus maintained that He had not come to abolish the law and the prophets but to fulfil them (Mt. 5: 17), so Paul asserts that 'the law and the prophets bear witness to' the gospel of justification through faith (Rom. 3: 21 f.).

Well into the second Christian century this solitary dignity is enjoyed by the OT writings. It has repeatedly been observed how impressive a number of educated pagans in the second century, like Justin Martyr and his pupil Tatian, were converted to Christianity, according to their own testimony, by reading the OT in Greek. By this time, of course, most of the documents which make up the NT had been in existence and circulation for decades, but they had not yet received general currency as a collection of writings standing alongside the OT as the volume of fulfilment alongside the volume of promise.

When, however, we speak of this unique status of the OT in the early church, we mean the OT as interpreted and fulfilled by Jesus. Church and synagogue shared the same sacred text (it makes little substantial difference if in some Greek-speaking areas the church's canon was slightly more comprehensive than that of the synagogue); but so diversely was that text understood by church and synagogue that they might almost have been using two different Bibles. In vain does Justin, in his *Dialogue with Trypho the Jew*, try to convince Trypho of the truth of Christianity by appealing to the scriptures which both acknowledge as divine: Justin's appeal presupposes an interpretation which Trypho cannot accept.

The interpretation may be summed up in the statement that Christ and the gospel are what the OT is all about. 'All the prophets testify about him that every one who believes in him receives forgiveness of sins through his name' (Ac. 10: 43). The prophets themselves may have 'searched intently . . . trying to find out the time and circumstances to which the Spirit of Christ in them was pointing' (1 Pet. 1: 10 f.), but those who witnessed the saving events had no need for such search or inquiry; they knew. The person was Jesus; the time was now. So completely does this understanding of the OT pervade the NT writings that it must go behind those writings to Jesus Himself, and this indeed is the testimony of all the Gospels and all the strata which may be discerned as underlying them. The bringing of good news to the poor, which according to an OT prophet characterized the proclamation of the acceptable year of the Lord (Isa. 61: 1 f.), is announced by Jesus as the essence of His own ministry: 'Today', He said, 'this scripture is fulfilled in your hearing' (Lk. 4: 18–21; cf. 7: 22). This, He made plain, is involved in the advent of that kingdom which, according to another OT writer, the God of heaven was to set up in days to come (Dan. 2: 44; 7: 14, 22, 27). He congratulated His disciples because they had lived to experience things which prophets and righteous men in earlier days desired in vain to see and hear (Mt. 13: 16 f.; Lk. 10:23 f.). And if His ministry was at last to be crowned by His death, this too—'that He must suffer much and be rejected'—was something that was 'written of the Son of man' (Mk 9: 12). Assured of this, He submitted to His captors with the words: 'but the Scriptures must be fulfilled' (Mk 14: 49).

His followers thus found the OT scriptures filled with new meaning as they unlocked their further mysteries with the key which their Master supplied. As their witness was perpetuated in written form, and the writings which perpetuated it were in due course collected and canonized in the NT, the authority of the OT was in no way diminished. When Marcion, in the first half of the second century, maintained that Jesus and the gospel were completely new, unrelated to anything that had gone before, and so denied that the OT had any right to be treated as Christian scripture, the church could find no place within its bounds for him or his views. Some of the arguments used to refute him may have been unintelligent, but it was a sound instinct that recognized that the gospel plant would not flourish more vigorously if it was severed from its OT roots.

THE WORD OF GOD IN THE OT

True, there has been a shift of perspective in the church since the early days when the OT was its only Bible, made intelligible by its fulfilment in Christ. Today the NT tends to be given priority over the OT. It will be widely agreed that a knowledge of the OT is necessary for the understanding of the NT. For one thing, it records the preparation for the gospel, the account of 'what has happened before', without which the gospel itself is not properly intelligible. Moreover, the NT is so full of OT quotations that a knowledge of the OT is as essential for its appreciation as a knowledge of the Greek and Latin classics is essential for the appreciation of (say) Milton. But for Milton the Greek and Latin classics carried no inherent authority; they provided an inexhaustible quarry of literary allusion. The OT allusions in the NT, on the other hand, are not there for literary effect; they imply the acknowledgement of the inherent authority of the OT. The NT writers regarded the substance of their message as being organically one with the message of the OT, so much so that OT and NT together may be viewed as two parts of one sentence, each part being essential to the understanding of the whole. This insight is expressed in Article VII of the Thirty-Nine Articles, which begins: 'The Old Testament is not contrary to the New; for both in the Old and New Testament everlasting life is offered to mankind by Christ, who is the only Mediator between God and Man, being both God and Man . . .'

The unity of the message of the two Testaments is not to be established by fanciful typological exercises which discover in the OT writings various NT doctrines of which neither the original writers nor their readers could have had any inkling. It can be more effectively demonstrated by the recognition of a recurring pattern of divine action and human response, such as is traced, for example, in 1 C. 10: 1–11 or Heb. 3: 7–4: 13.

Various attempts have been made to present this continuous message in such a way as to bring out its basic significance and its proper culmination in Christ. Of these attempts the most successful is probably that which presents it as the 'history of salvation' (*Heilsgeschichte*), the record of the saving acts of God which reaches its consummation in the saving work of Christ. God is repeatedly acclaimed in the OT as His people's 'salvation'. He manifests Himself in this character at successive epochs in OT history, but outstandingly so in the exodus from Egypt and the return from the Babylonian exile (cf. Exod. 15: 2; Isa. 45: 15–17). The record of the earlier of these deliverances provides a form of words in which to depict the latter, and the record of both provides in turn a form of words used in the NT to depict the saving work of Christ.

The salvation of God and the judgment of

God are in the OT two aspects of the same action: if He vindicated His name by allowing His people to go into exile when they rebelled against Him, He equally vindicated His name by bringing them back. Their salvation is His vindication (cf. Ps. 98: 1–3). In the climacteric act of the gospel the twin themes of salvation and judgment coincide: Jesus absorbs the judgment in His own person and thus accomplishes His people's salvation.

In this history of salvation divine act and prophetic word go hand in hand: neither provides a complete revelation without the other. The interrelation of the ministry of Moses with the deliverance achieved in the exodus is paralleled in the interaction of the ministry of later prophets with the acts of mercy and judgment which they proclaimed or interpreted. When we come to the NT consummation, redemptive act and prophetic ministry coincide in the same person—Jesus.

Some have found in the covenant theme a unifying principle for the OT record which leads on to the gospel fulfilment. The God of Israel is a covenant-making and covenant-keeping God: He enters into a personal relationship with men and women and undertakes to be their God on the understanding that they will be His people. In the days of Noah He makes a covenant with the whole human race (Gen. 6: 18; 9: 8–17); through Abraham He establishes His covenant with one particular family, with intimations of blessing for all other families (Gen. 15: 18–21; 17: 1 ff.; 22: 15–18); and when this family has grown into a nation He confirms His covenant with them at Mount Sinai on the morrow of their deliverance from Egypt, with a simple code of laws as the basic constitution of the covenant (Exod. 24: 3–8; 34: 10–28), and reaffirms it at Shechem on the morrow of their settlement in the promised land (Dt. 27: 1–28: 48; Jos. 8: 30–35; 24: 1–28). A later and more restricted covenant was that made with David, confirming the kingship over Israel to him and his descendants (2 Sam. 7: 8–17; Ps. 89: 19–37; 132: 11–18).

God's covenant with Noah receives little or no attention in the NT. 'The oath he swore to our father Abraham' (Lk. 1: 73) is viewed as fulfilled in the gospel of justification by faith (Rom. 4: 13 ff.; Gal. 3: 6–18); the covenant with David is seen (especially in the writings of Luke) to be fulfilled in the exaltation and sovereignty of Jesus (Lk. 1: 32 f.; Ac. 2: 25–36; 13: 22 f., 32–37; 15: 16–18). But the covenant of Moses' day is set in contrast with the eternal covenant inaugurated by Jesus and sealed by His blood; this latter covenant is identified with the 'new covenant' announced in Jer. 31: 31–34, which was effectively to displace the deficient and broken covenant made with the ancestors of Israel when God 'took them by the hand to bring them out of the land of Egypt' (cf. 2 C. 3: 4–18; Heb. 8: 6–9: 22).

Salvation history and covenant history are valuable clues to the Christian understanding of the OT and its place in the Bible as a whole, not least because they have not to be imported into the biblical record as organizing principles but are already present in that record. But they do not cover all the OT, and it is regrettable if their importance is exaggerated to a point where those parts of the OT which cannot conveniently be related to them are overlooked.

HUMAN RESPONSE IN THE OT

The 'wisdom books' of the OT cannot readily be brought under the heading of covenant or salvation history, yet they make their indispensable contribution to the message of the OT. The sage stood alongside the priest and the prophet as the communicator of divine truth to his fellows (cf. Jer. 18: 18). The wisdom literature of the Hebrew Bible has an international flavour about it, whether it deals with the observed regularities of life and nature (as in Proverbs) or with the deepest problems of human existence (as in Job). The later wisdom literature (*e.g.* Wisdom and Ecclesiasticus) is more closely tied to Israel's religious outlook and tends to identify wisdom with the law of Moses.

The OT records not only the revelation of Himself made by God in the course of His people's history, but also their response to it. Together with poetical books of the OT (preeminently the Psalter) the wisdom literature belongs largely to the area of human response to divine revelation. Men and women to whom God has made Himself known in personal experience as well as in national history tell what He has come to mean to them, and in their testimony we learn more of the ways of God with men—learn it, too, in such a way that the words of their testimony provide an acceptable vehicle for our own testimony to His dealings with us. This goes far to explain the perennial popularity of the Psalms as a vehicle for Christian praise.

OUR LORD AND THE OT

The Christian's assessment of the OT cannot be dissociated from Jesus' use of it. It is plain that He regarded it as the ultimate court of appeal. He quoted it to justify His own procedure and to expose the shortcomings of Pharisees and Sadducees alike. In it He found sustenance and refreshment for His soul; in it, too, He read the programme of His ministry and the will of God for His daily life and His crowning sacrifice. 'What was indispensable to the Redeemer', it has been well said, 'must always be indispensable to the redeemed' (G.

5

A. Smith, *Modern Criticism and the Preaching of the OT*, 1901, p. 11).

But while He drew indiscriminately upon Law, Prophets and Writings, He did not draw upon them undiscerningly. There is nothing wooden about His application of the sacred text, neither does He place it all on one dead level. The letter of the law must be subservient to the spirit of the law. The sabbath rest and the marriage relationship were instituted for the blessing of men and women, and are best observed when that purpose is promoted. Even Moses' assumption that divorce is permissible (Dt. 24: 1–4) is treated as a concession made because of men's 'hardness of heart'; He finds a more excellent way implied in the Creator's ordinance (Gen. 1: 27; 2: 24, quoted in Mk 10: 2–9). The literal observance of the sabbath law might give way to a higher necessity, as did the observance of the law relating to the bread of the Presence when David and his men were hungry (1 Sam. 21: 1–6, mentioned in Mk 2: 25–28). The law of 'eye for eye and tooth for tooth' (Exod. 21: 24) marked a substantial ethical advance at the time when it replaced the blood-feud with the principle of strictly limited requital, but to His disciples Jesus recommended the better principle of non-retaliation and, best of all, of requiting evil with good (Mt. 5: 38–48). He summed up the whole law (together with the prophets) in the twin commandments of love to God and love to one's neighbour (Dt. 6: 4 f.; Lev. 19: 18); any interpretation or application inconsistent with the law of love was accordingly ruled out (Mk 12: 28–31; cf. Lk. 10: 25–37).

He stood in the line of the great prophets of Israel, and treated their teaching in its own right, not as a series of footnotes to the law. Like them, he gave ethical (inter-personal) considerations primacy over ritual requirements (*e.g.* Mt. 5: 23 f.), in the spirit of Hos. 6: 6, 'I desire mercy, not sacrifice' (quoted in Mt. 9: 13; 12: 7).

Of all the prophets, the one who shows most affinity to Jesus is Jeremiah, the prophet of the new covenant, which insists on the inwardness of true religion. When Jeremiah looks back on the reign of King Josiah, what he finds most praiseworthy is not his cultic reformation but his righteous administration, his judging the cause of the poor and needy: it was in this that Josiah manifested his knowledge of God (Jer. 22: 15 f.). There is a striking resemblance, too, between Jeremiah's counsel of submission to the Gentile overlord of his day (Jer. 38: 17 f.) and Jesus' direction to render to Caesar what belongs to Caesar (Mk 12: 17) or His deprecation of the spirit of revolt against Rome which would one day lay Jerusalem level with the ground (Lk. 13: 1–5; 19: 41–44; 23: 28–31).

In fine, our Lord's use of the OT displays a creative and original exegetical method, which provides a standard and pattern for His followers; it 'is based on . . . a profound understanding of the essential teaching of the Hebrew Scriptures and a sure judgment of his contemporary situation' (T. W. Manson, *BJRL* 34, 1951–52, p. 332).

THE OT AS THE RULE OF FAITH

If the Bible is the Christian's rule of faith and practice, the contribution which the OT makes to his rule of faith has already been suggested.

It begins with God, presenting Him as one, as the Creator of the universe in general and of mankind in particular, as righteous and merciful in character and as desiring to see this character of His reproduced in men and women. When He is said to have created mankind in His own image this means (possibly among other things) that men are intended by Him to live in fellowship not only with one another but with Himself. They are to be responsive and responsible to Him, receiving His grace and giving Him their service, and exercising on earth the authority which He had delegated to them. When men revolt against His law they experience His judgment, but in the midst of judgment He does not forget to be merciful. Judgment, indeed, is His 'strange work' (Isa. 28: 21), alien and uncongenial to His nature, to which He girds Himself reluctantly, whereas He delights to show mercy and pardoning grace (Mic. 7: 18). All this is spelt out, not in the form of a theological system but in the historical context of His dealings with mankind, and especially with those whom He has called to be His own people.

If the OT uses anthropomorphic and anthropopathic language about God, this is more appropriate to the OT portrayal of His being and character than the use of metaphysical abstractions or of such mediaeval devices as the 'way of negation' or the 'way of eminence'. 'God is not a man' (Num. 23: 19; 1 Sam. 15: 29), for He is Creator and man is His creature, but man was made like God and is urged to be like God, so that the use of a common vocabulary for both God and man is but natural.

In some areas of the OT the relation between God and man is regulated by sacrificial and ceremonial legislation. It is noteworthy how speedily those who appreciated the redemptive efficacy of the sacrifice of Christ broke loose from this legislation. Some of them may have been antecedently disposed to view the temple ritual with reserve; but the implications of the work of Christ were decisive. What must have been for many Jewish Christians of the first generation a matter of spiritual instinct received classical demonstration in the Letter to the Hebrews, which presents a reasoned case for the abrogation of the whole system in Christ. Christians may well be thankful for the providence which led to the inclusion of this work in the NT canon: if the ceremonial law has been abolished in Christ we need not spend time in allegorizing its details so as to find in them some adumbration of His redemptive work. When the writer to the Hebrews compares the once-for-all sacrifice of Christ with the annually repeated sacrifice of the Day of Atonement, he emphasizes the contrast, not any resemblance, between the two. The NT stands in the tradition of those OT psalmists and prophets who knew how to draw near to God in heart-worship apart from priestly mediation (Ps. 73: 23–28) and recognized that He dwelt not in temples made with hands but with men and women 'of a contrite and humble spirit' (Isa. 57: 15; 66: 1 f.).

THE OT AND HUMAN CONDUCT

If the OT is used as a rule of conduct, it is easy to appreciate its fundamental insistence on justice and mercy, but it must be appreciated too that the practical application of these virtues was worked out in social contexts widely removed from our own. They had to be reapplied even in OT times when the pastoral way of life gave way to the agricultural and again when the agricultural economy was increasingly displaced by one that was urban and mercantile. This work of reapplication is still necessary in orthodox Judaism where the traditional law remains the norm for practice.

This means that the OT must be read in its historical setting if its ethical teaching is to be rightly appropriated. Jesus Himself distinguished His own interpretation of the law from what 'was said to the people long ago' (Mt. 5: 21 ff.) and rebuked those disciples who spoke of calling down fire from heaven to burn up some disagreeable people, after Elijah's example (Lk. 9: 52 ff.). It is anachronistic to judge Joshua or David by the standards of the Sermon on the Mount, or to think of Israel in the wilderness as a sort of Keswick Convention on the march. It is such anachronistic thinking that raises many of the 'moral problems' (as they are called) of the OT—problems which are readily dissolved when they are viewed in their contemporary situation, whether they be large-scale ones like the institution of the holy war and the 'ban' (ḥērem), exemplified in Jericho's devotion to total destruction, or small-scale ones like the prohibition of lending at interest to a fellow-member of the community. In the latter instance, what was a protection to the borrower at one stage of the economy becomes a hardship to him at a later stage, when he would have been only too glad to borrow at reasonable interest in order to embark on some advantageous enterprise.

In the former instance, war was regarded as an act of God of the same order as famine, plague, flood or earthquake. It took its toll, and passed on. Whereas such visitations are called 'acts of God' today in a technical and impersonal sense, they were generally recognized in OT times as forms of divine judgment (cf. 2 Sam. 24: 13; Ezek. 14: 21). In the NT, indeed, some of them are treated as adumbrations of the last judgment (cf. Lk. 17: 26–30), although the words of Jesus in Lk. 13: 1–5 serve as a warning against gratuitous conclusions about the sinfulness of the victims of such events (as indeed the book of Job does in the OT).

The history of Israel shows little enough of that calculated use of terrorism as an instrument of imperial policy which is so abundantly attested in the Assyrian annals. If some Israelite kings were tempted to use it on their own modest scale—as when David slaughtered two-thirds of the Moabite manpower (2 Sam. 8: 2) or Joab 'struck down all the men in Edom' (1 Kg. 11: 15 f.)—it was recorded without approval, if not with outright disapproval.

Within the historical narrative itself an ethical advance can be traced at times. The wiping out of Ahab's family by Jehu, encouraged by the leading prophets of the day and accomplished by treachery, becomes a century later an outrage bringing down divine vengeance in its turn on the house of Jehu (Hos. 1: 4). Elisha forbids King Jehoram to slay the Damascene prisoners-of-war, bidding him rather feed and release them (2 Kg. 6: 15–23). Amaziah is commended for not wiping out the families of the assassins of his father Joash, contenting himself with the execution of the guilty men themselves (2 Kg. 14: 5 f.).

In so far as moral judgments may be passed today on persons and actions of ancient history, they must be passed from a historical perspective. This will save us from the device (not yet wholly obsolete) of defending dubious actions of Hebrews in OT times with arguments which one would not dream of using when similar actions are performed by others, and from the equally unsatisfactory device of lending respectability to morally indefensible sentiments and deeds by allegorizing them. If the Canaanites slaughtered by Joshua or the workers of iniquity on whose heads certain psalmists call down the retribution of heaven are reinterpreted to refer to those spiritual enemies—the world, the flesh and the devil—with which the Christian must wage unceasing warfare, good and well; but it should not be supposed that this is the meaning of those OT passages. Such allegorization is no doubt necessary for devotional reasons in those Christian traditions which prescribe the regular repetition of the complete Psalter. Isaac Watts, paraphrasing Ps. 92: 11, may sing:

> *My inward foes shall all be slain*
> *Nor Satan break my peace again—*

but this is not what the psalmist meant when he said, 'My eyes have seen the defeat of my adversaries, my ears have heard the rout of my wicked foes.'

If we observe an ethical advance at certain stages of the OT narrative, or indeed an overall advance from beginning to end, it should not be supposed that one continuous line of progression can be traced from the earliest to the latest times. The patriarchal stories of Genesis reflect a level of civilized behaviour not easily matched during the settlement or under the monarchy. Even in the age of the monarchy, to be sure, the penalty imposed by King Asa on Maacah the queen-mother for her involvement in a Canaanite cult (2 Chr. 15: 16) seemed unduly lenient by the stricter standards of the annotators of the Geneva Bible (1560), who reproach him for giving way to 'foolish pity'.

Moreover, 'moral problems' of this order are not peculiar to the OT. When the actions in question are carried out for acknowledged political or military purposes they do not constitute *problems* in the ethical realm: we know too well how readily such purposes override considerations of humanity. But they do constitute moral problems when they take the form of terror in the name of God or in the interests of the 'manifest destiny' of a supposedly higher civilization, for it is there that considerations of humanity might be expected to be uppermost. True, the approaches to genocide in the history of Israel appear remarkably amateurish and ineffective when they are compared with the European extermination camps of the early 1940s or even, to look a little farther back, with the total disappearance of the Beothuks of Newfoundland or the Aborigines of Tasmania. Even so, the God revealed in the OT is just and merciful; His justice and mercy are the standards of His people's justice and mercy, and unjust or unmerciful conduct is inconsistent with His character. There are few finer expressions of this aspect of His character in the OT than the question with which He silenced Jonah's patriotic complaint: 'should I not be concerned about that great city?' (Jon. 4: 11).

This last reference reminds us that the God of Israel is 'the Judge of all the earth' (Gen. 18: 25); the OT depicts on a wide canvas His dealings with the nations at large over the centuries, 'ruling the kingdom of men and giving it to whom he will' (Dan. 4: 17, 25, 32). It anticipates Schiller's insight that 'the history of the world is the judgment of the world', but insists that this judgment is personally administered.

THE OT AND THE SOCIAL ORDER

It is emphasized at the outset of the OT that man is a social being. This is summed up in the Creator's statement in Gen. 2: 18, 'It is not good for the man to be alone'; it is also emphasized in the creation narrative of Gen. 1: 27, where 'man' whom God created is mankind, man in society: 'in the image of God he created him; male and female he created them'. The simplest social unit, the family, is quickly instituted: father, mother and children. Even Cain, driven from settled community life to pursue a nomadic existence, has not to endure his exile alone: not only does he marry and raise a family but he goes on to build a 'city' —a modest tent encampment, perhaps, but even so a setting where men, women and children could live in society (Gen. 4: 17).

Attempts to establish communities in independence of God are doomed to frustration because they lack cohesion, as was shown at Babel and later (Gen. 11: 1–9; Isa. 8: 9 f.); but His grace brings people together in families, tribes and wider groupings (Ps. 68: 6). The many genealogies in the OT books reflect this emphasis on family and tribal solidarity, in addition to serving as a skeleton to be clothed with living narrative. Appreciation of this is shown in the two NT genealogies of our Lord (Mt. 1: 2–17; Lk. 3: 23–38), which draw so largely on OT data. Indeed, family, tribal and national solidarity is stressed at times in the OT to a point which has been expressed in the phrase 'corporate personality'; this may prepare us for Paul's distinction of the two great human solidarities or corporate personalities 'in Adam' and 'in Christ' (Rom. 5: 12–19; 1 C. 15: 21 f.).

Moreover, man's responsibility not only to his fellows but to his environment is emphasized. There is a bond between people and land in the OT which the modern western reader finds it hard to appreciate; it is a bond, moreover, which is created and maintained by God. In Isa. 62: 4 f. it is depicted as a marriage bond. This bond applies intensively to one country the general creation ordinance of Gen. 1: 26–30, where man is granted over the earth and the creatures inhabiting it a dominion which is to be exercised in responsible trusteeship, not in selfish exploitation. Paul, in Rom. 8: 19–23, looks forward to the universal realization of this creation ordinance at 'the revealing of the sons of God'.

The social requirements of the law of God are emphasized in special detail for the life of His people Israel. The surrounding nations are expected to observe the basic decencies of good faith, consideration for the weak and respect for human dignity, and are reprobated when they violate them (Am. 1: 3–2: 3), but Israel's knowledge of Him and of His will is far greater than theirs and Israel's responsibility is correspondingly greater (Am. 3: 2). The reputation of Israel's God in the eyes of the other nations depends very largely on the behaviour of His people.

God's requirement of His people is summed up variously in the OT. We may think of the refrain of the 'holiness code' in the Pentateuch: 'I am the LORD . . . your God; you shall therefore be holy, for I am holy' (Lev. 11: 45). This holiness is a positive and all-embracing quality; its negative implications are corollaries of its positive essence. That positive essence is unpacked in such a declaration as that of Mic. 6: 8, 'He has showed you, O man, what is good; and what does the LORD require of you but to do justice, and to love kindness, and to walk humbly with your God?' The justice and kindness which the people of God are to show to one another is the reflection of the justice and kindness with which He has treated them. These qualities are applied not only on the main road of social ethics but in such out-of-the-way rules as the one forbidding a lender to retain overnight the outer garment which a borrower has left with him as a pledge, 'because his cloak is the only covering he has for his body. What else will he sleep in?' (Exod. 22: 27 f.).

The OT law of retaliation—'eye for eye and tooth for tooth' (Exod. 21: 24)—to which reference has already been made is more closely related to the golden rule than is often realized: 'Be done by as you did' is readily viewed as a corollary to 'Do as you would be done by'.

Even when the monarchy was instituted in Israel, the king was not above the law which regulated his subjects' lives. When Naboth refuses to sell his vineyard to Ahab, Ahab is annoyed, but does not think of violating Naboth's rights until Jezebel, who was brought up to a different idea of kingship, takes steps to secure the vineyard for her husband by a course of ruthlessness and perjury which called down the prophetic denunciation on the whole dynasty of Ahab (1 Kg. 21: 1–24). And when, in the next generation, increasing mercantile prosperity led to the emergence in Israel of a new moneyed class which could buy out the free smallholders and reduce them to the status of serfs, it was the prophets who condemned the breach of covenant involved in thus 'adding field to field' and 'grinding the face of the poor' (Isa. 5: 8; 3: 15; cf. Am. 4: 1; Mic. 3: 1–3). Such treatment of their neighbours was a sin against God.

In the relation of the people of God to the surrounding nations there is an unresolved tension in the OT. On the one hand, there are stern warnings against intermarriage and assimilation: Israel had been entrusted with a treasure—the knowledge of God—which could easily be dissipated or lost if she did not preserve her national and religious identity. Hence the call to Israel to remain separate from the other nations. At the same time, the treasure deposited with Israel was to be shared with others, that they too might come to know the living God. In the very early days of Israel's nationhood non-Israelite groups did join forces with her and enter into the covenant of Yahweh. But when Israel moved from the wilderness into Canaan, the attraction of the fertility cults practised in the settled land was so dangerous that a severe ban was imposed on making common cause with the Canaanites. Even so, some individuals, like Rahab and Ruth, not to mention the Gibeonites (Jos. 9: 3–27), acknowledged the greatness of the God of Israel and were admitted to the covenant community. But it was in the context of the Babylonian exile and return that Israel's mission in the world was more clearly expressed. When a substantial body of Israelites found themselves living as exiles in a non-Israelite community they were urged to participate in its welfare and pray for its welfare, yet not to be so involved in it that they cannot transcend its values (Jer. 29: 4–10). When permission to return from exile was granted, Israel's international responsibility was declared to be the world-wide impartation of the knowledge of Yahweh, whose action on his people's behalf showed that He alone was God (Isa. 45: 22 f.). Their restoration qualifies them to be His witnesses (Isa. 43: 10), but their mission is to be taken up and carried to its conclusion by the Servant of the Lord, who, in addition to fulfilling a ministry to Israel, is given as 'a light for the Gentiles', so that the salvation of God 'may reach to the ends of the earth' (Isa. 49: 6).

Alongside this outgoing emphasis, the period following the return from exile witnessed a new policy of segregation under Ezra and Nehemiah, which cannot have been easy to reconcile with the call to worldwide mission. The tension between the two survives into the NT, not only in the conflict between the wider outlook of Jesus and the separatism of the Pharisees, but also in the early church, in the conflict between the champions of the law-free Gentile mission and those Jewish Christians who believed that Gentile converts should be admitted to the believing community only with safeguards similar to those which governed the admission of proselytes to the commonwealth of Israel. The champions of the Gentile mission indeed appealed to the commission of the Servant of the Lord as their own commission (Ac. 13: 47). In this as well as other respects the portrayal of the Isaianic Servant may be seen as the climax of the OT in its function as preparation for the gospel.

BIBLIOGRAPHY

ANDERSON, G. W. (ed.), *Tradition and Interpretation* (Oxford, 1979).

BRIGHT, J., *The Authority of the OT* (London, 1967).

BRUCE, F. F., *The Time is Fulfilled* (Exeter, 1978).

BRUCE, F. F., *This is That* (Exeter, 1968).

EICHRODT, W., *Theology of the OT* (2 vols., London, 1961, 1967).

ELLISON, H. L., *The Message of the OT* (Exeter, 1969).

HASEL, G., *OT Theology* (Grand Rapids, 1972).

JACOB, E., *Theology of the OT* (London, 1958).

RAD, G. VON, *OT Theology* (2 vols., Edinburgh, 1962, 1965).

RAD, G. VON, *Wisdom in Israel* (London, 1972).

ROWLEY, H. H., *The Faith of Israel* (London, 1956).

ROWLEY, H. H., *The Unity of the Bible* (London, 1953).

VRIEZEN, T. C., *An Outline of OT Theology* (Wageningen, 1958).

THE TEXT OF THE OLD TESTAMENT

A. R. MILLARD

WRITING IN THE OLD TESTAMENT WORLD

When man invented writing he found a way to preserve his ideas and experiences that passed through the barrier of time. It was natural for the God who was prepared to speak human language to cause His words to be recorded by this human means. By His providence, the bulk of His revelation was given to a people who had inherited an alphabet ripe for universal use, so that any who wanted could learn to read the sacred books.

Moses is the first Israelite recorded as writing (Exod. 17: 14), and certainly he lived in a world where writing was well-known. Between 2000 and 1000 B.C. half a dozen or more scripts were used in Syria-Palestine. Most important of these were the 600 cuneiform signs of Babylonia, impressed with a stylus on clay tablets, and the 700 sign Egyptian hieroglyphic with its everyday cursive form, hieratic, written with pen and ink on paper (papyrus) and other smooth surfaces. Egypt's writing had little currency outside areas of strong and continued Egyptian influence, such as Palestine and the coastal cities of Phoenicia, whereas cuneiform was the international means of communication throughout the Near East. These, and all the other systems, were complicated, employed principally in administration, law, religion, and diplomacy, the virtual monopoly of the scribal class. A little before 1500 B.C. there grew up a rival that eventually supplanted all of them, the alphabet.

Probably familiar with Egyptian, the Semitic inventor(s) of the alphabet discovered how a small group of symbols could replace the cumbersome hieroglyphs: one sign was needed for each sound of the language, some 30 in all. The signs were pictures, chosen, we may suppose, on the acrophonic principle 'dog=d'. As no Semitic word can begin with a vowel, and as the vowels are subsidiary to consonants in the Semitic languages, though still necessary, so it was not vital to mark them. (Vowel signs were systematically established when the Greeks borrowed the alphabet about 900 B.C., for their language could not be written clearly without them.) By the end of the second millennium B.C. the alphabet was stabilized and beginning to oust the other systems. It had generated imitations at the hands of scribes trained in the Babylonian tradition who produced alphabets of cuneiform signs for use on clay surfaces, notably at Ugarit in Syria. Few though our examples of the infant alphabet are, they serve to show a wide use of writing made possible by the simplicity of the script, breaking the monopoly of the scribes.

WRITING IN ANCIENT ISRAEL

At the Conquest of Canaan, Israel took possession of towns where writing was known, and the simple alphabet was at home. History, law, prophecy, itineraries, accounts, tax-lists could all be recorded with ease (cf. Jg. 8: 14). Unfortunately, following Egyptian practice, the alphabet was normally written on papyrus, a vegetable paper that decays in damp soil, so we have no examples to show the range and style of early Israelite writing. Small specimens of ancient Hebrew do survive, written on more durable materials, pottery and stone, allowing us to see how it was used in everyday life, and to infer the existence of leather and papyrus scroll books. They are far from implying that everyone could read or write, but in the times of Isaiah and Jeremiah it seems likely there were few villages without one inhabitant who could do so. That impression is given, too, by the Old Testament, although any work of educated men, as that is, will tend to stress their skill!

This background helps us when we consider the origins and growth of Old Testament books. Valuable information can be drawn from the ancient documents themselves about the habits of scribes, and they may aid in detecting the types of error made as one generation copied the books of another. Even insignificant notes written on scraps of pottery display the skill of experienced efficiency, care to achieve legibility, an accepted mode of writing. Similar care can be traced in the Assyrian, Babylonian, and Egyptian literary manuscripts from 2000 B.C. onwards that supply a satisfactory analogy for Israelite practice. On one hand there is great attention to reproducing an older text exactly, perhaps with modernization of spelling, damage to the master copy being noted, lines counted, the scribe's name appended, and sometimes the name of a 'proof-reader', the source(s) of the master copy (or copies), the date, and the destination of the copy—king, temple, or individual. On the other hand, a composition might pass through editorial changes and revision so that several copies may vary widely. Where this is the case, the differences are often inexplicable or meaningless now, and follow no pattern; they are impossible to discover or predict from one text alone, a fact to be given especial weight in reconstructing the literary history of Old Testament writings.

For further reading on the subject of this section see 'The Practice of Writing in Ancient Israel', *The Biblical Archaeologist* 35 (1972), pp. 98–111; 'Approaching the Old Testament', *Themelios* 2 (1976), pp. 34–39, both by the present writer.

THE TRADITIONAL HEBREW TEXT OF THE OLD TESTAMENT

Writing existed in Israel, but we do not know how or when the books we have inherited were first recorded, for no copies are available earlier than the third century B.C. The oldest copies extant, the Dead Sea Scrolls, reveal a certain variety to be discussed below. They also reveal the existence, between 200 B.C. and A.D. 65, of the text-form known at a later stage as the Traditional or Massoretic Text (*MT*), upon which English translations are based.

From the days of the Exile Hebrew declined to the status of a minority language amongst the Jews, though a dialect persisted in Judaea, being replaced by Aramaic, the *lingua franca* of the Persian Empire. As the process continued, there was an increasing need to preserve the 'correct' pronunciation of the Hebrew Bible text in synagogue readings. To help the reader, some letters could stand as vowels (like y in 'quickly'), a usage starting in the Monarchy period and reaching its peak in Herodian times. By the seventh and eighth centuries A.D. more precise methods of marking vowels and accents were arising, which culminated in the scheme of points placed above, below, and within the letters used ever since to produce the approved sounds and intonation. Jewish scholars who applied this system to the consonantal text inherited rigid regulations designed to maintain precision in copying that parallel, and may derive from, ancient Babylonian attitudes. They also recorded variations in the written text handed down to them (the Massorah).

Some of these variations actually correct mistakes that had become enshrined in the written text, thus there stands at Isa. 49: 5 *lô* 'not', so AV, whereas the Massorah instructs us to read *lô* 'to him', so AV mg, RV, RSV, NEB, NIV, Dead Sea Isaiah Scroll A. Other notes offer alterna-

tive vowels for an ambiguous set of consonants, *e.g.* 2 Sam. 18: 13 where 'my life in jeopardy' or 'against his life' depend upon *napšô* and *napšî* respectively. The forms in the written text are termed *Kethîbh* 'written', and those noted by the Massorah in the margins *Qerē* 'to be read'.

Tradition also reported a few passages where the text had been altered to avoid unacceptable ideas, as in 1 Sam. 3: 13 where God says Eli's 'sons brought a curse upon themselves' (cf. AV, RV) instead of 'cursed me' (cf. RSV, NEB).

This Massoretic Text is represented to-day by a few manuscripts copied in the ninth and tenth centuries A.D., the major ones preserved in Cairo, Jerusalem, Leningrad, and London, and by all later Hebrew Bibles written or printed.

EARLIER TEXTS

Recovery of the Dead Sea Scrolls has proved the existence of other Hebrew texts beside the Traditional type in Palestine during the first century B.C. and up to A.D. 68. Attention has been drawn to these variant texts, inevitably, because they are new to us, but it should be observed they are in the minority amongst the Dead Sea Scrolls, and, furthermore, they are very fragmentary. Their differences from the Massoretic type are more than quirks resulting from scribal errors, although further study may show many are slips and not deliberate changes. (Thus the addition of Exod. 20: 11 to Dt. 5: 15 in one copy may be due to an unconscious mental association.) In the book of Jeremiah a small fragment seems to have a shorter text than the Massoretic, agreeing to some extent with LXX which is one-eighth shorter than *MT* in this book. (In Jer. 10 verses 6–8, 10 are omitted, 5 is placed after 9.) A text of 1 Samuel 1–2 does the opposite: it adds various phrases, some of them, again, found in LXX (*e.g.* 1: 25 appears to have begun 'They came before the Lord and his father slew the sacrifice as he would do year by year to the Lord'), some extra, as in 1: 22 where we are told explicitly Samuel was to be a Nazirite for ever, as implied by verse 11, and maintained by later Jewish tradition. What liberty scribes enjoyed in copying a biblical text, how free they were to add comments or explanations of this sort, or to omit repetitious phrases, and whether there were different classes of copy, as later when strict rules were enforced for producing texts for public reading, are questions to be answered in the future. Clearly there were various traditions of text, perhaps developed in separate communities (Palestine, Egypt, and Babylonia are proposed), not necessarily the same for each part of the Bible. When they diverged from the ancestral text common to all is unknown, and a matter connected with the history of the Old

Testament Canon recognition of the authority of the books (see below, p. 24).

TEXTUAL CRITICISM

These various types of text now revealed in Hebrew emphasize the value of textual criticism and complicate its practice. The purpose of the art is to recover as nearly as possible the words of the author or the first written form of the present book. Errors that have intruded over centuries of copying need to be detected and corrected wherever possible, additions traced and removed, and other alterations replaced. Unless based upon manuscript evidence, these activities remain theoretical, and may become very subjective.

Comparing one copy with another can disclose the mistakes of one scribe; if every copy is in agreement, detection of error is harder. Signs that something may be amiss are ungrammatical words, unintelligible words, difference from ancient translations (see below, p. 14) or quotations, unique features out of harmony with the text as a whole. Not one of these signs is conclusive; each case has to be weighed individually. Ancient translators may paraphrase, quotations may be inexact, an irregular or unintelligible feature may be proved acceptable by a new discovery. Nevertheless textual criticism has had many successes, giving us a clearer text, more likely to be authentic, and a better understanding of the existing words. Some examples will demonstrate the methods. Simple errors include

(a) confusion of similar letters such as *d* and *r*: Gen. 10: 4 'Dodanim': 1 Chr. 1: 7 'Rodanim'.

(b) transposition of letters, as in Ps. 49: 11 where *MT qirbām* is taken as 'inward thoughts' by AV (it means 'insides'), but should be read *qibrām* 'their graves' as RSV, NIV.

(c) mistaken repetition ('dittography'), *e.g.* 2 Kg. 19: 23 *MT brkb rkby* for *brb rkby* 'with my many chariots'.

(d) mistaken omission ('haplography') exemplified in many copies which omit Jos. 21: 36, 37 by a slip from the words 'the tribe of Reuben' to 'the tribe of Gad', cf. 1 Chr. 6: 63, 64. Dead Sea Scroll Isaiah A has a good case: the scribe slipped from 'house of the LORD' at the end of 38: 20 to 'house of the LORD' at the end of 38: 22, omitting verses 21, 22 entirely; they were added at a later date in the margin.

(e) incorrect separation of words, a prize example being Am. 6: 12 *MT bbqrym* AV, RV, NIV, 'will one plough *there* with oxen?'

to be read *bbqr ym* 'does one plough the sea with oxen?' as RSV, NEB, giving better sense and better poetry.

The degree of uncertainty increases with the length and complexity of any suspected error. Suppose the haplography in Isa. 38 (in (d) above), had persisted through all later copies, it could hardly have been rectified from the Hebrew alone.

Beside changes resulting from error, there may be deliberate alterations made to 'improve' the text. Pious replacements of 'curse God' by 'bless God', additional to those recorded in tradition noted above, can be observed in Job 1: 11; 2: 19; 1 Kg. 21: 10, etc., and of the god-name Baal by 'shame' in the personal names Ishbosheth (2 Sam. 2; cf. 1 Chr. 8: 33), and Mephibosheth (2 Sam. 9: 6; cf. 1 Chr. 8: 34). The parenthetical note, 'these names were changed', in Num. 32: 38 may be a directive to the reader to avoid pagan divine names. Notes like that, termed 'glosses', may bring in up-to-date information, although whether the work of the author or of a later scribe is often impossible to decide. Cases can be read in Gen. 14: 2, 3, 7, 8, 17 ('that is . . .'); Ru. 4: 7; 1 Kg. 8: 2 'the seventh month'. The possibility of extensive re-arrangements in the text, accidental or deliberate, in the way NEB maintains (in Isa. 27; 38; 53, for example), has to be allowed, but is a matter of opinion, and cannot be substantiated.

Where textual error does not seem likely, yet the text remains obscure, containing, perhaps, one of the 1500 unique words in the Hebrew text, discoveries in other ancient documents may shed light. Ugaritic, a language related to Canaanite, and Egyptian have preserved a word for ship that allows Isa. 2: 16, AV 'upon all pleasant pictures' to be rendered more satisfactorily as 'against all the beautiful craft' (RSV) or 'every stately vessel' (NIV).

All these methods have to be used cautiously, with attention to every alternative, with care to avoid forcing an alien meaning on to the text. The text has been preserved remarkably through many generations; it is a treasure to be prized, to be studied and repaired where time has brought small imperfections. It is not to be distorted or re-modelled to suit changing tastes or opinions. To those who are ready to listen respectfully it speaks its eternal message.

BIBLIOGRAPHY

See combined bibliography at end of The Ancient Versions, pp. 22–23.

THE ANCIENT VERSIONS

ROBERT P. GORDON

So long as the Jews remained in Palestine and spoke their mother tongue they had no problem in understanding their sacred scriptures. But already in the sixth century B.C., and long before the OT canon was complete, many Jews were to be found living far from their ancestral homeland. Some had been deported to Mesopotamia after the Babylonian capture of Jerusalem in 597 B.C., others had, about the same time, followed the long-established precedent of seeking sanctuary in Egypt. Yet even if this dispersal had not occurred the Jews could hardly have avoided exposure to the alien sounds of Aramaic and Greek in the centuries following the destruction of their state. The Babylonian hegemony in the Near East was short-lived; it was brought to a swift conclusion by the arrival of the Persians in Babylon in October 539 B.C. For the next two hundred years the Persians dominated the Near East, and under them Aramaic enjoyed unique status as the official imperial language. Whether in Palestine, or Egypt, or Mesopotamia, Jews found that it was necessary, not to say advantageous, to become proficient in the *lingua franca* of the empire. The archives of the Jewish community on the island of Elephantine in Egypt show the extent to which Aramaic had taken root in this corner of the empire in the fifth century B.C. And long after the Persians had been ousted by Alexander and the Greeks, Aramaic remained as a monument to Persian rule, being spoken and written in various parts of the Near East, Palestine included. Alexander's prodigious feats paved the way for the spread of the Greek language and culture in the orient, and no subject territory was more affected than Egypt and its new Greek-style foundation of Alexandria. It was in recognition of the needs of Aramaic-speaking Jews in Palestine and of Greek-speaking Jews in Egypt that the first attempts at translating the OT from the original Hebrew were made.

There are several reasons why scholars should be interested in the ancient versions of the OT. First, the translations are important for the study of the languages in which they are written. In each case they provide valuable information about the vocabulary, accidence and syntax of these languages at particular stages in their history. Secondly, no translation is made in an ideological vacuum. 'Many different factors leave their mark upon the work —the intellectual presuppositions which the translators inherit from their own age and culture, the religious and other opinions which they hold or to which they have to show deference, the prejudices and desires by which they are bound consciously or unconsciously, their education, their own ability to express themselves and the range of concepts in the language into which they are translating, and other matters besides.'[1] Moreover, professional objectivity and theological neutrality were not so highly prized among ancient translation panels —if such there were—as they usually are today. The idea of vicarious suffering was unacceptable to the Aramaic translators of Isa. 53, so they rewrote the chapter to suit their theology. Jerome, on the other hand, felt no compunction about introducing NT ideas into his Vulgate translation of the OT. When he translated Ps. 149: 4 ('he crowns the humble with salvation') as 'he will exalt the meek in Jesus' we need not imagine that it was his Hebrew which was deficient. It is possible to learn much about the theological stances and biases of the ancient translators, and of their constituencies, by comparing their work against the Hebrew original.

Thirdly, the ancient versions are based on Hebrew manuscripts older than the majority of the texts now available to us. This has been underlined by the publication of the Biblical texts from the vicinity of the Dead Sea; at many points the ancient versions, and especially the Septuagint, are found to agree with these texts against the standard Massoretic tradition. Here lies the explanation for the trend in modern English versions as noted by Kubo and Specht: 'In the OT, the Masoretic (*sic*) text is still basic but is challenged by ancient versions and the biblical MSS of the *Dead Sea Scrolls*'.[2] Usually it is not too difficult to reconstruct the underlying Hebrew (the German term *Vorlage* is often used to denote the source text) of a given rendering, and sometimes where the standard Hebrew text is obscure or impossible such retroversion will yield a better reading and an improved sense. There are, it is true, many pitfalls to be avoided in this kind of exercise; when the going was difficult the ancient translator could make 'silent emendations' just as readily as his modern confrère.[3] There is no substitute for intimate acquaintance with the translation methods and special features of a version if readings are to be correctly evaluated. Fourthly, NT quotations from the OT are quite frequently at variance with the standard Hebrew text. The explanation lies partly in the fact that the NT writers were more often than not quoting from a Greek translation, and there was no more a standard Greek tradition than there is a standard English Bible tradition. In the first century A.D. the so-called 'Septuagint' existed in several recensions; writers often had access to only one of these and were normally content to quote from their exemplar so long as it served their main purpose satisfactorily. In addition, there are a few places where it seems that writers or their sources have made use of the Aramaic paraphrases called 'Targums'. The tracing of quotations to their versional sources is often beset with difficulties and can only be helped by increased knowledge of the origins and development of the ancient versions in general, and of the Greek tradition in particular.

THE SAMARITAN PENTATEUCH

The Pentateuch is the only division of the Hebrew scriptures which the Samaritans hold to be canonical and authoritative. One of the consequences of the schism between the Jews and the Samaritans was that their editions of the Pentateuch were transmitted independently of each other from the second century B.C. at the latest. But while there can be no doubt about the antiquity of the Samaritan Pentateuch (henceforth denoted by SP), it is not nearly so old as the Samaritan community has always maintained it to be. Impossible claims are made on behalf of the Abisha[c] Scroll especially; it is said to have been copied by Abishua, Aaron's great-grandson (1 Chr. 6: 3 f.), in the thirteenth year of the Israelites' settlement in Canaan. This is unquestionably a piece of propagandist romancing calculated to bolster the claims of the Samaritan recension against its Jewish rival. Actually the scroll consists of two pieces sutured together, the older part (containing Num. 33: 1–Dt. 34: 12) copied as recently as the eleventh century A.D.

Strictly speaking, SP is 'not a version so much as a transcription'.[4] As the text-form of the Pentateuch which was transmitted in North Israel it has its peculiar characteristics, yet its disagreements with the Massoretic tradition can hardly be called substantial. For, while the differences between *MT* and SP number about six thousand, many of them are merely orthographical variations. In addition, SP has a tendency to simplify difficult forms and constructions and generally to make 'alterations typical of popular texts'.[5] Some of the remaining disagreements with *MT* are clearly the result of sectarian bias at work in SP. There are various

references, both explicit and implicit, to Gerizim, the holy hill of the Samaritans (cf. especially the interpolations after Exod. 20: 17 and Dt. 5: 21). Always the intention is to present Gerizim, rather than Jerusalem, as the divinely-chosen centre of worship in Canaan. At many points—the estimates vary between 1,600 and 2,000—SP agrees with the Septuagint against *MT*; sometimes the combined witness of the two may be used to correct *MT*, as at Gen. 4: 8 where *MT* lacks the words 'Let's go out to the field' (cf. NIV footnote). SP has not, however, been transmitted with the same accuracy and fidelity as *MT* and this, in addition to the obvious sectarian slant, accounts for its neglect by textual critics. Just occasionally an OT quotation or allusion in the NT is found to be in exclusive agreement with SP, notably in the account of Stephen's speech in Acts 7. In such cases we need not suppose that the NT writer was consulting SP. Rather, SP is the sole surviving witness to a reading which, doubtless, was once represented somewhere in the Septuagint, or even Targumic, tradition.

The first copy of SP to reach the west was brought from Damascus by Pietro della Valle in 1616, and the earliest printed editions were those in the Paris and London Polyglots (1632 and 1657 respectively). A separate edition was published in Oxford in 1790 by Benjamin Blayney. In those days SP was held in high regard and it took the researches and pronouncements of the great German critic Gesenius in the early nineteenth century to counter the unjustified claims which had been made for it. More recent investigation of the morphology of SP shows that it reflects the common Hebrew of Palestine between the second century B.C. and the third century A.D. With this evaluation the palaeographical studies of the American scholar F. M. Cross concur: the version is to be dated no earlier than Hasmonaean times.

THE SEPTUAGINT

The Septuagint is the doyen of the OT versions. In addition to the rights of primogeniture its uniqueness is assured by its constant deployment by NT writers and by the early Christians generally. Moreover, this version enjoys a special position in ancient Greek literature, for the Hebrew scriptures were 'the only oriental religious writings to achieve the distinction of translation into Greek'.[6] Properly the term 'Septuagint' applies only to the translation of the Pentateuch, but its use to denote the whole of the Greek OT can be traced back as far as Justin Martyr and Irenaeus in the second century A.D. The earliest account of Septuagint origins is given in the *Letter of Aristeas*, composed sometime in the second century B.C. *Aristeas* tells how, at the behest of Ptolemy Philadelphus II (285–247 B.C.), a team of seventy-two translators came from Jerusalem to Alexandria and translated the Pentateuch into Greek in seventy-two days. It is a desultory tale and contains a modicum of fact ensconced in a great deal of fiction. It is also an apologetic work and seems to have been written at a time when the accuracy of the Greek Pentateuch (at least) was being called in question. So the writer dwells on the impeccable scholarship of the translators and on the auspicious beginnings of their translation. In the next few centuries the legendary elements in the story became more numerous and more far-fetched, and, in some quarters at any rate, the claims made for the translation became more extravagant. For Philo of Alexandria, living at the beginning of the Christian era, the Septuagint was as much a product of divine inspiration as the Hebrew original and its translators had prophetic and priestly status. But there are details in the original *Aristeas* account which are usually deemed worthy of credence. It is very probable that the Pentateuch was the first part of the OT to be translated into Greek and that the work was carried out by bilingual Jews in Alexandria early in the third century B.C. It is not so likely, on the other hand, that Ptolemy Philadelphus was the instigator of the enterprise. Sufficient explanation for the undertaking is found in the existence in Egypt at this time of a large community of Jews who could speak only Greek. After the Pentateuch had been translated the rest of the canonical books will have been treated in the same way, so that by 100 B.C. a complete version of the OT in Greek was available.

The profusion of variant readings in the extant MSS of the Septuagint, and the proper method of accounting for them, is our next concern. The text of the Greek OT was never static; it was constantly being copied and subjected to revision in the interests of increased fidelity to the original Hebrew, or of an improved Greek style, or of a particular theory of translation. Thus a major uncial such as Codex Alexandrinus may incorporate different text-types and recensions, and all depending on the MSS available for individual books at the time of transcription. Some scholars, following the lead of the late Paul Kahle, have argued that the excess of variant readings is best explained on the assumption that there was no 'original Septuagint' (*Ur-Septuaginta*), but only a variety of independent translations out of which a standard text eventually emerged. Most Septuagintalists, while not excluding the possibility of early 'unofficial' attempts at translation, hold that the various texts and recensions are, in theory, traceable to a common source.

Jerome, in his *Preface to Chronicles*, speaks of three major recensions of the Greek OT which were acknowledged by the church in his day.

'Alexandria and Egypt recognize Hesychius as the author of their Septuagint; from Constantinople to Antioch Lucian the Martyr's version is acknowledged; the Palestinian provinces in between these use codices which were produced by Origen and published by Eusebius and Pamphilus. The whole world takes issue with itself over this threefold variety.' The study of the transmission-history of the Septuagint must begin with these three recensions, and particularly with the work of Origen. From about A.D. 230 to A.D. 245 Origen was engaged in the compilation of his Hexapla, a six-column edition of the OT in Hebrew and in Greek. It was a mammoth undertaking, but Origen was convinced of its usefulness; the Septuagint badly needed revision *vis à vis* the Hebrew text if it was to continue to be the powerful apologetic weapon which it had been in the hands of earlier generations of Christians. The first of the six columns of the Hexapla presented the Hebrew text of the OT, and the remaining five columns gave a transliteration of the Hebrew in Greek letters, the versions of Aquila and Symmachus, Origen's own reconstruction of the Septuagint, and, finally, the version of Theodotion. Using the Aristarchian symbols[7] Origen indicated Septuagintal additions to the Hebrew original and also the interpolated material with which he had corrected omissions in the Septuagint. Only a small proportion of Origen's work has survived. And while subsequent generations of scholars have been much in his debt it must be observed that, so far as his Septuagintal column is concerned, Origen 'tended to obliterate the most original and distinctive features of the Version'.[8] The policy of aligning the Greek to the Hebrew text with which Origen was familiar took no account of the changing, or at least changed, condition of the Hebrew since the time that the Septuagint had first been translated. Not only did the physical features of the earliest Septuagint become more blurred; the possibility of reconstructing Hebrew readings which antedated the standardization of the proto-Massoretic text became more remote.

Of the Lucianic and Hesychian revisions rather less is known. The former is associated with the name of an Antiochene presbyter who was martyred in A.D. 311/312. Lucian's interest was partly that of the literary stylist and his work shows a marked preference for the more classical Attic forms as against the common Hellenisms of the mainstream Septuagint tradition. In order to preserve ancient readings Lucian was happy to present a conflate text; his edition of the historical books ('the former prophets') is especially valuable as a reliquary of early readings. But there are indications from several sources—the Old Latin versions, Rylands Papyrus Greek no. 458, texts from Qumran Cave IV—that Lucian's proper due is that of a continuator rather than an innovator. 'We find in the Manchester Papyrus (no. 458) a text related to the Lucianic text of the Bible written some five hundred years before Lucian himself.'[9]

Hesychius was probably an Egyptian bishop living about the same time as Lucian. Although Jerome states that his revision became the standard text of the church in Egypt it has proved difficult to identify in the extant MSS. If more were known about the principles on which Hesychius carried out his revision the task of identifying Hesychian exemplars would be greatly simplified. Arguments for the Hesychian character of various MSS have been advanced at one time or another. A few scholars have gone so far as to suggest that the Hesychian recension is a figment of Jerome's imagination. There were, in any case, other revisions of the Septuagint besides those mentioned by Jerome, and one of the achievements of modern Septuagintal studies has been to isolate several of these. Without doubt the most significant advance here has been the identification of the so-called *Kaige* recension, precursor of the highly literal version of Aquila. The work of this school of translators is marked by such idiosyncrasies as the rendering of the Hebrew adverb *gam* by *kaige*, hence the name. The clue to the existence of such a recensional chain came with the discovery of the Greek Scroll of the Twelve (Minor) Prophets (the *Dodekapropheton*), fragments of which came to light at Qumran in 1952 and subsequently.[10] Père Barthélemy, the pioneer in this field, has claimed the version of Theodotion and various other texts and traditions within the Greek OT as being representative of the *Kaige* school.

As a translation of the Hebrew OT the Septuagint is best characterized as 'good in parts'. Because of the Pentateuch's primacy in the synagogue these books were, on the whole, treated with care and rendered fairly literally.[11] Other books such as Job, Daniel and Proverbs were handled rather more freely; in the last case Hebrew proverbs often appear in Greek guise. There are two Septuagint texts of Judges, but they are not independent versions: 'the one has used the other, or both stem from a common archetype'.[12] The translation of Isaiah is, somewhat surprisingly, of rather indifferent quality. Job and Jeremiah were translated from Hebrew texts which were significantly shorter than *MT*.

Probably the oldest extant Septuagint fragment is the Rylands Papyrus Greek 458 already mentioned. It is dated to the second century B.C. and contains parts of Dt. 23–28. Papyrus Fouad 266, with fragments of Genesis and Deuteronomy, is almost as old. From Qumran Cave IV have come fragments of Lev. 2–5 in Greek, and from Cave VII fragments containing Exod. 28: 4–7 and the apocryphal Epistle of Jeremiah (43–44); these are probably as old as the first century B.C. The principal uncials —the linchpin of Septuagint research—are the codices Sinaiticus (4th cent.), Vaticanus (4th cent.), Alexandrinus (5th cent.), Ephraemi rescriptus (5th cent.), and Marchalianus (6th cent.).

A number of ancient versions were based, in whole or in part, on the Septuagint, principally the Old Latin, Coptic, Armenian, Georgian, Gothic, Slavonic, Ethiopic, as well as certain Arabic translations. A few of these are of value for the light which they shed on their Greek originals, the most important in this respect being those in Ethiopic, Latin and Coptic.[13] The Sahidic Coptic version has lately enjoyed unaccustomed favour on account of its agreements with the already-mentioned *Dodekapropheton*. Several of the translations were produced to meet the needs of indigenous churches in situations such as are still encountered by modern missionaries. Ulfilas and Mesrop had to invent alphabets, the Gothic and Armenian respectively, before they could render the scriptures in the vernacular.

THE MINOR GREEK VERSIONS
Christian use—and misuse—of the Septuagint provoked the final estrangement between that version and the Jews, its erstwhile promulgators. But there was another factor in the changing Jewish estimation of the Septuagint. The process of standardizing the consonantal Hebrew text of the OT seems to have reached its climax by the end of the first century A.D. While Christians could, and did, use the Septuagint as though there had never been a Hebrew original, the position could not be the same on the Jewish side. There the gulf between the Greek and the stabilized Hebrew tradition was perceived to be too wide to be tolerated any longer. Earlier attempts to bring the Greek version into closer conformity with the Hebrew were now headed up in a version whose regnant principle was that of fidelity to the Hebrew *ad extremum*. **Aquila** issued his translation at some point in the early second century A.D., probably in Palestine. His response to the Christianizing of the OT was to produce a painfully literal rendering of the Hebrew original, representing nuances, etymologies, solecisms, and all. In following out this policy he was adhering to the exegetical principles expounded by his probable mentor, the famous Rabbi Akiba. We might compare Aquila's version with the English text of a modern Greek–English interlinear version of the NT, insofar as the absolutely literal rendition of the original is concerned.[14] And Aquila's work must have been intended for the same sort of restricted

readership. The Aquilanic version has largely perished, but enough fragments have survived to show how consistently the translation principles were applied. One of the most important of the witnesses to the version is the tenth-century Hexaplaric palimpsest discovered by Cardinal Mercati in the Ambrosian Library, Milan, in 1896. The palimpsest contains about one hundred and fifty verses from the Psalter, omitting only the first (Hebrew) column of the Hexapla as it was originally produced by Origen.

At least two other Greek translations of the OT were published in the period late second century to early third century A.D. Like Aquila, **Theodotion** appears to have built on foundations laid considerably in advance of his time, otherwise it would be very difficult to account for 'Theodotionic' readings which are already present in the NT and the apostolic fathers. Irenaeus informs that Theodotion was a Jewish proselyte and hailed from Ephesus. Origen obviously thought highly of his version, frequently using it to supply omissions in the Septuagint column of his Hexapla. Such was the superiority of Theodotion's rendering of Daniel that it almost completely ousted the feeble Septuagint version of the book; there are only two extant MSS to represent the latter. Theodotion's translation stands somewhere between the literalisms of Aquila and the stylishness of Symmachus. He had a disconcerting penchant for transliteration, especially of technical terms, and there are over a hundred examples of the phenomenon in the surviving portions of his work.

Symmachus, the third member of the trio, belonged to the Jewish-Christian sect of the Ebionites. His commitment to elegance of Greek style makes his version the complete antithesis to Aquila's, though there is evidence of his occasional use of the latter! In his attenuation of anthropomorphisms we can perhaps discover another expression of Symmachus's desire to present the OT to the Greek world in as favourable a light as possible, though it is also possible to put this tendency down to his acquaintance with, and respect for, rabbinic ideas on the matter. It is very difficult to pinpoint his date with precision; the early decades of the third century may not be far wrong.

THE ARAMAIC TARGUMS

Talmudic tradition associates the origins of the Targums with the occasion described in Neh. 8 when 'they read from the Book of the Law of God, making it clear (mg, "with interpretation"); and giving the meaning, so that the people could understand what was being read' (v. 8). This may well have been the first time that the Pentateuch was, at a public gathering, paraphrased in Aramaic for the benefit of those to whom the Hebrew was unintelligible. 'Targum' means 'interpretation' and we can readily imagine that in the early post-exilic days Aramaic 'interpretations' accompanied the reading of the Pentateuch in synagogue. At first the Targum will have existed only in oral form; it was forbidden to have a written Aramaic text alongside the Hebrew synagogue scroll, lest the authority of the original should appear to be compromised. There is a hint in a Talmudic story that some authorities may have looked askance at written Targums whether in or out of synagogue. The Mishnah (c. A.D. 200) lays down rules for the reading and translation of the scriptures in synagogue, and from these it is evident that greatest care was taken in the rendering of the Pentateuch. Indeed, the inclusion of lections from the Prophets and Hagiographa seems to have been a secondary development.

In spite of any discouragements there may have been, the task of committing the Targums to writing must have been begun in the pre-Christian era. Fragments of a Targum to Job which were discovered at Qumran have been dated to the middle of the first century A.D.; the form of Aramaic used would suggest the previous century as the time of the actual composition of the Targum. There is no such thing as a Targum to the OT; there are several Targums to the Pentateuch, a complete Targum to the Prophets, and individual Targums to most of the books of the Hagiographa. Targums Onkelos to the Pentateuch and Jonathan to the Prophets were accorded the status of official translations by Babylonian Jewry, though in origin they are as much products of the Palestinian synagogues as the remaining Targums. When they were brought to Babylon, probably sometime after the destruction of Jerusalem in A.D. 70, they were revised so as to agree more closely with the Hebrew original. Onkelos bears the marks of a particularly thorough revision and much of the distinctively Palestinian material was eliminated. The Pentateuchal Targums which were not subjected to redaction in Babylon are expansive and paraphrastic, valuable repositories of rabbinic tradition and lore. As well as the two complete Targums to the Pentateuch, Pseudo-Jonathan and Neofiti (identified as recently as 1956), the Palestinian Targum is represented by various fragments whose significance is none the less for the considerable difficulties which they pose. The Targums to the books of the Hagiographa seem, for the most part, to have been composed at a comparatively late stage. There are quite fundamental differences between the early Targum to Job represented in the Qumran fragments and the Targum which had previously been the sole Aramaic version of that book known to us.

There is a distinctive Targumic style which transcends the boundaries of the individual Targums; and because the Targums are interpretations, and not simply translations, there is all the more scope for these common characteristics to flourish. The synagogal *methurgeman* ('interpreter') considered it his duty to moralize, to contemporize and to bowdlerize, so that the average congregant might be aware of current orthodox teaching on matters of fundamental importance. A recurrent feature of the Targums is the use of anti-anthropomorphisms, as when 'the hand of the LORD' (Isa. 66: 14) is rendered in Aramaic by 'the might of the Lord'. Considerations of piety also forbade the *methurgeman* to say that Isaiah 'saw the Lord' (Isa. 6: 1); what the prophet saw was 'the glory of the Lord'. The *methurgeman* did not baulk at drastic simplification of the Hebrew if syntactical problems or factual discrepancies stood in his way. There were various ways of dealing with such situations. A difficult form might be treated as metathetical, and even where the text was straightforward the device of metathesis could be employed. At several points the Hebrew word *ya'ar* ('forest') is rendered as if it had been *'îr* ('city') just because it served the translator's purpose of actualizing the biblical reference. Sometimes, in accordance with the rabbinic principle of *gezērāh shāvāh* ('equal category'), an intractable word or phrase might be illuminated by reference to some other verse which bore overall resemblance to that being translated. Very often such problems were resolved by drawing on one of a number of stock words and phrases which recur throughout the Targums. Words like 'strength', 'falsehood', 'destroy', and phrases like 'rich in possessions', appear with remarkable frequency and have to be recognized for the translational ciphers that they are. There are also standard translations of particular Hebrew words. Wherever there is a reference to God's healing of Israel's wounds the Targum to the Prophets is inclined to represent 'heal' by 'forgive'. This accounts for the discrepancy between Mk 4: 12 ('and be forgiven') and Isa. 6: 10 ('and be healed'); the Gospel quotation is influenced by the Targum. Occasionally a word which is ambiguous is rendered so as to take account of both possibilities—a policy adopted on a much larger scale in the modern *Amplified Bible* ('startle *and* sprinkle' being one way of sorting the notorious crux in Isa. 52: 15!). Yet another feature of a modern version is anticipated in the Targums when, from time to time, they supply rubrics to indicate who is assumed to be speaking in a particular section. We may compare NEB's treatment of the Song of Songs. We find, for example, a cluster of such rubrics in the Targum to Jer. 8: 20–22. Verse 20 is prefaced by 'The congregation of Israel said', v. 21 by 'Jerusalem said', and v. 22 by 'Jeremiah the prophet said'. There are many similar inserts distributed throughout the Targums and there is reason to suspect that they were even more numerous at an earlier stage in the development of the Targums.

In the Targums we are introduced to the atmosphere of the Palestinian synagogue, especially in the sermonic and parenetic material of the more paraphrastic passages. And while the extant Targums certainly reached their final form in the Christian era perhaps the most crucial period of their development was in the inter-testamental era. The Targumic theological themes, and the favourite topics in the early synagogues, include the election of Israel, the preeminence of the Torah, the hope of messianic deliverance from foreign domination, the resurrection of the dead (whether a general resurrection or a resurrection of the righteous only), reward and punishment. 'You, O house of Israel, think that when a man dies in this world his judgment ceases'—which bears little relation to the Hebrew original of Mal. 3: 6—not only raises a point of contention between the Pharisees and the Sadducees in the late intertestamental period; it seems to take us right into the synagogue where the heterodoxy was being challenged. Judaism acquired for itself a considerable amount of eschatological paraphernalia during the inter-testamental period and the prominence of these themes in the Targums is no coincidence.

If both oral and written Targums circulated in the pre-Christian period we shall not be surprised to find echoes of them in the NT, always remembering that it was to the Greek Bible that the early church normally looked for inspiration. As well as the quotation from Isa. 6: 10 already mentioned, there are indeed a few other places where NT writers seem to be dependent on a Targum. The quotation from Deuteronomy in Rom. 12: 19 and Heb. 10: 30 finds its closest parallel in the Targums to the Pentateuch. Again, Eph. 4: 8 reproduces Ps. 68: 18 in a form which is found only in the Targum and the Syriac Peshitta. There may also be Targumic snatches in some of the speeches in the early part of Acts, as, for example, in Paul's synagogue sermon at Pisidian Antioch. Nor should the importance of the Targums for the study of the NT be limited to a few possible quotations. Concepts such as Gehenna and the Second Death find explicit formulation in the Targums and their use by NT writers can best be understood in the light of this and other relevant Jewish material. While the concept of the Second Death is known outside the Targumic corpus it is the latter which provides the most direct correspondence so far as the actual expression is concerned.

THE SYRIAC PESHITTA
(or 'VULGATE')

Syriac, a dialect of Eastern Aramaic, was the language of Mesopotamian Christianity for many centuries and is still spoken in some areas of eastern Turkey and northern Iraq. Christianity probably reached Mesopotamia during the first century, but, since there was already a large Jewish population in the region, it is difficult to know whether the translation of the OT into Syriac was first undertaken by Jews or Christians. Most scholars favour a Jewish provenance and this view seems to be supported by the incidence of Targumic and rabbinic elements in the translation; Christian translators might have adverted to a Targum from time to time, but they are unlikely to have depended on a Jewish version to the extent represented in the Peshitta. Opinion is also divided as to whether the Targumisms of the Peshitta Pentateuch are traceable to a Palestinian Targum or to the Babylonian Targum Onkelos. The former alternative is supported by the occurrence of some Palestinian (Western Aramaic) elements in the Eastern Aramaic of the Peshitta. On the other hand, the case for dependence on Onkelos has also been presented in convincing manner in fairly recent times. Here the Palestinian origin of Onkelos is offered as adequate explanation of the Western Aramaic features of the Syriac version. And in actual fact the gulf between the two points of view is not so great as is sometimes thought. If the Peshitta Pentateuch was translated in the late first century or early second century we need only state the choice as being, not between dependence on a Palestinian Targum and dependence on a Babylonian Targum, but between a Palestinian Targum specially imported for the use of the translators and a Palestinian Targum which was beginning to establish itself in Babylon and which would eventually gain official recognition there as Targum Onkelos. The onus of proof would then appear to rest with those who maintain that a Targum was specially imported for the occasion.

Illustration of the kind of circumstances in which just such a special importation could have occurred was indeed provided by the late Paul Kahle.[15] For Kahle the apparent dependence of the Peshitta Pentateuch on a Palestinian Targum required some special relationship between Mesopotamia and Palestine. This vital link he found to be the conversion of the royal house of the kingdom of Adiabene, east of the Tigris, to Judaism, and the subsequent close ties between Adiabene and Jerusalem in the decades before the latter's destruction in A.D. 70. After the conversion of the royal house, and in consequence of the existence already of a great number of Jewish converts in the area, a Targum will have been brought from Palestine to Mesopotamia specifically to aid Jewish translators working on a Syriac version of the Pentateuch. The theory has often been quoted in the absence of any certain information about Peshitta origins, but it remains quite unsubstantiated. We should note, moreover, that Kahle's reconstruction was necessitated by his—now widely rejected—view that Targum Onkelos was Babylonian *ab initio*. If all the Targums originated in Palestine—Onkelos as much as the others—then we do not need to resort to this kind of speculation to explain the Palestinian Targumic elements in the Peshitta.

So far we have been concerned only with the Pentateuch, but there is evidence of dependence on Targums in some other books of the Peshitta OT. This dependence is very marked, for example, in the Syriac translation of Malachi; in other books, such as 1 and 2 Samuel, there are Targumic features which may not add up to direct borrowing on the part of the Peshitta translators. As the version gained acceptance in the eastern churches the Targumisms tended to be obliterated and conformity to the Septuagint became the overriding concern. For all that, the Peshitta is in closer agreement with *MT* than is the Septuagint. The quality of the translation varies considerably from book to book, though we may remark on a couple of general characteristics: (1) a tendency to omit words or phrases which were unintelligible to the translators; (2) the translation of verses quoted in the NT, or of verses to which there is allusion in the NT, may be influenced by the NT reference.

The origins of the Peshitta were already proving intractable by the middle of the first millennium. We find Theodore of Mopsuestia at the beginning of the fifth century confessing that he had nothing to contribute on that subject. The earliest *dated* MSS are now housed in the British Museum; one dated A.D. 459/60 contains parts of Isaiah and a fragment of Ezekiel, and the other, copied in A.D. 463/4, contains the Pentateuch minus Leviticus. Research into the history of the version is hampered by the lack of a proper critical edition such as exists for most of the books of the Septuagint. To remedy this situation the International Organization for the Study of the Old Testament in 1959 authorized P. A. H. de Boer of Leiden to initiate a Syriac OT project, with the help of an international team of collaborators. The project's first volume devoted to a canonical book—1 and 2 Kings—was published in 1976. It would be a forlorn hope, however, to expect that the Peshitta's importance for textual criticism would ever approach that of the Septuagint.

Other Syriac versions of the OT such as the Philoxenian (early sixth century) and the Syro-Hexaplaric (A.D. 616–7) are Septuagint-based. The Syro-Hexapla, associated with the name of Paul, bishop of Tella, is a translation of the Septuagint column of Origen's omnibus edition of the OT described above, and is one of its most important witnesses. The so-called Christian Palestinian Syriac Version, of which OT lectionary portions are extant, is actually an Aramaic translation written in a modified Syriac script. A tentative dating between the fourth and sixth centuries is as much as present evidence warrants.

THE LATIN VULGATE

The Latin-speaking churches of North Africa and Europe (principally Gaul and regions of Italy) had their own translations of the Bible almost from their inception. Biblical quotations in the writings of Tertullian and Cyprian certainly indicate the existence of Latin renderings of both Testaments in the early third century. There is good reason to think that the history of what have become known as the 'Old Latin versions' goes back well into the second century. During the next two centuries there was a proliferation of Latin translations, all based on the Septuagint and yet exhibiting a wide divergence of readings. Such was the situation when, about the year A.D. 382, Damasus bishop of Rome commissioned his secretary, Jerome by name, to begin a revision of the Latin Bible. As far as the OT was concerned, Jerome's earliest efforts were aimed at establishing a Latin text which faithfully represented the Septuagint. But this phase of his work never reached completion; the more Jerome saw of the Old Latin the more he became convinced that what was really needed was a translation based on the original Hebrew, the 'Hebrew verity' (*Hebraica veritas*) as he called it.

Three centuries of Christian tradition stood in the way of such an undertaking as Jerome was now planning, for the Septuagint's divine inspiration was proclaimed and accepted in many quarters of the church. Discrepancies between the Greek and the Hebrew original hardly came into the reckoning since scarcely anyone knew Hebrew. Jerome was partly motivated by apologetic and missionary considerations, realizing that evangelism among Jews in particular was doomed to ineffectiveness so long as Christians adhered to translations which were unacceptable to their opponents. 'It is one thing to sing the psalms in churches of Christian believers, quite another to make answer to Jews who cavil at the words',[16] was how he saw it. So about A.D. 390 Jerome set about the work which was to become his most enduring monument. The first books which he translated from the Hebrew were Samuel and Kings and in the accompanying preface he presented his apologia for his work. The very title of this preface, *Prologus Galeatus* ('The Helmeted Prologue'), illustrates his wry sense of humour and also shows what sort of response he anticipated among the conservative ranks in the church. Not only text but canon was affected by this reversion to the Hebrew; the Greek apocryphal additions accepted in the Alexandrian canon were given short shrift under the new régime. Books such as Tobit and Judith were rendered from inadequate texts with lightning speed and minimal accuracy; others were not favoured with his attention at all.

In his translation of the canonical books, as also in his commentaries on them, Jerome often incorporates traditional Jewish explanations, especially if it is a question of geography or philology or something similar. At many points in the commentaries he acknowledges his indebtedness to his Hebrew tutor for a particular explanation or interpretation. (His acquaintance with Jewish learning can only have been enhanced by his departure for the east in 386. From this point on he made his home in Bethlehem, dying there in 420.) The cause of accuracy was also served by Jerome's constant recourse to the Old Latin versions, and also to the Septuagint and the minor Greek versions of Aquila, Theodotion and Symmachus. Slavishly literal or not, the work of Aquila earned high commendation from him. Jerome's own translation was pitched somewhere between the Aquilanic literalness and the freer thought-for-thought equivalences of some modern translations. From the introductions to the various books translated we can elicit information about Jerome's *modus operandi* and the order in which he tackled the books. After translating Samuel–Kings he worked on Job and the Prophets, then the Psalms and the books traditionally ascribed to Solomon. The books of Moses were among the last to be rendered, and the entire undertaking reached completion in 405.

As with most of the ancient versions, it is unwise to generalize much about the Vulgate OT. Different books exhibit different characteristics in translation. In one book Jerome may have relied upon an individual Latin or Greek version more than was his wont, or may have allowed himself more freedom of stylistic expression than usual. There is also what Roberts calls 'the tendency of Jerome to imitate in the Old Testament the Latin of the New Testament'.[17] By this means the scandal of the unfamiliar was, if not removed, at least reduced! Nor was Jerome averse to the practice of interpolating an occasional word to help his readers to a proper understanding of the text, or of eliminating repetitiousness in the interests of readability. We have already observed his predilection for Christianizing texts, especially those which seemed patient of a messianic interpretation. Thus the AV's misinterpretation of Hag. 2: 7 as a direct reference to the Messiah has the questionable—in this case—distinction of having Jerome for father.[18]

The expected opposition to the new translation did materialize, but by a gradual process between the sixth and ninth centuries the Vulgate attained to an unrivalled position in western Christendom, ultimately exerting great influence on the languages and literatures of western Europe. And once more the problem of divergent texts began to raise its head. One important factor was the contamination of the Vulgate from Old Latin texts which had not yet gone out of circulation. Finally, in 1546, the Council of Trent ruled on the desirability of having an accurate and authoritative edition of the Vulgate. The first response to this call, the Sixtine Edition issued by Pope Sixtus V in 1590, had such obvious shortcomings that a corrected version, the Sixto-Clementine Edition, was published by Clement VIII two years later. This latter edition has maintained its position until the present century; the Benedictine revision of the entire Vulgate commissioned by Pope Pius X in 1907 still awaits completion.

It is the ultimate irony that, within the Roman communion, Jerome's translation from the original languages of the Bible has for centuries been recognized as authoritative, and in such a way as to exclude further attempts to represent that same original yet more faithfully. The return to the original text as reflected in the Jerusalem Bible, the RSV Catholic Edition (now merged in the *Common Bible* of 1973) and the New American Bible is therefore to be warmly welcomed and encouraged—even if the battlelines must still be drawn over the issue of canon.

REFERENCES

1 E. Würthwein, *The Text of the Old Testament* (Oxford, 1957), p. 33.
2 S. Kubo and W. Specht, *So Many Versions?* (Grand Rapids, 1975), p. 13.
3 Cf. RSV's 'strike hands with foreigners' in Isa. 2: 6. There is no hint of the emendation of *MT byldy* to *bydy*; cf. AV 'children', as *MT*, for RSV 'hands'.
4 S. Jellicoe, *The Septuagint and Modern Study* (Oxford, 1968), p. 243.
5 Würthwein, *op. cit.*, p. 32.
6 S. P. Brock, 'The Phenomenon of Biblical Translation in Antiquity', *Alta* (The University of Birmingham Review), 2/8, 1969, p. 96.
7 Symbols used in Homeric criticism by the Alexandrian grammarian Aristarchus.
8 S. R. Driver, *Notes on the Hebrew Text and the Topography of the Books of Samuel* (2nd edn., Oxford, 1913 [reprint 1960]), p. xliii.

9 P. E. Kahle, *The Cairo Geniza* (2nd edn., Oxford, 1959), p. 221.
10 See D. Barthélemy, *Les Devanciers d'Aquila* (Leiden, 1963).
11 This does not apply in the case of Exodus, especially where the translation of technical terms is concerned. See D. W. Gooding, *The Account of the Tabernacle. Translational and Textual Problems of the Greek Exodus* (Cambridge, 1959).
12 Jellicoe, *op. cit.*, pp. 280 f.
13 The Armenian and Georgian versions may only have been *revised* on the basis of Greek texts.
14 We might also compare Robert Young's *Literal Translation of the Bible*. The comparison is apt in that Young, like Aquila, had a cherished translation theory—in his case affecting the rendering of the Hebrew *Waw Consecutive*.
15 *Op. cit.*, pp. 270 ff.
16 Cf. J. N. D. Kelly, *Jerome: His Life, Writings and Controversies* (London, 1975), p. 160.
17 B. J. Roberts, *The Old Testament Text and Versions* (Cardiff, 1951), p. 255.
18 For the correct rendering see RSV, and note the *cri de cœur* in the footnote to the verse in the *Amplified Bible*!

BIBLIOGRAPHY

General
BRUCE, F. F., *The Books and the Parchments* (4th edn., Basingstoke, 1984).
The Cambridge History of the Bible: Vol. I (ed. P. R. Ackroyd and C. F. Evans) Cambridge, 1970; Vol. II (ed. G. W. H. Lampe) Cambridge, 1969.
KAHLE, P. E., *The Cairo Geniza* (2nd edn., Oxford, 1959).
NOTH, M., *The Old Testament World* (Philadelphia–Edinburgh, 1966).
ORLINSKY, H. M., *Essays in Biblical Culture and Bible Translation* (New York, 1974).

Special Studies
(i) Hebrew Text
AP-THOMAS, D. R., *A Primer of Old Testament Text Criticism* (Oxford, 1965).
CROSS, F. M., *The Ancient Library of Qumran and the Biblical Text* (revd. 2nd edn., Grand Rapids, 1980).
CROSS, F. M., *Scrolls from the Wilderness of the Dead Sea* (New Haven and London, 1965).
HARRISON, R. K., *Introduction to the Old Testament* (Grand Rapids, 1969, London, 1970), pp. 211–259.
ROBERTS, B. J., *The Old Testament Text and Versions* (Cardiff, 1951).
WEINGREEN, J., *Introduction to the Critical Study of the Hebrew Bible* (Oxford, 1982).
WÜRTHWEIN, E., *The Text of the Old Testament* (2nd Eng. edn., London, 1979).

(ii) Samaritan Pentateuch
COGGINS, R. J., *Samaritans and Jews. The Origins of Samaritanism Reconsidered* (Oxford, 1975).
PURVIS, J. D., *The Samaritan Pentateuch and the Origin of the Samaritan Sect* (Harvard–Oxford, 1968).
WALTKE, B. K., 'The Samaritan Pentateuch and the Text of the Old Testament', ch. 14 in *New Perspec-*

tives on the Old Testament (ed. J. B. Payne; Waco, 1970).

(iii) Septuagint and Related Versions

JELLICOE, S., *The Septuagint and Modern Study* (Oxford, 1968).

JELLICOE, S. (ed.), *Studies in the Septuagint: Origins, Recensions, and Interpretations* (New York, 1974).

KENYON, F. G., and ADAMS, A. W., *The Text of the Greek Bible* (3rd edn., London, 1975).

GOODING, D. W., *Relics of Ancient Exegesis* (Cambridge, 1976).

TOV, E., *The Text-Critical Use of the Septuagint in Biblical Research* (Jerusalem, 1981).

WALTERS, P., *The Text of the Septuagint. Its Corruptions and their Emendation*, ed. D. W. Gooding (Cambridge, 1973).

(iv) Targums

BOWKER, J. W., *The Targums and Rabbinic Literature* (Cambridge, 1969).

CHILTON, B. D., *The Glory of Israel. The Theology and Provenience of the Isaiah Targum* (Sheffield, 1983).

CHURGIN, P., *Targum Jonathan to the Prophets* (New Haven, 1927).

LEVEY, S. H., *The Messiah: An Aramaic Interpretation. The Messianic Exegesis of the Targum* (New York, 1974).

McNAMARA, M., *The New Testament and the Palestinian Targum to the Pentateuch* (Rome, 1966/1978).

McNAMARA, M., *Targum and Testament* (Shannon, 1972).

(v) Peshitta

EMERTON, J. A., 'Unclean Birds and the Origin of the Peshitta', *JSS* VII (1962), pp. 204–211.

KOSTER, M. D., *The Peshitta of Exodus* (Assen, 1977).

LAMSA, G. M. (tr.), *The Holy Bible from Ancient Eastern Manuscripts* (Philadelphia, 1957).

ROBINSON, T. H., 'The Syriac Bible', ch. III in *The Bible in its Ancient and English Versions*, ed. H. W. Robinson (Oxford, 1940 [repr. 1954]).

(vi) Vulgate

KELLY, J. N. D., *Jerome: His Life, Writings and Controversies* (London, 1975).

SPARKS, H. F. D., 'The Latin Bible', ch. IV in *The Bible in its Ancient and English Versions*, ed. H. W. Robinson (Oxford, 1940 [repr. 1954]).

CANON AND APOCRYPHA OF THE OLD TESTAMENT

GERALD F. HAWTHORNE

DEFINITION OF TERMS

The word canon is derived from the Greek *kanōn*, a word which literally means a rod, a bar or a line, such as a mason's plumb-line. It was used to measure things or to keep an object on a straight course.

Metaphorically the word came to mean the standard by which people compared things and by which they judged their qualities or worth (cf. Gal. 6: 16). Sometimes canon referred to the rules of an art or trade, or the pattern used to guide the artisan. In sculpture, for example, the spearman, Polycletus, 'was regarded as the canon or perfect form of the human frame' (*TDNT*, 3.597). His figure was the sculptors' model of excellence.

From this metaphorical meaning came the idea of applying the word canon to a list of sacred writings that possessed special divine authority—an authority that gave these writings a normative quality. They became, therefore, the standard, the model, the paradigm by which the devout could evaluate other writings or ideas, and the rule by which they could regulate their own faith, teaching and practice.

It is this latter meaning we have in mind when we speak of the OT canon—a collection of writings inspired by the Spirit of God, holy, sacred, authoritative. This canon contains (1) the Pentateuch (Gen., Exod., Lev., Num., Dt.), (2) the Prophets: the Former Prophets (Jos., Jg., 1–2 Sam., 1–2 Kg.) and the Latter Prophets (Isa., Jer., Ezek. and the Twelve, i.e. the so-called 'Minor Prophets') and (3) The Writings (Ps., Prov., Job, Ca., Ru., Lam., Ec., Est., Dan., Ezr.–Neh. and 1–2 Chr.). Although at different times and in different places these OT books may vary in order or in number (the number of canonical books ranges from 22 to 39, depending on how they are grouped together), yet for Jews and most Protestants *all* of these books and *only* these books make up the OT canon—a closed and normative record of divine revelation.

Apocrypha also comes from a Greek word—the word *apokryphos*. Originally it meant 'hidden' or 'secret things', 'things obscure or hard to understand'. Eventually however, like the word 'canon', it became a technical term ap-plied to sacred and authoritative scriptures; it was so used by Jerome to designate those books which other church fathers had called 'ecclesiastical'—i.e. worthy to be read in church but not to be employed for the establishment of doctrine.

No one knows exactly why this word was chosen to describe these sacred writings. Possibly it was because some people considered them too sacred to be used by the common person or too deep or difficult to be understood by the uninitiated. Hence, they were kept hidden from him. Perhaps, on the other hand, it was because some thought them unworthy of being read along with the 'true holy scriptures', or as dangerous documents full of false and destructive teachings that should be kept secret from the ignorant masses who are easily led astray.

Whatever the real reason may have been, the term 'OT Apocrypha' now refers to the writings excluded from the Hebrew canon but included nevertheless in the canon of some Christians, especially that of Roman Catholics. These writings are 15 in number and include 1–2 Esdras, Tobit, Judith, The Rest of the Chapters of the Book of Esther, the Wisdom of Solomon, Ecclesiasticus, Baruch, A Letter of Jeremiah, The Song of the Three, Daniel and Susanna, Daniel Bel and the Snake, the Prayer of Manasseh and 1–2 Maccabees (cf. NEB). Only 8 of these books, however, show up in the table of contents of Roman Catholic Bibles (cf. JB), because 1–2 Esdras and the Prayer of Manasseh were not canonized by the Council of Trent (A.D. 1546) and are consequently omitted altogether, and because The Rest of Esther forms an integral part of Esther, while The Song of the Three, Susanna, and Bel and the Snake form an integral part of Daniel.

It should be noted that Roman Catholics prefer the expression 'deuterocanonical' to 'Apocrypha' for these books, not because by this term they consider them less inspired or less authoritative than the 'protocanonical' books (those of the Hebrew canon). They prefer it simply because this term highlights the fact that after doubt and dispute these books were finally defined and accepted as part of the canon but at a later date than that of the books of the Hebrew canon (cf. *New Catholic Ency-clopaedia*, 2.386; 3.29).

FORMATION OF THE OT CANON

The 39 books of the OT canon have been a part of the Christian Bible so long that we may have entertained the idea that God dropped all 39 books down from heaven bound in a single volume at one moment. But the very word 'canon' implies time and reflection and decision. Out of the many Hebrew writings composed during hundreds of years of Hebrew life, only some of them by divine providence and influence and human selection were chosen to be the standard, the normative rule for faith and practice. In other words the OT canon has a history.

(a) **Sources for the reconstruction of this history**

It is not at all easy to reconstruct a history of the formation of the OT canon, nor can this task be accomplished with certainty or exactitude. The reason for this lies in the sources we must use. They are sparse, vague and in some cases legendary. Their writers were not twentieth century critical scholars setting out to write at every step of the way a precise account of how and when each book of the OT was completed and acknowledged as inspired.

(i) **The OT.** One of these sources is the OT, but even the OT has little to say about itself—who wrote its different books, how and when they were finally assembled into an orderly corpus or what people were influential in the various stages of its development. For example, parts of the Pentateuch claim to be written by Moses: God's promise to blot out Amalek (Exod. 17: 14); the covenant-law of Exodus 20–24; 34 (note especially 24: 4 and 34: 27); the account of Israel's travels as recorded in Numbers (cf. Num. 33: 1–2); and if not the whole of the book of Deuteronomy at least chapters 27: 1–31: 9 (note 31: 9 ff.), etc. But nowhere within the first five books of the OT does it explicitly state that Moses was the author of the whole, the architect responsible for putting together and preserving in written form the ancient traditions of Genesis along with the new laws of God's covenant with Israel. Many times over such expressions as 'the LORD said unto Moses' occur throughout Exodus–Deuteronomy but although these expressions may argue for the inspiration of the Pentateuch they do not tell us clearly that Moses wrote down all that the LORD had said to him. Oral communication between inspired prophet and his fellow man was by no means a thing of the past.

Nor does any additional help concerning the final composition of the Pentateuch come from the later periods of Hebrew history. Certainly

the laws of Moses, even the written laws of Moses, are constantly referred and appealed to as an authoritative body of literature: Joshua (8: 34), Judges (3: 4), Kings (1 Kg. 2: 3; 8: 9; 2 Kg. 14: 6; 18: 4–6), Chronicles (2 Chr. 25: 4), Nehemiah (9: 14; 13: 1–2), etc.—all are witnesses to this fact. The sacredness of Moses' laws was unquestioned (2 Kg. 8: 9)—to obey them was to obey God. But again, these later writers tell us little of the composition of the Pentateuch as a whole. Almost every book in the OT pictures Moses as 'the fountain of Israel's law', and the prophets warned the nation against what would happen if it neglected the Law, but not one of them explicitly attributes to Moses anything more than the 'heart' of the Pentateuch—the covenant-law. On at least two occasions Israel promised to obey this Book of the Law that God had given them through Moses—once during Josiah's reign (2 Kg. 23: 2 ff.; 2 Chr. 34: 30 ff.) and again under Ezra and Nehemiah (Ezr. 7: 6, 14; Neh. 8: 1 ff.), all of which implies that this Law was regarded as canonical scripture. But what this Book of the Law consisted of no one knows—part of the Pentateuch surely, but possibly not the whole of it.

Hence the information gleaned from the OT permits only the following conclusions. It permits us to conclude that the *idea* of a canon is very old, going all the way back to the authoritative commands of God given to Adam, Noah, Abraham and especially to Moses, and that God could and did reveal his will in written form with the result that these written documents became sacred and normative. But it does not allow us to conclude with equal certainty what the extent of these documents were or that Moses was the author of the Pentateuch in all its parts, that he alone put this part of the canon together in its final form as known to us today.

What about the origin and formation of the so-called prophetic books of the OT? Again the witness of the OT to its own history—who wrote what books at what time and how they and they alone came to be considered sacred scripture—seems slight. For example, did Joshua the son of Nun write the book that bears his name? Perhaps. But no such claim for authorship comes from within the book itself. Nor is it possible to argue from Jos. 24: 26 ('And Joshua recorded these things in the Book of the Law of God') that 'the Book of Joshua was written by Joshua the prophet and added to the Pentateuch' (Harris, *ZPEB*, i, p. 715), because the expression, 'these words which were written in the law of God' refer only to the covenant Joshua made with the people of Israel at the end of his life and not to the book as a whole. Hence the question of authorship still remains in doubt and as a consequence

the answer to the question about when it was written is also unresolved.

What we have said about Joshua applies equally to the books of Judges, of Samuel and of Kings—the remaining 'Former Prophets'. Their authors are not identified and the date of their composition is not specified. If these books as we know them today were not written during the period they describe (as some presume), they are based, nevertheless, on documents that easily could have been written coincident with the events recorded in them—documents such as the Book of the Wars of the Lord (Num. 21: 14), the Book of Jashar (Jos. 10: 13; 2 Sam. 1: 18), a book written by Samuel about the rights and duties of kingship (1 Sam. 10: 25), the Book of the Acts of Solomon (1 Kg. 11: 41), the Book of the Chronicles of the Kings of Israel (1 Kg. 14: 19) and of Judah (1 Kg. 14: 29). It is a fact of history, however, that 'the Former Prophets' survived and became part of the OT canon, while their sources disappeared into oblivion. But why, especially since it is possible that some of these written sources were definitely prophetic in origin—The Chronicles of Samuel the Seer, of Nathan the Prophet, of Gad the Seer, of Shemaiah the Prophet, of Iddo the Seer, of Jehu the Son of Hanani (1 Chr. 29: 29; 2 Chr. 12: 15; 20: 34); and the Chronicles of the Seers (2 Chr. 33: 19)? And when did they become canonical? And under what circumstances? The OT does not itself answer these questions.

Nor does the OT fully answer these same questions when they are asked of the Latter Prophets—Isaiah, Jeremiah, Ezekiel and the Twelve. For the most part the message of the prophets was given orally (the Hebrew, *massā'*, 'lifting up' i.e. of the voice, found so frequently in Isaiah and translated 'oracle' implies a spoken word [of judgment]). Hence we are left wondering whether the prophet himself wrote the book that bears his name, or whether the job of collecting and writing down his oracles was left to his disciples, i.e. 'sons of the prophets' (cf. 2 Kg. 2: 3), to be done immediately (note that Baruch, the scribe, 'had written at Jeremiah's dictation'—Jer. 36: 4, 18, 27, 32; cf. also Isa. 8: 16), or at a later time. Although the information provided by the OT itself does not permit us dogmatically to say when each of these prophetic books was written or by whom, we can say that their very structure, built as it was around the expressions 'thus saith the LORD', or 'the word of the LORD came to the prophet', etc., marked them off as authoritative. And we can say too that this authoritativeness was enhanced when the prophets' predictive words of judgment came true in the national disasters that struck Israel and Judah and when the prophets' prophecies were quoted as the inspired word of the Lord

to be confidently depended on (cf. Ezr. 1: 1; Dan 9: 2; Zech. 7: 12, etc.). It was inevitable then that these books should become part of the OT canon.

What of the remaining books of the canon —Ruth, 1–2 Chronicles, Ezra, Nehemiah, Esther, Job, Psalms, Proverbs, Ecclesiastes, Song of Solomon, Lamentations and Daniel? The OT itself again has little or nothing to say about who actually wrote these books, or exactly when they were composed and took their place in the canon of scripture. Thus we are compelled to agree with the statement that while the OT 'legitimately ought to be allowed to define and describe canonicity, it has in point of fact almost nothing to say about the manner in which the holy writings were assembled or the personages who exercised an influence over the corpus during the diverse stages of its growth' (Harrison, p. 262).

(ii) **Sources outside the OT.** In spite of the fact that the OT has little to say about its own historical development, yet when the 39 books of the Hebrew canon were finally completed, it was they and not their underlying sources that the people preferred, accepted and used as sacred scripture. But when were these books completed and considered as canonical? Since the OT itself does not answer this question we must look elsewhere. In spite of the many external witnesses to the OT scriptures, the question is never really fully answered.

Our earliest witness to the completion of the OT canon is the Samaritan Pentateuch. According to Neh. 13: 28 and Josephus, *Antiquities*, 11.5.7–8, Nehemiah, about 432 B.C., chased the son-in-law of Sanballat the Horonite from Jerusalem, who then founded the religious community of the Samaritans in separation from the Jews. He built a temple on Mount Gerizim to rival the one in Jerusalem and took with him the sacred scriptures of the Jews. Since the Samaritan Bible consists only of the Pentateuch (with a modified book of Joshua—not, however, reckoned as part of the Bible—that included a history down to Roman times), it has been assumed by many that the later literature of the OT canon had not yet been developed or at least had not yet been looked upon as sacred. The difficulty with this assumption is that it is based on silence. Perhaps the Samaritans rejected the other parts of the canon because those parts championed the temple at Jerusalem and contained so many anti-Ephraimitic expressions (Bentzen, p. 35). The only certain fact is that at least by 432 B.C. the Pentateuch was completed and was looked upon as a unit and considered canonical.

The Septuagint (LXX), the first translation of the OT, is another early witness to the existence of a canon of scripture. This translation project took place in Egypt and was planned, according to legend, by Ptolemy Philadelphus (285–247 B.C.). *The Epistle of Aristeas* (c. 100 B.C.) narrates this legend, telling how 72 translators proficient in Hebrew and Greek were brought by Ptolemy to Alexandria and were accommodated on the island of Pharos where, in consultation with one another, they produced an agreed translation. Later traditions (recorded, *e.g.*, by Philo, Irenaeus and Clement of Alexandria) embellished the legend by describing how the translators were sequestered in 72 separate rooms, and produced 72 independent translations, each of which when examined agreed with the others word for word! If this story could be believed it would not only prove that the LXX was inspired but that the entire OT was recognized as canonical as early as 250 B.C. But it cannot be trusted to say more than that the translation project was begun sometime during the third century B.C.—begun no doubt with the Pentateuch. 'The lack of unity of plan in the books outside the Law indicates that probably many different hands at different times were engaged upon them' (Robinson, p. 556). The LXX, therefore, which probably took the greater part of a century (c. 250–150 B.C.) to complete, tells us little more than that the earliest canon of OT scripture was the Pentateuch.

Jesus ben Sira (c. 180 B.C.) wrote in Hebrew a book entitled Ecclesiasticus. In this work, the Law holds supreme place in the thought and admiration of Ben Sira (2: 16; 19: 20–24; 39: 1). Yet in chapters 44–50 he sings a 'hymn to the fathers' and praises the famous men of the OT from Enoch to Nehemiah indicating thereby that he knew of the existence of most if not all of the OT canon. Whether he thought of this canon as a 'closed' canon is another matter however. For in 24: 33 ('I will yet pour out teaching as prophecy and leave it for generations yet to come') Ben Sira seems to indicate that he thought of himself as an inspired person capable of writing normative truth that should be added to whatever canon there was.

The grandson of Jesus ben Sira translated Ecclesiasticus into Greek and added a prologue of his own. This prologue (c. 130 B.C.) is perhaps the earliest witness to the canonicity of the whole OT. It is certainly the earliest witness to the fact that the Hebrew canon was divided into three parts—Law, Prophets and Writings (Hagiographa). His words are: 'Whereas many and great things have been delivered unto us by the Law and the Prophets, and by others . . . the Law and the Prophets and the other books of our fathers . . . the Law, the Prophets and the rest of the books.' From these statements it is clear that the names he consistently gives to the first two groups are the standard technical terms used to denote the Pentateuch and the Former and Latter Prophets. But he describes the last group in such a general way that (i) he could be referring to that final miscellaneous collection of canonical writings now known as the Hagiographa and hence, he becomes a witness to a closed canon of 39 books, or (ii) he could be indicating that this last section was not yet complete and that the canon was still open in his day as in the day of his grandfather.

The texts from the caves of Qumran are an added early witness to the formation of the OT canon. These Dead Sea Scrolls belonged to a sect which separated from the rest of Judaism no later than c. 130 B.C., and occupied Khirbet Qumran for approximately 200 years. These scrolls contain quotations from most of the books of the OT. Investigations carried out on these quotations indicate 'that not later than about 130 B.C. the Law and the Prophets (in the Hebrew sense of the word) and most of the Writings (Hagiographa) were accepted and *regarded as canonical* with possibly some doubt about Ecclesiastes, Canticles, Esther and Ecclesiasticus' (Eybers, p. 36).

I Maccabees (c. 130 B.C.) is important because it singles out Daniel and the Psalms and apparently testifies to the fact that these books were treated as canonical in the second century B.C. I Mac. 1: 54 tells how Antiochus Epiphanes erected the 'Abomination of Desolation' in Jerusalem (Dan. 9: 24–27); I Mac. 2: 59–60 describes the deliverance of the three Hebrew children from the fiery furnace and Daniel from the lions (Dan. 1: 7; 3: 26; 6: 23) and I Mac. 7: 16–17 quotes expressly from the Psalms (Ps. 79: 2).

2 Maccabees (c. 124 B.C.) mentions two letters supposedly sent in 144 B.C. by Palestinian Jews to their brethren in Egypt. One of these, after some apocryphal stories about Jeremiah and Nehemiah, continues: 'The same things were also reported in the public archives and in the records relating to Nehemiah, and how, founding a library he gathered together the things concerning the kings and prophets, and the [writings] of David, and letters of kings about sacred gifts. And in like manner Judas also gathered together for us all those writings that had been scattered . . . by reason of the war that we had; and they remain with us' (2: 13–15).

The importance of these letters lies in the fact that, though they themselves may be spurious, they contain what seems to be a true recollection of an early stage in the formation of the OT canon. For the remark about 'the things relating to the kings and prophets' no doubt refers to the Former and Latter Prophets; 'the [writings] of David,' is an expression recalling the book of Psalms or some part of it; and the words, 'letters of kings respecting offerings', recollects those edicts of Persian kings issued in favour of the reconstruction of the temple as found in Ezra–Nehemiah. These remarks indicate that the books of the second division of the OT canon (the Prophets) and some from the third (the Hagiographa) were gathered together by Nehemiah to form part of a larger collection or library founded by him. Note, however, they link the name of Nehemiah (5th century B.C.) with preserving the canon, not with composing it or putting the final editing touches upon it. It is impossible to infer from these statements that Nehemiah had anything to do with canonizing even a part of the OT —only with recognizing that these books mentioned were authoritative and worth adding to those he already possessed.

Philo (d. *c*. A.D. 50) also is a witness to the tripartite division of the OT canon. He writes of 'laws, and the words foretold by the prophets, and hymns and other writings' (*De vita contemplativa*, 25). Yet for him the Law and the Law alone, was the super canon. He never gives an exegesis, in the true sense of the word, of a passage not found in the Pentateuch. He simply alludes to texts from other parts of the OT in the course of expounding sections of the Torah (Von Campenhausen, p. 14). His manner of quoting, however, is instructive. Even though he may have held that inspiration was not confined to the OT scriptures (Green, p. 130), yet he never once quoted from sources outside the canonical OT scriptures—not once from the Apocrypha. The canon he used, therefore, was essentially the canon of the Hebrew OT. Does action belie one's true creed?

The NT is perhaps the best early (AD 50-100) witness to a 'fixed' canon of OT scripture. Though more will be said about the relation of the OT to the NT later, note in passing that the NT writers refer to the OT as 'the scripture' (Jn 10: 35; 2 Pet. 1: 20), 'holy scriptures' (Rom. 1: 2), 'the Law' (Jn 10: 34), 'the law and the Prophets' (Mt. 5: 17), etc. The term 'Law' especially was a title that could be applied to any part of the OT (Jn 12: 34; 15: 25; 1 C. 14: 21). 'Such names or titles, though they do not define the limits of the canon, certainly assume the existence of a complete and sacred collection of Jewish writings which are already marked off from all other literature as separate and fixed' (Robinson, p. 558). Yet the one passage in the NT which gives clear evidence of the tripartite division of the OT (Lk. 24: 44), also sounds a note of uncertainty about the limits and contents of the third division. Instead of, 'The Law, the Prophets and the Writings', Luke says, 'The Law, the Prophets and the Psalms'. [Since Psalms heads up this third group, is it possible he was using it as a non-technical title for the whole?]

Flavius Josephus, the famous Jewish historian, a priest and a nobleman, wrote an important treatise in defence of the Jews. It was entitled *Contra Apionem*, and is dated *c*. A.D. 100. In this treatise is a section (1.8) of special interest for our discussion about the history of the canon and about the theory of inspiration and canonicity. Here is what he wrote: 'For we do not have vast numbers of books discordant and conflicting with one another. We have only twenty-two, containing the record of all time, books that are justly believed to be divine. And of these books, five are the books of Moses, which embrace the laws and the earliest traditions from the creation of mankind down to the time of his own death . . . From the death of Moses to the reign of Artaxerxes, King of Persia, the successor of Xerxes, the prophets who followed Moses wrote the history of the events that occurred in their time in thirteen books. The remaining four documents comprise hymns to God and practical precepts to men. From Artaxerxes to our own time everything has been recorded in detail. But these recent records have not been deemed worthy of equal credit with those which preceded them, because the exact succession of the prophets ceased. But what faith we have placed in our own writings is evident by our conduct; for though so long a time has now passed, no one has dared either to add, or to remove, or to alter a syllable. But it is natural for all Jews from their very birth to regard them as commands of God.'

There are several things to note from these remarks of Josephus. (i) For him the canon whose verbal form was inviolable was closed and in fact had been closed from the time of Artaxerxes (465–425 B.C.)—essentially the time of Malachi. 'The number of "reliable" books which allow for no alteration and are the code on which Jewish life is based . . . is final . . . and a sharp line is drawn between them and the numerous records of the period after Artaxerxes which cannot be fully trusted' (Katz, p. 76). (ii) This closed canon was a canon of twenty-two books arranged in three parts —five books of Moses, thirteen of prophets and four of hymns and practical precepts. Unfortunately Josephus does not state which books were included among the prophets or the hymns. Presumably, however, the thirteen books of the prophets included Joshua, Judges-Ruth, Samuel, Kings, Chronicles, Ezra-Nehemiah, Esther, Isaiah, Jeremiah–Lamentations, Ezekiel, Daniel, the Twelve Minor Prophets and possibly Job (or Canticles). The hymns and precepts then, would be made up of Psalms, Proverbs, Ecclesiastes and Canticles (or Job). If this presumption is correct, his OT canon would be identical with ours irrespective of how he arranged the books within it. [Note: According to this first century A.D. arrangement Esther, Ezra–Nehemiah, Daniel and possibly Canticles are included among the Prophets and not among the Writings as in the present Hebrew canon. This reflects a pre-rabbinic order 'which combines characteristics of the final Greek and Hebrew arrangements and is one of the various orders current in contemporary Palestine' (Katz, p. 77).] (iii) Finally, Josephus' remarks provide the first criterion for deciding whether or not a book is canonical, one of unquestioned authority: Was it written by a prophet? Josephus believed that from Moses to Artaxerxes there was an un-broken succession of prophets who wrote the history and thought of their own times, and that it was this that gave to his 22 books their intrinsic and unique holiness. With Artaxerxes, however, this prophetic activity came to an end. Consequently, although everything that happened from Artaxerxes to Josephus was recorded in detail, these later records were not considered of equal worth to the writings that had preceded them—they had no prophetic origin to make them trustworthy in the same sense. Josephus rests his case for this idea of canonicity on no authority other than his own. But this could be, and very likely is, because he was simply verbalizing a widespread current belief—a generally accepted idea that needed no proving.

Second Esdras (Fourth Esdras in the Latin) is a Jewish apocryphal book originally written in Greek at the end of the first century A.D. Although it is legendary in nature it seems nevertheless to reflect a genuine Jewish tra-dition that links Ezra in some literary way to the OT canon. In it Ezra laments that the Law had been burned in the destruction of Jerusalem and prays for the ability to rewrite it: 'Fill me with your Holy Spirit, so that I may write down the whole story of the world from the very beginning, everything that is contained in your law'. God answered Ezra's prayer and the story continues: 'I took with me the five men as I had been told, and we went away . . . On the next day I heard a voice calling me, which said: "Ezra, open your mouth and drink what I give you". So I opened my mouth, and was handed a cup full of what seemed like water, except that its colour was the colour of fire. I took it and drank, and as soon as I had done so my mind began to pour forth a flood of understanding, and wisdom grew greater and greater within me, for I retained my memory unimpaired. I opened my mouth to speak, and I continued to speak unceasingly. The Most High gave understanding to the five men, who took turns at writing down what was said, using characters which they had not known before. They remained at work through the forty days, writing all day, and taking food only at night. But as for me, I spoke all through the day; even at night I was not silent. In the

forty days, ninety-four books were written. At the end of the forty days the Most High spoke to me. "Make public the books you wrote first" he said, "to be read by good and bad alike, but the last seventy books are to be kept back, and given to none but the wise among your people. They contain a stream of under-standing, a fountain of wisdom, a flood of knowledge." And I did so' (14: 21–22; 37–48).

This passage, though hardly historical, pro-vides some interesting insights. It explains why the Law of Moses was not known to those returning to Jerusalem from their exile in Baby-lon. It joins with Josephus as one of the first two witnesses to the number of books in the OT canon. Whereas Josephus numbers 22 books, 2 Esdras gives 24, the number that corresponds with the regular Jewish compu-tation (Gen., Exod., Lev., Num., Jos., Jg., Sam., Kg., Jer., Ezek., Isa. , The Twelve, Ru., Ps., Job, Prov., Ec., Ca., Lam., Dan., Est., Ezr.–Neh. and Chr.). 2 Esdras seems also to equate the Law of God with the whole OT *e.g.*, the 24 books for 'public consumption' (plus the 70 other books that were written), and not to distinguish between the 'canonical' books and the 70 books reserved only for the wise in Israel as far as inspiration is concerned. And finally, 2 Esdras brings Ezra and his com-panions into close literary connection with the Law (cf. Ezr. 7: 6 and TB Sukkah 20a: 'The Law was forgotten out of Israel; Ezra came up and established it'). Could this be a fanciful way of saying that Ezra and the 'Great Synagogue' were instrumental in closing the Hebrew canon? Hardly. For 2 Esdras may indeed reflect a genuine tradition indicating that Ezra as scribe did editorial work on the canon, but it does not say categorically that he and his companions 'canonized' the scriptures.

For many scholars the councils held *c.* A.D. 90 in Jamnia (Jabneh), a place not far south of Joppa on the Mediterranean Sea, were decisive for canonizing the 39 books of the OT (see Bentzen, pp. 22–29; Von Campenhausen, p. 5). But too little is known about these councils to be so sure. What is known is that after the destruction of Jerusalem, Rabbi Johanan ben Zakkai asked permission from the Romans to establish his school at Jamnia. Here Rabbinic debates over whether or not the scriptures 'defile the hands' took place, and discussions about the canonicity of certain books—Ezekiel, Ecclesiastes, Canticles, Proverbs, Esther—went on from time to time. But 'the sources . . . do not preserve a record of any official canonical debate at Jabneh during Johanan's leadership'. From this 'it would appear that the frequently made assertions that a binding decision was made at Jabneh covering all scrip-tures is conjectural at best . . . Sounder scholar-ship is to admit ignorance and to allow the questions to remain as vague as the sources' (Lewis, pp. 126, 132). But from what little can be known it seems that the discussions at Jabneh centred more around which books should be excluded from the canon than which books should be included in it. Indications are that the canon was already fairly well defined before the meetings of the 'academy,' or 'court,' or 'school' at Jamnia took place. Questions, however, about the canonicity of Proverbs, Canticles, Ecclesiastes, Esther, Ezekiel and Jonah continued to be raised by Jewish leaders well on into the second century and beyond.

Our final witness to the formation of the canon is from the Talmud, a Jewish work consisting of (i) the Mishna (finished *c.* A.D. 200) and (ii) the Gemara, a gigantic commentary on the Mishna (finished *c.* A.D. 500). In the Babylonian Talmudic treatise called *Baba Bathra* (14b–15a) there is an extract, a famous unauthorized gloss (a *baraitha*), coeval with the Mishna (though not included in it) which among other things lists the books of the OT in much the same order as now found in the Hebrew Bible. In addition to the Book of Moses the order of the prophets is Joshua, Judges, Samuel, Kings, Jeremiah, Ezekiel, Isaiah [note the unusual order of Jeremiah, Ezekiel and Isaiah], the Twelve. That of the *Kethûbîm* [Writings, Hagiographa] is Ruth, Psalms, Job, Proverbs, Ecclesiastes, Song of Solomon, Lamentations, Daniel, the roll of Esther, Ezra and Chronicles.

This *baraitha* tells us too who wrote the OT books. Although this treatise is considered to be 'destitute of historical value, late in date and discredited by its own contents' (Driver, p. vi), it may, nevertheless, reflect accurately a belief held by many Jewish people in its own time and possibly centuries earlier. Undoubtedly it influenced the thinking of later writers about authorship and underscores the criterion for canonicity already expressed by Josephus: Only those works that can properly claim prophetic origin have a right to be included in the canon. 'Who wrote the books?' this *baraitha* asks. 'Moses wrote his book, the section about Balaam and Job; Joshua wrote his book and the last eight verses of the Torah; Samuel wrote his books, Judges and Ruth. David wrote the Psalms at the direction of the Ten Ancients . . . Jeremiah wrote his book, the book of Kings and Lamentations; King Hezekiah and his council wrote Isaiah, Proverbs, Song of Solomon and Ecclesiastes. The men of the Great Synagogue wrote Ezekiel, the Twelve Prophets, Daniel and Esther. Ezra wrote his own book and the genealogy of Chronicles down to his own period. Nehemiah completed it' (see Ryle, Excursus B, for the complete text. 'The separate books of the Pentateuch are not mentioned nor more than four of the Minor

Prophets; but the former are, of course, implied by the "Torah" and the latter by the "Twelve".').

Thus it is that this treatise contains interesting strange and sometimes incredible traditions about the authorship of the OT books. It is another witness to the three-part division of the OT, and it seems, along with 2 Esdras, to have provided the materials from which the Jewish scholar Elias Levita (1549) concocted his dubious theory that all the books and documents pertaining to the OT previously handed down separately were collected by Ezra and his companions (i.e. the men of the 'Great Synagogue'), arranged into the familiar three parts of the OT and closed so as permanently to exclude any other writings from this canon. But in actuality it provides no solid evidence with which we can confidently construct a reliable history of the formation of the canon.

(b) Summary and Conclusion

After this lengthy survey of the witnesses to the OT canon we still know very little about the canon—how it came to be, about the process of canonization: the writing, the collecting, the editing, the evaluating, the selecting, etc. —the when, where, why and under what circumstances these books of the OT came to be. We discovered that the OT gives no complete autobiography of its own existence from written document to completed canon. The Samaritan Bible tells us only that the Pentateuch was regarded as sacred and normative scripture by 432 B.C.—other books of the OT beside the Pentateuch may have been in existence long before then, but the action of the Samaritans tells us nothing about that part of the story. The LXX indicates that all of the books of the Hebrew Bible were in completed form and were considered worthy of translation by at least 150 B.C. Jesus ben Sira knew of the canon by *c.* 180 B.C. but apparently did not think of it as something final or closed. His grandson was the first to mention a three-fold division of the OT and he was supported in this by Philo (*c.* A.D. 50), Josephus (*c.* A.D. 100) and the later Jewish traditions found in the Talmud. 1 Maccabees (*c.* 130 B.C.) testifies to the canonicity of Daniel and the Psalms. Josephus and Second Esdras are the first to give the total number of books in the canon although they do not agree as to what this number was (24 or 22). 2 Maccabees (*c.* 124 B.C.), 2 Esdras (*c.* A.D. 100) and the Talmud's tractate *Baba Bathra* (*c.* A.D. 200) connect Ezra (and Nehemiah) in some literary way with the canon—a fact which indicates that there was a long-held belief that Ezra played an important role in the history of the canon. What that role was, however, is not made clear. The available evidence, therefore, gives no real history of the formation of the canon.

Modern critical scholarship has attempted to fill in the blanks (see Harrison, pp. 279–83 for summaries). Some of these attempts though enlightening are inadequate if for no other reason than that they do not allow for direct revelation from God. They view the canon as a purely human product from conception to completion, from written document to action of councils that pronounced it normative for synagogue or church. Other attempts fail because they do not allow sufficiently for the human element in the process of producing a canon. In light of this the following is a somewhat imaginative history of the OT based on the biblical texts and the traditions noted above. It tries to combine both the divine and human aspects of holy scripture.

The ancient traditions dating back to the beginning of time that concerned the creation of the world, the origin of life, the activities of the antedeluvian patriarchs, etc., were likely handed on with sacred carefulness by word of mouth from generation to generation over hundreds of years from widely diverse circumstances and geographical backgrounds. These traditions were a sort of canon, because those who passed them on—priests perhaps—must have believed they had their origin in direct revelation from God. As a consequence these 'priests' likely insisted that every minute detail be memorized and repeated with great care.

Eventually these many oral traditions, these sacred stories, circulating in different parts of the ancient world took on written form. No one can say for sure when this happened or who was responsible for doing it. It could have happened a millenium before Moses' day. 'Writing was known and practised in the ancient Near East long before the Hebrews took possession of Palestine . . . so that early claims that writing was unknown in Palestine in patriarchal times are quite unfounded' (Bainton, *IDB*, 4.909). Recent archeological discoveries by two Italian scholars, Paolo Matthiae and Giovanni Pettinato, of some 20,000 tablets at Ebla (near Aleppo in Syria) written in a new West Semitic dialect and dating *c.* 2400–2300 B.C. simply confirm this fact (see *Orientalia*, 44, 3 [1975], 337–74).

Whenever and by whomever these traditions were written they too were no doubt looked upon as 'canonical,' at least in the sense that they were treated as divinely inspired holy writings, authoritative accounts of the acts of God in history, of human origins and of the roots of Hebrew civilization.

At some point in time these traditions, or historical epics, were collected and brought together around a common theme—the covenant relation between God and man, finding their focal point in the Law of God, the Torah. There are reasons for believing that Moses,

from the human point of view, was the genius behind this integrative effort even though he may not have given the Pentateuch its final form: (i) he could have learned the ancient traditional stories of origins and of the patriarchs from his family for his early training was at home (Exod. 2: 9); (ii) he became the 'son' of Pharaoh's daughter (Exod. 2: 10) and as such could have learned to read and write and to become steeped in the arts and sciences of the ancient world with opportunities to probe into the distant past and encounter widespread ideas of primal origins; (iii) he was the Law-giver par excellence and is forever remembered as *the* one man through whom God chose to mediate His covenant law to His people; his name has long been associated with the first five books of the OT; (iv) the Law in general and the book of Deuteronomy in particular go back to an early period in Hebrew history—to a period certainly as early as that of Moses. The 'curse'-formula, for example, called down on the head of anyone who dared to add to or subtract from an authoritative divinely mediated written code (Dt. 4: 2; 12: 32), is also found in the law code of the Babylonian king, Hammurabi, whose reign may have been as early as 1792–1750 B.C. (see J. B. Pritchard, ed., *Ancient Near Eastern Texts*, 1950, pp. 178 f.).

Hence, 'since there is not a single passage in the whole Pentateuch which can be seriously considered as showing [late or] post-exilic influence either in form or content' (Albright, *From Stone Age to Christianity*, p. 345), it is not presumptuous or naïve to agree with the traditional view that Moses himself was the one who put together much of what we know today as the Pentateuch.

However much Moses wrote during his lifetime, it immediately became 'canon'—recognized by the people of Israel as authoritative, (i) because of its intrinsic worth and (ii) because of the stature of Moses. He was their towering leader of state, a man through whom God revealed Himself and gave His laws. In one sense Moses' writings became the normative expression of God's will for Israel for all time, the 'canon supreme' against which all other books of the OT had to be measured. It is held that these later books never reached the same status as the Law even though they were inspired, the products of prophets of acknowledged authority. Somehow the name, *qabbala*, 'tradition', was attached to them because someone believed that they did not add anything to the law but only interpreted it to their times (Bentzen, p. 33). In any case, in the threefold division of the canon, the Law (a term of such importance that it was applied to the whole of the Pentateuch) always is given first place.

But history interpreted as the acts of God did not stop with Moses. No doubt part of this continuous history was preserved in song and story and circulated orally. But there is no reason to assume that all events of importance were so preserved until a late date. Writing existed early, and the odds are that many significant early happenings were immediately recorded in this more permanent form. At first these recorded happenings may have existed as isolated stories circulating separately without any kind of framework to tie them together. Gradually they were accumulated and put into some sort of a collection. Books sprang up, like the Book of Jashar, the Books of the Acts of the Kings of Israel and of the Kings of Judah, the Chronicles of the Seers, etc. These books and chronicles were the precursors of and among the sources for the historical books of the OT. But when and by whom were these latter books composed? No certain answer can be given to this question. In light of the testimony of the OT to itself and the later traditions noted above, however, it is a distinct possibility that they came into existence, and were given much the same form that they now possess, between the eighth and sixth centuries B.C. at the instigation and under the supervision of the prophets, perhaps Isaiah and Jeremiah to name only two—God's seers, men of divine wisdom and insight. For this reason the many stories that had been coming into existence over the centuries and were forming a huge pool of amorphous information were now worked over by inspired men who selected from these source materials things that harmonized with the covenant-law, and chronicled the continuing relationship between God and His people. They wrote interpreted history and it is not surprising then that Joshua, Judges, Samuel, and Kings are called the 'Former Prophets' and were readily greeted as authoritative.

While supervising the writing of the Former Prophets, if not doing the actual writing themselves, the prophets were sounding God's warnings against Israel and calling the people to repentance. Their many oracles were oral for the most part and spoken at different times and to different audiences. But they were remembered and preserved. The 'sons of the prophets' (2 Kg. 2: 3) or personal scribes such as Jeremiah's Baruch (Jer. 36: 4) were no doubt largely responsible for their preservation (cf. Isa. 8: 16). Some prophets may have written their own books or at least supervised the collection of their oracles in their own times. But it is also possible that the writings of some of the Latter Prophets (Isa. , Jer., Ezek. or the Twelve) were edited and published at a much later time. Perhaps Ezekiel himself, the prophet of exile, came into the possession of many of these earlier oracles of the different prophets, recognized their inspired nature in that their predictions had come true, and put them into a semblance of order according to the names of the prophets who uttered them.

What part did Ezra play in the formation of the OT? A long standing tradition links him in a literary way with the canon (2 Esd. 14: 21 ff.; *Baba Bathra* 14b). Such traditions though clearly legendary often have some basis in historical fact. Is it possible that Ezra, priest and scribe skilled in the Law (Ezr. 7: 6) and his associates (Neh. 8: 9) did the final editing of the Pentateuch, and the final collecting and editing of the Former and Latter Prophets? This is not to say that he or the 'Great Synagogue' in any way canonized these books. For it is apparent from the Biblical texts that the Law was something very old, much older than Ezra, something that had a long standing authority in the thinking of the people of Israel. It is simply to recognize that some one or some group under God had to bring these diverse materials together and unite them around a common theme—the same theme that gave cohesion to the materials in the Pentateuch: God's covenant with His people. It is obvious that the various stories, laws, oracles, etc. found in the OT and written over a long span of years did not come together of their own accord. Such a pious and literate scribe as Ezra, with his learned companions (including Nehemiah; cf. 2 Mac. 2: 13–15), certainly was capable of accomplishing such a challenging task—a task so historically and theologically important. And if their work went beyond collecting and editing, it would only be 'to approve as canonical works that had for a long time been venerated as authoritative'—not in any way to give them authoritative status (Harrison, p. 283).

In any case, the Former and Latter Prophets together constitute the second part of the canon. Somehow, by divine direction, these were selected from a larger body of Hebrew literature, were acknowledged by the people of God as normative scripture and were universally used as such—possibly since the time of Ezra and Nehemiah, if not before. In the traditions about the canon these books—the Prophets—are distinguished from the Law on the one hand and the Hagiographa on the other.

The Hagiographa (*Kethûbîm*, 'Writings') is the third and final part of the Hebrew canon. That the OT was divided into three parts is not questioned by many people. But why it was so divided and what books were in each division is a matter of debate.

Perhaps on the one hand the three sections reflect three stages in the development of the canon, with the Hagiographa being the last and latest stage in a chronological sequence. Perhaps on the other hand the tripartite division indicates that the first two parts were written by men recognized as belonging to the prophetic order while the last, although written by inspired men, was written by men who were kings (David, Solomon), civil servants (Daniel), governors (Nehemiah), etc., and not prophets in the technical sense. No question of time then would be involved and it would be possible for much of the Hagiographa to have been written before the earliest documents of the writing prophets. There is no agreement among students of the OT canon about the answer to this question. If I must choose between the two alternatives presented here I choose the latter because (i) it is a reasonable alternative and (ii) it does not imply that the books of this division must necessarily be assigned a late date of composition—i.e. a date later than the time of Ezra.

What books are included in this third division? Again there is no certain answer. A fairly uniform Jewish tradition (Talmudic, Massoretic and the printed editions of the Hebrew Bible) places in it in varying orders of arrangement, Psalms, Job, Proverbs, Ruth, Canticles, Ecclesiastes, Lamentations, Esther, Daniel, Ezra–Nehemiah and Chronicles. Jesus' words, 'From the blood of Abel to the blood of Zechariah,' in Mt. 23:25 and Lk. 11:51 in part support this tradition [critical problems are involved in the Matthaean text, however], for His words could mean that the Pharisees must answer for all murders recorded in the OT *from beginning to end*—Genesis, the first book of His Bible, describes the death of Abel and 2 Chronicles, the last book of His Bible, the death of Zechariah (24:20–21). The grandson of ben Sira, the first person to mention the three-fold division of the canon does not tell us at all what books were in these divisions. The Evangelist Luke (24:44) mentions only the Psalms when he refers to the final part of the canon. And Josephus (*Contra Apionem*, 1.8) categorically states that the remaining books, after the Law and Prophets, were only four in number and that these four were composed of hymns and practical precepts.

Hence, it is quite impossible to speak with any degree of confidence about this third division, about what books belong in it, whether one, four or eleven (Ru., Ps., Prov., Job, Ca., Ec., Lam., Est., Dan., Ezr.–Neh. and Chr.), about when the books in it took final shape, or who the human instrument was who wrote them or collected them, or what the motive was for preserving them. Perhaps Ezra again was the key person, not only in collecting and editing, but in composing some of them as well. It is at least worth reminding ourselves that for many centuries the view prevailed that the canon of the OT was completed within the lifetime of Ezra, a view that has some biblical foundation (Ezr. 7:10, 25; Neh. 8:1 ff.; 9:3), but that was enlarged upon by statements

found in 2 Esdras and *Baba Bathra* (see above). But the fact of the matter is we just do not know enough to say with certainty that the canon was completed and closed by the time Ezra and Nehemiah left the scene. Hence it is possible to assume the canon was still developing in the period following their era. Certainly the books of the *Hebrew* OT were in their final shape by the second century B.C., for all of them were available for translation into Greek (the LXX), and every OT book but Esther was quoted in the scrolls of Qumran. But it is not certain that the books of the Hebrew OT alone were considered by all to be the sum total of divine revelation. Jesus ben Sira considered his sayings prophetic and worthy of a place alongside the prophets. Apocalyptic literature was being produced in this period and was vying for a permanent place in the religious literature of the Jewish people. There are hints, therefore, that the third section of the canon was still an open-ended thing in the days of Ezra and afterwards.

Eventually, however, in that mysterious way explained as the providential working of God, some writings were universally accepted as normative and others were not. Those writings comprising the Hagiographa, whether one in number or eleven, were accepted and used because of their self-authenticating character, because they were in harmony with the religious outlook already expressed in the Pentateuch and the Prophets, and because of their close associations with the worship of Israel, its national history and its revered leaders of the past. 'Unfortunately it is virtually impossible to be more specific than this about the processes by which the OT canon, or parts of it, became acknowledged as authoritative' (Harrison, p. 263). By A.D. 90 the 'school' at Jamnia had only to recognize and put their stamp of approval on a body of literature that already had been canonized by common consent and constant usage—a canon *de facto* that turned out to be the 39 books of the Hebrew OT. This is not to say that all these books were 'approved' once and for all without question. Ezekiel, Esther, Canticles, Ecclesiastes and Proverbs precipitated countless debates over whether or not they deserved a place in the 'canon'. For some scholars they contained contradictions or were liable to make an erotic impression on the immature or reflected mere Hellenistic philosophies or made no reference to the name of God. But by virtue of their own intrinsic worth they won their right to rank as sacred scripture along with the Law and Prophets.

THE SEPTUAGINT AND THE OT APOCRYPHA

As noted above (pp. 26–7) the first major Greek

translation of the OT, the Septuagint (LXX), was begun in Alexandria, Egypt under Ptolemy Philadelphus (c. 250 B.C.). Behind this translation project was not merely the desire to add to the accumulated literary wealth of the library in Alexandria, but more importantly to give Jews living outside of Palestine who no longer spoke or read Hebrew, a Bible in a language they could understand. The first books to be translated no doubt were the books of Moses. Eventually, however, the remaining books of the OT were also translated into Greek.

But interestingly the completed LXX not only contained the 39 books of the Hebrew canon; it also contained other books as well, books commonly called apocryphal—1–2 (3–4) Esdras, Tobit, Judith, the Additions to Esther, the Wisdom of Solomon, Ecclesiasticus, Baruch, the Epistle of Jeremiah, the Song of the Three, Susanna, Bel and the Dragon, the Prayer of Manasseh and 1–2 Maccabees—books that for the most part were written in Hebrew and translated into Greek. (Only Wis., 2 Mac. and Ad. Est. were originally composed in Greek [Sundberg, *CBQ*, p. 30].)

The history of the origin of this more inclusive Bible is shrouded in mystery. Some of the so-called apocryphal writings date possibly from the third or second century B.C.; others as late as the first or second century A.D. Some may have been written in Palestine, others in Mesopotamia or Alexandria. Some had wide circulation and because of their popularity were translated into several languages. All, however, found their way eventually to Alexandria and at some unknown time and manner were collected and combined into a canon of scripture larger than the Palestinian canon. Proof of this is the fourth century A.D. manuscripts of the LXX which, although they do not all agree on the exact number of writings, nevertheless combine the so-called apocryphal books with the 39 books of the Hebrew canon in such a way that one group of writings cannot be distinguished from the other.

Were these 'extra' books collected as sacred scripture by Alexandrian Jews who had a wider concept of canon and a broader view of inspiration than Palestinian Jews? It is not possible to say. On the one hand the Palestinian Jewish break-away sect, the people of Qumran, seemed to make little serious effort to distinguish sharply between the books of the Hebrew canon and other similar works (Harrison, p. 279; Sundberg, *CBQ*, p. 146). On the other hand the Alexandrian Jewish exegete, Philo, kept himself strictly to the Palestinian canon. Though in theory he refused to acknowledge that inspiration and revelation were limited to the period from Moses to Artaxerxes, yet in practice he quoted only from the 39 books of

that period—never once did he quote from any apocryphal book.

Nor is it possible to say that the gathering together of these 'apocryphal' books was done by a Christian or group of Christians. It is true that these writings first came to light as a collection in the great Christian Bibles of the fourth and fifth centuries (Sinaiticus, Vaticanus, Alexandrinus). But this fact says nothing about who brought them together, saw them as inspired scripture and blended them in along with the 39 books of the Hebrew canon to form a new and larger canon. We just cannot answer the question of the origin of the Apocrypha as a body of scripture.

The question of why the collection called the Apocrypha was ever brought together or recognized as sacred scripture is not easy to answer either. From an historical point of view it is invaluable because it throws light on the period between the Testaments. It provides much information about what happened to the nation of Israel between its return from the exile to the coming of the Romans, about the developing concept in Jewish thinking of life after death and the resurrection of the body, about issues still very much alive in NT times —law, good works, sin and its origin in the fall, the end of the world, etc. From an ethical and moral point of view much of it is on a very high plane, profitable for reading, beneficial as a model for life. Like the other writings of the OT, much of it is genuinely in harmony with the spirit of the Law. Hence, one is not at all surprised that these works were collected and preserved.

And yet for the Jews these writings, as important as they seem to be, did not 'defile the hands.' That is to say the Jews did not consider them inspired. Why? Again here is a question not at all easy to answer. Perhaps these writings did not 'defile the hands' because some of them contained errors—historical, chronological and geographical. Perhaps it was because others of them seemed to justify falsehood or deception. Perhaps it was because still others taught that salvation depended on deeds of merit (Green, pp. 95 f.). Perhaps the answer only lies in falling back on the providential acts of God. For whatever reason the fact remains that the apocryphal books were excluded from the Hebrew canon at least from A.D. 90 on, but included in the canon of the Christian church.

THE NEW TESTAMENT AND THE OT CANON

Recent studies show that for all practical purposes the Bible of the NT writers was the LXX (see E. E. Ellis, *Paul's Use of the Old Testament*). Since the LXX as it is known from fourth century manuscripts contained the Apocrypha along with the 39 books of the Hebrew canon, it is presumed that Jesus and His apostles accepted this larger canon without question—that Ecclesiasticus was as much sacred scripture for them as was Isaiah. Perhaps. But the following things should be noted before drawing any conclusions: (i) Although we know what the LXX contained as scripture in the *fourth* century, we have no way of knowing for certain what it contained in the *first* century. (ii) Jesus' terms for the OT correspond with the traditional terms describing the Hebrew canon: 'The Law,' referring to the whole of the canon (Jn 10: 34; Ps. 82), or 'The Law and the Prophets,' including *Kethūbîm* among the 'Prophets' (Mt. 5: 17; 24: 15), or as Luke has it, 'the Law of Moses, the Prophets and the Psalms' (Lk. 24: 44). (iii) As observed above (p. 33) Jesus' words, 'from the blood of innocent Abel to the blood of Zechariah' imply that 2 Chronicles (cf. 2 Chr. 24: 20) was the last book in His canon as it was in the Hebrew canon from Jamnia onwards. (iv) Although one cannot escape the fact that the NT contains quotations from and allusions to writings beyond those of the Hebrew canon, *e.g.* Paul quotes Aratus' *Phaenomena* (Ac. 17: 28) and Jude, the Book of Enoch (Jude 14–15), etc., yet not one of the apocryphal books is directly quoted as scripture (Geisler, p. 38) and no NT writer introduces his references to literary sources outside the Hebrew Bible with formulas to indicate he thought of them as inspired scripture. Formulas such as, 'It is written,' or 'the scripture says,' are used only to preface quotations from the 39 books of the Hebrew canon.

Thus, although the apocryphal books were in existence in the first century A.D., and probably formed a part of the LXX canon, and no doubt were known and used by some NT writers (cf. 1 C. 2: 9 with Sir. 1: 10; Heb. 1: 3 with Wis. 7: 25–27; Heb. 11: 35 with 2 Mac. 6: 18–7: 42, etc.; see Sundberg, *Old Testament of the Early Church*, pp. 54 f.), yet there is no clear evidence that the NT gave these writings the same status as it gave the writings of the Hebrew canon. In fact, the evidence points the other way. It seems to indicate that Jesus and the writers of the NT, while aware of the existence of the Apocrypha, deliberately chose not to recognize or use the Apocrypha as sacred scripture. It may not be possible to define with precision the concept of canon held by the scribes and Pharisees, the teachers of the law, in Jesus' day, or to determine in detail the contents of their canon. But it seems possible to say that the scriptures used by NT writers to explain the person and mission of Jesus were primarily those scriptures found in the Hebrew canon. In this sense we can say that for the writers of the NT the canon was closed—closed more by common consent and popular usage than by formal decree.

THE CHURCH AND THE CANON OF THE OT

If the NT quoted only from the writings of the Hebrew canon while merely alluding to the Apocrypha occasionally and without those formulas which denote inspiration, it is quite otherwise in the writings of the Fathers of the Christian Church. Clement of Rome (A.D. 95), for example, quotes from all three sections of the Hebrew canon—the Law, the Prophets and the Hagiographa—using formulas that indicate they possess divine authority. But he goes further than this and quotes also from the non-canonical writings, both the Apocrypha and the Pseudepigrapha, 'in a way not dissimilar to his use of the canonical writings' (Hagner, p. 111; see pp. 86–93). Interestingly though, Clement introduces no apocryphal writing with his special introductory formulas. But this is not regarded as significant since he employs these formulas with other non-canonical writings (Hagner, pp. 29–30). Polycarp, Barnabas, Irenaeus, Clement of Alexandria, Tertullian, Cyprian, Origen—Greek and Latin Fathers alike—quote both classes of books, those of the Hebrew canon and the Apocrypha, without distinction. Augustine (A.D. 354–430) in his *City of God* (18.42–43) argued for equal and identical divine inspiration for both the Jewish canon and the Christian canon: 'If anything is in the Hebrew copies and not in the versions of the Septuagint, the Spirit of God did not choose to say it through them, but only through the prophets. But whatever is in the Septuagint and not in the Hebrew copies, the same Spirit chose rather to say it through the latter and not the former, thus showing that both were mere prophets.' Augustine, though admitting to a difference between the Hebrew canon and the 'outside books,' nevertheless saw the former as appropriate for its time and the LXX as appropriate for the Church.

This acceptance of all books of the LXX as canonical persisted generally throughout the Church until the fourth century with possibly one exception. Melito of Sardis (d. *c.* A.D. 190) went from Asia Minor to Palestine and brought back from the East an official list of Hebrew scriptures. It contained 22 books essentially identical with the Hebrew canon, a canon that excluded the Apocrypha.

With few exceptions the Western writers continued even beyond the fourth century to regard the extra books of the LXX as equally canonical with those of the Hebrew OT. Three councils in North Africa (Hippo, A.D. 393 and Carthage, A.D. 397 and 419) included in their definitions of the OT both the protocanonical and the deuterocanonical books without distinction.

In the East opinion differed. Those writers such as Origen, Cyril of Jerusalem and Athanasius who had come in contact with the Hebrew concept of canon came to recognize a distinction between the two groups of writings. Jerome (d. A.D. 420), a Latin Father, because of his Hebrew studies, declared as aprocryphal all writings not contained in the Hebrew Bible. [Note: In spite of his theories on the canon he nevertheless included the Apocrypha according to church practice in his Latin translation of the Bible (the Vulgate).] Consequently in the thinking of some students of the canon 'the principal reason for the loss of authority suffered by [the Apocrypha] was that when the Jewish canon became known in the Church it was assumed *a priori*, that the Jewish canon was determinative for the OT of the Church' (Sundberg, *CBQ*, p. 152). 'Thus, in the early church the degree in which the Hebrew canon was esteemed determined the attitude adopted toward the Apocrypha' (Harrison, *ZPEB*, 1. 205).

With the discovery of the Hebrew texts and their translation and with the coming of the Reformation and its theme, *sola scriptura*, the whole question of what really constituted the holy scriptures was raised anew. Protestant leaders ignored traditional acceptance of all the books of the LXX and refused the status of inspiration to those books of the Vulgate not found in the Hebrew canon. Luther denied canonical status to the Apocrypha although he included them all (except 1–2 Esdras) as an appendix to his translation (1534). He called them 'useful and good to be read.' Calvin and his followers completely gave up the idea of canonicity for the Apocrypha and excluded them from the Bible because the Jews who had been entrusted with the oracles of God (Rom. 3: 2) had earlier rejected them from their canon. The Roman Catholic Church reacted quickly to all this and at the Council of Trent (1546) declared that the whole of the Apocrypha except for 1–2 Esdras and the Prayer of Manasseh were canonical and as fully inspired as were the other books of the OT.

In spite of this conflict of ideas the Apocrypha were included in many early English translations of the Bible, including the King James Version. Usually, however, they appeared with some sort of prefatory remark such as that these writings are valuable 'for knowledge of history and instruction of godly manners'. Later under Puritan pressure they were removed from between the covers of the Bible —an action reflecting the attitude contained in the Westminster Confession of Faith (1646–47) which stated that the Apocrypha were not 'to be otherwise approved or made use of than other human writings.' Today there is a revival of interest in the Apocrypha among Protestants as well as Roman Catholics. Editions of Protestant Bibles are once again appearing with the Apocrypha included in them. The apocryphal books, however, are grouped together by themselves after the 39 books of the Hebrew canon with their own pagination (see the Oxford edition of the NEB). The Apocrypha is now as easily accessible to Protestants as it has been to Roman Catholics.

CANON AND INSPIRATION

Fundamental to our understanding of canon is the doctrine of inspiration, by which is meant that sacred scripture is God's special revelation to mankind, that it is *the* trustworthy authoritative message from God, essential for a correct understanding of God and His acts and of ourselves and the meaning of our existence and that it was prompted by the Spirit of God, given to be obeyed as the voice of the living God (2 Tim. 3: 15 ff.).

This sacred scripture, however, was written down by human beings in human language at specific points in time and in particular geographical locations with all the limitations that humanness, language, space and time, societies and their cultures impose upon it. The Bible is seen, then, as the result of a joint effort on the part of both God and man in time and space —a product initiated by God and under His control, so that every part and form of it can be labelled 'God-breathed' (*theopneustos*, 2 Tim. 3: 16; cf. 2 Pet. 1: 21), but also a product of different men, living at different times and in different places, having differing personalities and outlooks, fears, aspirations, etc., so that every part and form also bears the stamp of humanness: *omnia ex Deo; omnia ex hominibus*.

God impelling men by His Holy Spirit, God working through and not in violation of human personalities, God initiating but also cooperating with holy men gave the world a body of literature that has become normative scripture. Inspiration preceded canonization. Inspiration, therefore, is the ultimate determining factor in deciding the extent of the OT canon.

But if the doctrine of inspiration includes both the divine and human factors, the idea of canonization does the same. The Spirit of God which worked through men in the composition of sacred scripture worked also in the hearts and minds of those who read and accepted them. If the OT canon is the result of the providential activity of a self-disclosing God, there is a very real sense in which it is also the product of the decisive action of thinking choosing human beings.

Since the idea of canon includes human choice, what factors went into making this choice? On what basis were certain books recognized as canonical and others not? Several criteria have been suggested.

(1) Only books written in Hebrew can be

recognized as authoritative. This criterion, however, does not account for the fact that books like Ecclesiasticus, Tobit and 1 Maccabees—books written in Hebrew—were excluded from the Hebrew canon, while Daniel, parts of which were written in Aramaic, was included.

(2) Only books whose contents harmonized with the Law can be considered canonical. It is true that from its origin the Pentateuch was considered normative, because it was recognized as *the* revelation of God to Moses. Hence, it is unthinkable that any book should be added to the canon that was contrary to its basic theme: God's covenant with His people. And no doubt this 'plumb-line' was used to judge all later writings. But certainly it cannot be the only criterion for deciding canonicity. There are books in the so-called Apocrypha which harmonize with the Pentateuch but were excluded from the Hebrew canon.

(3) Only books that were written before Malachi's time, the time when the voice of the Spirit stopped speaking or being heard, can be considered canonical. This was Josephus' view (*Contra Apionem*, 1.8). But it cannot account for the fact that many books written before this cut-off time—the Book of the Wars of the Lord (Num. 21: 14), the Book of Jashar (Jos. 10: 13), the Books of the Chronicles of the Kings of Israel and Judah (1 Kg. 14: 19, 29), etc.—were not preserved so as to become normative scripture. An early date is not an adequate criterion for canonicity.

(4) Only books written by prophets can be considered canonical—'propheticity is the principle of canonicity' (Geisler, pp. 43 ff.). Again it was Josephus who first put this criterion into words. Only those works which can legitimately claim prophetic origin have the right to canonicity (*Contra Apionem*, 1.8). Normative writings were inspired writings. And for Josephus, who may simply have been articulating the ideas of his times, the period of prophetic activity was a limited one. For him the unbroken succession of prophets extended only from Moses to Artaxerxes—the supreme fact that gave his 22 OT books (our 39) their normative value. No doubt this criterion played an important role in the selection process. On the one hand it accounts for the absence of the Apocrypha from the Hebrew list of OT books (they were written after the voice of prophecy ceased). But it cannot account for the fact that books expressly written by prophets and seers—The Chronicles of Nathan the Prophet, of Gad the Seer (1 Chr. 29: 29; 2 Chr. 12: 15), etc.—are not part of the canon.

(5) Only those books that demonstrated their value by religious usage, that gained their significance from close association with Israel's worship, can be considered as canonical. This criterion is good but inadequate. It fails to account for the fact that although Ecclesiasticus and 1 Maccabees had undoubted religious value for Judah both of these books failed to secure a place in the list of OT books (Harrison, p. 284).

(6) Only those books witnessed to by Jesus can be judged canonical. 'Without question our Lord believed all the OT books and so the entire OT itself to be the word of God. Inasmuch as he is the eternal Son of God his word is final . . . [He] placed the imprimatur of his infallible authority upon the OT scriptures in that he recognized them as divine' (Young, pp. 156–57). The difficulty with this kind of reasoning is manifold: (*a*) The attitude of Jesus toward the OT would not be of any consequence to Jews in determining the extent of their canon. (*b*) Jesus' remarks about the Law or the Law and the Prophets, His reference to Daniel the prophet and to the fact that 'the scripture cannot be broken' (Jn 10: 36), do not clearly tell us what books or how many actually were in His canon. (*c*) Jesus' attitude toward the OT scriptures, whatever books may have been included in them, did not canonize them or provide them with an authority they did not already have; His attitude merely shows He recognized their authoritativeness and their binding nature. (*d*) Even if one holds that Jesus put His imprimatur upon only the 39 books of the Hebrew OT, as is implied above, he must admit that this fact escaped the notice of many of the early followers of Jesus, or that they rejected it, for they accepted as equally authoritative those extra books in the wider canon of the LXX.

(7) Only those books can be judged canonical that are free from contradictions, inaccuracies, inconsistencies, peculiar practices, etc. On the basis of this criterion many of the Apocrypha certainly would be eliminated. Some apocryphal books abound in geographical, chronological and historical mistakes (Green, p. 195). Others support such new ideas as purgatory, prayer for the dead, remission of sins after death, etc. But if this criterion was (and is) used against the Apocrypha it might also have been (and was) used against the Hebrew Bible itself. Had the question of its canonicity rested purely upon standards such as this 'it is impossible to see how the Jews could ever have come to accept the OT books as being of divine authority . . . since the majority of the OT compositions were severely critical of the ancient Hebrews in one way or another' (Harrison, p. 284). And a criterion like this would have made it even more difficult for Christians to accept the OT as authoritative. Church history records that many early Fathers saw what they regarded as alien, cruel and peculiar practices in the OT —things unworthy of their understanding of

God, things they were forced to reject or allegorize or explain by typology.

If any one of these criteria is inadequate, what then was the basis of selecting some writings as sacred and normative and rejecting others? We cannot claim to give *the* answer. It may be a combination of some or all the criteria mentioned above. Yet the ultimate criterion is the intrinsic worth of the writings themselves, attested by what the Reformers called 'the inward witness of the Holy Spirit'. Their inherent authority, their own divine weight subjected reader or hearer to the judgment of God, forced him to recognize that these books were more than human in origin and led him finally to accept them for his standard of faith and practice. Whatever role the councils and synods may have played in the history of the OT canon they could never create this authority. They could only recognize it and submit to it. The canon is dependent not on church or council but primarily upon the Holy Spirit in the hearts of writers and readers. There is then something about the writings themselves that demands universal acceptance and usage and something within God's people that prompted them to say yes to this demand. If this is so perhaps we have reason enough for not considering the Apocrypha as canonical—valuable material for understanding historical backgrounds and for moral edification, yes, but not normative scripture. The Apocrypha seem never to have had sufficient weight of their own to be *universally* accepted by Jew and Christian alike.

BIBLIOGRAPHY

ALBRIGHT, W. F., *From the Stone Age to Christianity* (Baltimore, 1957).

ARCHER, G. L., *Survey of Old Testament Introduction* (Chicago, 1974).

BARR, J., *Holy Scripture: Canon, Authority, Criticism* (Oxford, 1983).

BECKWITH, R. T., *The Old Testament apocrypha in the New Testament* (London, 1985).

BENTZEN, A., *Introduction to the Old Testament* (Copenhagen, 1952).

BUHL, F., *Canon and Text of the Old Testament*, E.T. (Edinburgh, 1892).

CAMPENHAUSEN, H. VON, *The Formation of the Christian Bible*, E.T. (London, 1972).

CHARLESWORTH, J. H. (ed.), *The Old Testament Pseudepigrapha*, 2 vols. (Garden City, N. Y., 1983–84).

CHILDS, B. S., *Introduction to the Old Testament as Scripture* (London, 1979).

COATS, G. W., and LONG, B. O., *Canon and Authority* (Philadelphia, 1977).

DRIVER, S. R., *Introduction to the Literature of the Old Testament* (Edinburgh, 1913, reprinted 1972).

ELLIS, E. E., *Paul's Use of the Old Testament* (Edinburgh, 1957).

EYBERS, I. H., 'Some Light on the Canon of the Qumran Sect', in *The Canon and Masorah of the Hebrew Bible*, ed. S. Z. Leiman (New York, 1974).

GEISLER, N. L., 'The Extent of the Old Testament Canon', in *Current Issues in Biblical and Patristic Interpretation*, ed. G. F. Hawthorne (Grand Rapids, 1975).

GREEN, W. H., *General Introduction to the Old Testament: The Canon* (New York, 1899).

HAGNER, D. A., *The Use of the Old and New Testaments in Clement of Rome* (Leiden, 1973).

HARRISON, R. K., *Introduction to the Old Testament* (Grand Rapids, 1969; London, 1970).

HARRISON, R. K., 'Apocrypha', in *Zonderman Pictorial Encyclopedia of the Bible*, i (Grand Rapids, 1975).

KATZ, P., 'The Old Testament Canon in Palestine and Alexandria', in *The Canon and Masorah*, ed. S. Z. Leiman (New York, 1974).

LEIMAN, S. Z. (ed.), *The Canon and Masorah of the Hebrew Bible* (New York, 1974).

LEIMAN, S. Z., *The Canonization of Hebrew Scripture* (Hamden, Conn., 1976).

LEWIS, J. P., 'What do we mean by Jabneh?' *JBR* 32 (1964), pp. 125–132.

New Catholic Encyclopedia (New York, 1967), ii, article 'Bible', sections on 'Canon of the Old Testament' (J. C. Turro) and 'Apocrypha of the Old Testament' (C. Stuhlmueller); iii, article 'Canon, Biblical' (L. F. Hartman).

PFEIFFER, R. H., 'Canon of the Old Testament', in *Interpreter's Dictionary of the Bible*, i (New York, 1962).

ROBINSON, G. L., 'Canon of the Old Testament' in *ISBE*, ed. J. Orr, i (Grand Rapids, 1937).

RYLE, H. E., *The Canon of the Old Testament* (London, 1904).

SANDERS, J. A., *Torah and Canon* (Philadelphia, 1972).

SUNDBERG, A. C., *The Old Testament of the Early Church* (Cambridge, Mass., 1964).

SUNDBERG, A. C., 'The "Old Testament": A Christian Canon', *CBQ* 30 (1968), pp. 143–155.

YOUNG, E. J., 'The Canon of the Old Testament', in *Revelation and the Bible*, ed. C. F. H. Henry (Grand Rapids, 1958).

ARCHAEOLOGY AND THE OLD TESTAMENT

D. J. WISEMAN

Archaeology is the principal means of recovering the past by the discovery of ancient sites and by excavation finding the buildings, artifacts and written documents they once contained. In this way it provides a tool for the historian seeking to draw a picture of man and his activities and thought in a given period and place in history. Since the OT is itself a collection of writings within a precise life-setting, it is not surprising that the archaeology of Bible lands, mainly Syro-Palestine and its neighbours, which is colloquially designated 'biblical archaeology', has done much to help our understanding of the peoples, places, languages, traditions and customs among whom the Hebrews had their own special place.

While early, and some recent, exploration had interest in the Bible as a primary motive, modern archaeology has developed into a recognized and independent discipline using diverse methods to discover, date, examine, preserve and interpret its finds. Archaeology is not an exact science, though now a fast-moving field of contemporary research using methods of comparison and typology. Its results, with the general exception of documentary evidence, may be subjective, subject to changing interpretation or limited by lack of comparable material or even by the viewpoint and methods employed by the excavator. Nevertheless, certain principles of method or results now command widespread acceptance quite apart from any theological outlook, or lack of it, of the archaeologist himself.

The rôle of archaeology is confined to establishing the material background of a civilization. The ideas and thoughts of an ancient people may sometimes be reconstructed from these remains, but are more usually and reliably traced from their writings. Biblical archaeology has illustrated, explained and, though sometimes raising problems as yet unanswered, occasionally confirmed the biblical text. It does not, however, 'prove the Bible to be true'. OT writers select their facts and sources and words and often have spiritual insights and concerns which are beyond the scope of archaeology to question or confirm. Thus Biblical archaeology aims to illuminate

and supplement as well as to confirm, or more rarely correct, traditional interpretations. Since it introduces the reader to the contemporary background of the biblical writers it has become an indispensable, if not always essential, tool for the fullest understanding of the Bible.

i. Sites

It has been estimated that only about three per cent of the five thousand sites surveyed in Palestine or of the ten thousand ancient places in adjacent lands have been systematically examined. From these it appears that cities developed in the fourth millennium B.C., probably under Mesopotamian influence, though some like Jericho go back to the fifth millennium B.C. Places named in the early Genesis narratives—e.g. Nineveh, Calah, Erech, Erid(u), etc.—are attested as in existence by the third millennium. Places named in the patriarchal stories—e.g. Bethel, Shechem, Hebron (Kiriath-Arba), Sodom and Gomorrah —represent city-states whose existence is confirmed as a dominating feature of the period. About 1700 B.C. the massive defences of cities throughout the region were strengthened in face of new armaments (chariots and horses) and the incursions of the Hyksos (Sea-peoples). Such fortifications can be traced through Syria and Palestine (Dan, Hazor, Laish, Shechem, Tirzah, Gaza) and into Egypt. They were to be a source of astonishment to the incoming Hebrews (Num. 13: 28). Each city-state had its own ruler and tombs to bear witness to the wealth of the period. Later in the sixteenth century Megiddo, Jericho and Beth-zur were among the places apparently destroyed by the Egyptians following up the Hyksos. Their hold over the main strongholds of Palestine is seen also in the fourteenth century correspondence between the local rulers and the pharaohs (El-Amarna letters).

It is difficult to be sure that destruction levels at Tell el-Hesi (Eglon?), Megiddo, Lachish, Ashod and Hazor relate to the incoming Hebrews. There is no evidence of any occupation of Ai, and K. M. Kenyon claims to have found no trace of fallen walls at Jericho dated to this time (contrary to J. Garstang's earlier surmise), though there are signs of abandonment c. 1325 B.C., the time most generally attested from archaeological evidence for this event.

In the 'Philistine' period Gath, Gaza, Ashkelon, Ekron and Joppa are shown to be the principal and independent cities, and Philistinian-type decorated pottery, objects, coffins, pillars and temples are found. The latter are basically different from later temples. That at Tell Qasile explains Samson's action in grasping the two central pillars to dislodge them from their stone bases to bring down the roof single-handed (Jg. 16: 29). The Philistine penetration inland is marked by trade-goods found at Gibeah, Jerusalem, Beth-zur and Tell en-Nasbeh. Their monopoly in tempering iron led to military and economic superiority (1 Sam. 13: 18–22). In the monarchy iron replaced copper and bronze for agricultural implements as can be seen from the excavation of Saul's capital Gibeah (Tell el-Fûl), 3 miles north of Jerusalem, where the earliest Israelite fortifications have been traced.

Little remains archaeologically of the time of David unless the Jebusite glacis and the new wall at Ophel, 'the City of David', and the repairs at Beth-shemesh and Tell Beit Mirsim can be attributed to his defence against the Philistines. The later Iron Age shows an improvement in building techniques which coincides with the activity of Solomon whose gate-houses and buildings at Hazor, Megiddo and Gezer (so 1 Kg. 9: 15) have been discovered by Yadin. The so-called 'stables of Solomon' at Megiddo are now redefined as administrative offices or stores of the time of Ahab. Solomon's buildings in Jerusalem itself, including both the temple layout and the columned portico of his palace and its courts, follow the style of contemporary Syrian buildings already known from Alalah, Ugarit and elsewhere. His widespread trading activity is noted by a sherd inscribed 'gold from Ophir for Beth-horon' from Qasile. The implements used in the temple can be illustrated by those found at Hazor which include weights, shovels and even a snake on a pole (like Nehushtan, 2 Kg. 18: 4) and horned altars (2 Chr. 6: 13) found in contemporary temples at Arad and Beersheba. A broken Egyptian stela found at Megiddo and destruction levels at Debir and Beth-shemesh attest the raids into Palestine by King Shishak (Sheshonq I) c. 928 B.C. (cf. 1 Kg. 14: 25–26).

Rehoboam's reinforcement of the defences of Lachish and Azekah presupposes continued strife between Israel and Judah as do the reconstruction of Shechem, Gibeah, Bethel and Mizpah (Tell en-Nasbeh?). While 1 Kg. 16: 21–26 does not emphasize Omri as a builder, his work at Shechem and Tirzah (Tell el-Fara'ah) —the latter left half-unfinished in favour of his major construction of the new capital at Samaria—coincides with the biblical picture of his work there. Ivory decorations from his

houses (1 Kg. 22: 39; Am. 6: 4) and the massive pool in which his chariot was presumably cleaned down (1 Kg. 22: 18) have been uncovered.

The frequent contacts between Israel and Judah and their overlord kings in Assyria and Babylonia are the subject of direct reference in contemporary extra-biblical documents (see **ii.** below). Some of these are also supported by independent archaeological evidence. Thus, for example, Hezekiah's defence of Jerusalem against the Assyrians in 701 B.C. was made possible by his construction or adaptation of the Siloam tunnel rediscovered in 1838. This ancient water-conduit, '1,200 cubits long', gave access from within the city walls to an underground spring outside them (2 Kg. 20: 20; 2 Chr. 32: 30). The downfall of Judah is marked by the destruction of all the major fortified centres and by their abandonment. This is particularly noticeable along the southern border—Lachish, Azekah (Jer. 34: 7, Tell Beit Mirsim), Beth-Shemesh, Ramat Rahel and Arad. At Jerusalem mass graves outside the walls have been attributed to the sack of 587 B.C. During the exile Mizpah (Tell en-Nasbeh) continued as a poorly occupied town though the vineyards north of Jerusalem were still worked to supply Babylon. The splendours of Nebuchadrezzar's city can be judged from the extensive excavations of his capital with the palaces, temples and city occupied by him and Belshazzar, son and co-regent of his successor Nabonidus. Apart from a few inscribed tablets there is no evidence from Babylonia as yet of the Jews in exile. Their restoration to Judah can be seen in sparse re-settlements found at Gezer, Lachish, Bethel, Beth-zur (north of Hebron) and at Mizpah. However Judah did not recover its prosperity until the third century B.C.

ii. Inscriptions

Such archaeological evidence from site occupation is important but is more mute than the inscriptions which can be closely dated and more readily related to the text of the OT. In this way direct references to biblical events, places and persons are to be expected and are sometimes found.

The influence of the Babylonian cuneiform script first traced to c. 3500 B.C. is seen in Syria by 2500 B.C. At Ebla (Tell Mardiḥ); the scribes already use it to copy the same range of texts as those known both earlier and contemporarily in Babylonia itself. All types of recording, administration and school exercises (with their vocabularies and syllabaries reflecting the local Semitic dialect) are among the c. 10,000 texts found there. These show the scribes both composing and continuing the already long literary traditions. Instructions (similar to Proverbs), accounts of creation of a polytheistic nature similar to the later Babylonian epic beginning 'when on high . . .' (*enuma elish*) and an account of the Babylonian story of the Flood (Gilgamesh Epic), part of which was also found at Megiddo dateable to the fourteenth century B.C., are among them. This important collection, which includes hymns and prayers, commercial and state letters, royal edicts, covenant-treaties and other historical data as well as mathematical and medical texts, will prove important for the study of the background both of Gen. 1–11 and of the later patriarchal period. The geographical horizon of these texts does not extend to Canaan and Babylonia.

The Babylonian language and literature was commonly used throughout the ancient Near East during the second millennium B.C. when many thousands of texts, including 25,000 from Mari (Tell Hariri), provide a detailed picture of the period into which the patriarchs may well be placed. Language and customs are also well illustrated by the historical, legal and epistolary texts from Alalah (Syria) in the 18th–15th centuries, later Nuzi (Assyria, 15th cent.) and Amarna (Egypt, 14th cent.). Texts from Ras Shamra (Ugarit) include epics and myths (Baal, Aqhat, etc.) and others written in an alphabet using the cuneiform script. From the same city about the time of the entry of the Israelites into the promised land are texts written by bilingual scribes including the Flood story (with many similarities to Genesis but with polytheistic background and other significant differences), the Babylonian 'Job', hymns, prayers, proverbs and love lyrics (cf. Song of Songs) and the usual mass of legal and administrative records. The OT is thus to be viewed against a background of local literary traditions, using similar scribal methods (*e.g.* colophons) and genres to those employed by the Hebrews. The latter, however, is distinct both in its content and religious outlook. In every court and temple the written records precluded the necessity of relying upon writing down events only from later memory or from oral teaching and tradition which existed alongside the written word.

Thus by 1800 B.C. the Semitic alphabet is seen in jottings in the Sinai mines and by 1500 B.C. in Byblos as well as at Gezer, Shechem (a plaque) and Lachish (inscribed dagger). By the time the Hebrews entered Palestine Babylonian cuneiform, Egyptian hieroglyphs and hieratic, the Canaanite linear alphabet (the ancestor of the later Hebrew, Greek and Roman alphabets), an alphabet of 25–30 cuneiform signs related to that of Ugarit, the syllabic script of Byblos as well as scripts of Cypriot and Cretan type were in use. All of these could have been known to Moses through his Egyptian court education.

From the United Monarchy a few Semitic inscriptions have survived. One, an inscribed javelin head from el-Khadr near Bethlehem, may have belonged to a man following David into exile. A native inscription, the Gezer Calendar—a farmer's almanac or schoolboy's exercise—may date to Solomon's reign. Shishak's reliefs and texts on the walls of the Karnak temple of Amun at Thebes depict him beating Asiatic captives and list his conquests in Palestine. The usurper Omri (884–873 B.C.) is named in the Mesha' inscription (Moabite Stone, *c.* 830 B.C.) found in 1868. In this the king of Moab also tells how his father was defeated by Ahab but later regained his independence while Ahab was fighting Syria (2 Kg. 1: 1). 'Ahab the Israelite' is stated by Shalmaneser III of Assyria to have provided '2000 chariots and 10,000 men' for the coalition led by Irhuleni of Hamath and Benhadad II of Aram-Damascus (called Adad-idri or Hadadezer by the Assyrians). The Israelite contribution in chariots was the largest at the battle of Qarqar in 853 B.C. when the Assyrian advance westwards was checked for a while. Hazael had displaced Benhadad II by 843 B.C. and is called a usurper ('a son of a nobody') and 'our lord Hazael' on an inscribed ivory looted from Damascus by the Assyrian soldiers, and in historical texts. The Black Obelisk of Shalmaneser III (British Museum) shows the submission of 'Jehu son (dynasty?) of Omri' to the Assyrian king. This event is not mentioned in Scripture. A stone stela of Adad-nirari III from Rimah, west of Mosul, lists 'Yu'asu (Joash) of Samaria' as paying him tribute. To the reign of Jeroboam II (770–755 B.C.) may be assigned the 63 potsherds from Samaria which record wine and oil received as taxes paid in kind. There is also the seal of one of his officials 'Shema, servant of Jeroboam' not named in the Bible. Azariah (Uzziah) of Judah seems to have had a wide influence into Syria to judge from references to 'Azriyau of Yaudi' in contemporary Assyrian texts. The Hebrew inscription recording the removal of his bones to a new grave at Jerusalem is to be dated some seven hundred years later.

Menahem (*Menuhimme*) of Samaria, according to Tilgath-pileser III in his annals, joined Rezin of Damascus in bringing tribute to the Assyrians about 739 B.C. (cf. 2 Kg. 15: 37; 16: 5–9; Isa. 7: 1 ff.). The same historical annals name Pekah (*Paqaha*) as an ally of Rezin and tell how the Assyrians put Hoshea (*Ausi'*) on the throne of Israel ('the house of Omri'). The Assyrian annals for the year 731 name (Jeho)ahaz (*Yauhazi*) of Judah as paying tribute to Assyria along with Moab, Edom, Ashkelon, and Gaza (cf. 2 Kg. 16: 18). Further external testimony to his time are a seal of 'Ushnu, servant (official) of Ahaz' and a text from Nimrud, the capital of Assyria, listing tribute. Shalmaneser V claims to have begun the three-year siege of Samaria, an attack which seems to have been completed by Sargon II in 722/1 B.C. (hence the plural 'kings' in 2 Kg. 18: 10). The Babylonian Chronicle also records that Shalmaneser 'broke (the opposition of) the city of Shamarain (Samaria?)'. Sargon claimed to have taken 27,270 (or 27,290) 'men of Samaria' as prisoners, 'together with the gods in whom they trusted', thus verifying the polytheism so strongly condemned by the prophets. The same text describes the sack of Babylon in terms reminiscent of Isa. 13. The exiles from Samaria were taken to Gozan (Guzan, Tell Halaf) where documents soon show inhabitants bearing apparently Jewish names. Others may have been taken to Calah (Nimrud) where an ostracon lists West Semitic names like Menahem, Elisha, Hananel and Haggai.

The Siloam tunnel inscription records the meeting of miners excavating the 'last three cubits' from above and below when making the shaft of the 1200 cubit long water course used by Hezekiah to defend Jerusalem in 701 B.C. Sennacherib records this siege of Jerusalem when he 'shut up Hezekiah (*Hazaqiau*) the Jew in his royal city like a bird in its cage', but he makes no claim to any capture. In its more vivid account the OT gives the reasons why he failed to do so. Hezekiah's payment to him of '800 talents of silver and 30 talents of gold' is mentioned. Meanwhile the fall of Lachish to the Assyrian king is the subject of reliefs and inscriptions on the wall of Sennacherib's palace at Nineveh which show the deportees being taken away. Finds at Lachish attest the fierceness of the siege. The lintel of a tomb prepared for '(Shebn)ayahu who is over the house' (i.e. a royal steward) comes from a necropolis in the Silwan valley occupied by those of high rank. The text is the third longest monumental inscription in archaic Hebrew yet to survive. It supports the opinion that this is the tomb of the Shebna rebuked by Isaiah (Isa. 22: 15–16).

Esarhaddon of Assyria lists the tribute received from 'Manasseh (*Minse*) king of Judah'. The latter would also have been present at Calah in May 672 B.C. when the Assyrian king imposed a vassal-treaty on all his subjects, making them swear to be loyal to his sons as kings of Assyria and Babylonia. The text, with its covenant requirements or stipulations ('thou shalt . . . thou shalt not . . .') following a form basically unchanged from the second millennium, has done much to revive interest in the literary forms of ancient covenants as found also in the Ten Commandments and in Deuteronomy. Among other demands the vassals swear to take the god of Assyria as their god under threat of the reprisal of the sack of their cities and exile for their peoples for breaking any of the commands imposed. This type of text commences with a title and a historical prologue written or implied. It then gives the stipulations which the vassals have to acknowledge or repeat aloud; the arrangements for depositing a copy of the covenant in the vassal's sanctuary; and for its periodic public reading and renewal including the obligation to teach it to their sons and sons' sons for ever; the divine witnesses, the curses on the vassal should he transgress the covenant and blessings should he keep it (cf. Exod. 20–21; Dt. 1: 1–32, 47; Jos. 24).

The fiscal organization of Judah (*yhd*) required that taxes be paid in kind, and about six hundred stamped jar handles show that Hebron, Sokoh, Ziph and Mmst were collection centres from Hezekiah to the fall of Judah.

The Babylonian Chronicle gives an objective and reliable account of events for most years in the period 626–539 B.C. These include the Battle of Carchemish in August 605 B.C. and the defeat of the Syrians at Hamath which enabled the Babylonians to march unopposed through Palestine to the Egyptian border. Among the tribute brought in by many kings must have been that of Jehoiakim of Judah who remained faithful to Babylon for three years until the defeat of Nebuchadrezzar's army by the Egyptians recorded in 601 B.C. The Babylonians had marched to the west in 604 and 602 taking many prisoners who may have included Daniel and his companions. An Aramaic letter from Saqqara tells of the vain appeal of one city for help from Egypt. This may have been Ashkelon, Ashdod or Gaza; certainly the impending attack led Jeremiah to proclaim a fast (Jer. 36: 1 ff.).

The Babylonian Chronicle for Nebuchadrezzar's seventh year states that he 'called up his army and marched to the city of Judah (i.e. Jerusalem) and on the second day of the month of Adar (i.e. 16 March 597 B.C.) he captured the city and took its king captive. He appointed a king of his own choice (to rule) there; received heavy tribute and sent (the exiles) off to Babylon.' This provides clear evidence to compare with 2 Kg. 24: 10–17 and other OT passages. The precise date was not otherwise known to us but Jehoichin (*Yaukin*), king of Judah is named in texts from Babylon dated 595–570 B.C. as receiving rations from the royal stores there. Meanwhile his royal estates in Judah were managed until 587 B.C. by 'Eliakim, steward of Jehoiachin' whose seal is known from Debir and Beth-shemesh. The king chosen by Nebuchadrezzar to succeed Jehoichin was his uncle Mattaniah-Zedekiah (2 Kg. 24: 17). The last days of Judah until the fall of Jerusalem in 587 B.C. are graphically illustrated by the notes written on potsherds by the commander of an outpost of Lachish awaiting fire-signals (cf. Jer. 6: 1; 34: 7). Gedaliah's seal has been found at Lachish which must have been under his control, and that of 'Jaazaniah, minister of the king' at Mizpah (2 Kg. 25: 23; Jer. 40: 8). The impressions of the seals of Baruch, Jeremiah's scribe, and other individuals named in Jer. 36 have also been discovered.

Belshazzar's coregency with Nabonidus is attested in Babylonian inscriptions which also name the 'King of the Medes' who at this time can be none other than Cyrus who styled himself both 'King of Persia' and 'King of the Lands'. On this basis it has been suggested that Dan. 6: 28 be translated 'Daniel prospered in the reign of Darius even (i.e.) the reign of Cyrus the Persian' and that 'Darius the Mede' may well be a throne-name of Cyrus himself, since no Babylonian record survives of any ruler between Nabonidus-Belshazzar and Cyrus or between Cyrus and Cambyses (D. J. Wiseman, *Notes on Some Problems of the Book of Daniel*, London, 1965). Others identify Darius the Mede with a little known Gubaru/Gobryas, a governor of Babylon who is, however, never given the title of king (J. C. Whitcomb, *Darius the Mede*, Grand Rapids, 1959).

Cyrus records his proclamation restoring the temples of many deities and the return of the Jews after the Babylonian exile is in keeping with this. Papyrus letters from Elephantine in Egypt name both Sanballat and Johanan the high priest (Neh. 12: 22–25). Other opponents of Nehemiah, 'Geshem, King of Kedar', and 'Tobiah of Ammon' have left inscriptions. A recently published Babylonian 'dynastic prophecy' text gives details of the fall of Assyria, rise and fall of Babylonia and Persia and the rise of the Hellenistic monarchies. As in Daniel, though names of kings are not given there is enough circumstantial detail to identify the persons and periods described.

iii. The Dead Sea Scrolls and the OT

The chance find in caves near the Wadi Qumran north-west of the Dead Sea in 1947 led to the recovery of manuscripts which antedate the oldest *MT* of the OT hitherto known. Of some 500 manuscripts recovered from about 300 different caves in the neighbouring Judean hills a third are copies of the Hebrew OT and largely follow the traditional *MT*. They date from *c.* 250 B.C. (Exodus) to just before the fall of Jerusalem (*c.* A.D. 68). They show how accurately the scribes carried out the copying of earlier Hebrew texts. Others show marks of revision or are copies of various recensions which preceded or followed the Greek translations of the LXX *c.* 245 B.C. Aramaic and Samaritan writings were also found and deutero-canonical books (not accepted in the Jewish canon) in both Hebrew, Aramaic and Greek are also represented. The most copied books were Deuteronomy in the Pentateuch, Psalms

in the Writings and Isaiah in the Prophets. It is noteworthy that these books, used in the synagogue educational system of Palestine from 75 B.C., were the most quoted by Jesus Christ. The Qumran scrolls also illustrate the methods of exegesis used. Sectarian documents from the same finds include the *Manual of Discipline* and the *Temple Scroll* of the sect, generally and most plausibly identified as a branch of the Essenes. Though of much value in showing the continuity and variations in the OT texts, it is noteworthy that the fourteen copies of Isaiah have produced only about six agreed changes of a minor nature to the text as previously known. The primary importance of these scrolls is for NT studies.

iv. Evaluation

The foregoing is but part of the picture which may be reconstructed from the archaeological evidence. It can control extravagant and negative theories, both derived from established facts and from literary forms and interpretation. As it amasses new data constantly we 'must remember that the witness which archaeology and the texts afford is and always will remain incomplete . . . one must also admit that lack of archaeological evidence would not be sufficient in itself to cast doubt on the affirmations of the written witnesses' (R. de Vaux). Archaeology also raises problems which still await a final solution as, for example, the lack of evidence, despite extensive excavation, for occupation of Ai or Jericho at the time of the Hebrews' entry into the land, though different solutions may be justly proposed. It has solved a number of problems raised by critics, such as the existence and use of camels in Palestine in the early patriarchal period (Gen. 12: 16, etc.) or Tirhaqah's rule as early as 701 B.C. (2 Kg. 19: 9). It must be received as a valuable addition to our knowledge, but can never be a substitute for the Scripture itself. The Bible expositor and commentator needs to be constantly abreast of archaeological findings but never be its servant.

BIBLIOGRAPHY

Much new information is given as discoveries are made in special periodicals *e.g.* *The Biblical Archaeologist* (American Schools of Oriental Research); *Israel Exploration Journal*, *Iraq*, *Levant*, *Palestine Exploration Quarterly*, etc. Texts relating to the OT have been collected in PRITCHARD, J. B. (ed.), *Ancient Near Eastern Texts Relating to the Old Testament* (Princeton, 2nd edn., 1955) and *Ancient Near Eastern Pictures Relating to the Old Testament* (Princeton, 2nd edn., 1969), abbreviated in his *The Ancient Near East, an anthology of Texts and Pictures* (Princeton, 1973); and in THOMAS, D. Winton (ed.), *Documents from Old Testament Times* (London, 1968). A recent reliable compendium of biblical archaeological data is to be found in *The New Bible Dictionary* (Leicester, 2nd. edn., 1982) (or with illustrations in *The Illustrated*

Bible Dictionary vols 1–3, Leicester & Wheaton, 1980.)

ALBRIGHT, W. F., *The Archaeology of Palestine* (Harmondsworth, 1960).

AVI-YONAH, M., *Encyclopedia of Archaeological Excavations in the Holy Land* (London, 1976–77).

BRUCE, F. F., *Second Thoughts on The Dead Sea Scrolls* (Exeter, 1969).

BURROWS, M., *What Mean these Stones?* (London, 1957).

KITCHEN, K. A., *Ancient Orient and Old Testament* (London, 1966).

KITCHEN, K. A., *The Bible in its World* (Exeter, 1977).

MILLARD, A. R., *The Bible BC: What Can Archaeology Prove?* (Leicester, 1977).

MOOREY, P. R. S., *Biblical Lands* (London, 1975).

PAUL, S. M. and DEVERS, W. G., *Biblical Archaeology* (Jerusalem, 1973).

SANDERS, J. A., *Near Eastern Archaeology in the Twentieth Century* (Garden City, N.Y., 1969).

THOMAS, D. WINTON (ed.), *Archaeology and Old Testament Study* (Oxford, 1967).

THOMPSON, J. A., *The Bible and Archaeology* (Grand Rapids, 3rd edn., 1982).

WISEMAN, D. J., *Chronicles of Chaldaean Kings (626–556 B.C.) in the British Museum* (London, 1956).

WISEMAN, D. J. (ed.), *Peoples of Old Testament Times* (London and Oxford, 1973).

WISEMAN, D. J. & YAMAUCHI, E., *Biblical Archaeology: An Introductory Study* (Grand Rapids, 1979).

WRIGHT, G. E., *Biblical Archaeology* (London, 1962).

YAMAUCHI, E., *The Stones and the Scriptures* (London, 1973).

THE ENVIRONMENTAL
BACKGROUND TO THE
OLD TESTAMENT

J. M. HOUSTON

Studies of the environmental background of the Bible have gone through numerous phases of development. A primary interest has naturally been in the description of the land of Palestine itself. Geographical science itself has only matured in the last fifty years so that a satisfactory synthesis of landscape and culture is a recent development. But a topographical interest in the identification of Biblical sites, and a broad if hazy appreciation of the lie of the land in relation to settlements, the climate and its agricultural resources, and other broad appreciations of environment, have long attracted interest. Jerome expressed this at the beginning of the fifth century, when he prefaced his Latin translation of the Greek *Onomasticon* of Eusebius as follows:

Just as those who have seen Athens understand Greek history better, and just as those who have seen Troy understand the words of the poet Vergil, thus one will comprehend the Holy Scriptures with a clearer understanding who has seen the land of Judah with his own eyes and has come to know the references to the ancient towns and places and their names, both the principal names and those that have changed.[1]

And so for this reason, Jerome undertook his task. But accurate, empirical verification of place-names was impossible until the first systematic studies of Dr. Edward Robinson in the nineteenth century, who in the period 1838–56 had identified 177 out of the total 622 place-names in the Bible.[2] By 1889, 469 place-names had been located, largely as a result of the work of the Palestine Exploration Fund surveys.[3] The development of topographic mapping, including geological surveys,[4] then made it possible for the first reliable historical geography to be published, that of Sir George Adam Smith.[5] Since then new geographical studies, such as those of Abel,[6] du Buit,[7] and Baly,[8] and numerous atlas descriptions have added to the popular understanding of its terrain but scarcely contributed profoundly new insights.

A second phase of environmental background really began in 1890 with Sir Flinders Petrie's excavation of Tell el-Hesi, and the sensitive use of pottery chronology.[9] Now modern archaeological surveys of whole districts, as initiated by Nelson Glueck[10] and his successors help us to reconstruct the buried landscapes of past ages, illuminating the study of the processes of settlement over wide regions. This has been intensified in the last decade by the controversial issues raised by Alt,[11] Albright[12] and Mendenhall.[13] Their sense of *Territorialgeschichte* has contributed to much requestioning of traditional assumptions about the settlement of the Hebrews in Palestine. Israeli scholars like Yohanan Aharoni[14] and Samuel Abramsky[15] have added immensely to our understanding of the physical circumstances under which the social and religious life of Israel developed.

A third development has been that which sees the two environments of man as one: the social environment of man's own cultural achievement, blended with the physical environment in which man is set. That is, to see the inter-relationships of history and of nature as a whole, the one in which to the Hebrews God's imminence in events is linked with God's transcendence in the physical realm. To the Hebrews, there were no abstractions such as history or nature, for God's presence was recognized in the eventfulness and character of both.[16] But Biblical scholars have debated long on whether the uniqueness of Israel's faith was absolute or only derivative from differences with her neighbours and their cultures. Moreover, are the differences attributable to the respective physical-social environments, or is the uniqueness of Israel's faith and world-view a revelatory eventfulness? The answer depends in large measure on the presuppositions of the biblical scholars.

Scholars' presuppositions involve two aspects of the interpretation of the data. The first concerns causality. Is this world a closed system of cause and effect, so that 'natural' explanations are all one need look for, in terms of rational understanding? In past research, it was easier to identify those who took a positivist or

45

evolutionary approach because of the concerns for the origins of the religious consciousness or the origins of the texts. But now theological issues predominate, and biblical theology itself becomes a useful shelter behind which to hide one's viewpoint in expounding the views of the Israelites. Often what the lay reader wants to know is not how the phenomenon of creation was believed by the Israelites but whether in the 1980's this or that writer believes in it. The wind blowing over the 'Reed Sea' is a feeble explanation for the deliverance of Israel from Egypt at the Exodus. Eventually, we ask that the mythic trappings of contemporary explanation be honestly bared, to state in space and time what we literally believe took place. Historicist and geographic perspectives have, however, a concrete and particular eventfulness that the modern mind-set finds embarrassing, if not downright offensive, to the closed system thinking of the evolutionist and non-believer in the transcendent sovereignty of God.

The second concern of modern environmental studies is relating the spheres of the physical and social environments. Man-habitat-culture are inextricably one realm. For man perceives of his environment what his culture trains him to see, so that his culture is a filter or series of filters by which he selects what is meaningful and significant to him in his environment. Thus at one time it was popular to follow Gunkel and Gressmann in assuming that the mythological ideas of Old Testament creation and eschatology reflected borrowings from Babylonian sources. Now it is clear that the environmental and theological perspectives were fundamentally and consistently contrasted.[17] Likewise, as the distinctive ideas and religious life of Israel have been increasingly admitted, so has the antiquity of their expressions been pushed back rather than forward. So Wellhausen's 'Mosaic' legislation, as an innovation of the post-exilic period, is now discarded for more traditional dating. Behind this approach is the general interpretation of so many biblical scholars that Israelite religion is an organic outgrowth of the milieu of the ancient Near East. Some scholars point to monotheistic tendencies in other semitic peoples; others point out what they see to be pagan elements in the religion of Israel. This view is to be rejected flatly. Israelite faith is an original creation of God, and its monotheistic world-view has no antecedents in paganism. Israel's world was unique, notwithstanding its utilization of ancient pagan materials as sources of polemic and defence of its own faith.[18]

A third contemporary concern for clearer focus on environmental issues is to trace the remarkable unity of the Old Testament in the ethical responsibilities of Yahweh-Israel-the Promised Land. These provide us with fresh insights to the ecological crisis of our world today. For the perspective of how evil in the hearts of men influences and propagates sources of evil in the physical realm was well recognized by the prophets.

For man in his freedom is open to the world, not bound instinctually as all the animals are. Man is open to choice, open to meaning, so that he has to chart his course through reality as a cosmologist, who builds up space and time into a world-view that provides him with coherence and meaning, moral legitimacy and guidance. How he relates to the world, to society, and to God or the gods is thus all of a piece, so that the fragmented way in which modern, analytical thought would break up the cohesiveness of human existence is foreign to the ancient Near East as the setting of Israel's faith.

These perspectives contribute to the major environmental issues we can adopt in this survey of the Old Testament. They are as follows: the geographical setting of the Bible in the Near East and of the special role of the land of Israel; the cultural perspectives of its peoples, their religions and seductions to the people of God; the Hebrew settlement in the land, and the theological reality of the land of Promise; and the recurrent symbolism of environmental issues in the history of the Old Testament.

THE GEOGRAPHICAL SETTING OF THE ANCIENT NEAR EAST

Suspended between Europe, Asia and Africa, and between the seas of the eastern Mediterranean, Red Sea and Persian Gulf, the Near East is one of the most strategic areas of the old world. Whether man first appeared here or not, his first civilizations certainly occurred here in the river basins of Mesopotamia and the lower Nile. Although there are deserts occupying the south and east of this area, there are gradations towards more pluviose conditions northwards and westwards. In fact, there are six major types of terrain in the Near East, with their associated ecological and cultural distinctions.[19] Firstly, there are the riverine lands of southern Mesopotamia and the lower Nile, which are hot and with a low mean annual rainfall, but whose alluvial soils are rewarding when irrigation is practised. Here developed after the fourth millennium B.C. the two great riverine civilizations of Mesopotamia and Egypt. Secondly, south and west of Mesopotamia and surrounding the narrow thread of the Nile valley is the desert zone, which has been largely negative in character in the history of the Near East, a zone of nomadism, and trade, and usually a zone of lawlessness to the settled powers. Thirdly, there is the 'Fertile Crescent' called so by Breasted, because the long narrow coastal strip of Syria and Palestine along the better watered hill lands near the sea, together with the piedmont lands north-west of Aleppo and east beyond Kirkuk, consists generally of grassy hills and downlands, favoured by pastoralists and cultivators in antiquity. But east and south of this zone is the sterile steppe of Syria, the Jezirah, and the lands east of Jordan, traditionally a zone of nomadism. Fifthly, in the inward-facing flanks of the northern mountains that link the Anatolian and the Zagros systems, intermontane valley plains, well watered and once covered with a mixed oak woodland and natural grasslands, were probably the zone where cereals like barley and wheat were first domesticated. In the mountains of Galilee and Syria, there is a similar habitat. Finally, there are the mountain ranges of Anatolia and the Zagros, where the headstreams of the Euphrates and Tigris have their sources, and its inhabitants have practised highland economies.

After incipient plant-gathering, peoples had concentrated in the area. Between 10,000 and c. 5000 B.C., village communities developed in the hill lands surrounding the Fertile Crescent, in southern Anatolia, Syria, Palestine, and the highlands of Iraq and Iran. There, winter rains for cereals, pasture-lands for sheep, goats and cattle and a wide range of ecological conditions permitted a varied basis for cultural experimentation. Almost 1,500 years after early sites like Jarmo and Jericho had first been established, migrants had entered the riverine lands. It is possible village life took another thousand years to spread as far south as Khartoum (3300–3400 years B.C.), a further 1,500 miles to the south.[20] Meanwhile, by 3200 B.C. the Early Dynastic period had begun in southern Mesopotamia, and the first dynasty of Egypt began slightly later, c. 3100 B.C.

Although there is a comparable development of irrigation in these two river basins, their hydrological characters are fundamentally different, no doubt reflecting upon many of the sharp contrasts of culture that are recognizable between Egypt and Mesopotamia.[21] Egypt is the gift of the Nile, a single river which flows in a narrow alluvial tract never more than 30 miles wide, for some 500 miles between the delta and the tablelands of the Sudan. The Nile waters come from two great sources: the Blue Nile fed by the monsoonal rains of Ethiopian highlands, and by the other Nile rivers of east Africa, regularized by the marshes of the Sudd and the great reservoirs of Lake Victoria and Lake Albert. The lower Nile floods are remarkably predictable, fixing the annual agricultural calendar into three seasons: 'Inundation', from mid-July to mid-November; 'Coming Waters' (i.e. of the seed at the re-emergence of flooded lands) from mid-November to mid-March; and the period of drought, from mid-March to July. Man had a greater sense of confidence over the forces of nature, while the isolation of the area by deserts protected the Egyptian civilization more effectively from outside influences. The pattern of settlements was dominated by the trunk channel of the Nile, along whose bank were located many of the villages and the transient capital cities that tended to change with each Pharaoh's reign.[22] From the First Dynasty, annual records of the height of the Nile at each flood were kept, and tax records distinguished lowlands, regularly inundated, from highlands only under water with exceptional floods. Thus the seasonal pulse of the Nile was the measure of Egyptian sovereignty, to promote a totalitarian regime and mind-set, and a deification of the Pharaohs, all of which was foreign to Mesopotamian life.[23]

In the Mesopotamian environment, the lower Euphrates and Tigris combined to water the basin, in a more fluctuating uncertain regime. Annual high water occurs in May and June when the snow melt of Armenia combines with the spring rainfall maximum over eastern Anatolia, to feed the lower courses of the rivers in spate. Dependent upon the synchronization of these two climatic variables, there can be appreciable floods in the lower Mesopotamian plain. But the inter-annual irregularity of floods makes their control more difficult than in Egypt, while the high water peak in the height of summer (May–June) minimizes the efficient usage of water. The cereals are already growing in Mesopotamia when the floods arrive, while in Egypt, the cultivated fields are only sown with grain after the floods, and then have the cool season in which to grow. It is now known that much salinization of the soil occurred, with high water tables and intense summer evapo-transpiration. Professor Jacobsen has considered salinization to have been the primary cause of the northward shift of civilization, and the replacement of the Sumerian with the Babylonian.[24] A further feature of Mesopotamia is its exposure to highland raiders and to the migrations of varied ethnic groups, so that racial stock has been more hybridized and mixed than possibly in Egypt. There is altogether a much more insecure motif, physically, ideologically and culturally, in Mesopotamian society than in that of Egypt.

Between these civilizations and continents lies the land bridge of Palestine. It forms the western flank of the Fertile Crescent, bordering the eastern Mediterranean, although typically aloof from the ways of the sea. About 350 miles long and rarely wider than sixty miles before it encounters the desert, it extends from the Amanus and Taurus mountains in the north to Sinai in the south. With a kindly Mediterranean climate, with adequate winter rains and moderate summer heat,[25] together with a wide diversity of land-forms, this area though small in size has remarkable diversity of ecological niches and environments. Apart from the Jordan, its rivers flow intermittingly, but its porous, limestone hills are richly blessed with springs, and sub-surface water supplies have been an important factor for its societies. The coast has had relatively little influence on its culture, apart from the north where hills run transverse to the coastline to provide a few natural harbours such as Tyre and Arvad. But in Palestine proper, the exposed shoreline has lacked natural anchorages and shelter.

As a zone of passage between the two great civilizations of Mesopotamia and Egypt, as well as the theatre of struggle between the desert and the settled lands, trading transactions in times of peace have oscillated with military invasions or local enmity between nomads and cultivators in times of unrest.[26] Continued pressure by Semitic nomads from the desert has influenced the predominantly Semitic character of its inhabitants. But at least two tremendous displacements of whole peoples have swamped it in Biblical times: the Amorite peoples at the end of the third millennium B.C., and the Hebrew-Aramean wave of invaders in the last centuries of the second millennium B.C.[27]

Two great international highways have traversed Palestine in the biblical period, 'the way of the sea' (Via Maris) and 'the King's Highway'. The Way of the Sea was important at all biblical periods, and along it some of the most important cities of the country developed. It did not proceed strictly along the coast, and so its name reflected a northern viewpoint as in Isa. 9: 1, reflecting on its access to the Red Sea. Arvad, Tyre, Acco (Acre), Joppa and Gaza were all situated along it. But an inland branch followed on the western edge of the Shephelah via Aphek to Megiddo and thence to Hazor and on to Damascus. The second major highway, the King's Highway, stretched from Damascus in the north along the tablelands overlooking the Jordan via Ashtaroth, Rabbathammon, Bozrah, to Elath at the head of the gulf of Aqabah, with branches to Egypt and Arabia. Varying with the times, lesser internal routes linked the country, of which Aharoni has enumerated twenty-five as having some importance.[28] Their distribution, influenced by the physical accessibility of passes, dry valleys, and the outcrop of major springs and wells, has fixed the framework and the ranked hierarchy in importance of the towns and villages of Palestine.

The geographical influences on biblical history have been paradoxical. On the one hand, Palestine has been a country of isolated units, divided into petty tribal units and kingdoms, split, separated, isolated, by culture, and ethnic composition. So the regionalism associated with names and areas such as Galilee, Gilead,

Ammon, Moab, Edom, Philistia, Judah, Samaria, etc. has been profound and lasting. As early as the third millennium B.C., in the Early Bronze Age, there already existed significant cultural differences between the peoples of the mountain country and the plains. In passages like Jos. 12, there is enumeration of some thirty-one 'kings', each of whom ruled no more than one royal town and its satellite villages, a toparchical structure reflected in the Gospels in the parable of the talents. But alongside this intense parochialism and cultural fragmentation, there were also the massive impacts of the *Völkerwanderungen*, the march of armies, the constant oscillations of international influences between Egypt and Mesopotamia, and the rise or collapse of whole peoples. It was truly the cockpit of the ancient world.

Favoured as an agricultural land as early as the third and second millennia B.C., it was exporting oil and wine to Egypt. An Egyptian reference to it in the second millennium B.C., speaks of it as 'a goodly land, and contains figs and vines . . . its honey (dates) is plentiful and its oil immense; on its trees is every fruit; it has barley and wheat and its cattle are innumerable.'[29] So, too, the writer of Dt. 8: 7–9 could speak expansively of its productivity, while its forested mountains were distinctive (Jos. 17: 14, 19), and its mineral resources of iron and copper already exploited in the Negev, Edom, and Lebanon. And yet it was a poor land compared with the riverine civilizations, frequently afflicted by drought, facing unequal distribution of rain within adjoining districts (Am. 4: 7). Indeed, uncertainty of rain encouraged its people to trust God rather than their environmental resources (Dt. 11: 12).

CULTURAL PERSPECTIVES OF ITS PEOPLES

The natural frontiers of Palestine are geographical realities.[30] The western frontier is the Mediterranean; on the east, it is a climatic frontier, the Syrian-Arabian desert bordered more specifically by the watershed between the drainage flowing into the Jordan and those falling eastwards. The south-west is the River of Egypt, the Wadi el-Arish. Only in the north is the natural frontier not defined along its entire length, passing along the Litani, Hermon, and the watershed between the Yarmuk and the Oasis of Damascus. But it has been essentially an area of transit for trade and military influences.

The relief features of Palestine have been the stage on which differing cultural dramas have been played. The coastal plain, largely straight and unindented, has never given birth to a maritime civilization as other parts of the eastern Mediterranean have done. But agriculturally and in terms of trade, it has been the richest area, with the greatest diversity of cultures. Inland, the Shephelah represents the foothills of Judah, once clothed with woodlands and the scene of the struggles between the Israelites and the Philistines. The limestone backbone of the hills of Palestine lie toward it, divisible into four clear portions: the Negev mountains in the south, the hills of Judaea, of Ephraim, and to the north of Galilee. Beyond is the linear trench of the Jordan valley, divided into three parts: the Jordan rift, that includes the sea of Galilee, and Lake Huleh; the Dead Sea rift basin; and the Aravah desert, the most barren area of the country. East of the Jordan trench are the mountain plateaux of Transjordan, divisible into the mountains of Seir, Moab, Gilead and Bashan. They form a monotonous, rolling upland tract of semi-desert. These north-south orientated furrows and tracts of relief have provided a physical framework of great influence upon the settlement and life of biblical Palestine. Already by the third millennium B.C., there existed considerable ethnic diversities within the country, and independent cultural traits developed in the Canaanite period. After the Israelite conquest and particularly under the Israelite monarchy three ethnic elements became sharpened in contrast: the Phoenicians on the north coast, the Philistines on the southern and central coasts, and the Israelites in the Shephelah the western hills of Judah and Samaria, the Jordan valley and the western margin of the eastern tablelands of Transjordan.

A cultural perspective on the Old Testament must take into account three realities: the antiquity of its peoples and the migrations before biblical times; the remarkable diversity of cultures whose differences become more and more appreciable as researches are made; and the awesome pressures and therefore miraculous preservation of the uniqueness of Israelite faith in the midst of the nations. The Bible period in the Age of the Patriarchs begins about 2000 B.C. but the great civilizations of Mesopotamia and Egypt, between which the patriarchal wanderings were suspended, had existed 1,500 years before Abraham. Israelite settlement in the land of promise met with ancient towns and villages, as well as doubtless created many new ones also. But Jericho already existed as a settlement by about 8000 B.C. [31]

The cultural diversity of the Near East is attested in the Table of the Nations (Gen. 10), an ethno-geographical atlas unique in ancient literature, dating possibly as early as 1000 or even 1400 B.C. [32] Israel conceived itself as 'a congregation of peoples', groups representative of diverse families and clans. It was the uniqueness of Israel's covenant with God—there is no evidence any other people established a covenant with their Gods—with its roots in the historical event of the Exodus-redemption that gave birth to Israel as a 'nation'. [33] Subsequently, there were built up the necessary elements of nationality in common faith and custom, government and a defined territory (Dt. 32: 8, 9). Popular demand for a king like all the nations around them (1 Sam. 8: 5) led to territorial demarcation and inter-state diplomacy. So by the reign of Solomon, Israel was brought into contact and in dependence upon the many peoples who bordered its territory.

Biblical scholarship has shown the importance of separating the concept of 'Hebrews' from 'Israelites'. [34] The identification of the two terms occurs in the story of Joseph (Gen. 39: 14; Exod. 10: 3). But elsewhere the Exodus narrative indicates a large mixed group of non-Israelites also took part in the Exodus (Exod. 12: 38; Num. 11: 4). 'Hebrews', it is suggested, is a social rather than an ethnic term, and after Saul it practically disappears from the spoken biblical language. [35] Presumably, after the reign of David, who built up his organization of the state by assimilation, the democratic and religious character of the Israelites as 'sons of Israel' was more real. Thus their identity arose first as a sociological phenomenon rather than as an ethnic group, and then later their self-consciousness is developed around three primary issues: their covenant with God, the incomparable; [36] the historical experience of the Exodus-redemption; and their awareness of being the community of Israel.

Growing interest in ancient cosmologies indicates how fundamentally different Israelite faith was from the paganism of its neighbours, even though there were also sharp contrasts between the theologies of Mesopotamia and Egypt. [37] J. J. M. Roberts has recently argued that the radical contrast between 'the polytheistic gods of nature and the Israelite god of history must be softened considerably', in terms of the sense of history and the practice of divination among these ancient peoples. [38] But it is the gulf between Israel and the other nations that is far more obvious, in realms that still profoundly separate the minds of modern man. For all ancient thought lived in a closed system of the primordial realities of the coexistence of good and evil, and of determinism as the ultimate principle that influenced and disposed of the gods, as much as men. This is incompatible with the open view of a transcendent God who is prior to all else, who rules above and beyond all, who has made a good creation, in which evil is a subsequent intrusion. As Paul Ricoeur [39] and others have shown, this generates a profound contrast between biblical faith and all other systems of thought and faith. Moreover, the personal concern of God for His people, the uniqueness of His covenant with those responsive to Him, breaks down the inevitability of the fates, the cyclicity of time, and the materialism that infers the supremacy of matter over spirit. In these areas of faith, modern scientific man is as much under bondage to nature and nature's ways, as the devotees of the pantheons of Mesopotamia and of Egypt. For scientism is only an aggressive form of paganism.[40]

There is increasing awareness therefore, that most of the allusions and teaching concerning Israelite faith in creation were polemical against the false cosmogonies and cosmologies of the ancient world. This is the key to the biblical interpretation of God creating light prior to the establishment of the starry heavens (Gen. 1: 3, 14), and the polemics against astrology are very numerous in the Old Testament (Gen. 1: 14–18; Dan. 2: 10–19; Isa. 47: 13). At times, the references to Leviathan, Rahab and other mythical sea-monsters suggest deliberate denial of their existence as deities[41] (Pss. 74: 12–15; 89: 9–10; Job 3: 8; 7: 12; 9: 8; 26: 12–13; 38: 8–11; 41; Am. 9: 3; Hab. 3: 8–15), but more usually they are mentioned allegorically as being no more than God's creatures. The discoveries of Ras Shamra have greatly enriched our understanding of Canaanite religion, its obsession with the snake cult that shadows much Old Testament background, and its concern for the fertility rites of a harsh and climatically uncertain environment.[42] But the public stand of Elijah against the priests of Baal is only one of many polemics of the Old Testament against Baal and nature's ways. Elijah also learnt (1 Kg. 18) that God, as the Creator of all things, is in no way to be identified or confused with the works of creation; the Lord, therefore, was not in the wind, nor in the earthquake, nor in the fire (1 Kg. 19: 11). So too Hosea recognized that the corn, wine and oil, which the people presumed were the gifts of Baal, were in fact the provisioning of God (Hos. 2: 8–9); the vines and fig-tree were not the rewards of the lovers of the Canaanite deities (Hos. 2: 12).

It seems, therefore, as if Israel faced three dangers that provided a three-fold set of motifs to the moral and socio-political life of Israel: the seduction of the local Canaanite deities and their constant threat to domestic faith; the transcendent God who had called Abraham out of Mesopotamia to bind Himself in covenant to a faithful remnant; and the deliverance of Israel out of Egypt, whose totalitarian and monolithic traits were so implacably hostile to all that Israel's faith implied, that redemption and the historical eventfulness of the Exodus alone could save Israel.

THE SETTLEMENT IN CANAAN

In the future, as more archaeological data become available, the historical geography of the settlement in Canaan will take on a depth of perspective that is still shadowy and uncertain. But already certain issues are clear. Firstly, the invasion of the Israelites was not an isolated event; it was related to the great waves of expansion by Hebrew and Aramean tribes that exerted pressures over all the lands of the Fertile Crescent. For it was then also that the Ammonites, Moabites, and Edomites settled in Transjordan, and other peoples did likewise in Syria and the Euphrates valley. Secondly, the historicity of the Exodus is clearer. The mention of Ramses among the cities built by Israelite slaves (Exod. 1: 11) points to the beginning of the reign of Ramses II when he selected Tanis as his new capital. The Merneptah Stele indicates that the Israelites were in Canaan by c. 1220 B.C.[43] Glueck's archaeological surveys indicate that settlement was renewed in southern Transjordan only about the thirteenth century, after a long cessation.[44] The peaceful infiltration of the Israelites or the violence of their conquests varied geographically in different areas, and also varied with the historic sequence.

Alt envisaged the territorial division of Palestine in the Amarna period as follows:[45] fairly large territorial units and sparser population in the hill lands of Galilee, central Palestine and Judea; city states along the coast; city states in the Shephelah (Lachish, Gezer and Keilah); and a chain of city states from Acco to Bethshan in the plains of Megiddo, Jezreel and Bethshan, and another chain of city states from the coastal plain towards Jerusalem via Zorah and-Aijalon. Military pressures therefore varied from district to district, with a relatively peaceful expansion of colonization in the hill lands, much more resistance in the plains. Albright's archaeological interpretation is of violence and the destruction of many Palestinian cities.[46] Wright's more literary approach to the conquest suggests that the Israelite occupation took place in two stages.[47] The first stage was the destruction of Palestinian cities in the Israelite campaigns under Joshua against the southern part of central Palestine (Gilgal–Jericho–Bethel/Ai–Gibeon), against southern Palestine (Libnah–Lachish–Eglon-Hebron-Debir) and against Galilee (Hazor). This left untouched key centres and large numbers of inhabitants with whom the Israelites later had to come to terms. The second stage was during the period of the Judges when Israelite peaceful penetration of the wooded hill lands continued, but when planned attacks in numerous local conflicts also took place (e.g. Jos. 1–12).

While scholars differ as to the model of conquest and of the stages taken,[48] the extensive settlement of the hill country was doubtless facilitated by three factors. Firstly there was the patriarchal-tribal social organization of the Israelites which permitted guerrilla tactics of defence, better suited to small, unfortified settlements and dispersed groups of colonists. Secondly, the adoption of iron tools replacing the less strong bronze implements in the transition from the Bronze to the Iron Age would help the tasks of clearing the forests for agriculture.[49] Clearly, iron was still a Philistine monopoly but the Philistines were prepared to allow the Israelites iron agricultural implements although not arms (1 Sam. 13: 19–22). Thirdly, the invention of the plastered cistern in the Late Bronze Age,[50] adopted from the Canaanites, revolutionized the possibility of moving the centre of population densities from the spring-fed plains into the hill country and so cultivate lands never tilled before (see allusion to this technology in Jer. 2: 13).

Aharoni has pioneered in the historical geography of settlement, in using the biblical lists to map out the areas and Canaanite cities not conquered by the Israelites, as well as to define the tribal boundaries.[51] But much has still to be learnt about the history and sociological character of this period. Then for about one hundred and fifty years, the Philistines dominate the scene, especially in the Shephelah and coastal plain in the period between the Judges and the monarchy under David. Arriving several generations after the Israelites, they belonged to the wave of 'Sea Peoples' that migrated eastwards from the Greek mainland and islands into Syria and Canaan.[52] The voluptuousness of their women is the sad story behind Samson's life. David's victory over Goliath is much more than an epic story for it reflects the profound adjustment of Israelite theology and culture to face up to the Aegean concept of victory by championship, itself a challenge to the Israelite concept of the corporate personality of the people of Yahweh. Later in his reign, David took the Philistines wholly within his domain.

During the reigns of David and Solomon, the Israelite state reached its political and economic apogee. Geopolitically this is explained by their control of both the *Via Maris* and the King's Highway, thus enjoying absolute control over the major trade routes of the Near East. So the archaeological evidence reflects a sudden rise in the standard of living. But the prophetic denunciations reflect also in the subsequent period moral declension with this materialism. However, the trade routes were also the routes of armies, and so the Assyrian campaigns of Tiglath-pileser III and Sennacherib, the Egyptian invasion of 609 B.C., and then the victory of the Babylonian Nebuchadnezzar in 604 B.C., erased the last traces of Israelite–Judaean Independence.

THE PROMISED LAND

However, in exile as in occupation of the land, the Israelites developed a theology of the land whose features are not clearly understood today. And yet its application today has two powerful consequences: the relevance of Zionism in the state of Israel, and the challenge of environmentalists that the Judaeo-Christian tradition is responsible for the ecological crisis today. The former implies a reality that is perhaps misdirected from the reading of the Old Testament since it is the promise of God, reflective of His character, that is the basis, rather than a geopolitical structure. The latter accusation is unfounded if the theological understanding of creation and of man's dominion as steward is biblically understood.

There are other issues that also need to be denied. Following Mircea Eliade's views about religious sanctity too closely,[53] W. D. Davies in his important book *The Gospel and the Land* asserts the notion that Israel conceived of itself to be the centre of the earth.[54] Granted the term *omphalos* is once used (Ezek. 5: 5), but the mythological pagan view that temple or land had cosmic significance and sanctity *per se* is wholly foreign to the Bible. The centrality of Jerusalem and its temple was geographical not cosmological. The temple was a man-made house, in which God presenced Himself, even though the heaven of heavens could not contain Him (1 Kg. 8: 27). Likewise, while the Semites did have 'a feeling of a real and intimate connection with the land', and on occasion the Babylonian settlers in Israel were attacked by lions and other beasts because 'they knew not the manner of the God of the land' (2 Kg. 17: 24 ff.), yet there is no evidence that the Israelites thought of Yahweh as the local deity. Rather the Israelite exile in Babylon, looking towards the land of Canaan, could declare, 'I lift up my eyes to the hills—where does my help come from? My help comes from the LORD, the Maker of heaven and earth' (Ps. 121: 1–2).

But there is also the claim of Yahweh that the land, in which Israel lived, was Yahweh's, so that the Israelites were not possessors but 'aliens and my tenants' (Lev. 25: 23). Israel owned and could claim nothing. Moreover, as Buber has said, 'the very nature of the land of Canaan bears witness to the unremitting providence of God. And it is its nature that qualifies it to be the pledge of the covenant'.[55] God cares for the land, blessing it with rain (Dt. 11: 10–12), for the concept of nature is utterly foreign to biblical faith, nor is there an abstract world system, whether called cosmos or universe.[56] The radicalism of thought that sees in the Creator God the source and upholder of all phenomena gives no scope for any physical, autonomous system, called 'Nature'. Instead, the promised land dependent upon the faithfulness of Yahweh is seen within a triangular relationship.

Yahweh

Israel △ Canaan

Without Yahweh there could be no promise to Abraham, no promise of land, no fulfilment. Israel, too, was a variable in the situation, for as the benefactor of the covenant of God, it was the receiver of the law, so its enjoyment of the land was conditional on regulations for society and the land. If Israel disobeyed the commandments, then she could be expelled from the land (Lev. 10). But the land in which Israel was to dwell, was not based on recompense for legality, but upon the gracious will of God (Dt. 6: 20 ff.) So the land, won by conquest through the help of Yahweh, could also be lost if Yahweh withdrew His support (Jos. 23: 3, 9, 15–16).

A just relationship with Yahweh and the land was reflected also in a just society, established by the rule of law (Dt. 21: 5; 16: 18). Power was to be balanced between food producers and law-givers, so that Levites as the administrators of law were prohibited from being land-owners (Num. 26: 57, 62). Instead, they were set apart in certain cities (Num. 35: 1–8), supported in part by sacrifices and taxes (Num. 18: 21, 24). Poor tithe helped to redistribute wealth, and in addition the gleaning laws provided assistance for the needy (Lev. 19: 9–10; Dt. 24: 19–21). Zero interest rates also helped to control the accumulation of capital within the whole society, by use of the sabbath and jubilee years (Dt. 15: 1–10; 23: 19–20). It was a society of a work-leisure ethic, in which leisure was spent in the spiritual and educational needs of the society to give meaning to work and to one's existence, not the reverse as in a society compulsively addicted to work (Exod. 20: 9; Dt. 6: 6–9; 31: 9–13). Robert North is doubtful if this legislation was ever carried out, although it is clear that King Zedekiah put the ancient legislation again into effect in his reign (Jer. 34).[57] Isaiah too had the vision that renewal of God's people and renewal of history would be in the form of jubilee (Isa. 58: 6–12).[58]

It has been pointed out by Mendenhall, however, that a community based on values and covenant is sharply contrasted with a social control system organized and maintained by law.[59] That is to say, the kingdom of God is not a political state. It is not based on power, money or prestige but on the doing of love, justice and righteousness on the personal scale and not in the corporate organization. It is a community, called in grace, responsive in gratitude, active in free volition, binding each individual not by social organization but by 'the fear of the Lord', with a forward look to future hope, independent of all cultural and other social controls. Here is where biblical faith and practice transcends environmental controls, whether geographical or cultural, providing the people of God with a uniqueness and imperishable, lasting impact on all history. It is what Jesus preached and embodied.

The reality of the rule of God is meanwhile obscured by man's misuse of his mandate to have dominion over the earth. In the Song of the Seven Wonders, the psalmist praises God for putting at the disposal of man the sky, the earth, the water, the produce, the sun and the moon, the sea and above all else the gift of life itself (Ps. 104). Given the task of cultivating the given things of God's creation, as a gardener that tends the earth (Gen. 2: 15), man is exhorted 'Take care that the earth be able to support you, when your days and your children's days are multiplied' (Dt. 11: 16–21). So numerous precautions for the maintenance of God's creation are enumerated (*e.g.* Dt. 20: 19–20; 22: 6–8). But in the fall of man, in his greed and lust, the evil of man reflects upon the environmental deterioration (Isa. 22: 9–19; 24: 1–13). Exclusively economic, ecological, or political solutions today, cannot remedy the issues of the global environmental crisis we face, as the biblical principles of the Old Testament clearly demonstrate.

ENVIRONMENTAL MOTIFS OF THE OLD TESTAMENT

In conclusion, reference may briefly be made to environmental motifs of the Old Testament. This is a confused subject sometimes suggestive of a determinism of matter over spirit, of geography over history that is foreign to the Hebrew faith in the transcendence of God. It is further confused by the mesmerism 'nature' has had over the human mind since the dawn of civilization. The traits and contents of the physical universe are spelt out in man-made metaphors not reality itself. So man has made no progress in the human choice between God's *creatio ex nihilo* as the beginning of the universe, or the cyclical turnings of time. The infinite uncreated matter of Babylonian cosmogony, perpetually evolving, is not dissimilar to modern man's credulity about 'nature' and faith in 'nature's ways'.[60] Much theology too is confused in its thinking of the 'natural' and the 'supernatural'.[61] It is not peculiar that the natural environment is suited to mediate God as transcendent in the sublimity of the physical world, and as gracious in providing for man in the precariousness of human existence.

This is then a motif of the Bible, of the precariousness within which Israel was placed, between the wilderness and the garden,

Hebraic words for wilderness, steppe and desert are numerous, as the predominant characteristic of its environment. Moreover, its threat is more than physical, being viewed as evidence of a moral state, and of death. It is the realm of demons, of evil, and the scene of God's judgment (Ps. 106: 26 f.; Jer. 25: 38; Isa. 34: 13 f.). And yet it is the sphere of God's covenant in a twofold aspect: as a place of redemptive bliss, and as a place of testing and instruction (Dt. 32: 10 f.; Hos. 2: 14 f.; Jer. 2: 2). The Exodus wanderings are thus integrated into a whole series of lessons that Israel can learn from, both collectively as the people of God and as individuals. Today, it is a theological motif that has been most meaningful to those within the North American culture, since much of U.S. identity has been fashioned out of the wilderness motif which the Puritan founding fathers certainly recognized.[62]

The rise and fall of human enterprises and institutions within the Near East setting, is also clearly spelled out in the Old Testament. The conflict between Cain and Abel, cultivator and pastoralist, is typified. Invasions and conquests of nomadic peoples have interrupted the orderly development of irrigation and agriculture. The destruction of vegetation, soil erosion, and the decline of hydraulic works by silting, are well known in this environment. The holistic understanding of ecology has changed the modern mind-set radically in recent years, concerning the inter-dependence of life. But this is the atmosphere of the Old Testament, indeed much more fundamentally so, since ultimately it is recognized that disobedience towards God's orders and human pride are the cause of all ills. For the semitic thought of the Old Testament is not Greek thought, which so dominated western and latin Christianity, but totality thinking, concretely expressed and acted upon. So that man in community, and community under God, provide comprehensive and integrative frames of reference to provide *shālôm*, that typically biblical sense of peace, as health and wholeness, which is provided by righteousness and faith. For ultimately, the biblical sense of environmental controls and consequences is not that of nature, but of God the Creator-Redeemer.[63]

REFERENCES

1 Quoted by YOHANAN AHARONI, *The Land of the Bible* (Westminster Press, Philadelphia, 1967), p. XII.

2 J. M. HOUSTON, 'The Geographical Background in Old Testament Exegesis', *Trans. Victoria Inst.*, 86 (1954), p. 63.

3 Palestine Exploration Fund, *The Survey of Western Palestine* (London, 1881).

4 E. HULL, *Memoir on the Physical Geology and Geography of Palestine* (London, 1886).

5 Sir George Adam Smith, *An Historical Geography of the Holy Land* (London, 1894; 25th edition, 1931).

6 F. M. Abel, *Géographie de la Palestine*, 2 tomes (Paris, 1933).

7 M. du Buit, O.P., *Géographie de la Terre Sainte* (Editions du Cerf, Paris, 1958).

8 Denis Baly, *The Geography of the Bible* (Harper & Row, New York, 1974).

9 Aharoni, *op. cit.*, p. XIII.

10 Nelson Glueck, *The River Jordan* (Lutterworth Press, London, 1946); *Rivers in the Desert* (Weidenfeld & Nicolson, London, 1959).

11 A. Alt, 'The Settlement of the Israelites in Palestine', in *Essays in Old Testament History and Religion* (B. Blackwell, Oxford, 1966), pp. 133–69.

12 W. F. Albright, 'Archaeology and the date of the Hebrew conquest of Palestine', *Bull. Amer. Schools of Orient. Research*, 58 (1935), pp. 10–18; and 'The Israelite conquest of Canaan in the light of archaeology', ditto 74 (1939), pp. 11–23.

13 G. E. Mendenhall, 'The Hebrew Conquest of Palestine', *The Biblical Archaeologist*, 25 (1962), pp. 66–87.

14 Y. Aharoni, *op. cit.*

15 S. Abramsky, *Ancient Towns in Israel* (World Zionist Organization, Jerusalem, 1963).

16 H. Wheeler Robinson, *Inspiration and Revelation in the Old Testament* (Oxford University Press, Oxford, 1946), pp. 1–16.

17 John Bright, 'Modern study of the Old Testament Literature' in G. Ernest Wright (ed.), *The Bible and the Ancient Near East* (Doubleday Anchor Books, Garden City, New York, 1965), pp. 5–18.

18 Yehezkel Kaufman, *The Religion of Israel* (University of Chicago Press, 1960), p. 2.

19 Frank Hole, 'Investigating the origins of Mesopotamian Civilization', *Science*, 153, Aug. 1966, pp. 605–609.

20 Robert J. Braidwood, *The Near East and the Foundations of a Civilization* (Condon Lectures, Oregon, 1962).

21 J. M. Houston, 'The Bible in its environment', *The Lion Handbook to the Bible* (Lion Publishing, Berkhamsted, 1973), pp. 10–21.

22 David O'Connor, 'The geography of settlement in ancient Egypt', pp. 681–98; and H. S. Smith, 'Society and settlement in ancient Egypt', pp. 705–719 in Peter J. Ucko *et alii* (edit.) *Man, settlement and Urbanism* (Duckworth, London, 1972).

23 H. Frankfort *et alii*, *Before Philosophy, the intellectual adventure of early man* (Penguin Books, London, 1949), pp. 137–190.

24 T. Jacobsen and Robert M. Adams, 'Salt and silt in ancient Mesopotamian agriculture', *Science*, 128, Nov. 1958, pp. 125–57.

25 R. B. Y. Scott, 'Climate of Palestine' in George A. Buttrick *et al.* (eds.), *The Interpreter's Dictionary of the Bible* (Abingdon Press, Nashville, 1962), K–Q, pp. 621–626.

26 A. Reifenberg, *The Struggle between the Desert and the Town* (Jewish Agency, Jerusalem, 1955).

27 Emmanuel Anati, *Palestine before the Hebrews* (Alfred A. Knopf, New York, 1963), pp. 375–410.

28 Aharoni, *op.cit.*, p.40.

29 Quoted by Abramsky, *op.cit.*, p.20.

30 For brevity no attempt is made in this study to outline the physical geography of Palestine. For this background see Herbert G. May, *Oxford Bible Atlas* (Oxford University Press, 1962), pp. 48–53; Aharoni, *op. cit.* (ed.), pp. 19-38.

31 K. M. Kenyon, *Digging up Jericho* (Benn, London, 1957); see also Anati, *op.cit.*

32 J. Simons, *The Geographical and Topographical Texts of the Old Testament* (E. J. Brill, Leiden, 1966).

33 Delbert R. Hillers, *Covenant: the History of a Biblical Idea* (Johns Hopkins University Press, Baltimore, 1969).

34 H. Cazelles, 'The Hebrews' in D. J. Wiseman (ed.), *Peoples of Old Testament Times* (Clarendon Press, Oxford, 1973), pp.1–28.

35 George E. Mendenhall, 'The Apiru Movements in the late Bronze Age' in *The Tenth Generation* (John Hopkins University Press, 1973), pp. 122-141.

36 C. J. Labuschagne, *The Incomparability of Yahweh in the Old Testament* (E. J. Brill, Leiden, 1966).

37 See especially S. N. Kramer, *Mythologies of the Ancient World* (Doubleday, Garden City, New York, 1961), and Alexander Heidel, *The Babylonian Genesis* (University of Chicago Press, 1950).

38 J. J. M. Roberts, 'Divine Freedom and Cultic Manipulation in Israel and Mesopotamia' in Hans Goedicke and J. J. M. Roberts, *Unity and Diversity, essays in the history, literature and religion of the ancient Near East* (John Hopkins University Press, Baltimore, 1975), pp.181–190.

39 Paul Ricoeur, *The Symbolism of Evil* (Beacon Press, Boston, 1967), pp. 175–210.

40 See excellent survey on this theme in Stanley L. Jaki, *Science and Creation from eternal cycles to an oscillating universe* (Scottish Academic Press, Edinburgh & London, 1974).

41 Mary K. Wakeman, *God's Battle with the Monster: a study in biblical imagery* (E. J. Brill, Leiden, 1973); J. Day, *God's conflict with the Dragon and the Sea* (Cambridge University Press, 1985). See also Gerhard F. Hasel, 'The Polemic Nature of the Genesis Cosmology', *The Evangelical Quarterly*, 46 (1974), pp.81–102.

42 A. S. Kapelrud, *The Ras Shamra Discoveries and the Old Testament* (B. Blackwell, Oxford, 1965).

43 Pierre Montet, *Egypt and the Bible* (Fortress Press, Philadelphia, 1968), pp.16–34.

44 N. Glueck, *Rivers in the Desert*, pp.47–50.

45 A. Alt, 'The Settlement of the Israelites in Palestine', *op.cit.*

46 W. F. Albright, *The Biblical Period from Abraham to Ezra* (Harper Torchbooks 102, N. Y., 1963), pp.24–34.

47 G. E. Wright, 'The literary and historical problem of Joshua 10 and Judges 1', *Journ. of Near East. Studies*, 5 (1946), pp.105–14.

48 See especially: Manfred Weippert, *The Settlement of the Israelite tribes in Palestine*, Studies in Biblical Theology, second series, 21 (SCM Press, London, 1971), and P. W. Lapp, 'The Conquest of Palestine in the light of archaeology', *Concordia Theological Monthly*, 38 (1967), pp.283–300.

49 Aharoni, *op.cit.*, p. 219.

50 A. Barrois, *Manuel d'archéologie biblique*, 1 (Paris, 1939), p. 226.

51 Aharoni, *op.cit.*, pp.227–45.

52 Edward E. Hindson, *The Philistines and the Old Testament* (Baker Book House, Grand Rapids, 1971), pp.13–21.

53 Mircea Eliade, *The Sacred and the Profane* (New York, 1959), p. 20.

54 W. D. Davies, *The Gospel and the Land* (University of California Press, 1974), pp.7–10.

55 Martin Buber, *Pointing the Way* (Harper, New York, 1957).

56 P.van Imschoot, *Theology of the Old Testament*. vol.1 (Deseler, New York, 1965), p. 86.

57 Robert North, S.J., *Sociology of the Biblical Jubilee* (Pontifical Biblical Institute, Rome, 1954).

58 John Howard Yoder, *The Politics of Jesus* (Wm. B. Eerdmans, Grand Rapids, 1972), p. 37.

59 George E. Mendenhall, 'The Conflict between value systems and social control' in *Unity and Diversity*, pp. 169–180. See also his important study: *The Tenth Generation, the origins of the Biblical Traditions* (John Hopkins University Press, Baltimore, 1973).

60 N. K. Sanders (ed.), *Poems of Heaven and Hell from Mesopotamia* (Penguin, London, 1971), p. 70.

61 H. H. Farmer, *The World and God* (London, 1946), pp.51–67.

62 George H. Williams, *Wilderness and Paradise in Christian Thought* (Harper & Bros., New York, 1962).

63 See also W. Brueggeman, *The Land: Place as Gift, Promise and Challenge in Biblical Faith* (Philadelphia, 1977).

THE THEOLOGY OF THE OLD TESTAMENT

H. L. ELLISON

1. THE NATURE AND PURPOSE OF THEOLOGY

The theologian sets out to express in an ordered and systematic form all that may be known about God; this involves a consideration of the nature, purpose and behaviour of man as seen by God. True theology, in contrast to philosophy, psychology and allied disciplines, must be based on God's self-revelation.

In practice the resultant picture is always deficient in parts and gives the impression of contradiction in others. Hence the theologian normally tries to fill the gaps by logical deduction from the facts in his possession. Where these seem to be self-contradictory, the usual practice is to harmonize them by inferring wider truths which will include the apparent discords. In addition recourse is normally also had to man's observations, and there are few theologians who have not been influenced by the thought patterns and philosophies of the time.

God's revelation has, with a few possible exceptions, been given in specific historical circumstances against a specific background of culture and beliefs. This is true even of the universal revelation of God's eternal power and deity (Rom. 1: 20). In his search for the universally valid the theologian finds it necessary to try and strip away all that he considers particular, temporal and local. It demands the utmost skill and spiritual insight, however, to guarantee that essential parts of the revelation are not lost in this process.

It is not easy for man to acknowledge that because of his finiteness certain aspects of the divine nature and purpose are partially or even entirely hidden from him. As a result it is probable that every system of systematic theology—the term dogmatic theology is equally used—goes beyond the limits of what can be deduced with certainty from the biblical revelation.

(a) Theology and Philosophy

Since the amount of material at the theologian's disposal is wide and often, especially in the Old Testament, does not obviously conform to any discernible pattern, he feels compelled to try to make it fit some mould and principles of his own choosing.

While the Palestinian and Babylonian rabbis on the one hand and Paul and the other New Testament writers on the other sought these in Old Testament concepts, Philo of Alexandria (1st cent. A.D.) sought to convey the teaching of the Old Testament in terms of Greek philosophy, especially that of Plato. Most of the early Church Fathers, especially those who wrote in Greek, followed his example for the New Testament, and the tradition was followed by the mediaeval Schoolmen, though from the time of Albertus Magnus and Thomas Aquinas the influence of Aristotle became dominant and remains the philosophic basis for official Roman Catholic theology to this day.

The great theologians of the Reformation broke with this tradition, returning to the Bible concepts as basic. With the rise of humanism Liberal Protestant theology became increasingly philosophical; sometimes special stress has been laid on problems of epistemology, i.e. the problems of perception and communication. In most such cases the Biblical record is treated as an almost secondary authority, and great use is made of a false concept of 'progressive', or better evolutionary, revelation, though in most cases revelation is equated with man's discovery of God. For a true evaluation of the progressive element in revelation cf. T. D. Bernard, *The Progress of Doctrine in the New Testament* (1864).

(b) Theology and Preconceptions

Even when the Bible record is accepted unquestioningly as the source of a system of theology, there is almost unavoidably the assumption of some major doctrinal truth as the mould into which the whole body of truth has to be fitted. This helps to explain the very wide variations of theological outlook among those who unhesitatingly accept the authority of Scripture.

It should not be thought that this is specially a weakness of the intellectuals. Dispensational theology, for example, while originally propounded by academically trained men, is especially popular among people who would not be described as intellectuals, but it enables its adherents to produce a remarkably coherent, though often very partial, picture of the content of revelation.

2. BIBLICAL THEOLOGY

The term 'Biblical Theology' was coined by J. P. Gabler in an address given in 1787. Despairing, as he did, of reconciling Lutheran and Reformed (Calvinistic) theologies in Germany, he suggested that instead of the traditional systematic theologies, which had led to so much controversy, scholars should devote themselves to a Biblical Theology, which would be based solely on what the Bible had to say.

His suggestion did not meet with the success it deserved, because controversy shifted rapidly from traditional orthodoxies to the question how the Bible itself should be approached, when seen in the light of developing higher criticism. Old Testament scholars increasingly devoted themselves to depicting an evolutionary 'Religion of Israel', in which little internal unity could be found—a prerequisite for any theology—for it was seen mainly as man's varied discovery of God. In their study of the New Testament many scholars of the time had as their main concern the driving of wedges between Jesus and Paul and the other apostolic writers, and between the primitive and the sub-apostolic church. On the other hand, more conservative scholars were normally sufficiently satisfied with the system in which they had grown up not to want to leave or even modify it.

It is not chance that modern Biblical Theology really began with the Old Testament. The conservative tended to become bogged down in types and allegories, which deprived the Old Testament of much of its value and authority, while critical studies seemed to have deprived it of virtually all authority and value. A. B. Davidson, *The Theology of the Old Testament* (1904), was the first real indication of a new era. It is worth quoting his definition of Biblical Theology: 'In Systematic Theology, while Scripture supplies the knowledge, some mental scheme, logical or philosophical, is made into the mould into which the knowledge is run, so that it comes out bearing the form of the mould. In Biblical Theology the Bible is the source of the knowledge, and also supplies the form in which the knowledge is presented' (p. 1).

3. OLD TESTAMENT THEOLOGY
(a) The Development of Old Testament Theology

Professor Davidson's initiative was slow in bearing fruit and it had no direct successors. A new mood became clear after the first world war, due in part to the new Theology of Crisis, which took the Old Testament as seriously as the New. Most of the outstanding works on the subject produced on the Continent have been translated into English and are listed in the Bibliography. A number of English-speaking scholars have written valuable books which have taken into consideration the problems involved and are a preparation for something more inclusive and definitive. The great gain from these pioneering attempts at an all-embracing Old Testament Theology is that they have made clear how difficult the task is.

(b) The Presuppositions of Old Testament Theology

Whatever views a writer on Old Testament Theology may have on higher critical views, it should be clear that he considers the OT forms a coherent whole; in other words he need not be a conservative in his approach, but he does not accept the widely held view by liberals that any appearance of unity has been simply imposed on disparate elements by late editors. There will even then be distinctly varied approaches.

(i) There are some who will approach the OT from the standpoint of the NT and deal with it mainly or entirely as preparation. In other words they see the value of the Old almost entirely in its fulfilment and fulness in the New. Many of them are likely to go further and to see in Old Testament Theology—to use E. J. Young's phrase—'a useful handmaid to the discipline of Systematic Theology' (p. 110).

(ii) Many recognize that a unifying principle for the whole of OT revelation is not to be found within it. For that we must look to the NT. Yet it contains a valid and lasting revelation, which is not only presupposed in the New, but is normally necessary to its proper understanding. One who takes up this attitude may expect to be asked whether his final formulations are in harmony with the teaching of the NT, but he may not set out from the New and force the Old into the categories he has deduced from it. This is the standpoint adopted in this article.

(iii) A fairly general attitude of scholars writing on the subject is to take the OT by itself, ignoring the NT. Their experience has been, however, that whatever unifying element they choose from the OT they are unable to do justice to all its main aspects. This has been clearly shown by von Rad, who has been compelled to work on the basis of the theology of Israel's historical traditions and that of Israel's prophetic traditions without bringing the two into an ultimate unity.

(iv) A growing tendency is to accept that sufficient preparatory work has not yet been done on OT theology. So certain aspects only are dealt with. The works of H. Wheeler Robinson, H. H. Rowley and A. R. Johnson are of this nature.

4. THE CONCEPT OF REVELATION
(a) The Nature of Revelation

In contrast to the evolutionary and Hegelian

views that dominated OT studies for so long, but which are now being increasingly abandoned, the OT always depicts God as making Himself known to man. In the long line of His spokesmen, the canonical prophets, it is always God that takes the initiative. In contrast Jer. 23: 21 f. makes it clear that the popular prophets were, in fact, prompted by their own desires or psychic insights.

No clear explanation is ever offered of how the prophetic message came to the prophet, though the accompanying circumstances, especially at the prophet's call, are sometimes given, and Ezek. 2: 8–3: 3 makes clear, what should in any case be obvious, that the prophet had to assimilate the divine message. He was no mere speaking-tube. It is to be noted that the whole OT, apart from its third section, the Writings, is regarded as prophetic in nature, for Moses was the greatest of the prophets.

God's revelation is one of acts and words, which serve to interpret one another. This explains why the spoken revelation is almost always placed in a historical framework. There is no formulated doctrine of Inspiration as such, and it is apparently assumed that the written Scriptures will carry conviction to the one prepared to listen as surely as did the mighty acts and the spoken Word to those who first experienced them.

(b) The Sphere of Revelation
As said above, God's message came in a specific historical setting. Hence, though as real revelation it continues to have spiritual validity, it is never completely divorcible from its human context, or in other words, God in revealing Himself and His will does so in a human setting, which makes it also a revelation of human nature and behaviour as seen by God. He confines Himself to that which is within the sphere of man's possible experience and knowledge. Hence none of the problems which the philosopher is apt to raise about absolute truth are dealt with, nor are the doings of extra-terrestrial beings. In addition He uses human words and concepts, which as the vehicles of divine truth gradually acquire deeper meanings. Significantly too, revelation is not given until the situation of those receiving it makes it relevant.

(c) Progressive Revelation
What has just been stated makes the concept of progressive revelation inescapable. In addition, the two titles, Elohim and Yahweh, under which God was worshipped in Israel, implied a continuing revelation. The former may be fairly rendered 'The All-Powerful One' (see 5(a)); this presupposes that repeated acts of power will make His character and purpose ever clearer. The latter (see 5(b)) is explained in Exod. 3: 14, the Heb. being best rendered 'I will be what I will be'. This clearly suggests a

continuing revelation, which would not contradict that which had already been given. Hence the prophets, in contrast to the Wise, were less concerned with what had already been revealed, but more with expanding and deepening that which had already been made known. The OT concept of progressive revelation holds the middle ground between reading back later understanding of God into Israel's earliest ages and the rejection of the early history as unworthy of our spiritual consideration.

5. GOD—HIS NATURE AND ATTRIBUTES
God is referred to under two main names, or rather titles, Elohim and Yahweh. Though we can normally explain why one or the other is used, there are numerous cases where no reason can be given.

(a) The Title Elohim
Elohim is clearly derived from El, the name given to the king of the gods by the Canaanites, with Elôah, surviving mainly in poetry, as the connecting link. The lengthened form itself suggests majesty and this is increased by the use of the 'plural of majesty'—when used of the God of Israel, with few exceptions, it is used with a singular verb. In addition, however, the plural was probably intended to imply that every form of power is united in Him, in contrast to the common view that the various powers of nature were independent, though normally co-operating, entities. As Elohim God is the God of all the earth and all men and reveals Himself to all through nature and His mighty acts. The Israelite speaking to non-Israelites normally used Elohim, sometimes with the qualification 'God of heaven'.

(b) The Title Yahweh
Yahweh is the name of God within Israel, because of His revelation of Himself through Moses and the prophets, above all in the Torah; cf. the use of the two titles in Ps. 19. At the same time Gen. 4: 26 suggests that what is implicit in the title was partially apprehended from the earliest times.

Out of reverence Yahweh was replaced both in the reading of the Heb. Scriptures and in LXX by LORD, a practice followed in most Christian translations. Modern Jewish practice tends to use 'the Eternal'. Both are seriously misleading, for they obscure the fact that God made Himself known by a title, which stresses that God reveals Himself to men (cf. 4(c)), desires fellowship with men and that they may know Him. If in the OT the title is confined to Israel, it is because God revealed Himself to Israel, so that through Israel He might become known to all nations.

(c) God as Creator
The use of Elohim for the one true source of power in the world carried inescapably with it

the concept of Creator, and that from nothing, for it was impossible to grant to inchoate matter self-existence and power. In addition it followed that whatever powers there may be in nature were derived from Him, and that He is above and outside His creation, *i.e.* God controls nature but is not controlled by it. The unique use of Yahweh Elohim in Gen. 2 and 3 is to stress that the God of creation and of revelation are one.

(d) Monotheism

Such a concept of God's power and creatorship should in theory involve monotheism. In fact there are few, if any, indications of philosophical speculation on the subject. Acceptance of God's absolute power and of His grace displayed in the Exodus involved for those that received His revelation the impossibility of considering any other possible powers (Ethical Monotheism). This is found as early as Abraham. The dread of exile was not fear of passing from under God's rule, but of being separated from the land which He had given. In spite of Jewry's later use of Dt. 6: 4 as an affirmation of monotheism, first against paganism and then against tritheistic popular Christianity, its real meaning is probably 'Yahweh is our God, Yahweh alone'.

The frequent mention of 'gods' is no contradiction of this. It has already been remarked that Elohim means the powerful one(s), and so it is frequently used in this literal sense of beings, real or imaginary, to whom the nations attributed power, without normally any discussion of the validity of the title. The contempt implicit in its use is seen in its employment in Heb. for Ashtoreth in 1 Kg. 11: 5, 33, instead of a feminine. Some would see in Ps. 82 a degree of recognition of the pagan gods, but the term 'sons of the Most High' (v. 6; cf. 'sons of God' in Gen. 6: 2; Job 38: 7, etc.) points to angels being intended. The title 'sons of God' implies that whatever powers the angels may have derive from God Himself.

There is no suggestion of dualism, even in a modified form. Satan (Job 1: 6–12; 2: 1–7, Zech. 3: 1 f., 1 Chr. 21: 1) is a servant of God, even though a malicious one, and whatever power he can exercise is granted him by God. Similarly evil (1 Sam. 16: 14) or lying (1 Kg. 22: 22) spirits are in God's employment. The whole concept of dualism, especially in its Zoroastrian form, is flatly denied in Isa. 45: 6f. Though there is the beginning of the concept of 'spiritual hosts of wickedness in heavenly places' in Daniel, it is not elaborated. Though certain passages may be used by us to illustrate the fall of Satan, it is not clearly taught in the OT, where the stress is on human sin, not on events that preceded and influenced it.

e) The Metaphysical Attributes of God

Most systems of theology stress those concepts of God which are derived mainly from philosophy (metaphysics); they are, above all, His omnipotence, omniscience and omnipresence. These can easily be found in the OT, if it is treated as a collection of proof texts, but in fact they are normally taken for granted as being shown in the existence of Israel and of the individual; hence there is no consideration of the difficulties involved in the philosophical approach to these concepts.

The OT stresses the all-sovereignty of God, but does not raise the question of how this is compatible with man's freedom of choice. Traditionally El-Shaddai (Exod. 6: 3) has been translated as God Almighty, but this is improbable, and the exact meaning of Shaddai is unknown. The concept of sovereignty is rather suggested by Yahweh Tseba'ot (Lord of hosts, of all the powers in His heavenly and earthly creation). The miraculous is taken for granted, but with a few marginal exceptions it is seen not as a modification of creation but as its control, the means used being sometimes indicated. No answer is suggested as to why God tolerates evil (cf. Hab. 1: 13); at the same time He is seen as taking on Himself the ultimate responsibility for the suffering it brings to His creation (cf. Isa. 45: 5 ff.).

Equally the omniscience of God is taken for granted, but there is no suggestion that this is incompatible with human freedom. Indeed, in the prophets God is frequently depicted as though He did not know the future (cf. especially Jer. 18: 5–11), and it is the implication in the statement that God 'repented'. On the other hand there are references to God's knowledge of the individual (*e.g.* Ps. 139; Jer. 1: 5); there is no suggestion that His purposes can be thwarted, and occasionally exact dates are given for the future (*e.g.* Num. 14: 33; Jer. 25: 11 f.; Dan. 9: 2, 20). These two aspects are not contradictory but represent man's insoluble problem of reconciling God's foreknowledge and sovereignty with man's free will. There is no evidence, however, that it was felt to be a problem.

It is basic that God is greater than and outside His creation, yet He is omnipresent. This is achieved above all by two means, His angelic representatives, seen and unseen, and His Spirit. For the former see 5 (*d*). The Spirit of God can best be understood in most of its occurrences as the power of God exercised at a distance, and in poetic passages it is sometimes replaced by God's 'arm' or 'right hand'. The only passage that suggests the personality of the Spirit is Isa. 63: 10.

(f) God's Moral Attributes

Far more important for OT revelation are God's moral attributes. These are often given by direct revelation but they are substantiated by God's actions in the world and above all in the history of Israel. The key-passage is Exod. 34: 6 f. Not man's philosophical consideration of God but His treatment of sinful man is of most importance.

(i) *Holiness.* For the OT this goes beyond the almost universal realization of the separation of the divine from man which Rudolf Otto called the numinous. It is made clear by types, by God's actions, and by revelation (Isa. 6: 3 ff.) that this separation is due above all to man's sin. It is repeatedly stressed that this separation should disappear through Israel's (Exod. 19: 6) and the individual's (Lev. 19: 2) becoming God's possession and living accordingly.

(ii) *Righteousness.* This does not mean that God is bound by a law of His own creating, which He must enforce. Our modern concept of law is alien to the OT, and it is no chance that the word so translated (*torah*) really means instruction, though, since it comes from God, it is binding. Righteousness, when applied to God, means that the man who is prepared to approach Him humbly will always find Him completely consistent, and higher and better than he could have expected. It is expressed in the question, 'Will not the Judge of all the earth do right?' (Gen. 18: 25).

(iii) *Compassion, Mercy.* These concepts normally translate Heb. words from the same root as *reḥem*, the mother's womb. God's righteousness shows itself in a perfect understanding of and sympathy for His creation, including the animals (Jon. 4: 11; Ps. 104: 27–30).

(iv) *Grace.* Compassion leads in turn to great patience with the sinner, even though he is harming others. Punishment is normally deferred, so that man may repent. There is no suggestion that the forgiveness that follows is based on correct theology or sacrificial ritual. It should be noted that those incidents that especially raise objections today, *e.g.* the command to exterminate the Canaanites (Exod. 23: 23 f.; Dt. 7: 1–5) and Amalekites (1 Sam. 15: 2 f.), not only contain a moral purpose, but also ample time for repentance and change had been granted (cf. Gen. 15: 16).

(v) *Love.* While this term is used in the OT with, probably, all the shades of meaning we associate with it today, when it is applied to God, it never means purely an emotion, but always implies adequate action. It is used of God's choice of Israel, more rarely of a person (2 Sam. 12: 24 f.) or of a place (Ps. 87: 2). Then it includes all the faithfulness, preservation and care implied by election; cf. Jer. 31: 3. The failure to elect does not imply rejection; cf. Exod. 19: 5, where God's possession of the whole earth is stressed. So great are the privileges of God's electing love that not to experience it can be termed 'hate' (Mal. 1: 2 f.).

(vi) *The Covenant God.* God is depicted not merely as Creator, showing compassion to all He has made, but also as entering into a special relationship with it. This relationship is called a covenant, and it may or may not impose conditions on those with whom it has been made. Four covenants in particular need mention.

(a) *The Noachic Covenant.* In Gen. 8: 20–9: 17 we have a general covenant with Noah and his descendants and 'every living creature of all flesh that is upon the earth'. It is essentially a guarantee of God's faithfulness in preserving the earthly home of life from widespread natural disaster or from those reversals of natural phenomena to which geology bears testimony. No express conditions are stated.

(b) *The Covenant with Abraham* (Gen. 12: 1 ff.; 13: 14–17; 15: 5 f., 12–21; 17: 1–14; 22: 15 f.). The outstanding feature of this covenant is that it was made with an individual on the basis of his obedient faith; it was to extend to his descendants, and through them to mankind in general. Both in OT as a whole and in general Jewish thinking it plays a subordinate role to the next.

(c) *The Sinai Covenant* (Exod. 19: 3–8; 20: 1–17; 24: 1–11). Here the covenant was with Israel as a whole on the condition of a life lived on the level of the Decalogue. The conditions were broken almost at once, and the history of Israel was continued under the shadow of a broken covenant (Jer. 31: 32 JB, 'So I had to show them who was master'), yet in grace God remained faithful to His promises. The new covenant of Jer. 31: 31–34 is a renewal of this with a new Divine power.

(d) *The Davidic Covenant* (2 Sam. 7: 12–16). The promise made to David and his descendants had as its ultimate aim the setting up of God's perfect rule and so the bringing about of the purposes implicit in the three covenants already mentioned. The manner in which this covenant would be fulfilled would depend on the behaviour of the Davidic kings, but ultimate accomplishment was certain.

It is possible by pressing the evidence into a preconceived mould to deduce the idea of one all-embracing covenant, but there is no suggestion of this in the OT; cf. Rom. 9: 4 'the covenants'.

(vii) *Faithfulness.* This is regularly rendered 'truth' by AV, but this has been almost completely abandoned in modern translations, when it is used of God, and very often when referring to men. The OT is not concerned with absolute accuracy, the modern connotation of truth, but with the reliability of the one concerned. In the midst of a world of uncertainty, where experience shows us the folly of relying on circumstances or one's fellow-men, Israel discovered that God was completely reliable and consistent, i.e. trustworthy or faithful.

(viii) *Covenant Love, Loyal or Steadfast Love* (*ḥesed*). All these attributes, at least so far as Israel is concerned, are really summed up in *ḥesed*, which expresses the behaviour one is entitled to expect from one with whom one is in covenant relationship. It is found nearly 250 times, the vast majority of which refer to God's character and actions. When it is applied to man, RSV usually renders 'loyalty', and almost invariably 'steadfast love' when it is used of God. It implies God's complete loyalty to his covenant promises combined with a complete loving understanding of those with whom He has to deal. The somewhat freer and less consistent renderings of other modern translations produce a more attractive and melodious English for the reader, but miss the element of loyalty to the covenant. In the NT *ḥesed* is included in 'grace', which has taken on a wider meaning, for even those in covenant relationship with God do not merit His faithful love.

(ix) *Jealousy*. It is a pity that this term has become so debased in human contexts, for there is no adequate alternative in English, apart from the GNB paraphrase, 'I tolerate no rivals'. Unlike so many of the gods of the heathen, Yahweh is not supremely indifferent to man's behaviour and sufferings. When He sets His love on men, that love is absolute, and when there is a response to His love, He expects that it should also be absolute. That is why He expects standards from Israel He does not ask from other nations.

6. THE NATURE OF MAN
The OT concept of man, though not unique in most of its details, is so different to the concepts derived from Gk. philosophy, which have dominated Christian theological thought until recently, that it is not easy to make it clear in a few words.

(a) Man as a Unity
Man is bipartite, consisting of flesh (or body), which links him to his fellow-men and more remotely to all creation, and spirit, the breath of life, the gift of God, linking him to God. But when the two meet, they fuse into a unity called *nephesh*, misleadingly rendered 'soul' (Gen. 2: 7). The *nephesh* is the man as a whole. It is aware of and makes itself known to the world around through the body, while it is in contact with God through the spirit.

So real is this unity, that repeatedly parts of the body can be used to express the actions and purposes of the whole personality, and physical organs can be used to denote various functions of the inner man; *e.g.* the heart expresses intellect, will and emotions. For this reason too, while the weakness and transitoriness of flesh (body) is recognized, it is never depreciated, nor is there any suggestion of real existence in the future without it.

(b) Man in the Image of God
The term 'living *nephesh*' is used equally of animals and men (Gen. 1: 21, 24, 30; 2: 7, cf. NEB). The superiority of man is expressed by his being made in the image and likeness of God (Gen. 1: 26 f.). This is never described, but some of its implications are made clear. (i) Negatively, it does not suggest that man has spirit from God only in the way that animals have. The spirit or breath of life means that the fact of life is not merely an inevitable outcome of the evolutionary process but is God's gift. Nor is it suggested that God by nature has a form similar to man. Anything that might suggest that is merely an accommodation to human limitations (anthropomorphisms). (ii) Man is God's representative in this world and, as such, exercises a measure of dominion over it (Gen. 1: 26). (iii) Throughout the OT it is taken for granted that God and man can communicate. (iv) The whole material creation is transient and mortal, but man is capable of immortality—'the immortality of the soul', as normally understood, is not a Biblical doctrine. (v) God can reveal Himself adequately to man in human terms (anthropomorphisms), and may show Himself in visions, symbolically, in human form. (vi) There is no inherent contradiction between OT doctrine and the Incarnation. Rather, we gain the impression that the Incarnation was the ultimate purpose of man's creation.

ated the image of God, however much it may have marred it.

(c) The Fall of Man
No detailed description is given either of the world or of man before the Fall, because the subject is irrelevant to man as he is. But the commands to 'subdue' the earth (Gen. 1: 28) and to 'guard' the garden (Gen. 2: 15) imply resistance and danger. Equally the announcement of the penalty for disobedience (Gen. 2: 17) suggests the prior knowledge of the fact of death, which indubitably existed before the creation of man. The impression created, though not clearly stated, was that the garden was to be the centre from which the conditions of Paradise should gradually be extended over the whole world. Man was to be not merely the preserver of a God-created perfection, but also His fellow-worker in bringing creation to perfection.

The motive behind the Fall was the desire to be independent and self-sufficient, to be like God (Gen. 3: 5). It was irreversible, because Adam and Eve, while fearful of the consequences, were clearly not repentant in any true sense. In fact, though the argument from silence may be dangerous, there is no suggestion of any such repentance. The consequences of the Fall were, therefore, bound to continue, not so much because of physical inheritance, though this should not be completely ignored, as because of the fact that a child had to grow up in the narrow society of an imperfect family and in the wider one of an imperfect tribe and nation; cf. Gen. 18: 19 and the command to exterminate the Canaanites. Though the OT does not deny the reality of the individual or submerge him in the 'corporate personality' of his people, it makes it clear that he cannot insulate himself from his surroundings.

The Fall is not referred to elsewhere in the OT (modern translations are virtually certainly correct in rejecting the RV rendering of Hos. 6: 7, 'like Adam'), because, though man's imperfection and sin are taken for granted throughout, the reality of this could be learnt only by continued failure. Man is always tempted to believe that the entail of the past can be eliminated.

(d) The Fall—Its Results

Since there is no clear picture of what would have been, had man not sinned, we must infer the results of the Fall by putting various statements together.

(i) *The World.* Man partially lost his right of dominion, which was symbolized by the curse on the soil (Gen. 3: 17 ff.), which could be intensified by gross sin (Ps. 107: 33 ff.). Instead of bringing order and harmony to the animal world (cf. Isa. 11: 6 ff.), man brought unnecessary death to it, whether to provide clothing (Gen. 3: 21), sacrifice (Gen. 4: 4) or food (Gen. 9: 3). In addition judgments on man could involve death for the animals as is seen especially in the story of the Flood.

(ii) *The Dislocation of Society.* This is shown primarily by the disharmony in the family (Gen. 3: 7, 16)—note that GNB 'you will be subject to him' is correct; it is a statement of fact, not God's command. This disharmony led in due course to violence, murder, war and slavery. It was intensified by the confusion of languages and the resultant development of separate nations. The whole situation is aggravated by the apparent lack of purpose in the whole historical process in which man seems to be reduced to no more than part of the purposeless round of nature (Ec. 1: 2–11).

(iii) *Death.* We have no right to discount or explain away the statement, 'In the day you eat of it you shall die' (Gen. 2: 17). The concept of death in Heb. is wider than with us and involves essentially the inability to function. Physical death, the separation of spirit and body, is merely the logical and inevitable outcome of man's inability to carry out his true functions. Logically it would appear that when body and spirit separate, a man should cease to exist. There is very little information in the OT about man's state after death, but there is sufficient to show that a man's actions create a continuing personality. Since it is without a body, it cannot

function, and clearly the degree of consciousness in Sheol, the abode of the dead, is minimal. There does not seem to be any concept in the OT of a division within Sheol between the good and bad.

(iv) *Elemental Spirits.* The OT ignores, with very few exceptions, the names, titles, alleged powers and other details of the gods of the heathen, and so also of the demons (*shedim*, etc.), which are worshipped and apparently can exert power over those that do not serve Yahweh. There is no suggestion that they are fallen angels, but no explanation of their existence and power is offered.

(v) *Life after Death.* This is dealt with in the next main section 7 (*j*).

7. THE RESTITUTION OF ALL THINGS

The OT is essentially the story of the preparation for the reversal of the effects of man's fall and the harm it has done. Essentially this has had two sides. Man has had to learn the ineffectiveness of his own efforts and of his gods. Then Yahweh has had to display His power, His will and His purposes. To be noted is that the OT revelation of God's working is bounded by this world.

(a) From Adam to Abraham

Man left to himself reached a pitch of depravity where, with the exception of eight persons, he had to be wiped off the face of the earth. The memory of this judgment varied widely, but it seems universally to have imprinted on men the recognition that their gods placed limitations on their behaviour, and this led often to a high ethical standard, which was seldom observed for long in practice. This is not to suggest that there was a primaeval revelation going back to Adam. For this there is no evidence in the OT. It should not be overlooked that the ancestors of the patriarchs were idolators (Jos. 24: 14 f.).

(b) The Patriarchs

The stories of Abraham and his descendants to the fourth generation are not merely an account of how God prepared a people for Himself; they serve even more to stress the primacy of faith and trust in man's relationship with God. Christian presuppositions about Abraham's theological knowledge of God or Jewish ones about his keeping of the Mosaic Law find no support in the narratives. Apart from the birth of Isaac, there is little of the miraculous in them, for the faith described is based on God's promises and ongoing protection and not on His mighty acts.

(c) The Birth of a Nation

One cannot expect a nation to show the same degree of faith in God as an individual or small family group. Hence God had to reveal Himself otherwise to Israel than He had done to the patriarchs. We find the majority of OT miracles in the stories of Egypt, of the desert wanderings and of the conquest of Canaan. In them God displayed His control over nature and every natural force, whether deified or not. This was to give the certainty, at least to the faith of the prophets, that all Israel's sufferings, whether through disasters of nature or the victories of their enemies, must be the result of the people's sins and not of any weakness on Yahweh's part. Abraham's response to God's call could, with the passage of time, have been explained away as merely a subjective experience. The Exodus and the Conquest provided an unforgettable and undeniable factual basis for the history of Israel as God's people, in which the Exodus occupies the same position as the Cross and Resurrection in the history of the Church.

(d) The Law of Moses

The Law, or more accurately the Instruction (*torah*) given through Moses at Sinai and during the desert wanderings, was not intended as a legislative code to cover all possible contingencies then or later; it should have served as a guide to the type of life expected from a 'holy' people. The basis of the Covenant was the Decalogue (Exod. 20: 1–17), as is shown by its unique place in the Ark of the Covenant. Exod. 20: 22–23: 33, which is the rest of the Book of the Covenant (Exod. 24: 7), should be seen mainly as a commentary on the Decalogue. Much of it is modification of ancient Near-Eastern law, probably brought by Abraham from Mesopotamia. The same holds true of the laws of Leviticus and Deuteronomy; in the latter the Decalogue is again regarded as basic. If we make a comparison of these codes, it will be easy enough to discover areas of conduct which are not expressly dealt with.

In other words the Instruction (*torah*) was not intended to teach Israel, using its own wisdom, what God's will might be in every circumstance of life, but it was to be a light on man's path, which would enable God to guide both the individual and the people aright. It was also intended to reveal man's inability to observe God's will in his own strength—there was no power inherent in the Law—and so turn him in humility to God for aid. At the same time it was a turning point in human religion, for it provided for the first time a completely objective standard by which man could pass judgment on his own behaviour apart from the unreliable voice of conscience.

As with the civil law, the ritual regulations are based on those familiar to the patriarchs in Mesopotamia or Canaan. Again they have been modified to increase the worshippers' conviction of uncleanness and falling short, and of God's gracious willingness to restore communion. When they are viewed from the standpoint of the work of Christ, it is easy to see its

various aspects prophesied both in the sacrifices and the ordering of the Tabernacle. Since, however, there is no evidence that any understood the typology involved, and the prophets for the most part showed little interest in, and sometimes active hostility to, the popular use of the ritual, it is probably wiser not to include a typological interpretation of the ritual laws in a theology of the OT. Rather we should consider them as impressing on Israel the inadequacy of man's efforts to please God, even when the details of worship had been given by Him.

(e) From Joshua to the Babylonian Exile

From one point of view the end of Deuteronomy represents the climax of the OT. God had created His people, revealed His power and purposes to them and had brought them to the verge of the fulfilment of His promises. From then on it is a story of decline, in which the brighter episodes at the best halt but do not reverse the dominant trend downwards. Achan's sin, which leaves a lasting mark on Israel's subsequent history, is in some sense a parallel to the fall in Eden. The human choice of king and temple instead of Judge and Tabernacle simply made the final scene of loss of national freedom and exile only the more certain. The inherent fault in king and temple was that they limited God's choice of ruler, for the task became hereditary, and of place of worship, for the Temple could not be moved from Jerusalem.

(f) The Prophets

Parallel with this decline came the increasing revelation through the prophets—though it was all there in essence in the Law—insisting that God's primary demands on His people were justice, covenant loyalty alike to God and to fellow-man, and an unquestioning acceptance of God's will and standards. Without these the whole cultus, however valued, was merely an insult to God.

This went with a growing stress that this could not be attained by the people as a whole but only by a remnant, and that only through the work of God's perfect king (the Messiah, see 7 (*g*)). Against the background of exile it was further revealed that the accomplishment of God's purpose would involve a new covenant (Jer. 31: 31–34), which would be made effective only by the power of God's Spirit in the individual (Ezek. 36: 25 ff.), and by the work of the Servant of Yahweh in dealing with sin.

In other words God was using human failure, shown to be failure by the very existence of the Sinaitic Law, to demonstrate both the necessity and the methods of God's intervention and cure. For all that the experiences of the post-exilic period were needed to bring the lesson fully home, cf. 7 (*h*).

The prophets were also used to show the importance of the individual within the totality of the nation. Not even in the case of Jeremiah was the call to stand without other human aid interpreted to mean that he was to disassociate himself from his people, i.e. no warrant is given for individualism.

(g) The Messiah

The term Messiah, someone anointed, i.e. set apart for God's service, is hardly found in the OT as a technical term, except perhaps in Dan. 9: 25 f. Its elaboration belongs to the Inter-Testamental Period, yet the concept is clearly earlier. Primarily God's king is meant, of whom even David and the best of his successors were mere foreshadowings. There was, however, the expectation of a prophet at least as great as Moses (Dt. 18: 15, 18 f.). Equally Isa. 42: 1 shows that the title could be applied to the Servant of Yahweh—the putting of God's Spirit on him is equivalent to anointing—though he is never expressly identified with the King to come. The messianic hope could become a reality for the people as a whole only after it had become clear after Zerubbabel's death that there would be no merely natural restoration of the Davidic line. There is no clear evidence that language like that of Isa. 7: 14; 9: 6; Mic. 5: 2 was understood in any supernatural sense.

(h) The Return from Exile

The denial of national independence and of a Davidic king, combined with the removal of the splendour from the rebuilt Temple and the lack of the Ark, the sign of God's presence, were the outward indications that God's purposes would not be accomplished by the normal expressions of nationality or cultus. This was underlined by the fact that the majority of Jews lived outside the land. The Jews had become 'prisoners of hope', waiting for God's time of redemption. Where they went wrong was in the belief that they could hasten the day of deliverance by an increasingly meticulous observance of the Law of Moses.

(i) Rewards and Punishments

In the earlier books of the OT the rewards for obedience and trust were riches, or at least sufficient of the world's goods for an adequate life, health, children, triumph over one's enemies and a long life. Punishment for sin and disobedience was the deprivation of these things. The godly man, who had all these things, could as his physical strength failed him, depart in peace asking no more and knowing that in some sense he lived on in his descendants; cf. the institution of Levirate marriage (Dt. 25: 5 f.). Though it is not stressed, we must assume that this was the normal experience of the godly Israelite in the earlier period of his history. The story of Job receives much of its poignancy from the fact that even

his friends took for granted that his sufferings were irrefutable evidence that he was an outstanding sinner.

Gradually, as society grew more corrupt, the godly found themselves involved in the sufferings of their godless neighbours and discriminated against and wronged by evil men in high places. In fact, they had often to suffer more than the evil, until in many of the psalms 'poor' and 'afflicted' are virtual synonyms for 'godly'. This led to a very slow abandonment of the old concepts of reward and punishment, though they never entirely vanished in the OT, and men began to look for something beyond the grave to balance the inequities of this life.

(j) Life after Death

A man like Habakkuk faced with the collapse of society around him might put his faith in God as a sufficient answer (3: 17 ff.), while a Jeremiah, once exile had come to his people, could find satisfaction in God's coming redemption and restoration (31: 25 f.), but others found themselves looking for an answer beyond the grave. This hope took two forms, which are in no sense mutually exclusive.

For some, e.g. Job (19: 23–27), David (Ps. 139: 8) and Asaph (Ps. 73: 24 f.), there came the certainty that death and the conditions of Sheol could not end communion with God. They were so taken up with God, that the nature and conditions of continuing communion did not concern them.

Others thought rather of the coming time of God's universal rule, in which the curse would be removed both from nature and from Israel (e.g. Jl 3: 17 f.; Am. 9: 11–15; Isa. 2: 2 ff.; 11: 1–9). This would be preceded by judgment on the nations (e.g. Jl 3: 1 f.), and on the sinners in Israel (e.g. Mal. 4: 1). In some passages death is looked on as being deferred, as it was in man's early history (Isa. 65: 20), but in Isa. 25: 8 it is swallowed up for ever. The prophet, however, is not satisfied; the Servant of Yahweh's sufferings were far outweighed by the blessings they brought, but for the righteous as a whole there was very little that they had accomplished (Isa. 26: 16 ff.). So a future restoration of the nation seemed to him an inadequate recompense; hence to him was given the revelation that they would be raised to share in it (Isa. 26: 19), even as the Servant was to be raised (Isa. 53: 10 ff.). Though Ezek. 37: 1–14 refers in the first place to the return from exile, it is most unwise to rule out the thought of resurrection as well.

In Isa. 26 there is no thought of the resurrection of the heathen or the wicked within Israel (26: 14). It is only in Dan. 12: 2, written in the conditions of the exile and in the light of worse evils to come, that we have the resurrection of the wicked as well. It is not certain whether we have a foretelling of the raising of the good and bad only, leaving the mass of mankind in Sheol, or whether, as is more likely, 'many' means all (cf. Isa. 53: 12).

There is no doctrine of hell in the OT. In Isa. 66: 24, at one time a much quoted verse, the reference is not to the continuing personality (*nephesh*, cf. 6 (*d.* iii)) of the rebels but to their corpses. Apparently the suggestion is of a miraculous preservation of their bodies in the rubbish burning in the Valley of Hinnom as a reminder of past evil and to create abhorrence or disgust to all who see. Since the hope of resurrection is marginal in the OT, it is not to be expected that there would be any teaching about the fate of the wicked.

(k) The New Heavens and the New Earth
The combination of heavens and earth (Isa. 65: 17; 66: 22; cf. Rev. 21: 1) is to be understood as in Gen. 1: 1 or the world in its more immediate setting in space. The OT can go no further than seeing the perfecting of God's original creation and the accomplishment of His purposes in it. The fact that the NT opens up much wider vistas does not entitle us to assume that the OT revelation is no longer valid, and that this world is blotted out, once its purpose has been accomplished. Far rather, so far from redeemed man being removed to the throne of God in heaven the throne of God is to be with man; cf. Ezek. 48: 35. Though it is never given any explanation, it is clear that the world, both in its present and future state, has a lasting value and rôle in God's purposes.

8. THE THEOLOGY OF WISDOM
While the first two sections of the OT, The Law and the Prophets, are prophetic books and derive their inspiration from this fact, no prophetic claim is made by the Writings, except for a few of the psalms, *e.g.* 50 and 110. For all that, most of the books reveal a predominantly prophetic outlook. A notable exception is the three books it has become usual to comprise under the term Wisdom Literature, *viz.* Proverbs, Job and Ecclesiastes.

The accumulated experience of the generations was handed down by word of mouth and taught by the elders of the tribe to the younger men. At royal courts the councillors made a special study of traditional wisdom. Proverbs gives both the cream of Solomon's wisdom and collected sayings of the Wise. A basic presupposition is that true wisdom depends on the fear of the Lord. Granted that, human experience will be found to conform to a regular pattern in which the God-fearing can expect prosperity and success, while the foolish —not the mentally deficient but those in whom there is no fear of God—head for failure and ruin.

The one dissenting note is struck by Agur (30: 1-4, but perhaps on to v. 33). In strong terms he affirms that faced with heavenly wisdom he is no better than a beast. This is also the attitude of Job, which in Heb. stands immediately after Proverbs. Ecclesiastes, placed in the mouth of Solomon in his old age, when he had lost his fear of God, shows that the highest human wisdom, once the fear of the Lord is no longer present, is unable to construct any reasonable pattern out of human experience or to find a discernible purpose in it.

If we take these three books together, as well as a few of the psalms (*e.g.* 1; 37; 49; 78), we find that they affirm that man, because he is made in God's image, is able to discern the manner of God's working among men, provided that a due respect for God is present; where it is lacking, life becomes meaningless. To this Agur and Job object that God is too great for His ways to be really comprehended by men. In other words the wisdom books give a due place to man's observation and reason in the understanding of God and His works, but make it subject to a due respect for God and a recognition of human limitations.

While the personification of Wisdom (Prov. 8) may be rightly linked with the Word of the Lord (Ps. 33: 6; Jn 1: 1), there is no justification for interpreting it in a Trinitarian sense in its OT setting.

9. THE CHRSTIAN USE OF THE OLD TESTAMENT
(a) The Old Testament as Scripture
Paul's statement in 2 Tim. 3: 16 f. refers to the OT. Its implication is that Jesus the Messiah is its unifying factor and its fulfilment, and that the teaching of Jesus and His apostles is the guide to its understanding. The frequent quotations from the OT in all parts of the NT have less an apologetic purpose, though this is sometimes there, than the desire to show the vital link between promise and fulfilment. The NT books were written primarily for those who already were believers. Even when the OT was least known and least understood, the Church knew that it had to retain the OT, even when it might seem an advantage to drop it.

(b) Old and New?
Part of our difficulty about the use of the OT springs from the use of Old and New, when we speak of the testaments, or rather covenants. The usage is very early and is based on Heb. 7: 22; 8: 6 f., 13, which deal with the implications of Jer. 31: 31-34. But these passages are concerned purely with the priesthood and sacrifices of the Sinai covenant, which by their very nature were inadequate. We must not overlook that all the author's arguments are based on OT passages, which have retained their validity for him, while Jer. 31: 31-34 is clear that the newness of the coming covenant lies in its making real what the first covenant

could not achieve (cf. Rom. 8: 3 f.); *i.e.*, Sinai was a necessary step towards the complete revelation of God in Jesus the Messiah (cf. Gal. 3: 19–25). We need, therefore, always to remember that OT and NT are only convenience terms, and that the Bible is essentially a unity.

(c) Allegory, Typology, Analogy

The Bible is the account of God's redeeming work, through which God gradually becomes better known, cf. 4 (*a*) and (*c*). The much used modern term, 'salvation history' (*Heilsgeschichte*), is in fact an adequate description of a major part of its contents. Since, however, for many in the early Gentile church the gospel was the imparting of truth as a system rather than as a person (Jn 14: 6), progressive revelation could be ignored unless it could be expressed in terms of a rapidly growing systematic theology. For them the easiest way to rescue much of the OT was by allegory, by which a story or action could be interpreted in terms completely alien to the OT narrative. This approach had already been popularized by Alexandrian Jews, especially Philo. The only remotely analogous passage in the NT is Gal. 4: 21–26, but the essential features of the OT story are preserved by Paul.

Nearer to the spirit of Scripture is the interpretation of the OT by typology, i.e., the claim that God's cultic commands and ordering of events were intended to point to that which was to come. Its supporters appeal especially to Hebrews and 1 C. 10: 1–11. The weakness of this approach is that it minimizes the revelation to those who first received it, for there is no evidence that they were acting for the benefit of others who should come after them. In addition, anything that cannot be forced into the type tends to be ignored in exposition.

It is probable that in all these cases analogy is the best approach. This affirms that it is one and same God who is acting and speaking throughout Scripture, and that man's nature is unchanged, though his knowledge has increased. Hence there is an inherent oneness in God's actions, guidance and instructions. This does not offer an automatic solution to the problem passages of the OT, but once one accepts the facts of the situation described, which were not artificially created by God, as typology sometimes seems to suggest, one will recognize in them the unavoidable outcome of the meeting of human sin and God's righteousness. Analogy will also save us from the misuse of dispensationalism, which seems to suggest that God had different aims and standards at different stages in human history.

(d) Some Gains from the Old Testament Rightly Used

The OT will keep us from the idea that God's revelation is primarily one of right doctrine. It teaches that it is above all one of restoring a correct relationship between God and man in the course of salvation history. Correct doctrine is a great boon, but a true relationship with God is not necessarily dependent on it. It will also keep us from the modern tendency to judge other men's religions by the amount of truth and error we claim to find in them.

It saves us from the cult of the Greek lexicon and philosophy in our interpretation of the NT, for its language and outlook are firmly rooted in the OT. The same applies to efforts to understand the NT in terms of Hellenistic religion of first-century Judaism. The former is ignored, except in so far as the expanding church came into contact with it. The attitude of the NT to it is largely the same as that of the OT to the paganism that constantly threatened Israel. Though early Jewish writings illuminate the nuances of Jesus' and Paul's teaching, essentially the NT begins where the work of Ezra left off. It is worth remembering that the men of Qumran are not mentioned in the NT; there is no suggestion of the points that separated the Pharisees into at least two hostile camps; there are only two points mentioned as separating them from the Sadducees (Mk 12: 18; Ac. 23: 8).

The OT should keep us from the idea that right belief or 'charismatic' experience can take the place of right conduct, or that the NT is merely presenting us with a new and higher law. Above all it rules out any idea that man can ever find a place in which he can act independently of God.

The OT gives us a unique picture gallery of men and women who walked by faith with God. A closer appreciation of it would have saved us from an over-valuing of the ministry and of the showier spiritual gifts. There would have been less temptation to solve problems by fleeing from the world, and a greater appreciation of the fact that God is glorified by the doing of His will in the world. There would also have been less depreciation of the physical.

(e) The Interpretation of the Old Testament

While the OT must always be allowed to speak for itself, for it is a revelation of God, even though it looks to the future for its fulfilment, yet it must always be heard in the light of Jesus Christ. The Bible is one book, and none of its parts may be allowed to contradict another, even though they may speak with varying emphasis; it must not be forgotten, however, that seeming contradiction may be explained by a higher truth embracing both statements. Progressive revelation never means incorrect revelation, but only that it may be partial. When the perfect has come, it interprets the partial but does not abolish it, while the partial helps our understanding of the perfect.

BIBLIOGRAPHY

(Only works available in English are mentioned)

Survey

PORTEOUS, N. W., 'Old Testament Theology' in *The Old Testament and Modern Study* (Oxford, 1951).

General Outlines

CLEMENTS, R. E., *Old Testament Theology: A Fresh Approach* (London, 1978).

EICHRODT, W., *Theology of the Old Testament*, 2 vols. (London, 1961, 1967).

JACOB, E., *Theology of the Old Testament* (London, 1958).

KNIGHT, G. A. F., *A Christian Theology of the Old Testament* (London, 1959).

KÖHLER, L., *Old Testament Theology* (London, 1957).

VON RAD, G., *Old Testament Theology*, 2 vols. (Edinburgh, 1962, 1965).

VRIEZEN, Th. C., *An Outline of Old Testament Theology* (Wageningen, 1958).

ZIMMERLI, W., *Old Testament Theology in Outline*, E.T. (Edinburgh, 1978).

Special Studies

BAKER, D. L., *Two Testaments One Bible* (Leicester, 1976).

BARR, J., *Old and New in Interpretation* (London, 1966).

BRIGHT, J., *The Authority of the Old Testament* (London, 1967).

BUBER, M., *The Prophetic Faith* (New York, 1949).

DODD, C. H., *The Authority of the Bible* (London, 1929, 1960).

DODD, C. H., *According to the Scriptures* (London, 1952).

ELLISON, H. L., *The Message of the Old Testament* (Exeter, 1969).

JOHNSON, A. R., *The Vitality of the Individual in the Thought of Ancient Israel* (Cardiff, 1949).

KÖHLER, L., *Hebrew Man* (London, 1956).

ROBINSON, H. Wheeler, *The Religious Ideas of the Old Testament* (London, 1913).

ROWLEY, H. H., *The Faith of Israel* (London, 1956).

RUST, E. C., *Nature and Man in Biblical Thought* (London, 1953).

SNAITH, N. H., *The Distinctive Ideas of the Old Testament* (London, 1944).

TASKER, R. V. G., *The Old Testament in the New Testament*[2] (London, 1954).

VAN RULER, A. A., *The Christian Church and the Old Testament*[2] (Grand Rapids, 1971).

VISCHER, W., *The Witness of the Old Testament to Christ*, Vol. 1 (London, 1949).

THE INTERPRETATION OF THE OLD TESTAMENT

HAROLD H. ROWDON

The very name 'Old Testament' by which the first 39 books of the Bible are known, should alert us to the need for special care in interpreting them. The fact that they were written during the period when the 'old' covenant (=testament) was in force suggests that we who live under the terms of the 'new' covenant will view them in a 'new' light. Granted that a humble, believing attitude is called for, as well as careful attention to the grammatical sense, the literary form and the historical background, are there any further requirements for a Christian understanding of the OT?

Clearly, the NT has things to say that bear directly upon this question. For example, no-one who has absorbed the teaching of the NT in general and Galatians and Hebrews in particular is likely to observe the very precise instructions given in the OT regarding the practice of circumcision. How then are we to understand such instructions? Do they contain any meaning for the Christian, or are they now superfluous? And what about the rest of the OT?

Some—like Marcion in the second century—have rejected the OT completely, and have usually been repudiated by the Church as heretics. Others have stressed the parity of both testaments within the unity of divine revelation, on the basis that the new covenant is but a modification of the old and that both came from the same God (see, for example, A. A. van Ruler, *The Christian Church and the Old Testament*, Eerdmans, 1971). Many have agreed that there is an element of continuity, but have seen this in terms of the OT being an historical and theological *preparation* for the NT. Of these, some (*e.g.* O. Cullmann and A. Richardson) stress the view that the OT records God's mighty acts of 'salvation history'. There is, perhaps, a growing stress on the relationship between the testaments in terms of promise and fulfilment (see J. Bright, *The Authority of the Old Testament*, SCM, 1967). A. T. Hanson maintains that the connecting factor is the revelation of God's character (*Studies in Paul's Technique and Theology*, SPCK, 1974).

It has been very common for interpreters of the OT to look beyond the literal meaning of the text in the endeavour to find an interpretation that is in harmony with the NT revelation. The history of OT interpretation until modern times has largely consisted of discussion of the legitimacy of this 'allegorical' method of interpretation and attempts to discover guiding and controlling principles for its use.

This article will take the form of a brief historical survey, beginning with the ways in which NT writers used the OT and continuing with the history of OT interpretation in the Early Church, the medieval period, the Reformation and modern times. A concluding section will suggest some lines of approach to the task of interpreting the OT to-day.

I. The interpretation of the Old Testament in the New Testament

For a fuller discussion of the NT use of the OT, reference may be made to *A New Testament Commentary*, pp. 1110–18. Something, however brief, must nevertheless be said here about the exegetical methods used by NT writers.

Our OT was the Bible of the Early Church (Lk. 24: 44; 2 Tim. 3: 15 f.). The writers of the NT drew very heavily on the OT, and the number of quotations—let alone allusions—is legion. R. N. Longenecker has pointed out that *explicit* reference to the OT is concentrated in NT books addressed to audiences that possessed a Jewish background (*Biblical Exegesis in the Apostolic Period*, Eerdmans, 1975, pp. 210 ff.), but NT writings as a whole are shot through with allusions of one kind or another to the OT—even Paul's address to the Areopagus in Athens (Ac. 17: 22 ff.) contained some.

The methods used by NT writers to interpret OT passages provide a valuable starting point but not a terminus for our search for exegetical methods of handling the OT. For it should be said at once that NT writers occupied a unique position which marked them off from both contemporary Jewish exegetes and subsequent Christian exegetes. Like OT writers, they were prophets, and they were profoundly aware of being caught up in 'the supreme manifestation in history of the judgment and mercy of God' (C. K. Barrett, in *The Cambridge History of the Bible*, CHB I. 403). This gave them not only a sense of kinship with OT writers but also a community of theme. Unlike Jewish exegetes who were generally conscious of the absence of any prophetic voice, and in contrast to later Christian exegetes to whom the Holy Spirit was given to illuminate the sacred page in the sense of 1 C. 2: 12 f., the writers of the NT, like those of the OT, were directly inspired by the Holy Spirit who had been given to them for the purpose (Jn 16: 13). Their unique experience of the living presence of Jesus, through His Spirit, was therefore a determining factor in their OT exegesis. Their interpretations of the OT constitute part of the now completed revelation of Scripture. We cannot assume therefore, that the exegetical methods they used are necessarily the most appropriate ones for us to use to-day.

In order to understand those methods it will be helpful to pinpoint some of their basic presuppositions, and indicate how they affected their exegesis. The concept of corporate solidarity, which transcends the distinction between the individual and the group to which he belongs, enabled NT writers to transfer—without any sense of incongruity—what had been said in the OT of the nation of Israel and apply it to a single individual member of that nation—Messiah. There is also the presupposition of correspondences in history. This goes beyond mere analogies and illustrations, and means that, built into history by divine intent, events occurred which, in certain respects, reproduce previous ones and can therefore be interpreted 'typologically'. Thus, for example, the exodus of Moses' time was followed by another 'exodus' (the return from captivity), and yet another (salvation by redemption from sin). In this vein, Christ was seen as another 'Passover lamb' (1 C. 5: 7). Another presupposition of NT writers is eschatological fulfilment. This is the conviction that the Messianic age has been initiated (though it still awaits its final consummation) and therefore it is legitimate to apply to Jesus the OT messianic prophecies. A final example is the belief in the messianic presence which meant not only that the OT could be interpreted Christocentrically but also, as we have seen, that the messianic community was a prophetic phenomenon.

The actual exegetical methods used by NT writers include uncomplicated, literal exegesis. Just as Jesus had countered the devil by using Dt. 6: 13; 6: 16; 8: 3 in their plain and literal meaning, so, for example, Jas 5: 17 f. used Elijah's classic prayer as an example to be followed and Heb. 12: 16 adduced Esau's despising of his birthright as an attitude to be shunned.

In their exegesis of the OT, NT writers employed a number of contemporary Jewish exegetical methods, as Jesus had done. Like the rabbis, they do not appear to think it necessary always to quote the text *verbatim*. True, they may sometimes be using their own Greek version of the original Hebrew, or they may be following the text of an existing version other than the Septuagint, but the probability is that as often as not, the reason for their lack of concern with what we might call accuracy arose from the fact that precise verbal correspondence with the text cited was not considered as important then as it is now. (Even to-day the most exact scholars make use of paraphrase on occasion.)

From time to time, as in Rom. 10: 6 ff., NT writers utilized the 'pesher' form of running commentary on a string of OT passages. Frequently, they made use of various midrashic devices. Thus, for example, Paul used the method of analogy, i.e. the interpretation of the meaning of a word in one OT passage by its meaning in another (as in Rom. 4: 1–12) and the argument from the 'less' to the 'greater' (as in Rom. 5: 15–21; 2 C. 3: 7–18). He also used themes beloved by the rabbis (*e.g.* 1 C. 10: 1–4) and was fully prepared to argue *ad hominem* (*e.g.* Gal. 3: 19 f.).

NT writers obviously interpreted much of the OT as straightforward prophecy. Typological interpretation, which saw the recurrence of pattern in sacred history, is found fairly widely in the NT (*e.g.* 1 C. 5: 7). But the extent to which NT writers interpreted OT passages allegorically is hotly debated. Whether, and if so to what extent, the NT brings to light hidden meanings in the OT is uncertain. 1 C. 9: 9 f. and Gal. 4: 24 appear to be clear examples of allegorical interpretation. But it is arguable that the first passage consists of nothing more than 'mild allegorical exegesis' (Longenecker, *op. cit.*, pp. 126 f.) and that the second 'may well represent an extreme form of Palestinian allegorical interpretation that was triggered by polemic debate and is strongly circumstantial and *ad hominem*' (*ibid.*, p. 129). A. T. Hanson maintains that 'Paul only approaches the confines of allegory when he allows his typology to become too complicated; or when he is referring to a well-known text without reflecting very much on its exegetical implications' (*op. cit.*, p. 166). We may conclude with C. K. Barrett (who accepts the existence of some allegorical interpretation in the NT) that the characteristic NT estimate of the OT sees in it a combination of typology and prophecy (*CHB* I. 410 f.).

The regulative principle which controlled their use of the OT was undoubtedly conformity to what they knew of the life and teachings of Jesus Christ, and in particular His attitude to the OT (Mt. 5: 17; Lk. 10: 26; 24: 27, 44 ff.; Ac. 1: 3). 'In him', Longenecker asserts, 'they witnessed a creative handling of the Scriptures which became for them both the source of their own understanding and the paradigm [model] for their own exegesis of the Old Testament' (*op. cit.*, p. 51; cf. pp. 75–78).

Before leaving this part of the subject, we may well ask what were the specific purposes for which NT writers had recourse to the OT. First and foremost, they were concerned to show that the birth, life, death, resurrection and ascension of Jesus had been predicted in the OT. This comes out particularly clearly in Matthew (cf. 1 C. 15: 3 f.; Ac. 2: 16–36). In other words, they were concerned to relate the OT to the new situation created by the advent of Messiah in a way and for a purpose so different from that envisaged by contemporary Judaism. They also used the OT to establish norms of behaviour for the Christian community. Just as Jesus had appealed to Gen. 1: 27; 2: 24 when giving a ruling on divorce, so James used Am. 9: 11 f. to justify the admission of Gentiles to the Christian Church on equal terms with Jews (Ac. 15: 16–18) and Paul applied one OT Scripture after another to matters of Christian conduct (Eph. 4: 25 ff. provides numerous examples).

One thing that NT writers did not do to any significant extent was to anticipate some later Christian exegetes by importing into their understanding of the OT text completely extraneous ideas. Though it has been alleged by some scholars that, for example, the writers of John and Hebrews were indebted to Platonic thought for many of their insights, this is far from being proven. C. K. Barrett is undoubtedly right in saying, 'New Testament interpreters commonly move within the same general framework of thought as the Old Testament itself' (*CHB* I. 401).

II. The interpretation of the Old Testament in the Early Church

Broadly speaking, it would be true to say that the first few centuries of Christian history saw a growing use of the typological and allegorical methods of interpreting the OT. This resulted, in the first place, from the view that references to Christ—and the Church—are to be found everywhere in the OT. Augustine was to draw out the implications of this later, but as early as the end of the first century Clement of Rome discovered bishops and deacons in Isa. 60: 17. Apologetic needs deepened this conviction and led to more extensive use of the allegorical method. For one thing, Jewish repudiations of Christian interpretations of the OT stressed the literal meaning; for another, the second-century heretic Marcion rejected the OT altogether because of the moral and theological problems it posed. (His work, *Antitheses*, pinpointed the contradictions between the Old and New Testaments which the literal interpretation of the latter raised in his mind.) Opposition to such opponents of orthodox Christianity undoubtedly contributed to the growing use of the typological and allegorical methods. Already in the late first or early second century, the Epistle of Barnabas went as far as to deny that parts of the OT had ever been intended to be taken literally. For example, the taboo on eating pork had been intended to forbid association with 'swinish' men! Again, in reaction against Marcion, Irenaeus, writing in the late second century, saw typological correspondence not only between Adam and Christ but also between Eve and Mary and between the tree in the Garden of Eden and the cross on Calvary.

With the conversion to Christianity of men trained in Greek thought, and the emergence of Christian apologists eager to commend the faith to their contemporaries in a meaningful way, we find evidence of a further incentive to adopt a typological and allegorical approach to the OT. Here were men who, for evangelistic reasons, attempted to transpose the OT from its original Hebrew to a contemporary Greek idiom, thus making it both intelligible and (they hoped) acceptable to the Greek-speaking world. Chief among them was Origen, of whom R. P. C. Hanson says, 'he brought the touch of a master to what had hitherto been nothing much more than the exercise of amateurs' (*Allegory and Event*, SCM, 1959, p. 360).

Origen developed to a fine art the approach of his predecessor in the Catechetical School at Alexandria, Clement, and like him drew heavily from the methods of Philo, the Alexandrian Jew who had attempted to reconcile the Scriptures with Greek philosophy by means of the allegorical method of interpretation. Origen's thinking may be said to have started from two fixed points. He believed that nothing in Scripture was superfluous, without meaning or profit: he was intent on finding in Scripture those contemporary ideas that he believed to be true, even though they were not to be found on the surface of the Bible. With reference to the latter, R. P. C. Hanson goes as far as to say that 'he was consciously endeavouring to reconcile the text of the Bible with contemporary philosophy and was under the necessity of finding in the Bible by some means or other his philosophical speculations' (*op. cit.*, p. 362; cf. p. 214). From our present point of view, it should be added that Origen's use of allegorization enabled him to find Christian meaning in the OT. At the deepest level, the two testaments are not two, but one, for as Origen said in his commentary on Numbers, 'to us who understand [the OT] and expound it spiritually and with its gospel meaning it is always new' (cited in *CHB* I. 483).

Origen professed to be able to find three levels of meaning in Scripture—literal, moral and spiritual—and drew the analogy with the tripartite nature of man as he understood it

—body, soul and spirit. The literal meaning Origen associated with Judaistic exegetes, unintelligent literalists and simple folk generally, though he did admit that it is usually useful if kept in a subordinate position. Very occasionally, Origen refused to add to the literal meaning. Usually, he retains it, if only to encourage people to study the Bible and find something of value. Sometimes, he declares that the literal sense of a passage cannot possibly be intended to be taken seriously: it must be allegorized. So, for example, Origen refused to believe that we are intended to interpret literally the account of God walking in the garden, since this is something which could never have happened literally, God being spirit. Again, Origen evacuated of literal meaning ordinances in the law which he felt to be unreasonable (*e.g.* the prohibition of eating the kite, Lev. 11: 14—who would want to?) or impossible (*e.g.* the command to eat the chamois, Dt. 14: 5—an animal that Origen understood to be non-existent). In answer to the question why things of this kind were in the text, Origen replied that they were deliberately placed there by God in order to serve the same purpose as the 'stumbling-blocks' to faith found in creation—to stimulate enquiry and lead to the discovery of spiritual truth by means of the allegorical method of interpretation (R. M. Grant, *The Letter and the Spirit*, SPCK, 1957, p. 95).

The moral sense of Scripture Origen rarely used in his commentaries. It constitutes ethical or psychological teaching which is not specifically Christian in character and is usually absorbed into the third, spiritual level of meaning. Origen himself described this as an attempt to discover the fulfilment of types and the shadows of heavenly things to come and defended it on the ground that Paul both used it (Gal. 4) and asserted it in as many words (1 C. 10: 1–11; Col. 2: 16 f.). Despite the enunciation of various principles to govern allegorical interpretation, Origen's use of allegory 'breaks all rules and is unchartably subjective' (R. P. C. Hanson, *op. cit.*, p. 245). Genealogies, numbers and particular words provided fertile ground for Origen's allegorizing powers. For example, he usually understood the word 'horse' to mean 'voice', 'clouds' 'holy ones', 'well' 'the teaching of the Bible', 'leaven' 'teaching', and so on. Origen sometimes discovered different levels of allegorical meaning. Thus he found in the incident of Jeremiah at the potter's house (Jer. 18: 1–12) reference not only to the resurrection of the body but also to the bringing together of Christians and Jews in the Church (R. P. C. Hanson, *op. cit.*, p. 246).

It is hard to resist the conclusion that Origen's interpretation of the OT was arbitrary and even high-handed, despite his professed reliance on the guidance of the Holy Spirit. One

restraining influence on his spiritual ingenuity was his loyalty to the Church's rule of faith—the understanding of what had traditionally been believed by the Church, 'a kind of distillation of what the Church traditionally held to be the main purport of the biblical revelation' (*CHB* II. 176). On occasions, however, Origen was prepared to ignore and even to contradict this. We may conclude, then, with R. P. C. Hanson that 'what we see in Origen is an interaction between the Bible, the Church's interpretation of the Bible, and the insights of the individual scholar himself' (*op. cit.*, p. 374).

Despite the popularity of the allegorical method of interpreting the OT, some early Christian writers in the West, such as Tertullian and Cyprian, made little use of it, and a school of thought arose in the East—the Antiochenes—who were wary of it. Theodore, bishop of Mopsuestia (392–428), is a representative Antiochene. He rejected outright any allegorical interpretation which involved denial of the literal meaning of the text. He insisted that acceptable allegorization, such as that used by Paul in Gal. 4, must involve a comparison of real events in the past with others in the present. Such allegorical interpretation—more properly designated typological—is acceptable only if the type bears a real resemblance in its nature and effects to that which it signifies. So, for example, the blood of the passover is a type of the blood of the new covenant. As a further safeguard against fanciful allegorization, Theodore enunciated the principle that the exegete is justified in going beyond the NT use of the OT only if the OT text expresses its immediate meaning 'hyperbolically' (i.e. the phraseology goes beyond what the immediate reference would appear to require).

If Theodore places such severe restrictions on the use of the allegorical method, how does he relate the Old Testament to the New? Chiefly by viewing the OT as an unfolding historical development providing the background for God's new intervention in the person of Jesus Christ. Theodore stressed the difference between the old and the new, sometimes to an excessive degree. His stress on historical development prevented him from finding a full place in the canon of Scripture for much of the wisdom literature. Refusing to allegorize it, or give it any meaning other than the literal, he was unable to see how it contributed to the outworking of the divine purpose in history. And he is not altogether guiltless of importing into his understanding of the text ideas drawn from Greek culture. (For example, he understands man's creation in the image of God in terms of man's role as 'bond' of the cosmos, combining in himself the two realms of visible and invisible creation—a Greek rather than a Biblical notion.) Nevertheless, Theodore made an important protest against the excesses of Alexandrian allegorization. His fellow-Antiochene, John Chrysostom, showed the value of the approach for preaching, and his commentaries have a lasting value greater than those of Origen.

Jerome, the great Bible translator of the fourth century, made extensive use of the allegorical method in his earlier commentaries, and never ceased to regard it as legitimate and sometimes necessary. Like Origen, he held that to interpret some OT passages literally would be absurd or unedifying. As if God would have commanded Hosea, for example, to do something which is not honourable! Jerome recognized types in the OT, as well as straightforward prophecies, but he became somewhat wary of the allegorical method, and in his later commentaries made increasing use of the literal, historical approach.

Augustine, too, became more guarded in his use of allegory as time went on, and in place of the fairly free use of the device in his earlier commentaries became more guarded, though he continued to use allegorical interpretation, finding hidden meanings in the titles of psalms, the names of men and places and, above all, in numbers. Augustine, like Origen, believed that obscurities were divinely intended to stimulate thought. Similarly, he saw the rule of faith of the Church as a 'control'. Augustine insisted that the Bible was to be read and understood within the context of the Christian community. Difficult passages may be illuminated by clear passages elsewhere—a view contributed by Tertullian long before. In an effort to provide practical guidelines for distinguishing figurative from literal passages, Augustine insisted that anything that appears to attribute unrighteousness to God or the faithful, and anything that does not seem to conduce to good morals and true faith, must be interpreted allegorically. The ultimate criterion is that of love. If the literal sense tends to establish the reign of love it is the right one: if not, the passage is figurative. In this vein he asserted in his important work, *De Doctrina Christiana*, 'We must meditate on what we read till an interpretation be found that tends to establish the reign of charity' (cited in B. Smalley, *The Study of the Bible in the Middle Ages*, 1964 ed., p. 23).

III. The interpretation of the Old Testament in the Middle Ages

The dominant method of interpreting the OT during the period between the collapse of the ancient world and the Reformation was the allegorical one. During the earlier centuries of this long period, the study of the OT was undertaken largely in monasteries where the way of life favoured the contemplative approach to the text which is conducive to mystical, allegorical interpretation. The writings of the Antiochene school do not seem to have

been available in the West, and it was not until the twelfth century that a school of thought— the Victorine—began to stress the importance of the literal meaning of the OT. Albert the Great, and his more famous pupil, Thomas Aquinas, deeply influenced by the recently discovered thought of Aristotle, lent their great influence to the reaction against excessive allegorization, but so deeply rooted was this approach that it seems to have remained dominant until the Reformation period.

Writing in the fifth century, the monk John Cassian distinguished four levels of meaning in the OT—the literal, or historical sense, and three 'spiritual' senses, allegorical, anagogical and tropological. So, for example, Jerusalem is to be understood as a city of the Jews according to the literal sense. Allegory provides the doctrinal meaning, Church of God; anagogy draws out the heavenly meaning conveyed in Gal. 4: 26; tropology, which is concerned with moral meaning, sees Jerusalem as typifying the soul of man.

The works of Gregory the Great in the late sixth century, especially his commentary on Job, were to exercise tremendous influence on the attitude of medieval Biblical scholars towards the OT. Gregory paid scant attention to the literal meaning, but devoted great attention to the various spiritual senses, especially the tropological. Graphically, he described the functions of the various senses of Scripture in this metaphor: 'First we lay the historical foundations; next by pursuing the typical sense we erect a fabric of the mind to be a stronghold of the faith; and moreover as the last step, by the grace of moral instruction, we, as it were, clothe the edifice with an overcast of colouring' (cited in B. Smalley, *op. cit.*, p. 33). Gregory supported his tropological, or moral, interpretations by means of 'testimonies'. The interpretation which he gave to a particular text suggested another text containing a word which had the same spiritual meaning as the first. This gave rise to another, and another, until eventually Gregory formed a chain of parallel passages linked together by somewhat artificial and fanciful connections. Gregory brought all his learning to the task of Biblical exegesis, and used exegesis as the basis of all his preaching and teaching. In this, too, he deeply influenced medieval practice.

The venerable Bede followed this tradition faithfully. In the prologue to his commentary on Samuel he pointed out two reasons—an apologetic as well as a pastoral one—for the use of the allegorical method. 'If we seek to follow the letter of Scripture only, in the Jewish way, what shall we find to correct our sins, to console or instruct us, when we open the book of the blessed Samuel and read that Elcana had two wives?' (cited in B. Smalley, *op. cit.*, p. 36).

The allegorical method remained standard, though not without variation. Angelom of Luxeuil used as many as seven senses in his interpretation of the OT. But from time to time there were scholars who stressed the importance of the literal meaning and, implicitly or explicitly, frowned on excessive allegorical ingenuity. Miss Smalley has drawn attention to the importance in this connection of the Victorines, a succession of Biblical scholars associated with the Abbey of St. Victor at Paris, founded in 1110 (*op. cit.*, pp. 83–195).

Hugh of St. Victor stressed the importance of a proper understanding of the literal sense of the OT and prepared historical and geographical aids. It is interesting to note that he urged that, while literal study should begin with the OT and proceed into the NT, allegorical study should proceed in the reverse order. He insisted that allegorical interpretation needs to be undergirded by a knowledge of systematic doctrinal study. Hugh increased the importance of the literal, historical sense by bracketing it with the spiritual sense as leading to knowledge, in distinction from the third, tropological sense which leads to the practice of virtue. Andrew of St. Victor made no secret of his determination to expound the literal meaning of the OT, almost to the exclusion of any other. His work on the prophets set out quite deliberately to develop the literal exposition by Jerome. In his search for material to illuminate the OT in its historical sense he was not above availing himself of the wealth of Jewish learning, from which he drew extensively.

Despite the remarkably wide influence of Andrew's writings, the allegorical approach to the OT continued to exercise more influence than the literal upon the minds of medieval scholars. Thomas Aquinas, however, did make several vital distinctions which served to rehabilitate the literal sense. Commentators on the OT had long grappled somewhat inconclusively with the problem of whether metaphors and other forms of figurative language yielded any 'literal' meaning at all. (Theodore of Mopsuestia was among those who said that they did.) Aquinas boldly defined the literal meaning as the whole intention of the inspired writer, whether expressed in plain language or metaphorical. Drawing on Augustine's distinction between words and things, and fitting it into the Aristotelian framework that Aquinas incorporated into his thinking, he explained the allegorical sense by asserting that, whereas human authors express their meaning by words, God can also express meaning by 'things', i.e. historical happenings. The allegorical sense is therefore, for Aquinas, the

meaning which God has put into sacred history. In other words, the literal meaning represents what was in the mind of the sacred writer; the allegorical meaning discloses additional content which was in the mind of God when He inspired the particular passage of Scripture. The importance that Aquinas attached to the literal meaning of Scripture may be gauged from his dictum that while the spiritual interpretation is for the edification of the faithful, no argument may be deduced from it: only the literal interpretation is to be used for that purpose.

At least one late medieval writer, Nicholas of Lyra, set great store by the literal meaning of the OT, complaining that 'the literal sense is nearly suffocated among so many mystical expositions' (cited in *CHB* III. 79), but, as Miss Smalley has reminded us, we know so little about late medieval Biblical exegesis that generalizations are hazardous. Nevertheless, the chorus of denunciation mounted by humanist and Reformation writers of the late fifteenth and early sixteenth centuries against the excesses of the allegorists suggests that the literal meaning of the OT was in real danger of being submerged under a growing mountain of more or less fanciful interpretations. Geiler of Kaisersberg protested against exegetical methods which turned the Bible into a nose of wax.

IV. The interpretation of the Old Testament in the Reformation period

Foremost among the 'humanist' scholars of the Reformation period was Erasmus who, though his interest was in the NT, established canons of interpretation which were to influence study of the OT. Erasmus insisted that the literal, grammatical sense must be secured by the use of the best linguistic techniques available, and that the spiritual sense must be expounded in close relationship to this grammatical sense.

Luther went even further. He rejected outright the fourfold interpretation of Scripture by means of distinguishing the literal, allegorical, tropological and anagogical interpretations (the latter being what would be called in twentieth-century jargon 'eschatological'). He recognized that Paul had used allegory on occasions, and he was willing to resort to it in the pulpit, but he was opposed to any procedure that would undermine the literal sense of the OT, since he saw it as the history of Christ and of faith. In this he was undoubtedly reacting against those allegorizers who had evacuated the history of Israel of its basic significance. Antiochene typology was no more acceptable as a systematic scheme, since it, too, introduced the confusion of a double meaning and denied what to Luther was a fundamental principle—the historical presence of Christ in the OT. But, just as Luther was prepared on occasion to allegorize, so he was not doctrinaire in his attitude to typology. As R. H. Bainton puts it, to Luther 'Abel was not Christ, nor Isaac, nor Joseph and Jonah, and their experiences were not identical with his . . . But similarities of pattern were discernible' (*CHB* III. 26). 'The gain', to quote Bainton again, 'lay primarily in the relinquishment of a wooden schematization, with consequent freedom to roam and soar and indulge in interpretations, plastic, fluid and profound' (*ibid.*, p. 25). When he used allegory or typology 'it was for illustration: it was not a principle' (B. Hall, in *CHB* III. 87). Since the Spirit is one, Luther insisted, there cannot be a multiplicity of interpretations of Scripture. Following Lefèvre d'Étaples, he equated the literal sense with the prophetic and was therefore able to read the OT as a Christian book, finding Paul's theology in the Psalms and translating 'life' as 'eternal life' and 'the deliverer of Israel' as 'the Saviour' without introducing another sense as a formal principle. As Bornkamm has pointed out, Luther was able to do this because he directed his exegetical attention to those parts of the OT in which it was easy to find Christ (H. Bornkamm, *Luther and the Old Testament*, Fortress Press, Philadelphia, 1969, ch. 6; cf. E. G. Kraeling, *The Old Testament since the Reformation*, Lutterworth, 1955, pp. 16 ff.).

Though Luther saw Christ already present in the OT (though in veiled form, for in his own graphic phrase the OT was Christ's 'swaddling clothes') yet in other respects Luther saw a sharp dichotomy between the testaments. Law and gospel were poles apart for Luther, even though the former has a purpose which serves that of the latter. Here, as always, Luther's thought was dialectic and dynamic, in sharp contrast to that of later, Lutheran scholastics.

What Luther had said about the literal sense of Scripture Calvin underlined and enunciated in cool, rational form. Calvin aimed to set down the plain, sensible meaning of a passage, and to establish what the words mean in their context. 'He sought more frequently than most men of his age to interpret the writings of the Old Testament according to the circumstances and purposes of their own day, even though he always felt the gravitational pull of the needs of the analogy of faith' (B. Hall, in *CHB* III. 88). He set his face against allegory, and used typology sparingly. Like Luther, Zwingli and other major reformers, he insisted that what would nowadays be called the 'historico-grammatical' meaning is of fundamental importance to a right understanding of the text. Though his technical equipment for the task of exegesis was superb—and he was not altogether immune from the danger of his spiritual judgment being affected by it—he pleaded for the self-sufficiency of Scripture on the ground of the authenticating power of the Holy Spirit. Again, Calvin is at one with other reformers in urging that the enlightenment of the Holy Spirit is indispensable for a right understanding of Scripture, though he articulates the point more powerfully.

Calvin's view of the relationship between the testaments differed somewhat from that of Luther. For example, whereas Luther stressed the negative function of the law, Calvin emphasized its positive role. Since Calvin minimized the difference between Old and New Testaments it was easier for him than for Luther to interpret the OT without resorting to allegory and typology.

Something, however brief, must be said about the interpretation of the OT by Anabaptists. Very few generalizations can be hazarded about Anabaptists, since they did not constitute a homogeneous group. With regard to OT interpretation, interest attaches mainly to those Anabaptists who have been dubbed 'Spiritualists'. They distinguished between the letter and the spirit, not in the way of allegorists but in terms of a distinction between what they called the outer word—the Bible—and the inner word which God revealed direct to men. The Scriptures for them were at best an external witness and record of past revelation. Some draw attention to the apparent inconsistencies and contradictions between the two testaments, and whereas they tended to interpret the NT with extreme liberalism turned to spiritualization as the means of extracting meaning from the OT. To some extent theirs was an extreme form of reaction against current controversies. One of their number, Sebastian Franck, declared: 'I do not want to be a papist; I do not want to be a Lutheran; I do not want to be an Anabaptist.'

V. The interpretation of the Old Testament since the Reformation

While the Reformers had advocated the use of the critical faculties in the interpretation of the OT, they had pleaded for submission to the guidance of the Holy Spirit. True, this had not resulted in agreed exegesis, but it had acted as a curb against self-opinionated and cocksure attitudes. Subsequently, Protestant interpretation of the OT became stereotyped, if not fossilized. For example, Flacius Illyricus put Lutheran interpretation into a straitjacket with his influential *Clavis Scripturae Sanctae* (1562). But the sixteenth century saw the rise of philological and historical scholarship of a new order. Developments took place in both textual and higher criticism which foreshadowed the critical movement of the last two centuries. The federal theology of J. Cocceius severely modified the Reformed view of the virtual identity of the Testaments and led to an increased use of typological interpretation.

Above all, secular thinking, independent of ecclesiastical control, began to be applied to Biblical exegesis. The philosophy of Descartes undergirded an almost unlimited reliance on reason which led to critical attacks on the veracity of the OT.

In England, the eighteenth-century deists drew attention to apparent inconsistencies, contradictions, intellectual absurdities and moral ambiguities in the OT, and questioned its status as divine revelation. The crisis passed, but left its mark. Orthodox defenders of the faith against deism 'not only shared its presuppositions but accompanied its exponents much of the way' (W. Neil, in *CHB* III. 243). Thus Bishop Butler admitted the presence of difficulties in the OT and explained them by analogy with the flaws in nature (which was admitted by the deists to be the handiwork of God). On the continent of Europe, and particularly in Germany, deism had a considerable impact, leading to a downgrading of the OT. Lessing compared the OT to an elementary school book prescribed for the Jews but no longer required reading. Kant in *Religion within the Boundaries of Pure Reason* (1793) denied that the Jewish faith stands in any essential connection with Christianity. The attempt of early Christian writers to portray Christianity as a continuation of the old order was dictated by apologetic considerations.

It would be out of the question to attempt to survey the development of critical theories of the OT during the last two centuries. All that can be attempted here is to pinpoint some of the major background elements in the thinking of OT scholars, illustrate the results by reference to a few key figures, point out the existence of opponents to the dominant trend, and offer some observations on the present situation.

There can be no question that, fundamental to the modern approach to the OT (as to the NT) is a general reliance on the autonomous application of human reason to the task of understanding the text. Unfettered by ecclesiastical traditions and doctrinal formularies, the scholar uses current ideas and presuppositions to guide him to a satisfying interpretation. Among these presuppositions are theories of literary criticism. For example, in 1795 Friedrich August Wolf in his *Prolegomena to Homer* put forward the view that the Homeric poems originated in short lays or ballads, subsequently brought together to form the lengthy poems as we know them. This theory was applied by OT scholars to the documents of the Bible. Even more influential was the development of historical scholarship. The idea of history as a dynamic process from primitive beginnings to more advanced stages came to exercise enormous influence on OT scholarship. Hegel gave history a standing in philosophy and contributed a notion that was to influence some OT scholars (and, more importantly, some NT ones). This was the dialectic principle that a thesis gives rise to its antithesis, and from the inevitable clash between the two a synthesis emerges which combines elements from both thesis and antithesis. The idea of history as development was greatly strengthened by the evolutionary idea which, starting life as a scientific hypothesis, came to be applied in many other fields, including that of history. Modern science contributed to the formation of a climate of opinion which found the Biblical account of creation difficult—if not impossible—to accept, and discounted—if it did not deny—the miraculous and the supernatural. Belief in the universal reign of the laws of nature made it difficult for room to be found for anything that appeared to go against them. However, the dominance of immanentist philosophies for most of the period under review made denial of the supernatural more real than apparent! It was still possible to talk about the supernatural and yet look for it only *within* the natural.

Another solvent of traditional views of the OT (as of the NT) was the emergence of subjectivism in alliance with rationalism. F. E. D. Schleiermacher has been credited with uniting rationalism with the subjectivism of the Reformation. His *Christian Faith* (1821) had enormous influence and, according to A. R. Vidler, 'his works as a whole came to bear the same relation to subsequent Liberal Protestant theology as the *Summa* of St. Thomas does to Thomism or as Calvin's *Institutes* do to Reformed Theology' (*Christianity in an Age of Revolution*, p. 26). Already, Kant had denied that reason can lead to knowledge of anything deeper than *phenomena* (i.e. outward appearance) and had asserted that it is only through man's sense of unconditional moral obligation that theological or metaphysical certainty can be attained. Now, Schleiermacher based his concept of religion on the feeling of 'absolute dependence on God'. As a result, revelation was conceived to be not communication of knowledge but 'the rise of a new religious experience' (E. G. Kraeling, *op. cit.*, p. 59).

The interpretation of the OT in recent times has also been affected by the development of new areas of scientific study. It is well-known that archaeology has provided a good deal of evidence confirming the accuracy of OT history. This is not always the case, however. Furthermore, the first effect of the development of archaeology in the nineteenth century was to reduce the level of the history of Israel to that of any other Near Eastern people in ancient times. This, combined with the researches of anthropologists, sociologists and psychologists, facilitated the assimilation of the study of the OT to that of any other document surviving from the ancient world, and the implicit assumption that no unique feature was to be expected in it, other than what arose from the religious genius of the Hebrews.

The overall effect of the approach to the OT characteristic of the liberal Protestant scholarship based on these presuppositions has been well summed up by T. W. Manson as the placing between God and man of a plate-glass window that is soundproof (see C. W. Dugmore [ed.], *The Interpretation of the Bible*, ch. V).

Julius Wellhausen (1844–1918) may be said to have created the framework within which most OT scholars have worked in modern times. His theory had been anticipated by the Alsatian, Eduard Reuss, the German, K. H. Graf and the Dutchman, Abraham Kuenen, but Wellhausen argued the case with such force and developed its implications for the study of the OT in such a way that it is justifiably linked with his name. Developing theories of Pentateuchal criticism put forward by others, notably Eichhorn in his three-volumed *Introduction to the Old Testament* (1780–3), Wellhausen not only put forward a persuasive theory of the structure of the Pentateuch but also came to the conclusion that the prophets were the real initiators of Israel's religious development, that the OT legislation as we now have it came later, and that the Psalms and wisdom literature represent the crowning achievement of Israel's religious genius.

Theories such as these did not go unchallenged. Quite apart from opposition from those who shared the same presuppositions and the hostility of fellow-professionals (*e.g.* A. H. Sayce, Professor of Assyriology at Oxford), doughty defenders of the traditional approach to the OT raised their voices. In Germany, E. W. Hengstenberg, professor at Berlin, 1828–69, not only wrote learned works but also founded and edited an influential church newspaper. At Erlangen, J. C. K. von Hofmann provided 'next to Calvin . . . the most useful viewpoints for the defence and proper utilization of the Old Testament on a conservative basis' (E. G. Kraeling, *op. cit.*, p. 75). In England, E. B. Pusey, the high churchman who had studied in Germany and at first been attracted to the new views, wrote conservative commentaries on the prophets. Numerous replies to Wellhausen were written on a more or less scholarly basis by men like James Robertson, W. L. Baxter and, in America, W. H. Green. James Orr addressed himself to *The Problem of the Old Testament* (1906) and at a more popular level Sir Robert Anderson tried to counteract the effect of the new interpretations of the OT with titles like *The Bible and Modern Criticism* (1902) and *Daniel in the Critics' Den* (⁴1922).

In vain. The new approach, when it came, seemed to have come to stay (though its fruits often proved to be perishable). In Britain, progress was slow at first. It is of interest to note that in 1847, F. W. Newman, no longer a missionary associate of A. N. Groves but a thoroughgoing rationalist, published his *History of the Hebrew Monarchy* which claimed to find early Hebrew legends in the OT and discounted them as the product of primitive credulity. Ten years later, Samuel Davidson resigned his professorship at the Lancashire Independent College as a result of the uproar created by his contribution to the 10th edition of Horne's *Introduction to the Critical Study and Knowledge of Holy Scriptures* in which he was alleged to have denied the Mosaic authorship of the Pentateuch. *Essays and Reviews*, published in 1860, was the work of seven Anglicans, all but one professors or clergy. It included the latest in OT criticism and an essay by Benjamin Jowett arguing that the true distinctiveness of Scripture would appear only if it was interpreted 'like any other book'. Little or nothing was new, but the volume gave the appearance of being intended as a kind of public manifesto. Though it attracted intense opposition—led by men as diverse as E. B. Pusey and the seventh Lord Shaftesbury—the Judicial Committee of the Privy Council established the right for such views to be held in the Church of England. The extreme nature of the presentation of critical views of the OT by men such as J. W. Colenso, Samuel Davidson and —in the 1870s—T. K. Cheyne delayed the general acceptance of critical views for some time. But in the eighties S. R. Driver and T. K. Cheyne put forward new ideas with a degree of moderation and an appearance of evangelical faith. Also, in Scotland, W. Robertson Smith, professor of Hebrew and OT Criticism at the Free Church College in Aberdeen, a man whom Vidler described as 'an earnest evangelical who accepted the Calvinistic doctrines of the Westminster Confession' (*op. cit.*, p. 171) put forward advanced views on OT issues which led to a long drawn out trial for heresy that served to make those views more widely known and to arouse sympathy for him. (Later, Robertson Smith was to make important contributions to OT studies, through his application of anthropological theories to the study of early Hebrew religion, *e.g.* in his *Religion of the Semites*, 1889.)

Lux Mundi (1889), a volume of essays written by high churchmen, constitutes something of a landmark. Hitherto, high churchmen like Pusey and Liddon had been one with evangelicals in their opposition to the new views of the OT. Now, Charles Gore, Principal of Pusey

House, Oxford, in his essay on 'The Holy Spirit and Inspiration', was not only prepared to accept the non-historicity of Jonah and a late date for Daniel, but, more importantly, offered hints of a 'kenosis' theory to account for the apparent acceptance by Jesus of the historicity of Jonah. According to this theory, the divine Logos at the Incarnation 'emptied' himself of the metaphysical attributes of Deity, while retaining the moral and spiritual ones.

The new ideas about the OT—and the new approaches which underlay them—were gaining increasing acceptance around the world. In Europe, N. America and the overseas mission field, the story was the same. As a result, adjustments had to be made to concepts such as inspiration and revelation. For instance, in 1891, W. Sanday's Bampton Lectures on *Inspiration* admitted that the writers of the OT were inspired and that this experience constituted revelation, but maintained that the words in which they communicated that revelation were their own.

Subsequently, the activities of OT scholars have continued, unabated. Broadly speaking, the Wellhausenian reconstruction still holds the field, though it has suffered many modifications—some drastic—and may be said to survive only because of the lack of a comprehensive and convincing alternative—other than the traditional one! Among influential scholars of the present century reference may be made to Hermann Gunkel (1862–1932) who has directed attention away from written sources to oral tradition and, in particular, the development of sagas. This has led to new forms of literary criticism, notably tradition and redaction criticism, which is concerned with the editorial processes of committing oral tradition to writing, transmitting and modifying it.

VI. Conclusion

How are we to carry out the important task of interpreting the OT? We shall certainly wish to start in the way that Jesus and the apostles started, by recognizing that the OT is a revelation from God. Since it is—for us—a written revelation, there is a sense in which we can understand it only if we are prepared to pay attention to the words, grammar, syntax and the historical and cultural background of the writers. This is the grammatico-historical method of interpretation that was insisted upon by the Reformers. The fact that more recent Protestant scholars have often distorted this method by importing into it their own cultural presuppositions should not be allowed to prejudice us against it. The first aim of the exegete must be to listen to the words of the inspired writers of Scripture. The fact that he lives in an almost completely different culture is bound to introduce complications, but the effort must be made to hear the Scriptures—OT as well as

NT—in their original tone and setting. If he succeeds in doing so, he will be surprised at the extent to which he finds them speaking directly to his own situation, just as Paul and other NT writers found the OT revelation of God and His ways immediately relevant.

Not always. The OT is 'old', and we who have the benefit of the 'new' testament will read each in the light of the other. Not that we are likely to reject the OT outright, like a Marcion, or, more recently a younger Delitzsch or, to some extent, a Bultmann. It was not without reason that the Early Church accepted the OT as its Bible and retained it alongside the writings of the NT. Nor, it is to be hoped, will we circumscribe our use of the OT by looking there for nothing but revelations of 'Christ in the Old Testament'. We are not to imagine that the risen Saviour expounded the whole of the OT on the walk to Emmaus! The attempt to find intimations of Christ on every page of the OT has called forth immense ingenuity, but all too often it has gone hand in hand with the notion that the OT is a spiritual conundrum whose surface meaning is the property of the Jews and whose coded meaning belongs to the Christian Church.

This is not to say that Christ is not to be found in the OT. Of course He is. No-one who has read the NT seriously and takes it as authoritative can be in doubt about this. But does the fact that NT writers, using current methods of exegesis, were inspired to point out ways in which Jesus Christ was foreshadowed in the OT authorize us to add to their exegesis? A partial answer is provided by the principle that any such use of the OT should go no further than to provide illustration of truths about Christ clearly revealed in the NT. More than one evangelical writer has landed himself in formal heresy by unbridled use of the allegorical method of interpreting the OT. Another safeguard against abuse of the OT is a fairly strict adherence to the typological rather than the uncontrolled allegorical method. Granted that there is a recurring pattern in God's ways with men, we may expect to see significant features reappearing from time to time. But in drawing attention to these, we must be careful not to evacuate the text of its basic, historical meaning.

In the course of recent attempts to hold the testaments together, some have interpreted Scripture as the record of 'salvation history', and have been content to see it in terms of a succession of distinct stages in God's saving work. Others have stressed the theme of promise and fulfilment, not necessarily seeing the OT as nothing but promise and the NT as exclusively fulfilment, but seeing some fulfilment in the OT as well as the NT—and some promise in the NT. And, of course, there are the straightforward prophecies which, the NT claims, have been fulfilled in Christ.

The fact of the matter would seem to be that the two testaments are bound together in many ways. Differences and even sharp contrasts there are—within as well as between the testaments—but, since it is the belief of the Christian that they have not only human authors but also a single divine author, there is an underlying consistency between them. Just as the NT cannot be fully understood without reference to the OT, so the OT cannot be fully understood (in a Christian sense) without reference to the NT. The ultimate context of any passage of Scripture is the whole Bible. Among the links which bind the testaments together are clear messianic prophecies, obvious typological correspondence, and the enunciation of moral and spiritual teaching in the forms of admonition, narrative, poetry and the like, provided this is not transcended or modified in the light of the fuller revelation of God in the NT.

The task of the interpreter of the OT is not finished when he garners its harvest. To change the figure, he still has the formidable task of applying its teaching to life in the world of his own day. Just as the biblical languages have to be translated into the various vernacular languages of the contemporary world if they are to be intelligible, so the moral and spiritual teachings of the OT (as of the NT) have to be translated into contemporary cultural realities. Just as the exchange of the kiss of peace in NT times might, in some cultures today, be 'translated' into a friendly handshake, so the requirement that flat roofs be built with parapets to prevent people falling off (Dt. 22: 8) indicates a concern for public safety, and, particularly, prevention of needless loss of life, that can be 'translated' into many contemporary idioms.

We must not expect to find deep spiritual truth everywhere in the OT (or the NT). It was this expectation that led Origen, for example, to exercise his allegorical ingenuity to an extent that served only to turn the Bible into a book of conundrums. Many features of the OT which seem puzzling to Westerners today (*e.g.* genealogies) would have been meaningful to their original readers and form part of the 'package deal'. It is perhaps excessive attention to the individual words and phrases of Scripture at the expense of the overall thrust of passages and books that is responsible for this imbalance. Single words *can* be vitally important. But, on any account, some are more

important than others—and the same goes for passages and even books.

First, then, the OT should be interpreted on its own terms, in the endeavour to ascertain as accurately as possible what its first readers were intended to understand by the various documents as they appeared. Next, and most importantly for the Christian, it should be interpreted within the context of the complete Bible, so that what 'God spoke of old to our forefathers through the prophets' may be assessed in relation to what 'in these last days he has spoken to us by his Son' (Heb. 1: 1 f.). And serious attention should be paid, finally, to the 'plenary sense' which it has accumulated throughout the centuries as it has come to life with ever new relevance in the experience of the people of God.

BIBLIOGRAPHY

ANDERSON, G. W. (ed.), *Tradition and Interpretation* (Oxford, 1979).

BARR, J., *Old and New in Interpretation* (London, 1966).

BORNKAMM, H., *Luther and the Old Testament* (Philadelphia, 1969).

BRIGHT, J., *The Authority of the Old Testament* (London, 1967).

The Cambridge History of the Bible (3 vols., Cambridge, 1963–70).

CLEMENTS, R. E., *A Century of Old Testament Study* (London, 1976).

DUGMORE, C. W. ed. *The Interpretation of the Bible* (London, 1944).

GRANT, R. M., *The Letter and the Spirit* (London, 1957).

HAHN, H. F., *The Old Testament in Modern Research* (London, 1956).

HANSON, R. P. C., *Allegory and Event* (London, 1959).

HASEL, G. F., *Old Testament Theology: Basic Issues in the Current Debate* (Grand Rapids, 1972).

KRAELING, E. G., *The Old Testament since the Reformation* (London, 1955).

LONGENECKER, R. N., *Biblical Exegesis in the Apostolic Period* (Grand Rapids, 1975).

SMALLEY, B., *The Study of the Bible in the Middle Ages* (Oxford, 1952; paperback edition, University of Notre Dame Press, 1964).

STOLZ, F., *Interpreting the Old Testament* (London, 1975).

STUHLMACHER, P., *Historical Criticism and Theological Interpretation of Scripture*, E.T. (London, 1979).

THOMPSON, R. J., *Moses and the Law in a Century of Criticism since Graf* (Leiden, 1970).

WESTERMANN, C. (ed.), *Essays on Old Testament Interpretation* (London, 1963; American edition, *Essays on Old Testament Hermeneutics*, Richmond, Va., 1963).

INTRODUCTION TO
THE PENTATEUCH

DAVID J. A. CLINES

Form

The first five books of the OT, the Pentateuch, are essentially in the form of a *narrative*, running from the creation of the world to the death of Moses. This form immediately alerts us to the nature of these books. Though they contain a great deal of law, they are not in essence law-books; though they contain genealogies and speeches (the latter especially in Deuteronomy), they do not function merely as a record of the past or as address to the present. Fundamentally, these books tell a story, in which the doings of God with mankind and more especially with Israel his people are rehearsed. And that story does not exist for the purpose of entertainment, or even for the sake of curiosity about the past, but in order to instruct God's people about the nature of their God with whom they are still in relationship.

These books are called by the Jews the Torah. That term has traditionally been translated as 'law', and the view has been prevalent since pre-Christian times that such is what the Pentateuch essentially is. Since it has been universally acknowledged, by Jews and Christians alike, that the Pentateuch is the most important of the three divisions of the Hebrew canon (Torah, Prophets, and Writings), the OT as a whole has often come to be regarded as law. Thus, for example, Luther wrote in his *Preface to the OT* (1523): 'Know then that the OT is a book of laws, which teaches what men are to do and not to do, and gives, besides, examples and stories of how these laws are kept or broken; just as the NT is a gospel-book, or book of grace'. But such a view rests upon a misunderstanding of 'torah'; it does not primarily mean 'law', but 'guidance', or 'instruction'. So the stories of Jacob and Joseph are as much 'torah' as are the commandments given at Sinai, and the narrative of the crossing of the Red Sea (Exod. 14) as much as Moses' speech of encouragement to the tribes about to enter the land (Dt. 31).

'Torah' as 'guidance' appears in many different guises in the Pentateuch. Sometimes, indeed, 'torah' is explicitly directive, as in the Ten Commandments, which have the form of a chieftain addressing his tribe, or a king his subjects, or as in the many social laws, whether in the style of legal maxims (*e.g.* Exod. 21: 17) or of hypothetical cases (*e.g.* Exod. 21: 2–6). But at other times, it is reportorial, in the form of a table of nations (*e.g.* Gen. 10) or genealogies (*e.g.* Gen. 5) or of lists of booty (Num. 31: 32–47), and, more frequently, narrative, as in the greater part of Genesis and Exodus 1–19. The 'guidance' offered by the narrative portions of the Torah is indirect and inexplicit. In some cases we may be presented with models for imitation (as in the case of Abraham's faithfulness or Joseph's uprightness), but even here (and more especially in stories like those of Abraham's loss of nerve or Jacob's trickery) the narrator is more than a mere moralist; his story is often less didactic 'guidance' about personal behaviour than 'guidance' toward the reality of God who is working his purposes out through good men and bad.

Thus the Torah does not go about its task of offering 'guidance' by presenting a comprehensive set of rules for life; nor by developing a cohesive theological system; nor by telling the story of the past with reiterated clear applications of moral lessons for the present. Its guidance is manifold, and to a large extent indirect, for the reader is never allowed to forget that even its most directive 'guidance' is set within the framework of the narrative of Genesis to Deuteronomy. Everything is tied down to some point in time and space, not in order to render its teaching merely local and temporary, but to show that it offers 'guidance' and not 'law'.

Theme

Our first clue to the theme of the Pentateuch comes from the way it, and its various books, conclude. Remarkably, they do not come to an end at a point of rest or fulfilment, but on a note of expectation and tension. Thus Deuteronomy, and with it the whole Pentateuch, concludes with Israel on the point of entering the promised land. At its end it looks to the future with the farewell speech of Moses (31: 2–6) and the introduction of Joshua (31: 7 f.; 34: 9), who will lead Israel into Canaan. It does not leave the reader with a completed tale rounded off by the death of the hero of the work, but rather looks ahead to the development of the history that has only just begun. Even throughout the book of Deuteronomy, and not only at its end, this futuristic outlook is evident: its two most common phrases are 'go in and possess' (repeated 35 times) and 'the land which Yahweh your God gives you' (34 times).

If we turn now to the conclusion of Genesis, while it appears from the last verse of the book ('So Joseph died . . . and after they embalmed him, he was placed in a coffin in Egypt', 50: 26) that we have reached a point of repose, in the context of the previous verse that is plainly not so. For before his death, Joseph had assured his sons: 'God will surely come to your aid, and then you must carry my bones up from this place' (50: 25). So the coffin in Egypt is nothing permanent, but is meant, paradoxically, to direct the reader's vision toward the future.

The book of Exodus, also, concludes with an open-ended sentence: 'In all the travels of the Israelites . . . the cloud of the Lord was over the tabernacle by day, and fire was in the cloud by night' (40: 38): Israel is still on the march, still journeying. The exodus (the 'going out') has been accomplished, but there has not yet been an *eisodos* ('entrance').

Leviticus and Numbers, though apparently static and motionless with their accumulated weight of laws and cultic prescriptions, nevertheless sustain, by their conclusions, this impression of movement. Thus Leviticus is 'the command which the Lord gave Moses *on Mount Sinai* for the Israelites ' (27: 34), while Numbers moves the venue yet closer to the promised land, for it has consisted of 'the commands and regulations the Lord gave through Moses to the Israelities *on the plains of Moab by the Jordan across from Jericho*' (36: 13). Deuteronomy, though set in the same locale as Numbers, marks a progression upon Numbers because of its more forward-looking aspect that we have noted above.

So we are dealing in the Pentateuch with a story that has a certain dynamic quality and that, in spite of its leisurely pace and frequent halts, looks constantly toward the future. What then is the impetus that begins this pattern of movement?

The mainspring of the action of the Pentateuch is not to be found in the 'primeval history' (Gen. 1–11) with which it opens, for there the dynamic of the stories is provided by human (sinful) initiatives which are met by ever more gracious acts of divine forgiveness. Genesis 1–11 only serves to show that man's initiatives lead him deeper and deeper into sin. But in chapter 12, with the promise to Abraham, the initiative passes entirely into God's hands. From now on, the story will be, not of human initiatives prospered or judged by God, but of God's own fulfilment of his promise in spite of human doubts and antagonism.

The promise of Gen. 12: 1 ff. contains three elements: a posterity ('I will make you into a great nation'), a relationship ('I will bless you') and a land ('the land I will show you'). Elsewhere in the Abraham narratives the promise is repeated, with varying emphases: in 13: 14–17 the land and the posterity are stressed ('all the land that you see I will give to you and to your offspring forever', v. 15); in 15: 5 the posterity ('count the stars . . . so shall your offspring be'); in 15: 7–20 the land ('I am the Lord, who brought you out of Ur of the Chaldeans, to give you this land to take possession of it', v. 7), which will be given to Abraham's posterity ('to your descendants I give this land', v. 18); in ch. 17 the relationship, in the form of the covenant ('I will confirm my covenant between me and you', v. 2; 'I will establish my covenant . . . between me and you and your descendants . . . to be your God and the God of your descendants after you', v. 7), and the land ('The whole land of Canaan . . . I will give . . . to you and to your descendants . . . and I will be their God', v. 8). It is the fulfilment (and the partial non-fulfilment) of these three promises that may be said to be the theme of the Pentateuch.

The theme of *posterity* is plainly the theme of Genesis. The whole cycle of the Abraham narratives, to begin with, revolves about this subject. In these narratives the theme appears mostly in the shape of anxious questions: first, Will there be a son at all? and secondly, What will become of him? Will he survive to produce a posterity (cf. Gen. 22)? The other patriarchal tales continue to concern essentially the theme of the family and its preservation. Here lies the significance of the triple narrative of 'the ancestress in danger' (Gen. 12; 20; 26); it is important because the danger to the patriarch's wife is a threat to the fulfilment of the promise. Here too lies the significance of the barrenness of the wives of the patriarchs (Sarah, Rebekah, Rachel), and the significance of the famines in the land of Canaan (Gen. 12: 10; 26: 1; 41: 54) that threaten the survival of the patriarchal family. And yet the promise of posterity to Abraham is no empty one: it *has* been fulfilled at the birth of Isaac (Gen. 21), and, in a way, already at the birth of Ishmael (Gen. 16). Nonetheless, it has not been *fully* fulfilled: how many generations must it be before Israel numbers the dust of the earth?

The themes of the land and of the relationship also appear in Genesis in a minor role: the land that is given Abraham to possess is indeed explored and lived in by the patriarchs, but it remains the property of the Canaanites—except for one burial plot (Gen. 23: 17–20)! The patriarchal narratives take place outside the promised land almost as much as inside it, and the book comes to an end with the patriarchal

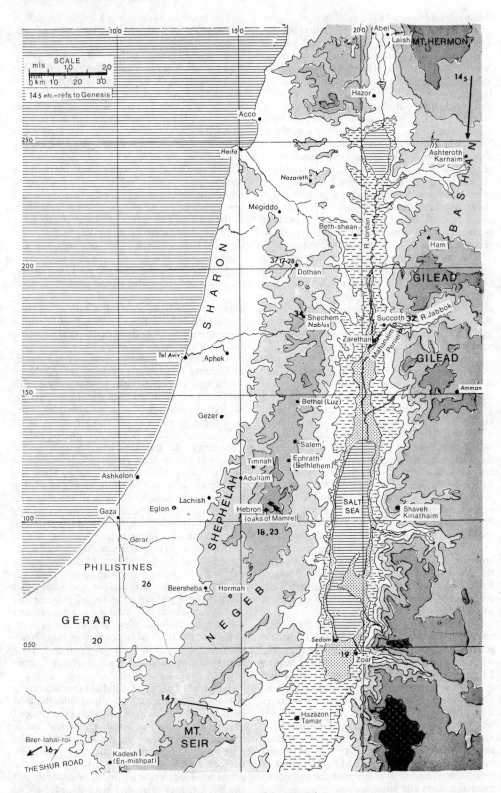

SCALE

mls 10 20
0 km 10 20 30

14,5 *etc.—refs.to Genesis*

MT. HERMON

Abel
Laish

14,5

Hazor

Acco

Haifa 250

Ashteroth
Karnaim

Nazareth

BASHAN

Megiddo

Beth-shean

Ham

SHARON

200

Dothan
37 17-28

GILEAD

R.Jordan

Shechem
Nablus
34

Succoth 32
R.Jabbok

Zarethan

Mahanaim
Peniel

GILEAD

Tel Aviv
Aphek

Amman

150

Bethel (Luz)

Gezer

Salem

SHEPHELAH

Timnah
Ephrath
(Bethlehem)

Ashkelon

Adullam

Lachish

SALT
SEA

Gaza

Eglon
Hebron
(oaks of Mamre)

100

Shaveh
Kiriathaim

Gerar

18,23

PHILISTINES

26

Beersheba
Hormah

GERAR

NEGEB

20

Sedom

050

19
Zoar

14

Hazazon
Tamar

Beer-lahai-roi
16
THE SHUR ROAD

MT.
SEIR

Kadesh
(En-mishpat)

Map 2—Canaan of the Patriarchs

family firmly outside the land and settled in Egypt. Only in the slightest degree has this element of the promise begun to be fulfilled. As for the promise of the relationship between God and the patriarchal family, that has indeed begun to take effect, but in different ways: Abraham enjoys an intimacy with God that allows him even to argue with the Almighty (Gen. 18: 22–33), and is in constant encounter with him; of Isaac we know only that Yahweh's blessing is on him (26: 12, 24); in the case of Jacob we may perhaps discern a maturing relationship with God, which however includes a promise on Jacob's part that betrays no recognition of the divine promise (28: 20 f.); with Joseph, though Yahweh is 'with' him (39: 2, 21), and he 'fears' God (42: 18), the relationship seems rather distant. In short, in the book of Genesis it is by no means established what the nature of that promised divine-human relationship is to be.

That element of the *relationship* between God and the descendants of Abraham is most clearly brought to expression in the books of Exodus and Leviticus. Both at the exodus and at Sinai it becomes plain what the promise meant by its words 'I will bless you', 'I will make my covenant between me and you', 'I will be your God'. The blessing of God comes in the form of salvation from oppression in Egypt and in the gift of the law; the covenant with the patriarchs provides the motivation for God's deliverance of Israel from Egypt (Exod. 2: 24 f.; 6: 4 f.) and it is ratified by the covenant of Sinai (chs. 20–23; cf. 19: 5; 24: 7 f.); the promise 'I will be your God' is made good by the exodus (6: 6 f.) and is amplified by the words from Sinai that begin 'I am Yahweh your God (20: 2). Leviticus spells out in detail how the relationship now established by God with Israel is to be maintained: the sacrificial system is to exist, not as a human means of access to God, but as the divinely ordered method by which breaches of the covenant may be repaired and atoned for. Throughout the 'Holiness Code' (chs. 17–26) of Leviticus it is precisely this matter of the relationship between God and Israel that is emphasized in the recurrent formula, 'Be holy because I Yahweh your God am holy' (*e.g.* 19: 2). Holiness here does not consist so much in ethical purity as in Israel's distinctiveness from the nations of the earth in its being a possession of Yahweh. It is, above all, the relationship with Yahweh with which Leviticus is concerned, as its summarizing conclusion shows: 'These are the commands which Yahweh gave Moses on Mount Sinai for the Israelites' (27: 34).

Yet, despite the fulfilments of the promise of a relationship that are to be found in these books, this is not a promise that can ever be totally fulfilled. For what is promised is not a contract that can be signed, sealed and delivered, and then stored away in the vaults of the past, but a personal relationship. Relationship is a dynamic term, for relationships cannot remain static. So at the exodus and at Sinai something is set in train rather than accomplished; the exodus is only a going out, and thus a beginning; the words of God from Sinai say 'You *shall* . . . you *shall* not'. Both Exodus and Leviticus, therefore, are pointing towards a future as yet unrealized, a future in which Israel has yet to discover what this promise of a relationship, 'I will be your God', will mean.

As for the promise of the *land*, it is in Numbers and Deuteronomy that this element of the patriarchal promise rises nearest to the surface. The census of the people with which the book of Numbers opens is no idle game undertaken to kill time in the monotony of the desert wanderings. It is portrayed as the initial preparation for the occupation of the land, for it is a census of all males 'twenty years old or more who are able to serve in the army' (1: 3); it is understood from the beginning that the land that is promised will nonetheless have to be fought for. And following that census at Sinai, all attention is focused on the land as the destination of the Israelite journeyings. Moses says to his father-in-law, 'We are setting out for the place about which Yahweh said, "I will give it to you"' (10:29); and they set out, the ark of the covenant and the cloud of Yahweh going before them (10: 33 f.). In the space of a couple of chapters, Israel is poised on the brink of Canaan, and the spies are sent out and actually enter the land (ch. 13). Thereafter the book revolves around the question whether and when Israel will enter the land: there is an attempt to return to Egypt, and a new commitment, too late, to go up to the land (ch. 14); there are commandments relating to the time 'After you enter the land I am giving you as a home' (ch. 15; cf. 15: 2); there is movement toward the land by a circuitous route (chs. 20–24); there are instructions about the extent and division of the land (ch. 34): Above all, there is the actual occupation of the land—that is, of that part of it lying to the east of the Jordan—by the tribes of Gad and Reuben and half the tribe of Manasseh (ch. 32; cf. 32: 33). So in Numbers the promise does not remain simply a promise for the future: it is partly fulfilled though largely not as yet fulfilled.

In Deuteronomy, as we have already noted, the emphasis is upon the land Israel is about to enter; its laws are 'the decrees and laws I [Moses] . . . teach you . . . that you may live and may go in and take possession of the land that Yahweh, the God of your fathers, is giving you' (4: 1; cf. 12: 1). In it Israel is addressed as a people who 'are now to cross the Jordan, to go in and dispossess nations greater and stronger than you' (9: 1). As it draws to a conclusion, Israel is given instruction about crossing the Jordan into 'the land Yahweh your God is giving you, a land flowing with milk and honey, just as Yahweh, the God of your fathers, promised you' (27: 3), and summoned to enter the land courageously (31: 1–6), while Moses is finally given a glimpse of the land he will never enter himself (32: 48–52; 34: 1–4). The promise of the land has begun to take effect, but for the most part its fulfilment still lies in the future.

The whole structure of the Pentateuch, then, is shaped by the promises to Abraham and their fulfilments, which are never final but always point beyond themselves to a future yet to be realized. The Pentateuch as a whole witnesses to a God who is ahead of his people, beckoning them into the future; the God of Abraham, Isaac, and Jacob is not a God of the dead, but of the living.

Origin

Questions about the origin of the Pentateuch bulk large in most 'Introductions' to the Old Testament. This is true of works of 'critical' scholarship, like those of O. Eissfeldt and G. Fohrer, and of conservative or fundamentalist works like those of R. K. Harrison or E. J. Young. It may be argued, however, that since solutions to the problems of Pentateuchal origins must remain to a large extent speculative or at least hypothetical, in the absence of any documents from which the Pentateuch might have been compiled, much scholarly activity in this area has been misdirected. It is more important, from both a literary and religious point of view, to attempt to interpret the Pentateuch as we have it than to debate questions about its literary pre-history. This is not to deny that the origin of the Pentateuch is a legitimate field of study, nor that reasonable hypotheses about the process of its formation can illuminate the text in its final form. The point at issue here is one of priorities.

Though the Pentateuch came to be known as the 'books of Moses' (since he figures more prominently than any other personage in the narratives, and since the law was mediated to Israel through him), the Pentateuch itself explicitly credits Moses with the authorship of only a relatively small part of its contents (Exod. 24: 4–8, referring to chs. 21–23, the 'Book of the Covenant'; Num. 33: 2, referring to ch. 33, the itinerary of Israel in the wilderness; Dt. 31: 19, 22, referring to ch. 32, the Song of Moses; and Dt. 31: 24 ff., referring probably to the Ten Commandments of 5: 6–21). That is not to say that Moses could not have been responsible for a much greater part in the composition of the five books, but simply that we lack conclusive indications. The custom of referring, in NT and Rabbinic times, to everything in the Pentateuch as the words of Moses (*e.g.* Mt. 8: 4; Lk. 20: 37; Ac. 3: 22) does not necessarily support the view that Moses wrote the Pentateuch, since 'Moses' had become a convenient way of referring to the first five books of the Bible (cf. Lk. 24: 27; 2 C. 3: 15). It seems unnecessarily sceptical, however, to deny that the work and teaching of Moses was the initial stimulus for the composition of the Pentateuch, and that a good deal of its contents beyond the passages explicitly ascribed to him may be authentically Mosaic; of how much of the Pentateuch this is true must remain a matter of opinion.

The overwhelming tendency in OT scholarship has, however, been to ignore the role of Moses in the composition of the Pentateuch and explain its origin as the outcome of a process of compilation of various documents from different periods in Israelite history. One of the first steps towards current theories of Pentateuchal origins was taken in 1753 by the French writer Jean Astruc in his *Conjectures on the original memoirs which Moses seems to have used in composing the Book of Genesis*; though not denying Mosaic authorship to Genesis, Astruc concluded that two documents, the one using the divine name Yahweh, the other the divine name Elohim ('God'), lay behind our present book of Genesis. Throughout the nineteenth century a number of documentary theories were developed, special attention being paid to differing linguistic usage and apparent narrative discrepancies in the various units of the Pentateuch. An important stage was reached in the work of W. M. L. de Wette (1807), who made the first firm link between a Pentateuchal source and Israelite history when he identified Deuteronomy as the Book of the Law used in Josiah's reformation (2 Kg. 22 f.) and further conjectured that Deuteronomy must have been composed about that time (621 B.C.). The classical form of the documentary theory of the Pentateuch was developed, in several works between 1876 and 1883, by the German critic Julius Wellhausen.

According to Wellhausen, the earliest source of the Pentateuch was the document J (so-called from its author, the Jahwist or Yahwist, who used the name Yahweh for God) from the ninth century B.C. The E document (from the Elohist, who employed the term Elohim for God) came from the eighth century, and the J and E sources were combined by an editor in the mid-seventh century. The Book of Deuteronomy (D), a separate source dating from 621 B.C., was added to the JE material in the mid-sixth century. The final major source, the Priestly work (P), was composed in the first half of the fifth century and combined with the earlier sources about 400 B.C. The Pentateuch as we know it thus came into existence no earlier than the end of the fifth century B.C.

This theory of the composition of the Pentateuch may still be said to be the consensus view among OT scholars, but many serious criticisms have been levelled at it, and the chorus of dissent has swelled markedly in recent years. Among those who still hold to its essential correctness, there has been a tendency to date the Yahwist's work a century earlier, in the time of the united monarchy, to favour an eighth rather than a seventh-century date for the composition of at least the core of Deuteronomy, and to allow that the Priestly work, set down in writing during the exile in the sixth century rather than after the exile in the fifth, may well preserve much older material.

Much more severe criticism has come from various quarters. Conservative scholars, including Protestant, Catholic, and Jewish writers, have repeatedly argued that the criteria used by the documentary school for analysing separate sources behind the Pentateuch are highly questionable, and that other reasons apart from differing sources could explain linguistic variations and apparent narrative inconsistencies in the Pentateuch. Evangelical scholars are not, however, committed to denying the propriety of seeking sources that may lie behind the Pentateuch nor to affirming that the Pentateuch as we now have it comes directly from the hand of Moses. Another type of criticism of the documentary hypothesis has come from those scholars, principally Scandinavian, who have stressed the role of oral tradition in the transmission of ancient narratives and have regarded as anachronistic the concept of the composition of the Pentateuch as an essentially literary process. While some of their criticisms have been extreme, their contribution has at least had the effect of stimulating interest in the pre-literary, oral phase of the transmission of the texts.

A more positive aspect of Pentateuchal source criticism, which in the past has often had a negative and destructive tone, has been the development in the last two decades of concern with the authors of the presumed sources of the Pentateuch as theologians who conveyed by their presentation of Israel's traditional history a message to their contemporaries. Thus the Yahwist's work has come to be seen as an address to the age of Solomon, urging Israel to prove itself to be a blessing to the nations in accord with the promise to Abraham of Gen. 12; the Elohist's work is an appeal to Israel of the ninth century to live in the 'fear' of Yahweh in the face of persuasive

alien cults; the Deuteronomist's work is a programme for national reform, emphasizing the unity of Israel and calling for a unified worship of Yahweh; while the Priestly work is addressed to the Babylonian exiles, re-iterating the authenticity of Israel's religious and cultic traditions and renewing the divine promise of blessing and superabundance in the land (Gen. 1: 26) to a generation who had all but given up hope for the future.

Nevertheless, even this welcome insistence upon the theological message of the Pentateuch still rests upon the analysis of the sources and the dating given them in the classical documentary hypothesis or some minor modification of it. All the signs at the moment are that this hypothesis is being thrown back into the melting pot and that no one can at present safely predict what the shape of Pentateuchal criticism in the next decade or two will be.

BIBLIOGRAPHY

From a conservative viewpoint

AALDERS, G. C., *A Short Introduction to the Pentateuch* (London, 1949).

FINN, A. H., *The Unity of the Pentateuch* (London, 1917).

HARRISON, R. K., *Introduction to the Old Testament* (Grand Rapids, 1969; London, 1970).

HUBBARD, D. A., 'Pentateuch', *NBD* (London, 1962), pp.957–64.

KIDNER, D., *Genesis. TOTC* (London, 1967), pp.15–26.

KITCHEN, K. A., *Ancient Orient and Old Testament* (London, 1966).

MANLEY, G. T., *The Book of the Law* (London, 1957).

YOUNG, E. J., *An Introduction to the Old Testament* (London, 1949).

Other Works

CLEMENTS, R. E., *A Century of Old Testament Study* (London, 1976).

BRUEGGEMANN, W. and WOLFF, H. W., *The Vitality of Old Testament Traditions* (Richmond, Va., 1976).

EISSFELDT, O., *The Old Testament. An Introduction* (Oxford, 1966).

FOHRER, G., *Introduction to the old Testament* (London, 1979).

FREEDMAN, D. N., 'Pentateuch', *IDB*, vol. 3 (New York, 1962), pp.711–27.

HAHN, H. F., *The Old Testament in Modern Research* (expanded edn.; Philadelphia, 1966).

KNIGHT, D. A., *Rediscovering the Traditions of Israel* (Missoula, Montana, 1975).

NOTH, M., *A History of Pentateuchal Traditions* (Englewood Cliffs, N.J., 1972).

VON RAD, G., *Old Testament Theology*, vol. 1 (Edinburgh, 1962).

WELLHAUSEN, J., *Prolegomena to the History of Israel* (Edinburgh, 1885; reprinted New York, 1957).

INTRODUCTION TO THE HISTORICAL BOOKS

L. O'B. DAVID FEATHERSTONE

In the middle of the fifth century B.C. Herodotus wrote a history of the wars between Greece and Persia which earned him the title 'Father of History', but about a hundred years earlier a history of Israel was published, which millions have read with profit. The books referred to in our Bibles as Joshua, Judges, 1 & 2 Samuel and 1 & 2 Kings were in their present form in Hebrew soon after the last event they record (2 Kg. 25: 27 ff.), which took place in the thirty-seventh year of the exile, or 561 B.C. They contain a prayer for those in exile (1 Kg. 8: 46–53), but no hint of the proclamation which Cyrus made in 538 B.C. (Ezr. 1: 1–4) authorizing their return to Jerusalem, and this encourages us to believe that the date these books were published was within ten years of 550 B.C.

An earlier edition of these books was almost certainly published just before the tragic death of King Josiah in 609 B.C. (2 Kg. 23: 29. So Snaith *IB*), or at any rate before the exile started in 597 (So Gray's introduction to 1 & 2 Kings). On the assumption that the book found in the temple in 622 B.C. (2 Kg. 22: 8) contained what we find in Deuteronomy, the whole collection has been called the Deuteronomic History of Israel. (See G. Ernest Wright & Reginald H. Fuller, *The Book of the Acts of God*, 1960, and Peter R. Ackroyd, *Exile and Restoration*, 1968.) It illustrates vividly the principles enunciated in Deuteronomy 28. 'If you obey . . . all these blessings shall come upon you . . . but if you will not obey . . . all these curses shall come upon you and overtake you.'

The books are in our Bible named after the main hero or heroes they speak about. These titles should not be taken to imply authorship. Joshua presumably did not write about his own death (24: 29). Judges 18: 30 must have been written at least three centuries after most of the judges were dead. Samuel's death is recorded at the beginning of ch. 25 of 'his first book', and the books 'of the kings' were clearly written about them rather than by them.

The book of Joshua lists the successes achieved in the conquest of Palestine under his leadership—first Jericho and the central highlands (1 to 9) then the south (10), and finally the north (11 & 12). This is followed by the statement (13: 1), 'There remains yet very much land to be possessed.' The responsibility of each of the twelve tribes is then set out (13 to 22). In the two speeches at the end of the book (23 & 24) the correlation between obedience and blessing, and between transgression and being consumed, are clearly stated.

The first chapter of the book of Judges paints a similar picture of successes, while stating explicitly that seven tribes did not drive out the original inhabitants of their territory. The plan for the chapters that follow is set out in 2: 11 to 19. 'The Israelites . . . forsook the LORD . . . and he sold them to their enemies . . . Then the LORD raised up judges . . . who saved them . . . but when the judge died the people return to ways even more corrupt.' This was true of Othniel, Ehud and Shamgar (3), Deborah and Barak (4 & 5), Gideon (6 to 8), Tola and Jair (10), Jephthah (11 & 12), Ibzan, Elon and Abdon (12) and Samson (13 to 16).

In the case of Deborah we have a prose version of the story (4), and an account in verse which looks as though it was composed at the time of the victory it describes. The way it speaks of Deborah, Jael, Sisera's mother and her ladies suggests it may well have been composed by Deborah herself.

The judges may in many cases have exercised their jurisdiction largely within the territory of their own tribe. Any overlap means that the period mentioned for each does not provide an absolute method for calculating the date of the fall of Jericho such as John Garstang attempted in 1931. Most modern writers accept a thirteenth century date for the Exodus and Conquest of the land, even though this makes difficult the interpretation of the chronological statements of Jg. 11: 26 and 1 Kg. 6:1.

The reason given by the sacred historian for success and failure was not an arbitrary one imposed without justification. The twelve tribes which made up the nation of Israel were held together primarily by their allegiance to Yahweh, and when that allegiance failed the source of their unity and strength was gone. The way the tribes could be called on to help, but might fail to come, is illustrated in Jg. 5:

16–17; 19:29–21: 12 and 1 Sam. 11: 7. Regular gatherings must have taken place three times a year (Exod. 23: 17; 34: 23 and Dt. 16: 16), but Samuel's parents must have been typical of many who came only once a year to the central sanctuary (1 Sam. 1: 3 and 2: 19).

The basic theme of the last five chapters of Judges comes in 17:6; 18: 1; 19: 1 and 21: 25. 'In those days there was no king in Israel; every man did what was right in his own eyes.' This does not mean however that the Deuteronomic historian believed that the country's problems were automatically solved when monarchy was introduced. To passages which indicate divine approval of Saul's appointment (1 Sam. 9: 1–10: 16; 11) he adds the warnings given by Samuel in chs. 8; 10: 17–27 and 12.

Although the analysis of 1 & 2 Sam. made by A. R. S. Kennedy in the Century Bible of 1904 has been much criticized, it still provides a working hypothesis which many are happy to accept. This assures us that 2 Sam. 9–20 and 1 Kg. 1–2 have come down to us virtually unchanged from the form in which they were presented by an eye-witness who wrote the history of David's court and of Solomon's succession as king. Two names have been suggested for this eye-witness. Duhm, Budde and Sellin each thought it was Abiathar, but August Klostermann's suggestion of Ahimaaz is an attractive alternative on the basis of 2 Sam. 17: 17–21 and 18: 19–32. Either is possible, neither is certain, but whoever it was he wrote an honest and revealing account of court intrigues in such a way that a spiritual and moral message comes across, which neither seventh nor sixth century historians needed to modify or expand.

It is now generally accepted that there was a great deal of literary activity during the reign of Solomon. Before his death it is almost certain that the story of the ark (1 Sam. 4–6) and most of the story of the origin of the monarchy had been recorded in more or less their present form. The account is factual and includes things that Saul did wrong, but through it all he remains 'the LORD's anointed'. To this basic material it looks as though comments and stories from other sources have been added which were more critical of the monarchy. The result is that we have a more complete picture of Samuel, Saul and David than would have been possible from any one source. E. J. Young and others have shown that it is unnecessary to speak of 'conflicting accounts'. It was possible for one writer to put in consecutive verses (1 Sam. 12: 12–13) two different points of view. Both were true!

Jos. 10: 13 and 2 Sam. 1: 18 both refer to the book of Jashar, and 1 Kg. 8: 12–13 may have come from the same source. Some have sought to identify it with 'the Book of the Wars of the LORD' of Num. 21: 14, but its size and scope are conjectural. 1 Kg. 11: 41 refers to 'the book of the acts of Solomon', 1 Kg. 14: 19; 15: 31 and a dozen other verses refer to 'the book of the annals of the kings of Israel', while 1 Kg. 15: 7 and another dozen verses refer to 'the book of the annals of the kings of Judah'. They were either the official records or a summary of them. They are not to be confused with the biblical books of 1 & 2 Chronicles.

Most of the material included about Solomon sets him in a good light, but criticisms of him are included in 1 Kg. 9 and become explicit in ch. 11. If there had been nothing to criticize, the kingdom would not have split in two so soon after Solomon's death.

In describing the two hundred years that followed, 1 & 2 Kg. devote more space to activities in the Northern Kingdom of Israel, including those of the prophets Elijah and Elisha, than to the kings of Judah, the descendants of Solomon who continued to reign in Jerusalem. All the northern kings did 'what was evil in the sight of the LORD', and the result, according to 2 Kg. 17, was the exile of northern Israel. High amongst the criteria by which the kings were assessed was whether they permitted the worship forbidden in Dt. 12: 2–6. The place which the LORD had chosen 'to make his habitation' was, in the eyes of those who backed Josiah's reformation, clearly Jerusalem, so the condemnation of those who set up or supported rival places of worship in the Northern Kingdom was almost a foregone conclusion, but immorality connected with worship was an additional basis for criticism. The facts recorded were carefully selected. Omri who founded not only a new dynasty but also the city of Samaria is dismissed in eight verses, whereas his son Ahab, because of his involvement in religious issues is mentioned in eight consecutive chapters.

Of the kings of Judah, Asa and his son Jehoshaphat are commended in 1 Kg. 15: 11 and 22: 43, while in 2 Kg. Joash (12: 2), Amaziah (14: 3), Azariah or Uzziah (15: 3) and Jotham (15: 34) all did 'what was right' but are criticised for allowing sacrifice in places other than the Jerusalem temple. Only Hezekiah (18: 3) and Josiah (22: 2) get full commendation on this basis.

The length of reign of each king is given and linked with the regnal year of his contemporary in the north or south. To fit these with events known from Assyrian records it is necessary to assume that some kings claimed as their own years which are also included in the reigns of their predecessors. A detailed examination of this problem is undertaken by Edwin R. Thiele in *The Mysterious Numbers of the Hebrew Kings* and his conclusions are followed both in the *NBD* and in Peake's Commentary (pp. 71 f.

1962). The dates given in the Chronological Charts at the end of John Bright's History of Israel are eight or nine years later from Jeroboam I to Zimri, and seven years later from Jeroboam II to the accession of Menahem. Bright's figures do not tie in as closely with Biblical data as do Thiele's, but have the advantage of being easier to remember. The key dates on his system are David's accession 1000 B.C., Solomon's 961, and the Northern Kingdom 922 to 722 B.C. There is full agreement on other key dates such as 701 for Sennacherib's invasion (2 Kg. 18: 13) and 597 for the exile of Jehoiachin and the beginning of the reign of Zedekiah, the last king of Judah (2 Kg. 24).

Jewish traditions hold that Isaiah and Jeremiah each wrote part of 2 Kings. The idea may have arisen from the similarity of 2 Kg. 18: 13–20: 19 to Isa. 36–39, and 24: 18 ff. to Jer. 52. In each case the relevant historical information appears to have been included as an appendix to the words of the prophet but there is no evidence that he was responsible for writing the record. 2 Chr. 26: 22 says Isaiah wrote the acts of Uzziah from first to last, but in 2 Kg. 15 only v. 5 contains information about Uzziah which is not of a routine nature.

1 Chr. 29: 29 refers to the Chronicles of Samuel, the Chronicles of Nathan and the Chronicles of Gad. 2 Chr. 9: 29 adds the history of Nathan, the prophecy of Ahijah and the visions of Iddo, and 2 Chr. 12: 15 adds the chronicles of Shemaiah and Iddo, while 2 Chr. 13: 22 speaks of the story of Iddo. Some hold that these are just different parts of the canonical books of Samuel and Kings, but as Iddo the seer is not mentioned in those books it seems preferable to accept that other material did exist which is no longer available. These references do not necessarily mean that the prophets named actually did the writing, but since each part of Samuel and Kings speaks of Yahweh's activity it is easy to see a reason for the Jews to speak of their historical books as 'the former prophets'.

The final incident in the Deuteronomic History (2 Kg. 25: 27 ff.) conveys a message of hope. Jehoiachin who had only reigned for three months in Jerusalem and then spent thirty-six years as a prisoner is released and given a place of honour among the other kings in Babylon. Humiliation had been followed by exaltation. Soon others would go out in joy, and be led forth in peace.

The story is taken further by 'the Chronicler' whose publication of 1 & 2 Chronicles, Ezra and Nehemiah is normally dated some time during the fourth century B.C. He starts his work with a résumé of events up to 1000 B.C., mostly in the form of genealogies. The information given in his first chapter is collected from Gen. 5, 10, 11, 25 and 36. Chapter 2 summarizes information from Gen. 35, 38, 46, Num. 26 and Ru. 4, and adds names not known from any other source. The sons of David listed in ch. 3 include those named in 2 Sam. 3, 5 and 12, and others also mentioned in 1 Chr. 14: 4 ff. The descendants of Solomon are traced to at least six generations after Zerubbabel, and both RSV and NEB follow the Greek text in v. 21, which gives us a total of eleven generations, and would take us into the third century B.C. We should not overlook the possibility that the list was extended to bring it up to date some time after the main work was published.

2 Chr. 36: 21 speaks of the confidence expressed in Jer. 25: 12 and 29: 10 that after 'seventy years' the exiles would be allowed to return. Daniel 9: 2 and Zechariah 1: 12; 7: 5 also refer to those prophecies, but for the Chronicler their fulfilment lay in the proclamation which Cyrus king of Persia made in 538 B.C. 2 Chronicles closes with it, Ezra opens with it, a slightly more detailed version is quoted in Ezr. 5: 13 ff., and the full decree is set out in Aramaic in Ezr. 6: 3–5. The Cyrus Cylinder, a contemporary inscription, shows that the Jews were not the only people to benefit from his enlightened policy.

Ezr. 3 records the laying of the foundation of the temple (c. 536) but, as 6: 15 shows, the building was not completed until twenty years later. The encouragement of Haggai and Zechariah, mentioned in Ezr. 5: 1 f., is fully confirmed from the books that bear the names of these prophets.

The Chronicler had a great affection for the temple, and the fact that Levites are mentioned 160 times in his writings compared with only three times in Samuel and Kings, and singers also get more mention in his books than anywhere else, suggests strongly that he himself was both a Levite and a singer. Levitical genealogies fill 81 verses of 1 Chr. 6 and most of chs. 23 to 26. Jewish tradition identified Ezra as the Chronicler, but most modern commentators reject this. Ezra's words however have been preserved for us in Ezr. 7: 27–9: 15, and Nehemiah's words in Neh. 1: 1–7: 5; 13: 6–31.

The date of Nehemiah's journey to Jerusalem is undisputedly 445 B.C., but three dates are possible for Ezra's arrival. In a 1958 Tyndale lecture J. Stafford Wright argued strongly for the traditional date, 458 B.C., the seventh year of Artaxerxes I, against those who maintained that it must be 398 B.C., the seventh year of Artaxerxes II. John Bright in his *History of Israel* shows that if we could in Ezr. 7: 7 f. read 'the thirty-seventh year' i.e. 428 B.C., the difficulties involved in each of the other views would be resolved. This is an attractive solution, but it means assuming that in both verses there were originally three consecutive words each starting with the Hebrew letter *shin* the first of which has dropped out.

Whichever date is accepted, the words 'after these things' in Ezr. 7: 1 mark a gap of at least two generations and possibly three or four. It would be helpful to have this gap indicated in printed versions of the book.

In the Hebrew Bible the writings of the Chronicler normally come at the end, and Ezra-Nehemiah is printed before 1 & 2 Chronicles. This suggests that the part of his work which covered the post-exilic period was first accepted as worthy of a place amongst the sacred scriptures, and then the value of the rest of his writing was recognized. The Greek translation preserved for us in the Apocrypha with the title 1 Esdras confirms that 2 Chr. 36: 21 was originally followed by Ezra ch. 1. If one person reads aloud Ezr. 1: 1–4, while others look at 2 Chr. 36: 22 f., it will become clear that 2 Chr. 36, the last chapter of the Hebrew Bible, ends in what was originally the middle of a sentence. The words, 'God be with him and let him go up' are good ones with which to end, but the fact that the sentence can be continued is a reminder of the continuing presence and activity of God.

There are only two books in the Hebrew Old Testament named after women. The book of Ruth tells a story set 'in the days when the judges ruled', but those days and their customs (*e.g.* Ru. 4: 7) had passed before the book was written. A similar change over the course of time is indicated in 1 Sam. 9: 9, and there are a number of parallels between the book of Ruth and the book of Judges which precedes it in practically all Bibles except the Hebrew. Nevertheless the fact that Ruth is found among 'the writings' rather than 'the former prophets' has led many to suggest that its publication is more likely to have been about the time of the Chronicler than that of the earlier historians. Some have suggested that it was intended as a race relations pamphlet or protest against the exclusion of foreign women from the Jewish community commended in Ezr. 10: 44 and Neh. 10: 30. Whenever or whyever the story was written it remains worth reading, and its heroine fully deserves mention in the New Testament genealogy of the Messiah (Mt. 1: 5; cf. Ru. 4: 18–22).

The book of Esther in most Bibles follows that of Nehemiah, but Ahasuerus, the Persian king mentioned throughout the book is to be identified with Xerxes who preceded the Artaxerxes under whom Nehemiah served. The Greek version of Esther which is translated in full in the NEB Apocrypha confuses the two. Between his third year (1: 3) and his seventh (2: 16) Xerxes was away fighting the Greeks. The climax of the story comes in his twelfth year (3: 7), i.e. 475/4 B.C.

The Hebrew version of Esther does not mention God or any religious practice other than fasting, although the Greek version mentions prayer repeatedly. A Greek footnote (Est. 11: 1 in the Apocrypha) refers to the translation of 'the preceding Letter of Purim' by Lysimachus being brought to Egypt in 114 B.C. How long before this the canonical story was written in Hebrew we do not know. L. E. Browne in Peake's Commentary (1962) refers to it scathingly as 'a novel with no historical basis'. Most of his arguments are from silence, and in contrast Joyce Baldwin (*NBCR*, 1970) lists five sources of information about Persian affairs during the fifth century BC, and concludes that the author knew as much as we do, 'and perhaps a little more, concerning the king, the city, and the situation about which he was writing'. Attempts to equate Mordecai with Marduk and Esther with Ishtar have for the most part been given up. The names may be explained in this way, but the characters are human beings and not pagan gods.

The book of Esther is not quoted in the NT, but is regularly read in Jewish synagogues at the feast of Purim in February or March each year. The children are encouraged to show their disapproval of Haman each time his name is mentioned. Those who accept the teaching of Christ will probably disapprove of Esther's request for an extra day of slaughter (9: 13), but cannot but admire her courage and the way the story is told.

Many of our neighbours will think it strange that we find help and encouragement in reading historical books first published well over two thousand years ago, but these books were written for our instruction (Rom. 15: 4) and can help us understand something of the ways of God, and serve Him more effectively.

BIBLIOGRAPHY

ACKROYD, P. R., *Exile and Restoration* (SCM, 1968).

ANDERSON, G. W., 'The Historical Books of the OT' in *Peake's Commentary on the Bible* (Nelson, 1962).

ANDERSON, G. W., *A critical introduction to the OT* (Duckworth, 1959).

BRIGHT, J., *History of Israel²* (SCM, 1972).

CLEMENTS, R. E., *Isaiah and the Deliverance of Jerusalem* (Sheffield, 1980).

EMERTON, J. A. (ed.), *Studies in the Historical Books of the Old Testament* (Leiden, 1979).

FRANK, H. T., *An Archaeological Companion to the Bible* (SCM, 1972).

GUNN, D. M., *The Story of King David* (Sheffield, 1978).

HARRISON, R. K., *Introduction to the OT* (Grand Rapids, 1969; London, 1970).

PAYNE, D. F., *Kingdoms of the Lord* (Exeter, 1981).

Rost, L., *The Succession to the Throne of David*, E.T. (Sheffield, 1982).

Wright, J. S., *The Date of Ezra's Coming to Jerusalem* (Tyndale Press, 1958).

Young, E. J., *An Introduction to the OT* (Tyndale Press, 1964).

See also relevant articles in *IB, ICC, NBC*[3]*, NBD* and *OTL*.

A NOTE ON OLD TESTAMENT CHRONOLOGY

F. F. BRUCE

The chronology of the OT presents many problems and uncertainties, and no attempt has been made in this regard to impose uniformity on the contributors to this commentary.

It is impossible to make any confident statement about the chronology of the period before Abraham: at the time of writing it is too soon to say what light may or may not be shed into this darkness by a study of the records discovered at Tell Mardikh in Syria (the ancient Ebla). Abraham is commonly assigned to the Middle Bronze Age, early in the second millennium B.C. (This dating, incidentally, was reached by blind reckoning in James Ussher's chronology, which brings Abraham to the promised land in 1921 B.C.)

The sojourning of the Israelites in Egypt can be dated only approximately. There is a wide consensus in favour of placing the Exodus in the 13th century B.C. (in preference to the 15th, which was favoured in the 1930s). The reference to Israel in Merneptah's victory stele (c. 1230 B.C.) seems to indicate that the Israelites had by this time reached Palestine but were not yet recognized as a settled community there. W. F. Albright interpreted the 430 years of Exod. 12: 40 f. as a reckoning according to the 'Era of Tanis' (c. 1720 B.C.) and so dated the Exodus c. 1290 B.C. in the reign of Rameses II. Another instance of reckoning according to the 'Era of Tanis' (Zoan) has been discerned in Num. 13: 22.

The figure of 480 years given in 1 Kg. 6: 1 for the interval between the Exodus and the founding of Solomon's temple may be regarded as the equivalent of twelve generations.

It is difficult to construct a chronological outline of the Israelite and Judaean monarchy from the biblical data alone because the totals of regnal years given in 1 and 2 Kg. for the northern and southern kingdoms from the death of Solomon to the fall of Samaria in the 6th year of Hezekiah (2 Kg. 18: 10) do not tally. The total for the northern kingdom during that period is 241 years, while that for the southern kingdom is 260. When there was no contemporary evidence (such as became available with the discovery of Egyptian, Assyrian and Babylonian records) to compare with those figures, the discrepancies might be equally well accoun... northern... by positing interregna in the southern kingdom or co-regencies in the... increased or... The northern total was thus... ally, it is now ev... uthern total reduced. Actually, it is now... kingdoms were m... that co-regencies in both inferred from the bib... frequent than might be inferred from the bib... data alone.

Shishak's invasion of Palestine, which took place in the 5th year of Rehoboam (1 Kg. 14: 25), is independently dated from Egyptian records and points to a date c. 930 B.C. for the disruption of the monarchy. David's reign thus began c. 1010 B.C. and Solomon's temple was dedicated c. 960 BC.

Assyrian chronology, from the early 9th to the late 7th century B.C., is accurately recorded by the *limmu* lists. The *limmu* was an official appointed annually who gave his name to the year in which he held office (like the eponymous archon in Athens and the consuls in Rome). These lists enable us to fix such dates as 853 B.C. for the battle of Qarqar towards the end of Ahab's reign (when he and other Syro-Palestinian rulers resisted the westward advance of Shalmaneser III of Assyria) and 841 B.C. as a *terminus ante quem* for the accession of Jehu (who in that year paid homage to Shalmaneser III), together with such later dates as 745 B.C. for the accession of Tiglath-pileser III (2 Kg. 15: 19, 29; 16: 7), 721 B.C. for the fall of Samaria (2 Kg. 17: 6), 711 B.C. for Sargon's capture of Ashdod (Isa. 20: 1), 701 B.C. for Sennacherib's invasion of Judah (2 Kg. 18: 13; Isa. 36: 1), and 663 B.C. for Ashur-bani-pal's sack of Egyptian Thebes (Nah. 3: 8–10).

When the Assyrian *limmu* lists fail, the Babylonian Chronicle takes over, enabling us to date the fall of Nineveh (Nah. 3: 1 ff.) in 612 B.C., the battle of Carchemish (Jer. 46: 2) in 605 B.C., the deportation of Jehoiachin (2 Kg. 24: 10–17) in March 597 B.C., the capture of Jerusalem by the Chaldaean army (2 Kg. 25: 3 ff.) in August 587 B.C., the accession of Evilmerodach (2 Kg. 25: 31) in 562 B.C. and Cyrus's capture of Babylonia in 539 B.C. The regnal years of the Persian kings, and of Alexander the Great and his successors after them, are sufficiently well fixed to date securely events that are certainly related to any of their reigns.

A Note on Old Testament Chronology

BIBLIOGRAPHY

ALBRIGHT, W. F., *From the Stone Age to Christianity* (Baltimore, [2]1946).

BICKERMAN, E. J., *Chronology of the Ancient World* (London, 1968).

BIMSON, J. J., *Redating the Exodus and Conquest* (Sheffield, 1978).

FINEGAN, J., *Handbook of Biblical Chrono[...]* (Princeton, 1964).

FREEMAN, D. N., and CAMPBELL, E. F., 'The [...]

[...]e Ancient Near East', in *The [...]t Near East* (Essays in Honor of [...] ology [...], ed. G. E. Wright (London, 1961),

Bibl[...]

W[...], and DUBBERSTEIN, W. H., *Babylonian [...]gy, 626 B.C.–A.D. 75* (Providence, R.I,

[...]LE, E. R., *The Mysterious Numbers of the Hebrew [...] Kings* (Exeter, [2]1951).

WISEMAN, D. J., *Chronicles of Chaldaean Kings* (London, 1956).

INTRODUCTION TO THE POETICAL LITERATURE

F. F. BRUCE

POETRY IN THE OLD TESTAMENT

Much of the wisdom literature of the OT is presented in poetical form. The main body of the book of Job is poetical not only in form but also in thought and language. The book of Proverbs, with parts of Ecclesiastes, is poetical in form even when the language, though pithy and epigrammatic, is prosaic. The Psalter is poetical throughout, as are also the Song of Solomon and Lamentations.

Many of the oracles in the prophetical books are poetical in form and language, and are rightly set as poetry in NIV and other recent versions. It is a precarious exercise, however, to use the alternation of poetical and prose sections in these books as a criterion for distinguishing between the contributions of authors and editors.

Apart from the regular oracles, we occasionally find a complete psalm incorporated in a prophetical book, like the prayer of Jonah (Jon. 2: 2–9) or the prayer of Habakkuk (Hab. 3: 2–19). A song of praise to the Creator (perhaps originally designed for the festival of Tabernacles) is dovetailed among the oracles of Amos (Am. 4: 13; 5: 8 f.; 9: 5 f.); its strophes are marked out by the refrain: 'The LORD is his name'.

Poems also occur from time to time in the narrative books. The threefold curse in the fall story of Gen. 3: 14–19 takes poetical form; so also do Lamech's vengeance-song in Gen. 4: 23 f., the birth-oracle to Rebecca in Gen. 25: 23, Isaac's blessing of his two sons in Gen. 27: 27–29, 39 f., and Jacob's blessing of his descendants in Gen. 48: 15 f.; 49: 2–27. The other books of the Pentateuch contain the Song of the Sea in Exod. 15: 1–18 (an expansion of Miriam's song in Exod. 15: 21), the oracles of Balaam in Num. 23 and 24, the Song of Moses in Dt. 32: 1–43, and the Blessing of Moses in Dt. 33: 2–29.

In Num. 21 there are some poetical fragments relating to the conquest of Transjordan, taken from a collection called 'the Book of the Wars of the LORD' (v. 14). A similar collection, 'the Book of Jashar', has provided the piece about the sun standing still in Jos. 10: 12 f., the 'lament of the bow' (David's dirge over Saul and Jonathan) in 2 Sam. 1: 19–27 and Solomon's oracle at the dedication of the temple in 1 Kg. 8: 12 f. It may have been from such a collection that the author of Judges derived the Song of Deborah in Jg. 5, where we find the most archaic Hebrew in the OT. David's song of thanksgiving in 2 Sam. 22 is duplicated in Ps. 18. In 2 Sam. 23: 1–7 we have a dynastic oracle comprising 'the last words of David'. The Chronicler incorporates selections from the Psalter in liturgical contexts in 1 Chr. 16: 8–36; 2 Chr. 5: 13; 6: 41 f.; 7: 3; 20: 21; he also preserves the oracle of Amasai in 1 Chr. 12: 18.

SYLLABIC RHYTHM

Old Testament poetry is characterized by recognizable rhythmical patterns which can be reproduced to a considerable degree in translation. Rhythm of sound and rhythm of sense combine to produce the poetical effect.

The rhythm of sound depends mainly on recurring patterns of stressed syllables. It is probable that unstressed syllables have a minor rôle to fill in this regard, but there is no agreement on what that rôle is. As for the pattern of stressed syllables, we may have a sequence of clauses (usually arranged in couplets) having two, three or four stressed syllables each (2:2; 3: 3; 4:4). Or we have an alternation of clauses with four and three stressed syllables (4: 3, like our common metre) or three and two stressed syllables (3:2). A sequence of such alternating clauses gives an elegiac effect. The 3:2 pattern is known as the *qînāh* or 'dirge' metre, because it is particularly common in laments, as in the book of Lamentations:

> How lonely | lies | the city
> once so full | of people! . . .

There are more elaborate patterns than these, but these are the most frequently occurring.

PARALLELISM

The rhythm of sense takes the form of 'parallelism'. 'Parallelism' is a stylistic form in which what is essentially the same idea is expressed twice over (or even more often) in parallel clauses or groups of clauses: the thought is the same, but the words are different.

The various types of parallelism are best described by means of actual examples. Three outstanding types are called complete parallelism, incomplete parallelism, and step-parallelism.

Complete parallelism. In complete parallelism we have two clauses (or pairs of clauses) where each significant term in the one corresponds to a significant term in the other. The parallelism may be *synonymous*, as in Gen. 4: 23 (in 4:4 metre):

Adah | and Zillah, | listen | to me;
wives | of Lamech, | hear | my words.

(Here 'wives of Lamech' is synonymous with 'Adah and Zillah', 'hear' with 'listen' and 'my words' with 'me', lit. 'my voice'.) Other examples are Isa. 1: 3b (in 3: 3 metre):

Israel | does not | know,
my people | do not | understand

or Ps. 27: 1, 3 (in each of these verses we have two parallel pairs of clauses in 3: 2 metre):

The Lord | is my light | and my salvation—
whom | shall I fear?
The Lord | is the stronghold | of my life—
of whom | shall I be afraid? . . .
Though an army | besiege | me,
my heart | will not fear;
though war | break out | against me,
even then will I | be confident.

This 3: 2 rhythm is not only characteristic of dirges (as we have said); in other places, such as Ps. 27, it can serve as the vehicle of joyful confidence and praise.

The parallelism may be *antithetic*, where the second clause (or pair of clauses) states the converse to the preceding one, as in Ps. 20: 8 (in 3: 3 metre):

They | are brought to their knees | and fall,
but we | rise up | and stand firm.

Isa. 1: 3b (already quoted) combines with Isa. 1: 3a to form a more elaborate structure of antithetic parallelism:

The ox | knows | his master,
and the donkey | his owner's | manger;
but Israel | does not | know,
my people | do not | understand.

Here the first two clauses, like the second two clauses, are in *synonymous* parallelism one with the other; but the second pair of clauses is in *antithetic* parallelism with the former pair.

The parallelism, again, may be *emblematic*; this adjective has been used to denote the construction in which one of the two parallel clauses presents a simile or metaphor describing the situation with which the author is actually concerned. A simple instance is Ps. 103: 13 (in 3:3 metre):

As a father | has compassion | on his children,
so the Lord | has compassion | on those who fear him.

Incomplete parallelism. Incomplete parallelism occurs where the second clause of a couplet does not exhibit a term of equivalent sense corresponding to each of the terms in the preceding clause. Thus, in the couplet already quoted from Isa. 1: 3a—

The ox | knows | his master,
and the donkey | his owner's | manger—

there is no verb in the second clause corresponding to 'knows' in the first clause. The verb, of course, can be understood perfectly well from the first clause; so far as sense is concerned, there is no need to repeat it (or a synonym). But metrical compensation for the missing term is made by the provision of an object with two stressed syllables in the second clause ('its master's crib') corresponding to the object with one stressed syllable in the previous clause ('its owner'). The same phenomenon appears in Ps. 1:5—

Therefore the wicked | will not stand | in the judgment,
nor sinners | in the assembly | of the righteous—

where, despite the omission of a verb in the second clause corresponding to 'will . . . stand' in the first clause, the 3: 3 rhythm is maintained by the use of a term with two stressed syllables in the second clause ('the assembly of the righteous') over against the single stressed syllable of 'the judgment'.

Alongside such instances of 'incomplete parallelism with compensation' there are many examples of 'incomplete parallelism without compensation'. If we consider Ps. 40: 2a—

He lifted me | out of the slimy | pit,
out of the mud | and mire—

we find no verb in the second unit corresponding to 'He lifted me' in the preceding unit (for no repetition of the verb is necessary), but the remaining words, 'out of the mud and mire', have exactly the same metrical value as their sense-counterpart, 'from the slimy pit', each of these word-groups having two stressed syllables. The couplet is the first of four (making up verses 2 and 3) in elegiac 3:2 rhythm, the rhythm in which practically the whole book of Lamentations is cast.

A fine example of the longer elegiac 4:3 rhythm appears in the vivid description of Chaos-come-again in Jer. 4: 23–26:

I looked | at the earth, | and it was formless | and empty;
and at the heavens, | and their light | was gone.
I looked | at the mountains, | and they | were quaking;
all | the hills | were swaying.
I looked, | and there | were no | people,
every bird | in the sky | had flown away.
I looked, | and the fruitful | land | was a desert,
all | its towns | lay in ruins

Here the impressiveness of the four elegiac couplets is enhanced by the solemn 'I looked', with which each begins, and by the solemn *coda* following the last of the four.

The first couplet of Lamech's vengeance-chant (Gen. 4: 23 f.) was quoted above as an instance of complete parallelism. The second and third couplets constitute examples of incomplete parallelism—without and with compensation respectively:

I have killed | a man | for wounding me,
    a young man | for injuring me.
If Cain | is avenged | seven times,
    truly Lamech | seventy- | seven times.

In both these couplets the second unit lacks a verb corresponding to that in the first unit, but there is no metrical compensation for the missing verb in the former couplet (the rhythm of the Hebrew is better represented if *yeled* is translated 'youth' rather than, with NIV, 'young man'), whereas in the latter couplet compensation is provided by 'seventy-seven times' with its double stress over against 'seven times' with its single stress.

An effective interchange of lines with three and two stressed syllables is combined with chiastic structure in Ps. 30: 8–10:

To you, | O Lord, | I called;
    to the Lord | I cried for mercy:
'What gain is there | in my destruction,
    if I go down | into the pit?
Will the dust | praise you?
    Will it proclaim | your faithfulness?
Hear, | O Lord, | and be merciful to me;
    O Lord, | be my help.'

Here there is a metrical 'inclusion' of two 2:2 couplets within two 3:2 couplets, and this coincides with a sense 'inclusion', in which a series of rhetorical questions (all implying the answer 'No') intervenes between a statement of the supplication in the first couplet and the substance of the supplication in the last couplet.

Formal parallelism. Occasionally, with a diminution of sense-parallels and a corresponding increase of metrical compensation the point is reached where parallelism in sense disappears altogether, and metrical balance alone remains, as in Ps. 27: 6 (in 3: 3 metre):

Then | my head | will be exalted
    above | the enemies | who surround me.

Step-parallelism. Sometimes part of one line is repeated in the next, and made the starting-point for a fresh step; this process may be repeated from the second to the third line. A good example of this is provided by Ps. 29: 1 f. (in 4: 4 metre):

Ascribe | to the Lord, | O mighty | ones,
ascribe | to the Lord | glory | and strength.
Ascribe | to the Lord | the glory | due his name;
    worship | the Lord | in the splendour | of his holiness.

Here the first three clauses exhibit step-parallelism; the fourth clause stands in complete synonymous parallelism with the third.

Another example comes in Ps. 92: 9 (in 3: 3: 3 metre):

For surely, | your enemies, | O Lord,
surely, | your enemies | will perish;
all | evildoers | will be scattered.

Here the first two lines exhibit step-parallelism; the third stands in synonymous parallelism with the second.

The 'archaic style' of this verse, noted in the commentary *ad loc.*, may be illustrated by a similarly constructed stanza from a hymn to Baal in the Ugaritic texts:

Lo, thy enemies, O Baal,
    lo, thy enemies thou shalt slay,
    lo, thou shalt destroy thy foes.

Another Ugaritic instance of step-parallelism is quoted from the Aqhat epic, where the son of Danel (cf. Ezek. 14: 14, 20; 28: 3) is addressed:

Ask for life, Aqhat, my boy,
    ask for life, and I'll give it you,
    life immortal, and I'll grant it you.

In sense rather than construction this is reminiscent of Ps. 21: 4, with its thanksgiving for the king (in 4: 4 metre):

He asked | you | for life; | and you gave it to him,
length | of days, | for ever | and ever.

Another form of step-parallelism might be recognized in Ps. 1: 1, if 'walk . . . stand . . . sit' represent three progressive stages in associating with the wicked. If, however, they are simply three different ways of describing that association, then we have regular synonymous parallelism.

STROPHIC ARRANGEMENT

One well-known instance of step-parallelism is integrated into a strophic structure: this is the repeated invocation of Ps. 24: 7, 9 (in 3:3:3 metre):

Lift up | your heads, | O you gates!
lift them up, | you ancient | doors!
that the King | of glory | may come in.

In the first response to the ensuing question from within ('Who is this King of glory?') there is a further occurrence of step-parallelism, in which 'mighty in battle' takes up and makes more specific the twin epithets 'strong and mighty' (Ps. 24: 8):

The Lord | strong | and mighty,
The Lord | mighty | in battle!

The repeated sequence of invocation, question from within, and response builds up a double strophe, with its concluding climax in verse 10 (in 2:2 metre):

The Lord | Almighty—
he is the King | of glory.

A common sign of strophic arrangement is the recurrence of a refrain. The threefold refrain in Pss. 42 and 43 (originally one psalm) marks the end of three successive strophes, at vv. 5 and 11 of Ps. 42 and v. 5 of Ps. 43. A similar strophic arrangement is indicated in Ps. 46 by the refrain in verses 7 and 11:

The LORD | Almighty | is with us;
the God | of Jacob | is our fortress.

Verses 1–7 probably consisted of two strophes, the transition from the one to the other being still marked by the notation 'Selah' at the end of v. 3, suggesting that the refrain was originally sung at this point too. Ps. 80 is divided into four strophes by the refrain in vv. 3, 7, 14a and 19:

Restore us, | O LORD God | (Almighty);
make your face | shine upon us, | that we
may be saved!

Similar refrains punctuate some of the prophetic oracles. One sequence of Isaianic oracles is punctuated by the refrain (Isa. 5: 25b; 9:12b,17b,21b;10:4b):

Yet for all this, | his anger | is not turned
away still his hand | is | upraised—

which has led to the view that in Isa. 5: 24 f. we have the conclusion of the sequence found in Isa. 9: 8–10: 4 (see the transposition of Isa. 5: 24 f. after Isa. 10: 4in NEB).

Strophic arrangement of at least a formal nature is involved in some of the acrostic schemes exhibited in Prov. 31: 10–31, in the first four chapters of Lamentations and in several of the Psalms—especially where three (as in Lam. 3) or eight (as in Ps. 119) couplets each beginning with the first letter of the Hebrew alphabet are followed by the same number beginning with the second letter, and so on to the twenty-second. (R. A. Knox's translation of the OT attempts to represent this Hebrew acrostic structure by a corresponding one in English.)

POETRY IN THE NEW TESTAMENT

Some of the poetical passages of the NT have always been recognized as such and have become traditional vehicles of Christian praise, like the canticles of Luke's nativity narrative—the Magnificat (Lk. 1: 46–55), the Benedictus (Lk. 1: 68–79), the Gloria (Lk. 2: 14) and the Nunc Dimittis (Lk. 2: 29–32)—and such hymns in Revelation as 'Worthy art thou' and 'Worthy is the Lamb' (Rev. 5: 9 f., 12) and the Hallelujah chorus (Rev. 19: 6). There is good reason to believe that the hymns sung by heavenly choirs in Revelation are echoes of those sung by the church 'militant here in earth' (or perhaps those sung below are regarded as echoes of those sung above).

Other hymns or rhythmical confessions of faith have been identified, with greater or lesser certainty, here and there in the epistles. The metre as well as the wording of Eph. 5: 14 suggests that this quotation (introduced by 'it is said') comes from an early Christian baptismal hymn. It is doubtful if we should recognize *poetry* in such passages as Phil. 2: 6–11, Col. 1:

15–20, 1 Tim. 3: 16 or the prologue to the Gospel of John: the structure of the Philippians and Timothy passages points in this direction, but their rhythms, like those of the other two passages, are *prose* rhythms. Poetry can be more confidently identified in the NT when the recognized rhythms of Hebrew or Greek poetry are present. The only instances of Greek poetical metre are quotations from Greek poets, as in Acts 17: 28 (Aratus, and possibly Epimenides), 1 C. 15: 33 (Menander) and Tit. 1: 12 (Epimenides). The characteristic forms of Hebrew poetry are plainly discernible in the Lukan canticles, and in the words of the annunciation (Lk. 1: 32 f., 35).

But the forms of Hebrew poetry appear preeminently in the teaching of Jesus, especially as recorded in the Synoptic Gospels. Perhaps one reason for his ready recognition as a prophet, over and above the evident authority with which he spoke, was the fact that his teaching was so regularly cast in the same moulds as the prophetic oracles of the OT. This incidentally made it easier to memorize them, but (more importantly) makes it credible that passages exhibiting this structure preserve—in translation at least—Jesus' *ipsissima verba*. Examples could be multiplied, but a couple will suffice, both from Matthew's version of the Sermon on the Mount.

The first is the strophe in Mt. 6: 19–21:

Do not store up for yourselves treasures on
earth,
where moth and rust destroy
and where thieves break in and steal.
But store up for yourselves treasures in heaven,
where moth and rust do not destroy
and where thieves do not break in and steal.
For where your treasure is,
there your heart will be also.

Here we have parallelism in sense, metrical structure (a–b–c, a^1–b^1–c^1, d–e) and even (when an attempt is made to turn the Greek back into Aramaic) rhyme.

The other is shorter, but is interesting because it includes a chiasmus (Mt. 7: 6):

Do not give dogs what is sacred;
do not throw your pearls to pigs.
If you do, they (the pigs) may trample them
under their feet,
and then (the dogs) turn
and tear you to pieces.

The structural pattern is a–b–b–a.

It is a pity that some more recent Bible translations, which have done so much to make the poetical passages of the OT visible to the reader, have not done the same for the teaching of Jesus in the Gospels.

BIBLIOGRAPHY

BURNEY, C. F., *The Poetry of our Lord* (Oxford, 1925).

GEVIRTZ, S., *Patterns in the Early Poetry of Israel* (Chicago, 1963).

GRAY, G. B., *The Forms of Hebrew Poetry* (London, 1915; New York, ²1972).

JEBB, J., *Sacred Literature* (London, 1820).

JOHNSON, A. R., *The Cultic Prophet and Israel's Psalmody* (Cardiff, 1979).

KOSMALA, H., 'Form and Structure in Ancient Hebrew Poetry', *VT* 14 (1964), pp.423 ff.

LOWTH, R., *Lectures on the Sacred Poetry of the Hebrews*, E.T. from the original Latin of 1735 (London, 1787 and later editions).

OESTERLEY, W. O. E., *Ancient Hebrew Poems* (London, 1938).

ROBINSON, T. H., *The Poetry of the Old Testament* (London, 1947).

SMITH, G. A., *The Early Poetry of Israel in its Physical and Social Origins* (London, 1912).

STUART, D. K., *Studies in Early Hebrew Meter* (Missoula, Montana, 1976).

INTRODUCTION TO THE WISDOM LITERATURE

F. F. BRUCE

The Old Testament includes three books which are distinctively known as 'Wisdom' books: Job, Proverbs and Ecclesiastes. In addition, the Psalter contains a number of compositions which have been called 'Wisdom' psalms (*e.g.* Pss. 4, 10, 14, 19, 37, 49, 73, 90, 112). The Septuagint includes further 'Wisdom' books which do not form part of the Hebrew Bible: Ecclesiasticus (the Wisdom of Jesus ben Sira, composed in Hebrew *c.* 180 B.C. and translated into Greek by the author's grandson half a century later), and Wisdom (composed in Greek by an Egyptian Jew in the first century B.C.). Baruch and 4 Maccabees (which illustrates from the Maccabaean martyrologies the triumph of right reason over the passions) also make a contribution to the wisdom literature of the Septuagint.

PRACTICAL AND REFLECTIVE WISDOM

In considering OT wisdom (Heb. *ḥokhmāh*) in its wider context, we may distinguish between practical and reflective wisdom, although there is no well-defined line of demarcation between the two.

Practical wisdom in any culture takes the form first of proverbial sayings which express in pithy terms observed regularities of nature or of human conduct: 'A red sky at night is a shepherd's delight' (cf. Mt. 16: 2) or 'A burnt child dreads the fire'. A more developed form is the riddle, fable or parable: well-known OT examples are Samson's riddle (Jg. 14: 12 ff.), the fables of Jotham (Jg. 9: 7-15) and Jehoash (2 Kg. 14: 9), and the parables of Nathan (2 Sam. 12: 1-4) and the wise woman of Tekoa (2 Sam. 14: 4-7). An example from one of the wisdom books is the story of the 'poor wise man' in Ec. 9: 13-16, probably based on a historical incident. One and the same Hebrew term (*māshāl*) does duty for both proverb and parable. The parable achieves its perfection in the Synoptic Gospels.

Reflective wisdom appears when the popular generalizations are seen to be inadequate to account for the perplexing facts of life, and problems such as the meaning of existence and the suffering of the innocent provoke thought at a deeper level.

WISDOM AND THE CREATED ORDER

When attempts are made to identify one central theme or principle around which OT theology may be organized, it is difficult to relate the wisdom literature to it. If the central theme be sought in the history of salvation, there is little enough of this in the canonical wisdom books. It reasserts itself, indeed, in the Septuagintal wisdom books: Wis. 10: 1 ff., for example, recounts the biblical story from Adam onwards in terms of the guidance of wisdom, with special emphasis on the Exodus narrative and the wilderness wanderings, but this note is absent from the wisdom literature of the Hebrew Bible.

If the central theme be sought rather in the covenant principle, it may certainly be agreed that the covenant established by the God of Israel with his people is the implicit presupposition of the canonical wisdom books, but they make no express reference to it. Here again the later wisdom books, identifying wisdom with the Mosaic law (cf. Bar. 3: 9-4: 4) and drawing a clear distinction between Israel and the other nations, differ from the earlier literature which is more international in character. It is not by chance that the hero of the book of Job is a non-Israelite, that Arabian and possibly Egyptian wisdom collections are incorporated in Proverbs or that Ecclesiastes has affinities with certain strands of Greek thought.

The God of Israel is not the God of Israel only; he is Creator of the world. His creation is there to be enjoyed and investigated, the study of creation unfolds the greater glory of the Creator, and this is a field of knowledge open to all. It is possible indeed to suppress the knowledge of God which is thus made available and to worship the creature in place of the Creator, but this is a perversion of the divine purpose in creation. Zophar the Naamathite may ask Job if he is able to 'find out the mysteries of God' (Job 11: 7), but his discouraging question is not to be treated as an inspired oracle imposing the answer 'No', for even if 'the mysteries of God' are inexhaustible, they are to be explored by man, and the highest function of wisdom is to guide man in this arduous quest, so that, as he seeks, he may increasingly find.

The wisdom theology of the OT is based on the assurance that wisdom is a gift from God, and is related to the age-enduring order of things in God's creation rather than to unique historical occurrences. Yet even wisdom theology discloses the salvation principle, arising out of man's encounter with creation in the fullest sense. God speaks through his works; he speaks through his dealings with men and women. To listen to his voice is the way to life; to ignore it is the way to ruin. It is by listening to it that men cultivate that 'fear of the LORD' which is 'the beginning of wisdom' (Ps. 111: 10; cf. Job 28: 28; Prov. 1: 7). The truly wise man is he who views life and the universe in this spirit of reverence, whereas the 'fool' is devoid of moral and religious sensitivity: when he says to himself 'There is no God' (Pss. 14: 1; 53: 1; cf. 10:4), he is not expressing intellectual atheism but ordering his life as if there were no God: 'there is no fear of God before his eyes' (Ps. 36: 1).

INTERNATIONAL WISDOM

The OT writers themselves recognize that wisdom knows no national frontiers. Some of Israel's neighbours are acknowledged to have a specially high reputation for wisdom. Solomon's wisdom was so exceptional that it is said to have been 'greater than the wisdom of all the men of the East, and greater than all the wisdom of Egypt' (1 Kg. 4: 30). The area where Job and his friends lived was renowned for wisdom: Jeremiah's oracle against Edom asks 'Is there no longer wisdom in Teman?' (Jer. 49: 7), while Obadiah to the same effect warns that when the day of reckoning comes Yahweh will 'destroy the wise men of Edom, men of understanding in the mountains of Esau' (Ob. 8).

In fact, apart from the oracles of Balaam (Num. 23: 7–24: 24), it is only in the wisdom literature that the utterances of non-Israelites are given canonical status in the OT. Job and his friends, as we have just seen, belong to Edomite clans, and the Israelite wisdom of Proverbs has appended to it collections of sayings by wise men and women from Massa in North Arabia (Prov. 30: 1–31: 9).

Parallels to the main varieties of OT wisdom literature are found in ancient Egypt and Babylonia, and at a later period in Greece. As early as the beginning of the third Egyptian dynasty (c. 2700 B.C.) Im-hotep, priest, physician and architect, is famed as the author of proverbs; two or three centuries later the maxims of Ptah-hotep constitute 'the earliest formulation of right conduct to be found in any literature' (J. H. Breasted, *The Dawn of Conscience*, 1935, p. 129). The collapse of the Old Kingdom (c.

2200 B.C.) led other Egyptian sages to a more pessimistic view of life, as they reflected on the vanity of worldly fortune, but one of them, Ipuwer, could look beyond present evils to the coming of a righteous king who would bring rest to men as a shepherd to his sheep.

There are some specially close parallels with 'the sayings of the wise' (Prov. 22: 17–23: 12) in those of the Egyptian sage Amen-em-ope, roughly contemporary with Solomon, which were arranged in thirty chapters (cf. the 'thirty sayings' of Prov. 22: 20). Whatever the relation between the two collections may be, the Hebrew 'words of the wise' are recorded in order 'that your trust may be in the LORD' (Prov. 22: 19); they are thus related to Israel's covenant faith.

As for Babylonian parallels, they provide several treatments of the theme of the righteous sufferer (which finds classic expression in Job), especially in the composition called, from its opening words, *I will praise the Lord of wisdom*, which describes the plight of a man whose experiences were quite similar to Job's (although the treatment is markedly inferior to that of the Hebrew book). Something of the pessimistic note of Ecclesiastes is anticipated in passages from the *Gilgamesh Epic* and from the *Dialogue of Pessimism*. In the latter work a Babylonian master and his slave discuss life and conclude that no values exist—in other words, that all is vanity.

There are periods in the history of many nations and individuals which dictate pessimism about any meaning or purpose in life. H. Ranston (*Ecclesiastes and the Early Greek Wisdom Literature*, 1925) adduced many striking parallels to Ecclesiastes from Theognis, a Greek poet who flourished c. 500 B.C. But here, as in parallels to other areas of the OT wisdom literature, it should not be hastily assumed that similarity in thought or even in expression implies direct dependence. Like occasions produce like effects over the whole world. Wisdom lore, both oral and written, is the fruit of experience and assumes (not without reason) that experience is not illusory but supplies valid evidence by which firm conclusions may be reached about God, man and the world.

THE WISDOM TRADITION IN ISRAEL

In addition to international and national wisdom, the OT bears witness to vigorous traditions of local or 'clan' wisdom. Of a city in the far north of Israel it is recorded that 'they were wont to say in old time, "Let them but ask counsel at Abel"; and so they settled a matter' (2 Sam. 20: 18). Reflections of such traditional wisdom have been pointed out in Amos and other pre-exilic prophets (cf. H. W. Wolff; *Amos' geistige Heimat*, 1964; D. A.

Hubbard, 'The Wisdom Movement and Israel's Covenant Faith', *Tyndale Bulletin* 17, 1966, pp. 3 ff.). The contribution of such wisdom to the teaching of the great prophets underlines the fact that Hebrew wisdom literature is stamped with Israel's faith in the one living and true God. Wisdom in biblical literature is divine wisdom; in man's deepest need the clearest and surest light comes from the knowledge of God. If OT wisdom does not make explicit mention of God's covenant with Israel, it finds a perfectly congenial setting in the records which are permeated with the covenant theme.

Solomon, whose excellent and far-famed wisdom is celebrated repeatedly in the narrative of his reign in 1 Kings, became the royal patron of wisdom literature. He himself is said to have 'uttered three thousand proverbs' and to have discoursed on natural history (1 Kg. 4: 32 f.). As late as the first century B.C. the author of the book of Wisdom thought it fitting to write in Solomon's name and to recast in terms appropriate to his own day the account of Solomon's prayer for wisdom given in 1 Kg. 3: 5–14 (cf. Wis. 7: 7–22). Indeed, about the beginning of the second century A.D. a collection of Christian hymns found currency as the *Odes of Solomon*—perhaps in tribute to the king whose 'songs numbered a thousand and five' (1 Kg. 4: 32). A later royal patron of wisdom literature appears to have been Hezekiah, to judge from the reference in Prov. 25: 1 to 'proverbs of Solomon copied by the men of Hezekiah king of Judah'.

While there was no lack of wisdom lore before the united monarchy of David and Solomon, its establishment marked the birth of an age of cultural enlightenment in Israel. Among the wise men at David's court mention is made of Ahithophel, whose counsel was 'like that of one who inquires of God' (2 Sam. 16: 23), and of Nathan, who is regularly designated 'the prophet' but who effectively moved the king to self-condemnation by his parable of the ewe lamb (2 Sam. 12: 1–6). Nathan may thus be reckoned among the sages as well as among the prophets. While sage, prophet and priest each had his own function and mode of communication, the three categories should not be so sharply distinguished that no overlapping between one and another is considered possible.

The place of the sage or wise man (Heb. *ḥākhām*) in popular esteem alongside the prophet and priest as a mediator of divine truth is indicated in Jer. 18: 18, where it is confidently asserted that 'the teaching of the law by the priest will not be lost, nor will counsel from the wise nor the word from the prophets'. The sages transmitted their wisdom from generation to generation; they had their schools, disciples, doctrines and collections of sayings, on which the OT wisdom writings have drawn.

CANONICAL WISDOM

The collections of sage utterances brought together in the book of Proverbs set forth the practical relevance of wisdom for ordinary life. God is known to be a righteous God, and his world is a moral world, characterized by temporal reward for justice and mercy and temporal retribution for wickedness and folly. But the more poignant and intractable problems of existence are not treated here. 'Proverbs seems to say, "Here are the rules for life; try them and find that they will work." Job and Ecclesiastes say, "We did, and they don't"' (D. A. Hubbard, *loc. cit.*, p. 6).

In the book of Job we meet the climax of a long process of wrestling with those problems. Earlier stages in this process are marked by what have been called the 'problem psalms'. Some of these psalms (*e.g.* Pss. 14, 19, 90) treat the problems calmly and almost philosophically: they contemplate the paradox of the world created by a good God and the perversity of man, who is part of that creation. 'The heavens declare the glory of God' and 'the law of the LORD is perfect', but as for man, 'who can discern his errors?' (Ps. 19: 1, 7, 12). But in other 'problem psalms' (*e.g.* Pss. 10, 37, 49, 73) there is a struggle with fear and doubt. The righteous suffer, the wicked prosper, and God apparently takes no action. 'Why, O LORD, do you stand far off? Why do you hide yourself in times of trouble? . . . Arise, LORD! Lift up your hand, O God. Do not forget the helpless' (Ps. 10: 1, 12). But the perplexity of the godly man is not left unanswered: everything that makes life worth living belongs to him who can say, 'God is the strength of my heart and my portion forever' (Ps. 73: 26).

But what if God seems to have abandoned the godly man? This is Job's situation. The book which bears his name propounds two crucial questions: (*a*) Will any man serve God for God's sake alone? (*i.e.* is there such a thing as sheer disinterested goodness?) and (*b*) Why should a godly man suffer? Satan asks the former question and is sure that the answer is 'No'; Job's maintenance of his integrity amid his distress proves that the answer is 'Yes'. But Job has no access to the heavenly council and, ignorant of the real cause of his misfortunes, is forced to endure his friends' reiterated contention that, since he is suffering, he must have sinned. Nevertheless he refuses to be persuaded by them and shocks them by challenging God to vindicate his own character (rather than Job's): at the end he is content when God speaks and he sees his experience in the perspective of the divine greatness.

Ecclesiastes has the form of a royal testament. It recommends wisdom as the only way to come to terms with the bleak realities of life —a cautious and unambitious wisdom, indeed, which finds contentment in the satisfaction of a day's work well done, the enjoyment of simple food and drink when one has thus acquired an appetite for them, and the pleasures of family life. It is best to be thankful for small mercies: the world is too full of injustice, the future too uncertain and death too final for the indulgence of high hopes, even if the Creator has 'set eternity in the hearts of men' (Ec. 3: 11). What would the Preacher have said to the man who can find no work, who has nothing to eat or drink, and who is forcibly separated from his wife and children? Nothing, presumably, but 'Utterly meaningless! Everything is meaningless' (Ec. 1: 2).

The canonical wisdom books, in their grappling with the problems of life on earth, do not call in a new world to redress the balance of the old. Once, indeed, Job in an upsurge of faith trembles on the brink of a new insight: out of my flesh if not 'in my flesh I shall see God' (Job 19: 26). But for the most part the quest is pursued within the limits of the present life. Only when we come to the late book of Wisdom do we find the concept of immortality freely invoked, and that under the influence of Greek thought.

NARRATIVE AND APOCALYPTIC WISDOM

Alongside the characteristic wisdom literature of the OT there is a wisdom narrative genre, more elaborate than the parable, exemplified particularly in the motif of the loyal Israelite who, exiled from home through no fault of his own, succeeds by wisdom in reaching a position of high responsibility and honour, in face of envy and malice. The prototype of this genre is the story of Joseph, 'discerning and wise' beyond all others, because of the Spirit of God within him, and therefore 'put . . . in charge of the whole land of Egypt' (Gen. 41: 38–41). The genre is specially common in relation to the exilic and post-exilic periods, as in the records of Daniel, endowed with 'insight and intelligence and wisdom, like that of the gods' (Dan. 5: 11), and Mordecai, whose careful forethought and prudent planning procured his advancement to be 'second in rank to King Xerxes' (Est. 10: 3). Samples of the genre outside the Hebrew Bible are the stories of Tobit and Ahiqar.

The book of Daniel illustrates the transition of narrative wisdom to apocalyptic wisdom: that apocalyptic is one development of wisdom literature is too often overlooked. Daniel's exceptional endowment with divine wisdom enables him to interpret Nebuchadnezzar's dreams and the writing on the wall at Belshaz-

zar's feast, as well as to maintain his integrity as a youth, when he is first brought to the Babylonian court, and in old age, when he emerges from retirement to exercise high responsibilities of state under Darius. The same kind of wisdom is illustrated in the Septuagintal additions which describe his exposure of the fraudulence of idolatry in the story of 'Bel and the dragon' and his vindication of Susanna's honour against her calumniators—the incident which gave rise to the proverb, 'A Daniel come to judgment'. But in the apocalyptic visions in the second half of the book, where Daniel requires the aid of an interpreting angel, the necessity of wisdom for grasping and imparting the divine purpose is emphasized: 'those who are wise [the *maskilim*] will instruct many' and, in spite of persecution and martyrdom, will rise at the end-time to 'shine like the brightness of the heavens' (Dan. 11: 33; 12: 3). 'None of the wicked will understand; but those who are wise will understand' (Dan. 12: 10). The same insistence on divinely inspired wisdom is maintained in NT apocalyptic; it is only by its means, for example, that the identity of the last imperial persecutor can be penetrated: 'This calls for wisdom. If anyone has insight let him calculate the number of the beast . . .' (Rev. 13: 18).

PERSONAL WISDOM

Wisdom is personified from time to time in the OT—personified as a woman, since the Hebrew word for 'wisdom' is grammatically feminine (like Greek *sophia* and Latin *sapientia*). She is pictured as a guide, philosopher and friend, as the donor of incomparable and imperishable wealth, as the mistress of a school where men are invited to learn the right way of life (Prov. 3: 15–18; 4:6–9; 8: 1–21). In Sir. 51: 23 such an invitation is issued in these terms:

Draw near to me, you who are untaught,
  and lodge in my school . . .
Put your neck under the yoke,
  and let your souls receive instruction;
  it is to be found close by.

There is a clear resemblance between these words and the gospel invitation of Mt. 11: 29, 'Take my yoke upon you, and learn from me', in which our Lord speaks in the rôle of Divine Wisdom.

Another form in which wisdom is personified in the OT has cosmic associations. The recognition that the wisdom of God is manifested in creation can readily be expressed in the statement of Prov. 3: 19(cf. Ps. 104:24):

The LORD by wisdom founded the earth;
  by understanding he established the
  heavens.

Let wisdom be personified, and at once she becomes the agent through whom the world was created. The best known instance of this portrayal comes in Prov. 8: 22–31, where Wisdom, brought forth by the Creator before the world's foundation, describes her presence with him—'I was the craftsman at his side' (Heb. *'āmōn*)—when he formed heaven and earth stage by stage and her joy in all that he made, including pre-eminently 'the sons of men'. In several strands of NT teaching this pre-existent wisdom, 'the Amen [an echo, perhaps, of the *'āmōn* of Prov. 8: 30], . . . the ruler of God's creation' (Rev. 3: 14), is not merely personified in a figure of speech but presented as really personal and as eventually incarnated in manhood in Jesus, who is therefore confessed as the 'firstborn of all creation', in whom, through whom and for whom the universe was brought into being, since 'he is before all things, and in him all things hold together' (Col. 1: 15–17; cf. Jn 1: 1–3; 1 C. 1: 24, 30; 8: 6; Heb. 1:2 f.). The OT portrayal of wisdom thus appears as an important root of NT christology.

BIBLIOGRAPHY

McKane, W., *Prophets and Wise Men* (London, 1965).

Noth, M., and Thomas, D. W. (eds.), *Wisdom in Israel and in the Ancient Near East* (Leiden, 1955).

Paterson, J., *The Book that is Alive* (New York, 1954).

Rankin, O. S., *Israel's Wisdom Literature* (Edinburgh, 1936).

von Rad, G., *Wisdom in Israel*, E.T. (London, 1972).

Whybray, R. N., *Wisdom in Proverbs* (London, 1965).

Whybray, R. N., *The Intellectual Tradition in the Old Testament* (Berlin, 1974).

Williams, J. G., *Those Who Ponder Proverbs* (Sheffield, 1981).

Zimmerli, W., 'The Place and Limit of the Wisdom in the Framework of the Old Testament Theology', *Scottish Journal of Theology* 17, 1964, pp. 146–158.

INTRODUCTION TO
THE PROPHETICAL BOOKS

G. C. D. HOWLEY

When the enemies of the prophet Jeremiah said 'Come, let's make plans against Jeremiah, for the teaching of the law by the priest will not be lost, nor will counsel from the wise, nor the word from the prophets' (18: 18), they briefly summarized the different sources of spiritual authority contained in the Old Testament. Priest, prophet and wise man represented three avenues along which the LORD spoke to His people during the centuries. Associated with each respectively was 'the law', 'the word' and 'counsel'. Priests exercised a teaching as well as a ceremonial ministry (Mal. 2: 6 f.), imparting the law. Prophets declared the oracle (word) of Yahweh, while the wise men imparted their wisdom and reflections upon truth. The three categories correspond with the three-fold division of the OT canon—Law, Prophets, Writings.

Prophecy proclaimed the word of God. This was expressed in two ways, which accord with the two sections of the prophetical books in the OT—the Former Prophets (Joshua, Judges, Samuel and Kings), which interpret history in the light of the purposes of God; the Latter Prophets (Isaiah, Jeremiah, Ezekiel and the Book of the Twelve), which record what was delivered to the people by the messengers of the LORD (Hag. 1: 13, RV).

There were prophets in evidence throughout OT times, though some were anonymous or less-known persons. Intimations of the will of God were rare in the later days of the Judges (1 Sam. 3: 1). Samuel, however, was favoured with a personal message from God, and as he grew the LORD revealed Himself increasingly to him (1 Sam. 3: 19–4: 1). He became the last and the greatest of the judges (Ac. 13: 20). He was the great reformer of the prophetical order, and encouraged schools of the prophets, being himself associated with a prophetic guild (1 Sam. 19: 20). He was afterwards regarded as the greatest figure since Moses (Jer. 15: 1). His work gave permanence and effectiveness to the prophetical functions, he becoming the real restorer of Israel's religion. From Samuel onwards God began to speak directly to the minds of men. The prophetic order can therefore be dated from Samuel's time. There are three references to Samuel in the NT from different men: Peter (Ac. 3: 24), Paul (Ac. 13: 20) and Hebrews (11: 32). 'The two great apostles appear to have regarded Samuel as a watershed in Israelite history' (E. F. F. Bishop, *Prophets of Palestine*, London, 1962, p. 28).

While men like Nathan and Gad probably functioned as court chaplains in David's day, the importance of the message communicated to David by Nathan (2 Sam. 7: 10–16)—which David described as 'an everlasting covenant, arranged and secured in every part' (2 Sam. 23: 5)—points to an even greater significance. The prophetic activity seen prominently in later centuries is exemplified by the ministry of Elijah and Elisha. These two men exercised an influential ministry, but they left nothing in writing. The literary prophets began with Amos, he and his contemporaries and their successors committing their messages to writing because of the permanent value of their ministry. They spoke to their generation, but their influence was destined to reach far beyond their own age; hence the importance of their place in the OT canonical books. The prophet was one who spoke on behalf of another, in this case on behalf of the living God. As Aaron became the spokesman of Moses (Exod. 4: 14 ff.), so the prophet filled the place of the mouthpiece of God to the people.

The prophet is variously described as seer (1 Sam. 9: 9, 19), man of God (1 Sam. 9: 6), messenger (Isa. 42: 19), servant (Isa. 42: 19), watchman (Ezek. 33: 7), man of the spirit (Hos. 9: 7). A seer had the capacity to discern beyond ordinary people. A watchman was a man on the outlook, watching for the hand of God at work. All were recipients of the divine word, set apart to deliver the oracle of the LORD to men. This they did by direct messages, by preaching sermons, by personal communications to individuals and groups. There were, however, false prophets active at certain times, which caused confusion among the undiscerning. Yet always the true prophets of God stood head and shoulders above the rest by virtue of their spiritual experience and their character.

The OT story unfolded against the background of world history. The whole range of the OT witnessed the rise and fall of great empires such as those of Egypt, Assyria, Babylon, Medo-Persia, with Greece and Rome figuring during the inter-testamental period. Kingdoms were consolidated, wars were waged, men rose or fell in the political spheres of the times, but all the time the internal history of the people of God was developing. The prophetic view of history was different from that of other oriental peoples: it was coherent, directed by general principles and in accord with a fixed plan.

The eighth century B.C. was a critical period. Messengers were sent by the LORD both to the northern tribes and to the southern people who centred upon Jerusalem. Amos and Hosea overlapped in their ministry, as did Isaiah and Micah in the south. This movement was destined to continue for fully three hundred years, eventually resulting in a remarkable collection of writings which brought much of the revelation of God to the people of Israel and reaching far beyond them to the whole of the Christian Church.

The period that saw the evolution of successive empires in the Gentile world covered a time of constant change in the affairs of the people of Israel. There was much social prosperity in the days of Amos; but there was also a tragic decay in spiritual values. There were extremes of wealth and poverty. Social disintegration went hand in hand with religious decline. Active religiosity abounded; the shrines had no lack of worshippers; people could be fastidious about ceremonial. Yet all this was marked, at the same time, by utterly false values attending the orthodox religion of the period. There was a contradiction between ceremonial and spiritual service, and much outward service to Yahweh without any heart (Mal. 1: 8, 13). During this long period there were many times when pure religion was no longer maintained —perhaps there was hardly a pretence of it. Many local shrines were probably overtly pagan, yet they were always busy (Am. 4: 4 f.; 5: 21–24; Mic. 6: 6 ff.). Cult priests would not reprove wrong practices (Am. 7: 10–13), and prophetic orders could be silent, merely time-servers and condoning evil.

Then there was the matter of political entanglements with foreign powers. The menace of Assyria was like a shadow in the sky for the people. They trusted in privilege as being the people of Yahweh, looking for deliverance (Am. 3: 1–7). They looked for the day of the LORD, when He would intervene for them and confirm the promises made to the patriarchs. That this was a false hope was declared with the utmost clarity by Amos (5: 18 ff.), who affirmed that the day would be one of darkness and not light. With a single message a prophet could shatter dearly-held hopes from the hearts of men. The surprising thing is the extent to which men were self-deluded, the great majority taking no notice of the prophetic warnings.

The prophets fitted into no single mould. The call of God came to noblemen and commoner, Isaiah seemingly being of noble stock, while his contemporary Micah was a countryman who moved among his own village people in his ministry. The call sometimes came to young men (Zech. 2: 4), as well as to those of greater maturity in age. What they shared in common was an experience of God that set them apart from their contemporaries through a distinctive knowledge arising from their encounter with Him. There were two main types of call: the visionary call, as seen in Isaiah and Ezekiel; and the call that came in the circumstances of ordinary life, exemplified by Amos and Jeremiah. Henceforth they became the messengers of the LORD.

Whether it was as in the OT days, or in our modern world, God is sovereign in the way He lays His hand upon His servants. In this respect ancient prophet and modern missionary stand on similar ground. From their early days God prepares men who are later to receive His word. Divine overruling can be discerned in the circumstances of their childhood, training, the obstacles they meet, and the way they each have to discover how to respond to events in their history. They will not necessarily be aware of any divine hand behind all, at first; this may surely be detected in the case of Saul of Tarsus—and parallels can be drawn between apostolic preparation for life and what happened in the lives of the OT prophets, who are our special interest in this article.

Despite all differences in these men or in their personal situations, certain fundamental elements marked them all. They were men of God's choice, fitted by Him for a special task, consecrated to Him from birth (Jer. 1: 5; cf. Gal. 1: 15). He had steered their course, gradually getting them ready for the eventual moment of truth when they would be clearly designated as having heard the word of the LORD and been called to their specific vocation. Themselves unaware of the God behind the scenes—though perhaps at times possessing a greater insight of Him, of His glory and His claims—when the actual time arrived, the experience would be overwhelming. Henceforth they had an assurance of God that stood them in good stead at all times, and particularly when they encountered adversity, domestically as Hosea, or at the hands of enemies, as Jeremiah.

This initial experience is vital to understanding both the men and their ministry. It was in harmony with each individual. Isaiah of Jerusalem was familiar with the temple, which was the place where he met with God. Ezekiel received his vision of the glory of Yahweh when far away from his homeland among the captives in Babylon. Jeremiah, a native of a small village and a priestly community, beheld familiar objects which became for him invested with a special significance (Jer. 1: 11–14). Habakkuk was like a watchman standing upon his tower (2: 1). In each case the prophetic call established their legitimacy, and led to the subsequent preservation of their integrity in difficult days. Their personalities could be discerned in the manner their call was received and responded to, as well as in the later events that befell them. All alike were the subjects of divine constraint, consecrated, equipped and upheld. With some it was for a brief period only, but with others—as in the cases of Isaiah and Jeremiah—the service of God covered long years, from young manhood into old age. As to the divine call, a writer has said: 'Yet the idea of God calling us goes to the heart of religion. God does more than wind up the watch of the world and let it run. He has a particular thing in mind for you and me to do. Not just Jeremiah, Paul or the apostles, but people in every age have had compelling convictions about the direction of their lives. One famous author once summed it up thus: God wants a different thing from each one of us, laborious or easy, conspicuous or quite private, but something which only we can do and for which we were created'.

Having received His call, each of the prophets pursued his task, normally acting individually. False prophets were found active in groups, sometimes large groups—as in the case of the prophets of Baal in the days of Elijah—but the true 'men of God' seem seldom to have crossed one another's tracks. An exception is found in the joint service of Haggai and Zechariah (Ezr. 5: 1 f.), during which time 'the elders of the Jews continued to build and prosper, under the preaching of Haggai the prophet and Zechariah a descendant of Iddo' (Ezr. 6: 14). There is no record of Isaiah and Micah acting together, nor of Amos and Hosea sharing in any way in their witness. On the contrary, they were usually solitary souls in their work.

'Tekoa is one Palestinian village which has retained its pristine name unchanged through centuries', says E. F. F. Bishop (*op. cit.* p. 175). He adds: 'Tekoa is rather lonely, though sufficiently set on a hill to be conspicuous from most directions . . . The view, once the place is reached, helps to an understanding of her prophet-son (despite his own self-witness). Amos came to be as detached as the village where he had been brought up.' By contrast, Zephaniah, who appears from his pedigree to have been a prince, a direct descendant from Hezekiah (Zeph. 1: 1), will almost certainly have lived in or near Jerusalem. We need not be surprised, therefore, that his message is directly addressed to the city and its people, with its mention of the Fish Gate and other specific places, and the warning that Yahweh 'will search Jerusalem with lamps' (1: 12 ff.).

The prophets differed greatly in temperament as well as in other ways. While we know little about some of them, a small number stand out from among the rest in their reaction to the discovery of their vocation. Isaiah was in close touch with the king and his court, mixing freely with the nobility. Hosea's domestic tragedy brought him the understanding of God as the divine Lover of His people. Jeremiah was deeply sensitive, and this characteristic is clearly seen in his early ministry. We can imagine his horror when he learned that the men of his own village conspired against him. God had a message for them: 'Therefore this is what the Lord says about the men of Anathoth, who are seeking your life, and saying, "Do not prophesy in the name of the Lord, or you will die by our hands"—therefore this is what the Lord Almighty says . . . I will bring disaster on the men of Anathoth, the year of their punishment' (Jer. 11: 21 ff.). Habakkuk wrestled with his problems, bringing them all into the light of the presence of God, ultimately reaching serenity in his spirit (Hab. 3: 17 ff.).

Of the two prophets who laboured together, Haggai was probably the older man, and Zechariah not only younger but extending beyond the period of the service of Haggai. Haggai is forthright, rugged in his call to put first things first. A realist, he was not easily to be turned aside from his plain-spoken message; while Zechariah an idealist, communicated verbal visions to grip the attention of the people, and encourage them to seek the way of the Lord. The blending of these diverse elements in their joint ministry led (as we have noted) to spiritual nourishment among the people of God.

The message of the prophets can be briefly summarized as (a) the revelation of the Lord, and (b) the recall to Him. This, however, is very much of an over-simplification. He was revealed in His nature and government, and the recall was with a view to re-establishing direct relations between God and His people. The message, then, was enshrined in the doctrine of God which the prophets proclaimed. They were reformers, not innovators: they stood in the mainstream of Israel's tradition. Their call was not merely to the Sinaitic covenant, which had been largely forgotten, but to a personal acknowledgement of and relationship with the living God Himself.

In an age of lowered values, Amos and his successors revealed God as transcendent. This divine transcendence was unfolded, so that the people might rediscover the greatness of their God. It was not sufficient to perform religious duties, for it was always the *heart* of man that God sought. The tragic fact was that the people had utterly wrong ideas of God—their God was too small. A classic illustration is found in the Lord's parable of the Pharisee and the tax collector (Lk. 18: 9–14). The Pharisee had a small conception of God, but large ideas about himself. He drew near to God in that spirit, thinking to impress the Almighty with his deeds. The tax collector, however, had come to realize the greatness of God and his own corresponding sinfulness. He came therefore as a penitent, seeking the mercy of God, and he received a blessing accordingly.

Through the prophetic era, it was characteristic of Israel to take their God for granted, and they were unprepared for the shock that came to them in the message: 'You only have I chosen of all the families of the earth; therefore I will punish you for all your sins' (Am. 3: 2). The divine supremacy and transcendence is declared in such words as these: 'For this is what the high and lofty One says—he who lives forever, whose name is holy: "I live in a high and holy place, but also with him who is contrite and lowly in spirit, to revive the spirit of the lowly and to revive the heart of the contrite"' (Isa. 57: 15). The nature of this transcendent God was revealed to the young Isaiah. He 'saw the Lord seated upon a throne, high and exalted; and the train of his robe filled the temple' (Isa. 6: 1). He was overwhelmed with this vision, and was unable to look up or speak to Him. Isaiah was reduced to a condition of despair until he had experienced the miracle of divine forgiveness and healing. He was in the presence of God who was the Holy One. Holiness means 'separatedness': for God to be holy meant that He was separate from man, essentially different. This did not mean that he stood aloof from men, as the prophetic oracle of Isa. 57: 15 makes clear. The proclamation granted to Moses centuries earlier declared Him as being infinitely superior to man, and yet to be disposed towards man in mercy (Exod. 34: 6 f.). His holiness is one of the primary revelations in the OT about God.

A second assertion was that He was righteous. 'Righteousness to the Israelite was no abstract principle or characteristic of an impersonal moral order. It is a definite quality of the Divine personality, standing over all norms and laws as well as in them. God is righteous in that He reveals to men what is right and helps to achieve the right which is due a righteous people' (G. E. Wright, *The Challenge of Israel's Faith*, London, 1946, p. 72). The righteousness of God is His self-consistency in His whole being. Just as Isaiah, who came to know Him as holy, declared God to be the Holy One of Israel, so Amos, with his insight into the righteousness of the Lord, was to call: 'But let justice roll on like a river, and righteousness like a never-failing stream'

(Am. 5: 24). Righteousness would be seen in 'the constant, personal intercourse between God and man in the realm of the will' (Wright, *op. cit.*).

Some exceptional experiences in life are a means of men learning more about God. This was the case in the affairs of Hosea, whose broken marriage, caused by the unfaithfulness of his wife Gomer, did not quench his love for her. On the contrary, he sought her even after her departure from his home (Hos. 1–3), and from his domestic sorrow there came to him the realization that his unswerving love for a faithless wife was but a faint reflection of the ceaseless love of Yahweh for Israel. From those clouded days was born the ministry of the prophet in which he affirmed what he had learned in the hard school of life—that the love of God for His people was constant, unaffected by their backslidings. If Amos cried for justice, Hosea—his contemporary as a prophet to the northern tribes—made the appeal of love.

The word *chesed*, usually rendered as 'mercy' or 'lovingkindness' in the older versions, is found in the RSV translated as 'covenant love' or 'steadfast love'. F. F. Bruce defines this as 'the attitude which God takes towards those to whom He has pledged Himself in solemn covenant (and which He expects them to show to Him and to one another)' ('The Sure Mercies of David': *Annual Lecture of the Evangelical Library*, 1954, p. 3.) Divine love is not merely a magnification of human emotional love, but a love that is based upon His promise, steadfast and unchangeable in character, reaching back to the promises made with the patriarchs and with David. Thus the translation 'steadfast love' that is found many times in the RSV (*e.g.* Hos. 6: 6, *et al.*). N. H. Snaith sums up the matter in this way: '*chesed*, in all its varied shades of meaning, is conditional upon there being a covenant. Without the prior existence of a covenant, there could never be any *chesed* at all' (*The Distinctive Ideas of the Old Testament*, 1944, p. 94 f.). It was because everything arose from the revelation of the character of God that He sought the response of His people in such words as, 'I desire mercy, not sacrifice, and acknowledgment of God, rather than burnt offerings' (Hos. 6: 6). Hosea with his sympathy and tenderness of heart, discerned that the ultimate truth about God was not His sense of justice but His infinite love.

Micah as an individual stands in contrast to his contemporary Isaiah, yet they are one in their realization of the degenerate condition of the people. Micah was a true son of the people, and called for a return to the old simplicities. His message reached its climax in the declaration of the divine will: 'He has showed you, O man, what is good, and what does the Lord require of you? To act justly and to love mercy and to walk humbly with your God' (6: 8). This summary of the requirements of true religion is thought by some (*e.g.* H. L. Ellison, *Men Spake from God*, 1952, p. 66) as virtually combining the teaching of his three great predecessors: to do justice—Amos; to love mercy (*chesed*)—Hosea; to walk humbly with your God, i.e. as befits His holiness—Isaiah. His prophecy draws to a close with a clear declaration of the God of Micah—'Who is a God like you, who pardons sin and forgives the transgression . . . ?' (7: 18). The deep impression his preaching made in his own age is shown by it being recalled a hundred years later in the days of Jeremiah (Jer. 26: 18), Hezekiah's reformation being apparently largely due to his ministry.

Such a brief consideration of the leading figures among the pre-exilic prophets does no more than glance at the men and their ministry. The lesser known prophecies of Zephaniah and Nahum concentrate respectively upon Jerusalem and Nineveh. Zephaniah points to a promise of salvation for Jerusalem and for the peoples of the earth, while Nahum's message is one of doom to fall upon Nineveh. The tension continues throughout his prophecy. Of Habakkuk as a person we know nothing. Yet there is a clear unfolding of his inner history contained in his writing. His personal problems as he considered the development of world events, and his experience of God during that time led to the message that became for him an anchorage, and has since become a means of universal comfort: '. . . the righteous will live by his faith' (2: 4). From this source the prophecy reaches down the centuries into New Testament times, and is echoed and quoted in the writings of Paul and the letter to the Hebrews (Rom. 1: 17; Gal. 3: 11; Heb. 10: 38).

Throughout the prophecies there is a mingling of stern and tender notes. In a different age and setting Paul wrote of 'the kindness and the severity of God' (Rom. 11: 12). His severity must never cause men and women to overlook His kindness or His longsuffering. The very fact that He sent a succession of His servants to the people over several centuries is evidence of the compassion of God for His erring people. There are those who affirm that the God of the Old Testament is different from the God of the New Testament: that God is stern, just and righteous throughout the OT, but that Jesus brought the new conception of the fatherhood of God. G. E. Wright gives this view little credence: 'Of all the misleading, inaccurate, and distorting generalizations this is one of the worst. It contains just the right mixture of truth and error to make it a devil's own brew of falsehoods!' (*op. cit.*). Jeremiah was the most reluctant figure among the prophets. This arose, not from unwillingness to serve God, but because of a deep sense of unfitness for such a heavy task. '"Ah, Sovereign LORD," I said, "I do not know how to speak; I am only a child"' was his first reaction to the divine call. But the call revealed his prior consecration to the office of prophet, and the consequent equipment that would be given for his ministry (Jer. 1: 4–8). He was destined to a life-time of virtual martyrdom through suffering. Yet while he lived to see the final break-up of Jerusalem, he became the greatest figure of his era, faithful to Yahweh to the very end. The youth was able to become 'a fortified city, an iron pillar, and bronze walls' against the whole land, the kings of Judah and all who ranged against him. 'They will fight against you; but they will not overcome you', was the divine promise (1: 18 f.).

'The Old Testament teaching about the law comprises two aspects which correspond to the two successive stages of its development' (E. Jacob, *Theology of the Old Testament*, E.T. 1958, p. 272). In the earlier stage the law could be defined as God's revelation to those who are in the covenant. The second stage 'can be characterized by the cleavage between the law and the covenant' (*op. cit.*). With the breakdown of the old covenant and the apostasy of the people, Jeremiah prophesied of the making of a new covenant. '"The time is coming," declares the LORD, "when I will make a new covenant with the house of Israel and with the house of Judah . . . this is the covenant I will make with the house of Israel after that time," declares the LORD. "I will put my law in their minds, and write it on their hearts; I will be their God, and they will be my people. No longer will a man teach his neighbor and or a man his brother, saying "Know the LORD", because they will all know me, from the least of them to the greatest . . . for I will forgive their wickedness, and will remember their sins no more' (31: 31–34). The law was written upon tablets of stone, never affecting their hearts, but the new covenant would be written upon their hearts. Within them would spring up a desire to fulfil the will of God because of the spiritual nature of the new covenant.

This was a change of a fundamental character. It looked on to the Christian era, and finds its fulfilment through the work of Christ at the Cross. A change of heart is of the nature of Christianity, as the apostle Paul expounded in his ministry of the new covenant. The coming of the Holy Spirit created men anew, so that it could be said of them, 'you show that you are a letter from Christ, the result of our ministry, written not with ink but with the Spirit of the living God, not on tablets of stone but on tablets of human hearts' (2 C. 3: 3). In the observance of the Lord's Supper the elements of bread and the cup become object-lessons to remind us of the central truth of Christianity: 'This cup is the new covenant in my blood . . . For whenever you eat this bread and drink the cup, you proclaim the Lord's death until he comes' (1 C. 11: 25 f.). Little could Jeremiah have foreseen that the covenant of which he told would be ratified in the blood of Jesus, and mediated by Him in His risen life (Heb. 8: 6–13).

Ezekiel was the great prophet of the Exile. He has been called 'the prophet of reconstruction', because despite his messages of judgment, he promised an eventual spiritual renewal of the nation, and the establishment of the new commonwealth (see F. F. Bruce, commentary on Ezekiel, p. 808 below). There is always hope, because there is always the living God who will not forsake His people. The climax of Ezekiel's prophecy affirms the divine promise, 'The LORD is there' (48: 35). This note of the ultimate realization of the presence of God among His people persists beyond the Exile. Zechariah and Haggai ministered in a period which Zechariah described as a 'day of small things' (4: 10). It was a period of spiritual depression; the people were a small minority and surrounded by their enemies. The messengers of Yahweh called for a restoration of right values, and prophesied that the glory of God would dwell amongst His people (Hag. 2: 9; Zech. 14: 16, 20 f.). He would 'shake the heavens and the earth, the sea and the dry land; and . . . all nations' (Hag. 2: 6 f.), to bring His purposes to fruition—a message that is echoed in NT times. There would be 'the removing of what can be shaken—that is, created things —so that what cannot be shaken may remain' (Heb. 12: 27). This unshakeable kingdom has become the inheritance of the people of God today.

The whole continuous build-up of the prophetic message was with the purpose of creating an awareness of God in His greatness and splendour, to bring about a wholehearted return to Him. Herein revival lies: there are no short cuts to this experience. Towering above all the differences of emphasis in the ministry of the prophets was an enlarged conception of Yahweh that could lead to repentance and full restoration to Him. Thus would the underlying purpose of God be realized, and in an ethical standard and experience, in a life that would be in harmony with His nature and His will.

The word was always greater than the person of its messenger. His task was to transmit the message without any addition of his own. Yahweh was seen as the sole author of history, human beings being the instruments of His word. The permanence of prophetic ministry was assured by a promise of prophetic succession (Dt. 18: 15–18). Such spiritual functioning was an essential for the people, as prophets

were their 'eyes' and their 'heads' (Isa. 29: 10), those through whom men might discern and learn from the divine point of view. The heavy responsibility of the prophets is suggested by the word to Jeremiah: 'I have made you a tester of metals and my people the ore, that you may observe and test their ways' (Jer. 6: 27).

The only explanation of the originality and creative powers of the prophets lies in their vision of God and their message arising from this revelation. Each of these men had a personal experience of God that accounted for his ministry. Each taught what he had learned from God: it could not have been humanly conceived or invented. The divine tenderness and love was expressed in such imagery as this: 'It was I who taught Ephraim to walk, taking them by the arms; . . . I led them with cords of human kindness, with ties of love' (Hos. 11: 3 f.). 'I have loved you with an everlasting love: therefore I have drawn you with loving-kindness,' (Jer. 31: 3). This essential originality sprang from the fact that the true prophets of God were men who stood in His council. The complaint against the false prophets was that they had no such privilege. 'But if they had stood in my council, they would have proclaimed my words to the people . . .' (Jer. 23: 22). In light of this we can understand the words, 'Surely the Sovereign Lord does nothing, without revealing his plan to his servants the prophets' (Am. 3: 7). The message could be communicated by oracle, vision, parable, sign, symbolism, poetry—all are used at some time or other in the ministry of the prophets of God. They were given special quickening of their faculties for the specific tasks they engaged in from time to time. Some of the phrases used give evidence of what took place: 'Thus says the LORD' . . . 'The oracle concerning . . .' . . . 'The word which Isaiah the son of Amoz saw' . . . 'Hear this word . . .' The receiving and delivery of every separate message must have been a memorable occasion for those servants of God, as once again they became vehicles through whom the word of God was made known to their fellow-men.

The prophetic messages arose from given historical situations, and were addressed, in the first place, to those occasions or persons. To grasp their true significance it is needful to isolate the fundamental principle from the immediate context. A prophet might address himself to a specific situation in the history of the nation, but the abiding truth enshrined in the message would remain for all time. Herein lies a unique element in the prophecies: there is never any doubt as to the sovereign rule of God in the world of today. The principles of His government unfolded in those ages are the same that mark His activity now among men. In this sense, God is not silent, despite the view of some that God has not spoken since the Cross. That view may be correct insofar as it refers to a visibe manifestation of God in the world. This will come at the End-time. But now, there is comfort in the knowledge of His invisible activity, His movements in history with a view to the eventual fulfilment of His eternal purpose.

Scholars have referred to the 'prophetic perspective', to the 'foreshortening of the prophetic horizon'. There were times when they looked forward to the day of the LORD, to the consummation of history. In so doing they would pass over the interval in time that stood between the immediate and the ultimate fulfilment of their ministry. The oracles of Isa. 40–66, at whatever point of time they were delivered, refer to the closing period of the Exile. Throughout the prophecy there is a looking forward to 'the age to come', in contrast to 'the present age'. There is no problem in this once we discern that there is an overlap between 'this age' and 'the age to come' . . . we may live our lives within the environment of this material world yet at the same time experience the powers of the age to come. It is a dual life, characteristic of those who experience a present knowledge of God. It is possible, thus, to understand the books of the prophets as we 'stand with them at their point of vantage, look at their particular history with them, and experience the challenge and immediacy of the will of God for that moment'. But we must also stand within our own history, and seek to find the immediate word of the Lord for us now, at this moment (Wright, *op. cit.*, p. 40). As we fulfil those two conditions, the truths the prophets reinforce will never remain merely abstract matters but become intimately related to life as we know it.

The final chapter in *The Doctrine of the Prophets* (A. F. Kirkpatrick, 1892) is entitled 'Christ the goal of prophecy'. Referring to the centuries of silence between the OT and NT times, the author comments: 'For if prophecy was, as it is professed to be, an inspired glimpse into the eternal present of the divine mind, it must needs foresee the divine purpose for mankind unfolding itself in time, and that foresight must in due course be realised in facts. When the curtain falls on the stage of Old Testament prophecy at the close of the fifth century B.C., we feel that the riddle waits for its answer, the drama lacks its denouement'. The New Testament explains how the first Christians regarded OT prophecy. 'The prophets who spoke of the grace that was to come to you searched intently with the greatest care, trying to find out the time and circumstances to which the Spirit of Christ in them was pointing when he predicted the sufferings of Christ and the glories that would follow. It

was revealed to them that they were not serving themselves but you, when they spoke of the things which have now been told you by those who have preached the gospel to you by the Holy Spirit sent from heaven. Even angels long to look into these things' (1 Pet. 1: 10 ff.; see also Lk. 24: 25 ff.; Ac. 3: 24 ff.). When the risen Lord taught His disciples along the road to Emmaus, He must have unfolded to them the secrets of OT messianic prophecy.

Approaching the OT with this knowledge, much can be discerned that, whatever its immediate bearing was, pointed to an ultimate realization in Jesus. In this way we understand the prophecies of the ideal king, the suffering servant, and many other elements that would find their substance in the advent and the kingdom of Messiah. 'For the testimony of Jesus is the spirit of prophecy' (Rev. 19: 10). Prophecy would prepare for Him, and it would bear witness to Him who was to be prophet, priest and king. The interpretation of prophecy in the NT was therefore Christ-centred, a typical apostolic sermon leading up to the words: 'All the prophets testify about him that every one who believes in him receives forgiveness of sins through his name' (Ac. 10: 43; cf. also Ac. 8: 30–35; 17: 3). We might add to our consideration those passages in the Gospels where OT prophecies are directly related to our Lord (Mt. 1: 22 f., *et al.*).

In addition to specific prophecies now regarded as messianic, there are passages in Lamentations—which strictly refer to the fall of Jerusalem—that have often been used concerning the passion of the Lord. A thoughtful comment on this matter says: 'As long as this is done reverently and knowingly, few would cavil at it . . . It is therefore entirely to be expected that in this book of the suffering for sin, there would be the frequent phrase that would remind the loving heart of a much deeper suffering' (Ellison, *op. cit.*, p. 154).

We have not included Daniel in this survey because of its apocalyptic character, and because it is not included in the section of the Prophets in the OT canon. Yet here too the vision of the son of man (Dan. 7) can be linked with other prophecies that point onward to Christ (see for example, Mk 14: 62).

In the dark days of the Jewish state, words were uttered that faith might grasp, one such message being found both in Micah and Isaiah: 'In the last days the mountain of the Lord's temple will be established as chief among the mountains; it will be raised above the hills and peoples will stream to it. . . The law will go out from Zion, the word of the Lord from Jerusalem . . .' (Mic. 4: 1–4; Isa. 2: 2 ff.). It was such prophecies amongst others that caused many devout people to be waiting for the fulfilment of the Davidic promises at the time when our Lord was born. Zechariah worshipped the Lord in his hymn of praise, 'because he has come and has redeemed his people. He has raised up a horn of salvation for us in the house of his servant David (as he said through his holy prophets of long ago) . . .' (Lk. 1: 68 ff.). It is evident that an understanding of OT prophecy is necessary for a realization of the full meaning of the NT.

Perhaps the final value of OT prophecy for us lies in the challenge of its devotional and ethical element. Throughout these writings the reader meets with assurances that faith can appropriate for the strengthening of spiritual life and hope. Such is the viewpoint suggested by the apostle Paul as he applies an OT psalm to our Lord: 'For everything that was written in the past was written to teach us, so that through endurance and the encouragement of the scriptures we might have hope' (Rom. 15: 4). A faith based upon the ongoing purposes of God as unfolded by the prophets will be strong, because it is built upon an unshakeable foundation.

BIBLIOGRAPHY

BISHOP, E. F. F., *Prophets of Palestine* (London, 1962).

CLEMENTS, R. E., *Prophecy and Convenant* (London, 1965).

CLEMENTS, R. E., *Prophecy and Tradition* (Oxford, 1975).

DAVIDSON, A. B., *Old Testament Prophecy* (Edinburgh, 1903).

DAVIES, E. W., *Prophecy and Ethics* (Sheffield, 1981).

EATON, J. H., *Vision in Worship* (London, 1981).

ELLISON, H. L., *Men Spake from God* (Exeter, [2]1958).

ELLISON, H. L., *The Prophets of Israel from Ahijah to Hosea* (Exeter, 1969).

ELMSLIE, W. A. L., *How Came Our Faith* (Cambridge, 1948).

GUILLAUME, A., *Prophecy and Divination* (London, 1938).

HEATON, E. W., *The Old Testament Prophets* (Harmondsworth, 1958).

JOHNSON, A. R., *The Cultic Prophet in Ancient Israel* (Cardiff, 1944).

KIRKPATRICK, A. F., *The Doctrine of the Prophets.* Warburton Lectures (London, 1892, [2]1897, reprinted Grand Rapids, 1958).

KUHL, C., *The Prophets of Israel*, E.T. (Edinburgh, 1960).

LINDBLOM, J., *Prophecy in Ancient Israel* (Oxford, 1962).

ROBINSON, H. W., *Inspiration and revelation in the Old Testament* (Oxford), 1946.

ROBINSON, T. H., *Prophecy and the Prophets in Ancient Israel* (London, 1923).

ROWLEY, H. H., 'The Nature of Old Testament Prophecy in the Light of Recent Study', in *The Servant of the Lord and Other Essays on the Old Testament* (Oxford, [2]1965), pp.95–134.

ROWLEY, H. H. (ed.), *Studies in Old Testament Prophecy* (Edinburgh, 1950).

SMITH, W. R., *The Prophets of Israel* (London, [2]1895).

SNAITH, N. H., *The Distinctive Ideas of the Old Testament* (London, 1944).

WACE, H., *Prophecy: Jewish and Christian.* Warburton Lectures. (London, 1911).

WESTERMANN, C., *Basic Forms of Prophetic Speech*, E.T. (London, 1967).

WRIGHT, G. E., *The Challenge of Israel's Faith* (Chicago, 1944).

YOUNG, E. J., *My Servants the Prophets* (Grand Rapids, 1952).

See also bibliographies to the individual prophetical books and to 'The Theology of the Old Testament' (p.84).

PART TWO
THE OLD TESTAMENT

GENESIS

H. L. ELLISON (Chapters 1–11)

and D. F. PAYNE (Chapters 12–50)

Note. Commentaries and books on Genesis are referred to by the name of the author. Full details are given in the Bibliography.

Name

Genesis is the first part of the Pentateuch, the five books of Moses. These are, however, regarded by the Jews as essentially one book, the division being originally for the sake of convenience. In the earlier days of writing it would have been very difficult to include the five books of the Law (Heb. *Tôrāh*, literally, Instruction) in one scroll for technical reasons. Traditionally the five sections are called in Heb. by the opening word, here *B⁰rēšît*; Genesis is the transliteration of the Gk. name used in LXX i.e. Origin.

Authorship

Certain portions of the Pentateuch are expressly attributed to Moses, *e.g.* Exod. 17: 14; 24: 3–7; Dt. 31: 24 f., but as a whole it is anonymous, and except in Deuteronomy, in his farewell address (chs. 1–11), the first person is not used for Moses. Historically, the use of the Pentateuch by the Samaritans makes it very difficult to place its present form later than the death of Solomon, when the North separated from Judah. Unless Mosaic authorship is rejected for *a priori* reasons, the simplest attitude is to regard Moses as responsible for the choice of the material, without affirming that he need have written it down himself. Certain portions were clearly passed down orally, whenever they may have been written down. A very few portions must have received their present form after the time of Moses.

There are those who maintain that most of the material of Genesis existed in writing before the time of Moses. Some base this on the theory that 'this is the account of' (2: 4; 5: 1; 11: 10, 27; 25: 12, 19; 36: 1, 9; 37: 2), variously rendered by NIV, is a colophon, or identifying phrase, of the type found on Mesopotamian clay tablets, marking the conclusion of a section, and that therefore these sections existed already on such tablets. However attractive this view, it faces major problems (cf. Kidner, pp. 23 f.). Then there is the view that Joseph produced a first edition of Genesis. He could have, but there is no scrap of evidence that he did. The genealog-

ies at any rate, and probably ch. 14, could well have existed in writing at a pre-Mosaic date. However the information was preserved, it seems wisest to regard the choice and arrangement of the material as the work of one man, *viz.* Moses.

The Structure and Purpose of Genesis

Genesis consists of two closely linked books. In chs. 1–11 we have the beginnings of man's history, in which we are told all that need be known to understand God's purposes of salvation; in chs. 12–50 we are told of the beginnings of Israel. But what we are given is virtually only salvation history (*Heilsgeschichte*, cf. *Theology of the OT*, p. 65). Even as the first book gives a minimum outline, so it is in the second, which is concerned mainly with the primacy of faith and of individual response. The genealogies serve a dual purpose. They stress the unity of mankind in his sin and failure, and that none fall outside God's care and grace. This means that in the truest sense the main purpose of Genesis is the revelation of the character and purposes of God and of man's fallen state.

The Main Problems of Genesis

More than any other book of the Bible Gen. 1–11 raises problems, which demand a high degree of secular knowledge and a series of special treatises for their answers, if indeed man with his limited knowledge can find them. This contribution to the understanding of Genesis is written from the standpoint, that a true grasp of its message is not dependent on scientific knowledge. While the writer has his views on many of these points, he has sought not to obtrude his views, for it would be intolerable pride on his part to do so, especially as he is no authority on most of the issues involved. So the textual comments will for the most part be confined to elucidating the meaning of the Hebrew text. For those wishing limited extra information the Additional Notes in Kidner will be found most valuable. In addition J.

Byrt has recently given us a well-balanced and informed survey of the main issues.

A warning is, however, in place. It is right and proper that those with scientific training should seek light on the secrets of nature and man's past from the Scriptures as well as from the evidence of the physical universe. They are both the work of the same God, and ultimately cannot be in conflict. But it must never be assumed that this information, incomplete by its very nature, and always liable to be modified as science advances, is a true understanding of the Scriptures and their purpose. We must never think that this world's wisdom and knowledge give a believer an advantage in the understanding of God's revelation, nor that ignorance is an aid to spirituality.

A. CREATION

There are here five main problems:

(i) *The Relationship of Gen. 1 and 2.* The commentary follows the commonly held view that the two chapters are looking at the same event, *viz.* the creation of man, from different points of view. There are those, however, who consider that these chapters are to be read consecutively with a considerable interval of time between them. This has recently been argued with much learning by E. K. V. Pearce.

(ii) *Gen. 1 and Science.* The commentary accepts that recent scientific research gives a picture that approximates to the order given in Gen. 1, and mentions only the main exceptions.

(iii) *Evolution.* Beyond drawing attention to the various verbs used to describe God's creative activity, the means used by Him are not considered, whether by special creation throughout, or by a God-guided evolution interspersed with creative acts. The Heb. is compatible with both views.

(iv) *The Meaning of Day.* In spite of the great deal written by some on the subject, it seems to be impossible to fix the meaning of 'day' (*yom*) with certainty in Gen. 1. While it could mean twenty-four hours, yet equally the whole creative act is one day in 2: 4 (Heb.), and in various statements about God's activity it is clearly a period. In either case, if the (unprovable) theory of days of revelation is correct (cf. commentary on ch. 1), the controversy ceases to have meaning.

(v) *Does Gen. 1: 2 Indicate a Reversion to Chaos?* The view, often called the gap theory, that Gen. 1: 2 indicates a gap between God's original creation and the creating of what now is, first became popular last century as an attempt to reconcile the view of a six-day creation and the existence of the fossils in the geological strata, which seemed to suggest very long periods of time. Quite apart from intrinsic difficulties (cf. Ramm, pp. 119–156), the Heb. of 1: 2 will not bear the meaning forced on it

by this theory (see commentary). Today this view is being increasingly abandoned by those who wish to harmonize Genesis with the geological record in favour of the view that the strata and their fossils were laid down by the Flood.

B. THE FLOOD

Until fairly recently the main sphere of controversy was whether the Flood was worldwide or confined to the area inhabited by man. Basically it involved theories of inspiration, for physical evidence was too scanty for a convincing answer. More recently, so especially Whitcomb and Morris, the view has been advanced that the Flood was of cosmic proportions and that the water-laid strata with their associated fossils are due to it. The Bible has nothing conclusive to say on the subject, and the arguments on both sides are based mainly on a selective use of the available evidence.

C. THE ANTIQUITY OF MAN

Man, as he is pictured in Gen. 4, can be traced back with reasonable confidence to the Paleolithic, *i.e.* at the end of the last ice age, about 8,000 BC, but the palaeontologist claims to have found traces of *homo sapiens*, i.e. man as we know him, in the Paleolithic period. Without expressing any opinion on this highly technical and controversial subject, it must be pointed out that not physical form or possible intellect but the essentially spiritual image and likeness of God made Adam true man.

D. CHRONOLOGY

For the Jew the year beginning in October 1976 was 5737 from the creation, while in the 17th century Archbishop James Ussher calculated that the creation must have been in 4004 B.C. There have been other estimates as well, which have based themselves purely on the statements of the Bible. In recent years, however, archaeology has been able to establish a chronology for the ancient Near East, which is accurate to a few years as far back as 2000 B.C. Before that the margin of error increases, but when the first wall of Jericho is dated by the radio-carbon method at something before 7000 B.C. this will be accurate to within a few centuries. There is ample evidence, that except where the text shows signs of corruption, the figures given are correct, but we cannot use them to construct a coherent chronological system, so this will not be attempted.

The Text of Genesis

As is the case throughout the Pentateuch the text of Genesis is very well preserved. In most of the cases where NIV, RSV and NEB depart from the *MT*, it is evident from the LXX and Samaritan editions that words have accidentally dropped from Heb.

ANALYSIS

I. THE BEGINNINGS OF MAN
(1: 1–11: 32)

Whatever view is taken of the relationship of the two accounts of creation (*Introduction, The Main Problems of Genesis*, A(i)), it is clear that the former is written from God's standpoint, while man is the centre of the latter. While the former leads up to the creation of man, its climax is God's satisfaction as expressed in the Sabbath. In the latter the climax is man's satisfaction as he finds his completion in the woman. It is only *a priori* considerations that will cause us to doubt that the latter has come down to us essentially from Adam himself; the former is obviously direct revelation.

i (a) Creation from God's standpoint (1: 1–2:3)

The suggestion that Gen. 1 is derived from Sumerian or Akkadian mythology, shows only how the refusal to accept revelation drives men to folly. No suggestion is made as to how all the gross polytheism was eliminated from poems like *Enuma elish* (*DOTT*, pp. 5–13, or A. Heidel, *The Babylonian Genesis*) and in the process an order of creation was laid down, unique in ancient literature, and not imagined by any outside the Hebrew tradition until modern times. To whom the revelation was given, we do not know. If we supply the name of Moses, it is merely because we know none more fitting. It is also impossible to say whether the revelation was purely verbal or mainly visual. There is much to be said for the latter view, which could mean that the seven days were days of revelation, but it must be insisted that this view, like any other, is unprovable.

The chapter begins with the simple statement 'In the beginning God created (*bārā'*) the heavens and the earth'. As in Jn 1: 1 there is no definite article with 'beginning'; the revelation is concerned solely with this world and as much of space as is intimately connected with it, 'the heavens and the earth'. While we are obviously intended to infer that whatever may have come earlier, such as the creation of angelic beings, was equally the sole work of God, the story, as throughout the Bible, confines itself to the area of human experience and activity (cf. Dt. 32: 8).

The translation offered by NEB, GNB, RSVmg, Speiser and many moderns goes back to medi-aeval Jewish commentators and is grammatically possible. It is, however, most unlikely that a chapter written in the lapidary style of Gen. 1 would start with such an involved sentence.

The verb rendered 'created' (*bārā'*), found 44 times in OT, is used only for God's activity and denotes 'the production of something fundamentally new, by the exercise of a sovereign originative power, altogether transcending that possessed by man' (Driver); it contains 'the idea both of complete effortlessness and *creatio ex nihilo*, since it is never connected with any statement of the material' (von Rad). It is used in 1: 21, 27 of the introduction of a new principle in the work of creation. While the opening verse may be intended as an introduction to the narrative as a whole, it is more likely that it refers to the inception of the creative process.

It has been argued by men of very different outlooks that we cannot conceive of the creation of chaos—'formless and empty'— appeal being often made to Isa. 45: 18. Many have used this argument to justify translating, 'and the earth *became* without form and void', cf. NIVmg, thus implying the destruction of the original creation, but this rendering flies in the face of Heb. syntax. In fact the use of 'chaos' rather prejudges the argument. When the building material of the earth came into being, only the eye of God could discern its ultimate purpose. By His Spirit He was sorting it out (v. 2). There is little to commend 'a mighty wind' (NEB, Speiser, von Rad); in the relatively few poetic passages where 'God' is used as a superlative, the context normally makes it clear. The sense is excellently given by 'the power of God' (GNB). The word for 'deep' (*tᵉhôm*) is linked by most with Tiamat, the goddess of chaos in Babylonian mythology. This is probable, but Israel's prophets were so convinced of Yahweh's omnipotence that they never hesitated to use old mythological terms as dead metaphors.

The first day (1: 3–5)

Light is one of God's outstanding attributes (Jn 1: 4 f.; 1 Jn 1: 5; 2 C. 4: 6). No suggestion is made as to where the light came from or how the darkness could coexist with it (cf. Jn 1: 5). The darkness persists within the area allotted to it by God, until at the consummation night disappears (Rev. 21: 25; 22: 5). The fact that the light but not the darkness is commended shows that God's method in creation involves the gradual elimination of the imperfect. This is also indicated by the order 'evening . . . morning' (v. 5), pointing to growing development from the less to the more perfect. The later Jewish method of reckoning the beginning of a day from sunset will have been derived from Gen. 1 and not the other way round.

3. And God said: what is said should express the speaker's thought and will (cf. Jn 1: 1 ff.). This was felt especially in Heb., where *dabar* signifies both a word and the thing named. For God there is no gap between thought, word and result.

4. the light was good (Heb. *ṭôb*): we are apt to use 'good' to express our acceptance; when it is applied to God's judgment, it means conformity to His will. The light was exactly as He intended it to be.

The second day (1: 6–9)
The separation of the atmosphere from the world. For an adequate understanding, it must be remembered that Heb. has no word for gas, a relatively modern coining. **6. expanse** is an attractive rendering of *rāqîaʿ*; the AV 'firmament' is more Latin than English (it derives from the Vulg.), and 'vault' (NEB, JB) and 'dome' (GNB) are only interpretations. Isa. 40: 22 shows that the OT does not necessarily think of a solid vault. Here (v. 7) and in vv. 16, 21 ('created'), 25, we have God's making along with His speaking. The most natural explanation would seem to be that it refers to God's further activity working on something that had come into existence by His command. This would leave room for a God-willed and guided development in that which He had brought into being. There is no divine commendation of the work of the second day, presumably because its work was completed on the third day.

The third day (1: 9–13)
The emergence of dry land. **11. vegetation:** 'grass' (AV, RV) includes the most primitive forms of plant growth; hence Speiser 'Let the earth burst forth with growth'.

The fourth day (1: 14–19)
It is here that the average modern parts company with Genesis. For him it is an absurdity that the sun and moon should come into being after the earth. The usual conservative answers, *e.g.* the sun had not been visible until then because of the clouds shrouding the earth, or that v. 16 is really retrospective (Leupold), have the disadvantage of being unprovable and to the sceptic implausible. It should be noted that **lights** (14, 16) is not the plural of **light** (3 ff.), but would be better rendered 'luminaries' or 'lamps' (von Rad), i.e. they should be regarded as mediators rather than originators of light. This, and the failure to mention sun and

moon by name, shows that there is a deliberate playing down of their importance in an age in which they were almost universally worshipped. They are mentioned because of the function they were to fulfil as the guides to the great and fundamental rhythms of life, which have a greater importance for the animal than for the vegetable creation. This view does not contradict the frequent affirmation that the work of the fourth day is in parallel to that of the first (e.g. Kidner).

The fifth day (1: 20–23)
Gen. 1 does not discuss the problem of where exactly life begins. For it, as for the OT generally, life involves the possibility of action and choice. So we have the term 'living creature' (AV, 'living soul'—*nepheš ḥayyāh*), expressly used of man in 2: 7 (NIV 'living being') applied to the whole of the animal creation, with its ability to create new life, cf. 2: 7; 7: 22.

So we are dealing with an entirely new development in the story of God's activity, and hence we find the word create (*bārā'*) once again, though no indication is given of the exact nature of God's action. **20. birds:** AV 'fowl', literally winged things; the term includes both the winged dinosaurs that preceded true birds and also insects.

The sixth day (1: 24–31)
On the sixth day the work of the fifth is continued on a higher level. The division of the animals is utilitarian rather than scientific, *viz.* those that would be domesticated (**livestock**), smaller animals (**creatures that move along the ground**) and **wild animals**. Then there is a sudden break. Instead of the divine fiat and the linking with what is already there, *e.g.* 'let the earth bring forth', there is an act of God to which He draws attention: **Let us make man** (26). Leupold still argues strongly for the traditional Christian view that the plural refers to the Trinity. This should not be completely rejected, but in its setting it does not carry conviction. The rabbinic interpretation that God is speaking to the angels is more attractive, for man's creation affects them (Ps. 8: 5; 1 C. 6: 3), cf. Job 38: 7. But there is no suggestion of angelic cooperation. Probably the plural is intended above all to draw attention to the importance and solemnity of God's decision.

The new element in the creation of man was that he was to be 'in the image and after the likeness of God', which would show itself above all in his dominion over the animal creation (26). In the immediate context it showed itself in his ability to have communion with God; ultimately, and perhaps most important of all, it made the incarnation of the Word of God possible. Other implications became clear in the course of continuing revelation.

There is a widespread tendency to regard the male as being in some way intrinsically superior to the female. For the effects of the Fall on relationship of the sexes see note on 3: 16. In God's purpose, however, the male and the female are part of the image of God in man. The resultant partnership, equality and voluntary subordination are in some measure a revelation of the Triune God's nature.

The divine judgment **it was very good** (31) causes many to picture Edenic conditions throughout the earth. But it means no more than complete conformity to God's plan; cf. note on v. 4. We should give due weight to the terms used in v. 28 **subdue** (*kābaš*), literally 'stamp on', and **rule over** (*rādāh*), literally 'tread down'. They show that God was presenting man with a major task. We cannot assume from v. 30, that in the original creation there were no carnivores (though this is maintained by Leupold).

The seventh day (2: 1–3)

So perfectly had God's purpose been accomplished that on the seventh day He *šābat*, i.e. ceased (NIVmg, NEB, Speiser), desisted (Driver), completed His work (JB), stopped working (GNB). In the context **rested** is inappropriate (2, 3), for it implies effort which is not otherwise suggested. We see from v. 2 that one could not affirm that God's work was **finished**, until He showed that it was by ceasing (cf. v. 3 mg.) from it (similarly in Exod. 20: 9 the keeping of the Sabbath is a sign, that all of a man's work has been done). That this desisting from creation is final is shown by the omission of any concluding mention of evening and morning. Hence there is no contradiction with Jn 5: 17, where the reference is to works of healing, not creation. Though clearly man in fellowship with God will keep Sabbath (cf. Heb. 4: 9 f.), in the sense of desisting from his own works, there is no evidence for a universal primaeval revelation; Ezra claimed that it was a revelation to Israel (Neh. 9: 14). The failure to realize that the proof of God's having finished was His Sabbath caused Sam., LXX, Syr., Jubilees to read 'on the sixth day' (v. 2), and this has been followed by NEB.

(b) Creation from man's standpoint (2: 4–25)

Whether v. 4 is taken as the conclusion of the former story of creation (SO NEB, JB, GNB, Wiseman) or as the introduction to the second story (SO NIV, RV, Kidner) is of little importance, unless with Wiseman the phrase **This is the account of . . .** is made a clue to the construction of Genesis. In fact (in opposition to *MT*), Skinner, Speiser, NEB, JB, GNB divide the verse between the two stories. It does not seem to make much difference to our understanding.

This story is fairly clearly placed in an arid region, watered only by repeated upsurging of underground water (cf. NEB) which would have made it cultivable, a fact apparently overlooked by Kidner, when he argues for a watery waste. There is, in spite of the arguments of Morris and Whitcomb, no real basis for the view that there was no rain until the Flood, nor is the language here really compatible with it, for it clearly implies that rain was something to be expected.

In the section 2: 4–3: 24 the Creator is called Yahweh Elohim, a title which is virtually unique. The reason for it is not difficult to find. Elohim stresses the power of God, and is the obvious usage in 1: 1–2: 3. Yahweh is God as He reveals Himself to man and cares for him. The double title is to stress that the God of creation is also the God who comes into relationship with man; it helps us also to avoid the type of criticism which contrasts the God of the Old with the God of the New Testament.

5. there was no man: man (*'ādām*) is mankind, including both sexes. It occurs as a proper name only from 4: 25 on, so HOS—its use as a name by NIV in 2: 20, 3: 17, 21; 4: 1 is mistaken. The term is linked with *'adāmāh*, 'tillable ground' (v. 7). Basic for OT concept of man is this verse, i.e. a body from the created world, linking him with all creation, breath, or spirit from God, giving him life and individuality, together create a psycho-somatic unity, a *nepheš ḥayyāh*, a living soul, a living being (cf. note on 1: 21 and Theology of the Old Testament, p. 55). The term **breath** (*nešāmāh*) is used here, rather than 'spirit' (*rûah*), probably to avoid the impression of suggesting that man was a semi-divine being.

Man was created in an arid region made cultivable only by the repeated swelling up of underground water. From there he was moved to a special **garden**, or rather 'park', to the east (vv. 8 f.) in Eden, an unspecified locality—commentators place it with equal confidence in the highlands of Anatolia or Armenia, or at the head of the Persian Gulf. Man was being given the task of extending the conditions of his home to the world around, a thought suggested by vv. 10–14, a section that has received no adequate physical explanation, possibly because of the effects of the Flood. It is to be noted that man had not only to till the garden but also to 'guard' it—**take care** is an unduly weak rendering of *šāmar* (cf. note on 1: 28); there was danger, unspecified, outside. **The Two Trees** (9). Scripture completely rejects the idea behind all magic, i.e. the superstition that man can force God's hand by any word, thing or action. It follows that the knowledge of good and evil as well as the gift of life were attributes God chose to give these trees and not part of their essence. We may even question whether accidental eating by man or beast would have had any effect. In other words, their action was sacramental (Leupold).

17. good and evil are widely regarded as meaning of moral right and wrong, but this is highly improbable. Had man not possessed a moral sense by virtue of his creation, one may question in what sense he was in the image of God. In addition, without such knowledge his disobedience could hardly have been regarded as sin in the full sense. As was pointed out on 1: 4, **good** need not have a moral sense, and the same is true of the use of **evil** (*ra'*); cf. Gen. 47: 9 (NIV 'difficult'), Isa. 45: 7 (NIV 'disaster'). Since man, unlike animals, was not created with an intuitive knowledge of what is good and bad for him, he was dependent on God for daily guidance. Whatever the reason (cf. 3: 22), the tree of life finds no special mention. The warning of the death penalty suggests strongly that the man knew the meaning of the word. It was human death, not animal death, that man's sin introduced into the world—there is nowhere a suggestion of animal immortality —so Adam may have met it in the world outside before he was transferred to the garden. Death for the OT means above all inability to function, and this was the chief result of man's disobedience; God's warning went into full effect. Man's physical death was merely the logical and inevitable sequel.

The Naming of the Animals (18–20). In the ancient world to give a person a name was a sign of authority over him (cf. 2 Kg. 23: 34; 24: 17). So the man's naming of the animals was the first recorded act of dominion over them. Since the account is man-centred, there is no reason to assume that this involved more than the animals indigenous to the area, or that their distribution was very different at the time —note that fish are not mentioned, nor apparently those included under 'creatures that move along the ground'. We are given no indication of the names, for man's first speech was certainly not Hebrew.

The Creation of Woman (20–25). The naming of the animals had impressed upon the man, that in all cases there were two sexes, often markedly different, but that he was alone. True partnership, in contrast to sexual instinct, must be based on a conscious need and desire. Man being in God's image—He is a Trinity—is by nature a social being. So solitariness is not good for him; v. 18 refers to both sexes equally! Since God's creative purpose involved from the first both male and female (1: 27), the first step to cure the aloneness was the creation of the woman to be his partner (so NEB); the Heb. implies the fitting into a unity in which each helps the other equally.

It must be seriously doubted whether *ṣela'* really means rib rather than side (cf. NIVmg). If it is side, then there are scientific secrets hidden here, which lie beyond the scope of this commentary. Unlike any other marriage,

Adam and Eve, though each found completion in the other, were essentially one being, which is the never completely achieved goal of every true marriage (v. 24, 'one flesh'); cf. Ac. 17: 26 (not AV). English is fortunate in being able to reproduce the Heb. assonance *'îš—'iššāh* by man-woman. In contrast to 3: 16 and most modern practice, the man should subordinate his interests to those of his wife (v. 24).

The virtually universal desire of fallen man to cover his body, at least in part, is paralleled by that which is hidden in his psyche, either knowingly, or in deceit of himself and others; i.e. the nakedness here is both literal and symbolic. In 3: 7 (*q.v.*) it seems to take on an even deeper meaning.

ii (a) The Fall of Man (3: 1–24)

1. the serpent: snake (GNB) would be a better rendering, for we are dealing with the normal Heb. word *nāḥāš*. While the link with Satan is implicit in v. 15 and explicit in the NT, it is not explained here. It is presented as the cleverest (Leupold) of the wild animals—there is no bad connotation in the word. The temptation is pictured as coming not from a superior being, but from an inferior, over whom the woman should have exercised dominion. How she heard it is unexplained. It must have been inherently natural, otherwise the shock would have put her on her guard. It seems clear that the voice was the expression of her inmost thoughts and desires. The punishment of the snake (v. 14) must not be understood as meaning that at one time it had legs. Rather, what had once seemed natural and beautiful would now be a perpetual reminder of what it had once done.

Is God Really Good? (1–5). The snake's opening words may be rendered 'Surely God did not tell you you must not eat of *any* tree in the garden'. It spoke as though an incredible rumour had reached it. The woman's answer was impeccable, but her tone of voice will have betrayed her willingness to doubt God's perfect goodness. Her mention of touching the tree must probably be laid at the man's door, as he thought that there might be a catch in God's gift, so it would be better for him to play for safety. With the doubt came the denial: you will not die; God wants to prevent your becoming like Himself. The rendering 'as gods' (AV, RVmg, NEB, JB) is possible, but not so apposite as **like God**. The temptation was to choose independence. The attractiveness of the tree (v. 6) was probably purely subjective. God had not made the temptation more difficult to resist. Evil desire always sheds a spurious attractiveness over that which is contrary to right.

Nakedness (6, 7). No motivation is suggested for the woman's giving the fruit to her husband and for his acceptance. Paul's categorical statement in 1 Tim. 2: 14 that Adam was not deceived, places the major blame on him, and implies that he acted with his eyes open. We may infer that he had already intended eating the fruit, or that he intended **to share his wife's** fate, rather than trusting God, though if the latter is the case, he soon forgot it (v. 12). Here the feeling of nakedness (v. 7) takes on an even deeper symbolic meaning. Both sought independence, but individuals can enjoy it fully, only if they are subordinate to a common centre of authority, which is ultimately God. As they 'liberated' themselves from God, they came into conflict with each other. The closer the relationship the more damaging the sin.

The Results of Sin (8–24). The fear of nakedness in God's presence (v. 9) was hardly a bodily matter; they knew that what they had done could not be hidden from Him. The major problem created by the story as it unfolds is why there is no suggestion of forgiveness from a God, who was to reveal Himself as 'slow to anger, . . . forgiving wickedness, rebellion and sin' (Exod. 34: 7). Why was there no second chance? The answer lies surely in the replies of the man and woman alike; there is not the least suggestion of penitence, or sign that they would have liked to return to complete dependence on their Creator. We see this in the penalties, which strike at the pride of those involved. The offer of Satan is repeatedly glory and power (Mt. 4: 8 f.) for those who follow him, but the result is always ultimately shame, as symbolized by the snake's walk and food. There is no suggestion that the snake's body was changed, but it took on a new meaning; cf. the rainbow (9: 11–15).

The Protevangelium (15). The germinal pronouncement of the gospel. The long conflict between those who are the children of God and the children of the evil one, which is one of the main themes of the OT, is here foretold. Not until the Virgin Birth could the full implication of the promise be understood (cf. Isa. 7: 14). The unfortunate translation by Vulg., perpetuated by R. A. Knox, 'she shall bruise your head', contributed largely to an over-estimate of the Virgin Mary. It should be noted that in contrast to the mediaeval misrepresentation of woman, attributing the main blame for the Fall to her (going back as early as Sir. 25: 24), an attitude unfortunately perpetuated in measure in the Reformation churches, God's promise sees her playing a main rôle in the coming conflict. Man's chief glory is his ability to exercise dominion, so he is humiliated by the rebellion of the soil. In spite of the advances of science, man has never been able to rely on controlling nature, its droughts and pests. Woman's main glory is that new life must come through her. This is not only linked from now on with pain but also with a deep, over-powering desire (the same word as in 4:

6) for her partner, something that lies behind so many broken marriages. In addition she is told that her husband will take advantage of it to rule over her. This is *not* a command, as it is normally rendered; NIV is correct with '**he will rule**'.

It is very widely held in Christian tradition that v. 21 refers to the divine institution of animal sacrifice (cf. note on 4: 3). If this were so, it is very hard to explain why something so fundamental is not made more explicit.

Expulsion from Paradise (22–24). The expulsion from Paradise is depicted as an act of grace. Endless life, which down the ages has been the dream of so many, would be an intolerable burden, if it had no attainable goal, for that depends on man's living fellowship with God (cf. Ec. 1). The motivation for the expulsion, which was obviously made known to man, was to impress on him that, though physical death would not come for many centuries, it was inevitable. In the discussion on 2: 16 f. it was argued that the function of the trees was 'sacramental', in which case a casual eating, in contrast to a deliberate one, would have no effect. The tree of life is never explained, either here or in Rev. 22: 2. Note that in contrast to the tree of the knowledge of good and evil, there was no prohibition of eating it.

The Cherubim (24). In the Tabernacle they formed the throne of God (Exod. 37: 7 ff.). In addition they were embroidered on the veil separating the Holy of Holies (Exod. 36: 35), symbolizing their role as guardians of God's throne, and it is in this capacity that they appear in Ezek. 1: 5 ff.; 10: 1 ff., and Rev.4:6 ff. They are best understood as the representatives of creation. They are the guardians of the tree of life, for they know that apart from the death of the Lord of Life, there would be no salvation for the world (Rom. 8: 18–23). Note that the **flaming sword** (24), not otherwise mentioned, was not held by the cherubim.

(b) **Cain and Abel (4: 1–16)**
We are now introduced to a series of events showing us how quickly the results of the Fall were revealed. As was said on 3: 7, the first effects of sin were seen in the family, and it is entirely consistent with this that the first murder is fratricide.

Murder occupied a unique position among sins in the OT. It is the only one for which there is a universal, mandatory death penalty, quite apart from the Sinaitic law (9: 6). This is mainly because it is the only act for which no form of reparation is possible, life being God's gift. Even the taking of animal life for food was to recognize this principle (9: 4).

1. With the help of the LORD I have brought forth a man: mediaeval commentaries, as well as some later ones, understood Eve's joyful words as meaning, 'I have gotten a man, even

Yahweh', as though she thought that Cain was the fulfilment of the promise of 3: 15. This is highly improbable, though it is a possible rendering of the Heb. On the other hand her recognition that her son was Yahweh's gift suggests a growing trust in God (cf. 4: 25).

The Brothers' Offerings (3–7). No suggestion of previous tension between the brothers is mentioned. The time came, when they brought an offering (*minḥāh*) to Yahweh. The word used means a gift, and is the regular word for tribute brought to a ruler. We should not import any redemptive meaning into the brothers' sacrifices, cf. 8: 20; they were the recognition of Yahweh's lordship. Both gave of what they had, and so Leupold is certainly correct in saying, 'Those who see the merit of Abel's sacrifice in the fact that it was bloody certainly do so without the least warrant from the text'. We are not told how Cain knew his sacrifice had not been accepted. The reason for the rejection is suggested in v. 6, 'If you do what is right'. The probability is that he resented having to accept God's lordship (cf. v. 13).

The Heb. of v. 7 is difficult, but we need not doubt that the general sense has been given by NIV (cf. NEB, GNB) when it sees sin personified as a ravenous beast. Speiser's rendering, 'sin is a demon at the door', is worth mentioning.

8. Cain said to Abel . . . 'Let's go out to the field': i.e. the open country. The addition to the Heb. text (cf. AV, RV text) is necessitated by Heb. linguistic usage, and is supported by Sam. and all the versions. It suggests that the murder of Abel was premeditated.

Cain's answer to God's question (9) shows that he had lost Adam's consciousness of nakedness before God (3: 10). That Cain felt no remorse is seen in his suggestion that God was being unfair to him (13). The putting of a mark, unspecified, on Cain (15) is no contradiction of what is said earlier about the mandatory nature of the death penalty for murder. Abel's blood was crying to God for vengeance (10) and therefore it was not the responsibility of others to take vengeance.

16. the land of Nod: i.e. the land of wandering, of nomads. **17. Cain lay with his wife:** there is no reason for questioning the traditional explanation that she was his sister (cf. 5: 4). **Building a city** ('îr): though NIV has normally retained the traditional rendering of 'city' for 'îr, it really means a fortified settlement, irrespective of size. Evidently a number of Cain's relations followed him. This is another downward step. Whether the wall was a protection against possible enemies or wild beasts, those who should have ruled show their fear of being ruled.

(c) **The Descendants of Cain (4: 17–26)**
Though, as a result of the Flood, Cain's descendants were to play no lasting part in human history, this genealogical list shows that they were not forgotten by God, and come as much within the scope of His salvation as others who died before the time of the Saviour.

The mention of the development of the arts and crafts seems to suggest that the effects of the knowledge of good and evil showed themselves especially among the Cainites.

19. Lamech: here we have the first mention of polygamy which, contrary to superficial, popular views, is far less common in the OT than is often supposed. When it is met, there is normally what seemed a valid reason for it, but none is here suggested. Lamech is claiming not a life for a life, but a life for a blow (cf. Exod. 22: 23 f.), and is even claiming divine sanction for his attitude.

The account of Cain's descendants breaks off here, because Lamech is a sufficient explanation of their disappearance.

(d) **Seth and his Descendants (4: 25–5: 32)**
The Worship of Yahweh (4: 26). Modern scholarship generally denies that the worship of Yahweh goes back to such an early date and bases itself on Exod. 3: 13 f.; 6: 3; but cf. Speiser, p. 37. If the records recovered for us by archaeology contain any mention of the name of Yahweh, it is at best in a shortened form. The most likely explanation would seem to be that offered by Martin Buber (pp. 48–55), that a primitive sacred call received a fuller meaning at the burning bush.

Adam to Noah (5: 3–31). The list of ten names in 5: 3–31 raises a number of problems of little spiritual importance. There is not likely to be any importance in the fact that a number of the names resemble those in the previous chapter, nor is there much value in finding possible Heb. meanings for the names, except in the case of Noah, for they were not originally Heb. More important, perhaps, is the length of life recorded for the ten figures in the genealogies, which range between 969 and 365 years. Various, mainly unsatisfactory, explanations have been offered. It is worth noting that in the Babylonian tradition the lives of the nine or ten antediluvian kings vary between 18,600 and 65,000 years. This shows that there was a tradition of antediluvian longevity, and it is easiest to assume that the effects of the Fall were slow in showing themselves except in the moral sphere.

MT gives 1656 years from the Creation to the Flood. Sam. and Jubilees (a second cent. B.C., non-canonical book linked with Qumran) reduce the figure to 1307, while LXX and Josephus increase it to 2242. Similar variations are found in ch. 11. There is general agreement that these variations are not accidental, but no adequate explanation for them has yet been offered. Only *a priori* prejudice will insist that

MT must be correct. This shows how hazardous chronological schemes can be.

No explanation is given for the long delay before Seth was born (5: 3). In the light of 5:4, it is unlikely that it was due to any impairment of Eve's fertility. Rather this is an example of God's deferring His activity in salvation until it is fully appreciated (cf. Isaac). It is not coincidence that it was Eve who recognized the significance of Seth, as is evident from her cry of joy over him (4: 25). We should assume that God made her realize that there was a special significance bound up with this new son.

The language of v. 3 must be taken seriously, also the fact that it is linked with Seth. Even on the godly line, in the line of salvation, the effects of the Fall become visibly obvious; it must not be understood to imply that the image of God had now vanished.

21. Enoch: the language used about Enoch is so cryptic that all speculation is out of place. It should not be forgotten that it is never expressly stated that Elijah did not die (2 Kg. 2: 9–14), though we are probably to infer it. The unprovable assumption that the two witnesses of Rev. 11 are Enoch and Elijah is based on a proper understanding of the theological problems involved. The most important point for us is that in Enoch's translation we have proof of the working out of Christ's redemptive power in the past. **29. Noah:** Heb. nōaḥ. Lamech links his name with Heb. nahēm ('comfort') and nūaḥ ('rest').

(e) **The Growth of Evil (6: 1–8)**
2. the sons of God: this term is used in the OT only of angelic beings, perhaps of higher rank. It was only because the possibility of sexual relationships contradicted the general concepts of angels, that early rabbinic expositors understood it to mean persons of high social class, i.e. there was a disregard of social differences, and very early the Church Fathers, followed by many of the Reformers, referred it to the descendants of Seth (so Leupold). The earliest Jewish interpretation was of angelic beings; so LXX, Jubilees, Enoch, Josephus (cf. 2 Pet. 2: 4; Jude 6). **4 Nephilim:** cf. Num. 13: 33, where they are giants, but here probably 'the fallen ones'. The obvious inference is that they were the offspring of the unions just mentioned, and the setting suggests that they were the ring-leaders in the evil being described. It also suggests that there was a reality behind the old mythological stories of amoral men of great strength. The mention that there were Nephilim later does not imply that they survived the Flood, but rather that the name lived on for men of great stature and strength as in Num. 13: 33.

The LORD's words in v. 3 are very difficult to translate and to interpret. The verb dūn (NIV 'contend with') is found only here and is rendered 'strive' (AV, RV) and 'abide' (old versions, RSV, NEB)—GNB paraphrases 'I will not allow people to live for ever'; JB has 'My spirit must not for ever be disgraced'. The force of **My spirit** is also not clear. We seem to have to choose between, 'My spirit shall not judge among mankind for ever' (Luther, Leupold), i.e. seek to restrain the growing evil (in which case the 120 years would be the period for repentance before the Flood came); or we can follow NEB, 'My life-giving spirit shall not remain in man . . . he shall live for a hundred and twenty years' (so essentially Speiser, JB, GNB). The objection that many of the post-diluvian ancestors of Abraham lived much longer is invalid, as Noah and his family had been taken out of the punishment for evil.

More important is God's judgment on man (5): his wickedness was great and 'every scheme that his mind devised was nothing but evil all the time' (Speiser). It is often suggested, especially by Jews, that the OT does not know the doctrine of original sin, or of man's essential depravity. Both are surely indicated here. So much is this the case that the rabbis based the doctrine of the yēṣer raʻ, the evil impulse which is in every man, on it—they balanced it, however, by postulating a yēṣer ṭôb, a good impulse nourished mainly by the study of Torah. Later, when faced by Christian teaching, they tended to soft-pedal the whole concept. The statement of God's grief (6) is typical anthropomorphic language, but bearing in mind the frequent criticisms of the God of the OT, it should be stressed that God is depicted as having no pleasure in the death of the sinner.

However this section is interpreted, it should be noted that man's sin is not laid at the door of the illicit breaking in of angelic powers; rather this was made possible by man's sin.

(f) **The Flood (6: 9–8: 19)**
Our interpretation of the Flood story will depend in great measure on how we understand the inspiration of the Bible's historical narratives. There is no doubt that it guarantees their accuracy, spiritually, at any rate. The qualification means simply, that the biblical narratives do not necessarily give the picture that would have been offered by a secular historian, had he been present. The vital question is whether the biblical narrator gives an accurate picture of events as they were known to him and as they were interpreted by the Holy Spirit, or whether he was given information by the Holy Spirit of facts he could not have discovered for himself. If we are to judge from later historical narratives, the former is correct, for the sources used by the later writer are often mentioned by name. It must not be overlooked that the Bible regularly uses popular, non-scientific language in describing natural phenomena. The wording of 2 Pet. 3: 5 f., so confidently appealed to in

this context, can be paralleled by passages like Ps. 24: 1 f.; Am. 7: 4. If we accept the latter view, we must believe from 7: 19 that the water washed over the highest peaks of the world, and in addition that every form of animal life, except for those in the Ark, ceased (7: 22). It seems probable that 'the universality of the flood simply means the universality of the experience of the man who reported it' (Ramm). In favour of this view, unless it is maintained that the distribution of animals in the world was at that time very different from what it was later, it relieves us from supposing that Noah fetched his animals from enormous distances and provided food for those demanding exceptional diets. There is no biblical warrant for the idea that God brought the animals to Noah.

The views of Whitcomb and Morris are not primarily based on biblical exposition, but on certain geological observations (cf. Byrt), and cannot therefore be treated here. It should, however, be noted that they virtually involve a re-creation, which would be in conflict with the message of the Sabbath (2: 1–3).

6: 14. an ark: Heb. *tēbāh*. The word in the Flood narrative is apparently of Akkadian origin; the same word is used in Exod. 2: 3, where it is certainly an Egyptian word; neither has any link with the ark of the covenant. Its size, assuming the cubit to have its later length of eighteen inches, was 450 feet by 75 by 45 high. It was not a ship in the ordinary sense; its purpose was to float and not to be navigated; hence Moffatt's quite appropriate rendering 'barge'.

If we ignore the general setting and the gross polytheistic distortions in the Babylonian Flood account, there are striking similarities between it and the Bible story (cf. Heidel, *The Gilgamesh Epic*). It is usually taken for granted that the Genesis story is derived from the Babylonian, but since we are dealing with living memories of a tremendous disaster, there is no valid reason why both should not be based on valid records of the event, though the Babylonian account is further from the reality, and contributes nothing to the Bible account.

16. Make a roof (mg, 'opening'): the meaning of the Heb. word *sōhar*, found only here, is uncertain. The most satisfactory explanation is that given by Driver: 'a kind of casement running round the sides of the ark (except where interrupted by the beams supporting the roof) a little below the roof' (so essentially GNB).

17. flood waters: Heb. uses *mabbûl*, which is found only of Noah's flood, cf. Ps. 29: 10. **18. I will establish my covenant with you:** there can be little doubt that this looks forward to 9: 8–17. Exod. 19: 5 shows how a covenant can be referred to before any of its details have been given (so Leupold). **19. two of all:** there

is no contradiction in the mention of 'seven pairs of all clean animals' (7: 2). While there is no need to assume that for Noah the division between clean and unclean was identical with that found in Lev. 11 and Dt. 14, such a division is virtually universal. Since it is based on food use, this is virtually a recognition that the beginnings of a meat diet preceded 9: 3.

On the supposition of a localized flood 7: 11 would seem to refer to a tidal wave sweeping water in from the Persian Gulf. This would help to explain why the ark finished up in the far north of the Mesopotamian plain. (Many suggest that dammed up water in the Armenian mountains, held by an ice barrier remaining from the last ice age, was also released, but this must remain supposition.) Such a sudden rush of waters helps to explain why no one was able to save his life.

7: 16. Then the LORD shut him in: the note of finality in judgment and protection could not be expressed more dramatically. The use of Yahweh here stresses the gracious protection.

The Flood lasted a year all but a month and a half (7: 11; 8: 13), of which forty days were of downpour (7: 12), the next 150 of inundation (7: 24): the slope of the Mesopotamian plain is so slight that the run off would be slow. The months are reckoned as having thirty days, but it is most improbable that any significance is to be read into this. To do so is to assume that an accurate measure of the month and year, in contrast to an approximate one, had already been calculated.

8: 4. the mountains of Ararat: Ararat, Assrian *Urartu*, is NE Armenia, near Lake Van. Mt. Ararat is *c.* 17,000 feet high, but the name was only later applied to this peak, and Heb. implies no more than a peak in this region. It is a gratuitous assumption of a miracle to make the animals find their way down through ice and snow from such a height.

Additional Note: Archaeological Evidence for the Flood

It caused a major sensation, when Sir Leonard Woolley claimed in 1929 that he had discovered indubitable evidence for the Flood during his excavations at Ur. Shortly afterwards S. H. Langdon made a similar claim for discoveries at Kish. Similar discoveries were made also at Uruk and Shuruppak, but it soon became evident that the flood strata at the various sites came from different dates. Details and literature can be found in Parrot. These discoveries proved that Mesopotamia had been subject to periodic major floods, none of which seem great enough to fit the Bible story, or even the tradition preserved in the Gilgamesh epic.

ii (a) God's Covenant with Man

8: 20. burnt offerings: consistent with the general tenor of Genesis, only burnt offerings, a recognition of God's sovereignty—not sin or peace offerings—are mentioned (cf. note on 4: 3). **21. Never again will I curse** (*leqallēl*) **the ground:** there are two words in Heb. rendered 'to curse' or 'cursed'. *'ārar* carries the same force as in English, cf. Gen. 9: 25, Dt. 27: 15, 16, etc., but this form of *qal* implies the utterance of a derogatory word (cf. Zech 9: 13, RSV). The implication here is that God had treated the ground as though it had no value. In contrast to Kidner, the promise was not based so much on the accepted sacrifice as on man's incorrigibility (Leupold), for punishment which is ineffective is not God's method. The promise of v. 22 is not one of complete immunity from natural disaster, but that it would not be universal nor destroy the normal balance of nature. There is nothing here to suggest that natural disasters are of necessity a sign of God's anger.

It is quite clear from 9: 1–3, that mankind now traces its origin to Noah, and so the original charge to Adam (1: 28) is repeated with significant changes. Noah was 'a righteous man, blameless among the people of his time' (6: 9), but the corruption around him had left its mark, if not on him, then on his sons. Though 'the image of God' (9: 6) was still there, it had been so marred, that man's dominion would be marked by fear and dread (v. 2), and the outward sign of this was man's using the animals for food, though the denial of blood (cf. note on 4: 1) was to underline man's fall from what he was at the first.

On vegetarianism as a possibly more healthy form of life the Bible has nothing to say. It certainly never suggests that it may be spiritually preferable, for such a concept belongs to 'the basic principles of this world' (Col. 2: 20–23), which in themselves have no value.

Many Christians support the maintenance or enforcement of the death penalty on the basis of v. 6. There can be no doubt that the concept of the sanctity of human life has greatly decreased in recent years, but there is considerable doubt whether the restoration of the death penalty would increase it again. Punishment for the sake of punishment is not God's method. **9: 11. my covenant:** Speiser gives the traditional definition: 'a solemn agreement between two parties, providing sanctions in the event of non-compliance'. Today, however, the concept of the 'suzerainty covenant' (Mendenhall) has been rightly popularized, which sees God acting unilaterally as sovereign lord, demanding only the acceptance and keeping of the covenant by the people (cf. Exod. 19: 5). The present covenant goes even beyond the typical suzerainty, for it was made with the animals as well, and so was an expression of the sovereign grace of God. **14. the rainbow appears in the clouds:** there is nothing in the Heb. to suggest that the rainbow was some-

thing new (so Leupold), but rather that a new meaning was given to it.

(*b*) **Noah and his Sons (9: 18–28)**
18. Shem, Ham and Japheth: in spite of Leupold's argument, v. 24 shows that Ham was the youngest; this seems to be supported by 10: 21, which makes Shem the oldest.
20. Noah, a man of the soil: NIVmg is preferred; cf. GNB 'Noah, who was a farmer, was the first man to plant a vineyard (so NEB, JB), though Leupold, 'Noah began as a farmer to plant a vineyard', is probably more correct. It is intrinsically improbable that wine was unknown before this, and the Heb. does not affirm this. Though it is not explicitly stated, it is generally assumed that Noah's drunkenness, though not his making of wine, was culpable (so Kidner, Leupold). **25. Canaan:** apparently Ham's youngest son (10: 2). No indication is offered why he and not his father should be cursed, nor why the curse should be on him rather than his brothers. Leupold's suggestion that it is a prophetic curse on what the Canaanites were later to be (but in Gen. 15: 16 it is the Amorites rather than the Canaanites) carries little conviction. Obviously he had done something despicable. The use of this passage to justify negro slavery and the superiority of the white man is as evil a misuse of Scripture as to justify antisemitism on the basis of Mt. 27: 25.

The blessing on Shem (26) suggests that Noah knew that he, more than his brothers, had accepted the knowledge of Yahweh passed on by his father. In spite of this, by the time of Terah and Abram, his descendants seem to have been idolaters (Jos. 24: 2). Japheth would enter blessing in the measure he accepted Shem's knowledge of God.

(*c*) **The Descendants of Japheth, Ham and Shem (10: 1–32)**
It has been shown that this chapter represents the world as it was known to Israel at the time of Solomon. Not all the nations known to Israel figure in it, and with our present limited knowledge, it would be impossible to fit some of the modern ones into it with any certainty. Once again we have an indication that inspiration is not concerned with the imparting of unknown facts of no spiritual importance. Those desiring further details are referred to *NBD* or other modern Bible dictionary.
9. Nimrod: see *NBD*. He was more than 'a mighty warrior'. GNB gives the sense, 'he became the world's first great conqueror'; he was also, apparently, the initiator of the Assyrian belief that a king among men had to show his right to rule by his prowess in hunting animals, especially lions. **before the LORD** is in the first place a superlative, implying a very great hunter, but it is probably also sarcastic—he showed his right to rule over the kingdom

he had created by force by killing the animal creation that God had entrusted to him. The OT nowhere shows any admiration for 'blood sports'. **15. Canaan:** linguistically the Canaanites, including the Phoenicians, were Semites, and Hebrew is derived from Old Canaanite, but so far as extant evidence goes, they were not ethnically Semites.

(d) The Tower of Babel (11: 1–9)

Before we are given Abram's ancestry, this story stresses why a new beginning had become necessary. The memory of the Flood (4) seems only to have acted merely as a call to show man's power in defiance of God. The living memory of what they did was preserved by the great *ziggurat*, 'a temple-covered artificial mountain' (Kidner), of Babylon. This followed the pattern set earlier, but no known relic of the Tower of Babel is left, nor is any likely to be found by the archaeologist, for the earliest levels of the city lie below the water-table of the plain. Studies of languages that were never reduced to writing have shown how quickly peoples with a common linguistic background have become unintelligible to one another. We have no indication of the identity of the pre-diluvian language, if it has indeed been preserved. God was acting in complete impartiality.

9. Babel: related here to *bālal* ('confound') and interpreted as 'confusion'. Babel is the universal OT form for Babylon (Akkadian *Bab-ili*, meaning the gate of God). The change was obviously deliberate.

(e) The Ancestry of Terah (11: 10–32)

Whatever may be thought of the figures given in ch. 5 for the lives of the pre-diluvian patriarchs, those given here—they show the same type of variants as in ch. 5 between *MT*, Sam., LXX and Jubilees—are completely inadequate to span the gap between the Flood and Abram, *c.* 2000 B.C. The name Eber has been found in recent excavations at Tell Mardikh in N. Syria (ancient Ebla), as the name of one of its kings. It is a serious misuse of archaeology to identify him with **Eber** (14 ff.), who will in any case have lived too early to fill the rôle being used. It shows merely that the name is of the type being used.

II. THE BEGINNINGS OF ISRAEL (12: 1–50: 26)

i. Abraham (12: 1–25: 18)

(a) Arrival in Canaan (12: 1–20)

Although Abram has been mentioned in the final verses of ch. 11, there is no doubt that ch. 12 commences a new major section of Genesis. It is now that the reader begins to discern the character and personality of Abram, as he takes on flesh and blood; it is now that Palestine at last comes into the story; and it is now that some of the great theological themes of the book reveal themselves clearly: the promised land, the promised people, and the response of

faith. There is a forward look to the whole narrative; not only do later events cast their shadows before them, but there is also a deeper and more spiritual dimension (cf. Heb. 11: 8–16).

1 ff. Abram was introduced to the reader in ch. 11 as without offspring, and resident in Haran, many miles north of Palestine. All this was to change, but by no accident of coincidence; it was in consequence of the plans of **the LORD** and the ready obedience of the patriarch. The call and promises constitute the election of God, though the term is not used; it was the sovereign unpredictable choice of God to single out Abram as the recipient of the message contained in vv. 2 f. The promise says little about **the land**, which he will soon see for himself; but the **great nation** lay far in the future, and indeed there was as yet no sign of any heir. Abram and his progeny will enjoy a great reputation, too; this God-given **name** contrasting with that sought by the men of Babel (11: 4). In this context, it is probable that the last clause of v. 2 means that Abram's name will 'be used in blessings' (NEB), and that v. 3 ends with the statement: by you all the families of the earth shall bless themselves. The last Heb. verb is ambiguous, and the LXX understood it to mean 'shall be blessed'; it is the LXX which is cited in Ac. 3: 25 and Gal. 3: 8. In any case, the ultimate blessing of mankind is implied if not stated.

4–9. The chosen family arrive at the promised land—**the land of Canaan** (5), as it would be known for many centuries yet. The family might be styled a clan (cf. 14: 14), but attention is drawn to Abram and the other two individuals who are prominent in the story. The land was by no means empty, as the note in v. 6 acknowledges, although there was evidently ample space for the newcomers. There were moreover a number of cities and sanctuaries, of which **Shechem** (6) and **Bethel** (8) were of special significance. They were to be no less important to Israel in later years, and we see Abram symbolically claiming them for the LORD, Israel's God. It was however the far south of the country, toward **the Negev** (9), which particularly suited the patriarchs with their flocks and herds.

Abram's age is given as **seventy-five** (4). Kidner points out that the patriarchal life-span seems to be approximately double today's norm; if we halve them we will get a better impression of the age, physical vigour, or beauty implied at various points in the narrative.

10–20. This is the first of three very similar narratives (see ch. 20; and cf. 26: 6–11). It is important to seek to see the function of each one in its own context. There is dramatic irony in this chapter; Abram has only just reached the land of promise when he is driven out of it by force of natural circumstances! No emphasis is laid on any lack of faith on his part, nor on his prevarication. The point is rather that he was at the mercy of events, of circumstances, and of stronger political forces; it could only be **the LORD** (17) who would rescue him from adverse circumstances. There was an important lesson here for Abram's descendants, who were all too often tempted to pride and self-sufficiency (cf. Jg. 7: 2).

(b) **Separation from Lot (13: 1–18)**
1–7. Abram now retraced his steps, via **the Negev** (1) as far as **Bethel** (3). The overriding theme is still the territorial issue: the patriarch had been shown that Canaan was to be his homeland, but he had yet to find a suitable home within it. At first the Bethel area proved attractive, but here problems arose (5 ff.), due to the very fact of the increasing prosperity of the family. The growing size of the herds (livestock of various kinds, cf. NEB, GNB) required a good deal of free range. There were two immediate disadvantages to the Bethel area: in the first place it was a fairly hilly region, with limited pasture lands; and secondly, earlier occupants were by no means absent from this part of Palestine (7). (Little is known about the **Perizzites**; perhaps they were to be found only in this particular locality.) It may well have been the attempt to avoid a clash with Canaanite neighbours which led to **quarrelling** between Abram's clan-group and that of Lot (7).
8–13. In geographical terms, the separation between the two men meant that Lot chose southern Transjordan as his domain, while Abram stayed in Palestine proper, west of the Jordan: this situation prefigured the later national situation, when Moab and Ammon (Lot's descendants) occupied southern Transjordan. This region was in general more fertile than most of Palestine—and v. 10 relates that its fertility was outstanding at this early date, comparable with that of Eden. Verse 13 anticipates chs. 18 f., but it serves to show that Lot made the wrong choice spiritually.
14–18. Abram, by contrast, is shown clearly that his choice is the right one. The divine promises of these verses recapitulate and emphasize those of 12: 2 f. The future growth of the population and territory of Israel are to be contrasted with Lot's progeny, two Transjordanian kingdoms which were always small and insignificant.

Abram is invited to traverse **the land** promised to him even more widely (17). No doubt he did; but v. 18 is content to name the place where he finally chose to settle, **Mamre** near **Hebron**. The **trees** there were probably already held to be sacred; as earlier at Shechem and Bethel, Abram here symbolically lays

claim to a sacred site for the worship of the true God.

(c) **The Battle of the Kings (14: 1–24)**
Gen. 14 is a unique chapter, which has occasioned a vast amount of discussion and dispute. It stands apart from all the other narratives about Abram, and presents him in a very different light; the peaceful patriarch is here a successful warrior. Theologically, it is not easy to see the purpose and function of the story. From a historical point of view, the chapter is tantalizing: one might have hoped that so much data about contemporary kings would have given us firm dates for Abram's lifetime, and further, that records from other nations would have given some confirmation of the events here related. Hitherto, however, neither hope has been realized. The lack of confirmation has led to increasing doubts about the historicity of the story. A particular difficulty is the unparalleled mention of a king of Elam campaigning so far from his own homeland; it is also surprising to find Mesopotamian powers at such an early date not only campaigning in Palestine but controlling part of it for twelve years or so (4). On the other hand, the most sceptical of scholars will usually admit that there are numerous details in the story which show genuine antiquity and realism. E. A. Speiser's treatment of the chapter is helpful; he has made the most of such archaeological evidence as is available, even though some of his arguments have been subjected to major criticism. Two points on behalf of historicity may be made: firstly, none of the details of the story has been disproved by any archaeological find; and secondly, whatever 'improbabilities' the chapter may contain, it is hard to imagine any plausible reason why such a story should have come into being if it had no historical basis whatever.
1–12. The link with the previous chapter is the mention of **Sodom** (2), followed up by reference to **Lot** (12). It is quickly shown that Lot's choice of terrain, despite appearances, had been far from ideal; not only was Sodom notoriously wicked, but its wealth proved a temptation to outside powers from as far afield as Mesopotamia. None of the invaders is known to us from other sources, unless perhaps **Tidal** is the Hittite king Tudkhalia I (c. 1700 B.C.); it is certain that Amraphel is not Hammurabi (an equation often made in the past). All four names are at least very appropriate for that era and that part of the world. Of their territories, **Shinar** (i.e. Babylonia) and **Elam** are well known; but **Ellasar** has not been identified, and neither has **Goiim** (which is the ordinary Heb. word for 'nations', and is not necessarily a placename here).

The five Palestinian kings (2) ruled in a specific region, **the Valley of Siddim**, apparently at the southern end of the Dead Sea (see notes on 19: 25); but evidently the confederate invaders had other foes, and they followed a curiously circuitous route (5 ff.) before joining battle with **the king of Sodom** and his allies: see map 24 in the *Macmillan Bible Atlas*. The invaders won, and **Lot** found himself a captive (12).

13–16. Abram now comes into the story for the first time; he need not have become involved, and his unselfish loyalty to his kinsman contrasts with the selfishness Lot had shown (13: 10 f.). The size of Abram's household (14) comes as a surprise; even so, he commanded no large army of 'retainers' (so NEB, correctly), and we should understand the sequel as a prolonged harassment of the confederates' rear, from **Dan** (at the time called Laish; cf. Jg. 18: 27 ff.) to **Hobah**. Thus rescued, **Lot** was free to return home to Sodom.

17–24. The question of relationships is a not unimportant aspect of the patriarchs' settlement in Palestine. In this chapter we see Abram in alliance with the people of the clans of the Hebron area (13), and in his activities on behalf of Lot showing himself a good neighbour to all the city states of Canaan. Two of the local kings responded warmly. Obviously **the king of Sodom** (17) was under obligation to Abram, and his offer (21) was natural enough; but Abram meant to be under no debt to any man —least of all the king of a city of Sodom's reputation (22 ff.).

The chief interest in the story centres on the other king, however: **Melchizedek** of Jerusalem (a name occasionally abbreviated as **Salem**, cf. Ps. 76: 2). There are several levels of meaning to be considered. On the purely factual level, the story is simple enough: a local Canaanite ruler makes a friendly gesture to the returning hero, provides a simple repast for his men, pronounces a blessing upon him, and receives a small share of the booty. Evidently the kingship of Jerusalem involved sacral functions. The deity worshipped by Melchizedek was 'Ēl 'Elyôn (**God Most High**); El was worshipped by the Canaanites as their supreme deity, as father and creator, and the title Most High was also well known to them. The wording of Abram's reply (22) makes it clear that this God worshipped by Melchizedek was none other than **the LORD**—the God who had appeared personally to him. The story would have been very different if Melchizedek had been a devotee of Baal!

At another level of meaning, there is undeniably symbolism here. The name Melchizedek can be translated 'king of righteousness' (cf. Heb. 7: 2), in marked contrast to the king of Sodom, whose name Bera (v. 2) apparently means 'in evil' (just as Birsha means 'in wickedness')—whatever the original sense and function of these names. Sodom was, as we know,

doomed; but Jerusalem (which figures nowhere else in Genesis) had a notable future marked out for it, as the city of God's choice and presence. It was wholly fitting, therefore, that the ancestor of Israel should stand under the blessing of the God already revered in Jerusalem.

If Abram thus represents the people of Israel, Melchizedek represents the future Davidic king (cf. Ps. 110: 4). Heb. 7, although its stress is more on the priesthood of Melchizedek, correctly recognizes his superior status *vis-à-vis* Abram. Thus Gen. 14 prefigures the rule of David and his descendants.

(d) **The Promised Land (15: 1–21)**
After the digression of ch. 14, the story reverts to the theme of God's promises to Abram; the new promise to act as Abram's **shield** (1) may well reflect on the military dangers exemplified in ch. 14. All the promises Abram had received, however, could only be dependent on his having an heir; but Sarai remained barren (11: 30). In the meantime proper legal provision had to be made, and it appears that Abram had already taken the steps normal in that part of the world at the time: he had 'adopted' a slave to become his **heir** (3). (See J. A. Thompson, *The Bible and Archaeology*, ch. 2.) This slave's name was **Eliezer**, but in view of difficulties and obscurities in the Heb. text, his exact position in the household (? steward) is uncertain and the reference to **Damascus** doubtful. Theoretically, at any rate, Eliezer could have provided Abram with heirs, but one can readily appreciate Abram's cry from the heart, '**what can you give me . . . ?**' In other words, 'what good will your reward do me . . . ?' (GNB). The gracious response set his mind at rest; his heir would be his own flesh and blood (4). But note that nothing is revealed as to the mother's identity!

Verse 6 is a key verse, drawing attention to Abram's faith and to the divine response to it. The three key terms are **believed, credited** and **righteousness.** The language is reminiscent of that of sacrifice and acceptance; cf. Lev. 7: 18; 17: 4, as the GNB paraphrase seeks to convey; but the basis of Abram's acceptance is not his sacrifices and altars but his faith, which means in context 'a consent to God's plans in history' (G. von Rad). For the more far-reaching implications, see Rom. 4, Gal. 3 and Jas 2: 14–26. It is the tranquil and obedient acceptance of God's plans (of history and of salvation) which places man in the right relationship with God.

7–21. Just as Abram had sought reassurance about his heir, so now he seeks reassurance concerning his territory, asking for some sign from God. We may reasonably assume that he had returned to Mamre, and he probably had limited horizons, looking for a territorial holding in that locality: the Heb. word translated **land** (7) is as vague as our word 'territory'. Later Abram was to acquire a small piece of land near Mamre by ordinary purchase (23: 16–20); the contrast here is startling. He and his **descendants** will be **given**—not sold—a vast territory, from the borders of **Egypt** to **the river Euphrates** (18). The lengthy list of individual peoples to be conquered or dispossessed (19 ff.) emphasizes the size and wonder of the promise. It was only in David's reign that fulfilment came; it should be noted that **the river of Egypt** (18) must be a boundary wadi (NIVmg) (probably the Wadi el-Arish), not the Nile. The total area is that of David's empire, not just of Israel's homeland.

This then, was the promise; but what of the sign? It was provided by **a covenant** (18), that is to say a solemn legal agreement, into which God voluntarily entered. The elaborate details of the ceremony (8–11, 17), which can be paralleled in a variety of ancient Near Eastern documents, emphasize both the solemnity of the undertaking and the gracious condescension of God, whose own presence is to be recognized in vv. 12, 17. Ever afterwards this covenant was to prove a reassurance and an inspiration to Israelites and Jews (not least in twentieth-century Zionism). The 'how' and 'when' of the promise, however, are entirely within God's control, as is at once demonstrated in vv. 13–16. Before the dimensions of the promised land are set out, the historical perspective is given priority. Abram's descendants face a very long wait, and bondage and oppression too, before the land will be theirs. The reason is noteworthy; nothing is said here of Israel's merits or shortcomings, but only of the demerits of **the Amorites** (16), the pre-Israelite population. Not until they deserve thorough-going punishment will they be conquered.

The time-scale envisaged is a puzzle, since four generations (cf. v. 16) is rather shorter than **four hundred years** (13). The Heb. word *dôr* usually means **generation**, but in this context 'lifespan' (i.e. of patriarchal dimensions) seems more suitable. See the note on Exod. 12: 40.

(e) **The Birth of Ishmael (16: 1–15)**
In spite of the promise of 15: 4, Sarai's barrenness continued, and **ten years** after his arrival in **Canaan** Abram still found himself childless (1 ff.). He had already explored one avenue to provide for an heir (see note on 15: 2 f.); now Sarai took the initiative, adopting yet another common practice of the time; copies of contracts have survived in which the wife placed herself under obligation to provide for an heir, if necessary, by supplying a slave girl to her husband. As Speiser points out, a legal situation ('as complex as it is authentic') is presented to the reader, and it is clear that all three parties

were not altogether blameless in the development of events. 'Beyond all the legal niceties,' says Speiser, 'are the tangled emotions of the characters in the drama.' Indeed, the story is an eloquent testimony to the heartlessness of the law and convention, and also to the psychological damage which polygamous unions so readily cause.

However, that is not the point of the story; and it is doubtful if Gal. 4: 23 gives us sufficient warrant to moralize over Abram's actions. (*Both* sons were born, literally speaking, 'of the flesh'; but Ishmael's birth was *only* 'in the usual way', as GNB renders it, whereas Isaac's came about 'as a result of God's promise'.) Abram, after all, had not been reproved for (temporarily) making Eliezer his heir; and he is nowhere reproved for engendering Ishmael, who in God's purposes was to be blessed and to father a great nation (cf. 17: 20). The point lies, rather, in the protracted testing of Abram's faith, and in the absolute sovereignty of God's choice, which could have rested on Ishmael—but did not.

Hagar's contempt for **her mistress** (4) led inevitably to the equally wrongful, harsh treatment of the girl by Sarai, while Abram opted out of a decision (6). Hagar's flight in the direction of her homeland (6 f.) followed, but she was intercepted by **the angel of the LORD**, speaking as His personal representative (cf. v. 13). The incident provided her with a name for her son-to-be; the name **Ishmael** signifies 'God hears' (11). One must not overlook the suspense and dramatic effect of the narrative, which scarcely hints throughout the chapter that Ishmael is not to be Abram's heir; in fact the promise of v. 10 points tantalizingly in the opposite direction. However, the description of Ishmael in v. 12 seems unsuitable for 'the son of promise'. The metaphor of **a wild donkey** may in part suggest nobility and courage, but the overall impression is of an unruly spirit of independence, setting him at odds with his **brothers** or kinsmen.

The incident provided also the name of a **well**, which commemorated the fact that God 'saw' as well as 'heard' (13 f.). The Heb. of these two verses is not without difficulties, but there is general agreement that the sense of Hagar's statement is much as NIV expresses it. The name of the well is rightly rendered in NIVmg 'the well of the Living One who sees me'. Thus the passage links the twin ideas of God's seeing and being seen (cf. 22: 14).

God's care for Hagar restored her to Abram's household, and the patriarch duly acknowledged and named his **son** (15). And so the matter rested for fully thirteen years (16, cf. 17:1).

(f) **The Everlasting Covenant (17: 1–27)**
Chapter 17 takes a step nearer the birth of the

son of promise. The promises of God become ever clearer and more detailed; and at the same time so do His demands. The twin poles of promise and obligation, of privilege and responsibility, are summed up in the word **covenant** (2). The question arises, what is the relationship between chs. 15 and 17? Both recount the making of a covenant between God and Abram. It is often asserted that they are parallel accounts, stemming from different literary sources or traditions (see p. 79). But on any view of the sources of Genesis, the writer must certainly have construed the two narratives as separate events, in view of the careful chronology which he offers the reader, and it is more satisfactory to view ch. 17, with Kidner, as a second stage in the divine covenant with Abram. Chapter 17 could be called a covenant renewal, just as Jos. 24 records a renewal of the Sinai covenant.

1–8. Again God **appeared** to Abram and addressed him directly; this direct experience may be termed prophetic (cf. 20: 7). The earlier divine promises are repeated and reinforced; but the big difference from ch. 15 consists in the obligation laid on Abram at the outset: **'walk before me, and be blameless'.** The two injunctions can be combined; their import is 'obey me in every respect' within the covenant commands (this was not a moral impossibility; cf. Phil. 3:6).

There is plainly a special interest in this chapter. In the first place, God revealed himself under a new name. **God Almighty**, Heb. *El Shaddai* (1). The exact meaning and origin of *Shaddai* remain uncertain, but the emphasis could well be on mightiness, as in the traditional rendering. The phrase differs from other similar divine titles in Genesis in that it cannot be attached to any specific location; the title therefore seems to describe God in His rôle of mighty helper to the patriarchs in their semi-nomadic wanderings (cf. Exod. 6: 3). In this context, it is asserted as the covenantal name; and at the same time Abram is given a new form of his name, for his covenantal name is to be **Abraham** (5). This change, as also that of Sarai to Sarah (15), betokened no actual change of meaning but rather a change of language or dialect; in both forms it means 'the father is exalted' (cf. *TDOT s.v.* 'Abraham'), but the longer form permits a word-play drawing in the sense of **many** (Heb. *hᵃmôn*, 5).

9–14. The sign of the covenant (11), i.e. the mark of obedience to it from the human side, is to be circumcision. The origins of this rite among other peoples are lost in the mists of antiquity, but it was normally a puberty or marriage rite (note Ishmael's age, v. 25). The distinctive feature in Jewish practice, based on the Abrahamic covenant, is its link with babyhood (**eight days old**, 12). Thus a Jewish child

is virtually born into the covenant, as he is into the Jewish community. Circumcision became especially important during and after the Babylonian exile. It is interesting to observe that this covenant was already open to others besides Abraham's descendants (12), and conversely, that his descendants by failing to practise circumcision could be **cut off** from the covenant **people** (14). Circumcision thus symbolized not a social kinship but an obedience to God's commands.

15–21. Once again the theme of the promised son is taken up, and it is at last revealed that **Sarai**, re-styled **Sarah**, is to be the **mother** (15 f.). The name in both forms means 'princess', and she no less than Abraham will give birth to royalty (16; cf. v. 6). The revelation is also given that the birth of the long-awaited son is only a **year** away (21), and Abraham is instructed to name him **Isaac** (19). This name means 'He (i.e. God) laughs', or as we should express it 'smiles upon him'. The name is seen as significant several times over in these chapters; here it is Abraham who laughs, in incredulous surprise (17). The reader is also reminded of the meaning of **Ishmael**, 'God hears', in v. 20. The two names serve to distinguish the future of the two boys and their descent: God has **heard** Abraham's plea for his first-born, and Ishmael will not be neglected by God nor despised by men—rather, a great international prestige awaits him; but the son of Abraham on whom God will *smile* is Isaac, for he alone will inherit the incomparable blessings of **everlasting covenant** relationship with God Himself.

22–27. The covenantal sign of circumcision is now implemented. It is emphasized that this sign was *not* limited to the seed of promise. This emphasis not only reflects on the historical fact that Ishmaelites and Arabs also practised circumcision, but also opens the covenantal door to those who are Gentiles (cf. Rom. 4: 9–12).

(g) Promise and Warning (18: 1–33)
Two distinct events are shown to be moving towards their foreordained climax: the birth of the promised son and the fall of Lot's chosen home, Sodom. Why should such disparate events coincide? The reason is that the long-awaited birth of Isaac, an event so full of joy and hope, stands in parallel and contrast to the birth—unheralded, unwanted and degrading—of the two ancestors of Moab and Ammon (19: 30–38), and the conception of the latter two boys was a direct consequence of the fall of Sodom. Chapters 18 and 19 are full of notable contrasts—*e.g.*, noon and night, righteousness and wickedness, generous hospitality and vicious ill-treatment of guests.

1–15. The impending events were heralded by a visit to Abraham of what he took to be **three**

men (2)—in fact, the LORD and two angels; cf. v. 33 and 19: 1. Taken by surprise as he clearly was, he reacted with all the instinctive and gracious hospitality for which Bedouin are still famous. When the hospitality had been equally graciously accepted, the divine promise of the birth of Isaac was renewed. This time it was **Sarah** who **laughed** (12), her incredulity evidently more deep-seated than her husband's. Thus the appropriateness of Isaac's name is again stressed; and further, the miraculousness of his birth is emphasized, especially in the challenging question, **Is anything too hard for the LORD?** (14). God not only predicted this birth but He alone made it possible.

16–21. The renewed promise of Isaac's birth was intended primarily as a challenge to Sarah's faith; as the spotlight now turns towards **Sodom**, the reader is given a new insight into the purpose of biblical predictions. Abraham was advised of the imminent danger to Sodom (vv. 20 f. must be addressed tó him, as GNB makes clear) for reasons which are detailed in vv. 17 ff. These reasons can be summed up in the single word 'covenant'; the covenant established (chs. 15, 17) between God and Abraham had expressed promises and obligations which could be fostered and furthered if God now revealed His plans. A covenant, moreover, is much more than a contract; it betokens a close and warm relationship, expressed here in the phrase **'I have chosen him'**, literally 'I have known him'. Their relationship is the basis for the description of Abraham as 'the friend of God' (Isa. 41: 8; Jas 2: 23). The continuing efficacy of the promises and the continuing importance of the obligations for later generations are plainly recognized in v. 19. The same combination of the themes of friendship, obedience, and revelation is to be seen in Jn 15:14f.

22–33. Abraham's concern for the welfare of his kinsman Lot was predictable, but he goes far beyond that in his pleading for the whole city of Sodom. In God's will, a righteous group may have a saving or preserving effect upon an unrighteous community. Abraham stopped at the number **ten** (32); in Isa. 53, as the JB footnote acknowledges, the 'many' are saved by the One. The passage is an illustration of how the nations could be blessed through Abraham (18).

(h) The fall of Sodom (19: 1–38)
Abraham's intercession for Sodom was unavailing; as v. 4 indicates expressly, there were not so many as ten righteous people in the city, and so the threatened doom must fall. The final demonstration of wickedness and the ensuing destruction of the cities of the plain are both portrayed in sombre colours, a frightening example for all time. The sequel (vv. 30–38) was equally grim, in a different way.

1–11. This paragraph draws attention, vividly, to the sin for which **Sodom** remains a byword. The Bible is quite unequivocal in its condemnation of sexual perversions of all kinds; there is, however, another dimension to the story which can easily be overlooked. The final, unforgivable sin was not that of the lust itself, but of a ruthless determination to harm and molest apparently defenceless people (strangers to whom every hospitality was due), in spite of the appeals made by Lot. He, it is clear, had not fallen into their ways; and yet his offer of his **daughters** (8) does him no credit, and made their later disrespect for his person the less surprising. The word translated **blindness** (11) is an unusual one, and Speiser's suggestion, 'blinding light' is attractive.

12–23. The angels showed every possible attention to Lot and his family. The fate of his daughters' husbands-to-be was not to be for lack of warning; but they, like Lot's wife, were too much attracted by all that Sodom could offer. The lesson is self-evident (Lk. 17: 32). It was their death which left the way open for the incest of vv. 31–35. Even Lot himself **hesitated** (16), but his righteousness is never in doubt (cf. 2 Pet. 2: 7 f.). His wish to reside at **Zoar** —however temporarily—was sufficient to save this **small** town from destruction (20; the name resembles and possibly means 'small').

24–29. The precise location of **Sodom and Gomorrah**, and the other cities of **the plain**, remains uncertain. The note in 14: 3 strongly suggests that at some time after the events now related, the waters of the Dead Sea covered the sites. If so (and archaeology has yet to solve the problem), the southern end of the Dead Sea must be meant. See J. P. Harland in *IDB* (*s.v.* 'Sodom') for discussion and map.

The whole Jordan valley is part of a rift valley, a major fault in the earth's surface; and it is reasonable to explain the destruction of the cities of the plain in terms of an earthquake, coupled with the ignition of sulphurous gases. Falling debris could have encased Lot's wife. For Genesis, however, the mechanics are beside the point; the important points are the divine principles of judgment and mercy. Lot was rescued for Abraham's sake (29).

30–38. **Lot** and **his two daughters** moved off into **the mountains**, presumably those to the east which later were named after Moab (cf. v. 37). We may assume that the nearby disaster frightened many people away from the area; even so, the older girl's remark in v. 31 is a gross exaggeration, even allowing for the ambiguity of the word rendered **around here** (perhaps 'in this land', with GNB footnote).

The girls' actions well illustrate the corrupting of an evil environment such as Sodom. The passage shows an interest in later times (38), however, which may suggest that the Moabites and Ammonites of a later period betrayed a sexual laxity thus typified by their origins.

Here again, Genesis reveals an interest in the symbolic or inner appropriateness of names. The name **Moab** (37) resembles closely the Heb. *mēʾāb*, 'from a father'; and **Ben-ammi** (38) signifies 'son of my kin(sman)'.

(i) Sarah in Danger (20: 1–18)

The moment is right, from the dramatic point of view, for the story of the promised son to reach its climax in the birth of Isaac, contrasting with the ill-omened births of 19: 36 ff. But to the reader's surprise there turns out to be one last hurdle: on the very eve of the conception of Isaac, it appears, Sarah was separated from Abraham and placed in another man's harem! No chronology is given, and it is quite permissible to suggest that the event took place rather earlier in Sarah's lifetime (in view of her age); if so, the story is placed here to emphasize once again the miracle of Isaac's birth (just as ch. 22, immediately after the account of his birth, demonstrates that only divine overruling preserved his life). The story is remarkably similar to that of 12: 10–20, and many commentators have suggested that it is a variant tradition of the same 'folktale' (and see 26: 1–16); conservative writers have been quick to point out how widely the details vary. The argument as such is a barren one, for neither proof nor disproof is possible; but it is certainly right to concentrate attention on the distinctive features of each story, and in particular to investigate the theological purpose of each.

A central motif of the chapter is the theme of guilt. Abimelech, is, in von Rad's words, 'objectively guilty, subjectively innocent'; while Abraham, however guilty of half-truths, is partially justified, and vindicated as a 'man of God' (**prophet**, v. 7), effective in prayer and intercession. There may be an intentional lesson here for later epochs; Abraham's descendants, however far from perfect, had a duty towards foreign peoples—even those with **no fear of God** (11)—and could bring an Abrahamic blessing upon them, and in doing so would be amply rewarded themselves.

1. Abraham has now left the Mamre area for **the Negev**; Gerar, in what was later Philistine territory, lay north-west of the Negev. **12.** This is the only verse in Genesis which justifies the claim that Sarah was indeed Abraham's **sister**, and some commentators take it as a lie on Abraham's part. If this interpretation is unlikely, it is nevertheless precarious to make this brother-sister marriage one of the major evidences for the historicity of these chapters. **16.** Despite some obscurity in the Hebrew (cf. NEB, JB), the purport is clearly to defend Sarah's reputation from the slightest hint of scandal. No doubt whatever must surround Isaac's birth. Such vindication may have been valuable

in later times, if other ethnic groups were inclined to view Israel's origins in the same light as those of Moab and Ammon.

(j) The Birth of Isaac (21: 1–21)

1–9. With no fuss or sentimentality, the long-heralded birth of **Isaac** is now recorded. The child was **circumcised** (4), in accordance with the instruction of 17: 12, and in due course **weaned** (8). The overriding theme of the first nine verses is that of laughter. The name 'Isaac' itself is thought to be an abbreviation for Isaac-el, i.e. 'God laughs', expressive of God's pleasure in the child and favour towards him. Both parents had already exhibited the laughter of surprise and incredulity (17: 17; 18: 12); Sarah now envisages the world as laughing with her (6: cf. NEB, GNB), in much the same spirit as the woman's friends and neighbours in Lk. 15: 9. The pleasure over any child was especially prominent at a weaning-celebration in the ancient East; thus v. 8 continues the motif of pleasure and joy. It is v. 9 which introduces the first sign of discord, reminding us of the existence of Ishmael and his mother. In the Heb. text, the verse ends with the single word *mᵉṣaḥēq*, translated **mocking** in NIV, 'laughing' (at Isaac) in NEB. It derives from the same verb again, and probably means 'laughing', but introducing a new and significant overtone, that of mockery (cf. Gal. 4: 29).

10–21. The sequel to the domestic friction was the departure of Hagar and Ishmael. Abraham's reluctance (11) re-echoes 17: 18; quite apart from his natural sentiments, he was no doubt concerned about the laws and conventions of the world in which he lived, for ancient documents have revealed that it was not normally proper nor legal to reject concubine and offspring in this fashion (cf. J. A. Thompson, *op. cit.*). However, Abraham was given divine instruction (12 f.) on the matter, which assured him that the rights of Ishmael were not in any danger—on the contrary, the sequel (15–20) ensured those same rights and prospects to the boy himself and to his mother.

Verse 21 shows Ishmael moving eastwards, to one of the areas where his descendants (various Arab tribes) were to roam and hunt in later centuries.

(k) Beer-sheba (21: 22–34)

Abraham remained in the Negev area for a time. In this rather arid region the wells of Beer-sheba were of great importance to man and beast, and it is not surprising that something of a boundary dispute should break out from time to time. In this case, both Abimelech (whose city lay well to the north) and Abraham were disposed to be conciliatory—in spite of the show of strength by the former, in bringing his military **commander** with him (22). A treaty was therefore concluded (32). Such covenants were accompanied by fixed rituals, in which sacrificial animals played a part (27); but the **seven ewe lambs** seem to have been an unexpected gift, not part of the ritual. The name **Beer-sheba** signifies 'well of the **oath**' (31); and the seven-fold gift was appropriate since the same word (Heb. *šeba'*) denoted both 'oath' and 'seven'.

Beer-sheba was to become an important city on Judah and Israel's southern frontier, and also an important sanctuary and place of pilgrimage (cf. Am. 5: 5; 8: 14), doubtless because of Abraham's connection with it. Here worship would be carried on in the name of *'El 'Olam*, **the Eternal God** (33); the planting of the sacred tree also symbolized long duration. The treaty, then, was meant to be valid indefinitely.

There is no evidence that the Philistines were already in Palestine. The reference to **the land of the Philistines** (34) is a purely descriptive and explanatory phrase, intended for readers at a much later date. The statement suggests that Abraham now moved north from Beer-sheba, towards Gerar.

(l) Provision and Sacrifice (22: 1–24)
Some years have elapsed, and Isaac is now old enough to ask questions. His quiet obedience to his father is however a minor aspect of the story, which concentrates attention on Abraham, for whom this was the supreme test of faith (cf. Heb. 11: 17 ff.). He was **tested** (1)— not tempted. Every parent can enter into his feelings; but it is important to observe that the premature death of **Isaac**, the **only son** of promise (2), would render null and void every promise God had made to him. To obey, then, would be to render the future meaningless; and yet he went without demur. Verse 8 may suggest that he already had a feeling that God would **provide** a way of escape. The word **provide** is indeed the linking theme of the whole chapter. This theme is plain enough in v. 14; it also underlies the name **Moriah** (2), which in Hebrew can be readily understood as 'place of provision of Yahweh'. (The name came to be associated with Jerusalem, cf. 2 Chr. 3: 1, but the vague reference here to **one of the mountains** prevents any certain identification of the location.)

9–14. Not till the last moment was Isaac 'redeemed', by means of an animal sacrifice; Israel was never to forget that the firstborn was a 'sacrifice' owed to the LORD; cf. Exod. 13: 1, 15. It must be remembered that Abraham, and Israel after him, lived in a world where human sacrifice was practised; and hitherto Abraham's God had not revealed His will in the matter. What is now made plain is that God's standards were no less exacting; but child sacrifice was permanently rejected. This lesson is secondary, however, being subordinated to the new aspects of God's character revealed to Abraham. Verse 14 concisely draws every possible lesson

from the name 'Moriah' and from the events there: God sees and He **will provide**; and as His provision is received, He Himself is seen. (The Hebrew verb encompasses *both* seeing *and* providing.)

15–19. Fittingly, since Isaac has now passed beyond the danger of death, the divine promises about him are renewed, and made the more sure to Abraham by an oath, on which Heb. 6: 13 f. provides sufficient commentary. Nothing whatsoever could now prevent Israel from becoming a great nation, which would conquer its **enemies** and yet be the source of blessing to **all nations**. Abraham's combination of faith and obedience (cf. Jas 2: 21–24) ensured all this.

20–24. This genealogical list may seem something of an anticlimax, but there is a clear purpose in the paragraph. Isaac was to be the forefather of a countless progeny; meanwhile God had 'provided' the mother, in the person of **Rebekah**. The other names may seem of minor interest, but, together with other genealogies in Genesis, they helped later Israel to understand its relationships to other peoples. This particular list relates to Syria (Heb. **Aram**) and associated tribal groups.

(m) The Purchase of Machpelah (23: 1–20)
The death of **Sarah** (1 f.) comes fittingly after the introduction of Rebekah to the reader. It appears that Abraham must have left Beer-sheba (cf. 22: 19) and returned to Mamre, which lay very near **Hebron**, then known as **Kiriath Arba** (see Jos. 14: 15). Mamre was apparently Abraham's chief centre, but his semi-nomadic life meant that he owned no property at all (cf. Ac. 7: 5). This situation was natural enough, and also a testimony to his faith (cf. Heb. 11: 8 ff., 13–16); but a corpse requires a permanent resting place! Abraham accordingly set about acquiring **a burial site** (20), and he selected the **cave of Machpelah** (9), near **Mamre** (19). This was to serve as the last resting place of most of the patriarchs; the site (probably authentic) can still be visited in Hebron to this day. It was Abraham's, and thus Israel's, first territorial holding in Canaan.

Most of the chapter is concerned with the details of the purchase, for the cave was owned by a member of a local group of **Hittites** (3). The OT references to Hittites are still puzzling, since it is well known that the Hittites were an important nation of Asia Minor, modern Turkey, and but for the OT we should not associate them with Palestine. It is disputed, therefore, whether there were, say, Hittite trading colonies in Palestine, or whether the biblical term refers to two quite separate peoples, one of which was a minor Canaanite group. The former view can at least be supported by the fact that some Hittite property documents from Asia Minor present some remarkable parallels to the story told here (*e.g.*

the specific mention of **trees**, v. 17). On the other hand, few if any of the details seem peculiar to the Hittites. See K. A. Kitchen, *Ancient Orient and Old Testament*, pp. 154 ff.

It is evident that with great courtesy and oriental skill in bargaining, **Ephron** coaxed Abraham into buying more than he had intended, and into paying a high price for it (10–16). But Abraham paid readily and without haggling; he was no man's debtor, and he acted indeed as **a mighty prince** (6). Later Israel could always be sure that Machpelah fully belonged to them; yet it was but the embryo of a much vaster inheritance.

(n) A Bride for Isaac (24: 1–67)

This, the longest chapter in Genesis, is devoted to a single theme, the choice of a bride for Isaac. The story is idyllic, and presented with outstanding literary skill; but it is far more than a charmingly told romantic tale. Its very length does something to balance the extensive narrative leading up to Isaac's birth; just as God had overruled in that matter, excluding every other potential heir of Abraham's, so now He overrules, in many small details, the choice of the 'only' son's only wife (in contrast to both Abraham and Jacob). We may see the chapter, then, as an object lesson in divine guidance; and it also illustrates that signs and indeed miracles may be seen in the minor details of life. There are four scenes to the story: the dialogue between Abraham and his servant (1–9), the meeting between the servant and Rebekah (10–27), the discussion in Rebekah's household (28–60), and Isaac's meeting with Rebekah (61–67).

1–9. The presupposition of the story is that Abraham had the right, and indeed the duty, as a wealthy man, to decide on a suitable bride for his son. Two motives governed his thinking: Isaac must not leave Canaan, but on the other hand he must not marry a Canaanite. (For Isaac to have returned to the Haran area would have been to put the clock back, so to speak.) The determination to keep the ethnic stock pure contrasts with Hagar's choice of an Egyptian wife for Ishmael (21: 21).

The **servant** (2)—possibly the Eliezer of 15: 2—agreed to his master's conditions, taking an oath in the most solemn manner (2, 9).

10–27. The scene shifts to northern Mesopotamia; the Haran area is intended (cf. 11: 31), although **the town** is not named (there was in fact a town called **Nahor**, but presumably here the name is personal; cf. v. 15). The servant's prayer recalled God's promises to Abraham (**kindness** denotes loyalty to a promise in v. 12). In naming a sign (14), he was in fact looking for 'a woman's readiness to help, kindness of heart, and an understanding for animals' (von Rad)—no bad choice!

God quickly overruled in the person of **Rebekah**, whose precise relationship to Abraham is spelled out; it may be noted that her father **Bethuel** (15) plays a minor rôle in the story, which suggests that he was very old and that his son Laban had become the effective head of the family. Rebekah proved to be the sort of person the servant was looking for, and very attractive besides (16). Her ready hospitality (25) clinched the matter for him, and he acknowledged that **the LORD** had **led** him 'straight' (GNB, for NIV **on the journey**) to the right household.

28–60. The hospitable words were put into effect (28–33), and the servant proceeded to explain his mission in full detail (34–41), and to relate fully how his prayer had been answered (42–48). In the face of these facts, neither Laban nor Rebekah's father could prevaricate, and permission for the marriage was readily given (49 ff.); besides, Laban was an avaricious man, as v. 30 has already hinted. Having received their consent and presented **costly gifts** (53), Abraham's servant showed a wish to depart much sooner than was customary in the 'timeless east'. Rebekah's readiness to break convention and go at once was a fresh confirmation of God's overruling.

61–67. Once again the narrator does not dwell on the length of the journey; all the emphasis in this chapter is on personal actions and reactions. **Isaac** now comes into the story, and conversely Abraham drops out of it. The scene is back in **the Negev**, probably near Beersheba. Here a man and wife met for the first time, and God's choice was ratified by the fact that without question or delay Isaac **loved her.** Verse 67 in the Hebrew text refers to **the tent** as Sarah's; this is probably the correct reading, emphasizing that Rebekah now takes Sarah's place as the mother of the chosen family.

(o) The Death of Abraham (25: 1–18)

The story of Abraham is now rounded off, with an account of his death and a full list of progeny. He had lived exactly 100 years in Canaan (v. 7; cf. 12: 4); and he had changed the political face of that and neighbouring countries, although the full results lay far in the future. The book of Genesis divides the whole of mankind into three groups (cf. ch. 10); but it offers another sort of tripartite division for Palestine and adjoining lands. One group consisted of the earlier inhabitants of the region (Canaanites, Hittites, etc.); a second comprised the various tribes and peoples descended from Abraham; and last—but very far from least —there was the nation of Israel itself, Abraham's most important group of descendants. Earlier chapters have introduced us to varied representatives of the first category; ch. 25 now lists for us numerous ethnic groups of the second category. This category in turn falls into three subdivisions: the descent of Keturah (1–4); the descent of Ishmael (12–18); and lastly the Edomites, who were descended from Esau (30). All of these were the future inhabitants of southern and northern Arabia.

Keturah (1) has not previously been mentioned, but her status seems to have been the same as Hagar's (**concubines**, 6); and we may well suppose that this union, like Hagar's, had taken place at a much earlier date in Abraham's life (cf. NIVmg). (Note that the paragraph is not dated in any way.) It was **Isaac** (5, 11) who received the full blessing, but no son of Abraham's went empty-handed (6). Ishmael's progeny, however, chose to live apart (see GNB of v. 18), in fulfilment of 16:12.

ii. Isaac, Jacob and Esau (25: 19–36: 43)
(a) The Birth of Jacob and Esau (25: 19–34)
A new major section of Genesis begins here, with the refrain 'These are the generations of . . .' (literally translated): Isaac is now the central character, and as the reader's attention is focused on him, it soon becomes clear that exactly the same principles of divine overruling and choice are operative. Rebekah is **barren** (21), as Sarah had been before her; and just as the divine choice had bypassed Ishmael in favour of the younger Isaac, so now the elder twin is to be inferior to his younger brother (see Rom. 9: 6–13). There is a difference, however: Esau's descendants, the Edomites, were to be much more closely associated with Israel than ever Ishmael would be (the Edomites would indeed be subservient to Israel; cf. v. 23, a prophecy which first came true in David's reign); and secondly, Esau, unlike Ishmael, himself took the initiative in losing **his birthright**, namely territorial greatness and political supremacy for his descendants.

The descriptions of Jacob and Esau prefigure the general characteristics of their descendants in several respects, such as the typical occupation and physical appearance of the Edomites. Symbolic appropriateness is also seen in their names. The name **Jacob** (26) probably meant, literally, 'He (God) protects'; but the theme of deceiving (cf. NIVmg) and the mention of the **heel** (the Heb. phrase ba'aqēb closely resembles the name Ya'aqōb) are seen as implicit in the name. Similarly the fact that **Edom** denotes 'red' is linked with Esau's predilection for the **red stew**.

The hereditary rights of a firstborn son were negotiable in those days; but to sell them so cheaply was a clear mark of contempt for them. Jacob's character, of course, was not wholly admirable, but at least he took the future seriously—a sign of faith (cf. Heb. 11: 8 ff., 21); it was Esau's supreme folly that he lived only for the moment.

(b) Isaac in Philistine Territory (26: 1–35)
It is surprising how little information Genesis offers about Isaac; in contrast to the many chapters devoted to Abraham, Jacob and Joseph, this is the only chapter wholly concerned with Isaac. It is therefore all the more surprising to find how many details of his career correspond closely with the stories of Abraham. The repetitive character of the chapter is intended to teach that 'the divine promise is renewed for each generation' (A. S. Herbert); this theme is explicit in vv. 3 f., and implicit throughout.

Yet there are distinctive elements. In going to **Gerar** (1, 6) and meeting with **Abimelech** and **Phicol** (26), and in passing off his wife as his **sister** (7), he was repeating Abraham's experience (see ch. 20); but he did not go like Abraham to **Egypt** (2; contrast 12: 10–20), nor was Rebekah taken like Sarah into the royal palace (8; contrast 20: 2). (A point of interest is that the word **caressing** in v. 8 is another word-play on the name 'Isaac'; exactly the same Heb. word occurs in 21: 9, see note.)

The **famine** conditions drove Isaac from the semi-arid Negev region (cf. 24: 62) into the more fertile and more populous area occupied by the precursors of **the Philistines** (1). There was plenty of scope for friction, and we may see Abimelech's warning to his people (11) as divine protection for Isaac and his family. Isaac now began to make the transition from semi-nomadism to farming (12), and his very prosperity was an added irritation to the local population, who had evidently taken steps to drive Abraham's descendants further away, by stopping up **the wells** for some distance around (15–18). The new wells were further sources of contention, as their names commemorated (19 ff.); but the blessing of God upon the offspring of Abraham already gave **room** and scope for both parties (22). There was a lesson here for later times; there was room in Canaan for both Israelites and Philistines, given goodwill on both sides. Abimelech, at least, was not slow to learn the lesson, and a solemn agreement was made between him and Isaac (26–33), which gave the name Beer-sheba a further appropriateness (cf. 21: 31). The word **Shibah** (33) must be another word denoting 'oath', a variant of the more common sheba.

Esau intermarried with the local population (34 f.). This not only contrasted with the marriages of Isaac and Jacob, but also had the effect of starting a breach within the family.

(c) The Forfeited Birthright (27: 1–45)
Esau had already forfeited the firstborn's share in his father's property (25: 29–34); now, in one of the most vivid narratives in Genesis, he also forfeits his father's testamentary blessing. The first loss had been largely his own fault, but this time he was indeed deceived (36), as he himself asserted in a bitter pun on his brother's name (see note on 25: 26). It is a story showing human behaviour and motives at their worst:

favouritism, deceit, foolish credulity, and murderous vindictiveness. Yet we see behind all the words and deeds the overruling hand of God, whose plans were not to be thwarted nor even endangered. There is a legal background to the story, in that the dispositions of a dying man had binding force in the culture of the day (cf. J. A. Thompson, *op. cit.*); and Isaac thought that he was dying (2), though in fact he lived for many more years. Besides, the spoken word then had a validity and permanence which is not true of our Western culture; neither blessings nor curses could be recalled. Isaac acknowledged this fact (33), even though it went against his inclinations. He had a love for Esau comparable with Abraham's for Ishmael; but in both cases God overruled, showing His sovereign choice and purpose.

Jacob's deceit was perhaps less blameworthy than his mother's, but he compounded a direct lie (19) with the near-blasphemous *double entente* (20), cf. GNB 'The LORD your God helped me to find it'. It may be noted that although the blessing was assured for his descendants, both he and Rebekah earned their own punishment, in an exile which lasted not the short **while** (lit., 'some days', 44) Rebekah expected, but many long years—mother and son never met again.

For Jacob's offspring, the blessing was to be fertility of ground and political dominance (28 f.). A like promise could not be bestowed on Esau's descendants, who would inherit the stony, infertile, mountainous country of Edom (39). (There is some ambiguity in v. 39, but the meaning must be that Esau will be denied **richness** and **dew:** so modern EVV, in contrast to the AV.) The very hostility of his environment, however, would make the Edomite a fighter, who would never readily nor for long accept Israelite domination (40).

Rebekah feared she might **lose both** her sons (45): the murder of Jacob, if it occurred, would call for vengeance and punishment, and so Esau too would be lost to her.

(d) Jacob at Bethel (27: 46–28: 22)

Having frightened Jacob into leaving home to seek refuge, Rebekah now coaxed his father into sending Jacob away from home to seek a suitable wife. Thus the chosen family was to preserve its racial purity through another generation; both Isaac and Jacob married wives from Abraham's kin in the Haran area (cf. v. 10)—a region known as **Paddan-aram**, 'the plain of Aram (Syria)' (2). Esau belatedly married another kinswoman of Abraham, in a rather pathetic and pointless attempt to win favour with his parents (6–9). Jacob's experiences are an interesting contrast to the events related in ch. 24, for Isaac himself had never left the promised land, and Abraham's servant had fetched Rebekah to Canaan with the very

minimum of delay; it was to be very different with Jacob.

The northward journey from **Beer-sheba** (10) took Jacob right by the site of Bethel, where he paused, reversing Abraham's route southward (12: 8 f.). Abraham had set up an altar, a precedent for later Israelite worship, but it was Jacob's link with the sacred site which was to make it such a very important sanctuary in the later northern kingdom. Verse 19 seems to distinguish the **place** (i.e. the sacred area, where the Bethel temple would be built) from the already-existing **city** (cf. 12: 8), which bore the name **Luz** until the Israelite conquest of Canaan (cf. Jg. 1: 23, 26), after which the name of the sanctuary became applied to the city as well. The name Bethel, 'the house of God', derived from Jacob's experience there (17). Jacob's dream not only impressed the awesome sense of God's presence upon him, but also revealed Bethel as a temple in embryo: the concepts of the day visualized a **stairway** (12, the rendering **ladder** (mg) seems less appropriate) linking a heavenly temple with the earthly temple where God (or gods, in pagan religion) deigned to meet His worshippers and receive their offerings. The **angels** go to and fro at His bidding in their tasks and ministrations (cf. Jn 1: 51). There are some interesting contrasts between Bethel and Babel; see *The Daily Commentary* (Scripture Union), vol. 1, p. 40.

Such then, was Jacob's first direct encounter with **the LORD**, who had similarly revealed Himself to **Abraham and Isaac** (13). He had made Himself *their* God, in a covenantal relationship (cf. Heb. 11: 16); we are told this of Abraham (chs. 15, 17), and we may infer it in the case of Isaac. Jacob in turn now made his covenant with God; for his part, he shows his character in the way he bargains (20 ff.), but the emphasis lies more on the promises of God (13 ff.), in which His earlier promises made to Abraham and Isaac's blessing upon Jacob (4) are both confirmed. An interesting feature of Jacob's response is his voluntary undertaking to tithe himself (22). The memorial **stone, set up as a pillar**, was well intended; but at a later date such pillars led to idolatry, due to the influence of Baal-worship (cf. Mic. 5: 13).

(e) Jacob's Marriages (29: 1–30)

Chapter 29 is an interesting account of human relationships. There is the charm of a love story, the pathos of an unloved wife, and the first episode in the relationship of two deceivers, Jacob and Laban. Behind all this we must see the hand of God, who had undertaken to care for Jacob (28: 20), and who purposed that Leah no less than Rachel should be a mother in Israel.

The story opens in a vaguely described region, somewhere in the **Haran** area (1, 4); it is evident that Jacob's meeting with Rachel was wholly a coincidence—from the human standpoint. He soon made a strong impression on the girl, showing a vigour and strength contrasting with the lazy attitudes of **the shepherds** (3, 8), as well as a warm affection towards his kinsfolk (11 f.). For her part, her beauty soon captivated the newcomer (17 f.). Her elder sister was less attractive, although the exact sense of the Hebrew is uncertain; probably the sense is that her **eyes** lacked lustre (cf. JB, NEB). It is also possible that the meaning is that though her eyes were 'lovely' (GNB), Rachel was even more beautiful; but it is not very likely that poor eyesight is meant, as NIV **weak** suggests.

We may be sure that in various respects these chapters reflect customs of the time and area; it is widely held that Laban was adopting Jacob as his heir (see notes on 15: 2 ff.). It may be that his own sons (31: 1) had not yet been born. On the other hand, we may easily take the chapter at its face value, and see Jacob as 'buying' his wives by servitude. Laban's deception, which can only have been possible because of the custom of brides' wearing thick veils (23, 25), secured Jacob's services for a second period of seven years (27, 30). Seven years' labour for a wife seems to have been a fairly high price at the time; so Laban did well for himself in gaining fourteen years in this fashion. Note that only a **week** (27) separated the two weddings; Jacob served his years for Rachel after his marriage to her.

Just as Sarah had had Hagar as a slavemaid, so both Leah and Rachel had their attendants. The two slave-girls are mentioned parenthetically (24, 29), in order to introduce to the reader all four of the women who were to be the mothers of the tribes of Israel. At a later date, no doubt partly because of such frictions as arose between Leah and Rachel, the law of Lev. 18: 18 prevented a man from marrying two sisters.

(f) **Jacob's Children (29: 31–30: 24)**
The birth of eleven sons and a daughter to Jacob is now recounted; at last the promise of a great nation (12: 2, etc.) begins to find its fulfilment. Even now the theme of barrenness is by no means absent, and it is emphasized from the outset (29: 31) that every son was a gift from **the LORD**. The large family, then, was His provision; but at the human, all-too-earthly level, the story is full of pathos. As H. C. Leupold has written, 'The house of the bigamist is a house divided against itself and the fruitful source of much mischief and the effectual disruption of all true discipline'. The argument over the **mandrakes** (30: 14 f.), a plant very popular as an aphrodisiac, well illustrates the unhappiness and the friction. The interpretation of the names is also related to

this ensuing rivalry. The footnotes in GNB make it clear that the interpretations are not scientific explanations of the names; some of the names may already have been ancient, their real meanings unknown. Some of them remain obscure. The interpretations given in Genesis, then, 'are not etymologies at all but expressions wrought into the form of proper names, expressing the sentiments or the hopes associated with the birth of these sons' (Leupold). The moral of the narrative is not simply a warning against bigamy; it is rather a warning against intertribal jealousies and frictions, to which later Israel would be all too prone. It is a human instinct to attach a special pride to the name of the clan, tribe or nation to which we belong; if later Israelites were tempted to exalt a tribal identity above that of the national interest, they should recall the interpretation of their names given here, which not only expressed a natural maternal joy in their existence but linked them indissolubly with their fellow Israelites of other tribal stock.

The sequence of the births is not without interest. Leah's first four sons (29: 31–35) are the names of the senior tribes in Israel; of the four **Judah** (35) was to be the most prominent. The tribes linked with the two slave-maids (30: 1–13) would be of lesser account, just as Ishmael was not to be compared with Isaac. (Note the same reason for concubinage as in 16: 1–4, namely barrenness or temporary barrenness; the idiom in 30: 3 means that Rachel would acknowledge Bilhah's children as her own.) Leah's last two sons were again minor tribes (30: 17 f.). Her daughter **Dinah** (21) is mentioned, to lay a basis for ch. 34. The last birth listed is by no means the least: Rachel's firstborn, **Joseph** (24), would be the most powerful of all, and the father of both Ephraim and Manasseh. Yet even that tribe should not be self-sufficient; the very name Joseph anticipated the birth of Benjamin (see 35: 16 ff.).

(g) **Jacob's Prosperity (30: 25–43)**
The long process now begins of Jacob's detaching himself from Laban. He himself could have left at once, for presumably the seven years' service to win Rachel had now been fulfilled, but if some such laws applied in the Haran area as that of Exod. 21: 2 ff., then he had no right to take his wives or children with him. Such was Laban's view of the matter too (cf. 31: 43); but at least Jacob could ask for permission to take his family with him. Laban was too shrewd to release such a profitable employee too readily, and in conversation emphasized the point that if Jacob left now, he would go penniless, for he owned nothing. So a bargain was struck which offered the younger man the opportunity of gaining wealth; Laban thus achieved six further years of Jacob's service (cf. 31: 41), while Jacob lost nothing but time,

emerging as **exceedingly prosperous** (43).

Once again we see the unelevating spectacle of two deceivers at work. The first ploy was Jacob's (32 f.), but his father-in-law swiftly outwitted him (35 f.). Jacob's second ploy was more subtle (37–42), involving some selective breeding, but based chiefly on the expectation that embryos in the womb would be affected by what the pregnant animals set eyes on. This common belief is now known to be quite unscientific, but it worked for Jacob! D. Kidner well comments, 'It would not be the last time that His [God's] part in a success would be much greater than it seemed to the observer'. Providentially, then, Jacob was not to leave the Aramaean region empty-handed, any more than Abraham had been the loser in Egypt (13: 1) or Isaac in Gerar (26: 12 ff.); but he still had the problem of getting safely back to the promised land with his family and his newly—acquired flocks and herds.

(h) The Flight from Laban (31: 1–55)

1–25. There were three reasons for Jacob's decision that the time had come to depart. Firstly, he was conscious of a growing hostility towards him (1 f.); and he could feel little affection towards a man who had acted as Laban had done (7). Secondly, his wives now showed a readiness to leave their home for an unknown land (14 ff.); it seems that their father had broken normal conventions in using up **what was paid** for them, i.e. the bride-price, which in this case had consisted not of a down-payment by Jacob but the profits of his long servitude. At any rate, they too felt alienated from Laban. In the third place, Jacob received clear directives from God (3, 11 ff.). The reference to **Bethel** (13) was to confirm that the God of his own personal experience (cf. ch. 28) was now unmistakably calling him back to the land of Canaan. Using deception to the last, Jacob seized an opportunity to leave (17 ff.); he went in flight (22) and the sequel quickly demonstrated that Laban might well have obstructed a more dignified departure. Laban took the trouble to pursue them, and might have acted more vigorously against Jacob than he did but for the divine warning of v. 24 ('Be careful not to threaten Jacob in any way', GNB). The confrontation took place in **Gilead** (23), the **hill country** to the east of the Jordan, some distance north of Mahanaim (cf. 32: 1 f.). Jacob's route was a more easterly one than had been taken by Abraham (12: 5–8).

26–42. A bitter argument ensued. Laban's reproaches in vv. 27 f. sound rather hypocritical, since it is hard to imagine that he would have released Jacob and his family at all, much less with such festivity. However, he could legitimately complain about the stolen **household gods** (30; cf. v. 19). Jacob was totally innocent of the theft, of course, and his vow (32) could

have cost the life of Rachel—if the gods had been found, but she herself ensured that they were not discovered (34 f.). We are never told of her motive for the theft; Laban's religious practices were clearly not those of the true worship of Yahweh (see also 30: 27), and the implication may be that Rachel had yet to be schooled in this respect (cf. 35: 2 ff.). On the basis of ancient Mesopotamian documents it has been argued that household deities also served a legal function, being roughly the equivalent of title deeds; but recent studies have thrown doubt on this interpretation. In any case, whether it was the religion or the property of her father that appealed to Rachel, neither would in fact benefit her.

Jacob's **angry** response (36–42) culminated in the reminder that Laban had been **rebuked** by God Himself. But for that fact Laban might yet have exacted retribution.

43–55. Instead, an agreement was reached and a **covenant** made. The solemnity of it is emphasized by the ritual of the sacrificial meal and night-watch (54) and by the binding oaths taken in the name of their respective deities. The verb **judge** (53) is plural, so that the text distinguishes between **the God of Abraham** and **the God of Nahor** (Laban's father); and we should probably re-translate **'the God of their father'** as 'their ancestral gods'. For his part, Jacob swore by the God of Abraham, who had also revealed Himself to Isaac; the circumstances of this revelation to Isaac are not recorded, but the unusual appellation **the Fear of . . . Isaac** must have arisen from it. The most durable witness to the covenant was the erection of **a pillar** (45) and a cairn (46); the latter was given two names, meaning the same thing, 'cairn of witness' in two different languages, Aramaic and Hebrew. Its purpose was that in perpetuity Aramaeans and Israelites should honour the boundary-line thus fixed between them (51 f.). The name **Mizpah** (49) also attached to the locality, which may well have been in the area of Ramoth-gilead, the disputed frontier-city of a later period (cf. 1 Kg. 22: 3): see *Macmillan Bible Atlas*, map 27. The name 'Gilead' itself bears some sort of relation to 'Galeed'; but the names differ not only in their vowels but also in their application, since the former denotes a region and a range of hills, the latter a specific site. 'Mizpah' was a common placename meaning 'Watchtower' (NIVmg); here the word-play depicts God as the One on **watch** at this frontier-post (49).

(i) The Meeting with Esau (32: 1–33: 20)

The setting of this narrative is Transjordan; Mahanaim (32: 2), the Jabbok (22), Peniel (31) and Succoth (33: 17) are all mentioned by name, and indeed each name is interpreted or reinterpreted with reference to Jacob's experience there. The first three, moreover, are linked with Jacob's experience of God; this Transjordanian territory was to form part of the land of Israel, but it would be under frequent pressure and attacked by other peoples (especially the Aramaeans, Ammonites and Moabites), and there is comfort and reassurance in the chapter for later Israelites. **Mahanaim** recalled the place where God had offered His protection; at **the Jabbok** and at **Peniel** Israel had **overcome** and gained God's blessing.

But in Transjordan there was at least to be no threat from Edom; the chief topic of chs. 32 f. is the reconciliation between Jacob and Esau, symbolizing their descendants in this region. It is of interest that in spite of his fears it was Jacob who took the initiative in approaching Esau (32: 3 ff.). He went on to take natural precautions in case Esau should prove vindictive (6–12); these included an earnest prayer, reminding God of His promises (cf. 28: 13 ff.). He then provided a handsome **'gift'** (13 ff.) in order to **pacify** (20) his wronged brother.

32: 22–32. The episode at **Peniel (Penuel** is an alternative form of the name) comes as a surprise to the reader, interrupting the story of the reunion of the two brothers. The name Peniel/Penuel signifies 'the face of God', reminding Jacob that he had no need to fear Esau when he was in the place of God's presence: thus the story tells of an answer to Jacob's prayer. The name **Jabbok** is meanwhile linked with the theme of wrestling, for **wrestled** (the Heb. word is *way-yēʾābēq*) is a wordplay on the name. The story of the struggle is skilfully told, so that the reader realizes the identity of Jacob's Opponent no more speedily than did Jacob. The upshot is the bestowal of a new and proud name upon Jacob: the first occurrence of the name **Israel** in the Bible. The original meaning of the name is probably 'God rules': without relinquishing the truth of this overriding fact of Israelite history, God deigns to let Jacob be the one to 'strive' (deriving from the same Heb. verb) and **overcome**. The old name 'supplanter' (cf. 27: 36) is thus itself supplanted, and Jacob moves on into a new phase of his life, **blessed** but yet humbled by a permanent limp (31). Verse 32 is in the nature of a footnote; this dietary abstention was a custom, not a law, and is nowhere else mentioned in the OT.

33: 1–11. While Jacob had paused in Mahanaim and Peniel, Esau had been making the long journey north from Seir or Edom (cf. 32: 3); and so at last the brothers met, still in the Peniel area. Jacob showed personal courage, though he took precautions for his favourite wife and son (1 ff.). Esau's large company (1) matched Jacob's for size (cf. v. 8); Jacob's very courteous (9) reply made it clear that there was no hostile

intent, indeed the opposite, on his side, and Esau too acted throughout in a friendly spirit. There is a graciousness and nobility in Esau's words; it is interesting to observe that Israel preserved as dignified a memory of the Edomites' ancestry as they did a contemptuous memory of the forebears of Moab and Ammon (cf. 19: 30–38). Time, then, had rectified Esau's vindictiveness; no doubt Jacob too had matured, losing much of his earlier deceitfulness, but G. von Rad is surely right to see the Peniel experience as having changed him: 'After his struggle with God, Jacob's relationship to his brother was settled'. Ch. 33 is undoubtedly intended to mirror 32: 22–32; it is no coincidence that Jacob describes Esau's face as like **the face of God** (10); cf. 32: 30.

33: 12–20. Esau took it for granted that Jacob would accompany him southward to Edom, but his brother had other ideas. With a last flash of his old deceitfulness, he first played for time (13 f.), residing for a while nearby—**Succoth** (17) was very near the Jabbok—and subsequently headed north-west across the Jordan to **Shechem** (18). Possibly he simply changed his mind, but more probably he never had the least intention of putting himself permanently in Esau's power.

Abraham had long before passed by Shechem (12: 6 f.), but Jacob planned to stay longer, as his property purchase shows (19). (It is uncertain what the value of the *qesitah* (NIVmg) may have been; NEB, indeed, understands the word to mean 'sheep'.) Like his grandfather he erected an altar, claiming the land for his God, who could now—since ch. 32—properly be called 'the God of Israel' (20, GNB).

(*j*) Conflict at Shechem (34: 1–31)

This unique chapter corresponds in some respects with ch. 14. There Abraham was confronted with a situation which led him to take military action; here two of Jacob's sons, also on behalf of a relative, take the sword. Abraham, however, had acted on the side of the peoples of Canaan, and had cemented good relations with them as a result; but by contrast the events at Shechem could only make Jacob's family **a stench to the Canaanites**, as Jacob himself expressed it (30). The chapter bears witness to evolving and changing relationships between Canaanites and 'Israelites' (to use the term somewhat anachronistically, but following the precedent set in v. 7). The chosen race, though still embryonic, was much bigger than it had been; property purchases had been made (33: 19), and the problem of intermarriage was bound to arise sooner or later. Had **Shechem** (here the name of a man, cf. v. 2) fallen in love with Jacob's daughter (3) and treated her respectfully, things might have turned out very differently; but his rape of **Dinah** (2) led inexorably to violence. He was a Hivite, a member of a pre-Canaanite Palestinian race, and it would seem that their lax sexual morals anticipated those of the Canaanites in later times. Probably the Israelite people were equally offended at the thought of intermarriage with uncircumcised people; their remarks were intended deceitfully, as is stated, but were not necessarily wholly untrue (13 f.). Circumcision had already become very important to them, and they could not have contemplated becoming **one people** (16) with uncircumcised groups, in view of 17: 9–14.

The sons of Jacob, then, demanded that the Shechemites should undergo circumcision. The Shechemites, for their part, were prepared to take this step, since they were persuaded that a closer relationship with the wealthy Jacob would benefit them too (9 f.); but dearly they paid for it (25–29). The chapter closes with two opposing viewpoints (30 f.):**Jacob** wanted peace at any price, while **Simeon and Levi** maintained that their murderous vengeance had been justifiable. Genesis later condemns their attitude (49: 5 ff.), but at this point the dilemma is left for the reader to solve for himself.

Chapter 34 is another narrative for which no chronological data are given, and it is possible to date it rather later than its present setting suggests; many scholars maintain that Simeon and Levi are already clans rather than individuals, in view of their attack on a whole city (25). In any case, the situation is plainly that of Genesis, not Judges: after the exodus and conquest of Canaan, Simeon settled much further south, and Levi was a priestly, non-territorial tribe. In the light of the numbers of men Abraham could command (14: 14), to say nothing of Jacob's great 'company' (33: 8), it would be wrong to insist that Simeon and Levi made their attack on the city quite unaccompanied; and while Dinah is undoubtedly an individual, it may be that she is singled out to represent a much bigger and wider problem. The name of the man who ravished her, after all, allows him to typify his whole city; and his father's name, Hamor, still attached to the dominant Shechemite clan as late as Jg. 9: 28 (see GNB). Reading Gen. 34 in these wider terms allows us to see it as a lesson to later Israel: treacherous violence against their neighbours was an over-reaction, but the alternative must not be a casual acceptance of Canaanite standards and a casual readiness to intermarry with Canaanites—both of which could lead to the submergence and ultimate disappearance of Israel as a distinctive people.

(k) Return to Bethel (35: 1–15)

The chapter depicts Jacob as moving southwards by stages from Shechem to **Mamre** (27); **Bethel** (6) is the halfway point and indeed the place of central importance. Jacob had long since promised to return there (28: 20 ff.), and made a vow to worship there the God who had appeared to him. The return to Bethel, then, has all the characteristics of a pilgrimage (2 ff.); it may be that Bethel afterwards became a centre of pilgrimage for people from the Shechem area, as von Rad holds; in any case, Bethel was certainly for long years the most important sanctuary in the northern kingdom, when many worshippers went there on pilgrimage. The self-purification would no doubt follow general patterns of behaviour; but here the stress lies on monotheism, as everything pagan was jettisoned. (It is thought that the **rings** in their ears were magical charms of some kind.) In a world of many deities and differing cults, nascent Israel was taught the nature and being of the true God by means of His self-disclosure—His names, His claims, and His promises. In this passage two divine names are used, **El-bethel** ('God of Bethel') and *El-Shaddai* (**God Almighty**), vv. 7, 11.

In vv. 1–7, the interest centres on Jacob's actions (although God acts in v. 5, protecting the pilgrims), while in vv. 9–12 we have the divine response, renewing the promises made to Abraham. The experience gave Jacob a fresh reason to set up a memorial **pillar** and to name the place **Bethel**(14f.); cf. 28: 17ff.

Rebekah's nurse (9), cf. 24: 59, is named nowhere else; one wonders why she had left Mamre. The only reason for mentioning her is the writer's interest in the place of her burial, near **Bethel.**

(l) Family Affairs (35: 16–29)

This passage consists of several brief paragraphs, in a sense disconnected, but together providing a useful transitional section in Genesis. Several stories are rounded off, as the death and burial of Rachel and Isaac are recounted; the birth of Benjamin completes the family of Jacob, so that now his **twelve** sons can be listed (22–26). (Verse 26 does not of course mean to suggest that Benjamin had been **born in Paddan–aram**, but that the other eleven brothers had been.) In a way the story of Jacob ends here; he lived for many more years, but he is no longer the centre of interest after this chapter; the focus of attention moves to his sons, especially Joseph. One son, **Reuben**, is already singled out for mention (22); the episode lays the foundation for 49: 3 f. Jacob's three eldest sons had now forfeited their birthright, giving pride of place to Judah.

It is puzzling why Rachel's death and burial should be linked with **Ephrath**, since she died **some distance** from it. Rachel's tomb was in Benjaminite territory (cf. 1 Sam. 10: 2), while **Bethlehem** (19) lay almost 20 km further south—beyond Jerusalem, in fact. Some scholars have looked for another place named Ephrath; an alternative possibility is that a road led directly from Bethel to Ephrath and bore the name **'the way to Ephrath'**, i.e. 'Ephrath Road'.

The mention of the ill-omened name **Benoni** (18), 'son of my sorrow', rather suggests that it was not forgotten, and was perhaps used in some circles in preference to **Benjamin**.

(m) Esau and Edom (36: 1–43)

An immediate difficulty confronts the reader in ch. 36; it seems impossible to reconcile the data given in vv. 2 f. with the earlier statements about Esau's marriages in 26: 34 f. and 28: 9. The omission of Judith's name here is of minor consequence; possibly she died, childless, at an early date. The real difficulty is that in 26: 34 Basemath was Elon's daughter, and in 28: 9 Mahalath was Ishmael's; whereas here **Basemath** appears as **Ishmael's** daughter, and a new name, **Adah**, is given to **Elon's** child. A simple expedient, adopted *e.g.* by Leupold, is to argue that Elon's daughter bore two names, Basemath and Adah; but it stretches credulity to maintain that Ishmael's daughter also bore the name Basemath in addition to Mahalath. It seems simpler to confess, with Kidner, that 'the lists have suffered in transmission'; but there is no way of knowing at what stage of transmission the variants crept in. The variations undoubtedly show that the accounts had an independent history; the brief earlier notices can readily have been transmitted in Israelite circles, but the full detail of ch. 36 strongly suggests that the lists it contains were compiled by Edomites. If so, the reign of David (when Israel conquered Edom) is a likely period for Israel to have had access to the data; v. 31 hints at this epoch. (Most evangelical scholars nowadays allow that some verses and sections of the Pentateuch were incorporated after the time of Moses: see p. 82.)

Verses 1–5 refer to births prior to the parting of the ways between **Jacob** and **Esau**, recounted in vv. 6–8. No hostility occasioned their final parting; somewhat as in the case of Abraham and Lot in ch. 13, it was the very God-given prosperity of the two men which forced them to separate. The chapter as a whole testifies to a brotherly interest in Edom on the part of Israel. Esau's chosen territory, unnamed in v. 6 (in *MT*, at least; the Syriac version names the **land**, and some modern versions follow it), was Edom or Seir, as the country came to be known. The name **Seir** (8), designating **hill country**, was linked with prior inhabitants of the land (20); cf. 14: 6. It is uncertain whether the **Horite** people were the 'Hurrians' known to us from other ancient sources; they were at any rate earlier inhabitants, unrelated to Abraham's family.

Verses 15–30 list names connected with Esau and the Horites. The term **chiefs** (15 and throughout the chapter) is an unusual one in

Hebrew, and some scholars prefer the rendering 'tribes' (cf. GNB); but 'chiefs' seems preferable, since another type of leader, **kings**, are listed in 31–39.

31–39. Edomite kingship is of interest; evidently there was no dynasty involved, and there was no fixed capital. The details suggest a non-hereditary, perhaps elective, monarchy, with each ruler making his own home-city his capital (much as Saul made Gibeah his administrative centre). **Shaul's** capital **Rehoboth** can hardly have been on the far-distant Euphrates *pace* RSV (37); the Heb. noun simply means **river** (although it often refers to the Euphrates), and it is best to render 'Rehoboth-on-the-River' here, with GNB and other Versions.

40–43. Since these **chiefs** follow the list of kings, it has been tentatively suggested that they were governors under the Israelite monarchy, following David's conquest of Edom.

iii. The Family of Jacob (37: 1–50: 26)

(a) Joseph's Dreams and their Sequel (37: 1–36)

The residence of **Jacob** in **Canaan** is briefly mentioned (1), by way of contrast to Esau's choice of Edom-Seir; the verse is parallel to 36: 6. Verse 2 begins with one of the formulaic verses of Genesis, and marks the start of the final section of the book, which mainly concerns **Joseph**, though most of the family of **Jacob** come into the story.

The story of Joseph will reveal how God overruled that the youngest son (Benjamin excepted) of the whole family came to take precedence over his brothers; the leading rôle exercised by the man Joseph prefigured the dominant rôle of the two 'Joseph tribes', Ephraim and Manasseh, in later Israel. These chapters, then, show that the principle of divine election is still active.

2–11. Three separate motives for the hostility and jealousy shown by Joseph's brothers are given: his tale-bearing (as they saw it), Jacob's favouritism, and finally the implication of the dreams. The first factor affected only four of his brothers, excluding especially Reuben and Judah, who showed more concern for Joseph than the others (see vv. 21 f., 26 f.). Jacob's favours were evident for all to see; the **robe** was not only ostentatious—it is still uncertain whether the Hebrew phrase refers to sleeves (RSV), as most scholars think, or to its being **richly ornamented** (so NIV and GNBmg)—but of royal character, to judge by the occurrence of the same description in 2 Sam. 13: 18 f. The robe was therefore as symbolic as the dreams. All the dreams in Joseph's story come in pairs, which confirms their significance and God-given character. Presumably Joseph's step-**mother**, Leah, is meant in v. 10.

12–28. These verses attest the continuing mobility of the family, with their herds and flocks. The story begins at Mamre (14; cf. 35: 27); it moves first to **Shechem**, and then even further north, to **Dothan** (17), an ancient city lying on the caravan routes. On the face of it, v. 28 refers to two caravans, one of **Midianite merchants** and the other of **Ishmaelites**: if so, a complicated tale emerges (why are the **Ishmaelites** mentioned first, in v. 25, if the other group were first on the scene?). It seems preferable to see the two names as synonymous, as *e.g.* in Jg. 8: 22 ff., and interpret the subject of the verb **pulled** as Joseph's brothers: as NIV and GNB. The acceptance of a slave-price for Joseph (28) would be a striking proof of his brothers' enmity.

29–35. The deed done, the brothers set about deceiving their ageing father; again we see how deceit marked the whole life of Jacob, and the deep sorrow it now caused him. His words in v. 35 mean simply that he would never cease **mourning** until he too died, not that he would still mourn in **the grave**, Sheol, 'the world of the dead' (GNB). (Note that this verse indicates that he had other **daughters** besides Dinah, the only daughter mentioned by name.)

Verse 36 anticipates ch. 39. The name **Midianites** at this point confirms the interpretation given above of v. 28.

(b) **Judah's Family (38: 1–30)**
This chapter seems at first a mere parenthesis in the story of Joseph. It serves to effect a neat dramatic pause, to be sure, as Joseph is, it seems, abandoned to his fate in Egypt; but that is by no means its sole function. In its own right, the narrative of ch. 38 gives us certain information about **Judah** and his progeny: it shows that already long before the exodus, Judah with his family separated from the other sons of Jacob and made himself at home in territories which would later belong to the tribe of Judah (1, 12); and it demonstrates afresh the fact of God's intervention and control in the chosen family. Judah's two firstborn were rejected, for different reasons; and God even showed which twin He selected—for **Perez** was to figure in the genealogy of the Messiah (Mt. 1: 3). The chapter does not directly point in a messianic direction; its concern is simply to emphasize God's overruling in the family. In context we can see yet another purpose in ch. 38; the casual immorality of Judah is contrasted by the remarkable moral rectitude of Joseph in ch. 39. Thus we can see why Joseph was to become more powerful than Judah, even though far in the future Judah would gain the greater honour and provide the royal line.

1–11. Judah's move into a new part of the promised land led directly to marriage with a **Canaanite** girl; the Bible makes no attempt to gloss over the mixed ancestry of the tribe of Judah. **Er**, the **firstborn** (3, 7), died early because of a **wicked** character, of which no further description is given. **Onan** suffered a like fate (9 f.), but in his case we know the reason: he persistently and maliciously cheated **Tamar** of her legal rights. The passage refers to the widespread practice in the ancient world known as 'levirate marriage'; this legal duty of a brother-in-law was intended to provide a widow with a son bearing her first husband's name and title. The responsibility could be financially onerous, and it is evident from this passage and also from the legal passage in Dt. 25: 5–10 that it could be very unpopular. Judah's reluctance to allow **Shelah** (11) to perform the duty was for a different reason, however, though he tried to deceive the widow about it.

12–23. In this all-too-human story we can observe both the determination of Tamar to have a son, come what may, and the casual self-indulgence of the new widower, Judah (12; **when Judah had recovered from his grief** refers merely to the period of mourning; cf. GNB). The passage bears witness to yet another convention of the times, namely the practice of cult prostitution. Quite apart from ordinary secular prostitution (which, alas, has flourished in all too many countries and epochs), there was in the ancient Near East a practice whereby respectable women might offer themselves to strangers as part of pagan rites and rituals, i.e. with no immoral intention. The Heb. word for **shrine prostitute** in 21 f. specifies this type of prostitution, though a more general term is used in v. 15. Judah, however, was presumably taking advantage of such practices, without any religious motivation, in view of his embarrassment in v. 23.

24–26. Tamar showed courage in keeping her secret till the last moment before a barbarous execution (suffered only by priests' daughters under later legislation; cf. Lev. 21: 9). The objects in her possession must have been very distinctive, and Judah **recognized them** without prevarication (26). His admission relates not to sexual morality but to the matter of Tamar's legal rights.

27–30. The **twins** born to Tamar were both given names relating to the circumstances of their birth; **Perez** signifies 'a breach,' while **Zerah** means 'brightness' or 'redness', with reference to the **scarlet thread.**

(c) **Potiphar's Wife (39: 1–23)**
The story now reverts to Joseph, whose fortunes are followed in detail through the rest of Genesis. The divine purpose is finally to be revealed clearly in 45: 7 f., expounded by Joseph himself; but at first Joseph sinks to the very bottom of the social scale, ending up in **prison** (20). The machinations of jealous brothers and an immoral Egyptian woman thus

put Joseph in a position from which his rise to power and influence could only be miraculous. Yet even in those days of slavery and imprisonment, **the LORD** allowed everything that he did to **succeed** (3, 23). In this chapter Joseph is the very model of the wise and the upright man; yet his successful career, both in Potiphar's house and in the prison, was due less to his character than to God's guidance: **the LORD was with** him (2, 21, 23). God's loyalty to him (**kindness**, 21) was reflected in Joseph's loyalty to his human employers, Potiphar and the keeper of the prison, both of whom could safely forget any business they had once entrusted to him. (Both Egyptians thus received their share in the worldwide **blessing** of Abraham; cf. v. 5.)

The attempted seduction of Joseph (6–12) contrasts with Tamar's successful seduction of Judah in ch. 38. Judah had voluntarily deposited with Tamar certain personal objects (38: 18); involuntarily, Joseph left **his cloak** with Potiphar's wife (12). Both women made the fullest use of these items. Potiphar's wife's favour turned to hatred (cf. 2 Sam. 13: 15), we may judge, for her accusations could well have resulted in Joseph's prompt execution. Some commentators have suggested that the fairly lenient punishment meted out to him indicates that Potiphar had doubts about his wife's veracity; but there is no other hint of such a motive in the story, and we should rather think of God's overruling. Potiphar's responsibilities evidently included control of the prison (cf. 40: 2 ff.). Not only did God mean to keep His servant alive, but planned to put him in contact with the king of Egypt, through the medium of one of **the king's prisoners** (20).

Many commentaries have noted that ch. 39 tells a story bearing close resemblance to an ancient Egyptian tale, the 'Story of the Two Brothers' (contained in *ANET*, pp. 23 f.). The stories are by no means identical, however, and few recent writers are inclined to make one dependent on the other. Seduction, attempted seduction, and false accusations, are age-old human misdeeds, and it would have been surprising if there were no parallels to Gen. 39.

(d) In Prison (40: 1–23)

Joseph was destined to spend some considerable time in prison (1; cf. 41: 1). The experience was to prepare the way for the next step in his career, though not in the way he hoped and expected. His very natural plea for help (14) fell on deaf, or rather, forgetful, ears (23). Thus once again it is emphasized that God and God alone controlled Joseph's affairs. The chapter also emphasizes that God alone could bestow the gift of the interpretation of dreams (8). Dreams play a relatively small part in the Bible as a whole, but provide a key motif in Joseph's

career. In general, the Bible does not suggest that they often convey guidance from God; their importance in this Egyptian milieu corresponds to the importance attached to them by the ancient Egyptians, who wrote 'scientific' treatises on their interpretation. The distress of the two high-ranking prisoners—they were both palace officials, whose 'offence' (cf. v. 1) may have been political—was no doubt due to the fact that in prison they were in no position to consult the experts on dream interpretation. Joseph's reply (8) is both polemic (contemptuous of such 'experts') and reassuring (since he is a man in touch with God).

The two dreams are rather similar, but provide an interesting contrast to those of Joseph himself (37: 5–11). The latter had needed no interpreter, for their import was all too obvious; the chief cupbearer's dream was not too obscure, but the significance of the **three branches** (10) puzzled him; but the chief baker's dream was more enigmatic altogether. Joseph's explanations indicated the very different fate that awaited the two men, but paid deference to the outward similarities by repeating a significant phrase: **Pharaoh will lift up your head** (13, 19). This idiom normally indicated favour, as in the cupbearer's case, but its meaning was to be more literal and fearful for the baker.

The brief sequel (20–23) demonstrates God's power, both in the exact fulfilment of the predictions and in the failure of human help for Joseph. The release of a prisoner on **Pharaoh's birthday** (20) is one of the details of the Joseph chapters which have been authenticated from Egyptian records, in this case the famous Rosetta Stone, which first provided the clue to the decipherment and understanding of the ancient Egyptian language.

(e) Pharaoh's Dreams (41: 1–36)

The centre of the drama now moves to the royal palace. There is little possibility of identifying the Egyptian king; Genesis is content to use the general term **Pharaoh.** He may have been one of the so-called 'Hyksos' dynasty (*c.* 1710–1570 B.C.), but even this much is far from certain. Since the last episode **two full years** had passed, and thirteen since Joseph had left home (cf. 37: 2; 41: 46).

1–8. Once again dreams feature prominently in the story. In the Egyptian environment, the king was bound to take the double dream very seriously; neither he nor the reader need doubt that they were God-given! His response was to consult the local experts, **the magicians and wise men**, but all in vain.

9–13. Joseph's time in prison had not been a mistake in the divine plan; **the chief cupbearer** at last remembered his obligation, at a very opportune moment. His remark about his **shortcomings** (9) is probably a reference to his earlier offence against the king rather than to his lapse of memory.

14–24. Joseph observed the correct court etiquette (for Egyptian customs differed considerably from Palestinian ones) and presented himself. The king had been led to think that Joseph was an expert in dream-interpretation, as if he had had a superior training to all the Egyptian magicians; but Joseph emphatically responded that he had no such abilities (16). The passage in effect promotes 'prophetic' inspiration, i.e. direct personal revelation from God, and subtly attacks the whole machinery of the dream-interpretation of the times. The king outlined the dreams; he was a kinder and more reasonable man than the Nebuchadnezzar of Dan. 2.

25–36. Joseph is enabled to interpret the dreams; **God** had determined the course of the immediate future (32), and He had graciously **shown to Pharaoh** His intentions (28). There is a new dimension to these predictions: Joseph's own dreams (ch. 37) had neither sought nor engaged any human co-operation; the royal officers' dreams (ch. 40) had left no opening for human intervention; but the prospect of seven years of prosperity permitted steps to be taken to alleviate the hardships of the subsequent famine. It seems probable that vv. 32–36 offer the fruits not of direct divine revelation but of Joseph's own shrewdness (in itself God-given, of course). Verse 34 makes it clear that the Egyptian king had total control over the farms and fields of Egypt; as K. A. Kitchen has expressed it, 'Joseph's economic policy . . . simply made Egypt in fact what it always was in theory: the land became pharaoh's property and its inhabitants his tenants (*NBD, s.v.* 'Joseph').

(*f*) Joseph's Exaltation (41: 37–57)
Pharaoh was immediately convinced, doubting neither the interpretation nor the advice he had received, and he readily perceived in Joseph the man to fill the proposed office. And so Joseph rose to a position of authority second only to the king (40). The general sense is clear enough, although a clause in v. 40 is obscure (**all my people are to submit to your orders:** see other versions), and the translation **make way** (Heb. *abrek* 43; see mg) is uncertain. The various symbols of office indicated in v. 42 attest the genuine Egyptian background of the Joseph story; pictorial representations of some of them are still extant (see *NBD*, fig. 122).

The honours bestowed on Joseph included a high-born wife (45); **On**, the city later known as Heliopolis, was central in the worship of Ra (or Re), the sun-god, the most important of the Egyptian deities. The meaning of **Zaphenath-Paneah** is still disputed (see K. A. Kitchen in *NBD, s.v.*). The final sentence of v. 45 refers to the extent of Joseph's authority (cf.

NEB), or less probably to the journeys he needed to make (cf. GNB).

Verses 46–57 describe the steady passage of time. Joseph ensured that the fullest advantage was taken of the seven years of plenty; domestically, too, they were **fruitful** years, as two sons were born to him. The second, **Ephraim**, commemorates this idea of fruitfulness; but there is dramatic irony in the first son's name **Manasseh**, since events were soon to show that Joseph had *not* 'forgotten' his **father's household**, i.e. his brothers.

Verse 54 introduces a new dimension to the **famine**, as it is revealed that **other lands** around were affected. Famine was all too common in the ancient East, but it was rare for both Palestine (for that is where the real interest is centred) and Egypt to suffer at the same time. Verse 57 is however unduly literal in the NIV; we need not suppose that the narrator was thinking of China or the Antipodes, but simply that throughout the relevant region the harvests were disastrously poor.

(*g*) The First Visit to Egypt (42: 1–38)
Whereas in recent chapters the interest has dwelt on Joseph and his rise to power, it now centres on the relationships, and the interplay of actions, between Joseph and his brothers, and between the latter and their father Jacob. God's overruling power is seen in the fulfilment of Joseph's dreams (6, 9).

Though Genesis does not make the point, no reader would doubt that it was God who destined and brought about the widespread famine; it was the famine in turn which brought about the reunion of Joseph with ten of his brothers. **Benjamin** (4) did not leave Canaan as yet, a fact which permitted Joseph to adopt the ploy of v. 15.

Joseph was probably not surprised to see his brothers, and at once recognized them (7); their failure to recognize him can readily be explained in terms of the twenty years that had elapsed, the fact that he spoke Egyptian (cf. v. 23), and their own belief that he was dead (13). His feelings towards them were not unmixed; while he could weep over their words (24), yet he could also adopt a harsh demeanour (7). We may justifiably think that the anxieties he caused them (to say nothing of Simeon's imprisonment) were no more than they deserved; yet two innocent men were also caused considerable mental distress, namely Jacob (36) and Benjamin (in ch. 44). Nor was his accusation of spying (9) truthful; it is pointless to dispute whether it was a natural anxiety in this period of Egyptian history or not, since it was in any case a trumped up accusation. Taking the story as a whole, then, the emphasis does not lie upon the (somewhat grudging) forgiveness exercised by Joseph, but on the divine principles of election and overruling, and to a lesser degree upon intertribal relationships; while 'Joseph' (i.e. Ephraim and Manasseh) emerged as the strongest tribal grouping in Israel, the vicissitudes of relationship between all the brothers and tribes resulted in jealousies and frictions and a measure of disunity in the era of the judges.

Reuben's confession (22) saved him from imprisonment (as the eldest); **Simeon** (24) accordingly took his place. Joseph's next reaction (25) can be interpreted as the act of a host, treating his brothers as guests; yet it was done in such a way that it was bound to puzzle them and cause them fresh anxieties (35). The episode ends with the very real anxieties of **Jacob** (36 ff.), who once again foresaw a wretched life this side of the grave (cf. 37: 35).

(h) **The Second Visit to Egypt (43: 1–34)**
Jacob was apparently prepared to sacrifice Simeon in order to save Benjamin, but ultimately his hand was forced by the persistence of the **famine** conditions (1). Even now he sought to avoid letting his youngest son go to Egypt, but Joseph had made his conditions perfectly clear, and Judah forced his father to face up to the realities of the situation. Both Reuben (42: 37) and now Judah (9) showed a willingness to suffer for the sake of the family which goes far to atone for their ill-treatment of Joseph; though it must be remembered they were precisely the two brothers who had earlier made some efforts to mitigate the other brothers' hostility to Joseph (cf. 37: 22, 27). Joseph's test of character was thus beginning to have its effects.

11–14. Jacob recognized that he must risk losing Benjamin (14), but took as many precautions as possible, by providing the proper gift to a high official demanded by oriental courtesy and by full restitution of the **silver** which had been mysteriously returned to them.

15–25. Returning to **Egypt**, the brothers met this time with a rather different treatment. Joseph himself would not meet them immediately, instructing his **steward** to act in his behalf; but they were received this time as honoured guests. As an Egyptian, the steward was careful to reassure them by reference to their own **God, the God of** their **father** Jacob, rather than any Egyptian deity (23). The prompt release of **Simeon** (23) must also have reassured them.

26–34. His brothers' humility once again proved the truth of Joseph's early dreams (cf. 37: 5–10). For his part, he came close to revealing who he was, both in the degree of interest he showed in Jacob's welfare and in Benjamin's arrival, and also in the knowledge he displayed of their order of precedence (33), which they could not fail to observe with **astonishment.** However, putting puzzlement and apprehensions aside, they settled down to enjoy their unexpectedly favourable treatment. The NIV

rendering that they **drank freely** (34) strikes the right note. GNB goes too far in implying they were 'drunk'.

The chapter ends by drawing attention to **Benjamin** (34), now shown signal favour by Joseph (his only full-brother). This episode contrasts with the events soon to befall him; and we may also notice that it did nothing to arouse the other brothers' jealousy. They had learned to feel a solicitude for Benjamin as a result of their unbrotherly attitudes and actions towards Joseph and their subsequent remorse.

(i) **The Final Testing (44: 1–34)**
The brothers' feelings towards Benjamin were soon put to an agonizing test, as we learn for the first time Joseph's real purpose in insisting on Benjamin's visit to Egypt. The unstinted hospitality they had received had set the brothers' minds at ease; it seems very probable (since no further mention is made of the matter) that on this occasion they knew that their money was being returned (1), in a final gracious gesture. The **silver cup** (2) was a different matter; its use in divination (5) is mentioned not as a detail of Joseph's religious practices, but in order to emphasize the enormity of the supposed crime. The theft of any religious object merited the death penalty (as the brothers themselves realized; cf. v. 9). In all innocence the brothers exposed Benjamin to the death penalty, but Joseph's steward offered a much more lenient alternative (10), designed nevertheless to isolate Benjamin from the others: would they abandon him to his fate? Joseph presently reinforced the temptation (17).

14–34. It was **Judah** who showed leadership, together with dignity and self-sacrifice, but we should not overlook the fact that the rest of the family expressed their assent by their silence. Judah could but acknowledge their **guilt** (16). He may have supposed Benjamin to have been guilty, but if so he was prepared to stand beside him; more probably he meant to indicate that this tragic turn of events, however inexplicable, could only be a sign of God's displeasure at their sinfulness; and we may also see the confession as not unrelated to their original sin against Joseph.

Judah's long speech (18–34) rehearses the earlier details of the story, as he knew it; Joseph's last word (17) had made reference to their **father**, so Judah did his utmost to elicit a sympathy for the old man from Joseph. In this he was certain to succeed, though he was not to know it. Two other noble qualities showed through his speech: his truthfulness and his unselfishness. Clearly he would now have become a **slave** himself (33) if only Benjamin could be spared.

The concern showed by Judah for both Benjamin and Jacob was important, not simply for the formation of his own personal character, but to lay a foundation for future relationships. It was later incumbent upon a powerful Israelite tribe like Judah to feel a keen responsibility for the weaker tribes like Benjamin and also for Israel as a whole. The responsible and thoughtful leadership shown by Judah in ch. 44 explains why his tribe was selected for subsequent leadership in Israel (see also 49: 8–12).

(j) Dénouement (45: 1–28)
The mention of his father finally compelled Joseph to reveal his identity; an intensely personal interview followed, from which every Egyptian and every intermediary were excluded. The brothers' initial reaction was speechless dismay (4)—not simply the shock of recognition, but some apprehension as to their fate now. Joseph had after all given them cause to fear him, and they had their consciences to wrestle with; much later on, they were still apprehensive (cf. 50: 15). For his part, Joseph said not a word about forgiveness, even though we may read his affections through his tears; his words in vv. 5–8 are of a more objective character, recognizing God's hand behind everything that had happened. *They* had been guilty of planning murder; but **God** had so manipulated events that the whole family would benefit. The themes of salvation are prominent, in the significant terms **remnant** and **survivors** (mg) (7). Joseph's high rank in Egypt (the phrase **father to Pharaoh**, i.e. his honoured counsellor, reflects Egyptian idioms) enabled him to provide salvation from the years of famine.

9–20. The next step was to arrange for Jacob and the whole family to come to Egypt (as predicted in 15: 13). Joseph's plan was for them to settle in **the region of Goshen**, near the royal court (10); the Delta region is indicated (probably the Wadi Tumilat), and the implied location of the capital in this part of Egypt is one pointer in favour of the Hyksos era (see note on 41: 1). As for the king, he reinforced Joseph's invitation, offering every honour and facility to the family (16–20). He said nothing about Goshen, however, and Joseph was later obliged to manoeuvre with some adroitness to achieve his wishes (cf. 46: 28–47: 6).

21–28. For the moment, then, Joseph's brothers left Egypt once more, laden with gifts. Jacob's incredulity was to be expected, but this time there was no note of sadness in his words, and he could anticipate his death without sorrow. The only jarring note in the paragraph is Joseph's final instruction to his brothers (24). The reference is probably to the recriminations in which they could well have indulged, since in giving their father the news that Joseph was still alive they must perforce admit the facts about their own misdeeds so long before. Their

conversation with Jacob is related very concisely (26 f.), but the reader need not doubt that Jacob, at some stage, would ask some awkward questions. While Gen. 45 teaches the reality of God's control in human affairs, the whole narrative demonstrates equally clearly that gross wrong-doing is not lightly to be forgotten, and that its after-effects are serious and far-reaching.

(k) The Family in Egypt (46: 1–34)
Invited by Joseph and encouraged by the Pharaoh, the whole family now took up residence in Egypt. Verses 1–7 describe the start of the journey, vv. 28–34 the arrival on Egyptian soil; the long intervening section, vv. 8–27, gives a much more detailed list of the family than we have encountered yet. It was important to Israelites of later centuries to have such detailed genealogies, so that they might trace their individual and clan histories; no less important is the theological purpose, namely to emphasize that *all* Israel went to Egypt, and *all* Israel was later rescued by God from servitude there. There has been much debate in academic circles as to which tribes and clans of Israel actually did experience a period in Egypt (a debate with very inconclusive results). A comparison of the figure **seventy** in v. 27 with the much larger number in 14: 14 readily permits us to suppose that by no means everybody attached to the wider patriarchal family went down to Egypt; but Genesis and Exodus are unambiguous in their assertion that every tribe of later Israel shared the same experience of God's salvation in the Exodus.

1–7. It was appropriate for Jacob to pause at **Beer-sheba**, which was not only the centre of much of Isaac's activities, but also the last outpost of the promised land. Abraham had been foolish to leave Palestine for Egypt in a famine situation (cf. 12: 10–13: 1), and Isaac had been careful never to leave Palestine, not even in the quest for a wife; it was fitting that Jacob should receive unambiguous divine guidance, reassuring him about what lay ahead. Verse 4 is a little obscure, when literally translated; GNB is clearer than NIV—'I will bring your descendants back to this land. Joseph will be with you when you die.'

8–27. The full complement in Egypt numbered **seventy** (27); but only **sixty-six persons** (26) made the journey. This enumeration is slightly puzzling, and it is to be remembered that certain adjustments need to be made. Joseph and his two sons did not of course need to make the journey; as for Benjamin, his youthfulness in recent chapters suggests that his large progeny (21) still lay in the future, and for all we know to the contrary, other grandsons of Jacob were as yet unborn. It may therefore be best to see the genealogy and the numerals as overlapping but not identical; the figure seventy, in particular, could well be a round number (LXX has 'seventy-five'; cf. Ac. 7: 14).

28–34. It is not quite clear, partly due to textual variations, what exactly **Judah**'s mission was (28). The GNB rendering at least makes good sense: 'Jacob sent Judah ahead to ask Joseph to meet them in Goshen'. At all events, there Joseph met the entourage, and there he was determined that they should remain; he was anxious for them to avoid the inveterate hostility of the city-dweller for the nomad (cf. v. 34), but it is evident that the matter needed to be broached with considerable tact and delicacy in order to gain Pharaoh's assent. By now Jacob and his family had begun to adopt a more settled way of life, but Joseph went out of his way to stress their pastoral mode of living. Clearly Joseph was resolved to prevent any disintegration of the family unit and any large-scale intermarriage with Egyptians.

Jacob could at last embrace the thought of death without sorrow (30); contrast 37: 35 and 42: 38, and compared Lk.2:29.

(l) **Joseph's Administration (47: 1–26)**
The severity of the famine is the background for two contrasting sections, vv. 1–12 and vv. 13–26. In vv. 1–12 we find the newcomers to Egypt honoured and cared for, given a **property** in the very **best part of the land** (11)—thanks to Joseph. The native Egyptians, by contrast, found themselves reduced by degrees to a position of state slavery (13–26). The chapter thus demonstrates once again the mystery of God's election and the magnitude of His deliverance.

1–6. Joseph's plans for his family were brought to fruition, Pharaoh readily permitting them to settle in Goshen. His final request to make use of **any among them with special ability** (6) was a tribute to Joseph's efficiency; but presumably the remark was treated as a mere courtesy and was not responded to.

7–12. Jacob himself was given the courtesy of an audience with the king. It was no doubt because of his great age that he pronounced a blessing upon Pharaoh, rather than *vice versa*. The patriarch's reply to the king's question about his age is interesting; it seems to reflect not only an increasingly shorter lifespan but also an unhappy awareness that Egypt was foreign soil. The many years spent by the patriarchs in Canaan had not transformed it into anything other than a land of **pilgrimage.** Jacob's words, then, had a regretful ring to them; but he still looked to the promised land, as v. 30 shows. Meanwhile he settled in Goshen, here styled **the district of Rameses** (11), a name the area acquired in the thirteenth century (the time of Moses).

13–26. Three stages can be seen in Joseph's dealings with the Egyptians. First they used up their **money** (14 f.), then they sold their **livestock** (16 f.), and lastly they had but their own persons to sell (19). Averse as we are in the modern world to the whole notion of slavery, we should not apply anachronistic standards to Joseph and consider his actions immoral; rather, the passage seeks to convey his skill in preserving life by every means possible. The 20 per cent tax was quite moderate in those times (26); and the principle of 'something for nothing' would never have been understood in the ancient world. Note the genuine gratitude expressed by the people in v. 25.

The NIV in v. 21 follows the ancient versions in preference to the *MT*; most commentaries and recent EVV agree with the NIV. The difference, though considerable in meaning, is slight in terms of Hebrew words.

This passage is one which clearly demonstrates the writer's knowledge of Egyptian affairs and practices; see G. von Rad, *ad loc.*

(m) **Ephraim and Manasseh (47: 27–48: 22)**
The affairs of the Egyptians were thus put in order by Joseph; the narrator's whole attention is now devoted to another people, namely the nucleus of a future nation, Israel, at present far from its promised territory. Appropriately, it fell to Jacob, the very personification of 'Israel', to order and arrange their future. Chs. 48 f. are accordingly devoted to his dying dispositions. Evidently Joseph at one point had his doubts about these arrangements (cf. 48: 17 f.), but we are to understand that Jacob was in his solemn words and actions guided by **the God** who, he said, had guided and **shepherded** his **fathers** and himself (48: 15).

47: 27–31. Jacob's first concern was to ensure that his own bones should not rest, even temporarily, in foreign soil: 'Israel' must rest in the promised land. (Symbolically, this was more important for Jacob than for Joseph; cf. 50: 26.) Once again the very strongest form of oath was taken (29; cf. 24: 2). Jacob's final action (31), in response to Joseph's oath, is of uncertain significance. The *MT* has the noun *miṭṭāh*, bed, but the LXX (translating from a MS without vowels) understood the word as *maṭṭeh*, **staff**, and Heb. 11: 21 follows the LXX rendering. It is difficult to decide which noun is original; Jacob is in bed in the next scene (48: 2), but not necessarily so at this stage in the narrative.

48: 1–7. As Jacob's final illness falls upon him, Joseph's two sons (cf. 41: 51 f.) are brought to the old man for his blessing. The whole chapter is concerned with them. Jacob first of all effectively adopts them (5), putting them on a par with his own two firstborn, while indicating that no later sons of Joseph should share their privileged position. For future Israel, this meant that the list of tribes and tribal holdings (as opposed to clans) was now closed with the names of **Ephraim and Manasseh.** Jacob's words (4) justified his decision: the promise of God to him at Bethel (=**Luz**) long before (ch. 28) had spoken of his many descendants, and Jacob saw in the concept of **fruitful**ness a pointer to Ephraim specifically, in view of the symbolic meaning of the name (cf. 41: 52). Verse 7, which at first sight seems pointless, may be part of his argument; the death of **Rachel** had meant that he himself could have no more sons, and so these two grandsons could properly be 'incorporated' with his own sons.

48: 8–22. The blessing is now pronounced. Jacob's opening question seems strange in the context; we may either assume that it is a *formal* question, for the act of blessing was formal and indeed semi-legal, or else we may take it that there had been an interval after vv. 1–7, and relate the question to Jacob's failing eyesight (cf. v. 10). Joseph carefully marshalled his sons into the correct position for Manasseh to receive the firstborn's blessing (13); it was Jacob who broke formality and normal procedures by **crossing his arms** (14). In reply to Joseph's protest (17 f.) Jacob showed prophetic knowledge. It was to be historical fact that Ephraim and Manasseh jointly should be the most powerful constituent part of Israel; and that of the two Ephraim should be the stronger. Hosea could refer to the whole northern kingdom as 'Ephraim' (see ch. 5, *passim*). Gen. 48 is concerned to show that all this would be no accident of history, but planned and foreseen.

In his words of blessing (15 f.) the name **Joseph** designates the two **boys**. By his reference to **the angel** Jacob 'calls to mind God's visible encounters with him at turning-points of his life' (Kidner). Throughout his life Jacob had been **delivered . . . from all harm**, but it may be appropriate to see a wider implication. Redemption (cf RSV) in the Bible begins at the physical level, and this is usually the primary sense in OT passages; but from the start God's deliverance was linked with questions of sin and obedience, so that moral aspects are implicit throughout.

God's promises through Jacob stressed chiefly the great prosperity and numerical strength of the two Joseph-tribes (16, 19), which would create a byword in Israel (20). In a final statement (21 f.) the return from Egypt is also promised, and Ephraim's tribal area hinted at. Jacob recalls an incident not otherwise recorded (unless ch. 34 is intended, as some commentators suppose), by which he had come to possess **the ridge of land**; the Heb. word is identical with the placename Shechem. (Jacob's bestowal of this territory on Joseph is recalled in Jn 4: 5.) Shechem would one day become the most important and the central city in the whole tribal area of Ephraim

and Manasseh (only later to be overshadowed by Samaria). So Jacob's words rather allusively suggest that Shechem was already in reserve, so to speak, for the newly-designated tribes.

(n) **The Blessing of Jacob (49: 1–28)**
Having thus made disposition regarding Ephraim and Manasseh, the dying Jacob turns his attention to all twelve of his sons. The so-called Blessing of Jacob is again prophetic, indicating something of the future character and experience of the tribes of Israel; Jacob's words are not merely foreseeing the future but also in a sense generating it (note how the patriarch speaks in v. 7). Many of the individual sentences are aphoristic in character, and we may well believe that they were rehearsed and repeated for many generations (the mottoes of Scottish clans and kings, *e.g., nemo me impune lacessit*, may provide a reasonable analogy). The sayings show various and varying features, sometimes word-plays, and sometimes animal symbolism. As befits aphorisms, the language is poetic, terse and allusive, and there are some added problems for the modern translator because of the great antiquity of the Hebrew.

1 f. The sayings relate to **days to come.** The period in view is for the most part the epoch of the judges and early monarchy; the preview is only partial, and the whole section is supplemented by the Blessing of Moses, Dt. 33. The end of time (as the AV rendering suggests) is not envisaged.

3 f. Recalling the event of 35: 22, Jacob predicts the loss of the pre-eminence which **Reuben**, as **first-born**, should have enjoyed among the tribes of Israel. Reuben virtually disappeared as a tribe during the judges period.

5 ff. The mantle of leadership would not fall on the next eldest brothers, either, for both **Simeon and Levi** stand condemned for their **violence.** They had already displayed their ferocity at Shechem (ch. 34), and v. 6 shows that it was a continuing characteristic, for which they were shunned by other Israelites. Simeon, like Reuben, was early overrun and dispersed to a considerable degree; Levi was to be 'scattered' in quite a different way, for it was the one tribe which had no territorial holding, but was allocated levitical cities in different parts of the country. Levi's important priestly functions were not divulged until that tribe had proved itself (see notes on Dt. 33: 8–11).

8–12. Judah, the next in age, had a glorious future in store—for Judah had already proved himself. This tribe is depicted as having the dignity and power of the **lion** (9), and as experiencing a miraculous material prosperity: the language of v. 11 is hyperbole, for to tie a **donkey** to a **vine** and to wash **garments in wine** are ridiculously prodigal actions. The sense of v. 12 is not certain, but probably it should be translated with NEB as a reference to a fine physical appearance. Judah, accordingly, will earn the **praise** (a word-play on his name; cf. Rom. 2: 29) of the rest of Israel, who will **bow down to** this dominant tribe (8). Verse 10 describes a growing pre-eminence for Judah; the symbols of **sceptre** and **staff** are not necessarily royal emblems (cf. Num. 21: 18), and they may be taken to presage a nobility (not yet royal) during the judges era; but the sequel would not only be royal but imperial, for **the nations** would seem to include nations outside Israel. Thus the prophecy anticipates the rise and achievements of David, who must be referred to by the words **until he comes to whom it belongs**—if indeed this is a correct translation of the clause. The promises to Judah were not completely fulfilled until the coming of the Messiah, of course; but it is difficult to be sure whether this passage already hints at such a fulfilment, or is content to look no further than David himself (just as the words about Levi conveyed no hint of that tribe's glorious priestly future).

The difficulty of interpreting v. 10 is compounded by the obscurity and textual uncertainty of the Hebrew, which appears to say 'until Shiloh comes' or 'until he (i.e. Judah) comes to Shiloh', cf. RSVmg. Elsewhere the name Shiloh refers only to a sanctuary in Ephraim, and it is virtually impossible to find any satisfactory meaning for it, literal or symbolic, in this context; besides, we should not expect to find any Israelite placename in the very general statements of Gen. 49. The view that Shiloh is a *personal* name, designating the Messiah, is almost impossible to justify; this interpretation became popular in Jewish and Christian circles, but it seems to have arisen less because of the Hebrew than because the Targum inserted the word 'Messiah' in its translation of this verse.

It seems significant that none of the ancient versions has the word 'Shiloh'. It may be that the vowels of the Heb. word in *MT* are incorrect—certainly they were not represented in writing in ancient times. A slight change yields the word *šellōh*, 'belonging to him'; this is the conjecture which the NIV has accepted. It can claim some support from the LXX and from the Syriac Peshitta, and the Targum may have based its reference to the 'Messiah' on such a reading. The strongest supporting evidence is Ezek. 21: 27, which could well be alluding to (and clarifying) this prophecy.

A very attractive alternative view (cf. NIVmg) derives from an old rabbinic interpretation. If 'Shiloh' was originally two words, not one, it could readily be vocalized as *šay lōh*, lit. 'tribute to him'; then the clause will mean 'until he comes to whom tribute belongs' (NIVmg). This interpretation seems to be gaining popularity, appearing for instance in NEB and GNB. Its chief

virtue is that it provides very close parallelism with the following clause; note how the GNB links the two clauses, 'Nations will bring him tribute and bow in obedience before him'. This interpretation, while not directly messianic in character, nevertheless envisages royal position (and not just over Israel) invested in the tribe of Judah.

13 ff. The oracles about **Zebulun** and **Issachar** testify briefly to the effects of the geographical situation of these two tribes-to-be. The former's interests would inevitably be maritime; while Issachar would prefer fertile land to a rugged independence. In being prepared to endure Canaanite domination, it would contrast very sharply with Judah.

16 ff. Dan will provide justice is a word-play in Heb. *(dān yādîn)*. In context, the saying makes Dan, though as small a tribe as Issachar, much more independent in character—ruling itself, and striking at any outside attempt to invade and dominate. Samson's career effectively illustrates the point. Verse 18 remains a puzzle to every commentator: its sense is clear, but not its relevance to the context. Perhaps the words are intended as those of Dan rather than Jacob, recognizing the severe pressures that Dan would suffer from powerful Philistine neighbours.

19 ff. The saying about **Gad** offers another pun (cf. NIVmg), and illustrates the pressures that tribe would undergo, in the area east of the Jordan; like Dan, it would show an independent spirit, striking back quickly. Fertility and rich produce would be the lot of **Asher.** The precise significance of the oracle on **Naphtali** eludes us (the NEB translates v. 21 quite differently), but its imagery may again relate to prosperity.

22–26. Joseph, like Judah, attracts a longer passage because of its importance. Chapter 48 was concerned chiefly with the mutual relationship of the two tribes which descended from Joseph; but here they are viewed as a unit (in central Palestine), prospering and seeking to expand (22), under severe pressure from the local population (23), but winning through with the help of God (24). The emphatic promise of **blessings** contrasts with the loneliness that the separate (NIVmg) individual had suffered in Egypt. Suffering will be replaced by glory. (Alternatively, the word 'separate' could denote a future prospect, that of being 'set apart' for special blessing; cf. GNB.)

27. The youngest, **Benjamin,** would engender a small tribe, but one which would be noted for its fierce prowess.

(o) The Death of Jacob (49: 29–50: 14)

49: 29–33. Jacob's last recorded words concerned his own future. The ancient Egyptians took great thought for the afterlife, and had an elaborate mythology concerning it; it is all the more remarkable that the dying patriarch was concerned simply that his bones should not lie in Egypt; he says not one word about Sheol or the life to come. The important thing was for the family to be together in death—laying claim, as it were, to the promised land. The purchase of **Machpelah** is recalled in detail (cf. ch. 23); a new detail is the mention of the death and burial of **Leah** (31).

50: 1 ff. It is well known that the ancient Egyptians were experts at **embalming**; in their own religious concepts, it was for the journey to the world of the dead, but in Jacob's case it was no less appropriate—for the cortège to Palestine. The length of the period of mourning (3) varied according to the importance of the deceased; for Jacob, it was of royal proportions, by Egyptian standards. (The seven day period of v. 10 is more typical of Israelite convention.)

4–14. Joseph was under solemn oath to perform his father's last wish, but he could not leave Egyptian soil without royal permission. This he sought through intermediaries (4) which suggests that he must for ritual reasons avoid the court while in mourning.

The route of the cortège is puzzling, **near the Jordan** (10 f.) has not yet been identified. The name **Abel Mizraim** (11) is yet another word-play; *'ābēl* is a noun meaning 'meadow' (or 'watercourse') and also an adjective, 'mourning'. Afterwards the whole family **returned to Egypt** (14), as they were under obligation to do. Had they remained in Canaan, they would have escaped the time of slavery that awaited them in Egypt; but it was the divine plan for them to undergo that servitude, and then to have the unforgettable, nation-making experiences of Passover and Sinai.

(*p*) The Death of Joseph (50: 15–26)

15–21. Jacob had been a powerful unifying influence on his sons, and his death could have been the signal for a rapid disintegration of the family. Moreover, **Joseph's brothers** still had a guilty conscience, patently; they had never before asked for forgiveness, it would seem from ch. 45. Another reason for their apprehensions was the long memory for vengeance that has often prevailed in the east (cf. Esau's words in 27: 41). It seems idle to speculate whether their story about Jacob's words was true or false (16 f.); certainly it must fairly represent his wishes, at least. Joseph's tears, when thus appealed to, gave them boldness to come in person before him (17 f.); once again we see them bowing down to him, even now fulfilling his dreams of long ago (37: 5–11). His reply is interesting; not one word is related concerning affection or forgiveness—although the comfort and reassurance of v. 21 may well imply such sentiments, spoken or unexpressed—but the whole argument concerns the purposes of God. Joseph's question, **am I in the place of God?**, does not of course deny that he had the power

of life or death; his point was that when God had shown so clearly His loving and saving purposes could he, Joseph, thwart them by any attack upon his brothers? It was rather his duty to **provide for** the whole family, putting past wrongs out of mind.

22–26. Joseph's life was shorter than his father's, and apparently shorter than his brothers' too. The span of **a hundred and ten years**, nevertheless, was fully appropriate, since it was held to be the ideal life span in Egyptian thought; and it was long enough for him to see and acknowledge the **third generation.** As an important Egyptian minister, he might well have been given a state funeral in the Egyptian style; but he showed a full determination to identify himself with his own kin. His adjuration shows too his firm conviction of God's continuing plans for His people: **God will surely to come to your aid** (24). His hopes were to be realized (cf. Exod. 13: 19; Jos. 24: 32). If Genesis stood on its own, it would end on a rather sad note; but Genesis is in fact simply the first volume of the history of salvation, and the **coffin in Egypt** was a promise for the future. Neither death nor Egypt could terminate the story, for God was a God of promise, and His people were men of faith (cf. Heb. 11: 22, and more generally Heb. 11: 13–16).

BIBLIOGRAPHY

Commentaries

CASSUTO, U., *Commentary on the Book of Genesis*, E.T. (2 vols., Jerusalem, 1961–64).

DAVIDSON, R., *Genesis 1–11*. CBC (Cambridge, 1973).

DAVIDSON, R., *Genesis 12–50*. CBC (Cambridge, 1979).

DRIVER, S. R., *The Book of Genesis*. WC (London, [2]1904).

GIBSON, J. C. L., *Genesis*. Daily Study Bible. 2 vols. (Edinburgh, 1981–82).

KIDNER, D., *Genesis*. TOTC (London, 1967).

KNIGHT, G. A. F., *Theology in Pictures: A Commentary on Genesis 1–11* (Edinburgh, 1981).

RAD, G. VON, *Genesis*. E.T., OTL (London, [3]1972).

SKINNER, J., *Genesis*. ICC (Edinburgh, [2]1930).

SPEISER, E. A., *Genesis*. AB (New York, 1964).

Other Works

BRIGHT, J., *A History of Israel*. OTL (London, [2]1972).

BUBER, M., *Moses*. E.T. (Oxford, [1947]).

BYRT, J., 'The Role of the Bible and of Science in Understanding Creation', *Faith and Thought*, 103, No. 3 (1976), pp. 158–188.

HEIDEL, A., *The Babylonian Genesis* (Chicago, [2]1954).

HEIDEL, A., *The Gilgamesh Epic and Old Testament Parallels* (Chicago, [4]1963).

HOLT, J. M., *The Patriarchs of Israel* (Nashville, 1964).

McKANE, W., *Studies in the Patriarchal Narratives* (Edinburgh, 1979).

MENDENHALL, G. E., *Law and Covenant in Israel and the Ancient Near East* (Pittsburgh, 1955).

MILLARD, A. R., and WISEMAN, D. J. (ed.), *Essays on the Patriarchal Narratives* (Leicester, 1980).

PARROT, A., *Abraham and His Times*. E.T. (Philadelphia, 1968).

PARROT, A., *The Flood and Noah's Ark*. E.T. (London, 1953).

PEARCE, E. K. V., *Who was Adam?* (Exeter, 1969).

ROWLEY, H. H., 'Recent Discovery and the Patriarchal Age', in Rowley, *The Servant of the Lord* (Oxford, [2]1965), pp. 283–318.

THOMAS, D. WINTON (ed.), *Documents from Old Testament Times. DOTT* (London, 1958).

THOMPSON, J. A., *The Bible and Archaeology* (Exeter, [3]1982).

THOMPSON, T. L., *The Historicity of the Patriarchal Narratives* (Berlin and New York, 1974).

VAN SETERS, J., *Abraham in History and Tradition* (New Haven and London, 1975).

WHITCOMB, J. C., and MORRIS, H. M., *The Genesis Flood* (Philadelphia, 1961).

WISEMAN, P. J., *Creation Revealed in Six Days* (London, 1949); revised edition in *Clues to Creation in Genesis*, ed. D. J. Wiseman (London, 1977).

WOOLLEY, L., *Ur of the Chaldees* (London, [3]1952).

EXODUS

ROBERT P. GORDON

The book of Exodus relates how God brought the nation of Israel into being by two creative acts. The first of these acts was the liberation of an enslaved multitude from the clutches of their Egyptian oppressors, the second was the binding together of these erstwhile slaves in covenant allegiance to Himself. No event in the later history of Israel can rank with the Exodus deliverance from Egypt or with the making of the Sinaitic covenant. No other book in the OT is so important as Exodus for the understanding of the vocation and destiny of the people of Israel. However, in recounting events which are determinative for the future Exodus does not divorce them from history already past. God's momentous intervention on behalf of the Israelites is portrayed as the fulfilment of covenant obligations undertaken in the days of the patriarchs. The approach of the climactic events which are described in the book is heralded in the words, 'God remembered his covenant with Abraham, with Isaac, and with Jacob' (2: 24).

For the Hebrews circumstances had altered greatly since the days when their illustrious ancestor Joseph had been acclaimed as the saviour of Egypt. It seems likely that Joseph came into prominence during that period of Egyptian history when the alien Hyksos were in control of the country. Like Joseph, these Hyksos were Semites who had come into Egypt from Palestine. They will have been all the more ready to elevate a slave like Joseph to such a high position if he was a brother Semite. For about a century and a half (c. 1720–c. 1560 B.C.) most of Egypt was subservient to the Hyksos dynasties (XV–XVI), until the house of Thebes headed a rebellion against the detested Asiatics. Thereafter the Egyptians resolved that they would never again submit to foreign domination: the creation of the New Kingdom (dynasties XVIII–XX), extending in its heyday to the river Euphrates, is usually regarded as an expression of this determination to keep the Asiatics at bay. Such is the background to the situation described in Exod. 1–2. The Israelites, who were of the same racial stock as the Hyksos, were multiplying at an alarming rate and constituted a serious threat to the national security. The maniacal attempt at genocide attributed to an unnamed king of Egypt was conceived because it seemed that history was about to repeat itself.

Moses was the man chosen to lead the Israelites out of the furnace of affliction. No matter about his feelings of personal inadequacy, he was ideally suited for the task. Brought up in courtly circles, neither his spirit nor his initiative had been destroyed under the taskmaster's lash. Moreover, the years spent in Midian saw him become familiar with the sort of terrain which the Israelites would encounter when they crossed the north-eastern boundary of Egypt. As the story progresses we can trace his development from reluctant spokesman to acknowledged prophet of God, even in the estimation of many an Egyptian (cf. 11: 3). Moses it was who first announced that God was about to fulfil His pledge to the fathers, who confronted the Pharaoh with repeated demands to release the Israelites, who subsequently led them to freedom, and who stood between them and God at Sinai when the commandments of God were presented to His covenant partners.

The latter part of Exodus (chs. 25–40) has as its major theme the construction of the Tabernacle and the installation of the priests who were to serve in this portable sanctuary. A cacophonous interlude comes in chs. 32–34 with the episode of the golden calf and the smashing of the covenant tablets. By divine grace, and in spite of human folly, the covenant was quickly renewed and the detailed instructions outlined in chs. 25–31 were put into effect (chs. 35–40). At Sinai God revealed Himself to Moses and the children of Israel in a singular way. This was the place where the whole nation entered into covenant relationship with God. The Israelites did not, however, take up residence there. Beyond the inhospitable desert lay the land of Canaan and that was their destination. Exod. 25–40 tells how Israel could experience the divine presence not only at the holy mount but throughout their peregrinations. The significance of the Tabernacle is announced early—'that I may dwell in their midst' (25: 8)—and the ensuing chapters show how, though endangered at birth, the covenantal relationship was established and the abiding presence assured. 'For throughout all their journeys the cloud of the LORD was upon the tabernacle by day, and fire was in it by night, in the sight of all the house of Israel' (40:

38). So Exodus reaches its conclusion and the original purpose of God is seen as having been fulfilled.

Traditionally the book of Exodus, like the rest of the Pentateuch, is attributed to the hand of Moses. There are indeed various references in the Pentateuch to his scribal activity (cf. 17: 14; 24: 4; 34: 27; Num. 33: 2; Dt. 31:9, 22, 24), and there is no reason to question the accuracy of these statements. In general, it would seem that Moses' relationship to the Pentateuch is like that between David and the Psalter (cf. Heb. 4: 7 where 'in David' probably means 'in the Psalter'). But whatever sources may have been used in the compilation of the Pentateuch—and modern literary criticism has devised its own methods of accounting for some of them—the decisive rôle of Moses in the formulation of the earliest Israelite creeds and laws is, in the present writer's estimation, incontrovertible.

The Exodus

The memory of the Exodus permeates virtually the whole of the OT. Not only that: when in the sixth century B.C. they found themselves exiled in Babylonia the people of Judah were encouraged to think of a Second Exodus which by its sheer magnificence would eclipse the memory of the earlier deliverance from Egypt. But the expectation was disappointed in the event and the Solomonic glory was not recovered when the exiles made their way back to Palestine after the edict of Cyrus. It took the fuller light of the Christian revelation to show that the hope of the Second Exodus was to be fulfilled at the spiritual level when, in consequence of our Lord's death and resurrection, liberation from bondage to sin would be proclaimed to every nation under heaven.

The book of Exodus contains no surfeit of chronological data from which we might deduce the date of the historical Exodus. If we were to take 1 Kg. 6: 1 au pied de la lettre we should conclude that the Exodus occurred 480 years before the foundation of Solomon's temple, i.e. about 1440 B.C. But we have cause to suspect that the figure of 480 is symbolical. Independent computation of the various figures given for the same period yields a total in excess of 550 years (cf. H. H. Rowley, From Joseph to Joshua, pp. 87 f.). The probable explanation of the larger total is that a clear distinction was not always preserved between concurrent and consecutive data. Most scholars nowadays agree that the sum-total of the Biblical evidence supports a thirteenth-century B.C. dating for the Exodus. The treasure-cities of Pithom and Raamses mentioned in Exod. 1: 11 are known to have been constructed in the reigns of the Pharaohs Seti I (c. 1303–1290 BC) and Rameses II (c. 1290–1224 BC). The Merneptah Stele (c. 1220 B.C.) includes Israel among the peoples of Palestine and therefore provides a *terminus ante quem* for the entry into Canaan. When allowance is made for the wilderness wanderings of the Israelites we may reasonably infer that the Exodus had taken place by 1260 B.C. at the latest.

This dating of the Exodus to the early thirteenth century B.C. accords well with the statement in Exod. 12: 40 f. that the Israelites were in Egypt for a total of four hundred and thirty years. (The round figure of four hundred years is given in Gen. 15: 13.) Assuming that this figure is not symbolical—and the existence of the minor variant in Gen. 15: 13 seems to warrant such an assumption—that would mean that Joseph was sold into Egypt early in the Hyksos era, a period which, as we have already suggested, provides the most likely setting for the Joseph story.

Considering the importance of the Exodus for Israelite religion and historiosophy the lack of corroboration of the Biblical account on the Egyptian side is, confessedly, surprising, the more so if the numbers involved had been as great as the OT seems to suggest (see below). The general picture of Asiatics coming into, and going out of, Egypt is illustrated in Egyptian records from various periods, so that in this respect the Exodus story is not at all improbable. But when the flight of individual slaves is occasionally logged in Egyptian reports (cf. Papyrus Anastasi V; see ANET[3], p. 259), we might expect some reference to the debouchment of hundreds of thousands of Israelites. A couple of points can be made by way of at least partial explanation.

It would be an understatement to say that a mass Exodus of Israelite slaves would represent a most grievous setback for Egypt and its king. This situation could be handled in one of two ways. Ancient monarchs had a capacity for writing up defeats as the most comprehensive of victories. The inconclusive battle which Rameses II fought at Qadesh (c. 1285 B.C.) is a case in point. Rameses does not spare the superlatives in describing how he overwhelmed the enemy. But with possession of both sides' accounts of the battle, and with some appreciation of the strategy and logistics involved, the modern student can take a different view of the famous encounter.

Another way of dealing with unpalatable facts was simply to leave them unrecorded. This kind of reaction is not peculiar to any particular period or country, as the following two examples will show. First there is the case of Tukulti-ninurta I of Assyria (1244–1208 B.C.), a contemporary of Rameses. A blanket of silence covers the last twenty-five years of Tukulti-ninurta's reign and 'the absence of royal records must be interpreted as a sign not of inactivity but of military defeat' (*Cambridge*

Ancient History[3] II: 2, 1975, p. 293). In fact the king's lack of military success seems to have been a major factor in his assassination. Our second example is from more recent history. When, for ideological reasons barely intelligible to Westerners, the government of the People's Republic of China imposed a news embargo following the Tangshan earthquake in July 1976, an attempt was being made to conceal the tragic fact that as many as half a million lives had been lost in the disaster. Information prejudicial to the national interest may sometimes have been treated in the same manner in the Egypt of three millennia ago.

According to Exod. 12: 37 'six hundred thousand men on foot, besides women and children' participated in the Exodus. Quite apart from the 'mixed multitude' also mentioned, this would mean a total of between two and three million people. Some, in an endeavour to render the statistics more credible, have urged that the word translated 'thousand' actually means 'clan' or 'leader, officer'. And it is true that *'eleph* can sometimes mean 'clan' (*e.g.* Mic. 5: 2) or, if revocalized, 'leader'. Recognition of these possibilities has contributed to an improved understanding of some OT references. The Exodus figures, on the other hand, do not lend themselves so readily to this kind of treatment. For example, the amount of silver mentioned in Exod. 38: 25 f. in connection with the census (cf. 30: 11–16) is obviously calculated on the understanding that the redemption money was paid by 603,550 individual males (38: 26). Probably the majority of OT scholars would accept that there was an Exodus, but many would argue that only a few tribes, perhaps Levi and the 'Joseph tribes', actually came out of Egypt under the leadership of Moses. Some incline to the view that migrations of Hebrews from Egypt to Palestine over several centuries have been telescoped into a single event of unparalleled significance. However, external support for either suggestion is, in the nature of things, hard to come by, so that the degree of idealization in the Biblical account cannot easily be assessed.

To speak of the whole complex of events which hinges on the Exodus, and of its relevance in any discussion of that subject, is beyond the scope of the present study. For the present we shall content ourselves with a reference to the 'Song of the Sea' in Exod. 15, and to its ancient, some would say contemporary, testimony to an event of fundamental importance for all the subsequent history of Israel. As with the resurrection of our Lord, attestation in secular sources is not the crucial factor; the sum of the events and developments fulcrate upon the one original Event is the best argument for its historicity.

The Divine Name

According to Exod. 6: 2 f. God said to Moses, 'I am the LORD. I appeared to Abraham, to Isaac, and to Jacob, as God Almighty, but by my name the LORD I did not make myself known to them'. This immediately raises a problem since the name Yahweh (better than 'Jehovah'; cf. commentary on Exod. 3: 15) occurs regularly in Genesis. Some scholars would add the further complication that the element *Yau* (or similar) in certain Amorite names of the second millennium is related to the Divine Name. (Similar claims are made in connection with personal names occurring in the third millennium Ebla texts, though the evidence has still to be adjudged by the scholarly world in general.) How then should we interpret Exod. 6: 2 f.? Several possible lines of approach have been worked out. One theory has it that 'name' in v. 3 really means 'character': although the name Yahweh was known to the patriarchs, their appreciation of God's character, as expressed in His name, was limited. According to another view the second half of v. 3 should be read as a question, 'and by my name the LORD did I not make myself known to them?' Neither of these attempted explanations has been received very favourably beyond conservative circles, and they do indeed suffer because of the unnatural strain which they impose on the Hebrew. That 'name' in Hebrew includes the idea of 'character' needs no substantiation here, but should the word be relieved of its primary significance so as to mean only 'character'? The second proposal has the air of the contrived about it; a rhetorical question of this type is not the most natural way of complementing the first half of the verse with its statement about God's revelation of Himself to the patriarchs as *El Shaddai*.

A quite different explanation constructed within the framework of the Pentateuchal documentary hypothesis has won wide acceptance among OT scholars. This says that Exod. 6: 2–30 is a parallel account to 3: 1–4: 31 and is excerpted from the Priestly source (P). The Priestly source is said to agree with the Elohist source (E) in representing the Divine Name as unknown before the time of Moses. Over against these stands the Yahwist source (J) which freely associates the Divine Name with the patriarchs and even with the pre-patriarchal era. Since there is a fair measure of agreement as to the extent of the Priestly source in Genesis we should be able to test this theory. But at once we encounter a difficulty. Where the Divine Name occurs in Genesis it is usually attributed to the Yahwist source, for it is the chief criterion by which that source is recognized. The chances, therefore, of finding material which is commonly ascribed to the Priestly source and which at the same time contains the Divine Name are almost non-existent by definition. But we can pursue our point a little further.

Much of the material in Genesis which is apportioned to the Priestly source consists either of genealogies, chronological details, or short snatches of narrative. Nevertheless, there are several longer pieces of narrative and we shall find it instructive to look at three of these. For convenience we shall make use of the tabular presentation of the documentary sources given by S. H. Hooke in *Peake's Commentary* (2nd ed., 1962, p. 176); cf. also J. Skinner, *Genesis* (*ICC*; 2nd ed., 1930, p. lviii). (i) Gen. 5: 1–32. Verses 1–28 and 30–32 are attributed to the Priestly source, but v. 29, which contains the Divine Name, is apportioned to the Yahwist. (ii) Gen. 7: 13–21. With the exception of vv. 16b and 17b the section is placed in the Priestly column. Verse 16b contains the Divine Name. (iii) Gen. 8: 14–9: 17. Apart from 8: 20–22 the block is assigned to the Priestly source. Verses 20–22 of ch. 8 are credited to the Yahwist; they have three occurrences of the Divine Name. We need not be surprised, then, to find that the Priestly material in Genesis reflects the view that the Divine Name only became known with the revelation to Moses. But rather than supporting the explanation of Exod. 6: 2 f. within the documentary construct, the evidence of our three 'Priestly' blocks might be turned against it. (Note also the possible implication of the name Jochebed in Exod. 6: 20, in a long 'Priestly' section; see the commentary *ad loc.*)

While, therefore, rejecting the documentary explanation of this particular problem we do accept the plain sense of Exod. 6: 2 f., *viz.* that the Divine Name was not used before the time of Moses among the Israelites' ancestors. The occurrences of the Name in Genesis, irrespective of sources, can easily enough be understood as scribal retrojections occasioned by its later currency in Israel. It was the same God who was active in all history and the character expressed in the Name remained unchanged from one age to the next. Even references such as Gen. 4: 26 and Gen. 22: 14, which might not seem at first blush to be explicable along these lines, can, we submit, be accommodated within this framework.

The Tabernacle

One of the effects of modern Biblical criticism has been to call in question the historicity of the Tabernacle as it is portrayed in Exod. 25–40. Many present-day scholars, indeed, would argue that these chapters are more of a theological essay than a historical record. They believe that the Israelites probably had a simple tent-shrine in the earliest phase of their history and that later writers invested it with some of the trappings and splendour of Solomon's Temple.

Evidence for this less ornate shrine they find, principally, in Exod. 33: 7–11, even though in its present context that particular tent is clearly to be distinguished from the Tabernacle. J. P. Hyatt goes so far as to call the Tabernacle 'an unrealistic and artificial structure that never existed except on paper'. But the arguments by which he supports his case are far from conclusive. It is somewhat surprising to find omissions and obscurities cited as an indication of fictitiousness. By such a standard we should conclude that Solomon's Temple never existed! And when we deal with 'the importation of later ideas into the account' we have to exercise care. It is true that, with the exception of the height, 'the dimensions of the Tabernacle are one-half those of Solomon's Temple', but the same facts could be expressed in the form, 'the dimensions of Solomon's Temple are double those of the Tabernacle', and a conclusion the opposite of Hyatt's could be drawn. More substantial is the objection by Hyatt and others that, at this point in their history, the Israelites would not have possessed the necessary skills and materials to enable them to construct a sanctuary as elaborate as the Tabernacle. Considerations such as are mentioned in 12: 35 f. and 17: 8–16 may have a part in relieving the difficulty.

We should also note that the Tabernacle is not entirely without parallel in the ancient Near East. Tent-like structures of a similar type are known from Egypt and Canaan in the third and second millennia B.C. Prefabricated tent-structures are attested in Egypt from the middle of the third millennium and these were for royal and religious use, especially in connection with funerary ritual. The portable pavilion of Hetepheres (*c.* 2600 B.C.), with its furnishings, is particularly well-known. Furthermore, the terms rendered by 'Tabernacle' and 'tent' in Exodus also figure in the fourteenth century (Ugaritic) account of the construction of Baal's sanctuary. Comparisons have also been made with the pre-Islamic Arab *qubbah*, a miniature red leather tent with a domed top, in which idols were carried. In this case, however, the evidence does not go back much before the middle of the first millennium B.C. But these are all incomplete parallels for that matter, and Noth's remark about there being 'no analogy to this astonishing construction anywhere in cultic history' retains a certain validity.

Significance of the Tabernacle

The detailed account of the Tabernacle given in Exod. 25–40 is not simply to be attributed to an ancient writer's interest in religious architecture. Its significance goes far deeper than that, and is primarily spiritual. While the OT does not give a systematic exposition of this spiritual significance of the Tabernacle and its furnishings we can appreciate in some measure what it represented to the average Israelite who saw it or who, in later times, learned about it from the ancient account. The Tabernacle was an object lesson which taught certain basic truths about God's character and about His relationship to His people. For example, the mere existence of an inner shrine housing the ark and the tablets of the law, and the inaccessibility of that adytum to all but the high Priest when he entered bearing sacrificial blood on the annual Day of Atonement, proclaimed in the boldest letters the holiness of God. Even the physical approach to the sacred tent witnessed to the same lofty requirement of holiness. Officiants in the tent had to approach it by way of the altar of burnt offering and the laver, reminders of the need for deliverance from the penalty and defilement of sin (cf. Heb. 10: 19, 22), before they could fulfil their priestly duties.

The Tabernacle taught other lessons which could hardly have escaped the notice of the attentive Israelite. One of the most elementary of these was that God is the source and sustainer of life. In the outer tent, the holy place, stood a table and a lampstand to underline this truth. The table on which was placed the bread of the Presence had its counterpart in Babylonian temples but had an entirely different significance. It did not speak of God's need of daily nourishment, but of His constant provision for Israel. The seven-branched lampstand was not just a luminary for the tent. It was a stylized tree and combined the ideas of light and life in such a way as to suggest that God was the source of both (cf. Gen. 1: 3; Jn 1: 4). In all, the symbolic value of the Tabernacle for the ancient Israelite was not inconsiderable. In the light of the various rituals performed in and around it that significance could not but become fuller and deeper.

In the NT this symbolic importance of the Tabernacle is, if anything, even more apparent. First, it was a 'copy and shadow of the heavenly sanctuary' (Heb. 8: 5), while its bicameral arrangement bore witness to man's alienation from God on account of his sin (Heb. 9: 8 ff.). But just as the portable shrine represented the divine presence to Israel, so that ultimate act of identification with men in the Incarnation is described in the Fourth Gospel as a 'tabernacling': 'And the Word became flesh and dwelt among us' (Jn 1: 14). Since John proceeds to speak of the glory associated with that revelation it is inconceivable that he was not making conscious reference to the Tabernacle. 'As the glory of God dwelt in the Tabernacle (Exod. 40: 34), so the Word dwelt among us' (C. K. Barrett). The fact is, however, that the NT mainly reserves the Tabernacle imagery for the occasion of the rending of the flesh of the Son of God, and for His post-resurrection life and ministry. Its ceremonial, especially on the Day of Atonement, anticipated the high-priestly work of Christ who entered once for all into the most holy place (Heb. 9: 11–14), now represents His people in that most sacred place (Heb. 6: 19 f.; 9: 24), and enables them also to enter the sanctuary by His blood (Heb. 10: 19–25). At Calvary Christ became the propitiatory (Rom. 3: 25; *hilastērion* there is the word translated 'mercy seat' in Heb. 9: 5), and by the rending of His flesh the obstructive curtain separating men from the divine presence was torn in two (Heb. 10: 19 f.). What the physical Tabernacle symbolized but was powerless to effect is now achieved within the framework of the heavenly sanctuary.

The writer to the Hebrews indicates that the typological significance of the Tabernacle extends beyond the use which he himself has made of it. Having enumerated the Tabernacle furnishings he adds: 'Of these things we cannot now speak in detail' (Heb. 9: 5) and 'the implication . . . is that the writer could have given such an interpretation of all the tabernacle furniture' (D. W. Gooding). Here then is an encouragement, a warrant indeed, to discover the typological import of the Tabernacle as fully as we can. But it is at this point that the subjective element comes to the fore and there are several considerations to be borne in mind. First, it must never be forgotten that the typological interpretations given in the NT bear their own authority; no subsequent interpretation can be authoritative in the same way. Secondly, the NT attaches significance to vessels and furnishings rather than to bars and bolts. Thirdly, the writer to the Hebrews was seeking to refute wrong doctrine and to buttress the faith of his addressees; an undisciplined typology would have achieved little with regard to these two worthy aims, and in this there is a lesson for us today.

Why then, it may be asked, are there constructional data in the account of the Tabernacle which appear to be redundant, if there is substance in the points just made? Are these details about pegs and cords and the like not recorded because they have their own typological significance? A helpful analogy—and it is no more than that—is suggested by Heb. 9: 9, where the Tabernacle is described as 'a parable (lit.) of the present age'. Now we do not normally expect to discover spiritual meaning in every detail in our Lord's parables. Some elements have an ancillary function; by themselves they hold no significance, yet without them the parables would be the poorer. The ancillary items in the Tabernacle account also have their functions to perform. There is, for example, a gradation in the metals used in the construction work. The closer the metal was to the most holy place the more precious it had to be ('preciousness proportionate to propinquity' is the principle). The gilding of the pillars at the entrances to the court, holy place and most holy place exemplify the same principle. In such ways the seemingly insignificant features contribute to an overall effect of no little importance.

Whatever the extent of our typological commitment we cannot expect to arrive at satisfactory interpretations if they are based on mistranslations or on misunderstandings of structural aspects of the Tabernacle. It is here that many older studies of the subject fall down badly. For this reason the commentary on these chapters pays particular attention to matters of cultural context, structure and design. Interpretations which are not founded upon an accurate appreciation of these same details are almost certain to be misinterpretations.

ANALYSIS

I. THE ISRAELITES UNDER OPPRESSION (1: 1–4: 31)

i. A New King in Egypt (1: 1–22)

Settled in Egypt under royal auspices, in the course of time the Israelites found that they could no longer bask in the reflected glory of Joseph. Several centuries had elapsed since the patriarch's death and the Israelite community had developed to the point where the native Egyptians regarded them as a threat to national security. When the rigours of corvée duty failed to have the desired effect the Pharaoh turned to more desperate measures. A programme of extermination was initiated, at first involving only the midwives who attended the Hebrew mothers (15 f.) but eventually requiring the co-operation of the entire native population (22). **5. numbered seventy:** LXX, a Hebrew MS from Qumran, and Ac. 7: 14 have 'seventy-five'. There are several possible ways of accounting for the variant traditions and neither figure represents the grand total of those who accompanied Jacob to Egypt. Neither his daughters-in-law nor his grand-daughters are included in the reckoning (cf. Gen. 46: 26). Verse 7 uses several verbs which occur in Gen. 1: 21 f. **multiplied greatly:** lit. 'swarmed'. **the land:** either Goshen or, by hyperbole, the land of Egypt (cf. Mt. 3: 5 f.) **8.** The **new king** was probably Seti I of the XIXth dynasty, who ruled *c.* 1303–1290 B.C. There is no need to interpret the verse as referring to the passing of the Semitic Hyksos dynasties in the sixteenth century. The memory of both Joseph and his great benefactions had perished as far as the Egyptians were concerned. **10. Come, we must . . . or:** the Hebrew wording recalls the scheming of the builders of Babel (Gen. 11: 4). Again the story centres on mortar and brick (14) and city-building (11); cf. Gen. 11: 3 f. But whereas the divine visitation was swift on that earlier occasion ('Come, let us go down', Gen. 11: 7) it was only after 'many days' (Exod. 2: 23) that God announced to Moses, 'I have come down to deliver' (3: 8). Like the builders of Babel, the Egyptians were concerned with

self-preservation; the presence of a potential fifth column in their midst was causing great anxiety (cf. 1 Sam. 29: 1–11). The Egyptian NE border was the most important strategically and it was in that region that Goshen was located. The Israelites were in an ideal position if they ever saw fit to side with an invading army and free themselves from the Egyptian yoke. **11.** Much of the Pharaonic construction-work depended on serf labour, whether by native Egyptians or settled foreigners. The Israelites were subjected to unusually harsh conditions of service for all that (cf. 5: 6–21). **store cities:** principally for the housing of food supplies and armaments; the NE Delta was fertile as well as strategically important. **Pithom** (Egypt. *Pr-itm*, 'House of [the god] Atum') was situated in the Wadi Tumilat and is probably to be identified with Tell er-Ratabah or Tell el-Maskhuta. **Rameses** is almost certainly the same as the *Pr-R'mssw* ('House of Rameses') mentioned in various Egyptian texts. Evidence published in 1975 strongly supports a location at Qantir, some fifteen miles to the south of San el-Hajar. **Rameses** was the Delta residence of Rameses II (*c.* 1290–1224 B.C.) in whose reign most of the construction seems to have been carried out. **15. Hebrew** has the same force as 'Israelite'. The term may be related to the Egyptian *'apiru* and the Babylonian *ḫabirū*, both of which are used to describe a widely-distributed class of semi-nomads whose presence in the near east in the second millennium was not regarded as altogether a blessing by the more settled urban communities. There is evidence for the presence of *'apiru/ḫabirū* in Egypt in the thirteenth century, but these are to be distinguished from the Israelite 'Hebrews'. While the Biblical term 'Hebrew' may, like its apparent cognates, include a social significance, it is almost always used in the OT in an ethnic sense. The Hebrew text as vocalized makes the **midwives** Hebrews (cf. NIV); some have argued that the Pharaoh would hardly have expected Hebrew midwives to carry out his instructions, and that 'midwives of the Hebrew women' would leave open the possibility that they were in fact Egyptian (so Josephus) and therefore more likely to comply with the king's diabolical demands. But if we let ourselves be guided by the names we shall conclude that they were Hebrews themselves. **16.** An outright attempt at genocide was the Pharaoh's response to the situation reported in v. 12. **17.** Providentially the matter was, for the time being, in the hands of God-fearing midwives. **19.** Perhaps the midwives were putting the Pharaoh off with a story, but it is also possible that childbirth came more easily to the Israelite women because of the harsh conditions to which they had become accustomed. The midwives' answer then bears witness to the Israelites' fecundity which has already been stressed several times (7, 9, 12). **21.** Fear of God had its recognition (cf. Gen. 22: 12; Heb. 5: 7); see Ps. 127: 3 and, by way of contrast, 2 Sam. 6: 23.

ii. The Birth of Moses (2: 1–10)

The writer concentrates on the child who will eventually be instrumental in the deliverance of the Israelites from Egypt; the names of the parents are not given; an elder sister is only mentioned for her part in the sparing of the child; Aaron, his senior by three years (cf. 7: 7), does not appear. The father's name is given as Amram and the mother's as Jochebed in 6: 20 (cf. Num. 26: 59); for another explanation see *NBD*, p. 795 (*s.v.* 'Moses', IIa). **2.** Ac. 7: 20 describes the child Moses as 'beautiful before God' (cf. Heb. 11: 23). **3.** As the child's lungs developed it became impossible to conceal him. **papyrus:** the strips would be woven together and then **coated** with tar (cf. Gen. 6: 14) to form a water-tight receptacle safe enough to hold the precious burden. This technique of waterproofing was standard over a wide area of the near east. Cf. Isa. 18: 2 for 'vessels of papyrus' which plied up and down the Nile in later times. That it is Moses' mother who makes the **basket** and carries it to the riverside is probably to be explained by the involvement of the menfolk generally in the serf labour. **reeds** is the word used in the expression 'Re(e)d Sea' in 13: 18. There are similarities between Exod. 2: 1–10 and the birth legends of other heroes of the ancient world. Legend had it that the great Sargon of Akkad (24th cent. B.C.) was put in a similar little chest by his priestess mother, and was left to float on the Euphrates. This kind of thing may have happened in real life from time to time, for legend is not divorced from ordinary human behaviour and circumstances. In the story of Moses the river episode is related to actual events—unless we adopt the view that the Pharaoh's order of 1: 22 is a literary contrivance to give the birth 'legend' credibility—and the depositing of the child by the river shows the mother complying with the royal decree, yet disregarding the essential point of that decree. **4. His sister:** probably Miriam (cf. 15: 20). **5.** As with most of the protagonists in this section, the name of **Pharaoh's daughter** is not given. Later tradition supplied her with several (*e.g.* Tharmuth in Jubilees 47: 5). The use of the definite article does not imply that the princess was the only daughter of the Pharaoh. She may even have been a quite minor princess born to one of the Pharaoh's concubines. **9.** We are perhaps to detect a touch of humour here; Jochebed is being paid from royal funds to look after her own child. **10.** By an improbable conjunction of circumstances Moses became 'instructed in all the wisdom of the Egyptians' (Ac. 7: 22). We are not told how long he remained in his mother's care; weaning might not take place until a child was about three years old (cf. 2 Mac. 7: 27 and 1 Sam. 1: 24). The name **Moses**, as the footnote indicates, is here connected with the Hebrew verb *māshāh*, 'to draw out'. The referent in **She named** could conceivably be Moses' mother, but is more likely to be the Pharaoh's daughter. If it is the latter it *might* be a difficulty that the princess is represented as being competent in Hebrew, or in a Semitic dialect close to Hebrew. Yet there is nothing improbable about the suggestion that a princess living in the Delta region, with its long history of Asiatic contacts, was acquainted with a Semitic dialect. Hyatt's exclamation at this point can only be taken as a sign of ignorance. One of Rameses II's daughters was called by the thoroughly Semitic name Bint-'Anath! An alternative explanation favoured by most OT scholars is that the princess actually called the child by a similar-sounding Egyptian name (appearing in such combinations as Tuth*mose*, etc.), and that the Hebrew explanation is by popular etymology. Kitchen, however, points out the difficulty that Egyptian *s* would in that case appear as *sh* in Hebrew *Mōsheh* ('Moses') but as *s* in the comparable Egyptian names Rameses and Phinehas (see *NBD*, pp. 794f.). [Philo and Josephus give the name a Coptic etymology, taking it to mean 'saved from water'—which etymology is indeed reflected in its Greek spellings.]

iii. Moses' Flight to Midian (2: 11–25)

11. had grown up: he was by now forty years old, according to Ac. 7: 23. It is the more remarkable, in that case, that he so readily identified with the oppressed Israelites. The statement that he **watched them at their hard labor** conveys the idea of a profound sympathy; it is the first act recorded of this man of God in the making, and is very significant. What was even more important was the fact that God saw the Israelites in their afflictions (25). **hitting** is the word translated **killed** in v. 12, but it is wiser to preserve the nuances.

12. Moses, David, Peter, and many another outstanding servant of God, had serious flaws in their characters. Moses recovered from this unpromising start (see Num. 12: 3). **14.** Moses' later reluctance to take on the task of leading the Israelites must have owed something to his experience of their ingratitude on this occasion. **15.** His flight was as much a matter of prudence as of fear. Heb. 11: 27 appears to refer to his departure from Egypt at the time of the Exodus. **Midian:** the Midianites were, according to Gen. 25: 1–6, the descendants of Abraham and Keturah. They were a nomadic people familiar with desert conditions (Num. 10: 29–32). In the period of the judges they appear as Bedouin cameleers who waged war on the Israelites (Jg. 6–8). Since relations between the Israelites and the Midianites were never cordial in the centuries that followed we can be sure that this account of Moses' association with them preserves an ancient and reliable tradition. While a location east of the Gulf of Aqaba may be correct for the later period, it may be that the Midianites were occupying part of the Sinai peninsula when Moses came into contact with them; the traditional siting of Sinai-Horeb rather depends on this assumption (cf. 3: 1). **17.** Water was precious and must often have been the subject of dispute (cf. Gen. 26: 17–22). The shepherdesses had apparently gone through the exertion of drawing the water from the well when their ungallant rivals interfered. Verse 18 indicates that this was not an unusual occurrence. **came to their rescue:** lit. 'delivered'; since it is most frequently used of God or of national deliverers raised up by God, we can regard its use here as programmatic, a hint of things to come. **18. Reuel:** Jethro in 3: 1; 4: 18. If Jethro did not have two personal names the alternatives seem to be: (i) that Reuel represents a variant tradition (Noth, Childs), or (ii) that it is a mistaken gloss based on a misunderstanding of Num. 10: 29 (Stalker), or (iii) that it is a clan name (Hyatt, Clements, following Albright). **19.** Moses was presumably still dressed as an Egyptian. **22. Gershom's** son Jonathan is mentioned in connection with the sanctuary at Dan in Jg. 18: 30. **23.** A **long period** passed and still there was no relief in sight for the stricken Israelites; not even the change of ruler brought any amelioration of their conditions. If the death of the king is taken as a serious chronological reference and the Exodus took place during the reign of Rameses II, then it is the death of Seti I to which allusion is being made. Verses 24 f. give intimation of a decisive change in the course of events.

iv. The Burning Bush (3: 1–12)
Like Jacob before him (Gen. 28: 10–17) and Gideon after him (Jg. 6: 11–24), Moses found his first direct encounter with God an unnerv-

ing experience (cf. v. 6). But if the human response in such a situation was stereotyped the divine purpose was mercifully consistent. Form criticism has drawn attention to the recurring constitutive elements of such 'call narratives' as we have here and in Jg. 6, Isa. 6, and Jer. 1. **1. Jethro:** cf. on 2: 18. **far side:** lit. 'back', i.e. west from the point of view of someone looking east. **Horeb** is an alternative name for Sinai, possibly connected with a Hebrew root meaning 'waste, desolation'. **the mountain of God:** surely to be preferred to 'the great mountain', though sometimes the word 'God' is used with superlative force (cf. Ps. 68: 15). The mountain is described thus proleptically, and not, we should imagine, because it was already a holy place for some tribe such as the Midianites. **2.** Verse 4 makes it clear that **the angel of the LORD** is none other than God Himself. The initial reference to **the angel of the LORD** is also dropped in the stories of Hagar and Gideon (Gen. 16: 11, 13; Jg. 6: 11, 14); we might also compare Abraham's encounter with God in Gen. 18: 1 f. Sometimes the angel is identified with God, as in Gen. 16 and Jg. 6, on other occasions such identification is impossible (cf. Exod. 33: 1 ff.; also 23: 20 f.). The concept of the angel of the LORD probably represents the nearest approach in the OT to the Christian revelation of the Divine Son. We may observe how, in direct analogy to the passages already cited, what is predicated of the Father in NT writings can also be predicated of the Son (cf. Jn 10: 30). The **flames of fire** symbolize the divine presence as in Gen. 15: 17 and elsewhere. Now the solemn covenant undertaking of Gen. 15: 18 ff. is nearing fulfilment. Natural phenomena (such as St. Elmo's fire or plant gas) and optical illusion are among the rationalistic explanations which have at one time or another been proposed for the 'burning bush'. These should not be discounted, but the emphasis in the story is on the fire as a divine symbol. In celebration of this occasion Dt. 33: 16 describes God as 'the Dweller in the bush'. **3.** The effect, and original intention, of the miracle was to win Moses' attention and prepare him for a new experience. The call and the response are expressed in conventional manner; cf. Gen. 22: 11; 1 Sam. 3:4. **5.** Cf. on v. 1. The **ground** was **holy** because of what was transpiring, not because of previous associations (cf. Joshua's 'holy ground', Jos. 5: 15). **6. God of your father** emphasizes that, although revelation is entering a new phase, it is the same God who is making Himself known. Verse 7 picks up 2: 25. **8. come down:** cf. on 1: 10. Canaan is presented in paradisial terms which heighten the contrast between it and the uncongenial terrain which the Israelites would experience *en route*. **Canaanites:** a comprehensive term for Semites living in Palestine, here possibly referring to lowland dwellers. **Hittites:** a Palestinian tribal group unrelated to the Anatolian Hittites who became an imperial power in the Late Bronze Age. (This is on the assumption that we have here a case of homonymy; otherwise the reference can only be to pockets of Hittites settled away from their homeland.) **Amorites:** properly those whose homeland was Amurru in Syria. **Amorites** and **Canaanites** are terms which are often virtually interchangeable; here the former may denote the inhabitants of the hilly regions of Palestine. **Perizzites:** may be connected with a Hebrew word meaning 'village'. **Hivites:** there is no external attestation of the existence of such people. This is not in itself problematical, but by a small emendation the word could in each of its occurrences be read as Horites (=Hurrians); cf. the case of Zibeon in Gen. 36—Hivite (v. 2) or Horite (vv. 20–30)? **Jebusites:** the people still in occupation of Jerusalem (Jebus) in the time of David (2 Sam. 5: 6–10). Verse 11 introduces a series of objections raised by Moses as he tries to extricate himself from the responsibility of leading the Israelites out of Egypt (cf. 4: 1, 10, 13). **12. I will be with you:** the use of the verb 'to be' perhaps anticipates v. 14 and the revelation of the divine name, but cf. the same promise in Jg. 6: 16. The **sign** given could only be appreciated when Moses had fulfilled the first stage of his commission. In this respect the signs given to Gideon (Jg. 6: 17, 21) and Saul (1 Sam. 10: 1–13) were of a different order. By so much did his experience of God surpass theirs.

v. The Divine Name (3: 13–22)

13. Moses' request is for rather more than another divine title, as v. 14 would indicate. The divine **name** would disclose something about the character of the God who had revealed Himself to Moses. **14.** Before the name is revealed an explanation of it is given. **'I am who I am'**—three words in the original—reveals and withholds at the same time. It does, however, establish the connection between the divine name Jehovah/Yahweh and the Hebrew verb 'to be' (*hāyāh/hāwāh*). The translation 'I will be what I will be' (cf. NIVfn) is also possible, and would make even more explicit the suggestion that God's character would be disclosed as events unfolded. As with the sign given in v. 12, Moses and the Israelites are being challenged to put God's word, and His character, to the test. **I AM** is not a translation of the divine name, which is not mentioned until v. 15, but is the first word of the interpretative **'I am who I am'** earlier in the verse. **15. LORD:** this is the traditional rendering of the tetragrammaton and the practice is at least as old as the LXX. The precise meaning of the name is much disputed, though there is no reason to doubt the connection with the verb 'to be' (v.

14 gives an explanation, not a translation). The consonants of the tetragrammaton are *Y-H-W-H*; the true vocalization is not known since ordinarily the name was not pronounced, the word *'Adōnāy* ('Lord') being read instead. Probably the form Yahweh is as near as we shall get to the original pronunciation. The English traditional form Jehovah cannot be right since it merely reflects the Jewish scribal practice of superimposing the vowel points of *'Adōnāy* on the consonants *Y-H-W-H*, in recognition of the fact that it was actually *'Adōnāy* that was read in synagogue. **18. a three-day journey** may be a literal triduum (cf. Gen. 22: 4?), or may denote a short period of indeterminate duration. The traditional site of Mount Sinai would not have been reached in three days. **21 f.** An enslaved people could not contemplate departure from Egypt without some provision for the journey (cf. 12: 35 f.). Slaves that they were, God was going to see to it that they enjoyed the same provision as would later be made for brother slaves within the community of Israel (Dt. 15: 13; cf. v. 15).

vi. An Unwilling Servant (4: 1–17)

Moses might have no doubts about the revelation of God which he had experienced, but he realized that his fellow-Israelites would not easily be persuaded that the God of the fathers had again visited His people. 'No frequent vision' (1 Sam. 3: 1) was as true of this period as it was of the last days of the judges. So Moses raises another objection to God's proposed course of action. The objection is met by a demonstration of the power of God and Moses is equipped with three signs (2–9) which would be sufficient to authenticate his claims in the eyes of his own people. **1.** Still the retort of 2: 14 must have rung in Moses' ears, even after the elapsing of years. On the former occasion he 'supposed that his brethren understood that God was giving them deliverance by his hand, but they did not understand' (Ac. 7: 25). **2 ff.** His shepherd's staff becomes a **snake.** The feat bears superficial resemblance to snake charming such as would have been practised in Egypt at that time; in this case the rod becomes a snake before the more familiar feat is performed (but cf. 7: 10 ff.). **5.** God takes into account the depressed condition and mentality of the Israelites; contrast Mk 8: 12. **6 f.** Instant cure, not to speak of creation, of leprosy (on which see the commentary on Lev. 13) might even have impressed the Egyptians as well as the Israelites. However, we do not read of this sign being performed before the Pharaoh. For instant affliction with leprosy as a divine judgment see Num. 12: 9–15. Miriam had questioned the uniqueness of Moses' experience of God, the very point that these three signs were meant to establish for all time. **9.** Performance of the third sign had to wait until

Moses returned to Egypt; he could not try it out in advance. This sign was really a miniature of the first plague which was inflicted on Egypt (cf. 7: 14–24). **10.** Moses persists with his contention that God has chosen the wrong man. Jeremiah also pleaded the excuse that he was not good with words (Jer. 1: 6); Paul, on the other hand, converted this liability (2 C. 10: 10; 11: 6) into an asset (1 C. 1: 17; 2: 1–5). Moses even confesses to a feeling of disappointment that his encounter with God has left him as ineloquent as before. This was his 'thorn in the flesh', though probably not Paul's; in both cases divine wisdom knew better. **11.** The answer, in the most comprehensive of terms, is that every condition of man is in the control of God (cf. Isa. 45: 7). **14. the Levite:** the designation may mean more here than simply 'descendant of Levi'; otherwise it seems superfluous where Moses the brother of Aaron is being addressed (but see Cassuto and Cole for attempts at explanation). **glad:** Aaron at least would welcome his brother and would offer moral support. **15.** Moses is still the one with whom God will communicate. **16.** When they address the Israelites Moses and Aaron will be in a relationship similar to that between God and His spokesmen the prophets (cf. 7: 1).

vii. Moses Returns to Egypt (4: 18–31)
18. Moses does not take Jethro into his confidence as to his real reason for going back to Egypt, perhaps because he still needs to be convinced himself of the viability of his mission. **19. the LORD had said:** cf. v. 27, with reference to Aaron. God is seen co-ordinating events even at this early stage in the deliverance. **20. and sons:** as well as Gershom (2: 22) there was Eliezer (18: 4). With vv. 19 f. cf. Mt. 2: 20. **21. But I will harden his heart:** while it is also said that the Pharaoh hardened his own heart (8: 15, 32; 9:34), we need not baulk at the implications of the present statement. Does it merely reflect the view that 'God is the first cause of everything' (cf. Cole and see on v. 11), or are we meant to understand that God was directly involved in the fortifying of the Pharaoh's resistance? Upon God ultimately rests the responsibility for the well-being of some and the discomfiture of others, and He is well able to bear it; cf. Rom. 9: 14–18. **22f.** The Pharaoh is to be cautioned at the outset as to the consequences of non-compliance with the divine command. Verses 24 ff. bristle with difficulties and have been the subject of many an article and paper. **24.** Having learned but lately that his enemies in Egypt can no longer harm him, Moses unexpectedly finds his life at risk from the God who has bidden him return there. Again it seems inadvisable to seek to eviscerate the statement that **the LORD met Moses and was about to kill him**, as though all that was meant was that he became dangerously ill. It is clear that Zipporah's action saved his life, precisely because it assuaged God's anger (**let him alone**, 26). The traditional, and still the preferred, explanation of the episode is that Moses had omitted to circumcise his son —because the family was living in Midian? —and the matter was being brought to his attention in a most compelling manner (cf. on 6: 5). **25. Zipporah** somehow understood the cause of her husband's predicament and, with a flint knife (cf. Jos. 5: 2), performed the circumcision. Thereafter the picture is rather obscure. Rather than saying that Zipporah touched **Moses' feet** the Hebrew actually says that she touched 'his feet', which could mean either Moses' feet or his son's. **feet** could also be euphemistic for 'genitals'. Zipporah's utterance, repeated in v. 26 almost as if it was proverbial, could mean that her husband whom she had almost lost was now secured for her on the basis of a blood-rite. Her words probably do not imply a rebuke of Moses. **27.** Brotherly solidarity marks Aaron's conduct at this stage (cf. Ps. 133: 1 f.). **29 ff.** The good offices of Aaron will have helped to elicit the correct response from the Israelites.

II 'LET MY PEOPLE GO'
(5: 1–11:10)
i. The First Interview with the Pharaoh (5:1–9)
This first audience with the king confirms all Moses' fears and misgivings. As a result of the intervention by Moses and Aaron the lot of the men in the labour gangs was made even less tolerable. But, as Cassuto well says, 'This account of initial failure in the execution of their mission heightens the dramatic tension of the narrative, and lends added emphasis to their subsequent success, which is described in the sections that follow'. Meanwhile Moses, who did not have the remaining chapters of Exodus before him, reacted in the only way he knew (22 f.). **1. This is what the LORD . . . says:** the characteristic formula of the later prophetic oracles. **'Let my people go':** cf. 3: 18. **hold a festival:** NEB has 'keep my pilgrim-feast'; it is the same Semitic root as appears in the Arabic *haj*, the Islamic pilgrimage to Mecca. For the Israelites the goal of the pilgrimage was Horeb (3: 12). **2.** The Pharaoh was accounted a god in Egypt and was unlikely to take to the peremptoriness of this particular oracular form. **3.** Ostraca from this period preserve work records which show that Egyptian serfs were in the habit of taking time off to attend to religious matters. **he may strike:** the king might be expected to have sympathy with this fear, since neglect of ceremonial obligations was thought to incur the wrath of the deity. **4.** But Moses and Aaron discover that they are dealing with an unreasoning tyrant who is obsessed with his

immigrant problem (cf. Cole). **5. the people
of the land** would be the servile element,
notably the Israelites. The Samaritan version
has a variant: 'now they are more numerous
than the people of the land', in which case the
expression would refer to the native Egyptians.
NEB has followed the Samaritan here, but we
cannot be certain that this is not another case
of the Samaritan smoothing out a difficulty (see
introductory chapter on 'The Ancient Versions'). **6. The foremen**, as vv. 14 f., 19 indicate, were Hebrews. **7 f.** From now on the
Israelites were to find their own straw and yet
maintain previous levels of productivity. Mud
from the Nile was put in wooden moulds and
left to dry in the sun; Hyatt notes that the
English word adobe, 'sun-dried brick', comes
via Arabic and Spanish from the Egyptian *db-t*.
Often chopped straw or chaff was mixed with
the clay to improve durability. 'Investigation
has shown that the straw yields organic acids
that make the clay more plastic, and its presence
also stops shrinkage' (K. A. Kitchen, *Ancient
Orient and Old Testament*, p. 156). Further illustration of the Egyptian preoccupation with materials and quotas comes from the Anastasi
papyri (13th century B.C.). **9. Lies** was the
Pharaoh's verdict on the claim of Moses and
Aaron to have had a divine revelation.

ii. The Oppression Intensified (5: 10–23)
12. As the supply of **straw** ran out the Israelites
had to make do with **stubble. 14.** There are
modern parallels for the way in which the
slave gangs were organized. Responsibility for
output was laid upon the Hebrew **foremen**
who **were beaten** when, inevitably, the earlier
quotas were not maintained. **15.** It was possible
in this period for even a slave to make direct
appeal to the Pharaoh if he had a grievance,
and the foremen take advantage of this concession. **16. but the fault is with your own
people:** i.e. in the Egyptian taskmasters who
refused to supply the straw. Another possible
rendering is: 'you have wronged your people'
(i.e. the Israelites, cf. 'your servants'). **21.** The
Pharaoh outmanoeuvred Moses and Aaron at
their first meeting; his achievement also included the discrediting of the two leaders in the
sight of the Israelites. **22 f.** Moses' expectation
of an instant deliverance (cf. on 4: 10) has been
laid in the dust. Yet if the divine intervention
had taken place at this point the declared purpose of God (9: 16; cf. Rom. 9: 17) would not
have been worked out so triumphantly.

iii. A Second Revelation to Moses (6: 1–13)
Moses' protestations are met with a reminder
of the special revelation which has been given
to him and a rehearsal of the promises made to
the fathers. But the down-trodden Israelites
have had their hopes raised once and then brutally dashed, and will not give ear to the reveries
of a Moses. For discussion of vv. 2 f. see the

introduction to Exodus. **1. will drive them
out:** cf. 12: 33, 39. **2. I am the LORD:** cf. vv.
6, 7, 8, 29. **3. God Almighty** is the traditional
rendering of the Hebrew *'El Shaddai*. More
probable is the suggested connection with the
Akkadian word *shadû*, 'mountain', especially
when we recall the Mesopotamian origins of
the patriarchs. 'God of the Mountain' or
'Mountain God' would be analogous to the OT
designation 'Rock' for God (so Cole). In Gen.
17: 1 God introduces Himself to Abraham as
'El Shaddai, and similarly to Jacob in Gen. 35:
11 (cf. 48: 3). Outside the Pentateuch the title
occurs mainly in Job, perhaps as a conscious
archaism. **4. covenant: established** with Abraham (Gen. 15: 18 ff.; 17: 1–14) and renewed
to Isaac (Gen. 26: 3) and Jacob (Gen. 35: 12).
5. remembered does not suggest a previous
lapse of memory, but intimates that the **covenant** undertaking is about to be fulfilled. Perhaps
this is the clue to the significance of that obscure
passage in 4: 24ff.; Moses, probably circumcised himself, was nevertheless culpable so far
as the covenant obligation of Gen. 17: 9–14
was concerned. As the instrument used by God
in bringing Israel into the covenant blessing he
more than anyone must fulfil the stipulations
imposed from God's side. **6. redeem:** 'the
Hebrew word used here denotes the right of
a member of a family to acquire persons or
property belonging to that family which was
in danger of falling to outside claimants' (Clements). For redemption of property see Lev. 25:
25, and of persons Lev. 25: 47 ff. Redemption
is one of the principal motifs in the story of
Ruth and Boaz (Ru.4: 1–12). The language of
redemption is also prominent in the development of the 'new Exodus' theme in Isa. 40–55
(*e.g.* 41: 14; 43: 1, 14). **7.** cf. Gen. 17: 8; Exod.
19: 5 f. **8. swore:** cf. Gen. 22: 15–18; 24: 7.
12. faltering lips: *MT* 'uncircumcised lips'
scarcely has a moral connotation as in the similar expressions in Jer. 6: 9 and 9: 26. Moses
again bemoans the fact that he is not a gifted
orator; his words have had no persuasive
power, even for his own people.

**iv. Genealogy of Aaron and Moses
(6: 14–27)**
As the saga is about to enter a new and, from
the Israelite point of view, more glorious phase
the family tree of Aaron and Moses is now
given. This genealogy serves. as a kind of
preface to the decisive chapter in the story of
deliverance: 'These are the Aaron and
Moses . . .', 'It was they who spoke to
Pharaoh . . .' (26, 27). Because of the subsequent importance of the Aaronite branch of
the family attention focuses on Aaron; nor was
the behaviour of some of Moses' descendants
such as would merit genealogical interest (cf.
Jg. 18: 30). **14 ff.** The first three sons of Jacob
are listed, following the order of Gen. 46: 8–

11, and then the family tree of Levi is given for a couple of generations. **20. Jochebed** may mean 'the LORD is glory'. Assuming that Moses did not rename his mother (cf. Num. 13: 16!), the name could be taken as evidence that the divine name Jehovah-Yahweh was known prior to the revelation to Moses, by some Israelites at least. But see the introduction to Exodus. The marriage of **Amram** to his **father's sister** would not have been permissible under the later legislation (cf. Lev. 18: 12). **Aaron** is mentioned first as being the elder son (cf. 7: 7). **23.** In consequence of the deaths of **Nadab** and **Abihu** (cf. Lev. 10: 1 ff.), **Eleazar** succeeded his father in office (cf. Dt. 10: 6). **25. Phinehas** ('the Nubian') and, probably, **Putiel** are Egyptian names. The incidence of Egyptian names in the tribe of Levi has often been noted by OT specialists. The genealogy poses a problem in that the sojourn in Egypt is spanned by only four generations and yet is said elsewhere to have been in the region of four hundred years (cf. Gen. 15: 13; Exod. 12: 40). But selectivity as a principle governing the construction of Biblical genealogical tables is well-known. Kitchen (*Ancient Orient and Old Testament*, pp. 54 f.) argues that Amram was the name of the family group to which Aaron and Moses belonged; Num. 3: 27 f., representing the Amramites as already numerous at the time of the Exodus, is cited in support of this view.

v. The Miracle of the Rod (6: 28–7: 13)

This miracle is quite distinct from the series of plagues soon to be unleashed on Egypt, and yet it introduces the conflict motif which permeates the next few chapters, as Moses and Aaron demonstrate the superiority of their God-given powers over the magic of Egypt. A similar feat, in legitimation of Moses' claims, had already been performed in the sight of the Israelites (4: 2–5). **30.** The protest of v. 12 is repeated. **1. like God:** primarily the comparison is meant to explain the working relationship between Moses and Aaron when they were in the Pharaoh's presence. But there may be more to it than that. The Pharaoh was a god in the reckoning of the Egyptians; so Moses is assured that he has divine authority for all that he says in the king's hearing. **prophet:** NEB 'spokesman' conveys the idea well. The conception of prophecy behind the statement is noteworthy; prophetic utterances are under the direct control of God. **2.** The demand is now for a full and final release of the Hebrews from bondage. **3. I will harden:** cf. on 4: 21. **4. my divisions:** cf. 13: 18. **7. eighty years old:** cf. Ac. 7: 23, 30. **11.** No suggestion is made as to the origin of the power by which the magicians achieve their effect; it could have been by sleight of hand (cf. Stalker). Jewish tradition had names for two of the magicians (cf. 2 Tim. 3: 8).

vi. The Nile Turned to Blood (7: 14–24)

This is the first of the ten plagues. The primary objective of the plague narratives is to show the superiority of the God of the Israelites over all the dark forces at work in Egypt. Rationalistic explanation of the chief elements in the first nine plagues is possible, and has the positive virtue of showing that the plagues bear a definite relation to the ecological conditions of the Nile valley. In that case the miraculous element in the accounts 'is to be found in their timing, intensity and distribution' (H. R. Jones, *NBC³*). Childs objects to conservative attempts at rationalistic explanation on the grounds that 'this genre of apologetic literature suffers from the strange anomaly of defending biblical "supernaturalism" on the grounds of rationalistic arguments'. Childs' objection involves broader issues than can be treated in the brief compass of the present commentary, but on one point we must express disagreement. It is unhelpful to attribute the rationalizing of elements in the plague storie to a desire to 'defend biblical supernaturalism'. The accounts of the plagues invite a measure of rationalistic explanation just because they describe conditions which, albeit in less extreme form, have prevailed in the Nile valley at one time or another. **15.** The Nile itself was considered a deity and the king's visit could have been for ceremonial purposes. Ceremonies in honour of the river were given special prominence during the period of inundation (see on v. 17). **16.** cf. 5: 1. **17. I will strike:** properly the pronoun refers to God; divine message and prophetic utterance are fused so as to be indistinguishable. **changed into blood:** verse 18 shows that an optical illusion such as deceived the Moabites on one occasion (2 Kg. 3: 22 f.) is not the likely explanation. **blood** need not be taken literally. When the Nile is in flood in July–September large amounts of red clay are brought down from the Ethiopian highlands, for a time producing the phenomenon of the 'Red Nile'. In the *Admonitions of Ipuwer* (possibly composed in the period 2,200–2,050 B.C.) the Egyptian sage complains about the social upheaval, distortion of values, and criminal violence of his day. At one point he bemoans the fact that 'the River is blood'. This may have to be interpreted in the light of another observation, that victims of violence were being thrown into the Nile. Even then it is possible that Ipuwer's acquaintance with the 'Red Nile' suggested the metaphor; he does in fact mention a little earlier that the river was in flood. **18.** Cf. Num. 11: 5 for the importance of **fish** in the Egyptian diet. According to one theory it was the presence of flagellates in the river, rather than an abnormal amount of suspended globules of clay, which caused the death of the fish. **19.** Egypt was, in the words of an ancient maxim, 'the gift of the

Nile'. Almost all the country's water came from the river. **even in the wooden buckets and stone jars:** lit. 'in trees and in stones'; NIV is a guess, but no better explanation has so far been offered. **22.** We are not told how the magicians obtained clear water nor, again (cf. v. 11), how they performed their 'miracle'—beyond that it was **by their secret arts.**

vii. The Plague of Frogs (7: 25–8: 15)
The plagues are not represented as being interdependent, but the possibility should not be ruled out on that account. Frogs were plentiful in the Nile valley, and especially after the inundation. The only other OT references to frogs are also in relation to the second plague (Ps. 78: 45; 105: 30). **8.** Cf. Gen. 20: 7. The Egyptian magicians were unable to disperse the **frogs** which they had helped to proliferate! **9 f.** The frogs are to be destroyed at a prearranged time as another sign of the greatness of the God of the Israelites. Moses proclaims the sovereign power of God to the Pharaoh rather as Isaiah did some centuries later to king Ahaz (Isa. 7: 11).

viii. The Plagues of Gnats and Flies (8:16–32)
16. gnats: NEB has 'maggots', while others prefer 'mosquitoes' or the like. If mosquitoes, the plague could be connected with an inundation of the Nile. Mosquitoes breed most happily in swampy conditions. The timing and the dimensions of the plague, nevertheless, do not permit of a rationalistic explanation. **19. the finger of God:** cf. 31: 18; Lk. 11: 20; another admission (cf. v. 8) is wrung out of the Egyptians. **20 f.** Many OT scholars regard the fourth plague as merely a variant account of the third. This does not seem to be the most satisfactory way of accounting for the similarity between the two plagues. Do we indeed need to account for the similarity? **21. swarms of flies:** the English phrase fills out the Hebrew word which basically means 'mixture'. The plague may have consisted of different types of insects. LXX has 'dog-fly'. Again we are dealing with a familiar feature of Egyptian life; cf. Isa. 7: 18 where the fly symbolizes the Egyptian army. **22. Goshen** was to be exempted from the troubles about to afflict the Egyptians. Because of its location in the NE Delta area it would have escaped the worst effects of any abnormal conditions brought about by the flooding of the Nile. **23.** But the distinction between the Israelites and Egyptians is not merely the result of chance climatic conditions. The greatest distinction of all, on the night of Passover (cf. 11: 7), will not permit even the semblance of a natural explanation. **distinction:** the Hebrew actually has 'redemption', which does not fit easily into the context. NIV represents a small emendation and is to be followed. **25.** The concession goes only

half-way to meeting God's demand. The Pharaoh will not risk losing his slaves by letting them go into the wilderness to worship. **26. would be detestable:** cf. Gen. 43: 32; 46: 34. Moses argues that his people would only incur the odium of the Egyptians since their sacrificial ritual involved the killing of animals which the Egyptians regarded as sacred. Others point out that the concept of animal sacrifice was acknowledged by the Egyptians, and suggest that it would actually have been the ritual, and the fact that the offerings were not being made to an Egyptian god, which would have provoked reprisals. **28.** The king capitulates, only to go back on his word again (32).

ix. Plagues on Cattle and People (9: 1–12)
3. plague: the word is no more specific than that. An outbreak of anthrax is a possibility, though v. 6 implies a sudden and widespread destruction of livestock. Only livestock **in the field** are said to have suffered; cf. on v. 6. **camels** were probably few in number in Egypt of the thirteenth century B.C. **4. a distinction:** cf. 8: 22 f. Apparently the Israelites still owned **livestock** in spite of their privations (cf. Gen. 46: 31–34). **6. All the livestock of the Egyptians** must either refer to animals in the field (cf. v. 4) or be treated as a case of hyperbole (cf. on 1: 7); vv. 19 f. refer to more cattle in the field. **8.** The next plague brings suffering for humans as well as animals. **9. boils:** Dt. 28: 27 mentions 'the boils of Egypt' as a scourge to be avoided. The word occurs several times in Lev. 13 among the symptoms of 'leprosy'. Nile scab and skin anthrax are among the closer diagnoses which have been offered. **11.** The magicians, who had already been forced to admit defeat (8: 18 f.), suffer the added indignity of contracting the plague just like the rest of the population.

x. The Plague of Hail (9: 13–35)
Announcement of the seventh plague is prefaced by some explanatory words for the king's benefit. He should by now have realized that all along he had been at the mercy of the God of the Hebrews. **14. send the full force:** NEB's 'strike home . . . against you' is excellent. **16.** Cf. Rom. 9: 17. The king was, all uncomprehendingly, helping to enhance the reputation (**name**) of God. **18.** Egypt did not experience hail-storms all that frequently; this one was to be of unparalleled ferocity. **19. livestock:** cf. on v. 6. Verses 19 f. introduce a new element. There was to be an opportunity for the Egyptians to protect themselves against the ravages of the hailstorm. Some Egyptians took advantage of the intelligence and cleared their fields of **slaves** and **livestock. 29. spread out my hands:** not the same expression as in v. 22. This is the attitude of prayer, as in 1 Kg. 8: 22, etc. **31.** An important time-marker is provided by the mention of **flax** and **barley.** These

would be at the stage described in January–February. **32. the wheat and spelt** came a month or two later.

xi. The Plagues of Locusts and Darkness (10: 1–29)

Impending events cast their shadow over the chapter. We witness a breakdown of morale among the king's courtiers. For a time they even manage to persuade their master to have second thoughts (7 f.). There are not-so-distant echoes—darkness (15, 21 ff.) and death (17)—of the fateful Passover night. The east wind fulfils a preliminary assignment as an instrument for the furtherance of God's plans (cf. 14: 21). **2.** God will be honoured not only in Egypt but also among future generations of Israelites as the Exodus story is told and retold (cf. 12: 26 f.; Dt. 6: 7, etc.). Rehearsal of the mighty acts of God was an essential feature of Israelite worship (cf. Jos. 24: 2–13; Ps. 78; Ac. 7: 2–53). **4. locusts** were a source of dread because of their destructive potential. Verse 5 gives a good account of the deleterious effect they would have on the land (cf. v. 15). **after the hail:** cf. 9: 32. **7.** The threat seems to have made an impact on the **Pharaoh's officials.** Devastation caused by an invasion of locusts would be the *coup de grâce* for a country already reeling under a plethora of woes. **9.** Moses' words ring with Churchillian defiance. He knows that the king presents no threat, and that the dénouement cannot be long delayed. **10 f.** Suspecting a darker purpose the Pharaoh refuses to allow the whole body of Israelites to go into the wilderness to worship. Women, children and possessions will be his security against duplicity. Worship at sanctuaries was a male prerogative, so why should women and children be released? **13. east wind:** migrations of locusts are affected by wind movement and direction. These particular swarms probably came from Arabia. Here we have a case of rationalizing, we might say, in the original account of the plague! **15. black:** the next plague is of intense darkness; 12: 29 is adumbrated in the eighth and ninth plagues. **17. forgive:** evidence of Moses' increased stature in the eyes of the king. **21.** The last of the 'natural' plagues sees the king at his most conciliatory (24), but it is not enough and it is too late. **darkness that can be felt:** a supernatural darkness, or possibly darkness caused by a *ḥamsîn* storm which arose at a signal from Moses. Ḥamsîn storms, which can last for as long as **three days** (22), bring great clouds of sand sufficient to obscure the light of the sun. **25.** NEB renders the verse so as to mean that the king must not only let the Israelites take their flocks and herds, but must also himself provide animals suitable for sacrifice. This may also be the intended sense of NIV which, however, is rather ambiguously expressed. Less likely is Cole's view that

the Pharaoh is being requested merely to 'allow Israel the means to sacrifice to YHWH by allowing them to take all their flocks and herds', for this is the point of the next verse (26). **29.** Moses' riposte was premature (cf. 11: 8; 12: 31).

xii. 'Yet one plague more' (11: 1–10)

1. and when he does . . . : NEB's 'he will send you packing, as a man dismisses a rejected bride' depends on emendation of the Hebrew; follow NIV. (Another matter: the original does not, of course, represent God as using a colloquialism such as 'to send packing'.) **2. silver . . . gold:** cf. 12: 35 f. and see on 3: 21 f. **3.** Recent events rather than royal upbringing will have accounted for the prestige enjoyed by Moses. Verses 4–8 are in the form of an oration delivered by Moses in the hearing of the Pharaoh. Cf. the comment on 10: 29; but it could be that 'ch. 11 has been constructed in topical and not chronological order' (Childs). Perhaps the speech originally formed part of the exchange reported in 10: 24–29. **5.** Notice of God's intention if *His* **firstborn** was not released had been served on the king before any of the plagues were inflicted (4: 22 f.). **6. loud wailing:** positions will be reversed when God intervenes on the side of Israel (cf. 2: 23). **7. a distinction:** cf. 8: 22 and 9: 4. The Egyptians will be taught a lesson about the uniqueness of the God of the Hebrews (8: 22), and will also discover that their erstwhile slaves are a nation apart. **8.** If the Pharaoh persists in his obstinacy his officials will by-pass him and appeal directly to Moses; they have already shown signs of impatience with his majesty (10: 7). Verse 10 draws a line between the first nine plagues, which are here summarized, and the tenth which is *sui generis*.

III. FROM EGYPT TO SINAI (12: 1–18: 27)

i. The Passover Instituted (12: 1–28)

The deliverance of the Israelites from Egypt was commemorated in two annual festivals. Because Passover was followed immediately by Unleavened Bread the two were sometimes treated as one (*e.g.* Dt. 16: 1–8), but they were quite distinct in character. Passover was a family festival originally observed without reference to altar, sanctuary or priesthood (note the absence of ritual prescriptions in the Levitical calendar at Lev. 23: 5). Unleavened Bread, on the other hand, had from its inception the status of a *ḥag*, i.e. one of the three annual pilgrim-festivals which had to be celebrated at a sanctuary (23: 14 f.). For the moral significance which Paul attached to the calendrical juxtaposition of Passover and Unleavened Bread see 1 C. 5: 7 f. It is the opinion of many OT scholars that Passover was an ancient pastoral festival which was invested with a completely new significeance in the light of the Exodus. This is a reasonable hypothesis—the analogy of the Israelite practice of circumcision suggests itself—but there is no clear evidence that this was the case. **2. the first month:** Abib (13: 4; 23: 15), later called Nisan (Neh. 2: 1; Est. 3: 7) and corresponding to March–April. Previously the Israelites may have observed an autumnal new year (cf. 23: 16; 34: 22, and the law of the jubilee in Lev. 25: 8 ff.). Cassuto maintains, on syntactical grounds, that v. 2 is not announcing a calendrical adjustment but is, rather, a statement of fact. ('You are now beginning to count a new year; now the new year will bring you a change of destiny', is his paraphrase of the verse.) There is something to be said for this view; cf. NEB's use of both the present and future tenses. **3. lamb:** the word is less specific; cf. v. 5 ('from the sheep or from the goats'). **4.** In later times a minimum of ten persons per **household** was laid down. **5. without defect:** cf. 1 Pet. 1: 19. **6.** No reason is given for the interval between selection (3) and the killing on **the fourteenth day:** perhaps it was to ensure that the animal was physically sound. **at twilight:** see the commentary on Lev. 23: 5. **7.** An apotropaic origin for this rite is often assumed; here it was certainly meant to be apotropaic in the sense that the judgment of God had to be averted. **8. roasted:** Dt. 16: 7 permits the boiling of the flesh of the Passover sacrifice, in accordance with the later custom for sacrifices generally (cf. 1 Sam. 2: 15, etc.). **bread made without yeast** figured in the Passover ritual as well as in the festival which followed it (14–20). The **bitter herbs** were later taken to symbolize the bitter experience of the Israelites in their servitude (cf. 1: 14). **10.** Cf. 23: 18; 34: 25. The flesh was not to be put to profane use. **11. in haste** also suggests a measure of trepidation. Isa. 52: 12, speaking of the 'Second Exodus', makes a point of deliberate contrast. **Passover:** 'passover victim', as in 1 C. 5: 7. The root also occurs in Isa. 31: 5 (*q.v.*), and this is probably the best clue to its meaning in Exod. 12; note especially 'I will pass over you' (13). There is little to commend the suggestion that the root from which we derive 'Passover' is connected with the homonymous verb 'to limp', and even less to support the idea that Passover originally involved some sort of 'limping dance'. **12. pass through** renders a verb quite unconnected with **pass over** in v. 13. **the gods of Egypt** were also to be brought into judgment. Their ineffectualness had been demonstrated in the earlier plagues when the natural forces thought to be under their jurisdiction were seen to be in the control of a greater power. **14. a day:** there is no obvious antecedent, but on the basis of vv. 17 f. we can confidently relate this verse to the observance of Unleavened Bread. In general

we have to bear in mind the Israelite method of reckoning days from sunset to sunset, and the fact that the Exodus actually took place on the night of the 15th Nisan. The festival of Unleavened Bread is commonly thought to have originated as an agricultural celebration; the Israelites are said to have taken over the festival when they settled in Canaan. In Exodus, however, Unleavened Bread has a purely historical association (cf. 12: 39). At the same time, it should be noted that the regulations of vv. 14–20 are addressed to a settled community; cf. especially v. 17 ('I brought') and v. 19 ('a sojourner or a native of the land'). **15. yeast** came to be associated with moral decay in both the NT and the rabbinic writings (cf. 1 C. 5:6 ff.; Gal. 5: 9, etc.). **17. your divisions:** cf. on 13: 18. In vv. 21–27 Moses issues instructions concerning the Passover to the leaders of the people. **22. hyssop:** identification is not easy; NEB has 'marjoram'. The reference to **hyssop** in John's crucifixion narrative (Jn 19: 29) is not without problems for the interpreter, but is certainly in keeping with the evangelist's presentation of our Lord's death in a paschal framework. **hyssop** was also used in certain purification rites (cf. Lev. 14: 4 ff.; Num. 19: 6). **Not one of you shall go out** clearly applies to later observances of Passover (cf. v. 31). **23. destroyer:** 2 Sam. 24: 16 speaks, with reference to another occasion, of 'the angel who was working destruction'. The **destroyer**, far from being opposed to God, is the agent of divine judgment. Verses 26 f. emphasize the didactic element in the Israelites' celebration of these epochal events (cf. 10: 2). Jewish observance of Passover still includes a series of questions and answers modelled on these verses.

ii. The Exodus (12: 29–51)

29. Attempts to find a natural cause for this the final plague are doomed to failure, that is if we take seriously the statement that it was the **firstborn** who were affected and that animals as well as humans were involved. **32.** The king has no alternative but to agree to the conditions laid down by Moses and Aaron. To his earlier request for Moses and Aaron to intercede with God for him (10: 17) he now adds a plea for their benediction. **35 f.** Cf. 1 1: 2. **37. Rameses** is the same as Raamses in 1: 11 (*q.v.*). **Succoth:** probably the same as Ṭkw(t), the name of a town or region, mentioned in Egyptian texts. It is possible that it was on the site of Tell el-Maskhuta; E. Naville equated Succoth with Pithom (cf. on 1: 11) but others have interpreted the evidence differently. Anastasi papyrus V (late thirteenth century B.C.) mentions Ṭkw(t) in connection with the escape of a couple of slaves from Egypt to Palestine; this is not surprising in view of its location near the NE border of Egypt. **about six hundred thousand men:** a remarkable number which has troubled commentators greatly; see the introduction to Exodus, particularly p. 151. **38. Many other people:** called 'the rabble' in Num. 11: 4. The Cushite woman whom Moses married (Num. 12: 1) may have been one of their number. **40. 430 years:** see the introduction to Exodus. [The reckoning has been related to the 'Era of Tanis'; cf. Num. 13: 22b.] Verse 42 speaks of reciprocal vigils. In future the Israelites will keep vigil on the night of Passover in gratitude for God's watchful protection during the judgment of Egypt. Verses 43–49 establish who can partake of the Passover sacrifice; the directions given here are, in part, addressed to the situation reported in v. 38. **44 f. A temporary resident** or **hired worker** cannot be treated as a permanent member of a family or of the community. A **slave** who has been **bought** is in a different position and may participate provided that he has been **circumcised. 46. not break any of the bones:** another parallel between our Lord's death and the Passover sacrifice which is brought out in the Fourth Gospel (Jn 19: 36). **48. alien** is not the same as **temporary resident** in v. 45, and implies more permanent residence. Again circumcision is put forward as the criterion for inclusion or exclusion.

iii. Commemorative Institutions (13: 1–16)

The separate topics of redemption of the firstborn (1 f., 11–16) and observance of the festival of Unleavened Bread (3–10) are linked in this section by the common theme of Exodus commemoration (8, 14). Childs has drawn attention to the structural parallelism between vv. 3–10 and vv. 11–16; compare v. 5 with v. 11, v. 8 with v. 14, and v. 9 with v. 16. **2.** Cf. 22: 29f. God lays claim upon those whom He has redeemed (cf. v. 15 and see 1 C. 6: 19 f.). Verses 12 f. indicate that the law of the first-born applied to males only. **4. Abib:** cf. on 12: 2. **6. seventh day:** 12: 16 also mentions a 'holy assembly' on the first day of Unleavened Bread. **9.** The Israelites did not look to religious markings or charms for inspiration, for they had come to know God through historical experience. Cf. on v. 16. **12. given over to the LORD:** lit. 'cause to pass over to the LORD'. There is a similar expression used in connection with child sacrifice as practised in pagan cults (see Lev. 18: 21; 2 Kg. 16: 3). Since there is every reason to think that the pagan ritual antedates the Exodus it is possible that the present use of the expression is investing it with a fundamentally new significance. **13.** The donkey was not included among the ritually clean domestic animals (cf. Lev. 22: 19). Because of its importance in other respects owners must often have exercised the option of redemption allowed here. The principle, though not the manner, of the redemption of the **firstborn of humans** is stated. A redemption

price of five silver shekels is given in Num. 18: 16 (cf. Num. 3: 46 ff.). **16.** The redemption of the first-born will be an unfailing reminder of the national redemption from Egypt. **symbol:** NEB has 'phylactery' (cf. Mt. 23. 5). Because Dt. 6: 8 and 11: 18 enjoin the binding of the words of God upon the hand it later became the practice to wear leather receptacles (t*ephillîn*) on the left arm and the forehead. These held pieces of parchment on which were inscribed the appropriate portions (*viz.* Exod. 13: 1–10, 11–16; Dt. 6: 4–9; 11: 13–21).

iv. To the Red Sea (13: 17–14: 4)

17. The most direct route to Canaan was along the Mediterranean coast, the route known to the Egyptians as 'The ways of Horus' and called here **the road through the Philistine country.** The main contingent of Philistines did not settle in the coastal belt of Canaan until some time later, so that it probably was not confrontation with the Philistines which was being avoided. But the direct route to Canaan would have been dotted with Egyptian garrisons and—supposing that they had overcome that obstacle—would have brought the Israelites into immediate conflict with the peoples of Canaan. **18. Red Sea:** The modern preference for 'Sea of Reeds' is not soundly based; see Davies (bibliog.). The term probably describes a stretch of water in the isthmus of Suez. Lake Menzaleh in the north, Lake Balah, Lake Timsah and the Bitter Lakes have all been nominated for the honour at one time or another. Certain identification of most of the places mentioned in this section is not possible, so that the itinerary is of little assistance in the locating of the 'Sea of Reeds'. **armed for battle:** cf. the use of the word 'hosts' in 12: 17, 41. NEB follows LXX in taking the word to mean 'fifth (generation)' but there is not much to commend this rendering (cf. also 'fourth generation' in Gen. 15: 16). The picture of warriors, women and children marching out of Egypt is not as unlikely as it may seem. In a relief from the Medinet Habu temple of Rameses III the bellicose Philistines are shown arriving at the frontiers of Egypt, warriors, families, ox-carts and all! **19.** Cf. Gen. 50: 25, and, for the thought, Gen. 24: 2–8; Heb. 11: 13. **20. Etham** has been connected with an Old Egyptian word meaning 'fort', though not all are agreed. If there was an Egyptian garrison there the change of direction ordered in 14: 2 f. would have an added explanation. **21 f.** Manifestations of the divine presence such as would mark the covenant-making ceremony at Sinai (cf. 19: 16 ff.) ensure that the people are led by the right way. The notice is timely, for the immediate circumstances (see 14: 1–18) would have suggested otherwise. **2.** None of the places mentioned in the verse can be located with any confidence. The first name is patently Egyptian and the other two are Semitic; they will all have been close to the Egyptian NE border. **3.** Cf. on 13: 20. The Pharaoh would receive intelligence leading him to suppose that the Israelites had reached an impasse and were easy prey.

v. The Crossing of the Sea (14: 5–31)
The Israelites' dilemma has been contrived in order to display once more the might and glory of God. The forces of nature are marshalled both to provide safe passage for the Israelites and to overwhelm with destruction the Egyptian detachments which have pursued them. See Ps. 77: 16–20. **5.** It was the realization that they had lost a sizeable proportion of their labour force which made the Egyptians decide to give chase. **6.** The Hyksos are usually credited with the introduction of the **chariot** to Egypt. By comparison, the Israelites' weapons must have been crude and inadequate. (Israel did not possess a proper chariot force until Solomon's reign.) **11.** This is but the first of many complaints which rang in Moses' ear during the wilderness wanderings (cf. 16: 2 f.; 17: 2 f., etc.). **12.** Something of this sort must have been said on the occasion described in 6: 9. **20.** Jos. 24: 7 recalls that on this occasion God 'put darkness between you and the Egyptians'. The latter part of the verse is difficult to translate and is usually emended to yield a suitable sense. **22. a wall:** 'This metaphor is no more to be taken literally than when Ezr. 9: 9 says that God has given him a "wall" (same word) in Israel. It is a poetic metaphor to explain why the Egyptian chariots could not sweep in to right and left, and cut Israel off; they had to cross by the same ford, directly behind the Israelites' (Cole). **24. the last watch of the night:** the night was divided into three (cf. Jg. 7: 19), so that the morning watch would extend from 2.00 a.m. till 6.00 a.m. Saul also found it an ideal time to belabour the enemy (1 Sam. 11: 11). **threw . . . into confusion** translates a word used particularly of God's routing of Israel's enemies (cf. 23: 27; Jos. 10: 10). **28.** Nothing in the account requires us to think that the king shared in the fate of his army, nor is there any historical evidence to support such an assumption. Considering the frequent mention of the Pharaoh in the plague narratives the absence of specific reference to him in chs. 14 and 15 must point in the same direction.

vi. The Song of the Sea (15: 1–21)
The great event of ch. 14 was celebrated in a hymn extolling the majestic power of God. By virtue of its poetic structure and frequent archaisms the poem invites recognition as what it claims to be, 'an early and authentic witness to the crossing of the Sea of Reeds by Israel' (W. F. Albright). Verses 1–12 celebrate the overthrow of the Egyptians in the sea and vv. 13–17 look beyond the wilderness to the settlement in Canaan. While it is possible to

treat the occurrences of the perfect tense in vv. 13–17 as so many cases of the 'prophetic perfect', it could be that these verses were added as a supplement to the original composition after the Israelites had entered Canaan. The 'Song of the Sea' has sometimes been explained as a later expansion of Miriam's 'song' of v. 21; this is based solely on the dubious principle of 'shorter is earlier'. **2.** LORD: in this case the shorter form Yah (as in *hallelu-jah*, 'praise the Lord') is used. **my song:** there is some philological support for NEB's 'my defence'. **my father's God:** cf. 3: 6, 15. **3. a warrior:** a fundamental conception of God among the Israelites; God was fighting with them in their 'holy wars'. **8. the blast of your nostrils:** the prose account talks of God causing a strong east wind to blow (14: 21). **9.** Any **spoils** worth the taking would only have been what had previously been obtained from the Egyptians (cf. 3:21 f.; 11:2; 12:35f.). **11.** God is unique; we should need to go to other passages, however, to find unequivocal expression of monotheistic faith. **12. earth** may sometimes mean 'underworld', like its cognates in Akkadian and Ugaritic. Either translation would be acceptable, though NEB retains 'earth'. **13. redeemed:** cf. on 6: 6. **holy dwelling** could denote Sinai (cf. Dt. 33: 2), or Zion (cf.2 Sam. 15: 25), or, since the word literally means 'pastoral dwelling', the whole land of Canaan (as in Jer. 10: 25; 23: 3). **14. Philistia:** the term can hardly have become current until after the main Philistine settlement in the twelfth century B.C. **15. melt away:** cf. Jos. 2: 9 ff. **17. the mountain of your inheritance:** a very similar expression is used to describe Baal's abode in a Ugaritic text (fifteenth century B.C. (?)). The remainder of the verse may have Zion in view, but some explain the references in a more general way. **18.** An affirmation of the kingship of God such as is common in the 'enthronement Psalms' (cf. Ps. 93: 1, etc.). Verse 19 is a prose appendix to the hymn. **20. prophetess:** presumably Miriam had the gift of ecstatic utterance. Cf. the cases of Eldad and Medad in Num. 11: 26 f., and note the implication of Num. 12: 2 with regard to Miriam. The women's victory dance was similar to that which greeted Saul and David after the killing of Goliath (1 Sam. 18: 6 f.).

vii. Food Miraculously Provided (15: 22–16: 36)
Much uncertainty attaches to the problem of the route followed by the Israelites after they moved on from the 'Red Sea'. The issue turns very much on where we locate Sinai, the mountain of revelation. This being so, it must be said that the traditional location of the mountain in the south of the Sinai peninsula still has many advocates. In the commentary we shall assume that the Israelites took the road which tradition

has ascribed to them, and first went down the western side of the peninsula. **22.** The **Desert of Shur** lay to the northwest of the Sinai peninsula, between Egypt and Palestine (cf. 1 Sam. 15: 7; 27: 8). **23.** Bitter water will not have been peculiar to Marah, but it was sufficiently bad to be enshrined in the name. The most common identification is with the modern 'Ain Hawarah. **25. showed** usually means 'instructed'; it is the same root which produces the word *tôrāh*, 'instruction, law'. Moses was instructed as to the properties of some tree or bush which would counteract the bitterness of the water. Parallels for this method of sweetening water have been cited, and in particular the Arabs' use of the barberry bush. Cf. 2 Kg. 2: 21 for the use of salt to purify undrinkable water (a case of 'homeopathic magic' according to Hyatt!). Jewish interpreters have discovered allusion to the law in the use of the verb translated **showed**, while many an earlier Christian exegete found the cross prefigured in the wood. Evidently the sweetening of the water was used as a parable of God's healing power (cf. v. 26). The plagues of Egypt would not trouble the Israelites if they continued to obey God (cf. Dt. 7: 15; 28: 27). **27. Elim:** another watering-place, possibly to be identified with Wadi Gharandel a few miles south of 'Ain Hawarah. **1. the Desert of Sin:** the name could be connected with Sinai; the two will have been adjacent wherever we locate the mountain. **2 f.** It was a barren place to which they had come and again the people gave vent to their feelings. Now they say that it would have been better if they had suffered **by the LORD's hand**—like the first-born of Egypt, presumably. The years of slavery and oppression seemed idyllic in comparison with their present state. Their chief complaint was about the lack of meat. 'Like all pastoralists, they were very loath to slaughter their beasts (cf. Num. 11: 22) . . .' (Cole). **4. rain down bread:** cf. Ps. 78: 24. **from heaven:** in presenting Himself to the Jews as 'the bread of life' our Lord drew a comparison between Himself and the manna sent down from heaven (Jn 6: 41). **5.** A special arrangement in recognition of the sanctity of the sabbath. See on vv. 22–30. **7. the glory of the LORD** was to be recognized in the miraculous supply of food as much as in the glorious manifestation of v. 10. If on this occasion the **grumbling** was met with a display of glory, it would not always be so (see Num. 11: 1). **8.** Quails for **meat** and manna for **bread** were God's gracious provision for their need (see vv. 13–36). Verse **10** reinforces the point of vv. 7 f. ('what are we?') in drawing attention away from Moses and Aaron and directing it to the LORD whose **glory** was being manifested **in the cloud** (cf. 13: 21 f.). **13. quail:** cf. Num. 11: 31–35. They are small gallinaceous birds

which migrate north from Africa and Arabia in the spring, some passing over the Sinai peninsula. They fly quite close to the ground and, especially when exhausted, are easy prey. Nothing else is said about them here, for the preoccupation is with the manna which was to be the Israelites' staple diet for the next forty years (v. 35; cf. Jos. 5: 12). **14. flakes:** a *hapax graphomenon* of uncertain meaning. NEB also has 'flakes' and JB 'powdery'. **15. What is it?:** in Hebrew, *mān hû'*. Actually the Hebrew for 'what' is *māh* (as in vv. 7 f.); the form *mān* is, however, paralleled in Canaanite texts of the second millennium B.C. Is this manna (cf. v. 31) related to the Arabic *mann* which is found in parts of the Sinai peninsula in early summer? The latter is an edible excretion produced by certain insects which live on the twigs of tamarisk trees (see F. S. Bodenheimer, 'The Manna of Sinai', *Biblical Archaeologist*, 10, 1947, pp. 2–6). While there are certainly features in common the preternatural elements in the account of the manna must not be overlooked; see especially vv. 18, 24, 26, 35. There was, too, an educative purpose behind the provision of the manna, according to Dt. 8: 3, 16; it was also 'spiritual food' inasmuch as it pointed beyond the merely physical and temporal (1 C. 10: 3; cf. Jn 6: 50 f.). **16. omer:** just over two litres. The term occurs only in this chapter, hence the explanatory addition of v. 36. It is not to be confused with the *homer* (which comprised 100 'omers'). **18. omer** in this case means a vessel holding exactly this amount. The verse is quoted in 2 C. 8: 14 f. in support of the Christian ideal of the voluntary equalization of wealth. **22.** Apparently the people were not expecting the double portion which came on the sixth day and went to Moses to seek an explanation. **23. Sabbath,** it is implied, was observed by the Israelites even before the giving of the Ten Commandments (ch. 20). This is the first occurrence of the word in the OT, though for the idea see Gen. 2: 2 f. **bake:** cf. Num. 11: 8. **24.** Manna baked or boiled on the eve of sabbath did not come under the prohibition of v. 19. **27.** It appears that these offenders were not punished; the law of Sinai had not yet been promulgated (cf. 31: 14). Contrast Num. 15: 32–36. **31. manna:** cf. on v. 15. **tasted:** see Num. 11: 8 for a slightly different description. **33.** This is the 'golden urn' of Heb. 9: 4. [It is said to have been golden in LXX, though not in *MT*.] The **jar** is not mentioned in connection with the most holy place in Solomon's temple (see 1 Kg. 8: 9). Stalker links its disappearance with the capture of the ark of the covenant by the Philistines (1 Sam. 4). **34.** We are to understand that the manna was placed **in front of the Testimony** (i.e. before the tables of the law) only when the tent of meeting had been constructed (see chs. 25–40). **35**. Cf. Num.21:5; Jos.5:12.

viii. Troubles at Rephidim (17: 1–16)
Problems familiar (1–7; cf. 15: 22–25) and un-familiar (8–16) confront Moses at this stage. **1. no water:** there are similarities between the present narrative (1–7) and an incident reported in Num. 20: 2–13 in connection with Kadesh. In particular, the reappearance of the name Meribah (7) in Num. 20: 13 has inclined many scholars to treat the two accounts as variant forms of a single tradition. On the other hand, problems concerning the provisioning of the Israelites must often have arisen during their term in the wilderness. It would be unwise to assume that the memory of only one such contretemps has been preserved. **from place to place:** fuller details are given in Num. 33: 12 ff. **Rephidim:** Wadi Refayid, according to tradition. Others (Noth, Clements) are favour-ably disposed towards an identification with the *er-rafid* mountain ridge to the east of the Gulf of Aqaba. **2. quarrel** and **put . . . to the test** are the verbs underlying the names Meribah and Massah in v. 7. **3**. Again the basest of motives is attributed to Moses (cf. 16: 3). Little did they know that before long it would be Moses' intercession which would save them from extinction (32: 9–14). **6. I will stand there before you:** cf. the people's question reported in v. 7. **Horeb:** a geographical datum usually given short shrift by commentators. Since the Israelites were still some distance from Sinai-Horeb the reference is indeed prob-lematical— unless we accept with H. R. Jones (*NBC*³) that the name 'here stands for some peak other than Sinai in the same mountain range'. For a comparatively recent illustration —in minor key, of course—of 'the water-holding properties of Sinai limestone' see *NBD*, p. 1253 [cf. on Num. 20: 11]. **7**. The conferring of two names on a single place is unusual and has often been put down to the conflation of two accounts of the same incident; cf. on v. 1. **8**. The Amalekites were a nomadic people who roamed the Negeb and desert re-gions further south. It was inevitable that be-fore long they would come into conflict with the Israelites; the meagre resources of the area would not suffice for both groups. If for the Israelites it was to be a war of attrition (cf. v. 16), the hostility was felt no less on the other side. The Amalekites harassed their rivals re-lentlessly on the road to Canaan and later showed themselves willing for every anti-Israelite enterprise launched by their neigh-bours (cf. Dt. 25: 17 ff.; Jg. 3: 13; 6: 3, 33; 7:12). **9. Joshua**, Moses' understudy, is mentioned for the first time (cf. 24: 13; 32: 17, etc.). It is noteworthy that the **staff of God** figures in both the episodes which this chapter links with Rephidim (cf. v. 5). **10. Hur:** Jewish tradition associates him with Miriam, either as her hus-band or as her son. **11**. This raising of the hand (strictly singular) is not likely to have been a gesture of supplication. Verse 9 indicates that, as on other occasions when God's power was being displayed, Moses was holding aloft the rod of God (cf. 9: 22 f.; 10: 12 f.; 14: 16). **12. hands:** 'Perhaps he alternated his hands in holding the rod' (Hyatt). **14. Write:** perhaps in the 'Book of the Wars of the Lord' (Num. 21: 14). **15. my Banner:** for the military sig-nificance of banners see Jer. 4: 21; 51: 12, 27; for the naming of altars see Gen. 33: 20, etc. **16. hands were lifted up to the throne of the LORD:** in supplication. But *MT* has 'hand' (sg.). Placing a hand upon the object, whether banner (cf. RSV) or altar (= 'throne'?), could signify the swearing of an oath (cf. Gen. 24: 2 f.). **from generation to generation:** cf. 1 Sam. 15: 1–33; 30: 1–20; 1 Chr. 4: 43.

ix. Jethro Meets the Israelites (18: 1–27)
Although Jethro had apparently not been en-lightened as to the real reason for Moses' return to Egypt (cf. on 4: 18), he had heard by now of the Israelites' departure from that land. After listening to an account of the mighty acts of God by which the deliverance was achieved (1–9) he was able to offer his son-in-law some practical advice which was gratefully received (13–27). The meeting of the two echoes Gen. 14: 17–20 and the story of the encounter be-tween Abraham and Melchizedek. Both Jethro and Melchizedek were 'non-Israelite' priests who came to offer their congratulations on hearing of God's deliverance of His servants; both were treated deferentially by the men of God whom they had come to greet (7; cf. Gen. 14: 20 and Heb. 7: 4–7); both blessed God for the exercise of His saving might. **1. Jethro:** cf. 2: 15 f. **2. had sent away:** because the underlying verb is occasionally used with the meaning 'divorce' one strand of Jewish tra-dition had it that Moses divorced **Zipporah**. However, the root has its usual significance, as in v. 27 ('sent . . . on his way'). **4**. This is the first reference to **Eliezer**, though note the plural 'sons' in 4: 20. **5. near the mountain of God:** cf. the reference to Horeb in 17: 6. Some take it that the Israelites were actually beyond Rephidim at this point (but see 19: 2). **7**. Interest centres on Jethro; Moses' wife and family are mentioned only in passing (5 f.). **the tent** will have been Moses' own tent, not the 'tent of meeting' of 33: 7–11. **8. all the hard-ships:** cf. the theme of vv. 13–26. **10**. Cf. Gen. 14: 20. **11**. Similar sentiments are expressed by Naaman the Syrian in 2 Kg. 5: 15. **12. brought:** the verb means, literally, 'took'. Jethro pro-vided sacrifices 'for God'; he may also have participated in the sacrificial ritual, though this is not required by the sense of the Hebrew. In view of our earlier comparisons with Gen. 14, advocates of the 'Kenite hypothesis' (*viz.* that

the Israelites learned to worship God as Yahweh from the Midianites/Kenites) might wish to make more of the statement that Jethro 'took' (lit.) sacrifices 'for God'. Melchizedek 'took' a tenth of all the spoils restored by Abraham (Gen. 14: 20 and especially Heb. 7: 6). In point of fact, the supporters of the 'Kenite hypothesis' interpret this verse to mean that Jethro was initiating the Israelites into the worship of Yahweh-Jehovah. The sharing of a meal **in the presence of God** may be a hint that the Israelites and Kenites entered into a covenant on this occasion (cf. on 24: 11); see Jg. 1: 16 (the Kenites were a Midianite tribe). **15. to seek God's will** means, in the first instance, to obtain an oracular decision. The Urim and Thummim (cf. 28: 30) provided one method of obtaining divine guidance. At this stage the Israelites will have had few if any written statutes and scarcely any experience in case law. For examples of especially difficult cases which could not be decided on the basis of earlier legislation see Lev. 24: 10–23; Num. 15: 32–36. **21.** Cf. Num. 11: 14–17. **officials over thousands:** some suggest that the organization of the people reflects Israelite military practice (cf. 1 Sam. 8: 12; 2 Kg. 1: 9). Exodus–Deuteronomy frequently draw attention to the military features of the Israelites' tribal organization in the wilderness period.

IV. THE GIVING OF THE LAW
(19: 1–24: 18)
i. The Theophany at Sinai (19: 1–25)
With the arrival of the Israelites at Sinai (1 f.) the primary purpose of the Exodus was nearing fulfilment (cf. 3: 12). But first there were preparations to be made. The theophany at the holy mountain was not an experience to be entered upon lightly; much of the chapter is concerned with the way in which the Israelites made ready to receive the divine revelation. **2.** As has already been indicated, the location of Mount **Sinai** is a question much debated. The weight of tradition favours Jebel Musa ('Mountain of Moses') in the south of the Sinai peninsula, while the claims of the neighbouring Ras es-safsafeh have also been pressed by some scholars. Some who think that Exod. 19 describes a volcanic eruption prefer to locate the mountain in NW Arabia, since there 'is no evidence for the existence of volcanoes in the peninsula of Sinai' (Hyatt). However, it is questionable whether our chapter is describing actual volcanic activity. Yet others adduce reasons for locating the mountain in the region of Kadesh-barnea, construing 3: 18 to mean that Sinai was much nearer the Egyptian border than is the traditional site. This view introduces unnecessary conflicts between the various sets of data given in the OT. Conclusive identification is impossible; the important thing is that

there was a Sinai. **3.** Any suggestion that God was thought to dwell on Mount Sinai is ill-founded if it is based on this verse. **4.** Cf. Dt. 32: 10 f. There is a covenant (or treaty) pattern discernible in vv. 4–8: proclamation of God's saving acts (4), statement of covenant conditions (5 f.), response by the other contracting party (7 f.). Cf. the introduction to ch. 20. **5. treasured possession:** used a couple of times of royal treasures (1 Chr. 29: 3; Ec. 2: 8). It is the word rendered 'jewels' in the AV of Mal. 3: 17. **the whole earth is mine:** 'implicit monotheism' (Stalker). High-sounding claims were made on the behalf of the gods of Babylonia and Assyria, but the gods could rise no higher than the military fortunes of their devotees. By contrast, the God of Israel was never more truly supreme than when His people were exiled and dispossessed. **6. a kingdom of priests:** the expression is unique in the OT, though cf. Isa. 61: 6. It is not that there was to be a priestly caste within the nation; rather, the whole nation was to enjoy priestly privileges and also to fulfil a priestly rôle in relation to the rest of the nations. 1 Pet. 2: 9 applies the term to the church, the 'New Israel' (cf. Rev. 1: 6; 5: 10; 20: 6). **9. trust in you:** cf. 14. 31. Verse 9b is almost the same as v. 8b; it is possible to treat it as resumptive. **10. wash:** cf. the purificatory measures undertaken by the Levites before their presentation to the LORD (Num. 8: 21). **11.** God only *appeared* at Mount Sinai; He did not *live* there after the fashion of the gods of Saphon and Olympus (cf. on v. 3). **12 f.** The rules are necessitated by the contagiousness of the 'holiness' of the mountain; it could even be contracted indirectly (13). **15.** Marital relations could disqualify a person from participation in sacred rites (cf. 1 Sam. 21: 5). Verse 16 portrays the theophany in terms of a thunderstorm. Because v. 18 seems to refer to volcanic eruption it is frequently argued that two distinct traditions of the theophany have been brought together to produce the present account. The two ideas are not mutually exclusive, both being for the more part conventional representations of the divine presence. **21.** The warning is repeated in v. 24 (cf. vv. 12 f.) to convey the absolute necessity of keeping within the appointed limits. **22. priests:** it would be surprising if the Israelites did not have some religious functionaries before the consecration of the 'Levitical priests'. The term may even be used proleptically of Aaron, Nadab and Abihu, in consideration of their later appointment to the priesthood (28: 1; cf. 24: 1 f., 9 ff.). In 24: 5 'young men' are instructed to offer sacrifices in connection with the covenant ceremony. **break out:** cf. 2 Sam. 6: 6 ff. **25. and told them** makes the most of the present text. A truer rendering would be 'and said to them', in which case Moses' words have been lost in transmission. (*MT* has suffered a similar accident in transmission at Gen. 4: 8, but there the ancient versions come to the rescue.)

ii. The Ten Commandments (20: 1-20)

The fundamental principles of Israelite religion are encapsulated in the Ten Commandments which were mediated to the people through Moses at Sinai. Taken in their proper setting they are the covenant terms imposed by God upon His covenant partners, for the record of the transactions at Sinai displays features which recur in the secular covenants and treaties of the times. The most fruitful comparisons have been made with the Near Eastern vassal treaty, which bound a subject state to an overlord with the promise of protection for as long as the treaty obligations were observed. At Sinai God, as overlord and saviour, dictated His terms, the people signified their acceptance, and a covenant was ratified (cf. 24: 7 f.).

That this 'Decalogue' is early is suggested by the absence of cultic requirements (it is sometimes called the 'ethical Decalogue' to distinguish it from the 'ritual Decalogue' of 34: 11–26); that it is not merely a law-code but a constitutive document is indicated by the form in which the demands are expressed and by the absence of penalties to be applied when the individual commandments were broken. There are other legal sections in the Pentateuch (*e.g.* the 'Book of the Covenant' in 20: 21–23: 33) which expound the principles enshrined in the Ten Commandments. The form in which the commandments are presented deserves further attention. Ancient Near Eastern laws are usually divided into two main categories: casuistic and apodeictic. Casuistic laws are most often expressed in the form 'When . . . , (then) . . .' (cf. 21: 7), and may have subsidiary ('if') clauses appended (cf. 21: 8–11). Apodeictic law deals in absolutes and is exemplified most clearly in the Ten Commandments. The latter are mainly in the form of prohibitions and are addressed to the individual Israelite. Only the fourth and fifth in the tabula are expressed as positive commands. Some scholars have surmised that even these were originally delivered as prohibitions and have sought by Procrustean means to make them conform to the general pattern. The Decalogue is repeated, with some minor differences, in Dt. 5: 6–21; the main divergences are in the treatment of the fourth and fifth commandments. It seems a justifiable inference that the commentary attaching to these commandments did not form part of the original communication; the commandments will have been expressed tersely and in such a way that they could easily be inscribed on a small tablet. Three different ways of extracting ten commandments (cf. 34: 28) from vv. 2–17 have evolved. In the present commentary we shall

regard v. 3 as the first of the series and vv. 4–6 as the second. **2.** In the above-mentioned vassal treaties the terms were normally prefaced by an account of the benevolent acts of the overlord towards his vassal. The reminder of God's acts of deliverance is brief by comparison, but serves a similar purpose. **3. before me:** various explanations of the Hebrew have been suggested; in other contexts the expression denotes hostility and mutual exclusion. Cf. 'with me' in v. 23. **4. an idol:** fashioned from wood or stone. In 34: 17 (*q.v.*) molten images are also banned. It is the making of images for use in worship that is proscribed; in this sense Israelite worship was aniconic. Whatever aberrations may have marred the nation's subsequent history, there is no evidence to suggest that images of Yahweh were ever made. **the waters below** perhaps reflects Hebrew cosmology, but subterranean springs and rivers could be intended. **5. them** could refer back to v. 3, though v. 4 effectively supplies a plural antecedent. **jealous** has unworthy connotations; God is *zealous* for His name and reputation. **the third and fourth generation** 'reflects the greatest probable extent of the range of members of any one family actually living together in one household' (Clements). **6. love** issues in obedience, and has its reward (cf. Jn 14: 21, 23 f.). **7.** 'It is unanimously agreed that this commandment protects the name of Yahweh from that unlawful use which could take place in the oath, the curse, and in sorcery, and, besides this, "wherever Israel in any way opened its doors to the cult of another deity"' (Stamm and Andrew). To invoke the name of God in substantiation of a claim which was mischievous or fraudulent was to invite the wrathful interposition of God Himself. See on Lev. 24: 16. Just as objectionable was the claim by certain false prophets that they were proclaiming 'the burden of the LORD'; the very use of the expression was forbidden (Jer. 23: 33–40). **8. Remember:** Dt. 5: 12 has 'observe'. The Babylonian *shapattu* was the name by which the fifteenth day of the month (full moon) was known. In spite of its apparent connection with the Hebrew *shabbāt* ('sabbath') the attempt to discover a relationship between the institutions represented by the two terms has proved rather unproductive. There is no reason to doubt that the sabbath was observed in the time of Moses, or before it for that matter. Verses **10 f.** give religious and humanitarian reasons for the institution of the sabbath. **11.** Cf. Gen. 2: 1 ff. In Dt. 5: 14 f. the humanitarian aspect is stressed ('that your manservant and your maidservant may rest as well as you'), and, in pursuance of the point, a reference to the Israelites' own experience of bondage in Egypt replaces the present argument from creation. This is in keeping with the humanitarian emphasis of Deuteronomy. Neither reason for the observance of sabbath is likely to have been included in the commandment as originally formulated (see above). **12.** A principle of broad application in the 'extended family' of early Israelite society. The **mother** as much as the **father** was to be honoured. Cf. the joint responsibility vested in the parents of the 'stubborn and rebellious son' (Dt. 21: 18–21). The commandment has not been abrogated in the Christian dispensation (cf. Eph. 6: 1 ff.). **13. murder:** the use of the verb *rāṣaḥ* in the OT is not restricted to one particular kind of killing. In its present setting it means something akin to 'murder'; there would be no point in legislating against unintentional homicide! Neither judicial killing by the state nor killing in war was covered by this interdiction. **14.** Intercourse with a woman unmarried and unbetrothed was not punished so severely as was adultery; note the difference in the penalties prescribed in 22: 16 and in Lev. 20: 10 (cf. Dt. 22: 22 ff.). Mt. 5: 27 f. goes right back to first principles. Verse **15** deals with theft in general. Some prefer to interpret it more narrowly of theft of persons (kidnapping; cf. 21: 16; Dt. 24: 7). Even in a Christian community the injunction may need repeating (cf. Eph. 4: 28). **16.** Lit., 'You shall not answer against your neighbour as a lying witness'. False evidence was not to be laid before the judges with the aim of securing the conviction of a defendant. **17. covet**, it is frequently claimed, looks beyond motivation to consequent action. But the normal sense of the verb and the use in Dt. 5: 21 of a synonym whose meaning is not in doubt tell against this view. Hyatt notes that 'the evil of covetousness was known and condemned long before the time of Moses, in Egyptian wisdom literature'. **house** is explicated by what follows; cf. the translation of 'houses' by 'families' in 1: 21. **20.** The very awfulness of the theophany would have the positive effect of discouraging the people from breaking the commandments laid upon them.

iii. The Book of the Covenant (20: 21–23: 33)

This is the name given, on the basis of 24: 7, to the collection of laws grouped together in the next three chapters. The laws are manifestly ancient, for the institutions which they presuppose are primitive. Points of contact with other law codes from the Near East can be discerned in plenty. This is exactly what we should expect to find since social needs and conditions varied little from country to country and from one era to the next. (The laws codified by the Persians in the late sixth century B.C. betray their indebtedness to the eighteenth-century Babylonian Code of Hammurabi [HC], which itself was a reformulation and development of earlier Mesopotamian case-law.) Throughout the Near East it was the king who was the arch-legislator and here we find a point of contrast rather than of comparison. The Israelites conceived of law as directly emanating from God. This conviction carried with it an inbuilt motivation to observe the state laws as being the revealed will of God; the observance of these laws was personally superintended by God Himself (cf. 22: 23 f.; 23: 7). Verses 22–26 have as their connecting theme the worship of God. **22 f.** God has spoken **from heaven** and has proclaimed His uniqueness; no idolatrous image is therefore fit to stand in His presence. **24. altar of earth:** of sun-dried bricks (adobe) or of packed earth. Examples of the former have been found on the sites of Canaanite sanctuaries. This is a very early type of altar; contrast 27: 1–8. **your burnt offerings and fellowship offerings:** the earliest types of offering; both are represented in the Ugaritic texts. **wherever:** there was as yet no central sanctuary. **25.** Only undressed stones were permitted in the construction of altars; cf. Dt. 27: 5 f.; Jos. 8: 30 f.; 1 Kg. 18: 31 f. Human hand or implement would convey defilement. Even the altar of burnt offering associated with the Tabernacle was the subject of an atonement rite (see 29: 36). **26.** Canaanite altars sometimes had **steps**. 'Steps are prohibited, because the command is addressed to the Israelite in general, who would sacrifice in his ordinary dress' (Driver). See also the comment on 28: 42.

Laws Concerning Hebrew Servants (21: 1–11)

2. Hebrew: cf. on 1: 15. **servant:** as was the case generally in the Near East, freeborn citizens most frequently fell into slavery through poverty and insolvency. But in Israel the status of such was not that of true slaves, since the bonds of brotherhood were not to be ignored. The Israelite **servant** was more of an 'indentured labourer' (Cole). At the end of the six-year period, or earlier if the jubilee supervened (cf. Lev. 25), the unfortunate regained his status without further obligation to discharge his debts. **4.** The **wife** was considered as the property of her master, inalienable even after marriage to a fellow-slave who subsequently obtained his freedom. **5 f.** Lifelong enslavement of an Israelite could only happen at his own request. The economic factor as much as professed love for a master must often have driven the Israelite slave to seek the security of a permanent contract. **before God** (fn.): to the sanctuary, in all probability. **door** and **doorpost** could refer either to the sanctuary or to the master's house. An instance of oath-taking at the gate of the chief temple of Eshnunna (Laws of Eshnunna, No. 37; see *ANET*[3], p. 163) illustrates the first possibility. Others associate the ceremony with the master's home because the slave is being admitted as a permanent member of the household. Dt. 15: 17 perhaps has a bearing on the matter: 'then take an awl, *and push it through his earlobe into the door, and he will become your servant for life*'. **7.** The difference consisted in the fact that the female slave was expected to become the wife or concubine of her master (10) or, failing that, of her master's son (9). **8.** If the master was unwilling to accord the woman the status of wife or concubine her rights were protected in law. She could be bought out of slavery by her relatives provided they had the capacity and the inclination. RSVmg 'so that he has not designated her' is also a possible rendering. NEB 'has not had intercourse with her' involves the transposition of two letters; the support of the Peshitta is not so unequivocal as the footnote suggests.

Assault and Injury (21: 12–36)

For various Babylonian parallels see the Code of Hammurabi, sections 195–214 (*ANET*[3], p. 175). **12.** The penalty might be applied by the community (cf. Lev. 20: 2) or by the avenger of blood (cf. Num. 35: 19; Dt. 19: 12). **13. God lets it happen:** a case of accidental or unaccountable homicide. Cf. the English expression 'act of God' and the similar formulation in HC 249: 'If a seignior hired an ox *and god struck it* and it has died, the seignior who hired the ox shall (so) affirm by god and then he shall go free'. **a place:** refuge could be sought at a local sanctuary (14; cf. 1 Kg. 1: 51; 2: 28) and, at a later stage, at one of the cities of refuge (Num. 35: 6, 9–34; Dt. 19: 1–13). **15.** 'If a son has struck his father, they shall cut off his hand' (HC 195). Here maltreatment of one's **mother** is included and a much more severe penalty attached. **16.** Cf. Dt. 24: 7. 'If a seignior has stolen the young son of a(nother) seignior, he shall be put to death' (HC 14). **17.** Cf. Lev. 20: 9 and the comment there. **18. fist:** there is some uncertainty about the word; NIV agrees with the LXX, but NEB prefers 'spade'. **19.** 'If a seignior has struck a(nother) seignior in a brawl and has inflicted an injury on him, that seignior shall swear, "I did not strike him deliberately"; and he shall also pay for the physician' (HC 206). **20.** The killing of a **slave** by his master does not seem to have been a punishable offence in other Near Eastern societies. Driver draws attention to the similar situation during the Roman republic. **21.** If a master occasioned indirectly the death of his **slave** his guilt would be harder to prove. Since the loss of a slave entailed a loss of capital this itself was a punishment. **22. and the court allows** renders an obscure expression; NEB has 'after assessment'. The assessment may have been related to the stage of embryonic development as in Hittite law (cf. Hyatt). **23 ff.** expound the

'Lex Talionis', the law of retaliation, which is found in other ancient codes. See on Lev. 24: 17–21. Verses **26 f.** add to the safeguards protecting the **servant** from harsh treatment by his master; cf. on v. 20. **28.** The goring **bull** is a recurring subject in the Near Eastern law-codes. **stoned:** as if guilty like a human (cf. Gen. 9: 5). **29.** If a human life is destroyed through sheer negligence on the part of the animal's **owner** both he and it had to die. In the non-Israelite codes the penalties were not so stringent where negligence was proved. According to the Laws of Eshnunna (No. 54; see *ANET*[3], p. 163) the owner had to pay two-thirds of a mina of silver. **30.** 'If, however, the penalty is commuted for a money payment, he shall pay in redemption of his life whatever is imposed upon him' (NEB). Normally the penalty for taking a life was incommutable. **32.** The life of a **slave** was not so highly valued as that of a free citizen; for the amount of the indemnity see Zech. 11: 12; Mt. 26: 15. **33 f.** Uncovered pits will have been a frequent source of annoyance in ancient Israel. The insouciant digger of the pit was allowed to keep the dead animal (cf. v. 36). **35.** 'If an ox gores an(other) ox and causes (its) death, both ox owners shall divide (among themselves) the price of the live ox and also the meat of the dead ox' (Laws of Eshnunna, No. 53).

Misappropriation of Property (22: 1–17)

1, 3b. The adjustment of the text as in RSV is certainly necessary. Otherwise we should have in v. 3 the unlikely proposition of a dead thief being sold because he was unable to make restitution (cf. AV). NIV avoids this by introducing a new subject in v. 36. A thief who could not make restitution was liable to enslavement (cf. 21: 2–6). **4.** A lighter penalty because the offence has not been compounded by the killing or selling of the **animal. 2. breaking in:** by digging through a mud-brick wall; cf. Ezekiel's acted parable (Ezek. 12: 1–7). **Bloodguilt** was not involved since the house-owner would find it difficult to know whether he was confronted by a mere thief or by a murderous intruder. **5. grazes:** the meaning has been disputed since ancient times; the verb may mean either 'graze' or 'burn' (cf. the rendering by **started the fire** in v. 6). NEB opts for the second alternative: 'When a man burns off a field . . .'. Whatever the cause of the damage, the responsible party had to **make restitution**; the livelihood of a family could be at stake. **7. double:** cf. v. 4. **8. the judges:** cf. 21: 6. The **owner of the house** could clear himself of any suspicion of peculation by invoking a curse upon himself (cf. v. 11). If he did not tell the truth it was expected that God would make the curse effective. From Nuzi comes a fine illustration of the way in which fear of the oath could serve the cause of honesty. In a case concerning the assignation of a female slave two of the litigants were ordered by the judges to substantiate their evidence: '"Go take the oath of the gods against the witnesses of Tarmiya." Shukriya and Kula-hupi shrank from the gods so that Tarmiya prevailed in the lawsuit and the judges assigned the female slave, Sululi-Ishtar, to Tarmiya' (see *ANET*³, p. 220). **9.** If an article has gone missing and the owner sees it in the possession of someone else the case must be decided at the sanctuary. **whom the judges declare guilty:** cf. on v. 8. Pronouncements may also have been obtained by use of the Urim and Thummim. **11.** Cf. on v. 8. **12.** Loss by theft was interpreted as a sign of negligence. **14. animal:** *MT* lacks the word, but NIV has the support of a Qumran text and of a couple of the versions. Responsibility for the injury or death depended on whether or not the owner was present when it occurred. **if the animal . . . the loss:** perhaps better, 'if he is a hired man, it comes in (i.e. out of!) his hire'; the hireling has the amount deducted from his wages. NIV means that the hirer took a risk in the first place and stands to receive no more than the original fee. Verses 16 f. are grouped with the preceding because the girl was, so long as she remained unbetrothed, her father's property (cf. Dt. 22: 28 f.). Even if the father refused to countenance the man as his son-in-law the **bride-price** had to be paid; the man's action had reduced the father's chances of receiving the marriage fee from an acceptable suitor. **17. pay:** Dt. 22: 29, dealing with rape, stipulates fifty shekels of silver.

Miscellaneous Regulations (22: 18-31)

Most are prompted by humanitarian considerations, but first there is notice of three capital offences (18 ff.). **18.** Cf. Lev. 19: 26; Dt. 18: 10-14; 1 Sam.28: 9. The verse implies that women especially were involved in sorcery; some cite Pughat in the Canaanite Aqhat legend (though see *NBD*, p. 726). Magic was widely practised in Mesopotamia and was proscribed in both Babylonian and Assyrian law. **19.** The imagery of bestiality pervades large sections of the Canaanite epic literature; cf. Lev. 18: 23 ff. **20. destroyed:** put under the 'ban' (cf. NEB); cf. on Lev. 27: 20 f. Others, with a measure of support in the versions, reconstruct the Hebrew thus: 'Whoever sacrifices to other gods (save to the LORD only) shall be put to death'. **21. you were aliens:** cf. Dt. 5: 14 f. Most of the laws in vv. 21–31 are of the apodeictic type; see the introduction to ch. 20. **25 ff.** To acquire wealth at the expense of the impoverished and insolvent is alien to the spirit of true religion. Lk. 6: 34 f. sets an even higher standard. **26.** Since the present law is concerned only with the poor in Israel (25; contrast Dt. 23: 20) a **cloak** would be the pledge most commonly available. 'But if this cloak had to be returned

each night (when its use was necessity, not luxury), its value as a pledge was minimal: it became purely a vexatious reminder of the debt' (Cole). Charging of interest was an integral part of Mesopotamian business life and readily tended towards usury, in the modern sense of the word. During the Persian period the Murashu family of Nippur acquired massive wealth by lending to local landowners in need of cash to pay their taxes. Their name has become synonymous with a type of profiteering which had raised its head in Babylonia during other periods when money was in short supply. **28.** Cf. 1 Kg. 21:10; Ac. 23:5. Lev. 19:32 also links respect for divine authority with regard for human authority. **ruler** in premonarchical Israel denotes the head of a tribe (cf. Num. 7). Verses 29 ff. deal with God's dues from Israel. **29. from your granaries** is an explanatory addition in NIV; **offerings** (lit. 'fulness') in Num. 18: 27 is used in connection with wine (cf. Dt. 22: 9). **or your vats:** again NIV expands; the Hebrew is lit. 'your tear', obviously in reference to some sort of natural juice or oil. The word appears only here in the OT with this kind of meaning, but is used five times in the Dead Sea 'Copper Scroll' (3Q15) in a similar way, with the possible meaning 'resin'. **firstborn:** cf. on 13: 13. **31.** Cf. Lev. 7: 24 and, for the reasoning, Lev. 11: 41–45.

Legal and Humanitarian Obligations (23: 1–11)

2 f. In a legal case some may be swayed by the crowd (2) and some few by feelings of pity (3). In both instances there is the danger that **justice** will be perverted. By the insertion of a letter **poor man** can be read as 'great man', a reading which some prefer because partiality towards an influential person is usually a much greater danger. Partiality towards either is forbidden in Lev. 19: 15. **4 f.** Perhaps by **enemy** an adversary at law is intended (cf. Mt. 5: 25 in NIV and RSV). **5.** Although there is some doubt about the way in which the verse should be translated the general sense is quite clear. Verse 6 discourages bias against the **poor** just as v. 3 forbade bias in their favour. **8. bribe:** cf. 18: 21. **those who see:** lit. 'clear-sighted'; cf. Samuel's challenge, 'Or from whose hand have I taken a bribe to blind my eyes with it?' (1 Sam. 12: 3). **9.** Cf. 22: 21. Verses **10 f.** treat of the sabbatical year; see on Lev. 25. There (v. 4) the reason given for its observance is religious, here it is humanitarian.

Cultic Prescriptions (23: 12–19)

12. Keeping of the sabbath is tied to the same humanitarian principle as in Dt. 5: 14. **refreshed:** cf. on 31: 17. Verse **14** introduces the three annual pilgrim-festivals. **15.** Cf. on Lev. 23: 6 ff. **empty-handed:** i.e. without an offering—perhaps of the first-fruits of the particular harvest associated with the festival. **16. Feast**

of Harvest: or, 'feast of weeks'; see on Lev. 23: 33–44. **17.** During the period of the judges there appears to have been only one major pilgrim-festival (cf. Jg. 21: 19; 1 Sam. 1: 3). **18 f.** Cf. on 34: 25 f. **fat,** the choicest part of the sacrifice (cf. Lev. 3: 16), would become putrid if left overnight.

The Epilogue (23: 20–33)
20. Cf. 14: 19; 32: 34. **21.** The **angel** is vested with divine authority, to the extent of being able to forgive sins. **my Name is in him:** this assertion virtually identifies the angel with God; cf. 33: 14. **23.** Cf. on 3: 8. **24. sacred stones:** orthostats sacred to Canaanite gods. Verses 25 f. outline the physical and material blessings which will assuredly follow if the Israelites remain loyal to God. **28. hornet:** cf. Dt. 7: 20; Jos. 24: 12. **29. wild animals:** precisely this situation arose at a later date (cf. 2 Kg. 17: 25). Settlers brought in by the Assyrians to replace Israelite deportees were troubled by lions for a time. The rationale behind the gradual conquest of Canaan is expounded further in Jg. 2: 20–3: 4. **31.** Cf. Gen. 15: 18–21. During the short-lived heyday under David and Solomon these boundaries were actually attained. **Red Sea:** here probably the Gulf of Aqaba. **Sea of the Philistines:** the Mediterranean. **the desert:** the desert region to the south of Palestine. **32.** God's covenant with Israel (24: 7) prevents them from entering into a covenant agreement with anyone else.

iv. The Covenant Ratified (24: 1–18)
1. worship at a distance: yet later they 'went up, and they saw the God of Israel' (9 f.). First the blood of the covenant animals had to be shed and the people united with God in a covenant rite (5–8). Eph. 2: 13 gives the NT counterpart to this. **2. Moses alone**, as the mediator of the covenant (cf. Gal. 3: 19), was allowed to approach the divine presence. **4. twelve stone pillars:** to signify the participation of all **twelve tribes.** For pillars and stones as witnesses to agreements see Gen. 31: 51 f.; Jos. 24: 27. **5. young men:** there were as yet no Levitical priests. The Hebrew word is sometimes used with a technical sense of 'knight' or 'squire'. **7. the Book of the Covenant** is the term usually applied to the preceding regulations (20: 21–23: 33) and is probably so used here. **8.** The remaining **blood** (cf. v. 6) was thrown upon the people who were thus joined to the altar (representing God). **the blood of the covenant:** words taken up by our Lord as He announced the new covenant which would be sealed by His own blood (cf. Mt. 26: 28; 1 C. 11: 25). As is well-known, the description of this occasion in Heb. 9: 18–21 incorporates elements from Num. 19 and the directions concerning the water of purification. **10. and saw the God of Israel:** the statement is bold, and yet the remainder of

the verse suggests that the vision was not so much of God as of His footstool. **a pavement made of sapphire, clear as the sky itself:** it is probably the **sky itself** which is being described! It formed the transparent (translucent?) footstool of the divine throne. **sapphire** seems to represent the familiar *lapis lazuli*, regarded as semi-precious throughout the Near East. Cf. the vision of the divine throne in Ezek. 1: 26. **11.** It was the usual practice to conclude covenant ceremonies with a meal (cf. Gen. 26: 30, etc.). As in the first celebration of the new covenant, only the beneficiaries will have shared in the meal (cf. Mt. 26: 26–29). The **leaders** may have shared in the fellowship offerings mentioned in v. 5 (cf. Lev. 7: 15 ff.). **12. the tablets of stone** contained the Ten Commandments (20: 2–17; cf. 31: 18; 34: 28). **13. Joshua:** cf. 32: 17, after the forty days and nights of v. 18 here. **14.** Cf. Gen. 22: 5. **16. settled:** the root whence the term *shekhinah* is derived. **17.** 'The terrifying God of Ex. 19 who appeared in his theophany has not changed. He returns at the end of ch. 24 once again in majesty and awe-inspiring terror. What has changed is his relation to Israel' (Childs).

V. INSTRUCTIONS CONCERNING THE TABERNACLE AND RELATED MATTERS (25: 1–31: 18)

i. Tabernacle and Furnishings (25: 1–27: 21)
The Materials (25: 1–9)
2. whose heart prompts him to give: according to 36: 2–7 there was no lack of people responding in this way; a similar spirit prevailed when the Second Temple was being built (Ezr. 1: 4; 2: 68 f.; 8: 24–34; cf. 2 C. 9: 7). **3. bronze:** 'copper' (NEB) is perhaps better; either is preferable to AV 'brass' (see *NBD*, p. 778). Copper was obtainable in the Sinai peninsula. **4. blue:** 'bluish-purple', 'violet'. **purple:** or 'reddish-purple'; these two colours were obtained from certain species of shellfish, notably the murex. **scarlet:** this dye was procured from an insect of the cochineal type. The colours associated with the immediate presence of God were neither drab nor dull. **fine linen:** both the term and the technique seem to have originated in Egypt. **goat hair:** lit. 'goats', but the reference will be to the **hair** (cf. LXX) which, on account of its durability, was popular in tent-making. **5. dyed:** lit. 'reddened' (cf. AV). **sea cows:** 'porpoise-hides' (NEB, cf. RVmg). There is a similar-sounding Egyptian word meaning 'leather', hence, presumably, NIV 'leather' in translation of the same Hebrew in Ezek. 16: 10. **8. dwell:** the root from which the term *shekhinah* is derived. This is a key verse in that it gives the reason for the Tabernacle's construction. **9. exactly like . . . the pattern:** cf. Heb. 8: 1–5; 9: 23 f.; because the Mosaic

Tabernacle was, in a sense, the earthly counterpart of the heavenly sanctuary it was doubly important to adhere to the directions given.

Ark and Mercy Seat (25: 10–22)

The instructions begin with the most holy place (the 'holy of holies') and work outwards. **10. chest:** this rectangular box, receptacle for the tablets of the law, measured approximately 3¾ feet x 2¼ feet x 2¼ feet. **11. pure gold:** possibly plates affixed by nails; it was the appropriate metal for the place of the divine presence. **molding:** an ornamental design ('cable-mounting'—Stalker) which was also a feature of the table and the altar of incense. **12.** There is no information elsewhere about the **four feet** of the ark. They would be small but sufficient to raise the ark from ground level. AV 'corners' (cf. LXX) is to be rejected. **15.** Whatever difficulties Num. 4: 6 may present (see *NBD*, p. 1158), 1 Kg. 8: 8 (as RSV) chimes in with the regulation given here. **16. the Testimony:** the tablets of the law which bore witness to the character and the requirements of the covenant-making God (cf. Dt. 10: 5). It was a common practice in the ancient Near East to deposit covenant and treaty documents in sanctuaries and in this respect the tablets of the Mosaic covenant were no exception. **17. atonement cover:** a compromise translation. Some take issue with the traditional 'mercy seat' on the grounds that the basic meaning is 'cover' or 'lid'. This etymology, however, is suspect (cf. Driver, *ad loc.*), and it is questionable whether the *kappōreth* was meant to serve as a lid for the ark. Propitiatory associations for the root *k-p-r* are not lacking in the OT, and the NT retains the LXX rendering by *hilastērion*, 'propitiatory', in Heb. 9: 5. Christ has become a propitiatory (*hilastērion*) to all who believe on Him (Rom. 3: 25). **18.** As in Gen. 3: 24 and Ezek. 28: 14 ff. the **cherubim** may have had a guardian function; such was the rôle of similar composite figures in other parts of the Near East. The direction of their gaze, however, was **toward the cover** (20), as if in contemplation of it. **19.** These figures were to be **of one piece with the cover,** which would naturally mean that they were to be 'made together, of hammered work, out of a single plate of gold' (Cassuto). Driver understands it otherwise: the cherubim were to be soldered on to the mercy seat so as to be inseparable from it. **22. I give you all my commands:** cf. Num. 7: 89. **between the two cherubim:** the invisible divine throne rested on the outstretched wings of the **cherubim** (cf. 1 Sam. 4:4; Ps. 80: 1). A representation of a royal throne supported by two cherub-like figures has been discovered at the site of the ancient Phoenician city of Gebal (Byblos).

The Table (25: 23–30)

23. The first of the items of furniture in the holy place to be described is the **table**, standing on the north side (26: 35). Such a table was among the spoils of war taken from Jerusalem by the Romans in A.D. 70 and is represented on the Arch of Titus in Rome (Driver, p. 273, has a reduced reproduction of this table taken from Reland's *De Spoliis Templi* (1716)). On it was placed the bread of the Presence (30), so that it was probably meant to portray God as the giver of food and sustainer of His people. There is no thought of providing food for God as was the custom in pagan temples. **24. molding:** see on v. 11. **25.** Round the table ran a golden rim about three inches high, to ensure that the bread of the Presence was securely placed. Another theory says that the **rim** (or 'frame') consisted of boards ('cross-stays', Driver) which joined the legs about half-way down and helped to stabilize them. The remains of such cross-stays are visible in the representation on the Arch of Titus. **27. Close to the rim:** the **rings** were to be placed at the tops of the legs **close** to the golden **rim** (or near the cross-stays; cf. on v. 25). **29. plates:** cf. Num. 7: 13. These were probably the containers for the bread of the Presence. **dishes:** used for incense according to Num. 7: 14 where the same word is in question. Frankincense was put on the bread of the Presence (Lev. 24: 7). The **pitchers** (cf. 1 Chr. 28: 17) held the wine used for libations (cf. Num. 28: 7, etc.). **30. the bread of the Presence** is so named because it was set out before the **Presence** (lit. 'face') of God. It consisted of twelve cakes baked from flour and arranged (hence 'the bread of the ordering' (lit.) in 1 Chr. 9: 32) in two rows (or piles; cf. on Lev. 24: 6) of six each. When they were replaced each sabbath they became the property of the priests (Lev. 24: 5–9; cf. 1 Sam. 21: 6; Mt. 12: 1–4). In Num. 4: 7 the cakes are referred to as 'the continual bread'.

The Lampstand (25: 31–40)

The lampstand (*menōrāh*) has frequently, and aptly, been described as a stylized tree. It is very difficult to be certain about some of the finer details, for the Hebrew is obscurely expressed at times. The lampstand removed from Herod's temple and portrayed on the Arch of Titus gives an overall impression of what is intended here. There were ten separate lampstands in Solomon's temple (1 Kg. 7: 49). **31.** NIV its **flowerlike cups, buds and blossoms** does not introduce any interpretative element —unlike NEB 'its cups, both calyxes and petals' —and is the better for it (even though it goes the way of NEB in almost all moderns in its handling of vv. 33 f.!). The issue is whether there were two parts to each almond configuration or three; it is important to translate the Hebrew of this verse literally so as not to prejudge the matter. **32.** It is probable that, as in the ancient representations, the **branches** rose to the same height as the central shaft. **33.** NIV, RSV, etc. explicate what is not necessarily in the Hebrew when they indicate that the **cups** *were* the ornaments, rather than parts of the ornaments. Ancient Jewish tradition is firmly in agreement with the tripartite division of the almond ornament and, as L. Yarden (see bibliography) has shown, such an arrangement as is favoured by most modern scholars would not have been acceptable to the compilers of the Talmud. There is neither necessity for, nor advantage in, Soltau's construing of the verse to mean '*three* bowls, a knop and *a* flower only in each of the six branches' (*The Holy Vessels*, p. 75). The **buds** were probably some sort of cup-shaped protuberance in the arms of the lampstand (cf. NEB 'calyx'); for **blossoms** NEB has 'petals'. **35.** There was to be a calyx (**bud**) just below the point where each pair of branches joined the shaft. **37. seven lamps:** they will have rested on the topmost ornaments of the shaft and branches. No further details of these **lamps** being given, it could be surmised that they were made of terracotta in accordance with normal practice. Cassuto thinks that they were not made of gold or this would have been specifically mentioned; but cf. v. 39. **so that they light:** there was little or no natural light in the holy place. Lampspouts and wicks were to be arranged in such a way as to shed light in front of the lampstand. **38. wick trimmers** and **trays** to hold the trimmings were to be provided.

Tabernacle and Tent (26: 1–14)

1. Strictly speaking, the **tabernacle** denotes the inner curtains described in vv. 1–6 and is carefully distinguished from the **tent**, the goats' hair covering which was spread over the **tabernacle** (see vv. 7–13). **2.** Since the structure stood ten cubits high (15 f.) and was ten cubits broad (see on v. 23), the inner **curtains** will have ended one cubit short of the ground on the north and south sides (cf. v. 13). Ten **curtains** each measuring **four cubits** in breadth would, when joined together, produce a piece sufficient to cover exactly the length (twenty frames each one and a half cubits broad; see vv. 16, 18, 20) and back (i.e. western end) of the Tabernacle. **3.** To make up the one great curtain two sets of **five curtains**, all of them sewn along their lengths, were joined by means of a series of picots and clasps. **7.** In much the same way the covering of **goat hair** (the **tent**) was to be made. **8.** Being **thirty cubits** in length the goats' hair curtains covered the top and two sides of the Tabernacle exactly. **9.** Eleven curtains each four cubits broad would yield a total span of forty-four cubits when joined along their lengths; this would be four cubits in excess of what was required to cover the top and back of the Tabernacle. Verses 9b and 12 give instructions as to how the extra

material was to be apportioned. A doubling of the **sixth curtain** at the front of the Tabernacle (accounting for *two* cubits; cf. on v. 12) will have provided a protective edging for the inner curtain; the extra two cubits of the **sixth curtain** were probably folded under the tabernacle curtain. **11.** The **clasps** which joined the goats' hair curtains were not visible inside the Tabernacle and were therefore made of **bronze** (or copper; cf. on 25: 3), in contrast with the clasps mentioned in v. 6. **12.** This verse is not without its difficulties; there would appear to be no room for a half-curtain to **hang down at the rear of the tabernacle** in that sense, since the **rear** would be fully covered already. Perhaps we are to understand that the surplus material lay on the ground; Cassuto refers to TB *Shabbath* 98b, where the tent is likened to a woman walking in the street with her train trailing behind her. Those who hold, with Kennedy, that the whole of the sixth curtain of v. 9 extended beyond the tabernacle curtain at the east end (i.e. folded and hanging down for two cubits as a sort of valance) have to treat the provision of this verse as a mistaken gloss. Soltau's explanation of the **half curtain** as a reference to the five curtains which were sewn together to cover the top and rear of the Tabernacle (*The Tabernacle*, pp. 48 f.) does not convince. 'Curtain' in this section means the individual lengths. The five curtains at the rear are included in the **tent curtains. 13.** In point of fact the goats' hair curtains extended to ground level on the north and south **sides. 14.** Two additional **coverings** (see on 25: 5) are mentioned but no further details are given. NEB ('a cover . . . and an outer covering') makes it clear that two **coverings** are intended. That they were **coverings** and not wrappers for the Tabernacle in transit (Cole) is indicated by 40: 19.

Frames and Bars (26: 15–30)

15. frames or planks (AV, RV, NEB) formed the supporting structure for the curtains and covers. It has been fashionable to translate by 'frames' since Kennedy's oft-cited *HDB* article appeared (see bibliography), but, attractive hypothesis though it is, absolute certainty has yet to be attained. Philological support from Ugaritic and Arabic has been summoned in more recent times; still the evidence falls short of proof. One advantage, among several listed by Kennedy, is that the beautiful inner curtains would be visible through the **frames** and not just at ceiling level, as would be the case with solid boards. **17. projections:** lit. 'hands'; these projections at the lower ends of the frames would fit into the silver sockets (19, 21, 25). According to Kennedy the word means 'uprights'—the upright spars which made up the frames. The translation would then run something like: 'two uprights per frame, each fitted to its fellow'. **19.** Each frame had two silver sockets (**bases**) to hold it in position. **23.** By means of these additional **frames** at either corner the back and sides of the Tabernacle were held together. Since the height of the Tabernacle was ten cubits and the length of the goatskin curtains was thirty cubits—enough to cover the top and two sides— it follows that the breadth of the Tabernacle was ten cubits (twenty cubits for the two sides and the remaining ten for the top (=breadth)). The six rear frames (22) will have accounted for nine cubits, possibly leaving the two corner **frames** to make up the remaining cubit. (Note that the thickness of the frames at the ends of the two sides may also have to be taken into account.) **24.** It is not at all clear how the corner frames were to be fitted. Kennedy's explanation is that these corner frames buttressed the frames at either end of the rear of the Tabernacle; they sloped upwards to the height of the **top** bar (cf. vv. 26–29) and its **ring**. Cassuto thinks that the corner frames were coupled ('twinned') with the end frames on either side by means of tenons and sockets. He understands **fitted into a single ring** to refer to the clamps which braced the pairs of corner frames. 'This was one of the customary methods used in Egypt to strengthen the corners of wooden structures; they were braced by a copper fillet that enclosed them like a ring.' It is an attractive solution to a very difficult problem. **25.** There were therefore **eight frames** in all in the rear wall. **26 ff.** Only one of the **crossbars**—the **centre** one (28)—extended the full length of side or rear, as the case might be. They were kept in position by the **rings** (29) affixed to the frames and themselves gave the whole structure stability.

Veil and Screen (26: 31–37)
The veil is the 'second curtain' of Heb. 9: 3. It proclaimed man's distance from God; the tearing in two of the curtain in the Herodian temple when our Lord expired (Mk 15: 38) announced the removal of a yet more ancient barrier. In Heb. 10: 19 f. the humanity and death of our Lord are viewed as a sanctuary curtain, but there is there no thought of obstruction, only of access. **31.** The **curtain** was to be tapestried just like the inner curtains of vv. 1–6. **33.** If we assume that the inner curtains reached to the ground at the rear of the Tabernacle it is not difficult to determine the position of **the clasps.** The curtain stretched for twenty cubits on either side of the **clasps**: these will therefore have been ten cubits from the rear of the Tabernacle. Since the **curtain** was hung from the **clasps** the most holy place must have been a cube, ten cubits in length, breadth and height (cf. on v. 23). The inner sanctuary of Solomon's temple was also in the shape of a cube (1 Kg. 6: 20). **33 f.** The only items of

furniture in the most holy place were the **ark of the Testimony** and the **atonement cover** which rested upon it. **35.** On the other side of the veil lay the holy place with its furnishings, the **table** and **lampstand**; there was also a golden altar, but it is not mentioned until 30: 1–10. **36.** This **curtain**, being more removed from the divine presence, was embroidered rather than tapestried. Cf. also the **bronze bases** (37) in this respect. **37.** Capitals for the **posts** are mentioned in 36: 38.

Altar of Burnt Offering (27: 1–8)
1. To the east of the door of the Tabernacle stood the **altar** of burnt offering, a small construction only **three cubits** high. **2.** The **horns** at the **corners** were of practical use in that the sacrificial animals could be bound to them. Miscreants would occasionally seek sanctuary at this altar by clinging to its horns (cf. 21: 14; 1 Kg. 1: 50; 2:28). **4 f.** Round all four sides of the altar, and about half-way up, ran a decorative projection—**the ledge** (5). While no function is mentioned in connection with the **ledge** it is usually assumed (*e.g.* Driver, Stalker, Childs) that it was for the priests to stand upon when offering sacrifice; Lev. 9: 22 is often cited in support. But it may be questioned whether such a platform was necessary in the case of an altar which stood four and a half feet high. Verse 5 shows that the **ledge** must have been about two feet from the top of the altar. See *IBD*, p. 25, for a photograph of a Canaanite incense altar complete with ornamental 'ledge' and note that the altar is about twenty-one inches high! The explanation of the ledge advanced here is also favoured by Cassuto. The **grating** extended from below the ledge to the ground; thus the lower half of the altar will have been encased in **bronze network**, perhaps for ventilation purposes. Much less satisfactory is the view that the ledge was on the inside of the altar shell and that the grating rested on it (though see Cole for a favourable presentation of the case). It is difficult to imagine how the rings of v. 4 were to fulfil their function if the **grating** was inside the altar. **8.** Because the altar as constructed was **hollow**, and in view of the regulation in 20: 24 f., it is sometimes suggested that the 'hollow shell' (NEB) was filled with earth or stones. It is perhaps significant in this connection that, unlike the altar of incense (30: 3), there is no mention of an altar top.

The Courtyard (27: 9–19)
9. It is impossible to be certain about the exact arrangement of the **curtains** which marked off the **courtyard**. The whole formed a rectangle one hundred cubits long by fifty cubits broad (18). It is nowhere stated that the distance between the pillars was five cubits—though that may have been the intention—nor is the total number of pillars given. The simplest arrange-

ment to represent diagrammatically would have been the most difficult to produce in practice, since it involves awkward fractions of a cubit for the distances between the pillars. According to this reconstruction the corner pillars are to be counted twice, once with the length and once with the breadth. On the north and south sides, therefore, there would be nineteen hangings on twenty pillars, on the west (rear) side nine hangings on ten pillars. A particular advantage of this scheme is that it makes it easy to take account of the data given for the east end (14 ff.), if the first and fourth pillars of the gate also served as additional pillars for the two 'shoulders' (which is how the Hebrew describes the sections at either side of the gate). A system based on a five cubit interval between the pillars is also possible and is adopted by Driver, Cassuto, etc. This requires that each side should have one more than the stated number of pillars, except that the last pillar in each case also serves as the first on the adjoining side. At the east end there is the slight complication that one set of hangings is supported by its own three pillars and by the first of the four gate pillars, while on the other side the screen is supported by the nearest shoulder pillar as well as the four specifically provided for it. The first of the schemes outlined above is in accord with D. W. Gooding's reconstruction as shown in *IBD* p. 1508. In *IBD*, p. 1510, there is a brief exposition of both schemes; the second diagram there follows the same arrangement as the reconstruction, but with a variant (and permissible!) disposition of the pillars and hangings at the east end. **10**. The **bands** may be ornamental fillets just below the capitals (cf. 38: 17, 19); the meaning is not secure beyond doubt, but it is less likely that some kind of connecting rod between the pillars (so JB) is intended. **19**. Guy ropes and **pegs** were used to keep the pillars of both Tabernacle and court firmly in position. The ropes are mentioned in 35: 18; 39: 40.

The Night Lamp (27: 20–21)
20. There is some difference of opinion as to whether this **light** is the golden lampstand which stood on the south side of the holy place; Lev. 24: 1–4 would appear to support the identification. To produce the **clear oil of pressed olives** the olives were, according to Mishnaic tradition, gently pounded in a mortar; ordinarily the oil would be obtained by crushing the olives in a stone press. **kept (burning)**: lit. 'continually', which is to be qualified by **from evening till morning** in v. 21; cf. 30: 7 f. and 1 Sam. 3: 3. The same word is used in connection with the 'continual (i.e. regular) offering'. **21**. The location of this lamp **outside the curtain** would also suggest that it is the golden lampstand which is meant (cf. on v. 20).

ii. Preparing the Priests (28: 1–29: 46)
(a) Robes and Insignia (28: 1–43)
The Ephod (28: 1–14)
Almost the whole chapter is devoted to a description of the high priest's attire; the simpler dress of the suffragan priests is detailed in vv. 40–43. **2. honor:** or 'beauty' (RSV). As in the fabric used for the Tabernacle curtains, we find that holiness and beauty are not incompatible —and this is especially true for such as are addressed in Heb. 12: 18–24. **4.** If the Talmudic statement on the length of the **sash** (thirty-two cubits, i.e. forty-eight feet) is anything like correct NIV is much to be preferred to RSV 'girdle'. **6 f.** Opinion is divided as to whether the **ephod** was a waistcoat or a loin-cloth. On the basis of 2 Sam. 6: 14, 20 (David's immodest display when 'girded with a linen ephod') it might be concluded that it was the latter. The boy Samuel wore an **ephod** in Shiloh (1 Sam. 2: 18) and the priests of Nob were similarly attired (1 Sam. 22: 18). **6.** Unlike the inner curtains of the Tabernacle, the **ephod** had gold threads woven into the familiar colours (see 39: 3). **7 f.** Whether waistcoat or loin-cloth, the garment was secured by **shoulder** straps attached to its upper **corners** (i.e. front and rear), and by a band tying it round the high priest's waist (8). **9 ff.** Affixed to the shoulder straps of the ephod were **two onyx stones** in gold **filigree settings** (11). Thus was symbolized the high priestly intercession on behalf of the individual tribes of Israel. Verses 13 f. give advance notice of the **settings** and **chains** by which the breastpiece of judgment was to be fastened to the ephod (see vv. 22–25).
Breastpiece of Judgment (28: 15–30)
15. The **breastpiece for making decisions** is so called because it contained the Urim and Thummim, the means by which divine guidance ('judgments') could be obtained. **breastpiece** translates a word of uncertain etymology and is suggested, rather, by the description which is given here and in the parallel passage in ch. 39. **16.** Made of the same material as the ephod (15), the breastpiece measured about nine inches **square**, and was **double**, i.e. folded in two to make a pocket. **17 ff.** Twelve precious **stones**, many no longer identifiable (NIV and RSV agree in seven cases out of the twelve), were to be set **in gold filigree** (20) and attached to the front of the breastpiece. **22 ff.** The breastpiece was fastened to the two filigree settings (13, 25), and so to the shoulder-pieces of the ephod, by means of two gold chains (14, 22, 24 f.). **26 ff.** A blue **cord** inserted in gold **rings** sufficed to fasten the lower corners of the breastpiece to the lower part of the two shoulder-pieces of the ephod. **30.** The **Urim and Thummim** were to be kept in the breastpiece pocket (cf. on v. 16). What precisely they were ('lights and perfections' as in RVmg is not

the only possible translation) and the method of using them are not known; but see I Sam. 23: 9–12 and I Sam. 14: 41 (as reconstructed in RSV, NEB with the help of LXX and Vulgate). Some method of drawing lots on a 'yes' or 'no' basis seems to be implied.

The Robe of the Ephod (28: 31–35)
31 f. This violet-blue **robe**, of a type worn by people of rank (cf. I Sam. 18: 4; Ezek. 26: 16), was drawn over the head in the manner of a S. American poncho (32). The **opening** was specially reinforced to withstand wear and tear (cf. NIV 'collar' in Ps. 133: 2). **32. collar:** Targum Onkelos renders by 'coat of mail' (cf. AV, RV) and this is now supported by the consideration that the same word occurs in Samaritan with this meaning. NEB 'with an oversewn edge' is based on a different etymology, as indicated in the footnote. **33 f. bells** and bobs (**pomegranates**) were arranged alternately so as to adorn the border of the robe. **35.** They had more than a decorative significance. 'Propriety demands that the entry should be preceded by an announcement, and the priest should be careful not to go into the sanctuary irreverently' (Cassuto). It may be that Jn 19: 23 has an allusion to the robe of the ephod.

Plate and Turban (28: 36–38)
36 f. Before the mention of the turban in its own right (39) come the instructions for the **plate** which was to be attached to it. The Hebrew word translated by **plate** probably means, basically, 'something shining' (*BDB*). Most often it has to be translated by 'flower' or 'blossom', hence NEB 'rosette'. **38.** Ritual exactitude is enjoined so that the people's offerings, as presented by the high priest, may be acceptable. The plate with its inscription in sacred characters (**as on a seal**, 36) would serve to compensate for any infringement of the ritual requirements such as the high priest might commit in the course of his duties.

Sundry Items (28: 39)
39. This kind of **tunic** resembled a cassock; as an item of clothing it was not restricted to the priesthood (cf. 2 Sam. 15: 32; Isa. 22: 21). Outside the inventories of priestly dress the terms for **turban** and **sash** occur only once (Ezek. 21: 26 and Isa. 22: 21 respectively), the **turban** with reference to a king and the **sash** in connection with a royal official of high standing.

Garments for the Ordinary Priests (28: 40–43)
40. The ordinary priests also wore **tunics** and **sashes** (same terms as for the high priest in v. 39). **headbands** may denote turbans of less elaborate style than the high priest's; according to 29: 9 and Lev. 8: 13 they were bound on to the head. Verse 41 anticipates the subject-matter of ch. 29. **42.** Ritual nakedness, especially for priests, was a feature of some

ancient religions; it was to be quite otherwise in Israel (cf. 20: 26).

(b) Directions for the Installation of the Priests (29: 1–46)
Washing, Robing and Anointing (29: 1–9)
1 ff. First details are given as to what will be required for the several sacrifices to be offered. **2.** These are three kinds of grain offering; cf. on Lev. 2: 10. **4.** Until Aaron and his sons have been washed and sacrifice has been made on their behalf they cannot enter the **Tent of Meeting.** Instructions concerning the laver are not given until 30: 17–21. There (vv. 20 f.) a regular washing of hands and feet before service in the Tabernacle or its court is laid down. We are probably to think of a washing of the whole body on this occasion; cf. Heb. 10: 22. Verses 5 f. seem to mention the regalia in the order in which they were to be put on (cf. Lev. 8: 7 ff.). **6. the sacred diadem** is the 'plate' of pure gold described in 28: 36 ff. NEB has 'the symbol of holy dedication'. **7.** Only Aaron is said to have been anointed, but see 28: 41; 30: 30; 40: 15. **9.** After **sashes** LXX lacks the words 'Aaron and his sons'. It is noticeable that the high priest's sash is not mentioned in vv. 5 f. (though included in Lev. 8: 7); the words in question could have been added in the Hebrew so as to make good the omission of the earlier verses. **ordain:** as in 28: 41 the Hebrew expression is lit. 'fill the hand'. The expression occurs in Akkadian texts from Mari (second millennium B.C.) in reference to the payment of fees for services rendered (cf. Noth). In the OT the expression may signify either the placing of a sacred object in the priests' hands as a symbol of office (Stalker), or the filling of the priests' hands with their first sacrifices (Driver, comparing v. 24). But it is also possible that the words had shed their original significance by this time and meant simply 'to install'.

Offerings for the Priests (29: 10–28)
10. The **bull** was offered as a sin offering (cf. v. 14). By laying their **hands** upon its **head** Aaron and his sons identified themselves with the animal. **12.** In Lev. 4: 7, referring to sins committed by a priest in office, the blood of the sin offering is put on the horns of the altar of incense. Here it is the altar of burnt offering which is intended; 'the priests, before their consecration is completed, are treated as laity' (Driver). **13.** See on Lev. 3: 3 f. **14.** This was the usual procedure for a priest's sin offering; cf. Lev. 4: 11 f. **15.** The second offering was a ram for a burnt offering (cf. v. 18). Unlike the bullock of the sin offering it was burned in its entirety, in keeping with Lev. 1: 10–13. **18.** NEB 'food-offering' assumes that the word translated by **an offering by fire** has connection with a homonym meaning 'food'. Verse 19 introduces the ram of ordination (cf. v. 22). **20.** In the application of the blood to the priests'

ears, thumbs and **big toes** the fact of their complete consecration to God was symbolized. The existence of a similar rite in connection with the cleansing of lepers (Lev. 14: 14–17) would not exclude a significance such as this in the case of priests on their day of installation. The holy bond between priest and **altar** was represented in the dashing of the remaining **blood** against the altar walls. **22.** Making due allowance for the occasion, the **ram for the ordination** was in effect a fellowship offering (cf. Lev. 3: 3 ff.). **thigh** is correct, as against 'shoulder' of AV, RVmg. **24. and wave them as a wave offering before the LORD:** the traditional explanation is represented by Stalker: 'The ceremony of "waving" meant that some parts of the sacrifice were swung or elevated towards the altar, signifying that they were given to God, and then swung back again, indicating that they were given back by God to the priests, for them to eat'. A quite different explanation was offered by Sir Godfrey Driver in *JSS*, I, 1956, pp. 97–105; it is represented here in NEB's 'and present them as a special gift before the Lord'. The so-called 'wave offering' is thus regarded as a special portion of the sacrificial animal which has been removed for presentation to God, and any idea of ritual movement is excluded. In support of this newer theory it has been pointed out that the idea of ritual movement agrees ill with the description of the Levites as a 'wave offering' in Num. 8: 11. **26.** Moses was acting as a priest on this occasion and was therefore entitled to share in the sacrificial animal, in accordance with the rules for the peace offering (Lev. 7: 31). **27 f.** According to vv. 22–25 the **thigh** was burned on the altar. The allocation of both **breast** and **thigh** to the priests is a feature of the *ordinary* **fellowship offerings** (28; cf. Lev. 7: 31 f.). **regular share** (NEB 'contribution') is to be preferred to AV 'heave offering'. The idea of ritual movement should certainly be abandoned in this case (cf. on the 'wave offering' in v. 24).

Sundry Regulations (29: 29–46)
29. Aaron's garments were to be passed on to his successors and just as his induction lasted **seven days** (30; cf. v. 35) so it is stipulated that his successors should observe the same initiatory period. **31 ff.** The remaining **meat** of the ram of ordination was to be boiled and then eaten together with the **bread** that was left in the basket (cf. vv. 2 f., 23); only the priests could participate in this meal (33). **36.** Made by human hands and unclean by association, the **altar** was fitted for sacred use by means of **sin offerings. 37.** A sin offering was to be sacrificed on each of the **seven days** of ordination. Once the **altar** had become **most holy** its holiness was transmissible; **whatever** ('whoever' is preferable) touched it passed into the realm of the sacred (cf. NEB 'forfeit as

sacred') and was at the disposal of God. **38.** The instructions now embrace the regular daily sacrifices; cf. Num. 28: 3–8. The word translated is **regularly** *tāmîd* and it became the accepted term for the 'continual (i.e. daily) offering.' **39. at twilight:** lit. 'between the two evenings'; see on Lev. 23:5. **40.** Cereal offerings (cf. v. 41) could be independent or, as here, supplementary sacrifices. **43. will be consecrated by my glory:** the Tabernacle will be hallowed by the divine presence (cf. 40: 34).

iii. Miscellaneous Instructions (30: 1–31:18)
The Golden Altar (30: 1–10)
1. Although the golden **altar** of **incense** was located within the holy place it is not so much as mentioned in 25: 23–40. It is commonly suggested that the altar of incense did not belong to the original Tabernacle, and partly for the reason that it seems to be included as an afterthought. This is a rather drastic conclusion to base on evidence so slender as we are considering. That the altar of burnt offering is referred to as 'the altar' from time to time does not necessarily imply that it was the only one associated with the Tabernacle; but it was the altar most commonly in use. Examples of incense altars dating from the early first millennium B.C. have been found at various Canaanite sites. Israel is as likely to have had such a feature in her cultic system at this stage as in exilic or post-exilic times, and perhaps more so. **2. two cubits:** about three feet high; the altar of burnt offering was three cubits (about four and a half feet) in height (27: 1). **3. molding:** cf. on 25: 11. **6.** The position of the golden altar in relation to the ark of the Testimony and the **mercy seat** is emphasized (cf. 40: 5). In 1 Kg. 6: 22 the incense altar in Solomon's temple is similarly described: 'the whole altar that belonged to the inner sanctuary he overlaid with gold'. Heb. 9: 3 f. ('the Holy of Holies, having the golden altar of incense') is perhaps to be understood in the light of such references. **9. any other incense:** the required ingredients are given in vv. 34–38. **other** (lit. 'strange, foreign') is the word used of the fire offered by Nadab and Abihu (Lev. 10: 1). **10. atonement** for the altar was made annually as part of the ritual of the Day of Atonement; opinion is divided as to whether Lev. 16: 18 f. is speaking of the altar of incense or the altar of burnt offering (see comment *ad loc.*). This was not, in any case, the only occasion on which the altar of incense was associated with blood ritual (cf. Lev. 4: 7, 18). Cassuto notes that this is the only article of the Tabernacle which is said to be **most holy:** 'so that no one should suppose, since it is dealt with last, that its sanctity is less than that of the remaining vessels'; but see v. 29.

Census Regulations (30: 11–16)
12. Census-taking was fraught with danger in

ancient Israel (cf. 2 Sam. 24). There are various suggestions as to why this should be so: a census could give rise to feelings of self-satisfaction and pride, or could bring the sins of individual Israelites before God's notice (Driver); taking a census implied a lack of faith in God (Cassuto); it represented an attempt to acquire comprehensive knowledge such as was only for God to possess (Clements). In the present context it seems clear that the primary purpose of the census was the assertion of God's rights among His people, and this fundamental aspect could too easily be overlooked. Num. 1 records how the command to take the census was implemented. **ransom:** each adult male (see Num. 1: 2) had to **pay a ransom** in order to preserve his life. Already at birth God's claim on the first-born males of Israel had to be met by the payment of a ransom (cf. 13: 13). **13. a half shekel** was the amount required on this occasion and it later became an institution in Israel (cf. Mt. 17: 24); it was a small amount payable by all without distinction: 'there was neither pauper nor patron in the cult in Israel' (J. Gray). **the sanctuary shekel:** different kinds of shekel were in vogue; 2 Sam. 14: 26, for example, mentions a 'royal shekel'. **15 f.** Since the levy had religious significance and the proceeds were put to a religious use (16) the imposition was the same for everyone. All benefitted equally from **the service of the Tent of Meeting.**

The Laver (30: 17–21)
The description of the laver (or 'basin') properly belongs to ch. 27 and the instructions for the court of the Tabernacle. It would be unwise to conclude from its present position that there was no laver used in connection with Tabernacle ritual (cf. the remarks on the altar of incense at the beginning of this chapter). Solomon's temple had ten bronze lavers (1 Kg. 7: 38 f.). **18 f.** Of unspecified shape (though the Hebrew root may suggest something round) and dimensions the **basin** was, like the altar of burnt offering, made of **bronze** (or copper, cf. on 25: 3)—solid metal in this case. For the source of this **bronze** see on 38: 8. Soltau (*The Holy Vessels*, p. 122) disputes the conventional representation of the laver as circular in shape on the ground that the same Hebrew word is used in 2 Chr. 6: 13 of a square(?) platform five cubits long and five cubits wide; but this is somewhat precarious (see *BDB*, p. 468). Since the priests were required to wash their **feet** as well as their **hands** (19, 21) there may have been taps in the **stand** for this purpose.

The Anointing Oil (30: 22–33)
25. blend: by boiling the aromatic ingredients in the hin (almost a gallon) of olive oil (cf. Job 41: 31). On the processes involved see Cassuto. **26 ff.** Not only the priests were anointed (30), but also the furnishings and utensils used in divine service. **29. most holy:** what was said of the altar of incense (10) can now be applied to all the vessels of the Tabernacle. **32.** Trading in spices in the near east was considerable and their domestic use for cooking and cosmetics commonplace, hence the need to guard the distinctiveness of the sacred blend.

The Incense (30: 34–38)
35. The mixture was **to be salted** because it was used in small amounts (cf. v. 36) and putrefaction must be avoided (cf. 29: 34; Lev. 2: 11). **36.** Some of the incense was beaten small and put in the vicinity of the altar of incense, before the ark of **the Testimony** (cf. on v. 6), to be used morning and evening (vv. 7 f.). It is less likely that this verse refers to the burning of incense in the most holy place on the Day of Atonement (Lev. 16: 12 f.). **37 f.** Cf. vv. 32f.

Master Craftsman (31: 1–11)
2. chosen is lit 'called by name' (NEB 'specially chosen'); cf. Isa. 45: 3. **Bezalel son of Uri, the son of Hur:** the same cluster of names, showing the same relationships, appears in 1 Chr. 2: 20 in the genealogy of Judah. **3. the Spirit of God:** present at the creation (Gen. 1: 2) and active in the sustaining of the world (Ps. 104: 30), the Spirit endows men with ability, whether to create, as here, or to administer, as Othniel (Jg. 3: 10). **6. Oholiab** means, appropriately in view of his work on the Tabernacle, 'The father is my tent' (cf. Bezalel, 'In the shadow of God'). **Also I have given skill:** it is characteristic of God to provide men with the means to fulfil His purposes (cf. Phil. 2: 13). **10. woven** represents a word of uncertain meaning; the root seems to be connected with the idea of plaiting.

Sabbath Observance (31: 12–17)
13. my Sabbaths: the obligation of sabbath observance has already been canvassed in Exodus (16: 22–30; 20: 8–11; 23: 12). After the announcement of the chief artificers responsible for the construction of the Tabernacle comes a reminder that the sabbath must be kept, even by those engaged in such a sacred task. And it is now stated that the sabbath is a **sign** of the special relationship which exists between God and Israel (cf. the sign of circumcision (Gen. 17: 11) proclaiming the covenant relationship into which Abraham was brought). **14 f.** Three times the penalty for profanation of the sabbath is stated so that all may appreciate the seriousness of such an offence. **17. rested:** properly 'was refreshed' (RSV) a striking anthropomorphism in view of the use of the same verb in 23: 12 in reference to the need of slaves and aliens to have refreshment on the sabbath. 'The language is purposely strong so that man may learn the necessity of regarding the sabbath as a day on which he himself is to rest from his daily labours' (E. J. Young).

The Tablets of the Testimony (31: 18)

18. This verse rounds off the account of the Sinai revelation and, by mentioning the **tablets of the Testimony**, prepares the ground for the next development in the story. We should doubtless understand the tablets as containing only the ten commandments, and that in their original form of terse command and prohibition (compare Exod. 20: 8–11 with Dt. 5: 12–15 for examples of commentary appended to a commandment). **the finger of God:** what Aaron did with his rod (8: 16–19) was described by the Egyptian magicians as the work of **the finger of God** (cf. also Lk. 11: 20). By itself, therefore, the expression indicates divine power and authority.

VI. REBELLION AND RECONCILIATION (32: 1–34: 35)

The Golden Calf (32: 1–10)

1. The people's demand and Aaron's acquiescence in it meant that even before the covenant stipulations were delivered to them in written form they had broken the first, second, and, possibly, the seventh (cf. on v. 6) commandments, and had also contradicted the covenant preamble (compare v. 4 with 20: 2). As a story of a people who 'turned aside quickly' (8) it has its NT counterpart (see Gal. 1: 6). **around Aaron** would be better rendered 'against Aaron' (cf. NEB 'confronted'). **2 f.** Just as personal property had been contributed for the erection and embellishment of the Tabernacle (25: 1–7; cf. 38: 8), so now a collection was made for a quite different, and totally unworthy, cause (cf. Jg. 8: 24–27). **4. fashioning it with a tool** suggests that the image was carved from solid gold; 'graving tool' is the word translated 'pen' in AV Isa. 8: 1. By a minor vocalic change **with a tool** can be made to mean 'in a bag', and, by a small leap of philological faith, 'in a mold' (SO NEB). **calf:** or 'bull-calf'. It is to be expected that the Israelites were familiar with the Egyptian and Canaanite bull-cults which flourished in the Nile Delta region. The Canaanite bull-cult of Baal was to prove a constant snare to them once they had settled in Canaan. **your gods . . . who brought you up:** but only one image was made. Many OT scholars regard this account as a protest against the bull-shrines set up by Jeroboam (1 Kg. 12: 28 f.). If this were the case we should have an adequate explanation of the plural reference (but see 1 Sam. 4: 7 f.). It is as likely, however, that Jeroboam was adopting the rallying call used on this occasion; the mention of the deliverance from **Egypt** is more likely to have originated at Sinai than on the occasion described in 1 Kg. 12. For all that, it is clear that Israel 'still looks for a god who acts, even if it be a false god' (Cole). **5. a festival to the LORD:** Aaron, a reluctant idolater, probably thought to contain

the error by associating the worship of Yahweh with the golden calf. **6.** Next day the Israelites **sacrificed burnt offerings and presented fellowship offerings** as might any Canaanite who knew nothing of the God of Israel; both types of offering (with the same Semitic root as the Hebrew in the case of the **fellowship offerings**) figure in the second millennium texts from Ugarit. **sat down to eat:** the normal accompaniment of fellowship offerings as prescribed in Lev. 7: 11–18. **indulge in revelry** may have a sexual connotation (cf. the same word translated 'caressing' in NIV at Gen. 26: 8). Usually, however, the verb is used without any such allusion, as in Gen. 21: 9. In 1 C. 10: 8 a quite separate instance of sexual immorality on the part of the Israelites is cited (*viz.* Num. 25: 1–18), even though the sin of idolatry has just been illustrated from the occasion described in these verses in Exod. 32. (Childs disagrees on this point, regarding the twenty-three thousand of 1 C. 10: 8 as a variant of the three thousand of v. 28 of this chapter.) Sexual licence certainly was a feature of the worship at the Canaanite bull-shrines. Whether Aaron and the Israelites thought of their bull-calf as a representation of Yahweh or as the throne which supported His invisible presence is hard to determine; either way their sin was of the utmost gravity. **7.** As in v. 1, though there for a different reason, the association of the Exodus with Moses' leadership has a derogatory ring. **your people** implies that God no longer acknowledges them as His. **8. have bowed down to it and sacrificed to it:** no matter about Aaron's attempt to syncretize the animal fertility cult and the worship of God, his 'feast to the LORD' (5) is dismissed as idolatry pure and simple. **10. I will make you into a great nation:** cf. Gen. 12: 2. For Moses it had been a great personal sacrifice to side with the Israelites (cf. Heb. 11: 24 ff.); now he was hearing of the possible extinction of his people and was being offered the chance to become a second Abraham. **11. your people** is Moses' answer to **your people** in v. 7. The deliverance of the Israelites from the Egyptian bondage was the measure of God's commitment to their cause. Why should God destroy them now? **12.** Also at stake was God's reputation. Even the Egyptians recognized the hand of God in the Exodus; if Israel were destroyed their erstwhile enslavers would conclude that God preferred to use His power for destructive ends. **13.** Thirdly, there were the promises made to the patriarchs. But could these not have been fulfilled through Moses who was no less a son of Abraham? No such thought occurs to Moses as he reminds God of the initial promise made to Abraham; and promise had been reinforced by oath (cf. Gen. 22: 16 ff.). Was the fulfilment now at risk in spite of the unconditionality of the promise? Judaism makes much of the merits of the patriarchs in explanation of God's covenant loyalty; the self-consistency of God is its true origin. **14. relented:** it is not implied that God's purposes are ever less than perfect (cf. Num. 23: 19). It is a description of God's attitude as seen from the human angle. Jn 6: 6 helps put the whole dialogue in its true perspective.

The Tablets Broken (32: 15–20)
15. inscribed on both sides: this was quite frequently the case with inscribed tablets. The tablets will have been quite small and were probably duplicates; on the latter point see M. G. Kline, *Westminster Theological Journal*, XXII, 1960, pp. 133–146. **16.** The phrases **work of God** and **writing of God** could mean that the tablets and their inscriptions were directly the product of divine creativity, or, since the Hebrew *'elōhîm* is used quite frequently with superlative force, that they were exquisitely done. See on 31: 18. **17. Joshua** had accompanied **Moses** for part of the way as his attendant (cf. 24: 13). **18.** Moses' reply is given in verse form; a certain amount of word-play is involved. **19.** Moses broke the tablets as an expression of his intense anger, but his action had a deeper meaning in that it proclaimed the annulment of the covenant just made. **20. burned** suggests to some scholars that the golden calf may have had a wooden core. The verb is not entirely inappropriate for an object of solid metal. The suggestion has been made —on the basis of a Canaanite text—that the collocation of the three verbs **burned, ground** and **scattered** is a conventional way of expressing complete destruction. **made the Israelites drink it:** this element is redolent of Num. 5: 11–31 and the trial by ordeal of a woman suspected of marital unfaithfulness. Verse 35 may bear some relation to this imposition. God is the jealous husband of Israel (compare Num. 5: 14 with Exod. 20: 5).

Aaron's Tale (32: 21–24)
22. prone . . . to evil is preferable to NEB's 'deeply troubled', though the word in question can sometimes bear the meaning 'trouble'. **24.** Moses had laid the blame for the people's aberration fairly and squarely on Aaron. The latter's defence—the autogenous bull-calf—may have been a case of 'eastern politeness' (Cole), but it is politeness to the point of deviousness; it is no better than Gehazi's answer (2 Kg. 5:25).

A Great Slaughter (32: 25–29)
25. were running wild: or, 'had cast off restraint'. **26. the Levites** were Moses' fellow-tribesmen and they had remained loyal to God during Moses' absence. **28. three thousand:** we are given no indication as to why these and no others were put to the sword. They may have been caught in the act of idolatry or may have been known as the chief advocates of

bull-worship. **29. You have been set apart:** the required sense can be obtained from *MT* without recourse to emendation, *pace* the footnotes in RSV and NEB; see Cassuto's explanation of *MT*. **against your own sons:** family relationships were subordinated to the service of God (cf. Dt. 33: 8 f.). The blessing consisted in the right to officiate in the Tabernacle (cf. Dt. 33: 10 f.; Num. 25: 10–13).

Moses Prays Again (32: 30–35)
32. the book: cf. Ps. 69: 28; 139: 16. The names of the living were inscribed in the divine register. Removal of a name meant forfeiture of life. In the NT the figure is applied to the life to come, as in Lk. 10: 20; Phil.4: 3. **33. Whoever has sinned** reflects the principle enunciated in Jer. 31: 29 f.; Ezek. 18: 1–4. **34 f. my angel:** cf. 23: 20, 23; 33: 2. **I will punish:** a threat of punishment in the distant future, to which v. 35 may or may not refer. Verse 35 could be intended to summarise all that has preceded: 'Thus (in the Levites' action) did the LORD smite the people' (**struck with a plague** translates a single Hebrew word).

God's Presence Withdrawn (33: 1–6)
1. you brought up: cf. on 32: 7. Reconciliation between God and His people is by no means complete. **to the land I promised on oath:** the force of Moses' argument in 32: 13 is acknowledged. **2.** Six of the 'seven nations greater and mightier' of Dt. 7: 1 are mentioned. **3. I will not go with you:** cf., with reference to a later situation, Dt. 1: 42. **I might destroy you:** because God is 'of purer eyes than to behold evil' (Hab. 1: 13). **6. at Mount Horeb:** the removal of the **ornaments**, which would have been a visible reminder of the Israelites' venture into idolatry, was not just a temporary measure. And, considering the people's capacity for aping their pagan neighbours, it would forestall any temptation to treat the ornaments as talismans. **Horeb** is another name for Sinai (cf. 3: 1; 17: 6).

A Tent of Meeting (33: 7–11)
For the view that this section preserves a tradition about the Tabernacle which has greater claims to authenticity than the rest of Exod. 25–40, see the introduction to Exodus. **7.** Now that the presence of God has been withdrawn we are informed of a provisional arrangement by which divine oracles were communicated to Moses. This **tent** differed from the Tabernacle in that it was pitched **outside the camp** (ct. Num. 2: 2, 17), and its location served to underline God's displeasure with His people. **9. the pillar of cloud would come down:** although God's presence had been forfeited by the commonalty of Israel it was not denied to Moses—a cause for jubilation among a chastened people (10). **11. face to face:** cf. Num. 12: 6 ff. **Joshua** served as verger in this temporary trysting-place.

A Prayer for God's Presence (33: 12–16)

12. whom you will send with me: so far God has only relented to the extent of undertaking to provide angelic assistance for the advancing columns of Israel. The prevailing uncertainties did not seem to tally with the favourable position which Moses was supposed to occupy. **13. your ways:** cf. Ps. 103: 7. In effect Moses is asking to know how he can conduct himself acceptably in the sight of God. Since Moses is the leader of the Israelites such a revelation will hold benefit for God's **people. 15 f.** Even after the assurance of the divine presence has been given (14) Moses reinforces his point that Israel has no *raison d'être* if God is not among them.

A Theophany Requested (33: 17–23)

18. show me your glory: cf. 16: 10; 24: 16. The request is for a theophany; the revelation of divine **glory** would assure Moses that his prayers had been answered. **19. all my goodness:** the gracious attributes and acts of God by which His character (**my name**) may be known. **on whom I will have mercy:** with the declaration of the attributes of grace comes the reminder that the exercise of them is God's prerogative entirely. **20. my face:** by this anthropomorphism the full disclosure of God is signified. But such a vision is beyond the capacity of mortal men to behold; cf. Gen. 16: 13; 32: 30; Jn 1: 18. **21 f.** There are noteworthy comparisons between these verses and Elijah's experience as recorded in 1 Kg. 19: 9–18. **23. my back** stands for a partial revelation of the divine glory. The section is strongly anthropomorphic without at all compromising the truth of the incorporeity of God.

The Theophany Granted (34: 1–9)

1. Chisel out: according to 32: 16 the first pair of tablets was 'the work of God'. **and I will write:** see the note on 31: 18. **3. No one is to come:** the restrictions are even more severe than on the occasion of Moses' first ascent (cf. 19: 24; 24: 1). Aaron had in any case disqualified himself from participation in the covenant renewal, even if it was only to accompany his brother for part of the way. **flocks** and **herds:** 19: 13; Heb. 12: 20. **5. and stood with him there and proclaimed** his name, **the LORD:** that the second clause agrees, *mutatis mutandis*, with 33: 19 ('and will proclaim . . .') suggests that God is the subject of both verbs here. Driver and Hyatt favour the construction of RVmg ('and he (= Moses) stood with him there, and called upon . . .'). In support of the first alternative Cassuto points out that **stood** represents the same verb as 'stand' in 33: 21 and 'present yourself' in v. 2 of this chapter, but in a different conjugation. As in the case of the original decalogue (20: 2), and in keeping with common Near Eastern treaty practice, the renewed covenant (cf. v. 10) is prefaced by a self-proclamation of the overlord. **6 f.** Here are 'The Thirteen Attributes' as they are known in Jewish tradition. In them the nature of God is revealed. 'It comes as near as the Old Testament anywhere achieves to providing a confessional definition of God. Characteristically it concerns itself with his attitude towards men' (Clements). Cf. 20: 5 f.; Dt. 5: 9 f.; Nah. 1: 3, etc. **7. to thousands:** and 'to a thousand generations' according to Dt. 7: 9. **he does not leave the guilty unpunished:** NEB 'and not sweeping the guilty clean away' is defensible, but NIV is to be preferred. There is some ambiguity about the meaning of the Hebrew verb in question. **9. our wickedness and our sin:** Moses associates himself with his wayward flock; cf. Dan. 9: 3 – 19.

Covenant Renewal (34: 10–28)

10. God first gives notice of what He intends to do on Israel's behalf—**wonders** which will eclipse the signs which accompanied the Exodus (*e.g.* Jos. 6: 1–27; 10: 12 ff.). **for you** refers to Moses and agrees with the special status of Moses in the whole matter of the **covenant** (cf. v. 27, 'a covenant with you and with Israel'). It is in the dispossessing of the peoples already in Canaan (11) that God will perform His **awesome** thing. **12.** Cf. 23: 32. **13.** Cf. 23: 24; Dt. 12: 3. **Asherah poles** were cult objects made of wood (whether poles or trees is uncertain) which were sacred to the Canaanite fertility goddess Asherah. **14.** On vv. 14–26 as a 'ritual decalogue' more ancient than the 'ethical decalogue' of 20: 3–17 see the discussion in Cole. **15. prostitute themselves:** a metaphor for idolatrous practices generally, and one not without literal significance where fertility cults were concerned. **they will invite you:** 1 C. 10: 27–30 shows how the same kind of situation could present problems for the individual Christian in first-century Corinth. How vulnerable the Israelites were in the face of such allurements was convincingly demonstrated in the affair of the golden calf. **17. cast idols:** corresponding to the prohibition on graven images in 20: 4. Perhaps the use of the term 'molten calf' in connection with Israel's sin (cf. 32: 4) accounts for the difference in emphasis. **18.** Cf. 23: 15. **19 f.** Cf. 13: 11 ff. The law of the **firstborn** is introduced in ch. 13 in the wake of the Exodus account; here it follows the regulations for the feast of unleavened bread (18) which had itself become so closely linked with the Exodus tradition. **21.** The sabbath law must be observed at all times (cf. 31: 13), including **plowing season** and **harvest** when the temptation to disregard it was strongest. **22. the Feast of Weeks** is the feast of harvest of 23: 16; it came seven weeks after the feast of unleavened bread (18). **the Feast of Ingathering** is another name for the festival of tabernacles (cf. 23: 16). **23.** Cf. 23:

17. Israel's religious calendar is presented in full in Lev. 23. **24. and no one will covet your land:** a word for the anxious worshipper along the lines of 1 Kg. 17: 13 and Mt. 6: 33. Cole remarks on the ease with which a farmer might move a landmark to the disadvantage of his more pious neighbour. Those living in outlying districts would be anxious lest in their absence some foreigner might seek to establish, or even to re-establish, a claim to a piece of ground. **25.** Cf. 23: 18. **the sacrifice from the Passover feast** corresponds to 'the fat of my feast' in 23: 18, but this law is specifically related to the Passover in 12: 10. **26.** Cf. 23: 19. God's generosity is acknowledged both positively and negatively—positively in the presentation of **firstfruits** and negatively in the eschewing of Canaanite fertility rituals. The previously assumed parallel between boiling a kid in its mother's milk and a reference in a Ugaritic text from Ras Shamra is now seriously questioned. **27. Write down these words:** cf. 24: 4, 7. These are the **covenant** terms outlined in vv. 12–26. **with you:** Moses was the mediator of the **covenant**; cf. on v. 10. **28. And he wrote:** the more natural implication is that Moses did the writing, since he is the subject of the verbs immediately preceding. But v. 1 is in opposition to this, and it may well be that the original subject (or even now the intended subject) of **wrote** was God. The matter hinges somewhat on the precise meaning of the phrases discussed in the commentary on 31: 18; 32:16.

Moses' Face Aglow (34: 29–35)
29. radiant: cf. Mk 9: 2 f. and parallels. The verb is related to the Hebrew word for 'horn' (cf. Hyatt's 'put out horn-like rays') and was misunderstood from early Christian times (already in the Vulgate), hence the common portrayal of Moses with a pair of horns in mediaeval art. **33. veil** only occurs in this passage and its precise meaning is not beyond doubt. Many see an allusion to a kind of mask worn by priests in certain primitive religions, but this cannot be advanced beyond speculation. Paul takes up the theme of Moses' radiant **face** and **veil** in order to expound the superiority of the 'dispensation of the Spirit' over the 'dispensation of death' (2 C. 3: 7–18). **34 f.** It would seem that, as on the first occasion (33), Moses did not normally veil his face until he had delivered the Lord's message to the people. The gap between Paul's 'rabbinical' explanation of the veil ('so that the Israelites might not see the end of the fading splendour', 2 C. 3: 13) and the original circumstances can thus be easily overstated. Furthermore, Paul shows himself aware of the original circumstances in which Moses felt it necessary to make use of the veil (see 2 C. 3: 7).

VII. THE INSTRUCTIONS CARRIED OUT (35: 1–40: 38)
i. Men and Materials (35: 1–36: 7)
Repetition of lengthy passages with or without modification is characteristic of Near Eastern literature in general. The recital of the offerings of the tribal leaders in Num. 7 well illustrates this feature; such repetition was not considered otiose or stylistically inferior—far from it. And when detailed instructions are recorded in the imperative the account of their execution is frequently given in the same terms. Anyone familiar with the Canaanite poems of Ugarit, to go no further, will not be surprised to find that Exod. 35–40 recounts in almost identical terms the carrying out of the directions of the preceding chapters (notably chs. 25–28, 30–31).

Sabbath Reminder (35: 1–3)
2. Cf. 31: 12–17; 34: 21. **3. Do not light a fire:** this prohibition is peculiar to this section, though it is reflected in 16: 23. It applied to the people of Israel **in** all their **dwellings** and was not merely a restriction on the burning of fires by those engaged in the making of the Tabernacle.

Request for Materials (35: 4–9)
This section corresponds to 25: 1–7 and differs from it in no significant point of detail.

The Sacred Inventory (35: 10–19)
This is a more detailed list than that given in 31: 7–11. **10.** Every **skilled** person was to be involved in the construction work, though under the tutelage of Bezalel and Oholiab (cf. v. 34). **18. ropes:** cf. on 27: 19.

Voluntary Offerings (35: 20–29)
The voluntary nature of the contributions is stressed throughout the section (21, 22, 26, 29). Men (23), women (25) and leaders (27) all showed a willing spirit.

God-given Skills (35: 30–36: 1)
Cf. 31: 1–6. Here it is emphasized that the necessary skills come from God, just as it was stressed in the previous section that the materials came from the people. Willingness and ability make a formidable pair. In the church it is too often the case that the willing are not able and the able not willing.

An Excess of Materials (36: 2–7)
2. and who was willing to come and do the work: those who gave up time and energy rather than material goods were also marked by a spirit of co-operation. **3. from Moses:** lit. 'from before Moses'. 'The picture is of the heap of materials lying *before* Moses' (Driver).

ii. Construction of Tabernacle and Furnishings (36: 8–38: 31)
The Tabernacle Constructed (36: 8–38)
Cf. 26: 1–37. There are no major differences between the two accounts. The instructions concerning the arranging of the goats' hair curtains (26: 9, 12 f.) are not repeated because

they do not affect the manufacture of the curtains. **38.** The capitals (cf. RSV) on the **posts** are not mentioned in 26: 37. 'There is a gradation in the gilding. The pillars at the entrance of the court have only silver gilding on the capitals (cf. 38: 19); those at the entrance to the Tent have gold gilding on the capitals only (cf. 36: 38); but those at the entrance of the Most Holy Place are entirely gilt with gold (36; cf. 26: 32)' (Stalker).

The Tabernacle Furnishings (37: 1–29)
The parallel material is in 25: 10–39; 30: 1–5. **1. Bezalel made the ark:** Moses was its maker according to Dt. 10: 3, but there it is probably a question of ultimate responsibility rather than of personal involvement. 'Exodus nowhere claims that Moses himself had personal artistic ability or skill' (Cole). **29.** 'A drastic abridgement of 30:22–38 (Hyatt).

The Altar, Laver and Court (38: 1–23)
Cf. 27: 1–8; 30: 17–21; 27: 9–19. **8. the mirrors of the women who served at the entrance to the Tent of Meeting:** a new piece of information which is usually regarded as anachronistic since the Tabernacle was not yet erected. **served** translates a verb more at home in military contexts and meaning 'to war' or 'to serve (in war)'; but see Num. 4: 23; 8: 24 for its use in connection with Levitical service. 1 Sam. 2: 22 refers to 'the women who served at the entrance to the tent of meeting'. Cole attempts to eliminate the anachronism by differentiating between this **Tent of Meeting** in Exod. 38: 8 and the Tabernacle. Cassuto, on the other hand, gives the verb the meaning 'to stand in array' and visualizes the women thronging to surrender their **mirrors** for the making of the **basin. 21. Ithamar** (cf. 6: 23; 28: 1) was in charge of the Gershonites and Merarites (Num. 4: 28, 33). The special appointment of the Levites has already received notice (cf. 32: 29) and no anachronism is involved here (*contra* Driver, Noth, Hyatt).

The Metals Used (38: 24–31)
24. the wave offering: cf. 35: 22. **25. who were counted:** cf. 30: 11–16. The total amount of **silver** was 301,775 shekels (3,000 **shekels** to a talent)—the amount to be expected from a poll of 603,550 men (26; cf. Num. 1: 46), if each gave the half-shekel (also known as a **beka**). The actual census did not take place until a month after the completion of the Tabernacle (compare 40: 2, 17 with Num. 1: 1 f.). For an ingenious attempt at harmonizing the data see Cassuto. **27. the bases for the sanctuary:** these are the **bases** of the frames over which the curtains were draped, and of the pillars on which the **curtain** was suspended. Forty-eight frames having two **bases** each (cf. 26: 15–25), and four pillars with a single **base** each (cf. 26: 32), make a total of 100 **bases**.

iii. The Priestly Garments (39: 1–31)
The divergences from ch. 28 are few in number and usually of no great significance. The punctiliousness with which the earlier directions were observed is emphasized in the seven occurrences of **as the LORD commanded Moses** (1, 5, 7, 21, 26, 29, 31). **3. sheets of gold:** there is no indication in ch. 28 as to how the **gold** was to be used in the making of the ephod. From thin plates gold filaments were to be cut and then worked in with the yarns. **30. the sacred diadem:** cf. 29: 6 and see on 28: 36 f.

iv. The Work Completed (39: 32–40: 38)
Moses Inspects the Work (39: 32–43)
Cassuto rightly draws attention to certain parallels between this section and Gen. 1–2. **32.** With the first part of the verse compare Gen. 2: 1. **43. Moses . . . saw:** cf. Gen. 1: 31. **So Moses blessed them:** cf. Gen. 1: 22, 28; 2:3.

Instructions for the Erection of the Tabernacle (40: 1–15)
After the Tabernacle furnishings were arranged (1–8) the anointing oil was to be poured on them and on Aaron and his sons (9–15). **2. on the first day of the first month:** this marks the beginning of the second year of the Israelites' wilderness wanderings (cf. v. 17; 12: 2). They had been in the vicinity of Sinai for nine or ten months (cf. 19: 1).

The Tabernacle Erected (40: 16–33)
The words **as the LORD commanded him** (Moses) occur seven times in these verses (19, 21, 23, 25, 27, 29, 32). **31.** Moses' name is included because he was acting in a priestly capacity (cf. 27, 29).

The Abiding Presence (40: 34–38)
So a major theme of the book of Exodus, the presence of God among His people (cf. 25: 8; 29: 45), is brought to its triumphant conclusion. The God who was revealed at Sinai would be with the Israelites wherever they went. **34.** This conviction was strengthened by the visible signs of the **cloud** and the **glory** which had been witnessed when Moses first went to receive instructions from God (24: 15 f.). **35. Moses** could not **enter:** cf. 1 Kg. 8: 10 f. **36 ff.** Cf. 13: 21 f.; Num. 9: 15–23.

BIBLIOGRAPHY

Commentaries
CASSUTO, U., *A Commentary on the Book of Exodus* (Jerusalem, 1967).
CHILDS, B. S., *Exodus: A Commentary*. OTL (London, 1974).
CLEMENTS, R. E., *Exodus. CBC* (Cambridge, 1972).
COLE, R. A., *Exodus: An Introduction and Commentary. TOTC* (London, 1973).
DRIVER, S. R., *The Book of Exodus. CBSC* (Cambridge, 1911).

ELLISON, H. L., *Exodus*. Daily Study Bible (Edinburgh, 1982).

HYATT, J. P., *Commentary on Exodus. NCentB* (London, 1971).

NOTH, M., *Exodus*. OTL (London, 1962).

STALKER, D. M. G., '*Exodus*'. *PCB* (London, 1962).

Special Studies

BIMSON, J. J., *Redating the Exodus and Conquest* (Sheffield, 1978).

CHAMBERS, L. T., *Tabernacle Studies* (Kilmarnock, n.d.).

CROSS, F. M., 'The Tabernacle', *Biblical Archaeologist* 10, 1947, pp. 45–68.

DAVIES, G. I., *The Way of the Wilderness* (Cambridge, 1979).

FINN, A. H., 'The Tabernacle Chapters', *JTS*, XVI, 1915, pp. 449–482.

GOODING, D. W., *The Account of the Tabernacle* (Cambridge, 1959). This study is concerned with the Greek text of the Tabernacle account.

GOODING, D. W., *art* 'Tabernacle', *NBD*, pp. 1157–1160.

HERRMANN, S., *Israel in Egypt SBT*[2] 27 (London, 1973).

KENNEDY, A. R. S., *art.* 'Tabernacle', *HDB*, IV, pp. 653–658.

KNIGHT, G. A. F., *Theology as Narration. A Commentary on the Book of Exodus* (Edinburgh, 1976).

KITCHEN, K. A., *Ancient Orient and Old Testament* (London, 1966).

KITCHEN, K. A., 'Some Egyptian Background to the Old Testament', *Tyndale House Bulletin*, 5/6, 1960, pp. 7–13.

MEYERS, C. L., *The Tabernacle Menorah* (Missoula, 1976).

MOTYER, J. A., *The Revelation of the Divine Name* (London, 1959).

NICHOLSON, E. W., *Exodus and Sinai in History and Tradition* (Oxford, 1973).

NIXON, R. E., *The Exodus in the New Testament* (London, 1962).

POLLOCK, A. J., *The Tabernacle's Typical Teaching* (London, n.d.).

RITCHIE, J., *The Tabernacle in the Wilderness* (Kilmarnock, n.d.).

ROWLEY, H. H., *From Joseph to Joshua* (London, 1950).

ROWLEY, H. H., *From Moses to Qumran* (London, 1963).

SOLTAU, H. W., *The Holy Vessels and Furniture of the Tabernacle of Israel* (London, 1851). Reference to Kregel edition (Grand Rapids, 1971).

SOLTAU, H. W., *The Tabernacle, the Priesthood, and the Offerings* (London, n.d.).

STAMM, J. J. and ANDREW, M. E., *The Ten Commandments in Recent Research* (London, 1967).

DE WIT, C., *The Date and Route of the Exodus* (London, 1960).

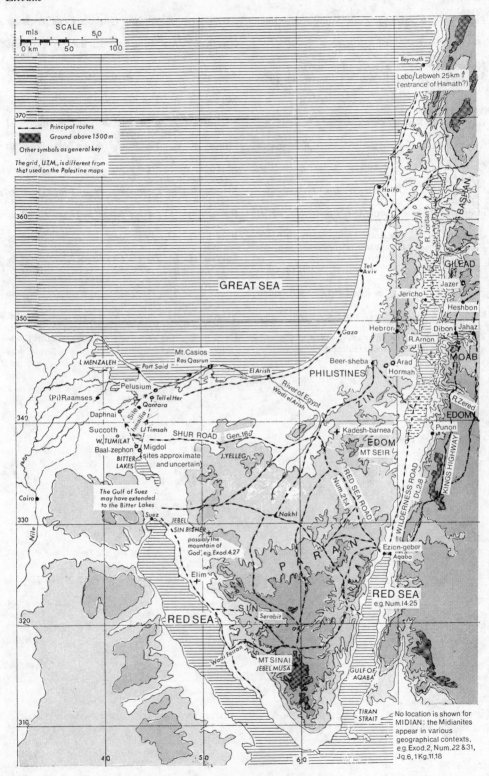

Map 3—The Sinai Peninsula

LEVITICUS

ROBERT P. GORDON

The third book of Moses is called 'the Levitical (book)' in the Septuagint and Vulgate versions; the English Bible tradition reproduces the exact form of the Vulgate (Latin) heading. It is not the most appropriate of titles, for the Levites are all but unmentioned in the book (but cf. 25: 32 f.). On the other hand, the subject-matter does very much concern the so-called Levitical priesthood, and to that extent it is acceptable. Leviticus purports to record regulations, principally of a ritual and cultic nature, which were committed to Moses at the tent of meeting (1: 1; cf. Exod. 40: 35) and on Mount Sinai (7: 38; 25: 1; 26: 46; 27: 34). On occasion Aaron is addressed, by himself (10: 8) or together with Moses (11: 1; 13: 1; 14: 33; 15: 1). 'Even the few passages, such as chs. 8 and 10, which are cast in the form of narrative do not aim at describing what once happened, but use this form in order to prescribe what is to continue' (A. C. Welch). (With this insight we can, for example, explain the apparent confusion between the priestly grain offering of installation and the daily grain offering in 6: 20.)

In Leviticus we are shown how Israel, now that the Tabernacle is completed, can fulfil its vocation and become 'a kingdom of priests, a holy nation' (Exod. 19: 6). For even the aberration of the golden calf and the selection of the tribe of Levi for priestly service did not exclude the individual Israelite from intimate involvement with the sacrificial ritual. Though many of the regulations are directed to the priesthood, the operation of the cult was no recondite matter. The major part of the laws of the offerings is addressed to 'the people of Israel' (1: 2), and certain duties, such as the killing of the sacrificial victim, are imposed upon them. What unifies this book which treats of such diverse subjects as sacrifice and skin complaints, food laws and festivals, is the conception of Israel as a people 'holy to the LORD' (cf. 20: 26). The claims of God upon His people extend far beyond the court of the Tabernacle. Even the seemingly petty distinction between clean and unclean animals has something greater in view—that Israel may be conscious of its separateness from all the other nations of antiquity. The practical holiness enjoined in Leviticus has a strong moral content: 'Here again we have evidence that the care for the poor inculcated in Deuteronomy is as clear here in Leviticus as there, and further, in Leviticus definite legislation is introduced in order to put the humanitarian principles into practice (N. H. Snaith on Lev. 27: 8). Where such a social conscience is in evidence holiness entails much more than ritual purity.

There is a fair measure of homogeneity about the book in its present form, as is evidenced by the interrelationship of laws and of whole sections. From time to time we come upon 'postscripts' (M. H. Segal) or 'colophons' (K. A. Kitchen); see 7: 37 f.; 11: 46 f.; 12: 7; 13: 59; 14: 54–57, etc. Segal suggests that scrolls containing separate groups of priestly *tôrôth* ('regulations') were used as manuals, with the 'postscript' acting in each case as a kind of title page. Such colophons, whether at the end of a document or at the end of each of its constituent parts, were commonplace in the ancient near east. A quite separate origin for chs. 17–26 was mooted by A. Klostermann in 1877. These chapters have much in common with the book of Ezekiel and lay special emphasis on holiness. On account of the latter feature Klostermann designated the section 'das Heiligkeitsgesetz' ('the law of holiness'). Chs. 19–22 in particular are imbued with the holiness principle (cf. 19: 2; 20: 7 f., 26; 21: 6 ff., 15, 23; 22: 9, 16, 32). Similar references are found outside the putative code, though not in such profusion (cf. 10: 3, 10; 11: 44 f.), so that the holiness factor cannot be the sole criterion by which the 'law of holiness' is distinguished from other material of a similar type. There is the additional problem that ch. 17, which has no trace of the holiness theme, has so many verbal and topical links with the preceding chapters as to appear misplaced in the 'law of holiness'. For that matter, indications of antiquity are as much in evidence in chs. 17–26 as in the rest of Leviticus, and it is increasingly recognized in scholarly circles that the nucleus of the Levitical legislation is to be dated to the formative years of Israel's history rather than to its period of exile and eclipse. The discovery of Canaanite cultic material in the Ras Shamra texts has played some part in this change of attitude towards the priestly corpus. 'The Ras Shamra texts further showed that a number of the technical terms connected with the sacrificial system and regarded as the invention of the priestly writers were already being used in Ugarit long before the period assigned to the priestly writing' (S. H. Hooke).

Nothing could be further from the viewpoint of Leviticus than the representation of its sacrificial order as 'man's expedient for his own redemption'. It is a basic presupposition of the book that sacrifice is a divine ordinance, the divinely-appointed way by which sinful men may approach a holy God. This is not to say that it is the ideal or perfect way of approach. It did not avail for high-handed sinning against God (Num. 15: 30; cf. Heb. 10: 26) and, as the NT clearly teaches, its value was entirely derivative and would have been non-existent but for the efficacious self-oblation of Christ. The institution of sacrifice lies in the distant, unrecorded past. In the OT we catch only glimpses of its practice in the primeval history. But we can certainly affirm that this institution was invested with divine authority in Israel. There, amidst all the crudities and superstitions which accompanied its observance in pagan cults, it taught moral lessons concerning God and His demands upon His creatures. Lev. 17: 11 presents the *raison d'être* of the sacrificial system: 'For the life of the flesh is in the blood; and I have given it for you upon the altar to make atonement for your souls; for it is the blood that makes atonement, by reason of the life'. The onus is on man to provide the means of atonement, but it is God who provides what man could never supply from his own resources. So it is with Christ the antitype of the Levitical sacrifices—Christ *'whom God put forward* as an expiation by his blood, to be received by faith' (Rom. 3: 25).

There are sporadic utterances in the prophetic writings which seem to repudiate the sacrificial system *in toto*. The references usually cited are Isa. 1: 11 ff.; 43: 23 f.; Jer. 7: 21 ff.; Hos. 6: 6; Am. 5: 21–25; Mic. 6: 6 ff. Jeremiah and Amos seem to be saying that the Israelites did not offer sacrifice during the wilderness period, the others that it would be better if their contemporaries abandoned their hecatombs and holy days in favour of right conduct and social justice. But it is unnecessary to interpret these fulminations as evidence of a rivalry between prophets and priests, or of a tension between word and sacrament; they must be viewed against the background of wholesale abuse of the sacrificial system in Israel. The average Israelite did not pause to consider that his ritual offerings to the God of the fathers were a mockery so long as his traitorous association with the Canaanite fertility cults persisted. Jeremiah and Amos are reminding their hearers that at Sinai God first enjoined obedience and then communicated the ritual law. The Hebrew phrase translated 'concerning' in Jer. 7: 22 would be better rendered by 'for the sake of': 'I did not speak to your fathers or command them for the sake of burnt offerings and sacrifices. But this command I gave them . . .'. Both Jeremiah and Amos show awareness of the wilderness tradition and it is most unlikely that they would be ignorant of the accounts which told of the offering of sacrifices during that period. 'On any view of the origin of the Pentateuch, the traditions current in Amos' day would have spoken of sacrifice in the time of Moses, and of the Patriarchs before him' (J. A. Motyer). This applies *a fortiori* to Jeremiah, and we need only think of the references to sacrifice in the Book of the Covenant (Exod. 20: 24; 23: 18) to appreciate Motyer's point. Not the principle of sacrifice, but the contemporary praxis, was what evoked the prophets' condemnation.

Nowhere in the NT, which is the full flowering of the prophetic insight, do we find the Jewish sacrifices regarded as anything other than a divine institution. Until 'the time of reformation' had come our Lord and His apostles participated in the Temple ritual. When the NT writers sought to expound the significance of Golgotha they most often did so in sacrificial terms derived from Leviticus and related priestly material. Already in the OT era the precedent had been established. 'It is no accident—that when priestly and prophetic religion meet in the figure of the Servant of the Lord in Is. liii the highest point of Old Testament religion is reached, as all that is valuable in cult is taken up into a person who both makes a sacrificial atonement (*hizzâ*, "lamb", "guilt-offering") and calls for the love and personal allegiance of the human heart' (R. J. Thompson). In the NT the physical perfection of the sacrificial animals is transposed into the moral flawlessness which characterized the great antitype (Heb. 9: 14; 1 Pet. 1: 19). Whereas those animal offerings 'could not perfect the conscience of the worshipper' (Heb. 9: 9), Christ entered the heavenly sanctuary through His own blood 'thus securing an eternal redemption' (Heb. 9: 12; cf. 9: 24–28; 10: 11–14). (Indeed, it is only by depicting our Lord as both sacrifice and sacrificing high priest that the writer of the letter to the Hebrews can take account of the full implications of His death.) Our Lord's death partakes of the nature of a sin offering (Rom. 8: 3; 2 C. 5: 21), being prefigured especially in the sin offerings of the Day of Atonement (Heb. 13: 11 f.), and in Him the festivals of Israel (cf. Lev. 23) find their consummation (1 C. 5: 7, 'Christ our paschal lamb'; 1 C. 15: 23, 'Christ the first fruits'). That our Lord died at Passover (Nisan 14) and rose from the dead on the Day of First Fruits (Nisan 16) makes the festival comparison peculiarly apposite.

There is also frequent reference in the NT to the concept of spiritual sacrifices—sacrifices which the Christian believer may offer to God acceptably in virtue of Christ's perpetually valid offering. See Rom. 12: 1; Phil. 2: 17; 4: 18; Heb. 13: 15 f.; 1 Pet. 2: 5; Rev. 8: 3 f., etc. This too has its roots in the OT (cf. Ps. 50: 14; 107: 22; 116: 17), and Jewish expressions of it occur in the Qumran literature as well as in the mainstream of rabbinism.

Some indication of our attitude towards the typological interpretation of Scripture has been given in the introduction to Exodus 25–40 (*q.v.*). As with the Tabernacle, so with the offerings: certain principles are being established and they are not dependent on the appli-cation of typical significance to every single detail of the ritual described. 'It is held, first, that in the character, action, or institution which is denominated the *type*, there must be a resemblance in form or spirit to what answers to it under the Gospel; and secondly, that it must not be *any* character, action, or institution occurring in Old Testament Scripture, but such only as had their ordination of God, and were designed by Him to foreshadow and prepare for the better things of the Gospel' (Patrick Fairbairn).

ANALYSIS

I. THE OFFERINGS (1: 1–7: 38)
i. General Regulations (1: 1–6: 7)
(a) **Burnt offerings (1: 1–17)**
The manual on sacrifice (1: 1–7: 38) is divided into two sections, the first and larger of which contains directions of interest to both priesthood and laity (1: 1–6: 7). Ch. 6: 8–7: 36, on the other hand, gives much information which would have concerned the priesthood only. Because the **burnt offering** was the Hebrew sacrifice *par excellence* it stands at the head of the list.
(i) **From the Herd (1: 1–9). I.** The mention of **the Tent of Meeting** indicates that the book of Leviticus is the sequel to Exod. 40: 34–38. **2. offering** is the word which is transliterated as *corban* in Mk 7: 11; it means '(that which is) brought near'. **flock** may mean either sheep or goats (cf. v. 10). **3. burnt offering:** the Hebrew term is *'ōlāh*, meaning 'what goes up'. It denotes a sacrifice which, apart from its blood (v. 5) and skin (7: 8), was wholly consumed on the altar. Sometimes the term *kālîl* ('holocaust') is used (e.g. Dt. 33: 10; Ps. 51: 19). The daily burnt offering—morning and evening—was a feature of the Tabernacle ritual (Exod. 29: 38–42; Num. 28: 3–8) such that the altar in the Tabernacle court was known as 'the altar of burnt offering' (compare Exod. 27: 1 with Exod. 38: 1). **without defect** can have only physical significance in this context; but there is a moral connotation when the same language is used of our Lord—the antitype of the burnt offering and of all the offerings (Heb. 9: 14; 1 Pet. 1: 19). **that it** (or 'he') **will be acceptable** is better than AV 'of his own voluntary will' (see already A. Jukes, *The Law of the Offerings*. pp. 50 f.). **4. He is to lay his hand:** on the Day of Atonement actual confession of sin accompanied this act (16: 21), and it is difficult not to see some hint of identification or representation wherever it occurs in sacrificial contexts (cf. 3: 2; 4: 4; Num. 8: 12). **to make atonement:** while the thought of sin in the offerer may not be prominent in the burnt offering it had the effect of expiating (again it is the root *k-p-r* which is in question; see on Exod. 25: 17) a man's inadvertent wrongs. **5. He is to slaughter:** the ordinary Israelite had to kill the animal which he brought for sacrifice; Ezekiel wished to reserve this task for the Levites (Ezek. 44: 10 f.). The priests were responsible for the killing of animals presented as national offerings (16: 11; 2 Chr. 29: 24). RSV 'throw' is preferable to **sprinkle** (cf. on 4: 6), since the **blood** was caught in a basin and dashed against the corners of the altar (cf. Zech. 9: 15). The AV and RV marginal references to Heb. 12: 24 and 1 Pet. 1: 2 are therefore inappropriate at this point. **6. skin:** according to 7: 8 the skin of the burnt offering was a priestly perquisite. **7. fire on the altar:** the

altar-fire was not allowed to go out (6: 13), yet must often have smouldered. Now the ritual revolves around the altar and it is the priests—**Aaron's sons**—who take precedence. **9.** The entrails and (hind?) **legs** must first be washed clean of excretive impurities before they can be placed on the altar. **burn** translates the root *q-ṭ-r*, which is the term for burning sacrifices on an **altar**; from the same root comes the word for 'incense', cf. here the pleasing **aroma** which ascended to God. For burning away from the altar, as in the case of the sin offering (e.g. 4: 12; see also Num. 19: 5, 8 in connection with the red heifer), the verb *ś-r-p* is commonly used. **offering made by fire:** NEB 'food-offering' connects the Hebrew with another root meaning 'food'; follow NIV. **an aroma pleasing:** this strongly anthropomorphic idea has travelled a long way in the history of religion, from Babel to Golgotha. A cruder, literal version is encountered in a Babylonian account of the flood, according to which the gods swarmed like flies to enjoy the goodly smell from Utnapishtim's sacrifice. In the NT we are told that 'Christ loved us and gave himself up for us, a fragrant offering and sacrifice to God' (Eph. 5: 2).
(ii) **From the flock (1: 10–13). II. the north side** is occasionally associated with the divine habitation (e.g. Job 37: 22; Ps. 48: 2). This is a new piece of information and should not be restricted to this category of burnt offering; burnt offerings, sin offerings and guilt offerings were all to be killed at the same place (see 6: 25; 7: 2; 14: 13).
(iii) **Of birds (1: 14–17). 14.** The **burnt offering of birds** was within the means of the poorer members of the community (cf. 5: 7; 12: 8; Lk. 2: 24). The poverty in question was of a material sort and does not lend itself to the kind of interpretation which would grade the worshipper in terms of spiritual development. Mary, who was among the spiritual élite, availed herself of this concession; see Lk. 2: 22 ff. **young pigeon:** lit. 'sons of pigeons', which may refer to genus rather than to age, in accordance with established Semitic idiom. **15. wring off the head:** not so in the case of the sin offering (5: 8). The **blood** was **drained out** by pressing the bird's body against the wall of the **altar**; there would be insufficient **blood** for it to be treated like that of the animal victims. **16. contents** is possible (cf. NEB, and RV 'filth'); RSV prefers 'feathers'. **ashes:** the word more often means 'fat' and here denotes the fatty ashes which were removed from the altar fire. **17. not severing:** cf. Abraham's treatment of the birds killed in the covenant ceremony described in Gen. 15: 9 f.
(b) **Grain Offerings (2: 1–16)**
The word translated **grain offering** can, in other contexts, mean 'present' or 'tribute' (e.g.

Jg. 3: 15; 1 Kg. 4: 21). Here it is intended as a present to God to secure His favour. Kurtz (cited in *NBD*, p. 1050) has noted the correspondence between the ingredients of the **grain offering** and the '*minḥāh* of the holy place' —the bread of the Presence, the oil for the lampstand and the incense on the golden altar. While the **grain offering** appears in this section as an independent sacrifice, it was often presented in conjunction with burnt offerings and peace offerings (*e.g.* Num. 28: 1–31).

(*i*) **Unbaked (2: 1–3). 1. someone** represents the Hebrew *nephesh*, frequently translated 'soul'. Often the word means no more than 'person' and hardly reflects the Greek concept of the soul. **grain offering:** 'meat' as in AV 'meat offering' used to mean 'food', but is now quite inappropriate in a rendering of *minḥāh*. **fine flour:** there is but one word in the original and it is better to omit **fine**; according to Jewish tradition the flour was sifted but was not ground **fine** (see Snaith, *NCentB*). **2. all the incense** was included in the 'token' (so NEB for **memorial portion**; see G. R. Driver, *Journal of Semitic Studies*, I, 1956, pp. 97–105) which was burned **on the altar. 3.** What remained of the grain offering became the property of the priests, and, as **a most holy part**, could only be eaten by them within the sanctuary precincts (cf. v. 10; 6: 16 f.).

(*ii*) **Baked (2: 4–10). 4. oven:** 'a portable stove or fire-pot' (*BDB*). 'The dough was stuck against the inner side of a clay cylinder, previously heated by a fire lit inside it' (Noth); there is a good illustration of this in *NBD* (1st ed.), p. 166. **cakes made without yeast:** from the derivation of the word for **cakes** it is often assumed that they were perforated. **mixed with oil** most naturally means that the oil was added to the dough before the baking process had begun. Thinner **wafers, spread** (lit. 'anointed') **with oil**, were also acceptable. **5. griddle:** a flat plate or pan made of iron (cf. Ezek. 4: 3).

(*iii*) **Additional Instructions (2: 11–16). 11. yeast** and **honey** were not permitted in cereal offerings because of their tendency to ferment. Two different words are translated by **yeast** in this verse; for the first NEB has 'anything that ferments'. **12.** But both of the forbidden ingredients could be brought **as an offering of the firstfruits**—with the proviso that they must not be burned **on the altar. honey** is mentioned as part of **an offering of firstfruits** presented at the instigation of Hezekiah (2 Chr. 31: 5); it could have been either grape syrup or bees' **honey. yeast** readily became a symbol of moral corruption in rabbinical and in NT thinking (cf. Mt. 16: 6; Lk. 12: 1; 1 C. 5: 6; Gal. 5: 9). **13. salt**, on the other hand, had a preservative value and its use with grain offerings was *de rigueur*. Animal sacrifices were also

salted (Ezek. 43: 24, and cf. the longer text of Mk 9: 49 as in AV), 'divine meals' being treated in the same way as common meals. Covenants sealed by sacred meals seasoned with salt were held to be irrefrangible (Num. 18: 19; 2 Chr. 13: 5). **14.** The restriction on presentation at the altar (v. 12) did not apply to grain offerings (cf. v. 16); **firstfruits** represents a different word from that similarly translated in v. 12 and is used, principally, of grain and fruit. The **heads** of grain would be roasted and then crushed.

(*c*) **Fellowship Offerings (3: 1–17)**
The word for **fellowship offering** may be associated with the Hebrew noun *shālôm* ('peace, prosperity, wholeness'), or with the verb *shillēm* ('to compensate'). It is normally used in the plural (*shelāmîm*) as here—with an abstract sense?—and very often in conjunction with the regular term for sacrifice (*zebhaḥ*). In the Ugaritic texts a cognate term, doubtless with similar meaning, appears to have been part of the regular sacrificial terminology. There were three categories of **fellowship offering**: votive offering, thanksgiving offering and free-will offering (7: 11–18). In this offering only were there portions for God, for the priests, and for the worshipper, so that communion has been regarded as an important aspect of it. (Milgrom points out, however, that the eating is done 'before the Lord' (Dt. 12: 7) rather than with Him.) The instructions in this chapter fall into two main divisions: vv. 1–5 concern offerings from the herd, vv. 6–17 those from the flock (subdivided into sheep and goats). 'The Peace Offering was not an offering to *make peace*, but an offering that celebrated and rejoiced in *peace already made*' (A. J. Pollock). As illustrative, perhaps, of this explanation of the peace offering we may note that the idea of 'atonement' is seldom, if ever, present; this is not the case with the other animal offerings (see 1: 4; 4: 26; 5: 16).

(*i*) **From the Herd (3: 1–5). 1.** The acceptability of a **female** animal makes for a notable difference between the fellowship offering and the burnt offering with which it has particular affinity in matters of ritual. **3. the fat that covers the inner parts** is 'the *omentum*, the membrane which encloses the intestines and in the case of a healthy animal has large pieces of fat clinging to it' (Snaith, *NCentB*). **4. the covering of the liver:** the caudate lobe, according to Snaith; for other possibilities see *NBD*, p. 703. D. M. G. Stalker (on Exod. 29: 13 in Peake's Commentary) suggests that the **covering** was burned as a protest against the widespread practice of hepatoscopy, in which the condition of the upper lobe of the liver was of great significance. **5.** A fellowship offering was normally to be preceded by a **burnt offering**, though it is possible that this requirement was met by the daily **burnt offering** of 6: 12.

(*ii*) **From the Flock (3: 6–17). 9:** the **fat tail** was a delicacy produced by a particular breed of sheep and could be so heavy as to prevent the animal from standing. It may be that the word translated 'upper portion' in I Sam. 9: 24 requires emendation to 'fat tail' (see J. Mauchline, *I and 2 Samuel, ad loc.*). **16 f. All the fat is the LORD's:** And so **fat**, as well as **blood** (v. 17; cf. 17: 12), was not to form part of the Israelites' diet.

(*d*) Sin Offerings (4: 1–5: 13)

The **sin offering** was concerned with both ceremonial and moral defilement. 'Purification offering' as a title has more to be said for it. Where the offence was of a moral character the general principle was that only sins of ignorance could be expiated (Num. 15: 30; cf. Heb. 10: 26). NEB so renders 5: 1–6 as to suggest that deliberate sins of concealment were expiable with sin offerings. This rests, however, on some dubious translation which is discussed in the commentary on those verses. The **sin offering** and the **guilt offering** are two of a kind; but, whereas the former dealt with offences against God, the guilt offering took more account of wrong done to one's neighbour (see 5: 14–6: 7). Regulations for the **sin offering** are laid down according to the status of the person(s) involved: vv. 1–12, the anointed priest, vv. 13–21, the congregation (necessarily implicating the priesthood), vv. 22–26, a ruler, vv. 27–35, one of the common people. Since the Hebrew word for **sin offering** is nothing but the regular word for 'sin' it is possible that 'sin' in one or two NT references may bear the Hebraic sense of 'sin offering'; see commentaries on Rom. 8: 3 and 2 C. 5: 21.

(*i*) **Of Priests (4: 1–12). 2. unintentionally** is lit. 'in error', whether 'through ignorance' (AV) or 'unwillingly' (LXX). With the exception of 6: 1–7 (*q.v.*) the general principle applies; only sins of this type are covered by the sin and guilt offerings. 'Jehovah, God of Israel, institutes sacrifice for *sins of ignorance*, and thereby discovers the same compassionate and considerate heart that appears in our High Priest, "who can have compassion on the *ignorant*" (Heb. v. 2)' (A. Bonar). **3. the anointed priest:** cf. vv. 5, 16 and 6: 22. The reference could be to the high priest or, since Aaron's sons were also **anointed** (Exod. 28: 41; 30: 30; 40: 15; Lev. 7: 36), to any member of the priesthood. As representatives of the people the priests could bring **guilt** on them, whether by their own actions or by misdirecting those who sought guidance from them. **6. sprinkle:** this is indeed the verb 'sprinkle'; see on 1: 5. **seven times:** cf. v. 17; 8: 11; 14: 7; 16: 14, 19; Num. 19: 4. **seven** being a sacred number —and not only in Israel—the suggestion is

probably of a complete cleansing being effected. **the curtain of the sanctuary** divided the holy place from the most holy place (Exod. 26: 33). A **blood** ritual was required in the holy place because of the sin of the priest who officiated there. **7. the altar of fragrant incense** was in the holy place, but on the Day of Atonement the blood ritual of the sin offering was also performed in the most holy place (16: 14). **8 ff. the fat from the bull of the sin offering** was treated exactly as in the case of **the fellowship offerings** (v. 10; cf. 3: 3 ff.). **11 f.** 'Here is the holy law exacting the last mite' (Bonar). The remainder of the animal was to be carried out to a clean place and destroyed (**burn** translates different verbs in vv. 10, 12; see on 1: 9). So was symbolized the complete removal of the sin which had necessitated the sacrifice. But the destruction of those parts of the animal which were normally eaten by the priests (cf. 6: 26) served to emphasize the seriousness of the fault (cf. also the offering of the congregation in this respect (vv. 13–21) and see 6: 30). The writer to the Hebrews relates all this to the sufferings of our Lord who 'suffered outside the gate' (Heb: 13: 11 f.).

(*ii*) **Of the Congregation (4: 13–21). 14.** The sin of the congregation is expiated by the sacrifice of **a young bull**, i.e. at the same cost as the sin of the anointed priest (v. 3). **15. the elders of the community** represent the congregation in the act of laying **hands** on the animal. **18. the altar that is . . . in the Tent of Meeting** is the altar of fragrant incense of v. 7. Verse 19 summarizes vv. 8 ff. **21.** Because the priest is himself a member of the congregation, and is, moreover, its representative, he is again denied a share in the meat of the sin offering (cf. on vv. 11 f.).

(*iii*) **Of a ruler (4: 22–26). 22. a leader:** this would refer to the tribal leaders, as in Num. 7, etc.; in later times it would include the king. **23.** A less costly sacrifice—**a male goat,**—is required. **24.** Like the **burnt offering** of sheep or goats this victim was to be killed on the north side of the altar of burnt offering (cf. on 1: 11). **25.** Because the anointed priest was not involved in the sin, either personally or jointly with the people, the blood was not sprinkled in the holy place (cf. vv. 6, 17) nor was it put on the horns of the altar of incense (cf. vv. 7, 18); it was put **on the horns of the altar of burnt offering.** The regulation of 6: 24 ff., 29 applied to what remained of the sacrifice; so also for offerings from any of the common people (vv. 27–31).

(*iv*) **Of an Ordinary Person (4: 27–35).** Either a **goat** or a **lamb** (vv. 27–31; 32–35) was acceptable; a yearling is specified in Num. 15: 27. The size and sex (**female**) of the animal mark it as the least valuable of the sin offerings and appropriate for the common people. Concessions to impecuniosity are made in 5: 7–13. In other respects the regulations agree with those for the sin offering of a ruler (vv. 22–26).

(v) **Offences requiring Sin Offerings (5: 1–6).** Four offences requiring expiation by sin offering are listed in a series of protatic clauses (vv. 1–4) and the procedure is then laid down (vv. 5 f.). **1.** It was an offence to keep silence if one had seen or heard something and had been put on oath **to testify** (**public charge** is NIV's rendering of a Hebrew phrase which means lit. 'sound of an oath'; NEB has 'solemn adjuration'). Cf. Jg. 17: 2; Mt. 26: 63 f. **he will be held responsible:** i.e. he shall be deemed guilty of an offence. Porter considers that the offence described in this verse is not in the same category as those of vv. 2–4, not being expiable by sacrifice. But it seems unnecessary to press the meaning of the clause that far. **2.** Uncleanness from contact with the carcass of any kind of animal (cf. Gen. 1: 24) is culpable. Noth thinks that vv. 2–4 do not refer to the person guilty of the original infringement but to someone who had knowledge of the infringement and did not enlighten the person concerned; these verses would then be envisaging situations similar to that of v. 1. While the Hebrew can support this interpretation it is not its more natural sense. **even though he is unaware of it** is better than NEB 'and it is concealed by him' (the latter making the act of concealment the real offence). The Hebrew construction is paralleled in 4: 13, where 'hidden from' is the only possible meaning and is implicit in NEB 'not known to the assembly'. **6. penalty:** for BH 'āšām RSV has 'guilt offering', which is the more usual meaning. There is indeed a close connection between the sin and guilt offerings, but the latter are not introduced until v. 14. Because the offences are not the most serious **a female . . . from the flock** is regarded as the appropriate sacrifice of expiation.

(vi) **Concessions for the Poor (5: 7–13).** A gradation in the value of the sin offerings, related to the importance of the persons involved, was evident in ch. 4. The concessions outlined in this section are for the benefit of the common people (4: 27–35) who might be too poor to bring even a **lamb** (note that the mention of a **lamb** in v. 7 picks up 4: 32–35 rather than 5: 6). **7. penalty:** this again translates the Hebrew 'āšām, as in v. 6. **the other for a burnt offering:** as 'an acknowledgement of gratefulness for the concession' (Snaith, PCB). The acceptance of one of the birds as a **burnt offering** showed that poverty was not a barrier to communion with God. **8 f.** The ritual of the bird for a sin offering differs from that for burnt offerings of birds (1: 14–17). In this case the head of the bird was not to be

severed, and some of its blood was to be sprinkled on **the side of the altar. 10. in the prescribed way:** in accordance with the prescriptions of 1: 14–17. **11. a tenth of an ephah of fine flour:** 'just the very quantity of manna that sufficed for each day's support' (Bonar) was required from the very poor. The absence of **oil** and **incense** marked this offering as different from the grain offering (cf. 2: 1). **12. memorial portion:** or 'token'; cf. on 2: 2. Although not a blood-offering in itself the token was burned on **top of the offerings made . . . by the fire,** suggesting that it was no less efficacious than the blood-offerings ('offering by fire' is 'used chiefly of offerings of animals' (BDB)). 'In this way, what appears to be an exception to the principle that "without the shedding of blood there is no forgiveness of sins" (Heb. 9: 22) really ceases to be an exception but rather serves to illustrate the principle of vicarious substitution which it is the main object of the ritual of sacrifice to illustrate and enforce' (O. T. Allis).

(e) **Guilt Offerings (5: 14–6: 7)**
The guilt offering has much in common with the sin offering, but it also involves the principle of compensation; it was required in cases where damage was done to an individual and it could be assessed in monetary terms. If it was impossible to make restitution to the wronged person or to his relative then the compensation went to the priests (Num. 5: 8). (i) **Offences in Holy Things (5: 14–16). 15. holy things:** most commonly the offence would consist in the withholding of offerings (tithes, firstlings, etc.) or in the presentation of offerings not up to the required standard, in either case **unintentionally. of the proper value in silver:** an appropriate safeguard considering the type of infringement being rectified. **the sanctuary shekel:** cf. on Exod. 30: 13. This sacred **shekel** was heavier than the commercial 'light' shekel. **16.** The offender had also to pay compensation (amounting to the value of what was withheld plus **a fifth**) **to the priest** because the priests had suffered loss in being denied their allotted portions from the **LORD'S holy things** (v. 15). (For details of priestly dues see Num. 18: 8–32.)

(ii) **Sins of Ignorance (5: 17–19). 17.** The principle is extended to include **what is forbidden in any of the LORD'S commands,** though strictly within the context of inadvertent wrong-doing. **18.** Since the offender may well not have been able to assess the amount for which he was liable there is no mention of compensation. This is what was known in later Judaism as 'the suspended guilt offering', because it was brought in cases where liability could not be absolutely proved. (iii) **Breach of Trust (6: 1–7). 2 f.** Various kinds of situations are envisaged in which an Israelite might cheat his fellow of property; such was primarily a breach of faith against the LORD (cf. RSV). **neighbour:** 'kinsman' or 'fellow-countryman' (NEB) would be better. It is surprising to find theft and oppression of one's fellow included in this list in view of Num. 15: 30. **5.** Restoration of the original amount plus a **fifth** must be made to the wronged party **on the day he presents his guilt offering,** or possibly, with AVmg, RV, 'in the day of his being found guilty'. **6.** Then the **guilt offering** could be presented; the principle of Mt. 5: 23 f. is reflected.

ii. Additional Regulations for the Priests (6: 8–7: 38)
The subject-matter of this section is summarized in 7: 37 f. The directions are for the more part addressed to the priests (cf. 6: 9) and, among other things, establish the rights of priests and worshippers to certain parts of the flesh of sacrificial animals.

(a) **Burnt Offerings (6: 8–13)**
Verse 9 refers to the regular evening **burnt offering** (cf. Exod. 29: 38–42) which was to remain upon the altar all night 'so that there would always be a sacrificial offering to preserve the bond between God and his people' (Porter). **10.** The priest who dealt with the ashes in the morning had to put on **his linen clothes** and **linen undergarments** (cf. Exod. 28: 42) while officiating at the altar—cf. the ritual of the Day of Atonement (16: 4). **beside the altar:** on the east side (1: 16). **11.** The linen garments were not to be worn outside the sanctuary precincts. **a place:** cf. 4: 12. **12.** Following the removal of the ashes the fire was to be replenished with **firewood** and the morning **burnt offering** consigned to the flames; afterwards other sacrifices, for individuals or for the community, could be offered as circumstances demanded.

(b) **Grain Offerings (6: 14–23)**
Verses 14 f. summarize 2: 1–3 with v. 14b a minor addition. **16.** All but the token (**memorial portion,** v. 15) went to the priests for food. As **most holy** (17; 2: 3) it had to be eaten **in the courtyard of the Tent of Meeting. 17. Like the sin offering and the guilt offering:** cf. 6: 29; 7: 6. **18. Any male:** cf. Num. 18: 8 ff. **20.** This verse embraces two quite different things, *viz.* the grain offerings to be presented on the occasion of the installation of a high priest (cf. 8: 26; 9: 17; Exod. 29: 23), and the daily **grain offering** (cf. v. 22). Because of this seeming complication many scholars are inclined to delete the words **on the day he is anointed** (cf. NEB). But it is probably too much of a coincidence that in Exod. 29: 38–42 there is a similar situation; there the law of the continual burnt offering follows immediately on the directions for the installation of the priests. **half . . . and half:** the whole of this cereal offering was burned (cf. v. 23), and not just a token (as

in 2: 2, etc.). **21. broken** is a guess since the Hebrew word is difficult to explain; NEB has 'crumbled'. **22 f.** The whole was to be burned because it was a priestly offering and the normal rules about priests' dues did not apply (cf. the similar kind of ruling in v. 30).

(c) **Sin Offerings (6: 24–30)**
25. the place the burnt offering is slaughtered: the north side of the altar (cf. on 1: 11). **26.** The priest was permitted to eat the flesh of sin offerings in which he himself did not have a personal interest (cf. on v. 30). As with the priests' share of the grain offering (v. 16) the eating had to be done **in the courtyard. 27 f.** Ritual 'holiness' could be contracted by touching the flesh of the sin offering. Deconsecration, to bring the person or object out of the realm of ritual obligation, would then be necessary. **30.** In the case of sin offerings for an anointed priest and for the congregation some of the blood was taken into the holy place (4: 5 ff., 16 ff.). The carcasses of such sin offerings were burned outside the camp and the priests, as themselves involved in what occasioned the offering, could not partake of the sacrificial flesh.

(d) **Guilt Offerings (7: 1–10)**
No details as to the ritual for the guilt offering had been given in 5: 14–6: 7. **2 ff.** The procedure for the ram of the guilt offering is virtually identical with that for the lamb of the peace offering (3: 7–11). **6 f.** As to priestly dues, however, the comparison is with the sin offering (cf. 6: 26, 29). **8 ff.** The mention of the priests' portions from the guilt and sin offerings (v. 7) leads to summaries of their dues in connection with the burnt offering (v. 8) and the cereal offering (vv. 9 f.).

(e) **Fellowship Offerings (7: 11–36)**
This offering is special because portions of it went to the offerer as well as to the priest. **12.** The thanksgiving category of fellowship offering was different from the votive and freewill categories (v. 16) in that unleavened **cakes** were to be presented in conjunction with it (for the kinds of **cakes** cf. 2: 4; 6: 21), and also leavened bread (13; cf. 2: 11 f.; 23: 17; Am. 4: 5). The latter was allowed because it did not go to the altar. **14. sprinkles the blood:** see on 1: 5. **15. eaten on the day:** cf. Exod. 12: 10, with reference to the Passover lamb. **16.** A further distinction (cf. on v. 12) between the thanksgiving and the other types of fellowship offering was that the latter could be eaten on **the next day** after the sacrifice. **18.** Noncompliance with these rules rendered the sacrifice unacceptable. **19 ff.** Both the **meat** of the fellowship offering (v. 19a) and those eating it (vv. 19b–21) must be ritually clean. Verses 22 ff. give regulations concerning the **fat** and **blood** of animals and do not relate specially to the fellowship offering. **23.** The **fat** of sacrificial

animals was invariably burned on the altar as God's portion (cf. v. 25). **24.** The **fat** of dead animals which had not been killed for sacrifice could be used for general domestic purposes, but was on no account to be eaten. **26 f.** cf. 3: 17. Verses **28 ff.** give directions concerning the priests' share in the flesh of the fellowship offering. **30. wave . . . as a wave offering:** NEB has 'presented as a special gift'; see on Exod. 29: 24. **31.** The **breast** of the so-called **wave offering** was shared among the priests but the **right thigh of contribution** went to the officiating priest (32 f.). **34.** Thus were the material needs of the priesthood to be met from generation to generation. **35. portion** is to be preferred to AV 'portion of the anointing' and RV 'anointing-portion' (RVmg 'portion'). **36.** As in the case of the regular grain offering (6: 20) there is a connection between these provisions and **the day** on which the priests **were anointed**. Verse 37 lists the offerings in the order in which they are treated in 6: 8–7: 36. The **ordination** really looks forward to ch. 8, though Porter thinks it may refer to 7: 35 f. **38. Mount Sinai:** a different location from that mentioned in 1: 1 in connection with the laws of 1: 1–6: 7.

II. THE PRIESTHOOD (8: 1–10: 20)
i. The Installation of the Priests (8: 1–36)
The chapter describes how the instructions given to Moses in Exod. 29 were carried out. Reference should be made to the commentary on Exodus for most details; only significant variations will receive attention here. The special position of Moses as officiant—and as recipient of priestly dues (v. 29)—should be noted.

(a) **Investiture and Anointing (8: 1–13)**
3 f. Now the presence of the **assembly** is emphasized. **8.** The **Urim and the Thummim** are not mentioned in connection with the **breastpiece** in Exod. 29: 5; see Exod. 28: 30. **9.** The refrain **as the LORD commanded Moses** recurs in the chapter (vv. 13, 17, 21, 29; cf. Exod. 39–40). **10.** For the anointing of **the tabernacle and everything in it** see Exod. 40: 9, where the installation of the priests is associated with the erection of **the tabernacle** (Exod. 40: 12–15). **11.** Cf. Exod. 29: 36; 40: 10 f. The sprinkling of the oil **seven times** was not mentioned earlier; cf. 14: 16, 27.

(b) **Offerings for Installation (8: 14–36)**
There were three animal offerings to be presented: the bull for a sin offering (vv. 14–17), the ram for a burnt offering (vv. 18–21), and the ram of ordination (vv. 22–29). **15. purify** is lit. 'sinned' (i.e. 'un-sinned'). The **altar** where the priests would be ministering had to be made ritually pure. **17.** In that the carcass of this animal was **burned up** it corresponds to

the sin offerings for priests or for the congregation as detailed in 4: 1–21. Verses 18–21 recount in terms similar to those of Exod. 29: 15–18 the offering of the ram of burnt offering. Verses 22–30, dealing with the ram of ordination, are in close agreement with Exod. 29: 19–26, the main difference being that the sprinkling of the priests' vestments (v. 30) is mentioned at an earlier stage in Exod. 29 (v. 21). **26.** Exod. 29 does not mention the placing of the cakes from the basket **on the fat portions and on the right thigh** before they were put into the hands of Aaron and his sons. **28.** It is evident that the right thigh was burned on the altar (cf. vv. 25 f.), whereas in the normal fellowship offering it was reserved for the officiating priest (7: 32 f.). **31. the meat:** of the ram of ordination; NEB adds 'of the ram' in explanation. **the bread:** cf. vv. 2, 26. Verses 33 ff. prescribe a seven-day initiatory period which the priests had to observe before entering on priestly service; cf. Exod. 29: 35.

ii. The Ceremony of the Eighth Day (9: 1–24)
Now that the seven-day initiatory period is over Aaron is ready to assume responsibility for the ritual aspects of Israel's worship. More offerings on behalf of the priesthood have to be presented (vv. 2, 8–14), and then the national offerings (vv. 3 f., 15–24). **3 f.** Virtually the whole gamut of offerings is required from the people; the guilt offering is not included because it was primarily concerned with offences involving compensation to one's fellow Israelite. **7. and the people:** their interests were represented in the priests' offerings as well as in the national offerings. The LXX variant is favoured by NEB ('and for your household'). Verses 8–11 are virtually a summary of 4: 1–12 where the rules for the priestly sin offering are given. Verses 12 ff. summarize 1: 10–13 (cf. 1: 3–9). **12.** Throughout the ceremony of the eighth day Aaron's **sons** act as assistants (cf. vv. 9, 13, 18). The next step was to present the national offerings: sin offering (v. 15), burnt offering (v. 16), grain offering (v. 17), and fellowship offerings (vv. 18–21). **16.** Perhaps in view of v. 24 NEB 'prepared' is better than **offered**—that is if v. 24 is to be taken as the finale of the eighth day. The same Hebrew verb is translated 'prepare' in NIV at Gen. 18: 7. **17. took a handful** is not the same expression as in 2: 2; 5: 12, and may imply that the whole **grain offering**, and not just a token, was **burned** on the **altar** (cf. 6: 23); but see on 10: 12 f. **22 f:** Two benedictions are mentioned, the first by Aaron as high priest (cf. Num. 6: 24 ff.) and then by Moses and Aaron conjointly. Porter compares the double blessing pronounced by Solomon at the dedication of the Temple (1 Kg. 8: 14, 55). **22. stepped down:** this need not imply that Aaron stood on an

altar ledge when he offered sacrifices; see on Exod. 27: 4 f. **24.** See the comment on v. 16. The reference is in any case to the national burnt offering, for the priests' offering had already been burned (vv. 13 f.). For the supernatural fire cf. Jg. 6: 21; 1 Kg. 18: 38; 1 Chr. 21: 26; 2 Chr. 7: 1. Divine recognition and approval are indicated; contrast 10: 2.

iii. Nadab and Abihu (10: 1–7)
The story of Nadab and Abihu, the two elder sons of Aaron (Exod. 6: 23; 28: 1), is to this section of Leviticus what Ac. 5: 1–11, the story of Ananias and Sapphira, is to the early chapters of Acts. For both accounts Moses' words to Aaron (v. 3) are the fitting commentary: 'This is what the LORD has said, "I will show myself holy among those who are near me"'. Compare v. 3 with Ac. 5: 11 and vv. 4 f. with Ac. 5: 6, 9 f. The episode also shares features with the account of Korah's rebellion in Num. 16. **1.** In what sense **Nadab and Abihu** were guilty of offering **unauthorized fire** is not clear. **unauthorized** is lit. 'strange', 'foreign', and the similar expression 'other incense' in Exod. 30: 9 is usually taken to refer to **incense** wrongly compounded, i.e. not as stipulated in Exod. 30: 34–38. Perhaps the **incense** was burned at the wrong time, or the **fire** was not taken from the bronze altar (cf. 16: 12), or some other breach of ritual was committed. Because v. 9 speaks of drunkenness it is a commonplace in Jewish tradition that Nadab and Abihu had acted under the influence of strong drink. **2.** The **fire** that signified divine approval in 9: 24 now issues in judgment. Cf. Exod. 32: 10; there was no time for Moses' intervention on this occasion. **3.** Like Eli on another occasion (1 Sam. 3: 18) Aaron could but acquiesce in the sentence of judgment on his own sons. As priests they had been especially near to God. For **remained silent** NEB has, with some justification, 'was dumbfounded'. **4. Mishael and Elzaphan:** cf. Exod. 6: 22. The provisions of 21: 1 ff. would have permitted Eleazar and Ithamar, the brothers of Nadab and Abihu, to remove the bodies, but these were exceptional circumstances and the remaining members of Aaron's family could not give place to natural sentiment in the normal way. **5.** The bodies, still attired in the priestly **tunics**, were carried **outside the camp** just like the carcasses of the sin offerings (same expression as in 4: 12, etc.). **6.** Now Aaron's other sons **Eleazar and Ithamar** come into prominence; hitherto Nadab and Abihu had taken precedence (cf. Exod. 24: 1, 9). They were not to mourn the loss of their brothers, neither by letting their **hair became unkempt** (cf. Ezek. 24: 17, 23) nor by tearing their **clothes** (cf. 2 Sam. 3: 31); cf. 21: 10 with reference to the high priest. **7. do not leave** echoes 8: 33 ff., but the chief comparison is with 21: 12.

iv. Rules for the Priests (10: 8–20)
9. It is specifically with priests acting in their official capacity that the prohibition on intoxicants is concerned (cf. Ezek. 44: 21). **10.** This was so that the critical faculties of the priests should not be impaired in such a way as to prevent them from distinguishing **between the holy and the profane.** By their abstinence the distinction would also be preserved for the lay worshippers, whether at the sanctuary or at home, for nothing less than the difference between the Israelite faith and the heathenish practices of Canaan was involved. **11.** Cf. Jer. 2: 8; Ezek. 44: 23; Mal. 2: 7, for the teaching rôle of the priests. Verses 12 f. possibly refer to the national **grain offering** of the eighth day; cf. on 9: 17. If the ordinary grain offering is in view nothing is added to 6: 16 ff. **12.** Since the **grain offering** is **most holy** it may only be eaten by Aaron and his sons. Verses 14 f. deal with the national fellowship offerings of the eighth day. **14.** In contrast to the grain offering the **breast** and **thigh** of the **fellowship offering** could be eaten **in a ceremonially place** and by any member of the Aaronic family, females included. **15.** As in 9: 21 both **thigh** and **breast** are regarded as a **wave offering**, though normally only the **breast** could be so designated (cf. 7: 34). In vv. 16–20 a procedural point arises over the disposal of the remainder of the second sin offering of the eighth day (cf. 9: 15). This national offering was treated 'like the first (i.e. the priests') sin offering' (9: 15). Normally priests were not permitted any portion of the national sin offering since they had an interest in it themselves by reason of their Israelite citizenship. **16.** Moses discovered that the general rule had been applied in this case—**the goat of the sin offering** had been destroyed (**burned**) just like the priests' sin offering (cf. 9: 11). **17.** But the national sin offering of the eighth day should have been treated differently from the usual national offering and in accordance with the ritual for a goat presented as an individual offering (cf. 4: 22–31). **take away:** it is implied that the eating by the priests formed part of the ritual of sin-removing (cf. NBD, p. 1052). **18.** In truth very little is said about the ritual for the national sin offering in 9: 15 and we might otherwise have surmised that it was treated *in every respect* like the first sin offering. But it is emphasized that its blood had **not** been **taken into the Holy Place.** A corollary of this is that the 'horns of the altar' in 9: 9 must be those of the incense altar in the holy place (cf. 4: 7, 18). Because there had been a separate sin offering for the priests on this occasion they were not represented in the national offering; they were therefore entitled to the flesh of the latter in accordance with 6: 26, 29 f. **19.** The answer which satisfied Moses

(v. 20) was that even when the correct ritual for the priests' sin offering and guilt offering had been observed **such things** as the destruction of Nadab and Abihu had **happened to** Aaron. Would partaking of the national sin offering have made much difference after such dreadful happenings? Milgrom suggests that the Nadab and Abihu episode made Aaron afraid to follow the usual practice lest the sin of the priesthood should add to the guilt of the laity.

III. CLEAN AND UNCLEAN
(11: 1–16: 34)

The priests' responsibilities were not limited to altar service. One of their tasks was 'to distinguish between the holy and the profane, between the unclean and the clean' (10: 10), and to this end directions are given in chs. 11–16. Various aspects of everyday life are covered and then the ritual for the Day of Atonement, the annual ceremony of purification for the nation, brings the section to its conclusion.

i. Clean and Unclean Creatures (11: 1–47)

This chapter treats at greater length than Dt. 14: 3–21 the subject of cleanness and uncleanness of animals. The primal divisions are observed: animals (vv. 2–8), fish (vv. 9–12), birds (vv. 13–19), and winged insects (20–23). It is difficult to discover a uniform principle according to which the creatures were pronounced clean or unclean. Habits, physical characteristics, cultic associations of an obnoxious type, valetudinarian considerations—none of these is sufficient by itself to account for the distinctions made. Another line of approach suggests that only perfect representatives of species were considered clean. Any hybrid creature was imperfect and unclean because it did not conform to type. The categories recognized in the animal creation are also held to reflect the tripartite division of human society (unclean—clean—priestly) presented in Leviticus. See the bibliography under Douglas (M.).

(a) Animals (11: 1-8)

3. The domestic **animals** kept by the Israelites would meet the requirements laid down here. Dt. 14: 4 f. actually gives a list of animals, both domestic and wild, which could be eaten. Verse 4 introduces a group of animals which lack one of the basic requirements and which were therefore to be regarded as **unclean**. **5. coney:** the rock badger; cf. Ps. 104: 18; Prov. 30: 26. **7.** Eating the flesh of the **pig** was considered particularly obnoxious (cf. Isa. 65: 4; 66: 17).

(b) Water Creatures (11: 9-12)

9. Again the criteria of admissibility are stated first; they apply to both salt-water and fresh-water fish. **10. swarming things:** the term is used of small creatures which swarm, whether on land, in the sea, or in the air; it is delimited here by **in the water.**

(c) Birds (11: 13-19)

Those regarded as unclean are named (cf. Dt. 14: 12–18), but certain identification is often impossible; generally speaking, they are birds of prey or they feed on carrion. Verses 13 f. mention various birds of the order of *falconiformes*. **15. raven:** i.e. all belonging to the family of *corvidae*. **16 ff.** Snaith (*NCB*) fits all the birds in these verses into the family of *strigidae*, but this is rather precarious in view of the wide translational differences among the ancient and modern versions.

(d) Winged Insects (11: 20-23)

20. A general prohibition on orthopterans is followed by a concession (21): orthopterans with **jointed legs for hopping**, i.e. saltatoria, could be eaten. **22.** These are specified as **locust**s of various kinds; cf. Mt. 3: 4. In all, nine different words for locusts are used in the OT, representing various types and various stages of development (cf. *NBD*, p. 47). **23.** AV and NIV add **other** to bring out what is doubtless the sense.

(e) Contact with Carcasses (11: 24-28)

24. Cf. v. 8. **by these** refers to what follows (though see NEB). Contact with a human corpse rendered a person **unclean** for seven days (Num. 19: 11, 16); uncleanness from an animal carcass lasted only **till evening**, when the next day began according to Jewish reckoning. **25.** Carrying involves closer contact than touching so that in this case the person's **clothes** must be washed. Verse 26 should probably be read in the light of vv. 24 f., otherwise it means that the mere touching of an **unclean** animal, even while it was alive, rendered the person **unclean** (so Noth). **27. that walk on all fours** could describe cats, dogs and bears (cf. Snaith (*NCentB, PCB*) and Noth), or even monkeys, according to Porter.

(f) Small Creatures and Carcasses (11: 29-47)

Not only people (v. 31) but objects (vv. 32–38) could become unclean by contact with the carcasses of a number of small animals of the rodent and lacertilian types. Such creatures are plentiful in Israel, so that the situations envisaged in these verses would often be difficult to avoid. **32. put it in water:** cf. v. 25. **33. break the pot:** cf. 6: 28. **35.** The **oven** would be made of clay (cf. on 2: 4). **36 f. water** and **seed** were precious and were partly exempt from the general regulation, except that uncleanness (38) did occur if the seed was wet and, in theory at least, absorbent. **39.** Contact with the **carcass** of a clean animal which dies of itself makes a person **unclean**, the more so if the **carcass** is eaten or carried (40). **41 ff.** Verses 29–38 have dealt with uncleanness conveyed by dead swarming creatures; now a general prohibition on the eating of these creatures is added. Verse 42 establishes what is meant by that moves about on the ground in the previous verse. **Whether it moves on its belly** refers to snake-like creatures (cf. Gen. 3: 14). **44.** Should the injunction to **be holy** be restricted to ritual cleanness, as is sometimes done? 'Be ritually clean, for I am ritually clean' seems inadequate. Avoidance of defilement through contact with **any** swarming **creature** points to higher truths. **45.** We should at least begin to think of moral content in the second occurrence of the injunction. Now it is linked with the Exodus deliverance and the electing grace of God. Verses 46 f. summarize the chapter.

ii. Childbirth (12: 1–8)

It may seem strange that the Israelites, who regarded offspring as the gift of God, should bring sin offerings after the birth of children. While the practice may appear to reflect the attitude of Gen. 3: 16 it is more probable that a sin offering was required on account of the disordered condition of the body as a consequence of childbirth. **2.** After the birth of **a son** a woman was considered ritually **unclean** for **seven days**, the same rules applying as for menstruation (15: 19–24). **3.** The rite of circumcision was practised widely throughout the Near East (cf. Jer. 9: 25 f.) and it was the covenant significance attached to it in Israel that was unique. It seems to have been an adolescence or marriage rite elsewhere, so that its association with infancy may be another distinctive feature of its observance in Israel. Presumably **the eighth day** was included in the **thirty-three days** of purification (4), making a total of forty days (cf. English 'quarantine'). **5.** In the event of **a daughter** being born the figures are doubled and the uncleanness lasts for eighty days. Various reasons for this difference are adduced—*e.g.* that the child is 'a future subject of menstruation' (Snaith, *NCentB*)—but Noth's remark about 'the cultic inferiority of the female sex' may be nearest the mark. **6 f.** The period of uncleanness is terminated in a simple ceremony in which a **burnt offering** and a **sin offering** are presented on the woman's behalf by the **priest. 7. flow:** lit. 'fountain'; cf. 20: 18; Mk 5: 29 (AV). **8.** A concession for the poor as in 5: 7. Mary the mother of our Lord could not **afford a lamb** and so availed herself of this concession (Lk. 2: 24; cf. 2 C. 8: 9).

iii. Cases of Skin Disease (13: 1–59)

The findings of various recent investigations of 'Biblical leprosy' tend towards the same conclusion: the 'leprosy' of Lev. 13–14 is, in most if not all cases, different from modern leprosy (*elephantiasis Graecorum*). This is hardly surprising since the term 'leprosy' is also used of a condition in clothing and in houses (13: 47–59; 14: 33–53). The word translated 'leprosy' covers a wide variety of skin disorders. Some

of these disorders are quite minor and NEB's rendition by 'malignant skin-disease' is unsuitable in view of the usual significance of 'malignant' in medical contexts. Indeed, in one of the most recent examinations of the Biblical data, E. V. Hulse ventures the opinion that vv. 1–28 of our chapter are describing psoriasis in its various forms. The use of the word 'leprosy' in the English Bible tradition stems from a mistranslation by the Septuagint and Vulgate. On the other hand, 'true leprosy certainly did exist in the Near East in New Testament times' (*NBD*, p. 459). Responsibility for declaring a person clean or unclean rested with the priests —this was their sole 'medical' function—and chs. 13–14 are essentially a diagnostic manual to aid them in their pronouncements.

(a) Diagnosis and Procedure (13: 1–17)
2 f. A case of 'leprosy' which first manifests itself as a mark on the **skin. 3.** If the **hair** on the **spot** is **white** and the **sore** subcutaneous then the **priest** must **pronounce** the man **unclean. 4.** If the tell-tale symptoms are absent the person must be quarantined **for seven days** and provided that there is evidence of improvement he must be quarantined for a second period of **seven days** (5; contrast the case of Miriam in Num. 12: 14 f.). **6.** If after a fortnight the mark **has faded** the man may be declared ritually **clean. 7 f.** Should the symptoms reappear a further inspection is necessary, for the chances are that the man has an **unclean** skin affection. Verses 9–17 are concerned with more advanced cases for which periods of quarantine would be superfluous. **10.** The presence or absence of **raw flesh** is the crucial factor, as vv. 14 ff. also indicate. **12 f.** Thus a man might be covered **from head to foot** with the white mark and yet be pronounced **clean. 16 f.** Regression in cases where there is **raw flesh** leads to a happier verdict.

(b) Recurrence of Symptoms (13: 18–23)
18 ff. Where there is a suspected recurrence of inflammation the priest is to look for the usual symptoms (cf. v. 3) and if these are present the person is **unclean. 21.** Quarantine regulations must again apply before an individual can be declared clean but it appears that this time a clean bill of health can be dispensed after only one seven-day period of confinement (23).

(c) Cases of Burns (13: 24–28)
The same symptoms are sought and the same regulations apply as in the previous section. The concern is with burns which turn septic (Snaith, *NCB*).

(d) Various Skin Diseases (13: 29–39)
According to Hulse vv. 29–37 describe favus ('a very severe fungus infection of the skin'). Verses 29 f. probably refer to tinea (cf. JB). In vv. 31–34 an impetiginous infection is implied. **31.** The absence of **black hair** would be a bad sign and would call for investigation. Instead

of **black** NEB has 'yellow', following LXX; the sense is little affected since either way there was need for further observation. **33.** Shaving round the affected area would make it easier to decide whether the itch was spreading. A second period of quarantine is required (cf. v. 5) to make absolutely sure that there is no uncleanness attaching to the infection. **35 f.** Even after the cleansing ritual has been observed the trouble could recrudesce, in which case the person should be declared unclean without further ado. **38 f. a harmless rash:** vitiligo may be intended. NEB 'dull-white leprosy' agrees with LXX; the translation is unfortunate.

(e) Cases of Baldness (13: 40–44)
40 f. No uncleanness attaches to baldness *per se*, but if it is accompanied by **a reddish-white sore** (42) that is a different matter.

(f) Unclean! (13: 45–46)
45. A person pronounced unclean by reason of a skin disease had to behave as if in mourning. His **clothes** and **hair** proclaimed his living death (cf. 10: 6). For the covering of the lips cf. Ezek. 24: 17, 22. **46.** Isolation **outside the camp** was the sentence for all those found to be ritually unclean (cf. 2 Kg. 7: 3); it was a misery sufficient to bring even Jew and Samaritan together (Lk. 17: 12–19).

(g) Discoloration in Clothing (13: 47–59)
47. mildew: NEB has 'stain of mould'. The external resemblance to the human diseases already discussed will have been responsible for the use of the term 'leprosy' (cf. RSV) with reference to inanimate things. **48. woven or knitted:** RSV 'in warp or woof' can have no sense, as Snaith (*NCentB*) rightly points out. (If the condition affects one it will affect the other!) **50 f.** The procedure is much the same as for human cases of skin disease. **51. destructive:** i.e. rotting. Verse 54 prescribes a second period of seven days comparable with that of v. 5. **55.** If the spot had **not changed its appearance** by this time the garment was declared **unclean**, regardless of whether or not the spot had increased in size. **56 ff.** Even if the spot is fading further steps are necessary before the garment may be pronounced **clean** (v. 58); it may still at this late stage prove to be unclean (v. 57).

iv. The Cleansing Ritual (14: 1–57)
(a) For Diseased Persons (14: 1–20)
3. The **priest** must **go outside the camp** because the man cannot be admitted until he has been pronounced clean (cf. 13: 46). **4. cedar wood, scarlet yarn and hyssop** were also used in the cleansing ritual of the red heifer (Num. 19: 6), being burned with the heifer to produce the ashes which were added to the water of purification. For **hyssop** in connection with cleansing see also Ps. 51: 7. In Jewish tradition the **cedar wood** was regarded as a

symbol of human pride, an interpretation which has commended itself to some Christian typologists. Interestingly, the **scarlet yarn** (lit. 'scarlet stuff of a worm') was understood by Jewish interpreters to symbolize humility (with emphasis placed on the *worm*); Christian interpreters with similar anagogical bent, but without reference to the Hebrew in most cases, have taken it to represent man's seeming greatness (for what else could **scarlet** denote?)! **5. fresh water** is lit. 'living water', water from a spring rather than from a well or cistern (cf. Jer. 2: 13; 17: 13). The water was probably in the **clay pot** when the bird was killed over it (so NEB). **7.** The release of the **live bird** symbolizes the removal of uncleanness from the man; cf. the 'scapegoat' on the Day of Atonement (16: 21 f.). **8 f.** Restoration to the community precedes restoration to full family life. The **seven days** are essentially a period of initiation and, as with the priests' initiation, they are concluded with an eighth day ceremony (10; cf. 9: 1 ff.). **three-tenths of an ephah:** probably a tenth for each of the sacrificial lambs (cf. Num. 29: 4). **12.** Although there were to be four offerings in all it is the **guilt offering** which receives most of the attention. In 5: 14–5: 7 the normal requirement for a **guilt offering** is given as 'a ram without blemish'. A man living outside the camp on account of ritual impurity would not have been able to fulfil his duties to God at the sanctuary; it is in this sense, perhaps, that reparation was being made by means of the guilt offering. **wave offering:** cf. on Exod. 29: 24. **14.** This singular rite also formed part of the ceremony of priestly installation (8: 23 f.). **15 ff. oil** is applied in the same way after it has been sprinkled **before the** LORD **seven times.** 18. Milgrom compares a Ugaritic ceremony of manumission; a female slave was freed when an officiant announced, 'I have poured oil upon her head and I have declared her pure'. **19.** Special attention has been paid to the rituals of the guilt offering and the anointing because of their distinctiveness. By contrast, we are not even told which of the remaining animals was presented as the **sin offering** and which as the **burnt offering**. On the basis of 4: 28, 32 we may surmise that the ewe lamb (v. 10) was for the **sin offering. 20.** It is possible that the whole **grain offering** was presented in association with the **burnt offering** (though see on v. 10); all of it was burned **on the altar**, in any case (contrast 2: 2).

(b) Concessions for the Poor (14: 21–32)
21 f. The concessions are as follows: a reduction in the amount of **flour** from three tenths to a **tenth of an ephah** and the replacement of the animals for the sin offering and burnt offering by **two doves or two young pigeons**, in accordance with 1: 14–17 and 5: 7–10. There

could be no concession affecting the main elements in the cleansing ritual, *viz.* the **male lamb as a guilt offering** and the **log of oil**. Otherwise the ritual is as in vv. 11–20.

(c) The Ritual for a House (14: 33–53)
The manifestations of 'leprosy' and the prescribed ritual are much the same as in the case of garments (13: 47–59). Again it is a question of chemical action or fungal growth (cf. NEB's 'fungus infection' in v. 34) which bears resemblance to the human diseases covered by the term 'leprosy'. **34. and I put:** all aspects of life, whether good or bad, are ultimately determined by God, the creator of life (see Isa. 45: 7; Am. 3: 6); so far is the OT removed from any thought of dualism. **37. greenish or reddish depressions** are the distinguishing marks as in 13: 49. **deeper than the surface:** this was the most important factor in determining whether a human condition was 'leprous' (cf. 13: 3, etc.). **45.** If there is a recurrence of the trouble after the measures of vv. 38–42 have been taken then the house must be destroyed. But if there is no fresh outbreak of the symptoms the **priest** may **pronounce** it **clean** (v. 48). The cleansing ritual is similar to that for a diseased person (cf. vv. 4–7).

(d) Summary (14: 54–57)
These verses summarize the contents of chs. 13–14, though minor summaries do occur earlier (13: 59; 14: 32).

v. Discharges (15: 1–33)
Verses 1–15 concern male discharges of a morbid type, vv. 16 ff. those of the normal type. Verses 19–24 deal with normal menstrual discharges, while vv. 25–30 are concerned with female discharges of an abnormal nature. Only in cases of abnormality was sacrifice required (vv. 14 f., 29 f.). **12.** Cf. 11: 32–38. Verses 13 ff. prescribe the course of action to be followed when the condition has cleared. A **seven** day period must be observed before a **sin offering** and a **burnt offering** are offered and a new beginning made (15); similarly in vv. 28 ff. **19.** Cf. 12: 2. 25 ff. Cf. Mk 5: 25–34.

vi. The Day of Atonement (16: 1–34)
This was the most important day in the Jewish religious calendar, the one day in the year when the high priest went into the most holy place with sacrificial blood. Because this was the occasion when a cleansing ritual was performed on behalf of the whole nation the details of that ritual are given here at the end of the section on cleanness and uncleanness (chs. 11–16) rather than in ch. 23 where all the annual festivals are enumerated. Such is its importance in Judaism that it is designated in Ac. 27: 9 as, simply, 'the fast'. Traditionally the period between New Year's Day, on the first of the seventh month, and the Day of Atonement, on the tenth of the same month, has been observed as a time of self-examination in anticipation of the great

day. The writer of the epistle to the Hebrews draws heavily on the ritual of the Day of Atonement as he demonstrates the superiority of our Lord's sacrifice over the whole of the OT sacrificial order (see especially Heb. 9). **1.** The death of Nadab and Abihu (10: 1 ff.) was graphic illustration of the dangers involved in approaching God's presence in the wrong manner. Milgrom thinks that vv. 1–28 refer in the first instance to the purification of the sanctuary after the sin of Aaron's sons. **2.** Entrance into the **Most Holy Place** was to be a privilege restricted to the high priest alone, and that only on very special occasions. **in the cloud:** of incense (v. 13). **3. sin offering:** see vv. 6, 11. **burnt offering:** see v. 24. **4.** Rather less than the full regalia of the high priest was to be worn on this occasion (cf. Exod. 28: 39, 42 f.). **8.** There are various possible explanations of **the scapegoat** see *NBD*, pp. 1077. AV 'scapegoat' goes back via Tyndale to the LXX and Vulgate. In later Judaism Azazel figures as a demon who taught men devious devices, but this is probably not its significance here (some scholars are, however, inclined to think that *MT* 'for Azazel' must have a personal reference —even if the 'person' be a demon—if it is to parallel **for the LORD**). NEB 'for the Precipice' has two points in its favour: (1) there is a similar-sounding Arabic word meaning 'rough place' (see *JSS*, I, 1956, pp. 97–105); (2) it was the custom in later times to push the live goat over a precipice situated three or four miles from Jerusalem. In the absence of a totally convincing explanation it should be said that there is some philological support adducible for the scapegoat tradition, as in AV and NIV. **13.** Protected from the sight of the divine majesty by **the smoke of the incense** the high priest could proceed with that part of the ritual which took place in the inner sanctuary (v. 14). Again the warning words **so that he will not die** (cf. v. 2) are uttered; contrast Heb. 4: 16. **14.** The atonement rite on behalf of the priesthood was completed by the sprinkling of blood on the mercy seat and also on the ground in front of the mercy seat. **15.** Now that he has offered sacrifice for his own sins the high priest can act on the people's behalf by bringing the **blood** of their **sin offering** inside **the curtain**. Our Lord was able to deal with human sin directly and decisively because of the very fact that He had no need to make atonement for any sins of His own (Heb. 7: 27). **18.** Next **the altar that is before the LORD** is the object of the high priest's ministrations. That this is the altar of incense and not the altar of burnt offering is suggested by Exod. 30: 10 (cf. also Lev. 4: 7, 18); most, however, understand the reference as being to the altar of burnt offering as in v. 12. **20 ff.** The idea of removing a nation's sins by transferring them to a live animal is very common in ancient texts; cf. also 14: 7. **21. both hands:** not just one hand as in 4: 4, 24, 33. **confess:** confession is seldom mentioned in connection with the presentation of animal sacrifices, but see 5: 5 and Num. 5: 7 f. **22. solitary place** is lit. 'a land cut off' (cf. Amplified Bible), i.e. a place of no return (cf. Ps. 103: 12). **24.** The burnt offerings were reserved until the ritual of the sanctuary was completed (cf. vv. 3, 5). **25.** Attired in his normal vestments the high priest not only presents the offerings of v. 24, but also burns **the fat of the sin offering** on the altar in accordance with the regulations given in 4: 8 ff. It is not clear which sin offering is intended—the high priest's (vv. 3, 6, 11–14) or the people's (vv. 5, 9, 15). Noth favours the former alternative. **27.** The carcasses are treated in accordance with the principle laid down in 6: 30 (cf. 4: 11 f., 21). **29. you must deny yourselves** primarily refers to fasting; the prohibition extended to all within Israel's borders, so that the resident alien, though not involved in the ritual, had to observe the fast. **31.** This day was to be observed as a **sabbath** so far as work was concerned. **34. once a year** stands in marked contrast to the multitudinous offerings brought throughout the year, and yet even this annual ritual represents ineffectual repetitiousness in the light of Calvary (see Heb. 9: 25 f.)

IV. THE 'HOLINESS CODE' (17: 1–26: 46)
i. Laws on Sacrifice (17: 1–16)
(a) **Concerning Animal Slaughter (17: 1–9)**
In this section directions are given concerning the slaughter of domestic animals for food. The requirement is that every slaughter 'should be undertaken as a cultic act' (Noth), and the reason is stated clearly in v. 7. **4.** Every animal for slaughter had to be brought to **the entrance to the Tent of Meeting**; a man was held to be guilty of murder if he did not comply. Dt. 12: 15–28, which permits the slaughtering and eating to take place 'within your towns' (v. 21), is addressed to a later situation. **6. sprinkle** should be 'throw'. Verse 7 shows what was likely to happen—and the implication is that it was already happening—in the absence of such regulations. **goat idols** were the demon-gods (cf. NEB 'demons') of rural mythology (cf. 2 Chr. 11: 15 and, possibly, 2 Kg. 23: 8, where NIV 'gates' could be read as 'satyrs'). In v. 8 the principle is applied to sacrifices proper (the **burnt offering** was entirely consumed and no part of it was used for food); these had also to be killed at the central sanctuary.
(b) **Prohibition on Blood (17: 10–16)**
Here, at greater length than hitherto (cf. 3: 17; 7: 26), the reason for the prohibition on blood is given. The Jewish practice of eating only kosher meat, i.e. meat from animals ritually

killed, finds its origin in this prohibition. Verse 11 expresses it all in a nutshell: **the life of a creature is in the blood** and, furthermore, it is the blood which God has appointed as the means of **atonement** (cf. Rom. 3: 25, 'whom God put forward as an expiation by his blood'). **13. any** (clean) **animal or bird** such as was not acceptable as a sacrifice and which had not been killed in accordance with vv. 5 f. could be eaten provided that its blood had been drained from it (cf. Dt. 12: 16, 24). **15.** To eat an animal which had died a natural or a violent death was to render oneself **ceremonially unclean.** Dt. 14: 21 forbids the Israelite to eat 'anything that dies of itself' but permits the **alien** to do so.

ii. Laws of Chastity (18: 1–30)
A fair proportion of the chapter (vv. 6–18) is concerned with the regulation of sexual relationships within the large family units that were characteristic of early Israelite society. **3.** Both **Egypt** and **Canaan** are mentioned, the former rather unusually in this context. The licentiousness of the Canaanites is often denounced in the OT; the mention of Egypt is especially apposite to vv. 6–18 in view of the common Pharaonic practice of marrying within the 'prohibited degrees'. **5. will live:** cf. Exod. 20: 12; Dt. 30: 15–20; Eph. 6: 2 f. It was precisely because of such irregularities as are about to be described that the Canaanites were under divine judgment (cf. vv. 24–28; Gen. 15: 16). **8. your father's wife** could as easily reflect a polygamous situation as a case of remarriage by a widower. **9.** Cf. Dt. 27: 22; 2 Sam. 13: 11 f. **born in the same home or elsewhere** is an unusual expression which may embrace legitimate and illegitimate offspring. Verse 11 is concerned with half-sisters, whereas v. 9 deals with sisters generally. Abraham's marriage to Sarah (cf. Gen. 20: 12) would not have been permissible by this later standard. Verse 16 does not conflict with the institution of the levirate (cf. Gen. 38: 7–11; Dt. 25: 5–10; Mt. 22: 23–28), since it was only meant to apply during the brother's lifetime. **18.** Again, and by definition, the prohibition applied during the wife's lifetime. Jacob's marrying both Leah and Rachel would have been in contravention of this law if it had existed at the time (cf. Gen. 29: 30). The term **rival wife** (see 1 Sam. 1: 6) hints at the domestic unhappiness which must often have accompanied polygamy; this unhappiness was institutionalised in the use of the term. Verses 19–23 are chiefly concerned with unnatural relations and acts. **21.** Cf. 20: 1–5. **to be sacrificed:** possibly to make them pass through fire as an offering to **Molech**, god of the Ammonites (1 Kg. 11: 7); see 2 Kg. 16: 3; 21: 6; Jer. 7: 31, etc. There is no mention of **fire** in the Hebrew text (cf. NEB: 'You shall not surrender any of your children to Molech'), but see 2 Kg. 23: 10 (and correct

Snaith (*NCentB*) on this point). Perhaps the practice involved some sexual perversion; otherwise it is difficult to account for the present setting of the prohibition. **Molech** has the consonants of a Semitic root for 'king' and the vowels of the Hebrew word for 'shame'. In the OT there are various instances of scribal disapproval being expressed in the vocalization of the originally unvocalized Hebrew text (*e.g.* the name Ashtoreth). **24 ff.** If the Israelites are guilty of the same sins as marred the Canaanite civilization let them remember what befell their predecessors in the land lest history repeat itself (cf. Rom. 11: 21).

iii. Rules and Regulations (19: 1–37)

A wide range of human activity receives attention in the chapter. There is no obvious connecting link, save that of the refrain, 'I am the LORD (your God)' (vv. 3, 4, 10, etc.). **2.** Cf. 11: 44 f. **3 f.** Several of the Ten Commandments are paralleled here; cf. Exod. 20: 3, 4, 8, 12. **respect:** lit. 'fear'; Exod. 20: 12 has 'honour'. **his mother and his father:** the order is uncommon in the OT, being found only in these chapters (Porter); see 20: 19; 21: 2. **gods of cast metal:** cf. Exod. 34: 17; Exod. 20: 4 has 'graven image', i.e. of wood or stone rather than metal. Verses **5 ff.** rule on the offerer's participation in his fellowship offering. **6.** According to 7: 15–18 the provision relating to eating **on the next day** applied to votive and freewill offerings but not to thanksgiving offerings. Verses 9 f. urge consideration for the **poor** and the **alien** at harvest-time; cf. 23: 22; Dt. 24: 19–22; Ru. 2: 1–23. It is possible that the practice originated in pre-Israelite times and concerned the harvest rights of fertility spirits. If so, the institution was now transformed beyond recognition. Verses 11 f. correspond, in part, to Exod. 20: 7, 15. **12. falsely:** NEB 'with intent to deceive'. **13. wages** had to be paid on the day on which they were earned (cf. Dt. 24: 14 f.; Mt. 20: 8). **14.** 'The deaf man cannot hear the curse and the blind man cannot see the obstacle. Thus both men are helpless and are therefore the special concern of God (Ps. 10: 14; 72: 12)' (Snaith, *NCentB*). **15.** Partiality towards the **poor** may interfere with the course of justice as much as may undue deference to the **great**. Verse 16b forbids anyone to bear false witness against a man on trial for his life; NEB has 'nor take sides against your neighbour on a capital charge'. **18. but love your neighbour as yourself:** cf. 1 Sam. 18: 1. For the NT quotations of this the second of the 'great' commandments see Mt. 22: 39 (and parallels); Rom. 13: 9; Gal. 5: 14; Jas 2: 8. NEB 'as a man like yourself' is slightly different and purports to represent the Hebrew idiom more accurately. This new-found insight was not applied by the NEB translators at 1 Sam. 18: 1, 3—far from it! **19.** Cf. Dt. 22: 9 ff. The distinctions

of nature are to be preserved. But the precise origin of these rules against mixtures is not known. Milgrom suggests that, in the case of garments, the prohibition arose out of the fact that the Tabernacle curtains and high priestly vestments were made from such a mixture; mixing of materials therefore was forbidden in the sphere of the profane. **20.** If the woman had been free Dt. 22: 23 f. would have been enforceable. In this case the woman is still her master's property and her fiancé cannot exercise the normal betrothal rights. **promised** is lit. 'assigned', so that the situation may, rather, be that the slave-woman has been assigned to concubinage but has not yet been claimed; so Snaith (*NCentB*). **21 f.** Because of her lowly status the slave-woman is not held responsible (contrast Dt. 22: 24), but the man must bring a **ram for a guilt offering** (cf. 5: 15). **23. regard its fruit as forbidden:** the Hebrew speaks of the trees being 'uncircumcised' for **three years. 24. an offering of praise** represents the same word as is rendered by 'festival' in the harvest setting of Jg. 9: 27. The Samaritan version has a variant reading which is adopted in NEB: 'and this releases it for use'. But NEB depends on a slight adjustment of the word-order and it is probably wiser to follow NIV. **25.** God's blessing would be upon the harvest in response to the people's acknowledging His prior claim on the fruit of the trees. Verse **26a** summarizes 17: 10–14. The LXX has 'upon the mountains' instead of **with the blood still in it** (lit. 'upon the blood')—a difference much more understandable in terms of the Hebrew words than of their English counterparts. The Greek would be referring to eating at pagan sanctuaries (cf. Ezek. 18: 6, 11, 15). **27 f.** These are mourning rites for the dead (cf. Dt. 14: 1; Isa. 15: 2; Jer. 9: 26; 25: 23; 48: 37). **28.** Cutting the flesh was a feature of the worship of Melqart (Baal in OT); see 1 Kg. 18: 28. There are various explanations of this self-disfigurement which have been advanced: to provide blood for a departed spirit, to render mourners unrecognizable to departed spirits, to drive away the spirits by the life-force resident in the blood, and so on. At Carmel the priests of Melqart were not, however, performing mourning rites. Verse 29 would include cultic prostitution such as was common among the Canaanites. **31. mediums:** necromancers like the so-called 'witch' of Endor (1 Sam. 28: 7). Verses 32 f. demand respect for the aged (and by the same principle for **God**) and for the **alien** (cf. Exod. 22: 21; 23: 9). **34.** The principle of v. 18 is extended to cover the Israelite's attitude to the stranger. Our Lord gave it an even wider application (Lk. 10: 25–37). **35 f.** Compare Am. 8: 5 for the abuses which could so easily arise in a society where even money, in the absence of proper coinage, had to be weighed. The **ephah** was a dry measure, the **hin** a liquid measure (cf. the NIV footnotes).

iv. Capital Offences of Various Kinds (20: 1–27)

2. A stricture against giving **children to Molech** has already been encountered at 18: 21. **4 f.** God appears as the defender of the helpless child, pledging Himself to execute judgment if the community turns a blind eye to a heinous practice. **5.** The **family** of the guilty person had also to suffer, possibly for connivance in the matter (but cf. Jos. 7: 24 f.). As Noth appreciates, if we were to accept the suggestion that the reference was originally to a Phoenician-type sacrifice—for which the name (unvocalized) was *mlk*—we should have to imagine that the OT writers misunderstood the practice. **prostituting themselves to Molech** certainly leaves the intention here in no doubt; this translation is much to be preferred to the alternative reading in the NEB footnote ('in his lusting after human sacrifice'). **6.** Cf. v. 27 and 19: 31. **9.** As in Exod. 21: 17 cursing one's parents is punishable by death (cf. Dt. 27: 16). It is commonly asserted nowadays that 'the spoken curse was an active agent for hurt' (*NBD*, p. 256). **his blood will be on his own head:** he is responsible for his own death and there can be no question of blood revenge. Verses 10–21 deal with sexual offences and their punishment. In ch. 18, where similar offences are discussed, there is no mention of penalties. **10.** That both parties came under judgment was not recognized by the accusers of the woman taken in adultery in Jn 8: 1–11. **12.** Verses **20 f.** do not demand the death penalty, but threaten childlessness—an extreme punishment nonetheless (cf. Num. 27: 2 ff.; Dt. 25: 6; Ru. 4: 10). **childless** may mean rather 'proscribed' (NEB); apart from Lev. 20: 20 f. the word occurs only in Gen. 15: 2 and Jer. 22: 30. **childless** would be appropriate in both of these references, though Jeconiah had sons (1 Chr. 3: 17 f.). **25 f.** By its observance of these laws Israel will maintain its distinctiveness among the nations. Verse 26 states the positive as well as the negative aspects of Israel's separation (**to me** and **from the peoples**).

v. A Holy Priesthood (21: 1–24)

Rules to safeguard holiness are laid down for the ordinary priests in vv. 1–9 and for the high priest in vv. 10–15. Verses 16–24 revert to the subject of the ceremonial fitness of the priests in general and rule on causes for disqualification from priestly service.

(a) The Ordinary Priests (21: 1–9)

1. unclean: By contact with corpses (cf. Num. 6: 9, 11 f.; 19: 11). **3.** A married **sister** would be counted as a member of her husband's family. **4.** The Hebrew is difficult. NIV has an indirect reference to the priest's wife who is not mentioned in vv. 2 f. (cf. AVmg). A commonly-accepted emendation of the Hebrew produces the reading: 'He shall not defile himself for a married woman' (cf. NEB). Thus v. 4 would refer to a married sister—and indeed to other married women in the family—just as v. 3 referred to an unmarried sister. **5.** Cf. 19: 27 f. **heads:** shaving the head as an act of mourning is what is forbidden (cf. Isa. 3: 24; 22: 12). **9.** Such a **daughter** would be a constant reproach to her father, a grave embarrassment to one functioning as a priest. For the punishment cf. 20: 14. Perhaps there was a special danger that priests, once they had forsaken the Lord, would involve their daughters in cult prostitution of the Canaanite type.

(b) The High Priest (21: 10–15)

Here the rules are, as we should expect, more strict. **10 f.** No outward signs of mourning (cf. 10: 6) are permitted, and no contact with corpses, no matter how close the relationship to the deceased. **12.** The high priest must not leave the sanctuary precincts during the period of mourning (cf. 10: 7). This restriction may only have applied to his leaving the sanctuary to pay his respects to the dead (so Allis, Porter). By contact with a corpse in its ritual uncleanness he could **desecrate the sanctuary of his God. 14.** To the restrictions imposed on the ordinary priests (v. 7) is added a prohibition on marriage to a **widow.** The high priest must marry within the priestly connexion and he must choose **a virgin from his own people.** Ezek. 44: 22 specifically allows the ordinary priest to marry the widow of a priest. **15.** A daughter might bring disgrace upon her father (v. 9) and a high priest—or any priest for that matter—could, by disregarding these rules, **defile his offspring,** rendering his male offspring unfit for service.

(c) Cases of Disqualification (21: 16–24)

Physical blemishes or defects may unfit a priest for service in the sanctuary. Some of the terms used are of uncertain meaning. **20. hunchbacked** and **dwarfed** may not be the correct translations. The terms may relate to the eyebrows and eyes respectively (so NEB, and cf. **who has any eye defect). 22.** But members of the priestly family who are debarred on this account are still allowed to partake of the priestly perquisites. **23. my sanctuary:** 'holy localities' or 'holy furnishings' (Noth); cf. Ps. 73: 17; Jer. 51: 51, where the same word also occurs in the plural.

vi. Holy Offerings (22: 1–33)

Verses 1–16 are for the instruction of the priesthood as to the eating of those parts of the sacrifices which were allocated by God for their use. The section on acceptable offerings (vv. 17–33) is also addressed to 'all the people of Israel' (v. 18).

(*a*) **Priests' Participation (22: 1–16)**
2. treat with respect translates the root *nāzar*, whence, possibly, the term 'Nazirite'. **3. cut off from my presence:** v. 9 makes specific reference to death as the possible outcome if the rules are not kept. Verse 4a contrasts with the provision of 21: 22; in this case the disqualification is full but not final. **8.** A higher standard is expected of the priest than the layman, for in this case eating animals not killed in the prescribed manner is absolutely forbidden. An ordinary Israelite who ate in these circumstances became unclean for a short period (11: 40; 17: 15). Verses 10–16 indicate those within the priestly circle who were entitled to a share in the offerings. **10.** An outsider is anyone who does not belong to the priestly circle as defined in the verses which follow. **guest:** a stranger temporarily resident in the community, here someone staying with a priestly family. Although a **hired worker** was not included, a **slave**, whether bought or **born** in the house, was permitted to share in the sacrificial food (11). **12 f.** Marriage to someone outside the priestly connexion meant that the daughter of a priest no longer had claim to support from the priests' sacrificial food. In certain circumstances it was possible for a woman to be reinstated in the priestly connexion (v. 13). Only the rights of *male* members of the priestly families are disclosed in 6: 18, 29; 7: 6. **14.** Cf. 5: 16; 6: 5, in the context of the guilt offering and the law of restitution. **15 f.** Responsibility for any profanation of holy gifts rested with the priests. Lack of vigilance on their part could involve Israelites in the kind of situation envisaged in v. 14.

(*b*) **Acceptable Offerings (22: 17–33)**
In general only offerings free of blemish and defect are acceptable, whether they be burnt offerings (v. 18) or fellowship offerings (v. 21). There is one exception to all this (v. 23). Failure to meet these requirements rendered a sacrifice inefficacious (cf. Mal. 1: 8 ff.). **18. for a burnt offering:** votive and **freewill** offerings were usually of the fellowship offering type (cf. v. 21). **21. fellowship offerings** were divided into three categories (cf. 7: 12, 16). The thanksgiving offering is dealt with in vv. 29 f. **22, 24.** Cf. 21: 18–21, there with reference to blemishes in priests. **23.** A distinction is made between the **freewill offering** and the votive offering in that an animal **deformed or stunted** is acceptable in the former case. The importance of repaying a vow in full is upheld. **24.** The verse need not imply a prohibition on the gelding of animals, as Josephus understood it to mean (*Ant.* iv. 8, 40). **27.** Another of the significant heptads in Leviticus (cf. 12: 2 f. and Exod. 22: 30). **with:** lit. 'under'. **28.** Cf. Dt. 22: 6 f. Some fertility rites involved sacrifices of this sort. **30.** Cf. 7: 15.

vii. The Religious Calendar (23: 1–44)
Israel's annual festivals are presented in the order of their occurrence, but first there is a mention of the weekly sabbath since it was a fundamental institution and was also the occasion of sacrificial offerings (cf. Num. 28: 9 f.). These are all embraced in the term **appointed feasts** (v. 2). The festivals have in some cases a historical significance, in others a purely agricultural significance. But it is possible that the festivals with historical significance (notably Passover, Unleavened Bread and Booths) were originally agricultural in character and assumed their historical significance after the events which they commemorate. For other festival lists see Dt. 16: 1–17; Exod. 23: 14–17; 34: 18, 21 ff. The special offerings appropriate to each festival are enumerated in Num. 28: 9–29: 38. In the NT several of the festivals are shown to have significance in the new order established by our Lord (*v. infra*).

(*a*) **Sabbath (23: 1–3)**
3. 'It is interesting to note that there is a reference to the sabbath in each of the four last books of the Pentateuch. Genesis presents the divine rest; the four remaining books emphasize the sabbatical legislation' (*NBD*, p. 1042). **any work:** the primacy of the sabbath is seen in the way in which the annual festivals tend to incorporate this feature (cf. vv. 7, 21, 25, 28, 31 f., 35 f., 39).

(*b*) **Passover and Unleavened Bread (23: 4–8)**
5. Passover was celebrated **on the fourteenth day** of the month Abib (Exod. 13: 4), later known as Nisan (cf. Est. 3: 7). For details see especially Exod. 12 and Dt. 16: 1–8. **at twilight** (cf. Exod. 12: 6) is lit. 'between the two evenings' and may mean between noon and dark or between sunset and dark, probably the latter (so NEB). Paul tells us in 1 C. 5: 7 that 'Christ, our paschal lamb, has been sacrificed'. **6.** Immediately following Passover came the **Feast of Unleavened Bread** (cf. Exod. 12: 14–20; 23: 15), in commemoration of the Israelites' hasty departure from Egypt (cf. Dt. 16: 3). For **seven days** unleavened cakes were to be the standard fare and the festival was to begin and end with a **sacred assembly** (7 f.). As this festival followed hard on Passover, so, Paul instructed the church at Corinth, should sanctified Christian conduct be their response to Christ's paschal offering on their behalf (1 C. 5: 7 f.).

(*c*) **First Fruits (23: 9–14)**
10 f. As token acknowledgment of God's provision of rain and harvest the Israelites were to participate in a ceremony of presentation of the **first grain** of the **harvest** in the presence of God (cf. Exod. 23: 19; 34: 26). Only after this rite had been performed were they at liberty to make use of the harvest themselves (v. 14). The

occasion of the presentation was **the day after the Sabbath**, which 'normative Judaism' has taken to mean the second day of Unleavened Bread—**Sabbath** referring to the first day of that festival (cf. v. 7). The Sadducees and others understood **Sabbath** in its usual sense of seventh day of the week and, since the Feast of Weeks comes fifty days after First Fruits and is therefore affected by the manner of reckoning employed, the issue was hotly disputed. **13. drink offering:** cf. Num. 15: 5 ff.; 28: 7, 31, etc. Post-biblical references would indicate that the **wine** was poured out at the base of the altar of burnt offering (Sir. 50: 15; Josephus, *Ant.* iii. 9, 4). According to the more usual method of reckoning First Fruits always fell on Nisan 16; this was the day of our Lord's resurrection and the significance of the date was evident to Paul as he wrote about His being raised from the dead as 'the first fruits of those who have fallen asleep' (1 C. 15: 20–23).

(*d*) **Feast of Weeks (23: 15–22)**
The festival is so named because it came **seven full weeks** after First Fruits (v. 15). It was also known as the 'feast of the harvest' (Exod. 23: 16) because it marked the end of the barley harvest (cf. Dt. 16: 9), and as the 'day of first fruits' (Num. 28: 26), since it heralded the beginning of the wheat harvest (cf. Exod. 34: 22). From the Greek for 'fifty (days)' (cf. v. 16) comes the later name 'Pentecost'. By a simple process of assimilation the feast of Pentecost, which occurred in the third month (Siwan), became recognized as the occasion of the giving of the law (cf. Exod. 19: 1). **15. day after the Sabbath:** cf. on vv. 10 f. **16. an offering of new grain** is, strictly, 'a new grain offering'. The Talmudic tradition is that this offering was of wheat, whereas that of First Fruits was of barley (cf. v. 13). **17. yeast** was permitted because the loaves were not burned on the altar (cf. 2: 12). Ordinarily, of course, **yeast** was used in the baking of food; the **two loaves** were food **for the priest** (v. 20). **21.** Pentecost occupied only one day in the festival calendar, but it was to be a day of joyful celebration (cf. Dt. 16: 10 f.). **22.** Cf. on 19: 9 f. While in one sense the verse 'does not fit in with the framework of a calendar of feasts' (Noth), the expression of concern for the deprived can scarcely be regarded as out of place when it is appended to a section on harvest festivals.

(*e*) **Feast of Trumpets and Day of Atonement (23: 23–32)**
These are the first two of the festivals of the seventh month. **24.** The 'Feast of Trumpets' marked the old New Year's Day and was still observed as the beginning of the civil year when the Babylonian spring year was adopted. **trumpet blasts:** The trumpet is still used to herald the Jewish civil New Year. NEB translates the word by 'acclamation', which is an accept-

able rendering in other contexts (*e.g.* 1 Sam. 4: 5 f.) but pays no heed to the ancient custom of trumpet-blowing on this occasion. **27 f.** The ritual of the **Day of Atonement** is outlined in ch. 16. Since this is a lay calendar the cultic details which were of concern to the priesthood are not repeated here. Lev. 25: 9 has the only other occurrence of the actual expression **Day of Atonement**. **deny yourselves:** abstain from food and normally pleasurable activities (cf. 16: 29). **32.** This use of **sabbath** to denote a solemn day of **rest** accords with the traditional understanding of the same term in v. 11 (see on vv. 10 f.). **of the ninth day:** since it was such a grave matter to be found in breach of the rules for the Day of Atonement (vv. 29 ff.) the exact duration of this special sabbath is made absolutely clear.

(*f*) **Feast of Booths (23: 33–44)**
This festival had both agricultural and historical significances. It was known as the 'feast of ingathering' (Exod. 23: 16; 34: 22) because it marked the end of the vintage and the end of all the year's harvests. The construction of booths ('tabernacles') recalled the time of Israelites' living in such flimsy shelters in the wilderness (v. 43; cf. Neh. 8: 14–17). If Day of Atonement was 'the fast' (Ac. 27: 9) the Feast of Booths was 'the feast' (1 Kg. 8: 2; Ezek. 45: 25); an especially great number of sacrifices were offered during the eight days of its observance (see Num. 29: 12–38). In Zech. 14: 16–19 it is seen to have apocalyptic significance. After the dreadful judgments of God upon the nations those who survive will be required to present themselves annually at Jerusalem to 'keep the feast of booths' (v. 16). **36.** There is no reference to an **eighth day** in Dt. 16: 13 ff., from which it is often inferred that this was a later addition to the festival. But Dt. 16 goes into very little detail about the observance of Booths and such a conclusion is too incautious. Jn 7: 37 ('the last day of the feast, the great day') probably alludes to this **eighth day** (cf. also Num. 29: 35; 1 Kg. 8: 66 (?); 2 Chr. 7: 9; Neh. 8: 18). **closing assembly:** Noth explains the word as meaning 'taboo day, special feastday'; NEB, on the other hand, has 'closing ceremony' (cf. Snaith, *NCentB*). The disagreement arises because of the uncertain relationship between the word and its basic root ('*āṣar*, 'restrain, close up'). Verses **37 f.** form an oddly-placed summary, since vv. 39–43 return to the subject of Booths. Perhaps vv. 39–43 were added later. **40.** The carrying of citrus fruits in a procession at Booths is attested for the later period (Josephus, *Ant.* xiii. 13, 5), and it is just possible that (choice) **trees** should be 'evergreens' (NEB goes so far as to say 'citrustrees'); there is Talmudic support for this explanation of the Hebrew. **branches:** cf. Ps. 118: 27. **42 f. booths** were used by workers at

harvest-time (Isa. 1: 8), but it is their association with the wilderness wanderings of the Israelites which is to be commemorated. The Pentateuchal traditions of the wilderness period speak of tents, though see Neh. 8: 14–17.

viii. Tabernacle Matters (24: 1–9)

2 f. Directions for the making of a lampstand for the Tabernacle are given in Exod. 25: 31–40, and the provision of oil for a **light** is mentioned in Exod. 27: 20 f., in terms very similar to those used here. In the present passage it is a regular supply of oil that is being ensured. **continually:** see on Exod. 27: 20. **4. The lamps:** see Exod. 25: 31 f. **the pure gold lampstand** is lit. 'the pure lampstand' as in Exod. 31: 8; 39: 37 (NIV as here in both cases). The use of **pure** in connection with various objects and commodities in Exod. 25–Lev. 27 suggests that here it refers to the material of which the lampstand was made (pure gold, as Exod. 25: 31) rather than to the lampstand's ritual cleanness (*pace* Snaith (NCB) and NEB). Verses 5–9 deal with the bread of the Presence (cf. Exod. 25: 30). Twelve loaves were regularly provided as food for the gods in Babylonian temples. In Israel, however, the twelve loaves of the bread of the Presence spoke of God as the Provider for all twelve tribes. 1 Sam. 21: 1–6 gives some insight into the practice at Nob in the reign of Saul. **5.** Neither the term 'bread of the Presence' nor any of its surrogates (cf. on Exod. 25: 30) is used in this section. On the other hand, this is the only place where the number of **loaves** is stated. **two tenths:** NIV adds, and doubtless correctly, **of an ephah. 6. two rows:** hence 'the bread of *arrangement*' (lit.) in 1 Chr. 9: 32, etc. (same Hebrew root). **the table of pure gold:** lit. 'the pure table'; see on v. 4 and cf. 2 Chr. 13: 11. Instructions for the making of this table are given in Exod. 25: 23–28. **7.** Cf. the cereal offering of 2: 1 ff. Noth takes v. 7a to mean that the bread was arranged in two piles (cf. RVmg). Snaith is divided between row (PCB) and pile (NCentB). The usual sense of the root and the meanings of its derivatives would favour **row**. The size of the cakes was large to judge by the amount of flour used. A token (**memorial portion**) of **pure incense** was to be offered and when the next sabbath came round the loaves were replaced and then eaten by the priests as **a most holy part** (9; cf. on 2: 3).

ix. A case of Blasphemy (24: 10–23)

Laws on blasphemy (vv. 15 f.) and retribution (vv. 17–21) are prefaced by a case of blasphemy on which a ruling was needed. Verse 22 ('one law for the sojourner and for the native') gives the common theme. **10. and an Egyptian father:** cf. Exod. 12: 38. The man was therefore a half-caste; 'generally speaking, blasphemy is committed by pagans' (NBD, p. 144, with various Biblical references). **11.** The man

blasphemed the Name, the sacred name represented by the tetragrammaton and later considered too holy to be pronounced at all. (Traditionally the word *'Adōnāi*, 'my Lord', is read wherever the tetragrammaton appears in the Hebrew text. In the LXX it is represented by *Kyrios*, 'Lord'.) **12.** Moses had no ready rule for dealing with this kind of case (cf. Exod. 18: 15 f.); Exod. 22: 28 forbids the reviling of God but attaches no penalty. The man's status as a half-caste also added to the problem. **16.** Blasphemy eventually included much more than the abuse of the divine **Name,** as is illustrated in Caiaphas' reaction in Mt. 26: 65 (cf. v. 66). This extension of the concept of blasphemy may be discernible already in this verse, for NEB has 'utters' for the two occurrences of **blasphemes,** and with quite good philological backing. It is indeed a different verb from that used in v. 15 and may be compared with Isa. 62: 2 ('and you shall be called by a new name which the mouth of the LORD will give (lit. 'utter')'). Verses 17–21 present the *lex talionis* ('law of retribution') in various of its applications; cf. Exod. 21: 23 ff.; Dt. 19: 21. This concept of retribution was not peculiar to Israel. It figures in the Code of Hammurabi which reflects Babylonian juridical procedure in the early second millennium BC but, as far as the economy of God is concerned, it was abrogated by our Lord (Mt. 5: 38–42). For all its savage aspect it could prevent the exaction of *more* than the equivalent of the damage originally inflicted. The possibility of monetary compensation for crimes except murder may account for the fact that instances of the implementation of this law are hard to find in the OT. **22.** The **alien** might benefit from special provisions on humanitarian grounds (*e.g.* 23: 22) but in the matters just discussed he is the same before the law as the native Israelite.

x. Sabbatical and Jubilee (25: 1–55)

These are extensions of the sabbath principle. Both biblical and post-biblical sources attest the Jews' observance of the sabbatical year at least (see NBD. p. 1043).

(a) The Sabbatical Year (25: 1–7)

2. The fact that the land was to **observe a sabbath to the LORD** shows that the sabbatical year had more in view than the condition of the soil. In a sense the institution of the sabbatical year was an assertion about the true ownership of the land (cf. v. 23, 'the land is mine'). Verse 5 forbids a systematic harvesting of the spontaneous growth of the fallow year. **6.** The **sabbath year** refers to this spontaneous growth; the uncultivated growth arising from the spillage of the previous harvest was to be available for all. Exod. 23: 10 f. mentions only the poor and the wild beasts as the intended beneficiaries of the institution.

(b) **The Jubilee (25: 8–12)**
8. After **seven sabbaths of years** came the sabbatical *par excellence*. **9.** Throughout the country the **trumpet** was to be sounded **on the Day of Atonement** (which came near the beginning of the old New Year; cf. on 23: 24) and the advent of the jubilee announced. This was the year above all when God laid claim to both land (v. 23) and people (v. 42); the land lay fallow (vv. 11 f.), that land which had changed hands was restored to its original owner (v. 13), and slaves could gain their freedom (vv. 39 ff.). 'Isa. 61: 1–3 is steeped in the jubilee phraseology, and Christ adopted this passage to explain His own mission (Lk. 4: 18 ff.)' (A. W. F. Blunt, *HDB* (one vol.), p. 809). **10. liberty:** the Hebrew word is related to an Akkadian term meaning 'release from obligations'. In Babylonia this was in the hands of the king who was expected to 'establish justice', commonly by a series of enactments at the beginning of his reign. **jubilee** derives from the Hebrew *yōbhēl*, 'ram, ram's horn' (though note that a different word is rendered **trumpet** (or 'horn' as in NEB) in v. 9). **11.** So far as the land and its usufruct are concerned the laws of the sabbatical year apply (cf. vv. 4 f.). This meant two fallow years in succession—for **jubilee** followed the sabbatical forty-ninth year —and v. 21 takes account of this situation, in principle at least.
(c) **Consequent Legislation on Property (25: 13–34)**
13. Land reverted to its original owner at **Jubilee**; in the last analysis it was inalienable. **15.** This meant that transactions were regulated according to the proximity of jubilee, for it was really a series of crops which was being bought or sold (v. 16). Such sales usually occurred when a family fell on hard times and the automatic reversion to original ownership set a limit to the duration of the penury and insolvency. Verses 14, 17 are addressed to those who might be tempted to make a fortune out of their fellows' misfortunes. The Lord is the protector of the dispossessed (Dt. 15: 9). **21.** In addition to what might grow of itself there would be sufficient **for three years** from the harvest of the **sixth year. 22.** The references to the **eighth** and **ninth** years support the view that vv. 20 ff. are talking about the sabbatical year, though some favour the jubilee. Against the latter view it can be urged that there would be no sowing in the eighth year since each jubilee was an eighth year following after the seventh sabbatical of the series. The data here can be easily appreciated on the assumption of a spring New Year, since the first sowing after the sabbatical would not be possible until late in the eighth year and harvesting would only begin in the **ninth**. But v. 9 indicates that the jubilee year—and therefore, we presume, the

sabbatical—began in the autumn. Whatever the solution to this problem, vv. 20 ff. are clearly an encouragement to give God His place and entrust the consequences to Him. Though they have nothing to do with conveyancing they prepare the way for the claim in v. 23, 'the land is mine'. **23.** The Israelites did not cease to be **strangers** and sojourners when they left Egypt and the wilderness behind them; now they were God's liferenters. **24.** The land was God's and He had allocated it according to His will and purpose. No temporary change in fortunes should be able to come between a family and its inheritance; there must always be a right of **redemption of the land**. This right existed independently of the law of automatic reversion in the jubilee year. **25. nearest relative** translates *gō'ēl*, 'kinsman redeemer' (cf. NEB 'his next-of kin who has the duty of redemption'). A *gō'ēl* was entitled to buy back property on behalf of an impoverished kinsman at any time (cf. Ru. 4: 1–4; Jer. 32: 6 ff.). **27. the balance:** the rehabilitated individual had to repay the original sum minus the total value of the harvests since the first transaction took place. The price would already have been calculated in accordance with vv. 15 f. Verse 28 establishes the principle of automatic reversion of land to its original owner in the jubilee year—if the property has not been redeemed already by a relative or by the original owner himself. **29. a house in a walled city** could be bought back but the **right of redemption** lasted for one **year** only. City dwellings did not properly belong to the sphere of land regulations. **30.** If unredeemed the house remained the property of the buyer in perpetuity; the advent of the jubilee year did not affect the situation. 'The jubilee reversion laws are evidently agricultural laws, and it was realised that they could not be applied in an urban community' (Snaith, *PCB*). **permanently . . . his descendants:** the Hebrew is strikingly similar to the phrasing of conveyancing documents found at Ugarit (latter part of second millennium). **31.** The same rules applied for **houses** in unwalled **villages** as for landed property. **32. houses** in the Levitical **towns** were in a different class from those of vv. 29 f. **33. So the property of the Levites is redeemable:** The Hebrew is far from clear; cf. RSV, inserting the negative, 'And if one of the Levites does not exercise his right of redemption'. **34.** Cf. Num. 35: 1–8.
(d) **Care for the Impoverished and Enslaved (25: 35–55)**
Verses 35–38 attach themselves to the jubilee laws because they also concern the needs of those fallen on hard times (cf. v. 25). **35.** An Israelite living as **an alien or a temporary resident** would benefit from the special provisions made for all such (cf. 19: 10; 23: 22).

This rather than the loss of civic rights (Snaith, *PCB*) is probably what is intended. **36. interest of any kind:** lit. 'interest and increase', denoting two types of repayment. The latter meant payment on an increasing principal, the former possibly involved the deduction of interest from the sum before it was advanced. Charging interest of fellow-Israelites is forbidden in the OT (cf. Exod. 22: 25; 23: 19), though it is permitted in the case of foreigners (Dt. 23: 20). Dt. 15: 1 f. provides for the remission of debts, or at the very least for their suspension, every seventh year. **38.** The common indebtedness of the nation to God should issue in social concern for the under-privileged (cf. 19: 34, 36; 25: 55). **39.** There was to be no such thing as an Israelite falling into slavery to another Israelite. Economic hardship might mean the selling of one's services to a creditor, but enslavement was strictly forbidden. **40.** Furthermore, the period of service must end at jubilee. Since Exod. 21: 2–6 allows a Hebrew servant his freedom after six years the present rule must have been applied when jubilee came before the completion of the six years. Verse 42 claims for God the service of all those who had been delivered from the Egyptian bondage (cf. v. 38). They were God's slaves (**servants**); cf. Paul's self-designation as a slave of Christ in the NT. **43. but fear your God:** cf. v. 36. **44 ff.** Non-Israelites, from within or without the community, could be acquired as slaves **for life** (v. 46); they were inheritable property and the jubilee regulation did not affect them. **47.** A resident alien prospers and acquires an Israelite as a servant. **48 f.** Redemption by a relative, or by the man himself from wages accruing, is permissible (cf. the law on property in vv. 25 f.). **50 ff.** Cf. vv. 15 f., 27.

xi. Reward and Punishment (26: 1–46)

Although not the closing chapter of the book of Leviticus, ch. 26 is a fitting coda to all the diverse themes of the preceding chapters. It was the wide-spread practice in the Near East to write a series of blessings and curses into a treaty or legal document in order to dissuade the parties from acting in breach of the agreement. And to this end it is invariably the curses which preponderate. This is the case here and in Dt. 28, the best-known Biblical example of the phenomenon. If the people of God walk in His ways they will enjoy the blessings, but if not, the most dire troubles lie in store.

(a) Conditional Blessings (26: 1–13)

1. Nothing idolatrous that human hands can fashion is to defile the **land** of Israel. An **image** could be made of wood, stone or metal. **sacred stone:** Moses erected twelve pillars in commemoration of the revelation at Sinai (Exod. 24: 4), following good patriarchal precedent (Gen. 28: 18). But the pillar came to have idolatrous associations, being sacred to the Canaanite god Baal, and was forbidden to the Israelites in the **land** (cf. Dt. 16: 22). Examples of these cultic pillars have been discovered on various Palestinian sites. **carved** translates a word of uncertain meaning, but it is possible to make a fairly good case for NIV. Porter thinks of a boundary stone on which there would be a representation of a deity. Verses 3–13 expound the blessings which God will bestow in recognition of Israel's faithfulness. **5.** One season of fruitfulness will run into the next; in Amos's celebrated words 'the ploughman shall overtake the reaper and the treader of grapes him who sows the seed' (Am. 9: 13). **13.** In Egypt the Israelites were pressed down by the heavy bar of the **yoke** of servitude. Now that has been removed and they can **walk with heads held high** as free men (cf. Zech. 1: 21).

(b) Punishment for Disobedience (26: 14–39)

The penalties increase in severity, culminating in cannibalism and exile. **16. wasting diseases, and fever:** the Hebrew terms occur only here and in the same context in Dt. 28: 22. **22. wild animals:** settlers in Samaria in the eighth century had to face this problem (2 Kg. 17: 25). **25.** Armies without and **plague** within will combine to prevent God's refractory people from escaping their punishment. **26. supply** lit. 'staff of bread'; cf. Isa. 3: 1; Ezek. 4: 16 f. **one oven** will be sufficient to **bake** what is available for the needs of **ten** households, and rationing will have to be introduced (**by weight**). **29.** Persistence in rebellion in the face of all the previous punishments would bring the people of Israel into such extremities that they would resort to cannibalism (for an example during a siege of Samaria see 2 Kg. 6: 24–31). **30. high places:** the word primarily means 'hill-top', and then a shrine erected on a hill-top. At one time the term had no distasteful connotations, for worship at a high place is associated with the prophet Samuel (1 Sam. 9: 12). **incense altars:** translated 'images' (AV), 'sun-images' (RV). The word occurs in several Palmyrene and Nabataean inscriptions, and denotes a pagan sanctuary; see J. Teixidor, *The Pantheon of Palmyra* (1979), pp. 66 ff. **idols:** NEB 'rotting logs'; the reference may be to the tree or pole sacred to the fertility goddess Asherah. **32. lay waste . . . appalled:** the same Hebrew verb is used to effect in two quite different senses. **34 f.** There will be trouble if the Israelites do not observe the land regulations of 25: 1–7. Such will be the devastation that amends will be made in one prolonged sabbath of fallowness (cf. 2 Chr. 36: 21). **36 ff.** Deportation will not end the horrors; outright extinction is threatened. **39b.** Punishment for the sins of previous generations will also be exacted, in accordance with Exod. 20: 5.

(c) Possibility of Restoration (26: 40–46)
40 f. Confession of guilt, both personal and
inherited, can turn away the divine anger and
bring to God's remembrance the benign intent
behind the patriarchal covenants (v. 42). **41.
uncircumcised hearts:** cf. Jer. 9: 25 f. **43 f.**
Only when judgment is meted out will God
in wrath remember mercy' (Hab. 3: 2). **45.**
Whereas the sore affliction would be 'vengeance for the covenant' (v. 25), it would also
be on the basis of covenant loyalty that God
would deal favourably with His people (cf.
Exod. 23: 22–33).

V. THE COMMUTATION OF VOWS AND TITHES (27: 1–34)
Many vows and dedications promised to the
sanctuary were commutable to monetary payments. The chapter deals with vows of persons
(vv. 1–8), dedications of animals (vv. 9–13),
and dedications of houses and land (vv. 14–
25). Vows could be made for various reasons,
and sometimes most injudiciously. Application
of a law of commutation would have prevented
the tragic sequel to the Jephthah story (Jg.
11: 29–40). Valuation of persons was strictly
according to sex and age (vv. 3–7). Such persons might have been promised to the sanctuary for special service (cf. 1 Sam. 1: 11); they
could be released from obligation by payment
of a sum of money. In the valuation for such
purposes it was the person's capacity for work
at the time of the valuation which was being
calculated. If we accepted the view that the
lower valuation put on women—approximately half of that for men—reflects a lower
estimation of womanhood, we should also be
forced to conclude that old age was not respected. Noth thinks that it is not just a matter
of single payments but of regular payments;
otherwise the highest valuation would have to
be put on children since, in terms of years, they
would have the greatest potential for work. **8.**
In cases of poverty the price of redemption was
fixed by **the priest** according to the means of
the person liable to pay. Verses **9 f.** establish
that a clean animal **that is acceptable as an
offering to the LORD** cannot be withheld
once it has been dedicated. Any attempt at
presenting a substitute for the original would
result in the forfeiture of both. **11.** An unclean
animal may be redeemed provided that **a fifth**
is added to the priest's valuation when payment
is made (13). **14 f.** The same rule applies for a
house as for the unclean animal of vv. 11 ff.
Redemption of land (vv. 16–25) is organized
according as the land is inherited (v. 16) or
bought (v. 22). The effect of the jubilee must
also be taken into account (vv. 17 f.; cf. 25: 15
f.). **16.** The amount of **seed** required to sow a
piece of land indicated the latter's size and
valuation was made accordingly. Verses **20 f.**
envisage a case of dishonesty in which a man
sells what he has already dedicated and therefore has no right to sell. Whether unredeemed
or sold dishonestly, land which is a man's by
inheritance and which he has dedicated to the
Lord cannot be repossessed in the **Jubilee.** As
something **devoted** to the Lord it is not affected by the jubilee legislation. **devoted** comes
from the root whence is derived the Hebrew
for 'ban', the setting aside of something for
God (cf. Jos. 6: 17) and irrevocably so (cf. v.
28). **24. bought** land could only be subject to
dedication and redemption until **the Year of
Jubilee**; then it was restored to the original
owner for whom it was a possession by inheritance. **26. a firstborn** could not be dedicated to
God because it was already His property (cf.
Exod. 13: 2; 34: 19). **27.** An unclean animal
was not usable for sacrifice and had either to
be redeemed or **sold** (cf. Exod. 34: 20). **28 f.**
Nothing devoted to God (cf. on vv. 20 f.) could
be redeemed, much less **sold. 29.** Saul was in
breach of this ruling (1 Sam. 15: 3, 9). **30 f.**
Tithes were redeemable at the usual rate if they
were of field-crop or fruit but tithes of animals
(32 f.) were not redeemable and the same sanction as in v. 10 could be applied in cases of
malfeasance.

BIBLIOGRAPHY

Commentaries
ALLIS, O. T., 'Leviticus', NBC³ (London, 1970).
BONAR, A. A., *A Commentary on Leviticus*⁴ (London,
  1861). References to first Banner of Truth Trust
  edition (London, 1966).
COATES, C. A., *An Outline of the Book of Leviticus*
  (Kingston upon Thames, n.d.).
HARRISON, R. K. *Leviticus TOTC* (Leicester, 1980).
KNIGHT, G. A. F., *Leviticus*. Daily Study Bible (Edin-
  burgh, 1981).
MILGROM, J., 'The Book of Leviticus', *The In-
  terpreter's One-Volume Commentary on the Bible*, ed.
  C. M. Laymon (London and Glasgow, 1972).
NOTH, M., *Leviticus*, E.T., *OTL* (London, rev. edn
  1977).
PORTER, J. R., *Leviticus*, CBC (Cambridge, 1976).
SNAITH, N. H., 'Leviticus', *Peake's Commentary on
  the Bible*, rev. (London, 1962).
SNAITH, N. H., *Leviticus and Numbers*, NCentB (Lon-
  don, 1967).
WENHAM, G. J., *The Book of Leviticus*, NICOT
  (Grand Rapids, 1980).

Special Studies
DOUGLAS, M., *Purity and Danger* (London, 1966).
DOUGLAS, M., *Implicit Meanings* (London, 1975).
DRIVER, G. R., 'Three Technical Terms in the Penta-
  teuch', *JSS* 1, 1956, pp.97–105.
FAIRBAIRN, P., *The Typology of Scripture*⁴ (2 vols.)
  (Edinburgh, 1864).

HULSE, E. V., 'The Nature of Biblical "Leprosy" and the Use of Alternative Medical Terms in Modern Translations of the Bible', *Palest. Explor. Quart.*, 107, 1975, pp. 87–105.

JUKES, A., *The Law of the Offerings* (London, n.d.).

KITCHEN, K. A., *The Old Testament in its Context* (London, n.d.). Reprint of articles in TSF Bulletin nos. 59–64.

LEVINE, B. A., *In the Presence of the Lord* (Leiden, 1974).

MILGROM, J., *Studies in Levitical Terminology I* (Berkeley, 1970).

MILGROM, J., *Cult and Conscience* (Leiden, 1976).

NEWBERRY, T., *Types of the Levitical Offerings*[3] (Kilmarnock, n.d.).

POLLOCK, A. J., *The Tabernacle's Typical Teaching* (London, n.d.).

ROWLEY, H. H., *Worship in Ancient Israel* (London, 1967).

SOLTAU, H. W., *The Tabernacle, the Priesthood and the Offerings* (London, n.d.).

THOMPSON, R. J., *Penitence and Sacrifice in Early Israel* (Leiden, 1963).

THOMPSON, R. J., *art.* 'Sacrifice and Offering', *NBD*, pp. 1045–1053.

YARDEN, L., 'Aaron, Bethel and the Priestly Menorah', *JJS* XXVI, 1975, pp. 39–47.

NUMBERS

T. CARSON

Title

The title 'Numbers' comes from the LXX and the book is so called because of the censuses recorded in chs. 1 and 26. The Jews call it *In the wilderness (bemidbar)* after the fifth word in Heb. This is the most suitable name as the book deals mainly with the wanderings of Israel in the wilderness.

Authorship

Space forbids an adequate discussion: the reader is referred to the OT Introductions by R. K. Harrison and E. J. Young and the articles in *NBD* and *ISBE*. We note however the following:

1. The authorship of Numbers is closely linked with the general authorship of the Pentateuch.

2. The Mosaic authorship of Numbers is accepted—not, however, in the sense that Moses necessarily wrote every word as we have it today. 'The position for which conservatives contend has been well expressed by R. D. Wilson, "That the Pentateuch as it stands is historical and from the time of Moses; and that Moses was its real author, though it may have been revised and edited by later redactors, the additions being just as much inspired and as true as the rest"' (E. J. Young, *Introduction to the Old Testament*, 1949, p. 51).

3. The essential Mosaic authorship is a natural inference from the book itself. About fifty times we read that the Lord spoke to Moses (*e.g.* 1: 1; 2: 1; 4: 1; 5: 1, etc.) and in ch. 33: 2 we are told that Moses wrote the record of Israel's journeys. Young (*ibid.*, p. 95) points out that the narrative contains names not found in the Pentateuchal narrative and 'since the presence of these names is an indication of genuineness— for why should anyone add them?—we may assume that we are dealing with a record which is indeed Mosaic, as it purports to be (v. 2). But if this record is Mosaic, then we have a strong argument for the Mosaic authorship of the other Pentateuchal narratives of the journeys'. The story of Balaam (chs. 22–24) is of course a section apart. Cf. 22: 4, note.

4. *NBD* (article 'Numbers' by N. H. Ridderbos), while assuming that the contents of Numbers go back to the time of Moses and noting that 'there are no *post-Mosaica* pointing unmistakably to a time much later than that of Moses,' adds: 'Various data point to a later time than that of Moses, or at least to another author than Moses; cf. 12: 3; 15: 22 f. (Moses in the third person); 15: 32; 21: 4 (perhaps the "book of the wars of the Lord" originates from post-Mosaic time), 32: 34 ff.'

In principle that statement is unobjectionable but not all scholars regard these passages as post-Mosaic. With regard to the use of Moses' name in the third person Latin students will remember that Caesar's name is used regularly in his *Commentaries* in the same way, and a modern missionary, C. R. Marsh, has written two books about his experiences in Algeria in the third person, calling himself Abd al Masih ('the servant of Christ'), for he felt that 'so much of it is of heartaches and tears, resolution and courage. To speak of such things among a few intimate friends is one thing,—to write of them for a wider circle is another' (*Too Hard for God*, 1970, introduction). On 15: 22 R. K. Harrison wrote: 'The objections raised in critical circles to the supposed non-Mosaic nature of Num. 15: 22 are much less assured, however, since the purpose of the reference was to stress the revealed origin of the sacrificial offering and its mediation to Israel through Moses. In such a case the allusion to Moses in terms of the third person would be entirely proper, although nonetheless emphatic' (*Introduction to the Old Testament*, 1970, p. 616).

5. The article by T. Whitelaw in *ISBE* and, more fully, in the *Pulpit Commentary*, is an excellent treatment from the conservative point of view. He emphasizes the author's acquaintance with Egyptian manners and customs and refers to legislation which obviously presupposes the wilderness (*e.g.* 19: 3, 7, 9, 14), to the antiquarian statement about Hebron in 13: 22 and to the lack of romancing concerning the years of wandering.

6. J. P. Lange's *Commentary* gives an impressive list of OT passages, commencing with Joshua, which reflect the matters recorded in Numbers, with the comment that a considerable part of the substance of Numbers can be recovered from these references.

The Number of the Israelites

One of the major historical problems of Numbers concerns the censuses of chs. 1 and 26. In ch. 1 the warriors from twenty years old and upward number 603,550 and in ch. 26 it is 601,730. On this basis the total population would be between two and three million. The same number (approximately) is given in ch.

11: 21 and Exod. 12: 37, and if the silver of Exod. 38: 25 is reduced to half shekels (cf. Exod. 30: 12) the number is exactly 603,550 (a silver talent being 3,000 shekels).

The credibility of these numbers has been called in question: in particular, J. W. Colenso subjected them to mathematical scrutiny in *The Pentateuch and Book of Joshua critically examined* (2nd edn., London, 1862). Stress has been placed on such matters as the rapid multiplication of the people, the crossing of the Red Sea in one night, the support in the wilderness and the difficulty of accommodating the people before Mt. Sinai or within the land of Canaan. These objections are discussed by T. Whitelaw in *ISBE*, pp. 2166–2167, and also in the *Pulpit Commentary* (v–xii), and by James Orr in *The Problem of the Old Testament* (1906), pp. 362 ff.

NBD (article 'Number' by R. A. H. Gunner) gives an outline of the problem and of some of the answers suggested, the most important being that 'a thousand' (*'eleph*) originally meant a tent group and has been misunderstood in the census lists, but recognizes that none are completely convincing. Reference should also be made to *NBD* (article 'Wilderness of Wandering' by K. A. Kitchen).

It is of course impossible to discuss the matter fully in a brief introduction (for the problem of the number of the firstborn see note at 3: 40–43) but we would point out that the census lists contain not only thousands but hundreds and in 1: 25 fifty and in 26: 7 thirty, that the numbers are totalled in both chapters, and that the numbers of ch. 1 are repeated in ch. 2, with sub-totals for each of the four camps, plus the grand total, and if these four chapters give a completely false picture of the numbers in the tribes, it does seem to deal a blow to the general credibility of the Pentateuchal data as they have been transmitted. For a critique of W. F. Albright's view (*From the Stone Age to Christianity*, 1940, p. 192) that the two censuses represent variant accounts of a census taken in the time of the United Monarchy see O. T. Allis, *The Five Books of Moses* (1943), p. 241. In the article 'Wilderness of Wandering' in *NBD*, K. A. Kitchen wrote: 'The apparently high figures are beyond absolute disproof, while no alternative interpretation has yet adequately accounted for all the data involved' (p. 1330). Cf. Exod. 1: 7–9; Dt. 1: 10.

The Desert
It has been thought impossible that such a large company of people should have been supported in the desert for forty years. But Whitelaw (*op. cit.*) argues that it should not be assumed that the region was as barren then as now. No evidence from the Bible or archaeology can be cited for this. See also *NBD* article 'Wilderness of Wandering' by K. A. Kitchen.

Special Features
1. The contents of Numbers are very varied. There is a mingling of laws, ritual, history, poetry and prophecy and the arrangement appears to be partly chronological and partly topical, subjects being introduced as suggested by the particular situation (cf. ch. 19).
2. There are several sections of priestly legislation. A comparison with Exodus, Leviticus and Deuteronomy will indicate a number of differences from the laws prescribed in Numbers. These will be commented on briefly in the notes (*e.g.* at 18: 18, 21).

Spiritual Teaching
1. *The Main Message*
Numbers emphasizes the holiness and faithfulness of the covenant-keeping God. Everyone with an infectious skin disease or a discharge, everyone unclean through contact with the dead, is to be put out of the camp, for the holy God dwells in the midst of it (cf. 5: 2, 3). Of that holiness the Nazirite is a living picture (cf. ch. 6). And so Numbers records God's judgment on the people because of their sin, for the holy God 'is a devouring fire' (Dt. 4: 24; cf. 11: 1–3, 33–35; 12: 10; 14: 34; 16: 31–35). Even Moses and Aaron were excluded from the land because they failed to vindicate God's holiness (cf. 20: 12, 24). But God did not reject the people. Although the unbelieving generation is to perish in the desert, He will bring their little ones into the land (cf. 14: 28–31). He abounds in steadfast love (cf. 14: 18) and He refuses to allow Balaam to curse them (chs. 22–24). And even those excluded from the land are not forsaken: His grace is still with them. Cf. the note at the beginning of ch. 33.
2. *Other Lessons*
Numbers is rich in types or illustrations of spiritual truth (see the article, 'The Interpretation of the Old Testament', p. 67). In fact the whole of the book may be regarded as typical. There is a nation of soldiers, a tribe of workers and a family of worshippers. In the light of the NT analogy between the desert wanderings and present Christian experience (cf. 1 C. 10: 1; also Heb. 3: 7 ff.), the camp arranged in perfect order around the tabernacle has been viewed as a picture of the church with Christ in the midst.
[NOTE. The high numbers of the Israelites in the desert, according to the census figures in Numbers and elsewhere in the Pentateuch, present a problem to which there is no agreed solution. The problem becomes specially acute at certain points in the narrative, such as Exod. 12: 37 and 14: 19–29, where we have to reckon with a body of people which could be got across the Sea of Reeds in one night—not merely armed men in military formation but women and children, with cattle as well. What the size of such a body might be can be esti-

mated by any one who has had experience in marshalling and moving large numbers of human beings. G. E. Mendenhall ('The Census Lists of Numbers 1 and 26', *JBL* 77, 1958, pp. 52–66) provides more solid evidence than was available to Flinders Petrie (*Egypt and Israel*, 1911, pp. 40–46) for holding that the noun *'eleph* ('thousand') meant, over and above its numerical value, (i) a subsection of a tribe and (ii) the contingent of fighting men which that subsection contributed to the army. Such a reinterpretation of *'eleph* in the Pentateuchal figures is less improbable than W. F. Albright's view (*From the Stone Age to Christianity*, 1946, pp. 192 f.) that David's census lists (2 Sam. 24: 9; 1 Chr. 21: 5) have been carried back to the time of the Exodus and the wilderness wanderings. In the Pentateuchal text as it stands the numerical value ('thousand') for *'eleph* is indicated by the correlation of the sum of half-shekels contributed to the tabernacle by the men of military age with the whole number of such men (Exod. 30: 11–16; 38: 25 f.). FFB]

ANALYSIS

I. THE PREPARATION FOR DEPARTURE FROM SINAI (1: 1–4: 49)

i. The First Census (1: 1–46)

A Census to be Taken (1: 1–16)

A census has already been mentioned in Exod. 30: 11–16 and, as the total is the same and as the present census was apparently conducted in one day (cf. vv. 1 and 18), it has been inferred that the earlier mention is an anticipation of this. Another census, taken thirty-eight years later, is recorded in ch. 26. The object of the first census was to organize the army in view of their imminent departure (cf. 10: 11); the census taken by David was also a military one.

1. The LORD spoke to Moses: these words are found some fifty-two times in Numbers. **in the Desert of Sinai:** cf. Exod. 19: 1; Lev. 7: 38. The location of Sinai is uncertain (see *NBD, s.v.* 'Sinai'). **in the Tent of Meeting:** cf. Exod. 25: 22; Lev. 1: 1. **on the first day:** the tabernacle had been erected a month (cf. Exod. 40: 17). Cf. 7: 1; 9: 1. They had been at Sinai about ten months (cf. Exod. 19: 1). After the legislative details of Leviticus the thread of the narrative is taken up again in Numbers. **2. by their clans and families** ('in the father's line,' NEB).

3. twenty years old and more: there is no specified age of retirement as with the Levites (cf. 8: 25), whose service must be marked by full competence; the census, however, is limited to those **who are able to serve in the army by their divisions:** it is the word used in 2: 4, 6, 8 of the companies around the four standards. **4–16.** From each tribe a man is chosen to assist Moses. These men are men-

tioned again in 2: 3 ff.; 7: 12 ff. and 10: 14 ff. For Nahshon and Amminadab cf. Exod. 6: 23; Ru. 4: 20; Mt. 1: 4; Lk. 3: 32, 33 and for Elishama cf. 1 Chr. 7: 26. Cf. also 1 Chr. 27: 16–22. Leah's sons are placed first, then the sons of Rachel and after that the sons of the concubines. Many of the names contain the name of God, *e.g.* Elizur, meaning 'God is a rock' and Shedeur, 'Shaddai is light'. **16. clans:** literally 'thousands'. Cf. Exod. 18: 21, 25 but the word does not appear to have here an exact numerical significance, being used sometimes of a military unit (cf. 31: 4, 5) and sometimes of a tribal unit (cf. Jg. 6: 15).

The Registration (1: 17–19)

Genealogies were important for Israel for the apportioning of the land, for the appointment of priests and Levites and later of kings and finally for the recognition of the Messiah (cf. Jos. 14–20; Neh. 7: 64; Mt. 1).

The Number of Each Tribe (1: 20–46)

	In the Wilderness of Sinai (ch. 1)	In the Plains of Moab (ch. 26)
Reuben	46,500	43,730
Simeon	59,300	22,200
Gad	45,650	40,500
Judah	74,600	76,500
Issachar	54,400	64,300
Zebulun	57,400	60,500
Ephraim	40,500	32,500
Manasseh	32,200	52,700
Benjamin	35,400	45,600
Dan	62,700	64,400
Asher	41,500	53,400
Naphtali	53,400	45,400
Total	603,550	601,730

20, etc. descendants: 'genealogical registrations' (NASB). For a general discussion of the numbers see Introduction. In the second census some tribes gained, some lost and there was a total loss of almost two thousand. Judah has the greatest number (cf. Gen. 48: 19, 20). Benjamin is the smallest except for Manasseh; the fall in Simeon's numbers is explained by 25: 6–18. It has also been suggested that the numbers for Ephraim and Manasseh have been accidentally transposed in ch. 26. In vv. 5–15 Gad is the eleventh place, but here in the third, doubtless because Reuben, Simeon and Gad formed one camp (2: 10–16). In 11: 21 and Exod. 12: 37 the total is 600,000, doubtless an approximation.

ii. The Levites (1: 47–54)
The Levites are not to be counted until later (chs. 3, 4). They are to be in charge of the tabernacle: to carry it, to tend it, to encamp around it, to take it down and set it up (50–51): **50. They are to take care of it. 51. Anyone else:** no one not of the tribe of Levi is allowed to approach to perform the duties just mentioned (cf. Lev. 22: 10). **52. his own camp . . . his own standard:** see ch. 2. **53. wrath:** i.e. divine judgment, such as followed the sin of Korah in ch. 16. **be responsible for the care of:** seems to refer to the furniture and equipment (cf. 8: 26). **53. the tabernacle of the Testimony:** so called because it contained the two tables of the testimony on which the ten commandments were written (cf. Exod. 25: 21; 31: 18).

iii. The Fourfold Camp (2: 1–34)
(a) The Standards (2: 1–2)
The people were to encamp, each by his own standard, 'under the banner of his patriarchal House' (JB). From vv. 3, 10, 18, 24, it appears that the other tribes took the standard of the leading tribe in their division. The ensigns were the smaller flags or banners which were carried at the head of the different tribes and subdivisions of the tribes (the fathers' houses).

The OT gives us no intimation as to the form or character of the standard (*degel*), while

rabbinic tradition, linking them with the four faces of the cherubim, is valueless.

R. K. Harrison has noted that the arrangement of the tribes in ch. 2 was long regarded by liberal critics as indicating the late date of the priestly material in the Pentateuch, but it is now known that Rameses II, the contemporary of Moses, used the same arrangement in his Syrian campaign (*Introduction to the Old Testament*, pp. 622–623).

(b) The East Camp of Judah (2: 3–9)
This consisted of Judah, Issachar and Zebulun. These were the first on the march. The leaders of the tribes are the same as in 1: 5–15.

(c) The South Camp of Reuben (2: 10–16)
This consisted of the tribes of Reuben, Simeon and Gad. These were second on the march. **Deuel** (cf. 1: 14; 7: 42, 47; 10: 20); an easy confusion between *d* and *r* in Hebrew explains why most MSS read Reuel here (cf. NIVmg and RSV text).

(d) The Levites in the Midst (2: 17)
See note on 10: 17.

(e) The West Camp of Ephraim (2: 18–24)
This consisted of the tribes of Ephraim, Manasseh and Benjamin. These were third on the march.

(f) The North Camp of Dan (2: 25–31)
This consisted of the tribes of Dan, Asher and Naphtali. These were last on the march.

The order of the tribes is the same as in 1: 21–43, except that Judah, Issachar and Zebulun take the lead instead of Reuben, Simeon and Gad.

(g) Summary (2: 32–34)
The total number, the special position of the Levites, encampment by the standards. Scripture does not make clear the exact position of the leading tribe in relation to the other two but the diagram below makes clear the general arrangement.

iv. The Family of Aaron (3: 1–4)
As the elder brother (cf. Exod. 6: 20; Num. 33: 39; Dt. 34: 7), Aaron was naturally chosen as the head of the priestly family, though Moses' activity at the covenant ceremony (Exod. 24:

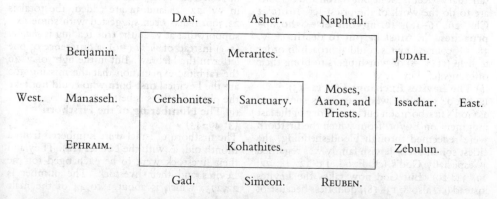

4–8) and at the consecration of Aaron and his sons (Lev. 8) shows that he was *de facto* the first high priest in Israel; cf. Lev. 10: 16–19. Aaron takes precedence over Moses. **the family of Aaron and Moses:** the chapter does not give simply the descendants of Aaron and Moses, as we would expect, but first of all the sons of Aaron (cf. Exod. 6: 23) and then the sons of Levi. Moses and Aaron became heads of the tribe of Levi **at the time the LORD talked with Moses on Mount Sinai. 3. ordained:** RV 'consecrated'; cf. Exod. 29: 1–37; Lev. 8: 1–36. The Heb. means to fill the hand, though with what is not specified; the term gradually lost its original force, and in Ezek. 43: 26 it is used even of the altar of burnt offering. It is probable that NEB 'installed' is a better rendering. **4. Nadab . . . Abihu:** see Lev. 10: 1–2. **they had no sons,** who might have succeeded to their priesthood. The words also explain why Eleazar and Ithamar were the only other priests **during the lifetime of . . . Aaron.** RV gives 'in the presence of', as if they were under their father's guidance. JB gives 'under'.

v. The Levites (continued) (3: 5–51)
(a) **The Levites given to Aaron (3: 5–10)**
5. Bring the tribe of Levi: cf. Exod. 28: 1. The term is a sacrificial one, denoting the presentation of an offering to God (cf. Lev. 3: 3, 7, 9, etc.) and the thought here may be that the Levites are first of all offered to the Lord (cf. 8: 13–16; 16: 9). Their duties are not here defined (7, 8) except that they were to have charge of all the furnishings of the Tent of Meeting (cf. vv. 25 ff. and 1: 47–51). They doubtless assisted with the sacrifices. See also 1 Chr. 23: 26–32 and 2 Chr. 29: 34. **9. they are . . . to be given wholly to him:** in the Hebrew 'given' is repeated. 'The repetition of *nethunim* here and in ch. 8: 16 is emphatic and expressive of complete surrender . . . The Levites however, as *nethunim*, must be distinguished from the *nethinim* (Ezr. 2: 58) of non-Israelitish descent, who were given to the Levites at a later period as temple slaves, to perform the lowest duties connected with the sanctuary' (Keil). None but Aaron and his sons are to do the work of the priest (cf. 16: 10; 2 Chr. 26: 16–18). **10. anyone else who approaches . . . must be put to death:** cf. v. 38. Of course Levites could approach in order to help (cf. v. 8) or worshippers to bring their offerings (cf. Lev. 1: 3).
(b) **The Levites Exchanged (3: 11–13)**
In Exod. 4: 22 the whole nation is spoken of as God's firstborn son but in memory of the last judgment on Egypt, from which the firstborn were redeemed through blood-shedding, the eldest son in every Jewish family was regarded as especially God's (cf. Exod. 13: 12, 15; 22: 29; 34: 20). But God now takes the Levites instead (cf. also 8: 13–18), doubtless because of

their relative faithfulness at the time of the golden calf (cf. Exod. 32: 27–29). Cf. vv. 41, 45; Dt. 33: 8–10; Mal. 2: 5. It was also fitting that the tribe that attended to the sanctuary should have this honour and that it should be the tribe of Moses and Aaron. **13. I am the LORD:** cf. 10: 10, used to stress the importance of a command.
(c) **The Levites to be Numbered (3: 14–20)**
The sons of Levi are to be numbered from a month old and upward (15), not from twenty years old as with the soldiers (1: 3), cf. vv. 40, 43 and 18: 16. The Levites commenced their work at the age of 30 (4: 3) or even 25 (8: 24) but God had them in view from the beginning.
(d) **The Number and Responsibilities of the Levites (3: 21–37)**
21–26. The Gershonites. These numbered 7,500 (22). They were to encamp on the west of the tabernacle (23). They were in charge of the curtains and coverings but not the framework (36). For details see at 4: 25–26.
27–32. The Kohathites. These numbered 8,600 (but see note at v. 39) and were to encamp on the south of the tabernacle. They were responsible for the furnishings and the curtain or veil. For details see at 4: 5–15. As the priests also belonged to the Kohathites, it is added that Eleazar was to have authority over the three families of Levi (32).
33–37. The Merarites. These numbered 6,200 and were to encamp on the north side of the tabernacle and they were to be in charge of the framework. For details see at 4: 31–32.
(e) **Moses and Aaron (3: 38)**
Moses and Aaron and his sons encamped on the east, i.e. at the front (cf. Exod. 27: 13). They were in charge of the ceremonial rites on behalf of the people. The 'sanctuary' here seems to include the outer court (cf. Lev. 12: 4). If any one else came near to perform such priestly service he would be put to death (cf. v. 10; 1: 51).
(f) **The Number of the Levites (3: 39)**
The total number of the Levites is given as 22,000, which is the correct number, as may be seen from vv. 43 and 46, but, if the numbers in vv. 22, 28 and 34 are added, the total is 22,300. It has been suggested with some LXX support that at v. 28 the true reading is *shālōsh* (=3) instead of *shēsh* (=6), a difference of one letter in the Hebrew. But in the light of v. 46 the rabbinic explanation that the missing 300 are the Levitical first-born who could not take the place of others is better.
(g) **The Numbering of the Firstborn (3: 40–43)**
The firstborn of Israel were numbered from a month old, as with the Levites (14). They and their livestock were to be exchanged for the Levites and their livestock. The number is 22,273, which is about 1 to 44 of the male

population instead of about 1 to 4, which might have been expected. One suggested explanation is that the command of Exod. 13: 2 was not retrospective but referred to those who were to be born from that time forward. Though this goes back to rabbinic exposition, it may be doubted whether it has any Scriptural support. The command in Exod. 13: 2 is linked with the first-born of Egypt (Exod. 13: 14, 15).

(h) **The Additional Firstborn (3: 44–51)**
There were 273 more firstborn than male Levites (46). Because they were not represented by Levites, they had to be redeemed with five shekels apiece (cf. Lev. 27: 6), **according to the sanctuary shekel** (47) or 'sacred shekel' (NEB). Cf. Exod. 30: 13. The former rendering 'probably presupposes that the standard weight was kept in the temple in accordance with a well-attested ancient custom' (*HDB*, vol. 3, p. 422). We are not told how the 273 were chosen, perhaps by lot. In Exod. 30: 11–16 all numbered in the census are redeemed with half a shekel but here only the firstborn are in view. In 18: 15, 16 there is a general command to redeem the firstborn but it was not necessary to redeem those who were replaced by Levites.

vi. Census and Service of the Levitical Families (4: 1–49)

(a) **The Kohathites (4: 1–20).** Cf. also 3: 27–32. In ch. 3 all the Levites were numbered from a month old (15) but here they are numbered from thirty years old to fifty in view of their service in the tabernacle (3). From 3: 17 it appears that Kohath was the second son of Levi but here the Kohathites come first, doubtless because they were in charge of the ark and the holy furnishings (5–15) and also because they were of the same tribal group as Moses and Aaron. **3. thirty:** thought to have been the age of full maturity (cf. Lk. 3: 23). In 8: 24 the age is given as 25, which was later reduced by David to 20 (cf. 1 Chr. 23: 24–32). The traditional explanation is that there was first of all a period of apprenticeship. In his comment on Jn 8: 57 Westcott referred to this verse and remarked that 'this age (i.e. 30) was the crisis of completed manhood'. See also note at 1: 3. **to serve** (cf. vv. 23, 30, 35, 39, 43) is really to serve in the army, as in 1: 3, for all divine service is warfare. **4. the most holy things:** here the furniture of the tabernacle. **5–7.** Cf. 3: 31. When the camp was to **move, Aaron and his sons** were to **take down the shielding curtain** which separated the holy place and the most holy (cf. Exod. 26: 36, 37), **cover up the ark** (cf. Exod. 25: 10–22) with the curtain, then cover that with water-proof **hides of sea cows** ('sealskin', RV; 'porpoise hide', NEB), spread over it a **cloth of solid blue**, 'a violet cloth all of one piece', NEB) and **put its poles in.** According to Exod. 25: 15 the poles were not to be removed, so it is thought that they were

removed on this occasion simply that the ark might be covered. The New Berkeley Version gives 'adjust'. Cf. 2 Chr. 5: 9. Normally the sons of Aaron were not allowed to go into the most holy place (cf. Heb. 9: 7) but here it was allowed because the cloud had departed (9: 17). For the coverings and colours see Note 2 at the end of the section. **7. the table of the Presence** was to be covered with **a blue cloth**. Upon it they were to place various ritual accessories and the bread and upon them **a scarlet cloth** and then a covering of **hides of sea cows** (7, 8). For the table see Exod. 25: 23–30; Lev. 24: 5–9. The **lampstand** and its accessories were to be covered with **a blue cloth** and then with **a covering of hides of sea cows**. It was then to be put **on a carrying frame** ('slung from a pole', NEB) (9, 10). Similar cloths were to be placed on the **gold altar** (11; cf. Exod. 30: 1–10) and the **articles used for ministering** (12). These may be any parts of the equipment not specified in vv. 7, 9, 14. They may have been articles connected with the altar of incense. A **purple cloth** was to be placed over the **bronze altar** of burnt offering, after the removal of the ashes. The **utensils** of **the altar** were to be placed upon it and then covered with **hides of sea cows** (13, 14; cf. Exod. 27: 3). The **Kohathites** had to carry all these by means of the poles but they were not allowed to **touch** them (15). Cf. 18: 3 and 2 Sam. 6: 3–7. From 7: 9 we learn that they were given no carts. For the bronze basin for washing see Note 1 at the end of the section.

Eleazar was to exercise a general oversight of the tabernacle and in particular to be in charge of the objects mentioned (16; cf. 3: 32). As the elder brother his service was more important than that of Ithamar (28, 33). **18–20.** The very life of the tribe (= 'branch') of the families of the Kohathites depends on the observance of the above commands. Aaron and his sons are to go into the sanctuary (5) but 'the Kohathites themselves shall not enter to cast even a passing glance on the sanctuary, on pain of death' (NEB). The language is stronger than in v. 15.

Note 1
In view of the words of v. 15, **all the holy articles**, it is astonishing that no mention is made of the bronze basin. The LXX and Samaritan Pentateuch add a verse, which editors regard as an interpolation, according to which the basin was to be put in a blue cover of skin and covered with a purple cloth. Most explanations for the omission of the basin are not satisfactory. Note the non-mention of the bronze altar in 1 Kg. 7 in contrast to 2 Chr. 4: 1. In both cases scribal accident may be the reason.

Note 2
The furnishings were covered with a cloth of

blue and then with goatskin, except the ark, the table of the Presence and the bronze altar. The ark had three coverings, also the table; the rest had two.

Some expositors attach precise meanings to the different colours but the ancients did not distinguish colours as sharply as we do. In Mt. 27: 28, for example, Jesus is arrayed in a scarlet robe; in Jn 19: 2 it is a purple one. Blue, purple and scarlet are used in Scripture as colours belonging to princes, nobles and palaces and it is doubtful if we are to see in their use in the tabernacle any symbolical significances beyond the exhibition of the manifold glory of God. It was fitting that distinctiveness should be given to the ark, the throne of God, with a covering of blue, to the table of His presence with the scarlet and to the altar of sacrifice with the purple.

(b) **The Gershonites (4: 21–28).** See also 3: 21–26. They were to carry all the curtains and coverings of the tabernacle as well as the curtains of the courtyard, and the **ropes** of the tabernacle (cf. Exod. 35: 18), though not the curtains of the courtyard posts (v. 32). In 7: 7 they are given carts. They are to be under the general **direction of Ithamar** (28). Cf. also v. 16. Ithamar had been a supervisor in the constructions of the tabernacle (cf. Exod. 38: 21).

(c) **The Merarites (4: 29–33).** See also 3: 33–37. The Merarites were to carry the woodwork of the tabernacle and the courtyard posts, **pegs** and **ropes** (cf. Exod. 27: 17; 35: 18), together with **all their equipment and everything related to their use**, *e.g.* rings, clasps (cf. Exod. 26: 29, 32). Cf. 3: 36, where the order is different. In the case of the Merarites, the various objects had to be assigned to particular people (32). In 7: 8 they too are given carts.

(d) **The Number of the Levites (4: 34–49)** The Kohathites numbered 2,750 (34–37), the Gershonites 2,630 (38–41), the Merarites 3,200 (42–45). It has been pointed out that the numbers correspond well with the total numbers in these families, though it is surprising that the Merarites have the smallest number in ch. 3 and the largest here. The total is 8,580 (46–49).

II. PRIESTLY LEGISLATION (A) (5: 1–6: 27)
i. The Cleansing of the Camp (5: 1–4)
2. Everyone with **an infectious skin disease** (cf. 12: 15 and Lev. 13: 14; older EVV render 'leper', but see commentary on Lev. 13,) **discharge** (cf. Lev. 15) and everyone defiled by **a dead body** (19: 11–22) is to be sent **outside the camp**. We would not be warranted in applying the words to the milder defilements mentioned, *e.g.*, in Lev. 15: 1–12. Leviticus only the excludes those with an infectious skin disease but, with the organiz-

ation of the camp, greater strictness is introduced. **dead body:** Heb. *nephesh*, 'soul', used for the whole man in Gen. 2: 7; that he is dead is indicated by his conferring of defilement. The reference is not to the body of an animal, as in Lev. 11: 24, 25, but to a human body, as in Lev. 21: 1–4; 10–12. **3. where I dwell among them:** it was God's presence in the midst that demanded holiness (cf. 1 C. 5).

ii. Restitution and the Priest's Portion (5: 5–10)
This passage is supplementary to the law of the guilt offering in Lev. 6: 1–7 (*q.v.*). Here it is added that if the injured person is dead, the restitution is to be made to his kinsman, or, if there is no kinsman, to the Lord in the person of the priest. The reference in vv. 9, 10 is not to sacrifices intended for the altar, which belonged to the priest only in part, but to 'dedicatory offerings, firstfruits and such like' (Keil).

iii. The Law of Jealousy (5: 11–31)
This section describes the trial of a woman suspected of adultery when there is no direct evidence against her, though her behaviour may have justified suspicion. According to R. K. Harrison, *Introduction to the Old Testament*, p. 624, it 'is distinctly reminiscent of the forms of treatment prescribed by the Babylonian priest-physicians of the second millennium BC', and there are similar rituals from elsewhere.

We might be surprised to find such a ritual here but we must remember that many ordinances of the Mosaic Law have parallels in heathenism, *e.g.* blood vengeance, sacrifice, slavery. In some of these instances God took the people where they were, freeing their customs from all superstitious and idolatrous associations and making them a vehicle of divine truth. In the case before us the terrifying nature of the trial would generally be sufficient to deter any but the innocent. The water itself had no power to produce the effects mentioned, which were the result of a divine judgment (21).

It has been pointed out that, unlike the trials of the Middle Ages, *e.g.* by fire and water, and heathen trials, this trial was not in itself injurious. A. R. Short in *A Modern Experiment in Apostolic Missions* (1920), p. 69, writing of early days in Africa, says: 'when anyone became ill or died, the fetish doctor would be called in, and he would indicate, by divining, the guilty party. The accused would be compelled to thrust his hands into a pot of boiling water: if the skin came off, he was condemned to a cruel death; if it did not, he was adjudged innocent'.

There is no record in Scripture of the trial being held. There were considerable developments in later post-exilic times. 'According to

the *Mishnah*, which devotes to this subject a special tractate (*Soṭah*), a wife could not be brought to this solemn trial unless her husband had previously warned her, in the presence of two witnesses, against intercourse with one whom he suspected, and also two witnesses had reported that she had contravened his injunctions . . . it is stated that, with the decline of morals in Palestine, the trial by the "water of jealousy" gradually ceased (in accordance with what we read in Hos. 4: 14), till it was finally abolished by Rabbi Jochanan, the son of Zacchai, some time after the death of our Lord' (A. Edersheim, *The Temple and its Services*, 1874, pp. 319–321). Cf. v. 13. If the ceremony seems to be partial towards the man, it must be remembered that the Mosaic law, because of the hardness of men's hearts, did favour the man:he was allowed more than one wife and could divorce his wife. Besides, the purity of the family was held to depend on the woman more than on the man and the law was a protection of an innocent wife. It also protected her from baseless and virtually insane jealousy.
12, 13. The case supposed is one where there is no witness. If the sin could be proved, the punishment was death (cf. Lev. 20: 10; Dt. 22: 22).
15. The man brings his wife to the priest and also a **grain offering** of barley flour. An **ephah** was equivalent to 22 litres (cf. 15: 4). Normally a grain offering of fine flour (cf. Lev. 2: 1) but barley flour was used by the poor and it here symbolizes the questionable nature of her life and standing before God. It is to have no **oil** or **incense** upon it, for signs of joy and festivity would have been inappropriate. From the man's point of view it is an **offering for jealousy**, from the woman's a **reminder offering**, recalling her sin if she is guilty. She is to **stand before the LORD** (16), i.e. before the tabernacle in which the Lord manifested His presence. **17. holy water:** it was probably taken from the bronze basin (cf. Exod. 30: 18). It is to be in a **clay jar**, for the same reason that they use the barley flour. The **dust** would remind one of the curse (cf. Gen. 3: 14) and would suggest a state of deep humiliation (cf. Ps. 72: 9; Isa. 49: 23; Mic. 7: 17), but it is sacred dust, because taken from the floor of the tabernacle (the tabernacle, unlike the temple, had no other floor; cf. 1 Kg. 6: 15, 30). The woman's hair is loosened (18) as a sign of mourning (cf. Lev. 13: 45) and of shame. She holds in her hand the **offering** (18, see v. 15), presenting to God the fruit of her conduct for His judgment, and the priest, as God's representative, has in his hand **the bitter water that brings a curse**. The water was not bitter in itself but, if the woman was guilty, it would cause bitter pain, as it brought the curse of God upon her (24).

19–22. The priest administers the oath. If the woman is guilty her **thigh** wastes away and her **abdomen** swells. 'Thigh' seems here to refer to the sexual organs. She is punished in the organs with which she has sinned. Others have suggested dropsy of the ovaries or ordinary dropsy.
21. curse and denounce: cf. Dt. 27: 15 ff.; Jer. 24: 9; 25: 18. **22.** 'So be it': cf. Neh. 5: 13.
23–28. The **curses** are written on a **scroll**, i.e. a piece of papyrus or leather, placed in the water, so that the water will be saturated with the curses (23). Verse 24 is anticipative. The drinking (26) implies a full acceptance of the curse if she is guilty (cf. Ps. 109: 18; Ezek. 3: 1–3; Jer. 15: 16; Rev. 10: 8). As the woman has taken the oath, **a memorial** portion of her **offering** ('so called because it was designed to bring the worshipper into the grateful remembrance of God, and to remind Him, as it were, of His promise to accept the service of His people rendered to Him in accordance with His command', Ellicott's Commentary on Lev. 2: 2) is burnt on **the altar** (26), and to prove the truthfulness or otherwise of her profession, she is made to **drink the water**.
29. This . . . is the law: cf. Lev. 12: 7; 15: 32. The section is formally closed and the thought added that, whatever the outcome, the **husband will be innocent of any wrongdoing**. It is this that justifies the supposition that the husband had been given some grounds for his jealousy.

iv. The Nazirite Vow (6: 1–21)
(a) The nature of the vow (6: 1–9)
The Nazirite vow was one of separation to God. 'Separation' is the key-word to the chapter, being repeated continually. 'Nazirite' (5, 8, 20) has the same meaning, as does also 'dedicate' (9, 11, etc.). RSV has gone further than most versions in bringing out the concept of separation, but is not entirely consistent. Either a man or a woman could be a Nazirite (2), but there is no example of a woman Nazirite in the OT. Am. 2: 11 ff., Lam. 4: 7 indicate that the practice was not rare and 'from references in Josephus it appears that Nazirites were a common feature of the contemporary scene' (J. D. Douglas in *NBD*).
2. The vow is called a **special** one (cf. Lev. 27: 2). In one sense every believer is meant to be 'special' (cf. Mt. 5: 46, 47) and therefore the Nazirite vow can have a general application. From another point of view some believers are called upon to make special sacrifices for the kingdom of God's sake (cf. Mt. 19: 11, 12; Rom. 14: 21) and to them the Nazirite vow has a special message.
There were three particular requirements of the vow. The Nazirite must abstain from wine and **other fermented drink** and anything associated with them (3, 4); his **hair** must not be

cut (5) and he must not touch a **dead body** (7, 9). Cf. Jg. 13: 4, 5, 7, 14; 16: 17–22; 1 Sam. 1: 11; Lk. 1: 15.

(i) Fermented drink was an intoxicating drink made from anything except grapes; sometimes it means fortified wine. The ban was not simply on intoxicants, but on everything derived from the vine. In practice, this meant a giving up of the only luxury readily available to all. In addition, Isa. 16: 7, Hos. 3: 1 suggest that the grape had special links with Baal worship. There is no suggestion that there was any ascetic purpose. The Nazirite continued to live a normal social life but for the term of his vow he was a living protest against that which excited sin (cf. Gen. 9: 20, 21; Prov. 31: 4, 5; Isa. 28: 7). Priests were forbidden to drink wine or fermented drink when they went into the tabernacle (cf. Lev. 10: 9). For the violation of this command cf. Am. 2: 12.

(ii) The simplest explanation of allowing the hair to grow would seem that it was the most obvious sign that an individual had taken the Nazirite vow. The fact that it applied to the woman as well suggests that the hair was allowed to float free; cf. Jg. 5: 2 (JB, NEBmg). (iii) Death being linked with sin brought defilement (cf. 5: 2 and the note there on *nephesh* which is here used in v. 6). The Nazirite was not allowed to become unclean by contact with his dead **father** or **mother** (7). In this the law for the Nazirite was the same as for the high priest (cf. Lev. 21: 1 1) and stricter than for an ordinary priest (cf. Lev. 21: 2, 3).

(b) **Defilement (6: 9–12)**

If the Nazirite is accidentally defiled by the dead, he is unclean till **the seventh day** (cf. 19: 11, 14, 16, 19; Lev. 14: 8, 9), when he shaves his head. The next day, the eighth, he brings **two doves or two young pigeons** (10), the cheapest blood offering (cf. Lev. 1: 14; 5: 7, 11; 12: 6, 8; 14: 22) **to the priest**. One is **as a sin offering** (11). The sin offering of Lev. 4 is for a sin committed unintentionally (2, 13, 22, 27); **suddenly** (9) assumes that such is the case here. The other is **as a burnt offering** (11), which was wholly for God (cf. Lev. 1: 9, 13) and was a fitting prelude to his reconsecration the same day. **11. make atonement for him:** in Lev. 1 and 4 atonement is linked with both the burnt offering and the sin offering. He also offered a guilt or trespass offering (12). The Nazirite offers the guilt-offering because of the delay in discharging his vow. The use of wine rather than accidental defilement is not mentioned, because it is assumed that a Nazirite would not deliberately break his vow.

(c) **The Conclusion of the Vow (6: 13–21)**

The vows of this chapter were for a set period. Later, men like Samson, Samuel, and John the Baptist were life-long Nazirites but only

Samson is expressly so called. (Samuel is so described at 1 Sam. 1: 22 in a fragment of *Samuel* recovered from Qumran Cave 4. Cf. R. K. Harrison, *Introduction to the OT*, p. 625.) In the case of Samuel it was on account of his mother's vow; in the case of the other two because of a divine revelation. At the end of the stipulated period he had to bring the complete range of Levitical sacrifices, apart from the guilt offering; cf. v. 12. For the meaning of these sacrifices cf. notes on Lev. 1–7 and Num. 15: 3–10 for the drink offering. The latter (17) prepares us for the fact that from then on the former Nazirite could drink wine again (20). The offering on the altar of the hair that had been shaved off (18) shows that the Nazirite's vow was something precious in God's sight.

The heavy cost of these sacrifices for the poorer Nazirite explains why in NT times charitable, pious Jews often paid for them; cf. Ac. 21: 21–24.

Some think Ac. 18: 18 refers to a Nazirite vow but Paul's head was not shaved at the door of the temple and there is no mention of the prescribed offerings. A. Edersheim, however, says that he might have cut off his hair at Cenchreae and brought it with him to Jerusalem (*The Temple and its Services*, p. 330). There seems no doubt about Ac. 21: 23–26, where Paul pays the expenses of four Nazirites who are about to discharge their vows.

v. **The Blessing of Israel (6: 22–27)**

The blessing is separate from the rest of the chapter. It is not the Nazirites who are blessed but the people of Israel. It is not recorded when the blessing was used. In Lev. 9: 22 mention is made of a blessing pronounced by Aaron but no words are given. Jewish tradition states that it was pronounced at the close of the daily sacrifice. Its position is specially appropriate, for it implies that God's blessing was available for all the people and was not confined to a special class like the Nazirites.

With v. 24 cf. Dt. 28 and Ps. 121. 'The face of God (25) is the personality of God as turned toward men' (Keil). Just as the light of the sun brings blessing to men naturally, so the light of God's face brings grace and favour spiritually (cf. Prov. 16: 15). Contrast the hiding of His face (cf. Ps. 30: 7). **26. make his face shine upon you:** 'The LORD look kindly on you' (NEB), i.e. may His loving care be directed towards you. **give you peace:** 'peace' is literally 'completion' and is the sum of all the blessings that God bestows on His people. A gradation may be seen from blessing generally to favour and finally the crown of peace. The name of Yahweh is repeated in each of the three verses: early Christian writers saw in the repetition an adumbration of the Trinity. **27. So they will put my name on the Israelites:** NEB gives: 'They shall pronounce my name over the Israelites'. But in Scripture God's name is so identified with His person that such a pronouncement linked the people with Himself, declaring them to be in covenant relation with Him. Cf. Dt. 14: 24; 28: 10; Isa. 63: 19; Rev. 3: 12 and the use of the divine name in Christian baptism.

III. LAST EVENTS AT SINAI AND PRIESTLY LEGISLATION (B) (7: 1–10: 10)

i. The Offerings of the Leaders (7: 1–88)
(a) Carts and Oxen (7: 1–11)
i. When: Heb. 'on the day when' (cf. RSV); if taken literally, these offerings took place before the census of 1: 1 (cf. 1: 1 and Exod. 40: 17). However, as they were not made on the one day (cf. vv. 11 ff.), and as the twelve leaders were appointed in ch. 1 and v. 2 refers back to ch. 1, it appears that 'day' must here be taken in a general sense, i.e. 'at the time that' (cf. Gen. 2: 4). For the anointing and consecration of the tabernacle cf. Exod. 29: 36, 37; 30: 26–29; Lev. 8: 10, 11, 33–35. Exodus mentions a seven day sanctification and anointing of the altar but Leviticus only one anointing of the tabernacle and altar, evidently referring to the first day. The leaders bring **six covered carts and twelve oxen** (3). **7. Two carts and four oxen** are given **to the Gershonites** (who carried the curtains and coverings; cf. 4: 25, 26), **four carts and eight oxen** to the **Merarites** (who carried the heavy framework; cf. 4: 31–32) (8), but none to the Kohathites, because they were in charge of the precious articles (cf. 4: 5–15), which had to be carried on **their shoulders** with due veneration (9). David sinned by allowing the ark to be carried on a new cart (cf. 2 Sam. 6: 3–8; 1 Chr. 15: 12–15). The carts are not mentioned in ch. 4, where the word 'carry' is used of the three families (vv. 15, 25, 31). The carts will hardly have been sufficient for all that had to be moved, especially under desert conditions. The exact nature of the carts is not clear. 'Covered wagons' has good authority. R. K. Harrison noted that ox-drawn wagons were used regularly in Syria by the Pharaohs from the time of Tuthmosis III (c. 1470 BC) onwards for several centuries (*Introduction to the OT*, p. 623). Keil believed that the offerings of vv. 12–88 were presented on twelve successive days because of the limited space upon the altar.

(b) **Other Offerings (7: 12–83)**
From v. 12 to v. 83 there is a record in similar language of the identical offerings of the twelve leaders, making it the longest chapter in the Bible, apart from Ps. 119. To us the record might seem unduly repetitious but the purpose may be to show that each tribe had an equal claim to the altar and that 'man may pass hastily

or carelessly over gifts and offerings, but God never can, never does and never will' (C. H. Mackintosh). The leaders are the same as in ch. 1 but the order is that of ch. 2.

The same offerings consisted of (i) a **silver plate** (cf. Exod. 25: 29); (ii) a **silver sprinkling bowl** (cf. Exod. 27: 3), both filled with **fine flour mixed with oil as a grain offering** (cf. Lev. 2: 4); (iii) a **gold ladle** (cf. Exod. 25: 29) **filled with incense** (this was a small, hollow vessel; RV 'spoon'); (iv) **one young bull, one ram and one male lamb a year old, for a burnt offering** (cf. Lev. 1: 2); (v) **one male goat for a sin offering** (cf. Lev. 4: 23); (vi) **two oxen, five rams, five male goats and five male lambs a year old** for a **fellowship offering** (cf. Lev. 3: 1, 6, 12; 7: 11 ff.; 9: 4). This (16) is the first of many places in Numbers where a goat is offered for a sin offering; cf. Lev. 16: 5; under desert conditions the goat was more readily available, but 'perhaps the choice of this animal implied its fitness in some way to represent transgression, wilfulness and rebellion. The he-goat, more wild and rough than any other of the flock, seemed to belong to the desert and to the spirit of evil' (R. A. Watson, *Numbers*, p. 355). **17. fellowship** (or peace) **offerings:** M. Poole thought these were more numerous because the princes and priests and some of the people made a feast before the Lord out of them and celebrated with great rejoicing (cf. Dt. 12: 7). For **Deuel** (42, 47) see note at 2: 14. Verses 84–88 contain a summary of the offerings.

ii. The Voice Speaking to Moses (7: 89)
Moses had authority to enter the most holy place (cf. Exod. 25: 22); cf. note on 3: 1–4. We are not told what Moses said but what he **heard.** Cf. Rev. 1: 12; 6: 6.

iii. The Lamps Lighted (8: 1–4)
For the **lampstand** see Exod. 25: 31–40; 30: 8; 40: 23–25; Lev. 24: 2 ff. It is the only part of the tabernacle furniture mentioned here. Although only **Aaron** is mentioned here, he was assisted by his sons in caring for the lamps (cf. Exod. 27: 21). **2. in front of the lampstand:** i.e. the lamps were to be positioned on the stand so as to throw their light forward, cf. NEB, JB, GNB. **4. hammered:** cf. Exod. 10: 2; 25: 18, 31; 37: 7. **the pattern:** cf. Exod. 25: 9, 40.

iv. The Consecration of the Levites (8: 5–26)
Moses officiates at the purification of the Levites, just as he had at the consecration of the priests (cf. Exod. 29; Lev. 8). The ceremony is much simpler than that for the priests. They are not said to be consecrated but cleansed and set apart. There is no anointing or investiture. Whereas the priests were washed (cf. Lev. 8: 6), and also the lepers (cf. Lev. 14: 8–9), the Levites were sprinkled with water (7) though here the difference may be due to the number

involved and their clothes were washed, which was the general requirement of worshippers (cf. Gen. 35: 2; Exod. 19: 10). **7. the water of cleansing:** literally 'water of sin', i.e. water to cleanse from sin (a similar expression is used to describe the 'water of cleansing' in 19: 9). It was probably taken from the bronze basin which was used for the cleansing of the priests (cf. Exod. 5: 17; 30: 18 ff.). But since we cannot be certain of chronological order, the rabbinic identification with the purification water of ch. 19 may be correct. The shaving (7) is the second stage of the purification but it is not as thorough as for the leper in Lev. 14: 8, 9. Part of the cleansing is done for them and part by them. One **young bull** is taken for a burnt offering and another **for a sin offering** (8, 12). The people of Israel lay their hands upon the Levites (10), a symbol of identification and transference (cf. Lev. 16: 21), 'in order that by this symbolic act they might transfer to the Levites the obligation resting upon the whole nation to serve the Lord in the person of its first-born sons, and might present them to the Lord as representatives of the first-born of Israel, to serve Him as living sacrifices' (Keil).

Just as the people laid **their hands** on the **Levites** (10), so the Levites were to **lay their hands on the heads of the bulls** (12), thus identifying themselves with the animals to which their sins were transferred, to make atonement for themselves.

14–19. Just as Israel is set apart from the nations (cf. Lev. 20: 26), so the Levites are set apart from Israel (14), but cf. Isa. 66: 21. They are to **come** (15) to the outer court of the tabernacle, for they are not allowed to go inside (cf. 4: 20). The Levites take the place of the **firstborn** (16–18). Cf. 3: 12. **19. as gifts to Aaron:** cf. 3: 9. **to make atonement . . . so that no plague will strike:** the Levites assisted the priests in their expiatory work but the thought here seems to be rather that, by encamping around the tabernacle, they prevented God's anger from falling on unauthorized persons who might approach (cf. 1: 51–53). 'The root *k-p-r-* is here used in its original non-religious sense: cover. The Levites act as a screen between the Holy Place and the common people' (N. H. Snaith *NCentB*); cf. 'and to protect the Israelites' (GNB).

20–22. These verses record the fulfilment of the previous commands, especially those in vv. 7, 10, 12, 13. **21. purified themselves:** literally 'unsinned themselves'.

23–26. The Levites are to serve in the tent of meeting from the age of twenty-five to fifty, when they retire from active service (cf. 4: 3). In v. 24 it is literally 'to war the warfare of the service' and in v. 25 'return from the warfare' (cf. 4: 3). After that they can still render assistance as required, but they **must not do the work:** the sense is given by NEB, GNB; they were to be available whenever there was special pressure of work.

v. The Passover (9: 1–14)

The first part of this chapter (vv. 1–5) predates the census of ch. 1 (cf. 1: 1) but it is related here because a supplementary passover took place after the census (11).

1. in the first month: Abib (in exilic and post-exilic times Nisan, after the Babylonian name), the spring month.

From Exod. 12: 25 it might have been inferred that they must postpone the passover till they entered the land, but the people are informed that they must keep it at Sinai. They did not leave Sinai till the twentieth day (10: 11). They were to keep it **in accordance with all its rules and regulations** (3). Cf. Exod. 12.

Some, however, were found unclean through touching a dead body (6), cf. note on 5: 2. Possibly these were Mishael and Elzaphan who buried their cousins Nadab and Abihu shortly after the erection of the tabernacle (cf. Lev. 10: 4, 5). It was natural for them to come to Moses, as it was through his command that they had become defiled. There was no special command forbidding the unclean to eat the passover but regulations such as Lev. 7: 20, 21 and 22: 3 seem to have been applied generally. The predicament was a serious one. If they failed to keep the passover, they would be cut off from their people (13); if they kept it in a defiled state, they would suffer the same punishment (cf. Lev. 7: 20, 21); so they consulted Moses who sought counsel from the Lord (6–8; cf. Exod. 25: 21, 22; Jos. 9: 14).

9–14. The answer was that unclean persons would be allowed to eat the passover in the second month. This was called by the Jews the 'little passover' and was said to last only one day. Hezekiah's passover was in the second month (cf. 2 Chr. 30: 2) but not Josiah's (cf. 2 Chr. 35: 1). It has been noted that v. 10 does not suggest anyone living permanently abroad; such persons could not keep the passover so long as the temple stood; after A.D. 70 there was no longer a passover lamb.

13. cut off from his people: cf. Gen. 17: 14; Exod. 12: 15; Lev. 20: 3, 5, 6, etc. Jewish tradition, probably correctly, understands this of death inflicted by God, not by a human tribunal. The 'alien' (14) is the proselyte of Exod. 12: 48, 49.

vi. The Cloud (9: 15–23)

These verses are an expansion of Exod. 40: 34–38. The pillar seems to have been fire wrapped in a cloud, God causing the cloud to be prominent by day and the fire by night. In Exod. 16: 10 the glory of the Lord is said to appear in the cloud and in 40: 34 the cloud covered the Tent of Meeting and the glory of the Lord filled the tabernacle. When they journeyed the cloud went before them (cf. Exod. 13: 21, 22), but in 14: 19 it stood behind them to protect them. When they encamped it was over the tabernacle (cf. Exod. 40: 38; Num. 9: 15, 16; 14: 14). It was not taken away during the desert wanderings (cf. Exod. 13: 22; Neh. 9: 19 ff.), but it seems to have vanished after the conquest of Transjordan; it reappeared temporarily at the dedication of the temple (1 Kg. 10, 11). Its departure (Ezek. 9–11; 10: 18, 19) was spiritual, visible only to the prophet. The glory of God dwelling in the midst of His people was called by the Jews the Shekinah (see R. A. Stewart's article 'Shekinah' in *NBD*).

15. the Tent of the Testimony: cf. 17: 7, 8; 18: 2. The tent is so called because the tables of the testimony on which the Ten Commandments were written, were placed in the ark in the most holy place (cf. Exod. 25: 16; 31: 18). The cloud covered the whole tabernacle and Moses could not enter because the cloud rested upon it (cf. Exod. 40: 34, 35). So the tent here seems to refer to the whole of the tabernacle; but the Lord's presence in the cloud appeared especially over the ark upon the mercy seat (cf. Lev. 16: 2). **16. the cloud covered it:** most ancient versions add 'by day' (cf. RSV, NEB). The **command** (18, 20, 23) was not the spoken or written word but the will of God as revealed in the cloud. **19. obeyed the LORD'S order**: 'remained in attendance on the LORD' (NEB). Cf. 1: 53.

22. a year: literally 'days', used of an indefinite period (cf. Gen. 4: 3), sometimes equivalent to a year and so translated here (cf. AV, RV, NEB, JB, GNB). 'The elaboration of the account (vv. 15–23), which abounds with repetitions, is intended to bring out the importance of the fact, and to awaken the consciousness not only of the absolute dependence of Israel upon the guidance of Jehovah, but also of the gracious care of their God, which was thereby displayed to the Israelites throughout all their journeyings' (Keil).

vii. The Silver Trumpets (10: 1–10)
The silver trumpet is shown on the Arch of Titus in Rome and on Jewish coins. It is described by Josephus (*Ant.* iii. 12. 6) as 'a little less than a cubit in length; the tube narrow, a little thicker than a flute, and just wide enough to permit the performer to blow it; while it terminated, like the other trumpets, in the form of a bell'. The Hebrew word (*hᵃṣōṣᵉrah*) is used here for the first time and is to be distinguished from the *shōphār*, a ram's horn used at the giving of the Law (cf. Exod. 19: 13 ff.), at the Year of Jubilee (cf. Lev. 25: 9), as a warning signal (Am. 3: 6), etc. R. K. Harrison (*Introduction to the OT*, p. 623) remarked that the silver trumpets have a decided bearing on the antiquity of the sources of *Numbers*. 'Such trum-

pets were in common use in Egypt during the Amarna Age, and some particularly elegant specimens that were interred with the pharaoh Tutankhamen (*c.* 1350 BC) were recovered by Howard Carter in the twentieth century'.

There were to be **two** of them (2). Later, however, the number may have been increased (cf. 1 Chr. 15: 24; 2 Chr. 5: 12). They were to be of **hammered silver** (2; cf. 8: 4). They were to be used for summoning the congregation and breaking camp (2). Both were to be blown to assemble **the whole community** and one to assemble **the leaders** (3, 4). The **east** and **south** sides are mentioned; LXX adds 'north' and 'west'. When **the assembly** was to be gathered a different trumpet signal was to be given (7). The trumpets were to be blown by **the priests** (8); cf. 31: 6. Since the word need not be confined to the two priestly trumpets, 2 Kg. 11: 14 and 1 Chr. 16: 42 need not refer to them. This (i.e. 'this sounding of the trumpets', NEB) was to be **a lasting ordinance** (8); i.e. 'a rule binding for all time' (NEB). They were to be used when the people went to war (9). Cf. 31: 6; 2 Chr. 13: 12, 14; 20: 21, 22, 28). However, at Jericho the *shōphār* was used (cf. Jos. 6: 4). The silver trumpets were used at the feasts and the beginning of the months only over the burnt offerings and fellowship offerings 10; hence they are not referred to in Lev. 23: 24. This was the only new moon that was also a feast day (cf. 28: 11; 29: 1; Ps. 81: 3). **they will be a memorial for you before your God** (cf. Exod. 28: 29): i.e. their purpose will be that God may remember you and bless you.

IV. FROM SINAI TO KADESH BARNEA (10: 11–14: 45)
i. The People Set Out (10: 11–36)
From this point to 14: 45 we have a new section of the book. The cloud had rested on the tabernacle for fifty days (cf. v. 11 and Exod. 40: 17). They had been at Sinai eleven months and twenty days (Exod. 19: 1). **12. the Desert of Paran:** 'situated in the east central region of the Sinai peninsula, north-east from the traditional Sinai and south-south-east of Kadesh, with the Arabah and the Gulf of Aqabah as its eastern border' (*NBD*). Cf. Gen. 21: 21; 1 Kg. 11: 18. This was not the next station but the third (cf. 12: 16; 13: 3, 26; 33: 16–18). The verse gives a summary of their journey up to this point. For the time taken see end of note at 13: 20.

Verse 17 provides an addition to the instructions of ch. 2. There the camp of the Levites set out after the camp of Reuben but here the Gershonites and the Merarites, who carried the tabernacle, set out after Judah. They went ahead so that the tabernacle could be set up before the arrival of the Kohathites (21). In v. 21 **holy things** is the regular word for the sanctuary, but, as the tabernacle when taken down was carried by the Gershonites and the Merarites (17), it must here refer to the holy furnishings that were carried by the Kohathites (cf. 3: 31 ff. and note on 4: 4).

29. Some take **father-in-law** to refer to **Reuel** rather than to **Hobab** his **son**, but in Jg. 4: 11 the word refers to Hobab and is generally so taken here. The Hebrew word *hōthēn*, however, need express only a marriage relationship and NEB gives 'brother-in-law' in both places. Hobab has not been mentioned before. The name Reuel is used in Exod. 2: 18 of the priest of Midian who became Moses' father-in-law but Jethro is his regular name in Exodus. (Reuel, however, may have been Jethro's father, who could also have been called Hobab.) He had returned home according to Exod. 18: 27. Here Hobab is said to be a **Midianite**. In Jg. 4: 11 his descendants are Kenites, who were a Midianite tribe. **do you good:** i.e. give him a share in the blessings that Yahweh would give them (32). Hobab refused (30) but, as his descendants are later mentioned in the land (cf. Jg. 1: 16; 4: 11; 1 Sam. 15:6; 1 Chr. 2: 55) it is possible that he afterwards consented. **31. you can be our eyes:** some think that Moses was wrong, as they had the guiding cloud, but Keil points out that the springs, oases and plots of pasture were often quite buried out of sight in the mountains and valleys, and therefore the cloud did not render a human guide unnecessary.

33. Sinai is called **the mountain of the LORD** only here. Elsewhere it is called 'the mountain of God', *e.g.* in Exod. 3: 1. **The ark of the covenant of the LORD went before them . . . :** cf. Jos. 3: 11. **to find them a place to rest:** cf. v. 36; Dt. 1: 33; Exod. 33: 14. NEB, following the Syriac version, says that the ark 'kept a day's journey ahead of them'. The 'three days' journey' of the first part of v. 33 would be the first stage, i.e. to Kibroth Hattaavah (cf. 11: 34, 35; 33: 16; Gen. 30: 36; Exod. 3: 18, etc.). Ibn Ezra suggested that it was only on this first stretch that the ark went in front and this is compatible with the Heb. syntax. **35–36.** The marches of the Israelites began and ended with prayer. The Lord is viewed as 'a man of war' (cf. Exod. 15: 3; 2 Chr. 6: 41, 42; Ps. 132: 8). The prayer of v. 35, echoed in Ps. 68: 1, was especially appropriate when the ark went before the armies of Israel in a holy war (cf. 1 Sam. 4: 3 ff.), and that of v. 36 on their victorious return.

Rise up . . . Return: Yahweh was envisaged as sitting invisibly enthroned on the ark.

ii. Taberah (11: 1–3)

The people complained about their **hardships** (1), probably because of the difficulties and deprivations of the journey (cf. vv. 4–6 and 21: 4). We are not told the origin of the fire (1).

The language is less definite than in Lev. 10: 2 but, wherever it came from, it was **fire from the LORD**. It **consumed some of the outskirts of the camp** but there is no mention of anyone being killed. It was a token of God's holy wrath and the fire died down in answer to Moses' intercession. The place was called **Taberah** or 'Burning' (cf. Dt. 9: 22). Taberah is not included among the stations in ch. 33. But there is no suggestion of any removal from Taberah to Kibroth Hattaavah between vv. 3 and 4. It has been noted that God's judgments after the giving of the Law are severer than before (cf. Exod. 14: 11–14; 15: 24, 25; 16: 2–8; 17: 3–7). For a record of God's judgments cf. Ps. 106.

iii. The Craving for Meat (11: 4–6)

The **rabble** or 'mixed multitude' (RV; cf. Exod. 12: 38) **began to crave** (cf. Ps. 78: 29 ff.; 106: 14). The Israelites wailed: cf. Exod. 16: 2, 3, where however wailing is not actually mentioned. The **meat** may include fish (cf. v. 5 and Lev. 11: 11). Poor Egyptians and other foreign slaves attached themselves to the Israelites. They claimed to have eaten **fish** in Egypt **at no cost**. 'The quantity of fish in Egypt was a very great boon to the poor classes . . . The canals, ponds and pools on the low lands continued to abound in fish even after the inundation [of the Nile] ceased' (Wilkinson, quoted in *ICC*, p. 103). The **melons** are water melons which have been cultivated from earliest times in Egypt. Herodotus mentions **onions** and **leeks** as common food of the workmen on the pyramids. He also mentions **garlic**. 'It will thus be seen that we have here a very vivid and true picture of Egyptian life, and, in particular, of the life of the lower orders' (*ICC*, p. 104). But they complain that now they have lost their appetite (NEB, 'our throats are parched') and wherever they look there is nothing but **manna** (cf. 21: 5; Ps. 22: 15; 102: 4). It has been objected that the people were rich in cattle (cf. Exod. 12: 38) but many were needed for sacrifice and they would not have lasted long if they had been used indiscriminately. Under desert conditions their number had doubtless decreased very considerably.

iv. Manna (11: 7–9)

Cf. Exod. 16: 14 ff. In Exod. 16: 14 the manna is said to be 'like frost on the ground' but in v. 31, evidently after it was gathered, 'white like coriander seed'. Here too it is compared to **coriander seed** (7), with the addition that it **looked like resin** (cf. Gen. 2: 12 'aromatic resin'). After the people prepared it, **it tasted like something made with olive oil** (8). In Exod. 16: 31 its taste was 'like wafers made with honey'. On the whole subject of the manna, including the spiritual teaching, cf. Patrick Fairbairn, *The Typology of Scripture* (1854), vol. 2, pp. 56 ff. No naturalistic explanation of the manna does justice to the Bible descriptions.

v. Moses' Complaint (11: 10–15)

The wailing among the people was universal and unashamed (cf. Zech. 12: 12), provoking the LORD's anger (10), which apparently did not actually erupt till v. 33. Moses was **troubled** or 'displeased' (RSV), 'partly for their great unthankfulness, partly, foreseeing the dreadful judgment coming upon them, and partly, for his own burden expressed in the following verses' (M. Poole).

Moses complains that God lays the burden of this people upon him. They were not his children that he should carry them to the promised land or find food for them or bear them alone (10–14). It is true that others had been chosen to bear the burden with him but that was only in smaller matters (cf. Exod. 18: 17–27). Moses' complaint was of course unreasonable but we must not condemn him because he fell short in 'casting his cares on the LORD' (Ps. 55: 22), for he was under great stress. It is worthy of notice, however, that the language has every mark of genuineness, for a later writer would hardly have attributed such words to Moses. Moses argues (12) that he is not Israel's mother. Why then should he play the part of a nurse? M. Noth says that in spite of the masculine form 'nurse' must here have a feminine sense. A slight change in spelling would give 'nursing (or foster) mother'. On the other hand AV, RV and *ICC* give 'nursing-father'. Cf. Dt. 1: 31; Ac. 13: 18 (RVmg); Isa 40: 11; 49: 22, 23. The ideas would then be that Israel is God's son (cf. Exod. 4: 22, 23; Dt. 32: 18; Hos. 11: 1) and therefore He is the appropriate nursing-father. Moses' two questions favour the feminine. **13. Where can I get meat . . . ?:** if Moses seems to have forgotten **The LORD will provide** (cf. Gen. 22: 14), we must remember that he is filled with despair and God appears to be doing nothing. Finally, like other great servants of God, he prays that he may die (cf. 1 Kg. 19: 4; Jon. 4: 1–3).

vi. The Seventy Elders (11: 16–17)

Seventy are to be chosen from **Israel's elders** to help Moses bear the burden of the people (cf. Exod. 3: 16; 5: 6; 12: 21; 24: 1, 9; Lev. 4: 15). The elders were the leading men from whom **seventy** had to be chosen. The Jews traced the origin of the Sanhedrin to these seventy but this is a typical piece of rabbinic whimsy. These seventy men must not be confused with the rulers of Exod. 18: 21–26, who would have been much more numerous. They were to receive some **of the Spirit** which was upon Moses (17). It is the gifts and power of the Spirit that are in view rather than His person. This did not mean that Moses was left with less of the Spirit.

vii. Meat Promised (11: 18–23)

The people are to eat meat for a month until they loathe it (19, 20). **18. Consecrate yourselves . . . for tomorrow:** they are to 'prepare themselves by purifications for the revelation of the glory of God in the miraculous gift of flesh' (Keil). Cf. Exod. 19: 10, 15; Jos. 3: 5.

They were to eat **not . . . one day** (19), as the previous year (cf. Exod. 16: 13) but **a whole month** (20). This however was too much for Moses' faith. **22. Would they have enough if flocks and herds were slaughtered for them?:** not merely the flocks of Israel (cf. Exod. 10: 9). **Would they have enough if all the fish in the sea were caught for them?:** the language is of course hyperbolical but the Lord reminds him that His **arm** is not **too short** (23: cf. Isa. 59: 1). The **six hundred thousand** of v. 21 is a round number (cf. 1: 46; Exod. 12: 37).

viii. The Seventy Chosen (11: 24–25)

Moses went out from the tabernacle, where he had spread his complaint before the Lord (cf. Exod. 25: 22), and gathered **seventy . . . of the elders** around the tent, in a semi-circle round the front of the tabernacle. **25. Then the LORD came down in the cloud and spoke with him:** cf. 12: 5; Exod, 33: 9; Dt. 31: 15. Normally the cloud was over the tabernacle (cf. Exod. 40: 38). The promise of v. 15 was fulfilled and **they prophesied, but they did so not do so again** (25). AV 'ceased' is misleading. 'The sign was granted on the occasion of their appointment to credit them in their office; it was not continued because their proper function was to be that of government, not prophesying' (*Speaker's Commentary*); cf. Heb. 2: 3, 4.

ix. Eldad and Medad (11: 26–30)

Eldad and **Medad**, who are otherwise unknown, **had remained in the camp** for some undisclosed reason; probably because they did not want the responsibility. It implies that they belonged to the seventy, used in vv. 24 and 25 in a general sense.

26. listed: literally 'written', indicating that Israel had learned the art of writing in Egypt. A young man told Moses, and **Joshua . . . who had been Moses' aide since youth** (cf. Exod. 17: 9–14; 24: 13; 32: 17; 33: 11; Jos. 1: 1) asked Moses to forbid them (28; cf. Mk 9: 38, 39). The other members of the seventy had been with Moses (vv. 16, 24, 25) when the gift of prophecy was bestowed on them. Eldad and Medad prophesying in the camp seemed to Joshua to be acting independently and so establishing a separate centre of authority, especially since they had disobeyed Moses' summons. But Moses was above jealousy and his reply is one of the noblest sayings of Scripture (29).

x. The Quail (11: 31–35)

The Lord brought **quail** to the camp by means

of a south-east wind (cf. Ps. 78: 26–31). 'Quails are twice mentioned in connection with the wilderness journeyings (Exod. 16: 13; Num. 11: 31, 32; Ps. 105: 40). Tristram has shown that they would naturally follow up the Red Sea to its bifurcation and cross at the narrowest part into the Sinaitic Peninsula. A sea wind would bring them in immense numbers into the camp which the Israelites occupied at that time. The miracle consisted in their being directed to the right time and place. Quails, when migrating, begin to arrive at night (Exod. 16: 13) and are found in large numbers in the morning (Num. 11: 31, 32). Their great exhaustion on their arrival makes it easy to believe all that is said in the narrative as to the numbers which the Israelites captured and the ease with which they were taken' (*HDB*, article 'Quails'). **31. brought them down:** the same word is translated 'scattered' in 1 Sam. 30: 16 and the traditional view is that in their flight they covered a day's journey on either side of the camp (for 'all around' cf. v. 24), at a height of three feet or so from the ground, thus being easily caught. **32. A homer** (= 'a donkey load') was ten ephahs (cf. Ezek. 45: 11), whereas an omer was a tenth of an ephah (cf. Exod. 16: 36). A homer was five to six bushels (*c.* 220 litres). In v. 33 some have sought a natural explanation, as if, *e.g.*, the plague was due to surfeit or food poisoning, but a divine judgment is clearly intended (cf. Ps. 106: 14, 15). **34. Kibroth Hattaavah:** 'graves of craving'. L. H. Grollenberg identifies the place with Ruweis-el-Ebeirig, north-east of the traditional Mt. Sinai. Hazeroth is generally identified with Ayin Khodara, an oasis with a well on the way from Sinai to Aqabah (cf. *NBD*).

xi. The Complaint of Miriam and Aaron (12: 1–16)

(a) The Nature of Their Complaint (12: 1, 2)

Miriam and Aaron complained about Moses' marriage to a Cushite woman. That this was not the main grievance, however, is evident from the next verse and from the fact that the Lord ignored it in his defence of Moses (6–8).

Miriam was evidently the instigator, for her name stands first (1) and **began to talk** is feminine and the punishment fell on her alone (10). Aaron was evidently carried away by his sister as he had been previously by the people (cf. Exod. 32). The name *Kushi* is linked with North Arabia (cf. Cushan, Hab. 3: 7), so it is quite possible that Zipporah is intended. Since this was a pretext, there are no reasons for inferring that it refers to a recent marriage. In view of the silence of Scripture it is unwise to jump to conclusions.

Verse 2, however, makes clear the real source of their grievance. Miriam was a prophetess (cf. Exod. 15: 20) and Aaron as high priest was able to wear the Urim and Thummim by which he was able to learn God's will for the people (cf. Exod. 28: 30) but in the previous chapter, with the appointment of the seventy, it was plain that Moses was regarded as the central-channel of divine authority; so Miriam and Aaron assert their equality (cf. Mic. 6: 4).

(b) The Meekness of Moses (12: 3)

That Moses should describe himself as **a very humble man, more humble than anyone else** (3), has struck many as strange. Some have explained it as the objectivity of an inspired man but it seems more natural to assume that it is an inspired addition, like the account of Moses' death in Dt. 34, which is why NIV brackets the verse. It is probably here said of Moses because of his silence under attack. The word refers especially to a person's attitude to God. It is his standing as God's representative that is being challenged, and he leaves his vindication to God.

(c) The Vindication of Moses (12: 4–10)

The LORD called to Moses, Aaron and Miriam to **come out** (i.e. from the camp, 11: 30) **to the Tent of Meeting** (cf. 11: 16), i.e. to the entrance to the court (4). **Then the LORD came down in a pillar of cloud** (cf. 11: 25 and Exod. 33: 9), and **stood at the entrance to the Tent**, i.e. at the entrance to the sanctuary, and Aaron and Miriam were commanded to come forward. There is no suggestion that they entered the sanctuary, or that there was a physical manifestation of God. The LORD then contrasts Moses with other prophets. He speaks to them in a vision (cf. Gen. 15: 1; 46: 2) or in a dream (cf. Gen. 20: 3; 28: 12; Dan. 8: 18; 10: 8) or in riddles, but with Moses who is entrusted with all God's house (i.e. not the tabernacle but the house of Israel: cf. Heb. 3: 3) the LORD speaks **face to face** (cf. Exod. 33: 11; Dt. 34: 10; 2 Jn 12; 3 Jn 14) and **clearly** (8). **he sees the form of the LORD**, not His essence but an outward manifestation (cf. Exod. 33: 20–23) which is different from that seen by prophets in a vision (cf. Ezek. 1: 26) and different also from a theophany (cf. Gen. 18: 1).

After delivering the rebuke of v. 8 the Lord departed, as is shown by the return of the cloud to its normal position. **10. there stood Miriam leprous, like snow:** that the punishment should fall on Miriam was natural because she was the chief instigator of the discontent (cf. v. 1) but it is likely that Aaron was spared so that the worship of the tabernacle should not be interrupted. With the judgment on Miriam cf. Exod. 4: 6; 2 Kg. 5: 27; 15: 5; 2 Chr. 26: 19, 20.

(d) The Healing of Miriam (12: 11–16)

Aaron pleads for his sister, identifying himself with her. **11. do not hold against us:** literally 'lay not sin upon us', the word for 'sin' meaning also 'sin's punishment', as in Zech. 14: 19. In his humility Moses, whose unique relationship to God she had questioned, also pleads for her (13), twice using a particle of entreaty. The JB renders: 'Please heal her, I beg you'. But the Lord insists that she must be humbled first. **14. If her father had spit in her face:** spitting was an expression of disapproval and disgust (cf. Dt. 25: 9; Job 30: 10; Isa. 50: 6). **would she not have been in disgrace for seven days?:** how much more when the anger of the Lord is kindled against her! So she must be excluded seven days from the camp where she had sought the highest place and she must be denied the privileges enjoyed by the lowest. Seven days was the initial period of exclusion for one suspected of having an infectious skin disease (older EVV 'leprosy') (cf. Lev. 13: 4) and then afterwards he had to stay outside his tent seven days (cf. 14: 8, 10). When she was healed she would doubtless be brought back according to the rites of Lev. 13 and 14. On the subject of 'leprosy' generally see notes on these chapters.

In v. 16 the people are said to have **left Hazeroth** (cf. 11: 35) and pitched **in the Desert of Paran.** From v. 26 of the next chapter it appears that the encampment was at Kadesh, which may be the same as Rithmah (cf. 33: 18).

xii. The Mission and Report of the Spies
(a) **The Spies (13: 1–16)**
The Lord tells Moses to send twelve men, a leader from each tribe, to spy out the land of Canaan. From Dt. 1: 22 it appears that the plan originated with the people. Many therefore have totally condemned it and compared it to the appointment of a king (cf. 1 Sam. 8–10). But it is questionable whether the present action was sinful. When Samuel heard about a king, he was displeased (cf. 1 Sam. 8: 6), and God confirmed that the motives were wrong; when Moses heard about spies, it seemed good to him (cf. Dt. 1: 23) and God made no criticism. Besides, Joshua, who was one of the original spies, himself sent spies later with beneficial results (cf. Jos. 2: 1). And while the mission to view Ai in ch. 7 was disastrous, it was because of the sin of Achan (v. 11). It remains true that 'divine help never dispenses with the wise, careful and zealous use of all human means and strength but rather demands it' (Kurtz). Cf. also ch. 21: 32. Probably Dt. 1: 32 does not refer to the sending of the spies but to their subsequent rebellion and refusal to go up (cf. vv. 26 ff.).

The names of the spies are given in vv. 4–16. They are not the same as the leaders in ch. 1. Of the twelve only **Caleb** (6) and **Joshua** (8, 16) are known to us from elsewhere. Caleb is mentioned here for the first time. From the fact that Caleb is called the Kenizzite (cf. 32: 12; Jos. 14: 6, 14) it is generally inferred that

he was originally a non-Israelite and later incorporated into the tribe of Judah (cf. Gen. 15: 19; 36: 11, 15). Joshua has already been mentioned (11: 28). Moses changed his name from Hoshea (= 'salvation') to Joshua (= 'Yahweh will save') (16). If Moses changed his name at this time, the earlier references must be proleptic but the new name may have been given earlier, *e.g.*, after the defeat of the Amalekites (cf. Exod. 17) and confirmed on this occasion or simply recorded (cf. the name 'Israel' in Gen. 32: 28; 35: 10). The tribe of Levi is omitted, as in ch. 1.

(b) **The Commission of the Spies (13: 17–20)**
The spies are told to go into the Negev and then into the hill country (cf. 14: 44). Negev in the Hebrew means 'dry' and it refers to the southern portion of Palestine. 'It covers approximately 4,520 square miles or nearly one half of the modern state of Israel' (*NBD*; cf. Jg. 1: 15; Ps. 126: 4). The hill country was the mountainous part of Palestine, occupied by the Hittites, Jebusites and Amorites (29). The words of Moses (18–20) do not seem to reveal a robust faith and may be contrasted with his words in Dt. 8: 7–9. It may well be that he was conscious that the moment of decision had come for the people, where not his faith but theirs would be decisive.

20. It was the season for the first ripe grapes: i.e. late July or August. 'They had left Sinai on the twentieth day of the second month (10: 11), or about the middle of May' (*Speaker's Commentary*).

(c) **The Mission of the Spies (13: 21–24)**
Verse 21 gives a general description of the reconnaissance from the south to the north, and some details are added in the following verses. It is possible also that the spies were not together all the time. They spied the land from the Desert of Zin in the south (cf. 34: 3; Jos. 15: 3), which is not to be confused with the Desert of Sin (cf. Exod. 16: 1), to Rehob in the north (cf. Jos. 19: 28; Jg. 1: 31), which is thought to be the Beth Rehob of Jg. 18: 28 and 2 Sam. 10: 6. **toward Lebo Hamath:** a town near the watershed between the Jordan and Litani rivers.

Two particular incidents are mentioned. **They went up through the Negev, and came to Hebron** (22). Hebron was an ancient city about sixty miles north of Kadesh. It is mentioned in connection with Abraham in Gen. 13: 18; 23: 19. 'The statement that it was built seven years before Zoan in Egypt probably relates its foundation to the "Era of Tanis" (c. 1720 BC)' (*NBD*). Zoan was the Greek Tanis in the NE of lower Egypt in the eastern part of the delta. **Ahiman, Sheshai** and **Talmai** were evidently chiefs of the Anakim; but they are obviously also clan names or titles, for they were driven out by Caleb over forty years later (cf. Jos. 15: 14). The descendants of Anak were proverbial for their gigantic size (28, 33; cf. Dt. 1: 28; 2: 10, 21; 9: 2). **23. carried it on a pole between them:** the *Pulpit Commentary* says: 'not on account of its weight but simply in order not to spoil it'. Stories are told of bunches of grapes in Palestine ten to twelve pounds in weight. **Eshcol** means 'cluster', hence the name of the valley (23, 24) near Hebron.

(d) The First Report of the Spies (13: 25–29)
Forty days later the spies returned to Kadesh. As often as 'forty days' is an approximation for over a month. Kadesh is not mentioned in v. 3 but see 32: 8. For Kadesh (26) see note on 20: 1. Their first report was quite factual and obviously agreed. It spoke of the **fruit of the land** (cf. Dt. 1: 25; Isa. 4: 2), of a land flowing **with milk and honey** (cf. Exod. 3: 8, etc.), but also of the strength of the inhabitants and the large and fortified cities, points which Moses had asked them to investigate (18, 19) and of the descendants of Anak (cf. 22). For further details of the five peoples, **Amalekites . . . , Hittites . . . , Jebusites . . . , Amorites . . .** and **Canaanites** consult *NBD* and D. J. Wiseman (ed.), *Peoples of OT Times* (1973), ch. 2, 'The Canaanites' (A. R. Millard); ch. 5, 'The Amorites' (M. Liverani). **the sea:** i.e. the Mediterranean.

NBC[3] notes that three features of the report are significant in the light of modern archaeological discovery. First, **milk and honey** is a traditional description of a fruitful land. Secondly, the reference to **fortified** cities is factual. Thirdly, the population was indeed a mixed one.

(e) The Second Report of the Spies (13: 30–33)
Caleb sought to quieten them. The reaction of the people was of utter consternation. Joshua is associated with him in 14: 6, 7, 30. From Dt. 1: 29 it is evident that Moses also remonstrated with them but Caleb took the lead. The other spies, however, now showed their true feelings. Note the contrast between vv. 30 and 31. Fear makes them embellish their first report and exaggerate. The people are not only 'strong' but **stronger than we are**. All the people they saw are **of great size** (32) and they themselves are as **grasshoppers** compared with **the descendants of Anak** (33; cf. v. 22). It is a **land** that **devours those living in it** (32), i.e. 'the land was an apple of discord because of its fruitfulness and, as the different nations strove for its possession, its inhabitants wasted away' (Keil); but cf. GNB. **33. the Nephilim:** 'giants' (LXX), mentioned elsewhere only in Gen. 6: 4. The spies evidently linked the sons of Anak with them.

xiii. Rebellion and Judgment (14: 1–45)
(a) The People Weep and Grumble (14: 1–4)
The report of the spies made the people lose heart (cf. Dt. 1: 27, 28). They grumbled against Moses and Aaron and even blamed God (2, 3; cf. Exod. 16: 2, 3 and contrast Exod. 15: 14, 15). They desired a leader to take them back to Egypt (4; cf. Neh. 9: 16, 17). At the time of the golden calf they turned to Egypt in their hearts (cf. Ac. 7: 39) but now they actually want to go back there. This was their crowning rebellion.

(b) Moses and Aaron (14: 5)
After an unsuccessful attempt to encourage the people (cf. Dt. 1: 29–31) Moses and Aaron fell on their faces, thus humbling themselves before God (cf. Gen. 17: 3, 17; Lev. 9: 24; Jos. 5: 14; 7: 6; Num. 16: 4, 22, 45; 20: 6). They did not do it privately but before all the people, thus identifying themselves with them in their sin and danger.

(c) Joshua and Caleb (14: 6–10a)
Joshua and Caleb **tore their clothes,** a sign of mourning (cf. Gen. 37: 29, 34; Lev. 10: 6; Jos. 7: 6; 2 Sam. 13: 31), and sought to encourage the people. **If the LORD is pleased with us** (i.e. if we do not alienate Him by rebellion), **he will lead us into that land** (8). **9. Their protection is gone:** 'protection' is the shadow that protects from the heat of the eastern sun (cf. Ps. 121: 5, 6; Isa. 30: 2, 3; 32: 2; Jon. 4: 6). Keil took it to refer to the protection of God, who was about to judge them (cf. Gen. 15: 16; Exod. 34: 24; Lev. 18: 25; 20: 23), but it could refer to the protection of their own deities (cf. Dt. 32: 30, 31). So *ICC*, JB, GNB. **10. But the whole assembly talked about stoning them:** it was probably not an order of the elders, but a spontaneous reaction of the people (cf. Exod. 17: 4; 1 Sam. 30: 6). In Israel stoning was the usual method of execution (cf. 15: 35, 36; Lev. 20: 2, etc.).

(d) The Glory Appears (14: 10b–12)
The cloud was continually over the tabernacle (cf. Exod. 40: 38) but here it evidently flashed with light at the entrance to the sanctuary (cf. 16: 19; 20: 6 and Exod. 16: 10; 33: 9, 10). With v. 12 cf. Exod. 32: 9, 10. God's purpose would not be deflected by their failure.

(e) Moses Pleads (14: 13–19)
Moses' reply is magnificent (cf. Exod. 32: 11–14). God's reputation will suffer among the Egyptians and the inhabitants of the land (cf. Exod. 15: 14, 15). They will attribute failure to God's inability (cf. Dt. 32: 26, 27; Jos. 7: 9; Isa. 48: 9, 11; Ezek. 36: 22, 23; Ps. 106: 23). So Moses prays for the people. **14. face to face:** literally 'eye to eye'. The same expression is found in Isa. 52: 8. **17. Lord:** Heb. *'Adonai* (= 'Sovereign Lord'). (But many MSS and some printed editions have Yahweh; this has been

followed by RSV, NEB, GNB; it is impossible to be certain which is the correct text.) The power is the power to forgive, as the next verse indicates. The latter part of v. 18 may not seem relevant to the plea for forgiveness but it is part of the revelation of Exod. 34: 6 f., and the whole must be quoted. Moses asks God to pardon the people (19) **in accordance with your great love**. The Hebrew for steadfast love (*ḥesed*) occurs most frequently in the Psalms and means 'steadfast love on the basis of a covenant'.

(f) The Lord's Answer (14: 20–25)

God promises to forgive the people but the rebels are not to enter the land. God's forgiveness does not always undo the consequences of His people's sins (cf. 2 Sam. 12: 13, 14; Ps. 99: 8; Heb. 3: 7–19). The meaning of v. 21 appears to be, not that God will be glorified by the punishment of the offenders but rather that His purposes will be carried out in spite of their sin. **21. as I live:** used as the formula of an oath (cf. Dt. 32: 40; 1 Sam. 14: 39, 45; 20: 3; Isa. 49: 18; Jer. 5: 2). **22. ten times:** marking completeness (cf. Gen. 31: 7), like our expression 'over and over again'. The rabbis however counted ten actual cases of provocation. Caleb alone is mentioned in v. 24 as not excluded from the land but Joshua's name is added in v. 30. The reason may be that Caleb took the initiative, while Joshua apparently hesitated for a time; cf. 13: 30 and 14: 6. **24. follows me wholeheartedly:** cf. 32: 11, 12; Dt. 1: 36; Jos. 14: 8, 9, 14. **his descendants will inherit:** in particular they inherited Hebron and the adjacent parts (cf. Jos. 14: 6–14; Jg. 1: 10–15). There is some considerable difficulty in understanding the point of the first words of v. 25. Some regard them as an interpolation. AV puts them in brackets. NEB and GNB link them with the previous verse, the meaning being that Caleb is to inherit the territory of the Amalekites and Canaanites. Others, as NIV, take them as the reason why the Israelites are to set out southwards. All contact with possible enemies was to be avoided. **the Red Sea:** cf. Exod. 10: 19; 13: 18, etc. The term Red Sea can generally be translated Sea of Reeds. The reference here is probably to the Gulf of Aqabah.

(g) God's Judgment (14: 26–35)

The people had spoken of dying in the wilderness (2). That is indeed to be their fate (28). All those twenty years old and over except Caleb and Joshua are to perish (29, 30). Cf. 26:63–65. Their children are to enter the land (31). Because of their age they could not be held so responsible. **29. every one . . . counted in the census:** cf. 1: 3. As the Levites were not numbered then (1: 47 ff.), it has been incorrectly inferred that they were exempt from the judgment. Support is believed to be given to

this inference by the presence of Eleazar in the land (cf. Jos. 14: 1). As he had been entrusted with the duties of the priesthood (cf. 4: 16), it is thought that he must have been over twenty. However there was no definite age requirement for the priests as for the Levites (cf. 2 Chr. 31: 17). It is noteworthy also that the exclusion of Moses and Aaron, who are distinguished from the congregation (26 ff.), is attributed to another cause (cf. 20: 12; Dt. 1: 37). **33. shepherds:** Heb. *rō'îm*, the ordinary word for 'shepherds', as in Ps. 23: 1 but, as shepherds are usually nomads (so JB) RV gives 'wanderers.' So also does NEB; GNB 'will wander'. Thus the iniquities of the fathers are visited upon children (cf. v. 18; Exod. 34: 16). **unfaithfulness** ('wanton disloyalty', NEB): indicating that their sin is regarded as a breach of their marriage to Yahweh (cf. Jer. 3: 6–14; Ezekiel and Hosea, *passim*). As the number of years from Kadesh Barnea till the extinction of that generation was thirty-eight (cf. Dt. 2: 14), it is evident that the forty years were counted from the Exodus. The forty years correspond to the forty days in which the spies searched the land (34). 'The period of forty years is, in the Old Testament conception, the life-span within which a man participates in the life of the community with full powers and full rights. After a forty-year sojourn in the wilderness the constituents of the community will be completely changed' (M. Noth).

(h) The Death of the Unworthy Spies (14: 36–38)

All the spies except Joshua and Caleb die by plague. The word for 'plague' is also found in 16: 48, 49, 50; 25: 8, 9, 18; 26: 1; 31: 16 and in Exod. 9: 14, etc. It is 'any form of death regarded as inflicted directly by Yahweh for an express purpose, whether for punishment or for some other reason' (*ICC*).

(m) The Presumption of the People (14: 39–45)

The people, realizing that they had sinned, are stricken with grief and they desire to go up to Canaan. But despite Moses' warning (41–43; cf. Dt. 1: 42) **in their presumption** (44: a rare word, implying self-confidence), they went up. The ark and Moses remained in the camp; the people were defeated and pursued as far as **Hormah** (44, 45; cf. Dt. 1: 44). Hormah (= 'Destruction') received its name on the occasion mentioned in 21: 3 (cf. Jg. 1: 17), which seems to have been misplaced; cf. note *ad loc*. **45. hill country:** cf. 13: 17.

V. PRIESTLY LEGISLATION (C) (15: 1–41)

i. Various Offerings (15: 1–21)

(a) In the Land (15: 1–2)

The close of ch. 14 tells of man's failure; the beginning of ch. 15 of God's faithfulness. His purpose is unchanged. He is going to bring the people into the land (2; cf. Rom. 11: 29). The laws of ch. 15 are addressed primarily to the new generation and there may have been an interval between chs. 14 and 15. The mention of the land also implies that these offerings were not made in the desert. Cf. also the introduction to ch. 33. It is to be noted also that it is the people that are addressed in this chapter and not Aaron (cf. 18: 1).

(b) **The Grain Offering and the Drink Offering (15: 3–10)**

The grain offering is treated in Lev. 2 but it is not there definitely linked with blood sacrifices. Some think that the offerings of Lev. 2 are meant to be independent of such sacrifices but there are very few examples in OT of independent grain offerings (cf. Num. 5: 15, 25; Lev. 5: 11–13; 6: 19–23). There is also no mention of a drink offering in Lev. 2. It is referred to in Gen. 35: 14; Exod. 29: 40, 41; Lev.23: 13, 18, 37; Num. 6: 15, 17. It had been required with the daily sacrifices and at the Feasts of Firstfruits and Pentecost. With v. 3 cf. Lev. 7: 16; 22: 18; and 23: 38. These offerings were **an aroma pleasing to the LORD** (3, 7, 10). The term is used in Lev. 1–3 of the burnt offering, grain offering and fellowship offering and in 4: 31 of the sin offering for one of the common people. Cf. Gen. 8: 21. The meaning of the drink offering is suggested by Jg. 9: 13 and Ps. 104: 15. The offerer rejoiced before the Lord who shared his joy (cf. Phil. 2: 17). As the offerings increased in size, so did quantities of the grain offerings and drink offerings (4–10). The offerers gave according to their ability. Cf. Lev. 5: 7–13. An **ephah** (4, 6, 9) was the equivalent of *c.* 22 litres (cf. 5: 15); 'ephah' is not in the original in the passage but it is assumed. A **hin** (4, 6, 9) was one sixth of an ephah. With this section cf. 28: 3–8.

(c) **One Law (15: 11–16)**

In these offerings there is to be the same law for the Israelite and the alien (cf. 9: 14). **13. native-born:** i.e. 'native Israelite' (NEB).

(d) **The Offering of a Cake (15: 17–21)**

When they come into the land they are to offer a cake (JB, GNB, 'loaf') from their first baking. It is an example of giving God the first-fruits of our wealth (cf. Exod. 22: 29; 23: 16, 19; Lev. 2: 14; 23: 9 ff.; Prov. 3: 9). Jewish tradition has followed this law both for the housewife and the baker. Cf. Neh. 10: 37; Ezek. 44: 30. **20. as an offering from the threshing floor:** cf. 18: 27; Exod. 22: 29; Lev. 2: 14. **21. throughout the generations:** i.e. for all time. Cf. Exod. 12: 14.

ii. **Unintentional Error (15: 22–29)**

If the congregation errs through inadvertence in not obeying these commandments by omission or commission (22), a young bull is to be offered for a burnt offering and a male goat for a sin offering. Cf. Lev. 4: 13–21.

If a private person sins unintentionally, he must offer a female goat a year old for a sin offering (27). Cf. Lev. 4: 27–35.

iii. **Defiant Sin (15: 30–31)**

If however a person sins **defiantly** (30) (NEB, 'presumptuously'; JB, GNB, 'deliberately'), he is to be cut off from his people (cf. 9: 13, note), because he **blasphemes the LORD** (cf. Lev. 20: 9; 2 Kg. 19: 6, 22; Ezek. 20: 27). **30. defiantly:** cf. Exod. 14: 8; Job 15: 25, 26; Ps. 19: 13; Heb. 10: 26.

iv. **The Sabbath Breaker (15: 32–36)**

This incident is doubtless recorded as an example of defiant sin, which explains the apparent severity of the punishment. It was a wilful act of rebellion. The death penalty had already been proclaimed for those who violated the sabbath (cf. Exod. 31: 15; 35: 2) but the method of execution had not been prescribed and more likely a ruling had to be obtained to decide whether **gathering wood** constituted 'work' within the terms of the ban; cf. J. Weingreen, *From Bible to Mishna* (Manchester, 1976), pp. 83 ff. **32. While the Israelites . . . were in the desert:** this has been thought to indicate a later hand. **33. the whole assembly:** i.e. the elders as the representatives of the congregation (cf. Exod. 18: 25, 26).

v. **Tassels (15: 37–41)**

The people are **to make tassels** (Heb. *ṣîṣîth*) **on the corners of** their **garments** and on each tassel a cord of blue in order to remind them of the commandments of the Lord. In later Jewish tradition the threads and knots were so arranged as to set forth various mystical meanings, even the 613 commandments of the law (cf. A. R. S. Kennedy's article 'Fringes' in *HDB*). Today, for most Jews, the tallith or praying shawl is the means by which the commandment is carried out, but the blue cord is not included, because of doubt how the dye is to be obtained. Every morning, when saying his prayers, he puts it on and after he dies he is wrapped in it (cf. Rabbi R. Brasch, *The Star of David* (1955), ch. 14). Cf. Dt. 22: 12; Mt. 9: 20; 23: 5; Lk. 8: 44. With v. 39b cf. Prov. 4: 25–27 and 1 Jn 2: 16.

In v. 41 the instructions are reinforced by the reminder of their relationship to the Lord and of what He has done for them (cf. Exod. 20: 2; Lev. 26: 13).

VI. THE REVOLT AGAINST MOSES AND AARON (16: 1–17: 13)

The date of the rebellion described in this chapter cannot be determined with any certainty. But there are no valid reasons for not seeing in it the reactions of desperate men after the debacle at Kadesh. Nothing else will explain the widespread dissatisfaction with Moses and Aaron.

We have in the story the meeting of two groups of malcontents, one religious, headed by Korah, the other civil, led by Dathan and Abiram. In the nature of things the former is regarded as the more serious. The two groups acted together.

i. The Rebellion (16: 1–11)
Four men are named as rebelling against Moses and Aaron. **Korah** was a Levite, **son of Izhar, the son of Kohath.** He was related to Moses (cf. Exod. 6: 18, 21). **Dathan, Abiram** and **On** were **Reubenites.** They may have been discontented because Reuben had lost the birth-right. The tents of the Kohathites and Reuben-ites were close to one another on the south side (cf. 2: 10; 3: 29) and disaffected ones would have the opportunity to confer together. On is not referred to again. It seems likely that he soon withdrew from the conspiracy. **2. they rose up against Moses:** i.e. 'rose in rebellion against Moses' (R. A. Knox). **well-known community leaders:** v. 8 implies that many were of the tribe of Levi but there were doubt-less also representatives of other tribes (cf. 27: 3). **3. They came as a group:** this may refer to all mentioned in vv. 1 and 2, although Korah and his men were probably the chief spokes-men. Dathan and Abiram apparently retired before v. 12, as they were not as interested in the priesthood as in Moses' civil authority. **You have gone too far!:** literally 'enough for you!' (cf. Gen. 45: 28). 'Enough of you and your pretensions' (Moffatt). **The whole community is holy:** Korah appears to be referring to Exod. 19: 6 and to be claiming the exercise of a universal priesthood instead of that of the family of Aaron. Of course he may have desired the high-priesthood for himself (cf. v. 10). **4. Moses . . . fell face down:** cf. 14: 5. The matter concerned God's honour, and Moses was leaving it to Him. **5. In the morning:** to avoid precipitate action. Perhaps On availed himself of the opportunity to repent. **holy . . . come near him:** the priests were consecrated and it was their special privilege to come into God's presence. Since they claimed to be priests, Moses bade Korah and his company to take their censers and offer incense and the Lord would show whom He had chosen to be priest (6, 7). No special, elaborate, religious articles need be understood by 'censers'. Moses repeats Korah's words of v. 3: **You have gone too far** (7). He then reproaches Korah and his accomplices for not being content with the privileges God has given them (cf. 3: 5 ff.; 8: 6 ff.). Korah himself, as a Kohathite, belonged to the most favoured family, which had charge of the sacred furni-ture (cf. 3: 31). But they were seeking the priesthood also and in so doing they were not really opposing Aaron but the Lord (11).

ii. Dathan and Abiram summoned (16: 12–15)
Moses sends for Dathan and Abiram but they refuse to 'come up', a word which 'is some-times used of going to a superior or a judge (Gen. 46: 31; Dt. 25: 7; Jg. 4: 5)' (*ICC*). **13. Isn't it enough that you have brought us up out of a land flowing with milk and honey . . . ?:** they seem to be echoing Moses' words of v. 9; they irreverently apply to Egypt the words that belong to Canaan and they charge Moses with wanting to **lord it** over them, showing that they were opposed to his civil authority. They suggest that Moses wants to **gouge out the eyes** of the men associated with them (14)—a phrase used literally in Jg. 16: 21 but here used figuratively in the sense of 'throw dust in the eyes', 'hoodwink' (NEB). Moses is very angry, for righteous anger is compatible with meekness. He asks God not to accept any offering that they might bring (15; cf. Gen. 4: 4). NEB 'murmuring' is based on an emended text, and is doubtful. If he had been a prince, he might have demanded tribute (cf. 1 Sam. 8: 11 ff.), but he had not taken so much as **a donkey** from any of them.

iii. Korah summoned (16: 16–19)
Moses repeats the command of v. 6. Korah and his company are to appear before the Lord (i.e. at the entrance of the tent of meeting; cf. v. 19; Exod. 29: 42; Lev. 1: 3, 5), with their censers the next day (16, 17). **19. When Korah had gathered all his followers:** to confront Moses and Aaron, **the glory of the LORD appeared** (cf. 14: 10).

iv. The Lord and Moses (16: 20–24)
The Lord commanded Moses and Aaron to separate themselves from the assembly that He might consume them, for plainly they were partakers of Korah's sin. **22. fell face down:** cf. 14: 5. Moses asks the Lord not to be angry for one man's sin. Of course more than one man had sinned but clearly Korah was the ringleader. The expression **God of the spirits of all mankind** (22; cf. 27: 16) describes God as the one who has given to mankind the breath of life and is therefore able to destroy it. As the result of Moses' intercession the assembly is spared and the judgment is confined to Korah, Dathan and Abiram and their companies.

v. Moses confronts Dathan and Abiram (16: 25–30)
As Dathan and Abiram have refused to go to Moses (12), he goes to them, followed by the elders (cf. 11: 16), 'for the greater solemnity of the action and for his own better vindication' (M. Poole). The assembly is warned to keep clear of the tents of the wicked men and touch nothing belonging to them, for they are under a curse (cf. Dt. 13: 17). Korah was with his followers in front of the tabernacle at the time, where his sons may have been watching, but

Dathan and Abiram and their families stood at the door of their tents, in defiance. Moses proclaims a test of his divine call. If the men die naturally, the Lord has not sent him but, **if the LORD brings about something totally new** and the earth **swallows them** and **they go down alive into the grave** (the place of departed spirits, corresponding to the Greek *hades*), then they have spurned not merely Moses but the Lord (29, 30; cf. v. 11; 1 Sam. 8: 7). **28. to do all these things:** *e.g.*, to bring the people out of Egypt, to lead them through the wilderness, etc.

vi. God's Judgment (16: 31–35)
Dathan and Abiram and the men belonging to Korah, i.e. his servants, are swallowed up and the two hundred and fifty offering incense are consumed with fire (cf. Heb. 12: 29). For an explanation on the physical level, which however does not eliminate the miraculous, cf. R. K. Harrison, *Introduction to the Old Testament*, pp. 629, 630. Korah was not swallowed up with Dathan and Abiram but burnt with the two hundred and fifty. At 26: 10 the Samaritan Pentateuch says: 'When the fire devoured Korah and the two hundred and fifty men'. (There is a reference in Jude 11 to false guides of a later day who 'perish in Korah's rebellion'.) From 26: 11 we learn that Korah's sons did not perish; no explanation is given us. On the other hand the children of the other two did perish (27, 32). Later the sons of Korah are a group of sacred musicians who are named in the title of several Psalms (*e.g.* 42–49). In 1 Chr. 6: 33, 37 the first place is given to Heman, a descendant of Korah and grandson of Samuel.

vii. The Censers Cover the Altar (16: 36–40)
The censers of the two hundred and fifty men are to be taken. They are holy because they have been presented to the Lord and so must not be used for any profane purpose (cf. Lev. 27: 28). For a similar reason the fire is to be scattered far and wide. The censers are to be hammered into sheets presumably as an extra covering for the bronze altar. They had been used to overthrow Aaron's office and are now to strengthen it. In v. 37 it is Eleazar rather than Aaron who takes up the censers, as the high priest must not be defiled by contact with the dead (cf. 19: 3; Lev. 21: 10–15).

viii. The Judgment of the People (16: 41–50)
The next day the people blame Moses and Aaron for the death of the rebels (41). This shows how widespread the dissatisfaction was. The cloud covers the tent of meeting and the glory of the Lord appears again (42; cf. v. 19). There has been no mention of the glory being removed from the tabernacle; so the meaning appears to be 'that at this time the cloud covered it in a fuller and much more conspicuous sense,

just as it had done when the tabernacle was first erected (cf. 9: 15; Exod. 40: 34) and that at the same time the glory of God burst forth from the dark cloud in a miraculous splendour' (Keil). God threatens to **put an end to them** (45; cf. v. 20). Moses and Aaron fall on their faces (cf. v. 22) but Moses no longer intercedes for them. 'All the motives which he had hitherto pleaded, in his repeated intercession that this evil congregation might be spared, were now exhausted' (Keil). So Moses commands Aaron to take his censer and make atonement for the people, for the plague had already begun (46, 47). This appears to be the only Scripture where atonement is directly linked with incense; cf. Lev. 16: 12, 13, which Moses probably had in mind. So the plague was stayed by the ministry of Aaron which had been despised (50). There was no repentance on the part of the people but there was the high-priestly intercession and, so to speak, the invocation of the mercy of the Day of Atonement. (On the nature of this and other OT plagues see A. R. Short, *The Bible and Modern Medicine* (1953), pp. 47 ff.)

ix. Twelve Staffs Placed Before the Ark (17: 1–7)
God had already shown who His priest was in ch. 16 by an act of judgment but it was proper that the people should also be convinced by a gracious miracle which better suited the ministry of Aaron.

Twelve rulers' **staffs**, were to be taken from the leading men, one for each tribe. Some have thought that there were twelve apart from Levi's but the text rather indicates that there were twelve altogether and so it is probable that the two tribes of Joseph were reckoned together, as in Dt. 27: 12. The names of the leaders were placed on the staffs (cf. Ezek. 37: 16). Aaron's name was on the staff of Levi; for although he was descended from the second son (cf. Exod. 6: 16–20), he was the priestly head and he needed to be vindicated against the rebellious members of the tribe. The staffs were to be placed in the Tent of Meeting in front of the Testimony, i.e. in front of the tables of testimony which were within the ark (cf. Exod. 25: 21), **where I meet with you** [plural] (4). The people did not have access into the most holy place but the Lord met them there in the person of Moses (cf. Exod. 25: 22) and of Aaron, when he entered with the incense and the blood of the sacrifices (cf. Lev. 16 and Exod. 29: 42, 43; 30: 6, 36). Note especially Exod. 29: 42: 'Where I will meet with *you*, to speak unto *thee*' (RV). He met the people through their representative. The staff of the man the Lord chose was to sprout and thus the grumbling would cease (5; cf. 16: 5, 7).

Some have made a distinction between the staff of Moses and the staff of Aaron as if the former was the staff of power and authority and the latter the staff of grace but a comparison of verses in Exodus shows that there was only one staff (cf. 4: 2, 17; 7: 10–12; 17: 5; 7: 19).

x. Aaron's Staff Sprouts (17: 8–9)

The next day it was found that Aaron's staff had **sprouted**. The short interval plainly indicates a miracle. And not only did it sprout; it **had budded, blossomed and produced almonds**. Thus Aaron's priesthood was vindicated as not only lawful but vital and fruitful. There is no indication from what kind of tree Aaron's staff had originally been taken.

xi. The Staff Put Back (17: 10–11)

The staff of Aaron is put back **in front of the Testimony** (cf. v. 4) as a sign to the rebels. The exact place it was put is not indicated. The matter is further discussed by F. F. Bruce at Heb. 9: 4 (*NICNT*).

xii. The People Despair (17: 12, 13)

God's judgment and the words of v. 10 fill the people with fear. The answer to the question of v. 13 is given in ch. 18. Aaron and his sons are 'to bear the responsibility for offences against the sanctuary' (1). Cf. v. 5. On these two verses the *Pulpit Commentary* says: 'These are the last wailings of the great storm which had raged against Moses and Aaron, which had roared so angrily at its height, which was now sobbing itself out in the petulant despair of defeated and disheartened men, cowed indeed, but not convinced, fearful to offend, yet not loving to obey'.

VII. PRIESTLY LEGISLATION (D) (18: 1–19: 22)

i. Priests and Levites (18: 1–32)

(a) The Duties of Priests and Levites (18: 1–7)

A summary is given of the duties of priests and Levites, partly to confirm the office of Aaron and partly to allay the fears of the people (cf. 17: 12, 13). **1. Aaron** and his **sons** and his **fathers' family** (i.e. the Kohathites who had charge of the sacred furnishings in contrast with the Levites in v. 2) are to **bear the responsibility for offenses against the sanctuary**. Defilement was unlikely to arise through acts of ignorance and carelessness, through the sins of the people (cf. 1: 51; Exod. 28: 38) and through the sins of the priests as they discharged their duties. The meaning is not so much that they are to be punished for these things, although punishment could be involved (cf. Lev. 10: 1–3), but they will take the guilt upon themselves (cf. Exod. 28: 38) and make atonement by the sacrifices, especially those on the Day of Atonement (cf. Lev. 16: 16 ff.); cf. also the priest's eating of the sin offering (Lev. 6: 25–30). Cf. also Lev. 10: 17. The remaining Levites are also to **join** Aaron and **assist** him (2). There is an allusion here to the meaning of

Levi (= 'joined'; cf. Gen. 29: 34 and Num. 1: 50–53; 3: 5–8, 21–37; 4: 1–33; 8: 19, 23–26). They are to perform their duties **before the Tent of the Testimony** (2), i.e. in the court but they are not to come near the furnishings or the altar under pain of death (3; cf. 4, 7, 22 and 1: 51; 4: 15). No one else is to assist the priests (4). The priests are to attend to the duties of the sanctuary and the altar or God's anger will again be upon the people (5; cf. 1: 53; 8: 19; 16: 35; Lev. 10: 2). The Levites are a gift to the priests (6; cf. 3: 9; 8: 16, 19) and their own priesthood is 'a service of' (7, Hebrew), i.e. an office bestowed on them by God's favour. **7. inside the curtain:** Heb. *pārōketh*, regularly used for the second curtain, that separating the holy of holies from the holy place. The verse is a summary of the priestly functions from the altar of burnt offering to the most holy place, where Aaron alone ministered. If anyone else came near to perform priestly duties, he would be put to death (cf. 2 Chr. 26: 17, 18).

(b) The Portion of Aaron and his Sons (18: 8–20)

The priests are to receive the portion of the offerings which is not burnt in the fire (8). **portion:** cf. Lev. 7: 35; NEB, 'allotted portion'. For the eating of the grain offering cf. Lev. 6: 16, the sin offering Lev. 6: 26 and the guilt offering Lev. 7: 6. The portion was to be regarded **as holy** (10). The males were to eat them (cf. Lev. 6: 18, 29; 7: 6). The most holy offerings could be eaten only by the priests alone in a holy place (see Lev 6: 16, 26; 7: 6); others could be eaten in any ceremonially clean place by the priests and their families (cf. vv. 11, 31, and Lev. 10: 12–14). The priests are also to have **whatever is set aside from the gifts of all the wave offerings** (11). The wave offerings are the breast and the thigh (cf. v. 18 and Exod. 29: 26–28; Lev. 7: 29–34; 10: 14, 15). These were to be eaten by the women as well as the men; **everyone in your household who is ceremonially clean may eat** them (11). The reference is to members of the household, not strangers or hired servants (cf. Lev. 22: 10–13). The firstfruits of oil, wine and grain are to be given to the priests (12; cf. Dt. 18: 4). **12. finest:** commonly translated 'fat', *e.g.*, in Gen. 45: 18 and Leviticus, *passim*. The firstfruits of all other produce, *e.g.*, from fruit-trees, are also to be given to them. This is in addition to Lev. 23: 10, 17. The amount is not specified. Cf. Exod. 22: 29; 23: 19; Lev. 23, 24; 26: 2, 10; 2 Chr. 31: 5; Neh. 10: 36–38; 13: 5, 12; Prov. 3: 9; Ezek. 44: 30. Verse 13b is like 11b. **14. Everything . . . that is devoted . . . is yours:** 'dedicated to God by vow or otherwise, provided it be such a thing as might be eaten or consumed by use; for the vessels or treasures of gold and silver . . . , devoted or dedicated . . . , were not the priests' but were appropriated to the uses of the temple' (M. Poole). **15. The first offspring of every womb . . . that is offered to the LORD, is yours:** cf. Exod. 13: 12; Lk. 2: 23. The firstborn both of man and the unclean beasts are to be redeemed. Originally the firstborn of a donkey had to be redeemed with a lamb or destroyed (cf. Exod. 13: 13; 34: 20) but later a commutation was accepted (cf. Lev. 27: 27). The redemption price of the firstborn of man at a month old is to be five shekels (16). Cf. Lev. 27: 6 and note at Num. 3: 44–48, where five shekels are paid for each firstborn not replaced by the Levites. The firstborn of clean beasts are not to be redeemed, for they are holy, i.e. dedicated to sacrifice (17; cf. Lev. 27: 26; Dt. 15: 19). Their flesh is to be for the priests, like the breast and thigh of the fellowship offerings (18; cf. v. 11). But Dt. 15: 19, 20 says that it was to be eaten by the offerers and their household (cf. also 12: 17, 18 and 18: 3). It would seem that the law was later modified. The offerings of v. 19 are the gifts mentioned in vv. 9–18. **19. an everlasting covenant of salt:** i.e. an indissoluble covenant. Salt was often used to ratify covenants. Cf. Lev. 2: 13; 2 Chr. 13: 5. Aaron did not enter the land but in v. 20 he is the representative of the priesthood. The priests, like the Levites, are to have no inheritance in the land, because God is their inheritance and their portion. Cf. vv. 23, 24; 26: 62; etc. In possessing God they possessed all things (cf. Exod. 19: 5).

(c) Tithes for the Levites (18: 21–24)

Instead of an inheritance in the land the Levites are to receive tithes for their service in the tabernacle (21). Tithes are mentioned in Gen. 14: 20; 28: 22 but now for the first time they are assigned to the Levites for their support, cf. Lev. 27: 30–33; Dt. 14: 22, 23. Some have seen a contradiction in Dt. 14: 22–29, where for two years the tithes are eaten by the worshippers at the sanctuary, the Levites being invited, and in the third year they are devoted at home to the Levites, orphans, widows and aliens. This festal or sacred tithe has been interpreted since post-exilic times as a second or additional tithe. Allowances must be made for the disturbed conditions of the Conquest, which are envisaged in Deuteronomy. The subject is discussed in *ISBE*, article 'Tithe', pp. 2987, 2988. If any other Israelites **go near the Tent of Meeting** (to do service), **they will bear the consequences of their sin and will die** (22; cf. v. 32; 1: 51; Lev. 19: 17; 22: 9). The duties connected with the Tent of Meeting are to be discharged by the Levites (23; cf. 1: 53 and 8: 19).

(d) A Tithe of the Tithe (18: 25–32)

Just as the people give one tenth to the Levites, so the Levites are to give **a tenth of that tithe** (26), to Aaron (28), i.e. to the priesthood (cf.

v. 20). Their offering is to be counted as though they had produced the grain and the wine themselves (27; cf. v. 30). The sacred portion which the Levites set aside for Yahaweh is to be from the best of the gifts that they receive (29). **31. anywhere:** cf. v. 10. If they fail to give a tithe of the best they receive to the Lord, they will **be guilty in this matter** and die, because they are profaning the holy things by keeping for themselves what should be given to the priests.

ii. The Ordinance of the Red Heifer (19: 1–22)

The chapter deals with the ordinance of the Red Heifer. We do not know when the ritual was inaugurated but it is generally associated with the mortality of 16: 49, as purification by methods hitherto prescribed would no longer be sufficient; but cf. note on 8: 7. For other references to defilement by the dead see on ch. 5: 1, 2. The treatment in P. Fairbairn's *Typology of Scripture* (1854), vol. 2, pp. 355 ff., is very illuminating.

A modern rabbinic opinion is, 'This ordinance is the most mysterious rite in Scripture' (J. H. Hertz). It is clear that its main purpose is to bring home to Israel that the whole of life is tainted with sin, which finds its expression in death. This is done in a way that would least disrupt daily life.

The chapter should be compared with the ritual of the heifer in Dt. 21: 1–9 and with the laws of uncleanness in Lev. 11–15. Cf. also Heb. 9: 13, 14.

(a) The Red Heifer (19: 1–10)

2. red heifer: a female is prescribed for the ceremony in Dt. 21: 3 and for the sin offering for one of the common people in Lev. 4: 28 but this is the only case where the colour of the victim is prescribed. **without defect:** AV and RV give 'without spot', which could refer to the colour—the rabbis said that two hairs of another colour would disqualify—but 'without defect' or 'perfect' is generally preferred. This is further defined by (without) **blemish. that has never been under a yoke:** cf. Dt. 21: 3; 1 Sam. 6: 7—either because a yoke would be regarded as spoiling it or, more probably, because it must be dedicated to God and must not be used for profane purposes. The heifer was to be given to Eleazar the priest rather than to Aaron because the high priest would have been defiled and not able to perform his priestly functions (cf. Lev. 21: 11, 12). The rabbis saw in the heifer a form of atonement for the golden calf, in which sin Aaron had been involved. The heifer was to be slaughtered **outside the camp** in the presence of Eleazar (3). NEB gives 'to the east of it'. The reference to **the camp** presupposes the desert as the place of the original observance. The flesh of certain sin offerings was burnt outside the camp, after some rites had been performed at the altar (cf. Lev.

4: 7–12; 8: 14–17; 9: 9–11) but here the whole is taken outside the camp. Eleazar sprinkles some of the blood seven times towards the Tent of Meeting (4) but he is apparently still outside the camp (vv. 3, 7). This is doubtless to indicate that cleansing comes ultimately from God and the mercy-seat in the tabernacle. 'Seven times' suggests completeness. **6. cedar wood, hyssop and scarlet wool:** the cedar has been thought to signify freedom from corruption, the scarlet life and health and the hyssop to have medicinal qualities (cf. v. 18). Other suggestions have been made and we cannot speak with certainty. In Lev. 14: 4 the use is different. With v. 7 cf. Lev. 11: 25, 28, 40; 15: 5, 6, etc. Contact with the heifer was defiling because it was a sin offering (8; cf. Lev. 16: 26). A man who is ceremonially clean is to place the ashes outside the camp (cf. v. 3) in a clean place (cf. Lev. 4: 12; 6: 11) **for use in the water of cleansing** (cf. 8: 7 and Zech. 13: 1). **it is for purification from sin (9):** literally 'it is sin'. AV and RV give 'a sin offering' (cf. v. 17). The virtue of the ashes derived from their connection with the sin offering. Contact with the ashes renders the person who gathers them unclean (10); 'for the defilement of the people, previously transferred to the heifer, was regarded as concentrated in the ashes' (*Speaker's Commentary*). **a lasting ordinance:** i.e. the foregoing regulations are perpetually binding. The only occasion mentioned for its use is in ch. 31: 19–24. The Mishna stated that only seven red heifers had been offered. The last red heifer was killed in the high-priesthood of Ishmael ben Phiabi (AD 58–60). **the aliens:** cf. 9: 14.

(b) **Personal Uncleanness (19: 11–13)**
Any man rendered unclean by touching the dead body of a man is unclean for seven days (11). He must **purify** (= 'unsin'; so also in vv. 13, 20; cf. 8: 21) **himself** on the third and seventh days (12). Uncleanness also lasted seven days for the birth of a male child (cf. Lev. 12: 2), for menstruation and other discharges (cf. Lev. 15: 13, 19, 24, 28). According to Keil, 'the selection of the third and seventh days was simply determined by the significance of the numbers themselves' (cf. *NBD* article 'Number' by R. A. H. Gunner). The defilement caused by touching the dead body of a beast lasted only until the evening (cf. Lev. 11: 24). The death of a man was the direct result of sin and so the sense of separation from God was more marked: hence the longer duration of the uncleanness. If a person neglected the rite, he defiled the tabernacle and was cut off from Israel (cf. note at 9: 13), because the water of cleansing (cf. v. 9) was not **sprinkled on him** (13; cf. v. 20). They would defile the tabernacle by being associated with it in their uncleanness (cf. Lev. 15: 31).

(c) **Uncleanness in the Tent or in the Open (19: 14–19)**
A dead body in a tent renders everything in the tent and even open containers unclean (14, 15). The latter would be polluted by the air (cf. Lev 11: 32). The rabbis equated tent with house and so LXX substituted 'house' for 'tent'. A priest would be allowed to come in only for a near relative and the high priest not at all (cf. Lev. 21: 1–4; 10–12). In the open contact with a dead body, a bone or a grave renders unclean (16). To avoid this uncleanness tombs were later painted white (cf. Mt. 23: 27; Ac. 23: 3). The rites of cleansing are described in vv. 17–19. **17. the burned purification offering:** i.e. the heifer that had been burnt for the removal of sin. The laws of purity are the most complicated part of rabbinic legislation.

(d) **Summary (19: 20–22)**
With v. 20 cf. v. 13; with v. 21 cf. vv. 8, 10, 19. **21. lasting ordinance:** cf. v. 10. The reference seems to be to the fundamental principle that the water of cleansing must be used to remove all ceremonial defilement. Verse 22 appears to refer to the uncleanness from a dead body (11, 16) rather than v. 21, for 'it is unreasonable that he who immediately touched the defiling thing should be no more and longer unclean than he who touched that person only' (M. Poole).

VIII. FROM KADESH TO THE PLAINS OF MOAB (20: 1–22: 1)
i. Kadesh, the Death of Miriam (20: 1)
The people came to Kadesh in **the Desert of Zin** (1; cf. 34: 3, 4) in the first month. It has generally been assumed that this is the first month of the fortieth year. The chapter reads like a succession of events, culminating in the death of Aaron (vv. 23–29), in the fifth month of the fortieth year (cf. 33: 38). The omission of the year is probably accidental. Some however have held that it was the first month of the third year and that v. 1 refers back to the journey of 12: 16. There is no suggestion in 33: 36–39 that Kadesh was their headquarters for thirty-eight years. It is simply mentioned as one of the forty-two stations and Dt. 2: 14 implies a general departure of the people from Kadesh at the beginning of the thirty-eight years. The reference to **the whole . . . community** (1, 22) is emphatic (cf. 13: 26 and 14: 1) and may indicate a re-assembling of the congregation which had been scattered in the wilderness. The organized camp may have consisted chiefly of Levites. **Kadesh** or 'Kadesh Barnea' (cf. 34: 4), originally En Mishpat (cf. Gen. 14: 7), was a well, a settlement and a desert region (cf. Ps. 29: 8), apparently in the north east of the Sinai peninsula on the edges of the desert of Paran and Zin. See K. A. Kitchen, article 'Kadesh', in *NBD*. **stayed:**

consistent with a shorter or a longer time spent at Kadesh. From 33: 38 it might be inferred that it was three or four months. Mourning for Miriam and waiting for the reply from Edom (14) may have caused the delay. Nothing is said of the circumstances of Miriam's death. If the fortieth year is in view, she must have been about a hundred and thirty years of age (cf. Exod. 2: 4 and Dt. 34: 7).

ii. Grumbling of the People (20: 2–5)
2. no water: there is no mention of a lack of water during their first stay at Kadesh. There may have been a temporary shortage of supply.
3. when our brothers before the LORD: the reference seems to be to those who perished in the rebellion of Korah (chs. 16, 17) 'by the Lord's visitation' (Knox).

iii. 'Speak to that Rock' (20: 6–13)
Moses and Aaron withdraw from the murmuring congregation and go to the Tent of Meeting, where they fall face down (cf. 14: 5) and **the glory of the LORD** appears (cf. 14: 10). Moses is commanded to take his staff and speak to the rock which will **pour out its water** (8). However, instead of speaking to the rock, he **struck the rock twice with his staff** (11). Nevertheless the water gushed out but, because of their sin, Moses and Aaron are not allowed to bring the assembly into the promised land (12). The passage should be compared with the incident in Exod. 17: 4–7, which took place not long after they came out of Egypt. The similarities between the two events are much smaller than the differences, and there is no justification for regarding them as duplicates of the one event. There is nothing remarkable that there should be a recurring lack of water in the desert (cf. Exod. 15: 22; Num. 21: 4, 5). There is no suggestion of violence done to the rock by its being struck. Moses was to strike the rock with the staff with which he struck the Nile (cf. Exod. 17: 5, 6). Plainly violence was not in question when he turned the waters of the Nile into blood (cf. Exod. 7: 19, 20). The reason for striking the rock was 'that the people might acknowledge him afresh as the possessor of supernatural and miraculous powers' (Keil). There is no real parallel with the incident described by C. S. Jarvis, *Yesterday and Today in Sinai* (1931), p. 156, where a sergeant of the Sinai Camel Corps caused water to flow from a rock by digging furiously with his spade. A. Edersheim, *Bible History*, vol. 1 (1875), pp. 186, 187, says that it seems strange that Moses should have been directed to take the rod if he were not to use it, but the staff was the symbol of the divine power. In Exod. 17: 6 Moses smote the rock but in vv. 9–12 he simply held the staff: the presence of the staff guarded the people against mistaking the true source of the miracle.

Paul refers to these incidents in 1 C. 10: 4.

Some have thought that he was following the rabbinical tradition that a literal rock followed the people but Paul speaks of a supernatural or spiritual Rock, i.e. Christ. If he had the rabbinical legend in mind, he applies it in his own way.

In what did the sin of Moses lie? The explanation is given in v. 12 and in Ps. 106: 33. He did not believe in God, to honour Him as holy (older EVV 'sanctify') in the eyes of the people. It seems that he did not believe that God would work a miracle without smiting the rock and so he missed a wonderful opportunity to demonstrate the holiness of God; for 'Jehovah's holiness is His supremacy, His sovereignty, His glory, His essential being as God. To sanctify Jehovah, therefore, is to assert or acknowledge or bring forth His being as God, His supreme power and glory, His sovereign claim' (*ISBE*, article 'Santification', p. 2682). 'By the waters of Meribah they angered the LORD, and trouble came to Moses because of them; for they rebelled against the Spirit of God, and rash words came from Moses' lips' (Ps. 106: 32, 33). It is plain that Moses' words were rash. He was not so wrong in what he said as in the manner in which he said it. If the people were not actually rebels at this moment, they were close to rebellion: and in saying **must we bring you water out of this rock?** (10) Moses was repeating what the Lord said to him in v. 8, and the **we** is not emphatic. It would seem that he was convinced that God would not give them water, for they did not deserve it, and that thereby he failed to honour God by giving a wrong concept of His character.

In spite of Moses' disobedience the rock yielded its water abundantly and **the LORD . . . showed himself holy among them** (13; cf. v. 12), but Moses and Aaron were forbidden to lead the people into the promised land (12), showing that blessing is not always a proof of divine approval. 'Trouble came to Moses because of them' (Ps. 106: 32; cf. Dt. 1: 37; 3: 26; 4: 21). 'Had the unbelief of Moses gone unpunished, the people would have been hardened in their own transgression. For their sakes therefore it was impossible to overlook it' (Dummelow's *Commentary*). It is not clear in what Aaron's guilt lay. Evidently he went along with Moses, without seeking to restrain or disapprove.

iv. Edom (20: 14–21)
Israel had refused the chance of invading Canaan from the south, the shorter and easier way, so God sent them the long way round (Dt. 2: 1). They asked Edom to give them a passage through their land; cf. Dt. 2: 2–6, where the proposal is attributed to the Lord's command and Jg. 11: 17, where Moab is included, and Num. 21: 21, 22, where a similar request is later made to Sihon, king of the

Amorites. The Edomites were descendants of Esau, the brother of Jacob (cf. Gen. 25: 20–28; 33: 1–17; Dt. 23: 7): hence **your brother Israel** (14). **16. an angel:** cf. Exod. 14: 19; 23: 20; 32: 34, but perhaps 'a messenger', i.e. Moses. They promise to drink no water without paying for it (16, 19). 'From the scarcity of water in the warm climates of the East, the practice of levying a tax for the use of the wells is universal' (Jamieson's *Commentary*). They will go along **the king's highway** (17): 'the name given to the direct road running from the Gulf of Aqabah to Syria, east of the Dead Sea and Jordan Valley. The route was in use between the 23rd and 20th centuries BC, being marked along its length by Early Bronze Age settlements' (D. J. Wiseman, in *NBD*). Edom, however, was churlish and refused to allow them to pass.

From Dt. 2: 4–6, 29 it appears that the Edomites, who repelled the Israelites on the western frontier, became alarmed when they appeared on their eastern or weaker side and actually traded with them. According to Dt. 2: 5 the Israelites were forbidden to contend with the Edomites because Yahweh had given the hill country of Seir to Esau as a possession but the king would probably not know or believe that.

v. The Death of Aaron (20: 22–29)
The people came to Mt. Hor, where **Aaron died** (28). His priestly garments (cf. Exod. 28) were placed upon Eleazar by Moses (cf. Lev. 8: 7–9), and he died **on top of the mountain** in the sight of all the congregation (contrast the death of Moses, Dt. 34). The people mourned for Aaron for thirty days (cf. Gen. 50: 3; Dt. 34: 8). Aaron was a hundred and twenty-three years old when he died (cf. 33: 39). His death stands in contrast with the unending priesthood of our Lord (cf. Heb. 7: 23, 24). Dt. 10: 6 says that he died at Moserah (cf. 'Moseroth', Num. 33: 30). Mt. Hor is an unidentified peak near Kadesh; the traditional site near Petra is impossible. **23. near the border of Edom:** perhaps to distinguish this mountain from the northern Mt. Hor in 34: 8. **24. gathered to his people:** cf. Gen. 25: 8, 17; 35: 29; 49: 29, 33; Num. 20: 26; 27: 13; 31: 2. The words are an intimation of life after death. In 27: 13 they are used of Moses who was buried alone and in Gen. 49: 33 and 50: 1–6 they are clearly distinguished from burial. **rebelled:** the very charge Moses had made against the people (10).

vi. Victory over the King of Arad (21: 1–3)
It is uncertain when this military operation took place. H. M. Wiener argued strongly that this section was misplaced; certainly it would have come better before ch. 13. For **Arad** cf. 33: 40; Jos. 12: 14; Jg. 1: 16. It appears to have been near the frontier of Judah and Simeon. For **Negev** cf. 13: 17. **Atharim** is the name of

a place at or near Hazazon-tamar. **3. Hormah:** from the same root as 'destroy' in vv. 2 and 3 (i.e. utterly 'devoted' to God). Cf. 14: 45; Dt. 1: 44; Jos. 12: 14. The victory here contrasts with the defeat of 14: 45. For Jg. 1: 17 see comments *ad loc. ICC*, however, suggests with good reason that the word is here used of the district.

vii. The Venomous Snakes (21: 4–9)
4. the people grew impatient on the way: This was one of the hottest and most difficult parts of the wanderings; in addition they had their backs turned on Canaan and might be resentful because they could not pass through the land of Edom. The new generation was not very different from the old and they complained **against God and against Moses**, describing the manna as **miserable food** (5; cf. 11: 6). **6. Then the LORD sent venomous snakes** among the people. They were so called because of the inflammation caused by their bite. The Arabah is said to abound with deadly snakes. The Hebrew word is *serāphîm*, 'burning ones' (cf. Isa. 6: 2; 14: 29; 30: 6). Verse 7 contains the first real confession in the book. But instead of the snakes being removed, a means of healing is provided in the form of a **bronze snake** resembling the snakes which had bitten them (cf. 1 Sam. 6: 5; Jn 3: 14, 15). Looking at the bronze snake is a picture of faith (8, 9). Later the bronze snake became a fetish and was destroyed by Hezekiah (cf. 2 Kg. 18: 4). In Wis. 16: 6 f. the bronze snake is called 'a token of deliverance . . . for he that turned toward it was saved, not by what he saw but by thee, the Saviour of all'.

viii. Various Encampments (21: 10–15)
In 33: 41–43 two intermediate stations are mentioned, 'Zalmonah' and 'Punon'. **10. Oboth:** the identification of the sites is uncertain. **12. the Zered Valley:** usually identified with Wadi el-Hesâ, which runs into the Dead Sea from the south-east. From Dt. 2: 14 ff. it is evident that it was an important stage in their journey for now they had left the wilderness of the wandering. **13. Arnon:** a river running into the east side of the Dead Sea opposite En Gedi (cf. Dt. 3: 12, 16; Jg. 11: 18 22, 26). 'The importance of the river is confirmed by the number of forts and bridges which are found there, the latter being mentioned by Isaiah (16: 2)' (R. J. Way, *NBD*). Nothing is otherwise known of **the Book of the Wars of the LORD** (14); it was evidently a collection of victory songs. **Waheb** ('watershed') seems to be the name of a town or fortress and **Suphah** the district. **15. Ar:** cf. v. 28; and probably Dt. 2: 36, 'the town in the gorge'. Before 'Waheb' we may have to understand a subject and verb, such as 'We (or the LORD) took'.

ix. The Song of the Well (21: 16–18a)
They come to a place where they find a well.

Hence the place was called **Beer** (16); cf. Beer-sheba. It does not say that the people dug it at this time. Verse 18 suggests that it had a history. The song itself may have been well known. The **scepters** and **staffs** may express the authority of the princes and nobles or there may be an allusion to a custom whereby the sheikh of a clan symbolically opened a well with his staff (cf. *ICC*).

x. Mattanah to Pisgah (21: 18b–20)
The people journey east to Moab to the north of the Arnon but the location of the places is uncertain (cf. *NBD*). **20. wasteland:** a term used especially of the arid land bounding the lower Jordan and east of the Dead Sea. 'Many scholars take Pisgah as the name applying to the mountain range in which the Moab plateau terminates to the west, the top or "head" of Pisgah being the point in which the ridge running out westward from the main mass culminates' (*ISBE*). A comparison with 33: 45–49 will show fewer stations than 21: 13–20.

xi. Sihon, King of the Amorites (21: 21–26)
Just as Israel had asked Edom to allow them to pass through their territories (cf. 20: 14–21), so they ask Sihon, king of the Amorites, and are met with a similar refusal. Previously they had been forbidden to contend with Edom, Moab and Ammon (cf. Dt. 2: 5, 9, 19) but this time they are told to 'begin to take possession of it and engage him in battle' (cf. Dt. 2: 24–37). **23. Jahaz:** site unknown; cf. Jos. 13: 18; 21: 36. In this battle Israel was victorious, took possession of his land and settled in all the cities of the Amorites (24, 25). **24. fortified:** RSV, JB, follow LXX, Vulg. in reading 'Jazer'. 'The statement in v. 25 that Israel settled in all the towns of the Amorites is somewhat anticipatory of the history itself, as the settlement did not occur till Moses gave the conquered land to the tribes of Reuben and Gad for a possession' (Keil). Sihon's capital was **Heshbon** (25), about sixteen miles east of the Jordan. Cf. 32: 37; Jos. 13: 26. **Sihon** had captured the territory of the Moabites as far south as the river **Arnon** (26). His territory extended as far north as the Jabbok (24; cf. Gen. 32: 22). Five princes of the Midianites were subject to him (cf. Jos. 13: 21). **24. to the sword:** cf. Exod. 17: 13; Dt. 13: 15; 20: 13. In Hebrew this phrase is literally 'to the mouth of the sword', from which it has sometimes been deduced that the blade of the sword was regarded as a kind of 'mouth'. But the idea is, rather, 'according to the capacity of the sword'. **25, 26.** 'The reference to **cities** in these areas is important in determining the date of the Exodus. There had been very few urban settlements in Transjordan for many centuries before about 1350–1300 BC' (J. A. Thompson, *NBC³*).

xii. A Ballad (21: 27–30)
27. poets: 'ballad singers' (RSV) 'bards' (NEB). The ballad seems first of all to celebrate the victory of the Amorites over the Moabites and then that of the Israelites over the Amorites. 'The children of Israel invite the Amorites to return and fortify the demolished fastness of their king, Sihon (27), exalting the monarch's prowess against Moab (28, 29), in order to bring into stronger light the valour of Israel, beneath which the invincible Amorite and his stronghold had for ever fallen' (30) (W. R. Smith, quoted in *ICC*, p. 300). **28. fire:** the conflagration of war. **29. Chemosh:** the chief god of the Moabites (cf. 1 Kg. 11: 7, 33), worshipped also by the Ammonites (cf. Jg. 11: 24). **30. Dibon:** four miles north of the river Arnon (cf. 32: 3, 34, etc.). **Medeba** was six miles south of Heshbon (cf. Jos. 13: 9, 16).

xiii. The Amorites and Og, the King of Bashan (21: 31–35)
While Israel was encamped, Moses sent spies (cf. 13: 2) to **Jazer** and the Israelites captured its surrounding settlements (cf. v. 25) and drove out the Amorites. From 32: 35 we learn that Jazer must have been destroyed. The country round about was very fertile and suitable for cattle and so attracted the tribes of Reuben and Gad (32: 1). Turning to the north, they slew **Og**, an Amorite king of Bashan, **at Edrei** and **took possession his land** (33–35). He was one of the giant race of Rephaites; Edrei was one of his two royal cities (cf. Dt. 3: 11; Jos. 13: 12). There was another Edrei in the territory of Naphtali (cf. Jos. 19: 37). Og's kingdom contained sixty fortified cities (cf. Dt. 3: 4, 5). His territory was given to the half tribe of Manasseh (cf. Dt. 3: 13), though it seems to have been only gradually settled. At this time Israel conquered the land of the Amorites from the Arnon Gorge to Mt. Hermon (cf. Dt. 3: 8). **Bashan** is often mentioned in Scripture as a place of extreme fertility (cf. Dt. 32: 14, etc.). In *HDB*, article 'Bashan', G. A. Smith wrote that the name was applied to territory north of Gilead and seems generally to have meant the whole of the most northerly of the three great divisions of Eastern Palestine. He also pointed out that the so-called 'giant cities of Bashan' of which J. L. Porter wrote (1877) are not older than the rise of Greek civilization in these parts.

xiv. Arrival on the Plains of Moab (22: 1)
1. the plains of Moab: cf. 26: 63; 31: 12, etc. It is a flat plain east of Jordan. This is the first biblical reference to Jericho.

IX. BALAAM (22: 2–24: 25)
With ch. 22 the last sections of the book commence, containing events that happened on the plains of Moab and the instructions given by Moses before the people entered the land.

Chapters 22–24 constitute a unique section, presenting us with a remarkable picture of a man called Balaam, who lived in Pethor in Mesopotamia or Aram (cf. 23: 7 and Dt. 23: 4), which was the original home of the ancestors of Israel. Although he lived outside the fold of Israel, he had some knowledge of the true God (cf. 22: 8, 13, 18, 19, etc., where he speaks of 'Yahweh') and is called in the NT 'a prophet' (2 Pet. 2: 16); but he also used sorcery and divination (cf. 22: 7; 23: 23; 24: 1 and Jos. 13: 22). R. K. Harrison (*Introduction to the Old Testament*, p. 630) has produced evidence to show that Balaam was a typical Mesopotamian diviner. How the oracles came into the hands of the Israelites is a matter of conjecture.

i. Balak Sends for Balaam (22: 2–6)
Although he had nothing to fear from Israel (cf. Dt. 2: 9)—but of that he was doubtless ignorant—Balak, king of Moab, was greatly afraid (cf. Exod. 15: 15) and sent messengers to Balaam asking him to curse the people of Israel. The Moabites and the Midianites are seen working together, which is not surprising, as they were neighbours (cf. Gen. 36: 35). Both are mentioned in vv. 4 and 7; v. 8 speaks of the 'Moabite princes' and 31: 8 of the 'kings of Midian' (cf. Jos. 13: 21). **4. who was king of Moab at that time:** 'As a post-Mosaic reference, either the single sentence was added, or it reflects the fact that the whole account was inserted in post-Mosaic times. Nowhere in chapters 22 to 24 do we have the usual formula, "God said unto Moses", found in every other chapter. This section, like the Book of Job, may have originated outside of Israel' (*Wycliffe Bible Commentary*, pp. 140, 141). **5. Pethor:** identified with Pitru on the river Sagur, near its junction with the Euphrates (cf. *NBD*). 'The journey from Pitru to Moab would be something like 400 miles and would occupy over twenty days, and from any place on the Euphrates the time-distance would not be appreciably less. The four journeys of the story would therefore have required about three months' (*ICC*). **6. those you bless are blessed . . . :** Balak had no doubt of the reality of Balaam's powers.

ii. The Elders and Balaam (22: 7–14)
Verse 7 shows that Balaam made a trade of his powers (cf. 2 Pet. 2: 15). He invites the elders to stay with him for the night. Perhaps he expects God to speak to him in a dream (cf. Gen. 20: 3, 6). Verse 12 is quite definite and Balaam should not have needed further guidance. **13. the LORD has refused:** Balaam appears to be quite willing. He omits all reference to cursing and the reason for the prohibition. This leads them to think that he desires a higher fee.

iii. Second Deputation to Balaam (22: 15–20)

Princes **more numerous and more distinguished**, and with greater promises, are sent to Balaam but he replies that he cannot disobey **the command of the LORD**, even if Balaam were to give him **his palace filled with silver and gold** (18). Note that he speaks of the LORD **my God** (18). In spite of the definite prohibition of v. 12 Balaam asks them to stay for the night, to learn more of the Lord's mind (19; cf. v. 8). God allows him to go, provided he implicitly follows His commands (20). But why the difference between vv. 12 and 20? In v. 12 we have God's highest desire for Balaam, that he should have nothing to do with the messengers of Balak. But Balaam was not ready for that; so the prohibition to go was withdrawn but the prohibition to curse retained, so that Israel might be magnified and Balaam himself given an opportunity to learn more about God.

iv. Balaam and the Donkey (22: 21–30)
22. But God was very angry when he went: Keil inferred from the Hebrew that it was not simply the fact that he went that aroused God's anger but his frame of mind (cf. v. 32). **the angel of the LORD stood in the road to oppose him:** the 'angel of the LORD' in the OT is sometimes a divine person but hardly here (cf. Gen. 22: 11, 12; 31: 11–13). Balaam at first did not see the angel. **24. between two vineyards:** the incident may have occurred in Moab, where vineyards were common (cf. Isa. 16: 6–11). These would be separated by walls (cf. Isa. 5: 5; Prov. 24: 31). The speaking of the donkey has caused considerable perplexity. When we are told that **the donkey saw the angel of the LORD** (23), it does not read like a subjective experience. 'The majority of writers and commentators who regard the narrative as historical have correctly interpreted the narrative as referring to a miraculous occurrence' (*ICC*, p. 335). Some have suggested that God conveyed the brayings of the donkey to Balaam in the form of human speech. This may point in the right direction, but, according to the narrative, the miracle was not in the ears of Balaam but in the mouth of the donkey (cf. 2 Pet. 2: 16).

v. Balaam and the Angel (22: 31–35)
Balaam's eyes are opened and he sees the angel. **32. your path is a reckless one before me:** cf. note on v. 22. The angel is there to thwart Balaam's mission, if necessary by death (33), and he warns him to **speak only what I tell you** (35; cf. 20). **34. I have sinned:** no deep contrition is observable.

vi. Balak Meets Balaam (22: 36–40)
36. town: NEB, GNB emend to Ar ('*îr* to '*ār*) (cf. 21: 15). **the Arnon:** cf. 21: 13. Balaam still does not give the reason why he cannot curse the people. In v. 38 Balaam uses *Elōhîm*, not Yahweh, in speaking with Balak. The use of the two names is a feature of this section and

has been held to indicate composite authorship but it would be quite natural for Balaam to use at times the name that specially indicated Israel's God and at other times the name that simply indicated the divine being. Cf. Albright's comment below. **39. Kiriath Huzoth:** identity uncertain. The sacrifices (40) were not thank offerings for Balaam's happy arrival but supplicatory offerings for the success of the undertaking before them. **40. princes:** Heb. *sārîm*, great ministers of state, not members of the royal family; cf. v. 21.

vii. The Oracles of Balaam (22: 41–24: 25)
In 1944 *The Journal of Biblical Literature*, vol. 63, published a paper by W. F. Albright, entitled 'The Oracles of Balaam', which was an outstanding contribution to the subject. The following extracts are of interest. 'The Greek text differs repeatedly from the Massoretic tradition in its use of divine names, and no attempt to distribute the prose matter between J and E has succeeded without a suspiciously large amount of emendation of divine names' (p. 207). 'There is nothing in the matter of the poems which requires a date in the tenth century or later for original composition' (p. 227). 'The Balû'ah Stele, from about the twelfth century BC, proves that there was already a well organized monarchy of some kind in Moab' (p. 227). 'The name [Balaam] is characteristic of the second millennium, and has survived in at least two place names, one of which is known to go back to the fifteenth century BC' (p. 232). 'We may infer that the Oracles preserved in Num. 23–24 were attributed to him from a date as early as the twelfth century, and that there is no reason why they may not be authentic, or may not at least reflect the atmosphere of his age' (p. 233).

(*a*) **Bamoth Baal (22: 41)**
Balak takes Balaam to Bamoth Baal ('High Places of Baal'), doubtless an ancient shrine, but chosen because it was the most convenient place for viewing the camp of Israel. It was necessary to see the people in order to be able to curse them. **he saw part of the people:** (literally 'edge', 'extremity') it appears that Balak brought Balaam nearer each time so that he might see the danger. Some however take the word here to refer to the far extremity and believe that he saw less each time so that their influence on him might be less; so NEB and apparently JB. The Hebrew word could refer to either extremity (cf. 23: 13). Chapter 24: 2, where he sees the actual encampment, seems to support the former view.

(*b*) **The Sacrifice (23: 1–6)**
'The nations of antiquity generally accompanied all their more important undertakings with sacrifices, to make sure of the help and protection of the gods; but this was especially the case with their ceremonies of adjur-

ation' (Keil). Balaam asks Balak to build **seven altars**, not as a mark of polytheism, but the number seven was sacred among many ancient peoples. The **offering** (3, 6) is literally a burnt offering, an ancient form of sacrifice that goes back to the patriarchs (cf. Gen. 8: 20). From v. 2 it appears that Balak the king acted as priest as well as Balaam. Balak is to **stay beside** his **offering** (3), 'as in God's presence as one that offers thyself as well as thy sacrifices to obtain His favour' (M. Poole). **3. Perhaps the LORD will come to meet with me:** from 24: 1 many have inferred that Balaam expected the Lord to communicate with him by means of omens. The expression 'is a technical one for going out for auguries or for a divine revelation' (Keil). Balaam spoke to God about the altars and sacrifices (4), apparently so that God might accept them and allow him to curse Israel but they were ignored and he was given a message to pass on to Balak.

(*c*) **Balaam's First Oracle (23: 7–10)**
7. Aram: 'In the OT Aram includes the northern part of Mesopotamia, Syria as far south as the borders of Palestine and the larger part of Arabia Petraea' (*HDB*). **the king of Moab:** cf. 22: 4 and Albright's note above. **the eastern mountains:** cf. Gen. 29: 1. The eastern mountains are here in contrast to the mountains of Moab (9). Balaam is not able to curse Israel because they are the object of God's favour and distinct from all other peoples (8, 9). **9. do not consider themselves one of the nations:** 'that has not made itself one with the nations' (NEB). This separation was not merely an outward thing. As Exod. 33: 16 and Lev. 20: 24, 26 show, it was primarily a separation to the LORD. When they lost their separation to the LORD, they also lost their outward separation; cf. Dt. 30: 3, where they are seen scattered among all nations on account of their disobedience. **10. the dust of Jacob:** cf. Gen. 13: 16; 28: 14. **the fourth part of Israel:** Israel was divided into four camps (cf. ch. 2). It is possible that Balaam could see only one, cf. 22: 41. But the meaning of the Hebrew word is uncertain. Traditionally it has been associated with the word meaning 'fourth part' or 'quarter' but the meaning may be 'dust clouds' (JB, 'cloud') as in Albright. LXX gives 'peoples' and NEB 'hordes'. **Let me die the death of the righteous** (*yᵉshārîm*), **and may my end be like theirs!:** 'righteous' is in the plural and would refer to the nation of Israel, God's Jeshurun (cf. Dt. 32: 15; 33: 5, 26). He would like to die like a pious Israelite, crowned with God's blessing. The **end** seems to refer to prosperity in his children; the thought of blessing beyond the grave could hardly have been in Balaam's mind. But he did not live the life of the righteous and therefore did not die like them (cf. 31: 8 and Jos. 13: 22).

(d) The Top of Pisgah (23: 11–17)

Balak takes Balaam to the top of Pisgah. It may have been the same spot from which Moses viewed the land (cf. Dt. 3: 27; 34: 1). **13. you can see . . . you will see:** taken by Keil as present, referring to the view upon Bamoth Baal (cf. 22: 41). So too JB. Certainly the top of Pisgah in Dt. 3: 27 gives an extensive view.

(e) Balaam's Second Oracle (23: 18–24)

As Balak was already standing (17), **Arise** (18) must be a command to rouse himself (NEB 'Up'). In v. 19 Balaam tells Balak not to expect God to **change his mind** (cf. 1 Sam. 15: 29). Scripture sometimes speaks of God changing his mind (older EVV 'repenting') (cf. Jer 18: 7–10) but this is God's 'unmovedness while others move and change. The divine finger ever points to the same spot but man has moved from it to the opposite pole' (A. Edersheim). **21. No misfortune is seen in Jacob, no misery observed in Israel:** so translated the words appear to mean that no misfortune or trouble is to come to Moab from Israel. The two Hebrew words, however, which are found together in other places (*e.g.* Ps. 10: 7; 90: 10; Job. 5: 6; Hab. 1: 3), may be taken in a moral sense, especially the first. AV and RV give 'iniquity' and 'perverseness', NEB 'iniquity and mischief', JB 'evil and suffering'. We suggest that this meaning is the right one. Israel is viewed as the holy nation to which the blood of the covenant has been applied (cf. Exod. 19: 5, 6; 24: 8). It is the ideal Israel rather than the actual that is in view. This interpretation seems to be confirmed by the second part of the verse: **The LORD their God is with them; the shout of the King is among them.** The people are seen in covenant fellowship with Yahweh. 'Shout' is the same word used in 29: 1 and Lev. 23: 24 of the blowing of trumpets; God is being acclaimed as king. **22. the wild ox:** 'probably the antelope, living wild in the scrub-covered hill-country with the goats and gazelle. It was among the animals which the Israelites were allowed to eat (Dt. 14: 5)' (A. R. Millard in *NBD*); but most identify it with the extinct wild ox. **23. There is no sorcery against Jacob, no divination against Israel:** 'The first word has to do with observance of birds or of omens generally and the second word refers to the casting of lots, *e.g.* by arrows (Ezek. 21: 21)' (N. H. Snaith, *NCentB*).

(f) The Top of Peor (23: 25–30)

Balak takes Balaam to another place, to **Peor** (28), in the hope that he may be more successful. Peor is 'a mountain somewhere to the north of the Dead Sea and opposite Jericho, described as looking toward the desert, but its location is not certainly identified' (*NBD*). Cf. 25: 3.

(g) Balaam's Third Oracle (24: 1–9)

Balaam gives up his sorcery (1; cf. 23: 23) and looks towards the desert where Israel is encamped on the plains of Moab (cf. 22: 1). He sees Israel **encamped tribe by tribe** (2; cf. ch. 2) and **the Spirit of God came upon him**. It is noteworthy that it is only after he has abandoned his auguries that it is said that the Spirit of God came upon him, as if he were a true prophet of Israel. In 23: 5, 16, it is said simply that the Lord put a message in his mouth. For other examples of unworthy men prophesying cf. 1 Sam. 19: 20–24; Jn 11: 15. **3. oracle:** a word generally associated with the name of Yahweh. **sees clearly:** the word occurs only here and in v. 15 and its meaning is uncertain. Some have thought that his eyes were closed in a state of ecstasy but cf. v. 4. JB gives 'the man with far-seeing eyes'. **4. God:** Heb. *'El.* Cf. 23: 22, 23. **Almighty:** Heb. *Shaddai*, a name by which God was known to the patriarchs and especially found in Job (cf. Gen. 17: 1; Exod. 6: 3; Job 5: 17, etc.). The tenses in v. 4 may suggest a custom. **falls prostrate:** cf. Ezek. 1: 28; Dan. 8: 17, 18; Rev. 1: 17. **whose eyes are opened:** we judge that it is the inward eye that is referred to (cf. Eph. 1: 18). **6. like valleys:** NEB choosing a rarer sense of the word, translates: 'like long rows of palms'. **gardens:** cf. Isa. 1: 30; 44: 4; 58: 11. **aloes:** well-known for their fragrance (cf. Ps. 45: 8). **the LORD planted:** like the garden of Eden (Gen. 2: 8). **7. Water will flow from their buckets:** 'The nation is personified as a man carrying two pails overflowing with water . . . that leading source of all blessings and prosperity in the burning East' (Keil). **greater than Agag:** it appears that **Agag** was a general name for the king of the Amalekites, as Pharaoh was for the king of the Egyptians. LXX renders 'Gog' (cf. Ezek. 38: 1). Cf. v. 20 and 1 Sam. 15: 8. For **king** cf. Gen. 17: 6; 35: 11. The first part of v. 8 repeats 23: 22, the second part leads on to the lion of v. 9. **arrows** probably represent weapons of war generally.

(h) Balak Dismisses Balaam (24: 10–14)

Balak strikes his hands together, which was a mark of anger, contempt or despair (cf. Job 27: 23; Lam. 2: 15; Ezek. 21: 17; 22: 13), and bids Balaam return home. Balaam reminds Balak of the words of 22: 18 and expresses his intention of returning home but first of all he will utter another oracle telling of Israel's dealings with Moab in the last days. 'last days'/'**days to come**' (NIV), older EVV 'latter days'—expressions constantly used in later biblical literature of the times of the Messiah, but earlier times may be included as pointing forward to those times.

(i) Balaam's Fourth Oracle (24: 15–24)

The oracle goes beyond Moab. It is divided into four parts, commencing with the words **he uttered his oracle** (15, 20, 21, 23). The first deals with Moab and Edom, the second with Amalek, the third with the Kenites and the fourth with great world powers. 'We have here a series of prophecies, commencing with the appearance of the Messiah and closing with the destruction of Anti-Christ. To this there is no parallel in Scripture, except in the visions of Daniel' (A. Edersheim, *Bible History*, vol. 1, 1875, p. 31). Verses 15 and 16 are the same as vv. 3 and 4 except for the words **who has knowledge from the Most High:** cf. Gen. 14: 19–22 and Dt. 32: 8. Balaam claims that he has had access to the secret counsels of God (cf. Job 15: 8).

(*i*) *A Star and a Sceptre* (*17–19*)
The primary reference in these verses may be to David, who defeated Moab and subdued the Idumeans (cf. 2 Sam. 8: 2; 11–14; Ps. 60: 8) but, as David points forward to great David's greater son, the prophecy of the star and the sceptre point also to Him (cf. Gen. 49: 10; Ps. 45: 6; Mt. 2: 2; Rev. 2: 28; 22: 16). 'This interpretation was so widely spread among the Jews, that the pseudo-Messiah who arose under Hadrian, and whom even R. Akiba acknowledged, took the name *Bar Cochba* (Son of a Star), in consequence of this prophecy' (Keil). NEB is probably correct in interpreting **scepter** (lit. 'rod') as 'comet'. Moab is naturally mentioned first because of Balak's desire to curse Israel and then Edom, their southern neighbour because they were also antagonistic (cf. 20: 20, 21). **17. foreheads:** or 'corners' (of the head): cf. Jer. 48: 45. NEB 'squadrons' is little more than a guess. If the translation **sons of Sheth** is accepted, the reference seems to be to an unknown tribe, akin to the Moabites. Some Jewish commentators understood it of the sons of Seth, the son of Adam, i.e. mankind, but that is inappropriate. Better mg 'noisy boasters' (cf. Jer. 48: 45) or NEB 'sons of strife', 'by which, according to the analogy of Jacob and Israel (v. 17), Edom and Seir (v. 18), the Moabites are to be understood as being men of wild, warlike confusion' (Keil). **Seir** (18) or Mt. Seir was the old name of Edom (cf. Gen. 32: 3; 36: 8; Dt. 2: 1). In Moses' time Israel was not allowed to fight against Edom (cf. 20: 21; Dt. 2: 4, 5) but the future is to be different. In v. 19 Balaam is still thinking primarily of Edom but the words may have a wider reference to Israel's dominion generally and to the destruction of all their enemies. NEB gives 'the last survivor from Ar shall he destroy' (see comment on 22: 36) but Moab has been dealt with in v. 17. Albright translated similarly but he assumed a transposition and placed the words after v. 17.

(*ii*) *Amalek* (*20*)
From Peor Balaam could see the country of the Amalekites which lay to the south (cf. 13: 29). **first among the nations:** Keil took it to mean that Amalek was the first of the nations to attack Israel (cf. Exod. 17: 8–16)—a doubtful interpretation. Balaam predicts ultimate ruin for Amalek, **first** and **end** being contrasted.

(*iii*) *The Kenites* (*21, 22*)
As the translation stands, the meaning appears to be that, in spite of their apparent security, the Kenites will be ruined and carried into captivity by the Assyrians or just possibly the Ashurim (Gen. 25: 3). Another translation, however, supported by the Palestinian Targum and Keil, says: 'Kain shall not be wasted until Asshur shall carry him away captive'. It is pointed out that the Kenites we read of in Judges were descendants of Hobab and friendly to Israel (cf. Num. 10: 29; Jg. 1: 16; 4: 11). So the words are taken to predict long-continued safety for them in contrast with the Amalekites. In **nest** there is a play on words, *qēn* in Hebrew meaning 'nest' (cf. Ob. 4; Hab. 2: 9). **set in a rock:** we cannot be sure what mountain fastness is referred to. The heights of En Gedi have been suggested, also Sela, later Petra. 'The name means "smith", and the presence of copper south-east of the gulf of Aqabah, the Kenite-Midianite region, confirms this interpretation' (J. A. Motyer, *NBD*).

The reference to **Asshur** in vv. 22 and 24 has been much disputed. It has been commonly believed to refer to Assyria, which is the Greek form of Asshur. Albright eliminated the reference by taking the word as a verb, 'I gaze', doubtless influenced by his desire to confine the references to people who were involved in this area in the 13th century B.C. NEB eliminates it in v. 22 but not in v. 24. Some have referred it to a local tribe (cf. Gen. 25: 3) but, as N. H. Snaith remarked, 'this tribe is too small here' (*NCentB*); this is true of v. 24, but not v. 22. M. Noth accepted the reference to Assyria but dated the words much later than Moses. If, however, the element of genuine prophecy is admitted, which Balaam's discourses certainly profess to be, we see no reason why the reference to Assyria should not stand, but there is some uncertainty in the interpretation of these oracles.

(*iv*) *Distant Judgments* (*23, 24*)
Balaam sees such universal judgment that he wonders whether anyone will be left alive (23). JB has 'The Sea-people gather in the north'; NEB renders: 'Ah, who are these assembling in the north . . . ?' This is based on a repointing and an emendation. **24. Kittim:** cf. Gen. 10: 4. 'The name seems to have come to apply to the whole island of Cyprus (Isa. 23: 1, 12) and then in a more general way to the coastlands of the E. Mediterranean. In Daniel's fourth vision . . . "the ships of Chittim" must be Rome' (T. C. Mitchell, *NBD*; cf. Dan. 11: 30). Tagum Onkelos renders 'Romans' here; the Vulg. has 'triremes from Italy'. In Macc. 1: 1; 8: 5 Kittim is applied to Greece. **Eber**, from which 'Hebrew' is derived, is thought to be a

poetical designation of Israel (cf. Gen. 10: 21, 25; 11: 14 ff.). The prophecy therefore may look forward to the overthrow of the Assyrians by the Greeks and Romans, the affliction of Israel from the same powers and the subsequent destruction of the Greek and Roman Empires.

It is noteworthy that v. 23 does not say that Balaam looked upon Asshur as he looked on Amalek (20) and the Kenite (21), for the Assyrian was in the distant future. The LXX reference to Og, taken up by JB, is also strange. NEB, following LXX, gives 'invaders' instead of **ships** (24).

(j) Balaam and Balak Part (24: 25)
25. returned home: 31: 16 suggests that he did not do so immediately but remained among the Midianites. The words may mean simply that he set off homewards.

X. ON THE PLAINS OF MOAB (25: 1–27: 23)
i. Israel and the Daughters of Moab (25: 1–18)
(a) Baal of Peor (25: 1–5)
At Shittim or Abel Shittim (cf. 33: 49), the last stage before Israel crossed the Jordan, the people were seduced into the immoral worship of the gods of the Moabites (2). Only one god, **Baal of Peor**, is mentioned in vv. 3 and 5. Baal means 'master' and the references seems to be to Chemosh, the chief god of the Moabites (cf. 21: 29). The actual mode of the execution is not indicated. **before the LORD:** cf. 2 Sam. 21: 6, 9, i.e. that he may see justice done. **5. Israel's judges:** cf. Exod. 18: 25, 26.
(b) Phinehas (25: 6–9)
Phinehas, the grandson of Aaron (7) executed summary judgment upon an Israelite and a Midianite woman—the Midianites and Moabites were working together (cf. 22: 4)—who, blatantly went into a **tent** (8), i.e. the inner part of the tent, evidently with immoral intent, while the people were weeping because of the anger of the Lord. **8. the plague:** not actually mentioned in the previous passage (cf. 14: 37; 16: 48–50). From Dt. 4: 3 we learn that all the males involved were destroyed and from Dt. 2: 14 ff. we would infer that they all belonged to the new generation, for they had passed the brook Zered (cf. Num. 21: 12). 'Upon this act of Phinehas and the similar examples of Samuel (1 Sam. 15: 33) and Mattathias (1 Macc. 2: 24), the later Jews erected the so-called "zealot right", *jus zelotarum*, according to which any one, even thought not qualified by his official position, possessed the right, in cases of any daring contempt of the theocratic institutions, or any daring violation of the honour of God, to proceed with vengeance against the criminals' (Keil). Phinehas, indeed came to be revered as the archetypal zealot for God. In Jos.

22: 30, 31 he is seen in a more conciliatory mood.
(c) A Covenant of Peace (25: 10–13)
Because Phinehas turned away God's anger (1 1; cf. Ps. 106: 23; Jer. 18: 20), God gave him His **covenant of peace.** For 'peace' cf. 6: 26. God gave to Phinehas a pledge of peace, a peace secured through the possession of a perpetual priesthood with its atoning sacrifices (cf. Jg. 20: 28). 'In accordance with this promise, the high-priesthood which passed from Eleazar to Phinehas continued in his family, with the exception of a brief interruption in Eli's days, until the time of the last gradual dissolution of the Jewish state through the tyranny of Herod and his successors' (Keil).
(d) The Guilty Ones (25: 14, 15)
The guilty pair were people of high standing. The man was **Zimri** whose father was one of the heads of the tribe of Simeon (cf. 1: 4). It is noticeable that the Simeonites declined in the second census more than any other tribe (cf. ch. 26). The woman was **Cozbi daughter of Zur**, one of the chiefs of Midian (15, 18). For Zur cf. 31: 8; Jos. 13: 21.
(e) Judgment on the Midianites (25: 16–18)
The Midianites are to be punished (cf. ch. 31). The Moabites are not mentioned; they had been motivated by fear, but there was no reason for Midianite involvement. It may also be inferred from the fact that it was the Midianites that Balaam counselled (cf. 31: 16) that they were the chief agents in corrupting Israel. They may also have had greater knowledge, with men like Jethro among them.
ii. The Second Census (26: 1–65)
From here to the end of the book we have preparations for entering the land. In this chapter there is a second census. There are similarities to the census of ch. 1 but there are also marked differences. The new generation is numbered, partly for military purposes (2), but also in preparation for entering upon their inheritance. Hence the various clans are mentioned and instructions are given for the division of the land among the different tribes (52–56). The military side is much more prominent in ch. 1.

Some tribes increased, including the three of the camp of Judah. Judah itself remained the largest (cf. Gen. 49: 8–12). Some decreased, including the three of the camp of Reuben. The greatest increase was in Manasseh (but see note on 1: 20 *seq.*) and the greatest decrease in Simeon (cf. 25: 14), and the total decrease was eighteen hundred and twenty. Cf. note on 1: 20–46.

The chapter should be compared with Gen. 46, Exod. 6 and 1 Chr. 4–8. In some cases names have been omitted, probably because the families had become extinct, and in a number of cases there are variations in the spelling. Some of these may have arisen in the course of transmission, others may be due to common variations in spelling of many names.

(a) **A New Census to be Taken (26: 1–4)**
Moses and Eleazar are commanded to take a new census **after the plague** (i.e. that mentioned in 25: 8, 9), which would account for the decrease in some of the tribes. They are to be counted from twenty years old and upward, **who are able to serve in the army of Israel** (2). **3. plains of Moab:** cf. 22: 1. **4. The Israelites . . . who came out of Egypt:** if it is objected that the people numbered on this occasion did not come out of Egypt, cf. 23: 22; 24: 8.

(b) **The Twelve Tribes (Excluding Levi) (26: 5–51)**
For the rebellion of Korah, Dathan and Abiram (9, 10) cf. chs. 16, 17. For **Korah** and **the line of Korah** (11) cf. note on 16: 31–35. **12. The descendants of Simeon:** cf. note on 25: 14. It was the only tribe not blessed by Moses in Dt. 33 and in the land it received a portion taken from Judah (cf. Jos. 19: 1). For **Er** and **Onan** (19) cf. Gen. 38: 1–10. **Makir** (29) had other children (cf. 32: 39, 40; 36: 1; 1 Chr. 7: 14–19). **33. Zelophehad:** cf. 27: 1 ff.; 36: 2 ff. Of **Dan** only a single clan is named, **Shuham** (42, 43). The mention of **Serah**, daughter of Asher (46), is noteworthy.

(c) **Division of the Land (26: 52–56)**
The land is to be **distributed by lot** (cf. Prov. 16: 33) and the inheritance named after the tribe. The size is to be according to population. From Jos. 15 and 16 we see that the portions for Judah, Ephraim and half Manasseh were made on a different basis.

(d) **The Levites (26: 57–62)**
The Levites are to be numbered separately, because they have no special inheritance in the land (cf. 18: 24) and from a month old and upward (62), as in 3: 39. For the service of the Levites cf. chs. 2–4. There are eight families in 3: 17–20, here five. **58, 59. Amram . . . Jochebed:** 'It is not certain that he [Amram] was literally the son of Kohath, but rather his descendant, since there were ten generations from Joseph to Joshua (1 Chr. 7: 20–27), while only four are actually mentioned from Levi to Moses for the corresponding period. Moreover the Kohathites at the time of the Exodus numbered 8,600 (Num. 3: 28), which would therefore have been an impossibility if only two generations had lived. It seems best to regard Amram as a descendant of Kohath and his wife Jochebed as a "daughter of Levi" in a general sense' (ISBE, article 'Amram'). But the genealogies and the chronological problems linked with them represent one of the most difficult areas in OT interpretation. **61. Nadab and Abihu:** cf. Lev. 10: 1, 2. With vv. 63–65 cf. 14: 28–32; Dt. 2: 13–15.

iii. The Daughters of Zelophehad (27: 1–11)

(a) **The Request (27: 1–4)**
For **Zelophehad** cf. 26: 33. According to 26: 51–53 the land was to be divided among the sons but Zelophehad had daughters only and they requested that they might have an inheritance. Without it they would have had no means of support or a marriage portion. **2. the entrance to the Tent of Meeting:** the place where justice was administered (cf. 11: 16, 26; 12: 4, 5). The point of v. 3 is that their father had died a natural death: he had not been in the rebellion of Korah and there was no reason why the divine displeasure should be visited on his descendants (cf. 16: 32, 33; Exod. 20: 5).

(b) **The Answer of the Lord (27: 5–11)**
Moses brought the matter **before the LORD**, i.e. in the tabernacle (cf. Exod. 25: 21, 22; Num. 7: 89) and it was decreed that, where there were no sons, the daughters should inherit or, if there was no daughter, his brothers, his father's brothers or his nearest relative (cf. Jos. 17: 3–6; Job 42: 15). See also ch. 36 for a modification. For the relation of this law to the levirate law cf. NBD, p. 789. See J. Weingreen, *From Bible to Mishna* (1976), pp. 86 ff.

iv. Joshua to Succeed Moses (27: 12–23)

Moses is told to go to a mountain of the Abarim range, apparently the range of which Nebo was the highest point (Dt. 32: 49). There he must die on account of the rebellion in the Desert of Zin **at the waters of Meribah** (cf. 20: 7–13). This command was not carried out immediately, for Moses is still commanding the people at the end of the book. It would appear that it was repeated in Dt. 32: 48–52. For its fulfilment see Dt. 34. **13. gathered to your people:** cf. 20: 24.

Moses' reaction is magnificent. He is not resentful or occupied with self but concerned only that the people should have a worthy leader to guide them. So the Lord commands him to appoint Joshua to succeed him. Joshua had long been associated with Moses (cf. 11: 28) and was with Caleb, the other faithful spy, one of the two numbered in ch. 1 who entered the land (cf. 26: 64, 65). **16. the God of the spirits of all mankind:** cf. 16: 22. **17. go out and come in:** the words refer to every-day life, whereas **lead them out and bring them in** 'signifies the superintendence of the affairs of the nation, and is founded upon the figure of a shepherd' (Keil). Cf. Jn 10: 3, 9. **18. without shepherd:** cf. 1 Kg. 22: 17; Mt. 9: 36. **in whom is the spirit:** cf. Gen. 41: 38; Dan. 5: 14. Spiritual capacity is intended rather than the person of the Spirit. There is no definite article in the Heb. ; cf. NEB. **lay your hand on him:** cf. Dt. 34: 9. As Moses handed on the priestly authority to Eleazar (20: 28), so he hands on the civil authority to Joshua. Moses is to commission Joshua in the presence of Eleazar **and the entire assembly** (19), in order that they might witness the ceremony and acknowledge Joshua as leader. Joshua is to have some of Moses' **authority.** He shall **stand before** ('appear before', NEB) **Eleazar the priest,** who is to learn God's mind by means of the **Urim** (21). The Urim is used for the Urim and Thummim; cf. note on Exod. 28: 30. Joshua is plainly inferior to Moses. He has some of his authority but he depends on the high priest, whereas Moses had immediate access into God's presence. Joshua failed to seek that counsel in Jos. 7: 3 and 9: 14, 15. The LORD does speak directly to Joshua in Jos. 20: 1. **21. at his command:** they were to follow the directions of the high priest after he consulted the Urim.

XI. PRIESTLY LEGISLATION (E) (28: 1–30: 16)
i. Seasonal Offerings (28: 1–29: 40)

In chs. 28, 29 we have a repetition, with supplementary additions, of instructions concerning offerings and feasts. These had doubtless been largely neglected during the thirty-eight years of wandering (cf. Introduction to ch. 33) and so they are now repeated to the new generation in view of entering the land (cf. Dt. 12: 8, 9). Special attention is given to the amount or number of the offerings. The offerings and feasts are treated in more detail elsewhere (cf. Exod. 12; Lev. 1–9; 16; 23. Cf. also Ezek. 45; 46). A different view from the above is mentioned in R. K. Harrison's *Introduction to the Old Testament,* p. 621.

(a) **The Offerings of the LORD** (28: 1, 2)
2. the food: cf. Ezek. 44: 7. God is viewed as feeding upon the offering; cf. Lev. 3: 11. There is thus communion between God and man. **my offerings made by fire** (2, 6, 8, 13, 19, 24): this is a general term to indicate the sacrifices which ascended by fire upon the altar (cf. Lev. 2: 2, 11, 16). It was also applied to the incense upon the bread of the Presence (cf. Lev. 24: 7). **an aroma pleasing to me:** cf. 15: 3–10.

(b) **The Daily Offering** (28: 3–8)
A lamb—NEB consistently with modern usage renders 'ram' throughout, for it was a male and a year old—is to be offered morning and evening **as a regular burnt offering** (cf. Exod. 29: 38–42; Lev. 6: 19–23). The offerings are to be accompanied by a grain offering of a tenth of an ephah of fine flour mixed with a fourth of a hin of olive oil (4, 5, 8; cf. Lev. 2 and Exod. 27: 20). For the **drink offering** (7, 8, 9, 10, 14, 15, 24, 31) cf. 15: 3–10. **7. sanctuary:** according to Exod. 30: 9 no drink offering was to be poured on the altar of incense; so it appears that it was poured on the bronze altar. **fermented drink:** 'may here be used exceptionally with reference to wine'

(ICC); cf. note on 6: 3. In Exod. 29: 40 a fourth part of a hin of wine is used with the daily sacrifice.

(c) **Sabbath Offerings (28: 9, 10)**
Sabbath offerings are here prescribed for the first time. For the 'grain offering' cf. 15: 3 ff.
(d) **Monthly Offerings (28: 11–15)**
Monthly offerings are also prescribed for the first time, much larger than the daily offerings and **a sin offering** as well as the **burnt offering** (15). The sin offering was for sins not expiated during the previous month. No mention is here made of the blowing of trumpets at the beginning of months (cf. 10: 10), as the emphasis is on the offerings. Eventually the first day of the month (i.e. the new moon) grew more and more into a feast-day, trade was suspended (Am. 8: 5), the pious Israelite sought instruction from the prophets (2 Kg. 4: 23), many families and households presented yearly thank-offerings (1 Sam. 20: 6, 29), the devout abstained from fasting (Jdt. 8: 6); it is frequently referred to by the prophets as a feast resembling the sabbath (Isa. 1: 13; Hos. 2: 13; Ezek. 46: 1). It is still observed, but not as a Sabbath, except in the seventh month.
(e) **The Passover (28: 16–25)**
The annual feasts are in two groups, those belonging to the spring and early summer and those of the autumn; cf. Exod. 12; Lev. 23; Num. 9: 1–14. Passover, Pentecost and Tabernacles were associated respectively with the barley, wheat and fruit harvests. No offerings are presented for the Passover itself but for the Feast of Unleavened Bread which followed. The offerings are the same as for the new moon and are repeated on each of the seven days (24). **24. the food for the offering . . . by fire:** cf. v. 2. The details of the offerings had not been prescribed before but the command for a sacred assembly, with no regular work on the first and seventh days, appears in Lev. 23: 7, 8.
(f) **Feast of Weeks (18: 26–31)**
The Feast of Weeks is also called the Feast of Harvest (cf. Exod. 23: 16), Pentecost (cf. Ac. 2: 1) and, as here, the **day of firstfruits.** Cf. also Lev. 23: 15–21; Dt. 16: 10. The offering made at the Feast of Weeks was the same as for the New Moon and the Feast of Unleavened Bread and was for one day only. 'The festal burnt offering and sin offering of this one day were independent of the supplementary burnt offering and sin offering of the wave loaves appointed in Lev. 23: 18 and were to be offered before these and after the daily morning sacrifice' (Keil).
(g) **The Blowing of Trumpets (29: 1–6)**
Chapter 29 deals with three feasts held in the seventh month of the sacred year (later called Tishri) or the first month of the civil year (our September–October). On the first day, still called New Year's Day (Rosh ha-Shanah),

there was to be a sacred gathering with abstinence from **regular work**. It was a day to blow the trumpets (cf. Lev. 23: 23–25). Trumpets were blown at every new moon (cf. 10: 10) but it was a special mark of this day. Actually the word 'trumpet' is not used here. NEB gives 'a day of acclamation' but the Jews have understood it to refer to the blowing of trumpets, the *shōphār*, made of ram's horn, being generally used rather than the *hªsosᵉrah* of Num. 10, which has never been used in the Synagogue. There were special offerings (2) in addition to the offerings of the new moon and the daily offerings (6; cf. 28: 11, 3).

(h) The Day of Atonement (29: 7–11)
On the tenth day there was to be a sacred assembly. They were to deny themselves and do no work (7). **7. deny yourselves:** cf. Lev. 16: 29; 23: 27. This was probably always interpreted as fasting (cf. Isa. 58: 3, 5; Ac. 27: 9). The burnt offerings of v. 8 appear to be in addition to the two rams of Lev. 16: 3, 5, just as the sin offerings of v. 11 are an addition to the sin offering of atonement of Lev. 16 and the daily offerings (cf. 28: 3). These offerings are the same as for the Feast of Trumpets (vv. 1–6). More details of the Day of Atonement are found in Lev. 16; 23: 26–32. It was always kept strictly as a Sabbath.

(i) The Feast of Tabernacles (29: 12–38)
The Feast of Tabernacles commenced on the fifteenth day and lasted seven days (12). On the first day there was a sacred gathering (12) and on the eighth **an assembly** (35; cf. Jn 7: 37); NEB gives 'closing ceremony'. On both days there was abstinence from **regular work** (cf. v. 1 and Lev. 23: 39). The eighth day 'only belonged to the Feast of Tabernacles as far as the sabbath rest and holy meeting of the seventh feast day were transferred to it; whilst, so far as its sacrifices were concerned, it resembled the seventh new moon's day and the day of atonement and was thus shown to be the octave or close of the second festal circle' (Keil).

A larger number of burnt offerings was appointed for this feast than for any other, because, as the feast of ingathering at the end of the year, when the fruit of their labour had been gathered in, it specially reminded them of God's goodness (cf. Exod. 23: 16). There is no explanation for the unique numbers ordered.

(j) Subscription (29: 39, 40)
The above offerings on behalf of the congregation are in addition to any offerings presented by individuals. Cf. 15: 3, 8; Lev. 22: 18, 21. Verse 40 in the Hebrew commences ch. 30.

ii. Laws Concerning Vows (30: 1–16)
Vows might concern the offering of some gift on the altar, abstaining from particular articles of meat or drink, the observance of private fasting or doing something for the service of God beyond what was required. Cf. Lev. 7:

16; 27: 1–13; Num. 6; Dt. 23: 21–23.

The heads of the tribes are addressed, as they would be responsible to exercise judgment in these cases (1). **2. a vow:** Heb. *neder*, the general word. A **pledge** ('*issār*) is found in OT only in this chapter, although the verb is often found meaning 'to bind'. The noun '*issār* was used by the Jews in a negative sense. NEB renders 'an oath to abstain from something'. With v. 2 cf. Ec. 5: 2–5.

Four distinct classes are mentioned: (i) a young woman in her father's house (3–5). If the father hears of (cf. v. 5) her vow and says nothing to her, her vow will be binding, but if her father disapproves of it on the day that he hears of it, it will not be binding **and the LORD will release her**, i.e. absolve her from the obligation and remit the punishment that non-fulfilment would incur. (ii) The second case (6–8) appears to be that of a married woman who vowed while she was still single. Her husband can annul it, once he hears of it, if he acts at once. **6. rash promise:** cf. Lev. 5: 4; Ps. 106: 32, 33; Prov. 20: 25. (iii) The third case (9) is of a widow or a divorced person. All her vows are binding. (iv) The fourth case is that of a wife in her husband's house (10–15). Here too the husband by his silence allows the vow and by expressing disapproval he disallows it. **13. deny herself:** cf. 29: 7. The meaning of v. 15 is that if a husband has allowed a vow by his silence (14) and later disallows it forcibly, he will bear the penalty due to his wife (cf. Lev. 5: 1; 4 ff.). All male vows, except those made by an under-age boy, are valid.

XII. ON THE PLAINS OF MOAB (continued) (31: 1–32: 42)
Chapter 31 describes the vengeance that was executed upon the Midianites (cf. ch. 25, especially vv. 16–18). Some verses, *e.g.* 7, 17, may give the impression that the Midianites were completely destroyed but, as they were powerful later (cf. Jg. 6), it appears that there were Midianites in other areas also. They were essentially nomadic.

i. The War Against Midian (31: 1–12)
'God's great care was to *avenge the Israelites* (2) and Moses' chief desire was to *avenge God* rather than himself or the people.' (M. Poole). **gathered to your people:** cf. 20: 24. **4. a thousand:** cf. 1: 16. The reference is probably to a military unit, approximately a thousand. **6. Phinehas:** for the choice of the high priest's son cf. 19: 3. It was not normal for a priest to be in charge of the army and it would seem that Phinehas was not chosen as commander but as inspirer; cf. Dt. 20: 2. **articles from the sanctuary:** the same expression as 'the holy articles' in 4: 15. It is likely that the ark was included (cf. 1 Sam. 4: 4) even though it is not mentioned by name. Others have thought of

the Urim and Thummim but these belonged to the high priest rather than to any other priest (cf. 27: 21). Others believe that they are identical with **the trumpets for signaling**, the **and** being explanatory. The war against Midian was distinctly a holy war. **7. every man:** i.e. all the adult males (cf. v. 17). **8. the kings of Midian:** according to Jos. 13: 21 they were 'princes of Sihon' and part of his government. This may explain how they dwelt in towns (10), whereas the Midianites were normally nomadic. **Zur** was the father of Cozbi (cf. 25: 13). For **Balaam** cf. v. 16 and 24: 25. There is no evidence that he actually joined in the fighting.

ii. The Anger of Moses (31: 15–18)
Moses is angry with the soldiers for sparing the women, who had been chiefly responsible for the sin at Peor (cf. 25: 1). Moses' meekness is not weakness. The command in v. 17 is severe but it is an example of what a 'holy war' involved. The example in 1 Sam. 15: 3 is even more extreme. The question is discussed helpfully by F. D. Kidner, *Hard Sayings* (1972), pp. 40–45. The young girls are spared (18). Being not yet corrupted, they could be assimilated into Israel. 'The male children, in order to secure the extinction of Midian, are to be slain' (*ICC*; cf. v. 17).

iii. Purification (31: 19–24)
The soldiers must remain outside the camp for **seven days** in order to purify those who have come in contact with a dead body. Their garments and other objects must also be purified. Cf. 19: 11–13, 18, 19, 22. The metals are to **be put through the fire** and also **be purified with the water of cleansing** (cf. 19: 9). What cannot stand the fire is to pass through the water. For the washing of the clothes on the seventh day cf. 19: 9. The rites of these verses go beyond those of ch. 19, probably because of the sin caused by Midian.

iv. The Spoils (31: 25–47)
The spoils are divided equally between the soldiers and the congregation (27, 29, 30); cf. 1 Sam. 30: 24 f. The soldiers in turn must give one part in five hundred to Eleazar the priest (29) and the congregation must give one part in fifty to the more numerous Levites (30).

v. The Offering of the Officers (31: 48–54)
Not a man is missing (49). The Midianites may have been taken by surprise but the complete freedom from casualties can be accounted for only by divine help. So the officers voluntarily bring an offering to the LORD to make atonement for themselves (50). They doubtless feel unworthy of God's mercy. The gold is brought into the sanctuary as a memorial for the people (54), i.e. to bring the people to remembrance before the LORD (cf. Exod. 30: 16).

vi. The Two and a Half Tribes (32: 1–42)
Reuben and Gad, who had been closely associ-

ated during the desert wanderings (cf. 2: 10, 14), ask to be allowed to settle on the east of Jordan on account of the great number of their cattle. They have often been popularly (if fancifully) regarded as typical of half-hearted Christians. They do not wish to go over the Jordan, which is viewed as typifying death to self and the entrance into the believer's full inheritance (cf. Rom. 6 and Eph. 2). Certainly their subsequent history throws doubt on the wisdom of their decision. On the other hand C. H. Waller in Ellicott's *Commentary* (on Jos. 22) wrote: 'Historically this [i.e. the blaming of them] is incorrect. God delivered the land of Sihon and Og to Israel; some one must inherit it. Again, the true eastern boundary of Palestine is not the Jordan but the mountain range of Gilead, which parts it from the desert which lies beyond.'

We would only add that the promises in Exodus were always of bringing the people into the land of the Canaanites, *Amorites*, etc. (cf. Exod. 3: 8, 17; 13: 5; 23: 23; 33: 2; 34: 11), and Transjordan was partly Amorite territory (cf. v. 33). Moreover, the fact that Moses agreed must not be overlooked.

(a) The Request of Reuben and Gad (32: 1–5)
1. very large herds and flocks: the great increase was doubtless due to conquest (cf. 31: 32–39). **the land of Jazer:** 'This is the land of the Jordan and to the south of the Jabbok, the northern half of the territory between the Jabbok and the Arnon. Thus the land of Gilead here must mean the southern half of this territory, though in verse 29 it includes the whole area between the two rivers' (N. H. Snaith, *NCentB*). See also S. Merrill in *HDB*, article 'Gilead'.

In v. 1 Reuben, the elder, precedes but in the rest of the chapter Gad comes first. Possibly Gad took the lead in this request. **3. Ataroth:** different from the Ataroth of Jos. 16: 2 on the other side of the Jordan. Cf. v. 34.

(b) Moses Remonstrates (32: 6–15)
Moses tells them that, if they do not go into the promised land, they will discourage their countrymen. He compares them to their fathers who were sent to spy the land but, after seeing it, discouraged the people from entering it (7–9; cf. chs. 13, 14).

(c) The People Reply (32: 16–19)
The people reply that they will not forsake their countrymen. They intend to build pens for their livestock and cities for their women and children and then they will join in the conquest of the land. Cf. Jos. 1: 12–18; 4: 12, 13.

(d) Moses Agrees (32: 20–24)
Moses agrees to their proposal, if they do as they have promised. **20. before the LORD:** the words may mean 'before the ark of the LORD',

which was the position of Reuben and Gad on the march (cf. 10: 18–20); this meaning seems to be supported by v. 17. Note that the sin of v. 23 is primarily a sin of omission and the meaning is not that their sin will be found out, for such dereliction of duty could not be hidden, but sin is personified as about to pursue, overtake and punish them (cf. Gen. 4: 7).

(e) **The People Reaffirm Their Intention (32: 25–27)**
In v. 17 they said 'ahead of (lit. before) the people of Israel' but now they take up the words of Moses **before the LORD**.

(f) **The Command of Moses (32: 28–32)**
Moses gives command concerning the tribes to Eleazar and Joshua and the **family heads**, for they were to be responsible for dividing the land (cf. 34: 17ff.).

(g) **They Receive Their Inheritance (32: 33–42)**
Moses gives them the kingdoms of Sihon and Og and there follows a list of their cities (cf. 21: 31–35). There is no mention of a request on the part of the half tribe of Manasseh. Moses here gives them a portion east of Jordan, while the other half had a portion on the west (cf. Jos. 17: 5–18). This division of the tribe is exceptional. Joseph had inherited the birthright (1 Chr. 5: 1), and so had Manasseh, his elder son; this was the first-born's double portion. **34. built up:** i.e. 'rebuilt' or 'repaired', a common use of the word (cf. v. 38 and 21: 30). R. K. Harrison regarded this section as 'a later scribal or editorial insertion to describe the outcome of the promises made earlier in the chapter to Moses' (*Introduction to the Old Testament*, p. 617). In v. 35 **Atroth Shophan** is in contrast to Ataroth (34). **38. these names were changed:** doubtless because they were names of heathen deities (cf. Exod. 23: 13). For the opposite cf. Dan. 1: 7. **Nebo** was 'the Bab. deity Nabu, son of Bel (Marduk), and thus descriptive of the power of Babylon itself (Isa. 46: 1)' (D. J. Wiseman, *NBD*). **Baal Meon:** also known as Beth Baal Meon (cf. Jos. 13: 17) and Beth Meon (cf. Jer: 48: 23). Cf. also 'Beon' in v. 3, which may be a transcription error for 'Meon'. **39, 40. Makir:** i.e. the sons of Makir or Makirites. **41. Jair:** a son of Manasseh on his mother's side (cf. 1 Chr. 2: 21, 22); he had joined the maternal tribe (cf. Dt. 3: 4, 14). **Havvoth Jair:** 'the villages of Jair' (cf. 1 Chr. 2: 22, 23). **Kenath:** 'It is usually identified with the extensive ruins at Qanawât, some 16 miles north-east of Bozrah' (*NBD*). Cf. 1 Chr. 2: 23.

XIII. ISRAEL'S JOURNEYS (33: 1–49)

The chapter is an itinerary of the journeys of Israel from Egypt to the plains of Moab. It is purely factual, there being no mention of failure and no reference to the generation of unbelief.

With the probable exceptions of the incident of the man gathering sticks on the sabbath day (cf. 15: 32–36) and the rebellion of Korah (cf. ch. 16), this is all the information we have of the thirty-eight years of wandering.

The reference to the land in 15: 2 implies that the offerings mentioned there were not made in the wilderness (cf. 28: 6). We know that circumcision was abandoned (cf. Jos. 5: 45) and we would infer that this was so also with the Passover. On the other hand God did not forsake his people in the wilderness: they still had the manna, Moses and Aaron, the tabernacle and the cloudy pillar (cf. Exod. 13: 22; Neh. 9: 19–21; Dt. 8: 2–5).

'The number of stations, which is very small for thirty-seven years (only seventeen from Rithmah or Kadesh to Eziongeber), is a sufficient proof that the congregation of Israel was not constantly wandering about during the whole of that time but may have remained in many of the places of encampment, probably those which furnished an abundant supply of water and pasturage, not only for weeks and months but even for years, the people scattering themselves in all directions round about the place where the tabernacle was set up, and making use of such means of support as the desert afforded, and assembling together again when this was gone, for the purpose of travelling farther and seeking somewhere else a suitable spot for a fresh encampment' (Keil). Many of the places mentioned in the chapter have not been identified.

The stations may be divided as follows:
(a) Egypt to Sinai (33: 3–15)
(b) Sinai to Rithmah (Kadesh) (33: 16–18)
(c) Rithmah to Kadesh (years of wandering) (33: 19–36)
(d) Kadesh to Shittim (33: 37–49)
In v. 2 note the reference to the Mosaic authorship. **3. Rameses:** cf. Exod. 1: 11; 12: 37. 'Most scholars believe that it was situated at or near Tanis' (*NBD*). **boldly:** cf. Exod 14: 8. **4. were burying:** new light is shed on the reason for the delay of the Egyptians. **gods:** cf. Exod. 12: 12; 18: 11. **5. Succoth:** cf. Exod. 12: 37. **6. Etham:** cf. Exod. 13: 20. **7. Migdol:** this site is probably to be identified with the Migdol referred to in Jer. 44: 1 and 46: 14 and in Ezek. 29: 10; 30: 6. **8. the Desert of Etham:** called 'the Desert of Shur' in Exod. 15: 22. Cf. Gen. 16: 7; 20: 1; 25: 18. **Marah:** cf. Exod. 15: 22, 23. 'Often identified with the modern 'Ain Hawârah' (*NBD*). **9. Elim:** cf. Exod. 15: 27. 'The Biblical references suggest that Elim is situated on the west side of the Sinai peninsula' (*NBD*). **10. Red Sea:** cf. 14: 25. **12. the Desert of Sin:** cf. v. 36 and Exod. 16: 1; 17: 1. **13. Dophkah . . . Alush:** these are not mentioned in Exodus. 'Some locate Dophkah at Serabit el-Khadim, an Egyptian copper- and

turquoise-mining centre where some of the earliest alphabetical inscriptions have been discovered' (*Oxford Bible Atlas*). **14. Rephidim:** the site is uncertain. **the Desert of Sinai:** cf. 1: 1. The stations up to Sinai are the same as in Exodus except for that by the Red Sea (10) and the two mentioned in vv. 12 and 13.

16. Kibroth Hattaavah: cf. 11: 34. For the omission of Taberah cf. 11: 3. **17. Hazeroth:** cf. 11: 35. It was 'a settlement at the north end of the present-day Gulf of Aqabah' (*NBD*). Most of the towns between Hazeroth and Moseroth (30, 31) cannot be identified. **18. Rithmah:** probably Kadesh. Cf. 20: 1.

23. Mount Shepher: Conder (article 'Wanderings' in *ISBE*, pp. 3067, 3068) identifies Shepher with a site sixty miles from Hazeroth. **30. Moseroth:** cf. 20: 22 and Dt. 10: 6. **Bene Jaakan . . . Hor Haggidgad . . . Jotbathah** (31–33) are not mentioned in chs. 20, 21. Hor Haggidgad is the same as Gudgodah (cf. Dt. 10: 7). **Jotbathah:** 'a land with streams of water' (Dt. 10: 7), 'probably the modern 'Ain Tābah, about twenty two miles north of Ezion Geber' (R. F. Hosking in *NBD*). **35. Ezion Geber:** a settlement at the north end of the present-day Gulf of Aqabah (cf. *NBD*, article 'Elath'). Solomon had great smelting works there. **Desert of Zin:** cf. 13: 21. **Kadesh:** cf. 20: 1.

Note the reference to the forty years and the age of Aaron (38, 39). Cf. Exod. 7: 7; Dt. 34: 7. For the death of Aaron on Mt. Hor cf. 20: 22–27 and Dt. 32: 50. On vv. 41–44 cf. C. R. Conder, *ISBE*, p. 3069. **Punon** 'is the modern Feinan, an area rich in copper ores, where mining has been carried on at various times in the past' (J. A. Thompson, *The Bible and Archaeology*, p. 70). **45. Dibon Gad:** cf. 21: 30; 32: 34. **46. Almon Diblathaim:** 'Almon of the double cake of figs' (cf. Jer. 48: 22). **47. the mountains of Abarim:** cf. 27: 12. From v. 45 to v. 49 four stations are mentioned over a distance of about twenty-five miles, whereas in 21: 13–20 'we read of a still more gradual and cautious advance in the Amorite lands' (C. R. Conder, *ISBE*, p. 3069). **49. Beth Jeshimoth:** cf. Ezek. 25: 9. 'Probably the modern Tell Adeimeh near the north-eastern shore of the Dead Sea' (R. F. Hosking, *NBD*). **Abel Shittim**= Shittim (cf. 25: 1; Jos. 3: 1). Beth Jeshimoth and Abel Shittim cannot be certainly identified. 'We have thus considered every march made by the Hebrews, from Egypt to Shittim, by light of actual knowledge of their route. We have found no case in which the stations are too far apart for the passage of their beasts and no discrepancies between any of the accounts when carefully considered' (C. R. Conder, *ibid.*)

XIV. DIRECTIONS IN VIEW OF ENTERING THE LAND (33: 50–36: 13)

i. The Destruction of the Inhabitants of the Land and their Idols (33: 50–56)

52. drive out: i.e. by destroying them (cf. Dt. 7: 1, 2). **carved images:** cf. Lev. 26: 1. **cast idols:** cf. Exod. 32: 4. **high places:** i.e. altars and other cultic installations often, but not necessarily, on hill tops. **54. by lot:** cf. 26: 53–56. **55. barbs in your eyes:** cf. Jos. 23: 13. The warnings of vv. 55 and 56 are new. The judgment predicted in v. 56 was carried out in the Assyrian and Babylonian captivities.

ii. The Boundaries of the land (34: 1–15)

(a) The Southern Boundary (34: 3–5)
In vv. 3 and 4 there appears to be a difference between **side** and **boundary**. If there is, it may be because much of the southern boundary, running as it did, through semi-desert, was vague. Cf. Jos. 15: 1–4, where the southern boundary is the boundary of Judah. **Desert of Zin:** cf. 13: 21. **the Salt Sea:** the Dead Sea. **Scorpion Pass:** cf. Jos. 15: 3. 'An ascent on the southern end of the Dead Sea between Arabah and the hill-country of Judah, identified with the modern Naqb essāfa' (*NBD*). **Kadesh Barnea:** cf. 20: 1. **Hazar Addar:** cf. Jos. 15: 3; probably identical with Hazron, which is there separated from Addar. **the Wadi of Egypt:** cf. Gen. 15: 18; believed to be the Wadi el-Arish but see *NBD*, pp. 353–4.

(b) The Western Boundary (34: 6)
'Except for a brief occupation in Hezekiah's day (cf. 2 Kg. 18: 8) this area was never in Israel's hands' (*NBC*³). Cf. Jos. 15: 12; Ezek. 47: 20. **the Great Sea:** the Mediterranean.

(c) The Northern Boundary (34: 7–9)
7, 8. Mount Hor: 'a mountain in northern Palestine between the Mediterranean Sea and the approach to Hamath, as yet unidentified' (*NBD*). Cf. Jos. 15: 5–11; Ezek. 47: 15–17. **Lebo Hamath:** cf. 13: 21. **Zedad** and **Ziphron:** not identified. **Hazar Enan:** 'enclosure of the Spring'. It may be Banias, 'though some identify it improbably with Qaratein, the last oasis before Palmyra' (*NBC*³). 'The geographical description of the northern boundary is so indefinite that the boundary line cannot be determined with exactness' (Keil).

(d) The Eastern Boundary (34: 10–12)
'It is impossible to trace this eastern frontier. All is uncertainty until the mention of the shoulder (ridge) east of the Sea of Galilee (*Chinnereth*, harp-shaped)' (N. H. Snaith, *NCentB*). **Shepham . . . Ain:** for suggested identifications cf. *NBD* and *ISBE*. Cf. also Jos. 15: 5.

(e) The Inheritance of the Tribes (34: 13–15) Cf. ch. 32 and Jos. 14: 1–5.

iii. The Dividers of the Land (34: 16–29)

In addition to Eleazar the priest and Joshua, one leader is to be chosen from each tribe to divide the land. This would secure the impartiality of the allotment. The only one of these leaders otherwise known is Caleb.

The boundaries in this chapter should be compared with those given in other places, which sometimes include the territories over which David and Solomon ruled.

iv. Levitical Towns and Cities of Refuge (35: 1–34)

(a) The Towns of the Levites (35: 1–8)

1. On the plains of Moab: cf. 22: 1. The Levites who had no special inheritance (cf. 18: 20, 23) were to receive forty-eight towns, including six cities of refuge for the killer (6). Cf. Jos. 21 and 1 Chr. 6: 54 ff. One reason for the distribution of the Levites throughout the land was doubtless to enable them to teach the law to all the people (cf. Dt. 33: 10). The towns were to be given to them in proportion to the size of the tribes (8). The Levites were evidently able to own their own land in these towns (cf. Lev. 25: 32–34). Verse 4 speaks of a thousand cubits as the measurement for the pasture lands and v. 5 speaks of two thousand cubits. The general explanation of Jewish writers is that the thousand cubits were for the cattle and the extra thousand for vineyards.

(b) The Cities of Refuge (35: 9–15)

Six **cities of refuge** for the **person who has killed someone** are to be provided, three on either side of the Jordan. Provision is made for three more in Dt. 19: 8, 9, if needed, but there is no record that they were ever built. Moses himself set apart the three east of the Jordan (cf. Dt. 4: 41–43); the others were set apart later (cf. Jos. 20: 7). The cities of refuge are also referred to in Exod. 21: 13; Dt. 19: 1–13 and Jos. 20: 1–9, where their names are given. They were naturally Levitical cities because they were dedicated (cf. Jos. 20: 7, where NEB gives 'dedicated') and because the priests and Levites acted as judges in such cases (cf. 17: 8, 9).

The custom of blood vengeance is very ancient and has been found among the Arabs in modern times. It could be eliminated only as a strong judicial system was set up; cf. David's inability to avenge Abner's murder in 2 Sam. 3: 28–34. Cf. 2 Sam 14: 7.

The word **avenger** (12; cf. Dt. 19: 6) is Heb. *gō'ēl*, the 'kinsman redeemer' of Ru. 3: 12, i.e. the nearest relative, cf. Lev 25: 25. **12. the assembly:** which would be represented by the elders, could refer to the assembly of the city of refuge or the assembly of the city from which the killer has come; probably both were involved.

(c) The Murderer (35: 16–21)

Murder is defined. The **avenger of blood** is to put the murderer to death.

(d) Unpremeditated Killing (35: 22–28)

Unpremeditated is defined. Cf. Dt. 19: 4–5. The killer is to remain in the city of refuge **until the death of the high priest who was anointed with the holy oil** (25): cf. Lev. 8: 12; 16: 32; 21: 10. Until the setting up of the monarchy, there was no other individual by which a new era could be reckoned. The influence of the Judges was rarely country-wide.

If the killer left the city of refuge before the death of the high priest, his life was forfeit (26, 27), for his life was no longer protected from the avenger.

(e) Additional Instructions (35: 29–34)

A person must not be put to death on the testimony of one witness (30; cf. Dt. 17: 6; 19: 15). No ransom is to be accepted for the life of the murderer (31) or to allow the killer to return home (32). Although the death was accidental, nothing must be done to minimize its seriousness; otherwise the land would be polluted (33; cf. Lev. 18: 24, 25; Dt. 21: 22, 23). God's presence in the land demands holiness (34). 'The money equivalent for a life was widely prevalent . . . Mohammed suffered the ancient practice of making a money payment to continue even in the case of wilful murder' (*ICC*).

v. The Law of the Marriage of Heiresses (36: 1–13)

(a) The Problem (36: 1–4)

In 27: 5–11 a decision was given that **the daughters of Zelophehad,** who had no brothers, should be allowed to receive their father's inheritance but the question is now raised: What if they marry? The inheritance would pass to the husband's tribe and thus the divinely arranged distribution of the land would be altered. Even the year of jubilee would bring no relief as it would in the case of property that was sold. With v. 1 cf. 26: 28–34 and also cf. 1 Kg. 21: 1–3.

(b) The Command of the LORD (36: 5–9)

Verse 5 implies that Moses brought the case before the Lord as he did in 27: 5 and the LORD commanded that the daughters of Zelophehad should marry within the family of the tribe of their fathers, thus keeping the inheritance of the family within the tribe (6). In vv. 7–9 it is made a general rule for heiresses in Israel. In v. 7 NEB gives 'a family' and in v. 8 'any family'.

(c) The Command Obeyed (36: 10–12)

The daughters of Zelophehad married the sons of their paternal uncles or possibly of their cousins (cf. Jer. 32: 12). The word may even mean a kinsman, as the Hebrew *dôd* is used of the male line of descent.

(d) Conclusion (36: 13)

A summing up of the laws received since their arrival on the plains of Moab in 22: 1. Cf. Lev. 27: 34. **the commandments and ordinances:** cf. Dt. 6: 1.

BIBLIOGRAPHY

Commentaries

BINNS, L. E., *The Book of Numbers*. WC (London, 1927).

COATES, C. A., *An Outline of Numbers* (London, 1937).

ELLICOTT, C. J., Ellicott's *Bible Commentary*, vol. 1 (London, 1882).

ESPIN, T. E., and THRUPP, J. F., *Numbers*. The Speaker's Commentary (London, 1871).

GRAY, G. B., *Numbers*, ICC (Edinburgh, 1903).

JAMIESON, R., FAUSSET, A. R., and BROWN, D., *Commentary on the Bible*, vol. 1 (Glasgow, 1863).

KEIL, C. F., *The Pentateuch*, E.T., vol. 3 (Edinburgh, 1868; reprinted Grand Rapids, 1956).

LANGE, J. P., *Commentary on the Holy Scriptures: Numbers- Deuteronomy*, E.T. (Edinburgh, 1874; reprinted Grand Rapids, 1956).

MACKINTOSH, C. H., *Notes on Numbers* (London, 1869).

MACRAE, A. A., 'Numbers' in NBC (London, 1953).

MARSH, J., 'Numbers' in *The Interpreter's Bible*, vol. 2 (New York, 1953).

NOTH, M., *Numbers*, E.T. OTL (London, 1968).

POOLE, M., *Commentary on the Holy Bible*, vol. 1 (London, 1683; reprinted London, 1962).

SMICK, E., 'Numbers' in WBC (London, 1963).

SNAITH, N. H., *Leviticus and Numbers*. NCentB (London, 1967).

STURDY, J., *Numbers*. CBC (Cambridge, 1976).

THOMPSON, J. A., 'Numbers' in NBCR (London, 1970).

WATSON, R. A., *Numbers*. EB (New York, 1903).

WENHAM, G. J., *Numbers*. TOTC (London, 1981).

WHITELAW, T., and WINTERBOTHAM, R., *Numbers* Pulpit Commentary (London, 1897).

Other Works

ALBRIGHT, W. F., 'The Oracles of Balaam', JBL 63 (1944). 207–233.

DAVIES, G. I., *The Way of the Wilderness* (Cambridge, 1979).

DEUTERONOMY

PETER E. COUSINS

To many readers of the OT, the Book of Deuteronomy appears rather unimportant. It apparently consists chiefly of history and laws; neither seeming very relevant to life in the Christian era, let alone in the twentieth century. In addition, most of both the historical and the legal material appears, in greater detail or with minor differences, elsewhere in the Pentateuch.

This adverse reaction must be called into question (so far as Christians are concerned) by the extensive use of Deuteronomy in the NT which contains over 80 references to the book. Our Lord relied upon it in his temptation (6: 13–16; 8: 3, cf. Mt. 4:4, 7, 10 and Lk. 4:4, 8, 12). He reaffirms the first and great commandment of 6: 5 (cf. Mt. 22: 37 f.; Mk 12: 29–33; Lk. 10: 27) and 18: 13 may be the seed from which grew a crucial demand in the Sermon on the Mount (Mt. 5: 48). Paul, too, found that Deuteronomy was closely related to Christian experience, as we may see from his use of 30: 12–14 (Rom. 10: 6–8); 32: 17–20 (Rom. 10: 19; 1 C. 10: 22; Rom. 12: 19); 27: 26 and 21: 23 (Gal. 3: 10, 13) and 25: 4 (1 C. 9: 9). Among other passages referred to in the NT are 32: 35 (Heb. 10: 30); 29: 18 (Heb. 12: 15); and 18: 15 (Ac. 3: 22; 7: 37) which has provided Christians with a basic concept for interpreting the work of Christ.

Judaism, too, draws deeply from Deuteronomy. The *Shema* recited morning and evening by observant Jews and having a religious significance comparable to that of the Lord's Prayer in Christendom, is composed of 6: 4–9 and 11: 13–21, together with Num. 15: 37–41. Saying grace after meals is justified by reference to 8: 10. In addition, several other Jewish observances derive from the book; wearing phylacteries (6: 8); the mezuzah (6: 9); and wearing tassels (22: 12). Evidence from Qumran suggests that Deuteronomy was one of the most popular books among the religious group that made its home there.

But quite apart from such matters of (important) detail, the book as a whole is of central significance in the OT. We shall refer later to its pivotal place in recent OT criticism. Even more momentous is its theological content. This is best understood with reference to the *form* of the book, as we shall now see.

Structure

At first sight, Deuteronomy is simply a series of addresses by Moses to Israel, together with various appendixes. An introduction (1: 1–5) is followed by a rather short first address (1: 6–4: 40) and a brief note about the cities of refuge (4: 41–43). The second address is much longer (4: 44–28: 67) and includes an extended legal section (chaps. 12–26). The third address (chaps. 29, 30) is an appeal to Israel to accept the covenant. The following chapters (31–34) seem to be appendixes; the appointment of Moses' successor (31), the Song of Moses (32), the Blessing of Moses (33) and the death of Moses (34). This arbitrary structure has attracted a good deal of attention, and it has been rather generally accepted by scholars that the book attained its present form only after a complex editorial process, extending over several centuries. Thus M. Noth sees the book as originally consisting of chaps. 5–26 and chap. 28 to which chaps. 27, 29 and 30 were added. At some time chaps. 31–34 were also attached, while 1: 1–4: 43 were written (he thinks) as an introduction to the so-called Deuteronomic History, extending from Joshua to 2 Kings.

During the last twenty years the problem of the structure of Deuteronomy has apparently been solved, and in a way that simultaneously vindicates its unity and illuminates its purpose. The book is very like the sort of treaty (or covenant) that was made in the second millennium B.C. between a suzerain (specifically, one of the Hittite kings) and a vassal. The implications are (a) that Deuteronomy presents the relationship between Yahweh and Israel in these terms, (b) that the book is a unity, since even what have often been regarded as later accretions contribute to the overall pattern, (c) that the book may be demonstrably earlier than most scholars have believed, if (as seems to be possibly the case) the treaty pattern followed is of a kind typical of the second millennium, rather than the seventh century or later, which is where 'critical orthodoxy' has tended to place the book.

Viewed in this way, Deuteronomy is organized thus:

1: 6–3: 29	Historical prologue, describing the 'political background' to the treaty
4: 1–40; 5: 1–11: 32	The basic stipulations of the treaty
12: 1–26: 19	Detailed stipulations

27: 1–26	Instructions about the recording (and periodic renewal) of the treaty
28: 1–14	Blessings invoked upon loyalty to the treaty
28: 15–68	Curses invoked for bad faith
29: 1–30: 20	Recapitulation of the terms in general
31: 1–34: 12	Provision for dynastic continuity of the treaty

Theology

In order to relate this 'suzerainty treaty' structure to the theology of Deuteronomy, we must take note of the place assigned to it in salvation-history. According to 1: 1, the treaty was presented to Israel by Moses in Transjordan, shortly before his death. The forty years' wandering was over, and a new generation facing the Promised Land was called upon to renew the Sinai covenant made with their parents, following the deliverance from Egypt.

Yahweh is presented as unique in being and power (6: 4; 35: 10, 14, 17). His power and love to Israel have been disclosed above all in the deliverance from Egypt and subsequent saving acts (4: 34–38). The future is secure: Yahweh promised Israel's ancestors that Canaan would belong to their descendants (8: 1; 9: 5). He will keep this promise and in doing so will judge the sins of the Canaanites (9: 4–7). His love and sovereign power mean that obedience to the covenant assures Israel of continued blessing in the land covenanted to her (11: 13–15; 28: 1–14).

So far as Israel is concerned, the relationship calls for utter and unconditional loyalty to Yahweh. This is why everything connected with pagan worship must be destroyed, including the 'high places' where Canaanite worship took place (7: 25, 26; 12: 1–7, 29–31) although these are significantly not mentioned by name. Cultic purity, however, is not enough. The laws in chaps. 12–26 demand loyalty to Yahweh in every detail of life. Above all, Deuteronomy calls for a response of love: love first of all to Yahweh as a response to his redeeming love (6: 4; 7: 7, 8) expressed in reverence for and obedience to his law (6: 4–9; 11: 13). No less important are love and humanitarian concern shown to the poor, the resident alien and even to animals (10: 17–19; 24: 10–22; 25: 4).

While obedience to the covenant will result in blessing, disobedience will bring a curse upon every aspect of the nation's life (28: 15–68). Hence the need for radical decision and commitment, expressed in the ceremony of covenant renewal (11: 26–29; 27: 9, 10; 30: 1).

Two elements in this deuteronomic theology present difficulties to many readers. One is the command to 'devote' to Yahweh (i.e. to

destroy) what other nations, including inhabitants of Canaan, would have regarded as the spoils of war. There are helpful discussions of this in *Hard Sayings: the Challenge of Old Testament Morals* by D. Kidner (Tyndale Press, 1972) and *The Goodness of God* by J. W. Wenham (Tyndale Press, 1974). The other is the closeness of the relationship affirmed in Deuteronomy between obedience (or disobedience) to Yahweh and material prosperity (or hardship). So marked is this feature that its presence elsewhere in the OT, particularly in the historical books, is commonly regarded as a sign of the work of 'deuteronomic' historians. Two general considerations are relevant here. First, that this principle is closely related to the absence from the OT generally of any clearly formulated belief in a life after death in which the injustices of this world would be redressed: for the OT, justice must be done in this life or not at all. Second, that since all forms of theism believe that the Creator of the world is also the source of all goodness, they also affirm a general (if not an invariable) link between obedience to his will and a degree of prosperity; it is the unrighteous who are 'going against the grain' of a morally constituted universe. The deuteronomic teaching on this has sometimes been regarded as an extreme expression of a fundamental general truth; sometimes it has been related specifically to Israel with the implication that in her affairs alone Providence ensured (for educative reasons) a closer correlation than elsewhere between obedience and prosperity.

It is thus difficult to exaggerate the importance of this covenant document as providing a means whereby God's people might understand their relationship to him and the significance of his commandments. Every aspect of community life, including the institutions of prophecy and of monarchy, are here revealed in the light of the covenant relationship. If it was indeed (a portion of) Deuteronomy that came to light during the Temple restoration in Josiah's reign (2 Kg. 22, 23 and 2 Chr. 34, 35), then history witnesses to the impact of the book upon the nation's life.

Date

For OT scholarship during the last century and a half, Deuteronomy has been no less significant in providing a bench line for the dating and assessment of many other books and hypothetical documents. It has generally been assumed first that 12: 1–14 demand the total centralization of the cultus at Jerusalem and secondly that non-pejorative references in other books to altars of Yahweh elsewhere must be dated at a period *before* Deuteronomy was promulgated. For most OT scholars, therefore, the book is to be dated (although not yet in its final form) at a time shortly before Josiah's reform.

It will have been, for example, the manifesto of the prophetic movement, or perhaps the product of Levites from the northern kingdom of Israel who came to Judah following the fall of Samaria. Not only the cultic provisions but also the general legislation are related to such hypotheses: detailed differences between the laws of 'JE' and those in 'P' may be explained (it is suggested) on the assumption that the legislation in 'D' represents a state of affairs intermediate between them.

These theories are by no means free from difficulty. If one of the principal purposes of Deuteronomy was to eradicate worship at the 'high places' and centralize it at Jerusalem then it is surprising to say the least, that the 'high places' are never specifically referred to throughout the book. There are also difficulties connected with the supposed role of the Levites. It is commonly claimed that before 621 B.C. all Levites were priests but that subsequently the country Levites who had officiated at the 'high places' were dispossessed and priesthood restricted to those at Jerusalem.

More generally, it is claimed that where ideas and vocabulary characteristic of Deuteronomy are found in historical books this indicates that a 'deuteronomic editor' has been at work revising and rewriting at a date subsequent to the supposed promulgation of Deuteronomy about 621 B.C. The book itself is not thought to have reached its final form until the exilic period.

That such hypotheses are not free from difficulty may be seen from their diversity. (For details, see the introductions to Thompson or Craigie, or any standard OT introduction such as that by G. W. Anderson.) At various times dates have been suggested in the eleventh, tenth, and sixth centuries B.C. Even scholars who agree on a seventh century date disagree considerably about the process whereby the book came into existence. In general, however, there has been an increasing tendency to recognize the presence in Deuteronomy of very ancient material.

Among scholars who have recently argued for a Mosaic origin are Kline, Manley, Thompson and Craigie. They have all agreed about the presence in the book of post-Mosaic elements such as chap. 34, and explanatory notes such as 3: 11. Some of the differences between 'JE', 'D' and 'P' legislation they would explain by reference to the intermediate nature of the period between the wilderness wanderings and a fully settled existence in Canaan. Thompson in particular, however, admits the possibility that original Mosaic material may under divine guidance have been interpreted and made more relevant to changing circumstances during succeeding centuries. (It would, indeed, be surprising if Hebrew law were unique in remaining unmodified by decisions about specific cases, especially since the Levites were entrusted with the God-given responsibility of deciding difficult cases.) On the other hand, so far as style and basic concepts are concerned, K. A. Kitchen has shown (in 'Ancient Orient, Deuteronomism and the OT' in J. B. Payne, ed., *New Perspectives on the OT*, Waco, 1970) that the ancient Near East offers other examples where a style continues unchanged for many centuries, so that there is no justification for ruling out the possibility that a document such as Deuteronomy might continue to influence Hebrew literature over a period of centuries. He also points out that the warnings in Deuteronomy of the danger of deportation and exile are thoroughly consistent with an early date since these possibilities are mentioned in ancient eastern inscriptions well before the time of Moses.

It has recently been suggested that Deuteronomy may have been compiled in the seventh century on the pattern of contemporary (Assyrian and Aramaic) suzerainty treaties rather than on that of second millennium (Hittite) treaties. The crucial difference between the two patterns is the presence in the earlier form of a historical prologue similar to that in 1: 5–4: 49 which has been said to be absent from the later pattern. The validity of this distinction has, however, been questioned, although without an agreed conclusion being reached.

Another comparatively recent theory is of interest even to those who are not convinced by it. Deuteronomy, it has been suggested, was written as an introduction to the 'deuteronomic history' contained in Joshua, Judges, Samuel and Kings. (It would follow from this that Numbers is not the fourth book of the Pentateuch but the last in the Tetrateuch.)

Whatever the objections to such a theory, it recognizes the theological and spiritual significance of a book that has too often been overlooked. There are various reasons for this neglect: in particular, the book has been misunderstood as a mere rehash of narratives and laws from elsewhere. The title 'Deuteronomy' has contributed to this misunderstanding. It derives from 17: 18, where the Hebrew phrase, 'a copy of this law', is mistranslated in the Septuagint as 'this second law' (*deuteronomion*). Although the Hebrew title ('ēlleh haddᵉbarîm—'these are the words'—cf. 1: 1) is not very illuminating, it does indicate the nature of the book as an address given to God's covenant people. Its message is in fact no less needed in the new covenant than in the old. As George Adam Smith wrote in 1918: 'Deuteronomy gives utterance to truths which are always and everywhere sovereign—that God is One, and that man is wholly His, that it is He who finds us rather than we who find Him; that God is Righteousness and Faithfulness, Mercy and Love, and that these also are what He requires from us towards Himself and one another; that His will lies not in any unknown height but in the moral sphere known and understood by all (30: 11–14)'.

ANALYSIS

I. HISTORICAL PROLOGUE TO THE COVENANT (1: 1–3: 29)

i. Introductory Note (1: 1–5)

As in other ancient suzerainty treaties (see introduction, p. 256) the speaker identifies himself (1). Moses demands Israel's allegiance on behalf of Yahweh. The time (3, 4) and place (1, 5) are defined, and although the places listed in v. 1 are not all known, v. 5 locates the scene.

2. It is not clear why this statement appears here; there may be a contrast between the eleven days required and the forty years taken. *Horeb* is the name given to the locality of Sinai in Deuteronomy except in 33: 22, cf. Exod. 3: 1; 17: 6; 33: 6; 1 Kg.19: 8; Ps. 106: 19; Mal. 4: 4. **all Israel:** a term characteristic of Deuteronomy.

4. Cf. Num. 21: 21–35.

5. expound: a rare verb, meaning to dig or to hew and thus to make clear. It thus points up the way in which the laws of Deuteronomy are first stated, then explained, then made the subject of exhortation.

ii. The First Attempt—Horeb to Hormah (1: 6–46)

Just as an ancient suzerain pointed out the benefits he had conferred upon a vassal, so Yahweh enumerates his saving acts, in the form of a historical retrospect (1: 6–8). (Thus he discloses himself not only in what he does but also in what he says.)

This is a sad story of failure. Twice the command comes to **go in and take possession** (8, 21), but Israel could not trust God for victory (26–33) and was thus unsuccessful when, disobeying the word of Yahweh (37), she tried to invade Canaan (41–46).

7. hill country of the Amorites: the central highlands. **Arabah:** apparently the area north of the Dead Sea. **the western foothills** (*šᵉp̄ēlēh*): the Mediterranean foothills. **Negev:** the southern area between these foothills and the desert. **The coast:** extended north towards Tyre. These ideal limits were never achieved, except perhaps in the reign of David.

9–18. This apparent interpolation (see Exod. 18: 13–27 and cf. Num. 11: 14) is in fact linked to v. 8b, since it records the fulfilment of Yahweh's promise to Abraham that his descendants would become a great nation.

15. The divisions refer to administrative units rather than to specific numbers.

16 f. We may note three important judicial requirements. Justice must be impartial, not favouring the rich and influential. Since it is an expression of God's concern for justice, it must not be influenced by threats. It applies equally to resident aliens as to Israelites.

19–46. These verses, paralleled in Num. 13, 14 tell a story of repeated rebellion and complaint (26–28, 32, 41–43) in spite of continued signs of God's goodness, love and protection (19, 25, 30–33).

31. To some extent, this reflects treaty terminology. But the love of God is a basic theme in Deuteronomy (see Introduction and cf. Dt. 8: 5; 32: 5, also Ac. 13: 18).

34–36. In judgment, Yahweh remembers mercy; indeed here and in v. 39 is seen the promise fulfilled in the deuteronomic covenant renewal.

37. In this context, no reference is made to Moses' sin described in Num. 20: 10–12, but he is involved in the sin of the covenant people; cf. 3: 26, 27.

38. your assistant: cf. 1 Kg. 10: 8 and Rev. 7: 9, 15.

41–45. Lost opportunities cannot always be made good. See Eph. 5: 15–17; Col. 4: 5; Heb. 3: 13–19; 12: 16, 17.

iii. Journey through Transjordan (2: 1–25)

This account parallels that in Num. 20, 21. It shows the nation avoiding conflict (4, 9, 19) or fighting (24 f.) in obedience to the guidance of Yahweh.

1–3. They had left Kadesh in a south-easterly direction, but later left the mountain range of Seir (Edomite country) and struck north towards Canaan once more. The precise route followed (cf. v. 8) is uncertain.

6, 7. These verses enunciate a basic principle. God's people may be helped by contact with unbelievers, but their trust is in God himself.

8. We turned from the Arabah road: i.e. they avoided the 'King's Highway' (cf. Num. 20: 17).

8b–9. Israel regarded Moab as well as Edom as having a special relationship since Moab was descended from Abraham's nephew, Lot (Gen. 19: 30–38); cf. v. 19.

10–12. An archaeological note, presumably from an editor. It would be interesting to know why these tall tribespeople were also known as **Rephaites** (see *NBD*), a word applied in Ps. 88: 10 and elsewhere to the shades of the dead. The reason may be that these early inhabitants of the land are thought of as long since dead.

13–19. The story continues, again recalling the

judgment that fell on the exodus generation (14, 15). **Ar** (18) may have been in the upper part of the Wadi Arnon.

20–23. Another archaeological note: for Rephaim see v. 11 and comment. **Caphtor** (23; cf. Jer. 47: 4; Am. 9: 7) is usually identified with Crete (**Caphtorites** may = Philistines). We may note the awareness of God's hand in the history of other nations (21, 22) but contrast v. 23.

25. Panic is commonly associated with the holy war (see on 20: 1–20).

iv. Conquest of Transjordan (2: 26–3: 11)

Two Amorite kingdoms are defeated: that of Sihon extended from the Wadi Arnon to the Wadi Jabbok; that of Og occupied Northern Gilead and Bashan. For this section see Num. 21: 21–35.

(a) The defeat of Sihon (2: 26–37)

26. offering peace implies the offer of a treaty. This would agree with 20: 10 and contrast with 7: 1, 2. The reason may be that Transjordan was not part of the land promised in Gen. 12; 15: 18–20. If so, the situation was changed by the hostility of Sihon (30, 32, 34–36).

27, 28. For these terms, cf. Num. 20: 14–21 and see Num. 21: 21–23. **road:** see on Num. 21: 22 for the King's Highway.

30. The hardening of Sihon's heart parallels that of Pharaoh's (Exod. 7–14). In each case, refusal to accept the divine message plays a significant part in the process of deliverance (cf. Rom. 9: 17; 11: 11, 25).

32. Sihon is defeated when he leaves the security of his encircling fortified position to give battle at Jahaz (perhaps the modern Jalul or a site near Madeba) which is mentioned also in the Moabite Stone.

34, 35. In accordance with the laws of the holy war (20: 1–20), all booty was totally destroyed. This *ḥērem* ('ban' in some versions) entailed dedicating all towns, animals, property and even people, who were potential slaves, to Yahweh for destruction (cf. Jos. 6: 21; 7: 20, 21 and 1 Sam. 15: 9 for infringements of the law). It is remarkable how easily many douce Bible-believing Christians seem to accept this appalling requirement. If we are not to go to the other extreme of striking it from God's Word as a tragic misunderstanding of his purposes, we must bear in mind the following considerations. (i) The future salvation of mankind depended on the preservation of God's self-disclosure in and to Israel. Jn 3: 16 depends on Dt. 20: 10–18. (ii) Archaeology has disclosed the appalling moral and religious contagion of Canaan at this period. (iii) In the circumstances, reform was out of the question; any influence would have been a negative one upon Israel. (iv) The 'hardness of heart' of the Hebrews reduced their guilt, and was a significant factor in God's working (Mk 10: 5).

(v) The *ḥērem* at any rate ensured that the Hebrews, unlike some more 'civilized' peoples, did not go to war for gain.

Has the *ḥērem* any relevance to the present age? Without attempting to blunt the edge of the issue by mere allegorizing, the Christian reader may find here a witness to God's unremitting and total opposition to evil, and to the need (cf. Mt. 5: 29, 30) to be ruthless in extirpating it from one's own life.

36. Aroer has been excavated. Perhaps the **town . . . in the gorge** was a suburb.

37. Cf. v. 9.

(b) The defeat of Og (3: 1–11)

3, 6. The *ḥērem* was observed.

5. These cities will have been (by modern standards) walled villages.

8, 9. For these alternative names for Mt. Hermon, see Ps. 29: 6; 1 Chr. 5: 23; Ca. 4: 8; Ezek. 27: 5. **Hermon** probably referred to the peak and **Senir** to the Anti-Lebanon range.

10. the table-land: i.e. the plateau of Moab.

11. If **Og** was the last of the **Rephaites** (see on vv. 10–12) he was not strictly an Amorite. His sarcophagus (**bed**) will have been made of iron-coloured basalt, like other large sarcophagi as found in Phoenicia. It was 13 or 14 feet by 6 feet, and at the time when these words were written could be seen in **Rabbah of the Ammonites** (the modern Amman).

v. The Conquered Land is Divided (3: 12–17)

It is not altogether easy to reconcile the information about tribal boundaries given in the various passages in Numbers, Deuteronomy and Joshua, perhaps because we do not understand them fully. Here two groups (**Jair** and **Makir**) within the half-tribe of Manasseh receive the northern part of **Gilead** and the whole of **Bashan** (13–15), while Reuben and Gad take the region north of **the Arnon**, including part of **Gilead** (12, 16). The meaning of v. 17 is not clear; it seems to define the limits of Transjordan, but some have suggested it refers to the area occupied by Gad (see Jos. 13: 24–28).

vi. Preparing to Cross the Jordan (3: 18–29)

The unity of God's people (a basic principle in both the Old and the New Testament) is emphasized here. The two and a half tribes who are to settle in Transjordan must help their fellows conquer the rest of the Promised Land (18, 20). The wives, children and cattle will have been protected meanwhile by the younger and older men and presumably by those referred to in 20: 5–8.

The prayer of Moses (23–29) is typical of the feelings of many who reach the end of life without seeing the completion of an enterprise they have seen well begun (24). Although it was his own sin that led to his exclusion from

Canaan (32: 51; Num. 20: 12), the responsibility of the people is emphasized here (26) and Moses' deprivation is seen as due to involvement in their sin. When Moses looked at the land from Pisgah this may have been understood as a formal taking possession of it (cf. 34: 1–4; Gen. 13: 14–17; Lk. 14: 18).

II. BASIC STIPULATIONS OF THE COVENANT (4: 1–11: 32)

i. Moses Appeals to Israel (4: 1–43)
In this final section of Moses' first address there are clear parallels with concepts found in Near Eastern treaties. 'The author of the treaty is named (1, 2, 5, 10), reference is made to the preceding historical acts, the treaty stipulations are mentioned, the appeal is made for Israel to obey, the treaty sanctions, blessing and cursing, are referred to, witnesses are mentioned (26) and the obligation to transmit the knowledge of the treaty to the next generation is stated (10)' (J. A. Thompson). The chief points made concern the importance of the Law (1–8), the sin of idolatry (9–24), the danger of judgment (25–31) and the goodness of God (32–40).

(a) God's Law (4: 1–8)
1. Hear now: comparable with the 'therefore' of Rom. 12: 1 as a link between God's saving acts and the responses of the redeemed. The command not to change what God has said (another reminder of the treaty aspect) is a recurrent biblical theme (Mt. 23: 16–26; Mk 7: 9–13; Rev. 22: 18 f.). The disaster of Baalpeor (3; see Num. 25: 1–9) shows the consequences of disobedience. But it is clear from vv. 6–8 that, far from being restrictive or a burden, God's Law is a sign of his love, and a means of blessing to those who live by it.

(b) The Sin of Idolatry (4: 9–24)
These verses are in effect a sermon on the Second Commandment. They hinge on the fact that at the supreme moment of salvation-history in the OT (comparable to Calvary in the new age) God's people **saw no form** (12, 15) but knew his presence through his spoken word demanding and defining covenant obedience.

9, 10. Here and in the following verses, it is implied that Moses' audience (ostensibly the children of the wilderness generation) **stood** themselves **at Horeb.** This is not an accidental error, but an affirmation of the contemporaneity of salvation. 'Were you there when they crucified my Lord?' asks the Negro spiritual, and faith replies 'Yes'.

13. It was natural to identify the covenant with the commandments, but this later led to a superficial and legalistic view of the covenant relationship. The **two stone tablets** may have been necessary because of the length of the content; more likely they correspond to the two copies commonly made of treaty documents.

16–19. Not only is God in his essence different from all that he has created; none can worthily symbolize him.

20. iron-smelting furnace: so great was the ordeal.

24. It is suggested that the word here translated **jealous** refers to an active zeal for righteousness. But Ca. 8: 6, which also conjoins it with fire, suggests an allusion to the intense and exclusive demands of God's holy and unselfish love.

25–31. There is no reason to see these verses as post- (or even immediately pre-) exilic. Defeat followed by deportation will have been familiar concepts many centuries earlier. What is significant is that Yahweh, unlike secular kings, might even forgive disregard of a solemn treaty (29–31).

(c) The Goodness of God (4: 32–40)
After a *negative* dissuasive in respect of idolatry there follows a *positive* incitement to loyal obedience. Israel's experience of salvation and of God's self-disclosure was unique (32–34). Arising from divine love (37), it showed his greatness (35) and should elicit obedience to his commandments (40). This passage shows clearly the essential continuity between the Testaments.

35. The mysterious holiness of deity (not generally associated in the ancient world with moral purity) was seen as a threat to humankind brought into contact with it (cf., *e.g.*, Gen. 32: 30); how much more when affronted by sin? The resolution of this discord is another great biblical theme.

35, 39. The monotheistic note sounded here may not imply the non-existence of other spiritual powers, but rather that they are of no account in comparison with Yahweh.

(d) The Cities of Refuge (4: 41–43)
See on 19: 1–9. The three cities mentioned here are in Transjordan, so that they could be set apart at this stage, whereas the others were established later (see Jos. 20).

ii. Introductory Summary (4: 44–49)
It is often suggested that these verses form the beginning of an original form of Deuteronomy (4: 44–30: 20). Whatever the explanation, vv. 41–49 appear as a parenthesis separating 4: 40 from its sequel in 5: 1. What follows from 5: 1 to 28: 68 takes the form of a second speech by Moses, following on the preceding one of 1: 6–4: 40.

44, 45. The four synonyms used in these verses are probably meant to imply the totality of the law. It is in principle (and sometimes in practice) possible to distinguish them: **law** (*tôrâ*) is teaching; **stipulations** (*ʿēḏuṯ*) are required by the covenant; **decrees** (*ḥōq*) have been written down; ordinances (*mišpāṭ*) are a judge's decisions.

48. Siyon: see 3: 9 and Ps. 29: 6; Zion (cf. AV, RV 'Sion', following *MT*) is clearly not intended.

iii. God and His People (5: 1–11: 32)

Before the exposition of the covenant law in 5: 12–26 comes this exhortation to covenant faith. Cunliffe-Jones sees it as a sermon on the First Commandment. It stresses the need for complete loyalty to Yahweh, and warns against self-righteousness and self-sufficiency. Love and reverence expressed in obedience are the response that God seeks.

AV and RV make clear what modern versions conceal, that singular and plural pronouns (thou/you) are used apparently at random in this section (see 6: 4–6: 5; 6: 13–6: 14; 6: 16 f.– 6: 17 f.). Many scholars think the singular is original and the plural a sign of later amplification, but K. A. Kitchen (*AOOT* p. 129) shows that such variation is a not uncommon feature of semitic style.

(a) The Heart of the Covenant (5: 1–6: 3)

For the Decalogue (6–21), see notes on Exod. 20: 1–17.

3. Cf. 4: 9 f.

4. face to face implies a direct personal relationship.

5. Moses is seen as mediator on several occasions. Here he is the one who interprets to Israel the voice of God, which they could hear (4, 22–27) but apparently could not understand.

6. This verse corresponds to the historical prologue of a suzerainty treaty. It is a reminder that God is known above all in saving his people.

7. A theme repeatedly stressed in Deuteronomy (cf., *e.g.*, 13: 1–18; 16: 1–22; 29: 1–29); indeed the whole book inculcates loyalty to Yahweh.

8. Cf. 4: 12–20; 7: 5; 12: 20, etc.

9, 10. Curses and blessings were normal in suzerainty treaties.

12–15. The slight differences in vv. 12–14 between this and the form in Exodus are not important. But the reason for obedience given in v. 15 is significant. Whereas the Exodus expansion points to God's rest from creation (Gen. 2: 2 f.), the emphasis falls here on man's rest in redemption. Rest for animals and servants mirrors the rest God wins for his people. Thus the OT calls upon man to rejoice on **the sabbath** in both creation and redemption.

16. Here too the Exodus material is further expanded.

17–20. It has been suggested that the brief form of these commandments may originally have characterized all.

21. The treatment in Deuteronomy of this, the only commandment referring exclusively to an inward disposition, differs in two respects from

that in Exodus. The **wife** mentioned in Exodus after **house** (which may mean 'household') is here placed first. Her unique position is further suggested by the use of two Hebrew verbs (**covet, desire**) one of which refers only to her, whereas Exodus subsumes all under one verb. This modification manifests a concern for women that is seen elsewhere in Deuteronomy (*e.g.* 21: 10–14; 22: 13–19; 24: 1–5). With vv. 22–27, cf. Exod. 19: 16 ff.; 20: 18 ff.

22. Both here and in Exod. 31: 18, the **stone tablets** are said to have been written by God. Passages such as Isa. 10: 5, to say nothing of Exod. 34: 28, may imply that God's agent was Moses. In any case, the phrase emphasizes the immediate divine authority of the Decalogue and the phrase **he added nothing more** suggests its primacy.

23–27. This expression of a universal human need for an intermediary between man and God, partially met by Moses (Gal. 3: 19), finds fulfilment in Christ (1 Tim. 2: 5; Heb. 8: 6; 9: 15; 12: 24).

29. There is a sad irony in this verse, in view of the repeated failures of the people of God.

5: 32–6: 3. In this exhortation, reference is made to the commandment (a fresh word; *miṣwāh* = 'charge', a formal injunction) Moses is about to give, expressed in the diverse laws of the covenant. Verses 32, 33 are typically deuteronomic in their warmth and urgency and stress on national and individual blessing as the fruit of obedience; cf. 6: 3.

3. milk and honey: this phrase, so often used in the OT, seems not altogether applicable to Canaan, but speculation about the reasons for its use has been ended with the discovery that it is a stock Middle Eastern literary motif, found in Egyptian and Ugaritic texts.

(b) The Great Commandment (6: 4–19)

Verses 4–9 are known to Jews as the *Shema* and are recited daily, with 11: 13–21 and Num. 15: 37–41, by men. Jesus quotes vv. 4 f., together with Lev. 19: 18, as the greatest of the commandments (Mt. 22: 36–40; Mk 12: 29–34; Lk. 10: 27 f.). The four words (Yahweh, our God, Yahweh, One) may be translated in various ways, but emphasize that Israel's God was not one of a pantheon, but sovereign and the object of entire devotion.

5. love: this transforms obedience from legalism into an expression of personal commitment. (But the word was also used of the suzerain—vassal relationship in some Near Eastern treaties; cf. 1 Kg. 5: 1.)

Emphasis on love as the basic element in Israel's relationship with God is distinctive of Deuteronomy and is an insight never fully understood and appropriated in the experience of God's people under the Old nor even the New Covenant. For **heart . . . soul . . .**

strength see 4: 29; 10: 12; 11: 13; 13: 3; 26: 16; 30: 2, 6, 10. For Hebrew thought, the heart is the centre of human being, including understanding and will as well as emotions. Soul is the principle of being, the source of life and strength. The reference to **strength** reinforces the demand. (When Christ adds 'mind' he is bringing out what is already implied rather than introducing something new.)

6-9. This total demand must never be overlooked. Not only is it to be upon the heart (cf. Jer. 31: 33), it must take first place in training children, in conversation (at home and outside) from the beginning to the end of the day; it should govern the senses, control behaviour, and direct life in the home and community. It is in the spirit of this that Paul can say: 'For me to live is Christ'.

8. hands . . . foreheads: the phylacteries (*t^epillîn*; Mt. 23: 5) are small leather cases containing this passage, together with 11: 13-21, Exod. 13: 1-10, 11-16, written on parchment. They are attached by leather straps to the left forearm and forehead of every Jewish male over thirteen at morning prayer (except on Sabbath and festivals).

9. doorframes: the same passages were attached in a small container (*m^ezûzāh*) to the doorposts. It is easier to decry the literalism of such practices than to emulate the devotion they express.

10-19. This section warns against the danger of forgetting God in prosperity (10-12). It adumbrates many of the book's characteristic themes: Yahweh's loyalty to his covenant with the ancestors (10, 18b); avoidance of idolatry (14); the material benefits of obedience (18); devotion to Yahweh (13, 17); the penalty of apostasy (15).

11. wells: these pits hewn out to hold water were, like the other items mentioned, associated with a settled existence, unlike the nomadic life of the Hebrews.

13. fear the LORD your God: cf. Mt. 4: 10 and Lk. 4: 8 for our Lord's use of this command to repel one of the wilderness temptations.

15. a jealous God: i.e. intolerant of all that prevents his people from enjoying the blessings his love provides; wrath is the obverse of holy love.

16. To **test** God is to try to force him to prove himself by imposing conditions upon him (see Exod. 17: 1-7). This Jesus refused to do (Mt. 4: 7; Lk. 4: 12).

(c) **Teaching the Covenant (6: 20-25)**
The home is the first setting for religious education. And the 'creed' to be recited (for other examples see *e.g.*, 25: 5-9; Jos. 24: 2-13) is no series of abstract truths but the 'old, old story' of the events that brought salvation. Integral to the situation are the divine commandments (24) which are indeed part of God's gracious

provision and bring blessing. This OT 'gospel' entails obedience.

25. The **righteousness** gained by obedience was not the *ground* but the *result* of deliverance (cf. Rev. 19: 8).

(d) **The Conquest of Canaan (7: 1-26)**
Although paganism is to be destroyed (1-5), Israel is not itself a righteous nation (6-16); its trust must be in God's power (17-26).

The Holy War (7: 1-5)
1. The national groups mentioned are Canaanite, including those **Hittites** (originally from Asia Minor) who had settled in Palestine. (But see note on Exod. 3: 8.)

2. For the holy war see on 20: 1-20.

3, 4. The prohibition is grounded not in race but religion, like its NT counterpart (2 C. 6: 14). Even apart from the restriction of the *ḥērem* in its most acute form to the nations mentioned in 20: 17, it is clear that the policy was not consistently implemented.

5. The **sacred stones** were probably associated with Baal and the wooden *Asherim* ('groves' in the AV) with the goddess Asherah (cf. Jg. 6: 25 f.; Jer. 2: 27 is probably ironic).

The Holy People (7: 6-16)
The injunctions in the previous section are grounded in Israel's position as God's own people. Not that this implies merit in them. Yet blessing will be theirs if they keep the covenant.

6. Israel is holy because she belongs to God who is distinguished by holiness from all that is created; she is 'set apart' rather than 'virtuous', although this too she must become. The idea of election (**chosen**) and of God's people as his **treasured possession** (cf. Exod. 19: 4 f.) are prominent also in the NT (cf. Tit. 2: 14; 1 Pet. 2: 9 f.).

7, 8. The mystery of grace is affirmed here (for another aspect of it cf. 9: 6). The God of the OT too chooses the weak (1 C. 1: 26-31) and to answer the question 'why?' in terms of his choosing the patriarchs merely pushes the problems one stage further back. Israel could say with Charles Wesley: 'He hath loved, he hath loved us, because he would love'. To redeem is to deliver (a person, animal or property) by means of payment. When used of the deliverance from Egypt, it loses to a great extent any reference to a price paid though some see this in **with a mighty hand.**

9, 10. These verses, incorporating (as many believe) words used for liturgical purposes, affirm God's loyalty to his covenant and his unshakeable opposition to evil. He is faithful (i.e. trustworthy) in love and judgment. **covenant of love:** Heb. *ḥesed*; this word, used some 245 times in the OT, and illustrated powerfully in the life of Hosea, refers especially to loyalty and love shown in an area of mutual responsibility such as family life. Yahweh shows it in his loyalty to Israel, in spite of the nation's repeated unfaithfulness.

13, 14. This is only one of many biblical passages which associate harmony in the infrahuman creation with human obedience to God. Quite apart from the reality of 'extraordinary' divine intervention, the study of ecology confirms the reality of this link. Similar lists of curses and blessings are found in 27: 11–28: 68 and there are parallels in contemporary suzerainty treaties.

15. For the diseases of Egypt we may cite Pliny's, 'Egypt, the mother of diseases'. But apart from the possible unhealthiness of the climate of Egypt, Exod. 15: 26 offers sufficient explanation.

16. See on 2: 34 f.

A Challenge to Faith (7: 17–26)
God has promised victory to his people, but the facts seem contrary (17). So the promises are reaffirmed, with additional detail (20, 22–24). There is a reminder of the power they have already seen at work (18, 19) and a challenge to future vigilance and loyalty (25, 26).

18. Under the new covenant it is the resurrection of Jesus that provides the decisive example of God's love and power.

20. There is no ground for interpreting the hornets literally: the reference may symbolize some form of God's activity on behalf of Israel. See *NBD*.

21–23. See on 20: 1–20. **22.** If the victory were too sudden and overwhelming, Israel would be unable to occupy all the settlements, so that wild animals would multiply.

25. The case of Achan (Jos. 7) illustrates this warning. Idolatry is as offensive and disgusting to God (**detestable**) as venal justice (Prov. 17: 15), commercial dishonesty (Prov. 20: 10) and religious insincerity (Prov. 21: 27).

26. Images are both disgusting and subject to the *ḥērem* (2: 23 f.).

(e) Lessons from the Past (8: 1–10: 11)
God's protection and loving discipline (8: 1–6) might well be forgotten in the prosperity of life in Canaan (8: 7–20). God's people do well to avoid self-righteousness (9: 1–5) and remember their own sinfulness (9: 6–10: 11).

Wilderness lessons (8: 1–6)
From Gen. 16: 7 to Rev. 12, the wilderness is a place where God meets man in discipline and deliverance.

2. The **desert** shows how deeply God's people are committed to him (cf. Hos. 2: 14).

3. The 'devotional' significance of the **manna** suggested here is not hinted at in Exod. 16 or Num. 11. For another interpretation, cf. Ps. 78: 24 f., also 1 C. 10: 3. The use of this verse by the Saviour (Mt. 4: 4; Lk. 4: 4) shows how it should be applied: to rebuke our own flabby materialism rather than to discourage us from supplying the needs of others. For related

thoughts, see 1 Pet. 2: 2; Jn 4: 34.

4. The only other biblical reference to this is Neh. 9: 21; this is providential care rather than a miracle.

5. These two great themes of sonship and discipline recur throughout the Scriptures, separately and entwined (Hos. 11: 1; Heb. 12: 5–11; Ac. 14: 22). God's practice has not changed.

The danger that prosperity may induce pride (8: 7–20)
This is vividly evoked in 32: 15. It leads to backsliding and to a judgment which is both divinely ordained and a 'natural' consequence of moral declension (19 f.).

7–10. This reads almost like a hymn in praise of Canaan. The **springs** contrast with the irrigation channels of Egypt; **iron . . . copper:** present in the Arabah; iron also near Mt. Carmel and Mt. Hermon. Verse 10 makes it clear that negative puritanism has no place in the Bible view of life.

12–14. The temptation to forget that wealth and prosperity are God's gracious gifts was not peculiar to Israel. Individuals and nations still forget their dependence on his bounty even when pollution and the suffering of the 'third world' reinforce this truth.

15. The almost supernatural terrors of the wilderness heighten the sense of God's powerful providence.

9: 1–6. In every way (as nations, as occupying walled cities, as individuals) the Canaanites had the advantage over Israel (1, 2). Only the power of Yahweh himself could defeat them (3). Yet so overwhelming a victory might lead God's people to think they merited what had been achieved (4), whereas it was the Canaanites, not Israel, who had got what they deserved (5, 6). The danger here is self-righteousness, rather than ingratitude and sloth as in the previous section.

Reminders of past failure (9: 6–10: 11)
The lesson of vv. 4 f. is continued. So far is Israel from being righteous that she shattered the covenant even at Sinai and survived only through the intercession of Moses (18 f., 25–29; 10: 10 f.). The passage is a sermon based on Exod. 24: 12–18; 32; 34—a striking example of the homiletic use of history.

10. Even today, faith uses such language: 'The Lord himself secured the visa for me!'

14. Moses declined this offer; the mediator of the covenant will not be blessed apart from his people. Solitary salvation is not a biblical concept.

17. According to contemporary ideas, this would signify the end of the covenant.

18, 19. The vicarious penitence and fasting of Moses provide a further link with the mediator of the new covenant.

20. The unique position of Moses and the desperate state of the people are seen in his interceding for the priest of Israel. This is not mentioned in Exodus.

21. This verse, like vv. 22–24, interrupts the narrative, which continues at 25.

22, 23. For these further examples of unbelief, see Num. 11: 1–3; Exod. 17: 1–7 and Num. 20: 10–13; Num. 11: 31–34; Num. 13, 14. Failure to trust God is the most serious of sins, because lack of trust destroys all relationships.

25–29. In pleading for Israel, Moses does not rest his case upon his own righteousness. Only the mediator of the new covenant could do this. Instead he speaks of the work God has already done (26, 29b): *Tantus labor non sit cassus.* He rests in the faith (the righteousness?) of Israel's ancestors (27); he reminds Yahweh that his honour is involved in the fulfilment of his declared purpose to save his people (28; cf. Ezek. 20: 9, 14, 22; Eph. 3; 10).

10: 1–5. This summary inevitably differs from the fuller narrative in Exodus; it is condensed for homiletic purposes. Elsewhere, the ark is regarded as the throne of Yahweh (Num. 10: 35 f.; 1 Sam. 4: 4). Here its role is explained in terms of the contemporary custom of preserving a copy of a suzerainty treaty within the shrines of the contracting parties.

3. like the first: God's grace is seen in fully restoring the broken relationship, as if the covenant had never been disrupted.

6, 7. This fragment of an itinerary, rather surprisingly inserted here, is closely related to Num. 33: 30–38.

8, 9. The reference to the ark explains the insertion of these verses which link with 1–5 (cf. Exod. 32: 25–29). **to carry the ark** was the privilege of the Kohathites who were non-priestly Levites (Num. 3: 31; 4: 15). **to stand before the LORD**, although used of many kinds of service in the OT, refers here to service in the sanctuary. **to pronounce blessings** was also a privilege (cf. Num. 6: 27). See also 18: 1–8.

(f) A Call to Commitment (10: 12–11: 32)

12. And now: introduces, as at 4: 1, a demand for personal decision, following a recital of what God has done. The issues involved are emphasized by the reference to blessings and curses which concludes the section (11: 26–32). In the Old Testament, as in the New, knowledge about what God has done and feelings of thankfulness or penitence are utterly futile if they do not bear fruit in obedience to God's revealed will.

What God requires (10: 12–22)

Commitment to God must be total (12 f.). Reasons for asking it are God's love in choosing Israel (14 f.); his being and character (17, 18); his redemptive and providential acts (21 f.).

12 f. For the question, cf. Mic. 6: 8. The demands for **fear** (respect, reverence) and **love** (see on 6: 5) are basic. They are bound to be expressed in a way of life defined in general terms as **to walk in all his ways** and **to serve** him; more specifically to **observe** his **commands.** These are no arbitrary expressions of divine sovereignty but **for your own good** (14 f.). The mystery of election (Jn 15: 16; Rom. 8: 28–30) is underlined by reference to God's transcendence (cf. Isa. 40: 12–26) and supplies the reason for commitment to him.

16. By means of a significant method of interpretation, the obstacle to obedience is identified. At the core of human nature (cf. on 6: 5) is resistance to God's will. Circumcision, practised by Israel's neighbours (except the Philistines) as a puberty rite (Exod. 4: 25), but by Israel from birth (Gen. 17: 11 f.), is here given a new meaning, not just as a physical 'badge' but as a symbol of opening up the heart to God. The same metaphor of opening and obedience occurs in Jer. 6: 10, Exod. 6: 12, 30. The idea of spiritual circumcision as characterizing the New Israel is taken up in Phil. 3: 3 and other NT passages. See also Jer. 4: 4; 9: 25 f.

17, 18. These verses express two aspects of God's character that we find hard to reconcile. He is supreme over all gods and (as the Exodus had shown) mighty and to be feared. His justice, unlike that of men, is not biased in favour of the powerful. Yet he is also (18) compassionate to the disadvantaged and in respect of them his justice is seen in redressing the balance of their deprivation. The resident **alien** is especially liable to be exploited (now as then) and so is especially the object of God's care. (For this emphasis, distinctive of Deuteronomy, see also 16: 11, 14; 26: 11; 29: 10–11; 31: 12.)

19. A further reason for showing concern for 'immigrants'. In Phil. 3: 20 and 1 Pet. 2: 11 God's people are seen as still being 'foreigners'.

Obedience and Blessing (11: 1–25)

The long sentence of 1–9 stresses the hearers' past experience of God's power in salvation and judgment and uses this as a reason for expecting obedience to be followed by blessing in the future. Verses 10–25 focus upon the future but make the same point.

2. For the apparent anachronism here, see on 4: 9 f.

3. signs. . . . things he did: a conventional phrase (often 'signs and wonders') for God's mighty acts. The three NT terms for miracles are 'mighty works', 'wonders' and 'signs' (Ac. 2: 22).

8, 9. Once more it is stressed that blessing is not automatic, nor linked to descent, but depends upon obedience.

10–15. In the Middle East, water is scarce and seasonal. In Egypt the supply depends upon human effort; water was raised from the Nile and directed through irrigation channels opened and closed by shifting earth **by foot.** Canaan relied more plainly upon God's decision to send or withhold the autumn and spring rains.

16, 17. Cf. Hos. 2: 8. This direct link between favourable weather and obedience to God corresponds neither to general human experience nor to Mt. 5: 45. It has been suggested that divine providence used this means of instructing Israel uniquely (cf. 1 Kg. 17 f.; Hag. 1: 1–11). Alternatively, we may use such a warning in the spirit of Lk. 13: 4 f.—all 'chance' events bringing blessing or disaster remind us of God's sovereignty and are a stimulus to thanksgiving or heart-searching and penitence.

18–20. These verses repeat 6: 6–9. It may be significant that their presence here separates the curse in 16 f. from the blessing in 21 ff.

24. This territory—from Sinai area and the Negev in the south, to the Lebanon range in the north, and from the Euphrates in the east to the Mediterranean in the west—belonged to Israel only in the time of David.

25. For the panic associated with the holy war cf. 7: 21–24 and Exod. 23: 27.

26–32. This final summary points up the significance of the curse and blessing in vv. 16 f. and 22–25. The mixture of curse and blessing is found in Hittite suzerainty treaties. It was also not unknown for a king, some time before his death, to cause his vassals to swear allegiance to his successor. Thus the covenant renewal ceremony under Joshua, the successor of Moses (Jos. 8: 30–35), may be anticipated here.

28. known: not just 'to be acquainted with' but 'to be personally involved with' (cf. Am. 3: 2).

29. See ch. 27. **Gerizim** and **Ebal** stand in the heart of Canaan on either side of the valley in which Shechem lies. **proclaim:** as in Jos. 8: 30–35. Gerizim is still a cherished site for the Samaritans (cf. Jn 4: 20).

30. This attempt to describe the position of the mountains, which would appear as a foot-note in a modern book, is rather obscure. **Gilgal** ('stone circle') may well not refer to the Gilgal near Jericho.

III. THE COVENANT LAWS (12: 1–26: 19)

This central section of Deuteronomy consists of laws to govern the life of God's people. Many of them are closely paralleled elsewhere, especially in the Book of the Covenant (Exod. 20: 22–23: 33), although half of the laws in this source are not found in Deuteronomy. Some are paralleled in the Code of Hammurabi, and it is difficult to doubt that Hebrew law as a whole was closely related to (although in significant ways different from) a general body of Semitic law. Several general observations may be made concerning the laws in Deuteronomy. (i) They are presented in a hortatory and

theological style rather than a purely legal one; their religious and ethical significance for the covenant people is made clear. Some situations (*e.g.*, civil wrongs leading to actions for damages) are omitted. Some laws are apparently included solely out of humanitarian concern. (ii) They sometimes differ from those of the Book of the Covenant by being modified so as to be more applicable to people (anticipating) living in a settled agricultural community. (iii) Unless they differ from every other body of law, they will include modifications and extensions, made over a period of time to meet changing circumstances and complex situations.

It is not always easy to understand the sequence and arrangement of this section. In general, 12: 1–16: 17 is concerned with worship; 16: 18–20: 20 with social organization; 21: 1–23: 1 with family law; 23: 2–25: 19 with laws of purity; 26: 1–15 describes two rituals; and 26: 16–19 is a closing exhortation.

i. The Law of the Sanctuary (12: 1–29)

Dt. 12 has come to be regarded as crucially important in any attempt to date the book or to trace the history of Israel's religious institutions. For these purposes, attention has focused on vv. 5, 11, 13, 14, 18, 21, 26, all of which restrict certain religious observances (specifically, sacrifice) to 'the place which Yahweh your God will choose out of all your tribes to put his name and habitation there' (5).

It is often suggested that this injunction cannot be ascribed to Moses, since episodes in Judges, Samuel and Kings (*e.g.* 1 Kg. 18) show that sacrifice might acceptably be offered in a wide variety of places. A direct commandment by Moses would scarcely (it is argued) have been ignored in this way. The conclusion has been drawn that throughout the time of the conquest and settlement and on through the period of the judges and the monarchy, sacrifice might be offered at local sanctuaries or 'high places'. This was supposedly the case until Josiah's reformation (2 Kg. 22, 23; 2 Chr. 34, 35) which included the destruction of all local sanctuaries and the deposition of the priests who officiated at them (2 Kg. 23: 5, 8, 13, 15, 19). Josiah's authority for these innovations, it is suggested, may be found in Dt. 12; on this view one of the principal objectives of those who wrote Deuteronomy, possibly in the ninth or eighth century BC, was to centralize worship at Jerusalem in order to eradicate the evils of syncretistic worship at the high places, which was so far (on this view) quite legitimate.

It is not easy to accept such an interpretation. First of all, and most obviously, Dt. 12 (indeed, the whole book) does not mention Jerusalem, a failure difficult to explain on the hypothesis under consideration. Secondly, the emphasis of ch. 12 is not on centralization (contrasting many sanctuaries with one) but on purity ('not as the Canaanites'—12: 2–4, 29–31) and order ('not wherever you choose'—12: 9, 13). Thirdly, there is no explicit reference to worship at the 'high places' (*bāmôth*), for which see note on Ezek. 20: 29, although one of the chief purposes of the writers was supposedly to achieve the destruction of these. (The non-cultic use in 32: 13; 33: 29 underlines this anomaly.) Fourthly, 16: 21 assumes a plurality of altars. Fifthly, 27: 1–8 enjoins the building of an altar not at Jerusalem, but on Mt. Ebal.

The truth about the centralization of Israel's worship (so far as it may be inferred) is more complex than suggested by the hypothesis referred to. There is no reason to doubt that a measure of centralization was present from the beginning of the conquest, since the tabernacle (situated at *e.g.* Shechem, Jos 8: 30 ff.; 24: 1 ff.; and Shiloh, 1 Sam. 1: 3) provided a natural focus for worship. It is equally clear that sacrifice was legitimately offered elsewhere (Exod. 20: 24), especially at places where God had revealed himself to the patriarchs (*e.g.* Bethel) or to later generations (Jg 6: 24). There is, however, no reason to think that worshipping Yahweh at Canaanite high places was regarded as acceptable, within the covenant.

Contrary to the general interpretation, it may well be that Dt. 12 was never intended to centralize the cultus. Just as 12: 5, 11, 14, 18, 21, 26 refer to 'the place' which Yahweh will choose, so 23: 16 refers to 'the place' which an escaped slave will choose to live in; but the second example shows that several different places may be in view, since the usage is distributive ('any place') not restrictive ('the one particular place').

Sacrifice at the Sanctuary (12: 1–14)

2. Shrines on **hills** are mentioned elsewhere in the OT but should not be confused with the 'high places' (*bāmôth*) of *e.g.* 2 Kg. 23: 5. Certain trees were also associated with worship.

3. Not the location only, but the style of Canaanite worship is to be avoided. The **sacred stones were** large upright stones, with phallic associations, possibly symbolizing Baal. **Asherah** were perhaps trees or wooden poles symbolizing Asherah, a mother- and fertility-goddess. By destroying these and the **idols of their Gods**, Israel would de-sacralize the sanctuaries and remove the temptation to worship the gods of Canaan.

4. The worship of Yahweh is to be clearly distinguished from that of other deities, presumably in respect both of locality and ritual.

5. It is the **Name** of Yahweh that will dwell wherever he chooses to reveal himself. (The word translated **dwelling** in the RSV is related to *shekinah* and 'tabernacle'; cf. Jn 1: 14.) This turn of phrase is often regarded as an eighth-century protest against a crassly superstitious view of Yahweh as himself inhabitating the Jerusalem temple, but is probably related to an Akkadian phrase which indicates a claim to sovereignty. The basic principle underlying the idiom is that the Lord is present as and where he discloses himself in sovereign love and grace.

6. This is an almost comprehensive list, although expiatory sacrifices (Lev. 4: 1–5: 16) are omitted. For **burnt offerings** see Lev. 1; for (communion) **sacrifices** see Lev. 7: 12–15; 22: 29, 30, and Lev. 7: 16, 17; 22: 18–23; for **tithes** and **firstborn** see 14: 22–29; the **vowed** and **freewill** offerings are described above as **sacrifices.**

7. Joy would be appropriate, not only in connection with worship but because the ability to fulfil this injunction would imply a settled status in the Promised Land, and the enjoyment of full deliverance.

8. It has been suggested that the phrase **do . . . everyone as he sees fit** may imply freedom (cf. Gen. 19: 8; 2 Kg. 10: 5) rather than licence (Jg. 17: 6; 21: 25). If liberty is meant, it is related to the fact that the desert period was not a time when cultic laws could be scrupulously observed. But a passage such as Jos. 5: 4–7 suggests that licence and laxity may be intended.

9, 10. Two such periods might have been the time after Joshua's successful campaign (Jos. 22: 4; 23: 1) or after David's victories (2 Sam. 7: 1; 1 Kg. 5: 3). But apparently neither opportunity was taken; and neglected opportunity proved (as it often does) to be disastrous.

12. This sounds more like an ideal than a literally practical possibility; some members of the household will have had to stay back with the animals and to guard the home. For **Levite** see on 18: 1–8. Since they taught the law in the villages of Israel (33: 10; 2 Chr. 15: 3; 17: 8, 9) and are specifically associated with Deuteronomy (31: 24–26), they may well have interpreted and updated it in later years.

13, 14. Whereas vv. 2–4 refer explicitly to Canaanite shrines and customs, these verses also prohibit (as does v. 5) individual or corporate innovation of a kind unsanctioned by the Lord. Both tendencies threaten the life and worship of God's people.

Sacred and ordinary meals (12: 15–28)

During the desert period, and while a legitimate sanctuary was near, the blood of a slaughtered domestic animal might easily be offered to God (27) and its flesh eaten in the context of a sacrificial feast, by members of the household who were ritually clean. This rule did not apply to animals such as **gazelle** or **deer** (15, 22) which were hunted, and might be killed some distance from the sanctuary. In a more settled situation, with the sanctuary at a distance (21), animals might be eaten without any religious or ritual consideration apart from the pouring out of the blood (16, 23–25). Special provision was made, however, for sacred meals at the sanctuary (26–28).

16. See Gen. 9: 4. God alone gives life to all living creatures. So the **blood** is sacred; it may not be manipulated for pagan rituals nor eaten (23–25).

20. In fact, meat was rarely eaten, except by the rich (cf. Am. 6: 4). Animals were kept for their produce, not their flesh. Meat was a luxury.

ii. The Sin of Idolatry (12: 29–13: 18)
The worship of Yahweh is to be different from that offered to the gods of Canaan (12: 29–32). Incitement to idolatry is to be firmly dealt with, whether it comes from a prophet (13: 1–5), a relation (13: 6–11) or a local community (13: 12–18).

30. While there is a great deal to be said for viewing the rituals of other religions with sympathetic insight, God's people in all ages have created appalling problems for themselves and distorted their own faith by incorporating alien practices and concepts.

31. For child sacrifice to Molech see Lev. 18: 21; Jer. 7: 31 and numerous references in 2 Kg. For the practice in time of national danger cf. 2 Kg. 3: 27. Archaeology confirms its prevalence in Canaan; it was a source of horror to the OT writers.

32. Cf. 4: 2; Rev. 22: 18 f.

13: 1–5. Dreams were regarded as a vehicle of revelation (Jer. 23: 25–32). But even if supported by miraculous powers, no prophetic oracle should be accepted if it entailed disloyalty to Yahweh. A later answer to an obvious question concerning the origin of the wonder-worker's power would be to ascribe this to demonic forces; but here the problem is solved by reference to the sole sovereignty of Yahweh, who brings it about as a test (cf. 1 C. 11: 19). The language of vv. 3, 4 is typical of Deuteronomy.

5. The provision for capital punishment here shows how absurd it is to treat 5: 17 as being in any simplistic sense an argument against the death penalty. The emphasis on purging the community of infection corresponds to Paul's demand in 1 C. 5: 1–13. Yet there is little evidence that the death penalty was generally exacted in this and in similar cases (17: 12; 19: 11–13; 21: 18–21; 22: 21–24; 24: 7) so that it has been suggested that the provision was intended basically to emphasize the gravity of the offence.

6–11. In view of the biblical emphasis on family life it is remarkable that loyalty to Yahweh takes precedence over family loyalty (cf. Lk. 14: 26). But the solidarity of the family (cf. Jos. 7) is grounded in the covenant.

9. The responsibility of 'casting the first stone' (see 17: 7) would both discourage careless accu-

sation and—unlike capital punishment today—make the 'executioners' personally involved in the sentence. Cf. Jn 8: 7; Ac. 7: 58.

12–18. The apostate city is to be subjected to the *ḥērem*, like Jericho. No personal gain will result (17) and the deserted city will become a *tell* (16), a mound formed by the ruins of the buildings. But a searching judicial enquiry must first take place (14); the roots of equity are found in the OT.

iii. Pagan Mourning Rites Forbidden (14: 1, 2)
Religion generally includes a cult of the dead, but anything of this kind is forbidden to God's people ('sons of Yahweh' is unique, though cf. Exod. 4: 22; Hos. 11: 1). Speculation about the meaning of the ceremonies is interesting but irrelevant; the point is that here, as in the OT generally, attention is focused on serving Yahweh in this life—a very different attitude from that of most religions. (But see Isa. 22: 12; Jer. 16: 6; Ezek. 7: 7.)

Clean and unclean food (14: 3–21)
The importance of these food laws (and rabbinic extensions of them) to the life of the Jews is well known. It is futile to seek detailed explanations for the inclusion and exclusion of creatures. We may suspect an avoidance of totemistic practices (the crow [14] was sacred to some Arab clans); hygienic implications are seen by modern readers (8); there is evidence that 21b (repeated in Exod. 23: 19; 34: 26) refers to a Canaanite ritual. But the Hebrews will not have looked for reasons—these were the divinely sanctioned and unalterable customs and taboos of the people, many of them doubtless observed from the distant past. Although in God's providence some did have hygienic value, they expressed and emphasized the uniqueness of the covenant people (2). They also witnessed to God's sovereignty over every detail of daily life. In both respects they teach an eternal lesson.

21. Blood would remain in such an animal (12: 23). If hygiene had been the chief consideration, concern for the resident alien or foreigner would have excluded their being offered it.

v. Tithing (14: 22–29)
It is not easy on any hypothesis to reconcile the various laws about tithing (see Lev. 27: 30–33 and Num. 18: 21–32; also Dt. 26: 1–15). A summary of the points at issue may be seen in Thompson, pp. 179–185. The general principle is stated in v. 22, and supplemented in v. 23 (which includes a reference to firstlings), vv. 24–26, 27–29. Gen. 14: 20 and 18: 22 show tithing as an ancient custom; Gen. 41: 34 (as well as extra-biblical reference) is a reminder that kings used this means of taxation. Important NT references are Lk. 18: 9–14; 1 C. 16: 2; 2 C. 9: 7. The principle of proportionate giving to God is not confined to the old covenant.

23. It is difficult to think that the whole tithe was to be used thus, even if passages such as 1 Sam. 9: 12; 20: 29 are related to this practice. **24–26.** This provision, a realistic one at a time when a central sanctuary was in view, is unparalleled in the OT. **27–29.** In every third year, special provision is made for local Levites. (But what, one asks, happened to priests at the central sanctuary in this year? Or to the local Levites and poor in the other two? Was the third year not simultaneously observed?)

vi. The year for cancelling debts (15: 1–11)
This passage begins with a brief statement of the law (1) followed by an explanation of it (2, 3) and an exhortation to obey it from the heart (4–11).
1. The practice is related in Exod. 23: 10–11; Lev. 25: 1–7 to letting the land lie fallow every seventh year.
2. But here the money-lending classes also make a 'sabbath' sacrifice. Verses 7–9 show that what is in view is complete remission of a debt contracted because of urgent need.
3. The provision is restricted to the covenant community.
4, 5. Again, the link between obedience and prosperity is stressed. Verse 11 shows a realistic understanding of what is likely to happen; cf. Mt. 26: 11.
6. A second basic principle: Not only are God's people to foster social and economic equality —they are not to put trust in unbelievers.
7–11. The generosity inculcated here has links not only with 2 C. 9: 7 but with the emphasis the Sermon on the Mount places on the importance of motive.

vii. Limitation of Slavery (15: 12–18)
Humanitarian concern (rare in ancient times as today but common in the OT) extends to debtors who have sold themselves as slaves. Women, of lower status in the parallel passage, Exod. 21: 2–11, are here treated like men. Not only are Hebrew slaves to receive freedom in the year of release; they must be given what they need to start a new life (13, 14). The reason is a theological one (15); belief inevitably affects behaviour.

The ceremony in vv. 16, 17 regularizes the position of a slave who values his place in his master's household (cf., *e.g.*, Eliezer, Gen. 24: 2 ff.) or who cannot cope with independence. In Exod. 21: 6 the ceremony of ear-piercing may be located at the sanctuary; here it is in the home. (There is nothing to be said for attempts to relate v. 17 to Ps. 40: 6.)
18. An appeal to reason and natural justice —the OT is not authoritarian, irrational and arbitrary, as often asserted by its enemies and sometimes implied by its friends.

viii. The Law of Firstlings (15: 19–23)
Cf. 12: 6, 7; 14: 23. Again, a brief statement

(19a) is expanded and applied. **19.** The firstborn belongs to God and is not to be used for economic gain. **20.** It is to provide a sacred (but doubtless an exuberant) annual meal at the sanctuary. **21.** Only the best may be given to God; cf. Mal. 1: 7 ff. **22, 23.** Cf. 12: 20–24; the blemish has desacralized the firstling.

ix. The Three Annual Pilgrimages (16: 1–17)
Just as Islam today has its *ḥaj*, or pilgrimage to Mecca, so Israel used the word *ḥāg* of these occasions when worshippers visited the central sanctuary. There is reason to believe that all three festivals (passover with unleavened bread, vv. 1–8; weeks, vv. 9–12; and booths, vv. 13–15) were connected with earlier agricultural festivals, which Israel was led to adapt and reinterpret as a commemoration of God's historical saving acts.

Passover and Unleavened Bread (1–8)
1. The antiquity of this law is shown by its using the Canaanite term, *Abib*, for March —April. The month was later known by its Babylonian name, *Nisan*.
2. Whereas passover had originally been a family festival, it is now linked to the central sanctuary. The historical books imply that this provision was largely ignored until the time of Hezekiah (2 Chr. 30: 26). In Exod. 12, the animal word used is to be a lamb, but here the technical word for **sacrifice** is employed and the victim may be from the **flock or herd** (see 2 Chr. 30: 24; 35: 7, though cf. vv. 1 and 6). This apparent innovation may be explained by Num. 28: 16–25.
3. The festival of unleavened bread was merged with the passover; it began on the fifteenth, the day after the passover, and went on for seven days. It corresponded to a widely observed festival associated with the barley harvest. But to Israel it spoke of a hurried journey, with no time for dough to be left to rise, and of the affliction in Egypt.
5, 6. The ceremony is centralized and thus sacralized. By NT times it was again eaten in the family but near to the sanctuary where the victim could be killed.
7. roast: Num. 11: 8 and 2 Sam. 13: 8 suggest the verb on its own may mean simply 'cook'. The reference to **tents** implies an early date.

The Feast of Weeks (9–12)
This was known also as 'the feast of harvest' (Exod. 23: 16) and 'the day of the first-fruits' (Num. 28: 26); later, from the fifty day period involved, as Pentecost. In the warmer parts of Palestine, barley ripens by April, but wheat rather later. Harvest would thus begin at the time of unleavened bread and end about seven weeks later. **10.** Once more, giving is to be proportionate; cf. v. 17. **11.** There is to be a shared feast. **12.** The festival is understood in terms of history and salvation, rather than

nature and fruitfulness (cf. the Christian interpretation of Easter).

The Feast of Booths (13–15)

Celebrations in autumn, to celebrate the harvest of olives and grapes and other summer fruits, were not uncommon in the Near East. In Lev. 23: 43 this is linked to the nomadic life-style associated with the exodus, but temporary dwellings in the fields may in any case have been appropriate during the harvest. **15. your joy will be complete:** cf. v. 11. The note of joy has too often been missing from the worship of God's new covenant people.

Summary: Annual Pilgrimages (16–17)

It may be significant that contemporary Near Eastern suzerainty treaties require vassals to report periodically to renew their oath of allegiance.

x. The Duties of Officials (16: 18–18: 22)

It is vital that God's people be rightly led and this section refers to judges (16: 18–20); the court (17: 8–13); kings (17: 14–20); priests (18: 1–8); and prophets (18: 9–22). The section 16: 21–17: 7, dealing with worship, appears to be misplaced from 12: 1–14: 21 but provides a reminder that sacred and secular were not divided in Israel; all authority came from Yahweh. It may also be significant that such pagan symbols as are forbidden in 16: 21 f. were associated with receiving oracles.

Judges (16: 18–20)

In 19: 12 and generally in the OT the local elders act as judges, though in 17: 8–13 there is provision for a central court of appeal (cf. 2 Chr. 19: 5–11). The role of **officials** is not clear. See Exod. 5: 6 f.; Dt. 20: 5 f.; 2 Chr. 34: 13 and 1 Chr. 23: 4; 26: 29. Verse 19 gives three brief apodictic rules about justice, expanded in 19d and applied in v. 20. **18. Judge . . . fairly:** still a rare blessing and not to be taken for granted. **17: 2–7.** See on 12: 32–13: 18.

The Central Court (17: 8–13)

Apparently the possibility of an appeal was not open to the accused (or the parties in dispute) but depended on the decision of the local judges to seek guidance from priests and (lay) judges at the central sanctuary, each group having a leader (9, 12). It is not stated whether the decision would be based on precedent or on use of the sacred lot, but it was to be received as coming with divine authority (12). Nor is it certain how such a court's jurisdiction related to that of the king. Verses 12, 13 offer a clear example of deterrent punishment.

The King (17: 14–20)

This is an amazing passage. True, suzerainty treaties might include stipulations about the choice of a king, but no other Near Eastern state would view its sovereign in this way. The monarchy is seen as permitted only, not ordained, by God (14, 15). The king (like a

greater King of Israel) is to be a fellow servant of the covenant (15), subject to its requirements (18, 19). Elsewhere, the king was God. In Israel, God was king.

15. This view of the monarchy resembles that of Hosea and 1 Sam. 8: 1 ff., 16, 17; cf. 1 Sam. 8: 11–18 and especially the example of Solomon. But such tendencies were common in the Near East. (Some centuries later, there were Hebrew mercenary soldiers in Egypt.) To behave thus implied lack of trust in Yahweh. **18–20.** A vassal king used to receive a copy of a suzerainty treaty; another would be placed in the shrine of the suzerain's god. 2 Kg. 11: 12 shows these stipulations being obeyed. Only the law of the covenant could preserve the king from the dangers of his position.

The Priests (18: 1–8)

The tribe of Levi had no tribal allotment, so special provision is made for their support (cf. 1 C. 9: 13, 14).

1. The priests who are the Levites: cf. 17: 9, 18; 24: 8; 27: 9. At 21: 5 and 31: 9 we find 'the priests the sons of Levi'. It is often suggested that all Levites were originally priests and that the designation of the sons of Aaron alone as priests was a later development, but this passage does not support the theory. All priests were Levites but not all Levites were priests, and we may translate here: 'the priests, the Levites—the whole tribe of Levi' (a similar construction occurs in 17: 1).

2. They did possess isolated settlements (Jos. 21).

3. Large numbers of right shoulder-bones have been found in a Canaanite temple at Lachish. The differences between this passage and Lev. 7: 28–36, Num. 18: 8–19 are not very significant; the priests' position may have varied locally or with time.

4. Cf. Num. 18: 12; 2 Chr. 31: 5 — the **wool** is mentioned only here.

6–8. These verses, which preserve the rights of Levites following the establishment of a central sanctuary, distinguish clearly between priestly and non-priestly Levites. Not only 10: 8; Num. 16: 9 but especially 2 Chr. 29: 11 show that the verbs in v. 7 need not imply priestly service. The Hebrew of v. 8b is not clear.

The Prophet (18: 9–22)

After a prohibition of the practices by which it was (and is) allegedly possible to gain supernatural knowledge (9–14) follows a promise that through the institution of prophecy Israel will have its own means of illumination (15–18). This obligates the nation to obey the word of Yahweh thus spoken (19) and to distinguish Yahweh's message from the words of men (20–22). **15. The LORD . . . will raise up . . . a prophet like me:** the promise has both individual and corporate significance. By NT times, it was understood of a precursor of the Messiah or of the Messiah himself (Jn 1: 21, 45; 6: 14; 6: 40; Ac. 3: 20–22; 7: 37, etc.).

16. It is remarkable that the only passage in the Torah which establishes prophecy as part of Israel's religion does so on this basis.

18. Cf. 17: 15; neither king nor prophet is above the covenant.

20–22. A difficult question (Jn 1: 19–25; Mk 12: 28). Two tests are stipulated—fulfilment of a prediction and loyalty to Yahweh. For other answers, see Jer. 23: 9–32; Ezek. 13; 19: 1–21.

xi. Criminal Law (19: 1–21)

Verses 1–13 deal with homicide; vv. 15–21 with witnesses; v. 14 is about boundary marks.

1–13. As in many decentralized societies, responsibility for avenging death by violence lay with the next of kin who might well act overhastily, even in a case of accidental death (4–6). Hence three cities are designated as sanctuaries (1–3), with the possibility of others being designated later (8, 9). This system is more fully described in Num. 35: 9–34 (cf. Exod. 21: 12–14). Jos. 20: 7–21: 40 describes how six were allocated, all of them Levitical. (If Dt. 4: 41–43 is an editorial note, then no more were envisaged.) The fact that the cities were Levitical and the right of asylum associated with the high priest (Jos. 20: 6) may indicate that they were regarded as an extension of the altar (Exod. 21: 14b). Murderers, on the other hand, might not use a city of refuge to escape justice (11–13). Such laws as these clearly antedate the rise of the monarchy and centralized government.

10. For this important idea, cf. v. 13; 21: 1–9; 22: 8; Gen. 4: 10–12; 2 Sam. 21: 1; Hos. 4: 2 f.; Lk. 11: 50 f.; Heb. 12: 24.

14. The **boundary stone** was of great importance in legal disputes and marked off land holdings dependent upon God's covenant gift.

15–21. A good example of a basic apodictic law ('A single witness shall not prevail against a man') with legal interpretation and homiletic application (19b–20).

15b. Cf. 2 C. 13: 1b; 1 Tim. 5: 19. **16.** The evil motives of the witness will, of course, appear only after investigation. **17.** A tribunal like that of 17: 9 ff. seems to be implied. **19b.** Cf. 13: 5 and other uses of this term, which is applied to practices attracting the death penalty, so that the 'false witness' may be thought to have himself sought the death of the accused. **21.** For the *lex talionis*, see Exod. 21: 23 ff.; Lev. 24: 17 ff.

xii. The Holy War (20: 1–20)

Until the early monarchy, military operations sanctioned by Yahweh were seen as a religious duty. (The concept was revived at Qumran, witness the document entitled: *The Warfare of the Sons of Light and the Sons of Darkness*.) From the evidence in Deuteronomy, Judges and 1

and 2 Samuel, we can build up a picture of the procedure. (*a*) Yahweh was consulted (1 Sam. 28: 5, 19, 22, 23). (*b*) The men of Israel were assembled and 'consecrated' (1 Sam. 21: 5; 2 Sam. 11: 11; Dt. 23: 9–14). (*c*) Victory was won, not by military strength, but by the action of Yahweh in demoralizing the enemy (Jg. 7; 1 Sam. 13: 15 ff.; 14: 6, 17; Jos. 10: 10; Jg. 4: 15; 1 Sam. 5: 11; 7: 10). (*d*) The spoil was subject to the *ḥērem* (see on 2: 34 f.) and belonged to Yahweh.

1. The untrained Hebrew foot-soldiers were no match for the armaments of Egypt (Exod. 14: 26–28) and Canaan (Jos. 11: 4; 17: 16; Jg. 1: 19; 4: 3). Later they acquired chariots (1 Kg. 4: 26) but to trust in these was proverbially to lack faith in Yahweh, who, like any other suzerain, was committed to support his vassals (Isa. 30: 16; 31: 1 ff.; Hos. 14: 3).

2. Priests and prophets and interpreters of omens regularly accompanied armies in the ancient world. Their role was seen as far more than merely psychological; they exercised an important influence on the outcome. Here the priest represents Yahweh's presence (cf. 1 Sam. 18: 18; 2 Sam. 11: 11).

5–7. Three points may be made about these exemptions. (*a*) They are probably rooted in ancient tabus which viewed individuals who had anything to inaugurate as being threatened by demonic powers. (*b*) Here they are of humanitarian significance, like so much else in this book. (*c*) Our Lord used similar examples (Lk. 14: 16–24) to show that no excuses exempt men from serving him. The **officers** (5) would in pre-monarchy days be tribal leaders (1: 15).

8. Cf. Jg. 7: 3. It is all too easy to demoralize God's people.

10–14. These comparatively lenient terms (especially so in view of contemporary practice) are to be offered only to enemies outside the promised land (15).

16–18. For the *ḥērem*, see on 2: 34, 35.

19, 20. There is no reason why Moses should not have known about siege warfare, since it was practised in Egypt and Canaan. But the prohibition in these verses—surely unique in the standing orders of any army—represents an ecological wisdom we are only now recognizing. Yet the argument deployed (19c) is not prudential, but recognizes the dignity of the rest of creation over against man.

xiii. Miscellaneous Laws (21: 1–25: 19)

It is hard to distinguish any pattern in this section although some laws are grouped together (*e.g.* 21: 10–21, family affairs; 23: 1–18, the purity of the community).

Unsolved Murder (21: 1–9)

This is clearly a very ancient ritual, nearer to magic than almost any other in the Bible, but lifted above magic by the liturgy of v. 8 and the application in v. 9.

2. The community which is threatened by the unexpiated blood is identified and accepts responsibility. **3.** The heifer, although not sacrificed, is chosen as if it were a sacrificial victim. **4.** Is virgin land chosen so that, like the virgin animal, it can accept the defilement of the bloodshed? Or so that the **blood**, transferred to the soil, need never be disturbed by the plough? Or is it seen as desert (cf. the scapegoat in Lev. 16: 22)? In any case, the death of the heifer is not sacrificial (but apotropaic?) since its neck is broken and no ritual is performed with the blood.

5. The priests are presumably connected with a local theophanic shrine; they will scarcely have travelled from the central sanctuary. **6.** This hand-washing is less of a formality than Pilate's; the threat of the unexpiated blood is keenly felt. **7, 8.** The purgation of v. 7 is transposed drastically by the appeal in v. 8 to the covenant relationship. **9b.** Indeed, since it is Yahweh who has provided the ritual, it is he who lifts the community's guilt. Corporate guilt is an alien concept to the modern world, but passages such as this challenge the reader to take it seriously.

Female Prisoners (21: 10–14)
It may be significant that both here and in vv. 15–17 the rights of a husband are delimited. But v. 10 places the law in a holy war context (20: 1) and the reference to woman in 20: 14, which applies to a distant city, may explain why 7: 3 is ignored.

12. The significance of these actions is unknown (but cf. 34: 8; Num. 20: 29). **13.** After a humane period of mourning and adjustment, the woman gains the full status of a wife. **14.** Consequently she may not be reduced to slavery. Here is another example of the higher status Deuteronomy gives women.

The Rights of the First-Born (21: 15–17)
Once more, a man is forbidden to behave arbitrarily. The ancient custom of favouring the first-born (Gen. 27; 48: 14) is here made obligatory. The absence of any reference to the situation envisaged in Num. 27: 1–11 is a reminder that Deuteronomy is preaching rather than legal code. These verses are a good example of how hate/love implies preference rather than emotional response (Mt. 6: 24; Rom. 9: 13). **17.** Cf. 2 Kg 2: 9.

A Rebellious Son (21: 18–21)
Here too the father's authority is limited. Only the community can deal with this offence which has passed beyond the jurisdiction of the family. Contrast Gen. 28: 24. Yet the father's authority is strengthened in this way, since the community stands behind him. Does this law underlie Isa. 1: 27? **19.** Both parents must agree about the seriousness of the case. **20.** Presumably other offences might be cited. **21.** In this case, the accusers

did not participate in the execution. There is no record of the procedure ever being invoked, but cf. Mk 7: 10 for a possible reference.

Exposure of a corpse (21: 22–23)
The reference is not to crucifixion, which was not a Hebrew punishment, but to exhibiting a corpse after execution (Jos. 8: 29; 10: 26 f.; 2 Sam. 4: 12; 21: 8 f.). The association of a curse with this is presumably because the criminal's fate demonstrates Yahweh's judgment against sin. But it is not altogether easy to see why this practice, which demonstrates that the land has been purged of evil, should defile it. Perhaps the sight is a witness to the sin of which the wrong-doer was guilty. It is not difficult, however, to see why this passage reverberated in Paul's mind (Gal. 3: 13).

Lost Property (22: 1–3)
Whereas Exod. 23: 4 ff. occurs in a legal context and states that even the adversary in a law-suit must be helped in this way, the law here is broader, since **brother** includes everyone of God's people.

Transvestism (22: 5)
Within living memory, this verse has been cited against the wearing of trousers by women; yet there has been no corresponding refusal to wear rayon/cotton or terylene/worsted mixtures (11). The practice referred to may have been thought to have magical effects. There is certainly evidence of transvestism and simulated sexual inversion being associated in the ancient world (as well as today) with sexual licence—and in a religious context.

Spare the mother bird (22: 6–7)
Another humanitarian law, with ecological value.

A safety regulation (22: 8)
Cf. Gen. 4: 9b. Factory acts have a biblical basis!

Unnatural combinations (22: 9–11)
See Lev. 19: 19. In the absence of any evidence, one must assume that magical practices of some kind are forbidden here.

Clothes with Tassels (22: 12)
In view of the tendency of Deuteronomy to supply theological explanations, it is surprising that the one in Num. 15: 37–41 is ignored here. The custom is perpetuated in the *tallith* (prayer shawl).

Six Marriage Laws (22: 13–30)
These laws are clearly linked by subject matter. Israel had high standards of sexual morality. Only one (30) is apodictic.
The bride accused of unchastity (13–21). The test, presumably the display of the blood-stained bed linen following intercourse, is not infallible but is used in other cultures also. If judgment goes against the groom, who would have sought the return of the bride-prize, he is both flogged and severely (28 f.) fined. He also loses the right to divorce his wife. But the guilty

bride is treated as an adulteress (22) since betrothal was binding (cf. Mt. 1: 19). Her father's responsibility is emphasized by the place selected for the execution (21). **21. a disgraceful thing** (*n*ᵉ*bālāh*): often euphemistically used of sexual offences (Gen. 34: 7; Jg. 19: 23; 20: 6-10; 2 Sam. 13: 12). It comes from the root n-b-l associated with *nābāl* (fool) as in Ps. 14: 1; 1 Sam. 25: 25.

Adultery (22). Explicitly forbidden in the Decalogue and destructive of family life, adultery was not always punished thus, to judge by Prov. 6: 25-35.

Seduction of a betrothed girl (23-27). The offence is treated as adultery, since the girl belongs to another man, but she is assumed to be innocent if the incident occurred in a remote place.

Seduction of an unmarried girl (28, 29). Uncomplicated by ideals of romantic love, and more realistic than Christians have sometimes been in evaluating sexual sin, the law simply demands payment of a bride price (though note the reason) and loss of the man's right to divorce.

Intercourse with a step-mother (30). Although some societies permitted this, and it is not unknown in the OT, Hebrew law forbade the introduction of sexual relationships into the extended family circle (Lev. 18: 6 ff.; Dt. 27: 20; cf. 1 C. 5: 1). Here, as elsewhere in this legislation, the law of Israel reminds permissive societies that monogamy and fidelity are divinely ordained for the benefit of society, that is, of men and women.

Exclusion from the assembly (23: 1-8)

Five apodictic laws (expanded in 4-6) define who shall be excluded from worship and social responsibility.

1. Perhaps because of imperfection (cf. Lev. 21: 16-23, although these verses are concerned only with the food offering). More likely because castration was a religious ritual in Canaan as elsewhere. Another viewpoint is seen in Isa. 56: 3 ff.; cf. Ac. 8: 27 f.

2. no one born of a forbidden marriage: Heb. *mamzēr*, which may refer to the offspring of incestuous unions or of mixed marriages.

3-6. Cf. Dt. 2: 18 ff., 29 and Num. 22-24.

7, 8. Edomites traced their descent to Esau. **third generation:** contrast vv. 2, 3. **abhor:** Heb. *ti'ēb*, 'to treat as if ritually impure'.

Purity of the camp (23: 9-14)

During war, Yahweh was especially present with his people, so precautions against offending him must be scrupulous. The non-ethical sense of 'holy' is clear in v. 14. While we may see the hygienic value of vv. 12-14, it will not have been apparent to ancient Israel. The law in vv. 10, 11 (cf. Lev. 15: 16) possibly indicates the awe attaching to life and reproduction.

Cultic and social laws (23: 15-25)

The refugee slave (15, 16). The slave of a foreigner is in view, since a Hebrew owner might claim the return of his property. No Hebrew may re-enslave the refugee. (Ch. 15: 15 is relevant here, and—to the Christian—Jn 8: 34.)

Religious prostitution (17, 18). Temple prostitutes, of both sexes and sometimes (men at least) practising homosexuality, were common in non-biblical religion and still exist (1 Kg. 14: 24; 2 Kg. 23: 7). The word used is *qādēš*/*q*ᵉ*dēšāh*, a holy man/woman. The practice is here forbidden nor may proceeds from it be dedicated to Yahweh.

Money loaned at interest (19, 20). This community knows nothing of co-operative trading ventures, let alone joint stock companies. Loans were normally for the relief of distress, and brotherly love forbade taking interest in such circumstances. Rates of 50 per cent are seen at Nuzi in the fifteenth century B.C. The foreigner, being a trader or merchant (cf. 'Canaanite' in Zech. 14: 21; Prov. 31: 24) is in a different category.

Vows (21-23). This is scarcely a law—another sign that Deuteronomy is not a formal lawcode. Cf. Ec. 5: 4 ff. It inculcates honesty before God and Ac. 5: 3 f. provides a salutary illustration.

A neighbour's crops (23-25). Here is a caring community, which yet prohibits exploitation of those who provide welfare (cf. the Pharisees' tendentious interpretation in Mk 2: 23-28).

Remarriage with a former wife (24: 1-4)

It is important to recognize that this law deals with one very special case only and in its complexity (the whole is one sentence, cf. Exod. 21: 1-6) assumes rather than promulgates a law of divorce. (Such a law is nowhere stated in the OT and must be inferred.) The law gives no reason why a man should not remarry his divorced wife upon the termination of her second marriage (4) but simply expresses abhorrence at the thought in two ancient formulae (4b; cf. 23: 18b and 22: 23). It has been pointed out that this prohibition would tend to stabilize the woman's second marriage and might restrain divorce.

1. indecency: lit. 'the nakedness of a thing'—not adultery (22: 22) nor necessarily any moral failing (cf. 23: 14 where the same term is used). By NT times the meaning had been forgotten. The **certificate of divorce** would (*a*) confer status on the woman (necessary in view of 22: 22) and (*b*) make it impossible for divorce to occur hastily, especially if a public official had to engross it. Yet not until he **sends her from his house** (formally) is the divorce complete. **3. dislikes:** Heb. 'hates'; cf. 21: 15-17. **4.** Both Hosea and Jeremiah found this relevant to their own experience and religious insight (Hos. 1-3; Jer. 3: 1-8).

Social Laws (24: 5–25: 4)
Exemption from military service (24: 5). Cf. 20: 7.
Respect for the family and the need to have
descendants takes priority over the Holy War.
The millstone sacrosanct (24: 6). The poor man is
protected by this law; were his creditor to take
the millstone, the debtor's family could not
prepare bread.
Kidnapping (24: 7). A restatement of Exod. 21:
16. Contrast Dt. 15: 22 ff. and note the severe
penalty for slave-trading and the 'purging' formula.
Laws about loans (24: 10–13). Again, the humanitarian concern of Deuteronomy appears. Even
the 'wealthy' creditor may not intrude into the
home of the poor borrower and if he takes
as a pledge the borrower's cloak, it must be
returned at evening (Exod. 22: 26, 27).
Rights of the day-labourer (24: 14–15). Once more
Yahweh appears as the protector of the defenceless. Whether a Hebrew or a resident alien, the
day labourer could not survive without money
to buy food and shelter for the night; 'he counts
on it' (GNB). God's people should not keep
creditors waiting for payment.
Personal responsibility (24: 16). See 2 Kg. 14: 6.
Although the OT assigns great importance to
corporate solidarity, the concept of personal
responsibility is very ancient. It is found also
in Hammurabi's Code, but there a son might
be executed if his father's negligence caused the
death of another man's son (2: 30). Ezekiel
(Ezek. 18) was thus enunciating no new principle when he (like Jeremiah) denounced the
fatalistic view that 'the fathers have eaten sour
grapes and the children's teeth are set on edge'.
For v. 17, cf. v. 13.
Laws of charity (24: 19–22). Part of the three
main crops (grain, olives, grapes) is reserved
for the poor—a form of welfare state in which
the deprived are able to profit by their own
efforts, as Ruth did, with some assistance (Ru.
2).
22. Again this motif recurs (see v. 18).
Corporal punishment (25: 1–3). Apparently a
judge could impose such a sentence (2) but
even a criminal must not be humiliated beyond
measure. As a 'fence' around this law, a limit
of 39 strokes was customary by the first century
A.D. (2 C. 11: 24).
The Ox in the Corn (25: 4). In spite of Paul's
question in 1 C. 9: 9, this law does show a
respect for animals similar to that in 22: 6 f.
Levirate Marriage (25: 5–10)
For other references to this practice, which was
not confined to Israel, see Gen. 38; Ru. 4 and
Mk 12: 18–27. It was designed to ensure that
the name of the dead man be perpetuated (6)
and his land not be alienated. The case of Ruth
is not altogether clear, since there was no
brother-in-law (Lat. *levir*) and the man who
should have acted as *gōʾēl* declined to do so.

9. For the transfer of a **sandal** in connection
with property rights see Ru. 4: 7; Ps. 60: 8.
Indecent Assault (25: 11–12)
Mutilation was a recognized punishment
among Israel's neighbours and (later) in Islamic
law but, apart from 19: 21, this is the only case
where it is prescribed in Hebrew law. The
severity of the punishment, and the present
context, may be explained by the possibility of
damage to the testicles (vv. 5, 6).
Fair trading (25: 13–16)
Cf. Lev. 19: 35 f., also (for use of dishonest
weights and measures) Am. 8: 5.
   Love to one's neighbour entails honest dealing. **15. just** (*ṣedeq*) is the word used for ethical
and judicial righteousness.
The Amalekites (25: 17–19)
This is not a legal regulation like those that
precede it but marks a transition from (chiefly)
ethical and social to ritual and liturgical requirements (26: 1–19). Since Amalek does not appear as an enemy of Israel after 2 Sam. 8: 12
this law would be irrelevant at a later date. The
tradition of a wanton attack on the rear of the
weary Hebrew fugitives is not mentioned in
Exod. 17: 8–16. But Am. 1: 3–2: 3 shows that
even those who are outside the sphere of special
revelation may be expected to **have fear of
God** and obey what Paul refers to (Rom. 2:
15) as the requirements of God's law written
(by common grace) in their hearts. Israel,
acting in accordance with the principles
of the holy war, is to be the instrument
of God's judgment (Ps. 149: 7; Isa. 41: 14,
15).

**xiv. Covenant Liturgies and Ratification
(26: 1–19)**
The legal stipulations of the covenant conclude
with two cultic liturgies (1–11, 12–15) and a
declaration of the ratification of the covenant
(16–19).
(a) **First-fruits liturgy (26: 1–11)**
It is not easy to reconstruct the law of tithes and
first-fruits. A first-fruits offering is associated
with each of the pilgrim festivals (Lev. 23: 9–
11; Num. 28: 26 and Lev. 23: 15–17; and the
first-fruits of wine could not be offered until
the Festival of Booths in the autumn). Cf. Dt.
16: 16 f. Perhaps the ritual of vv. 1–11 was for
a token offering in the autumn. In addition,
there is a difficulty about v. 11 which seems to
imply participation in a first-fruits feast
although these are reserved for the priests in
Num. 18: 13 f. But the greater abundance
of Canaan may have occasioned a change
in the law; in any case, it is not said that
the feast should be provided from the first-
fruits.
   The most remarkable feature of the liturgy
is the way it links the blessings of the soil,
not with cyclic natural forces (such as were
associated with Baal—see the amazing state-

ment in Hos. 2: 8) but with God's saving acts in history, and in particular with the exodus and the conquest of Canaan. In addition, by its focusing on the objective recital of what God had done for all his people it calls into question any tendency to reduce worship to the mere expression of subjective feelings.

Some scholars have seen significance in the fact that vv. 5–10 and some similar summaries (Jos. 24: 2b–13; 1 Sam. 12: 8; Ps. 136) make no reference to Sinai. But we need not postulate the existence of independent tribal traditions one of which knew nothing of Sinai, and which were merged only after the settlement in Canaan. This solemn recital is not necessarily to be regarded as an exhaustive credal declaration; it focuses above all on the gift of the land to landless nomads.

3. the priest: i.e. the chief priest of the central sanctuary. **4.** Either the priest's action at this point is imitated later by the worshipper (10) or the injunction of v. 10 is regarded as fulfilled by the procedure of v. 4.

5. Aramean: the reference is probably to Jacob, who, like Abraham, lived for a time in Aram-Naharaim, where the tribe of Terah came from (Gen. 11: 31). **wandering:** the word can mean either 'lost' or 'dying'.

6–11. The pattern of thanksgiving and worship transcends the ancient ritual. The worshipper remembers the plight from which God has delivered his people, his response to their cry for deliverance, his power in redemption, and the blessings he gives. All this prompts the worshipper to give in return, and to rejoice with others whom God has blessed.

(*b*) **Third Year Tithe Liturgy (26: 12–15)**
Although this tithe was allocated locally (12), the worshipper must nevertheless make a formal declaration, presumably while visiting the central sanctuary for a festival (13a), affirming that the tithe had been uncontaminated. The dialogue in Hag. 2: 10–13 (see also Hos. 9: 4) explains v. 14. This confession (unlike that in vv. 5–10) closes with a prayer for continued blessing (15).

(*c*) **Ratification of the Covenant (26: 16–19)**
Verse 16 refers directly back either to 12: 1, which begins the detailed covenant stipulations, or to 5: 1, which opens the whole section dealing with general principles. Verses 17–19 imply that a covenant renewal ceremony has taken place, of which no details are given. Israel has solemnly affirmed that she accepts certain obligations (17) and Yahweh has declared his purpose for the nation. He graciously acknowledges them as his people and guarantees them the blessings of the covenant (18, 19).

19. holy: both a fact—that Israel belongs to Yahweh—and a programme—to live in purity and righteousness.

IV. FUTURE COVENANT RENEWAL (27: 1–26)
It is not altogether easy to see why ch. 27 occurs at this point. The events to which it refers are all future, and in ch. 28 we return to the plains of Moab, for a series of blessings and curses concluding the covenant renewal ceremony. The transition from 26: 19 to 28: 1 is perfectly smooth. In addition, Moses is referred to in 27: 1 in the third person, for the first time since 5: 1. A partial explanation may be found by regarding ch. 27 as a 'document clause', incorporating within the covenant itself provision for its preservation and renewal. On this assumption it would be an integral part of the book and not (as is sometimes suggested) a later addition.

i. The Law to be Recorded on Stones (27: 1–8)
1. This refers in particular to the covenant renewal ceremony. The **elders** are associated with Moses, possibly because he would not be alive when the ceremony took place.

2–4. The repetitive style is typical of Hebrew writing. **on the day:** a generalized indication of time. The reference to **Mount Ebal** (4) shows that some days must elapse between crossing the Jordan and the prescribed ritual. (This should not be confused with the incident recorded in Jos. 4: 1–10.) Writing on a white-washed surface (2, 4) was typical of Egypt, rather than Canaan or Mesopotamia. The emphasis on understanding is important: 'Covenant consecration must be an act of intelligent, informed faith and devotion' (Kline). **Mount Ebal** (4) and **Mount Gerizim** (12) stood 40 miles north of Jerusalem and 20 miles west of Jordan, separated by a narrow pass. The Samaritans later claimed Gerizim as the true centre for worship (Jn 4: 20). Shechem, which lay at the eastern end of the pass, had powerful associations for Israel (Gen. 12: 6, 7; 33: 18–20; cf. Jos. 24: 32).

5–8. For the significance of this **altar** see the note on ch. 12. The prohibition of any **iron tool** may imply simplicity or it may be linked with the Hebrews' inability to work in iron; using iron might imply that the covenant depended on alien co-operation (Exod. 20: 25; 1 Sam. 13: 19–23).

ii. A solemn reminder (27: 9–10)
In the midst of the instructions for a future ceremony comes this reminder that Israel is already God's people. To **be silent** is common at the climax of a religious ritual (Neh. 8: 11; Zeph. 1: 7; Zech. 2: 13; cf. Hab. 2: 20). The verses emphasize several basic points: (*a*) present commitment rather than past experience, (*b*) obedience as fundamental to the covenant, (*c*) obedience as the consequence, not a condition of the covenant.

iii. A liturgy of cursing (27: 11–26)

This section has several surprising features: (*a*) it consists only of curses, in spite of v. 12. (*b*) The list of sins is highly selective, with some emphasis on sexual sin (20–23). (*c*) The common factor seems to be that these are sins performed in secret. (*d*) The relationship is not clear between this ceremony and Dt. 11: 29. (*e*) Nor are the details of the ritual clear. It has been suggested that the blessings may have corresponded to the curses as in 28: 3–6, 16–19. This so-called 'dodecalogue of Shechem' takes place alongside other lists of legal provisions collected for didactic purposes, *e.g.* the Decalogue (Exod. 20; Dt. 5) and the laws of Lev. 18: 7–18.

12, 13. The tribes associated with the curse are those descended from Jacob's concubines, together with Reuben, the renegade first-born, and Zebulun.

14. Levites: presumably those connected with the ark. **15–24.** God is concerned even with secret actions.

V. THE COVENANT SANCTIONS: BLESSING AND CURSES (28: 1–68)

In the overall covenant-treaty structure of Deuteronomy, this section appears as the normal declaration of covenant sanctions following the treaty stipulations. The way in which blessings (2–14) are outnumbered by curses (15–68) is paralleled in secular treaties. It also corresponds to the sad truth that for fallen man God's law brings a curse, rather than a blessing (Gal. 3: 10–14). On the association of material blessing with faith in God see p. 257.

The section should not be interpreted as a covenant renewal liturgy; the blessings and curses themselves are found succinctly stated in 3–6, 16–19. The rest is a sermon preached upon this text and characterized by the type of repetition common in the Near East.

i. Covenant blessings (28: 1–14)

These depend on obedience (1, 2, 13b, 14). Those listed in vv. 3–6 relate to urban and rural life, to domestic and agricultural work, and to everyday activities (6; cf. 31: 2). The 'commentary' in vv. 7–14 is chiastic in form (7/12b, foreign relations; 8/11, 12a, domestic affairs; 9/10, relationship to Yahweh).

ii. Curses for Disobedience (28: 15–68)

These verses are concerned with a basic biblical principle: that disobedience and refusal to trust God have disastrous consequences. The curses relate to many aspects of life: disease, drought, defeat in war, with its associated hardships, culminating in exile. But they are not listed in any discernible order. The 'kernel' (16–19) is not, for example, systematically amplified in the homiletic treatment that follows. Yet vv. 20–46 are roughly parallel to vv. 7–14 and a chiastic structure can be distinguished in vv.

25–37. Most scholars conclude that the section has undergone some amplification and this seems most likely. But it should not be assumed that the references to *e.g.* siege warfare (52) and exile (36 f., 41, 63–68) necessarily fall within this category. As K. A. Kitchen points out (*New Perspectives on the Old Testament*, ed. J. B. Payne, 1970, pp. 5–7), deportation and resettlement were no rarity in the ancient Middle East, being mentioned in documents of *c.* 1800 B.C. Nor was the besieging of cities an alien concept. Also to be rejected is the argument that the close parallels between vv. 20–68 and seventh-century Assyrian treaties prove literary dependence on these late sources. As P. C. Craigie points out *in loco*, although the presence of partially parallel material is not in dispute a more likely explanation is the continued existence of a body of common concepts expressed in treaties.

16–19. The curses mentioned correspond (though in a different order) to the blessings of 3–6.

20. confusion: cf., *e.g.*, Jos. 10: 10; Jg. 4: 15; 1 Sam. 5: 11; 7: 10, etc. The panic that should afflict God's enemies now afflicts his people.

21–26. These disasters correspond roughly to the blessings of vv. 7–13. The drought of v. 23, with the associated sand-storms of v. 24, are naturally linked with the diseases of humans and plants in vv. 21, 22. Defeat in battle is threatened in v. 25 and its sequel in v. 26.

22. drought (*ḥōreb*): this reading fits the context better than RSVmg, 'sword' (*ḥereb*). **25.** Cf. v. 7. Note in v. 10 the contrasting attitudes resulting from obedience or disobedience to God's word.

25–37. For the chiastic arrangement here cf. (*a*) 25a/36, (*b*) 25b, 26/37 (out of sequence), (*c*) 27/34, (*d*) 28/34, (*e*) 29/33, (*f*) 30/32.

29a. A graphic metaphor for blundering ineptitude. **30.** Cf. 20: 5–7.

45, 46. Cf. 29: 22–29. The curses are all but personified (cf. the Greek Furies). They serve as a warning to other nations.

47, 48. A grim choice; serve man must—either in joy and freedom or in bitterness and oppression. **49–51.** The sequel to disobedience is invasion by a foreign power described in conventional terms echoed in Jer. 5: 15. **52–57.** The horrors of a siege are vividly portrayed (in terms that would arouse protest from many believers today), cf. 2 Kg. 6: 28, 29; Jer. 19: 9; Lam. 2: 20; 4: 10; Ezek. 5: 10.

58–68. In the solemn summary that ends the section, the law is said to be written in a book, rather than spoken by Moses (58). We may think of 19: 18 f. or even of the Book of the Covenant (Exod. 24: 4, 7). The disasters mentioned are not arbitrary peevish gestures, but wholehearted expressions of the holy purpose of Yahweh who loves his people (62, 63).

Separation from the land is the inevitable result of a breach of the covenant whereby it was given (63b). GNB renders 65b: 'anxiety, hopelessness and despair'. Verse 68 may refer to enslavement following conquest or to 'normal' commerce (Ezek 27: 13; Jl 3: 6; Am 1: 9) but the victims are said to offer themselves and it has been suggested that **in ships** should be rendered (using a Ugaritic parallel) 'casually'. In any case, the symbolism is unmistakable: disobedience has brought the people of God right back to the bondage from which he delivered them.

Today we are more conscious of secondary causes leading to personal and social disaster. Our time-scale is different; we see blessing and judgment extending into a dimension beyond space and time. But judgment and chastisement —even in a temporal sense—are realities to the eye of faith.

VI. RECAPITULATION OF THE COVENANT (29: 1–30: 20)
The significance of this third address of Moses may be understood in various ways. Duplicate copies of treaty texts were quite common in the ancient world and this section may be such a summary. Or possibly ch. 29 is a summons to the covenant oath, which is finally taken in 30: 11–20. In either case, we have here a recapitulation of the theme of the book.

Certainly we can trace the familiar treaty pattern here. A historical review (29: 1–9) is followed by a statement of the nature of the covenant (29: 10–15) which passes into a 'curses' section (29: 16–29) and a promise of ultimate blessing (30: 1–10). Finally comes a challenge to commitment and the covenant oath (30: 11–20).

i Historical Review (29: 1–9)
1. In the Hebrew, this verse is 28: 69; it may be taken either with the preceding or with the subsequent section (cf. the transition between 4: 45 and 5: 1). The covenants of **Horeb** and **Moab** are distinguished but related. **3, 4.** Here is a basic biblical theme: even **signs and great wonders** will not evoke understanding and faith apart from God's self-revelation. If the parallels in Jn 2: 18–21; 6: 30 ff.; 9: 40, 41; 10: 38; 13: 7, etc, are here cited, this is not because there are no others, but as a sample of the many parallels which may be traced between Deuteronomy and the Fourth Gospel. **5, 6.** Cf. 8: 2–4. **7, 8.** Cf. 2: 32 ff.; 3: 1, 8, 12 f.; Num. 21: 21–35.

ii. The Essence of the Covenant (29: 10–15)
10, 11. The fact that the covenant involves the whole community is shown by the reference to children and resident alien workers. **12. a covenant:** lit. 'into the covenant of Yahweh your God and into his oath/curse'. The covenant included a legacy of blessing and also covenant obligations and sanctions. **15.** The thought here is of future generations who will be included within the covenant; cf. Jn 17: 20; 20: 29.

iii. Punishment for Disobedience (29: 16–29)
This section itself contains the elements of the covenant formula. It is addressed to the individual rather than the community corporately and warns that individual disloyalty (18) cannot be safeguarded by membership of the covenant community (19). In fact, the judgment experienced by such a person (20, 21) would ultimately be the destiny of the nation (22–28). **18. root:** idolatry and disobedience bear bitter fruit (cf., *e.g.* Hos. 10: 4; Am. 6: 12). For a NT application see Heb 12: 15. **19. watered land as well as the dry:** apparently a proverbial phrase, certainly indicating universality and possibly deriving from vegetation. **20.** Anger is often thought of as 'burning' in the OT. The extinction of the family name was dreaded by people whose belief in an afterlife was at best shadowy. **22–28.** There are parallels to this question in Near Eastern treaties. **23.** Cf. Gen. 19. **24b.** The Book of Lamentations answers this question and provides a commentary on this aspect of the covenant curse. The twentieth-century reader can fill out details of two thousand years of suffering and will relate it (with fear) to Mt 27: 25. **28.** The last phrase may point to later editorial work, though the concept of deportation was common in the time of Moses. **29.** God has revealed his law and his nature in the covenant. (Much more, Christians would say, in the New Covenant.) God's people should attend to these and not hanker for knowledge of his hidden purposes.

iv. Promise of Repentance and Forgiveness (30: 1–10)
It is remarkable that this section, unlike the rest of the book, consists of prophecy without exhortation. The language and ideas are strikingly paralleled in the later prophets (cf., *e.g.* Jer. 32), not least in those of the exile. While most scholars see this as proof of exilic origin or influence, conservative writers have suggested that later prophets will have been influenced by Moses. **1.** The judgments of 29: 21–28 have occurred. **2.** The first condition of blessing is repentance, a 'turning' (Heb *šûb*) corresponding to the 'turning' away from Yahweh that had occasioned judgment. **3, 4.** This gathering activity of God is typical of his salvation under both covenants. **5.** This return from exile in trustful obedience appears to have little in common with the Zionist movement of the twentieth century. **6.** Whereas in 10: 16 the Israelite

must himself circumcise his heart as an act of obedience, here the process is seen as a gracious act of God, closely related to the concepts in Ezek 36: 26; Jer 31: 33 and their NT parallels. **7.** Cf. Lam. 4: 21 f. **9.** Cf. Jer. 32: 41.

v. Appeal to Commitment (30: 11–20)
What God requires is neither incomprehensible nor unattainable (11–14). But only the hearer can decide to obey or disobey, a momentous decision (15–20). As it became increasingly clear (with the Exile and the New Covenant) that it is individuals with whom God deals, this challenge gained in relevance. As Kline points out in *WBC* (*in loco*), we are all exiles from Eden awaiting our joyful 'return' to the New Jerusalem.
11–14. It is natural to emphasize the remoteness of truth and wisdom from daily life and the difficulty of achieving them (Job 28: 12 ff.). But God's law was accessible to every Israelite (Ps. 19: 7–11). In Rom. 10: 6–8, Paul uses these words to illustrate the character of the new covenant, based on Our Lord's incarnation and the free offer of the gospel, in the power of the Spirit, all of which bring the **word . . . very near**.
15–20. The call to choose recurs throughout the Bible. It involves, not a mere momentary impulse, but commitment for a lifetime (16). The issues at stake could not be more serious: **life and death** or **blessings and curses**.

VII. THE CONTINUITY OF THE COVENANT (31: 1–34: 12)
The closing chapters of the book continue the covenant theme. Elements which occur here as well as in extra-biblical suzerainty treaties are: the appointment of (Joshua as) a dynastic heir (31: 1–8, 14–23); directions for the deposition of the treaty document (31: 9–13); the invocation of covenant witnesses (31: 24–29; 31: 30 —32: 29); the assignment of kingdom inheritance to the separate tribes (33); and marking the transition from the authority of Moses to that of his successor, an account of Moses' death (34).

i. The Recognition of Joshua (31: 1–8)
1. The LXX and evidence from Qumran support 'And Moses finished speaking . . .'. **2.** In Egypt, a wise man was conventionally thought to live 110 years (cf. Gen. 50: 22); Moses has surpassed this. He has in fact survived three (forty-year) generations. He is sufficiently strong for individual daily life (34: 7) but not for leading Israel. And he is forbidden to enter Canaan (3: 23–29; 32: 50–52; Num. 20: 11, 12). **3–6.** As always in the holy war, Yahweh leads his people.

ii. The Covenant Commemoration Ceremony (31: 9–13)
Just as a secular treaty document was placed in the sanctuary of the vassal, so the law is to

be kept in the ark (26). For the time of the commemorative ceremony, see 16: 13–15. Renewal as such is not implied, but God's people must periodically renew their own commitment and instruct the young (12, 13). Under the new covenant this is achieved by means of the Lord's Supper as well as by the preaching of the Word.

iii. The Formal Commissioning of Joshua (31: 14–23)
There is no need to distinguish diverse sources here. Joshua's role has been adumbrated in 1: 38; cf. Num. 27: 18–23. Now it is publicly stated that the time has come for him to assume his new role (7, 8) and a theophany confirms this and gives him a divine commission (14, 15, 23).
16–22. Intertwined with the 'Joshua' theme, in a manner typical of Hebrew style, is an introduction to the 'Song of Moses' which views it as corresponding to the secular covenant treaty motif of calling upon (the) god(s) as witness(es) to the terms of the covenant. **21.** God, who knows even the hidden tendencies within his people, provides in advance not only a warning but a means of restoring their faith. The role here assigned to the Song of Moses corresponds to that of the scriptures as a whole. Indeed, the words used in connexion with it in v. 19 are usually applied to God's law in the OT.

iv. The Song and the Law are Entrusted to Israel (31: 24–29)
24. There is no evidence to support changing *tôrâ* (law) here and in v. 26 into *šîrâ* (song). **25, 26.** Having been entrusted to the Levites, the law may well have been developed by them, most obviously by the addition of 32–34, and also by divinely sanctioned judgments concerning specific cases.
28. heaven and earth: see the introduction to 32: 1–43 and the comment on 32: 1–4.

v. The Song of Moses (32: 1–43)
In its context, this relates to 31: 28 f. and is in effect the witness of Moses to Israel, in terms which might apply to any period of the nation's history. In view of its developed literary characteristics and some of its theological content (cf., *e.g.*, v. 39 with Isa. 44: 6; 45: 5–7, etc.) many scholars have attributed it to the exilic period. But it contains archaic linguistic features, and several now date its original form as early as the eleventh century B.C. Its form resembles that of documents in which suzerains confronted erring vassals. This *rîb* ('controversy') form, exemplified from the eighteenth and seventeenth centuries BC, might well have been familiar to Moses. It generally commenced with an appeal to heaven and earth to witness the evil done by the vassal (cf. 1–4). This is followed by the plaintiff posing questions on which an accusation is based (cf. 5, 6). Next

comes a declaration of past benefits, received
by the vassal (cf. 7–14) and of his present
ingratitude (cf. 15–18). The *rîb* pattern would
end with a reference to the futility of other
alliances and a call to change policy or face
retribution. But in the Song of Moses vv. 26–
43 diverge from the *rîb* pattern, introducing
a word of hope and promise of deliverance.
Thompson suggests that an original Mosaic
utterance, freely based on the *rîb* form, has been
expanded and reapplied at a later date.
1–4. For the witness of **heavens** and **earth** cf.
Isa. 1: 2; Mic. 6: 1, 2. The words of the song
resemble **rain** and **dew** because they refresh
and renew the hearers, since they refer to the
character of Yahweh. He is as solid and trustworthy as a rock.
5, 6. The accusation (5) is followed by a question from the suzerain's messenger (6). **7–14.**
The Suzerain's kingly acts on behalf of his
vassal are enumerated under three heads: (*a*) **8,
9.** The *choice of Israel* is carried back to the
time when **the Most High** (*'elyôn*) allocated
boundaries to the nations (see Gen. 10). At the
end of v. 8 the RSV follows the LXX (later
supported by a Qumran MS) in relating this to
the activities of the heavenly council (cf. Gen.
1: 26; Job 1: 6; 38: 7; 1 Kg. 22: 19–22; Dan. 10:
13; Rev. 4: 2, 4[?]). For v. 9 cf. the frequently
misinterpreted Eph. 1: 18. (*b*) **10–12.** The *deliverance of Israel* is spoken of in three ways, being
compared to the care a man takes of the pupil
of his eye, the way an eagle teaches its young
to fly, and the guidance of a shepherd. **10a.**
Cf. Hos. 9: 10. (*c*) **13, 14.** The *conquest of the
Transjordan* (?) *hills* brought plentiful food, including wild honey and olive oil (13b).
15–18. The indictment of Israel is that in spite
of (or possibly because of?) her God-given
prosperity she forgot Yahweh and even turned
to other gods. **Jeshurun** seems to be a pet-name
for the nation—literally, 'the upright one'—
cf. 33: 5, 26; Isa. 44: 2. **sleek** may be rendered
'coarse'. For the gods of the heathen as **demons**
(a rare word used here and in Ps. 106: 37) see
1 C. 10: 20; for another view of pagan religion,
see Ac. 17: 23, 27. **18.** The motherhood as
well as the fatherhood of God is stressed here;
ignoring this aspect of God's nature has led to
an unbiblical emphasis on the Virgin Mary.
19–25. Sentence is passed on Israel for breaking
the covenant. **19.** Although Israel is sometimes
referred to as the 'son' of Yahweh (Hos. 11: 1)
it is rare for Israelites to be spoken of as his
children, particularly in terms of the covenant
(contrast Mal. 2: 10). **21.** Cf. Hos. 1: 9; 2:
23, GNB renders, 'so-called gods. . . . so-called
nation'. Attempts to date the poem by this
vague reference are unsuccessful. **22.** God's
wrath is boundless in its effects. **23–25.** The
curses recall those of ch. 28: disease, wild animals poisonous snakes, and warfare.

25. in their homes: where one would normally expect security.
26–38. Mercy will follow judgment. Throughout history, God has chastised his people (of the
old covenant and of the new) but has refrained
from destroying them. **26, 27.** This glimpse of
the struggle between mercy and justice resembles Hos. 11: 8, but the reason for divine
mercy is the one found in Ezek. 20: 9, 14, 22,
etc.—although Yahweh's 'name' is not mentioned here. Verse 27b also relates to Isa. 10:
7–11 which focuses not on a low view of
Yahweh's name, but on too high a view of the
power of his enemies. **28, 29.** Is Israel or are
her enemies said to be 'without sense' (GNB)?
Probably her enemies; they have no conception
of God's purpose in Israel's history. **30, 31.**
Israel's enemies should recognize the true significance of Israel's defeat, contrary to the covenant pledge of 28: 7. The enemies are judges
either (*a*) as sent by God for this purpose or (*b*)
as capable of passing a verdict on the strength
of the evidence in v. 30.
32, 33. The Bible never 'whitewashes' God's
instruments (Heb. 1: 12–17). Here **Sodom** and
Gomorrah connote evil, judgment and barrenness. **34, 35.** The conviction that divine
judgment is inevitable is not confined to Israel
(cf., *e.g.*, the Erinyes or Furies of classical
mythology). Here, with fruitful ambiguity, the
calamity may be seen as awaiting God's people
(23, 25) who must suffer first (1 Pet. 4: 17) *or*
as the destiny of God's enemies (36–43). **35.**
God's **declaration of vengeance** means deliverance for his people (Isa. 61: 2). This verse is
quoted in Rom. 12: 19 as a reason why God's
people should not themselves seek revenge. In
Heb. 10: 30 it is used as a warning against
apostasy. **36–38.** Not until God's people have
seen their own helplessness and the uselessness
of their false gods will he save them.
39. Words such as these (cf. 2 Kg. 5: 7; Ps. 104:
29 f.) underline the significance of the 'mighty
words' of Christ. **40–42.** Yahweh solemnly
swears by his own name (cf., *e.g.*, 2 Sam. 12:
5) that he will complete his work of judgment.
43. If such sentiments seem strange to Christians, the reason may be, not their great love
for their enemies, but their inadequate sense of
the destructiveness of sin. Ps. 104: 35 is not
misplaced and Rev. 6: 10 does not refer to
personal vengeance. It is remarkable that this
verse, which speaks of a new beginning after
deliverance should use the sacrificial word, *kipper* (=to cover, make atonement). The RSV of
v. 43 is based on the LXX, confirmed by a
Qumran MS (cf. Heb. 1: 6).
44–47. The prose framework of the Song is
resumed. It is no 'mere' poem but an expression
of God's will (46b), and God's law is not 'empty
words' (47, GNB) but a matter of life and death.
48–52. For **Nebo** see on 34: 1; also for the

command to **view Canaan.** The death of Aaron (also on a mountain) is described in Num. 20: 22–29; 33: 37–39. For a discussion of how Moses **broke faith** at Meribath-kadesh, see on Num. 20: 10 ff.; the episode is mentioned also in Dt. 1: 37; 3: 26; 4: 21 and Num. 27: 12–14.

vi. Moses Blesses Israel (33: 1–29)

In spite of its abrupt appearance at this point, the significance of this poem is plain. Since he is a **man of God** (1) his words will carry special power, so (like the dying Jacob; cf. Gen. 49: 1–27) he blesses his people before he leaves them. Yet both form and content are in some respects problematic. The blessings seem to have been encapsulated within a psalm (2–5, 26–29) which makes good sense on its own. Again, the (verse) blessings are generally supplied with a prose introduction. In addition, some of the 'blessings' are not blessings at all, *e.g.*, v. 22. And even the reader who is fully convinced of the reality of predictive *prophecy* may be surprised at the viewpoint *assumed* here. Simeon has apparently ceased to exist; Reuben is in danger; Dan has migrated to the North; Judah (briefly mentioned, without reference to its later royal associations) is in danger of being separated from the other tribes; Ephraim and Manasseh are pre-eminent. These circumstances are sometimes thought to imply an eleventh-century date, a possibility supported by the literary characteristics of the poem. Thompson suggests, 'It is not impossible that a sympathetic collector and editor of Moses' (original) utterances, who was true to the general spirit of Moses' blessings, might well have actualized Moses' words'. The verses contain a good deal that is obscure and modern translations and detailed commentaries are required for close study.

1–5. The majesty of Yahweh is described in terms of a theophany, like the sun rising on (significantly) Sinai; cf. Jg. 5: 4 f.; Hab. 3: 3. The reference here to **the holy ones** underlies the idea that the law was given by angels (Ac. 7: 53; Gal. 3: 19; Heb. 2: 2). Verses 3–5, interpreted by Craigie as Israel's response, refer to Israel's commitment at Sinai to God's law, seen as 'our most treasured possession' (GNB). **5.** The Hebrew supplies no subject here for **was king** (cf. NEB, JB); the reference might be to Moses. **6.** Although Reuben (here placed first as the first-born) appears in an idealized context in Ezek. 48: 7, the tribe disappears from history after the eighth century (1 Chr. 5: 18–22). Possibly we should render **nor let** as 'although'.

7. The military tone and hint of danger in this remarkably brief reference to the royal tribe (as it later became) may be related to its struggle with the Philistines. Craigie interprets it by referring to Judah's position in the van of Israel's forces (Num. 2: 9). Simeon, not mentioned in the blessings, was ultimately absorbed into Judah.

8–11. It is remarkable that vv. 8–10 are unlike the rest of the Blessing: spelling and word-forms suggest a later date, and the metre differs from that of v. 11, which resembles the rest of the poem. The **Thummim . . . and . . . Urim** were used by the priests in obtaining oracles (as in 1 Sam. 14: 41). In Exod. 28: 30 they are carried by Aaron in his breast-piece. For the episodes in v. 8b, see Exod. 17: 1–7; Num. 20: 1–3. They can be applied to the tribe as a whole only if Moses and Aaron are regarded as its representatives. In v. 9, by contrast, there is a straightforward reference to the incident in Exod. 32: 26–29. The prayer in v. 11 may relate to warfare or to some occasion when the tribe's priestly pre-eminence was under attack (cf. Num. 16: 1–11).

12. It is difficult to decide whether this refers to the position of the Temple, situated at Jerusalem in the hills of Benjamin's tribal territory, or to the security of the tribe, seen as carried like a child on Yahweh's back.

13–17. Like Gen. 49: 25 f., vv. 13–16 speak movingly of the fertility of the land allotted to the Joseph tribes, Ephraim and Manasseh (17b). Their military strength is also referred to in vv. 16b and 17 but here, as in Gen. 48: 14 ff., the supremacy of the younger (Ephraim) is affirmed.

16. the burning bush: Heb. *sᵉneh*; this may refer to Exod. 3: 2 ff., but since in early orthography the only consonants might have been *SN* the original meaning may have been 'in Sinai'.

18, 19. Gen. 49: 13 suggests that at some time Zebulun's territory extended to the sea, with its commerce and wealth of fish, but Jos. 19: 10–16 (17–23) implies that any benefit obtained will have been via exploitation of a trade route *from* the coast.

20, 21. Although v. 21b is obscure, there is a clear reference to Gad's strong tribal position east of Jordan (3: 12–16).

22. The comparison between Dan and a young lion from Bashan is straightforward, but it is not clear whether this should be related to the tribe's migration from the valleys of Aijalon and Sorek to the north (Jos. 19: 40–48; Jg. 18), since *bāšān* may here correspond to an Ugaritic word meaning 'viper', thus: 'who shies away from a viper' (cf. Gen. 49: 17).

23. Naphtali's tribal territory, near Galilee, is beautiful and fertile.

24, 25. Asher means 'happy' and the fertility of the tribal lands in the far north (renowned for olive trees) is also referred to in Gen. 49: 20. But a situation between Acre and Tyre carried a risk of attack and a need for strong defences. Is v. 25b a promise or a warning?

26–29. This concludes the hymn commenced

in vv. 1–5. The thought of v. 26 is found in Canaanite poetry but here refers to Yahweh's power in redemption. Israel's destiny involves warfare but also the peace of trustful dependence on Yahweh. Her uniqueness derives from his saving power (29a). **26. Jeshurun:** see v. 5 and 32: 15. **28. spring:** substitute the verb 'dwell' (*'an*) for the noun 'spring' (*'ayin*) and read, 'Jacob dwells'. **29. high places:** the sole occurrence of the word in Deuteronomy—and it is used in a non-cultic sense! (But some link it to a similar Ugaritic word meaning 'backs'.)

vii. The Death of Moses (34: 1–12)
The narrative is taken up from 32: 52. The story is told elsewhere in 3: 23–28; 32: 48–52 and Num. 27: 12–14.
1. This viewing of the land may have had legal significance, since a man would formally 'view' what he was about to possess (Gen. 13: 14 ff.). Although the full extent would not have been visible, the part symbolizes the whole, and the places mentioned can be located on the arc of a large circle, from north to south. **4.** God's people must trust, not in any human leader, but in Yahweh's covenant. **6.** Lit. 'one buried him'. It would be surprising if Moses had not been accompanied on this occasion. **9.** Yahweh has ensured the succession. But under the new covenant the one who redeemed God's people from slavery also brings them into the promised land. Emphasis is again placed on Moses' unique achievement and relationship to God. More than a thousand years would elapse before a 'greater than Moses' was to appear.

BIBLIOGRAPHY

Commentaries
CRAIGIE, P. C., *The Book of Deuteronomy*. NICOT (London, 1977).
CUNLIFFE-JONES, H., *Deuteronomy*. TC (London, 1964).
DRIVER, S. R., *A Critical and Exegetical Commentary on Deuteronomy*. ICC (Edinburgh, 1895).
HARRISON, R. K. and MANLEY, G. T., 'Deuteronomy' in *NBCR* (London, 1970).
KLINE, M., *Treaty of the Great King* (Grand Rapids), 1963).
KLINE, M., 'Deuteronomy' *WBC* (Chicago, 1962).
MANLEY, G. T., *The Book of the Law* (London, 1957).
MAYES, A. D. H., *Deuteronomy*. NCentB (London, 1979).
PHILLIPS, A., *Deuteronomy*. CBC (Cambridge, 1973).
VON RAD, G., *Deuteronomy*. E.T. (London, 1966).
SMITH, G. A., *The Book of Deuteronomy*. CBSC (Cambridge, 1918).
THOMPSON, J. A., *Deuteronomy*. TOTC (London, 1974).
WRIGHT, G. E., 'Deuteronomy' in *IB* (Nashville, 1953).

Other Studies
BALZER, K., *The Covenant Formula*. E.T. (Oxford, 1970).
CLEMENTS, R. E., *God's Chosen People* (London, 1968).
DUMBRELL, W. J., *Covenant and Creation* (Exeter, 1984).
KITCHEN, K. A., *Ancient Orient and OT* (London, 1966).
KITCHEN, K. A., 'Ancient Orient, Deuteronomism and the OT' in *New Perspectives on the OT*, ed. J. B. Payne (Waco, 1979).
MCCARTHY, D. J., *Old Testament Covenant* (Oxford, 1972).
MENDENHALL, G. E., *Law and Covenant in Israel and the Ancient Near East* (Pittsburgh, 1955).
NICHOLSON, E. W., *Deuteronomy and Tradition* (Oxford, 1967).
VON RAD, G., *Studies in Deuteronomy*. E.T. (London, 1953).
THOMPSON, J. A., *Ancient Near Eastern Treaties and the OT* (London, 1964).
WEINFELD, M., *Deuteronomy and the Deuteronomic School* (Oxford, 1972).
WELCH, A. C., *The Code of Deuteronomy* (London, 1924).
WELCH, A. C., *Deuteronomy, the Framework to the Code* (Oxford, 1932).
WENHAM, G. J., 'Deuteronomy and the Central Sanctuary' in *TB 22* (1971), pp. 103–118.

JOSHUA

JOHN LILLEY

Theme of the book

Joshua is a study in success, and in this respect it may be compared with Exodus and Acts. It should be read, therefore, by those who want to succeed. While much can be learned from failure, it is more inspiring and indeed more directly profitable to observe things being done well.

The subject of the book is the invasion and inheritance by Israel of the land promised to their forefathers. The term 'conquest' is somewhat misleading; on that level, success was qualified. Nevertheless, the People and the Land were brought together. In this, God's promise was fulfilled, and the faith of Israel was given a new dimension—which would never be lost entirely, and which has significance for Christian thinking too.

The place of Joshua in the Bible

To the Jews, Joshua is the first of the Former Prophets. These books teach the meaning of Israel's history down to the Exile; Joshua shows the establishment of the nation, in a position from which it defaulted and declined.

There are obvious links with Judges, which treats of that decline. Equally obviously there are close links with Deuteronomy, in subject-matter and language; and, less extensively, with Numbers. A whole generation of commentators based their work on projection of the accepted Pentateuchal sources into Joshua; this theory of a 'Hexateuch' is not dead yet, though Noth and the 'deuteronomic history' school have roundly condemned it. Most of the modern commentaries written or available in English follow Noth's lead; the writing of the Former Prophets is associated with the movement which led to Josiah's reforms, and Deuteronomy is seen as the prime expression of this teaching. This does not go far to explain the special affinities between Deuteronomy and Joshua; neither does it account for the clear division between the Law and the Prophets in Jewish tradition. The anonymous writer of Joshua was one of the Prophets; whether early or late, he knew and loved Deuteronomy as the Word of God.

The Book of Joshua as history

A modern historian would aim at a full and systematic account of the process of invasion and settlement. Our author had neither the training nor the information, nor (fortunately) the paper for such a task. He did have the inspiration of the Spirit; thus, within the limits of a scroll, he has given us those aspects of the story which matter most for spiritual instruction—and first of all, for the instruction of Israel while still under the old covenant. The author recognized the importance of the Land in God's purposes, and its importance to God's people; he explained how they came to be there, and related the occupation to the Israel of his day (compare Ezra for a post-exilic parallel). He understood the covenant God made with Israel, and the doctrine of the 'Holy War' which subordinated the pride and greed of man to the will of God. This view controlled his selection and his presentation; it will not satisfy the secular historian, but it is normative for a Christian even if he is interested in filling out the picture by historical research.

Arrangement and sources

It is noticeable that the author treats in detail the opening events, which are crucial historically and spiritually, and continues progressively in more summary fashion. It has been suggested that the detailed traditions were preserved at Israelite sanctuaries; this theory makes sense, but it should be remarked that (a) some commentators have made too much of the idea of aetiology, i.e. that stories were preserved, embroidered or even invented to account for place-names, etc.; (b) in so far as such theories discount the original unity of Israel, they create difficulties in relating (e.g.) Benjaminite Gilgal to Ephraimite Joshua. The records of the Covenant (Jos. 24) must have been a national possession, as was the Book of Jashar (10: 13, cf. 2 Sam. 1: 18). Various lists were used, selectively, in chapters 12–21; that of Judah includes (15: 61) places which probably only existed in the 8th century BC, and there are several opinions as to the date reflected by its organization. It is possible that the book was brought up to date from time to time, to maintain its relevance.

Historical background

The Egyptian hold on Canaan, which had been established by Tuthmosis III in the fifteenth century BC, slipped in the fourteenth (around the time of Akhnaten and the Amarna letters). Even the stronger Pharaohs of the Nineteenth Dynasty could do little more than secure the coast road to support the boundary of their sphere of influence; and from the time of Merneptah (c. 1230 BC), Egypt was in eclipse until the successful repulse of the Sea Peoples (with whom probably the Philistines were connected) by Rameses III in 1187. The Hittite Empire disintegrated in the same period. As the empires weakened, so their vassals (Canaanites and Amorites, respectively) disappeared, and the political and cultural scene changed.

The city-state was characteristic of Canaanite society. Typically it was ruled by a king, with a wealthy ruling class patronizing an advanced material culture and depending on serfs for agriculture and public works. Egypt had used this structure and had strengthened the authority of the 'royal cities', but had not always succeeded in retaining their loyalty (notably at Shechem). The Canaanite states had been in trouble with insurgents ('*Apiru*) since early in the fourteenth century. The Israelites and Philistines between them destroyed the southern Canaanites; their northern brethren took to the sea in earnest and became the 'Phoenicians' of classical history.

The Amorites are less easily identified (van Seters, *VT* 22, 1972, pp. 64–81). The term, in Akkadian ('westerner'), broadly indicated the peoples southwest of the Euphrates. There was a kingdom of Amurru, in the Hittite sphere, to which may have been related the short-lived kingdoms of Og and Sihon farther south. The Biblical usage seems to have been broader than the Akkadian, and is fairly set out in Num. 13: 29. Of the rest of the seven nations (Jos. 3: 10; Ac. 13: 19), little is known apart from scattered references.

Out of this melting-pot emerged 'a people not reckoning itself among the nations' (Num. 23: 9); capable of fratricidal war, yet always aware of kinship; prone to idolatry, but never able to escape the memory of a God whose form was not seen (Dt. 4: 12; 1 Sam. 3). The genealogical tradition and the Sinai covenant were alike essential to the formation of Israel. Noth's view, that Israel did not exist as such before the Settlement, is extreme and not widely accepted; the associated idea of comparing Israel to a Greek 'amphictyony' (a league with a religious centre) has not proved very helpful (B. Rahtjen, *JNES* 24, 1965, pp. 100–

104). We have very little detailed information, considering the time-scale, on how Israel developed from an invading army into David's people; but there is enough to show that the continuity is not a projection backward of later ideas.

Interpretation and Application

The fulfilment of God's promises, and the obedient faith by which they are received, form the main theme of Joshua. These principles may be taken historically, to see how God ruled and led his people in preparation for the coming of Christ; and typically, to illuminate Christian experience.

Historically, the book offers examples of faith, obedience, perseverance, and godly leadership. Even more important is the stress on 'inheritance' by the gift of God, and on the continuity of God's word and work through Abraham, Moses and Joshua. Perhaps the supreme lesson, reflected in Ps. 44: 1–8, is that God established his chosen people; the tragedy of Judges presupposes the victory of Joshua.

In the process, judgment fell on Canaan (cf. Gen. 15: 16; Lev. 18: 25). This has often been felt as a moral difficulty, but there could be no other way until the New Covenant brought in a published gospel and the outpouring of the Holy Spirit; to this the whole OT was leading. Rahab was an exceptional case, exemplifying the grace which would one day be open to all.

Typically, the NT guideline is Heb. 4: 8 ff.; the invasion was successful (see on 11: 23, 'rest'), but only a shadow of the heavenly inheritance. From this sprang a tradition of using the Land as a picture of heaven, the Jordan representing death. Clearly, such expositors must ignore the warfare in the land; indeed they can learn little from Joshua beyond the picture they have read into it. Expositors who draw lessons for spiritual warfare are on surer ground, but may still be found using the OT as a frame for setting out NT doctrine, rather than as a source for teaching the ways of God.

In the personal sense of 'type', we may well consider Joshua as a type of our Saviour, who bore the same glorious name for a similar, but transcendent, purpose.

ANALYSIS

I. INVASION (1: 1–11: 23)
i. Joshua commissioned (1: 1–18)
(a) Promise and instructions (1: 1–9)

The mantle of Moses falls on Joshua; an awesome inheritance, and not less so in retrospect, for the stature of the lawgiver did not diminish with the passing years. His title **servant** is found in Exod. 14: 31, Num. 12: 7 f. (a key passage), Dt. 34: 5; it occurs in Kg. and later books, and in Jos. frequently. The word ('*ebed*) means 'slave', but is often used of a king's officers, even of the highest rank. Joshua is given the title (Jos. 24: 29= Jg. 2: 8). The continuity of his service with that of Moses is stressed in this chapter, and recurs (esp. 3: 7; 4: 10, 14; 8: 30–35; 11: 12, 15, 20; freq. in 12–22; and, mainly by allusion, in 23). **aide** (NEB 'assistant'): cf. Exod. 24: 13; so of Elisha, 1 Kg. 19: 21; a term appropriate to personal domestic service (1 Kg. 10: 5), or to priests and others in the temple (Ps. 103: 21).

2. to the Israelites is not in the Gk., and some commentators excise it; but it serves to emphasize the ground of making the gift.

4. From the desert: the land is described by an axis from the dry valley at Joshua's feet, towards the **Lebanon** which is 'in his mind's eye' but not actually visible; to the right as far as the **Euphrates**; and to the left, to the Mediterranean. The RSV does not clearly distinguish the two areas.

Dt. 11: 24 is parallel but simpler; 'desert' there=Negeb. Cf. Gen. 15: 18, more general; Num. 34: 1–12, specific and more restricted.

the Hittite country—strictly, North Syria; the Assyrians used the term for Syria generally, and even for Palestine.

5. as I was with Moses (so 17; 3: 7; 4: 14): Moses was unique (Dt. 34: 10), but it must not be thought that the Lord's power or goodwill would be limited by Moses' removal. **with you:** this is the most treasured blessing (as its opposite is the most terrible disaster—'left him', Jg. 16: 20; 'turned away', 1 Sam. 28: 15). To Isaac (Gen. 26: 24) and Jacob (Gen. 28: 20) it meant security in a hostile environment; to Joseph (Gen. 39: 21), success in his work. For Moses (Exod. 3: 12), and now for Joshua, it was not enough to be sent with authority to do God's work, unless God would actually work with him. As experience deepens, so does the meaning and purpose of this simple idea (Exod. 33: 14–16). The promise comes to us in Mt. 28: 20; Phil. 4: 12 f. shows its effect.

6. Be strong and courageous: the law of Moses is not only the moral and ceremonial law, important as that will be for the good order and prosperity of the tribes, but all the instructions for government, warfare and social justice. To adhere to them will require moral courage and faith. Cf. Dt. 11: 18–25, 32: 47; but this exhortation is personal to Joshua.

8. your mouth: probably because silent reading was then almost unknown. Cf. Ac. 8: 30.

(b) The camps alerted (1: 10, 11)

10. the officers (*šoṭʿrîm*) are administrative (Gk. 'scribes') rather than commanders. **three**

285

days is clearly idiomatic for 'a few days' (cf. 2: 22, 3: 2). **take possession:** *yāraš* implies taking what was another's, by inheritance or succession; see Gen. 15: 7. *nāḥal* ('inherit', 6) stresses property rights (so KJV, 'divide').

(c) **The Transjordanians promise support (1: 12–18)**
Settlement east of the Jordan was a contentious issue from the first (see Num. 32). The area was not strictly part of the Promised Land (Num. 34: 12); and, while rivers are not always effective boundaries, the Rift Valley is a special case, and the land to the east is very different from Palestine proper (D. Baly, *Geog. of the Bible*, 1974, pp. 210 ff.). There was a real risk of separation (see Jos. 22). Yet Gilead and Bashan had fallen to Israel by the hand of God, and Moses had accepted the argument that it made suitable provision for the pastoral communities of Reuben and Gad. This conclusion is reflected in Dt. 3: 18 ff. (quoted here). The commandment is now grounded, first in promise (13), secondly in the appeal of brotherhood.

12. Manasseh: it appears from Num. 32 that the original parties to the settlement were Reuben and Gad, but that certain Manassite clans were recognized as occupying northern areas. This element is widely regarded as 'secondary' for purposes of source-criticism; commentators, *e.g.* Burney, attributed a Manassite

presence in Transjordan to eastward expansion (possibly implied in Jos. 17). Modern historians tend to think in terms of penetration (from the north-east?) by tribes later assimilated to Israel, as the Kenites were. Such movements doubtless occurred, but the Biblical tradition stresses the swift destruction of the old Amorite kingdoms by Israel.

14. east of: more correctly 'beside'; so Dt. 3: 8, of the East Bank, 3: 20, of the West. Theories of editing have been built on the traditional but incorrect rendering of *bᵉ'ēḇer* as 'across'; the preposition may need further indication as to which side is meant, for emphasis (15) or if the context does not make it obvious (*e.g.* 5: 1; 12: 1; 12:7, Heb.).

15. rest: this is the great theme of the Settlement (Dt. 12: 9 f.). The word is also used of the 'stopping places' (Num. 10: 33) and of the ark (1 Chr. 6: 31; Ps. 132: 8, etc.). It implies freedom from disturbance—freedom to work constructively (so 2 Chr. 14: 6 f., 'peace'). Referring to this, Heb. 4: 9 anticipates a 'sabbath rest' from the labour of pilgrimage.

ii. Reconnaissance of Jericho (2: 1–3: 1)
(a) **Rahab receives the spies (2: 1–7)**
1. Shittim: see Num. 33: 49, and map. The Wadi Nuseiriyeh, and other streams collecting rain from the edge of the plateau, make it possible to cultivate this part of the otherwise

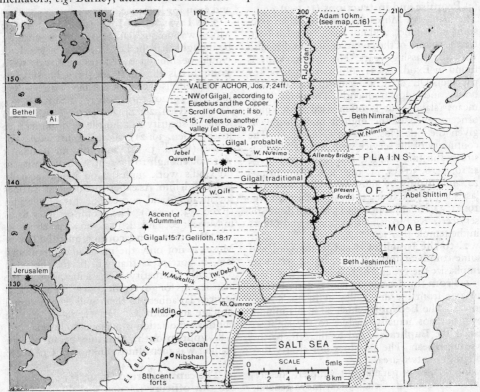

Map 4—Jericho

arid Rift. **look:** as far as Joshua knows at this stage, he will have to take Jericho by storm; the more information he can get the better. **prostitute:** the term may have meant 'innkeeper' (without prejudice to the question of morals); D. J. Wiseman, *Tyndale House Bulletin* 14, June 1964, pp. 8–11. **stayed:** yišk^ebû (lit. 'lay') has a wide range of meaning (v. 8 'settled down', NEB); here it only implies finding a place to sleep.

2. tonight: the whole action takes place at dusk; Rahab claims that the men decided not to stay, and left in good time to avoid finding the gates shut. Within an hour she had her opportunity and made her vital decision.

6. the roof was of course flat, and the usual place for drying grain or flax.

(b) Rahab wins a promise of safety (2: 8–16)

8. lay down: NEB 'had not yet settled', see on v. 1. Rahab was convinced by two kinds of evidence: (i) the demoralization around her; (ii) the facts of Israel's recent experience, testifying against her polytheistic background. Others believed and trembled; in her we see 'the work of faith'—confession (v. 11, using the formula which was doubtless an Israelite watchword, cf. Dt. 4: 39), and action (Jas 2: 25, cf. Heb. 11: 31).

10. completely destroyed: first mention of ḥērem, implying a religious motive rather than purely human conflict, and involving the people as well as the kings; hence the terror. See on 6: 17. **12. kindness:** the ḥesed which Rahab shows, and asks in return, is an act of goodwill, not of obligation ('mercy', Ps. 23: 6); but it also implies faithfulness in goodwill, once shown (hence NEB 'keep faith'). **15. part of:** lit. 'on the face of the wall', which was probably three feet or more of solid brickwork; see 6: 5.

16. the hills: the fretted gorge of the Wadi Qilt would provide ample cover, if scant food, till the alert was over.

(c) the sign of the scarlet thread (2: 17–21)

The twist of material would identify the house unobtrusively, but significantly to an Israelite search party; there is no question of identifying it from outside the city. **17. not . . . binding:** we will either discharge our obligations or be released. NEB paraphrases here. The spies trust that Rahab will not put the Jerichoans on their track before they have recrossed the Jordan.

The arrangement of the story should be noted. The previous paragraph (or episode; of course the original was not paragraphed) told how the agreement was made; this one describes the sign. It should not be read as if Rahab let the spies down and then parleyed with them! Neither is there a reason for visualizing two sources of the narrative. Episodic arrangement ('dischronologized', W. J. Mar-

tin, *VT Suppl.* 17, 1968, pp. 179 ff.) is characteristic of Hebrew; by failing to recognize it, commentators have often raised spurious difficulties.

(d) The spies get clear away (2: 22–3: 1)

three days: i.e. a few (see on 1: 10). **the road:** from Jericho along one of the wadis to the Jordan (v. 7). The spies might have been able to glean some tactical information, but their report on the enemy's morale is what matters to the story. Joshua now moves from settled quarters to an 'assembly area'.

iii. Crossing the Jordan (3: 2–5: 1)

(a) Preparations (3: 2–13)

This section leads up to the prophecy of v. 13, fulfilled in the next paragraph. Anticipation is skilfully built up by a succession of hints, *e.g.* in vv. 5, 8, 12. **2. three days:** see on 1: 10.

3. the ark played a special part in crossing the Jordan and in taking Jericho, the critical (and most fully-described) episodes of the invasion story. Here God opens the door for his people. So, in 9 out of 16 references (chs. 3–4), it is **the ark of the covenant of the LORD;** the covenant comprises the law, but is first of all the pledge of God's presence (v. 10).

4. NIV, RSV, transposing the half-verses, have altered the sense. The thousand-yard gap was not a mark of reverential awe, but a practical necessity for control of the operation, in view of the numbers involved. Even with the river drained away, the crossing must be at or near a ford to obtain reasonably firm ground.

6. Joshua said: next day, obviously. **7.** Joshua had been fully commissioned by Moses (Num. 27; Dt. 31) and was already exercising authority; but something more dramatic was needed before the mass of the people would accept him with real conviction. This was a by-product of the first test of the new leader; like the people, but in a special sense, he has not been this way before.

10. The list of seven nations occurs 23 times, with omissions and additions and in various sequences (R. North, *Biblica* 54, 1973, pp. 43–62). The **Hittites** are always named (cf. Ezek. 16: 3), though they had no kingdom south of Damascus; migrants may have formed colonies, or a class, within Amorite/Canaanite society (H. A. Hoffner, *Tyndale Bulletin* 20, 1969, pp. 27–37). **Hivites,** at Gibeon and in the north (11: 3), and **Jebusites,** may have been Hurrians (see on 9: 7). **Perizzites** were probably not an ethnic group (*NBD s.v.*). The **Girgashites** cannot be located, though the name occurs in Ugaritic and (possibly) Hittite.

12 anticipates 4: 2–4; although the episode of the stones is recounted in 4: 1–10, mention here is appropriate to Joshua's 'order of the day', and serves to link the whole account together.

13. heap refers to the water, rather than to

the dam; elsewhere only in the poetic accounts of crossing the Sea (Exod. 15: 8; Ps. 33: 7; 78: 13).

(b) The Jordan blocked (3: 14–17)

15. floodstage: lit. 'overflows its banks' (better than NEB 'reaches', cf. Is. 8:7). The flooding (described by Baly, *Geography*, p. 199) is due to the melting of the snow from Hermon in early summer. **16. in a heap:** see on v. 13. NEB 'as far as Adam' may reflect the Heb. (Qᵉrê) reading 'from'; 'at' seems to be original and better sense. **cut off:** drained away. The collapse of the bank at Adam, 16 miles upstream, was neither unnatural nor unique; the extraordinary thing was the timing. On a wider scale too, the timing of the crossing marks it as an act of God. The Jordan was fordable at other times (1 Chr. 19: 17). In flood, it could be crossed by strong men (1 Chr. 12: 15); but not by a baggage train, nor by the Levites with the ark. The Jerichoans must have felt safe—until it happened.

(c) The memorial of the crossing (4: 1–10)

This passage describes the first of several tangible witnesses to the word of God, and to the once-for-all experiences which could so soon be forgotten; cf. especially 8: 30; 24: 27. The memorial is to be simple, unpolished, directly connected with the event (v. 3). It is not even impressive in size; each stone can be carried by one man, and the group is only large enough to symbolize the equal interest of all the tribes (v. 5). The vital thing is that it should be preserved, and its meaning faithfully taught (v. 7; hence the sanctuary, 1 Sam. 10: 8, etc.).

9. that had been is not in *MT*. Joshua apparently replaced the stones with similar ones from the bankside; but the terms 'set up', 'to this day', have led commentators to refer the verse in its original form to the memorial. **10** is an explanation, not part of the narrative; it should include the phrase 'and the people (had) hurried over' (SO NEB). **just as . . . Joshua:** NEB omits, following Gk.; there seems to be no appropriate passage in the Pentateuch.

(d) The crossing completed (4: 11–14)

The episodic structure of the narrative is well illustrated here. This paragraph completes the account of the crossing as such, by specifically including the ark and the Transjordanians, and notes its importance for Joshua's career. There is no need to infer from v. 11, as Gray and others do, that vv. 15 ff. are from a different source.

11. watched: RSV 'before', i.e. in their presence; NEB omits, but without textual evidence. **12. armed:** cf. 1: 14; Exod. 13: 18; Jg. 7: 11. The exact meaning of *ḥᵃmušîm* is uncertain.

(e) The Jordan unblocked (4: 15–24)

Note the repetition in vv. 15–18, emphasizing the sense of control, and the solemnity of the occasion; cf. 3: 14 ff. **Testimony**, variant for

'covenant', refers to the engraved evidence (Exod. 34: 29). **19. tenth:** cf. 5: 10. **Gilgal:** see B. M. Bennett, *PEQ* 104, 1972, pp. 111–122. The traditional location (Grollenberg, *Atlas*, pl. 160) seems unlikely, in the absence of any remains. The memorial was probably a small cairn, later preserved in an enclosure; it is doubtful whether Gilgal could mean 'stone circle'.

24. you . . . fear: the Heb. vowels are anomalous and cast doubt on this rendering; NEB 'they' adopts vowels in line with the grammar of the preceding clause.

(f) Effect on the Canaanites (5: 1)

Here is one more sign, to add to those noted in 2: 10, that the 'powers that be' are for Israel. **Amorite:** the settled inhabitants generally; **Canaanite:** basically the dealers in purple dye, hence the people of the coast; but the term was used in a broader sense (11: 3), especially of the land (24: 3). See 'Historical Background'.

iv. Israel formally takes possession (5: 2–12) (a) The people circumcised (5: 2–9)

2. again (*šûb*): NEB 'seat yourself' (= *šēb*), as in Egypt pictures (*ANEP* 629). Heb. adds *šēniṯ* 'the second time', i.e. re-establish that all males are circumcised, as under the Abrahamic covenant. The practice, assumed in Exod. 12: 43–49 and commanded in Lev. 12: 3, had been suspended. The new Israel was in a sense, on probation, after their fathers had rebelled at Kadesh (Num. 14, to which this passage refers; 'us', in v.6, as in Num. 14: 8).

9. reproach of Egypt: although not part of the Sinai covenant, circumcision seals them as children of Abraham (and qualifies them to eat the passover). Now they can forget that they have been by turns refugees, slaves and fugitives; they can enter into their inheritance as a free people under God.

(b) The first passover (5: 10–12)

Appropriately, the Israelites celebrate and consecrate their arrival in the Promised Land by the Passover, recalling their deliverance. The reference to the manna may be surprising, as they had been living in agricultural land for some time; but it underlines the change in their way of life. KJV 'old corn' is misleading; the barley harvest was beginning (Lev. 23: 9–14).

v. Enlarging the bridgehead (5: 13–8: 29) (a) Instructions for attacking Jericho (5: 13–6: 5)

The commander of the army of the LORD appears simply as a man; once his person is established (5: 15), his directions are taken as from the Lord (6: 2). They are straightforward, and are faithfully carried out; the principal additions in the narrative turn on Joshua's speech, which is needed to interpret the events and to introduce the story of Achan.

4. seven priests: many commentators regard the priests, ark and trumpets as later 'priestly' embellishments of the story. It is of course possible to strip them out and leave a readable text; but the idea of the 'holy war' is basic to the whole tradition about Jericho. Cf. 1 Sam. 4 for another occasion when the ark was brought to a critical encounter. There are several minor peculiarities in the Heb. here, mostly relating to the trumpets and the ark, but these do not argue against the unity of the text. **trumpets of rams' horns:** *šōpᵉrôt (hay) yōbᵉlîm:* no distinction can be made between *šōpār* and *qeren* (v. 5); the **long blast** is the signal to attack.

5. collapse: so NEB; lit. 'upon itself'; strange pictures have been conjured up (and derided) on the basis of the traditional rendering 'flat'. Nothing remains of the 'Late Bronze' walls, and very little of the city (see on v. 26); but they must have been built on the ruins of earlier ones, which formed a sloping rampart round most of the city (see J. A. Thompson, *The Bible and Archaeology*, 1962, pp. 60 f.; K. M. Kenyon, *Archaeology in the Holy Land*, 1960, pp. 174–179).

(*b*) **Instructions followed (6: 6–11)**
7. armed guard: picked (and best-equipped) troops, as 4: 13; but not necessarily from the tribes of the Transjordan only, as NEB infers (presumably from that text). **8. blowing their trumpets:** this has been a contentious point of interpretation. From the silence of the people and from vv. 5, 16, commentators have inferred that there was an early account in which the trumpets also were silent, and that in later versions the priests' role was enhanced. Gray (NCentB) presents a significant shift from older documentary theories: 'Both the secular and sacred traditions served the purpose of the deuteronomic historian'.

(*c*) **The week of waiting (6: 12–14)**
While this doubtless helped to demoralize the Jerichoans, it also tested the discipline and faith of the Israelites. The sixth day shows no 'advance' on the first; so it often happens when we have to wait on the Lord.

(*d*) **The assault on Jericho (6: 15–21)**
16. See v. 5. **17. devoted to the LORD:** Heb. *ḥērem*. Lev. 27: 28 f., Mic. 4: 13 confirm the meaning 'devoted' or 'consecrated' (irrevocably). Cf. Dt. 13: 12–18, in the case of an idolatrous Israelite community. It must be shown that the motive is one of principle and not of cupidity. The consecration of Jericho amounts to offering the first fruits, acknowledging Israel's service and indebtedness to the Lord.

(*e*) **Rahab delivered (6: 22–25)**
It is not necessary to suppose that the entire circuit of the wall had collapsed (see on v. 5). **24. the LORD's house** could mean the tabernacle; or the author may simply have used the phrase current in his own day.

(*f*) **Joshua's curse on the city site (6: 26–27)**
This followed logically from the *ḥērem* (see on v. 17). It is remarkable that the ban was observed for some four centuries, till Hiel of Bethel broke it and the curse was fulfilled (1 Kg. 16: 34).

(*g*) **Achan breaks faith (7: 1)**
We now see (i) secret sin openly rebuked; (ii) one man's sin involving the community. This must be so if the community is truly holy, else the grace of God would be mocked. The verb *māʿal* is used almost exclusively for infidelity (to God; or in marriage, Num. 5: 12).

(*h*) **first assault on Ai (7: 2–15)**
Ai: for a review of the controversy arising from the absence of Late Bronze remains, see J. Callaway, *JBL* 87 (1968), pp. 312–320; *PEQ* 102 (1970), pp. 42–44. It seems that Joshua's target might have been an Iron Age settlement within the old city walls ('a few men', v. 3). However, D. Livingston (*WTJ* 33.1, 1970, pp. 20–44) has re-opened the question of the site of Bethel (and hence of Ai); see map. **near Bethaven:** the nearest inhabited site at the time of writing; cf. 1 Sam. 13: 5; later associated with Bethel, Hos. 4: 15. **5. stone quarries:** almost certainly, cliff quarries east or south of Ai. There is no suggestion that over-confidence (v. 3) caused the setback, but it did lead to deeper gloom. If we think the reaction (vv. 7–9) exaggerated, we might do well to examine critically the way we face disappointments. However, for Joshua it was not a case of 'taking the rough with the smooth'; at this stage, failure could only mean that the Lord had withdrawn his support.

(*i*) **Achan convicted and executed (7: 16–26) come forward:** presumably by representatives of the tribes and clans. **19. praise:** RV, NEB, confession, and so RSV in the parallel text Ezr. 10: 11; but 'praise', the usual meaning, is appropriate in these cases; cf. Ps. 50: 23. **21. Babylonia:** RSV 'Shinar'; perhaps read *śʿr*, 'woollen' (Gray, *ad loc.*); but Babylon was a cloth-weaving area.
24. the silver, etc.: even this is not restored to the treasury; everything is cast out as unclean, and no Israelite may profit by Achan's loss. The severity of the judgment is matched to the sense of the reality of God's presence with Israel (cf. Ac. 5, 1 C. 5). **25. stoned:** the normal method of execution by the community, who must take responsibility for purging the evil (Dt. 17: 7). **after:** implied; RSV follows Heb. Burning deprives of ordinary burial and expresses special horror of the sin (Lev. 20: 14, 21: 9). **them:** cf. 22: 20 'not . . . alone'. Inasmuch as a man was responsible for the actions of his household, they were accessories to his crime.

(*j*) **Preparing for the second assault (8: 1–9)**
Sin, being expiated, was put right away, and

confidence restored. Not only so, but Joshua received guidance to avoid the cost of frontal assault on this tricky objective. The use of the whole army was not a military necessity, but a commitment to the holy war; the spiritual issue is like that of Jg. 7: 2, but the practical conclusion is the opposite, because Israel's frame of mind (Jos. 7: 3) was different. **3.** The ambush is explained in some detail (logically following v. 2), and noticed again in v. 12. **thirty thousand:** v. 12 says 5,000. Scribal error must be presumed; 30,000 is improbable.

9. between Bethel and Ai: perhaps south of the height mentioned in Gen. 12: 8; not necessarily in a valley, but affording cover, and reached by a ravine. See on 7: 2.

(k) **Destruction of Ai (8: 10–29)**
10–13. Preparation for the attack. The first and last phrases, corresponding to vv. 3a, 9b, show the time-relation in these paragraphs. It is a question of narrative method rather than of sources. **14. a . . . place overlooking the Arabah** (om. NEB): Heb. *lammōʿēḏ*, 'to the meeting' (KJV 'appointed time'), cf. 1 Sam. 20: 35, is unnatural here; the emendation *lammōrāḏ*, 'to the descent' (as 7: 5) is justified. **17. or Bethel:** not in Gk.; probably not original, in view of vv. 9, 12. **18. javelin:** so 1 Sam. 17: 6, 45; Job 39: 23; 41: 29; hardly a 'dagger' (NEB). If this was a signal, it must have been relayed to the assault force; but Joshua may have been calling

on the Lord to stir them to action as arranged (8: 6 f.).

vi. Israel comes home again (8: 30–35)
The vale of Shechem was the very heart of Israel, geographically and emotionally; Gen. 48: 22 may well refer to it (cf. Gen. 34, 35: 1–4). Mystery surrounds the relations of Israel with Shechem, which apparently was captured or infiltrated by Hebrew invaders in the 15th century (the *ʾanšê ḥᵃmōr* of Jg. 9: 28?); this assembly can only have been made with the goodwill of the Shechemites. The altar stood on, and the curse (the larger part of the sanction, see Dt. 28) was pronounced from, Mt. Ebal, which is the higher mountain; the primacy of Gerizim rests on Samaritan tradition. In Dt. 11: 29 on to ch. 28, Moses commanded the promulgation of the law in the land, provided it in a teachable form, and prescribed the formula and ritual of the covenant. See further on ch. 24.

33. For the division of the assembly, see Dt. 27: 11 ff.; **formerly** ends Heb. sentence (NEB 'pronounced first'). The declaration of God's goodwill comes before the law. **34. the law, the blessings and the curses:** the three essentials of the covenant as enshrined in the 'Book of the Law' (see Lev. 26; Dt. 28).

vii. Breakout to the south (9: 1–10: 43)
(a) **Reaction of the Canaanites (9: 1–2)**
Note the skill with which the writer keeps the

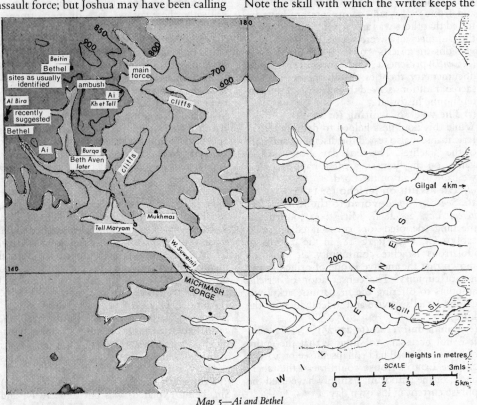

Map 5—Ai and Bethel

main subject in view. **west of the Jordan:** 'by', rather; see on 1: 14; cf. Isa. 9: 1. RSV omits 'and' after **foothills**, incorrectly (see on 12: 7). **about these things** (added in tr.): i.e. of Israel's progress.

(*b*) **Covenant with the Gibeonites (9: 3–15)** The Israelites make a second false move, this time through credulity and failure to seek guidance. However, God overruled and used the Gibeonite alliance to promote the next stage of the conflict (ch. 10).

Gibeon (see map): this impressive site has been partially excavated, with dramatic results (J. B. Pritchard, *Gibeon, where the sun stood still,* 1962). The 'Late Bronze' cemetery proves occupation in our period, if not so extensive as previously. Gibeon and the three lesser towns of the Hivite settlement (9: 17; 11: 19) occupied a strategic position on the northern boundary of Jerusalem (see further on 10: 1).

4. delegation: MT *wayyiṣṭayyārû* could be from words for 'ambassador' (KJV, J. Gray) or 'form' ('disguise', NEB). RSV reads *wayyiṣṭayyāḍû*, as in v. 12. **7. Hivites:** LXX = *ḥori* may represent the original form. The Hurrians were a Caucasian people who played a great part in the neo-Hittite and Mitannian kingdoms, and appear to have infiltrated into Canaan. **11. servants:** the visitors, though 'remote', ask for a covenant of vassalage rather than of equality (F. C. Fensham, *BA* 27, 1964, p. 97). This looks suspicious, but flattery wins the day.

14. sampled implies a communal meal, in itself a pledge of friendship; it may even refer to a covenant ceremony. **did not enquire:** this is of cardinal importance; it would have involved a reference to the priest. The principle applies equally to Christians. **15. the leaders of the assembly** are mentioned for the first time here (LXX, in v. 14), as the context becomes political rather than military. Modern commentators (*e.g.* M. Noth) tend to regard Joshua's part as a later addition; formerly 'the

elders' were regarded as late (*e.g.* by W. Rudolph). The issue is not solved by textual criticism (Noth, *ad loc.*). Scripture presents Joshua's position as compatible with responsible leadership in the tribes.

(*c*) **The trick discovered (9: 16–27)** **16, 17. three days, the third day:** see on 1: 10.

17. set out must be read with 10: 9, 43; we are not to imagine the whole nation as encamped at Gilgal, trying to live off the desert. Our text gives a sidelight on the infiltration which went on all the time, before boundaries were settled (cf. 11: 18, 18: 2). **22.** Although the elders are competent to take a decision on the spot, it naturally comes up to Joshua for confirmation.

(*d*) **The southern alliance counterattacks (10: 1–7)** **Jerusalem** had long been the paramount city of the region, though the number of city-states had increased since the Amarna period (Y. Aharoni, *Land of the Bible,* 1966, p. 195). It now entered into decline; sacked and abandoned by Judah (Jg. 1), it was occupied by Jebusite migrants till David's time. **the royal cities** included Gezer, Lachish and Jerusalem; despite its strength, the Hivite city had lesser status, probably acknowledging the king of Jerusalem as overlord. Beeroth and Chephirah, in enemy hands, would strangle Jerusalem's communications with the west.

(*e*) **The Battle of Gibeon (10: 8–15)** It is implied that Joshua came between the enemy and Jerusalem; hence the flight westwards. The hailstorm struck as the fugitives reached more open country, towards Azekah.

The record of the 'long day' has been much debated. Parallels have been found in Chinese, Egyptian and Mexican stories, but these will not coincide in date or time of day (E. W. Maunder, *JTVI* 53, 1921, pp. 120–148); and an astronomical aberration would not have gone unrecorded in Babylon. Attempts at interpret-

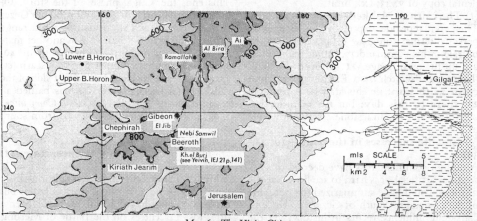

Map 6—The Hivite Cities

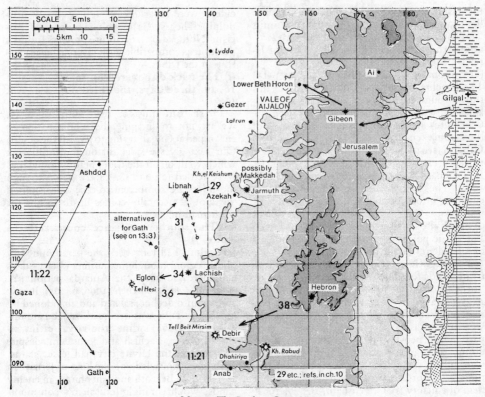

Map 7—The Southern Campaign

ing the poem, and especially the peculiar use of *dmm* ('be silent') of the sun, have ranged from eclipse (J. Sawyer, *PEQ* 104, 1972, pp. 139–146) to a curse on the gods of Gibeon (J. Dus, *VT* 10, 1960, pp. 353–361; see in answer J. Holladay, *JBL* 87, 1968, pp. 168–178). The one thing clear is that the Lord helped his people to exploit their victory; neither we, nor the inspired writer, can fully explain how this was accomplished. Verse 15 concludes the excerpt relating to the poem, unless it is an accidental copy of v. 43; LXX omits.

(f) The cairn at Makkedah (10: 16–27)
This vivid episode expresses the victory in personal terms; note how Joshua cared for the morale of his commanders, rather than building up his own image. **21. uttered:** lit. 'cut' (hence NEB 'scratch'); so Ex. 11: 7. **24. had come with him:** i.e. his staff or entourage. **27. there to this day:** but the memory has been lost, and the limestone cave is now one of many in the area.

(g) Israelite successes in the south (10: 28–39)
Although commentators have decried this account as artificial, it is hard to see how else the historian could have summarized the outcome of the campaign. South of Gezer, no trace of Canaanite influence recurs in history; yet the

main centres of the old regime are accurately identified here. It may be that for the purpose of this review Caleb's successes are included (cf. 14: 13; 15: 13–17); but 10: 3 mentions a king in Hebron, whose historical relation to the Anakite chiefs remains obscure. **38. turned around:** SW from Hebron. Debir was not on the way up from Eglon, but it commanded the approach from the lowland to the southern hills.

(h) Summary of the campaign (10: 40–43)
This ends the 'Gilgal phase' of the story. Of the southern Canaanite city-states, all but Gezer ceased to exist, and the Israelites could range through the hills. Settlement was another matter; but so far, the Lord had helped them. **40. slopes:** generally the upper part of a scarp (cf. 12: 3); here, the sparsely-settled east side of the hills. **41. Goshen** (cf. 15: 51) 'has baffled all commentators' (D. Baly, *Geog. Companion*, 1963, p. 68). The description runs from south to north.

viii. Victories in the North (11: 1–15)
(a) The North Canaanites concentrate (11: 1–5)
Jabin: the name recurs in Jg. 4. Tradition-study tends to assume only one historical Jabin, but the name could have been dynastic or even a title. Jos. 11 centres on the Battle of Merom,

while Jg. 4–5 is equally firmly linked to a very different battle in the Plain of Esdraelon.

Hazor is mentioned in Jos. 19: 36; it does not follow that Israel occupied it at an early date. The Middle Bronze Age city (=patriarchal age) was built on virgin soil. The Late Bronze city, presumably that destroyed by Joshua, is dated by Mycenaean pottery of about the 13th century BC; its description as 'the head of all those kingdoms' (10), i.e. those of E. Galilee, is confirmed by the excavations which uncovered a circuit wall enclosing an area many times larger than that of any other Palestinian city. The last Canaanite occupation, however, was mainly on the acropolis (Y. Aharoni, *Land of the Bible*, p. 207). **2. foothills:** SE of Carmel; the terrain is like the Judaean Shephelah (Baly, *Geography*, pp. 140 f.). **3. Jebusites:** usually following the Hivites in these lists (cf. 9: 1, 12: 8). It is interesting that the Jebusites are not linked to Jerusalem at this stage (see on 15: 63).

Hivites: cf. Jg. 3: 3. **Mizpah** (RSV 'Mizpeh' in v. 8), the 'watch-tower' overlooking the Huleh valley, cannot be located; the valley must be between Hermon and the Litani. **5. Merom:** the site has been much debated (see map); the 'waters' were probably nearby, not (as has been supposed) the outfall to L. Galilee.

Significantly, Jabin was tempted or compelled (by Israelite penetration?) to take the field and expose himself.

(b)Joshua defeats Jabin of Hazor (11: 6–9)
We are given virtually no details of Joshua's tactics. The essential points are that he was encouraged by the word of the Lord (cf. 1: 9; 6: 2; 8: 1; 10: 8); that he surprised and routed the enemy; and that he destroyed their horses and equipment, for which Israel had no use.

8. the east: this indicates that Merom lay well to the north, near a main east-west valley.

(c) Cities taken in the North (11: 10–15)
This paragraph covers the conquest of Galilee and of some of the Canaanite cities on its borders. The destruction of Hazor is well-known (see on v. 1). The unconquered cities (cf. Jg. 1: 27, 30–33) were in the Jezreel valley and by the coast. At v. 15 the author stresses his great theme, that the occupation was the Lord's promise and doing through Moses, worked out by Joshua's leadership in faith and obedience.

ix. Joshua's achievement (11: 16–23)
(a) Summary of the invasion (11: 16–20)
This paragraph should correct any impression that Joshua conquered the land in two campaigns. On the other hand, whatever penetrations may have been made (cf. ch. 17), the

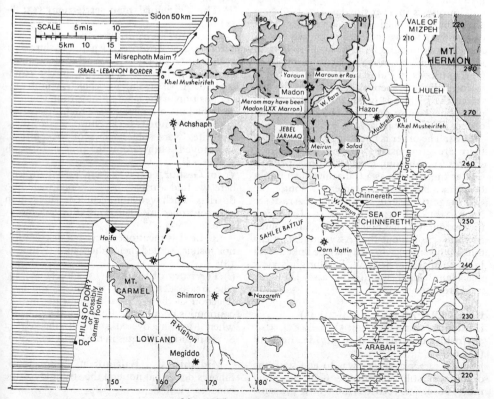

Map 8—The Northern Campaign

wars clearly put an end to the Canaanite social and political system. **16. their foothills:** see on v. 2.

(*b*) **Note on the Anakim (11: 21–22)**

This doubtless refers to Caleb's successes, here attributed to Joshua as overall leader. The Anakim were a symbol of terror to the early Israelites (Num. 13: 33, Dt. 9: 2). They may well have been foreign warlords, but the origin of the name is still a mystery.

(*c*) **Mission accomplished (11: 23):** see on v. 15. **the entire land** is a general statement of success (see Introduction); the author is here concerned with Joshua's very considerable achievement, not with the limits of it (13: 1). **rest from war** crowns that achievement (cf. 23: 1, Jg. 3: 11, etc.); now the people can cultivate the land and enjoy its wealth (Dt. 8: 7ⓕ).

II. THE ISRAELITE CONQUESTS (12: 1–24)

This short section links the two main parts of the book. Although in a literary sense the first section is complete in itself, ch. 12 rounds it off and joins it to the earlier conquests recorded in Dt. The schematic form is more akin to what follows. The overall effect emphasizes the unity of the book, composed as it is of very diverse material.

(*a*) **Conquests in Transjordan (12: 1–6)**

1. Arabah (KJV 'plain'): the dry valley floor; distinguish from the better-known Wadi Arabah south of the Dead Sea. (The) **Pisgah** is the plateau crest, not a particular mountain.

(*b*) **Conquests in Palestine (12: 7–24)**

8. foothills: the Shephelah, a hilly region between the highlands of Judah and the coastal plain; but see also on 11: 2. **the desert** is the eastern side of the Judaean ridge.

9–24. The order is not strictly geographical; there are grounds for relating it to literary sources (Y. Aharoni, *Land of the Bible*, p. 209). **Geder** (not known as a Canaanite city) might be Gerar, but this was rather far south; the Gk. suggests Goshen. **Hormah . . . Arad:** see Num. 21: 1–3, Jg. 1: 17. **Aphek . . . Lasharon** (in Sharon): Gk. has one king here, and counts Meron (v. 20) as one (but Assyrian texts mention *samsimuruna*). **Goyim** may be linked with Jg. 4: 2; Aharoni rejects W. F. Albright's view that Heb. 'Gilgal' was (in this case) Jaljuliyeh in Sharon; see map.

III. OCCUPATION (13: 1–21: 45)

i. Introduction (13: 1–14: 5)

(*a*) **Joshua commanded to divide the land (13: 1–7)**

Joshua's career as leader was to end with the occupation still incomplete. God promised more; but it was forfeited (note how the same material was used in vv. 2–6 and in Jg. 3: 3; cf.

Exod. 23: 30; Dt. 7: 22). Therefore (v. 7) Joshua must oversee the allocation of the area which was more or less effectively occupied.

2. Geshurites: cf. 1 Sam. 27: 8; not as vv. 11 ff.

3. Canaanite: it is likely that Philistine colonists (former 'Sea Raiders') gained control of this area with the goodwill of Egypt. **Gath** (cf. 11: 22) cannot be located with certainty. The prominent *Tell es Safi* has been favoured (lately by A. F. Rainey, *Eretz-Israel* XII, 1975, pp. 63–76), but there are good arguments for identifying it with Libnah. *Tell Areini* (129113), proposed by Albright, and renamed *Tell Gat* in 1948, proved to have been too small in the Philistine period. G. E. Wright proposed *Tell es Sheriah* (*BA* 29, 1966, pp. 78–86, and 34, 1971, p. 84, n. 20). The name was not unique (B. Mazar, *IEJ* 4, 1954, pp. 227–235). **Avvites:** 'villagers', Dt. 2: 23. The verse should end at 'south'. **4. from Arah** (*MT ûmecārāh*) 'cave'; LXX apparently read 'from Gaza', but a location near, or north of, Carmel is probably intended. **Gebal:** Byblos; (this) **Aphek** is inland from it; **Lebo** (RSV entrance) is near Baalbek in the valley. This survey corresponds to Num. 34: 7–8. The 'land that remained' was never occupied (cf. Jg. 3: 3); the minor initiative by Dan (Jg. 18) only emphasizes the failure of the nation.

(*b*) **The Transjordanian settlement (13: 8–14)**

Some words have dropped out of the text before v. 8. KJV exposes the gap; RSV slurs over it; NEB, NIV supply a reasonable conjecture, mentioning the other half–tribe. **9. the town** could be Aroer (again); its peculiar, commanding position in the bend of the Arnon could be described in both phrases (see map).

10. the Amorites: cf. Num. 21: 26; these Amorites were subject-allies of the Hittites, and moved southward in the time of Pharaoh Rameses II.

11. of Geshur, etc.: cf. 2 Sam. 13: 37. Already here we find a tribal area reckoned including districts which were not occupied. This region was controlled by Damascus after Solomon's time.

14. Levi is mentioned here because Moses, not Joshua, settled their inheritance (Num. 8, 18).

(*c*) **Territory of Reuben (13: 15–23)**

The area is described by its extent, and by a selection of the principal settlements; not by continuous boundaries. Reuben suffered badly when Moab recovered strength; the Mesha Stone mentions Gadites in the south (cf. Num. 32: 34).

Midianite . . . Balaam: cf. Num. 31: 8. Sihon's defeat did not end the struggle for the Medeba plain.

(*d*) **Territory of Gad (13: 24–28)**

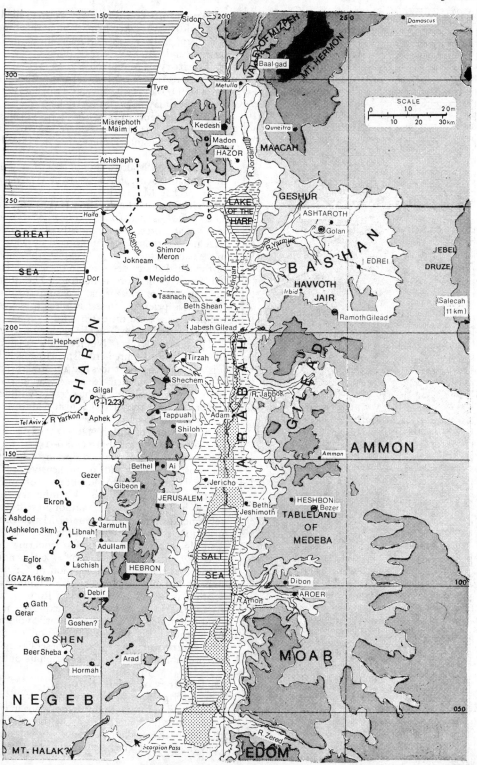

Map 9—Palestine and Transjordan

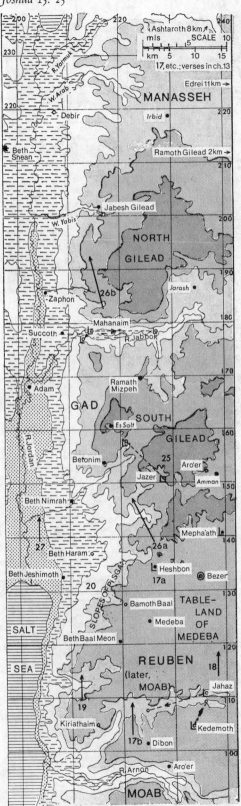

25. Ammonite country: as it was later called. No territory was taken from them at this time (Dt. 2: 19, cf. Jg. 11: 15, 26). **near:** lit. 'facing', see map and *NBD s.v.* 'Aroer' (2).

(e) **Territory of Manasseh (13: 29–31)**
See Num. 32: 39 ff. Here grain and cattle alike did well (D. Baly, *Geography*, p. 216); but later, the territory lay open to the Aramaeans.

30. settlements of Jair: *havvōt*, tr. 'villages' in Num. 32: 41 and elsewhere. **towns:** *'ir* means a defensible locality, not necessarily large.

31. half. . . Makir: despite consistency in the textual evidence, this seems to be a copyist's error for 'half Manasseh'.

(f) **Principles of the division (13: 32–14: 5)**
The author is particularly concerned *(a)* to stress that, directly or indirectly, the whole Israelite inheritance was authorized by Moses in the name of the Lord; *(b)* to explain the count of the tribal shares described in these chapters (14: 3–4; KJV 'therefore' is incorrect). The introduction here of Eleazar has led some to distinguish a 'priestly' interest in these passages; opinions vary as to the extent of the supposed post-exilic influence. The phraseology in several places recalls that of Numbers, the essential 'P' of traditional source-criticism. However, if it is admitted that the tribes had a central shrine —and few would deny this—it would have been inconceivable for Joshua to act without the priest, or for any Israelite historian to represent him as having done so.

ii. Settlement of Judah (14: 6–15: 63)
(a) **Caleb claims his share (14: 6–15)**
Before we come to the description of Judah, the most systematic and comprehensive of all, a special place is given to the fulfilment of God's promise to Caleb, Joshua's contemporary and fellow-heir (Num. 14). The author presents the settlements of Judah and Ephraim-Manasseh as prior to the formal division of the land (cf. 18: 5 and Jg. 1: 2); NEB is justified in rendering the opening verb of v. 6 'had come'. Comment is silenced at the sublime confession of Caleb's praise and faith. Of him also Paul could have written as he did of Abraham in Rom. 4: 20 ff. **12. the LORD helping me:** expresses not doubt, but Heb. *'ûlai* 'perhaps', faith avoiding presumption. For the Anakim, see on 11: 21. **rest from war:** cf. 11: 23. These passages are probably taken from fuller accounts of the wars.

(b) **Territory of Judah (15: 1–63)**
The description is in two parts: (i) vv. 1–20 correspond in format to the descriptions in ch. 18, but give the boundary only, with a note on the Kenite-Kenizzite inheritance (vv. 13–19). (ii) vv. 21–62 are a city-list in ten districts; LXX

Map 10—The East Bank

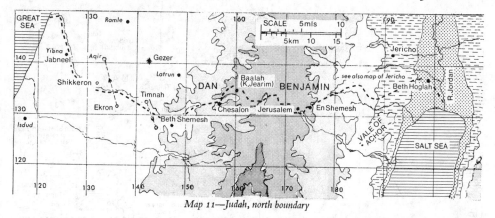

Map 11—Judah, north boundary

preserves an eleventh, the Bethlehem-Tekoa district, and there is reason to think that the scheme reflects a twelve-district organization of the kingdom of Judah with West Benjamin (under Jehoshaphat?). **3. Kadesh:** the name is preserved at *Ain Qedeis*, but *Ain Qudeirat* (5 m. north) is the principal oasis of the group.

12. The coastal area was never fully occupied; the boundary description, unlike the city-list, is a statement of intent rather than a record of an actual historical position. **4. their:** so LXX, NEB; Heb. 'your' is an interesting pointer to an original document similar, if not identical, to that used in Num. 34: 1–12.

18. got off: NEB 'broke wind', LXX 'cried out' (here and in Jg. 1: 14); Jg. 4: 21 'went down' (RSV), perhaps 'broke through', **she urged him:** some versions have the converse; either way, it seems that Othniel was unwilling to look a gift horse in the mouth. **32.** The discrepancy in the count indicates an unresolved problem in restoring the text. **36. Gederothaim** may be a later name for Gederah. **60. Rabbah:** probably Beth Shemesh (Egyp. *Rubute*). **63. Jebusites:** Jerusalem was, strictly speaking, in Benjaminite territory (so Jos. 18:

28); but the note here is relevant to Judah (see Jg. 1: 21, in its context). The Jebusite connection with Jerusalem reflects the times of the Judges; see Jg. 19: 10 f., 2 Sam. 5: 6, and note on Jos. 11: 3).

iii. Settlement in the Ephraim Hills (16: 1–17: 18)

(a) Territory of Joseph (Ephraim) (16: 1–10)

This section first takes Ephraim and Manasseh together (cf. 17: 14), and then treats the borders of Ephraim very briefly, compared with their description under Manasseh and Benjamin (17: 7–10; 18: 12–14). In turn, 18: 15–19 is rather less full than 15: 6–11. We may conclude that all these passages were abbreviated from full descriptions, to suit the author's purpose in each case. The primacy of Ephraim, prophesied in Gen. 48: 14, etc., was not yet realized. **8, 9.** Cf. 17: 7–9. The north-eastern extension of Ephraim follows the outcrop of a limestone which was favourable to olive-growing; the Kanah Brook formed a more artificial boundary (D. Baly, *Geog. Companion*, p. 75). **set aside:** perhaps in the region of Shechem (21: 20 f.); but see 17: 9.

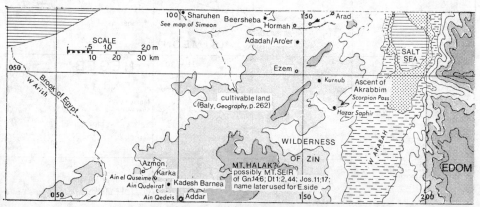

Map 12—Judah, South boundary

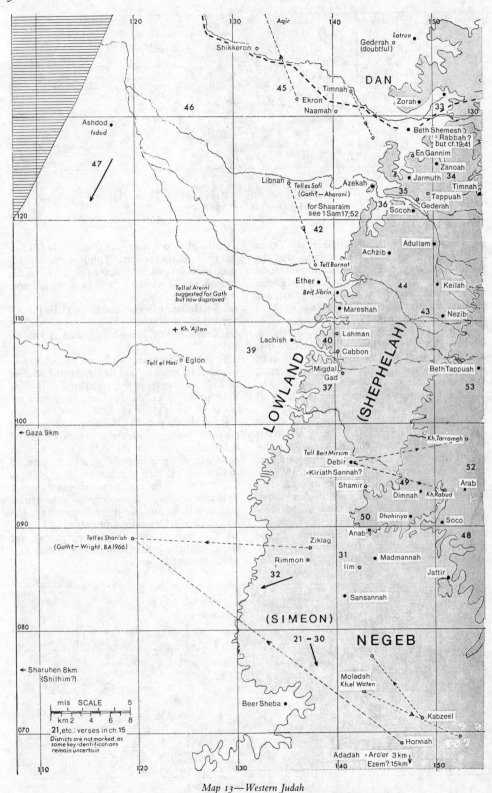

Map 13—Western Judah

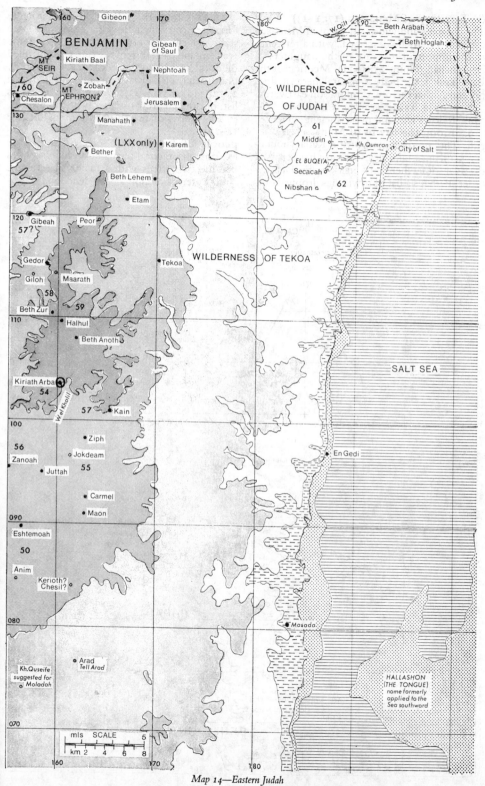

Map 14—Eastern Judah

(*b*) **Territory of Manasseh (17: 1–13)**
The complex and wide settlement of Manasseh can only briefly be described, with a reference to the important test case of the daughters of Zelophehad (Num. 27: 1–11). Mention of the East Bank settlement is natural here; it does not imply that there was migration eastwards.

7. people living (*yōšᵉbê*) is odd; NEB 'Yashub' follows LXX and other ancient evidence.

9. among the towns of Manasseh is difficult. The interpretation of the Kanah boundary is still uncertain; clearly it must have crossed the river somewhere. KJV, NEB keep the Hebrew order. Perhaps a list of towns has dropped out.

11, 12. Cf. Jg. 1: 27. The string of Canaanite fortresses (in which Egyptian garrisons were stationed till the 12th century), linking the western and eastern regions (11: 3), controlled the focal area of communications in Palestine. **Naphoth** (hill?), elsewhere only with Dor (11: 2, 12: 23, 1 Kg. 4: 11), which is **third** in this list; but the Hebrew number is not an ordinal.

(*c*) **Problems of northward expansion (17: 14–18)**
people of Joseph: lit. 'sons'. This passage explains in practical terms how the Josephites became two tribes with a major share in the land. In terms of God's providence and prom-

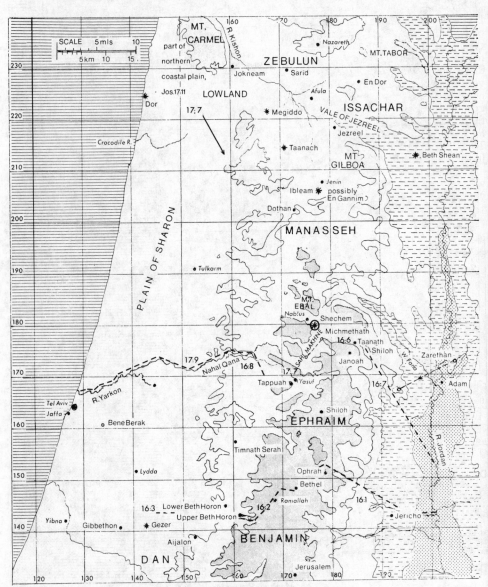

Map 15—Ephraim and Manasseh

ise, the explanation goes back to Gen. 48. Two distinct points are made and answered: (1) they needed more territory; (2) the best land, further north, lay in the valleys controlled by the Canaanite chariots. The mention of **Rephaites** (v. 15, cf. 12: 4) lends some support to the view that expansion was to be across the Jordan (cf. Jg. 12: 4; 2 Sam. 18: 6); but the main objective should have been to occupy the less fertile hills north of Shechem, and ultimately strangle the enemy cities below them (Y. Aharoni, *Land of the Bible*, p. 218; D. Baly, *Geography*, p. 169). **15 small:** 'âṣ, usually tr. 'hasten'; but LXX supports KJV, RSV.

iv. The other tribal areas (18: 1–19: 51)
(a) Conference at Shiloh (18: 1–10)
Having established the two main highland areas of occupation, Joshua sets about completing the job. An important function of leadership is to judge the right moment for imparting extra drive when enthusiasm is flagging; this involves not merely exhorting, but defining the next steps. The original lists were apparently groups of towns (v. 9); they were probably fuller than those now before us.

(b) Territory of Benjamin (18: 11–28)
This description is naturally similar to that of Judah (ch. 15; compare 18: 20 with 15: 12).

14. The lack of any detail on the 6 miles of western boundary may have something to do with the partial loss of Danite territory (Jg. 1: 34).

15. the west: Heb. 'went out to the sea', perhaps from the same original as 15: 11. **21.** Cf. 1 Kg. 1: 34.

28. Zelah. . . Kiriath: The text appears corrupt; this reconstruction gets the count right.

(c) Territory of Simeon (19: 1–9)
The list is similar to 15: 26–32; 1 Chr. 4: 28–33. For a full discussion, see W. F. Albright, *JPOS* 4 (1924), pp. 149–161; Y. Aharoni, *Land of the Bible*, pp. 104, 265 f. Simeon scarcely kept its identity after David's time, and is not counted in the division of the kingdom (1 Kg. 11: 32); the area became part of Judah (cf. 1 Sam. 27: 6; Gen. 49: 7; 1 Chr. 4: 39–43). Apart from Beersheba and Sharuhen (*Tell el Far'a*, destroyed by Shishak), hardly a town is certainly located.

(d) Territory of Zebulun (19: 10–16)
The description starts on the south side, and looks first west, then east and north. **11. near:** lit. 'facing' or 'by'. **12. Japhia** is generally taken as modern Yafa, though it looks out of place. Zebulun and Issachar covered a trade route from the north-east to Acco via the Kishon Gap (Gen. 49: 13; Dt. 33: 19).

(e) Territory of Issachar (19: 17–23)
The area includes hills less fertile than those of Zebulun, together with part at least of the Plain of Jezreel (cf. Gen. 49: 14 f.). **22.** This boundary probably stood the test of time; in the south, Issachar was more vulnerable.

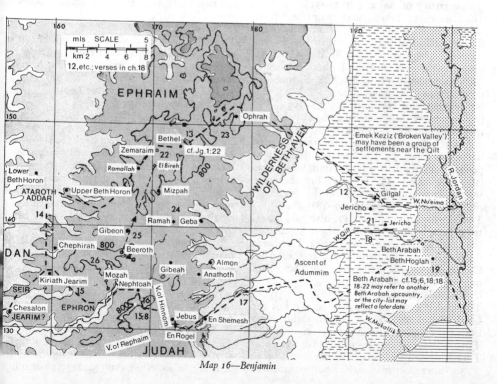

Map 16—Benjamin

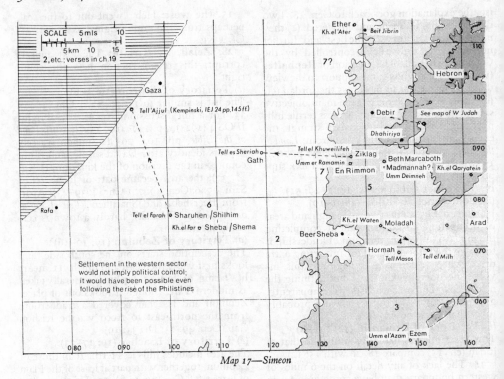

Map 17—Simeon

(f) **Territory of Asher (19: 24–31)**
The Canaanites (Phoenicians) maintained their
hold on the coast, Jg. 1: 31 f. Solomon gave up
the hinterland of Acco in return for Tyrian
support, 1 Kg. 9: 11. **26. Shihor**='marsh',
probably the outfall of the Kishon, but some
authorities locate it near Dor. **28. Sidon:** i.e.
their territory, inland of Tyre.

(g) **Territory of Naphtali (19: 32–39)**
In some ways the strongest area, but also the
most exposed to a northern enemy (2 Kg. 15:
29). The northern hills were heavily forested
in ancient times. **34. Jordan:** *MT* 'Judah' was
probably a scribal error for **Jordan**, which was
later re-inserted. **35.** The city list continues
where the boundary list leaves off.

(h) **Territory of Dan (19: 40–48)**
This is Samson's country. **47. but . . . territory** paraphrased; cp. KJV. The text appears
corrupt; LXX is similar to Jg. 1: 34. Har-heres
(in Judges) may be Beth Shemesh; the earlier
Canaanite city was destroyed, but Dan could
not keep their hold on the site.

(i) **Joshua's portion (19: 49, 50)**
The leader is served last (Mk 9: 35); but the
Lord secures his share. Even so, Joshua does
not retire to be waited on in idleness.
Timnath-serah appears to be a later form of
Timnath-heres ('Enclosure of the Sun', Jg. 2:
9); the alteration may have been intended to

remove the suspicion of association with idolatry.

(j) **Summary (19: 51)**
This note formally closes the account begun at
14: 1. The whole of the settlement, whether by
initiative or by allocation, is to be seen as
authorized and confirmed by the Lord.

v. The Cities of Refuge (20: 1–9)
(a) **The law of refuge (20: 1–6)**
See Num. 35: 9–28; Dt. 19: 1–13. **3. avenger
of blood** (NEB paraphrases): in primitive society this was a solemn duty of the next-of-kin,
as a sanction for the restraint of lawlessness.
However, he could not judge between homicide and murder. Before the monarchy, elders
were responsible for seeing that the sanction
was applied, but did not escalate into vendetta.
2 Sam. 14: 4–11 illustrates the shift away from
this principle when the 'King's Peace' operates.

6. stood . . . assembly suggests that the
man would be accepted formally on his return.
For the development of the law, see *NBD*
s.v. 'Cities of Refuge'. Bedouin custom grants
asylum for three days, without distinguishing
homicide from murder (J. Gray, *SVT* 5, 1957,
p. 174).

(b) **Six cities designated (20: 7–9)**
The three named in Dt. 4: 41 ff. are included.

7. Kedesh: Aharoni (*Land of the Bible*, p.
204) argues for *Kh. Qedish* (202237), assuming

that Barak's birthplace is the same Kedesh; but the former Canaanite city would have covered Upper Galilee more adequately.

vi. The Levitical settlements (21: 1–42)

(a) **The Levites claim their due (21: 1–3)**
This is the counterpart of 13: 14, etc. The town list dates from the United Monarchy (Albright, *Archaeology and the Religion of Israel*, 1946, pp. 121 f.), reflecting David's organization and settlement of the Levites (1 Chr. 23–24); the principle goes back to Moses (Num. 35), as we read here. 'With the aid of the Greek . . . we can eliminate nearly all differences between . . . Joshua and Chronicles' (Albright, *ibid.*).

(b) **Summary of the allocations (21: 4–7) from the clans** (vv. 5, 6 Heb.) is peculiar; NEB accepts an emendation in line with v. 7.

(c) **Aaronite allocation (21: 8–19)**
In view of Hebron's special status as Caleb's prize (14: 13 ff.), its allocation as a Levitical city called for special attention. The format of this paragraph is preserved in the shorter version, 1 Chr. 6: 54 ff.

(d) **Kohathite allocation (21: 20–26)**
Gezer was Canaanite till Solomon's day; the Philistines reclaimed **Gibbethon** soon afterwards (1 Kg. 9: 16, 15: 27). **25.** For **Gathrimmon** read Ibleam (1 Chr. 6: 70, Bileam).

(e) **Gershonite allocation (21: 27–33)**
Golan and **Be Eshtarah** (Ashtaroth) were lost to Syria by the time of Baasha, about 900 BC.

(f) **Merarite allocation (21: 34–42)**
Mesha occupied **Bezer** (then in ruins) and **Jahaz** *c.* 850 B.C. (*DOTT*, The Moabite Stone). For **Ramoth**, see 1 Kg. 22: 3.

vii. Conclusion (21: 43–45)

This corresponds to 11: 23, and amplifies it. **the land . . . forefathers** occurs 15 times in Dt., and similar phrases five more times. **rest on every side:** cf. Dt. 12: 10; 25: 19; 2 Sam. 7: 1.

44. not one . . . of them echoes Dt. 2: 36 and other passages, but is common Hebrew. **45.** Cf. 23: 14; above all details and difficulties, our author declares this as the most important fact.

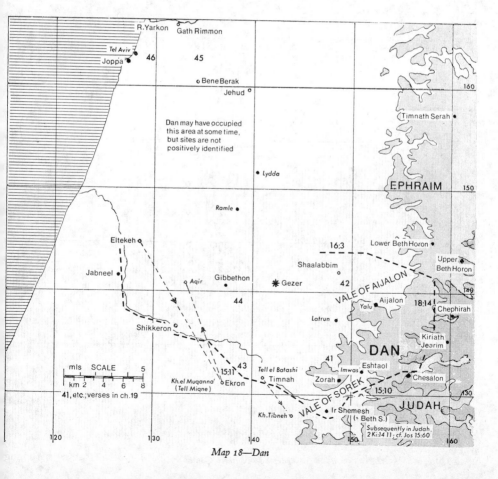

Map 18—Dan

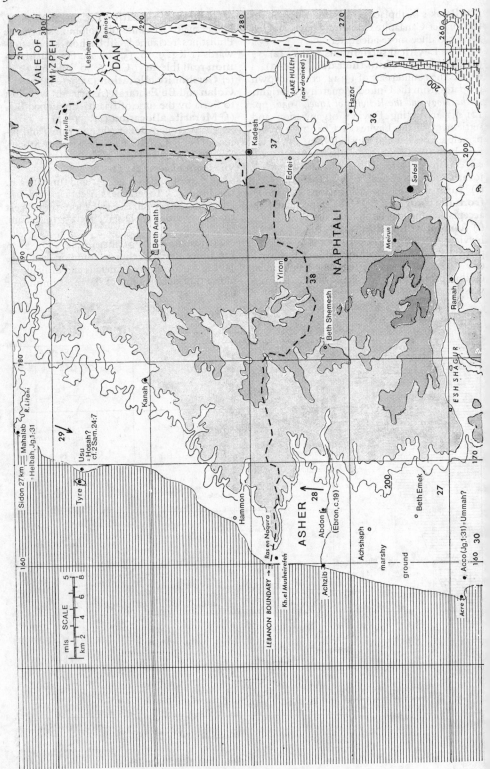

Map 19—Northern Galilee

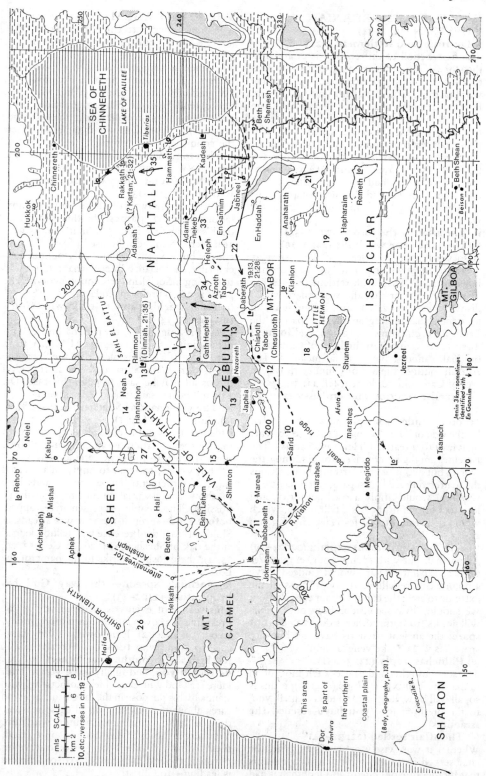

Map 20—Southern Galilee

IV. THE TRANSJORDANIAN QUESTION (22: 1–34)
i. Dismissal and settlement (22: 1–8)
The first section of this chapter is essential to the story of the invasion, answering as it does to 1: 12–18, and recording that God kept his word to those who kept faith with him. Note how vv. 2, 4 echo 1: 13, 15, 18, and the charge in v. 5 carries the same message as 1: 7. Verses 6–8 hang together; it is characteristic of Heb. prose to insert the reminder (v. 7) of the special position of Manasseh, so that the story can be read on its own. **your great wealth:** the eastern tribes had their inheritance, but they were not begrudged their share of the spoil which they had helped to capture in the west.

ii. The altar by the Jordan (22: 9–34)
(a) How the altar was built (22: 9, 10)
Associated with the release of the easterners was an incident which pointed up the problems inherent in the East Bank settlement—a sense of separation; fear that the westerners would disown them (vv. 24 f.); and, behind it all, an awareness that the region was not part of the Land (v. 19; cf. Num. 34: 12). **10. Geliloth:** (?) 'basins', cf. 'Galilee'; **in the land of Canaan**, if original, cannot have its usual meaning. The Arabah south of the Sea of Chinnereth was an area of Canaanite settlement (cf. 11: 3).

(b) Israelite reaction and embassy (22: 11–20)
11. on . . . side: NEB 'opposite'; Heb. *'el 'ēber,* 'to the side of', i.e. 'facing'. **12. to go to war:** or at least to threaten it; Heb. 'as an army'. The Israelites might be criticized for assuming the worst, but we must understand how serious the matter appeared. A separate altar (centre of worship) would imply a rival authority, and lead to a breach in the basic fellowship, which would be highlighted at festivals; cf. 1 Kg. 12: 25–33.

(c) The Transjordanians explain (22: 21–29)
The denial, put with such vigour, emphasizes that a separate altar would indeed have amounted to rebellion. It was tactless in the extreme to erect the copy without consultation; we should always consider how our actions will look 'from the other side'. **22. do not spare:** the ancient versions have 'let him not spare' (as v. 23, 'take vengeance').

(d) Phinehas' reply (22: 30, 31)
The sense of relief and praise is felt most of all in that **the LORD is with us** (cf. 1: 5); if this is so, all will be well. It is good to say 'thank you' to the brethren too (**you have rescued the Israelites**).

(e) The affair settled (22: 32–34)
Whether it was wisely or unwisely done, the altar served its purpose for a while. It seems that by the time of Gideon and Jephthah it had become no more than a story.

V. THE WAY AHEAD (23: 1–24: 33)
i. Joshua's charge to the elders (23: 1–16)
(a) The Lord's continuing goodness (23: 1–5)
The leader's approach is based on what his hearers know from their own experience. **5.** RSV justifiably uses future verbs; NEB (past tenses) tends to make Joshua give a more 'complete' view of the conquest than the text warrants. Though settlement is an established fact, the conquest is not complete (see on ch. 13), and has to some extent been anticipated in the division (v. 4).

(b) Exhortation to obey God and keep faith with him (23: 6–13)
The style naturally recalls that of similar exhortations in Dt. **7. names:** the thin end of the devil's wedge; cf. Eph. 5: 3 'hint'. **12. associate:** Heb. 'come' can be used of sexual intercourse; but NIV, NEB are probably right in generalizing, 'associate'. Intermarriage must lead to sharing in social and religious functions. The point is no less relevant today.

(c) Final warning not to trifle with God's justice (23: 14–16)
Every blessing implies the peril of 'greater condemnation'; cf. Lk. 12: 47 f.; Heb. 2: 1 ff.; 2 Pet. 2: 21. If a man is blessed in the Spirit, he must walk in the Spirit (Lk. 11: 24 ff.). God means all that he says (*e.g.*, in this case, Dt. 28); and he has said it in love, to save us.

ii. The Covenant at Shechem (24: 1–28)
(a) Convention (24: 1)
This chapter is not necessarily connected with the preceding (**then** is an inference). Some think it refers to the same ceremony as 8: 30–35, but vv. 13, 28 seem to imply an advanced stage of settlement. The account stands here to show the essential fulfilment of Joshua's mission. The people's representatives appear **before God**—even if the tent was already at Shiloh (18: 1), the Presence was acknowledged at the oak of Shechem (24: 26, cf. Gen. 33: 20; 35: 4); there Joshua speaks in the name of the Lord.

(b) Joshua's speech—'the way God has brought us' (24: 2–13)
This recital of events is characteristic as the preamble to a covenant (so, much more briefly, Exod. 19: 4; 20: 2). Israel owed its very existence to God, who **took . . . Abraham . . . led him . . . brought your fathers out . . . delivered you**, and finally **gave you a land**. Here is a God who can achieve something! who stands by his purpose in the long haul; and who cares about his people. For all these reasons, they can have confidence in a future with him. Yet there is more; having done so much, God, their creator, *commands* them now to serve his purpose, though they cannot yet see where it is leading—to Christ.

11. as did also is not in the Heb. ; some

think **Amorites . . . Jebusites** is a gloss (so NEB).

12. hornet: so traditionally, and in Gk.; only here and Exod. 23: 28; Dt. 7: 20. A similar word means 'leprosy'; NEB 'panic' (paralysis?). Garstang's reference to the Egyptian emblem is dubious; even punitive expeditions aimed to make Canaan secure as a buffer state against the Hittites. **two . . . kings:** LXX 'twelve'; it seems unlikely that Og and Sihon are meant (see v. 8). **Also** is not in Heb.

(c) **Joshua's speech—'Serve the Lord only'
(24: 14–15)**
Here is a mystery: God who creates and commands will not merely compel. He offers a choice, with the possibility that they might find it **undesirable**. Unless this choice is freely made, and worked out **with all faithfulness**, it will be nothing to God 'from whom all fatherhood . . . is named'. If God is so open, his agent cannot compel either, but only exhort and lead ('as for me'). **this day** a choice will be made; if it is by default, the local gods are bound to win.

(d) **Israel's response (24: 16–18)**
There can be no doubt of the reasonable answer. The power to stand by it will be tragically lacking under the Old Covenant (Rom. 8: 3; Heb. 8: 7); but the whole ministry of the judges and prophets witnesses that there was a genuine commitment which, in their better moments, Israel had to acknowledge.

(e) **Solemn affirmation (24: 19–24)**
The purpose of this seeming discouragement is to guard against a response of mere enthusiasm. Joshua faces the pastor's dilemma; it is his duty to persuade, but a decision induced merely by his persuasiveness will evaporate like dew. He can only remind them what is involved and with whom they have to do (see on 23: 14 ff.), and make the act as solemn (v. 22) and as honest (v. 23) as possible. **14. fear** is a Heb. technical term for worship, but it expresses an aspect which we ought not to forget (Heb. 12: 28 f.), however much the world rejects or misunderstands it.

(f) **The Covenant confirmed (24: 25–28)**
Whatever may be guessed or inferred as to a regular 'renewal ceremony', the verbs here refer to the original sealing of the covenant. **decrees and laws** (Heb. singular) may be collective (as Exod. 15: 25; Ezr. 7: 10) or refer to the covenant pledge itself. **26. oak:** *MT 'allâ*, only here, but similar to *'allôn*, 'oak'; NEB, LXX read *'ēlâ*, 'terebinth'. **27. are untrue:** NEB 'renounce'. The verb *kihēš* means 'deceive' (7: 11, 'lied'); cf. Isa. 59: 13, 'deny'; Jer. 5: 12. Turning away from God begins with fear, and a guilty conscience, and pretence (Gen. 3: 10). A tangible reminder witnesses silently to the covenant; so, down the ages, has the broken bread (1 C. 11: 26).

iii. **The passing of the leaders (24: 29–33)**
(a) **Joshua's death and burial (24: 29–31)**
Verses 28–31 are almost word for word (Heb.) as Jg. 2: 6–9, but arranged differently; in a small way, this illustrates an aspect of inspiration in the historical scriptures, in relation to the use of sources. **the servant of the LORD:** see on 1: 1. Only here is Joshua given the title.

30. Cf. 19: 49. Verse 31 concludes and sums up the message of the book. Success comes through the gift of God, with man's obedient and persevering response. The Israelite invasion of Canaan was never a complete success, and all too soon the vision and determination were lost; but the book attests that Joshua did fulfil his mission.

(b) **Burials of Joseph and Eleazar (24: 32, 33)**
Two footnotes: verse 32 records the fulfilment of Joseph's dying wish (Gen. 50: 24 f.; Exod. 13: 19). Verse 33 records the burial of Eleazar who, as Aaron's son and successor, had shared with Joshua the responsibility for the settlement. **silver:** cf. Gen. 33: 19; so Ac. 7: 16, but *qᵉsîṭā* was understood by LXX as 'ewe lamb'. **Gibeah** may mean simply 'hill'; 'town' is a reasonable inference. Aaron's family would naturally have lived near Shiloh till David's reign (see on ch. 21).

BIBLIOGRAPHY

Commentaries
BOLING, R. G., and WRIGHT, G. E., *Joshua. AB* (Garden City, N.Y., 1982).
BRIGHT, J., *Joshua. IB* II (Abingdon Press, New York, 1953).
GRAY, J., *Joshua, Judges and Ruth. NCentB* (Nelson, 1967).
MILLER, J. M., and TUCKER, G. M., *Joshua. CBC* (Cambridge, 1974).
SOGGIN, J. A., *Joshua.* Old Testament Library (SCM Press, 1972, tr. from French ed. 1970).
WOUDSTRA, M. H., *The Book of Joshua. NICOT* (Grand Rapids, 1981).

Historical Evaluation
ALBRIGHT, W. F., *Archaeology and the Religion of Israel* (Johns Hopkins Press, 4th ed., 1956).
BRIGHT, J., *A History of Israel* (SCM, 1960), pp.97–160.
BRIGHT, J., *Early Israel in Recent History Writing* (SCM Studies in Biblical Theology 19, 1956); a balanced assessment of recent trends.
GARSTANG, J., *Joshua–Judges* (Constable, 1931); to be used with caution in view of later developments in archaeology.
HARRISON, R. K., *A History of Old Testament Times* (Zondervan, 1957).
KAUFMANN, Y., *The Biblical Account of the Conquest of Palestine* (Magnes Press, tr. from Hebrew, 1953).

YEIVIN, S., *The Israelite Conquest of Canaan* (Netherlands Near-East Institute, Leiden, 1971).

Geography

ABEL, F. M., *Géographie de la Palestine* (French), (Gabalda, Paris; Vol. I, 1933: Vol. II, 1938, 2nd. ed. 1966).

AHARONI, Y., *The Land of the Bible* (Burns Oates, 1967; tr. from Hebrew ed. 1962).

BALY, D., *The Geography of the Bible* (Lutterworth, 1974); a systematic description of the land.

BALY, D., *Geographical Companion to the Bible* (Lutterworth, 1963); essays on particular aspects.

SIMONS, J., *Geographical and Topographical Texts of the Old Testament* (Leiden, 1959).

JUDGES

CARL EDWIN ARMERDING

Judges forms part of the official history of Israel, covering the period from the death of Joshua (1: 1; cf. Jos. 24: 29) to the birth of Samuel. The English title is derived from the Hebrew šōpᵉṭîm, a term signifying not so much the judicial role of a judge but rather his or her function as ruler, saviour or deliverer.

I. The Age of the Judges in History
(a) **Dating.** See 'Chronology of the Old Testament' article. Although the dating of the Exodus and Conquest is far from a settled issue, the majority of scholars (and this writer) hold to a 'late' or 'short' chronology which puts the Exodus sometime in the thirteenth century B.C. (See 'Chronology of the Old Testament', ZPEB, for evidence for the earlier date.) The period spanned by the judges is then between about 1250 and 1050 BC.

(b) **Historical Background.** Although never directly implicated in the stories of the judges, the chief external force in Palestine during the period was Egypt. On the short (or later) chronology, Judges begins during the dynasty of the great Rameses II (c. 1290–1224 BC), a time of considerable cultural and commercial intercourse between his country and Syro-Palestine. However, neither Rameses II nor the series of lesser monarchs who followed him had more than a passing interest in events off the main trade routes; hence, the lack of Egyptian presence in Israel during the period.

More in evidence are the local city-states and tribal kingdoms of Late Bronze – Early Iron Age Palestine. At the beginning of the thirteenth century there are Edomites, Moabites, Amorites and Ammonites in Transjordan, while Canaanites (later Phoenicians) and their allies (see 3: 3, 5 and n.) control the valleys to the north and the plain toward the coast. C. 1190 a new force appeared, with the arrival of a group of 'Sea People' known in biblical records as Philistines. Settling in five former Canaanite cities (Gaza, Gath, Ekron, Ashdod and Ashkelon), these Aegean warriors were to become the major foe of Israel from c. 1100 B.C. to the time of David. Although the process was slow, pressure from Philistines was partly responsible for the eventual consolidation of Israel and its abandonment of certain societal patterns and values which marked the time of the judges.

(c) **Numbers in Judges.** Various attempts have been made to fit the data of Judges into a comprehensive chronological scheme, usually following the longer chronology. But there is good reason to suggest that the various cycles are arranged theologically rather than chronologically, with some numbers which fit the schematic plan. Thus, for example, the major 'deliverer-judges' dominate the first period (see 'ANALYSIS') and to each is attributed a period of forty years (2 × 40 in one case) 'rest'. To these may be added Samson (½ of 40), Samuel (½ of 40), Saul (Ac. 13: 21), David (2 Sam. 5: 4), and Solomon (1 Kg. 11: 42). Other numbers follow a different system, but forty years of peace and deliverance seems to be a norm for a successful judgeship.

(d) **Concept of an Heroic Age.** The period of the judges cannot be understood apart from some consideration of the socio-political factors at work in the age. That it was an age differing widely from the centralized and disciplined picture given in the exodus and conquest narratives is immediately apparent. From the death of Joshua onwards, there is a complete change in the political and social sphere. When last seen in the Book of Joshua, the twelve tribes are gathered in Shechem renewing their covenantal unity before Yahweh, bound together by common loyalty to God, shrine and leader. By contrast, there is little in the Book of Judges that would demonstrate that even half of the tribes were able to act in concert, and the basic values expressed in society tend to be individualistic rather than corporate.

An age when political and social structure has given way to individualistic, charismatic leadership, with all of its attendant values and expression is commonly known as an Heroic Age. In the socio-political realm, the heroic age is generally characterized by various national movements, incorporating new people into the social unit, and a resultant unsettled pattern. The corporate, tribal, or national feelings that bind the social order have given way to an emphasis on personal leadership, often from the aristocratic warrior or landowner class. In the realm of personal values, individualism again predominates. Bravery, an exaggeration of physical prowess, an excess of passion, overwhelming hospitality and a commitment to romantic love—these are the ingredients that make up the heroic character. Music and poetry, the stuff of which oral epic is made, often mark the hero's life as much as his abilities in war or trading.

II. The Age of the Judges in Literature

Heroic society tends to preserve its history by means of the epic. In the usual epic form, exploits of the heroes are celebrated by the tribal bards, often by means of orally composed and recited poetry. Although the Book of Judges, like most of the Old Testament narrative portions, is largely in prose form, the presence of at least one poetic version (Jg. 5) suggests that such a form was originally considerably more widespread. In place of the court chronicler of a later age, or the Levitical scribe of the Mosaic era, we can imagine each tribe or village having its own bard whose job it was not only to entertain the townsfolk around the fire, but to preserve and transmit the historical memories of the group.

Such epic 'cycles' probably formed the earliest sources for the book of Judges. In our version, however, this material has been carefully woven together into a largely prose account of the period. At what time and by whom will never be fully known, but there are some characteristics of the composition that can give a measure of direction. First, the work is set out in a carefully considered theological framework, reflecting not only literary skill, but an easily discernible set of values. The pattern of the whole work is sometimes called an 'ABA' pattern; that is, there is a prologue and an epilogue, in the middle of which is sandwiched the main body of the composition. In the Prologue (1: 1–3: 6), the concern is to show the transition between the age of Joshua and the period of the judges, and to set forth the recurrent pattern of rebellion, defeat and oppression, deliverance, and finally renewed rebellion. Some of the material in ch. 1 clearly connects the story to the time of tribal conquest, but the outline is sketchy and seems merely to set the stage for a theological explanation of why the subsequent history was one of cyclic failure and success rather than Joshua's predominant success pattern.

In the Epilogue (17: 1–21: 25) the cycles of the judges give way to a series of accounts showing the depths to which the nation might sink. The incident of Micah, his ephod and Levite, the theft of the same by the migrating Danites and their rape of the city of Laish, together with the sordid tale of the Levite's concubine and the decimation of the tribe of Benjamin, serve to illustrate the repeated dictum, 'In those days there was no king in Israel; every man did what was right in his own eyes'. The stage is thus set for the transition to monarchy, a shift not fully completed until the days of Solomon. It is not unreasonable to think that the final editor or editors of the major part of Judges were themselves subjects of the

monarchy, possibly early enough so as not to reflect the subsequent division of the kingdom into North and South. In outlook they reflect the same values expressed throughout the great court history of Israel which we know as Samuel–Kings, although some concerns of the later books, *e.g.* centralized worship in Jerusalem, did not motivate the editors of Judges.

Between Prologue and Epilogue are set various cycles of epic material, the dating of which can never be resolved. While undoubtedly all of them represent very old poetic traditions, we should not expect prose narrative to reflect forms contemporary with the events. In one case, that of Deborah's Song (ch. 5), not only the content but the form in which it is presented, is now considered virtually contemporaneous with the events portrayed.

Additional marks of dates for component parts of the book may be found in individual details. Jg. 1: 21 seems written without knowledge of the Davidic conquest of Jebusite Jerusalem (*c.* 1004/1003 BC), while 1: 29 is similarly silent on the ceding of Gezer to Solomon by an Egyptian pharaoh (*c.* 950 BC). On the other end of the spectrum, the reference in 18: 30 to the captivity of the land shows that final editing of Judges, like the final version of the entire 'Deuteronomic History' (Joshua – 2 Kings) took place in the exile. That exilic editors would so carefully preserve earlier narrative as well as poetic portions is an indication of their conservative attitude toward traditions.

III. Judges in Biblical Theology

(*a*) **Its canonical context in the Old Testament.** From the above it should be clear that Judges forms part of a great theological history of Israel. The connection of Judges with what comes before (especially Deuteronomy – Joshua) and after (Samuel–Kings) is patently apparent. The theological conclusions can hardly be missed: obedience to God and His covenant will issue forth in blessing, while 'forgetting' God and His covenant will bring the curse of war and foreign oppression. But there is another side: God will not forget His people, even when they forget Him. There is, even in the cycle of repeated oppressions, an element of divine direction. God has, in fact, left the foreign nations in the land (and most of the oppressors are reasonably local foes) as an act of mercy, in order to teach the people what they need to know (2: 21–3: 6). And the face of the oppression itself, horrible as it was to endure, was a reminder that God's covenant could not be broached, but also that there was salvation to those who would cry to Him.

Along the way, the combination of heroic values with the Deuteronomic theology of history has created a picture which moderns find difficult to understand. Much of the activity, not only of the fickle and disobedient Israelites but even of their deliverers or judges, seems at variance with later ideals. It is true, as concluded in the Epilogue, that without a king a kind of undisciplined individualism reigned. In its finest hours, however, that individualism expressed itself through men and women who could rightly be called heroes of faith (cf. Heb. 11). To understand the ambivalence we must separate the theological concerns of the book as a reflection of both Deuteronomic covenant theology and post-Davidic ideals of theocratic kingship from the individualistic values of an heroic age. Neither societal pattern is considered, by itself, superior or God-ordained. Thus the heroic patterns of behaviour reflected in such charismatic but undisciplined characters as Samson and Jephthah can, under circumstances of covenantal obedience, reflect God's order for society. But when that order has broken down, and the individualism of Samson, Jephthah and their kind has become a barrier to obedience to the covenant, the need for a centralized power to keep the people in line is recognized. It is to the credit of the later editors, working with a sincere conviction that God's order required a king of His choosing, that they made no attempt to soften or eliminate the values expressed in an age that differed greatly from their own. Rather, they saw in a God-directed individualism the potential for great strength, a potential realized in a series of saviour-judge figures who were God's instruments for preservation of the nation in one of its most formative but difficult periods.

(b) **Use in the New Testament.** There are fewer than ten references to the Book of Judges in the New Testament. Most are allusions to events or persons in that period who are seen as in some way analogous to New Testament events or characters. Mary is compared in her blessedness to Jael, the wife of Heber who slew Sisera (Jg. 5: 24/Lk. 1: 42) but also to the barren mother of Samson to whom angelic visitation gave hope for a child (Jg. 13: 3/Lk. 1: 31). Likewise, John the Baptist, in the annunciation to Zechariah, is seen as a Nazirite like Samson (Jg. 13: 4/Lk. 1: 15), a thought echoed in the Matthean birth narrative of Jesus (Mt. 2: 23). Apart from that, there remain nothing but scattered references or obscure allusions to events like Samson's killing of a lion (Jg. 14: 5 f./ Heb. 11: 33). In truth, direct New Testament concern with the period is best summarized by the treatment given the era in Paul's speech at Pisidian Antioch: 'And after that, he gave them judges until Samuel the prophet' (Ac. 13: 20). In a similar sermon given by Stephen (Ac. 7) the period is passed over in silence. But to assume from this meagre reference that the period was unimportant for New Testament theology might be to draw a premature conclusion. As a part of the Deuteronomic history of Israel, the period of the judges was certainly known and respected by New Testament believers, and to attempt to isolate one era of that historical development from the whole would be wrong-headed. Little is made, except in Heb. 11 where Gideon, Barak, Samson and Jephthah are listed (v. 32), of the individual heroes of the period, but there is a constant awareness of the theology of covenant that lay behind the larger history.

(c) **Value for the church.** It is indeed strange that most Christian use of the Book of Judges is focused on the individual heroes, whose lives are sometimes held out as exemplary for Christians today. In fact, this aspect of things, which only the author of Hebrews saw fit to mention, is of considerably less importance for New Testament theology than is the covenant theology expressed in the editorial framework of the book. The new covenant community, like the old, is confronted by choices. Temporal existence and prosperity, while not in themselves expressive of the totality of the believers' hope, are not as incompatible with Christian eschatological concerns as has sometimes been alleged. The church of Jesus Christ is called upon to live in covenant obedience, to avoid the kind of conformity to the world that was a constant threat to Israel, and to look to God as the source of all physical and spiritual blessing. When we go awhoring after other gods, whether the Baals and Astartes of an ancient society, or the more subtle but equally tempting modern alternatives, we have turned from the Lord of creation and redemption to give love and service to that which is nothing. Turning from God's covenant was not simply a religious change of practice; it was a fundamental and revolutionary perversion of a correct understanding of the world. The ancients knew, as we often do not, that the world of harvests, the cycle of rain and sunshine, the very fruitfulness of the ground in yielding up its ores, was a function of God's grace and mercy. When these things were falsely seen as the product of nature religions or fertility cults, it was an expression of a fundamentally opposite world-view, one that had turned from our Christian understanding of a controlled universe under the hand of a Sovereign God, to a universe that could be manipulated by ritual adherence to cults of various deities, each of whom represented some independent aspect of that universe. There was no way an Israelite could serve both Baal and Yahweh; such service would require believing in two totally opposed ideas at one time. Likewise, the Christian church must realize it cannot serve God and the world. Either the conditions of the covenant are met, and the church goes forward, or it is in the grip of idols with all of the attendant decline and oppression that idolatrous forces carry in their wake.

But there is a message even for the church in decline. God hears the cry of the oppressed and will send deliverers. Even the most unlikely, perhaps a Samson or a Jephthah, may turn out to be God's instrument. He will choose the instrument; all we need do is recognize the problem. The book of Judges stands as an eloquent reminder that the Lord of history uses some unlikely candidates to do His work. True, we must view these men and women as part of their age, with its heroic values, but even then they are often persons with feet of clay. But, 'God raised them up'; who knows from what quarter He will send deliverance in our day.

IV. Historical Problems

(a) The office of Judge. Scholars have long wrestled with the vexing question of just what a 'judge' was and how he or she functioned in Israel. The chief data remain the texts of our book, a fact that gives scant comfort to the investigator. The term translated 'judge' (Heb. *šōpēṭ*) is not used widely, yet is a legitimate back-formation from the more general statement, 'X judged Israel' (the verb *šāpaṭ*). Language pointing to a 'saviour' or 'deliverer' function is equally prominent (verbal root *yāša'*) especially with regard to the major charismatic figures (Othniel, Ehud, Deborah, Jephthah) whose epic deeds constitute the core of the book's interest.

The problem is further complicated by the fact that two distinct kinds of 'judge' are evident, about one of which little or nothing is known. Chapters 10: 1–5 and 12: 8–15 recall five men, each of whom is said to have 'judged' Israel, but what facts are given tell us virtually nothing about the nature of their activities. Of the first one Tola, we read that he arose to save (*lᵉhôšiaʿ*) Israel, presumably following the Abimelech débacle, but nothing is known of the others. We are faced, then, with a list of such 'minor judges', as they have been called, sandwiched into a history made up largely of epic cycles recalling the distinctly occasional exploits of deliverer-heroes. The word *šōpēṭ* itself sheds no final light, for a study of its uses in the Old Testament together with its cognate parallels produces a semantic range broad enough to include the translations to 'judge' 'vindicate', 'rule', and even to 'deliver'. Theories have not been wanting, particularly to explain the minor judges. It has been widely held that they were 'law readers' and of a different order from the saviour figures, although with so little known of the activity covered in the statement, 'X judged Israel', which is applied

to both groups, it is difficult to see how such a conclusion may be defended.

About the major figures (Othniel, Ehud, Deborah and Barak, Gideon, Jephthah, Samson and Samuel) more can be said. Most were raised by a special outpouring of the Spirit of God, sometimes accompanied by divine visitation, in response to a military threat to the nation's existence. No office, in the usual sense, defined their role, but each in his own way became the 'deliverer of Israel'. Only when we assume a unity of the tribes which would understand destruction of one region or tribe as a break in the whole can we see how easily a regional saviour-figure could be brought into the tradition as a national hero.

(b) The extent of Israel. The scope of the judges' administration is clearer: they judged 'Israel'. That Israel included some entity broader than a single tribe is implicit in the term and supported by tribal lists and references as well. However, with the exception of the closing incident (Jg. 19–21) there is no unambiguous evidence that any judge of Israel functioned with reference to all twelve tribes. Even Samuel, the last and greatest of the judges, limited his annual circuit to Bethel, Gilgal, Mizpah and Ramah (1 Sam. 7: 16 f.), cities of the south central mountain region. For these reasons doubt has been expressed about whether any of the judges can be thought of as representing the nation as a whole in any form analogous to the role of a national leader.

(c) The nature of the tribal union. If it cannot be shown that any one judge provided a link between all the twelve tribes, we must ask further what was the real nature of the tribal federation in the period. The reigning hypothesis is still Martin Noth's comparison of the twelve-tribe league with similar confederations in Greece and other parts of the Mediterranean world. Although Noth's view of the settlement process departs widely from the Bible's own reconstruction, his 'amphictyony' (the Greek name for such a league) is built upon evidences which the Biblical record assumes. Basically, an amphictyony is a group of tribes or nations (often, but not always, twelve in number) gathered around a central sanctuary and making common cause in matters of religion and defence.

That Israel in the period of the Judges was such a league, or at least constituted itself under such an ideal, is assumed from the record of such twelve-tribal cooperation as the convenant ceremony at Shechem (Jos. 24) and the punishment of Benjamin (Jg. 19–21). Other than that, the details emphasize the fragmentation rather than the unity of the tribes.

ANALYSIS

I. PROLOGUE (1: 1–3)

i. Questions of Further Conquest (1: 1–36)
(a) Judean penetration in southern Canaan (1: 1–20). Chapter 1 sets the pattern of mixed success and failure, hinting at why some tribes failed and others succeeded. The overall picture is quite consistent with that of Jos., but in Jg. the failures are going to be emphasized as a background for God's delivering activity. The presence of Canaanite enclaves will be seen to have its own function (2: 22–3: 6), all of it within the covenant structure left as a legacy from Moses and Joshua.

1: 1. After the death of Joshua: the opening line (or title) ties Jg. to Jos. (cf. Jos. 24: 29–31) as a connected historical work. A detailed account of Joshua's death follows later (2: 6–10). Jg. is fundamentally an account of Israel's response to the loss of their powerful leader. **the Israelites asked the LORD, 'Who will be the first to go up . . . ?':** Jg. presents a picture of the conquest often thought to be at variance with the 'unified conquest' of Jos. 1–10. However, the editor of the Jg. material obviously intended these incidents to be seen as following upon the close of the earlier period; **first** refers not to the opening battle of the landtaking but to the initial thrust of the post-conquest operation. Cf. Jos. 13: 1 ff.; 15: 63 (agreeing with Jg. 1: 8); 18: 1–3, etc. Lacking Joshua, the tribes required an oracle to determine the order of battle (cf. 20: 18). The oracle may have been sought at a sanctuary, through the ark, or by the use of oracular devices, such as casting lots (cf. Jos. 7: 14 and Prov. 16: 33). **2. Judah:** together with Ephraim and Manasseh (the house of Joseph, v. 22), considered the leader of the tribes. **3. Simeonites:** Simeon was a blood-brother of Judah and later merged into that tribe. **territory allotted:** Heb. *gōrāl*. Basic to the narrative is Jos. 15 (on Judah) and 19: 1–9 (Simeon). God, as the sovereign, has set out the plan; the tribes merely 'possess' an allotment. **4. Canaanites and Perizzites:** two of the traditional 'seven nations' (cf. Dt. 7: 1 and Jos. 3: 10). Canaanite (with Amorite) is the more general term (Jos. 13: 4; Num. 13: 29). About Perizzites little is known. The term may be an appellative denoting 'dwellers in un-walled towns' (Heb. *p^{e}rāzôt*); cf. *AB*'s 'country bumpkins'. **struck down:** a general term for defeating an enemy. AV's 'slew' is misleading. **Bezek:** traditionally, Khirbet Ibziq, between Nablus and Beth-shean (see *MBA*, maps no. 57, 87). Judah then entered from the east and took a Canaanite city in Manasseh before sweeping south to Jerusalem. Cf. 1 Sam. 11: 8 which supports the northern location. **5. Adoni-bezek:** or 'the prince of Bezek' (*AB*). Cf. 'Adoni-zedek' (Jos. 10: 1, 3). LXX reads 'Adoni-bezek' in both accounts. The two stories have distinct differences. **6. cut off . . . :** mutilation is attested also in Mari on the Euphrates and in classical Greece. It disabled the victim as a fighter. Possibly ritual defilement was also intended, the reverse of Exod. 29: 20. (*NCentB*, Jos. Jg. Ru., p. 247). Adoni-bezek himself recognizes the justice in the judgment.

8. Jerusalem: an apparent conflict with Jos. 15: 63 and Jg. 1: 21. Two solutions have been current since Josephus or earlier: (*a*) Only the lower city was taken, the citadel remaining in Jebusite hands, and (*b*) the city was captured but not occupied. (See G. F. Moore, *Judges, ICC*, p. 21 and *LOB*, p. 197.) **fire:** Old Testament texts specify which cities were burned, cf. Jos. 6: 24 (Jericho); 8: 28 (Ai); 11: 11, 13 (Hazor). No archaeological record preserves this incident.

[R. Pearce Hubbard, 'The Topography of Ancient Jerusalem', *PEQ* (1966), p. 137, suggested that the Jerusalem of Jg. 1: 8 was a settlement on the south-western hill.]

9–20. Judean southern campaign: the hill country, the Negeb, and the lowland, or Shephelah (NEB) are distinct regions. The mountains from Jerusalem to Hebron, the semi-desert in northwest Sinai, and the low hills dividing the coastal plain from the mountains are meant. In neither Jos. 10: 40 nor here is the valley (Heb. *hā'ēmeq*) or 'coastal plain' confused with the Shephelah as is done by some commentators. Verses 18 f. deal with the plain, a region possibly included in greater Judah, but outside the limits of the normal tribal allotments. The impression is of a successful penetration by Judah (plus Calebites, Kenizzites, Kenites) in response to a divine direction. The nation is, so far, fully obedient to the command of the LORD. **10. Hebron:** Judah (cf. v. 20 and Jos. 15: 13 f.) took Hebron, the central city of the southern hill country. On **sons of Anak**, cf. Jos. 15: 13 f. **11. they advanced:** Heb.

'he went'. Cf. Jos. 15: 15–19. RSV and NEB harmonize the verb with v. 10 making Judah the occupier of Debir. It was, of course, Caleb the Judahite. **Debir:** a major city of the southern hill country originally called 'City of the Book'. Identified with Tell Beit Mirsim, eleven miles southwest of Hebron, but not in the hill country as Jos. 15: 49 would require. Recent challenges favour Khirbet Rabud, eight miles southwest of Hebron which permits a better identification of the 'upper and lower springs' of v. 15. **13. Caleb's younger brother:** RSV and the NIV are to be preferred to NEB, as the phrase can refer either to Othniel or Kenaz. **14. she urged him to ask:** NEB follows LXX, making Othniel the instigator of the request. The rest of NEB's reconstruction of the verse ('she broke wind . . .') has found little acceptance. **15. springs:** Heb. *gullôt*, possibly basins or pockets of subterranean water. Excavators of Khirbet Rabud found in a nearby ravine two wells which the Arabs call the 'upper and lower wells'. The reference to the springs increases the picture of blessing and fruitfulness.

16. Kenite: Exod. 18: 1, 12 and Num. 10: 29 ff. associate this clan with Midianites. Their name may signify an association with metalworking. Num. 10 demonstrates their knowledge of the desert and probably accounts for their covenant relationship with Israel. **City of Palms:** probably Jericho. **Arad:** probably not Tell Arad (Aharoni, *BA* 31 [1968], p. 31) but nearby Tell el-Milh. Cf. Num. 21: 1–3. **the people:** NEB 'Amalekites' represents an emendation of the text. **17. Hormah:** see Num. 21: 1–3. Related to verb *ḥāram* and noun *ḥērem*, which stood for a ceremonial total destruction of that which was 'devoted' to the LORD. **18. Judah . . . took:** LXX reverses the picture: 'Judah did *not* dispossess . . .'. Possibly these cities were taken or partially taken before 1200, after which date they became part of the Philistine pentapolis. See v. 19, where Judah did not dispossess those in the plain (NEB 'Vale'; see note on 1: 9–20), a reference to the area of these cities. **iron:** only later did David learn the secret of smelting from the Philistines (1 Sam. 13: 19–22).

(*b*) **Benjaminite failure (1: 21)**
The key phrase, 'the LORD was with them', from vv. 19, 22 is missing. This is the first real break in the pattern of obedience.

(*c*) **Josephite conquest of Bethel (1: 22–26)**
22. The house of Joseph: generally Ephraim and Manasseh, but can include Benjamin (2 Sam. 19: 20, where a Benjaminite, Shimei, is addressing David) or the northern tribes generally. **the LORD was with them:** as with Judah. *AB* follows LXX, 'Judah was with them', but this seems to ignore the obvious parallel with v. 19. **23. Bethel:** a major city (probably modern

Beitin, twelve miles north of Jerusalem) in central Canaan. Cf. Gen. 28: 19 and Jos. 18: 13 but also Jos. 16: 2. No conquest of Bethel is recorded in Jos. **24. how to get into the city:** Heb. $m^eb\bar{o}'$, not the gate, but probably an underground entrance. Cf. 2 Sam. 5: 8. **treated well:** Heb. 'do with you *ḥesed*'. The term has covenant overtone. See Jos. 2: 12. **26. Hittites:** probably a general name for north Syrians, not the earlier empire in Turkey. Nothing is known of 'New Luz'.

(d) Unconquered enclaves in northern Canaan (1: 27–36)
The remainder of Jg. 1 takes up the strain first noted in v. 21. The verbal form (Heb. *lō' hôrîš,* 'he did not drive out') implies that the tribe in question could and should have captured these cities. Their presence stood as a strong testimony to disobedience and its results. The cities form three distinct groups. **27. Bethshean, Taanach, Dor, Ibleam, Megiddo:** Dor, as a seaport, and Beth-shean at the confluence of the Jordan and Jezreel valleys, are joined together by Ibleam, Taanach and Megiddo, which guarded three great passes over the Carmel range, and effectively cut Israel's inheritance in two. **29. Gezer; . . . 35. Mount Heres** (prob. Beth-shemesh), **. . . Aijalon and . . . Shaalbim,** together with **Jerusalem** (21): these cities created a wedge between Ephraim and Judah in the south, probably accounting for the latter tribes' failure to be called to fight with Barak's army (Jg. 4–5). The remaining cities are in northern (Upper) Galilee or on the coast above Haifa. **34. The Amorites confined the Danites:** the lack of reference to Philistines points to an early date. Cf. ch. 18. **36. the boundary of the Amorites . . . from Scorpion Pass to Sela and beyond:** NEB changes **Amorites** to 'Edomites' (following LXX), thus explaining why a line which apparently ran from Beer-sheba to the Dead Sea and beyond is mentioned. In any case, the entire verse is problematical.

ii. Covenantal conclusions concerning further conquest (2: 1–3: 6)
This entire section connects ch. 1 with the cycles of judges beginning in 3: 7. Chapter 1 set the pattern but made only veiled reference to the covenantal contract or its central institution, the sanctuary. In 2: 1–3: 6 the covenant is reintroduced and the consequences of partial obedience are foreseen. The section falls naturally into four divisions, each of which turns the spotlight to a different participant in the drama. First Yahweh is seen (2: 1–5) affirming his covenant but modifying its effective working for the future. Then Joshua (2: 6–10), until now the spiritual force behind the conquest— even for a while after his death—is removed. Verses 11–19 summarize Israel's response

which forms the basis of the next 13 chapters. Finally, the role of the nations, hinted at in 2: 3, is given in full detail (2: 20–3: 6). This sequence provides us with an editorial summary of the ways in which God's covenantal work is being effected. Theologically it demonstrates that the covenant is dynamic rather than static, a response to, as well as a direction within, God's people. Although God is the dominant figure, there is a constant tension between His saving work and human initiatives.

(a) God's New Strategy (2: 1–5)
The new era begins with a shift of the sanctuary from Gilgal (cf. Jos. 4: 19–20; 5: 10) in the Jordan Valley, to a spot within the country proper. **Bokim:** 'Weepers'. Location is unknown, but the LXX specifies 'to Bochim and Bethel'; see note on 20: 18, 26. **the angel of the LORD:** no reference is here made to the ark, but both ark and angel (Heb. *mal'āk*, messenger) signify the presence of Yahweh without which no sanctuary could claim any legitimacy. **I brought you out of Egypt. . .:** a covenantal formula (cf. Exod. 19: 4; 20: 2; Jos. 24: 2–13, etc.). **2. you shall not make a covenant:** a covenant always contained stipulations, and Israel's responsibility is outlined in v. 2, as the basis for the curse to follow. Covenant relationship with the Canaanites would involve an acceptance of their deities, their agricultural and thus ceremonial practices, and their moral standards, all of which are incompatible with commitments already made to Yahweh. **Why have you done this?:** NEB's 'look what you have done!' or the *AB* reading, 'How could you do this?' brings out the flavour. For a nation to turn its back on its own God or gods was unthinkable, even by Near Eastern standards (Jer. 2: 10–13). **3. I will not drive them out:** expanded in 2: 21–3: 6. **they will be thorns in your sides:** lit. 'they will be to you as sides' (Heb. *ṣiddîm*). Cf. Num. 33: 55, 'as thorns in your sides', possibly the original of this text also. RSV changes 'sides' (*ṣiddîm*) to adversaries (*ṣārîm*), while NEB takes *ṣiddîm* from an original *ṣaddu* (Akkadian) meaning 'net' or 'snare' (see Driver, p. 6). NEB has paraphrased the entire sentence as a trapping metaphor, in which both the Canaanites and their gods participate in the ensnaring of Israel.

(b) Joshua's departure (2: 6–10)
The great leader is now formally ushered off the stage. 2: 6–10 ties Judges to the ending of Joshua (cf. Jos. 24: 28–31) and accounts for the change from a dominant conquest pattern to the pattern outlined in Jg. 2: 11–23. Verses 6–10a are quoted from Joshua; 10b is an editorial explanation of the failure of the 'third generation'. That this later generation did not know (NEB 'acknowledge', a common covenant word —cf. Am. 3: 2) Yahweh or his works is seen

as an inexcusable fault. No generation of God's people may long sustain its vitality merely on the strength of old traditions. **9. Timnath-heres:** cf. Jos. 19: 50; 24: 30, where metathesis has resulted in 'Timnath-serah'. The original form and location is still a matter of dispute.

(c) **Israel's pattern of response (2: 11–23)**
The covenant conditions have been restated, the great covenant leader is now gone, and Israel is left to see how she would respond. As it is the generation that 'did not know the LORD' which is in view, the result is predictable. A pattern of repeated cycles is set forth in vv. 11 – 23, serving as a summary of the action in the remainder of the book. The cycle moves from (i) rebellion (vv. 11–13) to (ii) defeat and servitude (vv. 14–15). From v. 18 and various later references we may assume that under the burden of its affliction the nation (iii) groaned, or cried to the Lord (cf. 3: 9, 15 and the earlier pattern observed in the prototype of all bondage, Exod. 2: 23). Finally, in response to the pitiful condition of Israel, the LORD (iv) raised up judges to deliver the people (vv. 16–18). The period of deliverance was at best a time of limited obedience (v. 17) and shortly after the death of each judge the cycle began anew (v. 19). Observable in the process is a progressive deterioration (v. 19 [NEB]: they 'would relapse into deeper corruption than their forefathers') a pattern basic to the theological direction of the book.

In the conclusion (2: 20–23), the editors give a theological rationale for the dominant pattern of failure and decline despite the presence of a series of deliverers. The terminology is again that of the covenant. We now see for the first time how even the partial nature of Joshua's conquest was an expression of Yahweh's covenant plan.
11–13. Baals (Heb. and NEB, plural 'Baalim'): although the Canaanite rain and fertility god Baal is the primary attraction for Israelite apostates, there were various local manifestations of this deity. Verse 13 couples Baal (sing.; *pace* RSV plural) with his consort Astarte (Heb. plural **Ashtoreths**), a pair well known for their fertility associations in the Ugaritic literature of North Syria. The cult of these two involved various immoral and degrading practices, all of which were a part of the religious system basic to Canaanite agriculture and its understanding of nature. With covenant Yahwism and its view of fertility, summarized in Dt. 28: 11 f., 23 f., there was no possibility of accommodation. **14–15. he handed them over . . . and he sold them . . . whom they were no longer able to resist:** victory or defeat, like fertility or drought, are seen to be a consequence of God's sovereign control of his universe. In the ancient Near East, various conflicting forces had to be consulted or pla-

cated in time of war; here the cause of defeat is clear and simple, **just as he had sworn to them** in his covenant (Dt. 28: 48), so it came to pass. **14. raiders:** NEB 'bands of raiders' captures both the original sense of the word and distinguishes the form of opposition in this period from the conquests of great empires which came later. **18. the LORD had compassion on them** (Heb. *yinnāḥēm*): NEB 'would relent' captures the flavour of the verb. God is seen throughout the Old Testament as free to change his effective direction in response to human need. **20. covenant that I laid down:** the covenant, like any ancient suzerain-vassal treaty, was initiated by the sovereign and obligatory for the vassal. **21. the nations:** the various Canaanite city-states, as listed in ch. 1. **22. to test Israel:** the presence of enemies is now seen to have a purpose, connected here with the conditional aspect of the covenant. Verses 20–23 form the transition to ch. 3: 1–6.

(d) **The nations remaining (3: 1–6)**
A second reason for the presence of non-Israelite elements is added and two lists of the nations remaining are given. As a natural conclusion the contracting of mixed marriages is noted, with the brief but pregnant comment: **and served their gods.**
2. only to teach warfare: cf. 2: 22 f.; 3: 4 and Exod. 23: 24 f. The skills of war-making, although not always valued by Christian ethicists, were a necessary part of existence in a hostile environment. **3. the five rulers of the Philistines:** 'lord' (Heb. *seren*), possibly related to Gk. *tyrannos*, a reflection of the traditional Aegean ancestry of this grouping of 'Sea Peoples' who settled on the coast in five principal cities, shortly after 1200 B.C. The list in v. 3 continues with mostly northern and coastal peoples, while the list in v. 5 is the traditional grouping less the Girgashites. See *NBD* for specific names. **to Lebo Hamath** (Heb. *Lᵉbô' Ḥᵃmāt*): NEB reflects the now commonly held belief that this is a proper name, modern Lebweh, 70 miles south-west of Hama (ancient Hamath). This often marks the northern boundary of ideal or expanded Israel (Jos. 13: 5; 1 Kg. 8: 65).

II. THE JUDGES (3: 7–16: 31)
Following the pattern set by the introduction, we are ushered immediately into the world of the judges. Although the outline is theologically rather than chronologically determined, the beginning with Othniel represents a link with the period of conquest. The whole book appears to divide naturally into two sections. The first five judges, all of whom, including the mysterious Shamgar, were deliverer-figures, represent a time when the land periodically enjoyed rest from conflict (Heb. *tišqōt*). (See 3:

11, 30; 5: 31; 8: 28.) In contrast, the latter period (8: 29–16: 31) is characterized by minor judges (see Introduction IV(a)) together with the rather unorthodox deliverers Jephthah and Samson. The land is never said to 'have rest' and the picture is one of increasing moral, political and military decline leading to the shameful climax of events in the Epilogue (chs. 17–21). The lesson is clear: a people which fails to give wholehearted obedience to the LORD can only sink lower and lower.

i. The period of 'rest': Othniel to Gideon (3: 7–8: 35)

This period is marked by the greatest exploits of the judges, both with respect to personal accomplishment and societal benefit. Through such heroes as Othniel, Ehud, Deborah, Barak and Gideon the chief 'raiders and plunderers' (2: 14 NEB; cf. 2: 16 'marauding bands') surrounding the infant nation were reduced and the people was allowed to take root in the land. This then, is appropriately set off from the later time of decline, beginning with the abortive attempt of Abimelech to change the direction of society from one of charismatic leadership, directly under God, to a form of hereditary monarchy.

(a) Othniel and Aram (3: 7–11)

Othniel is known for his connection with Caleb and the conquest of the Anakim in Southern Palestine (Jos. 15: 15 ff.; Jg. 1: 12 ff.), but the identity and location of his opponent continues to defy scholarly solution. In Othniel, however, the first 'deliverer-judge', raised up by the LORD and characteristically endued with His Spirit to confront a military oppressor, the pattern for all subsequent figures is established. The coming of the Spirit of God here must be seen as a special enduement of ability or skill and not necessarily as a personal relationship in the sense of Pentecost, though the OT never doubts that men and women of faith had a personal relationship with the LORD. **8. Cushanrishathaim:** the name, which means 'Cushan of Double Wickedness', is clearly an Israelite parody on some unknown original for which various suggestions have been given. **Aram Naharaim:** basic to the plausibility of any suggested identification of the ruler is some idea of where he came from. RSV 'Mesopotamia' carries a wrong connotation, with the literal 'Aram-Naharaim' (NEB and NIV) to be preferred. No kingdom of exactly this title is known, but 'Aram' or 'Syria of the Two Rivers' points to some place in north or even central Syria rather than to Assyria and Babylonia (see *NBD, s.v.* 'Aram, Arameans', 'Mesopotamia'). Attempts to change Aram to Edom, in keeping with Othniel's southern provenance, do violence to the text, and creative solutions have not been wanting that preserved the tradition of some northern penetration of

Palestine in either the 14th or 12th century B.C. See, *e.g.* A. Malamat, *JNES* 13 [1954], p. 231. **11. forty years:** see discussion of chronology in the Introduction I(a). Even if this is to be taken literally, it is not clear whether Othniel actually judged Israel all this time. The brevity of his notice does nothing to obscure his role as a courageous, exemplary man of God, ready to call the nation back to faith in Yahweh and obedience to his covenant.

(b) Ehud and Moab (3: 12–30)

Oppression next arises from a coalition of Transjordanian tribes led by Eglon, King of Moab. Its effect was felt mainly by the central hill dwellers, Ephraim and Benjamin. Reuben and Gad are not mentioned because they were powerless to do anything. The story, replete with classic epic detail, begins without some of the standard formulae of the Othniel account, and is an expression of the best of the storyteller's art. Qualities of bravery and leadership, together with an epic cunning or shrewdness, mark the hero. Although not said to be filled with the Spirit of the LORD, Ehud is plainly God's man for the job. **12. The LORD gave Eglon . . . power:** NEB 'he roused Eglon'. The ability of Moab is here characteristically seen as derived from Yahweh. No special piety or goodness is thus implied (cf. Dan. 4: 32). **13. Ammonites and Amalekites:** the former had settled in what is today Jordan while the latter was a nomadic southern tribe (see *NBD*). Together with Moab, they had felt the force of Israelite settlement. **attacked Israel:** the verb is used again in v. 29, there translated 'he killed'. AV renders 'smote' or 'slew'; the context must determine the nature and extent of the damage inflicted. **the City of Palms:** cf. 1: 16. Clearly Jericho, although the city itself may have been uninhabited at this time. Cf. NEB: 'Vale of Palm Trees'. The control of the lower Jordan valley was at stake. **15. the son of Gera:** probably a clan name. Cf. Gen. 46: 21 and 2 Sam. 16: 5. **the Benjaminite:** lit. 'son of the right', in contrast to **a left-handed man**: the sense of irony in the wordplay emphasizes the epic feature. **left-handed:** lit. 'drawn up or restricted in the right hand'. Left-handedness, an heroic quality in some ancient societies, is a mark of Benjaminites and is associated with their military prowess (1 Chr. 12: 2 and Jg. 20: 16). **sent him with tribute:** Heb. *minḥāh*, probably agricultural goods, necessitating a cadre of bearers. **16. a double-edged sword, about a foot and a half long:** cf. NEB: 'fifteen inches long'. Heb. *gōmed* (**cubit** in RSV) appears only here. NEB takes it to be the short cubit. Such a weapon could easily, especially on the right thigh, pass undetected. **19. idols:** NASB 'idols' or AB 'images' conveys the sense of the Heb. *peşîlîm*. These stones must have been a predominant landmark, possibly created from the stones set up by Joshua to mark the crossing of Jordan (Jos. 4: 19–24). **20. the upper room of his summer palace:** NEB 'roof chamber of his summer palace' takes the obscure Heb. *mᵉqērâh* as 'cool place', *i.e.*, 'summer palace'. **a secret message:** lit. 'a word from Elohim'. Note dual meaning, as this oracle could be a flattering prediction or a note of judgment. God's message may be a word of understanding or an active expression of his will. Eglon rose in anticipation, a detail vital to his impending demise. **22. which came out of his back:** Heb. is again difficult, but NIV and NEB's picture of the short sword protruding from behind is more accurate. LXX omits the phrase. Such details are characteristic of epic or heroic literature. **23. went out to the porch:** this room seems to have been some kind of platform with pillars or colonnades, but the exact escape route is unknown. **24. relieving himself:** lit. 'covering his feet' (cf. 1 Sam. 24: 3), a euphemism, clear in the context. **25. they waited to the point of embarrassment:** NEB, 'until they were ashamed' preserves the sense of the Heb. *bôš*. Cf. 2 Kg. 2: 17 and 8: 11 (Burney, p. 74). **27. blew a trumpet in the hill country of Ephraim:** while confusion reigned in Moab, Ehud quickly followed up the initial blow. Time only allowed for Benjamin and Ephraim to be alerted. **28. the fords of the Jordan:** seizing the fords put the retreating army in a vulnerable position and sealed the natural border against further penetration. No effort is made to relieve the tribes in Transjordan. **30. eighty years:** LXX adds 'And Ehud judged them until he died'. The period of rest is unusually long, and one must thus consider the victory of special significance.

(c) Shamgar and Philistia (3: 31)
This most enigmatic of references in Jg. has long fascinated scholar and layman alike. Possessed of a non-Israelite name (possibly Hurrian), said to be son of the Canaanite Baal-consort Anath (which NEB and others take to mean 'from Beth-Anath'), and remembered only for an unorthodox military conquest of six hundred Philistines, Shamgar is a strange figure. Current scholarship tends to regard Shamgar as a semi-nomadic mercenary engaged in opposing the earliest wave of Sea Peoples. He is remembered in the Song of Deborah (Jg. 5: 6).

(d) Deborah/Barak and Canaan (4: 1–5: 31)
Here we have the first large-scale operation against a major foe of all Israel. Furthermore, in the alliance of an Ephraimite judge (Deborah) with the northern tribes of Naphtali and Zebulun (Issachar and the Transjordanian tribes are also mentioned in ch. 5), we note the first time when 'Israel' specifically includes more than a regional grouping. That this battle was also

pivotal in the salvation-history of the tribes is clear; never again do Canaanite forces mount a full-scale battle with the growing nation of Israel. The battle is celebrated in two accounts: a sober prose statement, and a vivid epic poem. The two accounts present some internal difficulties, although so many details agree that suggestions pointing to two separate battles must be discounted. The entire episode bristles with historical and geographical difficulties, most of which would probably quickly fade if precise details of the period were known.

The prose account (4: 1–24)
1. the Israelites again did . . . evil: the standard introductory formula. **after Ehud died:** ties the history directly to Ehud, strengthening the conclusion that Shamgar 'delivered' but did not 'judge' Israel. **2. Jabin, a king of Canaan, who reigned in Hazor:** according to Jos. 11: 1–13, Jabin (there called king of Hazor) headed a coalition of Galilean city-states in a futile attempt to prevent Joshua's conquest of the area. Jos. 11: 10 f. records the destruction by fire of Hazor following the successful Israelite attack at the nearby 'waters of Merom'. Hazor is now clearly identified with Tell el-Qedah, a strategically-located site astride the principal trade route in northern Galilee just southwest of Lake Huleh. The excavator reports Bronze Age destruction by burning twice, the first *c.* 1500 B.C. (too early for the conquest) and the latter *c.* 1250–1200 B.C. From 1200 until Solomon created a major military and administrative centre in Hazor (1 Kg. 9: 15), there was no significant city on the mound (Y. Yadin, *Hazor*, Schweich Lectures, London, 1972, pp. 132, 134). In the second of two Judges-period strata there is a curious 'temple' or cultic building (*ibid.* pp. 132 ff.) but still no city that Yadin feels could be equated with a capital of Jabin. We should probably then see in Jabin a continuing representative of the old powerful coalition, but stress the role of Sisera as the true leader, a fact which accords well with the picture in Jg. 4 and 5. Hazor, which does not itself figure in the battle, may indeed have been but a village; however its earlier role as 'head of all those kingdoms' kept its memory and even precedence alive. **Sisera:** the name is non-Canaanite, and Sisera may have been a petty king (cf. 5: 19, 28) or a feudal chief of the 'Hazor coalition' whose family came either from Hurrian or Sea People circles. He, not Jabin, is the key figure in the story. **Harosheth-ha-goyim:** NEB 'of the Gentiles' translates Heb. *ha-goiim*. In light of the probable westward course of the battle, v. 16 would point to a location near Tell el-'Amr in the narrow defile of the Kishon Valley toward present-day Haifa. **nine hundred iron chariots:** cf. 1: 19. The figure of 900 probably refers to the entire coalition. In 1 Kg. 10: 26 Solomon

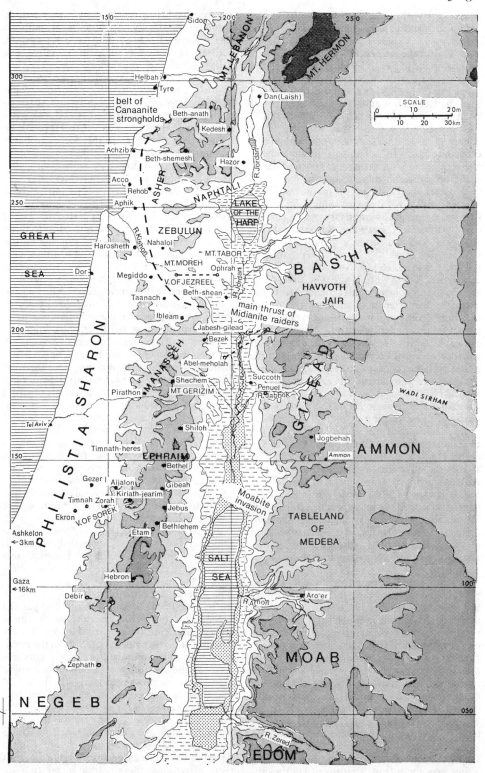

Map 21—Wars of the Judges

is credited with 1400 chariots. Both figures seem reasonable in light of Near Eastern documents.

4. Deborah, a prophetess: as the only woman in the line of judges and the only judge with whom prophecy is associated (until Samuel, but cf. Jg. 6: 8 for another prophet in the period), Deborah would be worthy of special mention even without her military exploits. The question she faced was whether Israel could exist as a nation split in two by a powerful Canaanite force. In calling for mobilization in Yahweh's name, she prophetically stood for all that God had set forth in his original covenant with Israel. **Lappidoth:** meaning 'torch' or 'flasher' (*AB*). That Barak, meaning 'lightning' is the same person is rightly labelled 'precarious' by Burney. **5. between Ramah and Bethel:** well-known centres of early Israel, six to twelve miles north of Jerusalem. Cf. Samuel's circuit, 1 Sam. 7: 16 f. **6. She sent for Barak . . . from Kedesh in Naphtali:** nothing is known of this general's antecedents. His home is usually identified with modern Tell Qades in Upper Galilee about five miles west-north-west of Lake Huleh. Aharoni suggests a location at Khirbet Qedish on the high slopes to the south-west of the Sea of Galilee east of the Valley of Jabneel (*LOB*, p. 204). Certainly this site is more appropriate as a venue for the muster (vv. 9 f.) as it is close to Mt. Tabor (v. 12) rather than fifty miles to the north in the centre of the Canaanite strongholds have been more suspicious of Jael's offer. **the great tree in Zaanannim:** identified only as 'near Kedesh'. The location is important to the narrative as it is the only clue to Sisera's escape route. Aharoni places it somewhere in the Jabneel Valley (*LOB*, p. 204), a low wadi system between Tabor and the hills on which his Kadesh stood. Sisera's retreat is then in a direction opposite to the army's. An alternative is to locate Zaanannim close to the northern Kadesh, and have two different cities in mind from v. 10 to v. 11.

12. they told Sisera: his intelligence system would have reported this. It signalled for him an opportunity to wipe out Israelite opposition in a central location, in much the same way as the great Saladin was later to trap the Crusaders on the Horns of Hattin.

14–16. The battle-cry is raised by prophetic utterance (typically in the ancient Near East an oracle was required), after which the conflict moves quickly to its conclusion. **15. the LORD routed Sisera:** both v. 14 and v. 15 stress Yahweh's role in the victory, although no mention is here made of the means. Simply, Yahweh routed (lit. 'confused') the army. On Barak and Deborah's part, the descent from Tabor kept them from a Horns of Hattin situation, but more importantly it set the battle in

the marshy fields near Kishon. Chapter 5: 20 f. fills in the details. Apparently a cloudburst turned the wadi into a raging torrent, sweeping before it all in its way. The further effect, in a valley which has only in recent years been drained to avoid the problem, was to create an instant quagmire in which chariots would hopelessly founder. The lightly-armed Israelites were in no way affected. **16. Barak pursued the chariots . . . as far as Harosheth-ha-goyim:** the rear of the force probably attempted to return westward through the increasingly narrow defile, possibly even trying to get through a pass in the Carmel range.

17. But Sisera fled . . . to the tent of Jael: probably in a northeastwardly direction, away from his army. It is often suggested that Hazor was his destination; there is no reason to think it was Jael's tent. **18. Jael went out:** her initiative is marked in the epic. Apart from her ultimate intention, revealed in due course, the gesture would be considered highly improper. **she put a covering over him:** Heb. *śᵉmîkāh*, a word used only here. 'Fly-net' has been proposed, but the need for concealment was paramount. **19. a skin of milk:** cf. 5: 25 where the second half of the parallel speaks of *hem'āh* (RSV 'curds'), the 'leben' or yoghurt of which Arabs are fond and which, some allege, has a soporific effect. **21. Jael . . . picked up a tent peg:** women generally put up the tents. **his temple:** a rare word. NEB 'skull', followed by 'his brain oozed out' in place of RSV 'it [the tent peg] went down into the ground' is based on a reconstruction which has not found great acceptance. **22. Jael went out to meet him:** as she had Sisera. Deborah's prophecy had come true; the glory was now shared by two women: Deborah, whose courageous call to a holy war had initiated the battle, and Jael, whose savage act of cruelty had finished it.

23. God subdued: the final comment is a reminder (as if any were needed) that such a battle is the LORD's. Verse 24 summarizes Canaanite decline in Galilee. No further reference to Hazor is made.

The Poetic Account (5: 1–31)

In ch. 5 we have not only a second and parallel account of the battle, but one of the most ancient and finest pieces of Hebrew poetry extant. Scholars agree that the bulk of the poem is almost contemporary with the events described, and it is often taken as more reliable than ch. 4. While appreciating the historical reliability of such a witness, we must keep two important factors in mind. First, poetic style is given to hyperbolé and figurative language. Second, a silence in the poem (*e.g.*, concerning Jabin) can only be taken as such—it is not a denial of the event or person so ignored. With these provisions, there is little in the two accounts that cannot comfortably be harmonized and nothing that requires an hypothesis of conflicting sources.

The poem (see *NBD*, 'Poetry', for comments on style), usually called 'The Song of Deborah' (though Barak is included in the title, but see v. 7, etc.), may be called a 'Victory Hymn' or 'Triumph Ode'. A popular suggestion sees in it a hymnic celebration as part of a covenant renewal ceremony (A. Weiser, *ZAW* 71 [1959] pp. 67–97), though evidence for such a setting must remain largely conjectural. The song gives full glory to Yahweh, the covenant-God of Israel, for the victory. The poem may be divided in various ways, but the dual themes of blessing and cursing seem prominent throughout. Blessing is given to Yahweh for his acts of old (4–5), for the volunteers who willingly come forth (2, 9), for the defeat of the enemy (19–22), and for the death of Sisera (24–27). Blessing is also specifically due to Jael (24–27) and Deborah, together with the tribes which heeded God's call to fight (13–18). Conversely, the curse is the lot of Meroz (23), the tribes which did not respond (13–18), Sisera (24–27), and Sisera's mother (28–30). Finally, all enemies of the LORD are cursed while those who love him are blessed as the sun rising 'in his might' (31).

Along the way a vivid picture is painted of conditions before, during and after the great victory of Yahweh over his most obstinate foe. Beginning with the resumé of life in the days of Shamgar (6–8), continuing to outline the order of battle as the tribes are called (12–18), and culminating in details of the rout at Kishon (19–22) and the death of Sisera (24–27), the poem concludes with the taunt-song over the latter's death. Although from the poem we can fill some gaps in our knowledge of the battle, its purpose is not to inform us but to elicit our praise. This it does in a profound yet simple way. **2. When the princes in Israel take the lead:** JB's 'the warriors . . . unbound their hair' reflects a possible reading for this difficult phrase, but evidence is lacking for an Israelite tradition of hairy warriors. The parallel phrase that follows is clear. **praise the LORD:** a key to the song's overall purpose. **3. Hear this, you kings! Listen, you rulers:** a good example of synonymous parallelism in which the second line restates the first. In the latter part of the verse we have a climactic or stair-like parallelism, in which each added line or phrase adds to the first. NEB preserves the flavour of the Hebrew. **4. LORD, when you went out from Seir:** in vv. 4 f. God is celebrated in a picture of his powerful theophany at Sinai. Such a recital of the past power of God in nature is common in psalm litany (cf. Hab. 3: 3–6) and appropriate here where God's control of nature is the key to

victory (vv. 20 f.). A severe storm is pictured, reinforcing the tradition of lightning and thunder in the Exodus account (Exod. 19: 16). At Kishon, in contrast to Sinai, it is the downpouring of rain that is decisive. **Edom:** reference to Seir and Edom has caused some scholars to seek Mt. Sinai to the east of the Arabah Valley. Cf. Dt. 33: 2; Hab. 3: 3 and Ps. 68: 7 ff.

6. In the days of Shamgar: Shamgar seems to be contemporary, strengthening the argument for dating both Shamgar and Deborah after 1200 when Philistines were in the land. **the roads were abandoned:** not 'highways' as in AV. The picture is of a time when societal breakdown kept the lucrative caravan trade from the hill country. Even travellers had to avoid the main roads. **7. Village life:** NEB 'champions' is from an Arabic root, which could also point to 'isolated villages'. The **Village life** would probably refer to the sturdy field-worker whose military exploits were celebrated in v. 11 where the word again appears. **8. war came to the city gates:** NEB 'they consorted with demons' is an attempt to make sense of a notoriously difficult text. The resulting parallelism is the strongest point of the reading. **9. My heart is with:** NEB turns the phrase to a vocative imperative: 'Be proud at heart'. If Deborah is the singer, either translation is fitting. **10. consider:** Heb. *sîhû*, meditate, ponder, recite. Both the rich (those riding) and the poor (those walking) were to recite the triumphs of the LORD. **11. the voice of the singers:** a difficult Hebrew phrase; cf. NEB where the exclamation 'Hark' precedes a reference to 'players striking up'. Why lyre-players are performing at the watering places is not clear. The last two lines stress the theme: the victories of Yahweh and his 'peasantry' (see note on v. 7).

13. the men who were left came down to the nobles: similarly NASB. NEB's alteration is not required. The **men who were left** (lit. 'survivors') depicts the sad state of Israel at the time. **came to me with the mighty:** Heb. 'to me' rather than 'for him'. NEB's 'as warriors' is equally possible. *AB*'s term 'knights' conveys the sense of Heb. *gibbôr*. **14–18. the tribal list:** this list expands the two-tribe army of 4: 6, 10 to include as respondents Ephraim, Benjamin, Machir (normally the eastern half of Manasseh, here probably western—cf. Num. 26: 29; 27: 1) and Issachar. Among those reproached are mentioned Reuben and Gilead (possibly Gad) in Transjordan, Asher up on the Phoenician coast and Dan, which appears still to be in its southern, coastal location. The reference to Meroz (v. 23) is unknown, leaving Judah and Simeon, both geographically remote, as the only tribes missing. **14. From Ephraim . . . Amalek:** lit. 'From

Ephraim their root (is) in Amalek'. Cf. Jg. 12: 15, but some scholars emend *'ªmālēq* to *'ēmeq* (vale). Changes of 'their root' are conjectural. **a commander's staff:** NEB 'musterer's staff'. lit. 'the pen of the scribe (*sōpēr*)', probably here one who mustered or counted the reporting volunteers. **15. Issachar:** although the battle was in her territory, ch. 4 strangely omits this tribe. From 5: 18 we see that Naphtali and Zebulun were leaders in the conflict. Possibly Issachar and others were called to join in a later stage of the battle. **princes of:** NEB, by rearranging the Heb. words, arrives at 'joined . . . in the rebellion'. RSV satisfies the Heb. NEB likewise finds a verb, 'stood by' in the second line. **much searching of heart:** cf. v. 16 (RSV) with NEB, which omits the second line. The Heb. text of the second line incorporates slight changes from the first. *AB* finds in the variation a word-play contrasting 'command-minded chieftains' to 'faint-hearted chieftains'.

17. Gilead: taken by many, including some ancient versions, as Gad. Cf. 10: 17 f. and 11: 1 where the equation is more difficult. **Dan:** reference is perhaps to Danites employed by Canaanite or Philistine merchantmen. Cf. ch. 18, apparently to be dated after Deborah. **19. the kings of Canaan:** Sisera and Jabin were leaders of a coalition. Canaan in the Bronze Age consisted of small city-states, each with a king. **Taanach, by the waters of Megiddo:** Taanach, a smaller residential city, together with the great administrative centre Megiddo five miles to the north-west, was located on the edge of the Carmel range overlooking the Kishon. Both were destroyed about 1125 B.C. (P. W. Lapp, *BA* 30 [1967], pp. 8 f.), possibly as a result of Deborah's victory. The **waters** undoubtedly refer to some marshy part of the Kishon near Taanach. (See D. A. Baly, *Geography of the Bible*, London, 1974, revd., pp. 125, 151.) **20. From heaven the stars fought:** there is no need to conclude that Israelites thought of stars as producing rain, although Ugarit provides some interesting parallels. The poetry merely points to a heavenly source for the discomfiture of Sisera.

23. to help the LORD: all members of the league owed primary fealty to Yahweh, as maker of the covenant. Likewise helping fellow-believers is not an option for the New Testament believer; it is his covenant-responsibility. Cf. 1 C. 12: 12–27. **24. most blessed of women:** Jael, despite the vicious nature of her violent act, kept covenant-faith with the nation to which her people had been joined. Heber's making of peace (Heb. *šālôm*, possibly a covenant term) with Jabin (4: 17) was a violation of his family's prior commitment to Yahweh. **26. she shattered and pierced his temple:** NEB 'she struck and his brains ebbed out'. See note on 4: 21. In an epic 'taunt song'

or 'victory hymn' such graphic description would be expected.

28–30. The note of irony and taunting predominates, not sympathy as some have suggested. **29. The wisest of her ladies:** their explanation, which is highly reasonable, heightens the irony. The reader knows Sisera will not return. **30. a girl or two . . . colourful garments:** the common fruits of victory.

31. So may all your enemies perish . . . : the Song concludes with a curse and a blessing. It is the logical conclusion to a hymn expressing covenant responsibilities to Yahweh and his people. The use of such a hymn in community prayers would be a natural extension of its purpose.

(e) Gideon and Midian (6: 1–8: 35)
The judgeship of Gideon is dealt with in considerable detail, marking as it does the close of the first period (see Introduction). The seven years of oppression (6: 1) are sandwiched between two forty-year periods of quiet (5: 31; 8: 28), the second of which is the last era so marked in the times of the judges. Apart from the minor judges, about whom little is known, only Jephthah and Samson appear as deliverers, neither of whose activities provided any substantial break in the pattern of decline. Gideon's deliverance, although a signal victory over a perennially-troublesome foe, still ended in disappointment. With the strange case of Gideon's ephod (8: 24–27) and the more tragic outcome of his son Abimelech's struggle for succession (8: 29–9: 57), the seeds of decline are planted. The twin themes of the later part of Judges (introduced in Gideon's time) are (i) religious apostasy arising from syncretistic practice and (ii) political instability resulting from the failure of judges to provide a continuing godly succession. The divine call, which rescued Gideon out of a syncretistic society, was not enough to keep him from returning to such practices at the end. In the second area, even his resolute affirmation of direct divine kingship (8: 23) did not prevent the tragic attempt at human succession that led to the ultimate breakdown of authority.

Gideon is at once the greatest individual hero of the epic and its most tragic figure. To see his great work of religious and military reform reduced to such proportions is a reminder that no generation or individual can rest on the activities of God in past time. The spiritual battle continued long after the Midianite hosts with their Bedouin allies had departed. 'The sword of the LORD and of Gideon' need not have lost its thrust; its cutting edge was blunted by disuse rather than opposition. We are reminded again that the greatest dangers for the people of God are internal; no Canaanite or Midianite army could withstand the force of the LORD's sword. But when the canker sores of internal decay are allowed to grow, the very instruments used by the LORD to repel the outward foe become useless.

Midianite oppression (6: 1–6). The standard formulae introduce the oppression, although Midian represents a different kind of conqueror. An Arabian tribe traditionally linked to Israel (Gen. 25: 2), the Midianites were nomads whose territorial range centred in Transjordan near the head of the Gulf of Aqaba. They were joined by Amalekites, an Edomite tribe (Gen. 36: 12, 16) an ancient foe of Israel (Exod. 17: 8–16), together with a group known as 'Sons of the East' (*Bᵉnê Qedem*), about whom little can be said (cf. 1 Kg. 4: 30; Ezek. 25: 1–10, etc.). The seasonal pattern of oppression reflected the nomadic way of life, in contrast to the continual expression of Canaanite strength dealt with in chs. 4–5. The attacks at harvest-time were, nonetheless, a fierce blow to life in the land. **2. prepared shelters for themselves in mountain clefts . . .:** probably for storing precious produce as well as to escape personally. Widespread starvation was the only alternative. **4. all the way to . . . Gaza:** lit. 'until your coming to Gaza', possibly a reference to a main road to that most south-westerly of cities. The raiders, entering from the north-east, despoiled the entire land. **5. camels:** contrary to a popular contention, the use of domesticated camels is documented from the beginning of the third millennium (*c.* 3000 BC) (see *NBD*, 'Camel'), although Jg. 6 may represent the first clearly military use of a large camel force.

Prophetic indictment (6: 7–10). Apart from Deborah the 'prophetess', this is the sole reference to a prophet in Judges. The speech of the prophet is cast in traditional prophetic form. The message likewise follows familiar patterns, and is an echo of the angelic pronouncement of 2: 1–3. It functions in the Gideon account as a reminder that the real problem, soon to be introduced in the narrative, was religious syncretism, not Midianite camels. **10. I am the LORD:** the self-identification of Yahweh, so characteristic of the Exodus deliverance under Moses (cf. Exod. 3: 13–16; 6: 7–8; 7: 5, 17; 12: 12; 14: 4, 18, etc.). The entire Gideon story abounds with allusions to the earlier salvation which for all subsequent generations became the prototype of God's saving work.

Gideon's call (6: 11–24). The narrative combines a portrait of Gideon, the potential hero, with the picture of a frightened fugitive meekly acquiescing in both his father's aberrant religious mores and the Midianite's control of the land. The angelic visitor seems more convinced of Gideon's valour than the hero himself. The call is accompanied by two assertions: (i) the LORD is with you (vv. 12, 16) and (ii)

you are a man of strength (vv. 12, 14). To the first Gideon puts an historical objection (v. 13) followed by a request for validation (v. 17), while to the second he expresses a personal reservation (v. 15). The historical objection is ignored, having just been dealt with in the narrative (vv. 7–10), while the personal objection is passed off with a further assertion, 'But I will be with you' (v. 16). The presence of God is the key theological point; affirmed by the prophet (vv. 8 ff.) to explain the oppression, and now by the angel to launch the deliverance. Again, the pattern reflects Exodus (cf. Exod. 2: 24 f.; 3: 12; 33: 14 f., etc.). The sign which confirms God's presence is both the willingness of the angel to remain and accept food (possibly an offering) and his demonstration of divine prerogative in the burning of the present (v. 21). The point of this sign, in contrast to the request for guidance later (6: 36), is to confirm in Gideon's mind who it is with whom he is speaking (v. 17).

11. the angel of the LORD: a common description of a theophany (cf. 2: 2; 13: 3, etc.), interchangeable with 'the LORD'. **the oak:** or 'terebinth'; possibly a sacred tree but more likely not seen as such here, for Gideon was threshing secretly in its vicinity. **Ophrah:** Aharoni (*LOB*, p. 241) has proposed modern Affuleh in the Jezreel Valley. **the Abiezrite:** a clan of Manasseh (v. 15 and Jos. 17: 2). **in a wine press:** such may be seen today, a simple trough in a large rock with a catchment basin. Presumably the public nature of most threshing floors made the wine-press location better. **to keep it from the Midianites:** NEB 'to get it away quickly' is possible. **12. mighty warrior:** 'You are a brave man' (NEB) fails to convey the sense of Heb. *gibbôr ḥayil*. Valour, but probably also a position of some rank in the community, is indicated (cf. v. 27). **15. my clan is the weakest . . . I am the least in my family:** Gideon, nevertheless, betrays his aristocratic background by calling ten of his father's servants. The true hero, though suitably modest, is not drawn from the lower classes. **18. offering:** Heb. *minḥāh*. Although the gift did become a sacrifice (cf. Gen. 4: 3 ff.; Lev. 7: 37), the word can also mean 'tribute' (see note on 3: 15) or merely 'gift'. The contents (v. 19) are not clearly sacrificial, although the amount (an ephah of flour equals about 45 pounds or 20 kilograms) would be excessive for such an occasion. **21. Fire flared from the rock:** by the touch of the angel the gift becomes a sacrifice. **22. Ah, Sovereign Lord . . . I have seen the angel of the LORD face to face:** Israelites believed that death would follow (cf. v. 23; also 13: 22 f. and God's word to Moses, Exod. 33: 20). The response in v. 23 'Peace to you' assures Gideon of the contrary. The reasoning of Manoah's wife (13: 23) would apply equally here. The word of the angel is then commemorated in an altar named 'The LORD is peace' (Heb. *Yahweh-šālôm*). **24. to this day:** clearly some time later. It was probably a centre for pilgrims.

Baal exposed (6: 25–32). Exposing Baal was necessary on two counts: (i) there must be a purifying of Israel prior to any foray against Midian, and (ii) Gideon himself is not yet a proven leader whose call to arms would be heeded. His boldness in purifying at least one village of its Baal-worship established the order of priority as well as raising Gideon to prominence. Even here, however, the later brilliance of Gideon's leadership is not yet in evidence. Gideon's father shares the spotlight in his solid and reasonable support for his son. **25. Take the second bull . . . the one seven years old:** the Heb. text, which is difficult, seems to point to two bulls, against the context which clearly has only one. NEB, by a slight emendation, reads 'a young bull . . . the yearling bull', which makes better sense. **cut down the Asherah:** NEB 'sacred pole' is to be preferred to the misleading 'grove' of AV. The Asherah was a cult object, probably representative of Astarte, the consort of Baal (see Dt. 16: 21 and Jg. 2: 11–13). **26. on top of this height:** NEB 'earthwork'. Some natural rock formation seems likely.

28–32. The powerlessness of idols to aid themselves is a favourite theme of the Old Testament (1 Kg. 18; 1 Sam. 5: 1–4, etc.). The Heb. text of v. 31 mockingly stresses the pronouns, 'Will *you* contend for Baal? Or will *you* defend his cause? . . . If *he* is a god, let *him* contend for himself . . . .' The name Jerubbaal (v. 32) completes the taunt. 'Let Baal contend', as the context demonstrates, is a challenge to the pagan god.

Invasion and response (6: 33–35). Both the religious reform and the fame of Gideon as leader must have spread through at least his own tribe, plus Asher, Zebulun and Naphtali (v. 35). Again, Issachar is not mentioned, but see note on 4: 6. The immediate motivation for Gideon's call to arms is clearly the charismatic enduement of Yahweh's Spirit (v. 34). **33. Valley of Jezreel:** Jezreel, the Heb. original of the Gk. Esdraelon, is here specifically the eastern part of the plain to the north of Mt. Gilboa. Chapter 7: 1 further delimits the action. **34. came upon:** lit. 'clothed itself with'. Cf. 1 Chr. 12: 18; 2 Chr. 24: 20. The sense is one of complete possession or identification. In 3: 10 a different verb is used.

Gideon's two fleeces (6: 36–40). The fleece is required as a pre-battle oracle (see 1 Kg. 22: 6–28). Cf. v. 17 (and comment) where the question is the identity of the messenger. The second sign (a dry fleece on a wet background) was the more obvious miracle. Such 'fleeces'

may represent a lack of trust, a possibility recognized by Gideon (v. 39). The receipt of the signs confirmed that this was the time to attack.

The final force shaped (7: 1–8). Verse 1 locates the two armies, with Gideon's conveniently placed by a spring, necessary to the subsequent narrative. The numbers are quickly pared from 32,000 to 300. Cf. Dt. 20: 8 where the morale factor is recognized as a disturbing influence in an army. The second test, despite a variety of homiletical suggestions to the contrary, seems to have been an arbitrary means of arriving at the required number. **1. the spring of Harod:** traditionally 'Ain Jalud, on the western edge of the Gilboa range overlooking the valley to the north. **the camp of Midian was north of them, in the valley near the hill of Moreh:** the valley is narrowed at this point by the presence of *Givat ham-Moreh* or 'The Hill of the Teacher'. It runs roughly east and west, creating an effective block from the valley northward toward Tabor, the Nazareth hills and the wadi systems running down toward the Sea of Galilee. On the southern slope, or in the valley below, the Midianite hordes were spread out. Gideon, like Barak (cf. 4: 14), began with the advantage of a higher location. **3. leave Mount Gilead:** lit. 'and depart from Mt. Gilead'. RSV changes Gilead to Gideon (as subject) and the verb *spr* to *srp* ('depart' becomes 'test', to conform with v. 4). NEB is content with turning the problematical 'Mt. Gilead' into 'Mt. Galud', agreeing with the Arabic name of the spring below (cf. note on v. 1, 'Ain J/Galud). We might expect 'Mt. Gilboa' for which there is no textual support. **5. those who lap the water with their tongues like a dog:** cf. v. 6, 'those that lapped, putting their hands to their mouths'. NEB makes the last clause apply to those on their knees, as lapping seems inconsistent with scooping up water in the hand. Perhaps the analogy of a hand with a dog's tongue (as a scoop) is more appropriate. **8. took over the provisions:** lit. 'and they took the provisions of the people', meaning that the 300 took what the 9,700 had brought (see NASB) including a good supply of jars and torches. **and trumpets:** those of the 9,700. Gideon's small band required an unusually large supply of 'non-military' goods. This, of course, was supplied by the larger contingent. The 9,700 then retired 'to their tents', a location from which they could be quickly recalled (v. 23).

The dream (7: 9–14). Dreams were often vehicles of divine revelation. This one, coming as it did to a member of the Midianite army, was especially convincing. **11. the outposts of the camp:** lit., 'the edges of the battle alignment'. Probably the sentries, although NEB, which separates the 'fighting men' from the rest of the camp, is not impossible. **13. A round loaf of barley bread:** NEB relates the opening word to 'stale' or 'dry', a suggestion that is gaining favour. It was able to roll and strike with some force. **14. this can be nothing other than the sword of Gideon:** barley-cake and tent are thus identified in the symbolism. **God has given . . . :** all ancient peoples believed in divine forces controlling battles; here the term for God is general.

The battle (7: 15–23). The message of the dream is followed by two acts: (i) Gideon bowed down (lit. fell down) in worship, the only appropriate response to the great impending work of God, and (ii) he returned to raise the battle cry. His battle plan appears to have been carefully worked out but whether it was indebted to his spiritual illumination we cannot say. The attack required close coordination and an element of total surprise, for which his 300 man force was ideal. The battle is clearly a 'War of Yahweh', as demonstrated in the war-cry of the soldiers (v. 20). Cf. 'The Book of the Wars of the LORD' (Num. 21: 14), which may have contained accounts of such battles. Proclaiming a Yahweh-war further tied the Israelite rebellion and its success to their re-affirmation of covenant loyalty to the LORD. Each soldier is required to stand faithfully (v. 21); it is the LORD who creates the conditions of victory (v. 22), a pattern oft repeated in Holy Writ (Jg. 4–5; Exod. 15, Rev. 19).

16. three companies: cf. 9: 43 and 2 Sam. 18: 2. **torches inside:** probably smoking firebrands from which a flame would burst out when waved in the air. **19. the beginning of the middle watch:** a division into three watches covered the dark hours. Thus, about 10 p. m. is implied. There would still be men awake. **22. turn on each other with their swords:** an army made up of various Bedouin tribesmen could hardly be expected to distinguish its friends from its foes under such circumstances. **Beth-shittah . . . Tabbath:** the precise route of the flight depends on identifications which remain uncertain. There may have been two groups, i.e., 'to Beth-hashittah in the direction of Zererah (or Zarethan)' and 'toward Abel-Meholah in the direction of Tabbath'. All of the army was headed for the fords of the Jordan.

The Ephraimite role (7: 24–8: 3). The largest tribe in the central hill country has not been called out, but now the flight of the routed Midianite army moves in its direction. After blocking the fords and slaying the two princes, they confront Gideon somewhere in Transjordan. Their anger at not being called up is assuaged by resort to diplomacy and the narrative moves on. **24. the waters of the Jordan ahead of them as far as Beth-barah:** unknown. Possibly a corruption of 'the fords of

. . . the Jordan', which are otherwise unmentioned. **25. Oreb . . . Zeeb:** cf. Isa. 10: 26 and Ps. 83: 11 f.

Gideon's pursuit of Zebah and Zalmunna (8: 4–21). Gideon and his band of 300 men have now undertaken to follow up the victory by destroying the leaders. It is clear that nothing short of the capture of these two nomad chieftains would convince the outlying tribes of the reality of the proposed new order. Apparently surprising the Midianites a second time deep in their own territory (the camp was 'off its guard', v. 11, lit. 'secure'), Gideon and his men took the leaders. Returning by the way he had come Gideon stopped to unleash his vengeance on the Israelite towns which had refused provision to his weary men. Finally, in vv. 18–21 we learn for the first time that Zebah and Zalmunna were, in some previous skirmish, responsible for the death of Gideon's own brothers, and the final act of the drama is more akin to ancient blood-vengeance than to the conduct of war.

Making allowance for the inability of ancient societies to undertake long-term incarceration and recognizing the inevitability of external harassment and internal civil strife as long as Zebah and Zalmunna were alive, we can better justify their execution. Gideon, in his own ultimate justification (v. 19), may have strayed far from the Golden Rule, but there were better reasons for their death at hand. The treatment of Succoth and Penuel, likewise, must be understood in light of its ancient context. The elders of those cities had not only shown a scepticism about the validity of Gideon's Yahwistic reformation but did all they could to insure its ultimate collapse, a clear violation of their Israelite loyalty oath.

5. Succoth: generally thought to be Tell Deir 'Alla just north of the Wadi Jabbok. Succoth, like Penuel, was well within Israelite boundaries and the cult centre may have been hostile to Gideon's reforms. **6. possession . . . in hand:** lit. 'Is a palm of . . . already in your hand?', which probably reflects the ancient custom of collecting hands of the slain. **Zebah and Zalmunna:** the names, like 'Cushan-rishathaim', are probably parodies contrived by the author, yielding the significance 'sacrifice' and 'protection withheld'. Their original form is unknown. **7. tear your flesh:** NEB 'thresh your bodies', i.e., use thorn bushes as a threshing sledge. **8. Peniel:** cf. Gen. 32: 24–32. Probably the twin site of Tulul ed-dahab on the Jabbok near Succoth. **9. When I return in triumph:** Heb. *šālôm*, better translated 'victory' than 'peace'. **10. Karkor:** in the Transjordanian desert 150 miles south-east of the Jordan fords. **11. east of Nobah and Jogbehah:** the former is unidentified. The latter is probably Khirbet el Jubeihat toward Amman from Succoth. **12. routing their entire army:** NEB 'army melted away', reflecting an Arabic root word, seems to fit the context.

13. the Pass of Heres: AV 'before the sun was up' is unlikely. The place is unknown. **14. a young man of Succoth:** Heb. *na'ar* may be a lad or a servant in a minor capacity. Cf. 7: 10. The incident reflects the spread of writing after the introduction of the alphabet *c.* 1400 B.C. **16. He . . . taught:** NEB 'disciplined', a change from 'flailed' in v. 7, which some ancient versions retain here. **18. at Tabor:** Mt. Tabor (cf. 4: 6), just north of Mt. Moreh. The incident is first introduced here. We now are shown a secondary motivation for Gideon's personal vendetta against the two kings. **19. the sons of my own mother:** uterine brothers. **20. Jether his oldest son:** for the kings to have been slain by a boy would have added disgrace to their death.

Gideon's tragic error (8: 22–27). The later life of the hero begins with one of the noblest refusals in biblical history. The Yahwistic theocracy is upheld, and hereditary kingship firmly rejected. But the rejection is immediately followed by a most odd request, the end result of which was to give that judge the trappings of an eastern monarch and provide a focal point for national religious unfaithfulness. The ephod gave to some of Gideon's own family ideas of kingship their father had rejected, while in the nation it aroused passions better satisfied by Canaanite religious practice. Abimelech's kingship and the worship of Baal-berith were the result.

22. Rule over us: Heb. *mᵉšol*. Three different words for rule are used in these two chapters. Gideon is never invited to be 'made king' (Heb. *mālak*), the word used all through Jotham's fable (9: 8–18), an honour which the editor of Jg. similarly refuses to Abimelech. **24. Ishmaelites:** both Midianites and Ishmaelites claimed descent from Abraham through different wives (Gen. 25: 2; 16: 15). Cf. Ishmaelites and Midianites in the Joseph story (Gen. 37: 25, 28). **26. seventeen hundred shekels:** from forty to seventy-five pounds, according to the light or heavy shekel. **27. made . . . an ephod:** a part of the priest's garments (Exod. 28: 28 f.; 35: 27; 39), to which the oracular Urim and Thummim were attached. Other passages pointing to the ephod as an article of clothing include 1 Sam. 2: 18; 22: 18 and 2 Sam. 6: 14. Less clear is this verse and Jg. 17: 5; 18: 14–18, in which some kind of molten image may be envisioned.

Gideon's closing years and the aftermath (8: 29–35). The summary of Gideon's family is likewise designed to introduce the Abimelech incident. The 'seventy sons' are contrasted with the one son of a concubine. Baal-berith is introduced and even more apposite is the comment in v. 35, 'and they did not show kindness to the family of Jerubbaal', a breach of covenant-fealty illustrated in ch. 9 and the subject of Jotham's fable. **29. went back home:** probably, established his own family unit, perhaps after the death of Joash. **31. concubine who lived in Shechem:** in addition to the many wives, itself a sign of Gideon's pretensions to royal status, he kept a concubine in a distant city. **Abimelech:** 'my father is king'. Attempts to find a pagan deity in the second element are unconvincing. 'My father' may refer to Yahweh or Gideon. **33. Baal-berith:** 'The Baal of the Covenant', connected with a shrine at Shechem (Jos. 24 and Jg. 9: 4). This god may have combined Israelite (Yahwistic) and Canaanite elements. **35. show gratitude:** NEB 'loyalty' expresses the covenant aspect of Heb. *hesed.*

ii. The period of 'decline': Abimelech to Samson (9: 1–16: 31)

In the later career of Gideon we readily observe the seeds of decline. Although set in the background from Abimelech until the epilogue (ch. 17–21), the question of kingship, on which the judges period would eventually founder, has been clearly and troublesomely introduced. The initial evaluation is negative, a view that requires modification later. Of more immediate destructive import is the renewal of religious syncretism, this time within the family of one of the deliverers. If the hero falls prey to such a snare (8: 27), what of the fickle mass? A third factor in the decline is the continued presence of non-Israelite forces, but the real problems are internal. In days of internal vitality, the people of God never have to fear the foe without, surely the lesson of the 'period of rest' (Jg. 3: 7–8: 28). Conversely, in a time of internal decay, there is little that can be done effectively to oppose 'foreign' influence. Within this period of steady decline, only two deliverer-judges appear, both of whom are shadowy, questionable characters. The 'minor judges', about whom we know so little, seem to provide what stability the period possesses.

(a) Abimelech: abortive kingship (9: 1–57) Abimelech's plot and coronation (9: 1–6). Although Shechem is well within the territory of Manasseh (Jos. 17: 2) its inhabitants clearly felt estranged from the Abiezrite clan of Gideon, an emotion exploited by Abimelech. The treacherous mission which followed almost succeeded, with the escape of Jotham set in contrast to the coronation in v. 6. The kingship of Abimelech, although probably limited in its scope to the immediate neighbourhood of Shechem (cf. 9: 41, 50, where only Arumah and Thebez are mentioned), was a definite movement away from the ideal kingship of Yahweh and as such figures large in the narrative. **1. Shechem:** the history of Shechem and early Israel is perplexing; although the chief city in north-central Canaan, no record of its conquest appears in Jos. and yet it is the scene of the covenant renewal in ch. 24. From the biblical account, as confirmed by the archaeological history of the site (Tell Balaṭa, just east of present-day Nablus), we may assume a continued Canaanite or mixed occupation into the Iron Age, in light of which the city's actions become clearer. **2. Ask all:** NEB 'whisper' reflects the conduct of this secret plot. **the citizens:** Heb. *ba'ʿalê* or 'lords of'. NEB's 'chief citizens' is better. The old Canaanite aristocracy was approached. Cf. 8: 14 where Succoth's officials (lit. 'princes', Heb. *śārîm*) and elders (*zᵉqēnîm*) make up the leadership. *Ba'ʿalê* may be a pun on the god of the town. **5. on one stone:** possibly in a kind of ritual act. Note how, of the seventy sons, paid for with seventy coins, one escapes. **6. Beth-millo:** lit. 'the house of the filling'. Often thought to be a filled part of a city (cf. 2 Sam. 5: 9; 1 Kg. 9: 15, 24), the Millo is here probably to be equated in some way with the Tower of Shechem (v. 46). **the great tree at the pillar:** NEB 'the old propped up terebinth'. Most moderns read Heb. *maṣṣēbāh* (pillar) in place of *muṣṣāb* (outpost, embankment) and relate it to Jos. 24: 26.

Jotham's fable (9: 7–21). Gideon's youngest son, clearly outflanked by the political-military power of his half-brother, resorted to a poetical masterpiece—the literary curse-form—to ensure the ultimate collapse of Abimelech's *coup d'état*. His call to the men of Shechem suggests that their claim to communicate with God was conditional upon their giving his fable at least a minimal hearing. The fable is easy to follow in its basic thrust: any tree with a useful function in the natural order would be too busy to leave its rightful work and 'sway over' the trees. Only the bramble, a low-lying scrub plant noted for spreading fire along the desert floor, has the temerity to accept the invitation. The picture is ludicrous: the one tree with no shade capability offers itself as shade; the one tree that has no function sees itself better than its brothers. But there is a more subtle point as well. In v. 15 the bramble says 'If in good faith' you are anointing me king, then come and take refuge, but 'if not, let fire come out . . . and devour . . .'. This is the crux of the matter of Abimelech's kingship: was it done 'in good faith'? For Jotham, however, the lack of 'faith' is not toward Abimelech but refers back to the breach of trust already shown toward Gideon's house (8: 35, developed in 9: 16–19). The contrast, cleverly constructed in the parable, ensures that the blessing offered for an act of faith, will be paralleled by a curse implicit in a breach of faith. The curse is cast in the mouth of the bramble (Abimelech) though his point of reference for 'good faith' is different. Since faith had already been broken (with Gideon

and his house) the curse and its result was inevitable.

7. the top of Mt. Gerizim: Boling (*AB*) suggests the ruin of old Middle Bronze buildings on a promontory 400 metres from the city as an appropriate pulpit. The actual 'top' of Mt. Gerizim (the mountain of blessing, Dt. 11: 29) is hidden from the city. **8. to anoint a king . . . Be our king:** see note on 8: 22. **15, 16. 'If you really want' . . . 'honourably and in good faith' . . . if you have treated him as he deserves':** all of these terms have covenant overtones. **17. my father:** Heb. *'ābî*, repeated in v. 18, in stark contrast to the claimed patrimony of Abimelech (my father is king), whose name appears frequently in the narrative. **18. slave girl:** Heb. *'āmāh*, a slur on Abimelech's mother's status. **19. be your joy . . . :** the same word of blessing used in v. 13, 'which cheers'. Only a useful tree (or legitimate king) could bestow such bounty. **20. let fire come out:** the fire devours from both directions, as both Shechem and Abimelech have broken faith. **21. Beer:** a common name, meaning 'well'. Unknown.

The curse fulfilled: Abimelech versus Shechem (9: 22–57). This long section, comprising various elements and activities, is tied together by v. 23 at the beginning and vv. 56 f. at the end. Although the curse was initiated by Abimelech and the men of Shechem, in swearing good faith falsely, and was articulated by Jotham in his fable, it is God who brings the curse to fulfilment. Thus, all that took place between Abimelech, the Shechemites, Gaal ben Ebed and the city of Thebez is merely a divine 'requiting' of the crime of the pretender and a 'turning back' of the wickedness of the men of Shechem (vv. 56 f.). The subtle interplay between primary and secondary causes is one of the distinctive features of biblical historiography, with neither element denied. The 'fire comes out' of Abimelech and the men of Shechem, but it is God whose 'evil spirit' sets them in opposition to one-another.

The initial plot is foiled (v. 25) because of an informer. At this point Gaal, 'son of a slave', appears to exploit the same argument about filial loyalty which had originally served the cause of Abimelech. If a partial pedigree is a sufficient credential, how much more a line going all the way back to Hamor (Gen. 33: 18–34: 18)? The second plot is likewise doomed because of an informer. Zebul, the ruler of the city, apparently an appointee of Abimelech (v. 28), saved the day with the suggestion that an early-morning raid would catch Gaal unaware. When Gaal was about to recognize the plot, Zebul first stalled him and then taunted him to fight Abimelech out beyond the protection of the city walls. A ruse the next day enabled Abimelech to gain entrance to the city. This time the city was razed and ritually defiled (sown with salt, v. 45). The 'Tower of Shechem' (probably the temple of El-Berith, v. 46) has been identified as the Middle Bronze–Late Bronze–Iron Age *migdāl* or fortress-temple at Tell Balaṭa. This final redoubt was burned, ending the history of the city for a considerable period. The end of Shechem (fire had come out) is now settled, but what of Abimelech? The second part of the curse is briefly but decisively recorded in the closing five verses of the narrative. Deprived of his strongest city, Abimelech attempted to expand his control to nearby Thebez. He was about to reduce it by burning as he did in Shechem, when his life (and the story) are abruptly terminated by a thrown millstone. Thus God is repaid and Jotham's curse has come true (vv. 56 f.).

22. governed: Heb. *yāśar*, NEB 'was prince over'. Cf. note on 8: 22. *AB* further reduces the phrase to 'was commander in Israel'. **23. God sent an evil spirit:** cf. Saul's experience (I Sam. 16: 14 ff., etc.). The Bible never visualizes the spirit world in terms of dualism. God rules all, good and evil. The spirit created the discord amongst the new allies. **25. set men on the hilltops to ambush:** the ambush was to catch Abimelech. He did not appear and their rapacity led to indiscriminate attacks on travellers, which let the word out. **26. its citizens . . . put their confidence in him:** Heb. *yibṭᵉḥû*, a term with possible covenant overtones. Cf. NEB: 'transferred their allegiance'. **27. and they had gone out into the field . . . :** this pagan harvest festival stands in strong contrast to the Israelite Feast of Booths with its positive thanksgiving and note of care for the disadvantaged (cf. Dt. 16: 13–15). **28. serve the men of Hamor, Shechem's father:** this sentence stands alone as an imperative in Heb. (cf. NASB, *AB*). There is no evidence for RSV or NEB's suggestion that Gideon's family served Hamor. The appeal is to serve the native line (represented by Gaal) in contrast to the half-breed foreigner: 'Why should we serve him?' **29. I would say:** following LXX. Heb. 'and he said' seems unlikely. **Call out your whole army:** NEB 'get your men together' is preferable. **stirring up:** Heb. *ṣārîm* is best seen as 'alienating' (NEB 'turning against'). **35. was standing at the entrance to the city gate:** at the time of Shechem's destruction (*c.* 1200–1150 BC) only the eastern gate was in use. Gaal would have been facing away from the mountains. **37. the centre of the land:** NEB: 'central ridge'; lit. 'navel'. *AB* favours Gerizim, the mountain south of the city, as this prominent landmark. The slope of Gerizim is today uneven, rocky and wooded, affording a plausible explanation for Zebul's 'shadow' ruse. **a company . . . the sooth-sayer's tree:** hardly the oak of v. 6 which was within the city. This fourth column had apparently crossed Gerizim toward present-day Nablus and was coming from the west down the pass. **41. in Arumah:** probably Jebel al 'Urma, a mountain across the valley to the east.

42. The next day: whether Abimelech was unaware of Zebul's pacification of the city, or whether the further raid was purely punitive, we are not told. Abimelech's petty response lost for him a golden opportunity to regain his influence in his chief city. **44. a position at the entrance to the city gate:** this time the object of the raid was to control entry into the city. **45. he destroyed the city:** recent work sets the date as 'early to middle 12th century BC' (E. F. Campbell and J. F. Ross, *BA* 26 [1963], p. 17). The city was not rebuilt until the time of Jeroboam I (1 Kg. 12: 25). **and scattered salt over it:** to create infertility. Possibly this was a ritual act. **46. the tower of Shechem:** NEB 'castle'. See comment above. **48. Mt. Zalmon:** recent opinion favours Mt. Ebal (R. J. Tournay, *RB* 66 [1959], pp. 358–68 and *AB*, p. 181). Tournay contrasts Jotham's speech on Mt. Gerizim (the mountain of blessing) with Abimelech's closing act on Ebal (the mountain of cursing).

50. Thebez: earlier thought to be modern Tubas, but now Tell el-Far'aḥ, six miles northeast of Shechem (*LOB*, pp. 242 f.), a Late Bronze Canaanite stronghold in the area. **53. an upper millstone:** a massive stone carried to the roof for the purpose. **55. when the Israelites saw . . . they went home:** the entire incident left no organization or movement. As so often in history, the death of a key man signals the death of his cause. Although called 'men of Israel' the group must have represented the mixed Canaanite-Amorite-Israelite population of the northern hills.

(b) **Tola and Jair (10: 1–5).** See Introduction, III(*a*). With Shamgar not really fitting any category, Tola and Jair become the first two minor judges we meet. It is perhaps significant that they fit into the 'declining' portion of the period; possibly through an administrative or legislative function they provided what stability the period knew. Of each judge it is said 'he judged Israel', but of Tola alone is there a record of his having 'saved' (*lᵉhôšîa'*) the nation. The introductory comment (10: 1) makes it patently plain that salvation was required after the sad collapse of both Gideon's and Abimelech's influence. Tola's origin (Issachar) and sphere of activity (Ephraim) span the geographical area affected by both. Gen. 46: 13; Num. 26: 23 and 1 Chr. 7: 1 confirm Tola's connection with Issachar.

Jair, although of Manasseh (Num. 32: 41), functioned in Gilead or eastern Manasseh. The strange notice given to his progeny, their cities and asses contains a subtle word-play (for asses, the unusual *ʿᵃyārîm*; cf. cities *ʿārîm*, although *MT* confuses the two). His burial place is typically noted. It may be modern Qamun, one and one-half miles west of Irbid in Jordan.

(c) **Jephthah: misdirected zeal (10: 6–12: 7)**. Chapter 10: 6–16 represents the standard formulaic introduction to a new section. The Baals and the Ashtaroth are seen as part of the 'gods of the seven nations' (cf. Jg. 3: 5 and note). The oppressors of this new era (v. 7) are both Philistine and Ammonite, the former appearing later in the text of the Samson cycle. Chapter 10: 8–9 sets the stage for the Jephthah deliverance, a strand picked up again in v. 17. Chapter 10: 10–16 is similar to earlier editorial notations, but with a new element. After all the previous acts of deliverance, beginning with the Exodus (v. 11), God has decided to intervene no more (v. 13). The drama builds with the ever-recurring question, 'Has God then forsaken his people?' (Rom. 11: 1). As always (and we, the readers, know already what the answer must be), the reply is 'God forbid'. The misery of Israel will always appeal to his heart, and v. 16 assures us that 'he became indignant' (NEB 'could endure no longer') over their plight. The stage is set for another deliverer to arise, and one is not long in coming.

Chapter 11: 1–3 is a flashback, introducing an unlikely hero. The son of a harlot, disowned by his family, Jephthah was still a man of standing (Heb., v. 1, *gibbôr ḥayil*; see note on 6: 12). His freebooting in the land of Tob must have demonstrated his leadership and charisma. Verses 4–11 see the hero brought back in triumph. The opening offer is made, the hero demurs, and the inducement is possibly made more attractive the second time (cf. 'leader' and 'head', note on v. 6). With suitable guarantees in hand, the hero and his suitors together approach Yahweh for ratification of the election. The LORD is called as 'witness' to the covenant, and the 'words' are deposited (orally or in written form) at Yahweh's shrine in Mizpah. The process reflects a subtle shift in the pattern of deliverance. With Othniel, Ehud, Deborah and Gideon, the initial approach seems to have been from the LORD. Here a human choice is merely ratified, although in light of 11: 29 we have no reason to doubt that it was.

The next item is to confront the enemy. Chapter 11: 12–28 shows by an extended argument from historical precedent that Jephthah, though a rough and rustic freebooter, could also engage his opponent using all the tools of logic and persuasion. (Cf. the eloquence of heroes in the Iliad and the Odyssey; also David, 1 Sam. 16: 18.) Jephthah's case turns on who has owned the land in question and when. When Israel entered Transjordan, the Arnon valley formed the border between Moab and her neighbour, the Amorite kingdom of Sihon (Num. 21: 13). Of Sihon Israel requested a free passage (Num. 21: 21 f.), the refusal which led to war and occupation of Sihon's territory from the Arnon northward (Num. 21: 32–35). The area had then been lived in by the tribes of Israel for a long time (300 years, v. 26) with no attempt by Moab, much less Ammon, to recover it.

Calling the gods of both parties to witness (for Chemosh, see note on v. 24), Jephthah avows that Yahweh must be the final Arbiter (v. 27). His decision is clear only in light of the subsequent battle. The argument, cast in legal language, is a masterpiece, but as in so many cases since, reason did not prevail. The narrative moves rapidly forward and events are covered with extreme brevity. Chapter 11: 29–33 tells of Jephthah's charismatic confirmation, his muster of the troops, his rash vow, and the rout of the Ammonites. The victory is final, and the credit is given to the LORD, but the narrative interest has now shifted to the vow, an ill-considered though well-meaning act of devotion. The 'first creature' (NEB, to be preferred to RSV **whoever** and NIV **whatever**) that comes out of the doors of my house, I will offer up as a burnt-offering. The hero's piety exceeds his wisdom.

Chapter 11: 34–40 carries the story to its pathetic conclusion. His only child, herself a model of pious submission, confirms his vow, wails her impending fate, and is memorialized in a continuing festival. The story is tenderly told, with emphasis on the emotions of both parties taking the place of gruesome details of the sacrifice. It stands as one of the most beautiful expressions of tragedy in the entire Bible. Finally, the Jephthah cycle is drawn to a close with an event reminiscent of Gideon's dispute with the Ephraimites (8: 1–3). Both the Ephraimite anger and Jephthah's reply show far less restraint than in the earlier episode. The ensuing internecine strife (12: 1–6) left Ephraim decimated and no doubt severely limited any subsequent influence which Jephthah's administration might have had outside of Gilead. The cycle closes (12: 7) with the standard formula for this latter portion of Jg.

10: 9. crossed the Jordan: probably no more than an occasional raiding and looting party. Neither Judah nor Benjamin figures in the battle while Ephraim seems to have been the subject of futile appeals for help (cf. 12: 1–3). **10. Baals:** a general term. Cf. note on 2: 11. **11. Egyptians . . . :** historical deliverances can be equated to this list only with some difficulty. The Egyptian reference is to the Exodus, the Amorite to Sihon and Og (Num. 21: 21–35), the Philistine possibly to Shamgar's victory (Jg. 3: 31), and the Amalekite to Gideon's campaign (Jg. 6: 3). Ammonites and Sidonians may have been part of Moabite (3: 13) and Canaanite (1 Chr. 1: 13 and Jg. 4–5) oppression. Maonites are, in this context, unknown. NEB follows LXX in reading 'Midianites'. **17. Gilead:** the lands in central Transjordan. Cf. 11: 1. **Mizpah:** meaning 'watchtower'. A common name, but Mizpah of Gilead is unidentified. **18. Whoever will launch the attack . . . ?:** cf. 1: 1. **head:** see note on 11: 6.

11: 1. mighty warrior: see comments above. *AB*'s translation 'knight' is appropriate, though anachronistic. **his father was Gilead:** many authorities see here a clan patronym rather than an individual father–son relationship (cf. 1 Chr. 7: 14–17). **3. land of Tob:** mentioned with Maacah, in 2 Sam. 10: 6–8. A Syrian town or district. Cf. David's early flight to the Philistines where he functioned as a freebooting mercenary chieftain. **5. elders:** returns to normal term for Israelite tribal or civic leaders. Cf. note on 9: 2. **6. commander:** NEB 'commander', Heb. *qāṣîn*, cf. with *rō'š*(RSV 'head', NEB 'lord') in v. 8. NEB (with *AB*, etc.) suggests that the second title offered carried a more permanent and judicial function than the first. **10. The LORD will be witness:** ancient covenants were witnessed by the deities. Lit. here, 'Yahweh will be a listener'. **11. he repeated all his words before the LORD:** Jephthah formally presents the matter in a Yahweh-shrine. Traditional ancient Near Eastern practice would have a written copy deposited.

13. the Arnon to the Jabbok, all the way to the Jordan: a large tract, bounded by two prominent transverse wadi systems on the north (Jabbok) and south (Arnon), incorporating the plain of the Jordan between. **17. Edom . . . Moab:** cf. Num. 20: 14–21 for Edom. From Num. 21: 11–20 and Dt. 2: 4–9 we imagine a similar request to Moab. Both kingdoms, which were related to Israel (Dt. 2: 8 f.), seem to have become settled in their lands shortly before the conquest. **19. sent . . . to Sihon:** the fuller account in Num. 21: 22 carefully delineates Israelite behaviour for the proposed passage. The refusal was unreasonable. Sihon's kingdom completely blocked Israelite entry to Canaan, leaving them no choice but to fight. No restrictions of kinship were in force. **24. your god Chemosh:** probably an *ad hominem* argument, as both parties agreed that their gods determined the fate of their territory (cf. the later Mesha stele, *ANET*[3], p. 320). To say that Jephthah believed in a territorial limitation for Yahweh simply does not follow. More problematical has been the attributing of the Moabite Chemosh to an Ammonite who normally venerated Milcom. Much nonsense has been swept away by Bol-

ing's recognition (*AB*, p. 203) that the historic circumstances of the land in question dictated that Chemosh and only Chemosh could be the subject of an appeal. The Ammonites, as more recent settlers, had to base their claim on former Moabite suzerainty which involved Chemosh, not Milcom. **26. Heshbon . . . Aroer:** cities on the plateau north of the Arnon. **three hundred years:** a round number. The figure represents all the 'oppressions' and 'rests' taken sequentially.

29. Spirit of the LORD: cf. 3: 10; 6: 34; 13: 25; 15: 14. **30. made a vow:** a normal procedure. It was the content that was foolish. **31. whatever:** Heb. *hay-yōṣē*, 'the thing or person coming out'. Animals, then as now, lived on the ground floor and in the courtyards. **a burnt offering:** NEB 'whole offering', Heb. *'ōlāh*. Cf. Lev. 1: 3–17. **33. Aroer . . . Minnith . . . Abel-Keramim:** only Aroer is known. **37. roam the hills, and weep with my friends:** NEB 'and mourn that I must die a virgin' conveys the sense. **39. did . . . as she had vowed:** the text unambiguously states that she was made an offering. This instance of human sacrifice is merely (and tragically) recorded and not condoned. The biblical attitude toward the subject is clearly antagonistic (Lev. 18: 21, etc.). **12: 1. Zaphon:** probably Tel el-Qos, in Transjordan north of Succoth. The battle was on Gilead's side of the river. **4. you are fugitives of Ephraim . . . :** NEB, with LXX, omits the entire taunt. The Heb. text remains a puzzle. **5. captured the fords:** to prevent the Ephraimite return. **6. Shibboleth . . . Sibboleth:** the pronunciation, not the meaning, is the key. Such simple tests have been applied to fugitives from time immemorial. **7. in a town in Gilead:** lit. 'in the cities of '. The site is unknown.

(d) **Ibzan, Elon and Abdon (12: 8–15).** The text turns to three 'minor judges' (see Introduction). The notations concerning each are consistent with earlier references (10: 1–5). **8. Bethlehem:** a common town name. Location uncertain. **9. gave . . . in marriage: . . . outside his clan:** lit. 'he sent outside'. The following line gives the sense. **12. Aijalon:** unknown, but not to be confused with the place of the same name in Dan. **13. Pirathon:** modern Far'atah, six miles south-west of Nablus, in a border area between Manasseh and Ephraim. **15. hill country of the Amalekites:** for a possible reference, cf. note on 5: 14.

(e) **Samson: wasted opportunity (13: 1–16: 31).** Continuing the picture of progressively greater decline, the narrative reaches the pinnacle of its epic detail. We know far more about Samson, the 'judge' who never really delivered Israel and whose most potentially fruitful years were cut off by his own folly, than we know about Othniel, Ehud or Deborah. There are perhaps several reasons. First, Samson's work stood to later generations as the opening round in the battle for survival against the Philistine menace (see Introduction, I(b)). From Jg. 14: 3 f. and 15: 9–13 it is clear that within both Dan and Judah Philistine domination had been accepted, a fact which constituted a greater threat to national existence than any previous oppression. Samson gave expression to the first true resistance to the encroachments of these powerful Sea Peoples. Second, Samson's life, although hardly acceptable by modern (or even monarchy) standards, represented the heroic ideal of courage, independence and pathos. Born after a miraculous annunciation, stirred from his youth by Yahweh's Spirit, a fighter, a lover, a clever rhetorician and even, despite great weaknesses, a man of the LORD, Samson stands as fit subject for a national epic. Finally, despite the positive values, Samson's life appears as the climax of the period of decline. It leads into the episodes of shame and debauchery with which the theologically-constructed narrative makes its final appeal for some stronger and more central authority. In this sense Samson's life is seen as one of great but wasted opportunity. With such credentials he might have delivered Israel, a claim never made for him. The times required more than a free-booting hero. Israel must be turned away from the individualism so exemplified by Samson, who even more than most of those he judged, 'did what was right in his own eyes'.

The epic begins with a standard formula (13: 1), continues with a detailed theophany and birth narrative (13: 2–24) and climaxes with Samson's Timnathite marriage and its consequences (ch. 14–15). Chapter 16 is an appendix comprising two accounts of Samson's loves, the second of which (Delilah) led to both his and the Philistine lords' downfall.

Chapter 13: 2–24 bears certain affinities to the Gideon account, although the differences far outweigh the similarities. The angel of the LORD is common to both but the manner of his coming and going is not. That the annunciation is given to a barren woman (13: 3) calls to mind Sarah, Hannah and Elizabeth, and heightens the sense of God's supernatural intervention. As with Gideon, the identity of the messenger is a question (cf. 6: 17 ff. and 13: 6, 16 f.), with His divine character finally evidenced by the acceptance of food in a distinctly worshipful context. Both the name (13: 6, 17) and the presence (13: 20, 22) of the LORD are ineffable, preserving the sense of awe toward the God whose every act of salvation is a wonder (13: 18 f.). The recognition that God has visited his people can lead to dismay or relief. In the presence of His holiness, Manoah can only think of God's awful judgment (13: 22), but his wife's reasoned reply reminds him that God

may appear for other reasons as well (13: 23). The chapter closes with the birth of the hero and his early stirrings toward God's task in the locality of his home.

13: 1. Philistines: Philistine, together with Ammonite, oppression marks the entire section (cf. 10: 7). The saga of the Philistines, who are the more troublesome foe, is placed in the second or climactic position. **2. Zorah:** a town from which the Danite tribal delegation is sent (18: 1 f.) to escape apparent Philistine pressure in the lowlands. It is modern Sar'ah on the north side of the Valley of Sorek. **from the clan of the Danites:** lit. 'the Danite family'. The normal word for tribe is not used, supporting the idea that ch. 18 precedes ch. 13 and only a clan or two remained. **5. a Nazirite . . . from birth:** cf. Num. 6: 1–21. Normally the vow was for a limited period. Samson's mother is warned about the provisions dealing with drink and the dead (vv. 4, 14), although for Samson the prohibitions seem chiefly to have concerned his hair (v. 5). **will begin the deliverance:** it is recognized throughout that the deliverance will be incomplete. **8. to teach us how to bring up the boy:** stress is here on his education. **12. what is to be the rule for the boy's life and work:** Heb. *mišpaṭ han-na'ar*. A text from Ugarit would favour the translation 'destiny of the child' (*UT*, p. 506). Now (cf. v. 8) Manoah wants to know in what way the boy will deliver Israel. **15. We would like you to stay:** there is a double thrust: hospitality demanded some provision for a stranger but, as in Gideon's case (6: 18 ff.), there is a hint already that the guest may be more than a stranger. The angelic response separated the messenger from Manoah (I do not eat **your food**) and enjoined him to direct any offerings to Yahweh. **17. What is your name?:** cf. Gen. 32: 29 and Exod. 3: 13, where the question is slightly different. The name would clarify the true identity of the caller and reveal secrets of the divine. Such a revelation is always veiled (v. 18, 'it is a name of wonder', NEB). **19. did an amazing thing:** Heb. 'and (he) was working wonders', presumably speaking of the angel. RSV also omits the next clause, 'while Manoah and his wife looked on'. **20. the flame blazed up:** contrast 6: 21. **24. Samson:** probably related to Heb. *šemeš* ('sun') although its precise meaning remains unclear. Attempts to connect Samson with a solar cult have failed for want of evidence. **25. the Spirit of the LORD:** cf. 3: 10; 6: 34, etc. There is no set formula for the Spirit's activity. **Mahaneh-Dan:** lit. 'the camp of Dan'; 18: 12 puts it higher in the mountains toward Jerusalem, but Eshtaol is closer to Zorah (probably modern 'Ešua', one and one-half miles northeast of Ṣor'ah).

Samson's marriage and its consequences

form the subject of the next block (chs. 14–15). Through this providential (cf. editorial comment, 14: 4) but heterodox liaison God opened the way for Samson to assume the office of judge. Of the three instances specifying spiritual filling, all are in this section (14: 6, 19; 15: 14) and they form something of an *inclusio*. The passage opens with a wilful demand for a bride (seen as God's providence) and closes with the formal rubric of judgeship. The proposed bride lived in nearby Timnah, and on one of his trips there Samson's first feat of strength is recorded (v. 6). The lion incident is a prelude to the later role of his Spirit-given strength, but also figures as the basis for the riddle whose secret is the key to all that follows. The large stakes set by Samson ultimately forced the hand of the Philistine 'hired men' who were facing financial ruin, and their action set a pattern for incidents yet to come. But more than that, the very success of their effort is one more link in the chain of Philistine disaster. Samson's weakness with women is exploited; he gives in at the last minute (14: 17). Apart from this failure, the story might have ended then and there. As it is, the first attack on a Philistine capital followed immediately, an attack carried out in the strength of Yahweh's Spirit (14: 19). Samson the deliverer is beginning to emerge.

Samson does not know that his bride has been given away, and ch. 15 begins with what may have been a normal conjugal visit in a marriage of what is called the *ṣadiqa* class. Here the wife remains at home and the husband visits periodically with a gift. It is clear that the father is embarrassed (15: 2), and may be claiming that Samson technically divorced his daughter. The whole incident sets the stage for the second attack on the oppressors, this time directed to their agricultural production at the vital harvest stage (15: 5). The Philistines, unable to confront Samson and perhaps recognizing the validity of his complaint (cf. 15: 3), wreak vengeance on the hapless bride and her family, an act which Samson swears to avenge yet once more (15: 7). His retreat is to a stronghold in Judean territory, and suddenly the feud becomes an international conflict. The men of Judah, who have little stomach for wars of liberation or charismatic heroes, would rather hand over Samson and keep the peace. The stage is again set for Samson's triumph and subsequent judgeship. Again, and for the last time (15: 14), the Spirit of the LORD has become his strength. In true epic fashion, a poem follows the victory. The hero's personal frailty is the subject of the short pericope with which the chapter ends (15: 18 f.). Samson is seen here as one who called upon God and knew His provision. Thus far providence has led him to a series of victories and a role as Israel's judge (15: 20).

14: 1. Timnah: Aharoni (*MBA*, Maps No. 79, 80; *LOB*, p. 267) favours modern Tell el-Batashi, about four miles down (northwest) the Valley of Sorek toward Ekron from BethShemesh. **3. uncircumcised:** the usual pejorative epithet of Philistines. Most other ancient Near Easterners were circumcised. **Get her:** v. 3 reverses the normal order: 'her! Get for me!' **She's the right one for me:** lit. 'she is right in my eyes'. A comparison with 17: 6 and 21: 25 leaps immediately to mind. **4. the Philistines . . . were ruling over Israel:** see Introduction, I(*b*). This event has been dated to the beginning of Philistine expansion inland, i.e., after *c.* 1080 B.C. **6. the Spirit . . . came upon him in power:** Heb. *tiṣlaḥ*, 'rushed upon'. Cf. expressions in 6: 34; 11: 29. The same verb is used in 14: 19; 15: 14 and here. **he told neither his father nor his mother:** possibly because it was a violation of his vowed status. **8. In it was a swarm of bees:** the carcass was old enough to have been picked clean and dehydrated. Honey was later taken by Jonathan for quick energy (1 Sam. 14: 24–30). **10. Samson made a feast:** lit. a 'drinking party'. Again, the vow seems not to have been a hindrance. **11. When he appeared:** Burney changes *r'h* (see) to *yr'* (fear). Because Samson was feared, there were thirty companions enlisted. The text is suitable as it stands. **12. Let me tell you a riddle:** lit. 'riddle a riddle'. Such devices were common in the ancient world, usually as a test of wit or skill. Samson's riddle is a perfect poetic couplet (3 + 3), the meaning of which would only be apparent to one familiar with the lion incident. (But cf. J. R. Porter, *JTS* n.s., 13 [1962], pp. 106–109, for another suggestion.)

15. On the fourth day: Heb. reads 'seventh day' but most translations follow LXX here. The exact course of events is still a bit confusing. **Coax your husband . . . we will burn you. . . . Did you invite us here to rob us?:** the companions now suspect that the whole thing may have been set up to make a tidy profit, and they hold the sponsoring family responsible. Their threatened punishment anticipates the fate of daughter and father in 15: 6. **16. Samson's wife threw herself on him:** a preview of the Delilah account. **I haven't even explained it to my father or mother:** cf. v. 6. His silence with his parents was for another reason. **18. What is sweeter . . . ?:** the solution is, like the riddle, in poetic bicola (2+2), as is Samson's reply (3+3). Porter (see note on v. 12) argues that one word with a double meaning ('honey' and 'lion') originally appeared at the end of both lines of the friend's response and was the key to the riddle. **19. Ashkelon:** one of the five capitals of the Philistines. This attack, spurred by Yahweh's third enduement, is the climax of the story. **20. wife**

was given . . . : sets the stage for the second deliverance (ch. 15). **15: 2. hated her:** *AB*'s 'you divorced her' takes 'hate' as a technical term used for divorce; cf. Dt. 24: 3. **3. I have a right to get even:** the verb *niqqāh* expresses 'being freed from one's obligation'. NEB removes the temporal clause following and translates 'this time I will settle the score (that is, free myself from continuing obligation to vengeance); I will do them some real harm.' **5. shocks:** the bundles of wheat already harvested (cf. v. 1). **6. burned her:** cf. 14: 15. **7. until I get my revenge on you:** their act of revenge incurred a further obligation for Samson (cf. v. 3). **I won't stop until:** stop the escalating feud. **8. in a cave . . . Etam:** a cave in the nearby Wadi Isma'in accessible through a narrow defile has been suggested.

9. Lehi: means 'jawbone' (vv. 15 f.); unknown locality. **10. to do to him as he did to us:** neither the Philistines nor Samson (v. 11) had heard of the Golden Rule. **14. Spirit . . . came:** this is the fourth and last time. The result is the closest to real deliverance Samson or Israel will know. **15. a fresh jaw-bone:** lit. 'moist'. A dry older bone would be light and brittle. **16. With a donkey's jaw-bone I have made donkeys of them:** a rhymed couplet with word-plays: *biʾlḥî haḥᵃmôr; hᵃmôr hᵃmōrātayim.* **killed a thousand men:** a great deliverance, but the lack of follow-up indicates both Samson's failure as a leader and the depth of Judean acceptance of its plight. **19. the hollow place:** lit. 'mortar', as in Prov. 27: 22, a circular bowl for crushing by means of a pestle. In Jerusalem, the Mortar (Heb. *maktēš*) was a district (Zeph. 1: 11). **En-hakkore:** 'Well of the One Who Calls'. Also means 'Well of the Partridge', which may have been original.

The last section (ch. 16), like chs. 14–15, moves the action back and forth from one of the five capitals (Gaza) to a border town in the Valley of Sorek, though the order is reversed (ch. 14–15, Timnah-Ashkelon-Timnah). Although each of the two incidents (the Gaza harlot and the Delilah affair) culminated in a victory of sorts, the effect is one of pathos rather than triumph. Certainly in neither case is Samson about his proper business of judging Israel, nor in any but the dying moment is the LORD called into the picture. How long Samson felt he could flirt with danger and retain his office we don't know, but when the secret of his strength was revealed, the presence of Yahweh departed (16: 20) and his role as judge formally ended. His final trip to Gaza might have been as conqueror; instead his sightless frame is dragged in chains to the grinding mill of the prison. The occasion is, naturally, for the Philistines one of rejoicing and they interpret the event as a victory for Dagon their god. The once-formidable Samson is reduced to an

object of sport, a game which led to their eventual undoing. Samson's final prayer is for vengeance—a continuation of the tit-for-tat feuding pattern. In death the tragic hero recoups something of his deliverer function, although all possibility of a continuing judgeship is forfeited. The story of Samson is the tale of what might have been. No potential saviour-figure offered more promise, yet none delivered less. Israel had sunk to a new low, and it only remained for two shameful incidents fully to expose their plight. With Samson the 'period of the judges' has come to an end.

16: 1. Gaza: modern Gaza, the most distant Philistine city from Samson's home. **2. all night:** repeated twice, modifying 'lay in wait' and 'kept quiet'. The confusion in vv. 2 f. has been cleared up by modern discoveries of Palestinian city gates of the period. With the gate securely locked, the Gazite horde apparently retired to one of the several spacious rooms in the gate-house until the gate reopened and the watch would be re-set. The two verbs, then, signify setting a watch and sleeping on it. **3. doors . . . posts . . . bar:** see 'Gate', *ZPEB*. **the hill that faces Hebron:** about thirty-eight miles from Gaza, mostly uphill. **4. valley of Sorek:** the Wadi es-Sarar, below Zorah, in which both Beth-shemesh and Timnah stood (cf. 14: 1). **Delilah:** the name has been identified as meaning both 'flirtatious' and 'devotee', the latter suggesting religious prostitution as her role. **5. Each . . . eleven hundred shekels of silver:** the total from five lords would be a very large amount. The specific weight of each piece is not known; in shekels the reward would seem excessive, even for such a service. *AB* changes 1000 (*'elep*) to 'unit' (*'alep*) and renders 'each man's unit, one hundred in silver'. **7. seven fresh thongs:** old gut would have been stronger. Samson seems to be suggesting that the gut had magical powers (*AB*). **11. new ropes:** already tried; cf. 15: 13. **13–14. into the fabric on the loom . . . the pin:** most modern translations include a long section from the LXX, apparently dropped from the *MT* (cf. RSV, NEB). The web was probably an upright loom. Moore (*ICC*, p. 354) suggests that Delilah wove the long hair into the warp, after which she beat it up hard and tight with the pin. The posts, which were fixed in the ground, were probably lifted clear by Samson when he awoke. **16. tired to death:** lit. 'his soul (or life) was shortened to (the point of) death'. The continued emotional barrage exhausted his powers of resistance. **18. she sent word to the rulers:** they had apparently tired of lying in wait. **the silver in their hands:** in such business payment is always in advance. **19. began to subdue him:** her evil device to discover whether his strength remained before summoning the Philistines. **20.**

he did not know: here is the real tragedy; cf. Num. 14: 40–45; Hos. 7: 9. **the LORD had left him:** his strength was only an outward sign of God's inner presence. **21. to Gaza:** the pathos heightens, the battered hero returns in shame through the repaired gate (cf. v. 3). **22. the hair . . . began to grow:** suspense: will long hair help when Yahweh is gone? **23. Dagon:** a West Semitic grain-god, apparently adopted by the Sea People upon their arrival in Palestine. **our god has delivered:** all ancients interpreted events theologically. The lines in both vv. 23 and 24 are cast in poetry (cf. NASB, *AB*). **25. they stood him among the pillars:** before Samson calls, God is preparing to avenge him. **26. that support the temple:** A. Mazar has illustrated this kind of a temple from Tell Qasile (*BA* 36 [1973], p. 43). A main hall had a roof supported by two wooden pillars set on round stone bases. The great number on the roof would have quickened the collapse. **31. He had led Israel:** better: 'he had judged'. His official role ended earlier (15:20).

III. EPILOGUE (17: 1–21: 25)

The closing section completes the 'ABA' pattern (see Introduction, II) in an epilogue which illustrates the natural outcome of a broken covenant. In place of the dominant 'rest' motif in chs. 3–8 or the 'he judges Israel' formula in chs. 9–16, we now find some variation of 'There was no king in Israel; every man did what was right in his own eyes' (17: 6; 18: 1; 19: 1; 21: 25). The editor has almost given up on the institution of judge. The people are fickle and the judges prone to human foibles, with Gideon, Jephthah and Samson examples on a descending scale of effectiveness. What follows is nothing less than the threatened dissolution of the society of tribal Israel, the complete reversal of God's unifying covenant with Moses and Joshua. Nothing but a king will stem the tide of anarchy.

The chapters divide into two main sections. Micah, his Levite and the Danites (chs. 17–18) begins with a family and ends with a peripheral tribe; the perversion of religious and social norms is spreading. Then, in a climactic finale (chs. 19–21), the rot spreads in concentric circles from a town to a full tribe whose position and influence was at the very heart of Israelite life. The outrage of Gibeah is the darkest moment of Israel's history, but in the ensuing civil strife there is also a ray of hope. The story ends with the covenant-league intact (just barely), its religious, military and social institutions having taken on new life. All is not lost. God has not cast off His people.

i. Micah's shrine: household apostasy (17: 1–13)

This short chapter is full of religious and social irregularities. A host of commentators have suggested that here we have a primitive, pre-levitical stage of evolution in Israel's religious life. But the point of the story is to contrast the scene with the norm; remove that fact and the account is irrelevant. The theft, curse, confession, blessing and resultant dedication of the image are merely an unflattering prelude to the establishment of an aberrant Yahweh shrine with an illegal priesthood (17: 5). This sets the stage for the entry of the Levite, whose normal function has fallen casualty to the general disorder. Micah, though by no means scrupulous about his shrine, but seeing a chance to lend it greater legitimacy, hires and consecrates the priest, and congratulates himself on having escaped his mother's curse and obtained Yahweh's blessing as well. Apostasy has become profitable; clergy and laity share its fruits.

17: 1. Micah: Here and in v. 4, *Mîkāyᵉhû*, everywhere else the shortened form *Mîkāh*. AB suggests an emphasis on the meaning 'Who is like Yahweh?' (*AB*: 'Yahweh the Incomparable') in the full spelling, an ironic contrast to the idol. **2. eleven hundred shekels:** 'silver pieces'; cf. note on 16: 5. **I heard you utter a curse:** both mother and son would respect the power of a curse. Perhaps the mother harboured suspicions of her son. **The LORD bless you, my son:** only a blessing could offset the previously uttered curse. The LORD is, of course, Yahweh. **3. I solemnly consecrate my silver:** the Heb. strengthens the affirmation (see NEB, NASB). **a carved image and a cast idol:** Heb. *pesel* and *massēkāh*. The first literally denotes something carved or hewn; the second a cast or moulded image. Later usage mixed the terms, and *AB*'s suggestion of a hendiadys (two terms with a single meaning) is reasonable. **I will give it back to you:** NEB has transposed this to the end of Micah's speech in v. 2. **4. two hundred shekels:** we are never told the whereabouts of the rest. **5. Micah had a shrine:** lit. 'a house of God (or gods)'; probably in existence prior to the theft. As 18: 22 shows, it served the entire neighbourhood. **ephod:** see 8: 27. **some idols:** the 'household gods' of Gen. 31: 19, 34 f., etc. The ephod and household gods may both have been used as oracular devices. **one of his sons . . . his priest:** family priesthood was not unknown in early Israel, although a Levite was to be preferred (v. 13).

7. A young Levite from Bethlehem in Judah: that a Levite would be considered of the clan (*mišpāḥāh*, not tribe) of Judah has a possible analogy in Samuel's situation (cf. 1 Sam. 1: 1 and 1 Chr. 6: 28). The Levites were intended to be spread throughout the other tribes (Num. 35: 1 ff. and Jos. 21: 1 ff.). **had been living:** Heb. *wᵉhû' gār šām*. NEB reconstructs the name Gershom from 18: 30; the prefixed 'Ben' ('son of') is an interpolation.

Others have found in *gār* a technical term signifying that Levites were in this period resident aliens and not Israelites. **8. Micah's house:** possibly here a village name: Beth-Micah (*AB*). Cf. 18: 14. **10. Live . . . be my father and priest:** not all Levites were qualified as priests and there is no indication this one was until he was consecrated by Micah (v. 12). The figure of priest as father (cf. the reversal in v. 11) is unusual, but cf. 18: 19. It seems to have been more than an indication of respect, but *AB*'s emphasis on the cultic diviner is without adequate foundation. The clause 'so the Levite went in' (NASB, AV) is omitted by RSV and NEB. Heb. *wayyēlek* can hardly mean 'went in'. **11. So the Levite agreed to live with him:** except for the name, identical to Exod. 2: 21 (Cassuto, quoted in *AB*).

ii. The Danite Migration: tribal apostasy (18: 1–31)
The chapter begins with the 'no king' rubric; we assume that given the presence of a king the Danite tribe would have been able to establish themselves in an inheritance. But the migration has, in this context, a purpose. In the Danites the apostasy of Micah will expand to a tribal heresy, even while the narrative is mocking Micah's feeble attempts to preserve 'my gods which I made' (v. 24). Also, by recounting the establishment of a Danite city and shrine in the very north of Israel, the later aberrations of Jeroboam (1 Kg. 12: 29 f.) are given a framework. What began as Micah's private heresy will, before the time the book is completed, have affected the entire northern kingdom. The chapter closes with a still greater tragedy. The Levite whose sons kept this shrine 'until the day of the captivity of the land' (v. 30) is now revealed to be a direct descendant of Moses (see note on v. 30). When a grandson of the great lawgiver is found leading a tribe and later a nation into Yahweh syncretism, what hope remains? There must be a king who would reign in righteousness; the alternative is anarchy and destruction.

   18: 1. the tribe of the Danites was seeking . . . a place of their own: cf. 13: 2. Originally assigned a place in the coastal plain (Jos. 19: 40–48), Dan was forced continually into the hills (Jg. 1: 34). In the Samson cycle he is pressed between the expanding power of the Philistine newcomers and the older tribe of Judah. Chapter 18 shows a small but representative group of this tribe establishing itself in what became its later territory (see note on v. 27). **they had not yet come into an inheritance:** NEB, although a paraphrase of the text, gives the sense. Grammatically the text is difficult. **2. all their clans:** omitted by NEB, with some MSS of LXX, Syriac. **Zorah and Eshtaol:** see note on 13: 25. **the house of Micah:** see 17: 8. Their arrival was the providential link in

a long chain of circumstances. **3. they recognized the voice** (NEB 'speech') **of the . . . Levite:** either his accent or his professional language. Alternatively, they may have known him personally. **Who . . . what . . . why?:** cf. Micah's questions (17: 9). His oracular function represented practical help in their mission. They needed to know whose oracle he was. His answer seems to have satisfied them, as they proceeded to inquire further. **6. Go in peace:** Heb. *šālôm*, welfare, success. Cf. note on 8: 9. **the LORD's approval:** NEB: 'in the LORD's hands'. Lit. 'before the LORD is your way'.

   7. Laish: cf. note on 18: 27. **living in safety . . . they were prosperous:** the Heb. text is problematical. Neither RSV nor NEB has attempted a full translation. A literal reading would be something like: 'dwelling in security, according to the manner (or "rule") of the Sidonians, quiet and secure, and there was no one humiliating (or "restraining") anything (or "for anything") in the land, a possessor (or "inheritor") of restraint.' The general picture is clear nevertheless; in many ways their life-style represents what Israel's should have been. **a long way from the Sidonians:** Laish was inland, across the Lebanon range from the parent city. It was probably built as a caravan city for Canaanite travellers. **no relationship with anyone:** or 'no covenant (Heb. *dābār*) with the Aramaeans' (NEB, with LXX, etc., read *'rm*, 'Syria', for MT *'dm*, 'man'). The Syrians were removed from Laish by the massif of Mt. Hermon. **8. How do you find things?:** lit. 'What . . . you?' Driver suggests a colloquial expression 'How have you fared?' NEB paraphrases. The report was most challenging and almost chiding. **11. six hundred men . . . armed:** the total number seems small. Verse 21 indicates the presence of a settlers group as well. **12. Kiriath-jearim:** west of Jerusalem, on the road from the old Danite territory. **Mahaneh-Dan:** not to be confused with that of 13: 25. **14. one of these houses:** NEB adds 'one of'. From v. 22 we assume a small settlement existed which Micah's shrine served. **ephod . . . cast idol:** see on 17: 3, 5. **18, 19. the priest said . . . they answered:** the protest is as feeble as the logic is corrupt. **20. the priest was glad:** quickly forgetting his benefactor, he merrily joins in the theft. **22. the men . . . were called together:** see note on v. 14. **23. What's the matter with you . . . ?:** The question and answer routine of vv. 23–25 is merely a ruse. Bullies delight in such repartee. **25. hot-tempered men:** NEB 'desperate men' forcefully represents the lit. 'bitter of soul'.

   27. attacked . . . and burned down their city: excavations since 1966 (see A. Biran, 'Dan', *EAEHL*, Vol. I, pp. 313–320) at Tell el-Qadi (Tell Dan) near one of the sources of the Jordan at the foot of Mt. Hermon have shed light on this event. A massive Middle Bronze earthen rampart was used in later periods in lieu of city walls. Danite occupation of the first Iron Age city probably came in the mid-twelfth century BC, when the city was rebuilt on older lines. **28. Beth-rehob:** lit. 'House of the Square'. Cf. 2 Chr. 32: 6. May be a city name; cf. Num. 13: 21. **30. Jonathan . . . son of Moses:** the Heb. clearly reads 'Moses' (*mšh*) but Jewish piety inserted above the line a nun (*mⁿšh*) to avoid such scandal in the reading. Cf. Exod. 2: 21 f. Moses' family is never glorified in subsequent tradition. **the time of the captivity:** probably 722/1 B.C. in the northern kingdom. **31. all the time the house of God was in Shiloh:** the first reference to this sanctuary (see 1 Sam. 1–3) which continued until destroyed *c.* 1050 B.C. The reference suggests an early date, with the end of v. 30 a later editorial insertion.

iii. The Gibeah Outrage: societal disintegration (19: 1–30)

The depth of degradation is indicated by two references. In 19: 30 those who 'saw it' (the eyewitnesses to the dismembered concubine) said 'Such a thing has never happened or been seen from the day that . . . Israel came up out of Egypt until this day'. And, *c.* 400 years later, the prophet Hosea likens Ephraim's depths of corruption to the 'days of Gibeah' (Hos. 9: 9; 10: 9). This incident (reflecting similarities with Gen. 19) was the low point of Israelite history from the Exodus to the Exile. It is for this reason placed at the end, the shameful climax of a period marked by covenant breaking and sin. Chapters 17–18 concerned a young Levite; here we have the story of an older Levite (Heb. '*îš lēwî*, 'a man, a Levite'). Again, the hill country of Ephraim and Beth-lehem figure in the account. And again there is a breakdown in standards, but the irregularities are social rather than religious. Time-honoured laws of hospitality and decency are flouted by the very ones whose covenant-loyalty should have guaranteed their conformity. Although the story culminates in the grievous wrong done to the Levite, he is pictured as himself partly to blame. The father-in-law, the servant and the old man are all seen in a brighter light, while the Levite's closing act of cruelty and contempt for his hapless concubine is hardly designed to elicit our sympathy, even when all cultural considerations have been made. But above all, it is the men of Gibeah who demonstrate the depths of evil in the story. The implied contrast with the pagan Jebusites is powerful: even those outside of Yahweh's covenant could hardly have sunk so low. The heinous sin could only call for judgment. The chapter concludes with a rallying of the tribal league to purge the blood-guiltiness from Israel.

19: 1. remote area: lit. 'backside of', probably the hill country off the main north-south road. **a concubine:** usually a second or lower-status wife (see *NBD*, 'Concubine'). **2. was unfaithful:** Heb. 'played the harlot'. RSV, NEB follow LXX. The context certainly favours the emendation, as she seems to have been the wronged party. **3. to persuade her:** Heb. 'to speak to her heart', a common idiom with an affectionate connotation. **She took him in:** RSV, again following LXX; cf. NEB and Heb., 'She brought him in . . .' Other than that, the girl does not figure in the story until v. 25. **he gladly welcomed him:** NEB 'who welcomed him'. Apparently the problem was a small one, and the girl's return had been an embarrassment to the family. The next few verses show the hospitality and leisure typical of the East, but also form a contrast with Gibeah's inhospitable actions. **4, 5, 8. three days . . . fourth day . . . fifth day:** a comparison with Jg. 14: 14 f. comes to mind. Perhaps the Levite should have kept a full seven-day feast. **8. Wait:** Burney argues for an indicative (so they tarried), as v. 9 indicates that the decline of the day was not a good time to leave, but there may be irony involved.

10. went towards Jebus: Jerusalem, six miles north of Bethlehem, was a Jebusite stronghold (v. 11) until taken by Joab (2 Sam. 5: 6–10). **11. the day was almost gone:** the Heb. is difficult, but NEB's 'weather grew wild and stormy' is conjectural. **12. we will go on to Gibeah:** another four miles north. Modern Tell el-Ful, Gibeah was destroyed *c.* 1100, probably in the battle described in these chapters. It was later Saul's capital (*EAEHL*, Vol. II, 444 ff.). Its location and topography would make it easy to defend. **13. Ramah:** probably modern Er-Ram, another two miles to the north. **15. sat . . . in the city square:** with his provisions (v. 19) he was obviously able to pay for lodging, and the code of Israel (and the East) demanded that he be received. The open square was no place to spend the night (v. 20). **18. house of the LORD:** RSV and NEB agree with LXX. Cf. Heb. 'to the house of Yahweh'. The text is not easily explained. **22. wicked men:** Heb. 'sons of Beliyya'al'. Etymologically 'Belial' is often related to the negative *b⁵lî* and the verb *yā'al*, giving 'worthless fellows'. 2 C. 6: 15 (Gk. *beliar*) reflects later writings when Belial is clearly a personal entity. **Pounding on the door:** NEB 'hurling themselves' conveys the reflective sense of the Heb. *hithpael*, and demonstrates the fury of their lewd desire. **so we can have sex with him:** prohibitions of homosexuality in Israel join with hospitality laws as a basis for the story (cf. v. 23, 'this vile thing'). **23. disgraceful thing:** Heb. *han-*

n°bālāh. AV's 'foolishness' lacks strength. NEB's 'outrage' is better. Even the ravishing of his daughter and the Levite's concubine was preferable to a homosexual violation of a guest. Cf. Gen. 19: 8. **25. the man took his concubine:** the Levite's insensitivity to his concubine (cf. v. 28) is another sub-theme in the account. **29. twelve parts:** cf. 1 Sam. 11: 7 and 1 Kg. 11: 30–39. The 'twelve pieces' has been seen as a later addition, as this is the first time in Jg. when all twelve tribes appear together. But the 'original' league of twelve is assumed throughout, especially if Jos.–Jg. be seen as a connected narrative. A piece to each tribe may have laid blood-guiltiness upon each. **30. Everyone who saw it said:** NEB (following LXX) adds an introduction to the speech, making the messengers say what follows.

iv. Civil War with Benjamin: the league collapsing (20: 1–48)
If the outrage of Gibeah represented the nadir of morality and ethics in Israel, certainly the civil war that followed may be called the darkest night of the nation's collective soul. Beginning as a purge of blood-guiltiness and proceeding along standard lines of covenant collective responsibility, the war exposed not only Benjamin's arrogance but the fragility of the entire league. The chapter begins with all Israel united. Though presented for theological reasons at the end of Jg. there is good reason to hold that this event took place much closer to the beginning of the period (cf. especially the reference to Phinehas, v. 28). Benjamin, although presumably invited, is missing and the rest are told the Levite's sad tale. It is clear (vv. 7 f.) that all Israel regard themselves as having incurred collective guilt which must be purged. To that end a battle plan is suggested (v. 9) and a supply organization set up (v. 10).

Naturally Benjamin must first be given the chance to rid itself (and thus all Israel) of the guilt. This could have been accomplished with little bloodshed (v. 13) and the 'evil put away', but when the Benjaminites chose to ignore the ultimatum, war became inevitable. Following usual practice, the tribes sought a battle oracle (v. 18), although the request, 'Which . . . shall go up first?' (reminiscent of 1: 1), assumes the rightness of going to war in the first place. This confidence, though justified (notwithstanding modern commentators) in light of the bloodguilt incurred, was soon to be shaken by successive defeats. Before the second round the more basic question is put (v. 23), while prior to the third and final battle there is a full assembly with sacrifices before the ark (vv. 26 ff.). In any case, the tribes realize that for some reason (possibly their own failure to keep the covenant sacrificial laws) the LORD has denied them the victory. The renewal of burnt and peace offerings in a genuine context of fasting and repentance is a key to their subsequent success against Benjamin.

Although details of the battle plan and its progress are somewhat confusing, the general outline is clear. The main army drew Benjamin out of Gibeah to the north (v. 31, 'to Bethel' and probably 'Gibeon' instead of 'Gibeah') while the ambushing party waited to the north-east (v. 34 'west of Geba', following RSV and LXX) until the signal to pounce on the undefended city. The general account (vv. 29–36a) concludes by noting that Yahweh was (for the first time) responsible for the victory (v. 35). Verses 36b–48 adds details of the ambush and its aftermath, including the sanctuary of a mere remnant in the rock of Rimmon (v. 47) and the decimation of all the towns of Benjamin, most probably under the Hebrew practice of 'the ban' (see note on 21: 11). The destruction is so complete that the problem now turns from preserving Israel free from blood-guiltiness to preserving the twelve tribes of the league. Has God raised up his people only to destroy them? Can eleven tribes be 'Israel' when there were twelve 'born' to Jacob? Has God cast away his people, whom he foreknew?

20: 1. from Dan to Beersheba: a standard editorial rubric, not necessarily determinative for dating this chapter *vis à vis* ch. 18. **Gilead:** all the Transjordan tribes. **as one man:** the key is the new-found unity, missing since ch. 1. **before the LORD:** usually indicates the presence of an oracle or altar, if not a full sanctuary. **Mizpah:** possibly Tell en-Nasbeh, eight miles north of Jerusalem. Cf. 1 Sam. 7 and especially 10: 17. **2. four hundred thousand:** on the large numbers, see note on 8: 10 and *NBD*, pp. 895–898. *AB* renders '400 contingents'. **13. wicked men:** see note on 19: 22. **15, 16. In addition . . . those living in Gibeah . . . seven hundred chosen men. Among all these . . . seven hundred . . . left-handed. . . .:** many scholars favour the idea that both groups of 700 were the same. See' NEB. **left-handed:** a Benjaminite heroic quality. See note on 3: 15. **sling:** a powerful weapon often used for large stones. Cf. 1 Chr. 12: 2. **not miss:** Heb. *ḥāṭā*, a frequent term for the act of sinning. **18. Bethel:** lit. 'house of God'. Although the tabernacle-sanctuary is usually called *bêt-'elōhîm* rather than the shortened *bêt-'ēl*, quite possibly the term here should not be taken as a place-name. No reason appears for a move from Mizpah (v. 1) to Bethel (cf. v. 26). **Judah:** cf. 1: 2. **26. Bethel:** *AB* suggests that only here does Bethel become a place-name, as the focus shifts to the ark, but the sole appearance of which is here. But nowhere else does Bethel appear to be the central sanctuary and it may be better to take all references as indeterminate. The ark is next mentioned as in Shiloh (1 Sam. 1–3). **28. Phinehas:** there is

no need to question that Phinehas here is the
grandson of Aaron (1 Chr. 6: 4), son of Eleazar.
The Shiloh priesthood (Eli) of 1 Sam. 1–3
comes from Aaron's other son Ithamar. **33.
Baal-tamar:** unidentified. **west of Gibeah:**
RSV follows LXX (cf. Heb. 'plain of Geba').
Geba (modern Jeba) was a short distance
north-east of Gibeah. NEB 'neighbourhood of
Gibeah' is an unnecessary emendation. **34. on
Gibeah:** lit. 'in front of', probably meaning
'east of'. **38. had arranged:** the sign was apparently the successful ambush (cf. v. 40). **42. the
men of Israel who came out of the towns:**
NEB follows Vulgate 'town', referring to the
ambush group. RSV and Heb. picture townsmen from cities on the route joining in. **43.
They surrounded:** RSV avoids Heb. 'surrounding', as surrounded men are not pursued!
NEB envisions the group 'hemmed in' and
driven as a solid mass to Geba (Driver, p. 20).
Gibeah: likely 'Geba' should be read. **45. rock
of Rimmon:** modern Rammun, a stronghold
four miles east of Bethel. **Gidom:** possibly
Geba. NEB 'cut down' is likewise conjectural.
48. towns: RSV has dropped the phrase *mēʿîr
mᵉtōm* ('entire city') in favour of *mᵉtîm* (men).
NEB 'the people in the towns' is closer to the
text.

**v. Final Conclusion: need for a king (21:
1–25)**
The restored unity of the tribes at Mizpah was
vital for the national survival and cleansing.
The oaths (vv. 1, 5) were undertaken in that
spirit; any violation of covenant unity called
for cutting off the offender and ensuring an end
to his posterity. The implications of this seem
not to have been worked out at Mizpah, and
only after the 'ban' led to the decimation of all
but 600 in Benjamin was it recognized that
this too left the covenant-league permanently
fractured. The indiscriminate killing and burning (20: 48) had left Benjamin with virtually
no tribe to reform. The solution was to apply
the same tactic to another group. Since the
hapless Jabesh-gileadites lacked tribal status
they were considered expendable. They are
placed under the same ban or *ḥērem* (see note
on 1: 17). The destruction of Midian (Num.
31: 17) provided the pattern for sparing only
the virgins, although in that situation the de-
flowered women were specifically charged with
the sin of seduction. That the slaughter did
not even resolve the problem (v. 14) seems
commentary enough. The second plot is pure
casuistry. The 'Big Oath' (*AB*) kept them from
'giving' their daughters but said nothing about
letting them be 'taken'. The scheme to collect
200 maidens from the Shilonites during their
yearly festival, though not apparently cleared
with them ahead (cf. v. 22), worked. The book
closes with the Benjaminites rebuilding their
shattered society. The final editorial comment

sums up the period, again from the point of
view of a later era. Even the purging of the sin
of Gibeah, and the fragile unity of the restored
covenant, is not enough. There must be a king
or at least someone with a strong central authority. 'Right' must be seen as conformity to
the covenant; not what seems to each man best
at the time. The stage is set for the rise of
Samuel, Saul and finally, God's chosen king,
David.

21: 2. weeping bitterly: cf. 2: 4 f. The
judges period begins and ends the same way.
4. built an altar, and presented: cf. 20: 26 f.,
where the offerings are already instituted in
'Bethel'. Possibly a place name is not indicated
in v. 2. **5. who from all the tribes:** Jabesh-
Gilead was not itself a tribe, but was part of
Manasseh's eastern half. **a solemn oath:** the
responsibility laid on all by the sign of the
bloody corpse was sacred and absolute. What
was being declared was a form of holy war, in
which all were bound to become participant or
foe. Verse 5 anticipates v. 8. **8. Jabesh-gilead:**
just east of the Jordan, north of the Jabbok.
The later inhabitants were closely allied to the
Benjaminite Saul (1 Sam. 11: 1–15 and 31: 11–
13. Cf. 2 Sam. 2: 4b–7). **12. took them to the
camp at Shiloh:** modern Khirbet Seilun about
three miles west of Lebonan (see detailed directions in v. 19). Although Shiloh was the great
central sanctuary of the period, the narrative
does not presuppose a knowledge of its location. **in Canaan:** as in Jos. 21: 2 and 22: 9
the contrast is between areas 'in the land of
Gilead' and those in Cis-jordan. **13. the whole
assembly . . . sent . . . an offer of peace:** this
was a formal statement of restoration (*šālôm*)
to full covenantal participation. The ban was
lifted. **17. must have heirs:** NEB takes *yᵉrûšat*
as a feminine collective: 'Heirs there must be
. . . .!' **19. the annual festival of the LORD
in Shiloh:** the account points to some local
Shilonite feast connected with grape harvest (v.
21). Cf. 1 Sam. 1: 3. **22. When their fathers
or brothers complain to us, we will say:**
NEB resolves the problem of who is speaking
by an emendation, 'complain to you, say to
them'. The text is confusing but the sense is
clear: the relatives of the stolen maidens are to
be let in on the casuistic plan. That is the end
of the matter; presumably they live happily
ever after!

BIBLIOGRAPHY

Commentaries
BOLING, R. G., *Judges.* AB (Garden City, N.Y.,
1975).
BURNEY, C. F., *The Book of Judges* (London, ²1930).
CUNDALL, A. E., *Judges,* in *Judges and Ruth* (A. E.
Cundall and L. Morris). *TOTC* (London, 1968).

GRAY, J., *Judges, in Joshua, Judges and Ruth.* New Century Bible (London, 1967).

MARTIN, J. D., *The Book of Judges. CBC* (Cambridge, 1975).

MOORE, G. F., *Judges. ICC* (Edinburgh ²1908).

SOGGIN, J. A., *Judges: A Commentary.* OTL (London, 1981).

Other works

AHARONI, Y., 'Arad: Its Inscriptions and Temple'. *BA* 31 (1968), pp.2–32.

AHARONI, Y., *The Land of the Bible* (London, 1966).

AHARONI, Y., and AVI-YONAH, M., *Macmillan Bible Atlas* (New York/London, 1968).

BALY, D., *The Geography of the Bible* (New York, 1957).

CAMPBELL, E. F., and ROSS, J. F., 'The Excavation of Shechem and the Biblical Tradition'. *BA* 26 (1963), pp.2–27.

DE GEUS, C. H. J., *The Tribes of Israel* (Assen, 1976).

DRIVER, G. R., 'Problems in Judges newly Discussed', *Annual of the Leeds University Oriental Society* 4 (1962–63), pp. 6–25.

LAPP, P. W., 'Taanach by the Waters of Megiddo'. *BA* 30 (1967), pp.2–27.

MACKENZIE, J. L., *The World of the Judges* (Englewood Cliffs, 1966).

MALAMAT, A., 'Cushan Rishathaim and the Decline of the Near East around 1200 B.C.' *JNES* 13 (1954), pp.231–242.

MAYES, A. D. H., *Israel in the Period of the Judges* (London, 1974).

MAZAR, A., 'A Philistine Temple at Tell Qasile', *BA* 36 (1973), pp.42–48.

PORTER, J. R., 'Samson's Riddle. Judges XIV.14, 18', *JTS*, n.s., 13 (1962), pp. 106–109.

TOURNAY, R. J., 'Le psaume LXVIII et le livre des Juges'. *RB* 66 (1959), pp.358–368.

WEIPPERT, M., *The Settlement of the Israelite Tribes in Palestine*, E.T. (London, 1971).

WEISER, A., 'Das Deboralied: Eine gattungs-und traditionsgeschichtliche Studie', *Zeitschrift für die Alttestamentliche Wissenschaft* 71 (1959), pp.67–97.

WRIGHT, G. E., *Shechem: The Biography of a Biblical City* (London, 1965).

RUTH

CHARLES A. OXLEY

Ruth is a story of delightful simplicity and purity, telling, mainly in conversation, of a mother, bereft of husband and sons, maintaining her faith in God; a daughter-in-law, bereft of her husband and childless, proving her devotion to her mother-in-law and to God, and an upright, generous farmer, blessed by his employees and by God. But for all its simplicity, the book poses several problems. (Cf. H. H. Rowley, 'The Marriage of Ruth', *The Servant of the Lord*, Oxford, 1965, pp. 171 ff.)

Fact or Fiction

The opening sentence gives the geographical and historical setting—Bethlehem in Judah in the days when the judges judged (1200–1020 BC) and the closing sentences fix the time to the third generation before David. Thus the return of Naomi to Bethlehem would be about 1100 B.C. But some commentators, notably O. Eissfeldt (*The Old Testament—an Introduction*, translated by P. R. Ackroyd, 1966, pp. 481 f.) and R. H. Pfeiffer (*The Books of the Old Testament*, 1957, p. 129), would separate the story from its connection with the family of David and see it as a folk-tale which, though linked with historical events, is for them 'pure fiction'. Others, notably E. J. Young (*An Introduction to the Old Testament*, 1953, p. 330) and G. T. Manley (*The New Bible Handbook*, 3rd ed., 1950), regard the book as a factual account of a sequence of actual events.

In support of the claim that Ruth is fictional, arguments advanced are (1) that the names of some of the characters fit too well. The aptness of *Mahlôn*, 'weakness', and *Kilyôn*, 'wasting away', not found elsewhere, suggests they were invented for the story, and the name *Naomi*, 'my pleasant one', though not invented, was chosen because it stands in antithesis to *Mara*, 'bitter'; (2) that Naomi, Ruth and Boaz are too good to be true and have been idealized; and (3) that a true account would have shown something of 'the rude, unsettled age of the Judges' (S. R. Driver, *Introduction to the Literature of the Old Testament*, 1898, p. 456). Against (1) it may be pointed out that Elimelech and Naomi might well have named their sons thus, particularly if the boys were sickly at birth, for *Mahlôn* would seem to be a participial form of *hālā'* or *hālāh*, 'to be sick, diseased, weak' (cf. Dt. 29: 21 (22)) and *Kilyôn* from *kālāh* 'pining', 'failing', esp. of the eyes (cf. Dt. 28: 65). Their early deaths support this possibility. Against

(2) and (3) it need only be said that the story is told simply and directly and any attempt to describe further the characters or the times in which they lived would have unnecessarily complicated the issue.

Arguments in favour of Ruth's historicity are (1) the book begins with the phrase *waye̱hî*, the normal way to begin historical narrative in Hebrew; (2) the author knew that at that time friendly relations existed between Israel and Moab (cf. 1 Sam. 22: 3–4) and when dealing with such customs as harvest gleaning by the poor, the application of the levirate marriage law, the obligation regarding retention of land within the family and customs associated therewith, the details are authentic; (3) to invent a Moabite link in David's ancestry and to incorporate the invention in a story would be highly unlikely (cf. G. Gerleman, *Ruth, BKAT*, 1960, p. 8); (4) as K. A. Kitchen states, the closing genealogy ties the narrative 'firmly into the family tradition of Judah and David' ('The Old Testament in its Context', 3, *TSF Bulletin*, No. 61, Autumn 1971, p. 8), and (5) in the genealogy of the Lord Jesus, Matthew and Luke both list Boaz and Obed, and Matthew adds 'by Ruth' (Mt. 1: 5). If the book of Ruth is fiction, the genealogy of the gospels is false.

Some scholars (E. König, A. Bertholet, S. R. Driver, W. R. Smith, L. B. Wolfenson, P. Joüon, M. Burrows and A. Vincent) argue that the genealogy of 4: 18–22 is a later addition. This is possible, but the *story*, as distinct from the *book*, ends with the words: 'and the women, the neighbours, gave him a name saying, "a son is born to Naomi"' and they called his name Obed' and the sentence continues 'he (is) the father of Jesse, the father of David'. Therefore the *story* would be incomplete without reference to Obed. But Eissfeldt goes further by removing also the latter half of verse 17 'and they called his name Obed . . .'. He thinks another name originally stood here, but was removed when the 'addition' was made (cf. Eissfeldt, *op. cit.*, p. 479). He draws attention to the unusual, perhaps unique, form of the verse, and following Peters (*Th. Rv.* 13, 1914, p. 449), suggests that the name in the original text was *Ben-no'am*, 'son of pleasantness'. A name bearing some relation to the declaration 'a son is born to Naomi' might have been expected, but *Obed*, 'servant', 'worshipper', is not inappropriate. Those who would disconnect the end of the tale from the line of David must answer the question, 'Why should a later hand gratuitously attribute Moabite ancestry to David?'—a question which raises wider ones: 'What is the purpose of the book?' and 'When was it written?'.

Authorship

A Jewish tradition (Talmud, *Baba Bathra* 14b) assigns the authorship to Samuel, but Samuel could hardly have written Ruth because (1) the custom of pulling off the sandal to confirm a transaction was said to have been no longer in use at the time of writing, thus some time must have elapsed (see 4: 7) though Driver suggests this may be an explanatory gloss (S. R. Driver, *op. cit.*, p. 455) and (2) the genealogy with which the book ends, implies that David was well known. In the absence of further evidence on authorship, it must be said 'author unknown'.

Date

We do not know when Ruth was written and widely differing dates have been suggested, *e.g.* the time of Samuel, the early monarchy, the reign of David, the reign of Solomon, the time of Hezekiah, the exilic and the post-exilic period. Arguments for a late date are based on (1) the belief that it was written as a tract in opposition to Ezra and Nehemiah in their stern measures against mixed marriages (Ezr. 10: 11; Neh. 13: 23–27); (2) that the 'breadth of outlook towards other nations' which appears in Ruth 'is more readily intelligible in a later than in an earlier period' (Eissfeldt, *op. cit.*, p. 483); and (3) the presence of several words and forms believed to be Aramaic and consequently thought to be late. Against (1) it must be said that anything less like a polemic tract in form and style could hardly be found, and, as Rowley has pointed out, it is just as easy to regard the book as a *defence* of the Ezra–Nehemiah policy (H. H. Rowley, *op. cit.*, p. 173, and his *Israel's Mission to the World*, 1939, pp. 46 ff.). Against (2) it must be asked, 'Where is the evidence for the alleged broadening of outlook toward other nations in the post-exilic period?' The exile intensified the consciousness of unique religious possessions which found expression in the restoration of the temple and its ritual. The rival Samaritan community was bluntly told, 'You have no portion, or right or memorial in Jerusalem' (Neh. 2: 20). Ezra believed that the survival of Judaism depended on their religious separateness and took strong action to prevent any intermingling of the Jews of Jerusalem with the 'people of the land'. Even two and a half centuries later, the Syrian attempt to Hellenize the Jewish religion resulted in the famous Maccabaean Revolt and as late as the first century A.D., Tacitus wrote, 'Among themselves they are inflexibly honest, and ever ready to show compassion, though

they regard the rest of mankind with all the hatred of enemies' (Tacitus, *Histories*, 5.5, Eng. trans. by Church and Brodribb, p. 195). The book of Jonah is regarded by some as evidence of the alleged 'broader outlook' of the post-exilic period, but the chief reason for ascribing a post-exilic date to Jonah is its 'broad universalism and tolerant humanity'! (cf. Eissfeldt, *op. cit.*, p. 405). On the other hand, a significant feature of the time of David is the extent of friendly relations with surrounding peoples. Against (3) the first point to be made is that the presence of Aramaic words or forms in a Hebrew document does not necessarily show that the document is of late origin. While it is true that Aramaic gradually replaced Hebrew as the common language after the exile, Hebrew from earliest times contained West-Semitic words and forms common to both Hebrew and its sister-tongue Aramaic. Furthermore, linguistic borrowing would result from association with Syrian Aram from the time of David. In any case, it is doubtful whether more than two or three of the words cited as late are genuine Aramaisms and these can more easily be accounted for as a scribal change or a gloss than by post-dating the whole book.

Positive evidence for a date during the reign of David is based on (1) the fact that the language and style of Ruth are classical Hebrew and, as S. R. Driver wrote in 1891, 'The general Hebrew style . . . stands on a level with the best parts of Samuel' (Driver, *op. cit.*, p. 454); (2) the presence of a number of archaic grammatical forms, particularly confusion of gender, found in the dialogue; (3) that the story is set in the form of an historical narrative and convincingly describes the characters and customs of the time; (4) that the kindness shown to Ruth is consistent with the general attitude to foreigners in the time of David, *e.g.* Moabites, 1 Sam. 22: 3; Gittites, 2 Sam. 6: 10; 15: 18, 19; Ammonites, 2 Sam. 10: 2; 17: 27; 23: 37; Cherethites and Pelethites, 2 Sam. 8: 18; 15: 18; Hittites, 2 Sam. 11: 3; 23: 39; and Archites, 2 Sam. 15: 32; (5) the absence of Solomon's name after David's would suggest a date during the reign of David or before Solomon was established; (6) the Talmudic tradition that Ruth originally formed part of Judges and that in the LXX, probably the earliest evidence for the order of the books, and in the Vulgate and subsequent Western translations, Ruth immediately follows Judges. Further evidence for the original placing of Ruth among the historical books comes from Josephus (*Contra Apionem* 1: 8), Melito of Sardis, Jerome (*Prologus Galeatus*) and a very old Hebrew-Aramaic list of Old Testament books. But in the Hebrew Bible Ruth is placed in the Kᵉtûbîm (Hagiographa or Writings), the third and last part of the Old Testament to be accepted as canonical. In the Babylonian Talmud, Ruth is first in the Kᵉtûḇîm before Psalms. Other lists place Ruth first of the Megillôt (the five 'Scrolls'). It is known that by the sixth century A.D., Ruth was in its present position in the Hebrew Bible, second in the Megillôt, and was read in the synagogue on the Feast of Weeks (Pentecost), which marks the completion of the barley harvest. Ruth was probably placed among the historical books first and later, when used liturgically, transferred to the Megillôt. If so, this would support an early date for Ruth. All this does not amount to proof, but the weight of evidence would seem to favour a date in the reign of David or Solomon.

The Purpose of the Book

The author did not state his purpose nor is it clearly evident in what he wrote. But there must have been some purpose even if it were the purely literary one of writing a pleasing short story. Some argue that Ruth was written to advocate a universalism which would embrace all foreigners, even those of Israel's traditional enemy, Moab; but in the story, the initiative is taken by Ruth, who, devoted to her mother-in-law, declares her allegiance to Naomi's God. Ruth is no missionary report. John Gray sees Ruth as a call to returning exiles in a time of restoration for faith in God, charity to aliens and 'loyalty to the good old social standards' (*New Century Bible*, Ruth, p. 402). Others argue that the whole point of the story is to account for the ancestry of David and to give a biographical sketch of his pious forbears. But the mention of David as the son of Jesse at the end of the story (4: 17b) and in the closing genealogy hardly stands out as the climax of the story. Driver sees a dual purpose: partly to supply an ancestry for David and partly to show how Ruth, a daughter of Moab, theocratically hostile to Israel, obtained an honourable position among the people of Yahweh (*op. cit.*, p. 454). Driver also sees a 'collateral didactic aim' to inculcate the duty of marriage on the part of the next of kin with a widow left childless. But as N. K. Gottwald comments, if Ruth is intended to revive or preserve the ancient custom of levirate marriage, it is not very clear in its depiction of the practice (Gottwald, *A Light to the Nations*, p. 518).

W. E. Staples has suggested that the book was composed as a midrash on a Bethlehem fertility-cult myth, with Elimelech representing the dying god, Naomi the mother-goddess and Ruth her devotee. Eduard Reuss (1804–1891) saw the story as a demonstration of a union, in the line of David, of Judah in Boaz and of Northern Israel in Mahlon, mistakenly equating *Ephrathite* with *Ephraimite* (though see

Jg. 12: 5; 1 Sam. 1: 1; 1 Kg. 11: 26). Ruth has even been seen as having a polemic purpose against Athaliah! Eissfeldt sees a similarity in purpose with the book of Job: restoration by God of what He has taken away after the endurance of suffering and trial. What K. A. Kitchen wrote of Jonah is also true of Ruth, viz. 'Once one discards the *straight* interpretation of this book as a plain narrative, then a chaos of rival interpretation ensues without any single clear solution' (Kitchen, 'The Old Testament in its Context', 4, *TSF Bulletin*, No. 62, Spring 1972, p. 6).

The present writer is convinced that the author was inspired to write the story of Ruth because it was a true story well worth telling. Its worth lies in its interesting facts about interesting people. That it contains much that is instructive, illuminating and uplifting is incidental, but all the more acceptable and enjoyable for being so. Among other things we see (1) that the LORD in His sovereignty was working out His cosmic purposes while intimately involved with persons who otherwise would have been ordinary; (2) that there is dignity and sacredness in much that we regard as secular and commonplace, even distasteful, *e.g.* work; (3) that the emergence of David was providential not fortuitous (G. T. Manley, *The New Bible Handbook*, p. 166); (4) that true religion is supranational; (5) that love has power to break through the barriers of alienations, hostilities and prejudices which we build high around ourselves; (6) that a foreigner who trusted in God and wished to be identified with the people of God was worthy of full acceptance; and (7) that all who put their trust in God's loving kindness (*hesed*) and who express it in their dealings with others will be richly blessed.

An interesting point is the function of the kinsman (*gō'ēl*), the light it throws on the statement that Yahweh was Israel's *Gō'ēl*, Redeemer (*e.g.* Isa. 41: 14), and the pointer it gives to redemption under the new covenant and to the Redeemer. Those who use Ruth to illustrate the NT gospel should point out among other differences that whereas Ruth had a legal claim on her kinsman, the sinner has no such claims on God's deliverance. And those who exercise their ingenuity here in allegorization would be better employed applying the real lessons of this story to today's problems (cf. H. L. Ellison, *The Message of the Old Testament*, p. 81). Ruth has particular relevance to the present time, when an unwillingness to put God first, others second and ourselves last results in the breakdown of family life, the loosening of family ties and the shirking of family responsibilities.

ANALYSIS

I. RUTH COMES TO BETHLEHEM (1: 1–22)

i. An Israelite family in Moab (1: 1–5)

A famine in the land of Judah caused **Elimelech** ('God is king'), his wife **Naomi** ('My pleasant one') and their sons, **Mahlon** ('Sickly') and **Kilion** ('Failing'), to leave their home in **Bethlehem** ('House of Bread') to stay in **Moab**, a plateau east of the Dead Sea. It is ironic that they should leave the 'House of Bread' in the land of promise for Moab, but **in the days when the judges ruled** there was religious apostasy and the Lord visited His people grievously. That they intended to return may be deduced from the use of the verb *gûr*, 'to sojourn, lodge'. Ephrath(ah) was an earlier name for Bethlehem (Gen. 35: 19; 48: 7; Mic. 5: 2 and see parallelism in 4: 11), hence the family is called **Ephrathites**. After Elimelech's death, Mahlon married **Ruth** and Kilion married **Orpah**; both brides were Moabitesses. The law did not prohibit marriage to a Moabite, but there were certain restrictions on Moabites' admission to the congregation (Dt. 23: 3; cf. Neh. 13: 23–30). Ruth and Orpah are not Hebrew names and the meanings are uncertain. **4. about ten years:** probably covered the whole time in Moab and the marriages may have taken place towards the end of this time. Mahlon and Kilion died. The narrator here focuses attention on Naomi, widowed, bereft of sons and in an alien land, all of which circumstances had religious significance.

ii. Ruth's determination to go with Naomi (1: 6–18)

Naomi decided **to return** to Bethlehem when news reached Moab **that the LORD had come to the aid of his people by providing food for them** (lit. *bread*). The verb 'visit', *p̄aqad̄*, can mean 'to come in blessing', often to end a time of trial, *e.g.* Gen. 21: 1; 50: 24, 25; Exod. 13: 19; Jer. 15: 15; 27: 22; 29: 10; esp. Ps. 65: 9. But the verb can also mean 'punish' as in Amos 3:2, 14 *et al.*

Naomi, not wishing to commit her daughters-in-law to life in an alien land, tells them to return to their own families. **8.** She acknowledges their kindness to their husbands and to herself and prays that the LORD will **show kindness** to them (show *ḥesed̄*, 'loving kindness', 'steadfast love') and grant them rest (*mᵉnûḥāh*, see 3: 1) in remarriage. (Note: *ḥesed̄* is a characteristic of the LORD Himself, expressed mainly in His covenant keeping. It is much stronger than *kindness*.) She kissed them goodbye, but they said they would go with her. Naomi, addressing them affectionately as **my daughters**, again advises them to go back. In a series of rhetorical questions, Naomi, with the levirate marriage provision in mind (Dt. 25: 5 ff.), argues that she cannot hope to bear sons to provide them with husbands and in any case they could not be expected to wait. **13.** The RSV translation conveys the thought that Naomi expresses regret that her daughters-in-law have been involved in her affliction, but

343

the Hebrew is 'for (it is) much more bitter for me than (it is) for you, for the hand of the LORD is gone out against me'. Her meaning seems to be 'I have lost husband and sons and am too old to remarry and have sons. You have lost husbands, but are young enough to remarry and have sons. Why share my affliction?' It is significant that Naomi does not attribute her affliction to chance misfortune but to 'the hand of the LORD', a common anthropomorphism for the LORD's over-ruling activity, acknowledged throughout the story. **14.** **Orpah**, evidently convinced by the argument, bade farewell and returned. It is unjust to blame Orpah for her decision. We do not know all the circumstances; for example, she may have known of Ruth's determination and that Naomi would not be left alone. But **Ruth**, with a stronger loyalty and closer bond of affection, **clung to** Naomi (*dābaq*, 'cleave', Gen. 2: 24; Ru. 2: 8, 21). **15.** Again Naomi encourages Ruth to return after her sister-in-law who was **going back to her people and her gods** (or 'god', Chemosh, Num. 21: 29), but Ruth, firmly resolved, expresses her determination in phrases of indescribable beauty. She declares her loyalty to Naomi, her willingness to identify with the people of Israel and her devotion to Naomi's God. Her promise is sealed with an oath invoking the LORD's judgment if she fails to fulfil it. This oath formula, possibly accompanied with a gesture, is found in full in Samuel and Kings but in abbreviated form elsewhere. **18.** Seeing the strength and character of Ruth's decision, Naomi **stopped urging her.**

iii. Naomi and Ruth arrive at Bethlehem (1: 19–22)

19. The arrival of Naomi and Ruth at Bethlehem caused considerable excitement. The women's question **'Can this be Naomi?'** suggests that the intervening years and her bereavements had altered her appearance. **20.** Naomi picks up the meaning of her name and replies, **'Don't call me Naomi** ('Pleasant'), **Call me Mara** ('Bitter'), **because the Almighty has made my life very bitter'.** This divine name *'El Shaddai* is nearly always used in God's dealings with individuals in affliction. (See Additional Note on *šadday* by L. Morris in *Judges–Ruth*, TOTC, 1968, p. 264.) **21.** The RSV translation **the LORD has afflicted me** is based on the Greek, Syriac and Latin emendation of the Hebrew text which is 'the LORD has testified against me', i.e. the LORD has demonstrated His displeasure with me, therefore do not call me 'Pleasant One'. The clause **the Almighty has brought misfortune upon me** completes the parallelism. Naomi exaggerates the adverse change in her circumstances. She went out with a full family but at a time of famine and though the LORD brought her back empty (i.e. bereft) of husband and sons, she came back with a devoted daughter-in-law, to sympathetic neighbours and at harvest-time. **22.** The narrator here seems gently to be making this point.

II. RUTH MEETS BOAZ (2: 1–23)
i. Ruth gleans in the fields of Boaz (2: 1–7)
1. Boaz, introduced as a relative of Elimelech, is described as **a man of standing**, Heb. *'ish gibbôr ḥayil*, usually translated 'man of valour' (cf. 3: 11, 'woman of worth', applied to Ruth). Both facts are significant, for Boaz, 'Strength' (see 1 Kings 7: 21), was legally and financially able to perform the part of the *gō'ēl*, 'kinsman' (see 3: 2). **2.** Ruth, aware of the legal rights of the poor to gather what was left by the reapers, set out to **pick up the leftover** ears of corn. Reapers were forbidden to reap to the very borders, nor might they be sent over the fields a second time (Lev. 19: 9; 23: 22; Dt. 24: 19). **3.** Ruth **as it turned out** came to a field owned by Boaz. As far as she was concerned it was by chance, but God overruled it: a fact which is not stated but everywhere implied. **4.** Something of the character of Boaz is seen in the greetings exchanged with his employees. **5.** Boaz asks his foreman, **'Whose** young woman is that?' (not 'who is that?'). **6.** He answered 'The Moabitess, who returned from Moab **with Naomi'. 7.** He continued that she had asked permission to **glean** and that she had worked with only a short rest. The Hebrew of this clause is uncertain: lit. 'this her sitting the house a little.'

ii. Boaz offers protection and shows kindness (2: 8–16)
8–9. Knowing of Ruth's loyalty to Naomi and to the LORD and aware of the possibility of her being driven off or molested, Boaz shows concern and advises her to glean with his maidservants and drink of the water, presumably, though Joüon thinks wine, drawn by his men and informs her that he has instructed them not to harm her. **10.** Ruth bowed **to the ground**, an action symbolic of humble gratitude. Her question contains cognate words in Hebrew, perhaps a play on words, lost in translation: 'Why do you *take notice* of me when I am *not-worthy-of-notice*?' **11.** Boaz answered that he knew of her dealings with Naomi and her faith in leaving her kindred and entrusting herself to an unknown people. The use of the infinitive absolute justifies **all. 12.** Boaz gives a blessing, significantly using the name **the LORD** (Heb. *Yahweh*), the covenant-keeping God. **wings:** a common figure for God's protective presence (cf. Ps. 91: 4; 17: 8; 36: 7). **13.** Ruth's reply is the equivalent of 'Thank you, sir'. Using the Hebrew idiom 'spoken to the heart' for **spoken kindly**, she calls herself his *šiphâh*, **servant**, more menial than *'āmâh* (cf. 3:

9). **14.** Boaz invites Ruth to join his party at meal-time and showed special favour by offering her freshly roasted **grain. 15–16.** Boaz instructed the reapers to let her glean **among the sheaves** rather than after the reapers and even to **pull out** for her some stalks already gathered into **bundles.**

iii. Ruth returns to Naomi (2: 17–23)
17–19. Ruth worked **until evening**, threshed the ears of barley and found she had gathered **an ephah**, equivalent to 22 litres or 4 gallons 6¾ pints. This, with what was left from the midday meal, she took to Naomi, who asked where she had gleaned and, realizing by the amount that someone had been specially helpful, added, **'Blessed be the man who took notice of you'.** Ruth told her it was Boaz. **20.** Naomi prays the blessing of the LORD upon Boaz and speaks of the LORD's **kindness** in not having forgotten **the living** (Naomi) **and the dead** (Elimelech, Mahlon and Kilion), by which she meant the LORD had fulfilled His covenant promise of *ḥeseḏ* 'loving-kindness'. Naomi went on to tell her that Boaz was a close **relative. 21–22.** Ruth told her of Boaz' instruction to stay **with** his **workers** until they had finished **harvesting** and Naomi agreed she should do so 'because in someone else's field you might be harmed.' (The verb *pāgaʿ* does not necessarily mean 'molest'.) **23.** Ruth did so through **the barley and wheat harvests**, i.e. April and May. (See *NBD* under 'Agriculture' and 'Calendar'.)

III. RUTH CLAIMS THE PROTECTION OF THE KINSMAN
(3: 1–18)

i. Naomi's advice (3: 1–5)
1. Naomi, characteristically in a rhetorical question, raises the matter of finding *mānôaḥ*, 'rest' (see 1: 9 for the almost identical word *mᵉnûḥāh*). This is not merely **a home.** It is an end to the uncertainties associated with the life of a young unmarried or widowed woman in that society and a 'settling down' with husband and the prospect of children, personal fulfilment and financial security. **2.** The point of her second rhetorical question is bound up with the function of the *gōʾēl*, 'next of kin'. The root verb means 'to serve as kinsman' whose responsibility it was to restore to a family property of which it had been dispossessed, to protect family rights and to avenge any wrong. The term was commonly used in civil law. Hence it meant 'to redeem' or 'buy back', 'to avenge' or 'vindicate'. Yahweh retained ownership of the land (Lev. 25: 23); thus it was not possible to buy land freehold. Israelites received the use and produce of the land by lot as an inheritance. In hard times, the leasehold could be sold, but it was the legal duty of the next of kin to redeem the property by purchasing it

and to restore it to the original owner or his heirs. If this were not done, the property was returned without compensation at the next year of jubilee (see Lev. 25: 10; 13–16; 24–28). It was the duty of a *gōʾēl* to marry the widow of his brother, if he should die childless, so that his brother's (or relative's) name should not be 'cut off in Israel'. Though these two institutions were not connected in the Mosaic law, they naturally came together and according to 4: 5 it was then the traditional practice to require the *gōʾēl* who redeemed the property also to marry the widow (or the heir's widow, as in this case) that the family might not die out but continue in possession of the property. **2b–4.** Naomi stated that Boaz would be on **the threshing-floor** that night and instructed Ruth to make herself presentable and at the right time and in an apparently appropriate manner present herself to him. **5.** Ruth agreed to do so.

ii. Ruth at the winepress (3: 6–13)
6–7. Waiting until Boaz had finished his meal and had lain down by the heap of grain, Ruth came silently and **lay down** at his feet. **8–9. In the middle of the night**, Boaz became aware of her presence and asked **'Who are you?'** Ruth told him and, using the euphemism **spread the corner of your garment over me**, asked him to marry her, adding 'since you are a kinsman-redeemer'. The word translated **the corner of your garment** is also translated *wings* 2: 12 but they are different figures. **10.** Boaz invokes on her the blessing of the LORD and praises her devotion saying, in effect, that her loyalty to her deceased husband in marrying a middle-aged *gōʾēl* to perpetuate his name and inheritance instead of seeking a husband from among the **younger** (lit. desirable) set was greater evidence of her devotion than that shown by returning with Naomi. **11.** Addressing her again as **my daughter**, he promised to discharge his responsibilities, adding **All my fellow townsmen** respect you, lit. 'all the gate of my people' (see Gen. 34: 24; Dt. 17: 2) **know that you are a woman** (or wife) **of noble character. 12.** Boaz emphatically acknowledges he is a **near of kin** but says there is one **nearer. 13.** He tells Ruth to lie until morning and promises with an oath to redeem the property if the *gōʾēl* with prior claim declines.

iii. Ruth returns to Naomi (3: 14–18)
14. To safeguard their reputations, Ruth left before there was sufficient light to recognize anyone. **15.** Boaz poured **six measures of barley** into her shawl. The measure is not specified but according to the Targum it was six seahs, a load of 88 lbs. **16–17.** Returning to Naomi, Ruth told her what had happened, adding that Boaz had sent the barley saying that she must not return empty to Naomi, who would no doubt recall her own complaint (1:

21). **18.** Naomi was confident that Boaz would deal with the matter that same day and told Ruth to 'sit still'.

IV. BOAZ MARRIES RUTH (4: 1–22)
i. Boaz assumed the right of redemption (4: 1–12)
1. Boaz took up a place at the town **gate**, where he met the nearer kinsman and called him over. The gate was the centre of town life, where legal business was transacted (see 2 Sam. 15: 2). It is significant that the name of the *gō'ēl* who declined to perpetuate the name of Elimelech to preserve his own is not mentioned. **2.** Boaz called ten **elders** as witnesses. **3.** Boaz informed the nearer kinsman that Naomi **is selling** the field-portion **that belonged to Elimelech**, but now seems to have been held in trust by Naomi for his heirs. The verb in Hebrew is in the perfect and would normally be translated 'has sold' but v. 5 shows the sale to be in the future and v. 9 that it was sold that day. Sometimes a perfect is used of an imminent action (cf. Gen. 23: 11). Naomi was offering the land to a *gō'ēl* before offering it to anyone else. **4.** Boaz gives him the opportunity to redeem the land, making it clear that should he decline, Boaz himself would redeem it. The man undertook to redeem it. **5.** Then Boaz informed him that in doing so, he must **'acquire'** i.e. marry Ruth **to maintain the name of the dead with his property. 6.** This effectively changed the whole position. Adding a piece of land to his property was one thing; taking on the responsibility of a (second) wife with the prospect of a son who would inherit the property was another. He passed the right and duty to Boaz. **7–8.** The transfer of this right was attested by the taking off and giving of a shoe—a custom which the narrator tells us had ceased by the time the story was written. **9–10.** Boaz declared the elders and the people **witnesses** that he had **bought** the inheritance of Elimelech and his sons and had acquired **Ruth** as his **wife**. The purpose is fully stated and the declaration ends as it began: **Today you are witnesses.** In the absence of written evidence of the transaction, sufficient reliable witness was essential. **11–12.** The people and the elders confirmed they were witnesses and added a traditional blessing: **like Rachel and Leah . . .** (the two wives of Jacob, to whom were credited the sons of their handmaids), a simile for fruitfulness. The adjective clause changes the figure to building a house, but house is a dead metaphor. A poetic parallelism ends v. 11 (see 1: 2). A further simile for fruitfulness is given—**like that of Perez, whom Tamar bore to Judah:** though the resemblance here lies in the similarity of circumstances and Perez' association with Bethlehem. (1 Chr. 2: 5, 18, 50 f.) The point is

made explicitly **Through the offspring** (lit. seed) **the LORD gives you** (i.e. Boaz) **by this young woman:** This suggests that Boaz may have been childless (see H. H. Rowley, *The Servant of the Lord*, pp. 192 f.).

ii. Ruth bears a son (4: 13–17)
13. Without details of the marriage ceremony, we are told Ruth became the wife of Boaz. The narrator, as did the people, acknowledges the conception and birth of a son as the LORD's gift. **14.** Likewise the women praise the LORD as they share Naomi's pleasure at the redemption and pray that the baby boy now referred to as the kinsman-redeemer will be famous throughout Israel. **15.** The prayer becomes a prophecy: **He will renew your life and sustain you in your old age.** Recognition of Ruth's loyalty is appropriately given as the story ends and the tribute, **better to you than seven sons**, is a powerful one, since seven sons was proverbially the perfect family (cf. 1 Sam. 1: 8; 2: 5). **16.** Naomi regarded the child as her own **and cared for him.** Legally she might have claimed him but it is clear that the basis of the relationship was love and joy. **17.** The townswomen recognized the special relationship between Naomi and the child and, perhaps in their excitement, even gave the baby a name: **Obed**, 'Servant' or 'Worshipper' (see Introduction).

iii. Genealogical note (4: 18–22)
Perez was the founder of the family of Judah to which Elimelech and Boaz belonged (Gen. 38: 29). Evidently several of the intermediate links have been omitted because the ten generations mentioned span more than seven centuries, from around 1700 to 970 B.C. The names mentioned in these verses reappear word for word in Matthew's genealogy of the Lord Jesus Christ. Ruth demonstrates that God overrules in the affairs of ordinary men and women as He works out His eternal purposes in the redemption of mankind.

BIBLIOGRAPHY

Commentaries
ATKINSON D., *The Message of Ruth. IVP* (Leicester, 1983).
CAMPBELL, E. F., *Ruth. AB* (Garden City, N.Y., 1975).
COOKE, G. A., *The Book of Ruth, Cambridge Bible* (Cambridge, 1913).
FUERST, W. J., *The Books of Ruth, Esther, Ecclesiastes, The Song of Songs, Lamentations. CBC* (Cambridge, 1975).
GRAY, J., *Joshua, Judges and Ruth*, New Century Bible (London, 1967).
KNIGHT, G. A. F., *Ruth and Jonah, TC* (London, 1950).

LATTEY, C., *The Book of Ruth*, Westminster Version of the Sacred Scriptures (London, 1935).

MORRIS, L., in Cundall, A. E., and Morris, L., *Judges and Ruth, TOTC* (London, 1968).

SMITH, L. P., 'Ruth', in *Interpreter's Bible*, II (New York, 1953).

Other works

ROBERTSON, E., 'The Plot of the Book of Ruth', *BJRL* 32 (1949–50), pp.207 ff.

ROWLEY, H. H., 'The Marriage of Ruth', *The Servant of the Lord and Other Essays on the Old Testament* (Oxford, 1965), pp.171 ff.

1 and 2 SAMUEL

LAURENCE E. PORTER

In the Hebrew Old Testament, 1–2 Sam., with Jos., Jg., and 1–2 Kg., are designated the 'former prophets' to distinguish them from the 'latter prophets' which we call the prophetic books. *Samuel* and *Kings* each originally formed one book; each became two books in the Greek OT on account of the length of the scrolls in common use. In the Hebrew the division was first made in the renaissance edition of Daniel Bomberg (Venice, 1516), though it occurs in MSS as early as 1477 (so L. H. Brockington in *Peake*[2]; Eissfeldt, Mauchline, *et alii* say 1448). In the Massoretic (Hebrew) text, 1–2 Sam. are simply 'Samuel', a title which cannot indicate *authorship*, since Samuel's death is recorded before the end of the first book; nor *subject*, since David plays by far the major part. In the LXX (Greek OT), 1–2 Sam. with 1–2 Kg. are entitled the books of the 'Kingdoms'; in the Latin they become the four books of Kings. And yet the name of Samuel is fittingly associated with the work; under God he brought the era of the Judges to its climax, and laid the foundation of the monarchy itself.

Composition and sources

Historical books in the OT can rarely be assigned to any particular date or author. In the ancient world authorship was not an exclusive property with financial worth as modern copyright law has made it, so nothing was gained by attaching one's name to one's composition. Then, the events recorded extend over a century. Many parts read like eye witness reports or contemporary documents; so the work contains not so much history composed from a study of sources, as a compilation of the sources themselves.

Critics differ as to exact details, but a multiplicity of sources is generally recognized, including sometimes variant accounts of particular events. The number of main sources is differently estimated by various scholars. R. H. Pfeiffer, *Introduction to the OT* (1941) sees two, one early and the other considerably later. A. R. S. Kennedy (pp. 13–26), on the other hand, distinguishes five:

S: The early stories of Samuel.
A: A history of the Ark of the Covenant.
M: A history of the monarchy favourable to it.
D: A history of the monarchy hostile to it, 'Deuteronomic' in outlook.

C: The history of David's court and the struggle for the succession.

Other views vary between these two, but most seem in agreement that:

1. There is some connection between the various sources used and the assumed sources of the Pentateuch.
2. The final compilation took place after the 'Deuteronomic' reformation of King Josiah in 621 BC, and reflects the moral and religious outlook of that movement. Such a view is not of itself objectionable; all historians start from their own particular philosophy of history. The historical books in general are imbued with the teaching of Dt. that the fortunes of the nation prosper in direct proportion to the people's obedience to, or apostasy from, Yahweh. But those critics go too far who suggest that the history is manipulated to fit in with this outlook.

For a fair statement of current critical views, see G. W. Anderson, *A critical introduction to the OT* (1959), pp. 71–81; for a more conservative approach, E. Robertson, 'Samuel and Saul' in *The OT Problem* (1946), pp. 105–136.

The Text

'The Hebrew text has come to us much corrupted in transmission, imperfect to a greater degree than that of any other part of the OT, with perhaps one exception' (H. P. Smith, p. vii). Indeed, there are few parts of the OT which show such divergences between the Massoretic (Hebrew) and the Septuagint (Greek; LXX) versions. Furthermore, there are also considerable variations between the readings of A (Codex Alexandrinus) and B (Codex Vaticanus) of LXX. Occasionally the Greek clearly preserves a more credible text and resolves some of the obscurities of the Hebrew text. But, as has been often pointed out (*e.g.* D. F. Payne, *NBC*[3], p. 318), it is a basic canon of textual criticism that the more difficult reading is more likely to represent what was originally written, since a less difficult may indicate deliberate simplification.

Mauchline (pp. 33 f.) notes that further light is shed on the text by some first century fragments discovered at Qumran. Though not very extensive, they lend some support to the LXX recensions, which is interesting since they represent a Hebrew text older than the Massoretic

—a Hebrew text, in fact, similar to that which the author of Chronicles knew.

Textual evidence at present available is of great interest, but does not permit of finality of judgment.

The books of Samuel as history

'The historical importance of the Books of Samuel must be evident to the least attentive reader. In them we have the only sources of information concerning the origin of the monarchy in Israel. How much this implies will be seen if we suppose the names of Samuel, Saul and David blotted out of our history of Israel' (H. P. Smith, *ibid.*). 1–2 Sam. are, indeed, generally regarded as of high historical worth. Their background agrees with what is known from other sources; evidence brought by archaeology for this period usually supports the scripture narrative. There are difficulties, to be sure, but had all incongruities been harmonized it would have rendered the history more suspect rather than more credible. The problem of suspiciously large numbers is referred to below.

The *chronology* of the period cannot be established with complete certainty. Some periods stated, such as the forty years' reigns of Saul (Ac. 13: 21, also Josephus, but not in OT) and David (2 Sam. 5: 4) overlapped by an extent impossible to determine. In these cases, furthermore, it must be recognized that forty was often used to denote an approximate round number. Chronological schemes are suggested in the various text-books; as an indication it might be mentioned that F. F. Bruce, *Israel and the Nations*, and the *New Bible Dictionary* (K. A. Kitchen, T. C. Mitchell) put the death of Saul at 1010 B.C. and of Solomon at 930 B.C. John Bright, *History of Israel*, who represents contemporary moderately critical scholarship, says 1000 B.C. and 922 B.C. respectively.

The books of Samuel as literature

These books, which tell of the establishment of the monarchy and the epic story of King David, are clothed in a style worthy of the literary renown of the 'sweet singer of Israel'. In the purely historical parts the description is vivid, the action fast-moving and the characterization superb. The court annals reveal a psychological insight no less perceptive than that of the greatest among modern creative writers. R. N. Whybray, *The Succession Narrative* (1968), contrasts these chapters with earlier biblical sagas which are in the nature of popular narratives and with history woven together from earlier sources; he sees here something more akin by its nature to the novel, assessable on the standards of the modern novel, the classical novel since the eighteenth century, 'a novel with a plot brought to a definite conclusion'. To use the word 'novel' is a little misleading, for the general reader associates novels with fiction, by definition that which is not true. But here no denial of historicity is implied; the term indicates the literary form and quality of the writing: a work may be a historical novel and at the same time history none the less. What Whybray says of the succession narrative is generally true of much of the rest of 1–2 Sam.

These documents contain also a considerable *poetic* element. The song of thanksgiving of Hannah (1 Sam. 2: 1–10) when she knew her prayer was answered is echoed in the spirit and sometimes the very language of Mary's 'Magnificat' (Lk. 1: 46–55). A moving elegy on Saul and Jonathan is in 2 Sam. 1: 19–27, and elegiac fragments in 3: 33, 34 (on Abner), and 18: 33; 19: 4 (on Absalom). 2 Sam. 22 reappears verbatim in the psalter as Ps. 18. The 'last words of David' (2 Sam. 23: 1–7) are a psalm not included in the psalter, but none the less poetic in atmosphere and literary form, recalling the oracles of Balaam in Num. 24. The lines centre on a beautiful description of the ideal ruler.

This poetic element is not restricted to purely poetic passages. The language of the entire work abounds in strikingly felicitous expressions, many of which in their AV translation have long been part of our literary heritage. A small selection will recall many phrases memorable still in the RSV: 'the glory has departed' (1 Sam. 5: 21), 'hitherto the LORD has helped us' (7: 12), 'a man after his (i.e. God's) own heart' (13: 14), 'the Glory of Israel will not lie or repent' (15: 29), 'there is but a step between me and death' (20: 3), 'bound up in the bundle of the living' (25: 29), hunted like 'a partridge in the mountains' (26: 20), 'a prince and a great man has fallen this day' (2 Sam. 3: 38), 'water spilt on the ground' (14: 14), 'as a bride comes home to her husband' (17: 3), 'a bear robbed of her cubs' (17: 8).

Characterization

This poetic strain derives to a great extent from David's literary and musical talents: it is fitting to notice here another feature of 1–2 Sam.— the author's gift for delineating the character of his *dramatis personae*. Outstanding are Samuel himself and the two kings. All are figures of heroic stature. Samuel's personal authority commands the respect of the whole nation; God's leading and commands govern his life, and he is zealous for God's honour. Saul, God's first choice for the kingship, is courageous, resolute, modest, and clearly a popular figure. David is a most attractive figure who could compel the affection and loyalty of those he led, a man of personal valour and military skill, whose generalship was matched by his statecraft in the establishment of the Israelite empire and the city of Jerusalem.

These are characters to rank with, nay, to overshadow, the great characters of epic and romance, like Alexander and Charlemagne. But the author of 1–2 Sam. is writing history, and not saga; he is careful to paint his heroes 'warts and all'. So Samuel fails catastrophically in the upbringing of his own sons, despite the tragic example of Eli. Saul's head was turned by his elevation and his personality suffered tragic deterioration. Even David, the man after God's own heart, allowed himself to fall into gross sin, adultery leading to contriving the murder of one of his captains.

The secondary characters too are individuals in their own right, all convincingly drawn. Eli the venerable priest and Nathan the faithful prophet; captains like the opportunist Joab, the ruthless Abner and the trusty Benaiah; princes like the grateful Mephibosheth, the feeble Ishbosheth, the insensitive Amnon, Absalom with his overweening ambition, and above all, David's friend Jonathan. Uriah the Hittite is clearly honest and loyal, but very dull; Nabal is dull without his virtues. Ziba is as crafty as Ahithophel, and the Old Testament surely has no villain more despicable than Doeg the Edomite. Of so many others there is no space to tell, but a word must be spared for the portrait gallery of women—Hannah and Peninnah, Michal, Abigail, Tamar, Bathsheba and others—comparable with that of Luke himself.

Critical questions

A commentary of this scope does not permit of adequate treatment of critical questions of date, authorship, composition, etc. For information on such matters, the student is referred to the detached essays elsewhere in this volume, and to works listed in the bibliography at the end of this introduction.

Two matters, however, seem worthy of special note at this point:

(a) 'Doublets'

Where a record has been compiled from several sources, it is clear that there may be traces of this in the resultant work. There may be passages showing an event from differing points of view, woven into one continuous narrative. But critics have tended often to see these differing points of view as plainly contradictory, not seldom on fairly unsubstantial evidence. The conduct of Eli and his sons is censured in a general statement in 1 Sam. 2: 12–25, and again by a visiting 'man of God' in vv. 27–36. H. P. Smith (p. 129) sees in 1 Sam. 13: 13 f. and 15: 28 two independent accounts of Yahweh's rejection of Saul, conveyed by Samuel at Gilgal, and yet each apparently unaware of the other. In this account of the institution of the monarchy in 1 Sam. 8: 9 many discern two completely irreconcilable stories (but see Commentary, *ad loc.*). In such cases it may be legitimate to see different stories

interwoven, but whether they are contradictory is another matter.

There is a second kind of 'doublet'; two stories presented as separate incidents in the OT narrative are seen by some scholars as duplicate accounts of the same event. Two accounts are given of David's coming to court (1 Sam. 16: 14–23; 17: 55–18: 5) but in one he comes as a hired minstrel, in the other as prospective son-in-law to the king—two distinct occasions, it might well seem. The same comment could reasonably apply to the two accounts of the negotiations for David's marriage to Saul's daughter (18: 17–19; 20) and these stories actually concern different princesses; to David seeking the protection of Achish (21: 11–16; 21: 7–28: 2); and especially to the two occasions when David, having Saul at his mercy, spared his life (23: 14–24: 22; 26: 1–25), concerning which Principal John Mauchline of Glasgow, writing as recently as 1971, maintains that two separate events are in view. Thirdly, some see a contradiction in the two accounts of Saul's death (1 Sam. 31: 4 ff.; 2 Sam. 1: 9 f.). Of course there is a contrast between the accounts, but only because the young man of 2 Sam. 1 is clearly lying in the expectation of a reward.

To sum up, it may be suggested that while 'doublets' of the kind suggested are not unknown in the literature of the ancient world, the tendency has probably been to claim for them too frequent a place in OT historical writing. It must also be borne in mind that in some cases in the *Samuel* writings textual uncertainties due to variant readings between *MT* and LXX render dogmatism impossible.

(b) Large numbers

Students have often been puzzled by the unexpectedly large numbers one meets in the OT. In Num. 1, for instance, military statistics are given which seem to envisage an Israelite population of over 2,000,000. So many could hardly have crossed the sea of reeds in one day.

It is generally assumed that the figures as they stand are inaccurate, but this is not to suggest that they are mere fiction; as J. W. Wenham suggests by way of comparison: 'no one in his senses would invent the story of a bus in which all 16,000 passengers were killed'. The numbers must have some significance; the difficulties arise from our way of understanding them. Several authors have studied the problem; among evangelicals R. E. D. Clark, 'The large numbers of the OT', *JTVI*, LXXXVII (1955), pp. 82–92, 146–152; and J. W. Wenham, 'Large numbers in the OT', *Tyn. B.*, 18 (1967), pp. 19–53. Wenham also has a summary in *The Lion Handbook to the Bible* (1973), pp. 191 f. Both hold that the Bible accounts are accurate, but may have suffered textual corruption or been wrongly understood.

Textual corruption. Sometimes a nought or noughts (as we should put it in terms of the arabic numeral system) has been added to a number: 2 Sam. 10: 18 tells of 700 chariots; 1 Chr. 19: 18 has 7,000. In 2 Sam. 15: 7 (*MT* and some LXX MSS), Absalom took forty years to work up his conspiracy; other LXX MSS, with Josephus, say more probably four years. Then again a numeral may drop out: 1 Sam. 13: 1 says that Saul was 'one year old', some LXX MSS give '30 years old'. There are also occasions when a numeral appears to have been changed for no clear reason: 800 in 2 Sam. 23: 8 becomes 300 in 1 Chr. 11: 11. Again, the noun to which a numeral is attached may undergo a puzzling change: 2 Sam. 10: 16's '20,000 footmen . . . and 12,000 men' become '32,000 chariots' in 1 Chr. 19: 7. Finally, the numbers in a list may be added up to a total different from that of the items enumerated.

The meaning of the root 'lp ('eleph, 'alluph, etc.)
The Hebrew root' *lp* in its various forms is found in many relevant passages. As a numeral it is often translated a 'thousand', though not infrequently it indicates merely a large number or a round number, much as we use 'thousands' in the plural. But it is also used for 'family' (Jg. 6: 15); 'clan' (Zech. 9: 7) or other social groups, or even military groups. A further extension of meaning includes leaders of groups; *alluph* can be a chieftain (Gen. 36: 15–43; AV, 'duke'), a captain over 1,000 troops, a professional or fully-armed soldier, or an officer in a general sense.

It has been suggested that the numbers of Num. 1 are much too large for the facts; they add up to over 600,000 men of military age, as well as the rest of the population. Yet, half a century before, two midwives were sufficient for the needs of the whole population! Attempts have been made to reduce the large numbers by interpreting 'thousands' as 'officers'; so in v. 20, 'forty-six thousand five hundred' could mean 46 officers and 500 men. Such calculations would clearly reduce the great numbers to more reasonable proportions, though we are not concerned here to prove that such an explanation furnishes the final solution

of the problem; other explanations have in fact been advanced for Num. 1. It is suggested, however, that the facts demonstrate that it may not be the large numbers which contradict commonsense and historical knowledge, but rather our imperfect understanding of the large numbers.

Notes are appended on selected passages in 1–2 Sam.:

1 Sam. 4: 'The Philistines . . . slew about 4000 men' (2); 'there fell of Israel 30,000 foot soldiers' (10). Wenham (*Tyn. B.*, pp. 42 f.) suggests that 30,000 is too large a figure, while the loss of 34 men (30,000 plus 4,000) might seem too small. Yet two factors are to be reckoned with: (a) 'we are approaching the period for which there is direct evidence that the initial brunt of the fighting was borne by representative figures' (cf. David and Goliath; the 'young men' of Abner and Joab, 2 Sam. 2: 14 ff.); and (b) so small a number could be serious in a day when the people were virtually unarmed (1 Sam. 13: 22).

1 Sam. 11: 8, 11: 330 professional soldiers could have relieved Jabesh-gilead; but to lead 330,000 men across the Jordan does not seem so practicable.

1 Sam. 13: 5: '30,000 chariots and 6,000 horsemen'. The Hebrew letter *lamedh* (our *l*) was used for 30; the final *l* of Israel could have been repeated, making 'one thousand' into 'thirty thousand'.

1 Sam. 15: 4 f.: '200,000 men on foot, and 10,000 men of Judah'. Wenham points out that this large force was in fact deployed against one fortified village; he proposes as more reasonable '200 footsoldiers and ten *'alluphim* of Judah'.

2 Sam. 17: 18: Ahithophel suggested sending a force of 12,000 men to pursue David, and yet when David gave orders to his army, 'all the people heard' (18: 5). Wenham thinks that 12,000 is too large a number to be within earshot, and the 20,000 casualties of 18: 7 too high also; he suggests 1,200 and 2,000 as more likely figures, and claims that they can be textually supported.

At all events, it would seem that here is a fruitful field for possible future study.

ANALYSIS

I SAMUEL

2 SAMUEL

I   DAVID MOURNS FOR SAUL AND JONATHAN (1: 1–27)

II   THE REIGN OF KING DAVID (2: 1–8: 18)
  i David king of Judah at Hebron (2: 1–4: 12)
   (a) David and Ishbosheth, rival kings (2: 1–3: 1)
   (i) Rival kings (2: 1–11)
   (ii) The first battle: Asahal dies (2: 11–3: 1)
   (b) David's sons: list I (3: 2–5)
   (c) The death of Abner (3: 6–39)
   (d) Ishbosheth assassinated (4: 1–12)
  ii David King of all Israel at Jerusalem (5: 1–6: 23)
   (a) David king of all Israel (5: 1–5)
   (b) Zion captured from the Jebusites (5: 6–12)
   (c) David's sons: list II (5: 13–16)
   (d) David victorious over the Philistines (5: 17–25)
   (e) The ark comes from Kiriath-jearim to the city of David (6: 1–23)
  iii David's dynasty, court and dominions (7: 1–8: 18)
   (a) The house of God and the house of David (7: 1–29)
   (b) War and Empire: 'The Lord gave victory to David wherever he went' (8: 1–14)
   (c) David's leading officers of state: list I (8: 15–18)

III   THE SUCCESSION NARRATIVE (9: 1–20: 26)
  i David's generosity to Mephibosheth (9: 1–13)
  ii David's great failure (10: 1–12: 31)
   (a) The Ammonite war (10: 1–11: 1)
   (b) David seduces Bathsheba, wife of Uriah the Hittite (11: 2–27)
   (c) Nathan's parable and David's repentance: Solomon born (12: 1–25)
   (d) The end of the Ammonite war (12: 26–31)
  iii The rape of Tamar (13: 1–14: 33)
   (a) Amnon assaults Absalom's sister (13: 1–22)
   (b) Absolom avenges his sister by killing Amnon, then flees (13: 23–37)
   (c) Through Joab's stratagem, Absalom is pardoned and restored to favour (13: 38–14: 33)
  iv The revolt of Absalom (15: 1–19: 43)
   (a) Rebellion breaks out (15: 1–12)
   (b) David a fugitive from Jerusalem (15: 13–16: 14)
   (c) Absalom in Jerusalem (16: 15–17: 23)
   (d) Absalom's fate (17: 24–18: 18)
   (e) News comes to David (18: 19–32)
   (f) David's grief and Joab's expostulation (18: 33–19: 8a)
   (g) David returns to his capital: Shimei, Mephibosheth, Barzillai (19: 8b–43)
  v Sheba rebels (20: 1–26)
   (a) Sheba's rebellion (20: 1–22)
   (b) David's leading officer of state: list II (20: 23–26)

IV   APPENDICES (21: 1–24: 25)
  i The famine and the seven sons of Saul (21: 1–14)
  ii Giant killers and Philistines (21: 15–22)
  iii David's Psalm of thanksgiving (22: 1–51)
  iv David's last words (23: 1–7)
  v David's mighty men (23: 8–39)
  vi David's census and the temple site (24: 1–25)

1 *Samuel*

I. ELI AND SAMUEL (1: 1–4: 1a)
i. The birth and dedication of Samuel (1: 1–2: 11)
(a) Elkanah and his family (1: 1–8)

1. A pious Ephraimite, Elkanah, went annually to worship at Shiloh where Eli and his sons ministered in the sanctuary. The harmony of his family life was disturbed by the rivalry of his two wives, Hannah the childless favourite and Peninnah who had children. Hertzberg (p. 66) comments: 'the history of the beginnings of the times of the kings opens with a narrative which bears all the external characteristics of an idyll. It does not however resemble the folk-tale with anonymous figures, as we are told the names of everyone involved.' The ancestry of **Elkanah** is given as far back as his great-grandfather; 'Ephrathite' (AV) signifies, as NIV, **Ephraimite**, of Ephraimitic descent, though 1 Chr. 6: 33 ff. suggests that the family had a Levite origin. **Zuph** gave his name not only to the Zuphites, but also to the 'district of Zuph' (1 Sam. 9: 5). **Ramathaim** is the dual form of Ramah, 'the height'; various places bear this name; Jg. 4: 5 mentions one 'in the hill country of Ephraim'.

2–3. Elkanah has two wives; polygamy was not forbidden but was bound to lead to domestic discord, especially where one was childless. The place of the family's annual pilgrimage was **Shiloh** between Bethel and Shechem, which, though Shechem and Mizpah were nearer, Elkanah no doubt chose because the ark was there. At Shiloh **Hophni and Phinehas, the two sons of Eli, were priests of the LORD** (3).

4–7a. When Elkanah offered sacrifice it seems that the wives and children received portions of the sacrificial meal, an occasion for Peninnah to taunt her rival with her childlessness. **5. double portion:** a phrase whose exact meaning has given rise to considerable discussion. Hannah is clearly the favourite, yet she receives only one portion. AV resolves the apparent contradiction by saying 'a worthy portion'; NIV says 'a double portion'; but there is no real authority for these readings, except one ancient rabbinic tradition. S. R. Driver (*Notes*, pp. 7 ff.) considers various possibilities, and decides in favour of the solution of the Gk. OT of adding a conjunction like 'although', 'howbeit', to underline the contrast between the two statements. RSV follows Driver: **although he loved Hannah**, with a marginal note 'Gk: Heb. obscure'. D. F. Payne (*NBC³*, *ad loc.*) suggests that Peninnah received the larger portion because Hannah 'has no mouths but her own to feed'. **7a.** 'Hannah's wound

was reopened annually on the occasion of the sacrificial meal at Shiloh' (McKane, p. 33). **7b. Therefore, Hannah wept and would not eat:** the tense of the verb here, says Driver, shows that the story is passing from what used to happen every year to what happened one particular year. Hannah gives expression to her grief, Elkanah seeks to comfort her.

(b) Hannah's prayer for a son is answered (1: 9–2: 11)

9–11. Hannah made her way to the Temple to pour out her troubles to the Lord. **when they had finished eating:** Hertzberg (p. 25) says that the text here is obscure and suggests that it implies that Hannah could not eat for grief. Eli the priest is named, as in v. 3, without introduction; some think he has been introduced in a passage now lacking, but other characters appear in the OT without introduction, as Elijah. **the LORD's temple:** clearly a more substantial structure than a tent or tabernacle; it had **doorposts** (9) and **doors** (3: 15); in vv. 7, 24, it is called the **house of the LORD**. It was above all the sanctuary where the ark of the covenant was lodged. The Jerusalem temple was, of course, not built until much later.

12–18. As she prayed, Hannah was observed by Eli from his seat near the sanctuary entrance. He judged the intensity of her emotion from her silent praying, but diagnosed drunkenness. Rebutting this charge, she told him of her troubles and of her vow to dedicate the child she was asking for to the Lord for the service of the sanctuary: 'no greater self-denial was possible' (Mauchline, p. 47). Eli spoke words of comfort and encouragement, and she left much happier.

19–20. With hearts full of worship and faith that their prayer would be answered they returned. When, in due time, a son was born, **she named him Samuel, saying, 'Because I asked the LORD for him'** (20). The etymology of the name is uncertain (it could mean 'name of God' or, conceivably, 'heard by God') but, as S. R. Driver says (*Notes*, p. 16), 'the name *šᵉmû'ēl* recalled to his [the writer's] mind the word *šā'ûl, asked*, though in no sense derived from it'.

21–28. Elkanah went to the next Shiloh festival alone, Hannah staying at home until the child was weaned, no doubt with due festivity (cf. Gen. 21: 8). The three then made the journey with offerings of a bull, flour and wine. **24. a three-year-old bull:** AV, RV have 'three bullocks', following the *MT*; RSV, NIV follow the Gk. (cf. the Qumran MS). Both renderings are possible; RSV, NIV is more probable. The child was handed over to Eli's custody.

2: 1–11. Hannah's song of praise is important both for its own sake, and also for its fore-shadowing of Mary's song in Lk. 1: 46–55. As Mauchline (p. 50) notes: 'Few comments are required on the text or the meaning of this psalm'.

ii. Samuel with Eli in the temple (2: 12–4: 1a)
(a) **Eli and his family (2: 12–36)**
Eli's family stands in striking contrast to El-kanah's. The pious and tender consideration of 1: 21 ff. are completely absent. Hophni and Phinehas were **wicked men** (AV, RV, 'sons of Belial'); **they had no regard for the LORD** (12). Meat bought for sacrifice they picked over, selecting the best, and ordered dis-obedience to the clearly stated Levitical direc-tions for sacrifice (Lev. 7: 31 ff.). Objectors received short shrift (16). In short, **they were treating the LORD'S offering with con-tempt** (17).

18. Samuel was ministering before the LORD—a boy wearing a linen ephod: he seems to be introduced at this point to highlight the contrast between the two families. His priestly status was marked by the **ephod**, in the OT either a skirt girt round the waist and worn by priests, or a cultic object (22: 18; Jg. 8: 27, 17: 15, etc.). Hannah and Elkanah visited him annually bringing a garment and receiving Eli's blessing. In due course, three more sons and two daughters were born to them. **21. the boy Samuel grew up in the presence of the LORD:** the boy's growth is noted as in the Gospel Luke notes the growth of John the Baptist (1: 80) and of Jesus (2: 40, 52).

The irreligion and immorality of Eli's sons became a public scandal, but the indignation of Eli's old age was ineffectual after a lifetime of disciplinary inaction. He challenged them with the rumours and warned them of God's inevi-table judgment but to little effect, **for it was the LORD's will to put them to death** (25); like the Pharaoh of the Exodus, their hearts were hardened.

27. Now a man of God came to Eli: an anonymous messenger from God occurs elsewhere in the OT; see Jg. 6: 8–10, 1 Kg. 13 *passim*, 1 Kg. 20: 13 ff., etc.; almost recalling the chorus in a Greek tragedy. This prophet challenged the people on behalf of Yahweh to confess His goodness (27–28), asked them why they behaved thus (29–30), warned them of inevitable judgment (31–33), and above all foretold that Eli's two sons would die in one day (34) and that he would be succeeded by **a faithful priest, who will do according to what is in my heart and mind** (35). A perma-nent dynasty of priests would follow, while Eli's progeny would be relegated to humili-ation (36).

The **faithful priest** would at first seem to

be Samuel, but he founded no priestly dynasty. Some see a messianic interpretation in v. 35, though in this case it is difficult to understand v. 36. Most scholars see a reference to the Zadokite priesthood (2 Sam. 8: 17, 15: 24, etc.); some indeed have gone further and said the passage must have been written in the time of the Zadokites, and in their support. This however is a purely subjective judgment, based on no textual evidence. Mauchline (p. 55) sums it up thus: 'It must be said that v. 35 by itself could be readily interpreted as having reference to Samuel as the faithful priest and his house as the one to be chosen for succession to the priestly office. Even the reference to **my anointed** in v. 35 does not rule out the refer-ence to Samuel. But the impecuniousness of the house of Eli which is described in v. 36 and which makes them come to the sanctuary to be accepted as pensioners or simply to receive alms, must mean that the **faithful priest** sig-nifies Zadok, **my anointed** is David, and the impecunious of the fallen house are either the family of Abiathar after his expulsion from priestly office (cf. 2 Kg. 2: 26–27), or the Levites whom Dt. 18: 6–8 authorized to serve the altar at the Jerusalem sanctuary and to have a provision made for them . . .'.

(b) **The call of Samuel (3: 1–4: 1a)**
General spiritual conditions are described, in-troduced by a third reference (see 2: 21, 26) to Samuel's growth. He is still a **boy**, but 'the term *na'ar* here applied to Samuel . . . is found applied to any age, from a new-born infant (4: 21) to a man of forty (2 Chr. 13: 7, cf. 12: 13)' (A. R. S. Kennedy, pp. 52 f., *note*).

Generally, nothing is happening spiritually, and direct revelation from God has ceased. **2.** Eli's sight is failing as Isaac's did with age (see Gen. 27: 1). **3. The lamp of God had not yet gone out** suggests a time near early morning; the lamp was either supplied overnight with one night's oil (A. R. S. Kennedy), or was extinguished at dawn (McKane). **4–10.** This night was different; Samuel's sleep was inter-rupted by a Voice calling: **Samuel!** Naturally, Samuel thought it was Eli, and ran to him. Eli disclaimed responsibility, as he did when the Voice called again, but the third time he grasped the identity of the Caller, and **realized that the LORD was calling the boy** (8). He instructed Samuel next time to reply, **Speak, LORD, for your servant is listening** (9).

10–14. The fourth call came 'Samuel! Samuel!'; Samuel was commissioned to warn Eli that *(a)* what God purposed would strike amazement and terror into all hearts (11); *(b)* everlasting punishment would visit Eli's house because of his sons' evil lives, and because Eli **failed to restrain them** (12–13); and it was too late to avert this doom by sacrifices (14).

15–16. Not surprisingly, Samuel was reluctant to communicate this sentence to Eli; he lay until the morning, and **he then opened the doors of the house of the LORD** (15). Did he linger over this daily chore to put off his embarrassing mission? But Eli insisted on hearing the worst: **Do not hide it from me. May God deal with you, be it ever so severely, if you hide from me anything** (17), an imprecation found in Ru., Sam., and Kg., but nowhere else in the OT. The old man heard and accepted God's judgment.

3: 19–4: 1a. Another note of Samuel's progress; he was recognized as a true prophet; the LORD was with him and **let none of his words fall to the ground** (19). Through him, God's authentic word came again to all Israel. So the little temple boy whose wakened ears had heard the voice of Yahweh became one of the earliest of the goodly fellowship of the prophets.

II. THE ARK OF THE LORD AND THE PHILISTINES (4: 1b–7: 1)
i. The Philistines invade Israel (4: 1b–5)
The name of Samuel disappears from the next three chapters, but two new names appear, the 'ark' and the 'Philistines'. The **'ark of God'** (3: 3) or **of the LORD's 'covenant'** (4: 3, 4, 5) is the central object of the tabernacle described in Exod., and is the throne where Yahweh Himself is present in the midst of His people (see notes on Exod. 24: 10–22; 40: *passim*; etc.; also K. A. Kitchen in *NBD*, *s.v.*, p. 82). It is part of the background of ch. 3; from ch. 4 onwards it becomes one of the chief elements in the story.

4: 1. the Philistines had long been, and were yet long to be, a thorn in the flesh of the Israelites. They were originally sea people from Crete and the rocky islands of the Aegean, and, no doubt in order to obtain food supplies, occupied and cultivated the fertile SW coastal strip of Palestine, to which, incidentally, they gave their name (Palestine=the land of the Philistines). The Egyptians drove them northwards up the coast where they established themselves in five cities, Ashdod, Ashkelon, Ekron, Gath and Gaza, though the order in 6: 17 may be preferred to an alphabetical order, under **rulers** (5: 8). See p. 62, article on the environmental background of the OT; also T. C. Mitchell in *NBD*, pp. 988–991, *s.v.* Philistines, and R. de Vaux, *Ancient Israel, Its Life and Institutions*, E. T, pp. 297–311.

1b–5. The story plunges without preamble into the Israelite–Philistine war, clearly the continuation or resumption of a campaign begun long before. The Philistines camped at **Aphek** (cf. Jos. 12: 18), the Israelites at **Ebenezer** (1). Neither site can be definitely identified. They were probably 'in the hill-country about 20 m. NW of Shiloh and overlooking the coastal plain, Aphek being two miles or so

NW of the other' (Mauchline, p. 69). Ebenezer cannot be the same as in 7: 12, since v. 6 suggests that the camps were within hearing distance. Moreover the name 'stone of help' seems singularly inept in view of what was to happen there. Battle was joined, and in the disastrous opening engagement Israel lost 4,000 men (2; cf. Introduction, p. 351). After a postmortem discussion, the elders decided that only the actual presence of the ark, which they regarded quite unspiritually to our ideas, yet quite in keeping with contemporary thinking, as a magic talisman, could ensure victory (3). It was brought, with Hophni and Phinehas in attendance, and thereon, the writer seems to say it with shame, **the LORD . . . enthroned between the cherubim** (4). Its arrival was greeted with a premature shout of victory (5).

ii. The ark of the Lord taken (4: 6–22)
The superstitious regard of the Israelites for the ark was shared by the Philistines, for the story of these people who had been miraculously delivered from Egypt and preserved throughout their long wilderness wanderings was, it is clear from the OT, well known to Israel's neighbours (cf., *e.g.* Jos. 2: 9 ff.). Consternation seized the Philistines, who cried **A god has come into the camp** (7). (Note that in the OT no enemies of God's people ever use the name Yahweh.) Realizing what they were up against, the Philistines encouraged each other to **Be strong . . .! Be men** (9), the only way to escape bondage to Israel.

10–11. Fighting began in real earnest; the Philistines were good soldiers, and routed the Israelites, leaving 30,000 footsoldiers dead on the battlefield, together with Hophni and Phinehas. Worst of all, **the ark of God was captured** (11), passing into the custody of the pagan foe.

12–18. 'The scene shifts from the battlefield to Shiloh . . . over 18 miles as the crow flies' (Hertzberg, p. 49). A **Benjamite** dressed for mourning ran the distance in one day to bring the dreadful news to Shiloh, where he found the aged Eli (he was 98) anxiously keeping vigil despite his blindness and awaiting news of how things had gone. He learned of the defeat, the enormous casualty list, even the death of his sons, but the loss of the ark was too much to bear. He fell from his seat, breaking his neck, **for he was an old man and heavy. He had led** (or judged) **Israel forty years** (18). Nowhere else is he called a 'judge', but he was in fact the link between the judges who preceded, and Samuel, the last judge and the first great prophet, and the founder of the monarchy.

19–22. The chapter ends with the harrowing story of how Phinehas's widow died in giving birth to a son whom, dying, she named **Ichabod** (Heb. *'i-kābōd*, 'no glory'). The glory had, in effect, departed from Israel; Driver

(*Notes*, pp. 49 f.) says that the word translated 'departed' is an ominous word in Hebrew and expresses 'is gone into exile'. He further suggests that this may have been the occasion of the desolation of Shiloh, still visible in Jeremiah's day (Jer. 7: 12 ff., etc.). (Archaeological evidence of the destruction of Shiloh was uncovered by Danish expeditions in 1926–32, but the data are insufficient to date the destruction.)

iii. The ark in the land of the Philistines (5: 1–12)

The Philistines took their sacred booty not to Ekron, which was nearer, but to Ashdod, their chief city and seat of a temple to their god **Dagon** (see K. A. Kitchen in *NBD*, *s.v.*, pp. 287 f.). Dagon, or Dagan, once connected with *dag*, fish; now more generally with *dāgān*, corn; was probably an agricultural deity. Place-names testify to his cult throughout Canaan. Jg. 16: 21 ff. tells of a temple and Dagon worship at Gaza.

2–5. The ark was set **beside Dagon** (2) in his temple, but ownership of the precious object brought its captors no joy, for **when the people of Ashdod rose early the next day** (LXX adds: 'they came to the house of Dagon and looked, and . . .'), **there was Dagon, fallen on his face on the ground before the ark of the LORD** (3). They had no doubt come to gloat over their enemies' loss; this contretemps must have made them very uneasy; Dagon's position suggests an attitude of respect, submission.

Nevertheless, they stood their god once more upon his feet; the next day not only was he fallen again on his face, but his head and hands were broken off as well (4). The next verse is rather obscure, but appears to refer to some custom, probably that referred to in Zeph. 1:9 and elsewhere.

6–9. This was not the only misfortune to visit the ark's captors; an epidemic of **tumours** (6) (AV, 'emerods', or haemorrhoids) broke out. The word 'tumours' gives a totally wrong idea; the affliction was almost certainly plague in its bubonic form. It was rodent borne; **rats** are associated with the buboes (6: 4 and the Gk. text of 5: 6). The enlarged inguinal lymph nodes ('in their secret parts', AV) are a classic feature of the disease, which is transmitted by the rat flea which the bearers of the ark carried with them from city to city. (Medical details here, and in discussion of Saul's deterioration, have been kindly suggested by Dr. J. K. Howard.) At all events, the Philistines withdrew the ark to Gath, leaving Ashdod to recover from its wounds.

10–12. The plague accompanied the ark to Gath, whose inhabitants sent it on to Ekron, where it was received with cries of panic and terror. 'Thus the God whom the Philistines think they have defeated is not defeated. He is the real Victor, who can give His people into the hand of the enemy and yet remain the Lord throughout' (Hertzberg, p. 55).

iv. The return of the ark (6: 1–7: 1)

(a) Preparations (6: 1–9)

The Philistines had had enough; after seven months they must get rid of their troublesome trophy. Priests and diviners said that if it were to be returned to Israel, it must be accompanied by a **guilt offering** (3), the 'trespass offering' of Lev. 5: 6, AV. The appropriate offering would be golden models of the rats and of the tumours. Some have suggested that the rats were a second and separate plague, but v. 4 says: **the same plague has struck both you and your rulers.** But the models recall Num. 21: 4 ff, where a bronze snake was made to allay a plague of snakes. Here there are five pairs of the models, one for each Philistine city. The matter is urgent, or theirs will be the fate of Pharaoh and of Egypt who hardened their hearts against Israel.

7–9. The offerings were to be placed with the ark on a new cart drawn by two hitherto unyoked cows who had calved. If these, forgetting their calves, made for Beth Shemesh, about 17 miles E of Ashdod, and just across the Israelite frontier, it 'could only be due to a special impulse from the God of the Hebrews' (A. R. S. Kennedy, p. 65) and all would be well.

(b) Beth Shemesh (6: 10–18)

The plan decided on was put into effect, and to the relief of the Philistines and the rejoicing of the Israelites, the cows made straight for Beth Shemesh, **keeping on the road and lowing all the way:**—a sign of their reluctance to abandon their young (Driver, *Notes*, p. 56). The Philistine lords were interested spectators.

13–15. The cart arrived while the people of Beth Shemesh were busy harvesting, and to their excitement and joy it came to rest in the field of a citizen, Joshua, where there was a great stone pressed into service as an altar. The wooden cart was broken up for the 'altar', and the beasts were offered in sacrifice. The presence of the **Levites** (15) poses problems. It is difficult to see why, if Levites were present, **the people of Beth Shemesh offered burnt offerings and made sacrifices to the LORD.** Some explain the difficulty by assuming that v. 15 is a later addition.

16–18. Verse 16 tells how the Philistine rulers, having fulfilled their role as observers, went home. Verses 17, 18 are in the nature of a summary; it is not necessary to see a contradiction between the **five** golden rats of v. 4, and **the number . . . according to the number of . . . fortified towns with their country villages** (18); '"a city and its unwalled villages" (or "a city and its adjacent territory") is commonly regarded as a unity' (Mauchline,

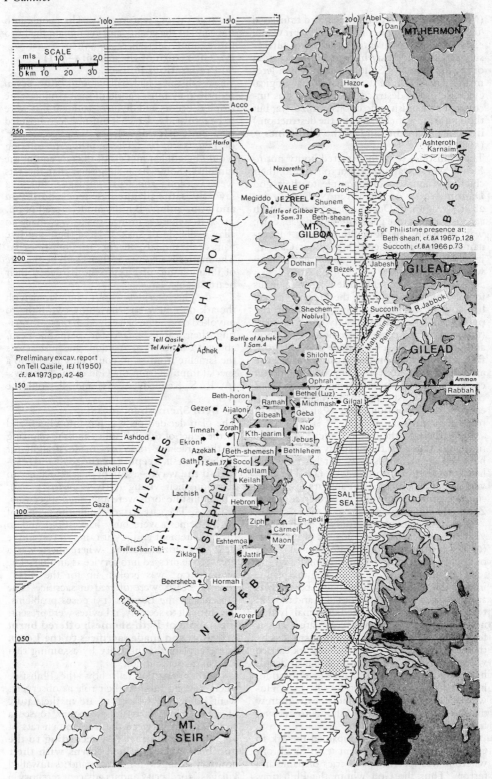

SCALE
mls
0 10 20
0 km 10 20 30

MT. HERMON
Abel
Dan
BASHAN
Hazor
Acco
Ashteroth
Karnaim
Haifa
Nazareth
VALE OF
En-dor
Megiddo JEZREEL
Shunem
Battle of Gilboa
1 Sam. 31
Beth-shean
MT.
GILBOA
For Philistine presence at:
Beth shean, cf. BA 1967 p.128
Succoth, cf. BA 1966 p.73
S
H
A
Dothan
Bezek
Jabesh
GILEAD
R
O
N
Shechem
Nablus
Succoth
R. Jabbok
Mahanaim
Peniel
GILEAD
Tell Qasile
Tel Aviv
Aphek
Battle of Aphek
1 Sam. 4
Shiloh
Preliminary excav. report
on Tell Qasile, IEJ 1 (1950)
cf. BA 1973, pp. 42-48
Ophrah
Amman
Rabbah
Beth-horon
Bethel (Luz)
Gezer
Aijalon
Ramah
Michmash Gilgal
Ashdod
Timnah
Zorah
Gibeah
Geba
Nob
P
H
Ekron
K'th-jearim
Jebus
Azekah
Beth-shemesh
Bethlehem
I
Gath 1 Sam. 17 Soco
L
Ashkelon
Adullam
Keilah
SALT
SEA
I
Lachish
S
H
E
Hebron
Gaza
T
Ziph
En-gedi
I
N
Carmel
E
S
Telles Shari'ah
H
Maon
Eshtemoa
E
Ziklag
Jattir
L
A
Beersheba
Hormah
H
N
R. Besor
E
G
E
B
Aro'er
MT.
SEIR

Map 22—Philistine Aggression

p. 81). The fact that Joshua's stone was extant in the author's day (18) has been adduced as evidence that the story is history and not folklore.

(c) Kiriath Jearim (6: 19–7: 1)

Israelites as well as Philistines must learn that it is dangerous to handle holy things unadvisedly. **19. God struck down some of the men of Beth Shemesh, putting seventy of them to death because they had looked into the ark of the LORD:** Driver says that the preposition translated **into** means rather 'in' or 'at'; the offence was probably the irreverent gaze of idle curiosity. McKane (p. 56) suggests 'gaped at'. The NIVmg and AV, following the Hebrew, give the number as 50,070, as does the Greek. But the Greek at all events cannot be correct, since it limits the slain to one family, the sons of Jeconiah! Moreover, the larger number is certainly greater than the entire population of Beth Shemesh. Josephus says 70, and it seems reasonable to accept this figure. RSV assumes that the 50,000 is an addition from an unidentifiable source; W. J. Martin (*Biblical Expositor*, i, p. 279) says: 'It is probably best to read: He slew 70 men, there being 50,000 men'. The lesson is clear; the death of 70 of the adult males of a small community was a fearful judgment; Israelites no less than Philistines must reverence the presence of Yahweh their Lord.

Awe-stricken, they asked their neighbours at Kiriath Jearim to relieve them of their responsibility. The ark was taken there, to the house of Abinadab whose son Eleazar became its guardian.

III. SAMUEL AND SAUL (7: 2–15: 35)
i. Samuel the judge of Israel (7: 2–17)

During the events of the three preceding chapters, Samuel has remained in the background; now, twenty years later, he returns to the centre of affairs. **2. It was a long time:** AV, 'the time was long'. Driver (*Notes*, p. 61) renders 'the days were multiplied and became twenty years', referring to a similar construction in Gen. 38: 12. Israel now sighed or **mourned** after the Lord. But their lamenting was not whole-hearted, they still had their Canaanite gods, **Baals and Ashtoreths**, and still knew Philistine domination. (For these two deities, see *NBD*, pp. 96 f., 115.) Samuel pointed them to the way of deliverance, to desert idolatry and return to Yahweh.

5–11. Samuel called the nation together at **Mizpah**, about 5 miles NE of Jerusalem, for fasting and confession, promising meanwhile to intercede for them. **6. they drew water and poured it out before the LORD:** a ritual found only here in the OT (but cf. 2 Sam. 23: 16). Most commentators seem agreed that this was not a libation, but a symbol of casting away their sinful ways; some have tried to relate it to the later rite of waterpouring at the Feast of Tabernacles (cf. Jn 7: 37).

It is at this point that we are told: **Samuel was leader of** (or 'judged') **Israel at Mizpah.** The Philistines, hearing of the assembly, began to muster their forces, driving the Israelites to plead more earnestly for Samuel's prayers. He set up the sacrifice of a lamb, a sacrifice that was interrupted by the Philistine attack. A violent thunderstorm simultaneously threw the attackers into confusion; they fled with Israel in hot pursuit as far as **Beth Car**, a location as yet unidentified.

12–14. Samuel celebrated Yahweh's intervention by the erection of a stone ('the stone of help') between Mizpah and **Shen** (RSV, reads 'Jeshanah' following LXX, Syr.; cf. 2 Chr. 13: 19), which he named **Ebenezer, saying, 'Thus far has the LORD helped us'** (12). This cannot be the Ebenezer of 4: 1, which is much too far from Mizpah. The Philistine rout was complete; never again were they to trouble Israel in Samuel's time, and Israel regained lost territory. It was God who restrained the Philistines, as also the **Amorites** (14) or Canaanites.

15–17. Samuel's position as a judge was established. 'The theocratic ideal has been realized. Under Yahweh, his true king, Israel is at peace from all his enemies within and without. Samuel is Yahweh's earthly representative, dispensing justice to a united Israel as did Moses in the birth-time of the nation (Exod. 18: 13 ff.)' (A. R. S. Kennedy, pp. 71 f.). He exercised his judicial functions on circuit between Bethel, Gilgal and Mizpah, and his home base at Ramah. Here also he built an altar where in addition to being judge it appears that he had succeeded to Eli's position as priest. He may, of course, have been just one of the many local priests at the various high places before the centralization of worship in the later monarchy.

ii. The institution of the kingship (8: 1–12: 25)

We now reach a turning point in the story. Israel is a theocracy, ruled by Samuel as judge (7: 15, 17) and priest (17). To ensure the succession after his death, he designated his sons as his successors, but they were ill-fitted and the people used this fact as a pretext for demanding a king, like all the other nations (8: 5). Chapters 8–12 record the transition from theocracy to monarchy and have provoked considerable discussion.

Much OT writing is clearly composed from various sources. But here many critics postulate sources that are highly contradictory. Some see Samuel as violently opposed to the establishment of a monarchy in some parts, and as favourable in others. Another criterion for distinguishing sources is the picture of Samuel himself, now as a national leader, now it is alleged as a local seer and fortune-teller. The division generally made is as follows (see G. W. Anderson, *Critical introduction to the OT*, pp. 71–81, for a useful summary): promonarchial (9: 1–10: 16; 11: 1–11); anti-monarchial (7: 2–8: 22; 10: 17–24; 12: 1–25). While recognizing that most text-books and commentaries adopt this view, one or two points are worthy of notice:

i. The late E. Robertson ('Samuel and Saul', in *The OT Problem*, pp. 105–136) said the alleged contradictions are often more apparent than real (see below, notes on 9: 11; 9: 16). It is fair to add that Robertson is not often quoted by contemporary critics.

ii. 'We should not overlook the fact that the accounts of the origin of the monarchy agree on important points. In every instance it is Yahweh who chooses the person of the king. He it is who lets loose the "wrath of God" which falls on Saul while ploughing; He enlightens Samuel on his sudden encounter with the unknown Saul and gives him the assurance that this is the *nāgīd* who is to rule Israel . . . Secondly all the accounts are aware that the king needs the consent of the people. This is given in the form of the acclamation, "Long live the king"' (Herrmann, *History of Israel in OT times*, p. 136).

iii. As to the dating of the sources, J. Bright (*A History of Israel*, p. 167) comments: 'It is unsound to dismiss the last of these narratives as a reflexion of subsequent bitter experience with the monarchy, as so many have done'. Herrmann (*op. cit.*, p. 66) adds, 'It is impossible to regard those passages which criticize Saul and his office as unhistorical and the others as historical; we can neither disregard the one in an attempt to construe the course of events nor use the other uncritically for this same purpose'.

A useful summary of the question will be found in D. F. Payne, 'The institution of the monarchy' in *NBC*[3], pp. 316 f.

(a) **The People demand a King (8: 1–22)**
1–9. Samuel's sons repeated the pattern of Eli's; they **did not walk in his ways. They turned aside after dishonest gain; and accepted bribes and perverted justice** (3). Yet Samuel appointed them his successors as judges. This was too much for the people who took advantage of the opportunity to demand a king **such as all the other nations have** (5), though McKane (p. 65) says that 'among the nations' would be preferable, meaning to provide effective leadership in a hostile world. Samuel, distressed by the request, laid the matter before the Lord, who instructed him to accede to their request, knowing that it was Yahweh Himself and not Samuel they were rejecting. At the same time, he must warn them of what a king would mean to them.

10–18. Samuel described in detail what they could expect from the king they wanted: **This is what the king who will reign over you will do** (11). They and their children will be impressed for military service (11–12a), for agricultural labour, the manufacture of arms (12b) and domestic service (13). Their lands and produce will be commandeered by the royal officials (14, 15); their servants and their stock will be taken over and they themselves enslaved (17). And it will be no use complaining: **When that day comes, you will cry out for relief from the king you have chosen, and the LORD will not answer you in that day.** That these predictions were fulfilled to the letter is no reason for assuming them to be written after Israel had experienced their truth.

19–22. Samuel's words fell on deaf ears; hearers refused to listen, saying: **'No! . . . We want a king over us . . .'.** One might wonder why, refusing Samuel's sons, they opted nevertheless for hereditary kingship!

(b) **Saul chosen and anointed (9: 1–10: 16)**
The scene changes to the Benjamite countryside; the actual place-name is not mentioned, it may indeed have dropped out of the original, which could have read: 'Now there was a man of Gibeah of Benjamin' (A. R. S. Kennedy, p. 77; so also D. F. Payne, *NBC*[3], p. 291). Gibeah was later called 'Gibeah of Saul' (11: 4). Saul's father was Kish, whose genealogy is traced back four generations to Aphiah. **Kish was a Benjamite, a man of standing** (AV: 'a mighty man of valour'). So the new dynasty was to be selected from the smallest tribe, not one of the great rivals, Judah and Ephraim. A king from either of these would have aroused the bitterest feelings in the other.

Saul is described in glowing terms; he was an **impressive young man**, surpassing all others in looks and in stature. **3–10.** 'A quaint, somewhat indefinite story' (Mauchline, p. 93). Saul and a servant were sent by Kish to find some lost donkeys. They went via the hill country of Ephraim, Shalisha, Shaalim and the territory of Benjamin until they came to Zuph, Samuel's country, perhaps twenty to thirty miles, but without success (3–4). Saul thought of giving up; his servant suggested consulting the local 'man of God' (6). Saul consented but raised the question of a fee; the servant produced a quarter of a silver shekel, a tiny sum, for the seer. Verse 9 is an editorial note that the **prophet** of the writer's days used to be called a **seer.** Off they went to find him.

11–14. Arriving at the town, they asked some teenage girls going to a ceremony whether the seer was in residence. E. Robertson (*op. cit.*) suggests that due to the ambiguity mentioned in v. 9, when Saul asked for the seer who lived at Ramah, the girls understood him to mean Samuel, the national prophet who had just arrived for a special occasion marked by a sacrifice (12) and a feast (13). It is at all events clear that Samuel had arrived from a journey (see v. 12; and Mauchline, p. 95). Saul and his servant went on as directed, and came face to face with Samuel, on his way also to the high place.

15–21. The day before, Yahweh had revealed to Samuel that on the following day He would send to him a Benjamite whom he was to **anoint** to be **leader over my people Israel** (16). The title is *nāgīd* (prince), not *melek* (king): Robertson says a prince is a charismatic leader raised up for a particular purpose—**he will deliver my people from the hand of the Philistines** (16), like the judges—and connotes no hereditary dynasty. When the two met, Yahweh revealed to Samuel that Saul was the designated *nāgīd*. Samuel made himself known to the young man and invited him to the feast, reassuring him that his father's donkeys were found. He continued, to the amazement of Saul: **And to whom is all the desire of Israel turned, if not to you and all your father's family** (20)? This Saul evidently understood as the kingship; he immediately protested his unworthiness, and the insignificance of his tribe and his family.

22–27. Samuel would have none of it, and set him in the place of honour at the banqueting table, seeing to it that he received the choicest portion reserved for an exceptionally distinguished guest, and, the feast over, a fitting bed. At daybreak, Samuel greeted him and set him on his way, first asking for a moment in private without even the servant's company.

10: 1–8. When the two men were alone, **Samuel took a flask of oil and poured it on Saul's head** (1). (For *anointing* in the OT, see R. de Vaux, *Ancient Israel*, pp. 103 ff.) To give confidence to the newly anointed that this was from the Lord, he was given three signs: on his return journey home,

i. Two men would meet him at Rachel's tomb with the news that, the donkeys being found, his father was now anxious about his safety.

ii. Three men on their way to Bethel to worship and carrying three young goats, three loaves and a skin of wine (cf. the beast, flour and wine of Hannah's offering, 1: 24), will greet them and give them two loaves.

iii. At Gibeah of God ('the hill of God', AV) he would meet a band of peripatetic prophets, and **the Spirit of the LORD will come upon you in power . . . and you will be changed into a different person** (6). Saul is to receive the endowment which the judges had known (Jg. 3: 10; 6: 34; 11: 29; 13: 25; 14: 6; 15: 14, etc.). **changed into a different person:** A. R. S. Kennedy (p. 85) comments that 'Saul's is the first conversion recorded in sacred Scripture'.

The mention of a Philistine garrison (5) reveals the extent of Philistine penetration.

Finally, Saul is to go to Gilgal and there wait seven days for the arrival of Samuel who will offer sacrifices there, **and tell you what you are to do** (8).

9–16. These signs duly took place, and Saul indeed prophesied, an event which caused raised eyebrows among those who regarded the wandering prophets as of very poor rank socially, and saw a rich man's son associating with them. **11. Is Saul also among the prophets?:** cf. 19: 23. **12. who is their father?:** meaning either that they come of no distinguished lineage, or that their fathers were no more prophets than Saul's father was. At last, Saul, back at home, reported on his search for the donkeys to his uncle, but, asked what Samuel had said, mentioned nothing **about the kingship** (16).

(c) Saul acclaimed (10: 17–27)
After the private anointing of Saul came public acclamation. The leader chosen by God must be accepted by the people. Accordingly **Samuel summoned the people . . . to the LORD at Mizpah** (17). His address began with a reminder of Yahweh's care for His people since the great deliverance of the Exodus (18) and recalled again that what they had done was an act of direct disobedience and rebellion against their God Himself, who had yet granted their request. **19. So now present yourselves before the LORD by your tribes and clans:** 'clans' is literally 'thousands' (see Introduction, p. 380).

20–24. The great assembly is described. Lots were cast to identify the man whom the Lord had selected; just as the guilty man Achan was found (Jos. 7: 16 ff.) and an apostolic replacement for Judas chosen (Ac. 1: 26). The casting of lots was in Israel no mere matter of chance or 'luck of the draw'; it was a prayerful exercise to find God's will (see J. Stafford Wright in *NBD*, p. 321). When the choice of Saul was announced, he was nowhere to be found; a further enquiry of Yahweh revealed that **he has hidden himself among the baggage** (22) where he was found and brought out. His physical presence proclaimed him a suitable leader; Samuel indicated that he was **the man the LORD has chosen**; and he was accepted by the people with public acclaim: **'Long live the king!'** (24).

25–27. Samuel now rehearsed once more **the regulations of the kingship** (25), and recorded his words on a scroll which was placed in the sanctuary: he **deposited it before the LORD.** He then dismissed the people to their homes; Saul went to his at Gibeah accompanied by **valiant men whose hearts God had touched** (26); 'men morally brave, loyal and honest (cf. Exod. 18: 21, 25)' (Driver, *Notes*,

p. 85). But there was a discordant note: **some trouble-makers** (cf. 2: 12), the very opposite of those just mentioned, **despised him and brought him no gifts** (27). Saul, waiting his opportunity, kept silence, as he had to his uncle in v. 16.

(d) Saul demonstrates his leadership (11: 1–18)

The new ruler soon had occasion to prove his mettle. **Nahash**, king of Ammon (later David's friend, 2 Sam. 10: 1 f.), besieged **Jabesh Gilead** on the eastern side of Jordan, some 23 miles SW of the Sea of Galilee. The inhabitants, cut off from the rest of Israel and uncomfortably placed between Aram on the N and Ammon on the S, sent a conciliatory message to the Ammonites offering to make a treaty, or covenant (Heb. b^erît), recognizing Ammonite suzerainty. Now b^erît signifies a solemn agreement between two contracting parties; not, as Hertzberg (p. 92) points out, an unconditional surrender. Nahash's reply was uncompromising: **'I make a treaty with you only on the condition that I gouge out the right eye of every one of you'** (2). Asking for seven days stay of execution to recruit assistance, which surprisingly the Ammonites granted (no doubt assured that Israel would not be able to help), they sent messengers to all the cities of Israel appealing for aid. They came to Gibeah, where the news aroused deep resentment.

5–11. Saul, returning from working on his farm, asked what all the excitement was about, and, learning the facts, experienced another infilling of the Spirit. In his righteous anger, he divided the carcases of two oxen into pieces, which he despatched by messengers throughout all Israel, calling on all in his own name and Samuel's to come and help, on pain of losing their own oxen by similar means. **Then the terror of the LORD fell on the people, and they turned out as one man** (7). The standard was raised at **Bezek** (8), 15 miles from Jabesh across the Jordan; 300,000 men of Israel and 30,000 of Judah gathered there. Most critics regard these numbers as highly exaggerated; Hertzberg, indeed, thinks that the word 'thousands' has been added. D. F. Payne (*NBC*[3], p. 292) comments: 'The numbers seem too high; since LXX presents even greater numbers, the text must have suffered early corruption in transmission'. A message of encouragement was sent to Jabesh, and a day or two later Saul divided his army into three groups; in the ensuing battle Ammon was routed.

12–15. The enthusiastic victors wanted vengeance on the men who had objected to Saul's kingship (10: 27), but Saul generously would have none of it (12, 13). Samuel invited the people to **reaffirm the kingship** at Gilgal (14). It seems unnecessary to regard this, as some critics have done, as a third account of the appointment of Saul; an act of confirmation and thanksgiving after the great victory would appear quite natural.

(e) Samuel hands over (12: 1–25)

Samuel's life-work was completed; he was ready to abdicate that the new leader might take over. He addressed the assembly of the nation (presumably that convened at Gilgal to 'reaffirm the kingship', though some have suggested that in fact it was at Mizpah, since his speech reads more naturally as a continuation of ch. 10) with his own defence of his life's work. It is a farewell sermon recalling that of Moses in Dt.: **Now you have a king as your leader. As for me, I am old and gray, and my sons are here with you. I have been your leader from my youth until this day** (2). He challenged the nation to show that he had been oppressive or unjust, offering to restore what he had robbed them of. The people protested that his rule had been righteous. He invoked the witness of God Himself; the people agreed: **'He is witness'**.

6–12. Samuel retraced Israel's history, showing Yahweh's goodness to them: **Now then, stand here, because I am going to confront you with evidence before the LORD as to all the righteous acts performed . . . for you and your fathers** (7). During their Egyptian bondage, He had heard and answered their cry and brought them into the land. In the time of the judges, despite their constant backsliding He repeatedly sent deliverers (including the rather surprising introduction of the name of **Samuel** himself; some see here an addition from a later hand, others a misreading for 'Samson'). When, more recently, Nahash had threatened, they demanded a king (is this, as has been alleged, a third account of how the monarchy began?). Here now in the person of Saul was what they had asked for.

13–18. Nevertheless, it was not too late to repent, and if they did so, things will go well (14), but if they continued in rebellion, the hand of the LORD **will be against you, as it was against your fathers** (15). RSV, following LXX, reads 'against you and your king', which is preferable as being more suitable to the context, see vv. 14, 25. To demand a king was still rebellious; Samuel drove the lesson home with a most impressive visual aid; at his prayer a great thunderstorm broke out (18). In this passage is the germ of much OT royal theology.

19–25. Terrified by this demonstration of Yahweh's might, they confessed their sins, and begged Samuel to pray for them: even though they had a king, as McKane (p. 88) says, Samuel was not redundant! He encouraged them to forsake their evil ways and return to Yahweh **—for the sake of his great name the LORD will not reject his people, because the LORD was pleased to make you his own** (22).

Samuel himself would continue to pray for them and to instruct them.

iii. Saul's campaigns (13: 1–15: 35)
(a) War breaks out with the Philistines (13: 1–23)

The account of Saul's active kingship begins with a sentence so corrupt in the extant Hebrew text as to have little meaning, as a comparison of AV, RV, RSV, NEB and NIV with their marginal readings will show.

AV	RV	RSV	NEB	NIV
Saul[a] reigned one year: and when he had reigned two years over Israel.	Saul was [a]thirty] years old when he began to reign and he reigned two years over Israel.	Saul was . . .[a] years old when he began to reign, and he reigned . . . and two[b] years over Israel.	Saul was fifty years[a] old when he became king, and he reigned over Israel for twenty-two[b] years.	Saul was thirty[a] years old when he became king, and he reigned over Israel for forty-two[b] years.
[a]Heb: the son of one year in his reigning.	[a]The Hebrew text has, Saul was a year old. The whole verse is omitted in the unrevised Sept., but in a later recension the number thirty is inserted.	[a]The number is lacking in Hebrew. [b]Two is not the entire number. Something has dropped out.	[a]fifty years: prob. rdg.; Heb. a year. [a]Prob. rdg.; Heb. two.	[a]A few late manuscripts of the Septuagint; Hebrew does not have thirty. [b]See the round number in Acts 13:21; Hebrew does not have forty-two.

Driver (*Notes*, pp. 96 f.) says, 'In form, the verse is of the type regularly followed in the Book of Kings in stating the age of a king at his accession and the length of his reign . . . although for some reason, the text as it stands is deficient'. In some Greek minuscules Saul's age at accession is given as thirty years; E. Robertson (*The OT Problem*, 1950, p. 125) suggested 52 years. Josephus (once) and Acts 13: 21 both say that he reigned for 40 years, a more likely figure for the reign of a king starting as a young man and ending with a son of full military age. (In another place Josephus gives him a 20 years' reign.) 'The whole verse', says Mauchline (p. 111) 'is missing in certain LXX Codices', including the earliest and most reliable ones.

The next recorded incident must have taken place considerably later, since Jonathan already leads an army.

Saul mobilized a force limited to 3,000 men, with two-thirds under his own command, the remainder under Jonathan's. Saul's headquarters were at Michmash; the battle terrain, including Bethel and Gibeah (more probably Geba) was in the Benjamite territory stretching some miles NW of where later Jerusalem stood. Jonathan had an early success over the Philistines which was widely publicized among the population, who rallied to Saul at Gilgal.

5–7. The Philistines mustered a new force of 3,000 chariots (Heb. says 30,000; see introduction, p. 351), 6,000 horsemen, and footmen innumerable in **Michmash, east of Beth Aven** (5). The effect on the morale of the Israelites was devastating; they sought safety in any available refuge or by flight to Gad and Gilead beyond the Jordan (7). Saul remained in Gilgal, those with him were **quaking with fear** (LXX has 'all the people deserted him in terror').

8–15a. Saul waited seven days fruitlessly at Gilgal for Samuel to arrive; meanwhile his men **began to scatter** (8), so he, a man of vigorous action, felt that something must be done. He ordered the burnt offering and the peace offering to be brought, and he **offered up the burnt offering** (9). No sooner done than Samuel appeared; Saul greeted him, only to be received with displeasure instead of the commendation he expected. He explained that the people were defecting and the Philistines pressing, and that he had **not sought the LORD's favour** (12). **13. You have not kept the command:** 'may be read, "Would that you had kept the commandment' (Mauchline, p. 113).

In view of this episode, Samuel pronounced God's sentence upon him: **your kingdom will not endure; the LORD has sought out a man after his own heart and appointed him leader of his people, because you have not kept the LORD's command** (14). This is the first mention of the so far unnamed David; Saul is reminded that the position could have been his. **15b–18.** Saul was left with 600 men. The Philistines launched a three-pronged attack, their hope of success all the greater because they had established a monopoly of the production of iron implements both agricultural and military. So when D-day actually dawned, Saul and Jonathan alone had swords and spears.

(b) Jonathan and the defeat of the Philistines (14: 1–46)

1–15. Jonathan, unknown to his father, who was at Migron near Gibeon with his advisers (including the priests), and to the people, took his armour-bearer to reconnoitre the enemy positions. They came to a pass dominated by two cliffs (4), impassable except by the most reckless. But Jonathan's trust was in Yahweh: **Perhaps the LORD will act on our behalf. Nothing can hinder the LORD from saving, whether by many or by few** (6). The foes are **uncircumcised**, the conflict a holy war.

The armour-bearer followed Jonathan implicitly. They would attract the Philistines' attention; if repulsed they would defer their attack, if invited to come up they would advance. Invited to climb the impossibly precipitous terrain, they met them in a narrow defile where they were able to kill twenty Philistines one by one as they advanced. The Philistines, incredulous that two men could wreak such havoc, assumed that the fugitives had regrouped. An earthquake increased their panic. **3. Ahijah:** of the priestly dynasty of Eli in **Shiloh**; he was **wearing an ephod**, or perhaps better, 'bearing the ephod' (23: 9 and 30: 7 clearly indicate something carried, not worn; but see note on v. 18). **15. the raiders:** those of 13: 17 returning home.

16–23. The victory and the Philistines' confusion could be seen across the valley from Gibeah, where Saul ordered a count of his forces to see who was missing; the absence of Jonathan and his armour-bearer was discovered (17). Ahijah was ordered to bring the oracle and seek divine guidance, but, the rout of the foe being visibly complete, Saul ordered him, **withdraw your hand** (19); consultation of oracles must yield place to action. Saul and his forces marched, joined by those who earlier had deserted or, though staying, trembled (13: 6). **So the LORD rescued Israel that day, and the battle moved on beyond Beth Aven** (23). **18. the ark of God:** this was in Kiriath Jearim, so many critics hold that the reference is to the 'ephod' (so LXX; cf. v. 3), a customary means of seeking God's will (see *NBD, s.v.* 'Dress'). But Hertzberg points out (pp. 113 f.) that 'it is quite remarkable that *ark* has been preserved at all, and this fact should at least tell against its being discarded too hastily'. **23. Beth Aven:** some prefer Beth-horon or Bethel. Certainty is impossible.

24–30. Saul's action after dismissing the oracle was ill-conceived; he banned all food for his men before sundown. Jonathan, unconscious of the decree, ate wild honey they found. His men, who abstained, told him: **Your father bound the army under a strict oath, saying, 'Cursed be any man who eats food to day'** (28). Jonathan was alarmed at the situation; he saw the folly of his father's action in depriving his soldiers of the bounty of the land flowing with milk and honey and thus impairing their strength for routing the foe.

31–35. Yet the victory was considerable; the Philistines were cleared from the 20 miles between Michmash and Aijalon. By nightfall the exhausted people **pounced on the plunder and, taking sheep, cattle and oxen and calves, they butchered them on the ground and ate them, together with the blood'** (32). Saul learned of this sin, not that they had broken his ban, which lapsed at nightfall (24),

but because in their hunger they ignored the ritual laws (see Lev. 17: 10–14; Dt. 12: 23; Ezek. 32: 25). To avert punishment, Saul built an altar, and saw to it that the ritual was observed. 'But note that, although the priest Ahijah was with Saul at this time, it was Saul who directed the slaughter of the animals and built the altar' (Mauchline, p. 119). Israel's priesthood does not seem yet to have become exclusive.

36–46. Saul proposed that, now the sacrifice had been offered, they should complete the annihilation of the enemy (36). The people agreed, but the priest suggested first seeking Yahweh's will, so Saul consulted the Urim and Thummim (see on Exod. 28: 30, p. 201), and received a neutral reply (37). He felt that divine silence indicated something wrong in the camp: **let us find out what sin has been committed today** (38). The culprit should die, even though it were Jonathan himself. None spoke, so Saul called for lots to decide whether he and Jonathan were at fault, or the people. (RSV in v. 41 restores the full text, as preserved in LXX (cf. NIVmg): part of it has been lost from *MT*.) Eventually Jonathan was indicated; he confessed that he had unwittingly broken his father's ban on eating. Jephthah-like, Saul found he had no option; thanks to his rash oath he must sacrifice his own offspring. But, as McKane (p. 99) says: 'Jonathan steals the thunder in this chapter as it is the intention of the author that he should'. His exploits had made him a popular hero; the people intervened and **rescued Jonathan, and he was not put to death** (45).

(*c*) **Summary of Saul's reign up to this point (14: 47–52)**
In ch. 15 we see Saul, proved unworthy of the kingship, set aside; in the last 6 verses of ch. 14 the author, or perhaps, as is often suggested, a later editor or redactor, summarizes the story so far.

47–48 tell of his military achievements. He fought against Moab, Ammon, Zobah (a small Aramaean kingdom), the Philistines and the Amalekites, and **inflicted punishment on them** (47). He delivered **Israel from the hands of those who had plundered them** (48). He consolidated his frontiers.

49–50 comprise family notes: Saul's sons, **Jonathan, Ishvi** (a contraction of Ishyo, or Ish-Yahweh—'man of the Lord', also called Ishba'al—see on 2 Sam. 2: 8), and **Malki-Shua:** his daughters, **Merab** and **Michal**, and his wife **Ahinoam**. His administration seems uncomplicated, only **Abner** son of Ner, the army commander, is named.

51 makes better sense if the AV/RSV rendering, which translates the Hebrew, is replaced by a reading from the LXX, which makes both Kish and Ner sons of Abiel, making Saul and Abner cousins (cf. v. 50, but contrast 1 Chr. 8: 33).

52 shows Saul not resting on his laurels, but constantly recruiting suitable talent for his standing army.

(d) War with Amalek: Samuel and Saul part (15: 1–35)

This summary is followed by an epilogue in ch. 15. In ch. 13 already Saul had learned that Yahweh intended to supersede him by **a man after his own heart:** now Samuel seems to offer him his final chance. Yahweh required the defeat and utter extermination of the Amalekites. Some have sought to justify Saul's leniency on the grounds of humanity, but this is hardly tenable. The complete destruction of the Amalekites was an example of *herem*, the 'devotion' of the entire spoil to Yahweh (cf. Jos. 6: 18; 7: 1, 11 ff.). Saul was fully aware of this; he had himself impetuously invoked it and been prepared to allow Jonathan to become its victim.

With 200,000 foot soldiers and 10,000 men of Judah (a division anticipating future events) Saul marched on Amalek. He warned the Kenites, connections of Moses who lived among the Amalekites (Jg. 1: 16) and then launched his offensive. Victory was complete, but **Saul and the army spared Agag** (9), the Amalekite king, and the pick of the livestock.

10–23. Samuel learned of Saul's incomplete obedience by Yahweh's direct revelation: **I am grieved that I have made Saul king, because he has turned away from me** (11). Samuel, angry and saddened, went to Saul who complacently asserted that he had obeyed orders. He had even erected a monument to celebrate the exploit (12). This complacency was soon shattered by Samuel's blunt question: **'What then is this bleating of sheep in my ears? What is this lowing of cattle that I hear?'** (14). Saul's stammered excuses were interrupted by Samuel's **'Stop! Let me tell you what the LORD said to me last night'.** He reminded the wretched man of all that God had done for him, making him king, and how in return he had deliberately disobeyed God's commands. **Why did you pounce on the plunder?** (19) he thundered. Saul tried to explain that the people had made him act as he had, intending to sacrifice the living animals **to the LORD your God** (21, cf. v. 30).

Samuel's reply was the sonorous psalm of vv. 22, 23: **'Does the LORD delight in burnt offerings and sacrifices as much as in obeying to the voice of the LORD? To obey is better than to sacrifice, and to heed is better than the fat of rams'**—a theme to be developed in years to come by Israel's great prophets.

24–31. Completely exposed, Saul confessed: **I have sinned. I violated the LORD'S command and your instructions. I was afraid** of the people and so I gave in to them (24). He begged Samuel to forgive him and accompany him to worship, thinking that this would put everything right, and failing to realize the gravity of his offence. Samuel refused Saul's request and reiterated: **the LORD has rejected you as king over Israel** (26).

The immediate sequel is not clear; NIV has: **As Samuel turned to leave, Saul caught hold of the edge of his robe, and it tore** (27). AV, RV, following the Hebrew, render 'As Samuel turned about . . . he laid hold upon . . .' NIV follows the general interpretation (*e.g.* H. P. Smith, p. 140) that Saul snatched Samuel's robe in order to detain him, but McKane (pp. 102 f.) argues that Samuel, not Saul, tore the robe. Mauchline (p. 125) defends the more traditional view. Some see in the tearing of the robe an acted parable like that of 1 Kg. 11: 30, 31.

Samuel was obdurate; not only was Saul dismissed, but Yahweh had given the kingdom **to one of your neighbours—to one better than you** (28). The verdict is irreversible: **He who is the Glory of Israel does not lie or change his mind; for he is not a man, that he should change his mind** (29). The dismissed king asked that at least Samuel would save his face before the people; the prophet agreed, showing that 'Samuel's sympathy with Saul was genuine' (Mauchline, p. 125).

32–35. The execution of Agag, shirked by Saul, was carried out by Samuel, who sternly reminded the Amalekite king that God's judgment had fallen upon him because of his own cruelty and sin. The final parting between Samuel and Saul is recorded, Saul to Gibeah and Samuel to Ramah, where he **mourned** Saul. **And the LORD was grieved that he had made Saul king over Israel** (35).

The Character of Saul

It will be useful to ask at this point what kind of man Saul was. Hertzberg (p. 123) asks: 'Is Saul the man after God's own heart? That is the theme of the Saul stories'. Most critics seem strangely disposed to whitewash him; Samuel, and even Yahweh, are against him. So H. P. Smith (pp. 97 f.), discussing the sacrifice he offered, says: 'What was Saul's sin in this matter is nowhere expressly set down, and it is difficult to discover anything in the text at which Samuel could justly take offence . . . it would not be impertinent to ask why Samuel had waited so long before appearing'. 'Samuel comes when all is finished', comments Hertzberg (p. 105), 'accuses Saul of disobedience, declares that Saul's kingdom will not continue, and that the Lord has sought out someone else, and departs. Saul, on the other hand, justifies his conduct in a modest and at all points irrefutable way'. To Mauchline (p. 113), Saul 'seems to come well out of the incident. Samuel's riposte sounds unconvincing to us'. McKane's view is more strongly expressed: 'It is doubtful whether 13: 7b–15a should be understood as late priestly propaganda representing a kind of clerical, closed shop attitude. If this is the intention of the passage, it is a clumsy and ineffective piece of work, for its effect is to enlist sympathy for Saul rather than for Samuel' (p. 93).

Are such views compatible with the Old Testament evidence? J. Bright (*History of Israel*, p. 170) says: 'Saul was a tragic figure. Of splendid appearance (1 Sam. 9: 2; 10: 23), modest (9: 21) and at his best magnanimous and willing to confess his faults (11: 12 f; 24: 16–18); always fiercely courageous, there was nevertheless in him an emotional instability that was to be his undoing'. This is a more balanced judgment. It is true that his frenzies, his alternations between black despair and moments of lucidity, became more obvious later in his career, yet already his character defects were apparent. He constantly acted rashly and thoughtlessly; his impatience at the delayed arrival of Samuel (13: 8, 9), his dismissal of the oracle he had invoked (14: 19), his ban on food for his men (13: 24); all were impetuous and led to great difficulties. Critics may justify his actions in ch. 13; but his own greeting to Samuel (13: 11) shows that he knew himself to be in the wrong; Eve-like he blamed everyone else—the people, Samuel himself, and the Philistines.

Saul's behaviour inevitably raises the question of his mental stability. 'Medically', comments J. K. Howard, 'he presents a very interesting case. The descriptions are quite classical of a severe manic/depressive illness with marked schizoid overtones. His paranoia, lack of foresight, faulty judgment, etc., are all classical signs'.

L. H. Brockington (*Peake*[2], p. 323) offers a balanced and objective comment: 'Saul, tired of waiting for Samuel, defies his spiritual power and offers sacrifice in his absence. Samuel regards this as an act of rebellion against God and solemnly rebukes Saul telling him that he will not now be the founder of a dynasty; God will appoint someone else to follow him on the throne'. In short, Saul is not without his fine qualities, otherwise how could God have chosen him as king? But, alas, he was *not* the man after God's own heart. His choice as king is difficult to understand. How could Yahweh select as king one predestined to failure? His call is, to the human mind, as incomprehensible as that of Judas Iscariot.

IV. SAUL AND DAVID (16: 1–31: 13)
i. David accepted and then rejected by Saul (16: 1–20: 42)
(a) Samuel anoints David (16: 1–13)

Samuel's position was difficult; Saul was still king by popular acclaim, even though rejected by Yahweh as charismatic leader. He had presided at the inauguration of the monarchy, and had placed Saul on the throne. Now Yahweh commanded him to anoint Saul's successor, a perilous assignment: **'How can I go?'** he asked when told to go to Jesse at Bethlehem taking his horn of oil since the new leader was to be one of Jesse's sons. He was to take a heifer for sacrifice, and assuring the elders of Bethlehem of his peaceable intentions, inviting them to sacrifice also, after consecrating themselves (i.e. ritual cleansing).

6–13. The story of David's anointing is familiar. On his arrival, Samuel first met Eliab, a tall and handsome young man (the description recalls our first view of Saul); Samuel assumes that his search for the man after God's heart is achieved. But Yahweh showed him his error: **Do not consider his appearance or his height, for I have rejected him. The LORD does not look at the things man looks at. Man looks at the outward appearance, but the LORD looks at the heart** (7). Abinadab, Shammah and four others were presented, but Samuel asked if there were any more. Jesse almost apologized: **'There is still the youngest . . . but he is tending the sheep'** (11). David was sent for; **he was ruddy, with a fine appearance and handsome features** (12).

Samuel's quest was at an end; he **anointed him in the presence of his brothers** (13, but see note on 17: 28). David received not only the unction, but like Saul before him, the Spirit's mighty investiture (10: 6, 10). Having confirmed Yahweh's choice, for he had no part in the choice, Samuel retired again to Ramah.

(b) David at Saul's Court (16: 14–23)

The Spirit not only came upon David, but also deserted his predecessor, leaving a vacuum filled by **an evil spirit from the LORD** which **tormented him** (14). 'The charismatic endowment reserved for the king of Israel has passed to David, leaving Saul not merely impotent, but demented and ravelled, so that he needs the solace of music' (McKane, p. 108). The evil spirit was **from the LORD**; no doubt in the sense that all things are within the ultimate control of Yahweh (cf. Isa. 45: 7; 1 Kg. 22: 19–23). The summoning of a musician, a man **who can play the harp**, was the prescription of his courtiers, familiar perhaps with similar phenomena; one of them with a solicitude recalling that of Naaman's slave-maid (2 Kg. 5: 2 f.) suggested a possible source of help. He had met or heard of David as a man of some parts, a shepherd not unversed in the military arts as well as musician. He was sent for, and came with gifts (bread, a skin of wine, and a young goat; cf. 1: 24; 10: 3) from Jesse, and soon proved indispensable to Saul, becoming his **armour-bearer** (21) or personal squire. He entered Saul's permanent service (22), and was at hand when the king's disorder recurred.

(c) David and Goliath (17: 1–18: 5)

'Chapters 17 and 18 seem originally to have existed in two different forms, a longer one represented by the present Heb. text and by some LXX MSS (notably the Alexandrian codex), and a shorter one represented by the Vatican MS of LXX. This latter omits 17: 12–31, 41, 50; 17: 55–18: 5. Each version offers an account that is complete in itself, although the shorter one minimizes the differences between the two traditions about David' (L. H. Brockington, *Peake*[2], p. 326).

1–11. This ch., like ch. 4, begins with Israelites and Philistines ranged for battle across the valley of Elah. The story needs no recapitulation, but some points call for comment. Details given about Goliath, his height—six cubits and a span (over 9 ft.), the specifications of his armour, sound circumstantial and may well rest on eye-witness testimony. Yet 2 Sam. 21: 19 says that *Elhanan* slew Goliath; AV says that Elhanan slew Goliath's brother, harmonizing with 1 Chr. 20:5 (see Commentary, *ad loc.*). Hertzberg (p. 139 n.) suggests that perhaps the name David itself may be a throne-name or title, since *dawidum* in the Mari texts means 'commander', and that his original name may be lost. But he doubts whether it could have been Elhanan.

12–31. Completely lacking in most LXX MSS; the English versions follow the Heb. David's visit with provisions for his brothers, like Joseph's generations before, is recorded, with his first sight of Goliath, the terror of the Israelites at his challenge, and Eliab's ill-graced welcome to David. Some think Eliab's sneer (v. 28) unlikely from one who had been present when David was anointed (16: 13), but Hertzberg (p. 139) for 'in the midst' reads '*from the midst*' in 16: 13, implying a measure of secrecy.

32–49. The arming of David and his single combat with the giant are described in dramatic detail. The youth volunteered where men of war had held back, assuring Saul that he was no stranger to fighting, having slain predatory lions and bears, and **this uncircumcised Philistine will be like one of them, because he has defied the armies of the living God** (36). Refusing the unaccustomed armour that Saul wanted to load on him, he **chose five smooth stones from the stream . . . his sling** was **in his hand** (40); the confident lad pitted his ease and rapidity of movement against the taunts and swagger of the Philistine: **the battle is the LORD's, and he will give all of you into our hands** (47). The outcome belongs to history.

50–54. The victorious champion disarmed and beheaded the enemy, the Israelites routed the Philistines, pursuing them to Gath and Ekron, and plundering their camp. David **put the Philistine's weapons in his own tent**; Goliath's sword was later in the tent-sanctuary of Yahweh (cf. 21: 9). The bringing of the Philistine's head to **Jerusalem** must have been after David's capture of that city (2 Sam. 5: 6–9).

55–58. Saul's reception of David has often been criticized on the ground that he would not need to ask who his own armour-bearer was. But the identity of David was not enquired into; that of his *father* was. Saul had promised (25) his daughter to whoever vanquished Goliath; enquiries into the pedigree of the king's potential son-in-law seem eminently appropriate.

18: 1–5. One of the pleasant little interludes in the book, telling of the covenant of friendship which Saul's son Jonathan made with David, investing him with his own robes and armour. Saul promoted him and **gave him a high rank in the army** (5), a popular appointment.

(d) David becomes son-in-law of the jealous Saul (18: 6–30)

6–11. These harmonious relations between the king and the young hero were not destined to last. Saul's hitherto concealed envy rose to the surface as he heard the women singing: **Saul has slain his thousands, and David his tens of thousands** (7). 'This threatened to embitter to the king more and more the whole triumph. A cruel jealousy boiled up within his soul' (F. W. Krummacher, *David the king of Israel*, p. 58). He was angry and displeased, and **from that time Saul kept a jealous eye on David** (9): an excellent description of the paranoid state.

The following day, Saul's evil spirit returned while David was playing the harp. Saul twice aimed his spear to pin him to the wall; David took successful evasive action.

12–30. Despite his jealousy, Saul needed David's support, so finding his daily presence unendurable he drafted him to the front with **command over a thousand** (13), 'a post of honour which was also one of danger' (Smith, p. 169). David was everywhere successful, **because the LORD was with him** (14), and he was universally popular. Saul promised him his eldest daughter as wife, with mixed motives; by encouraging him to **fight the battles of the LORD** (17) he hoped for his death at the hands of the Philistines, while during the wedding negotiations **Merab** was married to **Adriel of Meholah** (19). Meanwhile her sister **Michal** was in love with David; Saul decided to use her as a bait to lure him into the hands of the Philistines. News was leaked to David that Michal was his for the asking; a military exploit would be acceptable for the bride-price —all he needed to do was to slay a hundred Philistines and present their foreskins as evidence. Contrary to Saul's expectation, David easily brought double this tally and became his son-in-law. David's success and Yahweh's obvious blessing only caused Saul to be even more jealous. His forays against the Philistines continued to be uniformly successful.

(e) Jonathan as peacemaker between his father and David (19: 1–24)

Saul was not only jealous but also perturbed by the favour of Yahweh and of the people enjoyed by David; in this chapter are recorded four further attempts on David.

1–7. Saul instructed his household that David was to be eliminated. Jonathan first warned his friend to hide, and then reasoned with his father. David, he pointed out, had done nothing to offend the king to whom, indeed, he had rendered valuable services. Saul admitted his fault and withdrew his instructions; David returned to court.

8–10. David, successful again over the Philistines, was the object of a second murderous, but unsuccessful, attack by Saul (cf. 18: 10, 11).

11–17. A nocturnal attempt on David at home was foiled by his wife Michal, who facilitated his escape through a window (cf. Jos. 2: 15; Ac. 9: 24), replacing him in bed by an **idol** (16) and arranging the bedclothes to conceal the substitution. 'Image', Heb. *teraphim* (NIVmg) is a plural form with singular sense, usually meaning household gods, though some, *e.g.* W. F. Albright, have questioned the presence of such in the devout David's home. Discovering the deception, Saul scolded Michal: **Why did you . . . send my enemy away?** She lied that David had coerced her (17).

18–24. After his escape, David came to Samuel at Ramah; together they went on to **Naioth** (18), 'doubtless near Ramah; there was a community of prophets there, and we may assume that Samuel, free from responsibilities of national leadership, exercised leadership in that community' (Mauchline, p. 143). Saul immediately raised the hue and cry for the fugitive, and learning where he was, sent messengers to arrest him. They however met **a group of prophets prophesying, with Samuel standing there as their leader** (20), and were themselves inspired to join in the ecstatic prophesying, as did two further parties of envoys. Finally Saul went himself and fell under the spell; lying naked all day and night he **also prophesied in Samuel's presence** (24). Years before, Saul had met a similar group of prophets (10: 10–12), and receiving now as then the divine afflatus or some charismatic visitation, the same question was now asked: **'Is Saul also among the prophets?'** (24).

(f) David the fugitive and his friend Jonathan (20: 1–42)

As in the previous chapter, the writer is here concerned with David's departure from the court. 'We have already pointed out how important it seems to have been to the tradition to show that David's path to the throne was a legitimate one' (Hertzberg, p. 171).

1–11. David returned to discover from Jonathan exactly where he stood in relation to Saul, and why his life stood in danger. **'Never! . . . You are not going to die'**, declared Jonathan (2), explaining that his father confided in him and so he could keep David informed. But David thought Saul would keep his own counsel, knowing Jonathan's affection for him. His fears therefore were still very real: **there is only a step between me and death** (3). They immediately began to make plans; the next day David would absent himself on the pretext of a family sacrifice, and Jonathan would judge from his father's attitude how things stood. In moving terms, David asked Jonathan to be perfectly frank and pleaded that if he must die it might be at Jonathan's hand rather than Saul's. They went out **into the field** (11), i.e., the open country, to work out details.

12–17. Jonathan eloquently protested his loyalty to David and requested that when Yahweh gave him final victory, **do not ever cut off your kindness from my family— not even when the LORD has cut off every one of David's enemies from the face of the earth** (15). At his friend's request, David reasserted his love for him.

18–23. The details of Jonathan's plan now unfold. On the third day (19) David was to return to his hiding place and Jonathan, accompanied by a page, was to come and shoot three arrows. Should these drop short, all would be well; if they overshot the mark, it would indicate danger.

24–34. The scene returns to the palace. Saul noticed David's absence, but waited a day before enquiring the cause. Jonathan told him the prearranged story of a family sacrifice. Saul's temper blazed and he roundly abused his son; 'in his fury he slanders Jonathan's mother as well as Jonathan' (Mauchline, p. 148). He warned him: **'As long as the son of Jesse lives on this earth, neither you nor your kingdom will be established'** (31), and he hurled a spear at Jonathan as previously at David.

35–42. David was at the rendezvous; Jonathan's arrows overshot the mark. After the dismissal of the page they bid each other a highly emotional farewell (41). David departed, and **Jonathan went back to the town** (42). 'In the figure of Jonathan, the Old Testament has a real nobleman of high sensibility' (Hertzberg, p. 172).

ii. David exiled and persecuted (21: 1–26: 25)

(a) David at Nob (21: 1–9)

The court now barred to him, David went to **Nob**, where the descendants of Eli exercised the priesthood after the destruction of Shiloh. **Nob**, 'the city of the priests' of 22: 19, 'as Isa. 10: 32 shows, was a place between Anathoth (now 'Anāta, 2¼ miles NE of Jerusalem) and Jerusalem' (Driver, *Notes*, p. 172). The incumbent of the priestly office was **Ahimelech** (1) son of Ahitub, either a brother of Ahijah (14: 3) or else Ahijah himself, *melech* (king) and *Jah* (Yahweh) could be interchangeable synonyms. Ahitub was a brother of Ichabod, and therefore a grandson of Eli.

Ahimelech's trembling at the sight of David unaccompanied was due to astonishment rather than fear. David met him with equivocation; he had come, he lied, on behalf of Saul on a mission demanding utmost secrecy. He asked for food; the priest had only **consecrated bread**, which could be eaten only by the ritually clean. Being assured that as always on military expeditions David fulfilled this requirement, the priest gave David the **bread of the Presence** (6), AV 'shewbread' (see Lev. 24: 59; Exod. 25: 30).

7–9. The figure of **Doeg the Edomite** (7) is briefly introduced because of his future part in the story (see 22: 18 ff.). It is generally assumed that Doeg was detained in the sanctuary under some priestly discipline. The Edomites, descendants of Esau, were a continuous thorn in the Israelites' flesh; the very name would evoke a sinister presentiment in the mind of every reader. In v. 8 David asked Ahimelech for arms—**'Don't you have a spear or sword here?'** alleging that in the haste of setting out on the king's business he had forgotten his own. Ahimelech gave him Goliath's sword which was laid up in the sanctuary.

(b) David takes refuge with Achish at Gath (21: 10–15)

That day David fled from Saul and went to Achish king of Gath (10). In peril of his life, he sought refuge with the ruler of one of the cities of the Philistine pentapolis. This episode is not without its difficulties. First, David took refuge among the Philistines, the very people against whom he had spearheaded his own countrymen's attacks. Moreover, he wore the very sword which he had taken from their special champion in single combat. Some critics regard the story as straining credibility. A. R. S. Kennedy (p. 149) suggests that it is a *Midrash*, or later legendary accretion to history; Hertzberg (p. 182) remarks that the sword episode is 'not without its humour'.

Such strictures seem to overlook several considerations; (a) David did not voluntarily seek asylum among his people's enemies; he was driven by the inexorable need to evade the pursuit of Saul; (b) at Gath he behaved in a manner not calculated to gain a cordial welcome from Achish; and (c) he left Gath as soon as he could get away.

A more serious difficulty is that the Philistines are said to have recognized David, somewhat prematurely, as **king of the land** (11), perhaps because they had heard the song of the people (18: 7); certainly they can have known nothing of developments in the Saul—David struggle.

At all events, he escaped by feigning madness. 'David can therefore—though this is not expressly recorded—leave the court again without danger, without ending up in a Philistine troop or in the prison of Achish. The way God has prepared for him remains sure and opens up further' (Hertzberg, p. 183).

(c) David at Adullam and Mizpah (22: 1–5)

From Gath, David made his way to the **cave of Adullam** (Jos. 15: 35) in the Shephelah or lowland country, perhaps 12 miles SW of Bethlehem. Verses 4 and 5 speak of the **stronghold**; it has been much debated whether this word refers also to the **cave**, many arguments being adduced for and against.

Adullam proved an ideal headquarters for David and his followers, who became a sort of Robin Hood band. His family, including his parents, joined him, as did **all those who were in distress**, those rendered desperate by the demands of their masters (Smith, p. 203); **all those . . . in debt**, everyone who had a lender or creditor, cf. Isa. 24: 2 (Driver, *Notes*, p. 179); and all those who were **discontented**, 'those who had a chip on their shoulders, the people with real or imagined grievances' (Mauchline, p. 155). There were four hundred of them; David became their leader.

So perilous a refuge was hardly suitable for people so elderly as David's parents, so he took them to Moab, where the king granted them hospitality. His land had proved hospitable many years before to the family of Elimelech and Naomi (Ru. 1: 1 ff.); Ruth the Moabitess moreover was grandmother of Jesse, David's father.

It is at this juncture also that we first meet the prophet **Gad** (5) who told David that his place was not at Adullam, but in Judah. **Mizpah in Moab** (3) and the **forest of Hereth** (5); locations unknown.

(d) Saul's revenge on the priests at Nob (22: 6–23)

Meanwhile Saul was taking the keenest interest in David's movements. He **heard that David . . . had been discovered** (6): '"Discovered" reads a little oddly; a minor emendation gives "had joined up"' (D. F. Payne, *NBC*³, p. 299). 'Joined up' would suggest to Saul that David was no longer a lone outlaw but leader of a not negligible group. Saul was holding court **at Gibeah** seated **under the tamarisk tree on the hill** (6). AV, RV have 'in Ramah', but this is impossible if Gibeah is correct; RSV with RVmg has 'on the height'; Driver (*Notes*, p. 180) prefers 'in the high place'. Saul hurled vituperation at his courtiers—**men of Benjamin**, reminded them on which side their bread was buttered and challenged them to say why no one told him what David and his men were doing. **Doeg the Edomite** volunteered the information of what he had seen at Nob.

11–19. Saul was soon hot on David's trail; he summoned Ahimelech and his staff to appear before him. He accused him of conspiring with David against him, and feeding and arming the rebel, who was at that time biding his time to attack.

Ahimelech replied by a stout defence of David's loyalty; it was clear that he had known nothing of what had happened and that Saul's outburst had come as a complete surprise. But it was no use; Saul immediately ordered his guard to execute Ahimelech and all his colleagues. The guards demurred; Doeg enthusiastically carried out the commission. He killed **eighty-five men who wore the linen ephod** (18) and went to Nob to annihilate the total population of inhabitants and of livestock.

20–23. Abiathar, son of Ahimelech, alone escaped the massacre; he fled to David and told him what had happened. David felt that the real fault was his; he should have realized that Doeg would be driven by his smouldering resentment to seek his revenge at the first opportunity. He assured Abiathar that he would make the safety of the priest his personal responsibility.

(e) **David at Keilah (23: 1–14)**
News came to David of a Philistine raid on **Keilah** in the hill country about 3 miles south of Adullam. The village was built on a hillside whose terraced slopes were covered with corn (Driver, *Notes*, p. 183), making its threshing-floors an admirable target for the Philistine marauders. David **enquired of the LORD** (2) whether he should attack. We are not told of his method of enquiry, presumably the 'Urim-Thummim' type of lot-casting (see on 14: 36 f.). Yahweh's reply was affirmative. His men were nervous, so he enquired again; the order was confirmed and victory promised. He was to **go down to Keilah** (4), a phrase more appropriate if his base were further into Judaean territory than Adullam, which is 50 ft. lower than Keilah. The raid took place, victory was complete, numerous casualties inflicted, a rich booty of cattle taken and so David **saved the people of Keilah** (5).

6–13. Hearing of David's exploit, Saul was delighted, for Keilah was a walled township,

and he saw David as imprisoned there (7). Abiathar the priest, who had already joined David (22: 20), now came to Keilah bringing with him the ephod, so David was able again to consult the Lord. He asked whether rumours he had heard of Saul's approach were true, and whether the townsfolk would betray David to him. Receiving affirmative replies to both questions, David and his 600 men **left Keilah and kept moving from place to place** (13). Saul, realizing that his quarry had slipped through his fingers, gave up the hunt.

This marks a turning point in the story. David and his followers become fugitives and outlaws, relentlessly pursued by Saul and living a life of hardship and peril. The period is important in David's path to the throne, and more important for its part in his interior, spiritual development. Hunted by Saul like 'a partridge on the mountains' (26: 20), he learned that complete dependence and trust in God which permeate his psalms.

(f) **Saul pursues David: David spares Saul's life (23: 15–24: 22)**
15–18. God did not allow David to fall into Saul's hands, but his circumstances were not enviable. **David learned** (lit. 'saw', cf. AV, RV) **that:** RSV by repointing Heb. reads 'David was afraid because', which suits the context better (see v. 17). Jonathan came to his friend in his hour of need, **and helped him to find strength in God** (16), urging him not to fear. This visit must have brought strength and comfort to David; Saul's son assured him that his father would not find him, and David would become king (17). 'Jonathan', says McKane (p. 143), 'is closer to David in virtue of their covenant than he is to his father in virtue of blood'. D. F. Payne points out (*NBC*[3], p. 229) that 'Saul and his troops could not locate David, but Jonathan had no difficulty in finding his friend'. This is their last recorded meeting.

19–28. Meanwhile the Ziphites communicated to Saul the whereabouts of David hiding in their territory, offering to betray him. Saul thanked them graciously and asked for more details especially of his latest movements, needed because **he is very crafty** (22). When Saul arrived, David and his company had moved south to the wilderness of Maon. Saul was gaining on them when news came that the Philistines had again attacked, and he was forced to abandon the pursuit temporarily.

23: 29–24: 22 (cf. 26: 6–25). In Heb. , v. 29 is 24: 1. Saul's action against the Philistines completed, he came with 3,000 picked men to En Gedi determined to run David to earth. They came to the **Crags of the Wild Goats** (2): perhaps a description, perhaps a geographical name. Saul casually entered a cave where, unknown to him, David's group were resting.

They urged David to kill the unsuspecting king, since his delivery into their hands was God's doing. 'Yet David resists these pressures and refuses to take Saul's life' (McKane, p. 146). Instead, he stealthily cut off a piece of the king's robe as evidence that he could have killed him, but had refrained; Saul to him was still the Lord's anointed. He forbade his men to attack the king.

So David allowed him to leave the cave, and then calling after him by name he did homage, pleading with him not to heed detractors but to believe the testimony of his mutilated robe that David bore him no malice: **I am not guilty of wrong-doing or rebellion** (11). So why should Saul thus pursue after . . . whom? **A dead dog? A flea?** (14). He is happy to leave his cause with the Lord.

Saul was deeply touched by the incident and showed a flash of the warmth of heart that had made men rally to him in earlier days. He confessed to David: **'You are more righteous than I . . . You have treated me well, but I have treated you badly?** (17): adding, **'May the LORD reward you well for the way you treated me today'** (19). He acknowledged David as Yahweh's choice for the throne, and asked for clemency for his family after his death.

(g) **Samuel dies: David, Nabal and Abigail (25: 1–44)**
Samuel's death is recorded without reference to date or to his age. But the event is significant; for Samuel bridges the development from the theocracy and the judges to the monarchy and the great Old Testament prophets. Moreover it is clear that David, sorely beset by Saul, lost a pillar of strength in Samuel, 'a root which David had in Israelite soil was plucked up' (Hertzberg, p. 198).

1b–13. The next incident reveals the sort of life forced on David, without resources but with the responsibility for maintaining an increased force of 600 men (13; cf. 22: 2). He depended on what today might be called a protection racket. Most landowners paid the tribute he demanded, but one, **Nabal** of **Carmel** (not, of course, the Carmel in the north, but a place near Maon; cf. 15: 12), a wealthy flockmaster married to a beautiful wife, Abigail. At the time of sheep-shearing, normally a time of festivity, David sent ten young men to remind Nabal of his debt, requesting not money but hospitality for his troops. Nabal treated the application with scorn; so David called his men to action, 400 men marched with him, 200 stayed at base.

14–35. Abigail learned of David's intentions and was reminded of the very real protection he had given. Urged to take some action, and knowing her husband's obstinacy, she set out unknown to him for David's camp with don-

keys laden with copious provisions. David was preparing his revenge when she arrived, full of humility and apologies for her churlish husband: **'May my lord pay no attention to that wicked man Nabal. He is just like his name—his name is Fool, and folly goes with him.'** (25). 'Nabal' suggests one who has no regard for God or man (A. R. S. Kennedy, p. 165); the 'fool' who says in his heart, 'There is no God' (Pss. 14: 1; 53: 1) is a *nabal*. She offered her present, acknowledged the wrong that had been done to David and assured him of her confidence that he will live to become king; **the life of my master will be bound securely in the bundle of the living by the LORD your God** (29). She begged him not to burden his conscience in the day of his victory with blood shed without a cause.

Her pleading, added no doubt to her beauty and charm, won David's heart and forgiveness.

36–38. Back home, she found festivities in full swing, like the banquet of a king (36). Nabal was so drunk that she could not report on her mission until next morning. The news came as a great shock: **his heart failed him and he became like a stone** (37). Ten days later he was dead.

39–44. An appendix to the chapter tells of David's marriage to the widow Abigail; and a second union with **Ahinoam of Jezreel.** Meanwhile, **Saul had given his daughter Michal, David's wife, to Paltiel son of Laish, who was from Gallim** (44).

(h) **David spares Saul a second time (26: 1–25)**
The record now tells of David again sparing Saul's life, a story so similar to that in ch. 24 that it has been regarded as a 'doublet' or alternative account of an identical incident due to the compiler drawing on parallel sources of information. So Driver (*Notes*, p. 187) says: 'a different version of the same occurrences'. But here there are important differences pointing to different incidents. In the first, Saul went by chance, alone and unarmed, into a cave where David lay; in the second David reconnoitred the area in his search for Saul, finding him at night with his army and its commander Abner, sleeping **inside the camp** (7), armed with a spear. In the former, David cut a piece from Saul's robe, on this occasion he took the spear and jug of water from his bedside. 'The fact cannot be disregarded that the contrasts between the narratives are as notable and as widespread as the similarities; and, incidentally, there is no difficulty in supposing that there may have been two occasions, in different circumstances, when David spared Saul's life. The conclusion which is supported here is that there were two occasions' (Mauchline, p. 173).

1–5. It is again the Ziphites who inform on David's whereabouts. Saul with 3000 men set up a regular camp on the hill of Hakilah while David and his men from their mountain hide-outs watched Saul and Abner.

6–12. David's companions Ahimelech the Hittite and Abishai the brother of Joab went with him to surprise Saul in his sleeping quarters. Abishai urged killing him at once, but David again refused to **lay a hand on the LORD's anointed** (9), preferring to leave to Yahweh vengeance on Saul. Instead they took his spear and the water jug from his bedside, while **a deep sleep** from the LORD (12) fell upon Saul's men.

13–20. Out of reach, David hailed Abner, taunting him with his incompetence in guarding Saul, but 'more important than the comic deflation of Abner is the demonstration of David's innocence and magnanimity' (McKane, p. 157); Saul hearing David's voice and learning what has happened again protested his contrition. David pleaded for an end of Saul's pursuit: **'They have now driven me from my share in the LORD's inheritance and have said, "Go, serve other gods"'** (19).

21–25. Saul was again filled with remorse at his own wickedness: **'I have sinned. Come back, David my son. Because you considered my life precious today, I will not try to harm you again. Surely I have acted like a fool and have erred greatly** (21). David restored Saul's spear, kindly words were spoken on both sides, but both went their own ways at the end of the day.

iii. Saul's later years: David among the Philistines (27: 1–31: 13)

(a) David goes to Achish at Gath (27: 1–28: 2)

David had twice received Saul's assurances of goodwill, but did not feel easy: **'One of these days I shall be destroyed by the hand of Saul'** (1). He resolved to go back to the Philistines, out of Saul's reach. With his two wives and 600 men he went to Achish at Gath (cf. 21: 10–15); and **when Saul was told that David had fled to Gath, he no longer searched for him** (4). Such an influx into Gath could be an embarrassment for both sides; Achish allowed David the town of **Ziklag** (location unknown, probably about 13 miles south of Gath) where he stayed for 16 months. An interesting note says that Ziklag **has belonged to the kings of Judah ever since** (6).

8–12. David seems to have engaged in widespread slaughter and plunder as far as the Egyptian border. The arrangement suited Achish as well as David; the Philistine did not want a possible rival too near; David had no ambition to be a courtier in the palace at Gath, he wanted a base for military action. He successfully pulled the wool over Achish's eyes, giving him the impression that he was collecting his booty from his Judaean neighbours whereas in fact it was coming from Judah's enemies. The gullible Achish imagined that David was earning the reputation of a traitor to his people, thus barring the way to subsequent return.

28: 1–2. The Philistines were again preparing to mount a campaign against Israel. Achish informed David, and required him to march as his own **bodyguard for life** (2). It is not easy to understand or justify David's life of ruthlessness and deception and his association with the enemy; but he was living in highly perilous circumstances. The biblical account records, but offers no judgment.

(b) Saul at Endor (28: 3–25)

News of Samuel's death is repeated, not mere reiteration or doublet, but 'probably a necessary introduction here to the story of Saul's visit to Endor' (L. H. Brockington in *Peake*[2], p. 329). This is the account of the final decline of one who began well.

When His people entered the land God had sternly enjoined them to root out Canaanitish practices of spiritism and necromancy, for He Himself would speak to them through His prophet; to seek to know His plans by magical means was a 'detestable practice' (Dt. 18: 9–22). In early days, Saul had **expelled the mediums and spiritists from the land** (3), but his disobedience had caused a complete breakdown of communication from Yahweh. The three normal channels through which He spoke —dreams, consulting the Urim and Thummim, and the direct voice through the prophets (6)—were silent to Saul's enquiries. The Urim were in the custody of the priests: 'Having no priest with him since the slaughter of the priests at Nob, he could not consult the sacred lot; 22: 11–19 (Mauchline, p. 182).

8–19. In desperation, Saul, heavily disguised, visited a medium of whom he had heard at Endor, a few miles north of Shunem and Jezreel. The Philistines were lining up at Shunem, the Israelites at Gilboa. Driver (*Notes*, pp. 213 f.) suggests that the geographical details are inconsistent, and that 28: 3–25 should follow 30: 31. The medium received him suspiciously because her arts were illegal; promising her immunity, he asked her to call up Samuel. Terrified, she saw an apparition, **a spirit** (13). **14. 'An old man wearing a robe is coming up':** she realized the identity of her client. Saul prostrated himself before the conjured visitor, complaining that the word of Yahweh was no longer vouchsafed to him. Samuel replied that his questions had been answered already—and ignored, adding that the next day Saul and his sons would be killed and Israel's army fall to the Philistines.

20–25. Appalled and famished, Saul collapsed. Even in this crisis the gloom is illuminated by a gleam of compassion. The medium, failing to persuade Saul to take nourishment, was joined in her entreaties by his servants, and eventually he yielded. Bread was baked and a fatted calf roasted, and Saul and his men, refreshed, left—for the battlefield of Gilboa. Some have examined the incident for evidence of OT belief on the afterlife; but this seems unsafe since the episode is unique.

(c) **Philistine doubts about David (29: 1–11)**
The scene returns south to the Philistine coast; they were massing at Aphek to march north against the Israelites. **2. As the Philistine rulers marched with their units of hundreds and thousands, David and his men were marching at the rear with Achish:** 'military formations of differing sizes were passing in review, with David and his men bringing up the rear among the contingent of Achish' (McKane, p. 165). The other Philistine leaders asked: **'What about these Hebrews?'** (3). Achish proudly presented David as a valuable recruit to his service, but his colleagues did not share his gullibility. They were highly suspicious: **'Send the man back, that he may return to the place you assigned him . . . or he will turn against us during the fighting'** (4). They could not forget the songs celebrating David's victories against the Philistines (5; cf. 18: 7; 21: 11). The reaction of the fussy Achish borders on the comic; afraid of his colleagues he assured David: **'I have found no fault in you, but the rulers don't approve of you. Turn back and go in peace; do nothing to displease the Philistine rulers'** (6, 7). David, nonplussed at this turn of events, nevertheless agreed to leave at morning light next day. **So David and his men got up early in the morning to go back to the land of the Philistines, and the Philistines went up to Jezreel** (11).

David cannot have been pleased at this cavalier dismissal, but no doubt the hand of God was in it: 'David was spared, therefore, from having to take an active part on the Philistine side in the struggle against Saul and the Israelite tribes' (Noth, *History of Israel*, p. 181).

(d) **David marches against the Amalekites (30: 1–31)**
1–10. So David returned to Ziklag and found it sacked and all the inhabitants taken captive (including his own two wives) by the Amalekites, who had taken advantage of the absence of the Philistines. The effect on the returning warriors was devastating; the men, **bitter in spirit** (6), held David responsible. But with him, natural distress soon turned to action; **David found strength in the LORD his God** (6). Ordering Abiathar to bring the ephod, he enquired whether he should and could pursue the enemy successfully. Receiving a favourable reply, he set out with 600 men. At the wadi of **Besor**, 'one third of David's force is found to be too exhausted for further pursuit, a con-

dition by no means surprising, if they had just covered the 80 miles or thereby from Aphek to Ziklag in three days' (A. R. S. Kennedy, p. 184).

11–20. Pushing on, David's men overtook **an Egyptian in a field** (11), dispirited and starving after three days' fast. They fed him well, and interrogated him. He told them of a raid on **the Negev of the Kerethites and the territory belonging to Judah and the Negev of Caleb** and—worst of all (in the eyes of David and his men)—of the sack and burning of **Ziklag** (14). The **Negev** (see Driver, *Notes*, on 27: 10, p. 212, also p. 223) is properly 'the dry country', and so generally used of the south. The **Kerethites** were probably a sub-tribe of the Philistines; the name is probably connected with Crete (Caphtor), whence the Philistines originated. **The Negev of Caleb**, mentioned only here (but see Jos. 16: 19), is clearly the home of the Calebite clan to which Nabal belonged (25: 3). Assured his life would be spared, the Egyptian agreed to lead David to the marauders. They came upon them **drinking and revelling** (16) to commemorate their success over Judah and the Philistines. David's arrival took them completely by surprise; only 400 escaped, on camels; David recovered all the prisoners and booty intact, and in addition captured much spoil from the Amalekites. At the conclusion of the action, it was announced: **'This is David's plunder'** (20). To the suggestion that this sounds selfish, Kennedy (p. 185) says: 'a corrupt and unintelligible text is responsible'.

21–31. The sequel shows David acting judicially in two problems. First, **all the evil men and troublemakers** (22) among his followers wanted to share the spoil among themselves only, but David ruled that **the share of the man who stayed with the supplies is to be the same as that of him who went down to battle. All shall share alike** (24): this precedent was incorporated into Israelite military custom: **a statute and ordinance for Israel from that day to this** (25). Secondly, back in Ziklag, he sent shares of the spoil **to the elders of Judah, who were his friends** (26) in a dozen cities. He had the right to do this with 'David's plunder' (20), for it was not *herem*, 'dedicated' to Yahweh, as when Saul fought Amalek (ch. 15). Besides, it might dispose them to support his kingship later on.

(e) **The battle of Gilboa: Saul and Jonathan killed (31: 1–13)**
The Philistines were moving north from Aphek for their decisive attack (see ch. 9). The coast road to the plain of Esdraelon, which had been under Philistine control throughout Saul's reign, afforded them easy passage through friendly Canaanite and Phoenician territory and the plain was an ideal battle ground. It cut off

Saul's forces from the Israelites in Galilee, and it provided ample level ground to manoeuvre chariots (2 Sam. 1: 6). For an account of the battle, see J. Bright, *History of Israel*, pp. 173 f.

The chariots probably opened the attack on the Israelites on the lower slopes of Mount Gilboa; when they got too high the archers took over. Jonathan and his brothers, Abinadab and Malki-Shua, fell; Saul was badly wounded. To escape the final ignominy of mockery by captors, he asked his armour-bearer to kill him. The younger man had not the heart, so Saul committed suicide by falling on his sword, an example immediately followed by the armour-bearer. When the army realized what had happened, complete disintegration ensued: moreover, the Israelites who resided in the adjoining territory **abandoned their towns and fled. And the Philistines came and occupied them** (7).

One story remains—of kindliness and compassion bringing a solitary gleam into the desolate scene. The victors searched the battlefield according to custom to plunder the dead. Finding Saul and his sons, they took the armour to display in their temple of the Ashtoreths, the bodies they beheaded and hung on the walls of Beth Shan for all to see. They **sent messengers throughout the land of the Philistines to proclaim the news in the temple of their idols and among their people** (9). But the men of Jabesh Gilead (see 11: 1–13) remembered with gratitude Saul's kindness in bygone days, and **all their valiant men journeyed through the night to Beth Shan. They took down the bodies of Saul and his sons from the wall of Beth Shan** (12). The corpses were cremated and reverently interred; a week's fast marked their respect. In defeat and death, Saul still inspired affection in some people, as this story and that of the medium at Endor show. This is well brought out in the impressive character study of Saul by A. C. Welch in *Kings and Prophets of Israel* (1952), pp. 63–79.

2 Samuel

I. DAVID MOURNS FOR SAUL AND JONATHAN (1: 1–27)

The deaths of Saul and Jonathan opened David's path to the throne, but this was not his preoccupation when he heard of the tragic events on Gilboa. A dishevelled young refugee from the battlefield brought the news to him at Ziklag, reporting the rout of the Israelite armies, the enormous toll of casualties and the death of the two leaders. David demanded the source of his information. The young man, an Amalekite, told how he had come upon Saul, **leaning on his spear** (6), and hemmed in by chariots and horsemen; the defeated king had begged the Amalekite to slay him. He had done so, and taken from the body the crown and **the band on his arm** (10) and had brought these items of royal regalia to David, probably to curry favour as well as to substantiate his story. This account of what happened does not tally at all points with 1 Sam. 31: 1–6; some have attempted to harmonize the two passages, surely an unnecessary exercise. An informant who was looking to David for reward might have tinkered with truth!

He was motivated, as Hertzberg says (p. 236) by 'a mixture of grief and calculating hope'; he could hardly have anticipated David's reaction. The king and his courtiers tore their clothes and **mourned and wept and fasted till evening** (12). Then he turned upon the messenger: **'Why were you not afraid to lift your hand to destroy the LORD's anointed?'** (14). The Amalekite, an intruder in the army of Yahweh, boasted of slaying the king. David ordered his summary execution.

The rest of the chapter records the lamentation which David composed for the occasion, ordering that it should be learnt by the people. Our author's source for it is the **Book of Jashar**, a collection of national poetry mentioned in Jos. 10: 12 ff.; 1 Kg. 8: 12 f. The song is written in the Hebrew lament or elegy form (Heb., *qînāh*), which 'gives the poetry the character of a plaintive lilt' (McKane, p. 176). **19. How the mighty have fallen:** the theme of the poem at the beginning and end (27), as well as in the middle (25). The 'mighty' are primarily Saul and Jonathan; we are reminded of their heroism (22), the benefits they conferred on their subjects (24), and the very deep affection of David and Jonathan for each other. There is no moralizing or spiritualizing, just the overwhelming grief of a highly sensitive man. It is a passage of great literary beauty even in translation; its haunting cadences in the King James Version give it an imperishable place in English literature.

II. THE REIGN OF KING DAVID
(2: 1–8: 18)
i. David, king of Judah at Hebron
(2: 1–4: 12)
(a) **David and Ish-Bosheth, rival kings**
(2: 1–3: 1)
(i) **Rival Kings (2: 1–11)**

But life must go on, and David, who had long led a nomadic life, needed to settle. He enquired of the Lord; how we are not told. H. P. Smith (p. 266) thinks that 'the name was obtained by a process of exclusion like that used in discovering a person by lot'. He was guided to establish himself with his two wives, Ahinoam and Abigail, and all his followers in **Hebron** in the hill-country (Jos. 15: 45; 1 Sam. 30: 31); 'the most important town of the entire district' (Driver, *Notes*, p. 227). **then the men of Judah came to Hebron and there they anointed David king over the house of Judah** (4).

4b–7. David learned of the kindness of the men of Jabesh Gilead and sent them gracious thanks, praying that Yahweh would show kindness and faithfulness to them. He informed them that the Judahites had made him their king, and promised friendship to the Jabesh Gileadites. But the breach was far from healed.

8–11. Abner, Saul's commander-in-chief, rallied the North to Saul's surviving son **Ish-Bosheth**, whom he installed as **king over Gilead, Ashur, and Jezreel and also over Ephraim, Benjamin and all Israel** (9); he established a 'government in exile' out of Philistine reach. This division between North and South came to a head with the schism after the death of Solomon, but its origins date in reality from much earlier (see H. L. Ellison, *Prophets of Israel*, chs. i, ii). Ish-Bosheth was 40 (a pointer to Saul's age at his death), he reigned **two years** (10), though Hertzberg suggests that the clause originally read at the beginning of v. 12: 'he reigned two years when Abner . . . went out' (p. 250). **10. the house of Judah . . . followed David:** he reigned seven and a half years in Hebron.

Ish-Bosheth is the 'Esh-Baal' of 1 Chr. 8: 33; 9: 39; and probably the Ishvi of 1 Sam. 14: 49 (Mauchline, p. 203); his name was changed later to Ish-Bosheth, 'man of shame', because Esh-Baal is compounded with the name of the Phoenician god Baal. **9. Ashuri:** a name usually given to the Assyrians, obviously not intended here; probably a scribal error for the *Asherites* or the *Geshurites*.

(ii) **The first battle: Asahel dies (2: 12–3: 1)**
The northern forces under Abner and David's under Joab (1 Sam. 26: 6; his mother Zeruiah was David's sister, 1 Chr. 2: 16) met at the **pool of Gibeon:** 'a large reservoir which still exists' (H. P. Smith, p. 270). Arriving on opposite sides they parleyed across the water; Joab agreed to Abner's proposal that twelve picked men from each side should **fight hand to hand in front of us** (14). But the limited conflict got out of hand, and all the participants lost their lives. So great was the slaughter that its memory was preserved in a local place-name, **Helkath Hazzurim** (16): 'the field of sword edges'.

In the ensuing pursuit, Asahel, brother of Joab and Abishai and a noted athlete, was hard on the heels of the fugitive Abner. Abner, foreseeing the blood-feud that must follow if he were killed, advised Asahel to attack another

instead. But Asahel persisted, and Abner, 'presumably by stopping suddenly, lets him run on to the shaft of his long spear. We are to assume that this was not to kill him, but to make him unfit to fight. Unfortunately the spear touches the soft part of the abdomen. Asahel has been running so fast that the shaft goes right through his body and he dies on the spot' (Hertzberg, p. 252). Bystanders showed their respect by standing motionless.

2: 24–3: 1. Joab and Abishai took up the pursuit, and overtook Abner and his Benjamites at a strong position on a hill-top. Abner appealed to Joab to desist, pointing out the futility of fratricidal strife. Joab then called off the combat instead of fighting on through the night. The two armies returned to base and counted their casualties; the Davidites had lost 20 men including Asahel, the Benjaminites 360. The struggle continued: **'The war between the house of Saul and the house of David lasted a long time. David grew stronger and stronger, while the house of Saul grew weaker and weaker'** (1).

(b) **David's sons: list 1 (3: 2–5; cf. 5: 13–16; 8: 16–18)**
As the history of Saul is interrupted by a brief family register (14: 49–51), so here there is a list of David's sons, with the names of their mothers. They are said to be those born in Hebron, though Noth (*History of Israel*, p. 200) thinks some may have been born earlier. It is interesting to note that four wives are mentioned in addition to the two he brought with him to Hebron (cf. 2: 2).

The list of sons is as follows:
a. **Amnon**, son of Ahinoam. Later met his death as crown prince (ch. 13).
b. **Kileab**, another form of the name Caleb; son of Abigail; otherwise unknown.
c. **Absalom**, son of Maacah daughter of Talmai, king of Geshur; later led a rebellion against his father.
d. **Adonijah**, son of Haggith; briefly seized the throne before his father died.
e. **Shephatiah**, son of Abital, otherwise unknown.
f. **Ithream**, son of Eglah, **'David's wife'**. Why Eglah alone should be referred to as David's wife is puzzling; the other five were entitled to the same description. Hertzberg's view that she may have been the favourite wife, and H. P. Smith's that she was his half sister, have been discounted. Driver suggests 'some transcriptional corruption' (*Notes*, p. 246).

(c) **The death of Abner (3: 6–39)**
A sordid story of intrigue and murder follows. The ambitious Abner was taking advantage of conditions to consolidate his own position, even sleeping with Saul's concubine Rizpah. Control of the harem of a dead king gave a

strong claim to the succession also (cf. de Vaux, *Ancient Israel*, p. 116). Ish-Bosheth lodged his protest (7), without, however, accusing his general of ulterior political motives. Abner immediately made a blustering show of outraged dignity: **Am I a dog's head—on Judah's side?** (8). There is a pun on Caleb, the Hebrew for a dog, and the name of a clan of Judah; Abner was asking if he was to be treated as a mere Judahite. He reminded Ish-Bosheth of all his loyalty to Saul's house, and threatened that he might well go and place his services at David's disposal. **Ish-Bosheth did not dare to say another word to Abner, because he was afraid of him** (11).

Abner put his threat into effect and contacted David, offering to hand over the whole kingdom to him. His precise intentions are not stated clearly, but the outcome of the episode is that he 'played the role not only of founder but also of gravedigger of Ishbaal's kingdom' (Hertzberg, p. 257). David was cautious; he gave a restrained assent, subject to his ex-wife Michal, Saul's daughter, being returned to him (see 1 Sam. 18: 20; 25: 44). Ish-Bosheth agreed and took Michal from her husband, who could not disguise his grief, until Abner ordered him home.

17. Abner conferred with the elders of Israel: these, according to Hertzberg (p. 259), 'originally the "oldest" of both tribe and family, experienced and renowned (Job 29), apparently became an aristocratic group which by the pressure of events represented a sort of senate in town or tribe. The "elders of Israel" mentioned here (and at 5: 3; 17: 4, 15; 1 Kg. 8: 1) may be a nucleus drawn from the elders of the tribes'. Where the conference was held is not specified, it can hardly have been Ish-Bosheth's court. Abner went on south to Benjamin to recruit support, and then to Hebron to meet David, who feasted him and his companions. He promised to **assemble all Israel . . . that they may make a compact with you, and that you may rule over all that your heart desires** (21). David sent Abner away **in peace**, perhaps (though some discount this, *e.g.*, McKane, p. 195; H. P. Smith, p. 279) with a promise of responsibility at court.

Whether this be so or not, Joab who entered with his men **from a raid**, bringing **a great deal of plunder** (22), clearly thought his position threatened. Absent when Abner had arrived, he was disturbed by what he heard, challenging the king with the question of why he had behaved so. H. P. Smith (p. 279) says that Joab's anger was due to David's letting Abner go in peace, when as a kinsman of Asahel himself he should have taken action. Leaving the royal presence, Joab, unknown to the king, sent a message which reached Abner at the **well of Sirah** (26), which Driver (*Notes*, p.

250) identifies with 'Ain Sārah, about a mile north of Hebron. He returned, Joab met him and engaged him in private conversation, during which he killed him, **to avenge the blood of his brother Asahel** (27), in pursuance of the blood-feud which Abner had tried to prevent (2: 26).

David's reaction of extreme horror was immediate; he was no doubt apprehensive lest this act of wanton violence should be laid at his door. He protested his innocence, praying that God's judgment would fall on Joab, and invoking the most solemn curses on his house. The writer's final comment (30) links Abishai with his brother Joab in responsibility for the outrage.

David then ordered a public funeral for Abner, himself leading the mourning, again with a *qînāh* or lament of his own: **Should Abner have died as the lawless die? . . .** (33). Abner was a man of wisdom and experience who had been made to look foolish by Joab's unprincipled craftiness. After the funeral rites David fasted until sundown, a tribute which added to his already considerable popularity. He reiterated his respect for Abner: **'Do you not realise that a prince and a great man has fallen in Israel this day?'** (38). He spoke of his own loss, and again committed the matter of retribution to the Lord. He was too dependent on the support of **the sons of Zeruiah** to take any action against them.

(*d*) **Ish-Bosheth assassinated (4: 1–12)**
Ish-Bosheth's ramshackle kingdom did not long survive its main pillar, Abner, whose death caused not only grief but downright dismay. Baanah and Recab, two followers of Ish-Bosheth **who were leaders of raiding bands** (2), had had to leave their hometown of Beeroth for Gittaim, where they settled as **aliens** (3), a kind of second-class citizens. The only surviving member of the royal family was Jonathan's little crippled son, **Mephibosheth** (see below, ch. 9).

Baanah and Recab saw the opportunity of satisfying their grudge against Ish-Bosheth. Entering his almost unguarded house they quickly murdered him in his bed and travelled overnight with his head to present it to David; **'Here is the head of Ish-Bosheth son of Saul, your enemy, who tried to take your life. This day the LORD has avenged my lord the king against Saul and his offspring'** (8). They got scant thanks from David; recalling what he had done to the Amalekite who had brought the news of Saul's death he challenged them; how much more guilty were they: **wicked men** who had **killed an innocent man** in his own bed (11)? He ordered their immediate execution, and the ignominious exposition of their corpses, while giving orders for an honourable burial for Ish-Bosheth.

ii. David, king of all Israel at Jerusalem (5: 1–6: 23)

(a) David, king of all Israel (5: 1–5; cf. 1 Chr. 11: 1–3)

So Saul and his house had come to an end; no further obstacle stood between David and the throne of the whole nation. **1. All the tribes of Israel came to David at Hebron:** not surely the whole population, but representatives (cf. v. 3: **all the elders of Israel**). They brought their invitation to him to be their lord; 'here the promise to David is fulfilled: he becomes king over all the people' (Hertzberg, p. 266). During Saul's reign he had been their Moses and their Joshua: **'you were the one who led Israel on their military campaigns'** (2): Yahweh had promised him two offices; he was to be not only their **ruler**, but was also to **shepherd** them. 'This is the first use of this verb in the OT with reference to a king in Israel; it obviously demands of him a pastoral care of his people and not a despotic use of them' (Mauchline, p. 215).

David made a compact with the elders at Hebron and they anointed him; his reign had officially started. He was 30, and reigned seven and a half years in Hebron.

(b) Zion captured from the Jebusites (5: 6–12; cf. 1 Chr. 11: 4–9; 14: 1–2)

The first task to which David addressed himself was the provision of a capital for his kingdom. To have chosen a city with either northern or southern associations would inevitably have alienated large numbers of his subjects. An ideal site presented itself in Zion, the fortress city of the Jebusites who had hitherto resisted all the efforts of the invading Israelites to take it, and so was identified with neither north nor south. Attacked once more by **the king and his men** (6)—1 Chr. 11: 4 says 'David and all the Israelites'—they again showed resistance, sending a message to David which AV and RV report: '"Except thou take away the blind and the lame, thou shalt not come in hither": thinking, David cannot come in hither'. RVmg agrees more closely with NIV: **'You will not get in here; even the blind and the lame can ward you off.' They thought, 'David cannot get in here'** (6). David's assault succeeded; his strategy is described in v. 8, but, as A. R. S. Kennedy (p. 213) says, 'the first half of this verse is so corrupt as to have been long the despair of textual critics'. The general impression is of a frontal attack; for detailed examination see the larger commentaries. 1 Chr. 11: 6 f. says that Joab led the assault, thereby earning the command. The part played by the lame and the blind, says Driver (*Notes*, p. 260), lies behind proverbs excluding beggars later from the temple, though it is difficult to see the connection between 'the lame and the blind'

in verses 6 and 8. 1 Chr. 11 makes no reference to them.

But however uncertain the details, the result was evident; the city fell completely into David's hands. He occupied it and did a great deal of rebuilding to make it a capital worthy of his kingdom. **9. He built up the area around it, from the supporting terraces inward:** apparently beginning the fortifications later completed by Solomon (cf. 1 Kg. 9: 15, 24). The word translated 'inward' is the usual word for 'house', here as opposed to 'outside'. The account of the capture of Jerusalem is rounded off by an editorial note: **And he became more and more powerful, because the LORD, God Almighty was with him** (10).

11–12. Hiram king of Tyre contracted to send materials and workmen to build his palace; another editorial note comments: **And David knew that the LORD had established him as king over Israel and had exalted his kingdom for the sake of his people Israel** (12).

(c) David's sons: list II (5: 13–16; cf. 1 Chr. 11: 4–9; 14: 1–2)

3: 2–5 gives a list of the sons born to David in Hebron: now there is a further register of later additions to his family. An unspecified number of unnamed concubines (omitted in 1 Chr.) and wives are mentioned (13); by these more sons and daughters were born. The sons are listed: **1. Shammua; 2. Shobab; 3. Nathan; 4. Solomon; 5. Ibhar; 6. Elishua; 7. Nepheg; 8. Japhia; 9. Elishama; 10. Eliada; 11. Eliphelet**—eleven in all. 1 Chr. 14: 4–7 adds two more, Elpelet and Nogah, between numbers 6 and 7 in Samuel's list, and further substitutes 'Beeliada' for Eliada, 'so that David, like Saul, was easily able to give one of his sons a name compounded with Baal' (Hertzberg, p. 271). Of these sons Solomon is the only one who figures in our historical records; Nathan appears in the genealogy of Lk. 3: 31.

This list is a continuation of that in 3: 2–5, and probably comes from the same state archive.

(d) David victorious over the Philistines (5: 17–25; cf. 1 Chr. 14: 8–16)

News of David's anointing reached the Philistines; they were alarmed at this new development. A king at Hebron, sharing the rule with a rival in the north, was one thing; a king over the whole land was a far different matter. They sent out search parties, but, hearing of this, David **went down to the stronghold** (17). Most critics assume that the stronghold was Adullam; a minority suggest Zion but were this so the writer would hardly speak of 'going down'. **18. Now the Philistines had come and spread out in the Valley of Rephaim:** David, having consulted the oracle and received a favourable reply with assurance of victory, attacked and defeated them in a battle at **Baal Perazim**—'Lord of breaking out'—so completely that they fled, leaving their idols as spoils of war. Said David, **'As waters break out, the LORD has broken out against my enemies before me'** (20). 'He himself compares the break through to a phenomenon visible in hilly country during heavy rain. The water which pours down sweeps through and carries away any obstacles which may be in its path, banks of earth, hedges, walls, even a house built on the sand' (Hertzberg, p. 274).

But they massed again in the plain of Rephaim; the oracle directed David to change his tactics. There was to be no frontal attack this time, but a pincer movement **behind them and attack them in front of the balsam trees** (23)—better than 'mulberry trees' of AV, RV, though 'the authorities are not agreed as to the tree in question' (A. R. S. Kennedy, p. 217). A **sound of marching in the tops of the balsam trees** (24) was to be their signal to advance. It is Yahweh who goes ahead of His troops and who dictates the strategy that leads to David's complete victory; he **struck down the Philistines all the way from Gibeon to Gezer** (25).

(e) **The Ark comes from Baalah of Juddah to the city of David**
(6: 1–23; cf. 1 Chr. 13: 5–14; 15: 25–16: 3, 43)
David now had a capital city, and to it he brought the ark from Baalah of Judah, where it had long remained 'in 'Abinadab's house on the hill' (1 Sam. 7: 1). The parallel account in 1 Chr. is very similar, except that it is prefaced by the record of David's consultation 'with each of his officers' where the recovery of the ark was unanimously approved. In the *Samuel* account the initiative is David's; he sets out with 30,000 men, a figure often criticized as too high, though 'as Yahweh is a God of war such an escort is appropriate' (H. P. Smith, p. 291).

Hertzberg (p. 278) comments: 'it is not clear whether in the original context the mission was hostile, or whether it was cultic, and therefore peaceable'. The question of possible hostility arises because the region of Kiriath Jearim was under Philistine supervision, if not Philistine rule. **2. Baalah of Judah:** cf. 1 Chr. 13: 6, 'Baalah of Judah, Kiriath Jearim'. They were to bring back **the ark of God, which is called by . . . the name of the LORD Almighty, who is enthroned between the cherubim.** The sacred chest was placed on **a new cart** (3), undefiled by previous use and driven by Abinadab's sons, **Uzzah and Ahio** (or 'Uzzah and his brother', in the rendering suggested by RSVmg). The whole company, led by David, rejoiced with song and instrumental music. But the procession was interrupted by

tragedy: at **the threshing floor of Nacon**, the oxen drawing the cart stumbled and Uzzah presumably tried to steady the ark itself with his hand. The exact details are not clear. At all events, handling the sacred object cost him his life. David was indignant at the judgment, which seemed a bar to his ambition to place the ark in Jerusalem. He named the place **Perez Uzzah** (8): 'the breaking forth upon Uzzah', and abandoning his project, he deposited the ark with **Obed-Edom the Gittite** (10).

The ark brought blessing to its new resting-place, encouraging David to resume his project after three months. He celebrated the start of the journey with sacrifices and continued with rejoicing, music and dancing led by the king himself, **wearing a linen ephod** (14). 1 Chr. 15: 27 adds that he also 'was clothed in a robe of fine linen'. What he actually wore is not clear, for when the rejoicing throng reached Jerusalem, David's wife Michal saw him leading them, and despised him for **disrobing in the sight of the slave girls of his servants as any vulgar fellow would** (20): she evidently found his clothing inadequate, and was not slow to say so: **'How the king of Israel has distinguished himself today!'** she sneered, entirely insensitive to the religious dimension of his ecstasy. David replied that the very slave girls she thought would despise him would understand as she could not, and honour him for his emotions. As for Michal, she remained barren for the rest of her life (23); 'The natural understanding is that the estrangement was the reason for Michal's childlessness—not that she was stricken with barrenness by Yahweh, as some have supposed' (H. P. Smith, p. 297). Mauchline (p. 226) takes the contrary view, seeing as a penalty Michal's barrenness and the consequent final exclusion of the house of Saul from any part in the succession.

iii. **David's dynasty, court and dominions (7: 1–8: 18)**
(a) **The house of God and the house of David (7: 1–29; cf. 1 Chr. 17: 1–27)**
1–17. *David's desire.* This story differs little from its counterpart in 1 Chr. 17; David **was settled in his palace and the LORD had given him rest from all his enemies around him** (1). He grieved at the comparison between his own **palace of cedar** (2) and the temporary tent which housed the ark. He spoke with Nathan the prophet, 'a worthy successor to Samuel' (D. F. Payne, *NBC*³, p. 305), who assured him of God's approval for his scheme to build a worthy house for Yahweh. But with the night came a divine message to Nathan instructing him to reverse the counsel he had given to David. God, Nathan was reminded, had had no permanent house on earth, but since the Exodus, **I have been moving from place to place with a tent as my dwelling** (6). Nor

had He ever instructed His people to build Him a house. Then there was a personal message for David, reminding him of his call as a shepherd to lead the people, defeating all his foes before him. Israel will **'have a home of their own and no longer be disturbed'** (10). As for David building a house for Yahweh, 'Yahweh **declares to you that the LORD himself will establish a house for you'** (11). His son would succeed to the throne after him; the *nāgîd*, the prince or charismatic leader, was to found a dynasty under God's protection: **'I will be his father, and he will be my son'** (14). Even if David's son or any other of his future successors were to fail in his obedience, God would punish him severely, but he would not be cut off from the succession as Saul had been. **'Your house and your kingdom shall endure for ever before me; your throne shall be established forever'** (16).

This is one of the milestones of the OT revelation. The successive stages in the unfolding of God's redemptive purpose are marked by *covenants*, divine disclosures of God's sovereign forbearance and grace to man. To Noah (Gen. 9: 9–17) the promised deliverance from judgment is universal and unconditional; no requirements are imposed with the promise bestowed. To Abraham (Gen. 15) God indicated that the channel through which the nations were to be blessed was his seed, who were to be identified by the token of the covenant, circumcision (17: 9–14). At Sinai (Exod. 19; 20) a new covenant was pronounced by Yahweh to a people whom He had already redeemed from Egypt, a further manifestation of His grace, but with the Decalogue and its accompanying legislation, not merely the prerequisite for God's blessing but the definition of the personal holiness of the covenant people. There was an element of the conditional: 'if you will obey my voice and keep my covenant, you shall be my own possession . . . a kingdom of priests and a holy nation' (Exod. 19: 5).

With the establishment of David's kingdom came the covenant with David (see, *e.g.*, Ps. 89: 1–4, 26–37; 132: 11–18). The word 'covenant' does not occur in the present passage, but 'it is apparent from the other relevant passages that this is the basic annunciation to David of the covenant concerned' (J. Murray, *NBD*, p. 266). This covenant between God and His king is quite unconditional: 'Although obedience to Yahweh is demanded from succeeding generations of Davidic rulers, this is not envisaged as jeopardizing the continuance of the covenant. The purpose of referring to the divine chastisement of erring sons (vv. 14–15) is to reinforce the assertion that this will not lead to the annulment of the covenant' (R. E. Clements, *Abraham and David*, 1967, p. 54).

18–29. *David's worship.* The remainder of ch.

7 describes David's prayer of thanksgiving. He **went in and sat before the LORD** (18), meditating on his own unworthiness and insignificance and God's great goodness: **'Who am I, O Sovereign LORD . . . ? . . . you have also spoken about the future of the house of your servant'** (18, 19). He is completely absorbed by this wonder: **'What more can David say to you? . . . you have done this great thing and made it known to your servant'** (20, 21). He pours out his heart in praise: **'How great you are, O Sovereign LORD! There is no God but you, as we have heard with our own ears'** (22). No other nation has such a God as Israel, **'God went out to redeem as a people for himself'** (23). The tie between God and His people is indissoluble; He has promised an eternal kingdom to David's line, and because of so many promised blessings, **'so your servant has found courage to offer you this prayer'** (27).

Here we see the man after God's own heart communing with his God; we hear the breathings and the longings of the 'sweet psalmist of Israel'.

(b) War and Empire: 'The Lord gave David victory everywhere he went' (8: 1–14; cf. 1 Chr. 18: 1–13)

A summary of David's military exploits (1–14) and a register of his chief officials (15–18) round off the history so far. His campaigns consolidated his territories by the subjection of peripheral peoples. **1. the Philistines:** their defeat, recorded in more detail in 5: 17–25, is included for completeness. Hertzberg (p. 290) suggests reading: 'David, then, had defeated the Philistines'. **Metheg Ammah:** location uncertain; D. F. Payne (*NBD³*, p. 305) suggests Gath. **2. Moab:** the complete defeat of the Moabites was followed by a gruesome massacre of two in three of the prisoners, on the face of it an act of inexcusable cruelty. But the account is clearly fragmentary; a complete text might well modify the impression, which contrasts strangely with the hospitality of Moab in 1 Sam. 22: 3 f. **3. Zobah:** its defeat is identical perhaps with the event of 10: 6 ff. Zobah was one of the small states north of Israel forming the geographical territory of Syria, which did not become a political entity until centuries later (see K. A. Kitchen, *art.* 'Syria, Syrians', *NBD*, p. 1229). Hadadezer their king was going **to restore his control along the Euphrates River:** cf. 1 Chr. 18: 3 RSV—'he went to set up his monument' (perhaps a frontier pillar) there. David attacked, taking 27,000 prisoners and hamstringing all the chariot horses not required for his own service. Reinforcements from Damascus suffered a similar fate; David occupied the Syrian cities and exacted tribute. **6. The LORD gave David**

victory everywhere he went: he brought considerable spoils of gold and bronze to Jerusalem. **9. Hamath:** a strategic city on the river Orontes; cf. 1 Chr. 18: 9–11. **Tou** (cf. 1 Chr. 18: 9), king of Hamath, sent congratulations to David on overcoming Hadadezer, with presents of silver, gold and bronze, which David dedicated to the Lord with plunder from other campaigns. **13. And David became famous:** a second editorial comment. **13. Edomites:** he inflicted a crushing defeat on the Edomites in the **Valley of Salt** (probably near the Dead Sea, perhaps to the south of it) with 18,000 casualties and subsequent occupation (cf. the Massoretic heading to Ps. 60 for a slightly variant account).

(c) David's leading officers of state: list I (8: 15–18; cf. 1 Chr. 18: 14–17)
15. David reigned over all Israel, doing what was just and right for all his people: his aides are listed. **16. Joab** (cf. chs. 2; 3) was commander, **Jehoshaphat** son of Ahilud 'recorder' or annalist, **Zadok** son of Ahitub and **Ahimelech** son of Abiathar were priests. D. F Payne (*NBC³*) thinks that the order of Ahimelech and Abiathar should be reversed (see 1 Sam. 22: 20). **17. Zadok** first appears at this point; some think him to have been priest of a Jebusite shrine in pre-Davidic Jerusalem, but so dedicated a Yahwist as David would scarcely have selected such a priest. Others see him as a Yahwist priest from another sanctuary, perhaps Saul's nominee to succeed the Elides after their slaughter. **Seraiah** the secretary is the 'Shavsha' of 1 Chr. 18: 16. **18. Benaiah** son of Jehoiada commanded the mercenary groups of **Kerethites** and **Pelethites** —Cretans and Philistines, according to Mauchline. Finally, **David's sons were royal priests** (18mg): a puzzling expression; 1 Chr. 18: 17 has 'David's sons were chief officials at the king's side'. If David was acknowledged as heir to the priest-kingship of Melchizedek, some priestly functions, distinct from those associated with the ark, may have been discharged by members of the royal family.

III. THE SUCCESSION NARRATIVE
(9: 1–20: 26; see also 1 Kg. 1: 1–2: 46)
2 Sam. 9–20, with 1 Kg. 1, 2, are generally recognized as an independent unit of material. A. R. S. Kennedy calls it 'the history of David's court'; Otto Eissfeldt 'the succession story'; G. W. Anderson 'the court history'; others the succession narrative, the name given by R. N. Whybray to his exhaustive monograph (London, 1968).

Dr. Whybray discusses the narrative as history, as a literary composition, as a national epic, as a moral or religious tale, as political propaganda, stressing especially the first two aspects. He carefully tests the historicity by two

criteria; is it congruous with reliable external evidence? and is it inherently not improbable, congruent with the general course of history and of circumstances known to us, and without discernible motive for inventing or distorting facts? He concludes that the work is soundly based in history, and sees the author as an objective historian who admires David without whitewashing him, and who, rather than stating his own opinions of persons and events, allows them to speak for themselves.

He holds, however, that the writer's aim is not primarily historical but rather literary in that a central theme is pursued in a work of careful structure and great literary skill. This theme is the path that led to the firm establishment of Solomon on his father's throne. We see the elimination one by one of every royal prince who might be a rival contender, and the whole narrative is marked by skilful use of dialogue, profound psychological insight into character, and an effective mastery of style.

A careful examination of the passage as a literary whole, and of its similarity in outlook to Proverbs, leads to the conclusion that the succession narrative dates from early in Solomon's reign. Few, at all events, will quarrel with G. W. Anderson's description of this section as 'the supreme historical treasure of Samuel'.

i. David's generosity to Mephibosheth (9: 1–13)
Arrived at his plateau of stability, David's first thought was to honour the covenant he had made with Jonathan and his descendants for ever (1 Sam. 20: 42). It has been suggested that he may merely have been seeking the goodwill of Saul's surviving supporters, but the general impression that 1 and 2 Sam. give is of a man with a genuinely generous heart. Enquiries for any of Saul's house to whom he might show **kindness** (1), **God's kindness** (3), Heb. *ḥesed*, covenant love, produced a former servant of Saul called Ziba, who was able to tell David of the existence and the whereabouts of Jonathan's son Mephibosheth, who had been crippled as an infant when his nurse dropped him when fleeing after Saul's death (4: 4). The young prince's name was probably originally Merib-Baal (1 Chr. 8: 34; 9: 40a) or Merib-Baal (1 Chr. 9: 40b, *MT*); its meaning is uncertain, but the second half of the name, like that of Esh-Baal (1 Chr. 8: 33) was too unpleasantly reminiscent of the name of the pagan deity and was accordingly replaced by *bōsheth*, 'shame' (cf. 'the altars you have set up to burn incense to that shameful god Baal', Jer. 11: 13).

Ziba reported that Mephibosheth was living **at the house of Makir son of Ammiel in Lo Debar** (4), from where David ordered that he should be brought. Lo Debar has not been definitely identified, but is 'evidently in the region of Mahanaim. Jonathan's son had thus been hidden in the immediate vicinity of Ish-Baal's earlier residence' (Hertzberg, p. 300). He was duly brought and introduced into the royal presence; his natural nervousness was soon set at rest. All the personal estates of Saul and his family, David told Ziba, would be settled on Mephibosheth, who **'will always eat at my table'** (10). Ziba with his 15 sons and 20 servants were attached to Mephibosheth's household, an honour accepted with alacrity. 'David wanted Mephibosheth to regain status in the community' (Mauchline, p. 243).

Mica (12), Mephibosheth's **young son**, poses a question. Mephibosheth was five when Saul died (4: 4) which, with David's 7½ year reign in Hebron, makes him a young teenager when David moved to Jerusalem. The mention of his son must mean either that the invitation to court came when David had reigned several years in Jerusalem, or that Mica's name was added later to round off the record.

ii. David's great failure (10: 1–12: 31)
(a) The Ammonite war
(10: 1–11:1; cf. 1 Chr. 19: 1–20: 1)
The war with Ammon is detached from the list of campaigns in ch. 8, clearly because it is the background of the Bathsheba story. Nahash, the aggressive Ammonite king who besieged Jabesh Gilead at the outset of Saul's reign (1 Sam. 11: 1–11) died and was succeeded by his son Hanun. David had established friendly relations with Nahash (Saul's hostility to both being no doubt the bond) and sent messages of sympathy to his successor. But Hanun, like Rehoboam after Solomon's death, relied on his advisers, who questioned David's motives, suggesting espionage rather than genuine sympathy. The messengers were treated with indignity, half their beards shaved off and the lower part of their garments cut away. This humiliation no doubt vastly entertained the Ammonite spectators but David was naturally outraged. He spared the men's embarrassment by detaining them at Jericho until their beards were grown; meanwhile the Ammonites were shaken that David saw their coarse buffoonery (Hertzberg, p. 304) as a declaration of war. Hanun hastily recruited mercenaries from the Aramean states whose princes were perhaps, Mauchline (p. 245) suggests, glad to see Ammon as a strong buffer-state against David.

Joab and Abishai were in command of David's forces; they each took on half of the enemy line. Abishai's men lined up against the Ammonites and Joab's against their Aramean allies. The demoralized Arameans fled and the Ammonites followed suit, and Joab returned triumphant to Jerusalem.

Hadadezer of **Zobah** (8: 3–8) was not inclined to accept defeat, so he mobilized the Arameans **from beyond the River** (16) under his commander **Shobach** at **Helam** (location unknown, but probably east of the Jordan). These moves were reported to David, who mustered the Israelite forces and inflicted a devastating defeat on the Arameans, who lost 700 chariot teams and 40,000 foot soldiers (see NIVmg). Shobach was mortally wounded. The Arameans sued for peace terms, and from then on they **were afraid to help the Ammonites anymore** (19).

11: 1 reads ominously: **In the spring, at the time when kings go off to war:** instead of doing so himself, **David sent Joab out with the king's men**, staying in Jerusalem himself. Joab's army **destroyed the Ammonites and besieged Rabbah**, the Ammonite capital (modern Amman).

(b) David seduces Bathsheba, wife of Uriah the Hittite (11: 2–27)
At home in Jerusalem instead of leading his troops in their military engagement, David fell into a tragically compromising situation. Walking on his palace roof in the late afternoon his eyes were ravished by the sight of a beautiful woman who, presumably thinking herself unobserved, was taking her bath. Fascinated by the sight, David enquired and learned that she was Bathsheba daughter of Eliam, one of the thirty 'mighty men' (23: 34)—called Ammiel by transposition of the two elements in his name in 1 Chr. 3: 5—and wife of Uriah the Hittite, a soldier (probably a mercenary) in David's army. He sent for her and she became his mistress, and in due course was pregnant.

6–13. David, ever the man of action, sent to Joab requesting the presence of Uriah. Hertzberg (p. 310) suggests that this was to remove doubts about paternity when the child was born. The Hittite came; David enquired about Joab and the army, and the progress of the battle. He told him to go home **'and wash your feet'** (8): referring perhaps to ritual ablution connected with release from the vows imposed on a soldier engaged in a campaign (McKane, p. 229). At all events, the leave was followed by a present from the king, stigmatized by Mauchline as 'a very cheap trick intended to increase the sense of gratitude to David' (p. 249).

But Uriah had a high idea of the duties of a serving soldier, and returned not to his own home but to the military quarters, alleging that while **the ark and Israel and Judah are staying in tents** (11), and Joab and his army were encamped, it wasn't right for him to sleep with his wife. He stayed over a further night and was entertained by the king.

14–21. He left next day with a letter ordering Joab to put him **in the front line where the fighting is fiercest. Then withdraw from him so that he will be struck down and die** (15). The intrigue duly succeeded, though at the cost of the lives of some of David's other soldiers, sent in with Uriah to lend the exercise credibility. Joab foresaw that David would be angry at this, but he instructed his messenger to tell the king that Uriah was dead; hoping he would see the end as justifying the means.

22–25. The messenger did his work, and David accepted the story: **'Say this to Joab: "Don't let this upset you; the sword devours one as well as another. Press the attack against the city and destroy it." Say this to encourage Joab.'** (25).

26–27. Bathsheba observed the customary mourning suitable in the circumstances; the mourning completed David sent for her and married her, and a son was born. **But the thing David had done displeased the LORD** (27).

(c) Nathan's parable and David's repentance: Solomon born (12: 1–25)
The immediate sequel to David's lapse was the intervention of the prophet Nathan (see 7: 2, 4, 14), an interesting example of one mode of prophetic communication: the parable. The record of the incident begins with a clear statement that the author of the message was Yahweh Himself: **The LORD sent Nathan to David** (1). The story he told was of two men, one wealthy and the other poor; the latter owned a single ewe lamb, brought up as one of the family, his neighbour had **a very large number of sheep and cattle** (2). This did not prevent him, when a guest arrived unexpectedly, from commandeering the poor man's ewe rather than sparing a beast of his own for food. As king, David was accustomed to having law suits brought to him; listening to Nathan he was hearing a particularly oppressive case, and his verdict came swiftly: **'As surely as the LORD lives, the man who did this deserves to die! He must pay for that lamb four times over, because he did such a thing and had no pity'** (5, 6). 'Four times' follows the Heb.; Gk. has 'seven times'. Driver (*Notes*, p. 291) thinks that 'seven times' is original (cf. Prov. 6: 31), and was amended in agreement with the Mosaic law (Exod. 22: 1 = 21: 37, *MT*).

7–15a. Nathan made his point with dramatic and effective suddenness: **'You are the man'** (7). He went on to recall how God had given to David all that had been Saul's and much more, and yet David had sinned against Him in murdering Uriah **with the sword of the Ammonites** (9) and taking Uriah's wife for his own. Judgment will inevitably fall on him; **the sword will never depart from your house** (10): evil will be raised up against him from within his own family, neighbours will publicly take his wives, **You did it in secret, but I will do this thing in broad daylight before all Israel** (12). David confessed his sin

without any attempt at excuses. He clearly acknowledged himself as subject to God's law, and never showed the slightest resentment towards Nathan for his frankness. He was assured by Nathan of God's forgiveness, and that he would not die. Nevertheless his sin must be punished: **the son born to you will die** (14).

15b–23. The child born to Bathsheba was struck down, and died after a week, despite David's earnest prayers and fasting. His household were so moved by his grief that they dared not tell him when the child died. When he did know, to their astonishment, he ceased his mourning, washed and anointed himself, and **went into the house of the LORD and worshipped** (20): returning then to his normal life. When his servants failed to understand, he explained that as long as the child lived he entreated the Lord to spare him. **'But now that he is dead, why should I fast? Can I bring him back again? I will go to him, but he will not return to me'** (23). There can be no doubt of the deeply traumatic effect of the whole incident on David himself. 'Posterity, with a deep sense of what was appropriate, has regarded Ps. 51 as an expression of his experience' (Hertzberg, p. 316).

24–25. A second son was born to Bathsheba, Solomon, of whom it is recorded that **the LORD loved him** (24).

(d) The end of the Ammonite war (12: 26–31; cf. 1 Chr. 20: 2–3)
The Bathsheba story is told as an interlude in the history of the Ammonite war; the record in 1 Chr. 20 goes straight on from 2 Sam. 11: 1 to 12: 26. David's truancy from the battlefield in 11: 1 is put right by his return to command in 12: 29. Joab, who was successfully continuing his campaign against the Ammonites and had indeed captured their royal city of Rabbah, sent a message to the king: **'I have fought against Rabbah and taken its water supply. Now muster the rest of the troops and besiege the city and capture it. Otherwise I will take the city, and it will be named after me'** (27, 28). 'Joab's self-abnegation in this case should not be forgotten in our estimate of the character of this truculent but loyal subject' (Kennedy, p. 249).

David responded to the call and swiftly brought the battle to a successful conclusion; vv. 30, 31 describe the gains but contain some obscurities. First, the king's crown weighed a talent of gold (between 65 and 130 lb), a heavy burden for any monarch's head. But the Gk. (LXX) reads 'the crown of Molchom their king'. Molchom was the Ammonite god Milcom, so the crown could have been cultic rather than royal regalia. One possibility is that it was the **precious stones** (30) only that became part of David's regalia.

Secondly, v. 31 can be interpreted as meaning either that the Ammonites were subjected to fiendish torture, as AV and RV seem to imply; or that (following RVmg, RSV, NIV) they were condemned to forced labour. For the former view it can be said that such a gruesome massacre would not be out of keeping with the times (though not entirely consistent with the general OT view of David's character); for the latter it is adduced that the implements mentioned are industrial rather than military. The word translated 'brick-kilns' (suggesting burning to death) means rather 'brick-moulds', much less violent. A. R. S. Kennedy (p. 250) sums up the question: 'The [RV] text advocates torture, the margin hard labour. The latter is supported by the grammar and the lexicon, and is the view now generally accepted'. S. R. Driver discusses the verse exhaustively in his *Notes*, pp. 294–297.

iii. The rape of Tamar (13: 1–14: 33)

(a) Amnon assaults Absalom's sister (13: 1–22)

Amnon's sordid conduct and Absalom's violence are reported immediately after David's great sin, evoking two questions; to what extent the father's lapse contributed to the sons' wrongdoing, and how far the episode was due to David's indulgence and lack of discipline. At all events, the connection between moral failure and subsequent disaster is brought out, and all the more clearly since 'from this point to the end of ch. 20, this history of David's court is continued in precise chronological sequence' (A. R. S. Kennedy, p. 250).

1–6. Amnon and Tamar's full brother Absalom were David's eldest sons (3: 2, 3). Amnon's passion for Tamar seemed hopeless (v. 2), not because of this consanguinity (not an insuperable bar) but because as a virgin princess she lived in strict seclusion. But Amnon's cousin Jonadab resourcefully suggested a way of circumventing the restriction. Amnon was actually sick with passion frustrated; Jonadab advised exaggerating his symptoms and asking, when David came sick-visiting, for Tamar to be sent to nurse him and prepare tasty invalid food.

7–14. The ruse was tried and worked. Tamar came, and still exaggerating his symptoms, Amnon asked to be left alone with her. He begged her to feed him at his bedside and then invited her to have intercourse. When she refused, he took what he wanted by force despite her resistance and despite her pleas that he should ask David for her hand: her father would not refuse.

15–22. Having satisfied his lust, Amnon immediately lost interest: **Then Amnon hated her with intense hatred. . . . Amnon said to her, Get up and get out!'** (15). Tamar protested that putting her out was a greater wrong than that he had already done, but deaf

to her entreaties and showing scant respect to the **richly ornamented robe** (18) proclaiming her a virgin daughter of the king, he ordered his personal servant to put her out. She went away, displaying all the signs of her grief, rent robe, ashes on head and loud wailing (see de Vaux, *Ancient Israel*, p. 59).

Absalom was soon on the scene. He counselled his sister, despite Amnon's outrage against her and against himself, to wait until he had decided on his course of action. With his eye fixed firmly on his father's throne, he saw that his brother had played right into his hands. So he told Tamar, **'Don't take this thing to heart.' And Tamar lived in her brother Absalom's house, a desolate woman** (20).

The historian distinguishes carefully between the reactions of Absalom and of his father: **King David . . . was furious.** But **Absalom . . . hated Amnon** (21, 22). 'Anger breaks out, but nothing is done; David's love for his children (cf. later in ch. 19) has something unmanly about it. In Absalom there is a hate which he does not express, but which eats into him and is thus all the more dangerous. What David does not do, Absalom will do . . .' (Hertzberg, pp. 324 f.).

(b) Absalom avenges his sister by killing Amnon, then flees (13: 23–37)

23–29. For two years Absalom plotted his revenge, showing apparently little concern for Tamar's shame and distress. The time of sheepshearing came round, a time of rejoicing something like our harvest home (cf. 1 Sam. 25: 36). He invited to the festivities his father and **all the king's sons** (23). David excused himself, but promised Absalom that Amnon at least would be there—although in the event the younger sons were also present. Absalom instructed his servants to wait until Amnon was well under the influence of drink, and then to strike. This was done; the rest of the princes fled in confusion 'not on asses, but on mules as befitted their rank' (Mauchline, p. 262). The murder was clearly premeditated; the two years' delay indicates ambition as much as concern for his sister.

30–33. The news soon reached David in a highly embellished form: **'Absalom has struck down all the king's sons; not one of them is left'** (30). David's grief was overwhelming; he appears to have accepted the news at face value. Amnon's crafty counsellor Jonadab (13: 3, 5) urged him to view the matter sensibly, pointing out that Absalom had a motive for slaying Amnon, but not the others. 'Jonadab once again intervenes. He once again proves "his wisdom; but it is prompted by a guilty conscience" (Budde). The voice of reason speaks rightly and persuades the king' (Hertzberg, p. 327).

34–37. Absalom not unnaturally removed

himself from the scene, a fact mentioned three times (34, 37, 38). Some hold that this indicates textual confusion; Hertzberg (p. 325) transfers 34a to the middle of v. 29, but Mauchline (p. 263) more simply reads 34a as a continuation of 33: 'and Absalom has fled'. The rest of 34 is more difficult. The watchman in Jerusalem reports a company coming from the north, **in the direction of Horonaim:** NIV here translates the Gk.; the *MT* in this verse is briefer and less intelligible. The topography of the area makes the scene as described difficult to visualize. Hertzberg, following Alt and Eissfeldt, substitutes 'Bahurim' for 'Horonaim'. For further discussion, see Hertzberg, pp. 327 f. Jonadab reminded David that he had been right; but the fact that Amnon was dead did not diminish the lamentations. Besides the king's sons, **the king, too, and all his servants wept very bitterly** (36). Absalom's flight took him to Geshur in Transjordan, NE of Bashan, where he found refuge with his grandfather Talmai (3: 3) son of Ammihud, the king.

(c) **Through Joab's stratagem, Absalom is pardoned and restored to favour (13: 38–14: 33)**
David's duty was clearly to discipline Absalom, but **the spirit of the king longed to go to Absalom** (13: 39). The problem seemed insoluble until Joab took a hand, enlisting the help of **a wise woman** (14: 2), 'a person distinguished by her gifts and her authority' (Hertzberg, p. 331), from Amos's Tekoa, ten miles south of Jerusalem. She came, and on Joab's instructions disguised herself in mourning attire and told the king a circumstantial tale as Nathan had before. Her two sons had quarrelled and one was killed; the rest of the family demanded the death of the killer though this would mean the extinction of her husband's name and her own complete bereavement. David promised: **'Go home, and I will issue an order on your behalf'** (8), solemnly assuring her that no one would touch her surviving son.

She skilfully revealed that her story was a parable of his own conduct: **'When the king says this, does he not convict himself, for the king has not brought back his banished son? Like water spilled on the ground, which cannot be recovered, so we must die. But God does not take away life; instead, he devises ways so that a banished person may not remain estranged from him.'** (13, 14).

The woman made her excuses for her presumption: **'for my lord the king is like an angel of God in discerning good and evil'** (17). David made a shrewd guess: **'Isn't the hand of Joab with you in all this?'** (19). She confessed that it was, protesting none the less

David's superior wisdom.

David lost no time in sending for Joab and instructing him to bring Absalom back. Joab was delighted: **'Today your servant knows that he has found favour in your eyes, my lord the king, because the king has granted his servant's request'** (22). He then carried out the commission. But David's forgiveness was cautious and incomplete. Absalom, he said, was to live apart and not come into the royal presence.

This grudging forgiveness contrasts with Absalom's beauty and attractiveness; his hair especially was extraordinarily luxuriant. He had three sons and a daughter who inherited his own beauty and that of his sister Tamar, after whom she was named. Yet despite his advantages, Absalom was still rigorously excluded from the court, and Joab even refused to visit him when invited. Absalom therefore sent men to fire Joab's fields so that he had to come, even if only to seek an explanation. Absalom asked him to intercede with the king on his behalf; he felt he would be as well off back in Geshur, and pleaded to be restored to the royal presence. There was a show of reconciliation; Absalom was permitted to return, prostrated himself in submission and received the royal kiss of forgiveness.

iv. The revolt of Absalom (15: 1–19: 43)
(a) **Rebellion breaks out (15: 1–12)**
Back at court, Absalom proceeded to further his two aims, first to impress by his splendid entourage suited to the position he claimed as heir-apparent, and secondly to build up sufficient popular feeling to enable him to make a bid for the throne. Attended by a fifty-strong bodyguard he rode in a chariot, not usual in Israelite courts. Joseph in pagan Egypt (Gen. 41: 43) and later Adonijah (1 Kg. 1: 5) rode in similar style. Hertzberg comments: 'Absalom introduces strange customs which he perhaps learned from his grandfather the pagan king' (p. 336). He arrived early each day and stood **by the side of the road leading to the city gate** (2). Absalom asked each suppliant his tribe and his problem, and pointed to the inertia of the king's officers. How different were he king!— all then would get their rights; and he accepted obeisance when offered as though he were already king (5). So Absalom **stole the hearts of the men of Israel** (6).

This went on for **four years** (not 40, as AV and RV following Heb.), until Absalom felt able to strike. Begging David's leave to go to Hebron to pay a promised vow to Yahweh, he sent **secret messengers throughout the tribes of Israel to say, 'As soon as you hear the sound of the trumpets, then say, "Absalom is king in Hebron."'** (10). Conspiracy was afoot. The secret messengers 'were obviously intelligence officers, if not electioneering agents, whose job was to discover the possibilities of support for Absalom in the south and exploit it' (Mauchline, p. 271). Absalom had invited two hundred Jerusalemites who **went quite innocently, knowing nothing about the matter** (11). He shrewdly secured the adhesion of his father's counsellor, **Ahithophel the Gilonite**, grandfather of Bathsheba (if her father Eliam, 11: 3, is Ahithophel's son of that name, 23: 34). **Absalom's following kept on increasing** (12).

(b) David a fugitive from Jerusalem (15: 13–16: 14)

'David shows his true greatness on this his day of misfortune. He humbly bows himself under the bitter blow and leaves the future to the Lord, without, however, neglecting to take what steps he can' (Hertzberg, p. 341). He left Jerusalem precipitately, the only course open to him; but he still enjoyed considerable support. Absalom had not stolen *all* men's hearts! David's **officials** (14), his immediate entourage, remained loyal: **'Your servants are ready to do whatever our lord the king chooses'** (15). The sad procession set out, leaving **ten concubines to take care of the palace** (16). David **halted at a palace some distance away** to review the company as they passed. Besides his 'servants', six hundred Philistine mercenaries were among his following.

19–23. Among these Philistines was **Ittai** (19) of Gath, with whom David had had associations. He generously tried to persuade Ittai not to espouse his own very precarious cause, but Ittai would not go home: **'wherever my lord the king may be, whether it means life or death, there will your servant be'** (21). The king's flight evoked deep sympathy wherever he passed.

24–31. The priests Abiathar and Zadok, with the attendant staff of Levites, brought the ark from Jerusalem, but David, no doubt remembering the disaster at Ebenezer (1 Sam. 4: 11 ff.), ordered its return. Driver (*Notes*, p. 315) points out that apart from the list in 8: 17, this is the first mention of Zadok. Should Yahweh prove favourable to David he will worship again in Jerusalem; if not he will accept His will. He sent back the priests and their sons to await his return, while he went on. **30. David continued up the Mount of Olives, weeping as he went; his head was covered and he was barefoot. All the people with him covered their heads too and were weeping as they went up:** to add to his troubles he now heard of the defection of Ahithophel, probably his wisest statesman. He laid this matter before the Lord.

32–37. At the sanctuary summit of the mount of Olives, David persuaded another adherent, his friend Hushai (37), who wished to join him, to return rather to Jerusalem and join Absalom's staff as a spy, passing on information to David via the two priests and their sons Ahimaaz and Jonathan. Hushai's arrival at Jerusalem coincided with Absalom's triumphal entry.

16: 1–4. A little further on, Mephibosheth's steward, Ziba, met the king with a present of provisions recalling that of Abigail (1 Sam. 25: 10). The generous David did not suspect his crafty visitor's motives, in hinting even that his master had his eyes on the crown. Opinion as to the relative loyalty of Ziba and Mephibosheth is divided. Ziba's story, according to A. R. S. Kennedy (p. 269), is 'an *ex-parte* statement, almost certainly false in view of the greater verisimilitude of 19: 25 ff.' Mauchline (pp. 275 f.), Hertzberg (p. 345), and H. P. Smith (p. 347) agree; McKane (p. 225) and Brockington (*Peake*[2], p. 335) are suspicious of Mephibosheth. John Bright (*History of Israel*, p. 188n.) says: 'The behaviour of Mephibosheth is ambiguous. Though he later denied disloyalty, David apparently did not believe him.' At all events he finally gave half of Mephibosheth's estates to Ziba (19: 29); perhaps he still mistrusted the house of Saul.

5–14. David's next trial comes also from the house of Saul. As the royal cortège proceeded, **Shimei son of Gera** (5), met it at **Bahurim** (mentioned in the story of Michal's return to David, 3: 16) on the Jericho road **and cursed David**. His insults: **'Get out, get out, you man of blood, you scoundrel'** (7), and his taunt that David was suffering for what he had done to the house of Saul, were accompanied by volleys of stones. **Abishai**, Joab's brother, incensed at such rudeness, wanted to execute him, but David would have none of it. If his own son had risen against him, he said, why should not **this Benjamite** (11) curse him? Maybe Yahweh had bidden him. He would leave his case in the Lord's hands. The trek continued as far as the Jordan, and **there he refreshed himself** (14).

(c) Absalom in Jerusalem (16: 15–17: 23)

Meanwhile, in Jerusalem Absalom was setting up his government with Ahithophel as right hand man, but neither suspected the genuineness of Hushai's offer. Absalom asked him why he had not gone with David: **'Is this the love you show your friend?'** (17). 'No', came the glib reply, **'the one chosen by the LORD, by these people and by all the men of Israel—his I will be, and I will remain with him'** (18).

20–23. Absalom wanted to get things moving, and consulted with Ahithophel as to the next step. Advice was immediately forthcoming, namely that the pretender should have intercourse with the concubines his father had left behind (15: 16). To claim the king's harem, as Abner had sought to do (3: 7) and David himself had done (12: 8), was to lodge a strong claim to the succession (see R. de Vaux, *Ancient Israel*, p. 116). Hertzberg (p. 350) points out another implication of Absalom's action: 'Here, however, there is the added point that Absalom's predecessor was also his father. Reuben, who lies with his father's concubine, incurs a curse (Gen. 35: 22; 49: 3 f.) and loses the right of a firstborn'. That Absalom's deed was an act of policy and not merely of sensual satisfaction is demonstrated by its publicity: **they pitched a tent for Absalom on the roof** (22). Ch. 16 ends with a note of the high esteem in which both David and his usurping son held the wily Ahithophel.

17: 1–4. Ahithophel follows up his advice by suggesting that with 12,000 men he should pursue and strike down David **when he is weary and weak** (2). In the ensuing panic, David alone was to die: **The death of the man you seek will mean the return of all; all the people will be unharmed** (3).

5–14. Before committing himself, Absalom sent for Hushai to seek his counsel. Matching Ahithophel's oratory, Hushai declared: **'You knew your father and his men; they are fighters, and as fierce as a wild bear robbed of her cubs'** (8). Moreover, David, an outstanding soldier, will not be caught so easily. All available forces should be deployed and Absalom, not Ahithophel, should lead them: **'we will fall on him** [*scil.* David] **as dew settles on the ground. Neither he nor any of his men will be left alive'** (12). Flowery words seasoned with flattery carried the day against Ahithophel's wisdom. Hushai had served David well, and **the LORD had determined to frustrate the good advice of Ahithophel in order to bring disaster on Absalom** (14).

15–23. News of Absalom's strategic intention must be conveyed hotfoot to David. A glimpse is given of the efficient organization of the intelligence service. Hushai passed on his information via the priests to their sons Jonathan and Ahimaaz waiting at En-rogel on the southern outskirts of Jerusalem at the junction of the valleys of Kidron and Ben-Hinnom (Driver, *Notes*, p. 324). That the chain of communication was regularly established is indicated by the frequentative form of the verbs; the next link was the **servant girl** (17). On this occasion the young men were seen but managed to hide at Bahurim in the well of a sympathizer whose wife camouflaged their hiding-place from Absalom's scouts. The message they bore from Hushai urged David to act speedily; he suspected no doubt that Absalom might revert to Ahithophel's scheme. Happily David got the news and took evasive action, crossing with all his men over the Jor-

dan. Ahithophel realized that his plan was not being adopted, and that all had gone wrong. Clear-sighted, he saw that ahead lay only ruin, so he took his own life, joining the very small number of Old Testament suicides. Businesslike to the last, **he saddled his donkey and set out for his house in his home town. He put his house in order and then hanged himself** (23).

(d) Absalom's fate (17: 24–18: 18)
David established his base at **Mahanaim** (24), Ish-Bosheth's former headquarters in Transjordan (2: 8). Joab remained with him as commander; Absalom's was Joab's cousin Amasa, the son, according to the Hebrew, of Ithra 'the Israelite'. But in a list of Israelite officials, one is surprised to find one so distinguished from the rest. RSV, as also the parallel passage in 1 Chr. 2.17, has 'Ishmaelite', a much more likely reading. At Mahanaim, David was joined by Shobi an Ammonite, Makir the son of Ammiel of Lo Debar, Mephibosheth's former host, and the Gileadite Barzillai, who brought abundant provisions, **for they said, 'The people have become hungry and tired and thirsty in the desert'** (29).

18: 1–18. David took the initiative. He divided his forces into three well organized and officered groups, led respectively by Joab; his brother Abishai; and Ittai of Gath. He wanted to go with them himself but was dissuaded: **'You must not go out; if we are forced to flee, they won't care about us. Even if half of us die, they won't care; but you are worth ten thousand of us. It would be better now for you to give us support'** (3). He stayed at base, reviewing the forces as they went out to battle and recommending his commanders to deal gently with Absalom. In the ensuing battle the Israelites (Absalom's men) suffered an overwhelming defeat, losing no fewer than 20,000 men. **The battle spread out over the whole countryside, and the forest claimed more lives that day than the sword** (8).

9–18. The most notable victim of the forest was Absalom himself. Riding on a mule, he **happened to meet David's men** (9). Riding under an oak tree, he was caught up in the branches. His mule went on and he was left hanging. We are not told that he hung by the hair, but it is clear that he was so tightly held as to make escape impossible. News was brought to Joab who said that the prince should have been despatched; his killer would have been rewarded. But the messenger knew Joab well enough to reply that had he disobeyed David's wishes, **'you would have kept your distance from me'** (13). Expressing his impatience, Joab took **three javelins** and stabbed Absalom where he hung, his armour-bearers administered the *coup de grâce*. Joab **sounded**

the trumpet to recall his troops from pursuing the rebels and buried Absalom where he fell, in a big pit in the forest (17). A heap of stones was set up to mark the spot, and his followers dispersed in confusion. Having no son to bear his name (the three sons of 14: 27 must have died in infancy), Absalom had set up his own monument during his lifetime; a pillar in the neighbourhood of Jerusalem (cf. Gen. 14: 17 for the King's Valley) was still called 'Absalom's monument'. This stele has been much discussed by archaeologists.

(e) News comes to David (18: 19–32)
The king now had to be told. Zadok's son Ahimaaz volunteered to bear the tidings, but Joab hesitated, aware that David's satisfaction at the victory would be outweighed by grief at Absalom's death. He advised Ahimaaz to delay for a day, meanwhile sending a Cushite (Ethiopian), probably a slave: 'Go, tell the king what you have seen' (21). Ahimaaz still wanted to go; Joab finally yielded, pointing out that the mission would be unpaid. The Cushite took a direct but difficult route, Ahimaaz ran by way of the plain (23), a longer but easier way, and arrived ahead. Ahimaaz told his story first, saying that the king's enemies were routed; his guarded reply to David's enquiry about his son was interrupted by the Cushite's arrival with 'My lord the king, hear the good news!' (31). About Absalom the Cushite was enthusiastic: 'May the enemies of my lord the king and all who rise up to harm you be like that young man' (32).

(f) David's grief and Joab's protest (18: 33–19: 8a)
As Joab had foreseen, David's reaction was grief for his erring son: 'O my son Absalom! My son, my son Absalom! If only I had died instead of you—O Absalom, my son, my son!' (33). In this incident, as after the death of Saul and Jonathan at Gilboa, David appears 'as a man for whom private concern was more important than national emergency' (Mauchline, p. 289). The day of victory, when the people were naturally happy at the overthrow of a rebellion that had threatened the state as well as the throne, was turned by the king into a day of mourning: he cried aloud, 'O my son Absalom! O Absalom, my son, my son' (19: 4).

Joab remonstrated with him, pointing out the unfairness of his attitude to those who had risked their lives on his behalf. 'Today you have humiliated all your men, who have just saved your life . . . You love those who hate you and hate those who love you' (5, 6). David recognized the force of Joab's words and allowed himself to be persuaded to make a public appearance, taking his seat again in the gateway, where all the people came before him (8). Joab 'succeeds in raising the

king from his now completely inopportune sorrow, and has him watch the march-past of the warriors, thereby assuring them of his royal recognition of their deeds. And in this way the danger is overcome' (Hertzberg, p. 361).

(g) David returns to his capital: Shimei, Mephibosheth, Barzillai (19: 8b–43)
The immediate result of the rebellion and its collapse was confusion; the Israelites had fled home: 'it was a fluid situation, with no one actively in control in Jerusalem' (Mauchline, p. 290). Now that Absalom was dead, people looked back to the good old days of David's rule: 'So why do you say nothing about bringing the king back?' (10). David noted that while the Israelites (presumably the northerners) were making active arrangements for his return, his own tribe of Judah seemed apathetic. He sent a message to them by Zadok and Abiathar: 'Ask the elders of Judah, "Why should you be the last to bring the king back to his palace"' (11), reminding them that they had been first to make him king. As an inducement he offered Amasa Joab's post as commander, on grounds of kinship (13; cf. 17: 25), puzzling qualification seeing that it was shared by Joab! Says A. R. S. Kennedy: 'Joab had forfeited his sovereign's confidence by his flagrant disobedience of orders in the matter of Absalom. He who would command must first learn to obey' (p. 286). Amasa carried out his commission: He won over the hearts of all the men of Judah as though they were one man . . . Then the king returned and went as far as the Jordan. Now the men of Judah had come to Gilgal to go out and meet the king and bring him across the Jordan (14, 15). Crossing the frontier on his return journey, David was met in turn by three of those concerned during his flight from the capital:

(a) Shimei (16–23). Shimei had taken advantage of David's adversity to heap insults and curses on him (16: 5–14). Now the situation had changed he came to meet the king, arriving with a thousand Benjamites at the same time as Ziba. Cringing at David's feet, he implored him to forget his recent behaviour, pointing out that he first of all the tribe of Benjamin had come to do homage to the returning king. Abishai, brother of Amasa and Joab, nauseated by this craven *volte-face*, again (see 16: 9) wanted to slay him. But David would not agree; forbidding the execution he said his restoration should not be marred by bloodshed.

(b) Mephibosheth (24–30). Ziba, not Mephibosheth, had come to David during his flight (16: 1–4), hinting that Mephibosheth was less than loyal. The relative faithfulness of the two men has already been discussed *ad loc.*; here Mephibosheth states his case, which sounds reasonably convincing. But David was not completely convinced; he divided the estates between the prince and his servant. Mephibosheth was happy that the king was back: **My lord the king is like an angel of God** (27). He was content not only to accept David's decision, but willing that Ziba should have all: **'Let him take everything, now that my lord the king has arrived home safely'** (30).

(c) **Barzillai** (31–40). The record of the third of these personal interviews is entirely delightful. The wealthy octogenarian Barzillai, who had brought provisions for the fugitive king, **came down . . . to cross the Jordan with the king and to send him on his way from there** (31). David in return now invited him to Jerusalem; 'The invitation to Barzillai to spend the rest of his life at the court in Jerusalem naturally included his family, so that David's offer is far greater than appears at first sight' (Hertzberg, p. 367). But Barzillai excused himself on grounds of age and his natural desire to end his days in familiar home surroundings. He recommended **Kimham**, probably a younger son, to go in his place. David agreed, affectionately embraced the old man and completed his journey accompanied by all the people of Judah and half those of Israel (40).

41–43. David's Homecoming. This seems almost like a happy ending for the story. But a great catastrophe like Absalom's rebellion could not pass without leaving profound effects. There had long been undercurrents of jealousy and ill-feeling between north and south, Judah and the Ephraimite tribes (see H. L. Ellison, *Prophets of Israel*, chs. 1, 2). The two groups vied to be nearest the restored king. The Israelite faction complained to him that the men of Judah had stolen him away and had brought the king and his household to Jerusalem. (41) The Judahites claimed this was their right because of their blood-relationship to David, and yet they had not turned this to their own advantage. Israel pointed to greater numbers: **'We have ten shares in the king'** (43): saying they had first spoken **of bringing back our king.** The 'ten shares' have been seen as a reference to the yet future division of the kingdom (1 Kg. 11: 30, 31). L. H. Brockington (Peake[3], p. 336) prefers the LXX reading of this verse: 'and moreover, we are senior to you'. Noth (*History of Israel*, p. 58) holds that Simeon existed under the shadow of Judah, and seems to regard the ten as excluding Judah and Simeon. No settlement is recorded, but the seeds were sown of much trouble to come.

v. Sheba rebels (20: 1–26)
(a) **Sheba's rebellion (20: 1–22)**
Sheba, **a troublemaker** (1), son of the Benjamite Bicri, proclaimed a rebellion against David, calling on the Israelites, as Jeroboam did later (1 Kg. 12: 16), to 'resume their old tribal independence' (Driver, *Notes*, p. 340).

The identity of Sheba is uncertain but, according to Hertzberg (p. 371), his father Bicri's name, mentioned no fewer than eight times, may be related to that of Saul's ancestor Becorath (1 Sam. 9: 1). Israel rallied to the call; Judah remained loyal, they **stayed by their king all the way from the Jordan to Jerusalem** (2).

Back in his city, David's first thought was for the ten concubines he had left behind and who had been coveted by Absalom; he provided them with a securely guarded house but had no intercourse with them; like Tamar's their days were to pass **as widows** (3).

He now ordered Amasa to mobilize the men of Judah within three days and to take personal charge. Amasa did so, but not within the set time, thus giving Sheba an advantage. David sent him off to try to make up lost time; Joab and Abishai followed with **the Kerethites and Pelethites** (groups of mercenaries, perhaps Philistines, see 8: 18) **and all the mighty warriors** (7). The parties met at Gibeon, at the **great rock** (8), probably an altar (McKane, p. 278: he quotes also 1 Sam. 6: 18). Driver (*Notes*, p. 343) reads 'came, appeared' for **came to meet them**, suggesting that the meeting was not planned, but accidental. Joab, however, obviously wore hidden weapons—'like Ehud, Jg. 3', comments Hertzberg (p. 372)—and assassinated his unsuspecting 'brother'.

The pursuit of Sheba continued: **Then Joab and his brother Abishai pursued Sheba son of Bicri** (10): 'from this point, by his force of character and experience, Joab becomes the real leader of the expedition' (A. R. S. Kennedy, p. 293). David's followers seem to have hesitated as to their immediate loyalty, but after the removal of Amasa's corpse from public view they followed Joab. Meanwhile, **Sheba passed through all the tribes of Israel to Abel Beth Maacah and through the entire region of the Berites, who gathered together and followed him** (14). Abel has been identified with a site north of Hazor, some 5 miles west of Dan. Joab's troops besieged him there and threw up earthworks against the position. The siege was raised when a **wise woman** (16; cf. 14: 2–20) intervened, making terms with Joab who agreed to spare the city in return for her undertaking that Sheba's head would **be thrown to you from the wall** (21). The arrangement was honoured, the siege lifted, and the rebellion over.

The story of David's reign is virtually told; the story in 1 Kg. 1–2 of the final intrigues round his deathbed are part of the Succession Narrative, but belong in reality to Solomon's story.

(b) **David's leading officers of state: list II (20: 23–26; cf. 8: 15–18; 1 Chr. 18: 14–17)**
David had ridden the storm; all possible contenders had been eliminated. The same was

true also of Joab; like Ish-Bosheth, Amnon and Absalom, Abner and Amasa had paid with their lives for their ambitions. The story is rounded off with a list of officials similar to that at the end of ch. 8 which immediately precedes the Succession Narrative. Both lists begin with the name of **Joab** as commander; but in this new list the second name is **Benaiah son of Jehoiada**, another military official with charge apparently of mercenary units, who takes the place of Jehoshaphat (son of Ahilud) the recorder, demoted now to fourth place, below **Adoniram . . . in charge of forced labour** (24), a newcomer. Then follow **Sheva** the secretary ('Seraiah' in list I), retaining his fifth place, and the two priests, second and third in 2 Sam. 8 but sixth and seventh here. In list I they are 'Zadok the son of Ahitub and Ahimelech son of Abiathar'; in list II: **Zadok and Abiathar** (25). Abiathar is priest also in 17: 15; his son is Jonathan. Finally an eighth name, **Ira the Jairite was David's priest** (26), replacing David's sons as priests.

The list in 1 Chr. 18: 14–17 corresponds almost exactly with that in 2 Sam. 8: 15–18, except that the secretary is 'Shavsha' (clearly a variant spelling) and that David's sons are 'chief officials' instead of 'priests'. The differences between the first and second lists in 2 Sam. (and perhaps the puzzling differences between the names given to Zadok's priestly colleague) can be credibly explained by the passage of time. The difference of order points to a growing need for a more distinctively military administration.

IV. APPENDICES (21: 1–24: 25)

The last four chapters of 2 Sam. contain six disconnected appendices, arranged in symmetrical fashion. Two narratives of disaster (famine, 21: 1–14; plague, 24: 1–25) are separated by two catalogues of heroes and their exploits (21: 15–22; 23: 8–39), divided in turn by two of David's compositions, a psalm of thanksgiving (22: 1–51) and his 'last words' (23: 1–7).

It is impossible to assign these passages with any certainty to their chronological place in the main story of David's reign, though there are some indications. It is hardly likely, for instance, that the story of the hanging of Saul's sons in ch. 21 does not antedate David's kindness to Mephibosheth in ch. 9 (see 9: 1).

i. The famine and the seven sons of Saul (21: 1–14)

Famine had wasted the land for three years. David sought the counsel of the Lord as to the reason for the visitation, and learned that it was the bloodguiltiness of Saul which had brought it about. 'Few sections of the OT', says H. P. Smith (p. 374), 'show more clearly the religious ideas of the time. We see how Yahweh as the avenger of a broken covenant requires from the children of the offender the blood that has been shed'. The origin of the covenant in this case, the covenant with the Gibeonites, is recorded in Jos. 9. Saul, however, disliking the presence of an Amorite clan in the midst of the nation, **had tried to annihilate them in his zeal for Israel and Judah** (2).

David immediately consulted with the Gibeonites as to the satisfaction they required. They replied that they were not seeking blood-money, and that as Amorites they had no right themselves to take revenge by death upon Israelites. David, realizing that they were passing the matter back to him, asked: **'What do you want me to do for you?'** (4). They demanded the delivery to them of seven of Saul's sons who would be **killed and exposed before the Lord** (6). David acceded to their request, handing over two sons of **Rizpah** (see 3: 7) and five sons of Saul's daughter, **Merab.** The men were left where they were hanged, and Rizpah guarded their bodies from carrion birds and beasts of prey, until the October rains began to fall, showing that Yahweh had accepted the expiation and was once more gracious to His Land (A. R. S. Kennedy, p. 299).

David recovered the remains of Saul and Jonathan from Jabesh Gilead (see 1 Sam. 31: 12 f.): the bones of all were buried **in the tomb of Saul's father Kish, at Zela in Benjamin** (14). The site of Zela is unknown.

ii. Giant killers and Philistines (21: 15–22; cf. 1 Chr. 20: 4–8)

A selection of incidents follows, chosen to illustrate the heroism of individual warriors against the Philistines. Four episodes are recorded, introduced by the words: **and he became exhausted** (15). Mauchline (p. 304), following Driver (*Notes*, p. 353), sees this phrase as a corruption of a Philistine name; Hertzberg (p. 368), however, says: 'David's weariness is given as the occasion for a strong enemy warrior to kill him'. The parallel passage in 1 Chr. 20: 4–8 sheds no light on the matter, since it completely omits the first giant-killer.

(*a*) **Ishbi-Benob** (16), a Philistine of outsize proportions and weapons, was killed by Joab's brother Abishai while making an attempt on David's life, as a result of which **David's men swore to him** that they would not let him go out to battle with them: **'so that the lamp of Israel will not be extinguished'** (17). The 'lamp' suggests Yahweh's continuing presence in the midst of His people (cf. Ps. 132: 17).

(*b*) **Saph, one of the descendants of Rapha** (18) was killed by **Sibbecai the Hushathite** in a battle at **Gob** (Gezer in 1 Chr. 20: 4; 'Geth' [Gath] in LXX).

(*c*) **Elhanan** (19) slew **Goliath the Gittite.** This statement clearly raises the questions of its relation to the account of David's victorious combat with Goliath. See commentary on 1 Sam. 17: 1–11; for fuller treatment, D. F. Payne, *NBC*³, pp. 318 f.).

(*d*) An unnamed giant of great stature, and having the curious characteristic of an extra digit on each hand and foot, lost his life in battle at Gath at the hands of **Jonathan son of Shimeah, David's brother** (21). In 1 Sam. 16: 9, Jesse's third son is Shammah.

Verse 22 sums up the section: four giants of Gittite extraction **fell at the hands of David and his men.**

iii. David's psalm of thanksgiving (22: 1–51; cf. Ps. 18: 1–50)

This victory song, 'a sudden outpouring of the heart' (C. S. Lewis), recorded in ch. 22 is, except in very minor details, identical with Ps. 18, described in the psalter: 'For the director of music. Of David the servant of the LORD. He sang to the LORD the words of this song when the LORD delivered him from the hand of all his enemies and from the hand of Saul'. This is not a very exact indication of the date, except that the mention of Saul suggests that it was earlier rather than later in David's career. Most critics regard the psalm as Davidic, even those who deny Davidic authorship to almost all the psalms attributed to him in their superscriptions. Lewis sums up the position in his *Reflections on the Psalms*, p. 2: 'The Psalms were written by many poets and at many different dates. Some, I believe, are allowed to go back to the reign of David; I think certain scholars allow that Psalm 18 might be by David himself.'

The song looks onward and backward, to victories God has already given to His people, and to victories yet to come. For detailed comment on the text, see commentary on Ps. 18.

iv. David's last words (23: 1–7)

'The last words of David follow the royal psalm just as the blessing of Moses follows the song of Moses, and the texts have evidently been put together thus on purpose' (Hertzberg, p. 399). Unlike the composition in ch. 22, this short poem has no counterpart in the Psalter; nor is it paralleled in Chronicles. The introductory first verse recalls the prophecy of Balaam (Num. 24: 3, 15); from which Mauchline (p. 312) infers that 'we must see in it a traditional style of utterance'.

1. David is described not only as **son of Jesse**, but also as **the man exalted by the Most High** speaking of his enthronement; **the man anointed by the God of Jacob** (cf. 21: 51), and **Israel's singer of songs**: anointed and endowed by Yahweh. The last of these titles is debated; 'the "darling" or "favourite" (RSVmg) of the songs of Israel' is advanced as a more accurate rendering, suggesting that David was the theme rather than the author of the songs.

S. R. Driver (*Notes*, p. 357) says: '"the sweet *psalmist* of Israel" suggests much too strongly the unhistorical David of the Chronicles and the titles of the Psalms'; the more up-to-date Hertzberg (p. 401), on the other hand, says that 'sweet singer' is 'more probable'.

2–4. David now speaks of Yahweh, by whose Spirit he speaks (2). Yahweh is **the God of Israel** who has spoken, and **the Rock of Israel** (3a), an often-used Old Testament title (cf. Ps. 28: 1; 61: 2; 71: 3; 94: 22; 95: 1; etc.). The oracle of Yahweh Himself begins in 3b, with a commendation of the ruler governing his subjects justly in the fear of God, upon whom God's blessing falls **like the light of morning at sunrise on a cloudless morning, like the brightness after rain that brings the grass from the earth** (cf. Ps. 72. 6).

5. Such is the blessing that God has conferred upon David and his house, in making with him an everlasting covenant promising the permanence of his dynasty (7: 13, 16, etc.).

6–7. This bright prospect is contrasted with the outlook for **evil men**, theirs is not the portion of the 'grass sprouting from the earth', but of the thorns indicative of nature cursed by the Fall (Gen. 3. 18).

v. David's mighty men (23: 8–39; cf. 1 Chr. 11: 10–47)

There now follows the register of a kind of order of chivalry (so A. R. S. Kennedy, p. 308; D. F. Payne in *NBC*³, p. 313; Mauchline, p. 315; etc). This order had two classes, the **three** (18, 19, 23), and the **thirty** (13, 23, 24). 'Thirty' is a round number rather than a mathematical indication, v. 39 says: **thirty-seven in all**, though it would seem that the Thirty were replenished from time to time, as one man was killed (*e.g.* Asahel) and another was employed elsewhere (like Benaiah)' (D. F. Payne, *NBC*³, p. 314). The Chronicler places his almost identical list in ch. 11 of his first book, immediately after David's anointing at Hebron as king over all Israel and his capture of Zion.

8–12. The Three are named as

(*a*) **Josheb-Basshebeth, a Tahkemonite** (8),
(*b*) **Eleazar son of Dodai the Ahohite** (9, 10),
(*c*) **Shammah son of Agee the Hararite** (11, 12).

In 1 Chr. 11; 11, Josheb-Basshebeth is called 'Jashobeam, a Hacmonite'; LXX has a form which implies an original Ish-Bosheth or Esh-Baal. 'Hacmonite' may indicate his descent from the family of Hacmoni (cf. 1 Chr. 27: 32) rather than his geographical origin. Military exploits are attributed to each of the Three; in the cases of the second and third, against the Philistines. **8. eight hundred:** 'three hundred' in 1 Chr. 11: 11. 'The readings in this verse evidently varied before the time of the LXX, and there is no means of accounting for them.

Eight and three are interchanged elsewhere' (R. B. Girdlestone, *Deuterographs*, p. 27). **11 lentils**: 'barley' in 1 Chr. 11: 13.

13–23. Before formally listing the Thirty, the exploits of three individuals among them— Abishai, Benaiah, and one unnamed—are singled out. The three together overheard the yearning of David in the stress of the Adullam campaign: **'Oh, that someone would get me a drink of water from the well near the gate of Bethlehem'** (15), and hazarded their lives to satisfy his longing. Such devotion deeply moved David, who offered their gift as a libation to Yahweh: **'Is it not the blood of men who went at the risk of their lives?'** (17).

Abishai (18, 19) was **chief of the Three.**

Benaiah son of Jehoiada (20–23), from Kabzeel on the Judah–Edom border, **struck down two of Moab's best men.** Benaiah's other exploits include the killing of a lion in a pit **on a snowy day** (20), and the defeat of an **Egyptian** warrior in single combat (21). These feats put him in the first rank of the Thirty; **David put him in charge** (23; the 'Kerethites and Pelethites' of 8: 18; 20: 23).

24–39. These verses enumerate the Thirty. Few of the names given are mentioned elsewhere in the Old Testament. The first is **Asahel** (24), killed by Abner during the war with Ish-Bosheth (see commentary on 2: 12–3: 1), which implies that the Thirty must have existed very early in David's reign. 1 Chr. 11: 42–47 adds a few further names.

vi. David's census and the Temple site (24: 1–25; cf. 1 Chr. 21: 1–22)
The final appendix draws attention to the site on which the Temple was to be built. 'By the theophany here recorded, the threshing-floor of Araunah the Jebusite received a consecration which has made it holy ground not only for Judaism and Christianity, but for Islam as well' (A. R. S. Kennedy, p. 313).

The story begins: **Again the anger of the Lord burned against Israel, and he incited David against them, saying, 'Go and count Israel and Judah'** (1). 'Again' may suggest that the story continues 21: 1–14. The idea of Yahweh inciting David recalls the hardening of Pharaoh's heart (Exod. 4: 21, etc), and the lying heart in Ahab's prophets (1 Kg. 22: 22 f.). To OT writers men were subject to God's permissive will even when in rebellion against His sovereignty. We find this view difficult, as the Chronicler appears to have done: '*Satan stood up against Israel, and incited David to number Israel*' (1 Chr. 21: 1; cf. McKane, p. 203).

The organization of the census was entrusted to Joab, who nevertheless had his misgivings

(3, 4). However, the task was completed with thoroughness. Joab and his assistants crossed the Jordan and turned north as far as Dan, then west to Sidon and back as far south as Beersheba; in all they were away for **nine months and twenty days** (8). Back in Jerusalem, Joab reported the total number: **In Israel there were eight hundred thousand able-bodied men who could handle a sword, and in Judah five hundred thousand** (9). The Chronicler gives 1,100,000 in Israel and 470,000 in Judah, adding: 'but Joab did not include Levi and Benjamin in the numbering, because the king's command was repulsive to him' (1 Chr. 21: 5, 6).

By now, David also had his misgivings: **'I have sinned greatly in what I have done. Now, O Lord, I beg you, take away the guilt of your servant. I have done a very foolish thing'** (10). Yahweh replied to David's prayer by sending to him Gad the prophet, 'David's seer' (11; cf. 1 Sam. 22: 5) with a choice of three punishments from which one was to be selected: (*a*) three years of famine in the land; (*b*) defeat by his enemies for three months; (*c*) three days of plague in the land. David chose the third: **'Let us fall into the hands of the Lord, for his mercy is great; but do not let me fall into the hands of men'** (14). Judgment fell; no less than 70,000 men died in the land, but as the angel of affliction approached Jerusalem, **the Lord was grieved because of the calamity. . . . 'Enough! Withdraw your hand'** (16). The exact place where the plague was halted is named: **the threshing floor of Araunah the Jebusite.** David **saw the angel who was striking down the people** (17); his vision was so vivid that he broke down in confession and intercession: **'I am the one who has sinned and done wrong. These are but sheep. What have they done? Let you hand fall upon me and my family'** (17).

Gad visited David once more, with instructions to erect an altar on the site. He accordingly negotiated with Araunah for its purchase, with bargaining recalling Abraham's with Ephron in Gen. 23: 10–16. The vendor offered the land as a free gift, David insisted on paying a fair price; he would not sacrifice to the Lord what had cost him nothing (24). Fifty shekels of silver changed hands in return for the threshing floor and oxen for the offerings.

So the religious history of I–II Samuel, which began with the pollution of the cult by Eli's apostate sons, ends with the building of the altar which foreshadowed the Temple itself: **'Then the Lord answered prayer on behalf of the land, and the plague on Israel was stopped'** (25).

BIBLIOGRAPHY

Commentaries, etc.

ACKROYD, P. R., *The First Book of Samuel. CBC* (Cambridge, 1971).

ACKROYD, P. R., *The Second Book of Samuel. CBC* (Cambridge, 1977).

BROCKINGTON, L. H., 'I and II Samuel' in *Peake's Commentary on the Bible* (London, 1962).

DRIVER, S. R., *Notes on the Hebrew Text and the Topography of the Books of Samuel*[2] (Oxford, 1913).

GORDON, R. P., *1 and 2 Samuel. OT Guides* (Sheffield 1984).

GIRDLESTONE, R. B., *Deuterographs* (Oxford, 1894).

HERTZBERG, H. W., *I & II Samuel. OTL* (E.T. London, 1964).

KENNEDY, A. R. S., *I & II Samuel.* The Century Bible (Edinburgh, 1904).

KIRKPATRICK, A. F., *I Samuel, II Samuel. CBSC* (Cambridge, 1884, 1890).

MARTIN, W. J., 'I & II Samuel' in *The Biblical Expositor,* i (London, 1960).

MAUCHLINE, J., *I & II Samuel.* The New Century Bible (London, 1971).

McCARTER, P. K., *I Samuel. AB* (Garden City, N.Y., 1980).

McKANE, W., *I & II Samuel. TC* (London, 1963).

PAYNE, D. F., 'I & II Samuel' in *The New Bible Commentary*[3] (London, 1970).

ROBERTSON, E., 'Samuel and Saul' in *The OT Problem* (Manchester, 1950).

SMITH, H. P., *A Critical and Exegetical Commentary on the Books of Samuel. ICC* (Edinburgh, 1899).

WHYBRAY, R. N., *The Succession Narrative* (London, 1968).

General

ANDERSON, G. W., *A Critical Introduction to the OT* (London, 1959).

BRIGHT, J., *A History of Israel* (London, 1960).

CLEMENTS, R. E., *Abraham and David* (London, 1967).

DE VAUX, R., *Ancient Israel; its life and institutions* (E.T.[2], London, 1965).

DOUGLAS, J. D. (ed.), *The New Bible Dictionary* (London, 1962).

EISSFELDT, O., *The Old Testament, an Introduction*[3] (E.T. Oxford, 1965).

ELLISON, H. L., *The Prophets of Israel* (Exeter, 1969).

HERRMANN, S., *A History of Israel in OT Times* (E.T. London, 1974).

KRUMMACHER, F. W., *David the King of Israel* (E.T. Edinburgh, 1870).

MAY, H. G., *The Oxford Bible Atlas*[2] (London, 1974).

NOTH, M., *The History of Israel* (E.T.[2] London, 1960).

PAYNE, D. F., *Kingdoms of the Lord.* (Exeter, 1981).

WELCH, A. C., *Kings and Prophets of Israel* (London, 1952).

WENHAM, J. W., 'Large numbers in the OT', in *The Tyndale Bulletin*, 18, 1967, pp. 19–53.

WISEMAN, D. J. (ed.) *Peoples of OT Times* (Oxford, 1973).

1 and 2 KINGS

CHARLES G. MARTIN

INTRODUCTION

1 and 2 Kings (3 and 4 Kingdoms or Reigns in the Greek version) give a continuous narrative of the Hebrew monarchy from the time when David handed on a rich and extensive kingdom to the time of its final destruction. Four hundred years in little more than 50,000 words means a drastic reduction of detail. A parallel enterprise in British history is the Anglo-Saxon Chronicle which gives a year by year annal with the very occasional fuller incident. Kings adopts a very different principle of selection. Although the writer keeps rough track of time, he attempts no year by year coverage. Instead he writes 'history with a purpose' and the purpose is to show Yahweh, ruler of all powers and all history, displaying his character by his dealings with his covenant people. Hence many politically interesting or important matters are left out, and people and times are chosen for their religious and moral significance. The lesson is given explicitly (1 Kg. 2: 4; 3: 14; 6: 11–13; etc.) in terms reminiscent of Deuteronomy, and implicitly as progressive failure brings progressive decline. This so-called 'deuteronomist' stance has attracted much comment. Those who hold Deuteronomy to be a seventh-century product see Kings as a moralizing editorial work using some genuine historical material and some legend to illustrate the thesis. Such *a priori* treatment results in comments such as 'Dt. 17: 14–20 must have been written with Solomon in mind' (B. W. Anderson, *Understanding the OT*, 1957, p. 145), 'objective history obscured by Deuteronomist rationalization' (Gray, 28 f.), 'they pictured the ceremonies as they were practised in their own times' (Montgomery, 199). Those who accept Deuteronomy as substantially Mosaic and as representing a fundamental part of Israelite heritage, see Kings as giving a fair picture of events recorded, while accepting an editor who selected and arranged his material to point the moral of the sad story. A vast literature has arisen over these questions far beyond the scope of the present work. A brief commentary cannot continually pause to say 'Some scholars . . .' when the difference is one of presupposition, so it must be generally stated that the following notes are written from the standpoint that the Deuteronomic material was part of Israel's heritage and not an importation by a later author.

Author and Sources

'Editor' is too modern a term, and does injustice to the person who gave us Kings. Tradition ascribed the work to Jeremiah. Allusions here and there suggest it took its final form early in the exile, but nothing certain is known of its writing place or time of origin. Contemporary sources are referred to, including

The Book of the Annals of Solomon (1 Kg. 11: 41)

The Book of the Annals of the Kings of Israel (17 references)

The Book of the Annals of the Kings of Judah (15 references).

The opening chapters continue the style of Samuel and are apparently drawn from the same Court Narrative (ending at 1 Kg. 2: 46). The large sections dealing with Elijah and Elisha may draw on oral or written material from prophetic circles (certainly Elisha's exploits were being formally collected at an early date, 2 Kg. 8: 4). The final chapters may well be from the writer's own experience of those harrowing days. Some of the sources record 'miraculous' events which the author quite naturally accepts into his story of Yahweh's action. Modern readers may find this beyond their own experience but must let the writer tell his story and cannot expect lengthy discussion of everything unusual. The sources are very selectively used within a framework which tells the story king by king. For the divided kingdom the formula relates the two parts: 'In the nth year of King X of Israel/Judah, Y began to reign in Judah/Israel.' This is usually followed by the new king's age at accession (or designation as heir-apparent or co-regent), his mother's name, length of reign, and an assessment that he did what was right/evil in the sight of the LORD.

Chronology

Only at the very end of the story do we have a link with outside dating (2 Kg. 24: 12). Archaeology has furnished a mass of data—notably triumphal inscriptions and king lists—which allow cross-checking of dates, and also much light on customs, literature and culture of the times. In general it may be said that work on this material has increased respect for the author's sources, though difficulties of chronology remain. The major work by E. R. Thiele (*The Mysterious Numbers of the Hebrew Kings*, 2nd edn., 1965) has cleared many obscurities. Thiele compares the Kings records and shows how they reflect the various computational methods of the Ancient Near East—for example, whether or not the accession year of a king was counted as part of his reign—and also the custom of co-regency which started with David's designation of Solomon in his own lifetime. The finer points of chronological reconciliation were less important to the author than they seem to be to modern technical historians. What happened and what

it meant usually mattered more than the exact date. It may be that the 'Annals' the author consulted were more detailed in this respect. Perhaps it is significant that they have perished while the interpretation has survived. The same emphasis is preserved in the following notes and readers wishing to get help with particular chronological difficulties should consult the reference works quoted. Where necessary the following dating, taken from the *New Bible Dictionary*, has been used:

Egypt	Judah	Israel	Syria	Assyria
Sheshonq 945–924	Solomon 971/70–931/930			
	Rehoboam 931/30–913	Jeroboam I 931/30–910/09		
	Abijam 913–911/10	Nadab 910/09–909/08		
	Asa 911/10–870/69	Baasha 909/08–886/85	Benhadad I ?900–860	
		Elah 886/85–885/84		
		Zimri 885/4		
		Tibni 885/84–880	Benhadad II 860–843	
		Omri 885/84–874/73		
		Ahab 874/73–853		Shalmaneser III 859–824 Battle of Qarqar 853
	Jehoshaphat 870/69–848 (co-regent 873/72)	Ahaziah 853–852		
	Jehoram 848–841 (co-regent from 853)	Joram 852–841	Hazael 843–796	
	Athaliah 841–835	Jehu 841–814/13		
	Joash 835–796	Jehoahaz 814/13–798	Benhadad III 796–770	
	Amaziah 796–767	Jehoash 798–782/81		
	Azariah 767–740/39 (co-regent 791–90)	Jeroboam II 782/81–753 (co-regent 793/92)		
		Zechariah 753–752		
		Shallum 752		
		Menahem 752–742/41	Rezin 750–732	Tiglath-pileser III 745–727
		Pekahiah 742/41–740/39		
	Jotham 740/39–732/31 (co-regent 750)	Pekah 740/39–732/31		
	Ahaz 732/31–716/15 (co-regent 744/43 senior partner 735)	Hoshea 732/31–723/22		
		Fall of Samaria 722		Shalmaneser V 727–722 Sargon II 722–705

Egypt	Judah	Israel	Syria	Assyria
Osorkon IV	Hezekiah			
727–716	716/715–687/86			Sennacherib
	(co-regent 729)			705–681
Tirhakah 690–664				
	Manasseh			
	687/86–642/41			
	(co-regent 696/95)			Esarhaddon
				681–669
				Ashurbanipal
	Amon			669–627
	642/41–640/39			
				Fall of Nineveh 612
	Josiah			
	640/39–609			**Babylon**
	Jehoahaz			Nabopolassar
	609			626–605
Necho II	Jehoiakim			
610–595	609–597			Nebuchadnezzar II
	Jehoiachin			605–562
	597			
	Zedekiah			
	597–587			

Ethos and interests

To read a document compiled two and a half thousand years ago requires humility as well as imagination. These records sit in judgment upon us as much as we on them, and in so far as they claim to record a unique human experiment we cannot place them simply alongside political and social structures with which we are familiar. The Hebrew monarchy arose as a covenant (1 Sam. 12) built on a covenant at Sinai, built on a covenant with the patriarchs (2 Kg. 13: 23). The Davidic covenant (2 Sam. 7; 1 Kg. 8: 16–21) was superimposed on these. It is true that these covenants were misunderstood, forgotten and abused, but it is no service to the story to ignore them or suppose them a later fiction thrust incongruously upon the earlier actors in the drama. The story is about a community under Yahweh, Lord of history, concerned with relationships and righteousness as well as ceremonial. Hence the judgment upon each reign is of good or evil in the sight of the LORD. Religious condemnation sounds odd only to an age that separates symptoms from disease, that lets psychiatrists take over from priests and political columnists from prophets. But what people worship determines how they live and the distrust of the 'high places' was not a religious foible but a profound insight into human corruptibility at the deepest springs of understanding and response.

Kings deals with a small kingdom, not a twentieth-century global village. Dan to Beersheba was only 150 miles but still news could take several days at least and often weeks. Many a present-day school and playing fields covers more space than a Palestinian 'city' of those days. An agricultural society knows about seasons, growth and uncertainty more deeply than those whose food comes from the supermarket. Indeed, the growth of a cash-economy with its middlemen, bureaucrats and capitalists from Solomon on is an important factor in the story.

Incidentally to the main purpose of showing the grief and glory of the covenant people, there are several other questions raised: questions that linger in the mind, not just about Israel in the first millennium B.C. but about human society at large. Were the covenants mutually incompatible? Dt. 17: 14 f. suggests democratic appointment of the chief citizen under Yahweh. The dynastic principle (2 Sam. 7) is not always in conflict with this (*e.g.* 2 Kg. 21: 24) but could be. Here is a major tension between the ideals of charismatic leadership and constitutional authority. If the North clung to the first and the South to the second, who will say which fared best? The parallel problem of worship is focused in this history. Is a 'rule of saints' possible? What influence do rulers have—be they Jeroboam at Bethel, or Solomon, Manasseh or Josiah at Jerusalem? Was the centrality of Jerusalem God's ideal or the best in the circumstances? Solomon posed the question in 1 Kg. 8: 27. A later reply came in Isa. 57: 15. We still wrestle with the relation between personal piety and institutional religion.

Above all we feel progressively the tension of the divine long-suffering. 'They would not listen' (2 Kg. 17: 14) is a fundamental diagnosis of the human condition, amplified by prophetic anguish from Hosea and Jeremiah to Jesus on Olivet (Lk. 19: 41–44).

The following notes do not pretend to deal closely with matters of detail but to help the general reader listen to the author's story of 'your great name and your mighty hand and your outstretched arm' (1 Kg. 8: 42).

395

ANALYSIS

1 and 2 KINGS

1 Kings

I. COURT INTRIGUE AND A NEW KING (1: 1–2: 46)

The introduction of Abishag (1: 1–4)
1. King David was old (cf. 2 Sam. 5: 4): possibly about 70; Solomon might have been 20 and already married (comp. 14: 21 with 11: 42). Abishag is brought into the story because of her significance later (2: 17). **2. that our lord the king may keep warm:** there are parallels in other ancient texts to this unusual prescription.
Adonijah's bid for the throne (1: 5–10)
5. Adonijah, whose mother was Haggith (cf. 2 Sam. 3: 4): Chileab appears to have died young, so Adonijah was the oldest surviving son. Analogy with surrounding nations would have made him heir apparent, though no succession pattern was fixed in Israel. He and his advisers felt it wisest to force the issue. (Dt. 21: 15–17 refers to inheritance in general, not succession.) Saul and David were both charismatic leaders, acclaimed by the people as evidently God's kings, but the pattern was changing.
   chariots and horses (better, as JB, 'a chariot and team'): the same ostentation that Absalom had used (2 Sam. 15: 1). David was at best an over-indulgent father (6) and now so enfeebled that a power vacuum gave rise to palace cabals. Adonijah picked **Joab and Abiathar** (7), two trusty companions of David's in days gone by. Why they backed Adonijah is an enigma. Perhaps his extrovert character reminded them of the energetic young David they had so eagerly served. Perhaps they accepted the 'oldest son' principle and felt it was time for action.
8. Zadok . . . Benaiah . . . Nathan are identified as a rival party. The **special guard** were regulars, as distinct from the war-time levy which Joab commanded. Benaiah was in charge of the foreign mercenaries mentioned in v. 38 (cf. 2 Sam. 8: 18). **9. Adonijah then sacrificed sheep, cattle . . . :** all killing of meat was religious, so the feast was technically a sacrifice,

though at that time sacrifice was not restricted to priests. **En Rogel:** a spring in the Kidron valley about a quarter-mile outside the city wall. **10. he did not invite Nathan . . . :** because if he shared a meal with them he could not afterwards kill them when they became a threat to the throne.
The appeal to the king (1: 11–27)
Nathan appears as trusted adviser and plans his campaign with skill and speed. **11. the son of Haggith:** a shrewd play on harem jealousies. **13. Solomon your son shall be king:** no such exact promise is recorded but the oracle of 2 Sam. 7 could well apply to the *future* son; also, the Jerusalem-born son (when David was king of all the tribes) would be more appropriate than one born at Hebron (when he was king of Judah only). **Why then has Adonijah become king?** overstated the case since no anointing or crowning ceremony had taken place. **20. the eyes of all Israel are on you** suggests that David still retained the people's allegiance and that Adonijah was not a popular choice. Bathsheba follows this with a plea for personal safety: **I and my son Solomon will be treated as criminals** (21), a rival party likely to be eliminated. The magnanimity of David (2 Sam. 9) was not the usual behaviour of new kings. Nathan is announced—**Nathan . . . is here** (23)—as he did not have the same immediate access that Bathsheba enjoyed. The extreme court etiquette need not be ingratiating flattery of an old man, but contrasts sadly with Nathan's former directness (2 Sam. 12). He confirms Bathsheba's story, without the personal fear, and adds Zadok and Benaiah as loyal supporters.
David appoints Solomon (1: 28—37)
The king is stirred to activity, giving firm and exact instructions to establish a co-regency—something quite new in Israel, though current practice elsewhere. **28. Bathsheba** is recalled, having withdrawn during the conversation with Nathan. David swears **As surely as the**

LORD lives . . . (the same oath as 2 Sam. 4:
9) and recalls the Solomonic promise (29 f.).
His vigorous instructions indicate that he had
intended this all along and it was no feeble
falling for the suggestions of wily advisers. He
calls for **Zadok the priest** (32) who had been
in office jointly with Abiathar (2 Sam. 15: 24–
29 suggests David regarded Zadok as senior,
but 2: 35 suggests the reverse). David relies
upon his mercenary troops, **your lord's
servants** (33). These were **the Kerethites and
the Pelethites** (38), Cretan and Philistine
soldiers whose only loyalty was to the king
who paid them—another feature of Israel becoming 'like the nations'. Solomon was to ride
on my own mule (33) as symbol of succeeding
to the royal privilege. Horses had not yet become riding animals in Israel; most people rode
asses; mules were more rare (*e.g.* 2 Sam. 13:
29). **Gihon** was about half a mile N of En
Rogel but hidden from Adonijah's party by a
curve of the valley. **34. anoint him:** the exact
details of a full ceremony are given to put
the succession beyond doubt. The spontaneous
recognition of a charismatic figure (1 Sam. 11;
2 Sam. 5: 2) gives way to a political appointment. **35. I have appointed him ruler:** 'ruler'
(*nāgîd*) is the word preferred by prophets (*e.g.*
1 Sam. 13: 14; 2 Sam. 7: 8; 1 Kg. 14: 7) showing
the rôle, under God, of the chief citizen, rather
than 'king' (*melek*) which could easily degenerate into the tyranny of neighbouring monarchs.
over Israel and Judah: a double title which
raises the fundamental question whether there
ever was a truly *united* monarchy (see below
on ch. 12). **36. Amen! . . .** Benaiah gives
the loyal address of a professional soldier and
personal friend.

Solomon proclaimed king (1: 38–40)
The party **went down** the steep path down
the hillside to Gihon which was nearly at the
bottom of the valley (38). Zadok takes **the
horn of oil from the sacred tent** David had
pitched to house the ark (2 Sam. 6: 17) **and
anointed Solomon** (39), at once a civil and
religious action making him civil ruler and
sacred person (see 1 Sam. 24: 6 for David's
own recognition of this sanctity). Then **all
the people went up after him** (40), and the
popular ceremony is contrasted with Adonijah's private party of conspirators.

Adonijah's failure (1: 41–53)
The story conveys well the complete surprise
and alarm the feasters felt; their plans had been
completely overturned in the few hours they
had been feasting. **42. Even as he was speaking:** Jonathan's account contains detail after the
return of Solomon's triumphal party to the
city, so the **sound of the trumpet** (41) Joab
heard must be from the later proclamations in
the city. **Solomon has taken his seat on the
royal throne** (46) as the final act of initiation,

and the congratulations and David's response
(47, 48), make it plain to Adonijah that this
was no rival plot, but had David's full approval.
50. Adonijah was in fear of Solomon, as the
normal practice would be to kill off rivals to
the throne. Anyway he was caught in act of
treason, and relations between the half-
brothers may not have been cordial before. He
availed himself of the traditional sanctuary of
a holy place and **took hold of the horns of
the altar.** Solomon spares him with a caveat,
and he **came and bowed down to King
Solomon** (53)—a bitter reversal of the morning's hopes. **Go to your home:** not necessarily
house arrest, but a command to withdraw from
public life.

David's final charge to Solomon (2: 1–12)
The interval between 1: 53 and 2: 1 is not given.
It must have allowed time for the occasion
described in 1 Chr. 28–29 when they 'acknowledged Solomon . . . as a king second time'
(29:22) and for the earlier instruction about the
temple.
3. Observe what the LORD **your God requires:** given in terms similar to Dt., a refrain
which recurs throughout the history.
David's charge to Solomon to deal with **Joab**
and **Shimei** has been criticized as petty spite
—some have even suggested it is a later invention to clear Solomon of blame, but then the
reference to **Barzillai** is odd. More likely is
the view that David was anxious to hand on a
dynasty free from blood-guilt and curse. Solomon's words in vv. 33, 45 confirm this.
5. what Joab . . . did to me: RSV NEB continue
this by following an amended text to give
'innocent blood on the girdle of **my** loins'.
NIV follows Heb. with **belt round his waist.**
David's failure to deal with Joab at the time
was a major blunder, partly occasioned by the
uncertain law at the time about blood-feud;
now he urges Solomon to **Deal . . . according
to your wisdom** (16) and retrieve the situation.
7. show kindness to the sons of Barzillai:
the kindness (*ḥesed*) is the steadfast love based
on covenant (see 2 Sam. 17: 27–29; 19: 31–40;
esp. promise of 19: 33) and would be shown
by allowing him to **eat at your table**—i.e.
become pensioners of the royal household, not
necessarily live in Jerusalem.
Shimei's **bitter curses** (8) and David's forgiveness are recorded in 2 Sam. 16: 5–13; 19:
18–23. It is a pity he now feels that forgiveness
is less efficient than the sword at removing a
curse. Perhaps time had dimmed the humility
of 2 Sam. 16: 11, and popular superstition fed
his fear.
10. David rested with his fathers: a euphemistic formula used throughout Kings for death
(except those who died violently, *e.g.* 2 Kg.
12: 21; 14: 20). **and was buried in the City**

of David: beginning a custom that was followed for nearly all the kings of Judah. 12. Solomon sat on the throne: one Gk. MS adds 'being 12 yrs old'; Josephus gives 14 years. There is no firm evidence.

Solomon takes charge (2: 13–46)

13. Adonijah is either too cunning to fathom or incredibly naïve. Bathsheba clearly regards him with suspicion but sees nothing wrong with his request for Abishag. 15. things changed, and the kingdom has gone . . . (see 12: 15 for similar use of this root): Adonijah appears to accept the turn of events as the will of Yahweh. Although receiving his mother with delicate palace etiquette, Solomon predictably interprets the request as a claim to supersede David (see 2 Sam. 16: 22 for previous instance) though the story had earlier (1: 4) been at pains to deny that Abishag was David's concubine. 22. yes for him and for Abiathar . . . and . . . Joab: Solomon is sensitive about the rival group. Perhaps he is trigger-happy and jumped at a chance to rout possible opposition. 25. Benaiah . . . struck down Adonijah: apparently still in the palace where Adonijah had come to make his request.

Solomon spares Abiathar the priest (26) on religious and familial grounds, principally the former since you shared all my father's hardships applied equally to Joab. You carried the ark of the Sovereign LORD God may refer to the triumphant journey of the ark to Jerusalem (2 Sam. 6: 12). Some commentators give 'ephod', referring to Abiathar's sharing exile with David (1 Sam. 23: 6; 30: 7. NEB 1 Sam. 14: 18 gives 'ephod' for 'ark' on the basis of the Gk. text but there is no such textual justification here). Anathoth was a Levitical town (Jos. 21: 18) about 3 miles N of Jerusalem and a little beyond Nob where he had been brought up (1 Sam. 22: 11–20; cf. Jer. 1: 1). 27. fulfilling the word the LORD had spoken: through Samuel to Eli (1 Sam. 2: 31–36). The substitution of Zadok is not specifically mentioned here (see v. 35). If he is to be the 'faithful priest' of 1 Sam. 2: 35, it is suggested that the priesthood now returned to the line of Eleazar from a (usurping) Ithamar line (see NBD art. 'Eli'). 28. Joab . . . fled to the tent of the LORD, rightly fearing that Solomon would include him as a conspirator. Exod. 21: 12–14 shows limits applied by Hebrew law to the ancient practice of sanctuary. Some Gk. versions add, after beside the altar, 'and Solomon sent a message to the altar, Why have you fled to the altar? and Joab said, Because I was afraid of you and I fled to the LORD'. Benaiah, embarrassed by Joab's refusal to Come out, reports to the king for further instructions (30). Solomon rehearses Joab's guilt (cf. v. 5) and Benaiah accepts the royal judgment as overriding the traditional religious sanctuary. 33. on David

and to his descendants, his house and to his throne sounds almost an incantation, clearing the new dynasty of blood guilt. Joab was buried on his own land in the desert (34), getting at least an honourable burial after an exciting, and often honourable life. His strange hold over David, and final disloyalty, remain an enigma. desert: rough grazing land. Joab was a native of Bethlehem (2 Sam. 2: 32) about 6 miles from Jerusalem but may have had a personal holding on the outskirts of the city. Benaiah and Zadok are now officially placed in the offices they had held *de facto* during the co-regency (35). The priesthood is at the disposal of the king—another step down the slippery slope of being 'like the nations'. Only Shimei (36) remained from David's short-list. Solomon restricts him to Jerusalem (a tiny city about 30 acres) where he can be under close watch. He is not even to cross the Kidron Valley (37) to visit his estate at Bahurim, E of Jerusalem (2 Sam. 16: 5). Shimei, pleasantly surprised, agrees. What you say is good (38, better, with NEB, 'I accept your sentence'). He kept bounds for three years (39); then two of his slaves ran off to Achish (see NBD art. 'Slavery') who apprehended them under an extradition agreement (NBD p. 1197). Maybe Shimei had to collect them in person; maybe he had grown careless. Either way, when Solomon was told (41), he summons Shimei, carefully rehearses the agreement to make clear the legality of sentence, and adds again the matter David had dug up from under his forgiveness. The formula will be blessed . . . will remain secure (45) again like an incantation freeing the dynasty from curse. 46. The kingdom was now firmly established: indeed it was! But the reader feels exhausted rather than satisfied. A sad contrast with the magnanimity of the first king (1 Sam. 11: 11–15) but then, kingdoms 'like the nations' cannot be run on sentiment, and Solomon, son of the palace harem, had not come up the same hard way as the farmer's sons, David and Saul.

II. SOLOMON'S GLORY AND SHAME (3: 1–11: 43)

Solomon asks for wisdom (3: 1–15)

Solomon's marriage is referred to also at 9: 16 and 9: 24. Greek versions put 3: 1 and 9: 16 together after 4: 34 and start this section with the explanation of the sacrificial customs.

1. Pharaoh king of Egypt: probably Siamun, one of the last of the XXI Dynasty, then in decline (see NBD p. 345). For the Egyptians the alliance meant a peaceful and secure northern frontier, consolidating the foothold they appear to have esrablished by annexing Philistia on David's death. For Solomon, it was part of the policy of keeping by diplomacy the empire

David had won by the sword. Ironically, Siamun's treaty and daughter were worthless in halting the aggressive and disruptive policies of Sheshonq (Shishak) who began the XXII dynasty in 945 and invaded Israel in 925 (1 Kg. 14: 25).

Solomon . . . brought her to the City of David until his palace building was complete. The (favourable) story of Solomon's request for wisdom is prefaced with an explanation about the technically irregular place of worship. **2. The people were still sacrificing at the high places** because the centralizing of worship at Jerusalem was not completed until the reign of Josiah. The **high place** (*bāmôt*, 'hill shrines') became a by-word in prophetic rebuke as the Israelites fell into Canaanite practices associated with nature-worship at similar shrines. During the Settlement and early Monarchy (1 Sam. 9: 12; v. 2) there is 'no suggestion of idolatry but a light shade of disapproval' (see *NBD art.* 'High Place').

4. the king went to Gibeon, about 6 miles NW of Jerusalem, the **most important** (Gk. 'highest') **high place** where, according to 1 Chr. 16: 39; 21: 29, the brazen altar and tent of meeting from the wilderness days were kept. Gibeon, the crafty city (Jos. 9) had been allocated to the priests, descendants of Aaron (Jos. 21: 17). **Solomon offered a thousand burnt offerings:** RSV 'used to offer' could suggest a regular practice of worship at this shrine. **a thousand** means simply 'very many'.

5. the LORD appeared to Solomon . . . in a dream: as to Abraham, Isaac and Jacob and Samuel (Gen. 15: 12; 26: 24; 28: 12; 1 Sam. 3) the dream was a normal form of divine revelation but inferior to the direct prophetic word (Num. 12: 6–8) and, later, regarded with suspicion (Jer. 23: 25–32). Nathan had given God's word to David (2 Sam. 7: 4; 12: 1) but sadly neither he nor a successor appears to guide Solomon.

Solomon's request is a model of humble piety (vv. 6–9). **7. I am only a little child:** not literally young in years, but inexperienced in government (see Jer. 1: 6). **9. Give your servant . . . a discerning heart** (NEB 'a heart with skill to listen'): for Hebrew the heart was the centre of personal awareness and judgment, not of emotion, hence mind (RSV) is better. **discerning** is from root meaning 'to listen'; the ruler must have skill to listen before forming a judgment and so 'give a just hearing' (v. 11). **10. The LORD was pleased:** who added promises of all the less basic things Solomon might have asked. **12. a wise and discerning heart:** relates to practical wisdom, to assess people and situations, rather than the philosophical brilliance for which he is later celebrated (4: 31–34). The promise of longevity with its Deuteronomic condition **if you walk in my ways** (14) is a sad reminder that even wisdom does not guarantee persistence in godliness. **15. He returned to Jerusalem** where the **ark of the . . . covenant** was, sacrificed and celebrated, and then applied his new gift to the task of government.

Wisdom in action (3: 16–28)

Solomon's appointment had been political, at David's ruling, unlike the charismatic claims of Saul and David. The writer now gives an instance of the wisdom which showed the people that their new king was indeed fitted to rule (3: 28).

16. two prostitutes came to the king: all his people had immediate access. Prostitution was widespread in the ancient world. Even in Israel where 'the LORD' . . . detests' it (Dt. 23: 18) it was then, as now, an ever-present though disapproved part of the culture. Solomon's treatment of the case has become legendary. The true mother reacts convincingly as **she was filled with compassion for her son** (26, NEB 'moved with love for her son'). For Hebrew the seat of emotion was visceral: 'her bowels burned for her son'. Her love shows, too, in the use, in her plea **give her the living baby**, of a tender word (? 'bairn') in contrast to the formal 'son' when stating the case originally. Some Greek versions omit **living** to make clear that the dead child was not brought. (Josephus adds that Solomon ordered both children to be divided.)

Solomon's administration and power (4: 1–34)

1. ruled over all Israel: an early nationalistic term (as David, 2 Sam. 8: 15). Later **Israel** more often means the northern kingdom after the disruption. In spite of the emphasis on the united monarchy, it is doubtful if the unity was more than nominal (*e.g.* 2 Sam. 5: 5, 'all Israel and Judah', and the ease with which rebellions seemed to develop on north–south lines). Solomon's glory was principally displayed in the building and luxury at Jerusalem, but 'all Israel' helped pay for it, dearly.

2. these were his chief officials (compare lists for David's administration in 2 Sam. 8: 15–18 and (secondarily) 2 Sam. 20: 23–26): **Azariah son of Zadok——the priest** (see 1 Chr. 6: 8): If this list represents the administration of the later kingdom this could be the same Azariah, but then **Zadok and Abiathar** (4b) seem out of place. Another suggestion (Montgomery, pp. 114–115) is that **Elihoreph** (nowhere else used) is not the name of an official but an office, 'keeper of the calendar', so NEB gives 'In charge of the calendar, Azariah son of Zadok the priest', and makes **Ahijah the son of Shisha** the only 'secretary' (3).

4. Benaiah . . . commander in chief; as mentioned in 2: 35, no doubt still commanded the loyalty of the mercenaries, the Kerethites and

Pelethites, but now they shared him with the levy. One Gk. MS adds the surprising 'Eliab son of Joab over the host' after v. 6—perhaps a later note keeping the list up to date. **Zadok and Abiathar** as **priests** present a difficulty. Abiathar was banished from the priesthood (2: 27). The phrase may be an intrusion from 2 Sam. 8: 17. **5. Azariah son of Nathan—in charge of the district officers** (NEB 'superintendent of the regional governors'), a new appointment, not paralleled in David's court, though 1 Chr. 27: 2–15 suggests David's numbering of the people was connected with such administrative arrangement. **Zabud son of Nathan——a priest and personal adviser to the king** (as Gen. 26: 26), perhaps the nearest Solomon had to the candid friend Nathan had been to David. Lastly, the sinister **Adoniram son of Abda** (his Phoenician name did not help either) was **in charge of forced labor** (6). He is mentioned in 2 Sam. 20: 24 but since he survived in full vigour after Solomon's death (12: 18) it is doubtful if the levy was in fact begun in David's time.

Solomon's enlarged administration had to be supported and the **twelve district governors . . . who supplied provisions** were key figures in the structure. It has been suggested that Solomon deliberately crossed tribal boundaries to break down tribal loyalty, but more likely he simply aimed to get roughly equal numbers in the divisions and to take advantage of existing networks for collecting tax. **8. their names** are not in fact given, but only the patronymics. It is more likely that the list from which these were copied was torn on the right-hand edge than that the officers were hereditary at this stage (see JB). Since two were married to daughters of Solomon the list must be from the latter half of his reign. The position of Judah is not clear (RSV give 'over the land of Judah' at the end of v. 19 from one of various emendations to the text). Either Judah was free of impost or (more likely) v 19a is a repeat of v 13 so that Judah is the twelfth district with a single officer. **22. Solomon's . . . provisions** (possibly from an actual shopping list) was for **all who came to the king's table** (27), i.e. the growing number of his officers and pensioners. There was not only the maintenance of post and military horses (28)—the organization of a tightly knit, economically expanding state has to be paid for! By comparison with Nehemiah's provision for 150 (Neh. 5: 17) it has been calculated that Solomon was feeding at least five thousand people. The rest of the people **ate and . . . drank and . . . were happy** (20), they **lived in safety** (25) and the satisfying independence is reflected in **each man under his own vine and fig tree**. Not all the memories of Solomon's reign were bitter, and this picture of the good old days of security and prosperity recurs in the hopes for similar times again (Mic. 4: 4; Zech. 3: 10).

21. Solomon ruled: in the general sense of controlling trade routes and collecting **tribute** from the kings **west of the River** (24) who were otherwise autonomous. **Tiphsah** (Thapsacus), an important crossing town on the Euphrates river was about 400 miles as the crow flies from **Gaza**. Solomon did not control **the land of the Philistines** (21) who may voluntarily have accepted Egyptian overlords on David's death. This Egyptian bridgehead (see too 9: 16) proved a costly error when Shishak ended the Egyptian lethargy with his attack on Judah and Israel (14: 25).

29. God gave Solomon wisdom in fulfilment of the promise (3: 12) including nature-knowledge (33) and the practical wisdom enshrined in **proverbs** (see Prov. 25: 1). De Vaux connects **Ethan** and **Heman** with the Psalms ascribed to them (Ps. 88; 89) and regards **the sons of Mahol** (choir) as the choristers of Solomon's temple. It is significant, but sad, that no prophet appears in Solomon's court to balance his intellectual and cultural brilliance with reminders of humble duty as Nathan has done to David.

The planning and building of the temple (5: 1–9: 9)
Hiram's approach and treaty (5: 1–12)
These greetings from **Hiram** (1) link the previous section (34) with the major example of Solomon's wisdom, the building of the temple. Solomon used the opportunity to obtain Hiram's help in this project. **Tyre**, built on a rocky island just off the Phoenician coast was a rapidly rising power based on sea commerce and would be anxious to maintain good relations with Solomon in view of his control of trade routes. **Hiram had always been on friendly terms with David** (see 2 Sam. 5: 11 for earlier dealings) and knew (3) of David's frustrated desire to build a temple. The message through Nathan (2 Sam. 7: 4–13) did not mention **wars** and **enemies** (but see 1 Chr. 22: 8). **4. But now** the kingdom is settled and the long-deferred promise (**Your offspring . . .**, 2 Sam. 7: 13) can be fulfilled. **5. a temple for the Name of the LORD** was viewed with awe (cf. 8: 16) as a new departure. **the name** was a manifestation of personality, meaning far more to the ancients than to present-day people. The transcendent, unlimited Yahweh was in some way localized, available to his people in the house where he put his name (see below on 8: 29).

6. So give orders: a formal agreement to co-operate is requested, to which Hiram responds with joy (7) and acceptance (8). The **timber** was cut by **the Sidonians** (6), dragged down to **the sea** (9) and floated as **rafts . . . to the place you specify**. (According to 2 Chr.

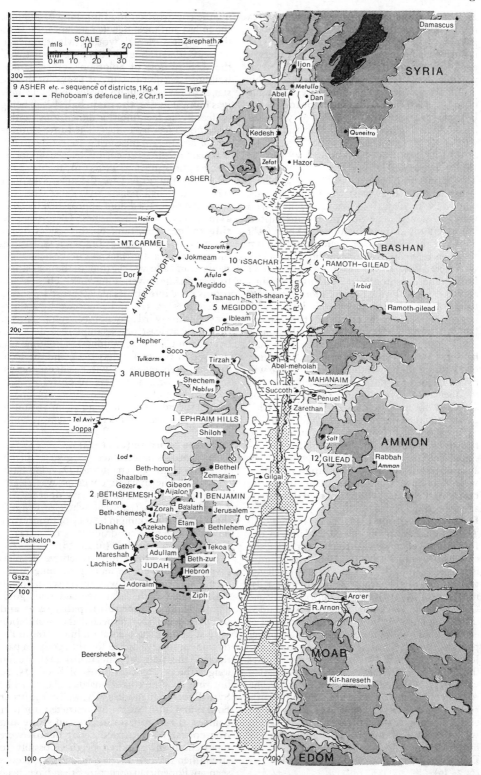

Map 23—Solomon's Districts

2: 16 this was Joppa and search in that area has uncovered confirming traces.) Solomon's payment in **wheat** and **pressed olive oil** (11) is more than enough to support the workers (a cor of wheat is about 8 cwt. or 400 kg.) so possibly Hiram exported the surplus as his profit on the deal. This mutually profitable treaty is described as bringing **peaceful relations** (12)—not the cessation of war, but harmonious relationships of trade and goodwill.

Solomon introduces a labour levy (5: 13–18)

This passage must be read with 9: 15–23 where a distinction is drawn between non-Israelites who were treated as serfs and Israelites who were 'no slaves'. The **Solomon conscripted labourers** NIV softens the 'forced labour' (as it translates the Heb. *mas* at Deut. 20:11; Jos. 17: 13 when referring to non-Israelites). Israelites were here allowed two months out of three **at home**, and one month **in Lebanon**, presumably as carriers for the expert Sidonian timberfellers. In the hill country of Judea a much larger number **removed from the quarry** (17) the stones and dragged them to the temple site: Palestinian limestone 'varies in colour and hardness, some very easily cut but hardening on exposure to the weather' (Gray). These will have included the permanent forced labour of the aliens. Verse 16 gives the **foremen** at 3300 and does not indicate their nationality. 2 Chr. 2: 18 (3600) says they, too, were aliens. 9: 23 mentions 550 Israelites. The stones were **removed from the quarry** (a relatively unskilled job) and **dressed** to fit together when assembled on site (17). **18. the men of Gebal** were also Phoenician and together with the **craftsmen . . . of Hiram** provided the necessary expertise.

Date of the temple (6: 1)

The foundation of the temple is dated to **the four hundred and eightieth year** after the exodus. It is impossible to say how this figure is arrived at (the Gk. variant 440 may be eleven generations of forty years from the priest list in 1 Chr. 6). K. A. Kitchen (*Ancient Orient and Old Testament*, 1966, pp. 72–75) gives extended discussion and concludes that the 480 years is 'some kind of aggregate' of overlapping periods which spanned the *c.*300 years. Josephus refers to a Tyrian king list which dates the foundation to the 12th year of Hiram—variously calculated at 957 or 967 B.C. The reference to **the fourth year of Solomon's reign** would give a date 967 if the 40 year reign is literally correct. A co-regency with David would alter this if Solomon's reign be taken as his sole reign.

Details of construction of the temple (6: 2–36)

'We actually possess in these chapters concerning the construction and furnishing of a temple the fullest and most detailed specification from the ancient Oriental world' (Montgomery). The close detail about the temple contrasts with the sketchy note of Solomon's other, larger, building. A cubit (2 Chr. 3: 3 says 'of the old standard') was about 18 inches so the Temple was modest in size, **the main hall** (*hêkāl*) being 90 feet by 30 feet (interior dimensions) with a **portico** 30 feet by 15 feet. The **inner sanctuary** (*debîr*, 16, 20) measuring 30 feet by 30 feet was part of the nave cut off by ornate doors. The height is given as 45 feet for the nave and vestibule, and 30 feet for the inner sanctuary which either had a space over (as 2 Chr. 3: 9 suggests) or a raised floor approached by steps as in similar Canaanite shrines. Three-storeyed **side rooms** were built on three sides of the temple (5, 6), each storey one cubit wider than the one below as the thickness of the main walls reduced and allowed the floor of the next storey to rest on the lower stonework. These storerooms were **five cubits** high (10) used as sacred storehouses (7: 51), and connected by a **stairway** (8—the word may signify a spiral staircase of which at least one example has been discovered in Canaanite building). The stone was **dressed at the quarry** (as 5: 18) and the accuracy of preparation is witnessed by the assembly with **no hammer, no chisel . . .** Dt. 27: 5 and Exod. 20: 25 forbad the working of stones for an altar but there is no reason to suppose this was extended to the temple building.

A divine promise (6: 11–13)

The record is interrupted to give a further reminder of the covenant with David (2 Sam. 7: 12 ff.). The dynastic covenant was clearly conditional—**if you follow my decrees . . . I will fulfil . . .** (12). The whole of Kings is the tragic outworking in history of progressive failure to meet the condition (2: 3 ff.; 3: 14).

Expensive furnishing (6: 14–38)

A lengthy and sometimes repetitive detail is given of the elaborate inner furnishing of the shrine. **18. no stone was to be seen:** for all was covered with cedar overlaid with gold. The carving of **cherubim, palm trees and open flowers** (29) respected the prohibition against human representation but were similar to contemporary shrines to other gods. In particular, the **pair of cherubim** (23) are no longer the reverent creatures of Exod. 25: 20 but huge sphinx-like guardians more like Syro-Phoenician models. The wall of the **inner courtyard** (36) was not restricted to four courses: **three courses of dressed stone and one course of trimmed cedar beams** were repeated to the required height (possibly to strengthen the structure against earthquake) as seen in Phoenician structures that have been excavated (and see 7: 12). **37, 38. the month** of Ziv (April–May) and the month of Bul (Oct.–Nov.) are given their Canaanite names which the eighth month explains in terms of the reckoning of the later monarchy and exile (see below on 8:2).

Solomon's other building at Jerusalem (7: 1–12)
A period of peace throughout the Near East allowed Solomon to devote twenty years and great wealth to his building projects. The hill north of Ophel was transformed from rough land around the threshing floor of Araunah the Jebusite into a complex of impressive buildings. Jerusalem became not only a city of strength but a city of splendour. Furthest north was the temple with either the bronze altar or the holy place sited immediately on the site of David's altar (2 Sam. 24: 18), probably where the present Dome of the Rock mosque now stands, the place traditionally associated with Abraham's offering of Isaac. Next below the temple was the palace in which he was to live and the palace . . . for Pharaoh's daughter (8). These living quarters were set further back and separated from the public buildings, the throne hall (7), the Palace of the Forest of Lebanon (2), 150 feet by 75 feet and used as a royal storehouse, with its extended porch, a colonnade 75 feet by 45 feet (6). So the temple, though ornately decorated, was only a small part of the total magnificence of the royal chapel, a few steps from the palace, even provided with a 'royal entry way' (2 Kg. 16: 18—possibly a later addition). Ezek. 43: 7–8 shows prophetic disgust at the arrangement.

The bronze furnishing of the temple area (7: 13–47)
13. Huram, the bronze-worker, half-Israelite, must not be confused with King Hiram. Sharing his Tyrian father's skill, his work follows Phoenician patterns. The citation highly skilled and experienced is reminiscent of Bezalel (Exod. 31: 4) though not specifically ascribed to the Spirit of God. 14. bronze was plentiful from Solomon's mines in the Arabah valley south of the Dead Sea. A bronze-working centre, identified by N. Glueck with Zarethan (7: 46) has been discovered E of Jordan where the deep layers of clay would facilitate making the large moulds needed for the pillars and Sea. The two bronze pillars (see also Jer. 52: 21–23) 24 feet by 69 inches diameter, hollow with thickness of 3 inches, were surmounted by capitals with interwoven chains (17). The detail is difficult—either 4 cubits of lilies (19) surmounted the 5 cubits of chainwork capital making the whole structure 27 cubits high, or, more likely, the capital was set in lilies that rose to within one cubit of the top. Albright and others suggest that these capitals contained fire which lit up the area and emitted smoke symbolic of Yahweh's presence. The names Jakin and Boaz (21) are much debated. R. B. Y. Scott argues from allusions in Psalms that the words were the start of two dynastic oracles such as 'He (Yahweh) will establish (thy throne for ever)' and 'In the strength (of Yahweh shall the king rejoice)'. The pillars, standing freely in front of the portico, were both a tribute to Huram's amazing technical skill and another parallel with Tyrian temples (as witnessed by a Sidonian coin discovery). The Sea of cast metal (23) and the ten movable stands of bronze each carrying its own basin (27–38, and see NBD p. 1244 for sketch) are minutely described. 2 Chr. 4: 6 says they were used for cleansing the offering and the priests. 25. twelve bulls: in threes facing the four points of the compass. Bulls were cult-animals of Baal worship but could well have symbolized to Israelites the omnipresence of Yahweh. The ornament of the sea was cast . . . in one piece with the Sea (24), a further indication of Huram's craftsmanship (a bath=22 litres, or 4.8 gallons). The desert basin (Exod. 30: 18) was simpler and less symbolically ambiguous, but if you employ an outside artist he will draw on his own culture for inspiration—you can rationalize it how you like. 40. the basins and shovels and sprinkling bowls of bronze were for offerings on the great bronze altar, ascribed to Huram in 2 Chr. 4: 1 but not included here (though assumed in 8: 22, 64). All these bronze furnishings stood outside the temple proper, in the inner court.

Golden furnishings of the shrine (7: 48–51a)
48. the furnishings that were in the LORD's temple were of gold. The golden altar (cedar wood, 6: 20, overlaid) for offering incense (cf. Exod. 30: 1), the golden table on which was the bread of the Presence (an elaboration of the provision in earlier Yahwist shrines; see 1 Sam. 21: 6) and the lampstands were in the hêkāl, and the minor utensils (also of gold) were for service connected with them. 51a. When all the work . . . for the temple of the LORD was finished: later the even greater efforts on the other buildings were completed. The economic and social significance was as great as the religious. For a country of less than a million inhabitants the building represented an immense investment of labour and natural resources, and was a prestigious demonstration of a booming nation. Socially it was evidence of Solomon's singleminded (if not ruthless) administration. It made Jerusalem the indisputable focus of the nation's political and religious life without, however, inspiring any national unity such as David's charisma had done.

Dedication of the temple (7: 51b–8: 66)
(2 Chr. 5: 1–7: 10)
51b. Solomon brought in the things his father David had dedicated: thus beginning

the transfer to the new sacred site. **the silver and the gold and the furnishings** would include those captured in David's wars (viewed as holy wars and so the spoils dedicated to Yahweh, 2 Sam. 8: 10–12).

8: 1. Solomon summoned . . . the elders: making the transfer of the ark to its new resting place a major civic and religious occasion. **the City of David** on the SE hill was much lower than the temple site, so **to bring up** exactly describes the operation. The occasion recalls David's bringing of the ark to Jerusalem (2 Sam. 6: 12–19; 1 Chr. 15) and Solomon hoped to make **the ark of the . . . covenant** once again a symbol of national unity. **2. the festival:** Tabernacles (*sukkôt* Dt. 16: 13, or ingathering, *'asip*, Exod. 23: 16), held after harvest ('at the end of the year', Exod. 23: 16) and marking the new year in the Canaanite reckoning used in the early monarchy. Later (possibly under Josiah) the Babylonian year, starting in March–April was adopted, hence the editor explains that the old **month** (*yerah*) of **Ethanim** was **the seventh month** (*hōdeš*) under the new reckoning (similarly at 6: 38 above). The time sequence is not clear. Either (*a*) the temple was finished in Bul of Solomon's 11th year and he waited 11 months to make the dedication coincide with the new year festival, (*b*) the temple was finished in Bul but the intervening time was occupied preparing the bronze furnishings, or (*c*) temple and furnishings were almost finished as people assembled in the last days of Ethanim, the arrival of the ark marking their final proclamation as complete in the first few days of Bul. If Tabernacles was connected with an enthronement ceremony of Yahweh, the occasion would be doubly apt, but there is no direct evidence for this from monarchy sources (see de Vaux, pp. 504–506).

Following the precedent set by David (1 Chr. 15: 14–15) **the priests took up the ark** (3) and its accessories and **the Tent of Meeting** (i.e. 'the tent that David had pitched for it' [2 Sam. 6: 17], not the Mosaic tent which 2 Chr. 1: 3 says was at Gibeon) to the accompaniment of sacrifice (cf. 2 Sam. 6: 13). The ark was installed **in the inner sanctuary** (*debîr*) with carrying **poles** left in place so that they would be **seen from the Holy Place in front of the inner sanctuary.** Possibly the poles were at right angles to the axis of the temple and the curtain across the narrow entrance was set back a little so that the pole ends (but not the ark) could be seen from the doorway. The ark contained the **two stone tables** (9). Heb. 9: 4 suggests other items had been *in* (not just *before*) the ark (see Exod. 16: 32–34; Num. 17: 10) but lost, possibly in some such incident as 1 Sam. 6: 19. **10. the cloud filled the temple of the LORD . . . the glory of the LORD filled his temple** in

an awe-inspiring and successful conclusion to the procession.

Solomon's acclamation and offering to Yahweh (8: 12–13)
The Gk. version puts vv. 12 and 13 at end of v. 53 and adds the line given in RSV so making the strong monotheistic couplet 'The LORD has set the sun in the heavens' (so Yahweh is greater than the sun which others worshipped) and **he would dwell in a dark cloud** (so Yahweh is ruler too of the storm clouds, symbol of the storm-god Hadad; see Dt. 4: 11; 2 Sam. 22: 10). Solomon then poses the problem of all shrines (see v. 27 below): **I have indeed built a magnificent** (or, 'royal') **temple, for you a place for you to dwell forever** (13).

Solomon's blessing (8: 14–21)
Solomon rehearses the national history as acts of **the LORD, the God of Israel** and puts the covenant **to . . . David** as, equally with the Sinaitic covenant, part of the divine election. **I have not chosen a city . . . for my Name to be there** (16, LXX adds 'but I chose Jerusalem', = 2 Chr. 6: 6) **but** (in contrast) **I have chosen David** who was not himself allowed to build the temple. **20. The LORD has kept the promise he made . . . I have provided a place there for the ark, in which is the covenant:** taking the history again back to its source in Egypt. Henceforth the national worship celebrated both Yahweh's initial choice of the nation and his choice of Zion and the Davidic dynasty (Ps. 68; 89; 132). Any doubt of the legitimacy of Solomon's succession was absorbed in a total theology of national election.

Solomon's prayer (8: 22–53)
22. Solomon stood . . ., spread out his hands: an attitude frequently shown in ancient near eastern art where suppliant stands before seated king or god. 2 Chr. 6: 13 gives details of a bronze platform (and says 'then knelt down', reconciling with v. 54 below). **the altar of the LORD** was not mentioned in the list of Huram's work.

The first section of the prayer (23–30) is a fine statement of God's transcendence yet covenant relationship with his people, and again links the Sinaitic and Davidic covenants. **23. there is no God like you** (reminiscent of Exod. 15: 11) **you who keep your covenant of . . . love** (see Exod. 34: 7; in *hesed*=loyal love, true to covenant promises). The Davidic covenant is again rehearsed (24–26) with the prayer that it may **come true. 27. But will God really dwell on earth?** shows a clear understanding that this house is no attempt to localize or limit the infinite God. Rather it is the place where God has **said, 'My Name shall be there'** (29, and see above on 5: 5 for **Name**). So the prayer is offered **toward this place** (29, 30, 35, 38, 42, 44, 48) or **in this** temple (31, 33) and Yahweh will hear **from heaven your dwelling place** (*šebet* possibly= place of enthronement). **30. when you hear, forgive:** because prayer would normally be a sign of repentance or humble acknowledgement (34, 36, 39, 50) seeking relief in various states and resulting in renewed reverence (40). Three other cases are envisaged: (*a*) the need for judgment, not forgiveness (32; see Exod. 22: 7–13 for example of this), **declare the innocent not guilty** (*ṣaddiq*, better: 'the one who is in the right') **and so establish his innocence** (the rightness of his cause); (*b*) the **foreigner** (*nokrî*, not a resident alien, but a visitor drawn by Yahweh's fame, as in the vision of Isa. 2: 2–4), who may also share Israel's reverence—in marked contrast to later narrowness; (*c*) the holy war (44) **wherever you send them,** where the prayer is **uphold their cause.** The calamities (33, 35) are seen as judgments. **33, 34. defeated . . . bring them back** may refer to prisoners carried off (as from the northern kingdom in 722 or by Sennacherib in 701). **35. no rain** was a frequent disaster and the marginal rainfall of Palestine made any failure the more serious. **37. famine . . . plague:** the result of failure or pollution of water. **locusts:** a pest to which Palestine and surrounding countries were specially vulnerable as locusts bred in nearby deserts. Jl 2 vividly describes one such plague. The list is charmingly and simply expanded to include **whatever disease . . . when a prayer,** all is assumed to be under the control of Yahweh who, **alone, know the hearts of all the men** (39). Even in distant captivity the people may **have a change of heart** (47; AV 'bethink themselves') like the later prodigal (Lk. 15) and **turn back to you with all their heart and soul** (*nepheš*= life force).

The prayer concludes with a further strong plea based on relationship with Yahweh. The king is **your servant** and Israel **your people** occupying a unique place in the divine plan: **you singled them out . . . to be your own inheritance** (53, see Dt. 32: 8, 9). The final ascription **O Sovereign Lord** (more correctly as JB 'Lord Yahweh') reaffirms the supremacy of Israel's God.

The kingly blessing (8: 54–61)

The attitude of reverent humility (54) changes to one of beneficent and impressive authority (55). Yahweh's faithfulness is both the subject of praise (56) and the spring of obedient living (58) that will bear witness to surrounding nations (60). **56. rest to his people . . . just as he promised** (see Dt. 12: 10) and **not one word has failed** (see Jos. 21: 45) reflect this strong historical sense of a developing divine purpose, hence the blessing. **57. May the Lord our God be with us, as he was with our fathers:** the behavioural condition is made

less harsh by the prayer **may he turn our hearts to him**, but reappears in its stark demand: **But your hearts must be fully committed** (61), the responsibility corresponding to the declaration **the Lord is God and . . . there is no other** (cf. Exod. 20: 3).

The language and ideas of the prayer and blessings are so close to those of Deuteronomy that some commentators regard these as late additions. It is by no means improbable, however, that Solomon knew the national history and its Mosaic roots. If he did say all this—and he may well have felt so after seeing 'the glory' (11)—then God gave him a real chance to return to humble piety and wisdom and undo the growing arrogance of seven years' royal building.

Final offerings and feast (8: 62–66)

The community emphasis (**the king and all Israel**, 62) is strong in this passage. Although later building dwarfed the temple and made it look like a royal chapel, the impression here is that it was all Israel's shrine to the true God. The **fellowship offerings**, too, symbolized fellowship with Yahweh and with each other. **65. the festival** was the new year festival of Tabernacles (see above on 8: 2) and may have been observed in settlements **from Lebo Hamath** (100 miles N of Galilee) **to the Wadi of Egypt,** or this could refer to the universal gathering at Jerusalem. **Seven days and seven days more, fourteen days in all** follows Heb. (RSV follows Gk. to give 'seven days' and so can translate Heb. normally as 'eighth' in 66, where NIV has the **following day**) of festival closed with the people **joyful and glad of heart,** a fitting end to an impressive ceremony. If only it had stayed that way!

The influence of the temple—alternately an object of neglect, devotion and false hope—is part of the following story. There is a feeling of unease that surfaces in Isa. 66: 1 and Ac. 7: 48, and it is noteworthy that the Letter to the Hebrews draws analogies, not from the temple, but the tabernacle. With the best of intentions a lot of Canaanite symbolism had been incorporated. The old Baalized Yahweh worship had at least a few footholds as subsequent relapses showed.

Yahweh appears again to Solomon (9: 1–9)

The earlier promises and conditions (3: 11–14; 6: 11–13) are repeated with greater urgency. **3. I have consecrated** answers the 'dedication' of 8: 63, and depends upon **my Name there forever,** i.e. the divine initiative rather than human cultus. Later superstitious trust (Jer. 7: 4) misunderstood this oracle. Yahweh's purpose for Israel was that they should be an object lesson to the nations of a stable society based on **integrity of heart and uprightness** (4). If they failed in that, they would yet testify to

Yahweh's moral character as a **byword** (*māšāl* —classic instance of general truth about life) and a **object of ridicule** (7). Responsibility is centred on the royal house (**you or your sons**, 6) but is extended to all the people (**they have forsaken**, 9) in line with the prophetic insistence on solidarity of people and king under God (1 Sam. 12: 14–15).

Solomon's commercial and public affairs (9: 10–10: 29)

Hiram's assistance had been paid for at the time (5: 11) so this transaction of **twenty towns in Galilee** (9: 11) must be connected with v. 14. Solomon needed to replenish his treasury and sold (or mortgaged) some territory. **towns** (*'ārîm*) is a general word used of any settlement, however small. Hiram was not pleased with the deal. **13. Cabul:** possibly a nickname, as Moffatt translates 'good for nothing'; Montgomery (following LXX) suggests 'border' (Heb. *gebûl*) or 'march-land'. Josephus refers to a Cabul in the area still in his time.

A formal list is given of the buildings and defence works on which Solomon used **the forced labour** (15), **the supporting terraces**, (or the Millo) a system of terracing supported by massive retaining walls which both fortified and enlarged Jerusalem on its steep-sided hill site, is witnessed by recent excavations. Excavations at **Hazor, Megiddo and Gezer** show a common design of gateway and confirm Solomon's strong fortification of these route-commanding cities. **Beth Horon** and **Baalath** (in the original Dan, Jos. 19: 44) guarded approaches from the west to the central hill country and **Tadmor** (or Tamar) **in the desert** completed the circle of defence at its southern end (18). The other **store towns** and **cities for his chariots** (19) are not specified but indicate the energy and thoroughness of Solomon's defensive policy. The parenthetic history of **Gezer** does not give the name of the Pharaoh or date of attack. Probably Siamun (see on 3: 1), having established a tentative foothold in Philistia, was glad to leave the ruined city to (the then friendly) Solomon. Solomon underestimated the significance of the Egyptian foothold but at least turned Gezer into a border fortress. The **slave labor force** (21) were Canaanites (see above on 5: 13–18).

Solomon's regular offerings **three times a year** (25)—at major festivals, as 2 Chr. 8: 13 elaborates—continued the national integration round the temple which was begun at its dedication. **burning incense:** NEB 'making smoke offerings'; text is obscure (see RSVmg; JB leaves a blank). **ans so fulfilled the temples obligations:** Heb. *šillam*='complete', or (occasionally) 'pay (vows)', so Gray suggests 'he used to discharge his vows'. JB gives 'he kept the temple in good repair'.

Solomon's sea ventures (9: 26–28 and 10: 11, 12, 22)

26. Ezion Geber (situated on caravan route from Arabia and developed by Solomon as a copper-smelting centre and port) was discovered by N. Glueck following the location here given **near Elath . . . on the shore of the Red Sea**. The **fleet of trading ships** (10: 22; 'a fleet of Tarshish', JB; 'a fleet of merchantmen', NEB; see NIV footnote) were large vessels for carrying ore or metal. Built and manned by Hiram's Phoenicians, **seamen who were familiar with the sea** (27, unlike the Hebrews) they did a three-yearly trading tour. **28. Ophir** is located in Gen. 10: 29 between Sheba and Havilah (i.e. S Arabia). Other suggestions are E Africa (a source of **gold**) or India (because the word for **apes** (10: 22) is of Sanskrit origin). **almugwood** (10: 11, 12, only use of word in OT) is mentioned in other texts as wood for high quality furniture, hence very suitable for ceremonial **harps and lyres**.

The Queen of Sheba visits Solomon (10: 1–13)

The nomadic Sabeans had settled in S Arabia (present Yemen) and prospered by developing caravan routes from the East (Hadhramaut) to Palestine, Egypt and Syria. Solomon's sea commerce was in competition and the queen's visit was in the nature of a trade mission—apparently successful (v. 13) though with some duties payable to Solomon (v. 15).

The incident is given as illustration of **the fame of Solomon**, his **wisdom**, building and retinue. **5. the burnt offerings:** discrepancy with Heb. text of 2 Chr. 9: 4 has prompted suggestion 'the way he went up (in ceremonial pomp to the temple)'. **6. The report . . . is true:** the queen pays warm tribute to Solomon's wisdom and magnificence. **8. How happy your men must be!** (so Heb.); RSV, NEB, JB 'wives' follow LXX as giving a more likely exclamation for a queen, especially as she goes on to mention **your officials**. Her **Praise be to the LORD your God** (9) could be the first response to the prayer of 8: 60. Yahweh's **love** for Israel is evident in giving them **justice and righteousness**.

Solomon's wealth (10: 14–29)

666 talents of gold (about 25 tons) has been regarded as exaggerated, but the whole record hangs together like an official list of wide and wealthy interests. The **shields of hammered gold** (16) were used on ceremonial occasions (14: 28) and the **throne inlaid with ivory** (18) and ornate setting added to the image of luxury and magnificence. Wealth begets wealth and the train of visiting admirers each **brought a gift** (25). Solomon's trade in **horses** and **chariots** was a new departure for Israelites and probably developed as he built up his own defence forces. Cilicians were famous horse-breeders; **Kue** is S of Taurus mountains. **Egypt** (28, also RSV, NEB) Heb. *miṣraim*, possibly should be *muṣri*, a district N of Taurus. JB gives simply 'from Cilicia' for the whole phrase.

Much of this wealth was absorbed in the vast building enterprises, much more in the ostentatious living of the king and his large army of retainers, but some spilled over to the nation as a whole and the memory is of **silver as common . . . as stone**; (27) and **cedar as plentiful as sycamore-fig** (see also 4: 20). The character of the nation was changed from the rustic simplicity of Saul's day and the stern expansion of David's. Imports of gold (even if much of it is locked up in shields and thrones) always produce inflation. In Solomon's Israel it added another factor, a class of individuals of great personal wealth apart from land. The traders and money lenders appear as principal exploiters in the later prophets. Their monopolist position had its beginning in Solomon's golden reign.

Inglorious end (11: 1–43)

The writer sets the stage for the disruption in ch. 12. In spite of the golden exterior all was not well. Peace had been assured through a network of alliances sealed by political marriages. Intrigue and opportunism had made rifts in the empire (vv. 14–40). The damage to the nation is seen both as a result of, and a judgment upon, the king's neglect of the Mosaic command.

1. King Solomon . . . loved many foreign women: LXX (followed by NEB) omits 'foreign' and adds v. 3a here, suggesting an official, approving record, before the editor's condemnation. The mention of **Sidonian** wives is attested by Menander of Tyre's statement that Solomon married a daughter of Hiram, and an **Ammonite** woman was mother of Rehoboam (14: 21). LXX adds 'Aramaean' to complete the count of surrounding countries. Polygamy was not forbidden (Dt. 21: 15) but appears to have been unusual among the common people (see de Vaux, p. 25). The numbers **seven hundred . . . three hundred** (3) may be compared with Ca. 6: 8 ('sixty queens, eighty concubines'). Montgomery gives a list of other recorded harems of prestigious size. **4. As Solomon grew old his wives turned his heart after other gods** gives the final result of the earlier disobedience against which the commandment (2) had warned: the pathetic sight of a man who could pray 8: 23 settling for 'no gods' of surrounding cultures. Verses 7, 8 describe his building for all his foreign wives, but v. 5 accuses him of personal idolatry too. **5. Ashtoreth** is the Canaanite fertility goddess Ashtart (with vowels of *bōšet*='shame') **goddess** (Heb. 'god', there is no fem. of the noun in Heb.) **of the Sidonians** but worshipped as consort of **Chemosh** (Moabite, 7) and **Molech** (Am-

monite, probably revocalized from *malik*= 'king'). **detestable god** (*šiqqûṣ* from root 'to abhor'): NEB gives 'loathsome god', LXX softens to (idol) 'god'. **8. burned incense and offered sacrifices:** Gray suggests the words are used contemptuously, 'making smoke and slaughter'. The whole passage oozes distaste for the alien cults. **The LORD became angry:** a sad irony after the prayer of 8: 46. **11. my covenant** which had been Solomon's boast is now his undoing. Judgment is delayed (12) and mitigated (13) **for the sake of David my servant and . . . Jerusalem** (cf. 1 Sam. 15: 27–28 for similar judgment).

Cracks in the empire: Hadad's escape and return (11: 14–22)

14. the LORD raised up . . . an adversary: *śāṭān*, used generally of opposition but later as proper noun for chief opposer of God. Political development is seen as God's judgment. The details of David's Edomite campaign are additional to 2 Sam. 8: 13–14 and the references to both slaughter (15, 16) and servitude (2 Sam. 8: 14) may indicate that the present record is a hyperbole. **Hadad** (v. 17 Adad, but there is no need to suggest two people) and his guardians, at least, survived and he arrived in Egypt as **only a boy** ('youth'). Pharaoh's cheerful shelter of potential troublers of Israel is seen also with Jeroboam (40) but vv. 21, 22 suggest he did not deliberately send Hadad back to stir up trouble. On the strength of Gk. reading 'Edom' for **Syria** (i.e. Aram) it is argued that v. 25b should come immediately after v. 22. So JB: 'This is where the harm of Hadad comes from: he loathed Israel and ruled Edom'. He may have had nuisance value but did not stop Solomon's copper and trading activities a little to the South.

Rezon of Damascus (11: 23–25)

23. Rezon took advantage of David's victory at **Zobah** (2 Sam. 8: 3); he and his **rebels . . . took control** at **Damascus** (24). David may have seen no threat in this but by Solomon's time the domestication of the camel was changing the trade routes and soon brought Damascus into prominence with a Euphrates crossing at Mari. Solomon however continued to use and fortify the old route through Hamath (2 Chr. 8: 3–4) leading to the Euphrates crossing at Tiphsah (4: 24): another lapse of judgment that had serious effects.

Jeroboam is designated king of ten tribes (11: 26–40)

26. Jeroboam was **an Ephraimite**—the jealous tribe (Isa. 11: 13) that had felt its share of harassment by Solomon's grandiose building and municipal enterprises. It is clear that the open division of the kingdom followed centuries of distrust and envy (Ellison, *The Prophets of Israel*, traces it back to the time of Achan). The mention of **the supporting terraces** may be to date the incident to the middle of Solomon's reign (9: 24); Shishak (40) began his reign in 945, Solomon's 25th year. **28. Jeroboam was a man of standing** (or, 'a man of property') and **did his work . . . well**, so Solomon put him in **charge of the whole labor force** (*sebel*, 'burden bearers' as 5: 15, not *mas*, 'levy') **of the house of Joseph** with status and contacts in **Jerusalem** (29). **Ahijah . . . of Shiloh** appears in ambiguous role: as prophet of judgment on Solomon, but of doubtful promise to Jeroboam (37, 38). The condition—and lack of anointing—contrasts grimly with Samuel's glad recognition of David when Saul had failed (1 Sam. 16: 12, 13). Shiloh was the home of the ark and centre of tribal league in earlier days. No doubt Ahijah shared the prophetic distrust of kings, especially kings like Solomon. The references are all to **my servant David** (32 ff.). The **new cloak** is likely to have been Jeroboam's (*MT* has 'now he had clad himself . . .') which would make the action of taking it off and tearing it even more dramatic. The alignment of tribes is problematic. The **twelve pieces** (30) hark back to the original twelve sons of Jacob. Joseph had become two tribes, Ephraim and Manasseh, and Levi was dispersed in various cities. So the territorial division at the settlement was into twelve areas and Ahijah's **twelve** may have been a defiant return to this league in place of Solomon's districts. Simeon had been absorbed into Judah (Jos. 19: 1–9) so the **ten tribes** (31) . . . **one tribe** (32) is difficult. LXX harmonizes with 'two cities' in v. 32. If Simeon is excluded (or counted as 'one' with Judah) the oracle suggests Benjamin joined the secession (see 12: 20 where LXX adds 'and Benjamin' to keep to its earlier *two*—yet *MT* has Benjamin in 12: 21). Benjamin, the tribe of Saul, might be expected to have strong ties with the north against Judah. Jericho was firmly attached to the north, but other cities (notably the Gibeon confederacy and Levitical cities) remained loyal to Jerusalem. The area became a frontier zone and scene of skirmish (14: 30). Gray suggests Simeon kept links with the north—because of pilgrimage to Beersheba in Am. 5: 5—so Benjamin is one tribe left to Judah. **34. I will have made him ruler:** *nāśî'*, less strong than *melek*=*king*. **all the days of his life** repeats the mitigation given in 11: 12. **37.** The promise to Jeroboam **you will rule over all that your heart desires** has an ominous ring. **king over Israel** (here used unequivocally of the northern tribes) loomed larger in Jeroboam's thinking than **if you will do whatever I command** (38). **40. Solomon tried to kill Jeroboam** when his spies brought him news of Jeroboam's reaction (v. 27). LXX has a long addition after 12: 24 about elaborate and unlikely preparations for revolt. The

suggestion that Jeroboam was 'politically unreliable' would have been quite enough to provoke Solomon's anger and Jeroboam's flight.

Death of Solomon (11: 41–43)
The formula **As for the other events** (41) summarizes each reign, giving parallel records. **43. Solomon rested with his fathers:** see on 2: 10. In spite of its glory 'Solomon's political kingship had sealed the doom of the kingdom' (H. J. Blair).

The disruption (11: 43)
11: **43. Rehoboam his son succeeded him as king**; the principle of succession is sonship, but whether the oldest is not stated, nor whether Solomon designated him. The usual annalistic detail is given with the short summary of his reign in 14: 21–31 after Jeroboam has been dealt with (contrary to usual practice by which the reigning monarch is dealt with first).

III. A KINGDOM DIVIDED
(1 Kg. 12: 1–2 Kg. 17: 41)
12: **1. Rehoboam went to Shechem:** as a matter of routine, but he, and all Israel, were completely outwitted by Jeroboam and his associates. It is unlikely a 'united monarchy' ever existed after Saul. The events of 2 Sam. 2: 1–11's hasty attempt at unity thwarted by Abner's ambition produced a 'dual kingdom', only partially healed by the invitation of 2 Sam. 5: 1–5. From his own Jerusalem (David's city) he was accepted by both north and south. No record is given of Solomon's specific acceptance at Shechem (the co-regency may have forestalled it). Rehoboam was aware of the old tradition, but clearly underestimated its significance. Already accepted by Judah, he presents himself to all Israel for their acknowledgement at the ancient covenant centre (Jos. 24).
2. Jeroboam . . . returned from Egypt (see NIV footnote) and joined **the whole assembly of Israel** (3), possibly as spokesman (v. 12), but v. 20 suggests he was not widely recognized. In any case he was *persona non grata* at court, and more likely egged on the legitimate aspirations of the leaders of the assembly. Rehoboam was taken completely aback by the rude reminder that this was no formal gathering and demanded **three days** (5) to decide. **6. the elders who had served . . . Solomon** were probably right. The people were not revolting; properly treated **they will always be your servants** (7). Predictably, the headstrong son of the harem followed the counsel of his peers, **the young men** (*y'lādîm*, used scornfully='the lads') **who had grown up with him** (8) and acted with arrogance in a situation that demanded tact. **11. scorpions** may refer to a particularly sadistic spiked lash. This ineptitude is seen as a **turn of events . . . from the LORD**

(15). Jeroboam could hardly have hoped the king would play so directly into his hands. The people reply in the revolutionary words: **What share do we have in David?** (16; see 2 Sam. 20: 1). **So the Israelites went home**, bewildered no doubt, and hoping for further parley. **18. Adoniram . . . in charge of forced labor** (perhaps the Adoniram of 5: 14) was the worst possible man to send and was **stoned to death**. Rehoboam could do nothing else but **escape to Jerusalem**. **19. So Israel has been in rebellion** (*pāša'*—a political use of a word usually meaning sin, rebellion against God). What started as a (fairly reported) demand for consideration ends as definite breach condemned as rebellion. Jeroboam is publicly acknowledged and made **king over all Israel** (20; now definitely excluding Judah: Benjamin's position uncertain as mentioned above). Verse 17 would follow more naturally after v. 20.

Rehoboam's attention to **Shemaiah the man of God** shows a readiness to accept that **this is my doing** (24); possibly he knew of the message to Solomon (11: 11). Of Shemaiah nothing is known except this incident and 2 Chr. 12: 5–8. LXX has a long addition after 12: 24 about Jeroboam's revolt and retelling part of the story, with Shemaiah for Ahijah (cf. D. W. Gooding, 'The Septuagint's Rival Versions of Jeroboam's Rise to Power', *VT* 17, 1967, pp. 73 ff.).

Jeroboam's reign (12: 25–14: 20)

25. Jeroboam fortified (i.e. *re-fortified*) **Shechem** at east end of pass between Mt. Ebal and Mt. Gerizim. An historic city commanding a major route, it was less easily defended than higher ground so the capital was later moved to Tirzah (14: 17) a few miles north, and later still to Samaria (16: 24). **Peniel**, E of Jordan on R. Jabbok, served both to safeguard travel and to provide a military presence in Gilead (which remained loyal to David in Absalom's rebellion). Ironically, Jeroboam probably used forced labour for this building. Realizing the precarious nature of his kingdom (and not trusting Ahijah's promise, 11: 38) Jeroboam deliberately sets about breaking the covenant centred on **the temple of the LORD in Jerusalem**. The temple not only made Jerusalem splendid by comparison with Shechem, but was a reminder of the Davidic covenant calculated to make the people return **to their lord, Rehoboam** (27). The institution of the alternative shrines reads much like Exod. 32: 4–6. The **golden calves** (bulls) (28) were not representations of deity but (as finds at Baal shrines show) the animals upon which Yahweh rode in triumph. Even so they were nearer Baal worship even than the stylized cherubim of the temple (6: 23–28). **29. Bethel** on the extreme S border was an ancient shrine with history

going back to Jacob (Gen. 28: 18–22). **Dan**, 100 miles N of Bethel at foot of Mt. Hermon, had a priestly tradition going back to the early settlement, perhaps even of Mosaic descent (Jg. 18: 30). JB 'the people went in procession all the way to Dan in front of the other' follows LXX suggestion of a ceremonial procession of the northern calf, perhaps after an inaugural ritual at Bethel (**calves**, pl. at v. 32). There is no MS authority for JB omission of **this thing became a sin** (30). **31. Jeroboam built shrines on high places**: dispersing the worship and making a reversion to Canaanite practices still more likely. Having no historic order to consider, Jeroboam **appointed priests from all sorts of people** (i.e. all classes—not 'the lowest' as AV) but excluded **Levites** as having allegiance to Jerusalem. The **festival . . . like the festival held in Judah** (32) was appointed a month later. This could still have been a harvest festival and Jeroboam may have acted quickly to get something public done to authenticate his kingship, especially if Rehoboam had been acclaimed at the Jerusalem festival a month earlier. The writer expresses his utter distaste: **sacrificing to the calves he had made . . . in the month of his own choosing** (32, 33). Jeroboam may have said, like Lenin, 'What else could we have done?' Ahijah might have told him if asked. But now the 'rebellion against the house of David' (19) is a **sin** against Yahweh (see below on 14: 7– 16). From here on the prophets had nothing but judgment to say to the northern kingdom until its end 200 years later.

Judgment at Bethel (13: 1–32)

The **man of God** from **Judah** (1) remains anonymous. His mission **by the word of the LORD** (2) is emphasized as a judgment on the new ritual right from the start. The burning of **human bones** was a fearful desecration, so the oracle spoke at once of the complete doom of Bethel and the survival of David's house (**name Josiah** may well be an updating by a later scribe, as **Samaria** in v. 32). **The altar** may have been of hewn stone or bronze shell filled with earth so its precise method of collapse is not known. In any case **the ashes** (*dešen* as Lev. 1: 16; 6: 10, connected with 'fat' parts of offerings) being scattered would invalidate the sacrifice. The double sign of palsy (4) and the collapsing altar deterred the king's arrogance and produced the pitiable plea **Intercede with the LORD your** (not 'my') **God**. The refusal of hospitality was an extreme action in the east and represented Yahweh's complete rejection of Jeroboam and Bethel. The miraculous is sparingly used, usually only in times of great crisis to underline judgment and sometimes, as here, to protect the messenger. The effect on the worshippers must have been staggering— a pity the man of God spoilt it by his delay (**sitting under an oak tree**, v. 14) and return. The **old prophet** (*nābî*) is distinguished throughout the story in contrast to **the man of God**. This could indicate disapproval of a cult-prophet connected with the Bethel shrine. The reason for his deceit is not clear; perhaps he wished to test the alarming word of the LORD against his local shrine. The shrine was outside Bethel so it must have been some time before he found the man of God (who could have been well back over the border into Judah if he had not tarried). The prophet claims revelation through **an angel . . . by the word of the LORD** (18) and later seems overcome by a genuine **word of the LORD** (20). The sad procession back to burial underlines the message: **the word of the LORD against the altar in Bethel . . . will certainly come true** (32). The tomb was still recognized in Josiah's time (2 Kg. 23: 17) 300 years later, by that time a testimony to judgment fulfilled.

Judgment confirmed (13: 33–14: 20)
33. Jeroboam did not change his evil ways: the momentary hope of Ahijah (11: 38) had gone for ever. JB catches the flavour: 'such conduct made the House of Jeroboam a sinful House', an OT instance of 'sin that leads to death' (1 Jn 5: 16); certainly no prophet would pray for him. The word for 'sin' (*hatṭa 't*) means 'missing the mark'—an apt summary of Jeroboam's misdirected efforts.

In sending to **Ahijah** at **Shiloh** (14: 2), Jeroboam showed the superstition of an anxious man, the ruler's fondness for a little gift: **ten loaves . . .** (3), and the illogical cunning of an habitual schemer: **disguise yourself** (2). Ahijah, now old and blind (4) shatters the disguise and gives his message of doom, this time without any ray of hope. At Shiloh he was close to the tradition of Samuel and the earliest shrine of Israel. He had spoken against Solomon's slide to diplomatic idolatry and now more sharply against Jeroboam's deliberate use of religion to bolster up a shaky regime. The new doom includes **scatter them beyond the River** and the cause here is religious (9, 15). Later prophets elaborated the social and moral consequences of religious decline. The doom is sealed by Abijah's death as his mother returns to **Tirzah** (17). **18. all Israel mourned for him** in sorrowful augury for the new dynasty since Abijah was apparently the firstborn and heir to throne. So **Nadab** became king upon Jeroboam's death (20).

Verdict on Rehoboam (14: 21–29)
The story interrupted at 12: 24 is resumed to give a verdict on Rehoboam's reign and include a few more incidents. **21. His mother's name** is given, reflecting the status enjoyed in the southern kingdom by the queen mother (not given for northerly kings as the hereditary principle was less significant). **22. Judah did evil**

in the eyes of the LORD: LXX gives 'Rehoboam' for **Judah**, specifying the king's part in the evil (as 15: 26, 34). 2 Chr. 11–12 gives more detail and refers to a good start spoilt by later apostasy. The sins cited are religious—**high places . . . sacred stones . . . Asherah poles** were the marks of Canaanite cultus condemned in Dt. 12: 1–3, which involved the ritual prostitution associated with nature religions. Ironically, the Heb. for **shrine prostitutes** is derived from the word for 'holy' (*qadeš*). Nature religions see holiness in being 'set apart' for ritual. Hebrew religion campaigned unceasingly for a moral as well as ritual element in holiness.

The invasion of **Shishak** (25), seen as divine retribution in 2 Chr. 12, is the only political event noted by the writer during Rehoboam's reign. It explains how the more wealthy southern kingdom came to be poorer and weaker than the northern. Shishak, in his inscription at Karnak (Thebes) lists 150 places from which he exacted tribute, including many in the North. Although Shishak failed to promote a more extensive Egyptian recovery, this raid was a disastrous reminder of Solomon's own proverb (Prov. 23: 4, 5). The north, with greater agricultural potential, recovered more quickly than Judah.

The incident of the **gold shields** being replaced by **bronze shields** (27) shows the continuance of ceremonial in which the king played a leading part but with the sarcastic overtone that it was a tawdry imitation of Solomon's splendour. Perhaps Rehoboam never really got over the illusions of grandeur he learned as son of the glittering harem. The **warfare . . . between Rehoboam and Jeroboam** (30) was rather a 'state of war' witnessed by border skirmish and mutual suspicion, a state of affairs that persisted until Assyrian pressure made agreement a political necessity fifty years later (15: 7, 16).

Abijah's reign (15: 1–8)
The synchronization with the **eighteenth year of the reign of Jeroboam** begins a method which continues to link the two kingdoms till the fall of Samaria. Some MSS give 'Abijam' for **Abijah**. **2. His mother's name** is given as **Maacah daughter of Abishalom**. If this is Absalom, David's son (see 2 Chr. 11: 20) his daughter would be much older even than Rehoboam. Josephus suggested 'granddaughter'. The **three years** comprise one full year and two parts. 2 Chr. 13 gives a longer and more rosy picture of Abijah's exploits, but Kg. judges that **his heart was not fully devoted** and the continuance of the dynasty is **for David's sake** (4).

Asa's reforms and politics (15: 9–24)
9. Asa became king just as the reign of the rival Jeroboam was coming to an end. **His**

mother's name, given as **Maacah**, raises some difficulty (v. 2, v. 8), but his grandmother may have retained for a time the status of queen-mother which was hers under Abijah. LXX gives 'Ana' here but not at v. 13. As a young man Asa showed considerable courage and conviction in reforming the worship and deposing Maacah from her position as **queen mother** (g^{e}birah='leading lady')—a drastic step as the position commanded great respect and power in the Near East. **A repulsive Asherah pole** (RSV abominable image for Asherah) translated two Heb. words. Sometimes the single Heb. word Asherah clearly means the fertility goddess of the Canaanites (1 Ki. 18: 19; 2 Ki. 21: 7). Sometimes it is used alone to mean the sacred pole which symbolised the goddess in Canaanite sanctuaries (Dt. 12:3; 1 Ki. 14: 15 and see NIV note here). **he did not remove the high places:** they remained a constant temptation to revert to nature worship but a decisive blow had been struck for a return to traditional Hebrew religion. It may be noted that the blow was struck by the king; no part is ascribed to the priests who should have been custodians of the cult. **Asa's heart was fully committed to the LORD** gives the overall estimate of his religious intentions. 2 Chr. 16: 10 indicates a later reluctance to suffer rebuke and LXX adds after v. 23 'in his old age he did evil'.

The conflict with **Baasha** arose after the ineffectual Nadab had been murdered. Baasha, a military opportunist, **fortified Ramah** (17) only 5 miles N of Jerusalem, controlling both north– south and westerly routes so that **to prevent anyone from leaving or entering the territory of Asa**. It is unlikely Baasha intended to launch an attack on Jerusalem itself and Asa's reaction overestimated the danger. Certainly it set a sad precedent of Hebrew calling on alien against Hebrew. **18. Asa took all the silver and gold**, undoing his virtuous dedication (v. 15) and sent it to **Benhadad . . . king of Aram**. Since its founding by Rezon (11: 23) fifty years or more before, Syria (the area based on Damascus, also known as Aram) had been growing more powerful and progressively encroached on the northern kingdom. Syria needed little persuasion to attack the N Galilee area, **Kinneroth** and **Naphtali**. **19. Let there be a treaty** (or 'There is a treaty') based on a **gift** (šōhad used generally for a bribe as Exod. 23: 8) shows the diplomat's pathetic optimism that the **treaty** he makes will be stronger than the treaty he asks Benhadad to **break**. The stratagem was successful and Asa resorted to the principle of levy to dismantle **Ramah** and build his own border towns **Mizpah** (=look-out post) and **Geba** a mile N of Ramah on a strong natural feature commanding the borderland. **23. all the other** events of Asa's reign . . . and the cities (see 2 Chr. 14) are only just noted. The historian is concerned only with the basic religious direction of the kingdom. It is certain Asa left the kingdom stronger and purer than he found it. The strength of his influence may be gauged from the fact that **Jehoshaphat his son** (24) is almost a lone case of succession in virtue as well as kingship.

The Northern Kingdom during Asa's Reign (15: 25–16: 28)
The record goes back to catch up what had been happening in the North during Asa's long and successful reign. By comparison it is a sad story of instability and ruin.
25. Nadab son of Jeroboam is dismissed with a cursory reference to his continuance in his father's evil and **his sin, which he caused Israel to commit** (26), the idolatries at Bethel and Dan. Nadab also starts the tale of assassination that marks the northern story, and stands in contrast to the dynastic principle and Davidic oracle that characterized the south. Nadab was victim of a coup by one of his generals while attacking **Gibbethon** (an indication that Nadab was not inactive). Baasha **killed Jeroboam's whole family** (29) a calamity which is seen as fulfilment of divine judgment passed by Ahijah on the sins of Jeroboam and his provocation of **the LORD, the God of Israel** (a reminder that even the schismatic northern tribes were viewed as under the promises and judgments of Yahweh's covenant). Baasha's brutal massacre was normal behaviour for a usurper. The fact that it was the predicated judgment does not gain him any credit, and his own downfall is partly due to this barbarity (16: 7b—the same pattern is shown by Hos. 1: 4 where Jehu's excessively bloody vengeance on the house of Ahab is denounced). The reference to Baasha's reign over **all Israel** (33) uses the term in a northern sense and shows that even Nadab's party accepted the new ruler. The prophetic rebuke from **Jehu son of Hanani** (16: 1) again uses the restricted **leader** (nagid) **of my people** (16: 2). Baasha would have preferred the absolutist **king** (melek) of his official title (15: 32). The repetition in v. 7 adds that he was **like the house of Jeroboam** and shows again that his massacre was no conscious blow for Yahweh but mere military opportunism. His reign of 24 years gets little mention, the border war with Judah and reverse at the hands of Syria having been already referred to at 15: 16–22. His son **Elah** is merely noticed (vv. 6, 8) before the fulfilment of Jehu's prophecy is given. **Gibbethon** (15) was still in Philistine hands and occupying the attention of the bulk of the forces, leaving **Zimri, who had comanded of half his chariots** (9) at **Tirzah**. The absence of patronym for Zimri **his servant** suggests he was an upstart, taking

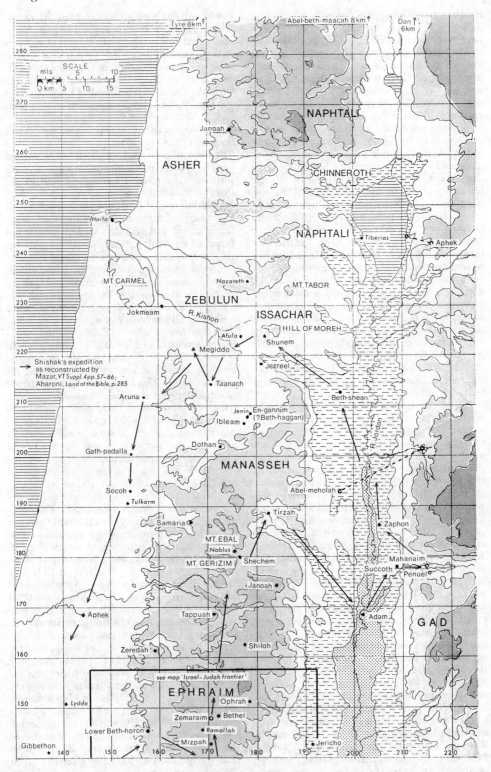

Map 24—The Northern Kingdom

advantage of a drunken stupor to succeed his master. The treachery passed into legend (2 Kg. 9: 31). Yet more blood flowed as **Baasha's whole family** fell (11). The reaction of the army at Gibbethon was immediate and Zimri's brief reign ended in inglorious suicide (18). The obituary (19) may seem an undue indictment of a 'reign' of only seven days, but emphasizes that Zimri was no reforming zealot but another self-seeking adventurer well prepared to accept the mould in which Jeroboam had cast the northern kingdom.

There followed four years (cf. v. 15 with v. 23) of civil war from which **Omri, the commander of the army** (16) emerged supreme and founded the most politically significant northern dynasty, which gave the kingdom the title in Assyrian records of 'the land of the house of Omri'. Nothing is known of **Tibni son of Ginath** (21) and speculation thrives. Omri is not a Hebrew name and his family is not given, so it has been conjectured he was of Canaanite origin or some other mercenary soldier championing a military party against a traditionally agricultural Hebrew party. **Tibni died** (22) either in the civil war, or opportunely by natural causes aiding Omri's purpose. Omri's **six years** in **Tirzah** (23) probably included the four of the civil war. His selection and fortification of **Samaria** (24) was a masterstroke giving the Northern kingdom a powerful and beautiful capital in a commanding situation. Excavations have revealed the scale of fortification and the three year siege before its final reduction in 722 B.C. is further witness to the strength of Omri's site.

Omri's brief seven years of sole rule were crammed with action which is only hinted at. He subdued Moab (as Mesha's inscription records); he established understanding with Syria, though at the cost of some territory and trading privileges (20: 34); he made league with Phoenicia, marked by the ill-fated marriage of his son **Ahab** to **Jezebel daughter of Ethbaal** (31). The writer is concerned less with political influence than covenant obedience and in that respect the new powerful dynasty was no better than the wrangling adventurers it succeeded. Indeed Omri **sinned more than those before him** (25). The schismatic worship devised by Jeroboam continued but the infiltration of Baal-worship (or the syncretistic worship of Yahweh with Baal-like ritual) was accelerated by the league with Sidon and the presence at court of Jezebel. The growth of the luxurious and powerful city of Samaria (his own property by purchase, v. 24) brought the same grandeur, ostentation and oppression as Solomon's Jerusalem had brought to the South. With Omri the northern tribes too began to taste the evil and pleasant fruit of politically successful kingship divorced from true religion.

Ahab and Jezebel and the emergence of Elijah (16: 28–22: 40)

As Asa's honest reign in Judah drew to a close, **Ahab son of Omri became king of Israel** (29), inheriting a firm and viable kingdom. The enthusiastic pursuit of Baal worship (vv. 31–33) cannot be blamed entirely on Jezebel though the fact that their sons had names compounded with -*iah* (contraction of Yahweh) suggests that Ahab still thought of himself as some sort of Yahwist.

34. Hiel of Bethel and his rebuilding of **Jericho** is cited as an example of the disregard of ancient divine curse, and also is evidence of expansion in Ahab's reign. **at the cost of his firstborn son Abiram** may refer simply to a fulfilment of Joshua's curse (v. 34b see Jos. 6: 26) or, less probably, to a foundation sacrifice of his son by the builder (JBmg).

Elijah confronts decadence (17: 1–19: 21)

Outwardly the northern kingdom prospered under Ahab. The capital grew more splendid with an ivory palace (22: 39), and many stables for the impressive cavalry force (Assyrian records of the battle of Qarqar in 853 B.C. speak of Ahab contributing 2,000 chariots and 10,000 soldiers to the coalition that temporarily halted the Assyrian expansion). Trade via Phoenicia prospered and agricultural produce was traded for prestigious luxuries of a growing upper class. As in the south, the economic divide between rich retainers of the king and poor smallholders was beginning and would soon widen to the gross exploitation denounced by Amos in the next century. Religion was splendid too with a garish house of Baal (16: 32), and Jezebel's hundreds of priests of Baal and Asherah (18: 19) like their later counterparts (2 Kg. 10: 22) went colourfully about their ritual.

Elijah in his garment of haircloth (2 Kg. 1: 7) was a fierce recall to the stern realities of Israel's desert origin and uncompromising monotheism. Yahweh was Lord of nature as of history and would not share his rule with Baal.

1. Elijah came from **Tishbe in Gilead** (RSV follows LXX; MT gives 'of the settlers'), not far from Jabesh Gilead. He breaks into the story, with no reference to family, occupation or earlier prophecy, but clearly has easy access to **Ahab**. He speaks as envoy of **the LORD the God of Israel** in direct challenge to Baal, announcing a trial of strength on Baal's vaunted character as storm and rain god. **neither dew nor rain in the next few years, except at my word**, struck at the source of Israel's prosperity. Thus Elijah was praying (Jas 5: 17) for national disaster. It would be an unequivocal statement of Yahweh's supremacy, as the prophetic word ruled out any idea that it was 'a chance' (see 1 Sam. 6: 9).

Two years of drought pass with no comment

except for examples of God's care for his prophet. At a time of religious crisis, with a man of such unusual commitment, extraordinary happenings are not surprising. The miraculous is only incidentally and tersely mentioned in the course of incidents that emphasize Yahweh's complete control and ability to provide for his prophet. **2. the word of the LORD came to Elijah** (and v. 8; 18: 1; 21: 17) in a manner not explained but with a certainty that is central to all prophetic activity. Discerning the true inspiration was a matter of importance (and even anxiety—Jer. 28). See below on 22: 24. **3. hide:** because at this stage the prophet's person was not inviolate as later became the case. **the Kerith Ravine:** a wadi E of Jordan, near Jericho, perhaps known to Elijah from shepherd days, provided the first refuge from Ahab. Gray argues for a reading 'Arabs' ('*arabîm*) for ravens ('*ōrᵉbîm*), not as a concession to rationalism but as parallel with the widow's later support. But **ravens** has complete textual support and is, in fact, no less likely than Bedouin offering flesh and bread in time of drought.

7. some time later the brook dried up, and the prophet shared the disaster he had predicted. The solitude and thought by Kerith gave place to sharing the hardship of a family in the disaster. Yahweh's authority is assumed, though how he **commanded** the **widow** (9) is not disclosed any more than how he commanded the ravens. Elijah trusted, braced himself for the 100–mile journey, and **went to Zarephath** (10), 7 miles S of Sidon in the territory of Jezebel's father but out of Ahab's jurisdiction. Jesus refers to this as an honour given to the Gentile widow but denied to the unbelieving Israelites (Lk. 4: 26).

The **widow** accepts the request **bring me a little water** as eastern courtesy even in time of drought, but expresses doubt about the further request for a **piece of bread** (11). Her oath **As surely as the LORD your God lives** (12) suggests she knew of Yahweh although living in Baal's city. Elijah's **Don't be afraid** is coupled with the test **first make a small cake of bread for me** (13) and the promise of v. 14. Just *how* the **jar** and **jug** were continually replenished is not stated, but many believers can sympathize with the joy and awe which Elijah and the family shared as day by day the promise was fulfilled (16).

The incident following is not directly related to the drought but reflects Elijah's character and power as God's agent. **17. the son of the woman became ill; and finally stopped breathing** (*nᵉšāmāh* as Gen. 2: 7, etc.) there is no evidence to determine whether death was apparent (as Josephus suggests) or real (as the mother and Elijah [v. 20] both believed). His revival (22) was rightly seen as a gift of God

through the prophet. Elijah's method as **he stretched himself out on the boy** (21) is recalled in Elisha's similar action (2 Kg. 4: 34) and shows his complete identification with the calamity, possibly intensified by the anguish of the widow's plaint **You have come to remind me of my sin and to kill my son** (18). The association of calamity with long-buried sin is a constant, and often superstitious, feature of popular religion. Elijah does not comment upon it but says simply **Look, your son is alive** (23). **22. the boy's life** (*nepheš*, 'life force') **returned to him.** The widow's response **Now I know** (24) shows inner certainty based on experience even greater than the steady daily provision.

Yahweh or Baal (18: 1–46)

The contest between Yahweh and Baal is resumed **in the third year** (18: 1). Josephus quotes Menander as saying there was a great drought of one year in the reign of Ethbaal of Tyre. The three and a half years of Lk. 4: 25 and Jas 5: 17 could reckon the usual six months dry season before Elijah made his statement (17: 1) when the October rains were due. Such a long drought reduced the land to an arid ruin. **2. the famine was severe in Samaria.** The king and his chamberlain take part in a search for grazing (5, 6). Did the royal horses get more care than the starving subjects? **1. Go and present yourself to Ahab** demanded rare courage from Elijah, made possible only by his faith in the promise **I will send rain. 3. Obadiah, who was in charge of his palace** (the same title is used in 4: 6) is introduced as a Yahwist who had used his position to mitigate **Jezebel's** attempts to **kill off the LORD's prophets** (4). No detail is given of her attempts and little is known of the prophets who were preserved or of their relation to Elijah. They were probably cult prophets attached to Yahwist shrines or maintained by the king (as in 22: 6). Obadiah seems uneasy in Elijah's presence (7) protesting his fidelity overmuch (13) and unable to grasp the situation. Perhaps calamity had made him a nervous wreck; perhaps he was not entirely easy in conscience in his role as chamberlain. Ahab's search for Elijah (10) summarizes three years of growing alarm as the king would gladly and illogically vent his frustration on the messenger of disaster. Elijah replies to Obadiah's anxious outpouring with the simple assurance **As the LORD Almighty lives, whom I serve, I will surely present myself to Ahab today** (15).

Ahab greets Elijah as **troubler of Israel** (17) with the typical obtuseness that cannot see beyond judgment to its moral cause. Elijah supplies what Ahab omitted: **you . . . and your father's family . . . have abandoned the LORD's commandments and have fol-**

lowed the Baals (18), and proposes a contest before **people from all over Israel** (19).

20. Mount Carmel was the western end of a ridge of hills whose ownership had been disputed by Tyre and Israel. The seaward end (W of traditional site in Elijah's memorial) was recognized Tyrian (and therefore Baal's) territory. The **prophets of Baal and . . . Asherah** would be challenged on their own ground. Ahab's compliance (20) shows the dominance of Elijah's personality. The exact nature of the contest was not disclosed but the priests showed remarkable self-confidence and compliance in appearing in force. Elijah challenges the lack of single-hearted commitment. **21. How long will you waver between two opinions?:** the verb *pāsaḥ* is used of the lame Mephibosheth in 2 Sam. 4: 4 and in Isa. 31: 5 of birds hovering. In v. 26 is describes the ritual dance. The figure may be of a cripple making his uneasy way on two crutches, or of a bird flitting from branch to branch. The uncompromising logic, **If the LORD is God, follow him; but if Baal is God, follow him**, struck at the root of the broadminded, inclusive culture Ahab had been fostering. The implications of monotheism sink in only slowly (see Ezek. 20: 39 and Mt. 6: 24 for other instances of the lesson). **22. I am the only one . . .** may refer to this particular confrontation with the many prophets of Baal or may be a comment on the tainted nature of other professed prophets of Yahweh.

The details of the contest show little difference in Canaanite and Hebrew preparation of offerings but the wild ritual of imitative magic contrasts sharply with Elijah's simple call to **sacrifice** (36). The end of the drought had been pronounced in the name of Yahweh (v. 1) so lest this should be ascribed to Baal the contest is made to turn on answer **by fire**. The crowd, previously silent (21) approve the terms: **What you say is good** (24). Elijah adds to the discomfiture of the Baal priests with some earthy humour (the first two phrases could mean that Baal was quite literally attending to nature). **28. they . . . slashed themselves as was their custom** (RSV reads the same verb, *gādad*, in Hos. 7: 14 in agricultural setting; usually it relates to mourning for the dead, *e.g.* Dt. 14: 1) in dervish-like oblivion to pain as they **continued their frantic prophesying** (29, a pejorative translation of the verb *nābā'* which covers prophecy very widely. JB 'ranted on'; NEB 'raved and ranted' are still less warranted. Possibly 'prophesying' within quotation marks would best represent the irony of the text). The doleful verdict of v. 26 is reinforced with the laconic **no response, no one answered, no one paid attention** (29).

30. Then Elijah said . . . Come near: in an invitation of open honesty. It was easy to taunt the ineffectual Baal; the real test of faith now began. He **repaired the altar of the LORD which was in ruins**, possibly an ancient shrine that had fallen into disuse, or been actively destroyed under Jezebel's regime. The **twelve stones** (31) were a silent reminder that the true Israel had been shattered by schism. The **water** probably was drawn from the sea and provided a three-fold guarantee against trickery. Elijah's brief prayer contrasts with the hours of Baal ritual and again involves the ancient covenant. **36. O LORD God of Abraham, Isaac and Israel:** not only Lord of nature, but of history and people. **37. Answer me, O LORD** contrasts with the **no answer** of v. 29 and the avowed reason is, not his own vindication but **so these people will know that you, O LORD, are God, and that you are turning their hearts back again** (NIV leaves little room for ambiguity. cp RSV 'thou hast turned their hearts back' JB 'you . . . are winning back their hearts'; NEB 'it is thou that hast caused them to be backsliders'). The translation turns on understanding Elijah's view of the situation. Was he optimistic that a dramatic sign would turn the people to Yahweh? More likely (as Jesus, Jn 2: 23–25) he despaired of any genuine repentance that way and wished them only to know that their decadence was not to be blamed on Baal or Jezebel but was Yahweh's doing, inevitably arising from their rejection of the ancient covenant and first commandment.

38. Then the fire of the LORD fell in such a demonstration of power that the people made the only possible response **The LORD he is God** (39). The fate of the **prophets of Baal** (40) was not unexpected. They and the people knew the stakes they were playing for. Elijah's championship of the desert covenant included also its rigid sanctions (Dt. 13).

Yahweh's vindication was not complete until the rains came and Elijah sends **his servant** (mentioned for the first time in the story) to watch for sign of the promised **heavy rain** (41). His attitude (42) may be one of emotional exhaustion or the 'prayed again' of Jas 5: 18. When the **small cloud** (44) finally appears the elation of victory gives him strength to run the 17 miles back to Jezreel as the king's herald.

The visit to Horeb (19: 1–18)

1. Ahab told Jezebel and the news only incensed her still further against Elijah. Not unnaturally **Elijah was afraid and ran for his life** (3), thus gaining the undeserved scorn of insensitive commentators. It was not pale cowardice but cold realism that prompted his withdrawal, first to **Beersheba** and then to **Horeb** (3, 8). If his request **that he might die** (4) showed undue self-pity, his analysis was sound. **I am no better than my ancestors** was true as far as bringing Israel back to faith.

Jezebel's message (2) was a solid reality. The people's frightened acclaim (18: 39) was not the same class of commitment and would soon pass. In his extremity, Yahweh again cared for the tired servant (5–7). EVV **an angel** obscures the ambiguity of Heb. *mal'āk* ('messenger' in v. 2). A kindly villager could have served unless Elijah needed some more numinous experience to renew his determination. **8. forty days and forty nights** recall Moses' receiving of the law (Exod. 24: 18). **Horeb, the mountain of God** would be about 100 miles across arid country. The site further reinforced the return to Israel's religious birthplace, and raised the question of how timeless principles given in the desert could be applied in the very different cultural conditions of prosperous settled agriculture (or modern industrial society). **10. I have been very zealous** (JB 'filled with jealous zeal') mirrors the second commandment (Exod. 20: 5). Elijah's was no petty envy of the place Baal held in Israel but a burning concern that Yahweh's supremacy should be known. Such zeal may not always be according to knowledge (see Jehu's use of the word in 2 Kg. 10: 16) but can be a wholly appropriate reaction (*e.g.* Ps. 69: 9 and Jn 2: 17). Elijah rehearsed the indignity Yahweh had suffered: **the Israelites have rejected your covenant** (LXX reads 'forsaken thee', but the reference to covenant is highly appropriate), **broken down your altars and put your prophets to death** (Elijah shows to Yahweh more of his concern for the prophets than he did to Obadiah; imperfect their witness may have been but their slaughter was a gross affront to Yahweh). **I am the only left** paints the blackest possible picture of Israel's decadence. **11. the LORD is about to pass by** (another parallel with Moses' experience; see Exod. 34: 6–7—comparison of that revelation with the present text is instructive), not in **wind, . . . earthquake** or **fire** which might have suited Elijah's fiery mood, but in **a gentle whisper** (or 'sound of silence', 12). The repetition (13, 14) reinforces both the urgency of Elijah's concern and the mystery of the divine permission of evil.

15. Go back does not introduce an answer to Elijah's theological problem. The storm and silence refuelled his conviction of Yahweh's mysterious supremacy. He must now continue as the agent of judgment. **the desert of Damascus** was to be the next hiding place and the long, 300 mile journey there would take him through **Abel Meholah** (16) in Manasseh near Jordan. **16. anoint** must not be pressed literally as only **Jehu** actually received the oil at prophetic hands (2 Kg. 9: 6). The verb (*māšah*) can indicate the appointment of which anointing was the symbol (*e.g.* Jg. 9: 8) and Isa. 61: 1 gives a parallel to its use here of the prophet **Elisha** as well as of Kings. **17. the**

sword of Hazael inflicted hurt on Israel after **the sword of Jehu** though they are given here in order of accession to kingship. It is not stated how **Elisha** was to **put to death.** Possibly the scourges are in a moral order: men might survive Syrian conquest; less easily could they recover from bloody civil war; none could escape the result of the divine rejection of the nation which Elisha would signify as he strengthened the remnant, the **seven thousand, all whose knees have not bowed to Baal** (18). **bowed . . . kissed** cover all shades of infidelity from the formal worship of casual attenders at Baal festivals to the priests who contorted their limbs in ritual dances.

19. So Elijah went from there carrying the stark outworking of judgment that was incipient in the tables of law Moses brought from the same mount. Paul (Rom. 11: 2–4) understood the deep anguish but sees the hope of restitution hidden from Elijah. In a different desert he arrived at a Christ-centred philosophy of history and saw hope beyond the 'casting away' that Elijah so vividly perceived at Horeb.

The call of Elisha (19: 19–21)

19. Elisha son of Shaphat is introduced as of good family, comfortably off (if the field that needed **twelve yoke of oxen** to plough it was a family possession) and able to afford an ox for celebration. **Elijah . . . threw his cloak around him:** in symbolic invitation to discipleship. There is no parallel or conflict with Lk. 9: 61–2—Elisha was not rushing to offer his services, but surprised at the invitation. Elijah deals gently with him and joins the happy rural celebration before they leave with the goodwill of the local community—perhaps some of the seven thousand.

Wars and prophets (20: 1–43)

The story leaves Elijah for the moment and deals with (possibly earlier) relations between Israel and Syria. Intricate debate has continued as to whether the Benhadad in ch. 20 is the same as, or son of, the Benhadad to whom Asa appealed (15: 18) and how the events can be fitted into Ahab's reign or should be ascribed to some other king of Israel. Here it is taken that Benhadad I of 15: 18 obtained some military advantage over Omri (20: 34) and that his son Benhadad II continued the policy of harassment in the middle years of Ahab's kingship. The détente of 20: 34b continued (see 22: 1) and strengthened into the alliance both kings shared against Assyria at Qarqar in the summer of 853. Thereafter Ahab resumed hostilities to retrieve Ramoth Gilead (perhaps promised but not ceded) and died there later in 853. Benhadad II was murdered by Hazael about 843 (2 Kg. 8: 15). **1. accompanied by thirty two kings:** a confederacy of tributary city states and sheikhs, unwillingly drawn into Benhadad's campaign and easily dispersed (25). Ahab at this time was reduced to vassal-status: **just as you say, my lord the king, I** am **yours** (4). The reason for his resistance is not clear. JB amends *MT* to give 'Your silver and gold are mine; you may keep your wives and children', so Benhadad's later message goes back on this agreement. NIV, RSV, NEB follow *MT* in which v. 3 is a general claim which Ahab accepts formally but he later resents the suggestion (6) that the city is open to general plunder. Ahab consults **the elders of the land** (7) and with their support refuses the indignity: **this demand I cannot meet** (9). His proverb in v. 11 (a pithy four words in Heb.) does him credit and enrages the drunken Benhadad. The mention of **a prophet** (13) recalls again the shadowy brotherhood of whom so little is known. Staunch Yahwist, in a nationalistic fashion, he wants Yahweh to be vindicated against the alien Syrians. By military victory **you will know that I am the LORD** with no moral overtones such as Ahab was wont to hear from Elijah. The dramatic reverse was achieved with tactics similar to Jonathan's at Micmash (1 Sam. 14). A suicide squad of **young officers of the provincial commanders** (14, 15, 17) goes out as if to surrender. **Ben-Hadad** gives his lordly orders (18) but as **each one struck down his opponent . . . Arameans fled** in general panic and the main army under Ahab completed the rout and collected spoil (21). **22. the prophet** warned Ahab to expect a Syrian return **next spring. 23. the officials of the king of Aram** offer the ingenious excuse that Israel's **gods** will be less at home in the plains. The more disciplined fighting force has experienced **officers** in place of laggard **kings** (24) and the battle is pitched at **Aphek** (unlikely to be the Aphek of 1 Sam. 29: 1 near Jezreel in the heart of Israelite territory; Gray suggests a town at the S end of L. Tiberias on the road from Damascus to Bethshan). The **man of God** (28) has the same concern as the prophet of the earlier incident: **you will know that I am the LORD** and the assertion of Yahweh's authority in both hill and valley. In the Syrian debacle, **Ben-Hadad fled** (30) but is encouraged to hope that **the kings of the house of Israel are merciful** (31). Mercy (*ḥesed*) implies loyalty to covenant rather than humanitarian feeling and the servants may have had an earlier Syro-Israelite agreement in mind. Ahab's reply **He is my brother** (32) showed acceptance in a suitably delicate diplomatic manner and spared Benhadad the necessity of humbling himself as his servants had done. Joining Ahab in his **chariot** (33) Benhadad hastens to make favourable terms. Ahab **let him go** (34), motivated by political considerations as well as a little magnanimity. A friendly Syria was a better

buffer between Israel and Assyria than a kingless defeated Syria.

But **one of the sons of the prophets** (35) did not agree. To him, Yahweh's honour demanded Benhadad's death and Ahab had **set free a man I had determined should die** (42). In fact there is no hint of any such divine 'determination' (Heb. *ḥerem*; see *NBD* p. 284a). Typically, the prophet enacts his message, forcing Ahab to give judgment against himself (40). The enacted incident was not actually analogous as Benhadad had not been similarly entrusted to Ahab. A **headband down over his eyes** (38) may have been necessary to cover a distinguishing mark of the sons of the prophets, hence the wounding incident which also gained him initial sympathy from the king as a casualty of the recent battle. The curse, **it is your life for his life** (42), shows the wide divergence of the theology of the nationalistic sons of the prophets from that of Elijah. To them, Yahweh was Israel's God and must strike down national enemies. To Elijah, Yahweh was Israel's God and was about to judge the house of Omri and the whole nation for moral and religious unfaithfulness to the covenant (21: 20–24).

Ahab and Naboth's vineyard (21: 1–29)

LXX puts ch. 21 immediately after ch. 19. In its present position it breaks two sections of Ahab's military exploits but has the effect of replying to the prophet's mistaken judgment of 20: 42.

Ahab again appears as weak rather than wicked. His **palace** in **Jezreel** (1) was a pleasant lowland residence he wished to extend. His request **let me have your vineyard** (2) is courteous enough and though Naboth appears scandalized at the thought of losing **the inheritance of my fathers** (3), it is unlikely such transactions were illegal at the time. (Transition from tribal organization to monarchy had weakened the force of Num. 36: 7–9, and Lev. 25 limits but does not prohibit sale.) Ahab however recognizes Naboth's right to refuse but **went home sullen and vexed** (4). **5. his wife Jezebel** had learnt her ideas of kingship in a different school. **7. Is this how you act as king over Israel?** In Tyre the kings were not so easily withstood and inadequate ideas of God bred wrong ideas about social obligation. **8. she wrote letters in Ahab's name** and her plot shows both Ahab's easy-going attitude to his responsibilities and the corruption of local government. The **elders and nobles** arranged the false trial; the **scoundrels** (10) were easily recruited. The semblance of legality achieved the grasping ruler's wish then as later—even to the more sophisticated techniques of the 20th century. The **nobles** (*ḥōrîm*) appear for the first time as a socially significant group (see Jer. 27: 20; 39: 6; Isa. 34: 12 for only other pre-exilic use). The charge, **cursed both God and the king** (see Exod. 22: 28; Lev. 24: 15, 16), brought death by stoning by the people **outside the city** (13). 2 Kg. 9: 26 associates his sons in his fate so there would be no survivor to inherit the land. **15. Get up and, take possession of the vineyard** may point to a custom that the property of those executed for treason went to the crown or be an instance of straight confiscation to which no one would object after Naboth's fate. **17. the word of the LORD came to Elijah:** who again comes into the story with dramatic suddenness. Cutting through the legalized trappings, like Nathan before him (2 Sam. 12) Elijah speaks directly to the king's conscience. **19. Have you not murdered** and also **seized?:** breaking both sixth and eighth commandments. Ahab's startled **So you have found me, my enemy?** (20) is a mixture of frustration and anger with a harrowed conscience. The encounter was heavy with menace and Elijah's terrifying denunciation (20–23) not only shattered Ahab but burnt into the memory of Jehu who had ridden the 20 miles down from Samaria with him (2 Kg. 9: 25). Again Elijah's condemnation is moral (not nationalistic): **sold yourself to do evil . . . caused Israel to sin** (20, 22). Ahab's repentance earned a personal respite, hence the doom, **dogs will lick up your blood——yes, yours!** was fulfilled in his son Joram (2 Kg. 9: 25 f.; but cf. 1 Kg. 22: 38 with note).

The parenthesis (25, 26) notes one major element in the charge against Ahab, and the one excuse. It was **idols** that led **the Amorites** into decline that cost them the land. Ahab accelerated a similar fate for Israel, **urged on** (the verb *sût* usually suggests persuasion against one's usual character) by **Jezebel his wife**. Omri's agreement with Phoenicia was at the price of one of the most disastrous marriages on record.

Ahab's death (22: 1–40)
After **three years'** cordiality (1) hostility with Syria is renewed (see above on 20: 1). The occasion is a visit by **Jehoshaphat king of Judah** (2) who is brought into the story before the chronological note in v. 41. Relationships between North and South have been much debated but the suggestion that Jehoshaphat was virtually a vassal of Ahab is mistaken. The marriage of Jehoram to Athaliah (2 Kg. 8: 16–18) sealed agreement between equals—and also spelt trouble for Judah when the firm piety of Jehoshaphat was removed. The dynastic stability of the south contrasted with the north and in face of Syrian pressure unity was politically essential anyway. Perhaps similar political considerations moved Jehoshaphat to keep such religiously alien company (see 2 Kg. 3: 14). Whatever the cause, Jehoshaphat at Ahab's court is not a happy sight and his **I am as you**

are (4) is shamefacedly qualified by the request **First seek the counsel of the LORD** (5).

So **the king of Israel brought together the prophets** (6), a motley band of **about four hundred men** with the same nationalistic outlook as the individual noted earlier (ch. 20). They were not necessarily time-serving men, but imbued with a zeal for the holy war—what was good for Israel was Yahweh's will—and seemingly unaware of deeper moral issues. **6. Ramoth Gilead** was part of Yahweh's territory so they unitedly advise **Go, for the LORD will give it into the king's hand**. Perhaps it was the manner or the very number of the voices that made Jehoshaphat uneasy and so brings **Micaiah son of Imlah** on the scene with Ahab's comment **I hate him for he . . . prophesies . . . bad** (8). However, Micaiah seems to be at liberty and **an official** is sent to find him, while the pathetically splendid scene continues at the **gate of Samaria** (10–12). The messenger, true to type, briefs Micaiah and tactfully advises him to **speak favorably** (13). The tone of his **Attack and be victorious** (18) must have been sarcastic and the king presses for **the truth in the name of the LORD** (16). Micaiah follows with the moving and controversial vision of disaster and the divine intention to **lure Ahab, into attacking Ramoth Gilead and going to his death** (20). The mystery of providence cannot be watered down and the Hebrew writers above all leave it stark and daunting (see above on 18: 37). The NT is no less sharp (*e.g.* 2 Th. 2: 11–12): '. . . the just law, the judgment of the skies: He who hates truth shall be the dupe of lies' (Cowper). Any attempt to exclude God from the process ends in dualism—the two opinions (18: 21) Ahab toyed with all his life.

24. Zedekiah makes the obvious retort, **Which way did the spirit from (or Spirit of) the LORD go when he went from me to speak to you?** raising the question of discrimination between rival prophecies. His own contribution (v. 11) showed signs of premeditation, possibly a vision of his own mind (Jer. 23: 16). Micaiah gives the Mosaic test (Dt. 18: 22). Events will show who is right: **you will find out** (25). The king's order, **Put this fellow in prison** (27), may have been partly to retain dignity and show determination to go to battle and partly pent up anger against Micaiah, who again claims events will vindicate him: **If you ever return safely, the LORD has not spoken through me** (28). The addition **Mark my words, all you people!** (not in LXX and omitted by JB, NEB) may come from a copyist who wrongly identified Micaiah with the canonical Micah (see Mic. 1: 2).

Ahab's misgivings are shown in his **disguise** (30; there is no suggestion that he hoped Jehoshaphat would suffer for him, as the Gk.

reading 'but you wear my robes' hints). The reason for the **king of Aram's** command **Do not fight . . . except with the king of Israel** (31) is not given. Probably he regarded the campaign as an act of treachery. The **bow at random** (34; a phrase that has passed into legend) gave the fatal wound. The king ordered, **get me out of the fighting** and with courage continued to direct operations **propped up in his chariot** (35). **that evening he died** and the battle was ended. **36.** '**Every man to his town, everyone to his land**': JB follows LXX in running 37a on to 36b: 'for the king is dead'. They brought him **to Samaria . . . and the dogs licked up his blood** (38), seen as a partial fulfilment of **the word of the** LORD in 21: 19. The reference to the **prostitutes** is obscure and some versions follow an emended text, 'they washed his armour' (as AV; cp NIV footnote). **Ahab rested with his fathers:** an unusual phrase for death in battle. Thus ends the story.

The record is an example of accurate relating of human complexity; the bravery in battle, the weakness, half excused by acknowledgement of Jezebel's evil genius, the stirring of conscience, anguished repentance, the underlying rejection of Yahweh's authority, all find mention. To attempt to disperse them among imagined contradictory sources is to lose a convincing picture of a 'doubled-minded man' (Jas 1: 7, 8).

Jehoshaphat (22: 41–50)
A brief but favourable comment shows Jehoshaphat completing the work of **his father Asa** (46). **the high places** remained, a snare the writer regretted, but they were accepted by even the most loyal Yahwist until Josiah's reformation. The **peace with the king of Israel** (44) has been noted above v. 2. **Edom** (47) reappears in Judah's history with reopening of trade disrupted by the activities of Hadad (11: 14–22) and Shishak's invasion. The **ships . . . were wrecked** and Jehoshaphat declined the help of **Ahaziah**, either regarding the wrecking as an ill omen, or reluctant to give free passage to Israelites through his territory (cf. 2 Chr. 20: 35 where the wrecking is a judgment on an earlier treaty with Ahaziah).

Abaziah (22: 51–53)
Ahaziah, Ahab's son and successor, had a short reign of two years, cut short by a fatal accident (2 Kg. 1: 2); he lived in the service of Baal **just as his father had done** (53).

2 Kings

Ahaziah and Elijah (1: 1–18)
Ahaziah's devotion to Baal is shown by his sending messengers, after his serious fall, to **consult Baal-Zebub** at **Ekron (Baal-Zebub=** 'lord of the flies', but may be a parody on Baal-zebul—'Baal the prince', or 'lord of the high place', a title of Canaanite Baal). Why so distant a shrine was chosen is not clear. **3. Elijah** intercepts the messengers, gives his message of doom and disappears. **5. The messengers** do not recognize Elijah but describe him by **a garment of hair and leather belt** and Ahaziah knows at once whom he is dealing with. The following incident is widely derided and certainly shows Elijah as a man of judgment rather than of grace. The 'innocent fifties', however, were willingly engaged in encompassing the death of a man whose character they must have known at least by repute. That the captain's **Man of God** (9) was said in scorn may be seen by the play on words in Elijah's reply **If I am a man** ('iš) **of God, may** ('eš) **come down** (10). The third group is saved by the captain's humble entreaty and Elijah, fortified by the message, **do not be afraid** (15), goes in person to deliver his rebuke to the dying king. The gruesome incident is included as part of the Elijah tradition and serves to mark out the awesome new character of prophet that he inaugurated. Certainly thereafter the prophet's person was inviolate in Israel.

17. So Ahaziah **died** and was succeeded by **Joram**, his brother (according to LXX and implied by his childlessness).

Elisha takes over (2: 1–18)
Elijah's departure from the scene is closely woven with Elisha's introduction as leading figure among the company of the prophets. As Joshua to the second Moses, Elisha was called to the difficult task of following the pioneer of a new stage in Israel's development. But whereas Joshua had presided over the settling of the land, Elisha prepared the remnant for the time when the people of Israel would follow the Amorites whose practices they had so lightly absorbed (1 Kg. 21: 26).

Both **Elijah and Elisha** (1) had premonition of the event as they went **from Gilgal** (not the better known low-lying town of Jos. 4: 19 etc. but a hill town between Shiloh and Bethel, possibly the one mentioned in Dt. 11: 30). **2. stay here**, was a test of Elisha's determination. **they went down to Bethel** (Gilgal was in fact slightly lower than Bethel but the route involved a final descent over the hill). A settlement of **a company of the prophets** (3) at

Bethel, the hated site of Jeroboam's pseudo-sanctuary, is here mentioned for the first time. They clearly acknowledge both Elijah and Elisha and also have premonition of the coming departure. **4. Jericho** had recently been rebuilt on the ancient mound by Hiel (1 Kg. 16: 34) in defiance of Joshua's curse. The prophetic settlement, traditionally known as Elisha's spring, was nearby and this is again the first mention of a prophetic community there. The final stage takes them **to the Jordan** (6) which parts in Elijah's last prophetic sign as he 'undoes' the victorious entry four centuries earlier. Finally he invites Elisha to **Tell me, what can I do** (9). **9. a double portion** (Dt. 21: 17) would mark Elisha as firstborn or leader among the prophets Elijah was leaving. Elijah leaves the matter in suspense: **If you see me when I am taken from you, it will yours** (10). The parting came as the fiery vision **separated them** and **Elijah went up in a whirlwind** (*not* the chariots). Elisha's cry **'My father, my father'** (in sense of reverence and dependence), **'the chariots and horsemen of Israel!'** (12) is echoed at his own death (13: 14) and has been interpreted as (*a*) an epitaph equating Elijah's value to Israel to more than military might or (*b*) elation at a worthy and triumphal exit, as though Elisha shared with the Negro spiritual the idea that it was the chariots and not the whirlwind that had carried Elijah home.

Elisha's confidence in the new power was now immediately tested. After the first **and struck the water** (14) Gk. adds 'and they [the waters] were not divided' to make clear that the river had resumed its flow during the time the prophets were on the eastern side. *MT* gives the same impression, without specifically making the addition. Elisha's question **'Where now is the LORD, the God of Elijah?'** is followed in Heb. by 'even (or also) he'. NEB relates this to Elisha: 'he too struck the water'. Gray adds it to the question: 'Where is Yahweh, the God of Elijah, even he?' **And when he had struck: when**, not in Heb. is added by NIV to make clear he did not strike twice. There is no explanation such as that offered in Jos. 3: 16 and indeed such a collapse of the bank would hardly account for two separate partings of the water. The religious significance clearly parallels the Red Sea and Jordan experiences of the advancing Israelites and symbolizes the unchanging power of Yahweh in changing circumstances.

The **fifty men** (17) would not have witnessed the whole event, but saw Elisha return over Jordan and recognized him as Elijah's heir, paying due respect (15). Their request to **seek your master** (16) is understandably resisted by Elisha, though by their persistence **he was ashamed** (17; NEB, 'had not the heart to refuse'). They **did not find him**, and like Moses

he had no known grave. As Elisha had realized (18b) there must be no backward look such as a venerated tomb might bring. Elijah's work was done; a fierce work of judgment that became symbolic (Mal. 4: 5–6), even idealized (Jn 1: 21), and seen at the end of the era in John the Baptist (Mt. 3: 1–10). After Moses and Elijah God had nothing fundamentally new to say until the coming of the one they joined on the mount of transfiguration (Mk 9: 4).

Reminiscences about Elisha (2: 19–8: 16)
Elisha began to follow Elijah towards the end of Ahab's reign (1 Kg. 19: 19–21). Elijah's departure was after Ahaziah's death, so Elisha's sole ministry spanned the reigns of Joram, Jehu and Jehoahaz. He died during the reign of Jehoash (13: 14) after fifty years of public life, a revered national figure whose exploits were proudly rehearsed (8: 4). The dozen or so incidents that are recorded are therefore spread over fifty years. No historical order is given, or can be clearly inferred. No principle of selection is given. Most of the incidents involve apparently miraculous acts and at one level indicate the casual public's interest in tales of extraordinary people. Probably 'the great things Elisha has done' were retold and preserved by the company of the prophets. At a deeper level the disjointed collection of stories poses a question of the author's intention. Those critics who on *a priori* grounds distrust miracle stories have to say why these particular accounts should have been invented and preserved. Those who are ready to accept them look for their purpose and, apart from many ingenious allegorical interpretations, two main suggestions can be made. Elisha is (*a*) the token of Yahweh's continued interest in the unstable politics of the dying nation and its neighbours (3: 4–27; 6: 8–7: 20; 8: 7–15; 9: 1–3) and (*b*) also the means of Yahweh's strengthening of the remnant to keep alive the true warm personal relationship of trust and reverence among the poor in spirit (2: 19–22; ch. 4; 6: 1–7; 8: 1–6). The stories of Naaman (ch. 5) and the Bethel urchins (2: 23–25) bridge the two categories. In all this Elisha must be seen against his times. The messenger was still to come who 'when they hurled their insults at him he did not retaliate' and the people of Bethel saw justice without mercy. The condemnation of Moab (like Amos's later pronouncements, Am. 1) showed a God who still used nations as his executioners. Although no historical sequence can be firmly inferred, the following table shows the position tentatively adopted in this commentary.

853	Assyrian advance temporarily halted at Qarqar
c. 852	Ahaziah dies. Jehoram becomes king 2: 19–22; 2: 23–25

campaign against Moab 3: 1–27
Elisha in Carmel and Samaria
    4: 1–7; 4: 8–37
famine (possibly 6: 24–7: 20 fits here)
    4: 38–41
    ?4: 42–44
Elisha in Damascus 8: 7–15

*c.*843 Hazael assassinates Benhadad II. Syria harasses Israel for forty years.

c. 841 Jehu assassinates Jehoram and becomes king.
Assyrians resume offensive and drive to Mediterranean coast.
Jehu pays tribute to Assyria.
Assyria not actively concerned in West for some years.
    8: 1–6; 4.42–44? 6: 1–7

814 Jehu dies and son Jehoahaz reigns
    6: 8–23

802 Assyrians besiege Damascus. Syrian pressure on Israel eased.

?800 Benhadad III succeeds Hazael

798 Jehoash succeeds Jehoahaz
    possibly 6: 24–7: 20
    Naaman's visit 5: 1–27

A spring is healed (2: 19–22)

If the incident follows immediately from 2: 18, **the city** (19) is Jericho. In this case the incident may symbolize the final lifting of the curse that had already worked itself out on Hiel (1 Kg. 16: 34). The request is made by **the men of the city**—not limited to the prophetic community—showing suitable deference (**our lord**). **the land is unproductive:** JB, 'the country suffers from miscarriages'. The verb **is unproductive** is used only of people, as Exod. 23: 26. The **new bowl** and **salt** (20) are accessories to the prophetic act and attempts at chemical explanations of the healing are unconvincing. **22. the water has remained wholesome to this day:** a continuing source of local gratitude to Yahweh and his prophet.

A curse at Bethel (2: 23–25)

23. From there Elisha went up links the two incidents and highlights the sudden change from grace and healing to curse and judgment. The **youths** were not innocent toddlers. Heb. *qāṭān* can mean 'small' as opposed to great in importance (18: 24), though usual of immaturity (1 Kg. 11: 17); *na'ar* is used widely of young men (*e.g.* 1 Kg. 11: 28; 2 Kg. 4: 22); *yeled*, **youths** in v. 24 is equally ambiguous (see 1 Kg. 12: 14). The context must decide and here suggests a gang of urchins lying in wait, coming out after he had passed (so that he **turned around**) and shouting abuse. **Go on up** is a sarcastic comment on the report of Elijah's departure. **baldhead** may refer to a prophetic tonsure or simply be coarse abuse. **24. he called down a curse on them:** *qālal*= 'speak evil of', Exod. 22: 28; Ps. 62: 4 not the

herem, 'ban', devoting someone to destruction (see on 1 Kg. 20: 42) and apparently went straight on his way. **bears** were common in the hill country at this time, a constant hazard, though the people and writer saw them as judgment. If the boys were reflecting their parents' contempt for the new prophet, Exod. 20: 5 might provide an appropriate commentary. **25. he went on to Mount Carmel:** where he appears to have had a residence (4: 25) and **returned to Samaria** (where he is seen at home in 5: 3 and 6: 32). It looks as though Yahweh's prophet was now able to live unmolested in Israel.

Joram's reign and the Moabite campaign (3: 1–27)

1. Joram is introduced with the usual synchronizing formula and though his reign is condemned there is some mitigation in that **he got rid of the sacred stone of Baal that his father had made** (2). **4. Mesha king of Moab** is known through his inscription (the Moabite Stone discovered in 1868) in which he attributes Omri's victory over Moab to Chemosh being 'angry with his land' and records gaining his independence **after Ahab died** (and see 1: 1) adding hopefully 'Israel hath perished for ever'. **he had to supply:** The enormous tribute seems more likely to be a single reparation than an annual impost, (as JB 'used to pay' suggests) and suggests Mesha 'was paying tribute of a hundred thousand lambs etc.' when he decided to rebel **against the king of Israel** (5). The message to **Jehoshaphat** and his response are much as before (1 Kg. 22) so they set out together with the **king of Edom** (probably the vassal deputy mentioned in 1 Kg. 22: 47). **Through the desert of Edom** (8) was a long detour, taking **seven days** (9) so that they approached Edom from the east (cf. v. 22). The lack of water seems to have been unexpected and was interpreted as a disaster brought about by Yahweh (perhaps by analogy with Ahab's campaign at Ramoth-gilead, 1 Kg. 22: 20). Jehoshaphat's enquiry shows that Elisha was in the company, though no reason for this is given. He is described as one who **used to pour water on the hands of Elijah** (i.e. was Elijah's servant) as it was early in Joram's reign and Elisha's own reputation had yet to be established. **13. Go to the prophets of your father and . . . your mother** echoes Elijah's stern attitude. The king temporizes with the plea that it is **the LORD** who is behind the calamity so a prophet of Yahweh is appropriate. Elisha's oath **As surely as the LORD Almighty lives** is another link with Elijah (1 Kg. 18: 15) and before that with the prophetic band at Shiloh (1 Sam. 4: 4). **14. I . . . have respect for the presence of Jehoshaphat king of Judah** shows that Elisha was no narrow northern nationalist. **15. While the harpist was playing the hand of the LORD came upon Elisha:** EVV follow a slight emendation of the text to give a solitary reference to music in prophetic activity at this time (see 1 Sam. 10: 5 for earlier reference). *MT* implies a practice ('whenever . . .'). There is no evidence that its purpose was to induce dervish ecstasy here; more likely it was to promote calm after the angry interview with Joram. The oracle of v. 16 is variously translated as imperative – **Make this valley full of ditches** (JB, 'dig ditch on ditch') or future (NEB, 'Pools will form', RSV 'I will make the dry stream bed full of pools'). The construction occurs in the oracle of 4: 43 which NIV, RSV, NEB, JB all regard as future ('they will eat'). So here NEB is preferable. **ditches** translates the unusual word *geb* ('cisterns', Jer. 14: 3). The promise of water is followed by the more weighty promise (18) to **hand Moab over to you** and the command to treat Moab with more severity even than was customary in the Hebrew settlement (see Dt. 20: 19–20 on sparing trees). The punitive mission escalates to a holy war, Yahweh executing justice in the manner of Am. 1 upon Mesha whose stele tells in detail how he had thrown off the Israelite yoke, in one town 'slaying all . . . for I had devoted them to destruction (*ḥerem*) for Ashtar Chemosh'. **20. The next morning . . . water flowing from the direction of Edom:** due probably to water running off the high ground after a sudden storm in Edom. Verses 21–24 rehearse the Moabites' preparations and their mistake as they see what they take to be **blood** (either the sun rising in the east over the water, or the red earth stirred up by the flow) and go **to the plunder.** The sacred ban is carried out to the gates of **Kir Haraseth** (see Isa. 16: 7). Mesha's desperate bid to cut his way out **to the king of Edom** (JB, NEB, 'to the king of Aram' [Syria] emends one letter to give better sense) is followed by his fearful sacrifice of **his firstborn son** (27). The result is given that **the fury against Israel was great**. The writer is unlikely to accept that the sacrifice was efficacious (though some Israelites may have done so). NEB paraphrases 'the Israelites were filled with such consternation at this sight' (but adds the RSV reading in footnote), and a reaction of awesome horror may have precipitated the withdrawal.

Elisha among the remnant (4: 1–44)
A series of incidents follows showing Elisha encouraging those that feared the LORD. They also provide incidentally a glimpse into everyday life in the countryside.

A widow in debt (4: 1–7)
1. my husband is dead: there is no direct evidence that he was one of Jezebel's victims. Note that there was no celibate vow for the company of the prophets. Their widows shared the desperate condition of all widows in the ancient world. **your servant . . . revered the LORD, but . . . :** gives an implied theology of material reward to which there are references both expectant and doubtful in OT (*e.g.* Ps. 37: 25; Ps. 73; Job 1: 10). NT references give no final answer (Mt. 6: 32, 33; Rom. 8: 18, 28) but encourage trust. Elisha does not comment on her **'but'**. He meets the need in a way that depends entirely upon her faith. The **creditor** (from *nāśāh*, lend on usury, as Jer. 15: 10) is spoken of disapprovingly in OT but was common practice in the ancient world (Exod. 22: 25; Neh. 5: 5–7). Slavery for debt was grudgingly accepted (Exod. 21: 7) with the softening legislation of release (Lev. 25). The blessing that Israel would lend to many nations (Dt. 28: 12) uses a word without usurious overtones, as in Ps. 37: 26; 112: 5). **2. what do you have in your house?:** typical of these stories in which relief comes from simple things readily to hand. **a little oil** Heb. 'Small phial of oil' emphasises how little. **4. shut the door behind you and your sons:** the privacy of the miracle is noteworthy. No public display; an unbelievable story, so the widow and her sons alone would share the secret fleeting experience of Yahweh's extraordinary provision. The prophet was not present so it was more than ever clear that the power was Yahweh's, available to humble trusting people. The continued act, **she kept pouring** (5), is a splendid instance of faith. **7. sell the oil** (an easy task with such a staple commodity), **and pay your debts:** JB, 'redeem your pledge'; NEB paraphrases more fully, 'redeem your boys who are being taken as pledges'. **live on what is left:** the abundance of God's giving (Mk 6: 43; Eph. 3:20).

A wealthy woman and her child (4: 8–37)
8. Shunem, N of Jezreel, was about 20 miles from Carmel where Elisha regularly visited and so **often comes our way** (9). The **well-to-do** (Heb. 'great' in status which might include wealth) **woman** showed hospitality which deepened to awe as she recognized him as **a holy man of God**. The discussion with her husband is a happy homely scene, though her later reluctance to tell him plainly of the child's death suggests that he was less keen to be identified with Elisha than she was. A **room on the roof** (10) was a permanent extra room. Some suggest this was because the holy man could not share with the ritually unclean family; more likely they just had not enough space. Elisha's offer to repay her for all her trouble shows some influence with **king** or **commander of the army** (13) and suggests a time when he had become a respected figure in Samaria. The woman is happy **among my own people**, showing the traditional contentment and solidarity of the tribal community. The gift of a child recalls the promise to Abra-

ham (Gen. 18: 1–15) but was more quickly fulfilled (17). The incident parallels the Elijah story (1 Kg. 17: 17). The child's sunstroke ends in his death, which the woman does not disclose to her husband. He is surprised at her visit to the prophet when **it is not the New Moon or the Sabbath**. (23; the reference to **New Moon** suggests a regular observance, perhaps merging with Canaanite custom. The Heb. word is usually translated 'month' and NIV is unusual in taking 'New Moon' as title of a festival (see Num. 10:10; 14:28) Moon worship (using different Heb. word) is mentioned at 2Ki. 23:5. The story aptly conveys the woman's purposeful and energetic preparation and journey to **Carmel**, a mixture of hope and bitterness, firmly controlled in the greeting *Shalom*, **'Everything is all right'** (26). **27. she is in bitter distress:** due to disappointed hope and the same doubt about Yahweh's goodness that the widow had experienced (v. 1). **the LORD has hidden it from me:** shows that prophets only had occasional clairvoyance, a special gift for special need. Usually as here, they awaited the unfolding of situations. **Gehazi** (here first mentioned as Elisha's servant) is dispatched with the **staff** (29), but the woman's insistence, **I will not leave you** (30), persuades Elisha to go in person. The ineffectiveness of the magical use of the staff contrasts with Elisha's prayer and intense personal involvement, perhaps recalling what he had heard of Elijah's similar incident (1 Kg. 17: 17–24). The effect is one of increased awe, **bowing to the ground** (37), with no recorded conversation. Again, the miracle is a secret affair with its own secret wonder. Perhaps she did tell her husband!

Death in the pot (4: 38–41)
38. Gilgal may be the site between Shiloh and Bethel mentioned in 2: 1, or near Jericho. It was a time of **famine**, a frequent calamity, hence the gathering of wild gourds by the inexpert prophet. The **wild . . . gourds** (39) are thought to be *citrullus colocynthis*, a yellow fruit with aperient qualities. The cry **death in the pot** (40) may be no more than a lighthearted 'They're poisoning us!' The handful of **flour** thrown into the pot is again a symbol of healing and provision. Attempts to explain it are unconvincing.

The firstfruits multiplied (4: 42–44)
42. Baal Shalishah shows an earlier place name (1 Sam. 9: 4) in the central hill country now compounded with Baal, probably on account of a shrine there. It is remarkable that the man brings **the bread from first ripe grain** (*bikkurim*) to Elisha rather than to a priest at the local shrine (Exod. 23: 19; Lev. 23: 20). The question **How . . . ?** (43) shows the same bewilderment as Jn 6: 9, but **he set it before them** (44) shows the same obedience of hopeful

trust. Elisha shares the gift and the sacramental meal is sufficient for all.

A Syrian healed (5: 1–27)
Since this story ends with Gehazi's withdrawal from public life (27) the incident must be placed late in Elisha's ministry. Syro-Israelite relations continued bad with border raids and periods of suspicious co-existence. **1. the LORD had given victory to Aram:** this gives the developing view of Yahweh as controller of all events, possibly here to discipline Israel, or perhaps Naaman was involved in withstanding the Assyrian assault on Damascus in 802 B.C. **he had leprosy:** NEB 'for his skin was diseased' is more accurate as Hansen's disease was not known in the ancient world. The word **leprosy** accurately conveys the social stigma involved, however. The **young girl** had been taken from some pillaged village to serve **Naaman's wife** (2) and shows not only charity but faith. **3. He would cure him** was a deduction from general report about Elisha (see Lk. 4: 27). **5. the king of Aram** misunderstands the message or refuses to deal below king level. His **letter** (the preliminary greetings are omitted and the quoted part begins 'and now . . .') causes confusion and the king of Israel's angry comment **he is trying to pick a quarrel with me** (7). Elisha retrieves the situation with his message **Have the man come to me** (8) and his terse treatment contrasts with display of an important soldier on an official visit. Naaman himself finds his expectations dashed. **11. I thought that he would surely come out to me:** conveys self-importance—'to a man in my position'. Understandably he finds the 25 miles journey to **Jordan**—a muddy meandering river—a humiliating suggestion. **13. his servants** perform their valuable service and, to his credit, Naaman changes his mind, goes, **and his flesh . . . became clean** (14). The return journey to Samaria was made in humbler mind. **15. Now, I know that there is no God in all the world except in Israel:** shows the idea of a localized God, but is a big step toward monotheism. The humble request **accept a gift** (Heb. 'blessing') is firmly refused. The further request for **as much earth as a pair of mules can carry** (17) again shows a localized Yahweh, so that Naaman can worship him on his own soil outside his territory. The conscientious difficulty of v. 18 is honestly expressed and has troubled many believers since, as they try to decide what is denial and what is responsible compromise in the course of duty. **Rimmon** is another name for Hadad, the Syrian title for Baal (cf. Tabrimmon father of Benhadad, 1 Kg. 15: 18). Elisha does not enter into discussion but gives the simple **Go in peace** (19).

The sad end of **Gehazi, the servant of Elisha** must be understood against a background of 15–20 years with the prophet, possibly living in a fantasy world of power and success just round the corner. Like Judas, his sin was not naked avarice (though his name in Heb. means 'avarice') but a more complex tangle of desires stemming from a failure to share Elisha's integrity. **20. my master was too easy on Naaman this Aramean** can be read to convey a lot of these frustrations. His reserve cracks; lies come easily (22) and he returns with his loot. Elisha's awareness unmasks his scheme. **26. Is this the time to take . . .** (JB, NEB follow LXX 'Now that you have taken the money, you can buy . . .') hints at the damage Gehazi had done. The open grace of Yahweh to an alien had been spoiled. Naaman was well pleased but would never know of the judgment on Gehazi whose failure, as so often, irretrievably marred a good act.

The borrowed axe (6: 1–7)
The disconnected incident reflects a peaceful time in the Jericho area. The reference to meeting **with you** (1) may be a courteous form of address, or show a settled ministry of Elisha in the area, concentrating on training the group. **2. Let . . . each of us . . . get a pole** (beam) **. . . there**, either to build a new refuge by Jordan, or get beams there to extend the existing accommodation. **4. And he went with them** and was at hand when the workman lost his axe. **6. Where did it fall?:** the close attention to the exact spot has suggested that Elisha in fact used his **stick** to thrust into the socket of the fallen axe so making it retrievable, but **threw it there** does not support this and the author clearly intends a miraculous impression. The religious significance is less clear, except as a reward to the workman's faith, and an addition to the shared wonder that fed the remnant's confidence.

War with Syria (6: 8–23)
This incident, including both Elisha's divine protection and humanity, cannot be definitely dated. Syria's ability to reach **Dothan** (about 12 miles from Samaria) shows a time when Israel's fortunes were at a low ebb—perhaps early in Jehu's reign after he had paid tribute to Assyria, or later when Jehoahaz was suffering under Hazael's unrelieved pressure. Assyria had other preoccupations from 840 to 810 and left Syria as Israel's main adversary. **9. the man of God**, later identified as Elisha (12), notifies **the king of Israel** of ambushes and movements of the Syrians. **11. the king of Aram** suspects treachery but is persuaded that **Elisha** is to blame. **15. early the next morning:** the city's predicament is clear and the servant expresses the fear of all: **Oh, my lord, what shall we do?** Elisha's reply (16) has been a cheer to many though less physically obvious than to the young man who saw **the mountains . . . full of horses and chariots** (which

take no further part in the story). The unexplained **blindness** enables Elisha to guide the raiders (who do not recognize his voice) the 12 miles **to Samaria** (19). The **king of Israel** treats Elisha with great deference (**my father**) even to the point of sparing hated enemies. **22. Would you kill men captured you have taken . . . ?** suggests a generosity towards prisoners which is put in doubt by the prophetic attitude of 1 Kg. 20: 42. LXX gives 'whom you have not taken', suggesting a more ruthless practice. *MT* (followed by NIV), however, gives more strength to Elisha's plea. **23. great feast** sealed the forgiveness—one could not kill anyone with whom one had eaten—and the Syrian raiders departed as friends.

A siege and its sudden raising (6: 24–7: 20)
The hostilities of v. 24 must be separated from the good relations of v. 23, probably by dating this in the reign of Benhadad II, predecessor of Hazael, so **the king of Israel** (26) would be Joram. The earlier agreement between Syria and Ahab did not last, and a lull in Assyrian pressure left Syria free to press claims against Israel. On this occasion **Samaria** was **besieged** with resultant **famine** and terrible suffering (28–29) at which the king's self-control snapped: **If the LORD does not help you, where can I?** (27) and he angrily determines to wreak his frustrations on Elisha. **25. a donkey's head . . . for eighty shekels and a fourth of a cab of seed pods** (edible bulbs, so JB 'wild onions') **for five shekels** denote severe famine prices by comparison with the later plenty (7: 1).

32. Elisha was sitting in his house, in respected audience with **the elders**, sharing in the calamity but a guarantee to the faithful of ultimate relief. His prescient reference to **this murderer** (lit. 'son of a murderer') might refer to his father Ahab's actions, or more likely be a Hebraism of character. **Is not the sound of his master's footsteps behind him?:** vv. 32, 33 telescope a series of events which ends with a confrontation of Elisha with the king. (the **messenger** follows Heb. and NIV then inserts **the king** to account for his presence at 7.2 RSV accepts correction of *melek* (king) for *mal'ak* (messenger) and so gives 'the king came down and said . . .') **33. This disaster is from the LORD** is not the acceptance of a judgment but an excuse for rebellion. **Why should I wait for the LORD any longer?** (JB 'Why should I still trust in Yahweh?') is a threat to renounce allegiance to Yahweh and therefore awe of his prophet ('wait for the LORD' is an expression of faith as Mic. 7: 7; Ps. 42: 5). Elisha gives a further proof of Yahweh's power with the double assurance **Hear the word of the LORD; this is what the LORD says** (7: 1) to the promise of plenty. **2. The officer on whose arm the king was leaning** (a close adviser, as

5: 18) derides the idea but is cut dead with the rebuke **You will see it . . . but . . . not eat**.

The **four men with leprosy** (NEBmg 'men who were suffering from skin diseases'; see above on 5: 1) are the first to realize what had happened. **6. The LORD had caused the Arameans to hear the sound of chariots**: Gray suggests 'rumour' for **sound**—an unusual but not impossible use of the word. **the king of Israel has hired . . .** reflects a practice in which the Syrians themselves had been involved earlier (1 Kg. 15: 18). **the Egyptians** (*miṣrayim*) **kings** are more likely *muṣri* (as 1 Kg. 10: 28), a nation north of the Taurus who later, under Benhadad III, feature as allies of Syria. The four men's fear that **punishment** ('evil') **will overtake us** (9) shows an awe inspired by unexpected good fortune which must be shared. **12. the king got up** and gave a reasonable interpretation of the Syrians' behaviour but was persuaded to check the story. The **five . . . horses** turn out to be only two and the riders **go and find out** and discover the extent of the Syrians' panic **as far as the Jordan** (13–18). **16. Then the people went out** and the word of Yahweh was fulfilled in both plenty and judgment (18–20).

The Shunammite's story resumed (8: 1–6)
The incident follows 4: 11–37 and the **famine** may be dated at the end of Joram's reign. The announcement is private to the woman, not a public challenge to Baal as in 1 Kg. 17: 1. H. L. Ellison suggests that a woman of such influence and wealth would have survived famine as long as any and the real reason behind the warning to leave was Elisha's knowledge of the bloodbath about to be released by Jehu. Shunem was near to Jezreel and few leading citizens were likely to survive. **3. she went to the king to beg for her house and land** which had apparently been confiscated. It seems she was widowed and so appeals in her own name. **4. the king** (probably Jehu) **was talking to Gehazi** and listening to the stories of Elisha, by now a national legend. At this opportune moment **the woman . . . came to beg** and Gehazi recognized her: **This is the woman**—and so her appeal was granted abundantly (6). Alternative dating of the passage after Elisha's death (as *e.g.* Gray) raises difficulties of identifying king, famine and dating the earlier incident.

Hazael's coup foretold (8: 7–15)
7. Elisha came to Damascus where apparently he was known and accepted, and perhaps at this juncture seeking refuge from Joram. The **gift** shows that Benhadad had not summoned Elisha but was taking advantage of an unexpected visit. **9. forty camel-loads**: a hyperbole signifying the honour in which Elisha was held. Elisha's reply (10) has suffered in the transmission of the text. *MT* has 'Go say, You shall

not (*lō'*) recover', but NIV, **'Go and say to him** (*lō*), **You will certainly recover'** is supported by a number of Heb. MSS and many versions. *MT* then represents an early attempt to avoid the appearance of a lie by the prophet. More likely, the prophetic insight deepened, with the hesitant **but . . .**, and as Elisha **stared . . . with a fixed gaze** and read Hazael's character he realized that though the illness was not fatal, he faced an ambitious assassin. Elisha weeps for his people, perhaps remembering the word of 1 Kg. 19: 15, and **the harm that you will do** (12)—the barbarities for which Amos later invoked judgment upon Syria (Am. 1: 3–5). NIV RSV (as against AV) correctly give Hazael's reply: **your servant . . . a mere dog**, not likely ever to wield influence to **accomplish such a feat** (13). An Assyrian inscription refers to Hazael as 'son of a nobody'. (AV 'Is thy servant a dog . . . ?' suggests Hazael is outraged at the slur on his character.) Elisha repeats his new terrible knowledge: **The LORD has shown me that you will become king over Aram** without specifically naming Hazael as assassin. Hazael could not wait for any other method of fulfilment, but himself treacherously kills the king. The **thick cloth** (Heb. *makbēr*, used only here) is disputed. Gray interprets it as 'netting (like a mosquito net) which one took and dipped and spread it before his face' and noticed that the king had died. The subject in **he took** is indefinite but Hazael fits the description best and it is not unreasonable to accept *makbēr* (from root *kābar*, 'to twist') as referring to bed coverings (*kebîr* is tentatively translated 'pillow' in 1 Sam. 19: 13 RSV and see RSVmg).

Jehoram king of Judah (8: 16–24 and see 1: 17)
It is confusing that two kings of the same name were reigning simultaneously in Israel and Judah for about three years. They also followed similar policies for **he** (Jehoram) **married a daughter of Ahab** (18), the disastrous political marriage which the good Jehoshaphat unwisely allowed. Athaliah is here called **daughter of Ahab** and NIV at v. 26 gives **granddaughter of Omri** (*MT* has 'daughter of Omri' which can idiomatically mean female descendant, though JB gives 'sister of Ahab' in v. 18 mg presumably as an alternative harmonization). Unfortunately the evil influence of Jezebel through Athaliah did not stop with only Jehoram doing **evil in the eyes of the LORD** (see 11: 1). Again the dynasty is saved **for the sake of David** (19), though **Edom rebelled** (20) after an exploit which nearly cost Jehoram his life as well as his province. The text of v. 21 is confused but it seems Jehoram and his chariots broke through a surrounding Edomite force, leaving the rest of the army to escape as best they could.

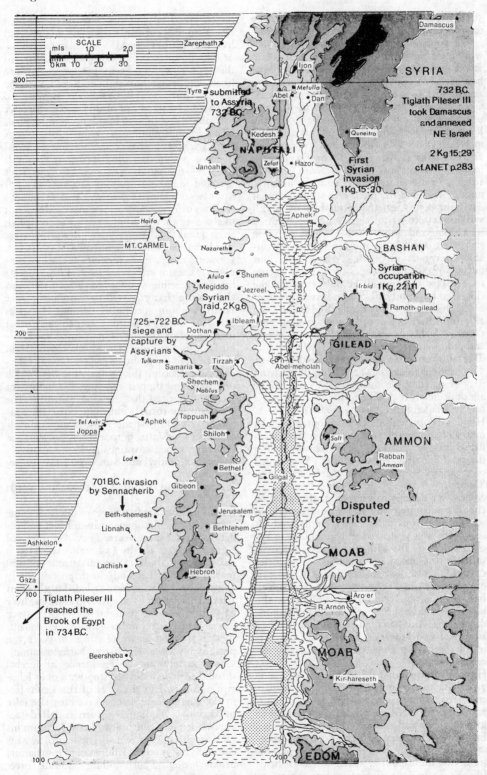

SCALE
mls   1,0   2,0
0 km 10 20 30

Damascus

SYRIA

732 B.C.
Tiglath Pileser III
took Damascus
and annexed
NE Israel

2 Kg 15:29
cf. ANET p.283

Zarephath

Ijon

Tyre submitted
to Assyria
732 B.C.

Metulla
Abel
Dan
Quneitra

Kedesh

NAPHTALI

First
Syrian
invasion
1 Kg.15:20

Janoah
Zefat
Hazor

Aphek

Haifa

MT. CARMEL

Nazareth

BASHAN

Afula
Shunem

Syrian
occupation
1 Kg. 22:11

Megiddo
Jezreel

Irbid

Syrian
raid, 2 Kg.6

R. Jordan

Ramoth-gilead

725–722 B.C.
siege and
capture by
Assyrians

Ibleam
Dothan

Tulkarm
Samaria
Tirzah

Abel-meholah

GILEAD

Shechem
Nablus

Tappuah

Tel Aviv
Joppa
Aphek

Shiloh

Salt

AMMON

Lod

Rabbah
Amman

Bethel

Gilgal

701 B.C. invasion
by Sennacherib

Gibeon

Jerusalem

Disputed
territory

Beth-shemesh

Bethlehem

Libnah

Ashkelon

MOAB

Lachish

Hebron

Gaza

Tiglath Pileser III
reached the
Brook of Egypt
in 734 B.C.

Aro'er
R. Arnon

Beersheba

MOAB

Kir-hareseth

EDOM

Map 25—Syrian and Assyrian invasions

Ahaziah king of Judah (8: 25–29)
24. Abaziah his son (sole survivor according
to 2 Chr. 22: 1) became king. His brief reign
is recalled primarily for its subservience to **the
ways of the house of Ahab** under the evil
influence of his mother **Athaliah**. His common
cause with **Joram the son of Ahab**, quite
apart from family ties, was dictated by Judah's
interest to contain Syrian expansion beyond
Ramoth Gilead (28). Joram's convalescence
at **Jezreel** becomes the occasion of Ahaziah's
further visit (29b) and involvement in Jehu's
purge (9: 27).

Jehu's revolt, purge and reign (9: 1–10: 36)
Elijah had understood the incurable nature of
the cancer of Baal worship (see on 1 Kg. 18:
37; 19: 16). Jehu's bloody purge, though an
inevitable judgment and in spite of the hopeful
10: 28, was as ineffectual as the Carmel drama
in reversing Israel's decline to oblivion. The
fast-moving narrative is a vivid commentary
on both the excitement and escalation of violence: the excitement of seeing Yahweh's judgment on blatant evil; the escalation until the
country was bereft of leadership and friends.
Certainly the massacre of Jezebel's kin would
have alienated both Phoenicia and Athaliah's
Judah, so that Jehu was obliged, in his first
year, to hurry with tribute to the Assyrian
Shalmaneser. The engraving on Shalmaneser's
Black Obelisk (*NBD* plate VII) of Jehu kneeling
is a fitting contrast to the swashbuckling commander driving furiously (9: 20) to set right
Israel's ills. Here is violence that judges but
does not heal. Only at Calvary did fierce judgment of sin bring restoration and health for
sinners.

The conspiracy (9: 1–37)
1. Elisha at last unleashes the judgment by
Jehu. The anointing ceremony was to be private (2) and with **oil** in the traditional manner
signifying that he is set apart to serve Yahweh
as **king over the LORD's people Israel** (6).
**4. So the young man . . . went to Ramoth
Gilead** which was apparently now in Israelite
control (see 14b). Jehu's question **For which
of us . . . ?** suggests he was not expecting the
honour, but he **went into the house** and heard
the decree and commission to **destroy the
house of Ahab** (7). Having delivered his oracle
of doom the young man, obedient to Elisha's
word, **opened the door and ran** (10), leaving
Jehu and his colleagues no chance of further
questioning. **11. Jehu went out to his fellow
officers:** an irony in view of his newly formed
intent to overthrow the **master**. They question
him about **this madman**. (from root *šāga'*, as
in 1 Sam. 21: 15 and below, v. 20) has been
taken as describing prophetic ecstasy, but is
more likely to represent the soldiers' contemptuous humour about the prophet's unkempt appearance and mysterious haste. Jehu's

reply shows similar light-heartedness—You
know what prophets are like!—but they reject
it: **That's not true** (Heb. 'Lie!') and Jehu shares
the oracle with them (12). **13. they hurried**
and enthroned him then and there on **the bare
steps** (Heb. *gerem* may refer to some now lost
architectural feature) with **trumpet** and acclamation, **'Jehu is king'** (see 2 Sam. 15: 10 for
the phrase which Gray and others link with
'enthronement' Ps. 47: 8; 93: 1). **14. So Jehu
. . . conspired:** his grandfather **Nimshi** seems
to have been renowned (see v. 20) though
his father's name is given here and at v. 2 as
Jehoshaphat. Verses 14b and 15a recapitulate
the history (8: 28–29) and explain why the king
was absent, thus facilitating the coup. **15. If
this is the way you feel** (*nephes*='spirit',
'whole-heartedness') i.e. if you really mean it,
don't let anyone slip out of the city. Jehu
plans complete surprise and rides pell mell 50
miles or more for Jezreel at the head of the
chariot column, leaving Ramoth Gilead to the
remaining defenders. The story vividly conveys the tension as the kings, unsuspecting and
unaccompanied (21) **rode out, each in his
own chariot . . . to meet Jehu. Have you
come in peace?** translates a single Heb. word.
RSV 'Is it peace?' might refer to events at Ramoth Gilead and show no panic. NIV more
likely refers to Jehu's reason for return to
Jezreel. Jehu's angry retort (22) **'How can
there be peace . . . ?'** gives vent to the pent-
up hatred of a loyal Yahwist against **the idolatry and the witchcraft of . . . Jezebel** (22).
idolatry (RSV harlotries) refers to the ritual
prostitution of Canaanite fertility worship;
witchcraft either to the rise of wizards and
augurs or to the seduction of Jezebel's 'cult of
softness'. With a final shout of **Treachery** (23),
Joram sank in his chariot. Jehu recalled the
oracle **I will make you pay for it on this
plot of ground** (26) and disposed of the body
accordingly.

**27. Ahaziah . . . fled up the road to Beth
Haggan:** i.e. towards Samaria, but after being
wounded by the pursuers he was taken NE to
Megiddo and died. NIV **'Kill him too!' They
wounded him** follows one variant of the text
(see RSVmg). Another variant has '"Him too!"
and they shot him'. (Verse 29 is an unexplained
intrusion into the story and conflicts with 8:
25.)

News of the murder of the kings must
quickly have reached Jezreel. Jezebel's careful
cosmetic preparations (v. 30) are puzzling. Perhaps, like Marie Antoinette, she had no idea of
popular feeling against her, or else resolved to
die fiercely and majestically. There is bitter
sarcasm in her **'Have you come in peace,
Zimri?'** (see 1 Kg. 16: 9–20; Zimri reigned
only a week). But Jehu's burning intensity
'Who is on my side? Who?' (32) drew the

unexpected support of the **eunuchs** and she fell to an ignominious and ghastly end. **34. Jehu went in** to eat and drink—not only a sign of callous indifference to an afternoon's bloodshed, but a seal of agreement with his followers and presumably local people who joined in the meal. It is significant that no one stirred in support of the hated Ahab dynasty. When the rough soldier remembers the due of **a king's daughter**, it is too late and the gruesome **word of the LORD** has been fulfilled (vv. 35–37).

The purge in Samaria (10: 1–28)
Samaria remained the capital and could withstand long siege, so Jehu resorted to a double guile. He plays upon the rulers' shock at news of the regicide and challenges them to **fight for your master's house** (3). Predictably, they weaken and offer parley. His terms are brutally carried out. At the gate of Jezreel with mock humility he admits '**It was I who conspired against my master . . . but who killed all these?**' combining both apparent Samaritan support and prophetic word (v. 10).

1. There were seventy sons of the house of Ahab: i.e. descendants. **2. your master's sons**: Ahab's grandchildren; the whole royal house would be covered by the term. Seventy is a conventional form for an indefinite large number (*e.g.* Jg. 8: 30). It is unlikely that v. 6 is a subtle ambiguity—**heads** could mean 'chief', i.e., bring the oldest sons—since in v. 8 Jehu clearly understands literal **heads. 6. the leading men of the city** were responsible for training the princes, and showed the cynical opportunism to be expected of those who learned their statecraft from Ahab and Jezebel (contrast the heroism of Jehosheba, 11: 2). Jehu, standing between the piles of heads at Jezreel, shows a macabre genius for frightfulness as a weapon. His blood-thirst extends beyond **the house of Ahab** to **all his chief men** (Gk. 'kinsmen') and even **friends** and **priests**. As Jezreel reeled under the shock, leaderless and numb, Jehu **set out and went toward Samaria** (12).

On his way to Samaria Jehu met **some relatives of Ahaziah**, apparently unaware of the recent happenings, and massacred them too (v. 14). He also **came upon Jehonadab son of Recab** (apparently alone since he joined Jehu in his chariot, v. 15b). Jer. 35 preserves the tradition of the Recabites and their style of life. In showing his **zeal for the LORD** (16) Jehu probably hoped to rally the support of the country people with whom the gentle Recabites may have had influence. On his arrival at Samaria, however, he showed himself in a totally different light, not as a religious reformer but as an ambitious usurper prepared to **serve** Baal **much** (18). With terrifying single-minded fanaticism that keeps no faith with heretics, Jehu lures **prophets, priests** and

ministers of Baal to their death, carrying his treachery even to the point of **making the burnt offering** (25). Such fanatical leadership never lacks its **eighty men** to do the killing and avenge outraged patriotism or religious feeling against the tyrant and renegade. **26. they brought the sacred stone** (*MT* 'pillars') **out . . . and burned it:** Baal shrines contained a stone pillar (*maṣṣēbāh*) and an Asherah (sacred tree or pole). Gray points out that 'the simplest way to shatter a massive piece of stone was to heat it and then throw water over it.'

Verdict on Jehu (10: 28–36)
28. So Jehu destroyed Baal worship: the judgment was efficient—even too efficient. (Cf. note on 1 Kg. 16: 7b and the judgment for 'the massacre at Jezreel' in Hos. 1: 4. The same principle is shown in Zech. 1: 15. Sinful men are intemperate agents of divine judgment.) But there was no healing, no positive turn to Yahweh. In spite of the guarded approval, **you have done well** (30), **the golden calves** remained, **the sins of Jeroboam son of Nebat, which he had caused Israel to commit sin** (29, 31) still did their deadly schismatic work, mixing Yahweh with natural forces and keeping the people from the (generally) purer worship of Jerusalem. The Phoenician Melkart Baal may have taken a knock but, as Amos shows, nature worship and attendant social evils were unchecked. The dwindling territory of Israel (v. 32; see on 1 Kg. 19: 17) under Syrian pressure was a symbol of decreasing spiritual strength. Jehu had stamped out one open evil; he had killed most of Israel's leaders in the process, and his **twenty-eight years** (36) were all too short to make good the damage. And as for stamping out the name of Baal, fifty years later people were still giving their children names linked with Baal nearly as often as names linked with Yahweh (witnessed by the Samaritan Ostraca, *NBD* p. 927). As the four-generation respite (v. 30) expired, and Hosea began his troubled prophecy, the calf-worshippers were well back in business at Samaria and Bethel (Hos. 8: 5; 10: 5).

Joash King of Judah (11: 1–12: 21)
11: 1. Athaliah the mother of Ahaziah was moved not only by maternal anger but by political opportunism. She all but succeeded in exterminating the Davidic line and, alone of northerners, was not overawed by the steady fulfilment of the promised stable dynasty in Judah (cf. Jehoash's gentler use of victory in 14: 13). **2. Jehosheba** (probably **the daughter of King Jehoram** by another wife) had survived one calamity (2 Chr. 22: 1) and now took the grave risk of defying the rampageous queen mother. She **took Joash** and hid him **at the temple of the LORD for six years** (3). 2 Chr. 22: 11 says she was wife of Jehoiada and so lived with her charge, without suspicion, in

the temple. **Athaliah ruled the land** in angry impotence, past childbearing herself and with no one of Ahab's line to import from Israel since Jehu had killed them all—and more. **4. In the seventh year:** when Jehoiada considered the time ripe, the hidden king was displayed. **the Carites** (mercenary troops from Cilicia) were **put under oath** and shown **the king's son**. The time chosen was **the Sabbath** (5) when the change-round of the three sections of the guard meant all would be available and and also all could move to their defensive positions without attracting notice. It was now also a time (possibly festival) when **the people of the land** were present in force (14)—landowning countrymen who were the 'silent majority' of nominal Yahwists. **10. the spears and shields that had belonged to King David** may refer to the ritual of 1 Kg. 14: 28. Onlookers would expect a royal visit from the palace to the temple to follow these preparations. The troops **stationed themselves . . . from the south side to the north side of the temple** (11) in a semicircle making it safe for Jehoiada to bring **out the king's son** (12). The king-making is given in detail. After giving the **crown** (*nezer* from root 'to separate', i.e. symbol of consecration to service of God and people) and **a copy of the covenant** (binding the new king to the national covenant in the spirit of Dt. 17: 18) he is **proclaimed** and **anointed** and hailed with **'Long live the king!'** The new king was **standing by the pillar** (one of the dynastic pillars Jakin and Boaz at the temple entrance; see on 1 Kg. 7: 21) **as the custom was** (14). **Athaliah** realized too late what was happening and went to her death. **17. Jehoiada then made a covenant** (Heb. 'the covenant' suggests this too was part of the custom; cf. 1 Sam. 12: 14): a three-way covenant **between the LORD and the king and people** and **between the king and the people**. So the tyrannous rule of Athaliah was replaced with the traditional Hebrew 'king under Yahweh'. **18. the temple of Baal** was torn down and **the priest of Baal** killed, more (it is to be feared) in a fit of nationalist frenzy destroying tokens of the hated tyranny than a genuine repudiation of nature worship (see below on 12: 3). Still there was only token bloodshed by comparison with the northern massacre (which was equally superficial). So the new king was installed in **the palace** and **took his place on the royal throne** (19), the final act of the ceremony (cf. 1 Kg. 1: 46). **20. all the people of the land rejoiced** that their ancient rights had been reaffirmed. It had been a risky day's work, but **the city was quiet**. The supporters of the old palace regime realized they had been outwitted. **11: 21. Joash did what was right in the eyes of the LORD . . .** because **Jehoiada the priest instructed him**

(12: 2; 2 Chr. 24: 17–25 tells a sad story of decline when the godly influence ceased). **3. high places** (see note on 1 Kg. 3: 2) were not regarded as illegal at this time but remained a constant snare. It was all too easy to slip into the nature and fertility rituals the Canaanites had practised for centuries at such shrines. Reforms in the temple did not always mean pure ethical monotheism at the outlying shrines.

The temple repaired (12: 4–16)
Joash took advantage of the priests' dilatoriness to get temple finances into his own hands. At first he instructed the priests to **repair . . . the temple** (5) out of **the money collected . . . received from personal vows . . . brought voluntarily** shows the variety of source. RSV follows an emendation: 'for which each man is assessed' which suggests a more formal arrangement. If dues were paid in money rather than kind the cash value must be agreed. *MT* gives simply 'the money which is brought . . .'). **5. every priest from one of the treasurers:** Gray suggests *each from his assessor* to match the earlier amendment and avoid any restriction to family or acquaintance. However **by the twenty-third year** they had **not repaired the temple** (6) and Joash took affairs into his own hands. **8. the priests . . . would not collect any more money** and **not repair the temple. 9. A chest** was set up to receive the money which was **counted** ('weighed', there was no coin at the time) by **the royal secretary and the high priest:** an early example of bureaucratic security happily offset by the honest **workmen** with whom no **accounting** was necessary, for **they acted with complete honesty**, a simple virtue which gave them an unexpected but undying memorial. The priests were not allowed to use the money for **any articles of gold or silver** (13) which might have left a loophole for fraud, but did retain their right to the **money from guilt offerings and sin offerings** (16; see Lev. 5: 16; offerings now in money, not kind). The story does the priests no credit, though the king may have been less than single-minded in his reaction.

Hazael's invasion and Joash's death (12: 17–21)
17. Hazael had made inroads against Jehu's Israel (10: 32–33) and now strengthened his rear before confronting the Assyrians on his northern border. His foray against **Jerusalem** seems rather half-hearted and he is easily bought off (18). 2 Chr. 24: 17–25 relates Joash's death to this incident and events arising from it, but here no cause is given for the conspiracy. **20. His officials** must have been agents of some enemy within the state, who were however unable to overturn the royal house (see 14: 5) **and Amaziah his son succeeded him as king** (21).

Jehoahaz king of Israel (13: 1–9)
The butchered and ennervated kingdom **Jehu**
left to his son **Jehoahaz** lay at the mercy of
Syria. The most energetic and godly of princes
would have been hard pressed to survive, and
Jehoahaz was neither. **2. He did evil in the
eyes of the LORD**, allowing, as his father had
done, the original snares of **Jeroboam**. The
battering from Hazael reduced Israel to little
more than a vassal state. The **fifty horsemen**
and **ten chariots** (7) were just enough to give
the puppet king pathetic pageantry on state
occasions. The reversal of fortune is seen as a
sign of **the LORD's anger** (3) which drove the
king to repentance. The parenthesis (vv. 5, 6)
preserves a tradition of help in response to his
repentance and Yahweh's concern for Israel.
The **deliverer** (5) may relate to the participation of Elisha referred to in 6: 8–23, or indirectly to the rise of Assyrian power under
Adad-nirari, but political reprieve produced no
deep religious reform (6). **5. the Israelites
lived in their own homes** (JB, AV, 'tents' is
more accurate) indicates sufficient security for
farmers to leave the protection of walled towns
and live by their fields in open country. But
the whole religious and social structure of the
country was tied to **the sins of the house of
Jeroboam** (i.e. shrines at Bethel and Dan) and
the **Asherah** which had apparently survived
Jehu's purge (10: 26 f.) remained.

**Jehoash (Joash) king of Israel (13: 10–14:
16)**
Information from various sources is woven
together, with some overlap (13: 12 f. repeated
at 14: 15 f.) to give an account of Israel's improving fortunes.

**10. the thirty-seventh year of Joash king
of Judah** (cf. 13: 1; 14: 1) suggests Jehoash
became co-regent at this time. Greek versions
make various attempts to harmonize the dates.
See above on 2: 19 for possible relation of
earlier incidents (6: 24–7: 20 and 5: 1–27) to
this period. **11. the sins of Jeroboam** still
provide the setting for this modest recovery,
so that there is a slightly ominous tone even
about the records of success (and see below on
v. 23).

14. Elisha is clearly a respected figure, perhaps in view of the incidents of 7: 1–20, and in
extreme old age he retains his prophetic vigour.
The chariots . . . of Israel . . . : recalls the
victorious title of Elijah (2: 12) and shows the
king's reverence—*You* are the source of Israel's
victory. Although Elisha was the symbol of
Israel's rejection (1 Kg. 19: 17) he yet put
responsibility firmly on the rulers. With **his
hands on the king's hands** (16) he sends **the
LORD's arrow of victory** speeding towards
Aram (17). But left to himself the king strikes
only three times (18) and earns the prophet's
rebuke. Elisha's passionate anger against

Yahweh's enemies (19) found little echo in the
politically conditioned mind of the king. A
subservient Syria might be useful. If he **completely destroyed it** there would be no buffer
between Israel and Assyria.

20. Elisha died, after half a century of loyal
service to Yahweh and despairing love to his
people, **and was buried**. The ensuing miracle
story is given without comment and its significance is uncertain. Perhaps the suggestion is that
Elisha's departing was, in its own way, as
remarkable as his master Elijah's. Raids by
Moabites indicate a grave in the Jericho area.
every spring: *MT* is difficult. JB gives 'every
year'. Gray gives 'at the end of the year' when
raiders were more likely to find harvest.

Verse 22 takes up the story after the interruption by the Elisha material, so JB 'Hazael . . .
had oppressed' correctly gives the pluperfect
force of Heb. The respite is because the LORD
was gracious to them and had compassion,
not (as 8: 19) for the sake of David, but because
of **his covenant with Abraham, Isaac and
Jacob** (23)—an important sign that the earlier
covenant with the patriarchs still applied to
Israel even in schism, and also that this covenant was a firm part of the tradition in the time
of the monarchy. **To this day** (omitted in
LXX) may be a later addition in view of the
deportation to Assyria. Many interpreters hold
that the patriarchal covenant was not broken
even by that calamity, or any of the following
2700 years, and understand Rom. 11: 15–22
accordingly.

24. Hazael . . . died: the last of the trio of
judgment pronounced in 1 Kg. 19: 16 f. Jehu's
intemperate zeal had torn the institutional vitals
from Israel; Elisha had established the idea of
a remnant in place of the religiously flavoured
nationalism of popular false hope; Hazael's battering had done greater apparent but less real
damage than these. Jeroboam II's long, seemingly prosperous rule, could be no more than
a stay of final execution.

Ben-Hadad either endured defeat at the
hands of Assyria or, more likely, inherited
the results of such a disaster from Hazael. (If
throughout the reign of Jehoahaz, v. 22, is
taken literally, Hazael must have survived until
798 after nearly 50 years of harrying Israel. On
the other hand there is a record of Jehoahaz
paying tribute to Adadnirari in 803 and Damascus suffered in the same Assyrian campaign.)
Hence **Jehoash . . . recaptured . . . the
towns** (25) and set Israel on the road to temporary recovery.

Amaziah king of Judah (14: 1–22)
The story of **Amaziah the son of Joash king
of Judah** is introduced with the normal formula but much of the material (8–14) carries
on the story of Jehoash of Israel from 13: 25.
If Joash's assassins (12: 20) hoped for a change

of policy they were disappointed. Although only 25 and sadly headstrong on occasion (v. 8) he established himself and **in everything he followed the example of his father Joash** (3). The historian is careful to point out that this was **not as David had done** and the **high places** still posed the fateful risk to true worship (4). It was apparently some time before he had **the kingdom . . . firmly in his grasp** (5) and then avenged his father on the assassins. The limit to vengeance (v. 6) was remarkable at the time. The reference to **the Law of Moses** (cf. Dt. 24: 16) is not to be lightly set aside as an editorial addition. Such humane treatment in time of crisis required a compelling basis and an ancient standard, often forgotten, shows through here. 2 Chr. 25 gives a much better account of the events summarized here and helps explain Amaziah's naïve challenge to Israel. The victory in **the Valley of Salt** (7; cf. 2 Sam. 8: 13) is described in the brief language of a formal annal without explaining its exact place or intention. If Amaziah was trying to free the way to Elath he was only partly successful as v. 22 ascribes that feat to his son.

Verse 8 resumes the story from a northern point of view, mildly contemptuous of Amaziah's challenge. **8. Meet me face to face:** an invitation to trial of strength (11), not simply a parley. Possibly a representative struggle was intended rather than a full-scale battle (as 1 Sam. 17: 8 f. and 2 Sam. 2: 14). **9. Jehoash . . . replied** in a scornful parable to avoid the confrontation. **10. Glory in your victory:** one word in Heb. capable of sarcastic overtones; cf. same verb in 2 Sam. 6: 20. The tone might be conveyed by 'Splendid!', or more exactly the contemptuous slang 'Big deal!' The sarcastic tone did not help and **Amaziah would not listen** (11). **Beth Shemesh (in Judah** distinguishes it from the northern town (Jos. 19: 38)) was about 15 miles W of Jerusalem and an important fortress on the Judah–Philistine border. It commanded the Vale of Sorek giving access from the coastal plain to Jerusalem. **12. Judah was routed**, Amaziah taken captive, and a token 200 yards of Jerusalem's wall dismantled. **14. He took all the gold and silver and all the articles . . . in the temple of the LORD:** 'Pillaging sanctuaries was just another custom of war' (de Vaux) but the fact that Jehoash was not afraid to do so in Jerusalem shows how far the sins of Jeroboam had moved the north from reverence for the ancient national shrine. But neither Jehoash nor Jehu before him pressed their advantage to overthrow the Davidic dynasty.

Verse 17 resumes the Judah story with mention of Amaziah's last **fifteen years**. Like his father, he fell to a conspiracy. His disastrous challenge and resulting loss of temple treasures

would have set both people and priests against him. In spite of flight to **Lachish** (19) he was assassinated and **Azariah** (= Uzziah, 15: 13 etc.) began his sole reign with the successful retrieval of **Elath** (22). The **sixteen years old** (21) must refer to his age on assuming co-regency in 791. When his father left him as sole ruler, Azariah was 40.

Jeroboam II King of Israel (14: 23–29)
Once again the prophetic priorities of the historian are clearly seen. Like the politically successful Omri (1 Kg. 16: 21–28), **Jeroboam son of Joash** gets short mention for his long and outwardly prosperous reign. The writer saves his space for more significant things like the obituary for Israel in ch. 17. **23. became king** refers to his sole reign and the forty-one years includes a ten-year co-regency with his father. **25. the boundaries of Israel** reached the former limits of David's glorious kingdom; **from Lebo [the entrance of** (or to)**] Hamath to the Sea of the Arabah** is here the proud measure of nationalistic success, but Amos was already pronouncing an equal doom (Am. 6: 14). How **Jonah . . . the prophet from Gath Hepher** (not far from Nazareth) came to prophesy this expansion or what terms were attached, we can only guess but a further reference is made to Yahweh's compassion (cf. 13: 23) which Jonah was less happy to see later applied to Assyria (Jon. 4). So even though **he did evil in the eyes of the LORD** (24) Jeroboam became Yahweh's deliverer and the unfruitful tree was spared yet longer. Politically the respite was due to Assyria's preoccupation elsewhere after crushing Syria. **28. he recovered for Israel both Damascus and Hamath, which had belonged to Yaudi:** NIV's guess at a difficult phrase. JB leaves a blank, 'how he . . . is not all this recorded'; NEB gives emendation to 'Hamath in Jaudi'. Both cities had owned David's rule. Damascus was a separate power when Amos spoke (Am. 1: 3) so the **recovered**, if correct, may refer to trading rights only. So **Jeroboam rested with his fathers** (29) and we are left to get further detail elsewhere. From the archaeologist's finds we know of Samaria's wealth and from Amos its oppression. As in Judah, so in Israel, monarchy had produced wealthy royal retainers and a class of *nouveaux riches* who exploited the poor until the class division was beyond peaceful healing (see de Vaux, p. 73). Religion was the lackey of the state. Rebuke was not welcome at the king's sanctuary (Am. 7: 13).

Azariah (Uzziah) king of Judah (15: 1–7)
Again a long and important reign is dismissed in few sentences. de Vaux suggests that **Azariah** was his birth name and Uzziah (v. 13) his coronation name (cf. Jer. 22: 11, Shallum for Jehoahaz of 2 Kg. 23: 34). The **fifty-two years** (2) included 24 as co-regent and 28 in his sole

right (767–740). He took his son Jotham as co-regent in 750 and it seems his grandson Ahaz took some responsibility in 744 possibly on Azariah's withdrawal from public life when he became a leper (5). **3. he did what was right:** making a unique hat-trick of 'good' kings, though each with the reservation about **high places. 5. the LORD afflicted the king:** but the details are not given here (see 2 Chr. 26: 16–21). **he lived in a separate house:** Gray prefers 'released from obligations'. The small palace discovered between Jerusalem and Bethlehem was thought a possible site but later excavations deny this. **Jotham had charge of the palace and governed** as co-regent. 2 Chr. 26: 6–15 also gives more details of Azariah's military and building exploits. Like Israel during this period, Judah enjoyed relief from outside pressure and was able to rebuild fortress and fortune.

The collapse of Israel (15: 8–31)
The house of Jehu met its inglorious end in **Zechariah son of Jeroboam** (8). After a mere **six months** of doing **evil in the eyes of the LORD** (9) he was struck down by **Shallum** (10). So the prophecies of Hos. 1: 4 f. and 2 Kg. 10: 30 (see v. 12) found their fulfilment. **10. In front of the people:** follows *MT* LXX in Ibleam (NIV fn) would make the retribution on Jehu's house even sharper (9: 27).

13. Shallum son of Jabesh: 'the son of a nobody' according to Assyrian records and so some regard **Jabesh** as place rather than person. He does not even get the usual assessment of good or bad on his one month (Heb. 'a month of days'='a full month', as AV, perhaps in mild scorn). He met his own violent end at the hand of **Menahem . . . from Tirzah** (14), the former capital. Menahem's barbarous treatment of **Tiphsah** (following *MT* but Tiphsah on Euphrates is unlikely. RSV follows Gk Tappuah a town a few miles from Tirzah). Gray suggests that the town was Shallum's home district. Alternatively, since Tirzah (Manasseh) and Tappuah (Ephraim) were on opposite sides of the tribal boundary, this may reflect inter-tribal struggle (see Isa. 9: 19–21) which followed the breakdown of Jehu's dynasty. This terror seems to have established Menahem's rule over **Israel** west of Jordan though **Pekah** (v. 25) may have exercised virtual kingship over Gilead on the east and dated his reign from the same time as Menahem—if his **twenty years** (27) are to be accommodated within the chronology. Within his diminished territory Menahem clung to **the sins of Jeroboam son of Nebat** (18). His already shaky kingdom suffered a further shock with the rise of **Pul king of Assyria** (=Tiglath-Pileser of v. 29), a vigorous and ruthless ruler who revived Assyrian strength in the west and led to Israel's final defeat. He appears as Pulu in the Babylonian

king list.' Pul's tactics show a change in Assyrian methods since the calculated brutality and terror of Adadnirari and his predecessors. Deportation rather than massacre became the lot of the defeated. So great a change requires a powerful cause and Ellison suggests Nineveh's narrow escape from destruction by the Urartu at the time of Jonah's prophecy. Assyria, he says, had been tempered into 'a rod that would chastise and not exterminate'. Pul's inscriptions mention tribute from Menahem, though the date is uncertain. Menahem appears to have acted in advance of direct demand so that the Assyrian king might help him to **strengthen his hold on the kingdom**. As is the manner of tyrants, Menahem extracted this bribe by taxation of **every wealthy man** (i.e. men of property—about 60,000 of them if a **talent**=3000 shekels). **20. So the king of Assyria withdrew** and Menahem died in peace.

23. Pekahiah . . . reigned two years with the now customary **evil** assessment. The only recorded event of his reign was its end, as **Pekah . . . one of his chief officers** took his chance, **conspired . . . , assassinated** him and **succeeded him as king** (25). So six 'kings' ruled in thirteen years and three died violently. Hosea's words 'they devour their rulers . . . and none of them calls on me' vividly describe those violent days and set the scene of his own sad life and prophecy (Hos. 7: 7). The uncertainty, corruption and treachery of these days are movingly depicted in Hosea and the final disintegration is rehearsed as a warning to Judah in Isa. 9: 8–10: 4.

Pekah's coup, cheaply and unexpectedly accomplished with only **fifty men . . . in the citadel at Samaria**, marked a rejection of Menahem's pro-Assyrian policy. The historian does not give here the detail of the Syro-Israelite attempt to induce Judah to join the anti-Assyrian league (but see below on v. 37 and 16: 5), but mentions its failure (29). Pekah receives the customary condemnation for **evil** and **the sins of Jeroboam** (28). In 734 **Tiglath Pileser** (Pul of v. 19) overran **Gilead and Galilee** leaving a trail of fire and destruction witnessed in archaeological finds, *e.g.*, at **Hazor** (29). **he deported the people to Assyria:** see above on v. 19 for this change in Assyrian tactics. With his anti-Assyrian policy in ruins Pekah was assassinated by **Hoshea son of Elah** (30) whose political vacillations (17: 1–6) brought the final destruction to Israel.

Jotham and Ahaz kings of Judah (15: 32–16: 20)
Uzziah (Azariah) had lived through many years of peace and reconstruction. His death was ominously marked by Isaiah's call to prophesy doom (Isa. 6: 1, 11) and **Jotham son of Uzziah** took control in dangerous times (32). The **sixteen years** are hard to fit into the

chronology (see 15: 30) and show some overlap with his father. **34. he did what was right in the eyes of the LORD:** the fourth generation of relative virtue (35). The brief record notes only his temple improvements (35) and the storm brewing in the north (v. 37). 2 Chr. 27: 3 f. mentions his defence preparations. Perhaps all was not as **right** in Judah as Jotham was, for we are told that **the LORD began to send** the marauders and certainly this crisis showed the faithlessness of Judah. The fateful hour found the young and intransigent **Ahaz** on the throne. His refusal to listen to Isaiah's advice is vividly recorded in Isa. 7: 1–8: 8. His Davidic lineage (16: 2) is contrasted with his conduct —like **the kings of Israel** (3). He is specially condemned because **he even sacrificed his son in the fire** (3). It has been debated whether these ancient Canaanite **detestable ways** were token dedication—'to pass through the fire' (3, NIV footnote) being analogous to passing through the water of baptism—but Jer. 19: 5 uses more direct language and see 2 Kg. 3: 27. Ahaz reacted to political peril with the most awesome religious ritual Jerusalem had ever seen—perhaps the frightful flowering of the seed planted by Solomon (1 Kg. 11: 7 and 2 Kg. 23: 10).

5. Rezin and Pekah were attempting to force **Ahaz** to join an alliance against Assyria, a piece of unrealistic nonsense-politics which, as Isaiah foresaw, was bound to fail (Isa. 7: 16–20). Ahaz was also under pressure in the south at **Elath** (6). The text has suffered, as **Aram** and Edom differ only slightly in Heb. and copyists have tried to make sense. (RSV gives 'the king of Edom recovered Elath for Edom') But if Judah was so weakened by attacks N. of Jerusalem **Rezin, king of Aram** could well have pushed down the Transjordan and captured **Elath for Aram** and let the **Edomites** live there under Syrian protection. The RSV emendation to *MT* suggests that Edomites themselves took advantage of Ahaz's trouble to regain the port. In this predicament **Ahaz sent messengers to Tiglath-Pileser** (7). His abject plea **I am your servant** and his **gift** (8) broke the long tradition of Judah's independence and isolation. From this time religious corruption in Jerusalem is linked with political vassalage. **9. the king of Assyria complied:** he was about to march anyway—and destroyed **Damascus**, deporting the survivors, and ravaged Israel (15: 29) and left Hoshea as his puppet in Samaria (15: 30; 17: 1). **10. King Ahaz went to Damascus:** to offer his submission and accept the Assyrian terms. The **new altar** after the Damascus **plan** was not a passing fancy but a symbol of vassalage. Politics and religion were closely linked. Yahweh, it was understood, bowed to Ashur as Ahaz to Tiglath-Pileser. Yahweh was not banished from his

temple but shared it with the victor's gods. The consecration of the new altar is given with detail which illustrates the sacrificial practice of the monarchy times: **burnt offering** ('ōlāh), **grain offering** (minḥāh), **drink offering** (nesek) and **fellowship offerings** (šelem) all feature in the cultic law (*e.g.* Exod. 29: 28–42; Lev. 1–3; 23) but now are offered on an alien altar. **14. the bronze altar** (see on 1 Kg. 8: 22, 64) **he brought** to **the north side** and relegated it to use in divination (**for seeking guidance**, 15), another Assyrian practice. **17. the sea** was remounted in **stone**, **the bronze bulls** being removed, possibly for tribute. Alterations in the palace and the temple entrance were also demanded by Assyria as tokens of demotion to subject-status. **18. the Sabbath canopy** is not elsewhere mentioned (JB gives 'the dais for the throne') but its removal probably showed further loss of royal privilege. The sad reversal of Judah's fortune after four God-fearing kings fulfilled Isaiah's direct warnings (Isa. 7: 17). Its effect on **Hezekiah his son** (20), who became co-regent in 729, was profound. But first we are given the last history of Israel and its obituary.

The fall and judgment of Israel (17: 1–41)

1. Hoshea son of Elah, the conspirator of 15: 30, **reigned nine years**, playing uneasy and futile politics. **the twelfth year of Ahaz** (see 15: 30) suggests that in some reckonings Ahaz's reign was dated from 745/4 (see above on 15: 2; Gray emends the text here to 'second', understanding a co-regency from 734). **2. he did evil . . . but not like the kings of Israel who preceeded him:** though we are not told in what way he improved. Dan was beyond his power, but there is no evidence to show that Bethel or Samaria improved religiously. **3. Shalmaneser king of Assyria** succeeded in 727. **Hoshea had been his vassal and had paid him tribute** as he had to Tiglath Pileser. A revival of Egyptian influence after long quiescence gave the drowning Israelites a straw to grasp but **So, king of Egypt** (now thought to be Osorkon IV) was a false hope (4). Hosea (7: 11; 12: 1) bitingly comments on the folly of the tiny Samaritan enclave pretending to negotiate. Hoshea **no longer paid tribute**, following the example set by Phoenician cities who hoped the change of Assyrian king would stop the westward pressure. Shalmaneser reacted punitively and Hoshea was **put in prison**, probably after he left Samaria to plead his case to the king. The kingless Samaritans held out for **three years** (5)—a tribute to Omri's skill in selecting the site and Ahab's in fortifying it —but were finally overcome and the leaders deported. Shalmaneser died during the siege, so Sargon claimed the victory and says he deported 27,290 inhabitants, leaving 'the rest' with a 'governor over them'.

7. All this took place because the Israelites had sinned: summarizing the writer's philosophy of history. Behind all the economic, social and political factors he sees the inevitable result of cultic corruption (8–12) and the neglect of **his decrees and the covenant** (15) with their healthy concern for social justice. More significant than Assyrian force of arms was the failure to live **in accordance with the entire Law** (13). Solomon had built Jerusalem's splendid temple but pandered to his alien wives' paganism (1 Kg. 11: 7 f.; v. 8b may refer to him among others), halting between two opinions. Jeroboam I claimed that his new cult was a fresh expression of the Exodus covenant (1 Kg. 12: 28) but in fact he **enticed** (or seduced) **Israel away from following the LORD** (21). His **two idols cast in the shape of calves** (16) had more in common with nature worship than with **the LORD their God, who had brought them up out of Egypt** (7) and led on to the excesses of v. 17—here ascribed to North as well as South (**all the starry hosts** refers to Assyrian practice, but is mentioned in Am. 5: 26 in his protest against the north).

Judah (13, 18 f.) should have learnt but the later editor notes (19 f.) that they fell eventually to the same judgment.

24. the king of Assyria followed the new practice of resettling conquered lands. This provided for gradual mixing of race and the erosion of national desire to revolt. The **lions** are interpreted (25 f.) as judgment because the new settlers did **not know what the god of that country requires**, so **one of the priests** was sent (or 'some priests', to agree with *MT* 'them'; see RSVmg, v. 27) to **teach them what the god of the land requires** at **Bethel**. The result was the mixture recorded in vv. 29–41.

33. they worshiped the LORD, but they also served their own gods: an epitaph for many societies since their day too. So arose the Samaritans, derided and despised by orthodox Jews (whom Jesus used to warn against a parallel confusion, Mt. 6: 24) but fiercely proud of their link with Moses and their version of the Pentateuch (see *NBD*, pp. 1131 f.).

IV. THE KINGDOM OF JUDAH ALONE (18: 1–25: 30)

Judah survived, albeit as Assyrian vassal, and had another 130 years of chequered history. During this time Assyrian power waned and finally passed to Babylon (612 and 605). Revival under Hezekiah and Josiah are religious bright spots in an otherwise gloomy record. More political detail is given so that the last 130 years of Judah gets more space than the previous 200 years.

Hezekiah's reign (18: 1–20: 21)

The **third year of Hoshea** (729 BC) must be the start of Hezekiah's co-regency and dates in vv. 1 and 9 start from then. **The twenty-nine years** (2) must refer to his sole reign from 716–687. The **fourteenth year** of v. 13 refers to his sole reign (i.e. 701 BC).

Verses 3–8 give a brief summary of his reign before the much fuller account (18: 13–19: 37) of how **he rebelled against the king of Assyria** (7). **He did . . . just as his father David had done** (3) without qualification since even the **high places** were removed, along with **the sacred stones** and **Asherah poles**, symbols of Canaanite religion. Even **the bronze snake Moses had made** was broken to end superstitious reverence (4). **it was called Nehushtan** (= bronze): so RSV, JB. NEB give 'they called it . . .', following Gk. *MT* gives sing. 'he called', as NIV fn. more likely as giving Hezekiah's comment 'It's only bronze, not god.' **5, 6. He trusted in the LORD . . . he held fast to the LORD:** reflect inner attitude, as **kept the command** reflect the outward result. **7. the LORD was with him** (as with Joseph, Gen. 39: 21 f.) and he prospered as witness his rebellion against Assyria and his defeat of the Philistines. 2 Chr. 29 elaborates on the reform. Isa. 20 and 30: 1–7 show the prophet's attempt to stop Hezekiah meddling in politics, especially with Egypt (a ten-year flirtation that nearly proved fatal). Sennacherib's own inscription shows that Hezekiah's attack on Philistia was connected with this intrigue and resulted in Padi king of Ekron being temporarily imprisoned in Jerusalem. The exact date when **he rebelled against the king of Assyria** is not given but the beginning of Sennacherib's reign saw him coping with rebellion in Babylonia (hence connection with Merodach-Baladan, 20: 12) and in Palestine, so it may have been then that the fateful decision was taken to refuse tribute.

Verses 9–12 rehearse the fall of Samaria briefly from Judah's annals, with the same moral as before: **they neither listened . . . nor carried . . . out** (12).

The defence of Jerusalem (18: 13–19: 37)

13. Sennacherib's attack **against all the fortified cities of Judah** took place in 701 and is described in lordly terms in his inscription. The Kings story emphasizes Yahweh's preservation of his city of Zion against the pagan invader and so gives only brief mention of the disaster in which it was set (13–16). Hezekiah's policy may have been religiously commendable and nationally heroic but it cost Judah dear. **Sennacherib . . . captured them** (13) covers the sorrow of the 'forty-six of his strong walled cities and innumerable smaller villages' mentioned in the inscription and of the host of captives. **Lachish** (14) features in a carving, on the palace wall at Nineveh, showing the city burning and the victorious king receiving homage.

Debate continues on ch. 18. Some suggest vv. 13–16 recount Sennacherib's 701 campaign and postulate a later siege in 688 referred to in 18: 17–19: 37. A single campaign can, however, be matched with all references, and v. 17 then shows a change of heart (or an act of treachery) by Sennacherib who, having received the tribute (16), turns again to demand entry to the city. The beleaguered citizens are stung by the treachery and so the earlier 'I have done wrong' (14) changes to fierce resistance. They had already improved their defences with the engineering feat of the new tunnel (20: 20) by which he brought water into the city.

17. the king of Assyria sent his supreme commander (the 'Tartan'), his chief officer (the Rabsaris) and his field commander (the 'Rabshakeh') to overawe the city. The section 18: 17–20: 19 is duplicated in Isa. 36: 1–38: 8 and 39: 1–8 where only the field commander, Rabshakeh, is mentioned. The speech is a model of pompous hectoring and abuse. 19. Say to Hezekiah (without any title) contrasts with the great king, the king of Assyria. Reliance on Egypt he quite reasonably ridicules. Reliance on the LORD he underrates—and misunderstands Hezekiah's purge of the high places (22), or subtly appeals to those who had been offended at Hezekiah's reform. He even claims Yahweh's authority for his campaign, speaking more truly than he knew (Isa. 10: 5 ff.), and promises the people peace and plenty after submission (31 f.) as have many tyrants since. His final argument (contradicting his third) is that no god is stronger than Assyria and it is impossible that the LORD could deliver Jerusalem (35). The people respond with silence (36), the courtiers with horror (their clothes torn, 37) and the king with humiliation in the temple and appeal to Isaiah (pray, 19: 4). His main concern is for the living God whom the field commander has mocked (4). Although Isaiah had criticized Hezekiah's politics and could have said 'I told you so', he sends a message of hope and prophesies judgment on Assyrian arrogance. 7. he hears a certain report: fulfilled in what Sennacherib received of Tirhakah the Cushite king . . . (9). It is now agreed (pace Bright, who held his 688 campaign theory partly on account of Tirhakah's youth) that Tirhakah was old enough to lead an Egyptian army (though he did not rule Egypt till c. 690) and powerful enough to cause Sennacherib to falter. The latter's death in his own country (see 37) happened 20 years later.

Verses 10–13 have been taken as a 'parallel account' to the field comander's speech but can stand as a second message, this time in writing, when the field commander . . . withdrew to Libnah (8) with the news of Jerusalem's defiance. It simply repeats the field commander's final argument: Did the gods of the nations . . . deliver them? (12). Hezekiah's reaction has gone into history as a model of humility and hope as he spread it out before the LORD (14) and prayed with sound theology —they were not gods (18)—and a jealous concern that all . . . may know that you alone, O LORD, are God (19; cf. 5: 15). His confidence is answered by Isaiah's declaration This is what the LORD, the God of Israel says (20), introducing a 'taunt song' in keeping with Isaiah's high view of Yahweh's transcendence as the Holy One of Israel (22). The field commander and his emissaries are cut down to size: your messengers . . . have heaped insults on the LORD (23). The arrogance becomes a tragic irony (cf. Isa. 10: 7–11). 24. I have dried up all the streams of Egypt: so NIV (with RSV) emends MT 'rivers of the fortress', but as Sennacherib had not conquered Egypt at this time, a future 'I will dry up' would be more appropriate. 25. I planned puts the boast of vv. 11–13 in perspective and my hook in your nose (28) becomes a biting judgment in view of Assyrian carvings showing subject kings being led in just this way. A message of encouragement is sealed with a sign ('ôt, sometimes, as 20: 8, but not always, miraculous) that normal growth of field and family would continue. Not more than two harvests would be lost.

It is from this time that the conviction of the inviolability of Jerusalem became de fide. 34. for my sake and for the sake of David my servant was given for hope in a dark day to a godly (if politically unwise) king. It became such a magical talisman that Jeremiah had later to campaign against it (Jer. 7). The dénouement came that night. On the large number (185,000) see NBD, p. 896. Heb. thousand ('eleph) looks very like 'alluph, 'commander', and '185 commanders' would match 2 Chr. 32: 21. Herodotus preserves a tradition of mice attacking the Assyrian camp and nibbling quivers and other equipment. Bubonic plague would fit both stories. All accounts agree that Sennacherib king of Assyria broke camp and withdrew home (36) and was murdered by his sons (37).

20: 1. In those days Hezekiah became ill and in answer to prayer had an extra fifteen years granted (6) which puts this incident at 702/701 just before Sennacherib's invasion. The change in the word of the LORD to Isaiah (1, 5) is directly related to Hezekiah's prayer and shows the Heb. idea of conditional prophecy as distinct from magical foretelling or divination. The healing was thorough, though beyond expectation of normal means (Pliny records the use of figs to draw ulcers) as with the use of oil in Jas 5: 14 f.

Hezekiah could not wait till the third day

(5) and requested a further **sign** (8), causing some commentators to doubt the continuity of the narrative. As with Ahaz (Isa. 7: 11), Isaiah leaves Hezekiah to choose the sign. The king avoids the **simple matter** and asks that **the shadow go back ten steps** (10). This much-disputed happening (see, *e.g.*, B. Ramm, *The Christian View of Science and Scripture*, 1954, pp. 111 ff. for various explanations) was a private sign to Hezekiah, of undisclosed duration. As he watched the **stairway** (Heb. *steps*) **of Ahaz, ten steps** formerly in shadow were illuminated, a vivid sign of extra time being given. It is arguable that, as so often, the prayed-for boon turned sour. The extra years were filled with enduring and making good the Assyrian ravages, and did little to turn the young Manasseh (who became co-regent in 696) from his pro-Assyrian paganism. Would things have been different if he had become a six year old king under his father's courtiers in 702? **12. Merodach-Baladan:** NIV, RSV, JB, NEB follow parallel in Isa. 39: 1; *MT* gives 'Berodach Baladan'. He ruled independently in Babylon from 720 to 709 and for a brief time in 703 before being again driven out by Sennacherib. **At that time** therefore poses a difficulty. A visit from the **messengers** in 711 would fit well with the conspiracies mentioned in Isa. 20 and the reference would be to an earlier occasion when **Hezekiah** had been **ill**. A later approach (701 or later) would indicate further machinations by Merodach-Baladan from his exile in Elam and the title **king of Babylon** then identifies him by his former position. **13. Hezekiah receeived . . . them:** the narrative conveys a pathetic naïveté matched by the tired, submissive comment **there will be peace and security in my lifetime** (19). The judgment (**carried off to Babylon**, 17 f.) has been challenged as later editing. Nineveh would have been more appropriate than Babylon to Hezekiah personally. It may rather be Isaiah's inspired reply to Hezekiah's naïveté: 'Yes, Babylon will revive, but what good will that do to Judah? You are not a valued ally but another fly to the spider.' Isaiah's isolationist policy was theologically based (Yahweh accepted no allies among pagan gods) but alternatives did not make even political sense.

21. Hezekiah rested with his fathers after a controversial and in many ways praiseworthy reign. He joins those whose piety we applaud but whose politics we distrust. To his credit he seems to have attempted some reform of social as well as religious abuse (Jer. 26: 17–19; Micah's protest was largely against exploitation by the rich).

Manasseh and Amon (21: 1–26)
Manesseh's **fifty-five years** (10 as co-regent, 45 as sole ruler) are remembered as the blackest page in all the history (v. 9 and see Jer. 15: 4).

The rise in Assyrian power made it inevitable that he should reverse the anti-Assyrian policy of his father, but the religious reversal was no token acquiescence to the overlord's customs but a hearty return to every kind of paganism. Canaanite **high places . . . altars to Baal . . . an Asherah pole** reappear along with Assyrian worship of the **starry hosts . . . sorcery, divination** and **mediums** (3–6). **6. he sacrificed his own son in the fire** ('passed his son through the fire'; see above on 16: 3) and by his idolatrous innovations desecrated **the temple of . . . the LORD** (7) which had started so hopefully with **David** and **Solomon** and which had just been the focus of Yahweh's deliverance (chs. 18, 19). **The Law . . . Moses gave** (8) was broken and the **prophets** (10)—no names or details survive—forecast complete ruin (11–15). Placed beside **Samaria** or **the house of Ahab** (13) **Jerusalem** now appeared their equal in apostasy and merited equal judgment. Religious apostasy affects other areas of life and it is not surprising that **Manasseh shed so much innocent blood** (16). Though few details have been preserved, the comparison with the northern kingdom, **Samaria** (13, **as Ahab king of Israel had done**), and the phrase **caused Judah to commit** (16), suggest the social evils that went with nature worship there flourished in Judah too. The abuses Micah condemned may have receded under Hezekiah but now returned in full force. Politically, Manasseh's reign was one of steady vassalage. Inscriptions of Esarhaddon and Ashurbanipal record his tribute. 2 Chr. 33: 11 ff. describes a deportation to Assyria and resulting penitence, and a prayer ascribed to him at this time is preserved in the Apocrypha, but the writer of Kings has selected enough (17) to show rampant apostasy and stops only to note his burial **in his palace garden** (18).

Amon his son gets even shorter mention (vv. 19–26). **21. He walked in all the ways of his father** and fell to a conspiracy of his **officials**. This must have been a palace intrigue rather than a popular uprising since **the people of the land** executed vengeance on the conspirators and **made Josiah his son king** (24).

Josiah's reign and reformation (22: 1–23: 30)
22: 1. Josiah . . . became king as Assyrian power was waning. Hence he was able to satisfy both the nationalistic longings of **the people of the land** (21: 24) who wished to throw off the alien yoke, and the religious desire to cleanse Judah of corrupt worship. 2 Chr. 34 describes stages in his reformation, but Kings gives a general approbation that he **walked in all the ways of . . . David** (2) and then goes straight to the events of the **eighteenth year** (3). The king urges forward the repairs to **the temple of the LORD** in terms

reminiscent of Joash's similar enterprise (12: 9–15). In the course of repairs **Hilkiah the high priest** (a rare use of the term in the time of the monarchy; see 25: 18) reports **I have found the Book of the Law** (8)—one of the most disputed documents in Old Testament studies. From the subsequent references and reforms it has been argued that part of Deuteronomy is meant. **8, 11. the Book of the Law:** the phrase occurs at Dt. 28: 61 and Jos. 1: 8. The title **the Book of the Covenant** (23: 2) links it with the Sinai history (Exod. 24: 7). The king's evident surprise and alarm (11) pose the question of the origin of the writing and why it was apparently unknown. Few writers today support de Wette's idea that it was a 'pious fraud' planted by priests wishing to reform the abuses of Manasseh's reign. More plausible are the suggestions (*a*) that Deuteronomy was preserved in the northern kingdom and brought to Jerusalem after the fall of Samaria by a refugee, or (*b*) that it was substantially extant in Samuel's time and some copy was deposited in the temple at the time of its dedication by Solomon (see on 1 Kg. 8: 54–61). Only a limited document is here in question as it was read publicly (11; 23: 2) in relatively short time (see Neh. 8: 3, 13 for a longer performance). Clearly it carried conviction in a way an entirely new composition would not and must have revived memories of ancient laws such as moved Hezekiah and Joash. The king's immediate reaction is alarm—**great is the LORD's anger**—suggesting that Dt. 28 was part of this book (13). Although Zephaniah and Jeremiah were active prophets at this time, he sends to **the prophetess Huldah** and receives a confirmation of judgment tempered by the promise that **your eyes will not see all the disaster** (20). Josiah died violently at Megiddo (23: 29) so **you will be buried in peace** (20) must be interpreted as 'before the final destruction'. An age which has little sense of the entail of sin or corporate responsibility finds Huldah's words harsh. But the Hebrew theology understood well that evil must work out in judgment, though individual repentance (19) might bring personal relief (cf. Jer. 39: 15–18). Nevertheless the response is not fatalism but action. Although reformation would not reverse the judgment it must be attempted out of loyalty to Yahweh (23: 1–3). In solemn concourse **the king stood by the pillar and renewed the covenant in the presence of the LORD** (23: 3). This would have been some time after the finding of the book as the king **called together** the leaders and prepared for his tour of purging and judgment (vv. 4–20) concluding with the **Passover** in the spring (21). The whole venture may have occupied several months. Some of the details reflect the provisions of Deuteronomy: the destruction

of **the Asherah poles** (6, 14), **altars** (12,15), **sacred stones** (14; see Dt. 12: 3); the suppression of **shrine prostitutes** (Heb. masc. pl. *haqqᵉdēshîm*, 7, covers male and female; see on 1 Kg. 14: 24) follows Dt. 23: 17; for **sacrifice to Molech** (10) and **mediums** (24) see Dt. 18: 10 f.; for worship of **starry hosts** (4, 11) see Dt. 17: 3. On the other hand Deuteronomy does not mention **high places** (5, 8, 9, 19, 20) or **the pagan priests** (*kᵉmārîm*, 5) and the provisions of Dt. 18: 6–8 were so modified that **the priests of the high places** (9) who were withdrawn from the rural shrines were not allowed to minister at **the altar of the LORD in Jerusalem**. It is doubtful whether Deuteronomy envisaged centralization of all worship at Jerusalem (in any case the central shrine in Deuteronomy is Mt. Gerizim, Dt. 27: 12). Dt. 12: 5–14 may be interpreted to mean 'not just any old shrine but one approved place in a locality'. G. T. Manley says 'not their number but their character' is in question (*The Book of the Law*, 1957, p. 132). Josiah may have misinterpreted Deuteronomy but it is more likely his centralizing at Jerusalem was undertaken for different motives. The outlying shrines had for centuries mixed Yahwism with Baal. Hezekiah's reforms (18: 4) had been short-lived. Josiah may have decided that complete suppression was the only answer and determined to keep the cult under his own control in Jerusalem. Not surprisingly, his action was still inadequate. As far as the people were concerned, Jeremiah rightly saw 'pretence' (Jer. 3: 10) and metal so base that refining was impossible (Jer. 6: 27–30). That he was unsuccessful is no reflection on Josiah's piety or zeal—but on the very possibility of a central shrine. Meeting occasionally at Gerizim or Shiloh to confirm the tribal league was one thing. The attempt to control worship even in the small area from Bethel to Beersheba was another.

The use of **human bones** (14, 16) was a desecration that would stop the shrines being used again. The reference to **the man of God . . . from Judah** (17), though commonly rejected as editorial, is a fitting commentary on the intervening 300 years (1 Kg. 13: 1–10). The **tombstone** (17) had borne its silent witness to the futility of the altar at Bethel, and **the men of the city** not unnaturally passed on the story. Josiah's purging tour of **the towns of Samaria** (19) shows his new freedom with the failing Assyrian influence—which also made more easy the eviction of Assyrian religious paraphernalia from Jerusalem.

21. the Passover: cf. Dt. 16: 1–8. There is no mention here of the feast of unleavened bread but the title **Passover** may include the complete ceremony. It was kept in the spring and was preeminently the celebration by united

Israel of their deliverance from Egypt. **22. not . . . any passover . . . since the days of the judges:** see Jos. 5: 10 for the last record. Kings is strangely silent about Hezekiah's Passover (see 2 Chr. 30) or any celebration during the monarchy. Some scholars hold that an enthronement festival in the autumn (after harvest) took over as the main religious celebration. If so the worship suffered great loss which the returning exiles did well to repair (Ezr. 6: 19 f.). Monarchy needed continually to be reminded of the deeper underlying dependence upon Yahweh and his deliverance.

Josiah receives his commendation—no **king like him** (25) but still **the LORD did not turn away from the heat of his fierce anger** (26). Judgment extends even to **the city . . . and the temple** (27), a lesson which Jeremiah fully understood (Jer. 7: 11–15) but the superstitious citizens refused.

Josiah's death at the hands of **Pharaoh Neco** is not explained. Nineveh fell in 612 and the Assyrians fell back to the Euphrates. In 609 Pharaoh Neco was going to their relief; so NIV **to help**, RSV *to* **the king of Assyria.** (Heb. *'al* often, *e.g.* 19: 22, but not always, means *against*, as AV here.) Why Josiah interfered is not clear. 2 Chr. 35: 21 gives a little more detail. Perhaps he had some league with the Babylonians or perhaps he had an inflated view of his ability to control passage through Palestine. His action served only to expedite Egyptian interference. **30. They brought his body in a chariot to Jerusalem,** and he was succeeded by **Jehoahaz** his son.

Jehoahaz and Jehoiakim (23: 31–24: 17)
Jehoahaz failed to follow his father's good example (32) and was deposed after **three months.** According to the Babylonian Chronicle Neco's campaign to the north lasted three months (July–Sept., 609) so he dealt with Jehoahaz on his way back to Egypt. Judah became tributary to Egypt (33), with **Eliakim** (another of Josiah's sons) as puppet king. The change of name to **Jehoiakim** (34) signified that he ruled as Neco's nominee. The amount of tribute ('*ōneš*, usually a civil punishment rather than war indemnity) is modest by comparison with that paid by Hezekiah (18: 14) and was met by tax on **the people of the land . . . according to . . . assessments** (see on 12: 4). **24:1 Nebuchadnezzar king of Babylon** began his reign in 605 a few months after inflicting a crushing defeat on the Egyptians at Carchemish. He overran Philistia in 604. **Jehoiakim became his vassal for three years** in a hurried and unwilling turnabout of political allegiance. In 601 Nebuchadnezzar fought an inconclusive battle (possibly referred to in v. 7) and returned to Babylon. Jehoiakim, in spite of Jeremiah's prediction (Jer. 25) took the opportunity and **changed his mind and rebelled against him.**

Unable at once to deal with the insurrection, Nebuchadnezzar sent raiding bands to harass Jerusalem (seen in v. 2 as a judgment from Yahweh). In spite of the gravity of the political situation, Jehoiakim is noted for his domestic wickedness, **he filled Jerusalem with innocent blood** (cf. Jer. 22: 13–19) and ended his evil reign just as Nebuchadnezzar was advancing on the city in December 598. His passing was so convenient that assassination has been suggested, but **rested with his fathers** (6) is not usually used of those who died violently. The very brief record can be amplified from the prophecy of Jeremiah.

Jehoiachin and Zedekiah (24: 8–25: 21)
8. Jehoiachin (=Jeconiah, Jer. 24: 1, etc.) **became king** and **reigned three months** while the city was under siege (Dec. 598–Mar. 597). Upon **king Nebuchadnezzar's** arrival (11) Jehoiachin **surrenderd. The king of Babylon took** him **prisoner,** along with his **mother . . . wives . . . his officials and the chief men of the land** and many others (15, 16) among whom was Ezekiel. Verses 13, 14 appear to be misplaced from the later destruction (**all the treasures . . . all Jerusalem**, were not taken at this time; cf. Jer. 27: 16–22).

17. the king of Babylon . . . made Mattaniah . . . king and the change of name to **Zedekiah** (*righteousness of Yahweh*) shows Nebuchadnezzar's sovereignty. Once again the futile hope in Egypt bedevilled the court. It seems that Isaiah's doom of blindness (Isa. 6: 9–10) had a political as well as religious fulfilment. In spite of Jeremiah's pleas (Jer. 27) **Zedekiah rebelled against the king of Babylon** (20) and precipitated the final siege and destruction. The 19–month siege and resultant **famine** (25: 3) ended with the king attempting to escape from the doomed city. He was overtaken, **captured,** sentenced, blinded and taken in **bronze shackles . . . to Babylon** (7). A month later (8) **Nebuzaradan . . . came to Jerusalem** with instructions to destroy the city. Many more were deported leaving only **the poorest people of the land** (12). The last traces of the splendour of Solomon (13–17) were taken as booty. Various officials were executed by the king of Babylon at **Riblah** (his headquarters in the west) presumably for implication in the conspiracy with Zedekiah and his pro-Egyptian allies. **So Judah went into captivity, away from her land** (21) and the tragic chapter of Hebrew monarchy ends.

Two paragraphs have been added to the story, possibly from Jer. 40 and 52 respectively, the stories of Gedaliah and of Jehoiachin's recognition.

22. Gedaliah was appointed **governor,** an honest man who was prepared to make the best of the situation under the Babylonians (24). With typical idiocy, he was assassinated and

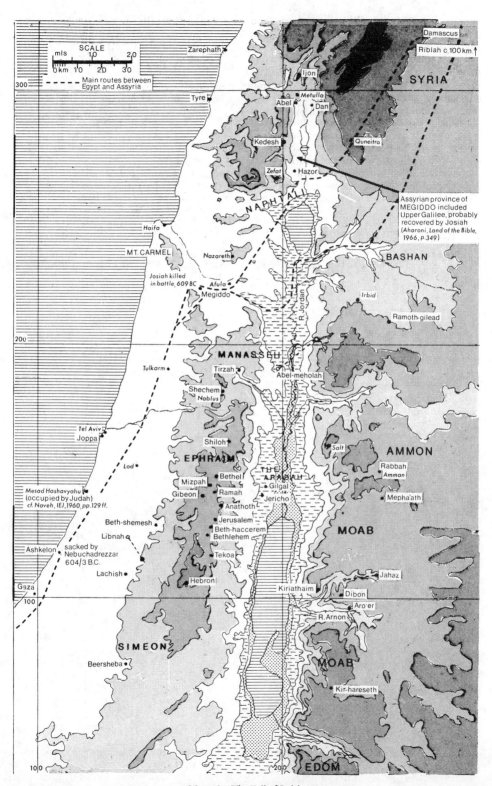

SCALE

mls
10   20

0 km 10   20   30

--- Main routes between
    Egypt and Assyria

Zarephath

300

Ijon

Riblah c. 100 km. ↑

SYRIA

Damascus

Tyre

Metulla
Abel
Dan

Kedesh

Quneitra

Zefat   Hazor

Assyrian province of
MEGIDDO included
Upper Galilee, probably
recovered by Josiah
(Aharoni, Land of the Bible,
1966, p.349)

Haifa

MT. CARMEL

NAPHTALI

BASHAN

Nazareth

Josiah killed
in battle, 609 BC
Afula
Megiddo

Irbid

R. Jordan

Ramoth-gilead

200

MANASSEH

Tulkarm

Tirzah

Abel-meholah

Shechem
Nablus

Tel Aviv
Joppa

Shiloh

Salt

AMMON

EPHRAIM

Lod

Rabbah
Amman

Mizpah   Bethel

THE
ARABAH

Mesad Hashavyahu
(occupied by Judah)
cf. Naveh, IEJ, 1960, pp. 129 ff.

Gibeon   Ramah
Gilgal

Mepha'ath

Anathoth
Jericho

Beth-shemesh

Jerusalem
Beth-haccerem
Bethlehem

MOAB

Ashkelon
sacked by
Nebuchadrezzar
604/3 B.C.

Libnah

Tekoa

Gaza

Lachish

Hebron

Jahaz

100

Kiriathaim

Dibon
Aro'er

R. Arnon

SIMEON

MOAB

Beersheba

100   200   EDOM

Kir-hareseth

Map 26—The Fall of Judah

439

the remnants fled from Chaldean vengeance to Egypt. A fuller account of the events is given in Jer. 40: 7–43: 7.

The happier paragraph tells of Jehoiachin's reinstatement in captivity. It has been suggested that this was added as an expression of hope for Judah, but no explanation is given. A remarkable confirmation of the **allowance** (30) comes from a Babylonian tablet which specifies rations for 'Ya'ukinu, king of the land of Yahudu'. The postscript ends with Jehoiachin enjoying his portion **as long as he lived** —the only king of Israel or Judah whose death is not recorded (perhaps because he was still alive when the books of Kings were completed).

BIBLIOGRAPHY

Commentaries

Burney, C. F., *Notes on the Hebrew Text of the Books of Kings* (Oxford, 1903).

Gray, J., *I and II Kings: Commentary* (London, [2]1970).

Montgomery, J. A., and Gehman, H. S., *The Books of Kings. ICC* (Edinburgh, 1951).

Robinson, J., *The First Book of Kings. CBC* (Cambridge, 1972).

Robinson, J., *The Second Book of Kings. CBC* (Cambridge, 1976).

Other Works

Bright, J., *A History of Israel* (London, [2]1972).

Ellison, H. L., *The Prophets of Israel* (Exeter, 1969).

Scott, R. B. Y., 'The Pillars Jachin and Boaz', *JBL* 58 (1939), pp.143 ff.

Thiele, E. R., *The Mysterious Numbers of the Hebrew Kings* (Exeter, 1965).

de Vaux, R., *Ancient Israel: Its Life and Institutions* (London, 1961).

Welch, A. C., *Kings and Prophets of Israel* (London, 1952).

1 and 2 CHRONICLES

J. K. HOWARD

INTRODUCTION

The two books of Chronicles are placed among the other historical books in the English Bible, but in the Hebrew Canon they are to be found in the third division, the Writings (*ketūbîm*) a fact that reflects their origin in the post-exilic community. The work of the Chronicler also includes Ezra-Nehemiah, the whole forming a composite history of God's people (essentially Judah, the faithful section of Israel) from the establishment of the Davidic kingdom to the development of a theocratic state under the reforms of Ezra after the Babylonian captivity (taking the view that historically the ministry of Ezra followed that of Nehemiah; see further the discussion of dating in the introduction of Ezra-Nehemiah).

The work of the Chronicler, understandably, has been greatly neglected. The books appear dull, they are full of uninteresting statistics, lengthy and detailed lists of religious forms and institutions, and are in striking contrast to the earlier historical books whose approach is much more in line with modern modes of historical thought. Nevertheless these books are of considerable importance. They supplement the material of Samuel and Kings, throwing additional light on what is at times a confused period of history. In addition an appreciation of the Chronicler's strong religious outlook and his purpose in writing, emphasizing the continuance of the community of God from the beginning of history through to his own time, together with the dangers of religious compromise, provides lessons from history, not only for his own generation, but for later generations as well, not least that of the twentieth century.

Authorship and Date

There can be little doubt that there is a unified authorship of the major part of both Chronicles and Ezra-Nehemiah. While there are certain later additions and expansions to the work, the basic material had been collected and edited by a single hand, writing at a specific time and with a definite purpose in mind. Traditionally the work has been ascribed to Ezra himself and there are certainly cogent reasons for dating the work in the Persian period. Considering the whole of the Chronicler's work together, the more important of these reasons may be stated briefly. The close relationship of the Aramaic of Ezra with that of the scrolls from the Jewish community of Elephantine in Egypt, which can be dated to the fifth century BC, together with the number of Persian words and the almost complete absence of Greek ones, especially in Ezra, points to a period before the overthrow of Persia by Greece. It is also possible that the Johanan mentioned at Neh. 12: 23 is the high priest of that name who is known to have held office around 410 B.C. Finally, the Chronicler's genealogy of the Davidic line (1 Chr. 3: 10–26) proceeds for only seven generations beyond Jehoiachin (598 BC). If an average of twenty-five years is assumed for each generation then the eldest of Elioenai's seven sons (1 Chr. 3: 24) would have been born about 420 B.C. and the youngest say between 410 and 405 B.C. The most likely date therefore for the completion of the work in the original form is about 400 BC, although later comments, additions and expansions have probably been added.

The date suggested for the work does not exclude the traditional authorship of Ezra, and indeed, a number of scholars, on the basis of language, style and specific interest, maintain that the writer of the 'Ezra memoirs' was also responsible for Chronicles. C. C. Torrey wrote, 'there is not a garment in all Ezra's wardrobe that does not fit the Chronicler exactly'. What is clear from a consideration of his work, however, is that the author was a man of wisdom and insight, a reformer who was concerned to ensure the progress of his people towards a theocratic ideal, a living religious institution that would be the centre of the nation's life. He thus rejected the political Messianism of Haggai and Zechariah, seeing not only its failure in the post-exilic community, but also the dangers to which it was likely to give rise in a nation within the Persian Empire. If the author was not Ezra, he was certainly a product of what may be termed the 'Ezra School'.

Purpose

It has been said that the Chronicler was not a writer of history in our sense of the term, but rather a commentator, one who felt free to reject material which did not fit in with his purpose and include other information that did. In other words 'the method of presentation is homiletical' (J. M. Myers); his concern is not historical but theological and the work provides 'the only instance of a Hebraic philosophy of history on an immense scale' (W. A. L. Elmslie). His concern is to interpret history to meet the needs of his own people, rather than to write history as an historian.

An understanding of his purpose can be seen only in the light of the political and religious situation of the latter half of the fifth century B.C. The initial hopes of a restoration of a Davidic king had long been dashed and by the time of Ezra's reform (possibly 427 BC) the political and economic situation had been largely stabilized through the work of Nehemiah. Ezra's task was to set up a local government within the Persian Commonwealth based on the Mosaic law. The city was rebuilt, the culture re-established and Jerusalem was once more the centre for both religious and legal authority, although the two can hardly be said to be separate.

The Chronicler saw that the only hope for the future lay in a strengthening of the religious institutions that had survived the Babylonian captivity. His desire was to strengthen the things that remained. His history therefore relates largely to the problems and the developments in the religio-social sphere, rather than those which were purely political.

His purpose was thus to demonstrate in the first place that the true Israel of God was the one perpetuated in the Davidic kingdom of Judah and now represented, in his own time, by the post-exilic community which derived from it. The Chronicler viewed the northern kingdom as apostate from the start and his attitude finds clear expression at 2 Chr. 10: 19. 'For him the Northern Kingdom was conceived in sin, born in iniquity and nurtured in adultery' (J. M. Myers). The division of the kingdom after the death of Solomon was, thus, much more than a political event. The Chronicler sees it as a deliberate rebellion against the divinely ordered Davidic dynasty and a forsaking of the one place at which the true worship of Israel may be offered. This separation of the northern tribes meant that they had removed themselves from the covenant community and were thus rejected by God. The true Israel of God is expressed in the tribes of Judah and Benjamin, together with the majority of the house of Levi and the few faithful ones from the north who came to Jerusalem 'to sacrifice to the LORD, the God of their fathers' (2 Chr. 11: 16). Furthermore, the period of the Chronicler saw an attempt to revive the northern community with its own centre of worship in opposition to Jerusalem. This Samaritan community presented marked dangers since it was based on the Torah, possessed a genuine Aaronite priesthood and was associated with a holy place of great antiquity.

The Chronicler sets his face, therefore, against the Samaritan community and its worship. From his point of view it was apostasy and the true Israel, centred in Jerusalem, dared not compromise with it. Only on the ground of humble submission to the true worship of God at Jerusalem could there be fellowship with the Samaritans. This anti-Samaritan feeling is probably reflected in 2 Chr. 11: 13–17; 13: 3–20; 25: 6–10, as well as in Ezra-Nehemiah (cf. also Jn 4: 20). The writer thus sets out to prove 'that in contrast to the godless Northern Kingdom, it is only the Southern Kingdom, Judah, with its Davidic dynasty and its Jerusalem temple, which is the true Israel, the legitimate bearer of the Divine rule which is achieved in the Kingdom of David, and that it is only the community of the Jews who returned from the exile, and not the religious community of the Samaritans . . . which faithfully maintains and continues this tradition' (O. Eissfeldt).

This underlines the second main purpose of the Chronicler, which was to emphasize that true worship must be centred in Jerusalem. The temple is the only authorized place where the worship of God could be carried out. This also explains the recurrent emphasis on religious institutions and the status of the Levites. The writer dwells on the place of the Ark, the temple itself and the chosen ministers of the Lord, seeing through these means the normal vehicle by which the will of God was made known. In so doing the writer also plays down the priestly functions of the king and instead concentrates organized worship in the hands of a religious establishment. Such an emphasis, although exclusive and restrictive, was nonetheless necessary in view of the social and political pressures being brought to bear upon the community. The Israel of God must be kept pure at any cost and its institutions required loyalty and devotion if they were to survive. His ideal would appear to have been a saved people, living under the obligations of God's Covenant in rigorous purity, conceived of largely in ritual and racial terms, and maintaining a sort of splendid isolation from all other peoples.

The Chronicler interpreted history with this end in mind and there can be no doubt that 'in his day his message rendered a most important service' (E. L. Curtis and A. A. Madsen). Although his viewpoint is limited and exclusive and far removed from the universalism and missionary vision of some of the prophets his work has an important place in the OT canon, for he 'is one of those through whom the great wealth of earlier thought came to be re-applied and re-assessed, so that it was meaningful not only for his generation, but for those that followed' (P. R. Ackroyd). Thus the Chronicler's history serves as a reminder of the continuing tension in God's new covenant community of the Church between exclusivism and institutionalism on the one hand and on the other that outgoing universalism which is more concerned with the out-working of the covenant in love, justice and integrity—in the spirit rather than the letter. His emphases on the requirement of the community to follow the paths of God and his demonstration that 'whenever men flouted what they believed to be the will of God the consequences were not trivial but disastrous' (W. A. L. Elmslie) have a permanent validity.

Literary Structure and Sources

The identification of sources and the literary structure of the historical books invariably presents problems of great complexity. The Chronicler often expressly states the source from which he is quoting whether it be official records, official lists or prophetic oracles. Much of this material may have come from the temple archives, rescued at the captivity and carefully preserved during the years of exile. He also had before him the great history of the people forming the books of Deuteronomy, Joshua, Judges, Samuel and Kings, as well as the Torah.

1 Chr. 1–9 is derived from Genesis to Joshua and the main portion of the rest of the work consists largely of sections of Samuel and Kings, frequently quoted verbatim. A number of traditions associated with prophetic sources are quoted at 1 Chr. 29: 29, 2 Chr. 9: 29, 12: 15, 13: 22, 20: 34, 26: 22 and 32: 32. Various official archives and records are quoted at 1 Chr. 9: 1, 2 Chr. 16: 11, 24: 27, 25: 26, 33: 18, 35: 27 and 36: 8. There are two other sources referred to as *midrāš* at 2 Chr. 13: 22, translated 'story', and 2 Chr. 24: 27, translated 'commentary'. These are the only OT occurrences of a word that became frequently used in later Judaism to describe rabbinical commentaries on Biblical material for the edification of the faithful. The meaning in these two places cannot be decided exactly, but they probably represent some sort of reconstructed history of Israel with various embellishments and explanatory notes added.

The fact that the Chronicler omits material merely indicates that it did not suit his purpose to include it, and in the same way his use of additional material to supplement his story is mainly in order to give further support to his main thesis. As was remarked at an earlier stage, the writer's purpose is homiletical and not primarily historical. He is concerned with the lessons that history provides for the people of his time and selects his source material accordingly.

ANALYSIS

1 CHRONICLES

1 Chronicles

I. PREFACE: THE GENEALOGICAL LISTS (1: 1–9: 44)

The material comprising the first nine chapters largely parallels similar genealogical lists in the Pentateuch and the other historical books. The Chronicler's main interest lay with the southern kingdom and he deals with other aspects of Israel's history and particularly the northern kingdom only as they particularly relate to Judah. The lists are not really an integral part of the work but may be viewed as an important preface, the purpose of which was to validate the lineage of David who occupied the central position in the work. Purity of family line was important to the post-exilic community and the Chronicler intends to show that David's lineage is impeccable as is the connected line of descent to the Jewish community of his own day. The lists provide, therefore, the Chronicler's understanding of the nature of God's people and His ongoing purpose in grace and redemption. The post-exilic community is thus seen as the true descendant of the Israel of God which lay in His purposes. There is consequently particular attention paid to Levi, Judah and Benjamin and to the descendants of David, for these comprise the true Israel with the Levitical priesthood as the only valid one and the house of David as the legitimate kingly line.

(a) Adam to Jacob (Israel) (1: 1–54)

The line from Adam to Noah is listed in only the barest detail and it is only with the sons of Noah that genealogies begin to be filled out in detail. The names **Tubal** and **Meshech** (5) occur in Assyrian inscriptions and letters from about the ninth and eighth centuries B.C. Gen. 10: 4 has 'Dodanim' for the Chronicler's **Rodanim** (7), probably Rhodes. The Aegean origin of the Philistines (**Caphtorites** at v. 12) is a tradition preserved also in Am. 9: 7. They were probably one of the group of 'sea peoples' who eventually managed to establish themselves along the Eastern Mediterranean seaboard following the loss of their original homeland consequent on the breakdown of the Mycenaean dynasty in the Greek area in the tenth century B.C. **Nimrod** (10) is characterized only as a **mighty warrior** (perhaps better, 'tyrant') and there is no reference to his being a great hunter.

The Chronicler's handling of the lists is interesting. He dealt firstly with side-lines (**Japheth** and **Ham**, vv. 5–16. and **Ishmael**, vv. 29–31) before concentrating on the main line which is his interest. His interest in one line of descent is seen also in his dismissal of **Keturah** (32–33) as merely Abraham's concubine, although the Genesis genealogy refers to her as his second wife, taken after Sarah's death.

In the Edomite lists (vv. 35–54), beginning with **Esau** and **Seir** and finishing with the various chieftains, **Timna** is given as a son of Eliphaz whereas the Genesis list states that Timna was his concubine. It is worth noting that the lists of chieftains give no indications of any dynasties and the impression is one in which the prevailing conditions were much as they were in Israel under the 'judges' with various leaders rising to prominence as conditions demanded it.

(b) The Line of Judah (2: 1–55)

The lists running from chs. 2 to 4 are more complicated than those in ch. 1 as the Chronicler has expanded them with material from additional sources to the main historical books. The writer's interests are clearly shown in his concentration on Judah (vv. 3–9) and the ancestors of David (vv. 10–17). It is also worth noting that the fact Judah married a Canaanitess does not affect his status in being the ancestor of David (v. 3). The persistent sin of **Er** and **Achar** brought the judgment of God upon them (vv. 3 and 7). To be within the covenant community does not automatically ensure salvation for while Yahweh is the God of mercy He is also the God of judgment.

The line of **Zerah** (6) is not given in full elsewhere and the probable interest of the writer lies in the connection of Zerah's line with the musical guilds. The transposition of **Achar** ('*ākār*) (v. 7) for Achan (Jos. 7: 1, 18, etc.) is probably deliberate to introduce a play on words as it has the same consonants as the participle '*ōkēr* (**disaster**); cf. the 'Valley of Achor' (Jos. 7: 26).

The list of David's ancestors (vv. 10–17) was obviously of primary importance, but it is interesting to note that while 1 Sam. 16: 10 f. and 17: 12 speak of eight sons of Jesse this list contains only seven names. Of interest also is the fact that only here is it learnt that Zeruiah and Abigail were David's sisters (cf. 1 Sam. 26: 6 and 2 Sam. 17: 25). They are introduced here because they will figure in the story of David at a later stage.

The remaining lists of this chapter are of interest largely for their historical and archeological value, and their association with the place names in the southern kingdom. The Caleb of this section is not of course the famous Caleb the spy (the son of Jephunneh) who is mentioned at 4: 15. **Havvoth Jair, Kenath with settlements** (23) might be better rendered, 'the tent villages of Jair and Kenath' and may reflect something of the semi-nomadic character of the southern tribes at this time.

(*c*) **The Line of David (3: 1–24)**
It is surprising that this section does not follow immediately on the list of David's ancestors at 2: 10–17. If, however, the whole section of genealogies is simply archival material that the Chronicler has added to his work with minimum editing, then the position is understandable. The lists vary slightly from those in Kings and Lk. 3 and this may simply indicate different traditions of reckoning the intermarriages in the royal family. A number of names also have variants in other places: for example, David's second son is called **Daniel** here (v. 1) but Kileab at 2 Sam. 3: 2. More interesting are the later variants: **Azariah** (12) is given his other name Uzziah in 2 Chr. 26 and 29 and Isa. 6: Jeconiah (16) is called **Jehoiachin** here and in 2 Chr. 38: 8 and **Shallum** (15; cf. Jer. 22: 11) becomes Jehoahaz. It is possible that these are examples of throne names. Other examples of this practice are: Jedidiah-Solomon, Eliakim-Jehoiakim and Mattaniah-Zedekiah. It is possible that even David is a throne name, his

original family name being Elhanan (see further on 1 Chr. 20:5).

Verses 15 and 16 are difficult verses. Josiah's son **Johanan** is not mentioned elsewhere and the suggestion has been made that he may have died before his father. The problem raised by the succession of Shallum-Jehoahaz in place of his elder brothers is discussed under 2 Chr. 36: 1 ff. The post-exilic line is traced in vv. 17–24 down to the writer's time (approximately 405 BC). **Shenazzar** (18) is the leader of the first return of the exiles, acting perhaps as regent for the young Zerubbabel who was not old enough to take charge of affairs in 538 B.C. His name is given as Sheshbazzar at Ezr. 1: 8, etc., and both forms are probably a corruption of the Babylonian *Sin-ab-usur*. There is a further difficulty at v. 19 where the father of Zerubbabel is given as Shealtiel whereas elsewhere it is Shealtiel, his older brother (Hag. 1: 2, 14; 2: 2, 23; Ezr. 3: 2; Neh. 12: 1, etc.). One explanation is that Shealtiel may have died early and his younger brother Pedaiah may have married the childless widow, in which case Zerubbabel would have been regarded as Shealtiel's son according to the rules of Levirate marriage (so W. Rudolph). The names of the post-exilic line are all common in the fifth and sixth centuries BC.

(*d*) **Southern Tribal Lists (4: 1–43)**
These are further pre-exilic lists of families with interesting traditions in regard to certain localities. The lists are derived from a number of sources, sometimes repeating what has gone before and also supplementing other material, in particular providing additional detail to the lists of ch. 2.

The list of descendants of **Ashhur** (vv. 5–8) is somewhat obscure although the place names have Judaean links (Tekoa, Zohar, etc.). The possible reason for the inclusion of this list is to validate the ancestry of the Tekoites who were prominent in the rebuilding of the walls of Jerusalem (Neh. 3: 5, 27). The short paragraph on **Jabez** (vv. 9, 10) reflects something of the Chronicler's theological interests and may well have been included for this reason. There is a play on words between Jabez and '*ōṣeb* (pain). His name was liable to bring him unpleasant consequences and, in popular thought, the circumstances could only be changed by giving another name, but the Chronicler emphasized that direct prayer can alter the fortunes of life for God listens to the prayer of the trusting person.

The remaining lists reflect both a partial migratory background and also the settlement of small industrial groups—potters, linen-makers—and probably refers more to the founding of trade guilds, whose names became associated with specific locations, than genealogies in the usual sense. The genealogy of **Simeon** (24–43) is very fragmentary and this reflects the fact that it lost its tribal identity very early, becoming absorbed into Judah (cf. Jos. 19: 1, 9; Gen. 49: 5–7). The final portion of the chapter deals with the Simeonite chiefs who were forced to migrate due to overpopulation and lack of pasture, suggesting a semi-nomadic type of life to a late date. The time of the migration is given as the reign of Hezekiah. The first move was westward to the area of Gerar—possibly a buffer state established by Shishak of Egypt (cf. 2 Chr. 14) and outside the tribal areas—and the second eastwards to the Akaba region where they displaced the remnants of Amalekites residing there since their dispersal by Saul and David.

(e) **Transjordanian Tribes (5: 1–26)**
In this section the virtually extinct tribes of Reuben, Gad and the half-tribe of Manasseh are dealt with. The fragmentary character of the information and its somewhat confused nature point to post-exilic conditions. The tribes had long since disintegrated and their records were lost, a point more or less admitted at v. 17 where the Chronicler notes that there were full genealogies in existence before the Assyrian conquest.

The loss of Reuben's birthright as eldest son of Jacob is related to his sin (Gen. 35: 22; 49: 4) and this is given as the reason for the rise of Joseph (v. 1) (see further J. M. Myers *ad loc.* and I. Mendelsohn, *BASOR*, 156, 1959, p. 38). The Reubenites appear to have remained as semi-nomadic herdsmen ranging over the whole area of the desert frontier (vv. 9, 10). The **Hagrites** (10) were Arabs who make their appearance on a number of occasions throughout Israel's history. According to Ps. 83: 6 they lived in the neighbourhood of Moab. The warfare mentioned may refer to Saul's Ammonite wars (1 Sam. 11).

The list of Gadites (vv. 11–17) does not correspond to other tribal lists (Gen. 46: 16; Num. 26: 15–18) and the Chronicler would appear to be using an independent source. Like the Reubenites, whom they eventually absorbed by the late ninth century BC, the Gadites were pastoral people and came into conflict with neighbouring Arabs over territorial rights (vv. 18–22). The conflict recorded here is possibly to be dated to the eleventh century B.C. and probably relates to a long period of border warfare against Arab incursions. The Israelites are stated to have gained the victory because God was with them and **because they trusted in him** (20).

The downfall of the Transjordanian tribal groups is dealt with according to the Chronicler's theology. Because they rejected God, He in turn raised up His own agent of judgment in the form of Assyria (vv. 25, 26). Their apostasy resulted in the Assyrian invasion and their loss of both political and ethnic identity. **Pul** and **Tiglath-Pileser** (the NIV uses the more accurate form of the name, as in 2 Kg. 15: 29, etc.) are not two kings but one. Pul (cf. 2 Kg. 15: 19) was his personal name which he retained as king of Babylon and Tiglath-Pileser represents his Assyrian throne name. The events refer to his campaign of 734 BC.

(f) **The Descendants of Levi (6: 1–81)**
This lengthy and complicated list probably has two main functions in respect of the Chronicler's own time. One is to record the various aspects of the functions of the Levitical orders and establish their proper status. The other is to record the legitimacy of the Zadokite priesthood. An essential element in the understanding of legitimacy was physical descent and thus genealogies are used as the means of showing historical continuity. The whole section appears to be a compilation of a number of separate and independent lists.

Verses 1–3 record the main family clans of the tribe of Levi and vv. 4–15 record the line of chief priests from Eleazar to the exile. No account is taken of Ithamar priests or interfamily connections and there is some evidence that the intention was to provide a balanced structure with Solomon as the centre point of reference, but the actual numbers are not completely clear. Verses 16–48 establish the main Levitical genealogies and also provide a schematic list of the singers built around the three sons of Levi. Two points are noteworthy here. The prophet **Samuel** (28) is here included in a list of Levites on the basis of function. He made sacrifices and thus, from the Chronicler's point of view, must be classified as a Levite. In fact he was an Ephraimite, but he is given Levitical descent by adoption to safeguard the legitimacy of his status in the eyes of the post-exilic community. The other point is the reference to the fact that it was David who produced the initial organization of the musical guilds (v. 31). The Chronicler draws attention to this tradition on several occasions and there is no good reason for discarding it, especially in view of David's known musical ability and interest and from what is known of contemporary Canaanite musical guilds from whom David may well have borrowed. Verses 48, 49 draw attention to the distinction between Levitical and priestly functions, more applicable to the post-exilic community, and lead into a further list linking Zadok with the priestly line of Aaron. The verses thus emphasize the importance of the Levites in the ordering of Israel's worship and underline the legitimacy of the Zadokite priesthood. The actual origins of Zadok remain obscure (see further H. H. Rowley, *JBL*, 58, 1939, p. 113, and note on Ezek. 44: 15, below).

The list of Levitical cities (vv. 54–81) probably indicates the arrangements at the period of the early monarchy, probably late in David's reign by which time the various Canaanite cities mentioned had been taken and before the tribal arrangement gave place to Solomon's administrative districts. The list includes also the cities of refuge as in Jos. 21, and indicates that the Levites were scattered throughout the whole land at this time.

(g) **The Northern Tribes (7: 1–40)**
These lists deal with the tribes of Issachar, Benjamin, Naphtali, Ephraim and Asher. While they mainly follow the genealogies of Genesis and Numbers there are a number of variations especially in names and numbers. The line of Issachar (vv. 1–5) is composed of two separate lists. The numbers do not tally, but this is probably due to the fact that they refer to tribal numbers at given times which may not be the same for all. The Benjamin genealogy (vv. 6–12a) is well ordered although again the numbers are higher than in Num. 1: 37 and 26: 41. The name **Elioenai** (v. 8) appears to be an anachronism as it does not occur before the period of the later monarchy and mainly in post-exilic times.

Verse 12b appears to refer to the tribe of Dan (cf. Gen. 46: 23; Num. 26: 42) although the name has dropped out. **Hushim** (or Shuham) was Dan's son and there is the added reference in the next verse to **Bilhah**, who was the mother of both Dan and Naphtali. The name **Aher** is difficult and a number of proposals have been suggested to emend the text here (see major commentaries ad loc.).

The section dealing with **Manasseh** (vv. 14–19) is somewhat obscure and there is some confusion over the exact relationship of **Makir** to **Maachah** (cf. vv. 15, 16). The genealogy of **Ephraim** (vv. 20–29) appears to have been derived from at least two separate lists which are not easy to reconcile. The time span allotted, however (ten generations), fits in with the known period between Ephraim and Joshua (about 250 years). The conflict with the **men of Gath** (probably the Gittaim of 2 Sam. 4: 3, between Gezer and Lod, and not the Gath of the Philistines) relates to the patriarchal period and a probable attempt at a westwards expansion of Jacob's sons in order to gain better pasture land. The failure of the attempt may have led to the settling of upper and lower Beth-horon which lay further east (v. 24). The genealogy of **Asher** (vv. 30–40) is given in remarkable detail considering its lack of status. Verses 30, 31 follow Gen. 46: 17, but the rest of the list has no parallel elsewhere in the Bible and the Chronicler must have had an independent source for this list.

(h) **The Benjaminites (8: 1–9: 1)**
This list of the family of **Benjamin** differs from that given at 7: 6–12 in a number of

respects and represents a different source—note the expression **father of** (vv. 33–37, and in Heb. at vv. 8, 9, 11) rather than 'son of' and the fact that here Benjamin is credited with five sons, but only three at 7: 6. There is evidence from these lists of a fairly extensive mixing of peoples. **Gath** (13) may again be Gittaim (cf. 7: 21).

The family of **Saul** (vv. 33–40) which completes the list seems to be based on two sources, one being the Samuel record (to v. 34) and the other a possibly post-exilic list which is being used to bring the genealogy down to the period of the Exile. There is a problem in respect of the exact relationship between **Ner** and **Kish**. According to 1 Sam. 14: 51 they were brothers, but here they are presented as father and son. A number of suggestions have been made to harmonize the records (see major commentaries ad loc.).

The whole list of genealogies is finally rounded off with a clear statement that all the lists given thus far related only to the pre-exilic period—**All Israel was listed in the genealogies in the book of the kings of Israel. The people of Judah were taken captive to Babylon because of their unfaithfulness** (9: 1). The post-exilic list of the inhabitants of the Jewish conclave based on Jerusalem occupies most of the rest of ch. 9.

(i) **The Citizens of Jerusalem and its Environs (9: 2–44)**
This chapter falls into three main divisions. Firstly there is a list of the heads of the first families to return (vv. 2–9). There were, apparently, representatives of the old northern tribes (**Ephraim and Manasseh**), but no details are given. This is followed by extensive details of the priestly and Levitical families with notes on their duties (vv. 10–34). **Temple servants** (neṯînîm) are also mentioned (v. 2) in the broad classification, but no lists are provided here. The title is restricted to the Chronicler's work in OT and the group probably represents the descendants of prisoners taken in the various wars, especially those of David and Solomon, dedicated to God and hence used as temple slaves in various menial tasks. The final verses (vv. 35–44) are almost exactly as 8: 29–38 and provide an account of Saul's ancestry as an introduction to the narrative section which begins at ch. 10.

The relationship of this chapter to Neh. 11 has always presented problems. The two lists most closely correspond in the names of the priests and Levites. Elsewhere there are considerable divergences, but it seems likely that they are derived from a common original list of all the heads of families who returned from the Exile. A detailed comparison of the Neh. list with that here will be found in J. M. Myers ad loc.

The expression **official in charge** (v. 11) was descriptive of both civil and religious officials. The heads of priestly families are all referred to as **able men** which may be variously explained as experts (i.e. in the temple service) or as men of standing. There appeared to be a twenty-four hour rota system for the gatekeepers. The chief gatekeepers were assigned to the four cardinal points of the compass and they were to be assisted **from time to time**, or better, 'round the clock' (v. 25), by those who lived out of town (**in their villages**), who served for a week at a time.

It is possible that the whole of this section from 8: 29 to 9: 33 is a later addition to the text. Verse 34 is almost identical with 8: 28 and occurs there as here as a transitional verse between the Levitical genealogies and the family of Saul.

II. THE UNITED KINGDOM
(1 Chr. 10: 1–2 Chr. 9: 31)
i. The founding of the Davidic Kingdom (10: 1–12: 41)
(a) The death of Saul (10: 1–14)

The Chronicler now begins to embark on his history and he introduces his account of the Davidic kingdom with a note on the death of Saul.

In view of the emphasis on David, Jerusalem and the cult it might be wondered why he should commence the story with Saul. The answer is probably theological. 'In Saul the Kingdom had made, as it were, a false start. Only Saul's death mattered because it had been a prelude to David's reign' (W. A. L. Elmslie). For the Chronicler the kingdom belonged to Yahweh and it is He who establishes it and chooses whom He will to rule over it. This outlook is seen for example in the very different version he gives of the words of 2 Sam. 7: 16 (= 1 Chr. 17: 14). It was important to show that the house of Saul came to an end because of Saul's unfaithfulness. It is God who chooses whom He will to rule over His kingdom and He chose David. Saul was rejected because **he was unfaithful** and because **he did not keep the word of the LORD** (13); for all his failures David maintained a close relationship with God and the kingdom is established in him and his line. The element of election is basic to the Chronicler's theology.

The story of Saul's final struggle against his lifelong enemies the Philistines is borrowed almost word for word from 1 Sam. 31: 1–13 (*q.v.*). The Philistines were attempting to wrest back control of the trade routes from Saul, and although Israel was defeated at Gilboa, it was a Pyrrhic victory for the Philistines. They had really been fought to a standstill and never advanced beyond this point. Furthermore the guerrilla forces under David were making effective inroads on Philistine power in the south at the same time.

Saul's death presumably came towards the end of the battle. The prospect of torture, mutilation and abuse (v. 4) was so horrifying that Saul was prepared to commit suicide rather than face it. Suicide is virtually unknown in the Biblical narratives, thus throwing into stark relief the frightful prospect that faced him. Even the Chronicler does not find this reprehensible in the circumstances.

The Chronicler states that all the sons of Saul perished, thus passing over the survival of Ishbaal and his attempt to continue his father's dynasty (2 Sam. 2: 4). As far as the Chronicler is concerned the fact that God has rejected Saul and his line means that they may be ignored. They have no part in the ongoing story of the true people of God.

The Chronicler also omits all reference to Ashtoreth and instead substitutes **their gods** (10), probably to avoid any reference to a goddess whose name was automatically associated with the immorality so roundly condemned by the prophets. **Dagon** is mentioned however; an ancient Akkadian god of vegetation. The reference to the exposure of Saul's skull in the temple of Dagon does not appear in the *MT* text of 1 Sam. Evidence from the Qumran texts would suggest that Chronicles is following a different Hebrew text of Samuel, which is closer to the LXX and attested in some of the Samuel fragments of Qumran. It is likely that where Chr. follows Sam. it is in fact providing a more faithful transmission of the original text of Sam. than the *MT*.

The omission of any reference to the cremation of the bodies by the loyal citizens of Jabesh Gilead may be religious in origin, since normally it was only certain types of criminals who were cremated (Lev. 20: 14, 21: 9; Jos. 7: 25).

The section concludes with the writer's comments on the reason for the rejection of Saul, in which three specific charges are laid against him, and for the choice of David (vv. 13, 14).

(b) David's rise to power (11: 1–9)

It is to be noted that the Chronicler omits totally the struggle between David and Saul and the remnant of his kingdom under Ishbaal. Such incidents are secondary to his purpose which is to concentrate only on the legitimate (i.e. Davidic) line. The section thus begins with the unanimous acclamation of David by the people, largely on the basis of his charismatic leadership in battle, already well proven. The Chronicler clearly assumes that his readers are aware of the full story (note the words **as the LORD had promised through Samuel**, v. 3). The important point in these verses is that it is **all Israel** who go to the city, whereas in 2 Sam. 5: 6 it is the **king and his men.** With this alteration of emphasis the Chronicler indicates that the holy city belonged to all Israel and that all had a share in it, both in terms of its religious and political significance.

Another emphasis here is the position of Joab who is always David's right-hand man and no reference is made to the curse that rests on him (1 Kg. 2: 5). According to 2: 16, Joab is David's nephew, which may well explain his unswerving and rather over-zealous loyalty.

For the details of the conquest of the Jebusite stronghold see notes on 2 Sam. 5: 4–10. Note again that David's progress is because **the LORD of hosts was with him.**

(c) David's Mighty Men (11: 10–47)

Most of this section is taken from 2 Sam. 23: 8–39 and the Chronicler has incorporated it into his narrative at this point to magnify David further and emphasize the support he received from the mighty men in carrying out the Word of God. The Chronicler thus emphasizes the unity of **all Israel** in this endeavour (v. 10). The list begins with the exploits of two of the three chief mighty men, **Jashobeam** and **Eleazar** (cf. 2 Sam. 23: 10–12 with vv. 13, 14). The locality of the exploits at **Pas Dammim** has dropped out of the Sam. passage. The story of the bringing of the water of **Bethlehem** is dealt with under 2 Sam. 23: 13–17.

Abishai is described as **chief of the three**, though he was not counted among them. For **Three** others read 'Thirty'; *cf.* RSV and see 2 Sam. 23: 18 f. It is significant that Joab's name is omitted entirely.

A comparison of the Sam. list with this shows a number of variants in names and spelling and one additional name in the Chronicler's list. The great majority of these men appear to have come from tribal areas of Judah-Simeon and the old area of Dan. Two are from mount Ephraim, one from the Jordan Valley, one from Benjamin and three from Transjordan. The picture is of strong and alert personalities mainly from David's own area who gathered about him because they saw in him the qualities of effective leadership that Saul so clearly lacked, especially in the later years of his kingdom. The idea of the thirty may be borrowed from Egypt as David uses Egyptian forms of administration on other occasions.

(d) The followers of David (12: 1–41)

These lists seem to be drawn from very early material. This section falls into two parts; a period when David was still an outlaw with his guerrilla forces established at Ziklag (12: 1–23) and the second part representing a census list of the forces that came to proclaim him king at Hebron (12: 24–41). The evidence of such large-scale defections to David indicates how it was possible for him to secure the throne immediately after Saul's death. The process, however, was under the hand of God, a point

the Chronicler emphasizes in the use of the words of Amasai, **For your God will help you** (12: 18).

The high quality of the men who had aligned themselves with David is emphasized to demonstrate the Chronicler's main point, that the best and most capable followed him because they recognized him as the chosen of the Lord. The followers from Benjamin are probably listed first due to the fact that they defected from Saul, a Benjaminite, and two of them actually from Saul's own district of Gibeah. They are thus given the place of honour.

The incident at 12: 17–19 was probably recorded because of the prophetic utterance of Amasai. It occurred in the 'outlaw period' and reflects David's suspicion of support from lesser individuals due to his having been already betrayed on three occasions (1 Sam. 21: 22, 23 and 26). The statement that **the Spirit came upon** (clothed) **Amasai** is a most significant conception of inspiration and is beginning to move in the direction of indwelling. The prophecy seems to have been originally a six-line stanza with the last line having dropped out, although Rudolph views it as a stanza of five half-lines of the style found in the Song of Solomon. It seems certain that a really ancient and otherwise unrecorded tradition is preserved here.

The list of units which came to David at Hebron presents a major problem in the large numbers recorded. One solution proposed by G. E. Mendenhall (*JBL*, **77**, 1958, 52–66) is that the word *'elep* translated **thousand** stands for a military unit and is based on social structure. This would mean translating 'the men of Judah . . . were six hundred units with eight hundred men' and so on. This may well indicate the age of the lists in that the term *'elep* was no longer understood by later writers. The main stress of the passage lies in the writer's inclusion of all Israel, including those who later became the northern kingdom, who came to Hebron to support David.

ii. David and the Ark (13: 1–16: 43)

(a) The first attempt to move the Ark (13: 1–14)

This section is paralleled in 2 Sam. 6: 2–11. The story of the ark is complex. It had been taken by the Philistines at the battle of Ebenezer (1 Sam. 5) and in view of the plague epidemic that struck the Philistine towns they returned it to Israel with a guilt offering (1 Sam. 6: 1–9). From then on throughout the reign of Saul it remained in obscurity in the house of Abinadab. David determines to restore the ark as the throne of Yahweh to its rightful place at the centre of Israel's civil and religious life, the implication being that Saul's misfortunes were occasioned by his neglect of God, symbolized in his lack of concern for the ark as the visible representation of His presence among His people. The Chronicler records David's good intentions here before the Philistine raids (note reverse order in Sam.), to illustrate why God was with him and brought him victory—his heart was in the right place. The Chronicler has adjusted the emphasis in the story to make it much more of a religious ceremony than the semi-military one recorded in Sam., for here it involves the whole convocation of Israel as well as the priests and Levites. All Israel is summoned from the river of Egypt (**Shihor**—an Egyptian word meaning 'pool of Horus' found elsewhere only at Jos. 13: 3; 1 Sam. 23: 3; Jer. 2: 18) to the Syrian border. The account reflects a post-exilic standpoint (note the use of the typical post-exilic phrase **the rest (of our brothers)** v. 2).

While the intention of David was right, his method of carrying it out was not. The Chronicler here wishes to emphasize that sacred objects must only be handled by those qualified to do so—it is part of his theological purpose in emphasizing religious institutions and the rights of the Levitical establishment.

Uzzah is thus killed as a result of failing to observe the commands of God (cf. 15: 13). The ark is kept in the home of **Obed-Edom** who may have been a Levite (Josephus records a tradition to this effect, *Ant.* 7.83), perhaps the same man who is mentioned in 15: 21, 24. If this is so then it may be that the Chronicler recounts the blessing of Obed-Edom as partly the result of the proper care of the ark by a properly qualified person.

(b) **Hiram's Mission and the Philistine Wars (14: 1–17)**
The material here follows a different order from Sam., but almost certainly neither is in chronological order in respect of David's reign. According to W. F. Albright, Hiram reigned about 969–936 BC, that is, his reign did not begin until the last decade of David's reign. Further, it is unlikely that David would have been involved in major building activities at this stage in his reign while he was still involved in a continuing warfare on all sides. It seems best to date the situation more as occurring late in David's reign, following his conquests and the subjugation of the Philistines, who were also Hiram's enemies.

The point of the Chronicler in recording the events here, however, is clear. He wished to show that God was with David in his enterprise in spite of the set-back over the ark. David is thus led to realize that he had been chosen as king because of the way in which the kingdom had been exalted. The purpose, however, was for the sake of his people Israel (v. 2), an excellent example of the biblical concept of election—not for privilege but for the benefit of others. The continued blessing of God is

also shown in the fact that **more sons** were born to him.

The attacks of the Philistines (vv. 8–17) are recorded as coming as soon as they learned that David was **king over all Israel** (a favourite expression of the Chronicler). They struck in the Valley of Rephaim and David, after securing God's advice, attacked them at Baal Perazim, so called from the battle in which the Philistines were torn asunder (cf. Perez Uzzah, 13: 11). The Chronicler's statements at v. 12 differ from the parallel at 2 Sam. 5: 21. It was quite unthinkable for him that David and his men would have done other than burn the idols. The second attack followed as soon as they had regrouped their forces and this time the defeat was even greater, the Philistines being pursued to the borders of their own country, thus clearing that section of Israel **from Gibeon to Gezer.** Not surprisingly, as the Chronicler states, the result of these victories was that the fear of David was **all the nations** (17).

(c) **David's plan for the removal of the Ark (15: 1–24)**
The emphasis in this section is very different from 2 Sam. 6. The Chronicler has added details of the number and family backgrounds of those who participated in the removal of the ark and there are also extended details of the arrangements for transport itself and the music to accompany it. The implication of v. 1 is that a considerable time had elapsed since the first attempt to bring the ark to Jerusalem, which is difficult to reconcile with the earlier statement that it remained at the house of Obed-Edom for only three months. It would appear that the Chronicler is seeking to emphasize that the ark was not moved until proper attention had been paid to the mechanics of the move and a proper **place** had been prepared to receive it. The use of this word (*māqôm*) suggests a holy place or shrine (cf. 21: 22, 25). The Chronicler lays great stress on the fact that only the proper persons should be invited and that it must be carried in the way specified by Moses (cf. Dt. 10: 8; Exod. 25: 13–14; 37: 4, 5). This is especially emphasized in v. 13—**the first time** the ark was moved was a disaster because the Levites were not present. Priests and Levites were thus summoned to sanctify themselves and their families and take charge of the transfer. David here acts through the proper ecclesiastical channels and the Chronicler thus presents a very different picture from the simple events recorded in 2 Sam. 6: 12.

Verses 16–24 deal with the musical arrangements for the procession and while at 16: 4 ff. the musical appointments take place only after the ark had been moved to Jerusalem, the Chronicler here has emphasized the tradition by pushing it back to the first great religious ceremonial connected with the establishment of the kingdom and its new capital. The musicians are both vocalists and instrumentalists, the latter are recorded as playing **lyres** (?zithers), **harps and cymbals.** The priests were the trumpeters. In addition there were the four porters to carry the ark and an overall master of ceremonies. The phrase in v. 22 could be rendered, 'Kenaniah, the Levitical chief of transport, was made director of transport because he was skilled at it'. The word *massā'* may mean 'music leader' or 'transport' and was perhaps deliberately chosen to show that Kenaniah was the director of the whole ceremony.

(d) The moving of the Ark to the city (15: 25–16: 3)

This section closely follows 2 Sam. 6: 12–19. The section falls into three parts, the procession to the house of Obed-Edom, the transport of the ark to Jerusalem and the accompanying ceremonies, and its installation in the special tent with the offerings and feastings. The Chronicler lists the king, the elders of Israel and the senior military commanders as well as the various religious officials as taking part in the procession and the associated ceremonies. He thus expands the Sam. narrative at this point and also departs from it in recording only one major sacrifice instead of those offered every six paces. The statement that David **wore a linen ephod** in addition to a **robe of fine linen** (v. 27) may be a later addition to the text on the basis of 2 Sam. 6: 14, for previously the writer has the king wearing only the normal priestly vestments. In the eyes of the Chronicler only the high priest was entitled to wear the linen ephod.

Although the Chronicler tones down the emotional display of the king during the procession, he records the reaction of Michal as further evidence of the contrast in outlook towards the ark between Saul and his family and David.

The arrival of the ark is the signal for general rejoicing with burnt offerings and peace offerings and a general feast. The implication of 16: 1 is that the offerings were prepared by the priests, but although he seems consistently to keep silent about the priestly role of the king, so apparent in Sam., Kings and Psalms, the Chronicler follows his sources in v. 2 where David performs both offering and blessing. Each person present received a share in the sacrificial meal—**a loaf of bread, a cake of dates, and a cake of raisins.** (The translation of **cake** is difficult. It only occurs here and the parallel passage in 2 Sam. 6: 19.)

(e) The appointment of the ministry (16: 4–6)

This short paragraph is significant in that it reveals again the Chronicler's constant stress on the Levites and their place in the cultus. If the arrangements described in the previous chapter may be thought of as an interim measure concerned simply with the removal of the ark to Jerusalem, then it would seem that the arrangements proved to be so satisfactory that they were made permanent. For the time being, however, there was to be a division of personnel between Gibeon and Jerusalem. The importance of Gibeon gradually declined, especially after the building of the temple, but at this time it ranked as the main centre of the cultus and it is not altogether clear whether any sacrificial worship was carried out at Jerusalem at this stage.

David's motives in bringing the ark to Jerusalem were not merely religious, but also political. In order to weld the northern and southern factions into a cohesive nation he required a central capital. This was afforded by Jerusalem which had been a Jebusite stronghold and without connections with Israelite tribes. The next step after the establishment of the city as a political centre was the reinforcement of its status in making it also the cultic centre for the nation.

(f) The Hymn of Thanksgiving (16: 7–36)

David's hymn of thanksgiving is composed of portions from a number of psalms (vv. 8–22= Ps. 105: 1–15; vv. 23–33= Ps. 96: 1b–13; vv. 34–36=Ps. 106: 1, 47–48). (For the interpretation of the hymn see comments on the relevant Psalms.) It is significant that the psalms used are among those that have become known as enthronement psalms. The Chronicler was probably relying on a well-established tradition at this point and it is conceivable that the triumphal carrying of the ark to Jerusalem set the pattern for the annual celebration at the autumn festival of Tabernacles.

(g) Provision for Ministry (16: 37–43)

The provisions for worship at Jerusalem in association with the ark are dealt with first and this may be of some significance in that it brings to the fore the importance of worship without sacrifice, a situation that gained increasing importance in the exilic and post-exilic periods. The tent for the ark was also going to be replaced by the temple under Solomon and once again the Chronicler is stressing that Jerusalem is the true cult centre, inheriting the tradition of the tabernacle situated at Gibeon which was now fast becoming an anachronism.

Sacrificial worship, however, was maintained at Gibeon in relation to the tabernacle and this is put under the charge of **Zadok.** The problem of the position and origin of the Zadokite priesthood, which eventually displaced the Aaronite priestly line of Abiathar, is highly complex and too involved for discussion here (see notes on ch. 6, above).

The final verse of the chapter is taken from

2 Sam. 6: 19, 20. It is noteworthy that the Chronicler makes no mention of the domestic quarrel between David and Michal (cf. 15: 29).

iii. David's desire to build the Temple (17: 1–27)

(a) His desire meets disapproval (17: 1–15)
The ark has now been transferred to Jerusalem and David is concerned to build a permanent shrine to replace the temporary tent in which the ark had been housed. Significantly, the Chronicler omits the comment of 2 Sam. 7: 1 to the effect that it was only after he had established his kingdom and subdued his enemies that his thought turned to the temple. The Chronicler gives the impression that David was immediately concerned with building the temple. Both accounts note the initial approval of Nathan, who was probably the head of the cultic prophets.

The Chronicler has laid more emphasis than Sam. on the subsequent prohibition (v. 4), although it is clear that it is not the actual building of the **house** that is in question, but the builder. Verses 5, 6 probably refer to the wilderness wanderings and the various early localizations of the shrine at Gibeon, Shiloh and Nob. Nathan's vision proceeds, however, with a word of promise. While David is forbidden to build a house for God, He will build one for David (v. 10). That is, He will provide a line of descendants whose task it will be to shepherd Israel. David has been a man of war engaged in subduing his enemies and ensuring that there will be peace for the development of stability and progress. The writer does not see this task as completed; hence the king must establish the nation and consolidate his position. This is the primary task; the building of the temple can wait until these settled conditions have been produced.

It is important that not too much weight is placed on vv. 11–14. While this section certainly possesses messianic undertones in the light of the post-exilic situation, the primary reference is clearly to Solomon. Nonetheless a close relationship between God and His anointed is posited (also reflected in the royal psalms) and he is viewed as the adopted Son of God to shepherd His people (**my son**, v. 13), for it is Yahweh who is King and Israel's king is His viceregent (cf. Pss. 2; 110). The throne and the religious institutions of the nation are thus closely connected, a characteristic of much OT theology.

In passing it may be noted that this concept also finds expression in the NT where David's heir is involved in building a temple—not now physical, but a spiritual house of God, being the community of the redeemed. Such a development is in keeping with the general NT view of a spiritual fulfilment of prophecy in Christ and His church.

(b) David's Prayer (17: 16–27)
David's response to Nathan's prophetic oracle takes the form of a prayer at the newly established Jerusalem shrine. David **sat before the LORD**, that is before the ark, viewed as Yahweh's throne. The text of the prayer is substantially that of 2 Sam. 7. It contains strong elements of confession and a conception of his unworthiness for the high destiny to which he has been called. Three elements stand out particularly, the greatness and uniqueness of God, His election and deliverance of Israel, and the continuity of the throne. Emphasis is also laid on David's faith and hope. The words **forever, established**, etc., mark the passage and this reaches its climax in the certainty expressed in v. 27.

There are some variations in this section from the Sam. parallel, which are quite likely due to the use of a different Sam. text from the *MT* and one more closely corresponding to those of LXX and the Qumran texts.

iv. David's campaigns (18: 1–20: 8)
The chief reason that David was not to build the temple was that he was a man of war and the Chronicler now proceeds to illustrate this point with an account of David's various wars.

(a) General Survey (18: 1–13)
The writer begins with the Philistine campaign. The success of the purely defensive wars mentioned earlier was not sufficient to provide the degree of security required. David takes the offensive although actual details are obscure. The Chronicler's statement that **Gath and its villages** were captured is his version of the difficult Metheg Ammah of 2 Sam. 8: 1, but as it was the centre closest to David's field of operation there is no reason why Gath should not have been captured. The defeat of Moab is passed over with no reference to the gruesome events of 2 Sam. 8: 2. The clash with the Aramaean states may have been the result of the Ammonite campaign. The Aramaeans had been steadily expanding from the beginning of the tenth century B.C. and it was more or less inevitable that they would come into conflict with David's own expansionist policies sooner or later.

Zobah (3) was the strongest of the Aramaean states at this time. It was apparently an area rich in copper and David is said to have taken large amounts of bronze as booty, later to be used in the temple.

The defeat of **Hadadezer** relieved the pressure on Hamath and the king, **Tou** ('Toi' in 2 Sam. 8: 9 f., see NIVmg) sent his son with a message of congratulation and a large present, which was solemnly dedicated to God in Jerusalem (v. 11).

The writer takes note of **Abishai's** conquest of **Edom** (for which David receives the credit in 2 Sam. 8: 13 f. and Joab in the preface to Ps.

60) and the overall impression is of a rapidly expanding sphere of influence. David does not seem to have incorporated the conquered states into an empire, but rather incorporated them into his realm as tributary states owing allegiance to David as 'head of the commonwealth'.

(b) **Note on the Organization of the Kingdom (18: 14–17)**
The rapid growth of David's dominion necessitated the development of a proper system of administration, a system which he largely based on Egyptian patterns. The Chronicler provides a list of the major departmental heads. The king was over all, **doing what was just and right**. **Joab** was the commander-in-chief of the armed forces, and **Jehoshaphat** was **the recorder** (mazkîr). This denotes an official with a wide range of duties largely related to ceremonial and protocol. **Zadok . . . and Ahimelech . . . were priests**, the former in charge of Gibeon sanctuary and the latter over that in Jerusalem. The **secretary** was **Shavsha** (2 Sam. 8: 17 has Seraiah, probably a Hebraicized form). His father is not noted indicating almost certainly that he was a foreigner and probably Egyptian (so R. de Vaux), perhaps specifically brought in to superintend the organization of the administration on the Egyptian pattern. The secretary was in charge of royal correspondence as the king's personal secretary, and the writer and publisher of royal decrees on the order of the king. He was also the bearer of diplomatic correspondence and at times acted as ambassador extraordinary. In charge of the elite corps of the king's bodyguard was **Benaiah**. The **Kerethites and Pelethites** (17) were the non-Israelite mercenary bodyguard. Their origin is uncertain although some think they may have been Cretans and Philistines. The king's sons are given key parts as administrators under the king. Here the Chronicler has changed the wording of 2 Sam. 8: 18 where they are said to officiate as priests, since he wishes to emphasize the 'official' priesthood rather than that attached to the monarchy.

(c) **The Ammonite Campaign (19: 1–20: 3)**
It is not altogether clear at what point in David's reign this major campaign took place. The Chronicler has already noted the defeat of the Aramaeans and he gives further details of how and why this conflict arose. It appears that the confrontation was due to the insult administered to David's good will embassy by the suspicious Ammonite king Hanun (v. 4). Although David did not immediately respond, there is no doubt that Hanun realized that he had precipitated trouble and consequently called on the Aramaean states for backing. The gross nature of the insult is apparent not only from the treatment afforded to the ambassadors

but also from the fact that David's actual words (v. 2) were 'I will do ḥesed with Hanun . . . as his father did ḥesed with me'. The term ḥesed (rendered **kindness**) is used of the covenant love of Yahweh to His people and reflects a deep devotion to a solemn mutual obligation. The Israelites had very deep feelings about such mutual obligations in serving a common cause —in this case apparently the fact that David and Nahash (Hanun's father) had joined together against Saul. To reject David's offer in such a way could only mean war.

The Ammonite campaign was very protracted and appears to have been fought in three phases. The initial battle resulted in the defeat of the Ammonites and the more local Aramaeans by the Israelite army led by Joab (vv. 6–15). Hanun then called on the more distant and powerful Aramaeans under Hadadezer to give him support and once again they were defeated, this time with David himself leading his forces (vv. 16–19). The result was the utter defeat of the Ammonite-Aramaean league, including the death of the Aramaean general Shophach. The Aramaeans under Hadadezer sued for peace and became David's vassals, thus bringing a solid block of territory under Israelite suzerainty, extending from the areas north and east of Lake Huleh, through the Antilebanon into the traditional area of Aram-naharaim beyond the Euphrates. There are differences in detail between the accounts in Sam. and Chr. more especially in regard to numbers (cf. 2 Sam. 8: 4; 10: 18).

The final stage of the campaign was the capture of Rabbah, the Ammonite capital (20: 1–4). It would appear that the siege of Rabbah had been delayed, perhaps due to the onset of winter, and David was content to wait until the following spring before instructing Joab to inflict the final blow. At any rate the point is made that the attack is launched **in the spring** (lit. 'at the turn of the year'). It would appear that two calendars were in operation, one with the new year in the spring and the other with the new year in the autumn, the respective festivals being Passover and Tabernacles.

David remained in Jerusalem, but the Chronicler studiously avoids any mention of the Bathsheba affair. Indeed it is noteworthy that David's private life is ignored completely. The Chronicler is concerned only with official matters and the rise and development of institutions. The result of these omissions has given rise to unevenness in the narrative, for although he gives Joab the credit of capturing the city, he has David returning to Jerusalem with the Ammonite crown (weighing surprisingly a talent of gold, approx. 75 lbs.) and other booty (cf. 2 Sam. 11: 1; 12: 26–31). The indication of v. 3 is that David made the local people break down the walls of their city or involved them in forced labour rather than that he inflicted some form of barbarity on them.

(d) Further conflict with the Philistines (20: 4–8)

It is likely that there were frequent 'incidents' involving the Philistines throughout the early years of David's reign. Three episodes are mentioned here, all of them centring about giants. In the first it is likely that **Gezer** (4) is correct against 2 Sam. 21: 18 (Gob). The Chronicler's statement that it was Goliath's **brother** that Elhanan slew avoids the apparent contradiction of 2 Sam. 21: 19 where Elhanan kills Goliath and 1 Sam. 17 where David is credited with the victory. **Lahmi** is probably a corruption of 'Bethlehemite' of 2 Sam. 21: 19. It is possible, however, that 2 Sam. 21: 19 preserves an old tradition that David's family name was Elhanan, and that he took the name of David as his throne name.

v. David and the Temple (21: 1–26: 28)

(a) The Census and the Temple Site (21: 1–22: 1)

The Chronicler has recounted how war booty had been set aside for the temple. Now he relates how the actual temple site was acquired. Unlike the author of Sam., the writer does not attribute to God the indiscretion of David in taking the census, but to Satan. It had become unthinkable for post-exilic Judaism to attribute evil to God (contrast Am. 3: 6). The idea of the **Satan** (Accuser) as a member of God's court, cast in the role of a sort of heavenly Director of Public Prosecution, was not new (cf. Job 1: 6 ff.; Zech. 3: 1). Here, however, he appears to some more as an opponent of God, a new development in Jewish thought, commonly (but not certainly) ascribed to the influence of Persian dualism. It has been suggested that his position is further emphasized by the omission of the article with his name, and thus becomes a personality with a will and purpose of his own opposed to the will and purpose of God. It is possible, however, that this should not be pushed too far and it seems likely that the Chronicler was still thinking in terms of Satan as an agent of God and thus avoiding the rather blunt statement of Sam. that it was God who tempted David. Here it is Satan's incitement (he **rose up against**—i.e. brought to mind, hence, tempted) that accounts for David's persistence in taking the census in spite of Joab's objections.

The specific reason for the census is not given, nor is it clear why this census was considered wrong, as a census for military purposes was authorized by God (Num. 24). It may be that the prophetic opposition arose from their sense of social justice. If the census was to be used as a basis for increased taxation of the people or as the basis of a corvée (forced labour), then it would clearly outrage the pro-phetic concept that justice and integrity should be the outcome of the relationship between the holy and righteous God with His people. It may be supposed that the outbreak of a severe epidemic was occasioned by the census takers moving from town to town, but the prophet Gad sees this as divine judgment to be averted only by confession and penitence. The nature of the epidemic is impossible to determine. The numbers quoted are extraordinarily high (v. 5). If, however, '*elep* is accepted as meaning simply a military or civil unit (see note on '*elep*, 'a thousand' at 1 Chr. 12: 24) it gives the figure of 1100 units for all Israel and 470 for Judah. This is about double the numbers given for the period of the tribal federation. The number in each unit was probably ten (cf. 1 Chr. 12: 24 ff.), thus giving a figure of 11,000 fighting men, a much more reasonable figure. The slight difference in numbers from the Sam. account is due to the Chronicler's omission of Levi and Benjamin (v. 6). The details of the census given in Sam. are also omitted as the main point of this section is the purchase of the temple site.

The Chronicler does not record how David came to see that he had been wrong to take the census. The Sam. parallel indicates that his conscience troubled him. The prophet Gad is directed to offer three alternatives to the repentant king (vv. 9–12). He chooses to put himself directly into the hands of God rather than face the humiliation of falling into the hands of his enemies. The result is the epidemic in which 70,000 died. Here again the figure should probably be understood as units—'70 units'. There was probably little to choose between in numbers of dead between the three-day epidemic or three years of famine.

The writer now reaches the point of the story in the staying of the plague and the choice of the temple site. David and his company are setting out for Gibeon in order to make sacrifice and seek counsel from God. The sudden appearance of **the angel of the LORD** (16) (seen now as a divine functionary rather than as a manifestation of Yahweh as in the earlier stories) causes the immediate necessity of calling upon God in repentance and confession and offering sacrifice. This was done at the site of the threshing floor of **Araunah** which David now buys. The story has close parallels with the Abraham-Ephron transaction (Gen. 23) and it may be no accident that there are these apparent and less apparent parallels in view of the tradition connecting the Mount Moriah of Abraham with the Mount Zion of David. The use of the word **site** (*māqôm*) suggests that there is here a remnant of an earlier tradition that it was already a holy place which was taken over as the site for Israel's national shrine.

The acceptance of the offering is confirmed

by the **fire from heaven** (26), a powerful attestation of divine approval (cf. Jg. 6: 21; 1 Kg. 18: 38; 2 Chr. 7: 1). God's wrath has been appeased, the plague ceases and Jerusalem is spared. The favourable response to the sacrifice indicated to David that this site should be the one for the temple and the future centre of both sacrificial and other forms of worship in place of the shrine at Gibeon. Hence David makes the proclamation of 22: 1. The whole story thus indicates how the temple site was chosen —it was not by chance but by God's intervention. There is also a clear illustration of the writer's major interest in the themes of failure and judgment; grace and restoration. The king paid heed to the prophetic rebuke, accepting the chastisement of the plague. He was, therefore, not merely pardoned, but also received a clear sign of divine favour.

(*b*) **Preparation for Building the Temple (22: 2–5)**
The remaining sections of 1 Chr. are largely devoted to detailing the preparations for the building of the temple. This section is concerned with the material preparations. There are no parallels to this section elsewhere, apart from isolated verses, and the Chronicler is utilizing some of his additional sources otherwise unknown. The verses describing the material preparations for building that David put in hand reflect a level of organization and administration in the kingdom only hinted at in 2 Chr. 24: 8, 15–18 and 22: 24. The census of the previous chapter is suggestive of a tighter bureaucratic control of the population and may reflect the increasing unrest within the empire in the latter part of David's reign, manifested in Absalom's rebellion, the Sheba uprising and the Gibeonite affair. Further, the scale of building envisaged by David for the temple, requiring vast amounts of materials, also required enormous manpower and necessitated the use of forced labour. The Chronicler makes this applicable only to foreigners: foreign labour gangs were sent to the quarries. The idea of using the free Israelite in a system of forced labour was clearly repugnant to the Chronicler (contrast 2 Chr. 2: 17 f. with 1 Kg. 5: 13), but that some sort of corvée was levied on the Israelites themselves seems clear from the fact that there was an official in charge of it (2 Sam. 20: 24).

The pre-occupation of David with establishing the kingdom and ensuring its safety rendered it impossible for him to do other than attend to the site and the collection of material so that his son Solomon would be able to proceed immediately with the actual building. According to this source David also wished to ensure that all the preparations were made on the ground of the immaturity of Solomon (v. 5). There is no indication of Solomon's age

when he attained the throne, but it is possible that there is a hint of co-regency here. He was made king before David's death (1 Kg. 1: 32–40; 1 Chr. 23: 1) although how long before is uncertain. According to 2 Chr. 3: 2 the building of the temple began in the second month of the fourth year of his reign. It could be argued therefore that there was a co-regency of four years. 'David's determination to have a temple built thus provides a possible motivation for a regency arrangement—to avoid a palace revolution that could jeopardize his plans' (J. M. Myers). The amounts of gold and silver collected, according to the Chronicler, represent astronomical figures. He is no doubt seeking to emphasize that David spared no expense in his preparations (approximately 3,775 tons of gold and 37,750 tons of silver!). The point is made, however, that this was only collected with **great pains** (14), a subtle implication that David's resources were slender compared with those of his son Solomon.

(*c*) **David's Charge to Solomon (22: 6–19)**
David's charge to Solomon (vv. 6–16) is couched in formal and solemn terms and bears some similarity to that recorded in 1 Kg. 2: 1–9, but the interest of the Chronicler is apparent here in ensuring the successful completion of the temple project. David has been unable to build it as he has been a man of war and caused much bloodshed. The Chronicler emphasizes a primarily ritual reason (v. 8) for his inability to build, whereas 1 Kg. 5: 3 simply states that he had been too busy fighting his enemies. In contrast Solomon is to be a man of peace. The play on words here is unmistakeable between **Solomon** (*šlmh*) and **peace** (*šlwm*) (v. 9). Solomon is charged to begin work straight away indicating that the charge has come at the very end of David's reign. The section concludes with a charge to the officials alone that they must stand by Solomon and provide him with all the help he requires. The public charge to the whole people with the ceremonial delivering of the king's testament to his son comes in chs. 28 and 29.

vi. The Temple Ministry (23: 1–26: 28)
(*a*) **The Levites (23: 1–32)**
Arrangements having been set in motion to ensure the completion of the temple itself, attention is now turned to the temple service. The Chronicler provides detailed lists of personnel and their functions in order that provision may be made for all aspects of temple worship. There is little doubt that these chapters form a single unit, although parts may belong to a later final writing of the book. The sources used by the Chronicler are not known, but are most likely derived from the temple archives. There is evidence, however, that the writer has developed them along his own lines, accommodating himself to the conditions of

his own time. In so far as the work of the Chronicler is an expositional commentary on Scripture this is valid practice, since the task of the expositor is to re-interpret Scripture for his own generation. The framework of the chapter follows the order of Ezekiel which may have provided the pattern for the Chronicler's arrangement.

The opening verses set the stage and introduce an order that could apply to the whole nation, based upon David's authority. His point is quite possibly to assert that the practice of his own time derives from liturgical practice under David and hence may claim this authoritative basis.

The provisions for the temple service begin with the Levites (v. 6) who are counted from **thirty years old or more** (Num. 4: 3 etc.). However, vv. 23–27 refer to numbering from **twenty years old.** This may reflect a later revision and the post-exilic situation. It is possible that the word *'elep* (**thousand**) should again be translated as 'unit', which would provide more probable numbers (see also comments on 12: 24 and 21: 5). The organization of the Levites was based on the three Levitical families and the details probably reflect the actual practice in the time of the writer, although the basic pattern may be attributed correctly to David. The whole passage points back to the beginnings of an organized clergy which developed in association with the needs of the temple. The reference to the **daughters** of Eleazar (v. 22) is of interest in that it suggests a claim to full status through the female line. The final section details the duties of the Levites (v. 27 should probably follow v. 24). God now **dwells** (25) or has taken up residence (*škn*) in Jerusalem. This is a significant term indicating the precise manner of divine residence and relates to the earlier understanding of the *miškān* —the tabernacling of Yahweh in the midst of His people. In view of this statement the vision of Ezekiel takes on an added significance (Ezek. 7–9) and represents a very different view from the other prophetic writings (cf. Deut. and Jer.) in which God is not so closely identified with Jerusalem and the temple.

The Levitical duties are subordinate to the priests—their job was to assist them (vv. 28 ff.), although they had responsibility for the direction of the music for the services. Generally the Levites were in charge of the material well-being of the sanctuary and its equipment, while the priests were more strictly the cultic personnel. This probably reflects post-exilic conditions, but the writer justly claims that what is being done in his age reflects the principles of service laid down by David.

(*b*) **Priests and other Levites (24: 1–31)**
The Chronicler's interest in the cult is evidenced by the fact that he provides no less than

six lists of priests or priestly families (cf. ch. 9: 10–12; Ezr. 2: 36–39; Neh. 12: 12–21) as well as numerous other references to them. Assisting David in the appointment of the priestly divisions is **Zadok** (representing Eleazar) and **Ahimelech** (representing Ithamar). According to 1 Sam. 22: 20 Ahimelech's father Abiathar was a grandson of Ahitub, a representative of the Elides who lost their position under Solomon (1 Kg. 2: 27). The Chronicler, however, relates Zadok to Ahitub and relegates Ahimelech to the Ithamar line. This probably reflects the ascendancy of the Zadokite priesthood which, from the time of Solomon, became the most important and influential group, although, at the same time, the account also reflects the successful struggle for full recognition by the Ithamar family which had apparently been confined to Levitical type duties.

The allocation to ministry was by lot (v. 5). Both lines of the priesthood are given equal ministry in theory (as at Exod. 28: 1 and Lev. 10: 6) so that the Chronicler can refer to them both as **officials of the sanctuary and officials of God** (5). The Chronicler indicates that the dominance of Eleazar (Zadokites) was due to their numerical superiority and consequently their group retained control of affairs. It should be remembered that the lists of names represent families rather than individuals as such, and a number of these families continued into NT times (*e.g.* Zechariah was of the line of Abijah, Lk. 1: 5).

The section dealing with the other Levites (vv. 20–31) appears to be a later addition to the list of ch. 23. It parallels that list, but takes it further, usually by one generation. However, the addition of a complete new line in the family of Merari would mean that a greater length of time than say 20–25 years has elapsed. The absence of the Gershon family is interesting.

(*c*) **The Singers (25: 1–31)**
In the same way as the priests and Levites the temple singers are also given status and an organization as official cult personnel. The appointments were made by David and the 'cult officials' and special emphasis is placed on Asaph, Heman and Jeduthan (Ethan) whose names are closely associated with the musical guilds. The relationship of these guilds to Zerah (2: 6) could suggest that their origin was pre-Israelite and that they were part of the local pre-settlement worship that was assimilated by Israel. The well known interest of David in music may well have been the factor which established them on an official footing and the evidence of the psalms reflects a close relationship between the organized worship and music in the early monarchy.

The second part of v. 4 presents interesting problems. The Chronicler has represented it as a series of names, but a strong case can be made out for viewing this as either a fragment of a psalm or a series of headings for classifying various psalms from a temple catalogue. The headings presumably became displaced at some stage and were read as a list of names. A minor change in vocal points and word division would give:

Be gracious to me, O Yahweh, be
    gracious,
My God art Thou,
I have magnified and will exalt my helper,
Sitting in adversity I said,
Give clear signs plentifully.

These may well have been originally references to the psalm types used and perhaps provide examples of the kind of inspired utterances which belonged to these Levitical singers. The last perhaps specifically related to collections of cult prophecies in which the singers were involved (for further details of this problem consult the major commentaries).

(d) Gatekeepers and Treasury Officials (26: 1–28)

The list of officials continues in descending order of importance to gatekeepers and treasury officials. While they may have been a lower order, their status is nonetheless important and they are accorded the status of Levites. This suggests that these lists may post-date the original Chronicler's history since apparently they were not accorded Levitical status in the immediate post-exilic period of Ezr.–Neh. (cf. Ezr. 2: 42, 70; 7: 24; 10: 24; Neh. 10: 20; 11: 19).

The lists of gatekeepers given here are similar to those given in Ezr. and Neh. but with expansions. The list seems to be a continuation of those of 9: 17, 18 and 16: 37, 38 with additional names added to bring it up to date at the time of the compiler and may be viewed perhaps as a later supplement. The family of Obed-Edom is given as sixty-two persons here, whereas at 16: 38 it is given as sixty-eight. His family may have been given the south gate which abutted onto the royal palace because of his close association with David. It is also to be noted that their functions were not to be restricted to gatekeeping, but they had additional duties to perform, **just as their relatives** (12). **16. To Shuppim:** an unintelligible intrusion arising from dittography from the last word of v. 15. **the Shalleketh Gate:** known only from this passage. It is possible it should be read 'the gate that leads to the road of ascent' (cf. Vulg., LXX). The word 'parbar', which NIV translates as **court**, (18) is also difficult. The word has been found on a Lydian inscription and on the 'copper scroll' of Qumran. The meaning may be 'treasury' or 'summer house'.

The treasury officials had two types of dedicated material to guard. There were the **treas-**uries of the temple of the LORD (22), including the implements of worship and the temple offerings (cf. 9: 28–29; 23: 28–29), and the **treasuries for the things dedicated** (26) which mainly consisted of war booty which had been dedicated to God. The references to the contributions of Samuel, Saul, Abner and Joab are noteworthy; perhaps they reflect the writer's interest in showing that 'all Israel' was associated with the religious institutions of the nation.

vii. The Administration of the kingdom (26: 29–27: 34)
(a) The Judiciary (26: 29–32)

This section bears no relation to the previous sections dealing with temple personnel, but has a place in the book in that it provides information about David's internal government and security arrangements. The source for the compilation of material may be **the annals of King David** referred to at 27: 24, probably conflated with material reflecting the writer's own situation. Secular affairs were under the Izharites and Hebronites, the latter having specific authority for the Trans-jordan area. The former group were responsible for **duties away from the temple** (29) although what exactly these were must be partly conjecture. According to 2 Chr. 19: 4–11 priests and Levites were appointed to judicial functions in the time of Jehoshaphat. Josephus (*Ant.* 4. 214) writes of two Levites being appointed as assistants for each judge and refers this practice back to Moses, indicating that in his time the practice was an old one. It is possible that the Izharites were thus some form of judicial functionaries.

(b) The Military (27: 1–15)

This list enumerates the divisional commanders, each of whom was called upon to serve for one month at a time. The list closely parallels that of David's mighty men (cf. 11: 11–47), but here they are commanders of divisions whose duty it was to serve the king in monthly relays. On the basis of '*elep* (thousand) meaning a unit, there is a total of 288 units, i.e. 24 units per month. If each unit had 10 men the impression is more of a personal bodyguard rather than a strategic military organization. There is more identification of family relationships here than in the earlier chapter and the variations suggest a parallel, but independent, source for this section. Verse 4 should probably read 'Eleazar the son of Dodai the Ahohite.'

(c) Tribal Governors (27: 16–24)

The list of tribal chiefs retains the twelve-tribe system, but uses a different order from the earlier lists and alters the actual tribal arrangements within the system. Asher and Gad are both omitted and to compensate for this Manasseh is divided into two districts. The tribe of Levi is retained and special mention is made of Zadok as an Aaronite. The fact that he does not appear to have been so regarded until the time of Ezra suggests that the list as it stands is a late compilation.

Verses 23 and 24 record the reason why no complete national census figures were available although there were such figures for special functionaries. The reasons cited are both religious in nature. On the one hand David believed the promise of God (cf. Gen. 15: 5) and on the other Joab was unable to complete the count because the wrath of God had fallen on the nation. This provides an interesting reflection on the account at 21: 5, 6: even an attempt at a census, such as is recorded there, does not accord easily with David's declaration of trust. **23. twenty years old:** this seems to have been the time when persons ordinarily entered into their civic responsibilities. Cf. Num. 1: 3 for a similar age limit; this was also the age for full participation in the Qumran community (note also 23: 23).

(d) **The Royal Estates (27: 25–31)**
The crown administrators appear to have been mainly concerned with looking after the royal storehouses in Jerusalem and the provinces and also with the management of crown property (farms, vineyards, etc.). Part of this began to accumulate in David's outlaw days and was largely the result of conquest. While the loose spoils of war were dedicated to God, land and other property, such as animals, were kept for the use of the court and required an extensive system for administration. There is no indication that there was taxation in David's reign and expenses were met from his private fortune and estates.

(e) **The Privy Council (27: 32–34)**
Side by side with the growing bureaucracy of public administrators and officials, David also had an inner cabinet of personal advisers. His uncle **Jonathan** is only mentioned here in the Bible. He and **Jehiel** (again only here) were responsible for the upbringing and education of David's sons. On **Ahithophel** see 2 Sam. 15: 12; 16: 15–17: 23. After his suicide he was succeeded by **Jehoiada, son of Benaiah**, known only from this passage. Hushai's title, **the king's friend**, may have been honorific, but more probably carried with it the function of a special personal adviser. **Abiathar** the priest had been an associate of David's for many years, but he is not referred to here as priest which is probably due to the Chronicler's tendency to emphasize the Zadok line as the legitimate priesthood and also, perhaps, because of Abiathar's later disgrace at the time of Solomon's accession.

viii. The End of David's Reign and the Accession of Solomon (28: 1–29: 30)
(a) **David's Final Instructions (28: 1–21)**
This section continues the story interrupted by the lists that have been introduced between

23: 2 and the opening of this chapter. The Chronicler informs us of what actually happened when David assembled the political and military leaders of the kingdom to witness the transfer of authority to Solomon. The Chronicler ignores the Kings source here and utilizes other sources which he expands into a unified narrative. His reason for not using the Kings account of Solomon's accession is probably because of the distasteful Adonijah affair and the palace intrigue associated with it. Solomon's accession was part of the divine plan and the Chronicler deliberately leaves out those elements of the story which are irrelevant to his main purpose.

David's address to his son is based on earlier sources, but the Chronicler's strong sense of election shines through here as elsewhere (vv. 4, 5). God had chosen Judah from the tribes of Israel, the family of Jesse from within that, David from among Jesse's sons and now Solomon from among the many sons of David, to occupy the throne and continue the dynasty. 'From the vantage point of the writer, such a succession of events were acts of God, not just circumstances of history' (J. M. Myers). However, the Chronicler also emphasizes the ethical content of election. The dynasty would not survive without the persistence of that relationship to God which had been maintained throughout the reign of David. The elements come out strongly: the concept of the king as God's son (v. 6 **my son**; cf. Ps. 2: 7, etc.) and the ethical principles of a right life upon which the former relationship was contingent (v. 7). Only if Solomon obeys the commandments of God will the succession be secure and the land belong to Israel forever. The Chronicler's lesson for his own time is clear.

The main aim, however, is the building of the sanctuary, the house of God, the symbol of His presence among His people. David thus proceeds to give specific directions in the form of a complete set of plans—for portico, temple, storehouses and other ancillary parts (vv. 11, 12) and the various elements of temple service and equipment (vv. 13–19). The amounts of gold and silver are set out in meticulous detail. (The account in Kings speaks only of gold and bronze.) The Chronicler points out that this was not merely a verbal set of directions but they were contained in a document (v. 19). Some such plan of the building may well have been preserved in the temple archives, but the Chronicler, in keeping with his main theme, wished to emphasize that this plan derived from God's inspiration. It came from **the hand of the LORD**. The comparison with Moses and Bezalel seems clear (Exod. 31: 1–11, etc.). For the Chronicler, David occupies the same position in regard to the temple as Moses did to the tabernacle. It is likely that this emphasis on divine direction is to be seen also at v. 12. AV, RV and NIV (**all that the Spirit had put in his mind**) give a better rendering than RSV ('all that he had in mind'). Heb. *rûaḥ* (spirit) is never used by the Chronicler other than in relation to God and it would seem that this verse is in keeping with the rest of the section in emphasizing that David's wisdom in drawing up the plans was an outcome of divine guidance. The very different emphasis from 1 Kg. 5 and 6 again underlines the Chronicler's preoccupation with the greatness of David.

There is a possibility that some of the description given here reflects the influence of Ezekiel, especially in relation to the **chariot, that is, the cherubim** (18, perhaps reflecting the throne chariot of Ezek. 1: 10; 43: 3–4). The final charge to Solomon (vv. 20, 21) is in order to impress on the young king and the people as a whole the seriousness of the undertaking upon which they have embarked. The language used reflects strongly that attributed to Moses in his charge to Joshua (Dt. 31: 6, 8; Jos. 1: 5) and again the parallel between Moses and David is emphasized. There is little doubt that this directive was for those who would be assisting Solomon as much as for Solomon himself, in order to inspire their loyalty and devotion to the cause.

(b) David's contribution to the Temple (29: 1–9)

This short section details David's personal contribution for the temple in terms of gold, silver, bronze, wood and stone, together with materials for mosaic flooring and various other precious materials. His concern for the project is so great that he had devoted his own personal **treasures** (*seḡullāh*) to the temple. On this basis he issued a challenge to the leaders of the nation similarly to devote themselves to God. The expression **consecrate himself** (5) literally means 'filling his hand' and was a technical term for the consecration of priests (Exod. 28: 41). RSV, on the other hand, interprets the phrases here to imply that the people's voluntary offering of their substance to God would constitute an act of consecration to Him. It is not merely the gift that is being dedicated, but also the giver. This is a concept developed further in the NT. The Chronicler records an enormous response and again there seems to be a link here with the voluntary giving of the people for the tabernacle. The Chronicler has allowed an anachronism to slip in as the **daric** (7) was a Persian coin. He was probably translating the sums involved into the monetary values of his own day. This passage and Ezr.–Neh. contain the first mentions of coinage in the Bible and it is unlikely that any coined money existed in the time of David. Once again the actual amounts are astronomical.

(c) David's Prayer of Thanksgiving (29: 10–20)

The willing generosity of the people called forth a prayer of thanksgiving from David. This is no empty gesture, but reflects the deep awareness that it was only because God had so abundantly blessed His people that such offerings could be given. The NIV paragraphs are not entirely satisfactory here. Verse 13 probably begins the second part of the prayer —**Now.** This introduces the main section. The sense of the whole is that David and the people have been giving thanks and praising God: **But** (emphatic) (v. 14) what is their status before Him? David proceeds to comment on this in a series of statements. All comes from God, for man is nothing, his days are no more than a transient shadow and lack security (*miqweh* or home abode, which RSV renders 'abiding', v. 15). God alone is the source of all things and thus He is providing for His own house, but He does so through the willingness of His people to offer themselves and their possessions to Him. David's prayer is that such a continued attitude of dedication to God with loyalty to His commands should mark both Solomon and the people. The concepts expressed have a clear validity extending on beyond the immediate circumstances. David finally called upon the people to **praise the LORD** and they did so in a spontaneous act of worship.

(d) Solomon's Accession (29: 21–25)

The accession of Solomon is pictured here as happening without any opposition, but the fact of such opposition is possibly in the Chronicler's mind when he lays emphasis on the fact that **he prospered and all Israel obeyed him** (23) and again **all of King David's sons pledged their submission** (24). There are certain differences from the account in 1 Kings, but the story is a unit setting forth the essential facts only. The Chronicler is not so much concerned with glossing over the unpleasant facts (his readers would know them anyway), but he was concerned to chronicle 'the history of the kingdom from a religious point of view and follows a straight line rather than detours that would detract from his objective' (J. M. Myers). The fact that **Zadok** acts as high priest and officiates at the anointing ceremony reflects the disgrace of Abiathar who took part in the abortive coup of Adonijah. The Zadokite line is now firmly in the ascendancy and will remain so.

(e) Summary of David's Reign (29: 26–30)

This is a summary of the barest facts only of the reign of David and simply rounds off this part of the narrative. Note again the emphasis that David had been king over **all Israel** (26), not even mentioning that the seven years reign at Hebron was only over Judah. This is indeed one of the few references to the early reign of David. As a good historian the Chronicler finally quotes his primary sources. Whether these were what are now the books of Samuel and Kings or whether they were archival material cannot be determined. The **kingdoms of all the other lands** (30) probably refers to the tributary kings of the empire.

2 Chronicles

ix. Solomon takes over the Kingdom (1: 1–17)

This section serves as a general introduction to the life and reign of Solomon. The Chronicler will emphasize mainly the completion of the building of the temple, the point to which he has been moving throughout his account of David's reign. Nonetheless, the notes on the wealth and honour of Solomon (to which he will return at ch. 9) serve to emphasize the fact that God was with him. His assumption of kingly power is described as being **established . . . over his kingdom**, a statement that may reflect the Chronicler's awareness of the struggle for power immediately after David's death.

The new king's first action is religious—an act of dedication involving both king and people (v. 3). It is represented here as an official act (1 Kg. 3: 4 suggests a personal act of devotion) taking place at the Gibeon sanctuary (still the official sanctuary for the kingdom, being the site of the old tent of meeting and using the original altar built by Bezalel). It is noteworthy that the Chronicler makes no reference to the high place nor sees any reason for the apologetic note of 1 Kg. 3: 3. The exile had shown the Jewish people that the presence of God was independent of place—and more important. The presence of God is here symbolized in the altar and confirmed in the revelation that Solomon receives.

The appearing of God to Solomon is based on the Kings parallel but is condensed and God here appears directly and not in a dream. There are slight alterations, although the ultimate significance both of Solomon's request and God's blessing is the same. The interesting omission is of Solomon's appearing before the Ark to offer sacrifice; an act which would not accord with the Chronicler's view of cultic duties. This constant playing down of the priestly role of the king has been noted earlier.

The account of the amazing wealth (vv. 14–17) derives from 1 Kg. 10: 26–29 with the additional mention of **gold, silver** and **cedarwood** (15). Cedar was a rare and highly prized wood; Solomon made it as common as the **sycamore** wood from the Shephelah. It is clear that Solomon was a great merchant prince who was able to turn every opportunity to advantage. He imported **horses** from Cilicia (there can be no doubt as to this rendering; Cilicia (**Kue**) is frequently mentioned in Assyrian documents from the ninth century BC) at the prevailing price ($m^e h\bar{i}r$) and chariots from Egypt, selling them through his agents to the Hittites and Aramaeans. The chariots were more expensive than horses due to the skilled workmanship required in manufacture whereas horses were simply bred without any of the modern concern for pedigree.

The wealth and wisdom of Solomon form a fitting start to the story of his reign indicating that God was with him to fulfil the divine promise of blessing.

x. The Building and Dedication of the Temple (2: 1–7: 22)

(a) Preparations for the building of the Temple (2: 1–18)

The really significant aspect of Solomon's reign is reached with very little attention being paid to the development of his armed forces and other aspects of the kingdom. Solomon gives the order for the work to begin on palace and temple, that is, the carrying out of David's blueprints. Although there are several references to the Palace (2: 11; 7: 11; 8: 1; 9: 11) nowhere does the Chronicler give any details of it. Palace and temple seem to have been a single complex of buildings and the temple was in some respects a royal chapel. Note how the Bethel sanctuary takes on a similar function for the northern kingdom (Am. 7: 13).

The enterprise was immense and labour was required as well as extensive organization. Labour was obtained by forced labour gangs (vv. 2, 17). The Chronicler tones down the Kings report (as he did for David's corvée) by restricting the work force to foreigners (perhaps prisoners of war). The Chronicler has also given credit to Solomon for his initiative in approaching Hiram of Tyre for men and materials. In the Kings account Hiram sends ambassadors of goodwill to Solomon and through these men Solomon makes his request. The Chronicler thus shifts the emphasis of the narrative and in fact all credit for the project is given to Solomon, although clearly this is to be read in the light of the previous planning laid down by David.

Solomon's letter (vv. 3–10) emphasizes the greatness of the house of God, but at the same time he recognizes that the God of Israel is the One who is too great to be contained in a house made by man, for the universe itself cannot contain Him. Before such a God even the mighty king Solomon pales into insignificance.

Solomon's first request is for a skilled workman able to direct his own craftsmen in their work (v. 7). In addition he required wood—**cedar, pine, and algum** (8). The latter was a precious wood used for furniture and the construction of luxury buildings such as temples and palaces. It was probably imported from Syria, although 2 Chr. 9: 10 has it coming from Ophir. The exact nature of the wood is unknown. In return for this help Solomon is prepared to send some of his workmen to assist in the preparation of timber and will provide food for their board. Hiram's reply (vv. 11–16) is worded more fulsomely than the Kings parallel and he agrees to provide the necessary help sending **Huram-Abi** (13), the son of a Tyrian father and a Danite mother (in Kings a Naphtali widow). Perhaps the Chronicler is drawing a parallel to Bezalel the craftsman of the tabernacle who was a Danite. The name Huramabi presents some problems. The Kings parallels (1 Kg. 7: 13, etc.) have Huram (NIVmg Hiram) and the text here may be translated 'Hiram my father', but king Hiram's father was Abihaal and would any way be an old man by this time and hardly the sort of person to be sent as a skilled craftsman. Rudolph points out that 'āb may also mean 'master' (Gen. 45: 8; Jg. 17: 10, etc.) and if this view is correct the meaning is probably 'Hiram my master (craftsman)'.

Hiram also urges Solomon to send his labourers without delay, together with the supplies for their keep. The timber would be shipped to **Joppa** and from there Solomon would be responsible for its transfer to Jerusalem. The provisions here are more definite than in Kings and Joppa is specifically mentioned since it was the nearest port to Jerusalem.

(b) **Construction of the Temple (3: 1–17)**
It is interesting to note that while the Chronicler maintains a dominant interest in the temple he shortens the description of the building itself. He is more interested in the institutions and worship associated with the temple than with its construction.

The temple site, **provided** by David (rather than where the Lord appeared), is identified with Mount Moriah by the Chronicler (not mentioned in Kings nor elsewhere). The site is thus associated with Abraham's offering of Isaac, perhaps because this site was designated 'the mount of the LORD' (Gen. 22: 14). The OT has numerous references to the 'mountain of the LORD' especially in the prophetic writings. The date on which work started corresponds to that in 1 Kings. The delay to the fourth year of his reign may have been due to problems in collecting the materials or the four years may represent a period of co-regency and Solomon began the work as soon as David had died. The Chronicler does not give the full measurements of the temple. The **old standard**

(3) was used for the cubit (i.e. equal to 20.5 ins.) and was also the one adopted by Ezekiel. The building consisted of three parts, a vestibule ('ūlām) or **portico** (34 ft × 17 ft), the aula (hēkāl), **main hall** (RSV 'nave') of the sanctuary (34 ft × 68 ft), and the inner shrine, the **Most Holy Place** (dᵉbīr) (34 ft × 34 ft). The inner shrine (literally oracle) was a cube possibly standing on a raised platform so that the whole building was 30 cubits high (so 1 Kg. 6: 2). The height of the portico given as a hundred and twenty cubits (4, NIVmg) is almost certainly an error. The original may have read twenty cubits for which a number of versions give some support. The portico was overlaid with pure gold, and the nave also, but here the gold was decorated with palm and chain designs. The decorations with precious stones may refer to some form of mosaic work on the cypress floor (so LXX). The whereabouts of **Parvaim** (6) from which the gold came is unknown. Only here is the amount of gold specified used to overlay the inner shrine. The two cherubs seem to have been cast in metal and overlaid with gold. (On cherubs consult standard Bible Dictionaries.) The curtain separating the nave from the inner shrine is based on that of the tabernacle and the description follows Exod. 26: 31–35. The Kings parallel has wooden doors separating the two rooms. The interesting features are the two free standing pillars. They were characteristic of Phoenician temples and Solomon has clearly borrowed from them, no doubt influenced by the fact that the chief architect was Tyrian. Indeed the whole pattern of the temple closely follows similar Phoenician and Canaanite structures of the period. (On the possible significance of the pillars see W. F. Albright, *Archaeology and the Religion of Israel*, 1942, pp. 144–148. On the temple structure itself see commentary on 1 Kg. 6.)

(c) **Furnishings of the Temple (4: 1–5: 1)**
The **bronze altar** (1) (not mentioned at 1 Kg. 7 where the verse has probably dropped out) stood about 17 ft high and must have either been approached by steps or perhaps more likely was in the form of a platform altar with a gradation of levels to the final one. The **cast metal sea** was obviously based on Canaanite patterns and may have been symbolic of the primeval waters or perhaps the life-giving waters provided by God for His people. It was supported by twelve bulls, for the Phoenicians the symbol of fertility and associated with the storm god Hadad who was responsible for bringing this life-giving rain. Solomon has adapted these concepts to the religion of Israel, for Israel's God was also the God of storms and thunder (Ps. 18: 10–13, etc.). The Chronicler simply says, 'something like oxen were under it round about' (RSV 'figures of gourds' is a reconstruction to fit with 1 Kg. 7: 24). The

compiler of Kings makes no mention of bulls or oxen and speaks of 'gourds under its brim' (1 Kg. 7: 24). The twelve bulls probably connect with the twelve tribes of Israel. The description is not easy to follow, but the general sense is clear. The variation in capacity from 1 Kings may be due to different shapes being envisaged, but a simple calculation suggests both figures are too large.

Ten basins were placed by the sea, five on the left and five on the right. They were for washing the burnt offerings (**rinse** only here and at Isa. 4: 4; Jer. 51: 34 and Ezek. 40: 38 and in the last instance used of offerings as here). For a description and details of the basins see 1 Kg. 7: 27–39. The symbolic nature of the decorations on the stands may have been the factor which led the writer to omit them. The **lampstands, tables** and **bowls** (7, 8) present problems. There was only one lampstand in the tabernacle and also in the second temple (1 Mac. 1: 21; 4: 49). 2 Chr. 13: 11 also refers to one lampstand but 1 Chr. 28: 15 and Jer. 52: 19 both speak in the plural. Here the Chronicler speaks of ten, together with ten tables, these presumably being for the slaying of sacrificial animals (cf. Ezek. 40: 38–43). They clearly had nothing to do with the Bread of the Presence.

The Chronicler speaks of two courts based on the Ezekiel pattern and the actual second temple. The term, **the large court**, is used only in Chronicles and Ezekiel. In the Kings parallels the inner court represents the space immediately adjacent to the temple and the great courtyard of 1 Kg. 7: 12 is the whole area around the palace/temple complex. The doors (v. 10) are not mentioned in Kings.

Huram (Huram-Abi at v. 16, see note on 2: 12) was in charge of the manufacture of all the various utensils which were cast in earthen foundries (v. 17) on the other side of Jordan. The bronze probably came from the recently excavated areas to the north of Elath on the Gulf of Aqabah. When the temple was finished, the consecrated gifts of David were moved into the treasuries (5: 1). No mention has been made specifically of these in the account of the building of the temple, but they are probably to be connected with the **upper parts** (RSV 'upper chambers') of 3: 9 and the 'side rooms' of 1 Kg. 6: 5.

(*d*) **The bringing-up of the Ark and the coming of God's glory (5: 2–14)**
This section falls into two parts, the description of the removal of the ark from its temporary resting place in the city to its permanent home in the temple (vv. 2–10) and the subsequent appearing of the glory of God as the indication that Solomon's work was accepted and the temple was in fact the habitation of Yahweh (vv. 11–14).

It is probably significant that the Ark is

brought into the temple on the feast of **the seventh month** (3), that is, the Feast of Tabernacles. Tabernacles was almost certainly the major festival of the early monarchy and echoes of the ritual and ceremonies are possibly preserved in a number of the Psalms. It appears to have been the feast that proclaimed Yahweh's kingship over His people and His world and the king was closely identified with the ceremonies as Yahweh's viceregent through whom He reigned over Israel. There are hints that the ark was carried in sacred procession at this time and thus the festival would have been a particularly appropriate time for bringing the ark, the chariot-throne of Israel's God, into His house. There are minor variations between the Chronicler and the narrative of 1 Kg. 8, particularly in the matter of who carried the ark. It is not entirely clear what the utensils were at v. 5, but it is likely that the reference is to those belonging to the original tabernacle sited at Gibeon, particularly in view of the use of the phrase **Tent of Meeting** (5) which is used only of the tabernacle.

Sacrifices accompanied the move, their number and size in keeping with the importance of the event (v. 6). The ark was put into the **Most Holy Place**, the central shrine of the temple, under the cherubs, whose wings formed a canopy for it (v. 8). The exact arrangement is not entirely clear, but it would seem that the ark was hidden by the curtain, although the poles projected through it, and the wings of the cherubs completely covered the ark above as their wings stretched from wall to wall. The statement that **they are still there today** (9) shows how closely the Chronicler followed his sources, since the ark was no longer in existence when he wrote. The ark contained only the tables of the law, although later accounts suggested that it also contained a pot of manna and Aaron's rod (Heb. 9: 4) probably on the basis of Exod. 16: 32–34.

The description of the coming of the glory of God contains considerably more detail than the primary source at 1 Kg. 8. This elaboration of the text is marked by brackets in RSV. The ceremony of installation was associated with music produced by the Levitical choir and orchestra, and by the priestly trumpeters, and may almost be seen as a sequel to the procession of 1 Chr. 15 and 16. The rendering of the psalm of praise was perfect and reflected, no doubt, the high degree of organisation and training that David had initiated. The coming of the glory of God was a cloud (cf. Isa. 6: 4; Ezek. 10: 4, etc.), demonstrating that God accepted Solomon's work and was seated upon His throne in His house.

(*e*) **Solomon's dedication prayer (6: 3–42)**
This section very closely follows its sources at 1 Kg. 8: 12–52, to which reference should be

made for detailed comments. 1 Kg. 8: 16 omits vv. 5b–6a and there are a few other minor variations, but essentially the text is the same. The prayer in effect consists of two addresses, one to the people (vv. 3–11) and the other a lengthy prayer addressed to God (vv. 12–42). The address to Israel underlines the faithfulness of God in the fulfilment of His promise to David. This fulfilment has been brought about by the action of Solomon whom God has graciously allowed to build the temple and for whom He has demonstrated His approval of the project by the appearance of His glory.

The second section is a long prayer which Solomon offers up while standing or kneeling on a **platform** (*kiyyōr*) in full view of all the people (v. 13). The exact function of this platform is not clear, but examples have been found in a number of countries in the area. Their use appears to have been restricted to dignitaries—kings, priests and others—and used for offerings and prayers to the deity. Just why Solomon used this is not clear; it may have been simply to make him visible to the whole gathering, or there may have been some religious significance, borrowed, like the temple design, from his Phoenician neighbours. Interestingly the Kings narrative omits all mention of the platform.

The content of the prayer is dealt with in detail at 1 Kg. 8: 22–52. The first part (vv. 14–21) consists largely of an ascription of praise to God, the one who has remained faithful to His covenant showing His steadfast **love** (*ḥesed*) to His people. On this basis Solomon makes his plea that the promises to David will never fail (v. 16). Yahweh is so great, however, that even the heavens cannot contain Him (v. 18) and while the temple will be the meeting place for God and man, the various petitions entreat Yahweh to **hear from heaven**. Of particular importance is the stress laid on the constant need for forgiveness and the principle of repentance for sin as the basis for forgiveness which is seen in each of the seven petitions in vv. 22–39. It is significant that each petition relates to national and community affairs, thus underlining the Hebrew concept of the importance of community over against modern concepts that overstress the individual. Verses 39–40 are a contracted version of 1 Kg. 8: 50–52.

The conclusion of Solomon's prayer (vv. 41, 42) does not occur in the Kings parallel. The wording is very close to Ps. 132: 8–11, one of the royal psalms which centre on the idea of the enthronement of the king as God's vicegerent over His people. The Chronicler presumably is utilizing one of his alternative sources at this point. It forms a fitting climax to the prayer and the Chronicler may well have felt this to be particularly relevant to his own time, especially v. 42.

(f) The dedication ceremony (7: 1–10)

The Chronicler once again follows his source (1 Kg. 8: 54, 62–66) very closely although with some rearrangement of his material, certain additions and some omissions. In place of Solomon's blessing of the people there is the account of the glory of Yahweh filling the temple and the fire from heaven consuming the sacrifice. This also occurred when David offered sacrifice on the threshing floor of Ornan to stay the plague and was evidence of the fact that God had accepted the sacrifice. The glory of Yahweh now filled the temple and the people worshipped Him in song. The title of the psalm given in v. 3 may represent the same as that at v. 6. A psalm title is in fact being quoted. The phrase might be better rendered 'the instruments of music to the LORD which King David had made to (accompany) "Give thanks to the LORD for His steadfast love endures for ever",'. The expression **opposite the Levites** could just refer to an antiphonal arrangement with trumpets sounding alternately with the voices, but more likely refers to the respective positions of priests and Levitical musicians. The Levites were apparently on the east side of the altar (v. 12) and the priests would thus have been on the west side, between the altar and the temple proper.

The **middle part of the courtyard** which Solomon consecrated because the altar was too small for the size of sacrifice being offered (v. 7) may well have been the original rock threshing floor on which David made his sacrifice.

The feast of vv. 8–10 was the feast of Tabernacles, possibly the major festival of the early monarchy, and the Chronicler stresses the size of the congregation that gathered. According to 1 Kg. 8: 66, Solomon dismissed the people on the eighth day, but here the eighth day represents the climax of the festival. The initial dedication of the temple had taken seven days and this was followed by the feast of Tabernacles, the total time for both being fifteen days with an additional day for the dismissal of the people. The reference to the **dedication of the altar** (9) includes the whole temple; the altar was the centre-point from the standpoint of Israel's sacrificial religion, for the place of sacrifice is the place of communion and forgiveness (see v. 12 and 1 C. 10: 18).

(g) The Lord's response to Solomon (7: 11–22)

Just as the fire coming down to consume the sacrifice was an indication of God's acceptance of it, and the coming of the glory of Yahweh to fill the temple was evidence that He approved of the place where He was to set His name, so the appearance of Yahweh to Solomon was an indication to him that his work had been accepted. Solomon is reassured that

God's blessing will rest on him and his dynasty, but the blessing is conditional. Sinfulness followed by repentance was certain to find forgiveness (v. 14); note the similarity in phraseology to the king's prayer. On the other hand a deliberate renunciation of Yahweh would lead inevitably to judgment and catastrophe with the land forsaken and the temple desecrated (vv. 19 ff.). It would appear however that the covenant between God and David (v. 18) is not affected by such judgment and there is no indication that the promise that **you shall never fail to have a man to rule over Israel** is other than unconditional. Some see here a definite messianic overtone (cf. Mic. 5: 2).

In view of the statement (v. 11) that both temple and palace had been completed before Yahweh appears to Solomon, it is not impossible that the reference to **this place** may refer to the whole temple/palace complex as the focal point of Yahweh's presence with His people. The temple signified His presence in terms of Israel's worship but the king's house was the place from which His anointed viceregent reigned over His people. Certainly the temple was only part of a gigantic building project and the view has been put forward that, at least during the reign of Solomon, the temple was little more than a royal chapel (see on 2: 1).

xi. Facets of Solomon's Reign (8: 1–9: 31)
(a) Domestic developments and administration (8: 1–18)
The section begins with a description of the large-scale building and fortification projects that Solomon undertook. In most respects the Chronicler follows 1 Kg. 9: 10–28, but at v. 2 there is a curious difference from the statement of 1 Kg. 9: 10 ff. There it is stated that Solomon gave Hiram twenty towns in Galilee in exchange for gold and silver. However, it is further stated that Hiram was not greatly impressed with the towns and this may explain v. 2 which records his returning them to Solomon as worthless. The state of the towns which annoyed Hiram, may also explain why **Solomon rebuilt the villages** and recolonized them. J. M. Myers makes the suggestion that in fact the towns had been given to Hiram as collateral until the final payment for the Phoenician raw materials could be made in gold, which would explain why they were given back to Solomon once the deal had been satisfactorily completed.

The capture of **Hamath Zobah** (3) is not mentioned in the Kings parallel. The name reflects conditions in the Persian period when Zobah was part of the province of Hamath and the Chronicler is using the name that would be more familiar to his readers. Hamath was, in fact, a friendly state in the time of David (2 Sam. 8: 9, 10) and it is likely that the friendship continued into the reign of Solomon. On the

other hand Zobah had given trouble to David (2 Sam. 8: 9; 10: 8) and it is possible that it had rebelled after his death, requiring Solomon's action recorded here. The building of **Tadmor** (4) may well have been as a fortress to protect the outskirts of his empire from Aramaean pressures. The Kings parallel refers to 'Tamar' (NIVmg) which was a small village in the south of the country, whereas Tadmor (the later Palmyra) was an important centre on the trade route to the east lying in the territory of Hamath Zobah, at the limits of Solomon's empire. **Beth Horon** was the gateway to the hill country some ten miles north-west of Jerusalem. The site of **Baalath** was in Dan, towards the coast, and its fortification may have been to ensure the continuing docility of the Philistine enclave. The phrase **all the cities for his chariots** (6) refers to those places mentioned in Kings such as Hazor, Megiddo and Gezer, at which Solomon's proclivity for building and fortifying is well attested by archaeology. Verses 7–10 describe the forced labour for the building projects. Both this passage and the parallel at 1 Kg. 9: 20–23 agree that the levy was confined to the remnants of pre-conquest inhabitants of the land and that Israelites were either soldiers or the overseers of the labour gangs. Note, however, 1 Kg. 5: 13 which the Chronicler has ignored earlier.

The short section about **Pharaoh's daughter** (11) only hints at the relationship with Egypt which is indicated at 1 Kg. 9: 16. There is also a significant change in wording here from 1 Kg. 9: 24. The Chronicler has Pharaoh's daughter **brought up** into her own special house which was separate from the palace/temple complex. The reason for this is almost certainly due to his emphasis on ritual purity (note the emphasis on **holy** in Solomon's words which does not occur in the Kings parallel), an outlook that led ultimately to the court of women in the temple of Herod.

The note on Solomon's arrangements for the various feasts and offerings follows 1 Kg. 9: 25 fairly closely except that the Chronicler makes no mention of the king offering incense, a priestly prerogative. Verses 13–16a are missing from 1 Kg. 9. The main point of the section is to emphasize that, with the completion of the building and the establishment of the sacrificial system **according to the requirement commanded by Moses** and **following the ordinance of his father, David**, Solomon had completed the house relating to the honour of God and fulfilled his father's commands.

The immense building programme which had now been completed must have made heavy inroads on the national exchequer and it is not surprising that Solomon embarked on an expedition to **Ophir** to recoup his losses (vv. 17, 18). **Ezion Geber** is at the northern end of the gulf of Aqaba and the remains of a large iron and copper smelting industry have been discovered there together with traces of a naval yard. It is likely that the finished copper goods from the area were used in highly profitable trading with Ophir, which is possibly to be located in present day Somalia. The copper mines appear to have been so profitable that, in spite of the prodigal expenditure in Solomon's building projects, he was saved from bankruptcy. The importance of this trading activity, in which Solomon was once again assisted by Phoenician expertise (the Tyrians were the best seamen of the time), was in breaking the South Arabian (Sabaean) trade monopoly over the land route which Solomon had by-passed. The visit of the queen of Sheba was a logical outcome in view of the threat Solomon posed to her own trade.

(b) The visit of the Queen of Sheba (9: 1–12)

This section follows very closely the source at 1 Kg. 10: 1–13. From the Chronicler's standpoint the story illustrated the glory of Solomon and in particular demonstrates the fulfilment of God's promise to him in providing not only wisdom to rule the people, but wealth and fame in addition (1 Chr. 1: 11, 12). God had thus shown Himself faithful to His covenant and promise. The underlying motive for the visit, however, clearly related to trade.

South Arabia was an important area, particularly active in regard to the spice trade, and the excavations at Marib, the capital of Sheba, indicate an advanced and progressive civilization. Trade was carried out throughout the area and northwards to Phoenicia and Syria. The sudden emergence of a new trading empire on the doorstep, already threatening their overland caravan route by inaugurating a sea link to the mineral wealth of Ophir, was sufficient to initiate high level diplomatic activity. The visit of the queen of Sheba thus takes on an added significance and it may be viewed, almost certainly, as a trade and diplomatic mission to establish some sort of agreement between Sheba and Israel.

The result of the visit was a declaration from the queen, extolling Solomon's wisdom. The view of the **wisdom of Solomon** expressed in vv. 3 and 4 seems to be essentially an administrative ability; he was able to organize and arrange, and a shrewd trader to boot, as the queen probably knew already to her cost! The Chronicler has departed significantly from his source at v. 8. At 1 Kg. 10: 9 Solomon sits on the throne of Israel, but here he sits on Yahweh's throne, **as king for the LORD your God.** The view of kingship here is a high one, according with the concepts expressed in the royal psalms that Israel's king is God's vicegerent. It is God who rules through His anointed

king. (Note also 1 Chr. 17: 14; 28: 5; 29: 23 and 2 Chr. 13: 8.) The visit ended with a mutual exchange of gifts, perhaps ratifying some form of agreement between the two nations. Verses 10, 11 seem out of context and are better related to v. 13, although the order is that of 1 Kg. 10.

(c) Solomon's wealth (9: 13–28)

The wealth of Solomon is described in vv. 10, 11 and 13–28. Verse 13 notes the annual revenue in gold—the colossal amount of approximately 25 tons. This did not include the revenue from **merchants and traders** (14) which was probably in the form of tolls and custom dues. In addition there appeared to have been some sort of tribute from the Arabian states, together with local taxes levied by the **governors of the land**, a term belonging to the Chronicler's time and used in explanation for his readers.

The **great throne inlaid with ivory** (17) was probably the showpiece used by the king when receiving dignitaries in audience. It is of interest that the Chronicler studiously avoids mention of the calf's head on the back of the throne (1 Kg. 10: 19), which would have resembled too closely the images that Jeroboam was to set up in Israel.

Solomon's shipping ventures with Hiram are of importance (v. 21). The Chronicler emphasizes the part of Solomon's fleet to the total exclusion of Hiram's (contrast 1 Kg. 10: 22). The expression **trading ships** is probably best taken to mean 'refinery fleet' (Akkadian *rašāšu*, to smelt) and refers to the ships which carried the smelted copper to Ophir and Punt—i.e. the East African coastline. Any centre for mining and smelting would simply be called Tarshish (see NIVmg). The sense then is that Solomon's refinery fleet, based at the refinery port of Ezion Geber, made a regular three year round trip bringing gold, silver, ivory and zoological specimens in return for iron and copper. The success of their trading voyages explains the abundance of gold and silver at the court (v. 20). The remaining verses (22–28) are further accounts of the magnificence of Solomon's reign. The size of the chariot cities is well attested by archeological work at Megiddo, Gezer and other places. The extent of his rule (v. 26) describes what was most probably a commercial and trading empire from which Solomon exacted various forms of taxation on the gold and passage of goods and on which he was able to impose restrictive trading practices to the benefit of Israel's treasury.

(d) The end of Solomon's reign (9: 29–31)

The various problems arising towards the end of Solomon's reign, and especially his political marriages which introduced alien religions into Israel, are omitted by the Chronicler. He refers, however, to his sources which include three prophetic records. Whether these may be identified with Kings or whether they were a common source for both historians is not clear.

III. THE DIVIDED KINGDOM—THE STORY OF JUDAH (2 Chr. 10: 1–36: 23)
i. The Reign of Rehoboam and the Rebellion of Israel (10: 1–12: 16)
(a) The Division (10: 1–19)

The accession of Solomon's son Rehoboam did not appear to be in question. There is a suggestion at v. 1 that there may have been a double coronation, one in relation to Judah and the other in respect of the northern tribes. David had united Israel and Judah largely through his personal charisma and this union continued through the strongly centralized reign of Solomon, but the ties were not strong, as the story indicates. The crown of Israel had to be received from the elders of the northern tribes and hence Rehoboam travelled to Shechem, the centre of the old tribal confederacy. The reference to **all Israel** thus relates to the northern tribes.

Before Rehoboam was made king, however, the demand was made that there should be some relief from the heavy burdens that Solomon had placed on the people in order to pursue his immense building programme. At this point Jeroboam comes into the picture (vv. 2 f). The Chronicler had omitted all reference to him in relation to Solomon's reign (except the allusion in 9: 29) and he had also made no mention of the discontent with Solomon's reign that developed during its latter phases and which is clearly indicated in the Kings account. The Chronicler knew it existed and so, it may be assumed, did his readers, but such conditions did not fit with the picture of an ideal king.

The actual events of the rebellion are discussed in detail under 1 Kg. 12: 1–20. It may be noted, however, that Rehoboam clearly had little appreciation of the depths of feeling of the people of Israel for, having delivered his ultimatum and provoked rebellion, he then sends almost certainly one of the best hated men in the kingdom, the man **who was in charge of forced labour** (18), to try to deal with it. It was only after he had been lynched that the king recognized the seriousness of the situation.

The Chronicler's viewpoint is made clear at v. 17—only those people of Israel who remained loyal to the Davidic dynasty were the true Israel. Verse 19 is simply a quotation from his source, although his retention of a statement that had little contemporary relevance for him in its original meaning may indicate that he was thinking of the developing theological split between north and south and the Samaritan schism of his own time.

(b) Establishing the Kingdom (11: 1–23)

Rehoboam's initial reaction to the rebellion was to resort to a military solution. He mustered 180 units (see note on *'elep*, a thousand, at 1 Chr. 12: 24) but he was prevented from putting his plans into operation by the intervention of the prophet **Shemaiah** (vv. 1–3). Again the Chronicler's viewpoint is underlined in the expression **all the Israelites in Judah and Benjamin** (v. 3 and 1 Kg. 12: 23). The description of the defensive arrangements (vv. 5–12) is unique to the Chronicler, indicating the fact that he was utilizing a variety of sources apart from Kings. All the places mentioned as fortress cities have now been identified (see L. Grollenberg, *Atlas of the Bible*, 1956). The cities form an interesting system of forts in the southern hill country or at its edge. Rehoboam was concerned at the likelihood of trouble with Egypt, now that the kingdom was weakened and divided. This trouble in fact occurred with Shishak's invasion described in 12: 1–5, but it is not clear whether the fortresses were built before or after this event.

The list of cities does not follow the expected sequence if the writer was enumerating them according to their geographical situation and this may be due to the fact that some of them were secondary forts, for use as supply centres or a second line of defence.

The migration of the priests and Levites (vv. 13–17) is based on 1 Kg. 12: 31–32 and 13: 33. The expulsion is not clear in Kings, but the implication is probably there and the Chronicler is not slow in seizing on anything that will magnify the sin of Jeroboam. Once again there is the emphasis on the fact that those of the northern tribes who really wished to follow in the way of Yahweh came south to the legitimate centre of Israel's religion (v. 16). There also appears to be an implicit assumption that only the laity were in rebellion and the loyalty of the levitical families to the central shrine was such that many suffered persecution and were prepared to relinquish all their worldly wealth to move south. This influx of faithful northerners together with the priests and Levites provided an additional stabilizing and strengthening factor to the southern kingdom (v. 17). It is not quite clear what is intended by the time limit **three years.** It may mean that the people of Israel only came to Jerusalem for a period of three years, that is, until Jeroboam had established the northern shrines or it may refer to the period that elapsed before Rehoboam's slide into apostasy began.

The short note on the family relationships of Rehoboam (vv. 18–23) is interesting in showing that he married his cousin, **Mahalath**, who was a great-granddaughter of Jesse through both her parents. Her father **Jerimoth** was presumably the son of a secondary wife or concubine of David as he is nowhere else listed. The Absalom who was the father of Rehoboam's second, but favourite, wife Maacah, was probably David's infamous son of that name. The eldest son of the favourite wife became the first in line of succession (v. 22). All his sons were placed in strategic centres throughout the kingdom (v. 23), to guard against disloyalty and possible revolt and thus secure his position. The final phrase is difficult. The phrase rendered in NIV as **took many wives for them** may be more literally rendered as he 'sought a multitude of wives', and it has been suggested that it might be rendered as he 'sought the multitude (of the gods) of his wives', and should thus be taken with the following verse (12: 1) describing the apostasy of Rehoboam.

(c) **Rehoboam's Apostasy (12: 1–16)**
This section utilizes 1 Kg. 14: 21–28 as a source, but the Chronicler follows his own order and interpolates some additional material, perhaps from the temple archives of Shemaiah's prophecy. In particular he gives a much fuller account of the Shishak invasion than the parallel passage in Kings (vv. 1–9).

Shishak was the first really strong pharaoh of the twenty-second (Bubastite) dynasty of Egypt. His aims were probably largely expansionist, over and above his intention to deal with Rehoboam. The invasion begins an era in which the two kingdoms of Judah and Israel were to be a buffer in the struggles of the major powers as well as, oftentimes, being pawns in their power games, falling within the sphere of influence of first this power and then that.

The invasion took place in Rehoboam's **fifth year** as king (c. 918 BC) and was clearly a full scale military operation in which the Egyptian troops were joined by large numbers of mercenaries from African territories to the south and west of Egypt (v. 3). Rehoboam's forces had to fall back on Jerusalem and the only way out of the situation was to become tributary to Shishak. (On the campaign itself see further NBD under Shishak.)

The major importance of the invasion, from the Chronicler's standpoint, was its theological significance, well expressed in the words of the prophet **Shemaiah** (v. 8). Judah had abandoned Yahweh and in turn He had abandoned them. It is made clear, however, that the function of the judgment was disciplinary and not retributive. The king and captains of Israel **humbled themselves** (7) and the ultimate catastrophe was averted, although not without cost. The principles enshrined in the Chronicler's story have an abiding relevance.

There follow a few more observations on Rehoboam's reign (vv. 10–14), mentioning the replacement of Solomon's gold shields for the temple guard, taken by Shishak, with bronze

substitutes. Again the Chronicler underlines his view that Judah escaped complete destruction because Rehoboam submitted himself again to Yahweh, although not completely (v. 14), and there was still some good in Israel. The reign is concluded with the usual reference to sources (v. 15). His son Abijah is called Abijam at 1 Kg. 14: 31 (see NIVmg). This may be merely a scribal variant or Abijah may be his throne name and Abijam the given family name.

ii. **The reign of Abijah (13: 1–14: 1)**
The assessment of Abijah in the Chronicler's history differs markedly from the Kings parallels. The latter has nothing good to say about him and states that he was only tolerated because of his fore-father David. The Chronicler however, gives no hint that he was anything other than a good king and the reason for this may lie in the fact that he was in arms against Jeroboam for most of his reign. To oppose those who are in open revolt against Yahweh must put him on the side of right as far as the Chronicler is concerned.

(a) **The Accession of Abijah (13: 1–3)**
A variant tradition is used here in regard to Abijah's mother. 1 Kg. 15: 2 and 2 Chr. 11: 20 give Abijah's mother as Maacah the daughter of Absalom. The matter is further complicated by the name of Asa's mother (15: 16). In view of the complexity of the family tree with so many different wives, concubines and children it is likely that there were a number of variant traditions and any solution can only be speculative. 'It is possible that in Kings the real name of Abijah's wife was submerged by the strong personality of his mother, Maacah' (Myers, p. 29), or Asa may have been a minor son whose mother had died leaving Maacah to continue as queen-mother.

(b) **The Israelite War (13: 4–14: 1)**
The speech of **Abijah** (vv. 4–12) in which he harangued the opposing forces of Jeroboam is used by the Chronicler to develop his own teaching on the apostasy of the northern kingdom. It may be viewed as the use of an historical illustration to deal with a situation prevailing in the writer's own time and the appeal of Abijah may be read as an appeal of the Chronicler to the Samaritan schismatics of that period. The northern kingdom was not merely in rebellion against David's dynasty, but against Yahweh Himself (the point of v. 5) and had adopted a corrupt and invalid religion (v. 8). The **golden calves** were probably designed originally as thrones or pedestals for the invisible presence of Yahweh and served the same function as the chariot-throne of the ark and the cherubim in the temple. The northern kingdom's downfall was thus assured. The downfall, however, was to be brought about by divine agency (v. 15) and the 'moral' of the

story is given further point at v. 18.

Zemaraim (4) was a border area probably near Bethel (cf. Jos. 18: 22). A **covenant of salt** was a perpetual covenant that could not be broken (Num. 18: 19; Lev. 21: 13). This reference to an eternal dominion for the Davidic dynasty is independent of Samuel and Kings. Whether the Chronicler means only to imply that Israel was Yahweh's kingdom ruled over by Yahweh's king, or whether there are Messianic overtones, is a matter of debate.

In view of the Kings assessment of Abijah's character the picture of him as 'a preacher and ardent upholder of the Levitical worship of Yahweh is an interesting touch of the Chronicler' (*ICC*). H. L. Ellison (*NBC*) makes the point that 'Abijah was far from practising what he preached (1 Kg. 15: 3); but what was settled religious policy in the north was still only an aberration in Judah'. The view of the disruption here is very much an oversimplification (vv. 6, 7). The impression that the whole affair was stage-managed by Jeroboam and a small group of malcontents (**scoundrels**) is not that given in the account of the rebellion. The use of the term **young** to describe Rehoboam (v. 7) probably means young in experience rather than age, but **indecisive** (lit. soft-hearted or timid) does not really describe his character unless the word is understood as implying weak in understanding. The use of the word **scoundrels** (lit. 'sons of Belial', but Belial is never used as a proper name in the OT, merely a synonym for lawlessness) to describe all the north is perhaps a rather sweeping condemnation in the light of ch. 10 and the Kings narrative. However, 'in the Chronicler's view, whatever may be the human justification, nothing could excuse the revolt against the Davidic line and the consequent religious apostasy' (A. S. Herbert in *PCB*).

The large number of the armies (compare the figures in vv. 3, 17 with those of the census in 1 Chr. 21: 5) and the killed should probably be thought of in terms of 'units' (see note on 1 Chr. 12). The reference to **five hundred thousand casualties** (17), if literal, would have resulted in far larger gains for Judah than a few border towns and villages (v. 19). The victory for Judah was divine in origin and the superior military strategy of Israel (vv. 13–14) was brought to nothing because **God routed Jeroboam and all Israel** (15; cf. also vv. 16, 18). The death of Jeroboam is viewed also as a stroke of divine judgment, but Abijah, on the other hand, knows the blessing of God, seen in the number of his wives and children (v. 21). The chronology varies from 1 Kg. 14 and 15 which makes Jeroboam survive Abijah by at least a year.

The conclusion of the account of Abijah's reign follows the Chronicler's usual practice of quoting his source—**the annotations** (*midrāš*) **of the prophet Iddo** (22). The use of the word *midrāš* probably indicates an expansion of a commentary upon an earlier document.

iii. The reign of Asa (14: 2–16: 14)
(a) The Early Years (14: 2–14)

The story of Asa's reign is given in much greater detail by the Chronicler than it is in Kings (1 Kg. 15: 11–24), although this narrative forms the basis of the Chronicler's account. The defeat of Abijah introduced a period of peace for **ten years** (1) which carried over into the reign of Asa. The Chronicler's verdict on his reign, that he did **what was good and right in the eyes of the LORD** (v. 2) relates principally to the religious reforms undertaken by him. As he was a boy when he came to the throne he would not have had the power to institute major reforms immediately, although this is the initial impression given. The chronology of Asa's reign in fact presents a number of problems (see below on 15: 19–16: 6). The reforms, however, are dated at 15: 10 as culminating in Asa's fifteenth year, by which time he was well established.

The reforms seem in part directed towards an increased centralization of worship in that he removed the **foreign altars and the high places** (3). In an earlier age the **high places** had been acceptable secondary centres of the worship of Yahweh. By the time of Asa, however, they had become associated with, or perhaps reverted to, the Canaanite fertility religions and the worship of the Phoenician mother-goddess Asherah (perhaps under the influence of the queen-mother, **Maacah**; see below on 15: 16). Set up on the high places were **sacred stones** (*maṣṣēbôt*, probably the symbols of the male element in nature), and the **Asherah poles** (*'ašērîm*), possibly wooden images of the goddess Asherah or perhaps a sacred tree. This religion was associated with sexual practices repugnant to the worshippers of Yahweh. The expression **foreign altars** (3) is probably to be linked with the **incense altars** (*ḥammānîm*) of v. 5. Several examples of these altars, usually with 'horns' at the corners, have been found in the excavation of Israelite towns from the period of the tenth to the seventh centuries BC.

The building of the fortified cities (v. 6) may have taken place after the Ethiopian war (below, vv. 9–15), and is a reflection of the unsettled conditions of the time (cf. 1 Kg. 15: 32). However, there is again an emphasis on the fact that God had given peace to the land as a result of the abandonment of paganism and a return to the Lord—**we sought him, and he has given us rest on every side** (7; cf. also v. 5). The rather odd phrase, **the land is still ours** (7) may be seen perhaps as a reminder to the reader that 'a time was to come when the land would be lost and the people of God exiled from it; possession of the land goes with obedience, with true searching for God' (P. R. Ackroyd). The large size of the standing army (v. 8) becomes more realistic if once again the word **thousand** is thought of as a 'unit' of unspecified size (see on 1 Chr. 12: 24). The high percentage of Benjaminites (almost 50 per cent) suggests that Asa maintained his hold on the total area taken by Abijah.

The reliance of Asa upon Yahweh is illustrated by the event of the conflict with **Zerah the Cushite** (9). It is probable that when Shishak withdrew from Palestine after the war with Rehoboam he left a group of mercenaries and their families to act as a sort of buffer on the southern edge of Judah. Zerah may have been the commander of the mercenary force. NIV here reads **Cushite** instead of 'Ethiopian' (cf AV, RSV). In this case, Zerah should be viewed as an Arabian (note Cushan at Hab. 3: 7 and Cushite at Num. 12: 1). Certainly an Arabian contingent seems to have been present (note **camels** at v. 15). The mention of the **droves of sheep and goats and camels** (15) may indicate that Zerah was simply trying to expand into fresh pasture lands, but the raid may equally well have been at the instigation of Osorkon I, Shishak's successor as Pharaoh, or perhaps in collaboration with Baasha of Israel.

The battle took place near **Mareshah**, about twenty-five miles south west of Jerusalem in the **Valley of Zephathah**, an unidentifiable location (LXX has 'in the valley north of Mareshah', which may preserve a better reading). The important feature of the battle, however, is its significance: as a result of Asa's prayerful trust **the LORD struck down the Cushites** (12), an element lacking in the later clash with Baasha.

(b) The Reformation (15: 1–19)
The reforms of Asa had been mentioned at the beginning of his reign as the basis on which God's blessing rested on him. Now the Chronicler gives a more detailed account and puts them into the context of the reign. It would appear from vv. 1 and 11 that the prophet **Azariah** addressed the king on his return from the defeat of Zerah. The address of the prophet (vv. 2–9) has been described as 'an excellent example of Levitical preaching' (so G. von Rad); that is to say the Chronicler has used the occasion to expand the address and apply the message to his own time. There are a number of allusions to the prophetical writings (Jer. 29: 13 f.; 31: 16; Zeph. 3: 16; Zech. 8: 10). The address has three main elements, an affirmation that Yahweh will be with the people as long as they are with Him (v. 2), a series of illustrations from history (vv. 3–6) and an exhortation (v. 7). It is difficult to be certain about the precise

background of vv. 3–6. On the surface it appears to relate to the situation in the latter period of the Judges (Jg. 17–21), but this seems to have little in common with the times of Asa and it may be that it refers more directly to the insecurity of the post-exilic period and the Chronicler's own time (cf. however 2 Kg. 14: 26).

The reforms which followed Azariah's address appear to have been thoroughgoing (vv. 8–15), taking in the whole territory of **Judah and Benjamin** as well as **the towns he had captured in the hills of Ephraim** (8). The **detestable idols** (8) were removed (cf. 1 Kg. 15: 12) and the altar repaired. This altar was the bronze altar that stood in the court-yard of the temple and the activities of the solemn convocation that took place in **the third month of the fifteenth year of Asa's reign** (10) probably included its rededication. The Chronicler mentions the support given by the faithful from **Ephraim, Manasseh and Simeon.** The mention of Simeon is difficult as the territory was in southern Judah. It may have been that the inhabitants of Simeon had become refugees (**who had settled**) as a result of Edomite expansion in the south, although Ellison (*NBCR*) views the reference as 'an unintelligent correction of an early scribal error'.

The completion of the reform was marked by a solemn convocation (vv. 10–15). It took place in the **third month** and may thus have coincided with the Feast of Weeks (Pentecost). The suggestion has been made (so P. R. Ackroyd) that there is an allusion to this at v. 14 in a word-play (*šābū'ôt*, the title of the feast, and *šāba'*, the verb 'to swear'). As the Feast of Weeks in later Jewish tradition (perhaps as early as the Chronicler) commemorated the giving of the law and the foundation of the national covenant, the choice of the third month was singularly appropriate to their rededication. The ceremony was marked by a renewal of the covenant (vv. 12–14), accompanied by the sacrifice of some of the booty taken in the campaign against Zerah (v. 11). Myers notes that the fact that 'the covenant was a sovereignly imposed affair may be seen from the threat accompanying it' (v. 13). The result of the people's faithfulness is that **the LORD gave them rest on every side** (15).

The earlier apostasy is directly attributed to the evil influence of the queen mother **Maacah** (16). (On the position of the queen mother see below on 22: 10–12.) She **had made a repulsive Asherah pole** (16), which might perhaps be rendered 'an unspeakable image of Asherah'. The image was destroyed and the remains burnt **in the Kidron Valley.** It is possible that there may have been some ritual significance in this (cf. 29: 16 and 2 Kg. 23: 4, 6, 12). Maacah is removed from her position of authority from which she had been able to exert a strong influence on the nation during the early years of Asa's reign. She presumably spent the rest of her life in isolation and disgrace.

The placing of the votive gifts (18) into the temple does not seem to relate to this context. The statement that **there was no more war until the thirty-fifth year of Asa's reign** (19) underlines its long and peaceful character and relates to the Chronicler's lesson that faithfulness to God brings its reward in peace, the general well-being and wholeness of the community (see 14: 6).

(c) **The War with Baasha and its aftermath (16: 1-14)**
The long peaceful era of Asa's reign came to an abrupt halt with the invasion of Judah by **Baasha king of Israel** (1). This is stated to have taken place in **the thirty-sixth year** of Asa's reign, a dating which immediately raises problems, since according to 1 Kg. 15: 33 and 16: 8 Baasha died in Asa's twenty-sixth year. A case has been made out for considering that the Chronicler's dating relates to the time elapsed from the division of the kingdom, putting this war in Asa's fifteenth or sixteenth year (so E. R. Thiele, *op. cit.*), but the case is more ingenious than convincing. However, there is some evidence from a stele of the reign of Ben-Hadad (*c.* 850 BC) that the Chronicler is correct (see W. F. Albright, *BASOR* 87, 1942, 23–29).

The precipitating factor was Baasha's fortification (v. 1) of Ramah, a town some ten miles north of Jerusalem and astride the main road. His main aim was probably to cut the trade route and also to prevent any movement of people south from his kingdom to worship at Jerusalem. Asa was in no position to lift the blockade and appealed to Ben-Hadad the king of Syria for help (v. 3), apparently on the basis of a long standing agreement (**my father and your father**). However, Asa stripped his treasury to ensure Ben-Hadad's intervention.

The result was as he wished; Ben-Hadad marched on Israel, invading the northern area. Essentially it was a diversionary tactic and the Syrian army does not appear to have penetrated any further south than the area above Lake Huleh. (Note, however, 1 Kg. 15: 20 which has 'Kinnereth' for the Chronicler's **store-cities** (4), suggesting that the Syrians may have penetrated as far south as Galilee.) The intervention was successful and caused Baasha to abandon his fortifications (v. 5) and Asa was able to re-occupy the area, using the materials of the abandoned fortifications of Ramah to fortify **Geba and Mizpah** (6) (sites uncertain).

The significance of this narrative lies in the fact that Asa had apparently lost confidence in the ability of Yahweh to protect him. It was a total reversal of the policy followed in the conflict with Zerah and calls forth the prophetic rebuke of **Hanani the seer** (vv. 7–10). Alliance with a foreign power set their gods on a level with Yahweh and inevitably this type of action was condemned by the prophets. The main point made here however, is Asa's lack of confidence. **9. the eyes of the LORD range throughout the earth:** cf. Zech. 4: 10. Such all-seeing power brings protection and help to those whose faith rests on Him (**fully committed to him**). Asa has **done a foolish thing** (cf. 1 Sam. 13: 13; 2 Sam. 24: 10; 1 Chr. 21: 8) and will suffer the consequences of his action in trouble for the rest of his reign (a marked contrast to the era of faith and confidence—14: 6; 15: 15). Read 'the army of the king of Israel' with LXX at v. 7, which is required by the context, rather than that of the **king of Aran.**

Asa's reaction to the word of the prophet is swift—he **put him in prison** (10), a further indication of his lack of faith. Those of the people whom he **brutally oppressed** (i.e. tortured) were presumably sympathizers with Hanani—perhaps an extremist group angry at the apparent cooling of Asa's zeal for Yahweh.

The Chronicler's notice of the reign ends with a reference to his sources (v. 11), not apparently equivalent to our book of Kings, and a note of Asa's death and burial. Even here Asa's lack of faith is mentioned in that he resorted to **physicians** and **did not seek help from the LORD** (12). The condemnation lies in the fact that the physicians would almost certainly have been pagan healers whose art would have been associated with a variety of undesirable practices rather than in any disparagement of physicians as such. It is not possible to diagnose the nature of the disease in his feet with any exactness, but as it lasted for two years before he eventually succumbed, it is possible that he was suffering from some form of gangrene, most likely arteriosclerotic. This would also explain the large amounts of **various blended perfumes** (14) used at the funeral which would have masked the unpleasant smell of gangrenous flesh.

iv. **The reign of Jehoshaphat (17: 1–21: 1)**
(a) **Its character and organization (17: 1–19)**
Jehoshaphat's reign is given considerable space by the Chronicler, and, in company with Hezekiah and Josiah, he ranks high in his esteem. Most of the material comes from sources other than Kings, although the little information given at 1 Kg. 15: 24; 22: 41–49 is utilized. However, the Chronicler's method of handling his material is very different from Kings and the narrative at 1 Kg. 22: 1–35 which there forms part of the story of Ahab is treated from the standpoint of a foolish alliance from which God rescued the good Jehoshaphat (see below on 18: 1–34).

The Chronicler begins by noting the necessary stages of fortification taken by Jehoshaphat at the beginning of his reign (vv. 1, 2). These were made necessary by the uncertainties of the relationship with Israel and clearly Jehoshaphat's first requirement was to consolidate his position in the country. The NIV may be at fault in its rendering **against Israel** (1). The term 'Israel' here seems more to refer to the southern kingdom and the northern kingdom is called **Ephraim** (2). The **towns of Ephraim** taken by Asa were in fact in the tribal territory of Benjamin. Hence v. 1 might perhaps be better rendered 'Jehoshaphat his son reigned in his stead and established his authority over Israel' (so Rudolph). The Chronicler was thus emphasizing the king's position as ruler over the true people of God.

The success of his rule was due to the fact that **in his early years he walked in the ways his father David had followed** (3). The fact that **he sought the God of his father** brought him **great wealth and honour** (5). The reforming work of Jehoshaphat is given only slight notice (v. 6) which suggests that it was little more than a correction of the slackness that had developed towards the end of Asa's reign.

Once the defence of the land had been organized, Jehoshaphat embarked on a major teaching mission (vv. 7–9). He placed this in the hands of a body of officials including laymen (**his officials**, v. 7), Levites and priests (v. 8). The prominence given to the groups of laymen is worthy of note in view of the Chronicler's general emphasis on the teaching of the law as a Levitical function. It is not clear what is to be understood by **the book of the LORD** (9). It could be the so-called 'Book of the Covenant' (see further *NBD* under 'Law'), but dogmatism is out of place.

At v. 7, the name **Ben Hail** (lit. 'son of might') does not occur elsewhere and the section should be read as LXX—'he sent his officials, outstanding men, Obadiah . . .' The name **Tob-Adonijah** (8) is an example of dittography from the accidental recopying of the two previous names.

The nations around Judah, noting the king's strength and its source, not only refrained from war, but also sent presents to Jehoshaphat. 'The attitude of the surrounding lands is the counterpart to the state of obedience and right conduct by the king' (P. R. Ackroyd). The Chronicler describes it as the **fear of the LORD** (10) and singles out two specific groups for mention—**Philistines** and **Arabs** (11), no doubt because of their traditional enmity against Judah. The result is that **Jehoshaphat became more and more powerful** (12).

Verses 12b to 19 record the military arrangements set up by the king. The section concentrates on the arrangements in Jerusalem and notes that there were two 'regiments', one from Judah with three commanding officers and one from Benjamin with two commanding officers. This standing army was **besides those . . . in the fortified cities throughout Judah** (19).

(b) **The Alliance with Ahab (18: 1–34)**

This story is taken over almost unchanged from 1 Kg. 22: 1–35. The prophetic element is important, in the courageous stand of Micaiah ben Imlah against the false prophets, but the Chronicler places the main emphasis on the position of Jehoshaphat. His alliance with the northern kingdom (v. 1) was a dangerous folly from which he was only rescued by the intervention of God, **the LORD helped him** (31). Furthermore, a marriage alliance with the house of Ahab was quite unnecessary since God had already given him **great wealth and honour** (1). The key to the whole section may lie in v. 2 where Jehoshaphat's action is represented as the result of being **urged** to go with Ahab. The word is stronger than NIV suggests and is used for seduction into apostasy at Dt. 13: 6—no doubt, for the Chronicler, a possible outcome of the alliance, but for God's intervention. The verb rendered **drew away** at v. 31 is the same as **urged** (2), perhaps deliberately. The lesson the Chronicler wished to underline was particularly applicable to his own time with the possibility of compromise with the north again in the form of the Samaritan community. The prophetic element of the story underlines the same message, for the insistence of Jehoshaphat on the presence of another **prophet of the LORD** (6) as opposed to **these prophets of yours** (22) places emphasis on the true religion of Jehoshaphat as opposed to the invalid religion of the northern kingdom. The Chronicler's lack of interest in Ahab is evidenced in his omission of the details of his death (1 Kg. 22: 35b–38). For details on this section see notes on 1 Kg. 22: 1–35. For **threshing floor** (9) read 'open space'—a sort of city square in front of the gate.

(c) **Further Reforms (19: 1–11)**

The safe return of Jehoshaphat is met by a prophetic rebuke from **Jehu the son of Hanani** (2). The implications of the previous chapter are now made clear. How could Jehoshaphat possibly have anticipated any good outcome from an alliance with the **wicked** and **those who hate the LORD** (2)? The debacle was inevitable, but the good deeds of Jehoshaphat will outweigh his folly (v. 3).

The reference to the goodness of the king forms the stepping-off point for a further account of his reforms. The judicial reform described in vv. 4–11 may well have been the result of a desire to strengthen the southern kingdom against the corrupting influence of

471

the north. The prophetic literature indicates a continuing need for such reforms of justice. The Chronicler's description tends to be in rather general terms. The people are **turned . . . back to the LORD** (4, note the word **again**, suggesting that this is an account of a later development and not merely an expansion of the reform of ch. 17). Justice is to be meted out in the **fear of the LORD** and hence, because it is God's justice that is being dispensed, there must be no perversion, partiality or taking bribes (vv. 6 f.).

In addition to the judges appointed in all the main cities (v. 5), Jehoshaphat also appointed a central court in Jerusalem to deal with major cases including homicide and appeals (vv. 8–10). The court had two divisions, one dealing with religious affairs (or perhaps the interpretations of the Mosaic code) under **Amariah the chief priest** and the other dealing with criminal and civil cases (or perhaps the administration of uncodified traditional law) under **Zebadiah son of Ishmael, the leader of the tribe of Judah** (11). The Levites were to act as bailiffs and general court officials. The official position of the **leader** is not clear. It is of interest to note how this reform of the legal system involves a delegation of responsibility from the king to his officials and a possible regaining by the priests of some of the authority they had lost in the highly centralized days of David and Solomon.

(d) The Moabite War (20: 1–30)

This story has no parallel in Kings; it is derived from one of the Chronicler's alternative sources and is included because of the way in which it illustrated the writer's understanding of God's ordering of men's affairs. Piety brings its reward and in time of crisis the community must rest its faith in God in whom alone victory and deliverance are to be found.

The invaders were a group of southern peoples, **Moabites and Ammonites** and **Meunites** (1). The identity of the latter group is uncertain but they are probably to be identified with the people of the Arabian kingdom of *Ma'ūn* who were the dominant South Arabian traders in the time of the Chronicler. They are mentioned elsewhere at 1 Chr. 4: 41; 2 Chr. 26: 7; Ezr. 2: 50; Neh. 7: 52. The invasion was mounted from the region of the Dead Sea (called simply **the Sea**, v. 2) and had reached En Gedi before the king had news of it. There was considerable alarm which resulted in the king proclaiming **a fast** (3) in which all the nation participated (v. 13). Thus while the **vast army** (2, 12) strikes fear into the king's heart, it also elicits the proper response on the part of king and people—they **seek help from the LORD** and **seek him** (4).

The congregation assembled at the **temple of the LORD, in front of the new courtyard**

(5). This is presumably the 'great court' of 4: 9, but the author may have in mind the design of the post-exilic temple with which the readers would be more familiar. The king offered a solemn prayer as his father Asa had done under similar circumstances (14: 11). The prayer contains allusions to Solomon's dedicatory prayer (vv. 8, 9) and also to the presettlement period of Israel's history (vv. 7, 10, 11). The word for **judgment** (9) by a transposition of consonants would give in the context a more credible reading of 'floods': 'the sword or floods'. The final appeal of the prayer underlines the king's awareness of his weakness in the face of the situation and his absolute trust in the reality of the power of Yahweh to deliver—**We do not know what to do, but our eyes are upon you** (12).

The answer of God comes in the form of a prophetic oracle delivered by **Jahaziel . . . a Levite and descendant of Asaph** (14) that is, a member of the Asaphite guild of singers. He appears to have been a cultic prophet, that is, a religious functionary who prophesied within a liturgical setting, and there is some evidence for these as a specific class of prophets within the sanctuary personnel. Some have suggested in fact that the Levitical singing guilds fulfilled a prophetic function (cf. 2 Kg. 23: 2 with 2 Chr. 34: 30). The name Jahaziel itself is significant, meaning 'God gives vision'. The important element in the oracle is that as far as Jehoshaphat was concerned, **the battle is not yours but God's** (15) hence **you will not have to fight this battle. Take up your positions; stand firm and see the deliverance the LORD will give you** (17; cf. Exod. 14: 13).

King and people respond to the word from God with an act of praise and worship (v. 18) and early the next morning set out for **Jeruel** (16) which lies south east of **Tekoa** (20) on the steep ascent from En Gedi. There is a strong suggestion from the whole account and the formation of Judah's army into a religious procession that the expedition is being viewed as a 'holy war'. By the time the army of Judah arrived on the scene the enemy had already destroyed themselves (vv. 23, 24). To ask how this came about is to miss the whole point of the Chronicler's story—**the LORD set ambushes** (22).

The victory was celebrated by claiming the booty which took three days, **there was so much** (25), followed by a service of thanksgiving in the **Valley of Beracah** (26). Beracah means 'blessing' or 'praise' and the verse may be intended to explain how this particular *wadi* got its name. The long term result of the victory was that **the fear of God came upon all the kingdoms** (29; cf. 17: 10) and the realm was at peace (v. 30; cf. 14: 6; 15: 15).

(e) The End of Jehoshaphat's Reign
(20: 31–21: 1)

The account of the last days of Jehoshaphat comes as something of an anticlimax. Verses 31–34 are largely a reproduction of the Chronicler's source in Kings with some minor modifications. Verse 33 is slightly altered from the source so that the blame is made to lie more definitely on the people and their failure to **set their hearts on the God of their fathers**. The references to the sources (v. 34) includes **the annals of Jehu son of Hanani** who is featured at 19: 2. The reference to the **book of the kings of Israel** is an interesting change from 1 Kg. 22: 45 and reflects the Chronicler's theology.

The abortive maritime adventure with **Ahaziah king of Israel** (vv. 35–37) appears in the same position as in the Kings narrative indicating the close following of his primary sources by the Chronicler. There is, however, a certain degree of reinterpretation, for the Kings story does not suggest that the venture was in association with Ahab's son, Ahaziah, and his later offer is roundly snubbed by Jehoshaphat (1 Kg. 22: 49). It may be that the Chronicler is utilizing additional material other than his primary source and it allows him to emphasize the point made by **Eliezer** the prophet (v. 37) that alliance with the wicked for trade is as equally displeasing to Yahweh as alliance for war (the theme of ch. 18). There is evidence that **Ezion Geber** was burnt down after the reign of Solomon and the allusion here may relate to the rebuilding known to have taken place in the ninth century B.C. when Jehoshaphat no doubt planned to redevelop the Red Sea trading routes.

The death of Jehoshaphat is recorded in the regular formula that concludes the story of nearly all the kings (21: 1) and this serves also to open the next narrative.

v. The reign of Jehoram (21: 2–20)

The account of Jehoram's reign in 2 Kg. 8: 17–22 is very brief and the Chronicler has clearly had access to additional sources and is thus able to elaborate on the bare facts of the Kings narrative.

(a) Jehoram establishes himself (21: 2–7)

It is worth noting that Jehoram was the brother-in-law of Jehoram of Israel through his marriage with Athaliah (v. 6) and the Chronicler has no doubts as to where the blame for his ways lay. The reign serves as an even more potent reminder of the dire consequences that follow alliances with evil than those recounted earlier.

It would appear that Jehoshaphat had put his sons in the various fortified cities of Judah to act as local administrators (vv. 2, 3; cf. 11: 23). He provided for them on a lavish scale, but the kingdom was reserved for the eldest son

Jehoram. As soon as Jehoram had established himself on the throne **he put all his brothers to the sword along with some of the princes of Israel** (4). Jehoshaphat is called 'king of Israel' at v. 2, in the Hebrew text. 'Israel' here is used in the sense of the true kingdom as elsewhere by the Chronicler.

The wholesale removal of all possible major sources of opposition (from v. 13 it seems certain that his brothers almost certainly followed their father and opposed Jehoram's Baalism) meant that Jehoram could pursue his religious policies, in which he was clearly under the influence of Athaliah and Jezebel. In spite of this apostasy, however, **the LORD was not willing to destroy the house of David** (7) on the ground of the **covenant** which is viewed by the Chronicler as unconditional.

(b) Rebellion of Edom and Libnah (21: 8–10)

The successful rebellion of two subject peoples, Edom and Libnah on the Philistine border, is seen as part of the judgment of God on Jehoram **because** he **had forsaken the LORD** (10). The account is not very clear—due, no doubt, to the rather confused text of the source at 2 Kg. 8: 21. What appears to have happened is that Jehoram and his army went to teach the Edomites a lesson only to find that the Edomites had **surrounded him and his chariot commanders** (9). Although he was able to **break through** it was nonetheless a defeat and resulted in an independent Edom. 2 Kg. 8: 21 makes the additional point that the rest of Jehoram's army fled, probably because they saw the king surrounded.

(c) Elijah's Letter (21: 11–15)

The result of Jehoram's religious policy was seen in the restoration of the high places that previous kings had destroyed. It is likely that he fostered a syncretistic religion which married Yahwehism to elements of Canaanite worship. It is interesting that he maintained names compounded with Yahweh for his children (v. 17 **Jehoahaz**, NIVmg). The king's apostasy prompts **Elijah the prophet** to send a letter pronouncing judgment on him and his family and foretelling his own death as the result of **a disease of** his **bowels** (15).

The Elijah letter presents certain difficulties which are not easy to avoid. In the first instance it seems certain that Elijah was not living as late as the reign of Jehoram of Judah. From 2 Kg. 3: 11 and the position of the translation story of 2 Kg. 2, it would seem that Elijah had departed either at the end of the reign of Ahaziah of Israel or at the beginning of that of Jehoram of Israel. In either case this would have been contemporary with Jehoshaphat and not Jehoram. On the basis of 2 Kg. 8: 16 it has been suggested that Jehoram was co-regent with his father for a time, but the text of this verse may be faulty. Certainly there is a problem about the statement of 2 Kg. 1: 17 which reports the accession of Joram of Israel in the second year of Jehoram of Judah. The other difficulty lies in the silence of Kings about this letter in view of the great prominence given to the Elijah/Elisha cycle of stories. It may be that the name of Elijah became attached to the letter because it originated from the prophetic guilds associated with him.

(d) **The last years and death of Jehoram (21: 16–20)**
The prophetic message was the prelude to the troubles which beset the last years of Jehoram. The kingdom came under attack from a combined force of **Philistines and Arabs** (vv. 16, 17). The phrase **who lived near the Cushites** probably relates to the settlers around Gerar from the time of Shishak (see note on 14: 8–14). The result of the raid was that the king's wives and all his sons except the youngest, who was probably too young to have been involved in the fighting, were taken as booty. The weakness of the kingdom is seen in that no punitive or recovery expedition was mounted. Jehoram's final days were lived in the shadow of **an incurable disease** (18) from which **he died in great pain** (19). The fatal condition seems to have been a massive rectal prolapse, probably strangulated, arising from some form of chronic dysentery or perhaps a massive rectal carcinoma. The final comment on Jehoram's reign is an evidence of the judgment that lay on him—**he passed away, to no one's regret** (20).

vi. **The reign of Ahaziah (22: 1–9)**
The Chronicler alone records the fact that it was the **people of Jerusalem** (1) who put Ahaziah on the throne. The significance of the statement is not clear, but it may have been an action by the people to try to stabilize a critical situation. The 'people of the land' ('am hā-'āreṣ) intervened on other occasions when the succession was in jeopardy (note 23: 20, 21; 26: 1; 33: 25; 36: 1). Whether that phrase may be viewed as having the same significance as the 'people of Jerusalem' is not clear, however; the present expression may represent the court faction acting hastily to prevent the 'people of the land' transferring the crown to another branch of the Davidic family as a result of their disgust with the policies of Jehoram.

The text of v. 2 has clearly suffered at this point. LXX gives 'twenty years old' and 2 Kg. 8: 26 gives **twenty-two years old**. The figure 'forty-two' (NIVmg) may be the result of the conflation of the two traditions. It would make the king two years older than his father.

Throughout the short one-year reign of Ahaziah, he followed a religious policy that was clearly the result of the domination of **Athaliah** who **encouraged him in doing wrong** (3)

and maintained the alliance between north and south. The Chronicler's condemnation could hardly be stronger—**he walked in the ways of the house of Ahab** (3). The account of Ahaziah's visit to his uncle Jehoram (Joram) of Israel and its consequences after the abortive joint expedition against **Hazael, king of Aran** (vv. 5–9) clearly presupposes a knowledge of 2 Kg. 8: 28–9: 28. (For detailed notes see commentary ad loc.) The mode of Ahaziah's death (v. 9) at the hand of **Jehu the son of Nimshi, whom the LORD had anointed to destroy the house of Ahab** (7) differs in detail from 2 Kg. 9: 27, 28. The weakness of the kingdom was now very apparent—there was **no one powerful enough to retain the kingdom** (9), because Ahaziah's own children were too young to rule and his brothers presumably had been killed by the Arabs (21: 17).

vii. **The interlude of Athaliah (22: 10–12)**
The ruthless action of **Athaliah** in butchering **the whole royal family of the house of Judah** was most likely designed to secure her position as regent and allow her to continue to enjoy the power she had obviously wielded as queen-mother. The queen-mother, as the king's mother and usually favourite wife of the deceased ruler, enjoyed considerable power and prestige (cf. 1 Kg. 2: 19; 15: 2, 10, 13; Jer. 13: 18), especially during the minority of her son. It has been argued that Athaliah had no intention of killing Joash, for without him she could not rule, and the reason for his kidnapping by the priests was not so much to save his life, but to provide the means of challenging her power when the time was ripe. On the other hand, she may not have been aware of the rescue of Joash and may have considered that she was reigning in her own right, but this was not the official view and the 'people of the land' were ready when the opportune moment arrived to put the true king on the throne. The heroine of this story was **Jehosheba** who was sister to Ahaziah and the wife of **the priest Jehoiada**. It is clear that the close blood-ties between the royal and high-priestly families were continuing.

viii. **The reign of Joash (23: 1–24: 27)**
(a) **The Crowning of Joash (23: 1–11)**
The narrative in this chapter closely follows its source in 2 Kg. 11: 1–20 (see commentary ad loc.) but there are points of interest in the Chronicler's handling of his material. Particularly worth noting is the important place given to the ecclesiastical authorities in keeping with his general emphasis. It is the **priests and Levites** who became the guards (vv. 4–8) because **they are consecrated** (cf. 2 Kg. 11: 4–8 where the guards are purely military). The people are to keep their proper place and **the LORD's command** (6 NIVmg) with respect to the temple must be obeyed. The Chronicler's

interest in the Davidic line comes out at v. 3 underlining his continuing emphasis on the temple and David as the founder of the kingdom of Israel. In keeping with his outlook he also states explicitly that it was **Jehoiada and his sons** (11) who anointed the young king. The **covenant** may have been a document enshrining a prophetic word establishing the king as God's viceregent, perhaps the 'decree of the LORD' of Ps. 2: 7, and thus the royal warrant.

(*b*) **Athaliah's response (23: 12–15)**
The source is followed closely in this section although again there are significant emphases in the Chronicler's version, particularly in the place given to the **singers** (13) and the sanctity of the temple shown in the strong words of Jehoiada, **'Do not put her to death at the temple of the LORD'** (14).

It is probably better to translate **the king, standing by his pillar** (13) as 'standing in his place', or even 'on his platform or dais' (note 2 Chr. 6: 13). The expression **out between the ranks** (14) is uncertain in meaning, but may mean no more than outside the temple precincts. **15. they seized her:** read with LXX 'they made way for her'.

(*c*) **The Reformation (23: 16–21)**
The first essential was to re-establish the covenant that **they would be the LORD's people** (16) and it showed the fact that a religious leader of worth had emerged with Jehoiada. The next stage was to remove all vestiges of the worship of Tyrian **Baal** (17) in the course of which **Mattan the priest of Baal** was killed. Mattan is a Phoenician name of this period and it is likely that he was from Sidon in common with Jezebel. At the same time the proper worship of Yahweh was restored **as written in the Law of Moses** and **as David had ordered** (18). This linking David and Moses as the founders of Israel's ordered worship is characteristic of the Chronicler. The other significant development was the reaffirmation of the full share of the Levites with the priests in the temple service. Then the king was escorted in triumph to his palace for the enthronement ceremony (v. 20). Not surprisingly **all the people of the land rejoiced** (21).

(*d*) **The period of reform (24: 1–14)**
The story of the reign follows its source at 2 Kg. 12 in general but with a number of significant variations suggesting additional sources. The most important of them relates to the apostasy of the king after the death of Jehoiada, which is not mentioned in Kings, the prophecy of Zechariah and the account of the Syrian war and the king's death. The Chronicler states that **Joash did what was right in the eyes of the LORD all the years of Jehoiada the priest** (2), whereas 2 Kg. 12: 2 makes the point that he did what was right throughout his reign

because of the firm grounding in the true faith that Jehoiada had given him.

The account of the restoration of the temple (vv. 4–14) follows the narrative of 2 Kg. 12: 9–16 in the main but with sufficient variations to make it possible that the Chronicler was drawing on another source. The appeal for funds to restore the temple occasioned by the neglect of Athaliah and her brood (v. 7) was made the basis of the head tax **imposed by Moses** (Exod. 30: 12–16; 38: 25–28) for the **Tent of the Testimony** (6). This point is not made in the Kings account, which also does not mention the dilatoriness of the original Levitical tax-collectors. The answer to the situation was **a proclamation** transforming what appears to have been a semi-voluntary tax into an obligatory one (v. 9). This had the desired effect and the people brought their tax into the temple, placing it in **the chest** provided. It is of interest to note that the Chronicler has moved the chest from 'beside the altar' (2 Kg. 12: 9) to **outside, at the gate**, no doubt to accommodate the story to the stricter temple regulations of his own time. The chest was emptied each day when it was full. The tax was sufficient to cover all the necessary restoration work together with a surplus (not mentioned in Kings) used for utensils (v. 14).

(*b*) **The apostasy and downfall of Joash (24: 15–27)**
The ideal situation presented at the end of v. 14 came to an end with the death of Jehoiada at the advanced age of **a hundred and thirty** (15); presumably a symbolic figure indicating the favour of God. The people also honoured him and buried him **with the kings, because of the good he had done in Israel** (again used here to speak of Judah, the true Israel).

At the instigation of the **officials of Judah** (17) the clock is turned back and there is a return to the worship of the Phoenician deities that had been so prominent during the ascendancy of Athaliah. These court officials may well have been part of the old regime and it is noteworthy that the tendencies towards the paganizing of Judaism generally derive from the court, not from 'the people of the land' who seem to provide a stabilizing and conservative influence. The outcome of such apostasy is seen as **anger** (18); essentially the outworking of the divine principle of retribution.

The king pursues his evil course in spite of the fact that God **sent prophets to the people** (19) culminating in the oracle of **Zechariah son of Jehoiada the priest** (20). For the significant statement **the Spirit of God came upon Zechariah** see note on 1 Chr. 12: 18. The principle of the words **Because you have forsaken the LORD, he has forsaken you** (20) reappears in NT (Rom. 1: 28). Instead of showing Zechariah respect, he is killed at the express command of the king (v. 21). The heinous nature of this act is magnified in view of the **kindness** of Jehoiada to Joash. The rendering 'kindness' for *ḥesed* is not really strong enough; it signifies a close bond of loyalty; the word being used for the 'covenant love' of Yahweh for His people. The killing of Zechariah in the temple is probably the incident alluded to at Lk. 11: 51 and Mt. 23: 35.

The downfall of Joash soon followed as the result of the Aramaean war (vv. 23–26). There are marked differences between this account and 2 Kings, and it is certain that the Chronicler is depending on another source—perhaps the **annotations** (*midrāš*) **on the book of the kings** (27). The Syrian army attacked at **the turn of the year** (23), that is in spring time, and with few men routed the **much larger army** of Judah (24). The defeat was a direct result of the disobedience of the people. The main points of contrast with the Kings account are the investing of Jerusalem and the wounding of the king (v. 25). Joash himself becomes the victim of a conspiracy and is murdered by two aliens. His death is portrayed as the direct result of his guilt in the death of Zechariah.

The story of the reign of Joash, showing 'how a good king, wisely guided, can so easily fall under evil influence and become apostate' (P. R. Ackroyd), is a good example of the Chronicler's purpose in using history for its spiritual and moral lessons.

ix. The reign of Amaziah (25: 1–28)
The narrative follows 2 Kg. 14: 1–20 in broad outline, but the main bulk of the story, relating to the Edomite campaign in vv. 5–16, is only mentioned briefly at 2 Kg. 14: 7. The Chronicler clearly had access once again to additional sources of information than what became the canonical books of Kings.

(a) The Accession of Amaziah (25: 1–14)
The opening defines the character of the king as one who did **what was right** but this is qualified almost immediately, **but not whole-heartedly** (2). The writer thus anticipated the later failure of the king. The execution of his father's murderers took place as soon as he had established himself, but in accordance with the Deuteronomic Law (Dt. 24: 16; cf. also Jer. 31: 29 f. and Ezek. 18: 1, 19 f.) he did not extend his judgment to the family. A difference is to be noted between human judgment, which was not to go beyond the guilty individual, and divine judgment, which might extend to the whole family for certain sins, as in the case of Achan.

(b) The Edomite Campaign (25: 15–16)
The brief mention of this campaign at 2 Kg. 14: 7 is considerably expanded by the Chronicler. His use of an alternative source here no doubt arises from the considerable religious interest contained in this narrative.

Amaziah prepared for the campaign by reorganizing his army and taking a military census (v. 5), apparently a standard procedure (cf. 1 Chr. 21; 2 Chr. 14: 8; 17: 14–19). In addition to the troops available from Judah he also hired **a hundred thousand fighting men from Israel** (6). These men were mercenaries, who, in addition to their basic pay, were to receive a share in the spoils of war. This note explains the situation of v. 13 (see below). The numbers in vv. 5 and 6 are best interpreted on the basis that the word *'elep* **(thousand)** means a military or civil unit of unspecified size (see 1 Chr. 12: 24 ff.).

The hiring of the northern mercenaries is the important religious point to be underlined. A message comes to Amaziah from a **man of God** (7), virtually a technical term for a prophet, that the reliance on the Israelite soldiers would be disastrous, **for the LORD is not with Israel.** To be assisted by, or rely on, this sort of help from the ungodly would bring inevitable defeat (v. 8). This lesson has been emphasized repeatedly in the previous accounts of the lessons to be learned from the lives of the kings of Judah. Note again how the message of God is brought to the king by a prophet (cf. 2 Chr. 12: 5; 15: 1; 19: 2; 21: 12; 24: 20).

When the king complained at the loss of the money paid to the mercenaries, the prophet assured him that **the LORD can give you much more than that** (9). The mercenaries, however, are greatly angered at their loss of expected war booty and in order to gain some recompense they raid some of the Judean communities near **Beth Horon** (13). **13. from Samaria:** probably in reference to their starting point, since they would hardly have raided their own territory. This action may have been recorded to indicate what the Chronicler saw as a punishment for Amaziah's initial faithlessness or for his subsequent lapse into idolatry.

The prophetic assurance that God does not depend on numbers to achieve His victory (cf. 13: 3–18) spurred on the king to undertake the campaign and the forces of Edom were destroyed (vv. 11–12). Large numbers of the enemy were killed, and the prisoners taken were executed by being thrown from **the top of a cliff**—a play on the word 'Sela' at 2 Kg. 14: 7. The change of name to 'Joktheel' (God destroys) mentioned there may be a hint at the events the Chronicler has recorded.

The sequel to the campaign (vv. 14–16) is of particular importance. Amaziah was apparently ensnared by his pride, for in transporting the gods of the conquered Edomites to Jerusalem, he was acting like one of the great oriental potentates who frequently did this for various reasons. Nowhere else is a Hebrew king reported to have done this and it is seen here as the reason for Amaziah's defeat by Israel. Once again a prophet intervened (v. 15), reminding the king of his folly and pointing to the impotence of the gods of Edom, which Amaziah's victory had demonstrated. The prophet was silenced— **Have we appointed you an adviser to the king?**— but makes a noteworthy retort—**God has determined** [counselled] **to destroy you** (16) because of his rejection of the prophet's advice and his worship of the Edomite gods.

(*c*) **The war with Joash of Israel (25: 17–28)**
The Chronicler's account follows 2 Kg. 14: 8–20 with only minor deviations. The defeat of Amaziah is seen as the result of his apostasy (v. 20) and his persistence in this ruinous course of action was part of God's purposes. Joash correctly understood the motive for Amaziah's desire for confrontation—**now you are arrogant and proud** (19). The courteous, but firm, reply from Joash to the presumptuous and arrogant challenge of Amaziah is worth noting. Amaziah refused to be deflected from his foolish course of action and the result was as the prophet had predicted. The army was defeated, the king humiliated, the treasuries sacked, hostages taken and part of the city walls were broken down (vv. 22–24). Verse 24 is a reminder that Obed-Edom's family were the hereditary guardians of the Temple treasury from the time of David. The defeat may have resulted in an increasing ineffectiveness in Amaziah's rule, as well as an unwelcome submission to Israel. The Chronicler's statement seems to suggest that the conspiracy (v. 27) began to develop soon after the defeat by Joash but that it took **fifteen years** to come to fruition. He was killed by the conspirators in **Lachish** to which he had fled and was buried in Jerusalem. RSV here reads 'city of David' (following 2 Kg. 14: 20) but *MT* gives **city of Judah**. Either is correct as Jerusalem was known as the 'city of Judah' in the Babylonian Chronicle.

x. The reign of Uzziah (26: 1–23)
(*a*) **Summary of the reign (26: 1–5)**
The section follows 2 Kg. 14: 21–15: 4 with the omission of Uzziah's failure to remove the high places (2 Kg. 15: 4) and the additional qualification that he only sought the Lord as long as his instructor, **Zechariah**, was alive (v. 5). It is of interest to note that Uzziah was made king by popular acclaim (v. 1) and it would seem that this was part of the successful conspiracy against his father.

The reign of Uzziah was marked by a major expansion of the kingdom of Judah. The Chronicler notes that **he rebuilt Elath** (Ezion-geber) (2). This important seaport had been lost to Judah in the reign of Jehoram (21: 8–10). Excavations in the area reflect three periods in the history of the port in the pre-exilic period —first in the time of Solomon, a second in the time of Jehoshaphat and the third period

contemporary with Uzziah. It remained under Judean rule until it was retaken by the Edomites about 735 B.C. The phrase **after Amaziah rested with his fathers** probably refers to the death of a king of Edom rather than Uzziah's father, perhaps the king who featured in the Edomite campaigns of the preceding chapter. The **Zechariah, who instructed him in the fear of God** (5), is otherwise unknown.

(*b*) **Uzziah's conquests (26: 6–8)**
'The first half of the eighth century, during which Assyrian pressure was withdrawn and the kingdom of Aram was relatively weak, was for both the Israelite kingdoms a time of internal prosperity' (P. R. Ackroyd). This freedom from the threats of the major powers led to a marked expansion and an attempt to reclaim the area lost to both Israel and Judah in previous reigns. The Chronicler utilizes sources other than Kings to give the picture of a south-western expansion into Philistine and Arab territory. The place names are all known except **Gur Baal** (7) which may not be an accurate transmission of the original. **Jabneh** is the later Jamnia and the meeting place of those who did so much to establish Judaism after the destruction of the Temple in A.D. 70. The **towns** (6) were probably forts built at strategic points to subdue the local inhabitants.

(*c*) **The Internal Developments (26: 9–15)**
The building activities throughout the reign of Uzziah are well attested by archeological discoveries, especially in the Negeb around Beersheba (see N. Glueck, *Rivers in the Desert*, 1958), where the **cisterns** (10) mentioned by the Chronicler have been found. They illustrate his point that Uzziah **loved the soil** (10), and made great efforts to establish and develop a sound agricultural economy. The conquests of Uzziah demanded a well organized and strong standing army (vv. 11–14). It would appear that the king reorganized the army, possibly in the face of the growing threat from Assyria. The equipment was **provided for the entire army** (14) by the king, in other words the troops no longer had to supply their own weapons, but were armed by the king. The nature of the **machines** (15) is not entirely clear, but were probably some kind of protective device or cover from which the defenders on **the towers and the corner defenses** could shoot arrows and hurl stones at their attackers. It is unlikely that they were propulsive weapons as catapults and similar devices were unknown at this period. The Chronicler's picture accurately portrays the internal prosperity of Judah through the long reign of Uzziah, matched by that of Israel to the north under Jeroboam II. The strength and security of the nation are put down to the fact that Uzziah **was greatly helped** (15)—that is to say, he received the

supernatural assistance of Yahweh for his faithfulness.

(d) Uzziah's downfall (26: 16–23)
The tragedy of Uzziah's reign was that **after Uzziah became powerful, his pride led to his downfall** (16). The particular incident which brought about his downfall was his entering the temple to **burn incense** (16). This action is described as being **unfaithful to the LORD his God.** NIV is not really correct here, AV translates as 'he transgressed against', but NEB gives a better rendering with 'he offended against'. The real point was the impropriety of his action in proudly usurping the role of the priests. **Azariah** with eighty other priests courageously stood up to the king (vv. 17, 18) and pronounced judgment on him. The Chronicler seems to imply that had Uzziah accepted the rebuke this would have ended the matter, but instead the king was angry (v. 19) and because of this **leprosy broke out on his forehead.** The word traditionally translated as 'leprosy' is not to be confused with the modern disease of that name. The biblical leprosy simply referred to a group of skin conditions considered ceremonially unclean before Yahweh. The records are so vague that it is almost impossible to be specific about actual diagnoses, although fungal infections, carbuncles, etc. are recognizable from the descriptions given. Uzziah's illness, which began on **his forehead** (19, 20), may have been no more than psoriasis which would have made him ritually unclean, the reason for his being **hurried out**, or it may have been some form of contagious skin disease. Because his illness made him ritually unclean he was forced to live in a **separate house** for the rest of his life, unable to enter the temple, and his son Jotham became regent (v. 21).

The story presents a number of problems. 2 Kg. 15 omits all reference to the reason for Uzziah's leprosy and there are many references to other kings carrying out priestly functions as part of their regal prerogative, although not the burning of incense. The Chronicler was perhaps viewing the episode from the standpoint of the legislation in force at his own time, but the essential point of the story is clear in emphasizing God's response to man's arrogance and pride.

The final note (v. 22) is of interest in crediting the prophet **Isaiah** with writing the story of Uzziah's reign. The king was not buried in the royal tombs but in a field beside them on the grounds that he suffered from 'leprosy'.

xi. The reign of Jotham (27: 1–9)
Jotham continued the religious policy of his father (v. 2) for which the Chronicler commended him and noted also with approval that he remembered his status as a layman and **did not enter the temple.** The reward for his doing **what was right** was prosperity and success. He embarked on an extensive building programme, no doubt a continuation of that of his father, which included the **Upper Gate** of the temple (v. 3), situated at the north entrance to the temple enclosure, and also extended the **Ophel** fortifications. The Ophel appears to have been some sort of defensive mound in the south of the city overlooking the Kidron valley. He also **built towns in the Judean hills** (4). These probably represented a series of fortresses designed for defence in case of attack and they seemed to be linked by a system of hill forts and watch towers **in the wooded areas.** This phrase may refer back to a programme of a re-afforestation that Uzziah had undertaken.

The description of most of this activity, together with the account of the Ammonite campaign (vv. 5, 6) was derived from sources other than 2 Kg. 16. Doubt has been expressed about the historical accuracy of this war since it is affirmed that Judah and Ammon had no common frontier at this time. However, as J. M. Myers points out, 'Israel was rapidly losing prestige and power after the death of Jeroboam II, in the wake of which the border people spilled over, as they always did, into the territory where the power vacuum existed'. The defeat of the Ammonites brought a massive tribute to Jotham for three years (v. 5). Whether they asserted their independence at the end of this time is not clear, but it may have been paid merely through the final years of Jotham's short sole reign. The **sixteen years** of his reign (vv. 1, 8) may have included the period of his co-regency with Uzziah and his actual reign may not have been more than seven years.

xii. The reign of Ahaz (28: 1–27)
(a) The character of Ahaz's reign (28: 1–4)
'The name Ahaz is surrounded by infamy as may be seen from this evaluation, but even more clearly from the references to him by Isaiah' (J. M. Myers). The reign of Ahaz was marked by a wholesale reversion to Canaanite religious practices, leading to the Chronicler's statement that he **walked in the ways of the kings of Israel** (2)—no greater condemnation could be made. The main statements are derived from 2 Kg. 15 with additional information which may derive from Isaiah. **3. the Valley of Ben Hinnom:** later simply the 'valley of Hinnom' or 'Gehenna', south of Jerusalem. The Phoenician/Canaanite practice of **sacrificing his sons in the fire** was particularly abhorrent to the prophets (cf. Mic. 7: 7; Jer. 7: 31).

(b) The Syro-Ephraimite War (28: 5–25)
The background for this section is 2 Kg. 15: 37; 16: 5 and Isa. 7. The essential point of the story is the **therefore** of v. 5. Judah's defeat represented the divine judgment for her apos-

tasy. The northern coalition defeated Ahaz, killing large numbers of his army, including a number of prominent persons in the kingdom (v. 7) **because** they **had forsaken the LORD** (6). 2 Kg. 16: 5 makes the point that Jerusalem was not captured.

The sequel to the defeat of Ahaz is the remarkable story of vv. 8–15 which centres on the prophecy of **Oded.** He is not mentioned elsewhere, but the story illustrates one of the Chronicler's themes that even when Yahweh was acting in judgment He was also concerned to show mercy. **The Israelites took captive** a large number of the people of Judah (v. 8). The prophet Oded does not question the defeat of Judah; that was Yahweh's judgment (v. 9) and Israel was simply His instrument in bringing it about. Israel, however, had gone beyond what was allowable and had acted in **rage**, intending also to **make the men and women of Judah and Jerusalem slaves** (10). This course of action would result in judgment upon themselves if it was pursued (v. 11). The prophetic word was obeyed and the Ephraimite leaders persuaded the army to give up the captives (vv. 12–14) who were returned to the south suitably clothed and fed (v. 15). It is of interest that the Chronicler has allowed the word **fellow countrymen** (RSV 'kinsfolk') (11) to stand, an indication of the faithfulness with which he has followed his source.

(c) **The appeal to Assyria (28: 16–21)**
Ahaz failed to learn the lesson of his defeat and appealed to man for help rather than God in spite of the pleadings of Isaiah (see Isa. 7). The weakness of Ahaz had resulted in others taking advantage of the situation (vv. 16–18) and throwing off Judean suzerainty. The appeal of Ahaz to **Tiglath-pileser** (20) appears to have been against Edom and Philistia rather than Israel and Aram. He no doubt hoped that Assyria's intervention would result in their return to Judah, but the Chronicler notes that Assyria **gave him trouble instead of help** (20) and **did not help him** (21). In fact Assyria, though it came to put down the rebellion of Edom and Philistia, did not return them to Judah, but organized them as Assyrian provinces. The resources of Judah had been severely depleted to no purpose as a result of the wrongdoing of Ahaz (v. 19).

(d) **The end of Ahaz's reign (28: 22–27)**
These verses give more detail of the total apostasy of Ahaz who **in his time of trouble** turned not to Yahweh, but to the gods of Syria who were viewed as superior as a result of the Syro-Ephraimite victory (v. 23). The whole country was turned over to foreign religious practices; the temple vessels destroyed and the temple itself closed (vv. 24, 25). Verse 24 appears to be an expansion of 2 Kg. 16: 18. The fact that Ahaz was not buried **in the tombs of**

the kings of Israel (27) is probably to be viewed as a further punishment for his apostasy.

xiii. The reign of Hezekiah (29: 1–32: 33)
The account of Hezekiah's reign differs very sharply from that given in 2 Kings. The Chronicler devotes four complete chapters to his reign, three of which are devoted to his reforms and the remaining chapter to mainly political matters. 2 Kings on the other hand only devotes one verse to Hezekiah's reforms and nearly three chapters to the mainly political aspects of his reign. Hezekiah's policy seems to be a mixture of nationalism and religious zeal, and clearly a major influence on his reign was that of the prophets, notably Isaiah and Micah. It cannot be mere chance that the king set his reforms in motion at the particular time when he was also taking steps to cast off the Assyrian yoke. Whatever steps may have been involved —and the Chronicler's record is not entirely clear as to the chronological order of events— it is obvious that Hezekiah's reform was an exceedingly thorough-going one and a precursor to that of Josiah nearly a century later.

(a) **The cleansing of the Temple (29: 1–17)**
It was no doubt a welcome task for the Chronicler to recount the good deeds of Hezekiah after the record of events that transpired under his evil father, Ahaz. According to the Chronicler (28: 24) Ahaz had closed the temple perhaps as a direct result of the Syrian interference in Judah's religious affairs. The first official move of Hezekiah was to restore the activities of the temple. **3. In the first month of the first year of his reign, he opened the doors of the temple of the LORD:** from the outset of his reign it was clear he was intending to reverse the total policy of his father in religious affairs. Verses 5–11 recount Hezekiah's address to the priests and Levites. The reason for the religious and political state of Judah lay in the fact that **our fathers were unfaithful** (6), which is followed by the moral logic of the **Therefore** of v. 8; because of their failure, the **anger of the LORD has fallen on Judah and Jerusalem.**

The first stage in putting things right was to cleanse the temple and restore the proper form of services. This could only be done by the proper religious officials, namely the Levites, and these respond in the proper fashion (vv. 12–15). The work was completed in record time (v. 17). **Everything unclean** (16) which was found in the house of the Lord probably relates to objects of pagan worship which had been introduced there by Ahaz. Once the temple had been cleansed Hezekiah was informed that all was now ready for a new start.

(b) **The re-dedication of the Temple (29: 18–30)**
Hezekiah's plan seems to have been to reestab-

lish the covenant relationship with Yahweh and this proceeded in three steps, the first being the cleansing of the temple and its reconsecration, the second the re-dedication of the temple and the third the people's response in bringing their offerings to God. The rededication of the temple began with Hezekiah making a **sin offering for the kingdom, for the sanctuary and for Judah** (21) in order to make atonement for the people who stood in great need of such sacrifice. The interesting point is the king's command (v. 24) that additional sacrifices were to be made for **all Israel.** This is a persistent feature of the Chronicler's account. Hezekiah's interest, however, includes not only the kingdom of Judah but also his brethren to the north. Verses 25–30 describe the congregational act of worship at which the burnt offering was made (v. 27), and in which the **whole assembly bowed in worship** (28) with the musical accompaniment of singers and trumpeters.

(c) **The offerings of the congregation (29: 31–36)**
The temple had now been properly dedicated and was ready for use, the people had been sanctified and the atonement sacrifices had been made. Hezekiah then called upon the people to **come and bring sacrifices and thank offerings to the temple of the LORD** (31). The overwhelming response to Hezekiah's appeal is seen in vv. 32–33 which details the large number of animals sacrificed and the point is made that **the priests were too few to skin all the burnt offerings**. The shortage of priests is used by the Chronicler to make the point that the Levites were more conscientious than the priests and, on certain occasions, were able to perform priestly functions (v. 34). The burnt offerings could not be eaten by the offerers but denoted a zeal for the worship of God. On the other hand the **fellowship offerings** and **drink offerings** (35) were partaken of by the worshippers and it is almost certain that the rejoicing on this occasion was associated with great festivities and feasting. Verse 36 makes the point that Hezekiah and all the people **rejoiced** at the restoration of the temple services and also at the speed with which the work had been accomplished.

(d) **Hezekiah's Passover (30: 1–31: 1)**
The next stage in the religious reforms of Hezekiah was the celebration of the **Passover to the LORD, the God of Israel** (1). It should be noted that the king **also wrote letters to Ephraim and Manasseh.** The northern kingdom had fallen by this time, but there still remained a remnant in that area and it was Hezekiah's purpose to unite them into an enlarged Judah to form once again a united Israel. Hezekiah no doubt felt that the time was opportune for such a move as Assyria was engaged

in problems elsewhere and could not turn its attention to what was essentially a bid for the full independence of Judah from Assyrian domination. That in the end the bid failed does not take away from the importance of the religious reforms that were undertaken at this time. The Chronicler utilized this historical situation is a sermon for his own time. The national significance of the passover lent itself admirably to the purposes of the king to bring all the nation once more under the one covenant, and the Chronicler was thinking, no doubt, of his own situation and his own appeal to the Samaritans of the post-exilic period to renounce their debased form of worship and become united in the true worship of Yahweh, centred on Jerusalem.

The preparations for the passover occupy vv. 1–12. It is to be noted that the festival was to be celebrated in the **second month** (2) largely as a result of the somewhat dilatory behaviour of the priests—**not enough priests had consecrated themselves**, nor apparently were there sufficient numbers of people in Jerusalem (v. 3). The king and his counsellors made a proclamation **throughout Israel from Beersheba to Dan** (5), the descriptive phrase is the reverse of the more normal order, Dan to Beersheba. The Chronicler probably thought from south to north rather than north to south. The proclamation is sent out by **couriers** (6) inviting all to join themselves in this great national celebration, but the response from the north was disappointing (vv. 10–11). The Chronicler remarks that only a few men from **Asher**, and **Manasseh** and **Zebulun** (11) actually went to Jerusalem. There was no response from the area of Ephraim, perhaps because the true followers of Yahweh had already moved into Judah, while the remainder cared little about the situation, or may have been afraid of the political implications of aligning themselves with Judah.

The actual celebration of the passover occupies vv. 13–22. The people came together to **celebrate the Feast of Unleavened Bread**, a clear indication that the two originally separate celebrations, the passover and unleavened bread, had become now so combined that they could no longer be distinguished. Verse 14 appears to relate more to the previous works of reform in the removal of the various pagan altars in Jerusalem, including the incense altars which were removed and thrown into the Kidron valley, an act which seems to have some form of ritual significance. The Chronicler makes the point as always, that what was done was according to the **Law of Moses the man of God** (16). The Levites are given prominence in that they appear to act on certain occasions for those who had not carried out the full ritual of purification (v. 17), thus the priests and

Levites are united in the service of God in the celebration of the passover. The importance of the Levites to the Chronicler is also borne out by v. 22, where Hezekiah **spoke encouragingly** to the Levites. The congratulation clearly indicates the esteem in which the Levites were held by the Chronicler.

The celebration of the passover departed from the normal practice in two important details. Firstly, the time of this celebration: **the fourteenth day of the second month** (15). This may reflect Hezekiah's desire to accommodate those from the north who appear to have celebrated the passover a month later to link with their autumn festival, held in the eighth month. It is interesting to note the difference in the approach between Hezekiah and Josiah (2 Kg. 23: 15, 16) who destroyed the altar at Bethel and brooked no link with the apostate north. The second point of difference was the exemption of those from the north from the ritual prescriptions and the fact that the king's prayer on their behalf was sufficient to allow them to approach God (vv. 18–20). 'In case of necessity, ritual could be set aside in favour of the worship of the broken and contrite heart' (J. M. Myers). This is an important point, for the Chronicler is often portrayed as a thoroughgoing ritualist but here he shows quite clearly that he abides by the prophetic concept that the true worship of God is not necessarily associated with ritual but with the correct attitude of heart and mind.

The intercession of Hezekiah on behalf of those who **had not purified themselves** (18) is a function which again reminds the readers of the activities of Solomon and is, perhaps, another indication of the way in which the Chronicler viewed Hezekiah. A further link with Solomon's activities is seen in vv. 23–27 where there is a second period of the festival: **The whole assembly then agreed to celebrate the festival seven more days.** This would remind the reader of the fact that Solomon celebrated for two weeks when the temple was dedicated. Here the second Solomon in Hezekiah similarly celebrated for two weeks following the rededication of the temple. In a similar vein the main theme of the celebrations is that of rejoicing, which is reiterated in several places throughout the context (vv. 25 and 26). Again the point is made that there had been nothing like these festivities since the time of Solomon (v. 26). The word **aliens** (25) is a term used in earlier stories to denote those members from other communities or nations who had settled in Israel and had accepted involvement in its life, being distinct from those who were simply visitors, such as traders. It is possible that the use of the word here is suggesting the presence of those people who at a later date would be referred to as proselytes,

i.e. Gentiles who took on the full duties and membership of the Jewish community. The text of the NIV (v. 26) is somewhat ambiguous and could be misunderstood to imply that there had been no passover celebrations since the time of Solomon. The real point of emphasis is that there had been no rejoicing, such as there was at this passover, since the time of Solomon. The immediate result of the passover celebrations was the final part of the reformation in the cleansing of the land (31: 1). This was an action on the part of all Israel, and just as Jerusalem had been cleansed before the festival, the whole land was cleansed from its various religious impurities which had been left over from the days of Ahaz. It is interesting that nothing is said here of the destruction of the bronze serpent mentioned at 2 Kg. 18: 4.

(*e*) **The re-ordering of the religious life (31: 2–20)**

This section continues the account of Hezekiah's reforms and details the new assignments for the priests and Levites (v. 2), new provisions for the offerings (v. 3) and various provisions for the religious personnel of the land (vv. 4–19). The details that are given add to the picture of Hezekiah not only as a second Solomon, but also in his administrative provisions as a second David. This is seen particularly in the considerable place which is given to the re-ordering of the priests and Levites (1 Chr. 23–26). Hezekiah is, in effect, affirming the old order which had been established on the commands of David. The priests were in charge of the offerings whilst the Levites attended to the music and administrative matters. The provision for the offerings (v. 3) underlines the royal contribution for the sacrifices, once again clearly following the precedent of Solomon. The next section (vv. 4–19) outlines the provisions that were made to ensure that the **portion due the priests and Levites** was provided in the proper way. At the king's command there was an abundant response from the people which was almost overwhelming. This consisted of the produce of the land (v. 5) as well as the general tithe of cattle, sheep and dedicated things. This willing and generous response of the whole community is obviously noted as an example for later generations. The tithes were gathered from **the third month** to **the seventh month** (7), and the immense stock-piles were then inspected by the king. When the large amounts were seen there was the proper response of giving thanks to God (v. 8).

Verses 11–19 detail the arrangements which were made for the storage and supervision of these tithes and contributions. The distribution was supervised by **Kore**, the **keeper of the East Gate** (14), assisted by a number of priests (v. 15). The register of Levites was according to function (**division**, 16) whereas the register of priests was according to families (v. 17). All required to be put on to a register in order that a fair and equal distribution could be made to the various families from the contributions that had been received. The unusual reference to **males three years old or more** (16) is generally amended to 'thirty years old and upwards' on the grounds that they were entering the house of the Lord in order to perform their duties. On the other hand, it appears from v. 18 that children were also involved in the distribution of the provisions and it may be that 'three' is in fact correct. A variation in the age on which the Levites entered upon their office is found at v. 17 where it is given as **twenty years old**. Elsewhere the age is given as 30 (Num. 4: 3) and 25 (Num. 8: 24); note also 1 Chr. 23: 3. The whole section is brought to a fitting conclusion with an assessment of Hezekiah's reign (v. 20). The verse relates to his reforming activities and notes his utter devotion to God and his service for the whole land, and because of this **he prospered.**

(*f*) **The Assyrian Invasion (32: 1–23)**
For full details of the campaign of Sennacherib in Palestine see J. Bright, *A History of Israel* (London, ²1972), pp. 282–286. The whole of this section has been very much telescoped, and would be virtually impossible to understand without the fuller account in Kings and the reference in Isaiah. The various Assyrian inscriptions which have been discovered also help to a better understanding of a difficult period. On the events associated with Sennacherib's invasion, see commentary at 2 Kg. 18 and 19. The Chronicler's handling of this material underlines his main interest in the religious matters associated with Hezekiah's reign, to which he devotes two chapters. The compiler of 2 Kings dismissed the reformation in a mere four verses (2 Kg. 18: 3–6). The Chronicler's description of the reign, however, needed to include a reference to the political events and this he has done in characteristic fashion, utilizing them to illustrate a religious message.

In view of the faithfulness and obedience of Hezekiah the Assyrian invasion may seem, at first, to be a strange reward. The Chronicler notes (v. 1) that it was **After all that Hezekiah had so faithfully done** that Sennacherib invaded Judah. At the end of this section (vv. 22 and 23) the Chronicler draws the lesson that is to be learned, namely, the faithfulness of God and the ultimate universal nature of His deliverance. The invasion might almost be seen in the Chronicler's terms as a test of Hezekiah's faith under dire circumstances.

It is interesting to note that the Chronicler speaks only of the Assyrian king **thinking to conquer** the fortified cities of Judah for himself. In fact contemporary records indicate

that Sennacherib took 46 cities, large numbers of prisoners, and gave some of Hezekiah's territory to the neighbouring Philistine kings, as well as laying a heavy tribute upon him. Verse 2 indicates, however, that Hezekiah recognized that Sennacherib planned to attack Jerusalem and he undertook the major defensive steps to secure the city against the invasion. The first was to organize his water supply (vv. 2–4). The reference to the **springs** probably includes, not only Gihon, but also En-rogel and possibly the Dragon's Fountain in addition. **4. the stream that flowed through the land:** not easy to identify, but it may refer to the conduits which carried water to a pool within the city (see Isa. 7: 3). Hezekiah later replaced these open water channels with the famous Siloam tunnel. At the same time that he established his own water supply for Jerusalem Hezekiah ensured that springs and wells outside the city would be stopped up to prevent the enemy from using them. The second line of approach was the strengthening of the fortifications of the city itself (v. 5) and then finally the whole country was set on a military footing, with reorganization of the army and an adequate supply of weaponry (v. 6). The Chronicler then introduces vv. 7 and 8, the characteristic address to the assembled company, in this case the combat commanders (v. 6). The opening is identical to the exhortations of Moses (Dt. 31: 6) and Joshua (Jos. 10: 25). The expression **for there is a greater power with us than with him** (7) may possibly connect with the Immanuel theme of Isa. 7: 14 although this cannot be proven.

The next phase was the message from Sennacherib which was sent during the siege of **Lachish** (vv. 9–19). The Chronicler does not mention the army which was sent with the ambassadors (2 Kg. 18: 17) and the message recorded here is a compilation of the speech of the commander (2 Kg. 18: 28–35) and the communication of Sennacherib himself (2 Kg. 19: 10–13). It is interesting that the Chronicler omits all references to Hezekiah's strength and to the Egyptian alliance which are mentioned in Kings. Verse 18 clearly refers to the speech of the commander who is not mentioned by title by the Chronicler. Verses 20–23 record the deliverance of the king and his people. At v. 20 Hezekiah is linked directly with **the prophet Isaiah**, and they are seen here to be joined in prayer together, possibly on the basis of 2 Kg. 19: 20. The narrative is highly compressed: there is no mention of the worry and anxiety that existed in Judah, nor of the king's lack of faith that is hinted at in 2 Kings. However the Chronicler is concerned rather with the outcome, namely, with the reward of faithfulness, and the deliverance of Hezekiah is seen as a direct intervention of God on his behalf.

This is presented as an immediate response to the combined prayers of king and prophet (v. 23) and Sennacherib returned **in disgrace** to face his own people and there is killed by one of his own sons. Verses 22 and 23 underline the religious message which the Chronicler sees in this story. Hezekiah is given **rest** (NIVmg) **on every side** (22) and **from then on he was highly regarded by all the nations** (23).

(g) Hezekiah's later years (32: 24–33)
This section deals with Hezekiah's illness and the end part of the reign in which Hezekiah like those before him fell into the sin of pride. The chapter ends with a note on the great wealth and honour which Hezekiah received during his reign. Hezekiah's illness (v. 24) is dealt with in more detail at 2 Kg. 20: 8–11. The **sign** refers to the sign of the sun-dial recorded in 2 Kings. Verses 25–26 require to be interpreted in the light of the story of the visit of the representatives of the kings of Babylon (2 Kg. 20: 12–19; Isa. 39: 1–8, and briefly mentioned at v. 31). At this time Hezekiah proudly displayed his treasures and his pride was bound to lead to disaster. The Chronicler notes, therefore, that **wrath was on him** (25), but goes on to note that the king **repented of the pride** (26). The disaster was foretold by the prophet Isaiah and relates to the eventual downfall of Judah.

The catalogue of achievements (vv. 27–31) demonstrates the blessings of God on the one who did that which was right in the sight of God. There is a certain degree of archeological evidence to support the overall features of a prosperous reign. The reference in v. 30 is to the famous Siloam tunnel. The visit of **the envoys of the rulers of Babylon** (31) is due to astrological interest in the sign of the sun-dial. The compiler of 2 Kings, however, relates the visit to a political mission during which Hezekiah displayed his treasures and wealth to the visitors. The Chronicler does not mention this: so far as his account is concerned, Hezekiah came out of this test with a clean record.

The conclusion of Hezekiah's reign (vv. 32–33) follows the general pattern that the Chronicler follows and makes particular stress on his **acts of devotion** as recorded by Isaiah. **32. the book of the kings of Judah and Israel:** this may well be the book of Kings that we know today.

xiv. The reign of Manasseh (33: 1–20)
The compiler of 2 Kings had no good word to say of Manasseh. The Chronicler, however, provides us with an account of Manasseh's repentance which is not found elsewhere. He also used this to draw out an important lesson for the people of his own time. The reign of Manasseh is initially one of total apostasy and a complete reversal of the practices of Hezekiah. The reasons for this may well have

been political. Hezekiah's reformation was a manifestation of the free spirit within the country that led to open rebellion against the yoke of a weakened Assyria. Manasseh, however, was faced with a very different situation. At the beginning of his reign Assyria was at the peak of its power and even Egypt had been brought under Assyrian influence. Manasseh's apostasy was almost certainly deliberate and reflected his subservience to Assyria. The Chronicler's story, however, with its record of his repentance, perhaps reflects a later situation when Assyria, with pressure from the Medes and the northern countries of the empire, was unable to give a great deal of attention to the west. Consequently, even though Judah may not have been actively involved in the rebellions of this time it is likely that Manasseh was at least sympathetic to the rebel cause. A return to the worship of Yahweh may thus reflect in the same way as Hezekiah's reform the spirit of rebellion within the nation.

Verses 1–9 give an account of the apostasy of Manasseh's early reign. It very closely follows the parallel text of 2 Kg. 21: 1–9. The record of the **detestable practices** (2) indicates that Manasseh's apostasy was essentially to re-introduce the Canaanite worship that had been removed earlier. Although the reference to **the starry hosts** (5) has been usually seen as an indication of Assyrian idolatry, there is ample evidence that such worship also formed part of Phoenician and Canaanite religion. Verse 10 indicates that the voice of prophecy was still to be heard, that the Lord spoke to **Manasseh and his people**, but the message was of little avail and from 2 Kg. 21: 16, would appear even to have been met with violence. The result was a period of judgment, the Assyrian yoke was once more brought upon the land and Manasseh was forced to submit to it. This act of submission (v. 11) most likely occurred at Nineveh. The word **Babylon** is probably generic, referring to the region of Mesopotamia rather than the specific city of Babylon, which was not the Assyrian capital. This event may possibly be dated to the year 672 B.C. at the time when Esarhaddon introduced a series of vassal treaties at the ceremony of the induction of the crown prince Asshurbanipal. Representatives of all the countries which owed allegiance to Assyria were brought together at the royal palace at Nineveh and there they were bound with particularly fearful oaths to support the crown prince after the death of his father. The name of Manasseh occurs on inscriptions of both Esarhaddon and Asshurbanipal. (On the other hand, Esarhaddon, unlike his father, paid respect to Babylon and may well on occasion have received foreign rulers there.)

The return of Manasseh to Jerusalem is seen by the Chronicler as a result of his repentance.

He **humbled himself greatly before the God of his fathers** (12) as a result of which God heard his prayer and **brought him back to Jerusalem.** The author of the books of Kings knows nothing of this repentance and Jeremiah also gives no indication of this and seems to suggest his sin remained throughout his reign (Jer. 15: 4). On the other hand, as has already been suggested, a change in the situation within Assyria itself may have resulted in drawing away Assyrian allegiance and a return to a more nationalistic attitude with which the worship of Yahweh would be associated. The main point in the section, however, is the religious message which the Chronicler underlined, using Manasseh as the type of the exile of all Judah. Because of his wickedness he was taken captive, but when he repented he was allowed to return to a period of restoration. The Chronicler may have used the episode as an allegory of Israel in exile. Because of its sin it had been taken to Babylon but now it has returned to the land. It was essential that the people continued in their attitude of repentance in order to maintain the restoration.

Verses 14–17 record the results of Manasseh's repentance seen in further strengthenings of the city defences, again suggestive of an act of rebellion against the Assyrian overlord. This was coupled with a removal of idols and pagan altars from the temple and the restoration of the worship of Yahweh in the city. Verses 18–20 are simply a summary of his remaining activities with a record of the sources from which the Chronicler has obtained his data.

xv. The reign of Amon (33: 21–25)

The Chronicler devotes little attention to this evil reign, a matter of five verses only. He underlined the point that Amon followed in the footsteps of his father with all its evils and apostasy. The result was that **his officials conspired against him and assassinated him** (24). The crisis resultant upon the palace revolt was dealt with by the **people of the land**, the free landholders of Judah who had acted in the past, and would act again in the future, in such times of crisis, to ensure that the Davidic dynasty continued. The exact situation and the significance of these events is not altogether clear, due to the very short note which the Chronicler has made.

xvi. The reign of Josiah (34: 1–35: 27)

(a) Josiah's reform (34: 1–33)

The reform, initiated by Josiah and linked to the finding of the law book in the temple, is given a great deal of importance in the narrative of 2 Kings. The Chronicler, however, does not place the same significance upon this event and there are certain differences in presentation in the two records. It is likely that both accounts are telescoped and have utilized different sources, presenting their data with different emphases, which would account for the apparent lack of harmony between the two records. It is likely that the early years of Josiah were, in fact, a regency, which was probably characterized by a degree of moderation and tolerance, but the time became increasingly ripe for a reform. The prophetic preaching which had been stifled in the earlier reigns, would now come into the open and the two prophets associated with the reform of Josiah were Zephaniah and Jeremiah.

Asshurbanipal died c. 627 BC, the twelfth year of Josiah's reign, and the year in which the reform really began (v. 3b). 'Both Zephaniah and Jeremiah spared no words in condemning the paganism of their day and in warning of the consequences of continued apostasy . . . now there were those who were ready to hear and obey. The time was ripe for both rebellion and reform, nevertheless, the call to reform was not primarily political, but religious, for it was voiced above all by those men who stood behind the law book which was produced in 622 B.C. (John McKay, *Religion in Judah under the Assyrians*, 1973, p. 43). Combining the two sources from 2 Kings and 2 Chronicles it is likely Josiah's reform occupied three stages. The first around 632–631 BC, the eighth year of his reign, was probably confined to court circles. The second stage around 628–627 BC, in the twelfth year of his reign, was the period in which the reform gathered momentum and extended to Jerusalem. It is likely that this was the period in which the temple clearing was begun and incidentally it coincides with Jeremiah's call to the prophetic office. The third stage, and perhaps the critical point of the reform, was in 621 BC, the eighteenth year of Josiah's reign when the law book, almost certainly Deuteronomy (as Jerome perceived in his day, c. A.D. 400), was discovered in the temple. This discovery gave both direction and authority to the reforming activities of the king.

Verses 3–7 record the beginning of the reform, and its first two stages in Josiah's eighth and twelfth years. The Chronicler makes the point that the reform sprang out of Josiah's correct attitudes; **while he was still young he began to seek the God of his father David** (3); thus even in the years of his childhood and inexperience he 'committed himself to that obedience which will lead to right action' (P. R. Ackroyd). A point of particular interest is the extension of the reform to the northern territory—**the towns of Manasseh, Ephraim and Simeon, as far as Naphtali** (6). The political overtones of such a movement north are quite clear and represent a deliberate attempt to restore the old Israel as a united kingdom and to the worship of Yahweh. Verses 8–13 introduce the beginning of the restoration of the temple. The Chronicler makes the important point that it was the king who took the initiative in restoring the temple as Hezekiah had done at a previous time (29: 3) and as David had done in planning the original building. The verses give an account of the various officials who were to supervise both the handling of the offerings and the work of repair. The list of officials and their names differs from that of 2 Kg. 22, suggesting a different source for the two accounts.

The discovery of the law book is recorded at vv. 14–21. This follows very closely the corresponding account in 2 Kg. 22: 8–13. There are, however, slight variations, for the Chronicler connects the discovery of the law book with the emptying of the money chests (v. 14). It is also significant that the Chronicler appears to give less importance to the discovery than the compiler of Kings. The Chronicler's account has the reformation already well in progress before the law book was found, although it gave form and content to the continuing work. The compiler of 2 Kings, however, sees the discovery of the law book as central to the beginning and continuance of the reform. No doubt these variations reflect the somewhat differing theological standpoints of the two authors. The prophecy of **Huldah** (vv. 22–28) follows almost exactly the text of 2 Kings. For the names of those who accompanied Hilkiah to visit the prophetess see 2 Kg. 22: 14. The prophecy was clearly an uncomfortable one, and this is underlined by the expression **all the curses** (24): cf. Dt. 29: 20.

The specific prophecy of v. 28 concerning the end of Josiah was not in fact fulfilled. It is interesting that the Chronicler did not revise the prophecy in the light of actual events, an indication of the faithful way in which such prophecies were preserved irrespective of the situation which followed them. The response of the king (vv. 29–33) was to summon the elders of Judah and Jerusalem for consultation which resulted in a renewal of the covenant relationship. Again the Chronicler follows quite closely his source at 2 Kings. The significant change is the substitution at v. 30 of **Levites** for the word 'prophets' at 2 Kg. 23: 2. It is suggested that this represents the Chronicler's view that the proclamation of the word of God, especially in terms of preaching, was in his time the prime function of the Levite. In other words, it is an interpretive change, indicating to the people of his own time that the prophetic function now lay in the hands of the Levitical community. The last part of v. 32 and all v. 33 is an expansion by the Chronicler indicating that the covenant applies to the whole of Israel.

(b) **Josiah's Passover (35: 1–19)**
This passage represents an expanded form of 2 Kg. 23: 21–23. It is interesting that the expan-

sions follow the Chronicler's specific interest in religious affairs for they relate to the ordering of officials and specific regulations regarding the details of ritual. Unlike the exception made by Hezekiah (30: 21), Josiah's passover was kept at the proper time, the **fourteenth day of the first month** (Lev. 23: 5). The Chronicler does not make reference to the relationship of the passover to the 'Book of the Covenant' (2 Kg. 23: 21) since he regarded the keeping of Josiah's passover as following the precedent of Hezekiah, hence not a new departure. The significance of the passover lay clearly in the elaborate ritual which now attached to it. The Levites, suitably sanctified and in their divisions (vv. 5, 6), were those who were to **slaughter the Passover lamb.** A note on their teaching function also occurs in v. 3. The provision of sacrificial animals (vv. 7–9) would suggest that the passover was associated with peace offerings and other forms of offerings as well as the specific passover festival. The whole account suggests a marked change in character from the early simple family feast to a centralized religious festival which under Josiah and in future years was to become the central feast of the year rather than the feast of tabernacles. The other clear change is in the introduction of **lay people** (7) indicating the increasing importance in the later monarchy and certainly in the Chronicler's time of the religious establishment as opposed to the ordinary people. For further comments on this section see the major commentaries.

(c) **The death of Josiah (35: 20–26)**
The brief phrase **After all this** (20) passes over the intervening twelve years from the keeping of the passover to the death of Josiah at the hands of Pharaoh Neco of Egypt in 609 B.C. The Assyrian empire at this stage was tottering and the new power was to be Babylon. Pharaoh Neco was allied to the Assyrians and it appears from this story that Josiah was apparently an ally of the Babylonians and he attempted to prevent Neco marching to the assistance of the Assyrians. There was an Egyptian garrison at **Carchemish** on the Euphrates and this withstood the Babylonians until 605 B.C. when Pharaoh Neco and his army were defeated (cf. Jer. 46: 2). The events recorded here had taken place some four years before Egypt's final defeat, and it would appear that Pharaoh Neco was on an urgent mission to assist the Assyrians whose forces at that particular stage were attempting to recross the Euphrates in an attempt to retake the city of Harran (see D. J. Wiseman, *Chronicles of Chaldaean Kings in the British Museum*, 1956, p. 19).

Pharaoh warned Josiah to keep out of the way; **it is not you I am attacking at this time** (21). The important point about these words is that they are delivered as coming from

God. Pharaoh Neco no doubt saw his march as being part of a divine mission, that is to say, a mission on behalf of his own Egyptian gods. On the other hand Yahweh had used foreign rulers to carry out his plans (note Isa. 45: 1; Jer. 27: 6) and v. 22 is quite explicit that Josiah should have recognized that the warning came from Yahweh. Neco may have been a strange mediator of the word of God but it should have been enough for a king of the spiritual sensitivity of Josiah. Josiah, however, failed to heed the warning and thus lost his life. Once again there is an explicit religious message in these verses. The death of Josiah caused profound sorrow throughout the nation (vv. 24, 25) and the prophet Jeremiah **composed laments for Josiah** (25). It would appear from v. 25 that the death of Josiah was regularly celebrated in a memorial service in later years. This passage contrasts with Jeremiah's injunction not to weep for Josiah (Jer. 22: 10).

xvii. The reigns of Jehoahaz, Jehoiakim and Jehoiachin (36: 1–10)

The last years of the kingdom of Judah are dealt with very rapidly by the Chronicler. A great deal of the material from 2 Kings is omitted although there is a certain element of interpretive comment by the Chronicler throughout this section. The period of the kingdom had come to an end and the history of the people of God following the exile will take on a new character and be upon a different basis.

(a) The reign of Jehoahaz (36: 1–4)

The people of the land (1), as in the case of Josiah (33: 25), acted in order to ensure the continuance of the line and put Jehoahaz on the throne. His reign is quickly passed over and it is worth noting that he was the last king of Judah to be invested by the people. Henceforth it would be Egypt or Babylon who appointed the kings, although the Davidic line remained intact until after the final siege of Jerusalem and the captivity. Egypt deposed Jehoahaz (v. 3) and put Jehoiakim his brother on the throne as king. It is possible that he was regarded as regent for the captive.

(b) The reign of Jehoiakim (36: 5–8)

Jehoiakim was the throne name of **Eliakim** (4) and he reigned for 11 years. He began his reign as an Egyptian vassal and remained so until the final defeat of Egypt and Assyria at the battle of Carchemish in 605 B.C. Jer. 23: 13–19 gives some idea of the conditions in the land during this period. The defeat of Egypt and Assyria gave Babylon a clear approach to the west and in the year following the battle of Carchemish, Nebuchadnezzar's army moved into Palestine. The result was that Jehoiakim was defeated and carried off to Babylon in **shackles.** It is likely that this is the episode referred to in Dan. 1: 1, although the Chronicler's reference is clearly independent of Daniel. The invasion is clearly

not that of 597 B.C. and it is not altogether easy to fit these events into the known chronology of the period. (See D. J. Wiseman, *Chronicles of Chaldaean Kings*, on this whole period.)

(c) The reign of Jehoiachin (36: 9, 10)

The Egyptians had managed to stem the advance of Babylonian power in 601 B.C. At that time Jehoiakim apparently withheld his tribute, but Nebuchadnezzar had merely withdrawn in order to strengthen his army and he returned in 597 B.C. By this time Jehoiakim was dead and the **three months and ten days** (9) was the period between the death of Jehoiakim and the capture of the city of Jerusalem by the returning army of Nebuchadnezzar **in the spring** (598–597 BC). The actual capture of the city was on March 12, 597 B.C. The Chronicler's statements in these verses coincide almost exactly with those in the Babylonian chronicles. Jehoiachin was deported to Babylon and the king of Nebuchadnezzar's choice, namely his **uncle Zedekiah** (cf. 2 Kg. 24: 17; 1 Chr. 3: 15 f.), was put over the province, as it now was, of Judah.

xviii. The reign of Zedekiah and the Exile (36: 11–21)

The Chronicler gives only the very barest outline of the reign of Zedekiah and the total collapse of Judah and the exile. Zedekiah was in fact a son of Josiah and may have been chosen for that reason. His eleven-year reign was essentially a disaster. It was marked by indecision and constant changing sides, partly no doubt due to the odd situation in which he found himself and the fact that Jehoiachin was still alive. There was also, no doubt, an important pro-Egyptian party within the country which influenced the situation and his eventual rebellion against Nebuchadnezzar. For the Chronicler, however, the important elements of the story were those which bear out its religious meaning. These verses in fact are not so much historical statements, but short sermons by the writer on the evils of the reign and the reasons for the exile.

The main blame lies on the king because he **did not humble himself** (12) and refused to follow the directions given by the prophets, particularly **Jeremiah.** Although the book of Jeremiah gives some point to the idea that Zedekiah was very much a captive of his own court, nonetheless the Chronicler rightly makes the point that the king lacked the strength to make any clear declaration for Yahweh and to follow what was right and proper. The end result was that **he became stiff-necked and hardened his heart** and that the whole people likewise were **more and more unfaithful** (14). Verses 15, 16 underline the Chronicler's emphasis on the mercy and grace of God in that He **again and again** (15) sent His messengers **because he had pity.**

Eventually, however, **there was no remedy** (16) and there follows the consequence in v. 17. This is the conclusion of moral logic; because they persistently rejected the way of God there was ultimately nothing for it but God's judgment upon the land and upon all in it. Verses 17–21 record the coming of Nebuchadnezzar, the destruction of Jerusalem and the eventual exile. There is significance in the Chronicler's statement that the **articles from the temple of God** (18) were taken for this was the primary moment of judgment; without these there could be no worship. This theme also points on to the eventual restoration, however, when those same vessels will be returned (Ezr. 1: 7 f.). Verse 21 links the words of **Jeremiah**, not only proclaiming judgment but also proclaiming the promise that after **seventy years** there would be recovery and restoration. The Chronicler understands this as a sabbath rest for the land and it is interesting to note that this concept is re-interpreted by Daniel (ch. 9) who saw the exile as not truly ending until there have been 70 sabbaths of years, that is 490 years, following the exile.

xix. The decree of Cyrus (36: 22–23)

These verses are simply the connecting link between Chronicles and Ezra-Nehemiah and are repeated at Ezr. 1: 1–4. Verse 22 has the first mention of **Persia** in any of the historical or prophetic books (except for Ezek. 27: 10 and 38: 5 which refer to Persia before its emergence as a world power). The return from the exile is presented as a fulfilment of **the word of the LORD spoken by Jeremiah** (22), a word which was for salvation as the previous one had been for judgment (Jer. 25: 11 ff.; 29: 10).

BIBLIOGRAPHY

Commentaries

ACKROYD, P. R., *I and II Chronicles, Ezra, Nehemiah. TC* (London, 1973).

COGGINS, R. J., *The First and Second Books of Chronicles. CBC* (Cambridge, 1976).

CURTIS, E. L. and MADSEN, A. A., *A Critical and Exegetical Commentary on the Books of Chronicles. ICC* (Edinburgh, 1910).

MYERS, J. M., *I and II Chronicles* (2 vols.). *AB* (New York, 1965).

RUDOLPH, W., *Chronikbucher (Handbuch zum Alten Testament)*. (Tübingen, 1955).

WILLIAMSON, H. G. M., *1 & 2 Chronicles. NCentB* (London, 1983).

Short Commentaries

BROWNE, L. E., in *Peake's Commentary on the Bible* (London, 1962).

ELLISON, H. L., in *The New Bible Commentary Revised* (London, 1970).

ELMSLIE, W. A. L., in *The Interpreter's Bible* Vol. 3 (New York, 1954).

Other Works, Papers, etc.

ACKROYD, P. R., *Israel under Babylon and Persia* (Oxford, 1970).

'The Theology of the Chronicler', *Lexington Theological Quarterly.* **92** (1973) pp. 101–116.

BRAUN, R. L., 'Solomonic Apologetic in Chronicles', *Journal of Biblical Literature.* **92** (1973) pp. 503–576.

FREEDMAN, D. N., 'The Chronicler's Purpose', *Catholic Bible Quarterly* **23** (1961) pp. 436–442.

HALLO, W. W., 'From Qarqar to Carchemish: Assyria and Israel in the Light of New Discoveries', *The Biblical Archeologist.* **23** (1960) pp. 31–61.

MCKAY, J., *Religion in Judah under the Assyrians* (Studies in Biblical Theology, Second Series No. 26). (London, 1973).

NORTH, R., 'The Theology of the Chronicler', *Journal of Biblical Literature.* **82** (1963) pp. 369–381.

PAYNE, D. F., 'The Purpose and Methods of the Chronicler', *Faith and Thought.* **93** (1963) pp. 64–73.

STINESPRING, W. F., 'Eschatology in Chronicles', *Journal of Biblical Literature.* **80** (1961) pp. 209–218.

WILLIAMSON, H. G. M., *Israel in the Books of Chronicles* (Cambridge, 1977).

EZRA

STEPHEN S. SHORT

AUTHORSHIP AND DATE

Originally the two books of Ezra and Nehemiah were continuous with each other, and were themselves a direct continuation of 2 Chr., as is evident in that Ezr. 1: 1–3a is practically identical with 2 Chr. 36: 22–23. The author can therefore be termed 'the Chronicler', and he incorporated into his work some autobiographical material of an earlier date written by Ezra and by Nehemiah. The last historical allusion in these books is to the high priest Jaddua (Neh. 12: 11, 22) whom the Chronicler mentioned, evidently, so as to trace the succession of the Jewish high priests up to his own time. Josephus (*Ant*. xi. 8. 4) states that Jaddua was high priest at the time of Alexander the Great (*c*. 330 BC). This was probably, therefore, the approximate time when the Chronicler compiled the books of Ezra and Nehemiah.

The chronology of the lives of Ezra and Nehemiah

Until fairly recently it had been universally assumed that the coming of Ezra from Babylon to Jerusalem antedated the coming of Nehemiah, after which they lived for a while in Jerusalem together. This is how the narrative is recorded in the Old Testament scriptures, and also by Josephus. Of late, however, doubt has been cast on this on account of one major consideration and a number of minor ones. The major consideration is that, knowing as we do that the high priest when Nehemiah was in Jerusalem was Eliashib (Neh. 3: 1), we are told in Ezr. 10: 6 that Ezra 'went to the room of Jehohanan the son of Eliashib' which was presumably in the temple precincts, and the assumption which is made (though the text does not state this) is that Jehohanan, seeing he had a room within the temple complex, must have been then the high priest; therefore Ezra's residence in Jerusalem must have been later than that of Nehemiah. How this new reconstruction of the history has been elaborated is as follows. It is postulated that the Chronicler (*c*. 330 BC) possessed certain documents relating to Ezra and to Nehemiah. But he did not appreciate that whereas the references to King Artaxerxes of Persia in the Nehemiah records related to Artaxerxes I (465–424 BC), the references to King Artaxerxes in the Ezra records related to Artaxerxes II (404–358 BC) (as is required by this historical reconstruction). So

he mistakenly related these latter to Artaxerxes I, and thus erroneously placed Ezra's coming to Jerusalem before that of Nehemiah. Nehemiah came to Jerusalem in the twentieth year of the reign of Artaxerxes I (Neh. 2: 1), *viz*. in 445 B.C. Ezra came to Jerusalem 'in the seventh year of King Artaxerxes' (Ezr. 7: 7) which, if this means Artaxerxes I was 458 BC, and if it means Artaxerxes II was 398 B.C. If Nehemiah came to Jerusalem in 445 B.C. and Ezra not till 398 BC, their activities in Jerusalem could not have overlapped, and hence the references to Nehemiah in the narrative of Ezra (Neh. 8: 9; 10: 1) and that to Ezra in the narrative of Nehemiah (Neh. 12: 36) have to be viewed as textual inaccuracies, even though the latter, in particular, seems integral to the story. Evidence, however, that the careers of these two leaders did overlap (involving Ezra coming to Jerusalem first) is to be found in such people as Meremoth the son of Uriah (Ezr. 8: 33; Neh. 3: 4) and Malchijah the son of Harim (Ezr. 10: 31; Neh. 3: 11) figuring in both narratives.

It should be appreciated that if the Chronicler published his book *c*. 330 B.C. (at the time of the high priesthood of Jaddua), and if he was indeed mistaken in placing the career of Ezra about a hundred and thirty years before that time, there would have been Jews aged between seventy and eighty who, having read this book, would inform the Chronicler that when they were children they saw Ezra and heard him read the law to the people. The fact that the Chronicler does not seem to have been challenged in this way suggests that he was not mistaken in his dating of Ezra's career.

Proof that a contingent of Jews did journey from Babylon to Jerusalem during the early part of the reign of Artaxerxes I is given by the statement in the letter of Rehum and Shimshai to Artaxerxes (4: 12), which belongs chronologically to the period between Ezr. 10 and Neh. 1, mentioning 'the Jews who came up to us from' and 'have gone to Jerusalem'. The reference could well be to the company which was led by Ezra.

Ezr. 10: 6 is not really decisive that Ezra's career followed that of Nehemiah. If Jehohanan —not, by the way, to be confused with Eliashib's grandson Johanan (the names are practically the same, but not the persons)—had been high priest at this time, as the reconstructed history assumes, this would surely have been stated. He would have been denoted not 'Jeho-hanan son of Eliashib' but 'Jehohanan the high priest'. Reference to Neh. 12: 22 indicates that the son of Eliashib who became high priest was Joiada, and that he was succeeded by Johanan (who may also have been called Jonathan, v. 11). The Elephantine papyri (fifth century BC) show that in 410–408 B.C. Johanan was the high priest in Jerusalem. The Jehohanan of Ezr. 10: 6 seems never to have been high priest. If Eliashib was aged about forty-five at the time of the story in Ezr. 10 (represented by the Chronicler as being *c.* 458 BC) he could well have then had a son (Jehohanan) who had a room in the temple; and it would have been quite possible for him in 433 BC, when aged about seventy, to have allowed Tobiah to use the temple tithe-room as described in Neh. 13.

The other arguments which have been advanced to support the conjecture of the career of Ezra postdating that of Nehemiah have little substance. (i) Attention has been called to the appearance of the name 'Nehemiah' in the list of the returned exiles in Ezr. 2: 2 (and Neh. 7: 7), referring to somebody who came to Jerusalem before Ezra did. But this, doubtless, was another person of the same name, for Nehemiah the governor did not return with Zerubbabel. (ii) Ezra referred in his prayer of chapter 9 to the fact that God had given them 'a wall of protection in Judea and Jerusalem' (v. 9); and some have suggested that the reference here is to the wall which had been built around Jerusalem by Nehemiah. But the Hebrew word used here is different from the Hebrew word translated 'wall' in the book of Nehemiah, and could stand also for a 'fence'. Since in Ezr. 9: 9 the term is related not only to Jerusalem but to Judea also, it must be used in a figurative sense and as simply meaning 'protection'. (iii) Weight has been attached also to the fact that Nehemiah is named before Ezra in Neh. 12: 26. There are listed here the gate-keepers 'in the days of Joiakim son of Jeshua the son of Jozadak, and in the days of Nehemiah the governor and of Ezra the priest and scribe'. But the fact that the phrase 'in the days of' is used only twice here shows that only two periods of time are indicated, that when Joiakim was high priest, and that when Nehemiah was the governor and Ezra was discharging the royal commission; and as to the latter of the periods it was natural to denote it by naming the governor first. This verse, therefore, instead of showing that Ezra lived later than Nehemiah, shows that they were contemporaries, which can only have been the case on the basis of the traditional chronology. It would therefore appear that there is no compelling reason for believing the Chronicler to have been grossly mistaken in his historical understanding of the period.

ANALYSIS

I   RETURN OF THE JEWISH EXILES UNDER SHESHBAZZAR (1: 1–2: 70)

II   COMMENCEMENT OF THE REBUILDING OF THE TEMPLE (3: 1–4: 24)

III   COMPLETION OF THE REBUILDING OF THE TEMPLE (5: 1–6: 22)

IV   RETURN OF MORE JEWISH EXILES UNDER EZRA (7: 1–8: 36)

V   EZRA'S HANDLING OF THE PROBLEM OF THE MIXED MARRIAGES (9: 1–10: 44)

I. RETURN OF THE JEWISH EXILES UNDER SHESHBAZZAR (1: 1–2: 70)
i. The decree of Cyrus (1: 1–4)
This was to the effect that the Jews in his domains might return to Judah and rebuild their temple. Its precise wording may have been drafted on Cyrus' behalf by a Jewish leader. By **the first year of Cyrus king of Persia** is meant the year when this Persian king conquered Babylon, *viz.* 538 B.C. Inscriptions show that Cyrus returned people of a number of nations who had been exiled to Babylon to their homelands, but his emancipating the exiled Jews was in fulfilment of God's promise through **Jeremiah** in Jer. 29: 10. Is it possible that his statement that **God . . . has appointed me to build a temple for him at Jerusalem** (2) was caused by his attention having been drawn to Isa. 44: 28 and 45: 13, as Josephus claims (*Ant.* xi. 1. 2)?

ii. The response to the decree (1: 5–11)
Those who availed themselves of Cyrus' provision belonged to the tribes of **Judah and Benjamin** (5) together with certain of **the priests and the Levites**. Israelites from the northern tribes had been in exile for 135 years

longer than these, and, through inter-marriage with people of other races may have largely lost their national identity. Cyrus handed back to the returning exiles the **articles** (7) which Nebuchadnezzar had plundered from the temple, both in 597 B.C. (2 Kg. 24: 13) and in 587 B.C. (2 Kg. 25: 13 ff.). Cyrus appointed as the leader of this company **Sheshbazzar the prince of Judah** (8). In 2: 2 the leader of the company is given as Zerubbabel, and some have therefore deduced that these were two names for the same person. But this is unlikely because in the narrative of ch. 5, whereas Zerubbabel was still then living, Sheshbazzar is referred to as though he was then dead (v. 14). Perhaps Sheshbazzar died soon after reaching Jerusalem and Zerubbabel took his place as the community's leader. If Sheshbazzar was the person denoted in 1 Chr. 3: 18 'Shenazzar' and who was a son of king Jehoiachin (also called Jeconiah), then Zerubbabel was his nephew (v. 19). Both 'Shenazzar' and 'Sheshbazzar' could go back to a Babylonian form Sin-ab-uṣur.

iii. Register of returning Jews (2: 1–70)
Chapter 2 provides a register of the Jews who returned from Babylon to Jerusalem in response to the decree of Cyrus. Presumably it had been preserved in the national Jewish archives, and the Chronicler discovered it and decided to reproduce it here in his narrative. The leader of the company is given as **Zerubbabel** (2). For his relationship to Sheshbazzar see note on 1: 8. The name Zerubbabel means 'seed of Babylon', indicating that he was born there. He is usually described as 'son of Shealtiel' (*e.g.* 3: 2). But 1 Chr. 3: 19 shows him to have been the son of Shealtiel's brother Pedaiah. Probably Shealtiel died childless, whereupon a levirate marriage (Dt. 25: 5 ff.) was contracted between Pedaiah and Shealtiel's widow, from whom Zerubbabel was derived, so that his actual father was Pedaiah, but his legal father was Shealtiel. **Jeshua** (2) was doubtless the high priest, 'son of Jozadak' (3: 2) whose name is given in the prophecies of Haggai and Zechariah as 'Joshua'. The **Nehemiah** mentioned in this verse cannot have been the national leader who arrived in Jerusalem about ninety-two years later. From v. 3 to v. 35 the returned exiles are listed according to the names either of their ancestors or of their towns of origin. Verses 36–39 refer to 4,289 returning **priests** (who would anticipate new opportunities for priestly service in a rebuilt temple). Verse 40 refers to the returning **Levites**, v. 41 to **the singers, the descendants of Asaph** (mentioned also in 2 Chr. 29: 30 and in the titles to Psalms 50 and 73 to 83); and v. 42 to **the gatekeepers of the temple.** From v. 43 to v. 54 **the temple servants** are enumerated, 'a body that David and the officials had established to assist the Levites' (8: 20). From v. 55 to 57 are enumerated **the descendants of the servants of Solomon** who were probably another group of temple labourers descended from the Canaanites mentioned in 1 Kg. 9: 21. From v. 59 are enumerated such returned exiles whose genealogy was uncertain. Some of them claimed to be priests, but **the governor** (63) ruled that they could not be consecrated as such until the divine will could be ascertained by using the sacred stones called **Urim and Thummim.** These had been kept in the high priest's breastplate pocket, but evidently they were lost when the temple was destroyed.

The total number of those who returned to Jerusalem at this time is shown in vv. 64 and 65 to have been thirteen short of fifty thousand. Many other Jews, however, remained in Babylonia, being comfortably settled there, and running thriving businesses which they were loath to abandon.

II. COMMENCEMENT OF THE REBUILDING OF THE TEMPLE (3: 1–4: 24)
i. The erection of the altar (3: 1–3)
The returned exiles no doubt knew that on the first day of the seventh month (when the Feast of the Trumpets was celebrated) burnt offerings were to be offered on the altar (cf. Num. 29: 1 f.). So **when the seventh month came** (which was in the autumn of 537 BC) they decided to erect the brazen altar and offer sacrifices on it. The Jewish leaders, therefore, **began to build the altar of the God of Israel to sacrifice burnt offerings on it, in accordance with what is written in the Law of Moses** (in Num. 29: 1–6). **3. They built the altar on its foundation:** i.e. on its original foundation, **despite their fear of the peoples around them.** Reference is made here to the hostility of neighbouring national groups, especially to the north, who resented the possibility of Jews in Jerusalem being restored to prosperity. So they put the Jews in fear. The belief of the Jews, however, was that by erecting the altar and making sacrifices on it God would be honoured and would protect, in consequence, His people.

ii. The resumption of the Mosaic religious ordinances (3: 4–6)
4. they celebrated the feast of tabernacles: it is stated in Lev. 23: 33 ff. that this feast, which lasted seven days, commenced on the fifteenth day of the seventh month. So it would start to be celebrated two weeks after the altar had been erected. They observed also **the regular burnt offerings** (5) as described in Exod. 29: 38–42. **5. the New Moon sacrifices:** these were not ordained in the Mosaic law, but new moon feasts were periodically observed before this (2 Kg. 4: 23; Hos. 2: 11; Am. 8: 5). **all the appointed sacred feasts of the LORD:**

including those which are described in Lev. 23.

Just as, when the first temple was built, timber from the cedars of Lebanon was floated down from the Phoenician ports to Joppa (1 Kg. 5: 8, 9), the same was done now (7), and the Jews made payment in kind from their grant from Cyrus.

iii. The laying of the temple's foundation (3: 8–13)

The foundation of the temple was laid by the Jews **in the second month of the second year after their arrival at the house of God in Jerusalem**, i.e. about six months after the events just described. **Jeshua** was in supreme charge of the rebuilding work, with **the Levites** under him. 2: 40 mentions two Levites: Jeshua and Kadmiel; and these are the men referred to in v. 9. Hence **Jeshua** in this verse (in contrast with v. 2) is not the high priest.

On the temple's foundation being laid the priests and Levites praised God using musical instruments (10). Whereas most of the onlookers **gave a great shout of praise** (12) when the foundation of the temple was laid, the older people **who had seen the former temple, wept aloud**, for it was obvious from the start that this new temple was going to be far less grand than was the earlier temple which had been built when the Jewish state was very prosperous and had great resources.

iv. Opposition to the returned exiles (4: 1–24)

Chapter 4 describes instances of opposition to the returned exiles on the part of their neighbours to the north. Verses 1 to 5 describe their opposition to the Jews as from the time when the Jews commenced to rebuild the temple (when Cyrus was king of Persia), and continuing for sixteen years till the second year of the reign of Darius I (522–486 BC). The account is rounded off (after vv. 1–5) with v. 24. The Chronicler, having recorded this campaign of hostility, decided that he would insert into his narrative here the story of certain later campaigns of hostility perpetrated by these neighbours to the north against the Jews. One of these is briefly recounted in v. 6, which occurred during the reign of Xerxes I, 486–465 B.C. (known also as Ahasuerus); chronologically this took place during the fifty-eight year interval between ch. 6 and ch. 7. The other is recounted at length in vv. 7–23, and occurred during the first half of the reign of Artaxerxes I (465–424 BC); chronologically this took place during the thirteen-year period which intervened between the end of the book of Ezra and the beginning of the book of Nehemiah.

(a) Opposition during the reigns of Cyrus, Cambyses and Darius I (4: 1–5)

Those who are called in v. 1 **the enemies of Judah and Benjamin**, and in v. 4 **the peoples around them** were the descendants of people who, after the Assyrians had defeated the northern kingdom of Israel and exiled most of its male population, were imported into the area of Palestine north of Judea and intermarried with those who remained (as described in 2 Kg. 17: 24). There was a succession of such importations, one by Esarhaddon (2; mentioned also in 2 Kg. 19: 39, and who reigned over Assyria from 681–669 BC), and another by **Ashurbanipal** (10), (669–627 BC). The community thus formed worshipped Yahweh (2), but were characterized by beliefs and practices which were inconsistent with this. Later they came to be known as 'the Samaritans'. They asked the Jewish leaders if they might cooperate with them in rebuilding the Jerusalem temple (2), claiming that there was no essential difference between their respective religious practices. But the Jewish leaders refused their request (3), their reason, no doubt, being because they considered these neighbours to be grossly in error as to their religious practices (2 Kg. 17: 32–34), and that to permit such cooperation would be likely to cause the faith of the Jews to become contaminated. The northern neighbours were affronted by this refusal, and conducted a campaign of opposition to the Jews which caused them to abandon for a while their work of rebuilding the temple (4–5).

(b) Opposition during the reign of Xerxes I (4: 6)

By the time that **Xerxes** became king of Persia the temple in Jerusalem had been completed for thirty years. But as soon as he came to the throne, **at the beginning** of his reign, the Jews' enemies tried to influence him against the Jews. It is not recorded here, however, that he heeded this slanderous accusation. Further information concerning the relationship of King Xerxes with the Jews is provided in the book of Esther.

(c) Opposition during the reign of Artaxerxes I (4: 7–23)

During the period of Ezra's authority in Jerusalem, prior to the arrival there of Nehemiah, a further letter of complaint against the Jews was written to the Assyrian king by their northern neighbours. It appears that the complaint was first made by **Bishlam, Mithredath** and **Tabeel** (7), whereupon it was taken up by certain higher officials, *viz.* **Rehum the commanding officer and Shimshai the secretary** (8), perhaps his personal secretary. The substance of the complaint was that the Jews in Jerusalem were rebuilding their city and raising up its walls (12), and they claimed that if the Jews were allowed to complete this work they would rebel against him, and **no more taxes, or duty will be paid** (13), causing **the king** to be **dishonoured** (14) and diminishing the domain over which he ruled (16). They told

Artaxerxes further that consultation of historical records would show that Jerusalem had proved to be **a rebellious city, troublesome to kings and provinces** (15). King Artaxerxes replied to this letter from Rehum and Shimshai saying that he had consulted the records in question and confirmed that the Jews in Jerusalem had repeatedly engaged in **rebellion and sedition** (19) so he authorized Rehum and Shimshai to **issue an order to these men to stop work, so that this city will not be rebuilt** (21); but he added the qualifying clause: **until I so order**, implying that he might, later on, revoke this decision. He did, in fact, eventually revoke it, when, in his reign's twentieth year, he authorized Nehemiah to organize the rebuilding of the city's walls (Neh. 2). Now, however, he ordered the rebuilding of the walls to be stopped; and on Rehum and Shimshai receiving the king's letter, having assembled an army, **they went immediately to the Jews in Jerusalem and compelled them by force to stop** (23). They did more, indeed, than Artaxerxes authorized, destroying that part of the wall which had already been built, and burning down the gates; and this was the destruction which was reported to Nehemiah in Susa as recorded in Neh. 1: 3.

The final verse of the chapter (24) has relation, not to the story just narrated, but to that of vv. 1 to 5. It recounts that, because of the obstructive actions of the neighbours to the north during the reign of Cyrus, the rebuilding of the temple **come to a standstill until the second year of the reign of Darius**, i.e. for sixteen years, until 520 BC.

III. COMPLETION OF THE REBUILDING OF THE TEMPLE
(5: 1–6: 22)
i. The resumption of the building of the temple (5: 1–2)
The discontinuation of the rebuilding of the temple was not only due to opposition by the Jews' northern neighbours; it was due also (as we are told in Hag. 1) to the Jews engrossing themselves with building luxurious houses for themselves. God chastised them for this materialistic attitude by afflicting their land with drought and famine. The prophet **Haggai** (1) brought this to the Jews' attention, with the consequence that the rebuilding of the temple recommenced (2).
ii. The authority for the rebuilding is questioned (5: 3–17)
The recommencing of the rebuilding of the temple would doubtless have infuriated the Jews' neighbours to the north, and it was probably these who induced **Tattenai** (who was governor of the whole satrapy of the Persian empire west of the Euphrates) to set about enquiring from the Jews as to what authority

they had for so acting (3). Tattenai and his entourage came therefore to Jerusalem for this purpose. It is probable that the Jews' leader Zerubbabel was terrified at this development, fearing that it would prevent the rebuilding of the temple from ever being finished. But the prophet **Zechariah** (1) assured him in the name of God that this great mountain would 'become level ground', and that as surely as Zerubbabel had laid the foundation of the temple he would bring it to completion (Zech. 4: 7–9).

In reply to Tattenai's questions the Jewish leaders told him that a long while before an earlier temple had stood on this site, which had been built by a famous Jewish king named Solomon, but that two generations ago their ancestors had so offended against their God that God had permitted Nebuchadnezzar king of Babylon to destroy it. So Nebuchadnezzar invaded the land, sacked Jerusalem, looted and then burned the temple, and exiled the Jews to his own country. But immediately Babylon was conquered by Cyrus, Cyrus issued a decree authorizing the Jews, not only to return to their land, but also to rebuild the temple; and these Jewish leaders stated that proof that Cyrus had authorized them to rebuild the temple was that they could produce the vessels which Cyrus gave them back so that they might be used in the temple when it was completed. So the Jews returned to Jerusalem, and laid the temple's foundation. But they had to admit that although the temple's foundation was laid as long as sixteen years before, still (as could be observed) the work was unfinished.

The decision of Tattenai, on hearing this statement by the Jewish leaders, was to ascertain from King Darius, to whom he was ultimately responsible, whether in fact a record could be found confirming that Cyrus authorized the rebuilding of the temple, as the Jews were claiming, and whether Darius himself was willing to ratify this. So Tattenai drafted the facts which the Jews had told him into a letter addressed to Darius (7 ff.), adding: **Now if it pleases the king, let a search be made in the royal archives of Babylon to see if King Cyrus did in fact issue a decree to rebuild this house of God in Jerusalem. Then let the king send us his decision in this matter** (17).

Tattenai's attitude toward the Jews was quite friendly, and he probably surmised that the charges he had been asked to investigate were groundless. He allowed the Jews, therefore, to continue with the rebuilding whilst the enquiry to king Darius was being made (5).
iii. Authority for the rebuilding is confirmed (6: 1–15)
The search for the decree of Cyrus which was made in the royal archives at Babylon (1) proved fruitless because this document had

been transferred, for some reason, to **Ecbatana** (2), the capital of Media, and the summer residence of the Persian kings (as distinct from their winter residence which was Susa, Neh. 1: 1). At Ecbatana, however, it was found, and its wording is given in vv. 3 to 5. The reason why its wording as given here differs from its wording as given in 1: 2–4 was because the latter had been drafted into the form of a public announcement to the Jews. The decree as found at Ecbatana contained brief details of the size and structure of the temple which was to be built, as well as authorizing the return of the temple vessels (3–5). Darius supplemented this original decree of Cyrus by decreeing himself that all the money and material provisions which the Jews needed so as to continue and complete the temple's rebuilding should be supplied to them (8–9), and that anyone who tried to hinder the work should be severely punished (11–12). All these instructions Tattenai and his associates put into effect (13). So the complaints of the neighbours to the north which had been aimed to obstruct the Jews in their rebuilding of the temple resulted ultimately in the Jews being greatly helped in their project. And they were further helped by the regular prophetic ministry which was carried out among them at this time by Haggai and Zechariah (14). The consequence was that **the temple was completed . . . in the sixth year of the reign of King Darius** (15), in 516 BC, four years after the rebuilding had been resumed. It is stated in v. 14 that **they finished building the temple according to the command of the God of Israel and the decrees of Cyrus, Darius and Artaxerxes, kings of Persia.** The inclusion here of the name Artaxerxes may have been because later on, as recorded in 7: 21–23, Artaxerxes made a contribution to the beautifying of the temple.

iv. The completed temple is dedicated to God (6: 16–18)
At the dedication of the newly-rebuilt temple, bulls, lambs and rams were offered on the altar (17), as had been done when Solomon's temple was dedicated to God (1 Kg. 8: 63), though the scale of the sacrificing was much smaller now, as the community was less wealthy than formerly. A duty roster was arranged for the priests and Levites (18).

v. The celebration of the Passover (6: 19–22)
19. On the fourteenth day of the first month, the exiles celebrated the Passover: this was the date ordained when the Passover was originally instituted (Exod. 12: 18), and it was eaten also by such Jews as had not been exiled and had now renounced all elements of heathen worship which might have crept into their religious practices (21). For seven days after that they celebrated the feast of unleavened

bread, as enjoined in Lev. 23: 6; **because the LORD had filled them with joy by changing the attitude of the king of Assyria** (22). It would have been more natural to have referred to Darius as 'the king of Persia'. But Darius was, of course, reigning over the territory which was formerly governed by the Assyrians; and it may be that the Chronicler deliberately called him here 'the king of Assyria' in order to make the point that Darius was making restitution for the destruction which had been wrought by a previous king of Assyria.

IV. RETURN OF MORE JEWISH EXILES UNDER EZRA (7: 1–8: 36)
i. Ezra's commission (7: 1–28)
The events of ch. 6 took place 'in the sixth year of the reign of King Darius' (v. 15), *viz.* in 516 BC, whereas those of ch. 7 took place **in the seventh year of King Artaxerxes** (7). On the presumption that the reference here is to Artaxerxes I (as has been argued in the Introduction), this means 458 B.C. Among the events which occurred during the intervening period of fifty-eight years (part of which was occupied by the reign of Ahasuerus), were those described in 4: 6, and those described in the book of Esther. It is probable that the prophecies of Malachi were delivered at this time. The names of the governors (Neh. 5: 15; Mal. 1: 18) of Judea following Zerubbabel are not known.

With this chapter there commences the recorded history of **Ezra** (1) and in vv. 1 to 5 his ancestry is given in seventeen stages back to **Aaron the chief priest** (5). If he had not possessed an ancestry such as this he would have lacked the authority he needed to fulfil the role in his nation's life which he undertook. This genealogy does not include every name in his line of descent, for between Aaron and Ezra were over forty generations. One major gap in this record is that between **Seraiah** (1) and Ezra. 2 Kg. 25: 18–21 relates that 'Seraiah the chief priest' was slain by Nebuchadnezzar shortly before the king sacked Jerusalem in 587 B.C. This was a hundred and thirty years before this story about Ezra. A fuller genealogy of Ezra is given in 1 Chr. 6: 3–15.

Ezra was not only a priest (descended from the original high priest); he was also a **teacher** (6), which means an instructor in and interpreter of God's law through Moses (10). The fact of his close contacts with King Artaxerxes seems to indicate furthermore that he was the Jews' representative to him at his court. At the Persian court his title **teacher of the law of the God of heaven** (12) may have been equivalent to 'secretary of state for Jewish affairs'.

It is to be presumed that Ezra, in Babylon, had heard that since the death of such able Jewish leaders as Zerubbabel, Jeshua, Haggai and Zechariah, the condition of those Jews who had returned to Judea was becoming unsettled and disordered. Ezra believed that this was because they were failing to obey God's law through Moses. Verse 25 shows that some of these Jews were entirely ignorant of these laws. Ezra explained this to Artaxerxes and asked that he, and certain fellow-Jews of his still in exile who were likeminded, might receive the king's authorization to travel to Judea with power to reform the abuses being perpetrated there, and enforce the observance of God's law through Moses. **6.** The outcome was that the king **granted him everything he asked:** Ezra must then have told Artaxerxes in greater detail what, in his opinion, needed to be done in Judea, and Artaxerxes accepted Ezra's advice and drafted it into the form of **the letter** (11) which is recorded in vv. 12–26. This letter authorized Ezra (*a*) to take money from Babylon to Jerusalem for the maintenance there of the worship of Yahweh (15–20); (*b*) to collect money for this same purpose from the Persian officials in Syria whom they would be contacting on their journey (20–21); (*c*) to have the priests, Levites and their helpers who served in the temple exempted from taxation (24); (*d*) to appoint magistrates throughout Judea who would be able to punish offenders with fines, imprisonment, exile or even death (25–26).

Verses 27–28 record Ezra's outburst of praise to God for so wonderfully disposing Artaxerxes' heart; and he explained this by saying: **'The hand of the LORD my God was on me'** (28). This figure of speech occurs frequently in the life-story of Ezra (7: 6, 9; 8: 18, 22, 31), and it occurs also in the narrative about Nehemiah (Neh. 2: 8, 18). There is probably an allusion here to the title Longimanus (so commonly latinized) which Artaxerxes I had selected for himself, meaning 'of the long hand'. He chose this title, doubtless, because of his outstretched hand being placed, figuratively speaking, on many distant nations. But the reasoning of Ezra was that, in a deeper sense, the Israelites existed under the outstretched hand of God. This expression of Ezra's is a further incidental indication that he lived during the reign of Artaxerxes I, and not of Artaxerxes II, whose title was Mnemon.

The journey of Ezra and his party from Babylon to Jerusalem, which is recounted in greater detail in ch. 8, is summarized in vv. 7–9, which relates that it took four months. From Babylon to Jerusalem direct was about 500 miles; but this route could not be taken because it lay across desert. The only practicable route was north-westwards up alongside the river Euphrates to the fording-place at Carchemish, and then south-westwards through Syria, a journey of about 900 miles.

ii. Ezra's journey (8: 1–36)

(*a*) **A list of the exiles who returned with Ezra (8: 1–14)**
Those who returned from Babylon to Jerusalem with Ezra are here classified under the heads of their respective families. About fifteen hundred Jews are mentioned; but because the word **men** is emphasized throughout the list, the entire company (including women) may have been about three thousand, far less than those returning under Sheshbazzar who numbered about fifty thousand (2: 64 ff.).

(*b*) **The recruitment of the Levites (8: 15–20)**
Ezra assembled the Jews who planned to accompany him beside **the canal that flows toward Ahava** (15). In v. 21 this is called **the Ahava canal**, implying that it took its name from a town situated on its course. Neither the town nor the river is mentioned elsewhere in Scripture, and their exact locations are unknown. As rivers sometimes change their course this one may not now exist. Probably it was a small river just north of Babylon which flowed into the Euphrates on which Babylon stood.

At the assembly point beside this river, Ezra **checked among the people** (15) and found that not a single Levite was among them. This was distressing to Ezra, because Artaxerxes had commissioned this company to go to Jerusalem in order to promote there obedience to the law of Moses with special emphasis on the rulings in that law relating to animal sacrifices (7: 17), which would involve much additional work for priests and Levites. Ezra knew, however, of a settlement of Levites at a place near by called Casiphia (the location of which is unknown to ourselves); so he sent thither a deputation of eleven men appealing to some of the Levites to join the company. Those who responded included about thirty-eight Levites (18–19) and **220 of the temple servants** (20).

(*c*) **The journey to Jerusalem (8: 21–31)**
Ezra had now to consider the safety of those who were journeying. Normally some visible protection would have been regarded as essential because of the danger both from wild beasts and also from armed robbers (31), and the more so when, as here, a large amount of treasure was being transported (25–27). The obvious resort would have been for Ezra to have requested from King Artaxerxes (with whom he was in great favour) an escort of soldiers and horsemen. But Ezra decided not to do this, feeling that it would undermine the testimony which, in previous days, he had borne to Artaxerxes concerning the faithfulness of God to those who trust in Him (22). So he, and the Israelites following his lead, **fasted** (as a sign of humility before God), and prayed (as an acknowledgment of dependence on God) (23), requesting from God **a safe journey** (21).

Ezra then **set apart twelve of the leading priests** (24), and **weighed out to them** the treasures which were to be carried (25), charging them to keep them safely till their journey's end (29).

The departure of the company from the river Ahava took place **on the twelfth day of the first month** (31). Since it was on 'the first day of the first month' that Ezra 'had begun his journey from Babylonia' (7: 9), the preparations beside the river Ahava must have occupied twelve days.

(*d*) **The arrival at Jerusalem (8: 32–36)**
After four months of travelling (7: 9) the company reached Jerusalem, and the fact of their being unmolested on the way (31) vindicated their faith in God's protecting care over them (21–23). The treasures which the priests had been carrying were reweighed to ensure that none had been misappropriated, and were then handed over to the temple staff (33, 34). The returned exiles, grateful to God for His preservation of them, sacrificed burnt offerings to Him (35). The decree of Artaxerxes (7: 12–26) was delivered to the rulers concerned.

V. EZRA'S HANDLING OF THE PROBLEM OF THE MIXED MARRIAGES (9: 1–10: 44)
i. Report to Ezra (9: 1–5)
The closing two chapters of this book form a sad ending to what is otherwise a happy and triumphant story. They describe what happened **after these things** (1), i.e. after Ezra and his company had reached Jerusalem which was in the fifth month of the seventh year of Artaxerxes' reign (7: 9). The story described in chs. 9 and 10 occurred in 'the ninth month' (10: 9) presumably of the same year. So the interval between the stories of ch. 8 and ch. 9 was probably four months. By saying to Ezra: **The people of Israel, including the priests and the Levites, have not kept themselves separate from the neighbouring peoples** (1), the officials meant that a considerable amount of intermarriage had taken place between the Jews in Judea and the pagan people around, this relating, presumably, more to such Jews as had been living in Judea all along to those who had but recently arrived there. The officials said further that those who had been guilty of these illicit unions had included not only certain of the priests and Levites, but also certain of the **leaders and officials** (2) who, because of their position in the community, should have set a good example to the rest. These, indeed, had **led the way in this unfaithfulness** (2) meaning perhaps the original offenders. The contracting of such marriages had been criticized also by Malachi (Mal. 2: 11), who probably prophesied during the fifty-eight year interval between ch. 6 and ch. 7.

God had forbidden the Israelites to intermarry with people of other nations (Exod. 34: 2 ff.; Dt. 7: 1 ff.) because He foresaw that this would result in the Jews' religion becoming corrupted by heathen ideas and practices, which became unhappily exemplified later on in the case of Solomon (1 Kg. 11: 1–8).

On Ezra hearing of these mixed marriages, he was overwhelmed with grief; and he expressed this in two ways, one of which was fairly common in a time of sorrow, *viz.* rending one's garments, and the other of which was unusual, possibly unique, *viz.* plucking the hair from one's head and beard. He realized that not only were these mixed marriages acts of disobedience to God's law, but that it was because of such acts of disobedience in former times that the Jews had been exiled to Babylon. So he **sat down appalled** (3) in the temple court. As the appointed hour approached at which the evening lamb was to be sacrificed on the altar, many Jews gathered to offer prayer, and they observed Ezra in his dejection. Then Ezra changed both his posture and his activity. Instead of sitting in silence, he knelt with his arms outstretched and started praying aloud.

ii. Ezra's prayer (9: 6–15)
Ezra's prayer on this occasion is one of the most moving of all the prayers which are recorded in Scripture. One of its characteristics is that although he himself was quite guiltless in this matter, he did not draw a distinction between himself the innocent one and his sinful fellow countrymen, but identified himself with them in their guilt. We may note what Ezra said:

(i) as to the fact of his nation's sin. He described the Jews' sin in v. 6 as being like a great flood which had reached the very vault of heaven and had submerged them.

(ii) as to the aggravation of their sin. He observed that (*a*) they had ignored God's warnings to them (10–12), and Ezra here alluded to those in Dt. 7: 1, 3, and 23: 6; (*b*) they had ignored God's judgments, Ezra showing in v. 7 that it was because the Jews had committed sin in a previous period of their history they had been divinely punished by being exiled to Babylon; (*c*) they had ignored God's goodness in their being restored to Judea, enabled to rebuild the temple, and protected from their foes round about (8–9). For a comment on the phrase **wall of protection** (9) see *Introduction*.

(iii) as to the consequence of their sin, Ezra concluded his prayer in vv. 13–15 by saying in effect: 'We Israelites are without excuse because of our sin; our desert is to be blotted by Thee out of existence; and all, therefore, that we can do in our plight is to cast ourselves on Thy mercy'.

iii. The people's repentance (10: 1–17)
When Ezra had completed his prayer, one of

those present whose name was **Shecaniah** spoke to Ezra and acknowledged with him the sin of the nation (2). He affirmed, however, that it was wrong to despair, believing that if the nation repented and turned from its sin, God would forgive them and restore to them His blessings. He therefore proposed that Ezra should take action by commanding the guilty men to put away all these wives and their children (3). This counsel which Shecaniah gave to Ezra might seem cruel and heartless; but it was felt to be essential if the Jewish faith was to survive. Moreover it seems that Shecaniah would himself be involved in the disruption of family life which would result, for his father, Jehiel the son of Elam (2), being one of the guilty men (26) would be required to separate himself from his wife and their children, including himself. Ezra agreed, therefore, to proceed, and he administered an oath to the Jews to ensure their cooperation (5). Then he left the temple court, and entered into a room belonging to **Jehohanan son of Eliashib** (6) (for further information about these men, see *Introduction*); but though he must have spent several hours up till then without food and water, because of his grief over the people's sin, he continued his fast. A public **proclamation** (7) was then made calling on all the returned exiles in Judah and Jerusalem to assemble in Jerusalem within three days. This, therefore, they did, gathering **in the square before the house of God** (9). Ezra indicted them with their sin, and told those who were

guilty to confess it, and to amend their ways by divorcing their foreign wives (10, 11). The people concerned, with the exception of just four men (15), agreed that this was necessary, but indicated that this could not be effected at that actual gathering, partly because so many men were involved, and also because of the inclemency of the weather at that time (13). It was **the ninth month** (9) *viz.* Kislev, which in our calendar would be December. It was 'the former rain' which fell in December, whereas 'the latter rain' fell at Springtime. What therefore was proposed was that the guilty persons should be tried by local judges in the places where they lived (14). This was done and it took three months (16–17).

iv. Register of those who had married foreign wives (10: 18–44)

Verses 18 to 44 consist in a list of those who were guilty. There were one hundred and eleven, consisting in seventeen **priests** (18–22), six **Levites** (23), one **singer** and three **gatekeepers** (24), and eighty-four others (25–43). It is stated concerning **the descendants of the priests** (18) that they offered to God a ram as a **guilt offering** (19), alternatively called 'trespass offering', and it is possible that each of the guilty persons did this too, as now they put away their foreign wives, **some of whom had children by them** (44).

BIBLIOGRAPHY

See under Nehemiah

NEHEMIAH

STEPHEN S. SHORT

Authorship and Date
see **Introduction** to the Book of **Ezra**.

ANALYSIS

I. NEHEMIAH IS INFORMED OF THE PLIGHT OF JERUSALEM (1: 1–11)

The story recounted in the book of Nehemiah commenced **in the twentieth year** (1) of the reign of King Artaxerxes I (2: 1), *viz.* in 445 B.C. The story recounted in the final four chapters of the book of Ezra occurred in the seventh year of that king's reign (Ezr. 7: 7). During the thirteen year interval between these stories, however, there occurred the event described in Ezr. 4: 7–23. It is narrated there how that 'in the days of Artaxerxes' the Jews in Jerusalem engaged themselves in rebuilding the city walls, which matter was reported to King Artaxerxes by their neighbours to the north, and of how Artaxerxes responded by commanding that 'an order be issued to these men to stop work, so that this city will not be rebuilt until I so order' (Ezr. 4: 21). The northern neighbours, consequently, hurried to Jerusalem 'and compelled them by force to stop' (Ezr. 4: 23), going so far, evidently, as to demolish the part of the wall which the Jews had built

and set fire to the newly-constructed city gates. One of the Jews in Jerusalem at this time was named **Hanani** (2), whose brother Nehemiah was living away in Babylonia, and who was in close touch with Artaxerxes through having been appointed **cupbearer to the king** (11). The duty of a royal cupbearer was to serve the king with wine, tasting it himself in his presence before so doing to prove that it was not poisoned. Only such men as were regarded to be completely trustworthy were appointed to this post. Very likely Nehemiah received the appointment when the king and himself were residing at Babylon. But Artaxerxes had a winter place of residence at **Susa** (1) east of the river Tigris and near the head of the Persian Gulf. Since the story of this chapter occurred in a winter month, **the month of Kislev** (1) —December in our calendar—Artaxerxes was staying at this time at Susa, and had taken with him there (among many others, no doubt) his Jewish cupbearer Nehemiah. Hanani, in Judea, felt that Nehemiah ought to be told of this recent destruction of the walls and gates of Jerusalem in case he might be able to make use of his close contact with Artaxerxes to prevail upon the king to adopt a more favourable attitude towards the Jews in Jerusalem. So Hanani and some like-minded companions of his made the journey of more than a thousand miles from Judea to Susa, and informed Nehemiah of the sorry plight of Jerusalem and its inhabitants (3). Nehemiah was distressed at the news, and prayed to God concerning the matter; and one of his prayers at this time is recorded in vv. 5-11. The prominence in this prayer of the element of confession of sin (6, 7) shows that Nehemiah did not view the overthrow of Jerusalem's walls as happening fortuitously, or simply being due to factors of politics or military might, but rather as God's judgment on the Jews for their sinfulness. In making this confession, Nehemiah, although personally a very upright man, associated himself with his nation in their guilt, saying: **I confess the sins we Israelites, including myself and my father's house, have committed against you** (6). Nehemiah recalled in his prayer God's promise to Moses recorded in Dt. 30: 1-5 to the effect that departure from God on Israel's part would result in their being exiled, but returning to Him would dispose Him to bring them back to their homeland (8, 9); and he testified to God's redeeming grace toward Israel (10). As Nehemiah proceeded with his prayer, the conviction became impressed on him that God wanted him to ask Artaxerxes if he might be released from his post of royal cupbearer, and be given authority to journey to Jerusalem and organize the rebuilding of the city walls. He realized, however, that this request might anger the king and bring punishment upon himself. So he prayed that when eventually he decided to broach the subject before Artaxerxes, the king's heart might prove favourably disposed towards him: **Give your servant success**, he entreated, **by granting him favour in the presence of this man** (11). His desire was that Artaxerxes might be divinely impelled to put into practical effect the qualifying clause which he had appended to his decree of Ezr. 4: 21 (quoted above) in which he forbade the city walls to be rebuilt until such time as he gave express permission for their rebuilding.

II. NEHEMIAH JOURNEYS TO JERUSALEM WITH THE KING'S COMMISSION (2: 1-20)

i. Nehemiah's request and the king's commission (2: 1-8)

Four months passed before Nehemiah obtained his opportunity to make his request to King Artaxerxes, this being the interval between 'the month of Kislev' (1: 1) and **the month of Nisan** (2: 1). Nehemiah was engaged in his customary duty of handing the king his wine. Normally when doing this, his demeanour, naturally, was that of cheerfulness; but on this occasion, because of his concern about the situation at Jerusalem, he was **sad**; and the king noticed this, and asked the reason for it (2). Nehemiah explained that it was because Jerusalem, where his ancestors had lived and died, had recently been ravaged; and on Artaxerxes asking him if there was any action he wished to take he expressed to him his desire to go to Jerusalem and repair the damage. In answer to Nehemiah's prayer, God disposed the king, not only to agree to Nehemiah's request, but to give him every conceivable help in the undertaking. In order that Nehemiah might not be molested on the journey (7) the king sent with him **army officers and cavalry** (9), a provision which Ezra, in somewhat different circumstances, preferred to do without (Ezr. 8: 22). The king granted Nehemiah's request also that **Asaph, keeper of the king's forest** (8)—probably the so-called 'Garden of Solomon' about six miles south of Jerusalem—might provide him with the **timber** he would need. We are informed (not here, but in 5: 15), that Artaxerxes went so far, at this time, as to appoint Nehemiah governor of Jerusalem, and he stipulated for how long he should act in this capacity before reporting back to him. The duration of this time is not stated; and it appears that Nehemiah did not, in fact, return to Artaxerxes for twelve years (13: 6). Probably a shorter period of time than this was originally specified, but it became progressively extended.

ii. Nehemiah's journey (2: 9 f.)

Nehemiah set out, therefore, on the long journey from Susa to Jerusalem. When he came to the region north of Judea which since the late eight century B.C. had been called Samaria (9), he encountered **Sanballat the Horonite and Tobiah the Ammonite official** (10). The Elephantine papyri, which consist in letters from and to Jewish colonists on the island of Elephantine in the Nile in upper Egypt written over the greater part of the fifth century BC, show that in 408 B.C. Sanballat was governor of Samaria, and he probably exercised the same authority there at this earlier time. (Indeed, in 408 B.C. he seems to have been quite old and to have delegated his authority to two of his sons.) The term **Horonite** may indicate that he came from Beth Horon in the district of Samaria. Tobiah seems to have been his subordinate, and the description of him suggests that originally he was an Ammonite slave. He may, at this time, have been ruling over Ammon east of Judea. Sanballat and Tobiah were greatly **disturbed** that Nehemiah had been appointed to restore Jerusalem from its degradation, for they felt that if Judah became strong, Samaria would be relatively weakened.

iii. Nehemiah inspects the walls (2: 11–16)

Three days after Nehemiah had reached Jerusalem he decided to make an inspection of the broken-down city wall, choosing to do this **by night** (12) so as to obviate attracting overmuch attention. Riding a donkey or mule, he commenced at the **Valley Gate** (13) near the city's southwest corner, and named after the Tyropoeon valley, and he proceeded eastwards for five hundred yards (3: 13), examining the wall from the outside, till reaching **the Dung Gate** through which the city's refuse was taken to the Valley of Hinnom. He continued alongside the city's east wall to **the King's Pool**, which was probably the pool of Siloam; but the wall here was so devastated that he had to dismount (14), and so he continued beside the ruined east wall overlooking the Kidron **Valley** (15) by foot. Having proceeded, presumably, to the city's northeast corner, Nehemiah **turned back** (15), which probably means 'retraced his steps', returning to **the Valley Gate** by the way he had come, and not inspecting on this occasion the north and west walls which perhaps he had already surveyed during the daytime.

iv. 'Let us start rebuilding' (2: 17–20)

The following day Nehemiah called together the Jewish leaders and told them of his intentions, and of God's help thus far, and they agreed to start rebuilding the walls without delay (18). But the enemies, Sanballat and Tobiah and **Geshem the Arab**, who may have ruled over Edom to the south, started to spread rumours that the Jews were planning a rebellion against King Artaxerxes (19), and they may have reminded these Jews of what happened when last they attempted to rebuild the walls (Ezr. 4: 12 ff.), to whom Nehemiah replied: **The God of heaven will give us success** (20).

III. THE BUILDING OF JERUSALEM'S WALLS (3: 1–6: 19)

i. The builders and their assignments (3: 1–32)

Chapter 3 describes how, under the superintendence of Nehemiah, different parts of the city wall at Jerusalem were rebuilt by various individuals and groups. Forty-two particular sections of the wall with its gates are mentioned, and they are traced round in an anticlockwise direction. The description starts with the repairing of **the Sheep Gate** (1) which was situated on the city's north wall and quite near its northeast corner. Verses 2–5 relate to the north wall extending westwards from the Sheep Gate; vv. 6–12 relate to the west wall, vv. 13–14 to the south wall, vv. 15–31 to the east wall, and v. 32 to the small section of the north wall between the northeast corner and the Sheep Gate. The Sheep Gate stood immediately north of the temple area, and through it sheep would be brought for sacrifice. It was therefore appropriate that its repairers should have been the priests under the leadership of **Eliashib the high priest**, who was the grandson of Jeshua and the son of Joiakim (12: 10), and who was mentioned before in Ezr. 10: 6.

The Jews in Jerusalem were assisted in their building operations by their fellow-countrymen who lived in the surrounding area, *e.g.* **the men of Jericho** (2), **the men of Tekoa** (5), the **men from Gibeon and Mizpah** (7), **the residents of Zanoah** (13) those of the district of **Beth Zur** (16) and **the district of Keilah** (17). The unanimity of the Jews in applying themselves to this task was almost total, the only exceptions of which we are told being the **nobles** from the city of Tekoa who **did not put their shoulders to the work under their supervisors** (5). The words 'under their supervisors' is a more probable translation than that of the AV and RSV: 'of their Lord', referring to God, possible though this is.

Men of various occupations joined in the work, not only priests (1, 22) and **Levites** (17), but also **goldsmiths** and **perfume-makers** (8), **merchants** (32), several exercising the office of **ruler** (12, 14, 15, etc.), and also some women such as the daughters of Shallum (12).

When Nehemiah organized the work he adopted the policy, wherever possible, of assigning a particular person to repair the part of the wall which was **opposite his house** (10, 23, 28, 29, 30), for this would encourage that person to work hard so as to ensure that his own home and family would be well protected. Some of the builders, having repaired one section of the wall, **repaired another section** (11, 19–21, 24, 27, 30). One of these was **Meremoth son of Uriah** (4, 21), who was probably the priest mentioned in Ezr. 8: 33 who, thirteen years before, received from Ezra and his party the treasures which these had transported from Babylon to Jerusalem. Another of them, **Malkijah son of Harim** (11), may well have been the person mentioned in Ezr. 10: 31 who, with many others, needed to separate himself from his foreign wife. As to **Meshullam son of Berekiah** (4), a marriage was contracted at about this time, probably, between his daughter and a man named Jehohanan who was the son of the Jews' enemy Tobiah the Ammonite (6: 18).

ii. Opposition to the building (4: 1–23)

Sanballat and his allies had adopted a hostile attitude to the Jews when he originally heard of their intention to rebuild Jerusalem's wall (2: 19). On hearing now that this intention was being implemented his hostility towards them increased, and **he ridiculed the Jews** (1), call-

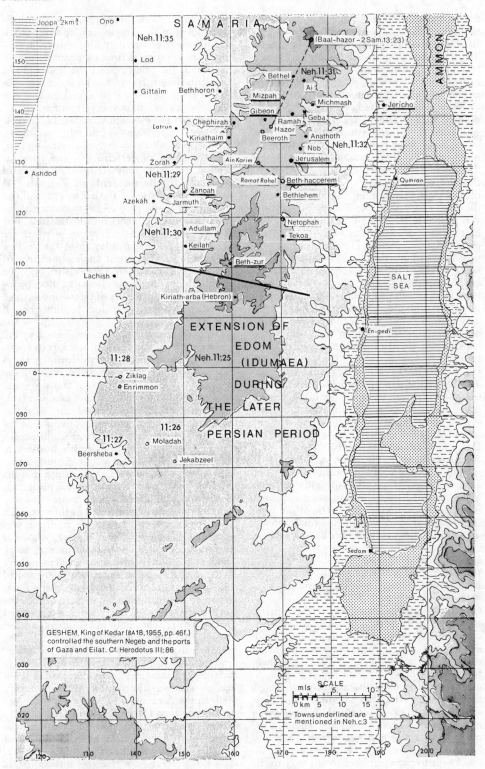

Map 27—The Restoration

ing them **feeble** (2), and mocking their procedure of using as materials for the new wall stones from the old wall, and **burned** ones at that, which might well be cracked and weak. The taunt of Tobiah was that so flimsy was this restored wall that a mere fox touching it would have enough impact to knock it down (3). The Jews, however, were not deterred by these jibes, and instead of answering back or retaliating they committed the matter to God in prayer (4, 5), and continued with the building (6).

Because of this Sanballat decided now to resort to physical attack. For this purpose he gathered together his allies, adding to his former ones (2: 19) **the men of Ashdod** (7) the ancient Philistine country to Jerusalem's west. The Jews had enemies now to the north (Sanballat in Samaria), to the east (Tobiah the Ammonite), to the south (Geshem the Arab), and to the west (the Ashdodites). Sanballat, their leader, could not formally declare war on the Jews, for Samaria and Judah both belonged to the Persian empire and were subject to Artaxerxes who had specifically authorized the rebuilding of Jerusalem's wall. But the enemies felt themselves able to engage themselves in sporadic terrorist activities against the Jews (8). Again Nehemiah prayed about the matter (9), and he exhorted his people to place their trust in God's invincible power which He could exercise on their behalf (14, 20).

He did not regard trusting in God, however, as being incompatible with taking sensible precautions against their being suddenly attacked. He knew that such attacks were likely because those of the workers who lived in the countryside around and came each day to Jerusalem to build repeatedly overheard the enemies' plans and were able to report them to Nehemiah (12). It was helpful to the governor to be able to receive these warnings; but before long he decided that, useful as it was, it involved danger, and that both for their own sake and also as an additional protection in the event of an attack being launched during the hours of darkness, all these provincial builders should remain in the city at night till the task was completed (22).

Not having a professional army, Nehemiah armed the builders. **Those who carried materials** (17) had a free hand, and in this they carried a weapon. The actual **builders** (18) had no free hand; so each of these **wore his sword at his side**: Nehemiah arranged also that a trumpeter should be constantly watching out for signs of the approach of the enemy, and that on seeing anything dangerous he should sound the trumpet, whereupon all the builders were to rally to the point where the threat was occurring (19, 20).

Having taken these precautionary measures the Jews applied themselves to their task with diligence. **6. the people worked with all their heart**, and they laboured from dawn to dusk (21). Even during the night none of them removed their clothes (23); and **each had his weapon, even when he went for water** (23). The Hebrew text of this final sentence of the chapter is mutilated. Rendered literally, it takes the form: 'Each one his weapon the water.' The RSV excludes the word 'water': 'Each kept his weapon in his hand' The AV excludes the word 'weapon', representing the text's meaning as being that builders wore their working clothes all the time except when they were washing from their bodies the dust and the sweat: 'Everyone put them off for washing'.

iii. Economic distress and Nehemiah's remedial measures (5: 1–19)

It was not only by external opposition that Nehemiah and the Jews were being hindered in their task but also by internal dissension. The fact that so many Jews were engaged in rebuilding the wall and therefore foregoing their normal means of livelihood brought financial hardship to the community. The reference in v. 2 is probably to those who were not themselves owners of land, and who hardly received enough food to keep themselves and their families alive. Others who did possess land had been compelled to mortgage it in order to obtain money for the purchase of food (3). Then there were landowners who, in order to be able to pay the taxation on their property which was levied by the Persians, had been compelled to borrow money at exorbitant rates of interest from Jews who were rich (4), and a consequence of this was that some of the poorer Jews were only able to make ends meet by selling their children into slavery (5).

Nehemiah was **very angry** (6) when he heard of how the richer Jews were exploiting their poorer brethren, and he charged them with **exacting usury from your own countrymen** (7), which was in breach of the legislation in Exod. 22: 25. He recalled to them that his own practice had been the very opposite of their own, and that whenever he had seen Jewish slaves offered for sale in a Gentile market-place, he would pay the ransom price and give them their liberty. But these Jewish nobles, on occasion, in order to make money, would sell poverty-stricken fellow-countrymen of theirs to heathen masters in the knowledge that Nehemiah, seeing their plight, would buy them back (8). This was not only morally wrong, Nehemiah said; it brought reproach on the Name of God (9). Nehemiah frankly admitted that there had been instances when he himself had done what these Jewish tycoons had been doing (as v. 10 seems to state); but he instructed now that all this profiteering should cease, and some priests were therefore summoned so that their promise could be made on oath (12). Nehemiah performed a bodily gesture, moreover, to symbolise the judgment of God on any who defaulted (13).

Nehemiah placed now on record the praiseworthy example he had set as governor of Judea. Most men in his position would have amassed money both for their personal salary and for that of their servants by additional taxation of the community, and this indeed was what had been done by **the earlier governors** (15). But though Nehemiah was entitled to do this, yet **out of reverence for God** and of his compassion for the needy people, he refrained. He deigned to involve himself, furthermore, in the physical work of building the walls, as did also his servants, and he resisted any temptation to make the purchase of cheap land at this time (16). He was very hospitable, moreover. When, for instance, certain Jews who wished to settle permanently in Jerusalem were still without homes there, he generously made provision for them (17). On one particular day, indeed, he arranged a huge banquet for his guests; and because the people were so heavily taxed on other accounts he paid for it all himself (18). All these deeds he wanted the Jews to remember; and he wanted God to **remember** them too (19).

iv. The wall completed in face of threats (6: 1–19)

The confederacy of the Jews' enemies, hearing that the Jews' rebuilding of the walls and gates of Jerusalem was almost completed (1), decided to make renewed efforts to hamper and demoralize them. Their use of ridicule had proved ineffective (4: 1–6), as had also their making of terrorist attacks on the builders (4: 7–23). The plan on which they therefore settled was to try to kill, or at least kidnap, Nehemiah himself. So they sent a message to him proposing that they met with each other on neutral ground and held a parley, under which circumstances they believed that Nehemiah could be seized or assassinated. The place they suggested for such a meeting was **one of the villages on the plain of Ono** (2), which was about twenty miles northwest of Jerusalem. Nehemiah realized, however, that this invitation concealed a plot against his life; so he replied to it by saying that he was too busy (3). Sanballat suggested therefore a later date for the meeting, but Nehemiah excused himself also from this; and the same thing happened twice more (4).

Sanballat sent his servant to Nehemiah next with an **unsealed letter** in his hand (5), written on papyrus, or leather, or pottery. It contained a totally false rumour about Nehemiah, and Sanballat wanted all who handled the letter to read it, so that the innuendo might spread around. In this letter Sanballat expressed concern about an idea that was abroad to the effect that Nehemiah intended to rebel against Artaxerxes of Persia by proclaiming himself **king in Judah**; and Sanballat suggested that they met so as to discuss how such a rumour could be prevented from reaching Artaxerxes' ears (6, 7). Again Nehemiah refused to meet Sanballat, and he sent him a curt reply saying that there was no truth in these allegations, they being Sanballat's own malicious inventions (8).

The final stratagem of the enemies against Nehemiah seems to have been on the initiative of Tobiah, for he is named, in this connection before Sanballat (12, 14). These two villains bribed (12) a false prophet in Jerusalem named **Shemaiah, who was shut in at his home** (10), probably meaning that he was in a state of prophetic ecstasy, to make a prophetic utterance to the effect that Nehemiah should seek sanctuary from danger in the holy place of the **temple.** Now none but priests were permitted to enter the temple's holy place (Num. 18: 7), and the purpose behind this ploy was to get Nehemiah discredited among the Jews by doing this unlawful thing (13). A true prophetic message Nehemiah would have heeded; but as to this oracle of Shemaiah's, Nehemiah knew that it was not from God, and quickly discovered that **Tobiah and Sanballat had hired him** to utter it. So he replied: **should one like me** (not being a priest) **go into the temple to save his life?'**

Shemaiah was not the only false prophet in Jerusalem who was opposed to Nehemiah; there were others, and also a false prophetess whose name was **Noadiah** (14). There were, indeed, **many in Judah** (18) who were hostile to the governor, this having been caused in part at least by two treasonable marriages, one between Tobiah the Ammonite and the daughter of a Jew named **Shecaniah**, and the other between Tobiah's son and **the daughter of Meshullam son of Berekiah** who had been actively engaged in the building of Jerusalem's wall (3: 4, 30). The consequence of this was that traitorous correspondence took place between **the nobles of Judah** and Tobiah (17).

Despite all, however, **the wall was completed on the twenty-fifth of Elul** (i.e. in October of 445 BC, Elul being the sixth month of the Jewish year), **in fifty-two days** (15). Whereas the rebuilding of the temple took twenty-two years (because after making a start the Jews became discouraged and ceased working till Haggai and Zechariah prophesied to them), the rebuilding of Jerusalem's city wall took just seven and a half weeks. **16. that this work had been done with the help of our God** was not only the testimony of the Jews themselves, but was the conclusion also of the Jews' special **enemies** at this time, and also of **all the surrounding nations.**

IV. A LIST OF THE EXILES WHO RETURNED WITH ZERUBBABEL (7: 1-73a)

i. Security precautions (7: 1-4)

Although the wall of Jerusalem had now been completely rebuilt, the city's security was not yet sufficiently ensured. Nehemiah took, therefore, some important measures by way of attending to this matter. He appointed two men to be in **charge over Jerusalem** (2), his own **brother Hanani**, who, a year before, had visited him at Susa, and had brought news to him of the city's plight (1: 2), and also **Hananiah** who already had been made governor of the fortress north of the temple. Hananiah was **a man of integrity, and feared God more than most men do**, and particularly than the 'many in Judah' who were bound by oath to Tobiah (6: 18). Nehemiah laid down also at what times of the day the city gates should be open, and when they should be shut (3a). He insisted furthermore that guards should be appointed to protect the city's private houses (3b). Nehemiah realized, too, that Jerusalem would be a safer place if it were more adequately populated, for at the present **there were few people in it, and the houses had not yet been rebuilt** (4). This last statement must be understood in a relative sense rather than in an absolute sense, for some houses there are referred to in v. 3, as well as in Hag. 1: 4. More houses were therefore needed in Jerusalem and more people to occupy them, for whilst the city had been unprotected by walls only small numbers had felt disposed to settle there, most of the Jews choosing to live in the district round about (73). Nehemiah's decision, accordingly, was to try to encourage some of these to establish their homes in the city itself; but he wished that only those of pure Jewish stock should do this.

ii. The list (7: 5-73a)

So he borrowed from the temple archives the register of those who had returned from Babylon to Jerusalem in response to the decree of Cyrus ninety-three years before (and which is recorded also in Ezr. 2, *q.v.* for comments) and he used this as the basis of his measures for the city's repopulation. That is why the list is inserted into the narrative again here in vv. 6-73.

The final sentence of this chapter belongs properly to the narrative recorded in the next chapter.

V. THE READING AND EXPOSITION OF THE LAW (7: 73b-8: 18)

i. Public reading (7: 73b-8: 12)

The events described in this chapter occurred **when the seventh month came** (7: 73), the month Tishri, the story recounted in vv. 1-12 taking place **on the first day of the seventh month** (2), the day when the Feast of Trumpets (Lev. 23: 23) was celebrated by the Jews. This was only a few days after the completion by the Jews of the rebuilding of the city wall, which occurred on 'the twenty-fifth of Elul' (6: 15), the sixth month.

The vocation of the priest Ezra, being a scribe, was 'to devote himself to the study and observance of the Law of the LORD, and to teaching its decrees and laws in Israel' (Ezr. 7: 10). To teach God's laws to those in Israel who did not know them was one of the purposes for which King Artaxerxes had sent Ezra from Babylon to Jerusalem (Ezr. 7: 25). He must therefore often have engaged in this duty between his own coming to Jerusalem in 458 B.C. and the arrival of Nehemiah in 445 B.C. Few of the Jews would possess personal copies of the scrolls of the law; so the main way in which they were able to become familiar with the law was by hearing it read publicly, and this was often done. Besides it having been done as described in detail here in ch. 8, there are further instances of this mentioned in 9: 3 and in 13: 1.

During the fifty-two days when the wall of Jerusalem was being built there would have been little or no opportunity for such convocations; but no sooner was the work finished than **all the people assembled as one man in the square before the Water Gate. They told Ezra the scribe to bring out the Book of the Law of Moses** (1): the fact that it was the people who asked Ezra to read to them the law shows that they were familiar with such sessions and benefitted from them. This particular convocation is described in detail because of the significance of its timing.

The Water Gate was the gate on the east side of Jerusalem through which the citizens passed when they descended to the spring Gihon to obtain water. At break of day the crowd assembled in the square on the inner side of this gate, and **from daybreak till noon** (3) they listened to Ezra and his fellow priests as they read from various scrolls of the Pentateuch. Doubtless there would have then been read Lev. 23: 23-25 describing the celebration of the feast of Trumpets on that particular day; but much moral instruction from different parts of the Pentateuch must have been read as well. **They read from the Book . . . making it clear and giving the meaning so that the people could understand what was being read** (8). As to the phrase **making it clear**, the mg suggests the alternative 'translating it,' but there is no evidence of the Jews in Jerusalem being unable to use a common language at this time. That there was a single 'language of Judah' is implied in 13: 24. It is best to regard the word as being used in its natural sense, of 'clearly'.

As the people listened to the reading of commandments in the law which they had failed to obey, they were **weeping** (9). Nehemiah, Ezra and the Levites appreciated their penitential response, but felt that as that day (the feast of Trumpets) was **sacred to the LORD** (9, 10, 11), it was a time for rejoicing rather than for weeping. So **all the people went away to eat and drink**, and to share their good things with others, (as in Est. 9: 19–22), **and to celebrate with great joy** (12).

ii. The Feast of Booths (8: 13–18)
On the following day, **the second day** (13) of the seventh month, the Jewish leaders **gathered around Ezra the scribe to give attention to the words of the Law** privately. Knowing that a fortnight later (starting on the fifteenth day of the seventh month) there would be celebrated the feast which is described in Lev. 23: 33 ff. in which the Jews commemorated God's care over their ancestors when they were journeying through the wilderness for forty years from Egypt to Canaan, they decided to read that passage carefully so as to ensure that how they had been observing it year by year conformed to the law's teaching. Instances of earlier celebrations of this 'feast of the seventh month' are referred to in 1 Kg. 8: 2 in the days of Solomon, and in Ezr. 3: 4 in the days of Zerubbabel. There is a further reference to this feast in Hos. 12: 9 where God told the northern kingdom of Israel that because of their sins they would be dispossessed of their homes and have to live in tents. He said: 'I will again make you dwell in tents as in the days of the appointed feast' (RSV). This shows that this feast was observed during the period of the Israelite monarchy, and that during the seven days the Jews lived in tents (mostly made from goat-skins). As now the Jewish leaders studied with Ezra Lev. 23: 33 ff., they deduced that, by rights, the people should dwell during this feast, not in tents, but in booths, made from the branches of trees (14). Instruction was therefore given to the populace that the celebration of the feast two weeks ahead should be observed in this way (15). This was done (16), and done for the first time since **the days of Joshua son of Nun** (17). **And their joy was very great.**

VI. THE RENEWAL OF THE COVENANT (9: 1–10: 39)
i. Confession of sin (9: 1–38)
The feast of booths which the Jews had just celebrated from the fifteenth to the twenty-second day of the seventh month was an occasion of rejoicing; but in the reading of the law day by day throughout its course (8: 18), and also, no doubt, at the 'assembly' on the eighth day, the Jews must have been convicted of many sins in their life, and of respects in which they had not adequately **separated themselves from all foreigners** (2). On, therefore, the following day, **the twenty-fourth day of the same month** (1), the Jews gathered together for a further convocation **fasting and wearing sackcloth**, and **confessed their sins.** For three hours they listened to further readings from the law, and for the next three hours they gave themselves to confessing their sin and worshipping God (3).

A long prayer is now recorded which is introduced in the RSV with the words: **And Ezra said** (6). These words are not present in the Hebrew text (for which reason they are omitted from the NIV and the AV), but they are found in the Greek LXX. They may well recall a genuine fact, in which event the story in this chapter and the chapter that follows should be regarded as centred on Ezra rather than on Nehemiah (as is also the story of the previous chapter).

As to the content of this prayer (6–37), after an acknowledgment of God's power and greatness (6), there follows a detailed review of certain of the significant events in the course of Israel's history. Emphasis is laid on God's unfailing goodness to them, and on their repeated sinfulness notwithstanding.

When the prayer had been concluded the Jews resolved to make **a binding agreement** with Yahweh their God (38). God's original covenant with Israel had been established and ratified at the foot of Mount Sinai (Exod. 24: 1–8). But its terms had not adequately been kept on the part of the Israelites. The covenant which was being made now was not a new one, but a renewal of the old one, as can be seen from an examination of its terms as recorded in ch. 10.

ii. The covenant sealed (10: 1–39)
Those who set their seal to the covenant are denoted in 9: 38 as leaders, Levites and priests of the Jewish community. In vv. 1–27 their names are mentioned following that of **Nehemiah the governor** (1), but they are given in the opposite order to that of the classification in 9: 38. As to the names listed down to v. 8, we are told: **these were the priests** (8); from v. 9 are listed **the Levites** (9); and from v. 14: **the leaders of the people** (14). Not only did these Jewish officials set their seal to this covenant, but **the rest of the people** (28) associated themselves with their action, included among them being **all their sons and daughters who are able to understand**, i.e. such children of theirs as were old enough to be able to enter intelligibly into what was taking place.

As to the content of what the Israelites now promised, this was both general and also particular. In general it was **to follow the Law of God given through Moses the servant of God and to obey carefully all the commands, regulations and decrees of the LORD our God** (29). But there were particular parts of the divine law which, on account of their having been neglected of late, needed special emphasis, and these are elaborated in vv. 30 to 39. They were as follows: (i) that they would not contract matrimonial alliances with the heathen (30); (ii) that they would refrain from trading on the sabbath day and other holy days (31); (iii) that they would ensure the adequate maintenance of the temple staff and services by regularly rendering their stipulated contributions (32–39), a resolve which they summarized by saying: **We will not neglect the house of our God** (39). It is sad to read in ch. 13 of how it was that when Nehemiah returned to Jerusalem for his second period of administration, having reported back to Artaxerxes in Babylon (13: 6), he found failure to have occurred at each of these points. Mixed marriages were occurring again (13: 23–28), the sabbath was being desecrated (13: 15–22), and the temple staff were failing to receive their requisite maintenance (13: 10–13).

The method by which the staff and services of the temple were to be maintained is given in some detail in vv. 32–39. It was to be (*a*) by the annual temple tax (32–33). The origin of this is described in Exod. 30: 11–16, before the temple was built. It consisted then in an occasional tax of half a shekel; but by now it had become an annual tax of **a third of a shekel . . . :** In New Testament times it was an annual tax of half a shekel (Mt. 17: 24); (*b*) by the provision of **wood** (34) **to burn on the altar of the LORD**, so that the altar fire might continually be kept burning (Lev. 6: 12); (*c*) by the presentation to the priests of **the firstfruits** of all that the Jews possessed (35–37a), and by paying the priests five shekels (Num. 18: 16) for the redemption of each firstborn son; (*d*) by the giving of **tithes** (37b–39), as was enjoined in Lev. 27: 30–33. The tithe (tenth part) of the land's produce was to be brought to the Levites; then the Levites were to bring **a tenth of the tithes** to the temple at Jerusalem for the maintenance of the priests; (cf. Num. 18: 25–28).

VII. LISTS OF JEWS IN JERUSALEM AND JUDEA (11: 1–12: 26)
i. Princes, priests and Levites (11: 1–34)
With the conclusion of the narrative of chs. 8–10 which centres on Ezra rather than on Nehemiah, the Chronicler continues from where he broke off at 7: 4, where he said that the city of Jerusalem 'was large and spacious, but there were few people in it'. There lived in Jerusalem **the leaders of the people** (1), but not many others. So to remedy this matter **the rest of the people cast lots to bring one out of every ten to live in Jerusalem**; then in addition to these who were forcibly conscripted to transfer themselves to the capital, some others freely volunteered to do this; and **the people commended all the men who volunteered to live in Jerusalem** (2). As for the Jewish leaders (mentioned in v. 1) who were already resident in Jerusalem, there are listed here those of them from the tribe **of Judah** (4–6), those from the tribe **of Benjamin** (7–9), **the priests** (10–14), **the Levites** (15–18), and **the gatekeepers** (19). The foregoing list is very similar to that which is recorded in 1 Chr. 9: 2–17. The **temple servants**, 'that David and the officials had established to assist the Levites' (Ezr. 8: 20), **lived on the hill of Ophel** (21) which means 'the mound' and was situated on the perimeter of the city to the southeast. To take care of the interests of all these the Jews had an official representative at the Persian court, namely **Pethahiah son of Meshezabel** (24); he was **the king's agent in all affairs relating to the people.**
ii. List of villages (11: 25–36)
In vv. 25–36 is provided a list of some of the **villages** (25) those where the Jews were now living, the towns in vv. 25–30 being within the former territory of **Judah**, and those in vv. 31–36 within the former territory of **the Benjamites** (31). Some Levites who had formerly lived in Judah lived now in Benjamin (36).
iii. Further lists of priests and Levites (12: 1–26)
Verses 1–7 list **the priests** who, ninety-three years before, journeyed from Babylon to Jerusalem with **Zerubbabel** and **Jeshua** (cf. Ezr. 2), and vv. 8–9 list **the Levites** who did so. The statement that **Bakbukiah and Unni, their associates, stood opposite** the Levites mentioned in the previous verse **in the services** (9) probably refers to the antiphonal singing of the two halves of a choir. Verses 10–11 record the high priestly line from Jeshua down to **Jaddua** (*c.* 330 BC), which presumably was the time when the Chronicler compiled this book. This is a continuation of the list of the high priests as recorded in 1 Chr. 6: 3–15. It would seem that the high priest **Jonathan**, the son of Joiada and the father of Jaddua, was alternatively called Johanan (22). As to the high priest **Joiada** the son of Eliashib, his brother was Jehohanan (Ezr. 10: 6). It is stated in 13: 28 that one of Joiada's sons (and a brother therefore of the high priest Jonathan) became married to a daughter of Sanballat.

Verses 12–21 give the names of the priests in the time of the high-priesthood of Jeshua's son **Joiakim**. Verse 22 states that a register of the heads of the priestly and Levitical families was preserved throughout the period from the

high-priesthood of **Eliashib** till that of Jaddua
in **the reign of Darius the Persian**, *viz.* Darius III (338–331 BC). Verses 23–24 mention
the Levites **up to the time of Johanan.** These
were recorded in the book of the annals,
which were certain official records. **24. as prescribed by David** whose instruction regarding
the rendering of praise to God in song is indicated in 1 Chr. 16: 4–6; 23: 30. Verses 25–26
name certain **gatekeepers** in two particular
periods, **the days of Joiakim** the high priest,
**and in the days of Nehemiah the governor
and of Ezra the priest.**

VIII. THE DEDICATION OF
JERUSALEM'S WALLS (12: 27–43)

There is described in vv. 27–43 **the dedication
of the wall of Jerusalem** (27) in which
thanksgiving was rendered to God for His
help in the rebuilding. For this ceremony the
Levites and the singers gathered from the surrounding towns into the city (27–29). The way
in which the priests and Levites **purified themselves** and **the people, the gates and the wall**
(30) may have been by the sprinkling upon
them of sacrificial blood. Nehemiah organized
two companies of princes, priests, Levites, musicians and singers to walk in procession around
the walls. Although the Valley Gate (cf. 2:
13), near the city's southwest corner, is not
specifically mentioned in this passage, it seems
clear that this was where the two processions
commenced. One of them was led by **Ezra**
(36), and these walked along the city's south
wall, past **the Dung Gate** (31), and then along
the east wall. The second procession was in the
charge of Nehemiah who walked at its rear
(38), and it proceeded along the west wall and
then the north wall. As they went they sang
praise to God with musical accompaniment.
The two companies reached finally the temple
area, **the house of God** (40), within the city's
northeast corner where **they offered great
sacrifices . . . and rejoiced** (43).

IX. ARRANGEMENTS FOR THE
SERVICE OF THE TEMPLE
(12: 44–47)

Verses 44–47 indicate how provision was made
for **the priests and the Levites** (44) and **the
singers and gatekeepers** (45), and it supplements, therefore, what is said about this in
10: 32–39.

X. NEHEMIAH'S SECOND PERIOD
OF ADMINISTRATION (13: 1–31)

When, in 445 BC, the twentieth year of the
reign of King Artaxerxes (2: 1; 5: 14), Nehemiah was appointed governor of Judea, it was
agreed that he should return to the king after a
certain period of time (2: 6). It was in fact only
after twelve years, in 433 BC, **the thirty-**

second year of Artaxerxes (6) that Nehemiah
returned to the king in **Babylon.** In due
course Nehemiah returned to Jerusalem to continue his work as governor of Judea. On resuming office he discovered to his anger that in
various respects the Jews in Jerusalem had become during his absence increasingly lax in
their moral and spiritual duties; and this chapter
recounts a number of instances of this.

The first of these instances related to the
tolerance which had been shown by a very
prominent Jew to a very prominent Ammonite. In a recent public reading of the law (as in
8: 1–8) attention had been paid to Dt. 23: 3–6
which decreed that because the Ammonites and
Moabites **had not met the Israelites with
food and water but hired Balaam to call a
curse down on them** (2), as is recounted in
Num. 22: 22–24, **no Ammonite or Moabite**
(1) should be given full rights of membership
in the Israelite community. And yet, during
Nehemiah's absence, no less a Jew than the
high priest **Eliashib** (an elderly man by now,
in view of Ezr. 10: 6), had given help to no less
an Ammonite than the enemy **Tobiah** (4), by
allowing him to store his household furniture
in one of 'the chambers of the house of the
LORD' (Ezr. 8: 29). This particular room in the
temple precincts was one which formerly had
been used for the storing of **the tithes of grain,
new wine and oil** for the temple officials; but
since tithing had been neglected of late it was
unoccupied, and hence available to be loaned
to Tobiah with whom Eliashib was somehow
closely associated (4). When Nehemiah
**learned about the evil thing Eliashib had
done** (7), he was **greatly displeased and
threw all Tobiah's household goods out of
the room** (8), and ordered that the room be
restored to its intended purpose (9).

The consequence of the practice of tithing
having been neglected of late, and the covenant
promises listed in 10: 35–39 been unfulfilled,
was that the temple officers were so poorly
maintained that, in order to secure a livelihood,
they were forced to abandon the sacred work
to which God had called them, and became
farmers (10). Nehemiah **rebuked the officials**
(11) about this matter, restored the temple officers to their sacred duties, reintroduced the
practice of tithing (12), and appointed four
reliable men to be **in charge of the storerooms** (13) who **were made responsible for
distributing the supplies to their brothers.**

Despite the Jews having covenanted in 10:
31 not to engage in commercial transaction on
the sabbath day they soon disregarded their
pledge. When Nehemiah had returned from
Babylon he saw **men in Judah treading wine
presses on the sabbath**, lading asses with various burdens and leading them into Jerusalem,
and also selling food (15). He saw them also

on the sabbath buying dried **fish and all kinds of merchandise** from certain men from the Phoenician port of **Tyre** who had a depot in Jerusalem. These practices should have been prevented by **the nobles of Judah** (17); so Nehemiah **rebuked** them. He ordered also that the main city gates should be kept closed from the evening when the sabbath began till the following evening (19), and as to certain smaller gates beside them which we have to assume remained open, Nehemiah appointed some of his servants to stand near them so as to ensure that no burden was brought into the city on the sabbath. There were certain merchants, however, who tried to break Nehemiah's blockade by setting up their stalls **outside Jerusalem** (20); but Nehemiah discovered them and threatened them with arrest; so they decided not to do this again. He replaced then his own servants as sabbath-day gatekeepers by **Levites** (22).

Despite the Jews having covenanted in 10: 30 not to contract matrimonial alliances with the heathen, this pledge, too, was soon disregarded by them, and Nehemiah discovered Jews who had married **women from Ashdod, Ammon and Moab** (23). As to those who had married women of Ashdod (on the coastal strip to the west, in the former Philistine territory), **half of their children spoke the language of Ashdod, or the language of one of the other peoples, and did not know how to speak the language of Judah.** Nehemiah spoke and acted towards them with considerable violence, and it is to be assumed (though it is not actually stated) that he ordered the offenders to divorce their foreign wives. The most flagrant instance of a mixed marriage was that between **one of the sons of Joiada son of Eliashib the high priest** (28) and a daughter of Sanballat. It appears that this man refused to obey Nehemiah's order to him to dismiss his wife; so Nehemiah **drove him** from his presence.

The final two verses of the book (30–31) describe some of the positive measures Nehemiah took by way of rightly establishing the service of God's house.

BIBLIOGRAPHY (EZRA AND NEHEMIAH)

Commentaries

ACKROYD, P. R., *I & II Chronicles, Ezra, Nehemiah. TC* (London, 1973).

BATTEN, L. W., *Ezra and Nehemiah. ICC* (Edinburgh, 1913).

COGGINS, R. J., *The Books of Ezra and Nehemiah. CBC* (Cambridge, 1976).

CLINES, D. J. A., *Ezra, Nehemiah and Esther. NCentB* (Basingstoke, 1985).

MYERS, J. M., *Ezra-Nehemiah. AB* (Garden City, N.Y., 1965).

Other Works

ACKROYD, P. R., *Exile and Restoration* (London, 1968).

ACKROYD, P. R., *The Age of the Chronicler*, Supplement to *Colloquium* (Auckland/Sydney, 1970).

ACKROYD, P. R., *Israel under Babylon and Persia. NCB* (Oxford, 1970).

BROWNE, L. E., *Early Judaism* (Cambridge, 1920).

COGGINS, R. J., *Samaritans and Jews* (Oxford, 1975).

COOK, J. M., *The Persian Empire* (London, 1983).

OLMSTEAD, A. T., *History of the Persian Empire* (Chicago, 1948).

ROWLEY, H. H., 'The Chronological Order of Ezra and Nehemiah', in *The Servant of the Lord and Other Essays on the OT* (Oxford, ²1965), pp.135–168.

ROWLEY, H. H., 'Nehemiah's Mission and its Background', in *Men of God* (London, 1963), pp.211–245.

ROWLEY, H. H., 'Sanballat and the Samaritan Temple', in *Men of God*, pp.246–276.

WRIGHT, J. S., *The Date of Ezra's Coming to Jerusalem* (London, ²1958).

WRIGHT, J. S., *The Building of the Second Temple* (London, 1958).

ESTHER

JOHN BENDOR-SAMUEL

CANONICITY

Esther is one of the five *Megilloth*, 'rolls' (cf. the books of the Law and the five books of Psalms). The five *megilloth* were associated with the Hebrew festivals as follows:

Song of Solomon—Passover (celebrating the Exodus)

Ruth—Feast of weeks (grain harvest and the giving of the law at Sinai)

Lamentations—Ninth of Ab (Fall of Jerusalem 587 B.C.)

Ecclesiastes—Feast of Tabernacles (grape harvest)

Esther—Purim (national deliverance).

The place and value of Esther have been debated vigorously by Jews and Christians. It appears to have been accepted at the Council of Jamnia in A.D. 90 when the Jewish canonization process was completed, though judging by two passages in the Talmud a few rabbis continued to have reservations, perhaps for theological reasons—the absence of the name of God, or Esther's marriage to a non-Jew, or because they rejected Purim as a pagan festival. It may also be significant that Esther is the only book of the Old Testament not found at Qumran.

In spite of these early doubts, Esther became one of the most popular books among Jews, with many commentaries (midrash) written on it. It is the only book outside the Pentateuch to have two Targums (Aramaic translations with expansions). There are more extant medieval manuscripts of Esther than any other Old Testament book, possibly because it was prescribed reading at Purim. Its popularity among a people who have experienced so much persecution over the centuries is hardly surprising for it is a record of deliverance from threatened extinction. It encourages the reader to expect a similar deliverance in his day and how often that encouragement has been needed.

Among Christians, Esther has been accepted as canonical very widely in the West and is almost always included in lists of canonical books which survive from the fourth century onwards. In the East, however, it was not universally accepted for some centuries. Athanasius (A.D. 367) gives it deuterocanonical status. It may be significant that the Western Church knew Esther through the Latin translations of the Septuagint which include additions to the text which mention God. From the seventh century, there seems to have been general acceptance throughout the church, though there continued to be those, like Luther, who questioned its value.

RELIGIOUS VALUE

The early doubts about its canonicity on the part of both Jews and Christians arise not from any question of the book's historicity but rather from the fact that it appears to be a wholly secular story with little religious or spiritual value. Whereas the king of Persia is mentioned 190 times in its 167 verses, the name of God does not occur once from start to finish. Nor are the Law and the Covenant mentioned at all. There is very little religious activity in the book, only fasting. Many Jews evidently found this absence of the name of God unacceptable and various additions were made at different points in the text, including prayers attributed to Mordecai and to Esther, a dream Mordecai had and its subsequent interpretation. These additions attempt to add to the religious value of the book by bringing God directly into the story.

There has been much speculation concerning the absence of God's name and of other distinctly religious elements. Some have suggested that since Esther was read aloud at Purim, a rather boisterous festival characterized by much drinking, it was thought inappropriate to mention God by name. More convincingly, others have suggested that this absence is due to the fact that the story was written in Persia soon after the events it describes and the author did not want to antagonize the Persians who worshipped Ahuramazda by mentioning Yahweh.

In many ways this doubt about the religious value of Esther is superficial since, even if God is not mentioned by name, the book displays a profound faith in Providence. The hand of God in history is there even if the name of God is not found. In 4: 14, when Mordecai asserts that if Esther is silent, 'relief and deliverance for the Jews will rise from another quarter', he is clearly referring to God. He goes on to suggest that Esther has become queen for just such an occasion as this—which clearly implies God's providential timing.

The whole sequence of events in chapter 6

points in the same way to God's hand. That crucial night it so 'happens' that the king cannot sleep, he 'happens' to call for the records, and of all the records, it 'happens' to be the account of Mordecai's action which saved his life that is read and then Haman 'happens' to be in court early. All these may be dismissed as coincidences by some but can only be regarded as God's providential ordering by the writer and most of his readers. There is no need to point out the obvious. Throughout the book the writer tells his story without explanations and embellishments. It is a fast moving tale with no time for any moralising.

While it is true that there are no direct references to religious observances in the book, it should be noted that in calling for a fast before she goes to the king, Esther is explicitly putting her case into the hand of God. Such a fast to be kept not only by her and her immediate companions and family, but also by all the Jews in Susa, would clearly include prayer to God. Mordecai is to call them together as an act of public recognition of their dependence upon God.

There is a basic trust in God underlying the whole book and the main characters are shown both to be dependent upon God and consciously to recognize their dependence upon Him. This is enough to give the book deep religious value. A book does not have to be full of references to God and of religious observances to have religious significance. The most moral stories need no moralizing. The various additions, though doubtless well motivated to increase the religious value of the book, add nothing.

HISTORICITY
Identification of the principal characters
One of the main problems in assessing the historicity of Esther lies in the identification of its principal characters—Ahasuerus, Vashti, Esther and Mordecai.

Ahasuerus has been identified in the past with Xerxes (486–465), Artaxerxes I (465–424) and Artaxerxes II (404–358), but there is little doubt that he should be identified with Xerxes. Note the following linguistic evidence:

Persian	Hebrew	Greek	English
khshayarsha	'ahashwerosh	xerxes	ahasuerus
artakhshathra	'artahshasta	artaxerxes	artaxerxes

What we know of Xerxes elsewhere is consonant with the picture we have of him in Esther.

Vashti is queen till 484 or 483 and Esther becomes queen in 480 or 479 and is still queen when the book ends. Neither name is found in secular records where, in the Greek of Herodotus and Ctesias, the queen's name is Amestris. Esther cannot be Amestris because Artaxerxes, who was the third son of Xerxes

and Amestris, was born in 483. So Vashti must be Amestris.

Amestris is known to have accompanied Xerxes on the Greek campaign and she later mutilated the mother of Xerxes' mistress. Stafford Wright speculates that Xerxes' original anger cooled down but was revived by this later incident which made the king decide finally to be rid of Amestris, using the previous incident as an excuse. This would explain the wording of Est. 2: 1 and the long four-year gap between the events of chapter 1 and the choosing of a new queen in chapter 2.

There is no further mention of Amestris in Xerxes' reign and she bore no more children after the date when Esther became queen. Almost nothing is known of the period between 479 and 465, the year when Xerxes was assassinated. Herodotus ends his account in 479 and Ctesias devotes but ten lines to the period between 480 and 465. Esther may well have died in this period without having any child. When Artaxerxes came to the throne, his mother reappears, and as queen mother (cf. Neh. 2: 6) regains power till her death in 424. Ctesias records her pressure on Artaxerxes for the beheading of 50 prisoners. This does not, however, prove or disprove that she was queen throughout Xerxes' reign. All that is recorded of Amestris in Herodotus and Ctesias accords with the character of the strong-willed Vashti.

These speculations prove little but do show that there is nothing in the secular records which cannot be harmonized with the Biblical record. The queen known to us in secular history is not Esther, but Vashti, and what little we know of the queen and her life is not at variance with the facts about both of Xerxes' queens contained in Esther. Nor is the linguistic problem insurmountable. Although at first sight the two names Amestris and Vashti (Washti in Hebrew) appear to have little in common, a study of the transliteration of names between languages shows they may be the same name. Since Greek has no *w* or *sh*, Herodotus could have substituted *m* and *s*, and then added a short *a* before the *m*. The *r* could have been in the Persian but lost in the Hebrew which has no -*tr*- sequence. We conclude then that Vashti is Amestris and that Esther does not occur in the very scanty secular records that have survived from this period.

Mordecai. There is no clear mention of him outside Scripture though in a list of three influential men in the early part of Xerxes' reign, Ctesias refers to 'Matakos' as the 'most influential of the eunuchs'. There is also mention of a Marduka, an accountant who was a member of an inspection tour from Susa, probably in the early years of Xerxes' reign. In Ezr. 2: 2 (cf. Neh. 7: 7) a Mordecai is listed as one who accompanied Zerubbabel on his return to

Jerusalem. Could it be the same man? Hardly, because Zerubbabel's return to Jerusalem was forty or fifty years before the events recorded in Esther.

Was Mordecai a eunuch? This would explain his access to the women's quarters. He appears to have been influential, or Esther would not have been one of those selected as a candidate for queen. Mordecai moves about freely in the palace area, a fact which his discovery of the eunuch's plot against Xerxes corroborates. It has been suggested that he had been in a high position at court but was temporarily in disfavour. This would explain both how he came to learn of the plot and why he was not rewarded immediately for his disclosure of the plot. Usually Persian kings gave immediate and lavish rewards for such loyalty. There are many such questions for which we have no evidence and no answer. This should at the very least make us very cautious in rejecting any part of the biblical record.

Neither Mordecai nor Esther is included in the list of famous people in the 'Praise of the Fathers' in Sir. 44–49—a fact which some adduce as evidence against their historicity. But this list is not exhaustive. Ezra does not occur either. Perhaps Ben Sira did not approve of Esther marrying a pagan king or thought Purim too worldly a festival.

Knowledge of Persian customs

There are many indications in the book that the author has an intimate knowledge of Persian life and times. Note the following:

1: 1. The extent of Xerxes' empire—it did stretch from India to Ethiopia. It has been objected that there were not 127 satrapies. This word is also used in 8: 9 and in Ezr. 5: 8 and Neh. 1: 3. Satrapies comprised several provinces, *e.g.*, the first satrapy comprised Mysia, Lydia, and part of Phrygia. Judah was part of the fourth satrapy. These 127 provinces may well have corresponded to the ethnic groups of the empire, whereas the 20 satrapies of Herodotus iii. 89 were larger groupings used for government and taxation purposes.

1: 3. The banquet in the third year corresponds to the great council called to plan the invasion of Greece.

1: 5–8. The arrangements for the banquet and the description of the fittings and layout of the palace conform to what is known of Artaxerxes' palace at Susa which was a restoration of the palace of Darius and Xerxes.

1: 14. The seven princes who formed the Council of State (cf. Ezr. 7: 14).

2: 16. The unexplained gap of four years between the banquet and Esther's accession corresponds to the period of the Greek campaign.

3: 2. Obeisance before the king and his favourite.

3: 7. Belief in lucky and unlucky days.

3: 13 and 8: 10. The courier post system.

4: 2. The exclusion of mourning from the palace.

5: 14. Hanging as the death penalty.

6: 8 f. Honouring a man by dressing him in royal robes. Horses wearing a crown.

Some general problems

Those who reject the historicity of the book often adduce the following as very improbable:

1: 1–3. The length of the feast—180 days, followed by a seven-day banquet. It seems legitimate, however, to understand that the council at which the king showed his leaders his glory and power lasted for 180 days and then ended with a seven-day banquet. Herodotus (viii. 8 ff.) refers to a special council of state which was held at Susa after the subjugation of Egypt to plan the invasion of Greece.

1: 12. Vashti's refusal to obey the king. Why should she refuse?

1: 19. The statement that the law of the Medes and Persians is unalterable is not corroborated outside the Bible. It is similar to Dan. 6: 9, 13, but is attested nowhere else.

1: 22, 3: 12, 8: 9. The despatch of letters in all the languages of the empire, instead of in Aramaic, the official language of the Persian empire, is not found outside the Bible.

2: 5. Mordecai could hardly have been carried away with Jeconiah in 597, and become prime minister in 474, 122 years later. The relative pronoun 'who' (at the beginning of 2: 6) could refer to Kish, the name immediately preceding it.

2: 17 The choice of Esther violates Herodotus' assertion (iii. 84) that the king had to choose his queen from one of seven noble families. But other well attested facts seem to contradict Herodotus on this point. Darius, for example, had other wives who were not from the seven noble families, including Xerxes' own mother. It is evident, then, that this limitation on the choice of a wife was not strictly observed.

3: 1. The appointment of a non-Persian to the very important position of prime minister (or grand vizier).

3: 12–13. For the king to give permission almost a year in advance for an entire people within his empire to be wiped out seems unlikely, and for him to allow the sort of fighting that is described in chapter 9 seems equally improbable.

5: 14. The enormous height of the gallows—50 cubits (over 75 feet)—seems unlikely, particularly when its construction took place in a hurry. But it is not impossible to conceive of many quite plausible explanations—a tree, or an existing building, or some high ground may have been used to ensure such a drop. In any case, the figure is not given as the precise height of the gallows. Haman's wife and friends suggest such a gallows be built and the king's eunuch refers to the gallows in 7: 9 in similar terms. The figure 50 may be used as a round number to convey the fact that the gallows was very tall.

Legendary character

None of these problems seems sufficiently serious to raise real doubts about the historicity of the book. They are, however, taken in conjunction with two more general objections by some scholars. The first such general objection is that certain elements in the story, especially the Vashti incident and the whole process of selecting a new queen, bear a striking resemblance to some legendary stories of the Ancient Middle East and especially to *A Thousand and One Nights*. Whatever the historical basis of *A Thousand and One Nights* may or may not be, there are historical parallels for such a search and selection elsewhere. This seems a very subjective basis for rejecting Esther.

Purim

The second general objection concerns the origin and nature of the feast of Purim. Some have rejected the historicity of Esther on the grounds that the book was written to justify the observance of Purim, a festival which many regard as originally a completely pagan feast. The secular character of Purim and the fact that it is 'not mentioned explicitly in any extant literature outside the Bible till the second century A.D. have been adduced to discredit its genuine institution as a Jewish feast at the time of Xerxes.

All sorts of theories have been advanced to account for its origin. Some have identified Purim with an earlier Jewish or Greek festival while others have picked a Babylonian origin. At least four different Babylonian festivals have been suggested at one time or another. Perhaps the most widely accepted theory today is that Purim is derived from the Persian New Year festival. But the evidence is very sparse and nothing can be said to be even remotely proved. Even the word *purim* is the subject of much speculation as the root *pur* is traceable in several languages. It seems fair to conclude that the surviving records of this period give us no real indication of the origin of Purim and that scholarly speculation to date is totally unconvincing.

It is true that Purim does have many secular characteristics, though it should not be forgotten that it is preceded by a fast and the whole book of Esther is read through in the presence of the whole household. Still, there are no special prayers or sacrifices and the Talmud permits drinking to excess. It is an occasion for much merry-making and the exchange of gifts. It may be noted, however, that the Christian festival of Christmas can be said to have similar pagan elements. The way a festival is celebrated does not necessarily discredit its religious origin or necessitate the rejection of the historical event it is said to commemorate.

As for the lack of reference to it, 2 Mac. 15: 36 refers to it implicitly when it states that the victory of Judas Maccabaeus on the 13th Adar 161 B.C. was on 'the day before Mordecai's day'. It is not referred to in Ezra and Nehemiah but they do not mention all the festivals of the law. Josephus does refer to it as *phrouraios* around the end of the first century. Where else could it be mentioned? So little has survived from these centuries that silence means little.

None of these objections seems substantial enough for us to reject the historicity of Esther. Some may assert that the evidence in favour of its historicity is not conclusive either. This may be conceded, but those who accept the general historicity of Scripture need have no hesitation in accepting Esther. To a very considerable extent the reader's presuppositions about Scripture will determine whether or not he accepts the historicity of the book. Such acceptance is not credulity. When the historical evidence is inconclusive, acceptance and rejection alike may be determined by theological convictions.

DATE AND AUTHOR

The type of Hebrew used in Esther is very different from the Hebrew of the second century B.C. which has been recovered from Qumran. This has compelled scholars to abandon the previously popular hypothesis of a late date for Esther. Increasingly a 4th or 5th century date is being accepted. Another piece of linguistic evidence supporting an early date is the absence of any Hellenisms such as are frequently found in 3rd and 2nd century B.C. writings.

The book makes no comment about authorship. The linguistic evidence and the detailed knowledge of Persian life that the book displays makes it likely that the author was a Jew living in Persia at a time not long after the events recounted in the book. The author may well have incorporated material originally written by Mordecai himself (cf. 9: 10).

ANALYSIS

I THE SCENE IS SET (1: 1–2: 23)
  i Queen Vashti is deposed (1: 1–22)
    (a) The banquet (1: 1–9)
    (b) Queen Vashti refuses the king's command (1: 10–12)
    (c) The king decides to depose Vashti (1: 13–22)
  ii Esther is chosen queen (2: 1–18)
    (a) The decision is made to find a new queen (2: 1–4)
    (b) Mordecai and Esther are introduced (2: 5–7)
    (c) Esther joins the candidates for queen (2: 8–11)
    (d) The procedure for the candidates (2: 12–14)
    (e) Esther is chosen queen (2: 15–18)
  iii Mordecai saves the king's life (2: 19–23)

II HAMAN'S PLOT IS REVEALED AND FOILED (3: 1–7: 10)
  i Haman plots to destroy the Jews (3: 1–15)
    (a) Mordecai defies Haman (3: 1–6)
    (b) Haman secures the king's consent (3: 7–15)
  ii Esther agrees to intercede (4: 1–17)
    (a) Mordecai mourns (4: 1–3)
    (b) Mordecai persuades Esther to intercede (4: 4–17)
  iii Esther goes to the king (5: 1–8)
  iv Haman decides to hang Mordecai (5: 9–14)
  v The king honours Mordecai (6: 1–13)
  vi The fall of Haman (6: 14–7: 10)

III THE JEWS TRIUMPH (8: 1–9: 32)
  i The Jews are permitted to defend themselves (8: 1–17)
    (a) Mordecai is promoted (8: 1–2)
    (b) Esther intercedes for her people (8: 3–8)
    (c) A new decree is written and despatched (8: 9–14)
    (d) The Jews rejoice (8: 15–17)
  ii The Jews triumph over their enemies (9: 1–15)
    (a) The Jews destroy their enemies (9: 1–10)
    (b) An extension at Susa (9: 11–15)
  iii The feast of Purim is instituted (9: 16–32)
    (a) A summary of the events of 13th and 14th Adar (9: 16–19)
    (b) Mordecai orders the celebration of Purim (9: 20–28)
    (c) Esther also orders its celebration (9: 29–32)

IV CONCLUSION (10: 1–3)

I. THE SCENE IS SET (1: 1–2: 23)
i. Queen Vashti is deposed (1: 1–22)
The historical setting is given: the time—the reign of Xerxes, and place—the palace of Susa. Against the background of his colourful and lavish palace, Xerxes' arbitrariness, hasty temper and precipitate actions stand out.
(a) The banquet (1: 1–9)
1. This is what happened, NIV translates the first word in Hebrew text, *wyhy* which usually links a book to a preceding historical account, and is the first word in Joshua, Judges, Ruth, 1 and 2 Samuel and also in Ezekiel and Jonah.

Xerxes, mg Ahasuerus (Persian Khshayârsha) means 'royal hero'. The author knew of more than one person with this name so he establishes which one is meant. See Introduction regarding the identity of Ahasuerus as Xerxes I (486–465 BC). **India to Cush:** a foundation tablet from Xerxes' palace at Persepolis lists the countries of Xerxes' empire. India and Cush (Ethiopia) are included. Herodotus also mentions that Ethiopians and Indians paid tribute to Xerxes and fought in his army. **one hundred and twenty-seven provinces:** *medînôt* are provinces, not satrapies, which are a larger unit

comprising several provinces; see Introduction.
2. At that time resumes the narrative which
had been interrupted by the identification of
Xerxes. **reigned from his royal throne**
stresses his royal authority. Some have interpreted this verse to mean that Xerxes was now
securely king, i.e. after he had successfully put
down the rebellions in Egypt and Babylon
which marked his ascent to the throne. **the
citadel of Susa** or 'the acropolis of Susa'. Susa
lies 200 miles north-east of Babylon and was
the ancient capital of Elam. Susa was one of
four Persian capitals, the others being Babylon,
Ecbatana and Persepolis. Heb. *bîrāh* means a
palace or fortress and refers not to the whole
capital but to the royal part of the capital.

3. banquet: see Introduction. The purpose
of this assembling of the great is not given
but may well have been to plan the campaign
against Greece. This would also explain
Xerxes' need to display his riches and power
so as to give his guests confidence in his ability
to defeat the Greeks. **military leaders:** Heb.
'army'. The Hebrew is uncertain since *ḥyl*
('army') is unrelated syntactically to the rest of
the clause. It is unlikely to mean the whole
army of 14,000 men, but probably the leaders
of the army. The LXX has a phrase which may
reflect an original Hebrew *wsry* 'and officers'.
**5. all the people . . . who were in the citadel
of Susa** refers not to all the residents of the
town, but to all who had come to the acropolis
for the council. **the enclosed garden:** *bîtan*
(Persian *apadana*) is a summer house—probably
an open colonnaded hall. **6. white and blue**
were the royal colours of Persia. The whole
description conveys something of the luxury
of the court. **7. wine:** drinking was the main
feature of Persian banquets. In the court there
was a great variety of very fine wine goblets
of which the Persians were understandably
proud. **8. each guest was allowed to drink
in his own way:** The normal custom was that
whenever the king drank, everyone drank. The
Persian court was noted for excessive drinking,
but the verse goes on to state that on this
occasion no one was compelled to drink. **9.
Vashti:** see Introduction regarding her identity. **banquet for the women:** Persian custom
did not make it necessary for men and women
to dine separately. Women were often present
at meals but Vashti chose to have her own
separate party for the women.

(*b*) **Queen Vashti refuses the king's command (1: 10–12)**
10. in high spirits: lit. 'the heart was good'.
The king was not drunk but he had drunk too
much to be completely sober. **Mehuman . . .
Carcas:** while none of these names has been
identified outside the Bible, they appear to be
Persian. A Carcas does occur in one of the
Persepolis treasury tablets. **seven eunuchs:** eu-

nuchs played a key role at court, not only in
supervising the harem but also in administration. **11. wearing her royal crown:** lit.
'with the turban of the kingdom' made of blue
and white cloth, the turban probably contained
a tiara. **her beauty:** Jewish commentators list
Vashti as one of the four most beautiful women
in history. **12. Queen Vashti refused:** no
reason is given but many have been suggested.
Since Josephus states that strangers were not
allowed to look at the beauty of Persian wives,
some have suggested that perhaps it was her
modesty that made her refuse to appear before
a group of men who had drunk more than was
good for them. Since the banquet probably
took place just before the birth of Artaxerxes,
some have suggested her pregnant condition
made her refuse. The king's request did not
violate Persian customs, however, and it was
expressed as a formal command conveyed by
the eunuchs, so Vashti's refusal was a flagrant
defiance of the king. **the king became furious:** a characteristic of Xerxes was his sudden
anger; cf. 7: 7. Note the parallelism (furious
. . . burned with anger) which is a common
feature of the book.

(*c*) **The king decides to depose Vashti
(1: 13–22)**
14. Carshena . . . Memucan: these names too
are unidentified elsewhere, but are probably
Persian names. **seven nobles** are mentioned in
Herodotus as principal advisors to the king.
Note the number seven again, a number of
special significance to the Persians. **had special
access to the king:** (cf. Herodotus iii. 84).
This was unusual because the Persian king was
usually inaccessible to his people. **were highest:** i.e. chief ranking officials of the kingdom.
16. not only against the king: Memucan
astutely plays down the king's personal anger
by suggesting this matter affects all his subjects.
19. Laws of Persia and Media: note the order,
in contrast to Dan. 6: 8, etc., reflecting the
greater prominence of the Persians at this
period. **cannot be repealed:** see Introduction.
The counsellors were anxious that the king's
decision be irrevocable since if Vashti regained
power they would be in great danger. **22. in its
own script . . . own language:** a considerable
number of languages and scripts existed in the
vast Persian empire. Decrees of Xerxes written
in Persian, Elamite and Babylonian as well as
in Aramaic have survived.

ii. Esther is chosen Queen (2: 1–18)
Mordecai and Esther are introduced and the
procedure for choosing the new queen is described. Esther wins the favour of the king and
is chosen queen.

(*a*) **The decision is made to find a new queen
(2: 1–4)**
1. Later: an indeterminate time, but it must
have been either within two years, i.e. before

Xerxes departed for the Greek campaign, or
else after four years, i.e. after the campaign.
anger subsided: it seems that Xerxes was beginning to relent regarding Vashti. **2.** Pages
address the king directly, but in the third person. Court etiquette demanded this. Only Haman in 3: 8 and Esther in 7: 3 presume to
address the king in the second person. The
king's attendants suggest new virgins to divert
the king and so save themselves from Vashti's
wrath.

**(b) Mordecai and Esther are introduced
(2: 5–7)**
5. Mordecai: derived from Marduk, the Babylonian god. That he should have had a heathen,
indeed an idolatrous, name is not surprising
since many Jews had a Hebrew and a Babylonian name; cf. Daniel and his friends. See
Introduction, on the identity of Mordecai. **6.
who had been carried into exile:** there is a
problem as to the antecedent of the relative
pronoun **who**—whether Kish or Mordecai, or
just the ancestors in general; cf. Gen. 46: 27,
where Joseph's sons were said to have come to
Egypt with Jacob. It can hardly be Mordecai
or else he would be about 119 when Esther
became queen; and Esther would at least have
been in her sixties. More probably **who** is
referring to his family. **7. Hadassah** in Hebrew
means 'myrtle'. **Esther** is possibly derived
from Ishtar, the Babylonian goddess of love;
others relate it to Persian *stāra*, 'star'.

**(c) Esther joins the candidates for queen
(2: 8–11)**
9. won his favour: Esther wins favour, i.e.
her conduct is good. It is not just that she has
good looks. She did not 'find favour', she 'won'
it by her character. **immediately:** Hegai gave
her preference over others and soon started
her on the 12 month beautification treatment.
seven maids selected: it seems these seven
were specially for her—another mark of
Hegai's favour. **10. Mordecai** in the Hebrew
text is in the emphatic position in its clause.
not revealed her nationality: Esther must
have eaten, dressed and lived like a Persian,
thus breaking Jewish dietary laws and other
customs. Presumably this was because Mordecai felt her Jewish descent would lessen her
chances of becoming queen. Some have criticized her as being 'worldy-wise', but this seems
a harsh judgment in the light of the circumstances that prevailed at the time.

**(d) The procedure for the candidates
(2: 12–14)**
13. Anything: emphatic, so stressing she got
everything she wanted, clothes or jewellery. It
is not known if she had to return it next morning or could keep it. **14. another part of the
harem:** probably refers to a different part of
the harem where the concubines were kept.

(e) Esther is chosen queen (2: 15–18)

15. Esther donned no special ornaments to
please the king. She was wise and cooperative
in accepting Hegai's advice (in contrast to the
headstrong Vashti). **16. royal residence:** better, 'king's apartment'—vv. 13 and 16. **seventh year:** i.e. four years after the Vashti incident, partly because Xerxes was away for two
years in Greece. **18. proclaimed a holiday:**
hanāḥāh means a causing to rest and could refer
to a remission of taxes, or of labour—hence a
holiday or an amnesty.

iii. Mordecai saves the king's life (2: 19–23)
Mordecai learns of a plot to assassinate Xerxes.
His disclosure of the plot saves the king. **19.
second time:** obscure. It could be a second
contingent for the queen contests or else a
retrogression in the story to the time before
Esther became queen. **21. guarded the doorway:** probably the king's private apartment.
at the king's gate: officials waited at the king's
gate and did not enter the palace until summoned. **21. conspired to assassinate King
Xerxes:** such palace plots were very common.
Xerxes was assassinated in such a court intrigue
some fourteen years later. **23. in the presence
of the king:** lit. 'before the king'. This may
be taken to mean either that the archives were
kept in the king's apartment, or that the writing
was done in his presence and at his direction.
Parallels to this official record of services rendered to the Persian king are found in Herodotus viii. 85 and Thucydides i. 129.

**II. HAMAN'S PLOT IS REVEALED
AND FOILED (3: 1–7: 10)**
**i. Haman plots to destroy the Jews (3: 1–
15)**
With the scene now set, the plot against the
Jews is described. Haman rises to power but
Mordecai defies him. In revenge, Haman extends his personal vendetta against Mordecai
to the whole Jewish people and secures the
king's consent to the destruction of the Jews.
(a) Mordecai defies Haman (3: 1–6)
1. after these events: gives no indication of
how long after. Esther was made queen in
479 and Haman's plot was in 474. There was
probably not a long gap between Haman's
promotion and Mordecai's subsequent defiance
leading to Haman's plot, so that Haman's promotion may well have been in 475. **Haman
son of Hammedatha:** nothing is known of
these names. Haman was a descendant of Agag,
the king of the Amalekites. The Amalekites
and Israelites were implacable enemies; cf. Dt.
25: 17–19. **higher than all the other nobles:**
Haman became prime minister. **2. knelt
down:** obeisance before high-ranking officials
was normal at court so that the king's order is
not surprising. Why did Mordecai refuse to
bow? Jews elsewhere bowed to rulers, *e.g.*
David to Saul, 1 Sam. 24: 8, cf. 2 Sam. 14: 4;

1 Kg. 1: 16; Abraham to the Hittites, Gen. 23: 7; Jacob to Esau, Gen. 33: 3. Presumably later, when Mordecai was prime minister, he had to bow before Xerxes. Probably he refused because Haman was an Agagite, and therefore an enemy. His conduct could be regarded as determined by nationalistic pride rather than by any religious conviction. There is nothing to indicate whether Mordecai was right or wrong in his attitude. That his attitude was also puzzling to later Jews may perhaps be deduced from the fact that it was thought necessary to justify Mordecai's refusal in the additions to the book.

3. The officials were concerned that Mordecai was disobeying the king. Perhaps they were treating this as a test case to see if Jews were exempt? Or did they disapprove of foreigners who disobeyed the king? **5. was enraged:** whatever the reason for Mordecai's defiance, Haman's violent reaction is inexcusable. **6. destroy:** meaning 'wipe out' occurs 25 times in ten chapters. **all the Jews:** Haman extends his hatred from one individual to the whole people.

(b) **Haman secures the king's consent (3: 7–15)**
7. they cast the pur: the subject of the verb is not specified, being third person singular. Probably an astrologer or magician cast **the lot** for Haman to find the propitious day for the extermination of the Jews. It is unlikely that the lot was cast each day for eleven months, but that the day was picked at one sitting. **in the first month:** the timing of the casting of lots may have been deliberate since according to the Babylonian religion, the gods met at the beginning of the year to decide men's fate. **Nisan:** the Babylonian equivalent of the Jews' Abib., i.e. March–April. **Adar:** February–March, eleven months later.

8. a certain people: Haman does not name them nor does he tell the king of his personal vendetta. It is in the best interests of the empire to get rid of this people. Haman makes three accusations against the Jews: (i) **dispersed and scattered:** these are not just synonyms. The first participle refers to their geographical dispersion through the empire, and the second to their separateness—unassimilated would be a good translation. (ii) **whose customs are different:** this was not unusual in the Persian empire which contained and was tolerant towards many minority groups. (iii) **who do not obey the king's laws:** this was the damning and untrue accusation. **9. ten thousand talents:** to the best interests of the empire, Haman adds a very substantial financial inducement to help sway the king; 10,000 talents was a very large sum indeed. Some idea of the size of such a sum can best be gained by comparing it to other amounts mentioned in Herodotus; *e.g.* the annual total revenue of the Persian

empire was 14,560 talents (Herodotus iii. 95). Strabo states that Alexander the Great's booty at Susa was 49,000 talents. This shows that either Haman was very wealthy or, more likely, that he expected a great deal of plunder from the destruction of the Jews. After the very expensive Greek campaign, this very attractive offer outweighed any hesitation the king may have had to the destruction of a large number of his subjects.

10. his signet ring: used for sealing the official documents of the king and so gave Haman complete authority to phrase the decree. **11. "Keep the money":** perhaps better translated 'Well, it's your money'. It is unlikely that the king refused the money. Rather it looks as if this was an Eastern bargain, cf. Abraham and Ephron (Gen. 23: 7–18). Mordecai in 4: 7 asserts that Haman will pay. Esther uses the word 'sold' in 7: 4.

12. orders: the decision was put into a legal decree and despatched throughout the empire. **secretaries** were stenographers, not the professional scribes. **13. couriers:** lit. runners, but they used a well developed system of horses stationed at appropriate intervals as mentioned in 8: 10, 14. This system enabled messages to be sent great distances very rapidly. **destroy, kill and annihilate all the Jews—young and old, women and children:** note the legal inclusiveness of all the categories. Such destruction was not unparalleled either in ancient times; cf. the Persian massacres of the Scythians, or in modern times, Hitler's slaughter of six million Jews. **15. spurred on:** why Haman should send the edict out in such haste eleven months before the slaughter remains a mystery. Perhaps he did not want to risk the king changing his mind and when he first began negotiations with the king he had not anticipated the lot falling so late in the year. **sat down to drink . . . bewildered:** drinking after concluding business appears to have been a Persian custom. Here it provides a most dramatic contrast. While kings and princes celebrate, ordinary citizens are in consternation.

ii. Esther agrees to intercede (4: 1–17)
When Mordecai hears of the decree, he enlists Esther's somewhat reluctant help. The queen, even after five years, is still very uncertain of her standing with the king and feels any approach to him is fraught with danger. She appears however, to accept Mordecai's suggestion that it is providential that she is queen at such a time and agrees to intercede on condition that the whole Jewish community first fasts on her behalf.

(a) **Mordecai mourns (4: 1–3)**
1. When Mordecai learnt of all: how did Mordecai learn all the details of the transaction including the sum promised, not just the published decrees? Presumably through friends at

court. **sackcloth and ashes:** tearing one's clothes and putting on sackcloth and ashes were the normal expressions of mourning. Such mourning could be deeply religious, as in Dan. 9: 3 and Neh. 1: 4. **2. no one . . . was allowed to enter:** apparently the wearing of sackcloth made a person ceremonially unclean, and therefore unable to enter the court. **3. great mourning:** the general mourning described here must have been for most Jews a religious act which would have been accompanied by prayer. That prayer or God is not mentioned here is certainly deliberate on the part of the author who consistently omits any reference to any religious act or idea.

(b) Mordecai persuades Esther to intercede (4: 4-17)

4. he would not accept them: Mordecai refused to stop his mourning. Why? Possibly Mordecai wanted to show that his grief was not merely over a personal matter but was of much greater significance in an unprecedented calamity. **6. the open square:** a traditional place for mourning. **7. the exact amount:** mentioning the amount indicated the seriousness of the crisis. Xerxes' personal greed added a new and frightening dimension to Haman's private vendetta.

10. to say: the author switches to direct speech for the rest of the exchange between Esther and Mordecai, thus heightening the dramatic effect. **11. one law:** apparently Deioces the first king of the Medes instituted this law which the Persians retained (cf. Herodotus i. 96–101). This law admitted of no exception. **thirty days have passed:** she fears she no longer enjoys the king's highest favour. Why did she not ask for an audience since the massacre was eleven months away? Perhaps she feared the request would be refused. **13. Do not think:** not necessarily a threat to Esther, but rather a factual reminder of the common danger all Jews faced. **14. from another place:** an allusion to God. See introduction for a fuller discussion. **will perish:** Mordecai is probably thinking of divine punishment if Esther disobeys God, not of some revenge of the Jews. **for such a time as this:** Mordecai clearly infers her accession to the throne was providential.

16. fast for me: Esther accepts the mission and now takes the initiative. In commanding a fast, Esther is seeking divine help. She is asking the Jewish community to intercede with God on her behalf. **night or day:** this was to be a very strict fast, observed through the night as well as the day. The fast lasted 40–44 hours—as Esther went to the king on the third day. Some idea of the seriousness with which Esther approached her task can be seen from the fact that she called for a fast right at the time of the feast of Passover—15 Nisan. **if I perish, I perish:** Esther still has natural fears but she is

willing to go all the same. As Moore so well adds, 'the rash man acts without fear, the brave man in spite of it'. **17. went away:** lit. 'he crossed'. Probably refers to the Ab-kharkha river which separated the acropolis from the rest of the town.

iii. Esther goes to the king (5: 1-8)

After her fast Esther decks herself out and goes to the king. When the king sees Esther standing in the court he welcomes her and asks what she wants. Esther invites Xerxes and Haman to come to a dinner. The king accepts the invitation. At the dinner Esther defers making her request, instead inviting the king and Haman to a second dinner.

1. royal robes: she discards her mourning and dresses as attractively as possible. **stood:** she went where the king could see her and summon her. From his throne-room he could see anyone approaching along the corridor leading from the women's quarters. **2. When:** Heb. *wyhy*, 'it came to pass', suggests she may have waited a little, so 'when finally . . .' **3. half the kingdom:** this is best regarded as oriental exaggeration which was not meant to be taken too literally, cf. Herod to Salome (Mk 6: 23). The king knew she must want something rather urgently to come to him, risking death.

4. Esther did not intercede for her people. Why? Possibly because she felt that this was not the right time or place. Since she had not been with the fickle king for thirty days, she probably felt she needed time to re-establish her influence with him. She may well have preferred a more private place for her request. Why did Esther invite Haman? To make the king pass judgment immediately on Haman, by confronting Haman in his presence? There have been many different reasons given. **5. bring Haman at once:** an escort to a banquet was an honour, not a 'constraint' on Haman's freedom. **7. my petition and my request is:** it almost looks as if Esther is about to state her request when she breaks off and invites the king and Haman to a second dinner when she will disclose her request. Why did Esther postpone her request a second time? Did her courage fail her?

iv. Haman decides to hang Mordecai (5: 9-14)

Haman's delight at being at the queen's dinner turns to wrath when he sees Mordecai on his way home. He gathers his friends and boasts of his power, but complains of his chagrin at Mordecai's defiance of him. His wife and friends suggest making a gallows and having Mordecai hung the next day.

10. Zeresh: an unknown name. **11. his many sons:** the Persians regarded a large number of sons as a great blessing. **14. a gallows:** perhaps a gibbet on which the victim would be impaled or crucified. **seventy five feet:** see Introduction.

v. The king honours Mordecai (6: 1–13)
The king's insomnia leads him to have some of the royal records read. The passage read concerns the incident when Mordecai discovered the assassination plot (cf. 2: 23). Xerxes asks if Mordecai has been rewarded. On hearing that no reward has been given, he asks who is in court. When Haman comes in, he asks him for advice on how best to honour a subject. Haman, thinking the king is referring to himself, suggests such a man be dressed in the king's clothes and be conducted round the city on the king's horse. Xerxes orders Haman to do this for Mordecai. Haman goes home mourning. His wife and wise men only make matters worse by saying that if Mordecai is a Jew, Haman will never succeed.

1. could not sleep: another providential event. **3. nothing has been done:** it was a point of honour for the king to reward such a benefactor. **5. Haman is in the court:** that only Haman was there confirms how early he had come to court to secure Mordecai's death. **6. rather than me:** Haman's pride leads to his undoing. **8. a royal robe:** this was indeed the highest honour. Herodotus (vii. 15–17) tells how Xerxes' uncle Artabanus was commanded by the king to put on the royal robes, sit on the royal throne and sleep on the royal bed. **a horse:** not just owned by the king, but one he had ridden. **crest:** Assyrian reliefs show horses wearing crowns. **12. head covered:** a sign of grief. **13.** Somewhat wise after the event!

vi. The fall of Haman (6: 14–7: 10)
Haman is still recovering from his humiliation when messengers come to summon him to the banquet with Xerxes and Esther. This time, Esther states her request—her own life and that of her people. When the king asks who has threatened it, Esther denounces Haman. The king is furious and goes out into the garden. Haman stays to plead with the queen for his life. The king returns and interprets this as an assault on the queen and orders Haman's execution on his own gallows.

14. hurried Haman: does not imply that Haman was late, or had forgotten the invitation. This merely stresses Haman's importance. **3. petition:** after the usual courtly introduction, Esther's request is dramatic and terse, perhaps reflecting her nervousness and tension. Esther not only unmasks Haman but also discloses her own race, identifying herself with her people. **4. sold:** probably refers to Haman's money offer. **destruction . . . slaughter . . . annihilation:** the same three words as in 3: 13. **no such distress would justify:** (cf. mg) a very obscure clause in the Hebrew as there is doubt over three of the six words in the clause! Perhaps the meaning is that Esther would not

have bothered the king with their little problems and so would have kept quiet if it had just been a matter of slavery and not death. **5. asked:** *wayyō'mer* could be translated 'exclaimed'. **6. The adversary and enemy!:** again a dramatic and terse reply. Who is it? 'An enemy! An adversary! **This vile Haman!'** **terrified:** better 'dumbfounded'; Haman was taken by surprise rather than struck by fear. **7. in a rage:** once again the king gives way to sudden and uncontrolled anger. **stayed:** Haman decided to appeal to Esther for mercy rather than follow the king and beg for mercy from him, perhaps because he knew from experience that the king's anger, once roused, was blind and ungovernable. Some commentators have criticized Esther for not interceding for him, forgetting that so long as Haman lived he constituted a deadly threat to her and her people. Though Haman seemed defeated at that point, were he to survive who could tell how soon he would be revenged. **8. falling on the couch:** Haman was prostrate before Esther, begging for his life when the king returned. Xerxes interpreted Haman's action as a violation of the strict rules concerning the harem. **left the king's mouth:** such an accusation was so serious that the servants treated Haman as a condemned man. **9. Then Harbona . . . said:** Harbona not only suggested a means for the immediate execution of Haman but confirmed the justice of his sentence by pointing out that Haman had intended to hang Mordecai, the man who had saved the king's life. **10. 'Hang him on it!':** this suggestion evidently appealed to the king as poetic justice and Haman's fate was sealed.

III. THE JEWS TRIUMPH (8: 1–9: 32)
i. The Jews are permitted to defend themselves (8: 1–17)
(a) Mordecai is promoted (8: 1–2)
1. the estate of Haman: since Haman had been executed as a traitor, his whole estate was forfeit to the king who gave it to Esther. His 'estate' included everything, all his property and wealth. **2. took off his signet ring:** Xerxes now made Mordecai his new prime minister, and Esther gave him Haman's property.

(b) Esther intercedes for her people (8: 3–8)
3. falling at his feet: Esther was not doing obeisance, but had collapsed in renewed anguish over the deadly decree which still doomed her and her people. The situation is still a serious one, as her conduct and words demonstrate. **4. extended the gold sceptre:** Xerxes is not pardoning Esther but encouraging her. **5. if it pleases the king:** Esther uses these standard court phrases to introduce her plea, but adds a feminine touch with a further phrase of her own 'if I am pleasing in his eyes'.

She is pleading as hard as she can and evidently still is not sure of the intentions of this capricious husband/king. **Haman . . . devised:** Esther astutely puts all the blame on Haman, thus conveniently forgetting Xerxes' own responsibility. **7.** Conscious of Esther's anxiety, the king lists all he has done for Esther and for the Jews so as to encourage her to believe he is well disposed to her, her people and her petition. **8. you:** emphatic in its position and followed by an imperative: 'you yourselves write what you want!'

(*c*) **A new decree is written and despatched (8: 9–14)**
9. twenty-third of Sivan: there is a gap of two months and ten days between Haman's decree and Mordecai's decree. No reason is given for this delay nor can it now be guessed. **10. fast horses:** the additional details here about the horses serve to emphasize the speed and reliability of the royal communication system. **11. to assemble:** The word here probably refers not just to the day but to the prior preparations that were necessary for the Jews to organize a successful defence. **protect themselves:** Mordecai solves the problem that Haman's decree cannot be revoked by adding to it a provision authorizing the Jews to defend themselves and to destroy any who might attack them. **destroy, kill, . . . annihilate:** note the similarity with Haman's decree. Full-scale retaliation was authorized. The irrevocability of Haman's decree makes it necessary for Mordecai to duplicate in reverse all its provisions, this inevitably giving the impression of a very harsh decree. When the day came, it is stressed that the Jews did not plunder their enemies.

(*d*) **The Jews rejoice (8: 15–17)**
15. the city held a joyous celebration: this would have included many Gentiles as well as the Jews. Perhaps like that of many a tyrant, Haman's fall was generally popular. **17. celebrating:** lit. 'a good day'. This would have been a religious festival for the Jews.

ii. The Jews triumph over their enemies (9: 1–15)
The 13th Adar, the day that was named as the day of their destruction becomes the day of triumph over their enemies. The people fear them and the rulers help them. They slay their enemies, including the ten sons of Haman, but they do not plunder. After receiving a report of the day's events in Susa, Xerxes grants Esther's request for a further day's extension to the fighting in Susa and the public hanging of Haman's sons. Elsewhere the Jews rest and celebrate on the 14th Adar.

(*a*) **The Jews destroy their enemies (9: 1–10)**
1. the tables were turned: the author deliberately avoids mentioning God. **2. those seeking their destruction:** retaliation was limited to those who actively sought to kill the Jews. **were afraid of them:** the Jews were now in favour at court and Mordecai had considerable power. Officials, therefore, supported them. **6. In the citadel of Susa** is in the emphatic position. It appears that the five hundred referred to were killed in the acropolis, not the main city. **7–10.** The names of Haman's sons appear to be Persian. As long as they lived Haman's sons constituted a potential threat to the Jews. **10. did not lay their hands on the plunder:** three times the writer repeats this. Though their enemies' booty had been given them, he evidently wants to stress that the Jews were fighting for survival, not for material gain. The Jews were not the aggressors but were defending themselves from their enemies.

(*b*) **An extension at Susa (9: 11–15)**
12. what is your petition?: evidently Xerxes realizes that Esther is not completely satisfied. He does not seem to be concerned at the slaughter of his subjects. **13. tomorow also:** why Esther asked for a further day's extension in Susa is not clear. There may be some contrast intended between the acropolis of Susa where there was fighting on the first day and the main town where there was fighting on the second day. Possibly their enemies had been very resistant in the acropolis and only on the second day did the Jews defeat their enemies in the main town. The public exposure of Haman's sons was intended as a warning and a deterrent to their enemies.

iii. The feast of Purim is instituted (9: 16–32)
After summarizing the events of the 13th and 14th Adar, the steps taken by Mordecai and Esther to establish Purim are described.

(*a*) **A summary of the events of 13th and 14th Adar (9: 16–19)**
16. seventy-five thousand seems a very large number and would suggest that anti-Semitism was quite prevalent in the 5th century B.C. Perhaps Haman's decree had inflamed hostility to the Jews. Many of the Jews' enemies must have hoped to destroy and plunder them but they were completely defeated. **plunder:** again their refusal to take any booty is stressed. **19. villages:** implies a distinction between those living in walled towns and others; whereas the previous two verses made the distinction between those living in Susa and others, unless all those outside the capital are included as 'villagers'. **presents:** (RSV 'choice portions') the exchange of delicacies became one of the main features of Purim.

(*b*) **Mordecai orders the celebration of Purim (9: 20–28)**
20. Mordecai recorded these events: this may refer to the whole story or more probably just to the most recent events which were the reason for the two days of celebration. **27. all**

who join them: 'all who should join themselves to them', i.e. all future converts. **without fail:** there is a great stress on all the Jews everywhere observing the days. This would seem to suggest that there was considerable reluctance on the part of some to celebrate Purim.

(*c*) **Esther also orders its celebration (9: 29–32)**

29. Queen Esther: evidently Mordecai's letter enjoining the observance of Purim was not completely successful, so Esther also wrote a letter urging its observance. **second letter:** probably refers to Queen Esther's letter which confirmed Mordecai's first letter. **30. words of good will and assurance:** Esther writes attempting to persuade rather than to command or coerce her people to observe Purim. **31. fasting and lamentation:** it became customary for the 13th Adar to be kept as a fast before the two feast days. **32. the records:** 'written in a book' confirms the likelihood that the author of Esther drew on written sources when writing his account.

IV. CONCLUSION (10: 1–3)

1. tribute: perhaps the king's income through the peaceful levying of tribute is mentioned here in contrast to the ten thousand talents Haman had promised him. Otherwise its mention may just be to indicate the king's prosperity. This prosperity is seen as a fitting outcome to the events of the book and also as enhancing the reputation of Mordecai the prime minister. **2. book of the annals:** another reference to the royal archives. **3. Mordecai . . . was second in rank:** the book closes with this tribute to Mordecai. Not merely a king's favourite, he was respected by his people and honoured for his successful administration. How long this continued is unknown. Mordecai's period of office must have ended before

Xerxes' assassination in 465 B.C. Almost certainly Esther had died or fallen from favour before then, too. But these historical details are outside the scope of this book which was written not to record the lives of the emperors, queens or prime ministers but a great national deliverance which would bring comfort and hope to millions of Jews through hundreds of years.

BIBLIOGRAPHY

Commentaries

ANDERSON, B. W., *The book of Esther, Introduction and Exegesis. Interpreter's Bible* III (New York and Nashville, 1954).

CLINES, D. J. A., *Ezra, Nehemiah and Esther. NCentB* (Basingstoke, 1985).

FUERST, W. J., *The books of Ruth, Esther, Ecclesiastes, Song of Songs, Lamentations. CBC* (Cambridge, 1975).

GORDIS, R., *Megillat Esther* (New York, 1974).

KNIGHT, G. A. F., *Esther, Song of Songs, Lamentation. TC* (London, 1955).

MOORE, C. A., *Esther. AB* (New York, 1971).

PATON, L. B., *Esther. ICC* (Edinburgh, 1908).

Other Studies

CLINES, D. J. A., *The Esther Scroll Its Genesis, Growth and Meaning* (Sheffield, 1984).

HOSCHANDER, J., *The Book of Esther in the Light of History* (Philadelphia, 1923)

NAISH, J. P., 'Fresh Light on the Book of Esther', *Espositor*, series 8, vol. 25 (1923), pp. 56–66.

URQUHART, J., *The Inspiration and Accuracy of the Holy Scriptures* (London, 1895), pp.288–339.

URQUHART, J., *The New Biblical Guide*, vi (London, 1898), pp.301–423.

WRIGHT, J. S., 'The Historicity of the book of Esther', in *New Perspectives on the Old Testament*, ed. J. B. Payne (New York, 1970).

JOB

DAVID J. A. CLINES

The Purpose of the Book

Every reader of this magnificent and timeless book realizes that its purpose is to deal, in dramatic form, with the problem of suffering. But it is important to understand exactly what the problem of suffering means for the author.

To many people of the modern world, obsessed with a need to discover the origins of things and convinced that by that method alone one can come to a true understanding of things, the problem of suffering is the question: Why does suffering happen? What is its origin and cause? and more particularly, Why has this suffering happened to me? To that question, serious though it is, the book of Job gives no satisfactory answer. Judged as an answer to the problem of the origin or reason for suffering, the book is a failure. To be sure, the question is ventilated, and partial answers are given by the friends: suffering comes about sometimes as punishment for sin, sometimes as warning against committing sin in the future and sometimes, as in the case of Job himself, for no earthly reason at all but in order to justify God's claim to men's disinterested love of himself. But the reader cannot learn from the book what is the cause of his own suffering, and it is much to the point that Job himself never becomes aware of the origin of his suffering. To him it remains a mystery to the last, and from that fact we may perhaps infer that the author does not regard this as the primary question about suffering.

A second problem about suffering is both raised and convincingly answered by the book: Is there such a thing as innocent suffering? The fact that we no longer doubt the existence of innocent suffering is partly due to the book itself; for the book speaks out clearly against all cut-and-dried theologies of guilt and punishment by its insistence that the Job who suffers is a righteous man. Not only the author (1: 1), not only Job himself (*e.g.* 6: 30; 9: 15), but also God (42: 7 f.) attest Job's innocence, and yet there remains a very natural human tendency to ask, when one suffers, What have I done to deserve this? The book of Job, without denying the possibility of fully deserved suffering, answers, Perhaps you have no need to blame yourself; suffering is not always a matter of desert. But even this question and its answer are a secondary issue in the problem of suffering.

The third, and essential, problem of suffering as expressed in the book of Job is, rather, an existential one, that is, How can I suffer? What am I to do when I am suffering? In what spirit can I go on suffering? By comparison with this question of existence the first question, about the origin of suffering, is virtually an academic one, and the second, about the existence of innocent suffering, is straightforward. This third question is the one that it takes the whole book of Job to answer.

Two different but complementary answers are given by the book as it portrays Job's reactions to his suffering. The first is expressed in the prose prologue of the first two chapters. Job's reaction to the disasters that come upon him is a calm acceptance of the will of God that is able to bless God both for what he has given and what he has taken away (1: 21), both for good and for harm (2: 10). The sufferer who can identify with Job's acceptance, neither ignoring the reality of suffering by escaping into the past nor so pre-occupied with the present grief as to forget past blessing, is fortunate indeed. Many sufferers do not come to acceptance so easily: they are rather a blend of Job the patient and Job the impatient. The second answer to the question, What am I to do when I am suffering?, emerges from the distress and turmoil of Job's mind as it is revealed in his poetic speeches. When acceptance is no longer, or not yet, possible and bitterness and anger and a sense of isolation from God, even persecution by God, are overwhelming, what Job does is what must be done, so the author would have us know. Job does not attempt to suppress his hostility towards God for what has happened to him; he will speak out 'in the anguish of (his) spirit' and 'complain in the bitterness of (his) soul' (7: 11). Above all, this is not some aimless venting of anger and frustration: it is directed towards God. Even though Job speaks rashly and unjustly of God, his protests are in the right direction; he realizes that it is God himself with whom he has to do. It is just because he calls upon God persistently that in the end God reveals himself to him (chs. 38–41) and Job's tensions are resolved by the encounter with God. And it is just because Job directs himself to God in his suffering, and not toward the secondary causes of his distress (the Sabeans, the natural forces) that God in the end can praise him for speaking of him what is right (42: 7 f.).

By all means, the book means to say, let Job the patient be your model so long as that is possible for you; but when equanimity fails, let the grief and anger and impatience direct itself and yourself towards God, for only through encounter with him can the tension be resolved.

The Origins of the Book

The chief clue we have to the origins of the book is the differences between the prologue and epilogue on the one hand and the speeches on the other. Not only is there the obvious difference of literary form, narrative prose being used in the prologue and epilogue and rhetorical poetry in the speech, but also minor differences occur: in prologue and epilogue the name Yahweh often occurs, while in the speeches only the names El, Eloah and Shaddai are used of God; there is no reference in the speeches to the cause of Job's misfortunes as portrayed in the prologue; Job himself is a quite different figure in the two parts, a patient sufferer who is commended in the prose sections, an impatient accuser of God who is condemned in the poetical.

Such differences have led many scholars to believe that there once existed a narrative, perhaps an epic, about the righteous sufferer Job long before the composition of the speeches. Job certainly appears in the prose sections as a figure of patriarchal times, and the reference to Job in Ezek. 14: 14 along with two other ancient heroes, Noah and Danel, suggests that the story of Job has a high antiquity. In addition we know of a number of literary parallels in ancient Near Eastern literature to Job or at least to the theme of a righteous sufferer, going back to the early second millennium BC.

There is every likelihood, then, that the story of Job was told for many centuries before the present book of Job was composed, probably some time between the seventh and the third centuries B.C. But it seems less likely that we should imagine that the prose framework of the book as we now have it ever existed independently of the speeches. Certainly the differences between the prose and the poetry are very much less significant than is sometimes supposed: for example, the name Yahweh could well be avoided in the dialogue because Job's friends are represented as non-Israelites; it is not surprising that the speeches proceed in total ignorance of the events in heaven that have brought about Job's sufferings, for if the ultimate cause had been known, there would have been no question to discuss; and there is no real conflict between Job's commendation and his condemnation, for they are upon different issues: in the matter of his integrity and disinterested piety Job is vindicated, while it is upon his ignorance of the divine purposes (38: 2) that God's condemnation falls. Indeed, it is improbable that the prose narratives ever formed an independent whole; the introduction of Job's friends in 2: 11 ff. is plainly designed to preface the speeches and Yahweh's address to the friends (42: 7 ff.) is unintelligible without the speeches. Since the author of the speeches must therefore be responsible for some at least of the prose narrative, it is not improbable that he is the author of it all.

Other parts of the book, such as the Elihu speeches (chs. 32–37), the Yahweh speeches (chs. 38–41), or at least the second of them, and the poem on wisdom (ch. 28), have been thought to be secondary additions to the poem. Some of these arguments have a certain weight, but it seems preferable to regard as the object of our interpretation the book that we actually have rather than hypothetical earlier versions of it. In what follows, therefore, the unity of the book, and especially of prologue, dialogue, and epilogue, has been assumed as fundamental for the interpretation of the book.

ANALYSIS

I. PROLOGUE (1: 1–2: 13)

In the prose prologue to the book are contained five scenes, artistically arranged: the first, third, and fifth (1: 1–5, 13–22; 2: 7–13) take place on earth, the second and fourth (1: 6–12; 2: 1–6) in heaven. Needless to say, Job and the other characters on earth remain ignorant of what transpires on the heavenly plane; it is only we, the readers, who are let into the secret of why Job is being made to suffer.

i. Scene 1: Job and his integrity (1: 1–5)

1. Job is introduced in the simple and direct style of the patriarchal narratives. **Job** is not an Israelite, it appears, for his homeland of **Uz** is most probably Edom (cf. the personal name Uz in the genealogies of descendants of Edom, Gen. 36: 28; 2 Chr. 1: 42), though some passages would tend to identify it with Aram (cf. Gen. 10: 23; 22: 21), to the north-east of Israel. Nevertheless, he is a worshipper of the true God, though he refers to him mostly as Elohim, 'God', and not as 'Yahweh', the personal name of God. That Job is a **blameless and upright** man, i.e. beyond reproach, not that he is sinlessly perfect, is affirmed by the narrator, by God (1: 8) and by Job himself (chs. 29 ff.).

2. The sequence of the verses suggests that even the number of his family, symbolically complete with **seven sons** and **three daughters**, ten in all, was the consequence of his piety. **3.** The same symbolically complete numbers occur in the idyllic picture of his possessions (note that his wealth is assessed entirely in terms of his animals and **servants**, or perhaps 'tillage', not monetarily): **seven thousand** and **three thousand** make the round ten thousand, while **five hundred** and **five hundred** make the round one thousand. The she-asses (not **donkeys** generally), valuable for their milk and their foals, are more precious than male asses; it is a different story with sons and daughters! The **people of the East** is the Israelites' term for the semi-nomadic and settled peoples east of the Jordan.

4. All the sons, doubtless married and each in his own **home**, would **take turns** in foregathering for convivial celebration; this sounds more like a whirl of social engagements than simply annual or birthday feasts. **5.** Plainly nothing disreputable attached to such feasts but Job's scrupulosity recognized that days of celebration could become almost unwittingly occasions for licence. Job acts patriarchally in offering sacrifices as priest on behalf of the family.

ii. Scene 2: The heavenly gathering (1: 6–12)

6. Corresponding to the innocent family gatherings there is taking place in heaven a far more momentous gathering, of the **angels**, lit. 'sons of God', God's courtiers (cf. also Isa. 6: 1; Jer. 23: 18, 22), among whom comes the **Satan**. The article before the term shows that this is not, properly speaking, the personal devil of Christian theology, but one of the servants of God with a role as investigator, adversary (cf. NIVmg) or even *agent provocateur*. Certainly it is not he who is the author of Job's misfortunes: Job's dealings are directly with God. **7.** The Satan's movements have not been idle wandering but a purposeful looking for failings. **8.** Job is God's boast; few are dignified by the title 'my servant' (*e.g.* 2 Sam. 7: 5; Isa. 42: 1). **9 f.** The Satan sharply questions, without any of the etiquette of courtly language, whether there is such a thing as disinterested piety. Cynicism about people's motives for religious belief can go too far.

iii. Scene 3: The first trial (1: 13–22)

This, the central scene of the prologue, is the most stylized. There are four messengers, who announce four disasters: the conventional number four (three plus one) heightens the tragedy (cf. Am. 1: 3), as does the fact that only one person survives each disaster. The calamities, two natural, two inflicted by men, strike from all points of the compass: the **Sabeans** (15) come from the south (Sheba), the **Chaldeans** (17) from the north; the lightning (**fire of God**, 16) from the storms that sweep in from the Mediterranean in the west, the whirlwind (19) from the desert in the east. The effect of the news upon Job is highlighted by the narrator's focus upon him rather than upon the scenes of the disaster themselves, and by the fact that Job has no time to recover from one shock before the next messenger arrives.

Job's reaction is not to blame natural events or human enemies (**the LORD has taken away**), not to forget God's blessing (**the LORD gave**), not to close his eyes to reality (**has taken**), but to bless the Lord for both good and evil (21). Yahweh's confidence in Job has proved justified.

21. Job's **mother's womb** to which he will return at death is probably to be understood as mother earth, out of which man was created.

iv. Scene 4: The heavenly gathering again (2: 1–6)

The former scene in heaven is presented again. Yahweh's report on Job is that **he still maintains** (lit. strengthens!) **his integrity**, i.e. his loyalty to God. The attack on Job has been as gratuitous (**without any reason**, ḥinnām, 3) as the Satan has denied Job's religion to be (**for nothing**, ḥinnām, 1: 9). Job will suffer any external hardship piously provided he is not physically afflicted himself. **Skin for skin** (4) suggests that Job has saved his own skin by piously accepting the death of his children; it will be a different matter if Job's own person is affected. This time the attack will have to come more directly from God himself: **stretch out your hand** (5).

v. Scene 5: The second trial (2: 7–13)

As if to speed up the narrative as it hastens to its critical point, Satan's exit **from the presence of the LORD** belongs to the account of the second trial; there is no interval of time between the permission and the affliction. The disease of **painful sores** (7) with which Job is smitten is clearly some skin disease; more specific identifications like elephantiasis or leprosy are hard to be sure about. Apart from the effect of itchiness, many other associated illnesses are complained of by Job in the course of the poem (see *e.g.* 7: 14; 19: 17, 20; 30: 17). Job is now an outcast, whether voluntarily or because of taboo laws, sitting **among the ashes** of the village rubbish heap.

Job's wife, whether out of hatred of God for what he has done to Job, or out of a desire that her husband's misery should be soon ended, urges him to **curse God** (9) and so bring death upon himself. Job does not reproach her for suggesting blasphemy, but for speaking **foolish** words; in his understanding God is as free to send **good** and **trouble** (i.e. harm) as he is to give and to take away (1: 21). In saying that Job **did not sin in what he said** (10) the narrator does not mean that he sinned in his heart; true, ch. 3 will show that Job found it far from easy to maintain his faith in God, and himself wished to be dead, but not through cursing God. Chapter 3 will make plain how different Job's response to calamity is from a fatalism that unquestioningly accepts all that happens as simply the will of God.

Job, being a chieftain of some eminence (1: 3), had friends in various countries, though we cannot with certainty identify their homelands. Their consolation of Job was well-intentioned, as is made clear by their sympathetic acts of grief, and their participation in his silent mourning for **seven days and seven nights** (13). Though their speeches did not reach to the heart of Job's distress, and he criticizes them sharply (*e.g.* 13: 4), their fault lies in their uncritical acceptance of orthodox theology and their inability to see that Job's is a special case.

II. DIALOGUE (3: 1–42: 6)
i. Job's soliloquy (first speech) (3: 1–26)

Job's first utterance, neglectful of the courtesies of oriental speech, is addressed to none of his friends, of whose presence he scarcely seems aware, but is a monologue, in which we suddenly plunge out of the epic grandeur and deliberateness of the prologue into the dramatic turmoil of the poem, from the external description of suffering to Job's inner experience. Though he will not curse God, he does curse his life; his soliloquy is one of the most poignant expressions of despair ever penned.

(*a*) **Curse on the day of his birth (3: 3–10)**
A curse usually pertains to the future; it is a sign of Job's despair that he utters this entirely futile curse on the past, which cannot be changed. He wishes that his birth-day could be blocked out (4–6a) so that it would not have come into the calendar of the year (6b, c); he longs that sorcerers who put a curse on days could have made it one of the unlucky days, in which successful conception or birth would not have taken place (8a, 10a).
8. Those who are **ready to rouse Leviathan** the sea-monster (cf. Ps. 104: 26; Isa. 27: 1) are magicians who believed themselves capable of arousing the dragon of chaos so that, perhaps, it would swallow up the sun, thus causing the darkness of eclipse. Some read 'sea' (*yām*) instead of 'day' (*yōm*). For calling on an expert in blessing and cursing, cf. Balaam (Num. 22 ff.). Job's language need not of course be taken as evidence of the poet's belief in the powers of such experts.

(*b*) **Wish that he had died at birth (3: 11–19)**
Since plainly such a curse had never been uttered, Job goes on to ask why, if he had to be born, he could not have died at birth (11a) or been still-born (16). The transition in grief from despair to questioning is a natural one, however different these moods may appear. Death is for him now sweeter than life, and he pictures the pleasures of Sheol compared to his present lot (13 ff., 17 ff.). There in the underworld there is quietness and **rest** (13, 17). The remainder of the picture of Sheol, with the equality of rich and poor, prisoner and taskmaster, small and great, is not really relevant to Job's point here, but is introduced because the poet is working with traditional material about the underworld; we have here the first of many *topoi* (passages dealing with a traditional theme) in a poem.
12. In Rome, and in Gen. 50: 23, the father received the new-born child on his knees as a token of legitimation, but it is perhaps the mother's knees (NEB) here (cf. Isa. 66: 12). **14.** Mesopotamian kings frequently boasted that they had rebuilt the ruins of famous cities of the past. **16.** Though this verse would seem to come more naturally after v. 11 (so NAB) or v. 12 (so NEB), it is a characteristic of poetic style in Job to pick up one motif after it has been interrupted by another.

(*c*) **The riddle of suffering existence (3: 20–26)**

Job's thoughts move to a wider question now: he does not only ask why, since he has been born, he has to go on living, but why it happens at all to mankind that they cannot always die when they are ready for it (20–23). So his soliloquy ends on a more general philosophical note. It is remarkable that he nowhere contemplates suicide.
23. Job's **way**, i.e. life, **is hidden**, in that he feels **hedged in** by God's attentions to him. 'The Satan saw God's *hedge* as a protection; Job finds it a restriction' (Andersen). **25. What I feared** or perhaps more generally, 'whatever I fear is the very thing that befalls me'.

ii. The first cycle of speeches (4: 1–14: 22)
(*a*) **Eliphaz's first speech (4: 1–5: 27)**
Eliphaz, like all the friends, intends to strengthen Job in his suffering, and no one brings a more comforting message than this friend. The essence of his first speech to Job is: You are a pious man, as we know well; there is therefore no need to lose heart, for the innocent never finally suffer. The key verses in his address are 4: 6 (**Should not your piety be your confidence?**) and 5: 8 (**I would lay my cause before him**). His message to Job is: Be patient.
(*i*) **You are a pious man (4: 2–6)**
Eliphaz's genuine concern for Job is clear in his deferential and almost apologetic opening words (2a). While his reminder to Job of how he himself has comforted many in a similar position (3 f.) could be taken as scornful (cf. **but now trouble comes to you**, 5a), it is better to read it as the mildest of reproaches. Job's only failing, at this stage, at any rate, is that he is **discouraged** (5). His very encouragement of others, as an act of true **piety** (lit. 'fear of God'), is itself a reason for confidence that God will soon restore him. Eliphaz does not doubt Job's piety (cf. 1: 1, where the same root for 'blameless' is used) and he believes firmly in justification by works (Terrien).
(*ii*) **The innocent never finally perish (4: 7–11)**
Quite apart from the fact that both Eliphaz and Job must have known innocent people who perished, i.e. died before their time—unless all such cases were explained away as due to some hidden fault—Eliphaz's encouragement to Job fails to speak to Job's condition. The comfort of v. 7 is all very well for a man who fears he may die, but Job is not in that company: he has already wished to be dead! In vv. 8–11 a traditional picture (a *topos*) of the fate of the wicked is painted. Eliphaz does not mean to imply that Job is among the number of the wicked; on the contrary, he is one of the righteous, so he need not expect to be **destroyed** or **perish** (9). There is no need to criticize Eliphaz's conviction, which is after all a Biblical principle (cf. Hos. 10: 13; Gal. 6: 7) that those who **sow trouble reap it**; even

though they may be as strong as lions (10 f.), the **breath of God** will consume them.

(iii) However, even the pious are not perfect (4: 12–21)

While for Eliphaz there is a clear distinction between the righteous and the impious, with Job on the side of the righteous, he feels bound to acknowledge that not even the pious are perfect, and so they must expect disciplinary suffering from time to time. Crucial here are vv. 17 ff.: 'Can mortal man be righteous before God' (RSV; it is not a matter of being **more righteous than** God) (17a)? This understanding, which goes beyond the traditional wisdom of the schools which saw morality entirely in black and white terms, Eliphaz has received by supernatural means, a **spirit** (15) that appeared to him in a dream (13) and delivered its secret message to him (12). Even God's heavenly servants, his angels, are not infallibly trustworthy (18; there is no thought of 'bad' angels here); how much less are mortal men, who, unlike the angels, can die within a single day (20a), even without being noticed (20b; Eliphaz does not mean unnoticed by God) and without ever attaining full understanding (21b).

(iv) Suffering, in fact, has to be expected (5: 1–7)

Suffering by way of punishment for wrongdoing is only to be expected, Eliphaz elaborates; men, being imperfect, bring suffering upon themselves (JB 'It is man who breeds trouble for himself' (7a), preferable to NIV **man is born to trouble**). This cycle of cause and effect is especially clear in the case of the wicked (2) whose unruly behaviour (NIV **resentment**) brings him to ruin. Verses 3 ff. simply develop this picture of the **fool**, and are not being applied to Job, though the reference to the fate of the fool's sons (4a) is rather insensitive in the circumstances (cf. v. 25). Now even the righteous, like Job, cannot hope to escape entirely from such suffering—affliction is not self-producing (6) but man-produced (7); there is no point therefore in Job's appealing for rescue to the angels (**holy ones**, 1), for they too are aware of this inevitable nexus of cause and effect. **5** is obscure, especially its second line; the general impression is that his wealth goes to feed others. **7. sparks** or perhaps 'eagles' (NEB, JB).

(v) To be practical, all you can do is to commit your case to God (5: 8–16)

Taking up his earlier theme that Job is essentially a pious man and so should not lose heart (4: 2–6), Eliphaz recommends patience to Job: if I were you, he says, I would leave my affairs in God's hands (8), for he is the great reverser of fortunes (11–16). Eliphaz embarks on another *topos*, this time about God's reversal of human fortunes; it applies to Job only in that Job has reason to hope in God that he too might be

treated like the **lowly** and **those who mourn** (11), like the **needy** and the **poor** (15 f.). This is the one piece of the friends' advice that Job does follow, **I would lay my cause before him**, though he hardly needs Eliphaz to encourage him to do so. His **cause** is both his parlous state of affairs and his 'case' (JB) in a more legal sense, which Job will be found laying before God as the dialogue proceeds (cf. 7: 11–21; 10: 18–22; 12: 18–23).

8. I would appeal to God is in contrast to any appeal to the 'holy ones' of v. 1. Verses 11–16 frame the destructive acts of God (12 ff.) with his saving acts (11, 15), so that the chief effect of this picture of God is to give **hope** to the **poor** (16; cf. and contrast Lk. 1: 51 ff.).

(vi) If you do so, God will restore you (5: 17–27)

If only Job will wait patiently for God to act, he will find that he is undergoing disciplinary suffering (17), and that 'he who wounds is he who soothes the sore' (18, JB); God is the 'Celestial Surgeon' (Stevenson). Again Eliphaz is carried away by the *topos* of 'the blessings of the righteous', a delightful poem in its own right, though singularly inappropriate to Job's situation when it comes to the promise that **your children shall be many** (25a)!

Verse 23a may mean that Job will 'have a covenant with the stones to spare your fields' (NEB). Verse 26 pictures beautifully the calmness of death at the proper age, unlike the premature death of the wicked. Verse 27, the conclusion to Eliphaz's speech, Rowley rightly characterizes as 'somewhat pontifical . . . a common mark of the closed mind'.

(b) Job's second speech (6: 1–7: 21)

It is perhaps something of a misnomer to call Job's speeches replies, for they frequently are not addressed to the friends but are monologues or addressed to God, and they rarely pick up the points that the friends have made. However, Job does not entirely ignore the friends (e.g. 6: 21–30), so it is convenient to regard his speeches as replies.

The structure of this speech is marked by the persons Job is addressing: in 6: 1–13, which is a soliloquy, he again expresses his wish to die (as in ch. 3); in 6: 14–30, which is largely if not entirely addressed to the friends, he expresses his disappointment in them and their comfort; and in 7: 1–21, all of which is apparently addressed to God, he forms his death wish into a complaint against the God who allows him to go on living.

(i) May God strike me dead! (6: 1–13)

Job's very lack of response to Eliphaz's speech is proof enough of how ineffectual Eliphaz's words had been. A person who feels as suicidal as Job will get little help from advice to be patient. Eliphaz has not plumbed the depths of Job's despair, so it is not surprising that Job, initially at any rate, ignores him, and re-iterates his wish to be dead. The key passage in this section is vv. 8 f.: **Oh, that I might have my request . . . that God would be willing to crush me . . . and cut me off.** If he could die now, before his suffering leads him into blasphemy, he could at least have the **consolation** of not having **denied the words,** i.e. 'decrees' (JB), commandments, **of the Holy One** (9). Eliphaz has called on Job to be patient, but patience requires a strength that Job does not have (11 ff.). Eliphaz has not recognized what a burden lies upon Job: if his **misery** (2) could be weighed it would **outweigh the sand of the seas** (3a); no wonder then that his words have been 'desperate' (rather than **impetuous** or even 'wild' (JB, NEB), for Job is apologizing for nothing, confessing to nothing in 3b). Just as in the prologue (1: 21; 2: 10), he recognizes that his suffering comes ultimately from God; here in the poem his pains are the result of the poisoned **arrows of the Almighty** (Shaddai) while the 'onslaughts' (NEB, better than NIV **terrors**) of God his enemy are set in battle array against him (4). His cries are not for nothing, any more than **donkey** or **ox** complain when their wants are satisfied. Job's needs have not been satisfied, however—at least not by Eliphaz, whose words are insipid and whose advice cannot be swallowed any more easily than can the vegetable or whatever substance it is that is translated **the white of an egg,** NIV, AV, JB ('the slime of the purslane', RSV; 'the juice of mallows', NEB; 6).

(ii) **You have been undependable friends (6: 14–30)**
Job has just complained that he has no strength in him to withstand constant pain (13), and now he will move on to complain that his friends have brought him no resources either. Verse 14 is a linking verse, in which Job indirectly charges his friends with having failed to pay him friendship's debt of **devotion,** the loyalty of friendship through thick and thin. In some versions (*e.g.* RSV 'He who withholds kindness from a friend forsakes the fear of the Almighty') a failing is itself a sin against God but NIV may be preferable in rendering '. . . **even though he forsakes** the fear of the Almighty'—a remarkable and impressive statement. (Job is of course not putting himself in the category of those who have abandoned religion.) Job goes on to compare his **undependable** friends to the undependability of the desert streams or wadis, which in the spring are full of water, but when needed most, in the summer, have dried up completely and prove a disappointment to travellers who seek them (15–20). **Now you too have proved to be of no help** (21a); they are **afraid** (21b) that if they identify themselves too closely with Job they too will come under God's judgment. They

treat him not as a friend but as some one who has asked for a loan: they offer plenty of advice, but no hard cash (22 f.)!

Job is prepared to be shown where he is in the wrong (24); if he is, 'fair comment can be borne without resentment' (25a, JB). But Eliphaz is implying, without making any specific accusation, that Job must have sinned in some way to be undergoing such suffering, and Job resents that implication. His '**integrity is at stake**' (29b); cannot he be relied upon to **discern** (30) the difference between undeserved and deserved suffering? Does he look like a liar, who covers up the truth (28)?

Verse 27 seems harsh and unjustifiable in the light of Eliphaz's mild approach to Job. Perhaps NEBmg is more on the right lines: 'Would you assail a blameless man? Would you hurl yourselves on a friend?'

(iii) **Why, O God, do you let me go on living (7: 1–21)?**
Though God is first addressed in v. 7, it seems sensible to take the statement in vv. 1–6 about the misery of his life as also directed toward God. Job's death-wish again asserts itself, but this time it is interwoven with the theme of the shortness of human life generally, and with an appeal to God to let him alone so that he may die in peace.

(a) *The brevity and misery of human life I know all too well (7: 1–10).* In reflecting upon his own misery, Job projects his own despair upon the nature of human existence generally: the common lot of mankind is **hard service,** and Job's experience, 'while exceptional in the intensity of his sufferings, is typical in the fact of suffering' (Rowley). His **days** that are **swifter than a weaver's shuttle** (6) are also the days of mankind at large, that **life is but a breath** (7) is the human lot and that **he who goes down to the grave does not return** (9) is common to mankind. And yet, paradoxically, life that is so brief can seem so tedious: the one event Job longs for—death—seems infinitely delayed, so that he is like 'a slave longing for the shade, or a servant kept waiting for his wages' (2, NEB). The nights are long (4b), the months are empty (3a), and he knows that he 'shall never again see good days' (7b, NEB). The only changes he knows are in the condition of his scabs, one day hardened over, another broken out with oozing pus (5; cf. JB).

(b) *Why do you not let me die here and now (7: 11–21)?* Job will address this powerful complaint and request directly to God (11). His complaint is that God, far from letting him alone, treats him like one of the legendary monsters of the deep, Yam (**the sea**) or Tannin (the sea **monster**), who had to be muzzled by God (cf. *e.g.* 38: 8–11 and Isa. 51: 9 respectively). It is ludicrous for God to imagine that Job poses any threat to his universe, yet he receives the same attention as did those forces of chaos (12). God never lets up in torturing Job (13 f.), so that Job would prefer death to life; he has no wish to go on living (**I would not live forever**, 16a). He resumes the theme of God's suffocating scrutiny of man with a parody of Ps. 8: in the psalm it is asked, 'What is man [so apparently insignificant] that you are mindful of him . . . care for him' (8: 4). Job, contrary to the spirit of the psalm, which goes on to declare man's pre-eminent place in creation ('ruler over the works of your hands', 6), asserts that man, and himself in particular, is indeed, and not only apparently, insignificant; God's 'mindfulness' of man and 'caring for' him is not for man's benefit, but a kind of sadistic torment by God (17 ff.). God gets to be too close for comfort (cf. Ps. 139: 1–5). Man is too insignificant to merit such close attention; so insignificant, indeed, that Job can question whether even a sin can be of such great consequence to God. Job is not admitting to being a sinner; he puts it hypothetically, 'Suppose I have sinned' (JB), 'how do I injure thee?' (20a, NEB). Is the sin of a petty human creature so important on the scale of the universe that God should have to make the sinner his mark or **target**? This is not an amoralist speaking, but a man suffering, unjustly he believes, and at the hands of an angry God, when his lifetime is virtually over and **soon** he will be dead and buried. So his request is that God should 'overlook' or 'tolerate' (JB, better than **pardon . . . forgive**, NIV, 21) any fault he may have committed (not that Job is confessing to anything!), since he is not worth worrying about.

(c) **Bildad's first speech (8: 1–22)**
Bildad too, like all the friends, believes that suffering is punishment, and that the death of Job's children is proof of that. His message to Job is: If *you* are innocent, you will not die. While Eliphaz assumed Job's general righteousness, Bildad urges him to search his soul, because through innocence alone he will be delivered from his calamities. The major part of Bildad's speech (8–19) elaborates on the theme that there is no effect without a cause, of which the conventional wisdom on the death of the wicked is a prime example. The speech concludes on a comparatively cheerful note: Bildad wants to leave open the question of Job's innocence.

(i) **Your children died for their sins; if you are innocent, you will not die (8: 2–7)**
Bildad's fundamental starting-point is that God does not **pervert justice.** If there has been suffering sent from God, some sin must have preceded it. This is exemplified in the case of Job's children (4). On the other hand, Job himself is not dead, so the possibility still exists that he is innocent of anything deserving of death. Job has only to **look to God** in prayer,

and **if** he is **pure and upright** his prayer will be heard. The rather tasteless reference to Job's **beginnings** in v. 7 is another instance of the rhetoric of the speakers carrying them away: Job's beginning was anything but small or **humble**. Everything is straightforward for Bildad: 'the simplicity of his words betokens the simplicity of his theology' (Andersen), that men's destinies are entirely in accord with their merits.

(ii) **There is no effect without a cause, as the case of the wicked shows (8: 8–19)**
Again the appeal to tradition (cf. 5: 27) shows up the inadequacy of the speaker's theology when faced with an unusual case. The proverbial expression of the theme 'no smoke without fire' in v. 11 introduces another elaboration of the traditional theme of the fate of the wicked. They are like the Egyptian papyrus plant: 'Pluck them even at their freshest; fastest of all plants they wither' (JB). Their confidence is **fragile** as 'gossamer' (NEB, 14); their growth like that of a lush plant that is not deeply rooted (16 f.). 'That is how its life withers away' (19 NEB) and other plants take its place.

(iii) **There is still hope for you (8: 20–22)**
Bildad ends on a hopeful note: **God does not reject a blameless man** (20a), and obviously Bildad believes that Job may yet prove to be such a man. But Bildad's wisdom is too shallow; it is 'helpful as a general guide to life; but trite, and even cruel, when the friends of God are the ones with the most trouble' (Andersen).

(d) **Job's third speech (9: 1–10: 22)**
With ch. 9 we reach the first truly difficult chapter of the book. Job's mood is certainly that of despair, but the question is to what extent he now doubts God's justice. He has already made no secret of the fact that he believes he is suffering unjustly; but that feeling we can attribute to his acceptance of the common theology of the time, that suffering is always deserved. Now, however, it appears, at least from our versions of the text, that he is charging God with 'cosmic injustice' (Gordis), i.e. that the particular suffering of the individual Job raises the question whether God is not in fact a quite amoral governor of the universe, from whom it is useless to expect justice (cf. *e.g.* 9: 16, 20, 24, 30 f.). Nevertheless it might be that his complaint does not reach as far as that, and that what he is protesting is that it is hopeless for a man to seek *vindication* from God, because no one is in a position to compel God to give him anything, not even the vindication he deserves. However ch. 9 is to be read, it is of the nature of a monologue, in which God is referred to in the third person, although occasionally (vv. 28, 31) he is addressed directly. Ch. 10, on the other hand, is consistently addressed to God, and renews Job's for-

mer plea (*e.g.* 7: 16) that God would leave him alone to die in peace.

(i) A man cannot prove himself in the right with God (9: 2–13)
The key to this strophe is the question, **How can a mortal be righteous**, i.e. declared righteous, justified (NAB), in the right (JB), or vindicated, **before God?** (2), a rhetorical question to which Job's fully developed answer is: in no way. Job is not speaking, as Eliphaz was, of how any one can be perfectly righteous before God, nor as Paul would, of how a sinner might be 'justified' or declared righteous before God, but of how a righteous man can be 'justified' or publicly vindicated by God. There is no way, Job says, that an innocent sufferer can compel God to demonstrate his innocence. That is because God is God and not man: he has limitless wisdom and power (4a), as is proved by his control of the universe. Job focuses upon the more negative aspects of God's power—**he moves mountains, shakes the earth, seals off the stars** (5 ff.)—not in order to picture him as a God of chaos (Habel) but to emphasize his freedom to act, whether for weal or woe (a point developed in 14–24). The freedom of God makes him incomprehensible (**cannot be fathomed**, 10; similarly v. 11), unaccountable (**who can say to him, What are you doing?**, 12) and uncontrollable (he does not **restrain his anger** once he has started on that course, regardless of the obstacles, 13).

3. he could not answer him one time out of a thousand: This is to be Job's experience when God does begin to question him (chs. 38–41). But perhaps the verse means 'God will not answer one question in a thousand' (NEB) for he is under no obligation to man. **7. it does not shine:** a reference to eclipses. **8. stretches out the heavens, etc.** are not destructive works, so Job is not referring exclusively to God's unattractive deeds, but to his **miracles** or 'marvellous' deeds (RSV) (10) in general. **9. the Bear and Orion, etc.:** groups of stars not identifiable with any certainty (cf. NEB). **13. Rahab** is a name (like Leviathan) for the legendary sea-monster of chaos with whom, according to some Hebrew folklore not found in the Bible, God did battle at creation (cf. on 7: 12). For the author of Job, this is no more than a literary allusion in passing; he does not lend his authority to the truth of the story.

(ii) Even if one could bring God to court, one would get no vindication (9: 14–24)
Job contemplates the possibility of bringing God to court in order to force him to deliver a public verdict of 'not guilty' upon Job. But that is really an impossibility, for various reasons: how could a mere man choose arguments (JB; NIV **words**, 14) to persuade God to come to court? How, if one did manage to enter into

dialogue with God, could one be sure that God was really listening, since he is crushing Job with a tempest (16b, 17a)? Even though he is innocent, in some way Job feels sure he would speak improperly, and so his **mouth would condemn** him (20); and in any case, one no more has a chance of issuing a summons against God than of using force against him (19). This movement of the speech concludes with Job once more asserting his innocence (21) and despairing of the possibility of vindication since God **destroys both the blameless and the wicked** (22b).

Several sentences in this strophe are very difficult, and cannot easily be harmonized with the interpretation given above, or with what Job says elsewhere. **15. I could only plead with my Judge for mercy** is what Bildad has recommended (8: 5) and is hardly Job's position. Perhaps the **not** of 15a should be carried on into this second line (Andersen). **16. he responded:** i.e. to my summons to appear in court. **20.** Job does not think that God would deliberately twist his words (so NEB), but that he would be so overawed and confused by God's presence (Rowley) that he would say something wrong. **21. I have no concern for myself** means 'I hold my life cheap' (NEB) and so have nothing to lose, and therefore can speak my mind. Verse 22 does not mean that God is immoral but that since as a matter of fact, according to Job's own experience, the destruction of good and bad alike comes from God, it is pointless for the good to expect or demand vindication. Verse 24 puts the same point another way: the wicked flourish in the earth, and judges seem to know or do nothing about it; God is surely at the back of that (24c) and therefore once again it is pointless to expect vindication.

(iii) A trial of law would do me no good, since there is no arbitrator (9: 25–35)
The key passage here is v. 33, where Job realizes that, because God is not a man (32), there is no one in a position above God **to arbitrate** and settle the dispute he has with God about his vindication. It is not a mediator between himself and God he wants (cf. AV 'a daysman') but someone who can impose his will upon God. Realizing that such a hope is vain, why does he not give in with good grace and resolve to put a brave face on his suffering and **smile** (27)? Because as soon as one suffering is past, another takes its place: God does not treat (rather than NIV **hold**) him as innocent, but sends further punishments. Even if he were to purify himself from all his supposed failings (30), God would proceed once again to blacken his character (31) by making him suffer further. Job is not charging God with injustice in general, but with the particular injustice of refusing to give a good name to a man who deserves it.

He holds fast his integrity still (2: 3). If God would only remove the suffering (**rod**, 34) away for a time, Job would feel more free to speak (35); as it is, he is afraid that any further appeal for vindication will only irritate God and bring down further wrath on himself.

35. but as it now stands with me I cannot: a very obscure phrase; NEB is most helpful with 'for I know I am not what I am thought to be', i.e. deserving of my suffering.

(*iv*) **I will speak in the bitterness of my grief to thee, O God (10: 1–22)**
Like so many of Job's speeches, this one ends with a passionate appeal directly to God. Job is not content to talk *about* God in the third person, but knows that since his dealings are with God himself, it is *to* God that he must direct himself. Here he reflects on the care and devotion God has spent upon his creation of him, and wonders whether 'all the kindness was but intended to make his present suffering the more acute' (Rowley). Various themes that we have met before are intertwined here with the new theme of God's creation of Job from clay and preservation of him (8–12) with a 'prodigal expenditure of skill' (Davidson): he has been **molded** from **clay** like pottery, **curdled** like milk being made into **cheese**, **knit together** like a weaver's handicraft and **given life**. Yet all along, it appears, God's purpose was quite other (13): **this is what you concealed in your heart . . . if I sinned, you would be watching me** (13 f.), so as to bring suffering upon him. Has Job now admitted to any sense of guilt? No, he means that whether he is wicked or innocent (14 f.) God's 'care' for him has been to make him his target (cf. 7: 20). God 'seeks out' iniquity in Job even though he knows that he is not guilty (6 f.). Was it for this that Job was born? Would not he have been better off never to have been born (18 f.; cf. 3: 10)? And cannot God now let him alone to live out his few remaining days in peace (20 ff.; cf. 7: 16, 19)?

This is the most serious accusation Job has yet made against God, but can Job be blamed for wondering what the purpose of an innocent life has been if it is to end in undeserved suffering with the odium of wrongdoing that is attached to suffering? It is not simply that Job hates suffering in itself. Of course he does, but what he most hates is that suffering is a condemnation of him. So his appeal in this second half of the speech is: **Do not condemn me** (2), i.e. 'Do not put me in the wrong' (NAB), and **tell me what charges you have against me** (2). The speech has been essentially about Job's vindication, and it is for that, rather than mere release from his sufferings, that he appeals.

(*e*) **Zophar's first speech (11: 1–20)**
Zophar is the most censorious of the three

friends. His message to Job is simple: you are suffering because God knows that you are a secret sinner (6); therefore repent (13 f.)!

(*i*) **God knows that you are a secret sinner (11: 2–12)**
Zophar is lacking any sympathy for Job's plight if he has heard in his outbursts only **all these words, and idle talk** (2 f.). He 'detaches the words from the man' (Andersen), for he, like the rest of the friends, remains entrenched in the view that suffering is inevitably due to wrongdoing. Since Job is not obviously a sinner, Zophar's 'insight' is that he must be secretly a sinner, whom God has found out. In spite of Job's claim—which he had never made in so many words, but which is a fair expression of his stance—that his **beliefs** or 'opinions' (NEB) are **flawless** and that he is **pure** before God, God knows—and somehow Zophar too has been let in on the knowledge—that Job is really a secret sinner. If the truth were known, it would doubtless be seen that God **has even deliberately forgotten some** of Job's sins (6c). Since God's mercy is well known, the chances are that Job is getting off lightly!

Zophar's reference to the wisdom of God leads him into a digression on that subject (7–12), all very unexceptionable, but beside the point for Job, who does not doubt God's wisdom for an instant. It exceeds the bounds of the universe: heaven, Sheol, earth, and sea (8 f.), and it searches out the iniquity of men (10 f.), no matter how well they think they have it covered.

4. beliefs: one would have expected rather a word for 'way of life' (which is how JB actually translates), but Zophar's point apparently is that 'in rejecting the theology of the friends Job was implicitly claiming superior understanding' (Rowley).

5. Oh, . . . that God would speak is just what Job would wish (cf. *e.g.* 10: 2). Verse 12 cannot be translated with any certainty; cf. NEB, NAB.

(*ii*) **Therefore you must repent! (11: 13–20)**
The **if** of v. 14 cannot be hypothetical, in view of v. 6c. Zophar exhorts Job to **put away** his **sin** (14) and then elaborates on the joys of the righteous (15–19), concluding with the conventional contrast of the fate of the wicked (20). Though Zophar's speech ends on that note, the emphasis in the second half of his speech is generally encouraging, for he assumes that Job could itemize his sins quite readily if he were prepared to search his soul and repent of his undoubted iniquity. Job's reply to such a misunderstanding of his situation will be caustic.

(*f*) **Job's fourth speech (12: 1–14: 22)**
In this speech Job addresses first the friends (12: 2–13: 18) and secondly God (13: 19–14: 22). The movement of thought, even within the

first section, is constantly away from the friends and towards God. Thus the gist of the whole speech is: I want nothing to do with you **worthless physicians** (13: 4); **I desire to speak to the Almighty** (13: 3).

(i) The friends and their wisdom compared with God (12: 2–13: 18)

Job begins by denying that his friends are any wiser than himself (2–12), and continues by contrasting their wisdom with that of God (13–25). No doubt, he begins sarcastically, **you are the people** (2, NEB 'you are perfect men' reads a different Heb. root), i.e. the only people who count, but **I am not inferior to you** (3). He is addressing all of them, though in v. 8 the verb is singular, so that he seems there to have turned his attention to Zophar. He is a man of importance, who has been able to call upon God and receive an answer (12: 4; cf. also ch. 29), but now has become a figure of fun as one despised by God (4). The relevance of vv. 5 f. is not clear, but in vv. 7 ff. he seems to be saying that the very animals have more wisdom in the sense of knowledge of God than do his friends. Certainly in vv. 13–25 we have a hymn on the **wisdom and power** of God (the two concepts are frequently combined and virtually identified at times in Job). What is fastened on are the destructive capabilities of God (e.g. 14, 16, 21), for it is from such destructive divine strength that Job is himself suffering. But the major point of the hymn is to affirm the wisdom of God over against the friends. The theme of contrast between the friends' wisdom and Job's is taken up again in 13: 1 f., and again the movement is away from the friends and disputes with them to a desire **to argue my case with God** (3b). Again the friends' wisdom is called into question—the wisest thing they could do is to keep quiet (5)—and Job asserts that it would not stand up to examination by God (6–12). The friends claim to be speaking for God, but in fact are speaking **deceitfully** for him (7). Therefore, Job reiterates, he proposes to address God, and that boldly (13–16), while the friends may stand by and listen to Job's vindication (17 f.), of which he is absolutely certain (18b). We note that, as in ch. 9, it is still vindication of his innocence that Job desires, and not at all simply release from his suffering.

12: 5 f. The relevance of these, and of several other verses in this section, is doubtful. Job seems to mean that the friends are displaying 'the theology of the prosperous, who can look down on the unfortunate and excuse themselves from giving sympathy by the assumption that they have brought it on themselves' (Rowley); in v. 6 then the thought of the prosperity of the wicked is evident, but neither verse is directly relevant to the subject of the wisdom of the friends (2–3). Verses 11 f. are

apparently an aside to the friends, v. 11 effectively a question meaning 'Is this not so?' and v. 12 a sarcastic reference to the friends' 'wisdom'. 13: 15a is probably best not understood as an expression of despair, but of determination: 'If he would slay me, I should not hesitate' (NEB; cf. NAB). AV 'yet will I trust in him' is not quite correct, for Job's 'trust' is rather in his own integrity.

(ii) A demand that God will declare what it is he has against Job, but ultimately that he will let him alone (13: 19–14: 22)

There are two thrusts in Job's address to God here. The first (13: 19–27) is a demand that God will bring out in the open what he has against Job; the second (13: 28–14: 22) is that he will leave him alone to die in peace. These two pleas have been heard before from Job (e.g. ch. 10).

(a) *What have you against me?* (13: 19–27). If our paragraph division is correct, associating v. 19 with vv. 20–27, Job first summons God to enter into a law-suit with him, with the purpose of pronouncing a verdict of 'innocent' upon Job (19). But two 'conditions' (NEB) must be observed, otherwise Job cannot believe the disputation will be fair (20): first God must take his 'heavy hand clean away from me' (NEB), and secondly he must **stop frightening me with your terrors** (21). If these two conditions are met, then God may begin the proceedings, or if he prefers, Job will do so (22). The language of the law-court is constantly being used here. What Job wants from God is the bill of particulars he has against him (23; not that Job is admitting to anything: he means 'what you claim are my sins', i.e. your reasons for making me to suffer). As it is, it seems to Job that God is making much ado about nothing (25 f.), punishing him for childhood errors (**the sins of my youth** is too formal), and, as we have heard before (e.g. 3: 23), constricting and confining him (27).

Verse 28 should probably be connected with the following chapter.

(b) *Why do you not leave me to die in peace?* (13: 28–14: 22). This poignant statement of the brevity of human life and the inevitability of death ends this long speech, concluding the first cycle on the note of despair with which Job started (ch. 3). That has remained his mood throughout, and the powerful and demanding appeals to God have not been signs of belligerency so much as of desperation. Man's life is all too short; is he really worth the scrutiny that God gives him (3; cf. 7: 17 f.)? Therefore, **look away from him**, Job cries, meaning to refer to himself so that he may enjoy the few remaining days he has allotted to him as **a hired man** (6).

The comparison of man's life with that of a tree (7–12) is one of the most beautiful passages in the book: **there is hope for a tree** of revivification (7); for man there is none, **till the heavens are no more** (12)—which is never, as far as Job knows. Job's thought trembles on the edge of a hope for resurrection: if only Sheol could be, not a final resting place from which there is no exit, but a hiding-place from God's scrutiny and consequent wrath (13), a place of **hard service** which would one day come to an end (14), a place from which God would be glad to reclaim a man, having given up scrutiny of any sins he might have committed, and having **sealed up** his transgressions **in a bag** (16 f.). But the hope is a vain one, as far as Job is concerned: **if a man dies, will he live again** (14a)? No! As mountains are worn away and soil is washed away, even the firmest hope of man is eroded by the bitter reality of death; **so you destroy man's hope** (18 f.). Man has no hope but to be **overpowered** finally by God (20), and brought to Sheol in loneliness, not even knowing what goes on above the ground, even if his sons come into honour (21); in his isolation **he feels but the pain of his own body, and mourns only for himself** (22). The Christian hope of the resurrection fulfils Job's trembling and rejected wish perfectly. Job would have been prepared to wait an eternity for his vindication (14), but without knowledge of resurrection he must demand that, if God is going to vindicate him, it will have to be on this side of death. That is why, perhaps, the book must end with the restoration of Job's fortunes in ch. 42.

14. NEB by transposing v. 12c to follow the question of 14a, makes Job answer his question as soon as he asks it. The Hebrew text, however, leaves it hanging in the air until v. 19c, so that the possibility may be fully explored.

iii. The second cycle of speeches (15: 1–21: 34)

(a) Eliphaz's second speech (15: 1–35)

Eliphaz has not abandoned the position he took up in his first speech (chs. 4 f.), that Job is a righteous man (the interpretation of 15: 5 is significant here), but here he is more reproving of Job for his refusal to respect the advice of his friends (9 f.) and to recall the blessings that God has given him (11).

(i) Job's lack of wisdom and sinful speech (15: 2–16)

Job is not behaving like a wise man with his multitude of windy words—not the first time such a reproof has been uttered (cf. 11: 2). What is more, in demanding vindication from God and in speaking of God's destructive power as he has (perhaps Eliphaz is thinking of 12: 13–25) Job is being irreligious (**you . . . undermine piety,** 4). In fact, he is uttering ideas that are positively wrong; v. 5 should probably be translated 'your mouth increases your wrongdoing, and your tongue chooses crafty words'

(cf. Andersen). Eliphaz does not mean, I take it, that Job's speech only adds to his former iniquity for which he is suffering, for he does not believe Job to be essentially a wicked man (cf. 4: 6); he means that Job's **mouth, tongue,** and **lips** (5 f.) are together leading Job into sin: his own language puts him in the wrong (**condemns you,** 6).

The same points, that Job is not wise but letting his tongue lead him into sin, are made by the second strophe (7–16). Job, for all his claim to knowledge (*e.g.* 12: 3; 13: 1 f.) is not the **first man** Adam, about whose superlative wisdom traditions are found elsewhere also in the OT (cf. Ezek. 28: 12 f.); nor does he **listen in on God's council** (8) like the primeval wise man 'on the holy mountain of God' (Ezek. 28: 14), or like even the prophets who thus have access to secret knowledge and the plans of Yahweh (Jer. 23: 18, 22); nor has he the wisdom of human experience that the friends enjoy by virtue of their greater age (9 f.). It is lack of wisdom, Eliphaz is charitable enough to think, that is leading Job into sin so that he is turning his spirit (**vent your rage**) against God (13). Returning to a previous affirmation, Eliphaz asserts that no man is wholly innocent, since not even the angels **(the holy ones)** are perfect (15 f.); Job must therefore expect to endure a certain amount of suffering (cf. 4: 17 ff.).

16. man who is vile and corrupt: this is not a personal insult directed against Job, but a statement, albeit an extreme one, of general applicability to men as contrasted with God.

(ii) The miserable life and fearsome fate of the wicked (15: 17–35)

It is not perfectly clear why Eliphaz chooses to elaborate on this theme. Some, who have thought Eliphaz to be convinced by now that Job must be an evildoer, have taken this as Eliphaz's prognostication of the fate in store for the wicked. Others, who see Eliphaz as mightily offended by Job's responses, take this poem as a warning shot across Job's bows. But it is also possible to understand the poem much more sympathetically: Job is *not*, Eliphaz has been maintaining, one of the truly wicked, and so this description is precisely what does not apply to him. Job has not, as Eliphaz imagines the wicked, suffered **torment all his days** (20) and Job is not, like them, hatching **trouble, evil** and **deceit** (35). He ought to recognize, then, that he does not belong to the **company of the godless** (34) and take care that he does not join their lot by his intransigence and defiance against God (25). This, however, is only one possible reading of the poem, and no doubt in the mouth of another of the friends it would have a rather different meaning.

Whatever the exact function of this passage, it is an elaborate character-study of the unrighteous, in which the first section (vv. 20–26) concerns his inner anguish of living constantly in fear of death, and the second section (vv. 27–35) deals with his ultimate fate of dying before his time (31 f.). Though Eliphaz characterizes this as **what wise men have declared** (18), it has to be admitted that there is a good deal of wishful thinking about both main themes of the poem, and that experience does not generally lend its support to Eliphaz's rather unconvincing picture.

(b) **Job's fifth speech (16: 1–17: 16)**
This is the most disjointed of Job's speeches so far. After the tirade that has by now become a ritual opening of all the speeches, Job delivers what is essentially a monologue, broken into by appeals variously to the earth (16: 18), to God (16: 7 f.; cf. AV; 17: 3 f.), and to the friends (17: 10). It is hard to follow any train of thought, but one new theme makes its appearance in this speech: Job feels himself persecuted by men as well as by God. Whether he has literally suffered physical abuse such as he describes (e.g. **men . . . strike my cheek in scorn**, 10) is hard to know; this is the conventional language of innocent sufferers in the Psalms (e.g. Ps. 22: 6, 16) where it may often be metaphorical; Job may also be partly referring to the assaults of his friends upon him; but that he has literally become an object of scorn to his acquaintances (17: 6) seems confirmed by the rather more matter-of-fact account of his sufferings in ch. 30. What matters most is that Job *feels* himself persecuted: not only has God made him his **target** (16: 12), as we have heard before (7: 20), but men also have persecuted him (16: 10) because he appears to be suffering deservedly at the hands of God. His physical appearance has become **a witness . . . against me** (16: 8), since most people associate sickness with sinfulness. And the upright, instead of sympathizing with his innocent suffering, **are appalled**, assuming that Job must be a grievous sinner indeed, 'and the guiltless man rails against the godless', i.e. Job whom he regards as godless, while 'just men grow more settled in their ways, those whose hands are clean add strength to strength' (17: 8, JB), being ever more convinced of the truth of their theology. The speech ends once more on the persistent note of hopelessness: 'All I look forward to is dwelling in Sheol' (17: 13, JB).

16: 2. miserable: rather, 'wearisome' (NAB), lit. 'comforters of trouble', i.e. who increase trouble. **9–14.** The metaphoric language is exceptionally rich: God is pictured as a wild beast (9), a traitor (11), a wrestler (12a, b), an archer (12c, 13a), a warrior (13b, 14) (Andersen). **11.** God and the wicked are on the same side in opposing Job! **18. blood:** unless covered, it cries to heaven for vengeance. **19.** Who the nameless heavenly **witness** is remains hard to say; possibly it is God himself whom Job has

confidence in to vindicate him ultimately. A simpler interpretation is offered by JB, which takes the 'witness' to be the cry of Job's blood which has reached heaven and translates v. 20a 'My own lament is my advocate with God'. **17: 3.** Job asks God himself to **give a pledge**, i.e. give a guarantee, for him and his eventual vindication, for there seems to be none left on earth who will **put up security'** any guarantee, of Job's innocence. If such had been Eliphaz's intention in ch. 15, he had not made it very plain. Verse 5 is very difficult; JB translates 'like a man who invites his friends to share his property while the eyes of his own sons languish, I have become a byword . . .'. **8.** Some find this a high point in the book, as a statement that 'righteousness is its own justification' (Gordis), but it seems preferable to see here the reaction of the self-righteous to Job's predicament. **13.** The **if** is hardly hypothetical, since his death seems imminent. NEB however seems to take 13–16 as some kind of life-wish on Job's part. **16. we:** this must mean 'I and my hope': hope is left behind at the doors of Sheol.

(c) **Bildad's second speech (18: 1–21)**
Apart from the usual insulting remarks with which the speeches of Job and the friends now typically open (2 ff.), Bildad's speech is entirely devoted to the theme of the fate of the wicked. Since Bildad's earlier speech (ch. 8) has called upon Job to search his soul, and has assured him that if he is innocent God will not reject him (8: 6, 20), we can only assume that the present speech is by way of warning to Job of what his fate will be should it transpire that he is one of those **who know not God** (18: 21). Other commentators take it for granted that since Bildad here holds out no hope for Job he has by now classified him among the wicked, but such is not the inevitable meaning of his speech. Certainly he paints a grim picture of the death of the wicked, with a special emphasis upon the activities of supernatural beings, the demons of death (11, 13 f.) who **startle** him, **devour** him and bring him to Sheol into the presence of the king of the underworld, **the king of terrors** (14).

4b, c. Bildad rebukes what he sees in Job as arrogance, a desire to conform the world to his own will, the foundations of the moral order being disturbed out of their places for Job's sake. It is true that Job is crying out for a shaking of the foundations, but only the foundations of the moral order as discerned simplistically by the wise men and their black-and-white theology of retribution. **11.** The **terrors** are virtually personified as the demons of death which go by the names of 'Hungry One' and 'Calamity' (Habel), two of the faces of death. **13. death's firstborn:** probably disease (cf. the parallelism). **14. the king of terrors:** Death, personified as ruler of demons of terror. **15.** The scattering of **burning sulfur** on his tent may be an allusion to some such natural disaster as befell Sodom and Gomorrah or a reference to the supposed disinfectant properties of sulphur, used to rid his house (**tent**) of the pollution his wickedness has brought upon it. **16.** The **roots** and **branches** of the wicked are metaphors similar to those we have met at 15: 30. Verses 18 f. are uncomfortably like what looks like being the fate of Job. In oriental thought a fate worse than death was to die without leaving any progeny, so that one's **name** (17) or fame perishes.

(d) Job's sixth speech (19: 1–29)
This speech contains one of the best-known lines in the book, rendered in AV as 'I know that my Redeemer liveth' (v. 25). Unfortunately the Hebrew text of this and the subsequent verses is extraordinarily difficult, so that the popular interpretation of the passage can hardly be supported. Nevertheless, there is a note of hope here expressed by Job in his future vindication when he will 'see' God, a proud claim. God has been his enemy, and has attacked him directly (6–12) and indirectly through the humiliation Job is suffering from his household and acquaintances (13–22). Yet the speech concludes, unlike all previous speeches of Job, not with despair, but with a confidence that is not reached again until his final speech (chs. 29 ff.; cf. especially 31: 35 ff.).

(i) God counts me his enemy (19: 2–12)
After the usual reproaches to the friends (2 f.), Job says that in any case, even if he has sinned, that is no business of theirs. That is a matter between a man and his God, and the role of friends is to offer encouragement rather than set themselves up as judges (4). Though Job's suffering can be made into an argument that he is a sinner (5), they should realize that the fact is that God himself **has wronged me**, i.e. has made me seem like a wrong-doer by sending entirely undeserved suffering (6). The image of God as Job's enemy is then further developed: when Job appeals for justice against unjust oppression with the cry of 'Violence!' (**I've been wronged**), there is no one to answer him, for God himself is the oppressor (cf. Jer. 20: 8). He calls out to a deaf universe (Habel). He feels constricted (8; cf. 13: 27), he has been made ignoble and dishonourable (9), he has been attacked as though by an army (10 ff.). Throughout his accusation, it is important to notice that Job maintains his position that it is God and God alone with whom he is having dealings.

6. God has wronged me: wrong refers both to his undeserved suffering and to God's delay in vindicating him. **7. there is no justice:** this does not mean that God is unjust, but that he is delaying the justice due to Job.

(ii) God has alienated my friends from me (19: 13–22)
Job feels deserted by all his household and his acquaintance, from his **wife** (17) to his brothers (13, 17b), his **kinsmen** (14), his **intimate friends** (14, 19), especially the three comforters (21 f.), and even to his **guests** (15a), his servants (15b–16), and **little boys** (18). This very moving picture of alienation is no fabrication; not only was his disease probably feared to be contagious, but also it was regarded as a sign of God's extreme displeasure of him. Hence Job must begin He (God) **has alienated my brothers from me** (13).

20. I have escaped with only the skin of my teeth, though it has become a proverbial phrase, is strictly unintelligible. Perhaps he means that he has escaped death only by the narrowest margin, but he is not really speaking about death. **21.** The friends, for all their advice, have lacked **pity** (cf. 6: 14). **22. Why will you never get enough of my flesh?**, i.e. 'why do you . . . insatiably prey upon me?' (NAB); they are his assailants, like God and his suffering.

(iii) Yet I am certain of vindication (19: 23–29)
Job utters the wish that his cry could be preserved (23 f.) so that **in the end** (25), whenever that may be, his claim to innocence may be vindicated. That, he is convinced, will come about and he will see God 'on my side' (RSV; rather than **with my own eyes** (27)) and no longer as his opponent. Now that he has uttered his conviction, no matter how improbable it seems, he can round on his friends and warn them to cease persecuting him (28 f.).

24. Some evidence exists for the practice of cutting an inscription into stone and then filling the letters with lead (see Rowley); whatever the custom, it is clearly an indelible method of recording that is demanded. **25. my Redeemer:** the language is legal: the redeemer is the 'vindicator' who will 'rise last to speak in court' (NEB). Job does not say expressly who he expects his vindicator will be; perhaps he knows, yet does not know, that it will be God. At the moment God is his enemy, so must not vindication come from another quarter? Yet on the other hand his hope is that he will see **God** 'on my side' (RSV) (26 f.). **26.** Job is not necessarily thinking of a vindication beyond death, though his language by no means rules that out. The destruction of his **skin** is what has happened already (there is no reference to 'worms' (AV) in the Heb.), and his hope appears to be that **in his flesh**, i.e. while he is still alive, he will see his vindication. The preposition **in** could also be translated 'apart from' (NIVmg) but Job will hardly have an expectation of bodiless existence. **27c.** Perhaps the line could be translated with NAB: 'My inmost being is consumed with longing'. **28b. the root of the trouble lies in him**, i.e. Job is the cause of his own suffering.

(e) Zophar's second speech (20: 1–29)

Zophar has been incensed by Job's maintaining his innocence, and now bursts out with a further speech on the fate of the wicked, which is no doubt directed against Job. In this second cycle of the dialogue, invention has deserted the friends, and each dwells in turn on the same theme. It is a powerful and terrifying picture that each paints, and they all are fine speech-makers. Yet once again the speech is pointless, remorselessly irrelevant to Job's true situation. Zophar's contribution develops three themes: the brevity of the rejoicing of the wicked, the self-destroying nature of sin, and the swiftness of the final destruction of the wicked.

(i) How brief is the happiness of the wicked! (20: 4–11)

The conventionality of Zophar's discourse is apparent from the start. Not only does he appeal to what has been known **of old** (4), but also his insistence that the **joy of the godless lasts but for a moment** is plainly contrary to observed fact; the wicked do prosper, and are not always cut off in the midst of their span of life. From a deeply religious point of view perhaps it can be seen that however long they live their joy is but momentary (cf. Pss. 37; 73), but when that insight hardens into a formal doctrine, as it seems to have here, it becomes absurd.

6. 'It is not Zophar's sermon against pride that makes him a false prophet, but his application of it to Job' (Strahan). **10.** There is the thought of retributive justice here: **his children** will have to beg from the very poor who begged in vain from their father.

(ii) Sin brings its own retribution (20: 12–22)

Wickedness, though **sweet in** the **mouth will turn sour** in the stomach, so that the fruit of wickedness, riches, is vomited up (12–15). Verses 12–18 are formed with a chiastic structure, so that v. 12 corresponds to v. 18, v. 13 to v. 17 and so on (Andersen). The paradox of sin is further developed by showing (20 ff.) how **in the midst of his plenty distress will overtake him** (22): he has been so greedy that he has consumed everything he could lay his hands on, and so has no **treasure** left to **save himself** with (20).

(iii) The sudden end of the wicked (20: 23–29)

Paradoxically, what the wicked will eventually be filled with is the **burning anger** of God (23). His end will be violent, as in war (24 f.), and his possessions will be destroyed (26 ff.). In the day of judgment (cf. 19: 29) **heavens** and **earth** will **rise up** to testify against his iniquity (27).

It is noteworthy, as Andersen points out, that Zophar's conception of the fate of the wicked shows him to be essentially as much of a materialist as the wicked man he so condemns. The loss of fellowship with God, which is what is making Job suffer, does not occur to Zophar as one of the self-induced punishments of the wicked. Everything for Zophar is on the level of possessions or physical life.

(f) Job's seventh speech (21: 1–34)

All three speeches of the friends in the second cycle have harped on the theme of the fate of the wicked; the final speech, that of Zophar, has gone so far as to maintain that the wicked enjoy the fruits of their sin for only a brief period, and are quickly cut off. Job concludes the cycle of speeches by denying the truth of these claims: on the contrary, he says, the wicked **spend their years in prosperity, and go down to the grave in peace** (13). Job's denial of the friends' doctrine is equally extreme, but his position seems closer to real life. In this speech, for the first time in the book, Job is addressing the arguments of his friends comparatively directly, his mood of despair is very much in the background, and there is no direct address to God. These differences from the usual pattern of the speeches do not indicate a development, however, but only a temporary change of style. The strength of Job's speeches remains his personal appeal to God, and their emotive quality lies in the mood of despair that pervades most of them. So his temporary movement in this chapter to the plane of more rational discourse is no improvement of his lot; but is satisfying to see the friends so tellingly answered on their own ground.

(i) Hear me, my friends (21: 2–6)

This elaborate introduction betokens Job's need to be heard on this subject where they have all been in agreement. To **listen** to him for once will be better **consolation** for Job than any amount of speeches (2). He has no doubt that the outcome of his speech will only be that they will **mock on** (3; the Heb. has the singular, but the plural is perhaps intended), for his **complaint** is not **directed to man** but against God, and he can expect no sympathy from upright men when that is the case. If they will really 'hear what I have to say' (5, JB; NIV **Look at me**) they will be so **astonished** at what he is about to disclose concerning the moral governance of the universe that they will **clap** their **hand over** their **mouth**, a gesture of amazed silence. It is awful enough for Job himself to contemplate (6), this truth that in God's world the wicked are allowed to prosper.

(ii) The wicked prosper; why so? (21: 7–16)

Job denies all that the friends hold dear on this subject. The wicked **live on** (7), 'they live to see their children settled' (8, NEB), their animals suffer no mishap (10), and they even blaspheme

God (14 f.). and survive. Job cruelly parodies Eliphaz's picture of the prosperity of the righteous (5: 17–27). This poem of Job's on the prosperity of the wicked is formed on a chiastic pattern, with v. 7 corresponding to v. 13, and vv. 8 f. to vv. 11 f. Within three verses Job contradicts Zophar (7; cf. 20: 11), Bildad (8; cf. 18: 19), and Eliphaz (9; cf. 5: 24). Job does not wish for prosperity on their terms (16), which includes a deliberate rejection of God (14 f.). The prosperity of the wicked can never be contemplated by a righteous person without a sense of outrage; so Job is not only asserting their prosperity, but prefacing to every statement of it: **Why?** (7).

(iii) How often do the godless suffer? (21: 17–21)

Not only do the wicked live prosperously; it is only infrequently that one sees the premature death of a wicked person (17). Job is thus contradicting Zophar (20: 5). In v. 19, NIV seems to be correct in adding the words **It is said** which are not in the Hebrew; the friends have fallen back on the defence: if the wicked themselves do not suffer, their children do. Job regards that as an evasion of the problem (19b).

(iv) It makes no difference, in fact, whether one is good or bad (21: 22–26)

Perhaps v. 22 may be understood as another unmarked quotation from the friends. Job, they will be implying, is impugning the wisdom and justice of God. Job replies that in fact it seems to make no difference whether a man is good or bad; the same fate happens to all. He does not appear to be contrasting here the prosperity of the wicked (23 ff.) with the **bitterness of soul** of the righteous (25), but to be saying that just as in death no moral differences between men explain their common fate, neither in life are such differences significant.

(v) Human experience testifies to the truth of Job's arguments (21: 27–34)

Job knows what his friends have been thinking (27) while uttering their apparently objective third-person statements about the fate of the wicked: the wicked suffer, Job is suffering, therefore Job belongs with the wicked. Eliphaz, we have argued, has been perhaps less convinced than the others that Job has done anything wrong; but the drift of Zophar's speech at least has been perfectly plain. Yet the friends' belief in the equation of suffering and sin, pointing to the disappearance of oppressive princes and of the wicked (28), is belied by common human experience. Ask any traveller, says Job (29), and you will hear of the **evil man** being **spared from the day of calamity** (30). 'No one denounces his conduct to his face' (31a, NEB), no one requites him for his deeds. In death as in life he is honoured by thousands and his tomb is guarded against grave robbers (32 f.). This common human experience fals-

ifies the theologies of the friends (34).

iv. The third cycle of speeches (22: 1–31: 40)

While in the first cycle the friends had their individual points of view, and in the second they all harped upon the fate of the wicked, each perhaps from a slightly different perspective, in the third cycle it is harder to see any logic in the speeches. Eliphaz apparently contradicts in ch. 22 his original position, Bildad delivers only the preface to a speech and Zophar makes no speech at all. It is possible that the text has suffered somewhat in transmission, and that originally the third cycle did contain three full speeches by the friends, together with replies by Job. But now it appears that they have run out of steam, and indeed there *is* nothing new to say.

(a) Eliphaz's third speech (22: 1–30)

(i) Is not your wickedness great? (22: 2–11)

In one respect Eliphaz's message in this speech is in perfect accord with his first speech (chs. 4 f.): he believes that Job **will be delivered through the cleanness of** his **hands** (30). His advice is to 'come to terms with God' (21, NEB). In another respect, however, Eliphaz seems greatly at variance with his former position: he apparently accuses Job of untold wickedness (5), mainly of the nature of social injustice (6–9). These are the most specific, most harsh, and most unjust words spoken against Job in the whole book, and it is strange to find them on the lips of Eliphaz, out of all the friends. The crimes they depict are just the kinds of behaviour that Job vigorously denies in his powerful protestations of ch. 31. Most commentators take Eliphaz's charges at their face value, but perhaps it is possible to read them somewhat differently. In all the cases that Eliphaz mentions it is the *neglect* of some social duty that he is charging Job with. Eliphaz is unlikely to have made the speech he did in chs. 4 f. if he believed that Job had actively **demanded security for no reason** (lit. without a cause), **stripped men of their clothing** (6), withheld **water** and **food** from the needy (7), allowed powerful men to seize the lands of others (8), and rejected the pleas of **widows** and the **fatherless** (9). Rather, since Eliphaz believes Job is suffering for some cause—momentary though the suffering may be (4: 5)— and since the cause cannot be found in any wrong that Job has done, for he seems to have done none, his sin must lie in what he has failed to do. To say that Job has **stripped** the poor **of their clothing** need not mean that he has actively done any such thing, but rather that he must have failed to offer clothing to some needy person; and so on. Doubtless, since Job is not absolutely perfect, there will be those untouched by his social concern; in hyperbolic oriental fashion Eliphaz pictures their plight as Job's wilful fault. Only thus can he explain why **snares are round about** Job and **it is so dark** (10 f.). From this perspective the meaning of vv. 2 ff. becomes plain. Eliphaz does not disparage righteousness or the fear of God, though he may seem to be doing so, but saying that it is not for Job's righteousness—which Eliphaz recognizes—that God **brings charges against** him (4), but for leaving undone those things that ought to be done (6–9). It is for that reason that Eliphaz is compelled to ask, **Is not your wickedness great?** (5); it must be, since he has no other way of explaining Job's suffering.

(*ii*) **God can see your secret sin (22: 12–20)**
It was Zophar originally who accused Job of being a secret sinner (11: 5 f.), but now we find Eliphaz warning Job that God must know of his sins of omission which Eliphaz has guessed at in the previous strophe. Job cannot hope to escape the penetrating insight of God who can **judge through such darkness** (13). Evil men have not found it possible to escape God's judgment; even though temporarily their houses were **filled . . . with good things** (18), they have been **carried off before their time** (16), to the pleasure of the righteous (19 f.). Eliphaz's excursus on the fate of the wicked functions here as a reminder to Job that no sins, even of omission, remain undetected by God.

(*iii*) **How you can be delivered (22: 21–30)**
Eliphaz speaks here in his former manner; he is basically on Job's side, and hopeful that Job can 'come to terms' (21, NEB) with God and so **be at peace**. Borrowing a theme from Bildad's first speech (cf. 8: 5 ff.), Eliphaz exhorts Job to **return to the Almighty** (23), i.e. repent, **find delight in the Almighty** (26), pray to him and **fulfill** his **vows** (27). Then all his undertakings will prosper (28), and Job will experience salvation and deliverance through **the cleanness of** his **hands** (29 f; the text does not seem to mean that some other guilty man will be delivered through Job's innocence as NIV says). Unlike the recent speeches of the friends, this of Eliphaz ends on an uplifting note—to which Job responds with even deeper despair. It is noteworthy that it is in the second cycle, when Job's lot is being more plainly associated with that of the wicked, that he shows some spirit (especially ch. 19), whereas the apparently more cheerful hope of a renewed relationship with God is what casts him into deeper despair. If there is anything in this variableness in Job's reaction, it signifies something that we know already, that Job has no doubts about his own essential righteousness, but is distraught by the apparent break in his relationship with God.

(*b*) **Job's eighth speech (23: 1–24: 25)**
There are two main themes in this speech of Job's: the first is Job's re-iterated appeal to God

for vindication, accompanied by an expression of the hopelessness of gaining access to God (ch. 23); the second is that of the plight of the innocent poor compared with the prosperity of the rich, a situation that God seems to do nothing about (ch. 24). All in all, though Job believes that if he could gain access to God he would be vindicated, he despairs of ever receiving such vindication, since God plainly does not hold days of assize (**times for judgment**, 24: 1) when wrongs are righted.

(*i*) **Oh, that I knew where I might find him (23: 2–17)**
If only he could gain access to God, the problem of his vindication would be solved, Job believes. God would not use violence with him (6a) but would listen to his protestations of innocence (6b) and would acquit him (7). But the trouble is that God is inaccessible: he is neither **east** nor **west**, neither **north** nor **south** (8 f.). Job has discovered only too well that God cannot be brought to account or brought to court (cf. 9: 2 ff., 19). And yet, if Job cannot find God, he knows that God can find him (10a; perhaps meaning 'he knows what he plans to do with me'), and that when God chooses to put him to the test he will **come forth as gold**, vindicated as innocent (10). For Job's life has been one of unimpeachable obedience to the commandments (11 f.). Nevertheless, he must confess his inability to compel God to vindicate him (**who can oppose him?**, 13). He is in dread (15) of the inscrutability of God that leaves a man in the dark for so long; nothing is straightforward with God; nevertheless, he will not be **silenced by the darkness** (17). The chapter is a fine statement of the impossibility of calling God to account, and one that handles finely the tension between a proper confidence in God and the appropriate awe at his freedom to do as he pleases.

(*ii*) **Why are not times of judgment kept by the Almighty? (24: 1–25)**
Job recognizes that his own case is not the only troubled one on earth. Looking beyond himself to the lot of both the innocent and the ungodly, he is compelled to wonder why God does not hold regular assize days, at which the anomalies in the moral governance of the world could be cleared up (1): **why must those who know him look in vain for such days** of judgment (1b)? Why on the one hand is the anomaly of the suffering of the innocent poor allowed to go on for so long? The poor have their landmarks removed (2; cf. Dt. 19: 14), their flocks seized (2b–3), their person insulted (4); they are reduced to gleaning the corners of the field (6), to sleeping without sufficient covering (7 f.), to working without adequate reward (11). The picture is a moving one; but God cares nothing for their suffering, apparently, for he **charges no one with wrongdoing** (12c). And why,

on the other hand, Job goes on to ask, is the anomaly of the successful evildoer allowed to exist (13–17)? Murderers and adulterers who love darkness rather than light are permitted to persevere, **friends** though they be with **the terrors of darkness** (17). It is the same question in its negative form. Job has moved beyond his own isolated case to raise the fundamental question of theodicy, i.e. of God's government of the world. It is a question that is comparatively marginal in the book of Job, and it does not receive a satisfying answer. That is because the book is much more concerned (see Introduction) with the question, How should one suffer?, than with the question, Why does God allow suffering? Yet the universal question of theodicy is never far from the surface in all of Job's speeches.

Some of what follows, in vv. 18–25, is so unlike Job's argument that one can only suppose that it must really be the friends who are speaking. The argument that nevertheless the guilty swiftly perish (18), that Sheol soon snatches them up (19), that their name is not remembered long (20), that though they may be prominent for a little time, they are soon cut off like heads of grain (24), is the friends' argument. We can either relegate these verses to the apparently missing end of Bildad's speech (ch. 25), or preferably, suppose that Job is quoting his friends in these verses, while in vv. 21–23 and in v. 25 Job speaks in his own person. RSV inclines to this view by adding 'You say' at the beginning of v. 18, though it attributes only vv. 18–20 to the friends. JB adopts the desperate solution of removing vv. 18–24 to follow 27: 23, while NAB marks off vv. 18–24 as poorly preserved in the Hebrew text and seeks refuge in the Latin version of Jerome (the Vulgate). NIV, unpersuasively, attributes these out of character verses to Job. Whatever is to be done about these difficult verses, Job's general stance is perfectly clear: God does nothing about the anomalies in the moral order of the world.

(*c*) **Bildad's third speech (25: 1–6)**
It appears that some disturbance has made its way into the text of Job at this point. Bildad's speech begins without the usual address, and is only five verses long, while a speech from Zophar is lacking altogether, though three speeches of Job follow and certain strophes attributed to Job sound very strange on his lips. Many scholars therefore suggest that Bildad's speech originally consisted of 25: 2–5 plus 26: 5–14, and that some disarrangement has occurred in the course of transmission of the text. As Bildad's speech now stands, it resembles some of the thoughts of Eliphaz, especially the view that as compared with God there is nothing in the created order that is perfectly **pure** (5; cf. 4: 17 ff.); if moon and stars are not

pure, how much less is man. The gulf that separates man and God is highlighted by Bildad's opening consideration of the might of God (2 f.), whose armies are without number (3a). The same theme of God's all-powerful rule is continued in 26: 5–14, if these verses also are to be attributed to Bildad.

(*d*) **Job's ninth speech (26: 1–14)**
Of Job's speech we seem to have in ch. 26 only the opening fragment, a taunt against Bildad, ironically accusing him of having been of no help to Job. Especially if Bildad's speech had included 26: 5–14, stressing the power of God, Job's reply is all the more apt. It is all very well, he means to say, to declaim about the majesty of God, but of what use is that to one like myself who is **powerless** (2)?; and how can your panegyric upon the wisdom of God (7, 12) serve to assist one like myself whom you claim to be devoid of wisdom (3)? Perhaps Job's speech is continued within 27: 2–6.

The remainder of ch. 26, which we have tentatively assigned to Bildad, is a reflection upon the wisdom and power of God (the two attributes are closely connected in Job). God is he who has been able to create the universe, hanging the earth upon nothing (7). Various aspects of cosmology are mentioned, many of them not to be found in the Genesis creation story, but obviously traditional accounts of the process of creation: so, for example, the building of the **pillars of the heavens** (11) and the inscribing of a a 'circle' (RSV), the **horizon**, (10) to lay out the plan of the universe. We have reference also to other creation stories, in which creation was spoken of as a victory by God over the monsters of chaos (**Rahab**, 12; cf. 9: 13; the **gliding** or flying serpent, Leviathan, 13; cf. Isa. 27: 1). God's continuing creative power is also mentioned, binding up **the waters in his clouds** (8), here thought of as the water-skins of the sky, and covering **the face of the full moon** (9) during the varying phases of the moon's cycle. Yet, and this is the speaker's chief point, these evidences of God's grandeur which are visible and known to men are but the **outer fringe of his works** (RSV 'outskirts of his ways') and convey only a **whisper** of the **thunder of his** actual **power** (14). Man cannot hope to comprehend the real God, but is given only a glimpse of him in so far as he has chosen to reveal himself.

(*e*) **Job's tenth speech (27: 1–28: 28)**
Again we face the problem of the correct assignation of these verses. While in 27: 2–12 we have the authentic voice of Job, there is some reason for suspecting that what follows in chs. 27 and 28 is not from his lips—otherwise he will be found in 27: 13–23 uttering the same platitudes on the fate of the wicked that the friends have uttered. It may be suggested that 27: 13–28: 28 preserves the third speech of

Zophar; it is noteworthy that the themes we find here, the fate of the wicked (27: 13–23), the secret wisdom of God (28: 1–27), and man's obligation to do righteousness and avoid evil (28: 28) have previously been made, more prosaically, by Zophar in 11: 7–20. Other scholars assign the verses differently, however, it must be acknowledged: Rowley, for example, follows the consensus in attributing 27: 7–12; 24: 18–24; 27: 13–23 to Zophar, regarding ch. 28 as an independent poem on wisdom.

(*i*) **Till I die I will not abandon my integrity (27: 2–12)**
The key note to this speech, as to so many others of Job, is that he will not abandon his claim to integrity. Though God has **denied** him **justice** (2), and though his friends continue to judge him to be in the wrong (5a), Job vigorously engages our sympathies by his affirmation that he intends to maintain his righteousness (6). Anyone who assaults Job's innocence thereupon has called down upon him the fate of the wicked (7), which, as everyone knows, is dire (8–10). Job has reached a state of knowledge by now about the uncompellable and inscrutable ways of God (**the power of God, the ways of the Almighty**, 11) that he is in a position to teach all comers what he has learned from experience. Yet the friends themselves ought already to have learned from observing Job all that he has to teach them (**you have all seen this yourselves**, 12); the only surprising thing is that their speeches have lacked any serious content (**meaningless** is the Heb. *hebel*, translated 'vanity' in Ec.; Job has already called the friends' words *hebel* in 21: 34).

(*ii*) **The portion of a wicked man (27: 13–23)**
After the passionate self-defence by Job, this strophe reads rather dully, being composed of the traditional material we have met so often before about the fate of the wicked. The difference in mood adds weight to the suggestion made above that this is no longer Job's speech, but perhaps Zophar's. The portion of a wicked man is here pictured in terms of what happens to his family, his wealth, and his own person: **his children, however many**, are multiplied only for the sake of **the sword** or **the plague** (14 f.), his wealth is left to others more righteous than himself (16–19), while he himself is carried off as if by **flood, tempest** or devastating **east wind** (20–23). If this is Zophar's speech to Job, it is plain that a good deal of the wicked man's portion has already been Job's lot, and the implication of the speech is perfectly clear and in line with Zophar's attitude throughout the book: 'God exacts of you less than your guilt deserves' (11: 6).

(*iii*) **Where may wisdom be found? (28: 1–28)**

The theme of this majestic poem, one of the great poetical masterpieces of the book, is that 'wisdom' is unattainable by man. By 'wisdom' is meant, not the practical kind of wisdom inculcated in the book of Proverbs, but rather wisdom as full and total understanding of the world and its order. This use of 'wisdom' would be very intelligible to the author of Ecclesiastes, who stresses that man 'cannot fathom what God has done from the beginning to end' (Ec. 3: 11; cf. 8: 17). This poem would sound somewhat strange coming from Job, since it is only by dint of lengthy divine argument (chs. 38–41) that he is brought to that recognition (cf. 42: 3); but more important than the question of which character in the dialogue utters the poem is its emphasis on the great gulf between human and divine wisdom.

The poet is not concerned to denigrate human wisdom in order to magnify the wisdom of God. His poem begins as a paean of praise to the ingenuity of mankind (1–11), and only then goes on to affirm that even so true wisdom eludes his grasp and is known only to God (12–27); to man is given, not 'wisdom', but the knowledge of God's law: what is wisdom for man is to live in **the fear of the Lord** (28).
(*a*) The wisdom of man (*28: 1–11*). The poet chooses only one example of human wisdom: man's ability to mine metals from beneath the surface of the earth. This is a particularly apt illustration of human wisdom, for it incorporates the theme of the search for what is precious. The Hebrew of the poem is rather obscure, partly because so little is known of ancient technologies of mining. All versions need to exercise some imagination to make sense of the details, but the general picture given by modern versions is clear. First, four metals for which men mine are noted. In v. 3 there seems to be a reference to the use of lamps underground. Verse 4 highlights the danger and remoteness of such industry, picturesquely describing the miner as he descends his shaft (**he dangles and sways**). This business of mining is a paradoxical process: on the surface the peaceful processes of agriculture go on, while underneath there may be a violent over-turning of obstacles to get at the metal (5). Man's ingenuity has created beneath the earth a path unknown to birds and beasts (7 f.). Unlike the animals, man is master of the earth (11); he can attack the sides of hills, 'upturning mountains by their roots' (9, JB); his eye is more keen than the falcon's (10, cf. v. 7), his paths more secret and remote than the lion's (10, cf. v. 8).
(*b*) *But where can 'wisdom' be found? (28: 12–28)*. Plainly the 'wisdom' that cannot be found by searching is something different from man's technological wisdom. The poet does not tell us directly what he means, but allows a sus-

penseful climax to build up which increasingly shows the impossibility of obtaining this wisdom. Its place is unknown (12), and so too the way to it (13); it cannot be valued in gold or silver or precious stones (15–19). The world itself does not know where it is to be found (14). Even the supernatural powers of **Destruction** (NIVmg) (lit. Abaddon, i.e. Sheol, the underworld), and **Death** know no more of it than a rumour (22). But God knows all about it (23), for in fact it is his own wisdom which he used in establishing the creation (24–27). It is inaccessible to man, this supernatural knowledge of the universe and its purpose and the laws that govern it; what has been given to man, however, is another kind of wisdom: a more manageable and practicable wisdom, a wisdom that consists in doing: the **fear of the Lord**, i.e. true religion, and **to shun evil** (28) is what constitutes wisdom for man. This poem can stand admirably by itself, but if it is to be read as concluding Zophar's final address to Job, its significance is to reject Job's claim to full understanding of the ways of the Almighty (27: 11) and to prescribe for Job, not a search for wisdom, but an endeavour after righteousness as his proper objective.

(f) **Job's eleventh speech (29: 1–31: 40)**
Job's powerful concluding speech has three movements: in the first he surveys in nostalgic mood his former happy circumstances before the hand of God fell upon him (ch. 29); in the second he portrays, in pathetic mood, his present isolation and degradation (ch. 30); in the third he pronounces, in defiant mood, a series of self-maledictions which come to a climax with a desperate appeal to be heard and vindicated (ch. 31). The presence of the friends is ignored completely, and God is not addressed: it is Job who speaks entirely of himself and about himself, and it is this concentration upon the one theme of his fate that makes this one of the most impressive and moving pieces of Old Testament literature.

(i) **Oh, that I were as in the months of old (29: 2–25)**
This nostalgic retrospect not only fills in the details of the picture of Job's life given us in the prologue, but also conveys the mood of what the life was that Job has now lost: of warm and dignified relationships. They were the days when **God watched over** him (2), the days of his **prime** (4), lit. 'autumn days', autumn being the season of maturity and of fresh growth when the new rains come. They were the days of prosperity, his flocks so plentiful that his **path was drenched with cream**, his olive trees so fruitful that the presses in the **rock poured out . . . streams of olive oil** (6). They were the days when respect was accorded him as the chief man, or sheikh, of his village, whose opinion carried most weight

at the meeting of elders in the village **gate** i.e. the open space near the entrance of the village (7–10). They were the days when he was in a position to bring assistance to the underprivileged, the **poor** and **fatherless** (12), 'those in extremity' (13, NAB), the **widow** (13b), the **blind** and the **lame** (15), the **stranger** whose rights he studied (16b; cf. NAB). The same two themes of his security and his prominent and positive rôle in society are then repeated in 18 ff. and 21–25.

It is noteworthy that for Job the blessings of his former life did not only include material prosperity and social honour, but, equally importantly, the possibility of doing good to those in need. Contrary to Eliphaz's guess that Job's sin must be acts of omission in the social sphere (22: 6–9), Job's present speech indirectly absolves him of any such failing: the privilege of wealth, in Job's eyes, was precisely that of being able to care for the needy. Job's pride in his achievement, as Andersen points out, was legitimate and not self-righteous: 'For Job to have adopted the posture of a cringing sinner would have been a species of self-righteousness for him'. Although from a Pauline perspective we know that in the strictest sense there is none righteous before God (Rom. 3: 10), the case of Job makes clear that we do wrong to pretend that men are as bad as they can possibly be or that men can never be innocent and righteous.

17. The **wicked** man is represented as a wild beast. **18. in my own house:** (lit. 'nest') a doubtful reading; other possibilities are 'in a ripe old age' (cf. Pope), 'with my powers unimpaired' (NEB), 'in honour' (JB).

(ii) **But now they make sport of me (30: 1–31)**
Now as Job compares his present lot with his past life the contrast could hardly be more extreme. Just as his former life consisted of a network of harmonious relationships with God, his fellows and the underprivileged, so his present condition is represented by the destruction of those relationships. Men now treat him with contempt (1–15; 24–31), while God has cast him off (16–23); in a way, however, they are one and the same experience, for it is God's doing that he suffers men's contempt (11). *(a) The worthless people who despise him (30: 1–8).* The first three strophes of this movement of the poem begin with **But now** (1, cf. 9, 16), highlighting the change in Job's condition. Job's attitude to those who despise him seems at first rather patrician: they are a **base and nameless brood** (8), the poor of the land who live on leaves and roots (as v. 4 seems to mean). Is it not precisely such people that Job would in former days have had a care for? Yes, and it is just for that reason that he is so scornful of their contempt now. Even those whom he previously treated with generosity have turned

on him and have regarded him as beneath themselves. It is their ingratitude that so moves him to wrath. The text of this strophe contains many difficulties, but the general sense is that among those who now regard themselves as superior to him, Job sees weaklings who, suffering **want and hunger** (3), have no strength for any productive work; they are the outcasts of society (8), yet their standing is higher than his.

(*b*) *The rabble who assault him* (30: 9–15). Job is now the butt of the scorn (**song . . . byword**, 9) of those whom he had once helped. They attack him, he complains (14); though there is no more physical assault involved than in his being driven forth from the company of men (12), the treatment he receives makes him feel like a city besieged (14), with its accompanying **terrors** (15). All this is because God has allowed and encouraged his assailants by unstringing his **bow** (metaphorical for his vitality) or loosing his 'cord' (RSV), a metaphor from the loosing of the tent-cord, which brings the tent down in a heap (11).

(*c*) *The suffering which God inflicts on him* (30: 16–23). Over and above the disgrace he now endures is the sheer physical suffering that has tormented him from the beginning. Day and night it gnaws at him like a monster (16 ff.). All of this is God's doing (19); yet appeals to him fall on deaf ears (20), for God too, like the unlovely rabble, has **turned on** him **ruthlessly** (21) and will inevitably bring him to death (23).

(*d*) *He must cry for help* (30: 24–31). Though he is convinced no good will come of it, he must cry out for help (24); he deserves help, since he has given it so freely (25), but when he **hoped for good, evil came**. This movement (ch. 30) of his speech ends with the recapitulation of his disgrace in the eyes of men, the theme with which it began: he is rejected by the assembly of his villagers (28) and consigned to the company of wild creatures (29). His skin turns black from his disease (28, 30) so that he is an object of loathing, and the music of his former life is turned to **mourning** (31).

(*iii*) **Oh, that I had my adversary's indictment!** (31: 1–40)
This final movement of Job's speech, in which he makes a solemn asseveration of his integrity, is in the form of a 'negative confession' in which he denies any crime that may be laid to his charge. If he has committed any of the sins mentioned, he prays that God will exercise the law of retribution and pay him back in kind. Such a catalogue of self-maledictions could be uttered only by a person completely convinced of his own integrity, and not surprisingly it comes to a climax (35 ff.) with Job's bold appeal for God to hear him and answer him with the appropriate punishment. At least let him have the indictment of charges that God holds

against him; he would be proud to carry about with him a document to which he could so confidently give an answer.

The crimes Job mentions give us an excellent indication of his own moral standards. In every case but one (that of idolatry, 26 f.) they are sins against one's neighbour; yet they are properly speaking also sins against God. The form of the oaths which Job takes is not always complete or systematic. They usually begin with **'if . . .'**, but in one case (1–4) a more positive statement is used; they usually conclude with **then** (*e.g.* 8, 10), but on occasion the corresponding retribution is left to the imagination (*e.g.* 33 f.). Since 35 ff. is clearly the climax of the poem, one would expect 38 ff., another oath of the usual type, to precede it; such a resumption of the main thread of the argument after the climax is not unknown in Job, but it is possible also that the placing of 38 ff. is due to a simple scribal slip.

(*a*) *Lust* (31: 1–4). Though the sin of adultery is mentioned below (9–12), here Job declares that he has not sinned by desiring a virgin, a temptation especially present to the owner of many servants, such as Job was. He has **made a covenant with** his **eyes** not to **look** with desire **at a girl** (1); as in the Sermon on the Mount, sin is seen to reside in the inward intentions of the heart, and not just in the outward act. Job's belief in the doctrine of retribution remains unshaken (2 ff.); his only complaint is that he is suffering from a malfunctioning of that moral law of the universe, suffering when he has not deserved to.

(*b*) *Dishonesty* (31: 5–8). Again sin is something that first occurs in the *heart* (7). The reference to the **scales** (6) and to the failure of his crops as the punishment for dishonesty (8) suggests that he is thinking primarily of **falsehood** and **deceit** (5) in business transactions.

(*c*) *Adultery* (31: 9–12). No code of laws such as the Ten Commandments is consciously being referred to in Job's protestations, but the crime of adultery was recognized throughout the Near East as a serious one (cf. 11 f.); it was often called 'the great sin'. The punishment in kind that Job calls down upon himself is either that his wife should be reduced to the lowest rank of servitude (cf. Exod. 11: 5), or perhaps that she should be taken in return by his neighbour (**grind** (10) possibly being a euphemism for sexual intercourse).

(*d*) *Injustice to servants* (31: 13 ff.). Here Job claims that he has gone beyond the call of the established duties of his time in treating any grievances of his servants as seriously as those of free men. He has not regarded his servants as chattels, though contemporary society would have entitled him to, but as fellow human beings (15), a remarkably sensitive ethical perspective.

(*e*) *Lack of social concern* (*31: 16–23*). Job has already portrayed his sympathy for the poor, the widow, the fatherless, and the stranger, the typical underprivileged persons of ancient Semitic society (29: 11–16). He reiterates this aspect of his behaviour, claiming that he had even taken orphans into his own household (18). He prays that if at any time he has **raised his hand against the fatherless** 'because I saw that I had supporters at the gate' (21, NAB) and that he could get away with injustice to the fatherless, retribution may fall upon the hand lifted in injustice and his **arm be broken off at the joint** (22). Fear of retribution from God has been a guiding instinct with him (23).

(*j*) *Avarice* (*31: 24–25*). Job now turns to further inward sins (cf. 1–4): the secret love of riches (24 f.), the worship of the sun and moon (26 ff.), pleasure at the downfall of his enemies (29 f.), any meanness through pretended ignorance (31 f.) or any other hypocrisy (33 f.). None of these denials is explicitly followed by a curse, but such is to be understood. In the present case, although Job has been exceedingly rich, his wealth has never become an idol in which he trusted instead of in God.

(*g*) *Idolatry* (*31: 26f.*). This is the only religious sin in Job's catalogue of crimes. Though adoration of the heavenly bodies was almost universal in the ancient world, for Job such worship would have been to serve the creature rather than the creator, and would have been **unfaithful to God on high.** The practice referred to in 27 is of throwing kisses to the moon as an object of worship.

(*h*) *Vindictiveness* (*31: 29 f.*). Not to rejoice over the downfall of the wicked once again goes beyond the ethics of Job's time; even the psalmists did not feel it wrong on occasions to be glad at the punishment of the wicked (cf. *e.g.* Ps. 54: 7; 118: 7; 137: 8 f.), but Job has followed the spirit of that law that enjoined giving help to one's enemy (Exod. 23: 4 f.; cf. also Prov. 20: 22; 24: 17 f.; 25: 21 f.).

(*i*) *Neglect of the needy* (*31: 31 f.*). Perhaps the thought of secret sins is still present here, in that Job may be thinking of occasions when he could have pretended not to know of cases of need. He has been generous to the needy not only in cases of obvious need (16–21) but also in cases when he has been the only one to know the need.

(*j*) *Hypocrisy* (*31: 33 f.*). Job is not even here admitting **sin.** He means, 'If I have committed transgressions and then attempted to hide them "as Adam did"' (AV, NIVmg). He denies that he has committed iniquity and then attempted to hide it for fear of the populace.

(*k*) *Job's final appeal* (*31: 35 ff.*). So formal has this oath of exculpation been that Job can conclude it with **I sign now my defense,** as though it were a written document. If only he could have, to match his own declaration of innocence, the **indictment in writing** from his **accuser,** i.e. the list of charges that God has against him. Far from being humiliated by it, he is so confident that all it could do is attest his integrity that he would **put it on like a crown** (36). He would **approach** God not as a criminal but as an innocent man who could **give an account** of anything that might be laid to his charge (37).

(*l*) *Exploitation of land* (*31: 38–40*). Job's final self-curse, perhaps accidentally transposed from another place in the chapter, calls down punishment upon himself if his land is able to testify that he has acquired it through oppression of its rightful owners (39). If that be the case, let retribution fall upon him, weeds springing up instead of **wheat** and **barley.**

v. The Elihu speeches (32: 1–37: 24)

(*a*) Elihu's first speech (32: 1–33: 33)

The view of most scholars is that the four speeches of Elihu are a later addition to the book of Job. Elihu is not mentioned in the prologue, and while it could be argued that this is nothing remarkable since it was to the author's dramatic advantage to have a fresh interlocutor appear at the end of the cycles of speeches, Elihu's absence from the epilogue is surprising. The Elihu speeches also delay Yahweh's reply to Job, which might have been expected directly after ch. 31; when Yahweh does reply (chs. 38 ff.) he addresses Job as if nothing had intervened. It is further often suggested that the Elihu speeches, in maintaining the purpose of suffering to be education, are at odds with the poet's intention to show that there is no real solution to the problem of suffering. Other factors sometimes mentioned, such as the stylistic peculiarities of the Elihu speeches and the laboured justification offered by Elihu for intruding into the conversation, are of minor significance in determining the question. In sum, the common judgment is that 'the speeches violently disturb the artistic structure of the original book' (O. Eissfeldt). They are to be understood, it is thought, as the attempt of a pious author to compensate for the failure of Job's friends to rebut his arguments and for the inconclusive nature of the divine speeches.

Defenders of the authenticity of the Elihu speeches have not, however, been lacking, but sometimes they have made exaggerated claims, such as C. Cornill's that the Elihu speeches are the 'crowning point of the book of Job'. R. Gordis has helpfully pointed out that the function of the speeches can best be understood as offering a human middle way between the position of Job and his friends. The friends have argued that God is just and that suffering therefore proves Job has sinned and that God is punishing him for it. Job denies both arguments, by insisting that his suffering is not the result of sin, and that therefore God is unjust. Elihu, who proclaims himself opposed to both Job and the friends (32: 6–12; 33: 5, 12; cf. the introductory narrative, 32: 2 f.), argues, by advancing his doctrine of suffering as discipline, that suffering need not be the penalty for sin already committed, but may be a warning, given in advance, to keep a man back from sin. In any case, the justice of God must not be impugned, as has been done by Job.

(i) Introduction (32: 1–5)

It is made very plain by the four-fold repetition of the word **angry** in what mood the young Elihu enters the conversation. He is angry at Job because he 'had made himself out to be more righteous than God' (2, NEB), i.e. the inevitable conclusion of Job's argument is that since he is in the right in his dispute with God, God must be in the wrong. This is something that Job had refrained from saying, so Elihu is putting words into his mouth quite unfairly here. NIV makes the reason for Elihu's anger rather less serious by translating **Job . . . justifying himself rather than God**, which is true enough, but hardly very blameworthy under the circumstances. Elihu is also angry at the three friends because **they had found no ways to refute Job** (3), i.e. had been unable to convince Job that God was not in the wrong. The anger of Elihu is plainly the anger of frustration, in that good manners dictated that the young should not speak before their elders.

(ii) Elihu's right to speak (32: 6–22)

The whole of this section is nothing more than a long-winded introduction of himself and defence of his participation in the conversation. Had the author previously given us grounds for analysing the characters of the participants in the debate, we would be inclined to find in Elihu a rather pompous young man, who promises far more than he is able to deliver. But perhaps it is unwise to pretend to draw character sketches of the speakers; it is their arguments rather than their personalities that catch the attention.

Elihu confesses his youth and voices his respect for the wisdom of age (6 f.), but takes courage from his belief that all are created with an equal capacity for wisdom (**it is the spirit in a man, the breath of the Almighty, that gives him understanding**, 8). Therefore it is not *necessarily* (one presumes he means to say) **the old who are wise** (9). So he is not afraid to declare **what I know**, (10). He has further been encouraged to enter the lists by the feebleness, as he judges it, of the friends' speeches (11 f.). He has gained the impression that they believe they have **found** true **wisdom** in Job and that only **God** may **refute him, not man** (13). Elihu is setting out to disprove that belief.

It is true that Job has not yet addressed him, but if he did, he would respond rather differently from the friends (14).

Turning now to Job (15), he points out the obvious and pronounces himself ready to speak (16 f.), being **full of words** (18), his mind being **ready to burst** with its multitude of thoughts (19) and needing relief from its frustration (20). Finally, as Rowley comments, 'Elihu gives himself another certificate, this time for impartiality': he will not treat anyone —and it is Job who has most to suffer from his tongue—with special respect (21); he is not **skilled in flattery**, so Job had better be prepared for some straight talking (22).

(iii) Why God brings suffering upon men (33: 1–33)

(*a*) *Elihu addresses Job* (33: 1–7). Elihu's wordy introduction continues. He claims no special wisdom apart from what can be acquired by every man in whom is the breath of the Almighty (4; cf. 32: 8). He calls upon Job to answer him (5), which Job should not find too difficult, since he, Elihu, will use none of God's strong-arm tactics; he too is a mere man, **taken from clay** (6). He is not being patronizing to Job when he says **no fear of me should alarm you** (7), but implicitly contrasting the weakness of his confrontation with the power of God from which Job has complained that he is suffering.

(*b*) *Job's accusations against God are unjust* (33: 8–13). Job has consistently maintained that God has denied him justice by refusing to defend his integrity, and that God's treatment of him has been that of an enemy (10 f.) rather than that of an impartial judge. In this Elihu intends to show that Job is **not right** (12), not by arguing—as the friends have—that Job is a sinner, but by showing that God sends suffering for other purposes, notably to warn man from committing sins in the future. In this way Elihu hopes to be able to show that both God's justice and Job's integrity can be maintained (cf. 12, 32).

(*c*) *Dreams are one way God has of speaking to man* (33: 14–18). Elihu will illustrate his interpretation of suffering by using the example of nightmares. They are one of the ways God has of speaking to man though men do not always recognize it (14). In dreams he sometimes **terrifies** men **with warnings** in order to turn men away from wicked deeds and to 'check the pride' (NEB) of men (17). This form of suffering is used by God to prevent greater suffering—the possibility of falling into **the pit**, i.e. death (18).

(*d*) *The imposition of suffering is another means God uses* (33: 19–28). Physical suffering is also used by God for the same purposes: to 'chasten' or warn a man lest he should commit some serious crime (19). Elihu develops the picture in the rest of the strophe. What often happens is a very severe illness, so that the man's **flesh wastes away** and his **bones . . . stick out** (21), and he is in danger of death (22). But it only needs a word on that man's behalf by one of the many mediatorial angels (23 ff.), and the man is healed and offers public thanksgiving for his restoration to health, as in the Psalms (*e.g.* Ps. 22: 22–25). He accompanies his thanksgiving with a confession of sin (27), even though it may only have been sin contemplated and not actually carried out.

(*e*) *Peroration (33: 29–33).* This strophe is mainly a recapitulation of what has gone before. God will give a man opportunity to repent several times (29), so that he can be delivered from destruction (30). Job is invited to reply (32), but if he has nothing to say, which he plainly has not, he should continue listening (31, 33). Elihu's purpose, he says again, is not to accuse Job of being a sinner, but to 'clear' him (32b) by explaining his suffering as God's discipline.

(*b*) **Elihu's second speech (34: 1–37)**
In this speech Elihu has ceased to address Job directly, and now appeals to the **wise men** (2) who could be the friends (in which case Elihu is being ironical), or a larger group of bystanders. His main point in this speech is that since God is just (10), any criticism by Job of what God does or fails to do is unjust. Elihu has now ignored Job's particular situation, and is trading in generalities.

(*i*) **Job is essentially irreligious (34: 2–9)**
Elihu begins by appealing to the **wise men** (2) to 'discover together where justice lies' (4, JB) in the matter of Job. At least Elihu does Job the honour of quoting his words, on occasion, and attempting to meet Job's arguments, which is more than the other friends have done. Here he takes up Job's claim **'I am innocent'** (5a; cf. 27: 6) and **'God denies me justice'** (5b; cf. 27: 2), i.e. has refused him justice by not vindicating him. Verse 6a should probably be translated 'should I lie against my right?' (cf. RVmg), i.e. 'should I confess to guilt when I am innocent?'. Elihu appeals to the audience to say if they have ever encountered a man like Job who **drinks** the **scorn** of his friends like water (7), and who by his claim that God has taken away his right has put himself in **company with evildoers**, who also charge God with injustice. Elihu argues that Job has by the statements of vv. 5 f. argued that **it profits a man nothing when he tries to please God**. This is unfair to Job. He *has* said that judgment does not always fall on the wicked (21: 7–34), and that trouble falls on good and bad alike (9: 22 ff.), but his whole behaviour has given the lie to Elihu's charge. His holding fast to virtue even when it has brought him no profit puts him in a far different

category from those who would glibly argue that virtue is useless. Job's perseverance in unrewarded virtue shows him to be anything but irreligious.

(*ii*) **God will not do wickedly (34: 10–15).**
The thrust of this strophe is that God will not be unjust (10, 12) and implicitly that therefore Job is wrong to charge God with any form of injustice. Elihu states God's justice in the conventional form of the doctrine of retribution (11), but not in order to equate Job with the wicked. God's justice is for Elihu an implicate of his being the **Almighty** who has **charge of the whole world** (13) and holds the breath of all living things in his hands (14 f.). But this, though a fine statement of the power of God, is really irrelevant to the question of his justice—unless perhaps Elihu means that 'might is right'.

(*iii*) **Shall one who hates justice govern? (34: 16–30)**
Elihu develops the foregoing argument, that the governor of the universe cannot be presumed to be unrighteous; God is **just and mighty** (17). He has the power to judge kings and nobles (18), to shatter them **without** need of **inquiry** (24) since he already knows their steps (21); he can overturn them in the night (25). His works of might are in strict accord with his justice: he shows no partiality to princes or the rich (19), he rewards men according to their works (25), and strikes men down for their wickedness (26) because they have disobeyed his laws (27) and oppressed the poor (28). The cryptic v. 29 is perhaps addressed more directly to Job, meaning: under these circumstances, if God **remains silent** and **hides his face** and does not produce vindication such as Job appeals for, who is in a position to **condemn**, i.e. say that he does what is unjust? Such is in any case the general theme of Elihu's address to Job

(*iv*) **But Job adds rebellion to his sin (34: 31–37)**
These verses are some of the most obscure in the book. One thing clear is that Elihu regards Job's constant demand for vindication as an adding of **rebellion** to **sin** (37), in that it puts God in the wrong. Elihu imagines the case of someone who has been punished for his sin and now comes to repent of it (31 f.). According to Elihu, Job's theology does not allow God to forgive such a repentant sinner, for Job would have a person who has suffered at God's hand demand vindication and reject forgiveness (33). If that interpretation of v. 33 is correct, Elihu is again unfair to Job, since Job does not maintain that all suffering is innocent. It is easy, however, to see how a person claiming that his own suffering is undeserved might be traduced by such as Elihu as affirming that all suffering is equally undeserved.

(c) Elihu's third speech (35: 1–16)
(i) What advantage has a righteous man? (35: 2–8)

Elihu's speeches are none too clear, but here he seems to be taking up again the claim he put in Job's mouth in 34: 9 that it 'profits a man nothing when he tries to please in God'. That is not Job's position, nor is it Job who asks **'What profit is it to me, and what do I gain by not sinning?'** (3). Elihu only imagines this to be Job's question. But he answers it for him by arguing that one cannot expect to be better off for being righteous (7); since God is so great, what happens on earth is of little concern to him (5), even if it is wickedness that happens (6, 8). This position, though reminiscent of Job's utterance in 7: 20, accords ill with Elihu's firm statement of the doctrine of retribution (34: 11), so his logic must be acknowledged to be rather weak.

(ii) Why is Job not delivered? (35: 9–16)

Since Job's complaint has been that God has taken away his right (27: 2), Elihu addresses himself to the question why Job has not been delivered from his affliction, having previously (ch. 34) dealt with the question whether God perverts justice by ignoring a just complaint. Here he takes the case of oppressed people who **cry out under a load of oppression** (9). They are not always delivered. Why not? Because something is lacking in their cry: it has been an involuntary cry and they have not addressed it to **God** their **Maker** who can reverse fortunes by giving **songs in the night** (10) and who can give greater wisdom to men than to the **beasts** and **birds** (11). They are not answered because in their **arrogance** they have neglected to cry to him (12); such cries are **empty**, and disregarded by God (13). The same is true of Job, says Elihu, who has been merely complaining of his suffering and not addressing himself to God (14 ff.). Once again Elihu misses the mark; he cannot have been listening to Job!

(d) Elihu's fourth speech (36: 1–37: 24)

This final speech of Elihu has two movements: in the first (36: 2–25, or perhaps 2–21), he reiterates his understanding of the function of suffering as discipline; and in the second he praises the power and wisdom of God in creation, which he regards as God's entitlement to be moral governor of the universe.

(i) The function of suffering as discipline (36: 2–25)

(a) Introduction (36: 2–4). Elihu's concern is still to speak **in God's behalf** (2) and to **ascribe justice to** his **Maker** (3), i.e. to prove that there has been no miscarriage of justice in Job's case. Since God is so far above men, he must **get** his **knowledge from afar** (3). He also assures Job that he, Elihu, has the answers; he is **one perfect in knowledge**, i.e. has accurate knowledge; he does not claim omniscience!

(b) Affliction as discipline (36: 5–16). Beginning with the case of the righteous as opposed to the wicked, Elihu asserts the usual wisdom doctrine that God **does not keep the wicked alive but gives the afflicted their rights** (6). His own contribution comes when he considers the case of the righteous who fall into suffering, a theme very close to Job's own situation. Elihu argues that the righteous in such cases (8) are being reprimanded for their transgression (past or future, the Hebrew does not make clear) and commanded to **repent of their evil** (9 f.). So suffering is divine discipline, a point we have heard already from Elihu (33: 15–30). If the righteous respond to such warnings, well and good (11), but if they do not, they suffer the fate of evildoers and **die without knowledge**, i.e. without having learned anything from the divine disciplining. The point of vv. 11 f. is then developed in 13–16: the ungodly when afflicted simply **harbor resentment** in their heart and **do not cry** to God **for help** (13); they die young and in shame (14). The godly, on the other hand, whose ears are opened to what God is teaching them by their adversity, are delivered (15). 'For you, no less, he plans relief from sorrow' (16, JB); Elihu seems to be expressing the hope that Job will be numbered among the latter.

(c) But Job is in danger (36: 17–25). Although Elihu has expressed his hope that Job will be counted among the righteous, all the current indications are that he is on the side of those who do not learn from their suffering, and is thus **laden with the judgment due to the wicked** (17). As a result, not even his **mighty efforts** will not keep him from **distress** (19). He needs to direct his plea to God, and to **extol** God's **work** in the midst of adversity (cf. 35: 10). Much of this strophe is far from intelligible.

(ii) The power and wisdom of God in creation (36: 26–37: 24)

The ensuing rather fine hymn on the creative power and wisdom of God is relevant to Elihu's speech only because he believes that it is God's creative power that gives him the right to be moral judge of the world. The present poem may thus be regarded as an elaboration of 34: 10–15. Thus although it is similar in many ways to ch. 38 at the beginning of the divine speeches, Elihu does not steal God's thunder, for he has a rather different point to make.

Elihu begins by affirming that **God** is **great**, the theme of the present poem; (lit. 'we know him not', i.e. completely) his greatness transcends our understanding.

(a) The clouds and the rain (36: 27–33). The wonders of the coming of rain are first referred to. Though we know far more than Elihu did about the movement of the clouds, there still remains deep mystery even on the simply

physical level. For Elihu, however, the wonders of rain and lightning go beyond their
meteorological aspects: they are one of God's
means of judging between peoples (31a), for
the same phenomenon can be both beneficent
(**provides food in abundance**, 31b) and destructive (he is 'the One zealous against evil',
33b, NIVmg).

(b) *The thunderstorm* (37: 1–5). The parallel in
Hab. 3: 6 indicates that it is the perception of
the living presence of God himself in the thunder and lightning that makes men tremble (1)
(Andersen).

(c) *The rain and snow of winter* (37: 6–13). The
winter storms, by which God 'shuts every man
fast indoors' (7a, NEB) and keeps wild **animals
in their dens** (8), do not only reveal God's
might in controlling (12) these forces that tame
both man and beast, but also express his wisdom in using the forces of nature for various
purposes, **whether to punish men**, or for his
own pleasure (**to water his earth**), or to **show
his love** for his creation.

(d) *The heat of summer* (37: 14–24). In the
phenomena of summer also are portrayed the
power and wisdom of God: in the **lightning**
of summer storms (15), the **clouds** so delicately
balanced (16), the hot **south wind** (17), the
blazing sky as hard as copper (18), the blinding
light of the summer **sun** (21). God's wisdom so
surpasses Job's that Job cannot even understand
how these phenomena work (15 f., 18), let
alone control them. So great is the **awesome
majesty** (22) of God, indeed, that Elihu asserts
that he is effectively unapproachable; he asks
Job, ironically, **to tell us what we should say
to him** (19a), but denies in the same breath
that it is possible to do so, 'for all is dark, and
we cannot marshal our thoughts' (19b, NEB).
To be blunt, although we can rest assured that
God **is exalted** both **in power** and **in justice**,
the fact is that the **Almighty** is **beyond our
reach**, i.e., we cannot have access to him (23).
This is the very position that Job has denied all
along by his repeated insistence that God
should personally answer his complaints. And
it is effectively refuted by the personal appearance made by God in the immediately subsequent chapter.

vi. The Yahweh speeches (38: 1–42: 6)
The speeches of Yahweh to Job are remarkable
both for what they omit and what they include.
First, it is surprising, but surely of the utmost
significance, that God makes no reference to
any sins or faults on Job's part such as the
friends persisted in attributing to Job and as
Job himself demanded to be told of. Clearly,
then, God holds nothing against Job; not even
his 'wild words' (6: 3, NEB) are a matter for
reproof. Above all, the importance of the divine speeches—for Job and for the message of
the book—is not so much what they contain

but the fact that they happen at all. Their very
presence shows that a person who determin-
edly calls upon God—even out of anger and
frustration—will find himself ultimately in
converse with God, in a conversation that leads
to the resolution of tension.

But these divine speeches are also striking
for what they contain. Far from taking up the
issues of innocence or guilt raised by Job, and
far from justifying the ways of God to man,
they deal wholly with the natural order, the
world of creation. Whether, as in the first
speech, God portrays the cosmic order and
parades before Job, so to speak, a menagerie of
his animal creation, or, as in the second speech,
he dwells with loving detail on the looks and
habits of the hippopotamus and the crocodile,
he speaks entirely of the world of nature, and
tells Job nothing he does not know already.
His purpose is not to give Job lessons in cosmology and natural history, and certainly not
to browbeat Job with dazzling displays of his
power and intelligence (which Job has never
for a minute doubted), but to invite Job to
reconsider the mystery and complexity and
often sheer unfathomableness of the world that
God has created. He expects Job to realize—
and Job is not slow at grasping the point—that
the natural order is analogous to the moral
order of the universe. Much of it remains beyond human comprehension, some of it seems
hideous, futile, or fearsome, but all of it is the
work of a wise God who has made the world
the way it is for his own purposes.

(a) **Yahweh's first speech (38: 1–40: 2)**
This speech consists largely of a series of questions addressed by God to Job. They are not
intended to humiliate Job by exposing his ignorance and inability to answer God, nor are
they designed to be such a display of God's
wisdom and omnicompetence as to require Job
to leave off his attempt to understand what is
happening to him. Rather, they challenge Job
to reconsider what he already knows about the
world that God has made, and to ponder its
mystery afresh. After the introduction in 38: 1
ff., God points Job's attention to ten features
of the natural order (38: 4–38) as exemplars of
its mystery, and to nine species from the animal
kingdom (38: 39–39: 30) to illustrate the mystery of created life. The final note struck by
God (40: 2) reminds us that the dialogue between God and Job is cast in the form of a
judicial proceeding (cf. also 38: 3), since that is
what Job has demanded (e.g. 31: 35); but the
purpose of the dialogue is not to establish guilt
or innocence, but to enquire after truth, to
expose the realities of created existence.

(i) **Introduction (38: 1 ff.)**
Job at last receives the reply he has so earnestly
desired: among his last words had been the plea
'Let the Almighty answer me!' (31: 35). Job's

appeals for a confrontation with God have throughout been couched in legal language: he has envisaged the calm and comparatively peaceful setting of a legal trial, but that is not the setting that Yahweh chooses. It is **out of the storm** that he speaks, for he does not so much wish to argue with Job as to convey to him how far beyond Job's range are the questions of the governance of the universe. The **storm** is traditionally an accompaniment of divine revelation (cf. *e.g.* Nah. 1: 3; Zech. 9: 14; Ps. 18: 7–15; 50: 3), and although it is terrifying, and has already figured in the book as a destructive force (1: 19), it means for Job that God does not intend to hold himself aloof from Job's sufferings but will meet him where he is and reveal himself to him. By addressing Job as one who **darkens my counsel with words without knowledge** (2) God does not belittle Job's intelligence, as the friends have sometimes done, but pronounces him to have no understanding of the divine plan (**counsel**) for the ordering of the universe. Job could hardly dispute the fact that his lack of insight into God's purposes effectively made those plans 'dark' and made God's dealing seem arbitrary. Again, in urging Job to **brace yourself like a man** (lit. 'gird up your loins') (the word has overtones of 'warrior' and the action is a preparation for a hard task or for battle; cf. Jer. 1: 17; Isa. 5: 27), God does not pour scorn upon Job, but encourages him to use all his mental strength to understand the message God will convey to him in indirect fashion. 'Job as man is not humiliated as a worthless worm, but confronted as one invited to dispute with God about cosmic mysteries' (Habel).

(*ii*) **Phenomena of earth and heaven (38: 4–38)**

(*a*) *The earth's creation (38: 4–7).* Here the creation of the world is portrayed as the erection of a building, with a **foundation** and a **cornerstone**, and built to plan with the use of a **measuring line**. The foundation and building of the earth was accompanied by the music of the **morning stars**, who are probably the same as the 'sons of God', the **angels**. (The laying of the foundation and the setting of the capstone were occasions for music and rejoicing, Ezr. 3: 10–11; Zech. 4: 7.) This is but one of the many biblical pictures of the creation drawn from the range of human creative work; it is not to be taken literally as the Hebrew conception of the structure of the universe. Its purpose, like that of the other rhetorical questions in the chapter, is not to humiliate Job but to bring him to reflect on the scope of God's abilities which are beyond his comprehension.

(*b*) *The creation of the sea (38: 8–11).* The sea is portrayed as having been born from the **womb** of an unnamed mother (8) and wrapped by God in a 'blanket of cloud' and 'fog' (9, NEB).

But it is also a threatening force that must be kept in its place, shut in with **doors and bars** (10). The phrase is reminiscent of the Babylonian creation story, in which the god Marduk having conquered the chaotic water monster Tiamat keeps her at bay by setting bars and posting guards, bidding them not to let her waters escape (*ANET*, p. 67); but there is no echo in Job of a conflict between Yahweh and the waters. Here God both protects (9) and controls (10 f.) the mysterious sea.

(*c*) *The Dawn (38: 12–15).* Even the coming of the dawn is beyond Job's comprehension, no matter how often he has observed it. NEB is probably correct in removing from these verses the references to **the wicked** (13, 15) which seem rather inappropriate, and in finding references to various heavenly bodies like the 'stars of the Navigator's Line' that 'go out one by one' (15) as the dawn breaks. Most picturesque is the line portraying the coming of day as bringing up 'the horizon in relief as clay under a seal, until all things stand out like the folds of a cloak' (14, NEB).

(*d*) *The Underworld (38: 16ff.).* Beneath the earth is a whole realm of creation unknown to man (in spite of his abilities in mining, 28: 1–11): **the springs of the sea**, the fountains of the great deep (Gen. 7: 11) which feed the waters of the sea, and the land of **death**, pictured as a city with **gates** (17) and 'doorkeepers' (17b, NEB), the 'janitors of Shadowland' (JB). The earth or 'land' whose expanse Job cannot comprehend is probably the land of death, the underworld.

(*e*) *Light and Darkness (38: 19ff.).* Light and darkness are viewed as separate beings who have their own dwellings assigned to them from the time of creation and to which they return at the due time. Job does not know how to 'escort' each 'on its homeward path' (20, NEB); unlike wisdom, God's master workman (Prov. 8: 22 f.), he was not even born at the time of their creation and assignment of dwelling-places (21). The irony of v. 21 is not so bitter if it is read as a question or as a hypothetical statement: 'If you know all this, you must have been born with them' (JB).

(*f*) *Snow (38: 22 f.).* Also beyond the reach of Job's knowledge are the **storehouses of the snow** and **hail** (22), reserved **for days of battle** (23) (cf. Exod. 9: 22–26; Jos. 10: 11; Isa. 30: 30).

(*g*) *Thunderstorm (38: 24–27).* The **east wind** is unlikely to bring thunder and rain, so JB may be right again in translating 24b 'when it scatters sparks over the earth'. The **channel** for the torrents of rain from the heavenly storehouse (25) is reminiscent of the 'floodgates' of heaven that are opened at the time of the Flood (Gen. 7: 11). A new point is introduced in vv. 26–27, which will be further developed in ch. 39:

it is stressed that much of what goes on in the created order does not happen for man's sake, but for the sake of other parts of God's creation, or simply because God wills it. Here it is the rain that falls on **a land where no man lives** and on **a desert** (26).

(*h*) *Rain* (38: 28 ff.). In Canaanite mythology, Baal, the storm-god, could be regarded as the **father** of **rain**, and one of his daughters was named Taliya, the **dew** (28). But here it is taken for granted that no satisfactory explanation can be given for the origin of rain, dew, or ice: it is beyond human understanding.

(*i*) *The constellations* (38: 31 ff.). Reference to various constellations between strophes dealing with the rain (28 ff.) and the clouds (34–38) may suggest that the heavenly bodies are here regarded as having some influence over the weather, though nothing in the text says so specifically. The 'sweet influences' of the Pleiades in AV (31) are only the invisible 'chains' (mg) that bind that cluster of seven stars together; and NIV's phrase **God's dominion over the earth** (33b) is misleading (the line is better translated, 'Can you, on earth, determine the laws that govern them?'). **Orion** (31) appears to be pictured, as in classical mythology, as a hunter with belt (**cords**) and sword. Identification of the other constellations is uncertain, though NEB takes **the Mazzaroth** as 'the signs of the Zodiac' and **the Bear** as Aldebaran (32). In this continuing series of rhetorical questions, Yahweh has been directing Job's thoughts to the fact that, whatever be the influence of the stars, Job has no influence over them, nor even any comprehension of the **laws** (33; 'laws of nature', NEB) that determine their movements.

(*j*) *The clouds* (38: 34–38). Job has no influence either over the coming of the rain or the appearance of lightning. Verse 36 is very obscure: do the 'clouds' and 'mists' (as the Heb. seems to mean) themselves have **wisdom** (even poetically speaking)? NEB finds a reference here to the wisdom of God shrouded in 'darkness' and 'secrecy', while NAB thinks the verse originally followed v. 40 and referred to the wisdom of the 'cock' who, in Jewish tradition, has been given the intelligence to distinguish between night and day (similarly JB). NIV's translation offers a sentence that seems out of place. The picturesque description of rain as caused by God's tilting the **water jars of the heavens** (37) is no more intended to be taken literally than is the reference to the 'channel' for the rain earlier (25).

(*iii*) **The animal creation** (38: 39–39: 30)
The remainder of the first divine speech directs Job to the animal creation—not to the animals well-known and useful to man, like sheep, ass and camel but to those that serve no purpose in the human economy and are, rather, mysteri-

ous, useless, or hostile to men. These too are part of God's creation though man may see no value in them or indeed may find them positively malevolent. It is the same with suffering: sometimes indeed it may have a recognizable purpose, but sometimes it may be just as enigmatic and hurtful to man as the wild animals can be. Nevertheless, it is part of God's order for the world, and he knows what he is doing in allowing it to be.

(*a*) *The lion and raven* (38: 39 ff.). The animal and the bird of prey are associated in the one strophe. The point is not that Job cannot **satisfy the hunger of the lions** (39), or even that it is God who **provides food for the raven** (41), but that there is a whole realm of God's creation that exists utterly independently of man.

(*b*) *Goats and hinds* (39: 1–4). Here too are animals quite inaccessible to man: the cycle of their life is unaffected by man's interference. They give birth and their young grow up without man's assistance or knowledge.

(*c*) *The wild ass* (39: 5–8). The **wild donkey**, exempted by God from service to man (5a), leads a free, though hard life, and is totally useless to man, unlike his domesticated cousin, the tame donkey driven through the noisy city streets (7).

(*d*) *The wild ox* (39: 9–12). An even greater gulf separates the domesticated ox from the *wild ox* or aurochs (not 'unicorn', AV), the most powerful of hoofed animals, though it became extinct in the 17th cent. A.D. The idea that he could be harnessed to the service of man is ludicrous.

(*e*) *The ostrich* (39: 13–18). If some animals are wild and free and untameable, others, like the ostrich, are simply ridiculous. Since this is not meant to be a natural history lesson, it does not matter that only the popular view of the ostrich as a cruel and feckless parent appears here; in fact only during the day are its eggs abandoned, and at night both cock and hen take turns at keeping the nest warm. Here the ostrich's reputation for folly (17a) is deployed to show that God has even created animals whose behaviour makes no sense—not by human standards, at any rate.

(*f*) *The war horse* (39: 19–25). At first sight out of place among the menagerie of wild animals, the war horse is included here because even he, though to some extent under man's control, has a strength and courage that imbue him with mystery. Even a creature so close to man can be ultimately incomprehensible to him: what gives the horse his **strength** (19), what is it in him that he **laughs at fear** (22), how does his urge to rush into battle arise (25)?

(*g*) *The hawk and eagle* (39: 26–30). Finally, Job's gaze is directed to the sky, to birds of prey, the hawk and the eagle (or, 'vulture', NEB); this strophe then balances that with which the animal series began (38: 39 ff.). Here are creatures that dart into man's ken from time to time (30) but who live their life for the most part in places inaccessible to man (27 f.). They serve no purpose in the human economy, they are predatory and unclean; yet they are created by God and their natural instincts (**wisdom**, 26) are implanted by him. If Job can accept that, he can accept also the fact that some cases, at least, of human suffering stem solely from the inscrutable wisdom of God.

(iv) **Conclusion (40: 1–2)**
The nuance of Yahweh's final direct address to Job is hard to grasp, but however ironical he may be about Job's inability to comprehend the totality of the divine plan (cf. 38: 2), he is never contemptuous of Job, nor does he seek to browbeat him into submission (cf. 38: 3). We may translate (following a suggestion of Andersen): 'Will he who disputes with the Almighty (Shaddai) give instruction, will he who argues with God give answer?' It is a simple invitation to Job the litigant to respond to Yahweh's speech.

(b) **Job's first reply (40: 3 ff.)**
Many commentators find here an expression of submission, humiliation and defeat on Job's part. He does indeed say, **I am unworthy** (lit. 'I am light'), in view of the limitations of his understanding borne in upon him by Yahweh's speech. But as yet he has nothing to **answer**; his case still stands. Though Yahweh has called upon him to reply, Job in effect invites Yahweh to continue his speech. Job will **put** his **hand over** his **mouth** (4), and as yet has nothing to add to what he has already said (5). His real response to Yahweh will come only in 42: 2–6; here he does no more than concede the strength of God's speech; he will wait for the peroration (40: 6–41: 34).

(c) **Yahweh's second speech (40: 6–41: 34)**
(i) **Introduction (40: 6–14)**
At first sight, God seems here to be browbeating Job with an assertion of his superior power. But not only would such an assertion cut no ice with Job (he had always conceded God's superiority [*e.g.* 9: 15–19]), it would also seem to be beside the point, since the issue is justice, not power. The thrust of the passage is perhaps best conveyed in the last sentence (14): that Job cannot of himself win vindication from God. Only one with power (**arm**, 9) like God and in physical control of the universe can have the authority to make judgments in the moral sphere also. Vindication of a man is a divine task, and Job has been encroaching on God's prerogatives by demanding vindication: by insisting upon his own righteousness, he **would discredit** God's **justice** (8), since the prevailing theology did not allow both innocent suffering and divine justice to co-exist. Job is at one with God in recognizing that only God can give him

the vindication he wants, but he has stepped beyond his created status in *demanding* anything, even vindication, from God. Read in this light, the divine exhortations of vv. 10–13 retain their irony, but they are far from being a cruel mockery of the feebleness of Job.

(ii) **Behemoth (40: 15–24)**
The second divine speech proves, as Job's non-committal reply (40: 4 f.) has led us to expect, to be no more than an extension of the themes of the first speech. Here, however, in place of the brief snapshots in ch. 39 of the animal creation, there are presented two panegyrics on Behemoth, the fiercest of the land animals, and Leviathan, the most dreadful of the sea creatures. If the earlier chapters concentrated more on the mystery of the animal creation, these chapters are concerned with the terror and monstrosity, and yet the splendour, of two of God's creatures.

Behemoth, meaning, as the plural of *bᵉhēmāh*, 'land creature', simply 'the great beast', has been variously identified as the crocodile (NEB), the wild buffalo (Pope), the hippopotamus (RSV and most commentators) or elephant (NIV) or as a mythical creature. Although the description of both Behemoth and Leviathan abounds in poetic exaggeration (*e.g.* 40: 18; 41: 19 ff.), it seems that real creatures made by God (15, 19) are in mind. Indeed, both creatures are also symbolic of primeval chaos, and their creation by God indicates his control of the chaotic powers that may threaten the stability of the universe. But they are as well real animals, it would seem, whom Job would know and recognize. Of such a creature, repulsive and hostile to man, God can say that **I made** him **along with you** (15), and even that he is **first among the works of God** (19), an allusion no doubt to Gen. 1: 21 where the 'great creatures of the sea' are mentioned first among the animals created by God. The point is that the world God has created contains not only man but also some beings inexplicably terrifying to man.

It is probably best to see in **behemoth** a description, poetically elaborated, of the hippopotamus. His chief diet is **grass** (15), his habitat in the **reeds** and **marsh** by the river (21). It is unexpected perhaps to find that the **hills bring him their produce** (20), though hippopotami are known to scramble up steep slopes in search of food. His strength is legendary (16 ff.), and he cannot be safely attacked by men (only his maker could vanquish him with a sword, 19b), let alone be caught with hooks or have a rope attached to him by his nose (24). A river in spate holds no terrors for him, and 'a Jordan could pour down his throat without his caring' (23, JB). The one doubtful element in the picture is that **his tail sways like a cedar** (17), since the tail of the hippopotamus is short and small; yet the thought may be in mind that even this comparatively insignificant part of the beast's anatomy is of exceptional strength.

(iii) Leviathan (41: 1-34)

While various authors have argued that Leviathan is a dolphin, a tunny fish, or a whale (as in NEB, transposing 41: 1–6 to follow 39: 30), the most widely adopted view is that he is the crocodile. It must be borne in mind that Leviathan figures in Canaanite mythology as Lotan, a seven-headed monster of the deep, and allusions to that mythological being are made in the OT (*e.g.* Ps. 74: 13f.; Isa. 27: 1). So **Leviathan** here, like Behemoth, has a symbolic value as a personification of chaos; but it is more probable that it is a matter of the real animal, the crocodile, being described in mythological and pictorial language than that the mythological creature is described in terms of the crocodile.

(a) *The uselessness of Leviathan (41: 1–11)*. The account of Leviathan is not arranged in any strict sequence, but this first section seems largely devoted to emphasizing that Leviathan has no practical usefulness for human beings. He cannot be caught (1) or tamed (2) or made docile and domesticated (3); he cannot be used in the service of men (4) or as a pet to entertain the children (5). He cannot serve as food for men (6), for, as the beginning of the strophe has already pointed out, he cannot even be caught (7 ff.). Anyone so reckless as to **lay a hand on him** would not do so a second time (8)! The mere sight of the crocodile is enough to turn away hopeful hunters (9). The final sentences (10b–11) of this strophe are rather obscure; in NIV they read as if God were saying that, if a man of courage is frightened away by the sight of a crocodile, only a fool would be reckless enough to approach God himself. But it seems unlikely that God is reproaching Job for approaching him even with his complaints, and it is preferable to take these sentences as referring to Leviathan; so JB: 'No one can face him in a fight. Who can attack him with impunity? No one beneath all heaven.'

(b) *The fearfulness of Leviathan (41: 12–34)*. The emphasis in this section of the poem lies on the fearfulness of various anatomical features of the crocodile. The highly poetic language and rhetorical fancies cannot be appreciated if literal exactitude is all the reader requires of literature. The **outer coat** (13), probably a coat of mail, is recognizable as the hard scales of the crocodile, his **undersides**, especially of his tail, are known to be **jagged potsherds** (30), and his motion in the water does indeed make **the depths churn like a boiling cauldron** (31). But one wonders whether the account of his breathing out fire (18–21) is meant to be taken very seriously. Rowley remarks that 'when the crocodile issues from the water, it expels its

pent-up breath together with water in a hot stream from its mouth, and this looks like a stream of fire in the sunshine', but poetry about the fire-breathing dragon like Leviathan should not be reduced to such a prosaic level. What matters in this poem in honour of the **king** of **all that are proud** (34), i.e. the wild beasts, is that the reader should be able to sense the awesomeness and grandeur of this creature that is so repulsive and hostile to man. Leviathan is the climax of Yahweh's speeches to Job, and the point of this strange excursion into the animal kingdom is not lost on Job: suffering is a crocodile, a hippopotamus, terrifying and mysterious, yet part of God's world and possessed of a peculiar splendour of its own.

(d) Job's second reply (42: 1-6)

Job's final speech, crucial though it is to the understanding of the dialogue between himself and God, is somewhat cryptic, and open to differing interpretations. What is clear, however, is that unlike his first speech of 40: 2–5, which was in effect not a reply but a refusal to reply, this speech evinces a real resolution of Job's dispute with God. It is resolved by Job's recognition of God's right to do what he does —even, though this is not said explicitly, to the extent of bringing suffering upon an innocent person. So what is new about Job's knowledge **that you can do all things; no plan of yours can be thwarted** (2) is not that God is almighty —Job has always known that—but that God's almightiness has an ineluctable purpose or **plan** in whatever he does. Job's complaint has been that his suffering made no sense—it was against the theological rules of guilt and punishment. Now he knows, through being led to consider the mysteries of God's animal creation, that his suffering makes sense to God. That is what matters to him, even though God has in no way explained or justified Job's suffering to him; it is enough for him to know that God knows what he is doing. This is why Job takes up God's earlier question, **Who is this that obscures**, by failing to recognize, the divine **counsel** or plan **without knowledge?** (3; see 38: 2); that, he now confesses, has been his mistake. To demand, as Job has done, an answer to the problem of suffering, is to intrude into an area beyond human comprehension: **I spoke of things I did not understand, things too wonderful for me to know** (3). Job has also demanded vindication from God; that he will receive in an unelaborate but emphatic fashion in vv. 7 ff., but that may wait, for more important now to Job than his public vindication is the fact that through his cries for a confrontation with God he has in reality met with God face to face. That God should actually have broken through the silence and have addressed Job, **'Listen now, and I will speak; I will question you, and you shall answer** me' (4; cf. 38: 3), and invited him into dialogue, is better than any vindication. Job can stand anything but being ignored by God. The personal experience of God (**now my eyes have seen you**, 5) transcends the suffering, the isolation and the sense of injustice as much as it transcends mere theory about God (**My ears had heard of you**, 5). While NIV and most modern versions have Job say, **I despise myself** (6), **myself** is not in the Hebrew, and it is more probable that he despises the words of abuse he has hurled at God. Likewise what he has to **repent** of is not any sin for which his suffering has come upon him, for it is axiomatic in the book that Job is no sinner; he can repent only of the extreme language, words 'without knowledge' he has uttered. But perhaps it is better still to take the word translated **despise** as 'melt', as did the LXX, i.e. 'I melt into nothingness', the feeling of a creature before his creator, and to take the word for **repent** as 'comfort', i.e. 'I am comforted though still sitting upon dust and ashes' (cf. 2: 8). What the friends have failed to accomplish through their presence (2: 11) and their speeches (cf. 16: 2; 21: 34) God has done by his personal intervention. Job is still suffering, still upon the ash-heap, but his bitterness is relieved and his tension is resolved by his encounter with God.

III. EPILOGUE (42: 7–17)

The dialogues of the book are over, and Job has received divine consolation enough for him to endure his suffering. The story of Job might have ended at that point were it not that one of Job's most insistent pleas has been for vindication, i.e. for public demonstration by God that Job is righteous and undeserving of his punishment. God is under no obligation to give Job that satisfaction and many innocent sufferers have been denied the happy outcome accorded to Job. Some scholars have thought the happy ending spoils the book of Job, in that it appears to revert to the old nexus between guilt and punishment, righteousness and blessing, that the book sets out to destroy. Is not the theology of the friends, that the righteous prosper, only confirmed by the epilogue to the book? No, for the friends insist that the righteous indubitably prosper, and the wicked inevitably come to an untimely end. The case of Job has proved how foolish any talk of necessity or inevitability in God's dealings with men is. But the epilogue wants to affirm, when all due allowance has been given to God to do as he pleases, that God delights to shower blessings upon one who serves him faithfully. This is by way of a bonus, an act of grace and not of compulsion on God's part. It is enough for Job that he has encountered God, but it pleases God to respond at the end to Job's pleas for vindication.

i. Vindication before the friends (42: 7 ff.)

In this charmingly ironic scene Yahweh emphasizes to the friends that it is Job, and not they, who have truly been **my servant** (repeated four times!), and that it is Job, and not they, who **has spoken of me what is right** (7 f.). What a remarkable, not to say comic, reversal of roles we find when punishment for the friends' folly is only averted by the prayer of the righteous and still suffering (cf. 10a) Job (8 f.)! Those who had felt so superior to Job are the ones who stand in need of forgiveness themselves; and Job is not only vindicated before them but becomes their champion. How can the friends' unexceptionable and respectful talk about God be termed **folly** when Job, whose speeches have been full of bitterness and hatred against God, is said to have **spoken** of God **what is right**? Only in this, that the friends spoke of God entirely in the third person, as an object, whereas Job insisted on addressing God personally. In a time of suffering, talk merely *about* God is folly; only a calling upon God, however bitter and violent, can be right, for it paves the way to an encounter with God.

ii. Vindication publicly (42: 10–17)

To the friends, the divine testimonial to Job (7 f.) has amply vindicated him, but in the eyes of his relatives and fellow-citizens the sign of divine vindication will naturally enough be the restoration of his fortunes. And his fortunes are restored in double measure (12); is there a hint here of compensation for the unwarranted loss Job had suffered (cf. Exod. 22: 4)? The comfort Job has received from his encounter with God (see on v. 6 above) is enriched by the comfort he receives from his relatives (11) now that he has been socially rehabilitated (contrast 19: 13 f.). The gifts of **silver** and **a gold ring** (11) are tokens of esteem rather than gifts to alleviate his poverty; his fortunes have already been restored (10). So wealthy does he become that there is sufficient inheritance for even his daughters to have a share!—daughters usually inherited only when there were no male heirs (Num. 27). The epilogue concludes on a note typical of the patriarchal narratives of Genesis: death at a ripe old age, **full of years**, is the final blessing of God. With this scene we are returned to the idyllic pastoral mood with which the book opened; within that stylized world, so far removed from our own, there has gone on beneath the surface a human drama that belongs to every age.

BIBLIOGRAPHY

ANDERSEN, F. I., *Job*. TOTC (London, 1976).

DAVIDSON, A. B., *The Book of Job*. CBSC (Cambridge, 1877).

DHORME, E., *A Commentary on the Book of Job* [on the text] (London, 1967).

ELLISON, H. L., *From Tragedy to Triumph: The message of the book of Job* (London, 1958).

GLATZER, N. M., *The Dimensions of Job* (New York, 1969).

GORDIS, R., *The Book of God and Man—A Study of Job* (Chicago, 1965).

HABEL, N. C., *The Book of Job. CBC* (Cambridge, 1975).

POPE, M. H., *Job.*[3] *AB* (Garden City, N.Y., 1973).

ROWLEY, H. H., *Job NCentB* (London, 1970).

STEVENSON, W. B., *The Poem of Job* (London, 1947).

STRAHAN, J., *The Book of Job Interpreted* (Edinburgh, 1913, [2]1914).

TERRIEN, S., 'The Book of Job', *IB* (Nashville, 1962), vol. 3, pp. 877–1197.

THE PSALMS

JOHN W. BAIGENT (1–72)

LESLIE C. ALLEN (73–150)

I. The Formation of the Psalter

The Book of Psalms is a collection of religious poems. (For the poetry of the Psalms see the article, Introduction to the Poetical and Wisdom Books.) The customary description of the Psalter in its present form as the hymnbook and prayer-book of the post-exilic temple cannot be far from the truth. But like any modern hymnbook its contents go back to diverse origins. It is divided into five sections or books, Pss. 1–41; 42–72; 73–89; 90–106 and 107–150. Each book concludes with a doxology added by the compilers, Ps. 150 evidently forming that of the fifth book and of the Psalter. Conversely Ps. 1 was probably composed or at least now functions as an introduction to the whole collection. This fivefold division may have been intended as an echo of and tribute to the five books of the Pentateuch, the basis of OT revelation.

Behind this fivefold division lies evidence of other, smaller divisions pointing to the existence of several earlier collections which were subsequently combined. There are duplicated psalms, notably Pss. 14 and 53, which must have featured in separate collections at an earlier stage. These two psalms differ in their divine titles, 'Yahweh' (EVV the LORD) and God (Heb. 'elōhîm) respectively. In fact 'Yahweh' is used predominantly in Pss. 1–41 and God in Pss. 42–83. This evidence shows the existence of at least two collections, generally called Yahwistic and Elohistic, emanating from circles with a different preference in addressing God, just as certain hymnbooks contain clear signs of editorial change on religious grounds cherished among particular Christian groups.

Psalm titles also indicate collections. Seventy-two out of the 150 are entitled **A Psalm of David**; most of these are in the first two books. There was evidently more than one Davidic collection: Ps. 72 ends with **This concludes the prayers of David the son of Jesse** yet over a dozen more appear later in the collection. Accordingly the note appended to Ps. 72 refers to an earlier self-contained collection. Then there are twelve psalms ascribed to Asaph and eleven to **the Sons of Korah**, evidently the repertoires of different temple choirs. There are fifteen Songs of Ascents (Pss. 120–134) and a number of what are called Hallelujah psalms (Pss. 104–106; 111–113; 115–117; 133; 146–150). Pss. 93–99 are a thematic collection, dealing with God as universal King or Judge.

The formation of the Psalter must have been a gradual process. The main period of composition appears to have been the four centuries of the Davidic dynasty (c. 1000 B.C.—c. 600 B.C.), but both then and during the exile and after the work of compiling and editing proceeded under the oversight of the Spirit of God until the completion of this inspired and inspiring monument to God's glory.

II. The Different Types of Psalms

Literature has its own conventions, and ancient Hebrew religious poetry was no exception. Obviously God can be addressed in two ways, in petition and in praise, and it is from these two basic forms that most of the psalmody of Israel developed. The development reached highly sophisticated and technical proportions.

1. A very common form of psalm is what scholars call a lament; a third of the Psalms belong to this category. It is a prayer to God for help in some crisis. There are two main types, the lament of the community, which uses the first person plural, and the lament of the individual, which uses the first person singular. Examples of the former may be found at Pss. 60; 79; 126 (cf. Jl 1–2) and of the latter at Pss. 3; 7; 42 f.; 88; 141. The laments of individuals are usually marked by general and figurative language rather than specific description: this feature made them suitable for widespread use, whatever the precise nature of the suffering. Laments tend to have five constituent parts, easily discernible in Pss. 79 and 102: a call upon God with an initial plea for help, an actual lament which describes the crisis, a profession of trust, a prayer and a promise of praise. Some laments go further and imply that a divine answer has been received part-way through, evidently through a temple prophet. This explains the dramatic change of tone which occurs in such cases as Pss. 6; 22; 28; 60 (cf. the comments on Ps. 85). In these instances lament turns into glad thanksgiving for God's

response. A related type of composition is the psalm of trust which expands an element of the lament into a distinct piece, *e.g.* Pss. 4; 16; 23; 125; 131.

2. After the lament the other great category of psalm is the song of praise. This takes two forms. One is the thanksgiving brought by an individual. It is the counterpart of the personal lament and the fulfilment of its promise of praise. The crisis is over, the believer has been delivered and he pours out before God an expression of gratitude as an accompaniment to his thank-offering. As in the lament, generalized language is used. 'The psalmist does not intend to relate what happened to him but to testify what God has done for him' (C. Westermann). Examples of this form are Pss. 18; 34; 116; 118. There are a few examples of communal thanksgiving, notably Pss. 124 and 129.

The other form of song is what is technically called a hymn: this form does not thank God for something He has just done, but praises Him more generally for His greatness and grace, exhibited in creation and in Israel's history. It usually opens with a call to praise, then gives the ground for such praise in a section introduced by **for** or in a series of Hebrew participles (relative clauses in the EVV), and ends with a renewed call to praise. Examples are Pss. 33; 36; 100; 103; 136. A special group using this form are the poems which celebrate God's kingship (Pss. 47; 93; 96–99). Scholarly controversy has raged over the setting and significance of these psalms and what links, if any, they have with a pagan New Year festival in Babylon. Many scholars associate these psalms with the Israelite autumn festival, the Feast of Tabernacles (cf. Zech. 14: 16); and some postulate an annual enthronement of Yahweh then, rather than simply a celebration of divine sovereignty.

Certainly the Feast of Tabernacles seems to have played a major role in the temple cult, i.e. the official, ritual worship operative in Jerusalem. There are gaps in our knowledge of ancient Israelite worship, and scholars have not been slow to suggest how they may be filled in the case of this festival. The view of a New Year enthronement ceremony including a dramatic conflict, with the king as the chief performer acting out a contest of defeat and victory and also celebrating his own enthronement, is associated with the name of the Scandinavian scholar S. Mowinckel. Most vigorously oppose his position, at least in its extreme form, for a number of seemingly valid reasons. Two German scholars, A. Weiser and H.-J. Kraus, are on safer ground in attributing to the Feast of Tabernacles distinctively Israelite roles. Weiser regards it as a covenant renewal ceremony with a reading of the Law (cf. Dt. 31: 10–13), while the enthronement of God and the king were

merely subsidiary themes. Kraus characterizes the festival as a celebration of the divine election of Zion and the Davidic dynasty. Psalms can be cited to support both views, though Weiser is generally held to ascribe too many psalms to his covenant festival. It is wise not to be dogmatic in defining the autumn festival in rigid terms, although kingship, covenant and royal Zion may well have all been among its varied themes.

Another group of hymns is in fact the Songs of Zion (Pss. 46; 48; 76; 87; 132; cf. 137: 3), which celebrate God's victory won at Jerusalem over His enemies. When the conquest actually occurred, in 701 B.C. or at an earlier period, is disputed, but it was regarded as a pledge both of God's choice of the capital as His home, and of His supremacy as Israel's Ally.

3. A further category, distinguished by subject matter and overlapping in type with the preceding groups, is the royal psalms. Their contents reveal that a Davidic king is speaking or is celebrated in terms of his special relationship to God. Examples are Pss. 2; 18; 45; 72; 89; 101; 110. There are other groups, less often encountered, such as psalms of access to the temple (Pss. 15; 24) and wisdom psalms which resemble the Wisdom Literature in their language and reflective and didactic tones (e.g. Pss. 1; 37; 73; 119; 127 f.).

In their present form the Psalms are intended for use in the cult, as indeed they still are in the Anglican tradition. It is a moot point how many psalms were composed expressly for cultic use, rather than re-used for that purpose. There is no reason to doubt that some at least originated as private prayers, but very many of them were originally composed for temple worship, even the 'I' psalms. There was ample opportunity for the individual to participate orally, as he brought his personal sacrifices and evidently in the course of public worship, to judge by a number of individual psalms which in part address the congregation (*e.g.* Pss. 32; 34; 73; 131) or are individual testimonies in a cultic setting (*e.g.* Pss. 92; 122).

III. Psalm Titles and Technical Terms
Just over three quarters of the Psalms are furnished with headings of various kinds. Most of the thirty-four which lack headings are in the fourth and fifth books. The headings appear to be not part of the actual psalms but subsequent annotations, which shed light on ancient traditions of worship and interpretation. They should be respected as part of the canonical text of scripture and not omitted as in NEB.

1. Descriptive terms are frequently used. **Psalm** occurs fifty-seven times: it is a religious song sung to musical accompaniment. **Song**, which appears thirty times, is a general term, but must have had some technical meaning.

Six psalms are entitled **Miktam** (Pss. 16; 56–60) and thirteen **Maskil**: the significance of both Hebrew words is uncertain, and larger commentaries may be consulted for suggestions. Also uncertain is the term **Shiggaion** (Ps. 7; see the commentary). Five psalms are entitled **A Prayer**, while Ps. 145 is called **A psalm of Praise**. This last term is also used for the Book of Psalms, literally Praises: it is to the LXX that we owe the English title. Ps. 45 is appropriately entitled **a wedding song**.

2. Personal names are often associated with the psalms that follow. **Of the Sons of Korah** (Pss. 42; 44–49; 84 f.; 87 f.) indicates the repertoire of a guild of temple singers (cf. 1 Chr. 6: 22, 31–33). The same is apparently true of the title **of Asaph** (Pss. 50; 73–83). He was appointed by David as the leading singer according to 1 Chr. 16: 4 f. Since Pss. 74 and 79 mention recent events obviously much later than David's time, the reference must be to pieces sung by the family choir founded by Asaph (cf. 1 Chr. 25: 1; Ezr. 3: 10). This is probably also true of the titles citing **Jeduthun** (Pss. 39; 62; 77; cf. 1 Chr. 16: 41), **Ethan the Ezrahite** (Ps. 89; cf. 1 Kg. 4: 31; 1 Chr. 15: 19) and **Heman the Ezrahite** (Ps. 88; cf. 1 Chr. 6: 33; 24: 4 ff.). The heading of the last mentioned psalm is interesting since it contains two names: evidently authorship is not in view, but the fact that the psalm featured in two choral collections.

Ps. 39 is likewise ascribed both to **Jeduthun** and to **David**, and this raises the question of the precise significance of the latter reference. That David composed psalms there can be no doubt: there is a strong biblical tradition to this effect outside the Psalter (*e.g.* 2 Sam. 1: 17 ff.; 23: 1; Am. 6: 5). On the other hand the fact that the LXX entitled Ps. 96 both as Davidic and 'When the house was built after the Exile' shows that by the time of the Greek translation (*c.* 150 B.C.) the heading was considered not necessarily to refer to authorship. It is possible that a nucleus personally composed by David grew into a larger collection still labelled Davidic (cf. the reference to **the prayers of David** in Ps. 72: 20 after a psalm ascribed to Solomon). Since 'David' could evidently be a title of a Davidic king (cf. Jer. 30: 9; Ezek. 34: 23; Hos. 3: 5), some scholars hold that the heading refers to a royal collection used by and for Davidic kings: J. H. Eaton's commentary has developed this viewpoint in detail. The allusions to David's personal experiences in the headings to fourteen psalms sometimes occasion difficulty in relation to their contents. Possibly in some cases at least they are later devotional suggestions seeking to throw light on David's life. One may compare the use of Pss. 96; 105; 106 in the account of David's bringing the ark to Jerusalem in 1 Chr. 16, which may be a

borrowing 'to illustrate the kind of rejoicing and praying that accompanied the ark rather than to record it verbatim' (D. Kidner). In a similar way could be interpreted the ascription of Ps. 127 (cf. Ps. 72) to Solomon, **the house** of v. 1 being re-interpreted of the temple, and of Ps. 90 to Moses on account of its affinities to Dt. 32 f. (For a literal interpretation of these headings see Kidner's Introduction, pp. 33–36, 43–46.)

3. Musical directions are sometimes given in the headings, and these reveal the importance attached to appropriate musical accompaniment in the worship of God. There is some doubt whether headings of this type refer to the following psalm or to the one before (cf. Hab. 3: 19). A term rendered **For the director of music** occurs in fifty-five headings: the RSV interprets as drawing the choirmaster's attention to the musical instructions that follow. Others understand the term to refer to a major 'choirmaster's collection' from which the psalms were taken, and which itself included the earlier Korahite and other collections.

Sometimes the accompanying musical instruments are specified: **with stringed instruments** occurs seven times and **for flutes** once (Ps. 5). A number of phrases beginning with **According to . . .** appear in the titles. These are generally taken, as by the NIV, to refer to well-known (secular?) songs to whose tunes the psalms were to be sung, but there is no certainty on this point. Two of them may be associated with the vintage festival, **Gittith** (Pss. 8; 81; 84) and **Do Not Destroy** (Pss. 57–59; 75; cf. Isa. 65: 8). Other titles are **The Doe of the Morning** (Ps. 22), **A Dove on Distant Oaks** (Ps. 56) and **Lilies** (Pss. 45; 69; 80; cf. Ps. 60). The NIV leaves untranslated similar, more obscure titles: **sheminith** (Pss. 6; 12), and **mahalath (leannoth)** (Pss. 53; 88): see the commentary for attempted elucidation.

Here may be mentioned **Selah** which occurs seventy-one times in the Psalter, mostly in the first three books. The LXX interprets as a musical interlude. The Hebrew word may mean 'lift up', as a direction either to the congregation to accompany the soloist or choir by lifting up their voices and joining in a refrain, or to the orchestra to strike up with their instruments. The term may also serve to divide a psalm into stanzas, although in the course of time it evidently became misplaced in some cases and even omitted. **Higgaion** which is added in Ps. 9: 16, probably means a murmur, referring perhaps to a quiet musical (cf. Ps. 92: 3) or vocal accompaniment.

4. Assignments to special occasions and purposes in worship are sometimes mentioned in the headings. Ps. 30 is probably directed to be sung at the festival of Hanukkah, the anniversary of the re-dedication of the temple (cf. Jn

10: 22), unless the title refers to the dedication of Ezr. 6: 16. Ps. 92 was evidently used in Sabbath services. Ps. 100 accompanied the thank-offering (cf. Jer. 33: 11), and Pss. 38 and 70 the memorial offering (cf. Lev. 24: 7). **A song of ascents** occurs in the headings to Pss. 120–134. The meaning of **ascents** is uncertain. The most popular view is that it refers to pilgrimage or procession up to the temple. Another suggestion, found in Jewish tradition, is that they were sung on a flight of fifteen steps in the temple court. Before being put together the individual psalms in the group appear to have had varied origins.

IV. The Christian and the Psalter

The commentary that follows is inevitably concerned largely with matters of exegesis, i.e. attempting to discover the writers' meaning and the significance for the people of their own times of what they wrote. There is no intention, however, to imply that the Psalms have nothing but a historical interest for the modern reader. On the contrary, it is recognized that the psalter is now part of the *Christian* Scriptures and as such must be read and used by the Christian in the light of the fuller revelation in Jesus Christ. (See also the article 'The Old Testament and the Christian'.)

For the purposes of this brief treatment, the Christian use of the Psalter may be divided into two aspects, the devotional and the didactic, although in practice they overlap.

1. The *devotional* use of the Psalter in both private and public worship follows the practice firstly of Judaism and then of Jesus and the early Church. The Psalms were not only chanted in the services of the temple and the synagogue, they also influenced the personal prayers of godly Jews (cf. Lk. 1: 46 ff., 68 ff.; 2: 29 ff.). A similar twofold use of the Psalms may be seen in the life of Jesus (cf. Mt. 26: 30; 27: 46; Lk. 23: 46) and in the practice of the Church (cf. 1 C. 14: 26; Eph. 5: 19; Col. 3: 16 and Ac. 4: 25 f.; 16: 25; Jas 5: 13).

The suitability of these magnificent poems as vehicles for the expression of the spiritual feelings of the Christian hardly needs any demonstration. The fact that the psalmist's description of his experiences is usually generalized and expressed in stereotyped language means that these prayers can be used by those who pass through similar but different experiences. Of course, the references to the election of Israel, the saving acts of God in her history, the choice of David and Zion and the hopes for the universal kingdom of God need to be understood in terms of the New Covenant, the redemption effected through Jesus Christ, and the Church as the new people of God (cf. 1 Pet. 2: 9 f.) and inheritor of the heavenly Jerusalem (cf. Heb. 12: 22 f.; Rev. 21: 2 ff.). Where the psalms have been adapted to be sung in metrical versions or as hymns based on them, this transposition into a Christian key has sometimes been made explicit: see, *e.g.*, 'The heavens declare Thy glory, Lord' (cf. Ps. 19); 'O bless the Lord, my soul' (cf. Ps. 103); 'This is the day the Lord has made' (cf. Ps. 118); and 'Jesus shall reign where'er the sun' (cf. Ps. 72). In fact the Christian rightly relates the whole Psalter to himself, to the Church and to Jesus Christ (see below).

Yet the Christian does face some problems when he attempts to make wholesale use of the Psalter, particularly in public worship. As H. L. Ellison writes, 'It should not be assumed that they are all necessarily suited to Christian worship. Even in the synagogue only about two-thirds are ever used in public'.

One problem concerns the element of *self-justification* found in some of the psalms (*e.g.* 7: 8; 17: 1 ff.; 18: 20 ff.; 26: 1 ff.; 44: 17 ff.; 59: 3 f.), which hardly seems to fit in with the Christian ideal of humility (cf. Lk. 17: 10; Phil. 3: 12 f.; 1 Jn 1: 8 ff.). Two things, however, should be borne in mind. Firstly, in some cases (*e.g.* 7: 3 ff.) the psalmist has been falsely accused and is simply protesting his innocence of those particular crimes (cf. Paul: Ac. 20: 26 ff.; 23: 1). Secondly, in others (*e.g.* 26: 1 ff.) the psalmist is claiming to be in a right relationship with God, i.e. to be one of the 'righteous', in contrast to the 'wicked' (see on Ps. 1). In neither instance is there any suggestion of absolute sinlessness. Nevertheless, it must be recognized that the language used is not Christian and that the NT equivalent is the confident assurance of the believer (cf. Rom. 8: 1, 33 ff.; Heb. 10: 19 ff.) who has been 'justified' by the grace of God, through faith and not by works (Rom. 3: 27 ff.; Eph. 2: 8 f.).

A more serious problem confronts the Christian in the so-called *imprecatory psalms* (*e.g.* 35: 1–8; 58: 6–9; 59; 69: 22–28; 137: 8 f.) in which the psalmist curses his enemies, calls down vengeance on them, often vindictively, and gloats over the prospect of their downfall. Again, it is important to try and understand the situation and viewpoint of the psalmist before condemning him out of hand. Whilst the desire for personal vindication and revenge cannot be ruled out completely, it is obvious that the psalmists took a wider view of the evil of their enemies. They saw it as a challenge to the divine government of the world. The enemies of the psalmist and of Israel are first and foremost the enemies of God, and the psalmist is more concerned for the honour of God than for his own (cf. 9: 16 ff.; 79: 9 ff.; 83: 16 f.; 139: 21 f.). It is inconceivable that the wicked should be allowed to continue in their rebellion against God. In the case of the wicked who are Israelites, the psalmists are implicitly appealing to God to carry out the threatened curses of the covenant (cf. Dt. 27: 24 f.; 28: 15 ff.).

It should be remembered, too, that the psalmists must see the triumph of right and the retribution of the wicked during *this* life, since they have no belief in judgment *after* death. Above all, it is vital to notice that the psalmists do not take matters into their own hands. They recognize that vengeance belongs to God (cf. 1 Sam. 25: 21 ff., 39). Nevertheless, the Christian is not able to adopt this kind of language in relation to his own enemies and persecutors. He has learned a better way from his Lord's teaching and example (cf. Mt. 5: 44 ff.; Lk. 23: 34) and from the NT generally (cf. Ac. 7: 60; Rom. 12: 14, 19 ff.; 1 Tim 2: 1–4). The most he can do is to re-apply these passages to the forces of evil in the world (cf. Eph. 6: 12 ff.) and to the sinful desires of his own heart (cf. Gal. 5: 16 ff.), using them as prayers that God will overthrow all that resists His will (cf. Gal. 1: 8 f.; 2 Th. 1: 7 ff.; Rev. 6: 10; 11: 17 ff.; 18: 2; 19: 1–6) and establish His kingdom of righteousness (cf. Mt. 6: 10; 2 Pet. 3: 13). (For a thorough treatment of this see Kidner, pp. 25–32.)

One further aspect may be considered a problem for the Christian: the almost total *concentration upon this life* and *absence of belief in a future life*. OT scholars differ over whether the psalmists ever express a hope of *life* after death (see the commentary on Pss. 16; 49; 73), but it is quite clear that normally the sights of the psalmists are set on this earthly life and that it is in this sphere that God's salvation and blessing (or judgment and punishment) must be experienced. To some extent the Christian can share this emphasis upon the importance of earthly existence, but he cannot share the psalmists' fear of death (cf. 6: 4 f.; 88: 1 ff.), unless perhaps he equates 'Sheol' with 'hell' or 'spiritual death'. The Christian reads and sings the Psalms in the light of the cross and resurrection of Jesus Christ, remembering that it is He who has 'destroyed death and brought life and immortality to light through the gospel' (2 Tim. 1: 10), and realizing that another dimension has been added to this life which means that questions of reward and vindication, judgment and retribution, may safely be left to the next life (cf. 2 C. 4: 16 ff.; Rom. 2: 6 ff.). In practice this is not such a problem and the Christian finds that many of the statements of confidence and hope for this life (*e.g.* 16: 11; 23: 6) can easily be extended to apply to the life to come.

2. The *didactic* use of the Psalter covers its employment both for theological teaching and for Christological testimony. The first aspect needs no elaboration here; the commentary itself provides this. It is not just the few obviously didactic psalms (*e.g.* Pss. 1; 19; 37; 111)

but all the prayers of the Psalter which constitute a comprehensive *education in the character of God and the nature of the life of faith*. The Psalms present a God who is not only the Saviour and Shepherd of His own people, but also the Creator and Sustainer, Judge and King of the whole world. The Psalms demonstrate, too, what it means to live as the people of God. In particular, the Christian has in the Psalter a 'school of prayer' (C. Barth), teaching him how to pray, when to pray and what to pray.

The evidential use of the Psalms as a *witness to Jesus Christ* is seen in the teaching of Jesus Himself (*e.g.* Mt. 21: 42; 22: 44; 23: 39; Lk. 24: 44 ff.; Jn 13: 18), in that of the apostles (*e.g.* Ac. 2: 25 ff.; 13: 33, 35 ff.; Rom. 15: 9) and particularly in the Letter to the Hebrews (*e.g.* Heb. 1: 6, 10–13; 2: 6 ff.; 5: 5 f., etc.). A number of different kinds of Psalms are involved. Some are royal psalms (*e.g.* Pss. 2; 18; 45; 110), which the Jews themselves eventually regarded as referring to the Messiah. Others are psalms of the righteous sufferer (*e.g.* Pss. 22; 41; 69) which apparently were never linked with the Messiah by the Jews, but were first used by Jesus as evidence that His sufferings were foreordained by God. Some are psalms of the godly man (*e.g.* Pss. 16; 40); another is a description of the true destiny of man (Ps. 8). Finally there are verses from psalms which originally referred to Yahweh Himself (*e.g.* Ps. 68: 18; 102: 25 ff.) that in the NT are applied to Jesus Christ (Eph. 4: 8; Heb. 1: 10 ff.).

A number of questions may present themselves to the thoughtful Christian. What is the nature of Christ's 'fulfilment' of the psalms? Is it the same in every case? Does it mean that they must be regarded as prophecies (*i.e.* predictions)? Can the somewhat limited usage of the NT be extended to cover other similar psalms or even the whole Psalter? To answer these questions adequately would require a more detailed discussion than is possible here (see Kirkpatrick, ch. viii). Briefly, it would seem most satisfactory to regard these psalms as containing expressions which were providentially overruled to prefigure or foreshadow the experiences of Jesus (see comments on Ps. 22) and His role in the history of salvation (cf. Ps. 2). The psalms of the righteous sufferer cannot be regarded as straightforward prophecies since they obviously refer in the first place to the experiences of the psalmist himself, and since not everything in them can necessarily be applied to Christ (see comments on Ps. 69). Similarly the royal psalms originally referred to the reigning Davidic monarch, and although Christ fully matches the ideal of kingship presented in them, this does not mean that every detail necessarily fits Him. It is therefore illegitimate to go to the Psalter for information about Christ which is not to be found in the NT; at the most it may be used to illuminate and confirm the witness of the NT.

If these principles are borne in mind, there is no reason why other royal psalms (*e.g.* Pss. 20; 21; 72), psalms of the godly man and of the righteous sufferer (*e.g.* Pss. 15; 35; 42–43; 54) and psalms relating to God as Creator, Redeemer and Judge (*e.g.* Pss. 23; 33; 96) should not be referred (at least in part) to Jesus Christ. Above all, whilst the Christian should always begin with the historical meaning of the Psalms, he should not stop there; he must read them in the light of the life, death, resurrection, ascension and second coming of Him in whom the whole Psalter finds its ultimate fulfilment.

Book One   Psalms 1–41

Psalm 1.   TWO TYPES OF PEOPLE

This psalm provides a fitting preface to the whole collection of psalms, whether it was written for that purpose or not. It is 'now meant to commend the study of the Psalter in particular as nourishment on the word of God' (Eaton). Though didactic rather than psalmodic (the metre, if any, is irregular), it may best be described as a 'wisdom song' (Weiser) and associated with 'the wise' (cf. Jer. 8: 9; 18: 18; Ec. 12: 9 ff.; Prov. 8: 1 ff.) whose function was to teach people 'to live their lives intelligently and on a moral and religious basis'(Weiser). It is not clear whether the psalm derives from Jer. 17: 5–8 or vice-versa. If the former, it is post-exilic; if the latter, it is pre-exilic. If it was used in the cult its context could have been the ancient pattern of curses and blessings (cf. Dt.27: 11–28: 6).

The psalm may be divided into two main parts (although some prefer three: cf. Weiser). Verses 1–3 paint the portrait of the righteous person: negatively, he does not follow the advice, share the way of life, or adopt the attitudes of the wicked; positively, he relies on the guidance of God and therefore fulfils his God-intended function. In contrast vv. 4–6 depict the doom of the wicked: they are empty, worthless, unstable and impermanent; their chosen way inevitably ends in ruin. The black and white division of mankind into **righteous** (Heb. *ṣaddîqîm*) and the **wicked** (Heb. *rᵉšāʿîm*), both words in the plural in v. 6, corresponds to the ultimate distinction between those who stand in a right relationship with God, with His law, and with their fellowmen, and those (whether Israelites or Gentiles) who deliberately reject these standards.

1. Blessed: Heb. *'ašᵉrê* (lit. 'Oh the blessedness(es) of'; probably a plural of intensity) should be distinguished from Heb. *bārûk* ('blessed': see on 26: 12). It denotes 'the praising of someone else for the blessing he has received or is going to receive' (H. Hartnell, in Weiser, p. 87) and may be paraphrased as 'how rewarding is the life of . . .' (A. A. Anderson) or 'to be envied is the man . . .' (W. Janzen; see Anderson, p. 58). 'Happy' (NEB; cf. RSV 144: 15; 146: 5) is not entirely satisfactory: by derivation it suggests a mood which is dependent on the chances and circumstances of life rather than a condition which results from the blessing of God. **mockers:** not found elsewhere in the Psalms but common in wisdom literature (cf. Prov. 15: 12; 21: 24). Instead of delighting in God's law, they make light of it and of those who follow it. **2. law:** Heb. *tôrāh* is lit. 'instruction', 'direction' or 'teaching' (cf. Prov. 8: 8). In the OT it refers to the revelation of the will of God through prophet (Isa. 1: 10) and priest (Dt. 17: 8–11); in specific regulations (*e.g.* Lev. 6: 9) and written law-codes (*e.g.* Exod. 24: 12; Dt. 29: 21); eventually it was used to denote the Pentateuch (Neh. 8: 1) and even the OT as a whole (Rom. 3: 9). (See also on Ps. 119.) Here the reference is probably to a written document which the righteous man (probably a scribe or a king; cf. Dt. 17: 19) would read to himself in a low tone (**meditates** is lit. 'murmurs') or recite from memory. It is implied that he intends to put it into practice (cf. Dt. 17: 19; Jos. 1: 8). **4.** For winnowing as a picture of divine judgment see Job 21: 18; Ps. 35: 5; Isa. 29: 5; Mt. 3: 12. **5. the judgment:** Heb. *mišpāṭ* can denote (as well as 'justice': see on 33: 5) the act or place of deciding, the verdict, the sentence, or the execution of the sentence, i.e. the punishment. Here it could refer to the final judgment of the Day of Yahweh (cf. Jl 3: 2, 12, 14) but more probably denotes continuous acts of divine judgment in the events of history (cf. Ezek. 23: 24) or God's verdict mediated through human agents (cf. Dt. 1: 17; 2 Chr. 19:8–11). The final result is always the purification of the people of God (cf. Mal. 3: 2 ff.), 'the company of the upright' (Ps. 111: 1). **6. watches over:** lit. 'knows', implies personal relationship, active interest, care, guidance, and even approval (cf. Ps. 139: 1–6; Am. 3: 2; Jer. 1: 5; Nah. 1: 7).

Psalm 2.   GOD'S KING

A royal psalm, most probably used at the enthronement of each Davidic king and possibly also at an annual celebration of his accession (see Introduction II. 2). It is not clear whether it was written specifically for a coronation, or perhaps at a critical point in the king's reign when he was menaced by a confederacy of kings from surrounding nations (cf. 2 Sam. 10; 1 Kg. 11: 14, 21, 23 ff.). The poet could have been the king himself—it has been attributed to David (so Kidner; cf. Ac. 4: 25) and to Solomon (so Kirkpatrick; cf. 1 Chr. 28: 6; 29: 22 f.)—or a court prophet or priest. Similarly we can envisage the king reciting the whole psalm (or a prophet doing it for him); alternatively, vv. 1–6 might have been spoken by the anointing priest and vv. 7–12 by the king.

There are four clear stanzas. Verses 1–3 describe the futile conspiracy of the earthly kings, whilst vv. 4–6 show the reaction of the heavenly King. In vv. 7–9 the Davidic king quotes his divine authorization, and the psalm ends (vv. 10–12) with the issuing of an ultimatum to the rebels.

This theological interpretation of the role of the Davidic king went far beyond the reality of the historical experience of monarchy. No king of Judah (not even David) ever exercised world-wide dominion. As the kings of Judah fell progressively more and more short of this ideal which was held before them, men looked into the future for the fulfilment of the divine promise to David (2 Sam. 7: 8–16; cf. Isa. 9: 7; 11: 1–5; Jer. 23: 5). After the fall of Jerusalem in 587 B.C. and the end of the monarchy psalms like this came to be understood and used in a prophetic and messianic way. The NT writers (and Christians generally) see the fulfilment of this psalm in the kingship of Jesus the Messiah (Ac. 4: 25–28; 13: 13; Heb. 1: 5; 5: 5; cf. Mt. 3: 17; Rom. 1: 4; Rev. 2: 26 f.; 12: 5; 19: 15). (See also Introduction IV. 2.) The Prayer Book appoints it for use on Easter Day.

1. Why expresses both astonishment that anyone could be so foolish as to revolt against God, and also confidence that such plotting is pointless (cf. Ac. 5: 39); the force of the **why** probably extends to v. 2. **plot:** the same verb as 'meditate' in 1: 2; cf. JB 'impotent muttering'. **2. take their stand:** lit. 'stand up', i.e. prepare for battle (cf. 1 Sam. 17: 16); cf. JB 'rising in revolt'. **and his Anointed One:** in OT times anointing served to consecrate objects (cf. Exod. 29: 36; 30: 26) or persons such as priests (cf. Exod. 28: 41), kings (1 Sam. 10: 1; 16: 3; 1 Kg. 1: 39) and possibly prophets (1 Kg. 19: 16; cf. 1 Chr. 16: 22). Here, as usual in the OT, the noun (Heb. *māšîaḥ*) refers to the reigning king regarded as a sacrosanct figure (cf. 1 Sam. 24: 6). It was only at a later date that the word came to denote the expected future Davidic 'Messiah' (see *NBD art.* 'Messiah'). **3. They say:** not in the Heb. This verse suggests the kind of rebellion of subject nations which frequently occurred in the ancient Near East when a king died and before the new ruler had established himself. **chains . . . fetters:** or 'bonds . . . cords' (RSV); probably a reference to the

leather thongs which secured a yoke to an animal (cf. Jer. 27: 2).

4. enthroned: lit. 'who sits' (cf. 11: 4). **laughs:** an anthropomorphism, stressing how ridiculous the hostility of God's enemies really is (cf. Ps. 37: 13; 59: 8; Isa. 40: 22 ff.). **the Lord:** NIV follows *MT* which has *'ᵃdōnāi* ('Lord', 'sovereign') but some Heb. MSS have *Yahweh*. **5. Then:** the turning-point in the crisis. **6. I have installed:** better, 'But as for me, I have installed . . .' **Zion:** originally the name either of the Jebusite fortress or of the hill on which it stood (cf. 2 Sam. 5: 7); then it was transferred to the temple hill (Ps. 132: 13; Mic. 4: 2) and finally to the whole of Jerusalem (cf. Isa. 10: 24; Am. 6: 1) as chosen by God to be His city (48: 1 f.). (See also *NBD art.* 'Jerusalem'.) **holy:** because it was the place where Yahweh, the holy God, manifested His presence symbolized by the ark, His earthly throne (2 Sam. 6: 2), at first located in the tent-shrine of David (2 Sam. 6: 17) and later in the temple (1 Kg. 8: 6, 13).

7. decree: Heb. *ḥōq* is translated 'statute' in Ps. 119. Here it probably refers to the divine oracle of 2 Sam. 7: 10–16 (known as the 'Davidic covenant'; cf. 89: 3) which may have been incorporated in a document (or charter) given to the king at his coronation. On that day (**today**) he became Yahweh's adopted **Son,** His legitimate earthly representative. **become your Father:** lit. 'begotten', does not imply physical descent or deification but adoption. The **I** is again emphatic (cf. v. 6). **8.** As 'son' he is also heir (cf. Gal. 4: 7); and since God's rule is worldwide, the king's inheritance is the whole earth. **9.** LXX has 'you shall shepherd them'; but the **scepter** or 'rod' seems to be the battle-mace rather than the shepherd's staff (cf. 23: 4). **dash:** 'effortless but complete destruction' (A. A. Anderson).

11. Serve: to submit politically to His vice-gerent implies also to worship Yahweh Himself. **11, 12. rejoice with trembling. Kiss the Son:** so *MT*; RSV has 'with trembling kiss his feet'. The text seems to have suffered some corruption here; it is unlikely that the Aramaic word *bar* ('son') would be used here when the normal Heb. word for 'son' (*bēn*) was used in v. 7. Many alternatives have been proposed: 'kiss sincerely' (Kidner); 'kiss the chosen one' (Smith); 'kiss the ground' (Ringgren); 'live in trembling, O mortal men' (Dahood); 'kiss the king' (NEB; mg 'the mighty one'). The ancient versions do not offer much help: LXX, Targ., Vulg. have 'accept correction'; Sym. and Jerome 'worship purely'. The simplest emendation (rearranging some of the letters) is that followed by RSV and JB. In the ancient Near East kissing the feet denoted an act of homage and self-humiliation (cf. Ps. 72: 9; 1 Sam. 10: 1). **12. he:** refers to God. **in your way:** 'in mid course' (NEB). **Blessed:** see on 1: 1. **refuge:** under His protectorate: the suzerainty of His king.

Psalm 3. A MORNING PRAYER FOR DELIVERANCE

This individual lament is the first of fourteen psalms whose titles relate them to events in the life of David (see Introduction III. 2). David's flight from Absalom is recounted in 2 Sam. 15: 13 ff., but this psalm makes no explicit reference to specific events recorded there. This means that it could be used by any individual Israelite to express his own predicament (*e.g.* false accusation or persecution); or the Davidic king, as representative of his people (cf. v. 8), could recite it on a day of national lamentation, when the land was suffering an enemy invasion.

It seems to divide into four stanzas, although there is no 'Selah' after v. 6. (On **Selah**, see Introduction III. 3.) Verses 1, 2 emphasize the seriousness of the psalmist's situation: he is surrounded by enemies who have already written him off. Verses 3, 4 express his confidence in the God who has protected him in the past and will surely do so again. Verses 5, 6 describe the experience of a night spent in peace because his mind was stayed on Yahweh. Finally, in vv. 7, 8 he calls on God for both victory and blessing.

1. The force of **how** probably extends to the following two lines. **2. of me:** lit. 'of my soul'. The Heb. *nepeš* is used in three main ways in the Psalms: (i) it denotes the principle of life in man, his essential vitality (Ps. 6: 4; 107: 5); (ii) it refers to the mental or psychological aspect of man, his personality, the seat of feelings, desire and will (Ps. 6: 3; 11: 5; 24: 4; 25: 1; 35: 13); (iii) with a pronominal suffix it acts as a periphrasis or emotional substitute for the personal pronoun: 'my soul' is 'I', 'myself' (so here and 6: 3, 4; 120: 2; etc.). In Gen. 2: 7 it corresponds to the English word 'being', and in references like Lev. 7: 20 and Ezek. 18: 4 to 'person'. Less common meanings include 'throat' or 'neck' (Ps. 69: 1), 'greed' (Ps. 17: 9), 'appetite' (Ps. 78: 18), 'desire' (Ps. 35: 25) and 'courage' (Ps. 107: 26). (See also *NBD art.* 'Soul'.) **God will not deliver:** lit. 'there is no salvation in God' (cf. v. 8). The saying presumably implies that the psalmist has sinned (cf. 2 Sam. 16: 7 f.; Job 8: 6) rather than that God is impotent (cf. Isa. 36: 15–18). **3. shield:** here the small, round, defensive shield (Heb. *māgēn*) used by the light infantry (cf. on 5: 12). **my Glorious one:** lit. 'my glory', either 'the one in whom I glory' (C. A. Briggs) or 'the one who restores my glory (i.e. honour, dignity)' (A. A. Anderson). **who lifts:** to lift the head was to restore to a position of freedom and dignity (cf. Gen. 40: 13; 2 Kg. 25:

27; Ps. 27: 6). **4.** The tenses of the verbs suggest repeated action in the past. The answer comes either in an oracle or in the act of deliverance itself. **his holy hill:** i.e. Mount Zion (see on 2: 6). **5.** In spite of his enemies and their views (cf. v. 2b) he experiences a restful night (the **I** is emphatic), supported as always (**sustains** is a continuous tense) by Yahweh's care. **6.** The 'many' of vv. 1, 2 have become an innumerable ('myriads' NEB) army arrayed in battle positions (cf. Isa. 22: 7), but he refuses to be scared.

7. Arise, O LORD: an Israelite war cry associated with taking the ark into battle (cf. Num. 10: 35; Ps. 68: 1). **Strike:** the psalmist may be remembering past experiences of God's deliverance, or expressing a future wish (cf. M. Dahood: 'O that you would smite . . . break . . .'). **on the jaw:** expressing contempt and insult (cf. 1 Kg. 22: 24; Job 16: 10). **break the teeth:** deprive of the power to harm (cf. Job 29: 17; Ps. 58: 6). **8. deliverance:** lit. 'salvation'; NEB 'victory' (see on 35: 3). For the thought of v. 8a cf. Prov. 21: 31. For the content of the **blessing** (see on 26: 12) of v. 8b cf. Num. 6:23–27.

Psalm 4. AN EVENING PRAYER FOR PEACE

It would be possible to classify this psalm either as an individual lament or as a psalm of confidence (see Introduction II. 1). Some (*e.g.*Kirkpatrick, Kidner) connect it with the same situation as that suggested for Ps. 3, i.e. Absalom's rebellion. Others see it either as the words of a leader of the community such as the king (J. H. Eaton) or the high priest (B. Duhm) during a time of famine or war, or as the prayer of an individual Israelite falsely accused of some crime (A. A. Anderson). In the latter case the psalm could have been used on occasions when legal cases were decided in the central sanctuary (cf. Dt. 17: 8–13; 19: 16–21) probably with an accompanying cultic act (cf. v. 5).

The psalm does not easily divide into stanzas. An alternative to the NIV would be to group the verses in pairs (Kirkpatrick) following the clue provided by the use of **Selah** (see Introduction III. 3); this seems less natural. The psalmist's cry for help (v. 1) is based on his past experience of God's deliverance when he was in a difficult situation ('hard pressed' NEB). In vv. 2, 3 he appeals to his adversaries: how can they pursue their false charges when it is obvious that Yahweh has been gracious to him and that therefore he is righteous? In the light of this he cautions his opponents to think again, desist from their sinful course, and withdraw their accusations (v. 4); then they must seek a right relationship with God (v. 5). Verse 6 seems to represent the discontent either of his opponents (A. A. Anderson) or of his friends (Kidner), whilst v. 7 (cf. Isa. 9: 3) expresses the glad satisfaction of the psalmist. Finally in v. 8 his confidence in God results in the assurance that he will have no sleepless night of worry and fear, but as soon as he lies down he will fall asleep, secure ('unafraid' NEB) in God's safe-keeping.

Title: see Introduction III. 1, 2, 3. **1. my righteous God:** lit. 'God of my righteousness' (see on 33: 5). Yahweh is the upholder of justice to whom he looks for his vindication (cf. 1 Kg. 8: 32). **Give me relief:** lit. 'you have enlarged me', 'given me room' (RSV), i.e. 'freed me'. NIV takes the verb as equivalent to an imperative (cf. v. 1a). **2. O men:** lit. 'sons of man'; prob-ably a reference to rich or influential members of the community (cf. on 49: 2). **3. godly:** Heb. *ḥāsîd*, one who practises *ḥesed* (see on 5: 7), i.e. one who is loyal to the covenant obligations in his relationships both with men and with God (cf. 18: 25; 86: 2; 109: 16), but especially one who is faithfully devoted to God's service. **4. In your anger:** lit. 'tremble' (cf. 'stand in awe' AV); NIV follows LXX 'be angry' as does Eph. 4: 26. **silent:** or 'still'. **5. right sacrifices:** either 'offered with the right ritual' or 'brought in the right spirit' and 'ac-companied by right living' (cf. Dt. 33: 19; Ps. 51: 19; 1 Sam. 15: 22; 2 Sam. 15: 12). **6.** Some (*e.g.* Kidner) take v. 6a as the wish of his friends, and v. 6b as the prayer of the psalmist. **good:** material prosperity (cf. v. 7), or even the rain that promotes it (cf. Dt. 28: 12; Jer. 17: 6). The **face** of God signifies both His presence and the expression of His feelings (cf. Num. 6: 24–26). To **let the light** of one's face **shine** (lit. 'lift up the light') is to 'smile' (Moffatt) or to 'show one's approval and favour' (cf. GNB 'look on us with kindness'; cf. Prov. 16: 15).

Psalm 5. A MORNING PRAYER FOR VINDICATION

This is an individual lament, the prayer of a man who has been falsely accused (cf. vv. 6, 9; cf. psalms of innocence like Ps. 26) or attacked by ruthless fellow Israelites (cf. vv. 4, 5, 10; Gentiles would not be eligible to enter the temple). If the psalm was composed by David (so Kirkpatrick, Kidner; but see Introduction III. 2) it could have arisen from his experiences at the court of Saul (1 Sam. 19; 20) or, more likely, from the time of Absalom's rebellion (2 Sam. 15–18; with v. 7 cf. 2 Sam. 15: 25; with v. 10 cf. 2 Sam. 15: 31). Its later cultic use could have been by the Davidic king, by an individual awaiting the decision of his case, or by a levit-ical singer on behalf of the whole congregation. Verse 3 suggests that it was used during the offering of the morning sacrifice (cf. Exod. 29: 39; 2 Kg. 3: 20; 16: 15; Am. 4: 4).

The five stanzas play on the antithesis be-tween the righteous and the wicked (cf. Ps. 1). The psalmist comes confidently to his God,

expecting both his spoken words (**cry** v. 2) and his unspoken prayers (**sighing** v. 1; 'inmost thoughts' NEB) to be heard and answered (vv. 1–3). The wicked, however, can expect no such welcome (either in the temple or in the law court) from a holy God who detests all forms of evil (vv. 4–6). It is because of their actions (cf. v. 10) that the wicked are refused entry to God's presence; yet the psalmist relies not on his good deeds (cf. Ps. 15; 24: 3–6) but upon the grace of God. This is the ground of his confidence that he will be vindicated (vv. 7, 8). A righteous God must not only protect the righteous man, but condemn and punish the rebels: justice must be seen to be done (vv. 9, 10). The divine defence of the righteous man should cause those who love and trust God to utter 'endless shouts of joy' JB (vv. 11, 12).

Title: see Introduction III, 1, 2, 3. **3. I lay my requests:** the Heb. text does not provide an object. The verb ('arrange', 'set in order') is used mainly either of sacrificial arrangements (cf. Gen. 22: 9; Lev. 1: 7, 8), hence RSV, NEB, etc. add 'a sacrifice'; or of presenting a legal case (cf. Job. 13: 18; 23: 4; 33: 5; 37: 19), hence NEBmg 'plea'. Other translations add 'my prayer' (AV, RV, GNB). The legal connotation seems to fit the context best. **wait:** lit. 'watch', 'look out'; more than waiting for an answer (cf. Mic. 7: 7); it expects a divine revelation or even a theophany (cf. Isa. 21: 6 ff.; Hab. 2: 1). **4. evil:** LXX, Vulg. read 'evil man' (cf. NEBmg). **5. who do wrong:** lit. 'doers of in-iquity'. They could be foreign enemies, crimi-nals, political opponents, or false accusers. S. Mowinckel believes that they are workers of magic who used sorcery to attack the psalmist. There is no reason to assume that the phrase means the same thing each time it occurs in the Psalms; the context usually indicates the exact connotation (cf. vv. 5, 6).

7. mercy: Heb. *ḥesed*. The basic idea seems to be 'firmness' but the usage often implies the existence of a covenant (cf. Ps. 89: 1 ff., 28). It is the 'loyalty', 'devotion', 'faithfulness' that is to be expected from someone with whom one is in covenant relationship (cf. 1 Sam. 20: 8). When used of God the word often contains an element of graciousness, since His covenant promises are totally undeserved (cf. Dt. 7: 6-9). It is also a quality that a man should display both to God and to his neighbour (cf. Ps. 109: 12; Hos. 6: 6). The word occurs in the Psalms more often than anywhere else in the OT. **house . . . temple:** it is just possible that David could have used such language of the tent-shrine of his time (2 Sam. 6: 17; cf. Gen. 27: 15; 1 Sam. 1: 7), but it would suit the Solomonic temple better. **8. in your righteousness:** either 'be-cause you are faithful to your covenant prom-ises', or 'by means of your acts of salvation', or 'along the path of the right conduct you have

marked out'. (See also on 33: 5.) **my enemies:**
lit. 'those who watch me'. **10. sins:** rather
'rebellions' (Heb. pᵉšā'îm). **11. name:** a shorthand for the totality of God's revealed character
(cf. Exod. 34: 5 ff.). Some transfer the phrase
spread your protection over them to v. 12b
and read 'you coverest him with a shield, and
crownest him with favour'. **12. shield:** Heb.
ṣinnāh; the large rectangular one which protected most of the body (cf. 3: 3).

Psalm 6. A PRAYER FOR HEALING

An individual lament. It is not certain whether
the psalmist is suffering from a long and severe
illness, aggravated by the taunts of his enemies,
or from enemy attacks which result in mental
anxiety and physical sickness. It is even possible
that any great misfortune could be described in
such terms. There is no clear evidence in the
psalm of authorship or date. Those who accept
Davidic authorship suggest either the time of
Absalom's rebellion (cf. Ps. 3) or after the
Bathsheba incident (2 Sam. 11). Delitzsch believed that Pss. 6, 38, 51, and 32 provide the
sequence of David's experience to the point of
his receiving the assurance of forgiveness. Pss.
6 and 38 would then reflect the process by
which God softened David's heart to receive
Nathan's rebuke (2 Sam. 12: 1–15). Although
in the first instance the prayer might have been
used privately, it would subsequently and normally be used in the temple, probably accompanied by sacrifice.

There seem to be four stanzas. In the first
(vv. 1–3) there is an implied acknowledgement
of sin (though not so explicit as in Ps. 38: 3 ff.;
cf. 32: 3 ff.) and therefore of the justice of God's
correction. There is certainly no protestation
of innocence (cf. Pss. 7; 26). The psalmist,
greatly shaken (**in agony** v. 2), throws himself on the mercy of God, pleading that he
should not feel the full force of God's fury. In
the second stanza (vv. 4, 5) he appeals to God's
covenant loyalty (**unfailing love** v. 4), His
'pledged goodwill' (Eaton). In other words, he
calls on God to be true to His revealed character
(cf. Exod. 34: 6, 7). His desire for life is not
simply selfish: it is a desire for God Himself.
He 'longs for a fresh lease of life in order that
he might be able to glorify God' (A. Weiser).
In the third stanza (vv. 6, 7) he emphasizes the
seriousness of his condition. The language may
be exaggerative and figurative, but he is not
being melodramatic when he talks about the
closeness of death (v. 5). In the final stanza (vv.
8–10) the psalmist completely changes his tune:
complaint and despondency give way to confidence and determination. Why? He has received the assurance that his prayer has been
answered. How? Was he given a specific
priestly (cf. 1 Sam. 1: 17) or prophetic (cf. Isa.

37: 15 ff., 21 ff.) oracle (cf. Ps. 12: 5; 60: 6 ff.),
or did it come from an inner assurance? Or did
he claim a personal conclusion from the general
assurance of salvation given to all worshippers
in the temple (cf. Ps. 107: 17 ff.)? We are not
told. What is clear is that 'the sure knowledge
that his prayer had been answered is not something which a man can work out for himself,
but is a gift from God' (Weiser).

This is the first of the 'Penitential Psalms' (6;
32; 38; 51; 102; 130; 143), so designated since
early in the history of the Church, although in
this case the penitence is not explicit. They are
all appointed by the Prayer Book for use on
Ash Wednesday. (See N. H. Snaith, *The Seven
Psalms*, London, 1964.) The language of the
psalm seems to have been echoed by Jesus on
a number of occasions (v. 3, cf. Jn 12: 27; v. 8,
cf. Mt. 7: 23; Lk. 13: 27; see also Introduction
IV. 2).

Title: see Introduction III. 1, 2, 3. **according
to sheminith:** lit. 'on the eighth'; LXX, Vulg.
'on the octave'. Possibly to be accompanied by
an eight-stringed instrument or to be sung by
a bass voice in the lower octave (cf. 1 Chr. 15:
21). **2. faint:** lit. 'growing weak' (cf. GNB 'worn
out'). **heal:** implies the need for forgiveness
(cf. 41: 4; 2 Chr. 7: 14). **bones:** the fundamental
part of the body used to stand for the whole
person (cf. 35: 9 f.) and particularly regarded
as the seat of health (cf. Prov. 16: 24, RV) and
vitality (cf. Ezek. 37: 11). **in agony:** 'disturbed', 'shaken' (cf. Gen. 45: 3). **3. My soul:**
see on 3: 2; here it may refer to mental anguish
in addition to the physical suffering of v. 2.
how long?: common in laments (cf. 74: 10;
79: 5).

4. Turn: i.e. away from wrath; or 'return'
to the sufferer (cf. Moffatt: 'Save my life once
more'). **unfailing love:** see on 5: 7. **5. no one
remembers you:** not necessarily the inability
to recollect, but to join in the worship of Israel:
the dead are outside the cultic sphere (cf. Isa.
38: 18 f.; Ps. 30: 9; 88: 5, 10; 115: 17). **the
grave** (mg. 'Sheol'): the realm of the dead (LXX
'Hades'). The etymology of the Heb. word
šᵉ'ōl is uncertain (see *NBD art.* 'Hell'). It seems
to have been pictured as a vast subterranean
cavern where all the dead exist as 'shades' of
their former selves (cf. Job. 26: 5 f.; Isa. 14: 9
f.; Ezek. 32: 17–32). **7. my eyes:** may be taken
literally (cf. 88: 9) or 'eye' may stand for the
whole person who has lost all his vitality. **foes:**
possibly the homonym 'adversity' (cf. NEB
'woes'). **8. you who do evil:** see on 5: 5.
away: they no longer have cause to persecute
him. **9. cry:** lit. 'favour' (related to 'mercy'
v. 2). **prayer:** plea for intervention. **accepts:**
either confidence for the future or equivalent
to a past tense. **10. turn back:** turn away from
the psalmist, or return to Sheol (cf. Gen. 3: 19;
Ps. 139: 15).

Psalm 7. AN APPEAL FOR JUSTICE

The title links this psalm with an otherwise unknown experience of David, presumably when he was an outlaw (1 Sam. 21–26) or just before (1 Sam. 18–20). Cush, a fellow-tribesman of Saul, apparently insinuated that David was plotting against the king (cf. 1 Sam. 22: 8; 24: 9; 26: 19). The psalm would then represent David's protestation of innocence and plea to God for deliverance (cf. 1 Sam. 24: 11–15). The later cultic use of this psalm (or its original setting if the title is discounted) would be when an accused man went to the temple to seek protection and obtain Yahweh's decision on his case, given through a priest or judge (cf. Exod. 22: 7–11; Num. 5: 11–31; Dt. 17: 8–12; 1 Kg. 8: 31 f.). The psalm, with its oath of purgation (vv. 3–5), would be recited by (or for) the accused and he would then wait for the divine acquittal (A. A. Anderson). It is also possible that the king recited this psalm at a time of national distress (Eaton).

After an opening invocation for deliverance (vv. 1, 2), the psalmist proceeds to declare his innocence in the form of a solemn oath (vv. 3–5, cf. Job 31). Then in vv. 6–11 he calls on God, the righteous Judge of all the earth, to pass His verdict and vindicate him, for he knows that he is in the clear. Verses 12–16 describe the inevitable fate of the wicked man and the self-destructive effects of his 'home-grown' evil. Finally (v. 17) the psalmist makes his vow to praise Yahweh for the deliverance which he is sure will come.

Title: see Introduction III. 1, 2. **Shiggaion:** meaning uncertain; it may refer to a type of psalm (free rhythm? lamentation? emotional song?) or to a kind of accompaniment (cf. Hab. 3: 1). **1, 2. pursue . . . they** (Heb. 'he'): it is unnecessary to emend either the noun to the singular (Weiser) or the verbs to the plural (RSV, NIV, GNB); such oscillation is quite frequent in the OT. **3 ff.** Such an oath of purgation may have been accompanied by the symbolic washing of hands (cf. 26: 6; Isa. 1: 15 f.). **4. him who is at peace with me:** 'my ally', or possibly 'him that rewarded me (with evil)'. **robbed:** lit. 'delivered'. Some (cf. AV, RV) take v. 4b as a parenthesis asserting that his conduct had actually been the opposite of what he was accused: 'I have even delivered the one who was my enemy without cause'. NIV is a possible alternative; but JB 'if I spared a man who wronged me' (cf. NEB) is less likely. **Selah:** see Introduction III. 3.

6. Cf. Num. 10: 35. **Awake:** God is inactive, as if asleep (cf. 44: 23). **7. rule over them:** reading šebāh ('be seated') for šûbāh ('return'); but cf. Num. 10: 36. **8. judges:** for the two words used in this verse see on 72: 2. Judgment involves both the vindication of the innocent and the punishment of the guilty (see on 33:

5). **my righteousness:** not a claim to moral perfection, only to be clear of the alleged offences (cf. v. 3; see Introduction IV. 1). **9. minds and hearts:** lit. 'hearts and kidneys', the seat of thoughts and emotions respectively. **12, 13.** The subject may be God (as supplied by RSV, NEB) but is more naturally the wicked man of v. 14: 'If he does not repent, but sharpens his sword, bends his bow and aims it (or 'fixes it'); then the weapons he has prepared will kill himself, and his arrows turn into fire-brands' (cf. JB). **14.** A vivid picture of the development of evil in a man's personality (cf. Job 15: 35; Isa. 33: 11; 59: 4; Jas 1: 15). **17.** If the psalmist was given the assurance that his appeal was granted (see on Ps. 6), this might be the thanksgiving itself, rather than a vow to be fulfilled later. **righteousness:** God remains true to the standard of His own revealed character (see also on 33: 5). **name:** see on 20: 1. **Most High:** see on 47: 2.

Psalm 8. MAN'S PLACE IN GOD'S WORLD

One of the hymns of creation (cf. Pss. 19; 104; 139). 'But nature is never praised for its own sake: there are no nature lyrics in the psalms. Nature is referred to only to the extent that it points to him who made everything' (H. Ringgren). This psalm would have been suitable on any cultic occasion, on the lips of the king or of any ordinary Israelite. It might have had a special use at the feast of Tabernacles (see on **gittith** below), and may have been chanted antiphonally (cf. **our**, v. 1, **I**, v. 3). The metre is irregular and the division into stanzas unclear.

The psalm opens with an exclamation (v. 1a): the singers are overwhelmed by the greatness and splendour of their divine Sovereign (cf. Isa. 6: 3). Even the inarticulate chorus of praise from the very young is a strong defence against the ancient enemies of God and silences all opposition (vv. 1b, 2). Verses 3–8 raise the question of man's place in the world. The 'paradox of man' (A. A. Anderson) is that compared with the vast universe in which he lives he is an insignificant speck of dust, and yet God has given him a dignity and supremacy out of all proportion to his size. Man is king of the earth, appointed to rule it for God (cf. Adam, Gen. 1: 28; 2: 15, 19 f.). Nevertheless, the greatness of man's status is no cause for the praise of man (cf. Swinburne's *Hymn of Man*: 'Glory to Man in the highest! For man is the master of things'); it only serves to emphasize the greater glory of the Creator (v. 9).

In the NT Jesus is seen as the second Man (or 'last Adam') who perfectly fulfils this statement of man's intended role (cf. Heb. 2: 6–9; Eph. 1: 19–22; 1 C. 15: 24–26). The Prayer Book suitably appoints this psalm for use on Ascension Day.

Title: see Introduction III. 1, 2, 3. **gittith:**
obscure; LXX has 'for the winepress' (cf. Moffatt 'vintage melody'), which might suggest its
use at the feast of Tabernacles (cf. Dt. 16: 13
ff. and see Introduction II. 2); on the other
hand, it could refer to a Philistine tune or
instrument (i.e. 'of Gath'). **1. LORD . . . Lord:**
Heb. *Yahweh . . .'adōnāi*, the proper name of
the God of Israel (see on Exod. 3: 15) and a
title indicating his position and authority as
sovereign lord. **name:** see on 20: 1. In vv.
1, 2 there are difficulties of punctuation and
translation. Verse 1a seems to be an introduction (cf. v. 9), but v. 1b could be taken with
it: 'Thou whose glory is praised in the heavens'
(Weiser; cf. AV, NEB). **You have set:** MT has
'set thou', but a change of one vowel gives 'is
repeated (in antiphonal song)' cf. 'is chanted'
(RSV). 'Thou hast set' is a possible emendation.
2. you have ordained: could be a new sentence (cf. RSV, GNB), but it is better to link it
with 'From the lips of . . .' **praise:** lit.
'strength', 'stronghold'; LXX 'perfected praise'
(cf. Mt. 21: 16) is a paraphrase. For the idea of
praise as a defence see 2 Chr. 20: 22. **enemies
. . . foe . . . avenger:** either the opponents of
Israel (cf. 44: 16) or the primeval powers of
chaos subdued at the creation (cf. Gen. 1: 2;
Ps. 74: 12 ff.; 89: 9 ff. Isa. 51: 9 ff.).

3. Cf. Isa. 40: 26. **fingers:** personal involvement in creation. **4.** Cf. Job 7: 17; 25: 6; Ps.
144: 3 f. **man . . . son of man:** Heb. *'enôš . . .
ben-'ādām*, two synonyms probably intended to
emphasize the frailty of mankind (cf. Gen. 3:
19; Ps. 9: 19 f.; 10: 18; 39: 11; 90: 3; 103: 15;
144: 4). **are mindful:** lit. 'remember', i.e. act
on his behalf. **care:** lit. 'pay attention to'. **5.
the heavenly beings:** or 'a god' (JB, NEB). The
Heb. *'elōhîm* (pl.) normally refers to 'God' (or
'gods') but apparently can also denote heavenly
beings (Ps. 82: 1; 86: 8; cf. Job 1: 6; Ps. 89: 6;
and see on 29: 1), hence LXX 'angels' (cf. Heb.
2: 7). If the mg ('God') is correct the allusion
would be to Gen. 1: 26 (cf. 1 C. 11: 7; Jas 3:
9). **glory and honor:** divine attributes (cf.96:
6). **6.** Cf. Gen. 1: 26 ff.; Ps. 18: 38; 110: 1; 1 C.
15: 27; Eph. 1: 22.

Psalms 9–10. JUDGE OF THE WICKED, HELP OF THE HELPLESS

It would seem that these two psalms were
originally one, as they are in some Heb. MSS
and in LXX and Vulgate (hence the different
numbering of the Psalms in some Bibles). This
is confirmed by the following: (i) Ps. 10 has no
title (a rare occurrence in Book I); (ii) an acrostic
scheme covers both psalms (on the use of acrostics see on Ps. 25): in Ps. 9 each stanza of two
verses begins with one of the first eleven letters
of the Heb. alphabet; Ps. 10 begins with the
twelfth letter and ends with the last four (the

middle has probably suffered some corruption); (iii) 'Selah' is not normally found at the
end of a psalm (9: 20); (iv) there are similarities
of language and contents (cf. 9: 9 and 10: 1; 9:
19 and 10: 12; 9: 5 and 10: 16). Those who deny
literary unity point to the change of mood
between Ps. 9 and Ps. 10: Ps. 9 is an individual
(or community?) thanksgiving; Ps. 10 is a lament. They suppose that Ps. 10 was written to
supplement Ps. 9. Such a mixture of types can,
however, be found elsewhere (cf. Pss. 22; 36)
and it seems best to treat these two psalms as
a whole (so JB, NEB).

Those who attribute these psalms to David
(see Introduction III. 2) see references to his
victories (2 Sam. 8), particularly over the Philistines and the Jebusites (cf. Ps. 10: 16), and
regard Ps. 10: 1–11 as a description of civil
disorders during David's reign (cf. 2 Sam. 3:
39; 15: 2 ff.). Others suggest that this poem
represents the prayer of the king, or leader of
the community, during a period of foreign (*e.g.*
Assyrian or Babylonian) domination. Alternatively, the psalm could have been used by any
needy person who came to the temple to seek
the help of God. The **wicked** (singular collective) in Ps. 9 are obviously the heathen nations
(vv. 4, 17); in Ps. 10 the word seems to refer
to particular men within Israel (but cf. 10:
16). Similarly, the terms **oppressed, afflicted,
helpless, needy, victims** (see notes below)
may refer to particular individuals within Israel, or to the whole covenant community,
describing not only its situation but also (ideally
at least) its attitude towards God (i.e. humility).

The psalmist begins with a promise to praise
Yahweh (9: 1, 2), because he is sure that He will
answer his prayer (vv. 3, 4). This conviction is
based on the past activity of God in the history
of Israel: the conquest of Canaan, or the victories of David (vv. 5, 6). The actual source of
confidence is traced to the nature and status of
Yahweh (vv. 7–12): King for ever (cf. GNB);
Judge of the world; Protector of the oppressed;
Avenger of blood (cf. NEB). Verses 13–20 enunciate the prayer of the needy person, with
further evidence of his confidence in Yahweh's
justice (vv. 15, 16 may refer to past events, but
the verbs could be prophetic perfects: see on
20: 6). Ps. 10: 1–11 continues the supplication
of the afflicted man, pouring out his deep concern about the self-confident and blasphemous
attitude of the wicked, and the success of his
schemes. Again (vv. 12–15) he appeals to God
to take drastic action on behalf of the weak and
under-privileged, again expressing his assurance that eventually Yahweh, the everlasting
King, must hear and answer.

Title: see Introduction III. 1, 2, 3. **1. wonders:** those acts of God which excite wonder,
whether considered 'miraculous' or not (cf.
119: 18): acts of creation (136: 4); judgment

(106: 7, 22; 78: 4); individual or national deliverance (71: 17). **3. turn back:** defeat (cf. 44: 10) or retreat (JB). The verbs in vv. 3, 4 could be read as present (JB) or future (NEB) tenses. **5. rebuked:** in actions not just in words (cf. 104: 7). The verbs in vv. 5, 6 could be taken as prophetic perfects (see on 20: 6) or as imperatives: 'rebuke . . . blot . . .' **name:** see on 41: 5. **7. throne:** in heaven (see on 11: 4), but also in the earthly temple (v. 11; cf. 76: 2; 80: 1). **10. know your name:** acknowledge God's nature and demands; live according to His will (cf. 91: 14; see on 20: 1). **seek:** see on 24: 6. **12. afflicted:** Heb. *'anāwîm*, lit. 'those who bow down', i.e. 'humble', 'meek'. A similar word occurs in v. 18 (*q.v.*); the two tended to be confused and to overlap in meaning.

13. gates of death: any experience of disease or calamity could be viewed as being at the threshold of death (cf. Ps. 107: 18; Isa. 38: 10), already in the clutches of Sheol (cf. 18: 5; 30: 3). **14. gates:** the centre of social and economic life (cf. 69: 12), they stand for the whole city (cf. 87: 2). **Daughter:** the city may be viewed as a mother, the inhabitants as her children (cf. 149: 2); here it is a personification of the city (cf. Isa. 1: 8). **16. Higgaion. Selah:** see Introduction III. 3. **17. the grave:** see on 6: 5. **17, 18. forget . . . forgotten:** disregard, forsake (cf. 8: 4) **18. needy:** Heb. *'ebyôn*, 'poor' (cf. 112: 9; 132: 15) and thus in need of God's help (cf. 12: 5). The word was later used as a self-description by the Qumran community and by an early Jewish-Christian sect (the Ebionites). **afflicted:** Heb. *'aniyyîm*, lit. 'those who are bowed down', i.e. 'humbled', 'afflicted' (see on v. 12).

10: 1. hide: see on 13: 1. **2. afflicted:** Heb. *'ānî*, singular of *'aniyyîm* (see on 9: 18). **3.** A difficult verse (cf. NEB). **boasts:** i.e. that he achieves whatever he wants. **blesses:** probably a euphemism for 'curses' (RSV; cf. Job 1: 5). **4.** Not a philosophical denial of God's existence (i.e. atheism), but a practical policy to live as though He did not concern Himself with human affairs (cf. vv. 6, 11, 13; 14: 1). **7. under his tongue:** i.e. kept in readiness (cf. 'on the tip of the tongue'). **8. victims:** an unusual word, probably 'unfortunate' (cf. JB 'out-of-luck'). **12. Lift up:** gesture of royal authority (Eaton). **forget:** see on 9: 17. **helpless:** see on 9: 12. **14. commits:** lit. 'leaves (himself or his cause)'. **fatherless:** representative of all underprivileged and oppressed (cf. 82: 3). **break the arm:** deprive of power. **17. afflicted:** Heb. *'anāwîm* (see on 9: 12). **encourage them:** 'give them courage' (GNB).

Psalm 11. UNSHAKEN COURAGE AND CONFIDENCE

This psalm of confidence is addressed not to God but to those well-meaning but faint-

hearted friends who had advised the psalmist to flee from his enemies. The writer's predicament is not clear: v. 2 may describe an attempt to assassinate him, or the mounting of a campaign of slander; v. 3 suggests a time when normal law and order have broken down. Those who link the psalm with an experience of David (cf. Title) refer to 1 Sam. 18: 12–29; 19: 11; or 27: 1 ff. Whether or not vv. 1, 4 imply that the psalmist has gone to the sanctuary for protection from his enemies (A. A. Anderson; cf. Exod. 21: 12 ff.; 1 Kg. 1: 50), the poem would be suitable for use by such a person as he waited in the temple for God to act on his behalf. The psalm has two parts: vv. 1–3 outline the situation as seen by the psalmist's friends: a time for panic and escape; vv. 4–7 describe the situation as seen by the psalmist: a time for trusting Yahweh the righteous, omniscient King.

Title: see Introduction III. 2, 3. **1.** Cf. Ps. 121: 1 f.; 1 Sam. 26: 20; Isa. 28: 16. **2.** Cf. Ps. 7: 13 f. Verses 2, 3 could be the psalmist's reason for refusing the advice given in v. 1, but they read better as part of the warning of his friends (RSV, JB, GNB). **3. foundations:** usually taken to refer to the social order (cf. Ps. 82: 5; Isa. 19: 10, 13; Ezek. 30: 4). **4. temple:** or 'palace'; it could refer to the earthly sanctuary (cf. Ps. 9: 11; Jer. 3: 16 f.), but here seems to denote the heavenly dwelling-place of God (cf. Ps. 18: 6; 47: 8; 103: 19: Hab. 2: 20). **observes:** the undercover machinations of the wicked (cf. **the shadows** v. 2) do not go unnoticed. **eyes:** lit. 'eyelids'; possibly a reference to the screwing-up of the eyes when scrutinizing an object. **5. his soul:** he himself (see on 3: 2). **examines:** a metaphor from metal refining (cf. Jer. 6: 27–30), it implies separation. **6.** Sudden and final judgment like that at Sodom and Gomorrah (Gen. 19: 24). **lot** ('cup'): that which is allotted by God, whether blessing (cf. 16: 5; 116: 13) or judgment (cf. Isa. 51: 17; Lam. 4: 21). **7. loves:** either 'delights to perform . . .' or 'delights to see men perform . . .'. **justice:** lit. 'righteousnesses' (see on 33: 5). **see his face:** have an experience of His presence and favour, especially in the sanctuary (see on 4: 6; cf. 17: 15; 24: 2; 27: 4; 63: 2). An alternative translation would be 'his face beholds the upright' (cf. AV, NEB).

Psalm 12. PROTECTION AGAINST PROPAGANDA

The original setting of this psalm is unknown. It could reflect conditions during the reign of Saul (cf. 1 Sam. 23: 11, 19 ff.; 26: 19) but would equally fit any time before the exile, especially the eighth and seventh centuries B.C. (cf. Hos. 4: 1 ff.; Mic. 7: 2 ff.; Isa. 33: 7–12; Jer. 5: 1–5). It was probably used in the cult as a lament of the community: with a leader (*e.g.* king) reciting vv. 1–4, the cry for help in the 'battle of words' (Kidner); a priest or prophet answering with the divine oracle of v. 5, the promise of salvation; and the community responding with the 'Amen' of vv. 6–8, the confidence that God's word is dependable in any situation.

Title: see Introduction III. 1, 2, 3. **sheminith:** see on Ps. 6. **1. godly:** see on 4: 3. The translation 'loyalty . . . faithfulness' (cf. NEB) is possible but unnecessary. **2. lies:** lit. 'utters emptiness'. **flattering:** lit. 'smoothnesses'. **deception:** lit. 'a heart and a heart', i.e. 'double thinking' resulting in 'double talk' (Kidner): hypocrisy. **3. lips:** a literary device (synecdoche) in which a part stands for the whole: the wicked are to be destroyed (cf. Am. 2: 3). **4. we own our lips:** i.e. our lips are 'our means of success' (Eaton); cf. NEB 'are our ally'. The power of words to exploit, control, and destroy is recognized throughout the Bible (cf. Dan. 7: 20, 25; Jas 3: 5 ff.; 2 Pet. 2: 1 ff.; Rev. 13: 5 ff.).

5. Originally an oracle given to the psalmist either directly (because he was a prophet himself; cf. 2 Sam. 23: 1 ff.) or through a priest or sanctuary prophet (cf. 1 Sam. 1: 17; 1 Kg. 37: 15 ff., 21 ff.). See also on Ps. 6. **weak . . . needy:** see on 9: 18. **I will protect . . .:** or 'I will place him in the safety for which he longs' (RSV, NEB). **6. flawless:** i.e. true, trustworthy. **silver:** in early times more precious than gold; and for use in commercial transactions its purity was important. **a furnace of clay:** possibly 'a crucible of clay' (Kidner); **7. us . . . us:** so some Heb. MSS and LXX; *MT* has 'them . . . him' (i.e. the 'weak' of v. 5). **such people** 'circle', 'assembly' (cf. 14: 5; 24: 6; Prov. 30: 11–14). **8. strut:** lit. 'walk'; cf. NEB 'flaunt themselves'. **what is vile:** lit. 'worthlessness'.

Psalm 13.   HOW MUCH LONGER LORD?

This individual lament could have been used in the temple by any Israelite who was either sick or being persecuted, or both. In addition, such a prayer could have been offered by the king as the representative of his people in a time of national distress. The situation of the original psalmist is not clear; he is obviously near death (v. 3) and oppressed by enemies (vv. 2, 4), but the relationship between the two conditions is not explained (see on Pss.6; 22). It would probably fit many experiences of David during the reign of Saul (see on Ps. 7).

The structure is straightforward: vv. 1, 2 use the customary style of laments (found also in Babylonian psalms) to express the deep sense of perplexity at the silence of God; vv. 3, 4 show that the psalmist has not given up all hope (cf. Luther: 'hope despairs and yet despair hopes'), for he prays for the mercy and justice of God; vv. 5, 6 conclude with an affirmation of trust and a vow of thanksgiving. The change

of mood in vv. 5, 6 may have resulted from an inner assurance that God had heard (see on Ps. 6).

Title: see Introduction III. 1, 2, 3. **1. How long:** lit. 'until when?' **forever:** 'utterly'. **hide your face:** the withdrawing of God's presence and help normally implied discipline because of sin (cf. Mic. 3: 4; Isa. 54: 8; 57: 17; 59: 2). The psalmist's enemies may have drawn that conclusion, but he shows no consciousness of sin (cf. 6: 1–3). **2. wrestle with my thoughts:** *MT* (NIV) suggests turmoil of mind. **every day:** lit. 'by day'; LXX adds 'and by night'. **enemy:** not necessarily an individual; here it is probably a collective (cf. v. 4). **3. Look on me:** lit. 'look' (cf. 10: 14), i.e. 'take note' (cf. **hide** v. 1). **Give light to my eyes:** i.e. 'give me life'. The eyes are the 'barometer of vitality' (A. A. Anderson); cf. Job 17: 7; Ps. 6: 7; 38: 10; 1 Sam. 14: 27, 29. **5. But I:** emphatic, 'But as for me, I . . .' **trust:** (JB 'rely'). **unfailing love:** see on 5: 7. **5, 6. my heart rejoices . . . I will sing:** or 'let my heart rejoice . . . let me sing' (cf. JB). **for he has . . . :** probably looking confidently to the future deliverance.

Psalm 14.   SINNERS ALL

This poem is more like a prophetic message (cf. references below) than a psalmist's lament, since God is not addressed. The life-setting of the psalm is not clear. Some think that the writer is describing a group (*e.g.* the ruling classes) within Israel who were victimizing the poor (cf. Am. 2: 6 f.; Mic. 3: 1 ff.; Isa. 3: 14 f.); others suggest that the psalm reflects the hardship of Israel in a godless and hostile world. Alternatively, vv. 1–3 may be seen as a description of mankind generally, and vv. 4–6 as referring to the godless within Israel.

The psalm may be divided into three parts: vv. 1–3 paint a picture of universal godlessness (cf. Gen. 6: 5; Hos. 4: 1 ff.; Jer. 5: 1 ff.; Isa. 59: 4 ff.; 64: 6 ff.); vv. 4–6 express astonishment at the lack of moral understanding displayed by the wicked who leave God out of their reckoning (cf. Jer. 5: 12; Zeph. 1: 12); v. 7 looks forward hopefully to the joyful restoration of God's people. Ps. 53 (*q.v.*) is another version of this psalm.

Title: see Introduction III. 2, 3. **1. The fool:** a collective, describing a class of men (cf. **they** v. 1b). Heb. *nābāl* does not connote a simpleton, but one whose moral thinking is perverse; he has deliberately closed his mind to the reality of God and to the implications of His moral rule (cf. Dt. 32: 5 f.; 2 Sam. 13: 12 f.; Isa. 32:6; Rom. 1: 19, 22, 28). **says in his heart:** i.e. 'thinks'. **no God:** see on 10: 4. **2. understand:** by submitting to God's authority (cf. 2: 10; 36: 3). **3. no one:** either among the wicked or, more likely, among mankind in general (cf. Ec. 7: 20; 1 Kg. 8: 46; 2 Chr. 6: 36; Ps. 143: 2;

Prov. 20: 9; Rom. 3: 9–20.). **4. evil doers:** see on 5: **5. learn:** either of their responsibility to God (cf. Isa. 1: 3) or of the coming judgment (v. 5). Some translate: 'Shall not all the evildoers be made to know (i.e. 'punished'; cf. Hos. 9: 7)?' **5. There:** in their chosen situation, imagining that they can evade the judgment of God. **company:** or 'assembly'; the fellowship (NEB 'brotherhood') of the godly. **6.** Weiser reads: 'Your plans against the poor will be confounded, for . . .' **poor:** see on 9: 18. **7. Zion:** see on 2: 6. **restores the fortunes:** not necessarily a reference to return from captivity (as AV, RV), but to a renewal of prosperity (cf. Job 42: 10; Ezek. 16: 33; Zeph. 2: 7). **Jacob:** see on 20: 1.

Psalm 15. WHO GOES THERE? CONDITIONS FOR COMMUNION WITH GOD

Archaeological evidence suggests that it was customary in the ancient Near East to inform worshippers of the cultic requirements (moral or ritual) necessary for admittance to a temple. This psalm could well have been used for such a purpose in the Davidic tent-shrine and subsequently in the Jerusalem temple (see also on Ps. 24). A group of pilgrims would approach the gate-keepers and ask for the conditions of entry (v. 1). Then a priest or Levite would give the answer of vv. 2–5b (cf. Mal. 2: 7). Although it is possible to find *ten* conditions here (cf. the decalogue of Exod. 20), it is better to see v. 2 as the actual reply and vv. 3–5b as providing a number of specific examples. Verse 5c could be a later addition when the psalm was used for didactic purposes. Similar 'entrance liturgies' may be found in Ps. 24: 3–6 and Isa. 33: 14–17; and prophetic teaching in the same vein occurs in Mic. 6: 6 ff.; Jer. 7: 1–11; Ezek. 18: 5–9; 44: 5 ff.

In the Prayer Book this psalm is set for Ascension Day; Christ is seen as fulfilling it when He entered the presence of God having lived a perfect human life (cf. Heb. 4: 14 f.; 7: 26).

Title: see Introduction III, 1, 2. **1. dwell** (cf. A. Maclaren: 'be guest') . . . **live:** the worshipper's ideal is to remain (like the priests and Levites) in the sanctuary all his life (cf. 23: 6; 27: 4; 61: 4; 84: 4). **sanctuary:** probably a reference to the tent-shrine erected by David to house the ark (cf. 2 Sam. 6: 17; 7: 6), but also applicable to the temple (cf. Ps. 27: 4, 5; Isa. 33: 20). **holy hill:** Mount Zion (see on 2: 6), sanctified by the presence of Yahweh. **2. blameless:** Heb. *tāmîm* means 'complete', 'without blemish', 'irreproachable'; not 'perfect', but 'having no outstanding fault' (cf. 19: 13), 'sound', having 'an undivided commitment' (von Rad; cf. Dt. 18: 13). Here it implies

integrity, sincerity, and whole-hearted devotion to God and to His law (cf. Gen. 17: 1; Ps. 119: 1). **truth:** what can be trusted. **from his heart:** cf. Ps. 12: 2; Isa. 29: 13.

3. neighbour: fellow-man. **casts no slur:** the exact sense is not clear; he does not repeat accounts of another's misfortune, or rejoice at them, or abuse him for it. **4. a vile man:** a notorious evil-doer who has evidently been rejected by God (cf. Jer. 6: 30); for the thought of v. 4a see Ps. 1: 1. **keeps his oath . . .:** cf. Lev. 27: 10. **5.** Taking interest from a needy person was forbidden in Israelite law (cf. Exod. 22: 25; Lev. 25: 36 f.) but allowed in business deals with foreigners (cf. Dt. 23: 20). Interest rates in ancient Mesopotamia could be as high as 50 per cent per annum. **accept a bribe:** corruption was a temptation for both judges and witnesses (cf. Exod. 23: 8; Dt. 16: 19; Isa. 1: 23; 5: 23; Mic. 3: 11; 7: 3). **never be shaken:** the man described will not only be admitted to fellowship with Yahweh in the sanctuary, but like any guest in the ancient Near East he will constantly be under his Host's protection (cf. Ps. 10: 6; 13: 4; 16: 8; 91: 1 f.; Prov. 10: 30; Isa. 33: 16; 1 Jn 2: 17).

Psalm 16. SATISFIED WITH GOD

This psalm of confidence seems to have originated in an experience of preservation from premature death (v. 10; cf. Ps. 38: 9–21), and is to some extent an act of thanksgiving for the past as well as an expression of trust for the future. It could easily fit David's experience as an outlaw (with vv. 4–6, cf. 1 Sam. 26: 19 f.).

The opening prayer and affirmation of faith (vv. 1, 2) imply that whilst a particular crisis may have passed, the psalmist is still in need of God's safe-keeping. Verses 3, 4 are difficult, but they seem to provide a contrast between the godly and the apostates (those who have been seduced by heathenism) in society; the writer identifies himself with the first group and dissociates himself from the second. (Verses 1–4 could be taken as one stanza.) Verses 5–8 express the author's awareness that having God he has all that he needs for a happy, contented, well-directed and secure life. Finally (vv. 9–11) he exults in the confidence that God will preserve him from death, so that he can live the more abundant life of one who is enjoying the presence and blessing of his God at all times.

Many commentators see in vv. 9–11 a belief (or hope) in life after death, either through resurrection (cf. Dan. 12: 2) or by translation into heaven (see also on Ps. 49: 15; 73: 24). This is probably going further than the psalmist's intention; his concern is with this life rather than with death and beyond (see Introduction IV. 1). The contrast is between life with God and life without God. Nevertheless, the implications of his trust in God point forward to the possibility of eternal life in the presence of God. 'The *hasid* (godly one) who is living by God, for God, and in God, no longer looks upon death as a threatening present reality; in the presence of the Living God it loses its importance . . . in some sense he lives in a sort of eternal present' (Martin-Achard, *From Death to Life*, 1960, pp. 151 f.). The early Christian preachers, basing themselves on the LXX rendering of vv. 8–11, saw these words as a prophecy of the resurrection of Jesus (Ac. 2: 24–31; 13: 34–37; cf. Lk. 24: 44 ff.). What the psalmist faintly hinted at becomes a reality for Christians through the work of Christ (cf. Jn 5: 28 f.; 6: 47, 54; 10: 10; 2 Tim. 1: 10; and see Introduction IV. 2).

Title: see Introduction III 1, 2. **2. I said:** so LXX, etc.; *MT* has 'thou (feminine *scil.* 'my soul') hast said'. **I have no good . . . :** *MT* has 'my good is not upon (or 'beyond') thee'. The sense is reasonably clear; cf. Weiser: 'my happiness depends wholly upon thee' (cf. 73: 25). **3.** The Heb. text is difficult; the NIV gives the most straightforward interpretation (cf. GNB). Other translations (cf. JB, NEB) take the **saints** (lit. 'holy ones'; cf. 34: 9) as pagan deities, and understand both v. 3 and v. 4 as referring to those who apostasize and worship other gods. **4. run after:** 'hasten after', 'exchange', or 'lust after'. **gods:** supplied to make sense. **sorrows:** cf. Gen. 3: 16; Rom. 1: 21–31. **libations of blood:** the exact nature of this practice is not clear (cf. Isa. 1: 15; 66: 3). **their names:** i.e. of foreign deities.

5. assigned: i.e. allotted. **portion:** land, property, or food. **cup:** see on 11: 6. **you have made secure . . . :** possibly 'thou art my lot for ever' (Weiser). **6. lines:** portions of land measured by a line (cf. Jos. 17: 5). In vv. 5, 6 the writer is spiritualizing an ancient tradition: when the land of Canaan was divided by lots to the Israelite tribes (Jos. 13: 14–14: 5; 18: 2 ff.; 19: 51) Levi was given no land; its portion and inheritance was to be Yahweh Himself (Num. 18: 20; Dt. 10: 9), i.e. they were to depend entirely upon Him for their living (cf. 73: 26; 119: 57; 142: 5). **7. counsels:** cf. v. 11a; given by oracle, in written law (cf. 73: 24) or through conscience (cf. **heart**). **heart:** lit. 'kidneys', centre of deep emotions and desires; here equivalent to 'conscience' (GNB). **instructs:** disciplines, corrects. **8. have set:** by observing His law; cf. 119: 30; 54: 3; 86: 14. **shaken:** see on 15: 5.

9. heart: see on 17: 3. **my tongue:** lit. 'my glory'; the Heb. consonants (*kbd*) could be read as 'my liver', a synonym for 'heart' (cf. Gen. 49: 6; Ps. 7: 5; Prov. 7: 23, RV, RV). **body:** lit. 'flesh'; the Heb. *bāśār* can denote the physical constituent of animals and men (cf. Gen. 40: 19) and therefore the body as a whole

(cf. 79: 2; 109: 24). It can also mean 'man' or 'mankind' (cf. 'all flesh', 136: 25; 145: 21). In this verse, however, it stands for the whole person (cf. 38: 3; 63: 1; 84: 2) and no contrast is intended with 'heart' and 'soul'. While there is often an emphasis on its weakness (cf. 78: 39; Isa. 31: 3), in the OT it is never regarded as intrinsically evil (cf. Rom. 8: 3 ff.). **10. abandon:** forsake, leave, abandon. **me:** lit. 'my soul' (see on 3: 2). **Sheol:** see on 6: 5. **godly one:** see on 4: 3. **Pit:** Heb. *šaḥat*, i.e. the grave; a synonym for Sheol (cf. 49: 9). LXX derived the word from the verb 'destroy', 'go to ruin', and translated it 'corruption'. **11. path of life:** 'that course of life which enables the godly to fulfil his destiny' (A. A. Anderson); cf. Prov. 4: 18; 5: 6; 9: 23; 10: 17; 15: 24. **presence:** lit. 'face' (see on 4: 6). **right hand:** cf. Prov. 3: 16. **fill me:** implies satisfaction (cf. 17: 15). **eternal:** probably 'as long as life lasts' (cf. Exod. 21: 6; see on Ps. 23: 6).

Psalm 17. A PLEA FOR VINDICATION

This individual lament (or psalm of innocence) would have been suitable for use in the temple by a falsely-accused man (see on Pss. 5 and 7), or by the king in particular as the representative of his people. Verses 3 and 15 may imply that the suppliant would spend the night in the sanctuary (cf. 2 Sam. 12: 6) and expect to receive the divine answer either in a dream (cf. 1 Kg. 3: 5) or through a priest or judge (cf. Dt. 17: 8–12) the following morning. The psalm could have originated during the period when David was an outlaw (cf. 1 Sam. 24: 12–15).

The sequence of thought is clear, despite some difficulties of translation in vv. 3 f., 14. In vv. 1, 2 the psalmist appeals to God to hear his plea for justice, and in vv. 3–5 declares both his innocence of the crimes with which he is charged (cf. 7: 3–5) and his general uprightness of life (but there is no claim to moral perfection). In vv. 6–9 he renews his supplication for protection, confident that he addresses a God of both power and love (v. 7a); whilst vv. 10–12 describe the relentless heartlessness of his enemies as they close in on him (cf. 1 Sam. 23: 25 ff.). Verses 13, 14 are a call for vengeance and retribution which will extend even to the next generation (cf. Exod. 34: 7). (On the vindictive elements in the Psalms see Introduction IV. 1.) The last verse (v. 15) is an affirmation (or prayer) that the psalmist will have the satisfaction of seeing God 'on his side' (cf. Job 19: 27), pronouncing in his favour, and thus assuring him of His continued presence and blessing (cf. 16: 11).

Title: see Introduction III. 1, 2. **1. my righteous plea:** lit. 'righteousness' (see on 33: 5); LXX adds 'my'. Weiser translates 'Hear me, O Lord of my salvation'. **2. vindication:** or 'sentence'; lit. 'judgment' (see on 1: 5). **see what is right:** i.e. the uprightness of the accused (cf. 11: 4 f.). **3. Though you . . . :** the verbs could be read as statements ('You try . . .') or as imperatives ('Try . . . visit . . . test'). **examine:** (cf. JB; Job 7: 18). **heart:** mind (thoughts) and will (choices). **nothing:** or 'no evil desire' (GNB). The Heb. is difficult; *MT* suggests 'nothing; my purpose is that my mouth shall not transgress' (cf. RV, AV). **night:** when men's thoughts roam freely.

4. Cf. 1 Sam. 25: 32 ff.; 24: 10 ff. **7. Show the wonder:** or 'make marvellous'; see on 9: 1 and cf. Gen. 18: 14 (RSVmg). **great love:** see on 5: 7; '. . . only a miracle of divine grace can save him' (Weiser). **by your right hand:** It could mean either 'by means of your power' (cf. 20: 6; 60: 5) or 'those who rise up against your power' (cf. RVmg), or alternatively, 'at your right hand', 'at your side we are safe' (GNB). **8. the apple of . . . :** lit. 'the pupil, the daughter of . . .'; it should be carefully guarded as a highly personal possession (cf. Dt. 32: 10; Prov. 7: 2; Zech. 2: 8). **wings:** cf. Ru. 2: 12; a reference either to the cherubim over the ark (cf. 1 Kg. 8: 6 f.; Ps. 61: 4; 80: 1) or to a mother bird (cf. Dt. 32: 11; Ps. 91: 4; Mt. 23: 37). **9. mortal:** or possibly greedy (see on 33: 19). **10. They close up their callous hearts:** lit. 'Their fat they have closed'; obesity is a picture of stubbornness and rebellion (cf. Dt. 32: 15; Ps. 73: 7; 119: 70; Isa. 6: 10; Jer. 5: 28). **11. They have tracked me down:** a slight emendation; *MT* has 'Our goings they have now surrounded' (cf. RV).

13. me: lit. 'my soul', i.e. 'me' (see on 3: 2). **14.** This verse is difficult. AV, RV, NIV understand it as a reference to the material prosperity of the worldly which contrasts with the spiritual satisfaction of the psalmist (v. 15). RSV, GNB, NEB take it as a prayer for vengeance. **15. I will . . . I will . . . :** or 'let me . . . let me . . .' **face:** see on 4: 6. **in righteousness:** 'for my vindication' or 'as the upholder of justice' (see on 33: 5), rather than 'because I am righteous' (cf. GNB, NEB, JB). **when I awake:** the verb can refer to resurrection (cf. Isa. 26: 19; 2 Kg. 4: 31; Dan. 12: 2), but here it is best taken in its natural sense. In the psalms the dawn is the time when God answers prayer (cf. 5: 3; 30: 5; 57: 8) and grants an awareness of His presence (cf. 139: 18), especially in the temple. **with beholding:** added to make sense; probably a spiritual perception rather than seeing a theophany (but cf. Num. 12: 6–8; Dt. 4: 12; 34: 10).

Psalm 18. THE SONG OF THE VICTORIOUS KING

This is a royal psalm of thanksgiving. The title relates it to the experiences of David and the contents might suggest that it was written in the period of peace between Nathan's oracle (2 Sam. 7; cf. 8: 1–14) and David's sin with Bathsheba (2 Sam. 11). In later years it would have been recited by a Davidic king on his return from battle, at a service of thanksgiving for victory; there is no evidence, however, for the suggestion that it accompanied a yearly dramatic ritual in which the king symbolically defeated his enemies (see Introduction II. 2). A slightly different version of this psalm is found in 2 Sam. 22.

The psalm divides into two main parts: vv. 1–30 and vv. 31–50. The writer begins (vv. 1, 2) with a series of metaphors to describe the source of protection and strength that God has proved Himself to be in his experience. Verses 3–6 briefly but forcibly refer to the extreme peril to which he was exposed and from which he sought deliverance. Verses 7–15 picture the divine intervention in terms of a storm theophany (manifestation of God), and vv. 16–19 tell of the resulting deliverance. Verses 20–30 see this deliverance as an act of vindication: evidence that Yahweh always deals righteously and faithfully with those who trust and obey Him. The second part of the psalm consists of a celebration of the triumphant career of the king who has the backing of Yahweh (vv. 31–45); his success is entirely attributable to the activity of his God, and so he concludes (vv. 46–50) with a paean of praise to the God who has committed Himself to bless the Davidic line (cf. 2 Sam. 7; Isa. 55: 3 f.).

Title: see Introduction III. 1, 2, 3. **servant:** see on Ps. 36 Title. **1. love:** an uncommon word, so some emend to read 'I will exalt' (cf. 30: 1); the verse is missing from 2 Sam. 22. **2. rock . . . rock:** the first represents Heb. *sela'* (cliff, crag), the second is the more usual word *ṣûr* (rock); cf. 1 Sam. 23: 25 ff. As a symbol of strength, reliability, faithfulness and unchangeableness, it became a divine appellative (cf. Dt. 32: 4, 31; 1 Sam. 2: 2; Ps. 42: 9). **fortress:** cf. 1 Sam. 23: 14. **horn:** symbol of strength (cf. the wild ox: 22: 21). **3.** If the verbs are understood as presents or futures, the verse can be taken with vv. 1, 2 (so NIV); if we translate 'I called . . . was saved' (Weiser), it links with vv. 4–6. **4. cords:** 2 Sam. 22: 5 reads 'waves' or 'breakers', a better parallel. **destruction:** Heb. *beliyya'al* (derivation uncertain), probably a synonym for **the grave** ('Sheol' mg) (v. 5; see on 6: 5). The king's battle with his enemies is seen as a struggle with the powers of death and chaos (see on vv. 7 ff.): in v. 4 they are like an overwhelming sea; in v. 5 they are compared to hunters lying in wait with nets and traps. **6. temple:** see on 5: 7; 11: 4.

7–15. Although it is possible that the writer could have experienced the intervention of God in a storm (cf. Jos. 10: 11; Jg. 5: 20 f.; 1 Sam. 7: 10), it is better to take this as an ideal description of a theophany (cf. 1 Kg. 19: 11 f.; Job 37: 1–38: 1; Ps. 29: 3–10; 50: 3; 97: 2–5; Ezek. 1: 44 ff.; Hab. 3: 2–15) based upon the manifestations of God in the past (cf. Exod. 15: 4–12; 19: 16 ff.; 20: 18; Jg. 5: 4 f.). Some suggest that there is also an allusion to Yahweh's primeval triumph over the powers of chaos (the 'deep' and the 'waters' of Gen. 1: 2, 6 f.). **10. cherubim:** here probably symbolizing the wind (see *NBD art.* 'Cherubim'). **14. arrows:** i.e. lightning. **15. sea:** so 2 Sam. 22: 16; *MT* here has 'waters'. **valleys:** cf. Exod. 15: 8; Ps. 104: 7; 106: 9. **16.** cf. v. 4. **19.** 'Distress' (v. 4) consists of being hemmed in by trouble; 'deliverance' means to be set at liberty and thus unrestricted (cf. 4: 1).

20–30. The purpose of these verses is to praise the faithfulness of Yahweh in keeping His covenant promises (v. 30; cf. Exod. 20: 6; Dt. 28: 1–14). The author is not claiming sinless perfection (on **blameless**, vv. 23, 25, see 15: 2), but a 'single-hearted sincerity in his devotion to God' (Kirkpatrick); cf. 15: 2 ff.; 17: 3–5; 24: 3–5. **25. faithful:** Heb. *ḥāsîd* (see on 4: 3). **26. crooked . . . shrewd:** or 'devious . . . crafty' (JB); cf. Lev. 26: 33 f.; cf. also God's dealings with Jacob (Gen. 29) and Balaam (Num. 22: 20). **27. humble:** Heb. *'ānî* (see on 9: 18). **28. lamp:** symbol of life and prosperity (cf. Job 18: 5 ff.; Prov. 13: 9); possibly read (with 2 Sam. 22: 29) 'you are my lamp' (cf. 27: 1). **29. advance against a troop:** or possibly 'break down the fence'; i.e. both lines may refer to scaling the walls of hostile cities (cf. NEB). **30. perfect:** Heb. *tāmîm* (the same word as **blameless**, vv. 23, 25). When used of God it points to the perfection of His righteousness and faithfulness: His utter dependability (cf. Dt. 32: 4). **word is flawless:** 'without dross' (JB); cf. 12: 6; 119: 140.

31–45. This section could be translated with future tenses (JB) or present (NEB, GNB). **31. Rock:** Heb. *ṣûr* (see on v. 2). **33. feet of a deer:** swiftness was essential to a successful warrior (cf. 2 Sam. 1: 23; 2: 18; 1 Chr. 12: 8). **34. bronze:** refers either to the arrows (NEB; cf. Job 20: 24) or to a bow strengthened with metal. **35. you stoop down:** lit. 'your meekness' (cf. AV, RV), seems to refer to Yahweh's condescension in raising a shepherd boy to the throne (cf. 113: 7 f.). A slight emendation would give 'your answering' (cf. RSV 'your help'). **41.** For examples of the heathen calling on Yahweh see 1 Sam. 5: 12; Jon. 1: 14; 3: 7 ff.; but followers of Saul may be intended here. **42. poured:** better 'crushed' (so 2 Sam. 22: 43) or 'trampled' (NEB). **43.** Cf. Ps. 2; 2 Sam. 8: 9 ff. **44. cringe:** see on 66: 3. **46. lives:** possibly an intended contrast with the dying and rising of Ba'al. **Rock:** see on v. 2. **47. avenges:** cf. Dt. 32: 35. **50. He gives . . . great victories:** lit. 'Magnifying the salvations of'; (on 'sal-

vation' see 35: 3). **unfailing kindness:** see on 5: 7; cf. NEB 'in all his acts he keeps faith with . . .' **anointed:** see on 2: 2. **descendants:** lit. 'seed'.

Psalm 19. A RESPONSE TO THE REVELATION OF GOD

The differences in style, metre and contents, and the abrupt ending of the first section, suggest that part of a hymn in praise of God in nature (vv. 1–6; cf. Ps. 8) has been combined with a hymn in praise of God's law (vv. 7–14; cf. Ps. 119). The justification for joining the two poems would seem to be that both deal with the revelation of the divine nature: the character of God is to be seen not only in the pages of Scripture but also in the book of Nature. As B. Ramm says, 'If the Author of Nature and Scripture are the same God, then the two books of God must eventually recite the same story' (*The Christian View of Science and Scripture*, 1964, p. 25). The psalmist may also have been influenced by the fact that in the ancient Near East 'sun' and 'justice' were thought of as belonging together; *e.g.* Shamash, the Mesopotamian sun-god, was considered to be the upholder of justice and righteousness (cf. the stele of Hammurabi; *DOTT* pp. 27 f., pl. 2; *ANET* p. 163; *ANEP* pl. 246). For the title see Introduction III. 1, 2, 3.

The psalm has inspired hymns like 'The heavens declare Thy glory, Lord' (Watts); 'The spacious firmament on high' (Addison); 'God of the morning, at whose voice / The cheerful sun makes haste to rise' (Watts); and settings like that in 'The Creation' by Haydn and a song by Beethoven. In the Prayer Book it is appointed for Christmas Day; the Incarnation being seen as the climax of God's acts of self-revelation.

The message of the skies (vv. 1–6)
The sun by day (cf. 136: 8) and the stars by night (cf. 136: 9; Isa. 40: 26) provide a continual (v. 2), non-verbal (v. 3), universal (v. 4) testimony to the splendour and power of God. The psalmist may have chosen to deal with the sun in more detail because it was regarded by many in the ancient world as a very important deity. He even seems to make use of the mythological imagery of the Babylonian hymns to the sun-God, Shamash (cf. *ANET* pp. 387 ff.); yet he makes it clear that the sun is simply a part of God's handiwork: it does not call men to its own worship but rather to the praise of the glory of the one and only Creator.

1. heavens: here the 'sky', not the dwelling place of God (cf. 123: 1). **God:** Heb. *'Ēl*, see on 50: 1. **the skies:** or 'expanse' (lit. 'beaten out'). The word derives from the early picture of the sky as a solid canopy over the earth (cf.

Gen. 1: 6 ff.; Job 37: 18) in which the stars are embedded and across which the sun makes its daily journey (vv. 5, 6), and with windows to let the rain through (cf. Gen. 7: 11). **4. voice:** NIV follows LXX which gives the required sense (parallel to **words**). The Heb. word (*qāw*) usually means 'line' or 'cord', but it may also have been used of a musical note or chord, hence NEB 'music'. 'Sound' or 'call' are other possible renderings. **4, 5. tent . . . pavilion:** the 'marriage-tent' (cf. Jl 2: 16) in which the bridegroom spends the night with his bride. (The Babylonian sun-god was regarded as resting during the night in the sea, lying in his bride-chamber in the arms of his beloved.) **champion:** or 'hero' (cf. Jg. 5: 31); a warrior needed to be a good athlete (cf. 18: 33). **6. circuit:** its 'turning-point' in the west (cf. Ec. 1:5).

The impact of God's law (vv. 7-14)
This poem may be divided into a hymn in praise of the law (vv. 7-10/11) and prayer for cleansing, power and acceptance (vv. 11/12-14). For the meaning of law (Heb. *tôrāh*) see on 1: 2; for the other synonymous terms in vv. 7-9 see on Ps. 119. The psalmist describes the character and effects of the law (vv. 7-11). If nature reveals the glory of *'Ēl* (v. 1) the creator God, then the law reveals the will and moral character of *Yahweh* (vv. 7 ff.), the covenant God of Israel, who gave the law (cf. **of the LORD,** vv. 7 ff.). The writer loves and treasures God's law, but he is far from being self-righteous or satisfied with a merely external observance of it. He finds the study of the law both challenging and disconcerting; he feels the need of inward cleansing and of power to overcome temptation (vv. 12, 13; cf. 51: 6 f., 10; 139: 23 f.). Acceptance by God must be an act of grace (v. 14; cf. 103: 8 ff.).

7. perfect: see on 18: 30. **reviving the soul:** restoring life and vitality (cf. 23: 3; Lam. 1: 11). **8. radiant:** 'bright' like the sun (cf. Ca. 6: 10); cf. 119: 6, 105, 130; Prov. 6: 23. **9. fear of the LORD:** here a synonym for the law (cf. Dt. 4: 10; Ps. 110: 10). **pure:** cf. 12: 6; Isa. 10: 1. **sure:** lit. 'truth' (see on 25: 5; cf. Jer. 17: 17). **10.** Cf. 119: 72, 103, 127, **11. great reward:** both material (cf. Prov. 22: 4) and spiritual (cf. vv. 7, 8). **12. hidden faults:** cf. Lev. 4: 1 ff., 13 ff.; Num. 15: 22 ff. **13. wilful sins:** lit. 'proudnesses'; either 'pride' (JB, cf. NEB) and the sins of proud defiance (cf. Num. 15: 30 f.) or 'arrogant men' (cf. 119: 21 f., 69 f., 85 f.). **blameless:** see on 15: 2. **rule over:** cf. Gen. 4: 7. **great transgression** (lit. 'rebellion', see on 32: 1): idolatry (cf. Exod. 32: 21, 30 f.; 2 Kg. 17: 11) or pride (cf. Gen. 3: 5 f.). **14. meditation:** see on 1: 2. **pleasing:** be received as a sacrifice (cf. Lev. 1: 3, 4; Ps. 51: 17; 119: 108; 141:2). **Rock:** see on 18: 2. **Redeemer:** Heb. *gō'ēl*, the next-of-kin who protects the

interests of his relatives (see on Lev. 25: 25; Job 19: 25; Isa. 41 :14).

Psalm 20.   A PRAYER FOR VICTORY FOR THE KING
The historical books of the OT give some idea of the preparations made before a king went into battle: the offering of sacrifices (cf. 1 Sam. 7: 9; 13: 9-12), the fasting and praying (cf. 2 Chr. 20: 3-12). Ps. 20 could well have been written for such an occasion. It is also likely that it would have been used (accompanied by appropriate ritual, cf. vv. 3, 5; 1 Kg. 22: 11 f.) at coronations (cf. Ps. 2) and celebrations of the king's accession, as well as at the regular temple services (cf. prayers for the Queen in Anglican services). Ps. 21 may be seen as a complement to Ps. 20.

The psalm has two main sections: vv. 1-5 constitute the community's intercession for the king, sung by the people or by the Levites on their behalf; vv. 6-8 express the confidence (voiced by a priest or possibly by the king himself) that victory is assured. The assurance was probably based on a prophetic or priestly oracle, given between v. 5 and v. 6, declaring that the sacrifices had been accepted and promising God's help (cf. 2 Chr. 20: 14-17). Verse 9 is a concluding prayer of the congregation.

Title: see Introduction III. 1, 2, 3. **1. name:** stands for the person (cf. 68: 4; 145: 1, 2), his revealed character (cf. Exod. 34: 5 ff.) and (particularly here and in v. 7) his active presence (cf. Exod. 23: 20 ff.; Num. 6: 27). See *NBD art.* 'Name'. **the God of Jacob:** although 'Jacob' can be used as a name for the nation, a synonym for 'Israel' (cf. 78: 5, 71; Isa. 41: 14), this title probably looks back to God's care for the ancestor of the nation (cf. Gen. 35: 3; Hos. 12: 2-6) whose name originally seems to have meant 'May God protect' (see on Gen. 25: 26). **protect you:** lit. 'set you up on high'. **2. sanctuary . . . Zion:** cf. v. 6, and see on 2: 6; 11: 4. **3. accept:** lit. 'find fat' (cf. Lev. 3: 16). **sacrifices . . . burnt offerings:** see on 40: 6. **Selah:** see Introduction III. 3. **5. victorious:** lit. 'your salvation' (see on 35: 3). **lift up our banners:** either a cultic act in which a symbol of the presence of Yahweh was exhibited (cf. Exod. 17: 15 f.; Num. 21: 8; 2 Kg. 18: 4), or a reference to tribal standards displayed when camping or marching (cf. Num. 1: 52; 2: 2 ff.; Ca. 6: 4, 10). LXX has 'we shall be magnified'.

6. saves: lit. 'has saved'; a prophetic perfect in which the future is so certain that it is described as if it had already happened; cf. RSV 'will help'. **anointed:** see on 2: 2. **saving power:** lit. 'acts of salvation' (see on 35: 3). **right hand:** the more active one, thus a symbol of power (cf. 118: 15 f.). **7. trust:** lit. 'make mention of' or 'remember' (cf. Jos. 23: 7; Isa. 48: 1); the verb in the first line has been supplied to make sense. **name:** see on v. 1; cf. 2 Chr. 14: 11. For the thought of the verse see Isa. 31: 1, 3. **9.** NIV follows LXX, giving a slightly better sense (cf. v. 6) than *MT* (NIVmg, AV, RV). **save:** Vulg. has 'God save the king.'

Psalm 21. BLESSINGS FOR THE KING

This royal psalm has been regarded by some as a thanksgiving for the king's victory, expressed *after* the battle (cf. vv. 1, 2, 4; 20: 4); others think that vv. 8–12 point to it being a prayer of confidence *before* a military expedition (cf. Ps. 20). It is probably better, however, to see this psalm as being used at a coronation (cf. vv. 3, 5) and on other occasions when the king was the centre of attention (see on Ps. 20).

There are two main parts: vv. 1–7 (sung by a priest or by the whole congregation) constitute a thanksgiving for all the blessings that Yahweh has granted to the king (and therefore to the people) as a result of the covenant with David (cf. 2 Sam 7; Ps. 89: 1 ff.); vv. 8–12 are either an oracle addressed to the king (so NIV, RSV, NEB), promising him triumph over all his enemies, or an expression of confidence addressed to Yahweh Himself (so A. A. Anderson). In any case, it is made clear that the king's success in battle will be entirely dependent upon the power of Yahweh, and He alone will receive the praise (v. 13).

Title: see Introduction III. 1, 2, 3. **1. victories:** lit. 'salvation' (see on 35: 3); here probably a reference to 'Victory' (NEB) in battle, but wide enough to include all Yahweh's 'blessings' (Weiser; cf. v. 3). **4. life:** in a narrow sense it could refer to preservation in battle, but in a wider sense it denotes a long and prosperous reign (cf. 1 Kg. 3: 11–14; Neh. 2: 3; Dan. 2: 4). It is unlikely that there is any thought of immortality (cf. 2 Sam. 7: 12) or even of living on in his descendants (cf. 2 Sam. 7: 29; Ps. 72: 17). **5. victories:** lit. 'salvation' (see on v. 1). **6. blessings:** see on 26: 12; the king receives peace, prosperity and fruitfulness from Yahweh in order to channel them to the land and its people (cf. 72: 15 ff.). **presence:** lit. 'face' (see on 4: 6; 16: 11). **7. unfailing love:** see on 5: 7; here a reference to God's loyalty to His covenant with David (cf. 89: 1 ff.). **9. fiery furnace:** possibly the picture of a burning city. **at the time of your appearing:** lit. 'at the time of your face'; either a reference to the 'presence' or to the anger (AV, RV, cf. 34: 16; Lam. 4: 16) of the king. **11. Though:** better 'For'. **13. Be exalted:** lit. 'Raise thyself'.

Psalm 22. FROM PERPLEXITY TO PRAISE

An individual lament (vv. 1–21) is followed by a confident vow of praise (vv. 22–31). The relationship between the two parts is not com-

pletely clear. The whole psalm could be a thanksgiving for deliverance, accompanied by a votive sacrifice (v. 25), in which case vv. 1–21 look back to the author's experience of suffering. It seems more natural, however, to assume that while the psalmist was expressing his anguish and pleading with God to deliver him, he received an assurance that God had heard and would save him (see on v. 21 and on 6: 8 ff.); and thus, in a dramatic change of mood, he looks forward to praising God in public and fulfilling his vows.

The psalm reads like the experience of a particular individual, and yet, because of the stereotyped language and imagery, it is difficult to determine the exact nature of his sufferings. Is he suffering physically because of the persecution of his enemies? Or has a severe illness caused his opponents to assume that he is being punished by God (cf. Job; Isa. 53: 3, 4) and that he is therefore 'fair game'? What is clear is that his sufferings, both physical and mental, are exacerbated by the feeling that God has abandoned him and refuses to answer his cries. Two features make this psalm unique: the psalmist does not protest his innocence (but it is surely implied in the **why** of v. 1); nor does he call for vengeance on his enemies (cf. Pss. 17; 69). The world-wide effects of his vindication (vv. 27 ff.) would seem more suitable if the psalmist were a king than if he were an ordinary Israelite. Yet it is not impossible that other individuals might make use of this psalm and relate it to their own troubles, and it could even have been used to express the feelings of the nation during a time of distress (*e.g.* the exile). The idea that it accompanied a symbolic humiliation and restoration of the king at an annual festival (see Introduction II. 2) is highly speculative.

Taking their cue from Jesus' quotation of v. 1 whilst on the cross (Mt. 27: 46; Mk 15: 34) and His post-resurrection teaching (Lk. 24: 26 f., 44 ff.), the NT writers see this psalm as a clear prefiguring of the passion of Christ and His subsequent vindication. The mockery of vv. 7, 8 was echoed by the priests (Mt. 27: 39 ff. and parallels); the division of clothing in v. 18 was fulfilled by the soldiers (Jn 19: 23 f.); vv. 14–17 could well depict the horrors of crucifixion, although they are not referred to in the NT; and the writer to the Hebrews (2: 1 f.) applies v. 22 to the glorified Jesus. Unlike the similar portrayal of the Suffering Servant in Isa. 52: 13–53: 12, this psalm does not offer any explanation of the purpose or significance of the suffering, nor does it appear to be a prophecy (i.e. prediction). The Christian may well believe that the description of a genuine experience of the psalmist was providentially controlled by the Spirit of God to provide a foreshadowing of the experience of Christ (see also Introduction IV. 2). Not surprisingly, the

Prayer Book appoints this psalm for use on Good Friday.

The dark night of the soul (vv. 1–21)
This puzzled cry of anguish consists of three sections, each of which contains a lament and a petition. Verses 1–5 contrast the psalmist's experience of the silence of God with the deliverance granted to past generations; vv. 6–11 contrast his present situation with his past experience of the protection of God: and vv. 12–21 describe his desperate plight in graphic imagery: he is very close to death, but still he cries for God's deliverance.

Title: see Introduction III. 1, 2, 3. **The Doe of the Morning:** possibly the name of a tune. LXX has 'concerning the help of the early morning'. **1. Why are you . . . :** lit. 'Far from my salvation (are) the words of my roaring', i.e. his crying has no effect. **3.** LXX has 'Thou art enthroned in the sanctuary, O Praise of Israel' (cf. Dt. 10: 21). **6.** Cf. Isa. 41: 4; 49: 7; 53: 3. **8. He trusts in the LORD:** lit. 'He rolled (*MT* 'Roll') on Yahweh'. The implied object of the verb could be 'himself' or 'his cause' (cf. 37: 5). LXX has 'He hoped in the Lord'. **12. Bashan:** the rich pastures east of Jordan produced strong, well-fed cattle (cf. Am. 4: 1). **16. they have pierced:** *MT* (NIVmg) seems to be corrupt. The versions suggest a verb: either (cf. LXX, Syr., Vulg.) 'pierced' (lit. 'dug') or (cf. Aq., Sym.) 'bind' (i.e. for burial). 'Cut' (cf. NEB) or 'tear' (GNB) are possible. **20. my precious life:** lit. 'my only one'; all he has left, his most precious possession. **power:** lit. 'hand'. **21. save me:** NIV provides good parallelism, but *MT* (NIVmg) may well be right. The one word in Heb. (*ʿanîtānî*) stands at the end of the verse and suggests a broken construction: 'Rescue me . . . and from the horns of the wild oxen—you have answered me!'

Daylight ahead (vv. 22–31)
Whether or not his situation has changed yet, the psalmist is now convinced that God has heard him and will deliver him. He envisages a great communal act of worship (vv. 22–26) when he gives his testimony (cf. 40: 9 f.; 66: 16 ff.) and makes his votive sacrifice (v. 25) in which all will share (v. 26). Finally (vv. 27–31), he foresees the outward spread of the story of salvation resulting in the conversion of the world, with all sorts and conditions of men, present and future, acknowledging the sovereignty of Yahweh. **22. congregation:** the worshipping community gathered in the temple, especially at a festival (cf. v. 25). **24. suffering:** LXX has 'prayer.' **25. From you comes:** i.e. 'You are the theme of . . .' (cf. JB). **I will fulfil my vows:** he will bring the thank-offerings promised during the time of trouble (see on 61: 5, and cf. 50: 14; 61: 8; 66: 13; 116: 14, 18); these would entail a sacrificial meal in which others could share (v. 26; cf.

Lev. 7: 6; Num. 15: 3; Dt. 14: 29; 16: 10 f.; 26: 12). **29.** A difficult verse: it is not clear whether it refers to the high and the low, the rich and the poor (especially those who, like the psalmist was, are close to death); or to the possibility of the dead worshipping Yahweh (cf. 6: 5; 30: 9). NEB gives a possible meaning. **rich:** lit. 'the fat ones' (cf. 17: 10). **30. future generations:** NIV follows LXX; *MT* has 'they shall come and proclaim . . .' **31. righteousness:** see on 33: 5.

Psalm 23. THE GOOD SHEPHERD
A psalm of trust which celebrates the gracious care of Yahweh; and in which the needs and troubles of the psalmist are touched on only incidentally. Most commentators find two pictures of Yahweh here: the Shepherd looking after His sheep (vv. 1–4), and the Host providing for His guest (vv. 5, 6). Certainly vv. 5, 6 do not maintain the sheep metaphor, but there is no need to assume the conscious introduction of another metaphor; the psalm is a unified expression of what God does for the psalmist. Verses 5, 6 suggest that it was written for, and most suitably used at, a sacrificial meal in the temple, probably a thanksgiving banquet (see on 22: 25; cf. 36: 8; 65: 4; 116: 17 f.) after an experience of deliverance.

It is not surprising, especially in the light of Jn 10 (cf. Heb. 13: 20; 1 Pet. 2: 25), that Christians have applied this psalm to Jesus Christ; nor that it has been paraphrased a number of times to be sung as a hymn: *e.g.* 'The Lord's my Shepherd, I'll not want' (Whittingham, etc.); 'The God of love my shepherd is' (Herbert); and 'The king of love my shepherd is' (Baker).

Title: see Introduction III. 1, 2. **1. shepherd:** used metaphorically in Israel and in other ancient Near Eastern nations as a title for a king or leader (cf. 2 Sam. 5: 2; 1 Kg. 22: 17; Jer. 23: 1 ff.; Ezek. 34: 1 ff.), it contains the ideas of authority and care. In the OT Yahweh is usually thought of as the shepherd of Israel, rather than of the individual (80: 1; cf. 28: 9; 100: 3; Isa. 40: 11; Jer. 23: 3; Ezek. 34: 11 ff.). **3. my soul:** see on 3: 2; 19: 7. **righteousness:** conveys the ideas of 'straightness', 'conformity to law', and 'deliverance' (see on 33: 5; 5: 8). **for his name's sake:** because it is His nature to do so (see on 5: 11; 20: 1). **4. the shadow of death:** the word 'death' may act as a superlative, i.e. 'total darkness' (cf. NIVmg), 'dark as death' (NEB). It could apply to any terrifying experience (see on 9: 13). **rod:** a club (often iron-tipped) used for protection from wild animals. **staff:** used for support and guidance. **comfort:** there is no promise of immunity from trouble or suffering.

5. enemies: presumably fellow Israelites, also in the temple. **anoint:** lit. 'make fat' (cf. NEB 'hast richly bathed'); not the word used for anointing a king but of entertaining a guest (cf. Lk. 7: 46). **6. love:** Heb. *ḥesed* (see on 5: 7). **follow:** 'or 'pursue' (cf. the enemies of v. 5). **I will dwell:** NIV follows the ancient versions; *MT* reads 'I shall return (to)'. In either case it expresses the worshipper's ideal of continual communion with God (see on 15: 1): 'your house will be my home as long as I live' (GNB). **house:** see on 5: 7. **forever:** lit. 'to length of days; cf. NEB 'my whole life long'.

Psalm 24. THE SANCTUARY OF THE GLORIOUS KING

This psalm would seem to be a processional liturgy used to accompany the bringing of the ark, symbol of Yahweh's presence (cf. 1 Sam. 4: 4, 21 f.; Ps. 132: 8), into Jerusalem and into the sanctuary. Whether or not it was written for the occasion described in 2 Sam. 6: 12–19 (cf. 1 Chr. 15: 1–16: 1 ff.) or that of 1 Kg. 8: 1 ff. (cf. 2 Chr. 5: 2 ff.), it will probably have been used at later annual celebrations of these events (cf. Pss. 68; 132). The LXX suggests that after the exile it was appointed for use on the first day of the week (associated with Creation).

There are three distinct sections: vv. 1, 2 are a brief hymn celebrating Yahweh's right to rule, since He is the Creator; vv. 3–6 are an 'admission liturgy' (see on Ps. 15) giving the conditions for the pilgrim's entry into the sanctuary, *viz.* purity in word, thought and deed; vv. 7–10 are a 'gate-liturgy' sung as the ark reached the entrance to the temple (or city); Yahweh's right of access is self-evident: He is the victorious King of Israel. The whole psalm is designed to be sung antiphonally. G. W. Anderson has drawn attention to the striking parallels between this psalm and Isaiah's vision (Isa. 6).

The Christian use of this psalm usually relates it to the entry into heaven of the risen and exalted Christ (cf. Heb. 9: 12, 24), and the Prayer Book therefore appoints it for Ascension Day. Some, however, have linked it with Advent or with Christ's triumphal entry into Jerusalem (cf. Mt. 21: 9 ff.). A number of hymns have been based on it, *e.g.* 'Lift up your heads, ye mighty gates' (Weissel); 'The golden gates are lifted up' (Alexander); 'The Lord of glory! who is He?' (Chapman); cf. 'Hail the day that sees Him rise' (C. Wesley, etc.); 'See the Conq'ror mounts in triumph' (Wordsworth).

Title: see Introduction III, 1, 2. **2. he:** emphatic. **seas . . . waters:** for the cosmological picture of the earth as a flat disc floating on a subterranean ocean, supported by pillars (the bases of the mountains) see Gen. 1: 9; 7: 11; Exod. 20: 4; 1 Sam. 2: 8; Ps. 18: 15; 136: 6; Jon. 2: 6. This verse may imply a victory over the powers of chaos (cf. v. 8; see on 18: 4, 7 ff.). **3. hill of the LORD:** see on 2: 6. **stand:** cf. 1

Sam. 6: 20. **4. lift up his soul:** see on 25: 1. **to an idol:** lit. 'the emptiness' (cf. JB 'worthless things'); possibly a reference to idolatry (cf. GNB; 31: 6). **5. blessing:** cf. Exod. 20: 6; Num. 6: 23 ff. **vindication:** lit. 'righteousness' (see on 33: 5). **6. the generation:** either 'company' or 'lot (portion)'; cf. NEB and see on 12: 7. **seek your face:** desire the presence and blessing of Yahweh (cf. Num. 6: 23 ff.; Ps. 4: 6; 11: 7; 17: 15; 42: 2). **God of Jacob:** see on 20: 1. NIV is probably right to follow LXX. **Selah:** see Introduction III. 3.

7. lift up . . . be lifted up: a call either to open wide or possibly to rejoice and be exalted at the honour bestowed. **8.** Cf. Exod. 15: 3, 18. **10. Almighty:** lit. 'of hosts' (Heb. *ṣᵉbā'ôt*), either the 'armies' of Israel (cf. 1 Sam. 17: 45) or the heavenly 'armies' of angels (cf. 1 Kg. 22: 19) or of stars and planets (cf. Gen. 2: 1). LXX has 'All-mighty' cf. 1 Sam. 4: 4.

Psalm 25. THE PRAYER OF A MAN IN TROUBLE

This individual lament is one of the nine alphabetic (or acrostic) psalms in the psalter. In Ps. 25 each verse begins with a different letter of the Heb. alphabet (in order), except for some slight irregularity. The acrostic may originally have been a pedagogic device for teaching the alphabet; but in these psalms it is probably intended as a mnemonic aid—unless it is simply a self-imposed artistic discipline (cf. the use of fugue as a form in music). The artificial scheme makes any development of thought very difficult. In this psalm the three themes of forgiveness, guidance and protection are woven together and constantly appear. However, a rough division into three sections is possible: vv. 1–7; 8–14/15; 15/16–22). The description of the psalmist's trouble is in such general terms that the psalm could be used by any worshipper; as Weiser says, '. . . it is by virtue of the universally applicable truths it proclaims a perpetual source of comfort for people who are lonely or forsaken'.

Title: see Introduction III. 2. **1. I lift up my soul:** he directs his whole being to God in trust (cf. v. 2) and prayer (cf. Lam. 3: 41). **2. put to shame:** misfortune will be interpreted as the punishment of God. **4 ways . . . paths:** cf. Dt. 9: 12, 16; 1 Kg .2: 3; Jer. 5: 4. **5. in your truth:** probably 'by means of your fidelity' (cf. v. 10) or 'in faithfulness to you' (cf. 26: 3), rather than 'in accordance with your teaching. Heb. *'emet* normally refers to a moral quality (i.e. 'reliability') rather than a simply intellectual quality (i.e. 'factuality'). **6, 7. Remember not:** to 'remember' is to 'take action in accordance with . . .' **love:** see on 5: 7. **rebellious ways:** see on 32: 1. **9. humble:** see on 9: 12. **10. faithful:** Heb. *'emet*; see on v. 5. **keep the demands of his covenant:** i.e. the stipulations of the Sinai covenant between Yahweh and Israel (see on Exod. 19: 5; 20: 1 ff.; 24: 3 ff.). **11. for the sake of your name:** see on 23: 3; cf. Isa. 43: 25. **12. fears:** a sense of awe which leads to willing obedience (cf. Job 1: 1, 8). **chosen for him:** i.e. the man must decide to follow the guidance given (cf. Isa. 48: 17). **14. confides in:** the Heb. word *sōd* includes both the ideas of 'confidential conversation and intimate relationship' (A. Bentzen; cf. 'sweet fellowship' 55: 14; 'council' Jer. 23: 18) and also the information conveyed (cf. 'counsel' Prov. 15: 22; 'plan' Am. 3: 7). **covenant:** the relationship and its obligations (see on v. 10). **21. integrity** (lit. 'blamelessness') **and uprightness:** here qualities of the psalmist (cf. 1 Kg. 9: 4; Ps. 18: 20 ff.) rather than of Yahweh. **22.** Possibly a later addition to adapt the psalm for congregational worship; it does not fit the acrostic scheme. **Redeem:** i.e. 'deliver' (see on 49: 7).

Psalm 26. THE APPEAL OF AN INNOCENT MAN

An individual lament or psalm of innocence (see on Ps. 7; cf. Pss. 5: 17) which gives no clue as to the nature of the psalmist's plight, whether he is being falsely accused, persecuted, or suffering from an illness. Consequently this prayer could be used by anyone in any sort of trouble. It could also have served as the pilgrim's confession at the temple gates, in answer to the demands of the door-keeper (cf. 15: 2 ff.; 24: 4 ff.). The psalm does not easily divide into stanzas. The opening prayer for vindication includes the author's claim to integrity, but he realizes the need to submit himself to the divine scrutiny (vv. 1–3). His negative protestation of innocence (vv. 4, 5; cf. 1: 1; 7: 3 ff.; 17: 3 ff.) is accompanied by a symbolic act of hand-washing (cf. Exod. 30: 19 ff.; Dt. 21: 6; Mt. 27: 24) and by joining in the worship at the sanctuary (vv. 6, 7). In vv. 8–12 he reiterates his appeal for deliverance, emphasizing his complete identification with Yahweh and with His people. Verse 8 has inspired the hymn 'We love the place, O God' by W. Bullock and H. W. Baker.

Title: see Introduction III. 2. **1. Vindicate me:** lit. 'Judge me'; a call for both justice and deliverance (see on 72: 2). **blameless:** lit. 'completeness', 'integrity' (see on 15: 2; 18: 20 ff.; cf. 1 Kg. 9: 4). **2. my heart and my mind:** lit. 'my kidneys and my heart' (see on 7: 9). **examine:** cf. 66: 10. **3. love:** see on 5: 7. **in your truth:** see on 25: 5. It is not clear whether the two qualities in this verse belong to Yahweh or to the psalmist. **4. deceitful men:** or 'worthless men' (NEB). **6. go about your altar:** probably a solemn procession (cf. NEB, JB), perhaps symbolizing petition (cf. 1 Kg. 18: 26; Ps. 118: 27). **proclaiming aloud . . . :** lit.

'making the voice of thanksgiving heard' (cf. RV). **7. wonderful deeds:** see on 9: 1. **8. love:** cf. 'abhor' v. 5; both words denote choice and appropriate action rather than simply emotion. **house where you live:** see on 5: 7. LXX has 'the beauty of your house' (cf. 27: 4). **glory:** the manifestation of divine holiness, power and presence in the sanctuary (cf. Exod. 25: 8 f.; 40: 34 f.; 1 Kg. 8: 11; 2 Chr. 5: 14; 7: 1 ff.) symbolized by the ark (cf. 1 Sam. 4: 21 f.; Ps. 24: 7; 78: 61; 132: 8) in the most holy place (cf. 1 Kg. 8: 6). **11. I lead:** or 'I will lead' (cf. v. 1). **blameless:** see on v. 1. **redeem:** i.e. 'deliver' (see on 49: 7). **12. level** (lit. 'upright') **ground:** 'safe from all dangers' (GNB) in the temple (cf. 122: 2). **great assembly:** lit. 'assemblies' (cf. 'company' v. 5, a similar word; and see on 22: 22). **praise:** lit. 'bless'. The original meaning of the Heb. verb *bārak* was 'kneel'. As the inferior kneels before the superior he receives his 'blessing' (Heb. *bᵉrākāh*) and in return 'blesses' the giver by offering praise and thanks and calling him 'blessed' (Heb. *bārûk*).

Psalm 27. NOTHING TO FEAR

A psalm of confidence in the protection of Yahweh (vv. 1–6; cf. Ps. 23) is followed by an individual lament (vv. 7–14) appealing to Yahweh for deliverance from malicious enemies. These may originally have been two separate psalms (cf. differences in style); but there are some points of contact (cf. v. 4 with vv. 8, 13) and they fit together well: the prayer of vv. 7–12 echoes the assurance of vv. 1–6. In the first section (vv. 1–6) the aggression of the psalmist's enemies is expressed in military terms; in the second (vv. 7–12) their opposition is more specifically described: they have unjustly accused him of some sin, so that even his own family may turn against him. The final section (vv. 13, 14) returns to the confident attitude of the first, and ends with an encouragement to hope (v. 14 may be a priestly oracle).

Title: see Introduction III. 2. LXX adds 'before he was anointed'. **1. light:** here a symbol of life (cf. 36: 9; 56: 13; Job 3: 20) and perhaps joy (cf. 97: 11; Isa. 9: 2) and salvation (cf. Isa. 58: 8). The 'Light of Israel' (Isa. 10: 17; cf. 60: 19 f.) is also the source of life and salvation for the individual (cf. Ps. 18: 28). **2. to devour my flesh:** NIVmg interprets on the basis of Dan. 3: 8; 6: 24; but *MT* (above) gives good sense: his enemies are like wild beasts out to destroy him completely (cf. 7: 2; 14: 4; 17: 12). **they:** emphatic. **3. army:** lit. 'camp'. **4.** See on 23: 6. **house . . . temple:** see on 5: 7. **beauty:** or 'graciousness' (cf. 90: 17); the splendour of the temple and its worship reflected the character of Yahweh. **to seek him:** lit. 'inquire', probably 'to seek an oracle' (i.e. a divine answer or decision). **5.** Cf. 91: 1 ff. **dwelling** (Heb. *sukkāh*) . . . **tabernacle:** here probably used of the sanctuary (v. 6; cf. 76: 2), a place of asylum (cf. Exod. 21: 13 f.; Num. 35: 9–34; Dt. 4: 41 ff.; 19: 4–13; 1 Kg. 1: 50). **6. tabernacle:** see on 15: 1.

8. The *MT* is difficult to translate with certainty. Heb. has 'To thee my heart said: Seek ye my face; thy face, Yahweh, will I seek'. NEB, JB resort to emendation. **face:** see on 4: 6. **Do not hide . . . :** see on 13: 1 (cf. 22: 24). **seek:** probably by offering sacrifice (cf. 2 Chr. 11: 16). **10.** Not necessarily literal: a picture of complete isolation and loneliness (cf. Isa. 49: 15). **receive me:** possibly 'adopt me'. **11.** This verse provided the inspiration for B. M. Ramsey's hymn 'Teach me Thy way, O Lord'. **way:** see on 25: 4. **straight path:** safe and firm (cf. 26: 12). **12. desire:** Heb. *nepeš* (see on 3: 2); here meaning 'greed' (NEB). **13. I am still confident:** *MT* has 'unless I had believed'. Perhaps we should understand 'I dread to think what would have happened unless I had believed . . .' **land of the living:** deliverance must come in this life (cf. 142: 5; and see Introduction IV. 1); there is no hope of vindication in Sheol (cf. 88: 5, 10). **14. Wait:** the assurance that the answer would eventually come (cf. 40: 1) provides the strength to endure (cf. Isa. 40: 31).

Psalm 28.   FROM PETITION TO PRAISE

This psalm follows the usual pattern of an individual lament, i.e. it has two distinct parts: vv. 1–5 express the psalmist's prayer for deliverance from an imminent and premature death, and for the punishment of the wicked; vv. 6–9 are a hymn of thanksgiving which assumes that the psalmist has received an answer to his prayer, or a clear assurance that he will (see on 6: 8 ff.; cf. Ps. 22). The exact nature of his trouble is not clear; it may have been a severe illness, unjust accusation, or persecution; Kirkpatrick suggests a plague which affected both the righteous and the wicked (cf. v. 3). The psalm is suitable for use by any Israelite (not just the king) in the temple (cf. v. 2). The final intercession for the nation (vv. 8, 9) may have been added to adapt the psalm for congregational worship.

Title: see Introduction III. 2. **1.** Cf. Lam. 3: 55 ff. **Rock:** see on 18: 2. **pit:** Heb. *bōr*, lit. 'hole', 'well'; a synonym for Sheol, the subterranean world of the dead (see on 6: 5; cf. 30: 3; 88: 4 ff.; 143: 7). **2. I lift up my hands:** the usual attitude of prayer, whether standing (cf. 1 Kg. 8: 22) or kneeling (cf. 1 Kg. 8: 54). **Most Holy Place:** the Heb. *debîr* was used of the inmost shrine of the temple (1 Kg. 6: 19 ff.; 8: 6 ff.), the equivalent of the 'Most Holy Place' in the tabernacle (cf. Exod. 26: 33 ff.). Here

the reference is to the earthly shrine (cf. 1 Kg. 8: 38) though it could probably also be applied to the heavenly (cf. 1 Kg. 8: 22). **3. wicked:** see on Ps. 1. **those who do evil:** see on 5: 5.

6. Praise: lit. 'blessed'; see on 26: 12. **7. shield:** see on 3: 3. **8. of his people** *MT* has 'of them'; NIV follows some Heb. MSS, LXX, Syr. **anointed one:** see on 2: 2. The welfare of the nation was bound up with the prosperity of the king. **9. inheritance:** cf. Exod. 19: 5; 1 Sam. 10: 1; 1 Kg. 8: 35. **be their shepherd:** or 'feed them'; cf. 23: 1 ff. **carry:** cf. Isa. 40: 11; 46: 3 f.; 63: 9. The welfare of the individual was bound up with that of the nation.

Psalm 29.   A HYMN TO THE KING OF STORMS

The similarities between this psalm and early Canaanite (Ugaritic) poetry suggest that the author was acquainted with such foreign literature; he may even have made use of a hymn extolling the might of the phoenician storm-god Ba'al-Hadad. If so, his purpose was polemical: in a deliberate rejection of Canaanite polytheism (cf. 1 Kg. 18: 21, 24; Hos. 2: 8) he insists that it is Yahweh, not Ba'al, who is King of the storm. It is possible, on the other hand, that this psalm was originally a battle hymn, written in the style of the earliest Hebrew (cf. Exod. 15; Jg. 5) and Canaanite poetry, celebrating an Israelite victory over the Canaanites (cf. 1 Sam. 7: 10). The LXX suggests that it was later sung on the last day of the Feast of Tabernacles, which in pre-exilic times may have been a New Year Festival at which the kingship of Yahweh was celebrated (see Introduction II. 2). The Talmud links this psalm with the Feast of Weeks (Pentecost).

The psalm has three sections: vv. 1, 2 provide an introduction, calling on the angelic hosts to acknowledge the majesty of Yahweh; vv. 3–9 describe a violent thunderstorm, coming from the north and passing to the south, as a theophany (see on 18: 7 ff.) or 'epiphany' of Yahweh displaying His majesty and power; vv. 10, 11 conclude with a statement of faith in the eternal sovereignty of Yahweh and an intercession for the people of God.

Title: see Introduction III. 1, 2. **1. Ascribe:** lit. 'Give'; JB 'Pay tribute'. **mighty ones:** Heb. *benê 'ēlim*, 'sons of gods (or 'God')'. In Ugaritic texts 'the sons of *El*' are minor deities of the pantheon, and some would take this verse as a challenge to the pagan gods (cf. NEB, GNB; 97: 7); but in the OT 'the sons of God' are created spiritual beings who serve in the heavenly council (cf. Job 1: 6mg; Ps. 82: 6; 89: 6, 7) as Yahweh's messengers (i.e. 'angels.'). The idea of heavenly beings does not detract from the uniqueness of Yahweh, but rather emphasizes it (cf. Isa. 6: 1–3). Here the thought may be that human language is inadequate to describe the glory of God (A. A. Anderson). **in the splendor of:** either a reference to the clothing of the heavenly worshippers (see NIVmg and cf. Exod. 28: 2), or, more likely, a description of God, i.e. 'in (or 'for') the splendour of (his) holiness' (cf. 1 Chr. 16: 29; 2 Chr. 20: 21, Ps. 96: 9; 110: 3).

3. The voice of the LORD: i.e. thunder (cf. Exod. 9: 23; Job 28: 26; 37: 4 f.; 38: 25; Ps. 18: 13) accompanied by destructive lightning (cf. vv. 5, 7) and hurricane winds (cf. vv. 8, 9). **the waters:** could refer to the Mediterranean Sea or to floods caused by the storm; but it is more likely a reference to rain-clouds seen as the chariots of Yahweh (cf. 18: 9 ff.; 104: 3b), or possibly to the waters above the firmament (cf. Gen. 1: 7; Ps. 104: 3a; 148: 4) viewed as symbolizing the powers of chaos (see on 18: 7 ff.). **5. Lebanon:** see *NBD*. **6. Sirion:** the Phoenician name of Mt. Hermon (cf. Dt. 3: 9). **9.** In line one NIV has a very likely emendation which provides a good parallel to line two. **in his temple:** see on 11: 4 (cf. Mic. 1: 2); this takes us back to v. 1. **10. the flood:** Heb. *mabbûl* is used elsewhere in the OT only of the deluge of Noah's time (Gen. 7–8), in which case we may translate here: 'Yahweh sat over (or 'at') The Flood; and Yahweh sits . . .' (cf. RV, JB). Alternatively, the reference might be to the waters of v. 3 (*q.v.*). **11.** The verbs could be read as statements: 'Yahweh will . . .' **peace:** Heb. *šālôm*; a comprehensive term whose basic meaning of 'wholeness' and 'harmony' widens out to include 'well-being', 'health', 'prosperity', as well as 'peace'.

Psalm 30. SORROW TURNED TO JOY

An individual thanksgiving of someone who has recovered from a serious illness (cf. Ps. 116; Isa. 38: 9–20); it was probably intended to accompany a thanksgiving sacrifice (see on 22: 25; 61: 5; 116: 17). The psalmist first (vv. 1–3) praises Yahweh for delivering him from death and healing him in answer to his prayers; and then (vv. 4, 5) he exhorts God's people to praise Him for His long-term mercy and grace which far outweighs any short-term wrath (cf. 103: 8 ff.; Isa. 54: 7 f.; Mic. 7: 18; 2 C. 4: 17). In vv. 6–12 he gives his testimony, addressed to God but intended also for the instruction of the godly. His suffering has taught him valuable lessons: in his success, affluence and healthiness he had begun to take things for granted (vv. 6, 7a; cf. Dt. 8: 11–20; 32: 15); but God allowed trouble to come into his life (v. 7b) and he suddenly became aware of his continual need of God's favour and protection (vv. 8–10). The answer to his prayers brought a dramatic reversal of his situation (v. 11) and convinced him that the praise of God must be his chief and constant occupation (v. 12).

The title (lit. 'A psalm—a song of the dedication of the house—of David') seems to contain a later addition which suggests that this psalm was used congregationally on the occasion of (and later in celebration of) the dedication of the Second Temple (Ezr. 6: 16) after the Babylonian exile. Alternatively, the reference may be to the purification and rededication of the temple in the time of Judas Maccabaeus (1 Mac. 4: 42–60), *c.* 164 B.C., after its desecration by Antiochus Epiphanes. According to the Talmud the psalm was used at the Feast of the Dedication (Heb. *Ḥᵃnukkāh*) which commemorated the events of 164 B.C.

Title: see Introduction III. 1, 2. **1. lifted me:** i.e. out of the Pit (v. 3; cf. 40: 2), like a bucket out of a well. **3.** In the OT death is seen as a disintegrating power which a sick person experiences, and Sheol as a sphere of influence into which he enters whilst still alive (cf. 18: 4 f.; 40: 2; 116: 3). Healing is thus a restoration to life (cf. Isa. 38: 16). **my soul:** see on 3: 2. **grave:** see on 6: 5. **pit:** Heb. *bôr*; see on 28: 1. **4. saints:** rather 'loyal ones' (Heb. *ḥᵃsîdîm*); see on 4: 3. **his holy name:** lit. 'the remembrance of his holiness' (97: 12; cf. 135: 13; Exod. 3: 15).

7. made my mountain stand firm: lit. 'for my mountain thou hast set up strength'. On the lips of the king this could refer to Zion, symbol of his own stability (cf. 1 Kg. 15: 4). **hide your face:** see on 13: 1; cf. 104: 29. **9. gain:** neither for God, for He loses a faithful worshipper (cf. 6: 5; 115: 17; Isa. 38: 18 f.); nor for the psalmist, for there is no hope of salvation in Sheol (cf. 88: 10 ff.; Isa. 38: 18). **pit:** Heb. *šaḥat*; see on 16: 10. **faithfulness:** Heb. *'emet*; see on 25: 5. **11. dancing:** a means of expressing worship (cf. 2 Sam. 6: 9, 14; Ps. 87: 7; 149: 3; 150: 4). **sackcloth:** symbol of penitence and mourning (see *NBD*). **12. my heart:** Heb. *kābôd*; see on 16: 9.

Psalm 31. A PRAYER IN TIME OF DISTRESS

This individual lamentation, in which thanksgiving also features prominently, has three sections. The first (vv. 1–8) expresses the confident prayer of a man hunted by his enemies (vv. 4, 8); it would fit the experience of David (cf. *e.g.* 1 Sam. 23: 15–29). The second (vv. 9–18) seems to be the lament of someone suffering from a severe illness (but see below), shunned by his friends (because they believe that God has forsaken him?—cf. Job), persecuted and falsely accused (cf. v. 20) by his enemies (cf. Ps. 6). This section finds echoes in the experience of Jeremiah (see references below). The third section (vv. 19–24) expresses the psalmist's praise either after the deliverance has been granted, or in confident anticipation of it (see on Ps. 6). Some have suggested that two psalms

(vv. 1–8; vv. 9–24) have been combined, since
the trouble seems to be different in the two
parts. It may be, however, that the second part
provides a more detailed account of the distress,
or a later stage in it. Verse 23 suggests that the
psalm (or just the thanksgiving?) was uttered
in public in the sanctuary; but it is not clear
whether the trouble has passed or was still
present (cf. Ps. 22).

Title: see Introduction III. 1, 2, 3. LXX adds
'(in a time) of extreme fear' (cf. v. 22). **1. Put
to shame:** see on 25: 2. **in your righteousness:** see on 5: 8. **2, 3. rock . . . fortress:** see
on 18: 2. **3. for the sake of your name:** see
on 23: 3. **4. trap:** cf. 9: 15; 25: 15. **5. I commit
my spirit:** i.e. 'I entrust my life for preservation'. The first line of this verse (with the
addition of 'Father') were the last words spoken
by Jesus on the cross (Lk. 23: 46); either because
He had the whole psalm in mind, or because it
was the common bed-time prayer of a Jewish
boy. **redeem me:** or 'ransom' (Heb. *pādāh*; see
on 49: 7); Heb. 'thou has redeemed' is either
a reference to past deliverance (see on 34: 12)
or a perfect of certainty: 'you will redeem me'
(see on 20: 6). **the God of truth:** see on 25: 5.
The meaning here is probably 'the true God'
(cf. 2 Chr. 15: 3) in contrast to the idols of v.
6. **6.** Cf. Jon. 2: 8. **I hate:** is possible (cf. 139:
21, 22), but the reading followed by RSV ('thou
hatest') provides a better contrast to v. 6b.
worthless idols: 'vanities of emptiness', i.e.
false gods who create false hopes (cf. Jer. 8:
19). **7. love:** see on 5: 7. **8. spacious place:**
see on 18: 19.

9. The suffering may be the result of the
malice of his enemies (cf. vv. 11–13) rather
than of disease. **my eyes . . . :** see on 6: 7.
soul: see on 3: 2. **body:** lit. 'belly'. **10. affliction:** NIV follows the versions because there is
no other indication that the psalmist is suffering
because of his sins (for MT cf. NIVmg). **bones:**
see on 6: 2. **11. the contempt:** other suggestions for avoiding the awkwardness of the MT
'exceedingly' include 'a calamity' (cf. Prov. 1:
26 f.) and 'a burden' (NEB). **12.** Cf. Jer. 22: 28.
13. Cf. Jer. 6: 25; 11: 9; 18: 23; 20: 3, 4, 10;
Lam. 2: 2. **15. times:** possibly 'fortunes' (NEB)
or 'my whole life' (A. A. Anderson). The first
line of this verse inspired W. F. Lloyd's hymn
'My times are in Thy hand.' **16. Let your face
shine:** i.e. 'smile' (cf. Prov. 16: 15); see on 4:
6; cf. 67: 1; 80: 3, 7, 19; 119: 135. This would
be a contrast to v. 11. **servant:** see on 27: 9.
unfailing love: see on 5: 7. **17. the grave:** see
on 6: 5. **18. righteous:** see on Ps. 1.

19. fear: see on 25: 12. **20. intrigues:** possibly 'slanderings' (Dahood). **accusing
tongues:** '(their) accusation' (A. A. Anderson).
21. Praise: lit. 'blessed'; see on 26: 12. **I was
in a besieged city:** cf. Jer. 1: 18; 15: 20. **22.**
Cf. 1 Sam. 23: 16. **23. Love:** see on 26: 8.

saints: rather 'loyal ones' (Heb. *ḥasîdîm*); see
on 4: 3. **proud:** cf. Prov. 16: 18. **24. be strong
. . . hope:** see on 27: 14.

Psalm 32. THE TESTIMONY OF A FORGIVEN SINNER

The second of the 'Penitential Psalms' (see on
Ps. 6) is really a psalm of thanksgiving; it
does, however, look back to an experience of
repentance. The psalmist had been suffering
because of his unconfessed sin (cf. Ps. 38); but
eventually he came to the point of confession
(cf. 2 Sam. 12: 1–13) and experienced the assurance of divine forgiveness. As a result he was
in a position to teach others the way of blessing
(cf. Ps. 1). The psalm was probably used in
temple worship when the restored sinner offered his song of thanks in the presence of his
fellow-worshippers (cf. 22: 22). It may have
been accompanied by the presentation of a sin-
offering (Lev. 4; 27–5: 19). In the Prayer Book
it is appointed for use on Ash Wednesday.

The poem may be divided into five sections.
Verses 1, 2 express the joyful relief of the
person who has been reconciled to God. Three
Heb. nouns are used to denote 'sin' and three
verbs to describe God's way of dealing with it.
The psalmist's 'rebellion' against the divine
authority has been 'lifted up' and 'carried away'
like a burden; his 'failure' to keep God's law
has been 'blotted out' from the sight of the
divine Judge; his 'crookedness', or 'deviation'
from the right path, is no longer 'counted'
against him—the debt has been cancelled.
There is no 'self-deception' because he has faced
up to himself and to his sin (cf. v. 5). Verses
3–5 describe first the effects of unconfessed sin
(vv. 3, 4 may refer to actual physical suffering
or to the pangs of conscience), and then the
result of a full and open confession. In vv. 6, 7
the writer presents the logic of his experience,
expressed as advice to any of God's people in
any sort of trouble. Affliction may well be
regarded as a pointer to sin; in which case the
prayer for deliverance must also be a prayer of
penitence. Verses 8, 9 could be the words of
the psalmist himself in his role as a teacher of
his people; but they are more likely to be a
divine oracle (cf. v. 8b) which the psalmist
received when he asked for forgiveness (see on
12: 5). Man is like a senseless animal when he
refuses to use his mind to grasp the divine will
and to follow it willingly (cf. 73: 22). Finally,
in vv. 10, 11 the psalmist summarizes his
'lesson' in a proverbial antithesis and calls on
God's people to make the sanctuary resound
with their songs of praise.

Title: see Introduction III. 1, 2. **1, 2. Blessed:**
see on 1: 1. **transgressions:** Heb. *pešaʿ*, lit.
'rebellion' (cf. NEB 'disobedience'). **forgiven:**
Heb. *nāśāʾ*, lit. 'lift up, carry'. **sins:** Heb.
ḥᵃṭāʾāh, lit. 'missing the mark'. **covered:** Heb.

577

kāsāh, lit. 'cover', 'conceal' (cf. v. 5; Neh. 4: 5). **count against:** Heb. *hāšab*, lit. 'think', 'reckon'. **sin:** or 'iniquity' Heb. *'āwôn*, lit. 'twisting' or 'going astray'. **in whose spirit:** LXX 'in whose mouth'. **3. my bones:** see on 6: 3. **4. my strength was sapped:** lit. 'my moisture (NEB 'sap'; i.e. 'vitality') was changed'. **Selah:** see Introduction III. 3. **5. cover:** (cf. v. 1). There must be no cover-up: God cannot 'cover' a man's sin until the man 'uncovers' it (cf. Job 31: 33; Prov. 28: 13). **guilt** (lit. 'iniquity' as v. 2) **of my sin:** an unusual expression (cf. NEB 'penalty of . . .'). Some read 'Thou hast pardoned my iniquity, my sin thou hast forgiven' (cf. JB).

6. godly: see on 4: 3. **while you may be found:** so the *MT* cf. 69: 13; Isa. 55: 6. **8. I will counsel . . . :** better 'I will counsel you, my eye (will be) upon you' (cf. 33: 18; 34: 13; Jer. 24: 6; 40: 4, Heb.). **9. but must be controlled:** the Heb. (lit. 'his ornaments must be held') is obscure, but the general sense is clear. NEB emends slightly to read, 'whose course must be checked'. **or they will not . . . :** better 'then nothing can approach you'; possibly misplaced from the end of v. 7 (cf. NEB). **10. unfailing love:** see on 5: 7. **11. righteous:** see on Ps. 1.

Psalm 33. IN PRAISE OF THE PROVIDENCE OF GOD

A congregational hymn of 'descriptive' praise which may have been composed for the great autumn (or New Year) festival which probably included a celebration of the renewal of creation and the covenant (see Introduction II. 2). This is one of the few psalms (cf. Pss. 1; 2; 10) in Book I which is not attributed to David in the *MT* (the LXX adds 'of David'). There is no evidence that the twenty-two verses were intended to correspond to the twenty-two letters of the Heb. alphabet (cf. Ps. 34).

The opening verses (vv. 1–3) exhort the worshippers to use every means at their disposal to praise God. The hymn proper (vv. 4–19) gives the grounds for such rejoicing. Yahweh's purposes are totally dependable and always for the best (vv. 4, 5). Westermann sees vv. 6–19 as a development of this double statement. Yahweh is not only the omnipotent Creator, whose active power is manifested in His word (vv. 6–9); He is also the Lord of history, whose purposes override all human planning (vv. 10–12), and whose omniscient providence makes earthly schemes and resources ineffective and redundant (vv. 13–19). The psalm concludes with an expression of confidence in Yahweh as the Protector of His people (vv. 20, 21), and with a prayer that His grace may be an abiding experience in the future (v. 22).

1. Sing joyfully: or 'Shout for joy to' (JB);

cf. 32: 7, 11. **righteous . . . upright:** the ideal characteristics of a worshipper of Yahweh (cf. Pss. 15; 24). **fitting:** praise 'comes well from' (NEB); cf. 147: 1. **2. harp . . . lyre:** two examples of the many instruments available for use in public worship (cf. 98: 5; 144: 9; 150; see *NBD* art. 'Music and Musical Instruments'). **3. a new song:** specially composed for the occasion, or celebrating the ever-new acts of God (cf. 40: 3; 96: 1; 144: 9; 149: 1; Isa. 42: 9, 10; 43: 18 ff.; 48: 6 ff.). **4. word of the LORD:** the expression of His will, and the means by which He effects His purposes both in creation (v. 6; cf. 147: 15) and in history (cf. Isa. 55: 10 f.). **5. loves:** i.e. loves to perform and uphold right and just deeds (cf. 99: 4; Jer. 9: 24). **righteousness:** Heb. *ṣᵉdāqāh* is conformity to a standard, whether social or divine. When attributed to God it denotes either His inherent moral uprightness and consistency, or His actions to maintain or bring about right relationships. It can therefore entail 'deliverance', 'vindication' and 'victory' for His people, and 'retribution' and 'punishment' for the wicked (cf. 22: 31; 40: 9 f.; 51: 14; 65: 5; 69: 27; 71: 24; 103: 6; 119: 75). **justice:** Heb. *mišpāṭ* often denotes the decision given by a judge, or practices which have become customary by habit or by legal decision. Used of God it carries a range of meanings similar to the word 'righteousness', and the two can thus be used as synonyms (see also on 1: 5). **unfailing love:** see on 5: 7. The 'covenant loyalty' of Yahweh toward Israel is extended to embrace the whole world (cf. Gen. 9: 9–17; Ps. 36: 5; 119: 64; 136: 1–9; Isa. 6: 3).

6. their starry host: sun, moon and stars (cf. Isa. 40: 26; 45: 12). **breath of his mouth:** a synonym for 'word' (cf. 147: 18). **7.** This verse could refer to the waters above the sky-vault (Gen. 1: 7) poetically viewed as an ocean, or to the separation of waters from dry land (Gen. 1: 9 f.; 7: 11; Ps. 78: 15). Some see the reference to Yahweh's mastery over the primordial sea (**the deep**; cf. Gen. 1: 2) as an allusion to His victory over the powers of chaos. **into jars:** *MT* 'as a heap' (cf. Exod. 15: 8; Jos. 3: 13, 16; Ps. 78: 13); NIV follows the ancient versions, reading the same consonants with different vowels. Dahood suggests 'in a pitcher' (cf. Job 38: 22, 37). **storehouses:** cf. 135: 7; Job 38: 22. **8. fear:** see on 25: 12. **9. he . . . he:** emphatic. **spoke:** cf. Gen. 1. **it came to be:** lit. 'it was' (cf. Gen. 1: 7, 9, etc.). **stood firm:** firmly established (cf. Isa. 48: 13). **11. purposes:** same Heb. word as 'plans' (v. 10). **12. Blessed:** see on 1: 1.

15. who forms . . . : only the Creator is able to read man's thoughts, because He 'formed' (cf. Gen. 2: 7) man's mind. **hearts:** see on 17: 3. **17. horse:** standing for 'chariotry' or 'military power' (cf. 20: 7 f.; Isa. 31: 1). **18.**

eyes of the LORD: providential care (cf. Ezr. 5: 5; Job 36: 7; Ps. 32: 8; 34: 15). **fear:** see on 25: 12. **unfailing love:** see on 5: 7. **19. death . . . famine:** caused by war, epidemic, drought, etc. **20. wait:** involving hope, trust and obedience (cf. 106: 13). **help . . . shield:** or 'our protective shield' (cf. Dt. 33: 29; Ps. 115: 9–11; see on 3: 3). **21. holy name:** see on 20: 1. **unfailing love:** see on 5:7. **even as:** or 'since'.

Psalm 34. THE VOICE OF EXPERIENCE

An individual thanksgiving, probably written to accompany the presentation of thank-offerings in the temple (see on 22: 25); but also containing a large didactic element, so that the experience of the psalmist becomes a testimony to future generations (cf. Ps. 32). This is an acrostic poem (see on Ps. 25), with slight irregularity. Despite the title (see below), there is nothing in the psalm specific to the events of 1 Sam. 21: 10–15 (cf. Ps. 56 title).

The poem is in three sections. Verses 1–3 form an introductory hymn in which the psalmist calls on others to join him in proclaiming the greatness of God. Verses 4–10 are his testimony to the goodness of God, which can be experienced by anyone who is prepared to 'make but trial of His love' (vv. 1–9 have been beautifully paraphrased by N. Tate and N. Brady in the hymn 'Through all the changing scenes of life'). In vv. 11–22 the psalmist speaks as a wisdom teacher (cf. Prov. 1–8), explaining the practical implications of what it means to 'fear Yahweh'. His black and white teaching (cf. Ps. 1) needs the counterbalance of the book of Job. There are several NT allusions to this Psalm; cf. 1 Pet. 2: 1, 3, 22; 3: 10–12; Jn 19: 36 (?). In the early church it was associated with the Eucharist (cf. v. 8).

Title: see Introduction III. 2. **When he feigned . . . :** lit. 'when he disguised (or 'altered') his judgment (or 'behaviour')'; cf. 1 Sam. 21: 13. **Abimelech:** either a copyist's error or an alternative name (or dynastic title, cf. Gen. 26: 1) for Achish (1 Sam. 21: 10 ff.). **1. Extol:** lit 'bless'; see on 26: 12. **2. My soul:** 'I' (see on 3: 2). **boast:** or 'glory' (cf. 105: 3; Jer. 9: 23 f.; Ps. 49: 6; 97: 7; Prov. 20: 14). **afflicted:** better 'humble' (see on 9: 12). **3. name:** see on 20: 1. **glorify:** lit. 'make great'.

4. sought: probably by visiting the sanctuary (see on 24: 6). **answered:** by an oracle, or by the act of deliverance itself. **fears:** better 'terrors' (NEB). **5. Those who look to him . . . :** *MT* has 'They looked . . . and were . . .': RSV ('Look to him, and be . . .') follows some Heb. MSS, Syr., Jerome (i.e. reading the same consonants with different vowels). **radiant:** smiling, delighted, joyful (cf. Isa. 60: 5). **6. poor:** see on 9: 18 (cf. Lam.

3: 1). **7. The angel** (lit. 'messenger') **of the LORD:** either the special manifestation of Yahweh referred to in *e.g.* Gen. 16: 7–13; Exod. 3: 2–6; Jg. 6: 11–23; 13: 3–20; or the angelic commander of the heavenly army accompanied by his celestial troops (cf. Exod. 14: 19; Jos. 5: 14; 2 Kg. 6: 17 f.; Zech. 1: 8–13). **8. Taste:** or 'judge' (cf. Prov. 31: 18). **see:** possibly a homonym 'drink deeply' (Dahood). **blessed:** Heb. *'aš^erê* (see on 1: 1). **9. Fear:** see on v. 11 and 25: 12. **saints:** lit. 'holy (or 'separated') ones'; here (cf. 16: 3) those who belong to Yahweh and stand in a special relationship with Him (cf. Exod. 19: 6; Lev. 11: 44 ff.). **lack nothing:** see 23: 1. **10. the lions:** the strongest hunting beasts (cf. 104: 21); LXX, Syr., Vulg. have 'the rich'; NEB takes as a homonym 'unbelievers'.

11. the fear of the LORD: that way of life which springs from a reverent acknowledgement of the holiness of God (cf. Prov. 1: 7). **14.** Cf. Job. 1: 1; Prov. 16: 6. **15. eyes:** see on 33: 18; and cf. the hymn 'There is an eye that never sleeps' (J. A. Wallace). **righteous:** see on Ps. 1. **16. face:** see on 4: 6; 13: 1. **17. The righteous:** *MT* 'Then they . . .'; NIV follows LXX, Targ., Syr., Vulg. **18. broken-hearted . . . crushed . . . :** either those who have lost all courage and hope (cf. NEB, GNB; 147: 3), or those who have been brought to the point of meekness and humility (cf. 51: 17; Mt. 5: 3). **20. bones:** see on 6: 2. **broken:** cf. 51: 8; Isa. 38: 13; Mic. 3: 3. **21. wicked:** see on Ps. 1. **21, 22. condemned:** lit. 'be (held) guilty' or 'punished'; some suggest 'destroyed' (cf. NEB 'brought to ruin'). **22. redeems:** see on 49: 7.

Psalm 35. THE PRAYER OF A FALSELY-ACCUSED MAN

This individual lament consists of three petitions, each ending with a vow of praise in view of the certainty of divine deliverance. There it no need to doubt that the psalm is a literary unity, describing the same experience from different aspects. Verses 1–10 are the psalmist's prayer for protection from those who are unjustifiably hunting him down. Verses 11–18 are a complaint about those who were once his friends but have now become his enemies. Verses 19–28 continue the psalmist's appeal to God, who is not only the righteous Judge (v. 24) but also the only 'truly reliable eye-witness' (A. A. Anderson; cf. v. 22), to vindicate him from all the false accusations of his opponents. The JB translation conveys very well the vivid and urgent expressions of the Heb. For a possible life-setting and use of this psalm see on Ps. 7. For a discussion of the imprecatory element (vv. 4–8, 26) see Introduction IV. 1.

Title: see Introduction III. 2. **1. Contend:**

or 'Oppose' (GNB); the verb usually refers to pleading a case in court, but sometimes to activity on a battlefield (cf. Jg. 11: 25) and this fits the imagery of vv. 1–3 better. **2. shield:** see on 3: 3. **buckler:** a shield to cover the whole body (see on 5: 12). **3. javelin:** *MT* is usually translated 'stop the way' (cf. NEB), but it may be the name of another weapon (JB 'pike'; GNB 'axe'). **my soul:** 'me' (see on 3: 2). **salvation:** the word (Heb. *yᵉšûʿāh*) covers the ideas of 'victory' (cf. 144: 10), 'vindication' (cf. 76: 9), 'rescue' (cf. 18: 19) and 'help' (cf. 69: 13). **5.** Cf. 1: 4. **angel of the LORD:** see on 34: 7; cf. 2 Kg. 19: 35. **7. pit:** makes better sense, transposed as it is from the preceding line cf. Jer. 18: 20. **8. them . . . they:** *MT* has 'him . . . he' (so NEB); NIV (with LXX, JB, GNB) takes the verse collectively. **9. my soul:** 'I' (see on 3: 2). **salvation:** see on v. 3. **10. whole being** ('bones'): see on 6: 2. **poor . . . needy:** see on 9: 12, 18.

12. my soul forlorn: lit. 'childlessness for my soul'; possibly we should read 'they seek for my life' (cf. NEB). **13. My prayers . . . :** cf. Isa. 58: 3, 5. RSV takes it as a reference to the psalmist's posture ('with head bowed') (cf. 1 Kg. 18: 42), but *MT* (NIV) suggests either that he would benefit from his own prayers, or that they went unanswered (cf. NEB). **15. stumbled:** sudden disaster (cf. Job 18: 12). **attackers:** lit. 'smitten ones'; some emend to 'strangers' (JB, GNB), but 'who smite me (with words) unawares' is more likely (cf. Dahood). **slandered:** lit. 'tore'. **16.** The Heb. is obscure: NIV following LXX makes good sense; NEB is less likely. Some find an allusion to sorcery (cf. Eaton). **17. ravages:** probably cognate with 'ruin' (v. 8); some suggest 'pit'. **life:** lit. 'only one' (see on 22: 20). **lions:** some read 'ungodly' (cf. NEB; and see on 34: 10). **18.** Cf. 22: 22 ff. **20. quietly in the land:** a unique expression; NEB 'peaceable folk'. **24. Vindicate:** lit. 'Judge' (see on 72: 2). **your righteousness:** see on 5: 8. **25. just what we wanted:** lit. 'our *nepeš*' (see on 3: 2). **26. distress:** lit. 'evil'. **27. vindication:** lit. 'righteousness' (see on 33: 5). **always:** lit. 'continually'. **exalted . . . :** lit. 'Let Yahweh be made great'. **well-being:** lit. 'peace' (see on 29: 11; cf. 119: 165). **28. speak:** lit. 'murmur' (see on 1: 2).

Psalm 36. THE WICKEDNESS OF MAN AND THE GOODNESS OF GOD

Each of the three parts of this psalm corresponds to a different psalm-type (see Introduction II); but there is no need to doubt its unity. Verses 1–4 are either lamentation or didactic (i.e. wisdom; see on Ps. 1) poetry, describing the godless arrogance of the wicked person (cf. 10: 4; 14: 1). Verses 5–9 are hymnic, praising the enriching and life-giving effects of the

goodness of Yahweh. (These verses form the basis of Watts hymn 'High in the heavens, eternal God'.) Verses 10–12 form a concluding prayer for continued protection. The speaker may be either a person pursued by the type of evil men he portrays in vv. 1–4 (cf. vv. 11, 12), or a representative of the community (perhaps the king himself) acting as its spokesman (cf. 'me' v. 11) or its teacher. Some suggest that vv. 5–9 point to the autumnal festival as its setting (see Introduction II. 2).

Title: see Introduction III. 2, 3. **the servant of the LORD:** although *ʿebed* is the ordinary Heb. word for 'slave' and as a self-description of a worshipper indicative of humility (cf. 69: 17; 135: 14), *ʿebed Yahweh* was an honorific title for the nation (cf. Isa. 42: 19) and for its distinguished leaders (cf. Dt. 34: 5; Jos. 24: 29; Ps. 89: 3). **1. An oracle . . . :** the *MT* is difficult, but it may mean that instead of the voice of God (cf. 2 Sam. 23: 1 ff.) the wicked man takes the promptings of Sin (personified) as divine utterances (cf. RSV). **my heart:** *MT* 'my', but some Heb. MSS (and the versions) have 'his', which gives better sense. **fear:** rather, 'dread' (cf. Isa. 2: 10; 19: 21). **2.** The text is difficult to interpret, but the sense seems to be that Sin deludes him into believing that God will not discover and condemn his evil-doing (cf. RSV). **3, 4. wicked:** or 'evil' (lit. 'trouble').

5. love: see on 5: 7. **reaches:** or 'is in'. **6. the mighty mountains:** lit. 'the mountains of God', probably a Heb. superlative. **justice:** lit. 'judgments'; bringing salvation to the godly (see on 33: 5; cf. 72: 1–4). **preserve:** lit. 'save', i.e. preserve the life of, provide for . . . (cf. Ps. 104). **7. shadow of your wings:** God's protective care (see on 17: 8). **8, 9.** The three essentials for life are food, drink and sunlight. **8. abundance:** lit. 'oil'; the picture may derive from the sacrificial meals in the temple (cf. Lev. 7: 11 ff.; Jer. 31: 14; see on Ps. 22: 26). **river:** cf. 46: 4; Ezek. 47: 1 ff. **delights:** Heb. *ʿēden*; cf. the garden of Gen. 2: 8–10. **9. fountain of life:** never-failing source (cf. Jer. 2: 13; 17: 13) of life (cf. Prov. 10: 11; 13: 14; 14: 27; 16: 22). **in your light:** the sunshine of God's face (see on 4: 6). **see light:** i.e. 'live' (cf. Job 3: 16; Ps. 49: 19). **10. righteousness:** (see on 33: 5); here probably a synonym for 'faithfulness'. **11. drive me away:** from home (cf. 109: 10), the temple (cf. 5: 4, 7) or the land (cf. 2 Kg. 21: 8). **12. See:** probably in imagination (perfects of certainty—see on 20: 6), or possibly symbolized in temple ritual. **evildoers:** see 5: 5.

Psalm 37. THE RECOMPENSE OF THE WICKED AND THE REWARD OF THE RIGHTEOUS

Weiser has described this wisdom psalm (see

on Ps. 1) as 'not so much a psalm as a collection of proverbs' like those in the book of Proverbs. The author is a man with the hard-won knowledge and experience of old age (cf. v. 25) who seeks to pass them on to the younger generation. His main aim is to encourage the godly to go on trusting God despite the apparent injustices of life, in which the ungodly seem to come off best. He does not deal with the theoretical problems involved, nor does he concern himself with the vindication of God's rule of the world (cf. Job). His purpose is more practical and pastoral: to help the faithful to come to terms with their situation by assuring them that any seeming injustice in life is only temporary (cf. Pss. 49; 73).

The psalm is an acrostic (see on Ps. 25) consisting of twenty-two stanzas, each having usually four lines and each beginning with a successive letter of the Hebrew alphabet. Consequently, there is little development of thought in the psalm. Most commentators divide it into four main sections; but three is equally possible (so Kidner). Verses 1–11 exhort the righteous to wait quietly with untroubled trust for God to recompense the wicked and reward the righteous. Verses 12–26 elaborate the contrast between the present and future situations of the righteous and the wicked. History proves that God can be trusted to deal with the wicked. Verses 27–40 emphasize that both the retribution of the wicked and the recompense of the righteous will be permanent.

The psalm inspired Paul Gerhardt to compose the hymn 'Befiehl du deine Wege', rendered in English by John Wesley as 'Commit thou all thy griefs' (some hymn-books start with the verse 'Put thou thy trust in God'). Mendelssohn provided a beautiful setting of vv. 1, 7 in his 'Elijah' (i.e. 'O rest in the Lord').

Title: see Introduction III. 2. Heb. has simply 'Of David'. 1. fret: suggests a mixture of anxiety and anger, resentment and irritation. NEB 'Do not strive to outdo . . . or emulate . . .' is unlikely; but vv. 3, 8, 27 do seem to imply that the righteous might be tempted to adopt the life-style of the wicked. who do wrong: see on 5: 5. 3. enjoy safe pasture: ambiguous Heb.; other possibilities are 'strive after faithfulness' or 'feed securely' (RVmg). 5. Commit . . . to: lit. 'Roll . . . upon' (cf. 55: 22). way: here probably 'destiny' (cf. JB 'fate'). 6. righteousness: see on 33: 5. 7. Be still: lit. 'Be silent'. 'The psalmist's conviction of God's ultimate, final intervention is so firm that he dares to wait . . . without trying to take the matter into (his) own hands' (Ringgren, p. 58; cf. 40: 1). 9. As the nations were cut off at the time of the conquest of Canaan (cf. Dt. 12: 29; 19: 1), so the wicked will be removed so that the righteous can enjoy

their inheritance in peace (cf. Prov. 2: 21; 10: 30). To inherit the promised land is to have the right to reside in Yahweh's land and thus to enjoy His care and blessing. 11. meek: 'humble' (see on 9: 12); in Mt. 5: 5 the 'land' becomes the whole 'earth' (cf. 2 Pet. 3: 13).

13. Lord: Heb. *'adōnāi*; see on 8: 1. laughs: see 2: 4. 18. known: see on 1: 6. 19. enjoy plenty: lit. 'are satisfied'. 20. the beauty of the fields: most modern translations understand a reference to flowers (cf. v. 2; Isa. 40: 6 f.); this is more likely than 'the fat of lambs' (AV). vanish like smoke: better, 'they come to an end in smoke' (cf. Mt. 6: 30). 21. do not repay: extreme poverty rather than dishonesty is evidently meant (cf. Dt. 15: 6; 28: 12, 44). 23. We should probably read (with a Qumran MS) 'By Yahweh are the steps of a man established, and in all his ways he delights'. 28. faithful ones: or, 'loyal ones' (see on 4: 3). They: many follow LXX^A and read 'The ungodly will perish for ever'. Cf. 1: 2–4. utters: meditates (lit. 'murmurs'); cf. 1: 2. 35. ruthless: 'acting like a tyrant'. flourishing . . . native soil: the *MT* could be so taken (cf. AV, RV), but is probably corrupt. Read 'towering like a cedar of Lebanon' (RSV following LXX). 37. future: the word usually means 'end', 'future'; but here (and v. 38) probably refers to descendants (see NIVmg and NEB, GNB, JB). The Israelite looked forward to living on in his children (cf. Dt. 25: 5–10; Isa. 66: 22; Ps. 109: 13).

Psalm 38. THE PRAYER OF A SUFFERING SINNER

This individual lament is regarded as the third of the 'Penitential Psalms' (see on Ps. 6). It is impossible to deduce from the psalm the exact nature of the trouble in which the psalmist finds himself. He appears to be suffering from an illness which causes his friends to treat him as a leper (cf. vv. 5, 11) and gives his enemies the opportunity to plot his destruction. Unlike Job in a similar situation, the psalmist is convinced that he is suffering as a result of his sins and the main point of the psalm is his confession of guilt and his plea for deliverance. The psalm has been attributed to David (see on Ps. 6) and to Jeremiah (cf. Jer. 20: 7–12), but in the latter's case there is no consciousness of sin. Others have seen the poem as an expression of the experiences of the nation (cf. Lam. 3). Whatever the origin of the psalm its presence in the Psalter shows that it could be used (probably with appropriate ritual—see note on the title) by anyone in serious trouble desiring to make confession. It is even possible that it was specially composed for such a purpose and that the stereotyped phrases were used to cover a range of experiences (cf. Ringgren, pp. 61 ff.)

The psalm may be divided into three main

sections, each beginning with an address to
God. Verses 1–8 describe the psalmist's physical and mental sufferings, seen as a punishment
from God; vv. 9–14 express his loneliness,
deserted by his friends and threatened by his
enemies; vv. 15–20 express his confidence that
God alone can and will deliver him, since he
has admitted his guilt and since the opposition
of his enemies is totally unjust. Finally, vv. 21,
22 conclude with a brief petition. The number
of verses may be intended to correspond with
the number of letters in the Hebrew alphabet,
but this is not an acrostic psalm.

Title: see Introduction III. 1, 2, 4. **A petition:** lit. 'to bring to remembrance'; to ask
God to remember is to ask Him to act (cf. Jer.
15: 15). RSV connects it with the offering of the
'memorial portion' (cf. Lev. 2: 2, 9, 16; 24: 7;
Isa. 66: 3). **1.** See on 6: 1–3. **2. arrows:** divine
judgment, particularly in the form of disease
(cf. Dt. 32: 23; Job 6: 4; Ps. 7: 12 f.). **3. body
. . . bones:** both can stand by metonymy for
the man as a whole, i.e. 'me . . . I'. (see on 6:
2; 16: 9). **sin:** see on 32: 1. **4. guilt:** see on 32:
1. For the picture of the consequences of sin as
a mighty flood engulfing the sinner cf. 69: 2,
15; 124: 4 f. **5. wounds:** not necessarily an
allusion to leprosy (cf. v. 11). **folly:** synonym
for sin (cf. 69: 5; Prov. 24: 9). **6. mourning:**
cf. 35: 13 f.; 42: 9; Isa. 58: 5; here apparently
the result of the burden of guilt. **7. searing
pain:** possibly a reference to fever (cf. NEB),
but more likely a general description of pain
and loss of strength. **10. the light from my
eyes:** either 'sight' or 'vitality' (see on 13: 3).
11. wounds: the word can denote leprosy (e.g.
Lev. 13: 2) but normally means 'affliction' in
general. **16. boast:** lit. 'magnify themselves'
(cf. Job 19: 5). **18. I confess:** lit. 'For I will
declare'. **troubled by:** lit. 'anxious because
of'. **19. vigorous enemies:** RSV emendation
('without cause') is supported by the parallel
without reason, but NIV follows MT which
could mean 'My enemies flourish and are
mighty', or 'The enemies of my life are
mighty'.

Psalm 39. LIFE IS TOO SHORT FOR
SUFFERING

This psalm has been variously described as
an 'elegy', a 'lament' or a 'penitential psalm'.
Despite the similarities in the situations of the
writers, it has none of the stereotyped phraseology of Ps. 38. As Weiser says, 'Its author is
of such an independent disposition and the
problem which agitates his mind is so closely
related to his entirely personal circumstances
that he throws over the restrictions which are
imposed upon him by the traditional forms and
in his strange dialogue with God provides us
with a deep insight into the struggles of his

soul in a way almost unique in the Psalter'. The
suffering of the psalmist, which he acknowledges is due to his sin (vv. 8–11), is exacerbated
not by the cruelty of others (as in Ps. 38), but
by the consciousness that life is so short and
man is so insignificant that there is nothing to
look forward to. Why should God bother to
discipline 'a creature as frail and fleeting as man'
(Kidner)? (Cf. Job 7: 17; Ps. 8: 4.)

The poem consists of four stanzas. Verses
1–3 provide the setting for the prayer. The
psalmist's determination not to complain to
God in the hearing of the wicked cannot be
maintained: after a mental struggle his
emotions get the better of him. In vv. 4–6 he
meditates on the brevity and frailty of human
life (cf. Job 7; Ps. 90) and the pointlessness of
worldly endeavour. In the light of these his
only hope is in God (v. 7). So in vv. 7–11 he
confesses his sin and pleads for an end to God's
disciplinary dealings with him. His final prayer
(vv. 12, 13) is based upon the transitoriness and
rootlessness of human existence. If God does
not save him soon he will have no life left to
enjoy! (Cf. Job 10: 20 f.) In contrast, the NT
sees this life in the perspective of eternity, and
provides the Christian with a hope that goes
beyond the grave (cf. Jn 12: 25; 2 C. 4: 16 ff.;
2 Tim. 1: 10; see also Introduction IV. 1).

Title: see Introduction III. 1, 2, 3. **Jeduthun:**
one of David's chief temple musicians (cf. 1
Chr. 16: 41). The reference here may be to a
guild of singers descended from him. (Mowinckel understands the word as 'Confession'.)
2. not even saying anything good: or 'I tried
to keep quiet without success' (cf. RSV). Some
find here a reference to the prosperity of the
wicked which only increases the psalmist's torment (cf. JB). **3. meditated:** sighed, groaned
(cf. 5: 1). **4 ff.** Weiser thinks that it is not
feasible to take this prayer as the sinful rebellion
and burning agony referred to in vv. 1–3. The
psalmist has not lost control; he speaks with 'a
calm and self-composed resignation'. **5. handbreadth:** the width of four fingers (cf. Jer. 52:
21). **breath:** 'puff of wind' (JB); cf. Ec. 1: 2,
14. **Selah:** see Introduction III. 3. **6. phantom:**
or like an image in a dream (cf. 90: 5). **He
bustles about, but only in vain:** perhaps 'a
mere breath are riches he heaps up' (cf. JB). **8.
transgressions:** see on 32: 1. **fools:** see on 14:
1. **10. scourge:** see on 38: 11. The nature
of his disease is not explained. **overcome:**
'exhausted' (NEB). **11. sin:** Heb. 'āwôn (see on
32: 1). **like a moth:** either a picture of the
destructive power of God (cf. Job. 13: 28) or a
reference to the brevity of the psalmist's life.
12. as an alien: Heb. gēr, a resident alien,
given a protected position (cf. Lev. 19: 33).
stranger: a less permanent resident; here a
synonym for gēr. **13. Look away:** a plea to be
spared further punishment (NEB 'Frown on me

no more'); cf. Job 7: 19; 14: 6. **I depart:** i.e. to
Sheol (see on 6: 5).

Psalm 40. DELIVERANCE PAST AND PRESENT

The first part of this psalm (vv. 1–10) forms
an individual thanksgiving, praising God for
deliverance from a serious illness. The second
part (vv. 11–17) is an individual lament in
which the psalmist cries for deliverance from
the trouble into which his sins have brought
him (cf. v. 12) and which his enemies are using
as an opportunity to destroy him (cf. vv. 14
f.). Verses 13–17 appear again, with minor
differences, as Ps. 70. It is possible that two
separate psalms have been joined together, perhaps by the addition of vv. 11–12 as a link.
Alternatively there is no reason why the psalm
could not be an original unity, part of it later
being used independently. For the sequence of
thanksgiving-lament see Pss. 9/10. The worshipper thankfully recounts a previous experience of salvation as the ground of assurance for
his present prayer for deliverance: 'what God
has done once, he can do again' (A. A. Anderson). Eaton thinks it likely that the psalmist
was the Davidic king representing his people
(cf. v. 5) in a festival liturgy. On the title see
Introduction III. 1, 2, 3.

A song of praise (vv. 1–10)

This section may be sub-divided into four
stanzas. In vv. 1–3 the psalmist describes his
experience of deliverance; vv. 4, 5 express what
he has learned from his experience; in vv. 6–8
he realizes that the only adequate response is
willing obedience to God; finally, vv. 9, 10
refer to the public testimony he has given to
the saving faithfulness of God. The writer to
the Hebrews (10: 5 ff.) attributes the words of
vv. 6, 7 (quoted from LXX) to Christ at His
entrance into the world to be the once-for-all
sacrifice for sins (see *NTC* on Heb. 10: 5 ff.).
The Prayer Book appoints the psalm for use
on Good Friday. (On the nature of Christ's
fulfilment of the Psalms see Introduction IV.
2.)

1. I waited patiently: lit. 'Waiting, I
waited'. The hopeful expectancy (see on 37: 7;
cf. 130: 5, 6; Hos. 12: 6) with which he looked
to God to answer His prayers for salvation (cf.
Isa. 25: 9) made it possible for him to endure
the period of waiting (cf. Isa. 40: 31). **2. the
slimy pit . . . the mud and mire:** pictures of
Sheol (see on 6: 5). Any disaster, but particularly disease, was regarded as involving the
sufferer in the sphere of death (cf. 2 Sam. 22:
5 f.; Job 33: 30; Ps. 30: 3; 69: 2, 14 f.; Jon. 2:
2, 7). Thus healing or restoration could be
described as deliverance from Sheol (cf. 1 Sam.
2: 6; Ps. 30: 3; Jon. 2: 7). **3. new song:** see on
33: 3. **4. Blessed:** see on 1: 1. **the proud:**
possibly 'idols' (GNB, cf. LXX 'vanities'). **false**

gods: lit. 'a lie'. **5. wonders:** past miracles (see
on 9: 1).

6. This is not a repudiation of sacrifice as
such, but a recognition that doing God's will
is more important than ritual observances (cf.
1 Sam. 15: 22; Ps. 50: 8–14; 51: 16 ff.; 69: 30
f.; Isa. 1: 11 ff.; Jer. 7: 21 f.; Hos. 6: 6; Am. 5:
21). Nothing less than his self-offering is a
fitting response to the grace of God (cf. Mic.
6: 6 ff.; Rom. 12: 1 ff.). **Sacrifice:** (Heb. *zebaḥ*,
lit. 'that which is slain') is a communion or
shared-offering (cf. Lev. 3). **offering:** (Heb.
minḥāh, lit. 'gift') can denote any offering, regarded as a gift to God, or in particular a cereal
offering (cf. Lev. 2). **burnt offerings:** (Heb.
'ôlāh, lit. 'that which goes up') are completely
burnt on the altar (cf. Lev. 1). **sin offerings:**
(Heb. *ḥaṭā'āh*, lit. 'sin') are expiatory sacrifices
(cf. Lev. 4). (For further details see *NBD* art.
'Sacrifice and Offering'.) **my ears . . .
opened:** (NIVmg) i.e. 'you have made me
obedient' (cf. Isa. 50: 4 f.; Jer. 6: 10). The Heb.
(pierced) is probably *not* a reference to the
piercing of the ear of a slave (Exod. 21: 6). **7.
Here I am . . . :** the words of a slave when
his master calls (cf. Isa. 6: 8). **in the scroll:**
probably the scroll of the Law (v. 8) in which
God's will for His slaves is expressed, rather
than a heavenly book which records men's
deeds (cf. 56: 8). The reference could be to the
coronation decree of the Davidic king (see on
2: 7). **written about me:** i.e. 'prescribed for
me' (cf. NIVmg; 2 Kg. 22: 13). **8.** Cf. 1: 2;
119: 11, 16, 47, etc.; Dt. 6: 6; Jer. 3 1: 33. **9.
righteousness:** see on 33: 5. **great assembly:**
see on 22: 22. **10. righteousness** see on 33: 5.
love: see on 5: 7.

A prayer for help (vv. 11–17)

The psalmist now appeals for the continuation
of Yahweh's saving goodness in his present
afflictions (vv. 11, 12); pleads for help and for
the downfall of his enemies (vv. 13–15); and
finally (vv. 16, 17) prays that the faithful may
continue to find their satisfaction in God, and
that he may not be forgotten but soon experience God's deliverance.

11. Some render this verse as a statement of
confidence: 'Thou wilt not . . .' (cf. GNB, NEB),
and see it as the conclusion of the song of praise
(vv. 1–10). **12.** The trouble is unspecified, but
acknowledged to be the consequence of his sin;
cf. GNB 'my sins have caught up with me'. **and
I cannot see:** cf. 6: 7; 38: 10; 69: 3. **16. seek:**
see on 24: 6. **be exalted:** see on 35: 27. **17.
poor and needy:** see on 9: 18.

Psalm 41. THE TESTIMONY OF A SICK MAN

There are three main sections in this psalm.
The middle one (vv. 4–10) is a lament in which
the psalmist prays for healing from some un-

specified illness, apparently due to his sin, and complains at the treatment he is receiving from both enemies and friends. The lament is introduced by a didactic section (vv. 1–3) extolling the blessings of the merciful man who enjoys the protection and care of Yahweh in every situation. The conclusion (vv. 11–12) expresses the grateful confidence of one who has experienced (or is certain that he will experience) the protection and care he has described in vv. 1–3. Verse 13 is not part of the original psalm, but a doxology which concludes the First Book of the Psalms (cf. 72: 19; 89: 52; 106: 48).

The relationship between the three sections of this psalm is not completely clear. The whole psalm could be an individual lament prayed during the illness; with vv. 1–3 as a statement of a general truth with which the psalmist contrasts his present position (translating v. 4 'But in my case, I say . . .') and upon which he bases his appeal (v. 10), and vv. 11, 12 being a statement of confidence (with verbs translated in the future tense—i.e. prophetic perfects: see on 20: 6). It is more likely, however, that the whole psalm is an individual thanksgiving probably recited in the temple (cf. v. 12) after deliverance had been granted, and accompanied by a thanksgiving sacrifice (see on 22: 25). In that case vv. 4–10 would be a description of the lament which the psalmist used when he was in trouble (the quotation marks should then continue from v. 4 to the end of v. 10); vv. 1–3 the words addressed to the listening worshippers (see on Ps. 34); and vv. 11, 12 the thanksgiving for restoration. Many commentators (*e.g.* Kirkpatrick) link this psalm (cf. Ps. 55) with the experience of David shortly before Absalom's rebellion (2 Sam. 13–18), regarding v. 9 as a reference to Ahithophel (2 Sam. 15: 31; cf. 16: 17).

Title: see Introduction III. 1, 2, 3. **1. Blessed:**

see on 1: 1. **regard for the weak:** NEB 'has a concern for the helpless' (Mt. 5: 7 reads like a paraphrase of this verse). **2. he will bless him:** lit. 'he shall be blessed' (the verb corresponding to the adjective of v. 1); the versions have 'he will bless him'. **desire:** Heb. *nepeš* (see on 3: 2), here meaning 'greed' (NEB). **3. restore him from his bed . . . :** a free translation based on the idea of 'changing' (RSVmg 'thou changest all his bed') his condition (cf. GNB); this seems more likely than the picture of a nurse making his bed (cf. NEB, JB).

5. his name: here probably 'the memory of him' (cf. 9: 5) rather than 'his posterity' (cf. 109: 13). **7. whisper:** cf. 2 Sam. 12: 19; here it could refer to the casting of magic spells (cf. v. 8). **imagine the worst:** rather, 'devise evil'. **saying:** not in *MT*. **8. vile disease:** lit. 'a thing of *bᵉliyyaʿal*' (see on 18: 4); probably a reference either to his sin (cf. Dt. 15: 9; Ps. 101: 3) or to a curse which has been put upon him (cf. NEB), operating as a fatal poison. **9. close friend:** lit. 'man of my peace', i.e. one with whom he had had a harmonious relationship (cf. 1 Sam. 18: 3; Jer. 20: 10); the reference here could be collective. **lifted:** lit. 'made great'; probably a picture of kicking or trampling on someone. In Jn 13: 18 this verse is applied to Judas Iscariot (see Introduction IV. 2). **shared my bread:** hospitality and sharing a meal create a bond of union and imply responsibility to protect and be loyal. **10. repay them:** see Introduction IV. 1. **11. pleased with me:** regard with favour. **12. integrity:** lit. 'blamelessness' (see on 15: 2; 18: 3). **presence:** lit. 'face' (see on 4: 6; 16: 11). **13. Praise:** Heb. *bārûk* (see on 26: 12). **Amen and Amen:** the response of the congregation (repetition for emphasis); Heb. *ʾāmēn* means 'truly', 'surely' (cf. Dt. 27: 15–26; 1 Kg. 1: 36). The doxology serves to conclude Book 1 of the Psalter.

Book Two Psalms 42–72

Psalms 42 and 43. PINING FOR GOD'S PRESENCE

There are good reasons for believing that these two psalms were originally a literary unity (cf. Pss. 9 and 10). Both have a common refrain (42: 5, 11; 43: 5); both are written in the same metre (*qînāh*); and both contain similar thought and language. In addition, Ps. 43 has no title (Ps. 71 is the only other psalm in Book Two without a title). It would seem that one poem has been split into two, probably for liturgical purposes. The psalm is clearly a lament, and probably an individual one; but some have suggested that it was a national lamentation recited by the king as the representative of his

people, perhaps when they were away on a military campaign (so Mowinckel). If it is an individual lament, the exact situation of the psalmist is not clear (cf. Ps. 84). He could have been one of the Jewish exiles in Babylonia in the sixth century B.C., or an Israelite refugee in some distant land during the period of the monarchy. Most would understand v.6 to mean that he was living in northern Palestine near the source of the Jordan, probably being a Levite (cf. title) exiled from the temple in Jerusalem, perhaps in the time of Jeroboam I (so Ellison; cf. 1 Kg. 12: 26 ff.; 2 Chr. 11: 13 ff.) or possibly in the time of Nehemiah (so N. H. Snaith, *Hymns of the Temple*, 1951, p. 43).

Our inability to tie down the exact situation of the writer hardly affects our general understanding of this beautiful psalm.

The poem falls into three stanzas. 42: 1–5 briefly describes the situation of one who is suffering from some unstated distress which causes his enemies to mock him. He calls to mind the joyful times in Jerusalem when the pilgrims flocked to the temple for the festivals, and yearns for the presence of God again. He clings to the hope that God will eventually rescue him and restore him to his post as temple-singer. 42: 6–11 underlines the severity of his predicament: he has experienced not only the awful proximity of death and the cutting taunts of his oppressors, but at times he has even felt abandoned by God Himself. Nevertheless, he cannot give up his hope in God. 43: 1–5 expresses his plea to God for vindication and deliverance which will result in his 'exodus' back to Jerusalem, once again to join in the praise of God in the temple. His prayer is undergirded by a deep certainty that God will not let him down. The main thought of the psalm has been beautifully paraphrased for Christian worship in the hymn, 'As pants the hart for cooling streams' (Tate and Brady).

Title: see Introduction III. 1, 2, 3. **42: 1. deer:** NEB 'hind', because the verb **pants** is feminine. **streams of water:** that do not dry up in summer (Jer. 17: 13; cf. 2: 13). **my soul:** 'myself' (see on 3: 2). **2. meet with God:** probably better read 'see the face of God': an expression for visiting the sanctuary and enjoying the presence and favour of God (see on Ps. 4: 6; cf. Gen. 43: 3; Ps. 84: 7). *MT* has 'appear before the face of God' which may be a scribal attempt to avoid the strong anthropomorphism which suggests that God can be seen (cf. an image of a pagan god). RSV 'behold the face of God' reads the same consonants with different vowels. **3. while men say:** following some Heb. MSS and Syr. *MT* has 'while one says'. **4. multitude, leading . . . :** two rare Heb. words. Possibly we should read either 'to the wonderful tabernacle (lit. 'booth'; cf. Ps. 27: 5)' with LXX (cf. JB), or 'how I used to go to the tabernacle of the Majestic One, even to . . .' (so A. A. Anderson). **festive throng:** or read 'the sound of pilgrims' (cf. NEB). **5.** NIV has conformed (probably rightly) the wording to 42: 11 (*q.v.*) and 43: 5.

6. This is most probably a description of northern Palestine from which the psalmist is speaking. NEB takes it as part of the word-picture of v. 7: his troubles are like the torrents of Jordan descending from the rocks of the Hermon range (the word **Hermon** is plural in Heb. here). **Mount Mizar** (lit. 'little mountain') is unknown; it may have been part of the Hermon range. **7.** God is the ultimate source of his troubles, whether or not they have been sent as a punishment (cf. 88: 7). Although the imagery may be based upon the geography of northern Palestine (cf. v. 6) there also seems to be an allusion to the mythological language used (*e.g.* in the Ugaritic texts) for the waters of chaos, the destructive powers of the underworld (i.e. Sheol; see on 6: 5). **Deep:** Heb. *tᵉhôm* (cf. Gen. 1: 2; 7: 4). **roar of your waterfalls:** lit. 'sound of thy waterspouts'; either the 'windows of heaven' (cf. Gen. 7: 4) or the channels of the primeval oceans of mythology. **8.** The verbs should probably be translated as past tenses: a reminiscence of the past days of happy fellowship with God (cf. v. 4; Isa. 30: 29). **love:** see on 5: 7. **9. Rock:** see on 18: 31. **forgotten:** i.e. failed to answer or act (cf. 13: 1 f.). **mourning:** see on 35: 14. **10. My bones suffer:** lit. 'with a shattering in my bones' (see on 6: 2). **11. my Savior:** lit. 'the salvations of my face'.

43: 1. Vindicate: lit. 'judge' (see on 72: 2). **ungodly:** 'disloyal', 'unfaithful' (cf. 4: 3); probably Jews. **men:** lit. 'man'; probably a collective. **mourning:** see on 35: 14. **3.** He asks to be led by God's Light and Truth as the Israelites were guided from Egypt to Canaan by a pillar of cloud and fire (cf. Exod. 13: 21; 15: 13). **holy mountain:** see on 2: 6. **4. harp:** Heb. *kinnôr* (see *NBD* art. 'Music and Musical Instruments'). **5.** See on 42: 11.

Psalm 44. THE PERPLEXED LAMENT OF A DEFEATED NATION

This national lament was no doubt composed during a time when Israel was suffering severe military defeats (cf. Ps. 60), and was originally used on a day of fasting called by the nation's leader in order to appeal to God for help (cf. 2 Chr. 20: 4 ff.; Jl 1: 14). The date of composition cannot be definitely fixed, but it seems more likely to have been during the period of the monarchy than in the post-exilic (Snaith) or Maccabaean (Calvin) periods. Two possible dates that have been suggested are the time of the crisis following Josiah's death (2 Kg. 23: 28 ff.) or during Sennacherib's invasion of Judah (2 Kg. 18: 13–19: 37).

The prayer is offered on behalf of the whole people by an individual—probably the king, but possibly the commander of the army or a religious leader—who speaks in the first person singular in vv. 4 ff., 15. The first stanza (vv. 1–8) is hymnic; it looks back to the saving deeds of God in the conquest of Canaan (vv. 1–3) and then uses that evidence as a basis for confidence and hope for victory (vv. 4–8. Note that it is difficult to know whether the tense of the verbs should be translated as present [NIV], past [JB] or future [AV, NEB]). The second stanza (vv. 9–16) recounts the present distress in the traditional form of a lament: they have been routed in battle (v. 10); some have been taken captive and deported to a foreign country (vv. 11 f.); the nation is scorned by her neighbours (vv. 13 f.); worst of all, Yahweh, their leader in past battles (cf. 1 Sam. 4: 3 ff.; 2 Sam. 5: 24), has apparently refused to help (v. 9). The third stanza (vv. 17–26) declares the nation's innocence of the charges of apostasy which might well have been levelled against it (cf. Dt. 4: 25 ff.; 6: 14 ff.), and its consequent perplexity at the present disaster (vv. 17–22), and ends with a passionate prayer for urgent help (vv. 23–26).

Title: see Introduction III. 1, 2, 3. **1. We have heard:** probably a reference to the cultic recital of salvation-history (cf. Ps. 78), possibly at a Covenant Renewal Festival (cf. v. 17; see on Ps. 50). **fathers:** cf. Dt. 6: 20 ff.; Jos. 4: 6, 21. **2. drove out:** lit. 'disinherited'. **planted:** cf. Exod. 15: 17; 2 Sam. 7: 10; Isa. 5: 1 ff.; Jer. 11: 7; 12: 2. **flourish:** 'spread out (like a plant)'; cf. Ps. 80: 8 ff. **3. arm:** i.e. 'strength'. **bring them victory:** lit. 'save them'. **right hand:** the more powerful (cf. Exod. 15: 6, 12; Lam. 2: 13). **light of your face:** God's favour and help (see on 4: 6). **4. King:** cf. 24: 7; 68: 24; 93: 1. **victories:** lit. 'salvations' (see on 35: 3). **5. push back . . . trample down:** as a wild ox (cf. Dt. 33: 17). **your name:** see on 20: 1. **8. Selah:** see Introduction III. 3. **12. sold:** like slaves (cf. Dt. 32: 30; Jg. 2: 14; 1 Sam. 12: 9; Isa. 50: 1). **14. byword:** or 'proverb' (see on 49: 4).

17 ff. 'Although the service of God is never perfect, it is possible to speak about loyalty and disloyalty to God, and therefore the claim of the nation need not be taken as an example of gross arrogance' (A. A. Anderson). **19. a haunt for jackals:** a proverbial expression for the wilderness as a place of ruin and devastation (cf. Isa. 34: 13; 35: 7; Jer. 9: 11; 10: 22). The meaning of the line is either that the country has been reduced to a waste or that the survivors have had to flee to the wilderness. **deep darkness:** *MT* has 'shadow of death' (see on 23: 4); cf. Isa. 9: 2; Ps. 107: 10, 14; Job 10: 21. **22. for your sake:** probably a reference to the fact that the reason for their suffering and its purpose are hidden in God (Weiser; cf. vv. 9–14) rather than the idea that they are suffering for their fidelity to God (A. A. Anderson); but cf. Paul's use in Rom. 8: 36. **23.** The puzzling inactivity of God is described in strongly anthropomorphic language which was probably not intended to be taken literally (cf. 1 Kg. 18: 27; Ps. 74: 11; 78: 65; 121: 4). **24. hide your face:** cf. Ps. 13: 1; 22: 24; 88: 14; Isa. 54: 8; 57: 17; Dt. 31: 17 f. **forget:** i.e. delay to take action about (cf. 9: 12). **25.** possibly a reference to the posture of sorrow and humiliation (cf. Dt. 9: 18; Jos. 7: 6; Ps. 119: 25; 137: 1; Isa. 47: 1). **26. Rise up:** possibly a reference to the Ark (cf.

Num. 10: 35). **redeem:** see on 49: 7. **unfailing love:** see on 5: 7.

Psalm 45. WEDDING SONG FOR A KING AND HIS BRIDE

There can be no doubt that songs like this were sung at royal weddings during the period of the Israelite monarchy. It is impossible, however, to identify the king for whom this particular song was originally composed—probably by a court poet or prophet. Some commentators favour a king from the northern kingdom (cf. v. 8) such as Ahab (cf. 1 Kg. 16: 31), Jehu or Jeroboam II; others feel that he must have been a Davidic monarch (cf. vv. 2, 6 f., 16 f. with 2 Sam. 7: 13 ff.) such as Solomon (cf. 1 Kg. 3: 1) or Jehoram (cf. 2 Kg. 8: 16). It is usually thought that the bride was a foreign princess (cf. v. 10), possibly from Tyre (cf. v. 12) or Egypt. At a later date, probably after the cessation of the monarchy, the psalm was given a messianic interpretation (so Targ.), the bride being taken as representing Israel (cf. Isa. 62: 5; Ezek. 16: 8–14). In Christian thought it has been applied to Christ (cf. Heb. 1: 8 f.) and to the Church as His bride (cf. Eph. 5: 23 ff.). Charles Wesley has given a superb Christian paraphrase of the psalm in his hymn 'My heart is full of Christ, and longs/ Its glorious matter to declare'. In the Prayer Book it is appointed for use on Christmas Day.

In v. 1 the enthusiastic poet introduces the subject of his song. The first part (vv. 2–9) addresses the king, finding proof of the divine blessing in his handsome appearance and gracious speech (v. 2); encouraging him to wage war against all falsehood, pride and injustice (vv. 3–5); and pointing to the splendour of his magnificent robes and the opulence of his court as evidence of his unique status as God's chosen representative (vv. 6–9). The second part (vv. 10–15) firstly addresses the bride, exhorting her to accept her new position with its consequent sacrifices and duties, but above all with its rewards and satisfactions, and yield herself to the king (vv. 10–12); then the poet describes the joyful occasion when she will be conducted into the palace to consummate the union with her royal husband (vv. 13–15). Finally (vv. 16, 17), the king is addressed again with a benediction which promises a permanent dynasty, universal rule and perpetual renown.

Title: see Introduction III 1, 2, 3. **1.** The poem is probably thought of as inspired by God and thus carrying the divine promise (cf. v. 17). **2.** Cf. 1 Sam. 9: 2; 10: 23; 16: 12; 2 Sam. 14: 25; 1 Kg. 1: 6; etc. Such language could easily become stereotyped and idealistic: '. . . it is doubtful whether *all* dynastic kings qualified as paragons of perfection' (A. A. Anderson). **forever:** see on 23: 6. **4. in behalf of . . . :** LXX and Vulg. have 'because of truth and meekness and righteousness'. The first line of this verse provided the inspiration for H. Milman's hymn, 'Ride on, ride on in majesty'. **5.** NIV reverses the order of the last two lines. **6.** Cf. 2 Sam. 7: 13, 16. Your **throne, O God** is supported by the ancient versions (cf. Heb. 1: 8). Although the Israelite king was not regarded as divine (as the kings of Egypt were), it is possible that he could be addressed as 'God' either in a form of Oriental hyperbolic language or as a representative of God (cf. Exod. 21: 6; 22: 8, 9, 28; Ps. 82: 6). The RSV rendering, 'your divine throne', is less likely but finds some support in 1 Chr. 28: 5; 29: 23. **scepter:** symbol of kingship. **7. anointing:** see on 2: 2. **God, your God:** the original form was probably 'Yahweh your God'. **8. palaces adorned with ivory:** cf. 1 Kg. 10: 18; 22: 39; Am. 3: 15; 6: 4; and see *NBD* art. 'Ivory'. **9. royal bride:** the bride rather than the queen mother (cf. Neh. 2: 6; Dan. 5: 2, 23). **Ophir:** the location of this source of choice gold is unknown (cf. 1 Kg. 9: 28; 10: 11; 22: 48; Isa. 13: 12). **10. Forget your people:** cf. Dt. 21: 13; Ru. 1: 16. **11. lord:** i.e. husband (cf. Gen. 18: 12; Jg. 19: 26, 27). **12. Daughter of Tyre:** probably a reference to the people (cf. 9: 14; 137: 8) rather than to the princess; in which case there is no necessity to regard the bride as Tyrian. **16 f. Your . . . you:** the pronouns are masculine and therefore refer to the king. **17.** The speaker is the psalmist, but he is probably to be regarded as speaking for God (cf. v. 1). **memory:** lit., 'name'.

Psalm 46. A MIGHTY FORTRESS IS OUR GOD

The origin of this psalm is often sought in some great deliverance such as that of Judah under Jehoshaphat (2 Chr. 20) or that of Jerusalem under Hezekiah (2 Kg. 18: 13–19: 36). Suitable though it would have been to use on occasions like these, there is nothing in the psalm that would tie it to a particular historical event. It may well be, therefore, that the psalm was composed to be used in the Jerusalem cult as part of the celebration of God's choice of Zion, and should be classified as a hymn of Zion (cf. Ps. 48 and Introduction II. 2).

The first stanza (vv. 1–3) envisages the ultimate world-catastrophe: the dissolution of the natural world by the forces of chaos. If such a cataclysm occurs, the confidence of God's people is that even at the end of the world God's powerful presence will remain like an unshakable rock. (The refrain of vv. 7 and 11, probably sung as a response by the congregation or by an antiphonal choir, seems to have been accidentally omitted after v. 3.) The

second stanza (vv. 4–7) depicts the peaceful refreshment of Jerusalem, the holy city, unaffected by the attacks of the nations who storm its walls, since it is defended by the God who lives amongst His people. The third stanza (vv. 8–11) points to the deliverances of God in history as pledges and foretastes of the day when God will finally destroy all warmongers and establish His eternal kingdom of peace on earth.

Luther's paraphrase *Ein' feste Burg ist unser Gott*, translated by Thomas Carlyle as 'A safe stronghold our God is still' and by F. H. Hedges as 'A mighty fortress is our God', expresses in Christian terms the same confidence in the reality of the protective presence of God with His people. (See also comments on Ps. 48.)

Title: see Introduction III. 1, 2, 3. **1. an ever present help:** i.e. He has fully proved Himself in the past to be a reliable help in times of trouble (cf. Isa. 55: 6). **2, 3.** The imagery in these verses seems to be based upon mythological descriptions of the primeval conditions at creation, when God conquered the forces of chaos (cf. Job 26: 5–13; Ps. 74: 12 ff.; 89: 8 ff.). **3. Selah:** see Introduction III. 3. **4. a river:** i.e. a perennial stream (not a wadi). The spring of Gihon, whose waters Hezekiah brought into Jerusalem by a tunnel (2 Chr. 32: 30), seems to have been used as a symbol of God's refreshing presence (cf. Isa. 8: 6 f.; 33: 21). There may also be a reference back to the Garden of Eden (cf. Gen. 2: 10). The blessing and joy of God's presence streams out from Jerusalem to the whole world (cf. Ps. 65: 9; 87: 7; Isa. 33: 21; Ezek. 47: 1 ff.; Jl 3: 18; Zech. 14: 8). **the holy place . . . :** LXX and Vulg. have 'the Most High has sanctified his habitation'. **Most High:** see on 47: 2 (cf. Gen. 14: 18 ff.). **5.** Cf. Jl 3: 17; Mic. 3: 11; Zeph. 3: 15. **at break of day:** lit. 'at the turn (i.e. dawn) of the morning' (cf. 1 Sam. 11: 9; 2 Chr. 20: 17; Ps. 5: 3; 17: 15; 90: 14; 143: 8). **6. are in uproar:** Cf. Ps. 2: 1 ff.; Isa. 17: 12 ff. **his voice:** cf. 29: 3–9. **melts:** i.e. in fear (cf. Exod. 15: 15; Isa. 14: 31). **7. LORD Almighty:** see on 24: 10. **is with us:** cf. Isa. 7: 14; 8: 8; 10. **God of Jacob:** see on 20: 1. **fortress:** lit. 'stronghold' (cf. 9: 1). **8. Come and see:** cf. 66: 3 ff. The saving acts of Yahweh may have been represented in a cultic drama. **9. bow:** symbol of military power (cf. 1 Sam. 2: 4). **shields:** MT is lit. 'wagons'. LXX, Targ. and Vulg. may be right in reading the same consonants as **shields** (cf. JB, NEB, GNB). **10. Be still:** probably a command to the nations to cease their fighting and to acknowledge the supremacy of God (cf. 1 Kg. 18: 37; Ps. 59: 13; 100: 3; Jer. 16: 21; Ezek. 6: 7, 13; 7: 27; 11: 10); or possibly directed to the people of God counselling them to reject all foreign alliances (cf. Isa. 30: 15). **11.** See on v. 7.

Psalm 47. KING OF ALL THE EARTH

This is one of a group of psalms (see also 93; 96–99) which celebrate God's kingship not only over Israel but over the whole world. There are three main ways of understanding this psalm. The *historical* interpretation sees it as a victory song in honour of a recent deliverance (*e.g.* the defeat of the Assyrians in the time of Hezekiah; cf. 2 Kg. 19: 35 ff.); the *eschatological* interpretation regards it as a hymn which anticipates the future establishment of the kingdom of God on earth; and the *cultic* interpretation understands it either as an enthronement psalm or as a psalm celebrating the kingship of Yahweh, used at the autumn New Year festival (see Introduction II. 2). If we combine these approaches, we may view the psalm as a hymn composed for use at the autumn festival and probably associated with a procession of the ark (cf. v. 5) into the sanctuary (cf. v. 8); celebrating not only the present kingship of God (v. 7), but also looking back to the past evidences of His sovereignty in history (vv. 3, 4) and looking forward to the future when His reign would be universally accepted (vv. 8, 9). Each of these aspects may possibly have been represented in the liturgy by dramatic actions.

Christian interpretation, taking its cue from v. 5, has often linked this psalm with the ascension of Christ: cf. hymns like 'God is gone up on high' by C. Wesley, and 'God is ascended up on high' by H. More.

Title: see Introduction III. 1, 2, 3. **1. Clap your hands:** cf. 2 Kg. 11: 12; Ps. 98: 8. **shout:** cf. 1 Sam. 10: 24. **all nations:** all the nations (perhaps represented by the people of Israel) envisaged as joining in the acclamation of God. **2. Most High:** '*Elyôn* was the ancient name for '*Ēl*, the high god of the Canaanite pantheon, and also the name of the chief deity of the Jebusite cult in Jerusalem before the time of David (cf. Gen. 14: 18–24). When used of Yahweh it stresses His supremacy over all the other gods (cf. Ps. 95: 3). **The great King:** the self-designation of the Assyrian kings (cf. 2 Kg. 18: 19). **3.** Most probably a reference to the conquest of Canaan (cf. 44: 1 ff.) and possibly also to the victories of David. The verbs could, however, be translated as present (JB, NEB) or future (RV) tenses. **4. chose:** cf. Dt. 7: 6 ff.; 14: 2; 32: 8 ff. **inheritance:** the promised land. **pride of Jacob:** Canaan was the 'proud possession' of Israel (cf. Dan. 8: 9). **loved:** see on 26: 8.

5. This could be a reference to God ascending again into heaven after His descent to earth to deliver His people (cf. Isa. 31: 4), but it is more likely to refer to a procession of the ark (symbol of Yahweh's presence) up to the temple (see on Ps. 24). **shouts:** cf. Num. 23: 21. **trumpets:** particularly used at the New Year (cf. Lev. 23:

24; Num. 29: 1) and at coronations (cf. 1 Kg. 1: 39; 2 Kg. 9: 13; 11: 12). **7. a psalm:** Heb. *maskîl* (see Introduction III. 1); the meaning here may be 'skilfully' or 'with understanding'. **8. God reigns:** see on Ps. 93: 1. **holy throne:** either in heaven (cf. Ps. 11: 4) or above the ark in the sanctuary (cf. 1 Sam. 4: 4; 2 Sam. 6: 2; Ps. 80: 1; 99: 1; Jer. 3: 16 f.). **9.** It may be that some representatives of foreign nations were occasionally present at festivals in Jerusalem, in which case their presence could be viewed as symbolic of the time when all peoples would come to worship Yahweh (cf. Isa. 2: 2 ff.; Zech. 8: 20 ff.). **as the people:** NIV supplies 'as'; possibly 'with' should be read (cf. GNB, NEB). **Abraham:** cf. Gen. 17: 4; 18: 18. **Kings:** or 'shields' NIVmg, symbolizing 'rulers' (cf. 84: 9; 89: 18).

Psalm 48. THE GOD OF ZION

Like Ps. 46 this psalm may well be classified as a hymn of Zion, provided that it is remembered that it is the God of Zion, rather than Zion itself, who is the focus of attention. The older commentators saw Pss. 46–48 as a trilogy celebrating the miraculous deliverance of Jerusalem under Hezekiah (2 Kg. 19: 35 ff.). More recently it has been suggested that these psalms belong to the ritual of the autumn New Year festival (see Introduction II. 2 and comments on Pss. 46; 47). If so, then Ps. 48 could well have been used to accompany or precede a procession round the walls of Jerusalem (cf. vv. 12 f.). The procession itself may have been part of a cultic drama in which the divine defence of Jerusalem against the attacks of the nations (vv. 4–7) was made a present reality (cf. vv. 8, 9). 'This psalm . . . tells us something of the psychological effect of a great festival on the participants, of the rejoicing, enthusiasm, and deep gratitude called forth by that which the cultic performance actualized' (Ringgren, p. 17).

Verses 1–3 weave together the two strands of the praise of God and the glorification of Zion. Verses 4–7 depict a scene of the banding together of hostile kings against Jerusalem, a situation which, whilst it could be illustrated from Judah's history (see below), is more likely a 'typical, traditional, half-mythological' description (cf. Ps. 2: 2) which is 'meant to assert that no enemies, be they ever so strong, will be able to do any serious harm to those who are on the Lord's side' (Ringgren, p. 106). Verses 8–11 express the joyful reaction of those who witness the presentation (or listen to the recital) of the protective and saving acts of God. Finally in vv. 12–14 the worshipping pilgrims are called to take part in a thanksgiving procession (cf. Neh. 12: 27 ff.) around the walls of Jerusalem which would 'impress the picture of the holy city upon their memory as deeply as possible' (Weiser) so that they will be able to tell their children at home that the God of Zion is the eternal protector of His people.

Christian interpretation applies this psalm to the Church (cf. Mt. 16: 18) as the NT counterpart to Zion (cf. Heb. 12: 22). John Newton's hymn 'Glorious things of thee are spoken', though primarily based on Ps. 87 and Isa. 33: 20 f., illustrates very well the Christian use of the hymns of Zion. (See also Introduction IV. I.) The Prayer Book appoints the psalm for use on Whitsunday, regarded as the birthday of the Church.

Title: see Introduction III. 1, 2. **2. Mount Zion:** see 2: 6. **Zaphon** (Heb. ṣāpôn): Mount Zaphon was regarded in the Ugaritic myths as the dwelling-place of the god Ba'al-Hadad (cf. Isa. 14: 13 and cf. Mount Olympus as the home of the Greek gods). The meaning here seems to be that Zion is the true 'Far North' (cf. NIVmg), i.e. the dwelling-place of Yahweh. **the Great King:** see on 47: 2. **4 ff.** These verses could refer to definite historical events such as the Syro-Ephraimite alliance (2 Kg. 16: 5) or the Assyrian attack under Sennacherib (2 Kg. 18: 13–19: 36; cf. Isa. 10: 8); but more likely refer to a 'symbolic or dramatic representation of God's victory over his enemies' (Ringgren, p. 16). **7. by an east wind:** or 'As the east wind shatters . . .' **ships of Tarshish:** large sea-going vessels, probably named after the smelted metal they were designed to carry, or possibly built in Tartessus, a Phoenician colony in Spain (see *NBD art.* 'Tarshish'). The reference here may be symbolic of the enemies of God (cf. 72: 10) and particularly of their wealth, power and pride (cf. Isa. 2: 16). **8. Lord Almighty:** see on 24: 10. **Selah:** see Introduction III. 3.

9. meditate on: or 'picture' (lit. 'make like'); cf. NEB 'we re-enacted the story . . .'. **unfailing love:** see on 5: 7. **10. name:** see on 20: 1. **right hand:** God's power. **righteousness:** see on 33: 5. **11. villages of Judah:** her towns and villages (cf. 97: 8). **judgments:** the punishment of her enemies was also the deliverance of Judah. **12.** After a siege it would be necessary to inspect the city to see that it was unharmed; but here the reference is probably to a cultic procession. **13. ramparts:** the sloping bank (or bulwark) which protects the foot of the walls. **citadels:** heavily fortified parts of the palace. **14. For this God is our God:** or 'Such is God' (NEB). All the strength of Zion points to the protective power of God. **guide:** possibly the picture of a shepherd (cf. 77: 20; 78: 52; 80: 1). **even to the end:** a slight emendation supported by LXX, Vulg; *MT* reads 'unto dying', the significance of which is not clear. Some consider it part of the title of Ps. 49; others suggest the translation 'against Death' (cf 49: 14).

Psalm 49. MAN'S FINAL DESTINY

The opening verses suggest that this is a wisdom psalm (see Introduction II. 3), written for the instruction of men rather than the praise of God; and the contents confirm this by displaying a number of parallels with such wisdom literature as Job, Proverbs and Ecclesiastes. The author, who probably lived after the exile, grapples with the problem of the inequalities of life (cf. Pss 37 and 73) and presents a solution which came to him after a period of meditation.

Verses 1–4 form an introduction in which the psalmist calls on everyone (not just the people of Israel) to listen to his teaching (cf. 78: 1 ff). The psalm then falls into two main sections, each ending with a similar refrain (vv. 12, 20). In the first section (vv. 5–12) the writer demonstrates the limitations of wealth: it can buy neither lengthening of life nor release from Death. In the second section (vv. 13–20) he describes in more detail the inevitable fate of the oppressive rich who, when the day of swift and brutal retribution arrives, have to leave everything behind; but he finds consolation in the belief that God can rescue the poor and upright man from the grasp of the underworld (v. 15).

Verse 15 is theologically the most important statement in the psalm, providing the answer to the negative of v. 7; but its precise meaning is not clear. Does the writer simply envisage deliverance from an untimely death such as the wicked meet (see on Pss. 16 and 37; cf. Job 15: 32; Ps 18: 4 ff.; 30: 2f.; 73: 17 ff.; 86: 13; 102: 24; 103: 3 ff.; 116: 3, 8; Isa 38: 10; Jer 17: 11)? Or does he believe that he will escape death, either by being 'taken' into God's presence *before* death (cf. Gen 5: 24; 2 Kg. 2: 11) or by being 'raised' from Sheol *after* death (cf. Isa. 26: 19; Dan. 12: 2)? The problem that faces the psalmist would seem to need a solution which involves a different destination for the righteous and for the wicked (cf. Lk. 16: 25); but whether he has reached that answer, which is rarely found in the OT, is not absolutely certain (cf. Ps. 73). What is clear is that the psalm teaches that 'in death itself the difference between the man who serves God and the man who scorns Him is made apparent. The psalmist is sure that his God will not let him suffer the fate of the impious; through faith, he asserts that God will be with him, the hand of Sheol is impotent against the presence of Yahweh with those who are His own' (R. Martin-Achard, *From Death to Life*, 1960, p. 157). (For the Christian approach to this psalm see Introduction IV. 1.)

It should be noted that there are a number of textual problems in this psalm which means that the translation in places cannot be more than tentative.

Title: see Introduction III. 1, 2, 3. **2. low and high:** lit. 'sons of mankind (Heb. *'ādām*) and sons of a man (Heb. *'îš*)'. The context seems to demand a contrast (see on 4: 2; 62: 9), but the meaning may simply be 'all mankind, every living man' (NEB). **rich and poor** (Heb. *'ebyôn*): practically equivalent to 'unjust and righteous' (see on 9: 18). **3. utterance:** or 'meditation', see on 1: 2. **heart:** see on 17: 3; cf. 45: 1. **4. proverb:** Heb. *māšāl* (cf. Prov. 1: 1) can also mean 'taunt' (Ps. 44: 14), 'allegory' (Ezek. 17: 2) and 'oracle' (Num. 23: 7). Here it may mean a 'didactic poem', a 'wise saying' or 'instruction' received by inspiration (cf. Ps. 78: 2). **expound:** or 'solve', lit. 'open'. **riddle:** or perplexing problem (cf. 1 Kg. 10: 1). **harp:** music is used either to induce ecstasy (cf. 1 Sam. 10: 5; 2 Kg. 3: 5) or to accompany the instruction (cf. NEB).

5. deceivers: those who 'dog his heels' (cf. JB) and seek to supplant him (cf. Gen. 37: 36; Jer. 9: 4). **6.** Wealth itself is not condemned (cf. 1 Tim 6: 17). **7. redeem:** (Heb. *pādāh*). The verb is used in the OT for the rescue of a slave or captive (Exod. 21: 8) and the redemption of a person or animal from death (Exod. 13: 13; 21: 30) by payment either of a substitute or of money (Exod. 13: 13; Num. 18: 15 f.). It is also used figuratively to denote deliverance from any sort of trouble (cf. Ps. 26: 11; 78: 42; 119: 134). **a ransom:** lit. 'his ransom' (Heb. *kōper*) or 'the price of his life' or 'his substitute payment' (cf. Exod. 30: 12f.; Num. 35: 31; Prov. 6:35; 13:18). **8. ransom:** or 'redemption' (Heb. *pidyôn*); cf. Exod. 21: 30. **9. decay:** see 16: 10 on 'the Pit'. **10.** Cf. Ec. 2: 14 ff. **foolish:** see Prov. 1: 7. **senseless:** see Prov. 12: 1. **12.** Cf. Ec. 3: 19; here the statement seems to apply to the wealthy and wicked.

13. sayings: lit. 'mouth'. The difficult phrase could be translated 'Thus end those who are pleased with their own talk' (Weiser). **Selah:** see Introduction III. 3. **14. the grave:** see on 6: 5. **death:** in Ugaritic literature Mot (Death) is the god of the underworld (cf. Job 18: 13 f.; 28: 2; Jer. 9: 21; Hos. 13: 14). **feed on them:** or possibly read 'be their shepherd' (RSV). **in the morning** NIV follows *MT* which makes fair sense (cf. Mal. 4: 3); 'morning' is the time for judgment or vindication (cf. 17: 15; 46: 5). **15. redeem:** see on v. 7. **my life:** 'me' (see on 3: 2). **take:** the same verb as in Gen. 5: 24; 2 Kg. 2: 3 ff. **16. Do not be overawed:** cf. v. 5; possibly 'Do not envy' (NEB; cf. 73: 3). **17.** Cf. Job 1: 21; Ec. 5: 15. **19. he:** *MT* 'you' or 'she'; RSV follows LXX, Vulg. **generation of his fathers:** cf. Gen. 49: 29. **never see the light:** Cf. Job 17: 13; Ps. 88: 12. **20. without understanding:** *MT* has 'does not understand' (cf. JB 'Man in his prosperity forfeits intelligence').

Psalm 50. GOD'S ASSESSMENT OF HIS PEOPLE'S WORSHIP

The form and content of this psalm resemble those of the oracles of the prophets (cf. Isa. 1: 10–20; Am. 5: 21–24). It could have been originally delivered by a cultic prophet during a religious festival in Jerusalem, perhaps one associated with the renewal of the covenant (see Introduction II. 2). Some would place it either in the time of Hezekiah's religious reformation (2 Kg. 18: 4 ff.) or during Josiah's reformation and covenant renewal (2 Kg. 23).

There is a clear structure. Verses 1–6 form an introductory hymn which describes the impressive appearance of God, coming as Judge to call to account those who are under a special obligation to Him. The first part of the divine rebuke (vv. 7–15) deals with the dishonouring of God in the sacrificial cult. In spite of all their religious zeal the people are failing to take seriously the *spiritual* nature of God. They are behaving as though He needed their gifts; as though outward ritual were enough to satisfy Him. The second part of the divine rebuke (vv. 16–21) deals with the dishonouring of God in the everyday lives of those who have taken part in the worship of God. There is no question of ignorance of God's law: they can recite the commandments from memory word perfect. What is condemned is the superficial, legalistic, casuistical approach which claims to know and obey God's law, but in practice manages to evade and completely disregard its clear demands. They are failing to take seriously the *moral* nature of God. As a conclusion, vv. 22, 23 issue the Judge's final warning. He has the authority and power either to carry out the sentence on the guilty or to vindicate those who honour Him not only with their lips but also in their lives.

Title: see Introduction III. 1, 2. **1. The Mighty One, God, the LORD:** Heb. *'Ēl 'elōhîm Yahweh* (cf. Jos. 22: 22). *'Ēl* (possibly derived from a root meaning 'to be strong' or 'to be first') was the general Semitic word for 'God' and the name of the chief god of the Canaanite pantheon; *'elōhîm* (plural) was used for 'God' (possibly plural of intensity) or 'gods'; *Yahweh* was the distinctive name of Israel's God (see on Exod. 3: 15). LXX, Syr., Vulg. translate 'The God of gods, the Lord' (cf. 84: 7). **2, 3.** The theophany emanating from Mount Zion (cf. Am. 1: 2) is described in terms of that at Mount Sinai (see on 18: 7–15). **Zion:** see on 2: 6. **perfect in beauty:** cf. Lam. 2: 15; Ps. 48: 2. **shines forth:** cf. 80: 1; 104: 2. **4.** In the Hittite treaties (covenants) heaven and earth, mountains and rivers are among the witnesses to the treaty. Here they are called on to witness that the oath has been broken (cf. Jos. 24: 26 f.; Isa. 1: 2 ff.; Jer. 2: 4 ff.; Mic. 6: 2 ff.). **5. consecrated ones** (Heb. *ḥasîdîm*):

ḥesed is the ideal characteristic of a covenant people (see on 4: 3; 5: 7). There may be a touch of irony here (cf. v. 16). **made** (lit. 'cut') **a covenant:** a reference either to its original ratification (cf. Exod. 24: 5 ff.) or to a recent renewal (cf. Jos. 24: 25 ff.; 2 Kg. 23: 1 ff.). **by sacrifice:** cf. Gen. 15: 9 ff.; Jer. 34: 18; Exod. 24: 5 ff. **6. Selah:** see Introduction III. 3.

7. I am God: perhaps originally 'I am Yahweh' (cf. Exod. 20: 2; Dt. 5: 6). **8. sacrifices . . . burnt offerings:** see on 40: 6. **10.** Cf. 1 Chr. 29: 14; Dt. 10: 14; Ps. 24: 1. **on a thousand hills:** or 'on my mountains in their thousands' (cf. NEB). **12, 13.** Cf. Dt. 32: 28; Lev. 3: 11; 21: 6 ff.; Num. 28: 2; Ezek. 44: 7. **blood:** cf. Gen. 9: 4; Lev. 1: 5, 11; 3: 5; 17: 11; Dt. 12: 23, 27. **14.** It is difficult to decide whether to translate 'Sacrifice a thanksgiving offering' (cf. Lev. 7: 12; 22: 29; Ps. 56: 12; Am. 4: 5) or 'Offer a hymn of thanksgiving' (cf. Ps. 26: 7; 42: 4; 69: 30). **vows:** probably to offer sacrifices (see on 61: 5; cf. 22: 25 f.; 56: 12). There is nothing in the psalm to suggest that sacrifice itself is being repudiated (see on 40: 6 ff.). **16.** Some of the 'consecrated ones' (v. 5) are **wicked. 17. instruction:** cf. Prov. 12: 1. **my words:** cf. Exod. 34: 28; Dt. 4: 13; 10: 4. **18. you throw in your lot:** lit. 'your portion is . . .' (cf. 119: 57). **20.** Cf. 2 Sam. 16: 1-4; 1 Kg. 21: 8-14; Jer. 9: 4; Mic. 7: 6. **21.** NEB 'and shall I keep silence?' is possible. **22. forget:** cf. Jg. 3: 7; Dt. 8: 19; Job 8: 13. **23. thank offerings:** see on v. 14. **honors:** cf. Mal. 1: 6.

Psalm 51. A PRAYER FOR FORGIVENESS

This individual lament is most suitably called a 'Penitential Psalm' (see on Ps. 6). The heading links it with the experience of David recorded in 2 Sam. 11-12, and it obviously fits that situation to a large extent, being an expansion of David's confession of 2 Sam. 12: 13. But some commentators are doubtful whether the psalm should be attributed to David (see Introduction III. 2). The religious ideas are said to fit better an origin in the seventh or sixth centuries B.C., resembling as they do the teaching of Jeremiah and Ezekiel. H. H. Rowley suggested that the psalm was composed with David in mind, to be used by others who were conscious of similar flagrant sins (*From Moses to Qumran*, 1963, p. 96). J. I. Durham recommends that 'it is best to refrain from dogmatic conclusions concerning this psalm's authorship, either to identify it with David or to deny that it relates to David's experience'. Verses 18, 19 are usually regarded as a later addition (exilic or post-exilic) adapting the psalm for congregational use. Some (*e.g.* Eaton) think that it was originally intended to express the penitence of the community, uttered by its representative (king, governor or

high priest). In the synagogue it may now be recited on the Day of Atonement, and in the Prayer Book it is appointed for Ash Wednesday.

The psalm opens (vv. 1, 2) with urgent pleas for forgiveness, based upon the psalmist's knowledge of the merciful character of God (cf. Exod. 34: 6 f.). The genuineness of his confession is demonstrated by his profound understanding of the true nature of sin in its outward, inward and Godward aspects (vv. 3-5). Verses 6-12 express his deep desire for inward cleansing and spiritual renewal; whilst vv. 13-17 declare his determination to show his gratitude not only in humble thanksgiving, but also in a public testimony to the saving acts of God (cf. 9: 1 f.; 22: 25; 40: 9 f.). The conclusion (vv. 18, 19) asks that God will enable Jerusalem to be rebuilt so that the cultic observances, impossible to carry out during the exile, may be resumed, to the pleasure of God.

Title: see Introduction III. 1, 2, 3. **1. have mercy on:** or 'be gracious to'; the verb usually expresses the attitude of a superior to an inferior, carrying with it the idea of unmerited favour. **unfailing love:** see on 5: 7. **your great compassion:** lit. 'the multitude of thy mercies'; 'mercies' here represents a word which in the singular usually means 'womb' (cf. Isa. 49: 15) or 'bowels' (cf. Phil. 2: 1, AV), thus it signifies deeply-felt compassion. **blot out:** as from a book (cf. Exod. 32: 32; Neh. 13: 14). **transgressions . . . 2. iniquity . . . sin:** see on 32: 1 f. **wash:** the verb is used of washing clothes by treading them (cf. Exod. 19: 10, 14; 2 Sam. 19: 24; Jer. 2: 22). **cleanse:** a cultic term (cf. Lev. 13: 6, 13, 17). **3. I know:** or 'I acknowledge' RV (cf. Isa. 49: 12). **4.** Sin, even when directed against one's fellow man, is in the last analysis rebellion against God: 'sin is ultimately a religious concept rather than an ethical one' (Weiser). Cf. 2 Sam. 12: 13; Gen. 39: 9; Prov. 14: 13; 17: 5. **so that:** his confession of culpability reveals the justice of God's punishment (cf. Jos. 7: 19). **justified:** lit. 'clear'. **5.** There is no suggestion here that the processes of birth or conception are sinful in themselves, nor that the birth of the psalmist was illegitimate. 'The Psalmist confesses his total involvement in human sinfulness, from the very beginning of his existence' (A. A. Anderson). This is not offered as an excuse, but rather as an additional evidence of his utter sinfulness (cf. 58: 3).

6. truth: see on 25: 5. **wisdom:** see on 111: 10. **7. cleanse:** lit. 'un-sin' (cf. Num. 8: 21; 19: 12 ff.). **hyssop:** symbol of cleansing (cf. Exod. 12: 22; Lev. 14: 1 ff.; Num. 19: 6, 18). **wash:** see on v. 2. **snow:** fairly rare in Palestine (cf. Isa. 1: 18; Exod. 4: 6; Num. 11: 10; 2 Kg. 5: 27; Lam. 4: 7; Dan. 7: 9). **8. Let me hear:** RSV

has 'Fill me', but *MT* (RSVmg, NEB, GNB, NIV)
makes good sense: the psalmist will not be
truly happy until he hears a divine oracle giving
him absolution (cf. 2 Sam. 12: 12). **bones:** see
on 6: 2 (cf. 38: 3). **rejoice:** 'jump for joy' or
'dance' (NEB). **9. blot out:** see on v. 1. **10.**
Forgiveness is not enough. 'Unless a radical
change is wrought by God, the future will be
but a repetition of the past' (A. A. Anderson).
Cf. 1 Sam. 10: 6, 9; Jer. 32: 39; Ezek. 11: 29;
36: 25 ff. **Create:** the subject of the verb (Heb.
bārā') is always God; the result is always something completely new (cf. Gen. 1: 1; Isa. 45: 8;
48: 6 f.). **heart:** the whole of a man's inner life,
but especially his will (choices) and his mind
(thoughts). A **pure heart** probably means an
undivided will or single-mindedness in doing
God's will. **spirit:** probably a synonym for
'heart' (cf. v. 17), but with some emphasis on
attitudes and motivation. A **steadfast** ('loyal',
GNB) **spirit** desires to please God (cf. v. 12).
11. presence: lit. 'face'; the reference here may
be particularly to taking part in temple worship
(cf. 42: 2). **do not take:** cf. 1 Sam 16: 14 (cf.
15: 24 ff.). **your Holy Spirit** (or 'spirit'): the
phrase is found in the OT only here and in Isa.
63: 10 f., where it seems to denote the presence
of God amongst His people. **12. joy:** 'the joy
in the helpful nearness of God is the actual
motive-power of the new way of life which
the poet here envisages' (Weiser). Cf. 13: 5 f.;
35: 9. **salvation:** see on 35: 3; here not simply
forgiveness but the blessings that follow.
14. bloodguilt: lit. 'bloods'; a reference
either to murder (cf. 2 Sam. 12: 14 ff.) or to
impending death (cf. 30: 9) as the punishment
for sin. **righteousness:** see on 33: 5. **15. open
my lips:** he is unable to worship God in his
sinful condition (cf. Isa. 6: 5; Ezek. 16: 23; Ps.
66: 18). **16, 17.** An absolute repudiation of all
animal sacrifices cannot be intended (see on
40: 6 ff.). There were no atoning sacrifices
prescribed for deliberate sins (cf. Num. 15: 30
f.) like murder and adultery; the sinner could
only throw himself in penitence upon the
mercy of God (cf. Hos. 14: 1 ff.; Jl 2: 12 ff.).
17. *MT* has **the sacrifices of God**; NIVmg is a
possible emendation (cf. NEB). **spirit . . .
heart:** see on v. 10. Cf. Isa. 57: 15; Ezek. 11:
19; 36: 26. **18. Zion:** see on 2: 6. **walls:** may
refer not only to the defences of the city restored under Nehemiah in 444 B.C. (Neh. 1:
3; 2: 17; 6: 15 f.), but also to the walls of the
temple which was finished under Zerubbabel
in 515 B.C. (Ezr. 6: 14 f.). **19. righteous:** either
the proper sacrifices offered at the appropriate
times (cf. NEB, GNB), or those offered in a right
spirit (cf. Dt. 33: 19; Ps. 4: 5). **whole burnt
offerings:** see on 40: 6. *MT* has 'burnt offering
and whole burnt offering' which may be an
explanatory gloss for 'righteous sacrifices'.
bulls: very costly sacrifices.

Psalm 52. TRUE AND FALSE SECURITY

The first part of the psalm (vv. 1–7) is like an
individual lament, but it is addressed to the
wicked man who is oppressing the righteous,
not to God Himself. It is reminiscent of the
prophetic message of judgment on the individual (cf. Isa. 22: 15–19). The second part (vv. 8,
9) is like a psalm of trust or of thanksgiving.
Its life-setting is not clear; Weiser believes that
it was used when the evildoer was arraigned
before the congregation, cursed and then expelled from the community. The speaker
would be a prophet or priest as representative
of the people. The heading (see Introduction
III. 2) links the psalm with an incident in the
life of David (1 Sam. 22: 9–19), but some of
the contents (*e.g.* the apparent reference to the
Temple in v. 8, and the lack of any reference
to the savage slaughter at Nob) make such an
identification difficult for many.

Title: see Introduction III. 1, 2, 3. NIV expands the difficult *MT* to make three lines, and
reads *hesed 'ēl* as **disgrace [in the eyes] of God**.
RSV 'against the godly' (cf. NEB) assumes that
the two words have been transposed and
wrongly vocalized. Perhaps they should be
omitted as a gloss. Yet *MT* can make fair sense:
'Why do you boast, great man, of your evil?
God's love is eternal (GNB cf. AV, RV), i.e.
nothing the tyrant does can shake God's faithfulness to His people. **2.** Cf. Prov. 18: 21. **who
practice deceit:** cf. 101: 7. **3. falsehood:** i.e.
slander (cf. 119: 29; Exod. 23: 1–9). **truth:** lit.
'righteousness'. **Selah:** see Introduction III. 3.
4. love: see on 26: 8. **harmful word:** i.e. that
is destructive (cf. 35: 25). **5. tent:** i.e. 'home'
(cf. Job 18: 14; Ps. 132: 3). It is unlikely to refer
to the temple (as Weiser suggests). **uproot:** cf.
v. 8; 1: 3. **6. righteous:** see on Ps. 1. **fear:** be
filled with awe (cf. 34: 9). **laugh:** probably not
malicious joy (cf. Prov. 24: 17) but gladness
that God has vindicated the godly (cf. 54: 7)
and that evil has not triumphed (see Introduction IV. 1). **by destroying others:** or 'in his
desire' (cf. Prov. 10: 3; 11: 1); GNB 'looked for
security in being wicked'. RSV 'in his wealth' is
a possible emendation.
8. The security of the godly is in marked
contrast to the insecurity of the ungodly (cf.
vv. 5, 7). **flourishing** (or 'spreading') **olive
tree:** i.e. a luxuriant one; the olive is evergreen
(cf. Jer. 11: 16; Ps. 1: 3; 92: 12 ff.). **in the house
of God:** it is not known whether trees actually
grew in the temple area. The phrase could refer
to the whole land (cf. Hos. 9: 15). **unfailing
love:** see on 5: 7. **for ever:** see on 23: 6. **9.
you have done it:** or 'acted' (cf. 22: 13; 118:
24). **I will hope:** (*MT*) makes good sense: cf.
JB 'and put my hope in . . .' **name:** see on
20: 1. **in the presence of your saints:** i.e.
before the worshipping congregation. For

saints or 'the godly' (Heb. *ḥᵃsîdîm*) see on
4: 3.

Psalm 53.   SINNERS ALL
This is another version of Ps. 14 (*q.v.*). Apart
from slight details, the main differences are the
use of *Elohim* ('God') instead of *Yahweh* and a
variant version of v. 5 (Ps. 14: 5, 6).

Title: see Introduction III. 1, 2, **3. mahalath:**
obscure, but possibly the name of a tune (cf.
Ps. 88) or of the accompanying instrument ('to
the flute'). **5. where there was nothing to
dread:** or 'where no terror was', i.e. before,
or at the time. **those who attacked you:** *MT*
'your besieger' (cf. rsvmg; 'the enemies', GNB)
which may point to a military situation for
which Ps. 14 was modified.

Psalm 54.   AN APPEAL FOR HELP
The historical note in the heading links this
psalm with the period of David's flight from
Saul (cf. 1 Sam. 23: 19; 26: 1). Another possibility is that it represents the prayer of someone
who has been falsely accused (cf. vv. 1, 3; Pss.
5; 7). The Prayer Book appoints this psalm for
use on Good Friday (see Introduction IV. 2).

The structure is that usually found in an
individual lament. In the opening verses (1, 2)
the psalmist cries for help and appeals for a
hearing. Then (v. 3) he describes the cause of
his trouble, and expresses (vv. 4, 5) his trust in
God and his confidence (or desire) that God
will destroy his enemies. Finally (vv. 6, 7) he
vows to show his gratitude in cultic acts and
accompanying words of thanksgiving, for he
is sure that God will save him.

Title: see Introduction III. 1, 2, 3. **1. by your
name:** an active power (see on 20: 1). **3.** (1
Sam. 23: 15) **strangers:** *MT* (NIV, cf. rsvmg)
suggests either 'foreigners' or those 'estranged'
from God (cf. Isa. 1: 4). rsv has 'insolent men',
the reading of some Heb. mss and Targ. (only
one letter different from *MT*). **Selah:** see Introduction III. 3. **4. Lord who sustains:** Heb.
ᵃdōnāi. MT (rsvmg 'with those who uphold')
suggests that God also uses others to help His
servant (cf. 1 Sam. 23: 13; 2 Sam. 23: 8 ff.). **5.
Let evil recoil:** 'The evil will return to . . .'
NIV, NEB, JB, GNB translate as a wish: 'May . . .'
rsv 'He will requite' follows the traditional
reading (cf. LXX 'he will return'). **those who
slander:** lit. 'those who watch me'. **faithfulness:** lit. 'truth' (see on 25: 5). **6. freewill
offering:** lit. 'freeness'; a reference either to
sacrificing 'freely' or to a type of sacrifice which
is offered voluntarily and not as a result of a
vow (cf. Lev. 22: 18–30; Num. 15: 1–6). **your
name:** see on 20: 1. **7. he has:** the perfect tenses
in this verse are probably anticipatory (see on
20: 6). **in triumph:** supplied to complete the
sense (cf. 52: 6, 7); cf. GNB 'I have seen my
enemies defeated'.

Psalm 55.   OPPRESSED AND BETRAYED—BUT GOD SUPPORTS
This individual lament is the 'spiritual case-
history' of a man who learned how to cope
with life's burdens (cf. L. Griffith, *God in Man's
Experience*, 1968, pp. 90 ff.). Attempts to connect this psalm with David's experiences during the rebellion of Absalom, and especially
with the treachery of Ahithophel (2 Sam. 15–
17), or with the period of Saul's persecution (1
Sam. 19–27), though attractive, are incapable
of proof. It is better to admit that we have
no idea of either the historical setting, or the
personal circumstances of the writer, that gave
rise to this moving *cri de coeur*. The emotional
strain under which it was written not only led
to fluctuations in mood and style, but has also
helped to create difficulties in translation and
interpretation. Inevitably, Christians have
often seen the psalm as a foreshadowing (or
even a prediction) of Christ's experience of the
treachery of Judas (cf. 41: 9) and the opposition
of the Jewish leaders (see Introduction IV. 2).

The psalmist begins (vv. 1, 2) with a passionate appeal to God to hear and answer his prayer.
Then (vv. 3–5) he describes both the causes
and the effects of his trouble. In vv. 6–8 he lays
bare his initial 'gut-reaction' to his problems:
he felt that he could not cope with them and
wanted to run away and leave them as far
behind as possible (cf. 11: 1; Jer. 9: 2). Instead
he turns to God (vv. 9–11) with a cry for
judgment on those who are wreaking havoc in
his city. His fierce outburst continues with
the revelation (vv. 12–14) that amongst his
opponents is one who has been his most intimate and trusted friend. Again (v. 15) he calls
for the destruction of his enemies. In vv. 16–
19 his mood changes and he expresses his assurance that God will answer and deliver him; but
he still cannot get over the fact that his friend
has deceived and betrayed him (vv. 20, 21).
His final consolation (v. 22) comes in words
which may have been the oracle of a cultic
prophet (see on 6: 8 ff.): God gives His servants
the strength to bear their burdens, if only they
will commit them to Him; He does not intend
them to be finally defeated (cf. 2 Cor. 4: 8 f.).
The psalmist finishes (v. 23) with the conviction that God will judge the wicked, and with
a final determination that whatever happens he
will trust God. (On the imprecatory elements
in the psalm see Introduction IV. 1.)

Title: see Introduction III. 1, 2, 3. **1. do not
ignore:** see on 13: 1. **2. my thoughts trouble:**
lit. 'I am restless'; cf. JB 'I cannot rest from
my complaining'; GNB 'I am worn out by my
worries'. **4. terrors of death:** or 'deadly terror'
(cf. Exod. 15: 16). **6. dove:** cf. Jer. 48: 28.
7. desert: an uncultivated region which can
include steppe-land and pasture as well as desert

593

(see *NBD*). **Selah:** see Introduction III. 3. **9.
Confound their speech:** possibly translate,
'Confuse and divide their speech, O Lord' (cf.
Gen. 11: 5–9; Ps. 12: 3 f.). **9–11.** JB personifies
the nouns: 'Violence . . . Strife . . . Malice . . .
Abuse . . .', etc. **11. streets:** or 'market place',
probably the meeting place of the legal assembly. **12. if a foe were raising himself
against me:** lit. 'one who hates me (who)
magnifies (himself) against me.' **14. fellowship:** Heb. *sôd* (see on 25: 14). **15.** Cf. Num.
16: 31 ff. **the grave:** see on 6: 5. **evil finds
lodging among them . . .:** cf GNB 'Evil is in
their homes and in their hearts'. **17.** Whenever
he prays (cf. 119: 164; Dan. 6: 10) God will
hear. **18. he ransoms:** lit. 'redeems' (see on
49: 7). **from the battle . . . :** or 'from the
hostilities against me'. **19. enthroned:** cf. Dt.
33: 27; Ps. 9: 7; 29: 10; 74: 12. **who never
change their ways:** the *MT* (NIV, RSVmg) is
difficult, but suggests either 'no change of heart
for them' (JB) or 'because they have not received
a retribution' (A. A. Anderson). **Selah:** occurs
in the middle of the verse in *MT*. **20. My
companion:** supplied to complete the sense;
MT 'He'. **friends:** lit. 'those at peace with
him'. **covenant:** a solemn promise made binding by an oath (with God as witness) resulting
in a relationship with mutual obligations. **22.**
This verse (together with 16: 8; 108: 5; 25: 3)
is beautifully set to an older German chorale
by Mendelssohn in his 'Elijah'. **cares:** lit. 'what
is given', i.e. 'lot', 'portion' (cf. 11: 6), 'fortunes' (NEB). LXX (quoted in 1 Pet. 5: 7 as
'anxiety') has 'care'. **righteous:** see on Ps. 1.
23. pit of destruction: lit. 'well of the pit'
(LXX 'the pit of destruction'): see on 28: 1; cf.
16: 10; 49: 9.

Psalm 56. FAITH BANISHES FEAR

The psalm may be divided into two stanzas (vv.
1–4; 5–11), each containing a brief lamentation
and an expression of confidence in God, and
each ending with a similar refrain (v. 4; vv. 10,
11); with a concluding thanksgiving (vv. 12,
13). As with some other individual laments (see
on Pss. 22; 28; 31), it is not clear whether this
is the prayer of a man *during* his afflictions—in
which case vv. 12, 13 represent his assurance
that he will soon be delivered (see on 6: 8
ff.)—or the thanksgiving (accompanied by a
thank-offering; cf. v. 12) of a man *after* he has
recently received deliverance—in which case
vv. 1–11 are a quotation of his original prayers
(cf. 30: 8 ff.; 41: 4 ff.).

The situation envisaged in the psalm may
have been physical attack or false accusation.
The words could well express the sentiments
of David at Gath (1 Sam. 21: 10–15). Some
believe that the psalm is a national lamentation
(cf. 'peoples', v. 7), perhaps spoken by the king
as representative of his people. The later title

in LXX ('For the end, concerning the people
that were removed from the sanctuary . . .')
suggests that it was used as a prayer of the
nation in exile. Translation and interpretation
are complicated by several difficulties in the
text.

Title: see Introduction III. 1, 2, 3. **When the
Philistines . . . :** not stated in 1 Sam. 21: 10
ff., but possibly implied in 22: 1 (cf. 'escaped').
1. be merciful: see on 51: 1. **hotly pursue:**
or 'pant after'. **2. slanderers:** see on 54: 5. **in
their pride:** lit. 'height'; GNB (cf. AV) takes it
as a reference to God ('O Most High') and
transfers it to v. 3; NEB translates v. 3a 'Appear
on high (cf. 68: 18) in my day of fear'. **3. When:**
lit. 'The day that'. **4. word:** God's promise, or
a prophetic message of salvation (cf. 130: 5). **I
will not be afraid:** cf. 27: 1, 3. **mortal man:**
lit. 'flesh', man in his weakness (see on 16: 9;
cf. 78: 39; Isa. 31: 3).

6. They conspire: following Targ.; *MT* has
'They stir up strife'. **7. On no account let
them escape:** NIV slightly emends *MT* which
suggests 'in spite of iniquity shall they escape?'
(NEB). RSV 'recompense them for their crime' is
a more likely emendation. **8.** 'Sleepless nights
and many hours spent in torment and weeping
are not endured in vain as far as God is concerned. Suffering, as it were, is capital invested
with God, booked by him . . . and collected
by him' (Weiser). **Record my lament:** or 'take
account of my wandering (or 'lamentation')'.
Are they not in your record?: possibly an
explanatory gloss on the alternative reading
(see NIVmg), 'Should this not be "in thy
book"?' (cf. Mal. 3: 16; Dan. 7: 10; Job 19: 23).
10, 11. See on v. 4. **12. under vows:** lit. 'Thy
vows . . . are upon me' (see on 61: 5). **thank
offerings:** or 'thanksgivings' (see on 50: 14).
13. Cf. 116: 8 f. **soul:** 'life' (see on 3: 2). **and
my feet from stumbling:** cf. v. 6; this may
be another explanatory gloss (cf. v. 10),
'Should this not be "my feet . . ."?'. **walk
before God:** live conscious of His presence
('face', see on 4: 6) and in accord with His will
(cf. Gen. 17: 1). **light of life:** or 'light of the
living' (see on 27: 1; 36: 9; cf. Job 10: 21; Ps.
116: 9).

Psalm 57. SHELTERED FROM
FEROCIOUS ENEMIES

The combination of a lament (vv. 1–6) and a
thanksgiving (vv. 7–11) linked together by an
identical refrain (vv. 5, 11) provides a close
parallel to Ps. 56 (*q.v.*), and again raises the
question whether the psalm represents a man's
prayer *during* (cf. vv. 1–4) his troubles or *after*
(cf. v. 6) he has been delivered (see on Pss.
22; 28; 31; 56). The traditional phrases and
stereotyped images make it difficult to reconstruct the personal circumstances of the psalmist: is he being physically attacked (cf. vv. 3, 6)

or falsely accused (cf. vv. 4, 6)? The heading associates the psalm with David's experience as an outlaw (cf. 1 Sam. 22; 24). Others suggest that it could be the lament of a king spoken in the sanctuary, where he was spending the night (cf. vv. 1, 8; 2 Sam. 12: 16); or possibly a national lament offered by a leader on behalf of the whole people (cf. v. 9). Title: see Introduction III. 1, 2, 3. **1. Have mercy:** as 56: 1, 'Be gracious' (see on 51: 1). **my soul:** 'I' (see on 3: 2). **in the shadow . . . :** see on 17: 8. **the disaster:** lit. 'destructions' (cf. 52: 2; 55: 11). **2. Most High:** see on 47: 2. **who fulfills his purpose for me:** NIV supplies **his purpose**; or translate 'who avenges me'. **3. rebuking . . . :** or 'he will reproach him who pants after me' (cf. 56: 1). **Selah:** see Introduction III. 3. **love:** see on 5: 7. **faithfulness:** lit. 'truth' (see on 25: 5). **4.** Cf. 7: 2; 10: 9; 17: 12. **5. Be exalted:** GNB 'Show your greatness' (cf. 7: 6; 18: 46; 21: 13; 46: 10; Isa. 2: 11 ff.). **glory:** see on 26: 8; cf. Exod. 14: 4, 17 f.; Lev. 10: 1 ff.; Ps. 97: 2–5; 138: 5. **6.** Cf. 7: 15; 9: 15; 31: 4; 35: 7 f. **my soul:** 'I' (see on 3: 2); LXX has 'they have bowed down my soul'. **7–11.** Cf. 108: 1–5. **7. steadfast:** calm trust and constant loyalty (cf. v. 6; 112: 7 f.; 78: 37). **8. my soul:** lit. 'my glory' (see on 16: 9). **I will awaken the dawn:** instead of letting Dawn (personified: cf. Job 3: 9; 38: 12; 41: 10; Isa. 14: 12) wake him. Dawn is the time of deliverance (cf. 17: 15; 46: 5). **10.** See on v. 3; cf. 36: 5. **11.** See on v. 8.

Psalm 58. GOD WILL JUDGE THE WICKED

The understanding of this psalm depends to a large extent on the interpretation of vv. 1, 2. Are the words addressed to *divine beings* ('gods', RSV, JB) or to *human judges* ('rulers', NIV, NEB, GNB; cf. RSVmg)? Those who support the former suggestion (*e.g.* Weiser, A. A. Anderson) point to passages where God is depicted as surrounded by divine beings (or angels) who do His bidding (cf. Job 1: 6; Ps. 82: 1, 6; 1 Kg. 22: 19; Isa. 6: 1 ff.) and particularly to the idea of guardian angels of the nations (cf. Dt. 32: 8, LXX; Dan. 10: 13, 20 f.; 12: 1) whose duty was both to judge rightly and to see that justice was done and respected on earth (cf. v. 2b; see on Ps. 82). According to this view vv. 3–9 refer to the whole mass of evildoers on earth. Those who support the latter suggestion (*e.g.* Kirkpatrick, Kidner) either point to passages where human judges are apparently addressed as 'gods' (cf. Exod. 21: 6; 22: 8 f., 28; Dt. 19: 17; Ps. 82: 1, 6) or argue that the word here (Heb. *'ēlîm*) does not mean 'gods' but 'mighty ones' (cf. Exod. 15: 15; 2 Kg. 24: 15; Job 41: 25; Ezek. 17: 13; 32: 21). According to this view, vv. 3–9 refer particularly to corrupt human judges. The second view would seem to be simpler and perhaps more convincing.

The psalm could be an individual lament but is more likely a national lamentation, since there are no personal allusions. In vv. 1, 2 the psalmist (or God?) charges those who should be upholding justice with complete failure to fulfil their duty: instead of restraining evil they are initiating it. Verses 3–5 describe the evildoers in terms which emphasize their innate wickedness. Verses 6–9 are a prayer of malediction, calling down a seven-fold curse on the evil-doers. (On the textual problems in these verses see below.) Finally (vv. 10, 11) the psalmist looks forward to the day when God will fully recompense the wicked (cf. Isa. 24: 21) and demonstrate openly that there is indeed justice in the universe (cf. 94: 2; 128: 2; Isa. 3: 10 f.). (On the imprecatory psalms see Introduction IV. 1.)

Title: see Introduction III. 1, 2, 3. **1. rulers:** MT *'ēlem* ('silence'? cf. RV), which hardly makes sense, has been read as *'ēlim* ('gods' or 'mighty ones'). See the discussion above, and cf. 82: 1, 6 (which have *'lōhîm*). **2. mete out:** lit. 'weigh out' (cf. Job 31: 6; Ps. 62: 9; Prov. 16: 2). **3.** Cf. 51: 5. **wicked:** see on Ps. 1. **go astray:** or 'are estranged' (cf. Isa. 1: 4). **4a. venom:** i.e. slander, lies, cursing, etc. **4b, 5.** '. . . all snakes are deaf . . . and the charmer holds their attention by the movement of his pipe, not its music' (G. Cansdale, *Animals of Bible Lands*, 1970, p. 206). Snake-charming (cf. Ec. 10: 11; Isa. 3: 3; Jer. 8: 11) may have been used to obtain oracles. **6. teeth:** see on 3: 7; cf. 57: 4. **7. vanish like water:** cf. Job 6: 15 ff.; 2 Sam. 14: 14. **when they draw the bow . . . :** NIV tries to make sense of the difficult MT. RSV 'like grass let them be trodden down and wither' is a fair conjecture. **8. like the slug:** the suggested translation 'miscarriage' (cf. NEB) fits the context better (cf. Job 3: 16; 10: 18 f.; Ec. 6: 3). **9.** Again MT seems to be corrupt; with a small emendation it can be translated 'Before they perceive it, he will tear them up like thorns, like weeds he will sweep them away in his burning anger' (cf. NEB). **10. righteous:** see on Ps. 1. **bathe their feet . . . :** an experience of the total defeat of evil (cf. 68: 23; Job 29: 6).

Psalm 59. PROTECT ME, O MY STRENGTH!

This is the individual lament of a man who is innocently persecuted by wicked and ruthless men (apparently of his own nation). Despite the vivid poetic imagery, however, it is difficult to reconstruct from the psalm the exact personal circumstances of the writer: v. 3 suggests physical attacks, whilst vv. 7, 12 suggest false accusation, slander, cursing, etc. From the references to the people of Israel (vv. 5, 11, 13) and their enemies ('the nations', vv. 5, 8) some have deduced that this is a national lamentation;

but it is better to regard these as evidences that the psalmist made his petition in the sanctuary in the presence of the congregation, and therefore incorporated into his prayer the needs of the community as a whole. The words 'my people' (v. 11) may suggest that the speaker is a king or governor and that he is speaking as the representative of his people. Those who accept the historical origin given in the heading (cf. 1 Sam. 19: 11–17; but see Introduction III. 2) believe that David may have later adapted the psalm for liturgical use.

The psalm has been carefully constructed with two main sections (vv. 1–10; vv. 11–17), each ending with a similar refrain (vv. 9, 10; v. 17), and each sub-divided with a similar description of the enemies (vv. 6, 7; vv. 14, 15). As is usual in a psalm of lament, it contains not only petitions (vv. 1, 2; 4b, 5; 11–13) and references to the psalmist's situation (vv. 3, 4a; 6, 7; 14, 15), but also expressions of confidence that God will deliver (vv. 8–10; 16, 17) and vows to offer thanksgiving (vv. 9; 16, 17).

Title: see Introduction III. 1, 2, 3. **1. protect me:** lit. 'set me on high' (cf. 'fortress', vv. 9, 16, 17). **2. evildoers:** see on 5: 5. **bloodthirsty men:** lit. 'men of blood'. **3. Fierce:** lit. 'strong'. **offense . . . sin:** see on 32: 1. **4. I have done no wrong:** lit. 'without iniquity' (see on 32: 1). **Arise:** see on 44: 23; cf. 7: 6. **to help me:** lit. 'to meet me' (cf. v. 10). **5. God Almighty:** see on 24: 10. **show no mercy . . . :** lit. 'be not gracious to all . . .' **Selah:** see Introduction III. 3. **6. dogs:** the pariah dogs of the eastern town usually slept in the sun during the day, and then at night prowled about in packs looking for food; they frequented the rubbish dumps and were regarded as unclean and savage (cf. 22: 16). **7. they spew:** possibly 'foaming at the mouth', i.e. rabid (cf. JB). **they spew out swords:** *MT* makes good sense (cf. 52: 2; 55: 21; 57: 4). **they say . . . us:** supplied to bring out the meaning (cf. Job 24: 15); but it might be the words of the psalmist: 'For who is paying any attention?' **8. laugh:** see on 2: 4. **9. O my Strength:** NIV follows some Heb. MSS, LXX, Targ., Vulg. *MT* has 'His Strength'. **I watch for you:** so *MT* which makes good sense (cf. JB, NEB); RSV has 'I will sing praises' from Syr. following v. 17. **10. go before me:** cf. 21: 3; Isa. 21: 14. **gloat over:** see on 54: 7. **those who slander:** see on 54: 5.

11. do not kill them: since this seems to contradict v. 13, some translate 'Do indeed slay them' (cf. JB) or read as a question (NEB). The point seems to be that their punishment must be seen as a divine judgment (cf. v. 13; Exod. 9: 15 f.; 1 Sam. 17: 46; Ps. 58: 7–10), not as an accident. **make them wander:** 'scatter them', 'cause them to wander' (cf. Num. 32: 13). **13. Jacob:** see on 20: 1. **15. howl:** NIV follows LXX,

Vulg.; *MT* 'they tarry'. **16. strength:** the same word as in vv. 9, 17. **love:** see on 5: 7. **morning:** traditionally the time of deliverance (cf. 17: 15; 46: 5), or a reference to spending the night in prayer in the sanctuary (cf. 2 Sam. 12: 16).

Psalm 60. THE PRAYER OF A DEFEATED PEOPLE

The situation which originally gave rise to this psalm was obviously a heavy defeat for the Israelite army, probably from Edom (cf. v. 9). In deep distress the people—represented no doubt by their king or leader (cf. v. 9)—uttered this national lament, probably accompanied by fasting (see on Ps. 44). If we follow the attribution of the heading (see below), then we must assume that Edom attacked David's army in the rear whilst they were preoccupied with the Syrians. An alternative historical setting might be that referred to in 2 Kg. 8: 20 ff., but otherwise the occasion cannot be identified.

Verses 1–5 describe the catastrophic effects upon the nation of their recent defeat, which they attribute, not to the foreign enemy, but their own God. They are convinced, nevertheless, that He has not given them up for good and therefore they approach Him in a spirit of confidence, assured that He will deliver those who are still in a special relationship with Him. (Note that the question of whether they deserve their suffering is not raised; cf. 44: 17 ff.) The lament is followed by an encouraging oracle (vv. 6–8), probably spoken by a prophet, which emphasizes God's lordship over both Canaan and the surrounding lands, and thus constitutes a promise of victory. (It may be that this is a quotation of an earlier oracle, possibly associated with the periodic renewal at the sanctuary of Yahweh's distribution of the land: cf. Dt. 31: 3 ff., 10 ff.; Jos. 24: 8 ff.; Num. 24: 17 ff.) Finally, in vv. 9–12 the commander-in-chief prays for success in the forthcoming campaign against Edom, aware of the doubts and uncertainties, and yet confident that if God is truly with them they will be victorious. (Note vv. 5–12 reappear in 108: 6–13 applied to another context.)

Title: see Introduction III. 1, 2, 3. **Lily of the Covenant:** lit. 'Lily of Witness'; probably the name of a tune. **when he fought . . . :** see on 2 Sam. 8: 3–8; 10: 6–18; 1 Chr. 18: 3–6; 19: 6–19. **when Joab . . . :** see on 2 Sam. 8: 13 f.; 2 Chr. 18: 12 f.; cf. 1 Kg. 11: 15 f. **1. burst forth:** lit. 'broken us' (cf. Jg. 21: 15). **3. shown . . . desperate times:** lit. 'make . . . see hard things'; but possibly it should be translated 'made . . . drink a cup of bitterness' (cf. NEB). **wine:** cf. Isa. 51: 17, 21 f.; Jer. 13: 13; 25: 15 ff.; Ps. 75: 8. **4. banner:** here a signal for flight (cf. Jer. 4: 6). **to be unfurled against the bow:** better, 'to flee from the bow' (LXX), AV

is also possible. **Selah:** see Introduction III. 3.
5. those you love: the people of God (cf. Dt.
33: 12; Isa. 5: 1; Jer. 11: 15). **be delivered:** lit.
'saved' (see on 35: 3).

6. from his sanctuary: the literal translation
('by his holiness') is probably better (cf. 89: 35;
Am. 4: 2): God swears by Himself (cf. Am. 6:
8), and His essential nature (holiness) makes it
impossible for Him to break His promise (cf.
Num. 23: 9). **6, 7.** For the places mentioned
see *NBD*; they are representative of the whole
territory of Israel. **7. my helmet:** lit. 'the
protection of my head'. **scepter:** or commander's 'staff'; a symbol of authority. **8.** The
places mentioned were part of David's empire
(cf. 2 Sam. 8: 1–14). **washbasin:** a picture of
menial service. **upon . . . I toss my sandal:**
either a symbol of taking ownership (GNB; cf.
Ru. 4: 7; Dt. 11: 24) or (translating with Kirkpatrick, 'unto . . .') a picture of the master fling-
ing his sandals to the slave to carry or clean (cf.
Mt. 3: 11). **over Philistia . . . :** NIV follows
Syr. and 108: 9; *MT* has 'Philistia, shout because of me' (cf. JB, GNB). **9.** The speaker is
probably the king or leader of the army. It
seems that another attack on Edom is planned.
fortified city: possibly Petra, the capital of
Edom (cf. Ob. 3). **10b.** Cf. 1 Sam. 4: 3 ff.; 2
Sam. 5: 24; Ps. 44: 9. **11. against the enemy:**
or 'from trouble' (cf. JB). **help of man:** lit.
'salvation of man' (cf. 33: 16 f.; 146: 3). **12.
gain the victory:** i.e. perform deeds of valour;
JB 'fight like heroes' (cf. 1 Sam. 14: 48; Ps. 118:
15 f.). **trample down:** see on 44: 5.

Psalm 61. SECURE ON THE ROCK— SAFE IN THE TENT

One view of this psalm sees it as the lament of
an individual (possibly a Levite?) far from the
temple (v. 2; cf. Ps. 42/43); another view is that
it is the thanksgiving of a worshipper in the
temple (vv. 4, 5), recalling his earlier prayer
for protection (vv. 1–3; see on Pss. 56; 57).
As so often in these laments the cause of the
psalmist's distress is not specified (see on vv.
2, 3). The inclusion of an intercession for the
king (vv. 6, 7) is fitting since he was regarded
as the channel of divine blessing and protection
to the nation (cf. 28: 8; 72: 1–17) and thus to
the individual Israelite.

Those who follow the attribution of the
heading place the psalm either during Absalom's rebellion (2 Sam. 15–19) or at a time
when the king was away on a campaign (cf.
Pss. 20; 60). If the psalm is Davidic, vv. 6, 7
may be seen either as the king's prayer for
himself and his dynasty (cf. Jer. 38: 5 for a
king's reference to himself in the third person),
or as a later addition for congregational use
(Kidner). After the exile the psalm was used as
a prayer of the dispersed nation and the king

of vv. 6, 7 was interpreted as the Messiah (so
Targum).

Title: see Introduction III. 1, 2, 3. **2. from
the ends of the earth:** a reference either to a
distant place (cf. Dt. 28: 49; Ps. 46: 9) or to the
underworld (cf. Exod. 15: 12; 1 Sam. 28: 13;
Ps. 63: 9; Isa. 29: 4). **as my heart grows faint:**
either 'when my courage fails' or 'when my
vitality is ebbing away', i.e. Sheol has begun
to take hold on him (see on 40: 2). **the rock:**
see on 18: 2; cf. 18: 31, 46. **higher than I:** or
possibly 'too high for me', i.e. to scale in his
own strength. **3. refuge . . . strong tower:**
cf. 9: 9; 18: 2; 46: 1, 7; 48: 3; 59: 9, 16 f.; 62: 7
f. **the foe:** could be a reference to Death (cf.
49: 14).

4. I long to . . . and . . . : or 'I will . . . I
will . . .' **tent:** see on 15: 1. **forever:** see on
23: 6. **wings:** see on 17: 8. **Selah:** see Introduction III. 3. **5. vows:** used to offer thanks-
offerings (cf. Lev. 7: 11 ff.; 22: 18 ff.; 27: 1–
25); but in the psalms they are not so much
conditional promises of gifts (cf. the 'bargains'
of Gen. 28: 20 ff.; Jg. 11: 30 f.) as expressions
of certainty that God will answer prayer and
give deliverance (cf. 22: 25 f.; 50: 14; 56: 12).
the heritage: or possibly 'the desire' (cf. NEB).
fear your name: exhibit the reverence due to
a holy God (cf. 34: 7, 9); for **name** see on 20:
1. **6. Increase the days:** lit. 'add days to the
days of ' (cf. 2 Kg. 20: 6). **for many generations:** cf. 1 Kg. 1: 31; Neh. 2: 3. **7.** Cf. 89:
36. **in God's presence:** enjoying His favour
and blessing (cf. 56: 12). **love:** see on 5: 7.
faithfulness: lit. 'truth' (see on 25: 5). **8. vows:**
normally paid once for all (see on v.5). **your
name:** see on 20: 1.

Psalm 62. NO OTHER HOPE

In this individual psalm of confidence the exact
circumstances of the psalmist may not be clear,
but what is patently obvious is his absolute
trust in God. In the first half of the psalm (vv.
1–7) the description of his plight—harassed by
ruthless and treacherous enemies (vv. 3, 4)—
is sandwiched between a double expression of
his certainty about God (vv. 1–2, 5–7). There
is no need for him to keep on crying to God;
he is so sure of the dependability of God that
he is content silently to await God's deliverance
(cf. 40: 1; 123: 2). Then (vv. 8–10) he turns
to his fellow-worshippers (suggesting that the
psalm is being spoken in the sanctuary) and
exhorts them to rely on no one but God. Any
other possible grounds of confidence—
whether human power or material resources—
are illusory. Finally (vv. 11, 12), like a wisdom
teacher, he recounts the lessons that he has
learned from divine revelation—either through
a prophetic oracle or from the cultic recital of
God's mighty deeds (cf. Ps. 136): that God is
both able and willing to keep His covenant

promises and to ensure that the wicked are punished and the righteous rewarded (cf. Exod. 20: 5 f.; Dt. 28).

Title: see Introduction III. 1, 2, 3. **1. alone:** the Heb. *'ak* comes six times in this psalm, at the beginning of vv. 1, 2, 4, 5, 6, 9; it denotes emphasis ('surely', 'truly') or contrast ('but', 'only'). **my soul:** 'I' (see on 3: 2). **finds rest** lit. '(is) silence' (cf. v. 5). **salvation:** see on 35: 3. **2. rock . . . fortress:** see on 18: 2. **shaken:** JB 'I can never fall'; GNB 'I shall never be defeated'. **3. throw him down:** or 'that you may murder him'. **leaning wall:** a description of the persecuted man, close to death (cf. Jer. 15: 20). **tottering fence:** 'broken down parapet' (A. A. Anderson). **4. his lofty place:** a reference either to the special social position of the psalmist or to the spiritual dignity of any God-fearing man (cf. v. 7). **Selah:** see Introduction III. 3.

5. See on v. 1. **Find rest, O my soul:** lit. 'be silent, my soul'. **6. shaken:** or 'moved' (the same word as in v. 2). The omission of 'greatly' here (cf. v. 2) is probably not significant; some translations omit it from v. 2. **7. salvation:** see on 35: 3.

9. Lowborn men . . . the highborn: lit. 'sons of mankind (Heb. *'ādām*) . . . sons of a man (Heb. *'îš*)'; there is not necessarily a contrast here (cf. NEB, GNB; see on 49: 2). **on a balance:** cf. Prov. 16: 2; 21: 2; 24: 12; Dan. 5: 27. In Egyptian thought the gods weighed a man's heart after death to assess his worth; here judgment takes place before death (cf. Job 31: 6). **11. One thing . . . two things:** a repetition for emphasis (cf. Prov. 6: 16; 30: 15 ff.; Am. 1: 3 ff.), or equivalent to 'many things' (cf. Job 33: 14; 40: 5). **12. loving:** see on 5: 7. **reward:** cf. Prov. 24: 12.

Psalm 63.   THIRSTY FOR GOD

The author of this psalm was obviously a man who knew his God intimately, and for whom the experience of God's presence and favour meant more than anything else in life. Even the pressing problem of those who were persecuting him has to take second place (vv. 9–11) to the expression of his longing for God Himself (vv. 1–8).

The heading (see below) links the psalm with the experience of David, probably intending his flight from Absalom and his army (cf. 2 Sam. 15: 23–28; 16: 2, 14; 17: 2 f., 29) rather than from Saul and his men (cf. 1 Sam. 23: 14; 24: 2), since in v. 11 he seems to refer to himself as king (see on Ps. 61). Whilst the contents of the psalm would seem to fit such a life-setting quite well, many modern commentators see the psalm either as the lament of an accused man (cf. v. 11) longing to be once more in the temple enjoying the protection of God, or as a prayer of thanksgiving offered in the sanctuary

by someone who has already experienced the assurance of God's deliverance (cf. Ps. 61). The early Church adopted it as its morning psalm (see on v. 1).

Title: see Introduction III. 1, 2. **the Wilderness of Judah:** cf. Jg. 1: 16; 15: 61; and see on Ps. 55: 7. **1. I seek:** the verb is connected with the Heb. word for 'dawn' and probably implies the idea of turning to God with eagerness in the early hours (cf. 57: 8; 130: 6; Prov. 1: 28; 7: 15; 8: 17) hence LXX 'I cry to thee early' (cf. AV). **soul . . . body:** i.e. the whole person (see on 3: 2; 16: 9; cf. 84: 2). **weary land:** a description of the psalmist's inward condition rather than of his outward circumstances (cf. 143: 6; Isa. 33: 2). **2. seen:** probably not a claim to having seen a vision or theophany (cf. Isa. 6: 1 ff.), but to having experienced the presence of God through the cultic worship (cf. 42: 2; 84: 7) and having received God's help (cf. 5: 3; 27: 4; Hab. 2: 1). **glory:** see on 26: 8. **3. love:** see on 5: 7. **better than life:** i.e. life is not worth living without the covenant loyalty of God. **4. praise:** lit. 'bless'; see on 26: 12. **in your name I will lift up my hands:** see on 28: 2; 20: 1.

5. my soul: i.e. 'I' (see on 3: 2). **satisfied:** cf. 36: 8. **the richest of foods:** 'marrow and fat' stand for the choicest forms of food (cf. Gen. 45: 18); in fact, fat was forbidden to the Israelites (cf. Lev. 3: 16; 7: 23). **6. think of:** ('meditate') see on 1: 2. **7. my help:** the underlying thought may be the function of the sanctuary as a place of asylum (see on 27: 5). **shadow of your wings:** see on 17: 8 (cf. 36: 7; 61: 4). **8. my soul:** i.e. 'I' (see on 3: 2). **clings to:** 'follow hard after' (cf. Jer. 42: 16) or 'cleave to' (cf. Gen. 2: 24; Dt. 4: 4; 10: 20; Ru. 2: 8; Ps. 91: 14; 101: 3; Jer. 13: 11). **right hand:** see on 44: 3. **9. depths of the earth:** i.e. Sheol (see on 6: 5; cf. 55: 15; 86: 13; Isa. 44: 23; Ezek. 26: 20). **10. food for jackals:** the desecration of a corpse was considered a shameful punishment (cf. 1 Sam. 31: 10 ff.; 2 Kg. 9: 36 f.; Am. 2: 1). **11.** Cf. 61: 6. **by God's name:** lit. 'by him'; either by Yahweh (so NIV, NEB, GNB; cf. 1 Kg. 8: 31) or by the king (cf. Gen. 42: 15 f.; 1 Sam. 17: 55; 25: 26; 2 Sam. 11: 11; 15: 21). **praise him:** lit. 'glory', i.e. 'boast'. **will be silenced:** lit. 'stopped', i.e. they will be proved wrong (cf. Job 5: 16; Ps. 107: 42).

Psalm 64.   A PRAYER FOR GOD'S SWIFT RETRIBUTION

The author of this individual lament seeks divine protection from the threats and plots of his enemies; though it is not clear whether they have actually begun to affect him yet. It is not possible to discover the original life-setting, but the psalm could have been used by any persecuted man.

Like other similar laments (cf. Pss. 5; 7; 10; 12; 57), it begins with a brief petition to God (vv. 1, 2) and then concentrates on a vivid description of the undercover machinations (cf. 11: 12) of the psalmist's opponents (vv. 3–6), who kid themselves that God cannot read their thoughts. Verses 7–9 express the psalmist's certainty (for this use of the perfect tense see on 20: 6) that God will speedily cause the schemes of the wicked to rebound on them and bring about their downfall (cf. 7: 15 f.). The result will be that the nation as a whole (or possibly, all the world; cf. Isa. 26: 9) will recognize that God does rule and judge. Finally (v. 10), the psalmist calls on all God's faithful people to act on what they have learned about Him: humbly to trust Him and proudly to praise Him. (Note: the text is somewhat obscure in places and thus translation and interpretation are difficult.)

Title: see Introduction III. 1, 2, 3. **1. as I voice my complaint:** i.e. 'as I complain': his 'lament' (NEB) concerns the persecution of his enemies, not the providence of God (cf. 1 Sam. 1: 16; Ps. 55: 17). **protect . . . hide:** these could be translated as confident futures: 'thou wilt protect . . . thou wilt hide' (Kirkpatrick). **2. hide me:** see on 27: 5; 63: 7. **conspiracy:** or 'council' (Heb. *sōd*: see on 25: 14). **wicked . . . evildoers:** see on Ps. 1; 5: 5. **noisy crowd:** or 'turbulent mob' (NEB); cf. Dan. 6: 6, 11. **3 f.** The imagery probably refers to slanders and false accusations rather than to magic spells or curses (so Mowinckel); cf. 55: 21; 57: 4. **4. the innocent man:** see on 15: 2. **without fear:** i.e. of God (cf. Dt. 25: 18; Ps. 55: 19); possibly read 'without being seen' (cf. NEB). **5. they encourage each other:** or 'they encourage themselves in' (RV; cf. JB, GNB). **snares:** cf. 7: 15; 9: 15; 35: 7; 140: 5; 142: 3: 1 Sam. 18: 21. **Who will see them?:** i.e. God (cf. 59: 7); MT (NIV) would refer to the snares. **6.** A difficult verse. **We have devised:** MT lit. 'We are complete . . .'; GNB makes good sense: 'We have planned a perfect crime'. **Surely the mind . . . :** a comment either of the plotters or of the psalmist (cf. GNB); it may be a proverb (cf. Jer. 17: 9).

7–9. Some (*e.g.* Weiser) translate with past tenses as reporting a retribution already effected; the whole psalm being the worshipper's testimony after his prayer had been answered (cf. Pss. 56; 57). **8. he will . . . bring them to ruin:** MT lit. 'they have made him stumble'; possibly translate (Eaton): 'by their tongue they bring him down upon themselves'. **shake their heads:** cf. 22: 7; Jer. 31: 8; 48: 27; or possibly translate 'flee away' (cf. NEB). **9. ponder:** or 'understand'. **10. Let the righteous:** or 'The righteous will' (JB, GNB); for **righteous** see on Ps. 1. **rejoice in the LORD:** i.e. because He rules and recompenses righteously (cf. 5: 12;

32: 10; 58: 11). **praise him:** lit. 'glory', i.e. 'boast'.

Psalm 65. PRAISE FOR THE GOD WHO SENDS THE RAIN

Whilst it is possible to view this psalm as a harvest festival thanksgiving psalm, used either at the feast of Tabernacles (Exod. 23: 16; Dt. 16: 13–15; see Introduction II. 2), the feast of Weeks (Exod. 23: 16; 34:22; Num. 28: 26 ff.; Dt. 16: 9–12), or the feast of Unleavened Bread (i.e. the offering of the first-fruits of the barley harvest; Lev. 23: 9–14; Dt. 26: 1–15), it is more likely that it was written as a national psalm of thanksgiving for use in the spring, after a time of drought and famine—or at least a delay of the rains—seen as a divine punishment for sin (cf. v. 2; Dt. 28: 22 ff.; 1 Kg. 8: 35 f.; Jer. 14: 1 ff., 19 ff.; Am. 4: 7 ff.).

The psalm has three main sections. In vv. 1–4 the community gathers in the temple to fulfil the vows that they had made to God when they prayed in their recent distress. They rejoice that He is God who answers prayer, who grants forgiveness and all the blessings of His close presence amongst them. In vv. 5–8 they sing praises to God as Saviour and Creator: the one who works both in history and in nature to control the powers of chaos and to bring safety, security, peace and joy to the whole world. The concluding section (vv. 9–13), with a change of metre, paints a vivid picture of the blessings of fertility as God sends the rains and prepares the land for the harvest, transforming the barren ground into lush green pastures. (Note: it is not clear whether this section should be read as a description of what had already happened— 'You have visited . . . you have crowned . . .' — or as an anticipation of what was confidently believed to be on the way.) W. C. Dix made vv. 12, 13 the starting-point of his fine harvest hymn 'To Thee, O Lord, our hearts we raise'.

Title: see Introduction III. 1, 2, 3. **1. praise awaits you:** MT has lit. 'For thee silence, praise' (cf. 62: 1); RSV (cf. NEB, JB) follows LXX, Syr., Vulg. (cf. NIVmg and 147: 1). **vows:** see on 61: 5. **2. all men:** lit. 'all flesh' (so AV, RSV), either all Israel or the whole of mankind. **3. sins:** lit. 'iniquities'; see on 32: 2. **transgressions:** see on 32: 2. **overwhelmed by:** cf. NEB 'are too heavy for us' (cf. 38: 4; 40: 12). **atoned for:** or 'blot them out' (JB, NEB).

The basic meaning of the Heb. verb *kipper* may have been either 'to cover over' or 'to wipe off'. Its main use in the OT ('to make atonement') describes the removal of the effects of sin, usually by cultic (i.e. sacrificial) means (cf. Exod. 29: 36; Lev. 4: 20; 16: 10; 17: 11) but also by intercession (cf. Exod. 32: 30) or by payment of a ransom (cf. Exod. 30: 16). The subject of the verb is usually the man who offers the sacrifice, but sometimes (as here) it is God who 'atones', i.e. forgives (cf. Dt. 21: 8 f.: Ps. 78: 38; Isa. 6: 7; 43: 25). **4. blessed:** see on 1: 1. **choose:** cf. Dt. 7: 6 ff.; 14: 2; Ps. 78: 70; 89: 3; 106: 23. **bring near:** cf. Num. 16: 5; Ps. 15: 1 ff.; 23: 6; 24: 3 ff.; 84: 2; 96: 8. **the good things of your house:** probably a reference to the sacrificial meals in which worshippers joined (cf. 22: 26; 23: 5; 36: 8; Jer. 31: 14) but no doubt including the idea of spiritual refreshment. **your holy temple:** lit. 'the holy place of thy temple' (see on 5: 7).

5. awesome deeds: cf. Exod. 34: 10; 2 Sam. 7: 23; Ps. 47: 2; 66: 3; 68: 35; 76: 7; 89: 7; 96: 4; 99: 2 f.; 106: 21 f.; 145: 6. **of righteousness:** lit. 'in righteousness' (see on 33: 5); RSV 'with deliverance', NEB 'with victory'. **hope:** or 'confidence' (cf. 40: 4; 71: 5). **ends of the earth . . . farthest seas:** i.e. the whole world (cf. v. 8; 72: 8). **6. mountains:** the most solid parts of the earth (cf. 18: 7; 46: 2 f.). **armed:** as a warrior prepared for action (cf. 93: 1; Isa. 51: 9 f.; Eph. 6: 14). **7.** Cf. 89: 9; 93: 3; 104: 5–9. **seas:** probably a reference to the waters of chaos (Gen. 1: 2 ff.; see on Ps. 18: 7 ff.; 29: 3, 10). **8. your wonders:** the 'extraordinary' acts of God in nature (cf. Exod. 7: 3; Dt. 4: 34; 26: 8; Ps. 78: 43; 86: 17) rather than the 'natural' wonders of creation. **where morning dawns and evening fades:** lit. 'the outgoings' or 'portals' (JB) 'of the morning and evening'; cf. Job 38: 19 f. The reference here is probably to the whole earth from east to west.

9, 10. See *NBD art.* 'Rain'. **9. You care for:** lit. 'you visit' (cf. Gen. 21: 1; Exod. 13: 19; Ps. 8: 4). **water:** NIV follows the ancient versions; *MT* has 'makes it abundant' (cf. NEB). **streams of God:** probably a reference to the source of rain (cf. NEB; Job 38: 25; Gen. 7: 11; 8: 2). **10. level its ridges:** i.e. breaking up the clods of earth. **crops:** i.e. the sprouting of the new seed. **11. . . . the year with your bounty:** lit. 'the year of your goodness', i.e. the spring and summer rains were the climax of a whole year of God's blessing. **your carts:** lit. 'your tracks'; probably a reference to the storm clouds (cf. 18: 10; 68: 4, 17, 33; Isa. 66: 15). **12. The grasslands . . . overflow:** better 'they (the tracks of God) drop on the pastures . . .'; or possibly emend to 'the pastures . . . shout for joy' (cf. 96: 12; 98: 8; Isa. 55: 12). **desert:** see on 55: 7.

Psalm 66. COME AND SEE WHAT GOD HAS DONE

There are two main approaches to this psalm. One sees it as primarily an individual thanksgiving (vv. 13–20) for deliverance from some personal trouble (vv. 14, 17–19), with an introduction (vv. 1–12) taken over from the liturgy of congregational worship (perhaps from an annual New Year festival—see Introduction II.

2). The other regards it as a national thanksgiving after a deliverance from some unspecified distress (vv. 9–12), the speaker in vv. 13–20 being the king (or some other leader). Some commentators go further, believing that it fits the experience of the people of Judah and Jerusalem under Hezekiah, when they were delivered from Sennacherib king of Assyria (Isa. 36–37).

The psalm falls into three main sections. The first (vv. 1–7) summons the world to worship God and acknowledge His great power, having seen what He did for Israel when He brought them out of Egypt, through the Sea of Reeds, and over the river Jordan into Canaan. The second (vv. 8–12) continues the call to the nations to praise God, this time for His deliverance of His people from the severe trials and distress through which they have recently passed (cf. Ps. 67; Isa. 37: 20). The third section (vv. 13–20) expresses the thanksgiving and testimony of an individual (probably the national leader) as he enters the temple to fulfil the vows made when he called on God during his time of trouble.

Title: see Introduction III. 1, 3. **2. glory:** see on 26: 8 (cf. 96: 3). **name:** see on 20: 1. **offer him glory and praise:** lit. 'make glory his praise'. **3. cringe:** feigned (i.e. unwilling) homage (cf. Dt. 33: 29; Ps. 18: 44; 81: 15). **awesome:** cf. 65: 5. **4.** The verbs might better be rendered as futures, or as a summons: 'Let . . . worship . . .' **name:** see on 20: 1. **Selah:** see Introduction III. 3. **5. Come and see:** may refer to symbolic acts performed in the temple during the recital of the salvation-history (cf. 46: 8), or indicate that the worshippers regard themselves as present in imagination at the events being recalled (cf. v. 6c). **awesome:** see on v. 3 (cf. Exod. 15: 11; Jer. 32: 19). **6. waters:** probably the Jordan (cf. Jos. 3; Ps. 114: 3, 5), but it could refer to the Sea of Reeds ('Red Sea', Exod. 13: 18; cf. Exod: 14: 22) as the first line does. **come, let us . . . :** the worshippers speak as though they were involved in the events of the Exodus (cf. Dt. 5: 3). **7. his eyes:** cf. 11: 4.

8. praise: see on 26: 12. **10.** Cf. Job 23: 10; Ps. 26: 2; Isa. 1: 25; 48: 10; Jer. 6: 29; Zech. 13: 9; Mal. 3: 3. **11. into prison:** cf. Job 19: 6; Ezek. 12: 13; 17: 20. **burdens:** or possibly 'chains' (Targ.). **12. ride:** or 'drive' (i.e. in chariots); such might be the fate of survivors in a battle (cf. Isa. 51: 23; Am. 1: 3). **fire . . . water:** symbols of extreme danger (cf. Isa. 43: 2). **place of abundance:** *MT* (NIV and RSVmg) could imply 'abundance' (cf. 'wealthy place', RV), but RSV is probably right in its slight emendation ('spacious place'; cf. NEB 'liberty'); LXX has 'refreshment' or 'rest'.

13. burnt offerings: see on 40: 6. **vows:** see on 61: 5. **14.** Cf. Jg. 11: 35 f. **15.** Cf. Lev. 22:

18 f. **an offering:** lit. 'smoke' (RSV); cf. Exod. 29: 18; the Heb. word can also signify 'incense' (cf. Exod. 30: 1 ff.; Ps. 141: 2; Isa. 1: 13). **16.** Cf. 22: 22; 34: 11. **fear God:** cf. 34: 7, 9. **17. his praise was on my tongue:** lit. 'praise was under my tongue' (see on 10: 7). **18.** Cf. Isa. 59: 2 f. **If I had cherished:** lit. 'If I had seen . . .' **sin:** see on 32: 2. **LORD:** should be 'Lord' (i.e. Heb. *ᵃdōnāi*, not *Yahweh*). **19. listened:** or 'heard' (i.e. answered). **20. Praise be:** lit. 'Blessed'; see on 26: 12. **who has not . . . :** lit. 'who has not turned aside my prayer or his steadfast love from me'. **my prayer:** might be a gloss from v. 19 (cf. NEB). **love:** see on 5: 7.

Psalm 67. THE PRAISE OF THE GOD WHO BLESSES

This psalm is usually regarded (on the basis of v. 6a) as a harvest thanksgiving song sung at one of the three main Israelite agricultural festivals (see on Ps. 65), most likely the feast of Tabernacles (see Introduction II. 2). If so, the emphasis is upon the future experience of God's favour rather than the past evidence of His blessing in the harvest. But if vv. 6, 7 are taken as referring to the future (see below), the psalm may be regarded as a national lament or prayer, asking not only for God's blessing in the material prosperity of the nation (vv. 1, 6, 7; cf. Dt. 28: 2–14; Ps. 115: 12–15), but also for the universal recognition of God's praise-worthiness (vv. 2–5). As in Ps. 66, the evidence of God's goodness towards His people is envisaged as winning the nations to His service. Above all, the psalm should be seen as an elaboration of the priestly blessing (cf. Num. 6: 24 ff.) echoed in v. 1, and no doubt heard regularly in the worship of the temple, the effects of which are seen as spreading out to the whole world. The psalm is beautifully paraphrased by H. F. Lyte in the hymn 'God of mercy, God of grace'.

Title: see Introduction III. 1, 3. **1. gracious:** see on 51: 1. **bless:** see on 26: 12. **his face shine:** i.e. 'smile' (JB); see on 4: 6; 31: 16. **Selah:** see Introduction III. 3. **2. salvation:** see on 35: 3. **3. peoples:** all the nations of the world. **4. rule:** or 'judge' see on 72: 2. **guide:** 'lead' or 'care for' (cf. 23: 3; 78: 14, 52 f.; 107: 30). **6, 7.** The perfect tenses could be translated as futures (see on 20: 6): 'The land will . . . God will . . .'; or as jussives (cf. v. 1): 'May the land . . . may God . . .' **7. ends of the earth:** i.e. the whole world (cf. 65: 5; 72: 8). **fear him:** cf. 34: 7, 9.

Psalm 68. GOD'S TRIUMPHAL PROCESSION

This is one of the most difficult psalms in the Psalter both to translate and to interpret. Attempts to find a life-setting range from suggesting a particular historical occasion (*e.g.* 2 Sam. 6: 12–19; 1 Kg. 8: 1 ff.; or 2 Chr. 30) to the idea that Ps. 68 is really a catalogue of some thirty poems, each listed by citing its first line or stanza. The most satisfactory suggestion seems to be that it is a processional song, intended to accompany a festival procession (possibly during the autumn festival—see Introduction II. 2) probably headed by the ark as a symbol of God's presence (cf. v. 1 and see on Ps. 24) and celebrating the triumphal kingship of Yahweh. In later Judaism Ps. 68 was used in the Synagogue at Pentecost, which included a commemoration of the giving of the Law at Sinai (cf. vv. 7, 8). In the Christian Church it has been associated with the ascension of Jesus (cf. v. 18; Eph. 4: 8 ff.) and also used on Whitsunday (see Introduction IV. 2). Verse 18 forms the starting-point of A. T. Russell's hymn 'The Lord ascendeth up on high'.

Inevitably, any attempt to trace the progression of thought in this psalm must be tentative and generalized. The prelude (vv. 1–6) calls the people to the worship of the God who protects them from all their enemies and cares for them in all their troubles. The worshippers begin (vv. 7–18) by reliving the mighty deeds of God in the *past*: the Exodus from Egypt (vv. 7–10), the conquest of Canaan (vv. 11–14) and the choice of Zion as God's earthly habitation (vv. 15–18). They then (vv. 19–27) rejoice in the *present* assurance of God's presence, power and willingness to help, symbolized by the triumphant procession of the ark into the sanctuary. Lastly (vv. 28–35), they look to the *future* and anticipate God's final victory and universal sovereignty.

Title: see Introduction III. 1, 2, 3. **1–3.** The verbs can be translated as affirmations, either in the present tense ('God arises . . . '; cf. NEB) or in the future ('God will arise . . . '; cf. GNB). **1.** This echoes the signal given whenever the ark set out (Num. 10: 35; cf. 1 Sam. 4: 3). **2. smoke:** a picture of what is unstable and unsubstantial (cf. 37: 20; 102: 3; Isa. 51: 6). **wicked:** see on Ps. 1. **3. righteous:** see on Ps. 1. **4. his name:** see on 20: 1. **extol him:** the verb (lit. 'lift up') has no object; it could be 'highway' (RSVmg, NIVmg, JB; cf. Isa. 40: 3; 57: 14; 62: 10) or 'your voice' (cf. NEB; cf. 93: 3). **on the clouds:** cf. v. 33; NIV is slightly preferable to 'through the deserts' (NIVmg), though both are possible (cf. v. 7). In Ugaritic literature Ba'al is called 'the Rider of the Clouds', i.e. the giver of rain (see on Ps. 29; cf. 18: 10 f.; 104: 3). **LORD:** here *yāh*, the shorter form of Yahweh (see on Exod. 3: 15). **5.** Cf. 72: 2, 4. **his holy dwelling:** either heaven (cf. Dt. 26: 15) or the temple (cf. v. 16). **6. lonely:** those who are 'lonely' and 'friendless' (NEB). **with singing:** a possible translation based on Ugaritic; or 'to prosperity' (RSV), cf. GNB 'into happy freedom'. **rebellious:** i.e. stubborn Israelites (cf. Dt. 21: 18; Ps. 78: 8; Isa. 30: 1; 65: 2; Jer. 5: 23; Hos. 4: 16).

7–8. Cf. Jg. 5: 4 f. **7. Selah:** see Introduction III 3. **8.** Cf. Exod. 19: 16 ff.; Ps. 18: 7–13. **9.** Possibly a reference to the provision in the wilderness (cf. Exod. 16: 4; Ps. 78: 24, 27). **your . . . inheritance:** either Israel or the land of Canaan (cf. 28: 9). **10. poor:** see on 9: 18. **11. the word:** possibly a reference to the thunder (cf. v. 33b; 29: 3–9) which puts the enemies to flight (cf. Jg. 5: 20 f.) or to the oracle given before the battle (cf. Jg. 4: 6). **those who proclaimed:** the Heb. is feminine, thus GNB 'many women carried the news' (cf. Exod. 15: 20 f.; Jg. 11: 34; 1 Sam. 18: 6 f.; 2 Sam. 18: 19 ff.). **12. divide the plunder:** cf. Jg. 5: 30. **13.** A difficult verse. The meaning may be that although some tribes stayed away from the battle (cf. Jg. 5: 16) the Israelite soldiers returned laden with booty such as gold and silver figures of a dove (possibly the symbol of Astarte, goddess of love). Alternatively, this verse may be a description of the women of v. 12, dressed in their recently acquired ornaments. **14. Almighty:** Heb. *šaddai* (see on Gen. 17: 1; Exod. 6: 3). **Zalmon:** lit. 'Dark Mountain' (JB); probably east of Jordan (cf. v. 15; see *NBD*). **15. majestic mountains:** lit. 'mountain of God', a Heb. superlative. **Bashan:** a kingdom east of the Jordan (see *NBD*; cf. 22: 12). **16.** Mount Zion was not the highest mountain in Canaan; its importance rested solely in Yahweh's choice, not upon its size (cf. Isa. 66: 1 f.). **17. chariots:** cf. 2 Kg. 6: 17; Isa. 66: 15; Ezek. 1: 4 ff.; Hab. 3: 8; Zech. 14: 5. **the Lord has come from Sinai:** a fair emendation (cf. Dt. 33: 2; Jg. 5: 4; Hab. 3: 3); *MT* could be rendered (so A. R. Johnson) 'the Lord is amid them, the God of Sinai is in the sanctuary' (cf. v. 8). **18. from men:** cf. Jg. 5: 12; 2 Sam. 8: 11; 1 Kg. 4: 21; cf. GNB 'from rebellious men'.

19. Praise be to: lit. 'Blessed'; see on 26: 12. **daily:** may connect with 'Praise be to' rather than 'bears'. **bears our burdens:** or 'carries us' (cf. Exod. 19: 4; Dt. 1: 31; Ps. 28: 9; Isa. 40: 11; 46: 1–4; 63: 9). **20.** Cf. 1 Sam. 2: 6. **21. crush the heads:** utterly defeat (cf. 74: 13; 110: 6; Hab. 3: 13). **hairy crowns:** possibly a reference to letting the hair grow to increase strength in holy wars (cf. NEB; cf. Dt. 32: 42; Jg. 5: 2 NEBmg). **go on:** i.e. continue (cf. JB 'the man who parades his guilt'). **22. them:** supplied to make sense; it is not clear whether it refers to the enemies (cf. Am. 9: 2 f.) or to the scattered Israelites (cf. Isa. 43: 5 f.; 49: 12). **Bashan:** here seems to stand for the 'highest heights' (cf. v. 15). **23. plunge:** NIV rightly emends (cf. 58: 10). **the tongues of your dogs . . . :** this may be a proverbial expression for retribution (cf. 1 Kg. 21: 19; 22: 38; 2 Kg. 9: 36). **24. my King:** a well-known title for deities in the ancient world; a frequent title for

Yahweh in the psalms (5: 2; 10: 16; 24: 7, 8, 10; 29: 10; 44: 4; 47: 2, 6; etc.), but not so common elsewhere in the OT. **25. with:** *MT* 'around'. **26. praise:** lit. 'bless, see on 26: 12. **in the great congregation:** or 'in companies'. **the LORD:** should be 'the Lord' (Heb. *'adōnāi*, not *Yahweh*). **in the assembly;** or 'from the fountain,' i.e. all true Israelites. **27.** The four tribes mentioned (two from the south, two from the north) probably represent all twelve (but cf. Jg. 5: 14, 18). **Benjamin:** possibly first because Jerusalem was counted as in its territory. **princes:** leaders, not members of the royal family. **the great throng:** translation uncertain; one Heb. MS has 'in their coloured garments' (cf. JB).

28. Summon your power: *MT* 'Your God has commanded strength'; NIV follows many Heb. MSS, LXX, Targ., Syr., Vulg. **29. Because:** or 'from', linking it with v. 28 (cf. JB). **temple:** see on 5: 7. **30. the beast:** or 'the wild beast'; probably a reference to the hippopotamus or crocodile as a symbol of Egypt (cf. GNB; Ezek. 32: 2). **bulls . . . calves:** kings and their people. **Humbled . . . scatter:** the Heb. is difficult; RSV may be closer with 'Trample under foot those who lust after tribute'. **31. Cush:** Heb. *Kûš*, i.e. 'Nubia' (NEB). **33. with mighty voice:** cf. 29: 3. **34. majesty:** or 'dignity' (cf. Dt. 33: 26). **35. awesome:** cf. 65: 5. **in your sanctuary:** cf. v. 5; *MT* (RSVmg) suggests 'as he comes from' (NEB; cf. 20: 2). **Praise be:** lit. 'Blessed'; see on 26: 12 (cf. 89: 52; 1 Chr. 16: 36).

Psalm 69. THE CRY OF A LONELY SUFFERER

This individual lament is the prayer of a man *in extremis*, suffering in every possible way: physically, mentally, socially and spiritually. The descriptions he gives are not, however, explicit enough to enable us to build up a detailed picture of his troubles. It seems clear that he is suffering from some severe illness (vv. 1–2, 14–15) which he regards as a divine chastisement (v. 26) and therefore confesses his sins (v. 5), although they are probably sins of ignorance and inadvertence. His suffering is exacerbated by the unjust accusations of his enemies (vv. 4, 14, 18 ff., 26) who persecute him (and possibly imprison him; cf. v. 32) for his devotion to God (vv. 7, 9–12), and by the unsympathetic attitude of his family (v. 8). On top of all this, he is concerned that if God does not answer his prayers, others will be in danger of losing their faith (v. 6; cf. v. 32). The psalmist's prayer is for a speedy end to his sufferings (vv. 1 ff., 13–18, 29) and for vengeance on his enemies (vv. 22–28; cf. Ps. 22). (On the problem of vindictiveness in the Psalms see Introduction IV. 1.) At v. 30 the psalm changes to a vow of thanksgiving (vv. 30–33) and an exhortation to praise (vv. 34–36), addressed to his fellow-worshippers in the Temple (cf. v. 32). The psalmist had probably received (by an oracle?) assurance that deliverance was on the way (see on Ps. 22).

Attempts to identify the author and historical situation break down through lack of concrete evidence. On the traditional attribution to David see Introduction III. 2. A popular alternative suggestion is Jeremiah (cf. Jer. 11: 18 ff.; 12: 1 ff.; 15: 10 ff.; 17: 12 ff.; 18: 18 ff.; 20: 7 ff.). If vv. 34–36 are not a later addition (cf. 51: 18, 19) the psalmist could have been a Jew anxious for the rebuilding of the Temple after the Exile (cf. v. 9) or critical of the ritualistic worship of his time (cf. vv. 22, 31). Whilst it would be possible to envisage the psalm being used to express the feelings of the nation in a time of trouble (*e.g.* the Exile), the idea (cf. Eaton) that it was used to accompany the symbolic humiliation of the king at the autumn festival (see Introduction II. 2) is highly speculative.

After Ps. 22 this is the psalm most frequently quoted in the NT (see marginal references), especially as a pre-figuring of the sufferings of Jesus, although this does not mean that the whole psalm should be applied to Him as though it were a prophetic prediction (see on Ps. 22 and Introduction IV. 2). The confession of v. 5 cannot be placed on the lips of Jesus; and instead of the curses of vv. 22 ff., He prayed 'Father, forgive them . . .' (Lk. 23: 34). Not surprisingly, the Prayer Book appoints the psalm for Good Friday.

Title: see Introduction III. 1, 2, 3. **1, 2.** The **waters** and **miry depths** are probably a picture of the powers of chaos and death, i.e. of Sheol and its sphere of influence (cf. vv. 14 f.; see on 40: 2; cf. 18: 4; 2 Sam. 22: 5 ff.; Ps. 130: 1; 144: 7). **1. neck:** possibly the original meaning of Heb. *nepeš*, often translated 'soul' (see on 3: 2). **4. what I did not steal . . . :** RSV unnecessarily changes a statement (cf. NIV, RV, JB) into a question. The phrase may have been a proverbial expression for injured innocence (cf. Lev. 6: 5; Ps. 35: 11; Jer. 15: 10). **5. folly:** a synonym for 'sin' (cf. Ps. 38: 5; Prov. 24: 9). **not hidden from you:** cf. 19: 12 f.; 139: 23 f. **6. LORD** (i.e. *Yahweh*) **Almighty:** see on 24: 1. **who seek you:** see on 24: 6. **9. insults:** same word as **scorn** (vv. 10, 19). **10.** The exact translation is uncertain, but NIV gives the likely sense. **11. sackcloth:** see on 30: 11. **people make sport:** cf. Job 30: 9; Ps. 44: 14. **12. gate:** centre of business, justice and community life (cf. Gen. 23: 10 ff.; Dt. 21: 19; Jos. 20: 4; Ru. 4: 11 ff.; 1 Sam. 4: 12–18). **13. in the time of your favor:** i.e. when God deems best (cf. JB; cf. Ps. 31: 15; Isa. 49: 8). **love:** see on 5: 7. **thy faithful help:** lit. 'in the truth of thy salvation' (see on 25: 5; 35: 3);

the phrase can be taken with v. 13 (NIV, JB) or v. 14 (RSV). **14. mire . . . waters:** see on vv. 1, 2. **15. pit:** see on 28: 1 (cf. 55:23; Prov. 30: 15 f.; Isa. 5: 14). **16. mercy:** lit. 'compassions'. **17. Do not hide . . . :** i.e. 'do not withdraw thy favour' (see on 4: 6; 13: 1). **18. rescue** Heb. *gā'al* denotes 'protect' or 'deliver' as by a next-of-kin (see on 19: 5; cf. 103: 4; 119: 154). **redeem:** or 'ransom me' (Heb. *pādāh*: see on 49: 7). **20. scorn:** same word as **insults** v. 19, cf. v. 19. **I looked for sympathy:** or 'I waited eagerly (for someone) to show sympathy'. **21.** A picture of scornful treatment. **gall:** (LXX) probably from a plant (cf. Hos. 10: 4). **vinegar:** sour wine, unfit to drink.

22. The reference is probably to sacrificial meals in the Temple by which the hypocritical wicked would deceive themselves that they were in fellowship with God (cf. Paul's use of this verse in Rom. 11: 9). **may it become retribution:** *MT* has 'for peace (pl.)'. NIV follows LXX ('for requital'); RSV follows Targ.; 'let their sacrificial feasts (i.e. peace offerings) be a trap'. **23. backs:** the seat of man's strength and vigour (cf. Dt. 33: 11; Job 40: 16). **25.** Cf. Job 18: 17 ff.; Prov. 14: 11. **26.** NIV follows the Heb., but RSV is probably right to follow the versions (cf. JB). **27. Charge them with . . . :** cf. NEB 'Give them the punishment their sin deserves'. **do not let them share . . . :** lit. 'let them not come into your righteousness' (i.e. salvation: see on 33: 5). **28. book of life:** OT references seem to envisage at least two kinds of books: one recording the name and deeds of all living people (Ps. 51: 1; 109: 13 ff.; Neh. 13: 14), another containing the names of the righteous (Isa. 4: 3; 56: 5; Dan. 12: 1; Mal. 3: 16; cf. Rev. 3: 5; 13: 8). To be **blotted out** implies retribution and death (cf. Exod. 32: 32 f.). **29. in pain and distress:** see on 9: 18.

30. name: see on 20: 1. **thanksgiving:** see on 50: 14. **31.** See on 50: 8–15; 51: 15 ff. There is a word-play here: God prefers a **song** (Heb. *šîr*, v. 30) to an **ox** (Heb. *šôr*). **with its horns and hoofs:** i.e. 'full-grown' (GNB) and ritually clean (cf. Lev. 11: 3–8). **32. poor:** see on 9: 12. **seek God:** see on 24: 6. **may your hearts live:** i.e. 'take courage' (cf. NEB). **33. needy:** see on 9: 18. **his captive people:** lit. 'his prisoners' (cf. 68: 6); possibly a reference to the Exile (cf. Isa. 42: 7, 22). **35. Zion:** see on 2: 6. **rebuild . . . :** best fits the Exile and after (cf. Isa. 44: 26; 61: 1; Ezek. 36: 10), but could rather refer to the Assyrian invasion in the time of Hezekiah (2 Kg. 18: 13 ff.; Isa. 1: 7 ff.). **36. children:** lit. 'seed'. **love his name:** see on 26: 8; 20: 1.

Psalm 70. AN URGENT PLEA FOR HELP

A variant of 40: 13–17 (*q.v.*), probably duplicated for use as an individual lament and included in a separate collection of psalms.

Title: see Introduction III. 1, 2, 3, 4. **1. Hasten:** RSV has 'be pleased', borrowed from 40: 13. **2.** A shorter version of 40: 14. **3. turn back:** RSV 'be appalled' conforms to 40: 15 (cf. NEB). **4, 5.** Slight differences from 40: 16 f.

Psalm 71. THE PRAYER OF AN OLD MAN

The author of this psalm seems to be an old man (cf. vv. 9, 18) persecuted by enemies (vv. 4, 10, 13) who believe that he is vulnerable (v. 11), either because of his natural weakness or possibly because he is suffering from an unspecified illness which has brought him close to death (cf. v. 20) and which they take as evidence that he is a sinner (cf. Job). His prayer, which is a mixture of lamentations and expressions of confidence and praise (see on Pss. 22 and 41), is like a tapestry woven out of his reminiscences of earlier psalms such as Pss. 22; 31; 35; 38; 40; 109 (see references below) and backed by the experiences of a life-time (cf. also Ps. 86 and Jon. 2: 2–9). The psalm is probably exilic or post-exilic. Some have attributed it to Jeremiah. LXX adds a title: 'By David; of the sons of Jonadab, and of the first that were taken captive' which suggests that the psalm was used to express national feelings during the exile (cf. v. 20, RV).

1–3. See on 31: 1–3a. **3. rock of refuge:** so many Heb. MSS, LXX, Targ., Vulg., Syr. (cf. 31: 2); *MT* has 'rock of habitation' (cf. 90: 1). **to which I can always go:** NIV follows *MT*; cf. NEB and RSV mg. RSV 'a strong fortress' follows LXX and 31: 2. **4. wicked:** see on 1: 4 ff. **5, 6.** Cf. 22: 9, 10. **5.** 'OT hope is not wishful thinking, but . . . God-inspired certainty . . .' (A. A. Anderson); cf. Jer. 29: 11; 31: 17. **6. you brought me forth:** the meaning is not certain; another possibility is 'my strength' (cf. LXX 'my protector'; cf. NEB, GNB). **7. portent:** NEB 'a solemn warning' (cf. Exod. 7: 3; 11: 9; Dt. 6: 22). The psalmist has probably been regarded as an example of divine punishment (cf. 31: 11; Dt. 28: 46). **8. splendor:** 'honour' or 'renown' (cf. Dt. 26: 19; Prov. 28: 12). **9.** Cf. Isa. 46: 3 f.

12, 13. Cf. 22: 11; 35: 4, 22, 26; 38: 21 f.; 40: 13, 14; 109: 29. **13. covered:** i.e., with disgrace (cf. 109: 29). **15. righteousness:** see on 33: 5. **salvation:** lit. 'salvation' (see on 35: 3). **measure:** a rare Heb. word, related to the verb 'tell'. **16. I will come:** i.e. to the Temple to offer praise. **I will proclaim:** lit. 'I will cause to remember', i.e. 'make mention of . . .'. **righteousness:** see on 33: 5. **17. marvelous deeds:** see on 9: 1. **18.** Cf. v. 9; 22: 30. **your power:** lit. 'thy arm' (cf. 37: 17). **19. righteousness:** see on 33: 5. **the skies:** lit. 'the height'. **20. me . . . my life:** another reading (*Kethibh*) is 'us . . . us' (so RV). **depths of the earth:** i.e. Sheol (see on 6: 5; 63: 9). **bring me**

up: i.e. he is already in the sphere of death's influence (cf. 18: 4 f.). **21. honor:** lit. 'greatness'. **22. faithfulness:** lit. 'truth' (see on 25: 5). **Holy One of Israel:** seldom found outside Isaiah (see on Isa. 1: 4; cf. Ps. 78: 41; 89: 18). **23. I:** lit. 'my soul'; see on 3: 2. **24.** Cf. 35: 4, 26, 28; 40: 14. **tell:** lit. 'meditate' (see on 1: 2). **your righteous acts:** lit. 'thy righteousness' (see on 33: 5).

Psalm 72. BLESSINGS ON GOD'S KING

The original life-setting of this royal psalm was probably the enthronement of the Davidic kings, and possibly also the yearly celebration of their accession at the New Year Festival (cf. Ps. 2 and see Introduction II. 2). *MT* attributes the psalm to Solomon; Targ. has 'By Solomon, spoken in prophecy' (i.e. of the Messiah). LXX (cf. AV) has 'For Solomon' (a possible rendering of the Heb.) and some have suggested that it was written by David (so Calvin) or even by Solomon for himself. The association with Solomon may, however, simply be a deduction from v. 10 (cf. 1 Kg. 10: 1 ff., 22) and it is better to admit that we do not know the name of the author (probably a court poet) or of the king for whom it was originally written.

After the opening petition (v. 1), the bulk of the psalm may be regarded either as an intercession (or blessing), with the verbs translated as jussives ('may', 'let', as RSV), or, with the verbs taken as futures (as AV, RV), as a confident prediction (or prophecy) based upon the assurance that God would answer the prayer of v. 1. (NIV, NEB, JB, GNB give a mixture of the two.) The main part of the psalm may be divided into four stanzas. Verses 1–7 deal with the relationship between the king and his own people, praying that he may be the channel of divine protection and blessing to his nation. Then vv. 8–11 ask that his kingdom may be world-wide and that he will receive universal homage. However unlikely this might seem for a king of Judah (but cf. 1 Kg. 10: 23 ff.), it was the logical goal for one who was regarded as the vicegerent of Yahweh, King of the universe (cf. Ps. 2: 6 ff.; 1 Chr. 28: 5; 29: 23; 2 Chr. 9: 8). Verses 12–14 remind the king that despite his important international position, his primary duty is to be a father and shepherd to the lowliest of his people; in fact, this is to be the basis of his world-wide renown. The psalm concludes (vv. 15–17) with prayers for the welfare of the king, the prosperity of his land, and the perpetuation of his memory, as God fulfils through him the promise made to Abraham (Gen. 12: 2 ff.; 22: 18). The doxology of vv. 18, 19 is probably a later addition (cf. 41: 13) as also is v. 20 which marks the close of the Second Book of the Psalter (see Introduction I).

The language of the psalm, addressed as it is to the far from perfect rulers of Judah, might seem extravagant. This may be partly because certain ideas and phrases have been borrowed from ancient oriental hyperbolic 'court style', but largely because the poet has in mind a picture of the ideal king based upon the nature of the kingship of God Himself. It was inevitable, therefore, particularly after the cessation of the monarchy at the Exile, that this psalm should be applied (cf. Targ.) to the coming Messiah (see on Ps. 2 and Introduction IV. 2). It is surprising, however, in the light of its obvious applicability to Jesus, that no use is made of it in the NT. Nevertheless, the early Church used it for Epiphany (cf. vv. 10 f.; Mt. 2: 1–11), and it forms the basis of hymns like 'Hail to the Lord's Anointed' (Montgomery) and 'Jesus shall reign where'er the sun' (Watts).

Title: see Introduction III. 2. **1. your justice:** NIV follows the Versions; *MT* has 'thy judgments'. *MT* suggests the handing over of the written law to the king at his coronation (cf. Dt. 17: 18 ff.; 1 Sam. 10: 25; 2 Kg. 11: 12); NIV suggests the gift of being able to judge rightly (cf. 1 Kg. 3: 9, 28; Isa. 11: 2 ff.; 28: 6) which offers a better parallel to **your righteousness** (see on 33: 5). **royal son:** i.e. the 'king' of the first line. **2. judge:** Heb. *dîn*, a synonym for the more frequent *šāpaṭ*, both conveying the two aspects of defending, delivering, or avenging, punishing. **righteousness . . . justice:** see on 33: 5. **afflicted ones:** see on 9: 18. **3. prosperity:** Heb. *šālôm*; see on 29: 11. **the fruit of righteousness:** or read 'in righteousness', i.e. prosperity will come to the land through the king's righteous rule (vv. 1, 2). **4. defend:** or 'judge' (Heb. *šāpaṭ*), see on v. 2. **afflicted:** see on 9: 18. **children of the needy:** cf. Ps. 94: 6; Isa. 1: 23; 10: 2, see on 9: 12. **5. He will endure:** NIV (cf. v. 15) follows LXX and Vulg. (cf. Dt. 17: 20; Isa. 53: 10); *MT* (NIVmg) is well

represented by GNB 'May your people worship you as long as the sun shines'. **6.** Cf. 2 Sam. 23: 4; Isa. 32: 2; Hos. 6: 3. **mown field:** here probably before it is cut (cf. NEB). **7.** Cf. v. 3. **the righteous:** *MT* has 'the righteous man'; RSV 'righteousness' follows some Heb. MSS, LXX, Syr., Vulg.

8. from sea to sea: probably a reference to the whole earth (cf. Mic. 7: 12; Zech. 9: 10), rather than any particular seas (cf. Exod. 23: 31). **the River:** usually denotes the Euphrates (cf. Gen. 15: 18; 31: 21; 2 Sam. 10: 16). **9. The desert tribes:** *MT* suggests 'beasts of the wilderness' (cf. JB), but the reference may be to wild Bedouin tribes (cf. LXX, Vulg., NEB 'Ethiopia'). **10. Tarshish . . . Sheba . . . Seba:** remote places with which Solomon traded (1 Kg. 10: 1 ff., 22); see *NBD*. **distant shores:** islands and coasts of the Mediterranean. **12. needy . . . afflicted:** see on 9: 12, 18. **14. rescue:** Heb. *gāʾal*, see on 69: 18. **blood:** i.e. 'lives' (GNB). **precious:** cf. 1 Sam. 26: 21; 2 Kg. 1: 13 f.; Ps. 9: 12; 116: 15. **15.** Cf. 1 Sam. 10: 24; 2 Sam. 16: 16; 2 Kg. 11: 12. **gold from Sheba:** representative of all kinds of tribute (cf. v. 10). **bless him:** the people will either bless the king or call down God's blessing on him (see on 26: 12). **16. tops of the hills:** usually the least fertile parts. **Lebanon:** see *NBD*. **let it thrive . . . :** *MT* is difficult; NIV omits 'from the cities' (cf. RSV, AV) **17.** Cf. Job 18: 19; Ps. 89: 36 f.; 1 Kg. 2: 12, 45. **name:** see on 20: 1. **may his name endure:** *MT* has 'may his name have issue (or 'branch forth')'; but one Heb. MS and the Versions read 'his name shall endure' (cf. JB, NEB). **call him blessed:** or 'happy' (the verb is cognate to 'aš‌erê: see on 1: 1). **18. Praise be:** lit. 'Blessed'; see on 26: 12. **marvelous deeds:** see on 9: 1. **19. name:** see on 20: 1. **Amen and Amen:** see on 41: 13. The doxology forms the conclusion to Book II of the Psalter.

Book Three   Psalms 73–89

Psalm 73. FAITH REBORN

In the temple services there was evidently room for a period of open worship in which individuals gave testimonies to their fellow-believers of God's dealings with them, as in the old Methodist class meetings. Here the psalmist candidly relates an experience of crippling doubt from which he eventually emerged spiritually enriched.

Conclusion (v. 1)

God is good is no mere cliché but a mature conviction grounded in experience. In similar vein Dostoevsky could say: 'It is not as a child that I believe and confess Christ. My hosanna is born of a furnace of doubt.'

The problem stated (vv. 2–14)

He has not always been so sure. Recently he **almost** lost his faith. Around him he **saw** irreligious, self-centred folk who enjoyed *šālôm*, peace and **prosperity:** for them all was well. Health and uncommon happiness was theirs. What was the secret of their success? Not good, spiritual lives, to be sure. They brazenly flaunted their arrogance, and it was their habit to ride roughshod over others' rights. **Their** beady **eyes bulged** (NIVmg) 'through folds of fat' (NEB), as they busily schemed. Superior and cynical, they engaged in malicious talk and threats. To all around they dictated their orders, and God they dismissed as an irrelevance. Was not the **Most High** God too transcendent to care, to be bothered with mankind? A convenient theology, for it left them practical atheists, free to do as they liked. No wonder they attracted popular support among God's **people**, who 'turn to them and lap up all they say' (JB; cf. RSVmg). Even the psalmist was drawn to this easy way of life devoid of moral and religious scruples. Its advantages were obvious: they had all the luck, wealth galore and never a worry. Was he not wasting his time obeying his conscience and washing his **hands**? Where did it get him? All the blows from which the others were exempt (v. 5) came his way. God seemed to have a down on him, for trouble dogged his steps all the time.

The psalmist had obviously been trained in the wisdom schools which produced such works as Proverbs, Job and Ecclesiastes. The wisdom teachers sought to relate religion to life and its problems. Traditional belief regarded wealth as God's blessing upon the righteous and trouble as His punishment for impiety. But increasingly there were seen to be exceptions to this rule of faith, which brought agony and torment to the orthodox believer. It is this problem that the psalmist brings into the open, for the benefit of his fellow-believers and as part of an act of worship. Both they and God were present in the sanctuary, and he turns from one to the other in the psalm (cf. v. 28). He tries to square facts and faith in a topsy-turvy world where the moral God seemed absent and rampant evil was allowed. 'Virtue in distress and vice in triumph make atheists of mankind' (John Dryden). How could one go on believing?

The solution sought and found (vv. 15–20)
He was saved from the brink (cf. v. 2) by his fellow-believers, 'the family of God' (NEB). There seemed a barrier between him and his God in his present frame of mind. But the reality of his fellowship with his brothers in the faith checked him from the conclusion of his human logic. How could he let them down? They were God's grappling iron to pull him back to Himself. But he was still a long way off; an unscalable mountain lay between. 'I found it too hard for me' (NEB), he says.

He eventually attended a festival service at the temple, and during the worship discovered that light which 'surprises the Christian while he sings' (W. Cowper). Many psalms imply that in the temple the wonders of God's grace and the **terrors** of His judgment were celebrated as powerful factors. At such services God revealed Himself as sovereign judge and saviour, to prompt His people's praise, warn against infidelity and assure the oppressed of vindication. Then it was that the scales fell from the psalmist's eyes and he was granted an experience of the God 'who when the godless do triumph, all virtue confounding, / Sheddeth His light, chaseth the horrors of night, / Saints with His mercy surrounding' (J. Neander, tr. C. Winkworth). Converted again to God's point of view, he took to heart what he had heard rehearsed in the temple service, the reality of divine power and the judgment for the wicked (cf. Job 27: 13–23). He applied it to his irreligious and immoral contemporaries. The successful lives of those whom he had envied were built on quicksand and had no permanent security in God's world. The **Lord** (cf. JB) was biding His time, as if asleep. He could be trusted to intervene, alert and active (cf. 35: 23; 78: 65). Then will temptation's 'fancies flee away', as unreal as in a nightmare. 'Fading is the worldling's pleasure . . . / Solid joys and lasting treasure / None but Zion's children know' (J. Newton).

Lasting treasure (vv. 21–28)
The psalmist confesses his former blindness as to his relationship to God, as a believer. His earlier evaluation of what was worthwhile (v. 13), he admits to be based on materialistic premises ill befitting one made in God's image. He belongs to God, and God it is who holds him in a strong grip that will never let him go, counselling him aright and promising a glorious destiny. How can personal fellowship with a living God perish in Sheol? The psalmist struggles with the concept of an afterlife in God's presence with an exploring logic based on faith. Is not knowing Him eternal life (Jn 17: 3)? The only vocabulary at his disposal is **take**, 'receive', used of the translation of Enoch and Elijah (Gen. 5: 24; 2 Kg. 2:1).

None but God, nothing else, can satisfy him. His faith is no longer conditioned by material factors. Though his human frame lose its vitality, in God he will continue to find his source of spiritual life (cf. 2 C. 4: 16–18). 'He is all I ever need' (GNB) is his devout confession. Those estranged from this source of life are necessarily doomed. But the psalmist finds satisfaction in close fellowship with God at the temple worship. Here he has come as a consequence of his commitment, in order to **tell** what God has done for him, and to proclaim it to be of a piece with His great deeds of salvation for His people.

Psalm 74. ANCHORS IN THE STORM

Why, why? is the agonized cry of the suffering community (vv. 1, 11), as of many a sufferer since. It is not so much the 'why?' of enquiring minds as the cry of aching hearts reacting to chaos and confusion. God is viewed as the unseen, sovereign controller of human experience. To Him therefore must come the appeal, invoking His love and power as steadying anchors in the storm.

Appeal to the Good Shepherd (vv. 1–3)
Disaster has struck, and to a supremely religious people it can be a sign only of divine rejection, a terrible contrast to His earlier work of election. They echo the age-old Song of Moses (Exod. 15: 13, 16 f.), laying claim to its affirmations as the people whom God once **purchased** and **redeemed**. We are the heirs, they imply, of those who in the Exodus received the gift of covenant relationship. Scripture comes to life as God's contemporary people appropriate its ancient truths. **Zion** too played a vital role in his purposes as the 'mountain' made for His 'abode'. Now shockingly **the sanctuary** lies in **ruins**; God's home on earth is a ghastly monument to **enemy** action. Can God stand aside? The situation is complex: if they are victims of God's wrath, God too is victim of the invader's destruction.

Details of the havoc (vv. 4–8)
They pour out the sorry tale in prayer, thereby bringing some relief to their shattered minds. The problem is not only theirs, but God's. It is **your foes** who are responsible, committing sacrilege in damaging the temple. In this respect God is on His people's side as they mourn. There is something here of the faith of Rom. 8: 35–39. Here is 'tribulation' indeed. It is a tragedy comparable to the disciples' despair that Jesus, antitype of the temple (Jn 2: 19), should be crucified.

Probably this was part of Nebuchadnezzar's second and fatal attack on Jerusalem in 587 B.C. as reprisal for rebellion (2 Kg. 25). The temple where hitherto the faithful had sung songs of praise was recently resounding with raucous shouts of triumph as the enemy **roared**. The vandals held nothing sacred in their murderous resolve and impious outrage. Sacred sites throughout Judah suffered at their hands, and holy beauty was wantonly destroyed.

Renewed appeal (vv. 9–11)
Festivals and daily services, outward symbols of faith, were held no more. God was silent: no **prophets** brought reassurance (cf. Lam. 2: 9) like Isaiah in an earlier period (*e.g.* Isa. 7: 16; 8: 4; 37: 30). God was absent: where was His outstretched arm, why did He not assert His power?

Praise of God's power (vv. 12–17)
The psalm-leader is prompted to break into song. His faith rises above the despair of the congregation, calling them back to renewed confidence in his **king**. Faith must have the last word, not sight. **You, you**, he exclaims, countering **they, they** of vv. 4–8. However strong they are, God is stronger. The vocabulary of ancient Near Eastern lore is applied as metaphor to the Exodus. Pagan religious poets

traditionally described their god's victory over **the sea** and monsters like **Leviathan**. Israel triumphantly claimed such language for what Yahweh accomplished on their behalf when the Red Sea was divided and corpses of Egyptian oppressors were thrown up on the shore, when water was provided in **the desert** and Jordan was dried up. And this Lord of sacred history is also the powerful God of creation and providence.

A last appeal (vv. 18–23)
To such a God the people bring fervent prayers. 'Thou art coming to a King, / Large petitions with thee bring' (J. Newton). Surely Yahweh will vindicate His **name** and not let **the enemy** insult Him with impunity. They feel helpless as a **dove**, a defenceless prey. But they are not alone: their cause is **your cause**. The onus rests upon the **covenant** God to intervene. And this prayer of faith had its eventual reward. After the exile temple and society rose again from their ruins.

God's people can still appeal to His love and power revealed in dynamic event, to Calvary love and to resurrection power (Rom. 5: 8; Eph. 1: 19 f.). These believers have left an example in claiming for themselves a renewal of divine power and ancient grace, not selfishly but for God's own glory.

Psalm 75.   THE SILVER LINING
The people's praise (v. 1)
The theme of their worship is God's **wonderful deeds**, His historical acts of grace on Israel's behalf. This introduction is surprising: in view of the crisis mentioned later, urgent prayer might have been the community's first word. Theirs is the uncommon faith of Habakkuk (3: 17 f.) and of Paul and Silas who praised in prison in the dark (Ac. 16: 25).

God's oracle (vv. 2–5)
Here is another surprise. Appreciation of God's power might have given way to supplication (cf. 74: 12–23). Instead, a divine message breaks in, illustrating the glorious principle that 'before they call, I will answer' (Isa. 65: 24). Doubtless a prophet on the temple staff was inspired to interrupt (cf. 2 Chr. 20: 14). God knows all about His people's problem and intends to deal with it. They are victims of proud and **wicked** men. The Judge of all the earth has not abdicated control but will intervene in His own good time. When moral foundations are undermined through violence and injustice, God it is who providentially restores the balance, capping a 'thousand-year Reich' with a Nuremberg. Israel's faith is bolstered by His warning to their oppressors: they cannot with impunity toss their **horns** defiantly against God.

The prophet's commentary (vv. 6–10)
The inspired message is now expounded. **God**

... **judges** takes up v. 2, **he exalts** vv. 4 f., **wicked** and **horns** v. 5, and **it is God** recalls **it is I**, v. 3. God is the arbiter of human destiny, it is reaffirmed. Lasting blessing comes from no human source, only from God. Human life is the scene of divine adjustment; the NT adds another dimension, a Last Judgment of unsettled scores.

Even now the **cup** of judgment is in Yahweh's hand, ready to be administered to the people's foes and send them reeling as with a heavy blow. This OT metaphor has sacred significance for the Christian. It was echoed in the Gethsemane prayer of Jesus (Mk 14: 36), who 'drained the last dark drop'.

The prophet reinforces the oracle with a confident promise of perpetual praise when it is fulfilled. God will keep His word, performing the threat of v. 5 and blessing His people. Thus is concluded the third reaction to the crisis. The community's resolve to 'praise Him for all that is past' and God's own word of assurance are followed by this call to 'trust Him for all that's to come' (J. Hart).

Psalm 76. GOD'S VICTORY

'The strife is o'er, the battle done' (F. Pott): the triumph of resurrection hymns echoes this OT counterpart. Like Pss. 46 and 48 it proclaims a decisive victory won at Jerusalem. Originally it probably celebrated David's capture of the Jebusite city and his defeat of the Philistines who came to their allies' aid (2 Sam. 5). This ancient event was immortalized as an archetype of God's supremacy and as a pledge of its recurring and ultimate demonstration. When Judah and its monarchy were weak, the faithful would derive fresh hope from singing such a psalm. When the Assyrians failed to capture Jerusalem in 701 B.C., its escape must have given new relevance to this old hymn. Worshippers in the temple were proud to stand in the city of God. It thrilled them with a reminder of God's dominion, established in principle when He won Jerusalem for Himself and quelled all opposition. For the seer of Revelation these sentiments were transformed into Christian hope for the future (Rev.21:2; 22: 3; cf. Heb. 12:22, 28).

God's renown (vv. 1–3)

The people of God throughout their land acknowledge and celebrate His fame as Lord of **Zion**. It is Israel's privilege that within its territory God has deigned to make His earthly home. **Salem**, once possessed by Jebusite kings (Gen. 14: 18), has passed into the hands of the God of **Israel**. There He dwells among His people. He is there by right of conquest. All the military power of men had proved useless against His omnipotence. Such is the greatness of Israel's God.

God's power (vv. 4–6)

What chance could any mortals have against this eternal Light, the God who is **resplendent**? **Mountains** which have stood **majestic** from time immemorial seem to shrink before the grandeur of the Ancient of Days. No wonder experienced troops were totally defeated, **still** before Israel's Champion. The reference is to a type of holy war in which God fought for His people, causing 'a panic confusion and demoralization of the enemy, whose effect was to paralyse their confidence in their fighting powers' (G von Rad; cf. Exod. 15: 14 f.; 23: 27 f.; 1 Sam.7: 10). The God of Exodus power, who 'threw the horse and its rider' into the sea (Exod. 15: 1), had proved no less victorious in the promised land.

God's intervention (vv. 7–9)

From ancient events are deduced principles of divine activity in both vv. 4 and 7. Those who oppose Him cannot hold their own. The God whose home is **heaven** as well as Zion spoke, and such was the power of His word that the forces of **the land** ceased their raging forthwith. Like an Israelite judge sitting to hear evidence and rising to his feet to deliver his verdict, God **rose up** and dealt with the oppressors of His people. His past action carries with it the implicit certainty that He can and will act thus whenever necessary.

Homage to God (vv. 10–13)

Future implications come to the fore, as in v. 7. Rebels against God will be forced to acknowledge His authority. He will use their very rebellion to enhance His glory. In view of God's sovereign control over their foes His people are urged both to promise and to bring offerings as tokens of their own reverent submission and grateful homage. His entourage, Israel at worship, is exhorted to show tangible appreciation of their awe-inspiring God, who time and again **breaks the spirit** of foreign rulers who could conquer His people and their land.

For God's OT people Jerusalem had sacramental significance for the land and for national life. The ancient conquest of the capital carried strong covenantal overtones as a crucial event laden with guarantees for the future. It was the D-day which promised an eventual V-day, like the cross and resurrection, at which God in principle 'disarmed the principalities and powers . . .' (Col. 2: 15).

Note: v. 10. The exposition follows the RSV and NIV mg, but the text and interpretation are by no means clear. Contrast NEB and GNB.

Psalm 77. FAITH'S VICTORY

The psalmist reports to the congregation the trial to which his faith was subjected and how he came through it. Disaster had overtaken the nation; this sensitive individual took to heart its troubles and felt their brunt upon his own soul.

Summary (v. 1)

His prayer was eventually answered. 'I cried aloud to God . . . and he heard me' (NEB) is his testimony. Outwardly nothing changed, but he received a fresh conviction of God's ultimate purposes, and his anguish left him.

Earlier anxiety (vv. 2–10)

The psalmist's experience is better represented with past tenses (NIV, JB, NEB, cf. AV). This is a flashback describing his previous torment. There was a time when to **remember God** was a source of inconsolable sorrow. He could not sleep, and indirectly God was responsible by letting him down, as he thought. Nights were spent in prayer, but there were times when his grief was too deep to be put into words. He could not help comparing bygone **days** glorified in sacred saga with the miserable fate of his country at the moment. It created serious repercussions in his mind and grave doubts concerning God. 'My spirit asked this question' (JB; cf. NIV, AV), he says, or rather a shattering volley of questions. About the existence of God he has no doubt, but as to His providential dealings with Israel he is myst-ified. Once the nation basked in God's favour and covenant **love**, had a firm place in His affections and enjoyed promised blessing. Those good old days seemed at an end **for-ever**. Could it be that God had thrown His people over? Did his **promise** count for nothing? What did it all mean? And 'what hurts me most' (GNB), he says, is the conviction that God's **hand** had lost its ancient power where His people were concerned. No longer was it true that 'no word from Thee can fruitless fall' (H. Twells). (This comment is based on RSV rendering of v. 10. NIV treats it as the beginning of the next paragraph.)

Renewed assurance (vv. 11–20)

The psalmist thinks again. Still he dwells upon olden times, but now they grip his soul. The events of sacred history kindle a fire and by its glow he catches a fresh sight of the God behind them. He is matchless, without rival. His ways are characterized by holiness, in the primary sense of transcendent power (cf. Isa. 6: 3). The great archetypal event of the Exodus, when He laid claim to the whole nation, both Israel and Judah (cf. Ob. 18), is a permanent witness to His election. No, God had not changed.

He meditates not now with gloom but with adoring wonder upon the miracle of the Ex-odus. Probably he quotes from an ancient hymn in verses 16–20: they are in a different metre from the foregoing and archaic in tone. The Exodus is dressed in the majestic language of theophany. The OT often represents in such stylized grandeur God's intervention in history (cf. Jg. 5: 4 f.; Ps. 18: 7–15; Hab. 3: 3–10).

Water, the symbol of chaos and forces hostile to God (cf. 74: 13), shrank away in fear when He appeared, and so the Red Sea was crossed. His dread coming to aid His oppressed people is described in terms of a furious thunderstorm. Amidst **whirlwind** and between flashes of lightning dark was 'His path on the wings of the storm' (R. Grant). Ahead of His people God 'strode across the sea' (JB), too sublime for mortal eye to see, but revealing Himself to trusting Israel in an experience of His presence and power. Nor did He abandon them on the far shore but like a shepherd led His human flock safely through the perilous wilderness under the charge of appointed leaders.

And so the psalm ends. The psalmist needed no other argument. It was enough that God had revealed Himself—once and for all—on Israel's side. The beginning guaranteed the end. The dynamic landmark of the Exodus was a signpost that pointed unerringly on, an earnest of faith's fulfilment. In a sense the promised land still lay ahead, and the psalmist soldiers on in the darkness, daunted no more but with firm step and a light ablaze in his heart, sure that 'he who began a good work . . . will bring it to completion' (Phil. 1: 6).

Psalm 78.   THE LESSONS OF HISTORY

The people are assembled, probably in the temple at a festival. A spiritual leader takes the opportunity to preach a sermon from history. He does not give a straightforward historical account nor does he concentrate solely on the mighty acts of God, of which the people at worship often heard. Instead he considers the topsyturviness of Israel's history, for his hearers to take both encouragement and warn-ing therefrom. He knew only too well the truth of the cynical observation that the one thing to be learned from history is that people learn nothing from history. But he pleads for hind-sight to become foresight as he traces God's hand in the twists and turns of Israel's journey through time.

A sacred duty (vv. 1–8)

He craves a hearing for his **parables**, a 'story with a meaning' (NEB) or moral that he would tell concerning 'mysteries from the past' (JB). There were sharp tangents and dead ends in the history of God's people. In one sense he had nothing new to say, only a reminder of the old, old story of God and His acts of wonder-working power achieved on Israel's behalf. In fact there was a twofold tradition which had to be handed down from generation to **gener-ation**, a heritage of grace and **law**. The two were linked, for the law stood four-square upon grace. Redeeming grace was but the his-torical prologue to and justification for God's demands upon His people (Exod. 20: 2). The first was meant as motivation for the other so that the contemporary heirs of this double tradition might trust in their great God and obey His revealed will. But there was a sombre side to this religious tradition, meant not to demoralize but to deflect from the same old mistakes as Israel's ancestors made. 'These things occurred as examples and were written down as warnings for us' was Paul's echo (1 C. 10: 6, 11).

Remember Ephraim (vv. 9–11)

The psalmist breaks off to give an illustration of the grim consequences of ignoring past history. He mentions an incident doubtless notorious to his hearers, when the tribe of Ephraim, for a long time Israel's leading tribe, 'turned tail when the time came to fight' (JB), fine archers though they were. Why did God not bless them with victory? Because they had deliberately disregarded God's grace made so plain long ago, and they failed to derive from it an incentive to live in harmony with His will as revealed in the **law**. So theirs was the **covenant** curse of military defeat (Lev. 26: 17; Dt. 28: 25). 'How shall we escape if we ignore such a great salvation?' (Heb. 2: 3) is the psalmist's implicit warning.

Grace abounding (vv. 12–16)

What was the grace that they spurned? It was their ancestors' witnessing of the plagues in **Egypt**, the crossing of the Red Sea, guidance through the wilderness by **cloud** and fire, and the provision of water at Rephidim (Exod. 17: 6) and Kadesh (Num. 20: 10 f.). These are for the psalmist some of 'the glories of my God and King, / The triumphs of His grace' (C. Wesley; cf. v. 4).

Grace despised (vv. 17–33)

The inconstancy of the Exodus generation (v. 8) is resumed and expanded. It was a feature of the wilderness journeyings. They dared to defy the **Most High** after their wonderful escape from Egypt, 'deliberately challenging God' (JB for **put God to the test**). 'They unbelievingly and defiantly demanded instead of trustfully waiting and praying' (Delitzsch). They were sceptical of His power to save by providing food despite His provision of water, which they grudgingly admitted. Their doubts as to God's ability to **spread a table** contrast sharply with the simple faith of 23: 5. Yahweh reacted in exasperation, on the one hand making His displeasure known (Num. 11: 1) and on the other raining upon them not only **manna** but also quails, driven off course as they migrated north after the winter. Then, angry still, He did not allow them to glut their avarice before He killed their best men (Num. 11: 33 f.). Incredibly they still refused to **believe**, to take seriously God's claims upon them, and so that generation was destroyed as unusable and un-

worthy of His promises (Num. 14: 22 f.). 'He snuffed out their lives' (NEB).

Where sin abounded . . . (vv. 34–42)

There was a temporary response: the survivors came snivelling back to Him. But it meant little. Professions of God as their mainstay, their champion, came too easily to their lips (cf. Isa. 29: 13; Hos. 6: 1–4), and were belied by their obvious infidelity. **Yet** God went on caring for His covenant people despite their failing to keep their side of the **covenant**. **Merciful**, He forgave. Swallowing His anger, He mitigated His punishment. He was mindful of their frail mortality. What were they but gusts of **a passing breeze**? So He gave them another chance. Yet his magnanimity was excuse for playing Him up further. Times without number they 'tried his patience' (NEB), heedless of the hand (**power**) which had protected them **from the** Egyptian **oppressor** (cf. Dt. 4: 34).

Exodus power (vv. 43–51)

What had this mighty hand done? It had brought the plagues upon Egypt as God's means of rescuing Israel. He was behind the natural calamities which had befallen the Egyptians. They were His 'messengers of evil' (NEB, v. 49). The climax came with the slaying of **the firstborn**, a final Hiroshima blast to break the stubborn oppressor.

Led home by the Shepherd (vv. 52–55)

God took as much care of His covenant **people** as a shepherd does his **flock** when he escorts them to fresh grazing land. He protected them from the perils behind and before in the form of pursuing Egyptians and waiting Canaanites. Israel's pilgrim fathers were brought safely to their destination, God's own country, the mountainous land of Canaan (**hill country**, JB 'highlands'), won by right of conquest. He it was who 'allotted the nations' 'lands to Israel as a possession' (NEB) and distributed them among the various **tribes**. Along with the Exodus, these were the landmarks of grace to which Israel looked back, monuments to a God of power and covenant love. All this He had done for them.

Outworking of the covenant curse (vv. 56–64)

Israel's early history in Canaan was the wilderness pattern (vv. 17, 32) all over again. **Like . . . fathers** like sons—they had rebellion in their blood. How illogical and perverse in view of God's mercies, which constituted an appeal for total obedience (Rom. 12: 1)! In Israel's hands God's plan to bless a covenant people misfired because they themselves failed to hit the intended target. The obligations of the covenant law were blatantly ignored during the Judges period. Conforming themselves to the Canaanite world, they put other gods before **the Most High** and resorted to 'heathen places of worship' (GNB). They thereby entered the shadow side of the covenant out of the sunshine of His favour (cf. Exod. 20: 3–5; Jg. 2: 11–15). He turned against His ungrateful, apostate people and abandoned them to Philistine attackers. In the territory of Ephraim **Shiloh**, religious centre of the tribal federation of Israel, was overrun. The ark, symbol of God's **might** and glorious presence on earth (**among men**), was allowed to fall into pagan hands. Ichabod—the glory departed (1 Sam. 4: 17, 21 f.)! God was no longer in their midst; so, deprived of their supernatural Ally, victory was no longer theirs (cf. vv. 42 f., 53–55). The Philistine foe was the rod of His anger (cf. Isa. 10: 5); he was allowed to invade, burn, kill and so disrupt social life that the norms of marriage, religious and funeral rites were no longer possible.

A new beginning (vv. 65–72)
From the ruins rose phoenix-like a new society under God. Inexplicably, beyond all the bounds of obligation or reasonable expectation, sacred history started again, at a diifferent point. It was God who took the initiative. The contrast of the former inactivity and the new intervention of **the Lord** is daringly described in terms of a drunken warrior who awakes from his intoxicated stupor and is master of his fighting faculties once more (cf. 35: 23). The Philistines were overthrown, the ark came back —yet not to the sanctuary of Shiloh (**the tents of Joseph**). **Ephraim** lost its old supremacy. Instead the ark went to a new home, **Mount Zion** or Jerusalem. **Judah** became honoured host to the ark. To house it the temple was built, a magnificent structure modelled upon God's sanctuary in 'the high heavens' (RSV; cf. NIV; lit. 'the heights'), a permanent sanctuary which would last as long as **the earth**. God **chose** not only a tribe and a place for special blessing but also a man, whose glorious mission it was to continue the shepherding work of his Master (vv. 52–54). The clock of grace started again under **David**. By strange irony the shepherd boy was taken to be royal shepherd of God's people. His humble training stood him in good stead: his rule was marked by 'unselfish devotion' (GNB) to God and by efficient leadership. There is here a hint at the Davidic royal line as the established channel of God's dealings with His people.

So the psalmist traces his nation's chequered history up to the point which set a pattern for the present. He has grappled with history's surprises and found the winding river of God's purpose eventually dominating the terrain of human waywardness. He cannot see round the corner to further mysteries that lie ahead, the destruction of the temple, the overthrow of the monarchy and the exile of Judah. He is mercifully spared the knowledge of such catas-

trophes, but had he lived through them he would have seen the new relevance of his warning reference to the Ephraimites as turning their backs upon history and upon God (vv. 9–11) and would have clung still to his basic tenet of the victory of divine providence. At every turn God confronted His people, whether as Saviour or as Judge.

Centuries later Paul was to continue the psalmist's quest for meaning in history. In Rom. 9–11 he tussled with a similar conundrum as he contemplated the reversed roles of Jew and Gentile in God's contemporary purposes. He drew three similar conclusions: an unshaken faith in divine sovereignty, however unsearchable God's judgments and inscrutable His ways (Rom. 11: 33), a continuing conviction that the Davidic Messiah was for evermore the catalyst of human destiny (Rom. 9: 5; 10: 4, 9, 13) and a deep respect for the kindness and severity of God. 'Continue in his kindness; otherwise you too will be cut off ' is his word of caution to presumptuous Gentile Christians (Rom. 11: 17–22).

12. Zoan: possibly the store city and royal city Raamses (Exod. 1: 11), was in the eastern part of the Nile delta. **44–51.** Six of the ten Egyptian plagues of Exod. 7–12 are cited. **47. sycamore-figs:** 'fig trees' (GNB). **48.** JB and NEB follow some ancient textual evidence which refers to a further plague, the fifth one of Exod. 9: 1–7. **65b.** More probably 'like a warrior overcome (formerly) by wine' or 'excited by wine' (GNB; cf. JB, NEB).

Psalm 79. THE HOLOCAUST
All the symbols of security were shattered—nationhood, the capital, even the temple. Judah's erstwhile allies had deserted her. Alone she had faced the foe—and lost. Survivors of the enemy's bloodbath looked to God, their only hope in a cruel, friendless world. Behind them lay the grim tragedy of 587 B.C., Nebuchadnezzar's historic siege and invasion of Jerusalem. Ahead of them lay a questionmark over their own and their nation's survival. Heartbroken, a group gather round the ruined shrine and lay their anguish before the God of Judah.
The tragedy described (vv. 1–4)
As a logical lead-in to the following appeal the tale of woe is told in such a way as to stress God's own involvement in the debacle. Not merely the Jews but indirectly their God had suffered at the hands of their enemies. **Jerusalem** had been reduced to **rubble**, but beyond human tragedy Judah's foes had by this act been guilty of trespass upon God's property and of sacrilege in His sanctuary. When the lives of countless Jewish resisters were held cheap, when their massacred bodies were thrown outside the city like so much offal and denied decent burial, God was affected, for

were not the victims of such subhuman treatment His **servants** and bound by covenant ties to Him (**saints**)? Was He not their liege Lord, morally obliged to intervene on their behalf? Judah's neighbours looked on and laughed— the last straw of humiliation. Edom, Ammon and Moab offered no help, no sympathy, but only jeers and gibes. The divine implications of this experience are left unmentioned to be drawn during the appeal (v. 10).

The appeal (vv. 5–12)

The situation can scarcely be endured. In agony the people cry out **How long?** But so strong is their sense of God's sovereignty that they see the hand of God even in this crisis. Yahweh would not have allowed all this to happen unless He Himself had some purpose in it. Behind Nebuchadnezzar can be only His enabling, just as Assyria of old was the rod of His anger (Isa. 10: 5). The fires that had raged over Jerusalem's landmarks (2 Kg. 25: 9; cf. Ps. 74: 7) were symbols of His passion (**jealousy**). God is both the Enemy who has vented His anger and the Friend whose help is sought. Judah had been by no means guiltless, but a large measure of guilt attached too to the foreigners who had battened on God's people and destroyed their homeland. Infidels, they worshipped their own gods and gave no allegiance to Yahweh. Surely they could not go scotfree (cf. Isa. 10: 5–19)?

In history one generation has often suffered for the misdeeds of its predecessors, and Israel was very conscious of the chains of solidarity which bound generation to generation (cf. Exod. 20: 5 f.). From one point of view it was an overwhelming backlog of sin which fell upon the nation (cf. Lam. 5: 7) and could have removed every trace. But the survivors plead for mitigation, that they may not suffer further on this account. If their plea is granted, they admit that it will be undeserved. They ask for His **mercy**, and that soon, so that God may be like the father in the parable who had 'compassion and ran and kissed' the prodigal (Lk. 15: 20). Down and out as they are, will not God at least feel sorry for them?

They have another, more compelling argument in their armoury—for in their extremity they are pounding on heaven's doors and bombarding God. The derision of surrounding states (v. 4) is directed not merely against Judah but against Judah's God. He is surely weak and helpless beside the Babylonian and allied deities who had empowered Nebuchadnezzar's army —so they reasoned with their sneering question **Where is their God?** God's honour is at stake. From past experience His people know Him to be their powerful Saviour, but His reputation (**name**) is now poor in the eyes of neighbouring states. It is on this account that His people plead for **help** and for dismissal of their guilt that

stands in the way. The time is now ripe for a mighty demonstration to contemptuous neighbours that God does not stand idly by when His **servants' blood** is spilt. Many of them are **prisoners** of war with a death sentence on their heads, but beyond their pitiful weakness the eye of faith can see the strong **arm** (power) of their God with potential to rescue them. Their **neighbors** have had the impudence to speak insolently against the sovereign **Lord**, and must be paid back for this outrage. They deserve nothing less than the traditional severe punishment of sevenfold requital (cf. Gen. 4: 15; Lev. 26: 18).

A promise of praise (v. 13)

The community express their faith in the God who has made them His covenant **people** and taken them into His care as their Shepherd. They have every confidence in Him in view of their relationship with Him. What will they be able to do in return for His anticipated intervention? They pledge their hearts to Him in unceasing thanksgiving. When the nation is restored to security, the new story of His grace will be added to the long list of saving events as a permanent part of the people's heritage of praise.

Note: v. 12. The fold of the robe over the chest served as a pocket in which to carry money, etc. (cf. Prov. 17: 23).

Psalm 80.   THE BROKEN VINE

Paul's aching 'desire and prayer' for his Jewish brethren 'that they may be saved' (Rom. 9: 1– 3; 10: 1) is prefigured in this Judean psalm sung in the Jerusalem temple (v. 1b; cf. 2 Kg. 19: 14 f.) concerning the northern tribes whose realm had fallen to the Assyrians. It was probably composed in the reign of Hezekiah or Josiah when there was a strong movement for national integration (cf. 2 Kg. 23: 15, 29; 2 Chr. 30). There is no malicious, self-righteous criticism, only a sense of tragic void and a yearning that those whom God had joined together should be re-united in the vine (cf. the olive tree in Rom. 11: 17–24), 'that they may be one' (Jn 17: 11, 22).

The lost sheep of the house of Israel (vv. 1–3)

The decimated **flock** pray to the divine **Shepherd**, the God whose royal power and glorious presence among His people was symbolized in the **cherubim**-topped ark. They look for His radiant appearing (cf. Dt. 33: 2; 2 Th. 1: 7) as champion of His own. The prayer for restoration to their former state of blessing (cf. v. 10 f.) runs as a refrain through the psalm (vv. 3, 7, 19, cf. 14 a). Laying hold of the priestly benediction upon Israel, they long for God to smile upon them in favour again (Num. 6: 24–26; cf. Ps. 67: 1).

A frowning providence (vv. 4–7)

Their doctrine of God was too great to allow that the situation was out of His control. He held their **enemies** on a leash. But 'how much longer, Lord God Almighty' (GNB), are their prayers to be rejected? Sorrow was 'their daily bread' (NEB) given to them by God. 'You let the surrounding nations fight over our land' (GNB, cf. NIV, RSVmg, JB), is their complaint as they feel the smart of humiliation.

The broken vine (vv. 8–13)

Land and people went together in God's covenant, and on this ground they plead for re-occupation of lost territory. The past triumphs of His grace they proclaim in the parable of the **vine** (cf. Isa. 5: 1–7; Hos. 10: 1; Mk 12: 1–12; Jn 15: 1–11). 'The figure is expressive of the divine purpose, choice and care, and of Israel's destiny to expand and bear much fruit for God. It also expressed the people's unity, a single organism transcending the generations' (Eaton). If God was His people's shepherd, He was also their gardener. Like weeds other **nations** now cover holy **ground**, but in hope the praying community look back to God's work of grace when He prepared the garden and cared for His beloved vine. From Lebanon's gigantic **cedars** to the southern **mountains**, from the Mediterranean **sea** to the **River** Euphrates once stretched God's vineyard (cf. Dt. 11: 24), in the days of the Davidic empire. The present is an incomprehensible travesty of the past. Unprotected by God, His land and people are now the weak prey of every foe, who, unclean as any wild **boar** (Dt. 14: 8), tramples down the vine. But the political problem is at heart a spiritual one: **Why have you ...?**

A plea for renewal (vv. 14–19)

Heaven represents not only divine power but the gulf which yawns between them and their absent God. Yet they adduce two motives for His intervention, both with reference to His **right hand**. First, His was the initial responsibility for planting the vine and so the report of its destruction must move Him to action. 'He is not one to begin a great work and lose interest in it' (Kidner; cf. Phil. 1: 6). If the people have erred and merited God's frown, guilt attaches to Israel's enemies too. The second appeal is based upon the Davidic monarchy, whose reign had been made sacrosanct by divine decree of honour (cf. Pss. 2; 89: 21; 110: 1). It was God's declared will that the king should be strong in His service, and viceroy of a mighty realm. To God's act they solemnly vow to react with perpetual loyalty. The gift of new life will be used as an opportunity for appreciative worship. The initiative lies with the Almighty God; they are helpless till His mercy's beams gladden their eyes and warm their hearts.

Psalm 81.   NOT THE LIP OF PRAISE ALONE

Israel's obligation to worship (vv. 1–5a)

The background is the autumn festival, a complex of sacred events inaugurated by the one-day Feast of Trumpets on the first of the month (**New Moon**; cf. Lev. 23: 24; Num. 29: 1 ff.) and concluded by the week-long Feast of Tabernacles from the fifteenth (**full moon**; cf. Lev. 23: 34; Num. 29: 12 ff.). Every resource of voice and instrument is to be used to acclaim God as the source of all strengthening grace. Laid upon His people is this sweet burden of praise, a charge dating back to the time of the Exodus, when to save Israel from their enemies God 'attacked' (GNB) or 'went to war' (JB) against **Egypt** in the plagues. Thus behind the **ordinance** towers the grace of God as the great motivation for praise.

Israel's obligation to walk in God's ways (vv. 5b–16)

A prophet intervenes (cf. 75: 2; 1 Sam. 15: 16), constrained by God's uncanny **voice** (NIVmg) to his heart. The message begins with an elaboration of divine grace. He freed His people from virtual slavery, their forced labour as coolies on Egypt's building sites. This was no matter of ancient history: in principle God's present people were there, and the benefits of His Exodus blessings still accrued to them, centuries later (cf. Am. 2: 10; Eph. 2: 4–6). He revealed Himself in benevolent action, responding to their cries, and in solemn word, when He made a covenant with them at Sinai, manifesting His unseen majesty in **thunder**. Moreover, be it noted, He revealed Himself at **Meribah** in holy sentence of judgment (Num. 20: 13). This awesome Lord lays claim upon His people's allegiance, an allegiance wider than worship. If the festival is God's 'solemn charge' (v. 5, NEB), so too is this wider claim (v. 8 'I give you a solemn charge', NEB: the same Heb. root is used). The Ten Commandments are echoed in v. 9 f. (cf. Exod. 20: 2 f.) in anticipation of a theme of the festival, the giving of the Law (cf. Dt. 31: 10 ff.).

There was a time when grace was taken for granted, continues the prophetic message with a ring of yearning pathos (cf. Mic. 6: 3): the wilderness generation chose their own wayward path to destruction. Lest history repeat itself, a warning is given to the present generation of God's people (cf. 1 C. 10: 6–12). They stand at the crossroads, to choose God's will or their own. 'There are only two kinds of people in the end: those who say to God "Thy will be done", and those to whom God will have regretfully to say, "Thy will be done"' (C. S. Lewis). His will is best for them, for it spells their blessing. His power is at the disposal of an obedient people, ready to give the victory, as of old (v. 5), God's victory in which they may share (cf. Rom. 8: 37). The dark picture of conquest and subjection serves to enhance a glorious prospect of peace and plenty, if only . . .

Psalm 82.   THY KINGDOM COME

This psalm reads like an ancient exercise in communication. By blatantly speaking after the manner of men the psalmist endeavours to mediate divine truth. For argument's sake he concedes the concept of a polytheistic pantheon —that it may ultimately be denied. In hard-hitting polemic he seizes the pagan religious system as spoil for Yahweh, proving its inadequacy from its results.

The impeachment (vv. 1–5)

In prophetic fashion the psalmist paints a heavenly picture of the **great assembly** presided over by Israel's God (cf. 1 Kg. 22: 19 ff.; Job 1: 6 ff.). Surprisingly the supernatural beings present are not angels gathered to learn His will but **the gods** of the nations (cf. Dt. 4: 19; 29: 26; 32: 8). Nor is this an ordinary council meeting: it is a trial, and God presides not as chairman but as judge. At this celestial Nuremberg He impatiently accuses the various national deities of misrule, of abuse of the powers delegated to them. Their showing was deplorable: there was little premium on morality in pagan cultures, highly religious though they were. But Israel's God had a passion for social justice, as His prophets stressed. Injustice, partiality, ignoring the underprivileged who could not stand up for their rights—these were indictable offences in the eyes of Yahweh. He demanded high moral standards and social responsibility. Yet these whom men worshipped served to undermine 'the very basis of earthly society' (JB).

The verdict (vv. 6, 7)

A death sentence is passed (**I said**; cf. NEB and 2 Sam. 19: 29 AV). Despite their supernatural rank and immortality, they are to be stripped of their privileges and suffer the degrading penalty of death. Like the victims of a political *coup d'état*, they would **fall** into the infernal abyss (cf. Isa. 14: 9, 12–15). In plain terms this is an assurance of God's sovereignty. All the rivals of Yahweh were in reality His servants, ultimately accountable to Him and holding a temporary brief.

A Prayer (v. 8)

The psalmist adds a fervent Amen to the divine pronouncement. He urges that the true Lord of **the nations** may soon take over in direct rule. In faith he can transcend the dominant world view held by his pagan contemporaries. 'They will say of me, "In the LORD alone are righteousness and strength . . . Bel bows down, Nebo stoops low"' (Isa. 45: 24; 46: 1).

Strange though the psalm appears at first reading, in similar vein the NT celebrates the triumph of Christ over 'the rulers and authorities', 'the spiritual forces of evil in the heavenly realms' (Eph. 6: 12; Col. 2: 15; cf. Jn 12: 31). Their doom is sealed; the end is in our Lord's hands (1 C. 15: 24).

Jewish tradition applied the psalm to human judges, despite v. 7. Jn 10: 34 f. may (but not necessarily) reflect this later exegesis, in which case it is used as an *argumentum ad hominem*.

Psalm 83.   POWER MADE PERFECT IN WEAKNESS

Judah is in danger of being invaded and destroyed by an overwhelming coalition of nations. The occasion is unknown; it was probably in the eighth or seventh century B.C.

The present crisis described (vv. 1–8)

God's people hammer on the doors of heaven in urgent prayer. The threat to the chosen nation is indirectly a threat to God Himself. How can He stay inactive? For Judah's **enemies** are His enemies: inasmuch as they plot **against** His **people**, they plot against Him (cf. Mt. 25: 42–45). In simple faith they relate the political problem to God. For He had covenanted to take care of Israel and placed them under His special protection. So, with their very existence at stake, they claim His aid and warn Him of their enemies' presumption. A hostile ring encircled them. To the east **Moab** and **Ammon, the descendants of Lot** (Dt. 29: 19), are the chief protagonists, while in the south looms **Edom** with a number of nomadic satellites. On the western horizon are **Philistia** and **Tyre**, while from the north come Assyrian reinforcements to the coalition, perhaps from **Assyria's** Palestinian provinces.

Past aid invoked (vv. 9–12)

But if the local coalition has a strong ally in Assyria, Judah has a stronger, who proved His power in ages past. 'Thine arm, O Lord, in days of old, / Was strong . . . Be Thou our great Deliverer still' (E. H. Plumptre), is their prayer. They hark back to the Judges period centuries before, to the defeat of the Canaanites under Deborah and Barak (Jg. 4, 5) and of the Midianites under Gideon (Jg. 7, 8). God had protected His sheep when trespassers tried to take over His **pasturelands**.

Imminent help requested (13–18)

Now that history was repeating itself, they looked to the same God to intervene afresh. The leader of the praying community feels moved to add his personal plea: **O my God.** The God of past holy wars is passionately implored to lead His people to new victory, and to put panic into the hearts of their enemies. May humiliation lead to positive homage, when the broken survivors acknowledge Yahweh's supremacy and worship Him as Lord of the world. Israel by faith are already assured of His glory, however grim and hostile are their circumstances. They long for faith to pass into sight, that the kingdom of the world may soon become in fact the kingdom of their Lord (Rev. 11: 15).

Psalm 84.   A PILGRIM'S TESTIMONY

This song rivals Paul's letter to the Philippians as an expression of spiritual joy and devotion to the Lord. A visitor to the autumn festival publicly testifies what it means to him to worship God in the temple at Jerusalem. Among English paraphrases the best-known is probably 'Pleasant are thy courts above' (H. F. Lyte).

God's house (vv. 1–3)

'How I love your temple!' (GNB) is the pilgrim's confession, inspired by the fact that in the OT it is the appointed place where God uniquely reveals Himself. So it holds a special place in his heart. To worship there thrills his soul and satisfies a deep desire, for here he meets **the living God** in fellowship. He feels a rapport with the very birds nesting in the precincts: he too knows the homing instinct that brings him back here again and again. His personal faith and reverence ring out in the way, so beloved by George Herbert, in which he addresses his Lord, 'my God and King'.

The happy pilgrim (vv. 4–7)

It is not his privilege to be on the temple staff and give life-long **praise**, which is far better (cf. Phil. 1: 23). But he enjoys a second best which is not to be despised, regular seasons of worship in the temple. For him and likeminded folk pilgrimage is a pledge of their dependence upon God and this is why their 'hearts are set on the pilgrim ways' (NEB). On the way the sun-scorched scenery in the late summer would be depressing to any ordinary traveller, as he plods through 'the thirsty valley' (NEB). But for the pilgrims earth around is softer green. They have spiritual refreshment of which the world knows nothing. In their hearts they relish the prospect of communion **before God in Zion**. As they draw near their journey's end, however far they have come, instead of feeling weary, they renew their **strength** (Isa. 40: 29 ff.; cf. Phil. 4: 13).

God's king (vv. 8, 9)

Jerusalem housed both the temple and the palace: royalty and religion were twin channels of God's purposes for His people. Reverence for the divine King (v. 3) necessitated respect for His human representative, who reflected His protective power (cf. v. 11). God's smile on the king (the **anointed one**, a type of Christ) spelled prosperity for the nation.

The happy believer (vv. 10–12)

The psalmist knows his priorities. He turns his back on the world's wicked ways, tempting as they are, and willingly exchanges them for the pearl of worshipping his God. He finds in Him true security and abundant blessing, to which a life of moral integrity is the key according to the covenant. What a privilege it is to commit one's life to God Almighty (cf. Phil. 1: 29)! He could not always stay on this mountain top of spiritual experience, but when he returned through the valley he would take back with him a renewed vision, and a stimulus to obey God's will.

10. Render with NEB 'linger by the threshold' (cf. JB, GNB). The priestly office of **doorkeeper** was highly respected and denied to the psalmist (cf. Jer. 52: 24). **11. sun:** better 'battlement' (JB, NEB), alongside **shield:** both protect from danger.

Psalm 85.   A DIALOGUE WITH GOD

The God of yesterday (vv. 1–3)

The worshipping community, in dire need, turn to their God in prayer and plead His past grace, perhaps the return from Babylonian exile, though modern scholarship is not so certain on this point as a former generation was. His previous salvation is prized as a basis for present hope that He will prove a Saviour still (cf. Phil. 1: 6). Very conscious of their sinfulness, they realize that it was all of grace, for they deserved God's destructive **wrath**.

The needs of today (vv. 4–7)

Things have now gone very wrong for them, and they feel that the lack of a right relationship with God is the root problem. They cast themselves upon Him as their only means of help (**God our Savior**); they appeal to their covenant relationship with Him (**your people, your unfailing love**). How they need their God! The joyless pressures of their present life drive them back to Him for renewal and fresh reasons for praising Him.

God's all-sufficiency for tomorrow (vv. 8–13)

A temple prophet (cf. 75: 2; 81: 5) delivers God's reassuring answer, a single yet comprehensive word, **peace**. **He promises peace** to His covenant people bound in fellowship to Him (**saints**). It spells an end to the broken relationship and the beginning of a new wholeness and true fulfilment. The prophet turns preacher and expands the basic message. He qualifies the promise with a condition: 'if only they renounce their folly' (JB; cf. NIVmg, GNB). Forgiveness of sin (v. 2) is not to be presumed upon, as if one could complacently go on sinning with a view to further forgiveness. God's saving help is promised to those who worship Him in spirit and honour Him; it is they who are to experience His powerful presence (**glory**). Such **faithfulness** will pave the way for His **unfailing love** (cf. v. 7): a right attitude of heart and life will find God's **peace** (cf. v. 8). 'Man's loyalty will reach up from the earth and God's righteousness [saving righteousness (cf. Isa. 45: 8; Rom. 3: 21, 24)] will look down from heaven' (GNB, v. 11). This beautiful harmony between God and His people would be sacramentally revealed in blessing upon the **land** and its crops, in accord with the OT covenant (cf. Dt. 7: 12 f.). So God would reveal Himself to them, and **righteousness** on both sides and between them would be the sign of His coming to make His home with them (cf. Jn 14: 23).

Psalm 86.   GRACE ABOUNDING
Pleas for help (vv. 1–7)
The psalmist persistently implores God to hear him in his need (cf. Lk. 18: 1–7). Each plea is matched with a claim; the claims gradually rise from self-orientation towards a focus upon God Himself. Their relationship is that of **servant** and **Lord**: the vassal affirms his loyalty and claims the aid of his Overlord. 'Helpless and weak' (GNB, v. 1) and joyless too, he asks to be given 'reason to rejoice' (JB, v. 4). Ultimately, he realizes, it is God's grace which can be his only plea. He appropriates a statement from a well-known creed of Israel (cf. Exod. 34: 6), concerning the riches of His grace to any suppliant. He derives comfort from his knowledge that God is one who answers prayer.
How great Thou art! (8–13)
The psalm moves into a hymn of praise. Rising above his trouble (cf. Ac. 16: 25), with a heart at leisure from itself, he worships his Lord. Such is His matchlessness that nothing else than universal adoration will adequately reflect His worth (cf. Rev. 15: 3 f.). From the general he sanely descends to the particular, making his individual response to God's greatness in a prayer for instruction in faithful living and for single-minded obedience. Still on the personal level, he gives **praise** for previous proof of God's grace in his own life, in rescue from mortal danger.
Further appeals (vv. 14–17)
God can do it again: 'I was delivered . . . The Lord will rescue me' (2 Tim. 4: 17 f.). Faced with brutal violence from 'people to whom you mean nothing' (JB), the psalmist leans upon divine grace, quoting again and at greater length from Israel's traditional confession of faith. He renews his vassal claim and asks for strengthening and a clear demonstration of God's 'goodness' (GNB) by reversing the situation (**comforted**, cf. Isa. 40: 1 f.) in his favour.

Psalm 87.   ZION, CITY OF OUR GOD
The chosen city (vv. 1, 2)
What a privilege to come to **Zion** to worship! Pagan religions each had their holy mountains, the homes of their gods (*e.g.* Mt. Olympus),

but the true **holy mountain** was the site of Jerusalem, where Yahweh revealed Himself in a special way. He had chosen it rather 'than any other place in Israel' (GNB). Just as Israelites flocked there from other towns, so it was the logical venue for pilgrims the world over, a veritable Mecca in God's purposes.
God's word expounded (vv. 3–6)
The psalmist has watched foreign pilgrims (not tourists!) visiting Jerusalem, and he hails the sight as prophecy beginning to come true, the realization of a **glorious** prediction which God had spoken of Zion through His prophet (cf. Isa. 2: 2–4; Zech. 9: 12 f.). The prophetic oracle is quoted in v. 4. Formerly it could be said of Israel 'You only have I known of all the families of the earth' (Am. 3: 2), but God had a greater purpose, for were they not all to be blessed through Abraham (Gen. 12: 3)? Other nations may join the intimate circle of God's covenant favour. No longer could it be said that all Egyptians (**Rahab**, cf. Isa. 30: 7) and Babylonians, Philistines and Phoenicians, even black-skinned people from far-off Ethiopia (**Cush**) (cf. Jer. 38: 7 ff.; Ac. 8: 27) were 'excluded from citizenship in Israel' (Eph. 2: 12), for some at least were present at the festival as believers, and any narrow exclusivism was overruled by this prophetic word. They were there by right of adoption; each could claim 'Of Zion's city / I through grace a member am' (J. Newton).

The psalmist goes on to expound the prophecy in vv. 5 f. He emphasizes the right of foreigners to be there as naturalized citizens of Zion, in order to quell any vestiges of nationalism. Foreign proselytes share as much as any native in the religious security transmitted through Jerusalem the golden. As Yahweh makes up the register of His kingdom (cf. Exod. 32: 32; Isa. 4: 3), He does not begrudge a place in the list to foreigners who by their faith have been **born** anew and so qualify for membership.
A sacred song (v. 7)
One of the festival songs was coming true in a new way. There was evidently a song which spoke of the river of Paradise in Jerusalem, God's latter-day Eden, and viewed this river as the spiritual source of Israel's life (cf. 36: 8; 46: 4; Ezek. 47: 1–12). Now its tributaries were starting to flood the world with the water of life (cf. Isa. 2: 2). Hallelujah!

The psalmist is a remarkable herald of the NT revelation. Probably not without opposition, as his very emphases suggest, he calls Israel to embrace God's wider will, eventually fulfilled through Christ in the Church. For the Christian the concept of Zion is lifted to a higher plane (cf. Jn 4: 21; Phil. 3: 20; Heb. 11: 10, 16; 12: 22 f.).

Perhaps the original order at the beginning

was vv. 2, 1, 5b (cf. NEB). **5.** LXX refers to Zion as 'mother': JB and NEB follow this textual tradition (cf. Gal. 4: 26).

Psalm 88. THE SLOUGH OF DESPOND

The speaker is walking through the valley of the shadow of death in this 'saddest psalm in the whole Psalter' (Kirkpatrick).

Praying about the problem (vv. 1–9a)
Three times in the course of the psalm the sufferer cries to God for **help**. His reaction to his constant affliction (cf. vv. 15, 17) has been to turn constantly to God, but so far his prayers have gone unanswered. His situation is desperate: he is as good as dead. For all the satisfaction he gets out of life he might just as well be in Sheol or **the pit**, the realm of the dead, where according to the OT one lived a shadowy, weak existence (cf. Isa. 14: 9 f.), **cut off** from life, from fellowship with God and certainly from His 'protecting hand' (JB) or **care**. God, he feels, is responsible for banishing him to this bleak and barren exile; he is the victim of divine hostility, which, as a believer, makes his plight harder to bear. He suffers from loneliness, deprived of his friends. They shun him like the plague to avoid the spiritual contagion of this man upon whom God's blessing has ceased to rest. He is locked in a dungeon of despair (cf. Lam. 3: 7), sunk in lack-lustre apathy.

Forlorn questions (vv. 9b–12)
But he does not stop praying. If God does not answer, his only prospect is actual death and the impossibility of renewed blessing. The questions in vv. 10–12 all expect the answer 'No'. Earthly life, generally speaking, is in the OT the context of God's wonderful acts of covenant **love**. The psalmist cannot face death and **Destruction** ('Abaddon', NIVmg; cf. Rev. 9: 11), which lacks any positive elements and where people are shadows of their former selves. Life here and now glitters with divine possibilities and with opportunity for **praise**. 'There cannot be such a thing as true life without praise. Praising and no longer praising are related to each other as are living and not living' (C. Westermann). The psalmist's high opinion of earthly life contrasts with his view of the hereafter. To die was to be forgotten by God and man. It was not given to every saint to rise to the heights of 73: 24, 26.

A final appeal (vv. 13–18)
His only hope is to pray on, to try to get through to this God who seems to have **rejected** him, the sovereign Arbiter of human experience. His suffering is no recent phenomenon: chronic ill-health has been his lot since a boy. He goes on to repeat obsessively previous themes of divine victimization and human loneliness, tied to his treadmill of sorrow.

Against the sombre background of this psalm the Christian can better appreciate the NT's shout of joyful praise that 'our Savior Christ Jesus' has 'destroyed death' (2 Tim. 1: 10). His resurrection has opened the floodgates of eternal life: 'Where, O death, is your sting?' (1 C. 15: 55 f.; cf. Heb. 2: 14 f.). The psalmist's pessimism is now a theological impossibility, ever since Jesus took over, as it were, this 'archetypal cry of suffering' (Eaton). If emotionally any Christian still passes through such deep waters, He supremely understands (Heb. 2: 18). But although the psalmist's evaluation of death has been transcended, his view of life's potential has not.

18. Render 'Darkness is my one companion left' (JB, cf. GNB; cf. vv. 6, 12) or possibly 'Thou hast . . . parted me from my friends' (NEB; cf. v. 8).

Psalm 89. FAITH'S PERPLEXITY

Nowhere is the paradox of faith and sight, divine promise and human experience, more pronounced. Both extremes stand under the power of God, of that the psalm has no doubt (cf. vv. 19, 38), and both are taken equally seriously. The incomprehensible riddle of providence is laid before God, for Him to resolve. The community (cf. v. 17 f.), led by their king (vv. 1, 50 f.), have gathered for praise and prayer, greatly burdened with national calamity and its implications for the Davidic monarchy.

Praise of God's loyalty and love (vv. 1–18)
The king challenges his dire circumstances with a defiant song of adoration. This hymn at the outset introduces the key words of the psalm, **great love** and **faithfulness**. 'God's gifts and his call are irrevocable' (Rom. 11: 29): on this promise the king is standing concerning God's grace and dependability. They are of eternal validity; they reflect the heavenly and divine. Specifically he has in mind the Davidic covenant, the promise of a dynasty which would never die (cf. 2 Sam. 7).

The king's praise is in tune with the celestial hymns of Yahweh's angelic courtiers, who pay Him homage and sing of His power and constancy, acknowledging His unrivalled perfection. He is the Lord of the created world. Even the cruel **sea** obeys Him. Mention of the sea prompts a snatch of pagan lore, plundered for Yahweh, concerning His victory as Creator over the watery forces of chaos and its allied monsters (cf. Job 26: 12 f.; Ps. 74: 13 f.; Isa. 51: 9). The universe is a wonderful edifice commemorating His power. The majestic mountains are His handiwork. His rule over the world is no despotic tyranny but firmly based upon His attributes of moral goodness, reliability and loving care. Yahweh's people have been let into such secrets as these. Their privilege it is both to join in jubilant acclamation of Him as King without an equal (cf. 92: 2 f.) and to experience His **favor** within their lives (cf. Num. 6: 25). No wonder they are moved to praise. He is the source of all their **strength**; they have access to His power. And the God-appointed channel of His gracious help is none other than the Davidic **king**. He is the pivot of divine blessing upon the nation. So at the very heart of Israel's vitality and faith stands God's covenant with David.

The glorious revelation (vv. 19–37)
God's ancient word is poetically narrated: the prose form of this royal theology appears in 2 Sam. 7: 8–16. David, the archetype of God's royal representative among men, founded an institution which would never pass away. God's power (**arm**, v. 21; cf. v. 13) and victory (v. 23; cf. v. 10) were promised to him and to his descendants. Just as God was King of the world, so too would be the Davidic king, with a realm stretching across the Semitic world, from the Euphrates and its tributaries to the Mediterranean **sea**. His would be a unique relationship with God. As focal representative of the nation in His sight, he would bear the special title of **firstborn** (cf. Exod. 4: 22) and look to God as adoptive **Father** and protector (cf. Ps. 2). Covenant obligations were laid upon each successor, but God's initial promise to David would ever stand firm. Individual defaulters would not go unpunished, but no human weakness could impair the immortal word, which was backed by God's very character.

The ugly reality (vv. 38–45)
The promised ideal seemed to have suffered eclipse before the stark experience of king and country. God had **renounced** His inviolable **covenant** (cf. v. 34), it is claimed: this is the pith of the problem. What the king had recently undergone could by no stretch of the imagination be called remedial punishment, on the lines of v. 32. The country lies in **ruins**, looted by any who cares to trespass (cf. 80: 12). The **crown** is held in contempt by neighbouring kings. Victory promised to him had passed to his **foes**, it is remarked with bitter irony. Military defeat and loss of royal power are his lot, counteracting all God's precious promises. The king himself has become 'old before his

time' (GNB) because of the humiliation which attacked not merely his self-esteem but the very word of God. Nor is the naïve conclusion drawn that another power than God's has been at work: Israel's instinctive faith in divine sovereignty over human experience forbids it. God's power is not in question; it is the matter of His promised patronage of the Davidic monarchy that makes His suffering people falter.

A prayer for restoration (vv. 46–51)
The king cannot solve the mystery, he can only lay it before God. He pleads the shortness of **life** and the certainty of **death**. Time is running out; if God does not act in mercy soon, he, the accredited heir of promise, will never experience the triumph of God's word. He is a pitiable travesty of all His faithful promises, denied 'those earlier signs of your love' (JB). Supposed to be the highest of the kings of the earth (v. 27), actually he is humiliated and bears the brunt of foreign ridicule. His final word, **your anointed one**, is a climactic appeal to his personal role as the repository of divine promises and human hopes.

This question-mark placed against the Davidic monarchy was destined to grow larger as Judah shrank in power and was dragged into exile. Nor did the return to the land bring consolation, although the problem was temporarily alleviated by re-interpretation of the Davidic promises (cf. Isa. 55: 3–5). But hope was never lost of a Messiah, a Christ, an anointed king of David's line who would perfectly embody all the ideals of scripture. The NT proclaims that Jesus is this very one (Lk. 1: 32 f.; Ac. 13: 22 f.). He has laid claim to be rightful successor to the old promises, and in His hands they have grown to cosmic proportions (cf. 'firstborn' in Rom. 8: 29; Col. 1: 15; Rev. 1: 5). Ironically this psalm in which suffering and glory jostle sets a mysterious pattern which was followed by the Heir: 'Here is your king' was spoken of one wearing a crown of thorns.

47b. I.e. 'that you created all of us mortal' (GNB). **51. every step** i.e. 'wherever he goes' (JB, GNB); possibly render 'heels', i.e. as he flees. Verse 52 is not part of the psalm but a doxology marking the end of the third book of the Psalter (cf. 41: 13; 72: 18 f.).

Book Four   Psalms 90–106

Psalm 90.   LIFE'S EITHER-OR
A long period of national calamity (v. 15) drives God's people to reflect upon the meaning of life in the light of the nature and purposes of God, and to hope prayerfully for better things.
An affirmation of faith (vv. 1, 2)
God is the point of reference with which the

psalm begins to discuss its problem. As His people's 'eternal home' (Isaac Watts), He has ever been the focal point of Israel's existence. The present generation under stress are not alone: they grasp with relief their precious heritage of close attachment to the God of the covenant (cf. Dt. 33: 27). They express their sense of awe at their God whom time and space do not hold captive. Greater than the impressive **world** around, He antedates the immemorial **mountains** nor will He ever cease to exist. This is their **Lord**, they affirm in proud praise.

A meditation on man's finiteness (vv. 3–6)
The sombre fact of human mortality stands out all the starker against the background of divine infinity. **Men** walk across life's stage for a moment, clay puppets doomed to disintegrate into **dust** when their tiny part has been played (cf. Gen. 2: 7; 3: 19). Their built-in obsolescence contrasts with God's eternity. From His heavenly throne not only are men as small as grasshoppers (Isa. 40: 22), but their timescale is minute to Him. He surveys human history spread before Him like a map. A whole millennium is only 'a yesterday now over' (JB) or a four-hour watch to a sleeping man. A quick succession of pictures of transitoriness flash by, reinforcing their message: a flood (**sweep away**; cf. GNB), a 'dream' (RSV; lit 'sleep'; NIV adds **of death**), vegetation in the sun-baked east.

A confession of sin (vv. 7–12)
The psalm is no product of fatalistic cynicism. Mortality is not only a divine decree but a phenomenon for which man is responsible. It is interpreted as the result of sin: there is an essential link between mortality and morality. The change to **we** in this section acknowledges the community's sense of involvement and guilt. The underlying rationale is the OT covenant promise of long life as the corollary of obedience (Exod. 20: 12; Dt. 5: 33; cf. Rom. 6: 23; 1 C. 11: 30). This is why, they confess, our vitality has deteriorated to 'a whisper' (GNB) so that in our failing years we are already like the ghosts we are to become in Sheol (cf. Isa. 29: 4). Though we may live to seventy or even eighty years of age, our lives are treadmills of **trouble** and frustration, and all too soon we are whisked away.

This pessimistic assessment of life is by no means the psalmist's last word but a realistic prelude to a true optimism. It is because men live for the moment, leaving God out of account and failing to 'consider . . . the sternness of God' (Rom. 11: 22) that they are forced to draw this dismal conclusion. His wrath is to be taken seriously as a proper reverence towards Him demands. Only He can **teach** how to 'make the most of the time' (Eph. 5: 16) and to spend it wisely. 'How blest is life if lived for Thee!'

A prayer for blessed lives (vv. 13–17)
All the foregoing has been a basis for this appeal. God's **servants** cannot live aright without God's gracious help. They have already suffered long and have just confessed their sin. Now they plead for mitigation of their punish-

ment. They pray that a new day of grace may dawn for His people so that living yields joyful praise (cf. Dt. 26: 10 f.; Ps. 85: 6) instead of worried prayer. They have endured days of **trouble**, the disaster of divine punishment, but now they plead for God to relent and to restore them, for the God who wounds can also heal (cf. Isa. 30: 26). They long for God to **show** Himself in **splendor** among them and in the ongoing experience of the community. Apart from His gracious **favor** all they attempt is labour in vain (cf. 127: 1). God's blessing is the secret of purposeful living and of work that lasts (cf. 1 C. 15: 58). Gone now is the pessimism of vv. 3–12: life under God's lordship (cf. v. 1) means joy and fulfilment.

Note: v. 10. In the light of anthropological archaeology seventy years was not the average age but a standard limit which some might reach.

Psalm 91. THE SHIELD OF FAITH
A believer has come to the temple to worship. The priestly blessing he receives (cf. 1 Sam. 1: 17) abounds in a rich profusion of metaphors, promising deliverance from every type of danger.

The divine protection (vv. 1–13)
To **dwell in** God's **shelter** refers primarily to frequenting the temple, but it alludes also to the worshipping attitude of heart which finds its security in God (cf. 27: 4 f.). **The Most High** and **the Almighty** are ancient titles for God and have a traditional, venerable ring. They suggest that 'our fathers' God . . . their dear abode, / We make our habitation' (T. H. Gill). The testimony of faith in v. 2 is resonant with personal pronouns.

The man who puts his trust in God is given assurance of deliverance from peril, instanced in vv. 3, 5–7. No 'hidden dangers' nor 'deadly diseases' (GNB) will be allowed to harm him. Like a strong, formidable eagle protecting its vulnerable young from attack, God will keep His child safe under His **wings** (cf. Exod. 19: 4; Dt. 32: 11; Ru. 2: 12; Mt. 23: 37). Divine loyalty to the covenant guarantees safety. Whatever uncanny forces men were or thought themselves prey to, whether the night-demon Lilith (Isa. 34: 14) or the sinister **arrow** of sunstroke at dangerous **midday** or the plague unleashed at night (cf. Isa. 37: 36), God is the effective answer to all such fears, whether rational or irrational. However strong the battle, however long the list of casualties, the believer will survive unscathed. When God's justice is seen to be done on the **wicked**, he will **observe** unharmed.

Summarizing vv. 1–8, the next two verses crystallize the assurance of protection for the obedient believer and his family ('home' NEB, GNB; cf. Exod. 20: 6). God's tender care is such that He even supplies a celestial bodyguard around the believer, who carry him along the rock-strewn road. Allusion is made in v. 13 to the religious lore of the ancient Near East which spoke of gods killing dragons and other beasts (cf. 74: 13 f.). God's victory becomes that of the man of faith: he enters into God's own triumph as he faces life's threats (cf. Rom. 8: 37).

The divine promise (vv. 14–16)

The priest receives a message from God Himself to transmit to the believer before him. In solemn echo it corroborates what the priest has said. To the person whose faith 'clings' (JB) to God and will not let Him go (cf. Ru. 1: 14, 16 f.) and who has entered into an intimate knowledge of God, comes an assurance of deliverance. His prayers for help will not go unheeded: God's own presence will fend off **trouble**. He will 'lift him beyond danger' (NEB, **deliver**) and grant him the covenant blessing of **long life** (cf. Dt. 6: 2) and saving help.

The psalm speaks of physical safety as well as spiritual. It is a vivid reminder that the OT covenant concerned the body as much as the soul. This note, although not absent from the NT (cf. Mt. 6: 33; 2 Tim. 4: 18), is muted there (cf. Mt. 10: 28; Lk. 10: 19 f.). Rom. 8: 35–39 is the spiritual heir of this beautiful psalm.

> Safe shall be my going,
> Secretly armed against all death's endeavour;
> Safe where all safety's lost; safe where men fall;
> And if these poor limbs die, safest of all
>
> (Rupert Brooke).

'It is impossible that any ill should happen to the man who is beloved of the Lord . . . Ill to him is no ill, but only good in a mysterious form. Losses enrich him, sickness is his medicine, reproach his honour, death is his gain' (C. H. Spurgeon).

The rabbis took the psalm as messianic (and some modern scholars regard it as a royal psalm). The temptation story reflects this contemporary understanding. Jesus rejects Satan's seductive use of vv. 11 f. (Mt. 4: 6 f.): it is not a promise to the foolhardy and self-willed.

The syntactical problem in vv. 1–3 is best resolved in the NEB: 'You that . . . , who say . . . , he himself will snatch you away.'

Psalm 92. THE RELEVANCE OF WORSHIP

The psalmist has been attending the festival services at the temple. He has heard once more the sacred saga of God's triumphant grace. These are his personal reflections.

A personal Amen (vv. 1–4)

He has taken part in the regular round of worship to the accompaniment of the temple orchestra. Now he raises his own Amen of appreciation. God's attributes of **faithfulness** and covenant care have especially struck him. It has thrilled his heart to hear of God's celebrated **works** in creation and providence (cf. 74: 12–17; 77: 11–20).

God's power and wisdom (vv. 5–9)

He expresses his awe at the grandeur of God's activity and the profundity of His purposes (cf. Rom. 11: 33). Mysterious indeed is His providence at times. By no means all are convinced of the interpretation which believers put upon life, for not all have that true wisdom that begins with the fear of Yahweh (Prov. 1: 7). But now the psalmist can view with equanimity the prosperity of the wicked. His time in the temple has been well spent, teaching him afresh the truth of the judgment of God, one of the sacred themes of worship (cf. 73: 17–20). When he sees **the wicked** 'grow like weeds' (GNB), he is unperturbed. His eye of faith, made keen in the sanctuary, can see God's cloud of judgment on the distant horizon. **Grass** is a deliberately ill-omened comparison: it reflects not only luxuriance but transitoriness in its eastern setting (cf. 90: 5). Destruction is built in, as it were, and certain. By contrast God is supreme and eternal. Verse 9 has an archaic style. It may be a snatch of a traditional hymn recently sung, cited to confirm God's triumph.

A personal testimony (vv. 10, 11)

It is all true, affirms the psalmist. God's grace and judgment, themes of sacred song, have come true in his personal experience. He can testify how God has graciously supplied him with vigour and vitality. **Exalted** (v. 8) echoes **exalted** (v. 10) (the same Heb. root is used in both cases), as if to say that the psalmist shares something of the supremacy of his God (cf. Rom. 8: 37). He gratefully records the overthrow of his personal adversaries and sees it as God's power and judgment at work, and so an application of v. 9.

The elixir of life (vv. 12–15)

God's own people do not suffer the fate of premature death. Not grass but long-lived trees are the best description of their vitality. The secret is their gathering regularly in the temple for worship. This is a congenial environment, a good soil that communicates God's resources and makes life fruitful and satisfying. All such worshippers enjoy the covenant blessing of a ripe **old age** (cf. Dt. 34: 7; Ps. 91: 16). Theirs is 'the fruit of lips that confess his name' in praise (Heb. 13: 15). Here in the temple they are ready to proclaim ('eager to declare' NEB) that God is **upright**, 'straight in his dealings with others' (A. A. Anderson), 'always to be relied on' (Oesterley). The psalmist has come back to the theme on his heart at the beginning, God's faithfulness (v. 2). He is pure rock with never a flaw or fault, reliable to the core (cf. Dt. 32: 4). And, affirms the psalmist, unable to resist a final personal note, He's **my Rock**.

The psalmist's assurance must have encouraged many a Hebrew saint in his faith. Like the previous psalm, it has a notable this-worldliness about it, especially in its final part, which is transcended by the NT truth of a heavenly sanctuary, where the tree of life flourishes and God's servants shall worship Him for ever (Rev. 22: 2 f.). But even now 'the Church with psalms must shout' (G. Herbert).

Psalm 93.   STILL ON THE THRONE
This noble hymn of praise celebrates the kingship of Israel's God, along with Pss. 47, 96–99 (see the Introduction). His victorious domain, established in various spheres, is joyfully acknowledged by His followers, for whom it spells security and reflected triumph.

The King of creation (vv. 1, 2)
The LORD reigns is a declaration of allegiance to Yahweh (cf. 2 Sam. 15: 10; 2 K. 9: 13), the conviction of His absolute power. His attributes of **majesty** and **strength** are described as royal robes: they are His 'habits'. He is monarch by virtue of His work of creation. He it is who has made the world secure and immovable. Creation is proof of the antiquity of His kingship: He is no *parvenu* pretender to another's **throne**, here today and perhaps overthrown tomorrow. His kingship is rooted in the remote past, as stable as His created **world**. Your rule is one in which we can have complete confidence, Israel thankfully confesses to their God.

The King of Providence (vv. 3, 4)
A note of urgency and suspense is sounded: opposition rears its ugly head, and in alarm the community turn to their God afresh. The **seas** or 'ocean currents' (NEB 'ocean') speak of hostility and evil (cf. Rev. 21: 1). But paradoxically the language has a reassuring ring: pagan lore of divine triumph over the forces of chaos is echoed and applied metaphorically to any menace to God's rule over the earth (cf. 74: 13 f.). The sinister threats roaring in His people's ears fade to a murmur by contrast with the thunderclap of God's majesty (cf. Isa. 17: 12–14). He 'biddeth them cease, / Turneth their fury to peace, / Whirlwinds and waters assuaging' (J. Neander; tr. C. Winkworth). Praise to the Lord!

The King of His people (v. 5)
This is the One who has graciously revealed Himself to Israel, His will in the law and His presence in the temple throneroom. His spiritual 'laws' (GNB), the covenant terms, emanate from this same God: they are as reliable as the natural laws of the world. Who dare rush into His presence? Special preparations are necessary if any would approach this awesome, sovereign God in worship (cf. Isa. 6: 1–5).

Psalm 94.   IN THE SPIRIT OF BONHOEFFER
God's people are in the grip of an oppressive, Nazi-type regime. As a representative of the community the psalmist brings their case to the appeal court of heaven, and in his own name he challenges the government and encourages the persecuted people.

Prayer and problem (vv. 1–7)
Wicked men are in power, but the speaker knows of a higher authority to whom he may report their misdeeds and request their removal. He prays to the moral God of earthly providence to intervene and restore the social equilibrium. They are acting like little gods, abusing their power at their subjects' expense. God must surely do something, for it is His own chosen **people** who are suffering. Although throughout the ancient Near East protection of the underprivileged was held to be a sacred duty of leaders, **widow**, orphan and resident **alien** (JB 'guests') were being massacred. When confronted with a charge of this sacrilege, the authorities shrugged it off, brazenly holding that God turned a blind eye to their conduct and took no notice.

Rebuke and reassurance (vv. 8–15)
It is they who ought to be taking notice! Using the style of wisdom teachers, the psalmist bravely challenges the government. He calls them **fools**: they lack the wisdom which is based on reverence for God (Prov. 1: 7).

They are making the mistake of underestimating Him and forgetting the implications of His creation of **ear** and **eye** (cf. Prov. 20: 12). He it is who has given all **nations**, not only Israel, a responsible awareness of His moral will (cf. Rom. 1: 20; 2: 14). Their conclusion that God does not matter has no substance: it is just 'a puff of wind' (JB, NEB).

Still using wisdom language, he turns to encourage his suffering brothers, first via a 'horizontal' prayer and then directly. Despite the contrary example of the men in power, how good and wise it is to learn of God in submissive obedience! In the Word 'springs of consolation rise / To cheer the fainting mind' (A. Steele), as it assures of divine realities. It helps the believer to hold on in faith and hope **till** God's justice catches up with the miscreants and they are toppled. Of one thing they can be certain: God's faithfulness to His victimized chosen ones (cf. v. 5). True **judgment** will eventually be done, never fear, and the **upright** will be rehabilitated.

Testimony and trust (vv. 16–23)
The psalmist reports a clash he himself recently had with the authorities. He stood alone, and yet survived the ordeal. Or rather he was not alone, for God helped him through (cf. 2 Tim. 4: 16 f.). He thought himself on his last legs, but God's covenant care sustained him. He

finds divine encouragement for the future in this personal escape from death, although he has plenty to worry about. But it is a matter of simple spiritual logic that God cannot possibly be on the side of the present government who have brought in oppressive measures legalizing their conduct. They are using the lawcourts as a tool of flagrant injustice and outright murder. But once more he alludes to his personal experience of God's strengthening grace and bases upon it his conviction that evil will not always be rampant. Without a doubt **our God** (cf. vv. 5, 14) can be trusted to stem this tide of **wickedness. 1.** Recent study suggests that vengeance is more precisely 'vindication', i.e. deliverance for the oppressed and punishment for their oppressors. **7, 8.** NEB 'pays no heed. Pay heed yourselves'. The Heb. verb is significantly repeated. **10a. disciplines:** rather 'instructs' (JB, NEB); similarly in v. 12. **16.** JB and GNB rightly take the verbs as past.

Psalm 95. OBEISANCE AND OBEDIENCE

The chosen people have gathered in Jerusalem to celebrate a festival. The contents of the psalm appear to indicate that the renewal of the covenant is to be the theme of the ensuing service. But first their hearts need to be prepared.

Worship of the God of creation (vv. 1–5)
Before entering the temple the devout encourage each other to join in God's praises, joyfully 'acclaiming' (JB) Him as their **Rock**, their faithful Protector. The theme of their praise is His rôle as sovereign Creator. Proof of His regal supremacy lies in His creative work (cf. 93: 1 f.). No other nation worships a God of whom it may truly be said that He has the whole wide world **in His hand**. The underworld was commonly thought of as beyond the gods' reach and high **mountain peaks** were held to be the abodes of the gods: the psalm deliberately denies both beliefs. Yahweh has sole and complete jurisdiction over both areas. He has Manufacturer's rights of control.

Worship of the God of the covenant (vv. 6, 7a)
'Come in' (JB), the cry rings out again, come into the temple and pay adoring homage to Yahweh. He it is who made Israel into a national entity: the chosen nation owes its origin to His grace. **Our God**—his **people**, the two-sided covenant formula (cf. 81: 10 f.) is savoured with relish. He is their Good Shepherd, they 'the people he pastures, the flock he guides' (JB). All His covenant care is evoked by the pastoral imagery.

Warning of God's covenant claims (vv. 7b–11)
But the relationship has created a claim upon Israel as well as bestowing care. If God is to be worshipped aright, there must be a due sense of responsibility, the twin of privilege. So a temple prophet brings God's realistic word for the hour (cf. 81: 5b–16). The covenant grace and law to be proclaimed in the festival confront Israel with a crucial choice, to go God's way or to follow their ancestors' precedent in stubborn rebellion and ultimate destruction. **Today** is the existential moment of opportunity which demands a response for or against God. 'See to it, brothers, that none of you has a sinful unbelieving heart, that turns away from the living God' (Heb. 3: 12). They had spoken of their protecting **Rock** (v. 1): then let them heed the lesson of the rock of provision at Strife Camp (**Meribah**) and Testing Place (**Massah**) not long after the covenant was promulgated at Sinai. They wrongly 'challenged' (JB, NEB) God, doubting His goodness and making arbitrary demands that He prove His power. 'If we were for ever testing the love of our wife or husband and remained unconvinced after years of faithfulness, we should wear out the utmost human patience' (C. H. Spurgeon). Such behaviour was all the more reprehensible in that they had witnessed the miracles of the Exodus and His earlier provision.

The congregation had spoken of themselves as God's flock (v. 7). Then let them heed **his voice** (Jn 10: 3 f., 16). And let them beware lest they have cause to say 'We all, like sheep, have gone astray, each of us has turned to his own way' (Isa. 53: 6). The forty-year wilderness wandering to oblivion was fitting reprisal for the wandering hearts of their forbears (cf. Heb. 3: 10) from whom God withdrew His blessing in repugnance. They were categorically barred from entry into 'the land of rest I had for them' (JB, cf. GNB; cf. Dt. 12: 9 f.). The incident is mentioned as an implicit warning, made explicit in Heb. 3: 7–4: 13. The Lord's **rest** is only for those who take His yoke of obedient service (Mt. 11: 28 f.). The choice still stands, the rest which results from trust and obedience or self-destructive wandering wherever fancy leads.

Psalm 96. OUR UNIVERSAL GOD

The hymn 'Let the song go round the earth, / Jesus Christ is Lord' (Sarah G. Stocks; in the last verse: 'Jesus Christ is King') is modelled upon this psalm and the following two. If that Christian cry has a presumptuous ring in the ears of a world peopled with Buddhists, Moslems, atheists, etc., this psalm is even more daring in pitting the God of the little Hebrew nation against the pantheons of Canaan, Egypt and Mesopotamia, and envisaging the world's past, present and future as in His mighty hands.

Praise to the world's Creator (vv. 1–6)
The excited call goes out with repetitive insistence: **sing** the praises of Yahweh, Israel's God. It is to be **a new song**. Just as His care is new

every morning (Lam. 3: 23), so His praise must be ever new. Israel worships as representative of **all the earth**, firstfruits of a worshipping world (cf. v. 3). They have received His saving help down the ages. **His marvelous deeds** in part they know from the record of creation and in part have experienced in a whole calendar of events from the Exodus onwards. Israel is to exist in the world as a vocal witness of this heritage and experience of God. In a practical sense there is little missionary spirit in the OT: Yahweh's universality is a matter of doctrinal faith and visionary hope, rather than a present challenge to outreach. By Israel's very worshipping in the temple a divine bridgehead was established in the world which afforded a promise of universal rule.

Why should Israel expect other nations to worship their God? Did they not have **gods** of their own? But these are dismissed as nonentities. This is Yahweh's world. He, not Baal nor Marduk, is alone the **great**, awe-inspiring Creator and there is no real alternative to Him. So 'loud must be his praise' (JB). The **splendor** and **majesty**, the power and glory which are His attributes, are poetically portrayed as His royal retinue in the temple throneroom (cf. Isa. 6: 1 f.).

Praise to the world's Creator and Judge (vv. 7–10)

Again a threefold summons to the whole world rings out, to echo and acknowledge these supreme attributes of His. He is worthy of nothing less than that all humanity should **worship** and reverence Him. **Offering** has a double sense, religious and political, of sacrifice and tribute, to be brought in token of vassalage to the divine King (cf. 68: 29). Israel is again the herald, now of the message of His royal status. His right to the throne depends upon two great factors, creation and judgment. In creating the world He 'hath 'stablished it fast by a changeless decree' (R. Grant), secure against any threat. He it is who maintains the moral order as well as the physical, and intervenes to correct oppression. 'The order of nature in creation and the order of history in judgment are planned by God in such a way that they are tuned to each other and supplement each other, both being directed towards their common goal, and that goal is the realization of the "righteousness of God" in his plan of salvation' (Weiser). So 'with the story of His worth / Let the whole world ring!' (S. G. Stocks).

Praise to the world's Judge (vv. 11–13)

The psalm rises to a crescendo in a call to **joy** and jubilation, addressed to the universe for all God's creatures to take up, animate and inanimate. In Israel's contemporary world, as in the modern world, there were many evidences of disarray. But Israel, no less than the Church, looked forward to a divine coming when the universal ravages of sin and violence would be gloriously set right. 'The creation waits with eager longing' to 'be set free from its bondage' (Rom. 8: 19 f.). This stained **world** is to be restored so that it perfectly reflects God's righteous rule. In faith the suffering world is called to anticipate the joy of this great event.

Psalm 97. THE RIGHTEOUS KING
God's glorious appearing (vv. 1–6)

Every saving advent of God in the past and future is summed up in this stylized picture of divine intervention, in which God proves Himself victorious King over evil and catastrophe (cf. 18: 1–19; 50: 3). Judah for one recognizes Yahweh as King, but to deem this sufficient would do Him an injustice. Only the acclaim of all humanity would adequately reflect His glory. So the rest of the world, including the far-flung Aegean **shores**, is invited to share this thrilling affirmation that Judah's God **reigns**.

Their transcendent God is surrounded by an awesome aura of mystery (cf. Dt. 4: 11). **Righteousness and justice** are like the carved figures that support a monarch's **throne**, for His rule is based upon these traits. He is not static and remote, but intervenes in this world, enveloped in searing **fire**, 'the splendour of light', and in holy goodness which destroys those who would dispute His rule (cf. Exod. 19: 18). His coming is like a terrific thunderstorm which leaves men aghast. So terrible is this God who comes that the very **mountains**, bywords for stability and strength, quake and quail before this source of eternal power. For He is no less than **the Lord of all the earth**. The heavenly phenomena of clouds, thunder and lightning serve as heralds of His coming to establish **righteousness**, while all mankind are awed witnesses of His glorious appearing. **Righteousness**, a key term of this and other psalms of kingship, refers to God's plan of redemption whereby His own attribute (v. 2) may be echoed and realized on earth.

This magnificent word-picture is intended as a vehicle of praise, an attempt to reflect the dynamic grandeur of God: 'Almighty, victorious, Thy great name we praise' (W. C. Smith). The NT descriptions of Christ's Second Coming are significantly based in part upon such OT pictures as this one.

Reactions to His appearing (vv. 7–12)

So dynamic is the impact of His coming that all idolaters are confounded. The empty bubble of their pride in false religion is burst at last. They are forced to confess the inferiority of their own deities to Yahweh. But **Judah's** capital and her sister cities **rejoice**, their faith vindicated by God's **judgments**, the acts by which He carries out His verdicts upon men.

This faith of theirs is expressed in v. 9, faith in their God as an **exalted** Being whose power extends over the whole world. Beside Him the seeming power of the god of the mightiest nation on earth fades into insignificance.

Yes, this is our God, Judah affirms. His kingship consists not only of His omnipotence as Lord of all the earth, but also of His covenant relationship with Judah. He has decreed that His righteousness, which in grand event He has manifested on earth from time to time and will manifest again (vv. 2, 6), should be embodied in Judah. They are to be an obedient, **righteous** people, in whose hearts righteousness dwells. Upon them rests the obligation to **hate evil**, for they are in covenant relationship (**faithful ones**) with the God of goodness and right. But this burden is light, for it is coupled with God's loving protection. **Wicked** men are still about, although the voice of faith celebrates their overthrow. Yet God **guards** His people, insofar as they are obedient. Not for them the darkness of destruction but covenant blessing which makes them radiant and rejoicing. The world does not yet **rejoice** in Judah's God (v. 1), but His people are to inaugurate the vision (cf. Mic. 4: 1–5). This too is their obligation, to bear witness to Him by rendering **praise** in worship.

Psalm 98. IN EVERY CORNER SING

This psalm, the twin of Ps. 96, celebrates the kingship and victory of Israel's God. Past, present and future are telescoped together in a grand hymn of faith.

Adoring the Victor (vv. 1–3)

The religious community is exhorted to **sing a new song**, in fresh appreciation of all that God has done. After the short summons to praise the rest of the stanza is given over to the grounds for it. The wonders of creation and of all His providential dealings with His people down the centuries provide background material for their hymn. The highlights of their history have been the manifestations of divine power. 'His the triumph, His the victory alone'; it has all been due to His enabling grace (cf. 1 C. 15: 10). Many have been the occasions when their God demonstrated His saving help and made plain to the rest of the world His claims where Israel is concerned (**righteousness**). He has kept faith with His covenant partner and actively implemented (**remembered**) His promises. There can be no soul in the world whom the news of His countless victories has not reached (cf. Dt. 2: 25; 1 Chr. 14: 17; 2 Chr. 32: 23; Ac. 26: 26).

Acclaiming the King (vv. 4–6)

The second stanza begins and ends with a note of acclamation (**shout for joy**: 'acclaim' JB, NEB). The ceremony of acclaiming a newly installed human king (cf. 1 Sam. 10: 24; 2 Kg.

11: 12, 14) is re-enacted in the temple and transferred to Yahweh. The whole world, as yet represented by Israel, is urged to recognize His royal authority and to submit to it. The cheering and fanfare of **trumpets** which belong to the civil ceremony are echoed in the songs of the congregation and the music of the temple orchestra. That Israel alone should hail Him is not enough: their God is no local princeling but lays claim to **all the earth**. The covenant relationship with Israel (v. 3) is not exclusive but the prelude to the universal extension of His majesty. For faith it is but a short step from the inauguration of God's rule to its consummation (cf. Rev. 1: 1, 3).

Awaiting the Judge (vv. 7–9)

Every part of the natural world is invited to make its contribution to this universal acclaim. The **sea**, the land, the **rivers**, the **mountains** are all encouraged to be joyously alive with the sound of music. All creation is bidden join in Israel's symphony of praise, for the day of its rehabilitation is at hand (cf. Rom. 8: 19–23) when the King comes to set up His just rule. His righteous claim will be substantiated, no longer limited to Israel (v. 2) but extended world-wide. The Christian Church takes up the cry and, fusing the OT ideals of divine and Davidic kingship, sings 'Hail to the Lord's anointed . . . Righteousness in fountains / From hill to valley [shall] flow' (J. Montgomery).

Psalm 99. WORSHIP THE KING

This is the last of the psalms of kingship which praise God's rule not only over Israel but over the other nations. Its keynote is holiness.

The God who rules the world (vv. 1–3)

Here is God's holiness as expressed in His worldwide dominion. A proper response to the kingship of Yahweh would be awesome respect from the whole of humanity. So **great** is Israel's conception of Him. In staggering faith they speak of **Zion** as His world capital. There in the temple He **sits enthroned**, His invisible presence conceived to be above the sphinx-like **cherubim** whose wings overshadowed the ark. Majestic and awe-inspiring in His self-revelation (**name**) to Israel, He is worthy of universal acclaim. He is **holy**, in the original sense of possessing transcendent power and divine otherness (cf. Isa. 6: 3).

The God who rules Israel (vv. 4, 5)

God's holiness is revealed in His establishment of law and order. He has created a society (**Jacob**) in which His might is used not despotically but in the service of right. He has set up a state governed by His laws, and in the course of Israel's history has seen to it that **justice** was done. This prompts Israel's praise and homage at the sacred ark (cf. v. 1; 1 Chr. 28: 2; Isa. 6: 1).

The God of royal clemency (vv. 6–9)
God's holiness has been revealed in the history of His gracious dealings with Israel. Favourable response to suppliants was a royal attribute (cf. Jer. 37: 20) in which their God was not found wanting. There is a brief survey of the effective ministry of intercession of great men of God, leaders and mediators who not only represented the nation's cause to Him, especially in face of enemy attack (cf. Exod. 17: 11; 1 Sam. 7: 8–11), but received and preserved His covenant terms. So awesome is their King that personal audience is impossible: He communicated via **the pillar of cloud** which symbolized both His presence and His inaccessible majesty (Exod. 33: 9; Num. 12: 5; cf. 1 Sam. 3: 3 ff.).

In v. 8 occurs a devotional change to direct address: the God of the past is **our God** still. His ancient treatment of His people carries an implicit hope that the present generation in their difficulties may also experience God's grace and royal pardon, and that He will listen to their intercessors (cf. Jl 2: 17; Rom. 8: 34; Heb. 4: 14–16). With awesome wonder they worship in Jerusalem the God who is so far above them and yet so near.

6. Render 'Moses and Aaron among . . . and Samuel among . . . name, called . . .' (cf. NEB). **8.** In the context **their** is probably an objective pronoun. Render 'and an avenger of wrong-doings done to them' (R. N. Whybray; cf. NIVmg).

Psalm 100.   THE OLD HUNDREDTH
This invitation to praise is similar to that in 95: 1–7a. It is designed to prepare the hearts of the congregation for subsequent worship.
Hallelujah to our Shepherd (vv. 1–3)
The psalm is addressed throughout to God's chosen people; in the first line Israel is representative of **all the earth**. The people are summoned to the service of 'worship' (NEB, GNB). **Joyful songs** are to be the response to what God is and does: joy inspired by Him is to return to Him. Worship is to flow first from the realization of Yahweh's deity: it is tantamount to a renunciation of other gods and a vow of renewed allegiance. Appreciation of His covenant relationship is to be a related motivation. Here too praise and commitment are one: 'We belong to him' (JB, GNB). They completely depend upon Him for their spiritual existence, as the people formed by Him to declare His praise (Isa. 43: 21). To Him they owe both their beginning and the continuing blessings along the way as 'the flock which he shepherds' (NEB).
Hallelujah to our good God (vv. 4, 5)
Soon the congregation will pour through the **gates** and into the open **courts** of the temple. What will stir their hearts to **praise**? Above all God's goodness, one of a number of OT

counterparts to grace in the NT: 'How good is the God we adore, / Our faithful, unchangeable Friend!' (J. Hart). The whole future of His people lies secure in His hands, for He always cares (1 Pet. 5: 7).
Note: **3.** The alternative Heb. reading 'and not we ourselves' (AV) is less fitting in the context.

Psalm 101.   THE KING'S OATH
This is a royal psalm, pledging the king's intention to serve the One whose viceroy he is (cf. v. 8). It has been called 'the king's mirror': it preserves a challenging ideal to any in positions of leadership, whether civil (cf. Rom. 13: 1–7) or ecclesiastical (cf. 1 Pet. 5: 1–4).
The twofold theme (v. 1)
The Davidic covenant bestowed great privilege upon him (cf. 89: 19–37), but it also imposed heavy responsibilities, personal loyalty (**love**) to the covenant and social **justice** (cf. 1 Kg. 9: 4).
Personal loyalty (vv. 2–4)
The king promises moral integrity as a constant principle of his life. His motivation is that he may thereby experience God's presence in blessing (cf. Jn 14: 23). He renounces any 'sordid aim' (NEB) and claims that faithlessness will be anathema to him. He will embrace not wrong but right as his standard in ruling.
Social justice (vv. 5–8)
The king, as head of the judiciary, was obliged to maintain the covenant laws. This obligation he now gladly shoulders. Slander would be ruthlessly put down as a bane to society. Proud men, whose self-importance exceeded their social value, would be firmly put in their place. An equitable society was his aim, where reward was based on merit. It lay within the king's power to create an élite by bestowing rank and position upon his subjects. The members of his administration would be people of integrity and religious faith. Traitors and liars would not be welcome at court nor keep their posts for long. At the **morning** law sessions in Jerusalem, where the king would handle the more difficult cases, he promises to rid the country of the criminals brought to the capital for trial (cf. 2 Sam. 15: 2 f.; Jer. 21: 12).

Psalm 102.   FRUIT FROM BARREN GROUND
Suffering is an inescapable human experience. This lament, as it is technically called, is a sufferer's cry for help to the God who has previously revealed Himself as favourable. As the heading implies, its aim is 'to lay one's inner sufferings before the one who alleviates suffering, heals wounds and dries tears' (Westermann).
The appeal (vv. 1, 2)
The sufferer craves a hearing. He yearns for the light of God's **face** in renewal and blessing

(cf. Num. 6: 25). He cannot endure his desperate plight much longer.

The problem (vv. 3-11)

His sufferings are primarily physical, a demoralizing fever which has stolen his appetite (cf. JB, GNB, v. 4) and left him 'nothing but skin and bones' (GNB, v. 5). In a culture where ill-health was viewed ominously as a punishment for sin, he found himself isolated and cold-shouldered. Rivals made it an occasion for one-up-manship and cruelly misused his name (cf. a Jonah, a Jeremiah). But worst of all to endure were the spiritual implications of his suffering. If God is the Lord of providence, how could the sufferer avoid the conclusion that God had discarded him, a victim of divine displeasure? So he mourned, overwhelmed by this cruellest cut of all.

Hope for the future (vv. 12-22)

The psalmist sets his own suffering against a tragic background, the experience of the religious community to which he belonged. Evidently Jerusalem lay in ruins, mere **stones** and rubble. God's people still loved their blitzed city. They clung to divine promises about **Zion** and confidently held their fulfilment to be imminent. The guarantee of this hope lay in God's everlasting sovereignty (v. 12) and His covenant relationship. Israel, His covenant partner, was intended to be the earthly mirror of His **glory** before mankind. A despised, destroyed Zion—God's 'agency' on earth—was a contradiction in terms and by no means His last word. His **destitute** people's **prayer** would find an answer. This communal confidence brings comfort to the psalmist, for the God of Israel is also the God of the Israelite.

Forgetting his anguish for the moment, he enthusiastically throws himself into this vision of the future. That God still has a use for His people he cannot doubt. In anticipation he hears already the Hallelujahs of a myriad host of Gentiles and Jews, gathered in Jerusalem and looking back to the time—still future to the psalmist!—when God intervened in grace and liberated His oppressed, **condemned** people. This is an exultant faith which, rising above circumstances and human logic, clings to the God of hope (cf. Rom. 5: 2-5; 15: 13).

A fresh appeal (vv. 23, 24)

But a 'not yet' anchors him to the painful present (cf. Rom. 8: 18-25). Men of Israel were prepared to face eventual death and Sheol with serenity (cf. Gen. 25: 7). But they jibbed at a premature death, an eventide at noon (cf. v. 11). Since God's own life lasts for ever (cf. GNB), the poet craves a small share in God's eternity, so that he at least may live to a ripe old age.

Praise and comfort (vv. 25-28)

The point just made is expanded. God is the great Creator, older than **the earth** and **heavens**. Aeons old, they seem to be everlasting, but the Creator must be greater than His creation and outlive it. Material things are prey to time's ravages, but God is essentially immortal and immune from decay. By the covenant God had linked Himself with His chosen people and shared Himself with them: because He lived, they would live also (cf. Jn 14: 19), protected by Him. This guarantee the psalmist hugs to his heart as a hope that he in his suffering may personally find it coming true.

Verses 25-27 are applied to Christ in Heb. 1: 10-12 and v. 27 is echoed in Heb. 13: 8. This Christological understanding was facilitated by the medium of the LXX, where God speaks directly from v. 23 onwards, addressing one who is explicitly called 'Lord' in v. 25. The passage is regarded as a heritage to be claimed for Christ, as the divine Creator (cf. Heb. 1: 2 f.). In turn the Christian community and its individual members are heirs to the hopes expressed in the psalm as the antidote to despair (cf. Heb. 12: 3, 12, 22-24; 13: 14).

Psalm 103. AMAZING GRACE

Ancient Israel had the delightful custom of incorporating personal testimonies into public worship (cf. Ps. 73). Here an individual's thanksgiving to God before the congregation develops into his leading them in worship. The speaker draws three concentric circles of praise, personal, communal and universal (cf. 22: 22-31).

Praise for personal experience (vv. 1-5)

The psalmist enthusiastically urges himself to thank God for five blessings. Far from ignoring His **benefits** and taking them for granted (cf. Lk. 17: 15-18), his whole being praises God with respectful awe. Pride of place is given to His solution of the worst problem, sin. The context reflects the frequent OT link between sin and sickness (cf. 1 C. 11: 30). Evidently the author has recovered from a serious illness and so premature death. He translates his relief into praise. He sees this deliverance as but one instance of God's lavish giving of gifts fit for a king and total enrichment of his life.

Praise for God's dealings with Israel (vv. 6-18)

The community's experience of divine grace is the psalmist's own, writ large (vv. 4, 8). Israel, so often the **oppressed** pawn of political powers, had seen God's grace in her history. Long ago **Moses** had pleaded with Him in terms of v. 7 (Exod. 33: 13) and God had revealed Himself to him in terms of v. 8 (Exod. 34: 6). This latter text the poet proceeds to expound in vv. 9-18.

Grace sums up God's dealings with His people. He is **slow to anger** (9), **abounding in love** (10 f.; cf. Ezr. 9: 13). His grace exceeds the largest dimensions known to man (cf. Eph.

3: 18 f.). He is 'kind' (GNB, v. 13; the Heb. verbs echo **compassionate** in v. 8). 'Father-like, He tends and spares us; / Well our feeble frame He knows' (H. F. Lyte). The Creator who sternly imposed sin's penalty (Gen. 2: 7; 3: 19) became the God of the covenant, the kindly Father of His people (Exod. 4: 22; Hos. 11: 1, 3 f.). Verses 15–18 expound further the theme of steadfast **love** or covenant faithfulness. It is contrasted with man's inherent mortality. Like a wild **flower**, he is gone with **the wind**. Generations come and go, but one factor which survives from age to age is this divine love. It guarantees the survival of the people of the **covenant**, as from father to son the same constant relationship with God is handed on. It is essentially a two-way relationship: it calls for a response of obedience and loyalty (cf. Hos. 6: 6).

Universal praise (vv. 19–22)
Israel at worship often celebrated Yahweh's kingly power **over all** (cf. Ps. 93; 95–99; Isa. 6: 3, 5). This theme the psalmist weaves into his thanksgiving, for God's power backs up His grace and makes it strong (cf. v. 11, especially in NEB). Nothing less than the praise of angelic **hosts** and of all the creatures of realm can adequately reflect His greatness. Will not the little voice of the individual believer (cf. vv. 1–5) be lost in this universal chorale? By no means. 'Ransomed, healed, restored, forgiven, / Who like thee His praise should sing?' (Lyte).

1 C. 15 and Eph. 1–2: 10 are good passages to read alongside this psalm. The Christian reads it with new insight into God's grace and so should respond with even greater gratitude. A new dimension of life has been revealed in Christ, banishing fear of death's **pit** and ensuring the survival not only of the covenant community (cf. 102: 28) but of every individual member down the ages.

Psalm 104.   GENESIS SET TO MUSIC
The author of this beautiful poem has been called 'the Wordsworth of the ancients'. It is a solo hymn of praise offered in the course of communal worship, his **meditation** (v. 34) upon God's mighty power and loving care mirrored in the world around. It echoes the themes of the first chapters of Genesis: the relation between them is 'like that of a coloured picture to the clear lines of a woodcut' (Weiser). There are striking parallels between this psalm, especially vv. 10–14, 20–27, and the Egyptian Hymn to Aten as the source of all life. The Hymn was composed by Akhenaten, alias Amenhotep IV, Pharaoh in the fourteenth century B.C., who scandalously abandoned the traditional religion of Egypt and practised monolatrous worship of the sun-god Aten. It is possible that the psalm was influenced indirectly or, less likely, directly by the Hymn, as certainly Prov. 22: 17–24: 22 was by Egyptian teaching, in which case, as D. Kidner concluded with reference to the Proverbs material, an Egyptian jewel has been taken, re-set by an Israelite workman and put to finer use. Then the psalmist deliberately corrected the Hymn by downgrading the role of the sun. Alternatively 'Akhenaten's religion, being certainly in some respects like that of the Jews, set him free to write poetry in some degree like theirs' (C. S. Lewis).

The King of creation (vv. 1–4)
The poet urges himself to praise his God and proceeds to do so. 'How great Thou art!' is the adoring cry wrung from his **soul**, as he sees God's 'power throughout the universe displayed'. God is King and the world is His realm. His royal robe is the **light** of Gen. 1: 3. Upon the firmament of the sky, erected as effortlessly as any nomad would his **tent**, He has built His palace, above the heavenly **waters** (cf. Gen. 1: 6–8). The **clouds** are His royal **chariot**, the **wind** His Pegasus. The elemental forces of nature are but His minions, at the service of His majesty.

The stable earth (vv. 5–9)
The modern scientific world-view is different from that of the ancients, who thought in quaint terms of an oil-rig structure miraculously fixed in the subterranean ocean. But modern man must share the psalmist's reaction of awe and trust towards the God who has fixed the orbit of the planet earth and, moreover, made it capable of supporting life. The primeval world, a watery mass, had first to be cleared of water to make it habitable (Gen. 1: 2, 7, 9). God accomplished this Herculean task simply by issuing an order. His 'word / Chaos and darkness heard, / And took their flight' (J. Marriott). The water receded, 'cascading over the mountains, into the valleys' (JB, cf. NEB, GNB) and retreating to its permanent place, the sea bed (Gen. 1: 9). The cruel sea is kept at bay, and **the earth** has been made safe to live in.

The home of beast, bird and man (vv. 10–23)
The psalmist paints some delightful cameos of nature, in praise of its Creator. Water, the potential enemy of terrestrial life, has been harnessed to become its means of sustenance, serving God by serving His creatures. The **springs** supplying water from the subterranean ocean and issuing into rivers, are supplemented by rain from the celestial ocean (cf. Gen. 2: 5 f.; 7: 11). God's providential control and care are thus revealed. The rain is the result or **fruit** of His personal activity. He is not remote from nature: it is but a step from its phenomena to God Himself (cf. Rom. 1: 20).

Vegetation such as **grass** and cereals is God's

gift to animals and mankind. Vineyard, olive grove and cornfield are pledges of His caring and proofs of His wish for man to be healthy, happy and high in morale. **Trees** are the home God has given to **the birds**; mountainous terrain unsuitable for human habitation is His home for certain **wild** animals. The poet has no selfish view of nature as wholly man's to exploit and spoil. He would have regarded conservation as an obligation arising from a divine pattern imposed upon the world. From this standpoint he can lose even a natural fear of ferocious **beasts** and view the lion's **roar** as akin to prayer (cf. Job 38: 41; Jl 1: 20)! Beasts prowling at night are the counterpart of men at work by day, all sharing in a divinely programmed cycle of activity. Human work belongs to a God-ordained pattern (cf. Gen. 2: 15; 3: 23). The **sun** and **moon**, far from being deities, as Israel's neighbours imagined, are but God's clock and calendar for His animate creation (cf. Gen. 1: 14).

The sea (vv. 24–26)
The psalmist pauses for a general reflection: 'What variety you have created, arranging everything so wisely!' (JB) Wherever he looks he is prompted to praise the Creator. The **sea**, traditional object of awe and even dread to Israelite landlubbers, he brings within the scope of his adoration. In similar vein Paul could weave negative and hostile elements into his praise (Rom. 8: 35–39). The poet sketches the sea's vastness and its teeming life, its population of foreign **ships** and marine monsters. His fear of the latter is transmuted by the remarkable portrayal of **the leviathan** as a frisky, puppy-like creature, as much a product of God's creative work as anything else.

The divine life-force (vv. 27–30)
All creatures, great and small, depend upon God. He is their father-figure and they are members of His vast family. His personal, sustaining care is the ultimate source of their **food** supply. They are at the mercy of His generous **hand** or averted **face**. The power of life and death are His, for God's 'breath' (v. 30, GNB; cf. NEB) is the secret of physical life (cf. Gen. 2: 7; 6: 17). Whenever this life-force is withdrawn, the animate reverts to **dust** (cf. Gen. 3: 19). Each new generation is evidence of a continual process of creation, replenishing human and animal stock.

Praise of God's power (vv. 31–35)
The poet hopes that God's glorious power will never cease to be revealed in the natural world. He prays that, as once God took delight in His creation (Gen. 1: 31), so His creatures may continue to receive His smile of favour. How wary man should be: one look from Him and the **earth** quakes, one touch and the **mountains** erupt (cf. 97: 4 f.)! For himself the psalmist takes a vow of lifelong **praise**. He offers

these reflections of his as a sacrifice acceptable, he trusts, to God, and as an aid to the congregation's worship (**Praise the LORD.**). His final prayer is that the man-made flaws in God's beautiful handiwork may be removed. Those who by flouting God's moral order deliberately spoil the harmony of creation forfeit their God-given privilege of sharing in it. But the psalmist cannot end on such a sombre note: **praise**, personal and communal, is man's due response to so great a God. Parts of the psalm have been paraphrased in Sir Robert Grant's hymn 'O worship the King' and in W. C. Smith's 'Immortal, invisible, God only wise'.

Verse 4 is quoted in Heb. 1: 7 from the LXX.

Psalm 105.   GOD IS FAITHFUL
The people of God have met to worship Him. This psalm is intended as a vehicle of their praise. Its overall theme is God's faithfulness to His promises (vv. 8, 42). Israel's sacred history is sketched in such a way as to reinforce the spiritual lesson that He is utterly trustworthy and able to save and keep.

The call to praise (vv. 1–6)
Israel is invited to return **thanks** to God and to worship. Part of this worship would be testimonies to His salvation, not individual but national. They would look back to the historical creation of His covenant people, as this psalm does, and bring it home to their own hearts. Beyond their frontiers were pagan **nations**, but Israel was an enclave where the true God was honoured. They know His **name** to be praiseworthy, for He has revealed to them His personal character and purposes. So they are called to meet with Him in joyful thanksgiving and to appreciate afresh His power and **face**. Contemporary bearers of a living heritage which stretches back to Abraham's day, their privilege it is to look back with gratitude to the laying of their spiritual foundations as God's own people.

The covenant concerning the promised land (vv. 7–11)
Yahweh is the covenant God of Israel (cf. Exod. 20: 2). To establish the covenant He made use of His universal authority, shaping the fortunes of Egypt for Israel's benefit. If His people are urged to **remember** (5, Heb. *zikᵉrû*), He never needs urging to remember His promise to the patriarchs (8, Heb. *zākar*). An essential part of this reiterated promise concerned **the land of Canaan** as Israel's destined possession (cf. Gen. 17: 8; 26: 3; 28: 13).

Waiting for the promise (vv. 12–25)
For many generations the promise was a matter of faith, not sight. To the landless patriarchs, a handful of aliens and nomads among the various Canaanite states, the hope was an unattainable dream. But even then God was at work, protecting His people's ancestors and so

preparing for its fulfilment. When kings such as Pharaoh and Abimelech would endanger the succession, He intervened and kept them sacrosanct (Gen. 12: 17; 20: 3). Although the ancestors were forced to leave the land, as if the promise was nullified, He was in fact controlling nature and history according to His purposes. He paved the way by the career of **Joseph**. Joseph's experience was that of Israel in miniature. Promised future greatness (Gen. 37: 5–11), he nevertheless had patiently to undergo trial and testing before it all came true.

Through the life of this individual God was encouraging His own to maintain their larger hope. He used Joseph's eminence as a means of preserving and blessing His people (cf. Gen. 45: 7 f.). Divine blessing, as often, came in the form of physical fertility (cf. 127: 3 and comment), thereby fulfilling another element in the patriarchal promise, unmentioned earlier (cf. Gen. 12: 2; 22: 17). These were omens to hearten Israel's forebears and to sustain them through coming misfortune. God was sovereign even where Egyptian enmity was concerned: paradoxically it was the intended means of eventually fulfilling His plan of blessing.

The powerful prelude to fulfilment (vv. 26–36)

If Joseph was God's man for an earlier crisis (vv. 16 f.), **Moses** and **Aaron** were raised up for this hour of need. God revealed His power in Egypt in order to execute His covenant plans (cf. v. 7). Plague after plague came at His command, in reprisal for the rebellion of the Egyptian vassal of this Overlord of the nations.

Homeward bound (vv. 37–45)

The Exodus spelled the beginning of Israel's nationhood and heralded the dawn of the day of promise. God's blessing was evident then, in the form of material wealth and physical enabling. He had made it plain to Egypt that the Israelites were no ordinary people but under His special protection. He went on guiding and supplying their everyday needs in abundance. The psalm stresses the basic theme that this experience was the outworking of God's faithfulness to His ancient promise.

They were liberated from Egypt with a song on their lips (Exod. 15) and with **joy** that was to be echoed down the ages till the present generation took up the strain (v. 3). Canaan and its assets were theirs at last, not won by their own achievement but bestowed as God's gifts (cf. Dt. 6: 10 f.). Redeemed by divine initiative and recipients of divine grace, what was there for Israel to do? Nothing but to show their gratitude by complying with God's revealed will, constrained by His faithfulness. Religious praise (cf. vv. 1–6) and moral obedience were to be their twin response to the finished work of their covenant God, who had kept His promise.

It takes little to translate this psalm into Christian terms. At the sacred feast of the Lord's Supper God's people are bidden remember the establishment of the new covenant, promised through Jeremiah long before (1 C. 11: 25 f.). The death and resurrection of Jesus are the focal points of God's revelation of His purposes for the Church, to be treasured and cherished as eternally valid and relevant for contemporary living. The letter to the Hebrews takes up the specific theme of the psalm and gives it a Christian extension. The promise to Abraham was not exhausted by Israel's temporal occupation of the land. Canaan is a shadow of the reality, a heavenly country, which is to be the final destiny of God's people of the covenants old and new (Heb. 3: 7–4: 11; 11: 13–16, 40; cf. Lk. 1: 72 f.).

28–36. The order and number of the plagues of Exod. 7–12 here appear differently: the ninth is mentioned first and the fifth and sixth are omitted.

Psalm 106. TEARFUL TRUST

This psalm, like the last, reviews Israel's history, but it presents the reverse side of the coin. The sin of God's people is stressed, in tones of confession. But real as their sense of sin is, they are overwhelmingly conscious of God's steadfast **love**, His covenant love which will not let them go. This is the lifeline at which they clutch. It is the ground of their hope that He will save from national distress caused by their sin.

The grace of God (vv. 1–3)

The people are a pitiable remnant: the majority of the nation have been dispersed by the exile (v. 47). Yet the opening theme is not a prayer about their dire need, but praise expressing a conviction of God's faithfulness upon which they depend. 'How good is the God we adore, / Our faithful, unchangeable Friend!' (J. Hart) is their glad thanksgiving. He is 'high above all praise', for no expression of **praise** can adequately match His great deeds, especially those done on Israel's behalf. Yet the people are aware that God's grace is not something to be cadged or exploited. They understand that it imposes obligations and demands an appropriate lifestyle.

A solo prayer (vv. 4, 5)

The worship leader slips in his own plea, which in itself is a measure of the faith underlying the psalm. The nation's future prospects are bright: that is beyond question for the believing community. But he pleads that he personally may be privileged to share in God's future blessing of His **chosen** people. **Remember me** is his entreaty: the penitent thief was later to echo his words and their spirit (Lk. 23: 42).

Sin and salvation (vv. 6–46)

The community humbly confess their sin to

God, in time-honoured words used by King
Solomon (1 Kg. 8: 47). Their wickedness is of
a piece with that of their ancestors. History has
a habit of repeating itself, especially in spiritual
matters. The people look back to the glorious
beginning of their national history and find
even the Exodus to be sin-stained. Just as the
fall of Adam was in one sense the fall of every
man (Rom. 5: 12) and mirrors as an archetypal
event a pattern which all have separately followed, so the basic events of the Exodus, wilderness wanderings and entry into the promised land set the tone of Israel's subsequent
history. Other historical psalms attribute to the
Exodus, etc. a once and for all significance for
election and salvation, but this one exposes
their shadow side. Similarly Christians look
back to the Cross as a signpost both to God's
saving love and to their sin (Rom. 5: 6–8). So
the community who first used this psalm point
the finger of accusation at themselves even as
they accuse their **fathers**.

God's 'many acts of faithful love' (NEB, v. 7)
in protecting His people from the plagues and
delivering them from Egypt are mentioned to
show the exceeding sinfulness of their sin (cf.
Rom. 7: 13, AV), to enhance its shocking character (cf. Exod. 14: 11 f.). But, thank God, where
sin abounded, grace much more abounded.
He went on saving His people, obviously not
because of any merit of theirs but **for his
name's sake**, to win renown for Himself by
others' acknowledging His **mighty power** (cf.
Exod. 14: 18). From this angle the Exodus
constituted a key factor for the future: it revealed God as the Saviour of His sinning
people. Not that this truth was to be claimed
presumptuously, but it did provide hope for
the penitent. Too it was able to create a new
context for the exercise of faith and **praise** (cf.
v. 47; Exod. 15). The implicit prayer is that
God may be proved a mighty Saviour still.

But sin kept on knocking at Israel's door
and found ready admittance every time. In the
wilderness they 'challenged' God (JB, v. 14),
and received a two-edged settlement of their
complaints (Num. 11: 4, 31, 33 f.). **Dathan** and
Abiram mutinied against the God-appointed
leaders and had to be exterminated (Num. 16).
At Horeb (Sinai), of all places, even while
God was revealing Himself and His will, the
people's career of ingratitude reached on all-
time low, in the calf incident (Exod. 32: 1–6).
No wonder Israel stood on the brink of disaster
as a result. But **Moses**, the covenant mediator,
threw himself into **the breach**, like a brave
soldier defending a gap in the defences of a
besieged city. And so they were reprieved
(Exod. 32: 11–14).

But they had not learned their lesson. They
actually 'rejected' (GNB, v. 24) the **land** of
promise with all its desirable qualities. Cow-

ardly disbelief was their reaction to God's invitation. 'They stayed in their camp' (JB) and
'muttered treason' (NEB, cf. Dt. 1: 21–32). They
fully deserved God's curse barring them from
the land, a curse whose long-range effect Israel
had recently experienced (v. 47, cf. Dt. 4: 27).
Next, they defected from God's service and
got involved in pagan rites to 'lifeless gods'
(NEB, cf. Num. 25: 1–3). Again Israel was
spared only by an intercessor's entreaties (cf.
the Servant's task in Isa. 53: 12). A living
memorial to **Phinehas** existed in the people's
midst, the special priestly rank of his descendants (cf. Num. 25: 11–13): this was God's
accolade of appreciation (cf. Gen. 15: 6). **Meribah**, which means 'strife', was the scene of
further trouble, with tragic repercussions, for
the people's provocation led to **Moses'** own
fall from grace (cf. Num. 20: 2–13).

And when they did enter the land, what
then? It proved a disaster, for it exposed them
to fresh temptations to idolatry, child sacrifice
and a whole gamut of pagan practices. Israel
disobeyed God and broke her marriage vows,
becoming 'unfaithful to God' (GNB, v. 39; cf.
Jg. 1: 21; 2: 3, 17; 3: 6). Here again ancient
history held up a mirror to more recent happenings. The psalmist deliberately paints the
Judges period in terms of the fateful last pre-
exilic centuries (cf. 2 Kg. 17: 17; 21: 16; Jer. 3:
1–3). The period was a pendulum of punishment and reprieve (cf. Jg. 2: 11–19). Israel
suffered national humiliation—no stranger to
more recent generations, including the psalmist's own. Not that the other nations had an
inherent right of superiority—let alone their
gods—but God permitted it as reprisal for Israel's spiritual and moral crimes. Again the
national sin appears all the blacker in the context of God's saving help (v. 43; cf. v. 7). What
brought about changes for the better in Israel's
experience? Humanly speaking, it was the
people's penitent **cry** to God (cf. Jg. 3: 9; 6: 7)
that triggered off a mitigation of their bitter
lot.

A cry for help (v. 47)

The religious community dare to take those
past deliverances as precedents for their own
future. They bring their personal cry to the
God of the covenant (47, cf. v. 45). What they
now need so badly is for God to relent again and
to implement His covenant love vouchsafed so
long ago (cf. Neh. 9: 6–37). They plead for
renewed national identity, for restoration of
God's people to their land. They vow thanksgiving if their prayer is answered, promising
to make God's **praise** their pride (cf. NEB). The
psalm has come round full circle to the theme
of praise (cf. vv. 1 f.). The community wait,
fully aware of their sin and its wages. But,
conscious too of their Saviour, they have cast
themselves upon Him in hope.

Paul applied this psalm to a wider setting in Rom. 1, seeing its saga of human failure and divine abandonment and wrath as a pattern which came true in the experience of the Gentiles (compare v. 20 with Rom. 1: 23; v. 41 with Rom. 1: 24, 26, 28; vv. 23, 32, 40 with

Rom. 1: 18; v. 39 with Rom. 1: 26 f.).

26. Raising the hand was a gesture used to reinforce an oath (cf. Rev. 10: 5 f.). Verse 48 is a doxology marking the end of the fourth book of the Psalter (cf. 41: 13; 72: 18; 89: 52).

Book Five   Psalms 107–150

Psalm 107.   THANKSGIVING AND PRAISE

Israel is gathered at the temple for a service of thanksgiving. Individuals are to have the opportunity of testifying to God's help in particular difficulties, by oral statement and by sacrifice (v. 22). Then the whole community will cap their thanksgiving with a general outpouring of praise. These two parts of the service are reflected in this psalm. Initially four groups of people are called upon to give their testimonies to answered prayer (vv. 4–32); later the congregation sing a hymn celebrating God's providential control of nature and human affairs (vv. 33–43).

The people's duty (vv. 1–3)

The religious community owes its entire existence to God's goodness. The exile has come—and gone. In fulfilment of such prophecies as Isa. 43: 5 f. the Hebrews have been restored from their dispersion throughout the ancient world and are in 'enemy' hands (NEB, cf. JB, GNB) no longer. Their God has **redeemed** them, claiming them back as His own. Standing as they are on redemption ground, they have an obligation to return **thanks** to Him for constancy to His covenant promises. The standard call rings out in v. 1 (cf. 106: 1), and the congregation are invited to take the words of praise upon their own lips, reciting them after the priest (cf. 118: 2).

But the call to thanksgiving is not exhausted by citing the corporate grace of God. Ordinary life has its reasons for gratitude. Everyday occurrences of divine help are worth voicing in testimony before God and the congregation. They are not directly of national importance, but they mean much to the individuals who have experienced them.

God guided the lost (vv. 4–9)

Travellers were out in the wilds, hopelessly lost and far from any 'inhabited town' (JB). Their supplies of food and drink had run out; they were demoralized and helpless. No, not helpless, for they could take their problem to God in prayer. Like countless believers before and after them, they had their prayer answered. With His help they tried again and were **led**, they believed, **straight** to civilization and shelter. These travellers were in the temple that day, and they were bidden come forward and

confirm this miracle of providence and the evidence that God is able to meet the material needs of His people.

God liberated prisoners (vv. 10–16)

Some ex-prisoners were there that day. There was good cause for their being sent to prison. They had committed crimes; they had sinned against the God of law and order. Chained down there in the dark dungeon, they too had lost their morale and their hope of tasting freedom. Humanly speaking, there was **no one to help**. In ancient society prisoners were apt to be forgotten and left to rot, serving indefinite sentences (cf. Gen. 40: 23). Suddenly they found themselves free. They could explain it only as divine answer to their prayer. They too are urged to acknowledge openly their debt to the God who can break prison **bars**.

God healed the sick (vv. 12–22)

Another group was there, who till recently had been unable to attend any services in the temple because of illness. Their appetites gone, they were 'nearly at death's door' (JB). They admitted, reported the priest, that their maladies were the result of **their iniquities**, and that they fully deserved them. They 'were fools, they took to rebellious ways' (NEB, v. 17). In the OT sickness is often linked with wrongdoing (cf. Jn 9: 2). 'Although this view is not the whole truth (cf. Job), many a sick person needs to have his sins forgiven more than he needs anything else' (Rhodes). These too turned to prayer. Normally one would visit the temple and plead for a priestly oracle to be granted, promising recovery. Instead it was **sent** to their sickbeds (cf. Isa. 38: 4 f.), and they soon knew the joy of God-given vitality and health. Now it is their turn to identify themselves and add their 'Amen' to the priest's report, with **thank offerings** and solo **songs**.

God rescued seamen (vv. 23–32)

Members of the merchant navy were there that day, with a thrilling story to tell, especially to Hebrew landlubbers. They had run into a storm in the Mediterranean (**the mighty waters**) and were able to experience at first hand the awe-inspiring rage of nature's forces. But for them it was God's **wonderful deeds**, not simply as created long before but acting out His direct behest. Israel did not shrink from viewing Yahweh as God of the unwelcome storm as well as God of the welcome sunshine. At the mercy of giant **waves** 'they lost their nerve in the ordeal' (JB). Their expert 'seamanship' (JB, NEB) was no good to them now. But their eventual testimony is the same as that of the preceding groups, far different though their need was. God's power is a match for any crisis. 'Those in peril on the sea' found that God heard them when they **cried** to Him (cf. Mk 4: 35–41). The **storm** subsided, miraculously to their eyes, and they reached their port safe and sound. Now they can give public testimony at the service attended by **the people** and their civil leaders.

The God of ecology (vv. 33–38)
It is not for every one to undergo dramatic experiences such as these. But all can find common ground in praising God, *e.g.* for His providential control of nature. He is the Lord of the **desert** and the **rivers**. Let those who live in fertile territory beware lest they leave Him out of account. They may find their water supply drained away and their fields turned into saltflats (cf. Sodom and Gomorrah). Men knew of land which used to be dry and barren, but now it was blossoming like the rose (cf. Isa. 41: 18). This must be God's work, giving 'the hungry a home' (NEB) and enabling His people to recolonize the land. These colonists enjoyed covenant blessing (cf. Lev. 26: 4, 9; Dt. 28: 4) in respect of crops, cattle and population.

The God of the weak and needy (vv. 39–43)
The ups and downs of life—more prevalent in rugged ancient civilizations than in today's comparatively cocooned western one—were not outside God's control, avow His people in praising faith. To be nobly born was no guarantee of a lifetime of nobility. Contrariwise He can lift up the underprivileged to high blessing as well as demote **nobles**. He compensates for life's inequalities, to the delight of the believer and the chagrin of God's enemies.

These themes of praise are also lessons for the **wise** to take to heart, those whose attitude to life is founded upon respect for God (cf. Prov. 1: 7). God protects His own and is constant in His care.

Psalm 108.   OLD, YET EVER NEW
Psalms 51: 7–11 and 60: 5–12 are here combined. There is no need to repeat a full exposition. A new crisis prompted the re-use of Ps. 60, a prayer grounded in God's promise. Evidently the grim beginning of that psalm was felt to be less suitable to the new occasion. The thanksgiving of Ps. 57 was substituted for it: with its celebration of God's **steadfast love** and closing appeal to His **glory**, it directed attention to God and provided hope that He would help.

This combination illustrates how Scripture can come to life as it is applied to new situations in the experience of the believer and the church. Interestingly, in the setting of Ps. 60 verses 7–9 already harked back to an old promise of God. The Bible speaks again and again to the hearts of His people.

Psalm 109.   ON TRIAL FOR MURDER
This psalm is an individual's lament to God. It has some unusual features, which are best explained by assuming that it was uttered at a religious court where he stood on trial (cf. Exod. 22: 8 f.; Dt. 17: 8–13). Before the priestly judges, who represented God, he claims his personal innocence and lays counter-charges against the plaintiffs.

A plea for justice (vv. 1–5)
The psalmist pleads for acquittal. He is guilty of none of the charges. His previous life has been marked by **praise** to God and so, it is implied, by devoutness. He is not one of those people who live irreligious lives and resort to God only in times of crisis, as a pilot resorts to his parachute. So he pleads as one who can claim vindication, as an intimate devotee. The accusations against him lack foundation. They are a pack of lies. In fact they are an unwarranted, shocking **return** for his **friendship** and prayers of intercession for the plaintiff's welfare.

His accusers' malevolence (vv. 6–19)
It is possible to interpret this section as the psalmist's ranting against one of his accusers, whom he singles out from the rest. More likely he is quoting their own intent and charges against himself (cf. JB). In vv. 2–5 and 20 ff. his opponents are mentioned only in the plural, so that the singular pronouns here more naturally refer to the psalmist. Their accusation and **evil** are specified twice, in vv. 4 f. and 20, serving as a framework for his citation of them in these verses. Moreover the 'curse' of v. 29 would be a weak anticlimax after the dire imprecations of this section, if the psalmist was responsible for both.

Evidently his accusers had planned to bring trumped up charges against him and to attack him by means of legal prosecution (cf. 1 Kg. 21: 8–16; Mk 14: 55–64). They hoped that his very plea of 'not guilty' would incriminate him in court. So great was their hatred that they wished a string of evils upon him. They wanted him to die a premature death, after losing his 'job' (GNB, v. 8). For his children they wished a beggar's lot, for him bankruptcy and penury. They wanted to see him an ostracized figure, in a close-knit society where the loner was doomed. In a culture which prized the handing down of the family **name** through the generations, they wished for its extinction. In a religious community, where the solidarity of the family was held to affect the fortunes of future generations (cf. Exod. 20: 5), they wanted God to do His worst.

On what grounds did they utter these spiteful curses against the psalmist? He is not afraid to cite them. They accused him of failing to meet the neighbourly obligations which the covenant laid upon members of the chosen nation, in response to God's own covenant love (**kindness**, Heb. *ḥesed*; cf. Jer. 2: 2; Hos. 4: 1 f.). According to his adversaries he had heartlessly hounded his **poor** victims **to** their **death**. This charge is closely linked with the following references to cursing. Apparently he is accused of witchcraft, of laying curse-spells upon his victims (cf. Gal. 5: 20). They had tried to invoke counter-curses against him, in reprisal for his alleged regular 'habit' of cursing. They wanted it to recoil upon him and to hold him closely in its grip.

Renewed pleas (vv. 20–29)

These quoted sentiments are such an affront to the truth that their proponents themselves deserve to suffer them. He appeals to his divine Judge to live up to His revealed character (**name**) and covenant care (Heb. *ḥesed* again). He is acutely conscious of his need and helplessness apart from God. A **shadow** of his former self after all the worry, he feels at his opponents' mercy. They can flick him off like an insect on a coat, and dispose of him. He has been **fasting** in preparation for this religious trial (cf. 69: 10 f.) and so he feels physically weak. He has to bear their taunts, as they mock him, confident of their own success.

So he throws himself upon God's **love** in urging that there be no miscarriage of justice. The unfortunate death which is the basis of the legal charge (cf. v. 16) was no fault of his own, but an act of God. As he assures himself of the truth, his confidence grows. His accusers' threats mean nothing to him: it is the blessing of God that is his concern. As a loyal **servant** of God, his cause is God's cause, and so he hopes for a happy verdict. If justice is to be done, his opponents should lose their case and face the humiliation of failure.

A vow of praise (vv. 30, 31)

The psalmist promises not to forget this boon, after it is granted. He will testify to his appreciation of God's help before the community at worship in the temple (**the throng**). He has the assurance that he will win the day. Does he not know that God comes to the aid of the underdog, as his legal advocate? His Judge is also counsel for his defence (cf. Isa. 50: 8 f.; Rom. 8: 33 f.).

Verse 8 is applied to Judas in Ac. 1: 20 as warrant for posthumous forfeiture of his apostleship to a successor. Like all the psalms of innocent suffering this psalm finds its loudest echo in the experience of Jesus. Accordingly Judas is the fitting heir of this particular curse,

as history's supreme embodiment of infidelity (cf. vv. 16, 20).

Notes: **18. entered . . . like water:** there may be an allusion to the ordeal by 'the water of bitterness that brings the curse' (Num. 5: 16–28). **31.** Evidently in court both the counsel for the prosecution (v. 6; cf. Zech. 3: 1) and that for the defence stood on the **right** of the accused.

Psalm 110. PRIEST AND KING

Parts of this psalm are very precious to the Christian who has learned from the NT to apply them to the work of Christ. Behind this fullness of meaning lies a long pre-Christian history. Unfortunately its original significance is not at all clear in places: this is evident if the possible interpretations of the text in the NEB are contrasted with those of the NIV. For simplicity's sake the NIV will be followed. In origin this was a royal psalm uttered by a court poet in honour of the Davidic king, evidently on some notable occasion such as his coronation. Two divine oracles are quoted, and each in turn is amplified by the psalmist.

God's invitation (vv. 1–3)

The first sacred oracle which the poet takes up is an assurance of prestige and power. The king is invited to a place of honour next to God Himself, for he functions as God's representative and viceroy upon earth. In ritual terms the enthronement beside Yahweh may allude to the king's customary position by 'the pillar' in the temple (cf. 2 Kg. 11: 14; 23: 3). Victory is assured (cf. Jos. 10: 24). Foreign enemies often exploited the unsettled period of a new reign of an inexperienced king, but he is encouraged by a promise of divine aid (cf. 2: 8).

The psalmist proceeds to expound the implications of the oracle. The **scepter** with which the king has been invested is destined to journey far, as it were. From the royal and religious capital God will extend his dominion and make it radiate out among his hostile neighbours. The king is assured that he will have the loyal backing of the **troops**. They will enthusiastically identify themselves with their royal commander. The **young men** (NIVmg) of the country will assemble early on the **day of battle**, fresh and full of vigour, to fight for their liege lord.

God's promise (vv. 4–7)

The second oracle is a solemn pledge of the king's sacred role in the purposes of God. Once a Jebusite king had ruled in Jerusalem, who was 'priest to God Most High'. Abraham met and paid his respects to **Melchizedek**, an ancient member of this royal line (Gen. 14: 18–20). When David conquered Jerusalem, he added the privileges of Jebusite kingship to his Israelite crown rights. The king of Israel, reigning from Jerusalem, was thus nominally a **priest**, a sacred mediator between God and his people. In practice little use seems to have been made of this honour (cf. 2 Sam. 8: 17 and contrast 2 Chr. 26: 16–21; it may be for this reason that the psalmist does not go on to give a direct exposition of his second oracle). The permanent nature of the divine investiture is stressed. God would have no second thoughts. Unlike the Jebusite dynasty, the Davidic one was never to be superseded.

The king's endowment with the Jebusite royal title apparently reminds the psalmist of the original conquest of Jerusalem which made it possible. He sees in this victory an assurance of God's continuing help in days to come. Whereas in v. 1 the **right hand** refers to divine honour, here it symbolizes divine protection. As the narrator of David's military campaigns had made clear, the secret of his success was that God was with him (2 Sam. 5: 10; 8: 6, 14). The power was His. So it would ever be. The great Lord of hosts would work with the king's army and guarantee their triumph (cf. 2: 5, 8 f., 12).

Verse 7 evidently refers to the king, although direct address is expected. It may allude to the king's refreshing himself while on the march. It is more likely that it refers to a royal ceremony at the spring of Gihon near the temple, during which the king ritually drank from the sacred fountain and symbolically received the vital resources necessary for his reign (cf. 1 Kg. 1: 45). Thus strengthened, thereafter he would enjoy an abundance of life. While his foes were doomed to lie prostrate (v. 1), his destiny was a life of triumph.

This psalm had its own glorious destiny—to speak of greater things than terrestrial gains in the eastern Mediterranean, important as these were in the divine plan of history. With the eclipse of the Davidic dynasty this composition was re-interpreted of a king yet to come, God's Messiah. By the first century A.D. the messianic interpretation was standard. Jesus echoed this understanding of the psalm when he challenged His contemporaries and showed them that on their own premises the Messiah had a higher standing than they were prepared to admit (Mk 12: 35–37; cf. too Mt. 26: 64). Following the lead of their Lord, the apostles freely applied v. 1 to Him and to His exaltation in heaven. It holds the record of being the OT text most frequently cited or alluded to in the NT (cf. Ac. 2: 34 f.; 1 C. 15: 25; Eph. 1: 20; Col. 3: 1; 1 Pet. 3: 22). By this means they established the truth that 'The highest place that heaven affords / Is His, is His by right' (T. Kelly). The writer to the Hebrews made much of this psalm; he developed the application of v. 4 to Christ's exercise of a heavenly, non-Aaronic priesthood after the sacrifice of Calvary (Heb. 1: 3, 13; 5: 6–10; 6: 20–10: 21).

Psalm 111. TRUTH APPROPRIATED

This and the next psalm form a complementary pair. They are both acrostic poems, consisting of eleven lines of which each half-line begins with a successive letter of the Hebrew alphabet. The initial Hallelujah stands outside this acrostic scheme.

The psalmist has been attending one of the great festivals at the temple. He testifies what it has all meant to him, in a solo recited to **the assembly**. In Israel's worship there were sometimes those who honoured God with their lips, while their hearts were far from Him (Isa. 29: 13). This worshipper at least has been worshipping in spirit and truth; he has found **delight** in the sacred themes and responded in devotion with **all** his **heart**.

He is grateful that God has instituted the feasts whereby 'he allows us to commemorate his marvels' (JB, v. 4). His **wonders** have just been experienced afresh in worship. They are the sacred history which was Israel's foundation stone—the Exodus (cf. Exod. 3: 30), the trek through the wilderness and the gifts of the Law and the promised land. This cluster of events was ever celebrated as the touchstone of God's power and purposes for His chosen people. They revealed Him to be their King, endued with the royal attributes of glory and majesty. They showed His tender care and His **righteousness**, here in the sense of covenant faithfulness. His provision of quails and manna in the wilderness was a pledge of His continual keeping of the **covenant** promises ever since. His laws given at Sinai were prized as Israel's national and religious constitution and as the embodiment of God's own moral character for His people to share (v. 8; cf. v. 7).

What can the psalmist say to these things? In them is revealed God's being as **holy** in His transcendence, and so man can react only with reverence and awesome wonder. True reverence is in fact the starting point for an ability to cope with life's meaning and problems (**wisdom**, cf. Prov. 1: 7; 9: 10). Such secrets are opened not to the mystic nor to the philosopher but to the willing practitioner of God's commands (cf. Jn 13: 17). His people are to respond to His revelation and **redemption** with obedience and unending **praise**. The psalmist envisages his own psalm as a new link in an ever-growing chain.

5. provides is better rendered more literally 'provided' (cf. AV). **8b.** More probably 'made with truth and uprightness': cf. NEB 'their fabric goodness and truth'. **9f. awesome** is 'to be feared': it is echoed in **fear**.

Psalm 112. TRUTH APPLIED

This acrostic psalm takes up where the previous one left off. In all probability the same poet was responsible for both. It is an exposition of Ps. 111: 10 and also an application of God's own attributes to the believer. In terms of Eph. 2: 4–10, if Ps. 111 celebrates God's grace, this one commends the good works which are its intended corollary.

God can rightly be praised only by him whose total life is marked by reverence and willing obedience. Such a man enters into the joy of the OT covenant promises of material prosperity. His family would share his blessing (cf. Exod. 20: 6). Not only does God's **righteousness** endure for ever (111: 3), but so does his own, here in the developed sense of God's intended ideal of a blessed life, right in every respect. Moreover he becomes a **light** shining in the darkness, encouraging and helping others in distress. He reflects like a mirror God's own attribute of kindly generosity (111: 4) and is a living channel of God's goodness. Rich as he is, he is no grab-all miser, but freely shares with the have-nots what God has given him. Blessed, he becomes a blessing to others. He does not override the interests of his fellows but 'runs his business honestly' (GNB).

Come what may, he is **steadfast** with a God-given security and people would never forget his good example. To be sure, he is not immune from life's shocks, but his faith holds him fast. 'Steadfast in heart, he overcomes his fears' (JB). In the light of v. 1 the psalmist's message is: 'Fear Him, ye saints, and you will then / Have nothing else to fear' (N. Tate and N. Brady). He would know success in his life and command the respect of others. The picture of prosperity as the reward of virtue is enhanced by the final reference to the frustrated envy of the **wicked man** who sees none of his ambitions come true.

The NT with its more other-worldly orientation sets less emphasis on earthly reward (but see Mt. 6: 33; 2 C. 9: 11; Phil. 4: 18 f.). The broad principles of the psalm still stand, however. In particular God's gift of material prosperity creates an obligation for the Christian too (cf. 1 Tim. 6: 17–19). Paul quotes v. 9 in 2 C. 9: 9 as an illustration of a 'cheerful giver'.

Verse 4 is ambiguous; in the context more probably the believer is described (cf. JB, NEB, GNB). In v. 4 language elsewhere used of God (cf. 18: 28; 27: 1) is transferred (cf. Mt. 5: 14; Jn 8: 12; Phil. 2: 15).

Psalm 113. OUR GOD'S GLORY AND GRACE

This is the first of the 'Hallel' psalms (Ps. 113–118) which were sung regularly at all the great Israelite festivals. By the first century A.D. they were chanted around the table at the family celebration of the Passover, the first two psalms at the beginning and 115–118 at the end. Thus they were a feature of the Last Supper in the upper room.

Invitations to Praise (vv. 1–3)
The repeated cry rings out to the worshipping community to lift up their hearts in **praise**. Three times they are urged to bless God's **name**, the whole revelation of His character and will. How can He be praised enough? To do it adequately would take the rest of time (cf. Eph. 3: 18) and the concerted tongues of all creatures on earth (cf. 48: 10; Mal. 1: 11). No lesser response in space or time is worthy of Him. The group who met were not thereby excused from praise, but assured all the more of their own obligation to play their part there and then.

Incentives to praise (vv. 4–9)
Israel's God, Yahweh, is greater than all else which stands for power. Imperial **nations**, imposing and often menacing to little Israel, were nothing compared with the great Lord of history. The world of nature, majestic and awe-inspiring to the observer (cf. 8: 3), must be less than the One who created it all. Yet He is no remote Being. Amazingly His **glory** serves to enhance His matchless grace. He stands not only supreme but unique, as the God who 'sets his throne so high but deigns to look down so low' (NEB). Great as He is, He **stoops** in grace to our world, to where we are. By way of illustration the psalmist harks back to Hannah and to her song of praise (1 Sam. 1–2). From her experience he observes that God can miraculously give new life. The happy **mother** whose yearning has at last been satisfied and deprivation removed has cause to praise, for the God of the universe is also the God of the family. From Hannah's song the psalmist takes up the theme of rescue (1 Sam. 2: 8). God cares for the **poor** wretch who scavenges in the rubbish dump outside the village, the suffering outcast for whom society has no room (cf. Job 2: 8). When later they find themselves rehabilitated and restored to honour, they too have reason to praise—'ransomed, healed, restored, forgiven'. The God of the universe is also the God of the **needy** individual. Such a God as this deserves our proud **praise**.

Psalm 114. THE EXODUS SET TO MUSIC

This, the second of the Hallel psalms, looks back to the basics of Israelite faith, the source of Israel's understanding of herself and her relation to God. It handles its sacred theme unusually, with a whimsical sense of humour.
The birth of the nation (vv. 1, 2)
Israel thought of herself as essentially a liberated, redeemed people. They recalled with gratitude the time when the burden of foreign oppression rolled away and they became free —not free in any anarchical sense, but free to

enter God's service. By the Exodus they became a holy people who worshipped Yahweh as their God and a vassal people who owned Him as their King (cf. Exod. 19: 6; Rev. 1: 6).

The miracles of the Exodus (vv. 3, 4)

The crossing of the Red Sea and the Jordan and the earthquake of Mount Sinai (Exod. 14: 21 f.; 19: 18; Jos. 3: 14–17) are the events he celebrated in song. Something happened then. It was so tremendous that its witnesses retreated in shocked alarm. The Red Sea 'ran away' (NEB), the **Jordan** 'stopped flowing' (JB) and seemed to shrink **back**, while the **mountains** jumped into the air like any startled sheep!

Questions asked (vv. 5, 6)

What could it have been? What was the matter? Let's ask them, suggests the psalmist. By faith the years roll away and the worshippers feel themselves present at the very scene as if it had all just happened.

The answer supplied (vv. 7, 8)

This is the focal point of the psalm, for which the foregoing has prepared. God, hitherto only indirectly referred to (**God's**, v. 2), is now dramatically disclosed as the divine Hero of the Exodus, whose presence with His people caused such consternation. The 'Master' (JB) was there in power. Ever since, Israel had never been alone but stood in His protecting shadow. The whole world is invited to share nature's ancient concern at so great a God who revealed Himself in their midst in history and continually reveals Himself in their worship at the temple. He is a wonder-working God who can turn barrenness into blessing for His people (cf. Exod. 17: 6; Num. 20: 11).

2. **Judah** and **Israel** are probably synonymous here.

Psalm 115.   THEIR HELP AND SHIELD

Psalms 115–118 are the second part of the Hallel group (see the comment on Ps. 113). They were the 'hymn' sung at the end of the transformed Passover meal in the upper room (Mk 14: 26). God's people are in a situation of distress and weakness. They bring their petitions and praise to Him as One who is able to help them. Depressed by their external circumstances, they recover their spiritual morale in the temple.

Appeals to God's honour (vv. 1, 2)

Allusion is made to their need by citing the mocking taunt of surrounding pagan states. God's reputation is at stake, and this is the community's noble concern rather than any self-seeking. They take their stand upon the promises of God and His covenant relationship with them.

Praise of God's power (vv. 3–8)

The sarcastic question of v. 2 is taken seriously. **Our God** is in the supreme place of supernatural power (cf. Eph. 1: 20–23). And what of their gods? If they are anything like their representations, they are a sorry bunch—dumb, blind, deaf and in fact devoid of any senses. Their devotees inevitably 'grow to be like them' (NEB; cf. 2 Kg. 17: 15; Jer. 2: 5), impotent and divorced from reality. What an implicit contrast to the true God and to the potential of those who **trust in** Him!

Encouragement to faith (vv. 9–11)

Evidently a priest takes up the theme of **trust** and applies it to the congregation in their need. He calls upon laity and priests alike, upon the whole revering community (cf. v. 13; 22: 23). Their God is able and willing to **help** and defend them.

Assurance of God's blessing (vv. 12–15)

The priest continues. He has received an assurance that God will honour His promises (cf. v. 1). The covenant community who have heeded his call to trust can confidently expect the gift of abundant life, which **bless** in the OT generally implies. He puts upon them a priestly blessing (cf. Num. 6: 23–27) which echoes a traditional promise of increase in population (cf. Gen. 22: 17; Dt. 1: 11). The nation was apparently numerically small at this time (cf. perhaps Ezr. 9: 8, 15), and the renewal of the ancient promise meets them at the point of their contemporary need.

Avowal of praise (vv. 16–18)

Just as the priest took up the congregation's words (vv. 8 f.), so now they smoothly take up his. Yahweh claims for Himself the divine sphere of **the heavens**, and so He possesses transcendent power (cf. v. 3). And He it is who has entrusted **the earth** to mankind as His stewards (cf. Gen. 1: 28). The uncompromising implication is that He is the sole God and has a unique claim to men's gratitude. True, that privilege is temporary (cf. the comments on Ps. 88), but this is all the more reason why the present generation of God's people should use every opportunity for praise. To **extol the LORD** is the natural response to His blessing (cf. Eph. 1: 3).

Psalm 116.   THINKING AND THANKING

This beautiful psalm of thanksgiving owes its charm to the psalmist's experience of God's grace and its spiritual impact upon him. The precise nature of his particular crisis is not clear: there are hints of sickness (v. 3) and persecution (v. 11). Psalms of this type, far from wallowing in personal details, focus attention on what God has done. The psalmist brings his thank-offering to God and just before the sacrifice utters this prayer and testimony in front of the congregation.

Rescue (vv. 1–4)

Answered prayer prompts the psalmist's declaration of **love**, in response to the divine initiative (cf. 1 Jn 4: 19). He nearly died, **death** lurked so close. Like an animal caught in a trap, he felt doomed–till his desperate cry was answered.

Reflections (vv. 5–11)

The incident serves to illustrate God's attribute of grace. Here is a lesson for all believers to learn (**our God**). When any are at their wits' end and cannot cope with the problem (**simple-hearted**), God's way is to come to their aid—this the psalmist has proved. God has taken away his source of anxiety (cf. 42: 5) and now he may enjoy a new peace of mind and 'a heart at leisure from itself'. He challenges himself to enter into this blessing and to relax, for the human mind does not quickly lose its habit of worrying and needs urging to keep pace with reality. God's bounty is such that instead of **death** life is his experience; instead of **eyes** full of **tears**, eyes fixed upon God as his Guide and Teacher; instead of **stumbling feet** a sure **walk** which is marked by obedience to God (cf. Gen. 17: 1; 48: 5). Finally, he implicitly encourages others to hold on to their faith, especially in times of crisis. Faith in humanity may prove bitterly disappointing, as it did for him, but faith in God never goes unrewarded.

Reaction (vv. 12–19)

The psalmist is bewildered as to what would be an adequate response to God's deliverance. But the unpayable nature of the debt does not absolve him from making what contribution he can. Shortly he is to offer a libation of wine as part of the thank-offering ritual (Num. 28: 7). The **cup** will be a testimony to God's **salvation.** He will engage in worship (**call on the name**). He will publicly fulfil the private promises he made in his time of trouble, to bring a thank-offering. He has learned by experience that the premature death of God's people 'costs Yahweh dear' (JB; cf. 72: 14) and that He is quick to avert such a tragedy. Liberated, the psalmist gratefully re-dedicates himself to His service. As Charles Wesley paraphrased, 'the mercy that hath loosed my bonds/Hath bound me fast to Thee'.

10. The quotation in 2 C. 4: 13 follows the LXX. **15.** For the Christian God sometimes has a greater blessing (cf. Phil. 1: 21–23).

Psalm 117.   A THOUSAND TONGUES

This is the shortest psalm in the Psalter. It is a hymn of praise sung by the Israelite community. It bases its theme on the favourite text of post-exilic Israel, Exod. 34: 6, the description of God as 'abounding in steadfast love and faithfulness'. Yahweh had once and for all revealed Himself to His people as a God who made promises of grace and kept them. How can they praise Him enough? Rhetorically they

enlist the aid of **all** other **nations**, wishing for 'a thousand tongues', as it were, to sing their 'great Redeemer's praise' (Charles Wesley). Unwittingly they thus let loose in the world an invitation which later enabled the Gentiles to share in covenant grace (cf. Rom. 15: 8–12). Israel's would-be hired choristers eventually became her partners in faith.

2. great: literally 'strong' (NEB), as in 103: 11. The Christian is reminded of the final proof of divine love as 'strong as death' (Ca. 8: 6) and even stronger (Rom. 8: 37; 1 C. 15:55–57).

Psalm 118.   ON THE VICTORY SIDE

This Psalm evidently originated in victory celebrations of Israel's king and people (cf. 2 Chr. 20: 27 f.). Later it was probably used in periodic commemorations of God's past goodness to the Davidic dynasty and to Israel. It is the last of the Hallel psalms (see the comments on Ps. 113; 115), sung in the home at Passover time. According to Jewish tradition it was used at the Feast of Tabernacles, to which v. 27 points. It was a processional psalm begun outside the gates of the temple and continued inside (vv. 19 f., 26).

A call to praise (vv. 1–4)

A priest opens the psalm by inviting a response to God's abiding goodness. He challenges first the laity to take up his cry, then his fellow priests, and finally solicits a resounding shout from one and all (see on 115: 9–11).

The king's testimony (vv. 5–18)

A new voice speaks. The king bears witness to God's saving help in time of dire need and reflects upon lessons learned from the experience. His natural fears were overcome and proved groundless. Next time panic will not so easily grip him. This past proof of God's powerful support provides comfort for the future. 'The psalmist here speaks like a champion, throwing down the gauntlet to all comers, defying the universe in arms' (C. H. Spurgeon). Recourse to human allies, which once seemed so obvious, is a poor second to a practical faith in God (contrast 2 Kg. 16: 5–7; Isa. 7: 1–13).

He sets in dramatic contrast the crisis and its sequel. Swarms of foreign **nations surrounded** him and seemed likely to overwhelm him. But prayer and trust in God's power were the weapons that brought him victory (cf. 1 Sam. 17: 45). Like King Asa he did not go forth alone against the foe: strong in God's **strength**, he rested on Him and went in His **name** (2 Chr. 14: 11). In v. 14 Moses' famous victory song comes alive again and becomes his own (cf. Exod. 15: 2). The song of believers is a golden chain down the ages: 'We raise it high, we send it on—/ The song that never endeth' (T. H. Gill).

He quotes the army's songs of triumph

which gave testimony to God's enabling, and he thereby acknowledges in turn that 'every victory won' is 'His alone' (H. Auber). Having looked death in the face (cf. v. 13), his renewed lease of life means opportunity for praise of his Saviour. He can even incorporate the crisis into his praise as evidence of God's chastening hand to bring him back to His will (cf. 89: 30–33; 2 Sam. 7: 14 f.).

Knocking at the gates (vv. 19, 20)

The king requests admission to the temple through the **gates** which only those right with God in heart and life may enter. His call to the priestly gate-keepers receives an answer affirming the king's condition (cf. Ps. 15; 24) and implicitly inviting him in.

The prayer and praise of king and congregation (vv. 21–29)

Inside the temple the victorious king gives all the credit to his God, echoing v. 14. Evidently quoting a proverb, he contrasts his unlikely prospects before and during the battle with its glorious climax. The people take up the theme, tracing the king's triumph to God's enabling and deeming it a miracle. They urge each other to celebrate this happy **day** of victory 'on which the LORD has acted' (NEB). They pray that this **success** may be no isolated incident but the pattern of days to come.

In response the priests pronounce a blessing upon the king and his entourage, doubtless in terms of Num. 6: 24–26. Thereupon the people pledge their faith in Yahweh as **God** indeed and express their joy that He has 'made his face to shine' upon them and so given them **light.** Then the priests call the people to process through the temple and up to **the altar,** their waving branches touching and seemingly joining as they walked (cf. Lev. 23: 40). Like the people, the king pledges his own trust in God. The initial priestly voice rings out again at the end. By granting victory God has revealed His goodness—let **thanks** return to Him.

Like the other royal psalms, this one was inherited by the Messiah and came remarkably true in His experience. The allusion to vv. 25 f. at the triumphal entry is significant (Mk 11: 9 f.; cf. Lk. 13: 35. 'Hosanna' is the equivalent of **save us,** now used as a joyful cry of acclamation). Jesus applied vv. 22 f. to a greater conflict and conquest, His coming passion and resurrection (Mk 12: 10 f.), and Peter proudly echoed his Lord's usage in Ac. 4: 11. These verses became an important part of the NT messianic stone theme (cf. Eph. 2: 20 f.; 1 Pet. 2: 4–8).

22. the capstone was a well-squared, massive stone, which ensured the stability of the two adjoining walls.

Psalm 119. THY WORD IS TRUTH

This psalm, by far the longest in the Psalter, is an elaborate acrostic. It consists of twenty-two stanzas, corresponding to the letters in the Hebrew alphabet. Each stanza has eight two-part lines beginning with the same letter. This feat of artistry is a literary monument raised in honour of God's revelation to Israel. It glories in the **law** as God's communication of truth (v. 160) with regard to doctrine and ethics. The **law** refers not merely to legislation nor probably to the Pentateuch alone, but comprehensively embraces all that God has made known of His character and purpose, and what He would have man to be and do (cf. Rom. 3: 19). The Torah is viewed here not as a burden (contrast Ac. 15: 10) but as a lifeline to God and a demonstration of His grace and guidance.

In celebrating God's revelation the poet rings the changes by employing eight synonymous terms, in each of which a particular shade of meaning may be detected. The **law** (*tōrāh*) is divinely revealed teaching. **Statutes** (*'ēdōt*) are God's covenant terms for His people to observe. **Precepts** (*piqqūdīm*) are detailed rules for life. **Commands** (*miṣwōt*) express the insistent will of a personal God who is Israel's Lord. **Decrees** (*ḥuqqīm*) are rulings written down and prescribed for permanent observance. **Laws** (*mišpāṭīm*) are verdicts of the divine Judge covering a full range of circumstances. **Word** or **words** stands for two terms. The first (Heb. *dābār*) refers to the communication of God's will to His people, while the second (Heb. *'imrāh*) often has the connotation of **promise** and is sometimes so rendered. To this list may be added **ways,** a pattern of life based on God's will (cf. Dt. 5: 33).

From one point of view the psalm is a hymn in praise of God's revelation. From another it is a prayer expressing man's continual need of the Good Shepherd's care (cf. vv. 19, 176). The **law** is no do-it-yourself manual which God has handed over to man to use as best he can. It is the written part of a lifelong teach-in. With it comes the assurance of His living presence with the believer, prompting, warning, promising, enabling (cf. vv. 150 f.). The author is no dilettante composing poetry in a secluded ivory tower. He is caught up in the hurly-burly of life. Much of the psalm reflects a situation of tension and distress. The psalmist turns to the God of the Word, appealing to His written promises and craving His aid.

Magnificent as it is, the psalm creates problems for the expositor. Sometimes verses go in pairs, at times there is a longer run of related material. Very often the verses express separate sentiments, hinged to their neighbours solely by the initial letter of the line and by mention of God's law or the like. Some commentators optimistically attempt to label each stanza with a distinctive theme. They tend to achieve this end at the expense of majoring in a few verses and ignoring the contribution of the rest. It is better to view the psalm as a kaleidoscope of varied, often recurring topics and to examine it thematically.

A thread which runs right through the poem's rich tapestry is an appreciation of the value of God's revelation. It is **sweeter than honey** (103) and better than money (14, 72, 127). It is the author's **delight** (47, 70, 111, 174) and desire (20, 40, 131). It evokes his **praise** (7, 54, 62, 164, 171 f.) and his **love** (48, 97, 113, 140, 162 f., 167; cf. too 46, 129, 152). No wonder that he mulls over it and takes it to heart (11, 13, 15, 55, 148). But by himself he cannot fathom its depth of meaning and scope, and so he prays for insight and the ability to apply its challenge to his daily life (12, 18, 27, 32–34, 66, 73, 108, 124 f., 135, 144, 169). Because he sets such store by the Word, he turns to the One who gave it, appealing in his time of trouble to His character and promises expressed there (25, 28, 41, 49 f., 58, 107, 116, 149, 154, 156). Yet he is mature enough to realize that there is spiritual value in suffering and that it can be God's school (67, 71, 75).

He recognizes the obligation to stay loyal to God through thick and thin, and he reports to Him that despite intense persecution and harassment he has not let his Lord down (51, 60 f., 69, 83, 87, 95, 109 f., 141, 143, 157, 161). His implicit hope is that God will stand by him in his hour of need. In fact his obedience is often the basis of an explicit appeal to Him (22, 30 f., 38 f., 42, 58–60, 84–86, 94, 121 f., 132, 153, 159, 173, 176). He knows that it is irrational to live heedless of God's will and then to expect Him to help him. Other people's disobedient lives grieve him as tragic (53, 136, 139, 158) and fatal (21, 118 f.), for only obedience can give a sense of relief (45) and ensure security (165) and the enjoyment of salvation(155).

He is aware too that deliverance will itself create further obligation and so he promises obedience if his present needs are met (8, 17, 88, 115, 134, 145 f.)—as past needs have been (26, 65). He promises praise as well (170 f., 175). He pledges himself to live henceforth a life honouring to God and His Word (15 f., 23, 44, 57, 78, 106, 112). Ample incentives to a godly life lie in the greatness of God (64, 73, 89–91, 168) and in His moral goodness (68, 137 f.). Yet he knows all too well that his own resolve will come to nothing unless his Lord undergirds it with His strength (5 f., 10, 29, 35–37, 80, 117, 133).

To this end God's **word is a lamp to** his **feet** (105, 128, 130). He rejoices that it has sustained him in the past (92) and been a source of hope (49) and comfort (50, 52), of practical wisdom (24, 98–100, 104) and a satisfying life (93). And it is the basis of his hope for the future (43, 76, 81 f., 114, 123, 147, 166, 170).

Although this poet has much to say of his personal faith, experience and hope in relation to God, he is no individualist. He appreciates the fellowship of kindred spirits (63, 74, 79). He commends a life of trust and obedience, yearning that others may tread this path (1–4, 9).

19. stranger: one devoid of rights; cf. v. 54; 39: 12; Lev. 25: 23; 1 Pet. 2: 11.

Psalm 120. A BURDEN LIFTED

Here begin a group of fifteen psalms (Ps. 120–134) which each bear the title **A Song of Ascents.** The meaning of **ascents** is uncertain, but the most plausible view is that it refers to pilgrimage up to the temple in Jerusalem, so that these are pilgrim songs. Before being put together for this purpose, they appear to have had diverse origins. This one was primarily an individual's thanksgiving for answered prayer. Many Israelites at the feasts would not only engage in communal worship but take the opportunity to bring their personal problems before the Lord in prayer and await his answer (cf. 1 Sam. 1:3–18).

Answered prayer (vv. 1, 2)
'I called to the LORD . . . and he answered me' (NEB, cf. AV, RV) is the psalmist's glad testimony. It seems to allude to a priestly oracle recently given to him in assurance that God would solve his problem. He has been the victim of **lying** and misrepresentation. Like many, he has proved by bitter experience the untruth of the adage, 'Sticks and stones may break my bones, but words can never hurt me'. But now, after unburdening himself to God and receiving the divine assurance, he feels vindicated in his soul and cowed no longer.

Divine justice (vv. 3, 4)
Verse 3 echoes the oath formula 'May God do so to me and more also . . .' (cf. 1 Sam. 3: 17; 2 Kg. 6: 31). Here the NEB renders the verse: 'What has he in store for you . . . ? What more has he for you?' Evidently the psalmist's persecutors invoked curses upon themselves to impress others with the 'truth' of their own wrong claims against him. The psalmist reminds them of the strong language of their perjury and warns that they can expect a self-invoked doom. Since they have shot their vindictive words at him, sharp as any arrow (cf. 64: 3; Jer. 9: 8), their prospect is divine **arrows** of judgment and firebrands of destruction as hot as any made from **broom** charcoal.

A sheep in the midst of wolves (vv. 5–7)
Life has been very difficult, complains the psalmist. People around him have treated him like an enemy and not as one of themselves. It has been like living among a lot of heathen foreigners: they have not behaved at all like decent Israelites. It takes two to keep the **peace,**

and for his part he has done all he could (cf. Rom. 12: 18). But they have ignored his peaceful overtures. Burdened with this situation, of being a dove among hawks, he has come and cast his anxiety upon God (1 Pet. 5: 7) and received strong comfort.

4. broom wood provided charcoal which gave out a fierce, long-lasting heat. Verse 5 is metaphorical and explained in v. 6 (cf. JB, GNB). The people of **Meshech** lived between the Black Sea and the Caspian, while **Kedar** was a Bedouin tribe in the Syro-Arabian desert. The inhabitants of these widely separated areas are selected as examples of foreigners with whom an Israelite would not feel at home but in danger.

Psalm 121.   ABLE TO KEEP
This psalm can be regarded as the OT equivalent of Phil. 4: 7. Its keynote is struck by the word **watch over**, which occurs five times. It evidently became a pilgrim song; in origin, as the dialogue form seems to indicate, it was probably an interchange between an Israelite believer and a priest on duty at the temple, whose blessing he sought (cf. Ps. 91).
The source of help (vv. 1, 2)
The speaker is or expects soon to be in a situation of stress. His question exposes his anxiety and sense of inadequacy. To the pilgrim **the hills** would be the mountainous area of Jerusalem, in whose temple he would soon be worshipping God and nurturing his faith. To the psalmist the mountains may have been the scene of a dangerous journey which he dreaded (cf. vv. 6, 8) and for which he sought assurance that he would not walk alone.

Even as he questions, his faith provides its own answer. He can reassure himself with a declaration of trust. The omnipotent God of the created universe is the God of the individual. His faith is grounded in the truth, simple yet so profound, that 'God who made the earth, The air, the sky, the sea/ . . . Careth for me' (Sarah B. Rhodes). Yet he still seeks confirmation in the spirit of the cry 'Lord, I believe. Help thou my unbelief'.
The safety of the believer (vv. 3–8)
The priest soothes with a benediction this man in whose heart faith and fear are tussling: 'May He bless you with security' (cf. JB, GNB and Num. 6: 24). God is not made in the image of man, whose attention lapses after a while. This Sentry never dozes on duty! As **Israel's** Guardian He has proved His ever-watchful care. And the God of the people is no less the God of the individual. His protection is promised. He is like **shade**, a metaphor whose force only those who have lived in hot climates can appreciate. He ever stands by as a bodyguard. The physical peril of sunstroke (cf. 2 Kg. 4: 18 f.) and the mental peril of moonstroke are warded off by

this priestly announcement. If this particular believer was ready to voice further fears, they are quelled by a comprehensive assurance. The keyword **watch over** is continually repeated for its therapeutic value. His journey is under God's blessing. Travelling mercies are promised, including a safe return. And the great journey of life henceforth is likewise to be shared with the Shepherd who cares and keeps (cf. Ps. 23; Jn 10: 9). Who need fear with such assurances as these?

6. The **moon** has often in men's history been feared for its effect upon the mind and nervous system: cf. the word 'lunacy'. In Mt. 4: 24; 17: 15 'epileptic' is literally 'moonstruck'.

Psalm 122.   THE HOLY CITY
This is a further pilgrim song, composed for this very purpose, unlike the earlier ones in the series. An Israelite has come up to the capital with a local group to attend one of the festivals in the temple. On his arrival he is overwhelmed by the scene and occasion. He expresses his thoughts to his fellow-pilgrims, as his full heart glances back, around and forward.
Pilgrimage to Jerusalem (vv. 1, 2)
He thinks back to the joys of anticipating and preparing for this event. To the duty of worship (v. 4) his spirit had responded with a glad Amen. He had looked forward so much to this pilgrimage—'and now we are here, standing inside the gates . . . !' (GNB, cf. RV) They have arrived at last, and the singer expresses for them all the excitement they each feel.
Appreciation of Jerusalem (vv. 3–5)
Jerusalem was a magic word which conjured up a world of meaning for the Israelite. By its compactness as a built-up, walled **city** it stood as a symbol of the people's religious and political security. It had taken over from Shiloh and other earlier cultic centres the role of sanctuary of the federation of tribes (cf. Dt. 12: 5–7). There the different tribal groups converged. As they worshipped together, they realized their overall oneness as the people of **the LORD**. Upon them all as members of the covenant people rested the obligation of praising His **name** (a compound term for God's self-revelation and His presencing Himself among His people). Jerusalem was also revered as the political capital of the theocracy and the home of justice. Its 'tribunals' (JB) were renowned as a court of appeal where every king worth his salt guaranteed that justice would be done (cf. 2 Sam. 8: 15; 15: 2; Jer. 21: 12). Jerusalem stood for God's claims upon Israel in the areas of worship and social order.
Prayers for Jerusalem (vv. 6–9)
The psalmist does not forget his manners. It was the custom to utter greetings of **peace** on entering a home or community (cf. 1 Sam. 25:

6; Mt. 10: 12 f.). In this case it is especially appropriate, for it echoes the popular linking of the name of the city with the Hebrew *šālōm* (cf. Heb. 7: 2 and contrast Lk. 19: 41 f.). The pilgrim's prayer, which he urges his companions to echo, is that Jerusalem may by God's grace live up to its name. Ancient communities lived under the threat or fear of invasion, and for Jerusalem to fall would spell the collapse of the nation. It was the pulsing heart of the country and the fount of its vitality.

It was the embodiment of God's purposes for the nation. So the psalmist strongly binds around it in his prayers a threefold cord of **peace.** This touchstone of blessing affected the lives of all of his Israelite **brothers.** It deserved stability and prosperity, if it was to be a worthy setting for God's jewel, the temple.

So the singer returns to his opening theme. It is his proud privilege to be one of the guests at God's earthly home.

Isaac Watts' hymn, 'How pleased and blest was I', admirably re-interprets this psalm for Christian worshippers. For such, Jerusalem is a cipher for 'the unity of God's people in worship and communion, the throne-centre of God's Anointed, the fountain of life flowing from God's presence' (Eaton). God's present word is expressed in Heb. 12: 22–24.

3. closely compacted together: cf. the usage of the same verb in Exod. 26: 11 ('fasten . . . together').

Psalm 123. FINDING GRACE TO HELP

The community is suffering beneath the oppressor's heel. They bring their urgent prayers to God in a lament. This is the original setting of what later became a pilgrim song of trust.

The throne of grace (vv. 1, 2)
The people's representative begins with a personal expression of his dependence upon and trust in God, thus betraying his suitability for the task of prayer leader. The God to whom he looks is the King of heaven, more than able to meet any earthly need. His humility and respect are shared by the oppressed community. A fine word picture is used of **slaves** whose trained **eyes** follow every move of **their master**, waiting for the slightest gesture of his wishes. So they fix their spiritual gaze upon God. They await their Master's merciful intervention, laying claim to the covenant relationship (**our God**).

In time of need (vv. 3, 4)
The repeated plea for **mercy** and the turning to God in direct prayer (contrast v. 2) reveal their agitation and keen sense of need. Their suffering has become too much for them in intensity and in duration. They are the despised victims of proud oppressors whose lives of ease and plenty (cf. RSV) are a cruel mockery of their own deprivation. Having laid their problem before God, they wait with a hope that soars above their circumstances.

This short poem is a beautiful illustration of the spirit of Heb. 4: 16. Verse 3a in the Greek form of the *Kyrie eleison* has been a traditional prayer of the Church.

Psalm 124. THE BROKEN SNARE

In origin this was a communal thanksgiving. The nation gathered to praise God for dramatic deliverance from a recent crisis which threatened their entire existence. Later the psalm was used as a pilgrim song which summed up generally God's 'help in ages past'.

The human danger (vv. 1–5)
The precentor sings the first line, then the congregation take up the strains. The effect of the repetition is to stress that 'we have no help but Thee'. To dwell on what might have been is often an unrealistic, fruitless exercise. Here it is used to good effect. The community contemplate the dire alternative. 'Did we in our own strength confide, / Our striving would be losing' (Martin Luther). Death in the OT is sometimes pictured as a ravening monster (cf. Prov. 1: 12; Isa. 5: 14) or drowning **waters** (cf. 69: 2, 15). The pictures are applied to the nation's enemies, **men** through whose furious attack death's powers were at work. Tales were doubtless told of travellers swept away by a **torrent** swollen after heavy rainfall: God's people were saved in the nick of time from no less a fate.

The divine deliverance (vv. 6–8)
The divine name repeated at the outset comes to the fore again. Survival and present safety are traced back to God's hand and will. He snatched them from the jaws of these beasts of prey. He broke the **bird** trap and set His people free. To Him be the glory! The psalm closes with an affirmation of trust: 'Our Helper He, amid the flood / Of mortal ills prevailing' (Luther). They have proved God to be their Saviour, re-using His creative power (cf. 1 Pet. 4: 19). With this proof they face with confidence whatever the future holds.

Psalm 125. ANCHORED TO THE ROCK

Judah was evidently under the control of a foreign power, with whom some Jews, virtually denying their ancestral faith, were happy to collaborate. From within such an uneasy atmosphere comes this psalm of confidence, composed to reassure anxious hearts. It stands upon divine promises associated with the OT covenant. Its NT counterpart is 2 Tim. 2: 12, 19.

Faith's firm foundation (vv. 1–3)
Isaiah gave the assurance in time of crisis that those who stayed firm in faith would stand

firm in fact (Isa. 7: 9). The psalmist encourages his fellow-believers in similar vein. He draws upon the traditional picture of impregnable Zion (cf. Ps. 46; 48; 76; Isa. 28: 16). 'Solid joys and lasting treasure / None but Zion's children know' (J. Newton; cf. Heb. 12: 22). **Jerusalem** stands within a circle of hills; to the eye of faith this became a symbol of Yahweh's protective power that **surrounds his people** as a promise for today and every tomorrow. Oppressive foreign rule had placed its heavy hand **over the land** promised to faithful Israel (cf. Jos. 14: 1–5), but the assurance rings out that it would not always be so. God would not permit believers to be pressurized into abandoning their faith by too long a trial (cf. 1 C. 10: 13).

Faith's fervent prayer (vv. 4, 5)
But already the pressure is heavy. So the psalmist briefly turns from the congregation to address God directly, pleading His help for the faithful who in heart and life are endeavouring to maintain the **good** standards of the covenant (cf. 1 Sam. 12: 23). At the moment the collaborators seem to be on the winning side, but the poet warns that their abandoning the traditional faith must eventually spell their sharing the oppressors' punishment: nominal membership of the covenant nation counts for nothing. For him, as for Paul, 'a man is a Jew if he is one inwardly and circumcision is circumcision of the heart' (Rom. 2: 29). So in the closing benediction he prays not for every Judean but for the faithful. **Israel** is equated with **those who trust, the righteous**, the **good** and the **upright.** Upon all such falls this benediction of security and fulfilment. When Paul echoed it in Gal. 6: 16, he was mindful of its context, whether he meant by the 'Israel of God' Jewish Christians or, more probably, the whole 'family of believers' (Gal. 6: 10; cf. 4: 26–31).

Psalm 126. COUNT YOUR BLESSINGS
This pilgrim song had its origin in a time of national distress. It is a poignant medley of joy and sorrow, with the same threefold pattern as Ps. 85. It recalls past blessing, pleads for its renewal and records the divine reply to the plea.

Praise for the past (vv. 1–3)
In the light of v. 4 'restored the fortunes' (NIVmg) is a wide phrase. Here it is probably applied to the return from Babylonian exile. The community, burdened by trouble as they are, remarkably relive the wonder of that miraculous event. Surprised by **joy**, they were scarcely able to believe their eyes—it was all too good to be true (cf. Lk. 24: 41; Ac. 12: 9). Even Gentiles were impressed and admitted that Israel's God must be responsible for this miracle. Not to be outdone by pagans, Israel

echo in glad and simple testimony their indebtedness to God's power.

Prayer for the present (v. 4)
The retrospect has served both as a reminder that God is able to save His people and as an implicit appeal for Him to act again on their behalf. The post-exilic community experienced difficulty and frustration. **Great things** gave way to a 'day of small things' (Zech. 4: 10). So the community pray for heavy showers of blessing. In the rainy season the dry wadis of **the Negev** turned into torrents of water: their parched lives need similar reviving.

Promise for the future (vv. 5, 6)
A temple prophet answers their prayers. In Canaan and Egypt **sowing** was traditionally associated with sorrow as a time of death (cf. Jn 12: 24; 1 C. 15: 36). This proverbial saying is taken up in sympathetic reference to the people's plight. They are plodding wearily through their problems and toiling for a better society. The reassuring promise comes that their labour will be not in vain but an investment. The **seed** of sorrow will yield a fruitful harvest of joy and hope come true (cf. Gal. 6:8f.).

  6. **seed to sow:** read 'bag of seed' (NEB).

Psalm 127. THE LIFE OF FAITH
Ancient Israel was called to view secular life as sacred. Daily life was to be lived under the eye of God and each activity squared with the divine will (cf. Dt. 6: 6 f.). Since under the old covenant earthly life was the arena of divine salvation and judgment, it was the Israelite's prime duty to relate every human concern to Yahweh. The good things of life were traced back to His generous hand in praise; failure was a tell-tale sign of His displeasure. This simple philosophy proved inadequate, and even in the OT and certainly in the NT it is qualified by a more complex teaching (cf. Job; Hab. 3: 17 f.; Rom. 8: 35–39). But it proved a good working principle for life, and so it can be still (cf. Mt. 6: 33).

At work (vv. 1, 2)
Two examples of necessary labour are mentioned. Houses needed to be built to replace the tumbledown and to cater for new families.

  At night someone had to **stand guard**, the sentry on the city wall to warn of enemy attack. But activities crucial for the survival of the family and community were liable to failure, unless Yahweh was taken into account (cf. the covenant curse of Dt. 28: 30). 'Apart from me, you can do nothing' (Jn 15: 5) is the covenant rule: only if God is in the enterprise will all be well. Three times for emphasis the verdict **in vain** is passed upon human self-sufficiency (cf. 33: 16 f.). God and man are involved together in the covenant, and no man dare dispense with the senior Partner. The longest working hours spent in drudgery are no guarantee of success: God's grace is the secret. Not that laziness is the human corollary, but working with reliance upon One whose own work is the decisive factor (cf. 1 C. 15: 10; Phil.2: 12 f.).

At home (vv. 3–5)

The first half of the psalm taught by means of warning; the second teaches by commending. The theme, the boon of the family as God's gift, has a slightly ironic ring in these days of overpopulation and birth control, but its setting is an ancient community in constant need of replenishment against the ravages of disease, war and undernourishment. A bevy of sons born not too late in life was asset indeed, for they would be old enough to protect their father in his declining years. Against the onslaught of misfortune they would be a strong defence. If he were accused in the lawcourt held inside the city **gate**, they would rally round, ensuring that he was treated fairly and protecting his interests in a way denied to loners in society like widows and orphans (cf. Isa. 1: 23). Let such a proud father rejoice, for he has received 'a gift from the LORD' (NEB, cf. Gen. 33: 5; Dt. 7: 13). The family is endorsed as the basic unit of society, a divinely intended source of comfort and strength and, conversely, sphere of responsibility.

Note: Verse 2b is difficult. It may mean that God so blesses a normal day's work that overtime is unnecessary and one's opportunity for sleep is not curtailed nor is one a victim of insomnia through anxiety. Possibly the Heb. word for **sleep**, here spelt unusually, is an Aramaism meaning prosperity.

Psalm 128. GODLINESS WITH CONTENTMENT

Here is an example of priestly teaching given at a festival to the gathered people. The seemingly anonymous crowds are made up of individuals dear to God, each bearing a responsibility towards Him and a potential for rich blessing.

A beatitude explained (vv. 1–4)

The secret of blessing, stresses the psalmist (vv. 1, 4), is a life dedicated to God in reverent obedience to His moral will. What is this blessing? The unsophisticated answers unfolded in vv. 2 f. have scant affinity with the glossy dreams of modern materialistic man. It is the contented enjoyment of the **fruit** of honest **labor** (contrast Lev. 26: 15 f.; Isa. 65: 21 f.). It is the domestic satisfaction of a wife and family. The **vine** and **olive** not only stand for fertility, here sexual, but also implicitly trace it back to God as His gift (cf. Dt. 8: 7–10).

A benediction (vv. 5, 6)

The homely scene earlier described has nothing in common with a 'little box' mentality. It is integrated with a strong community spirit. At the hub of Israel's national life stood **Jerusalem**, its throbbing heart not only politically but religiously. There stood the temple, God's earthly home, and from it radiated out His blessing upon the worshipping pilgrims from all over the country. Only if the holy city remained and prospered, could individuals continue to experience this blessing. The worshippers are made conscious of an essential link between private life and this focal point of communal, religious solidarity. There is felt to be no incongruity in juxtaposing a personal boon of living long enough to see one's grandchildren and a prayer for blessing upon God's people as a whole.

This psalm has much to teach the restless, individualistic modern westerner. It is true that it shares certain limitations with Ps. 127, but if it is not the whole of the story, it is a part to be taken seriously. 'Even the fact that many godly people have to struggle with sorrow does not nevertheless invalidate the other truth that whenever happiness enters a home it is gratefully and humbly enjoyed as a gift from God' (Weiser).

Psalm 129. ANTIDOTE TO DESPAIR

The post-exilic community clustered around Jerusalem is the victim of oppression. In God's presence they encourage themselves and plead for the non-fulfilment of their foes' designs.

Comfort from the past (vv. 1–4)

The precentor breaks the depressed silence of the gathered people by bidding them join with him in looking back and setting their present ordeal in the perspective of history. Persecution is no stranger to God's folk (cf. 1 Pet. 4: 12). The nation, here personified, has undergone perennial suffering ever since its earliest history, back in Egypt (cf. Hos. 2: 15; 11: 1). As it were, 'they scored my back with scourges' (NEB, cf. Isa. 51: 23). But though often knocked down they were never knocked out, to use J. B. Phillips' paraphrase of 2 C. 4: 9. What was the secret of such resilience? The recital of suffering culminates in a testimony to the Saviour. Loyal to the covenant, God each time broke the yoke of oppression. A whole history of liberation is compressed into this grateful testimony, resonant with implications for their present distress.

'Confound their politics' (vv. 5–8)

Zion is here the touchstone of God's purposes. Its opponents find themselves the losers. As Israel's lot had so often been tragedy capped by triumph, so their appropriate experience would be initial success culminating in failure. May unrealized potential be theirs, like seedlings with no depth of soil (Mk 4: 5 f.; cf. 2 Kg. 19: 26)! The agricultural metaphors are developed into a reference to the harvest blessing (Ru. 2: 4). The attitude of others to God's people determines His attitude to them. 'Who-

ever touches you touches the apple of his eye'
(Zech.2: 8; cf. Mt.25: 31–46, esp. 34, 41).

Psalm 130. THE RICHES OF HIS GRACE

An individual Israelite takes part in a temple
service, confessing his need and sense of sin,
and casting himself upon God's grace. The
psalm became a pilgrim song which fittingly
prepared for subsequent worship of a holy
God.

A prayer for mercy (vv. 1–4)

The psalmist is overwhelmed; he feels out of
his depth, as it were. He pleads with God to
meet his need. He is convinced that his own
sin is responsible for the plight he is in, and
confesses it implicitly in vv. 3 f. If God kept a
strict tally of men's sins, there would be no
hope for anybody, for 'all have sinned' (Rom.
3:23; cf. 1 Kg. 8:46; Ps. 143:2). The psalmist is
conscious of a gulf which divides men from
God and not merely men in general but especially himself. The answer lies solely in God's
quality of **forgiveness.** Yet his attitude is far
from Heinrich Heine's cynical deathbed claim,
'God will forgive me. It is His job'. The aftermath of forgiveness is to be holy awe. His
reaction will be not complacency (cf. Rom. 2:
4) but devotion and obedience.

A pastoral message (vv. 5–8)

The poet turns to the congregation and shares
with them his personal **hope.** He is waiting for
the assurance of sins forgiven via a **word** of
pardon delivered by the priest in the **morning**
(cf. 107: 20; 143: 8; Lam. 3: 57). For this assurance he **waits more** ardently than a man on
night duty waits for the long, dark hours to
pass. His experience has taught him a message
for his fellow-worshippers, for his sinfulness is
not confined to himself (v. 3; cf. Isa. 6: 5).
God's **redemption** is not a solo performance,
at the Exodus, but a deliverance from sin's
bondage which God is able to grant whenever
the need arises. Such is his trust in this God
who places His power at the service of His love
that he is convinced that He will liberate His
people from the penalty and power of sin.

Christ gave a new dimension to the truths
of this psalm. Eph. 1: 7 takes up its key words
and relates them to Him. More exactly 1 Jn 1:
8–2: 2 is its NT counterpart, assuring that the
despair and inadequacy of believers find their
remedy in God's grace.

Psalm 131. CHILDLIKENESS

An individual brings his simple contribution
to a temple service. It is a profession of faith
and submission. He has realized the value of a
quiet trust in God and the folly of pretentious
pride. He does not 'busy' himself (NEB) with
things that are beyond him. He does 'not have
the restless will/ That hurries to and fro, /
Seeking for some great thing to do/ Or secret
thing to know' (Anna L. Waring).

This position has not been won without a
struggle with his headlong **soul.** He hints that
many a storm of self-seeking has had to be
overcome. He has come through to a mature
relationship of resting in God. He compares
himself with **a weaned child** 'in its mother's
arms' (JB), no longer fretting for its mother's
milk and craving for its own desires to be
satisfied but finding contentment in a cuddle
and the nearness of love.

Like Ps. 130 this poem moves from prayer
to exhortation. From the maturity of his faith
the psalmist counsels the congregation to foster
an attitude of trusting **hope.**

Psalm 132. A RELIGIOUS PAGEANT

This pre-exilic composition belongs to a ceremony commemorating David's moving of
the ark to Jerusalem. It falls into two halves:
prayers for the reigning king are offered in the
context of the ceremony (1–10) and are then
answered affirmatively (11–18).

David's promise concerning the ark (vv. 1–5)

God is urged to bless the present king because
of the work of the founder of the dynasty (cf.
v. 10). **David** laboured strenuously (**hardships**) to bring up the ark from Kiriath Jearim
and to plan a permanent home for it in the
form of the temple (2 Sam. 6–7; 1 Chr. 28–
29). He made a solemn promise not to rest till
these ambitions on God's behalf were fulfilled.
The Champion of the covenant people
(**Mighty One of Jacob**, an ancient title, cf.
Gen. 49: 24) deserved nothing less.

The procession and public prayers (vv. 6–10)

The sacred journey of 2 Sam. 6: 12–15 was
evidently re-enacted in the commemoration. A
choir play the part of David and his men, who
heard of the neglected ark's whereabouts while
in Ephrathah, the area of Bethlehem, David's
home, and went to Kiriath Jearim (**Jaar**) to
transport it to Jerusalem. The choir encourage
their fellow-worshippers to process to the
temple to conclude the ceremony before the
ark, the **footstool** of God's throne (cf. 1 Chr.
28: 2), after it has been installed afresh in the
Holy of Holies. But as yet it waits to be carried
in the procession. Verse 8 is uttered as the ark
is lifted (cf. Num. 10: 35), addressing the God
whose presence and power in Israel it symbolized. The hope is expressed that its bearers may
be deemed qualified to perform their sacred
task (**righteousness**, contrast 2 Sam. 6: 16 f.),
while the people, God's 'loyal servants' (NEB)
(**saints**) sing His praise. The final prayer reverts
to the opening theme (v. 1) of the reigning
king's welfare.

God's promise concerning the dynasty (vv. 11, 12)

In the rest of the psalm a temple prophet brings the divine answer to the prayers, confirming anew God's promises of old. His goodwill towards the king is grounded in a general guarantee of the permanence of David's royal line (2 Sam. 7: 12–16). For their part each of his descendants is obliged to obey God's covenant laws (cf. Dt. 17: 18–20; I Kg. 8: 25; 2 Kg. 11: 12; Ps. 89: 31 f.). The solemn promise of vv. 11 f. matches David's in vv. 2–5.

God's presence in Jerusalem and patronage of the king (vv. 13–18)

Now the prophet relays the reply to the themes of vv. 6–10. The permanence of the dynasty depends upon God's presence in **Zion** (**For**). It is indeed His chosen home, as v. 8 claimed. 'God is here and that to bless us' (J. L. Black) can be His people's cry as they gather in worship. His presence spells material and religious blessing for the people and their priestly channels of grace. In fulfilment of the covenant with **David**, God's **anointed**, divine right undergirds the present occupant of the throne in a position of power (**horn**) and stability (an ever-burning **lamp**, cf. Lev. 24: 2; I Kg. 11: 36). Victory and success would mark his reign.

The psalm is remarkable for the way in which the venerable past is blended with the here and now. The worshippers are no antiquarians pathetically trying to revive a bygone past. They are conscious that in a past era their God once and for all revealed His will in deed and word and that it is their privilege and responsibility to identify with that revelation. The king is the decisive gauge of his subjects' fortunes, just as Christ, the last Davidic **horn** (Lk. 1: 69), is for the Church.

Psalm 133.   ALL ONE IN THE LORD

The opening verse is a wisdom saying which originally discouraged **brothers** from setting up separate households and so dividing the family estate (cf. Dt. 25: 5). Here it is put to a wider use, as v. 3b and the religious nature of the comparisons in vv. 2–3a reveal. From all over the country pilgrims would converge on Jerusalem to celebrate the festival in worship. The crowded, Keswick-like scene was a fine representation of the **unity** of the covenant community, bound by a common faith.

The psalmist searches for pictures to convey his appreciation of this fellowship. The quaintness of the first can be partly dispelled for the Christian by comparing the woman's beautiful act of pouring spikenard over Jesus' head (Mk 14: 3, 6). Here the reference is to the fragrant anointing **oil** (Exod. 30: 23–25) poured over the **head** of a new high priest (**Aaron**), consecrating him for his religious office. It would trickle **down** his uncut **beard** (Lev. 21: 5) on

to his magnificent **robes** (Exod. 28; 29: 5–7). The ceremony would evoke a multiple response, sensual, aesthetic and devotional, and no less is the impact of the pilgrim crowds upon the psalmist's heart. The second picture reflects appreciation of refreshing **dew** during the bone-dry months (cf. Hos. 14: 5). The **dew of Hermon** was evidently an expression for a heavy deposit.

The gathering in **Zion** is no mere nationalistic demonstration but the seeking of God's appointed means of grace for the renewal of **life** in its fullness. **For** justifies the pictures: the priestly oil stands for **blessing** and the dew for **life** in store for God's family.

Psalm 134.   THE CIRCLE OF BLESSING

This composition was evidently used at a series of night services which according to Jewish tradition were held during the Feast of Tabernacles (cf. I Chr. 9: 33; Isa. 30: 29). Its two parts, linked by the lop-sided ambiguity of the Heb. verb *bārak*, 'bless' (cf. Eph. 1: 3), are an interchange between congregation and priests. (NIV renders the two usages of *bārak*, vv. 1, 3, as **Praise . . . bless**.)

Blessing God (vv. 1, 2)

The priests are urged to represent the congregation in a verbal outpouring of adoration and a physical gesture of raising **hands** (cf. I Tim. 2: 8) towards the Holy of Holies where God was symbolically enthroned.

God's blessing (v. 3)

They make a response by conferring a blessing upon the congregation (cf. Num. 6: 23–26).

From the temple in **Zion** issues blessing which will accompany the pilgrims as they eventually return home. Emanating from the Maker of the world, it knows no limits (cf. Eph. 3: 20).

Psalm 135. HALLELUJAH

This festival hymn celebrates the majesty and grace of Israel's covenant God. The weather phenomena cited in v. 7 may identify the occasion of its use as the autumn Feast of Tabernacles. It begins and ends with an enthusiastic Hallelujah.

The first call to worship (vv. 1–4)

The congregation (cf. 113: 1) is urged to sing God's praises. OT worship was never a vague, emotional outburst, but was logically grounded in the person and/or work of God. Of the reasons here given the first is a general one of glad appreciation of God's self-revelation (**name**). The second is the community's election and the fact that they belong to Him (cf. Dt. 7: 6; I Pet. 2: 9). They gratefully look back to the time when the great transaction took place, at Sinai (Exod. 19: 3–6).

God's revelation in creation and history (vv. 5–14)

A soloist sings of his own conviction of the majesty and uniqueness of **our Lord.** The whole universe, assigned by other nations to a pantheon of **gods,** is at the sole service of His sovereign will. The rainy season with its storms and **wind** is under His providential control—not, it is implied, that of the Canaanite Baal, as his devotees claimed. He is also the Lord of history, architect of the great saving events of the Exodus and Canaan's capture (cf. Ac. 4: 24, 27 f.). **Sihon** and **Og** in the Transjordan played an important role in Israelite tradition, as the first kings to be conquered (Num. 21: 21–24, 33–35). God shaped the course of history for the benefit of His covenant **people,** to give them the promised **land.** This proud citation of ancient exploits is no pathetic preoccupation with bygone glories. God's historical revelation of His nature and will is always relevant and deserves perpetual commemoration in worship. 'An almighty Saviour is the Saviour still.' His past patronage of His people is a guarantee that He will undertake for them in the future too (cf. Dt. 32: 36; Rom. 5: 9 f.; Gal. 2: 20).

A jealous God (vv. 15–18)

The hint of vv. 5–7 is now developed. The gods of the surrounding **nations,** ever a temptation to Israel (cf. Dt. 6: 12–15), are formally renounced. Thereby praise of the true, living God and a declaration of trust in Him are implicitly proclaimed. These verses are almost identical with 115: 4–8 (see the comments there).

The final call to worship (vv. 19–21)

Each sector of the religious community is urged to make its own contribution to the service of worship so as to ensure a harmony of praise to the utmost (cf. Rom. 15: 6). Layman, Aaronite priest and his assisting Levite—the whole community in fact (see on 115: 9 f.)—gathered in the temple, God's earthly home, are bidden to **praise** their Host.

3. that is pleasant: 'it (i.e. **his name**) is lovely' (cf. AV, RV).

Psalm 136.   EVER FAITHFUL EVER SURE

Like the previous psalm this is a song praising God for His revelation in creation and history. It is antiphonal: the first half of each verse would be recited by a priestly singer, and the refrain chanted by a choir or the congregation (cf. 2 Chr. 7: 3; Ezr. 3: 11).

Invitation to thanksgiving (vv. 1–3)

Praise in the OT is not sentimental or vague but solidly grounded in particular, practical and personal aspects of God. His benevolence

and omnipotence here come to the fore; together they guarantee the permanence of His love.

Love in creation (vv. 4–9)

Creation is celebrated as an extraordinary achievement illustrating both the power and intelligence of God. A number of its phases are selected as a host of reasons for praising the Creator. But the most important lesson of creation for the psalmist is His 'bountiful care' which 'breathes in the air, . . . shines in the light' (R. Grant). The truth that 'He with all-commanding might / Filled the new-made world with light' (John Milton) is interpreted as a revelation of His **love.** This goes far beyond natural theology: it depends upon a knowledge of God as Saviour, and it is this knowledge that in retrospect casts its warm hue over the stark phenomena of nature and invests them with new meaning.

Love in history (vv. 10–22)

For the secular historian history is a blend of chance and human personality, but to the worshipper it is God's stamping His own purpose and personality upon human experience. Here it is traced in Israel's national experience of the Exodus, the wilderness trek and the entry into Canaan. These are great archetypal events which, like the crucifixion and resurrection of Jesus in the NT, reveal and pledge God's permanent love for the people of the covenant. Each detail is attributed to the loving care of the divine Guardian and Guide.

Redeeming and sustaining love (vv. 23–26)

Verses 23 f. are either a summary of the foregoing or a reference to the later event of the return from exile. God's remembering is His acting upon a past promise or in accord with a relationship previously established. It is thanks to Him that Israel came to enjoy freedom and victory over heavy odds. Nor is His blessing merely a thing of the past or confined to Israel. The final proof of His care, a choice which may point to the harvest festival as the background to this psalm, is the provision of **food** for all creatures (cf. 104: 27 f.). His providential love overflows the covenant people and embraces the world. The closing call in v. 26 rounds off the psalm, reverting to vv. 1–3. The choice of the post-exilic title **God of heaven** is dictated by a desire to echo v. 5. The vast, mysterious **heaven** above symbolizes the power of God which, far from presenting a lowering threat, serves to undergird His love and confirm its effectiveness.

6. See the comments on 24: 2; 104: 5–9. **15. swept:** literally 'shook off ' like an insect (cf. 109: 23).

Psalm 137.   BITTER MEMORIES

The historical books of the OT tend to be

written in a restrained, unemotional style. This psalm of lament uncovers the personal experience and feelings of a Jewish exile who, now home again (cf. **there**, vv. 2, 3), relives the traumatic events of the period of deportation in Babylonia and the fall of Jerusalem which triggered it. The key words linking the three sections are **remember** and **Jerusalem** (or **Zion**). It is a poignant medley of love and hate.

A scene of grief (vv. 1–4)
Beside one of the tree-lined canals of Babylonia (cf. Ezek. 3: 15), a group of Jews just 'sat and wept' (GNB). Their grief was no mere homesickness. They were haunted by memories of **Zion**, bitter-sweet memories of festivals and fellowship with God and believer, and tragic ones of the ruins to which God's earthly home and the capital of His realm had been reduced. The group, perhaps temple musicians in the old days, had their harps with them, not in their **hands** but hung upon the branches, for they had no heart for music. Rubbing salt into their wounds, their Babylonian guards had sarcastically asked them to entertain by singing **one of the songs of Zion** celebrating Jerusalem's glory (cf. Pss. 46; 48; 76; 87). They refused to cast God's pearls before swine. They felt that this was neither the time nor place for sacred songs. The misery of vv. 1–3 is accentuated in the Hebrew by constant repetition of the ending *-nu* (**we, our**), which has a ring of pathos as in Isa. 53: 4–6.

A vow of loyalty (vv. 5, 6)
The psalmist now speaks as an individual, thus registering his heightened emotions. His pledge of constant love for **Jerusalem** is as solemn as any marriage vow. He invokes upon himself the penalty of physical handicaps (cf. Mt. 5: 28–30), so that he would never 'be able to play the harp again' or 'to sing again' (GNB). This is more than patriotism: the city is a symbol of the divine presence and praise. His faithfulness to it would be a measure of his faithfulness to God Himself.

A prayer for retaliation (vv. 7–9)
Restored to their homeland, the exiles witnessed again the desolation they remembered. It was not till twenty-two years after the initial return in 538 B.C. that the devastated temple was rebuilt. The psalm evidently belongs to the intervening years when every glance brought a reminder of the catastrophe of 587. Feelings ran high against Judah's brother nation Edom, who betrayed their kinship by looting captured **Jerusalem** and handing its refugees over to the enemy (cf. Ob. 11–14). God is asked to adjust the balance of justice by punishing the collaborators. An even greater degree of guilt was attached to Babylon, here personified. The divine principle of 'an eye for an eye' (cf. Exod. 21: 24; Dt. 19: 21) is invoked. Ancient warfare was cruelly waged against the next generation

by destroying babies (cf. Hos. 10: 14; 13: 16), and in the light of v. 8 this had been Judah's experience. 'The imprecation holds up a mirror to the Babylonian atrocities against Jerusalem and flashes the scene back on to the perpetrators as their coming recompense' (Eaton). Perhaps the psalmist is consciously quoting prophecy (cf. Isa. 13: 16; Jer. 51: 56). His enraged outburst transcends vindictiveness, for his human feelings are inextricably mingled with a passion for God's honour and justice.

Psalm 138. PRAISE FOR ANSWERED PRAYER
Despite difficulties of text and interpretation, it is reasonably clear that this psalm is an individual's song of thanksgiving. Some scholars attribute it to a Davidic king, while others consider that the psalmist speaks in the name of the post-exilic community, thanking God for release from exile.

Divine love (vv. 1–3)
The psalmist is in the **temple** forecourt with his face turned towards the main building (cf. 1 Kg. 8: 29). He is there to express his thanks to God, putting his **heart** and soul into his **praise.** Probably as a preface to a thank-offering, he bears witness to answered prayer and gratefully records God's enabling.

He openly defies the **gods** of pagan nations, proud of this practical proof of the superiority of his own God. Yahweh has given a demonstration of His loyal **love**, and proved the supremacy of His self-revelation (**name**) and promises.

Universal hope (vv. 4–6)
Painfully aware of the inadequacy of his little contribution of praise to so **great** a God, he looks forward to a time when every monarch on **earth** will bow the knee in homage and lift voices in **praise** to Israel's God, **when they hear** His revelation (cf. 102: 15). Such praise will be more worthy of His majesty. The wonder of it is that despite His supremacy He is so approachable—provided that He is approached in a humble frame of mind (cf. Lk. 18: 14).

Personal faith (vv. 7, 8)
As he faces the future, he affirms his trust in this great God. He realistically acknowledges that he has not seen the last of **trouble**, but he has the assurance of a **life**-giving God behind him, ready to intervene on his behalf. The psalmist has a part to play in God's overall **purpose**, and He can be trusted to bring it to fruition (cf. 57: 2; Phil. 1: 6). Expressing to the end his dependence upon God, he closes with a prayer (cf. 33: 22). As a piece of God's workmanship, he claims His continuing care (cf. Eph. 2:10; 1 Pet. 4:19).

1. gods: possibly 'angels' (LXX, JB). **6. knows:** possibly 'humbles' (NEB).

Psalm 139. HONEST TO GOD

This psalm falls into two parts, vv. 1–18 and 19–24. Had it ended at v. 18, it might seem to be a reverie on God's attributes in relation to the believer. But the sequel belies the apparently rarified tone of the first part.

Taking the psalm as a whole, its setting is best viewed as a religious court (cf. Ps. 109). The psalmist is protesting his innocence before almighty God who knows him through and through, is never absent from his side and has superintended his life from its beginning (cf. Jer. 12: 3; Jn 21: 17; 2 C. 11: 31).

God's omniscient care (vv. 1–6)

The author has gladly submitted to the divine scrutiny. He is 'uncovered and laid bare' to His eyes (Heb. 4: 13). Every detail of his daily routine is known to Him, every fleeting thought, every unspoken **word**. He cannot keep anything back from God, for He is close by, protectively covering him with His **hand** (cf. Exod. 33: 22). He reacts to God's omniscience with awesome wonder: it is beyond his ken and too sublime to comprehend.

God's omnipresent care (vv. 7–12)

The psalmist develops the thought of v. 5. Wherever he might wander, God would always be **there**. He acknowledges that it would be no good trying to run away from God, even if he wanted to. If he cannot hide anything from Him, he cannot hide himself either. God's **hand** would always be there to guide him aright, whether he went up to the **heavens** or down to **Sheol** (NIVmg), to the far east or the distant west (cf. Jer. 23: 23 f.). Nor is He a mere man from whom one can hide in the dark! The poet has a strong sense of God's **presence** and, it is implied, his life has been lived in the light of this consciousness (contrast Job 22: 13 f.).

God's omnipotent care (vv. 13–18)

Like Jeremiah, the poet realizes that before God formed him in the **womb** He knew him (Jer. 1: 5; cf. Job 10: 8–12). The formation of his unborn embryo he ascribes to the personal activity of God, and again his reaction is one of thrilled awe and wonder. Every part of his physical frame is known to the divine Maker. Not only the constitution but the career of the poet is an open book to Him, and in fact already written down in God's ledger of human destiny (cf. 56: 8; 69: 28). Such foreknowledge and forethought are overwhelming to him. In adoration he confesses himself unable to comprehend God's greatness (cf. 40: 5; Rom. 11: 33–36). He implicitly contrasts God's full knowledge of his own **thoughts** (v. 2) with his inability to grasp those of his Maker. Still reverting to the first part of the psalm, he continues the theme of v. 3. The sequel to God's awareness of his **lying down** is His presence at his bedside in his waking moments. It is to

this God who is so near and knows him so well that the subsequent appeal is addressed (cf. 119: 150 f.).

Appeal to the caring God (vv. 19–24)

The psalmist claims that he is the victim of violence and prays for God to intervene on behalf of himself, the innocent party. God's own honour is at stake, for He too has suffered at their hands. The suppliant declares himself loyal to God and totally opposed to their **evil** schemes. 'Evil for him is no abstract idea; it is embodied in evil men' (Kirkpatrick). He reverts again to an opening theme and welcomes a fresh examination as to whether he is telling the truth or if he has followed a path that is 'hurtful' (RSVmg) to others. Above all he commits himself positively to God's leading (cf. v. 10) **in the way** that is eternally right, whatever men may say or do.

9. LXX, followed by JB, NEB, GNB, is preferable: 'If I lift my wings to the dawn or dwell . . .' **14.** RSV is probably correct in following the ancient versions: 'for thou art fearful and wonderful.' **15. in the depths of the earth:** JB paraphrases 'in the limbo of the womb'. There may well be an echo of the ancient belief in the first man's conception in mother earth (cf. Job 1: 21). **17. precious:** rather, 'hard' (JB), 'difficult' (GNB). **23. anxious thoughts:** i.e. in reaction to the critical situation. **24. offensive:** possibly 'idolatrous'. Some scholars consider that the psalmist is accused of idolatry.

Psalm 140. THE POWER OF PRAYER

The psalmist has been maliciously slandered and cruelly pressurized. In this lament he brings the problem to God and pleads for His intervention. The literary style is marked by rich imagery, drawn from war, hunting, etc.

A cry for help (vv. 1–3)

A strong sense of need grips the author. He is at the mercy of these trouble-makers who have been waging against him a campaign of calculated provocation. They have stung him to the quick with the venom of their slander. His only hope is to appeal to the divine Judge for protection.

A second cry (vv. 4, 5)

The appeal is repeated in desperation. It is intensified by development of the lament. With the cold determination of the hunter his victimizers have been callously creating situations of torment and harassment in his daily life.

A prayer of proven faith (vv. 6–8)

Thus far the bulk of the psalm has been given over to an elaboration of personal suffering. Now the element of prayer is expanded as the psalmist centres his thoughts upon God and what He means to him. He recalls the ties of devotion and submission which link him with his LORD. Having in the past acknowledged

God's claim upon his life, he can now himself claim God's active care and concern. He has proved His saving help and can look back to times of danger when He protected him (cf. Eph. 6: 17; 1 Th. 5: 8). Now he needs again this divine support. He pleads for the malicious intent of his persecutors to be frustrated.

A prayer of retribution (vv. 9–11)
Appealing to the divine principle of justice, an eye for an eye (see on 137: 8 f.), he prays that the fate which they openly wish for him may redound upon themselves. He urges the execution of deserved punishment, such as Sodom-like fire (cf. 11: 6) or a seismic chasm into which Korah's company fell to their deaths (cf. 55: 15). Enjoyment of God's gift of **the land** was a privilege forfeited by individual disobedience to His claims (cf. Exod. 20: 12); the psalmist's enemies were surely included in that category. Reverting to the principle of exact retribution, he argues that their own evil (vv. 1 f.) and hunting him down should find their nemesis.

A statement of confidence (vv. 12, 13)
Coming to God in prayer like this has given him an inner strength and poise he did not possess before. The frantic cries of the opening part of the psalm have gradually given way to a firm conviction that God, as Israel's King, is the effective Judge and Saviour of **the poor**. In His court of appeal claims neglected by the human establishment find a satisfactory solution. The psalmist looks forward to the time that would **surely** come, when **the righteous**, so often synonymous with **the poor**, would 'have good cause to thank' Him (JB) in glad testimony to His saving grace. The future is theirs, along with the right to worship and to live on in His land (contrast v. 11; cf. 25: 13; 37: 9). So he encourages his own heart and the hearts of his fellow-worshippers.

Verse 3b is quoted in Rom. 3: 13 in a catalogue of OT statements about human sin.

Psalm 141. FOES WITHOUT AND WITHIN
This is a man's cry for help. He has enemies out to destroy him, but he is well aware that he also has an enemy within, a mind easily tempted to wrongdoing. From both he begs God for deliverance.

An urgent prayer (vv. 1, 2)
The psalmist craves a hearing and intimates his dire need. Will God accept his **prayer**? The temple offerings He does deign to accept from priestly hands, and the man hopes that the prayer offered with his own outstretched **hands** will prove acceptable too (cf. Rev. 5:8).

Power to withstand (vv. 3–5)
He asks God to control his speaking and thinking. He knows the havoc caused by unwise words slipping out (cf. Prov. 13: 3), and he

needs this strong Ally to help him **guard** his tongue. He knows too the dominant pull of his **heart** towards involvement in **evil** and association with wrongdoers. He resolves to leave their circle with its lavish hospitality (cf. 23: 5) and to learn to prize rather the kindly reprimand of **righteous** folk (cf. prov. 9: 8). Thus he will live more nearly as he prays.

A fate to avoid (vv. 6, 7)
It is difficult to make sense of these verses in the present Heb. text. The NIV attempts to reconstruct it. The psalmist appears to be looking ahead to the disastrous end of the godless, possibly to encourage himself in the stand he is taking.

A way of escape (vv. 8–10)
Evidently he now has the wrath of his former companions to contend with (compare v. 9 with v. 4). He looks to God for help and confesses his trust in Him. His enemies are like cunning hunters and he is the object of their manhunt (cf. 140: 4 f.). His only weapon against them is a prayer for justice to be done, so that they fall victim to their own scheming and he survives unscathed.

Psalm 142. NOBODY CARES
Prayer changes things, beginning with the state of mind of the praying man or woman.

The psalmist moves from depression and frustration to a point of positive hope and healthy trust in God.

An initial cry (vv. 1–3a)
Loudly and despairingly he announces his intention to **tell** his troubles to God. He is at the end of his emotional tether, but finds some comfort in the fact that God already knows and understands (cf. Mt. 6: 32). Yet it is a spiritual paradox that prayer does not therefore become unnecessary. God still wants to hear and the believer certainly needs to pray.

Negative circumstances (vv. 3b, 4)
He explains his dire situation. Caught in a **snare** set by his enemies, he cannot get out of his plight by himself nor will anyone help him. There is nobody to 'befriend' him, nobody who 'cares about' him (JB). He stands alone.

Positive prospects (vv. 5–7)
'Other refuge have I none, / Hangs my helpless soul on Thee' (Charles Wesley) is virtually his trusting cry in his extremity. God is 'all I want in this life' (GNB), he testifies. He pleads his weakness and implicitly confesses God's sovereign power. He promises that once God lets him out of this trap, this **prison** of trouble (cf. 88: 8; Lam. 3: 7), he will bring to the temple his thank offering with a testimony of praise to Him as Saviour. By faith he revels in the prospect of there celebrating God's bounty in renewed fellowship with His people.

The heading applies the psalm to David's experience at Adullam (1 Sam. 22: 1), its sentiments being judged suitable to that occasion (cf. Ps. 57). **4.** In court the counsel for the defence stood on the **right** (cf. 16: 8; 109: 31). **refuge:** represents a different Heb. word from that in v. 5: it is better rendered 'way of escape' (NEB).

Psalm 143. AT THE END OF MY TETHER

An individual delivers his lament in the temple before awaiting a reassuring oracle to be issued next morning (v. 8).

Prayer (vv. 1, 2)
The psalmist, in dire need, realizes that he cannot pressurize God to help him by appealing to his own merits. His only claim is to a covenant relationship with his God (**servant**, cf. v. 10), initiated and maintained by divine grace. He appeals to God's **faithfulness**, to His attribute of being true to His covenant promises and ready to set right and vindicate His own (**righteousness**). He is well aware of the danger involved in bringing himself to God's notice and thus exposing himself to the divine scrutiny. Such is his sense of awe and consequent sense of his own inadequacy. The reference to human waywardness (cf. 130: 3; 1 Kg. 8: 46) is no shoulder-shrugging excuse, but expresses a conviction of the power of sin.
'*One* way is left open to him: to give himself up wholly to the grace of God' (Weiser).

Predicament (vv. 3, 4)
The psalmist explains his plight in general but strong terms. He has been the victim of ruthless persecution. His varied allusions to death in v. 3 underline its devasting effect upon his life. He stands in death's shadow, already weakened and without vitality, **like** the helpless ghosts imprisoned in Sheol (cf. 88: 3–8, 10–12). This harrowing experience has left him 'dazed with despair' (NEB).

Precedent (vv. 5, 6)
His hope is set in the God who once and for all revealed Himself in action as His people's Saviour and Lord (cf. 77: 11–20). He takes comfort in recalling the ancient precedents of God's proving His powerful aid. It is not to the labour of his own hands that he appeals, to 'fulfil Thy law's demands' (A. M. Toplady, v. 2) in self-justification, but to the achievement of God's **hands**. Nothing in his **hands** he brings, but stretches them out empty in a yearning gesture of need and dependence upon God, fully aware of his own barrenness (cf.42: 1 f.).

Petitions (vv. 7–12)
He is so weak, he needs help before it is too late and he actually dies. He pleads with God not to refuse to answer his urgent prayer.
Evidently oracles of help were delivered to individuals by the priests on **the morning** after their prayer of laments was offered (cf. 90: 14), and the psalmist desires this favourable

response. Verses 8–10 cap each petition with a mention of personal trust. This faith is not intended as a meritorious virtue in its own right but as a confession of helplessness. The psalmist needs advice and instruction to be included in the oracle of response. But that alone would be insufficient: to know what to do, valuable as that is, is nothing without the power to turn knowledge into achievement. So he pleads for God to manifest Himself to him as a personal guide, just as He had done for Israel of old (cf. Neh. 9: 20), and to clear out of the way Mount Frustration and Mount Difficulty.
He appeals to God's name, His revealed character as true to the covenant and loyally **unfailing** to His own. He enlists God's aid to fight his battles for him against those who, unlike himself, have not pledged their lives to God and stand outside the covenant circle.
Charles Wesley's hymn, 'Jesu, Lover of my soul', captures remarkably the spirit of this psalm for the Christian. Paul was well aware of its spiritual message concerning sin and faith. In Rom. 3: 20 he refers to v. 2 after showing the universality of human sin (cf. 3: 9). Man's only hope is to throw himself upon God's free promise of salvation. To the righteousness of v. 1 the apostle turns in Rom. 3: 21 (cf. 1: 17): in Christian terms it means God's undertaking personally to set sinful man right with Himself, an opportunity to be appropriated 'through faith in Jesus Christ'. God's **righteousness** in this sense is the remedy for unrighteous man.

Psalm 144. KING AND COUNTRY

The first part of the psalm, vv. 1–11, echoes portions of Ps. 18. A Davidic king speaks in his role as representative of Israel, seemingly in the late pre-exilic period in view of the language used. He praises God and prays for His aid. In the second part, vv. 12–15, God's blessing is invoked upon His people. As a theocracy Israel looked to their God for prosperity and for wise government, which was mediated through the human king.

The king's praise (vv. 1, 2)
Such martial skills and exploits as he has achieved are gratefully traced back to God as their only source. 'Every virtue' he possesses 'and every victory won . . . / Are His alone' (H. Auber). He is a kindred spirit of Paul: 'By the grace of God I am what I am' (1 C. 15: 10).

The king's surprise (vv. 3, 4)
He humbly expresses his amazement at God's grace, in terms of 8: 4. How can it be that he, a mere mortal (cf. Neh. 1: 11), should be so favoured? Why should God 'notice' him (JB, GNB) or pay him such attention? Like his fellows he is of himself so little and insignificant, 'no more than a puff of wind' (NEB, cf. JB, GNB).

The king's prayer (vv. 5–8)
Matching the monarch's humble view of him-

self is his correspondingly exalted view of God (cf. 2 C. 4: 7). He who has experienced His help on previous occasions now requests His intervention in a new crisis. He paints the prospect of divine aid in terms of a theophany, a breaking into time and space of a colossal, eternal energy with devastating effect. This picture of divine power serves as an assurance that, great as the king's enemies are, his God is greater still and able to subdue them. His serious plight is described first as **mighty** (or 'deep' JB, GNB) **waters** and then more literally as pressure from foreign powers who think nothing of breaking solemn treaties.

The king's promise (vv. 9–11)
He makes a vow to sing in the temple a solo **song** of praise, newly composed for the occasion, after God has come to his assistance. He assures himself that assist He certainly will, in the light of precedents in the past history of the Davidic dynasty and in his own experience as the contemporary wearer of the crown (cf. Ezek. 34: 23; Hos. 3: 5). But threat of foreign invasion looms large. To relieve his anxiety the king understandably repeats the poignant details of his plight in a renewed appeal.

The people's prospects (vv. 12–15)
The king's subjects trustingly leave to his care the immediate matters of foreign politics. They look beyond the present crisis to creative hopes of renewed prosperity and security in everyday life. In the OT economy material blessings are naturally ascribed to God's generous hand, and sought afresh from Him. The nation's future is represented by sturdy boys and strong, beautiful girls, who can work together to build a better nation. But only God gives such increase. They pray too for an affluent society. **Filled** barns have their dangers (Lk. 12: 16–21), but accepted in trust and used for good, they are welcome tokens of God's covenant grace. Wealth, represented by large flocks and herds, and civil order are both boons indeed. There is an implicit suggestion that Judah at this time enjoyed neither. Yet they ingenuously look to their God to supply this lack, as conscious as their king (vv. 1 f.) of their dependence upon Him. More prized than the gifts is the Giver Himself, the God of the covenant.

2. my loving God: lit. 'my steadfast love'. RSV ('my rock') emends in accord with 18: 2; 2 Sam. 22: 2. NEB keeps the Heb. and renders 'my help that never fails'. **8, 11.** The raising of the **right hand** was a gesture accompanying an oath (cf. Dt. 32: 40). **14.** Possibly the middle part should be rendered as JB 'and may there be an end to raids and exile' (cf. AV, RV).

Psalm 145. TELL OF HIS MIGHT, SING OF HIS GRACE
Like Ps. 111, 119 this one is an acrostic. Yet its thought is not in bondage to its form: it man-

ages to develop pretty freely. It is a solo hymn intended to stimulate the congregation to appreciate and praise God's kingship. This is the theme explored in the song. A royal crown spells power and exaltation over one's subjects; it also obliges its wearer to care for their welfare. On these two counts God is praised in alternating fashion for His greatness and goodness. The psalm has an exuberant ring, typified by the frequency of the word **all.** Its stress on kingship and the implicit reference to the harvest in vv. 15 f. suggest that it was sung at the autumn festival, the Feast of Tabernacles.

Royal greatness (vv. 1–6)
The title **King** broaches the overall theme. The psalmist pledges lifelong commitment to praising God for His self-revelation (**name**). An initial reason appears in v. 3: the vastness of God's power. The awe inspired in modern man by the vast universe is paralleled here by the reaction to God's magnificent **greatness** (cf. Rom. 11: 33, 36). This attribute the soloist has learned from the heritage handed down to each fresh **generation** of His people, the account of His kingly **works** in creation and redemption (cf. 74: 12–17; 95: 3–7). To this tradition every generation was obliged to respond with praise, and the psalmist willingly owns himself part of this living chain of worship (v. 6).

Royal goodness (vv. 7–9)
There is a caring side to God's kingship, and this too is part of the heritage, the old yet new 'story' for men to 'recite' (NEB). God blesses His subjects and is loyal to His royal responsibilities (**righteousness**, cf. v. 17; 116: 5; 143: 1). The credal statement of Exod. 34: 6 is quoted in v. 8; it was a favourite text of post-exilic Jews. 'Steadfast love' (RSV) is strictly a covenant term, but it gradually burst its national bonds and was used of God's common grace to all creatures, as here in the light of v. 9. (The book of Jonah is a commentary on vv. 8 f.) The King of creation is lavish with providential gifts.

Royal greatness (vv. 10–13a)
Accordingly all His creatures (NEB, GNB) are obliged to praise, not only His covenant people (**saints**). As bearer of the tradition of God's revelation Israel is witness to neighbouring nations of His power in creation and covenant history. Their message is that the world is their God's realm and that He is implicitly sovereign even now (cf. Dan. 4: 3, 17, 34f.; Rom. 13: 1–6).

Royal goodness (vv. 13b–20)
The divine King is true to His obligation to care especially for the oppressed (cf. 72: 4, 12–14). His subjects throughout creation 'look hopefully' (GNB) to Him in dependence, and it is from His generous **hand** that all **food** comes. It is implied that an acknowledgement of the Provider in praise must complete the cycle

of growth and consumption. From material blessings the psalmist returns to the note of v. 14, specifically mentioning God's role as helper in time of danger. He is ever within earshot of a sincere **cry** for help (cf. Phil. 4: 5b–6). He fulfils the royal duty to maintain moral order in society, promoting the welfare of the obedient **who love him**–and, it is implied, keep His commands (Exod. 20: 6; 1 Jn 5: 2)–and wielding providential justice against those who flout the divinely appointed moral order.

Finally the psalmist reverts to his opening point (vv. 1, 2, 6). However, his personal **praise** is woefully inadequate by itself. He yearns to stand among a congregation made up of **every creature**: only thus could God be worthily honoured.

Verse 13b, lacking in the mainstream Heb. tradition, is rightly restored to this alphabetic poem. It supplies the missing couplet starting with the letter 'n'.

Psalm 146. PRAISE AND TRUST

This is the first of five Hallelujah psalms, each one set in the framework of a communal call to praise at beginning and end. This psalm unusually combines personal praise with an exhortation to trust God. The psalmist thereby expresses his awareness that praise must be the fruit of a living commitment, if it is to be meaningful.

A promise to praise (vv. 1, 2)

Congregational **praise** is the sum total of the worship rising from individual hearts. Far from being an observer of others worshipping, the poet determines to share in it personally. Such is his appreciation of God that lifelong praise must be his response.

A plea for faith (vv. 3–5)

Realistically he knows that the hearts of some attending the service may be far from Him (Isa. 29: 13). He takes the opportunity to expound the nature of faith, negatively and positively. Personal trust in Yahweh, the God of the covenant community (**Jacob**), is an asset indeed: 'Happy the man whose hopes rely/ On Israel's God' (Isaac Watts). Humanism is essentially doomed. To commit oneself wholeheartedly to one's fellows leads to a dead end. Any man or group of **men** are transitory, and so are their philosophies and panaceas.

Promptings to praise and faith (vv. 6–10)

The bard lists what he prizes in the character and activity of God. His work in creation reveals His omnipotence. He is also the God of the covenant, and here His faithfulness comes to the fore. Where His people are concerned, God has shown Himself able to meet every kind of need, social, physical and economic. 'None shall find His promise vain' (Watts). Accordingly the needy individual, whatever his need may be, is implicitly urged to relate it

trustingly to God and, after his particular need is met, to return praise to Him.

The psalmist hints at the moral responsibility laid by God upon His people: He expects certain standards, and frustration is the lot of those who disregard them. But he cannot leave the theme of God's patronage of the needy. His last instance concerns the three types of (potentially) deprived groups in the Judean community, the resident **alien** who lacked civil rights, and the **widow** and orphan who were liable to exploitation. But God was their champion. And if He can and does meet such needs as these, no kind of need is beyond His help. In a word He is King, powerful and, unlike human leaders (vv. 3 f.), permanent. **Zion**, as His capital and the meeting place of the worshipping community, has cause to be proud of such a praiseworthy God and to feel secure in Him.

4. the ground: i.e. 'the earth he came from' (JB). There is a sombre play on the words man (*'ādām*) and earth (*'ªdāmāh*), bringing out human inferiority and inadequacy (cf. Gen. 3: 19).

Psalm 147. HIS POWER AND HIS LOVE

This post-exilic psalm of praise is a medley of two interwoven themes, God's great power and His gracious patronage of the covenant people. Its setting was probably the autumn Feast of Tabernacles in view of the references to the harvest (v. 14) and to the law (v. 19; cf. Dt. 31: 10 f.). It has three stanzas, each beginning with a fresh call to praise.

God's redemptive care for Israel (vv. 1–6)

The return from exile is chosen as the basis for a worshipful meditation on God's being and purpose. The Jewish community, rebuilt and restored, is a living testimony to His strong and tender care. The heartbreak of exile (cf. 137: 1–4) has been replaced by the healing comfort of being home again. It calls for Hallelujahs from His grateful people. The transcendent **power** that controls **the stars** (cf. Isa. 40: 26, 28) has been exerted on their behalf, in the overthrow of Babylon and the rehabilitation of downtrodden Israel.

God's providential care and Israel's response (vv. 7–11)

The covenant God (**our God**) is celebrated as the great Provider for bird, beast and man. The dramatic contrast of the Palestinian seasons and scenery is traced to His providential control. The rain after months of drought and the new green mantle for the bare earth are gifts from Him. Nor is man the sole recipient of such care, for God also sustains the lower orders of animate life. If He bestows providential care (**unfailing love**) upon His people, their proper response is reverent awe and continual trust rather than relying upon any **strength** of their own (cf. Isa. 40: 29 ff.). The tragedy is that men lose their sense of values and are more prone to find their sufficiency in the amassing of armaments—strong cavalry and infantry forces (cf. Isa. 31: 1).

God's providential and spiritual care for Israel (vv. 12–20)

The security and wellbeing of the post-exilic community are divine gifts to be acknowledged with gratitude. The recent good harvest did not just happen or depend upon man's efforts, but was the outworking of God's loving care. The seed was 'watered / By God's almighty hand; He sends the snow in winter, / The warmth that swells the grain, / The breezes and the sunshine, / The soft refreshing rain' (M. Claudius, translated by Jane M. Campbell). The omnipotent **word** that brought creation into being (Gen. 1: 3 ff.) is at work still, controlling the seasons and weather. **Snow, frost and hail**, comparatively rare phenomena in Palestine, excite Israel to awesome wonder and praise of God. It is **his icy blast**, eventually to be thawed by the warmth of **his breezes.**

But this providential **word** does not stand alone: it has a spiritual counterpart in the special **word to Israel**, the revelation of God's will for their lives in the laws of Sinai, traditionally read at the Feast of Tabernacles. What a unique privilege is theirs! The **decrees** are thus themselves an incentive to obedience.

13. strengthens . . . blesses: better 'has strengthened, has blessed' (cf. NEB). **17b. who can withstand:** perhaps the text originally read 'the water stands frozen' (NEB).

Psalm 148.   UNIVERSAL PRAISE

This exuberant hymn of praise consists of two stanzas with a parallel structure. An extended call to praise, enumerating those summoned (vv. 1–4, 7–12), is followed by the ground and theme of praise (vv. 5 f., 13 f.).

Celestial praise (vv. 1–6)

The heavens and their denizens are urged to make their contribution to a universal chorale. The angelic retinue in God's heavenly temple and palace comprise a choir praising their Lord and King (cf. 103: 20; Isa. 6: 3). The sky's lights are personified, together with the towering **heavens** and the celestial **ocean**, which was credited with storage of rain (cf. 104: 3; Gen. 1:6 f.; 7: 11; 8:2). One and all they are challenged to **praise** God for their creation and preservation, for their endowment with particular functions and unique roles by the great Creator. They can each one tell the glory of God and proclaim His handiwork (19: 1). Just as an exquisite piece of craftsmanship serves to bring glory to the craftsman, so the appointed purpose of the created world is to glorify God

by reflecting His power and glory. The works of creation by fulfilling their divinely allotted function exist as eloquent testimonies to God's revelation of Himself (**name**).

Terrestrial praise (vv. 7–14)

From the heights (v. 1) the psalmist descends to the depths, the **ocean depths** and the earth. 'The heavens are not too high . . . The earth is not too low' for praise (G. Herbert). Even the giant whales (cf. Gen. 1: 21) are monuments to His power and testify to it. The phenomena of extreme weather conditions communicate His transcendence and proclaim His might and will. 'All creatures great and small', from 'the purple-headed mountain' to 'each little bird that sings' (Mrs. C. F. Alexander) attest landscaping artistry coupled with a keen eye for detail.

Coming to mankind, the climax of creation, the bard calls upon all, whether high or low in rank, old or young, male or female, to bring their distinctive, conscious praise. Probably in v. 12 he is eyeing the religious community gathered in Jerusalem for worship (cf. Jl 2: 16 f.). Israel serves to represent mankind in their praise (cf. 96: 1–3). Reason enough for praising lies in His intrinsic sovereignty and supremacy above all the elements of **earth and heavens** listed earlier. Whatever power each possesses is delegated from Him. A more intimate reason is His bestowal of victory and vitality (**horn**, cf. 92: 10) upon **his** chosen **people**. Bound as they are in covenant relationship with Him (**saints**), they have been given ample cause for **praise.** Privileged to draw near to this Fount of every blessing and to enjoy communion with Him as a nation of priests in Jerusalem, the special place of His presence (cf. 73: 28; Exod. 19: 6; Dt. 4: 7), their joy and duty it is to sing Hallelujah.

The intimate turn taken by the psalm at its close reminds the Christian of the progression from old song to new in Rev. 4: 11; 5: 9 ff.

Psalm 149.   FIRSTFRUITS OF VICTORY

The composition of this psalm was evidently inspired by a national victory. As the people praise God for it, they look forward to the future, final triumph of His purposes.

A victory won (vv. 1–4)

The first half of the psalm is an extended call to worship, explained in v. 4. A recent military success prompts **a new song**, for it is by no means the people's achievement but the result of divine aid. The community worshipping in Jerusalem (**Israel, the people of Zion**) recall that in fact the nation owes its very existence to their God and **King.** He it was who made a rabble of slaves into a cohesive nation (cf. 95: 6; 100: 3). The God of the Exodus has proved to be with them still, and they are urged to join in the religious dance and to sing to the music of **tambourine** and strings (cf. Exod. 15: 20; Jg. 11: 34). This is to be their response to God's favour in 'conferring victory on us who are weak' (JB), who in their weakness depend upon Him (**the humble**).

Victory to come (vv. 5–9)
As the service of worship continues, members of the congregation fling themselves 'prostrate before God' (JB) in devotion, and then evidently engage in a sword dance as they sing. Their **swords** are as it were **double-edged** in symbol as well as in fact: they not only commemorate the recent victory but ceremonially enact the full and final victory which God's people would one day enjoy. The OT traditions of Holy War are echoed here, and the conviction of a war to end all wars when God's justice would be upheld and the forces of evil laid low once and for all. Was not this **sentence** 'decreed' (NEB)? The Law and the Prophets contained divine guarantees of such a glorious finale (cf. Dt. 20: 1–4; 32: 41 f.; Isa. 45: 14; Jl 3: 9–16, 19–21). Yesterday's victory, celebrated in today's praise, was a stepping stone to the promised triumph of the end time. And in God's **glory** manifested on that day His own people would have the privilege of sharing. Hallelujah!

The theme of Holy War is developed in the NT to a spiritual, cosmic level. The Church is called to wage it with the sure knowledge of eventual victory (cf. 2 C. 10: 4 f.; Eph. 6: 11–17; Rev. 12: 10 f.).

1, 5, 9. saints: Heb. *ḥᵃsîdîm* refers to those bound in covenant relationship with God. This term is also rendered 'the faithful' and 'godly' elsewhere. **5. beds:** probably the places where they lie prostrate in worship (cf. JB, NEB); possibly it refers to divans on which one reclined at sacred meals.

Psalm 150. A CRESCENDO OF PRAISE

This final psalm not only brings to a close the special group of praising psalms (Pss. 146 ff.), but probably stands also as a doxology to the fifth book and indeed to the entire Psalter, just as the earlier books had their shorter doxologies (41: 13; 72: 18 f.; 89: 52; 106: 48).

The 'where' of praise (v. 1)
The people of God are gathered for worship in the temple, **his sanctuary.** It is the centre of the world, the place where earthly **praise** ascends to Him. The call rings out to Israel to represent the world in praising. Their Hallelujahs blend with those sung by the celestial host (cf. 148: 2) in the grand 'vault' of heaven (NEB).

The 'why' of praise (v. 2)
God's **acts of power** are those so often celebrated in Israel's psalmody; His acts of creation and of deliverance and preservation of the

chosen nation (cf. 74: 12–17). Like a range of spotlights they cast their concerted beams upon God Himself, highlighting His 'immeasurable' (NEB) **greatness** as Lord of creation and Lord of sacred history.

The 'how' of praise (vv. 3–5)
Every instrument in the temple orchestra is bidden play its distinctive part, whether percussion, wind or **strings.** Together with sacred **dancing**, they create a loud symphony of **praise**, in response to the glory of God, rising to a magnificent crescendo with **the clash of cymbals.**

The 'who' of praise (v. 6)
'All that hath life and breath, come now with praises before Him' (J. Neander, translated by C. Winkworth). Every voice is to fulfil its highest function by praising its Creator, from whom it derives its breath. This OT challenge has come ringing down the centuries. 'Let the Amen sound' in turn from His New Testament people!

BIBLIOGRAPHY

Commentaries
ALEXANDER, J. A., *The Psalms* (1850, reprinted Grand Rapids, 1975).
ALLEN, L. C., *Psalms 101–150.* Word Biblical Commentary (Waco, Texas, 1983).
ANDERSON, A. A., *Psalms.* New Century Bible (London, 1972), 2 vols.
ANDERSON, G. W., 'The Psalms', *Peake's Commentary on the Bible* (London, ²1962), pp.409–443.
BRIGGS, C. A. and E. G., *The Book of Psalms. ICC* (Edinburgh, 1906, 1907), 2 vols.
CRAIGIE, P. C., *Psalms 1–50.* Word Biblical Commentary (Waco, Texas, 1983).
DAHOOD, M., *Psalms I: 1–50; Psalms II: 51–100; Psalms III: 101–150. AB* (New York, 1966, 1968, 1970).
DURHAM, J. I., 'Psalms', *Broadman Bible Commentary,* vol.4 (London, 1972), pp. 153–464.
EATON, J. H., *The Psalms.* TC (London, 1967).
ELLISON, H. L., *The Psalms.* Bible Study Books (London, 1968).
KIDNER, D., *Psalms 1–72; Psalms 73–150. TOTC* (London, 1973,1975).
KIRKPATRICK, A. F., *The Book of Psalms.* CB (Cambridge, 1902) (reprinted Grand Rapids, 1952).
KNIGHT, G. A. F., *Psalms.* Daily Study Bible. 2 vols. (Edinburgh, 1982).
RHODES, A. B., *Psalms.* Layman's Bible Commentaries (London, 1961).
ROGERSON, J. W., and MACKAY, J. W., *Psalms. CBC.* 3 vols. (Cambridge, 1977).
TATE, M. E., *Psalms 51–100.* Word Biblical Commentary (Waco, Texas, 1984).
WEISER, A., *The Psalms,* Eng. trans. by H. Hartwell. OTL (London, ²1979).

General and Special Studies

BARTH, C. F., *Introduction to the Psalms*, Eng. trans. by R. A. Wilson (Oxford, 1966).

JOHNSON, A. R., *Sacral Kingship in Ancient Israel* (Cardiff, 1955).

LEWIS, C. S., *Reflections on the Psalms* (London, 1958).

MOWINKEL, S., *The Psalms in Israel's Worship*, Eng. trans. by D. R. Ap-Thomas (Oxford, 1962), 2 vols.

RINGGREN, H., *The Faith of the Psalmists* (London, 1963).

WESTERMANN, C., *The Praise of God in the Psalms*, Eng. trans. by K. R. Crim (London, 1966).

PROVERBS

CHARLES G. MARTIN

Invoked or not, God is present. So said the inscription on Jung's door in Zurich and it is a remarkable commentary on his study and service of humankind. Some things simply are so; the archetypes reappear; healing is possible. The quotation also provides a clue to the book of Proverbs.

The Hebrew Old Testament is divided into three sections—the Law, the Prophets and the Writings, answering to the three groups of leaders, priest, prophet and wise (Jer. 18: 18). Even the casual reader must sense that the Writings are very different from the other two sections. There is history in Chronicles, Ezra–Nehemiah and Esther, but it is not quite like the history of Exodus or Kings. The Psalms overarch the whole of the Old Testament, giving cultic form, personal experience, history, pageant and wisdom. Then there are Job, Proverbs and Ecclesiastes. Ecclesiastes is short, and disturbs the reader only after close study and much thought. But there is quite a lot of Proverbs and the longer you live with it, the more the 'difference' hovers in the mind until it is almost tangible. One surprising clue is the use of the words 'holy', 'holiness', which appear only three times (see on 20: 25; 30: 3). Chronicles, Ezra and Nehemiah have a lot of references to holiness—mostly the holy place, or holy people, but holy by reference to God who is transcendent, glorious, jealous. Esther in its strange way mentions neither God nor holiness, though clearly God is present in a dialectic more subtle than any Marx imagined. Job follows its theme with occasional mention of God and holiness alongside its preoccupation with human *angst* and suffering. Ecclesiastes is sharp and provocative, an appendix to Job. But Proverbs is seemingly so pious, godly and commonsensical. It only slowly becomes clear why the editor has so little interest in the seraphim's cry of 'Holy, holy, holy'; 'worshipping the LORD in the beauty of holiness'; or even (when you look closely) any worship at all. (See note at 2: 8.)

Proverbs is about life and living it the sensible way. The world was made by wisdom (ch. 8) and those who follow wisdom will find that the world fits them, and fosters their efforts. Wisdom is God's workman (8: 30) so the fear of the LORD is the first step toward wisdom (9: 10), the ground and origin of all knowledge (1: 7) and a fountain of life (14: 27). Wisdom, in fact, writes the handbook, the instruction manual for use in God's workshop. If fools despise wisdom and instruction they come to ruin in all the tragic and colourul ways Proverbs describes. Those who read and practice, who listen to the wise father, will prosper in the end, and generally now as well. To follow instructions, it may help if you know the manufacturer. But people can recognize wisdom without recognizing the LORD whose fear is its beginning, and certainly without a personal experience of holiness. It is not nationalistic; there is no awe-struck terror before the burning Mount and hardly any reference to the Covenant. It is a book for all races. It reflects the world as seen by the pragmatist. Its wise and witty sayings 'work'. They work because that is the way the LORD has set things up. Even if people do not invoke that creatorial power, His creative and sustaining wisdom goes on giving them a world where wisdom operates, where things can make sense to man. Proverbs is the scrapbook of common grace. Alexander Maclaren described it as portable medicine for the fevers of youth, and with medicine what matters is that you take it whether you know the doctor or not. Proverbs reflects the wisdom writings of many peoples and is a worthy reminder that all men share some basic insights into their situation, their 'human condition'. Its wisdom may be followed for the wrong reason—self-interest, because wisdom 'works' —but as William Temple said 'The art of politics is so to arrange matters that self-interest prompts what justice demands'. Christians may follow Proverbs' advice for deeper reasons; they may even find the 'pay-off' an embarrassment. They may find Proverbs very this-worldly, with references to the hereafter so few that some commentators deny there are any at all (see on 11: 7). But they too can read with profit and joy, a wry smile or pang of sorrow, and enjoy many a finely balanced saying to keep them thinking about the world and its varied dwellers.

There are links of course with great OT words—righteousness, uprightness (see on 8: 15–21) and justice because these are deep truths about man's true goal and direction. The motto (1: 7; 9: 10) also provides a firm tie with the rest of Scripture. The fear of the LORD is an elusive concept. It is certainly not terror, nor even a numinous dread (see on 28: 14). It is a reverent awareness about reality, the very opposite of arrogance and *hubris*. It is the acknowledgement of a boundary to human choice or discovery. Von Rad describes it as 'a limit to empirical wisdom; on the boundary, submit to God' and McKane comments that this is 'not a contradiction of self-hood but a discovery of the self'. Those who spend all their time challenging the fences never learn how to enjoy the field. Those who live in fear of the LORD find a service that is perfect freedom and a confidence that gives liberty. It guided the Israelite midwives (Exod. 1: 21), under-girded justice (Exod. 18: 21) and the humanitarian laws (Lev. 19: 14, 25; 25: 17) and the monarchy (1 Sam. 12: 14; 2 Sam. 23: 3). It shines in the ideal ruler (Isa. 11: 2 f.). In the New Testament this fear is again man's proper acknowledgement of who he is (Lk. 12: 4 f.; 2 C. 7: 1; Eph. 5: 21).

1 Pet. 2: 17 repeats Prov. 24: 21 and the command 'Fear God' is part of the everlasting gospel (Rev. 14: 7). This fear may be faintly realized and poorly articulated; the use of 'God-fearing' as a term of less understanding or commitment than 'Christian' is an illustration. But invoked or not, God is present and wisdom lies in acknowledging this. The late twentieth century faces a crisis here. The commonsense of Proverbs is welcome, good social cement. But a society that is less and less sure of God finds the basis of morality and community crumbling. Those who put out the stars have nothing to steer by. Christians may rejoice that, invoked or not, God is present and that there is in man a *mind* (see 4: 23) that can respond.

Does Christian faith go beyond Proverbs? Yes, insofar as it gives deeper motivation. The prudential advice of Proverbs seems almost calculating beside the spontaneous self-giving of Christian love. Christ brings not only new motive but new power to carry it out (Rom. 5: 1–5). For all that, Christians need Proverbs if they are to be wise as serpents and harmless as doves; if they are to walk in wisdom towards others, not as fools but as wise. Proverbs still describes the world in which we live. It is a good handbook, even for the Maker's sons.

Authorship and Date

The ascription to Solomon (1: 1) acknowledges him as the principal source and inspiration of wisdom and literature in Israel. During his reign strong ties were formed with Egypt (1 Kg. 3: 1) and there was wide knowledge and free trafficking of ideas among the wise (1 Kg. 4: 31) like the international confraternity among scientists in our own day. The headings ascribe some groups especially to Solomon (10: 1–22: 16 and 25: 1–29: 27, edited under Hezekiah's direction). Anonymous wise men are quoted (22: 17–24: 22 and 24: 23–34). Agur

and Lemuel (30: 1; 31: 1) are also mentioned. Other sayings were apparently added (see on 30: 1). At what stage the final editing was done cannot finally be determined. It is becoming increasingly evident that Wisdom literature was part and parcel of the ancient world and Kidner argues that in the case of Proverbs 'its contents could all have been in existence, though not all gathered into one book . . . in Solomon's lifetime'.

Two other ancient wisdom collections that have been of special interest to scholars are the Egyptian Teaching of Amenemope and the Assyrian Words of Ahikar. The first could well have been earlier than Solomon; the second unlikely to date before 700 B.C. Both show close, even verbal, parallels with the sayings of the wise (22: 17 ff. see notes) and possible allusions elsewhere. The use made of these sayings in Proverbs, however, suggests that the editor felt able to use and modify them very freely, or even that they had been absorbed into Hebrew versions of the common near eastern wisdom and used from thence, rather than slavishly copied from other written collections.

Other commentators argue for revisions, bringing the (predominantly secular) Wisdom from many sources increasingly into line with Israelite theology, and so regarding references to the LORD as later revisions. But while there may well have been minor revision and some rearrangement, there is no reason to doubt that in Israel the wisdom tradition developed and grew in the context of God, the LORD who created all things, directs history, and whose eyes are in every place, keeping watch on the evil and good.

Text and Style

The reader may be apprehensive at so many footnotes (fn. in commentary) and fear that if so many emendations in NIV footnotes are necessary the text must be in a poor state. Difficulties of translation are always great in bridging centuries and trying to get alongside a different culture. In the case of epigrams the difficulties are greater still. Consider our own 'Least said, soonest mended', and similar common sayings. Their power is in their terseness, but that very terseness leaves much to be understood. Most of the Proverbs consist of couplets, metrically balanced pairs consisting of three or four Hebrew words each. The order may not be decisive and verbs may be left out (see notes on 10: 6; 27: 19 for example). Add to this that some of the words may be unusual, perhaps used for the sake of a pun, and the translator's task is difficult indeed. It is not surprising if he resorts to small alterations here and there which seem to make a more balanced saying, or better sense (see *e.g.* note at 12: 12). NIV—and even more so NEB—have felt free to modify not only the vowels, but the consonants quite often, especially if one of the versions (early translations in Greek, etc.) supports the alteration. The AV tried to stay with the Heb. text wherever possible. In the present commentary difficulties of text have been noted, and where NIV or NEB has taken what appears to be too ready a recourse to a version or emendation attention is drawn to other possible solutions.

The style is metrical and epigrammatic. JB captures this well on occasion (12: 24; 16: 1; 21: 4) but finds it impossible to maintain throughout. NIV goes for smoothness and intelligibility, which gets across the antithesis or parallel. A major distinction of literary type can be seen in the type of verb used. The so-called 'Sentence Literature' uses verbs in the indicative, to state the two sides of any idea: 'A soft answer turns away wrath, but a harsh word stirs up anger'. That's how it is. Think about it. By contrast the 'Instruction Literature' uses verbs in the Imperative: 'Do not exploit the poor because they are poor and do not crush the needy in court'. The distinction can be seen clearly in ch. 22 where the style changes at v. 16. The Instruction Literature is expanded in the first nine chapters to give extended advice and exhortation on a variety of topics. Elsewhere it is in the form of a single imperative, followed by a statement explaining the reason for the instruction (see note at 22: 17).

McKane identifies three types among the sentence literature: sayings concerned with the education of the individual for a successful and harmonious life; sayings concerned with the community and the effect on it of good or bad behaviour by individuals; sayings concerned with God, a 'moralism which derives from Yahwistic piety'.

Classification, however, is of largely academic interest, and the present commentary does not attempt to look at the sayings by type, or by subject matter. Proverbs is a patchwork. As the man said when he started reading a dictionary, 'It keeps changing the subject'. And the very change is what makes it such a joy. Over and over again, from every possible point of view, in every possible situation, the basic principles of living are thrust at us; sharply, sadly; cryptically, humorously, directly, suggestively, proverbs are 'friends that feelingly persuade me what I am'. The book is not to be read through at a sitting, as if to follow an argument. It is to be enjoyed in small doses; to be thought over, savoured in the mind; to be worried over until some meaning is grasped; to be remembered as a jog to the conscience or a spice to the conversation.

ANALYSIS

I. INTRODUCTION AND MOTTO (1: 1–7)

The proverbs gives the book its name in Hebrew as in English. **of Solomon** refers to him as principal author and inspiration of such literature in Israel. Heb. *māšāl*, 'proverb', has a root meaning of 'comparison' and is used of both the extended allegory of Ezek. 17: 2 ff. and the colourful simile of 10: 26. It is used also for the evocative catch-phrase (*e.g.* 1 Sam. 10: 12), the moral maxim (1 Sam. 24: 13) or even a taunt (Isa. 14: 4; Hab. 2: 6). The majority of sayings in this book, however, are 'comparisons' in the sense of two statements put side by side either in antithesis (*e.g.* 10: 10, 11, 12, 22)—a contrasting pair to emphasize significant difference—or synonymous (*e.g.* 10: 18)—a poetic repetition—or, less frequently, as a development (*e.g.* 29: 1). All are easy to remember, simplistic even, like moral news headlines. **1, 2.** The purpose of the collection is stated with a fascinating list of key words. **wisdom:** Heb. *hokmāh*, the general term, very occasionally used in the sense of 'crafty' (2 Sam. 13: 3) but in Prov. always in a praiseworthy sense. **discipline:** Heb. *mûsār*, one of the sterner ways wisdom is gained, with overtones of correction if necessary (see 22: 15). **understanding words of insight:** the verb (*bîn*) and noun are both from the root 'to discern'. This is a grasp of the reality of a situation (a Scot might say 'canny'), distinguishing what matters from what is peripheral. **3.** The content of this instruction and insight is spelt out in four large sections: **prudent** (from root *śākal*='to behave oneself wisely' as in 1 Sam. 18: 30) is seen as success and prosperity (17: 8). It has the ambiguity of prudence or 'knowing one's way around' with all the temptation (Gen. 3: 6) or possibilities of growth (21: 11) that phrase includes. Perhaps Jesus' words in Lk. 16: 8 give the taste. **what is right:** Heb. *ṣedeq*, an expression of God's nature, 'that standard by which God maintains the world' (Snaith), and very often linked with **just** (*mišpāt*), a word which has a secular use as custom (1 Sam. 2: 13) but more generally a moral use as pronouncement, such as a judge might make, and pre-eminently God's declared will (Ps. 19: 9

and Ps. 119 *passim*). **fair:** Heb. *mēšārîm*, from a root meaning 'upright', 'even', emphasizes impartiality, which was all too often lacking in the 'justice' of the time. **4. prudence for giving to the simple: prudence:** Heb. *'ormāh*, a word which has 'crafty' connotations in earlier writing (*e.g.* Jos. 9: 4) but has a slightly better value in Prov. (1: 4; 8: 5; 8: 12) and is contrasted here (and at 8: 5) with the **simple** (*pty*) whom we meet frequently in the Psalms (19: 7; 119: 130) and Proverbs—not the moral implication of 'fool' but certainly ill-fitted for survival in real life; shiftless, gullible, almost a 'sucker'. The parallel **young** emphasizes inexperience and rashness that need knowledge (*da'at*, a general word for stored information and experience, possibly 'know-how' and, distinct from wisdom, Ec. 1: 16) and **discretion**, a neutral word describing a capacity to devise whether for good (2: 11) or evil (12: 2).

Not only the simple and young are in mind. **the wise** and **the discerning** will **add to their learning** (*leqah*)—a word connected with 'taking' suggesting that knowledge is to be accepted from God. It is connected with process rather than content of learning—**get guidance. get** (*qānāh*, usual word for 'buy'): see 4: 7 and note.

The section closes with four subjects for study and understanding: **proverbs** (as v. 1), **parable** (the only other use at Hab. 2: 6 suggests 'satire'), **the sayings . . . of the wise**, much venerated in the ancient world, and **riddles** (trick or difficult questions, Jg. 14: 12; 1 Kg. 10: 1, or dark sayings, Ps. 78: 2).

The Motto

7. The advice of Proverbs is summed up in the well-known motto. **The fear** (*yir'āh*) **of the LORD**, as Proverbs will teach us, is no abject dread, but a relationship of reverence, openness and obedience that brings strength and life (14: 26, 27) and is the foundation (**beginning** [Gen. 1: 1]='ground' rather than commencement) of a coherent world-view worthy of the title **knowledge**. As for **fools**, they are all that is opposite to this growing, strengthening relation. They come in three sorts in Proverbs (*kesîl*, *'ewîl* as here, and *nābāl*) but all are characterized by obstinacy, a wilful and insolent refusal to listen to the wisdom of others or the command of God. **despise**: this verb sums up their attitude; the concordance entry for 'despise' illustrates exactly the sort of person Proverbs has in mind (Esau, Gen. 25: 34; Michal, 2 Sam. 6: 16; Sanballat, Neh. 2: 19, Haman, Est. 3: 6).

II. A FATHER'S WARNING AND ADVICE (1: 8–9: 18)
i. Parental instruction (1: 8–19)
8. your father's instruction . . . your mother's teaching: although Proverbs describes a man's world with advice for **my son** (daughters feature only once, 31: 29) the mother occupies a place of honour and respect. The family is a crucial unit of growth, instruction and discipline. In this secure setting the growing youth can gain real adornment and reward (9). The perennial danger is that the alternative will prove more exciting and **sinners entice** (10). The advice **do not give in** is backed by a typical piece of wisdom: their wanton violence (11) and robbery (13) are cut to size and their unthinking folly exposed. Even **birds** (17) can look after their own interest better than can these men who cannot understand that **they waylay only themselves** (18). History since then has only confirmed the truth of v. 19 (see Lk. 12: 15).
ii. Wisdom's appeal (1: 20–33)
Wisdom is personified (as in 8: 1–36; 9: 1–6), adding dramatic power to an urgent plea for attention, and a serious search for knowledge and the fear of the LORD. The appeal is wide and public, **in the public squares at the head of the noisy streets** at **the gateways of the city**, where business and legal affairs brought people together. The **simple ones** (as v. 4) and fools (as v. 7) are joined with **mockers** who feature throughout Proverbs as arrogant mischief-makers. They are reproved for wilful disregard of wisdom's offers (24, 25, 29, 30). The picture is not of an anguished search for elusive truth but of a reckless indifference to the open statement of the truth. The subsequent panic-stricken 'search' will be fruitless (28–30) —a principle which can be derided but not avoided (2 Th. 2: 11 f.). **I will laugh . . . I will mock** (26, and see Ps. 2: 4) is not a cynical indifference to people but the vindication of wisdom in the face of insolent rejection. The element of derision or taunting cannot be eliminated from the OT (*e.g.* Ps. 52: 6 f.) and the desire to do so may reflect a casual attitude to truth rather than real charity.
iii. Seeking and finding wisdom (2: 1–22)
1 ff. The verbs **accept** (1) . . . **store** (1) . . . **call out** (3) . . . **search** (4) are more than the parallelism of Hebrew poetry. They underline the involvement and effort needed both to obtain and retain wisdom. The comparison with **silver** and **treasure** highlights the indolence so often shown to the really valuable. **5.** The **fear of the LORD** (as 1: 7) with its reverence and awe is linked with **the knowledge of God** as God opens his character and purposes to those who seek him.

6. The LORD gives wisdom and again (as in 1: 24) it is God who takes the initiative. He requires of the recipients, not intellectual ability, but moral attitudes of uprightness, blamelessness, justice and faithfulness (7, **his faithful ones**, Heb. *ḥasîdîm*, those who show *ḥesed*, 'loyal love' to the covenant).

In NT 'saints' represents *hagioi* which draws attention to their separated character. LXX used *hagios* to translate the Heb. *qādōš* which describes God's otherness (Isa. 6: 3, etc.) and when applied to people stresses their separation to God. Used of *things* it marks the separation of holy from profane. Proverbs uses *qādōš* 'holy', only twice (9: 10; 30: 3; LXX gives *hagios* both times), and *qōdeš*, 'holiness' once (20: 25 (NIV 'dedicate'), where LXX gives the verb *'hagiazō*, 'sanctify'). In later Jewish thought holiness came to be identified more with obedience and loyalty to the law (*tōrāh*) and less with cultic purity and separation. Thus loyalty to the Law was the hallmark of the Hasidim from whom the Pharisees developed. For Proverbs therefore, *ḥasîdîm* (NIV **faithful ones**) are those who are loyal to God's wisdom. Proverbs uses *ḥesed* ('loyal' to covenant) frequently (3: 3; 11: 17; 14: 22; 16: 6; 19: 22; 20: 6, 28; 21: 21; 31: 26) where LXX uses *eleēmosynē* ('mercy') restricting it to an inter-personal relationship rather than relationship to God. NIV usually translates *qōdeš* in OT by 'holy (one)' (AV sometimes gives '*saints*'), but is not so consistent with *ḥasîdîm*—'faithful' (2 Sam. 22: 26) 'the godly' (Ps. 4: 3; 12: 1; 32: 6), 'saints' (Sam. 2: 9; Ps. 30: 4; 31: 23). As with the Beatitudes (Mt. 5: 3–12) the reward (9) is reward only to those who already seek these moral qualities (see Mt. 13: 12).

The poetry opens out the nuances of pleasure, security and guidance (10, 11).

12. save you introduces another pungent comment on the evil with its particular **delight** and **perverseness** (14, AV 'frowardness', it is the way **evil** twists good things to wrong ends and Proverbs picks out many instances; see 6: 12 f. and note).

16. It will save you from the adulteress: this is the first of several warnings against the **adulteress** (5: 3–23; 6: 20–35; 7: 1–27; 9: 13–18) and **the wayward wife**. Both words are commonly used for stranger, alien (Dt. 14: 21; 1 Kg. 11: 1) but when in the feminine gender as here, likely to mean 'estranged from husband', i.e. an adulteress. She is a 'stranger' also in that she has no claim upon the affection or attention of those she seduces. The reference to the **partner of her youth** would strengthen this view and the forgotten **covenant** would refer to her marriage vows of the law of the covenant (Exod. 20: 14). Less likely is the allegorical view which sees in the passage a rebuke of religious unfaithfulness. The personal degeneration (18, 19) following sexual promiscuity is heavily underlined as a sanction, no doubt often ignored then as now, but remaining a moral fact even if disregarded (see 7: 24–27 and note).

Verse 20 gives the positive benefits of wisdom. **walk:** characterizes the OT view of the godly life. It is a progress, in the company of **good men** on the **paths of the righteous**, with the typical gain and loss—**remain . . . be cut off** (21, 22). It is naïve to dismiss this down-to-earth assessment as either not true to life or outmoded OT materialistic outlook on life. Whatever the NT adds in terms of considerations of a less material nature, there is still impressive evidence that, in general, integrity 'pays' better than treachery, and uprightness better than wickedness, even in human terms. The fact that this may become an unworthy motive is no reason for denying the principle and throughout Proverbs we shall find it over and over again.

iv. The outworking of wisdom (3: 1–35)
The rewards of wisdom and the fear of the LORD figure largely in this account of how the wise father's teaching works out in practice. The blessings are various and incidental—the famous hedonistic paradox that pleasure and well-being come not by being sought but incidentally in the pursuit of some other value. **prolong your life . . . prosperity** (2) **health, . . . nourishment** (8) happiness (13) security (23) confidence (24) as well as more tangible things like **barns . . . filled** (10) and **favour and a good name in the sight of God and man** (4, and cf. Lk. 2: 52; Ac. 2: 47; Gen. 39: 1–4). The outworking of wisdom demands loyalty and determination (3) **trust** (5) and humility (7).

3: 5. Trust in the LORD is the secret of the wise man. It is to be wholehearted and full-time, **in all your ways**—a rebuke to the part-time godliness which does **lean on** our **own understanding** when paths seem familiar. To **acknowledge him** (usual verb for 'know', as 1: 2) is not mere assent but personal awareness of God that leads to obedience and praise (Ps. 100: 3; Jer. 31: 34). **he will make your paths straight** is, again, 'reward' only for those who want what is right (**make straight** occurs again as such a reward in 11: 5; 15: 21 and see Isa. 45: 13). **9. Honor the LORD:** the sacrificial requirements of Exod. 23: 19 and Dt. 26: 9–11 were examples of proper acclaim and respect (Heb. *kābad* as Exod. 20: 12). Our treatment of our possessions may be formal or ceremonial but *can be* an expression of our high regard for God. It is the motive that counts (Mk 12: 41–44; 2 C. 9: 7). **11. the LORD's discipline** is as much part of life for the godly as the filled **barns** (10) and is a mark of caring relationship, as the quotation in Heb. 12: 5–6 emphasizes. The eulogy of **wisdom** (13–20) celebrates its suitability in both man and God. To man **she is a tree of life** (18). For Proverbs as for OT generally, this includes more than length of days. It is a metaphor of quality and fulfilment (19: 23) and a symbol of growth, freshness and fruitfulness. In the LORD, wisdom is seen in his work of creation (19, 20, and see 8: 22–31 and note). **the earth . . . the heavens . . .** and **the deeps** need not be brutally forced into service to show a primitive three-storey cosmology. To the ancients, as to Paul (Rom. 1: 20), many modern scientists or the heavenly company (Rev. 4: 11), creation can defy exact description yet evoke praise.

In everyday life **sound judgment and discernment** affect attitudes and actions in both broad intention and specific deed. **you will go on your way in safety** (23; 4: 26) expresses a popular OT metaphor. The godly life is a steady progress, a characteristic life style—as is the contrary 'way of the wicked' (2: 12; 4: 19; cf. Ps. 1: 1–6)—which need not be disturbed by **sudden disaster** (25) since the outcome is in the LORD's keeping (26). Such confidence is shown in just and considerate living (27, 28, and see Lev. 19: 13), a relationship of trust with **your neighbor** (28, 29; 24: 28; 25: 9) and uprightness (32) which has no need to envy those whose short-cuts of violence, scorn or folly will end only in disgrace (35).

v: The precious heritage of wisdom (4: 1–27)
3, 4. my father . . . taught me: underlining the OT principle that truth and history are maintained through the family. Our age of rapid change could well re-learn the lesson of the unchanging **commands, and live**. So the father urges his son to value his heritage and strive to make it his own. **7. though it cost all you have, get understanding: get** translates the verb usually given as 'buy'. This 'getting' is a costly business and requires not academic ability but a willingness to make an effort, to learn and do what is right. Verses 10–19 develop the OT theme of the 'two ways' (see on 2: 20; 3: 23). **11. the way of wisdom . . . straight paths:** contrasts with **the path of the wicked . . . the way of evil men** (14). In each case there is commitment to a direction, a steady style of life. There is a sharp objectivity about this throughout Proverbs completely different from the modern subjectivity that leaves everyone to choose for himself. Whatever anyone thinks (14: 12), it does not change reality.

The LORD is the ultimate arbiter (see on 5: 21; 15: 9; 16: 2). Jesus uses the figure in Mt. 7: 13 f. Learning is a two-way process. **I guide you . . . and lead you** (11) describes the investment of care and time of the instructor; **accept** (10), **Hold on to** (13), **make level** (26) describe the corresponding involvement of the learner. There is an urgency about the passage which challenges slackness or indecision in moral education. **18, 19. the light . . . deep darkness:** a basic biblical contrast, rich in meaning (Gen. 1: 18; 2 C. 4: 6; Jn 1: 5; 3: 19). The steady growth in the light gives hope and fulfilment; the tragic irony of v. 19b is written over many clever schemes of the wicked from that day to this.

The closing verses (20–27) repeat the need for personal involvement, a complete dedication of heart, speech, eyes and feet in the way of wisdom. The emphasis on the importance of **words** reflects the fundamental message of Dt. 8: 3. It is here, not in material things, that **life** subsists. Hence the urgent plea: **Do not let them out of your sight** (21), **Put away . . . perversity** (24), **look straight ahead** (25), **make level** (26), **Do not swerve** (27). **23. Guard your heart**—this verse does not teach the circulation of the blood (before William Harvey!) but the importance of a constant mind. The **heart** (Heb. *lēb*) is not the seat of emotion or goodwill (as current English 'his heart is better than his head') but the centre of personality, decision, understanding; so NIV sometimes translates 'judgment' (6: 32; 7: 7). Hence **it is the well-spring of life**, for good or ill (Mk 7: 21–23; Phil. 4: 7). This verse could be 'the scripture' Jesus referred to in Jn 7: 38.

vi. The counterfeit and the real in marriage (5: 1–23)
The father again warns his son against the seduction of **an adulteress** (3) and her smooth and alluring speech (see 2: 16 and note). **4. but in the end** puts a major consideration. Instant pleasure or fascination blinds the dupe to the harsh reality. Wisdom weighs not only the immediate gain, but the end (Num. 23: 10; Ps. 37: 37 f.; 73: 17; Prov. 5: 11; 14: 12; and often). **5. her steps lead straight to the grave:** (mg. 'Sheol', AV variously 'grave', 'hell', 'the pit') is the OT antithesis of life, not necessarily with any idea of torment, as NT 'Gehenna', but of futility, inactivity, death (cf. 1: 12; 7: 27; 9: 18; 15: 11, 24; 23: 14; 27: 20; 30: 16). Verse 6 may refer to the pupil ('thou' as AV) or the adulteress (**she**, NIV)—the Heb. tense does not distinguish. In either case, there is a refusal to take heed, an aimless way of life. **she knows it not:** an example of 4: 19 (NEB 'does not care' would be an unusual use of the verb). **7. now then, my sons:** the exhortation widens to include, perhaps, the more settled married men as well as the gormless youth. Unchastity

is folly now and ruin later. Hence **Keep to a path far from her** (8) matches the earlier **maintain discretion**. A continued self-discipline is required. **Your lips may preserve knowledge** (2) and **listen . . . what I say** (7) suggest the power of thought and idea to guide action, as Jesus powerfully taught in Mt. 5: 27–29. Gen. 38: 16; 39: 12 well illustrate the writer's theme. The consequences are spelt out: loss of reputation (9), loss of wealth (10, either because the lawful husband claims damages, or costly presents are wasted on the mistress), depression (11, not necessarily disease; see Ps. 73: 26), bad conscience (12, 13) and public disgrace (14). **9b. years:** NIV follows *MT*; NEB 'honour' follows an amended text. **one who is cruel** occurs at 11: 17; 12: 10; 17: 11. Kidner suggests here 'blackmailer'. By contrast vv. 15–20 celebrate the satisfaction and fruitfulness of true marriage. The pattern **Drink . . . let . . . may . . . may** (15, 17, 18, 19) is best maintained by translating v. 16 as advice rather than question (so NEB 'do not let your well overflow into the road'). The passage then uses the imagery of **cistern, springs, fountain** to describe sexual satisfaction in marriage, rather than the wastefulness of promiscuity. Verses 18, 19 share the OT open delight in the physical joy of marriage (cf. Ca. 4) and this suggests NIV is right in translating **breasts** rather than 'affection' (RSV following alternative vocalization as 7: 18), contrasting more sharply with v. 20. Verses 21–23 link together these prudential considerations with the **view of the LORD. he examines all his paths:** the verb suggests assessment, weighing. God's moral governance is often referred to in this way, as though he watched the inexorable outworking of the **cords of . . . sin** (see 15: 3; 1 Kg. 16: 7, etc.; 2 Chr. 16: 9; Ps. 34: 15). NEB transposes 6: 22 to be read between 5: 19 and 5: 20 but there is no textual warrant for this.

vii. Straightforward living (6: 1–15)
Three vivid paragraphs advise the young man to avoid liability for the debts of others, to work diligently at his own affairs, and to deal honestly. Proverbs is strongly against being **security for your neighbour** (17: 18; 22: 26 f.) or for a stranger (11: 15; 20: 16). The taking of pledges was a natural precaution (Gen. 38: 17), particularly perhaps with alien traders, but lenders in the ancient world could drive hard bargains and Israelite law attempted to control abuse (Exod. 22: 25–27; Dt. 24: 6, 12, 17), but these laws were often neglected (Am. 2: 8; Neh. 5). In an agricultural community, even more than our own, inability to pay could be the lot of the best intentioned, so Proverbs counsels caution. **What you have said** can bring you into **your neighbour's hands**, so hasten and get clear of the obligation (6: 2 f.). This does not mean heartless indifference to

the need of a neighbour (or enemy, 25: 21) but any help should be voluntary and proportional to resources.

6. The **sluggard** is one of the sharply drawn (even over-drawn) figures Proverbs uses to point a lesson (6: 6, 9; 10: 26; 13: 4; 15: 19; 19: 24; 20: 4; 21: 25; 22: 13; 24: 30; 26: 13–16). Shiftless, self-excusing, half-hearted or bone idle, he is the opposite of all that Proverbs understands about getting on with the business of living in a purposeful, organized, thrifty way like **the ant**. For the use of natural history by the wise men of old see 30: 24–31; 1 Kg. 4: 29–34.

12. a corrupt mouth and the wink, nudge and gesture that go with it, provide an excellent example of the perverseness that Proverbs deplores (see 2: 14). The pleasure and security of normal converse are twisted to bring **dissension** among others and **disaster** to the sower. The tragic result of such behaviour comes **suddenly** and **without remedy. A scoundrel** (12) translates Heb. 'man of Belial' (as 16: 27; 19: 28); av 'naughty' gives the sense in its old meaning of naught, nothingness, no-good. Evil is emptiness, absence of worth or good. In NT Belial is used of the devil as opposed to the fullness of Christ (2 C. 6: 15).

viii. Things the LORD hates (6: 16–19)
The OT pulls no punches about God's opposition to evil (Dt. 16: 22; Isa. 1: 14; Am. 5: 21) and his people are called to similar definite attitudes (Ps. 139: 21; Prov. 8: 13; Am. 5: 15). **detestable to him:** expressing the distastefulness and outrage of the things mentioned. The concordance list of the word **detestable** shows this sense of things that violate human decency, community and the basis of life as God intended it. So the **seven** evils destroy society by misusing the good capacities of **eyes, tongue, hands, heart, feet, witness** and confidence.

ix. Further warnings against adultery (6: 20–35)
Verses 20–23 form an extended introduction to serious thought and steady purpose, a readiness to heed **commands, teaching** and **corrections.** (NEB transposes 6: 22 to follow 5: 19; see note on 5: 19.) **23. lamp . . . light:** cf. Ps. 119: 105; these words follow the metaphor of 4: 18 f. and vividly describe the way in which the commandment shows up the true nature of blandishments of the **immoral woman** (NIV follows *MT*; NEB 'wife of another man' follows LXX; a small emendation would give the same formula as 2: 16; 7: 5). It is clear from v. 26 that no casual liaison is intended but a determined **adulteress** (Heb. 'a man's wife'). **Do not lust. . . in your heart** (25) pushes the attention back before the deed, as does NT (Mt. 5: 28; Mk 7: 21; Jas 1: 14, 15). **26a.** NIV is one attempt to make sense of a difficult line; RSV, equally possibly, gives 'a harlot may be hired for a loaf of bread'. **32. a man who commits adultery**

lacks judgment summarizes the torrent of warning analogies in vv. 27–35. As in 5: 10–14, momentary pleasure cannot be compared with lasting disgrace (30, 33), fury and possible revenge by the outraged husband (34, 35) and punishment. **destroys himself:** might allude to the death penalty (Dt. 22: 22) though there is no evidence this was commonly, if ever, carried out. **himself:** Heb. *nepeš*, cf. 1: 18 (AV 'soul'), an inclusive word, not a detachable spirit, but rather 'life force' or 'what makes him a person'. See Mk 8: 36, 37 for similar dificulties of translation in NT.

x. Further warning against the adulteress (7: 1–27)
The theme is developed with a dramatic poem showing how helpless the young pleasure-seeking innocent is to meet the wily wife who fills her idle moments with polished and sophisticated seduction while her husband is away. Hence the urgent plea to **keep my commands and you will live** (2). Moral education that puts all responsibility and decision on young shoulders could profitably learn from this direct, even authoritarian, counsel. Experience may bring mature ability to make one's own judgments (Heb. 5: 14) but meanwhile a firm framework may **keep you** (5) and is not to be derided.

The poem describes the seduction, smooth as a modern advertisement. There is even a religious touch (14). The peace-offering (see Lev. 7: 16) had to be eaten the same day and hence she needed company, and she offers the contemptuous but prudent assurance that the husband is well out of the way. The alluring picture is shattered with the simile **like an ox going to the slaughter** (22). The promised pleasure and love is shown for the tawdry imitation it is. **23. it will cost him his life:** Heb. *nepeš* (see on 6: 32; 2: 18); even if not literally punished with death, he will never be the same man again. 1 C. 6: 12–20 argues the case even more strongly for Christian believers, in a society quite as sexually promiscuous as our own or that of Proverbs'. Custom or condoning cannot make twisted relationships right, or undo the physical and psychological consequences.

24–27. The moral is emphasized again. **Do not let your heart turn to her ways:** don't underestimate the power of a seducing woman (26) but look beyond the passing allurement to the tragic consequences.

xi. Wisdom states her case (8: 1–9: 18)
The introductory section (1: 8–9: 18) ends with a powerful positive statement, gathering up the hints scattered throughout the section (1: 20–23; 3: 13–20). No longer by contrast with the crooked and perverse, but in forthright, direct terms, wisdom claims to fit the universe, to be evidently the key to life and understanding, as

it was fundamental to its creation (22). Wisdom fits man to be truly man (32–36) in open fellowship and contentment (9: 1–6).

(a) Wisdom's call (8: 1–5)
Above the babble of conflicting greeds, **wisdom calls out** (1). To rouse people from their indifference or low-level satisfactions, **understanding** has to **raise her voice.** As in 1: 20, the call is widespread (2, 3): **men.** in general, even **simple** and **foolish** men (5) are urged to pay attention, for this wisdom is no esoteric philosophical system but down-to-earth common sense. It has to do with moral standards (6–14), the purpose and goal of social and personal life (15–21) and a proper response of wonder and worship to the universe around us (22–31).

(b) Wisdom and godliness (8: 6–14)
The description of wisdom has a wholesomeness and refreshing quality like a sea breeze after the stuffy atmosphere of the scheming world. Powerful words drive the lesson home. **what is right:** Heb. *yāšār*, a great OT word, the 'upright' of 2: 7; 3: 32; base of the 'equity' of 1: 3; the standard by which all is judged Ps. 19: 8; 1 Kg. 15: 11, etc. There is finality and objectivity in biblical wisdom which contrasts with the relativistic and subjective morass of much 20th century opportunism. **8. just:** Heb. *sedeq* as 1: 3 note. **9. right:** as 24: 26 (NIV 'honest'); 2 Sam. 15: 3; Isa. 30: 10, the simple, obvious truth, even if unpalatable. **13. hate evil:** see on 6: 16. NEB relegates 13a to a footnote, possibly as gloss from 3: 7 or 16: 6, but there is no MS evidence, and no need to exclude reference to **the LORD** from this expansion of wisdom. Familiar nouns are recalled as wisdom names those who share her house: **prudence** (as 1: 4), **knowledge** (1: 4), **discretion** (1: 4, here pl.), **sound judgment** (2: 7), **understanding** (1: 2) are joined by **counsel** (advice freely offered, but coloured by its source, 1 Kg. 12: 13, 14; Ps. 1: 1; 33: 11; bad men may still have the power to give good counsel, 2 Sam. 16: 23) and **power** (the might or strength to get things done, though floundering without wisdom, Ec. 9: 16) to give a balanced, many-sided tool-kit for dealing with life.

(c) Wisdom and society (8: 15–21)
Most of these qualities are seen in the ideal ruler of Isa. 11: 2 f., a beautiful instance of how things are when **kings reign** and **princes govern** by wisdom. Riches, . . . honor, . . . righteousness, . . . justice, . . . wealth are the rewards of such wise rule (Isa. 11: 4–9). The **wisdom** is the root from which wealth grows and hence more valuable than its fruits. The comparison with **gold** and **silver** (10, 19), generally reckoned the durable and valuable things, highlights the real value of what is intangible and lasting (by comparison with which they are 'perishable', 1 Pet. 1: 18).

(d) Wisdom and creation (8: 22–31)
This passage is often read as if it referred prophetically to Christ, the wisdom of God (1 C. 1: 24) and the word by whom all things were made (Jn 1: 1–3). There is a strong connection in the development of Jewish thought between this passage, through two books of the Apocrypha (Ecclesiasticus 24 and Wisdom of Solomon 7) to Philo of Alexandria (early 1st century) who attempted to join Hebrew and Greek world-views with the idea of a principle of wisdom (*logos*, word), an emanation from God by which the world was made. But Philo's *logos* was impersonal and 'spiritual'. So when John speaks of the Word (*logos*, Jn 1: 1) he reinstates the true Hebrew idea of a personal, creating God and 'uses Philo's word to reject Philo's thought'. This passage achieved notoriety in early Christian argument when Arius (4th century) quoted the LXX in support of his view that Christ, God's wisdom, was first-begotten in the sense that he was first, in point of time, to be created (a point of view that might be borne in mind by any who wish to apply this passage directly to the pre-incarnate Christ).

22. The LORD possessed me: follows Vulg. RSV 'created' follows LXX. The Hebrew (*qānāh* as 4: 7) usually means 'get' as by purchase (Jos. 24: 32), and hence what is got is numbered among one's possessions. Occasionally the getting is by giving birth (Gen. 4: 1) or by (implied) creation (Gen. 14: 19); 'brought me forth' (mg., cf. 24, 25) may follow this idea. The emphasis, as here, is on the fact that wisdom belongs to the LORD, not on how or when it came so to belong. The primacy of wisdom to the creation, **before the world began . . . before . . . before** (25). . . . **before** (26), sets the universe in a fresh light. Here is no random happening but ordered, premeditated development. 'The laws that make the universe a cosmos, not a chaos, are expressions of the divine mind' (Westcott). This gives solidity, significance and pattern to the universe and sets the poet free to rejoice in it with evocative word and metaphor. The detail is to be enjoyed in this way, not pressed into service to support particular cosmologies (as 28, 29 to show a supposed three-tier system—see note on 3: 19 f.—or 27b to prove the earth is round). There are suggestions of bounty (24), meticulous care (26), superabundant power (27b), 'girdled the ocean with the horizon', NEB) and control (29; see Job 38: 4–11; Ps. 33: 6–7). In all this God's wisdom rejoiced, **delighting in mankind**, a unique feature of the biblical account of creation. Man is not God's drudge in the world, but object of favour and joy. 'With joy thou saw'st the mansion where the sons of men should dwell' (Lady Campbell).

(e) **The lesson enforced (8: 32–36)**
The examples have been spelt out, the supremacy and suitability of wisdom displayed, so now wisdom urges **listen to me . . . be wise . . . watching daily at my doors**. This will produce happiness (32) **life . . . and . . . favour from the LORD** (35). The contrast is again drawn between **life** and **death**, growth in harmony with the true nature of things and the rejection that **harms himself** (36) a violation of the personality (AV 'wrongeth his own soul', see Num. 16: 38 and Prov. 6: 32 note).

(f) **Two invitations and their results (9: 1–18)**
1–6. Wisdom's final appeal is cast in the form of an invitation to a feast, open to all, in terms reminiscent of Jesus' parable (Lk. 14: 16–24). Over against this is a final appeal from her rival the **woman Folly** (NEB 'Lady Stupidity') with exactly similar invitation (16) but utterly perverted result. Instead of the open fellowship of the meal shared with wisdom (5) there is the furtive conspiracy of v. 17, **stolen** perhaps suggesting that evil is parasitic upon good; even the pleasures of sin depend upon God's good creation for any enjoyment they may bring.
13. undisciplined: RSV 'wanton' follows amended text. AV 'simple' follows *MT*, using the same word as for her victims. She is no better than they.

Between these two invitations are sandwiched two sorts of person. The **mocker** (1: 22; 3: 34) reappears in all his intolerance of correction, with his companion the **wicked man** (3: 33) who meets arguments with violence. Against this is set **a wise man** who learns and prospers.

Verse 12 is a sobering motto—your attitudes affect *you* most of all.

III. THE PROVERBS OF SOLOMON
(10: 1–22: 16)
After the lengthy introduction we reach the proverbs proper, the catchy couplets that keep wisdom alive in the mind. Chapters 10–22 contain the first selection attributed to Solomon, not arranged by subject, and with occasional repetition, shots for the locker of the young man who has been prepared by the introductory appeals to seek wisdom and live by it. Several of the themes dealt with at length before will appear in specific application, and other maxims are added as the sage ranges widely over human life and society.
10: 1. Our attitudes affect us (9: 12) but others too. Effect on **father** and **mother** is still a valid consideration. The basic wisdom or folly may be seen in industry or idleness (5).
2, 3, 4. General principles for which Proverbs is often derided (see note on 2: 20). Specific cases may seem to contradict, but there is no denying the natural flow of events which the

prudent man will take into account. At a deeper level, **the LORD** has not abdicated control. There is also the hint that all reality is not seen, the **value** and **death** may have deeper meaning than the casual onlooker imagines. AV 'the LORD will not suffer the soul of the righteous to famish', while not dividing *soul* as a separate entity, suggests there is more to man than stomach (Dt. 8: 3); see note on *nepeš* (6: 32). The verses echo a deep-seated human intuition; cf. the popular saying 'no good will come of it'. **6, 7.** The contrast between the evergreen, growing nature of righteousness and the decaying, life-denying nature of wickedness. **Blessings:** a fragrant word, as a glance at the concordance will show. There is richness, fruitfulness and relationship. **violence:** same root as 8: 36 (NIV 'harms'); not necessarily physical assault, but any of the malicious ways in which one may 'do violence' to another. Verse 6b illustrates a difficulty in translating these sayings. Many are carefully balanced pairs of three Hebrew words. The order of the words does not always distinguish subject and object clearly and this has to be inferred by the translator. So RSV gives 'the mouth of the wicked conceals violence', reversing the NIV translation.
8. a chattering fool: literally 'a fool of lips'— a loud-mouth. Folly is often noted for its noise by comparison with the quiet humility of wisdom (19). He who knows least shouts loudest.
9. integrity: brings security in that sense that there is nothing to hide; **he who takes crooked paths** is always trying, ineffectually, to cover his tracks. **10.** RSV follows a sentence inserted by LXX to make a balanced couplet: 'the sly hint brings trouble but the straightforward way is better'. NIV follows *MT* which repeats 8b and seems disjointed.
11. Again the contrast between life-giving abundance and withering evil. Verse 11b repeats 6b. **a fountain of life:** a frequent metaphor (13: 14; 14: 27; 16: 22), pointing to the abundant giving of God (see Ps. 36: 9 and Jn 4: 14).
12. Hatred stirs up dissension: by making everything public, provoking confrontration. **love covers:** not by excusing, but by keeping matters discreetly until reconciliation is achieved (see 11: 13, and Jas 5: 20; 1 Pet. 4: 8 for NT quotation).
13. him who lacks judgment: lit. 'heart', Heb. *lēb* (see note on 4: 23). This character often meets us in Proverbs (10: 13; 11: 12; 12: 11; 15: 21; 17: 18; 24: 30). He won't learn and must be driven like a mule (Ps. 32: 9). Verse 14 repeats the lesson of v. 12. Wisdom acts like love; the fool's babbling has the same effect as hatred.
15, 16. Proverbs speaks realistically of the facts. There *is* strength in wealth, though v. 2 and v. 16 suggests it means wealth honestly earned;

poverty does put people at risk. It does not follow from these facts that one should put confidence in riches (1 Tim. 6: 17) or oppress the poor (14: 31). **16. punishment:** Heb. 'sin' as the contrary of **life** shows the wider meaning Proverbs gives to life. **17.** The metaphor of **the way** (see on 3: 23) emphasizes the folly of refusing correction.

18. LXX has 'righteous lips', possibly because the given text seems difficult. **lying lips** can stand, however, with the general meaning that the hater must either dissimulate or speak his **slander** and look a **fool**.

19–21. An example of wise dealing (see 1: 3; **wise** is the same root as 'prudent'). On restraint rather than prattle see v. 8. When the **righteous** (see on 8: 8) speaks it is worth waiting for and will **nourish many**. By contrast the wicked and senseless show their emptiness.

22. A well-known proverb of trust in God's beneficence. The Hebrew is emphatic: **the blessing of the LORD,** it (alone) **makes rich. he adds no trouble:** this rendering leaves the initiative with God, and is better sense than the alternative suggested in RSVmg.

23. Another contrast between a **fool** and the **man of understanding** is what they enjoy.

24, 25. In both short and long term **the righteous** has security. His ultimate **desire** is to see God and be established for ever. By contrast **the wicked** man faces the future with **dread,** not **desire.** As he fears, **the storm** removes him, but leaves the righteous unmoved (and see v. 28).

26. The **sluggard** (see 6: 6) is as irritating and useless to others as he is a burden to himself.

Verses 27–30 celebrate the certainty that comes from **the fear of the LORD. life, . . . prospect, . . . refuge, . . . never to be uprooted:** contrasting with the emptiness and hopelessness of **the wicked. the wicked will not remain in the land:** see 2: 21. This may refer to the covenant promise of Canaan, though Proverbs is not nationalistic and the phrase may be rather a picture of rootlessness. **31, 32.** The **perverse tongue** (see on 2: 12) is again contrasted with straightforward speech that informs and pleases.

11: 1. The **scales** and **weights** were crude by comparison with modern scales and lent themselves to fraud (Am. 8: 5; Mic. 6: 11 show instances in both northern and southern kingdoms). The proverb underlines the important OT view of **the LORD** as interested in the ordinary affairs of the market place. Dishonesty there is as much **abhorred** as an idol in the shrine (Dt. 7: 25; 25: 13–16).

2. pride is cut to size in Proverbs (13: 10; 21: 24; 16: 18; 29: 23). Here it is the presumptuous attitude, impatient of restraint (the same word as Ps. 19: 13), and contrasts with **humility:** the only other use of this word shows it as a man's proper attitude before God (Mic. 6: 8).

3–9. Seven sayings all contrasting, in different ways, two sets of people. On the one hand **the upright, . . . the righteous, . . . the blameless,** enjoy guidance (3), a **straight** way (5), and deliverance (4, 6, 8, 9). On the other hand **the unfaithful, . . . the wicked, the godless man** reap destruction (3) **are trapped by evil desires** (6), get into **trouble** (8). Individual comparisons are worth pondering. This is no list of 'goodies' and 'baddies' but penetrating study of things that build up and break down the person. Verse 4 turns the screw of 10: 2 tighter—even if honestly gotten, **wealth** will be shown as inadequate in **the day of wrath.** **7.** The Heb. text has suffered in transmission. NEB omits **wicked** (on the view, Whybray suggests, that OT does not teach life after death, rather than on MS evidence) and so reads 'When a man dies, his thread of life ends'. Heb. *tiqwāh,* regularly meaning **hope** (AV 'expectation'), is used once (Jos. 2: 18) for 'cord', hence NEB 'thread of life'. NIV of v. 4 and v. 7 can, however, be maintained and link with other faint clues in OT of hope beyond death (*e.g.* Job 19: 25–27; Isa. 53: 11). Verse 8 is poetic justice as, *e.g.* Exod. 15: 9 f. **9.** The meaning is that **knowledge** is the best way to deal with slander against a **neighbour. The righteous** finds the facts and so **escapes** from being misled, or possibly is able to rebut a slander against himself.

10–11. The social effects of righteousness. The modern reader is likely to imagine the **city** as much larger than it was. The commonest word ('*îr*) can apply to even unwalled small settlements. The word here (*qeret*) often denotes strength (cf. the cognate *qiryāh,* 10: 15; 18: 11). The other main emphasis is on community. Modern sprawling conurbations will not know the same sense of mutual dependence and relationship as 5000 people in a 'city' of 20 acres. Even so the proverb holds true and is another incidental illustration that sound morality meets human need, however much criticized by individuals.

12–13. The way of wisdom seems so obviously right, though against all common practice and inclination. Belittling and talebearing come easily but the reaction of the **man of understanding** and one who is **trustworthy** is clearly better.

14. A common theme of Proverbs (15: 22; 20: 18; 24: 6). Wisdom is not proudly isolated but prepared to take counsel (see note on 8: 14). **15.** See 6: 1–5.

16. NIV translates *MT* but avoids an ambiguous couplet by inserting **only,** assuming that a contrast is intended between grace and mere **wealth** to which no **respect** may belong. Perhaps the meaning is that grace brings reward as surely as violence. NEB and GNB follow an addition in LXX of two lines to give a pair of balanced couplets. NEB also gives an unusual twist ('bold' instead of **ruthless**) to give 'Grace in a woman wins honour, but she who hates virtue makes a home for dishonour. Be timid in business and come to begging; be bold and make a fortune'.

17–19. The consequences of the two ways of life are again contrasted in terms of effects on oneself. As with many proverbs, the comparisons are sharply drawn: **benefits . . . harm, deceptive wages . . . sure reward, truly righteous . . . pursues evil**, and they deepen in meaning as they are turned over in the mind.

20, 21. Another expression of the LORD's assessment of attitudes: **perverse** (AV 'froward'; see on 2: 12), **detests** (see on 6: 16). This assessment works out in the fabric of life, hence the assurance of v. 21—an expression of confidence in final justice as much as an observation of the general run of life. **be sure:** Heb. 'hand on hand', as our 'here is my hand for it'.

22. A sharp opposite to v. 16 and an example of an extended simile unusual in this group of sayings (another example is in 10: 26).

23–31. The end of rival life-styles is described under various heads. Verse 23 gives the overall picture and v. 31 concludes with the usual Proverbs expectation that conduct is requited on earth. This is worked out in the contrast between liberality (24, 25) and miserliness. Cf. 2 C. 8: 8–15, which urges liberality following the example of Christ. The result here, **gains even more . . . poverty**, is a statement of common observation rather than motive, and is still admitted in Phil. 4: 16–19. The monopolist's temptation to make a profit from scarcity contrasts with the public acclaim given to a generous dealer (26). False trust **in his riches** contrasts with natural growth (28); folly and trouble (29) gain nothing but righteousness yields lasting fruit (30).

27. NEB 'if a man pursues evil it turns upon him' (see AV) gives the sense. **30.** RSV and NEB follow Gk. to avoid seemingly harsh use of 'a wise man takes away lives'. NIV **he who wins souls is wise** is at least possible. The phrase 'take souls' can be a euphemism for murder (1: 19), but is also used metaphorically (6: 25). The promise 'you will be catching men' (Lk. 5: 10) would provide a NT parallel. **31.** 1 Pet. 4: 18 quotes LXX of this verse, making **receive their due** 'hard to be saved'.

12: 1. discipline: the instruction (*mûsār*) of 1: 2 with its overtones of correction (3: 11). Proverbs is up to date in its emphasis on the wisdom of accepting correction (15; 9: 8; 19: 25; 6: 23; 13: 18) and the folly of those who 'won't be told' (1: 7).

2. favor: a rich word, including both the benefit to the one favoured (acceptance, as Isa. 58: 5; 49: 8) and the delight of the one who shows favour (11: 1; 12: 22).

3. Continuance and root: a fundamental consideration of Hebrew poetry and wisdom (Prov. 12: 7, 12; Ps. 1: 3; 15: 5; 21: 7; Jer. 17: 7 f.). The figure is continued in the NT (Eph. 3: 17).

4. A wife of noble character (celebrated at length in 31: 10–31) is here commended for the dignity and credit she adds to her husband in contrast to the **disgraceful wife** that is a constant erosion of his position. **noble character** (*ḥayil*) is a wide word, variously translated strong, valiant, rich, great, able. Ruth 3: 11 illustrates the meaning here.

5. plans (cf. 16: 3; 20: 18); **advice** is the 'guidance' of 1: 5, so both words are neutral (see 6: 18). **righteous** or **wicked** men use or abuse these faculties which they have as made in God's image (see Jer. 29: 11; Job 37: 12, and note on 8: 14).

6. As 11: 9. The sense may be either that **the upright** intervenes and **rescues** men who are slandered, or that uprightness is the best defence against slander.

7. See on v. 3; **the house of the righteous** reflects the idea in Hebrew and other ancient cultures of a man's continuance in his posterity (see 2 Sam. 7: 25–29).

8. See 13: 15. The **wisdom** is the 'wise dealing' of 1: 3 (see note). Proverbs either states a general rule or says how things should be in society. 1 Sam. 18: 5, 14–16 (where RSV has 'had success' for 'dealt wisely') shows how mixed things can be. Verse 9 gives a barbed illustration. People see through empty pretensions.

10. A remarkable example of the hedonistic paradox noted at 3: 2; **the wicked** in selfish determination is cruel to the animal that serves him. The **righteous man cares** (=knows, understands, as 3: 6) **for the needs of his animal** and his wholesome regard for even the animal will bring the reward of better service.

11. See 28: 19. A reminder that the world must be used the right way. **He who works his land** follows the divine ordinance of Gen. 2: 15, confirmed after the Fall (Gen. 3: 23). The verb (*ābad*) is the usual word for 'serve', and the concept of 'serving the land' could profitably be revived in our own age with its **chase of fantasies.**

12. Text corrupt leading to widely different translations. RSV takes one emendation ('the strong tower of the wicked comes to ruin') to make a balanced couplet. NIV tries to make sense of *MT*.

13, 14. Two more sayings on one of Proverbs' favourite themes (10: 11, 20, 21, 31, etc.) and another example of the inevitability that links action and result. **trapped . . . fruit:** contrasts the misfiring of a perverse scheme with the flow of action in accordance with nature. Evil backfires; good flows on to satisfaction.

15. a wise man listens: could almost be a sub-title for Proverbs. By contrast the isolation of the **fool** is pitiful. What **seems right to him** cuts him off from seeing the truth, but does not alter it (16: 25).

16. the prudent man: Heb. *'ārûm*, here and at v. 23. He has the 'prudence' of 1: 4 (see note) and so acts for his best interest. **overlooks:** the same Hebrew word as 'conceals'(v. 23); it does not have overtones of hauteur.

17–19. True and false speech are contrasted for social significance in court (17) and endurance (19), and rash and wise words for their personal effect (18). Verse 17 is not a tautology—**a truthful witness** habitually can be relied on in court to give honest evidence. **pierce like a sword . . . healing:** graphically descriptive of the bane or balm that words can bring.

20. Sharply different aims reflect inner **deceit** and the (surprising) opposite **joy** as both motive and outcome. The **peace** is Heb. *šālôm*, also wholeness. NEB catches the fullness with 'seek the common good'.

21. Cf. Ps. 91: 10 where the inference is that the LORD guards the righteous. So here both parts talk about results and not just 'happening'. The pagan Philistines knew the difference between ill-fortune and judgment (1 Sam. 6: 9). **22.** See 6: 17. The contrasting virtue is now given as his **delight. 23.** See v. 16. **24.** The lot of the **diligent** (see 10: 4; 12: 27; 13: 4; 21: 5) and of **laziness** (10: 4, 19: 15, like the 'sluggard' of 6: 6—see note) is developed. Not only is there a difference of wealth (10: 4) but of position. The **slave labor** or corvée (Heb. *mas*) was Solomon's own inglorious introduction to Israel (1 Kg. 5: 13).

25. One of Proverbs' common sense observations about the springs of mood and behaviour (see 18: 14). **a kind word:** appropriate, encouraging, just, such as Solomon's counsellors recommended to the headstrong Rehoboam (1 Kg. 12: 7).

26, 27. The Heb. text is difficult in both verses. **26. is cautious in friendship:** RSV and NEB follow an amendment. NIV, like GNB, tries to make sense of the *MT* 'spy out' (as in Jg. 1: 23) which could mean 'look out for' and gives a balanced couplet. **27. does not roast:** NEB 'puts up no game' and NIV relate the *MT* to two possible roots (NIV choosing a root translated 'scorch' at Dan. 3: 27). RSV follows LXX 'will not catch'. The general sense remains—a further development of slothful and diligent (see v. 24) —satisfaction demands effort of some kind.

28. The first half is clear. **In the way of righteousness** (see on 2: 20) **is life:** this leads us to expect the antithesis of RSV. The Heb. text is obscure and NIV, just as likely, gives the parallel **along that path is immortality.**

13: 1. A reference to **a wise son** (cf. 10: 1) introduces another selection of the father's in-

struction. There is no Heb. verb in the first half of the couplet. NIV supplies **heeds** from Gk. which matches (rather prosaically) the second half.

2, 3. Wisdom in speech. The text of v. 2a is difficult (NIV, RSV, NEB represent different guesses) but there is a clear contrast between fruitful words that satisfy and **the unfaithful** man whose words conceal **violence** (see on 10: 6). **craving:** NIV gives an unusual translation (but cf. Ps. 35: 25), of *nepeš* (see on 6: 32); NEB paraphrases, 'violence is meat and drink for the treacherous' and suggests the inner character of insincerity. Verse 3 follows Proverbs' prudent caution about speech. Rashness can lead to ruin.

4. Another sketch of the sluggard (6: 6). He **craves and gets nothing**. His idleness can't stop him wanting things, so his state is even more pitiable.

5. NIV contrasts the attitude of **the righteous** with how **the wicked** behave. The second half could as well be 'makes offensive (cf. Exod. 5: 21) and **brings disgrace**' (as 19: 26), which directs attention to the 'smear' effects of **what is false.**

6. Another variation on a familiar theme with **guards** and **overthrows** giving the powerful contrast.

7, 8. The ambivalence of wealth is keenly observed. Verse 7 may be a detached observation that appearances can mislead, or a deeper lesson about true riches (Rev. 3: 17). Verse 8 has a double meaning: the poor lack the security wealth brings the rich, but the poor are free from the anxieties wealth brings.

9. A good example of the genius of Proverbs in showing the superabundance which characterizes virtue. **is snuffed out:** not balanced simply by 'will keep burning', but by the more vital **shines brightly** (RSV 'rejoices'). Light is much more than the absence of darkness.

10. An expansion of 11: 2 (see note). **Pride** is arrogantly self-sufficient.

11. Dishonest money: AV, 'by vanity . . . by labour', still gives the modern sense—easy come, easy go.

12. A shrewd observation that has passed into common speech. The modern emphasis on the need for achievement simply picks up a very old fact about human nature.

13. He who scorns, like the insolent (v. 10), appears in his true folly in Proverbs. Here he **scorns instruction**, and this is the root of his attitude to others (14: 21, see note; 1: 7; 23: 22). **instruction . . . command:** the covenant basis of Israelite wisdom.

14. The subtlety of evil with its **snares** is a frequent biblical theme (Exod. 23: 33; Dt. 7: 16; Prov. 29: 6, 25; Rom. 7: 11). The defence is in the **fountain of life** which comes from **the teaching of the wise.**

15. See 12: 8. The second half in RSV 'the way of the way of the faithless is their ruin'—less well known than AV, 'the way of transgressors is hard'—does justice to the treachery (as Ps. 25: 3; Jer. 5: 11; 12: 1) of the faithless. **is hard**: following Gk. Kidner suggests another slight amendment to give 'will not last' cf. NIVmg.

16. expose: catches the ironic situation. Only **the fool** is fooled.

17. When diplomacy was conducted almost entirely by personal **envoy**, the quality of the messenger was crucial. All the modern paraphernalia of communication have not made this ancient wisdom obsolete.

18. The theme runs through Proverbs (1: 25 f.; 10: 17; 12: 1; 15: 5) that **discipline** and **correction** are goods to be welcomed, not affronts to be resisted.

19. Verse 19a is similar to 12b. The second half does not provide a clear contrast, so NEB offers 'Lust indulged sickens a man; stupid people loathe to mend their ways'—but with no MS support.

20–22. The results of association. Choose your friends carefully (see 1 C. 15: 33); **a companion of fools** not only becomes foolish but **suffers harm**, shares **misfortune** and leaves his **wealth** to **the righteous**. The reward of **wise, . . . righteous** and **good** continues to **children's children**.

23. This would be a commentary on the grasping landlord (GNB 'unjust men keep them from being farmed', and cf. Isa. 5: 8). **injustice**: NIV gives the usual sense of the word *mišpāṭ* (see on 1: 3); AV 'want of judgment' could mean that the poor man's patch does not feed him because of his own mismanagement.

24. This much quoted maxim has given Proverbs (and the OT view of the family) a harsh image. It is true Proverbs does believe in corporal punishment—by a diligent parent (19: 18; 23: 14; 22: 15). Proverbs also believes in the caring, supportive family (4: 3, 4) and the discipline is to be seen in this context—as with the LORD's discipline (3: 11 f.).

25. See 10: 3.

14: 2. See 3: 32. The contrast between the **devious** (3: 32 'perverse') and upright springs from radically different attitudes to the LORD. Deviousness (2: 15; 3: 32 and here) has the sense of 'leaving the straight way'.

3. rod: a rare word (see Isa. 11: 1); the sense 'shoot' could give 'pride sprouts from the lips of fools'. If it is taken as a rod of correction, then his words themselves destroy his pride. **back**: NIV requires an unsupported alteration. **the lips of the wise protect them**: as 11: 9; 12: 6.

4. An example of how translation is influenced by what you think the lesson is. *MT* gives 'where there are no oxen, a manger of grain'. The letters for grain could give the adjective 'clean', so NIV **the manger is empty** and AV has 'the crib is clean'. RSV, NEB try to preserve the couplet by accepting an emendation to 'there is no grain', making the first half say the same as the second half. But the *MT* can stand with the sense: you can have no oxen and keep your grain, but the ox will give abundant crops for the sake of what he eats. **5.** See note on 12: 17.

6. A mocker seeks wisdom and finds none: a tragic commentary on the self-destruction of those who will not take wisdom seriously. See on 1: 22–26 and Gal. 6: 7.

7. An example of Proverbs' cool approach. **stay away**: tersely sums up the fruitless situation. **8.** NEB refers both to the effect on the actors. 'A clever man has the wit to find the right way; the folly of stupid men misleads them'. NIV leaves open the question as to whom the fools deceive. The **prudent** (see note on 12: 16—not quite 'the clever' of NEB) will **give thought** (see on 1: 2b) **to their ways**—i.e. their life-style—looking below the surface for the deeper issues.

9. NIV, RSV and NEB give guesses at a difficult text. The verb **mock** is singular. *MT* gives 'fools' and 'sin' (or sin-offering) as the nouns. **goodwill** can be used of acceptance through sacrifice (Lev. 23: 11 and see on 12: 2) so one meaning could be: the sin offering is no good to fools but brings acceptance to the upright. There is, however, a good case for AV 'Fools make a mock at sin' (GNB 'foolish people don't care if they sin') since the pl. noun with singular verb can mean 'every fool scorns guilt (or the guilt-offering)', with the response 'but among the upright there is favour (or acceptance)'. Gen. 4: 7 is a possible illustration.

10. The OT is very much aware of shared emotions and responsibilities—the so-called 'corporate personality' which sees everything in its social context—but there are occasional flashes of individual self-consciousness. There is a depth of **bitterness** and **joy** which is known inwardly and alone (see 1 C. 2: 11).

11. Another example of the general Proverbs view of life (see 10: 2 note). **house . . . tent** may suggest the pilgrim character of the upright, but see Ps. 84: 10.

12. A fundamental commentary on the human condition (repeated in 16: 25). **seems right**: a pathetic epitaph on the efforts of both rash and careful, the arrogant (Rom. 1: 22–28) and the fearful. Human judgment is limited by lack of full knowledge both about present facts and long-term consequences. The humble response of Jer. 10: 23 is more appropriate.

13. The wisdom literature includes a few such pessimistic asides (Ec. 2: 2; 7: 3), an antidote to over-emphasis on pleasure and happiness. But Proverbs does recognize times of joy (*e.g.* 5: 18 f.).

14. Each day adds to the store from which **faithless** and **good** have to satisfy themselves. In Mt. 12: 35, Jesus gave the corresponding outward result. Here the inward resource for the individual himself is emphasized.

15–17. Three words of caution. It is no accident that the stored wisdom of all cultures usually urges pause and restraint. Pause to weigh what you hear (15), what you can safely do (16), where your temper may lead you (17). **A simple man . . . a fool . . .** and **A quick-tempered man** are only too natural.

18. The end of things must be borne in mind. Here (and at v. 24) it is in the figure of reward and acclaim for the **prudent** and wise, while **the simple** and fools reap **folly**. **inherit** (cf. Exod. 23: 30); the Heb. word can be used figuratively of storing up (Jer. 16: 19).

19. Proverbs shares the OT confidence in vindication of goodness—perhaps delayed but ultimately inevitable (Ps. 37: 5 f.). Est. 6: 6–11 would no doubt appeal to the writer as an excellent example.

20, 21. Things as they are and as they should be. Verse 20 is a simple statement of sycophantic society which has not changed much over the years. More serious is the deeper analysis of v. 21. The dislike may be contempt. **despises:** a base word (see on 1: 7 and 11: 12; 'derides' is the same Heb. word), striking at the very root of common humanity (22: 2; Mal. 2: 10; Jas 3: 9) and meriting the apparently harsh rebuke of Jesus (Mt. 5: 22b) and the judgment of v. 31.

22. plot: describes a human potential that can be used for **good** or **evil**. **love** is the steadfast love (Heb. *hesed*), one of the great virtues men can share with God (Ps. 103: 4).

23. A pithy appeal for action rather than words!

24. See on v. 18. **25.** See on 12: 17.

26, 27. Two sayings about **the fear of the LORD**, bringing **security** and **life** (see on 10: 27). The confidence is firmly rooted in the assurance of life and the two verses contrast with the sad v. 12.

28, 35. The first of many sayings about **a king** (16: 10, 12, 13, 14, 15 and many others) perhaps reflecting wryly on Solomon's own experience. His son Rehoboam knew the bitterness of v. 28b (1 Kg. 12: 16 f.), and Jeroboam (1 Kg. 11: 28, 40) ironically knew both parts of v. 35.

29. See note on v. 17. The complete answer to v. 17a is given here. **A patient man** is frequently commended (15: 18; 16: 32) and shares a celebrated character of God (Exod. 34: 6; Ps. 103: 8).

30. Sound psychology! The **envy** is the 'jealousy' of 6: 34 and is the self-destructive way of dealing with injury or want. **A heart at peace**, in a similar situation, brings growth.

31. See v. 21.

32. have a refuge: usual NIV translation for Heb. *hāsāh* which AV usually gives as 'trusts'. The trust which the righteous have even in death cannot be cut out of the OT (see on 11: 7).

33. See NIVmg. If **not** is omitted (as *MT*) the couplet is an expansion, not a comparison. Even among fools wisdom cannot fail to be recognized.

34. A much quoted and penetrating test of national greatness, abundantly attested throughout history. The **disgrace** is the 'poverty' of 28: 22 (*heser*; all versions give this rather than *hesed*, 'loyalty', *r* and *d* are very similar in Heb.).

35. See on v. 28.

Chapter 15 presents more about words.

15: 1. A gentle answer (usual word for 'tender', Gen. 18: 7, metaphorically 'weak', 2 Sam. 3: 39 and see 1 Chr. 29: 1) contrasts with the **harsh word**, and is a good example of Proverbs' desire to 'cool it'. The **gentle answer** need not give away a position. It is conciliatory, not compromising. By avoiding a show of strength it may keep negotiation at a level where true meeting of minds is possible. A text for the *envoy* of 13: 17 (see 2 Kg. 18: 26 for an example) and modern-day diplomats and interviewers too! Col. 4: 5 f. is a NT application.

2. The tongue of the wise: not only instructive but also good to listen to. Proverbs itself shows the quality in high degree, the well-turned, considered phrase contrasting with the **folly** which **fools gush out**.

4. A tongue that brings healing: It is more than the 'soothing word' (NEB), a positive healing (13: 17; 12: 18; 16: 24 use the same word). **a tree of life:** fits this idea of health and provision (as 3: 18, and see Rev. 22: 2) and could serve as a symbol for all who devote themselves to counselling and healing with words. By contrast, perverse, twisted speech **crushes the spirit** as confidence is lost. Another social benefit of wise speech is to **spread knowledge** (7), a positive contribution to stability and community. The parallel of **lips** with **hearts** emphasizes the lesson of 4: 23 (see note).

3. See on 5: 21. **everywhere:** including Death and Destruction (see v. 11).

5. A variant of the theme of 13: 1 with the added hope of still further advance since **shows prudence** could be translated 'will learn prudence' (as 19: 25).

6. This is not a straightforward 'Righteous men keep their wealth but wicked men lose theirs' (as GNB). The **righteous** live happily with their **treasure**, but to **the wicked, income** ('harvest', 14: 4; 'wealth', 3: 9), even if honestly obtained, does not give peace and plenty but **trouble**. Not that the wealth is bad; the wicked cannot cope with it. Lk. 12: 13–31 is a NT illustration. Greed or injustice make matters worse and **trouble** ('*ākar*) has over-tones of the story of Achan (Jos. 7—see pun in Jos. 7: 24 f. and 1 Chr. 2: 7) whose avarice brought trouble to his house. See 10: 2 and note, and 11: 17; 11: 29; 15: 27 for connected sayings.

8, 9, 26. On **detests** see 6: 16 note. **sacrifice . . . prayer:** not necessarily contrasted. Both were acceptable if sincerely given. The LORD's outrage at insincere sacrifice is a familiar prophetic theme from 1 Sam. 15: 22 to Am. 5: 21 ff. Gen. 4: 4, 5 is an illustration. See 14: 9 and note. The way of wisdom and the prophetic word have much in common.

9. way . . . pursue: following earlier symbols of two life-styles (see on 4: 10–19). The two springs of conduct will be seen in the **thoughts** (plans) (26).

10, 12. A progression. He who goes astray needs **discipline** (see note on 1: 2) but **hates correction**, rejects it, and so **will die**. The **mocker** (12) seems the more pathetic in his impatient refusal of the reproof that could save his life. **10. the path:** an alternative word to 'the way' of v. 9, but as it is used once (Jg. 5: 6) of caravan routes (AV 'highways') NEB gives 'main road'.

11. An extension of 5: 21 and 15: 3. **lie open** emphasizes the folly of trying to hide from God. The earlier verses emphasize God's steady watching and weighing of actions. **Death** (Heb. Sheol) (see on 5: 5) and **Destruction** are the abode of the dead where there is no activity or praise (Ec. 9: 10; Ps. 88: 10 f.) but they are not beyond God's knowledge. See Job 26: 6; Ps. 139: 8.

13, 15. Two sayings about the influence of mood. **happy heart . . . heartache** reflect usual Heb. usage of **heart** (*lēb*; see on 4: 23) for the self or central person (cf. 'you are not your usual cheerful self'). It is the inner disposition rather than material surroundings that are really important. **oppressed** (often translated 'needy', as in 14: 21) contrasts with **cheerful** ('good') rather than rich. Phil. 4: 11–13 shows the lesson well-learnt.

16, 17. Two homely applications of vv. 13, 15. The **fear of the LORD** and the **love** make simple things abundantly adequate. The **turmoil** is not the 'calamity' of v. 6 but confusion (as 1 Sam. 14: 20), lacking the certainty and direction that come from **the fear of the LORD**. With v. 16 cf. Mk 10: 23.

14. The *karma* of **knowledge and folly.** Each progresses by its own nature along its own road (Mt. 13: 12).

18. Another instance of Proverbs' advice to 'cool it' (see on v. 1 and 14: 29). Stirring up **dissension** is easy but useless. Mt. 5: 9 gives the contrary virtue.

19. The **sluggard** is contrasted with the **upright** (NEB follows LXX, 'diligent', to give a more obvious pair) because he is basically dishonest in his self-excusing laziness (see refs. at

6: 6). He cannot reverse nature, however, so things go from bad to worse as **thorns** take over.

20. The first half repeats 10: 1, but the second gives a sad view from the other side. The mother's sorrow (10: 1) is pushed aside by the base son who **despises** (see on 14: 21).

21. The man **who lacks judgment** is the same as 'he who chases fantasies' (12: 11); NEB 'empty-headed' gives the sense excellently. His light, happy-go-lucky attitude contrasts with the steady progress towards a goal of the **man of understanding** who **keeps a straight course** (Heb. *yāšar*, see note on 8: 6).

22. See 11: 14. NEB makes the contrast one of time rather than number of advisers: '. . . with long planning they succeed'.

23. Very different from the joy folly brings to the empty-head of v. 21 is the pleasure of making **an apt reply.** The Heb. 'answer of the mouth' (cf. 16: 1) must be interpreted by the context. NEB gives 'a man may be pleased with his own retort' and so creates an antithesis with 'how much better is a word in season'. NIV makes the two parts parallel. GNB conflates the two parts: 'What joy it is to find just the right word for the right occasion!'

24. the path . . . upward gives another clue that life will not end with death. It has been suggested that **upward** and **going down** are later additions and Proverbs says only that the wise man will avoid a premature death, but this is on *a priori* rather than textual grounds.

25, 27. Another parallel with prophetic literature. In spite of its matter-of-fact observation of things as they are (see 13: 23) Proverbs recognizes that **the LORD** is on the side of the threatened poor (cf. Isa. 5: 8 ff.). **27. bribes:** an endemic evil in the ancient world, judging by ancient law codes that prohibit them. The line between 'gift' and 'bribe' may be a fine one and the word used here (*mattānāh*) is more generally 'gift' (Gen. 25: 6; Ps. 68: 18). Here and at Ec. 7: 7 the line to **bribes** is clearly crossed. The more usual word for bribe (*šōḥad*) is used in the law (Exod. 23: 8; Dt. 10: 17; 16: 19) and prophets (Isa. 1: 23; Mic. 3: 11). McKane suggests Proverbs accepts it as 'part of practical wisdom' (17: 8; 21: 14) but those observations can equally be understood in the light of the condemnation here. **trouble:** the *'ākar* of 15: 6 (see note). **26.** see on vv. 8, 9.

28. The heart (Heb. *lēb*; see note on 4: 23) is the spring of what is said (Mt. 12: 34 f.), so this saying amplifies 10: 11, 20, 21, etc. The second half strengthens v. 2b.

29. See on vv. 8, 9. The irony is that the wicked *want* **the LORD** to be **far from** them (Job 21: 14), not realizing their desolation.

30–33. A group of sayings loosely connected by the benefits of openness. **A cheerful look** may be in a friend or messenger who brings

good news. To be open to **life-giving rebuke** introduces you to the stimulating company of **the wise**, and the **humility** proper to **the fear of the Lord** brings its reward of **wisdom** and **honour** (22: 4; 18: 12). **He who ignores discipline** stands out in his self-rejecting folly. **despises:** not the contemptuous word of 14: 21, but 'rejects'—almost 'throws himself away'. See on 4: 32 for **self** (*nepeš*).

16: 1–9. The Lord in charge. All these sayings (except v. 8 and possibly v. 6) pose the question of the relation between man's decision and God's control of events.

Man may plan (1, 9), conduct his own self-assessment (2), behave how he will (4, 5, 7), but in some sense the issue is decided by **the Lord**. Man proposes, God disposes. In common with OT in general, proverbs makes no attempt to solve the riddle of freedom and determinism. In various places both truths are presented as spurs to actions and curbs on human pride. Here the idea of the Lord's supremacy is to reassure and encourage so that you will **commit to the Lord whatever you do** (3, the same idiom as Ps. 22: 8). **the reply of the tongue:** see on 15: 23. This could be decision or final word. Without this all merely human plans are futile as Mic. 3: 7 scathingly observes. **4. his own ends:** the same word as 'answer' (1), with the sense 'to answer the situation'. Things in God's world fit together; there are no loose ends; **even the wicked** are in the plan, raising the problems of Rom. 9: 14–20. RSV is right to give 'its purpose', not **his own ends** (Living Bible, AV 'himself'). It is the cohesive structure of the world that is emphasized, not God's direct interference in events.

It would suit our logic more easily if **a day of disaster** was made for **the wicked**, but the Heb. world-view sees nothing difficult about the converse. Job wrestles with the problem of trouble befalling the *righteous*. **2. motives are weighed by the Lord:** cf. 21: 2; 24: 12; the idea is of a norm, measure in general (as Exod. 5: 18) rather than specifically referring to weight. It is God's norm that matters, not how a man judges. There is no need to force an allusion to the Egyptian God of Wisdom, Thoth, weighing the hearts at death.

6. Through love and faithfulness (see 14: 22) **sin is atoned for** uses the standard word for **atone** (*kāpar*, Lev. 4: 20, etc.). This is not to put the onus for release upon the offender, nor to belittle ritual, but to emphasize the sincerity of attitude which is the core of true religion; as in Mic. 6: 6–8. By such fruits, too, the truly repentant are marked out (Lk. 7: 44–50). **avoids:** NIV is strangely inconsistent in translation of this word, giving 'shun' (3: 7), 'turn from' (22: 6); **avoids** (as in 13: 14; 15: 24; 16: 6) is less definite and obscures the decision and

action involved. It is definite rejection, not skirting round, of evil that **the fear of the Lord** requires.

7. The man who is right with God becomes a centre of reconciliation. **peace:** Heb. *šālôm*, the wholeness and harmony which spreads from the individual to wider influence in society (Jas 3:18).

8. Another **'better . . . than'** saying that would go well with 15: 16 f.

10–15. A good kingdom. God's rule in human affairs is mediated through the ideal **king**. The Heb. ideal king was no autocrat, but God's appointee, God's gift to the people, and himself God's servant (Dt. 17: 14–20). In such a condition his decisions and **justice** will be reliable (10), trade will be justly administered (11), **righteousness** will give stability (12; cf. 14: 34), true men will gain their just respect (13) and his **wrath** will make people take notice (14); **life** and **favor** will flow from his presence (15). **10. speak as an oracle:** the only favourable use of Heb. *qesem* ('divination', Dt. 18: 10), it must take its sense from the context here (see 1 Kg. 3: 16–28 for an example). Ps. 72 shows similar hope for ideal kingship and Isa. 32: 1–8 gives it expression in the Messianic hope.

16. get wisdom . . . choose understanding: see on 4: 5, 7. Such 'getting' needs purpose and readiness to spend effort. The comparison **better** repeats a general theme (see 8: 10 f.).

17. avoids: see note on v. 6. **The highway** (as Num. 20: 19, cf. 15: 10 note) has a metaphorical use as an open, straight way that gives security and hope (Isa. 11: 16; 35: 8). The second half is no mere prudential advice to 'keep out of trouble' (NEB 'watch your step and save your life'). **guards his soul** (*nepeš*): a broad phrase. Ps. 121: 7 f. has the flavour, which might include our phrase 'maintains his integrity'.

18, 19. A plea for humility, both by the oft-quoted observation of v. 18 and the **better . . . than** saying matching 15: 16, 17. **the oppressed:** Heb. *ʿanāwîm* (14: 21; 15: 15; 22: 22; 30: 14; 31: 9); those who are not only lacking in financial means (as is implied by the alternative word, *rāš*, 14: 20; 22: 2) but also in self-regard. The modern emphasis on powerlessness and underprivilege is close to the OT view. God is on the side of the poor (Ps. 140: 12; 34: 6) and against their oppressors (Isa. 3: 15). Jesus' words in Lk. 6: 20 are an apt though surprising summary.

20. NEB creates an antithesis with 'The shrewd man of business will succeed well but . . .'. NIV **whoever gives heed to instruction** is equally likely, and heeding the word then gives rise to the trust of the parallel second half.

21, 23, 24. Taken together these sayings give a picture of considered and persuasive speech;

good ideas, well conveyed. **promote instruction** (*leqaḥ*, learning, as 1: 5; see note) refers to the learning process, rather than what is learnt. It can have a sinister meaning (7: 21 'persuasive words'); 'taking words' would preserve the ambiguity and leave the context to decide. On its own v. 21b could be prudential advice to the salesman, but vv. 23, 24 give a fuller view. **sweet** and **healing** (see on 15: 4) are happily blended in **pleasant words**. What is good for you can be enjoyed too.

22. Understanding (*śekel*, 'wisedealing'; see on 1: 3) is the *giving heed* of v. 20 and joins the list of attitudes that make for life (10: 11; 13: 14; 14: 27) while the **folly . . . of fools** is their own rebuke. **25.** See on 14: 12.

26. A realistic, if unromantic, view of work. The converse is given in 21: 25. OT and NT both take such a view, acknowledging the need for labour, but resisting its exploitation (Dt. 24: 14 f.; Prov. 20: 13; 1 Tim. 5: 18; 2 Th. 3: 10). In a wider sense the saying might apply to less material incentives. For some 'fame is the spur'. **appetite** is another unusual translation of *nepeš* (see on 6: 32); cf. our 'inner man'.

27–30. Ways of causing trouble (see 6: 12–14). **A scoundrel** (see 6: 12 note), **. . . A perverse man, . . . A violent man** and the shifty secretive man all contribute to the breakdown of trust, friendship and peace. Whether by bitter invective (27), quiet slander (28) or the swashbuckling that entices (29: see 1: 10), society is weakened. **plots:** the usual Heb. word for 'digs' as 26: 27, so NEB 'repeats evil gossip'—'digs up trouble'. **30. He who winks:** the furtive gesture should put you on your guard.

31. Gray hair (='old age', Gen. 15: 15) was given respect in the ancient world (Lev. 19: 32). The second half repeats the conviction of 3: 2 (see note).

32. A striking simile reinforcing the lesson of 14: 17, 29. Proverbs is not a military manual and does not have much to say about the **warrior** (*gibbōr* as in 1 Kg. 1: 8, etc.). It does know a lot about human nature and the difficulty of self-control. To control the **temper** needs both the determination of **a warrior** and the wit of **one who takes a city.**

33. The chapter ends where it began with God in charge. **The lot** (Heb. *gôrāl*) is nearly always used in a ceremonial setting to discover God's will (Lev. 16: 8, etc.; 1 Sam. 14: 41 NIVmg gives a fuller instance). The other, later, usages where it seems to apply to secular setting still have overtones of God's control (Jl 3: 3; Jon. 1: 7). The practice was accepted in NT times (Ac. 1: 26) but not, apparently, after the coming of the Spirit—though we are not told exactly *how* 'the Holy Spirit said . . .' (Ac. 13: 2). **but** makes the proverb a riddle; it could be 'and', so making a straightforward statement: that's how guidance comes.

17: 1. feasting (Heb. *zebaḥ*, as in 7: 14; 15: 8) is the usual word for sacrifice of peace-offering (cf. mg Lev. 3: 1, etc.). Family or community festivals were closely linked with worship (1 Sam. 20: 6) which could be mixed with strife, then as now. The saying may simply contrast **strife** with **quiet**, or, following Proverbs' reserve about ritual, be suggesting that quiet meditation would be better than a noisy 'religious' occasion. **2.** See 12: 24. **A servant** could have considerable influence and certainly **rule over a son** during the latter's minority. There is no OT law to support the second half, though it may well have happened in celebrated cases and given rise to the proverb, a welcome acknowledgement that ability could match privilege.

3. See 16: 2. **the LORD tests the heart:** not to catch out or condemn, but like the workman who refines **silver** and **gold**. The simile is a hopeful one for the individual (Ps. 139: 23; Job 23: 10). For the nation there was judgment (Jer. 6: 27–30) but later hope (Zech. 13: 9). The same simile appears also in NT at 1 Pet. 4: 12 f.

4, 7. A deep-rooted principle of character and result. **A wicked man** and **a liar** respond to their own sort; **Arrogant** (mg. Eloquent) and **lying lips** are similarly incongruous to **fool** and **ruler** respectively.

5. He who belittles (11: 12) and despises (14: 21) may go on to oppression (14: 31) or be one who **mocks the poor.** The insult is the same. To be glad at calamity is an all-too-human failing. It was curbed by the law (Exod. 23: 4 f.) and Jesus' teaching goes even further and requires positive help (Mt. 25: 31–46), as does 14: 31b.

6. The reciprocal regard of old and young is an ideal that needs restatement amid talk of a generation gap. The vigour and vitality of the **children's children** are the continuance of the old man's life, and his experience is a resource in their development.

8, 15, 23. See note on 15: 25, 27. **A bribe** is the usual force of Heb. *šōḥad*—a 'gift' to obtain favour beyond one's rights, or, more bluntly, **to pervert the course of justice** (23). Proverbs usually takes the line that crime does not pay, though here (8) as elsewhere there is the realistic observation that sometimes crime seems to pay—at least for a time (14: 12). **a charm:** NEB 'works like a charm', conveying the smoothness of corruption. The receiver is even more directly condemned, by **the LORD** (15) and by his own secretiveness (23; 21: 14).

9–14. Personal relationships develop along clear principles. **9. He who covers over** (cf. 10: 12) an offence seems weaker, but keeps **friends.**

10. A rebuke may be less dramatic than **a hundred lashes** but achieves more positive results. **11. rebellion:** easy to stir up, but the violence escalates as **a cruel official** is **sent against him**; better stop at **the beginning** (14). The unpredictability of the **fool** makes him a greater menace than an enraged animal (12). The perverseness that returns **evil for good** (13) brings its own judgment (see 2 Sam. 3: 26–29; 12: 11–15 for two examples in David's life).

14. like breaking a dam makes good sense of an uncommon verb (2 Chr. 23: 8 'dismiss'= let go) and there seems no need for NEB's unusual crime, 'stealing water'.

16. A down to earth recognition that teaching can be wasted on **a fool**. This is not a snobbish elitism, because (as always in Proverbs) the fool gets himself into this situation by his own stubbornness. **he has no desire:** reflecting his lack of will rather than lack of ability.

17. A friend (neighbour) is valued for his constancy. Proverbs knows all about fickle friends (18: 24), sycophantic friends (19: 4), but also the strong and true friends (27: 6; 27: 17 NIV 'another') who really **loves**. The family support is most welcome, and most noticeable in **adversity**. A proverb for today when family and neighbourhood are threatened by mobility and individualism. **18.** See on 6: 1 ff.

19, 20. As in vv. 9–14, a way of life brings its consequence; **sin** ends in **a quarrel**. Verse 19b gives the same lesson in a cryptic way: **builds a high gate** can symbolize many attitudes that bring **destruction**, the ostentatious pride of Nebuchadnezzar (Dan. 4: 29–32), the selfishness of Jehoiakim (Jer. 22: 13–19) or the proud display of Hezekiah (2 Kg. 20: 12–19). The **perverse heart** and **deceitful tongue**, too are subject to this overriding providence, and 'come to no good' (NEB).

21, 25. See on 15: 20. **a fool for a son** (Heb. *kesîl*) and a **fool** (*nābāl*, see on 1: 7) are both a loss to themselves and a grief to others. Parental grief over unfulfilled hopes is an old sorrow. **22.** See on 15: 13, 15. **23.** See on v. 8.

24. No one drifts into wisdom: **keeps . . . in view** describes both the determination and the concentration required. **a fool** lets his attention wander aimlessly.

25. See v. 21. The **grief** here is the 'annoyance' of 12: 16 or 'ill-temper' of 21: 19. The relationship causes friction as well as sorrow.

26. The Heb. of this verse begins with 'also' (or 'even' as v. 28) as if this followed a similar proverb, perhaps v. 15 or (as Kidner suggests), 18: 5. **innocent** refers to character, **officials** to rank (as 17: 7, 'ruler'). The principle may seem obvious but every human administration needs reminding of it, from Dt. 1: 16 ff. to 1 Pet. 2: 14. One of the crises of our own time is how to establish such moral common places in the absence of the fear of the LORD.

27, 28. More advice to 'cool it' (see on 15:

1; 16: 32). **with restraint** (as 10: 19) deals realistically with his human nature (Jas 3: 3–10). **Even a fool** can earn some credit by silence (a proverb of international currency).

18: 1. Various translations represent various guesses at a difficult text. **pursues selfish ends:** Heb. 'seeks desires'—RSV, NEB follow Gk. to get a rare word, 'pretext', (as in Jg. 14: 4 where the LORD sought an 'occasion' against the Philistines). The meaning is then that the estranged or isolated person makes any excuse to break with others. GNB paraphrases *MT*: 'people who do not get along with others are interested only in themselves' (which seems rather trite); JB 'Who lives by himself follows his own whim'. The proverb, like the behaviour of those who are **unfriendly**, is difficult to understand.

2. airing his own opinions: Heb. *lēb*, 'heart', 'mind'—a subtle dig at the self-revealing nature of foolish talk. The **fool** 'declares himself' by his chatter.

3. This could be a parallelism, observing that wicked or shameful behaviour earn the contempt of society. But **contempt** is the base 'despising' of 14: 21, so the first line could be a 'What goes with what' saying (as 17: 19 f.). The second line then contains a backlash— contempt is part and parcel of wickedness, 'but' (equally possible as **and**) so do shameful deeds (**shame**) and public **disgrace** go together.

4, 6, 7, 8. More about words. They can be **deep waters** (see 20: 5) that hide as much as they show; a spring or **fountain** feeding a river at which all can drink (**bubbling brook** is too poetically dramatic for Heb. *naḥal* which is used for the 'brook' Kidron and similar watercourses). NEB reverses the phrases in v. 4 to give a parallel to 15: 2, 28. Foolish words bring **strife** to others (6) and **undoing** to oneself (7). The fascination of malicious gossip shows words at their most subtly destructive (see 16: 28; 26: 20)—like the leisurely relish of a delicacy they are slowly absorbed in the mind. **choice morsels:** from a Heb. root used only here and 26: 22. AV 'wounds' connects with it a different root meaning 'burn'.

9. Heb. begins with 'again', 'even', suggesting that this followed a similar saying. It carries the condemnation of the sluggard even further (13: 4). His idle refusal to produce his share puts him in company with the positively destructive. **one who destroys:** a strong phrase (AV 'great waster'), an example of the varied use Proverbs makes of Heb. *ba'al*, from the simple 'man' (22: 24) to 'owner' (3: 27 RSVmg, and even 'owner' of a wing in 1: 17!). In 12: 4 and 31: 11 it is 'husband'. Here and in 24: 8 the force 'master' fits well—master-waster, master of mischief. It is in this sense of 'master' that the word named the Canaanite god Baal.

10, 11. Two sorts of security. The sayings contrast the true **strong tower** with the imagined refuge of **wealth** (**safe . . . unscalable** translate the same Heb. word, so the contrast is sharpened). **The name of the** LORD signifies his attributes and character.

12. See 15: 33; 16: 18.

13. General advice to think before speaking (cf. v. 2) but particularly against prejudiced or thoughtless verdicts by judges.

14. See 15: 13. Another ancient observation of the power of mind over body. **A man's spirit** (Heb. *rûaḥ*) is sometimes indistinguishable from his 'self' (*nepeš*, as in 6: 32). When they differ, *nepeš* is 'life force—what makes him alive' and *rûaḥ* is 'driving force—what keeps him going'. **sickness** can be transcended by the determined will, but a **crushed spirit** lays bare inherent human weakness. Where it is the result of repentance, it is acceptable to God who can give healing (Ps. 51: 17).

15. Knowledge grows. See Mt. 13: 12.

16–18. Ways of settling dispute. **gift:** Heb. *mattān* (see on 15: 27), the neutral word but the context here plainly shows it gets quick attention. When the **case** begins, first impressions can mislead, before **another** has opportunity for cross-examination—a specific example of the general principle in v. 13. **the lot . . . settles** (18): see on 16: 33. This is the only reference to such settlement in private suits. It is a problem of all societies to develop legal systems that settle legal issues **between strong opponents**. If they do not (as here) accept God's judgment (as witnessed by **the lot**), there must be some other principle regarded as superior to both contenders, and this is hard to find.

19. Half a dozen different translations reflect an uncertain text. RSV, JB, GNB accept an amendment based on Gk. to give 'helped'. NIV, NEB and AV attempt to make sense of *MT* with **'An offended brother'** and there is a good case for the resulting parallel. The most difficult rifts to heal are those within the family.

20, 21. An expansion of 12: 14 gives a cryptic saying. **a man's stomach** suggests that v. 20 refers to one who talks for a living, as NEB 'his lips may earn him a livelihood'. But taken with v. 21 there is a hint of both the seriousness (**life and death**) and the unavoidable consequences of speech. So GNB gives 'You will have to live with the consequences of everything you say'.

22. Proverbs has high praise for a good **wife** (5: 18; 12: 4; 31: 10 and see note on 14: 1). **receives favor from the** LORD echoes 8: 35 and with 19: 14 shows that a successful match is God's gift, as at the first (Gen. 2: 22 f.). Paul recognized the overriding consideration, 'only in the Lord' (1 C. 7: 39). NEB 'earns' for **receives** obscures this.

23. Not only the content but the manner of speech is worth comment. The saying notes objectively the vast difference of attitude springing from the division of **rich** and **poor**—a difference that seems stupid in the light of 22: 2; 1 Sam. 2: 7, and far from the grace of the gospel (1 Tim. 6: 17 f.).

24. The Heb. is difficult. RSV changes one letter to read 'these are' for **a man of**. For **may come to ruin**, RSV follows Gk. instead of *MT* 'will be broken'. AV 'a man who has friends must show himself friendly', makes reasonable sense of the first line, but then the second half is a weaker antithesis. **a friend** (line 2): lit. 'one who loves', a stronger word than the 'neighbour' of line 1 NIV **companions**. Also **sticks closer** is a strong word (used of Ruth; Ru. 1: 14), so it would seem that the first line should be some foil for a statement in the second line of true loyalty from a real friend. Driver suggests 'There are friends who do nothing but chatter, but . . .'.

19: 1–3. Folly exposed. **Better** (1)—but not necessarily 'better off' (Kidner). This puts the record straight from 18: 23; in fact NEB follows some MSS to change **fool** to 'rich' (as in 28: 6) to make the reversal even plainer. The contrast, however, is at a deeper level of personal quality. Not just the 'honest . . . lying' antithesis (as GNB) but **blameless** (as 2: 7; 10: 9 integrity, openness, simplicity in the best sense, Gen. 20: 5) against **perverse** (as 2: 15, devious, furtive, relying upon duplicity). Verse 2 begins in Heb. with 'also', expanding the 'better' of v. 1. **knowledge:** bringing caution and sound judgment which will be missed by hasty action. **miss the way:** accurately gives the meaning of a common Heb. word for 'sins'. But fools never learn. When the inevitable **ruin** strikes, it is **against the** LORD (emphatic in Heb.) they rage, instead of learning their lesson.

4–7. Relationships gone wrong. Another rider to 18: 23 f. on how **wealth** distorts relationships. The pseudo **friends** (4) desert the **poor** for the wealthy—whether he is honestly generous (6) or more ambiguously **gives gifts** (see on 15: 27)—while the **poor man** (7) is deserted even by his family. In this context, v. 5 could imply that the **false witness** was bribed. Such perversion of justice would destroy society and so cannot **go unpunished**. It was in this context that the famous 'Eye for an eye' was given (Dt. 19: 16–21). The third line of v. 7 can be a further sorrow of the poor man. NEB follows Gk. to add another line and make a separate couplet: 'Practice in evil makes the perfect scoundrel; the man who talks too much meets his deserts.'

8. He who gets wisdom: lit. 'gets heart' Heb. *lēb*; see on 4: 23, 10: 13; 17: 18 RSV 'judgment'; 15: 32 'understanding'. Perhaps 'common-sense' or 'a sound mind'. The saying repeats the profit from such an attitude as against the self-destruction referred to in 8: 36. Verse 9 repeats v. 5. **10.** See 17: 7; 26: 1 for other

sayings about what is **not fitting**—innate repugnance to social misfits. The idea of 'what
is fitting' is part of the equipment of the wise
man in many cultures and is one of the voices
of experience that must not be lightly dismissed. To describe it as 'conservative' or 'inarticulate' does not lessen its authority.

11, 12. See 14: 29. Men reflect the character of
God when they show **patience** and **overlook
an offence.** Such magnanimity is prudent
(**wisdom**) but also morally elevating (**his
glory**). So the **king** is reminded (12) that **his
favor** may gain greater result and renown than
his **rage**—something Rehoboam might have
learnt with profit (1 Kg. 12: 6–18).

13, 14. Happy and unhappy families. The grief
of 17: 25 may become **ruin** if the foolish son
handles any of the estate. The **prudent wife**
(see on 18: 22) is contrasted both with the
'nagging wife' (13, NEB) that wears a man
down, and also with 'things' that are **inherited.** She is a special gift **from the LORD.**
The two halves of v. 13 seem ill-assorted. Each
half has a proverb to itself (17: 23; 27; 15).
Wives have been known to nag the father over
the behaviour of foolish sons.

15. Laziness is a characteristic of the sluggard
(see 6: 6) from which the Heb. noun is formed.
The **shiftless man** is slack (10: 4, same Heb.
as **shiftless**) and even deceitful (Ps. 120: 2).
Here he goes hungry; in Ec. 10: 18 uncomfortable. His troubles are always slightly over-
drawn, adding humorous point.

16–19. God's word in life. Verse 16 is a variation of 13: 13. The 'respect' of that verse
leads to obedience in the one who now **obeys
instructions,** to his own well-being (cf. v. 8).
The grim alternative is given in v. 16, **will die.**
The principle is worked out in three areas—
the underprivileged, the family, the violent.
17. kind to the poor: the beneficent provisions
of Dt. 15: 10 f. would have brought joy to
giver and receiver alike. **18. Discipline your
son for in that there is hope:** before he gets
to the desperate stubbornness of Dt. 21: 18–
21.

18b. NEB 'be careful not to flog him to death'
gives one meaning; the other is that failure to
discipline may destroy him.

19. A hot-tempered man ('a furious man') is
likely to fall foul of the laws against violence
(Exod. 21: 18–27) with their **penalty,** and it is
useless to help him out.

20. Either a reminder of the importance of
the end, or a heading to a fresh collection of
sayings.

21. A reminder of God's providence. See on
16: 1–9.

22. Various translations show a difficult text;
lit. 'A man's desire is his loyalty'. NIV makes
good sense and adequate balance with the
second half (see 19: 1).

23. The fear of the LORD leads to life: in
modern jargon it is 'life-orientated', not the
inert tradition its critics imagine. The second
half is confused (lit. 'full will remain will not
be visited by evil'). NEB 'he who is full of it will
remain untouched by evil' gives the sense and
with the first half matches the NT view (1 Tim.
4: 8).

24. Another pen-sketch of **the sluggard,** too
idle even to eat and a symbol of those who start
an enterprise and lack determination to finish
(Lk. 14: 29). NIV rightly gives **dish** (the word
occurs in 2 Kg. 21: 13) rather than AV 'bosom'
(which suggested he was too lazy to cover his
mouth when he yawned).

25, 29 (and see 21: 11). Proverbs endorses the
'example' or 'deterrent' use of punishment, as
evidenced in the law (Dt. 13: 11) and included
in NT (1 Tim. 5: 20). The biblical view that
judgment is God's (Dt. 1: 17) gave a strong
base to recognize both the offender's guilt and
his dignity as a person, and also the need to
reinforce standards. Without such a base, modern penology wobbles between 'making an
example', 'teaching him a lesson' and 'helping
him back into society'. The way of reasoned
correction is of course ideal, but only works
with **a discerning man.** Proverbs deals realistically with life (29; 10: 13; 17: 10). **learn
prudence:** see on 1: 4. This is a general use of
the word and there seems little need for NEB's
unusual 'he resents it like a fool' which gives a
different antithesis altogether.

26, 27. These unlikely sounding activities of
the shameful **son** appear to relate to an attempt
to take over the family estate. So JB gives 'He
who dispossesses his father and drives out his
mother'. The **shame** and **disgrace** (see 13: 5)
are the worse for being caused by **a son** and
are more than the disapproval of society. The
use of the word in Isa. 1: 29 f.; Ps. 71: 24 gives
a hint of a more personal loss. Verse 27 may
be a comment on v. 26.

28. Another comment from the lawcourt (see
on 12: 17; 14: 5; 25: 18). **A corrupt witness**
(Heb. 'witness of Belial'; see 6: 12) **mocks at—**
and makes a mockery of—**justice,** as the base
fellows ('sons of Belial') worked Jezebel's foul
will on Naboth (1 Kg. 21: 10). **29.** See v. 25.

20: 1. The temperance slogan. As a glance at
the concordance entry for **wine** will show, the
OT knows of both joy (Ps. 104: 15) and sorrow
(Gen. 9: 21) through **wine.** In a culture where
it was a normal beverage, it was specifically
forbidden to priests on duty (Lev. 10: 9) and
Nazirites (Num. 6) and drunkenness was a
well-known hazard. **whoever is led astray:**
not only **is not wise,** but can work social havoc
and disaster (Isa. 28: 7 f., RSV 'stagger from
wine', is the same phrase as here). Proverbs
gives nine references out of ten to support the
temperance lobby and those who plead for

'responsible use' should be as balanced as the OT in their awareness of human frailty (see 23: 29–35). Eph. 5: 18 gives an even better way. Verse 2 repeats 19: 12a and recommends appropriate caution.

3. Common values overturned again. The quarrelsome loud-mouth is a **fool**. The man who gives **strife** a rest (**avoid** is from the same word as 'Sabbath'!) is not a weakling, but shows **honor** (as in 3: 35; 11: 16; 15: 33 where also we see values turned right way up).

4. **The sluggard** finds the world a hard place, but seems foolishly hopeful enough to seek **at harvest time. looks:** the usual Heb. word for 'ask'; perhaps he is begging for help from his neighbours, with the same response as the foolish girls in Mt. 25: 8 f.

5. Wisdom is not always on the surface; you have to **draw** it **out** and this needs the **understanding** that Proverbs is all about. The **man of understanding** (*t^ebûnāh*, from the same root as 'to understand words of insight', 1: 2 note) treads his discreet way through Proverbs and is worth a study on his own (15: 21; 10: 23; 11: 12; 17: 27; 3: 13 ff.) He **will draw out** the **purposes**, but will still need to assess it, because **the purposes** are the 'counsel' of 8: 14 (see note). This verse does not mean that everyone is a well of wisdom waiting to be tapped —contrary to some theories of education.

6. A proverb for advertisers! **unfailing love** (*ḥesed*) and **faithful** (*'^emûn*, cf. 'amen' in NT) are two great OT words of reliability—the loyal love that keeps the covenant and the steady (Exod. 17:12) dependability that undergirds society (12:17 'honest') and delights the LORD (12: 22 'faithfully').

7. The entail of good, as of evil, is very real to the OT (Exod. 20: 5 f.). Our hurrying age could well ponder the long term effects of character more deeply. There is more to be left to the children than money.

8. As with the 'city' of 11: 10 (see note) the modern reader is likely to underestimate the influence of the **king to judge**. 1 Kg. 3: 16 shows that even two harlots had immediate access to Solomon's judgment, so the ability to assess **with his eyes** was a most powerful factor. While there are obvious limits, those who deal face-to-face with people develop skills of assessment beyond the spoken evidence.

9. This humble confession contrasts with the complacency of 16: 2. Only God assesses truly (5: 21; Ps. 19: 12) as only God can forgive.

10. See 11: 1.

11. The OT has a great realization of the potential of **a child**—Heb. *na'ar* can be anyone from a baby (1 Sam. 1: 22) to a young man (1 Sam. 14: 1). They are not mini-adults but at each stage show their character by their **actions**. JB 'play' is a pleasant suggestion though hard to justify from the text. A case could be made for 'from infancy' (instead of **by his actions**). The proverb would then give a happier version of Ps. 58: 3.

12. This could be a straightforward acknowledgement of the wonder of creation—a text for Fact and Faith films. More deeply, it might be about response—**ears that hear** and **eyes that see** speaking of spiritual perception (Isa. 6: 10) which ultimately comes from God (Mt. 16: 17). **13.** More advice to the sluggard (see on 6: 6–11).

14. A humorous comment on the Eastern bazaar; still as true in today's second-hand car markets. More seriously it nags us to keep 'accepted' business practices under review; it is easy to slip over the line between bargain hunting and deception.

15. Even in prosperous times **knowledge** holds its value. Solomon's early reign was marked by both parts of the saying (1 Kg. 4: 29 f.; 10: 27) but sadly they go out of balance towards the end.

16. See on 6: 1–5. Proverbs is in general against suretyship, especially here with a third party who might be an alien trader. **wayward women:** the NIV follows the Heb. which as in the parallel 27: 13 is feminine, so could possibly refer to a pledge given to a harlot, as Gen. 37: 17, 18. **hold it in pledge:** RSV reads 'him' though there is no reference to such a custom. As NIV translates the second half repeats the first. For the law about taking garments in pledge see Exod. 22: 26–7.

17. The whole truth—not the half-truth given by Lady Stupidity in 9: 17.

18. See 11: 14. More advice about planning and forethought. Jesus used the theme to show what discipleship needs (Lk. 14: 31 f.).

19. The first line repeats 11: 13a. A gossip. Malice (11: 13), fascination (18: 8) or aimless chatter (**talks too much** is linked with 'simple', Heb. *pty*; see on 1: 4) all undermine the privacy which is essential to a confident and respectful society. **so avoid:** keep your own counsel.

20. The law was plain (Exod. 20: 12; 21: 17). Even if by the time of Proverbs the penalty was never exacted, the moral condition was **pitch darkness**. The commandment is still valid, even though NT adds a note to the father (Col. 3: 20 f.).

21. See 13: 11 and note. Here it is not just wealth but **inheritance, quickly gained**, perhaps unscrupulously (as in 19: 26, see note; Gen. 25: 33; 27: 19) or thoughtlessly (Lk. 15: 12) but with the same loss **at the end**.

22. A remarkable series of sayings, belying the harsh legalistic image the OT has for some. This verse and 24: 29 go beyond the obvious 17: 13, and 25: 21 advises positive benevolence towards an enemy. Rom. 12: 19–21 puts it in

NT setting, with the same reason ('leave room for God's wrath', NIV). So here **wait for the LORD** stops hasty action and gives the confidence that **he will deliver you**, whatever happens to the enemy. **23.** See v. 10 and 11: 1.

24. A reflection on the providence mentioned in 16: 1–9 and 19: 21. There is no Heb. for **directed**, so that dependence on **the LORD** is even greater and more emphatic (lit. 'from the LORD a man's steps'). The response is one of humility (Ps. 139: 1–6; 2 Chr. 20: 12) and a rebuke to brash self-confidence (Jas 4: 13 ff.). **his own way:** may be God's way, inscrutable to man, or possibly man's **own way** which he is not able to understand fully or plan wisely without God's help.

25. vows: a common feature of the ancient world, and often a snare. Jephthah is the most startling example (Jg. 11: 34–40) but the provisions of Num. 30 show that vows might bring unforeseen obligations. The Pharisees developed a casuistry on the matter which Jesus condemned (Mt. 23: 16–22). Jesus called for simple, direct speech that could be trusted (Mt 5: 33–37). **dedicate:** Heb. *qōdeš*, RSV says 'it is holy', in Proverbs only here; cf. *qādôš* in 9: 10; 30: 3. See introduction. It is noteworthy that Proverbs seems to be little interested in the idea of holiness. Its use here is in the ritualistic, almost contagious (see Hag. 2: 11–13), use of the word. What is holy in this sense, is set apart, dedicated to a religious use. It can become mere ceremonial, though the emphasis upon the distinctive nature of what was holy was intended to teach moral lessons about the transcendence of the God whose service was holy (Lev. 19: 2; 1 Pet. 1: 15 f.).

26, 28. The ideal **king** is **wise**, and not only **winnows out the wicked** (as v. 8, discriminating between false and true) but takes action against them. **drives the threshing wheel over them:** may refer to the rolling of grain on the threshing floor which crushed corn from husk so that they separated easily on winnowing. **Love and faithfulness:** which bring blessing to the individual (14: 22; 16: 6) and also supply the support of the state. **love** repeated from the first half (Heb. *hesed*, see note at 14: 22) includes the idea of 'loyalty' and refers to the covenant nature of Hebrew monarchy (see Dt. 17: 15–20)—the king's loyalty to his subjects as well as their loyalty to him.

29. Strength for the day—the vigour of youth and the experience of age are each worthy of respect and not to be set in competition. Joy in the **strength** of youth is an often-neglected OT theme (Ps. 19: 5; Ec. 11: 9).

30. See on 19: 25. The fact that punishment is necessary to clear the account is deeply rooted, though challenged by current penology. The word for **cleanse away** (only in first half, **purge** is inserted for the sake of English sense

in second half) is a rare and late word that has to do with ceremonial or ritual purification (Est. 2: 3; Lev. 6: 28 'scour') so does not speak of atonement, but the removal of social stigma.

21: 1. The divine providence extends to kings (see on 20: 24 and 16: 1–9). The classic examples are Cyrus, for blessing (Isa. 45: 1–7), and Pharaoh, for judgment (Exod. 7: 3–5).

2. See 16: 2.

3. A truly prophetic word in the Wisdom literature. **sacrifice:** Heb. *zebaḥ* (see on 17: 1; 15: 8). It can be no better than the one who brings it, often insincerely (v. 27). **right and just:** hallmarks of right relationship with God (see on 1: 3). The principle is deeply rooted in OT; *e.g.* 1 Sam. 15: 22; Isa. 5: 7; Jer. 4: 2; Mic. 6: 6–8. For Solomon the phrase was particularly memorable (1 Kg. 10: 9).

4. Haughty eyes (one of the *detestable things* of 6: 17) **and a proud heart** use two normal words for high and broad. The moral use picks out an overweening self-esteem (Ps. 101: 5; Dt. 8: 14), in current idiom 'too high and mighty'. Yet this self-importance is admired as a strong stance for living—**the lamp of the wicked**. The proverb is then a sober illustration of Mt. 6: 23.

5. Cautious planning again (12: 24; 13: 11; 28: 20; 29: 20).

6–15. Observations on law and order. Bribery (6; see on 15: 27; 17: 8, 23) does the receiver no lasting good. **7. violence** is self-destroying (see Mt. 26: 52), as history ancient (Exod. 15: 9 f.) and modern bear witness, and as politicians fear from more sophisticated means of making war. A terrible price to pay for refusing **to do what is right. 8. devious . . . upright:** the age-old antithesis (see on 8: 6). The **guilty** person never does things the straightforward way. Amos's plumbline (Am. 7: 7 f.) is a symbol of how God's straight standard shows up the crookedness of social injustice. If the **quarrelsome wife** (9) is litigious (as the use of the word at 18: 18, 'disputes', suggests), the saying fits well here, and the advice is to find your own small room rather than contest the case. Even the law court can be a place where **the wicked** can indulge his appetite (**craves** as Dt. 12: 20) for revenge without mercy (10).

Verse 11 returns to the moral of 19: 25 and sees the social benefit of justice being seen to be done. Verse 15 carries this further to compare the reactions of the **righteous** and **evildoers** (see 11: 10).

12. The Righteous One: not explained. NIV takes it to be God, working out his purposes (see on 5: 21). Otherwise (as mg) it would refer to a righteous judge who has to pass judgment (**takes note**='acts prudently'; see on 1: 3) on **the house of the wicked**.

13. the poor: a constant concern of OT (see on 14: 31; 19: 17). A judge should have been the first to support them but often **shuts his ears** (Isa. 10: 2; Lk. 18: 2–5). The saying could apply more widely to all who could, but do not, hear. Lk. 16: 19–31 is a classic case.

14. gift . . . bribe: see the two words noted in 15: 27. **in secret** makes it clear the transaction is a shady one, perhaps to avoid just punishment (not always successful, 6: 35!). On a personal level 1 Sam. 25: 18 ff. shows a more commendable example.

16. An isolated and cryptic saying. It is not clear if we are dealing with a rebel or an ignoramus. NEB takes the latter with 'A man who takes leave of common sense'. His fate is obscure, too. **the dead:** the mysterious *repa'im* (as 9: 18), not the ordinary 'dead' of (*e.g.*) Ru. 4: 10. JB gives 'shades' (as Isa 14: 9). Perhaps attention is drawn to his present aimless existence as well as his bad end (1 Tim. 5: 6).

17. loves: a strong word (as 17: 17) showing the grip *la dolce vita* has—and the cost.

18. a ransom: a sum of money for release (connected with verb 'to make atonement'); it has caused perplexity among translators. It is unlikely that **the wicked** and **unfaithful** suffer for the benefit of **the righteous** and **the upright**. With 11: 8 it might mean that the righteous escape and the wicked suffer, but the two happenings are not related, certainly not in a substitutionary way. More likely, as JB suggests; 'The wicked man is the price to be paid for the virtuous', and so turns the proverb into a meditation on the mystery of freewill. Is virtue worth evil which is the logical correlate of freely chosen good actions?

19. A variant of v. 9.

20. a foolish man devours it: the story of many a wasted inheritance. By contrast the rewards of **righteousness and love** (21) are lasting (Mt. 6: 19–20).

22. Not a physical assault, but a strategy—a fifth-column spreading uncertainty (NEB), or the general planning his attack. Ec. 9: 14–16 gives the same lesson from the point of view of the defenders—wisdom is better than might.

23, 24. An expanded version of 13: 3 with a fuller description of the arrogant **mocker** (see note on 1: 22).

25, 26. The two sayings are connected. The **sluggard** is so far gone that **his hands refuse to work**—even the urge of appetite seems too weak (16: 26), yet still he **craves** (13: 4). The **righteous** can keep himself—and others (Eph. 4: 28).

27. how much more so when brought with evil intent: perhaps to impress others, or to allay suspicion (see 15: 8). 7: 14 could come under the condemnation. It is just possible there is a reference to the fertility worship that was mixed with Yahwism, since the **evil intent** is the 'lewd acts' of Ezek. 22: 9; ch. 23.

28. The antithesis 'the words of an obedient

man' (mg) with the **false witness** may mean that the untrue evidence will fail (as it did in Mk 14: 59) rather than that the person himself will **perish**. Both may be true. An 'obedient man' is one who heeds the law, or heeds wisdom, as in 8: 34 where the same construction is used. NIV text consigns both the **false witness** and **whoever listens to him** to destruction.

29. If connected with v. 28 mg, this contrasts the way the two witnesses give their evidence. More generally, it shows the folly of brashness. **an upright man gives thought to** either his own ways (and so proceeds with more reserve) or examines the case so brashly put forward by his opponent (as in 18: 17).

30, 31. A further call to humility in the face of the providence of **the LORD**. In thought and in action the issue is with him. Verse 30 is a standing refusal to those who want the wisdom of Proverbs (or any other part of Scripture) without the LORD.

22: 1. A good name (**good** added from Gk., not in Heb.) and **to be esteemed** may be at the level of popular acclaim, or of acceptance with God. Either way, the intangible asset is preferred to the more tangible **riches**.

2. The final exposure of the folly of snobbery (see on 14: 20, 21; 18: 23). This is the true ground for a welfare state (Dt. 24: 17–22). A secular society is hard pressed to find any idea powerful enough to make the **rich and** the **poor have** it **in common**.

3, 4. Verse 3 is another comment on the **prudent** and his foil **the simple** (see on 1: 4). Cheerful optimism that takes no thought for danger will **suffer for it**. The pairing with v. 4 shows that **humility** is nothing to do with the simple. **Humility** is a steady and thought out response to the truth about life and God. Joined with **the fear of the LORD** (though **and** is not in Heb.) it yields **wealth and honor and life**. NEB, JB supply 'is' instead of **and** after **humility** and so (rather implausibly) make the fear of the LORD part of the reward (see 15: 33).

5. the wicked shares the difficulties of the sluggard (15: 19), though **thorns** is a rare word that may mean 'hooks' and so (with **snares**) symbolize the difficulties in which he is caught, for all his scheming. But **he who guards his soul** (as 19: 16) avoids the danger.

6. Ancient wisdom about education. **Train** is the word used for 'dedicate' (1 Kg. 8: 63; cf. the festival of dedication, Jn 10: 22), so this is a religious duty, not an economic preparation. **in the way he should go:** this means that the education should fit the child, not the child be fitted into the system. It also calls for individual attention to individual aptitudes, but assumes some agreed goal by which **the way** can be determined. Such training is a true preparation for life. Verse 15 with its doctrine of 'original folly' (Whybray) guards against an idea that children are stores of goodwill that have only to be drawn on (see 13: 24). The **discipline** have been overdone in the past, but cannot be dismissed.

7. A matter-of-fact observation. It is the job of good government to see that the **rule** does not become oppression, nor the slavery cruel. See Am. 5: 11–15.

8. An example of moral consequence: **the rod** is used for sceptre (Ps. 45: 6), so it could read 'His reign of terror will come to an end'. In any case, **fury** cannot reverse the natural law.

9. Another moral consequence (11: 24, 25): **generous** lit. 'a good eye' which is a symbol of generosity, as an evil eye ('stingy', 23: 6) is a Hebraism for miserliness. Note Mt. 20: 15 mg. 'is your eye evil . . . ?'

10. quarrels is a common word for judgment or cause, so the scene may be the court. LXX has 'Cast the scoffer out of the council', followed by NEB to give a second line: 'if he sits on the bench he makes a mockery of justice'. The general meaning is clear—a persistent troublemaker must be dismissed.

11. Ideal courtier for the ideal king. The combination of generous **speech** and pure **heart** is more than just the persuasiveness of 16: 21 (see note).

12. See 5: 21; 15: 3. An encouraging reassurance that **knowledge** does not stand frail and friendless. **The LORD** watches to see eventual justice done. See 1 Sam. 3: 19 for an example.

13. Another excuse from **the sluggard**.

14. See the fuller treatment of the **adulteress** and her way in chs. 2, 5, 7. The new idea here is that to fall into it reflects the anger of **the LORD**. 5: 21 f.gives a clue as to how this comes about.

15. See on v. 6.

16. AV, NIV make this one saying with the common penalty **both come to poverty**, suggesting that providence will not allow the schemer to profit (21: 30). NEB, JB make two sayings: 'Oppression of the poor may bring gain to a man, but giving to the rich leads only to penury'—a semi-humorous comment that bribing the rich does not pay.

IV. THE WORDS OF THE WISE
(22: 17–24: 22)

This collection of sayings shows a different literary type from the 'sentences' of the preceding section. These proverbs are all cast in the form of Instructions, with verbs in the imperative, usually supported by a clause explaining the wisdom of following the instruction. Sometimes the explanation runs on into another verse. NIV follows an amendment of *MT* to give **thirty sayings** (20). (*MT šilšôm*, 'the third day ago'; Qerê (marginal correction) *šālišîm*, 'officers' (? 'leading ideas'), and *šelōšîm*,

'thirty', all have the same Heb. consonants). The reading **thirty sayings** has received support, too, because the Egyptian *Teaching of Amenemope* (see introduction) has thirty chapters, some of which match the sayings of this section, as far as 23: 12. The thirty sayings are numbered serially in GNB. Most of these topics have been dealt with in the previous proverbs (cf. NIVmg). With a slightly longer treatment some pithy remarks are made, but the pace slows and some sayings seem almost heavy beside the sharpness of earlier epigrams.

22: 17–21. Introduction. LXX has **the sayings of the wise** as title and continues with 'Incline your ear and hear my words.' 2: 2–5 gives a similar introduction to a block of instructions. Wisdom is not for the hearer alone, but to be **ready on your lips** (18) **to give sound answers** (21) to others; not for idle curiosity but **that your trust may be in the LORD**.

SAYING 1. **22 f. in court** lit. the gate: the place of trade and justice in the ancient world (Am. 5: 10) where the **poor** and **needy** would seek redress. For the idea of **the LORD** contending a cause see Mic. 6: 2; Ps. 74: 22 for himself, and Ps. 35: 1 for others. In him **the poor** have a powerful attorney who will turn the tables and **plunder** the plunderers.

SAYING 2. **24 f.** Company. The matter has been dealt with at length (1: 10–19). **or you may learn:** violence is easily admired and copied by the thoughtless. The Egyptian has a chapter beginning: 'Do not associate with a hothead'.

SAYING 3. **26 f.** Suretyship (see on 6: 1–5). Similar advice, with a dry warning—**your very bed . . . snatched from under you**.

SAYING 4. **28.** The **boundary stone** (repeated at 23: 10). Boundary marks were important in the ancient world, as witnessed by the Israelite Law (Dt. 19: 14; 27: 17; and see Prov. 15: 25) and the Egyptian parallel: 'Do not carry off the landmark, nor disturb the position of the measuring line'. The Heb. word is generally used for boundary, but this could be marked in various ways—by a cairn of stones (Gen. 31: 51), a stone (Jos. 15: 6) or a hedge (Isa. 5: 5). There might also be other prominent features by reference to which boundaries were determined. **set up by your forefathers:** shows respect for ancient agreement and settlement (see on 23: 10 f.).

SAYING 5. **29.** The good worker. The Egyptian has 'scribe', but the Heb. word can be used of all crafts (Exod. 20: 10). The phrase **serve before** implies a court appointment, either domestic (1 Sam. 8: 16) or artistic (1 Kg. 7: 14). The lesson is that kings recruit the best—as 1 Kg. 11: 28 ironically recalls.

SAYING 6. **23: 1–3.** Etiquette for the new boy at court. **note well what is before you:** and don't let the feast weaken your concentration as a negotiator, if that is what you came for.

Alternatively (see mg) 'note . . . who', and don't forget you are in the king's presence. Curb your appetite. The warning against **delicacies** is not clear, nor why they are **deceptive food** (Heb. 'bread of lies'). **given to gluttony:** *ba'al nepeš* (see note on 18: 9 for Heb. use of *ba'al*, 'master'); perhaps near in sense to Phil. 3: 19.

SAYING 7. **4 f.** Warnings against slaving for **riches** are as widespread in literature ancient and modern as is the disregard with which they are treated. Here it is the uncertainty that is stressed, **fly off like an eagle** (Egyptian has 'geese') **to the sky**. Mk 4: 19; 10: 23 show even greater risks.

SAYING 8. **6–8.** A thumbnail sketch of the miser. **stingy** (Heb. 'evil eye'; cf. 22: 9): he begrudges everything. The visit will be **wasted** time (8) and leave a bad taste in the mouth, literally and metaphorically.

SAYING 9. **9.** Dealing with **a fool**. This is one half of the paradoxical advice of 26: 4 f. Speaking to him is worse than useless since **he will scorn**. Schoolteachers may too readily quote Mt. 7: 6 but there is truth in it.

SAYING 10. **10 f.** The **boundary stone** (as 22: 28) stands for God's ownership of the land. To tamper with it is arrrogant disregard of his order. It was **the fatherless** who were most liable to oppression if the law was not upheld (Lev. 25: 25). The **Defender** is the *gōʾēl* ('kinsman', 'redeemer') and this is a special case of the general principle of 22: 23. Here the LORD plays the part of the kinsman who safeguards the inheritance. Ruth (esp. ch. 4) shows the law at work. The *gōʾēl* had the right to redeem property or person, or to avenge blood (Num. 35). God takes the title in his relation with his people in Isa. (41: 14, etc.; see concordance, *s.v.* 'redeemer'.)

SAYING 11. **12.** A general comment like the introductory 22: 17. GNB takes it as the 11th saying.

SAYING 12. **13–14.** Ancient wisdom about education was the same in many parts (13: 24; 22: 15). The *Words of Ahikar* (7th century B.C.) have a close parallel to v. 13 but nothing as positive as 22: 6. No doubt Moses profited under similar treatment (Ac. 7: 22). **he will not die:** not just 'it won't do him any harm' but 'it may teach him a lesson that will ultimately save him from ways that lead to death' (note parallel of **die** in v. 13 with **death**, mg Sheol in 14b).

SAYING 13. **15 f.** One incentive to study is a proud parent. **My inmost being** (Heb. 'kidneys', AV 'reins'): used as seat of emotion, as **heart** (*lēb*) is seat of reason and will. Together they make a full personal response (*e.g.* Ps. 7: 9; 26: 2; Jer. 17: 10) and may underlie the imagery of Heb. 4: 12.

SAYING 14. **17–18. envy:** a destructive passion, robbing the envious of trust and **hope**, as well as embittering relationships. It is the 'pain that he has it' rather than jealousy ('pain that I have not') and may cloud a right assessment of what it is that he has (see 24: 1 f.). Ps. 37 is an extended meditation on the subject. NEB 'emulate' for **envy** gives the outcome, not the inner thought represented by Heb. (*qānā'*). **hope:** NEB gives 'thread of life' (see 11: 7 note).

SAYING 15. **19–21.** Watch your company—again (see 22: 24 f.). Not only the violent but the bibulous corrupt. This expands the general warning of 20: 1 (see note). Verse 20 may be the basis of the gibe against Jesus (Mt. 11: 19). The link of **drunkards and gluttons** reminds us that temperance is not only about alcohol.

SAYING 16. **22–25.** GNB makes all this the 16th saying. NEB makes verses 22, 24, 25 the 15th saying and v. 23 the 16th saying to keep the numbers straight (see on v. 12). **Listen to your father** reinstates the commandment (Exod. 20: 12) positively against earlier denunciations of breach (15: 20; 17: 25). Verse 24 repeats the substance of verses 15 f. The joint gladness of **father and mother** (25) gives an insight into the OT home—the mother as chattel is an inaccurate stereotype. (Gk. has no 'mother' in 25a but the idea is maintained in 25b.)

SAYING 17. **26–28.** In spite of many sermons, v. 26 is not an evangelistic text but a plea for close attention (as Paul's plea to his child in the faith, 2 Tim. 3: 10–14). If it is the happy father of v. 25 who is speaking, then his example will be as important as the appeal to reason (**heart**). NIV **keep to** follows an emendation; 'delight in' is equally likely and means, 'be as happy as I am in lawful marriage' (see 5: 15–20 for a similar argument). **a deep pit:** animal trap (Jer. 18: 22), metaphorically used of Sheol in 1: 12. **multiplies the unfaithful** (treacherous): sin does not stand alone; adultery involves deceit and disloyalty.

SAYING 18. **29–35.** More about liquor. A vivid description of a drunkard's sorrows, both the hangover (29) and the incapacity (33–35) and the fatal fascination (35b).

SAYING 19. **24: 1 f.** See on 23: 16–18. There the answer is trust in the LORD and hope for the future. Here it is a simple appeal to the wrongness of evil, spelt out in v. 2. The strongest motive is not always self-interest. Intuitive revulsion against **violence** and **trouble** can still be powerful.

SAYING 20. **3 f.** See 14: 1. The positive benefits of **wisdom, understanding** and **knowledge** may be the literal furnishings of the **house**, or symbolically the character and relationships that fill out the family who live there.

SAYING 21. **5 f.** Wisdom is better than strength. See note on 21: 22. Verse 6a repeats 20: 18b; v. 6b repeats 11: 14b.

SAYING 22. **7.** Not only in waging war, but in

counsel at **the gate**, wisdom is essential. The **fool** has nothing to contribute—and may even thereby gain some credit (17: 28). **too high** ('exalted', as in Isa. 6: 1): the same word as 'haughty' (21: 4), showing the fine line between glory and arrogance—to exalt wisdom is good, but the tone of voice in which v. 7a is spoken could show a haughty self-opinion. Est. 6: 6 gives a wryly humorous example of the line being crossed.

SAYING 23. **8 f. schemer** (lit. 'master of mischief'; see note on 18: 9): more plain speaking and an appeal to the instinctive rejection of the **schemer** and **mocker**. **detest:** the 'evil intent' of 21: 27 (see note), a moral outrage that cannot be excused.

SAYING 24. **10. trouble** is the test—a text for Outward Bound enthusiasts. There is a pun, as **small** and **trouble** are similar in Heb. Perhaps 'a tight corner need not cramp initiative'.

SAYING 25. **11 f.** Responsibility for others. The biblical answer to 'Am I my brother's keeper?' is consistently 'Yes!' from Gen. 4: 9 f. to Rev. 19: 2. Here the excuse (12a) suggests they 'did not want to be involved'. More specious modern arguments like 'leaving people to choose for themselves' must be tested in the light of him **who weighs the heart** (see on 16: 2). 2 Tim. 2: 24–26 and Jude 22 f. show the principle being applied. Whether **those who are being led away** deserve it or not, they must be given help and support.

SAYING 26. **13 f.** Sweet food for body and mind. See 15: 4 note. With v. 13 see Ps. 19: 10. Verse 14b repeats 23: 18, possibly copied here in error as it makes an unusual (three-lined) saying, and does not add to the idea of **future**.

SAYING 27. **15 f.** Respect for the person is carried a stage further to protect his **dwelling**. The resilience of **a righteous man** is attributed to God's care in Ps. 37: 23 f. and Mic. 7: 8. 2 C. 4: 9 shows the NT experience.

SAYING 28. **17 f.** Another of the sayings which refute a bloodthirsty stereotype of the OT (see on 20: 21 and v. 29 below). Again the inner attitude is in question, and **the LORD will see**. This response to a personal **enemy** must be separated from the people's gladness when tyranny is overthrown (11: 10b) though the separation may be hard to achieve. Jesus gives a moving example personally (Jn 13: 26) and collectively (Lk. 19: 41–44). **turn away his wrath:** suggesting that it will recoil upon the head of the gloating onlooker. The words of Ahikar, 'Envy not the prosperity of thine enemy and rejoice not at his adversity', link this saying with v. 19.

SAYING 29. **19f.** See on 23: 17 f. and 24: 1 f. **the lamp of the wicked:** see on 21: 4. The emphasis is again on the **future**.

SAYING 30. **21 f.** A plea for good citizenship. In Israel **the king** was not as autocratic as in some

neighbouring systems, but still the LORD's anointed is to be honoured. 1 Pet. 2: 17 carries the principle into the Roman rule. The second line may be the corollary—'the rebellious' could be unstable individuals or even revolutionaries. The **destruction** could then arise either from those who change or from **the LORD and the king**, when this would be an OT parallel to Rom. 13: 1–4. GNB: 'have nothing to do with people who rebel against them; such men could be ruined in a moment'. There is little to support NEB's wholesale change of sense to 'Fear the LORD and grow rich'.

V. MORE WORDS OF THE WISE (24: 23–34)

A small separate collection of instructions added as an appendix, including a single aphorism (27), some sayings about justice (23–26, 28, 29) and a story-instruction (30–34) in the style of 7: 6–23.

23–26. The universal cry for justice. **peoples will curse, nations denounce:** appeals to a universal revulsion against crooked judges. NEB, 'all nations . . . all peoples' gives the force though there is no 'all' in Heb. This important principle may be called a categorical imperative, or common sense, or the law written within the heart (Rom. 2: 15) and it is part of the beneficent Creator's common giving to all. The Mosaic law (e.g. Dt. 16: 18 f.) gave it a covenant setting, linked to the character of God (Exod. 34: 7), in a fuller understanding of man's nature and place in the universe. Verse 23 is similar to 18: 5; 28: 21, but only half the couplet has survived. **26. kiss on the lips:** Proverbs and OT in general knows both true and perfidious instances of this sign of true friendship. The lesson here is that **an honest answer** is the truest sign of friendship you can offer.

28 f. Words and attitudes go together. Whether **without cause** means 'unless you have to' (as 3: 30—NIV 'for no reason'), or 'falsely' (as Gk.) the saying marks the seriousness of giving evidence. The extension to inner motive in v. 29 foreshadows the argument of Mt. 5: 21–48. See on 20: 22.

27. Good advice to the new tenant, but with a general lesson. Attend to the future productivity before your own comfort. **build:** more than making basic shelter (NEB, 'establish house and home'); it can even include starting a family (Gen. 30: 3; 1 Sam. 2: 35).

30–34. A marvellous example of a 'tale with a moral' summarizing what has already been said about the **sluggard** (see on 6: 16).

VI. HEZEKIAH'S EDITION OF SOLOMON'S PROVERBS (25: 1–29: 27)

25: 1. These are more (see 24: 23) form an appendix to the main collection in chaps. 10–

24. copied: Heb. *he'tîq*, more usually 're-moved', so the emphasis may be on arranging rather than just transcribing, and this is borne out by grouping into subjects more than in the earlier sections. **Hezekiah** (716–687 B.C.) is described as an energetic and (certainly at first) godly **king of Judah**. There is no record in Kings of his literary interests, but his confidence in God's purpose for Jerusalem may have led him to look into its history and early kings. **2–7.** Kingship in the ancient world has its mystery and the aura of being 'more than just an ordinary person'. The anointing in Israel was a sign both of subservience to God and grace from God (see on 16: 10–15). So there the king will **search out a matter** and translate his wisdom into a refining process (4) that establishes **his throne** in **righteousness** (5). Modesty at court may reflect wry memories of Solomon's or Hezekiah's own dealing with upstarts. Jesus makes it a parable of the need for humility in everything. (Lk. 14: 10 f.). Heb. qualifies **a nobleman** with 'whom your eyes have seen' (cf. mg), but NIV follows Gk. in attaching this clause to v. 8, making a better balance to both verses. **before a nobleman:** possibly NEB gives the correct sense, 'to make room for a nobleman' (i.e. in the face of a more worthy person).

8–28. Mainly about words, in dispute, in counsel, on business, in advocacy, for cheer, for irritation. The relation between one person and another is most of living, so it is no wonder that in all cultures popular wisdom is full of advice about how to make friends and influence people.

8–12. Quiet discussion is more powerful than open accusation. Mt. 5: 25 points the same lesson and Job 22: 21 extends it to God. Those who are always wanting to 'bring the Press in' might remember this section. Such brash action may lose the golden moment to give **A word aptly spoken**, and will certainly make an angry rather than **a listening ear**. It is a pity that some modern media encourage experts in confrontation rather than **a wise man's rebuke**. The whole imagery of vv. 11, 12 is of charm, courtesy and gentle strength. These are the things that build up personal relationships. **13 f.** In business **a trustworthy messenger**, though ordinary and drab, is preferable to the colourful but empty boaster. The farming similes catch the flavour of both exactly. 2 Sam. 18: 19–32 shows the two types, though in less happy situation.

15 f. The power of persuasive speech has been noted already (see on 16: 21–24). 'How to say' could become more important than 'what to say'. Verse 16 corrects over-emphasis on rhetoric and flowery speech (see v. 27). Tertullus (Ac. 24: 2–4) might have taken note. It is possible that v. 16 is a warning against greed

or over-indulgence but v. 27 seems to link **honey** with speech.

17–22. How to treat a neighbour. Consideration is the core of good neighbourliness.

17. Seldom set foot: Seldom translates the only such use of a word from root 'precious' (Isa. 13: 12 'make . . . rare' is nearly the same) in the sense of 'rare'. So **Seldom** does not convey the subtlety of the saying—perhaps 'Make your visits welcome, a (rare) treat to your neighbour'. This is as much a matter of manner as of frequency. We can have **too much** even of infrequent visits from bores. Friendship can be destroyed violently by **false testimomy** or gossip (18), painfully by faithlessness (19) or thoughtlessly by not recognizing how the other feels (20). Truth, **reliance** and fellow-feeling are what make real neighbours. **20. soda** with vinegar would give a neutralizing action. Verses 21–22 (see on 20: 22) are not unique to Heb. wisdom; Babylonian *Counsels* (possibly much older than Solomon) advise 'Requite with kindness your evil-doer . . . nurture him'. (Confucius, however, did not agree: 'With what, then, would you requite good?') This is another example (as 24: 24) of a principle recognized by many, even if fulfilled by very few. See 2 Kg. 6: 20–23 for one successful application. **and the LORD will reward you:** this again puts the commonsense virtue in a wider context.

23–26. Damaging words, cheering words, and mixed words. **a sly** (lit. 'secret') **tongue:** one that spreads malicious gossip and slander. The **angry looks** may come from the person slandered, or those who believe the evil report. (**a north wind** does not normally bring rain in Palestine, so perhaps the saying originates elsewhere.) Verse 24 repeats 21: 9. The **good news** (25) might be brought by the faithful messenger (13) and is just as cheering to the receiver as the message is to the sender. When **a righteous man . . . gives way** (26, 'slips' as in Ps. 94: 18) the damage is great. His usual good character gives credence to his compromise. **muddied spring** (see uses of the word in Isa. 57: 20 and Ezek. 34: 18): the very opposite of the still waters the good shepherd finds for his flock (Ps. 23: 2).

27. See on v. 16. The Heb. is difficult. NIV makes one guess. RSV renders the second line as 'so be sparing of complimentary words'.

28. The opposite of 16: 32. The imagery of the vulnerable **city** is very telling. The quick tempered man is at everyone's mercy.

26: 1–16. Various kinds of fool. All sorts of folly are illustrated in this collection of shrewd observations. See on 1: 7 for the three sorts of fool. In this section he is *kesîl* all the time, but no great significance can be attached to this. He needs correction and guidance (3) not promotion (1, 8). Talking to him is a frustrating but unavoidable affair (4, 5). He can't be trusted with a **message** (6) or value a **proverb** (7, 9). He is a danger to himself and to others (10) and is not likely to learn any better (10, 11). In all this we are both warned against our own potential folly, and helped to deal with the fools we meet.

1. rain in harvest: a disaster as well as unfitting (cf. 1 Sam. 12: 16 f.). The promoted **fool** will do actual damage. The droll picture of the **stone** caught up in the **sling** (8) sums up the uselessness of a fool in a position of responsibility. Verse 2 is either a refutation of superstition—fools might be afraid of some random **curse**, but judgment is not capricious—or, alternatively (with NEB) the **curse** is abuse which fools give without cause, and it will achieve nothing. **3. halter:** shows that **whip** is not for punishment, but the thought of motivation and control is uppermost.

Verses 4, 5 are not naïvely contradictory, but amount to 'It needs insight to talk to a fool; sometimes humour him, sometimes rebuke him'.

Verses 7, 9 have identical second lines but two lessons. The fool cannot use a proverb properly and either will hurt himself (RSV, 'a thorn that goes up into the hand') or others (NIV, **a thornbush in a drunkard's hand**, as a weapon). Only the wise have the skill and sensitivity to make the most of a proverb (Ec. 12: 11).

10. Like an archer who wounds (NIV) and 'The great God that formed' (AV) show how wildly guesses at a difficult text can vary. The Heb. *rab*, usually 'great' (no Heb. here for 'God'), is occasionally **archer** (Jer. 50: 29; cf. also, in a compound phrase, Gen. 21: 20).

13–16. The sluggard reappears with his foolish excuses (see 22: 13), with his slow start to the day (14), self-defeating idleness (15) and cast-iron defence against criticism (16). There is an obstinacy about his lethargy that is a moral, not a temperamental, failure.

17–28. Envy, wrath and all uncharitableness. A collection of sayings about things that destroy relationships. There is the meddler (17), the shameless double-crosser (19), the **gossip** (20) and the stirrer (21). Beneath it all is hatred and ill will, **an evil heart** (23) that twists praise into flattery (28) and openness into guile (26).

18 f. Our age is not the first in which 'joking' erodes honesty. The reckless refusal to act seriously destroys the mutual trust upon which society rests.

20–22. All gossips and journalists should memorize these sayings—**quarrel** and **strife** have to be kindled and fuelled. They can also be averted and quenched (15: 1). Unfortunately we all like the **choice morsels**. (Verse 22 repeats 18: 8 and NIV gives correct translation as against AV 'wounds'.)

23–26. The **glaze** (see mg) involves a change of Heb. consonant and gives point to a saying about hypocrisy (see Mt. 23: 25–28). Hatred leads to dissembling (24), which rots the basis of human society. There is still the overriding conviction that his wickedness will be exposed and will recoil upon himself (27) but meanwhile he works ruin (28). The belief in justice (27) is seen also in the *Words of Ahikar*: 'He that digs a pit for his neighbour will fill it with his own body'. Another common-sense view (see on 24: 24), part of the furniture of the universe which men cannot dispense with.

There is less evident grouping in chap. 27. It is a patchwork of sharp sayings about personal attitudes and social relationships. JB's short but stylized couplets convey the disjointed but polished images. As in chap. 26 there is no specific mention of God, but this moral governance is behind the common wisdom.

27: 1. Warning against cocksureness is matched by other ancient wisdoms, expanded by James (4: 13–16), and a needed reminder today.

4. In Proverbs **jealousy** is always bad (3: 31; 6: 34; 14: 30; 23: 17; 24: 1, 19). Elsewhere it can be used of zeal or single-mindedness for good or ill (2 Kg. 19: 31; Ps. 69: 9). 'The LORD is a jealous God' (Exod. 20: 5) and his single-minded thrust of truth and loyalty drives unremittingly against both the disloyalty of his people (Ezek. 16: 35–42) and their oppressors (Ezek. 36: 1–5). In fallen man this capacity for passionate commitment often lacks good content and so drives him on in baser rivalry with his fellow. It is a 'moral inversion' in which God-given power is channelled to diabolical ends. See 2 C. 7: 9–13 for a happier example.

5. hidden love (JB 'voiceless love'): loses its strengthening and healing power. The essence of love is to be shown (Rom. 5: 8). The attempt to balance vv. 5, 6 by translating 'pretended love' cannot be supported. Verse 6 stands on its own as another comment on open rebuke.

6. faithful is a strong word (Ps. 19: 7; Prov. 11: 13 'trustworthy'), used of God (Dt. 7: 9), the utterly reliable One. 'Amen' (Rev. 3: 14) is from the same root. NEB 'well-meant' is too insipid. There is a depth of solid concern that makes **the wounds** a healing ministry.

7. The wider meaning is well known to 'poor little rich children' to whom nothing brings pleasure.

8. strays: conveying the idea of aimlessness. There is praise for the determined pilgrim but not for the wanderer. Caring for one's own is a Christian duty (1 Tim. 5: 8) so the **nest** may be a significant parallel.

10. The three lines are unusual and may suggest a displacement or loss. NEB relegates the second line to a footnote, but still has no easy pair. The first two lines could stand together with the sense: 'If you have a real friend you can go to him in trouble—he will be better even than a brother' (see 18: 24). The third line is then a disconnected saying (with an exact parallel in the *Words of Ahikar*).

11. Reverts to the earlier motif of the wise father instructing his son (10: 1, etc.).

12. Repeats 22: 3.

13. See note on 6: 1–5. **wayward woman:** Heb. is feminine singular, 'a foreign woman' (see note on 20: 16).

14. A humorous picture of ill-timed bonhomie.

15 f. See 19: 13; 21: 9; 25: 24. The **quarrelsome wife** is impossible to restrain—a surprising but apparently perennial index of man's failures to fulfil the ideal of Gen. 2: 23; or even, after the Fall, of Gen. 3: 16. I Pet. 3: 1–7 shows a happier possibility.

17. one man sharpens another: weaker than AV 'a man sharpens the countenance of his friend'. There is a keenness and alertness that comes from good friendship. This is the positive possibility of which I C. 15: 33 is the negative.

18. A proverb of reward for duty done. Both verbs have the idea of 'guarding' more than 'tending'—i.e. preserving from harm or neglect rather than supplying needs. So NEB 'guards the fig tree . . . watches his master's interest' is more accurate. **eat its fruit . . . be honored:** rewards proper to the service rendered. A cash economy may obscure this.

19. The cryptic Heb. is reflected by various translations. The verbs have to be inferred (lit. 'As the water the face to face, so the man's heart (mind) man'). NIV **a man's heart reflects the man** focuses attention on the inner self (as in I Sam. 16: 7) but this hardly matches the sort of 'reflection' of the first part. NEB 'one man's heart answers another's' introduces two people. JB stresses the difference, not similarity, 'As no two faces are ever alike, unlike too are the hearts of men'. The text is worth pondering. It can prod us to think about individuality and relationship. The reflection is recognizably me, but not me. So I recognize you as my fellow, but not my copy.

20. Death and Destruction (mg 'Sheol and Abaddon') (15: 11 and 30: 16): symbols of perpetual dissolution, the opposite of God's work of creation. Two ideas are mixed. There is no clear picture of torment (see on 5: 5) such as 'Gehenna' has in NT, but the bleakness of destruction that gets no satisfaction from what it destroys—insatiable appetite with no pleasure in eating. The 'bottomless pit' of Rev. 9: 1, etc., follows this imagery. Some modern existentialist writing gives the flavour and also extends it as the proverb: **neither are the eyes of man.** Cf. G. K. Chesterton's comment on the barbarians: 'They only saw with heavy eyes, and broke with heavy hands'.

21 f. Two illustrations about basic nature. The refiner shows the signs of pure metal, so **praise** tells about a **man.** Pounding may break fine but does not alter nature. **like grain with a pestle** is one word in Heb. and distorts the metre. NEB, JB omit it.

23–27. A disconnected pastoral exhortation. The continuing fruitfulness of a well cared-for farm is contrasted with diminishing capital or uncertain honour. Trade and administration are necessary but no society should forget that it relied ultimately on a fruitful earth. **a crown:** may be the symbol of honour in general; if literal, the sentence fits less well and does not follow the Davidic hope of 2 Sam. 7: 13 (followed in 29: 14).

Chapter 28 comprises a collection of sayings loosely grouped around the social and individual results of character.

28: 1–5. The wicked and righteous in society. **The wicked** (1) is easily startled and, by inference, more easily moved than **the righteous** whose clear conscience gives him boldness. (See Neh. 6: 11 for an OT example and Eph. 6: 14 for a NT one.)

2. many rulers: reflecting the instability of war or intrigue. Hos. 8: 4 comments on such a sorry condition—the north Israelite kingdom had six kings in thirty years. The antithesis between **is rebellious** and **understanding** (*bîn* as 1: 2) illustrates the meaning Proverbs gives to the latter. **order:** this rendering of Heb. *kēn* (translated 'base' in Lev. 8: 11) makes good sense of the MT, though NEB, JB despair unnecessarily and follow LXX.

3. A ruler: NIV takes one possibility. NIVmg 'a poor man' the more likely, more startling picture of unexpected and unnatural suffering (Mt. 18: 28–31 includes it in a parable).

4. the law: Heb. *tôrah*, used four times absolutely in Proverbs (cf. vv. 7, 9; 29: 18, elsewhere, *e.g.* 13: 14, as law, or teaching, of the wise), usually denotes God's law, especially as given through Moses. If it has this force here, then the link is with the Hebrew culture rather than general wisdom literature. NEB 'lawless . . . law-abiding' are too general. **praise the wicked:** a stark statement of the subjectivist morass that follows when absolute standards are rejected.

5. Continues the theme with the specific example of **justice.** The difference of direction between **evil** and **those who seek the LORD** radically effects understanding (*bîn* as v. 2). To evil men justice might be expedient, but they cannot operate at the deeper level of truth. **fully:** not simplistic or arrogant, but a plain statement of possibility (see I Jn 2: 20 where there is good support for 'you know everything').

6–11. The effect on the individual. **blamelessness** (6), observance of **the law** (7), uprightness (10) and **discernment** (11), are again shown as qualities that build up the person, irrespective of external circumstances. This is the way the universe runs; other ways lead to loss of fancied wealth (8), safety (10) or hope (9).

6. where ways are perverse: only here and at v. 18 in OT the Heb. **ways** is in the dual number. The perversity is two-faced unreliability, or the instability suggested by Bunyan's Mr. Facing-both-ways.

8. The general moral has been given positively and negatively in 13: 22; 19: 17. The particular reference here is to **exorbitant interest** forbidden in dealings with fellow-Israelites (Lev. 25: 35–38) but not with aliens (Dt. 23: 19 f.). NEB gives 'lending at discount or at interest' to distinguish the technical terms. In the first you actually get less than the value of the bond (like a discounted bill); in the second you pay extra as interest.

9. See 21: 27; 15: 8.

10. See 26: 27 for evil backfiring upon the doer. **leads:** causes to leave the path, used literally in Dt. 27: 18; it suggests taking advantage of the unsuspecting (cf. Jesus' condemnation of similar action in Mt. 18: 6).

11. The **rich** and **poor** contrast simply emphasizes the supremacy of **discernment sees him through:** may be a legal term (as in 18: 17), so the rich man does not have it all his own way in court.

12. The social effects of morality. See on 11: 10.

13. A memorable statement of a great biblical principle (see Ps. 32: 3–5). The context must decide the use of **conceals** (kāsāh). At 17: 9 (NIV 'covers over') it is a proper reaction to another's wrong; in Ps. 32: 1 there is happiness when God 'covers' sin; here it is fruitless for a man to conceal his own **sins. confesses and renounces:** brought powerfully together (see Lev. 26: 40–42). One is useless without the other (Jer. 7: 10). See Num. 5: 7 for the interweaving of social and religious factors in wrong-doing.

14. NIV supplies **the LORD** (not in Heb.) and makes this sound like a motto of 1: 7; but the verb **fears** is not the 'reverence' (yir'āh) of 1: 7, but the 'dread' (paḥad) of Hos. 3: 5; Mic. 7: 17. The corresponding noun is given by NIV as 'calamity' at 1: 26, but the numinous 'Fear' of Gen. 31: 42 gives a better antithesis to the barefaced brashness that **hardens his heart.** NEB 'scrupulous in conduct' has little to commend it.

15 f. The terror of tyranny. The verses reflect the desperate experiences of many **a helpless people** in the ancient world and since. Cf. the story of Confucius and the woman whose family had been killed by tigers, but still lived in tiger-ridden country in exile: 'Oppressive rulers are more cruel than a tiger.'

17. Another example of how translation is affected by presuppositions. The Heb. is literally: 'A man oppressed by blood of life (human blood) to pit will flee; do not uphold him.' NIV, JB take 'to the pit' to be symbolic of **till death,** and 'flee' to **be a fugitive,** linking the proverb with Gen. 4: 13–16. JB follows the parallel with Cain even more closely by making the last phrase 'Do not lay hands on him'. NEB regards the saying less profoundly and gives 'will jump into a well to escape arrest'. NIV, JB reflect more authentically the OT (and ancient wisdom) sense of dread of being **tormented by the guilt of murder** (see 1 Kg. 2: 5; Mt. 23: 35).

18. See on v. 6 for **ways are perverse** (i.e. 'two ways'). **suddenly:** Heb. 'in one' can stand as JB: 'he who wavers between two ways falls down in one of them.' For line 1 see v. 26.

19. Good husbandry contrasted with the folly of 12: 11 and its result. **abundant food** is matched ironically with **have his fill of poverty.**

20, 22, 25. eager to get rich may be dishonest (as v. 20 suggests) or **stingy** (22). Either way his goal eludes him and he **stirs up dissension** (25). The **faithful** (see on 20: 6) **man** may not reap material riches but will **be richly blessed.** The trust (25) is confidence ('boldness' of 28: 1) which makes both evil and niggardliness unnecessary.

21. The first line repeats 18: 5. The second line is not about hunger driving desperate men to **do wrong,** but a satirical reference to judges who can be bribed even with **a piece of bread** (see Am. 2: 6).

23. A typically pragmatic proverb. Straightforwardness pays in the long run—though NT would add a better motive (Eph. 4: 25).

24. A proverb reminiscent of the 'Corban' scandal of Mk 7: 9–13 and an example of the dull conscience (30: 20). **him who destroys:** as in 18: 9 and possibly including self-destruction (6: 32).

26. He who trusts in himself (Heb. lēb as 4: 23) presumably won't bother to listen to advice. There is a self-confidence which is arrogant folly. **he who walks in wisdom:** suggesting a steady progress (as 10: 9; 14: 2; 19: 1). See Eph. 5: 15. **is kept safe:** will escape by his careful attention. A different word is used in v. 18 where 'deliverance' comes from outside, though God may not be named as the source. Mordecai gives an example in Est. 3: 1–6.

27. See on 11: 24–26 and 19: 17.

28. An expansion of v. 12b.

Chapter 29 consists of a final selection of sayings with no apparent grouping. Several echo earlier proverbs but the general effect is of a wide ranging commentary on the individual and society at large.

29: 1. The 'just law and judgment of the skies'

with which the collection began (1: 24–26). Pharaoh is the prime example (Exod. 7: 3; 8: 15); another is the Israelite nation (Neh. 9: 29). **suddenly . . . without remedy:** add to the fearfulness of the divine retribution (6: 15; Rev. 18: 10–17). To be **without remedy** is the deepest doom (2 Chr. 36: 16; Isa. 6: 10; Jer. 19: 11, 'cannot be repaired').

2. A variant of 11: 10.

3. Line 1 follows 10: 1a. Line 2 shows the neglect of the father's advice (5: 7–11) without the happier ending of Lk. 15: 30.

4. justice: the codification of righteousness in civil affairs (see on 1: 3), good for both kingdom and **king** (16: 12). NIV gives the opposite as the man **who is greedy for bribes** (JB 'extortioner') which is unusual for Heb. *t^erûmāh* ('offering' or 'oblation'). Both he who tries to offer and he who accepts a bribe are threats to a stable society, but the use of a normally cultic word is odd. Gk. suggests a slight change to give 'deceiver'.

5. Flattery is no real service; see 28: 23.

6. sing and be glad. emphasizes the liberty of the **righteous** in contrast to the ensnared state of the **evil man**, but a small change would give 'runs' for **sing** and make a more balanced couplet. So JB gives 'the virtuous runs on rejoicing'.

7. justice: a legal term (as 20: 8 'to judge' and see on 22: 10). AV 'the cause of the poor' gives the sense. The **wicked**, typically, see no sense in such an argument.

8. A saying in the spirit of 15: 1–4. **stir up:** gives an interesting idea of the use Proverbs makes of this verb, usually about speech in bad context (6: 19; 14: 5; 19: 5, 9). The root means 'puff' (Ps. 10: 5; Ca. 4: 16) and may be connected with the blacksmith's bellows (Isa. 54: 16). **Mockers** fan discord all over the **city**. Ac. 9: 1 gives a NT example of this usage.

9. A contribution to the paradox of 26: 4, 5. **goes to court** means a legal case, and the proverb suggests it is a waste of time prosecuting a **fool**, because **there is no peace**, either in the hearing or, more likely, no satisfactory end to the case.

10. A disturbing comment on wickedness. A **man of integrity** is a standing rebuke that cannot be tolerated (v. 27; Am. 5: 10). **Seek to kill the upright.** MT could be rendered, as NEB 'the upright set much store by his (the blameless man's) life'.

11. See 14: 17, 29.

12–21. A group of sayings showing the general theme of government and control.

12. Courtiers tell the **ruler** what he wants to hear; hence the corrupting effect if he **listens to lies**. The positive answer is in v. 14 (see on v. 4 and 16: 10–13). The common humanity of all classes and stations of society (13) is an important result of the doctrine of creation (see

Mal. 2: 10 and note on 22: 2). Government will never become oppression where this is understood.

In the context of the family (15, 17) and the household (19, 21) Proverbs counsels firm treatment but with the final purposes of **wisdom, peace, delight**. Otherwise no one takes any notice (19) and **grief** ensues in the end (21), though the meaning of Heb. *mānôn* (**grief**), used only here, is uncertain.

16. The state needs not only righteous leadership but inspired guidance (18). NEB 'no one in authority' does not give the usual force of **no revelation** ('visions' as 1 Sam. 3: 1). **revelation:** the clear knowledge of God's will for the immediate situation. **the law** (*tôrāh*, see on 28: 4): the record of past revelations. In days of renewed charismatic experience, this proverb reminds us to keep the law and prophecy together and not in tension if **the people** are to grow responsibly. **cast off restraint:** 'running wild' as in Exod. 32: 25—this Sinai incident is itself a sad example of the proverb.

20. See 15: 2; 26: 12b.

22–26. The collection ends with some home truths about **anger, pride**, dishonesty and the **fear of man** upon individuals and those around them, and the sharply contrasting blessing of him who **trusts in the LORD**. No man is an island; his **anger stirs up dissension** (22); his **pride** or humility will have its effect (23); misguided loyalty to a dishonest friend puts a man at odds with the law (24); **Fear of man** (25) or the favour of **a ruler** (26) are dangerous beside the safety and **justice** the LORD gives.

27. See on v. 10.

VII. THE SAYINGS OF AGUR AND OTHERS (30: 1–33)

It is not clear how this selection of sayings originated. The title **The sayings of Agur** may apply only to vv. 1–4, vv. 1–9 or vv. 1–14. LXX divides the sayings, putting vv. 1–14 between 24: 22 and 24: 23, and 30: 15–31: 9 between 24: 34 and 25: 1.

30: 1. Agur son of Jakeh: an otherwise unknown wisdom teacher, who commends himself warmly to us by his humble piety before **the Holy One** (3). **an oracle** mg Massa suggests a family or place (Gen. 25: 14) but the usual meaning, **an oracle**, is more likely as it fits better with **declared** (*n^e'um* as Jer. 1: 8 and *passim*). Nothing is known of **Ithiel and Ucal.** The consonants of the Heb. text can be read to give 'I have wearied myself, O God, I have wearied myself, O God, and come to an end' (Kidner, p. 178). LXX gives the quite different introduction 'This is what the man said to those who trust God'.

2–4. By comparison with God's wisdom and transcendence, humility is the only proper attitude for man. In the sanctuary this becomes plain (Ps. 73: 15–22). **the Holy One:** used only here and at 9: 10 in Proverbs; in both places the honorific plural is used (unlike the singular which is used in Isa. 1: 4, etc.). It is worthy of comment that Proverbs is so little interested in such an important OT idea. The appeal is to utility and commonsense, not the covenant relationship with the holy God (Lev. 19: 2). The fear of the LORD (1: 7) is a proper reverence, acknowledging the power and wisdom that controls the universe, but it is not the shattering awareness of God's otherness that Isaiah knew (Isa. 6). See further comment in Introduction.

4, 5. In language reminiscent of Job (chs. 38, 39) this comes as near anything in Proverbs to showing God's transcendence, but still it is as Creator of all things rather than as morally supreme. See Ec. 5: 2 for another example of this in the Wisdom literature.

5, 6. God's **word** leaps the gorge of man's ignorance and provides a tried refuge. **is flawless** (JB 'unalloyed'): a word from the goldsmith; unlike the mixture that is human nature (Jer. 6: 27–30), God's **word** is pure all through (Ps. 12: 6). **God** (*'ᵉlōah*) is the word used widely in Job. The similar phrases in 2 Sam. 22: 31; Ps. 18: 31 substitute 'LORD' (Yahweh) for **God**. **Do not add** is more general than Rev. 22: 18 and though still posing the question of *how* we recognize genuine words it should give caution to those who vaunt additional writings as equal in authority to Holy Scripture.

7–9. Safety first morality. A keen awareness of human frailty can lead to an escapist desire for peace and a quiet life. Even the OT is more robust in places (*e.g.* Ps. 62: 10; Ps. 23: 4), prepared to face extremes, while Paul exulted in them (Phil. 4: 11–13). But Jesus still taught his disciples to pray 'Lead us not into temptation' (Mt. 6: 13) and the line between believing boldness and over-confidence is a real one. **10.** Even **a servant** (slave, Heb. *'ebed*) has dignity and it is an enlightening study to trace the word in OT (Exod. 20: 10; Dt. 23: 15, etc.). A slave was not an expendable chattel in the sight of the LORD. The formal **curse** was frequent in the ancient world (*e.g.* execration texts) and the OT in general regards them lightly (see on 26: 2). But when the curse is a cry to the LORD it is powerful (Dt. 15: 9; Jas 5: 4).

11–14. Four denunciations linked by the introduction, **There are those who** (lit. 'a generation . . .'). No judgment is given. The fourfold arrogance is simply held up to opprobrium.

15 f. A sharp, even bitter, comment on insatiability is introduced with the bloodsucking **leech** and the continual cry, **Give, Give.** (The text is cryptic: 'to the leech two daughters,

give, give'.) **three . . . four:** a poetic introduction as in Am. 1: 3. There follow the ever open **grave** (mg Sheol; see on 27: 20) **the barren womb** ('closed', as in Gen. 20: 18), sad symbol in OT of unfulfilled womanhood, the parched ground and the devouring **fire**. Behind all these may be seen the unsatisfied human spirit (Jn 4: 13) or the grasping avarice which itself makes its own satisfaction impossible. Compare Buddhist *dukkha*, the unending hopeless longing, root of all suffering.

17. An expansion of 20: 20. Possibly an imagined scene in the desolate **valley** where the rebellious son met his death (Dt. 21: 18–21). **18 f.** Another foursome, this time linked by deep wonder at everyday events. The ancients were often better observers than we, less hurried, more detached, and here more questioning and questioning at a deeper level. The writer is not asking for explanations in terms of aerodynamics, flotation or hormones. He quietly meditates the mystery and fittingness of the world around him. **way** (Heb. *derek*) is ambiguous enough to provoke thought, and the **man with a maiden** sufficiently different from the other three to make the common factor elusive—movement that leaves no trace? grace and ease? mastery? things you wouldn't believe if you hadn't seen them?

20. By contrast with the gentle and fascinating 'way of a man with a maiden', **the way of an adulteress** is void of conscience, grace or meaning. **eats:** may refer to her adultery, or a meal with her client. Either way, **I've done nothing wrong** shows a rationalization that is darkness indeed (Mt. 6: 23).

21–23. Four things linked by the notion of hopeless incongruity—things that just will not do because people are in situations they have not the skill to cope with. The **servant** will never have character or experience to rule (Felix, Ac. 24: 27, is an example, described by Tacitus as exercising 'the power of a king with the disposition of a slave'; and see 19: 10). The **fool** (*nābāl*, the loud-mouthed churl, typified by Nabal in 1 Sam. 25) cannot cope with a full stomach. The **unloved woman** will find it hard to forget bitterness and scheming, and Sarah as **mistress** learned how rudely her **maidservant** could behave in triumph (Gen. 16: 1–4).

24–28. Get organized. Four examples to point the lesson that size and strength are not everything. Practical wisdom includes foresight (25) finding security (26; Mt. 7: 24), discipline (27), persistence (28). Each creature shows a restriction—**little strength, . . . little power, . . . no king . . . can be caught in the hand**, yet an achievement suited to its capacity.

29–31. Four things **stately in their stride** (AV 'comely in going' is more picturesque) do not have any evident moral significance. Perhaps a

wry reminder that others beside kings can have a distinctive gait—a text for goose-stepping Führers, and other pompous people. (Kidner comments that in modern Hebrew the word for **strutting rooster** means 'a starling'.)
32 f. Things are what they are. Folly and scheming cannot win, so **clap your hand over your mouth** (an expression of humble repentance, Job. 40: 4). **churning . . . twisting . . . stirring up** (RSV correctly gives the monotony of Heb. by translating 'pressing' thrice) has the ring of inevitability. The wise will take account of the certain end of actions and not produce **strife**. In Heb. **nose** and **anger** are similar so the pun makes the saying the more memorable.

VIII. THE WORDS OF LEMUEL (31: 1–9)

31: 1. The words of Lemuel: an isolated oracle (see on 30: 1 for **oracle**). Nothing else is known of this king or **his mother**. Advice to princes is found in Egyptian and Mesopotamian writings. The sentiments here echo what has been said already in Proverbs. The appeal (2) is both as mother and dedicator (**vows**). Such a child of love and purpose must not think of sexual folly (5: 8–17) or drunkenness (20: 1) but strive for justice (29: 14). **5. lest they drink and forget:** drunken oppression is a sadly recurrent element of history (see Isa. 5: 22 f.). Verses 6, 7 probably provide a sarcastic comment on the folly of drunken kings rather than serious advice to let the **perishing** drown his sorrows. **8. destitute** (Heb. 'sons of perishing'): orphans who also would have no one to plead their **'rights'** (='cause' as 29: 7).

IX. THE GOOD WIFE (31: 10–31)

The famous eulogy of the good wife is an acrostic of 22 sayings, each verse beginning with a letter of the Hebrew alphabet in order. Modern Westerners may notice in this paean of praise a lack of emphasis on relationships or romance. It is not only praise of the ideal wife but also advice to would-be husbands of the 'Can she cook and can she sew, Billy boy?' type. Love in marriage is not often remarked in OT (Gen. 24: 67; 29: 18, 20; 1 Sam. 1: 5; 18: 20; Ec. 9: 9; Est. 2: 17) and occasionally unworthy miscalled 'love' is noted (7: 18; 1 Kg. 11: 1). But Proverbs does show joy and passion (5: 15–19) and respect for the mother and wife as a woman of worth (see 12: 4 and note), often pointing out how fortunate the husband is to have so good a partner (18: 22; 19: 14; 31: 12).

The acrostic is clearly about a woman of position and ability in her own right. She has a large household, ample means, land and vineyard, knowledge and charm. She is diligent, wise, and caring.

11. Her husband has full confidence in her: the same word is used of trust in the LORD (16: 20). **lacks nothing of value** is not an obvious translation (NEB 'children are not lacking' is even less obvious). **lack** (as Ps. 23: 1) can indicate need or want. **value** ('spoil') can include captured girls (Jg. 5: 30), so this could possibly mean he will want no concubines; more likely (as 16: 19) it is an expression of simple contentment. **husband** (Heb. *ba'al*): see note on 18: 9.
12. She brings him good is prosaic and sounds as if he gets a good bargain; but Heb. *gāmal* (**brings**) can be a fuller word; 'deal bountifully' (Ps. 13: 6) conveys a little more of the glad goodwill with which the **good** is done.
13–19. A fascinating picture of the role of the lady of the house in the ancient world, active in planning, trading, spinning, providing.
20. She fulfils the earlier exhortations to care for **the poor** (14: 21, etc.).
21. clothed in scarlet: usually a sign of prosperity (2 Sam. 1: 24) rather than warmth. The noun is plural; LXX and Vulgate (using different vowels) give 'double', so NEB 'two cloaks'.
25. Strength and dignity appeal to us as very appropriate to such a lady. We may be less happy with **laugh at the days to come**. Laughter (*śāḥaq*) is often derisive (1: 26) but can refer to innocent and commendable rejoicing (8: 30 f.). AV gives 'she shall rejoice in time to come'. NIV may be an expression of confidence.
28. She receives the respect and praise she deserves, hinting that her training of the household (22: 6) has avoided the tragedies of 10: 1; 15: 20; 29: 15, etc.
30. The Song of Solomon shows that **Charm** and **beauty** can be appreciated. The point here is that they *can* be **deceptive** and **fleeting** by comparison with the fear of the LORD. Modern readers who may think this is a rather unromantic view are welcome to have beauty and charm in their list of desirable qualities provided they keep the other twenty qualities given here on their list as well. So Proverbs ends where it began, with the supremacy of the fear of the LORD.

BIBLIOGRAPHY

Commentaries
JONES, E., *Proverbs and Ecclesiastes.* TC (London, 1961).
KIDNER, D., *The Proverbs.* TOTC (London, 1964).
MCKANE, W., *Proverbs: A New Approach.* OTL (London, 1970).

Oesterley, W. O. E., *The Book of Proverbs. WC* (London, 1929).

Scott, R. B. Y., *Proverbs and Ecclesiastes. AB* (Garden City, N.Y., 1965).

Whybray, R. N., *The Book of Proverbs. CBC* (Cambridge, 1972).

Other Works

Thomas, D. W. (ed.), *Documents from Old Testament Times* (London, 1958)—for examples of other Wisdom writing in the ancient world.

See also bibliography to article 'Introduction to the Wisdom Literature' (p.120).

ECCLESIASTES

DONALD C. FLEMING

The meaning of the book

Probably the chief problem confronting us in reading Ecclesiastes is how we should read it. Should we take it at face value or should we read certain passages as ironic or sarcastic? Is the author defending the orthodox viewpoint or is he challenging it? Does he believe all he says or is he raising hypothetical arguments and then answering them? Do the apparent contradictions betray a real inconsistency or can they be explained as part of the author's argument? Is there but one speaker in the book or do we have a dialogue between a worldly-wise cynic and a pious believer? The possibilities are numerous, a fact reflected in the great variety of interpretations offered in every era, from ancient to modern.

The essential point to bear in mind in reading Ecclesiastes is that it belongs to that literary genre known as Hebrew Wisdom. The author is not a prophet who speaks from the standpoint of divine revelation, but one of 'the wise' who reasons his teaching from what he observes and experiences. He does not demand obedience by announcing, 'Thus saith the Lord', but seeks to instruct and persuade by appealing to his hearers' understanding.

As in much of the wisdom literature, there may be nothing particularly religious about the author's statements at all (cf., for example, the non-religious, down-to-earth practicality of many of the sayings collected in Proverbs). We are no doubt at variance with the sage's intentions if we read his book as if it were a collection of pious reflections on the abiding worth of the 'spiritual' life in contrast to the transitoriness of earthly desires. Our author has not set out to comfort the hearts of the faithful by assuring them that, in spite of the apparent futility of life, all is well if one has faith in God. Rather, he faces squarely the anomalies of life and seeks to find some meaning to existence; then, on the basis of his reasonings, he offers advice to his hearers.

The author is not a mystic but a hard-headed realist. He has no time for cant. If we may make a comparison with the book of Job, he stands not with the orthodox whose well-rehearsed platitudes remove all problems, but with Job, whose experiences drive him to seek different answers.

For all his earthiness and scepticism, the author of Ecclesiastes is by no means an atheist, not even a humanist. In fact, it is his belief in God which gives him his interpretation of life. That interpretation we understand, in summary, as follows.

Any apparent 'plus' in life is cancelled out by the ultimate certainty of death (2: 14, 18; 5: 16; 6: 1–6). It seems that man is the victim of inexorable fate. But is he? The author does not see it in such impersonal or pessimistic terms. For him God is the controller of life and death; everything is determined according to His purposes (3: 14; 8: 15). True, those purposes may be unknowable (3: 11; 11: 5), but that is no cause for despair. The meaning of life may be hidden from man, but the author, in spite of his occasional moments of frustration, never really doubts that such a meaning *does* exist (3: 11; 8: 16 f.; 9: 1). Man's duty is not to search after what God has kept to Himself, but to enjoy what God has given to man, namely, life (3: 12 f.; 5: 18 ff.). Therefore, let man face life not with dread but with joy. Let him find enjoyment in the world God has created for him and in all his activities in that world (2: 24; 9: 7 ff.); not, however, in the sense that he abandons himself to the pursuit of pleasure for its own sake without any consideration of higher values, but in the sense that he accepts life, with both its plus and its minus elements, as the gift of God, the Creator (11: 8–12: 1). Moderation and self-discipline there must be (7: 14–18), but one's basic attitude must be positive. It is full-blooded enjoyment that the author counsels, not passive resignation; for once a person has declared himself for God, he must make judgments on the issues that confront him in God's world. Let him, then, choose wisdom rather than folly, righteousness rather than wickedness, life rather than death (7: 12; 8: 8; 9: 4).

These positive injunctions are balanced, however, by some solemn observations of the realities of a workaday world. The author's insistence upon the proper enjoyment of life is because life is brief and because it is given by God as a gift, not because those who do good are always rewarded and those who do evil are always punished. He knows that this is not so (8: 14). Yet though he cannot understand God's working, again he does not reject it. He cannot explain how unjust men are allowed to prosper, but he does not lose his faith in God. He makes no claim to have found the answer to the problem of suffering and evil, but he nevertheless is assured that God is a good Creator, in the enjoyment of whose gifts man can find at least some significance to life (3: 11 ff.).

The author rejects the traditional wisdom of the wise with its neatly ordered solutions to life's problems and its confident assertions of how and why God acts. The highest wisdom to which man can rise is to face the fact that he is merely a creature and that true wisdom rests only with God. God is sovereign and God is Creator: on these two basic facts, without developing his theology further, the author has constructed his philosophy of life.

Authorship and date

The name Ecclesiastes is an English transliteration of the Greek title given to the book by the translators of the Septuagint. The Hebrew word from which the translators derived this title is *qōhelet*, the name by which the author of the book calls himself. What the author had in mind in choosing *qōhelet* as his pseudonym is difficult to ascertain. The word has to do with summoning or gathering a congregation. Possibly it signified one who called or, more likely, addressed a gathering of people, hence (via the Greek *ekklēsiastēs*) the well known English title, 'the Preacher'. If 'preacher', then he is, to say the least, a most unorthodox one. Other suggestions such as philosopher, lecturer, debater, or teacher are probably closer descriptions of the position adopted by the author.

There has been much debate over the identity of the author. Today, virtually all Old Testament scholars, even the most conservative, are of the opinion that a king who lived in the 10th century B.C. could not have been the author of Ecclesiastes. They claim that the Hebrew is far too late and points to a time when Aramaic was becoming the popular language of Palestine. Some have even argued that the book was written originally in Aramaic then translated into Hebrew. Gordis, however, argues convincingly against this, adding the suggestion that the author most likely spoke both Aramaic and Hebrew, but wrote his learned works in Hebrew, albeit with an Aramaic flavour. Hebraized Aramaic words and constructions, plus the presence of Persian loan-words and the apparent influence of Greek on the language, seem to support a date of writing somewhere in the 4th or 3rd century B.C.

The tradition of Solomonic authorship stems from the biographical details of the first two chapters. It seems our author has followed the not uncommon practice of identifying himself with some well known figure in order to give point to his argument. In these two chapters he places himself in the position of Solomon (though it should be noted that he nowhere calls himself Solomon) whose wisdom, indus-

try, wealth, and general life-style provide the author with a fitting background for his opening reflections on the saying (possibly also from Solomon), 'Vanity of vanities, all is vanity'. This section (1: 12–2: 26) is but one of many short essays which the author has brought together in his book (see *Composition and Style* below) and it is in only this section that he assumes the Solomonic identity. His acid comments elsewhere on the injustice, folly, oppression, and ruthlessness of rulers hardly reflect the viewpoint of a king (*e.g.* 3: 16; 4: 1, 13–16; 5: 8; 8: 3 ff.; 10: 4–7, 16–20).

Anonymity of authorship is no barrier to our understanding the book's teaching. The worth of a book derives from the truth inherent in it, not from the name of the author.

Little is known of the personal life of the author. Being one of the wise, he no doubt belonged to the upper classes and most probably lived in Jerusalem (note his assumption that his readers attended the temple and his familiarity with life at the higher levels of government: 5: 1, 2, 8; 8: 2 f.; 10: 4). He would have taught in one of the wisdom schools there, and this book indicates something of the content and style of his teaching (12: 9 f.). We gather from his writing that he was a very observant, very sensitive person, though at the same time he had a robust zest for the good things of life. He had a wide experience on which to draw to illustrate his teachings. His nostalgic comments on the enjoyments of youth (11: 9) and his moving description of the decline of old age (12: 2–7) suggest that he wrote his book in his later years.

Composition and style

It must be admitted that the author of Ecclesiastes made no effort to summarize his teaching in the form we have outlined. His book in parts seems to have little logical progression of thought, being, it appears, a collection of some of his philosophic reflections in later life. However, there does seem to have been an effort to arrange the essays in some sort of sequence. The opening section (chs. 1 and 2) provides a fairly straightforward presentation of the author's theme. The essays which follow are restatements, evaluations, or developments of this theme, and each touches in some way on one of the author's basic considerations, such as the futility which death brings to life, the God-given duty to enjoy life, the tragedy of folly, etc. There are variations in style from essay to essay: reflections in the first person, exhortations in the second person, general comments on life, and pithy wisdom sayings.

The apparent inconsistencies between the various sections of the book have given rise to many theories of reconstruction and analysis. Various schemes of multiple authorship have been suggested but have not proved convincing. A more popular theory is that one or more of the conservative wise men worked over the original radical writing, inserting orthodox aphorisms at appropriate points to tone down the author's heterodox statements. By contrast, we believe that the more orthodox statements are part of the author's argument. After all, he did belong to the school of the wise, even if he was regarded as a renegade, and it is natural that he should draw on the fund of wisdom

sayings available to him. His thought-processes, vocabulary, and literary style reflect the environment in which he was trained.

Modern scholars are increasingly returning to the view that the book is from one hand, and that all the inconsistencies must be accepted as an essential part of the author's thesis. Possibly there are editorial notes at the beginning and end of the book (1: 1; 12: 9–14), in which case the book proper begins and ends with the theme, 'Vanity of vanities, all is vanity'.

ANALYSIS

I ACCEPT WHAT GOD GIVES AND ENJOY IT (1: 1–4: 16)
    i The world as it appears (1: 1–11)
    ii The search for a purpose to life (1: 12–2: 26)
    iii Everything happens at its appointed time (3: 1–15)
    iv There is no moral order in the world (3: 16–4: 3)
    v The futility of achievement (4: 4–16)

II MAKE THE MOST OF LIFE'S VARIED CIRCUMSTANCES (5: 1–10: 20)
    i Advice about religion (5: 1–7)
    ii Wealth is useless without contentment (5: 8–6: 12)
    iii The value of wisdom in an imperfect world (7: 1–14)
    iv A warning to avoid extremes (7: 15–29)
    v Compromise is the way to survive (8: 1–9)
    vi There is no justice in life (8: 10–17)
    vii In view of death, enjoy life (9: 1–12)
    viii Wisdom is better than folly (9: 13–10: 20)

III HAVE A POSITIVE ATTITUDE TOWARDS LIFE (11: 1–12: 14)
    i Have boldness in spite of uncertainty (11: 1–8)
    ii The enjoyment of life is a responsibility (11: 9–12: 8)
    iii Final comments (12: 9–14)

I. ACCEPT WHAT GOD GIVES AND ENJOY IT (1: 1–4: 16)
i. The world as it appears (1: 1–11)
Looked at from one point of view, life certainly does not seem to have much purpose. A man works hard all his life but gains nothing by it. In the end he dies and loses all. The same thing happens generation after generation; nothing changes (1: 1–4). The sun rises and sets, then the next day rises again—and so it goes on, day after day. The wind blows but is never exhausted, circling round to follow the same course all over again. Year after year rivers empty their waters into the sea, yet the rivers never dry up and the sea is never full (5–7). There is nothing but constant, weary movement, yet nothing really changes, nothing satisfies. The past will be repeated in the future; but the past is soon forgotten, and the same fate awaits the future (8–11).

1: 1. See Introduction. **the Teacher:** the Heb. *qōhelet* is a feminine participle form, which suggests that originally it probably signified an occupation but later came to be applied to the person engaged in that occupation. **2. meaningless:** vanity, breath; i.e., without substance, empty, transient. **3. under the sun:** on the earth; life in the world of men. See also on 2: 19. **5.** After completing its day's travel, the 'weary' sun **hurries** back to its starting point, only to repeat the process next day, and every day. In other word, it gets nowhere! **8. wearisome:** both to the man who observes the phenomena and to the phenomena themselves. Nothing man says, sees, or hears can explain this futile toiling in nature's monotonous round. **11. no remembrance of men of old:** i.e., people too easily forget what happened in past generations. It is because of this that things appear to them as new (v. 10).

ii. The search for a purpose to life
(1: 12–2: 26)

Speaking as Solomon, the author now describes his own painful experience as he went about the frustrating business of trying to find a meaning to life. First he tried the way of wisdom, only to be driven to the conclusion that all man's activity is, in the long run, futile. Man cannot change what fate has determined (12–15). The author used his great learning and experience to study not only wisdom but also its opposites, but he still found no answer to his problem. His experiment with wisdom led only to greater frustration and misery (16–18).

Continuing his search, the author then turned to pleasures of various kinds, but he found nothing of enduring worth (2: 1–3). He used his resources and know-how to construct lavish buildings and to provide himself with luxurious gardens and farms; he amassed a personal fortune; he equipped his household with everything he needed for a life of uninhibited pleasure (4–8). At the time, all this activity brought a certain satisfaction, but as he looks back the author confesses that it was all to no purpose. He was no nearer to finding life's supreme good (9–11).

Solomon's wealth and achievements were unsurpassed. No one could do more than he had done. But if even he found that all this brought no lasting satisfaction, what chance is there for anyone else? The author therefore turns to consider wisdom and folly once again (12). Obviously, wisdom is better than folly: what is perfectly clear to the wise man, the fool can not even see! On the other hand, what lasting benefit does wisdom confer? For the wise man dies just like the fool and both alike are soon forgotten (13–16).

The futility resulting from the fact that the advantage of wisdom over folly is cancelled by death is enough to make the wise man hate life (17).

Not only has wisdom no advantage over folly, diligence has no advantage over idleness. Conscientious hard work leads in the end only to despair. A man uses all his intelligence and skill in his work, toiling at it by day and worrying about it at night, but when he dies all that he has built up passes to someone who did not work for it and who may even ruin it (18–23).

All this drives the author to the firm conclusion that God intends man to enjoy the good things of life and find enjoyment in his work. This is God's gift. The person who accepts this gift pleases God; to him God gives the means to enjoy His gift. The person who does not accept pleasure as God's gift (but pursues it as a goal to be attained by his own efforts) displeases God and is branded a sinner. All he builds up is ultimately lost and he discovers, to his despair, that life is futile (24–26).

1: 13. wisdom: i.e. intellectual enquiry, which the author finds inadequate for an understanding of life's meaning. Elsewhere he commends wisdom (practical wisdom) as being of value in the affairs of everyday life (*e.g.*, 2: 13 f.; 7: 11 f.; 8: 1–5; 9: 13–18). **heavy burden:** 'to be afflicted with' (Gordis); 'a grievous affliction' (Scott); 'a miserable fate' (GNB). **14. chasing after the wind:** lit. feeding on the wind, i.e., futile. **15.** probably a quotation; so also v. 18. **17. madness:** revelry, recklessness, wickedness; applied here to the author's thought rather than his conduct. Experiments with the latter are described in the next paragraph, 2: 1–11. **18.** The greater the wisdom, the greater the feeling of frustration.

2: 1. test you with pleasure: the test and the results are given first (vv. 1 f.). Verses 3–11 fill out the details. **3. my mind still guiding me with wisdom:** his indulgence was not complete abandonment. He was able to form a judgment on developments arising from his experiment. **5. parks:** Heb. *pardesim*, plural of *pardes*, a loan-word from Persian *pairi-daeza*, '(royal) enclosure', whence also comes Gk. *paradeisos*, used in LXX of the earthly Eden (*e.g.* Gen. 2: 8; Ezek. 28: 13) and in NT of the paradise above (*e.g.* Lk. 23: 43; 2 C. 12: 3; Rev. 2: 7). **7. slaves:** both born into his household and acquired from elsewhere. They would be needed in large numbers for his grandiose enterprises. **9.** The author adds point to his argument by emphasizing that this unrivalled capacity to pursue pleasure as a worthwhile object of human endeavour was utilized according to the best wisdom available. **10.** Wisdom told him to use his fortune to gain maximum pleasure from life. He did, and it brought some satisfaction. But that was the only reward; it soon wore off. The ultimate good still escaped him (v. 11). **reward:** elsewhere 'lot' (3: 22; 5: 18 f.), 'portion' (9: 9).

12. the king's successor can do no more than Solomon did; the new king is doomed to the same futility. **15 f.** The author did not have available to him the New Testament teaching on life after death with its retributions and rewards. Even if he did he would not have used it to provide some glib answer to the problem before him. Death, and the vague, shadowy existence of Sheol which lay beyond it, was not something to look forward to (see 9: 10).

18. things I had toiled for has the meaning of 'that which is achieved by toil', 'that which is earned'. It is the *fruits* of one's labours that are left to another, hence the despair of v. 20. **19. under the sun:** in this context, 'during my lifetime' (Scott). **22. striving:** mental strain deriving from the futile wisdom of v. 19. **23.** A remarkably apt description of modern man. It is the ceaseless, driving activity of laying plans, setting goals, expending effort, fulfilling ambitions which drives the person to **pain** and **grief.** Contrast this with the peaceful enjoyment of work in v. 24. The former is man's torture of himself; the latter is God's gift.

24. There is no suggestion that pleasures mentioned hitherto were 'man-made' but the pleasures in this verse are 'God-given'. The author makes no distinction between secular and sacred, since all come from God. Rather the distinction is between pleasure pursued as a goal in life and pleasure accepted from God's hand as a natural consequence of His creation. It comes when it is not sought for in itself. **25.** 'All power to experience the sensation of eating and drinking comes from God' (Jones). **26. sinner:** used here not with its conventional meaning of 'opposite of righteous' but as the equivalent of the person who wastes his energies on futile pursuits. He is a sinner because he displeases God, in contrast to the one who **pleases** Him. He misses the enjoyment God desires for him; the other finds it. This 'sinner' is the frustrated 'seeker-after-life's-meaning' of the author's narrative. He loses to others the benefits he imagined he was accumulating for himself (cf. v. 26b with v. 21) and concludes again that 'all is meaningless' (cf. v. 26c with v. 21b). Gordis comments that whereas conventional wisdom declares that the sinner is a fool, here the fool is a sinner.

iii. Everything happens at its appointed time (3: 1–15)

In ch. 1 the author had contemplated the apparent futility of life in the light of the repetitive cycle in the natural world (see 1: 2–11). In ch. 3, ignoring for the time being the conclusion reached in 2: 24–26, he goes back to take another look at the meaninglessness of existence, this time in the light of that fixed order of events into which all man's activity fits according to God's pre-ordained plan. It is but wasted effort for man to try to improve his lot, since everything will continue to happen at the particular time God has determined it to happen (3: 1–9).

This awareness of an inexorable fate creates feelings of bitter frustration, for though man's mind reaches out after the eternal it is not able to grasp it. Man can still not understand God's ways. Since God has designed each happening to fit perfectly into its appropriate setting, man should accept whatever circumstances God sends him and find pleasure in them (10–13). But the realization that he cannot alter what God has prescribed, even if he wants to, keeps him in a state of fear before God (14, 15).

3: 1. time: Heb. *z⁰mān*, a late Aramaism (found also in Ezr. 10: 14; Neh. 10: 34; Est. 9: 27) meaning here 'a fixed or appointed time'. **season:** a time when something occurs or happens. The words are used in vv. 1–8 not in the sense that there is a time and place for

everything, but in the sense that everything happens at the appointed time which has been determined for it. That this is the meaning is confirmed by the author's sardonic question in v. 9 and the conclusions he draws from it in vv. 10–15. **2.** Then follows a list, arranged in seven pairs of opposites, representative of the whole range of activities which fill up a person's life. **5. scatter stones . . . gather them:** early Jewish commentators understood this as a metaphor for engaging in or refraining from marital intercourse, an interpretation supported by the second part of the verse.

11. The author is confident that life has meaning. What disturbs him is that man cannot find out that meaning. **made everything beautiful in its time:** referring to events rather than materials. **eternity:** Heb. *hā'ōlām*; the most disputed word in the book. Differences of interpretation have to do with the varying usages of the word in Biblical and non-Biblical Hebrew, the alternative vocalization of the Hebrew consonants, and the peculiar character of the author's thought. Interpretations gather around three main ideas: (i) eternity, the notion or conception of eternal things, an urge to omniscience, the divine quality in man; (ii) the world, worldliness, the love of the world, a sense of the sum total of past and future events; (iii) forgetfulness, ignorance, darkness, an enigma, toil. **12, 13.** See on 2: 24–26. **14. revere him:** 'fear before him' (RSV). The author's frame of mind suggests a beaten-into-subjection fear, resignation, rather than the reverential 'fear of the Lord'. **15.** The endless cycle, the constant repetition in God's ordering of human affairs; an echo of the concluding observation in the parallel passage in ch. 1 (cf. 1: 9–11).

iv. There is no moral order in the world (3: 16–4: 3)

Though well aware of the fixed order of God in human affairs, the author at the same time observes that there seems to be no moral order in the world around him. For example, wickedness and injustice abound (16). A person might find comfort in the thought that God will put everything right in some judgment day in the after-life (17); on the other hand, there may not be an after-life. Maybe God is trying to show men, by the common fate He has determined for them and beasts, that really they are no better off than the animals. And who can *prove* that men have life after death anyway? The best a man can do, concludes the author, is to enjoy life while he can (18–22). Not all, however, can enjoy life. The unhappy victims of oppression would be better off dead, better off still had they never been born (4: 1–3).

3: 16. An allusion to corruption in judicial and administrative affairs. **19. breath:** or spirit (v. 21); cf. wind (1: 14). See also on 12: 7. **22.**

Enjoy the present, for who knows what will happen after death? **4: 1. oppression:** tyranny; exploitation of the disadvantaged by those with power and influence. **2.** Cf. 9: 4 ff.

v. The futility of achievement (4: 4–16)
Various examples are now given to illustrate the uselessness of so much of man's hard work. First there is the case of the man who can never relax and enjoy his work because he is continually driving himself in order to be ahead of his competitors (4). Another does not work at all and ultimately destroys himself (5). Both extremes should be avoided. Better that a man be relaxed and enjoy what he does than drive himself on by ambition only to create difficulties for himself (6).

Another unhappy example is that of the man who lives alone without family or friends and wears himself out making money. He himself has no time to enjoy the fruits of his labours and he has no dependants who will enjoy them after him (7, 8). Various proverbs are added to show that one who cuts himself off from others is really harming himself, for co-operation with others increases a person's security (9–12).

Probably no one experiences the futility of achievement more than the great man who falls from power. He may have risen from poverty and imprisonment to overthrow a long established king who, because he would no longer listen to advice, had become a fool in his old age (13, 14). Yet even this brilliant youth will find that the acclaim with which he was greeted by his subjects will not last for ever. When he is dead he will soon be forgotten (15, 16).

4: 4. envy: rivalry; i.e., competition spurs him on to greater output and a higher quality of work. **5. folds his hands:** cf. our 'twiddles his thumbs' (Ryder). **ruins himself:** lit 'eats his own flesh,' i.e. starves. **8. he asked:** not in the original but supplied to make up the sense, introducing the quotation which follows.

12a. 'If a man is alone, an assailant may overpower him, but two can resist' (NEB). **13–16** is probably best understood as a parable, a typical 'rags to riches' story, though many suggestions have been made as to the historical identity of the people involved. **14. within his kingdom:** presumably the kingdom into which the youth was born and which he was destined to rule. **15. the youth:** Heb. 'the second youth' (RSVmg). Not a third person introduced into the story, but the youth of v. 13 f., 'the lad who was second', 'the old man's successor' (Gordis). **16. no end to all . . . before them**. The idea is similar to that of 1: 3 f.; 1: 9 ff.; 3: 15: in the endless cycle of generations, a man's fame is nothing: those who come before him do not know of it and those who come after him have forgotten it.

II. MAKE THE MOST OF LIFE'S VARIED CIRCUMSTANCES (5: 1–10: 20)

i. Advice about religion (5: 1–7)
It is natural that in dealing with the practical aspects of life the author, being a teacher, should have something to say on religious matters. First he warns against thoughtless participation in temple rituals. The person is a fool who offers a sacrifice without either an understanding of what he is doing or a desire to learn the implications of his religion (5: 1). A person thinking of making a vow must consider his vow carefully before pronouncing it before the Almighty. Too many words will lead to a foolish vow just as too much work will lead to a night of foolish dreams (2, 3). Vows are not compulsory, but once made they have to be carried out. Making excuses to the temple official about a broken vow will not help a person escape God's punishment (4–6). The more reason, therefore, to fear God and avoid irresponsible speech (7).

5: 1. Guard your steps: be careful! Remember, you are going to worship God. **listen:** implying understanding. **3.** It is not uncommon for an author to quote a current proverb in its entirety, though his chief concern may be with only part of the proverb (in this case, the latter part). **6. the messenger:** probably the priest or official whose responsibility it was to collect payments due to the temple. **7.** The text seems to have suffered in transmission. Possibly it is a proverb, used similarly to that in v. 3. It would then be apposite to vv. 4–6 as v. 3 is to vv. 1, 2.

ii. Wealth is useless without contentment (5: 8–6: 12)
The author now moves on to note the dangers created by greed for money, and points out that the imagined benefits of wealth, sometimes ill-gotten, sometimes ill-used, are but an illusion. To begin with he cites corruption in government. Each official extorts as much as he can, since other officials in the echelons above him are waiting for their 'cut' from the proceeds. It is therefore not surprising that the poor and defenceless suffer most from such a system (8). Since all cultivated land is subject to royal taxes, the grasping officials have ample opportunity to grab their share of the profits (9).

Yet wealth does not satisfy, because the more a man has, the more he wants. The rich man sees his prosperity build up only to be spent on others. He lies awake at night worrying while the labourer sleeps soundly (10–12). He may even lose his accumulated wealth in an unsuccessful business venture, ending up with nothing to pass on to his son in spite of a lifetime of hard work (13–17). Life is short and a man should find enjoyment in the things God has given him—food, possessions, work. This is God's will. The joy comes from Him (18–20).

However, not all who have the wherewithal can enjoy it. A person who has all the good things of life may die without having enjoyed them and someone else gains the benefit (6: 1, 2). A man may live long and be prosperous, but if he fails to enjoy what he has, then a still-born babe, never having seen the light of day, is better off than he (3–6). No matter how much a man works to provide for himself, he is never satisfied. What use is it, therefore, for him to be continually striving to improve his lot in life? It is better that he should find enjoyment in what he has than that he should reach out constantly for more (7–9). After all, he cannot change the course of events which God has determined. It is wasting words to argue with God, either about what is best for man during his short life on earth, or about what will happen after he dies (10–12).

5: 9. The text has suffered in transmission and is variously translated. NIV, followed above, seems best suited to the context. **11.** More wealth, more parasites; more possessions to look at, but less enjoyment. The author's standpoint among the upper classes is reflected here, also in vv. 12, 14a. **17. in darkness:** so stingy that he ate his food in the dark to save oil but the meaning could be metaphorical, *viz.*, in bitterness and gloom. **18.** Conventional wisdom taught that he who fulfils God's will is happy; Ecclesiastes, that he who is happy is fulfilling God's will (see note on 2: 26).

6: 3. does not receive proper burial: he has the disgrace of dying forgotten. **4, 5. it:** the still-born child. **its name is shrouded:** it leaves no name behind. It is forgotten. **6. the same place:** Sheol, the world of the dead. 'Both the foetus and the man who lives for two thousand years end in Sheol, and the shorter journey is preferable, says Qoheleth' (Jones). **7.** A proverb; so also v. 9a. The author builds these loosely connected proverbs into a coherent argument (see above). **9.** 'Better a joy at hand than longing for distant pleasures' (Gordis). **10. named:** determined. The author summarizes by returning to one of his main themes. **12. life** is **meaningless:** because it is determined from outside and man can do nothing to change it.

iii. The value of wisdom in an imperfect world (7: 1–14)

In a series of proverbs, some borrowed and others his own, the author faces up to the realities of life and makes some suggestions. He realizes that life has to be lived in spite of its misfortunes, and that to expect perfection is to invite disappointment. He therefore recommends attitudes which will help a person to accept life's circumstances, for better or for worse, and make the most of them.

A good reputation is desirable but can never be permanently secured till the person has completed life satisfactorily. His deathday, then, is more important than his birthday. It is the climax of his life: his good name is at last safe (7: 1). Better, therefore, to live with a view to the certainty of death than to waste life in empty frivolity (2–4).

The sincere rebuke of a wise man is better than the empty praise of a fool, but even a wise man can become a fool if he allows himself to become corrupted by greed (5–7). A man with patience will wait for the outcome of a matter. He will not be prematurely boastful, will not lose his temper, and will not try to escape present frustrations by the foolish wish to bring back the past (8–10). Wisdom and wealth, when used together, can improve the quality of a person's life and also give him greater security (11, 12). But whatever circumstances a man finds himself in, he must accept them as sent by God and not try to change them. He must remember that he cannot understand the meaning of the complex events of life, but he can at least enjoy the good that comes to him (13, 14).

7: 1. name: reputation. **fine perfume:** its significance in the proverb is its pleasant odour. Often in this section the author appears to quote a common proverb, then add his own comment, often introduced by 'for'; *e.g.*, v. 2a is the proverb, v. 2b his comment. **2. better to go to a house of mourning:** because of the reminder it gives that death is the inevitable end of man. **3. heart:** in Hebrew connected more with the mind than with the emotions. Sobriety is conducive to the improvement of the mind, levity is not. Likewise v. 4 contrasts the wise mind and the foolish mind.

5. song of fools: praise of fools. **6.** Foolish talk and laughter generate nothing but noise. **10.** Cf. 1: 9–11; 3: 15. **11.** Either (i) wisdom is good when one has the means to enjoy it, *e.g.*, Solomon (1: 12–2: 26); therefore, too bad for the man who is wise but poor; or (ii) an inheritance should be utilized with wisdom, otherwise it may be foolishly squandered. **those who see the sun:** the living. **12.** 'Wisdom is better with an inheritance . . . for there is the double protection of wisdom and money, and the advantage of knowing that wisdom preserves the lives of those who possess it' (Gordis).

iv. A warning to avoid extremes (7: 15–29)

The author observes that righteousness does not always lead to happiness nor wickedness to suffering. The righteous may die prematurely; the wicked may live long. This prompts the author to suggest a middle course, where one's enjoyment of life will not be ruined either by an over-zealous concern for righteousness and wisdom or by a too tolerant attitude towards wickedness and folly. The person who avoids both extremes and who obeys God will be successful in the end (15–18). Certainly righteousness and wisdom are preferable to sin and folly, but a person should also face up to the plain fact that everyone sins sometimes. No one can argue with this, for every man knows that he himself is guilty of the sins he sees in others (19–22).

Again the author points out how he searched for the meaning underlying all existence, but he found it beyond the capacity of man to comprehend. Absolute wisdom was beyond his reach (23, 24). So he turned his attention to the realm of human conduct. Here at least he could see the advantages of wisdom and reason over folly and madness (25). His unfortunate experiences with women provided him with one example of folly. With charm they enticed him only to deceive, leaving him with a feeling of bitter distrust. He concludes that a wise man is rare enough, but a wise woman is non-existent (26–28). For this he blames not God, but man, who has been too smart for his own good (29).

7: 15. I have seen: though the doctrine of the 'golden mean' was widely known in the world of Greek philosophy, our author develops the idea against the background of his own thought and experience. **16. over-righteous . . . overwise:** the warning is against extremism. Religious fanatics (v. 16) as well as criminals (v. 17) bring disaster. **18. the one . . . and . . . the other:** hardly referring to righteousness and wickedness; more likely a generalism pointing to the middle path. **will avoid all extremes:** This free translation of a difficult idiom probably catches the sense intended by the author. **19. ten rulers:** possibly a reference to the ten-man form of government in cities of the Greek Empire. **20. righteous man:** connected with the 'wise man' of v. 19. To the author righteousness is inseparable from wisdom, and wickedness from folly (cf vv. 15 ff., 25).

23. all this: referring to what follows. **25. to search out . . . the scheme of things:** to seek to reach a conclusion. So also v. 27. **26. sinner:** as opposed to the man **who pleases God.** It is the way each finds his enjoyment which makes the difference. See note on 2: 26. **28.** If women have a low rating in the author's judgment, so too do men—only one better over a sample of a thousand! **29. mankind . . . men:** Heb. *'ādām*, mankind as a whole, not men in contrast to women.

v. Compromise is the way to survive (8: 1–9)
Wisdom enables a man to see below the surface of things and to know what is the right way to act. It will teach him that it is better to act

graciously than to be harsh and unbending (8: 1). For example, if he is in the king's service he will do whatever the king commands, even if it is unpleasant. After all, he *has* sworn obedience. Also it is wise (and safe) not to stand around showing displeasure towards an absolute monarch whose word is final (2–4). The wise man need not fear the difficult situations which arise, for wisdom will always show him the way out. He will know when and how to act (5, 6). Yet a man's actions are always accompanied by some uneasiness, for he knows that he cannot foresee the future, that he has no control over life or death, and that wrong-doing is never the solution. Just as there is no escape from battle, so there is no guaranteed success to the wrongdoer (7, 8). Such are the problems one faces when ruled by a dictator (9).

8: 1. explanation: 'meaning' or (in this context) 'solution'. **brightens a man's face:** gives the appearance of graciousness, whatever his inner feelings may be. **hard appearance:** anger, aggressiveness, a determination to have one's own way. **2.** Again the author's upper-class background is reflected. Perhaps his pupils were being trained for some royal court. **oath:** oath of allegiance to the king sworn before God. **3.** 'Show no impatience towards the king and do not persist in a thing if it displeases him' (NEB). **6. misery:** better 'trouble' (RSV). Perhaps the verse means that although troubles and failures are inevitable, there is sure to be a loophole somewhere, so that a wise man will find his way out'. More likely, however, it connects with the following verse and has to do with man's ignorance of the future. **8. wind:** alt. 'spirit' (NIVmg), i.e. the spirit of life in man. **no-one is discharged in time of war:** variously translated and interpreted. Either 'man has no immunity from war' or 'man has no control over war'.

vi. There is no justice in life (8: 10–17)
Often it is difficult to see any principle of justice operating in the world. The wicked go unpunished and even when they are dead and buried people still praise them in the very place where they did their evil (10). To our author it appears that this lack of retribution encourages people to sin. Cynically he observes that the more they sin, the longer they seem to live (11, 12a). The author knows the conventional explanation, namely, that in the end those who fear God will prosper while the wicked will be justly destroyed (12b, 13), but he also knows of many cases where good men suffer while evil men prosper (14). This, however, is no reason for a man to want to opt out of life, for this he cannot do; but he can, and should, find positive enjoyment in what God has given him in life (15). Better this than to spend weary days and sleepless nights searching for answers

which cannot be known. Only God knows the meaning of His own actions (16, 17).

8: 10. The text is obscure, and the reconstructions and interpretations numerous. The point seems to be that neither in life nor in death did justice catch up with these evildoers. **12. Although:** better, 'for' or 'because', making this a subordinate clause of v. 11. **I know that** begins a new sentence. The author quotes (with disapproval) the accepted maxims (vv. 12b, 13). That he does not accept these pat answers is clear from his own comments which precede (vv. 10–12a) and follow (v. 14). The traditional teaching no more satisfies our author than it did Job. **14. is . . . meaningless:** 'makes no sense' or 'is immoral' (Scott's attempts to catch the particular shade of meaning here).

vii. In view of death, enjoy life (9: 1–12)
Continuing his consideration of the lack of any moral order in life, the author finds only limited consolation in the knowledge of God's overruling control, for a man has no way of knowing whether the things which happen to him are a sign of God's pleasure or displeasure. The same fate, death, comes to all men, whether they are good or bad (9: 1–3). The advantage is not that of the good man over the bad, but of the living over the dead. The living can still know and do things, but the dead are useless and forgotten (4–6). Therefore, a person should get out of life, and put into it, as much as he can while he can, for there will be no further opportunity after death (7–10). So much in life seems to depend on chance. Those who deserve success miss out; those who do not deserve calamity are suddenly overtaken by it (11, 12).

9: 1. all this: connecting with the previous verses. **love or hate:** i.e., God's love or hate, His approval or disapproval. The future, which is as uncertain for the righteous as it is for the wicked. The only certainty is death (v. 2 f.). **4. dog:** most despised of beasts in the East; **lion:** noblest of beasts. **5.** The author tempers the 'hope' of the previous verse: certainly the **living** have knowledge—they know that they too will die! **the dead know nothing:** the context (or one look at a corpse) makes the meaning obvious. The dead can no longer join in the everyday activities of life (v. 6b). **7.** Not unbridled pleasure for its own sake, but an enjoyment of the good things of life as God's gift. **God favors,** or approves of, such enjoyment. (See on 2: 24–26; 3: 12, 13; 5: 18, 19.) The enjoyment is full-blooded (v. 10a). **8. clothed in white . . . oil:** signs of rejoicing. **10.** See on 2: 15 f. **11, 12.** The four examples are given not to commend sloth, weakness, laziness, or folly, but to point out that misfortune often besets those deserving of success.

viii. Wisdom is better than folly (9: 13–10: 20)
In this section the author seems to have brought together a number of illustrations and proverbs which, though typical in style of the conventional wisdom teaching, are used by the author in a way consistent with the theme of his book. He begins with a simple story illustrating how a man by his wisdom may save a city, though if he has neither wealth nor power he will soon be forgotten, even by those whom he has saved (13–16). Men may brag and boast and display their might, but it is the quiet word of wisdom which saves (17, 18).

Through a little foolishness much good can be destroyed. Foolishness inclines a man always to do the wrong thing and marks him out as a fool in the eyes of everyone (10: 1–3). By contrast the wise man always knows how to act. A wise courtier, for example, will not panic at a display of temper by the king, but will maintain his composure and thereby avoid making a serious mistake (4). Unfortunately, fools often get into power while more capable men are not given a chance (5–7). Not only in the king's service, but in most things one does, there is an element of danger. Therefore, it is wise always to be careful and to be well prepared, otherwise anticipated success may end in disaster (8–11).

A fool talks without thinking of the consequences of his words and so brings about his own undoing. He wearies himself with endless talk about matters which it is not possible for man to know. He is so stupid that 'he doesn't even know the way to town' (12–15). Rulers who are immature and irresponsible, who use their position solely for their own comfort without consideration for the needs of the people, are a curse to the country they rule. Not so those who are well-born and who discharge their responsibilities with dignity and self-control (16, 17). Idleness brings deterioration. The lazy person must remember that if he wants to enjoy the good things of life he must have the money to buy them (18, 19). The wise man will learn to control his thoughts and his speech, and so keep out of trouble. He will bear in mind that 'walls have ears' (20).

9: 13 ff. Though the story illustrates that wisdom is better than might (vv. 16a, 18a), it also illustrates what has gone before (v. 11). The suggestion that the **poor wise man** was Archimedes, who helped Syracuse by his **wisdom** when it was besieged by the Romans in 212 B.C., is improbable by reason of date and other circumstances.

10: 1. As a few dying flies can spoil good perfume, so a little folly can spoil the good that has been created by wisdom. **2. right . . . left:** in ancient cultures associated respectively with skill and awkwardness, hence approval and disapproval, hence right and wrong. **3b.** Meaning: 'By his behaviour he proclaims his own folly;' not 'He calls everyone else a fool.' **4 ff.**

A further indication of the social background of both the author and his students; see on 8: 2. Note also vv. 16f., 20 below. **8. a pit:** to trap wild animals. These verses have to do with occupational hazards, not tricks against one's neighbour. The lesson: Take care! **a wall:** stone walls were likely hiding places for snakes. **10.** Why use a blunt axe? It is wiser to sharpen the axe beforehand and save energy. The lesson: Always be properly prepared. So also in v. 11: 'Knowing how to charm a snake is of no use if you let the snake bite first' (GNB).

15. he does not know the way to town: probably an idiom implying great stupidity. **16. servant:** rather 'child' (mg) meaning an inexperienced youth. **feast in the morning:** the wrong time for revelries; a sign of decadence in government. **17. of noble birth:** a man properly bred for the position in contrast to the immature upstart of v. 16. **eat at a proper time:** cf. v. 16. **19. laughter:** pleasure. **answer:** it is money which provides the food and drink just mentioned, therefore money can help towards enjoyment. See also 5: 19; 7: 11. **20. in your thoughts:** the danger of harbouring evil thoughts is that one may, in an unguarded moment, blurt out what will later be regretted. **in your bedroom:** in privacy. **a bird on the wing . . . :** probably a folk saying.

III. HAVE A POSITIVE ATTITUDE TOWARDS LIFE (11: 1–12: 14)
i. Have boldness in spite of uncertainty (11: 1–8)
As usual, the author will not countenance a passive attitude towards life. He admits that life is uncertain, but that is no reason to refuse to act positively. Whatever a man decides to do he must work at it boldly in spite of the risks, believing that it will bring the desired results in due course. However, he should spread his resources and not concentrate them in one place. Then if he is overtaken by some misfortune he will not lose everything (11: 1, 2).

Nature itself shows a man that there are many things over which he has no control and which he does not know. If he waits till he is certain before taking action he never will take action (3–5). His attitude must be positive. He must be diligent and optimistic (6). Just as the farmer must spend his day working in spite of his uncertainty about the weather, so a man must make the most of his opportunity to enjoy life while the light of life's day lasts. For the long night of death is approaching (7, 8).

11: 1 has been variously interpreted. Traditionally it was understood to refer to generosity: he who is generous to others will one day be the recipient of generosity himself. In the light of the context it seems more likely to refer

to business ventures. **upon the waters:** some see here a reference to overseas trade. **2.** 'Don't put all your eggs in one basket.' **seven . . . eight:** An idiom meaning 'several', 'many'. **3.** Man cannot alter the laws of nature. 'What is to happen will happen, and what has happened must be accepted' (Scott). **4.** Do not put off necessary activity with the excuse that you are not sure whether conditions will be favourable. **6. both will do equally well:** note the author's optimism, in contrast to the pessimism he is so frequently accused of. He does not consider the possibility that both might do badly! **7, 8.** Life is compared to the light of day, death to the darkness of night.

ii. The enjoyment of life is a responsibility (11: 9–12: 8)
To the author the enjoyment of life is not something about which a man can be indifferent. It is not something he can leave to chance, with the vague hope that maybe some day enjoyment will come his way. He has a positive responsibility to enjoy life now, and God will call him to account for the way he responds to this responsibility. It is particularly important for a person to understand this while he is still young, and so avoid misusing his physical and mental powers by futile pursuits. For he will find that his capacity for the true enjoyment of life will be gone before he realizes it (9, 10).

Let the young man remember that God is the Creator—the Giver of life and all good things—and so let him enjoy God's world and God's gift of life as He intended them to be enjoyed. It will be too late when old age comes and the sunny days of life are gone for ever (12: 1, 2). The author likens the decline of old age to the deterioration of a once stately house. The old man, shaky, bent, half blind, half deaf, unable to sleep well, afraid of heights, and fearful of imaginary terrors, has lost his zest for life (3–5). Finally, death overtakes him. He is (to use another comparison) like a broken bowl or a shattered water jar. Life has come full circle. It leads, in the end to nothing (6–8).

11: 9. Be happy: continuing the theme of v. 8 that the enjoyment of life is an imperative. **10. meaningless:** the familiar word 'vanity', which in this context has the meaning of 'a fleeting breath' (Gordis).

12: 1. Creator: not merely a synonym for God, but an emphasis on the fact that He is Creator. The verse is the climax of the author's repeated injunctions to enjoy the Creator's gifts (*e.g.*, 2: 25; 3: 13; 5: 18 f. See also Introduction: *The meaning of the book*). **2–6.** Though there has long been general agreement that we have in these verses an allegory of old age, there has been no agreement as to its details. Schemes which attempt to make all the details fit a consistent picture throughout, while ingenious, are entirely unconvincing. (A. D. Power has collected and itemized a total of 176 suggested equivalents!) It is doubtful that the writer intended all the details to be understood allegorically. To make matters worse, he has mixed his pictures and inserted a few literal descriptions. Yet in spite of all this the general drift is clear. **2.** The fading light of old age; no chance now that the clouds will pass away or that the sun will shine again. **3.** The features of the run-down house answer to the failing powers of the decrepit old man (or woman)— trembling hands, crooked legs, too few teeth, dimmed eyesight, and failing hearing (4). **4. rise up at the sound of birds:** he is unable to sleep well. **songs grow faint:** he has lost his ability to sing or power to appreciate music. **5. the almond tree blossoms:** his hair turns white. **the grasshopper drags himself along:** he is bent up and walks only with great difficulty. **desire no longer is stirred:** he has no more sexual appetite, or 'caperbuds have no more zest' (NEB). **eternal home:** death. **6.** There are two pictures of death here: (i) The cord holding the lamp is cut, whereupon the lamp falls and its bowl is smashed; (ii) The wheel used in drawing water from the well breaks and the pitcher is smashed. **7. the spirit returns to God who gave it:** all life belongs to God. It comes from Him and it is terminated when He determines.

iii. Final comments (12: 9–14)

The change from first to third person suggests that these biographical footnotes may have been added by another writer, probably one of the author's contemporaries, perhaps one of his former students. Not only did our author teach professionally in the wisdom schools, he also taught among the common people. He prepared his teaching carefully, selecting traditional wisdom sayings to combine with his own, and presented it in a way helpful and instructive to his hearers. But he never twisted the truth to suit his own purposes (9, 10). The writer adds the comment that such wisdom teaching, whose real source is God, both stimulates the hearers and remains firmly fixed in their minds (11).

A warning, however, is necessary, for excessive study can be harmful, particularly if one ventures beyond the teachings laid down by the wise (12). The fear of God and obedience to His commands are still basic to all man's behaviour, and God will hold him accountable for his actions (13, 14).

12: 9–14. Gordis sees here only one editorial addition. Rankin sees two: a first disciple's praise (vv. 9–11) and a second disciple's warning (vv. 12–14). Eissfeldt also sees two, but beginning at v. 12, *viz.*, v. 12 and vv. 13, 14. **9. people:** in contrast to the sons of the rich who attended the wisdom schools. **set in order:** including the idea of composing. **11. one Shepherd:** God. **12. My son:** a common form of address from teacher to pupil. **be warned . . . of anything in addition to them:** a doubtful translation. Possibly it should simply be translated, 'One further warning' (NEB), referring to what follows in **13, 14.** Man's enjoyment of life as God's gift does not excuse him from obedience or exempt him from judgment.

BIBLIOGRAPHY

Commentaries

BARTON, G. A., *The Book of Ecclesiastes.* ICC (Edinburgh and New York, 1908).

FUERST, W. J., *The Books of Ruth, Esther, Ecclesiastes, Song of Songs, Lamentations.* CBC (Cambridge, 1975).

GORDIS, R., *Koheleth: the Man and his World* (New York, 1969).

JONES, E., *Proverbs and Ecclesiastes.* TC (London, 1968).

POWER, A.D., *Ecclesiastes* (London, 1952).

RANKIN, O. S., 'Ecclesiastes' in *IB*, V (New York, 1956).

RYDER, E. T., 'Ecclesiastes' in *Peake's Commentary on the Bible*[2] (London, 1962).

SCOTT, R. B. Y., *Proverbs/Ecclesiastes*, AB (New York, 1965).

Other works

CASTELLINO, G. R., 'Qohelet and his Wisdom', *CBQ* 30 (1968), pp.15–28.

GINSBERG, H. L., 'The Structure and Contents of the Book of Koheleth', in *Supplements to 'Vetus Testamentum'* 3 (1955), pp.138–149.

OSBORN, N. D., 'A Guide for Balanced Living', *The Bible Translator* 21 (1970), pp.185–196.

SCOTT, R. B. Y., *The Way of Wisdom* (New York, 1971).

VON RAD, G., *Wisdom in Israel*, E.T. (London, 1972).

WRIGHT, A. G., 'The Riddle of the Sphinx'. *CBQ* 30 (1968), pp.313–334.

WRIGHT, J. S., 'The Interpretation of Ecclesiastes'. *EQ* 18 (1946), pp. 18–34, reprinted in *Classical Evangelical Essays in OT Interpretation*, ed. W. C. Kaiser (Grand Rapids, 1972).

SONG OF SONGS

R. W. ORR

Authorship and date

The Song is from the school of Solomon, being of the genre of Wisdom. The situation has a parallel in the recognition of David as founder and patron of the school of psalmody. Allusions to Solomon in The Song show him as a distant figure, and a poor example for lovers. We must look to a later age for the author—a conclusion strengthened by the existence of at least two words in The Song belonging to a later period (the Persian word translated **orchard** [4: 13] and the Greek for **carriage** [3: 9]).

The poet's name has not come down to us. Indeed many scholars, as recently as Gordis in 1974, insist that The Song has no single author, but is a collection of lyrics from many places and different periods. If however the reader can perceive an overall design, then he will feel that he has the best proof possible that he is dealing with the work of one hand. The use throughout The Song of a common stock of vocabulary and ideas tends to the same conclusion. The recurring motifs and images, usually given a piquant new twist on their second or third use, furnish important clues to the structure. They are many, and include: apple tree (2: 3; 8: 5), left arm and right (2: 6; 8: 3), I charge you (2: 7; 3: 5; 8: 4), my beloved, like a gazelle (2: 9; 2: 17; 8: 14), vines in bud (6: 11; 7: 12), let me hear your voice (2: 14; 8: 13), my lover is mine (2: 16; 6: 3; 7: 10), until the day breaks (2: 17; 4: 6), I looked for him (3: 2; 5: 6), I brought him into my mother's house (3: 4; 8: 2; cf. 8: 5), majestic as . . . (6: 4; 6: 10), pomegranates in bloom (6: 11; 7: 12), desert (3: 6; 8: 5).

We know the poet only as one who delighted in the gentle side of nature, and who wrought and polished his verses with loving care. He was apparently a man of wealth and culture, able to exercise discerning appreciation of the good things of life. Herbert conjectures that the author may have been a woman. It is certainly true that The Song regards marriage sensitively from the woman's point of view; and there is of course value in looking at a familiar subject from another viewpoint. But another possibility may be borne in mind: that the poet wrote The Song for his only daughter. His wife was dead, and the many tender references to her are in the way of recapitulating in the daughter their own joys remembered in tranquillity. His generous heart says, We had

our day, and it was good; blessings now on the young folk.

The poet's world was a pleasant place indeed. This fact in itself tends to limit the date of composition to one of the more peaceful periods of Israel's history. There is fairly strong evidence for the 4th century B.C. After the reign of Solomon it was not until the advent of the Medo-Persian empire that the whole land of Israel was at peace under one government. Under the *Pax Persica* one might freely visit the whole land as the poet did, from En Gedi to Lebanon.

Herbert and Henshaw favour a third century date, but this does not allow much time for the recognition and inclusion of The Song in the LXX around the end of that century. Another opinion is that the mention of Tirzah in parallel with Jerusalem (6: 4) places it in the first 30 years of the 9th century, when Tirzah was capital of the northern kingdom. It does seem, though, that the literal meaning of Tirzah (charming) is sufficient reason for its choice by the poet; moreover it avoided the odious name Samaria.

There is indeed a poetry of place names. Who has never felt its power transmute timetables into high romance? Even artificial coinages may have this quality, evoking a range of emotions from delight to horror. '. . . and there upon the grass among elanor and niphredil in fair Lothlórien . . .'; 'Gorgoroth, the valley of terror in the land of Mordor . . .' (J. R. R. Tolkien, *The Lord of the Rings*, pp. 370, 421). In The Song, place names redolent of Israel's history and of scenic interest combine with euphony worthy of Tolkien himself.

1: 14 **En Gedi:** a delightful oasis at the mouth of a wadi in the middle of the west coast of the Dead Sea—perhaps the scene of the song.

4: 1 **Gilead:** the upland pastures on the east of the Jordan.

4: 8 **Lebanon, Amana** (Abana: 2 Kg. 5: 12), **Senir** and **Hermon:** the mountain ranges west of Damascus. There is conscious art in the piling up of these names, and in their association with **lions** and **leopards.** To transpose into a Scottish idiom: from Stornoway to Inverary, by Dunvegan and the Kyle of Lochalsh —rocks of the grey seal, corries of the red deer.

6: 4 **Tirzah** and **Jerusalem:** Tirzah was a pleasant small town in the hill country of Israel north of Shechem, and capital of Israel for the period between Solomon and Omri, when it was replaced by Samaria. Since Tirzah means charming (somewhat like royal Balmoral) we may again transpose the whole verse: Beautiful as Balmoral, majestic as Edinburgh, wi' a hundred pipers and a' and a'.

7: 4 **Heshbon:** a town on a hill near Mt. Pisgah, east of the north end of the Dead Sea, and once the capital of the Amorites. **Damascus:** the Syrian capital.

7: 5 **Carmel:** a hill jutting into the Mediterranean, and overlooking present-day Haifa.

Interpretation

The Song appears to the uninstructed reader to be a frank and uninhibited love song, showing the path of true love by many a winding path from ardent desire through ecstasy to blissful fulfilment. Yet one's sense of the fitness of things immediately rejects this as being all too human. The Song is after all a book of the Bible, and must have a spiritual purpose. Then how are we to read it?—as an allegory—and then whether of history or of spiritual truth? Or as a parable, in which the general idea of earthly love points to something higher? Is it perhaps a drama, and if so has it two, three or four main characters? Or is it just a loose-leaf folder of poems which might as easily be shuffled into some other arrangement? And who is the Solomon referred to? and the Shulammite? These considerations moved Aglen to write that The Song 'holds without question the first place among the puzzles of literature'; and the judicious Rowley observes that 'no book of the OT has found greater variety of interpretation'. This variety is illustrated in the three most recent treatments of The Song in the Scripture Union daily readings. B. C. Aldis (1949): The historical king Solomon is the hero, who woos a country girl under the guise of a shepherd. J. Stafford Wright (1954): Solomon is the villain, who tries in vain to win a country girl from her shepherd lover. H. L. Ellison (1970): The Bible's glorification and justification of pure love within marriage, which embraces the physical as well as the spiritual.

These, however, are mere samples of the range of interpretation. The Song has been viewed as a *historical writing*: Solomon's defence of his marriage with Pharaoh's daughter. It has also been regarded as a *historical allegory*, which when it trenches upon the future becomes somewhat of an apocalypse. The Targum viewed The Song as an outline of the history of Israel from the Exodus to the messianic age. Early Christian writers saw in it the Church under both the Old and the New covenants. Cocceius read the history of the Reformation into The Song: it is John Wyclif who is 'terrible as an army with banners', and Martin Luther whose 'nose is like a tower of Lebanon'.

Much more widely The Song has been read as *devotional allegory*, celebrating the mutual love of God and His people. This was the standard pre-Christian interpretation. 'Rise up my love, my fair one' was a summons to captive Zion to return from the Babylonian exile. 'It eased the conscience of the pious, who were thus relieved of the embarrassment of apologizing for the presence of apparently secular poetry' (Jastrow, p. 9). To the same effect Aglen: 'The history of the interpretation of the book from the earliest times has been a long apology to account for its place in the sacred Canon'. Christian scholars such as Cyril of Alexandria reinterpreted according to their own interests; and so 'the voice of the turtle' became the preaching of the Apostles, and the announcements 'I have come into my garden' and 'Eat O friends' came to refer to the Incarnation and the Lord's Supper. Cyril also found that 'the bag of myrrh that lies all night between my breasts' was none other than Christ ensconced between the old and the new scriptures. These examples are culled from Rowley (pp. 200–208), who remarks sagely, 'That we, for our profit, may rightly find in the images of The Song, as in all experience, images of things spiritual, does not mean that it was written for this purpose'; and again 'We must distinguish between what is devotionally profitable, and what is exegetically sound' (p. 211). The chapter headings of the AV (1611) are a good example of the allegorical interpretation.

Chapter I. 1 The Churches loue vnto Christ. 5 Shee confesseth her deformitie, 7 And prayeth to bee directed to his flocke. 8 Christ directeth her to the shepheards tents. 9 And shewing his loue to her, 11 Giueth her gracious promises. 12 The Church and Christ congratulate one another. Chapter II. 1 The mutuall loue of Christ and his Church. 8 The hope, 10 and calling of the Church. 14 Christes care of the Church. 16 The profession of the Church, her faith and hope. Chapter III. 1 The Church her fight and victorie in temptation. 6 The Church glorieth in Christ. Chapter IIII. 1 Christ setteth forth the graces of the Church. 8 He sheweth his loue to her. 16 The Church prayeth to be made fit for his presence. Chapter V. 1 Christ awaketh the Church with his calling. 2 The Church hauing a taste of Christes loue, is sick of loue. 9 A description of Christ by his graces. Chapter VI. 1 The Church professeth her faith in Christ. 4 Christ sheweth the graces of the Church, 10 and his loue towards her. Chapter VII. 1 A further description of the Church her graces. 10 The Church professeth her faith and desire. Chapter VIII. 1 The loue of the Church to Christ. 6 The vehemencie of loue. 8 The calling of the Gentiles. 14 The Church prayeth for Christes comming.

We find this devotionally profitable indeed, for do we not feel ourselves to be 'loued with everlasting love'? But its being exegetically sound is another question. Matthew Henry writes on 2: 9: 'They saw him looking through the windows of the ceremonial institutions and smiling through those lattices; in their sacrifices and purifications Christ discovered himself to them, and gave them intimations of his grace. In the sacraments Christ is near us, but it is behind the wall of external signs, through those lattices he manifests himself to us; but we shall shortly see him as he is'. Excellent! but Matthew Henry did not find these insights in The Song; he imported them from elsewhere.

Other readers will find their own love object. Roman Catholic interpreters see a reference to the Immaculate Virgin in the salutation 'You are all fair, my love; there is no flaw in you'. A contemporary Urdu writer, relying on Muhammad's descent from Ishmael through Kedar (cf. 1: 5), identifies the Beloved with the prophet of Islam (Abdul Aziz Khalid, *Ghazalul-ghazalat*, Lahore, 1972, p. 128).

The harm caused by treating The Song as a devotional allegory is that it not only uses The Song to shadow forth God's love, which is so abundantly declared elsewhere in story and in psalm; it uses it up entirely, and so misses its intended purpose. There is no other book of the Bible which is devoted to the subject of married love, and so an important element of biblical wholeness may be lost.

Parable differs from allegory in that a spiritual lesson is conveyed, not by each detail in turn, but by the writing taken as a whole. Exegesis on this line will understand the poem in its literal meaning, and in addition will find overtones of the love of God. Scriptures will come to mind such as 'The two will become one flesh. But he who unites himself with the Lord is one with him in spirit' (1 C. 6: 16b, 17). This approach will commend itself to many thoughtful readers. Its first step is of course a study of The Song in its straightforward sense.

We may dismiss the discussion of *heathen fertility rites* as being an academic exercise leading to uncertain conclusions about literary sources. Of much more interest is the work of J. G. Wetzstein (1873), introducing the *Wedding Feast* theory, later taken up and elaborated by E. Renan. It is based on the parallels observed between material in The Song and traditional Syrian wedding customs. In Syria, village weddings take place mostly in Spring, and during the week-long festivities the groom and his bride are treated as king and queen. However, not content with these general insights (which can in any case be derived from The Song and from general biblical background), this and the previous school have gone too far toward making a pagan carnival of the occasion. In addition, the reconstruction by Renan and others is impossibly complex.

We conclude this survey by considering The Song as *drama*. It may have two characters (Solomon and a country girl), three (a triangle including the Shepherd Lover), or four (the Shulammite introduced to aid Solomon by trying to seduce the faithful shepherd). Of these, the *Shepherd Lover* theory has gained widespread acceptance, and is well presented by J. A. Balchin. The difficulty about this is the need to impose quite arbitrary interpretations. Who would have guessed, for example, that although 1: 16 appears to be the girl's response to the king's endearments of 1: 15, she is really thinking of her absent lover?

So we return to the *literal* view: that the Song of Songs is simply love's old sweet song between a lover and his lass. Perhaps we were too hasty in assuming that the Holy Spirit would have nothing to say to us about this human love, and about that covenant of faithfulness which is the basis of human society. Could it be that our difficulty in accepting it in its plain meaning within the covers of our Bible stems basically from an uneasy conscience not yet reconciled and renewed in this area, ever crying in petulance, Why hast Thou made me thus? 'The Song comes to us in this world of sin, where lust and passion are on every hand, where fierce temptations assail us, and try to turn us aside from the God-given standard of marriage. And it reminds us, in particularly beautiful fashion, how pure and noble true love is' (E. J. Young, *Introduction to the OT*, 1949, p. 327).

We shall therefore read The Song as a set of idylls in praise of married love, with dramatic development from desire to fulfilment. This purpose is sufficient in itself, for its teaching on the sanctity and joy of ideal love, and its imperatives of chastity and life-long faithfulness, contribute significantly to the completeness of scripture. The devotional use is secondary, and without any explicit warrant from the NT (for it is nowhere quoted). The Song does provide, in evocative phrases and striking figures, rich vocabulary for devotional use, and good lines for hymns. But as a complete work it belongs to the home rather than to church, and is for personal rather than for congregational reading.

But perhaps the Synagogue has found the happy mean, for by ancient custom it is sung by a cantor on the eighth day of Passover each year—an ideal method of keeping its message alive without the dangers of over-exposure. For we need The Song. God the saviour of all men gives to us The Song in these days of confusion and desperate need, to show to our jaded and cynical age the life-long joys of wedlock after God's own purpose. Yet there has always been an element of resistance to the plain meaning of The Song. In 1567 Luis de

Leon was brought before the Inquisition for declaring that it dealt with human love. May latter-day commentators be preserved from such a fate!

Marriage: the background and the tensions

The choosing of a suitable partner was always considered to be the responsibility of parents. No doubt the entreaties of love-struck youth sometimes guided the process, but that was only the occasional triumph of nature over social convention. Courtship as we know it did not exist. An arranged marriage generally took place when the boy was in his late teens, and the girl a little younger.

The giving by the groom's family of the *mohar*—more happily called bride-gift (Mace) rather than bride-price—and its acceptance by the bride's parents formally constituted an indissoluble alliance between the two families in their children. This differs from modern engagement in that *this* was 'the point of no return' (F. F. Bruce); it awaited only the festive bringing home of the bride to make the marriage fully effective. If we call the first stage 'betrothal', and the second 'marriage', we still have to remember that the betrothed pair were irrevocably committed to each other. The degree of intimacy considered quite proper for them would not be appropriate for a Christian engaged couple under our present conditions. (I am indebted to Mr. H. L. Ellison for material in these two paragraphs.)

The Song is to be thought of as the awaking and ripening of mutual affection between a lad and a girl already betrothed, leading on to the bringing of the bride to her new home, with its happy sequel. An arranged marriage may become, and indeed ought to become, a love-marriage.

From the earliest days of biblical thought, the bride's desire is recognized as nothing less than the law of her constitution as woman: made for her man, she is incomplete without him. In The Song, no shadow of the Fall blights their Eden. Her husband's response to her yearning is not, as in Gen. 3: 16, the exercise of his authority, but his own answering desire. After the Fall, the relationship was locked into the pattern in which the life of the man is work-oriented: he finds satisfaction in his craft. The woman however finds her fulfilment in marriage. It is this psychological asymmetry which fuels the dominance of the man in the partnership. The Song however celebrates an experience of Eden Revisited.

The poet uses the artist's right of selection to deal solely with the *delights* of marriage. That wedlock in this hard world brings cares and hazards, to say nothing of downright distress, is not discussed. Its ecstasies transcend our common experience too. Just as for us the devotion of a psalmist or the zeal of an apostle are matters more of aspiration than of experience, so is it with this vision of ideal marriage. Our circumstances and endowments have been sadly reduced since the gates of Eden closed upon us. But the vision is a noble one, and all true lovers are granted glimpses which validate the truth of it.

Another question is bound to suggest itself to the Christian reader. Does not our Lord, and following Him Paul, recommend by both example and teaching the single state in preference to marriage? How does this square with the glorification of marriage in The Song?

Well, let the other side be put too. Our Lord reflected dignity upon family life by subjecting Himself to the conditions of the home in Nazareth, with parents, brothers and sisters. He bestowed a blessing by His presence and gift at the wedding in Cana. And when the question arose of renouncing marriage for the sake of the kingdom of God, our Lord declared that this is not for all, but only for those enabled by God to accept it (Mt. 19: 10 ff.). And it is Paul who finds in marriage a parable of the love of Christ (Eph. 5: 21–33).

Even so, Paul does show definite reluctance to allow his active fellow-workers to marry. They will certainly have his prayers, and even his blessing, but he won't dance at their wedding. This was precisely paralleled last century in the British occupation of India: empire-builders like Sandeman regretted when their subalterns married, knowing that they could no longer be expected to show the same single-minded commitment to the cause. The parallel is clear: the Church was at war and distress was imminent. Paul had learned from his Lord that the daughters of Jerusalem would soon have good cause to weep for themselves and for their children. Dean Alford declared that the man who marries conforms to God's pattern for man, but those who for Christ's sake abstain from marriage conform to the pattern of our Lord Himself.

To take another example: many (but again not all) Christians find compelling reason to forswear alcohol, even though the Bible, including The Song, hails wine as one of God's good gifts. Where the enemy is seen to gain advantage, sanctions are applied—even sanctions that hurt.

And so abstinence is not in itself virtuous; it is noble only in as far as it is, in the circumstances, a realistic response to the demands of war. There must be, for the duration, a point of iron somewhere in our lives; for demobilization cannot be until our Lord returns, and the trumpet sounds the victory. Yet far, far more than all considerations of policy is the Christian's engagement to follow the Crucified.

My Lord, my Saviour, when I see thee wearing
  Upon thy bleeding brow the crown of
    thorn,
Shall I for pleasure live, or shrink from
  bearing
Whate 'er my lot may be of pain and scorn?

(Jacques Bridaine, 1701–67)

We all know something of both delights and denials, the tension being adjusted for each of us by a distinctively personal equation.

A final question: are the delights of the senses for this world only, or is it possible that the pleasures at God's right hand are for the whole man, and are aesthetic as well as intellectual and spiritual? The answer can hardly be in doubt. We can look forward to a more robust humanity in that life with God for which He is preparing us, when this present phase of struggle and tribulation lies behind us. Marriage and procreation belong entirely to this world (Mt. 22: 30). Yet experience and expression of personal affection will be *more* characteristic of the incorruptible state than of the present, when indeed they must be curbed and even denied. Because of the real dangers of misunderstanding and misuse, the holy kiss urged by both Peter and Paul is now generally reduced to J. B. Phillips's celebrated 'hearty hand-shake all round', or even evaporates into an holy smile. In that vigorous immortality which is God's final intention for us, we shall live and love, work and worship, to the full.

The imagery of The Song is not eidetic; by this is meant it does not, like much modern writing, draw the picture in such realistic detail that the reader imagines himself a participant. Rather is it impressionistic: the symbolic imagery cools the imagination, and raises the thought to the level of idealization. The communing of Bride and Groom is far above mere carnal commerce; it is charged with the psychical energy of nuclear fusion released when two hearts, distanced by the Creator when He made them male and female, approach each other for union in a life-long bond.

ANALYSIS

VI ALL CHOICE FRUITS (7: 10–8: 14)
    i New as well as old (7: 10–8: 4)
    ii In travail (8: 5)
    iii Love is strong as death: a parenthesis (8: 6–7)
    iv Our little daughter (8: 8–12)
    v Happily ever after (8: 13–14)

TITLE (1: 1)

The incomparable **Song**, in the manner of **Solomon** (i.e. in the Wisdom class of literature). Heb. *lišlōmōh* can also mean to, for, or concerning Solomon. NEB has 'The Song of all songs to Solomon'. But some modern scholars regard the title as meaning that it is an anthology of many originally independent songs. Jastrow counts 23 such, while Gordis makes it 30.

I. YEARNING AND RESPONSE (1: 2–11)

In this whole section the groom is absent. The third person pronoun is used, **Let him kiss me.** This once established, the more ardent second person is used (cf. Dt. 32: 15 AV for a similar switch of person), yet all the utterances must be thought of as reverie, soliloquy or apostrophe of the absent lover.

i. Her desire (1: 2–4)

The desire is hers, ordained by God (Gen. 3: 16). The Bible regards the woman, whether in her faithfulness or her folly, as equally with the man a sexual being. Yet she looks to her lover for the initiative. A kiss on the cheek is the time-honoured salutation of friends; **kisses**: many kisses, are for lovers. She would receive these offerings of love with her lips, like **wine.** The interests of poetry and of precision suffer alike in the use of **you** in place of the old, intensely personal 'thou'; but it is a loss that cannot be helped. We who still use the old forms for liturgical purposes are the last generation to do so. We are already a minority, and we mourn our passing.

3. perfumes is an improvement on the old 'ointments', though probably they had an olive oil base. Attar or otto, as in 'attar of roses', is a Semitic word which conveys the idea. Just to repeat his well-loved name, and so remember his graces and commend him to others, seems to fill the house with fragrance. The devotional use is not far to seek.

The problem of interpretation becomes critical with 1: 4 **Take me away with you.** Those who favour the shepherd theory find much of their strength in this verse. Balchin writes convincingly: 'She yearns for her shepherd lover and even though he is absent she calls longingly for him and pleads that he take her

away. It is the king who has brought her into his chambers; she has not come willingly. She speaks to her lover as though she were alone with him'. This is an attractive approach to the problem of the book; later however it becomes difficult to maintain consistently. On our view, the girl imagines herself already ensconced in the apartment of her **king**, her own Prince Charming.

ii. Dark yet lovely (1: 5, 6)

Delighted anticipation now gives way to questionings about her own attractiveness, addressed to the girls, who in their attendance upon the bride are exalted to the temporary dignity of **daughters of Jerusalem**. Her outdoor work in the family **vineyards** has tanned her skin (and the East loves a fair complexion). The hard-headed brothers, with a view to the family fortune, had kept her at work to the detriment of her own **vineyard** ('My face is *my* fortune, Sir, she said'). She is able however to reassure herself. **Dark** indeed she is, like the goathair **tents** of the Bedouin desert-dwellers, **Kedar** and **Salma** (see mg.), but **lovely** too, like a well-fashioned tent.

iii. Where is my lover? (1: 7, 8)

A paragraph division might well be placed after 1: 6, to show that the girl now turns in thought to her lover. She wants to find him, yet fears to wander **like a veiled woman**, blinded and in mourning, not knowing where he is. 'Share my work', he says; **follow the sheep and graze your goats**, and you shall find me. The more they can share each other's interests and work, the more satisfaction they will find. The lost loveliness of the archaic 'O thou whom my soul loveth' (AV) contrasts with the crudity of NEB in 1: 7.

iv. His response: jewels for the fair (1: 9–11)

The girl is not the only person to be thinking about someone else. Now we have her lover's reverie: he is thinking of the most splendid spectacle he has ever seen—the prancing steeds of **Pharaoh's** cavalcade, the very embodiment of grace enhanced by adornment. Those who have seen horses pull only brewery drays or milk floats may need to be reminded that the horse of antiquity was the valued possession of kings. The lad announces his intention of paying a glad tribute in **gold** and **silver** to adorn his bride. It should be noted that the regular usage of The Song is that the groom refers to the bride as **my darling** (beginning with 1: 9), while she refers to him as **my lover** (from 1: 13).

II. THE FIRST LOVE OF ALL
(1: 12–2: 17)

> *Two little children, seeing and hearing,*
> *Hand in hand wander, shout, laugh, and*
> *sing.*
> *Lo in their bosoms, wild with the marvel,*
> *Love, like the crocus, is come ere the*
> *Spring.*
> *Young men and women, noble and tender,*
> *Yearn for each other faith truly plight,*
> *Promise to cherish, comfort and honour;*
> *Vow that makes duty one with delight.*
> *Oh, but the glory, found in no story,*
> *Radiance of Eden unquenched by the Fall;*
> *Few may remember, none may reveal it,*
> *This is the first first-love, the first love of*
> *all.*

(Coventry Patmore, 1853)

Sometimes we older folk wrong our lads and lasses in not recognizing and respecting this beautiful first-love. Here at any rate we have it, the bright shoots and tender buds of simple delight in each other. There is the innocence of children, albeit ripening for something else, in their call to each other: 'Under the greenwood tree, who loves to lie with me'.

i. Under the greenwood tree (1: 12–2: 7)
The **bed** (16) is of course the greensward, and the massive trunks of **cedar** and the over-arching branches of **fir** (17) make a delightful bower for this picnic. The five senses combine to make Eden again of that woodland glade. The **perfume** of v. 12 is nard (cf. Mk 14: 3). It was an imported perfume, to be had from the same shop as the little sachet of gum **myrrh**, worn on a string round her neck (but down out of sight) by any girl who cared about being attractive. 'Close my love is to my heart as the cluster of myrrh that lodges in my bosom all the night through' (Ronald Knox). Natural grace allied itself with fragrance in the **henna blossoms** of their Palestinian vineyard with which she compares her lover: the Flower of En Gedi.

He knows where there is **an apple tree among the trees of the forest** (2:3) and leads her there. 'Apple' is of course a catch-all term for fruit, and the apples we know did not grow in Israel at that period. Ellison prefers to translate 'orange', and the picture is indeed a lovely one: ripe oranges in Spring, 'golden lamps in a green night'. But perhaps *apricot*, which even in the wild state affords a profusion of sweet fruit, is a better guess, and as good a picture. So the shade of the tree makes a **banquet hall**, with apricots for each course,

and kisses for wine to help them down. Tyndale (1534) has a somewhat different scene: 'He brought me into his wyne seller: and his behauer to mewarde was louely'.

At the heart of this little idyll is a repeated pledge of mutual love, first in the positive mode, **how beautiful you are** (15, 16), and then in the comparative (2: 2, 3). The girl responds to his adoration with a modest 'I am only a little crocus' (2: 1 mg)—the meadow saffron which grows in **Sharon**. 'I'm of no more account than the ordinary anemone that blossoms red in every valley'. We must note that **rose** and **lily**, like apple, are general terms; the translations followed here are more exact. It is of especial interest that the common 'lily of the field' (Mt. 6: 28 f.) in which our Lord saw surpassing beauty was probably this very scarlet anemone. 'A mere anemone!' comes the gallant response. 'Compared with you, the other girls are no better than **thorn** bushes.' This leads on to the banqueting house scene, where the beloved is seen as excelling the other young men as the apricot tree excels the common woodland species. There is a proverbial saying in the East that the tall date palm gives fruit but no shade; the spreading pipal gives shade but no fruit. Happy those who sit under an apricot tree, blessed with both shade and fruit. The shade-giving fruit tree is the person who affords both protection and instruction. They are rare, but the beloved is one such. She will linger with delight upon that scene, for it portrayed her beloved so perfectly, and that was the moment when love came like a crimson dawn to her heart. The idyll closer with longing for the caresses of the beloved (2: 6), but for this she must wait. This is the use made here of the earnest charge to the probably frivolous **daughters of Jerusalem, Do not arouse or awaken love:** i.e. beware of arousing passion prematurely; don't urge youth into behaviour for which the time has not yet come. The charge will be repeated twice in different contexts (3: 5; 8: 4), and the three occurrences bring a range of lessons for the proprieties of marriage: maturity, privacy, temperance.

> *Here cherries grow that none may buy*
> *Till Cherry-Ripe themselves do cry.*

In the Heb. **by the gazelles** and **by the does of the field** some (*e.g.* JB) have heard an echo of a similar-sounding adjuration 'by the Lord of Hosts'. If so it is a reminder that it is God himself who has made us male and female, and we are answerable to Him. But the overt appeal is to the example of the timid and graceful little deer, which teach us that the time of love will come in due season.

ii. The season of singing (2: 8–15)
Like the cuckoo in England, **the cooing** of the migratory doves announces that Spring has come to land and to heart (a different word

from that tr. *dove* in 2: 14 etc.). The lithe, active lad, nimble as a deer, comes one fair morning to call his love to the delights of a day in the orchards and vineyards, at a season so much in accord with their own joy. No comment is needed on these charming lines, except in the final verse (15), which commentators find 'cryptic' (JB), 'difficult and unrelated' (Herbert), 'not easy to grasp' (Balchin)—and so it gets loaded with ethical and religious significance. Yet after all it may be no more than a rollicking game, a merry rough-and-tumble among the vines.

> *A-hunting we will go.*
> *We'll catch a little fox*
> *And we'll put him in a box*
> *And never let him go.*

(The thieving fox appears as a motif in Hellenistic pastoral poetry—one of a number of fascinating features which that poetry has in common with The Song.)

iii. Not yet (2: 16, 17)
Our interpretation of these verses hinges on the decision whether it is night or morning when the *day breathes* (so the Hebrew). The majority of commentators decide, strangely enough, for evening; but that is surely the time when shadows *gather*. GNB is clear: 'until the morning breezes blow and the darkness disappears.' We understand the sense to be: (the girl speaks) 'Day is done, my lover. We have had a wonderful time together, and it's time for you to go home now. Another day will come, and at last *the* day will come. Of course we belong to each other, but in the meantime have patience, and be off to your flocks on the flowery meadows. Be a dear deer, and leave as you came. Goodnight.'

III. THE DAY OF HEARTS' REJOICING (3: 1–5: 1)
i. Nightmare: lost before possession (3: 1–5)
The girl's yearning for her lover found expression night after night (for the word **night** is in the plural) in a vision of terror: **I looked for him, but did not find him.** This dramatic tension sharpens the ecstasy of ultimate fulfilment.

By the delicately indirect device of this dream, their long-awaited joy is sketched in anticipation. The dream admits no impediment between the moment when **I found** him: and **I brought him to my mother's . . . room.** There is nothing furtive about it; everything is done with the approval of the family, and the girl delights in taking the same place in the onward march of life as her mother occupied one generation earlier. 'And now, O daughters of Jerusalem, the day was yours, but the night is ours, so you may go. Just as no foot can follow the shy gazelle, and no eye observe what passes in their remote covert—so grant us too the right of privacy. Let no-one disturb us in our seclusion' (3: 5). It was only a dream, but its fulfilment was near.

ii. The day of rejoicing (3: 6–11)
The general sense is clear enough: the girl is carried in procession to the home of the boy's parents. We see the groom in his kingly state as Solomon-for-the-day (9, 11), but we do not see his bride, as today she is modestly veiled (4: 3), and travels in the litter which her own Prince Charming has sent for her. Today for the first time she is called **bride** (4: 8). The **carriage** (literally *bed*, carried by means of poles) is home-made; **'Solomon'** himself had expended a great deal of labour on it, and the girls had made the inside fittings all very splendid. As a special touch of class it is given a fancy Greek name in v. 9; RSV conveys this by using the Portuguese-Indian word *palanquin*.

The young men too had their appointed part: for the day they were the **sixty warriors, the noblest of Israel.** They had sallied forth to accompany the palanquin, all armed with **swords**, or what would pass for swords. No doubt they took turn in carrying the bride while the long, merry train traversed stretches of **desert**, and wended its way along dusty roads **like a column of smoke**. The two families apparently lived in adjacent fertile valleys separated by a considerable hill. At its lowest point, the path crossed over the dusty, stony tail of the hill ('the desert'), which was visible from both homesteads (3: 6; 8: 5). The lad had disdained the path for himself, and taking the shortest way had bounded over the hill like a gazelle (2: 8). Now there, at the boy's home, is 'Solomon's mother' (a thousand times happier than poor old Bathsheba in her palace intrigues), blushing and smiling for the part she has to play. She welcomes the bashful bride, and congratulates her son, who only now actually appears, by crowning him for the happiest day of his life.

The transfer of the girl to her new home with the groom's parents would normally precede the intimacies of marriage. In several Bible histories, as that of Jacob (Gen. 29), circumstances demand some other arrangement; but the general rule is (to quote Derek Kidner, on Gen. 2: 24) 'leaving before cleaving'.

iii. 'How beautiful you are, my darling': groom praises bride (4: 1–15)
The allegorical method can find the whole counsel of God in every dimple of each anatomical system. In a canto like this, the ingenuity of the preacher gets full play, and not seldom the bounds of congregational propriety are breached. I remember a homily centred upon the bride's navel (7: 2). For an hour the preacher took us on a conducted tour in Urdu of the torrid zones north and south of that equator,

to the displeasure of elders and parents present. Some readers know that the agony can be experienced in English too. These passages are not suitable for reading in church, and Scripture Union wisely omits them from the family readings.

The first Bible word for the private relation of husband and wife is 'to know' (Gen. 4: 1 AV), a word which involves the whole personality, with unveiling and opening on the one hand, appreciation and appropriation on the other. The fourth chapter of The Song is the first of such unveilings. Any hand but a poet's would mar it.

> *Her goodly eyes like Saphyres shining bright,*
> *Her forehead Yvory white,*
> *Her cheekes lyke apples which the Sun hath*
> *rudded,*
> *Her lips lyke cherryes charming men to byte,*
> *Her brest lyke to a bowle of cream uncrudded,*
> *Her paps lyke lyllies budded,*
> *Her snowie neck lyke to a marble towre;*
> *And all her body lyke a pallace fayre,*
> *Ascending up, with many a stately stayre,*
> *To honors seat and chastities sweet bowre.*

(Edmund Spenser, 1552–99)

The groom now anticipates the approaching night (4: 6) with a playful taunt phrased as a triumphant echoing retort upon the girl's earlier 'not yet' admonition of 2: 17. 'Come to me' may be the sense rather than **come with me**; the names of forbidding mountain peaks **Lebanon, Amana, Senir**, and **Hermon** with the mention of **lions** and **leopards** being used to hint at the distances which had separated the lovers, and the dangers now safely passed. These features are to be thought of symbolically—even personally—rather than geographically; and the same is true of the gentler contours of the **mountain** and **hill** of fragrance. The clue to **mountain of myrrh** is in 1: 13.

Modern translations no longer exhibit the one-eyed marvel of the AV (4: 9) but the anticlimax present in RSV is made even more explicit in GNB: 'The look in your eyes . . . and the necklace you are wearing'. The flow of the poetry requires some such rendering as

> *With only a glance of your eyes*
> *And the merest movement of your neck*
> *You have captivated me.*

The **garden locked**, the **spring enclosed**, are the offering of her virginity which the girl brings to her husband. There is moreover **a well of flowing water** for life-long delight (cf. Prov. 5: 15–19).

iv. Drink your fill, O lovers! (4: 16–5: 1)
The hour for the consummation of love has come: **Let my lover come into his garden**. The invitation is accepted: **I have come into my garden, my sister, my bride**.

The closing couplet, variously interpreted as being addressed to the wedding guests, or to all lovers everywhere, is surely in fact a benediction upon the bridal pair: **drink your fill, O lovers!** The word **O friends** does not forbid this interpretation any more than **sister**; indeed both words belong to the same circle of ideas. Any good girl has a deep emotional need of her father's approval before giving herself unreservedly to her husband. Our Heavenly Father does this for us in The Song.

IV. ALL RADIANT IS MY LOVER (5: 2–6: 3)
i. Nightmare: lost after possession (5: 2–8)
'Too good to be true' is the logic here, and the old dream of fear comes back in a new form. Yet there is a difference, for now the bride admits his right of access even after she has retired for the night. Love's communing is but thinly veiled in dream language. The problem with which the dream wrestles is that she is over much concerned with her own comfort and convenience, and inconsiderate of needs which only she can meet. She fears that her inability to respond immediately to his advances may cause trouble between them. But love is patient and kind, and love will not fail. She faces up to her problem and learns her lesson.

ii. 'My lover is radiant': bride praises groom (5: 9–16)
'To find detailed comparison with Christ at this point does injustice to the text, and leads to an erotic appreciation of the Son of God'. We find ourselves here in hearty agreement with Balchin, who goes on to point to the vision of Christ in Rev. 1: 1–26 as a suitable text for devotional reflection.

Her prince is a manly man, with his bushy black **hair**, and sideburns like flowerbeds. As her adornment emphasizes her womanhood, so his is distinctively masculine. The **milk** in which the **doves** bathe is probably the cascades of a waterfall; his quick glances remind her of birds in their wheeling flight to and from the dark cavern behind the fall. Pale **lilies** would make a poor palette for lips; it is of course the scarlet anemone which is in mind. His **legs** are sturdy enough. In short, his appearance is virile, and majestic like the **cedars** in **Lebanon**. His discourse too is most engaging (16).

iii. I rest in his love (6: 1–3)
This brief exchange between the girls and the bride gives an opportunity for her to reaffirm the confident assurance of her husband's faithful love which her dream seemed to question. He has gone, and the girls have as much chance of finding him as the bride has. He has gone *to pasture his flock*: she replies [the tr. **browse** is inappropriate]; he is at his own proper work in the flower-spangled meadows. But more—he has gone **to gather lilies** ('he told me so'), and the bride has no doubt who will get his

love-posy. She repeats that well-remembered affirmation made after their wonderful Spring day together, but significantly changes the order: **I am my lover's and my lover is mine**. They belong entirely and unreservedly to each other, so long as they both shall live. 'However intimate we are with a friend, or however close our spiritual communion with a fellow Christian, there always remains a last barrier of reserve which falls only in the marriage bond . . . An image of the complete self-giving and trust of faith, and so a training for them: this is the place held by the sex instinct in the Bible' (Paul Tournier, *A Doctor's Case-book*, SCM, London, 1954, pp. 64 f.)

V. O QUEENLY MAIDEN! (6: 4–7: 9)
i. My one and only: groom praises bride (6: 4–10)
In response, the groom now declares his proud love of his bride. **Beautiful as Tirzah . . . lovely as Jerusalem:** he claims that she combines the graces of the northern and the southern kingdom, and recalls the stirring moment of her arrival, surrounded by the sixty valiant youths, 'striking awe like a bannered host' (Jastrow).

The harem of **sixty queens and eighty concubines**, though far short of the Solomonic tally of 700 and 300 (1 Kg. 11: 3) is still barbaric enough; the **virgins beyond number**—poor lasses!—are the girls who wait upon the queens, and will in due course be promoted to be concubines. All envy the one-and-only.

The last lines of 6: 4 and 6: 10 represent the same two Heb. words, context suggesting in the one case a military host, in the other a celestial host.

ii. Surprised by love: a parenthesis (6: 11, 12)
This brief lyric is quite difficult; it may be the bride's reminiscence of the moment when suddenly she realized how much she loved the youth who was destined to be her **prince**. Immediately her imagination had raced ahead: she would be his queen, at his side. The reference to **the new growth in the valley** and **the vines** suggest that the occasion was the Spring picnic already described (cf. 2: 13).

iii. 'King held captive': groom praises bride (6: 13–7: 9)
Who is the **Shulammite**? The usual answer, which appears to underline the NIV tr, is that she is none other than the bride. But as the title occurs only once, and that near the end of The Song (6: 13), the identification is insecure. Doubt increases when one considers that Solomon, the arch-polygamist, is regarded in a poor light in The Song, and that 'Shulammite' is simply the feminine form of Solomon— the Solomoness, so to speak. The name was rendered in Greek by 'Salome'. By one of

history's curious tricks, there is a Salome in the NT (though actually named only by historians). She was the daughter of Herodias who danced so shamelessly for Herod and his guests (Mk 6: 22). So we shall understand the verse as a disavowal: though the bride's charms are being described, yet she is no Salome dancing for the troops, while they cry:

> 'Turn, turn, O Salome,
> turn, turn, so that we can see you'.

The description of the bride continues in terms which are more impressionistic than realistic; like all good art, they evoke admiration without passion. Take for example **Your waist is a mound of wheat, encircled by lilies**. Realism is found indeed in the colour (for wheat-coloured is even today in the East the approving description of somewhat fair skin), and perhaps in the rounded contours and finely granulated texture. But the image is that of a mound of winnowed grain in a harvest-thanksgiving context, set about with flowers in token of festal joy. So the notes are fertility and joy. The point of comparison for the **navel** seems to be the knotted blind plug of a wineskin formed when a limb of the goat-skin is securely tied off. Every link with the girl's mother is tenderly dwelt upon; yet it is observed that she has her own distinctively personal blend of qualities. This difficult verse is brilliantly turned in GNB to avoid the ugly word *belly*, (NIV **waist**), but the result is teasingly obscure.

> A bowl is there,
> that never runs out of spiced wine.
> A sheaf of wheat is there,
> surrounded by lilies.

East of Suez (but west of Peking) a good bold **nose** is considered attractive; the usual phrase is 'a nose like a sword'. NEB puts it well: 'Your nose is like towering Lebanon that looks towards Damascus. You carry your head like Carmel'. In the concluding verses (7: 6–9) the groom's appreciation of this further unveiling of his bride's charms is followed by joyful appropriation.

VI. ALL CHOICE FRUITS (7: 10–8: 14)
i. New as well as old (7: 10–8: 4)
It is the bride now who is the speaker, rejoicing in their utter unity in trust and love. If, as it appears, the marriage feast has now come to an end, it is only the beginning of a love-life. **let us go . . . There will I give you my love.** She makes it her care, as well as her joy, to be the chief delight of her husband's life.

13. At our door, in the recesses of the eaves, she **stores every delicacy**: not only Spring's love-apples (the **mandrakes** of Gen. 30: 14 ff.), but also the more mellow autumn fruits. Love is for life, and there is a sweet ripening of love in the fall of life, which Spring could hardly imagine possible. This touches one of the most urgent needs of our day: to strengthen marriage so that it weathers out the storms of half a century and more; that when the afterglow of sunset fades at last, the couple will still sit hand in hand to take goodnight of each other. In youth, ecstasy; in age, serenity. Both are good, and which is better, only God knows.

Thoughts of her **mother** (8: 1 f.) throng the young wife's changing day-dreams, and yearning thoughts of children at their **mother's breasts**. Then she herself becomes the mother, and sees her beloved as a child to be kissed at any and all times, and be fed at *her* breasts with what she fancifully calls **the nectar of my pomegranates**. The truth is that she wants a boy, in the image of her own Prince. She loves her husband with renewed ardour, for it is through him that this gift will come.

The third adjuration **not to arouse or awaken love until it so desires** (4), being set within an established marriage situation, may perhaps be in the nature of a wise observation that not too much should be grasped after; the spontaneous upsurge of desire can be awaited. C. S. Lewis, a noble lover indeed, has something in his *The Four Loves* to the effect that Venus is no infallible goddess; she has a way of failing utterly when most is expected of her. But what of that? Lovers will find each other again.

ii. In travail (8: 5)
This charming one-verse lyric harks back to that romp in the greenwood long ago, with apricots for the banquet and kisses for wine. That is when **I roused you** to love, says the Prince, and my fruit was sweet to your taste (2: 3–7). Now your step is slower, for you are carrying our babe under your heart. Now as we cross the **desert** to your family's home (from the distance I saw the dust rise like a column of smoke from the wedding palanquin just here!), you walk **leaning** upon me (she is going back to her old home to have her baby). **There . . . there** now, we have arrived.

iii. Love is strong as death (8: 6, 7)
This parenthesis marks the passage of the waiting time. **Place me like a seal**, bearing my name and likeness, as a locket upon your **heart** (inwardly), as a signet upon your **arm** or hand (publicly): an avowal that your heart and arms are for me alone. For love demands all, and will have all. Its fiery flashes are not merely a **blazing fire**, but a very flame of JAH. Its fire is not simply, to use our worn-down phrase, awfully hot; it is *aweful*, as carrying the divine imperative and sanctions (Mal. 2: 14 f.). Let no-one trifle with this awesome elemental power. 'Were a man to offer all the wealth of his house to buy love, contempt is all that he would purchase' (JB).

iv. Our little daughter (8: 8–12)
When love meets love, breast urged to breast,
   God interposes
An unacknowledged guest,
And leaves a little child among our roses.
We love, God makes: in our sweet mirth
God spies occasion for a birth.
Then is it His, or is it ours?
I know not—He is fond of flowers
      (T. E. Brown, 1830–97)

In reading this as the birth announcement we are continuing on an independent path. But indeed there is no well-marked path. Agley speaks for many when he says, 'We might wish this conclusion away or in some other part of the poem'. Most present-day commentators see it as a harking back to the bride's childhood, and to the care which the calculating brothers took of their potentially valuable little sister. Gordis understands that it is the girl's many suitors who speak, complaining of her immaturity. Hudson Taylor sees under this figure 'the elect of God who are not yet brought into saving relation to Him'.

We are keeping within the accepted lexicon when, relying upon the poetic flow of The Song, we select something like 'a precious little girl' as the appropriate sense of **young sister**. "*āḥ* and *'āḥōth*: brother/sister, develop the parallel meanings of friend, neighbour, and beloved' (Gordis, p. 31). We have then the following result: 'It's a girl—the little darling! She is so tiny now, but in due course she in her turn will come to her spring-time, and her lover will seek her. We must take good care of her as she grows up. **If she is a wall**, firm and dependable, well able to look after herself, we shall adorn her suitably. But **if she is a door** easily moved and receiving all and sundry, we shall have to restrain and protect her'.

The wife to her husband: '**I am a wall**: I have kept myself for you. Have you not found me utterly dependable? Have I not brought you the glad contentment of *shalom*?' The husband to his wife (taking up her last word): '**Solomon**, did you say? No *shalom* there! A veritable **Baal Hamon**: lord of crowds and confusion. Solomon was a wealthy man, with more vineyards than he could enjoy. He let them out at twenty per cent. **You, O Solomon** may have your wealth and your women; the keepers are welcome to their twenty per cent. **My vineyard** is **my own** (it's my own sweet wife I mean). I am the true Solomon, for I have peace.' (Perhaps this reflects back some light upon the title, 1: 1.). The Heb. word tr. **mine to give**=at my own disposal. It is unthinkable that the lover should give it away!

v. Happily ever after (8: 13, 14)
In this final brief canto, house and garden are full of merry bustle, with Mother's voice the one which commands attention. Enters Father.

The echoes of 2: 17 and 4: 6 in the final verse complete the sequence (for the **spices** of 8: 14 are the myrrh and frankincense of 4: 6): 'There was a time when you sent me out of the house at night to my sheep on the meadows. Then came the day of our joy, and that day has not yet passed away. You have a word for everyone in the family; have you something to say just for me?' She has: **Come away, my lover**; and his answering ardour will not fail.

BIBLIOGRAPHY

AGLEN, A. S., 'The Song of Solomon', in *An Old Testament Commentary for English Readers*, ed. Ellicott, C. J., vol. IV (London, 1882).

BALCHIN, J. A., 'The Song of Solomon', in *NBC*[3] (London, 1970).

CARR, G. Ll., *The Song of Solomon. TOTC* (Leicester, 1984).

FUERST, W. J., *The Books of Ruth, Esther, Ecclesiastes, Song of Songs, Lamentations. CBC* (Cambridge, 1975).

GORDIS, Robert, *The Song of Songs and Lamentations* (New York, 1974).

HENSHAW, T., *The Writings* (London, 1963).

HERBERT, A. S., 'The Song of Solomon', in *Peake's Commentary on the Bible*[2] (London, 1962).

JASTROW, Morris, Jr., *The Song of Songs* (Philadelphia, 1921).

KNIGHT, G. A. F., *Esther, Song of Songs, Lamentations. TC* (London, 1955).

LEWIS, C. S., *The Four Loves* (London, 1960).

MACE, David R., *Hebrew Marriage* (London, 1953).

MONRO, Margaret T., *Enjoying the Wisdom Books* (London, 1964).

POPE, M. H., *Song of Songs. AB* (Garden City, N.Y., 1977).

RENAN, E., *Le cantique des cantiques* (Paris, 1860).

ROWLEY, H. H., 'The Interpretation of the Song of Songs', in *The Servant of the Lord, and Other Essays on the Old Testament*[2] (London, 1965), pp. 195–245.

SCHONFIELD, Hugh J., *The Song of Songs* (London, 1959).

TAYLOR, J. Hudson, *Union and Communion* (London, 1894).

ISAIAH

DAVID F. PAYNE

Isaiah's Life and Times

Isaiah son of Amoz was born in the middle of Uzziah's long reign (c. 791–740 B.C.), in an era of apparent stability and relative prosperity for Judah. He seems to have lived in the capital, where he may have been of aristocratic family; on the other hand, his prophetic status itself can have given him his ready access to the royal court. His call to prophetic office came in the year of Uzziah's death (6: 1). His marriage must have taken place not long afterwards, possibly in the reign of Jotham (c. 740–732 B.C.). He had at least two sons, to whom he gave the symbolic names of Shear-jashub (7: 3) and Maher-shalal-hash-baz (8: 1–4), who were in boyhood and babyhood respectively at the time of the Syro-Ephraimite invasion (c. 735/4 B.C.).

This invasion illustrates the effects of the growing menace of Assyria, whose armies now posed a frequent threat to the small states of the Levant, including the kingdoms of Israel, Judah and Damascus. Israel and Damascus combined forces to resist the Assyrians, but when Ahaz of Judah (c. 744–715 B.C.) wisely refused to join the ill-fated coalition, they attacked and invaded Judah. Ahaz, in alarm, took the irrevocable step of appealing to the Assyrian king for aid, in spite of Isaiah's strong warnings against any such move (cf. ch. 7).

The upshot was that Judah was reduced to the status of the unwilling vassal of Assyria, while Israel suffered much harsher treatment, beginning with the loss of much of her territory in c. 733 B.C., and culminating in the siege of Samaria and the fall of the kingdom a decade or so later. The fall of her sister-kingdom must have increased Judah's fears of Assyria, but also her hostility to the conqueror. During Hezekiah's reign (c. 729–686 B.C.) there were several moves to rebel against Assyrian domination. Hezekiah looked for allies, one of whom was Merodach-baladan, a Chaldean who managed to seize and hold the throne of Babylon for some time (721–710, and again in 705–702 B.C.), till finally driven out by Sennacherib: see ch. 39. Hezekiah thought the moment propitious for revolt in 704, but in 701 the forces of the Assyrian king devastated Judah and crushed the rebellion, though not without disaster to his own armies (cf. 37: 36). Isaiah warned against all such alliances and revolts, but he predicted that God would pro-

tect Jerusalem itself. He was not hostile to Hezekiah, who was a much more devout king than his immediate predecessors.

Whether Isaiah lived on into the reign of Manasseh or not cannot be said. Later Jewish tradition claimed that he did so, and was martyred by Manasseh; but there is no contemporary evidence to support the story.

For the chronology of Isaiah's epoch, see p. 109, N.B. The dates given above are based on the assumption of coregencies.

The Book and its Authorship

The traditional Christian (and Jewish) view of the authorship of the book is simple enough: one man, the eighth-century prophet Isaiah, wrote every chapter of it. Outside conservative circles, however, modern biblical scholarship holds a much more complex view. While there are disagreements on some details, most scholars would accept some such picture as the following: the oracles of Isaiah himself are contained in chs. 1–39; chs. 40–55 are largely the work of a sixth-century, exilic prophet; chs. 56–66 include the oracles of at least one more man, who worked in Palestine in the late sixth century; and the whole book also incorporates many editorial passages, usually brief but some quite lengthy. In particular, chs. 24–27 and chs. 36–39 are rarely held to be Isaianic; the latter section is biographical, virtually identical with 2 Kg. 18: 13–20: 19 (from which it may be drawn) and can readily be interpreted as the work of an editor who wished to round off the story of Isaiah and also to provide a transition (see ch. 39) to chs. 40 ff., in which Babylon is such a major topic. Chapters 24–27 are characterized as 'apocalyptic', and since it is usual to date anything of an apocalyptic nature in the late postexilic period, many scholars have considered these chapters to be perhaps the latest part of the whole book. The date of Isa. 24–27 cannot be considered in isolation from the date of Daniel (see the introduction to Daniel); if the traditional sixth-century date of Daniel is accepted, there will be little difficulty in attributing this earlier apocalyptic material to Isaiah.

In general, there are two rather different issues involved: first there is the basic question whether the prophetic literature as a whole contains any editorial material, and secondly it has to be decided whether the oracles in the book of Isaiah seem to be the work of one prophet or of two or more.

There can be no doubt at all that in some sense the book contains editorial material. The prophets were primarily 'preachers'; that is to say, their original ministry was oral. Their oracles, delivered orally in specific situations to specific audiences, needed no editorial material; but when these oracles were brought together and committed to writing, a certain amount of additional material, to provide amplification, explanation, and connecting links between oracles, was inevitable. (A very clear example of such material can be seen in 16: 13 f.) The real question, therefore, is whether, and to what extent, the prophets served as their own editors. In general, there is very little evidence on which to decide this question. Many scholars agree that Isaiah himself edited a number of his early oracles, forming a document referred to as his 'testimony' (8: 16); this verse also mentions his disciples, however, and it is widely believed that the *final* editors of prophetic books were not the prophets themselves but their schools of disciples. Perhaps the question is not particularly important; the doctrine of inspiration is not endangered, for the God who inspired the prophets can have inspired their disciples and editors just as readily. At any rate, several evangelical writers have found no difficulty in envisaging such editorial activity; see especially *NBD*, *s.v.* 'Isaiah, Book of'.

But whether or not there were editors, were there two or more further prophets whose work is incorporated in the later part of the book? The arguments about this are of two kinds, doctrinal and evidential. Many evangelical writers have taken the view that the NT settles the issue, since citations from every part of the book are there attributed to 'Isaiah' by name (see *e.g.* Rom. 9: 27 ff.; 10: 16–20, where there are quotations from Isa. 1: 9; 10: 22 f.; 53: 1; 65: 1). However, the case is not proven; it can be argued that the NT never discusses the question of authorship, and that in all cases the NT writers were simply using accepted modes of reference. (It is true, nevertheless, that in NT times nobody, to our knowledge, ever questioned the unity of the book of Isaiah.) Another doctrinal argument must be dismissed out of hand, as irrelevant; there is a widespread impression that to 'believe in' more Isaiahs than one automatically constitutes a denial of predictive prophecy. This is simply not true, for the plain fact is that *all* scholars are agreed that chs. 40–66 contain a good deal of prediction; the question at issue is a different one, namely whether it is long-range or short-range prediction. Neither view in itself constitutes a denial of the miraculous, whatever may be the doctrinal opinions of individual scholars.

Since then the doctrinal arguments are not watertight, the issue ought to be decided on evidential grounds. Many arguments have been used, for instance detailed analyses of style and language, on which longer commentaries must be consulted; but the basic point of controversy is a simple one. Virtually all commentators agree that chs. 40–55 predict the fall of Babylon and the subsequent release of the Jewish exiles from the standpoint in time of the exilic situation. In other words, the fall of Jerusalem (587 B.C.) is described as a *past* event, the fall of Babylon (539 B.C.) as a *future* event (see *e.g.* 51: 17–20 and 47: 1–5 respectively). The question is therefore whether God's messenger in these chapters was actually living during this interval, or whether the prophet is Isaiah himself, some 150 years earlier, not only predicting the end of the Exile but also putting himself mentally in the actual position of the exiles. We will not deny the latter possibility if we are prepared to accept the miraculous; on the other hand, the name of Isaiah never once occurs after ch. 39, and such a long, sustained transposition in time (so to speak) is absolutely unique. The fact must be faced that no hint is ever given in these chapters that the predictions are long-range; for instance, Cyrus is quite casually named in 44: 28 and 45: 1 as if every reader would already know who he was (contrast the wording of 1 Kg. 13: 2, where Josiah is a figure in the indefinite future). Hence the attractiveness—to many scholars, at least—of the view that chs. 40–55 contain the oracles of an anonymous sixth-century prophet. Such a prophet is conjectural (though it is widely held that 40: 6 ff. briefly describes his call to prophetic office) and anonymous, so that he must be called 'Second Isaiah' (or 'Deutero-Isaiah') for convenience. The chief argument against such a hypothesis is in fact this anonymity; if there was indeed such a remarkable prophet, ministering in Babylon to the exiles, how can it possibly have happened that his very name, and every recollection of· him, became lost? Admittedly, any prophet in Babylonia predicting the fall of Babylon would have been obliged to adopt some means of secrecy for his own protection.

The traditional view of the unity of authorship raises a further question which has often been overlooked by conservative writers. How, it needs to be asked, were the messages to the exiles conveyed to them? It is insufficient to say that the whole book of Isaiah must have been complete and available to them, for two reasons. Firstly, there are passages which are explicit directives, applicable to a specific point in time; how would exilic readers of an old book have known when to obey the injunction of 48: 20, for example? (Any exiles who had sought to obey this command 25 years too early would have provoked immediate and severe retribution from the Babylonian authorities!)

Moreover, many of the prophet's oracles and arguments are clearly *in response to* statements and complaints made by the exiles (*e.g.* 40: 27; 45: 9 ff.; 49: 14); his arguments would have lost much of their point and effectiveness if they had been known beforehand. Secondly, very few people, especially in exile, could have had access to large, laboriously written documents; the prophetic message would of necessity have been publicly proclaimed if the whole community were to hear it. Thus the only reasonable probability seems to be that some unknown person brought the oracles of chs. 40–55 to the attention of the exiles in Babylonia, *c.* 540 B.C. Very probably he would have declaimed many of the prophetic words when the community there met together for prayer and worship. We seem, then, to be compelled to conjecture the existence of a 'Second Isaiah', if not as the author, at least as the mediator and spokesman of chs. 40–55.

The same general considerations also apply to chs. 56–66. Here the prophetic words are addressed to Jewish people in Judah shortly after the Exile, and many scholars have conjectured that there was yet another prophet, 'Third Isaiah' (or 'Trito-Isaiah'), if not several men, in that era. If such a view be rejected, once again some mediator or spokesman of these oracles too must be allowed for.

The Servant Poems

Four passages in the second part of the book have given rise to protracted discussion and controversy. They are 42: 1–4; 49: 1–6; 50: 4–9; and 52: 13–53: 12; though other verses and passages (*e.g.* 61: 1 ff.) are sometimes linked with them. They are commonly known as the 'Servant Songs'. Elsewhere in the prophecy Israel is named as the Lord's 'servant' (*e.g.* 41: 8), but the Servant in the so-called Songs is portrayed rather differently, even if similar language is used here and there. If these passages still refer to the nation (as has been held by most Jewish and not a few Christian writers and commentators), we must at least say that there is *some* difference between the two portraits of Israel. The passages themselves do not identify the Servant, unless 49: 3 does so; but the word 'Israel' in this verse has again been a matter of considerable debate. (It could be a scribe's erroneous addition, since one Hebrew MS omits the word; or—more probably—the name could here function as a designation for a leader in Israel.)

The NT sees in Jesus the fulfilment of some of these passages, especially 52: 13–53: 12 (cf. Mt. 8: 17; 1 Pet. 2: 24 f., etc.). On this basis, the passages may well be labelled Messianic. We should pause, however, before making the simple equation 'Servant = Messiah'; the important question is not so much 'Did Jesus fulfil the role of the Servant?' as 'What sort of role did He fulfil as the Servant?' The NT, after all, shows Him fulfilling a number of OT roles, including that of Israel (see Mt. 2: 15, and cf. Hos. 11: 1). In other words, there may be no essential conflict between identifying the Servant as Israel and finding the role's fulfilment in Christ.

Many other views have been propounded; see the survey (up to 1955) in C. R. North, *The Suffering Servant in Deutero-Isaiah*[2] (London, 1955). Hypotheses that the Servant was some historical individual, such as Hezekiah or Jeremiah, are rarely entertained today, though it is very possible that in sketching his portrait the prophet drew upon the historical experience of individual Israelites. The autobiographical hypothesis (which was mooted by the Ethiopian eunuch, Ac. 8: 34) still has its occasional supporters; the fact that the Second and Third Songs are couched in the first person singular is the chief basis for it. But all such views face the insuperable obstacle that the Servant is, so to speak, larger than life; no historical individual in the pre-Christian era lived up to such claims. Other hypotheses can safely be set aside as most unlikely.

The Servant's role seems to be depicted as partly royal, partly prophetic. The picture may owe something to Moses and something to David—indeed, the very term 'Servant of the Lord' is applied in the OT to these two individuals far more than to anyone else. The passages, then, may well be saying that Israel's future leadership, beyond the Exile, will centre upon a person at once kingly and prophetic—and, not least, suffering. Such terms as 'king' and 'anointed' may have been avoided quite deliberately, partly because the word 'king' would have conveyed too stereotyped an impression for an exilic audience (one recalls how careful Jesus was in His use and avoidance of the same terms), and partly because the prophet did not wish to predict a speedy restoration of the Davidic dynasty in postexilic Jerusalem, which many hoped to see but looked for in vain. We can thus explain the lack of precision in these prophecies, and also the degree to which the prophet's thought oscillates between the future nation and the future Servant, since it was only through the returning exiles and the restored Israel that the Messiah would eventually come. The true, divinely-appointed leadership lay buried within the historical continuum that was Israel. In some sense, then, the Servant is both Israel and the Messiah. The great insight in the prophet's portrayal of the Servant is the central significance given to suffering.

The Teaching of the Book

The teachings enshrined in the book of Isaiah are wide-ranging and not easily summarized. Approached chronologically, they revolve around three different historical situations: Judah under Assyrian dominance (chs. 1–39), the Exile in Babylon (chs. 40–55), and Judah in the early postexilic era (chs. 56–66). In other words, the book contains the messages provided for three quite different generations. However, the book may also be approached as a whole, in which case it may be divided in different ways; for instance R. K. Harrison strongly advocates a twofold division (drawn from W. H. Brownlee), in which chs. 1–33 are almost exactly paralleled by chs. 34–66 (see his *Introduction to the Old Testament*, pp. 788 f.). Most scholars continue to feel, however, that the book is best understood in terms of the usual three-fold division.

Two themes in particular serve to unite the book. The first is the theme of the holiness of God, indelibly impressed on Isaiah's mind at his call (6: 3) and frequently recalled in a phrase characteristic of this book but rare elsewhere in the Bible, 'the Holy One of Israel' (1: 4, etc.). The second prominent motif is that of Zion-Jerusalem, which was both the political centre of the nation and also the site of the temple's location. Isaiah had a clear awareness of what holiness meant—above all an utter moral uprightness—and a powerful conviction that Jerusalem, as 'the holy city', ought to demonstrate the sort of holiness that characterized its God. It was only too obvious that contemporary Jerusalem not only fell short of such a standard but indeed exhibited the very opposite condition (a state of affairs epitomized in 5: 7), even though the citizens tried to hide the fact under a gloss of outward piety and propriety. Isaiah's first purpose, then, was to strip off the veneer and reveal the truth, to make it clear that a holy God could not tolerate such a situation indefinitely, and to indicate something of God's purposes for Jerusalem, both in the short term and in the more distant future. Punishment and purification were essential and inevitable.

The punishment would fall in the sphere of international politics; but many of Isaiah's contemporaries failed to see God's hand either in the shaping of historical events or in the activities of foreign nations. The prophet was therefore impelled to emphasize God's power throughout the world (already impressed upon the prophet at his call; cf. 6: 3). And since God was in control of the whole human situation, political intrigues and machinations were foolish, and indeed betrayed a lack of faith in the Lord of history. Hence the call to faith (especially 7: 4, 9).

The situation would seem to demand final punishment, the annihilation of an intransigent people; but God was 'the Holy One *of Israel*', who could not abandon His own people, and in the specific situation of Isaiah's own day would not abandon His city either. Of His

people, a remnant would survive (see note on 7: 3); and in a land ravaged by Assyrian armies Jerusalem itself would escape destruction (29: 5 ff.; both predictions had been fulfilled when 1: 8 f. came to be written). Afterwards, out of the holocaust would come, in due time, a purified people in a truly holy city under a king greater even than David (9: 2–7; 11: 1–9). Although many of Isaiah's oracles related to specific historical situations, and must be seen against that background, there was and is a timeless quality about these themes seen as a whole. 'Jerusalem' came to be a synonym for God's worshipping people, who in every age need, if in differing degree, the warnings, the rebukes, the reminders, the appeals and the promises offered in Isa. 1–39. The chapters were committed to writing, both as a testimony to the accuracy of Isaiah's predictions and because of the abiding value of his teachings.

In chs. 40–55 a new historical situation is envisaged; the punishment has now fallen, and the name 'Jerusalem' now refers not only to the city (in ruins) but to its survivors deported far away to Mesopotamia. The chief thrust of the message now is therefore different from that in chs. 1–39; stern denunciation has given place to hope and comfort (40: 1, etc.). Yet there is continuity. The hope for the distant future expressed in the earlier chapters could now be a hope for the immediate future—provided that God's people seized the opportunity. God is still presented, emphatically, as Lord of history, even though the chief stress lies now on His role as Saviour of His people. The prophet is less concerned with the divine choice of Jerusalem than with the motifs of creation and exodus, because he sees in them the chief proof of God's power and willingness to save. Another change of emphasis, as compared with chs. 1–39, is to be found in the different picture of the Coming One: whereas the divine choice of David's line is explicit in chs. 9 and 11, such passages as ch. 53 lay stress not on royal position and millennial peace but on suffering and sacrifice. Israel's own sufferings during the Exile in fact prefigured those of the Servant of the Lord. Restored and purified, God's people could engage in a worldwide mission, consonant with the character of their God, whose glory and dominion were universal (an emphasis which continues right through the book).

If the message of chs. 40–55 was equally timeless in many respects, it had an immediacy about it which could have presented problems of understanding if chs. 56–66 did not follow. A partial return from Babylon had taken place, but early postexilic Jerusalem did not immediately see the dramatic fulfilment of all the promises of chs. 40–55. Chapters 56–66 are therefore important, for above all they show how God's promises and purposes were to be appropriated and furthered in a depressing situation and in hard times. Salvation is still seen as God's chief work, but it is the deliverance not from Exile but from all the problems of the period which is now in view. To obey God now means not to depart from Babylon but to depart from evil behaviour and from negligent patterns of worship. Thus the final chapters of the book widen the horizons of 'salvation', and imply a longer gap between the hardships and humiliation of that period and the glories of the future 'Jerusalem'. If chs. 1–39 above all invite readers to subject themselves to a rigorous critical self-examination, and chs. 40–55 above all challenge readers to make a ready response to the summons of God, chs. 56–66 offer modes of thought and patterns of behaviour appropriate to every age as the people of God move, however slowly, towards the fulfilment of His purposes and their destiny.

ANALYSIS

I. ORACLES FOR JUDAH AND JERUSALEM (1: 1–12: 6)

The first 12 chapters of Isaiah contain both a record of his teachings and some account of one period of his life; most of the material dates from the early part of his ministry. The central theme is the religious and moral condition of Jerusalem; the prophet offers a searching analysis of the Jerusalem in which he lived, and contrasts contemporary grim realities with the future glorious future God has planned for the city. Many short oracles have been brought together in order to present this contrast fully and effectively.

i. Jerusalem, Present and Future (1: 1–5: 30)

Chapters 1–5 contain no biographical material; they serve as a preface to the book, and draw attention to the serious state of affairs in Judah and Jerusalem. What the prophet endeavoured to bring home to his contemporaries in a variety of ways and on many separate occasions, is presented as a whole to the reader, giving us an impressive picture of the society in which Isaiah lived. For this society, the prophet predicted first punishment and then transformation.

(a) The Title (1: 1)

The opening verse introduces the reader to the prophet—his family, the sphere of his ministry, and his era (see the Introduction). The term **vision**, in view of its scope, means something like 'revelation' rather than a single visionary experience; it is a term which authenticates the prophet and his prophecy. It is probable that this title relates to chs. 1–12 only, in view of the phrase **concerning Judah and Jerusalem**; chs. 13–23 are oracles, bearing individual titles, concerning foreign nations.

(b) Judah's Sickness (1: 2–31)

The chapter introduces the reader to the situation which confronted Isaiah throughout his long ministry; a sombre picture of Judah's sins and shortcomings is built up, by the use of brief paragraphs from the prophet's preaching. Verses 7 f. relate to the situation which followed the invasion of Sennacherib in Hezekiah's reign, in 701 B.C.; but we cannot date most of the short oracles brought together in this chapter. They are couched in a variety of forms. Verses 2 f. are reminiscent of the lawcourts (the **heavens** and the **earth** are called upon as witnesses), and so too vv. 18 ff. (**reason**—i.e., present arguments). Other parts of the chapter are laments (4–9, 21 ff.); the **Ah** of v. 4 and the **See how** of v. 21 are the language of lamentation. Thirdly, there are oracles of direct challenge to the nation (10–17, 24–31).

The gloomy picture is neither impersonal nor completely hopeless; time and time again the prophet makes a direct appeal to his people,

to listen and to change their attitudes and behaviour. While the precise situation left behind by Sennacherib's armies was transitory, the general political future for Judah was to be one of weakness and danger, invasion and conquest, for centuries to come; and Judah's apostasy and social injustices also lasted a very long time. Hence the prophet's words had a function and appeal in Judah long after their original setting; and indeed his words constitute a challenge to any community in any epoch.

2–23. To extend the prophet's metaphor, we might describe vv. 2–9 as the diagnosis of the nation's sickness, vv. 10–23 as the prescription for healing, and vv. 24–31 as the prognosis. The sickness is twofold: it is moral and religious (2 ff.) and also physical (5–9). The loving relationship between God and His people has been breached by the wilful obtuseness and disobedience of the latter. Isaiah stresses from the outset the holiness of God; **the Holy One of Israel** (4) is a key-phrase in the whole book. The physical disaster, on the other hand, must have been only too obvious to all; Jerusalem had escaped capture, but the rest of Judah was laid waste by the Assyrian armies. By skilful comparisons, the prophet vividly depicts this situation (8) and subtly underlines the moral cause of the disaster by reference to the evil cities **Sodom** and **Gomorrah** (9 f.). Many Jews would have found such a comparison objectionable; did not the nation punctiliously observe all the ritual requirements of the worship of God? True, responds Isaiah; but God rejects the whole paraphernalia of external observance unless it is accompanied by social justice and consideration for the underprivileged (17). This was a constant theme of all the eighth century prophets (*e.g.* Hos. 6: 6–10; Am. 4: 1–5; Mic. 3: 9 ff.). It is striking that the charge of gross infidelity to God (**harlot**, v. 21)—more typical of Hosea than Isaiah—is based on social injustice, rather than on the idolatry first mentioned in v. 29.

The prophet offers the nation a choice (18 ff.). Jerusalem and Judah may be freed from their **sins** and may enjoy prosperity **if** (and only if) the nation chooses the path of **willing** obedience. Otherwise nothing but warfare and invasion can be expected (20).

24–31. In this paragraph there is nothing conditional; the ultimate, unswerving intentions of God for His holy city are stated clearly. Jerusalem's real **enemies** (24) were not external, but those inside the capital who had emptied it of justice and right dealings. The city's need, therefore, was not peace but **righteousness** and **justice**; it required purging and purifying, till it could truly be named **the Faithful City**. In this context, **redeemed** (27) is roughly equivalent to 'purified'. Finally, the accusation of idolatry is made (29 ff.); the details mentioned relate to the Canaanite fertility cult practices. (The sense of these verses is made clearer in NEB.) Isaiah offered no hint of when this transformation was to take place; in effect, his words constituted an appeal to his contemporaries to initiate the transformation.

(*c*) **The Day of Judgment (2: 1–22)**

1. This new title is generally thought to relate to chs. 2–4, whereas 1: 1 is of wider application. Isaiah may well have issued a collection of his warning oracles in written form long before the end of his ministry; if so, this title once stood at the head of such a document.

2–5. The theme of Jerusalem's future is taken up again, in a hymnic oracle which also appears in Mic. 4: 1 ff. Isaiah seems to have taken the passage from Micah, adapted it slightly, and added v. 5, which serves as a transition to the following oracle. Alternatively, both prophets may have drawn the passage from a well-known hymn in current temple usage.

The last days is a vague phrase, comparable with our 'in God's good time'. The time-scale, then, is not revealed, but God's purpose for Jerusalem is made plain: it will be exalted above all rival sanctuaries, and so attract the whole world as worshippers. Taught by God, the nations will then have every dispute peacefully settled, and universal peace will ensue. It is doubtful if v. 2 is predicting geographical changes; **mountains** here signify places of worship (*e.g.* Mount Sinai, Mount Olympus).

'When will all this be?' readers have always wanted to know; the prophet in effect poses a different and more challenging question: 'What are *you* doing to bring it to pass?' Verse 5 reminds the reader that present-day Jerusalem, full of injustice and bloodshed, was far from attracting foreigners to the **law** of God or **the word of the LORD** (3). The challenge remains relevant to every Christian community; His word is still **the light** by which His people are to **walk.**

6–22. Verses 6–21 are one oracle (note the refrain in vv. 10, 19, 21), to which v. 22 has been appended. The poem may be divided into three stanzas, as in RSV. It serves as a contrast to vv. 2 ff., where Jerusalem's happy future was depicted; now the reader is reminded that God will one day bring fearful punishment upon all who now oppose His will, whether such men are pagans or disobedient Israelites. The prophet is warning not just Judah but all Israel, the whole **house of Jacob** (6), as also in v. 5.

6–9 are addressed to God, but the tone is not that of private prayer; it may well be that Isaiah was playing a leading role in a gathering for worship, a festival assembly when the theme of God's coming as king and judge was acknowledged and celebrated. Thus after addressing God in vv. 6–9, the prophet turns to the congregation and warns them of the implication of God's coming. Jerusalem and Judah are accused of idolatry (8), in plain language, but the initial accusation is more obscure (6 f.); v. 7 refers to materialistic self-reliance—the prosperity was based on social injustices, moreover; v. 6 refers to foreign influences, but it is not clear whether commerce or religion is in view (contrast NEB with NIV). The material well-being alluded to in v. 7 suggests a very early date in Isaiah's career, before the prosperity of Uzziah's reign had ebbed away.

10–17. At all events, the situation is beyond forgiveness (9); punishment must inevitably come. This is depicted by Isaiah in poetic imagery, of God's arrival in storm and tempest, sweeping down from the north (**Lebanon**); God's agent of punishment was in fact to be the Assyrians, whose armies descended on first Israel and then Judah from the north. The OT prophets foresaw and described more than one day of the Lord (cf. v. 12); the advent of the Assyrian armies on the Palestinian states was one such 'day'. It was a day now all too close at hand for the northern kingdom.

18–22. One particular effect of the divine judgment is singled out for mention; it was idolatry (v. 8) which had caused God's anger, and it was only fitting that His punishment would strike at **the idols**, which for all their costliness would be abandoned, thrown away as useless when terror struck.

22. The last verse, an addition to the oracle (whether addressed to the congregation or the reader), is an appeal, not to reject idols (as we might have expected), but to **stop trusting in man.** Idols, after all, are all-too-human creations, and the more serious and pervasive danger to God's people in every age is that they will be swayed by the fashions and views and achievements of men. Even the most influential men in society are but mortals, of no special significance in God's sight, we are reminded. The verse also provides a transition to ch. 3.

(*d*) **The Breakdown of Society (3: 1–4: 1)**

1–15. The theme of leadership unites three separate oracles, 1–9, 10 f., 12–15. The contemporary leaders of Jerusalem are rebuked, and the nation warned that worse is to come; even oppressive rulers are better than the leaderless anarchy which faces Judah.

1–9. This oracle may have been addressed to the court, but it is noteworthy that nothing is said about the king. Isaiah foresees the day when the land will be bereft of men of experience and knowledge, amid famine conditions. The vivid picture implies the situation that would follow invasion and deportation. The Assyrian armies regularly left devastation in their wake; they would deport the leading citizens and administrators of states they viewed as rebellious, though often leaving a native king to rule his ruined land. In such a situation, says the prophet, the citizens will be desperate for men to take the lead, and will choose the most reluctant fellow with the slightest claim to advancement (6 f.). Possibly the **cloak** was a very slight mark of distinction; or possibly it was a poor enough garment, but better than nothing. 7a is difficult, cf. RSV and NEB but probably the sense is roughly 'I am not the man to remedy (the situation).'

The oracle concludes (8 f.) with a condemnation of the whole present administration; once again the comparison with **Sodom** is made (cf. 1: 10). The leaders are evidently brazen in their sins; the very 'look on their faces' betrays them. It should not be overlooked that the trusted leaders include **the skilled craftsman and the clever enchanter** (3), who were apparently preferred to the priesthood as a source of guidance.

10 f. These two verses are of completely general application, reminiscent of many passages in Proverbs; cf. also Ps. 1. The prophet here adopts the role of a teacher, encouraging and admonishing his hearers. In the context, however, he may be addressing the national leaders, bringing a word of encouragement to the godly among them.

12–15. Verse 12 seeks to make explicit the present predicament of the ordinary citizen; but there are problems of Hebrew text and language. The meaning is either that the administration is weak and effeminate (so NIV), or else that 'money-lenders' and 'usurers' dominate the scene (so NEB). In any case, the leaders **lead you astray**.

The brief oracle that follows (13 ff.) is an effective climax; Isaiah utilizes the language of worship, which recalled—perhaps at the great festival each new year—that God would arise to judge the nations, the word translated **people** being plural in the Hebrew. **The LORD takes his place** as judge; but this time the judicial verdict is pronounced against **the people**, or rather the people's **elders and leaders**, whose rapacity has brought such distress to **the poor**. (We must be careful not to let familiarity with the phraseology dull our appreciation of the final accusation of v. 15.) The mention of **my vineyard** (14) is probably intended to show that property-owners have suffered, as well as the poorer classes; on the other hand, it may be a metaphor for the nation as a whole, as in 5: 1–7.

3: 16–4: 1. This oracle, which seems to reflect a period of peace and prosperity early in Isaiah's career, provides an appropriate sequel to the condemnation of the (male) leaders of society earlier in ch. 3; the prophet now points an accusing finger at the luxuries and the pride of the society women. He breaks off the poem to give a catalogue, in prose, of some of their costly adornments (18–23). It was not so much the ostentation that offended the eighth-century prophets as the fact that the money which paid for the luxuries had been extorted from the poor; cf. Am. 4: 1. Isaiah predicts that the public ostentation will be replaced by public humiliation; the last clause of v. 17 either means nakedness (as in RSV, JB) or else a brand on the forehead (cf. NEB).

Reverting to verse, the prophet's thought moves from the society women to Jerusalem as a whole (to which the pronoun **she** refers in v. 26). So many of the men will die in **battle** (25) that **women** will become desperate for the lowliest status in society (4: 1)—the very reversal of their present lofty position, with its ostentatious status symbols.

(e) **The Restoration of Society (4: 2–6)**
4: 2–6. The section is rounded off with a passage promising salvation for Jerusalem. Except that it is prose, it corresponds exactly to the opening passage in the section, 2: 2 ff. Its imagery is quite different from 2: 2 ff., on the other hand, and most modern commentators think that vv. 5 f. (if not the whole passage) reflect an eschatological viewpoint of considerably later date than Isaiah's era (see Introduction). Against a late dating, it may be argued that 2: 1–4: 6 is a well-structured unit, dating from Isaiah's lifetime and perhaps 'published' separately (see note on 2: 1), and that this passage is integral to the whole.

The passage picks up the theme of the women castigated in the preceding section (4). Of the menfolk, only **survivors**—of **holy** character—will remain; the women will be cleansed in heart, after the severe **judgment** God will inflict. But when God's **day** comes, and judgment is past, He will provide at the same time visible signs of His presence and the protection from all foes which His people need (5 f.); and then (2) everything that the Lord has planted shall prosper, **beautiful and glorious**. (In context, it seems that **the Branch** here does not refer to the Messiah as in 11: 1.) The image of the book of life (3) may also be found in Ps. 139: 16; Rev. 20: 12–15; that God had destined a specific remnant to survive the political disasters ahead was one of Isaiah's reiterated themes (see the comment on 7: 3).

It is to be observed that in his treatment of the future, here and elsewhere, Isaiah brings together both conditional and absolute predictions, both literal and symbolic, and moreover both near and far-distant in the time-scale of history. To say that the time-scale was not revealed to the prophet is true enough, but puts the emphasis in the wrong place; the lessons of the various predictions consisted of warnings, threats, promises, encouragement, or comfort, and some sense of urgency and immediacy was essential if they were to have any effect.

(f) The Song of the Vineyard (5: 1–7)
This song is one of the finest examples of the prophet's art and skill in the whole book of Isaiah. In structure it resembles the joyful songs which must have been common enough at harvest, or vintage festivals; but a 'sour' note soon creeps in, in the last phrase of v. 2, **bad fruit** (a single word in Hebrew). Isaiah's hearers, whom we may imagine to have been gathered to make festival, will have pricked up their ears at this point. Who, in any case, was the unlucky 'friend' (so JB, for NIV **the one I love**) he was talking about? Some more discerning listeners may have begun to think in metaphorical terms, for lovers and brides could be described as vineyards (cf. Ca. 8: 12)—was the prophet referring to some friend's faithless wife?

At this point (3) Isaiah begins to speak in the first person, as if the troublesome **vineyard** was his own. He asks his audience for advice (one is reminded of Nathan's parable, 2 Sam. 12: 1–7). His own proposed remedy must have struck his hearers as drastic in the extreme; and was the prophet really proposing to bring about a localized drought (6), as Elijah had once commanded a much more serious drought (1 Kg. 17 f.)? Not until v. 7 is the truth revealed: **the LORD** is the owner, and **Israel** and **Judah** jointly His **vineyard**. The perversion of **justice** is the burden of God's complaint through the prophet; this lesson is inculcated in a memorable word-play, for in Hebrew 'justice' is *mišpāṭ*, 'bloodshed' *mišpāḥ*, and 'righteousness' is *ṣᵉdāqāh*, while 'a cry' of distress, is *ṣᵉʿāqāh*. The words are remarkably similar, but the realities behind the words are the greatest possible contrasts.

Such was the accusation left ringing in the Jerusalemites' ears—truly an unpleasant taste in the mouth at a vintage festival!

This parable in song laid the foundation for the Parable of the Wicked Husbandmen (Mk 12: 1–9).

(g) A Six-fold Verdict (5: 8–23)
This section of six woes follows very aptly on the Song of the Vineyard, which refers briefly in pictorial form to the glaring defects in society. The woes proceed to make detailed accusations, and to name the punishment which must surely follow. As in chs. 3 f., the picture of carefree luxury suggests an early period in Isaiah's ministry.

One of the major problems in Israelite society (in both kingdoms) was the question of property. All too readily society polarized, into the great landlords on the one hand and the poverty-stricken peasants on the other. (See Kaiser's commentary for a helpful discussion of Judah's economy.) To some extent this process was inevitable, but it was undoubtedly acceler-

ated by land-grabbing activities on the part of some rich men—who are reprobated in v. 8. The threat in v. 10 is of a very poor harvest; **A ten acre vineyard** will produce approximately eight gallons of wine, while the grain harvest will be a mere tenth of the **seed** sown.

The rapacity of the rich landlords was compounded by their godless debauchery (11 f.) and their mockery at, and perversion of, the truth (18–21). With such men at the head of society, the prophet laments, the whole people is doomed—**to exile** (13). It is **the understanding** of God that is lacking. Verses 14 ff. are a parenthesis, discoursing in more general terms on the fate of the **nobles** of Jerusalem and on God's pleasure in **justice** and **righteousness** (contrasting v. 7); v. 17 depicts vividly the depopulation of Judah which exile will bring. Verse 18 offers a vivid portrayal of the efforts some men will go to in order to break God's laws.

In the final woe (22 f.) Isaiah pours scorn on the impotent judges, who lacked the will or the courage to withstand bribery and corruption; there was only one activity in which they could claim expertise!

(h) The Lord's Anger (5: 24–30)
Isaiah may originally have spoken the words of vv. 24 f. in a different context; note that NEB has transferred these verses to follow 10: 4. Verses 26–30 are again a separate oracle. Nevertheless, the arrangement of ch. 5 makes good sense as it stands; the woes of vv. 8–23 lead naturally to an expression of the divine anger (24 f.), and the final paragraph portrays in vivid detail the human agents (though without naming them) of God's punishment upon His people. Verse 25 ends with familiar words, which serve as the refrain of the long passage 9: 7–10: 4. Hence, the decisions of NEB and various commentators to transfer this verse (and perhaps vv. 24, 26–30 too) to follow 10: 4. In the present context, the verse links v. 24 with vv. 26–30: God's people have rejected His law and have already suffered for it, but His righteous anger will lead to further punishment yet. The punishment recalled in v. 25 is most probably the devastating Assyrian attack on the northern kingdom by Tiglath-Pileser III in 734/3 B.C. God's hand **is still upraised**, i.e. 'raised to strike' (JB).

26. The **nations are** not named, but are evidently from far away. If vv. 26–30 were originally an oracle against the northern kingdom, then Isaiah would certainly have had Assyria in mind; and indeed Assyria was to reduce Judah too to straits, even though it was the Babylonians, from equally far away in Mesopotamia, who would ultimately lay Jerusalem in ruins. In any case, the efficiency, vigour and might of the Mesopotamian armies is vividly portrayed—a fearful warning to those who disobeyed the God of Israel. Isaiah emphasizes in v. 26 that He is in full control of international history; the Assyrians march at His bidding. This lesson, developed in 10: 5, was very necessary in an era when many Israelites would have automatically assumed that the gods of Assyria governed the fortunes of that powerful nation. In today's world, nobody thinks in polytheistic terms any more; but 'market forces', the 'demon' Communism, and other impersonal forces are often viewed as the controlling powers of our world.

ii. Isaiah and King Ahaz (6: 1–12: 6)

The core of chs. 6–12 is widely thought to consist of Isaiah's 'testimony' (8: 16), a document which he himself drew up as an indictment of the infidelity of court and nation. Whereas chs. 1–5 have depicted the general moral decay of the nation, chs. 6–12 are concerned to show how God's word was disobeyed in a specific historical situation, namely the sudden crisis caused by the invasion of Judah by Israelite and Aramaean armies. The autobiographical material demonstrates how powerfully Isaiah himself strove to persuade the king to adopt different policies, and so serves to emphasize that Jerusalem's leaders did not fall into casual and unconscious infidelity, but with full deliberation and forethought rejected God's word to them.

All this sombre material still stands as a warning, but a more rounded picture is given to the reader by the fact that some of Isaiah's most joyful predictions stand alongside the denunciations.

(a) The Prophet's Call to Office (6: 1–13)

In this chapter we meet the prophet himself for the first time. In the following chapters we find a few other episodes of his life and activity, and it is often suggested (*e.g.*, by Kaiser) that 6: 1–9: 7 was the 'testimony' referred to in 8: 16. Certainly it is the most personal section of the whole book (except for chs. 36–39, which relate to a very late period in Isaiah's ministry). On the other hand, it is unnecessary to suppose that the narrative of the prophet's call must have stood originally at the head of the document containing it, however logical this may seem to us. Much of the material in chs. 2–5 is also of an early date in Isaiah's ministry, and some of it too may have formed part of his 'testimony'.

It is occasionally questioned whether the commission of ch. 6 was necessarily the prophet's inaugural call; but there is no good reason to doubt it (see the discussion in Young, *ad loc.*). Moreover, Isaiah 6 can be compared with the call narratives of both Jeremiah and Ezekiel; the three passages have the remarkable common feature that the prophet in each case is warned, at the very outset of his ministry, of the hostile reactions he will encounter (cf.

Jer. 1: 18 f.; Ezek. 2: 4–7). R. E. Clements has suggested that this repeated feature was intended 'to allay the objection that if the message had truly come from God the people would have listened to it. . . . These narratives show that the refusal to listen to the prophet does not cast doubt on the truth of the prophet's words, but rather confirms it' (*Prophecy and Tradition*, p. 35).

C. R. North has pointed out that the outstanding emphases in Isaiah's theology are already explicit or implicit in the account of his call (*IDB* ii, p. 733, *s.v.* 'Isaiah'). He lists these emphases as Yahweh's sovereignty, Yahweh's holiness, human sin, faith in Yahweh, the remnant and the Messiah. **1–8.** Isaiah's vision is described. For all we know the whole experience may have been visionary, and **the temple** (1) may mean God's heavenly dwelling-place; but it is tempting to believe that Isaiah was physically present at the Jerusalem temple at the time, and saw a spiritual reality denied to the rest of the worshippers (note v. 10), most of whom were only too content with the externals (cf. 1: 10–17). The **smoke** (4) may relate to altar fires; did the altars themselves tend to hide God from His worshippers' eyes?

God is seen as the eternal King, enthroned in the midst of His courtiers (perhaps in itself a traditional picture; cf. 1 Kg. 22: 19), in contrast to the king of Judah, **Uzziah**, the end of whose long and prosperous reign was in sight. The courtiers and leading men of Judah have already been depicted as wicked and doomed (3: 14 f., 4: 14); the courtiers of Yahweh, by contrast, are concerned only with His holiness and glory. They are called **seraphs**, a term unique in the Old Testament to this passage; elsewhere the Hebrew word denotes serpents, as in Num. 21: 6, and it is possible that the creatures are envisaged as winged serpents.

The seraphim's three-fold cry **'Holy, holy, holy'** (as Calvin acknowledged, there is no reason to find here an allusion to the Trinity) gives emphasis by repetition, and the prophet's very natural and proper reaction was to sense and confess his own uncleanness and that of his people. The reference to **unclean lips** is not of course to imply that their deeds were holier than their words; the lips are singled out for mention because the spoken word was a prophet's business—thus Isaiah acknowledged his unworthiness to be a prophet; it is interesting to note the similarities and contrasts between Isaiah's call and Jeremiah's (cf. Jer. 1: 4–10). Unlike Jeremiah, Isaiah showed a quick readiness to act as a prophet once his lips had been symbolically cleansed.

9–13. The actual teachings which the prophet was to transmit to the people of Judah are not indicated here (they can, after all, be found in the rest of the book); it is rather the *effect* of these teachings which is laid before the reader. From hindsight, we know that all too few in Judah did heed Isaiah's words, and that a long era of political disasters for Judah began during the course of his ministry. But Isaiah himself did not need hindsight; at his very call it was made clear to him that his ministry would be remarkably unsuccessful in his own generation, but that the very failure was ordained by God: indeed, in God's eyes it would be no failure. Paradoxically, his failure to persuade his audience would prove him to be a true prophet!

We must not try to soften the theological difficulty by talking about the 'permissive' will of God; the disobedience and subsequent punishment of His people was not peripheral but central to the divine plan. On the other hand, we are not to suppose that God forced would-be-obedient Israelites into disobedience. A parallel may be found in the early chapters of Exodus, where Pharaoh is sometimes said to have hardened his own heart (*e.g.* Exod. 7: 22 f.), and sometimes to have had his heart hardened by God (*e.g.* 9: 12). In Isaiah 6, the theological point is that wilful men, for all their arrogance, were impotent to thwart the intentions of the Almighty.

Isaiah's response (11) was tantamount to a plea on his people's behalf; but the plea was unavailing. The only gleam of hope appears at the end of v. 13, a verse which is both obscure and textually uncertain. The start of the verse offers no hope; if as many as a **tenth** of the population survive the invasion and deportation of vv. 11 f., they will not be safe, for fresh disaster will strike. On the other hand, even a felled tree leaves a **stump** behind, which may prove the **seed**-bed for fresh growth. In RSV, the last sentence of the verse is outside the quotation marks; in other words, it is an editorial comment on the simile in the commission. The NEB omits it altogether, since it is missing from the LXX. The verse as a whole may be compared with 10: 33–11: 1 (*q.v.*). **The holy seed** is probably both the Messiah and the righteous remnant of God's people.

(*b*) **The Appeal to King Ahaz (7: 1–9)**
The outward failure of Isaiah's ministry, predicted at his call to office, was signally exemplified a few years later, at the time of the Syro-Ephraimite War, when the king of Judah himself proved blind to political realities and deaf to the word of God. Chapter 7 thus illustrates ch. 6. The story is told for the benefit of the reader, and therefore includes elements of expansion and explanation; for instance, Ahaz will have known only too well the situation outlined by Isaiah in vv. 5 f.

The kings of Damascus (**Aram**, v. 1) and Israel were seeking to make common cause against the Assyrians, and to unite the Palestin-

ian states in their confederacy. Judah, under King Ahaz, wisely resisted the diplomatic pressures, but the immediate sequel was that the Syrian and Israelite armies invaded Judah and attacked Jerusalem: the year was *c.* 734 B.C. Ahaz himself was to be replaced by a Syrian nominee, **Tabeel** (6); well might he and his people take fright (2). Isaiah, however, far from being apprehensive, had nothing but contempt for the petty kingdoms to the north; even the spelling of the names **Rezin** and **Tabeel** was deliberately inaccurate and derisive (*e.g.* Tabe-al—as in AV, correctly—means roughly 'good-for-nothing'!). His graphic phrase **smoldering stubs of firewood** (4) is plainly contemptuous.

The scene of the confrontation between Ahaz and Isaiah lay just outside the city, on the east (see map, p. 748); it is highly probable that the king was inspecting the city's water supply, always a serious problem in time of siege. (A generation later, Hezekiah constructed the Siloam tunnel in order to improve the water supplies, in readiness for Sennacherib's siege; whenever Jerusalem was surrounded on all sides, the place where Ahaz and Isaiah met fell into enemy hands; cf. 36: 2.)

Isaiah was instructed to take his son **Shear-Jashub** with him (3), no doubt as a tacit sign to Ahaz. The name means 'a remnant shall return', a name which primarily symbolized the threat of disaster (specifically, deportation or exile), though a note of muted hope is not absent. The boy was apparently no longer a babe in arms, and we may suppose that he had been born shortly after Isaiah's call, and given a name expressive of the threat to Judah described in 6: 11 ff. The name now took on a special significance. Hitherto, Judah had scarcely attracted Assyria's attention but, frightened by the Syro-Ephraimite invasion, Ahaz now proposed to solicit Assyria's aid (cf. 2 Kg. 16: 7 f.), thereby making Judah a vassal of the imperial power. Any future revolt against Assyria would invite invasion and deportation by way of punishment; thus the name 'Shear-Jashub' took on a relevance it had not had before.

The purpose of Isaiah, accordingly, was to dissuade Ahaz from seeking Assyrian support, and to persuade him to share Isaiah's own firm faith in Israel's God. First he uttered God's solemn promise that the warlike intentions of Damascus and Samaria would come to nothing. Verse 8 is difficult: in the first place, the introductory **for** (NIV) has to be rendered 'even though' to give any logical sequence of thought; secondly, the mention of **sixty-five years** is not easy to explain, and is perhaps a slight error in the Hebrew for 'six or five years' (i.e. 'five or six years'), which makes much easier sense (so JB; but longer commentaries should be consulted). The general sense of vv. 8 f. seems to be that **Rezin** and **Pekah** may have the full resources of their kingdoms behind them, but they are still powerless in reality. It may also be implied that Rezin and Pekah are the legitimate rulers only of their own realms—and that Ahaz is the legitimate 'head' of Jerusalem and Judah (cf. J. A. Motyer, *Tyndale Bulletin* 21, 1970, p. 121).

The final challenge thrown at Ahaz and his advisers is another of Isaiah's brilliant word-plays: **If you do not stand firm in your faith** (Heb. *ta'ᵃmīnū*), **you will not stand at all** (Heb. *tē'āmēnū*). See JB and NEB for two different attempts to reproduce the word-play in English. The word of God was clear: the choice was between faith (in God, not Assyria!) and permanent loss of political independence and stability. Faith in God was just as positive and decisive a policy as was a costly appeal to Assyria.

(c) The Sign to Ahaz (7: 10–17)

Probably some little while elapsed before the prophet returned to the king with a fresh word from the Lord; at least, so the note of impatience in v. 13 suggests. The historical setting is unchanged; the threat posed by the Syrian and Israelite invaders is still frightening Ahaz and his advisers. By now Ahaz must have made up his mind to appeal to Assyria for military assistance, and that is why, with a show of piety (cf. Dt. 6: 16) he declined to seek **a sign** from God (12). The last thing he wanted was tangible proof, by a sign such as lightning or earthquake, that he had made the wrong decision. Thus he rejected God; note how the phrase **your God** in v. 11 becomes **my God** in v. 13.

Isaiah had previously promised that the plans of Rezin and Pekah would come to nothing (v. 7); he now reiterated this prediction (16), in terms clearly implying the terrible effects of the coming Assyrian invasion of Damascus and the northern kingdom of Israel, and then immediately proceeded (17) to prophesy that the arrival of the Assyrians in force would spell worse trouble for Judah too than she had ever known in her history as a separate kingdom. (The last phrase of v. 17 was not part of the spoken oracle, but was added for the reader's benefit.) Thus, what began as a promise ended as a threat; the temporary relief occasioned by the fall of Judah's present enemies would be more than offset by the domination and oppression of Judah's new 'friend' and ally, Assyria. The temporary relief would, like the proverbial lull before the storm, merely herald the disasters to follow.

King Ahaz chose to ask for no **sign**, for he knew it would almost certainly be an embarrassment to him; but God chose nonetheless to provide a sign, which could not be overlooked by the king or his advisers and entourage. (Such is the sense of the **house of David**, v. 13; cf. v. 2.) The sign was to be that of the birth of **Immanuel** (14).

Scarcely any verse in the Bible has been more debated and discussed than Isa. 7: 14. The chief controversial issues are as follows:

(a) In what precisely does the 'sign' consist? Virginal conception? The birth? The name? The changed situation?

(b) Does the Hebrew noun *'almāh* signify 'young woman' (RSV) or **virgin** (AV, RSVmg, NIV)? And is the woman concerned a specific individual, or is the reference general?

(c) Does the annunciation phrase itself imply royal birth or not?

(d) The birth is clearly future; but has the conception of the child already taken place (as in NEB), or not (as in NIV)?

(e) Does the passage demand an immediate fulfilment or not?

(Longer commentaries and Bible dictionaries should be consulted for the detailed arguments about these questions.)

However, certain points can be made with a fair degree of conviction:

(a) No Christian who takes Mt. 1: 20–23 seriously can deny an ultimate fulfilment in Christ; but two options still remain open, namely a single fulfilment, in Christ, or else a double fulfilment; one in the lifetime of Ahaz, the other the Messianic fulfilment. The latter option in fact seems preferable, in view of the following considerations.

(b) The word 'sign' (Heb. *'ōt*) requires a reasonably early fulfilment; a prediction may be long-term, but a sign is by definition a pointer in the contemporary situation towards a more distant event. See especially F. J. Helfmeyer, *TDOT* i, *s.v.* *'ôth*.

(c) Despite several attempts to demonstrate otherwise, it remains very doubtful whether the Hebrew word *'almāh* signified *only* a 'virgin'. Certainly it was a term which *included* virgins; but it cannot be restricted to them.

(d) In a context where names clearly functioned as signs (Shear-Jashub in 7: 3, and Maher-Shalal-Hash-Baz in 8: 1–4), it is highly probable that it was the name 'Immanuel' rather than the child's conception or birth, which was to be the sign.

(e) It seems probable, though not certain, that the Hebrew construction suggests that Isaiah was referring primarily to a young woman *already* pregnant; virtually the same construction occurs in Gen. 16: 11 (*q.v.*).

(*f*) No natural exegesis can apply v. 16 to a far-distant future.

(*g*) It is not very likely that Immanuel was to be Isaiah's own child, since his son Maher-Shalal-Hash-Baz was probably conceived and born during the same political crisis (8: 1–4). It is even less likely that Immanuel was to be a son of Ahaz, since in that case the king could easily prevent the sign coming to pass, simply by giving the child a different name. It is certainly true that we never hear of a child of either Isaiah or Ahaz who bore the name Immanuel.

On the basis of these conclusions, we can interpret the passage as follows. Ahaz had refused to seek a sign, since he knew in his heart that such a sign would prove that Isaiah was right. But a sign was to confront him nevertheless; it was this, that before nine months could elapse the Syrian and Israelite invaders would have departed so dramatically that many mothers-to-be in Judah would name their newborn sons **Immanuel**—'God is with us'. (The name Ichabod, 'the glory has departed', cf. 1 Sam. 4: 21 f., provides a helpful comparison and contrast.) In other words, 'Immanuel' would become a very popular child's name in the year ahead. However, the name would be a sign or proof to Ahaz, not that the Syro-Ephraimite threat had already vanished (that fact would be self-evident), but that the God who was thus acknowledged to be 'with' His people was purposing to bring grave trouble on them, through the agency of the Assyrians. When would this threat be fulfilled? Within a very few years, says Isaiah—before children now in the womb could grow to years of full discrimination (16). (The prediction of v. 15 is further explained in vv. 21 f.)

The choice of the name Immanuel would be a mark of faith on the part of the mothers (contrasting with Ahaz's lack of it); and it was the faith of such simple, devout folk which would ultimately be rewarded. Isaiah here and elsewhere predicts the survival of a remnant, through whom God's own choice as King and Messiah would one day come. Judgment could not be God's *last* word for His own people; the day would come when (not any young woman but) the virgin would conceive and bear the Son whose name would signify the final and definitive salvation of His people (Mt. 1: 21). Then at last God's presence would be with His people in a very different and more wonderful way, experienced not in the sudden absence of Judah's enemies but rather in the abiding presence of the Son of God.

(*d*) **The Threat to Ahaz (7: 18–25)**
The chapter ends with four short oracles, which Isaiah may have uttered on different occasions, but which together serve to amplify the threat of v. 17. The main thrust of the prophet's words is to show Ahaz and Judah the nature of the threat posed by Assyria, though it is made clear that Assyria will not act as a free agent but as God's instrument to punish Judah.

18 f. Not only Assyria but Egypt will, overruled by God, bring trouble upon Judah. Egypt was noted for its flies, Assyria for its bees, and God is depicted as a bee-keeper whistling for his bees to follow. Plainly, Judah is to be the land infested by the two; the picture may be of the two nations fighting each other in Palestine, or else of two of Judah's 'allies' preying upon her.

Verse 20 very cleverly shows the folly of Ahaz' action in 'hiring' the Assyrians from beyond the Euphrates (**the River**); Ahaz wanted them to carry out one relatively minor operation (i.e. the defeat of Rezin and Pekah), but the truth was that they would know no such limits to their interference in Palestinian affairs. The **hair of your legs** means pubic hair, and the picture thus conjured up is that of utter humiliation.

Verses 21 f. serve to amplify v. 15. An apparently idyllic picture is used to show a Judah which is largely depopulated and which has reverted to nature. **curds and honey:** a sign of natural plenty, but in this context implying the loss of what would nowadays be called the benefits of civilization; living on potatoes and blackberries might be a modern parallel.

Verses 23 ff. again depict a land which has reverted to nature; v. 24 implies that wild animals are infesting some areas of the depopulated Judah. The disaster of 701 B.C., at the end of Isaiah's ministry, must have produced such results in various parts of the land.

Note that the last two oracles both state or imply Isaiah's remnant theme; despite the extent of the disasters to come, some of God's people would survive.

(*e*) **Comfort and Warning (8: 1–10)**
1–4. The symbolic action of Isaiah here briefly described was intended to reinforce the comforting part of the message of ch. 7, namely the forthcoming utter defeat of the two small nations at present attacking Judah. His second son's name, given at birth, was **Maher-Shalal-Hash-Baz**, meaning 'Speed-spoil-hasten-plunder' (NEBmg), and signifying the speed with which Damascus and Israel would fall prey to the Assyrians (cf. 7: 16). To give added weight to the symbolic name, Isaiah made out an ordinary property deed in the name of Maher-Shalal-Hash-Baz, and had it properly attested, to symbolize the transfer of the riches of Damascus and Israel to **the king of Assyria** (Tiglath-pileser III).

5–10. Just as in ch. 7 we find themes of promise and threat intertwined, so again in this passage, which begins with a note of warning and ends on a strong note of hope. It is not quite clear at what point the change of tone occurs (see commentaries, NEB), but the NIV rendering may reasonably be followed.

The oracle (5–8) must have followed the final decision of King Ahaz to invoke Assyrian military assistance against Rezin and Pekah; this was taking a sledgehammer to crack a nut, says the oracle, contrasting Jerusalem's relatively small water supply with the mighty Euphrates. **6. the waters of Shiloah:** Gk. Siloam; here symbolizing God's supply and protection for His people—despised and rejected by them. (NB. The Siloam tunnel was not constructed till a generation later.) The Assyrian forces, invited into Palestine by Ahaz, would know no boundaries, but would 'flood' Judah too. Judah is described as **'your land, O Immanuel'**, i.e. the land where so many young mothers were rejoicing in the belief that God was with them (see the discussion on 7: 14, above).

Here the oracle ended, on a frightening note; but for the reader a brief hymn (9 f.) was inserted at this point, picking up the theme of God's presence. The hymn is very similar to Ps. 46; it may have been composed by Isaiah at a later period in his ministry, or he may have quoted it from a well-known psalm of his day. It provides comfort whenever human enemies threaten to overwhelm God's people; in the long run, no godless empire can prevail. It was the sort of hymn which would have been used at Ahaz's coronation (see notes on Ps. 2); but the king had lost faith in the God who laughs at the machinations of godless peoples.

(*f*) **Darkness descends . . . (8: 11–22)**
As Isaiah rounds off his **testimony** (16), he gives first of all an explanation for his attitude in the present political crisis (11–15). God had spoken to him directly, warning him to avoid the prevalent fears and fancies of the populace. The passage is a trifle obscure, presumably because we no longer know exactly what rumours (*e.g.* **conspiracy**, 12) were circulating in Jerusalem. (The NEB offers clearer sense, but is too speculative.) For Isaiah and like-minded people (the imperatives of vv. 12 f. are plural), who truly feared God and worshipped Him in truth, God's presence would afford **sanctuary** and a **rock** of protection; for the rest of the nation, north and south, the very fact of God's presence would bring punishment, as they fell captive (15) to Assyria. This dichotomy of attitudes did not cease in Isaiah's time; see the NT treatment of vv. 14 f. in Rom. 9: 32 f. and 1 Pet. 2: 8. The prophet then gave instructions to **seal** up his teaching (**law**, 16); he would no longer preach to deaf ears, but would leave a book of **testimony**, consisting very probably of chs. 6 ff. and perhaps some earlier oracles, to prove the truth of his warnings and of God's

word when the predicted historical events came to pass. Moreover, he and his two sons, with their symbolic names, would be living reminders in Jerusalem that God had spoken (18). Many people would turn to superstitious rites for guidance (practices long since condemned; cf. Lev. 19: 31), at which the prophet expresses his indignation: the **people** should **enquire of their God**, not the **dead**! But let Isaiah's disciples (cf. v. 16) turn to his written teaching, (NIV **law**) for no-one who consulted mediums and wizards would receive any light of guidance (20). (For other possible ways of understanding vv. 19 f. see EVV and longer commentaries.) Far from gaining light, the bulk of the nation would find themselves in the increasing darkness of frightening conditions, brought about by the Assyrians (21 f.).

Note: v. 18 is cited in Heb. 2: 13, and applied to Christ; G. F. Hawthorne's discussion of the passage should be consulted, p. 1510 herein.

(*g*) **A Great Light (9: 1–7)**
In his 'testimony', Isaiah had built up a frightening picture of the darkness and distress about to descend upon both Judah and the northern kingdom. That could not be his last word, however; at some later point in his ministry, perhaps on the occasion of the birth or the accession of a royal prince of David's line (cf. v. 6), he gave expression to the joyful oracle of vv. 2–7. The theme is certainly that **there will be no more gloom** (whether or not this is the correct rendering of v. 1), not even for those northern areas wrested from the northern kingdom by the Assyrian Tiglath-pileser III in 734–732 B.C. Isaiah expresses his hope in hymnic fashion, and stresses the certainty of it partly by the use of past tenses (or rather the Hebrew equivalent of past tenses), and partly by reference to the will of God (v. 7).

Verse 1 is notoriously difficult to translate; see EVV and commentaries for the various possibilities. The reference to **Galilee**, with its mixed population, is clear enough; cf. Mt. 4: 15 f. It must have been difficult to envisage any hope for it in Isaiah's time; the source of hope was that God purposed that a king of David's line should one day rule over an Israel restored to its full dimensions. (This is implicit in the reference to David's **kingdom** in v. 7.)

Verses 2–7 are not as such directed towards the fate of northern Israel, but predicate just as much hope for Judah; no doubt as a spoken oracle the passage was addressed to Judaean ears. The first element in the **great light** predicted will be the fall of the oppressor, *viz.* Assyria, who must be defeated no less decisively than **Midian** had been (cf. Jg. 6 f.). Only then can disarmament take place (v. 5) and peace reign.

Verse 6 depicts the coming King in four rôles. Contemporary kings of Judah had been disastrously advised, and powerless in warfare; they had been anything but fathers to their people, and they had achieved neither peace nor prosperity. Isaiah portrays a king who will not be a failure in any one of these respects. Had any human king ever fulfilled the predictions, we would need to translate 'in battle God-like', with NEB, instead of **Mighty God**, and 'long-lived' for **Everlasting**; the Hebrew permits such variation. But as applied to Christ, the more natural rendering is plainly the more appropriate.

Note where Isaiah's emphasis lies: the kingdom of the future will be characterized above all by **justice** and **righteousness**, in glaring contrast to Isaiah's contemporary Judah (cf. 5: 7), and indeed to every human kingdom in some degree.

(*h*) **The Downfall of the Northern Kingdom (9: 8–10: 4)**
In this long poem (marked by a refrain, 9: 12, 17, 21, and 10: 4; see also 5: 25), the prophet reverts from the glorious future hope to the present realities of God's anger against the northern kingdom. It was in *c.* 722 B.C. that **the day of reckoning** (10: 3) finally came for the northern kingdom, through the agency of the Assyrian armies. The first enemies of Israel to be mentioned are, however, not the Assyrians, but **Arameans** and **Philistines** (9: 12), and in 9: 21 civil war in Israel, and hostilities with **Judah**, are mentioned. It is possible that Isaiah is recapitulating the whole history of the northern kingdom in this passage (see Kaiser for details), but it seems simpler to suppose that he is portraying the increasing political chaos of the last decade of the northern kingdom's existence.

9: 9–12. Samaria, far from being humbled by the depredations of Tiglath-pileser III in 737–732 B.C., **with pride and arrogance** shows delusions of grandeur, quickly dispelled by local enemies. In 9: 13–17 we see the country so bereft of leadership (even lying prophets would have been better than no prophets, v. 15 suggests!) that **every month speaks vileness** (or 'folly', cf. RSV). The whole land is doomed; not even the **fatherless and widows** can be rescued, in spite of God's general concern for such. The folly leads in turn to the total anarchy depicted in 9: 18–21. Yet in the anarchy there were still some men in positions of influence who abused their power to feather their own nests at the expense of the **poor** and the **widows** (10: 1–4). It is to these unjust law-makers that the prophet directs his final words of warning and rebuke. Perhaps there was still time for them to have repented had they wished; otherwise, they faced certain death or deportation (10: 4).

(*i*) **The Limits of Assyria's Power (10: 5–34)**

5–19. The northern kingdom had fallen before this oracle was pronounced. Assyria had been appointed by God as His agent to punish Israel and Judah (cf. 5: 26, 7: 18); but by *c.* 715 B.C. the arrogant attitude and behaviour of the Assyrians had become scarcely tolerable (12), and Isaiah here pronounces the woe upon them which God had declared. **Samaria** and many other cities of Syria and Palestine (9) had fallen to Tiglath-pileser III and his successors, and now Jerusalem was under threat (10 f.); the Assyrian king who speaks in v. 8 may have been either Sargon in 713–711 or Sennacherib in 701 B.C. (cf. 37: 10–13).

Just as many years before Isaiah had tried to instil faith and courage into Ahaz, so now again he endeavours to comfort and strengthen his fellow-citizens in the face of imminent danger. He tells them first that the Assyrians had gone beyond the bounds of their divine commission (6 f.) and goes on to indicate how they in turn will be punished by God (16–19). He stresses more than once that the Assyrians are no more than a tool in God's hand (5, 15), however powerful they may appear to human eyes.

20–34. The link between the preceding passage and vv. 20–27a is provided by the words **remaining** and **remnant** (19 f. same Heb. word), and by the future frame of reference. Assyria is to be reduced to a remnant in God's good time; but the prophet had previously indicated, especially in the symbolic name of his son Shear-Jashub (7: 3), that *Judah* too would be reduced to a small number of survivors. However, Judah's **remnant** was a sign of hope, for it was a remnant that would **return**; Isaiah is probably here using the word in two senses; of literal return from exile and deportation, and of spiritual return to God. The last sentence of v. 22 is somewhat unclear; 'A destruction has been decreed that will bring inexhaustible integrity' (JB) may represent the meaning.

Ultimately, the oracle declares, God will **carry out the destruction** of all His enemies (23), on a world-wide scale; but that event, so long delayed since Isaiah prophesied, might offer too little hope to a suffering people. So the oracle goes on to predict that **very soon** (25) the Assyrian yoke will be lifted. Many listeners must have been doubtful whether mighty Assyria could ever be thwarted; hence, the reminder of God's past deliverance of His people from Egyptian and Midianite oppression.

In vv. 27b–32 the prophet paints a terrifying picture of an enemy—undoubtedly the Assyrians are meant—advancing from the north upon Jerusalem. In their major attack on Jerusalem in 701, the Assyrians in fact approached from a different route; so it is best to view the passage as imaginative rather than predictive—Isaiah is vividly reminding his people how easily and rapidly the Assyrians could reach the very gates of Jerusalem, and by implication showing that Yahweh was the only possible source of hope. Political alliances could achieve nothing useful against Assyria. Only **the LORD Almighty** is able to bring the might of Assyria crashing down like a tree or a forest.

Some commentators take vv. 33 f. as a brief oracle threatening Judah; the metaphor of the trees then lays a foundation for the imagery of 11: 1. More probably, however, the chapter division is correct, and the two verses relate to the fall of Assyria; v. 19 used the same imagery with reference to Assyria.

(*j*) **God's future King (11: 1–16)**

1–9. Disaster ahead has now been prophesied both for Judah and for Assyria; but beyond Judah's time of trouble lies glorious hope. The disaster will bring low even the line of David, it is implied by the reference to the **stump of Jesse** (1); but from that line shall come God's ideal ruler. The theme of 9: 6 f. is thus resumed; once again **righteousness** (5) and peace (6–9) are stressed. The coming king will be thoroughly equipped for his task by **the Spirit of the LORD** (2), which has long since empowered David himself (cf. 1 Sam. 16: 13); and (no less than Solomon) he will show perfect **justice** (4) in his administration. We do not know at what juncture in his ministry Isaiah uttered this oracle, but we can clearly read between the lines the contrast with the present king on Judah's throne, and the present conditions prevailing. Ahaz was probably the king at the time, rather than Hezekiah, who did show many godly features.

The era of peace (6–9) is seen to benefit all nature, world-wide. The prophet's primary interest centres on the situation in Jerusalem (the **holy mountain**) but he sees the whole **earth** in harmony together and in harmony with God (9).

10–16. Though a separate poem (indeed vv. 10 f. seem to be two short independent oracles), this passage continues the theme of vv. 1–9. The coming king, called now **the Root of Jesse**, will ensure that **the earth will be full of the knowledge of the LORD** (9) by drawing all men to himself. People of all **nations**— even **Assyria!** (16)—shall look to him; hence he is described as a **banner** (10). Changing the figure slightly, the prophet then depicts the king as raising **a banner** (12), as a sign to bring all the exiles of Israel and Judah home. The reunited people of God will forget their ancestral rivalries (13), and will take military action only against the intransigent foes of Israel (14 f.). (The **slopes of the Philistines** is either their 'flank' (NEB) or the western 'slopes' (JB) of their territory.)

The dispersion of Israel and Judah depicted

in v. 11 looks far beyond the actualities of Isaiah's time: see Introduction.

(*k*) **A Thanksgiving Hymn (12: 1–6)**

The first major section of the book of Isaiah (chs. 1–12) ends in hymnic fashion: those who see God's blessings come to pass will give Him due praise. As so often when Isaiah is looking into the future, however, he is not unmindful of the present; v. 2, for instance, reminds us of the fear displayed by Ahaz and his court (cf. 7: 2), and it serves as a challenge to God's people in any age, to put aside fear and to trust in God who is the sole author of salvation.

The call to put fear aside is followed by a call to praise (4 ff.), introduced by a reference to **the wells of salvation** (3). The phrase may be simply metaphorical, but is perhaps an allusion to the water drawn from Gihon annually at the joyful feast of Tabernacles. As surely as the feast comes round each autumn, so surely will salvation come for the harassed people of God. Thus, the prophet seeks to reassure the **people of Zion** (6) and instil into his fellow citizens his own confident faith in **the Holy One of Israel**. With this phrase, so characteristic of Isaiah, the section is brought to an end.

II. ORACLES ON FOREIGN NATIONS (13: 1–27: 13)

It is interesting to speculate to what extent foreign peoples and nations were aware of the oracles about them by the prophets of Israel and Judah. It may very well be that the primary intention of such oracles was by way of instruction, warning or hope to God's people themselves.

Brought together in these chapters, however, the prophetic oracles give an over-all impression of God's universal rule. Chapters 1–12 have spoken of the future of Jerusalem and Judah; chs. 13–27 go on to reveal something of God's wider purposes.

i. God's Word to the Nations (13: 1–23: 18)

Although the precise purpose of the individual oracles in this section may differ somewhat, together they present two lessons in particular: foreign oppression will cease, and foreign (potential) allies will fail. There is thus a message of hope for God's people when oppressed by foreign powers, and a message of warning that their reliance should be placed only in God, not in political intrigues and alliances. Thus the prophet's advice to Ahaz (ch. 7) is in effect re-emphasized in a wider setting.

(*a*) **The Oracle concerning Babylon (13: 1–14: 27)**

The longest of the oracles concerning foreign nations, this prophecy can be split up into the following component parts: (*i*) 13: 1, title; (*ii*) 13: 2–16, the fall of all empires; (*iii*) 13: 17–22, the fall of Babylon; (*iv*) 14: 1 f., the salvation of Israel; (*v*) 14: 3–21, Israel's taunt against the king of Babylon; (*vi*) 14: 22–27, the fate of Babylon and Assyria. It is very likely that most of these sections were originally separate oracles, directed to different situations in the prophet's career. Sections (i) and (v) (which now provide the literary framework for the rest) could have been uttered at any time during Isaiah's lifetime; Assyria was frighteningly strong at the start of his ministry, and all powerful by the end of it. These two oracles' primary purpose was to give comfort and assurance to the arrogance of Judaea. Section (ii) contrasts the arrogance of Babylon with the fate in store for it; this oracle could well have served as a warning to Hezekiah to avoid any alliance with Babylon, whose king Merodach-Baladan (see 39: 1) tried in 705 B.C. to implicate Judah in an ill-fated revolt against the Assyrians.

The taunt-song (14: 4b–22) once stood alone, as a spoken oracle, and voices an anger against the Babylon monarch which would have been inappropriate for Merodach-Baladan (who moreover was not a king who 'made kingdoms tremble', 14: 16). Most commentators have associated this passage with a later era, when the kings of Babylon had replaced the Assyrians as rulers of the whole Near East; many scholars have therefore attributed the taunt to a sixth-century writer and denied it to Isaiah while evangelical commentators generally treat the passage as long-distance prediction.

Other commentaries again have seen the taunt as addressed to a king of Assyria rather than Babylon; in fact, as Erlandsson has emphasized, the king of Assyria bore the additional title 'king of Babylon' during the greater part of Isaiah's career. In any case, it is doubtful if the passage is concerned with a *specific* king; it is the generic world-ruler who is the object of the prophetic taunt. Probably, then, the taunt was another of Isaiah's oracles intended in the first place to give comfort to those of his own day and succeeding generations who were suffering from the arrogant cruelties of Mesopotamian emperors.

Section (iii) forms part of the prose introduced to the taunt-song; these verses (1–4a) were probably never a spoken oracle, but were written to give a fresh setting to the taunt.

The prophecy as a whole (13: 2–14: 27) may now be briefly considered; in this wider context, the name 'Babylon' is probably already symbolic, as in the NT (cf. Rev. 18), of the godless world-empire of any era. The ultimate downfall of man's proud empires is the teaching of the passage as a whole; once God has given His people their final salvation, never again shall they find themselves at the mercy of the arrogant whims of any human ruler.

(*i*) **13: 1.** The section **concerning Babylon** is

described as an **oracle**, or 'pronouncement'; the Hebrew word is *maśśā'* which in other contexts means 'burden'. Hence the AV rendering. The oracle came to the prophet in a vision (cf. NEB).

(*ii*) **13: 2–16.** God Himself is the speaker, placing the impending fall of Babylon in the setting of His final judgment upon the Gentile nations, **the day of the LORD** (6). The general picture is similar to that of Jl 2 (*q.v.*); for the concept of the day of Yahweh, see the notes on Am. 5: 18 ff. Here we see God, at the head of His own host, summoning the nations to battle; God's warriors are not defined, but are simply characterized as **holy ones** (JB 'sacred warriors'). The mustering (2–5) is followed by a description of the terror to be felt by the nations (6 ff.). Then at last the **day** of battle comes, a disaster of not only worldwide but cosmic dimensions (cf. vv. 10, 13). In all this vivid and terrifying passage no explicit reference is made to Babylon, unless the phrase **the gates of the nobles** (2) is a pun on the very name Babylon, which in the language of Babylonia meant 'gate of the gods'. It is made clear in v. 11 that God's foes are the **evil** and arrogant, an apt description of Babylon in its heyday, but equally applicable to a long succession of earth's proud empires.

(*iii*) **13: 17–22.** Now the oracle is directed against Babylon specifically; the first proper name mentioned is that of the **Medes** (17), who played a growing role in Near Eastern politics from the time of Isaiah, and who with the Persians brought about the fall of the Babylonian empire in 539 B.C.

The Chaldeans (19 mg) were a people who had gained a leading position within Babylonia by the time of Isaiah; Merodach-Baladan (cf. 39: 1) and Nebuchadrezzar were both Chaldeans. It was under Nebuchadrezzar (605–562 B.C.) that Babylonia reached its zenith of power, pomp and splendour, but his empire fell only a generation after his death. The city itself survived until towards the time of Christ, when it became the abandoned site described in 20 ff. The first stage of the fulfilment of the oracle may perhaps be seen in the devastating Assyrian attack on Babylon in 689 B.C. (cf. Erlandsson); the prophet himself may have lived to witness this event (note the statement **her time is at hand**, 22). It is the arrogance of Babylon for which the city is condemned (19). Its fate is to be totally deserted, even by wandering nomads (20), and left as the haunt of wild creatures.

(*iv*) **14: 1 f.** Even in this brief passage we may see the double frame of reference; if Isaiah's first thought was for the restoration of the northern kingdom, in the wider context we must understand **Israel** in the wider sense; when man's empires are finally overthrown,

God's whole people will be restored. Verse 2 is partly symbolic, depicting the tables turned on former oppressors. God's purposes for the heathen were not total annihilation, for some would join Israel in the true worship of God; this theme, present but rarely stressed in the OT (see however 56: 6 ff.), is a major doctrine in the NT.

(*v*) **14: 3–21.** It is important to realize that this poem is not the plain language of prosaic description but a highly pictorial **taunt**, a parody of a lament. In deeply sarcastic vein, the prophet pretends to feel sorrow for the dead king, and to treat seriously the claims to divine status which were made by the kings of Assyria and Babylon alike (12 ff.). The king is acclaimed as **morning star, son of the dawn**, a phrase which equates him with a deity worshipped by the Canaanites, and no doubt well known by name to the people of Judah. (The AV term 'Lucifer' also refers to the daystar; it is inappropriate to the passage to think that Satan is meant.) The **mount of assembly on the utmost heights of the sacred mountain** (13) refers to the Canaanite equivalent of the Greeks' Mount Olympus, the home of the gods. Thus, the king is depicted as a resplendent deity—but one who, like the day-star each morning, fades swiftly into insignificance and oblivion! He falls headlong from the height of human power and acclaim to the grave—and beyond. If we seek a specific historical setting for the taunt-song, the death of Sargon II (705 B.C.) seems particularly appropriate, for he died in battle outside Assyria and was buried far from his capital. Thus his funeral lacked the pomp and ceremony accorded even to the minor kings of his day (cf. vv. 18 f.). The event is shown to symbolize a deeper reality. In **the grave** (Heb. Sheol, 15, which is here as elsewhere a sort of combination of the grave itself and the after-life, see especially vv. 9, 11), the dead and humiliated king is an object of wonder (16). The point emphasized is the contrast between his past glory and his ultimate humiliation, between this world's acclaim and the judgment of God; cf. Lk. 16: 19–31. The prophet makes two further points. He draws attention to the joy and the peace which follow the tyrant's death (7); even the forests of **Lebanon** (8), so often raided for timber by conquering Assyrians, are now at peace! Hope for exiled **captives** (17) is by implication linked with this motif; this feature of the poem again points to Sargon, who had conquered Samaria in 722 B.C. and boasted of the number of exiles he deported from Israel.

The second point provides the note on which the poem ends; it is that such tyranny inevitably brings disaster, ultimately, upon the tyrant's own nation (20 f.). Both Assyria and Babylon so perished, one after the other.

The poem, then, though composed in celebration of the death of a specific tyrant, proved to be and may be read as a prediction of the fall of every human tyrant and his fate in the after life. *Sic transit gloria mundi.*

(*vi*) **14: 22–27.** Both of the great powers of Mesopotamia are the object of the prophet's condemnation, in this final paragraph of the oracle against Babylon. First Babylon itself is referred to (22 f.) in a brief prose summary of 13: 17–22. The final oracle (24 f.) reverts to poetry, and predicts the defeat of the Assyrian armies in the land of Israel; such a promise must have given much hope to Judah during the latter part of Isaiah's ministry. It was partially fulfilled in 701 B.C. (cf. 37: 36 f.), but the Assyrian **yoke** was not lifted till late in the seventh century. However, the final two verses of the whole section (13: 1–14: 27) place the specific promises of vv. 24 f. within the wider context of God's **purpose . . . for the whole world**. God's suffering people must therefore have patience; meanwhile they can be sure that no imperial power can **thwart** His plans.

(*b*) **Concerning the Philistines (14: 28–32)**
The reader's attention is now directed away from the empires of Assyria and Babylon to a series of smaller states in Judah's immediate vicinity. Philistia attracts a brief and somewhat cryptic oracle from Isaiah. **Ahaz** was pro-Assyrian in his policies, but his successor Hezekiah was not, so the Philistines soon after the death of Ahaz (28) sent an embassy (**envoys**, 32) to try to enlist Judah's support in a confederacy against the Assyrians. Verse 29 seems to imply that an Assyrian king (**the rod that struck** the Philistines) had recently died; but the prophet warns that future Assyrian kings and armies—described in a kaleidoscopic series of images—will be even more harsh in their treatment of Philistia. (For **darting, venomous serpent**, cf. D. J. Wiseman, *Tyndale Bulletin* 23, 1972, pp. 108 ff.) Thus Philistia is doomed for its anti-Assyrian policy; but Judah may rest content, a God-ordained **refuge** (32) where even **the poor** and **needy** will be cared for (30). The implication is that Judah must avoid any involvement in the Philistine policies. Thus once again we find Isaiah counselling faith in God and expressing his distrust of political alliances.

The date of the death of Ahaz is not certainly established (see notes on 1 Kg. 16: 1 f.). The Assyrian **rod** may be either Tiglath-pileser III (d. 727 B.C.) or Shalmaneser V (d. 722 B.C.).

(*c*) **Concerning Moab (15: 1–16: 14)**
The pronouncement about Moab consists of a long poem (15: 1–16: 11), with a brief concluding statement (16: 12), and then a short prose oracle, which is explicitly stated to be later than the long poem (16: 13 f.). Isaiah could have uttered both pronouncements, at different oc-

casions in his long career, or else the long poem could be his and the prose oracle God's word through a later prophet; more probably, however, Isaiah is here quoting a much older oracle, to which he adds his own postscript. In other words, he is endorsing the older word of the Lord, which had foretold disaster for Moab, and confirming that it will come true within three years. The older oracle may perhaps date from the reign of Uzziah's contemporary, Jeroboam II king of Israel, who had campaigned widely in the territories east of the Jordan (cf. 2 Kg. 14: 23 ff.); under pressure from Jeroboam, the Moabites might well have made an appeal to the people of Judah (cf. 16: 1), who had recently been invaded by Israel themselves.

15: 1–9. The opening section of the poem is descriptive of the suffering of the Moabites. Some of its chief cities are pictured in ruins (1), while panic reigns throughout the land. The citizens endeavour to escape from the country with such belongings as they can carry, desolation in their rear (6 f.). So great is the distress that the onlooker is moved to pity (5), but God's own comment on the situation (9) predicts even more suffering to follow: the **lion** may be understood literally, or figuratively of human attackers.

16: 1–11. Despite their hardships, the Moabites can find sufficient **lambs** (1) to send as a gift and bribe to Jerusalem. While the Moabite women wait in trepidation (2), an embassy goes to Jerusalem and begs for asylum for all **the Moabite fugitives** (3 f.). To bolster up their plea, they pay lip-service to the belief that once their unnamed **oppressor** has gone from the scene, a successor of **David** will rule once more (i.e. in Moab). Their final words in v. 5 are doubtless intended to flatter the present king in Jerusalem.

It is evident that the Moabite pleas were rejected; vv. 6 f. must represent the reply given to their envoys, pointing out their past **insolence** towards Judah, and also the fact that their words can never be believed. The plea rejected, nothing remains for Moab but such misery and suffering as again moves the poet to pity (8–11).

16: 12 ff. Isaiah adds his Amen to the older prophecy; if Moab once again appeals to Judah, even offering worship to God in Jerusalem, 'he will gain nothing' (12, NEB). Thus, the prophet reapplies the poem to his own day. If the point itself had said not a word as to when the disaster would fall, Isaiah can now reveal the divine word that **within three years** Moab will be utterly broken, its population reduced to a pitiful remnant (13 f.). He presents this threat as if it were a legal contract, **as a servant bound by contract would count them.**

We do not know enough of Moabite history to ascertain when Isaiah uttered this oracle of doom. The general tenor of his words was probably a warning to Judah against making common cause with the Moabites against Assyria.

(*d*) **Concerning Damascus—and Israel (17: 1–14)**
Although there are four separate literary pieces in ch. 17, they all focus on the same historical situation, the invasion of Judah by the armies of Damascus and Israel in 734 B.C. The prophet seeks to reassure and guide the terrified people of Judah (cf. 7: 2) in several ways. In the opening oracle (1–6) the certainty of doom is pronounced, first for **Damascus** (1 ff.—hence the title), and then, in equal measure, for the northern kingdom, **Ephraim**. Isaiah's attention centres on the latter, and putting Damascus aside, he goes on to contrast the northern kingdom's present **glory** and pride with its imminent future, reduced to negligible proportions comparable with the pitiful quantities of **grain** and **olives** that are left behind after harvesting. (The **Valley of Rephaim**, well known to Jerusalem's citizens, adds a vivid touch to a vivid picture.) The prose passage (7 ff.) reinforces the threat of doom for the northern kingdom (8) and reveals that God plans to punish them for their idolatry and neglect of Himself; it is punishment with a purpose, for when calamity strikes they will think again of **their Maker** (7 f.).

Two brief poems conclude the chapter. The first (10 f.) continues the charge of idolatry, now addressing the northern kingdom directly. Isaiah has singled out a specific type of pagan worship, the Adonis cult (Adonis may in fact be named—see JB, NEB) in which the forced growth of **plants** (as described here) had symbolic value. Isaiah neatly finds a quite different symbolism, the lack of any **harvest** (cf. v. 6). The second poem (12 ff.) is reminiscent of Ps. 2: 1 ff. and Jl 2: 1–11, and was intended to give courage to Judah when threatened by any and every foreign army; God would protect His own even if the whole world descended upon Jerusalem! How much more, then, would He put the puny armies of Damascus and Israel to flight; they would disappear overnight (14).

(*e*) **Concerning the Ethiopians (18: 1–7)**
Chapters 18 ff. are all concerned with Egypt, but ch. 18 names the people of **Cush** (or Ethiopia), because it was an Ethiopian dynasty which came to power in Egypt in 715 B.C. Evidently the Ethiopian king of Egypt, Piankhi, had sent **envoys** (2) to the king of Judah, Hezekiah; we can be certain that their purpose was to involve Judah in a coalition against the Assyrians. Isaiah warns Hezekiah against any such folly, by providing God's answer to the ambassadors. They are to **go** back home, to their **land** renowned both for its profusion of insects (1), and also for its **tall** and warlike people (2). For all their

military prowess and their distance from Assyria, the people of Ethiopia are not safe; God Himself has spoken (4 ff.), and it is a word of doom and destruction. The self-description of the Lord (4) is striking; He is the objective onlooker, unaffected by the intrigues and conflicts of men on earth.

Verse 7 is addressed to the reader, not to the envoys; it looks beyond the immediate fate of the Ethiopian and Egyptian armies (defeated by the Assyrians in *c.* 701 B.C.). Ultimately, the prophet reminds his readers, God intends that even such a distant nation as the Ethiopians shall worship **the LORD Almighty**, bringing their offerings to the Jerusalem temple. God's final purposes in history are those of a worshipping people drawn from all nations; cf. 66: 23.

(*f*) **Concerning Egypt (19: 1–20: 6)**
Egypt is now named in plain language, and is the subject of the whole chapter, which consists of an oracle in verse (1–15), supplemented by five short prose pronouncements regarding Egypt's future.

19: 1–15. The poem has three stanzas, which all present the same picture of doom about to descend on Egypt, a doom which is ordained and controlled by the Lord (1). The first stanza depicts civil war, culminating in the rise of a **fierce king** (4), i.e. a 'cruel' king (NEB). The native Egyptian religion will provide no rescue or relief. Various possible historical settings for this oracle have been considered, but the disorders preceding the accession of the Ethiopian Piankhi in 715 B.C. seem to provide the most appropriate fulfilment.

The second stanza (5–10) describes a further disaster, showing in detail how the Egyptian economy would break down, due not to warfare but to the failure of the annual flooding of the **river** i.e. the Nile, on which Egypt's whole fertility and prosperity have always depended. Thus the accession of the fierce king of v. 4 would bring no stability to the country; indeed, the last stanza (11–15) presents dramatically the helplessness of the king, by indicating the total lack of advice that is available even to his **wise counsellors**. The only wise words they could have offered would have been to explain that the hand of Israel's God was behind Egypt's troubles (12). Verse 15 contains a proverbial description of total helplessness.

We may see in this oracle Isaiah's determination to persuade the court of Judah not to embark on any alliance with Egypt against Assyria.

19: 16–24. Just as ch. 18 ended with an appendix (v. 7) which set out God's purposes beyond judgment and disaster, so now this chapter, at greater length, looks beyond the historical events of 715 B.C. and outlines something of the divine plan for Egypt. The five paragraphs may date from different periods,

but together they build up a clear picture of God's intentions. The first section (16 f.), as J. Mauchline very reasonably suggests, most probably points to the events of 701 B.C., when **terror** in the **land of Judah** (cf. 2 Kg. 19: 6 f., 35) fell upon the Assyrian king Sennacherib at a time when Egyptian armies had failed to achieve anything against the Assyrians.

The next two sections (18, 19–22) together depict the Egyptians as gradually coming to acknowledge Israel's God as theirs, in consequence of His dealings with them in history (22). At first only a few **cities** will turn to Him; the reference to the **City of Destruction** is rather obscure. *MT* reads 'City of the Sun' which may be designed to show that Yahweh's influence will reach even to the city named after Egypt's most important deity, the sun-god Re. The developments mentioned in vv. 19 ff. may well imply that Jews were to take the physical signs of the worship of Yahweh to Egypt.

By NT times a very large number of Jews had taken up residence in Egypt (a process which may have begun as early as Isaiah's time) but the passage clearly posits a wholesale turning of the Egyptians to God, such as has never yet taken place.

The final two paragraphs (23, 24 f.) continue to look beyond any historical events known to us; above all, their symbolical teaching is important. The ancient world was not ill-supplied with trade-routes, though no doubt the road from Assyria to Egypt was long and arduous. The existence of the **highway** between them implies in this case not the march of armies but peaceful and prosperous intercourse —with no barriers between. Between the two lay Syria and Palestine, but— says the prophet —that territory will be fragmented no longer, but will consist of a united **Israel** (of Davidic dimensions) on a par with the mighty imperial powers. Harmony reigns between the three states, for all worship the same God, whose temple lies in Jerusalem, which makes Israel **a blessing on earth**. The passage attests the prophet's startling faith (in an era when Judah was so puny and powerless) and also his breadth of tolerance (to which Jonah's views about Assyria are in complete contrast).

20: 1–6. This brief chapter, which begins in biographical fashion, shows how far Isaiah went in his endeavours to persuade Hezekiah against relying on Egyptian promises. The new Ethiopian rulers of Egypt were deeply involved in the revolt of **Ashdod** (a Philistine city), which was attacked and fell to the Assyrians in 712/11 B.C., and evidently Hezekiah was very much inclined to join in the fruitless revolt. The chapter reveals that fully **three years** prior to the fall of Ashdod the prophet had been a walking symbol of utter humiliation and destitution on the streets of Jerusalem. Unexplained, the **sign** of his **going around stripped and barefoot** could well have portended Judah's own fall and exile, and certainly this possibility is lurking in the background of the symbol. However, the sign is now explained as directed against Egypt. When the Assyrians rout the Egyptian armies, taking many deportees, all those who formerly put their faith in Egypt will be **afraid and put to shame.** (**The people who live on this coast** include both Philistines and the people of Judah.) In other words, *now* is the time to draw back and be wise; once Egypt is defeated, her allies in Palestine will have no hope of escaping from Assyrian vengeance.

Thus the three chapters relating to Egypt end on a note which reveals clearly where the prophet's emphasis lies: it is not the fate of Egypt but the fateful choice of Judah which is uppermost in his mind.

(*g*) **Another Oracle on Babylon (21: 1–10)**
The reader's attention is now taken back to Mesopotamia, with another oracle against **Babylon** (cf. chs. 13 f.). The name Babylon is withheld till v. 9, so that the oracle seems particularly obscure to modern readers; it was probably intended to be cryptic even to the prophet's first hearers, no doubt in order to compel their careful attention. The title's reference to **the Desert by the Sea** is itself puzzling. (It is the first of a series of strange titles and appellations; cf. 21: 11; 22: 1; 29: 1; 30: 6.) The phrase may be better translated 'maritime plain', reflecting the Assyrian name for Babylonia (cf. JB). A case can also be made for omitting the word **Sea**, thus getting a simpler title, 'a wilderness' (see NEB). The word **desert** later in v. 1 is the same Hebrew noun.

The oracle first (1 f.) portrays a **looter**, as fearful as a storm in **the southland** (the wilderness area to the south of Judah), who is finally identificd as the troops of **Elam** and **Media**. An attentive listener should immediately have thought of Babylon as the city under **siege**. The prophet then describes his own **horror** at the vision he has seen (3 f.), in marked contrast to the unconcerned feasting of the **officers** of Babylon, who ought to have been preparing for battle (5). These two themes recur in the book of Daniel; cf. Dan. 5: 1–4; 10: 8–11. Finally, the prophet depicts himself as the Lord's **lookout** (6–9; cf. Hab. 2: 1), who sees and announces the fall of **Babylon** and **its gods**. His message is addressed to the suffering people of Judah (10).

Most commentators make this oracle refer to events of sixth century B.C., when Babylon fell to the Medes and Persians; many scholars accordingly, date it in the sixth century. Erlandsson, however, gives detailed arguments for placing the oracle in *c*. 700 B.C.; in such a

context, the chief point of the prophecy would have been to warn Hezekiah of the folly of resisting Assyria. The lack of any reference to Assyria is surprising, but may be due to the cryptic character of the oracle. (See Introduction.)

(*h*) **Concerning Edom and Arabia (21: 11–17)**
Two brief oracles relate to the regions to the south east of Judah, first Edom (also known as **Seir**), then northern **Arabia**. The oracle against Edom (11 f.) is even more cryptic than the earlier part of the chapter. The title refers to **Dumah**, which was a town in Edom; the name was probably chosen because in Hebrew *dūmāh* means 'silence'. The answer given to the Edomite question, after all, was not very informative. The question was a commonplace one, a simple request to know the time; but it must here symbolize the **'night'** of Assyrian oppression. It is not easy to date such a brief and cryptic oracle, but if we may link the two oracles together, the campaigns of Sargon II in 715 B.C. provide a very likely historical background.

The oracle concerning Arabia (13–16) is plain enough. The **heat of battle** (15) threatens the rich **caravans** of the Arabian traders, and even the more warlike Arabian tribes will be decimated within a single **year.** (See note on 16: 14.)

(*i*) **Concerning Jerusalem (22: 1–25)**
The two sections of this chapter both relate to affairs in Jerusalem; in this respect ch. 22 stands apart from the rest of chs. 13–23, which otherwise consist of oracles against foreign peoples. The feature linking ch. 22 with this wider context is probably the background common to so many of the oracles in chs. 13–23, namely the threat posed by Assyria, which was to be God's instrument of punishment upon many peoples in the Near East in this epoch (cf. 10: 5).

1–14. The first oracle in the chapter accuses Jerusalem of callous and unthinking revelry (13), despite the fact that so many disasters had just occurred. The setting can only be the sequel to Sennacherib's siege of Jerusalem in 701 B.C. Before Sennacherib's precipitate departure from the scene (cf. 37: 36), the Assyrian king had rampaged through Judah, causing death and destruction everywhere, and evidently many had died of famine in the capital (2). But instead of mourning and repentance, the Jerusalemites were so relieved that they shouted the news from **the roofs** (1), and proceeded to feast off the few surviving animals (13), no doubt endangering further lives by this gluttony. It seems very likely that the aristocracy and the court, in particular, are the object of Isaiah's denunciations. The pronouncement of the divine anger in v. 14 is very strongly worded, and we must assume that the men so denounced had been guilty of bringing the full weight of the Assyrian armies down upon their country. The prose section (8–11), expanding the oracle, tells how they had planned and made the Siloam tunnel instead of seeking guidance and help from God. God is described in v. 11 as He who had **planned** all that had happened, namely the **day of tumult** (5) which had afflicted Jerusalem in 701 B.C. Verses 5–8 describe the Assyrian siege of Jerusalem, in terms which to us are slightly obscure but must have been clear enough at the time. **Elam** and **Kir** were foreign contingents of the Assyrian army, while **the Valley of Vision** (1, 5) is a word-play on the name Valley of Hinnom (or Gehenna) just outside Jerusalem; Jerusalem as a whole is meant by the phrase. **8. the Palace of the Forest:** the armoury erected by Solomon; cf. 1 Kg. 7: 2; 10: 17.

15–25. Another oracle follows, denouncing a high official of Judah, the **steward Shebna**. The general historical setting seems to be the same as for vv. 1–14; we know from 36: 3 that Shebna held a somewhat lower post in 701 B.C., so evidently this oracle dates from a year or two earlier. We may then safely conjecture that Shebna was one of the chief culprits in persuading Hezekiah to revolt against Assyria (and was subsequently demoted). The only explicit charge made against Shebna, however, is that he planned for himself an ostentatious **grave** (16). No doubt this action typified the man's whole attitude in a self-centred heedlessness of the plight of his country and his fellow-citizens. Isaiah only mentions the tomb in order to emphasize how useless it will be; for God's plan is that Shebna will die in exile, far from his chosen burial place (18). Before his death, he will suffer the indignity of demotion from the high post of being **in charge of the palace**, i.e. comptroller of the palace.

The vivid comparison of Shebna to a **ball** (18) is matched by that of **Eliakim** (20), his successor, to a **peg** (23) in a wall; Shebna can swiftly be uprooted, but Eliakim will be firmly established in the same office. The importance of the post is indicated, indeed emphasized, by the description of its authority in v. 22 (a verse which provides the basis for Rev. 3: 7).

Possibly vv. 24 f. represent a later statement by the prophet. He now sees that Eliakim showed selfishness too, in blatant nepotism; Isaiah therefore neatly extends the metaphor of the peg, and reminds Eliakim that pegs too can readily be removed.

For other interpretations of the information about Shebna, see *IDB, s.v.* 'Shebna'.

(j) Concerning Tyre and Sidon (23: 1–18)
The final chapter in this major section of the book of Isaiah is devoted to Phoenicia, whose chief cities were **Tyre** (1) and **Sidon** (2). The people called themselves 'Canaanites'; hence, the use of the name Canaan in v. 11 (NIV **Phoenicia**, cf. mg); often in the OT, as in this chapter, 'Sidon' means the country as a whole. The passage reflects the great prowess of the Phoenicians in maritime commerce, and also the colonies which they founded right across the Mediterranean as far as Spain. But from *c.* 700 B.C. their decline began, and this was rightly foreseen by Isaiah, as his oracle (vv. 1–12) makes plain. The Assyrians first put pressures on them, and then under the Babylonian empire they were again under attack; the island part of the city of Tyre, however, was never captured by any foe prior to Alexander the Great in 332 B.C. Thus the fulfilment of the oracle was progressive, in all taking more than three centuries.

Verses 1–4 recall the rich trade between Phoenicia and Egypt (**Shihor** is thought to be synonymous with **the Nile**), and bewail the ultimate fall of the city of **Tyre**. Many of its citizens have fled to **Cyprus** (1, 12). (The largest ships of the time were called **ships of Tarshish.**) The rest of Phoenicia looks on in dismay (2, 4). **Egypt** is distressed, because of the loss to herself of the lucrative trade with Phoenicia; but evidently Phoenician colonies like **Tarshish** (Tartessus in Spain) no longer had to help the mother city (10). The decline of Phoenicia, says Isaiah, will be no mere chance of history; it is the Lord's set purpose. The chief cause of God's anger was the commercial pride, the soulless self-aggrandisement of Phoenicia (8 f.).

Verses 3–18 are basically in prose, though including snatches of poetry, and are later. After Sennacherib's severe harassment of Phoenicia in 701 B.C., Tyre's trading was very largely disrupted for almost exactly seventy years, when the decline of the Assyrian empire permitted its commercial recovery. Late in his ministry, then, the prophet foretold the city's recovery (15 ff.), portraying Tyre as a **prostitute** plying her trade and singing in the streets. Verse 18, with a marked change of tone, reveals that ultimately it is God's purpose that the richest pagan city (symbolized here by Tyre) will be pagan no longer, but will dedicate all its resources to the worship of God. There is an allusion here to the part played by Tyre, centuries earlier, in the erection and embellishment of Solomon's temple.

Verse 13 (with which v. 14 is to be taken) is extremely difficult, in terms of both text and translation. If RSV or NEB is correct, then the verse can only date from the time of Nebuchadrezzar's attack on Tyre (see notes on Ezek. 26 ff.), for it reflects on the fact that Babylon, not **Assyria**, had fulfilled Isaiah's oracle. (In that case, the verse must have been a marginal comment which by later scribal error gained admission to the text of Isaiah.) But NIV (cf JB) follows another possible rendering; see in particular the discussions by Erlandsson and Young. No certainty is possible.

ii. God's Word to the World (24: 1–27: 13)
This section is often called 'the Apocalypse of Isaiah'. The scene is now cosmic, and the time reference the future. As elsewhere in Isaiah, close study shows that separate short oracles have been brought together to give a wider picture. The downfall of all that is hostile to God, the blessings in store for God's own people, and His ultimate purposes for Jerusalem (27: 13), are the predominant themes, which give both comfort and assurance to His faithful people in times of political hardship or disaster. God is presented as in full control of the whole of the world and the whole of time.

(a) **Worldwide Judgment (24: 1–20)**
Hosea, prophesying a generation or two earlier than Isaiah, had mourned over the chaotic moral condition of the northern kingdom, and predicted the utter ruin of the land (Hos. 4: 1–10). Isa. 24: 1–20 takes up the theme, v. 4 in particular recalling Hos. 4: 3, but extends the scope of the prophecy to the wide world. The imperial powers like Assyria must one day suffer God's punishment; while the small nations like Judah were already suffering His punishment, inflicted by means of the Assyrians. So the prophecy brings all the threads of chapters 13–23 together; vv. 1–3 and 14 reveal the coming universal scope of the punishment decreed by **the LORD** (3). Verse 2 emphasizes that every class of society will be affected; and at the end of the day the 'remnant' will be very small indeed (6, 13). The lament (4–12), which is embedded in the prophecy, provides the explanation for the world-wide disaster to come: the earth's **people . . . have disobeyed the laws** of God (5). They have broken **the everlasting covenant** (cf. Gen. 9: 16); the punishment is depicted in terms which contrast with the Flood of Noah's day, for it is a picture of terrible drought. The lack of **wine** (7–11) typifies the failure of all vegetation as well as the loss of every source of joy. Every **city** is abandoned to **ruins** (10, 12), as the citizens search hopelessly for food in the countryside. Verses 17–20 resume the same theme of disaster to come, again in language which recalls the Flood story (18; cf. Gen. 7: 11).

Verses 14 ff. pick out a specific group of people (**they** is emphatic at the beginning of v. 14), presumably the remnant implied in v. 13, whose experience is very different. They **shout for joy**, in every part of the world; it is evidently those who worship the God of Israel who have survived the holocaust. The note changes markedly in the middle of v. 16; although the exact sense of the second half of the verse is uncertain (see EVV), we should

probably take it as an introduction to vv. 17–20, not as a postscript to vv. 14–16a.

(b) **The Faith of the Future (24: 21–25: 5)**
The future downfall of the earth's unrighteous, godless systems will not result in a spiritual vacuum. Idolatry will perish with those who practise it; the prophet sums up idolatry in terms of the worship of stars (**the powers** of **heaven**), **sun** and **moon** (21 ff.). The OT frequently recognizes the spiritual reality of idolatry; idols in themselves have no reality, but the power of idolatry, over the minds and actions of men, was self-evident in the ancient world. The NT stresses the satanic and demonic aspects of idolatry; see especially Eph. 6: 12. Rev. 20: 1 ff., 7 is based on v. 22.

Idolatry, then, will ultimately bow down to **the LORD Almighty** (23)—a phrase which emphasizes God's control of all powers of the universe. At this point the cosmic picture is put aside, for the Lord has chosen to **reign gloriously** not in the majesty of the heavens, but in **Jerusalem**, before ordinary human beings faithful to Him. The mention of **elders** recalls Exod. 24: 1 ff.; cf. also Rev. 4: 4.

The promise of v. 23 is fittingly followed by a hymn of joyful praise (25: 1–5), which the prophet may well have composed to be used in the worship of his day. Those who truly believe that God will act and bring His plans in history to fruition, may already enter into the good of them; to the eye of faith, the downfall of the enemies of God's people has already happened. It is Judah, dominated and oppressed by the Assyrians and their successors, who are here described as **the poor** and **needy** (4); the **foreigners** are the oppressors of every era, beginning with the Assyrians. The passage thus had not only future but permanent relevance; in the context of worship **the noise of the foreigners** is already hushed.

(c) **The Lord's Banquet (25: 6–12)**
The three paragraphs (NIV) of this final part of ch. 25 may have been originally independent (*e.g.*, vv. 10 ff. seem to incorporate an oracle against Moab), but placed together, in this general setting, they continue the theme of the blessings in store for God's people, and set in contrast the fate in store for such as Moab. The unifying phrase is **this mountain**, harking back to 'Mount Zion' (24: 23), with which the lowly degradation of Moab to **the very dust** is contrasted. God's people are declared to be drawn from **all peoples** (6), joining in the wonderful banquet prepared by Him. Not only will sorrow be permanently removed from the scene, but **death** itself (the '**sheet**' of v. 7) is to be banished (cf. 1 C. 15: 54; Rev. 21: 4)—a vision of the future given to very few OT writers. The final defeat of death is the ultimate **salvation** of God's people, as they gratefully acknowledge (v. 9).

To modern readers, vv. 10 ff. make un-pleasant reading, and are something of an anti-climax. Two things must be said in partial explanation: firstly, that **the manure** (Heb. *madmēnāh*) is a word-play on the Moabite place-name Madmen, which explains the ima-gery chosen; and secondly, that in the context Moab must be used to typify all the inveterate enemies of the people of God, partly for histori-cal reasons, and perhaps partly because the name Moab so closely resembles the Hebrew word for 'enemy', *'ōyēb*. The chief point of the passage is that God will **lay low** all human **pride** which opposes itself to God's plans and God's people.

(d) Songs of Hope and Trust (26: 1–21)

In several respects ch. 26 parallels ch. 25, and so reinforces its message; nowhere in Scripture is a better example of comfort provided in difficult days by a consideration of the future. Verses 1–6 contrast two cities, in a **song** per-taining to a future day. The first—Jerusalem, obviously—is a **city** of such secure **peace** that **the gates** may be freely opened, in tranquil **trust** in the Lord's deliverance. (Note that the exact sense of v. 3 is uncertain; see NEB, JB.) The message for the *present* was clearly that the down-trodden people of Judah should here and now repose such trust on their God, who would one day lay **low** the other **city**, i.e. the capital of the world-empire, and permit His own **oppressed** and **poor** people to tread it down, in turn.

Verses 7–19 revert to the present day, in a passage which blends the themes of lamen-tation and trust. **The wicked** are perversely blind to God (10), whereas **the righteous . . . wait** for God to act; in the meantime the **name** of God and the memory of Him (cf. JB) suffice for them (7 f.). They believe implicitly that God will increase **the nation** and restore its **borders** (15; cf. 9: 3)—permanently removing the **other lords** who had oppressed them (13 f.). Verses 16 f. emphasize not only the **distress** which had been suffered, in vivid pictorial language, but also acknowledge the past vain struggles of the people of Judah (under Ahaz and Hezekiah, in particular) to rescue them-selves. Many had died in the years of strug-gling; but they are not beyond hope, for death is itself to be defeated. The prophet draws out the implications of 25: 8 in v. 19, which also provides a deliberate contrast with v. 14: today's oppressors are doomed, but yesterday's and today's martyrs **will live**! Few OT writers were granted this glimpse beyond the grave (cf. Dan. 12: 2); the general picture of the after-life, both in Israel and neighbouring lands, was of a shadowy existence in a depress-ing, dusty underworld; but with another characteristically vivid metaphor, the prophet visualizes life-giving and light-bearing **dew**

penetrating as it were through the dusty earth into Sheol.

The prophet does not dwell on this revel-ation; instead, he gives practical advice for the present time (20), and appends a final assurance that God will punish today's evil men (21). God's people can successfully **hide** from their human foes; but those enemies will not ulti-mately be able to hide their sins and bloodshed from God's all-seeing eye.

(e) Restoration and Worship (27: 1–13)

The NIV lay-out makes it clear that this chapter consists of several distinct paragraphs; there is a continuous thread of thought, but no doubt we have here what were originally quite dis-tinct oracles. Verse 1 predicts the fall of God's enemies; vv. 2–11 promise happier days for both Judah and Israel but take a realistic look at the contemporary condition, contrasting its future with the present condition of an un-named city; and vv. 12 f. predict the return of all Israelite exiles to their own land, and their worship in Jerusalem.

Verse 1 draws on the language of ancient Canaanite myths, in which **Leviathan** and **the monster** (Rahab) were enemies defeated by the god Baal; almost identical descriptions are found in the Ras Shamra texts (see *DOTT*, pp. 129 f.), and it is clear that Isaiah was using expressions very familiar to his audience. Equally plainly, the prophet is using this language metaphorically, to describe historical enemies of Yahweh. **Leviathan** may well sym-bolize Assyria, and **the monster** Egypt; other equations have been suggested, but this in-terpretation provides a perfect balance in vv. 12 f.

Verses 2–6 pick up the theme of 5: 1–7, promising that Judah (by implication) will eventually be **a fruitful vineyard** (2) and that Israel will yield a miraculous abundance of **fruit** (6); in the meantime God tends His vineyard with every care, and pleads with His people to respond to Him.

Verses 7 ff. acknowledge that God has af-flicted the former northern kingdom severely, not so much in punishment as with a purpose—the end of idolatry—in view; v. 7 implies that God's punishment of His enemies is recogniz-ably of a different order from His disciplining of His own people. (The beginning of v. 8 is obscure.)

Verses 10 ff. again mention an unnamed **city**; this is possibly to be interpreted generi-cally (see note on 24: 10), but the language used in v. 11 is more appropriate to God's people than to pagans, and therefore Samaria is prob-ably intended (Jerusalem is less likely in the present context). If so, the lack of God's **favour** is not to be permanent, in view of the promises of vv. 9, 12.

12 f. Using two different metaphors, the

prophet predicts the return to the land of Palestine of those who had gone to **Assyria** as deportees and to **Egypt** as refugees when the northern kingdom fell in 722 B.C. Verse 9 had foretold the cessation of Israel's idolatry; v. 12 goes further, and says that Israel's future place of worship will be neither Dan nor Bethel but **Jerusalem** in Judah.

Thus the cameos of the future of chs. 24–27 end with the theme of the future purified and unified worship of God, centred on Mount Zion.

III. JERUSALEM UNDER ASSYRIAN DOMINATION (28: 1–39: 8)

The structure of this section resembles that of chs. 1–12; here too a collection of oracles is followed by a biographical section in which prophet and king are brought together. The king is now Hezekiah, and probably most of the oracles in these chapters date from the later years of Isaiah's ministry. Although Jerusalem is once again the central theme, there is a wider perspective in that the section begins with the fall of the northern kingdom and ends with the exile to Babylon. The prophetic teachings largely reinforce those of earlier chapters: the political situation varies, but God's word is the same.

i. Oracles of Warning and Promise (28: 1–35: 10)

There is no clear pattern in these chapters, but a certain progress of thought is visible. Chapters 28–32 contain miscellaneous oracles, chiefly of warning or rebuke. Chapter 33 is a psalm, which renders thanks to God for His deliverance hitherto; and chs. 34 f. look into the future, anticipating the downfall of God's enemies and the final deliverance of His people.

(a) Rebuke to the Kingdom of Israel (28: 1–13)

The passage is a warning oracle to the northern kingdom (**Ephraim**), in which is incorporated a separate message of hope (5 f.) to a small number who will survive, the **remnant** of God's **people**. The oracle probably dates from the earlier part of the reign of Hoshea (c. 732–722 B.C.), when many citizens of the northern kingdom were in a state of ill-founded euphoria. Isaiah took particular exception to the drunken revelling that was typical of the day; the **drunkards** seem to be depicted as wearing garlands (NIV is clearer than RSV in v. 1, but RSV may be correct, if we can assume that **the head of a fertile valley** meant Samaria). The garlands lead the prophet to build up an agricultural picture, by which he predicts the fearful **hail storm** that is coming (i.e. the Assyrian conquest) and the all-too-brief 'harvest'—the lull before the storm. But by contrast, God will Himself be an unfading garland to the faithful

remnant, granting them all they need (in some future day).

Continuing his attack on the heedless revellers, Isaiah makes the damning statement that neither **priest** nor **prophet** in the northern kingdom was any better than the ordinary citizen (7 f.). Verses 9 f. are most probably the contemptuous rejoinder of the prophets whom Isaiah was attacking; Isaiah, they claim, is treating them as if they were tiny children. There are difficulties in translating v. 10 (cf. EVV) but the accusation is either that Isaiah was babbling, or else (more probably) that he was trying to teach them their ABC.

Very well, Isaiah retorts in vv. 11 ff., if the people of Israel will not listen to his elementary teaching, they will perforce learn a harsher lesson—taught by the Assyrians, those men of **strange tongues**—which in fact derives from Yahweh Himself. The tragedy is that God had formerly offered them a message of comfort and consolation; but they had been deaf to it (12; cf. especially Mt. 23: 37).

(b) Rebuke to the Kingdom of Judah (28: 14–22)

If vv. 1–13 castigate the blind guides of the northern kingdom, vv. 14–22 bring the rebuke home to Judah, and specifically to the leading politicians in **Jerusalem** (14). These could be the men who gave Ahaz such foolish advice in 734 B.C., but more probably they are the counsellors of Hezekiah, who scoffed at Isaiah's advice and advised Hezekiah to join in the ill-fated revolt against Assyria in 705 B.C. In v. 15 Isaiah characterizes their whole attitude (they did not actually *speak* thus, of course): their predictions of what will happen are sheer **falsehood** (and self-deception), and they seem to imagine themselves immortal. Isaiah counters this attitude by offering them an oracle from **the LORD**. The oracle (16 f.) is important in NT usage (Rom. 9: 33; 1 Pet. 2: 4–8); though enshrining a permanent truth, its immediate import was one of promise and challenge comparable with the message to Ahaz in 7: 4, 9. The **stone**, the **sure foundation**—symbolizing God's protection in the Assyrian assaults soon to fall on Judah—is the promise depicted as inscribed on the stone: **'the one who trusts will never be dismayed'**, i.e., he will not show faithless agitation (so Young). The final verb of v. 16 is textually uncertain; 'waver' (NEB) is conceivably the correct sense; cf. 7: 9. (The NT 'put to shame' is derived from the LXX, which is interpreting rather than translating.) Verse 17, which continues the building metaphor, makes it clear that the **stone** symbolizes protection, by the contrast between the true and the false **refuge**. The false counsellors will be **beaten down** by the Assyrian **scourge** (18). Verse 20 is thought to have been a popular saying, and is used here to describe the same loss of adequate protection. Verses 21 f., recalling how God had wonderfully protected His people in earlier days (cf. Jos. 10: 1–11; 2 Sam. 5: 17–25), reveal that now it is that same God's determined **decree** to bring **destruction against the whole land**, however **alien** to His ultimate purposes for His people. The decree of judgment is not yet irrevocable, for v. 22 incorporates an appeal to heed the prophet's words, even yet.

For a comprehensive list of other interpretations of v. 16 see Kaiser *ad loc.*

(c) **The Parable of the Farmer (28: 23–29)** The oracle of vv. 14–22 had acknowledged that punishment of His own people was God's 'strange' and 'alien' deed; evidently it was too strange a concept for many in Judah to understand or accept: would God *really* bring disaster on His own people? Isaiah, therefore, reinforces his arguments and predictions by using a parable about farming; in general, the farmer's profound skill (26) in cultivating the soil is not doubted by other people. The lesson is, then, that the God who teaches the farmer is no less wise and skilful in his own 'husbandry'; one is inevitably reminded that Judah was God's 'vineyard' (5: 1–7). Emphasis is laid upon the fact that farmers, to get the best results, must apply a variety of different procedures (some of which might puzzle an inexperienced onlooker). In particular, farmers have to apply a measure of violent activity to achieve results (27 f.); but they dare not overdo the use of force or everything would be lost (v. 28 is clearer in NEB). God, then, must treat His own people severely; but His actions have a purpose behind them, and He will certainly not carry the punishment too far. The prophet rounds off the parable with a reminder (29) that **the LORD** not only excels **in wisdom** in general, but is **wonderful in counsel**, i.e., in offering the right practical advice, through His prophets, in serious political crises. The phrase stands in contrast to the false counsellors of vv. 14 f.; and it recalls and reinforces 9: 6.

(d) **The Assyrians and Jerusalem (29: 1–12)** This section brings together three or perhaps four separate messages intended for the people of Jerusalem: vv. 1–4, 5–8 and 9–12, of which vv. 11 f. are in prose and are probably in the nature of a footnote. The first two oracles can best be understood as having been uttered at sacred festivals.

Verses 1–4 pronounce woe upon Jerusalem, and convey a warning of Sennacherib's siege of the city in 701 B.C., viewed as God's punishment of His own people. Jerusalem is described as **the city where David settled**, when he had taken it from the Jebusites, to provide a contrast with the present situation, when God's punishing army **will encamp** outside the very

same city. It is also called by the cryptic name **Ariel** (another of Isaiah's puzzling titles; cf. 21: 1), a Hebrew term which seems to have had at least two different meanings, one of them 'altar hearth', which fits this context well. In other words, Jerusalem was noted for its altar fires and sacrifices; during Sennacherib's siege, fire and bloodshed of a different sort will characterize it!

Verses 5–8 take up the theme of the first oracle, but now offer hope and salvation: in more prosaic language, Sennacherib's forces will not in the end be successful, since God will take action against them (in turn), and the Assyrian armies will fade away like **a dream**; see 37: 36 f. for the fulfilment of the promise. The promise is set in the context of God's ultimate victory against *all* Gentile enemies, which many scholars believe to have been a major theme of the annual new year ceremonies in the Jerusalem temple (see notes on Ps. 2). Jerusalem had brought grave trouble upon herself; but God would never permit her to be obliterated, and in Isaiah's day He would not so much as allow her to fall captive to Assyria.

Verses 9 f., addressed to false **prophets** who were blind to reality, must come from a slightly earlier period in Isaiah's ministry, presumably at the time when Hezekiah was beginning to plan revolt against Assyria, encouraged by inept counsellors and misguided prophets. Verses 11 f. are a deeply sarcastic addition to the oracle of vv. 9 f. Evidently these prophets still experienced visions, but everything was a **sealed scroll** to them; and even worse, their 'revelations' revealed nothing whatever to those who listened to them. (The **scroll** is not meant literally.) 1 Kg. 22: 5–23 gives the most detailed OT description of the activity of false prophets.

(e) **The Certainty of God's Plans (29: 13–24)** This passage too is composed of several short oracles, originally unconnected. The phrase **upside down** (16) provides something of a unifying theme, for we read of perverse human behaviour, on the one hand, and of transformations effected by the Lord, on the other.

The first oracle (13 f.) recalls a theme from 1: 10–15, namely the perversity of hypocritical worship; in punishment, God will turn human wisdom into folly, and bring shock after shock upon Jerusalem (v. 14 must be predicting unpleasant surprises, not miracles of salvation; see NEB). The historical setting is the period immediately before Hezekiah's revolt, when Judah's most trusted politicians were led into the folly of conspiring with Egypt against Assyria. The next oracle (15 f.) alludes to these secret intrigues with Egypt, which were conducted behind Isaiah's back; this he interprets as an attempt to **hide their plans from the LORD**. Such folly is tantamount to accusing the

Creator of lacking wisdom and understanding. Verse 17 foretells a transformation, but it is disputed whether desolation or the very opposite, miraculous fertility, is meant; probably we should take the verse with what precedes, and understand it as predicting the imminent, disastrous invasion by the Assyrians of Palestine, via **Lebanon**; see NEB.

Verses 18–21 change the tone from judgment to hope, looking beyond the Assyrian attacks to a happier future, when God will overturn present conditions. The oppressed will **rejoice**, while the oppressors will be removed from the scene. Although the promise is general, the warning implicit in v. 21 applied with special force to the unjust judges of Judah (cf. 1: 16 f., 21 ff.).

It is difficult to find a precise historical background for vv. 22 ff. This oracle too promises transformation, this time for Israel rather than Judah; v. 23 perhaps alludes to the Assyrian deportation from the northern kingdom after the fall of Samaria. Verse 24 clearly indicates that Isaiah was very dissatisfied with present-day attitudes in Samaria.

It is not clear why **Abraham** is mentioned (22), nor what is meant by his redemption. It may refer to the fact that God had brought him all the way from Mesopotamia to Canaan; this would have special point and relevance if indeed v. 23 does have in mind Assyrian deportations of citizens of Israel from Palestine to a variety of places in Mesopotamia. (In the OT, this Hebrew word for 'redeem', *pādāh*, normally means to rescue, often for a price; the nearest parallel to this passage is 1 Kg. 1: 29.)

(f) **The Folly of Human Plans (30: 1–17)**
Four oracles relating to the period of Hezekiah's revolt against Assyria are here brought together: vv. 1–5, 6 f., 8–14, 15 ff. The first two are both protests against the policy of seeking Egypt's help against the Assyrians. Even Ahab had been prepared to consult prophets of Yahweh before embarking on a potentially disastrous campaign (cf. 1 Kg. 22); but evidently Hezekiah's counsellors took pains to avoid hearing the Lord's word through His true prophets (2). The phrase **'forming an alliance'** (1) probably implies secrecy (cf. 29: 15); it is an unusual phrase, which seems to be a metaphor from weaving a web. Egypt had often enough failed to give promised military aid to her protégés; but a new dynasty there, which had extended the country's size and frontiers (cf. v. 4), may have inspired fresh confidence in her ability to keep her promises. Isaiah (rightly, as events soon proved) maintains that Egypt's **help is utterly useless** (7).

Both oracles are to the same effect, but the second is altogether more poetic and allusive than the first; no doubt the intention was to attract greater attention from a **rebellious** audi-

ence. The title (6) is another cryptic one (see 21: 1), explained by the rest of the verse: Judah's envoys are visualized as making an arduous journey through **the Negev** (i.e., for secrecy avoiding the main coastal road) to Egypt, laden with bribes. (See note on 14: 29 for the **darting snakes**.) Yet the expensive and dangerous journey is in vain, for Egypt is a veritable monster of chaotic power—but she achieves nothing. **Rahab** was a primeval monster who was defeated by Baal according to Canaanite religious beliefs; the name is also applied to Egypt in Ps. 87: 4 (and perhaps Isa. 51: 9f., *q.v.*).

In the third oracle (8–14) the prophet concentrates his attack upon people like Hezekiah's advisers who shut their ears to the word of God through the prophets (**this message** in v. 12 may mean prophetic warnings in general). He castigates their attitude to the prophets in vv. 11 f.; as in 28: 15, Isaiah is putting into words what they *meant*, not what they actually said. But God's word is not so easily avoided or overthrown; punishment will surely come, as suddenly as a **wall** collapses, as irrevocably as **pottery** is smashed (13 f.). The certainty of God's word coming true is symbolized in the instruction to **inscribe** the oracle (8); if the word translated **'scroll'** should in context be better rendered 'inscription' (NEB), it is historically the fact that the oracle and its fulfilment remain as **an everlasting witness** in a Book!

The fourth oracle is more general in character, but is particularly apt as a condemnation of Judah's panicky attempts to get Egyptian military support against Sennacherib, and as a prediction of the speed and effectiveness of the Assyrian invasion. The picture of Judah in isolation, abandoned by all allies, is especially vivid and compelling.

(g) **The Promise of Deliverance (30: 18–33)**
This passage can be taken as a single unit, which falls into two natural sections (18–26, 27–33), which were probably originally separate. Verses 19–26 are in prose, but vv. 29–33 seem to be in verse (so also JB, NEB). Verse 18 is in verse, and serves as a transition from the warnings of vv. 1–17 to the consolation and hope of this passage. This sudden change of tone is typical of much of the book of Isaiah; indeed, it is also a characteristic of the book viewed as a whole. Verse 18 suggests that it is precisely the hopeless isolation of Judah in the face of the Assyrian assaults which brings about the change of circumstances and the change in the divine message. 'Thus far and no further' sums up the divine intentions for Assyria. It is clear that the immediate promise was the rescue of Judah from the Assyrian armies; but the prophecy looks far beyond that to the Golden Age (23–26), with a miraculously watered and productive land of Israel. The fulfilment of

the former is to be the proof of the eventual fulfilment of the latter.

Verses 19–22, though predictive, still convey a down-to-earth picture of the present situation. Judah's people are not yet ready to **cry** to the Lord, despite their 'prison fare' (cf. 1 Kg. 22: 27), which may imply conditions of siege, and they are still idolaters. But the time will come when they acknowledge Yahweh as their true Teacher, and will be prepared to follow His guidance through the **teachers** he sends. Verses 23 ff. may suggest that at the time of the oracle God had sent a measure of drought and famine; but v. 26 seems wholly figurative.

The final oracle of the chapter (27–33) draws on the language of worship; indeed, vv. 27 f. seem to belong to a temple hymn (whether quoted by Isaiah or composed by him), looking forward to Yahweh's coming, as if **from far**, to deliver His people and defeat the Gentile **nations** (cf. Ps. 2; Hab. 3). **The Name of the LORD** signifies the tangible reality of His presence, in certain OT passages such as this; cf. 59: 19. Verses 29 f. take up the language of a **holy festival** (probably Passover) when God's **majestic** visitation of His people at Mount Sinai was celebrated and recalled (cf. Exod. 19: 16 ff.). At Mount Sinai God had visited Israel in love; but on this occasion, while in Jerusalem the festival is celebrated with **tambourines and harps**, God will be visiting punishment upon **Assyria**, which no longer acts as His **rod** (as in 10: 5) but is smitten by it (31 f.). The final verse, 33, plainly predicts the utter defeat of the Assyrian **king** (see 37: 36); but its language adopts a word-play upon another cultic theme—not this time the true worship on Mount Zion but the idolatrous worship at Topheth, just outside Jerusalem, in which children were burned in sacrifice to the god Molech (strictly, Melech), (NIV **the king**) cf. Jer. 7: 31 f. Ahaz was one king who sacrificed his son in this grim cult (cf. 2 Kg. 16:3).

(h) Divine Protection for Jerusalem (31: 1–9)

This chapter forms a fitting climax to Isaiah's recorded preaching in the circumstances of Hezekiah's revolt against Assyria. Two oracles are brought together, the first pronouncing woe upon Hezekiah's pro-Egyptian advisers (1–3), the second promising salvation to Jerusalem from the Assyrian invader (4 f., 8 f.). The latter oracle incorporates an appeal to respond to God (in prose, vv. 6 f.).

The first oracle (1–3) contrasts the power and wisdom of **Egypt** with those of God, from whom the pro-Egyptian party chose not to **seek help**. These counsellors of Hezekiah naturally hoped that the Egyptian armies would bring disaster to Assyria; Isaiah replies that the Egyptian forces were far from invincible, and

predicts that God will bring **disaster** upon them—and their allies, i.e. Judah.

The oracle promising salvation for Jerusalem (4 f.) and disaster for Assyria (8 f.) begins with two vivid but startlingly different similes. Both stress that God will not abandon **Mount Zion**, any more than a **lion** will desert its hard-won **prey** or a mother-bird its fledglings. It is Yahweh and no human army (certainly no Egyptian one!) who will defeat Assyria (see 37: 36). The Assyrians' **'stronghold'** may allude to their king, Sennacherib (though note NEB). The oracle ends with a reference to the altar **fire** at the temple, making it a symbol of the **furnace** of God's anger against Assyria.

The oracles thus offer both warning and promise to Jerusalem; the appeal (6 f.) is made to the whole nation, and probably dates from the period after 701 B.C., when in spite of the disaster suffered by Sennacherib's army, both Judah and northern Israel lay firmly in the Assyrians' grip. The prophet now recalls the word of God that Assyria—not just a single Assyrian army—must **fall** (8); but God is biding His time, because of the sins of Israel and Judah, their rebellion and their idolatry. Thus the chapter provides a good example of the way in which the oracles of the Lord could be used and re-used in changing circumstances, finding more fulfilments than one; and it also shows how the heart of the prophets' message was basically one of appeal.

(i) 'The Fruit of Righteousness' (32: 1–20)

The chapter falls naturally into three sections: vv. 1–8, 9–14, and 15–20. The first two were originally independent, but the third was written to be a continuation of the second. The first oracle is one of hope, the second is of warning and rebuke, and the third section reverts to the note of hope. Thus as a unit the chapter is one of joyful hope, though incorporating a warning, and the general effect is one of both comfort and challenge.

Verses 1–8 can be understood in two ways. When originally delivered as a spoken oracle, very probably at the accession of Hezekiah as king of Judah, it constituted an appeal: *every* new **king** and his **rulers** should make it their aim to **reign in righteousness** (1). If they proved willing to live up to this responsibility, they would provide every benefit to their citizens (2 f.) and at the same time restrain evil in society (4–8). The first verses could as easily be translated '*If* a king reigns in righteousness . . . *then* each will be . . .'. But even Hezekiah failed to live up to the very high standards set, and his successor, Manasseh, was one of the worst kings Judah ever had; thus, as part of the finished, written prophecy, the oracle undoubtedly takes on a messianic function, reinforcing 9: 6 f. The passage thus offers hope for evil times, while never losing its appeal and challenge to every ruler and indeed every evildoer.

Verses 9–14 constitute a general warning to the people of Judah, addressed especially to the **complacent** womenfolk of the land (cf. 3: 16–4: 1), who ought instead to be mourning and bewailing the situation. Disaster will fall **in little more than a year** (10), and luxurious cities and mansions will be deserted (13 f.). It seems probable that this oracle anticipated the devastating attack of Sennacherib on Judah in 701 B.C., when only Jerusalem itself escaped major damage.

The final section (15–20) indicates that the **forever** of v. 14 has a limit (the various Hebrew terms rendered 'for ever' in EVV have a more indefinite connotation than the English equivalent); thus the time of disaster for Judah, though long lasting, was not to be permanent. It is God's promise that eventually conditions of utter peace and wonderful prosperity shall bless His people, and even the animal kingdom will benefit. As so often in Isaiah, however, the most prominent theme is neither peace nor prosperity, but **righteousness**. The passage also stresses that no human king will inaugurate this millennial era; the agent of blessing will be **the Spirit** of God (15) cf. Jl 2: 28 f.; Ac. 2: 16 ff. In the OT the operation of the Spirit is chiefly to empower leaders of Israel and to inspire prophetic spokesmen (cf. Jg. 6: 34; 2 Sam. 23: 2, etc.); but here **the Spirit** is to be **poured upon us**, namely upon *all* God's people.

In this section of hope and blessing, v. 19 seems strangely out of place, with its apparent message of destruction. The first two words of the Hebrew text are uncertain, and the NEB offers an attractive reinterpretation of the verse: 'It will be cool on the slopes of the forest then, and cities shall lie peaceful in the plain.' Some such rendering fits the context much better.

(*j*) A Thanksgiving Hymn (33: 1–24)

There are many echoes of the Psalms in this chapter (listed by Kaiser), and many commentators agree that it was written as a hymn, i.e., to be used in worship at the temple. The date and authorship have been more in dispute, but the miraculous deliverance from Sennacherib in 701 B.C. may well have occasioned this thanksgiving psalm. The **destroyer** of v. 1 is then either Sennacherib himself, or more probably the Assyrians in general.

The psalm begins by pronouncing **woe** upon the enemy (1), and proceeds to offer prayer and praise to the **exalted** Lord (2–6); these themes were the twin sources of Judah's consolation and thanksgiving. In this context, **the fear of the LORD** (6) denotes the worship of Yahweh in Jerusalem, seen as **the key to** the **treasure** He gives His people.

Verses 7 ff. recall, in the style of a lament,

the desperate situation which the enemy had caused, v. 9 referring to various regions affected by the invading army. Verses 10 ff. offer the reply which God had made to His troubled people; the enemy are addressed in vv. 11 f. Then in v. 13 God calls on the rest of mankind to **acknowledge** what He had **done** for Judah.

In vv. 14 ff. Isaiah's keynote, righteousness, again appears. All Judah owe God a debt of thanksgiving for deliverance, but not all—by any means—are godly enough to be worthy to enter the temple courts (cf. Ps. 15). But those who are truly grateful may show it by amendment of life; gratitude demands it and, moreover, divine promises commend it. These promises are outlined in vv. 17–22: the enemy, whose presence was still (even after 701 B.C.) so obvious and so hateful (18 f.), will ultimately be banished, leaving a land with wide horizons, and then with undivided minds the worshippers will be able to **see** their God **in his beauty** (17). (This concept of 'seeing' God belonged especially to the sanctuary, to the realm of worship.) God, worshipped as judge, king and saviour, will provide perfect peace to the city of His sanctuary (20, 22). All will experience physical and spiritual well-being (23 f.).

Two verses (21, 23) introduce imagery of the sea and ships, and are rather puzzling, perhaps because we no longer understand fully the allusions. Verse 21 promises the **broad rivers and streams** which the thirsty land of Palestine so conspicuously lacks (cf. Ezek. 47: 6–12); but the prophet assures his listeners that the stream will not permit the war-galleys of any enemy to invade Judah. Verse 23a (which should perhaps be taken with v. 21; cf. JB) seems to address any such potential enemy, giving warning that invading ships will be damaged and make no headway (cf. Ps. 48: 7).

(*k*) The Downfall of God's Enemies (34: 1–17)

Chapter 34 reflects the age-old hostility between Judah and **Edom**, and is undoubtedly based upon an oracle against Edom, predicting its utter abandonment and desolation. Many historical circumstances must have given rise to such prophetic oracles against the Edomites (cf. especially Jer. 49: 7–22, where again **Bozrah**, a placename in Edom, is used as a synonym for the land as a whole). Here, however, the picture is cosmic (see v. 4), and most commentators agree that 'Edom' represents **all** the **nations** hostile to God (2); ch. 35 goes on to show the opposite side of the coin, namely the future blessings of the people of God. Undoubtedly the chapter is full of imagery, and it is not easy to know how literally it was meant to be taken; the ultimate total defeat of all that is opposed to God is the chief lesson of the passage. See also 63: 1–6.

Verse 1 adopts language appropriate to the

lawcourts: **the world** is summoned to hear the divine verdict and sentence. Verse 2 recalls the language of psalms such as Ps. 2, which similarly depicts Gentile nations in deliberate hostilities against 'the LORD and his anointed'; and v. 3 recalls Ps. 97: 5. The enemy is shown to be more-than-human in v. 4; it may be that the original reference was to the gods worshipped in Edom, but the theme of the destruction of these heavens and this earth ultimately requires the glad promise of Rev. 21: 1. The theme of the fate of **the sky** is not further explored here; attention is at once directed to the earth beneath, **Edom** being named for the first time in v. 5. Verses 6 f. portray the coming **great slaughter** in terms of sacrifice; it will be as if the Edomites are sacrificial victims on altars to Yahweh. Verses 9 f. apply to Edom language drawn from the fate of Sodom and Gomorrah (cf. Gen. 19: 24–28); while a different picture (vv. 11–17) is drawn from the fate predicted for Babylon in 13: 20 ff. Both pictures portray total desolation; the stress on the full complement of wild beasts (15 f.) is meant to mirror the total absence of human beings, and v. 17 shows God allotting Edom as a sort of promised land for wild creatures. Verse 11 again uses the language of earlier Scripture; the words **chaos** and **desolation** are the 'without form and void' of Gen. 1: 2. The verse is a clever paradox, depicting God as taking building instruments and careful measurements in order to produce—**desolation**! (The last line of the verse is unclear, however; cf. NEB.)

In sum, then, every human foe of God will one day be utterly banished from the scene. The reason is supplied in v. 8; God's people, epitomized in the term **Zion** as His enemies are in the term **Edom**, cannot be for ever at the mercy of the merciless, nor can those who have harassed and hounded them remain for ever unpunished. The **day of vengeance** and of **retribution** will surely come.

(*l*) Restoration and Transformation (35: 1–10)

'Vengeance' today has a negative and unproductive ring about it, but a comparison of ch. 34 with ch. 35 shows that **vengeance** and **retribution** belong together; note 34: 8; 35: 4; 61: 2. The world cannot be put to rights and the era of peace brought in without both the banishment and punishment of the wicked and also the blessing of **the ransomed of the LORD** (10). Chapter 34 has depicted the former; ch. 35 now presents the latter, in a poetic oracle of glowing joy. The passage has many links with later chapters (cf. 40: 1 f., 5, 9 ff.; 42: 20; 43: 20; 51: 11), and its earliest, partial fulfilment will have been the return from the Babylonian exile which is the major theme of chs. 40–55. (Note the use of the word **'return'** in v. 10.) Verses 1 f., 6 f. are the mirror image of the

horrors of desolation in 34: 9 f. The thick woods of **Lebanon** and other areas on the borders of Palestine will characterize the Promised Land too, and in the transformation **the glory of the LORD** will be revealed. The transformation of all nature will benefit humankind too (3–6); a transformation which the ministry of Christ adumbrated, in His many healings. Verse 9 contrasts with the picture offered in 34: 11–14, and may well point to the actual state of affairs which large-scale depopulation brought upon Judah during the period of the Babylonian exile. Verses 8, 10 show **Zion** (as the place of God's presence and His worship) as the goal of all His people. Their route to the Temple is described in language reminiscent of the special roads which were built in different parts of the ancient world for processions to and from pagan temples.

Thus, the language of temple processions and of return from exile is blended together in order to show the ultimate perfect joy and tranquil prosperity of the people of God.

ii. Isaiah and King Hezekiah (36: 1–39: 8)

These four chapters are almost identical with 2 Kg. 18: 13–20: 19, and there can be no doubt that either the book of Isaiah drew upon 2 Kings or *vice versa* (see Introduction). In 2 Kings the chapters serve a generally historical purpose, and readers should consult the commentary on 2 Kings for detailed discussion of historical questions and issues (see pp. 434–6). We may legitimately find a different purpose and emphasis here. In the first place, the emphasis rests more on the prophet and his words than on the interplay of historical events; and secondly, the section serves as a transition from a situation of Assyrian dominance to one of Babylonian dominance. In their biographical interest, chs. 36–39 resemble chs. 6 ff.

(*a*) Sennacherib's Siege of Jerusalem (36: 1–37: 38)

This section, which tells of Sennacherib's attack on Judah in 701 B.C. and its sequel, is identical with 2 Kg. 18: 13–19: 37, except that 2 Kg. 18: 14–16 are here omitted. If the omission is significant, it may be intended to divert attention from the straits to which Jerusalem was reduced and to centre it upon the boastful Assyrian words uttered by **his field commander**. Although at first (36: 10) the Assyrian officer claims to be acting on Yahweh's behalf, his later words deny the power of the Lord to save His people (36: 18 ff.) and even accuse the Lord of deceiving them (37: 10).

The prophet Isaiah is not mentioned until 37: 2. His response reinforces the more general oracles earlier in the book. First, he gives assurance to Hezekiah that he need not fear the Assyrians, for God has simple and straightforward plans for banishing their armies from Judah and bringing Sennacherib's life to an end

(37: 6 f.). Then, in reply to Hezekiah's prayer for deliverance (16–20), Isaiah voices an oracle from the Lord condemning the arrogance of Assyria (22–29). This oracle is amplified by explicit promises of divine protection for Jerusalem (30–35). This narrative ends with the fulfilment of the promises of v. 7—the Lord 'confirming His word by signs following'; Kaiser points out the contrast between the results of Hezekiah's prayer to Yahweh and Sennacherib's prayer to his deity, who was plainly unable, even in his own temple, to deliver the Assyrian king from death.

(n) Hezekiah's Illness (38: 1–22)

The chapter parallels 2 Kg. 20: 1–12, with one major change, *viz.* the inclusion here of Hezekiah's psalm (vv. 9–20). The psalm ends with the expectation of the king's recovery and his renewed worship at the temple; these features have been thrown into relief by placing vv. 21 f. in their present position, and displacing them from their strict chronological setting (contrast the position of 2 Kg. 20: 7 f.).

The psalm reinforces the impression of ch. 37 that Hezekiah was a man of prayer, and underlines the fact that God answers prayer. A contrast with the faithlessness of his predecessor Ahaz may well be intended. Ahaz had refused to seek a sign (cf. 7: 12), and consequently brought disaster on himself and on Judah; Hezekiah of his own initiative asks God for a sign, and his life is miraculously prolonged. This contrast would again give point to the arrangement of this chapter, ending as it does with reference to the **sign**. (We should not therefore rearrange the chapter, as do NEB and some commentaries.) Verse 22 furthermore provided a promise for later eras of Judah's history, especially in the exilic period, when **the temple of the LORD** lay in ruins.

The psalm may be classified as an individual psalm of thanksgiving, comparable with, *e.g.*, Ps. 9 f.; 18; 32. It expresses its author's confidence that the Lord saves him from illness and death (20), and he looks back (in serene trust) on his earlier distress (10–15). He now sees value both in the past suffering and in the future years added to his life (16–19). (Note that v. 16 is obscure in Hebrew; the NEB rendering is clearer than NIV.) The final verse of the psalm could equally well be translated by a present tense, 'the LORD saves me . . .'. It is entirely possible that the psalm came into regular use in temple worship; in such a setting the future tense will have been more appropriate, as worshippers looked expectantly forward to God's help in times of trouble, gaining confidence from Hezekiah's experience. If this conjecture is right, we can see that the psalm would have offered an added dimension of faith and comfort in later, troubled epochs.

Thus, in one or two respects Isa. 38 antici-

pates, or at least adumbrates, the exilic situation; such a situation is to become patent in ch. 39.

(c) Hezekiah and Babylon (39: 1–8)

The chapter parallels 2 Kg. 20: 12–19. It deals with an incident earlier than Sennacherib's campaign of 701 B.C., which was the subject of chs. 36 f., but it stands appropriately enough at the end of the narratives about Hezekiah and Isaiah, since it points forward explicitly to the Babylonian exile (vv. 6 f.). In its own day, Isaiah's oracle may have been understood to mean that the Assyrians would in due course deport the royal family—and many others besides—from Judah and place them in Babylon, which was also a rebellious vassal of Assyria at the time. (Similarly, the exiles from Samaria had been settled not only in Assyria itself but in other subject territories such as Media; cf. 2 Kg. 17: 6.) But history records that it was not the Assyrians who brought this disaster upon Judah, but the Babylonians themselves, when they succeeded the Assyrians as masters of the Near East, approximately a century later.

On this sombre note, with a submissive but not unselfish Hezekiah, the first major part of the book of Isaiah ends.

IV. THE RETURN OF THE EXILES (40: 1–66: 24)

At this point in the book, the scene shifts dramatically. In ch. 39 we met Babylonian envoys in Jerusalem; in chs. 40 ff. we are concerned with Jewish exiles in Babylonia—as predicted in 39: 6 f. The prediction was not fulfilled all at once; there is a time-lag of well over a century between the situation of ch. 39 and that presupposed in ch. 40 (see Introduction). From one point of view, chs. 40 ff. supply the proof that the prophecies of Isaiah were amply fulfilled. From another point of view, these chapters provide a new message, one of hope and comfort for God's people in times of hardship and despair.

The section falls into three natural subdivisions, chs. 40–48, 49–55, and 56–66.

i. The Departure from Babylon (40: 1–48: 22)

The condition of the Jewish exiles in Babylonia shortly after 550 B.C. must have been one of hopeless despondency; they felt themselves to be trapped, far from home, and abandoned by their God. The years of exile had dragged on for about half a century. By now some Jews were convinced that the gods of Babylon had proved too strong for Yahweh, and were inclined to turn to Babylonian idolatry; while even the more faithful were convinced that God had abandoned them to their fate, and had inflicted the exile as a permanent punishment upon His people. Lam. 1 should be carefully studied if we wish to gain an insight into the thoughts and feelings of devout Jews of this period; and it is precisely to such thoughts and feelings that Isa. 40 responds. It is widely supposed that passages from Lamentations were used in worship; and it may well be that the oracles of chs. 40–55 were declaimed to the exiles in their gatherings for prayer and worship. The very first word, repeated for emphasis, strikes the note that they most longed and needed to hear: **Comfort!** (contrast Lam. 1: 2).

(a) The New Message of Comfort (40: 1–11)

This prologue to chs. 40–55 as a whole begins to spell out the details of what the divine message of comfort has to offer. The passage is a vivid one, characterized by two notable features. The first is the sequence of imperative verbs, **Comfort . . . speak . . . proclaim . . . prepare**, etc.: the call is not to passive resignation but to positive and wholehearted action. The second is the series of voices, some of them unidentified; most probably the scene envisaged is the heavenly court, much as in 1 Kg. 22: 19–23, and the voices of vv. 3 and 6 are those of angelic beings. In v. 6 the response to one such voice comes from the prophet himself, according to NIV (following LXX and the Isa. Scroll); the Hebrew (Massoretic) text is slightly different, and makes the verb impersonal (so AV, NEB), though the prophet may still in fact be meant. In v. 9 there is again uncertainty (this time a matter of translation rather than text), as to whether the bringer of **good tidings** *is* Jerusalem, or is sent to Jerusalem (note NIVmg). All the speakers, then, except God Himself (v. 1), are kept in the background; the spotlight falls on the message rather than the messengers. Nor are the people addressed ever specified; the imperatives are plural in vv. 1–5, and probably the widest possible audience is envisaged. The command to **Cry out** (6) is masculine singular, and almost certainly addressed to the prophet; while the feminine singular commands of v. 9 are best explained as addressed to **Zion/Jerusalem** (as in NIVmg). The question arises what is meant here by Zion/Jerusalem. It seems most probable that the prophet uses the term to mean both the literal city and (more particularly) the exilic community, most of whom were Jerusalemites by origin; thus in v. 9 the exiles are entrusted with a message for **the towns of Judah**.

The first word to the exiles (1 f.) is one of reassurance: God has neither abandoned His **people** (they remain His, and He is their God) nor inflicted permanent punishment on them—the punishment is now complete! (The **double** penalty may refer to the destruction of Jerusalem and the long period of the exile; but it

probably means no more than 'in full measure'.)

The prophet next adopts the language of worship (3 ff.), recalling both the pagan processional highways of Babylon and elsewhere, and also the expectation in Jewish worship that God would 'arrive' in person, revealing His presence to His worshipping people. The exiles need not envy the splendour of heathen processions in Babylon; their own God is coming, and the whole world will see His **glory** revealed. It is for them to help **prepare the way** for Him; for the exiles, **the desert** was the wide expanse of the Syro-Arabian desert which lay between Babylonia and Judah (see map, p. 753). God's **glory** would be seen, in other words, in His control of history, bringing His own people back from exile to Judah (vv. 9 ff. confirm that this is the meaning); but they must willingly co-operate, setting out in faith for the homeland. This call into the desert was not of course meant literally, as it had been for the Israelites leaving Egypt centuries earlier, an occasion the prophet undoubtedly had in mind.

Such, then, was the prophet's message to the exiles; but his words had significance for later periods, for the return from exile was but the beginning of the world-wide revelation of God's glory. We see its fulfilment reported in Mt. 3: 1 ff., in John the Baptist's preparation for the advent of the Messiah. (Note that in Mt. 3: 2 and parallels, the sense is slightly different; it is no longer the preparation but the 'voice' which is in the wilderness. This NT wording follows the LXX rendering of Isa. 40: 3.)

Verses 6 ff., quite apart from the textual uncertainty referred to above, are unclear in their sequence of thought. Not improbably, the whole of the second part of v. 6 represents the prophet's initial reply to the command '**Cry out**'; his question '**What shall I cry?**' can be taken to be despondent in tone, and the statement that follows undoubtedly strikes a pessimistic note—it may have been a popular saying about the brevity of life (akin to the longer passage in Ec. 1: 2–11), i.e., why bother to undertake a prophetic ministry? Verses 7 f. are then to be understood as the response; the transience of life cannot be denied, but it is in any case God alone who terminates life, while on the other hand His word—entrusted to His prophets—is neither transient nor insignificant.

The final paragraph of the section (9 ff.) reverts to the theme of the good news for Judah and her exiles. The theme of the divine 'epiphany' is again prominent, but now it is God's **power** which is emphasized. The exiles needed to be reminded that their God was omnipotent (however powerful the gods of Babylon may have seemed to be); yet His might did not alienate Him from His own people, who were His prized possession (His **reward** and **recompense**), the **flock** whom He tended with individual attention and care.

(b) God's Greatness and Power (40: 12–31)
It is evident from the tone of this section, marked as it is by a series of challenging questions, that the exiles were not automatically inclined to credit the power and love of Yahweh their God to which vv. 10 f. had referred. Verses 12–26, therefore, emphasize His incomparable power and greatness, and vv. 27–31 stress His willingness to extend that power to those who trust in Him. This passage is often termed a 'disputation' by modern scholars; the exiles had to be challenged in their thinking and to be persuaded of the truth of the divine promises.

Verses 12–17 remind the exiles of Yahweh as Creator—a theme they must often have voiced in their worship, but the implications of which they had largely forgotten. Nobody, human or superhuman, and certainly no Babylonian god, had stood beside Him when He created the universe and set human history on its course. The Creator God, therefore, stood incomparably far above the mightiest created phenomenon (*e.g.*, **Lebanon**) and the mightiest **nations** too. Even mighty Babylon is **before him as nothing**.

Verses 18 ff. explicitly contrast the living, dynamic Creator God with the passive images of Babylonian gods. Verses 19 f., like 41: 6 f., may have been drawn from a longer poem in which the prophet condemned and ridiculed idolatry. The first part of v. 20 is very obscure in Hebrew, but the general sense of the paragraph is plain enough. See NEB for an alternative rendering.

Verses 21–24 return to earth, so to speak, and contrast God's power with that of earthly **rulers**. Babylon's apparently mighty kings were soon to be overthrown, as later chapters (especially 45 f.) reveal. Verses 23 f. are a reminder that the Creator is also the Lord of history. Verses 25 f. briefly revert to the superhuman level, and remind the exiles that the stars, so important in Babylonian astrology, were but the handiwork of Israel's God, and testify to His power, not their own.

Verses 27–31 again stress the power of God in creation, this time countering an explicit complaint made by the exiles (v. 27). Far from ignoring and disregarding them, their omnipotent God now offers to His depressed and despondent people in exile all the **strength** they need, and not least the power of mobility (v. 31), for the journey from Babylon back to Judah is never far from the prophet's mind. Those **who hope in the Lord** shall find a **strength** for action beyond ordinary human expectation (v. 30).

(c) 'Do not fear' (41: 1–29)
The theme of God's power continues through this chapter, which lays stress upon God's control of history (past, present and future), in order to allay the fears of the exiles. Structurally, the chapter consists of two 'trial speeches', separated by oracles of promise and comfort. The 'trial speeches' are a dramatic way of drawing the exiles' attention to the falsity of the claims, whether implicit or explicit, of Babylon and its gods; the prophet pictures God as bringing the nations and pagan deities to court, and throwing a challenge to them to which (as it proves) they have no reply. (Note that the second line of v. 1 seems somewhat inappropriate to its context; the emendation accepted by NEB and many commentaries is very plausible.)

The first challenge (1–7) is addressed to the nations in general, although Babylon would be foremost in the prophet's mind. They are challenged to say who it was had raised Cyrus of Persia (2) to prominence and given him victory after victory (cf. mg.). It was certainly none of the defeated **nations** who had done so! It was of course **the Lord**, Israel's God, who had controlled human history from its inception up till now (4). The nations' fear of the advance of Cyrus is emphasized (5 f.); v. 7 seems to show their hasty and pitiful attempts to construct idols to help them.

Since Israel's oppressors are thus reduced to trembling, Israel in turn has nothing to **fear** (10). God promises His people all the help and strength they need, reminding them of His goodness long ago to **Abraham**, who had been safely guided from Babylonia to Palestine just as the exiles now would be, for they too were designated as God's **servant**, God's **chosen** people (8 f.).

Verses 11–16 extend the argument that no nation, certainly not Babylon, will prove powerful enough to obstruct the exiles. Even if the latter were worms in their own estimation (14), they would be transformed into a people capable of overcoming every obstacle. Verses 17–20 seek to remedy the exiles' fears about the difficulty of the journey home. The God who had long ago supplied all the needs of Israel in the wilderness of Sinai would work even greater miracles now.

The second challenge (21–29) is addressed to the pagan gods whose pomp and ceremony in Babylonia no doubt had tended to impress many a Jewish émigré. Ancient documents testify to the many predictions made by the spokesmen of Mesopotamian deities. But had any Babylonian deity ever successfully predicted *any* historical event? The acid test, says the prophet, is whether any of them had ever predicted the rise of Cyrus (25). The very career of Cyrus was proof enough that Yahweh, who had predicted it through His prophet, was in

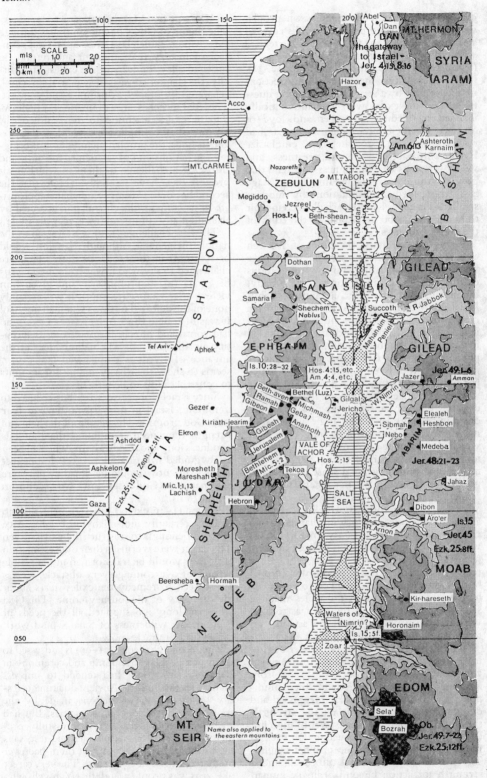

Map 28—The Land of the Prophets

control of history, and that all the gods of Babylon were **false**, mere **wind and confusion** (29). The logic of this 'trial speech' was inescapable; every thoughtful and perceptive Jewish exile could only take comfort, and face the future with renewed faith and courage. If anyone should be disposed to transfer their fears from Babylon to Cyrus, however, he is told that Cyrus is but the servant of Yahweh, **who calls on my name** (25). (See further on 44: 28.)

(d) God's Servant: His Mission (42: 1–4)

A new theme is now introduced in a passage commonly known as the First Servant Song (see Introduction). It is quoted in its entirety in Mt. 12: 18–21, which sees its definitive fulfilment in the ministry of Christ. It originated as an oracle, linked closely with the other so-called Servant Songs (49: 1–6; 50: 4–9; 52: 13–53: 12), but rather distinct in character from the passages in which it is now embedded. Its chief purpose, evidently, is not to identify the Servant of the LORD, but to make clear something of his character and calling. The word **servant** (1) might elsewhere denote a humble and lowly position, but undoubtedly here it is an honoured title, descriptive of leadership. The servant is publicly designated and acknowledged by God (1), he is granted the permanent indwelling of the **Spirit** of God (2) —reminiscent of the judges of old, though their experience of the Spirit was of temporary duration—and he is to exercise a world-wide mission. The language seems to link kingly and prophetic characteristics in a role reminiscent of that of Moses. It is as if to say that the Second Exodus, such a major theme in these chapters, will require a Second Moses.

In its present position, the oracle offers a contrast to two other 'servants' of God, namely Cyrus, so prominent (though not yet named) in ch. 41, and Israel as a whole, described in 42: 18–25. Cyrus was raised up by God to be a military conqueror; but the Servant will exercise a gentle and considerate role of a very different character (2 f.). Moreover, what he will establish **on earth** is not a rigid, inflexible legal system (contrast Dan. 6: 8) but divine **justice** and guidance (4). (The word translated **justice** probably means something like 'the will of God' in context, while **law**, Heb. *tōrāh*, basically denotes the guidance offered to worshippers through priests and prophets.)

The prophecy waited centuries for its fulfilment in Christ; but we should partly see it as a challenge and a programme of action, addressed primarily to those in positions of leadership among the exiles, and not least to the descendants of David there. They were not to be overawed by Cyrus and other world-conquerors, nor were they to be **discouraged** by the glaring problems and difficulties they

seemed to face (4). The first step towards the establishment of God's will **on earth** must be the return to the homeland, which only they could organize; the definitive step in the establishment of His will would be the ministry of the perfect Servant-Messiah.

(e) The Ministry of Deliverance (42: 5–9)

The passage does not make it clear who is being addressed, and more than one possibility is open (*e.g.*, some commentators think Cyrus is in view). Most probably, however, we should see the paragraph as linked with vv. 1–4, and so addressed to the exiles, and especially to the leaders among them. This interpretation can be supported not only by the argument from position and sequence of thought, but also by the fact that the same themes are stressed as in chs. 40 f., namely God's power as seen in creation (5), His incomparability and incompatibility with idols (8), and His ability to foretell future events (9)—lessons which the exiles were evidently slow to learn. In v. 9 the prophet's argument is that the God who had foretold many events in past history was now offering **new** promises (of release from exile), which were equally to be believed and trusted.

In this setting of reminders about God's power and promises, the exiles are challenged to consider the role God intended for His people (6 f.). They longed for their own release; but the will of God is that they should see an obligation to preach release (of a different, less concrete, character) to the world. That is the purpose for which God has **called** and **will keep** them; in a word, to provide **light for the Gentiles**. The exact meaning of the phrase **a covenant for the people** (literally, 'a covenant of people') is obscure, and has been much debated; the NEB rendering ('a light to all peoples'), though simpler, is not very likely to be right. Perhaps the meaning is that Israel is destined to bring to all peoples not only the **light** of God's presence with them but the possibility of a **covenant** relationship with Him. Once again in this paragraph, we see that God's role for His people remained very largely unfulfilled until the perfect work of Christ; the release from exile could only presage the release of all men from the bondage of 'nature's night'.

(f) Promise and Rebuke (42: 10–25)

The promises of God referred to in v. 9 lead on to a glad hymn of praise (10–13), reminiscent of such psalms as Ps. 96 and 98. The hymn calls on peoples outside Israel (Arabia and Edom are alluded to in v. 11, while **the islands** in v. 12 are more general) to join in the praise of Israel's God: thus once again Yahweh is exalted, to the detriment of foreign deities. Verse 13 vividly depicts Yahweh in action, and vv. 14–17 develop this theme, though still in very pictorial language. There are several contrasts to be noted: first, God's recent inaction (i.e. during the exile) is contrasted with His coming powerful activity; secondly, His help for His people (**the blind**) is set against His hostile deeds (the imagery is of the east wind from the desert, v. 15); and lastly, His people, as they follow His guidance, are contrasted with idolaters, whether Babylonian or Jewish.

The last section of the chapter (18–25) takes a realistic look at the wilful blindness of so many of the exiles. The word **blind** is a sub-theme of the chapter: in vv. 6–16 it contains no rebuke, but simply recognizes the helpless condition of people without the guidance of God, but here (18 ff.) we find unwillingness, not inability, to see. This wilful disregard of God's summons is particularly reprehensible in those who have been called to special service (19). (The meaning of Heb. *meꞏšullām*, NIV **the one committed to me**, has yet to be satisfactorily explained, although the word was common enough as a proper name, Meshullam; see NEB and commentaries.) Verse 21 is presented as a contrast to **this . . . people** (22); it must therefore be making the (permanently valid) point that God's written word and spoken oracles have a perfection never remotely matched by the lives and conduct of His people, sad to say.

The chapter ends by emphasizing that Israel's sufferings in exile had been due to the very disobedience which they were still displaying (24 f.); v. 23 is a plea to change their attitude.

(g) The Promise of Release (43: 1–21)

The rebukes (rare in these chapters) give place again to comfort. The promise of release from exile is once more the prophet's theme, but it is now both widened and deepened. It is widened, since the dispersed of Israel in all quarters of the globe, not merely in Babylon, are to be brought back home (5 ff.); it is deepened by the emphasis upon God's special love for His own people (3 f.). The language is pictorial, but the underlying reality is that, whereas the Jewish exiles were to be freed and helped by Cyrus, the African continent, specifically **Egypt**, was to suffer invasion and conquest by Cyrus' successor, Cambyses. The love of God, thus to be displayed in history, is the sufficient answer to all the exiles' fears (1 f.). Note: the NEB rendering of v. 4 can hardly be right.

Again describing the exiles as **blind** and **deaf** (8; cf. 42: 18 f.), the prophet envisages them as 'led out' (*scil.* from Babylon) for a special purpose, that of being God's **witnesses** in a court scene (10). The other party in the case, it is implied but not stated, are pagan gods, who are challenged to find **witnesses** to their ability to predict the future (9). By this mode of argument, the unique power of Yahweh is argued and emphasized (10–13); the paragraph culminates in underlining God's ability to lay low

any empire, and the next oracle (14–21) makes it specific that it is **Babylon**, and its Chaldean (cf. mg.) rulers, who are to fall. (So much is clear, in spite of the obscurities in the Hebrew of v. 14.) This fresh deliverance of Israel is cast in terms of the exodus from Egypt long before, so often rehearsed in Jewish worship in times ancient and modern; in effect, however, the prophet tells the exiles to forget the exodus (17), because their own future experience will be even more wonderful. There is significance in the description of Israel as 'created' (15) and **formed** (21); it serves to confirm the unchangeable purpose God had for His people. The **praise** of God (21) was never far from the prophet's thoughts and modes of expression.

(h) Former Unfaithfulness (43: 22–28)

The final section of ch. 43 concerns itself with the failures in Israel's former praise of God. The passage is set out as a court scene, like vv. 8–13, but now Israel is not a witness to God but appears as His opponent (see especially v. 26). Clearly, some exiles denied that their deportation to Babylon had been deserved; had they not always worshipped God faithfully, with a devotion to the point of sheer weariness? This claim is emphatically rejected by God; on the contrary, they had **wearied** Him with their constant **offences** (24). It hardly suits the general context to make vv. 22 ff. refer to the exilic period itself, when of course sacrificial worship in the Jerusalem temple was a physical impossibility; rather, we should give emphasis to the repeated **me**—i.e., the many sacrifices and devotions had never reached God, because of the sins that accompanied them. Verse 27 recalls the sinfulness of national leaders from the very first (probably the **first father** means Jacob himself), and v. 28 confirms the justice of the punishment which has befallen Israel. (The **dignitaries** are probably the kings of Judah, who were in some sense attached constitutionally to the **temple**.) Signal punishment was deserved and had fallen; and yet God's verdict is—forgiveness (25)!

(i) Israel's God and Babylon's Idols (44: 1–23)

This section consists of two oracles (vv. 1–5, 6–22); a short hymn of praise is appended (v. 23). The second oracle incorporates a long satire on idolatry (vv. 9–20), which seems to be in prose.

1–5. The first oracle is one of hope and promise, to allay the exiles' fears (3). The chief point of it is that Israel has a future—she is still God's servant, with a mission to perform. Her future will be one of material and spiritual prosperity, so much so that non-Jews will voluntarily attach themselves to Israel and to her God (5). **Jeshurun** (2) is a rare synonym for Israel, perhaps a name of pride, derived from a word meaning 'upright' (cf. Dt. 32: 15; 33: 5, 26).

6–20. The second oracle also counteracts exilic timidity (8), this time by throwing out another challenge to the gods of Babylon. Above all, the Babylonian religion had failed by its total inability to predict the fall of the Babylonian empire.

We can only assume that the sheer outward pomp and splendour of Babylonian worship was making a considerable appeal to Jewish exiles. The long digression (9–20) is a brilliant attack, not upon Babylonian religious thinking as such, but upon the idols themselves; the purpose of the satire is to persuade the exiles that an idol is neither more nor less than a block of wood. The sheer contrast with the living though unseen God of Israel is implicit throughout.

21 ff. The prophet concludes his oracle with a plea to the exiles to remember their calling, to turn their backs on idolatry and, forgiven and delivered, to dedicate themselves to God. As so often, he ends on a note of praise (23); this hymn speaks of the deliverance from exile as if it had already taken place (**'redeemed'**, cf. v. 22). To the dejected Jews in Babylon, the statement that God would display **his glory in Israel** must have been a wonderful and yet challenging promise.

(*j*) Cyrus as God's Appointed King (44: 24–45: 13)

The prophet now builds up to a climax, centring on the person of **Cyrus**, now named for the first time (44: 28; 45: 1). The message is a startling one; previous foreign conquerors had been recognized by the prophets as God's agents (*e.g.*, Nebuchadrezzar, cf. Jer. 25: 9), but Cyrus was to be and to do something more remarkable. It was not God's intention to return the throne of Judah to the descendants of David in the immediate future; but Cyrus, foreigner and pagan though he was, was to do for Judah more or less what David had done long before! He was to allow the exiles to return, and to permit, and indeed help to finance, the rebuilding of the temple (cf. Ezr. 1).

This remarkable message was carefully built up, in such a way as to compel the exiles' attention. The first part of it (44: 24–28) is addressed to them, and emphasizes the power of God as shown in creation (24) and history (27, which is probably a reference to the exodus). The fact was that pagan oracles (so optimistic about Babylon!) were to be proved false (25), whereas Yahweh's oracles to **his messengers** the prophets had time and time again come to visible fulfilment. On this basis, the prophet's comforting promises about **Jerusalem** are to be believed (26). Then who will carry out this **purpose** of the Lord? No king

of Judah, but rather **Cyrus** of Persia (28)—whether the exiles liked it or not! The term **shepherd** was a common metaphor for kings, cf. Ezek. 34.

The second part of the oracle (45: 1–7) is directly addressed to **Cyrus**, given now the title **anointed**, hitherto reserved for those of Israelite descent: an honourable title indeed (1). The pattern adopted for this oracle, moreover, is that used in Ps. 2 and Ps. 110, as the exiles would at once have perceived. The victories and successes predicted for Cyrus were the necessary prelude to his future benefits to Judah —as v. 4 makes clear. Plainly, it is not expected that Cyrus will adopt the Jewish faith (4); he is merely the instrument of the divine purposes for His people, and indeed for the world (4, 6). The last verse of the oracle emphasizes God's total control of history; victory and defeat, **prosperity** and **disaster**, alike come from Him (7).

Once again, a short burst of praise (8) is employed to round off an oracle; once again, the promise is spoken of as if it had already taken place.

9–13 are an appendix to the Cyrus pronouncement, and reflect the incredulity with which some of the exiles greeted the oracle. The prophet accordingly challenges his audience: it is God Himself whom they have the temerity to question and criticize (9 f.)! He reiterates his message: God, the almighty Creator, has plans which only Cyrus can fulfil (12 f.). Note that there are textual uncertainties in vv. 9, 11, but NIV may in general be followed. **13. righteousness:** Heb. *sedeq*, used often in chs. 40–55 with some such sense as 'victory'; A. S. Herbert paraphrases the phrase here as 'for my triumphant purpose'.

(*k*) The Nations and God's People (45: 14–25)

This section comprises several brief oracles by the prophet (cf. the NIV paragraph divisions). Their common theme is the future of other nations and their relationship to Israel.

14–17. A previous passage (43: 3 f.) predicted the Persian invasion of Egypt; taking up the theme, the prophet now foresees the day when such peoples (and by implication many other nations) will bring their wealth, not reluctantly to brutal conquerors, but willingly to the land of Israel (their **chains** metaphorical), simply because the true God, hitherto hidden from other nations, will be seen in Israel. It will be a day when idolatry and idolaters will be **put to shame**. Verse 17 then stresses the bright future of **Israel** itself, permanently safe from foreign attacks.

Verses 18 f. confirm the purpose of God, again in a way designed to counter the exiles' doubts and objections. The God who had not only **created** the world but planned its future (i.e., He did not leave it in the state of chaos depicted in Gen. 1: 2) *still* has purposes for His world—and He has continually revealed them to His people through His prophets. This assertion is appropriately followed by another attack on idolatry (20 f.), since idols never predicted any historical event.

The final verses (22–25) remind the exiles that God had long since determined (as, *e.g.*, Ps. 2 indicates) to bring all the peoples of the world into subjection and obedience to Himself. So the nations are already invited to **turn** to God; if they now choose to worship Him, they will be **saved** from the fate that the enemies of His people must one day face. Such was the meaning of vv. 22 f. in historical context; but we can legitimately see in them a true *praeparatio evangelica*; cf. Rom. 14: 11; Phil. 2: 10 f. Verses 24 f. summarize the teachings of this section. We should probably delete the phrase **of me** (24), cf. NEB; there is textual doubt about it.

(*l*) The Folly of Idolatry (46: 1–13)

Chapter 45 has offered the exiles a clear-cut choice: they must decide between identifying themselves with Babylon and its gods, on the one hand, and looking expectantly for Cyrus of Persia to act as Yahweh's agent, on the other. Chapter 46 now reinforces that message; as elsewhere, it is likely that separate oracles have been brought together to function as a sermon. Verses 5 ff. are a general attack on idolatry, emphasizing the sheer helplessness of idols and their inability to aid any worshipper; but vv. 1–4 are a specific attack on the chief deities of Babylon, namely **Bel** (better known as Marduk) and **Nebo**, predicting their coming helplessness when the armies of Cyrus advance on Babylon. Both oracles show how utterly different Yahweh has always been to His people.

The third section of the chapter (8–13) is a further reminder to the exiles that their God had **from ancient times** accurately predicted future events; their unwillingness to credit His promises now, to the effect that Cyrus (described as **a bird of prey**, 11) will bring about their deliverance, is sternly rebuked (8, 12). Despite their blind disbelief, the salvation is certainly coming, in the very near future, with consequent blessing for **Israel** (13).

(*m*) The Impending Fall of Babylon (47: 1–15)

This longer oracle is the only example of a denunciation of a foreign nation in chs. 40–55. It is the logical sequel to the promises to the exiles of the rise of Cyrus; his rise meant Babylon's fall, inevitably. Thus the oracle is by implication a message of hope to the Jews (cf. v. 4). It is a skilful poem, employing imagery and irony very effectively; the sarcasm of v. 12 bears comparison with Elijah's mockery in 1

Kg. 18: 27. Note how Babylon is depicted as a queen—dethroned, and reduced to the status of a slave-girl (Jerusalem's fate would be the very opposite; cf. 52: 1 f.).

The passage reflects the cruelty of Babylon (6), its arrogance (7 f., 10), and its devotion to astrology and magical practices (12 f.). The prophet is also careful to explain the motivation of God's control of history (6). The Babylonian captivity had been ordained as the divine punishment of Judah, and to that extent Babylon had been no more than His agent; but the merciless treatment shown to the exiles in turn merited divine retribution. The chapter ends on a note of the uselessness of Babylonian worship; **'there is not one that can save you'** (15), Babylon is told. If so, there is none who can *prevent* the salvation of the exiles!

(*n*) The Summons to Depart (48: 1–22)

This final chapter in this part of the book is puzzling, since it combines the themes of hope and promise which are characteristic of chs. 40–48 with words of condemnation and rebuke (which some commentators have found out of place and attributed to a later editor). It is also unclear whether we have a single oracular poem or a collection of several short oracles. Thirdly, there are some textual uncertainties.

It seems best to take the chapter as a single poem, and to explain the unusually large element of criticism and censure in terms of the audience addressed. In chs. 40–47, the prophet evidently was speaking primarily to those Jewish exiles who, though wavering, had not forsaken their God, and who would be willing to heed his message; ch. 48 is addressed to the whole nation (cf. v. 1) and recalls the sins which had brought it to political disaster, namely the combination of formal, insincere worship (1 f.) and idolatry (5). Earlier prophecies and Israel's past hostility to the prophets are also recalled (3 f.). How different things could have been (17 ff.)!

The nation has been punished (10), but is still obstinate and treacherous (8). Nevertheless, for His own purposes God proposes to act for their salvation (9), and He now brings them the startling news of the fall of **Babylon** and the victories of Cyrus (14 f.). God is the speaker throughout most of the chapter, but the prophet suddenly interjects a sentence at the end of v. 16, presumably to show the fulfilment of God's plan to give His people warning of Babylon's impending fall.

The fall of Babylon will provide the exiles with a second exodus (20 f.). This call to leave Babylon is the climax of chs. 40–48. Those who obey will have nothing to fear as they embark on the difficult homeward way (21); but those **wicked** enough to reject God's instructions to leave Babylon are forfeiting the prosperity they might have (22). (The Hebrew

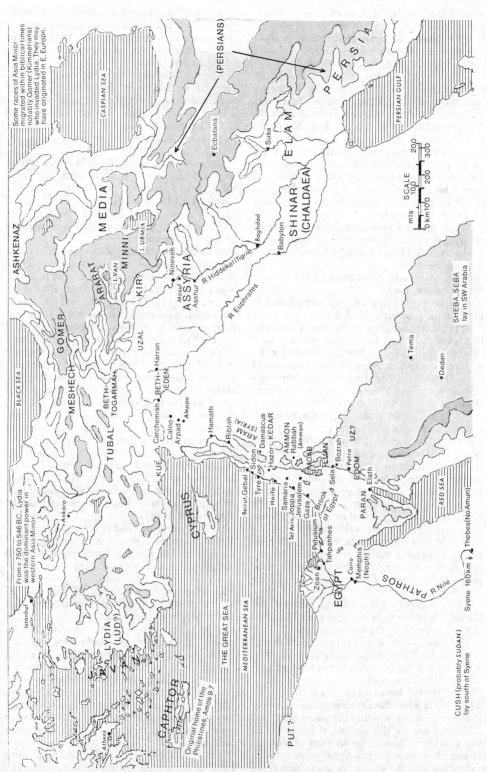

Map 29—The World of the Prophets

Some races of Asia Minor migrated within biblical times notably Gomer (Kimmerians) who invaded Lydia. They may have originated in E. Europe.

From c 750 to 546 B.C., Lydia was the dominant power in western Asia Minor.

CASPIAN SEA

ASHKENAZ

GOMER

MESHECH

ARARAT

MINNI

MEDIA

KIR?

L.VAN

L.URMIA

Ecbatana

(PERSIANS)

PERSIA

ELAM

Susa

SHINAR (CHALDAEA)

PERSIAN GULF

SCALE

mls 100 200 300

0 km 100 200 300

BLACK SEA

TUBAL

BETH-TOGARMAH

UZAL

Carchemish BETH-EDEN

Harran

Calno

Arpad

Aleppo

Hamath

Riblah

Mosul Nineveh

Asshur

ASSYRIA

R. Hiddekel (Tigris)

Baghdad

Babylon

R. Euphrates

Istanbul

Ankara

LYDIA (LUD?)

J A V A N

Athens

CRETE

CAPHTOR

Original home of the Philistines. Amos 9.7

KUÉ

Beirut, Gebal

Tyre Sidon

Haifa

Tel Aviv, Joppa

Gaza

Samaria

Jerusalem

Brook of Egypt

AMMON (Amman)

Rabbah

Damascus

ARAM (SYRIA)

Hazor

KEDAR

MOAB

EDOM

Sela

Petra

UZ?

Bozrah

TEMAN

Elath

PARAN

Tema

Dedan

SHEBA, SEBA lay in SW Arabia

CYPRUS

THE GREAT SEA

MEDITERRANEAN SEA

RED SEA

Zoan

Pelusium

Tahpanhes

Cairo

Memphis (Noph)

EGYPT

R. Nile

Thebes (No Amun)

PATHROS

Syene 160 km ↓

CUSH (probably SUDAN) lay south of Syene

PUT?

word *šālôm*, NIV **'peace'**, is more aptly translated 'prosperity' in vv. 18 and 22.)

ii. The Return to Jerusalem (49: 1–55: 13)

Chapters 49–55 are addressed to the same
people as chs. 40–48, the Jewish exiles in Babylon. There is now a change in emphasis, rather
than in the message itself. The exiles' attention
is drawn away from their unhappy situation in
Babylon, and directed towards the homeland,
and in particular to the mother-city. In prosaic
fact, Jerusalem lay in ruins during the exilic
period; but the prophet is confidently looking
forward to its restoration and its future glories.
This message was one of permanent validity—
setting hope and confident expectation in front
of God's people in times when their vision
tended to be limited.

These chapters also contain three passages
descriptive of 'the Servant of the LORD'; here it
is the future leadership of God's people which
is the theme.

(a) God's Servant: the Scope of His Ministry (49: 1–6)

The future well-being of a reunited Israel is
much in the prophet's mind, but vv. 1, 6 make
it clear that the blessing of the world is no less
important to him. These twin themes here
constitute his message; but the vehicle for the
message is a speech by an unnamed servant of
God. This second 'Servant Song' (see Introduction) is placed on the lips of the servant presented to the reader in 42: 1–4 (see comments
ad loc.). Once again it can be seen that he is *both*
a prophet (cf. especially Jer. 1: 5; 20: 7–11) with
a powerful tongue (v. 2), *and* a political leader
(vv. 5 f.) of royal dimensions. Prophets before
the exile had been persistently ignored and
sometimes abused by Israel and Judah; here we
find envisaged a coming prophetic leader, at
present hidden from them (2), who will with
God's help persevere until not only Israel but
the world is blessed with **salvation**. The vision
evidently looks beyond the return from exile
(5). It is again a vision of a second Moses;
and again from hindsight we can see that the
prophecy was never fulfilled until the coming
of Christ.

Verse 3 entitles this coming **servant** the
'Israel' who will bring glory to God, in
marked contrast to the historical Israel.

The second half of v. 5 is parenthetical, and
is sometimes thought to be misplaced (cf. NEB);
it shows that the servant's **spent strength** (4)
has now been renewed.

(b) The Joyful Return (49: 7–13)

The **This is what the LORD says** makes it clear
that v. 7 begins a new and separate oracle; it is
addressed not to 'the servant of the LORD' of
vv. 1–6 but to Israel, **the servant of** foreign
rulers. It is nevertheless appropriate enough
following v. 6; the first stage in the blessing of
the world is to be the glorification of Israel (7),

and that in turn cannot occur till all the exiles
return from Babylon and every other point of
the compass (12); **Aswan** was probably the
most southerly point to which Jewish people
had then penetrated.

Above all, however, it is the exiles in Babylon who are addressed; they must make ready
to **'Come out'** from Babylon, and make the
difficult journey home, serenely confident of
God's help on the way (9 ff.). As so often, the
prophet breaks into a hymn of praise at the
prospect (13).

Verse 8 spoke originally of **the day of salvation** from the power of Babylon, but it held
the germ of a greater promise, cf. 2 C. 6: 2. The
latter part of the verse picks up the language of
42: 6 and reapplies it to Israel, viewed as the
embodiment of God's **covenant** to **the people**
of the whole world.

(c) The Restoration of Zion (49: 14–23)

The attention now moves from the exiles in
Babylon to the fate of the mother-city in Judah,
Zion (14). Jerusalem lay in ruins, almost deserted, from 587 B.C. onwards, and the citizens
who came to worship God in the ruins of the
temple must have voiced sentiments such as
Lam. 1: 1; 5: 20. The present oracle responds
to such despairing plaints, with a message of
miraculous hope. The vivid imagery, picturing
Zion as a **bereaved and barren** woman (21)
about to become a **bride** (18) and acquire a
large family, heightens the contrast between
the present and the future. First the foreign
garrisons will leave and the city will be rebuilt
(17), then its population will multiply pro-
digiously (19 f.), and finally that population
will be swollen by returning exiles brought
home by humbled foreign rulers (22 f.). Incredible? God's challenge to faith is clear and unmistakable: **those who hope in me will not be
disappointed** (23).

(d) The Power of God (49: 24–50: 3)

Evidently, some exiles *did* find such predictions
incredible. The prophet here seeks to support
the promises with logic and reason. First, the
power of God is asserted against those who are
too overawed by the might of Babylon (49:
24); God had been known since ancient times
as **the Mighty One of Jacob** (cf. Gen. 49: 24),
and had long since—at the exodus—shown
Himself as **Savior** and **Redeemer** (49: 26).
Mighty as Babylon is, divided she will fall; the
conventional metaphors in v. 26 refer to civil
war. In 50: 2 f. the same theme of God's power,
revealed especially at the exodus, is again emphasized; the setting envisaged is a law-court,
in which God's challengers have no **answer** to
give to Him—indeed, they do not even make
an appearance!

50: 1. A reply to the belief that God must
have finally abandoned His people in exile and
cast them off for ever. To answer this convic-

tion, two frequent OT metaphors are cleverly utilized. Firstly, if God had been Israel's 'husband' (Israel being viewed as the exiles' **mother**), then He could not have divorced her without providing documentary evidence (cf. Dt. 24: 1–4); then the marriage is still valid! Secondly, God had often enough 'given' His people into the hands of oppressors (cf. *e.g.* Jg. 6: 1), but had any payment ever been made? Then God has the right to retrieve His own 'property'! (If the exiles were minded to blame God for their troubles, however, let them recall that the temporary 'divorce' and 'sale' had been entirely due to Israel's past **sins**.)

(e) God's Servant: His Perseverance (50: 4–11)

We are presented in vv. 4–9 with the picture of a prophet, persecuted and taken to court. The use of the first person singular has led some commentators to take the poem literally —i.e., that the author ('Second Isaiah', on this view) was so treated by the Babylonian authorities. It is true that the poem bears comparison with the plaints of another prophet, Jeremiah (cf. esp. Jer. 11: 18 ff.; 20: 7–12); but it seems better to follow the majority of exegetes and see the passage as a sequel to 49: 1–6, or, in other words, as the third 'Servant Song' (see Introduction), to which 52: 13–53: 12 is, in turn, the sequel.

The speaker, then, is the unnamed Servant of the Lord, depicted in the role of a prophet; in this Servant poem, no royal traits are referred to. He is a mediator of the word of God (4), who is humiliated by men (6) but wholly undeterred (5). The outstanding point of contrast with other prophets, notably Jeremiah, is his willing assent to suffering and shame, a theme amplified in ch. 53. His confidence in his final vindication is unshakeable (9).

Such will be the true prophet, as opposed to the many false ones Israel had known. In future the nation will be well advised to look out for and to heed such a **servant** of God (10). Verse 11 is addressed as a stern warning to the disobedient; but the metaphors are no longer clear to us. Some pagan rites could be meant. The contrast is at any rate clear enough; the obedient will know the **light** (Heb. '*ōr*, 10) of God's provision, but the rebellious will have to endure the **light** (Heb. '*ūr*, more accurately rendered 'flame', v. 11) of the fires of **torment**.

(f) Comforting Promises (51: 1–52: 2)

The appeal of 50: 10 is reinforced with a threefold poem (possibly three separate poems with a similar theme), each section prefaced with a call to the exiles to pay heed (1 ff., 4 ff., 7 f.). Verses 9 ff. are a response, calling on God to act; and vv. 12–16 are a divine promise of help and deliverance. A key word in vv. 1–8 is the Heb. *ṣedeq*, which the NIV renders by

righteousness; vv. 5, 8 its sense may rather be 'deliverance' (cf. RSV).

Verses 1 ff. are an encouragement to have faith in the joyful future that is promised in v. 3. **Abraham** is **the rock** from which they **were hewn**: and he—the father of faith— even before Isaac's birth had the courage and vision to believe that his seed would reach national dimensions.

Verses 4 ff. stress how **speedily** God's promises of deliverance are to be fulfilled. The parallels with 42: 1–4 are striking, and remind the exiles that God's purpose in saving them is the blessing of the world. Verse 6 affirms that **the heavens** and **the earth** are less stable than God's promises. Verses 7 f. go on to urge the exiles to trust those promises, putting aside any fear of **men**, who are after all far more transient than the material universe.

The exiles' appeal for God to act (9 f.) may have been drawn by the prophet from their worship. The highly poetical language recalls the language of ancient myths about the creation of the world as the Canaanites envisaged it, myths in which a deity defeated a **monster** named **Rahab**, which symbolized primeval chaotic waters, and created an ordered world upon the dry land that emerged. But in Israelite usage 'Rahab' was sometimes a pejorative term for Egypt, and this is likely to be implied here: the exodus is once again in the prophet's mind. Verse 11 is picked up from 35: 10, and introduces the words of comfort and promise which follow.

Verses 12–16 pick up some earlier themes of the chapter. The transience of man and the power of God are once again set in contrast. The practical promises of v. 14 are underpinned by the words of v. 16 which stresses the protective care of God and the continuing privileges of His **people**.

The exiles' appeal to God for help (51: 9) is answered by a double appeal to *them* to act (51: 17; 52: 1). The appellation **'Jerusalem'** is used both of the exiles themselves (51: 17) and also of the future **city** (52: 1). Both are promised a future very different from the past distresses, which are summed up in v. 19 as the double disaster of the **destruction** of the city and temple, and the death of many citizens in conditions of siege and warfare. The imagery used is that of somebody **made to stagger** (17) as if intoxicated; the language recalls the laments of Lam. 1 f.

The present situation, then, is soon to be reversed (22 f.). The response required from the exiles is basically a change of attitude—to be fully ready to respond to the divine call to action, putting behind them their fears, their self-pity and despair. 52: 1 is not so much a call to holiness as a promise that in a future day

Jerusalem will be wholly free from foreign and pagan overlords.

(g) The Exiles' Arrival at Jerusalem (52: 3–12)

The climax of this passage is the affirmation: **the LORD . . . has redeemed Jerusalem** (9). Both the city itself and the city's long-lost 'children' in exile are about to be restored; the call to praise (in advance of the event!) is wholly appropriate. In this joyful context, the prophet takes his last look at Babylon, which he does not even deign to name (it is meant by the **here** of v. 5 and the **there** of v. 11). The prose meditation of vv. 3–6 looks back at past history, and emphasizes that no oppressor of Israel, past or present, has had any claim upon them; that is the point of the repeated **for nothing**. And just as **Egypt** and **the Assyrian** had been forced to cease their oppression, so now the people of God can look forward to immediate deliverance from Babylon. They must make immediate preparations to **depart** (11).

This message is enshrined in a vivid oracle (7–12), which describes the joy of the restored Jerusalem in terms of messengers to the city being greeted by its **watchmen**. The return of the exiles is depicted as a solemn and sacred procession (11); it is as if God Himself returns with them (8)—as their King (7). The final verse alludes to the **haste** and **flight** involved long before in the first exodus; the new exodus will be even more wonderful!

(h) God's Servant: His Suffering and Triumph (52: 13–53: 12)

As 52: 11 f. have presented the climax of one chief strand in the prophet's teaching, namely the imminent departure from Babylon, so 52: 13 dramatically introduces the passage which provides the climax of his other main theme, that of the ministry of the Servant of the LORD. 52: 13–53: 12 is commonly called the Fourth Servant Song (see Introduction); it picks up and concludes the message of the earlier passages (42: 1–4; 49: 1–6; 50: 4–9). The speaker is God Himself in 52: 13 ff. and 53: 11 f. (from **'by his knowledge'**), announcing the future glory of the Servant; while the prophet is probably the speaker (for his people) in 53: 1–11 (to **'be satisfied'**), reporting on the sufferings of the Servant. (Alternatively, Gentiles may be the speakers.)

It is impossible for any Christian to read the passage without immediately thinking of its fulfilment in Christ, many centuries later; and unconsciously we fill in any 'gaps' in the account. The prophet himself never named the Servant, nor even identified him plainly as the Messiah; his description of the sufferings combines the language of sickness with the language of judicial punishment (and his readers might have understood either or both

as pictorial); he gives no hint of the method by which the death of the Servant would give place to new life and glory; and above all he gives no indication of the time-scale involved. Such details, then, were not what the prophet set out to impart to his hearers or readers. Above all, he wanted to impress two types of contrast upon his readers: one is the contrast between deep suffering and subsequent triumph; the other is the contrast between the attitudes adopted towards the Servant before his glorification and those adopted subsequently. In other words, the reader's attention is directed partly to the central figure, and partly to those affected by his ministry.

52: 11 ff. The Servant, who was similarly presented to us **(See)** in 42: 1, and who has since spoken of his experiences (49: 1–6; 50: 4–9), is now promised the highest ultimate majesty. As his sufferings give way to glory, the **kings** of the **many** nations who previously **were appalled** at the sufferings are shown to be dumbfounded at his exaltation. Notes: (i) **act wisely:** the Hebrew verb may also mean 'will prosper' (mg.) and here the sense of success is clearly uppermost; (ii) the parenthesis in v. 14 seems incomplete in Hebrew; one possible solution, often adopted, is to transfer the statement to follow 53: 2, cf. NEB; (iii) **sprinkle** is the usual sense of the Hebrew verb, it is true, but 'startle' (RSV) may be right and offers better sense in context.

53: 1 ff. These verses look back to the Servant's humiliation, depicted in terms of sickness. The natural reaction to such sufferings is to turn away from the sufferer (2); but, more than that, it was commonplace in the world of ancient Israel to reject and despise people in deep suffering, since it was viewed as a sure sign of God's displeasure, as the book of Job testifies. But a very different explanation is appropriate for the Servant's humiliation—so different that the onlookers are incredulous at the news (1). They are forced to review their thinking, not only because of what they are told but because of **the arm of the LORD**, i.e. the revelation of God's power in turning the Servant's dishonour into glory and power.

53: 4–9. The explanation is now given: the Servant's sufferings were not because of his own grievous sins, as everyone would have supposed, but entirely and unambiguously on behalf of others—for **my people** (8), the prophet acknowledges. They had sinned (5 f.), he had not (9); their sins had brought deep affliction upon him, but they—the guilty— reaped not retribution but blessing (5). The picture of illness changes in v. 7; the Servant is now portrayed as a man on trial for his life, innocent but nevertheless condemned and executed. This change is intended not so much to predict the exact nature of Christ's sufferings as to highlight the character of the Servant; he is not really like a patient and resigned sick man, merely stoical in suffering, but someone who quite deliberately chooses not to defend himself from false accusations, condemnation and execution. Only by silently accepting the suffering could he bring blessing to others.

Notes: (i) v. 8 is notoriously problematical, both as to text and meaning; the NEB rendering ('Without protection, without justice . . .') has much to commend it, except that the first phrase is more probably 'after arrest and sentence' (NEBmg); (ii) **and with the rich in his death** (9): here, too, there are difficulties, and the meaning may well be 'and his tomb with evildoers', an exact parallel with the first line.

53: 10 ff. The changing attitudes of human beings are now set against the unchanging attitude, acts and purpose of God. It was **the will of the LORD** that the Servant should suffer, as **a guilt offering**; it was equally His will that the Servant should go on to triumph like a conquering king (12). Thus, beyond the grave he must **prolong his days**, in God's purposes, and **see his offspring** (another human picture). The emphasis lies less on the Servant's triumph, however, important as it is, than on the blessing it too will bring to others: **transgressors** will be interceded for, **the sin of many** borne; **many** indeed shall be **justified**.

Notes: vv. 10 f. are again very difficult to understand in full detail, because of uncertainties of text and language. The NEB rendering should be studied carefully; it is better than NIV in some respects, but not entirely satisfactory. It utilizes textual evidence from the Dead Sea Scrolls.

What was the relevance of this whole passage to the exiles? First and foremost, it offered them hope and assurance: the nation, soon to be restored, would in due course have its king. He would be powerful enough to silence the kings of the nations, yet righteous enough to satisfy all God's stern demands (cf. Jer. 23: 5 f.). Above all, he would bring healing and righteousness to the nation which had so signally lacked it in centuries past. Secondly, the passage called them to a path of duty: as the New Testament commentary on this passage expresses it, 'Have this mind among yourselves . . .' (Phil. 2: 5). We find here a general truth that suffering is often God's way to success (as He sees success), and with it an implicit call to look back on the sufferings of the past (*e.g.* the years of exile) and to draw benefit and profit from them. There is also an implied call to seek, here and now, the righteousness of God's provision. Finally, we should not overlook the fact that the promise of the advent of the Servant-Messiah to serve and rule his people reinforced the call to leave Babylon (52: 11). What God wanted to see was

His people back in their own land, reunited, rebuilding, and seeking to tread the paths of righteousness (cf. 55: 3–7).

(*i*) **Jerusalem's Future Prosperity (54: 1–17)**
In vv. 1–10, the attention reverts from the Servant's future glory to the present desolation of the Jews, personified as a **barren** (1) and **deserted** (6) woman. The themes are similar to those of 49: 14–26; once again we have a prophecy which clearly responds to the lamentations voiced by the exiles. The message is not only one of hope and comfort but, more than that, it is a call to praise (1). The promises made are two-fold: firstly, the decimated nation is going to recover fully from the disasters of the sixth century B.C., recovering all its lost territory and seeing a rapid repopulation; and secondly, the disaster that the Babylonian exile had been was one which would never recur. The exiles should look back on the past decades as a mere **moment** in time (8), and look forward to the **everlasting kindness** of their God in the bond of the covenant relationship (as unbreakable as the marriage bond; cf. v. 5). (See NEB for a more intelligible rendering of v. 6.) Verses 9 f. underwrite these promises with a divine oath, recalling God's promise long before never to permit a second Deluge (cf. Gen. 9: 8–17).

The emphasis in this passage is wholly on the promises of God; but the motif of the marriage-covenant relationship in itself implies a call to fidelity. There is thus a conditional element in the promises, an element which becomes more explicit in ch. 55.

In vv. 11–17 the future glory and security of Jerusalem is the theme. The city will be inviolable, for it is under the protection of the God who controls all history (15 ff.). Safe from hostile attack, it may safely be ornamented with dazzling gems (11 f.)—a city surpassing in splendour even Babylon in its heyday. Its 'masons' (NEB—probably a preferable reading to **sons**) shall be **taught by the LORD** (13), like Bezalel of old (Exod. 31: 1–5). The spiritual aspect is no less important than the material, however; such a **heritage** belongs to those who are **the servants of the LORD** (17), to those **taught** by Him (13), and re-**established in righteousness** (14). Thus, in this oracle too, we find the paradox of God's unalterable purposes side by side with conditional promises. The restored Jerusalem of post-exilic times was lacking in ornate splendour and by no means inviolable; thus, the divine promise awaited fulfilment in a different era; cf. Rev. 21. The message for the exiles, however, was that it was open to them to claim the fulfilment of every promise.

(*j*) **A Challenge to Heed the Promises (55: 1–13)**
The message to the exiles (chs. 40–55) con-

cludes with a vivid and effective appeal (vv. 1–9), and a solemn yet joyful promise (vv. 10–13). The words of v. 1 are obviously metaphorical, probably recalling the cries of street-vendors; but these wares are free! The appeal is basically a call to leave Babylon, with all its enticements (characterized as **what does not satisfy**), and trusting in God, to make the arduous return journey to Palestine (2 f.). The 'Promised Land' is still the land of promise (2, 13), both from the material and the spiritual point of view; if the exiles heed and obey the summons, then they 'may have the very fullness of life' (Whybray, paraphrasing the rather misleading phrase **that your soul may live** of v. 3), cf. Jn 10: 10.

Verses 3 ff. are of special interest in this context; they are not so much a promise as part of the prophet's appeal. The exiles would be inclined to look for a human leader, another **David**, for selfish reasons; instead, they are told that they have a duty to carry out David's functions, to the world. The functions in question are those not only of prince (**leader**) but instructor (**commander**—NB, not a military term as in English) and indeed **witness** to the power of God. As C. R. North has commented, these terms imply moral leadership, not dictatorship. In this way the timeless promises made to David (cf. 2 Sam. 7) are reaffirmed to the Jewish people, not however as a promise to them but as a call to glorious service. (The promise of the Messiah may very well be implicit, but it is not the point of this passage.)

Verses 6–9 reinforce the same appeal. Israel had for centuries 'sought' God in the sanctuary, from which the exiles had been separated by many miles; but He may now be sought and **found** by them, for **he is near**, waiting to rescue them from Babylon. It means raising their sights from Babylon's transient splendour to the realities of God's imminent deeds in history (through Cyrus). With this summons comes the promise of full **pardon** for the sins which had taken them to Babylon in the first place.

Verses 10–13, by way of epilogue, insist that all God's promises to the exiles are irrevocable, as unvarying as the pattern of nature (10 f.). Yet nature itself can and will be transformed (12 f.); the poetic language of the hymns of Israel (cf. *e.g.* Ps. 96: 11 f.) can become a miraculous reality, when God reverses the effects of the Fall (cf. Gen. 3: 17 f.), to the blessing of man and His own glory. When this miracle occurs it will be irreversible (13); but it cannot even begin to occur until the exiles turn their backs on Babylon, from which they now have the opportunity to **go out in joy, and be led forth in peace** and prosperity (12).

iii. Judah after the Return (56: 1–66: 24)
The final section of Isaiah consists of oracles

and teaching addressed to those who lived in Judah shortly after the exile, towards the end of the sixth century B.C. There is little that is distinctively new in the general tenor of these chapters; the new features (such as the discussion of fasting in ch. 58) are chiefly due to the need to adapt the same sort of *teachings* to a different *situation*. The theme of a glorious future is now especially prominent; to those who lived in a period of instability and hardship, and who were aware that many of God's promises remained as yet unfulfilled, this note was vital. The book thus ends by offering both exhortation and inspiration: a discouraging today is to be lived in the light of a glorious tomorrow.

(a) The Basis of Worship (56: 1–8)
This passage concerns itself with two different groups of people: Jews in their homeland (1 f.), and foreign converts also in Judah (3–8). Verses 1 f. pick up the theme of **righteousness** from ch. 55, but the appeal is no longer to seize God's sudden, climacteric opportunity to leave Babylon. God had withheld from the Jews in early post-exilic Judah (late sixth century) many of the promises contained in chs. 40–55, but His full **salvation** was available if His people showed themselves obedient to His will. Their obligations concerned both worship and ethics (epitomized in v. 2); these constitute the **righteousness** of everyday living.

But if many Jews were failing in both respects, a number of foreigners, notably some of the **eunuchs** who were Persian officials and administrators in Judah, were attracted to Israel's faith. The old law of Dt. 23: 1–6 had barred such people from the sanctuary, in order to protect its ritual purity; the time has now come to put the emphasis on spiritual readiness for worship. Foreigners who have demonstrated their sincerity (4), and **who bind themselves to the LORD** (6—probably circumcision is implied), are invited by God Himself to His temple when rebuilt (515 B.C.). The prophet not only authorizes this change of practice, but also looks forward to a much-enlarged worshipping people of God (8). Jesus, citing v. 7, similarly enjoined that no hindrances should obstruct devout Gentiles from worship at the temple (Mk 11: 15–19). Note that the privilege of temple-worship more than offsets the very natural human psychological problems felt by eunuchs (5).

(b) Rebuke and Comfort (56: 9–57: 21)
The true worship called for in 56: 1–8 is now contrasted with the actual state of affairs which prevailed in Judah shortly after the exile. The nation's leaders were for the most part (though we may presumably exculpate Haggai, Zechariah, Zerubbabel, and others) lazy, self-seeking and avaricious (56: 9–12), while many of the

ordinary people were guilty of apostasy and idolatry (57: 3–13).

The oracle against national leaders (56: 9–12) adopts pastoral imagery. The 'flock' of Judah can freely be raided (9), because the prophets who ought to be giving warning are **blind** and **mute** (10), while the politicians (**shepherds**) are too busy feeding themselves (11). Verse 12 seems to be quoting a popular drinking-song. (In v. 10 the first word should read 'his' and may refer to **Israel** or to God.) The figure changes in 57: 1 f., a brief passage designed to reassure **the righteous** that however neglected and maltreated they may be under present conditions, they will know full **peace** (=well-being) in due course, whether in this life or hereafter. The text and meaning of these two verses are not at all clear; see other EVV for alternative renderings.

In 57: 3–13 we have a detailed oracle of judgment upon idolatry, depicted as harlotry, a typical OT figure. Verse 4 reveals something of the scorn with which such people treated devout men and true prophets and hence God Himself. The general character of the idolatry is clear: it was the old Canaanite fertility cult, with all its sexual rites and rituals, together with child sacrifice to **Molech** (5, 9). The latter cult was celebrated especially in the Valley of Hinnom, just outside Jerusalem. Verse 8 mentions some domestic **symbols**, probably also of sexual character. Verse 10 shows how persistent all this idolatry was, in spite of its meagre rewards (see NEB for a possibly superior rendering); and it was all done in a spirit of self-righteousness, as the sarcasm of v. 12 makes plain. Finally, the prophet links the inevitable prediction of doom for idolaters with reassurance and promise for the righteous. The promise may be compared with Mt. 5: 5.

57: 14–21. The theme of promise continues, probably addressed particularly to exiles who had returned from Babylon and were distressed by the evil leadership and prevalent idolatry in post-exilic Judah. Such evils were **the obstacles** (14) in the way of the complete fulfilment of the promises which had been received by the exiles while in Babylonia; cf. 40: 3 ff. God insists that His anger which had brought about the exile as punishment was over (16 ff.); He had now fully determined to bring well-being and prosperity (**peace**) to His people, although the wicked among them could of course expect nothing of the sort (20 f.). The **greed** (17) of pre-exilic Judah is singled out for mention because that was the sin all too prevalent again now; cf. 56: 11.

Verse 15 recalls ch. 6, but the absence of any mention of the temple is noteworthy, and suggests that there was considerable corruption in the post-exilic temple worship. The devout could nevertheless meet with their God, since His eternal dwelling was not only in heaven above, but also in **lowly** hearts (cf. Mt. 5: 3).

(c) **Fasting and Sabbath Observance (58: 1–14)**
Oracles are here brought together on two closely related topics, the observance of fast-days (1–12) and the Sabbath (13 f.). The historical situation envisaged is the very early post-exilic period, when much rebuilding still needed to be carried out (cf. v. 12), and when fast-days seem to have been a prominent feature of worship (as also during the exile, but not earlier). The prophet challenges the people's thinking on both observances; his words must be as arresting as the **trumpet** (1) which was regularly sounded at the start of sacred days (cf. Ps. 81: 2).

The prophet analyses their practice of fasting, responding to their complaints that God has paid no attention to it (3), and finds two faults: in the first place, their observance is quite insincere (2 ff.), and secondly, it is unaccompanied by any concern for the needy (5 ff.). It is evident from vv. 5 ff. that God's 'choice' is genuine self-denial rather than ceremonial and ostentatious fasting; cf. also Mt. 25: 35 f. If the people are prepared to remedy these faults, then earlier promises (cf. especially 52: 12) will yet be fully granted—not now in the literal journey from Babylon to Judah, but in the metaphorical journey of life and conduct (8–12). Several other metaphors are used to emphasize the prosperity and well-being that are conditionally available to them.

The **Sabbath** (13 f.) also came to prominence in the exilic and post-exilic period, but evidently its observance was half-hearted and careless. This must be remedied, but not in any kill-joy fashion; it is a day intended to be a **delight**, and it offers promises (cf. Dt. 32: 13). Verses 13 f. are better translated in the NEB.

(d) **A Confession of Sin (59: 1–21)**
Although the contents of this chapter are easily understood and defined, its form and function are somewhat puzzling: who are addressed in v. 2, and who are the speakers in vv. 9–15? The passage may constitute a sermon for the people in post-exilic Judah, incorporating their response in confession of sin; but an attractive possibility is that the chapter was written to serve a purpose in their worship. If so, vv. 1–8 are a reminder (to be read or declaimed in public worship) of the people's sins and misdeeds; vv. 9–15a provide the response which they are encouraged to make publicly, and vv. 15b–20 (again, to be declaimed) offer both warning and promise, according to the people's future deeds.

Verses 1–8, then, contain an indictment of the whole nation, though the misdeeds which are enumerated are mainly those of leaders and judges. Verse 1 implies that people were blaming God for the hardships of the time; the real reasons, however, were the facts expressed in v. 2.

In vv. 9–15a we have a confession of sin appropriate to the situation. Here there is no attempt to shift the blame, whether in God's direction, or on to the shoulders of the ruling classes alone. It has to be admitted that **righteousness stands at a distance**, and that **truth is nowhere to be found**.

God's response to the situation is outlined in vv. 15b–20. Evidently **no one**, not even the governor nor the high priest, had the courage to attempt to **intercede** and change the situation. God Himself must therefore act, punishing the guilty and blessing the godly. Here the scene suddenly broadens out, bringing other lands (**the islands**) into the survey, and anticipating God's final deeds on Mount **Zion** (cf. Rom. 11: 26).

Verse 21 is a brief prose appendix, not concerned with Judah's sins, but looking forward to the outpouring of God's **Spirit** upon His people; cf. Jl 2: 28 f.

(e) Jerusalem's Future Glory (60: 1–22)

This superb poem, describing the glories of the future Jerusalem, had not been fulfilled by NT times (cf. Rev. 21), nor has it yet come to fruition. Nevertheless, we must not divorce its message from the situation of the late sixth century B.C.; it offered a total contrast to that situation, and so provided a stimulus and a target—as well as a promise—to that generation. That is why they were directly addressed —**'Arise, shine'** (i.e., arise with beaming faces). They were invited to apprehend the available **glory of the LORD** (1). The language of vv. 1 ff. is drawn from the rising of the sun.

Behind the promises of most of the chapter we can recognize the realities of the early post-exilic situation. Pitifully few exiles had returned (4), the country was poverty-stricken (5), with all too few sacrificial animals (7) to offer at a rebuilt but far-from-glorious temple (8, 13). (The places named in vv. 6 f. were famed for their **camels** and sheep respectively.) It was not for another 75 years or so that the Persians permitted the rebuilding of the city walls (10); the Jews were politically helpless, a tiny state (22) dominated by an all-powerful Medo-Persian empire (12, 14). Verse 15 reveals explicitly the contempt and neglect suffered by Judah in this period; labour was hard, and the evidence of past **destruction** all too plain to see (17 f.). All these difficulties and problems were to be removed or remedied; or rather, the situation was to be totally transformed. Humiliation would give place not to insignificant mediocrity, but to unimaginable glory.

It may be that the original oracle consisted of vv. 1–18; at any rate, vv. 19 f. seem to look to a more distant, unearthly future (unless we

are to view the language as that of hyperbole) and may indicate a later meditation on the same theme. Verse 21 reveals why the promises of the chapter have waited so long for fulfilment; the material blessings must be accompanied by inward righteousness, that God might **display** his **splendour**. That is why the last statement of the chapter strikes such a paradoxical note: God will not delay in the fulfilment of what He promises, and yet He will not act until 'the fullness of time' (NEB).

(f) 'The Year of the LORD's Favour' (61: 1–11)

It is generally agreed that the imagery of this chapter is based on that of the year of jubilee (see Lev. 25): a **year** of liberty and restoration is to be proclaimed (1 f.), when the present troubles of Judah will be reversed (3 f.).

Verses 5 ff. foresee the time when Israel will at last fulfil its destiny, becoming 'a kingdom of priests' (Exod. 19: 6), other nations willingly supplying their material needs. All oppression will then be a thing of the past (8), as Israel comes into the good of God's **everlasting covenant** (8 f.). The chief ends in view are universal **righteousness and praise** (11).

In v. 1 and again in vv. 10 f. we find the first person singular used. Some exegetes think that the same speaker is intended throughout; it is more likely, however, that the speaker in v. 1 is the prophet himself, while in vv. 10 f. Israel is the speaker, rejoicing in her future **garments of salvation**. Although vv. 1 f. are reminiscent of 42: 1, we need not think here of the 'suffering Servant'; the speaker is one who bears the authentic marks of the prophet, who is thus authorized to announce the 'jubilee year'. The time of fulfilment was, as we know, long delayed, and it fell to a greater Prophet to announce the eventual arrival of **the year of the LORD's favour** (see Lk. 4: 16–21).

Note: **the day of vengeance** is not intended as a contrast to **the year of the LORD's favor**. In Hebrew, the noun *nāqām* has a wider and less negative meaning than English 'vengeance', and in this context would be better rendered 'restoration' or 'restitution' (cf. 35:4). At the same time, the release of the oppressed necessarily implies the punishment of the oppressors (cf. 63: 4).

(g) The Certainty of God's Promises (62: 1–12)

Although many commentators think the speaker in vv. 1, 6 is the prophet, it seems more likely that it is God who says **'I will not keep silent'**, rebutting a frequent complaint of ancient Jewish people in hard times (cf. Ps. 28: 1). The promises made to the exiles in Babylonia in chs. 40–55 had only very partially come true by the last quarter of the sixth century B.C., and despondency and disbelief were prevalent in Judah. This chapter responds to such a situation, promising in God's name that all the present ills will pass away, and that the earlier promises will yet be wonderfully fulfilled; there are therefore many echoes of earlier chapters, especially 40: 1–11.

The promised brightness and beauty (1 ff.) must have contrasted with the ruined buildings and walls all too visible in and around Jerusalem; similarly the picture of a busy, happy, populous country (4 f.) must be set against the pitiful handful of people who were there at the time. The names used in v. 4 (see NIVmg) were probably all well-known girls' names (*e.g.*, for Azubah (**Deserted**) see 1 Kg. 22: 42), here skilfully applied to Zion, again personified as a woman. The picture of a woman's **sons** marrying her (5) is startling; a slight alteration of the Hebrew yields 'so you shall wed him who rebuilds you' (NEB).

Using fresh imagery, the prophet now urges the people to a life of prayer (6 f.); they are to be **watchmen** (elsewhere prophets would be meant) and 'recorders' who remind their Employer of His commitments (the Hebrew word *mazkîr*, still the word for a 'secretary', literally means 'one who reminds . . .'). Only by urgent prayer will the grave shortages caused by the rapacity of **foreigners** (whether Persian officials or Edomite infiltrators) be remedied (8 f.).

A final call to positive action (10), coupled with renewed promises (11 f.), rounds off the section.

(*h*) The Destruction of God's Enemies (63: 1–6)

This vivid short oracle stands as an appendix to the promises of chs. 60 ff. The removal of all the hardships and the transformation of adverse circumstances have been repeatedly foretold, with the assurance that the nations will help God's people (60: 10; 61: 5). Briefly, 60: 12 has warned the disobedient nations that their rôle is to be a different one—that of signal punishment. This is now the theme of 63: 1–6. **Edom** is singled out for mention, since her treatment of the Jews and of Judah was so hurtful and so deeply resented in the sixth century (see Ps. 137: 1, 7 ff.); but it is widely agreed that Edom is here a symbol of all the inveterate enemies of God's people. Indeed, the NT supports this interpretation: see Rev. 19: 15. See also ch. 34.

The passage is a dialogue, as it were between a sentry (one of the 'watchmen' of 62: 6, perhaps) and a blood-spattered warrior, who is speedily recognized as God Himself. God stands **alone** (3), because no human agency had lifted a finger to stop the oppression of His people (5). Verse 4 recalls the promise of 61: 2, where too **the day of vengeance** and the **year** of release are but two sides of the same coin.

(*i*) A Prayer for Speedy Deliverance (63: 7–64: 12)

At this point we encounter a sudden, marked change of mood. Chapter after chapter, section after section, has been offering the post-exilic generation promises of deliverance and of a glorious future; the prophet has been speaking to the people in God's name. Now we find the people addressing God, the prophet acting as *their* spokesman instead, a true mediator. The whole of 63: 7–64: 12 is a prayer for help; in structure it is a psalm, very similar to Ps. 44; its content may be compared with the whole book of Lamentations. Probably the prophet composed it expressly to be used in worship. In its setting in the book, the psalm is a plea that the divine promises, already given, may speedily come to pass (64: 12). The historical setting envisaged is plain: Judah and Jerusalem are in ruins, the temple not yet rebuilt (64: 10 f.).

63: 7–14. The psalm opens with a confession of faith, recalling God's loyalty to His covenant with Israel at Sinai (that is the connotation of **kindnesses**, 7) and Israel's frequent disloyalty (10). History had shown God alternately rescuing His people (9) and then being compelled to punish them (10). NIV, AV and RSV are almost certainly wrong at the start of v. 9; most EVV now follow the LXX—the Hebrew seems faulty —and read 'It was neither messenger nor angel but his presence that saved them' (JB). Verses 11–14 recall particularly the days of **Moses** and Joshua (who led Israel to rest in the Promised Land). There is some emphasis here on the powerful presence of the **Holy Spirit**. Probably v. 11 should begin, '**Then his people recalled**', and not as mg.

63: 15–19. The prayer solemnly acknowledges that Israel's disloyalty of old has not ceased, and that the disasters of the sixth century B.C. are but well-merited punishment (17 f.). To this confession, the prophet adds several points: (i) God's fatherhood—greater far than that of **Abraham** or Jacob—is such that even erring sons may expect signs of His love (16); (ii) God's inaction could endanger His own reputation (19); (iii) God could prevent His people's sins, if He so willed (17; cf. Mt. 6: 13).

64: 1–7. The prayer now asks explicitly for God to act (1 f.); the visible signs of His presence are what the people long to see. The prophet recognizes that of course God's own person is invisible (3 f.). Having thus called on God to act, the prophet swiftly reverts to the motif of sincere confession of sinfulness.

64: 8–12. Finally, the prophet stresses the severity of God's punishment, in itself an implicit plea to Him to act, as are also the direct questions of the last verse. He again emphasizes that God is His people's Father and Maker (8); in other words, God may be relied on both to love them and to mould them as He will. He cannot abandon them!

(j) The Destiny of Faithful and Faithless Jews (65: 1–25)

Throughout chs. 60–64 the themes have been national; the prophet has offered the whole nation God's promises of full salvation, and provided them with a communal prayer that God would speedily fulfil His word. In ch. 65, the prophet faces the contemporary reality that Israel was a divided nation (cf. ch. 57): by no means all the people were worshipping the God of Israel, and yet there was also a faithful section of the community. In vv. 1–7 the prophet accordingly castigates the rebellious idolaters among them, and warns that God's punishment must one day fall. However, the innocent are not to suffer with the guilty; indeed for the time being the guilty will escape punishment because of the godly (8–12; cf. Mt. 13: 28 ff.). In due course, however, those who worship the god **Destiny** will encounter their well-merited destiny (note the word-play, reproducing the Hebrew, in vv. 11 f.); and just as certainly the godly will come into full blessing. (**Sharon** was already famed for its fertility, while the arid **Achor** would yet be 'a door of hope' (see Hos. 2: 15).) Verses 13–16 (perhaps a separate oracle) stress the certainty of the same future destinies, as an encouragement to the godly and a stern warning to the apostate.

The final oracle in the chapter (17–25) ignores the idolaters and reinforces God's promises to His faithful people. It is doubtful if v. 17 envisages the destruction of this universe; more probably the prophet is promising its transformation, in an era when all the **former** troubles shall be forgotten. The picture drawn for us is, at least in part, that of a second patriarchal age, with all its remarkable serenity and longevity. The idyllic picture in v. 25 is implicitly messianic, since it is taken from the messianic prophecy in ch. 11 (it abridges vv. 6–9). The overall effect of this picture of the future is not other-worldly; as so often with passages of this character, its starting-point is things as they were, the starkly contrasting realities of the late sixth century B.C. All the hardships which then distressed godly people would one day be totally removed; God had promised!

(k) Final Promises and Stern Warnings (66: 1–24)

The NIV paragraph divisions, together with the alternation between verse and prose sections, serve to draw attention to the fact that ch. 66 contains a considerable variety of material; oracles and parts of oracles have been brought together to present the final lessons of the book. In general, the same theme predominates as in ch. 65, namely the gulf between faithful and faithless Jews, and between their respective destinies.

Verses 1–6 anticipate the rebuilding of the temple under Haggai and Zechariah, but warn that neither the rebuilding itself nor the offering of many sacrifices at the new temple will in themselves be pleasing to God, who after all needs no temple made with hands (1). What God wishes to see is the man who is **humble** and obedient to His **word** (2); insincere worship is no better than blatant idolatry (3 f.), especially when it is coupled with hostility towards the devout (5). Hypocrites of this sort will eventually (though not before **the temple** is rebuilt, evidently) be punished (6).

Verses 7–16 revert to an earlier theme, the future well-being of Jerusalem, depicted in terms of a mother and her offspring; the metaphor is sustained to the end of v. 14. The comforting paradox of vv. 7 f. is intended to draw attention to the miraculous speed with which the now ruined, almost deserted, city will be restored, regaining population and prosperity. **11. in her overflowing abundance:** more probably 'her plentiful milk' (NEB). These blessings of God's faithful people will at the same time mean the signal punishment of **his foes** (14 ff.).

Verses 17–24 are also concerned with the fate of rebellious Jews, especially those guilty of degrading and idolatrous practices (17). (It is not certain what rite is meant by **one in the midst**; some have suggested that the practice mentioned in Ezek. 8: 7–13 is in view.) The very last sentence in the chapter (24) is a stern warning to such rebels. Two happier motifs are also incorporated, however. There is the renewed promise to faithful Jews that the nation shall be restored, the exiles brought home from every quarter of the globe (19), and never again dislodged from their inheritance (22). Finally, we find the promise that from the Gentile **nations** shall come those who will be prepared not only to aid Israelites (20) but to worship Israel's God; for it is His will that all mankind shall one day **bow down before** Him (23). In this community of the faithful, birth is no barrier (21); and thus the Church is prefigured. The book of Isaiah thus ends with a warning to Jews that 'not all who are descended from Israel belong to Israel' (Rom. 9: 6), and an appeal to all men, 'Do not be faithless, but believing' (Jn 20: 27).

BIBLIOGRAPHY

BLOCHER, H., *Songs of the Servant* (London, 1975).
BOER, P. A. H. DE, *Second Isaiah's Message* (Leiden, 1956).
CLEMENTS, R. E., *Isaiah 1–39. NCentB* (London, 1980).

ERLANDSSON, S., *The Burden of Babylon* (Lund, 1970).

GRAY, G. B., *A Critical and Exegetical Commentary on the Book of Isaiah* (chs. 1–27 only), *ICC* (Edinburgh, 1912).

HERBERT, A. S., *The Book of the Prophet Isaiah. CBC* (2 vols., Cambridge, 1973–75).

JONES, D. R., *Isaiah 56–66 and Joel. TC* (London, 1964).

KAISER, O., *Isaiah 1–12: a Commentary. OTL* (London, ²1983).

KAISER, O., *Isaiah 13–39: a Commentary. OTL* (London, 1974).

KISSANE, E. J., *The Book of Isaiah* (2 vols., Dublin, 1941–43).

KNIGHT, G. A. F., *Deutero-Isaiah: a Theological Commentary on Isaiah 40–55* (New York and Nashville, 1965).

LEUPOLD, H. C., *Exposition of Isaiah* (2 vols., Grand Rapids, 1968–71).

MCKENZIE, J. L., *Second Isaiah*, Anchor Bible (Garden City, 1968).

MAUCHLINE, J., *Isaiah 1–39. TC* (London, 1962).

NORTH, C. R., *Isaiah 40–55.* ²*TC* (London, 1964).

NORTH, C. R., *The Second Isaiah* (Oxford, 1964).

NORTH, C. R., *The Suffering Servant in Deutero-Isaiah*² (London, 1956).

SIMON, U. E., *A Theology of Salvation: a Commentary on Isaiah xl-lv* (London, 1953).

SMART, J. D., *History and Theology in Second Isaiah* (London, 1967).

SMITH, G. A., *The Book of Isaiah*, 2 vols. (London, ²1927).

SMITH, S., *Isaiah Chapters XL-LV* (London, 1944).

VINE, W. E., *Isaiah: Prophecies, Promises, Warnings* (London and Edinburgh, 1946).

WESTERMANN, C., *Isaiah 10–66. a Commentary. OTL* (London, 1969).

WHYBRAY, R. N., *Isaiah 40–66. NCentB* (London, 1975).

YOUNG, E. J., *The Book of Isaiah. NICOT* (3 vols., Grand Rapids, 1965–72).

JEREMIAH

DONALD WISEMAN

The book is named after the prophet Jeremiah who was the Lord's main messenger to Judah and the surrounding nations *c.* 626–580 B.C. It is placed consistently as the second in the canonical order of the major prophets, between Isa. and Ezek. In LXX *Ieremias* occupies the place it holds in the EVV.

The Times of Jeremiah

Jeremiah lived in a period of repeated political and moral crisis in Judah. Upheavals internationally were caused by the decline and fall of the Assyrian empire and the subsequent rise of Babylonian power which was opposed by Egypt, with Judah the weak, and often dependent, small hill-state between them, which was eventually crushed. Ashurbanipal's death (*c.* 627) encouraged moves for independence by Egypt and Babylon and no less by Josiah. The call of Jeremiah may have coincided with threats of a Scythian invasion from the north or an impending Babylonian advance. Soon afterwards the discovery of the Law-book in the temple led to Josiah's reforms. The part Jeremiah played in these is not explicitly stated, but most think that initially he participated, stressing the covenant relationship between God and His people (11: 1–8) but later, seeing the superficial effect (7: 1–20), he stressed that faith in God expressed in life was more essential than mere ritual observance.

The Babylonian Chronicle affords a unique contemporary insight into the principal events of this period. Assyria was defeated by an alliance of Babylonians, Medes and wandering tribes' people (Manda, Scythians?), Ashur and Calah falling in 614 B.C. and Nineveh itself two years later. The Assyrians retreated to Harran where they were initially supported by Necho II of Egypt (610–594 B.C.), despite Josiah's fatal attempt at intervention by his attack on the Egyptian garrison at Megiddo. Subsequently Judah lost much of its independence (2 Kg. 23: 29 ff.) for Jehoahaz II, son of Josiah, was replaced by his elder brother Jehoiakim and Judah came under strong Egyptian influence. He seems to have engaged in lavish building projects in the city and temple (22: 13–19) and Jeremiah's opposition following the battle of Carchemish in August 605 B.C.—characteristically outspoken as in his temple sermon (7: 1–8: 3)—set out to warn against the false hopes of peace and prosperity and trust in the temple *per se* to save them. In

that year the Babylonians swept the Egyptians back to within their borders and in the following year campaigned in Syria, at which time Daniel and other Judeans were taken to Babylon.

Jeremiah anticipated the onset of the Babylonians and the sack of Ashkelon in 604 B.C. (47: 5–7), as had Zephaniah (2: 4–7). A fast was proclaimed (36: 9) but the lesson had no lasting effect. Jehoiakim, a vassal of Nebuchadrezzar II of Babylon (36: 9–29), changed sides in 601 B.C. when the Egyptians defeated the Babylonian army (2 Kg. 24: 1). As Jeremiah predicted, the Babylonians despatched local garrisons with troops from Syria, Ammon, and Moab to raid Judah pending their own punitive expedition (2 Kg. 24: 2).

By December 598 B.C. the Babylonians were ready to punish Jehoiakim. 'In the month of Kislev of his seventh year the Babylonian king mustered his troops and marched to Syro-Palestine. He besieged the city of Judah and on the second day of the month Adar he captured the city and seized its king. He appointed there a king of his own choice, received its heavy tribute and sent them to Babylon' (*Babylonian Chronicle:* B.M. 21946, 11–12). This reliable extra-biblical account records the capture of Jerusalem on 16/17 March 597 B.C., the seizure of Jehoiachin and his replacement by the Babylonian nominee Mattaniah-Zedekiah, the youngest son of King Josiah (1: 3) and uncle of Jehoiachin (2 Kg. 24: 17), and the beginning of the exile, all subjects of Jeremiah's prophecies. False prophets predicted that the exile would last only two years and raised popular opinion against Jeremiah. Such assertions he specifically answered to the exiles in Babylon in a letter full of common-sense and wise counsel (ch. 29) and by his symbolic action in Zedekiah's fourth year (ch. 28) when the false prophets supported pro-Egyptian activities. Jeremiah was against such disloyalty to agreements freely entered into with Babylon. However, rebellion there in 595/4 B.C. raised hopes of renewed freedom and representatives from Edom, Ammon, Moab, Tyre and Sidon came to Jerusalem to discuss its possible extension (27: 3). The prophet compared those in Jerusalem (ch. 24, 'bad figs') with the faithful remnant in exile.

In 589 B.C. Hophra came to the throne of Egypt and intervened in Palestinian affairs much as had his father Psammetichus II (594–

589 B.C.). Zedekiah's negotiations with him were interpreted by the Babylonians as rebellion, so in 588 B.C. they moved first against Syria and then south into Judah. Lachish (Tell ed-Duweir) and Azekah (Tell ez-Zakariyah) SW of Judah were encircled. The Lachish Letters vividly portray the anxiety of the garrison. News came of an Egyptian intervention in 587 B.C. and the Babylonians moved from Jerusalem to meet and rout them (37: 3–8). The Jerusalemites, feeling the danger past, released their slaves (34: 8 ff.) but contrary to Jeremiah's advice reenslaved them and continued to resist the Babylonians (37: 3–10; 38: 14–23). When the prophet tried to leave the city he was arrested and imprisoned as a deserter (37: 11–21) and held until the city fell in 587 B.C. and Zedekiah taken away, blinded and captive.

The Babylonian commander ordered Jeremiah's release and he joined the newly appointed governor of Judah, Gedaliah, at Mizpah (40: 6). But when Gedaliah was assassinated the group fled to Egypt to avoid Babylonian reprisals. These occurred with a further deportation of exiles from Jerusalem in 581 B.C. Jeremiah, with Baruch, was forcibly carried off to Egypt where traditionally he is said to have been stoned to death at Tahpanhes a year later by Jews who rejected his further condemnation of idolatry (44: 24).

Jeremiah's character and message

The personality of Jeremiah, through his many personal references ('I' is more frequent in Jer. than in any other OT prophet) comes out strongly. His association with Anathoth (1: 1; cf. 1 Kg. 2: 26–27) has led many to assume that he was of a priestly family. He was humble and yet reluctant at his call (1: 6; cf. Isaiah, Amos, Hosea). He was outspoken, like Micah (26: 16–18), and capable of strong denunciation of evil and hypocrisy. He interceded for friend and foe alike (15: 11; 18: 20) and when God's word through him was one of judgment he was broken-hearted over his people's apostasy (7: 16; 11: 14; 14: 11).

For his action in denouncing faith in the temple and institutions rather than in God Himself, Jeremiah was increasingly subject to persecution and imprisonment (20: 1), yet continued to speak out (20: 7) despite the threat of death (37: 12). He was consistently opposed to false prophets who were to be distinguished by the fact that God had not sent them (23: 21), nor were they advised of His counsels (23: 18, 22); their ideas were their own (23: 25–31) so they had no divine authority and were without true knowledge (14: 18) and propagated lies (5: 31). Their word would fail. The word of the true prophet, like Jeremiah, would be substantiated by the life of the messenger and his communion with the One who sent him, and

by the effect of his message (23: 13–22). God's word is not at man's disposal (23: 18) and can be given a man against his wish (26: 6–7). It can be like a crushing hammer (20: 7–9; 23: 29), for which action a prophet may have to wait long (15: 10–25).

Jeremiah demonstrated his personal faith in the word given him by his purchase of family property at a place then occupied by enemy forces (ch. 32), and his practical wisdom in his letter to the exiles (ch. 29) and his foresight in committing his prophecies to writing as a means of their preservation (ch. 36). He was often a lonely witness and was forbidden to marry (16: 1–4), yet was thoughtful of those who helped him *e.g.* Ebed-Melech (39: 15–18) and his secretary Baruch (45: 22–5). His poetic sense is outstanding as is his use, like Ezekiel, of visual aids in preaching.

As a prophet emphasizing repentance and personal religion, he was a sensitive man of deep emotion and insights. He dwelt upon the revelation of God in nature (8: 7; 12: 9; 17: 11; 22: 23; 48: 28), drawing for illustration upon the almond tree, the boiling kettle and farm-life. Jeremiah was 'God's man and a true patriot'. His purpose was to lead God's people to better things. For them he intercedes that judgment may be averted (14: 7–15: 9). He speaks feelingly of them as God's chosen people, holy (2: 3), a chosen vine (2: 21; 12: 16), God's loved ones (11: 15; 12: 17) and inheritance (12: 7–9), flock (13: 17) and firstborn (31: 9).

Jeremiah saw that God was ever a God of mercy calling for repentance despite the inevitable outcome of the people's idolatry and forsaking of His law. He was not against sacrifice and ritual but saw that this could only be valid as it is reflected in a state of heart and life reflecting a true covenant relationship with God (7: 2; 31: 22). The new covenant (31: 31–34) would make God's people a universal blessing (33: 6–9) and he spoke much of the terms which signify the covenant relationship. He stressed the knowledge of God as the One who knows (29: 23) and foreknows. Lack of such knowledge is a mark of the failure of Israel (8: 7), the priest (2: 8), the 'poor' (5: 4) and the godless (4: 22), and can only be reversed by means of the new covenant which will itself be marked by the knowledge of God (31: 34). God is the creator of all (27: 5), including nations which are His instruments (27: 6; 31: 35–37). He is just, righteous and loving (9: 23–24). Jeremiah's writings are also distinguished by his sensitivity to sin and judgment. The latter is in major part self-imposed as a consequence of sin which is the refusal to know the Lord, shown in forgetting (2: 32; 3: 21) and leaving Him (2: 17–20), in rebellion, infidelity and sickness of heart (3: 22).

Jeremiah looked forward to the Messiah, the

Righteous Branch (23: 5–6; cf. 3: 16–17), the descendant of David, 'the LORD *our* righteousness' (33: 16) who alone would bring peace to a penitent people (33: 8, 14–16). Messiah's rule would be a blessing not only to his own city and people (31: 12–14) but also to others (16: 19; 30: 9; 33: 5). More immediately he saw the rebuilding of a holy Jerusalem (31: 23–40).

It is small wonder then that when men sought to compare Jesus Christ, sorrowing over the unrepentant and doomed nation, they did so with Jeremiah (Mt. 16: 14). When Christ cleansed the temple he quoted Jer. 7: 11 and Paul applied the lesson of the potter's house (Jer. 18: 1–11) to the Jews of his day (Rom. 9: 20–24). Of the forty quotations from Jer. by NT writers the majority are associated with the fall of Babylon (cf. Rev.).

The Arrangement of the prophecies

The book is an anthology of Jeremiah's prophecies and experiences. The main arrangement seems clear: (i) the prophecies concerning Jerusalem and Judah (chs. 1–25); (ii) biographical narratives involving Jeremiah and prophecies of salvation for Israel and Judah (chs. 26–45); (iii) prophecies concerning foreign nations (chs. 46–51), and a historical appendix (ch. 52). Cf. also ANALYSIS below. Within this arrangement, however, no precise chronological principle is followed, though there is some grouping according to the reign in which they were made:

Josiah	1: 1–19; 2: 1–6: 30; 7: 1–10: 25; 18: 1–20: 18.
Jehoahaz	none
Josiah or Jehoiakim	11: 1–17: 27.
Jehoiakim	25–26; 35–36; 45–48.
Jehoiachin	31: 15–27.
Zedekiah	21–24; 27–34; 37–39; 49–51.
Gedaliah (& Egypt)	40–44.

The composition of the book has been much discussed. Critics vary in the prophecies they assign to Jeremiah. Some consider the personal biographical sections to be the work of an author or editor who was not Baruch and would reject the third source or sections in the 'Deuteronomist' style, *e.g.* beginning 'the word which came to Jeremiah from the LORD', as authentic and impose a late date upon them largely because they put a late date upon this style of Hebrew. Such language in both poetry and prose is used over the centuries for the law and temple and would be well known to Jeremiah as almost certainly the standard

traditional Hebrew from the tenth century at least (so also S. R. Driver, *op. cit.*, xli–xlvi). This theory would, moreover, require the belief that a later editor changed the words of Jeremiah from the first to third person. Though Aramaic was increasingly common in Jeremiah's time its scant use (*e.g.* 10: 11, possibly a marginal note) is another indication of Jeremianic authorship.

Some designate chs. 30–31 (or 33) as the 'Little Book of Comfort' and others chs. 37–45 as the Passion Story of Jeremiah by Baruch. There is no justification for the theory which allows only the poetic passages as original to Jeremiah, nor is it possible, other than subjectively, to reconstruct the scroll dictated to Baruch by Jeremiah (36: 1–2). There is no need, nor satisfactory reason, to doubt that Jeremiah committed his main sayings from *c.* 626–604 B.C. to writing in the way stated. Others could have been added and written down by Baruch while he and Jeremiah were in Egypt. The selection and arrangement could have been done with Jeremiah's advice. While scholars' theories differ, the coherence of language, thought and teaching in all sections is a powerful argument, if one is needed, for the Jeremianic authorship.

The Text

Hebrew MSS from Qumran, dated at latest A.D. 68, support the *MT*, while at least one fragment (4Q Jer[6]) shows that some recensions were current which follow a shorter text known from Gk. (LXX). The latter is about one-eighth shorter than Heb. *MT*—i.e. *c.* 2,700 words or the equivalent of 6–7 chapters. Most of these omissions are minor and due to the individual translator(s) into Gk., to shortening of the text (*e.g.* chs. 27–28), omission of doublets (8: 10–12; 30: 10–11), or a few omissions by error (*homoeoteleuton*), *e.g.* 39: 16–20; 33: 14–26; 39: 4–13; 52: 28–30. Though the LXX also adds about 100 verses there can be no support for any general claim that the Gk. text is superior to the *MT*.

The most notable variants are the placing of the prophecies concerning the nations in the LXX after 25: 13 in the order Elam (49: 34–39), Egypt (ch. 46), Babylon (50: 1–51: 58), Philistines (ch. 47), Edom (49: 1–6), Kedar (49: 28–33), Damascus (49: 23–27) and Moab (ch. 48). It has been suggested that this rearrangement was made when Persia was the major world power and so Babylon was placed after Egypt (E. J. Young).

ANALYSIS

I. PROPHECIES CONCERNING GOD'S ACTION AT HOME AND ABROAD
(1: 1–45: 5)
i. The Call of Jeremiah (1: 1–19)

The title (1–3) gives the prophet's name ('Yahweh exalts' or casts down) and location 4 miles north of Jerusalem (Anathoth=mod. 'Anāta). **2–3.** Emphasis is on God as the source of the prophet's vocation and of his repeated inspiration from his call in Josiah's **thirteenth year** (c. 627 B.C.) to the exile at the hands of Nebuchadrezzar II in the autumn of 587 B.C. (a) **The divine call (4–5).** This comes from God personally as part of His eternal plan involving Jeremiah in a widespread ministry—

to the nations (5), **to everyone I send you to** (7) as shown by the range of the prophecies in this book. Vocation is part of God's foreknowledge (**knew**) and action when he **set apart** and 'made' him a prophet.

(b) **The divine equipment (6–10).** Jeremiah thought he was 'too young' (Gk.) or a 'young man' without sufficient qualification or experience. He may have been about 20 years old. Such objections God overrules by His authority (**command**) and the promise and assurance of His continuing and sustaining presence. Note the simple and direct language used to the newly commissioned, cf. the 'Do not be afraid' to Abraham (Gen. 15: 1), Moses (Dt. 3: 2), Mary (Lk. 1: 30), or Paul (Ac. 27: 24). The

touched . . . mouth (9) indicates both cleansing (as Isa. 6: 7) and enabling. The prophet's words must be identical with God's word. Their effect (10) will be destructive, then constructive, giving ground for hope following judgment. To **destroy, overthrow** (NEB, demolish), (re)**build, plant** foretell the course and theme of the prophecies (cf. 18: 7, 9; 24: 6; 31: 28; 42: 10).

(*c*) **Confirmation of the Call (11–16).** The two visions are given to confirm the call and encourage a reluctant prophet. They also served to authenticate his commission to others since, like Amos (1: 1; 8: 1) and Isaiah (2: 1) he could add **I see** to 'I heard'.

(*i*) **An early vision through nature (11, 12).** The sprig of **almond** blossom (lit. 'waker', *šāqēd*), the harbinger of spring and coming fruit, is interpreted by a play on words as God is 'watchful' (*šōqēd*) to keep His promise and fulfil his word. For Jeremiah's appreciation of nature see also 2: 10; 8: 7; 12: 8; 14: 4–6. (*ii*) **A later vision through events (13–16).** This introduces also the theme of the first group of prophecies (chs. 1–24)—judgment from the north (i.e. Assyria, Babylonia and possibly the Scythians) which would result in the siege and sack of Jerusalem. The large boiling cauldron **tilting away from the north** tells how the attack will be southwards through Syria. The self-imposed judgment is due to forsaking God and consequent idolatry. In God's universal rule and sovereignty (15, 16, note **all**)—the theme also of chs. 46–51—he would use existing forces as his agent for punishment (cf. 3: 18; 4: 5).

(*d*) **Call to action (1: 17–19).** Response to Yahweh is to be total and immediate obedience. Anyone who 'is ashamed to stand forth with the word will soon have no word to proclaim' (Cawley). The prophet must be fearless and stand firm, confident in God's victorious presence despite opposition which will inevitably arise from every class. The **people of the land** (18) may here refer to the principal landowners rather than to the general populace.

ii. First Message: A warning of judgment (2: 1–3: 5)
These earliest messages are typical of all in condemning Israel's apostasy (2: 1–3: 5) and in pronouncing the consequent judgment of God with a series of calls to repentance (3: 6–6: 30). The appeal to past history is directed to the capital Jerusalem itself (1–3). Israel once showed 'unfailing devotion' (NEB) and love to God and therefore followed him persistently. She was thus considered separate and **holy**, like the first fruits (Dt. 26: 1–11).

(*a*) **The appeal to common sense (2: 4–13).** Has God ever forsaken his own people? Yet the people (5), priests and rulers (8) all fail to ask if the LORD is still their God (**Glory**, 11)

and perennial (**living**) source of life (13). All failure was due to forsaking God and His law (8) and so they had polluted (**defiled**) his land (7) by relying on **worthless** (unreal, unsubstantial) gods and false prophets (8). This was something no pagan nation anywhere, whether in the west (Kittim, Cyprus) or east (Kedar in N. Arabia) would ever do (10–11). The LORD therefore lodges a formal complaint or call to answer a case (**bring charges**) before witnesses, but the charge is unanswerable. The **heavens** (Dt. 32: 1; Isa. 1: 2) and the earth are the two witnesses usually invoked. For the vivid picture of men's failing water-supplies contrasted with God's bountiful provision (13) cf. Isa. 55: 1; Jn 4: 10–14; Rev. 21: 6.

(*b*) **Apostasy in Israel (2: 14–19).** The downward course of sin is traced. Slaves were either purchased or born into slavery (homeborn). The LORD had redeemed Israel from the first state in Egypt (Exod. 20: 2), yet now by political alliance they had opened the way to attacks on Judah from the south, from the Delta capitals of **Memphis** (Heb. *Noph*) and Daphnae (**Tahpanhes**) and placed themselves under the power of the major states of the day. The threat from Assyria, whose symbol was a lion, led to the fall of the northern kingdom in 722 B.C. after which the land was invaded by lions (15, cf. 2 Kg. 17: 25). The new slavery resulted directly from a futile submission to Egypt (the 'black' Nile) and Assyria (River Euphrates). **17–18.** The decadence is thus self-afflicted and results from wilful disobedience. When the Lord led (Gk. omits this) Israel turned away. **19. backsliding** (here 'turning away') is a key theme in Jer. 3: 6–8, 11, 14–22; 5: 6; 31: 22). It is synonymous with forsaking the Lord and occurs when due awe and reverence of God (**awe of me** is a strong term as in Gen. 31: 42) is absent.

(*c*) **Degeneration in Israel (2: 20–28).** From steadfast love for God (2) Israel long ago had abandoned the controlling protection of the law and covenant (**yoke** and **bonds**) to indulge in illicit relations with the false gods (usually Canaanite Baals) and the perverse practices required by their worship. This is consistently pictured in OT as fornication. **21.** Jeremiah frequently emphasizes his point by asking questions. Since the **choice** (*šōrēq*) **vine** had now run **wild** (as seen by Isa. 5: 1–7), the only course open is to uproot it. **22.** Sin is indelible. **23–25.** The call to change direction requires recognition of the fruitlessness, aimlessness and hopelessness of life despite its seeming busyness in the determination to sin. Israel is compared with a she-camel or donkey on heat madly rushing around in search of new mates. **25.** In contrast it seems that no effort would prevent her going after **foreign gods**. **26.** None of the classes leading the nation into error (cf. 5, 8) show embarrassment at turning for help in times of disaster to the very God they have rejected. In this way they bear witness to His existence and ability to help. To lead them to true repentance the prophet ironically challenges them to ask their new masters for help. (*d*) **Complacency in Israel (2: 29–37).** Calamity and divine punishment have not yet taught the people to heed God's word. Jeremiah pleads with them to remember the LORD and so become aware of their guilt. Yet they still plead innocence (35) as no pious Hebrew should (cf. Ps. 51: 4). If they forget God (31–32) and reject the clear evidence against them (33–35) judgment must inevitably follow (36–37). **37. hands on . . . head** were one sign of shame (2 Sam. 13: 19). (*e*) **Continuing infidelity (3: 1–5).** The once close relationship (2: 1–3) is now a marriage broken by Israel's unfaithfulness. Dt. 24: 1–4 forbad a divorced man to remarry his wife following her adultery, since this would defile him (Hos. 4: 2 f.) and pollute the land and nation (2, cf. 2: 7). Sin against God's law was openly marked by His withholding rain and prosperity (3, Dt. 11: 14). **4–5.** God is never taken in by merely professed devotion. The inability to match word with action contrasts with God's own nature and practice and is always rebuked (Isa. 29: 13; Mt. 15: 8). Conformity between life and lip is an essential characteristic of the true God-fearer (Mk 7: 6).

iii. Second Message: a call to repentance (3: 6–6: 30)
To the warning of judgment is now added the promise of pardon if repentance is genuine. Some consider this prophecy to be a collection made up from several sayings. Even if so the whole forms a remarkable united message.
(*a*) **The guilty sisters (3: 6–20).** The theory that these verses interrupt the connection between v. 5 and v. 21 is contradicted by the continued reference to themes already introduced in ch. 2 (*e.g.* harlotry, 3: 6, cf. 2: 20). 'Apostate Israel' fell in 722 B.C. but this failed to move her sister-state Judah to repent. Judah is therefore held to be the more guilty. A moving call to repentance is given to the northern tribes, now in exile, and others in the devastated land (12–13).
The summons to return is based on a restored relationship—**I am your husband**. Restoration will result in (i) right leadership. Shepherds are figurative for kings throughout Jer. and Ezek. The presence of the enthroned LORD will require no additional symbol of His presence (*e.g.* the ark as the throne of God) or His law (15–17). (ii) restoration and unity (18–19) which foreshadows the new Israel with the new Jerusalem (Gal. 4: 26; 6: 16; Heb. 12: 22; Rev. 21: 12, 14, 22). God's glory will be

self-evident witness drawing in all nations (3: 17; 4: 2). (*b*) **The way of repentance (3: 21–4: 3).** Weeping exiles hear the call to come home and respond accordingly. The restoration of Israel should encourage Judah to emulate them with its promise of faithfulness restored (22), renewal of the covenant relationship and trust in the Lord rather than in the hill-defences or hill-shrines of Baal. Confession of sin must be total, recognizing sin for what it is: folly, wasted opportunities and inheritance (cf. Jl 2: 25), lack of hope, ingratitude and disobedience (24–25). **24. shameful gods** is the worship of Baal, a phrase sometimes used to avoid pronouncing the detested name of Baal itself. **4: 1. return:** the answer to the question raised in 3: 1 (cf. v. 22), must be (i) positive—**to me** (emphatic); (ii) negative—action undoing the past by removing false gods and all that goes with them; (iii) moral determination (**no longer go astray**)—not merely outward resolve—issuing in a law-abiding life (2). (*c*) **Destructive war is coming (4: 3–31).** First, a plea for repentance before the anticipated and imminent invasion. The people must act to remove obstacles to the word taking root and so personally rededicate themselves to the Lord (Dt. 10: 16). Then, anticipating no response to this, the prophet sees the attack by the Babylonians (according to some, the Scythians) as divine judgment ('**I**', 6, 8). The result is an attempt at defensive action (5–6), alarm and fear (8–9). **10. I said:** since Jeremiah never preached such peace it may be right to follow some texts 'some say', a reference to former prophets (*e.g.* Isa. 37: 33–35) or to false prophets (cf. 6: 14; 1 Kg. 22: 22). The approaching destruction is compared to the threatening clouds of a scorching 'sirocco' wind from the desert (11–13) sweeping in from the north (Dan) and reaching to the north of Jerusalem (15, Ephraim), Jeremiah was appalled at what he saw: Judah's failure to repent (14), the horror and inevitability of the doom (18), its extent reversing the very order of God's creation (23–26; cf. Gen. 1: 2 f.) and man's futile efforts to stem it (30–31). **19.** The prophet identifies himself with the sufferings of those he addresses: 'the throbbing of my heart' (NEB). **22.** It is all the more horrifying in that the causes of all this were the ignorance and stupidity of God's own people who, having the law, should know better (cf. 5: 21). As ever the Lord's drastic treatment is tempered with mercy (27–28), but no mere flattery will divert the instrument of justice (30–31). **30.** Jerusalem still plays the harlot, enlarging the eyes by painting with antimony (2 Kg. 9: 30) and searching for allies (**lovers**). (*d*) **Unlimited corruption (5: 1–9).** The prophet looks urgently at the justice of such coming judgment and fails to find one righteous person whose presence might justify its diversion (cf. Gen. 18: 16–33). The LORD is also vindicated by the people's failure to be corrected when they break the law *e.g.* in the matter of false oaths (2). While the **poor** might possibly be excused by ignorance of His law, this would not hold for **the leaders.** Yet both alike are equally stated to have broken the covenant (5, cf. 2: 20) and perverted what has been given them by God. The resulting judgment is therefore argued to be just and no forgiveness is possible for **such a nation as this** (6–9).

(e) **A call to the destroyer (5: 10–19).** The destroyer is summoned to ravage land and people on the grounds of their proven faithlessness (11), false swearing and disbelief that God would act (12) despite the clear statements of Jeremiah and Zephaniah that He would do so (13). The contemporary Babylonian Aramaic speech seems not to have been readily understood in Judah at this period, as was also the case in Isaiah's time (Isa. 36: 11).

(f) **Wickedness abounding (5: 20–31).** Further evidence of Israel's guilt. The greatness of God as creator, sustainer, giver and avenger is contrasted with the meanness of man. When God's judgment, involving exile (19), is questioned, the moral reasons behind such a punishment are restated. The sovereign God who set a boundary to the sea cannot be thwarted by man's wrong exercise of freewill. The latter results in all kinds of sin, stubbornness and hostility, backsliding (23), lack of fear of God and perversion of the right (24). Sin withholds good from the doer (25) and from those to whom, according to law and justice, good must be shown and done (27–28). The Hebrews regarded the **heart** as the seat of understanding more than of feeling (Job 12: 24) and 'fatness' (28) as a mark of self-indulgence associated with impiety (Job 15: 27; Ps. 73: 7). Yet **my people love it this way** (31). False prophets win wide acclaim while a true prophet is too uncomfortable to be popular (cf. Lk. 6: 26).

(g) **The alarm sounded (6: 1–8).** The attack from the north clearly foretold in 1: 13; 4: 6 and justified (ch. 5) is now focused on its target Jerusalem. Jeremiah, using the vividly imagined speech of defender and attacker, orders the former to retreat. His neighbours (Benjaminites) who had already withdrawn to Jerusalem were now to move 12 miles south (Tekoa) from which position they could watch for the fire-signal from Ramat-Rahel (**Beth Hakkerem**), the highest hill between Jerusalem and Bethlehem. This would herald further dispersion into the desert or into the Judean hills in face of the ferocious determination and uncertainty of timing of any attack (4–5).

(h) **Another appeal is rejected (6: 9–15).** The same God who gives the warnings also orders preparation for the assault on His own city. Despite this a further appeal to repent and return is made. Amid the destruction (**cut down . . . trees,** 6) search is still made for a repentant sinner, but, alas, there is no **remnant** (9). The failure to keep God's word results in total destruction which falls, in the words of the curses (cf. Dt. 28: 20; 8: 10–12) upon all classes of law-breakers, their property, means of livelihood and families. Jeremiah thinks of those least able to help themselves (11) when exile and extinction comes. **11.** Perhaps read with LXX 'I will pour out'. When false teachers deceptively proclaim a false peace (13–14), the Lord still offers complete rest (**16. your souls**= Heb. 'yourselves', but cf. Mt. 11: 29). **15.** The stress is on the fact that they should have been **ashamed** of the abominable things they did.

(i) **The appeal to history (6: 16–21).** The basis of God's relationship with His people is still the ancient path of His law expressed in their history and religion. Despite the warnings of the prophets (**watchmen**) the people refuse to obey (17). The description of the invasion is taken up again (17–25). **18.** 'Know of a certainty and take heed what is going to **happen to them.**' The nations and the whole world (**O earth**) will be witness. **20. Sheba** in SW Arabia was a centre for the trade in incense used in sacrificial rituals.

(j) **The cruel enemy (6: 22–30).** The description of the Chaldean (Babylonian) enemy begun in 4: 5–7; 5: 15–17; 6: 1–8 is here further expanded (and is repeated later 50: 41–43). It is so terrible that Jerusalem is to don mourning garb (26). **25. terror . . . on every side** is a characteristic Jeremianic phrase (cf. 20: 3; 46: 5; 49: 29; also Lam. 2: 22; Ps. 31: 13). The first prophecies show that Jeremiah was well aware of his rôle as 'fire' testing the nation. Their refusal, however, means that the process is not completed and the people are **rejected silver** and, as such, are rejected by the great Assayer.

iv. Fateful reliance on the Temple (7: 1–8: 3)
The central temple was held to be sacrosanct. It was thought that the LORD would save it, His city and His people because His name was there, as He had done in the days of Hezekiah when the Assyrians besieged the city in 701 B.C. Since there is no clear mention of an immediate Babylonian threat, some interpret these messages (to 10: 25) as addressed to those showing mere outward signs of reform under Josiah; others link them with a harvest festival at a later time of uncertainty following Jehoiakim's accession (i.e. *c.* 608 B.C., cf. 26: 1). Trust in the temple itself becomes idolatry. Once again the people are urged to a true

repentance shown by a life according to God's requirements, otherwise destruction and exile are inevitable.

(a) **Warnings against mere cultic worship (7: 1–20).** A forceful message to **reform your ways and your actions** (3), i.e. 'settled habits and the separate acts which go to form them', another characteristic phrase of Jeremiah (cf. 18: 11; 26: 13; 35: 15), is directed to those primarily concerned as worshippers entering the temple court (cf. 26: 1). The expansion of this appeal (5–7) emphasizes that the right way of life must be shown in right social action. Godless dealings end in hurting the **innocent** as shown in the judicial murders (shedding of **blood**) carried out by Jehoiakim (cf. 26: 23). **3.** Rising early and speaking, sending, etc. is characteristic of the urgency and diligence of Jeremiah in carrying out his mission (cf. v. 25; 11: 7; 25: 3–4; 26: 5; 29: 19; 32: 33; 35: 14–15; 44: 4 and elsewhere as a reminiscence of Jeremiah. [2 Chr. 36: 15]). **4. The temple of the LORD** may be repeated as the ecstatic cry of thoughtless temple-worshippers whose theology is so summarized, or for greater emphasis, or as a slogan of the false prophets. Even true statements can become a living lie through misuse. God's house ceases to be His if it is taken over as a refuge by those who continue in sin (10). Certainly God sees what happens and condemns it (cf. Mk 11: 17; Lk. 19: 46). **12–15.** He is no respecter of buildings misappropriated as a **den of robbers** (emphatic), nor does He condone idolatry of any kind (16–20). The illustration given is the sack of **Shiloh** north of Bethel (cf. 26: 6) by the Philistines *c.* 1050 B.C. as attested also by archaeological evidence of the ground plan which copies the tabernacle. Even though the symbol of God's presence (the ark) was there (Jos. 18: 1; 1 Sam. 1: 13) God abandoned it (Ps. 78: 60). **16–20.** The people's action is past praying for ('**I will not listen to you**'). Their persistent idolatry works as much against themselves as against God. **18.** The worship of **the Queen** (LXX 'hosts') **of Heaven** marked the reintroduction of the Canaanite (Ashtoreth) or Babylonian goddess (Ishtar) as part of astrology (= Venus), a practice condemned throughout the OT (cf. 8: 2; 44: 17).

(b) **Obedience and/or sacrifice? (7: 21–28).** Some would interpret v. 22 as showing an ignorance of the fundamental Mosaic laws, but the prophet's present concern is with priorities. Proper sacrifice (as opposed to the false non-God-directed acts of v. 18) is subordinate to, as well as a consequence of, true obedience. The overriding requirement is to keep to the love and obedience to God demanded by the law and covenant (cf. Mic. 6: 1–8). **27–28.** Since the people continually fail to respond, the preacher needs encouragement to persist

despite the known outcome of his present mission.

(c) **Mourning (7: 29–8: 3).** Not only the land but now the temple itself is defiled. This causes the prophet to call for national mourning (29) and to look to **the days** that **are coming** for the result (trace this recurring phrase in 9: 25; 16: 14; 19: 6; 23: 5–7; 30: 3; 31: 27, 31, 38; 33: 14; 48: 12; 49: 2; 51: 47,52). God makes the punishment fit the crime. Those who undertook pagan dedications and sacrifices on the city's burning rubbish-heaps (Topheth) would themselves not even be buried in such unhallowed ground. They would lie unburied or disinterred there, exposed to the very elements they vainly worshipped. Such is the ultimate shame and horror. Mass graves filled with bones found in the environs of Jerusalem may be the archaeological attestation of the fulfilment of this prophecy in 589–7 B.C. (as again in A.D. 70).

v. Tragic disobedience ends in doom (8: 4–9: 22)
(a) **Return (8: 4–7).** The pleading poem recapitulates the state of the people and the Divine plea to return. (**Re**)**turn** (Heb. *šub*) occurs six times in vv. 4–7. If anyone **turns away** from God can he **turn** back? The illustration chosen is of the birds which do, contrasted with the war-horse which does not. The people's answer is ignorance, alienation and covenant-breaking (so they **do not know**, 7).

(b) **Leaders and led both fail (8: 8–9: 6).** To declare trust in the word of God when it is rejected is a mere lie. Leaders bear a heavy responsibility; their effectiveness will be known by their fruit. Some take the **wise men** to be a separate class from **the scribes** (active in Josiah's reign (2 Chr. 34: 13) and now mentioned as such for the first time), but this is unlikely. These with the prophets and priests united in proclaiming a false peace (cf. 6: 13–14; LXX omits 10–12) will all be included in the punishment. Their lack of fruit means that even that with which they have been entrusted by God will be taken away (cf. the parable of the talents, Mt. 25: 28; Lk. 8: 18). **14–17.** The north is already lost and further retreat is impossible. The need for **healing** recalls Israel's earlier punishment at the poisoned waters of Marah (Exod. 15: 23) and the poisonous snakes of the desert from which there was deliverance (Num. 21: 6–9). But now 'they shall bite you beyond power to heal' (so LXX 17–18).

8: 18–9: 1 (=*MT* 8: 18–23). The first two commandments have been broken (no other God). This glimpse of Jeremiah's agonizing compassion reveals his sympathy despite the just condemnation of the once holy city (as Christ in Mt. 23: 37–38). **18.** Possibly 'Through lack of healing my pain increases'. **20.** Opportunity for repentance can pass (Mt.

27: 1–15; Heb. 12: 17). Harvesting is in April–June with **summer** fruit gathering in August. This may refer also to the fact that the campaigning season was now over and Egypt had failed to help her vassal Judah. **22.** The prophet's rhetorical questions imply the answer of (i) the law and (ii) the Lord Himself (3: 22; 17: 14; Dt. 32: 29).

9: 2–6. Adultery breaks the seventh commandment (2) and the prevailing treachery and deceit the ninth. As a consequence sin abounds, expressed in lying speech (5, 8) and ending in everyone 'playing the Jacob' (i.e. **deceiver**, 4, cf. Gen. 27: 36) and being alienated from God. Compare Jas 3 for the social effects of sin.

(*c*) **Despite His pity God must punish (9: 7–22).** Vindication (7–9, 12–16) is interspersed with calls for lamentation (10–11, 17–22) by the women for whom mourning will be no mere professional but a personal concern (cf. Lk. 23: 27–28). A serious famine or epidemic following a siege may be in mind.

vi. The LORD is Sovereign (9: 23–10: 25)
23. This may take up from v. 12. The only ground for boasting is a personal knowledge of God and His loving-kindness (NEB 'unfailing devotion'), **justice and righteousness**. This is the principle of true wisdom both in national, church and personal affairs (cf. 1 C. 1: 30–31; 2 C. 10: 17). Without this those bearing an outward sign of association with the covenant are in fact outside it (25). With v. 26 cf. 49: 32. Israel will be treated no better than those outside nations whose case will be taken up in chs. 46–52.

Such a knowledge of God is distinct from a foreign astrology (10: 2) and 'the helpless idols made and moved by man' (3–9).

6–16. This strong denunciation of idolatry may well reflect the words of Isaiah (40: 18–20; 44: 9–20; 46: 5–7) and expands Ps. 135: 5, but there is no ground for rejecting these verses as later than Jeremiah. **9. Tarshish:** possibly Tartessus in Spain (LXX Carthage), others explain as 'cargo (ore-carrying) ships'. **Uphaz:** 'refined' rather than an error for Ophir. **11.** This verse is written in Aramaic, perhaps as a popular answer to idolaters, or an additional (marginal?) explanation to foreigners. The prophet stresses the uniqueness of the LORD God as maker and upholder of all (6–16). He is different. As 'Jacob's creator' (16, NEB) He must be all men's strength and stay.

17–25. In a final plea the prophet identifies himself with the suffering people as the exile begins and they pass through the country occupied by nomads. The coming doom stimulates a prayer which the nation should have made in submission (23), accepting correction before it is too late (24) and only then praying for the enemy's defeat (25) as promised in the law (Dt. 30: 1–10).

vii. Fourth Message: the covenant (11: 1–12: 17)
(*a*) **The covenant proclaimed (11: 1–8).** Judah is warned of the need to keep the covenant God gave their fathers, otherwise the judgment curses it contained, foreshadowing punishment on the disobedient, will be proclaimed and enacted. The phrase **this covenant** (2) may well refer back generally to that made at Sinai (4), though most argue that it is to the book of the law (usually, but not certainly, identified with Dt.) discovered by Hilkiah in the reign of Josiah and made the basis of his reforms *c.* 621 B.C. (2 Kg. 22–23). Some date this prophecy to the reign of Jehoiakim before the Babylonian defeat of Egypt at Carchemish in 605 B.C.

2–5. The old Sinaitic covenant required constant renewal, as *e.g.* by Josiah (2 Kg. 23: 2–3). As with all ancient Near Eastern treaty-covenants it contained curses on the disobedient (3) and promises of blessing for the obedient (5); it arose from a specific historical situation (4, **I brought . . . out of . . . Egypt**); its main purpose was a stable relationship within law between the sovereign and vassal (at Sinai uniquely **you . . . my people, I . . . your God**). Ratification was by public assent, **Amen**, and taking action according to the stipulations listed in the covenant (5). **4.** The **furnace** for smelting iron became a symbol of the suffering of slavery (Dt. 4: 20; 1 Kg. 8: 51; Isa. 48: 10). **5. a land flowing . . . :** part of the original covenant mentioned outside the Pentateuch only here, 33: 22 and Ezek. 20: 6, 15. **6–8.** The covenant required constant proclamation of its demands of obedience and the dangers of disloyalty. While God has always kept His sworn promise (**the land you possess today**) the people had neglected theirs (5–6). **6.** Nothing is known elsewhere of a preaching mission by Jeremiah outside Jerusalem. **7–8.** are abbreviated by LXX to 'yet they did not obey'. The **words** (NEB terms) having been violated by apostasy, nothing is left but the implementation of the promised curse on the evildoer.

(*b*) **The covenant broken (11: 9–17).** God already sees that, despite the recent public and all too temporary covenant renewal ceremony under Josiah, there is a plot (Heb. 'bond') to rebel and return to the old ways of idolatry (9–10). The people have disregarded their history. Judgment is both divinely inflicted and self-inflicted, so it is hypocritical to pray to God for deliverance or to enter His temple for worship (14–15; cf. 7: 16). **12–13.** The no-gods cannot **help them**, despite their numbers and the multiplicity of street shrines and altars **you have set up . . . to that shameful god Baal**. More than 880 such altars are attested in contemporary Babylon. **15.** Heb. is obscure, 'what business has my cherished one in my temple when she perpetuates vile schemes?' . . . will you rejoice when disaster strikes?' Ritual is no shield in a time of catastrophe. God's plan for His own loved (15) people (16, the flourishing **olive tree**) was far different. The allusion here is to the deliberate burning down of olive-trees when they become fruitless (cf. Jn 15: 2, 6; cf. Rom. 11: 17).

(*c*) **Plots against the prophet (11: 18–12: 17).** In this foretaste of the opposition Jeremiah would have to face the language echoes Isa. 53. **18–23.** Though he was unwittingly in danger, like a wandering **lamb**, God tells him what is coming (19). It may be that the prophet (18–19a), then the people (19b), then God (21–22) are the speakers. In the plot by relatives and neighbours to kill him Jeremiah prefigures Christ who said that a prophet has no honour in his own country and that a man's foes shall be those of his own household (Mt. 10: 36). Note the similarities: (i) suffering as a lamb (19), (ii) his life sought by men of his own town and (iii) his message rejected.

The opposition at Anathoth may in part have a historical basis. The priests of the house of Abiathar were deposed in favour of the sons of Zadok and settled there under the dominance of Jerusalem (1 Kg. 2: 26 ff.). Moreover the prophet will have supported the suppression of their local shrine during the reforms of Josiah. The appeal for divine **vengeance** (20) is not so much for personal reasons (cf. Ps. 139: 19–22) as a vindication of God's message through His messenger (21). It is promised (21–23) and was fulfilled in the later Babylonian attack. **19. the tree and its fruit:** or food (some read 'sap'). The Targum interprets this as 'let us put poison in his food'. **23.** Cf. Ezr. 2: 23 which shows that 128 persons returned to Anathoth after the exile.

(*i*) **The Confessions of Jeremiah (12: 1–6).** In conversation with God Jeremiah faces the agelong question of why the godless prosper and the faithless thrive. Nevertheless he sees he must commit himself to the foreknowledge and righteousness of God (3; cf. Gen. 18: 25). Yet why should nature suffer for man's disregard of the Almighty (4)? God's answer is to brace Jeremiah for yet fiercer, and often subtler, opposition from his family who trick him and hound him out (6). Their treachery will contrast unfavourably with the prophet's steady faith. **5.** If he stumbles now at home how will he fare later at Jerusalem? We can learn that 'God never calls a man to contend with horses until He has practised him with footmen; that God never yet sent a man into the wilds of Jordan until He had trained him in the land of peace' (G. C. Morgan, *Studies in the Prophecy of Jeremiah*). The **thickets:** the luxuriant flood plain round Jericho haunted, as it was until a

century and a half ago, by lions and other wild animals (cf. 49: 19).

(*ii*) **The Lord's lament (12: 7–13).** The vivid pictures used here of the state of the rebel nation can be paralleled in other prophecies; a devastated **house** (or temple), cf. Mt. 23: 38; a rejected wife (3: 1); a marauding **lion** (8); an alien **bird** (or possibly 'hyena's lair', NEB), robbed by predators (9); a devastated **vineyard** (10–11; cf. Isa. 5: 5–7); a plundered region (12) and a good crop swamped by **thorns** (13). The use of the prophetic perfect in reference to a future state sees the coming action by God as already fulfilled. This is the Lord's answer to any complacency but note how it is marked all through with an intensive pathos (**my . . .** seven times). **10.** The rulers (**shepherds**) may be the enemy kings who complete the destruction, or the Judean leaders (cf. 2: 8) who misled the nation initially and so opened the way to them.

(*iii*) **The restoration of the nations (12: 14–17).** When Jehoiakim rebelled in 601 B.C. in favour of Egypt, the Babylonians sent **wicked neighbors**, Syria, Moab and Ammon, to inflict damage on Judah. They thus became a divine agent for punishment (2 Kg. 24: 1–2). Yet God, the supreme ruler of all nations, indicates a possibility of return for those peoples who will share the same fate as Judah in exile at the hand of the Babylonians (chs. 48–49). The terms will be the same—a repudiation of Baal-worship, repentance and entering into a new covenant relationship with the Lord God (16) so that He can rebuild and restore (17, cf. 1: 10).

viii. Enacted warnings (13: 1–27)
Actions speak louder than words and were often so employed by prophets like Jeremiah (19: 1–15), Isaiah (20: 1–6), Ezekiel (4: 1–3) and others (2 Kg. 13: 14). All the warnings now given show the separation of the nation from its God and the consequent punishment inflicted.

(*a*) **The first warning: a sign (13: 1–11).** The soiled **linen belt** is clearly shown by the explanation given (8–11) to symbolize the close intimacy the people once enjoyed with their Lord (11). This had been marred by contact with pagan and idolatrous streams of influence which had destroyed the people's pride in their God and so soiled them, His name and glory through apostasy. The nation, like the garment, is now good for nothing and will be soiled in exile (9–10). **1.** The order not to let the belt **touch water** may have been to show that it was brand new. **4. Perath** (*prt*): is probably the reference to a cleft (4, *perat*) by the stream at Wadi Fara (Parah, Jos. 18: 23 and so a play on words), 3 miles east of Anathoth (so Gk. Aquila). It is not impossible, however, that the Euphrates is meant. Either would provide the same lesson. There is no need to follow some critics (*e.g.* Mowinckel) in assuming that it was a visionary experience.

(*b*) **A second warning: a parable (13: 12–14).** The seemingly incongruous saying or proverb (12) about the full wine skins, usually symbolic of joy and economic prosperity, is explained (13) as the wrath of God falling on every section of society. (Such explanations are the true distinguishing mark of any ancient parable.) The judgment will make them drink the cup of His anger and in their subsequent drunken stupor their own judgment will be blurred and mobility impaired at a time of crisis. They will fail to distinguish between friend and foe (14, **smash . . . against** is used of breaking bottles in Ps. 2: 9) and will be like defenceless men (Isa. 51: 17; Ps. 60: 3). Drunkenness was a social evil in biblical times also (Gen. 9: 21–25; 1 Sam. 25: 36 ff.; Rom. 13: 13) and a characteristic of pagan worship.

(*c*) **Third warning: a sermon (13: 15–27).** The danger of pride and self-trust is emphasized. The appeal is based on God's own majesty (15–16) which is always seen as incomparable with the Baals, and is followed by a declaration of the love which yet lies behind the foreboding messages (17). The king and queen-mother are called to account for the state of the nation (18–21). These are usually identified with Jehoiachin and Nehushta in 597 B.C. (2 Kg. 24: 8–16) but could equally well refer to Jehoahaz and Hamutal in 608 B.C. or to Jehoiakim after the defeat of Egypt by Babylon (605 or 601 B.C.). **16.** The people are compared to travellers overtaken by the dark among the hills. **21.** The reference may be to Hezekiah of Judah's erstwhile wooing of Merodach-Baladan II of Babylon despite Isaiah's warning (2 Kg. 20: 12–19). **23.** The figures describe the impossibility of Judah changing her idolatrous ways of her own accord. **22–27.** Woe upon Jerusalem whose sins have now taken on the indelible character of sin. Yet Jeremiah never gives up hope and envisages a time of cleansing through exile (27).

ix. Fifth message: the great drought (14: 1–16: 21)
This consists of statements of the situation (1–6) followed by a dialogue between God (1, 11; 15: 1) and the prophet speaking on behalf of the people (7, 13).

The drought and famine is vividly described as it affects all classes of people (2–4), animals (5–6) and the environment on which they depend. The city and whole countryside are affected. Such a calamity is not to be taken as 'natural' but as an expression of divine disfavour of, and judgment on, sins (Dt. 11: 13–17; 28: 23). It should bring a nation to prayer and repentance. Whether the prayer (7–9; cf. 20–22) is one that ideally they should have prayed, or did pray, or was prayed by a godly

remnant or by Jeremiah on behalf of his people, knowing that confessed sin brings forgiveness (1 Jn. 1: 9), is open to interpretation. The basis of it is true repentance (**we have sinned against you**) which claims the special relationship between God and his chosen people which, if broken, affects His **name** (9, includes 'reputation'). The prayer still savours of trust in the LORD's presence in His town and temple (**we bear your name**) and so will have encouraged those still relying on this (cf. ch. 7). The dominant note of Jeremiah's faith in the Saviour, the **hope of Israel** (8; 17: 13), is introduced. The question is how God can act as if He were a mere passing stranger and not a permanent resident among them (8). **10–12.** The Lord's reply concerns the people (10). The lack of movement and direction of will shows them to be still in their sinful state and God's holiness and justice must reject them utterly. Despite his compassion Jeremiah must not even plead God's name (7, 21) since salvation is impossible without signs of repentance. No mere sacrifice will avail of itself (12) to avert the doom cited by Jeremiah's characteristic phrase (30 times he uses **sword . . . famine . . . plague**, cf. 16: 14, etc.; Ezek. 14: 21).

That they may have been misled by ritualistic priests (11) or false **prophets** (13–16) is no excuse. The latter are defined for the first time as lacking commission by God and truth in their message, which can be shown to be false by their valueless predictions being overturned. Such false prophets are active before the close of any dispensation (Mt. 24: 21). **18.** Political disruption has a spiritual cause.

Heb. may mean 'they wandered off to a land with which they were unfamiliar'.

19–22. When faced with death everywhere Jeremiah, like Abraham (Gen. 18: 22–33), Moses (Exod. 32: 11–13) and Samuel (1 Sam. 7: 5–9, cf. Ps. 99: 6), renews his supplication (cf. 15: 1). It is a model, acknowledging the sovereignty of God and man's sin and pleading God's name and power (19). **21. your glorious throne** could refer to the city and temple and heaven (cf. 7: 12; Ps. 11: 4; cf. Heb. 8: 1).

(*a*) **God's final word (15: 1–9).** Moses' successful intercession, like that of Samuel, rested on the willingness of the people to cooperate. That is now lacking. 'Let my people go' into the desert indicates that 'the disease (sin) can only be cured by the surgery of exile' (2–9). It takes up their dismissal by Pharaoh (Exod. 12: 31). To be unburied (3) is the greatest humiliation (cf. 34: 2–22). The extent of the calamity is shown by reference to the number of widows and to the mother of seven (normally a sign of prosperity and ensured succession, 1 Sam. 2: 5) having no survivors (9).

(*b*) **Jeremiah's lament and the Lord's rebuke (15: 10–21).** The conversation between the Lord and His servant (cf. 14: 1 ff.) is resumed. Jeremiah bemoans his life and lot under strong opposition (10). He was now a curse to those he would help. **11.** Heb. is difficult. RSV 'So let it be, O LORD' is interpretation of *MT 'āmar*, 'the LORD *said*'. **13–14.** These two verses are no insertion (cf. 17: 3–4) but essential here to show that the continued stubbornness of the people will be no match for the Babylonian's at that time strengthened with weapons including better iron (12, from Anatolia) and bronze than available to Judah. **15–21.** The Lord's comfort is assurance that though Jeremiah will be a prisoner he will be consulted by his captors (11–14); he must not despair, for he will get not vengeance (only ultimately) but restoration and recommissioning as God's spokesman (as Moses, Exod. 4: 16) and be a bulwark against sin. The Lord's initial promise to him (1: 18) will be fulfilled as he acts. That Jeremiah's prayer (15) is quoted (Ps. 69: 7) shows how well he had appropriated God's word (16; cf. Ezek. 3: 1–3; Rev. 10: 10). **18.** God is not a fickle little **brook**.

(c) **Jeremiah's life to be an enacted sign (16: 1–21).** The prophet is told to act contrary to popular custom and (i) not to marry (2–4) because death will strike every family in Jerusalem; (ii) not to take part in the funeral rites (5–7), including the customarily self-inflicted wounds, shaving the head and the offering of food and pouring of libations to mark continued association with, and respect for, **the dead** (7); (iii) not to participate in joyful occasions (8–9) for such would cease to exist. This interpretation is more likely than that which sees here specifically the covenant-signs taken by Christ to commemorate His death (Lk. 22: 19–21), or finds this merely a meal for the comfort of the mourner (2 Sam. 3: 35; 12: 17) for such were condemned (Dt. 26: 14). But the people who have hitherto failed to learn the lesson of their history would have to learn it through the hard school of exile. The message of hope always breaks through Jeremiah's gloom—here foreseeing a new exodus. The restoration will ultimately include Gentiles as well as Jews (14–15). This is no mere scribal interpolation from 23: 7–8 but is integral to the forward-looking message of the prophet in diverse circumstances. **21.** This verse continues the threat from vv. 9–12.

x. Sixth message: the outcome of sin (17: 1–27)

1–4. Judah's sin is indelible, like writing cut in hard stone with an iron stylus tipped with emery (cf. Job 19: 24). This reference to stone tablets and inscribed altars should remind them of the Law of God. Instead 'indelible sin, inevitable loss' is linked with the constant memory of idolatrous altars and *'ašerîm* (not AV 'groves', but wooden pillars symbolic of the goddess

Asherah) condemned by the spiritually minded (2 Kg. 21: 3, 7). **8. fear:** Heb. *yîrā*; AV see (*yir'e*) represents the Massoretic pointing. The law leads to (i) curse on those who disregard it—illustrated by withered tamarisk (EVV **bush**) which has no prospect of improvement (5–6); (ii) blessing on the one rooted in God—illustrated by the well-watered **tree** (7–8). Faith, or lack of it, is always shown by its fruit (5–8), as is the outcome of the heart and of the law (9–10). **9. The heart** of man **is deceitful** (the same root and meaning as Heb. Jacob) and incurable (so 15: 18; 30: 12; RV, NEB, 'desperately sick'). **11.** The illustration of **a partridge** (sand-grouse?) is used as this was thought to hatch the eggs of other birds (as said of the cuckoo). Unjustly acquired **riches** may disappear when counted on for security. Only God can deal with the heart (9–10). Rev. 2: 15 applies v. 10 to Christ in acknowledgment of His Deity. Trust in things, including riches (11) cannot meet man's basic need. A true view of the sovereign God will cause us to turn to Him for healing and salvation (13–14). Only this way is hope, for calamity awaits those who reject Him (13). **13. in the dust:** i.e. ephemeral, like writing which will disappear as opposed to the enduring character of that which is 'written in heaven' in the book of life (Isa. 4: 3; Mal. 3: 16). Jeremiah under persecution, questioning and mockery (15, 'If only it would happen' rather than **Let it now be fulfilled**) identifies himself with those who trust (14–18), though he too must face the outcome for those who do not (16–17). He does not ask for calamity to fall on his own people but for just retribution on those who mock.

17: 19–27. Part of the neglect of God has been caused by, and shown in, neglect of His day, the **Sabbath**, and the law which safeguards it. Jeremiah, standing where he can observe this and make an illustration of it to a ready audience (cf. 7: 2; 17: 19) declares this to be an example of breaking God's law, the punishment for which could yet be averted by true repentance. The majority of scholars take this passage as post-exilic because of the resemblance to the legalism of Neh. 13: 15–22. Nehemiah, Amos (8: 5) and Jesus Christ (Mk 2: 27) all stressed that the practice of sabbath law keeping ideally demonstrated a right attitude of heart. Ellison has shown that, since sabbath-keeping requires the self-denial of ceasing from ordinary business, Jeremiah, who constantly stresses spiritual religion and denounces formalism, is asking for that here and for no mere outward observance. **23.** LXX adds 'more than their fathers'.

xi. Seventh message: the potter and plotters at work (18: 1–23)

The figure of the Potter vividly underlines the omnipotence of God over men His creation (cf.

Isa. 29: 26; 45: 9; Rom.9: 21). But, like the NT parables, not every part must be pressed for its symbolism, for neither nations nor men are lifeless lumps of clay and life depends on the response men make to God's plan. The principles on which He works are stated and are important for the understanding of all prophecy. The accent here is on the failure to make the vessel (4, **marred**, Heb. 'disfigured'). It is God who moulds, breaks down (ch. 19) and rebuilds. His power is not exercised arbitrarily (11) and the possibility of renewal by God is conditional on a change of heart. Here the offer is met by sarcasm and rejection (12). Such conduct is unnatural and is as irrational as it is tragic (13–14), so the prediction of judgment must stand (15–17). **3. at the wheel:** Heb. 'the two stone-wheels', the lower being turned by the potter's feet or hand to spin the upper. **4. seemed best:** Heb. *yāšar*, 'is/was right'). **11. preparing:** the Heb. word is from the same root as 'potter'. Exile will remould the nation. **14.** Translation uncertain. The snows and streams of Lebanon are perennial yet the people forget the eternal God for 'empty' (vain, **worthless**) gods (15). **16.** These are expressions of horror and dismay at destruction when God turns His back (17, cf. 2: 27). **20. evil:** Heb. includes 'calamity' as v. 17, Isa. 45: 7.

Jeremiah has subtle opponents who either seek to entrap him with his own words (18, LXX 'let us heed his words') as some did with Jesus Christ (Mk 12: 13), or to ignore him (*MT* as NIV). He had spoken openly against priests, wise men and prophets (4: 9; 8: 8–9), yet they were confident that the old established order would remain (NEB 'there will still be priests to guide us'). They would use Jeremiah's words as a basis of a charge of treason against him for 'undermining the morale of the people'.

Jeremiah's cry for vengeance (19–23) has been thought by some commentators to be so uncharacteristic as to be the work of another. But though more passionate perhaps than other utterances (*e.g.* 11: 20; 17: 14–18) this is to be understood not so much as a call for any egotistical vendetta as pleading for the vindication of the divine law. Jeremiah has already been told not to pray for the people (14: 11; 15: 1) and they have since refused the offer of remaking by the Potter. He asks now for the curses imposed by the law on the sinner to be made effective (21–23; cf. Dt. 28: 15 ff.). **20. my life:** Heb. *napši*, 'myself'.

xii. Eighth message: the broken waterpot (19: 1–15)

The previous potter's lesson was for the prophet himself and emphasized the pliable nature of the situation and the possibility of remedy. This is a public statement of the irreparable and irremediable situation (10–11). The message demands faith from its deliverer who is to go (2, 4) before being told what to say. In the presence of witnesses representing people and priests Jeremiah goes to the south east of the city, to the dumps used for depositing broken potsherds as well as the scattered garbage and the bones of criminals. The site was also used for the constant burning of rubbish (*Tophet*) and for rituals to the god Molech and so had become a picture of Gehenna (hell). **3–9.** Many, following the LXX, think this summary of past oracles (cf. 7: 31–33) an insertion. However, the repetition here, perhaps taken from the so-called Memoirs of Baruch, gives added force to the parabolic warning of what God was 'about to bring' (Heb., 3: 15) on Jerusalem and Judah. For such symbolic actions cf. Isa. 20; Ezek. 4: 1 ff. etc.; Ac. 10: 21. **3. kings of Judah** may refer to the coregency of Jehoiachin with Jehoiakim *c.* 607–598 B.C. **7. will ruin** or 'tip out' (*baqqōtî*) is a dramatic play on words as the prophet emptied the bottle (*baqbuq*) before smashing it, as God would His holy city (12), once a 'noble vessel' to witness to Him (2 Tim. 2: 20). This clearly spoke of the forthcoming complete break-up of the family and community (9, cannibalism, against Dt. 28: 53). **10–13.** Jerusalem will burn like the pagan altar it has become—cf. slaughter, burning (12), and 'offering up' (13). **14–15.** The prophet ensures that the message is heard by all by repeating its substance at his usual open-air stand.

xiii. Persecution becomes a witness (20: 1–18)

Public witness produces an immediate reaction from Passhur the chief temple official responsible for order, who was also a priest (1) and a prophet (6). He is carefully distinguished by his family name *ben-Immer* from another of the same name in 21: 1; 38: 1. No public scourging or mockery in a cramped position on a scaffold (like the cross) to the north of the temple would make the prophet change his message (2); nor would release from persecution (3) do so. Jeremiah publicly identifies Passhur with the Babylonian calamity by renaming him 'Terror on every side' (cf. 6: 25), a play perhaps on *māgōr*, 'made an exile', or on Passhur as 'torn away' (?). Note the precise prophecy that Passhur would not be killed but exiled, that he would see his friends killed (4), that royal treasures would be taken (5), and that Babylon would be the destination—both facts mentioned for the first time. The absence of reference to temple vessels may point to the earlier captivity of 597 B.C., for by 594 B.C. Passhur seems to have lost office (29: 25). Passhur's action against God's messenger identifies him as a false prophet himself, a state proved by the subsequent fulfilment of the prophecy.

This is one of the most personally revealing

passages in prophetic literature. At his blackest hour, perhaps while still imprisoned in the stocks, Jeremiah complains vigorously that God has **deceived** him (7, 10, Heb. 'misled', 'seduced'). He was not a prophet of his own choice; at his call the Lord had 'overpowered' him and promised him both His authority and His words (1: 6–10). Now he was laughed at for his witness which had been largely one of warning of violence and destruction (8). 'People are amused but not convinced.' Nothing had happened quickly to prove him right. His inner urge was to continue, for a true prophet cannot contain God's message within himself (9). However, opposition, including that of friends he trusted, has turned his own words back against him (3, cf. 10). The return of confidence in vv. 11–13 may have been occasioned by his release or by the prospect of it. The LORD is a strong 'fear-inspiring **warrior**' so ultimate victory is assured. This term 'warrior' is used of the LORD in 14: 9 (cf. Ps. 24: 8; Isa. 42: 13). The upsurge of depression in vv. 14–18 can readily be understood in such circumstances and in so highly sensitive a person. The Bible is realistic in its description of the way God's people may encounter periods of distress and despair and even desire to die, like Job (3: 1 ff.) and Elijah (1 Kg. 19: 4). **16.** The overthrow of Sodom and Gomorrah was so well-known as to be a matter of common reference (23: 14; 49: 18; 50: 40; Dt. 29: 23; Isa. 13: 19, etc.).

xiv. Ninth message: the choice of life or death (21: 1–10)
Early in the last Babylonian siege (c. 589 B.C.) Zedekiah sends to Jeremiah hoping for word of a miraculous delivery (4) as had happened at the Exodus and again under Hezekiah in 701 B.C. In a prolonged siege such enquiries are to be expected and the incident in 37: 3–10 is not a doublet of this section but was occasioned by a temporary relaxation in the siege when Egyptian forces under Hophra advanced against the Babylonians (also called Chaldeans at this time after their dominant tribe, 4). It has been suggested that this chapter follows the preceding one because of the occurrence of the name Passhur, though here it refers to a different person (cf. 20: 1). Jeremiah's reply is factual, fearless and direct. It adds specific predictions to those previously given. God will not save but will fight against His own city and people (5–6, 10). Judah will be rendered so powerless that the enemy will easily get in (4). In the previous siege of 701 B.C. the Lord had used pestilence as a means to save them (2 Kg. 19: 35), now it would be used to decimate and devastate them. Nebuchadrezzar II (the W. Aramaic variant is Nebuchadnezzar) of Babylon is God's agent and to fight against him is to fight God (6–7).

The choice of the two ways—**life** and **death** —follows Dt. 30: 15, 19 (cf. 1 Kg. 18: 21) and is a challenging picture used also by Christ in Mt. 7: 13. **9.** These words encouraging defection were subsequently taken as the basis for the charge levied against Jeremiah. **escape with his life:** i.e. 'he shall take home his life, and nothing more' (NEB). The metaphor occurs again in 38: 2; 39: 18; 45: 5.

xv. Prophecies relating to kings and false prophets (21: 11–25: 38)
It is uncertain whether these prophecies are arranged in any chronological order.
(a) **A governor's duty (21: 11–14).** Even now the rulers are urged strictly to observe the law and justice which alone can divert doom and disaster which follows as the reward for evil (11–12). The exercise of law and order (yāšār – 'right') is a primary responsibility of any one in authority (2 Sam. 15: 4). Failure means that the whole land, hill and plain (13), will be ravaged. This declaration seems to be a synopsis of the message to all the kings to whom Jeremiah preached (13–14; cf. 1: 2–3). **12. every morning:** here possibly denoting the urgency. **13.** The rulers relied on their defences as they did on the impregnability of the Temple.
(b) **Zedekiah (22: 1–9).** The words of 21: 11–12 are now made personal to each of the last five kings of Judah. Here at the palace gate where right judgment should have been dispensed Jeremiah proclaims the royal duty of ensuring justice and social rightness. Righteousness alone 'exalts a nation' and maintains the proper dignity of king and people alike (4). Failure to carry it out at every level results in degradation and desolation (cf. 17: 25). Christ's message to Jerusalem was similar (Mt. 23: 28, 38).
Verses 1–9 are possibly addressed to Zedekiah (if so, not in chronological order; but cf. 23: 1–8). **5.** The Lord can only swear by Himself as originator of the covenant (Heb. 6: 13–18). Part of the royal palace was 'The House of the Forest of Lebanon' (1 Kg. 7: 2–5); **fine cedar beams** (7) might be here a metaphor for pillars of society.
(c) **Jehoahaz (22: 10–12).** Jehoahaz (**Shallum**) succeeded his father Josiah who died at Megiddo while vainly attempting to oppose the Egyptians in 609 B.C. He reigned for three months before being deported by Necho to Egypt where he died (2 Kg. 23: 31–34). The people are told not to **weep for the dead**, i.e. Josiah, whose death in battle is preferable to Shallum's. He was to be the first king of Judah to die in exile, but at this time (11), c. 602 B.C., was still alive.
(d) **Jehoiakim (22: 13–23).** Shallum's elder brother was a vassal of Necho, whose oppressive actions are contrasted with the just reign of

his father Josiah (2 Kg. 23: 34–37). To pay his dues and for purposes of self-aggrandisement he imposed forced labour-service (13) contrary to the law (Dt. 24: 14). Elaborate and ostentatious buildings attributed to him have been excavated at Ramat Rahel. But a fine palace never of itself made a good king. **Jehoiakim** was a fierce opponent of Jeremiah and of his teaching (ch. 36). Failure to express the knowledge of God in practical daily activities, i.e., true religion (16; cf. Jas 1: 27) would in his case also mean that proper religious rites would not be performed at his coming death (18–19; as also foretold in 8: 1). If vv. 20–23 refer to Jerusalem then the **shepherds** would be her rulers. It may however tell of those watching on the high points on Judah's boundaries to the north (**Lebanon**), north-east (**Bashan**) and south-east (**Abarim**, 20) and seeing in 601–597 B.C. the failure of their **allies** to stem the Babylonian advance and thus their subsequent deportation (22).

(*e*) **Jehoiachin (22: 24–30).** Jehoiachin, whose personal name was (Je)**coniah** (24: 1), an intimate possession of God and bearing his authority (**signet ring**; cf. Hag. 2: 23; *NBD* pp. 1154–5) succeeded his father Jehoiakim in December 598 B.C. After only three months he and his mother Nehushta were deported to Babylon (2 Kg. 24: 8–16) where he remained for thirty-seven years. His presence there is attested in Babylonian tablets dated 595–570 B.C. which list rations supplied to him (*Ja-ú-kîn* of *Ja-hu-du*) and his (seven) sons (**children**, 28; cf. 1 Chr. 3: 17). He never returned from Babylon though given a measure of freedom under Evil-Merodach (=Amēl-Marduk), Nebuchadrezzar's successor there (52: 31–34). He was therefore written off from the list of kings of Judah. **29.** When men will not listen to, or obey, God, the earth is called to witness (as in 6: 19).

(*f*) **Word to the leaders of the state (23: 1–8).** Though generally addressed to all rulers (**shepherds**, 22: 22) this passage may well also contain a specific message to Zedekiah (cf. 22: 1–9), whose name, 'The LORD is my righteousness/vindication' has a similarity with, but in his person not the same character as, the future Messiah-King (6, *Yhwh ṣidqēnū*—'**The LORD Our Righteousness**'). Here Jeremiah clearly looks beyond the immediate history to the time when the Ideal King—the True Shepherd—would reverse the actions which mark all false shepherds (2), **scattered . . . driven . . . away . . . not bestowed care on** (cf. 2: 8; 10: 21), and would **gather . . . bring . . . back . . .** and **tend them** and provide security and well-being for His people (3–4). Thus is foreshadowed the work of the good Chief Shepherd for His people (Jn 10: 1–18). Unlike the weakling Zedekiah, the puppet-king set up

by Nebuchadrezzar of Babylon, Jesus Christ is a real king ruling according to the divine choice and law who is Himself counted as our righteousness (1 C. 1: 30–31) and imparting righteousness (Eph. 2: 8) and the Spirit who alone enables men to live aright.

5–8. The messianic prophecy begins with 'Look, the time is coming' which sixteen times Jeremiah uses to introduce a message promising hope for the future. The **Branch** is a title of Messiah as the final King of the Davidic line (33: 15) who will be one with God Himself (Isa. 4: 2); a Man and a Servant (Zech. 3: 8; 6: 12). It describes the new growth springing from a cut down tree (Isa. 11: 1, 5). He will reunite the people (8) as Christ alone can by the blood of His new covenant which makes the ideal of Sinai a reality. Henceforth the LORD would be remembered more from His work as leading the new 'Exodus' (cf. Lk. 9: 31) which will eclipse the earlier one from Egypt. The restoration from exile in Babylon is little compared with that greater restoration from the exile of sin.

(*g*) **Word to the religious leaders (23: 9–40).** Jeremiah's complaint (9–10) is justly based on a right conception both of God's holiness and the false prophets' failure. The latter is explained as (i) a corruption of life with its consequent anarchy affecting the law and the land (9–15); (ii) a corruption of the word and message; when compared with the Lord's word this leads to (iii) inevitable judgment (16–22) for claiming falsely to be the bearer of God's word (23–40).

9–15. *lanneḇī'îm* can be translated **Concerning**, 'about' or 'against' **the prophets**, but may be a short title (cf. 48: 1, 49: 1). The complaint is endorsed by God who speaks to Jeremiah and all the people. The self-righteous prophets of Judah condemned Israel's prophets for their pagan Baal orgies which had been punished by the sack of Samaria. They appeared to be unaware that even in Jerusalem's temple (11) pagan rites were practised and idolatry (**adultery**, 14) condoned and illegal practices followed that rendered them already judged and prepared for the forthcoming sudden destruction such as had fallen on **Sodom** and **Gomorrah.**

16–40 is a crucial passage for understanding the nature of true and false prophecy. Outwardly little distinguishes them. But the false prophet (i) bends his message to what the people want to hear and makes no moral demands: with unfounded optimism he promises peace to those who despise God's Word and deliverance from divine wrath to those who insist on their own path and resist His revelation (17); (ii) uses conventional phrases claiming divine authority (21, 31, 34) but has no first-hand commission or experience of it (22,

30) and is without a manner of life which matches the message (22); (iii) the source of his inspiration was himself and not God (16, 21, 27, 32). The **heart** is Heb. *lēb*, 'mind' (17, 26). Note that dreams (25) are not of themselves condemned as a means of revelation and were so used by God (*e.g.* Gen. 37: 5 ff.; Dan. 2: 3 ff.). Self-originated ideas are condemned. The false prophet was absent from God's **council** (18, 22, the consultative assembly of 1 Kg. 22: 19 ff.) the word being used of intimate conversation and fellowship (Ps. 55: 14). Such prophets can be tested by results, lies make men **forget** God's **name** (27, character, fame) and men as a result of this act without **benefit** (32). Such men are uncommissioned (21–32) and must not be listened to, they are **godless** (11).

By contrast the true prophet is described: (i) he learns direct from God's intimate council (18); (ii) his message is faithfully delivered (28) and always causes men to turn from evil (22); (iii) he does not avoid the truth of the wrath of God on sin (19–22). God's word is always effective, being nourishing like wheat, purifying like fire and powerful like a heavy sledgehammer (so Heb. , 28). **30–32.** The omnipotent and omnipresent God (23–24) heeds the misuse and misrepresentation of His name and makes a threefold declaration, with reasons, why he is **against** the false prophets (30–32). His judgment on them (33–40) here rests on the double meaning of **oracle** (*massā*) which is both a solemn utterance and a literal burden, something lifted up (cf. v. 39), carried. The special 'solemn utterance' is reserved for the men to whom God trusts His message. Otherwise it 'will make nonsense of the words of the living God' (36, NEB). The misuse of the term 'oracle' has so lowered its currency that it is to be avoided.

(*h*) **The figs (24: 1–10).** After the capture of Jerusalem on 16 March 597 B.C. the leaders, including Jehoiachin and skilled professional and craftsmen, were taken to Babylon (1; cf. 2 Kg. 24: 10–17). Those who remained with Zedekiah, or had escaped to Egypt, must have adopted a superior attitude, considering themselves the 'good' and fortunate ones. Jeremiah argues that they had not been taken as they were so rotten (9) and, like good early ripe figs of June—a delicacy (cf. Isa. 28: 4) and harbinger of spring and the coming plenty—the 'good' were stated to be the exiles who would in time be replanted and revivify the land. This would happen when they were reborn in heart unity with God (32: 39) and truly repentant and thus prepared to keep the old covenant terms. These aimed at fellowship with God. Note the increasing emphasis on the new conditions which would soon be declared as the new covenant (31: 33; cf. Ezek. 36: 26–27). All this foresees

the good results of Jeremiah's teaching in the lives of the exiles (ch. 29). The wickedness of those remaining in Judah is also attested by Ezekiel (chs. 8–9; 22–23). This will bring upon them the further hurt in the judgment of the final siege of Jerusalem in 589–7 B.C. (9, cf. 43: 1–4) as Christ also foretold it would under the Romans (Mt. 23: 28). **1. the LORD showed me:** the secret of the true prophet (also of Am. 7: 1, 4, 7; 8: 1) contrasts sharply with the source of inspiration of the false prophets (23: 32). **3.** God tests us against the earlier object lessons He has given (cf. 1: 11–13). **8.** A Jewish colony is known in Egypt (Syene) before 525 B.C. which had a distorted form of Yahwehworship. These earlier colonies of Jewish refugees in Egypt were probably founded by those who left with Jehoahaz in 608 B.C. reinforced by others anticipating the Babylonian assaults after 605 B.C.

(*i*) **The end coming (25: 1–14).** The date of this important prophecy which foretells the seventy year captivity is given precisely. The twenty-third year of Jeremiah's ministry in which he was openly acknowledged as **the prophet** (2; cf. 1–5) coincided with the decisive battle of Carchemish in 605 B.C. when Nebuchadrezzar II defeated Necho II of Egypt (46: 2). Though still unheeded (4), the prophet's message is the same (5–7). The consequences of refusal to hear God's voice are now given as the failure of happiness, daily livelihood and inspiration (**light**, 8–10). All this will be brought about by the Babylonian invaders (the 'evil of the north') and by their vassal tribes led by Nebuchadrezzar **my servant**, used by the Lord as His agent of judgment (8, cf. 4: 5 ff.). Yet with the warning of judgment comes a note of hope in the limit of time set for captivity (11), though seventy years ensured that few if any of the exiles would return. The period ended *c.* 536 B.C. with the return of exiles following the decree of Cyrus ordering the return some time after his capture of Babylon in October 539 B.C.

This chapter further illustrates the way God speaks to His people. First, by the word through His spokesmen (1–7), corresponding to the revelation in the Bible and proclamation in preaching. Then through the contemporary history. Often thoughts of unfounded and fancied security for God's people (the church) are overthrown by the lesson of judgment. In the end the sin of the pagan instruments used at the time by God (12–14) must be judged according to God's own standards in His written revelation (15–38). **3. I have spoken . . . again and again:** this may account for the repetitive nature of some of Jeremiah's sayings. **7.** Idolatry is trusting in **what your hands have made** (cf. 14). **13.** The LXX inserts modified chs. 46–51 after the first part of this verse and makes v. 13b the superscription to the prophecies of the nations (i.e. omits v. 14; see INTRODUCTION).

(*j*) **The cup of wrath (25: 15–29).** This section introduces the prophecies against the named nations (25: 15–38). The scope of the Lord's fury embraces *all* nations beginning with Jerusalem and Judea and then 'the uttermost parts of the earth' (18–26; 28: 33). The intoxicating cup as a symbol of divine wrath is used by Jeremiah (13: 12 f.; 49: 12), Isaiah (51: 17, 22), Zechariah (12: 2) and the Psalmist (75: 8) and has been compared with ancient trials by ordeal (cf. Num. 5: 19–27; Isa. 51: 17). All the places and peoples mentioned (omitting Damascus, 49: 23 f.) are the subject of special prophecies in chs. 46–51. After Judah the list groups places affected by direct Babylonian campaigns (*e.g.* Egypt in 601 B.C. and Dedan, Tema and Buz in Central Arabia—all mentioned in contemporary inscriptions). **The people left at Ashdod** are so noted (20) because the city had been sacked by Psammetichus I of Egypt a decade earlier. For all, the coming judgment is inevitable (27–29). **15.** Wine and drunkenness are often used as a picture of staggering under judgment. **20–26. all the kings of . . . :** this repeated phrase has caused some commentators to reject these verses as late, but such phrases occur in contemporary historical texts. **26. Sheshach** (*MT šešak*) is generally taken to be an *Atbash* cryptogram in Heb. for Babel (using A = Z, B = Y etc.); it may equally be an older name for Babylon itself.

(*k*) **Universal destruction (25: 30–38).** In separate poetic passages which reiterate the warnings (30–32) and describe the inescapable horrors of the destruction to come (34–38) Jeremiah boldly stresses both the indictment of the LORD, the Judge of all the earth, against all nations and individuals for their wickedness (31) and the fierceness of the divine anger (37–38). The noise of all this is likened to the battle-cries of warriors mixed with the shouts of men treading out blood-red grapes (cf. Isa. 63: 1). The bodies of the victims will be spread over the ground like manure (33). The leaders **(shepherds)** will be **like** sacrificial rams (Heb. *keʼēlē*), which is better in context perhaps than **like fine pottery** (*MT, kikeʼlī*). All this is 'because of the devouring (all consuming) **sword** and **fierce anger of the LORD'** (37, 38).

xvi. The outcome of the temple-city (26: 1–28: 1).

(*a*) **The personal consequences of the temple sermon (26: 1–19).** Jeremiah's statements, given in full in 7: 1–8: 3, are repeated here in summary form (cf. 25: 4–7). Persecution was inevitable because he did not retract a word the Lord had told him to say. The comparison with the lowly ill-fated shrine at Shiloh in Ephraim was not flattering. The

threat against the temple was prejudged by the religious leaders before their civil counterparts (11) as blasphemy and so worthy of death. A similar charge was brought against other prophets and against Jesus Christ (cf. Exod. 22: 28; Mt. 26: 60). Rescued from lynching by the mob (9), like Stephen (Ac. 6: 13), Jeremiah is given a fair trial at the court convened at the New Gate—either that built by Jotham (10; cf. 2 Kg. 15: 26–35) or another name for the Benjamin Gate (cf. 17: 19). He uses the opportunity of defence before witnesses to reaffirm his God-given unchanged message and to challenge the people to ensure that justice is done (12–15). If innocent blood were shed this would be a further call for divine requital (cf. Mic. 3: 12). Some high officials at least recognized this, quoting the precedent of Micah (3: 2) whose message accorded with that of Jeremiah and yet had brought repentance and reform under Hezekiah and had averted judgment (18). It is of additional interest that this shows that for a century Micah must have been openly accepted as a prophet and his words kept. Like Jesus Christ before Pilate (Lk. 23: 22), nothing worthy of death is found in Jeremiah.

13. relent expresses the divine change of activity worded in such a way as to bring the action within man's comprehension and experience. **19.** For Hezekiah's reform see 2 Kg. 18: 4; 2 Chr. 29–31.

(*b*) **The case of Uriah (26: 20–24).** Perhaps to contrast the prophet Jeremiah who stood his ground with one who fled, Baruch recalls the otherwise unknown **Uriah** whose outspoken words had resulted in his death. This makes it clear that there were other faithful prophets whose words and works are not included in the selection of Scripture, despite his being the only recorded case of a prophet being executed (cf. Heb. 11: 37). Tur-Sinai has tried to identify Uriah with the unnamed prophet mentioned in a Lachish letter.

Jehoiakim as a vassal of Egypt would have had extradition rights. Jeremiah's freedom (24) only temporarily averted danger. This may have been because he was placed under the protection of Ahikam ben-Shaphan who had himself been involved in the Josianic reform (2 Kg. 22: 12–14) and was the father of the pro-Babylonian Gedaliah (39: 14; 40: 5). **22. Elnathan:** possibly father-in-law of Jehoiachin (2 Kg. 24: 8). **23.** Uriah's deportation from Egypt contrasts with Jeremiah's later importation there.

(*c*) **Plotting rebellion (27: 1–11).** Chapters 27–29 (with many variants in LXX) enlarge on ch. 23 and relate to the days of Zedekiah (i.e. after 597 B.C.). Certain literary characteristics have been noted: *e.g.* Nebuchadrezzar for Nebuchadrezzar (except 29: 21) and the addition of *the prophet* after Jeremiah's name, perhaps as opposed to the many false prophets. Here he aims to show that to plot against the powerful Babylonian would be of no avail. On this he addresses the ambassadors of Judah's five nearest neighbours then visiting Zedekiah's court (1–11), king **Zedekiah** himself (12–15), the **priests** (16–22), the **prophets** (28: 1–16) and the Jews in exile (29: 1–32).

According to the Babylonian Chronicle for 595 B.C. Nebuchadrezzar remained in Babylon owing to the outbreak of a local revolt, though eventually the leaders were caught and executed. In Egypt Necho II had died in 594 B.C. and been succeeded by Psammetichus II, who was himself engaged in a war in Ethiopia. Thoughts of an anti-Babylonian coalition, similar to that formerly centred on Hezekiah against Assyria, may have drawn Edom, Moab, Ammon, Tyre and Sidon to meet Zedekiah in the following year. Jeremiah takes the opportunity by demonstration, wearing a typical slave's yoke as imposed by Babylonians, and by addressing the envoys to warn them against any such plan. He argues not on the basis of political expediency but on the sovereign word and power of Israel's unique God who has already planned to give their **countries** (6, LXX 'the earth') into Babylonian hands. The details are given in the individual prophecies of chs. 47–49. Observe how throughout Nebuchadrezzar is under God's control (6, **my servant**; cf. 25: 9), despite his seeming immediate power—but his own time of punishment will come (6–7). The pagan **prophets**, *diviners*, dream-interpreters, astrologers and **sorcerers** (whose contemporaries in Babylonia are well attested in many documents; cf. 29: 8) have consulted their local deities but are not to be trusted. This is consistent with the OT attitude that they produce 'lies'. Such methods are forbidden by the law and are distortions of the true means of knowing God's will. **1.** 'Jehoiakim' (AV) does not fit the context, so it seems, in view of 28: 1 and other Heb. MSS, Syr. and Aquila versions here, that **Zedekiah** should be read (as NIV).

(*d*) **A word to Zedekiah (27: 12–15).** The message to the king is similar, but it must have taken courage to urge Judah's continued subordination to Babylon in face of the royal policy of the time and of the more popular line taken by the many false-prophets. Once again the latter are marked by their lack of divine commission, by reaction like the pagans to the prevailing situation, by encouragement of resistance to the divinely ordered phases of history and by their results. They will be involved in the very doom their lies sought to evade.

(*e*) **A word to priests and people (27: 16–22).** A prevalent saying of these same false prophets was that the sacred temple **vessels** taken off with Jehoiachin (Jeconiah) to **Babylon** in 597 B.C. would soon be returned and so signify the speedy restoration of the exiles and of the temple. This is shown to be another lie. Reinforcing his previous message, Jeremiah declares that concern should be with the immediate facts, that a revolt would cause a further Babylonian invasion and the removal of the remaining temple furniture. The larger and less mobile objects had been left there when the smaller vessels had been looted in the first attack. All the temple treasures were indeed removed in 587 B.C. (22; 52: 27; cf. 2 Kg. 25: 13–17), but ultimately restored as foretold (Ezr. 1: 7–8). This specific prophecy is coupled with yet another word of hope in eventual restoration (19–23). **18–19** are not contradictory or ironical, because repentance might yet avert divine wrath. Note how a true prophet like Jeremiah was prepared to face the verdict of history.

(*f*) **Challenge to a false prophet (28: 1–17).** This chapter in Heb. (*MT*) is much fuller than in the Gk. (LXX) translation. It affords a rare insight into a contest between a true and an (otherwise unknown) false prophet, both affirming that they speak in the same LORD's name. Hananiah of Gibeon (5 miles NW of Jerusalem) stakes his reputation on a certain return of Jehoiachin, the exiles and Temple treasures within **two years** (1–4). Jeremiah's reply worded 'Certainly, would that God would do so' (6) reveals his personal desire yet at the same time his doubt, and is followed by reference to previous true prophets whose word of doom had been shown true in the subsequent event (7–9; cf. 26: 18). Hananiah, like Jeremiah, used visual aids to reinforce his own message (10; 27: 2). He probably broke the wooden yoke off Jeremiah's neck roughly, though perhaps formally in the manner used of releasing slaves publicly. Jeremiah realized that the Lord had told him to wear it as a symbol of the diametrically opposed truth—bondage, not release (10–11). That he did not reply immediately need not denote a faltering faith. He would realize that the mass of people (5) believe what they want to hear and that now was no time to speak and cause an unnecessary rebuff or hardening of the heart against God's word. The true prophet may find himself in a minority of one (but with God on his side; cf. 1 Kg. 22). He may also have felt the need to wait for specific reassurance from the Lord in face of the other's claim to be speaking for the same Master (cf. 12–13). So, probably wearing new **iron** yoke-bars to indicate the fierce oppression to be expected in exile, he directly accuses Hananiah of being a false prophet. His accusation is that Hananiah was not sent by God, did not declare the truth but a lie, and was a rebel against the Lord (15–16, and so subject to the punishment foretold for divine law-breakers). Moreover this would be demonstrated by Hananiah's death two months later in the same year (594 B.C.). All would immediately see the proof of the truth and effectiveness of God's word (17), as in the sudden death of Pelatiah (Ezek. 11: 13) and Ananias and Sapphira (Ac. 5: 1–11). Hananiah 'was conscientious, but his conscience was not fully illumined. He thought too much of Israel's privilege and too little of Israel's responsibility. He did not take all the facts into account: he was deceived by his own heart.'

xvii. A letter to the exiles (29: 1–32). This chapter deals with the situation in Babylon at the time Hananiah was the spokesmen for the false prophets (ch. 28). Jeremiah takes the opportunity of a diplomatic mission to Babylon sent by the vassal king Zedekiah of Judah to his overlord Nebuchadrezzar to send letters to the exiles by the hands of two of his friends Elasah, brother of Ahikam (cf. 26: 24), and Gemariah (cf. 36: 10). His letter directs the exiles to settle down (3–7) and pay no attention to any of their local false prophets who followed the Hananiah doctrine in saying that the captivity would be of short duration (8–9). The addressees are those leaders, civil and spiritual, and all who had accompanied Jehoiachin into exile (1; cf. 2 Kg. 24: 17–20). With good common sense he argues that they must adjust themselves to the circumstances in which God has placed them. Babylon is a picture of the world in which we live. He does not call for any compromise in any matter of religious faith but does insist on right relationships within the family and community. We must pray for the welfare (wholesomeness in every aspect, physical, moral and spiritual) of the state with which our own well-being is inextricably linked (7; cf. Gen. 18: 23–33; Mt. 5: 13–16). He stresses that such a life is part of the Lord's good plan for His own and that it is only for a limited time (10–11). The seventy years must be well spent in turning back to God's unfailing mercy (the time implies a continuing educational programme for this throughout the generation). When they are restored to God He can restore them to their promised inheritance (10–14). Because we 'have here no continuing city' does not mean that God may not call us to continue to live in the city.

Jeremiah taught this also to combat the view that only in Jerusalem could the LORD be truly worshipped. He is as accessible in Babylonia as in Judah. **15–19.** This paragraph is addressed to those about to follow into exile and takes up again the idea that those not yet in exile would be punished. Jeremiah is in effect reminding them (and probably also those already in exile) of the parable of the good and bad figs (17; cf. 24: 8). **20–23.** The words of false prophets may

often be accompanied by evil living which the omniscient God observes (23, 'I am the knowing One'). Their false message and activities will bring them into conflict with the authorities. Their execution will only bring additional hardship on all God's people. Their proclamation of the hope of restoration is not only false in substance but also in the timing it gives. It also assumes the wrong basis for its fulfilment. Many argue like this today.

24–28. A letter from Shemaiah, one of these false prophets in exile, quotes in reply from one of Jeremiah's own letters (28; cf. v. 5). The effect of this letter reaching the senior priest in Jerusalem from a recognized 'prophet' in Babylonia (31) is further action against Jeremiah (24–29). His spirited reply (30–32) is a prediction that Shemaiah and all his family will perish (the direct curse formula), as had Hananiah, before the Lord brings about the return of His people. This would be another signpost that God was vindicating His word. **8. the dreams you encourage them to have:** i.e. you tell them what they want to hear (cf. Isa. 30: 9–11). **16–20.** These verses are omitted by LXX, but the repetition here (cf. 24: 1–10) may be to counter the continuing arguments of the false prophets in Babylonia as in Jerusalem. **22. Zedekiah and Ahab:** Nothing further is known of these two. For the use of fire as a punishment see Dan. 3: 20.

xviii. Messages of hope and blessing (30: 1–31: 40).
Chapters 30–33 contrast with the rest of this book. They also appear to interrupt the material taken to be Baruch's biography of Jeremiah. Yet the theme of the promise of restoration from captivity forms a genuine sequel to chs. 25–29 which concern the duration of it. The so-called 'Book of Consolation' (chs. 30–31) reiterates ideas already introduced, e.g. **return** (3: 6–18) and the salvation of the Lord. The words concern all the people of Israel (**Jacob**). Note also **Ephraim** (31: 18–22). The messages have thus been variously dated early, when Josiah was moving in the north against Assyria (c. 619–612 B.C.), to the dark days of Zedekiah before the final collapse of Judah, or to an even later time (usually by those who make comparisons with Isa. 40 ff. which they assume to be post-exilic). The whole is unquestionably Jeremianic. In any event the change of note is from primarily one of necessary judgment to one of hope following expiation through the suffering of exile.

(*a*) **Restoration foretold (30: 1–11).** Restoration follows disciplining. It means rest, peace (10), God's unbroken presence (11) and full **health** (17). That it is also freedom from slavery is demonstrated by the breaking of the Babylonian yoke from off the exiles. The Lord alone can do by right (8–9) what Hananiah sought to do by force (28: 10–11). The super-scription of the new writing (1–3)—writing implies a witness to a certain fulfilment (36: 2) —summarizes the whole hope. God will re-store all His people to all their possessions according to all His promise. He sympathizes with the suffering being endured by His own, which is, however, limited in measure (4–8). This hurt of judgment (**a time of trouble for Jacob**, 7) is part of the just and predicted punishment incurred by disobedience, with-drawing from God and failure to serve Him and thus maintain His peace (10–11). History had shown this in the case of Jacob (Israel). Suffering, as often, is illustrated by childbirth (8). Its aim is to teach obedience (cf. Heb. 5: 8) and to lead to salvation. Note alongside this the promise of the ideal kingship to come (9; cf. 23: 5; Hos. 3: 5; Ezek. 34: 23; 37: 24 f.). This was partially fulfilled in Zerubbabel leading the return and more fully in Christ (Heb. 1: 8). **10–11.** These verses are omitted here by LXX and recur in 46: 27–28.

(*b*) **Restoration of the wounded (30: 12–17).** The reason for, and result of, the punishment (exile) described in v. 11 are now clearly stated. The Lord uses a **cruel** enemy (14) as His agent of wrath against sin which is incurable (12–15). Sin always results in injury and distance between a man and his fellows (14–17). The situation is hopeless apart from the gracious act and promise of God (17). The latter includes the punishment of those who hurt His people (16, 20). In the NT this is viewed as the faithless (14, **allies** and neighbours of Judah) being brought into captivity to Christ by conversion (cf. Am. 9: 12 as quoted in Ac. 15: 17). Note here the assurance of physical and spiritual healing, an idea to be taken up later (cf. 8: 22; Jl 2: 25).

(*c*) **Restoration for Jerusalem (30: 18–34).** This passage is similar in theme to Isa. 35. The divine restoration will be physical (17), territorial (18), economical (18–20), govern-mental (21) and spiritual (22). All this will fulfil the covenant promise (22; cf. Gen. 17: 7; Exod. 6: 7; Lev. 26: 11–13; Dt. 7: 3; 2 Sam. 7: 24). The new city state will surpass the nation's splendour at its zenith under David and Solo-mon. The prince and ruler will be one of their own flesh and blood and at the same time a priest (21; cf. Ps. 110; Heb. 7: 17–21). Verses 23–24 (cf. 23: 19–20) are a reminder that one cannot just eliminate the idea of judgment for those who do not return (note emphasis on **turn back**) in a euphoric hopeful future. The time of the promise is yet to be.

(*d*) **Restoration through the New Covenant (31: 1–40).** The whole of this magnificent chap-ter throbs with the great hope of the restoration of all God's people. **1–6.** The covenant, sum-marized in 30: 22 and outlined in 31: 31–34, is

shown to include **all the clans of Israel** (1). This is the response to the royal proclamation of 3: 12; Israel will be prominent among the returnees. The captivity of Israel and the de-portations from Samaria will be looked on as past (exile) and as another **wilderness** experi-ence (cf. Hos. 2: 14–16; 11: 4). The curse will be removed and the land will be fruitful as originally (contrast Dt. 28: 30, 39) and individ-uals will enjoy the results of their labour. The schism between Israel (**Ephraim**) and Judah (possibly also a reference to Samaritans and Jews, 5–6) will be healed. The former will come to Jerusalem to unite in worship at the Jerusalem temple. Some members of the northern kingdom may well have returned with the party from Babylon; others had stayed in the land (Ezr. 6: 21). There is no warrant for interpreting this restoration only of the diaspora descendants of Israel. A final and fuller fulfilment in the new Jerusalem (and thus in the church) is foreshadowed.

The **new covenant**, like the old, is based on divine **favor** (2) and **love** (3) as detailed in verses 31–34. It will enable those unable to make progress by their own efforts to do so by divine enabling (8). The way home is described as continuing repentance (9). The restored nation will be cared for by the good Shepherd (10; cf. Isa. 40: 11), and abundant supplies will be available for the sacrifices (14). This loving-kindness of God will be witnessed by the remotest nations (10–14) as they see how the same God who scattered is now their gath-erer, redeemer and ransomer (11). **2–3.** Heb. is obscure; cf. RV which complains that God's love was confined to the distant past ('of old'). The answer is that it is **everlasting** (3). Or read **from afar** (NIVmg), i.e. heaven.

Rachel, the mother of Benjamin and Joseph (and so Ephraim) is depicted as bewailing her sons and the attempt to destroy the promised line (15). But she is now comforted by the promise of their return (16–22). Ramah (15) is either the site 5 miles N of Jerusalem near Anathoth (Jn 18: 25) or the place of similar name near Bethlehem associated with Herod's slaughter of children in his attempt to kill the promised Messiah (Mt. 2: 17–18). It was at Ramah that the exiles were gathered prior to deportation (40: 1). God will wipe away all tears (Rev. 7: 17). The mention of Rachel intro-duces the thought of **Virgin Israel** (21) as still God's loved bride (3) who pleads to be taken back (18). Verse 22 has been subject to much discussion: **a woman will surround a man** (Heb. 'shall compass, go round about') perhaps means 'woos' rather than that a paradise situ-ation is envisaged where a female (*neqēbāh*) can protect any virile male (*geber*). A traditional Christian interpretation is that a woman's womb shall (miraculously) bear a son: this would foretell the incarnation of Christ (cf. Gen. 3: 15; Isa. 7: 14; Mt. 1: 23).

23–30. The prophecy of vv. 21–25 was revealed in a dream (26; cf. Zech. 4: 1). The Lord's blessing will be on those He restores for they will be just, holy, diligent and satisfied (23–25). On their return the loss will be made up by rapid increase (27–28). **27–28.** These vv. are reminiscent of Jeremiah's call, for the LORD is still watchful (*šōqēd*) over His word to carry it out (1: 11, 12). **28–30.** The emphasis in the new state will be on individual responsibility. **29.** This was probably a well known proverb expressing a fatalistic scepticism (cf. Ezek. 18: 2).

31: 31–37. The idea of a **new covenant** is first stated as such here. It will unite divided people (31)—just as it does OT and NT. The law will be seen as grace. The compulsion of the law will be replaced by the willing consent of the heart (mind, 33), for the new covenant is one of the Spirit rather than the letter (2 C. 3: 6). The effect will be a realization of the unchanged ideal and plan of a close relationship between the LORD and His people (33). To **know the LORD** (*yāda*') implies the close binding union through the covenant (Exod. 6: 7; 7: 5, 17; Dt. 7: 9). An individual, without human mediation, will know God personally through His removal of the sin-barrier that has separated them from Him (34): thus the New Testament (=New Covenant) which was brought into effect through the atonement of Jesus Christ. This passage is quoted in Heb. 8: 6–13; 10: 14–18 and applied to the church. The security of the covenant is the faithfulness of the Creator, whose mercies never fail (35–37; cf. 33: 19–22). This is a classic passage for understanding the Lord's unchanging nature as the God of order (hosts) in heaven and earth. This is basic to His being as God of law and love. His covenant and His love are consistent.

31: 38–40. The points mentioned identify the extent of the future restored city of Nehemiah and of the eternal city of God, the New Jerusalem (Rev. 21: 9 ff.). It is measured to the north (NE—**Hananel**, NW—**Corner Gate**), possibly to the east and west (**Gareb** and **Goah** are unknown) and to the south. The **valley** of Hinnom (40; cf. 7: 31) was to the south where rubbish and the ashes of pagan sacrifices were dumped.

xix. Prophecies in Zedekiah's day (32: 1–34: 22)

(a) Faith demonstrated in adversity (32: 1–44)

(i) The purchase (1–15). This chapter is dated to 588/7 B.C., Zedekiah's tenth year, when the siege of Jerusalem had already lasted one year (1; cf. 39: 1) and was about to end in disaster (2 Kg. 25: 1–3). Jeremiah was arrested when trying to go through the ring of enemy posts which hemmed in the city (24; cf. 37: 11–14). His principal adversary was the king who charged him with his apparent defection to the enemy, his outspoken belief in an imminent Babylonian victory and with urging the uselessness of resistance and predicting the downfall of the monarchy (3–5). Prisoners were held in a temporary guarded camp set up in the palace garden (cf. Neh. 3: 25). Before attempts were made to silence him, the prophet takes the opportunity of a visit from a relative to show his faith in the future restoration of the land. Divine guidance came to him through the revealed word confirmed by the event. This urged him to faith in his Lord as the One who will restore His people from exile to their own rightful possessions (6–8)—the theme of chs. 32–33. **Anathoth** (7) was already in enemy hands and so no member of the family or anyone else would readily purchase the property. It was offered to Jeremiah to keep it within the family (Lev. 25: 25–28). Following the full and customary legal procedures (9–12) he pays the full and fair price, publicly weighing the silver according to the normal method of payment between strangers (cf. Gen. 23: 16). Also in the conventional way he takes measures to preserve the title deeds for future verification (13–15). Whether the documents were written on papyrus (as is most likely because the witnesses wrote (12)), or were on a clay tablet sealed within its own envelope on which was written a duplicate 'open' text as LXX on v. 11 may well indicate, the object is clearly to prepare a long term witness which would survive the exile and be available for regaining title to a reoccupied land. This widespread practice is attested frequently in documents and storage jars recovered by archaeologists. A similar story is told of Rome in 211 B.C. when Hannibal's camp-site outside the beleaguered city was readily bought as a mark of faith in a coming independence (Livy xxvi. 11; Florus ii. 6). Lest the interpretation be not clear Jeremiah makes a statement of his intention on the authority of God. Note the increasing use made of the title LORD Almighty (15, 18; cf. 21: 35). The record is made by **Baruch** (12) who is mentioned here for the first time. He was to play an important part in preserving Jeremiah's precise words (cf. 36: 4).

(ii) The prophet prays and God answers (32: 16–44). Aghast at what he has done Jeremiah prays for reassurance (16–25). He bases himself on the nature of God, omnipotent (17) and omniscient (19) as He has already shown in history. God has intervened in the past despite the people's repeated failure to trust him (20–24). **Nothing is too hard** (i.e. exceptional as well as difficult) for God to do (17, 27; cf. Gen. 18: 14). When the prophet looked for a creative, and therefore effective (Ps. 33: 9; 148: 5), word

from God in his immediate situation, all he
receives is a command to act in faith as if
the land of Judah, now being punished, had a
glorious future. This is faith (cf. Heb. 11: 6).
Many commentators argue that vv. 17b–23 are
a liturgical addition reminiscent of Dt., yet they
are the essential background to the question
implied in v. 25.

God's answer (26–44) opens with a reference
to Jeremiah's own prayer (27; cf. 17, 24) assuring him that he had been heard. God, not the
Babylonian, is the supreme Lord of history
(17); He is acting in power, not in weakness,
in rewarding the city with **fire** (29), **sword,
famine** and **plague** (36; cf. 14: 12; these with
the Flood are typical of divine judgment). Judgment will fall on all sinners. Persistent refusal
through life from youth (30) to heed the frequent calls to repentance (33), coupled with
open pagan practices (28; cf. 19: 13) can have
only one result—divine wrath (30–32, 37). All
this is God at work, 'plucking up and pulling
down' (1: 10).

Yet how wonderfully God's mercy is shown
to work through judgment (Rom. 11: 32–36).
Both are God's work. In His answer (36–44)
the Lord emphasizes rebuilding and replanting
(41). Judgment is a necessary prelude to restoration (42) when He will work unity between
God and His people and among themselves
singleness of heart to **fear** His name (Ps. 86:
11) and give the power to love accordingly (39,
singleness of heart and action). Thus hope
is founded on the new covenant. **38. they will
be my people, and I will be their God**: a
summary of the covenant (cf. 31: 22) in which
He will bring them back. The object of such
restoration work includes security (37), revital-
ized personal relationships (38), the preservation of God's people through their dependence on Him (38–40) and the full outworking
of His good for theirs (41). Note the strongly
worded promises (thirteen times **I will**) and
the **assuredly** and **with all my heart and soul**
(41, only here of God). Yet another result will
be restored economic prosperity when Jeremiah's deed purchasing the family property,
now seeming such a loss, will be shown publicly to be a certain gain.

(b) **God the restorer of fortunes (33: 1–
26).** The changing moods of hope (1–13) and
seeming despair (14–26) have led many commentators to reject vv. 14–26, which is not in
the Gk. translations, as absent from the original. However, they realistically accord with
the situation. Sin, punishment, cleansing and
restoration (1–9) are followed by joy, praise to
God and peace (10–13) and, as in ch. 23, all
these blessings stem from the promised Messiah of David's line who is **Our righteousness**
(14–16). When He comes kingship and priesthood will be enduringly united (17–22). The

promises God made cannot be thwarted by any
dire events the nation may undergo (23–26).
The subdivisions followed here are those often
given in the prophets (**This is what the LORD
says**).

(i) **The restoration of the people (33: 1–9).**
Jeremiah is reassured of the LORD's sovereign
power as the One who **made the earth** 'and
fashioned it firmly' (2, LXX; cf. *MT* 'who does
it'). He had only to ask to receive (3; cf. Mt.
7: 7). Prayer is linked with the revelation of
unsearchable things (*MT* $b^e s ̣ u r o t ̄$; rather than
RSV 'hidden', $n^e s ̣ u r o t ̄$). The question in the
prophet's mind is how can God restore the
prosperity of Judah after all that has happened?
The answer given is: (i) Rebuilding can only
follow the destruction of sin (4–6). The Babylonians are the instrument for the latter. Yet
there certainly will be both rebuilding and an
end of sin. All calamity is remedial in intent.
(ii) God **will heal** (6; cf. 8: 23) and **cleanse** the
sin (8; cf. 31: 34). Jerusalem will then be a true
witness to God's power and provision again
(9).

(ii) **The restoration of the land (33: 10–13).**
The fall of Jerusalem and the blessings of the
New Covenant are both assured here (10). The
contrast between the soon present reality and
the coming restoration is vivid; goodness
(=prosperity also) and joy instead of gloom
and sorrow, homelife instead of exile, and
worship in the temple (Ps. 106: 1; Ezr. 3: 11)
instead of crying in a pagan wilderness. The
material prosperity will be seen in fertile Judah
again (12–14 also presupposes 32: 44 and the
vindication of Jeremiah's purchase-deed).

(iii) **The restoration of the king (33: 14–26).**
Jeremiah has already foretold the renewal of
the royal line in which a king will rule justly
and here he repeats 23: 5. The Messiah bears
the royal name and title—the righteous new
'Shoot' (**Branch**) who will bring peace and
security—and gives His name to His city and
people. *Yhwh-ṣidqēnū* here foreshadows the
identity of the redeemed Church and individuals with Christ 'who is made unto us
righteousness' (1 C. 1: 30; 2 C. 5: 21). The
participants in the covenant must display the
same character (holiness and righteousness) as
their Master. The security of the promise is
illustrated by reference to earlier unbroken
covenants: (i) Davidic (17; cf. 2 Sam. 23: 5); (ii)
the priesthood (18); (iii) day and night (the
divinely instituted 'natural law' as promised to
Noah in Gen. 8: 22; cf. v. 20). Christ, like
Melchizedek, unites the offices of king and
priest (Heb. 7: 1, 17–25) and ideally believers
must reflect this (cf. Rev. 1: 6). His sacrifice
completed everything foreshadowed by the Levitical priests. Ideally church and state work
together (note king and priest, 21). **22–26.** The
Davidic covenant is here worded to show it

continues from the earlier one made with Abraham (cf. Gen. 15: 5; 22: 17). This is used as an answer to those who argue that God has abandoned both Israel and Judah.

(c) **A last word to Zedekiah (34: 1–7).** The attack by the Babylonians and their allies on Judah began successfully in late 589 B.C., following Zedekiah's rebellion. The outlying towns and villages (including Anathoth) were quickly overrun. **Lachish and Azekah** (7, modern Tell ed-Duweir and Tell ez-Zakarīyah, c. 30 and 15 miles SW of Jerusalem respectively) are mentioned in the contemporary Lachish Letters (*e.g.* No. IV) as apprehensive of the coming attack and in communication with each other by fire signals. However, Nebuchadrezzar did not yet advance further south, perhaps because of help to Jerusalem promised by Hophra of Egypt. It may well have been in a temporary lull in the siege caused by this threat to the Babylonian invaders that Zedekiah received Jeremiah's message concerning the fate of both the capital and of himself (1–7). The wording of his personal encounter with Nebuchadrezzar (3, 'your eyes shall behold the eyes of the king of Babylon') might have been taken later to be a prediction of his own blindness (39: 5–7). If he had ceased resistance as now advised this might have been avoided. There is no need to emend vv. 4–5 to read 'obey the voice of God so **you will not die by the sword**' (as some do since LXX omits v. 4b; cf. 38: 17). Zedekiah's death (5) is nowhere detailed, but the burial with full military honours accords with 2 Chr. 16: 14.

(d) **A broken covenant (34: 8–22).** The temporary slackening of the siege (21–22) would raise false hopes of successful help from Egypt. It may have induced the men of Jerusalem to go back on a **covenant** solemnly sworn in the temple (15, 18; cf. Exod. 20: 17) to keep to the Hebrew law enacted at the time of the Exodus (Exod. 21: 2; Dt. 15: 12) to ensure the freedom of the individual forced to place himself under a master to pay off a debt. It is a typical human reaction to danger to show sudden zeal to keep a neglected law of God (here, Exod. 21: 2; Dt. 15: 12). Their purpose might have been to increase manpower for defence or to allay the possibility of defection to the enemy. Hebrew slaves should have been granted liberty (8, *derôr* denotes a release from slavery and debt by royal proclamation, cf. Babyl. *andurārum*) after six years, i.e. every seventh year (13–14).

The coming captivity will be God's judgment on those who take away **freedom** from their fellows (i.e. thus break God's law). God will grant **'freedom'** to the 'natural forces' of punishment to deprive the transgressors of the **'freedom'** of life (17). **18–20.** The party to a **covenant** was made to **walk between its pieces** of the animal sacrificed in its ratification

(Gen. 15: 9–11, 17 as also Babyl. texts from Mari). At the same time they invoked on themselves a similar fate if they failed to keep the stipulated conditions. **20–22.** To lie unburied was an ignominious fate for any Semite (cf. 15: 3).

xx. Prophecies in Jehoiakim's reign (35: 1–36: 32)

This begins another cycle of prophecies (to ch. 44; see INTRODUCTION). Chronologically these events follow ch. 26.

(a) **The Recabites (35: 1–19).** In contrast with a vow not kept (ch. 34), the story of one loyally maintained in adversity and therefore commended is given in this chapter. Attacks by raiders, including groups from Moab and Ammon (11; cf. 2 Kg. 24: 2), were instigated by the Babylonians in 599–597 B.C. since they themselves could not then punish Jehoiakim's defection following the setback they had suffered at the hands of the Egyptians in 601 B.C. This forced **the Recabites** to retreat from the desert into Jerusalem for protection. These were a subdivision of the Kenites (Jg. 1: 16; 1 Chr. 2: 55), early associated with Israel, who had settled in S. Judah (1 Sam. 15: 6; Jg. 4: 17). This clan or group (2, **family**) had been founded by J(eh)**onadab the son of Recab** who supported action against the wicked dynasty of Omri and all Baal worshippers (2 Kg. 10: 15–31). They were worshippers of the LORD (Yahweh), ardently against any apostasy and devoted to the nomadic way of life in protest at the evils of civilization. This reaction against the ills of society was expressed negatively by retreat to the desert. For almost three hundred years their group had kept to their strict vows and way of life (6, 14; cf. the Nazirites). Jeremiah's invitation to the temple precincts was to test them deliberately before witnesses. The latter included the important official who, as 'Keeper of the (Temple) Doorway' (4; cf. 2 Kg. 25: 18), was responsible for preventing any unworthy person entering the holy Temple. Contrast Christ's action as expressed in Eph. 2: 14; Heb. 10: 19. **12–19.** The Recabites' refusal to **drink wine** is taken as a direct object lesson for Judah. They had kept tenaciously to a purely human command over succeeding generations, but the people of Judah as a whole had refused to keep the law of God given at Sinai. Verse 15 is Jeremiah's summary of the teaching of former prophets (cf. 18: 11; 25: 5–6). So the Recabites will have their reward from God. It will be similar to that granted to those who keep His covenants assuring an unbroken succession (*e.g.* to David)—the privilege of serving God (19; cf. Dt. 17: 12; 1Kg. 17: 1).

(b) **The Scroll (36: 1–32).** This chapter affords a unique insight into the way the words of a prophet were spoken, written down and preserved. It will be noted that the written and oral traditions were identical (4) and accurately transmitted (18). Response to God's word varies from awe (16) to opposition (23), but despite any seeming ineffectiveness the LORD ensures continuity (29–31) and ultimate fulfilment (32). God chose to commit His word to writing (as His Word to flesh) and not to begin anew with each succeeding age. It is opposition which here leads to the word being enforced and enlarged.

(*i*) **The first written edition (36: 1–7).** The date was 605/4 B.C. following the Babylonian victory at Carchemish and throughout Syro-Palestine. The origin of the written word was a divine command to write (2). The contents were **all the words** God had spoken through His prophet concerning Israel (LXX reads 'Jerusalem') and Judah. There is no indication whether this was everything throughout Jeremiah's ministry thus far (626–605 B.C.) or selections from it (cf. ch. 32), i.e. up to 25: 1–13 (note 'this book'), which was written at the same date. Jeremiah was now in hiding (5, 19, 26) rather than yet imprisoned ('*āṣūr*, 5, 26, is however so used in 33: 1; 39: 15; cf. 37: 4). He may have been disbarred from the Temple following 20: 1–21: 6. The purpose of inscripturation is to inform everyone of the will of God and to call for repentance (3). Written words both control and emphasize spoken statements.

(*ii*) **Reading the written word (36: 8–26).** The method by which the prophecies were written down is openly stated—dictation, the use of a competent secretary, using contemporary scribal methods (4, 17–18). The work may have taken some time (9; cf. 1). The time chosen for the public reading was a fast (9) when the people would gather at the temple —probably at a time of national crisis after December 604 B.C. Babylonian and Egyptian texts may indicate that this was after the fall of Ashkelon to the invading Babylonians in that month. The place was by the main gate by which everyone had to pass into the inner court (**upper courtyard**, 10; cf. 1 Kg. 6: 36), perhaps in the office of a sympathizer with Jeremiah, for if **Gemariah son of Shaphan** was the same as in 26: 24 he would be a brother of Ahikam.

The written word needs to be complemented by oral testimony (11–13), which must itself be checked against Scripture (14–15). The effect of the reading is to be noted—some respond to it with respect (16) and appreciation of its urgency and relevance to the present situation. Those, like Jehoiakim, who are habitually unsympathetic will be roused to cold-blooded contempt and opposition (20–24, the scroll is gradually destroyed). Jehoiakim's reception of the scroll contrasts with that given to the book of the law by Josiah (2 Kg. 22: 11). The small group of those who urge caution, having been

previously moved by the reading (25), may have advised Jeremiah and Baruch to go into hiding. Overall is the protecting hand of God which limits opposition (26). **23.** Wheeled 'braziers' standing on special tracks before the throne are known from palaces excavated in Syria and Assyria. The **scribe's knife** was used both to cut the papyrus sheet and to sharpen the reed brush-pens.

(*ii*) **The scroll rewritten (36: 27–32).** The second edition included material identical with the first (28) and was soon made with the aid of a divinely inspired memory (cf. Exod. 32: 19; 34: 1). Some additions, probably chs. 25–34, were added as well as a subscript outlining the prediction of Jehoiakim's fate known, except for 20: 18–19, only from this passage (cf. 2 Kg. 24: 6). His successor Jehoiachin reigned for only three months and ten days. Neither physical nor human barriers can ultimately prevail against the divine word. Contempt cannot nullify it, for 'the word of the LORD endures for ever' and the one who despises it will perish (30–31; Rev 22: 19).

xxi. The siege and fall of Jerusalem (37: 1–39: 18)
(*a*) **Jeremiah's first imprisonment (37: 1–21).** Chapters 37–38 continue the intimate details of the personal history of Jeremiah during the siege of Jerusalem. They could only have originated from his own hand. The situation is similar to 21: 1–10 and is introduced by a review of Zedekiah's policy which showed no change of heart (1–2).

In 588 B.C. the pharaoh (=king) Hophra (Gk. Apries) of Egypt marched in support of Zedekiah's rising against Babylonia. The news caused the **Chaldeans** (Babylonians) then besieging Jerusalem to withdraw and thus encouraged the inhabitants to expect a permanent relief rather than a temporary respite. Zedekiah secretly asks Jeremiah to intercede with God (3) and enquire about the future. This is a testimony to the prophet's unswerving faith. But God does not relent while people fail to repent, so the reply offers no hope for the city (7–10). God gives the prophet a confirming revelation which will prepare him for further opposition. In choosing **Jehucal**, an opponent who called for the prophet's death (38: 4) and **Zephaniah** who had earlier heard Jeremiah's view (3; cf. 21: 1), Zedekiah was at least tactless in his choice of messengers.

In the interval in the siege Jeremiah demonstrates his trust in the eventual outcome by going north (13, **Benjamin Gate**) to Anathoth to take up his newly purchased field (32: 7). He was falsely charged with deserting to the Babylonians (11–14) and imprisoned. The place for this, in a cistern beneath a house, may have been because the usual prisons were already full of deserters, or to isolate him (38:

6, 13). Although he had advised others to surrender to minimize the horrors at the fall of the city, he himself, like Jesus Christ, identified himself with his own people and stayed with them (11–15). The leaders who had once protected him (26: 16; 36: 12) may have been deported by this time (14–15).

When Zedekiah approaches him again, perhaps hoping for word of some miraculous delivery of the city as in 701 B.C. (Isa. 37), Jeremiah is prepared (cf. 6–10). He fearlessly shows how the false prophets had misled the king and that Jerusalem will fall, however weak the enemy might seem to be (10). In view of this the king is forced to grant lessened restrictions despite the famine conditions. Three round flat loaves of bread were a sufficient meal for a hungry man (21; cf. Lk. 11: 5–6).

(b) **Further imprisonment and release (38: 1–13).** The rejection of the written word (ch. 37) is followed by further opposition to the messenger who now brings a final warning. Despite its similarites with 37: 11–21 this may well be a separate incident nearer to the time of the fall of the city. This account alone has the demand for execution, and different questions and reasonings as well as different places listed.

Jeremiah has access to the public from the stockade, so he courageously repeats his prophecy of doom. His message remains unchanged and his statement of 21: 9 is now used against him (cf. Christ in Mt. 26: 61). The four witnesses (1) include those who may have been hostile to him already, **J**(eh)**ucal** (37: 3), **Gedaliah**, probably not the later governor (chs. 40–41) but the son of **Passhur** named earlier (21: 1–3) and here. In their view Jeremiah was a traitor. Like Pilate, Zedekiah is too weak to oppose popular clamour (4), though he knows the prisoner to be innocent. The misinterpretation of the motives of those who speak in God's name is to be expected (4). The king dare not let a holy man be put to death and a 'natural death' would be the more easily explained. He may have believed that so long as the prophet was alive there might be some hope of divine intervention on behalf of the city. Jeremiah's experience in the dungeon is that of Lam. 3: 53–57. The location of the cistern within the stockade (6) need not contradict the statement that he was earlier in an official's house (37: 15). Many such interconnecting storage places for rain water are known from underground Jerusalem.

Ebed-Melech ('Servant of the King') was a **Cushite** slave who may well have risen to an official position (7, cf. 29: 2; Gen. 39: 1; Ac. 8: 27). His ability to gain audience of the king could have been due to this or to the fact that the king sat at the gate to judge any case brought to him (7). He courageously intercedes on what appear to be simply humanitarian grounds. **10. thirty:** read 'three' with RSV (Heb. *šlšm*). Note the care to use cloth taken from the temple or palace storeroom (Heb. 'underneath the treasury') to assist a weakened man being hauled up (11–13). For all this God himself will reward Ebed-Melech (39: 15). The various imprisonments and releases, vividly recorded from first hand evidence, mark stages in God's care for His own witness (cf. 36: 26).

(c) **A secret interview (38: 14–28).** Once again Zedekiah sends for Jeremiah. This time he meets him at a temple entrance (probably the royal entry of 2 Kg. 16: 18). Jeremiah wisely demands assurance of security in view of the known hostility of the king towards him (15). This is given in the standard solemn Hebrew oath formula, 'By the life of the LORD who gives us our lives' (16, NEB). Should Zedekiah break his word it would be assumed that he would be put to death by God for doing so. In contrast Jeremiah assures him that his life would be spared if he surrendered to the Babylonians. The king, however, fears ill-treatment at the hands of the pro-Babylonian Judeans who have already defected. Life depends on God, not man (20). Note that no promise is made of protection from ill-treatment and that this second call to Zedekiah to surrender is reinforced by reference to what may have been a common taunt-song which put the king in the same position as that in which Jeremiah had been (22–23). The threat to the royal family should there be further stubborn resistance was later carried out (39: 6). Zedekiah's sin would be a direct cause of Jerusalem's downfall (23, Heb. 'you shall burn this city'; RSV, NEB read the passive). **24–28.** Were the news of the secret interview to become known Jeremiah's life and Zedekiah's position could have been placed in danger. The excuse for it, prepared and given (26), was a half-truth (cf. v. 17) and necessary (27). 'Sin among men often creates positions where there is no perfect solution or way out' (Ellison). So Jeremiah was held safe in the stockade until the city fell.

(d) **The fall of Jerusalem (39: 1–14).** This dramatic event, so momentous in the history of God's people, is recounted four times in Scripture (here; ch. 52; 2 Kg. 25; 2 Chr. 36). With it the prophecies made over the preceding forty years now come to pass. The eighteen month siege (c. January 588–July 587 B.C.) takes its toll through famine and the Babylonians make a breach and the weakened defenders capitulate. The enemy sets up a military command post in the centre gate (3). Their names and titles are Babylonian. **3. Nergal-Sharezer:** because of the repetition here some read this as identical with the Babyl. *Nergal-šara-uṣur* = Neriglissar 'the prince of Sinmagir', the **high official** (RSV 'Rab-mag', i.e. the chief *emuqi*) or army commander who was to become king of Babylon (559–556 B.C.). The **chief officer** (RSV 'Rab-saris', Babyl. *rab ša rēši*) is mentioned in contemporary Aramaic documents.

Because vv. 4–13 are omitted by LXX and vv. 1–2 seem to intervene between 38: 28 and 39: 3 some take the latter as an insertion (RV treats vv. 1, 2, as a parenthesis), but they are a necessary historical introduction in this chapter which is a collection of data, some treated in more detail in the next section. RSV transposes v. 3a from the end of ch. 38 to make a smooth sentence. Verses 4–10 are covered in greater detail in 52: 7–16.

4–8. The fate of Zedekiah is as prophesied (cf. Ezek. 12: 12–13). He was later deported to Babylon (2 Kg. 25: 7) where he died (52: 11). Full details are given in 40: 1–6. Zedekiah, alas too late, seems to have shown initiative in attempting an escape. **5. Riblah:** 200 miles north, the Babylonian headquarters in Syro-Palestine (cf. 2 Kg. 23: 33 and Babylonian texts). The **king's garden** was near the Pool of Siloam (cf. Neh. 3: 13). The city had a double line of walls. The Arabah was the valley running down to the Dead Sea. **9–10.** This describes the final deportation; the majority of the leaders and skilled men (52: 15) had gone ahead with Jehoiachin in 597 B.C. Even now a small 'remnant', **the poor people**, remain (10).

(*e*) **Appendix: a promise to Ebed-Melech (39: 15–18).** Provision is made for the African slave who had helped Jeremiah. He does not forget Ebed-Melech (38: 7–13), though many do forget those who aid them in times of dire trouble. His kindness to God's servant in his time of need is recognized by God (15) and considered as an act of faith in God (18). This was the base of his salvation (cf. Ac. 16: 31). 'As you did it to one of the least of these my brethren, you did it to me' (Mt. 25: 40). He is promised security for himself in the unpromising conditions of the coming chaos (this section is therefore to be dated before Jeremiah's release). A coloured Cushite slave could have expected no mercy, especially from the Babylonians who might have taken him to be pro-Egyptian.

xxii. The later biography and final messages of Jeremiah (40: 1–45: 5)
The personal narrative of the prophet's life is carried on after the fall of Jerusalem in 587 B.C., both in Judah (chs. 40–42) and in Egypt (chs. 43–44).

(*a*) **Deciding the future way (40: 1–6).** The final stages of the siege and collection of prisoners was left to **Nebuzaradan** (=Babyl. *Nabū-zēr-iddin*) who was in charge of the Babylonian garrison. Nebuchadrezzar appointed **Gedaliah** (5) to be governor of the district with

his seat at Mizpah, NW of Jerusalem (either 5 miles at Nebi Samwīl or 8 miles at Tell en-Nasbeh). His position is confirmed by a seal impression from contemporary Lachish inscribed *lgdlyh š'l hbyt* ('belonging to Gedaliah who is over the House', i.e. chief minister). Nebuchadrezzar himself had returned to Babylon, but the Babylonians clearly realized that they were God's own instrument for punishment (2). There is no need to attribute these views to some later Jewish writer. Jeremiah appears to have been caught up with the refugees and prisoners being deported and may have been rescued from among them by Gedaliah's action. He certainly received the word of prophecy right up to the end of his ministry (1) and his decision to remain with the 'remnant' was doubtless influenced by his faith that the adjacent land would be reoccupied (32: 15) as it was apparently also untouched by war (12).

Jeremiah's choice was bold and patriotic (6) though he well knew that the hope of the future of God's people lay with the exiles in Babylonia (24: 4–7). He chose to stay as guide to the very people who had persistently rejected him (10).

(*b*) **Gedaliah as governor (40: 7–12).** For a while it seemed that there was hope for those who remained. There was sustenance available in July/August (the **summer fruit**, 10, 12) for the city had fallen between the fifth (1: 3; 52: 12) and seventh months (41: 1). Gedaliah's leadership was such as to inspire foresight and confidence (9–10) and he was joined by those who had fled to Moab (11; cf. 27: 3) and Ammon (14), and who perhaps, like the Recabites (35: 11), had been displaced by the invaders (12).

(*c*) **The plot against Gedaliah (40: 13–16).** Gedaliah's weakness was a seeming inability to judge the character of the people around him. Among those joining him was **Ishmael** (14), a remote member of the royal line of David, who was perhaps aggrieved at not having been made governor himself and believed Gedaliah to be a traitor since he was trusted by the Babylonians. The Ammonite king **Baalis**, otherwise unknown, may have wished to enlarge his territory and so wanted Gedaliah out of the way. Nevertheless, a man in a position of authority, like Gedaliah, needs to watch carefully lest he rejects sound advice, falling into the very attitude ('speaking falsely', 16) of which he accuses others.

(*d*) **The outcome of the plot (41: 1–18)**
(*i*) **Gedaliah assassinated (41: 1–10).** Johanan's suspicions (40: 15) were confirmed. Within less than three months—if **seventh month** refers to the same year 587 B.C. (cf. 39: 2); though others interpret as in the following year—Ishmael murdered Gedaliah. Ishmael was not a Babylonian official; **one . . . officers**

(NIV) is omitted by LXX and 2 Kg. 25: 25; MT 'and some royal officials', may refer back to Baalis. The total number of the party is not stated. They were sufficient to overwhelm eighty men (5, 7). The dastardly act violated the laws of hospitality ('eating together', 1) which protected both host and guests. The Jews and Babylonians with him were probably killed to remove all witnesses, though they must have resisted, and to gain time to further the rebellion (3-4). This plan was thwarted by the pilgrims passing on the way to worship at Jerusalem. They attest the continuing faith of the loyal remnant in Israel after the fall of Samaria in 722 B.C. At Mizpah they would get their first sight of the ruined city—though their prior signs of mourning (4) may mean that they already knew of this, yet still wished to go there.

Murder, like all sin, leads to further sins, hypocrisy and deception (6, **weeping**) and greed (8). Except for the ten who escaped by revealing that they had supplies of the kind the rebels lacked, all were murdered. The bodies of those killed 'because of Gedaliah' (9 MT, AV) were hidden in a cistern typical of the hill-towns—made by Asa to supply Mizpah with water *c.* 900 B.C. (cf. archaeological discoveries at, *e.g.*, Gibeon). Ishmael then attempted to abduct the survivors, among whom must have been Jeremiah, Baruch and other witnesses (10). This tragedy brought to an end any hope of revival in Judah. It has long been commemorated by later Judaism by a fast in the seventh month (October; cf. Zech. 7: 5; 8: 19).

(*ii*) **The remnant rescued (41: 11–18).** Johanan, suspicions against the Moabites vindicated, takes swift action to rescue those Ishmael had led off, including the royal princesses whom the merciful Babylonians had entrusted to Gedaliah's care. This he did at the cistern of Gibeon (now excavated at El-Jīb; cf. 2 Sam. 2: 13), but the murderer himself escaped (15). The inclusion of **soldiers** (16; cf. v. 3) is unlikely, and this is probably to be read as 'men' here. The fear of Babylonian reprisals for the murder of their nominee Gedaliah was real (17). It led to a change of plan and route. Near Bethlehem, the 'inn' (so RVmg, AV 'habitation', NIV **Geruth**, others 'sheepfolds' (Heb. is uncertain)), was an appropriate stopping-place to discuss future plans. **Kimham** was the son of Barzillai rewarded by David for his help while an exile in the same area (2 Sam. 19: 37–38).

(*e*) **Which way to go? (4: 1–43: 7)**
(*i*) **Jeremiah consulted (42: 1–6).** This is the first reference to the prophet since the flight from Mizpah. Men without true faith often seek God only in times of trouble. Jeremiah was obviously well known as a consistent witness who would know God intimately for there

was unanimity in approaching him. They assumed that only a prophet could 'enquire of God'. Though previously forbidden to pray for the people (7: 16; 11: 14; 14: 11) Jeremiah was now free to do so. He first demanded unity and refused to think of God as 'his' alone and not 'theirs' also (3–5, **your God**; 6, **our God**). He is LORD God of all (18). Realizing, as the sequel shows, that their mind was already made up, he then requires a solemn oath, equivalent to the response God demands to His covenant, that whatever God commands they will do (5–6). This is the only valid basis for seeking guidance of the Lord. The names here vary in the sources (1). **Jezaniah** (following *MT*) is called Azariah in LXX and 43: 2 (RSV, JB follow). It is, however, not unusual for men to have more than one name.

(*ii*) **The answer (42: 7–22).** The delay in answering (7) may have been to test their sincerity. The prophet puts the people's request to God in their own words (9; cf. v. 4). God's reply is clear, consistent, anticipates their probable decision, and accords with His previous words (10; cf. 1: 10). It is not Nebuchadrezzar but God who is in control (12). The Babylonians have already shown clemency and to stay in the land was a reasonable course to adopt. The prophet therefore (i) *assures* them of salvation and security if they obey (11); (ii) *warns* of the consequences of disobedience (13–18), stressing that in Egypt (always typical in OT of life outside God's will) everything that had befallen Judah and that they had sought to escape would befall them there—war, panic, hunger (14), and death (16–17); (iii) *commands* them emphatically not to go down to Egypt (19); (iv) *reveals* the deceit of a heart which asks for guidance when it has already made its decisions (20–21). The answer ends with a reaffirmation of the results which would follow a departure for Egypt (22; cf. vv. 16–17). **12. restore you to your land:** 'dwell in' (*MT*; cf. RSV 'remain in') is only a difference of Heb. vocalization.

(*iii*) **God's word rejected (43: 1–7).** Despite their promise (42: 5–6) the group refused to accept divine guidance. Various excuses might vainly be put forward for taking a contrary course. They accused Jeremiah of speaking lies (2), when what they had once trusted in had been shown to be lies (27: 10, 15–16; 28: 15) by the recent events which had been predicted by the very person they now accuse. They invented a story that he was under the influence of pro-Babylonian **Baruch** (1–3) who had presumably argued independently for staying in the land. This group showed no change of attitude from that which led to the fall of Judah. They were presumptuous (2, **arrogant**) for ranking themselves against God's authority. But no excuse can disguise that their decision was a flaunting disobedience to the voice of the Lord (7). Like Christ (Mt. 26: 60–63), Jeremiah appears to have remained silent in face of false accusations. So the unwilling prophet is taken to Daphnae (**Tahpanhes**, 7; cf. 2: 16) on the NE border of Egypt, *c.* 27 miles SW of Port Said. Tell Defneh was excavated by Flinders Petrie in 1886.

(*f*) **The Babylonian defeat of Egypt is predicted (43: 8–13).** The excavations of Tahpanhes revealed a large paved area outside 'the palace-fort' (Elephantine Papyri) which has been identified with **the brick pavement** (9, *MT* 'brick-terrace' or 'platform'). The Hebrew for **royal canopy** (10) is unique (literally 'glittering tapestry'?). Jeremiah uses the symbolic act of burying something beneath the platform to indicate that the Jews in Egypt would be under Babylonian domination (10).

He predicts the horrors they had sought to avoid including deportation of themselves and of the Jews who had fled before them to Egypt (40: 11–12); Josephus *Ant.* x. 182). Babylonian inscriptions attest an attack in 568/7 B.C. when Amasis (570–526 B.C.) was defeated (cf. Ezek. 29: 19 f.; 30: 24–26). In front of the 'House of the Sun-god' (12, Heb. *Beth-Shemesh*, here distinguished from the place of the same name in Judah), the famous temple of On at Heliopolis (near Memphis and modern Cairo), was a row of obelisks (13, *MT* 'images') of which only one now remains. Others are now in London (Cleopatra's Needle), Paris and Istanbul.

(*g*) **The Lord's recent activity in Judah (44: 1–6).** Jeremiah's last message to the Jews (*c.* 585 B.C.) is addressed to those in Egypt at Magdal, E. of Tahpanhes (so Amarna texts; cf. Ezek. 29: 10; 30: 6), at nearby **Memphis** (*Noph*, 2: 16), and in **Upper Egypt** or Pathros, (Egypt. *p'trs*; Babyl. *Paturisi*), 'land of the south' (cf. v. 15) as opposed to Lower Egypt (see *NBD*, p. 938). It is possible that all were assembled for some purpose (15) or received the message in a letter. That there were Jews in the region is attested by the Elephantine Papyri. Some think that the diffuse nature of this chapter is due to later expansion, but the versions do not support this and it could equally well be the verbal account of a speech.

Jeremiah reviews what God has done to Judah (2). He reminds them of God's characteristic patient pleading, and the people's persistent refusal to listen (6), and pleads with them not to succumb to the fascinations of the surrounding idolatry. If they do so, the same judgment as had befallen apostate Jerusalem and all Judah would be theirs.

(*h*) **Appeal to the remnant (44: 7–14).** The appeal in vv. 7–10 is to demonstrate that continuance in sin will produce continued judgment. Their action is due to their having forgot-

ten the lesson of the past failure and its consequences. Sin is always an act against oneself (7) as well as against God (10). Judgment is therefore to be 'cut off' and to suffer a belittled international reputation (8). The Lord is ever concerned that there be a **remnant** (7; cf. 10, 14), but they are without repentance, shown by no humility, no awe of God and no effective law (10). The latter has been clearly set before them at Josiah's reform and subsequently (9: 13; 26: 4).

(*i*) **The Final message (44: 15–30).** The **wickedness** of the **wives** (9) was stimulated by their worship of the mother-goddess; **Queen of Heaven** (17) applies equally to the Canaanite Astarte, the Babylonian Ishtar or the Egyptian Hathor, if not here used as an epithet of the moon. Their view that so long as they had carried out these practices all had been well (18) is negated by history. These cults were probably originally Babylonian cults involving libations, sacrifices and making votive cakes bearing an image of the goddess of birth (a star, LXX, Targum; cf. 7: 18). The men may well have been influenced by such superstitions (19) and their plea of ignorance is denied (15) for without the men the women could not have made a vow (Num. 30: 4–17; cf. v. 9). Ironically the women are told to go ahead with their vows (cf. v. 17 *every word* is a solemn vow) which will be worthless as no one will be left alive (26). The part played by the women in refusing God need not indicate any special movement led by the royal princesses (Skinner). Woman's influence is powerful and can be used for much good. A remnant would survive to bear witness to the truth of the word of God and Jeremiah (28; cf. v. 14).

Jeremiah's final word is similar to his first. God is **watching** ('wakeful') over His word (27; cf. 1: 12; 31: 28) to bring about the predicted and just punishment on broken vows (25; cf. v. 27). None would be left alive to use the name of the LORD in oaths (26). History will show whose word will stand (28–29). The sign given (30) was a specific prediction of the death of Hophra, who was strangled to death by his enemies to whom he was handed over fourteen years later (570 B.C.) by his successor Amasis (Herodotus ii. 161). Jeremiah pointedly does not say that he would be captured by the Babylonians.

Nothing further is said of the fate of Jeremiah. Baruch may have died about the same time and no record remains. Tradition holds that the prophet was stoned to death by the Jews in Egypt.

(*j*) **A word for Baruch (45: 1–5).** Jeremiah does not forget those who helped him and, like Ebed-Melech whose personal prophecy is appended in 39: 15–18, passes on a word to his faithful secretary. As with the commencement of the prophecies grouped together in chapters 1 ff., 25 ff., 35 ff., this is dated to Jehoiakim's fourth year (605/4 B.C.). It forms both a fitting appendix to ch. 44 and introduction to the prophecies concerning the individual nations whose fates are recorded separately in chs. 46–51. The Babylonians will overrun all the peoples who surround Judah. Amid all this it is God who speaks to the individual whose moods He knows (2). **Baruch** could well be depressed at the prophecies of doom he had to record (3) and perhaps also at the treatment of his master. He is reminded that God's sorrow is the greater at having to destroy what He has created. Baruch will suffer exile but not loss of life. Jeremiah's deep personal and spiritual concern for his employee is clear. Verse 5 can be translated 'and you ask for mighty acts?—do not. Though behold I am bringing disaster upon everybody, says the LORD, I will let you take (capture) your life as a prize wherever you go'. **1.** The words referred to must be those of the burned scroll (36: 2–4) since the whole book of Jeremiah was not completed until *c.* 560 B.C. (52: 31–34). **4.** *MT* begins 'Thus you shall say to him' (i.e. Jeremiah as the medium of God's message).

II. PROPHECIES CONCERNING FOREIGN NATIONS (46: 1–51: 64)

These 'oracles' (*massā*), spoken **concerning** (Heb. uses *l* 'with reference to' or *'el* or *'al*, 'about', i.e. not necessarily 'against') the Gentile nations, are arranged geographically, beginning with Egypt (46: 2–28) and then moving to Philistia (47: 1–7), Moab (48: 1–47), Ammon (49: 1–6), Edom (49: 7–22), Syria (49: 23–33), Elam (49: 34–39) and finally Babylon (50: 1–51: 64). For the variant order in the Gk. translations see INTRODUCTION.

These show that the same principle applies to God's dealings with Israel's neighbours as to His own people. He must punish sin. He is sovereign in the affairs of all men whether they recognize Him or not. These prophecies also have a typical, spiritual application such as pervades Scripture. It can best be seen and interpreted by the later references to these same nations, *e.g.* parallel quotations from chs. 50–51 with Rev. 11: 8; 17–18 show Babylon as a type of the way of life that continues into our own age. Note how many characteristics of these nations can still be met with today. Though many critics debate the Jeremianic authorship of some of these prophecies (*e.g.* 50: 1–51: 58) there is no substantive evidence to deny this. He had been called to address all nations (1: 5, 10) and does so in the lively manner employed also by Isaiah (chs. 13–27) and Ezekiel (chs. 25–32).

i. Egypt (46: 1–28)

Egypt was the ancient dominator of S. Palestine even before the Mosaic period. Josiah had recently been killed opposing her army (609 B.C.) and now in August 605 B.C. (2) Egypt had been defeated at the battle of Carchemish, an event which shook the Near Eastern world of that day (12). The reliable Babylonian Chronicle tells how the Egyptians fled when Nebuchadrezzar, co-regent of Babylon (2), 'beat them to non-existence'. Those who escaped were overtaken near Hamath and defeated 'so that not a single man escaped to his own country'. Jeremiah sees the troops called up for battle (3–4) and then their dramatic flight from the banks of the river Euphrates (5–6, NEB). Archaeological evidence shows that the small shield (3, *māgēn*), the larger rectangular one (*şinnā*), the helmet (4) and the coats of linked armour scales were the contemporary defences of the soldier. Also that the army included Greek (**Lydia**) as well as men from the Sudan (**Cush**) and Libya/Somalia (**Put**, 9). Egypt, like Gilead, was famous for medicine and 'full of physicians' (Herodotus ii. 84) but these were of no avail (11). **13–28** have been dated by some to 604 B.C. or to a later Babylonian attack on Egypt in 568 B.C. (cf. 43: 8–13). The king of Egypt was a worthless ally—an empty vessel—and so is called by a name symbolic of a great disaster (17; cf. 20: 3) variously translated 'King Bombast' (NEB), 'Much-noise-but-he-lets-the-chance-slip-by' (JB), 'Crash' (Driver) or 'Loudmouth' (Harrison). His failure to grasp the opportunity is described as the **serpent** (i.e. royal insignia) **fleeing away** (22). This may refer also to the event described in the Babylonian Chronicle for 601 B.C. when 'the king of Babylon . . . took the lead of his army and marched to Egypt. The king of Egypt heard it and mustered his army. In open battle they smote each other and inflicted great loss on each other. The king of Babylon and his troops turned back and returned to Babylon.' The damage to the Babylonians was so great that the next year had to be spent in re-equipping the army. Elation at this event was such that Jehoiakim rebelled against his overlord (2 Kg. 24: 1). Jeremiah seems therefore to have been led to predict once again the ultimate defeat of Egypt (25–26a), though adding a word of ultimate restoration to the Egyptians as an introduction to a similar note of hope for Israel herself in these tumultuous times (28–29). **15. Why will your warriors be laid low?** RSV follows LXX reading, 'Why has Apis fled?' (*nāş ḥāp*): RV renders *MT nishap*, 'swept away'. Apis was the strong bull of Osiris.

Egypt in OT often stands for the world which bids us turn to it for help, though we have come out from its domination (*e.g.* Num. 11: 5; 1 Kg. 3: 1). We must remember that it is always a broken reed (37: 6) and can never save God's people (37: 5–8). In this chapter, as often, the unreliability of Egypt is contrasted with the reliable God who will restore His people (27–28).

(ii) Philistia (47: 1–7)
The date of this prophecy is variously interpreted. Some posit an Egyptian attack on **Gaza** (1), said to have occurred when Necho II retreated after the battle of Carchemish (but the interpretation of Herodotus (ii. 159)—Kadytis as Gaza—is questionable). Lipinski has shown that this reference (1) is before the Egypto-Babylonian war of 601 B.C. Gaza was certainly besieged and taken by Alexander in 332 B.C. and, as Amos (1: 6–7), Zephaniah (2: 4) and Zechariah (9: 5) prophesied, it was destroyed by Alexander Jannaeus in 93 B.C. The context of v. 5 indicates, however, that **Ashkelon** on the seashore (5) had been cut off from both its traditional northern (Phoenician) allies Tyre and Sidon (4) and from 'the rest of their valleys' (so AV, Heb. 'im'qam). The latter might be translated 'the remains of their strength' (cf. 49: 4). RSV follows an LXX interpretation 'Anakim', as a play on the Goliaths now laid low. The Anakim were the early inhabitants of the region (Num. 13: 28–37; Dt. 2: 21; Jos. 11: 22) but may have been a title (rank) rather than reference to physique (*VT* 15, 1965, 468–474). According to the Babylonian Chronicle for 604 B.C. Nebuchadrezzar 'marched to the city of Ashkelon and captured it in the month Kislev. He took its king prisoner and carried off booty. He then turned the city into a mound of ruins and a heap of rubble and then in the month Šebat marched back to Babylon.' The king, nobles and sailors from Ashkelon are specifically mentioned in a list of prisoners held in Babylon in 592 B.C. A papyrus letter (found at Saqqâra) appealing for help against the advancing Babylonians may have come from Ashkelon about this time.

Philistia, the home of the Philistines who originated in 'the island of Crete' (**coasts of Caphtor**, 4) were the closest neighbours ('the unconverted in the visible church who oppose spiritual principles') who oppressed God's people. With such the LORD has a perpetual quarrel (6–7) and they have nothing on which to rely in a time of judgment. Gaza (Jg. 14: 10–11) and Ashkelon are here seen as being overwhelmed in the same swift flood (2) from the north (i.e. Babylonians, 1: 14) as devastated Egypt (46: 8). Panicking parents would not even stop to take their small children with them (3). All is a picture of coming divine judgment. The sword of the LORD never rests and it is vain to cry for help (6–7).

(iii) Moab (48: 1–47)
The devastation to overtake **Moab** is announced in a collection of prophecies. Moab, with Ammon and Edom, was instigated by Babylon to raid Judah as a reprisal for Jehoiakim's rebellion in 601–597 B.C. (2 Kg. 24: 2), pending her own punitive expedition. Moab had been warned earlier by Jeremiah of inevitable judgment at the hands of Babylon (9: 26; 25: 21; 27: 1–7). Here he quotes freely from Isaiah's prophecies to the same end (chs. 13–16). According to Josephus (*Ant.* x. 181 f.) the Babylonians overran Moab *c.* 581 B.C. Cf. Ezek. 25: 8–11.

Moab's representative characteristics are trust in her own strength, her strongholds and treasures (7), her pride in herself (29) in defiance of the LORD (42) which led her to gloat over the misfortunes of Israel and Judah (27) but reflect her historical relations with those states. She owed her origin to Lot (Gen. 14: 37) and originally occupied the high fertile plateau as far north as Heshbon (2; cf. Num. 21: 15–16) and beguiled Israelites into idolatry (Num. 25: 1–3). The Israelites conquered the area north of the river Arnon which Reuben occupied for a time and built the town of Nebo (2, Num. 32: 3, 38). After many wars she was made a vassal of David (2 Sam. 8: 2) until king Mesha's revolt against Israel (2 Kg. 3: 4). She gained her independence from Assyria *c.* 627 B.C. Further warnings of judgment on her are given by Ezekiel (25: 8–11), Amos (2: 1–3) and Zephaniah (2: 8–11).

(a) Judgment on Chemosh, god of Moab (48: 1–10). Kiriathaim (1), 6 miles NW of Dibon, and **Horonaim** (3, Hauronem) are mentioned in Mesha's inscription (the Moabite Stone). The destruction is envisaged as far-reaching. **Heshbon** (2, mod. Hesbān) has been excavated, but **Madmen** (2) is unlocated—unless, as some (LXX), we read Heb. *gm-dmm tdmm*, 'also (thou) shalt be utterly silenced'. The practice of taking the gods of the conquered, especially nomadic, peoples, is attested in Assyr. annals (cf. v. 7). **7.** Chemosh (also mentioned in the Moabite Stone, see *NBD* p. 835) was the principal deity of Moab (*Kamus*; cf. Num. 21: 29). His complete defeat is emphasized in this fine poetic passage. This will be an added condemnation for the vile cult practices (2 Kg. 23: 13). Her land will be depopulated, for **in Heshbon men will plot her downfall** (2, Heb. *b'hešbôn hēš'bu*—a play on words). **6.** Safety lies only in retreat into the remoter desert (*MT* 'Aro'er can be translated 'heath' (AV, RV) or 'tamarisk'; RSV, JB **wild ass** and NEB 'sandgrouse' follow LXX interpretation). **9.** salt: Heb. *ṣīṣ*, some infer from Ugaritic a reference to sowing salt over the site of destroyed cities (mg; cf. Jg. 9: 45). Perhaps translate 'to set up a gravestone (LXX *sēmeia*, implying Heb. *ṣiyyūn*; cf. 2 Kg. 23: 17) for Moab for she shall be completely ruined'. **10.** The call to God's workers never to slack even in the terrible work as agents of judgment.

(b) **Moab's security disturbed (48: 11–20).**
Moab had never previously endured exile but
this is now forecast (11–12). Trust in their god
Chemosh (13; cf. v. 7) would prove as vain as
had the Israelite reliance on the calf worship at
their local 'house of god' (Bethel, 13). They
too had suffered exile (1 Kg. 12: 29; Am. 4: 4;
5: 5; 7: 13). The picture of the sudden evacu-
ation and destruction is based on the famous
Moabite wine trade. This would run to waste
and be shattered (11; cf. 32–33). Verses 17–20
are a lament on the fall of Moab couched in the
language of Deuteronomy (e.g. 32: 35). **18. on
the parched ground:** reading ṣāmēʾ as Isa. 44:
3; for AV 'sit in thirst' (MT ṣāmāʾ)', cf. Syr. 'in
filth'. Dibon is modern Diban, 13 miles east of
the Dead Sea.
(c) **Destruction everywhere (48: 21–27).** A
prose section lists the towns overrun and by
which her strength (**horn,** 25) was broken.
Judgment is all inclusive and thorough. Those
who despised Israel would become despicable,
a concept resumed in Rev. 1: 7 (cf. Mk 15: 27–
32). Moab will be made drunk but not with
her own wine (cf. 11–12).
(d) **The proud humbled (48: 28–39).** Jeremiah adapts the earlier words of Isa. 16: 6–12
in another lamentation (28–33), followed by a
description of the practice (34–39). The crushing of the country and its hopes is marked by
the fall of additional places. **Kir Hareseth** (31)
may be the modern Kerak, 8 miles east of the
Dead Sea (i.e. **sea,** 32) and the Qrḥḥ of the
Moabite Stone. **32. Jazer** was 10 miles north
(cf. Num. 21: 32), **Sibmah** 3 miles NW and
Elealeh (34) 2 miles north of Heshbon. **sea of
Jazer** follows MT but yām (sea) is omitted by
Isa. 16: 8 and LXX (cf. RSV). **Eglath Shelishiyah**
(34, NIV) is taken as a proper name, AV translates
'heifer of three years old'.
(e) **Final judgment (48: 40–47).** The **eagle**
represents Nebuchadrezzar of Babylon (cf. 49:
22) acting as agent for the LORD against whom
Moab has vaunted herself (42). Balaam's
prophecy against Moab (Num. 21: 28; 24: 17)
will be fulfilled. Refugees seek shelter in various places but in vain (43–45; cf. Isa. 24: 17–
18). Yet God's mercy is present in judgment
with a promise of restoration similar to that
given Israel and Judah. Though Moab would
cease to be a people (42), as to this day, it would
be repeopled and become a place of refuge
(47; Dan. 11: 41). Verse 47b is an interesting
colophon indicating the end of the copied text
(cf. 51: 64; Ps. 72: 20; Job 31: 40) and is not a
later editorial mark.
iv. Ammon (49: 1–6)
Ammon (east of river Jordan and north of
Moab) is condemned for greed, especially in
the accumulation of land (cf. Gal. 6: 8; Mt. 6:
9 ff.). The northern part from Heshbon to the
river Jabbok was occupied by **Gad** (1; cf. Jos.

13: 14–28) until they were ousted by the Assyrian invasion of 733 B.C. (2 Kg. 15: 29). Ammon, here personified by her chief deity **Molech** (1; MT here malkām, 'their king'), then
took over (cf. Am. 1: 13) much as she sought
to do in Judah after 587 B.C. (cf. 40: 13–
16). So the question is asked (1) 'has Israel no
children of its own that the Ammonites should
have taken possession of this portion of its
territories?'. Ammonites were regarded as the
product of incest (Gen. 19: 38).
2. Rabbah of the Ammonites: Heb.
Rabbath-bnê-ʿAmmōn; the capital is now ʿAm-
man, capital of Jordan (Gk. Philadelphia) on
the river Jabbok 14 miles NE of Heshbon and
24 miles east of the river Jordan. **a mound
of ruins:** Heb. tel. **villages:** Heb. 'daughters'
denotes the surrounding dependent villages.
3. walls: MT baggᵉderōt, the stone sheepfolds
characteristic of the area. **Ai** is not otherwise
known as a place in Jordan and may here be
revocalized 'ī, 'ruins', i.e. Heshbon on the border shared with Moab (48: 2) 'is laid in ruins'.
4. your valleys: Heb. ʿamāqīm implies 'your
strength'. Once more a prophecy ends with a
promise of restoration (45: 5; 46: 26–27; 48: 47;
49: 39). Ammon flourished until the second
century B.C. under the Tobiad family and with
Nabatean trade.
v. Edom (49: 7–22)
Edom, formerly Seir (Gen. 22: 3), lay south
of Moab and SSE of Judah. It was originally
occupied by Esau and his descendants (10). The
northern tribe and capital Teman (7; cf. Job 4:
1) took their name from Esau's grandson (Gen.
36: 1). It extended south to Aqabah and included many rocky areas and fortresses, e.g.
Bozrah (13), modern Buṣaira, recently excavated c. 20 miles SE of the Dead Sea, and
Sela, **the rocks** (16), Petra with its gorge (Sik)
leading to Umm el-Buyara, a one-thousand
foot high fortress citadel. **Dedan** (8), modern
al-ʿUlā, lies south of Edom and was a flourishing caravan centre mentioned in Babylonian
texts.
All of Edom must share the LORD's wrath
with Israel. If Israel had to drink the cup surely
Edom cannot escape it (12; cf. 25: 15). This was
also predicted by the contemporary prophets
Ezekiel (25: 13) and Obadiah (1–6; paralleled
here in vv. 14–16, 9–10 but it is not possible
to say which, if either, prophet borrowed from
the other). Edom in OT is characterized like
Esau by a boastful wisdom (7; cf. Job 2: 11; 15:
18; 1 Kg. 5: 10) which leads to a contempt of
God. The punishment for such is to be made
foolish and driven out of the rock-fortresses on
which they rely. No place will be untouched
(10); there will be no hiding-place and no note
of hope (as offered, e.g., to Moab, 48: 47).
Though the exercise of His justice may cause
hapless widows and helpless orphans (11), God

in His mercy will care for them (Ps. 68: 5). The prophecy was fulfilled when Edom was taken over by the Nabateans in the third century B.C. Those who fled to S. Judea (Idumea—the birthplace of the Herods) were subordinated by Judas Maccabeus (1 Mac. 5: 65). **12.** The **cup** of the wrath of God (25: 15, 28) is a vivid picture of judgment (Isa. 51: 17; Rev. 14: 10). This has led some to date this prophecy after the catastrophe in Jerusalem in 587 B.C. Verses 17–22 are in poetry (contra RSV); cf. 19: 8 and 50: 40; chs. 44–46. **18. Sodom and Gomorrah** are the classic example of God's overthrow of a sinning people (cf. Gen. 10: 19; 14: 2–8; Dt. 29: 23; Isa. 13: 19; Jer. 23: 14; 50: 40; Lam. 4: 6; Mt. 11: 23; Jude 7). **19.** What ruler can defend his people against **me**? **21. Red Sea:** better, Reed Sea (Heb. *yam sūp*), i.e. marshes by the Bitter Lakes.

vi. Syria (49: 23–27)
Judgment will extend to the north where **Damascus**, the capital of Aram (Syria) and her former associates, the frequently allied city-state of **Hamath** (Ḥāma), 110 miles to the north, **and Arpad** (Tell Erfād), 95 miles to the north, with their local rulers and gods (2 Kg. 18: 34; Isa. 10: 9; 36: 17) will be overthrown. The Babylonians under Nebuchadrezzar did this in 595 and 594 B.C. (Babylonian Chronicle). They elsewhere name these states among tribute paying vassals, much as the Assyrians had earlier incorporated Arpad (738 B.C.), Damascus (731 B.C.) and Hamath (720 B.C.) into their highly developed provincial system. Syria traditionally joined Israel when it was convenient, and so must now share in the judgment she had suffered. **23.** NEB 'tossed up and down in anxiety like the unresting sea'. **25.** This appears to have been spoken by the inhabitants of Damascus who today describe their city as 'Paradise'. The *MT* **'not** (Heb. *lō*') **abandoned'** should be translated as *lō*' (emphatic) —'how completely deserted the city is!' There is no need to identify **Ben-Hadad** (27) since this dynastic name was held by at least three kings, most notably the contemporary of Ahab (1 Kg. 15: 18; 20: 1; 2 Kg. 6: 24; 8: 7; 13: 3). **27.** Cf. Am. 1: 4.

vii. The Arabs (49: 28–33)
Kedar in its restricted sense is a nomadic tribe in the Syro-Arabian desert but is often used as a collective term for the bedouin generally. They were large-scale sheep-breeders (Isa. 60: 7) and skilled archers (Isa. 21: 16–17) and some have described them as symbolic of those who snipe at God's people. **Hazor** (30) is probably not the renowned city of the north but the Arabs living in open village settlements (cf. v. 31), as the word *ḥāṣēr* and LXX imply; 'remote' (30, **in deep caves**) in the desert. They will be robbed of their wealth—tents, vessels and camels (29: 32). Jeremiah warns of impending

raids against them—if v. 32 is a call to the Babylonians—or unsuccessfully undertaken by them. The prophecy was fulfilled in Nebuchadrezzar's sixth year (599/8 B.C.) when the Babylonian Chronicle relates that the king of Babylon in Syria 'sent out companies and scouring the desert they took much plunder from the Arabs, their possessions, domestic animals and gods'. The Babylonians did the same in 581 B.C. **29.** Was **Terror on every side** a common war cry? (cf. 6: 25; 20: 3, 4, 10; 46: 5). **32 mg.** The custom of cutting the corners of the hair, common among Arabs, was forbidden to Jews (Lev. 19: 27) because of pagan associations (cf. 9: 26; 25: 13).

viii. Elam (49: 34–39)
This brief prophecy was perhaps part of a warning to Zedekiah against siding with the rebellions which were spreading throughout the Babylonian empire. According to the Babylonian Chronicle **Elam**, the ancient kingdom east of Babylonia, attacked Nebuchadrezzar but when he advanced against them the king of Elam fled in panic in 596/5 B.C. and in the following year an internal revolt in Babylonia itself was suppressed. The Elamites were long famous as bowmen (35; 50: 9; 25: 25; cf. Isa. 22: 6) against the western kingdoms (*e.g.* Gen. 14: 1 ff.) so have been called the 'anti-church militant'. They were dispersed among other nations by Persians and Medes as well as by the Babylonians (36) and formed part of the forces which occupied Babylonia in 539 B.C. is no evidence that Nebuchadrezzar himself entered Susa (Sushan), the Elamite capital, as had his earlier namesake Nebuchadrezzar I *c.* 1100 B.C. and the forces of Assyria in 640 B.C. The **throne** set **in Elam** (38) is either that of judgment (cf. 1: 15; 43: 10) or the *MT* may be revocalized 'I will make the throne of Elam desolate'. **39.** Elam's recovery may be attested by Ac. 2: 9.

ix. Babylon (50: 1–51: 64)
The long final prophecy concerns the principal opponent of God's people, Babylon—representative of the world system which both attracts and persecutes the people of God. Rev. 17–18 (parallel to chs. 50–51) shows that the spirit of Babylon lives on. Objection has been taken to the Jeremianic authorship of these prophecies on several grounds: (*a*) at the time they were written (593 B.C., cf. 51: 59–60) they did not express the prophet's known viewpoint. He was then urging submission to Babylon (chs. 27–29), whereas here there is hope of an imminent end to the city and of speedy release; (*b*) the historical situation viewed the temple as violated (50: 28; 51: 11) and the Jews in exile (50: 4, 17; 51: 34). On these and other grounds the majority of scholars date the prophecy to *c.* 538 B.C. Against these arguments it must be recognized that (i) these facts

are predicted and predictable; (ii) though repetitive (perhaps for emphasis the fall of Babylon is mentioned eleven times, of the city of Babylon nine times and the return of Israel nine times) the style and quotations are Jeremianic. The sayings also closely resemble the earlier prophecies of Isaiah (chs. 13–14) and parts of Ezekiel; (iii) the purpose of the prophecy is expressly stated to be for the comfort of those already in exile in 593 B.C. or soon to follow them (51: 62); (iv) Jeremiah is stated to be the author (51: 60).

(a) **Babylon will fall (50: 1–20).** Babylon is characterized by her principal deity (2) **Bel**, 'Lord' is now a title of the god **Marduk** who with her mere 'idol-blocks' will be put to shame. **1.** The Chaldeans (Babyl. *Kaldaia*) were the native tribe who under Nabopolassar in 627 B.C. won independence from Assyria and inaugurated the renowned Neo-Babylonian (Chaldean) Dynasty which under his son Nebuchadrezzar II (605–562 B.C.) dominated the ancient Near East until Babylon fell to the Median federation under Cyrus in October 539 B.C. The latter are the foe from the north (3, 9) who are summoned to attack Babylon (14–16) now doomed (11–13). Babylon will suffer as had Judah (1: 13). Amid these events the 'Israelite' exiles will show the first stages of a penitent heart by returning to the Lord's covenant (cf. 32: 40) and so the LORD will be able to bring them back to Jerusalem. **6–7.** For the simile of the lost sheep, led astray from truth and hope by their leaders (shepherds), cf. 23: 1; Mk 6: 34; Jn 10: 12. **8–13.** The inhabitants or foreigners are told to **flee**. This may be advice to the Jews since the simile of male goats leading the flock is compared with Israel going first into exile (17). This section is also the first summons to the powerful nations of the north (9), named in 51: 27–29 and including skilled bowmen (cf. 49: 35) to act on behalf of the LORD (**1**) against the very people who had enslaved His own. The dire punishment Babylon had inflicted on others—Judah and Jerusalem (18: 16; 19: 8) and Edom (49: 17)—will fall on her. Note how her international status is reversed (12) and the prospect this gives of approaching freedom.

Verses 17–20 describe the reaction of God's people to the fall of Babylon. Just as Assyria fell to the Babylonians (and their Median confederates) in 612 B.C. in judgment for their deporting the northern tribe of Israel from Samaria in 722 B.C., so now Babylon will fall to Cyrus the king of the Medes and Persians. The effect of exile will be cleansing and restoration of the remnant. All this is portrayed as future blessing in the time of the Messiah (20, **In those days, at that time**).

(b) **Call to vanquish Babylon (50: 21–32).** National armies are consciously or uncon-

sciously to act as the weapon of divine vengeance (cf. 28) against Babylon (25) and the reason as always is given (24, 29). The reversal of rôles is emphasized. Babylon, **the hammer** (23), once God's own instrument (25: 9) is itself to be beaten in its entirety (21–27). **Merathaim** (21), 'two rebellions', may be an allusion to the deportation of the Jews under Jehoiachin and Zedekiah as well as to S. Babylonia (Babyl. *māt mārratu*—'the salt-sea land' and **Pekod**, 'punishment' (cf. 27) to the main tribe east of Babylon (Ezek. 23: 23; Babyl. *Puqudu*). The development of the trail of destruction is precisely traced (26–32). The proud and self-sufficient will fall (29–32). The young warriors (**bulls**, symbol also of the Babylonian god Marduk) will be slaughtered (27, 30) but the once oppressed peoples held there will be free to worship (28). **21. them:** some understand 'their remnant', reading *'aḥᵉrītām* for MT *'aḥᵉrēhem*, lit. 'after them' (cf. RSV). Verse 30 is repeated from 49: 20.

(c) **Babylon devastated (50: 33–46).** By contrast those who depend on God will be delivered, freed by the new conquerors. The LORD of hosts is always stronger than those who may hold His people in their grip (33). It is the duty of the nearest kinsman to avenge the wronged (34). The LORD does this for His people (Isa. 47: 4; 48: 20). Babylon will fall by the **sword** (35–37) and by **drought** (38). The latter may refer to the diversion of the river Euphrates, thus drying up essential water supplies to the city and its flood barrier defences, which enabled the invading Persians to enter the city unopposed in 539 B.C. The invaders are noted for their cavalry (42) and Elamite bowmen (29; cf. 49: 35). Thus everything on which Babylon depended (35–38) is removed and nothing left (cf. Rev. 18: 16–20). All go down to final destruction (39–43). **41–43.** Cf. 6: 22–24. **44–46.** Though this may look like one nation prevailing over another it is the LORD's work. These verses are adapted from 49: 19–21 with **Babylon** substituted for 'Edom', **Babylonians** for 'Teman', **nations** for 'Red Sea'. The lion which formerly figured Nebuchadrezzar now typifies Cyrus (Isa. 44: 24–45: 6).

(d) **God's plan concerning Babylon (51: 1–19).** The prophecy against Babylon continues by using the emphasis of various literary forms (cf. the climactic metaphor of vv. 20–23 and the taunt-song of vv. 41–43). Here the device is used in which expressions have a double meaning, partly by the use of a cypher interchanging letters called *Atbash* (see 25: 26 for explanation). Thus **the people of** (1), literally 'the heart of those who come against', as AV, stands for 'Chaldeans' (Heb. *kasdîm*); **winnow** (2) for 'strangers' (similar Heb. root) and 'Sheshach' (AV, RV, cf. NEB) for 'Babel' (41), i.e. **Babylon**. The lesson is clear. The once glorious Babylon is now incurably sick. Nothing and none can heal her (8–9; cf. 8: 22; 46: 11). The end will come suddenly before anyone has time to lift the bow or don armour (3). This in fact happened at the fall of the city, and the reading 'unto' (*'el*) is preferable to 'not' (*'al*); 'Let the archer draw . . .' (J. Bright). The only hope of escaping the judgment is to **flee** (6). This underlies the later prophecy of Rev. 17: 2–4; 18: 2–3 where the spirit of Babylon as affecting all nations and driving them to madness (7–8) is applied to the world system of the last days. God's moral purposes are to be seen in history. It is the LORD who sets the final Medo-Persian attack in progress and Babylon is warned by Him (an act of mercy) to prepare for the end (11–14). Babylonian texts (Nabonidus) show that the title 'king of the Medes' (11) was correctly in use in 544 B.C. (probably of Cyrus). **13. many waters:** of the Euphrates (cf. Rev. 17: 1). Babylon in Rev. is the spurious bride. The Lamb's bride dwells by life-giving waters. The sovereign power of the LORD of hosts, and not that of the idols, rules over nature and the affairs of men. This is stressed by a repetition from 10: 12–16 (15–16). The living Lord, in contrast to dead idols (15–18), is our inheritance and we are His (19).

(*e*) **God's instrument (51: 20–24).** Babylon will not fall by chance or by mere changing political and economic circumstances. The LORD Himself is against the city and wields the battle-axe against her. This is Cyrus who followed Nebuchadrezzar II of Babylon as 'The Hammerer' of nations (cf. 50: 23). In his turn Nebuchadrezzar had but followed Assyria in this rôle (Isa. 10: 5). Those who would interpret this as Israel must do so in a spiritual sense for otherwise such action was never literally fulfilled. **23. governors . . . officials:** Both terms are common Akkadian (Assyro-Babylonian) designations of provincial officials.

(*f*) **Agents against Babylon (51: 52–33).** The complete devastation of Babylon is emphasized again (26, 29) and is described as the reward for past sin (Dt. 32: 35; Rom. 12: 19). **25. destroying mountain** seems to be an epithet of Babylon: **mountain** is used both of strength and temple and contrasts with the mountain of the LORD (Isa. 2: 2). Babylon will become as ineffective as an extinct volcano. Verse 26 contrasts Isa. 28: 16 and the lasting foundation stone (1 Pet. 2: 6–8). The agents used by God will include many allies of **the Medes** (28; cf. v. 11), Urartu (**Ararat**—later Armenia), and their neighbours the Mannai (**Minni**) and Ashguz (**Ashkenaz**, cf. Gen. 10: 3) between Lake Van and Lake Urmiyeh in NW Persia—all mentioned in Assyrian inscriptions. Under

their **commander** (Heb. *tipsar*, cf. Nah. 3: 17; Assyr. *dupsar* 'scribe' as a high military official) they will swarm like locusts against once fertile Babylonia (27). The city's renowned postal system (31) helps spread the fear and panic of the end (cf. Lk. 21: 26). Cyrus, 'the king of the Medes' (28, so LXX and singular verbs) devised a surprise night attack through the dried up river-bed, having diverted the river Euphrates (the **river crossings**) and the water-defences (32, cf. 36) or **marshes** (Heb. *'agammim*, 'pools') which, according to Daniel (ch. 5), Herodotus and Cyrus inscriptions, brought down Babylon quickly and dramatically. The **king** who was informed (31) was probably Nabonidus, who was captured and exiled to Carmania, or his co-regent Belshazzar who was killed. The picture of the devastation by **fire** spreading to the surrounding reed-marshes (so AV 'reeds', 32) to envelop the refugees is likened to a harvest in which Babylon herself is reaped on a well-trodden **threshing floor** (cf. Isa. 17: 3).

(*g*) **Jerusalem's case against Babylon (51: 34–44).** The 'inhabitress of Zion' relates the terrible deeds Nebuchadrezzar had done to her which are to be avenged (34–35). The very horrors inflicted on Jerusalem will now befall Babylon. It will be a jackal-infested ruin, a curse instead of a praise (37–41). But here, unlike Jerusalem, there is no prophecy of restoration. The picture is of **a serpent** (NEB 'dragon', Heb. *tannin*, used of large river or sea creatures like the crocodile, Ps. 74: 13) which swallowed God's people (cf. Rev. 12: 4) but is now itself destroyed and forced to disgorge its prey, as the fish did Jonah. The language is also reminiscent of sacrifice, cf. vv. 35, 40; Heb. 'my wrong and my flesh', i.e. my torn and injured body. For the **blood** to **be on** a person is to take full responsibility (cf. 2 Sam. 1: 6; 1 Kg. 2: 37; Mt. 27: 25). **39** may reflect Belshazzar's feast on the night the city fell. Verses 41–43 are a taunt-song. For Sheshach=Babel, cf. 25: 26; 51: 1. **The sea** (42) is the overwhelming enemy invader (cf. 46: 7; 47: 2).

(*h*) **More judgment on Babylon (51: 45–53).** God's people have no place in the doomed city and so must come out (45–50). They must remain calm amid violence, rumour and revolution (46; Mt. 24: 16). While it may seem that evil triumphs (51) and Babylon's defences reach to heaven they are so strong (53, an echo of the Babel builders) her 'high towers' (NEB—perhaps the ziggurat temple-towers) are not impregnable and God will have the last word (51–58) and condemn Babylon and her images (47, 52). Though the prophecy was fulfilled within a few years the message of the 'last days' is particularly applicable today. Like the exiles (50) we must ever remember the Lord and His word. Even if the memory is tinged with shame, as theirs of the temple (51), we can rest assured that there will be **retribution** (56). Verse 49 is variously translatable: 'Even Babylon must fall for Israel's slain just as the whole earth's slain have fallen for Babylon' (Harrison; cf. RV, NEB); or better, 'Babylon in her turn must fall because of those slaughtered in Israel, just as through Babylon there fell men slaughtered all over the world' (JB).

(*i*) **The Fall of Babylon (51: 54–58).** This is now viewed as complete and may reflect the actual happening of the night of the capture (*e.g.* v. 27 and Belshazzar's feast). Note the repetition of the conqueror's name as **LORD Almighty** (57–58). The 25 foot wide double defence walls known from excavation and from Herodotus (i. 178 ff.) were in fact demolished by Xerxes in 485 B.C. All Babylon's work was 'for emptiness' (i.e. in vain) and her people's efforts over generations vanished in a moment, like a puff of smoke (cf. Hab. 2: 13).

(*j*) **The action taken with the written prophecies (51: 59–64).** As with earlier prophecies (*e.g.* 18: 1–17) this one is reinforced by act and word (63–64; cf. Rev. 18: 21). The scroll (or copy) written in 594/3 B.C. by Jeremiah probably refers to the whole book (rather than chs. 50–51 alone), the purpose of which was to be read aloud (63) and to be the comfort of the exiles (Rev. has a similar purpose). On this cf. E. W. Nicholson, *Preaching to the Exiles* (Oxford, 1970).

Jeremiah took advantage of the journey to Babylon by **Seraiah** (59) who was the brother of his friend and scribe Baruch (32: 2) and the **staff officer** (so NIV, not 'quiet prince' AV). LXX makes him 'commissioner of tribute' sent by Zedekiah, whose journey to Babylon at this time is otherwise unknown. The symbolic action and ritual word (64) emphasized the perpetual destruction by God of the greatest world power of the OT era at its capital on the river Euphrates. **62.** 'and they shall be weary' (*MT*, AV echoes from v. 58; LXX, RSV, JB, NEB omit). **64. Thus far . . .** is a colophon or editorial note to mark off Jeremiah's own words from the appendix (ch. 52) which was taken from other historical sources (2 Kg. 24–25).

III. A HISTORICAL APPENDIX (52: 1–34)
i. The Fall of Jerusalem (52: 1–30)

This was probably added to show how Jeremiah's principal and constant prophecy of the coming fall of Jerusalem was fulfilled. Verses 1–27 are taken almost verbatim from the state records used by the compiler of 2 Kg. 24: 18–25: 21 (see commentary there) and are added here much as 2 Kg. 18–20 are in Isaiah (chs. 36–39). The details of the temple furnishings taken as spoil (17–23) are particularly relevant since their restoration after the seventy years'

captivity (Ezr. 1: 7–11) had been the main argument in oppositon to the false prophets (ch. 28). Some of the major differences between this and other accounts (*e.g.* ch. 39) are noted. **4–16.** This section appears in abbreviated form in 39: 1–10; vv. 7–11 provide more information than Kgs. on Zedekiah's torture and imprisonment. The siege lasted from January 588 (4) to July 587 B.C. (6)—the reckoning here being according to the Babylonian calendar year beginning March/April. **12. tenth day** (cf. 2 Kg. 25: 8, 'seventh day') perhaps includes the time between Nebuzaradan's arrival and the firing of the city. Verses 17–23 supplement the list of temple spoil given in 2 Kg. 25: 13–17. The larger articles (*e.g.* the 10 cubit diameter laver, **bronze Sea**) were broken up for transportation (17) and the smaller items taken for their value as gold and silver (19). For a description of the two large freestanding bronze pillars from the front of the temple (20; cf. 1 Kg. 7: 15–22) see *NBD* p. 593. **23. on the sides:** Heb. *rūhāh*, NEB 'exposed to view'; some read 'space' (*rewah*). **24–27.** Cf. 2 Kg. 25: 18–21. Execution was confined to those who were instigators of Zedekiah's rebellion or considered to be representative of the people in this. **Seraiah** was a grandson of the high-priest Hilkiah under Josiah (1 Chr. 6: 13–15) and **Zephaniah** an important anti-Babylonian leader (cf. 29: 24–32; 37: 3) and deputy to the high priest. **28–30** is a unique source. The variation in number of prisoners may be due to listing only the males taken in 597 B.C. whereas 2 Kg. 24: 14, 16 shows that complete families from Jerusalem numbered more than 18,000. Regnal years here follow the Babylonian system, thus **seventh year** of Nebuchadrezzar 598/7 B.C. (cf. 2 Kg. 24: 12, 'eighth', because the event recorded follows the change of year a few days after the fall of the city) and **eighteenth year** (29) is the 'nineteenth' of Jer. 52: 12. The total in verse 30 may include captives from Egypt.

ii. There is still hope (52: 31–34)

This is the first step in the promised restoration. As with other accounts God's punitive action on His own people ends with words of mercy. 2 Kg. 25: 27–30 shows how Jehoiachin was released on parole by Nebuchadrezzar's successor Evil-Merodach (=Amēl-Marduk, 'servant of the god Marduk'), king of Babylon 562–560 B.C.; see R. H. Sack, *Amēl-Marduk* (1974). Babylonian ration lists attest the presence of Jehoiachin and other Judeans fed by the king in Babylon in 595–570 B.C.

BIBLIOGRAPHY

BRIGHT, J. *Jeremiah*. Anchor Bible (New York, 1959).
CAWLEY, F., and MILLARD, A. R. 'Jeremiah' in *The New Bible Commentary Revised* (London, 1970), pp. 626–658.

CUNLIFFE-JONES, H., *Jeremiah*. Torch Bible (London, 1960).

ELLISON, H. L. 'The Prophecy of Jeremiah'. A series of exegetical articles in *The Evangelical Quarterly*, 31 (1959)-40(1968).

HARRISON, R. K., *Jeremiah and Lamentations. TOTC* (London, 1973).

HYATT, J. P., and HOPPER, S. R., 'Jeremiah', in *IB* V (1956), pp.999–1142.

LESLIE, E. A., *Jeremiah* (New York, Nashville, 1954).

MUILENBERG, J., 'Jeremiah', in *IDB* II (1962), pp. 823–835.

NICHOLSON, E. W., *Jeremiah 1–25; 26–52.* Cambridge Bible Commentary on the NEB. (Cambridge, 1973, 1975).

NICHOLSON, E. W., *Preaching to the Exiles* (Oxford, 1970).

PATERSON, J., 'Jeremiah', in *Peake's Commentary on the Bible*[2] (London, 1962), pp.537–562.

ROBINSON, H. W., *The Cross in the Old Testament* (London, 1955).

THOMPSON, J. A., *The Book of Jeremiah. NICOT* (Grand Rapids, 1980).

WISEMAN, D. J., *Chronicles of Chaldean Kings (626–556 B.C.)* (London, 1956).

WISEMAN, D. J. (ed.), *Peoples of Old Testament Times* (Oxford, 1973).

YOUNG, E. J., *An Introduction to the Old Testament* (London, 1956), pp.223–233.

LAMENTATIONS

W. OSBORNE

Literary Form

Little more than a cursory reading of the book is required before the 'lament' nature of the poems becomes evident. Yet a more careful examination of the text is required to specify the exact nature of each of the five poems. The poems vary quite considerably in form, even though they are woven about a common theme.

The history of lament literature can be traced back some 4,000 years to the Sumerians, who composed dirges following the destruction of certain famous cities in Mesopotamia. Two of the best known of the extant Sumerian laments, 'The Lamentation over the Destruction of Ur' (cf. *ANET* pp. 445–63) and 'Lamentation over the Destruction of Sumer and Ur' (cf. *ANET* pp. 611–19) have been examined for their similarity to Lamentations. Some of the phrases are indeed strikingly similar, but it is unrealistic to imagine a direct borrowing by Lamentations. Mesopotamian influence on the literary development of Syria–Palestine was considerable, and apposite phrases entered the repertoire of Palestinian scribes over a long period of time. Indeed many of those phrases in Lamentations said to be derived from Sumerian models are already paralleled in the writings of earlier Israelite prophets. Prophetic use of the 'lament' forms already involved using the traditional forms of dirge employed in the community, and in some cases transforming them. Thus funerary dirges, personal laments, communal laments, etc. are employed by the prophets to lend persuasion to their arguments. One significant transformation of the funerary dirge was its use in a satirical fashion. Here a lament is composed in the past tense as though the person were already dead, to indicate the certainty of his demise. Normally composed and executed by professional mourners, the laments were rigidly patterned to ensure that no part of the ritual was left out. Characteristic of many forms of the lament is the tendency to heighten the loss by constant reference to a glorious past *e.g.*, 'How the mighty have fallen! . . . Saul and Jonathan, beloved and cherished' (2 Sam. 1: 19–27).

In Lamentations the rigidity of the forms of personal laments, communal dirges, etc. is broken down, and the forms are much more fluid; indeed, only ch. 5 conforms to the traditional structure of the community lament.

The reason for this will be discussed under 'authorship' and also in the commentary.

Historical Background

There is little debate concerning the events described in the poetry of the laments. The Babylonian destruction of Jerusalem in 587 B.C. is the occasion for these bitter dirges and their assessment of the significance of those bewildering events. Judah had survived a period of Assyrian pressure during which Samaria had fallen, and had only recently enjoyed a revival of religion under Josiah during which the significance of the temple in Jerusalem had been stressed to the detriment of local syncretistic shrines. All this tended to create a climate of opinion in which Zion was seen as inviolable, since she possessed all the symbols and hence assurance of God's continued presence and favour. It was against this mistaken notion that Jeremiah campaigned so vigorously, insisting that the symbols meant nothing when divorced from 'true religion' (Jas 1: 27).

Authorship and Date

The position of Lamentations immediately after Jeremiah in our English versions is due to the tradition, adopted by the LXX and other ancient versions, that Jeremiah was the author. Rabbinic authors refer to the book simply as 'Lamentations' (*qînôt*) or 'How!' (*'êkāh*), and in the Hebrew Bible it is placed with the 'Writings'. It is easy to see how Jeremiah has become the principal contender for authorship. In 2 Chr. 35: 25 he is said to have composed laments on the death of Josiah which 'became an ordinance in Israel'. Nothing, however, in Lamentations can be taken to refer to Josiah's death in 609 B.C., and other features of the book are frequently taken to imply that Jeremiah could not have been the author. Chief among these considerations are sentiments which seem to many to be ill suited to Jeremiah's stance. It is asserted that he would not have written 4: 17 'we **watched** for a nation that **could** not save' since he opposed reliance on Egypt (Jer. 2: 18; 37: 5–10). Further, the elevated estimate of Zedekiah, '**our very life breath**', is regarded as strange, given Jeremiah's dealings with this king (37: 17). In short, the sentiments of the writer seem more like those of the hopes of the people whom Jeremiah denounced than the sentiments of the prophet as outlined in his prophecies. This is not a decisive argument, however, when it is considered that in Lamentations the writer is at pains to stress the *corporate* nature of the nation. In the final analysis no definite conclusion as to authorship can be maintained.

It is generally agreed that the book was written not long after 587 B.C. The vivid descriptions of the misery of the city have all the marks of an eyewitness. The different forms employed in the five poems has suggested to some scholars a plurality of authors, but the consistent use of the alphabetical form and a unity of viewpoint together with repeated use of prophetic phrases and reference to their covenant warnings suggests a single author. Further the book is symmetrical, and the types of laments are chosen to conform to this symmetry. The central chapter contains the kernel of the book couched in the form of a modified individual lament. It is sandwiched on either side by two chapters full of the misery and despair of laments to emphasize, using a familiar form of the prophets and full of prophetic

allusion, the vindication of the prophetic warnings. Yet being so sandwiched, the central chapter with its note of hope is set in stark relief. For the significance of the choice of the form of lament for each chapter see the commentary.

Poetic Structure

The first four chapters are acrostics, i.e. each verse begins with a letter of the Hebrew alphabet in turn so that each chapter has twenty-two verses (except ch. 3 where every letter of the alphabet is used to begin three consecutive lines, hence 66 verses); cf. Ps. 119. Various reasons have been suggested for this device, some quite fanciful, but it seems quite likely that this rigid structure is being used as a control in what is clearly a highly emotive and potentially erratic situation. Ch. 5 does not employ the alphabetic device but retains the twenty-two verse arrangement.

The rhythm is 3+2 or *qînāh* metre, with variations of 2+3 and 3+3.

ANALYSIS

I   FIRST LAMENT (1: 1–22)
  i The Present Distress: (a) An Onlooker's View (1: 1–11)
  ii The Present Distress: (b) Zion's Assessment (1: 12–22)

II   SECOND LAMENT (2: 1–22)
  i Judgment in the Household of God (2: 1–9)
  ii The Cost of False Confidence (2: 10–13)
  iii The Source of False Confidence (2: 14–17)
  iv Yahweh, Zion's True Confidence (2: 18–22)

III   THIRD LAMENT (3: 1–66)
  i A Man of Sorrows (3: 1–21)
  ii A Time to Hope in God (3: 22–39)
  iii A Time to Take Stock (3: 40–54)
  iv A God Ready to Answer (3: 55–66)

IV   FOURTH LAMENT (4: 1–22)
  i The Glory is Departed (4: 1–16)
  ii Broken Reeds: Faithless Friends (4: 17–22)

V   FIFTH LAMENT (5: 1–22)
  i Oh That We Had Never Sinned! (5: 1–18)
  ii But God, Rich in Mercy (5: 19–22)

I. FIRST LAMENT (1: 1–22)
i. The Present Distress: (a) An Onlooker's View (1: 1–11)
1. How (*'êkāh*): the genre of the poem is immediately obvious from the use of this term. It is employed frequently in the prophetic lament

literature (cf. Isa. 1: 21; 14: 4; Jer. 48: 17). See the introduction. There follows a carefully arranged sequence of images designed to heighten the contrast between Jerusalem's present misery and her former glory. This is a feature typical of Near Eastern lament literature in general. Given the vivid and detailed nature of the description, it is generally agreed that the poet must have been an eyewitness of the events. The destruction which called forth this moving account is clearly that wrought by the Babylonians in 587 B.C. There is no valid reason to see in ch. 1 any reference to the earlier attack of 597 B.C. (*contra* Wood). The speaker in vv. 1–11 is an onlooker, possibly the writer himself, or even one of the 'passers by' of v. 12 being used as a literary ploy. The derision of outsiders following the humiliation of the sinful nation is already a feature in the prophetic literature, where it is regarded as a consequence of breach of Yahweh's covenant (cf. Dt. 29: 24 ff.; 1 Kg. 9: 7 ff.). **full of people—deserted, great—widow, queen—slave:** the contrasts are extreme. Childlessness, widowhood and slavery in the Ancient Near East were fearful conditions, dreaded by all, even the humblest. How incredible that it should have happened to one so notable (the personified Jerusalem)! **2. her lovers:** those who wooed her into alliance against the Babylonians (Jer. 27: 3) have now left her to lament alone, or even joined the Babylonians in their invasion. **3. After affliction:** the NIV translation of this verse depends on reading the Hebrew preposition *min* 'from' as causal, because of affliction. It seems better to give it its more usual force 'out of, from', and regard the whole verse as referring to events in Judah's past. She has finally suffered the ultimate punishment of exile from her sacred soil, even though her history of disobedience to Yahweh has meant that her existence has often been one of **affliction and harsh labor**, even when as an independent nation she dwelt **among the nations**. 'Rest' in the land was a clear sign of God's favour towards His people, and failure to achieve that rest implied His disfavour (cf. Heb. 4: 8–10). **4.** Deprived of access to their holy city, the pilgrims no longer throng her roads on their way to the set feasts. The tense of the verbs has changed from the perfect of the previous verse. Participles now indicate the continuous nature of the mourning and desolation felt by the cities' inhabitants, particularly those once busily involved in these joyous festivals. **her maidens grieve:** the Hebrew depicts the maidens 'grieving' (*nûgôt*) over departed joy. **5.** The reason for Zion's startling reversal in fortune is not hard to find. **the LORD has brought her grief because of her many sins: sins** translates Heb. *pešaʿ*, 'rebellion' which, although it is originally a term used in international politics, came to signify disobedience to the terms of the covenant with Yahweh. Hence the consequences outlined in this verse—**her foes have become her masters** and **her children have gone into exile**—are punishments laid down for breach

of covenant in the Pentateuch (Dt. 28: 14; Lev. 26). This theme will be forcefully developed in the poems which follow. **6.** The city's lost glory is best illustrated by the plight of her nobility. Once the leaders of a prosperous nation they are become like frightened animals, too weak and fearful of their pursuers to even stand still to find pasture. **7. Wandering;** the MT reading is *merûdāh* 'homelessness'. The phrase is best rendered 'in her time of affliction and homelessness', and is meant to contrast Jerusalem's present pitiable condition (cf. the same terms used at Isa. 58: 7) with her **treasures** of former days. A too rigid view of the poetic structure has forced various commentators to delete one or other of the four lines in this verse to make it conform to the three line scheme of the other verses of this chapter. **8.** The reading **unclean** is achieved by emendation of *niddāh*, which is better rendered 'object of scorn'. Zion's sin has not only affected her political life, but now also her religious prerogatives are lost. **her nakedness:** the term is designed to express her low standing, even loose living, and hence by extension her idolatry in which she **sinned greatly. 9.** This insidious evil has polluted her, and brought about an unexpected ruin. The cry from Zion is meant as a quotation to reflect the surprise of the city at her overthrow. Note that while vv. 5–7 reflect her political distress and vv. 9 ff. her religious plight, the interjections by Zion in v. 9 and v. 11 reflect the nature of *her* concern. **10.** Even the temple, which was the symbol of Yahweh's presence and Israel's privilege, has become defiled by the entry of forbidden aliens. **11.** Jerusalem's former glory, both secular and sacred, is forgotten in her preoccupation with mere survival.

ii. The Present Distress: (b) Zion's Assessment (1: 12–22)

12. In the aftermath of the destruction the city has had time to assess the situation, and determine causes. The true source of her trouble is perceived: this is what **the LORD brought on me in the day of his fierce anger**. The opening words of the verse are lit. 'not to you' giving rise to the NIV's improbable **is it nothing to you?** The appeal to uninvolved onlookers for a sympathetic appraisal occurs again at Job 21: 9; Lam. 2: 15; cf. Mt. 27: 39. **13–15.** The true horror of the situation has begun to dawn on Jerusalem, not only because all she boasted in is gone, and she is treated as a captive animal, but the cause is now all too clear: **my sins . . . have come upon my neck** (14). For the summoning of an assembly as the occasion for such a judgment cf. 1 Kg. 21: 9 ff. **16–17.** The utter helplessness of Zion is now emphasized by the city herself, and by the author's comment which represents a kind of crisis point in the development of Jerusalem's appreciation that from here on she knows that **The LORD is righteous** (18). cf. RSV 'in the right'. From this point on each element of her disastrous overthrow is seen in the solemn light of her rebellion against Yahweh (18–20). There is no plea for restoration or grace in ch. 1; this will develop gradually only after the full horrendous consequences of Zion's sin are unfolded. The only appeal she feels able to make in terms of justice is for punishment to be meted out to her enemies who behaved so cruelly towards her (21–22). **20. death:** it is best to render 'plague', another possible rendering of Heb. *māwet* (cf. Jer. 15: 2; 18: 21).

II. SECOND LAMENT (2: 1–22)
i. Judgment in the Household of God (2: 1–9)

The second ode will expand upon the nature of Yahweh's work of destruction in Zion as it affects both chosen people and places. Each verse depicts in detail the fearful destruction of all those institutions and material blessings which should have symbolized Zion's special covenantal prerogatives with Yahweh. Such symbols are, however, illusory when the very basis of the covenant relationship in Zion's devotion to Yahweh is completely absent. Thus each of the verses 1–8 begin quite specifically by attributing the fearful devastation of all that Zion held dear to the action of Yahweh, her Sovereign Lord. **1. covered . . . with the cloud of his anger:** better rendered 'disgraced' (taking *ya'ib* as from the same middle yod verb as the Arabic *'aba*). This agrees well with the sentiments which follow for **the splendor of Israel** has been **hurled down**. The phrase **from heaven to earth** is used to imply the most extreme fall imaginable (cf. *e.g.*, Prov. 25: 3), while Israel's **splendor** comprised all those gifts lavished upon her by God which set her apart from other nations and signified divine election. Specially prominent among these were the temple and its furniture, **his footstool**, yet not even this caused God to turn away His wrath. The elect have frequently to learn that election is often a costly blessing, for God exercises a special scrutiny over His elect. **2 ff.** Yahweh is now depicted as a furious warrior who by his irresistible power has brought to an end all that Judah trusted in for the future. It is a pathetic condition for the people of God who had misplaced their trust to rely on **princes** (2), **horn** (mg. strength) (3), **palaces** (5), **strongholds** (5) and even God's **dwelling** (6, now the temple, the outward sign of God's presence) and its officials, and **appointed feasts** (6) instead of on Yahweh Himself. All these things are meaningless without true trust and worship, so **The LORD has rejected his altar** and **abandoned his sanctuary** (7). The **shout** is now not the joy of a

feast, but the enemy in the Holy Place itself—and Yahweh Himself has done it! Indeed just as He was able to approve the original building of the temple complex (1 Kg. 9: 3), He **'stretched out a measuring line'** like a workman about to destroy in a systematic and deliberate fashion the **wall around the Daughter of Zion. 9. the law is no more:** because those responsible for teaching the people God's law (*tôrāh*) are all gone into exile.

ii. The Cost of False Confidence (2: 10–13)
10. elders of . . . Zion . . . young women of Jerusalem: probably meant to indicate the entire population remaining in the city. They are a pitiable group for whom the poet weeps, for they are so dispirited and bereft of material goods they can only sit around and watch their children die from hunger. There seems to be no hope of remedy: **Your wound is as deep as the sea. Who can heal you?**

iii. The Source of False Confidence (2: 14–17)
The nation had been led astray by **visions . . . false and worthless** mediated by the professional prophets (cf. Jer. 23: 9 ff.). Their confidence in ultimate deliverance despite their mode of life was misplaced. What was needed was an exposing of **sin** so as to **ward off your captivity** (14). Zion's enemies will mock her because of her confidence and pride, now that she is destroyed. Their most fervent desires have been fulfilled: **this is the day we have waited for** (16). Now the full extent of Yahweh's destructive purpose is displayed **which he decreed long ago** (17), namely in the covenant curses (cf. Lev. 26: 14 ff., Dt. 28: 15 ff.).

iv. Yahweh, Zion's True Confidence (2: 18–22)
18. The first line of v. 18 is difficult in the *MT*. The AV reflects the difficulty while the RSV has resorted to considerable emendation to produce its version, and the GNB's 'let your walls cry' is of little help. The entire verse and the one following are nevertheless a call to the city to be in earnest about seeking the Lord Himself as the only true source of confidence. Harrison, in fact, reads the **wall of the Daughter of Zion** in apposition to **the LORD**, symbolizing His protective strength for the city. **19. for the lives of your children:** introducing the petition of Zion outlined in vv. 20–22. Zion's petition is a cry for mercy out of a growing sense that all she laboured for in producing prophets, priests, maidens and young men has proven to be in vain—all is lost for in **the day of the LORD'S anger** the foundation for such labour was false (1 C. 3: 10 ff.).

III. THIRD LAMENT (3: 1–66)
The identity of the sufferer (the **I**) in vv. 1–39 has been the focus for a great deal of discussion

and conjecture, and various individuals have been suggested, chiefly Jeremiah, while the idea of a collective 'I' in which Zion speaks under the guise of an individual has found acceptance. Not only the identity of the sufferer but the relation of this chapter to the rest of the book is at issue. Occupying as it does the focal point of the book, the third dirge contains an essential core of hope of restoration in God's good time. There is a symmetry about the book which highlights this present chapter, sandwiched as it is between two blocks of material with a dominant and vivid description of despair. The writer has throughout chosen to express himself in traditional forms (cf. introduction), and the one most suited to continue the lament genre and yet introduce the essential element of hope is the personal lament with its frequent theme of 'certainty of hearing'. This is a feature in psalms of personal lament where the subject inevitably comes to an assurance that his cry will be heard. The form is common enough *e.g.* in the Psalms, but the writer has modified it, as indeed he has other traditional forms, to his particular purpose. No specific individual is intended, nor indeed is it necessarily a communal 'I', but the 'certainty of hearing' motif is introduced by the literary form and then applied to the 'we' of vv. 40 ff.

i. A Man of Sorrows (3: 1–21)
Much of the language used to describe the afflicted individual is reminiscent of the 'Psalms of Lament', in fact v. 6 is a direct quotation from Ps. 143: 3, with the first two words transposed for the acrostic. Unlike the psalms, however, the sufferer in this chapter is under punishment by Yahweh Himself, hence his ability to transfer the picture with its lessons to the nation. **21. Yet this I call to mind, and therefore I have hope** represents a syncopation by the writer. The rigid structure of the triple acrostic of this section imposed a strain on the writer and the reader. It is relieved by the writer when he ensures that divisions of thought and literary form frequently do not coincide. Hillers points out how frequently this 'syncopation' occurs in the book *e.g.* 3: 3, 6, 12, 18, 42, 48, 60 and 2: 8, etc. In the present verse the last thought of the section vv. 19–21 (Heb. *zayin*) is syncopated and forms a bridge with what follows to introduce the element of hope.

ii. A Time to Hope in God (3: 22–39)
The emendation in the *MT* to produce the RSV rendering of 22a is slight and is suggested by the Targum and Peshitta. The sandwich of despair in which this section is deliberately placed makes its sentiments regarding God's faithfulness all the more forceful (this is a frequent device in Hebrew poetry). In fact it stands out as a moving statement of the certainty of God's ultimate purposes of good for

man (cf. Rom. 8: 28). God's anger is the passing phase, His mercy is always available. But He is the Sovereign Lord who dispenses His gifts in His own appointed time. Punishment may be designed to educate, and this is best for a man **while he is young** (27). In any event, Yahweh does not **willingly** (better 'wilfully') **bring affliction or grief to the children of men** (33). Yahweh does not behave unjustly towards men to deny them rights, but His concern involves dealing with the just and the unjust, and hence **calamities and good things** come from Him (38). **39.** The mention of **a man punished for his sins** leads into the next logical sequence.

iii. A Time to Take Stock (3: 40–54)
40–48. The mention of sin and punishment in v. 39 provides the basis for linking what has gone before with the experience of Judah, hence the 'we' passages begin. If all that has gone before is true of individuals then why not also of communities? This leads to an exhortation to a sincere repentance—**Let us . . . return to the LORD. . . lift up our hearts and our hands to God** (40, 41)—and gives rise to the communal prayer of confession that follows. **48.** Another example of syncopation in which the community prayer is lost and the individual reappears to complete the literary form of individual lament in the following verses. **49–54.** The form of individual lament is again taken up in typical language so as to lead to the 'certainty of a hearing' in which God will answer the individual and take up his cause.

iv. A God Ready to Answer (3: 55–66)
Now that the parallels in experience have been established between those served by the individual laments and Zion, the poet is free to complete the form and expect the nation to follow the parallel, through to the point where Yahweh will certainly answer the penitents' cry. **59. Uphold my cause:** introducing the idea of God as a judge prepared to punish the guilty party. This brings the poem into line with Zion's request for a consistent application of God's judgment, which she feels will involve her enemies, a feature already expressed by her at the close of ch. 1.

IV. FOURTH LAMENT (4: 1–22)
In keeping with the symmetry of the book this chapter is designed to correspond closely to ch. 2. Just as in ch. 2, so here, the former glory of the nation is forcefully contrasted with its present misery, and the officials, especially the professional prophets (4: 13; 2: 14), are castigated for their deception of the people. Yahweh's anger is also clearly seen as the reason for the present distress (cf. 3: 6, 11, 16).

i. The Glory is Departed (4: 1–16)
This section is divided into three subsections by vv. 6, 11 and 16, attributing each description

ultimately to Yahweh's anger. **1–6.** This subsection deals with the **sons of Zion**; once as precious as gold, they are now discarded as dross. **sacred gems** (Heb. holy stones): referring not to the temple blocks but, as J. A. Emerton suggests (*ZAW* 79 (1967) 233–36), holy (*qōdeš*) is to be equated with Akkadian, Arabic and Aramaic cognates to mean 'jewel'. Thus 'precious stones' corresponds to the **pure gold** of v. 1a. The neglectful attitude of **ostriches** (3) toward their young is proverbial (Job 39: 13–18). Mention of the fearful destruction of **Sodom** (6) highlights again the use of images from the covenant warning passages (cf. Dt. 29: 22). But Zion's sin is so great that the punishment is far more appalling (cf. Mt. 11: 20 ff.), and wrought by the hands of wicked men, not God. **7–11.** This subsection deals with the leaders who were once so proud and easily recognized by their grooming, and are now **not recognized in the streets** but share the common fate and common appearance. The NIV **princes** is actually 'nazirites' in the *MT*, but the sense of the term here appears to be one of nobility as, *e.g.*, in Gen. 49: 6 where Joseph is the *nāzîr* of his brothers (cf. Dt. 33: 16). Their appearance is so affected by the awful **hunger** to which the city is subjected. These vivid and fearful pictures have all the stamp of an eyewitness account. There are times when the survivors almost appear to have the worst of the bargain. **11. consumed her foundations:** takes up the architectural metaphor, and corresponds to its use in 2: 8 ff. **12–16.** So impressive were Jerusalem's defences that no one could readily conceive of her being captured, but she fell from internal weakness caused by **the sins of her prophets and the iniquities of her priests** (13). Those who especially charged to instruct the people in God's requirements for purity have failed, and now they are **defiled with blood** (14), and themselves the source of uncleanness. Thus the people seeing the priests defiled by contact with dead bodies (Lev. 21: 1 ff.) will not go near them, and they find no place at all to employ their talents. **16. The LORD himself has scattered them:** even as in ch. 2, the Lord will not now regard religious symbol or office as a substitute for righteousness.

ii. Broken Reeds: Faithless Friends (4: 17–22)

As in ch. 2, misplaced confidence was bitterly rewarded: **we watched for a nation that could not save** (17). Despite Jeremiah's warnings, the nation looked to Egypt for help against the Babylonians (Jer. 37: 7), but it was futile. The wall was breached and all resistance came to an end. The king and his soldiers fled the city but were caught in the plain of Jericho where Zedekiah was taken prisoner (Jer. 52: 6–9; 2 Kg. 25: 3–6). The expressions **our very**

breath and **under his shadow** (20) as applied to the Judean king are ultimately derived from Egyptian usage associated with the Pharaoh. The high-sounding titles were of little comfort when the king lay bound in a Babylonian prison. Egypt and Zedekiah were not the only source of disappointment; Edom has actually rejoiced to see the downfall of Judah (Ob. 10–16). This was an act of extreme treachery from a 'brother', and Zion is consoled to think that while her own punishment has justly run its full course, the same justice would yet be meted out to Edom (21).

V. FIFTH LAMENT (5: 1–22)

This fifth lament differs from the others in a number of respects. Firstly it no longer employs the acrostic form even though it is made up of twenty-two verses. It is an example of a 'community lament' like those found in Pss. 44; 60; 74; 79; 80 and 83. The symmetry of the book is maintained in that ch. 5 is designed to balance ch. 1 to a considerable extent, and many of the sentiments of ch. 1 will again be taken up here. The great change, however, is that this final chapter now includes the hope of the individual (cf. ch. 3) transferred to the community in general. In a sense Zion no longer 'sits lonely' but is the 'we' of ch. 5, devastated to be sure, but no longer devoid of hope.

i. Oh That We Had Never Sinned (5: 1–18)

3. fatherless . . . widows: echoing the situation in ch. 1 after the destruction of the city. Babylonian rule is established and has proven harsh: **we are weary** (5). On **no rest** (5) see 1: 3. As in ch. 1 there is a reflection on their past misdeeds among the nations. The sentiment of v. 7 is not intended to mitigate their present responsibility, but in keeping with the 'communal' sense of the poem points out the inevitable consequences of our actions on our fellows. The community has come to appreciate the deep significance of her sin by its consequences: **woe to us, for we have sinned!** (16; better 'alas that we ever sinned!'). All she treasured most is lost, and the section ends in a climax of loss, for even **Mount Zion . . . lies desolate** (18).

ii. But God, Rich in Mercy (5: 19–22)

Though the symbols of His presence are gone, Yahweh remains, and despite Israel's subjugation He still rules over all men. As Israel experienced His restoring power **of old**, so they may still pray in hope: **Restore us to yourself** (21). The final verse with its recurring discordant note has caused the synagogue in its services to repeat v. 21, to end on a note of hope. But vv. 20–21 constitute a microcosm of the entire book; hope sandwiched between despair gleams all the brighter.

BIBLIOGRAPHY

FUERST, W. J., *The Books of Ruth, Esther, Ecclesiastes, Song of Songs, Lamentations. CBC* (Cambridge, 1975).

GORDIS, R., *The Song of Songs and Lamentations* (New York, 1974).

GOTTWALD, N. K., *Studies in the Book of Lamentations. SBT* 14 (rev. ed., London, 1962).

HARRISON, R. K., *Jeremiah and Lamentations. TOTC* (London, 1973).

HILLERS, D. R., *Lamentations. AB* (New York, 1972).

KNIGHT, G. A. F., *Esther, Song of Songs, Lamentations. TC* (London, 1955).

KRAUS, H. J., *Klagelieder* (Threni), Biblischer Kommentar (Neukirchen-Vluyn, 1968).

MEEK, T. J., and MERRILL, W. P., *The Book of Lamentations. IB* VI, (New York and Nashville, 1956).

RUDOLPH, W., *Das Buch Ruth—Das Hohe Lied—Die Klagelieder*, Kommentar zum Alten Testament Deutsch (Gütersloh, 1962).

WOOD, G. F., *Lamentations*. Jerome Bible Commentary (London, 1969).

STEPHENS-HODGE, L. E. H., *Lamentations. NBCR* (London, 1970).

EZEKIEL

F. F. BRUCE

The Man and the Book

Ezekiel, member of a priestly family attached to the Jerusalem temple, was one of the exiles taken to Babylon with King Jehoiachin in 597 B.C. In the fifth year of his exile he was called to the prophetic ministry, and exercised that ministry for over twenty years. His prophecy was directed mainly to his fellow-exiles in whom, he believed (as his elder contemporary Jeremiah also did), the hope of Israel's future rested. It is they who are addressed throughout as 'the house of Israel', the nucleus of the restored nation.

For the first six years his message was predominantly one of disaster. The established order in Judah and Jerusalem was doomed: the exiles had to realize this and not put their trust in a sudden reversal of fortune and an early return home. But after Jerusalem was taken and its temple destroyed by the Babylonian forces, his message became one of restoration. In the arrangement of his prophecies the messages of doom (chs. 1–24) are separated from the messages of hope (chs. 33–48) by a series of oracles against foreign nations (chs. 25–32).

The book of Ezekiel (with Isaiah, Jeremiah and the Twelve) belongs to the Latter Prophets, the second subdivision of the Prophets, which in turn is the second of the three divisions of the Hebrew Bible. Its canonicity must have been established well before the Christian era. Yet rabbinical tradition asserts that at one time there was talk of its being withdrawn from public use. The chariot vision of ch. 1 gave rise to a school of speculative mysticism which, it was feared, might be a menace to orthodoxy. (In due course, indeed, this mysticism made a major contribution to mediaeval kabbalism.) Some rabbis insisted, therefore, that Ezekiel's chariot vision should be read or expounded in school only to students of the highest maturity, and that it should not be included in the synagogue lectionary. Again, some of the ritual prescriptions for the age of restoration in Ezekiel's last vision (chs. 40–48) were inconsistent with those laid down in the Pentateuch, and no harmonization seemed to be possible. 'When Elijah comes', said some pious scribes, 'he will explain the discrepancy.' Happily, it was not necessary to wait so long: a special blessing is pronounced on one Hananiah the son of Hezekiah (a rabbi of the generation c. A.D. 70–100, who also defended the chariot vision

against the charge of leading people into heresy), because he sat up night after night, burning the contents of 300 jars of oil, until he found a way to interpret Ezekiel so that he did not conflict with Moses (TB Ḥagigah 13a, b).

Date and Composition

Until the 1920s there was almost unanimous agreement that the book of Ezekiel was substantially a literary unity, containing the oracles of one man who lived among the Jewish exiles in Babylonia in the first half of the sixth century B.C. This agreement was shattered in 1924 with the publication of G. Hölscher's *Hesekiel, der Dichter und das Buch* ('Ezekiel, the Poet and the Book') and for about a generation a wide variety of views about the date and the composition of the book was ventilated. It was dated at various points between the seventh and the third centuries B.C., and even when a genuine core of prophecy was ascribed to the historical Ezekiel, this was confined to the poetry in the book, amounting to 170 verses, according to Hölscher, or to some 250 verses, according to W. A. Irwin (*The Problem of Ezekiel*, 1943).

Then there was a marked return to a recognition of the exilic setting and essential unity of the book. This is the position adopted here, and it no longer calls for defence against a contrary dominant position.

How long or short an interval separated Ezekiel's visions and oracles from their being recorded in their present form is uncertain, but it was probably not more than a generation. We do not know if Ezekiel had one particular secretary to whom he dictated his messages as Jeremiah dictated his to Baruch (cf. Jer. 36: 4, 32), or if he had disciples to whom, like Isaiah a century and a half before, he committed them for safe keeping (cf. Isa. 8: 16). Some of the sections dated before the fall of Jerusalem include passages which reflect the conditions of the later exile: these may have been added by way of interpretation. Ezekiel's oracles, like Jeremiah's (if we follow E. W. Nicholson, *Preaching to the Exiles*, 1970), may have formed the basis of exhortations addressed to the exiles in the generation after they were first uttered, to keep them in remembrance of the prophet's lessons and the hope of restoration which he proclaimed after the final disaster in Jerusalem. What we should have in the book in that case is not an 'authentic' kernel and 'inauthentic' additions (as Hölscher and others maintained) but a living and on-going interpretative activity in close relation to the prophet himself, setting forth in explicit detail the meaning and relevance of his message.

Place and Personality

As for the place of Ezekiel's prophesying, some of his symbolic actions and oracles against Jerusalem—*e.g.* his mimic siege in 4: 1 ff. and departure as for exile in 12: 1 ff., and especially his 'visit' to the city in chs. 8–11—are so direct and realistic that many expositors have inferred from them that he was present in the city for at least part of the last six years of Zedekiah's reign. But this inference is unnecessary. It was for the exiles that Ezekiel's symbolic actions were designed, in order to convince them that Jerusalem was doomed; and the 'visit' of chs. 8–11 is expressly said to have been paid in a state of ecstasy—when, as the prophet says, 'the hand of the Sovereign LORD' fell upon him. Moreover, in describing Jerusalem in chs. 8–11 he was describing a city with which (including the temple area) he was quite familiar, since he had left it only six years before the 'visit'. But if (as seems most probable) the account of his ecstatic levitation and transportation is to be taken as the record of what he consciously experienced, then it provides some insight into the peculiar character of his prophetic calling and inspiration and perhaps also of his personality. The aphasia which he underwent (apart from the divine 'opening of his mouth' to deliver oracles) from the time of his call until he received the news of the city's fall (3: 26; 24: 27; 33: 21 f.) is also relevant here. It is precarious indeed to try to psycho-analyse Ezekiel on the evidence of the book which bears his name, but his neighbours felt that they had a strange man in their midst. No doubt some degree of spiritual kinship with Ezekiel is a powerful asset in understanding and expounding him. Thus, among his many commentators, it has been suggested (by J. Patterson, *The Goodly Fellowship of the Prophets*, 1948, p. 295) that 'perhaps none were better qualified to interpret this bizarre personality than the quaint and peculiarly competent A. B. Davidson' (who in 1892 produced the volume on Ezekiel in the old Cambridge Bible series).

Ezekiel entered so completely into the purpose of God that his own words, actions and way of life were caught up into it and became instruments of its accomplishment. At the same time he was emotionally one with his afflicted fellow-countrymen, not only the exiles but the beleaguered inhabitants of Jerusalem. 'No prophet, not even Jeremiah, so completely identified himself with the sins and sufferings of Israel as Ezekiel. In that extraordinary communication in ch. 4, the prophet, as Son of Man, is instructed to lie for 390 days on his left side and bear the iniquity of the house of Israel, and then for 40 days on his right side to bear the iniquity of the house of Judah. Many unsuccessful attempts have been made to give an intelligible meaning to these figures, but they need not concern us here; what is significant is that the Son of Man, as God designates the prophet, undergoes in his own person, as the representative of his people, a sin-bearing which strains the imagination' (S. H. Hooke, *The Kingdom of God in the Experience of Jesus*, 1949, p. 61).

The Message of Ezekiel

It is noteworthy how many gospel themes and images are anticipated in Ezekiel: the good shepherd, the river of life, the holy city—to mention but a few. Like his fellow-prophet Jeremiah, and like the Lord of the prophets six centuries later, Ezekiel begs his hearers to turn back from their sinful and disastrous ways—for 'why will you die, O house of Israel?' (33: 11).

This appeal is made to individuals and community alike. Ezekiel has been charged at times with teaching an atomistic ethic (cf. 18: 1–29; 33: 10–20), and indeed he does justly emphasize personal responsibility in situations where individuals were prone to blame their troubles on handicaps arising from heredity or environment; but he makes it quite plain at the same time that national and civic groups have a corporate responsibility, which may extend over many generations.

When Ezekiel is called the father of Judaism (i.e. the spiritual ancestor of Ezra's settlement), this sometimes carries with it the subjective value-judgment that Israel's post-exilic religion represents a decline from the higher pre-exilic level, and that Ezekiel is in measure responsible for this decline. Recognition should rather be given to Ezekiel as the preacher of the new birth and the clean heart, the prophet of that coming age of the Spirit in which the righteous requirements of the law would be fulfilled by those who, in Paul's words, 'do not live according to the sinful nature but according to the Spirit' (Rom. 8: 4). Ezekiel was a priest as well as a prophet, and his vision of restoration concentrates on the new temple and its ordinances of worship. But these are the material symbols of inward holiness.

He takes up the refrain of Israel's law of holiness: 'Be holy; because I, the LORD your God, am holy' (Lev. 19: 2), which remains the principle of Christian living in the NT (1 Pet. 1: 15 f.). If he insists on physical separation and on ceremonial and cultic purity, these are to be external signs of the divinely-wrought cleansing within. Ezekiel knew from first-hand experience how harmful physical contact with pagans and paganism had been to the cause of true heart-religion in pre-exilic Israel.

Like Isaiah, he had a tremendous sense of the

holiness of God, coupled with a passionate appreciation of His eagerness to bestow His pardoning grace. For Ezekiel, as for Isaiah, judgment is God's 'strange work'—alien and uncongenial to His nature. Yet, when His people act wickedly and refuse to repent, acquiescence on His part would give them and others the impression that He is ethically indifferent. He visits them in judgment to remind them of His holiness and to vindicate His name, so that 'they shall know that I am the LORD' (6: 10, etc.). But when the judgment, long delayed, falls at last, when their homeland is devastated and they themselves are dispersed among the nations, acquiesence on His part in this state of affairs would give them and others the impression that He was unable or unwilling to help His own people. He visits them in blessing, with the assurance of restoration and the establishment of a new order in which they will do His will from the heart. Once more His holiness is declared and His name vindicated: 'Then they will know that I am the LORD their God for though I sent them into exile among the nations, I will gather them to their own land' (39: 28). This is the climactic occurrence of the recognition formula so frequently repeated throughout the book whether Israel or the nations be addressed. In righteousness and mercy God makes Himself known on earth, for the knowledge of God is the chief end of man.

ANALYSIS

I. THE CALL OF EZEKIEL (1: 1–3: 27)

i. Time and place (1: 1–3)

1. In the thirtieth year: Ezekiel's inaugural vision has a twofold dating. The dating in v. 2 is immediately intelligible, but the epoch from which **the thirtieth year** is reckoned is uncertain. The prophet might be indicating his age: in the year in which he would normally have entered upon his priestly service (cf. Num. 4: 3) he found himself called to a different ministry. W. F. Albright (less plausibly) suggested that **the thirtieth year** is reckoned from the same epoch as the other dates in the book and marks the time when the compilation of Ezekiel's oracles was completed (i.e. 568 B.C.), or when Ezekiel dictated them from memory to a scribe, as Jeremiah dictated his to Baruch (Jer. 36: 1–4). **by the Kebar River:** i.e. the 'great canal' (modern Shaṭṭ en-Nil), which left the Euphrates just north of Babylon and flowed by Nippur (*c*. 60 miles S.E. of Babylon) back into the Euphrates south of Ur. The **exiles** were those residing at Tel-abib (see 3: 15). It was in this depressing situation, far from his home, that he saw **the heavens . . . opened** and **visions of God**—meaning (as the analogy of 8: 3; 40: 2 indicates) divinely granted visions.

2. On the fifth of the month: if the month was 'the fourth month' (Tammuz), as in v. 1, then the date was July 31, 593 B.C., for **the fifth year of the exile of King Jehoiachin** ran from Nisan 1 (April 30) of that year to Adar 29 (April 18), 592 B.C. Jehoiachin's exile, we know from a contemporary Babylonian source, began on Adar 2 (March 16), 597 B.C. The Babylonian authorities continued to give

him some recognition as king in exile, and so apparently did his fellow-exiles; in acknowledgment of the actual circumstances, however, Ezekiel dates his visions in terms of Jehoiachin's exile, not his reign. His reign had lasted little more than three months (2 Kg. 24: 8; 2 Chr. 36: 9). For his successor Zedekiah see 17: 13 ff.; 21: 35. **3. the word of the LORD came:** a common OT expression for the prophetic experience (cf. 1 Kg. 17: 8; Hos. 1: 1). Less frequently do we read outside Ezek. that **the hand of the LORD was upon** a prophet; when the expression is used of Elijah (1 Kg. 18: 46) or Elisha (2 Kg. 3: 15), it indicates a special supernatural empowerment; in Ezek. it denotes the onset of prophetic ecstasy.

ii. The inaugural vision (1: 4–28a)

The description of Ezekiel's inaugural vision is one of the most difficult passages to translate in the whole OT; the rendering in the NEB is outstandingly successful and illuminating. But the main lesson conveyed by the vision is clear: the God of Israel is not tied to His temple in Jerusalem. His throne, equipped with wheels and upborne by the cherubim, is mobile; He can and does manifest His presence to Ezekiel in Babylonia as readily as He had manifested it (say) to Isaiah in Jerusalem (Isa. 6: 1 ff.); He is the God of heaven and earth.

4. a Windstorm: a storm cloud shot through with lightning flashes formed a traditional vehicle for a theophany in Israel; cf. Exod. 19: 16–18; 1 Kg. 19: 11 f.; Ps. 18: 7–15; 68: 7–10. If on this occasion it came **out of the north**, the presence of Yahweh presumably followed the same route to Babylonia as the exiles had previously taken, and the local divinities could not impede his progress. The **four living creatures** (5) are identified in 10: 1 ff. as cherubim, composite forms symbolizing the winds or, more generally, the forces of nature which bore up the God of Israel as he rode upon the clouds (Pss. 18: 10; 68: 4) and supported his invisible throne in the holy of holies in Jerusalem (1 Kg. 6: 23–28). Before the establishment of the Jerusalem temple, Yahweh of hosts was known in Shiloh as he 'who is enthroned between the cherubim' (1 Sam. 4: 4), and he continued to be worshipped under that title in Jerusalem (Pss. 80: 1; 99: 1). In Ezekiel's vision it is emphasized that his throne is not stationary; it can move in any direction— forward, backward, sideways, upward or downward. As in earlier (Ps. 68: 17) and later (Dan. 7: 9) theophanies, it is a chariot-throne (cf. 1 Chr. 28: 18).

The word rendered **glowing metal** (4, 27), Heb. *ḥashmal*, is of uncertain meaning; NEB translates here 'a radiance like brass' (LXX *ēlektron*, Vulg. *electrum*). G. R. Driver suggests that the imagery of Ezekiel's vision 'will have been suggested to him, as so often, by some familiar object or process, here the work of a Babylonian brass-founder' (*VT* 1, 1951, p. 62). This is at least preferable to discerning here the description of a dynamo, not to speak of a space-ship. **7. their legs were straight:** like those of a human being, though their feet were cloven. **like burnished bronze:** NEB, better, 'like a disc of bronze'. **13. torches:** cf. the 'blazing torch' which symbolized the divine presence in Gen. 15: 17. Verse 14 is absent from LXX.

16. chrysolite: NEB 'topaz.' **18. Their rims were high and awesome:** render, with NEB, 'All four had hubs and each hub had a projection which had the power of sight'. **20, 21. the spirit of the living creatures was in the wheels:** so that the wheels functioned as animated extensions of their bodies.

22. what looked like an expanse (or 'vault' of heaven): Ezekiel's firmament, **sparkling like ice**, is probably identical with John's 'sea of glass, clear as crystal . . . mixed with fire' (Rev. 4: 6; 15: 2); Ezekiel saw it from beneath, John saw it from above. The details of the vision are based in part on the vision of the God of Israel described in Exod. 24: 10. There Moses and his companions saw 'under his feet . . . something like a pavement made of sapphire, clear as the sky itself'. So here Ezekiel sees **above the expanse . . . what looked like a throne of sapphire**, or *lapis lazuli* (26). But whereas no attempt is made in Exod. 24: 10 to portray the God of Israel himself, Ezekiel tells how **high above on the throne was a figure like that of a man**. If man was made 'in the image of God' (Gen. 1: 27), then it is not

inappropriate that, in default of complete silence about the appearance of God, he should be depicted anthropomorphically, at least in the language of tentative analogy. So in Dan. 7: 9 ff., while the 'Ancient of Days' is differentiated from the 'one like a son of man', he takes his seat on a fiery throne equipped with wheels, and his raiment and hair are described. **28. Like the appearance of a rainbow:** the reference to the rainbow may well recall to us its covenant significance in Gen. 9: 12–17 (where it is dissociated from theophanic language).

iii. The prophet's commission (1: 28b–3: 15)

Having seen the vision of God, Ezekiel now receives his prophetic commission. He is to be God's messenger to the people of Israel, exiled in Babylonia, but he is not promised that any heed will be paid to his message; indeed, from the description of those to whom he is sent, he might well despair of any response. But the messenger's duty is to deliver his message faithfully; the responsibility of paying heed to it rests with the hearers.

1: 28b. the appearance of the likeness of the glory of the LORD: the multiplication of qualifying terms has a reverential purpose; Ezekiel will not claim to have seen God directly. The **glory of the LORD** is his presence or *shekhinah*, as in Exod. 34: 18; 40:34f.;1Kg.8: 11.

2: 1. Son of man: Heb. *ben 'adam*, the regular form of God's address to Ezekiel. It means 'man', 'human being', perhaps emphasizing the prophet's creaturely weakness by contrast with the divine glory (cf. Ps. 8: 4). **2. the Spirit came into me:** practically synonymous with 'the hand of the LORD was upon' me (1: 3). The consequent divine empowerment is shown in that the Spirit, as he says, **raised me to my feet:** he had very naturally fallen prostrate before the vision of the glory of God, but when a man who has thus humbled himself is raised to his feet by God, he can stand foursquare in the face of every adverse wind that blows. **3. I am sending you to the Israelites:** primarily to the exiles in Babylonia (3: 11) who, for all their rebellious attitude, nevertheless constituted the remnant in which the hope of national survival was embodied— the 'good figs' of Jer. 24: 5–7 (cf. 'the house of Israel' in Ezek. 3: 1, etc.; 11: 15; 37: 11). And however **obstinate and stubborn** (4) they might be in face of Ezekiel's warnings, the event would prove to them, even against their will, that in him they had **a prophet among them** (5). **6. briers and thorns are all around you and you live among scorpions:** a metaphorical description of his uncomfortable situation as he prophesied to people who would prefer not to hear him (cf. Isa. 6: 9 f.; Jer. 1: 19).

8. eat what I give you: the mournful burden of his message is depicted as the text of **a scroll** (9), which he must digest before communicating it to others (cf. 3: 10). **10. on both sides of it were written words . . .** like the scroll of Rev. 5: 1. Scrolls normally had writing on the inside only, but here the doom-laden contents overflow on to the other side: no room is left for human additions to the divine judgments. **3: 3. it tasted as sweet as honey in my mouth:** cf. Pss. 19: 10; 119: 103; Jer. 15: 16 ('When your words came I ate them . . .'); Rev. 10: 8–11 (the resultant inward bitterness which John experienced is not mentioned by Ezekiel, but it may be imagined).

3: 6. they would have listened to you: for the greater readiness of Gentiles to hear the message of God cf. Jon. 3: 5; Mal. 1: 11; Mt. 11: 20–24; Rom. 10: 20 f. **9. like the hardest stone, harder than flint:** cf. Jer. 1: 18 for a similar assurance to Jeremiah; also the Servant's language in Isa. 50: 7. **11. the Sovereign LORD:** Heb. *'adonai Yahweh* (so frequently in Ezek.).

12. the Spirit lifted me up: cf. 8: 3; 11: 1, 24; 37: 1; 40: 1 f. Ezekiel's susceptibility to ecstatic transport is reminiscent of Elijah (1 Kg. 18: 12; 2 Kg. 2: 16). **a loud rumbling sound:** cf. 1: 24. **14. in the anger of my spirit** (LXX omits **bitterness**): in the tense exaltation which was the consequence of **the strong hand of the LORD upon** him. **15. the exiles . . . at Tel-abib:** cf. 1: 1. The Akkadian *til abubi* ('mound of the deluge') was used of mounds covering ancient ruined cities, believed to be antediluvian. Tel-aviv is thought by some to have been a kind of concentration camp for deported Jews employed on the irrigation system of Babylonia. It has given its name to modern Tel Aviv (interpreted as 'hill of spring'). After **the Kebar River** RSV omits the clause in *MT* which means 'who were dwelling there' or 'where they dwelt'; render: 'And where they dwelt there I sat overwhelmed among them' (AV 'I sat where they sat'). **overwhelmed:** NEB 'dumbfounded'. **seven days:** cf. Job 2: 13, where Job's friends sit with him in silence for this length of time, which was the period of mourning for the dead (Gen. 50: 10; 1 Sam. 31:13).

iv. Ezekiel the watchman (3: 16–21)
The substance of this paragraph is repeated in 33: 1–9. The sentinel who fails to give warning of approaching danger is personally responsible for the ensuing disaster, but if he gives due warning, his hearers bear the responsibility themselves, if they fail to pay heed to him.

20. When a righteous man turns from his righteousness: the possibility of a good man falling into sin, as well as of a sinner repenting of his wickedness, is treated in greater detail in 18: 5–29 (cf. 33: 12–16).

v. Ezekiel's dumbness (3: 22–27)
The prophet's dumbness and consequent inability to reprove his people present problems. If his dumbness persisted without intermission for the six or seven years which elapsed until he received news of the fall of Jerusalem (24: 25–27; 33: 21 f.), he could hardly have fulfilled his commission to be a warning voice to the house of Israel. Perhaps his dumbness was broken only when he was given a divine message to proclaim and returned when it was completed: this indeed is the implication of v. 27.

22. the plain: the flat area contrasted with the mound on which the exiles had their settlement. It may have been here that Ezekiel saw his original vision, since he had to travel from there to Tel-aviv (3: 12–15). **24. inside your house:** it appears to have been in the Tel-aviv settlement (cf. 8: 1, and note on 12: 5). **25. You . . . they will tie with ropes:** denoting the divine constraint, as in 4: 8. **you cannot go among the people:** except, presumably, at the command of God; the symbolic actions of 4: 1–5: 4 were carried out in public as 'signs' to the beholders (4: 3).

II. THE EXILES WARNED OF JERUSALEM'S DOOM (4: 1–7: 27)
i. Four symbolic actions (4: 1–5: 4)
The symbolic actions of 4: 1–5: 4 set forth the impending siege and fall of Jerusalem. Such actions, performed by the prophets of Israel (cf. Isa. 20: 2–4; Jer. 13: 1–11; Hos. 1: 2 ff.) were an integral element in the self-fulfilling word of God which they were given to communicate and helped to ensure the accomplishment of what they symbolized.
(a) *The mimic siege* (4: 1–3). Ezekiel draws a plan of Jerusalem on a tile and surrounds it with imitation ramparts, entrenchments and other apparatus of a siege. He himself acts the besieger.

2. build a ramp up to it . . . :. for the reality cf. 17: 17 and 21: 22 (Nebuchadrezzar's siege of Jerusalem); 26: 8 f. (his siege of Tyre). **3. an iron pan:** 'an iron griddle' (NEB), to represent an 'iron curtain' cutting off the city. **a sign to the house of Israel:** to warn the exiles not to place their hopes in the survival of Jerusalem (cf. Jer. 29: 1 ff.).
(b) *The prophet's vigil* (4: 4–8). Ezekiel is not only to play the part of besieger; he is to 'bear the punishment' of the northern and southern kingdoms successively by lying beside the miniature Jerusalem for many days on his left side and then for a shorter period on his right side (left and right in Hebrew usage corresponding to north and south respectively).

4. bear their sin (iniquity): cf. the Servant's role in Isa. 53: 11 f. **5. three hundred and ninety days:** NEB adopts the LXX reading 'one hundred and ninety days'. It is difficult to decide between the two readings because of uncertainty about the reckoning of the 390 or 190 **years** of Israel's punishment. The 390 years might be reckoned from the beginnings of apostasy under Solomon (1 Kg. 11: 4 ff.) to the impending fall of Jerusalem; it is more difficult to discern a starting-point for the 190 years with the same terminus. A starting-point for the 40 years of Judah's punishment (6) would be equally unascertainable: it is probably a coincidence that 40 years elapsed from the call of Jeremiah (Jer. 1: 2 f.) to the fall of Jerusalem. If the 40 years be added to the 390, the resultant 430 years could reach back approximately to the time when Jerusalem first became Israel's capital city. Attempts to make Ezekiel's call or the siege of Jerusalem the starting-point of the periods indicated are even more unsatisfactory. But the **days** of Ezekiel's vigil may have corresponded to the actual duration of the siege. It began on January 15, 588 B.C. (24: 1 f.; cf. Jer. 52: 4) and ended on July 29, 587 B.C. (Jer. 39: 2; 52: 6), but did not last continuously for 560 days; it was raised temporarily because of the approach of an Egyptian army (Jer. 37: 5 ff.), so that its effective duration may have approximated the 430 days of Ezekiel's acted siege. **6. a day for each year:** for the principle cf. Num. 14: 34.

(*c*) *Polluted siege-rations* (4: 9–17). The stringencies of the siege and the conditions of exile made it impracticable to observe the laws forbidding food that was ritually unclean: Ezekiel's acted parable is enforced by the divine injunction to restrict himself to siege-rations and to prepare them in a manner that involved their ceremonial pollution, especially for a priest.

9. wheat and barley, beans and lentils, millet and spelt: whatever kinds of grain were available, inferior as well as superior, had to be scraped together to bake a daily allowance of 8 ounces of indifferent bread. Baking with a mixture of cereals was perhaps ritually forbidden, like sowing with a mixture of seeds (Lev. 19: 19). **11. a sixth of a hin:** Jerusalem's water supply was limited; hence in siege conditions it would be rationed to a little over a pint (three quarters of a litre) a day. **13. In this way the people of Israel will eat defiled food:** animal dung (15), mixed with straw, was used as fuel for baking bread on stones, but human excrement (12) was ritually unclean and was therefore to be buried out of sight (Dt. 23: 12–14). **14. I have never defiled myself:** Ezekiel's protest is echoed by Peter in Acts 10: 14. **I have never eaten anything found dead:** prohibited in Dt. 14: 2. **or torn by wild animals:** prohibited in Exod. 22: 31. **foul flesh:** such as the flesh of peace-offerings from the third day onward (Lev. 19: 5–8). **16. I will cut off the supply of food:** For the scarcity of bread

during the siege cf. Jer. 37: 21; 52: 6; Lam. 2: 12; 4: 4, 9; 5: 10. **in anxiety . . . in despair:** the increasing food-shortage would be accompanied by terror at the thought of what would happen when the besiegers broke into the city (cf. 12: 18 f.).

(*d*) *The prophet's hair divided* (5: 1–4). As the fourth symbolic action Ezekiel cuts off his hair and beard and then divides it into three parts, of which one part is burnt, one is cut up with a knife and one is scattered to the winds. A few hairs remain protected in his lap, but even of these some are later thrown into the fire. Only the merest remnant of hair is left, and this is a sign of the fate of the people of Jerusalem.

5: 1. a sharp sword: the use of a sword as a razor may emphasize the conditions of war. Shaving the head could be a sign of captivity and enslavement, as in Isa. 7: 20. **4. A fire will spread from there to the whole house of Israel:** LXX reads 'and you shall say to all the house of Israel' (introducing vv 5 ff.); *MT* may have been influenced by 19: 14.

ii. The symbolic actions explained (5: 5–17)
The prophetic sign is followed by the prophetic word: action and speech together constitute the prophecy. The city portrayed on the tile is Jerusalem, destined because of her rejection of the law of her God to suffer siege, famine, destruction and depopulation.

5. . . . which I have set in the center of the nations: for the belief that Jerusalem was the centre or 'navel' of the earth cf. 38: 12 (a similar belief regarding Shechem is attested in Jg. 9: 37; as for the corresponding belief among the Greeks, the stone navel of the earth is still to be seen at Delphi). **6. more than the . . . countries around her:** because they had not been blessed with the knowledge of God granted to Jerusalem; cf. 16: 48–52; Am. 3: 2. **laws . . . decrees:** case-laws (*e.g.* Exod. 20: 3–17; 21: 1–22: 17; 23: 4 f.) and apodictic or categorical laws (*e.g.* Exod. 22: 18–23: 3; 23: 6–19) respectively. **9. all your detestable idols:** the term rendered 'detestable' is used technically in the 'Holiness' and Deuteronomic law-codes, exceptionally frequent in Ezek., denoting both moral and ritual outrages (cf. 16: 1). **10. fathers will eat their children:** cannibalism during the siege of Jerusalem is mentioned in Lam. 4: 10 (cf. Dt. 28: 53–57). **11. as surely as I live, declares the Sovereign LORD:** an adjuration specially common in Ezek. **you have defiled my sanctuary:** details are given in 8: 5 ff. **12. a third . . . :** this explains the three-fold division of the prophet's hair in the fourth symbolic action (5: 1–4). The burning of one-third denotes **the plague or . . . famine:** the cutting up of one-third denotes slaughter **by the sword;** the scattering of one-third denotes dispersion **to the winds** (cf. v. 10), and even those thus dispersed will

be in further danger from the **sword. 13. they
will know that I the LORD have spoken:** a
combination of two recurring affirmations in
Ezek.—'they (you) will know that I am
Yahweh' (cf. 6: 7, 10, 14) and 'I, Yahweh, have
spoken' (cf. vv. 15, 17). **15. you will be** *(MT*
'it shall be') **a reproach and a taunt . . . :** cf.
Dt. 28: 37; 29: 22–28. **17. wild beasts:** not
previously mentioned among the visitations of
judgment; cf. 14: 15.

iii. Denunciation of the mountains of Israel (6: 1–14)

From prophesying the doom of Jerusalem in
particular Ezekiel now addresses the whole land
of Israel, making special reference to its mountains, for they were the principal sites of the
bamoth—the local sanctuaries or 'high places'
(cf. 20: 29)—at which so much degenerate
worship was practised (cf. Hos. 4: 13). Josiah's
reformation, nearly thirty years before, had
included the abolition of the high places (2 Kg.
23: 13, 15, 19 f.), but it did not command the
sympathy of the people, and after his death the
old practices returned (cf. Jer. 11: 13; 17:
2 f.). The prophet's words of denunciation are
confirmed by appropriate actions of hand and
foot (11).

(a) Disaster threatened (6: 1–7). **3. the ravines
and valleys:** for **high places** were to be found
there as well as on **the mountains and hills,**
e.g. in the valley of the son of Hinnom, to the
south of Jerusalem (Jer. 7: 31 ff.). **4. incense
altars:** this is the most probable sense of *ham-
manim*, small altars sometimes placed on top of
altars of burnt offering (2 Chr. 34: 4). **I will
slay your people in front of your idols:**
Heb. *gillulim*, a derogatory term (meaning
something like 'dungheaps'), much favoured
by Ezekiel. The corpses of the worshippers
would expose the powerlessness of the idols.
**5. I will scatter your bones around your
altars:** cf. Josiah's action in 2 Kg. 23: 20. **6.
your altars will be laid waste and devastated:** altars belonged to the essential equipment of high places. NIV **devastated** represents
the reading of the ancient versions for *MT* 'held
guilty' (AV, RV 'cease'). **7. you will know
that I am the LORD:** a recurrent recognition
formula in Ezek. (cf. vv. 10, 13, 14).

(b) A remnant will survive (6: 8–10). **8. some
. . . will escape the sword:** cf. 5: 3. **9. their
adulterous hearts . . . have turned away
from me:** lit. 'their heart which has departed
like a harlot from me' (cf. AV, RV); this language
for idolatry is elaborated in 16: 15 ff.; 23: 3 ff.,
after the precedent of Hos. 1: 2 ff. (cf. Exod.
34: 15; Lev. 17: 7; Dt. 31: 16; Jer. 2:20; 3: 1,
etc.). **10. And they will know . . . :** here the
knowledge involves repentance and recognition of the truth and righteousness of God.

(c) Words reinforced by deeds (6: 11–14). **11.
Strike your hands together and stamp your**
feet: these actions express malicious joy in 25:
6, but here they express confirmation of the
divine oracle, like the arm-baring of 4: 7 and
the sword-brandishing, thigh-smiting and
hand-clapping of 21: 8–17. **sword . . . famine
. . . plague:** cf. 5: 12, 16 f. **12. he that is far
away . . . near . . . survives** (by the pestilence) **. . . spared** (from the sword): these
terms together convey the comprehensiveness
of the coming disaster. **13. under every
spreading tree:** cf. Dt. 12: 2; 1 Kg. 14: 23; 2
Kg. 16: 4; 17: 10; Isa. 57: 5; Jer. 2: 20; 3: 6; 17:
2. The trees provided shade and helped to mark
sacred spots; they were not themselves objects
of worship. For the wording of this verse cf.
20: 28. **14. from the desert to Diblah** (mg
'Riblah'): from the southern to the northern
boundary of the land of Israel. At Riblah on
the Orontes, near the Syro-Israelite frontier
(Num. 34: 11), the king of Egypt had bound
and deposed Jehoahaz in 608 B.C. (2 Kg. 23:
33; cf. Ezek. 19: 4) and there, in 587 B.C., the
king of Babylon passed sentence on Zedekiah
(Jer. 52: 26 f.).

iv. The day of wrath (7: 1–27)

This chapter is commonly—and no doubt
rightly—interpreted as a poem, although it is
not printed as such. There are three strophes,
each ending with Ezekiel's characteristic recognition formula (4, 9, 27). The theme is the
imminence of Israel's doom: 'the end has come'
(1). This theme is repeated because of the
people's unwillingness to believe that disaster
was so near (cf. 12: 21–28). So the prophet
particularizes the disaster: idolatry will be punished (3 f., 8 f.), pride and violence will be
avenged (10 f.), commercial enterprise will
wither away (12 f.), there will be no heart for
resistance to the enemy (14), sword, famine
and pestilence will do their worst (15), and
those who escape will fare no better than those
who succumb (16 f.). The rich will be reduced
to beggary; money will be useless, for there
will be no food to buy with it (18 f.). The
temple will be profaned and pillaged (22);
pagans will take possession of their property
(21, 24). No counsel adequate to the catastrophe will be forthcoming from their traditional advisers (26); their rulers will be at their
wits' end themselves and unable to provide
protection or guidance (27).

(a) First strophe (7: 1–4). **2. The end:** the word
qes is the same as that used to a similar effect
in Am. 8: 1–3. The **end** of divine forbearance
means the beginning of judgment.

(b) Second strophe (7: 5–9). **5. This is what the
Sovereign LORD says:** this strophe is in large
measure a repetition of the previous one. **7.
upon the mountains:** perhaps as the chief sites
of the high places (6: 2 ff.), but LXX omits the
phrase (cf. emendation in NEB).

(c) Third strophe (7: 10–27). **10. Doom:** re-

peated from v. 7. The meaning of Heb. *ṣephirah* is uncertain in these two places, but 'doom' (cf. NEB) is most probable (the RSV addition of the pronoun 'your' is unnecessary). **the rod:** cf. 'rod of wickedness' (11). **11. Violence has grown into a rod to punish wickedness:** LXX renders 'violence has arisen and will break the rod of the wicked one'; the verse has baffled translators. **12. wrath is upon the whole crowd:** omitted in LXX, perhaps because even then the Hebrew defied translation. **13. as long as both . . . live . . . will not be reversed:** omitted in LXX. **not one of them will preserve his life . . . :** perhaps 'no man whose life is mere iniquity will hold his own' (see NEB for another possible translation). **14. for my wrath is upon the whole crowd:** omitted in LXX as in vv. 12, 13; but here it is more intelligible. **15. Outside is the sword, inside are plague and famine:** a description of siege conditions (cf. 6: 11). **16. All who survive and escape:** cf. 5: 3 f. **like doves of the valleys:** omitted in LXX. **moaning:** the Syriac version reads 'they will die' (if we adopt LXX and Syriac readings, the meaning is 'all of them will die, every one in his iniquity'; cf. NEB). **17. every knee will become as weak as water:** LXX implies incontinence through terror (cf. NEB). **18. shaved:** like **sackcloth**, a sign of mourning (cf. Isa. 3: 24; 15: 2; 22: 12; Jer. 16: 6; Am. 8: 10), forbidden in Dt. 14: 1. **19. it has made them stumble into sin:** NEB 'their iniquity will be the cause of their downfall'. **20. Their beautiful jewelry:** gold, jewels, etc. **22. my treasured place:** the temple, possibly the holy of holies (cf. Ps. 74: 1). **23. prepare chains:** NEB 'clench your fists' (another symbolic action, as in 6: 11). **the city:** Jerusalem. **24. their sanctuaries:** cf. Am. 7: 9; both there and here the reference is to local sanctuaries ('high places'). There could even be a contrast between '*their* sanctuaries' and '*my* treasured place (22). **25. terror:** NEB 'shuddering'. **26. prophet . . . priest . . . elders:** for a similar three-fold division cf. Jer. 18: 18, where the people insist that no such failure as that indicated here will befall them. **the law:** Heb. *torah*, 'instruction' (NEB 'guidance'); teaching was a priestly duty (cf. 44: 23; Dt. 33: 10; Mal. 2: 6 f.). **27. the people of the land:** here set over against **the king** and **the prince** (or governor). At this period the phrase is used of the common people in distinction from the court, the priests and the prophets (the 'establishment'); cf. 22: 29; 45: 22; 2 Kg. 16: 15; Jer. 1: 18,etc.

III. JERUSALEM REVISITED
(8: 1–11: 25)

We now move forward fourteen months, and have the record of five visions (with ac-

companying oracles) granted to Ezekiel during an ecstatic visit to Jerusalem. As the visions proceed, the *shekhinah* leaves the temple and city in a succession of movements.

i. Idolatry in the house of God (8: 1–18)

The divine glory which normally shone from the holy of holies was no longer there: Ezekiel saw it in the temple precincts, ready to leave the apostate sanctuary. Canaanite and foreign cults which Josiah had abolished thirty years before were now reinstated: far from the temple constituting a protection to Jerusalem, as in Isaiah's day (Isa. 31: 8 f.; 33: 17–22), its pollution now ensured the city's downfall as well as its own (cf. Jer. 7: 4, 8–15).

(a) Ezekiel transported to Jerusalem (8: 1–4). **1. In the sixth year . . . :** September 17, 592 B.C. LXX has 'the fifth month' for **the sixth month** of *MT*. **I was sitting in my house:** cf. 3: 24. **the elders of Judah:** the leaders of the 'house of Israel' at Tel-aviv (cf. 3: 1, 15), who had evidently paid heed to Jeremiah's letter (Jer. 29: 4–7) and settled down to some kind of ordered community life in exile. **2. a figure like that of a man** (so LXX, as though reading '*ish* for *MT 'esh*, 'fire'): cf. the description in 1: 27. **3. what looked like a hand:** the phraseology avoids too anthropomorphic a portrayal of God. **took me by the hair of my head:** imitated in later deuterocanonical and uncanonical literature. Ezekiel in retrospect knew that this was an ecstatic experience: it was **in visions of God** that he was transported to Jerusalem, which was perfectly familiar to him, city and temple alike. **the inner court:** cf. 1 Kg. 7: 12. This, the goal of his visit, is mentioned here in anticipation of v. 16; before reaching it he stopped at three intermediate stages (vv. 5, 7, 14).

(b) First detestable thing (8: 5 f.). Four 'detestable things' are disclosed to the prophet, each succeeding one worse than its predecessor. **5. the gate of the altar :** perhaps the north gate of the city, receiving its name from an altar which stood there (cf. Jer. 11: 13) in honour of the **idol of jealousy,** the Canaanite fertility goddess Asherah (2 Kg. 21: 7; 23: 6), depicted in relief on a slab set in the wall, and so called by Ezekiel because it provoked Yahweh to jealousy (cf. Exod. 20: 5; Dt. 32: 16, 21). It has been mentioned by anticipation in v. 3, the last clause of which is rendered 'to rouse lustful passion' in NEB.

(c) Second detestable thing (8: 7–13). **7. the entrance to the court:** the gateway into the forecourt of the palace, south of the temple area. **8. dig into the wall:** thus enlarging the **hole** so as to make **a doorway** large enough to pass through. **9. see the wicked and detestable things:** their nature is disputed, but the **crawling things and detestable animals** (10) are reminiscent of illustrated manuscripts of

the Book of the Dead and point to an Egyptian cult, amalgamated syncretistically with **all the idols of the house of Israel**. This act of worship took place secretly, within doors, perhaps reflecting the clandestine negotiations going on between the Egyptian court and Zedekiah, in breach of his oath to Nebuchadrezzar. **11. seventy elders:** representing the whole nation (cf. Exod. 24: 1, 9; Num. 11: 16). **Jaazaniah son of Shaphan:** his participation was particularly shocking if he was the son of that Shaphan who, as royal secretary, read the newly discovered lawbook to Josiah (2 Kg. 22: 8–10). **12. each at the shrine of his own idol:** or 'carvings'; the words as they stand might mean that each practised this worship at home as well as in the **darkness** within the temple precincts (the reference may be to an inner chamber known to Ezekiel). **they say, the LORD. . . has forsaken the land:** if so, it was because of these very 'detestable things'.

(*d*) *Third detestable thing* (8: 14 f.). **14. women . . . mourning for Tammuz:** Tammuz (Sumerian Dumuzi) wooed and won Inanna, the Sumerian goddess of love (Akkadian Ishtar), and died in consequence. His death was celebrated at the height of the summer heat, in the month which bore his name (approximately July). He was later identified with the Syrian Adonis, 'the one beloved by women' (Dan. 11: 37).

(*e*) *Fourth detestable thing* (8: 16–18). At last Ezekiel is brought into the **inner court** of the temple (cf. v. 3), where, **between the portico** of the holy house **and the altar** of burnt-offering, he sees **twenty-five men . . . their backs to the** sanctuary, facing **east** and **bowing down to the sun** (16), presumably at sunrise. Solomon's Phoenician architects may have orientated the structure with this in mind, in conformity with their native use. Sun-worship had been practised in the Jerusalem temple before Josiah's reformation (2 Kg. 23: 5, 11). We are reminded of Josephus's description of the Essenes of his day, who took the eastward position at morning prayer, 'as though entreating the sun to rise'. **17. putting the branch to their nose:** a gesture or ritual of uncertain identification, perhaps idolatrous in character and thus defiant or contemptuous in intention (cf. LXX 'turning the nose up', 'sneering'). NEB, less probably, has 'even while they seek to appease me' (cf. the classical use of olive branches in supplication).

ii. Death in the city (9: 1–11)
Sentence of death is pronounced on Jerusalem, and executed as soon as the righteous are sealed against destruction. Those who are thus sealed constitute a saved, and saving, remnant.

2. six men: it is doubtful if we should add the **man . . . who had a writing kit** (palette with ink-well and pen) to these six summoned

to execute divine vengeance on Jerusalem, in such a way as to see here the first recorded occurrence of the seven angels of destruction (cf. Rev. 8: 2; 15: 1); the man dressed as a scribe is distinguished from the six. **the upper gate:** built by Jotham (2 Kg. 15: 35); cf. Jer. 20: 2. It is apparently identical with the gate of 8: 14. **the bronze altar:** the altar of burnt-offering, as in 8: 16 (cf. 1 Kg. 8: 64; 2 Kg. 16: 14). **3. went up . . . to the threshold:** the first stage in the departure of the *shekhinah* from the inner throne-room (cf. 10: 18 f.; 11: 22 f.). **4. put a mark:** *taw*, the last letter of the Hebrew alphabet, then written in the form of a cross. It served the same kind of protective purpose as the mark on Cain (Gen. 4: 15) and the blood-stains round the door at the first Passover (Exod. 12: 22 f.). **on the foreheads:** cf. Rev. 7: 3, where the servants of God are so sealed against the impending judgments. **6. do not touch anyone who has the mark:** cf. the preservation of the 7,000 who had refused to worship Baal in 1 Kg. 19: 18, and the preservation of Jeremiah at the fall of Jerusalem (Jer. 39: 11–14). The indiscriminate slaughter in this vision corresponds to what happened in the sack of the city (cf. Lam. 2: 21). **Begin at my sanctuary:** because that was the centre and source of the 'detestable things' (cf. Lam. 4: 13). For a NT echo see 1 Pet. 4: 17. **the elders:** those of 8: 11, but LXX 'inside the house' implies the men of 8: 16. **7. Defile the temple:** i.e. with bloodshed. **8. Ah Sovereign LORD!:** cf. the pleas of Amos (Am. 7: 2, 5) and Jeremiah (Jer. 14: 19–21); since Moses (Num. 14: 13 ff.) intercession had been part of the prophet's ministry. **the entire remnant:** all those left after the deportation of 597 B.C. In fact a remnant was spared: that was the point of the sealing. **9. The sin is exceedingly great:** bloodshed and **injustice** in the **land** and **city** were as abominable in Yahweh's sight as idolatry in the temple. **The LORD has forsaken the land . . . :** cf. 8: 12. **10. I will not spare . . . :** cf. 8: 18.

iii. Fire in the city (10: 1–22)
If in the second vision of the present series the prophet saw the people of Jerusalem put to the sword, in the third he sees the city itself set on fire.

1. the expanse that was over the heads of the cherubim: not the gold-plated cherubim in the holy of holies but the 'living creatures' of Ezekiel's inaugural vision (1: 5 ff.), now for the first time in Ezek. called **cherubim**. For the **expanse** or platform cf. 1: 22 ff. The 'living creatures' reappear as supporters of the departing *shekhinah*. For the **throne of sapphire** cf. 1: 26. **2. the man clothed in linen:** the scribe who in 9: 11 has announced the completion of his former mission; now he is commanded to take **burning coals** from the chariot throne (cf. 1: 13) **and scatter them over the city** like incendiary bombs. For NT parallels cf. Lk. 12: 49; Rev. 8: 5. The historical fulfilment is recorded in Jer. 52: 13. **3. on the south side of the temple:** the action has thus far taken place on the north and east sides. **4. the glory of the LORD rose . . . :** cf. 9: 3. **The cloud filled . . . :** as at the original dedication of the temple (1 Kg. 8: 10 f.). **5. The sound of the wings:** cf. 1: 24. **7. one of the cherubim reached out his hand:** for the living creatures' hands cf. 1: 8.

9. I looked . . . : in vv. 9–17 details of the inaugural vision (1: 15–21) are repeated, to emphasize the identity of the cherubim here with the living creatures of that vision (cf. below, vv. 15b, 20, 22). **13. the wheels . . . being called . . . "the whirling wheels":** two Hebrew words for 'wheel' are used in chs. 1 and 10, *'ôphan* and *galgal*; NIV distinguishes them by rendering the latter 'whirling wheel' (NEB 'circling wheel'), but this verse emphasizes that it is the same wheels that are denoted by either word. **14. Each of the cherubim had four faces:** this verse is probably displaced (it is absent from LXX). For **cherub** read 'ox', as in 1: 10. **19. the cherubim . . . stopped at the entrance to the east gate:** ready to bear the glory of the God of Israel across the Kidron valley to the Mount of Olives (11: 23). The **east gate** (cf. 40: 6; 43: 1–5; 44: 1–3) was the main entrance to the temple precincts (cf. Pss. 24: 7, 9; 118: 19f.).

iv. Denunciation of false counsellors (11: 1–13)

The prophet's attention is directed to those men of influence in Jerusalem who express confidence in the city's prospects and dismiss prophecies of woe. It is difficult to fit this vision into the chronological sequence of its context: it may be recorded here because of its related subject-matter.

1. the Spirit lifted me up: cf. 3: 12, 14; 8: 3. **the gate:** cf. 10: 19, but there is no mention here of the cherubim or the *shekhinah*. **twenty-five men:** as in 8: 16, but a different body of men. **Jaazaniah:** distinct from his namesake in 8: 11. **leaders of the people:** NEB 'of high office'. **3. Will it not soon be time:** (LXX 'is not the time near . . . ?') is preferable to NIV mg; **to build houses** is a sign of security, normality and expectation of long residence; cf. Jeremiah's advice to the exiles (Jer. 29: 5). Such a sense of security is probably expressed in the metaphor: **this city is the cooking pot, and we are the meat**—i.e. we are as safe as meat in a cooking pot. In another context the proverb might mean 'we are in danger of being cooked alive'; but that would not be appropriate here. **7. The bodies . . . are the meat:** it is uncer-

tain whether **The bodies** should be understood as the victims of these leaders' ruthlessness or as those doomed to be slain by the sword at the capture of Jerusalem. **this city is the pot:** Ezekiel develops this figure along different lines in 24: 3–14. **I will drive you out of it:** the city will afford them no protection; they will be led away for execution. **10. I will execute judgment on you at the borders of Israel:** at Riblah (cf. 6: 14). **13. Pelatiah son of Benaiah died:** Ezekiel in his vision saw him die; whether or not he actually died at that moment is uncertain, the more so as Ezekiel has just predicted his death (with that of his colleagues) at the hand of the Babylonians. It may be that his death in Ezekiel's vision confirms the sure fulfilment of that prediction when the time comes. **Will you completely destroy . . . ?:** cf. 9: 8. Pelatiah's name means 'Yahweh preserves (a remnant)'.

v. The promise of restoration (11: 14–21)

It is emphasized afresh that the hope of Israel rests in the exiles, not in the people of Jerusalem: the exiles will be restored and cleansed, so as to become once more God's covenant-people. This promise anticipates the fuller statement in 36: 16–32.

15. They are far away from the LORD: the implication of the Jerusalemites' words is that the presence of Yahweh is confined to the land of Israel (cf. 1 Sam. 26: 19); those who have been deported to a far country may therefore be written off. **This land was given to us as our possession:** cf. 33: 24. **16. I have been a sanctuary for them:** Yahweh can dwell among His people in a foreign land, as truly as He can forsake His dwelling in Jerusalem. **for a little while:** for the duration of their exile or 'in (some) small measure' (cf. mg). **17. I will give you back the land of Israel:** to **you**, the exiles, and not to the present population of Jerusalem. **19. I will give them an undivided heart** (the seat of the will), **and put a new spirit** (the principle of life) **in them:** cf. Ps. 51: 10. For **an undivided heart** LXX has 'another heart' (reading Heb. *'aḥer* for *'eḥad*). Although Ezekiel does not use the word 'covenant' here (but see 16: 60; 34: 25; 37: 26) this passage (like its expansion in 36: 16–32) is his counterpart to the 'new covenant' oracle of Jer. 31: 31–34, where God undertakes to put his law within his people and write it on their hearts. **a heart of flesh:** echoed by Paul in his exposition of the new covenant (2 C. 3: 3). A **heart of flesh**, unlike a **heart of stone**, is responsive to the will of God. No better commentary can be found than C. Wesley's hymn, 'O for a heart to praise my God'. **20. They will be my people, and I will be their God:** the ancient covenant-oath (cf. Lev. 26: 12; Hos. 2: 23; Jer. 7: 23, etc.; and in NT 2. C. 6: 16; Rev. 21: 3).

vi. End of the ecstatic visit (11: 22–25)

Ezekiel sees the *shekhinah* depart not only from the temple but from the city: both are now left desolate. Then he returns (as he had come) 'by the Spirit of God' and rejoins the exiles.

23. the mountain east of it: the Mount of Olives, from which in 43: 2 the **glory of the Lord** returns to the new temple. **24. the Spirit lifted me up and brought me . . . in the vision:** cf. 8: 3; his return, like his coming to Jerusalem, was ecstatic. **the vision I had seen went up from me:** he returned from his ecstatic to his normal state of consciousness.

IV. THE FALL OF JERUSALEM DEPICTED AND FORETOLD (12: 1–15: 8)

i. Two symbolic actions (12: 1–20)

To the symbolic actions of 4: 1–5: 4 two more are now added: first comes the action and then its explanation.

(*a*) *Leaving home* (12: 1–16). Ezekiel obeys the command to dig through the mud-brick wall and carry his household stuff out through the hole in the sight of his neighbours.

2. a rebellious people: cf. 2: 3–7. **They have eyes to see but do not see and ears to hear but do not hear:** cf. Isa. 6: 9 f. Until they were convinced of the city's doom, the exiles would go on expecting an early return home. **3. belongings for exile:** the bare minimum; it would have to be carried on the exile's own shoulder all the long way. But it appears that the symbolic action denoted not primarily being led off into exile but attempting to escape from the enemy under cover of darkness. **to another place:** probably to someone else's house in the settlement, far enough from his own for his removal to be witnessed by his fellow-exiles.

The people naturally asked him **'What are you doing?'** (9); by way of answer he tells them that **the whole house of Israel** resident in Jerusalem will go into exile (11) and that **the prince** himself (for the title cf. 21: 25) will carry out his baggage **at dusk**, covering his face, as Ezekiel had done (6), to disguise himself, 'that he may not be seen by any eye' (12, LXX). Nevertheless he will be caught and taken captive to Babylon. **13. my net . . . my snare:** cf. Lam. 4: 20, 'The Lord's anointed, our very life breath, was taken in their pits'. **but he will not see it:** a reference to Zedekiah's being blinded by the Chaldaeans (Jer. 52: 11). The account in Jer. 52: 7–11 of Zedekiah's attempt to escape by night, his being overtaken in the plains of Jericho, punished by Nebuchadrezzar at Riblah (cf. Ezek. 6: 14) and imprisoned in Babylon 'till the day of his death' is a grim commentary on this oracle. **14. I will scatter . . . his staff and all his troops:** cf. Jer. 52: 8, 'all his soldiers were separated from him'. **I will pursue them with drawn sword:** cf. 5: 2, 12. **16. I will spare a few of them:** these are the survivors of the siege and destruction of the city, who joined in exile their brethren who had been carried away with Jehoiachin (Jer. 52: 28–30) or were dispersed elsewhere, and experienced repentance and eventual restoration.

(*b*) *Eating and drinking with trembling* (12: 17–20). This further symbolic action has affinities with that of 4: 9–17. As there the prophet ate siege rations, prepared under siege conditions, so here he is commanded to eat and drink and **tremble . . . and shudder** (18) to depict the **anxiety and . . . despair** of the Jerusalemites under siege (cf. 4: 16), as they contemplate the ruin of their city and land (19). The explanation of both symbolic actions ends with the promise that they will **know that I am the Lord** (20; cf. v. 16).

ii. Two popular sayings refuted (12: 21–28)

(*a*) *The fulfilment never comes* (12: 21–25). The **proverb** of v. 22 seems to mean 'Day succeeds day, but these prophecies of doom are never fulfilled'. Jeremiah, throughout his forty years' ministry in Jerusalem, endured frustration because his hearers refused to believe that his warnings of disaster would ever come true, and Ezekiel's hearers appear to be infected with the same wishful thinking. The prophetic word or vision might be potent at first, they thought, but if it was not fulfilled immediately, its potency faded. The prophet's reply is that **every vision will be fulfilled** (23), lit. 'the word (i.e. substance) of every vision', **without delay:** Yahweh will **fulfil** it in their days (25).

(*b*) *It will not happen yet* (12: 26–28). The second popular saying admits that the prophetic vision will be fulfilled, but in the distant future. This delusion is countered, like the previous one, with the assurance that the fulfilment will come without delay.

iii. Three denunciations of false prophecy (13: 1–23)

One reason for the people's unwillingness to believe the prophetic warnings was the pervasiveness of the 'false prophets' who kept on plying them with 'smooth things' (Isa. 30: 10) instead of telling them the unpalatable truth. The prophets here denounced by Ezekiel are those against whom Jeremiah had to contend in Jerusalem (cf. especially Jer. 23: 9–40).

(*a*) *First denunciation: the self-commissioned messengers* (13: 1–9). **2. prophesy against the prophets of Israel:** the majority of them belonged to professional guilds (called in earlier days 'the sons of the prophets'), some of which at least were attached to sanctuaries (cf. A. R Johnson, *The Cultic Prophet in Ancient Israel*, 1944). **who prophesy out of their own imagination:** instead of speaking 'from the mouth of Yahweh' (cf. 3: 16; Jer. 23: 16). **3.**

who follow their spirit: instead of the Spirit of Yahweh (cf. 11: 5, 24). have seen nothing: instead of a true vision of God (cf. 1: 1). 4. like jackals among ruins: helping on the destruction by their burrowing instead of repairing the wall to make it withstand a hostile assault, which was the work of a true prophet (5; cf. 22: 30). 6. divinations a lie: divination, resorting to various devices (mostly of pagan origin) to foretell the future, was forbidden in Israel (Dt. 18: 10–14); true prophecy came by divine inspiration, not by manipulation. They say, "The LORD declares": cf. 22: 28; Jer. 23: 31. the LORD has not sent them: cf. Jer. 23: 21, 32. 9. they will not belong to the council of my people: they would be excluded from the true Israel of God and would not enter the land with those who returned from exile.

(b) *Second denunciation: the daubers with whitewash* (13: 10–16). The state of Judah and Jerusalem is like that of a tottering wall; the false prophets, instead of taking remedial action, conceal its precarious condition by covering it with a coat of whitewash and thus render its collapse more certain. Five centuries later, the Qumran community applied the same denunciation to the Pharisees, the 'expounders of smooth things', as they called them (CD 1: 18; 8: 12). The 'covering with whitewash' is the false prophets' assurance of 'Peace', when there is no peace (10; cf. Jer. 6: 14; 8: 11; Mic. 3: 5), 'saying that all is well when all is not well' (NEB). The rain in torrents, hailstones and violent winds which bring down the wall (11–14) denote the divine judgment which is to come upon Judah and Jerusalem. The false prophets are justly overwhelmed in the ruin which they did so much to expedite.

(c) *Third denunciation: the hunters of souls* (13: 17–23). The women against whom this oracle is directed prophesy out of their own imagination (17) like their male counterparts (2) but, instead of helping the people of God, they ensnare their lives (18, 20) and thus precipitate their destruction. The magic charms which they sew on all wrists and the veils or shawls which they make of various lengths for their heads (18) evidently belong to the paraphernalia of witchcraft; their appropriate use was thought to preserve or take away people's lives, and may well have done so where their efficacy was believed in (19). The gravamen of the charge against them is that they have disheartened the righteous and encouraged the wicked (22), but the power of God is mightier than witchcraft: He will expose their pretensions and deliver their victims.

iv. Idolatry among the exiles (14: 1–11)
Not only were there false prophets in Judah and Jerusalem; among the exiles too there were those who tried to seduce their fellows into adopting the religious practices of their Babylonian neighbours. When the elders of the exilic community came to consult Ezekiel about the will of God, he could not do as they asked because they cherished idolatrous tendencies in their hearts; the only answer they could get would be a direct one of judgment from God Himself.

1. elders of Israel: cf. 8: 1, where, however, they are called 'the elders of Judah'. 3. wicked stumbling blocks: NEB 'the sinful things that cause their downfall' (cf. 7: 19), here referring to idols (*gillulim*, as in 6: 4). 5. recapture the hearts: NEB 'grip the hearts' —so as to cause fear and consequent repentance. 7. When any Israelite . . . : the language is reminiscent of the case-laws of the Holiness Code (cf. Lev. 17: 3, etc.). any alien living in Israel: in this context these resident aliens may be proselytes (cf. 47: 22 f.). 8. I will set my face against that man . . . : for the penalties of idolatry cf. Lev. 20: 3, 5, 6; Dt. 13: 1 ff. an example and a byword: cf. 5: 15; Dt. 28: 37; Jer. 24: 9. cut him off from my people: expel him from the covenant-community of Israel. 9. I, the LORD, have persuaded that prophet: in order to test His people, as in Dt. 13: 3. Cf. the 'lying spirit' sent by divine permission to mislead Ahab's prophets so as to 'lure' him to his fate at Ramoth-gilead (1 Kg. 22: 20–23). The verb *pittah*, translated 'lure' there, is rendered 'persuade' here, and 'deceive' in Jer. 20: 7, 10, where Jeremiah's opponents hope he may be 'deceived' in his prophesying, so that he may come to grief, and he himself fears that this has actually befallen him: 'O LORD, you deceived me, and I was deceived.' 10. the prophet will be as guilty: the prophet's doom at the end of v. 9 is that of the general idolater in v. 8 (cf. Jer. 14: 15 f.). 11. They will be my people and I will be their God: the covenant promise, as in 11: 20.

v. Jerusalem's plight irremediable (14: 12–23)
That the presence of righteous men in a community, especially if they are powerful intercessors, can protect it against disaster is a recurring OT theme: the classical instance is the divine assurance to Abraham regarding Sodom (Gen. 18: 23–32). But Jerusalem's plight is now so desperate that even the presence of the most righteous men who ever lived could not save it from famine, wild beasts, the sword or pestilence. The same theme finds expression in Jer. 15: 1–4, where Moses and Samuel (prevalent intercessors indeed) play the part that Noah, Daniel and Job play in the present passage.

13. cut off its food supply: cf. 4: 16; 5: 16. 14. Noah, Daniel and Job: three men outstanding for righteousness; for Noah cf. Gen. 6: 9; 7: 1 (yet the only persons delivered by his righteousness were his own family), and for Job cf. Job 1: 1, 8 (and 42: 8, 10, where he prays

effectually for his three friends). **Daniel** (Heb. *dan'el*; NEB 'Danel') is spelt differently from the name of the hero of the book of Daniel, Ezekiel's contemporary, and is possibly to be identified with a figure comparable in antiquity with Noah and Job—the Danel who is celebrated in Ugaritic literature of the 14th century B.C. as a righteous and wise ruler, who judged the cause of the widow and orphan (cf. 28: 3). (It may be a coincidence that one 'Danel' is mentioned in Jubilees 4: 20 as the uncle and father-in-law of Enoch.) If this identification can be upheld, then all three righteous men in this passage are non-Israelites (unlike the Israelites Moses and Samuel in Jer. 15: 1), but if they lived in Jerusalem their righteousness would avail to save their own lives only—not even (by contrast with the Flood narrative) the lives of their families. This may anticipate the ethical individualism emphasized in 18: 1 ff.; 33: 10–16.

21. my four dreadful judgments: summarizing what has been threatened in greater detail in vv. 12–20. Three of the four—**sword, famine . . . and plague**—have been mentioned in the oracles of 5: 12 and 6: 12, and the other—**wild beasts**—in that of 5: 17. **22. if there should be left in it any survivors:** cf. 12: 16. Here the survival of a few people from the siege and sack of Jerusalem is not so much an act of mercy to the survivors themselves as a source of consolation to the exiles: when they see the survivors and hear their harrowing experiences they will be glad they had gone into exile already and will understand that God has had a purpose in it all.

vi. The parable of the useless vine (15: 1–8)
Jerusalem is here compared to a vine that yields no grapes. Such a vine is good for nothing else: the only thing to do with it is to burn it. For the picture of the vine cf. Ps. 80: 8–19, with the related picture of the vineyard in Isa. 5: 1–7. These OT pictures are reflected in the NT in Mk 12: 1–9; Jn 15: 1–8 (where Jesus, as the 'true vine', embodies the true Israel).

2. how is the wood of a vine better than any . . . trees . . . ?: the vine is cultivated for its fruit alone (cf. Jg. 9: 13); its wood is useless for anything but fuel. Once it could be said, 'Israel was a spreading vine; he brought forth fruit' (Hos. 10: 1); that was no longer true. Jerusalem had been exposed to the fire of judgment a few years previously, when Jehoiachin and the flower of his subjects were carried into exile (2 Kg. 24: 10–16): it was now like a **charred** vine. If its wood was good for nothing before that, how much more worthless was it now! Let it be abandoned completely to the fire (cf. Ps. 80: 16; Jn 15: 6; Heb. 6: 8).

The parable is set out in vv. 1–5; the application to Jerusalem follows in vv. 6–8. **7.**

Although they have come out of the fire: Heb. 'though they have escaped'. Jerusalem escaped destruction when the Chaldaeans besieged it in 597 B.C., but next time there would be no escape: the city would become a ruin and **the land desolate** (8).

V. ALLEGORY AND EVENT (16: 1–19: 14)
i. The unfaithful bride (16: 1–63)
The delinquency of Jerusalem is now portrayed in a powerful and, indeed, revolting allegory. The city is compared to a baby-girl exposed at birth without the normal minimum of attention. Yahweh took pity on her, adopted her and brought her up and, when she became nubile, made her His bride, decking her with garments and ornaments fit for a queen. But instead of showing gratitude and fidelity, she turned to prostitution and committed fornication with strangers—Egyptians, Assyrians and Chaldaeans—enticing them and even bribing them to become her lovers (1–34). In real life such a woman could not escape the penalty reserved for an adulteress: public exposure and stoning (35–43a). Jerusalem's sisters, Samaria and Sodom, had behaved disgracefully and been punished for it; yet by comparison with her outrageous conduct theirs appeared positively innocent. So much the more certain and overwhelming would her punishment be (43b–52).

Yet for Jerusalem, as for Samaria and Sodom, there was hope of ultimate restoration. Yahweh in grace would remember His covenant with her and re-establish it in perpetuity, although she had violated her pledge to Him (53–63).

The portrayal of Yahweh's covenant with His people in terms of the marriage bond appears in Hos. 2: 4 f. and Jer. 2: 2 (cf. also Isa. 50: 1; 54: 6 f.; 62: 4 f.). The Hosea precedent in particular seems to have influenced Ezekiel: there, as here, apostasy and idolatry on the part of Yahweh's people are stigmatized as fornication and adultery (cf. Jer. 2: 20–3: 5). The analogy was all the more apt because of the part which ritual prostitution played in much fertility worship.

2. confront Jerusalem with her detestable practices: this language no more implies the prophet's presence in Jerusalem at the time than the language of the oracles against Tyre (26: 2 ff.) or Egypt (29: 1 ff.) implies his presence in those places. **3. your father was an Amorite and your mother a Hittite:** yet the Jews charged the Samaritans with being half-breeds! Jerusalem was a Canaanite city until David's reign, and as its inhabitants were not expelled or destroyed it retained much of its non-Israelite character. The Amorites (cf. Jos. 10: 5) and Hittites (cf. 2 Sam. 23: 39) may represent the Semitic and non-Semitic elements in its indigenous Jebusite population. **4. cut:** better 'tied', with NEB. The salting of a new-born child, after washing and before swaddling, was —and still is—believed to strengthen it.

6. 'Live . . .': MT continues, 'I caused thee to multiply . . .' (so RV); NIV has 'I made you grow' (lit. 'I made you grow'); NIV has 'I made you grow' (lit. 'I gave thee', possibly 'I will make thee'). Render perhaps: 'Live, grow up; I will make you like a plant of the field'. **7. the most beautiful of jewels:** lit. 'ornament of ornaments', i.e. the full beauty of womanhood. **8. gave you my solemn oath:** the Sinai covenant is treated as Yahweh's marriage contract. **10. covered you with costly garments:** This may be the earliest biblical reference to silk (Heb. *meshî*), produced by silkworms from the leaves of the white mulberry and imported from the Far East. **15. But you . . . a prostitute:** a reference to foreign alliances. **17. You . . . made for yourself male idols . . . :** a reference to the foreign cults which had to be accommodated as part of the foreign alliances. **20. you took your sons and daughters:** for child immolation cf. 2Kg. 16: 3; 21: 6; Jer.7: 31; see further Ezek. 20: 25 f., 31; 23: 37, 39. **22. in all your detestable practices:** lit. 'with' all your abominations, i.e. in addition to them she was guilty of ungrateful forgetfulness (cf. NEB). **24. mound:** NEB 'couch'. **a lofty shrine:** Heb. *ramah*, NEB 'high stool'. The *ramah* in the allegory corresponds to the *bamah* (cf 20:29) in the reality; as the former was used for public prostitution, the latter was used for public idolatry. **26. the Egyptians:** cf Isa. 18: 1 ff; 31: 1–3; Jer 2: 18, 36; 37: 5 ff. for the recurring and fatal temptation to trust in Egypt. Egypt regularly used Judah and the other small states of S. W. Asia as pawns in its moves against the Mesopotamian powers, and as regularly let them down (cf. 29: 6 f; Isa. 36: 6). Here there may be a special allusion to the Egyptian blandishments which at this very time were leading Zedekiah to break his oath (cf. 17: 15) as they had led the northern king Hoshea to do so at an earlier time (2 Kg. 17: 4). **27. the daughters of the Philistines:** ie. the five Philistine cities. The Philistines were pagans and non-Semites, yet even they are represented as being **shocked** at Jerusalem's conduct. The reference may be to Sennacherib's invasion of Judah in 701 B.C. (2 Kg. 18: 13 ff.; Isa. 36: 1 ff.); he claims to have given some cities of Judah to Ashdod, Ekron and Gath. **28. the Assyrians:** as when Ahaz sent an embassy to Tiglath-pileser III in 734 B.C. (cf. Isa. 7: 17; 8: 5–8).**29. Chaldea** (NIV mg): as when Hezekiah concerted anti-Assyrian plans with Merodach-baladan (2 Kg. 20: 12–19; Isa. 39:1–8). **30. brazen:** NEB 'imperious' is nearer the sense ('bossy', perhaps). **33. you give gifts to all your lovers:** actually, the 'presents' sent to foreign allies by way of tribute, but in the allegory the harlot is pictured as preposterously hiring her lovers instead of being hired by them (34).

36. This is what the Sovereign LORD says . . . : the punishment of the wife who turned harlot was stated more concisely in Hos. 2: 3; here it is elaborated, each aspect of her unfaithfulness being matched by an aspect of punishment (for death by stoning cf. Dt. 22: 21).

44. 'Like mother, like daughter': Jerusalem is a worthy daughter of those earlier inhabitants of Canaan whom the land 'vomited out' because of their abominations (Lev. 18: 25, 28). **46. your elder sister was Samaria, . . . your younger sister was Sodom:** Samaria's conduct, though culpable enough to bring disaster upon her, was less culpable than Jerusalem's (cf. 23: 4, 11; Jer. 3: 6–11). It may seem odd to treat Sodom as a sister of Jerusalem and Samaria, but she shared the same Canaanite ancestry, being 'younger' in the sense of 'smaller'. For a comparison of Sodom with cities of Israel to Sodom's advantage cf. Mt. 10: 15; 11: 23 f. **47. You not only walked . . . :** NEB in a superior rendering treats this as a question: 'Did you not behave as they did and commit the same abominations?' **51. Samaria did not commit half the sins you did:** cf. the allegorical representation of Samaria and Jerusalem as Oholah and Oholibah in 23: 1–49.

53. I will restore the fortunes . . . and your fortunes along with them: even for Jerusalem there would be restoration, as for Samaria and Sodom, when shame at her wretched state allegorically depicted in vv. 35–43a brought her to repentance. **56. You would not even mention your sister Sodom . . . ?:** a sad situation indeed, in which the formerly unmentionable Sodom was displaced as a by-word for wickedness by the city of God, and that on the lips of the heathen Philistines and Edomites!

60. I will remember the covenant I made with you in the days of your youth: at the beginning of the wilderness wanderings (cf. Exod. 24: 3–8; Jer. 2: 2 f.). **I will establish an everlasting covenant with you:** cf. 11: 19 f. (where the word 'covenant' is not used); 2 Sam. 23: 5; Isa. 55: 3. **61. give them to you as daughters:** Jerusalem will regain her status as mother-city of the people of God (cf. Gal. 4: 26). **not on the basis of my covenant with you:** but by a new divine act of sheer grace. **62–63. you will know that I am the LORD, . . . when I make atonement for you for all that you have done:** because God is 'rich in mercy' (Eph. 2: 4; cf. Ps. 130: 7 f.; Mic. 7: 18–20).

ii. The two eagles and the spreading vine (17: 1–24)

The first part of this chapter propounds an **allegory** (vv. 1–10); the explanation of the **allegory** follows (vv. 11–21), and there is appended a promise of a happier future in terms of the imagery used (vv. 22–24). The allegory or parable describes members of the animal and plant worlds behaving as animals and plants do not naturally behave: the actions ascribed to them are those of the real-life situation which they symbolize. This real-life situation is the vacillating policy of Zedekiah which led to his downfall.

(*a*) *The allegory* (17: 1–10). **3. A great eagle:** Nebuchadrezzar, king of Babylon, well represented by the king of birds. **Lebanon:** the home of the **cedar**. Since the **cedar** here is the dynasty of David, **Lebanon** is used metaphorically for its seat in Jerusalem. **4. he broke off its topmost shoot:** a reference to King Jehoiachin (cf. 1: 2), who was carried into exile (597 B.C.) **to a land of merchants** (Babylonia, cf. 16: 29), to **a city of traders** (Babylon). **5. he took some of the seed of your land:** NEB 'he took a native seed', i.e. Zedekiah, whom Nebuchadrezzar appointed to govern Judah and Jerusalem in Jehoiachin's place (2 Kg. 24: 17). **by abundant water:** in a well-irrigated seed-bed. **like a willow:** Heb. *ṣaphṣaphah* occurs here only, and the sense may be '(he made it) a fruit tree'; the introduction of a willow simile into the description of a vine is inappropriate. **6. a low, spreading vine:** a reference to the lowly status of Zedekiah as the Babylonian king's vassal. **under it:** NEB, better, 'beneath him'—beneath the eagle in the allegory, beneath Nebuchadrezzar in historical fact.

7. another great eagle: Pharaoh, king of Egypt, whether Psamtek II (595–589 B.C.) or his successor Apries (589–570 B.C.), the 'Hophra' of Jer. 44: 30. Pharaoh enticed Zedekiah from his sworn allegiance to Nebuchadrezzar, promising him protection and provision. **stretched out its branches:** i.e. its rootlets, through which the vine gets its moisture. **from the plot where it was planted:** i.e. from the land of Judah. **8. It had been planted** i.e. 'though it had been planted (by Nebuchadrezzar) in good soil' (as already said in v. 5). **9. Will it not be uprooted . . . ?:** the agent is not stated but is, by implication, the eagle (Nebuchadrezzar). **It will not take a strong arm:** the deposition of Zedekiah would require no great effort. **10. Even if it is transplanted:** or 'though it has been (trans)planted' (cf. v. 8). **the east wind strikes it:** the hot wind blowing across the desert from Babylonia.

(*b*) *The explanation* (17: 11–21). **12. The king of Babylon . . . carried off her king and her nobles:** cf. 2 Kg. 24: 11–16. **13. made a treaty with him:** a reference to the vassal treaty imposed by Nebuchadrezzar on Zedekiah, who was required to swear fealty to him in the name of Yahweh. This oath may have been confirmed by the change of name (2 Kg. 24: 17) from Mattaniah ('gift of Yahweh') to Zedekiah ('righteousness of Yahweh'). **He also carried away the leading men of the land:** in fact, by removing the wisest counsellors he unintentionally exposed Zedekiah to the influence of his ill-advised pro-Egyptian courtiers, which brought about his rebellion (15) and ruin (16). **15. horses and a large army:** for horses from Egypt see Dt. 17: 16; 1 Kg. 10: 28 f.). **16. he shall die in Babylon:** cf. 12: 13. **17. Pharaoh with his mighty army . . . will be of no help to him:** although Zedekiah's agreement was probably made with Psamtek II, it was his successor Apries (Hophra) who first sent military help, but by then the siege of Jerusalem had already begun: the Egyptian approach made the Chaldaeans raise the siege, but only temporarily (Jer. 37: 5 ff.). **20. I will spread my net for him . . . :** practically a repetition of 12: 13. **21. all his fleeing troops shall fall by the sword . . . :** cf. 12: 14; 2 Kg. 25: 5 (Jer. 52:8).

(*c*) *The noble cedar* (17: 22–24). **22. I myself will take a shoot . . . :** the figure of the **cedar** for the dynasty of David is resumed, but now it is no 'great eagle' but the God of Israel Himself who undertakes to **break off** one of its **topmost shoots** and plant it **on the mountain heights of Israel** (23), i.e. in Jerusalem (cf. 40: 2; Isa. 2: 2; Mic. 4: 1). **23. it will produce branches and bear fruit:** cf. v. 8, but this is no vine but a **splendid cedar**, the promised Prince of the house of David (cf. 34: 23 f.; 37: 24 f.), the 'righteous Branch' of Jer. 23: 5 f., whose name 'The LORD Our Righteousness' (*Yahweh ṣidqenu*) proclaims that he will maintain the faith betrayed by Zedekiah, who proved so false to his name. **Birds of every kind will nest in it . . . :** similar language is used of the Babylonian monarchy in Dan. 4: 12, 21. Here the world-wide sway of the messianic kingdom is denoted. **24. All the trees of the field:** i.e. all the rulers of the earth, and the nations which they govern (cf. Dan. 2: 44; 4: 25 f., 32, 34 f.).

iii. Personal responsibility (18: 1–32)

When hardship came, in the form of invasion, siege and exile (as at this time) or otherwise, there was a tendency among those who experienced it to say that the sins of the fathers were being visited on the children, that they themselves were suffering not for any fault of their own but because of their ancestors' misdeeds. This attitude could find some support in the decalogue (Exod. 20: 5; cf. 34: 7) and in the near-contemporary judgment of Jeremiah and the author of Kings that the apostasy of Manasseh, less than a century before, could be expiated only by foreign domination and exile (Jer. 1: 15 f.; 5: 1–17; 17: 1–4; 2 Kg. 21: 10–15; 22: 16–20; 23: 26 f.; 24: 1–4). But, when indulged to excess, it tended to destroy all sense of personal responsibility; hence Ezekiel presents a counterbalance to it in what has been called the 'moral atomism' of this chapter. In itself this 'moral atomism' would be as one-sided as the attitude which it aims at correcting, but when its corrective purpose is recognized its appropriateness to the current situation can be appreciated. That one man can 'bear the punishment' of others was known to Ezekiel himself (4: 4–6) and was to be exemplified supremely in the Servant of the LORD (Isa. 53: 11 f.). The contents of ch. 18 are later summarized in 33: 10–20.

(a) *A misleading proverb* (18: 1–4). **2. 'The fathers eat sour grapes, and the children's teeth are set on edge':** i.e. the children are paying the penalty for their fathers' actions. The proverb is quoted also in Jer. 31: 29 f., and similarly rebutted: 'every one will die for his own sin; whoever eats sour grapes, *his* own teeth will be set on edge.' **4. every living soul belongs to me:** each separate person (Heb. *nephesh*) is a distinct creation of God; the person who **sins** (and not his descendants) **will die** (or otherwise suffer) for his sin.

(b) *Moral change from generation to generation* (18: 5–20). **5. Suppose there is a . . . man:** This is the regular introduction to case-laws in the Israelite legislation (cf. Exod. 21: 7, 20, 26, 33; 22: 1, etc.). The details of conduct in vv. 6–9 which make a man **righteous** are especially characteristic of the Holiness Code (Lev. 17–26), though they are found in other parts of the Law also. **6. eat at the mountain shrines:** probably a reference to sacrificial meals at the high places (cf. 6: 2 ff.; 20: 28 f.), forbidden by implication in Dt. 12: 2–28. Josiah had abolished worship at the high places (2 Kg. 23: 8 ff.) but his reforms were short-lived. **lift up his eyes:** cf. Ps. 121: 1, probably to be rendered 'Shall I lift up my eyes to the hills?'—the implied answer being 'No'. **or lie with a woman . . . :** cf. Lev. 18: 19; 20: 18. **7. returns what he took in pledge:** cf. Exod. 22: 26 f.; Dt. 24: 10–13. **8. does not lend at usury:** cf. Exod. 22: 25; Lev. 25: 36; Dt. 23: 19; Ps. 15: 5. **9. he will live:** cf. Lev. 18: 5, 'the man who obeys them will live by them'.

10. Suppose he has a violent son . . . : the righteousness of the father cannot be credited to an unrighteous son. It is those who do the works of Abraham that are Abraham's true sons (Jn 8: 39). **12. does detestable things:** i.e. idolatry. **13. he will surely be put to death:** an echo of a recurrent legal formula (cf. Exod. 19: 12, etc.). **his blood will be on his own head:** cf. Lev. 20: 11 ff. He (and no one else) will be responsible for his death, the

penalty for his own misconduct.

14. But suppose this son has a son . . . : the wickedness of the father cannot be debited to a righteous son. **20. The soul who sins is the one who will die:** repeated from v. 4. Each generation stands on its own feet in respect of reward or punishment for righteous or unrighteous behaviour. **The son will not share the guilt . . . :** laid down as a legal principle in Dt. 24: 16 and historically exemplified in 2 Kg. 14: 6; here stated to be a principle in God's dealings with men.

(c) *Moral change within one person's lifetime* (18: 21–24). A wicked man who repents of his wickedness and practises amendment of life will be forgiven (21 f.); cf. the Chronicler's account of King Manasseh (2 Chr. 33: 12 f.). Conversely, a formerly righteous man who turns to iniquity and idolatry will suffer condign retribution (24); cf. the account of Joash, king of Judah (2 Chr. 24: 17 ff.). But in this paragraph the main emphasis lies on God's eagerness to pardon: as all the great prophets insist, he has no **pleasure in the death of the wicked** (23; cf. v. 32).

(d) *The divine vindication* (18: 25–29). **25. 'The way of the Lord is not just':** because, as they thought, He made the children suffer for their fathers' sins. But He replies by repeating the substance of vv. 21–24, with a reversal of order, to emphasize that His ways are indeed just, because He enforces personal responsibility; what injustice there is lies in their ways, not in His.

(e) *Call to repentance* (18: 30–32). **30. then sin will not be your downfall:** lit. 'and you will have no more stumbling block of iniquity' (cf. 7: 19; 14: 3 f., 7). The troubles through which they were passing made them complain that God was unfair: 'Repent', says God, 'and put me to the test; put off your rebellious attitude **and get a new heart and a new spirit!'** (31). Cf. 11: 19 f.; 36: 26 f., where this is God's gift to His repentant people. **32. For I take no pleasure in the death of anyone:** cf. v. 23. It is because God delights in mercy that His plea is so urgent: **Why will you die? . . . Repent, and live** (cf. 33: 11).

iv. A dirge for the royal family (19: 1–9) The disasters that befell recent kings of Judah are described in terms of the misfortunes of a brood of lion whelps.

2. What a lioness was your mother among the lions!: the mother is the nation or tribe of Judah—whose emblem (as it happens) was a lion (Gen. 49: 9; Rev. 5: 5)—rather than the queen-mother Hamutal (2 Kg. 23: 31; 24: 18). **3. She brought up** (better, 'exalted') **one of her cubs:** Jehoahaz, who succeeded his father Josiah in 609 B.C. (2 Kg. 23: 30). **He learned to tear the prey:** neither in Kg. nor in Chr. are such details recorded of his three months' reign as are hinted at here. **4. he was trapped in their pit:** cf. Lam. 4: 20 (of Zedekiah), but the imagery is used here because it is suitable for the capture of a lion. **They led him with hooks:** cf. 2 Kg. 19: 28; Isa. 37: 29 (of Sennacherib); 2 Chr. 33: 11 (of Manasseh). **to the land of Egypt:** Pharaoh Necho, as part of his reprisals against Judah for Josiah's ill-starred attempt to bar his way at Megiddo, deposed Jehoahaz and carried him in fetters into lifelong imprisonment in Egypt (cf. Jer. 22: 10–12), setting his brother Jehoiakim on the throne in his place (2 Kg. 23: 31–34). **5. she took another of her cubs:** probably Jehoiakim. The description of his activity in vv. 6–8 may suggest that after Necho's expulsion from Asia by Nebuchadrezzar in 605 B.C. (2 Kg. 24: 7), Jehoiakim tried to extend his realm at his neighbours' expense, until they banded together, captured him and brought him before Nebuchadrezzar (who at this time made an annual incursion into the area). If so, Nebuchadrezzar appears to have reinstated him as his sworn vassal. His withdrawal of allegiance some years later led to the investment of Jerusalem in 597 B.C. and the surrender and exile of his son Jehoiachin, who had just succeeded him (cf. 1: 2). Many commentators identify this second cub with Jehoiachin (supposing Jehoiakim to have been passed over in silence), but the language of vv. 6–8 does not fit him at all. If Jehoiachin be indeed intended, this language must belong exclusively to the figure of the young lion.

v. Another dirge for the royal family (19: 10–14)

The theme is the same, but the picture changes from a lioness and her cubs to a vine and its branches.

10. Your mother was like a vine: the mother is still Judah; for the simile cf. 15: 2; 17: 6. **11. Its branches were strong . . . :** NEB, better: 'It had stout branches, fit to make sceptres for those who bear rule' (a reference to successive kings of Judah). **12. But it was uprooted in fury:** a description of the overthrow of the Judaean monarchy. **The east wind made it shrivel:** as in 17: 10, the east wind is Nebuchadrezzar. **13. planted in the desert:** exiled. **14. Fire spread from one of its main branches:** from its stem; a reference perhaps to Zedekiah's rebellion against Nebuchadrezzar, which led to the wiping out of all his family (2 Kg. 25: 7; Jer. 52: 10 f.).

VI. THE LAST DAYS OF JERUSALEM (20: 1–24: 27)

i. A record of unfaithfulness (20: 1–44)

We move on a year, and come to a further group of oracles, more ominous, if possible, than the preceding ones; for now, it appears (cf. 21: 18 ff., 25 ff.), Zedekiah's breach of treaty has become known to Nebuchadrezzar, and Nebuchadrezzar has determined to take decisive action against Jerusalem: the fall of the house of David is inevitable. The first in this group of oracles takes the form of a divine retrospect of Israel's unfaithfulness 'from the time they left Egypt until now' (cf. Num. 14: 19).

(a) *The elders' inquiry* (20: 1–3). **1.** The date is August 14, 591 B.C. **the elders of Israel:** cf. 14: 1 (also 8: 1). **3. I will not let you inquire of me:** the reason has been given in 14: 3.

(b) *Unfaithfulness in Egypt* (20: 4–8). **4. Will you judge . . . ?:** Ezekiel is invited to concur with God's judgment (cf. 22: 2; 23: 36). **confront them with the detestable practices of their fathers:** not now depicted allegorically, as in ch. 16, but historically. **5. I am the LORD your God:** cf. the message with which Moses was sent back to them (Exod. 3: 14 f.); the actual wording recurs throughout the Holiness Code (cf. Lev. 18: 2, 30, etc.). **6. a land flowing with milk and honey:** cf. Exod. 3: 8, etc.; the phrase implies a rich pastoral (rather than agricultural) economy. **7. get rid of the vile images:** their involvement in **the idols of Egypt** is not explicitly recorded in the Pentateuchal narrative, but the Hebrews' worship of 'other gods' at a still earlier date is recalled in Jos. 24: 2, 14 (with a bare reference in the latter verse to idolatry in Egypt, which might, however, refer to the continuation in Egypt of earlier Semitic practice).

(c) *Unfaithfulness of the first wilderness generation* (20: 9–17). The wilderness period is not here envisaged as one of honeymoon innocence, as it is in Jer. 2: 2 and Hos. 2: 14 f.; but the presentation in this chapter is quite in line with the Pentateuchal narrative and is echoed in Stephen's speech (Ac. 7: 39–44), with its interpretation of Am. 5: 25–27. **9. for the sake of my name . . . :** i.e. my reputation; cf. Exod. 9: 16; Jos. 7: 9 (and, for the sense, Num. 14: 13–16; Isa. 43: 25; 48: 11). **11. the man who obeys them will live:** an echo of Lev. 18: 5 (cf. Lk. 10: 28; Rom. 10: 5). **12. I gave them my Sabbaths, as a sign between us:** i.e. a token of the covenant; cf. Exod. 31: 13–17. **I the LORD made them holy:** cf. Exod. 31: 15; Lev. 20: 8; 21: 8, 15, 23; 22: 9, 16, 32. **13. they utterly desecrated:** instead of 'keeping it holy' according to the commandment (Exod. 20: 8; Dt. 5: 12). **15. I swore . . . that I would not bring them into the land:** cf. Num. 14: 22 ff.; Ps. 95: 11.

(d) *Unfaithfulness of the second wilderness generation* (20: 18–26). Only the children who came out of Egypt survived to the end of the wilderness wanderings (Num. 14: 31, 33), but they are described as being no better than their parents. They in their turn rejected the same ordinances as were given to their parents. **23.**

I swore . . . that I would disperse them: cf. Lev. 26: 14–39; Dt. 28: 15–68; 32: 26. **25. statutes that were not good:** the divine **laws**, ('the man who obeys them will live by them', 21), became by misuse a means of death, rather than life (cf. Rom. 7: 10, where the application indeed is different from Ezekiel's). **26. I let them become defiled . . . the sacrifice of every firstborn:** for example, they misapplied Exod. 13: 2 ('Consecrate to me every firstborn') and similar commandments, although Exod. 13: 13 makes it plain that this 'consecration' does not involve child-sacrifice, which is expressly forbidden in Lev. 18: 21. They reckoned that the sacrifice of the firstborn (cf. Mic. 6: 7) was even more pleasing to God than their redemption (cf. Exod. 34: 20b). Ezekiel's contemporary prophet represents Yahweh as saying that this abomination was 'something I did not command, nor did it enter my mind' (Jer. 7: 31; cf. 19: 5; 32: 35). In view of Ezekiel's own language in v. 31 below (cf. 16: 20), he plainly understands the divine action here as penal; cf. Ps. 18: 26 ('to the crooked you show yourself shrewd'); Rom. 1: 24, 26, 28 ('God gave them over . . . to sexual impurity'). Ahaz and Manasseh are said to have sacrificed their sons (2 Kg. 16: 3; 21: 6). **that I might fill them with horror:** and so produce revulsion.

(*e*) *Unfaithfulness in the promised land* (20: 7–29). After their settlement in Canaan, the Israelites took over the Canaanite sanctuaries and fertility-cults. **28. high hill . . . leafy tree . . . fragrant incense:** cf. 6: 13. **made offerings that provoked me to anger:** an idolatrous **offering** which provoked Yahweh to anger (this clause is absent from LXX). **29. this high place:** NEB 'hill-shrine'. For a full discussion see P. H. Vaughan, *The Meaning of 'bāmâ' in the OT*, 1974. The Heb. term *bamah* is here derived by paronomasia from *mah* ('what?' or 'where?') and *ba* ('going'), so as to make it mean 'a place where people go'.

(*f*) *Unfaithfulness even in exile?* (20: 30–31). The elders are asked, as representatives of the exiled community, if they will persist in their ancestors' idolatry. If the answer were left to themselves, it would be 'Yes'—the reason for Yahweh's refusal to **let you inquire of me** is, as in 14: 2–5, their 'setting up idols in their hearts'. But Yahweh will deal with them sovereignly, purging them of rebellion by the judgment of exile and restoring them to serve Him in the holy land.

(*g*) *Judgment and restoration* (20: 32–44). Whatever idolatrous tendencies the exiles may cherish, God will check them; with a firm and irresistible hand He will turn them into the way of obedience, so that when they are brought back to their own land it will be as Yahweh-worshippers. **33. with a mighty hand and an out-** **stretched arm:** as at the Exodus (Dt. 4: 34, etc.). **I will rule over you:** He had been their King since the Exodus (Exod. 15: 18; 1 Sam. 8: 7; Ps. 47: 6 f., Isa. 6: 5, etc.), but henceforth He would exercise His kingship more absolutely than ever before. In fact, after Jehoiachin (1: 2), Ezekiel rarely (as in 17: 16; 37: 22, 24) gives the title 'king' to any ruler of Israel (cf. 21: 25), even to the coming prince of the house of David (cf. 34: 24; 37: 25; 44: 3, etc.). **35. the desert of the nations:** a figurative wilderness this time, perhaps, but it would be the site for their new **judgment**, as **the desert of the land of Egypt** (36) was for their forefathers' judgment. **37. I will take note . . . as you pass under my rod:** MT continues 'and I will bring you into the bond of the covenant' (so RV). The shepherd counted his sheep ('by number', so RSV, preferring LXX to MT), holding his **staff** over them as they entered the fold one by one; any that did not belong to his flock would be rejected. Thus the flock of God would be 'purged' of rebels: what would happen to these is not made plain. **39. Go and serve:** NEB, better, 'Go, sweep away'. **you will surely listen to me . . . :** NEB, better, 'you will never be disobedient to me or . . .'. The exiled community, purified by judgment in exile and purged of its rebels, will be restored to **the land** of Israel and **serve** the God of their fathers on His **holy mountain** (Zion) with appointed **gifts** and **offerings** (40). They themselves will be acceptable to Him by means of (rather than **as**) **fragrant incense** (41); their sacrifices will be approved because they are offered by people who desire to do His will from the heart. **41. I will show myself holy:** lit. 'I will let myself be sanctified'; His holiness, which had been vindicated by the punishment of His apostate people, will now be vindicated in the sight of the nations (cf. Ps. 98: 2 f.) by the restoration of His repentant people. **44. for my name's sake:** cf. vv. 9, 14, 22.

ii. Four sword oracles (20: 45–21: 32)
The four oracles in this section are linked together by the theme of the 'sword' which is found in each.

(*a*) *A sword against Jerusalem* (20: 45–21: 7). The last five verses (45–49) of ch. 20 in the English versions appear more appropriately as 21: 1–5 in MT.

46. set your face toward the south: three Hebrew nouns for **south** are used in this verse: 'Teman' (so NEB), *darôm* and Negeb. All three are here used in the general sense of **south:** as one approached the land of Judah by the regular route from Babylonia, one went from north to south (via Carchemish). Similarly in 26: 7 the king of Babylon comes to Tyre 'from the north'. The southland is compared to a forest about to be completely destroyed by fire. But the fire is kindled by Yahweh; in reality, the southland is about to be invaded by the Babylonian army, and the sword which it wields is the sword of Yahweh (21: 2–5).

21: 2. To the three terms for 'south' in 20: 46 correspond **Jerusalem**, **the sanctuary** and **the land of Israel**, all of which are to be devastated by the **sword** which **the LORD** Himself has **drawn . . . from its scabbard** (5). **3. righteous and wicked:** the counterpart of the 'trees, both green and dry' in the forest fire metaphor of 20: 47. **6. groan with broken heart and bitter grief:** as the people of Judah and Jerusalem would do under invasion and siege. Cf. the symbolic actions of 12: 17 ff. **7. every knee become as weak as water:** cf. 7: 17.

(b) *The song of the sword* (21: 8–17). The song itself (vv. 9b, 10) may be a traditional one: on Ezekiel's lips it acquires a new and doom-laden significance.
10. polished to flash like lightning: cf. Gen. 3: 24; Dt. 32: 41; here, as there, the **sword** is Yahweh's. **Shall we rejoice in the scepter of my son, Judah? The sword despises every such stick** is unintelligible; cf. the conjectural rendering in NEB. The *MT* here ('Ah! the club is brandished, my son, to defy all wooden idols!') The meaning may be that nothing made of wood, whether for offence or for defence, can resist this **sword**, which Yahweh has whetted and burnished and put into **the hand of the** Babylonian **slayer** (11), to be used **against** His own **people, . . . against all the princes of Israel** (12). **12. Therefore beat your breast:** a gesture of grief (cf. Jer. 31: 19). Whatever v. 13 may mean, it echoes the closing words of v. 10. **14. strike your hands together:** a vigorous action, to accompany and imitate the execution of the sword. It may even be, as NEB suggests, that Ezekiel himself is to 'swing' a **sword**, cutting **to the right, then to the left** (16); the prophetic action, like the prophetic word, is self-fulfilling.

(c) *The king of Babylon's sword* (21: 18–27). Ezekiel pictures Nebuchadrezzar and his army marching south from Carchemish through Syria until he comes to a fork in the road. Shall he fork right for **Jerusalem** or left for **Rabbah** (modern Amman), capital **of the Ammonites**, who evidently had rebelled against their Babylonian overlord about the same time as Zedekiah (cf. vv. 28–32; 25: 1 ff.; Jer. 40: 14; 41: 15)? In order to determine which of the two ways to take, Nebuchadrezzar casts lots by approved methods: (i) divination by means of two **arrows**, one marked 'Jerusalem' and the other marked 'Rabbah', so that whichever came out from the quiver first would supply the answer; (ii) the consultation of an oracle by means of **idols**, the exact nature of which is no longer known (cf. Jg. 17: 5; 1 Sam. 15: 23); (iii) hepatoscopy, the examination of **the liver** of sacrificed animals (many clay liver-models,

divided into zones to provide guidance for such inspection, have been found in Babylonia; cf. the bronze Etruscan model from Piacenza). The unanimous response is **Jerusalem** (22), so to Jerusalem he marches to lay siege to it. Even pagan divination is overruled by the true God for the accomplishment of His purpose.
19. the sword of the king of Babylon: this key-phrase links the present oracle with the preceding and following sword-songs. **23. to those . . . :** to the people of Jerusalem, who live in a fools' paradise, the ruin of their city will seem incredible; but Yahweh remembers their breach of the **allegiance** which they **have sworn** and has decreed its capture.

25. O profane and wicked prince: Zedekiah was specially responsible for the breach of the oath of allegiance which he had personally sworn (cf. 17: 15). He is called **prince of Israel**, not king (*nasi'*, not *melek*): Jehoiachin's kingship continued to be recognized (cf. 1: 2); see also note on 20: 33. Zedekiah's doom is sealed. The **turban** and **crown**, the insignia of royalty, will be taken from him (26) and will remain without a wearer **until he comes to whom it rightfully belongs** (27)—an echo, perhaps, of Jacob's blessing of Judah in Gen. 49: 10 ('until he comes to whom it belongs'). The reference is probably to the Davidic ruler in the age of restoration (cf. 34: 23 f., etc.); see note on 17:23.

(d) *A sword-song against Ammon* (21: 28–32). Even if Nebuchadrezzar dealt with Jerusalem first, the Ammonites in their turn would soon feel the edge of his **sword** (28)—or rather the sword of Yahweh (as in v. 3), for Nebuchadrezzar is but a sword in Yahweh's hand (cf. Isa. 10: 5).
28. about their insults: i.e. their malicious exultation over the fall of Jerusalem (cf. 25: 3). NEB understands Heb. *herpah* otherwise and renders 'to their shameful god'—i.e. 'Molech, the detestable god of the Ammonites' (1 Kg. 11: 5). **29. you . . . you:** the sword is apostrophized; the **false visions** and **lying divinations** deny that it will fall on the Ammonites. **it will be laid:** lit. 'to lay you' (still addressing the sword). **30. In the place where you were created . . . I will judge you:** from here to the end of the chapter **you** (as the Heb. forms make plain) is consistently the sword, i.e. Nebuchadrezzar. When he has accomplished Yahweh's work of retribution, he and his empire will also endure divine judgment by means of other instruments—**brutal men** (31) or 'barbarians' (LXX)—to be raised up for the purpose. Thus the 'sword' which was 'drawn' in vv. 3–5 is at last 'returned' **to its scabbard** (30).

iii. Three more oracles against Jerusalem (22: 1–31)
Ezekiel is called upon not only to enter into the

afflictions of his people by 'bearing their sin' (4: 4–6); but also to view them from the divine perspective and share in pronouncing their judgment (cf. 20: 4).

(*a*) *The bloody city* (22: 1–16). Manasseh had 'filled Jerusalem' with 'innocent blood' (2 Kg. 21: 16) and polluted it more than all his predecessors with idolatry (2 Kg. 21: 2–15); and more recently Jehoiakim had imitated him in the limited measure that was open to him (Jer. 26: 20–23). **2. confront her with all her detestable practices:** cf. 16: 2; 20: 4. **7. they have oppressed the alien:** resident aliens were under Yahweh's special protection (Exod. 22: 21; 23: 9).

The offences listed in vv. 6–9 embrace those which we distinguish as ethical and ritual, like those listed (negatively) in 18: 5–8. They violated the consistent teaching of the law and the prophets, and made Yahweh **strike** His **hands together** in anger (13). Perhaps the specific mention of **unjust gain** at this point implies that by clapping His hands He makes it vanish. The citizens' **courage** (lit. 'heart') will fail when He begins His work of judgment (14). **16. When you have been defiled in the eyes of the nations** (NEB 'I will sift you'): jealous as He was for the honour of His name (cf. 20: 9, etc.), Yahweh was prepared to let it be **defiled**—for a time—when the nations saw His people scattered and concluded that He was powerless to save them. But the scattering was remedial in intention (15), and the holiness of His name would yet be vindicated (36: 23).

(*b*) *The smelting furnace* (22: 17–22). The 'uncleanness' of v. 15 is compared to **dross** so pervasive that nothing but long and intense heat in the **furnace** of **wrath** can consume it and leave the modicum of pure **silver** to emerge after the smelting. Jerusalem, swollen with the influx of people from the surrounding countryside, besieged and destroyed, is itself the furnace. For the same figure cf. Isa. 1: 22a, 25; 48: 10; Jer.6:27–30; 9: 7; Zech. 13: 9; Mal. 3: 3.

(*c*) *Princes, priests, prophets, people—all unrighteous* (22: 23–31). The leaders of the people have betrayed their trust: the **princes** are guilty of robbery, violence and bloodshed (25, 27), the **priests** have profaned the holy ordinances (26), the **prophets** have prophesied falsely (28); for the daubers with **whitewash** cf. 13: 10–16.

24. a land that has had no rain or showers: Rain is a symbol of divine grace. Jerusalem and Judah are compared to a spiritual desert. **29. The people of the land:** the freeborn citizens, who follow their princes' example. **30. I looked for a man:** despite what has been said in 14: 12–20, about Noah, Daniel and Job, it is implied here that one righteous man might yet have availed to check the collapse of the state. If it be asked why Jeremiah could not fulfil a

prophet's rôle (cf. 13: 5), and mend **the wall and stand in the gap**, the answer may be that he had not the public status necessary for such a rôle. He himself had not found such a man in Jerusalem (Jer. 5: 1). The ruin had developed so far that no one with less than kingly authority could be expected to take any effective action—and if Josiah's action had proved ineffective, no help could now be looked for from the royal house.

This whole section (vv. 23–31) echoes the oracle of Zeph. 3: 1–8, pronounced at least a generation earlier.

iv. Two disgraceful sisters (23: 1–49)

The style of this chapter is very similar to that of ch. 16, but there are two important differences in content: not Jerusalem only, but Samaria and Jerusalem, are portrayed as breaking their marriage vows (cf. Jer. 3: 6–14); and the adultery in this chapter symbolizes not primarily idolatry but foreign alliances (which indeed involved the acknowledgment of the gods of the allied nations). Their allegorical names **Oholah** and **Oholibah** (4) are traditionally interpreted as 'Her tent' and 'My tent is in her', but they are not so vocalized in *MT*. It may seem strange that **Oholah** should be called **the older** (cf. 16: 46), since Samaria was first founded by Omri between 880 and 875 B.C. (1 Kg. 16: 24); but all that is meant is that the northern kingdom was larger and more powerful than the southern (cf. 16: 46).

(*a*) *A bad beginning* (23: 1–4). For their harlotry **in Egypt** (3) cf. 20: 7 f.

(*b*) *Samaria's unfaithfulness* (23: 5–10). The foreign alliance which brought the northern kingdom down was made with **Assyria**. Jehu paid tribute to Shalmaneser III in 841 B.C., regarding it probably as an insurance against aggression from Damascus, and Menahem followed his example by paying tribute to Tiglath-pileser III a century later (2 Kg. 15: 19). **mounted horsemen** (6), as distinct from chariotry, was a novelty which impressed the people of Samaria as it later impressed the Jerusalemites (v. 12). But **the Assyrians** reduced the territories of Zebulun and Naphtali to provinces of their empire in 732 B.C. (2 Kg. 15: 29) and treated the rest of the northern kingdom similarly nine years later, ultimately storming Samaria itself in 721 B.C., after a three years' siege (2 Kg. 17: 4–6).

(*c*) *Jerusalem's unfaithfulness* (23: 11–21). Jerusalem watched Samaria's depravity and decided to go one better. She too entered into treaty relations with **the Assyrians** (12), first (it appears) when Ahaz enlisted the help of Tiglath-pileser III against the Syro-Ephraimite alliance (2 Kg. 16: 7 ff.), although Isaiah warned him against the fatal consequences of doing so (Isa. 7: 17, 20). After the Assyrians came the **Chaldeans** (14). The Chaldaeans lived in southern

Babylonia, by the Persian Gulf. Merodach-baladan, who tried to involve Hezekiah in an anti-Assyrian alliance (2 Kg. 20: 12 ff.; Isa. 39: 1 ff.), was a Chaldaean, and it was a Chaldaean dynasty that established the Neo-Babylonian Empire (626–539 B.C.) which was dominant in the years of Ezekiel's ministry. At this time therefore **Chaldeans** tended to become a synonym for **Babylonians** (15). The portrayal of **men . . . portrayed on a wall . . . in red** (14) is illustrated by mural paintings uncovered in Mesopotamia (cf. the decoration of Jehoiakim's palace, Jer. 22: 14). Jerusalem entered into treaty relations with Babylon when Nebuchadrezzar II imposed tribute on Jehoiakim (2 Kg. 24: 1); then she yielded to the blandishments of **Egypt** (19) and rebelled against Babylon (cf. 17: 15 ff.).

(*d*) *Jerusalem's doom pronounced* (23: 22–35). Jerusalem's breach of treaty will be avenged by her **lovers** (22), i.e. **the Babylonians and all the Chaldeans** (23); the latter term is used here in its original, more restricted sense: **Pekod and Shoa and Koa** were all in the Chaldaean homeland. **all the Assyrians:** much of the former Assyrian territory now belonged to the Babylonian Empire. **24. with weapons:** MT *hōṣen* is unknown (RSV renders 'from the north,' following LXX; NEB 'with war-horses'). **25. They will cut off your noses . . . :** as in 16: 37 ff., the destruction of Jerusalem is compared to the punishment meted out in some parts of the Near East to an adulterous wife. **28. those you hate:** the effect of the revulsion and **disgust** of v. 17. The judgment-poem of vv. 32–34 portrays Jerusalem as draining the **cup** of wrath which had previously been drunk by Samaria. (*e*) *Their unfaithfulness and doom recapitulated* (23: 36–49). Ezekiel is invited to acquiesce in the judgment of the two sisters (36; cf. 20: 4; 22:2).

39. they sacrificed their children: cf. 20: 26. **41. you sat on an elegant couch:** cf. 16: 24 f., 31. **incense and oil . . . me:** cf. 16: 18. **42. rabble:** NEB 'Sabaeans' (from S. W. Arabia). **45. women who shed blood:** cf. 22: 2 ff. **49. you will know:** here the pronoun **you** refers to Ezekiel's hearers: in the three preceding clauses it refers to the unfaithful women.

v. Jerusalem besieged (24: 1–27)
The date (Jan. 15, 588 B.C.) is that given in Jer. 52: 4 for the beginning of the siege of Jerusalem. Ezekiel learns it **this very day** (2) by **the word of the LORD** (1); in default of such supernatural communication it was several months before he received news of the fall of the city a year and a half later (33: 21).
(*a*) *Allegory of the meat in the pot* (24: 1–5). The leaders of the people had previously boasted that the inhabitants of Jerusalem were as safe as meat in a cooking pot (11: 3); but what would happen to them when the **pot** was **put**

on the fire and the contents thoroughly boiled? (*b*) *The corroded pot* (24: 6–14). In a variation from the preceding allegory, Jerusalem is now compared to a corroded **pot** from which the **deposit** and **impurities** adhering to it must be burnt away. The rust and filth are the bloodshed and idolatry of which the city has been guilty. To get rid of them scouring will not suffice; the pot must be heated red-hot: a fearful prospect for those within.

6, 9. Woe to the city of bloodshed!: The denunciation once uttered against Nineveh (Nah. 3: 1) now falls on Jerusalem. **Empty it piece by piece . . . :** a reference, as in 11: 7, to the deportation of the inhabitants (it has been suggested that this sentence belongs to vv. 3–5). **7. she poured it on the bare rock:** where it could not be absorbed or covered by earth; uncovered blood cries for vengeance (cf. Gen. 4: 10; Job 16: 18; Isa. 26: 21). **10. mixing in the spices:** G. R. Driver tentatively emends to 'stew the stew' (*Biblica* 19, 1938, pp. 175 f.). **11. set the empty pot:** LXX omits **empty**. The boiled meat in the pot is burned to a cinder by the fierceness of the heat and, added to the other encrustations, must be completely cleansed away by the fire.
(*c*) *Death of the prophet's wife* (24: 15–24). The prophet who was invited by God to join Him in judging the people must now manifest his solidarity with his people under judgment. His wife, **the delight of** his **eyes**, is to be taken from him by death, but he must exhibit no sound or sign of mourning (cf. Jer. 16: 5 ff.). His neighbours will ask him why he is acting so strangely, and he will tell them. When Jerusalem's day of desolation comes, when the temple, **the delight of** its **eyes** (21), is destroyed and its children killed within it, the blow will be too unimaginably overwhelming to be expressed by any of the conventional tokens of grief. We may recall another Son of Man, to whom indeed the authority to execute judgment was given, but who was afflicted in all His people's affliction and absorbed their judgment in His own person.

17. Keep your turban fastened . . . : mourning for the dead was normally marked by going barehead and barefoot. **the customary food of mourners:** so RSV for 'bread of men'; the reference may be to the funeral feast, provided for the **mourners** by friends, which ended the period of fasting for the dead. **24. Ezekiel will be a sign to you:** cf. 12: 6. This is the most personal and poignant of all his acts of prophetic symbolism. Only here, apart from 1: 3, is **Ezekiel** mentioned by name. This is the subscription to chs. 1–24 as 1: 3 is the superscription.
(*d*) *Promised end to the prophet's dumbness* (24: 25–27). From the day after his wife's death (vv. 18b–24) until news came of the fall of Jerusalem

Ezekiel remained dumb—he had not even any further oracle to deliver to his people (cf. 3: 25–27). With the investment of the city the judgment had fallen: now let it work. For the coming of the **fugitive** with news of the capture of the city and Ezekiel's consequent release from dumbness see 33: 21 f. **26. on that day:** NEB 'soon'; actually, it was some months after the fall of the city that he received the news (contrast v. 2 above).

VII. ORACLES AGAINST FOREIGN NATIONS (25: 1–32: 32)

The oracles against foreign nations were uttered at various times, but their introduction at this point in the arrangement of the book provides a dramatically effective interlude between the beginning of the siege of Jerusalem (24: 1) and the news of its fall (33: 21 f.). Such oracles have a comparable position in Isaiah (13–23) and perhaps in the original order of Jeremiah.

i. Oracle against Ammon (25: 1–7)

This oracle appears from the language of v. 3 to belong to the period immediately following the destruction of Jerusalem and its temple in 587 B.C.; it continues the denunciation of Ammon in 21: 28–32. The Ammonites (25: 3), Moabites (25: 8), Edomites (25: 12), Philistines (25: 15) and Tyrians (26: 2) are all rebuked for their unneighbourly rejoicing over Jerusalem's fate. **4. the people of the East:** the Bedouin of the Syrian desert (cf. v. 10). **5. Rabbah:** the Ammonite capital (modern Amman). **7. you will know that I am the LORD:** like other nations (cf. vv. 11, 17), the Ammonites imagined that the collapse of the Judaean monarchy meant the eclipse of the God of Israel; they would be compelled to acknowledge His power.

ii. Oracle against Moab (25: 8–11)

The Moabites, sister-nation to the Ammonites (cf. Gen. 19: 37 f.), would share their judgment (cf. Jer. 27: 3; Zeph. 2: 8 f.). According to Josephus (*Antiquities* x. 181 f.), Moab and Ammon were conquered by Nebuchadrezzar in 583 B.C. **8. Moab and Seir:** so MT; LXX omits 'and Seir' (i.e. Edom; cf. vv. 12–14). **9. the flank of Moab:** its northern border, protected by the three **towns** mentioned. **at its frontier towns:** NEB 'from one end to the other'.

iii. Oracle against Edom (25: 12–14)

Of all Judah's neighbours, the Edomites acted most outrageously at the time of her downfall, occupying the cross-roads to cut off the retreat of her fugitives, and are therefore most severely reprobated (cf. Ps. 137: 7; Jer. 49: 7–22; Ob. 1–21). A further denunciation of Edom appears in 35: 1–15. **13. from Teman to Dedan:** from north to

south of the Edomite territory. **14. by the hand of my people Israel:** the pressure of the Nabataean Arabs pushed the Edomites from their earlier homeland west into the Negeb, where they were subjugated and judaized by John Hyrcanus (134–104 B.C.).

iv. Oracle against Philistia (25: 15–17)

The Philistines occupied part of the Judaean territory which Nebuchadrezzar gave them. **16. I am about to stretch out my hand against the Philistines:** cf. Jer. 47; Zech. 9: 5–7. **I will cut off the Kerethites:** a play on words in Hebrew (**cut off** and **Kerethites** have roots of identical form, *krt*). For **Kerethites** (Cretans) as a synonym for **Philistines** cf. Zeph. 2: 5; see also 2 Sam. 8: 18, where the Kerethites and Pelethites (a variant form of 'Philistines') constitute David's bodyguard.

v. Oracles against Tyre (26: 1–28: 19)

Tyre, the greatest Phoenician seaport, with one harbour on the mainland and another on its almost impregnable island-fortress, had acknowledged the suzerainty of Babylon after Nebuchadrezzar's victory at Carchemish (605 B.C.), but later (594/3 B.C.) joined neighbouring states in a conspiracy to throw off his yoke (Jer. 27:3). According to the historians Menander and Philostratus, quoted by Josephus (*Apion* i. 156; *Antiquities* x. 228), Nebuchadrezzar besieged Tyre for 13 years (*c.* 585–572 B.C.); cf. Ezek. 29: 18. That he established some kind of authority over Tyre is implied by the mention of a Babylonian high commissioner for Tyre alongside its native king in an inscription of 564/3 B.C.

(*a*) *The fall of the city foretold* (26: 1–21). In this group of four oracles, particular prophecies of the damage to be wrought by Nebuchadrezzar (vv. 7–11) are interspersed with more general threats of utter destruction, such as Tyre did not experience until it was taken by Alexander the Great after a siege of seven months in 332 B.C.

1. the first day of the month: the month is not specified. If, with some LXX witnesses, we read 'the first month' (so NEB), the date is April 23, 587 B.C., but v. 2 may indicate a date after the capture of Jerusalem three or four months later. **2. The gate** (lit. 'gates') **to the nations is broken:** with the fall of Jerusalem and the Judaean kingdom a customs barrier between Tyre and the lands farther south was removed; Judah's devastation would thus be Tyre's 'replenishment'. The wording of vv. 3–6 (which may be a later doublet of the oracle of vv. 7–14) refers to the destruction of the island-fortress of Tyre, which Nebuchadrezzar did not achieve: it was achieved by Alexander when he used the rubble from the ruins on the mainland to build a causeway out to the island. **6. her settlements on the mainland:** Phoenician cities which acknowledged the leadership of Tyre. Their overthrow would isolate the island city.

7. From the north I am going to bring against Tyre . . . : for the language cf. Jer. 1: 13–15 (of an attack on Jerusalem); 50: 3, 9 (of an attack on Babylon). **Nebuchadnezzar king of Babylon, king of kings:** as he might be designated in an official proclamation. **8. raise his shields:** like the Roman *testudo*; under the protection of the interlocking shields the **battering rams** could be safely used **against** the city **walls** (9). **12. into the sea:** better, 'into the midst of the sea' (cf. NEB). **13. your noisy songs . . . the sound of your harps will be heard no more:** echoed in the dirge over apocalyptic Babylon (Rev. 18: 22).

15. Will not the coastlands tremble . . . ?: the fall of a great commercial city brings dismay to all those who traded with her; here the Aegean cities are pictured as going into mourning for Tyre. **17. a power on the seas:** Tyre's economic empire extended over the Mediterranean (where Carthage was colonized by her in the 9th century B.C.) as far west as the Straits of Gibraltar and beyond.

19. when I bring the ocean depths over you: Tyre will be overwhelmed by the primaeval ocean (Heb. *tehôm*; cf. Gen. 1: 2); i.e. she will be lost in oblivion; the same idea is involved in her going down **to the pit** (Heb. *bôr*, 20), the nether abyss. Cf. what is said of Egypt in 31: 14–18; 32: 18 ff., and of Babylon in Isa. 14: 15 ff. **20. take your place:** so LXX for *MT* 'I will give beauty' (the result of wrong division of words).

(*b*) *The wreck of the good ship Tyre* (27: 1–36). In this lament the island of Tyre is pictured as a gallant merchantman that founders in the high seas complete with ship's company and cargo. Verses 4–7 describe her workmanship, vv. 8–10 her crew, workmen, merchant-sailors and mariners.

3. gateway: lit. 'entrances', a reference perhaps to Tyre's two harbours. **you say . . . 'I am . . .':** read perhaps 'you are a ship' (Heb. *'oni*, 'ship', for *'ani*, 'I'). **4. your domain:** here used of the sides of the ship. **5. Senir:** Amorite name for Hermon (cf. Dt. 3: 9). **6. Cyprus:** Heb. *Kittim* (originally the name of the south Cypriot city Kition). **7. Elishah:** Alashia, a city on the east coast of Cyprus (mod. Enkomi). Both Elishah and Kittim are listed among the 'sons of Javan' (Greece) in Gen. 10: 4. **8, 9. Sidon . . . Arvad . . . Gebal** (Byblos): Phoenician cities which supplied the ship's crew. **10. Persia, Lydia and Put:** the last two appear to have been Libyan peoples (cf. Gen. 10: 6, 13) and so probably was the first; NEB 'Pharas' is preferable to NIV **Persia**. **11. Helech:** NEB 'Cilicia' (cf. Assyrian *Hilakku*). **Gammad:** of uncertain identification; perhaps to be located in North Syria. NEB in-

cludes vv. 10 and 11 in the poetical structure of vv. 3b ff.

Verses 12–25a constitute a prose insertion into the dirge; they provide valuable information about Mediterranean commerce in the 6th century B.C. **12. Tarshish:** the Phoenician port of Tartessus in southern Spain. **13. Greece:** originally Ionia, the Greek settlements in W. Asia Minor. **Tubal and Meshech** regularly go together, in OT (cf. 32: 26; 38: 2) as in the Assyrian records (*Tabali* and *Mushku*) and Herodotus (*Moschoi* and *Tibarēnoi*). **Tubal** was a comprehensive term for the neo-Hittite states of E. Asia Minor; **Meshech** corresponded roughly to Phrygia. **slaves:** cf. Rev. 18: 13. **14. Beth Togarmah** (cf. 38: 6): Assyrian *Til-garimmu*, N.E. Asia Minor (traditionally identified with Armenia). **15. Rhodes:** so LXX for *MT* 'Dedan' (cf. the oscillation of the initial letters of Dodanim, Gen. 10: 4, and Rodanim, 1 Chr. 1: 7). The Rhodians acted as middlemen, as did also the men of **Aram** (16, for mg 'Edom') for the wares here associated with their name. **17. Judah and Israel:** in the days of Solomon (1 Kg. 5: 11) as in those of the elder Agrippa (Ac. 12: 20) Tyre and the other Phoenician cities depended on Galilee especially for **wheat** and other agricultural produce. **From Minnith:** the meaning of Heb. *minnith* (RSV 'olives') and *pannag*, **confections** (RSV 'early figs', NEB 'meal') is uncertain. **18. Helbon:** N.W. of Damascus, still a centre of grape-growing. **wool:** NEB 'wool of Suhar' (a sheep-grazing area N.W. of Damascus). **19. Danites and Greeks:** (*MT* 'Vedan and Javan' (RV)) is unintelligible; A. R. Millard (*JSS* 7, 1962, pp. 201 ff.), followed by NEB, suggested 'and casks of wine'. **Uzal:** Izalla (NEB), between Harran and the Tigris, famed for its wine. **20. Dedan:** in N.W. Arabia (cf. 25: 13; 38: 13). **21, 22. Kedar** ('black'—the land of black tents) lay in N. Arabia, **Sheba and Raamah** in S. Arabia, through which passed the trade-routes for Indian spice. **23. Canneh:** unidentified. **Eden:** south of Harran (cf. Am. 1: 5, 'Beth Eden'). *MT* adds 'the traffickers of Sheba'. **Kilmad:** read with NEB 'all Media'. **25. ships of Tarshish:** a generic term for large merchantmen. **serve as carriers:** *MT* 'were your caravans'. **with cords twisted and tightly knotted:** (24) or, 'in plaited and twisted ropes'.

The dirge is resumed in v. 25b (NIV resumes it with v. 25a). **26. the east wind:** blowing from the mainland, a reference to the Babylonian attack. **28. the shorelands will quake:** NEB, better, 'the troubled waters tossed'. The boats which pulled away from the holed ship, after picking up men, shook and shivered as the rowers strained under their officers' command (cf. S. Smith, 'The Ship Tyre', *PEQ* 85, 1953, p. 108). **29. the mariners . . . will stand on the shore:** perhaps in Egypt (cf. S. Smith, art.

cit., p. 109). **30. roll in ashes:** NEB 'sprinkle themselves with ashes'.

32. As they wail . . . they will take up a lament: vv. 32b–34 form an 'included dirge' within the main dirge of vv. 3b–11, 25b ff. The dirge is possibly sung by those who have escaped from the wreck. **35. their faces are distorted:** NEB 'their hair stands on end'. Despite the NIV punctuation, v. 36 may be the prophet's summing up; 36a anticipates 28: 19, while 36b repeats 26: 21.

(c) The doom of the ruler of Tyre (28: 1–19). This section comprises two oracles against the ruler of Tyre as the personal embodiment of the city-state: in the former (vv. 1–10) he is designated **ruler** (Heb. *nagid*); in the latter (11–19) he is designated **king** (*melek*). The ruler of Tyre at this time was Ithobal II (an earlier bearer of the name is mentioned as Jezebel's father in 1 Kg. 16: 31). Like many other Near Eastern kings in antiquity he was considered a manifestation of divinity. **2. I am a god:** or 'I am El' (the head of the Canaanite pantheon). **on the throne of a god in the heart of the seas:** the island of Tyre is here (uniquely) portrayed as the divine dwelling-place (contrast v. 14). **3. wiser than Daniel:** Heb. *dan'el* (cf. NEB), proverbial for wisdom as well as for righteousness, as in 14: 14, 20. The wisdom celebrated here is the practical wisdom deployed in the acquisition of unprecedented commercial prosperity (4 f.). **7. foreigners . . . , the most ruthless of nations:** the Babylonians, as in 30: 10 f., 31: 12. **8. the pit:** Heb. *shaḥath*, not *bôr* as in 26: 20, but similarly meaning the place of destruction beneath the earth (cf. Ps. 16: 10). The king's island-fortress will become his tomb. **10. the death of the uncircumcised:** a shameful death (NEB 'strengthless'); the Phoenicians and the Egyptians (cf. 32: 19) practised circumcision, but their circumcision, in a manner of speaking, would be reckoned to them as uncircumcision: both would fall before the uncircumcised Babylonians.

In the second oracle the fall of the king of Tyre is described in terms of the expulsion of primal man from paradise, according to a Phoenician version of the Eden story. In this version primal man is royally crowned and adorned, unlike the unclothed Adam of Gen. 2: 25; but his regalia symbolize the dominion conferred on man in Gen. 1: 26–28. 'The real prototype of the king was Adam, God's vicegerent, with his dominion over the world' (H. L. Ellison, *The Centrality of the Messianic Idea for the OT*, 1953, p. 14). In the Phoenician story, as in its Hebrew counterpart, the root sin of primal man was pride, for which he was expelled from Eden by the **cherub** that guarded it (16; cf. Gen. 3: 24) and consumed by fire (18, a feature absent from the Hebrew narrative).

This passage has contributed some details to the traditional picture of the fall of Satan. **12. the model of perfection:** lit. 'the signet of perfection'; for the metaphor cf. Jer. 22: 24; Hag. 2: 23 (NEB, otherwise, 'you set the seal on perfection'). **full of wisdom:** for the wisdom of the first man cf. Job 15: 7 f. **13. every precious stone:** the nine jewels listed in *MT* appear on the high-priestly breastplate (Exod. 28: 17–20); LXX here lists all twelve of them. The ruler of Tyre, like primal man, was priest as well as king. **14. anointed as a guardian cherub:** NEB 'a towering cherub as guardian'; LXX omits both adjectives. **the holy mount of God:** the Phoenicians regarded Mt. Zaphon, in N. Syria, as the home of the gods, like Olympus in Greece (cf. Isa. 14: 13, 'the . . . heights of the sacred mountain'). **the fiery stones:** variously interpreted, but David Qimḥi's explanation of them as jewels (the material or decoration of the priest-king's palace?) is as reasonable as any. **16. Through your widespread trade . . . :** Tyre's commercial prosperity induced arrogance, which is here viewed as a reproduction of the first man's sin. Verses 16–18 combine features of the Paradise analogy with those of the historical situation. **18. you have desecrated your sanctuaries:** by dedicating in them treasures acquired by violence and injustice. **19. you have come to a horrible end . . . :** cf. 26: 21; 27: 36. Each of the three groups of oracles against Tyre is concluded with this refrain.

vi. Oracle against Sidon and message of hope for Israel (28: 20–26)
Sidon, with its two harbours, lay on the coast some 25 miles north of Tyre; it was involved with Tyre in the revolt against Nebuchadrezzar of 594/3 B.C. (cf. Jer. 27: 3), but was reduced by him a few years later. Here it is threatened with judgment by plague and sword; the familiar recognition formula is used in vv. 22 and 23.

The recognition formula is also used twice (vv. 24, 26) in the brief message of Israel's restoration which is appended to the words of doom against Tyre and Sidon. In mercy and judgment alike Yahweh manifests His glory, that all **the nations** may see it (cf. Pss. 98: 2; 126:2b).

vii. Oracles against Egypt (29: 1–32: 32)
As in the days when the Assyrian empire extended to the Mediterranean seaboard (cf. Isa. 31: 1–3), so in the era of Babylonian hegemony the Egyptians depended on their Syro-Palestinian neighbours to pull their chestnuts out of the fire and constantly incited them to revolt against their Mesopotamian overlords. It was with Egyptian encouragement that Zedekiah forswore his allegiance to Babylon (cf. 17: 15 ff.). When Jerusalem was besieged, Pharaoh Hophra, called Apries by the Greeks

(589–570 B.C.), created a diversion which led to the temporary suspension of the siege, but soon withdrew his forces (Jer. 37: 5 ff.). It was about this time that some of the following oracles were uttered.

(a) *Oracle against Pharaoh* (29: 1–16). The date (v. 1) is January 7, 587 B.C. **3. you great monster:** as Egypt was pictured as Rahab, the monster of chaos (Pss. 87: 4; 89: 10; Isa. 30: 7), so Pharaoh was portrayed as Leviathan, her dragon-associate, traditionally killed and given as food to 'the creatures of the desert' (Ps. 74: 14). But here Leviathan becomes a crocodile (cf. Job 41: 1), hooked with a gigantic gaff and thrown up on dry land to be devoured by beasts and birds of prey. **The Nile is mine:** arrogance is the undoing of Pharaoh, as of the Tyrian king. **4. with all the fish . . . :** Pharaoh's subjects.

7. you broke, and their backs were wrenched: NEB (better) 'armpits'; the same criticism of Egypt's unreliability was voiced by the Assyrian Rab-shakeh over a century earlier (2 Kg. 18: 21; Isa. 36: 6). **10. from Migdol to Aswan:** from the Asian frontier to Aswan, at the first cataract of the Nile, the southern limit of Upper Egypt: south of that lay Ethiopia or Nubia (NIV transliterates **Cush**). The desolation of **forty years**, with the depopulation of the Egyptians (10–13) did not take place: for the non-fulfilment of the worst predictions of doom against Tyre and Egypt see H. L. Ellison, *Ezekiel: The Man and his Message*, 1956, pp. 102–105 (and cf. Jer. 18: 7–10; Jon. 3: 4–10). **14. Upper Egypt:**

(b) *Egypt a recompense for labour lost over Tyre* (29: 17–21). The date of this oracle (the latest of Ezekiel's dated oracles) is April 26, 571 B.C., about a year after the end of the siege of Tyre. Because Nebuchadrezzar derived no profit worth mentioning from his thirteen years' siege of Tyre, he will recoup his losses from the plunder of Egypt, whose aid to Tyre may have supplied a *casus belli.* **18. every head was rubbed bare and every shoulder made raw:** from the carrying of loads for military operations. **20. I have given him Egypt:** Nebuchadrezzar invaded Egypt in 568/7 B.C., but the extant records do not indicate how extensive his victory was.

Like the oracle against Sidon (28: 24–26), this oracle ends with a word of encouragement for Israel (v. 21). **a horn:** a symbol of strength (cf. Ps. 92: 10; Lk. 1: 69). **I will open your mouth:** cf. 24: 27; 33: 22.

(c) *The judgment of Egypt* (30: 1–19). **3. the day of the LORD** for Egypt will be her time of judgment. **Cush** (4) was used in parallelism with **Egypt** from the time of the Ethiopian (25th) dynasty (715–663 B.C.); cf. Isa. 20: 3 ff.; Nah. 3: 9. For **Put** and **Lydia** (5) cf. 27: 10; **Libya** represents the unintelligible *MT Kub.*

6. from Migdol to Aswan: cf. 29: 10. **9. messengers:** cf. Isa. 18: 2; these **messengers** sail up the Nile **in ships** (*MT*) to warn **Cush** in **her complacency** of the approaching destruction.

11. the most ruthless of nations: cf. 28: 7, and for the general sense cf. 29: 19 f. **12. I will dry up the streams of the Nile:** i.e. the delta (cf. Isa. 19: 5 ff.; 11: 15), on which the life of Egypt depended.

13. the idols, and . . . images are 'great men' and 'princes' in LXX, whence NEB 'lordlings' and 'princelings'. **Memphis:** NEB (transliterating Heb.) 'Noph', the capital of Lower Egypt, 16 miles south of Cairo. **No longer will there be a prince:** i.e. of a native Egyptian dynasty. This was the situation for many years after the Persian conquest of Egypt in 525 B.C. **14. Pathros:** Upper Egypt, as in 29: 14. **Zoan:** Tanis, otherwise Avaris, a Hyksos foundation of *c.* 1720 B.C. (cf. Num. 13: 22), later rebuilt as a frontier fortress by Rameses II (Exod. 1: 11). **Thebes:** NEB (transliterating Heb.) 'No' (cf. Nah. 3: 8), the capital of Upper Egypt. **15. Pelusium:** a frontier fortress near the Mediterranean, in the N. E. corner of the delta. **Thebes:** here rather, with LXX, 'Memphis' (so NEB 'Noph'). **16. Pelusium:** here rather, with LXX and NEB, 'Syene' (Aswan). **Memphis will be in constant distress:** NEB 'and flood-waters shall burst into it'. **17. Heliopolis:** 6 miles north-east of Cairo. **Bubastis:** (modern Tell Basta), 40 miles northeast of Cairo. **18. Tahpanhes:** known to the Greeks as Daphnae, whence modern Tell Defneh in the canal zone. It was the scene of Jeremiah's oracle of judgment against Egypt (Jer. 43: 8–13), which may have been fulfilled in 568/7 B.C.

(d) *Pharaoh's broken arm* (30: 20–26). Egypt's weakness is described in terms of a fracture of Pharaoh's arm, which incapacitated him from wielding his sword. The date (v. 20) is April 29, 587 B.C. The breaking of Pharaoh's sword-arm is perhaps the defeat of his army which attempted to relieve the siege of Jerusalem (17: 17); he was no longer in a position to offer battle to the Babylonians, and their eventual attack on Egypt would be like the breaking of his other arm. **21. bound up for healing:** NEB (following LXX) 'with dressings and bandage' (i.e. poultices and a rollerbandage).

(e) *The fall of the cedar* (31: 1–18). This oracle, dated June 21, 587 B.C. (v. 1), is introduced with the quotation of a poetical description of the rise and fall of the Assyrian Empire in terms of a majestic cedar of Lebanon. The cedar, nourished by the nether streams, flourished in imperial splendour and provided shelter for bird and beast (6), like the tree which the king of Babylon saw in his dream in Dan. 4: 10 ff.

(cf. also Ezek. 17: 22 f.). No tree in Eden, **the garden of God** (9; cf. 28: 13; Gen. 2: 8 f.) could rival it. But because of overweening arrogance it was felled by divine decree (10–14), and Pharaoh is warned that what had happened to Assyria 25 years before will soon happen to him.

3. Consider Assyria: MT 'behold Assyria'. RSV emends to 'I will liken you to', but **Assyria** is supported by LXX and is retained by NEB (cf. AV, RV). **11. the ruler of the nations:** Nebuchadrezzar, as in 29: 19 f.; 30: 24 f. **according to its wickedness:** here the historical reality has invaded the parabolic language. **12. the most ruthless of foreign nations:** cf. 28: 7; 30: 11. The Babylonians, who had joined with the Medes in destroying Nineveh in 612 B.C., will overthrow the power of Egypt. **14. no other trees . . . are ever to tower proudly:** the fall of Egypt will warn the other nations not to aspire to excessive greatness, but to remember their own mortality.

The concluding paragraph (15–18) combines parabolic and literal terminology. As the forest of Lebanon is pictured as going into mourning for the fall of the great cedar, so the fall of Egypt will make **the nations tremble** (16). **17. its allies among the nations:** render with NEB 'were scattered among the nations'. The references to **the grave** and **the pit** (16 f.), where the king of Egypt is to **lie among the uncircumcised, with those killed by the sword** (18), anticipate the oracle of 32: 17–32. **18. Pharaoh and all his multitude:** catching up the introductory words of v. 2.

(f) *Another oracle against Pharaoh* (32: 1–16). The first part of this oracle (vv. 1–9) reproduces the imagery of 29: 1–5. Here too Pharaoh is compared to a dragon-like **monster** (*tannîn*) or crocodile with its habitat in the Nile, netted this time (not hooked, as in 29: 4) in the divine seine and thrown up on land to be the prey of birds and beasts.

1. the twelfth year: some LXX and Syriac witnesses read 'the eleventh year', which would yield the date March 15, 586 B.C. instead of the less probable March 3, 585 B.C. **2. a lion:** lit. 'a young lion' (Heb. *kephîr*), appropriate enough for the vigorous Hophra, although the transition to **monster** is abrupt. **a monster in the seas:** cf. Isa. 27: 1, but here the sea is the Nile (as in Nah. 3: 8). **3. With a great throng of people:** cf. the 'fish' of 29: 4 f. **7. I will cover the heavens . . . :** such darkness is, in biblical prophecy, a frequent concomitant of political convulsions (cf. 30: 18; Isa. 13: 10; Jer. 4: 23; Jl 2: 31; 3: 15; Mk 13: 24; Rev. 6: 12).

The second part of the oracle (vv. 10–16) repeats the substance of the first in non-symbolical terms: the divine judgment against Egypt will take the form of Babylonian invasion, slaughter and captivity. The Nile will

flow quiet and clear, untouched henceforth by man or beast.

12. most ruthless of all nations: repeated from 28: 7; 30: 11; 31: 12. **16. the lament:** cf. the pictorial mourning of the forest of Lebanon for the fallen cedar in 31: 15 ff.

(g) *Egypt in the underworld* (32: 17–32). The prophet himself is bidden to sing Egypt's dirge (18). A nation which has lost its independent identity is compared to a former potentate in the realm of the dead, stripped of vitality, power and wealth (cf. 26: 20; 28: 8; Isa. 14: 15 ff.).

17. In the twelfth year: LXX adds 'in the first month' (cf. RSV). The date is April 27, 586 B.C. **18. the pit:** Heb. *bôr* (as in 26: 20), synonymous with **Sheol** (21mg). **19. the uncircumcised:** the Egyptians were circumcised, but their circumcision does them no good in Sheol; they must lie there along with the uncircumcised Assyrians and others (cf. 28: 10; 31: 18). **21. the mighty leaders will say of Egypt:** the *'elê gibbôrim* (plural of *'el gibbôr*, rendered 'Mighty God' in Isa. 9: 6), who still exercise some kind of authority even in Sheol (cf. v. 27), mark the arrival of Egypt, become as weak as the rest of 'the strengthless dead' (NEB); cf. Isa. 14: 9 f. Among them is **Assyria**, destroyed in 612 B.C., despite the **terror** it had spread throughout the nations (22 f.). **Elam** too **is there**, conquered by the Assyrians in 645 B.C. (24 f.). **Meshech and Tubal** (cf. 27: 13) had participated in the Scythian invasion of 626 B.C., which had caused great panic in Syria and Mesopotamia; they too were now at peace (26). The **warriors who have fallen** (27) are perhaps the Nephilim (cf. Gen. 6: 4; Num. 13: 33); these heroes of antiquity had received honourable military burial, unlike those whose fall is commemorated in this dirge, and may be identical with the 'mighty leaders' of v. 21. **Edom** (29) and **the princes of the north**, including **the Sidonians** (30; cf. 28: 20–23) and other Phoenician powers, have also reached Sheol in advance of Egypt. **30. They lie uncircumcised:** read 'with the uncircumcised'; the Phoenicians, like the Egyptians, practised circumcision (cf. 28: 10). **31. Pharaoh will see them and he will be consoled:** a ruler who cherished military and imperial ambitions on earth cannot complain of not finding worthy companions in Sheol.

VIII. THE HOPE OF RESTORATION (33: 1–37: 28)

i. The watchman's commission (33: 1–20)

This section provides a literary transition from the oracles against foreign nations (25: 1–32) to the news of Jerusalem's fall (vv. 21 f.) and the ensuing messages of restoration. Much of its material has appeared in earlier contexts in the book (cf. 3: 16–19; 18: 21–32), but here it is all presented in (presumably) its original form as a literary unit.

2. When I bring the sword against a land: military attack is a form of divine visitation (cf. 14: 17, 21). The appointment and responsibility of a **watchman** in such circumstances is set forth in general terms in vv. 2–6. In vv. 7–9 the prophet is appointed **a watchman for the house of Israel**; these verses have already appeared as 3: 17–19.

10. Our offences and sins weigh us down: this complaint provides the occasion for the immediately following reassurance. **11. I take no pleasure . . . :** the parallel in 18: 23 is given the form of a rhetorical question, 'Do I take any pleasure . . . ?' Verses 12–20 have been anticipated in 18: 21–30. This evangelical note is specially appropriate to Israel's present situation. The memory of their fathers' sins and their own might well have led them to despair but for the assurance that the past can be forgotten, the slate wiped clean, and a new beginning made.

ii. News of Jerusalem's fall (33: 21 f.).
The date in *MT* (Jan. 8, 585 B.C.) is surprisingly late, as Jerusalem had fallen on July 29, 587 B.C., nearly eighteen months before (Jer. 39: 2; 52: 6). Some witnesses (including a few Hebrew and LXX MSS and the Syriac version) read 'the eleventh year' instead of **the twelfth year** (21); the date would then be Jan. 19, 586 B.C. **22. the hand of the LORD was upon me:** cf. 1: 3. **I was no longer silent:** at the time of the city's investment Ezekiel had been told that when a fugitive brought him the news of its fall his **mouth** would be **opened** (24: 25–27); this promise was now fulfilled (cf. also 3: 25–27).

iii. Warning to those left in Judah (33: 23–29)
Those who were left in Judah after the deportation were a pitiful remnant, 'the poorest people of the land' (Jer. 52: 16), yet in their own eyes they were **many** in comparison with **Abraham**, who **was only one man** and yet **he possessed the land:** they reckoned therefore that **the land** was thenceforth **our possession** (24; cf. 11: 15). But the future belonged not to them but to their exiled brethren: they themselves were destined to be diminished yet further by **sword**, **wild animals** and **plague** (27; cf. 5: 12, 17; 14: 21) because of their persistence in moral and cultic **detestable things**, such as have been denounced above in 18: 10–13. There was a later deportation of Judaeans in 583/2 B.C. (Jer. 52: 30). **25. you eat meat with the blood:** forbidden to mankind in Gen. 9: 4 and to Israel in Lev. 17: 10 ff., etc.; the counterpart in Ezek. 18: 11 is eating 'at the mountain shrines'. **28. the mountains of Israel:** cf. 6: 2 ff.

iv. Admonition to the exiles (33: 30–33)
Only those who truly loved God would possess the land, and even the exiles had a long way to go before they were ready for restoration. They loved to hear Ezekiel's latest oracle (30), but they did not take his words to heart; they were more concerned with material **gain** (31). They listened to what he said as one might listen with pleasure to a beautiful singer or a well-tuned **instrument**, but it made no practical difference to their conduct (32). Yet his message would come to pass, and **then they will know that a prophet has been among them** (33; cf. 2: 5).

v. The Shepherd of Israel (34: 1–31)
The motif of the shepherd-king was widespread in the ancient Near East, not least in OT. It is more than a coincidence that the two greatest leaders of Israel in OT times, Moses and David, served their apprenticeship as shepherds. Yahweh, Israel's supreme King, is also the Shepherd of Israel *par excellence* (cf. Ps. 80: 1; 100: 3; Isa. 40: 11); this is the rôle in which He speaks throughout the present oracle. (*a*) *Denunciation of the worthless shepherds* (34: 1–10). The kings and princes of Israel are denounced as false shepherds who fleeced and devoured the flock of God entrusted to their care instead of tending them, with the result that the sheep were scattered all over the earth. This section is echoed in Zech. 11: 15–17 and more especially in Jesus' reference to those hirelings who 'creep and intrude and climb into the fold' and in the hour of danger leave the sheep to be worried by wolves (Jn 10: 12 f.).

6. My sheep wandered . . . over all the mountains: cf. the language of Micaiah in 1 Kg. 22: 17 and Jesus' compassion on the multitude 'because they were like sheep without a shepherd' (Mk 6: 34)—like an army without a captain.

(*b*) *Yahweh seeks out His scattered flock* (34: 11–16). Whatever the hirelings might do, the God of Israel will perform the part of a true shepherd to His flock, gathering them together, feeding them with **good pasture** (14) and tending those of them that need special care (cf. Ps. 23). Similar language is used in the gospel parable of the lost sheep (Mt. 18: 12 f.; Lk. 15: 3–7); here the reference is to the restoration from exile.

6. I will search for the lost: cf. what is said of the Son of Man in Lk. 19: 10. **the sleek and the strong I will destroy:** these are presumably the sheep's assailants. LXX reads 'the strong I will watch over' (cf. RSV).

(*c*) *The fat sheep and the lean sheep* (34: 17–22). Even among the sheep judgment must be carried out: the stronger were bullying the weaker, monopolizing the **good pasture** and trampling the remainder underfoot, pushing their way first to the drinking-places and churning up the water that was left—a parable of social injustice in Israel (cf. 22: 3–12). The oppressors must be punished and their victims defended.

(*d*) *The 'one shepherd'* (34: 23 f.). In place of the hirelings who proved unfaithful to their charge, God will set over them a new shepherd, whom he calls **my servant David** (cf. 37: 24 f.)— the messianic **prince** (cf. Jer. 23: 1–6). Great David's greater Son here bears his ancestor's name (cf. Hos. 3: 5; Jer. 30: 9). The parable of the good shepherd in Jn 10: 1–16, which has this oracle as its OT background, implies Jesus' claim to be the Davidic Messiah: the 'one shepherd' of Jn 10: 16 is a deliberate echo of the same phrase here in v. 23 (see also 37: 22– 24). So also the close relation between **I, the Lord**, and **my servant David** in v. 24 is reproduced in the close relation between the Father and the Son in their joint protection of the sheep in Jn 10: 27–29.

24. prince: Heb. *nasi'*, as later in 37: 25; 44: 3, etc. It is doubtful, however, if 'king' (*melek*) is avoided here as a matter of principle; it is used in the parallel statement in 37: 24.

(*e*) *Paradise regained* (34: 25–31). In the time of restoration peace and plenty will be established, with life-giving showers (26) and rich harvests (27).

25. a covenant of peace: cf. 37: 26 (also 16: 60, 62). The conditions of the new covenant are mentioned more frequently in Ezek. (cf. 11: 19 f.; 36: 25–27) than the actual term **covenant** is used. **rid the land of wild beasts:** cf. Lev. 26: 6, similarly in a 'covenant' context. **29. a land renowned for its crops:** *MT* 'a plantation for renown' (cf. AV 'plant of renown', at one time misinterpreted as a messianic designation); LXX 'in hope of peace' (reading *shalôm*, 'peace', 'prosperity', for *MT shem* 'name', 'renown'). **30–31. they . . . are my people, . . . and I am your God:** the essence of the covenant (cf. Lev. 26: 12). **sheep of my pasture:** *MT* adds 'men' (i.e. 'you are my human flock').

vi. The doom of Edom (35: 1–15)
The restoration of Israel has as its counterpart the desolation of her enemies, here represented by Edom, already the target of a denunciatory oracle in 25: 12–14. Edom's spiteful behaviour in the day of Judah's desperate need was specially reprehensible because of the close kinship between the two peoples. The Edomites occupied the southern part of the kingdom of Judah, which was consequently known in Graeco-Roman times as Idumaea. Their former home territory, **Mount Seir**, was for its part later occupied by the Nabataean Arabs, who established their capital in Petra, the former Edomite stronghold of Sela (cf. Ps. 60: 9; Jer. 49: 16; Ob. 3). In due course Edomites (Idumaeans) and Nabataeans, together with other

small ethnic groups in that area, lost their separate identity. See J. R. Bartlett, 'The Moabites and Edomites', in *Peoples of OT Times*, ed. D. J. Wiseman, 1973, pp. 229 ff.

2. Mount Seir: NEB 'the hill-country of Seir', the highlands to the east of the Arabah, the original Edomite territory (cf. Gen. 27: 39 f.; 32: 3 ff.; 36: 6 ff.). **3. I will . . . make you a desolate waste:** cf. Mal. 1: 2b–4. **10. These two nations and countries will be ours:** the reference is to the two Hebrew monarchies, Israel and Judah; seeing the territory of the latter depopulated, like that of the former nearly a century and a half earlier, the Edomites planned to take 'vacant possession'. **the Lord was there:** and therefore the land was at His disposal, not theirs (cf. Lev. 25: 23), and He would reunite north and south (cf. Ezek. 37: 15 ff.). **14. While the whole earth rejoices:** NEB 'the whole world will gloat over you' as Edom had gloated over the downfall of Judah and Jerusalem (cf. Ob. 12 f.).

vii. New hope for the mountains of Israel (36: 1–15)
In 6: 1–3 **the mountains of Israel** were apostrophized in terms of denunciation because of the idolatry practised on them. Now they are apostrophized in tones of consolation: although they are at present occupied by alien invaders, because their rightful inhabitants are in exile, yet the invaders will soon be expelled and the rightful inhabitants restored to cultivate them and reap fruitful harvests from them.

2. the enemy: pre-eminently the Edomites, as v. 5 indicates; the boast **'The ancient heights have become our possession'** repeats the substance of 35: 12. **3. hounded you:** NEB 'trampled you down'. **5. In my burning zeal:** lit. 'in the fire of my zeal'. When Yahweh's land and people were objects of derision, His own reputation was dragged in the mire; the 'zeal' with which He vindicates His people against the enemy is His concern for His own name and character and pledged word (cf. vv. 7, 20–23). The **scorn** heaped on Israel by the aliens will recoil on themselves (v. 7). **that they might plunder its pastureland:** NEB renders alternatively 'to hold it up to public contempt'. **7. I swear:** lit. 'I have lifted up my hand (cf. NEB; Gen. 14: 22). **13. 'You devour men . . .':** as though the mother country were a cruel stepmother; cf. the spies' evil report of the promised land in Num. 13: 32. **15. cause your nation to fall:** better, 'bereave your nation', as in v. 14.

viii. A new heart and new spirit (36: 16–32)
The people have been polluted by immorality and idolatry; they must undergo a radical cleansing within. Such a cleansing is here promised: it will be accompanied by the impartation of a new nature. The language and thought are

akin to Ps. 51: 10, 'Create in me a pure heart, O God, and renew a steadfast spirit within me'—although there the cleansing is personal, whereas here it is corporate. The substance of this passage has appeared above in 11: 16–20.

20. and yet they had to leave his land: as though their God could not protect them against the Babylonians. His **holy name** was thus **profaned**, and required to be vindicated in the sight of the nations (cf. Ps. 98: 1–3; Isa. 48: 11). **25. I will sprinkle clean water on you:** the language is reminiscent of the 'water of cleansing' prescribed in Num. 19: 9, but that removed external and ceremonial pollution: this is symbolical water and effects inward cleansing (cf. Heb. 9: 13 f.). This thought is taken up in the fountain image of Zech. 13: 1 and later provided scriptural authority for proselyte baptism. It may also have influenced the baptism of John; if so, he makes a distinction between his own administration of water and the spirit-baptism which his successor would administer (Jn 1: 26, 33). The **water** of v. 25 and the **new spirit** of v. 26 are conjoined in the description of the new birth in Jn 3: 5. **26. A new heart . . . :** cf. 11: 18 with notes *ad loc.* The **new spirit** is shown in v. 27 to be God's own spirit: they will thus be able to keep His covenant (cf. Jer. 31: 31–34); they will be confirmed in the occupation of their land and enjoy peace and prosperity there (28–30). The God of Israel will be glorified in His purified people. **31. you will remember your evil ways:** divine grace produces an awareness of past ingratitude. 'In the NT, religion is grace, and ethics is gratitude' (T. Erskine).

This promise was a favourite with the rabbis, who looked for its fulfilment in the messianic age, when the 'evil impulse' would be eradicated and unprecedented fertility enjoyed. In Christian theology it greatly influenced John Wesley's doctrine of the clean heart.

ix. The cities rebuilt (36: 33–38)
Here is a further picture of Paradise regained (cf. 34: 25–31). The desolate land of Israel will be **replanted**; its cities will be **rebuilt and be filled with flocks of people**.

37. I will yield to the plea of the house of Israel and do this for them: 'When God designs to bless his people, he sets them a-praying for the blessing which he desires to give them' (Matthew Henry).

x. The valley of dry bones (37: 1–14)
(a) *The vision* (37: 1–10). The vision of the valley of dry bones is perhaps the best-known scene in the whole book of Ezekiel. On previous occasions when **the hand of the LORD was upon** Ezekiel, or he was transported **by the Spirit of the LORD**, what he saw was factual enough (cf. 8: 1, 3 ff.), but the present vision is purely symbolical. As the following interpretation makes plain, the restoration of

life to the bones is a parable of Israel's national resurrection (vv. 11–14); but in course of time it naturally came to be treated as a parable of personal resurrection, as can be seen in the wall-paintings of the synagogue at Dura-Europos on the Euphrates (3rd century A.D.). **2. that were very dry:** it is emphasized that every vestige of life had long since departed from them. **4. 'Prophesy to these bones . . .':** the most unpromising congregation that any preacher ever addressed; but the thought is echoed in our Lord's words in Jn 5: 25, 'the dead will hear the voice of the Son of God, and those who hear will live'. **9. Come from the four winds, O breath:** it is helpful to remember that one Hebrew word, *ruaḥ*, does duty for 'breath', 'wind' and 'spirit'; cf. the one Greek word *pneuma* in Jn 3: 8, 'the *wind* blows wherever it pleases . . . ; So it is with every one born of the *Spirit*'. The influence of this section of Ezekiel is so pervasive in Jn 3: 3–8 that it is no wonder that Jesus expressed surprise when Israel's teacher failed to grasp the allusion (Jn 3: 9f.). **10. breath entered them:** as when the Creator breathed into the first man's nostrils the breath of life, 'and man became a living being' (Gen. 2: 7).

(b) *Its interpretation* (37: 11–14). The dry bones represent **the whole house of Israel**, northern and southern kingdoms together. Humanly speaking, any hope of national revival is as much out of the question for them as for any of the other ethnic groups which lost their identity as a result of deportation. But the sovereign act of God will revive them and restore them to their **own land**. The message is identical with that of 36: 22–32.

12. your graves: perhaps the lands to which they had been exiled (cf. v. 21). **14. I will put my Spirit** (*ruaḥ*, 'breath') **in you:** cf. 36:27.

xi. National reunion (37: 15–28)
The political division which followed Solomon's death (1 Kg. 12: 16–20) had its roots in the period of the settlement. The attempts by Hezekiah (2 Chr. 30: 1 ff.) and Josiah (2 Kg. 23: 15 ff.) to repair it were short-lived. But Ezekiel, like Elijah three centuries before (1 Kg. 18: 31), thinks in terms of 'all Israel' and foretells the effective mending of the breach in the time of restoration (cf. Isa. 11: 13). So, in post-exilic and NT times, Israel was held in principle to comprise all twelve tribes; cf. Mt. 19: 28 parallel Lk. 22: 30; Ac. 26: 7; Jas 1: 1; Rev. 7: 4–8; 21: 12. Ezekiel's prophecy is accompanied by an act of prophetic symbolism, the joining together of two 'wooden tablets' (NEB), inscribed respectively 'Judah's ' and 'Joseph's ', so as to form a single folding tablet. As one united nation Israel will dwell in their own land, governed by the prince of the house of David.

16. a stick: anything made of wood; LXX 'a

rod' (like the tribal rods or sceptres of Num. 17: 1 ff.). For **Joseph:** because he was the father of **Ephraim,** the leading tribe in the northern kingdom. **22. one nation:** echoed in the 'one flock' under 'one shepherd' of Jn 10: 16. **one king:** cf. v. 24; Ezekiel normally uses 'prince' (*nasi*'), as in v. 25 and 34: 24, rather than 'king' (*melek*), except in reference to Jehoiachin (cf. 20: 33), but **king** may be used here because of the proximity of **kingdoms. 23. They will be my people, and I will be their God:** covenant-language, as in v. 27; 11: 20; 34: 30 f. **24. My servant David:** cf. 34: 23 f. **26. a covenant of peace:** cf. 34: 25. **an everlasting covenant:** cf. 16: 60 (also Isa. 55: 3, in association with the fulfilment of the dynastic promises made to David). **put my sanctuary among them forever:** cf. v. 28; elaborated in 40: 5–44: 31. **27. My dwelling place will be with them:** cf. the name of the city, 'The LORD is there', in 48: 35, and the NT counterpart, conjoined with the covenant formula, in Rev. 21: 3. **28. I the LORD make Israel holy:** cf. 20: 12; Exod. 31: 13; Lev. 20: 8; 21: 8, 15, 23; 22: 9, 16, 32.

IX. GOG AND MAGOG (38: 1–39: 29)
i. Oracles against Gog (38: 1–39: 20)
Soon after the people of Israel are restored to their land they are exposed to one final threat: a horde of aggressors from north of the Fertile Crescent, led by one Gog, will invade their land to attack and plunder them as they live peacefully in settlements as yet unfortified. Ezekiel's parents could have told him how, shortly before his birth, the Scythians had spread panic by such an incursion from the north. On this occasion, however, the God of Israel will come to His people's defence and annihilate the enemy horde. Gog's invasion cannot be identified with any known historical event; the attempt to interpret the passage with reference to Alexander the Great (cf. L. E. Browne, *Ezekiel and Alexander*, 1952) founders on the undoubted fact that Alexander and his followers did not meet their end on the 'mountains of Israel' (39: 4).
(*a*) *First oracle against Gog* (38: 1–13). **1. set your face against Gog:** the name, though not the person, is identical with Gyges (Assyrian and perhaps Lydian *Gugu*), founder of the Lydian dynasty of the Mermnadae (7th century B.C.). **the land of Magog:** not certainly identified, and perhaps a derivative of **Gog.** Later Jewish tradition identified it with Macedonia. **Magog** is listed in Gen. 10: 2 among the sons of Japheth, along with **Meshech and Tubal,** and since their location is known (cf. 27: 13), Magog was presumably in the same general area, perhaps Western Asia Minor (cf. 39: 6). **chief prince:** cf. AV; this is preferable to 'prince of Rosh' (LXX; RV, NEB), which complicates the

geographical data by taking Heb. *rôsh* ('chief', 'head') as another unidentified place-name. **4. I will turn you around, put hooks in your jaws:** cf. the language addressed to Pharaoh in 29: 4, but the warning to Sennacherib in Isa. 37: 29 provides a closer parallel. See 39: 2 with note. **5. Persia, Cush and Put:** if, with NEB, we render 'Pharas' as in 27: 10, then three African groups are intended (cf. 27: 10; 30: 4 f.), unexpected as it may be to find them supporting a mainly Anatolian army. **6. Gomer:** i.e. Cimmerians (Assyrian *Gimirrai*), also listed as a son of Japheth in Gen. 10: 2. In the 8th century B.C. invading Cimmerians overran Armenia and gravely weakened Meshech and Tubal; then, according to Herodotus (iv. 12), they settled in Northern Asia Minor. **Beth Togarmah:** cf. 27: 14. In Gen. 10: 3 Togarmah is a son of Gomer. **8. In future years:** a variant of 'in the latter days' (cf. v. 16), referring to the time of Israel's ultimate deliverance (and her enemies' downfall). **10. thoughts will come into your mind:** that the invasion is planned by Gog does not conflict with his being brought against the land by the divine overruling (vv. 16 f.); his thoughts as well as his actions are foreordained. **unwalled villages:** the fortification predicted in 36: 35 (cf. 48: 30 ff.) has not yet been effected (cf. Zech. 2: 4). **a peaceful and unsuspecting people:** like the men of Laish in Jg. 18: 7 and the Arabs in Jer. 49: 31. **12. the center** (Heb. *ṭabbûr*, 'navel') **of the land:** cf. 5: 5 (with note); 40: 2. **13. Sheba and Dedan and the merchants of Tarshish:** cf. 25: 13; 27: 22, 25; they are spectators here, not participants. (It may be an unworthy suspicion that credits them with hopes of profiting by Gog's **plunder.**) **her villages:** so LXX for *MT* 'its young lions' (NEB by an emendation renders 'her leading merchants').

(*b*) *Second oracle against Gog* (38: 14–23). Verses 14–16 repeat the substance of vv. 8 f. **16. when I show myself holy through you:** that the God of Israel uses the opposition of His people's enemies to make His ways the more widely known is declared to Pharaoh in Exod. 9: 16 (cf. Rom. 9: 17).

17. Are you not the one . . . ?: cf. NEB (following LXX) 'When I spoke in days of old through my servants the prophets, . . . it was you whom I threatened to bring against Israel.' The reference probably includes 'the Assyrian' of Isa. 10: 5–32; 31: 8 f., and the northern invader of Jer. 4: 6–29. (But for Ezekiel there is no question of Gog's being the instrument of divine judgment against Israel, as those earlier invaders were.) Similarly Ezekiel's denunciation of Gog provided a precedent for the downfall of the last 'king of the North' in Dan. 11: 40b–45, and in the Qumran texts the downfall of both Gog and the 'king of the

North' is reinterpreted of the extermination of the 'Kittim' (Romans). LXX makes Gog the leader of the locust swarm of Am. 7: 1, taking it as symbolical of a human army and identifying it with the invading locusts from the north of Jl 1: 4–2: 20. **18. my hot anger will be aroused:** in the following verses all the forces of nature are mobilized to be the instruments of the divine judgment against Gog (cf. the fire from heaven which consumes the post-millennial 'Gog and Magog' of Rev. 20: 8 f.).

(c) Third oracle against Gog (39: 1–16). This oracle recapitulates the emphasis of the first oracle against Gog (38: 1–13) and amplifies the threat of annihilation. The enormous number of troops at Gog's command is indicated by the prediction that it will take seven months to collect and bury their bones, while their discarded weapons will keep the Israelites supplied with firewood for seven years.

2. I will turn you around: repeated from 38: 4, but while there it may be an echo of Isa. 37: 29 ('I will make you return by the way you came'), as though Gog is on his way back from the southernmost limit of his advance when disaster overtakes him, here the expression is introductory to his being dragged **along** and brought up **from the far north** (cf. 38: 15) **against the mountains of Israel**. W. Zimmerli may be right in wondering whether both here and in 38: 4 there is a hint of an earlier Gog of the past now brought back to lead this last invasion. **4. On the mountains of Israel you will fall:** which he intended to attack (v. 2). The cause of his fall is direct divine action (cf. v. 3). **6. I will send fire on Magog:** Gog's homeland will also be visited in judgment. The addition of **the coastlands**, i.e. the Aegean shores and islands (cf. 26: 15; Gen. 10: 5), supports the location of **Magog** in Western Asia Minor. **7. my holy name . . . :** cf. 36: 20–23. **the Holy One in Israel:** a variant of the characteristic Isaianic title, 'the Holy One of Israel'.

11. I will give Gog a burial place: the only memorial he will have **in Israel**, for all his ambitions. **the valley of those who travel east:** better, 'the valley of Abarim' (NEB), i.e. Peraea; cf. 'the mountains of Abarim', which included Mt. Nebo (Num. 33: 47 f.; Dt. 32:49). **east toward the Sea:** i.e. the Dead Sea (cf. 47: 8 ff.). **it will block the way of travelers:** NEB 'all Abarim shall be blocked'. **Hamon Gog:** i.e. 'Gog's Horde' (NEB). **14. to cleanse the land:** unburied corpses defiled the land. **16. a town called Hamonah:** unidentified.

(d) A sacrificial feast (39: 17–20). The horrific invitation in this paragraph (reproduced in Rev. 19: 17 f.) amplifies what is said in v. 4 about the birds and beasts of prey feeding on Gog's fallen army. Here the army is described in terms of sacrificial animals: **rams and lambs,**

goats and bulls—all of them fattened animals from Bashan (18.) **fat** and **blood** (19) were not eaten by Israelites, but these feasters have no such scruples, even at what God calls **my table** (20).

ii. Further promises of restoration (39: 21–29)
The promises here summarized have been developed in 36: 16–38; 37: 11–14. **24. I hid my face from them:** cf. Isa. 8: 17. With the outpouring of God's Spirit (cf. 36: 26 f.; 37: 14; Jl 2: 28–32), His favour is restored to His people. The overthrow of Gog will confirm the lesson already taught by Israel's exile and subsequent restoration: God's purpose is that Israel and all the nations may know that He is Yahweh—may see His name vindicated and His character manifested. It was His righteousness, not His weakness, that sent His people into exile; and it is His righteousness that has brought them back.

X. THE NEW COMMONWEALTH (40: 1–48: 35)
In keeping with the close association between people and land throughout the OT, a purified people implies a purified land, and this is the subject of Ezekiel's last vision. Within the holy land lies the holy city, and alongside the holy city, but separate from it, stands the new temple, the holiest place of all—because the divine glory which had abandoned the first temple returns to take up its abode there (43: 2–5; 44: 4). 'I will put my sanctuary among them forever', God had promised, and then 'the nations will know that I the LORD make Israel holy' (37:26,28).

The limits of this commentary permit only the most cursory examination of the dimensions and other details of the following description.

i. The new temple (40: 1–4: 20)
The date of this vision (v. 1) is April 28, 573 B.C., if **the beginning of the year** means 'the first month' (so LXX).

(a) The temple mount (40: 1–4). **1. the hand of the LORD was upon me:** cf. 1: 1; 8: 3; 37: 1. **2. visions of God:** cf. 1: 1; 8: 3. **a very high mountain:** 'the mountain of the LORD's temple' which is to be 'established as chief among the mountains' (Isa. 2: 2; Mic. 4: 1), perhaps identical with 'the center of the land' or 'the navel of the land' (38: 12). **buildings that looked like a city:** not the holy city itself, but the temple complex, so described because of its imposing appearance. **3. a man whose appearance was like bronze:** a celestial being (like the 'man' in Dan. 10: 6, who had 'arms and legs like the gleam of burnished bronze'), **with a linen cord** for longer measurements (cf. 47: 3) **and a measuring rod** for shorter

ones (cf. v. 5). **the gateway:** presumably the 'gate facing east' (v. 6).

(*b*) *The east gate* (40: 5–16). The **long cubit** was *c.* 21 inches (as against the ordinary cubit of *c.* 18 inches); the **wall** surrounding **the temple area** was therefore *c.* 10 feet 6 inches in height and thickness (5). (Its other dimensions are given in 42: 20.) The elaborate east **gateway**, described in such detail (vv. 6–16), fortified with guard-rooms on either side, is similar to the Solomonic gateways at Megiddo and Hazor and may well have the dimensions of the east gateway of the first temple. The function of this gateway is indicated in 44: 1–3.

(*c*) *The outer court* (40: 17–27). Ezekiel's temple has the same basic ground plan and orientation as Solomon's temple (1 Kg. 7: 12)—outer court, inner court, and holy house (as one moves from east to west). Ezekiel is led into the **outer court** through the east gate, and then inspects the north gate (vv. 20–23) and south gate (vv. 24–27) which also gave access to it. In the outer court the people were to gather for worship.

(*d*) *The inner court* (40: 28–37, 47). The **inner court**, to which only priests were to be admitted, had south, east and north gates of its own, through which it was entered (by priests only) from the outer court: they had the same general dimensions as the gates leading into the outer court. The inner court was 100 cubits (175 feet) square; in it stood **the altar** of burnt offering (cf. 43: 13–17), in front of the entrance to the holy house.

(*e*) *Sacrificial arrangements* (40: 38–43). The description of the inner court is interrupted by an account of sacrificial arrangements in the vestibule of its north gate, followed by a reference to priests' rooms. Among the animal sacrifices specified in v. 39 the peace offering (cf. Lev. 3: 1 ff.) is notably absent; but see 43: 27.

(*f*) *Rooms by the gates* (40: 44–46). By the inner sides of the north and south gates were two rooms for priests. The **priests who have charge of the temple** (45) are the non-Zadokites (cf. 44: 14); those **who have charge of the altar** (46) are **the sons of Zadok** (cf. 44: 15 ff.).

(*g*) *The temple portico* (40: 48 f.). After inspecting the courts Ezekiel is taken to the temple proper, the holy house, which comprised (from east to west) portico, holy place and holy of holies. The portico (*'ûlam*) measured 20 cubits from left to right, like that of Solomon's temple; from front to back (12 cubits as against 10) it measured rather more than Solomon's (1 Kg. 6: 3). **48. the jambs:** NEB 'a pilaster'. **49. there were pillars:** like Jachin and Boaz in Solomon's temple (1 Kg. 7: 15–22).

(*h*) *The holy place and holy of holies* (41: 1–15a). **1. the outer sanctuary:** Heb. *hêkal* ('palace',

'great house'), NEB 'sanctuary'; the holy place, the main compartment of the building, is meant. **2. the entrance was ten cubits wide:** four cubits less than the gateway of the portico. The wall between the portico and the holy place must have jutted in from north and south to leave an entrance of 17½ feet. The length and breadth of the holy place, 40 cubits by 20 (v. 2), and of the holy of holies, 20 cubits by 20 (v. 4), were as in Solomon's temple (1 Kg. 6: 2, 17, 20) and later in Herod's temple (Josephus, *War* v. 215 f., 219). **3. he went into the inner sanctuary:** i.e. the holy of holies. Ezekiel could not follow him here, priest though he was; the high priest alone of mortal men might enter the holy of holies (Lev. 16: 2 ff.; Heb. 9: 7), although Ezekiel nowhere distinguishes him from the other priests. The entrance to the holy of holies (6 cubits) was in its turn narrower than that to the holy place; like the entrance to the holy place, it was closed by folding doors (vv. 23 f.), no mention being made of a curtain or veil. **5. the side rooms:** NEB 'arcades'; their details are obscure, but the general pattern of Solomon's temple is followed (1 Kg. 6: 5 f., 8, 10) as later in Herod's temple (Josephus, *War* v. 220 f.). They surrounded the wall of the temple proper on the north, west and south sides. **8. raised base:** or 'pavement' (NEB), presumably the elevation reached by the 'ten steps' of 40: 49 (mg). **12. The building facing the temple courtyard on the west side:** the purpose of this building, 'at the far end of the free space' (NEB), is unspecified (it may have been the 'court' of 1 Chr. 26: 18).

The floor space of the holy place and holy of holies was 60 by 20 cubits (as in the temples of Solomon and Herod), but when the vestibule, the thickness of the wall, the side chambers and their outer walls, and the yard to the north were added, the total structure occupied a square of 100 cubits (175 feet), equivalent in area to the inner court (40: 47).

The height of the holy house is not given. Cyrus's decree authorizing the building of the post-exilic temple (Ezr. 6: 3) specified a height of 60 cubits (twice that of Solomon's temple, 1 Kg. 6: 2) and a breadth of 60 cubits (unless the text originally ran 'its breadth [twenty cubits and its length] sixty cubits').

(*i*) *Interior decoration and equipment* (41: 15b–26). The portico, holy place and holy of holies were panelled inside with wood, the panelling being ornamented with alternate carvings of palm-trees and two-faced cherubim (unlike the four-faced cherubim of 10: 14—but those were three-dimensional). Similar decoration was used in Solomon's temple (1 Kg. 6: 29). **22. There was a wooden altar:** the table of showbread; cf. the 'altar of cedar' in Solomon's temple (1 Kg. 6: 20b). The table in the Mosaic tabernacle was smaller (Exod. 25: 23); the dimensions of that in Herod's temple are not given (Josephus, *War* v. 217). **23. The outer sanctuary and the Most Holy Place:** i.e. the holy place and the holy of holies. **25. a wooden overhang:** NEB 'a wooden cornice'; the meaning of the Hebrew word is unknown.

(j) *The priests' rooms* (42: 1–14). These rooms, which the priests used for sacrificial meals, storage and robing (vv. 13 f.), were situated to the north of the western building of 41: 12; to the south of it stood their kitchens (46: 19 f.). Many of the details are quite obscure. **13. the priests who approach the LORD:** the Zadokites (cf. 40: 46; 43: 19; 44: 15 ff.). **the grain offerings** (*minhah*), **the sin offerings** (*hatta'th*) **and the guilt offerings** (*'asham*): the burnt-offering (*'ôlah*) is not mentioned here, as it is in 40: 39, because it was completely consumed; and the peace offering (*shelamim*) was eaten by the worshippers (cf. 46: 24). **14. these are holy:** and might communicate holiness to the people who were admitted to the outer court if they were worn there (44: 19).

(k) *Overall dimensions* (42: 15–20). The whole temple area, outer and inner courts together (with the holy house and other buildings), stood on a square of 500 long cubits (875 feet), surrounded by the wall already mentioned in 40: 5, an external token of that **separation** which was essentially inward and spiritual. According to the Mishnah tractate *Middoth* these were the dimensions of the temple area as extended by Herod; those given by Josephus (*Antiquities* xv. 400) are somewhat smaller (about one furlong square), while the walled area of the present Haram esh-Sherif is substantially larger. Hecataeus of Abdera (4th–3rd century B.C.) reported that the temple area in his day measured 5 **plethra** (500 feet) by 100 cubits (quoted by Josephus, *Apion* i. 198).

ii. The returning glory and call to holiness (43: 1–12)

(a) *The returning glory* (43: 1–5). Nineteen years before, Ezekiel had seen the divine glory, up-borne by the cherubim, leave the polluted temple and hover over the east gate before leaving the precincts and the city altogether (10: 19; 11: 22 f.). Now, through the east gate **the glory** returns and fills the new temple, as it had formerly filled the tabernacle (Exod. 40: 34) and the first temple (1 Kg. 8: 10 f.). After the return from exile Yahweh commanded that the new temple be built, 'that I may take pleasure in it and . . . appear in my glory' (Hag. 1: 8 RSV).

2. the glory of the God of Israel came **from the east:** Ezekiel had last seen it over the Mount of Olives (11: 23). **like the roar of rushing waters:** cf. 1: 24. **3. the vision I had seen when he came to destroy the city:** the vision of 8: 1 ff. **the visions I had seen by the**

Kebar River: the inaugural vision of 1: 1 ff. **I fell face down:** cf. 1: 28. **5. the Spirit lifted me up:** cf. 8: 3. **the glory of the LORD filled the temple:** this is the climax of Ezekiel's prophetic experience; what follows is by way of corollary. For the Christian counterpart to this indwelling glory cf. Jn 1: 14; 2 C. 3: 7–4: 6.

(b) *Call to holiness* (43: 6–12). Because the God of Israel resides among His people, they must be holy as He is holy. The holiness of His dwelling-place is emphasized not only by the encircling wall of 42: 20 but by the establishment of an unoccupied space between it and all other buildings (cf. 45: 2). Solomon's palace, his Egyptian queen's residence, and other royal structures were enclosed in one court along with the temple (1 Kg. 7: 1–12), and the temple was polluted by the idolatrous practices which went on in them under some of his successors, as well as by the 'funerary monuments'—a more probable rendering of *peger* than **lifeless idols** (9)—of the kings. Such a risk must no longer be run. The whole temple mount is to be **most holy** (12)—reserved for God and His worship.

6. I heard one speaking to me from inside the temple: the voice is God's (cf. Lev. 1: 1). **7. this is the place of my throne . . . forever:** cf. Ps. 132: 14 for similar words in reference to the pre-exilic city. **10. that they may be ashamed of their sins:** the divine presence among the people does not guarantee their holiness but challenges them to holiness. The portrayal of the new temple in all the details of its structure and service will provide them with an object lesson in holiness. So, in the NT order, 'God's temple is sacred, and you are that temple' (1 C. 3: 17).

iii. The altar of burnt offering (43: 13–27)

(a) *The dimensions of the altar* (43: 13–17). The **altar** of burnt offering in the inner court was mentioned briefly in 40: 47. It is now described as having the form of a ziggurat with three layers in addition to **the gutter on the ground** (14), lit. 'the bosom of the earth'—probably sunk in the ground one cubit deep to collect the blood, with **a rim of one span** (13; NEB 'handbreadth') surrounding it to prevent the blood from spreading outwards. The topmost layer was the **altar hearth** (Heb. *har'el*, v. 15, or *'ar'el*, v. 16), on which sacrifices were consumed; it was equipped with **four horns** (15; cf. Exod. 27: 2; 1 Kg. 1: 50f.). The **ledge** of v. 17 is the upper or **smaller ledge** of v. 14; the dimensions of the lower or **larger ledge** (16 cubits square?) may have fallen out. LXX renders **ledge** (Heb. *'azarah*) by *hilastērion*, used in the Pentateuch (Exod. 25: 17, etc.) for the 'mercy seat' (*kapporeth*); cf. Heb. 9: 5.

13. one cubit wide: NEB (better) 'projected a cubit' (as also in v. 17). The whole altar, exclusive of the base and the horns, was 10 cubits (17½ feet) high. It was ascended by **steps** from the east (v. 17); the officiating priests would then face west. Contrast the ban on altar steps in Exod. 20: 26.

(*b*) *The consecration of the altar* (43: 18–27). The altar must undergo a week-long ceremony of cleansing (lit. 'un-sinning') and atonement (Heb. *kipper*, v. 20) with sin offerings and burnt offerings—a much more elaborate ceremony than the simple consecration of Exod. 40: 10. Then, from the eighth day, the regular sacrificial services can be conducted on behalf of the people.

18. sprinkling blood upon the altar: cf. Exod. 29: 16, 20, etc. **19. you are to give:** 'you' is singular, but the reference is general; Ezekiel was now 50 years old and the likelihood of his surviving to minister in the new temple was remote. **27. fellowship offerings:** providing fellowship meals, in which the worshippers shared.

iv. The closing of the east gate (44: 1–3)
After the divine glory had entered by the east gate (43: 1–5), it was kept closed; no mortal might use it henceforth, apart from **the prince** (3). One might identify him with 'my servant David' (34: 23 f.; 37: 24 f.), but he is scarcely a messianic figure; his duties are more like those of a lay ecclesiastical commissioner. He is permitted to enter and leave by the east gate when he eats his share of the peace offerings which he brings **in the presence of the LORD** (3; cf. 45: 16 f.; 46: 2, 8). His sacral privileges are restricted indeed as compared with those of the earlier David, who on special occasions wore a priestly vestment, offered sacrifices and blessed the worshippers (2 Sam. 6: 14, 17 f.), went into the tent that housed the ark and 'sat before the LORD' (2 Sam. 7: 18) and conferred priestly status on his sons (2 Sam. 8: 18). The Qumran order for the new age, in which the Davidic Messiah is subordinate to the priesthood, is based on Ezekiel's blueprint.

This passage may have given rise to the tradition that, when the Messiah comes, he will enter the temple by the east gate, for which reason the Golden Gate in the east wall of the Haram esh-Sherif is permanently closed.

v. The law of the priesthood (44: 4–31)
(*a*) *Qualifications for priestly service* (44: 4–16). The holiness required by the presence of the divine glory is again emphasized, with renewed insistence on separation. In pre-exilic days various kinds of service in the house of God had been performed by non-Israelites, such as the Gibeonites (Jos. 9: 23, 27) and Carites (2 Kg. 11: 4, 19; cf. the denunciation of 'all who avoid stepping on the threshold' in Zeph. 1: 9). Their description as **uncircumcised in heart and flesh** (9) implies impiety (cf. Dt. 10: 16; Jer. 4: 4) as well as literal uncircumcision. They cannot be allowed in the new temple: foreigners

must be excluded (contrast Isa. 56: 6 f., where Yahweh's temple is to be called 'a house of prayer for all nations'). This exclusion was enforced in the second temple from Nehemiah's day (cf. Neh. 13: 4–9); in NT times non-Israelites might enter the Court of the Gentiles, recently enclosed by Herod, but they might not penetrate the barrier into the sacred precincts proper, on pain of death (cf. Ac. 21: 28 f.). But it is plain from 47: 22 f. that the exclusive policy in Ezekiel's vision is not motivated by national chauvinism.

The service which had once been done by foreigners was henceforth to be discharged by those **Levites** who had shown themselves unworthy of sacrificial functions by their participation in idolatry (v. 10). They might slaughter animals for private worshippers (v. 11) and perform other temple duties (v. 14) but not minister at the altar (v. 13). The dominant view is that these Levites had been priests at the local sanctuaries throughout the land which Josiah closed in 621 B.C., in the course of his reformation (2 Kg. 23: 5, 8), and that they were transferred to the central sanctuary at Jerusalem in accordance with Dt. 18: 6–8, but were prevented by the existing Jerusalem priesthood from sharing their prerogatives (cf. 2 Kg. 23: 9). This remains hypothetical. The Jerusalem priests themselves had not been guiltless in the days of apostasy: under Ahaz, for example, the priest Uriah co-operated in the setting up of an Assyrian altar in the temple (2 Kg. 16: 10–16), and the various pagan installations which Josiah removed from the temple and its vicinity (2 Kg. 23: 4, 6 f., 11 f.) had not remained there without priestly acquiescence. Ezekiel indeed knew of 'detestable things' perpetrated or permitted by the temple staff in his own lifetime (8: 3ff.).

One group of Jerusalem priests, however, **priests . . . Levites and descendants of Zadok**, had not been compromised in this way (15). Zadok, the founder of their line, exercised a priestly ministry at David's court, alongside Abiathar, scion of the former Shiloh priesthood (2 Sam. 8: 17; 15: 24 ff.). There is no substantial evidence for the theory that Zadok belonged to the pre-Israelite priesthood of *'El 'Elyôn* ('God Most High') in Jerusalem. Under Solomon, Abiathar was demoted (1 Kg. 2: 26 f.) and Zadok, who had anointed Solomon king (1 Kg. 1: 39), became undisputed priestly leader (1 Kg. 2: 35). His family remained in office in Jerusalem until the destruction of Solomon's temple in 587 B.C. When Zerubbabel's temple was built seventy years later, it was the Zadokite family that supplied the successive high priests from Jeshua the son of Jehozadak to Onias III and his brother Jason, who were deposed the one after the other by Antiochus IV (*c.* 170 B.C.). After that a Zadokite high-priesthood was maintained in the Jewish temple at Leontopolis in Egypt until Vespasian closed it in A.D. 71. The Qumran community regarded the Zadokites as the only legitimate high priests and refused to recognize the non-Zadokite high priests who, until the revolt of A.D. 66, held office in Jerusalem. The Zadokites are given a Levitical lineage in 1 Chr. 6: 1–15, 50–53.

(b) *Priestly regulations* (44: 17–31). The regulations about the priests' dress and life-style are similar to those of Exod. 28: 40–43; Lev. 21: 1–23, etc., with some variations.

19. so that they do not consecrate . . . : cf. 42: 13 f.; 46: 20. **21. No priest is to drink wine . . . :** cf. Lev. 10: 9. **22. They must not marry widows . . . :** in Lev. 21: 13 f. this restriction applies only to 'the high priest, the one among his brothers . . .' (cf. Lev. 21: 7 for marital restrictions applicable to priests in general); Ezekiel, however, makes no mention of a chief priest. **23. They are to teach my people . . . :** for the teaching ministry of the priests cf. Dt. 33: 10; Mal. 2: 6 f.; for their judicial functions cf. Dt. 17: 8 ff. **27. he is to offer a sin offering:** cf. Lev. 4: 3 ff.; Heb. 5: 3; 7: 27. **28. I am to be the only inheritance; . . . no possession:** but in 45: 4 f.; 48: 11–14, the priests and Levites have a 'sacred district' allocated for their residence. **29. everything in Israel devoted to the LORD:** i.e. 'devoted to God' (NEB), Heb. *ḥerem* (cf. Lev. 27: 21, 28 f.). **31. The priests must not eat anything . . . found dead or torn:** cf. 4: 14. In Lev. 7: 24 this provision applies to all Israel.

vi. The holy district (45: 1–8)
In the reallocation of the land of Israel among the tribes (cf. 48: 1–7, 23–29) there is to be a reserved zone of national territory, slightly south of centre, stretching from the Mediterranean to the Jordan, 25,000 cubits (about 8¼ miles or 13.6 km.) from north to south. Directions regarding it are given here and (more fully) in 48: 8–22. In the middle of this zone is the **sacred district**, 25,000 cubits from west to east, divided into two parallel strips, each 10,000 cubits from north to south. The more northerly of these strips is allocated to the Levites for their residence (v. 5); the more southerly to the Zadokite priests (3 f.). In the centre of the Zadokite allocation is the temple enclosure (cf. 42: 15–20), with an unoccupied space 50 cubits wide all round it, outside the encircling wall (v. 2). To the south of **the sacred district** another strip, also 25,000 cubits from west to east but only 5,000 cubits from north to south, contains **the** capital **city** in the centre, on a square of 4,500 cubits (cf. 48: 30 ff.), with the city lands lying west and east of the city itself (v. 6); the city allocation does not belong to any tribe but to all Israel (i.e. it is federal territory). The temple is thus quite

separate from the city. The remainder of the reserved zone, the territory west and east of the holy district and the city allocation, bordering on the Mediterranean and the Jordan, comprises the 'crown lands', the allocation for **the prince** (vv. 7 f.).

vii. Sacral ordinances (45: 9–46: 24)
(a) *The prince's duties* (45: 9–17). The provision of a 'civil list' for the prince means that he and others in authority will have no more excuse for exploiting or oppressing the people (v. 9). The maintenance of administrative justice involves the use of just and agreed weights and measures (vv. 10–12; cf. Lev. 19: 35 f.; Dt. 25: 13–16; Prov. 11: 1; contrast Am. 8: 5). The people's **offering** (income tax) is fixed at one sixtieth of the harvest and one out of every 200 sheep; this is to be handed over to **the prince**, who is responsible to provide the public sacrifices out of it (vv. 13–17).

11. The ephah and the bath: the former was a dry measure, the latter a liquid measure, each about 4½ gallons or 20 litres, one-tenth of a **homer** (which etymologically meant an ass load) or, for liquid measure, of a **cor** (14). A **hin** (24) was one sixth of a **bath**. **12. The shekel** weighed 0.4 ounces or 11.4 grams; it comprised **twenty gerahs**. A **mina** comprised **fifty shekels:** it was conveniently reckoned with 'weights of ten and twenty-five and fifteen shekels' (NEB). **17. drink offerings:** libations of olive oil (cf. vv. 14, 24).

(b) *The sacred calendar* (45: 18–25). The calendar which Ezekiel had known in the pre-exilic use of Jerusalem (cf. Lev. 23) is to be considerably modified. On Nisan 1, around the time of the spring equinox (which may have been Ezekiel's New Year's Day), the sanctuary is to be cleansed (lit. 'un-sinned') by a **sin offering** (vv. 18 f.), and another sacrifice for the same purpose is to be offered on Nisan 7—or rather, as LXX reads, 'on the first day of the seventh month', i.e. Tishri (v. 20). The **Passover** of Nisan 14, with the following week of **bread made without yeast**, remains essentially unchanged (vv. 21–24), as also does the autumnal festival of Tabernacles six months later (v. 25), except that throughout both these weeks of pilgrimage **the prince** has to provide **sin offerings** as well as **burnt offerings, and grain offerings** (vv. 22–25). The sin offerings presented on these occasions appear to take the place of the one annual sin offering on the Day of Atonement (Lev. 23: 26–32). There is evidently no mention of Pentecost (cf. Lev. 23: 15–21).

(c) *Further princely duties* (46: 1–18). The weekly **Sabbath** and **the New Moon** (first day of each month) are marked by the opening of the east **gate of the inner court** (1). The **prince**, having entered the outer court by its east gate (cf. 44: 3), approaches the east **gate of the**

inner court, but does not pass through it (only the priests may enter the inner court). There he presents prescribed sacrifices as the people's representative, handing them over to **the priests**, whose prerogative it is to **offer** them on the altar (vv. 2–8). The prince then leaves by the east gate of the outer court; his departure, like his arrival, coincides with that of the people, but they use the **north** and **south** gates of the outer court (vv. 9 f.). Further details of the prince's temple duties are given in vv. 11–15.

The prince's gifts to his sons from his own landed property belong to them inalienably (since they are members of the royal house); similar gifts to his servants revert to the royal house in **the year of freedom** i.e. the jubilee year (Lev. 25: 8 ff.). No land might be alienated in perpetuity from the family that originally owned it, whether the royal family or any family of the common people (vv. 16–18).

(d) *The priests' kitchens* (46: 19–24). The distinction between the priests who minister at the altar and those **who minister at the temple** (24) is maintained even in the kitchen arrangements: the former boil the sacrificial flesh and **bake the grain offering** for their own consumption in kitchens behind the temple, at the west end of the inner court (cf. 42: 1 ff.); the latter boil **the sacrifices of the people** in kitchens situated in the corners of the outer court. The priests' sacrificial food was specially holy, and if it were cooked in the outer court it might communicate holiness to (**consecrating**) **the people** (20), like the vestments of 44: 19.

viii. The river of life (47: 1–12)
The theme of **the river** rising in the temple mount and flowing down the Kidron valley to the Dead Sea in rapidly increasing volume is developed most fully by Ezekiel, but it is not peculiar to him. Joel tells how 'a fountain will flow out of the Lord's house and will water the valley of acacias' (Jl 3: 18), and in Zech. 14: 8 there is a description of 'living water' flowing out from Jerusalem on the day of the Lord, one branch entering the Mediterranean and another the Dead Sea. In Ezekiel's vision vegetation springs up along the banks of the river, and the water in the Dead Sea is made **fresh** and teems with **fish**, apart from outlying **swamps and marshes** (11), from which **salt** will continue to be collected.

In the NT this vision is realized in the fulfilment of our Lord's prophecy of the outpoured Spirit in Jn 7: 37–39 (it is to one or another of the OT passages just mentioned that reference is made in His words, 'as the Scripture has said') and, in greater detail, in John's vision of the 'river of the water of life' which flows 'from the throne of God and of the Lamb' through the midst of the new Jerusalem, providing sus-

tenance for the tree of life whose leaves are 'for the healing of the nations' (Rev. 22: 1 f.; cf. Ezek. 47: 12). In a Christian sense Ezekiel's river thus serves as an apt symbol of that life in the Spirit which the gospel holds forth as God's free gift to all believers.

8. the Arabah: the depression in which the Dead Sea lies. **10. En Eglaim:** uncertain, but perhaps to be identified with Ain Feshkha, 18 miles north of **En Gedi**.

ix. The division of the land (47: 13–48: 29)
(a) *The frontiers of Israel* (47: 13–20). The land is delimited on the west by the Mediterranean and on the east by the Jordan and Dead Sea. Its northern frontier runs eastward from a point on the coast north of Tyre, via **Hazar Enan** at the foot of Hermon, to **the entrance to Hamath** (mg) or **Lebo Hamath**, probably in the vicinity of Riblah (cf. 6: 14). The southern frontier runs from **the Wadi of Egypt** (Wadi el-Arish) on the west, via **Meribah Kadesh** (cf. Num. 20: 1–13), to **Tamar** (19), perhaps the Hazezon Tamar of Gen. 14: 7, south-west of the Dead Sea.

(b) *Provision for resident aliens* (47: 21–23). The national territory provides a home not only for **the tribes of Israel** but for the **aliens who have settled** down and brought up families in the land (cf. Lev. 19: 33 f.; 24: 22). They are to be treated **as native-born Israelites** and given allocations with the respective tribes among which they reside (vv. 21–23). In the following centuries this provision was interpreted of religious proselytes (cf. 14: 7).

(c) *The tribal zones and the reserved zone* (48: 1–29). The land is to be divided into thirteen parallel zones, each stretching from the Mediterranean to the Jordan and Dead Sea. One of these (described in detail in vv. 8–22) is the reserved zone already specified in 45: 1–8, including the 'sacred district', the city with the city lands, and the prince's estate; the others are divided among the twelve secular tribes, Manasseh and Ephraim having a zone apiece (cf. 47: 13). Seven tribal zones are to the north of the reserved zone and five to the south of it. The arrangement of the tribal territories deviates from that specified in earlier OT records: in particular, Benjamin now lies south of Judah (with the reserved zone between them), whereas formerly it lay to the north (with Jerusalem between them).

Nothing is said of the breadth from north to south of the twelve tribal zones, whether it was the same for each or varied from one to another, so no inferences can be drawn respecting the exact location of the reserved zone and the holy city: in any case, such a schematic division of the land does not encourage precise geographical calculations. Attempts have been made by means of such calculations to show that Shechem, not Jerusalem, was to be the site of the new temple. It is incredible that a Jerusalem priest, as Ezekiel was, should have entertained such a revolutionary proposal without drawing specific attention to it and justifying it.

x. The holy city (48: 30–35)

The location of the **city** has been given in 45: 6; now its dimensions are given, together with an account of its **gates—three gates** on each **side**, twelve gates in all, each named after one of the tribes of Israel, like the twelve gates of John's new Jerusalem (Rev. 21: 12 f.). Ezekiel, perhaps deliberately, refrains from calling the new city Jerusalem: **the name of the city from that time on will be** *Yahweh-shammah*, **The LORD is there** (35)—and that is adequate reason for calling it the holy city.

> *Jehovah founded it in blood,*
> *The blood of his incarnate Son;*
> *There dwell the saints, once foes to God,*
> *The sinners whom he calls his own.*

> *There though besieged on every side,*
> *Yet much beloved and guarded well,*
> *From age to age they have denied*
> *The utmost force of earth and hell.*

> *Let earth repent and hell despair,*
> *This city has a sure defence;*
> *Her name is called 'The Lord is there',*
> *And who has power to drive him thence?*

As William Cowper acknowledged in these lines, Ezekiel's prophecy is part of the Christian Bible, and as such bears witness to Christ. The Christian lessons of Ezekiel's new commonwealth are plainly drawn out in the Apocalypse. John depicts 'the holy city, new Jerusalem', which is the glorified community of the people of God. Because this community as such is God's dwelling place among men (Rev. 21: 2 f.), there is no need of a separate temple. If, as Ezekiel says, 'The LORD is there', then in John's eyes 'the Lord God Almighty and the Lamb are its temple' (Rev. 21: 22). In the present gospel order, Ezekiel's new temple, city and commonwealth are all alike realized in that 'dwelling in which God lives by his Spirit' (Eph. 2: 22) which anticipates the accomplishment of the eternal purpose when, in the fulness of time, all things are united under Christ as their true Head (Eph. 1: 9 f.; 3: 9 f.).

BIBLIOGRAPHY

Commentaries

*CARLEY, K. W., *The Book of the Prophet Ezekiel*, CBC (Cambridge, 1974).

COOKE, G. A., *The Book of Ezekiel*. ICC (Edinburgh, 1936).

CRAIGIE, P. C., *Ezekiel*. Daily Study Bible, (Edinburgh, 1983).

EICHRODT, W., *Ezekiel: A Commentary*, E.T. (London, 1970).

FAIRBAIRN, P., *An Exposition of Ezekiel* (Edinburgh, 1851; reprinted Grand Rapids, 1960).

GREENBERG, M., *Ezekiel*, AB. 2 vols. (Graham City. N. Y., 1983–00).

*STALKER, D. M. G., *Ezekiel*. TC (London, 1968).

*TAYLOR, J. B., *Ezekiel*. TOTC (London, 1969).

*WEVERS, J. W., *Ezekiel*. NCentB (London, 1969).

ZIMMERLI, W., *Ezekiel*. E.T., Hermeneia, 2 vols. (Philadelphia, 1979–83).

Other works

ACKROYD, P. R., *Exile and Restoration* (London, 1968).

CARLEY, K. W., *Ezekiel among the Prophets* (London, 1975).

ELLISON, H. L., *Ezekiel: The Man and his Message* (London, 1956).

GUTHRIE, T., *The Gospel in Ezekiel* (Edinburgh, 1863).

HOWIE, C. G., *The Date and Composition of Ezekiel* (Philadelphia, 1950).

NEWBERRY, T., *The Temples of Solomon and Ezekiel* (London, 1887).

ROBINSON, H. W., *Two Hebrew Prophets: Studies in Hosea and Ezekiel* (London, 1948).

ROWLEY, H. H., 'The Book of Ezekiel in Modern Study', in *Men of God* (London, 1963), pp.169–210.

*Those commentaries marked with an asterisk are designed for the general reader. Of the others, that by Zimmerli is by far the best in any language.

The Julian equivalents given for Ezekiel's dates are based on R. A. Parker and W. H. Dubberstein, *Babylonian Chronology, 626 B.C.-A.D. 75* (Providence, Rhode Island, 1956).

DANIEL

A. R. MILLARD

Few figures in the OT are as familiar as Daniel, a man uprooted from his home, educated in an alien society, who kept an unswerving loyalty to the God of his people. His ability and the integrity inspired by his faith took him to high offices of state. Called to do the impossible, to tell the king his dream, his faith was rewarded with divine insight, saving him from death. Under the normally kind Persian rule he would not compromise even for a month, and his enemies knew he would not. His faith was neither ostentatious nor secret, but steadfast, ready to give account when asked, even to rebuke a king for heedless sacrilege. Fitted for the greatest ministerial responsibilities in the state, he was also fitted for the unique responsibility of receiving and presenting revelations about his nation in international affairs for centuries ahead.

Daniel's faith reflects the theology of the book. His prayer in ch. 9 continues the attitude of Deuteronomy: God's chosen people could enjoy their promised land so long as they were obedient; their continuous, wilful, disobedience sent them into exile. Yet the punishment would have an end; indeed, the agents of the sentence were limited and controlled by God, as had the Assyrian, so the Babylonian would crash, and all who tried to pass the limit. Truly the sentence would expire, the people of God would see His kingdom established, but not in Daniel's day. For he was shown the triumph, certain as it was, to be delayed. Human empires had a further lease on the rule of Israel, from the kingdom of gold through the silver and the bronze to the iron and clay. A definite end there would be; then human pride would be abolished at a blow. In this lay Israel's ultimate hope. For the exiled and oppressed the very example of Daniel could encourage; the affirmation of his friends could be their motto (3: 17, 18). Whereas Ezekiel, for example, envisaged a Jerusalem of greater glory, the prophecies of Dan. 2 and 7 embrace a more spiritual 'kingdom', the national names of Jerusalem and Israel being absent. The important element was the certainty of God's purpose reaching its goal, including justification of the faithful in everlasting life.

As the Ancient of Days, God wears as great an aura in Daniel as in any part of the OT. He is displayed as the world-ruler, majestic, dealing with mortals through His agents, the angels. At the same time, He is concerned for the welfare of His worshippers, the uncompromising, those who know Him by His covenant name (ch. 9). For them He meets faith with faith by revelations of the future. Unrevealed, who could know if God altered His plans? By disclosing them He showed His readiness to stand by His word, by fulfilling them stage by stage—Daniel witnessed Babylon's fall—He demonstrated His constancy. World empires could not continue indefinitely, no human state could ever reach complete control for man could not control himself; in the end God would be seen triumphant.

Man, then, appears as God's creature, whether Jew or Gentile. If a great king was humbled for his pride, the lesson was there for every man. Daniel and his friends are models. The case of Darius paints man as basically ignorant of God, yet able to understand when told about Him, and to turn acceptably to Him once his self-importance has been swept away. For the faithful is the promise of eventual victory.

Daniel and History

The stories of Dan. 1–6, set in the sixth century B.C. present certain problems when read in the light of other records. Most students of the book feel those are errors that would be intolerable in a contemporary writing but could arise three centuries or so later. Consequently chs. 1–6 are commonly regarded as written by a second century B.C. author, using slightly earlier sources. The date is bound up with the question of Daniel's prophecies discussed below (Vision and Prophecy). Some of the problems are major matters, some technical details. Any study is vitiated unless allowance is made for the paucity of evidence: first hand records from the Persian chancelleries are few and specialized; the Babylonian kings have left very incomplete accounts of their reigns; outside the OT no Jewish texts survive for the period. Some paths toward answers are offered here; they should not be thought definitive.

i. Nebuchadnezzar's madness is recorded by Daniel alone, although other vague stories from antiquity may refer to it. Lacking any relevant records from the latter part of his reign, it is improper to discard this one. Amongst the Dead Sea Scrolls were recovered fragments of a tale about Nabonidus, father of

Belshazzar, telling how he was healed of an ulcer by a pious Jew. Nabonidus spent ten years in northern Arabia, far from Babylon. Suggestions that Dan. 4 echoes the desert sojourn or the Nabonidus story are probably trying to weave incompatible threads.

ii. Belshazzar king of Babylon was known only from Dan. until cuneiform texts recovered from 1854 onwards named him as son of Nabonidus, last king of Babylon. He is never entitled 'king' in these texts, yet he exercised royal authority during his father's absence, and is named beside him in oath formulae. Now Dan. is not a product of the traditional Babylonian scribal schools, nor is it written in Babylonian. The word 'king', moreover enjoyed a wider use than in English. In ch. 5 Belshazzar is represented as son of Nebuchadnezzar; again a looser use of 'father' may be involved than English can allow, as attested in Hebrew. Nothing is known of Nabonidus' wife, Belshazzar's mother; it is quite possible she was a daughter of Nebuchadnezzar. See further *EQ*, 49 (1977) pp. 71–72.

iii. The Medes figure in Dan. as a major power, usually linked with the Persians (6: 8, etc.). Darius who took over Babylon is termed 'the Mede'(5: 31; 9: 1). In Isa. 13: 17; 21: 2; Jer. 51: 11, 28, Medes are foreseen as conquerors of Babylon. Beside Dan. these passages are invoked as evidence for Jewish belief in a Median Empire, headed by Darius, between the Babylonian and the Persian. Surviving Babylonian, Persian, and Greek records prohibit such an insertion, and they are beyond doubt. Accordingly, the Median Empire is adjudged a misunderstanding of the second or third century B.C., after Persia had fallen. A powerful Median state did exist in western Persia, participating in the sack of Nineveh (612 B.C.), defeated by Cyrus the Persian in 549 B.C. and added to his realm; Cyrus was probably grandson of the conquered Median king Astyages. Loss of independence did not bring loss of Median identity or influence. Cyrus made the Median capital Ecbatana his seat (cf. Ezr. 6: 2) and adopted the Median system of government, even borrowing the word 'satrap' from the Median dialect. The word order 'Medes and Persians' (5: 28, etc.) maintains their importance, and Greek writers could call the great Persian war 'the war with the Medes' (Thucydides 1: 14). Daniel's vision of the ram is explained as embodying both Medes and Persians (8: 20); the Medes are not a separate state. The identity of 'Cyrus the Persian' and 'Darius the Mede' is discussed below, but with the foregoing in mind, there is a possibility of the ethnic terms being loosely interchangeable (cf. English–British). If this be the case, Media cannot be counted as a separate entity in equating the kingdoms of chs. 2 and 7. See further Young,

pp. 275–94, and, arguing for a Median Empire, Rowley, *Darius the Mede*.

iv. Darius the Mede, 5: 31 reports, 'took over the kingdom, at the age of sixty-two' upon the death of Belshazzar. Since Belshazzar and his father Nabonidus were succeeded by Cyrus the Persian in 539 B.C., Darius has been confidently dismissed as unhistorical (see Rowley). If Medes and Persians can be so closely related as proposed above, the hypothesis of D. J. Wiseman becomes attractive: Darius was another name for Cyrus (cf. NIV mg at Dan 6: 28). The syntactic parallel between 6: 28 and 1 Chr. 5: 26 where two names of one king are cited is the basis for the theory, along with a hint from a Babylonian text that Cyrus may have been known as king of the Medes. Greek sources report Cyrus' age as about 60 at the fall of Babylon, with indirect support from Persian practice. See D. J. Wiseman, *Notes . . .* 9–16; for other views J. C. Whitcomb, *Darius the Mede* (Grand Rapids, 1959).

Other historical difficulties are noted in the Commentary.

The Languages of Daniel

Dan. 1: 1–2: 4a and 8–11 are written in Heb., the intervening chs. in Aram., the *lingua franca* of the Babylonian and Persian Empires. The reason is unknown; speculations range over different sources, loss of a complete Heb. version, attempt to restrict access to the semipolitical prophecies, the Heb. introduction fitting the book for Scripture, a bilingual composer—and many Jews were bilingual—passing easily from one language to the other.

Comparison with the Heb. of the rest of the OT and the Aram. preserved in other documents led to characterization of both languages as later than the sixth century B.C., more appropriate to the second. Recent studies invalidate the linguistic arguments, especially in showing the Aram. is most likely to belong to the sixth to fourth centuries B.C., although it could just be later. The Persian loanwords are quite at home in a sixth century context, and even the three Greek musical terms do not force the date to be lowered. See the detailed investigation by K. A. Kitchen in D. J. Wiseman and others, *Notes . . .* pp. 31–79; his results have been accepted by leading linguists.

Vision and Prophecy

Accounts of dreams and their interpretations are known from the third millennium B.C. onwards; Joseph and Daniel were two of many, though more successful (see A. L. Oppenheim, *The Interpretation of Dreams in the Ancient Near East*, Philadelphia, 1956). Those in Dan. differ in having long-distance aims beside their immediate relevance, except for Nebuchadnezzar's second dream. Revelations, symbolism of beasts, great conflict and divine triumph at the end are features shared by Daniel's visions and writings from the last two centuries B.C. and the early Christian period called 'apocalyptic'. Dan. is often claimed to be the pioneer of the class. Attentive reading of *I Enoch, Jubilees,* or the *Testaments of the Twelve Patriarchs* will reveal the common ground and numerous points of difference (standard translations in R. H. Charles, ed., *Apocrypha and Pseudepigrapha of the Old Testament,* Oxford, 1913). Montgomery called Dan. 'the connecting hinge between the Heb. Canon and later Apocalyptic', and even his position is thought to over-emphasize the apocalyptic aspects by recent writers (see Porteous, Heaton; also L. L. Morris, *Apocalyptic,* London, 1973). Affinities with the Prophets are prominent; Isaiah and Jeremiah had visions concerning their people's future distresses and restoration. Dan. belongs to a time when no national Israelite state existed, no Davidic ruler had to be recalled to covenant duties, so it prepares for a kingdom of God transcending physical limitations.

No other prophecies in the OT have aroused such dispute as Daniel's. The major question is about their authenticity. Did Hebrew prophets speak of events far in the future, or only to their immediate circumstances? The distinction between interpretations of Dan. is this: prediction or retrospection. Almost every other debated matter in the book depends on the answer to this one.

i. Daniel as Predictive. Judaism and the Christian Church at large have held the book to be wholly the work of a Jewish exile living in Babylon in the sixth century B.C. His prophecies were revelations granted by the God of Israel to His devoted servant.

ii. Daniel as Retrospective. Jerome, *c.* A.D. 400, designed his commentary on Dan. to refute a third-century philosopher Porphyry. He had assigned Dan. to the second century B.C. on the ground that predictive prophecy was impossible, the 'visions' were actually narratives of recent history. Attitudes similar to Porphyry's were expressed occasionally over the next 1500 years, then spread widely in the nineteenth century and are now standard for the majority of OT scholars.

The principal reason is the accurate description of events during the first half of the second century B.C. notably in ch. 11. Porphyry's rational recoil from predictive prophecy is sufficient argument for sceptics. Christian scholars who support the same date argue that, for a sixth-century B.C. work, Dan. is out of harmony with the other prophets in concern for far distant affairs and details, culminating in ch. 11, and in lack of interest in its contemporaries. Historical, linguistic, and other arguments drawn in to bolster this position have been discussed above and in the Commentary. None of these compels a second century B.C.

date, as admitted long ago by S. R. Driver (*Introduction to the Literature of the Old Testament*[9], London, 1913, p. 509). The present work adopts the traditional stance.

The Unity of Daniel

There is little need to posit compilation from various sources for a sixth-century B.C. composition, although some have supposed ch. 11 was re-written after the Maccabaean success. For a second-century B.C. product the likelihood of earlier sources is great in chs. 1–6, although the supposed historical and linguistic difficulties have restrained many from visualizing a time much earlier than the fourth century B.C. For a defence of a second century B.C. unity see H. H. Rowley, *The Servant of the Lord and Other Essays*[2] (Oxford, 1965), pp. 249–280.

As the book stands its various parts are interrelated by the person of Daniel and by the dates given to events and visions (the latter being fictitious on the later date for the book). Nebuchadnezzar's dream-image prepares for the visionary kingdoms, the suffering of Daniel and his friends for the endurance and faith required in the persecutions later forecast. The concept of God, the Universal Ruler who cares for His people is the same throughout.

Daniel in the Canon

Hebrew and Christian traditions differ, placing Dan. in the Writings and the Prophets respectively. Priority belongs to the Hebrew, yet Daniel undoubtedly exercised a prophetic gift and can hardly be distinguished from the other Prophets except in the exclusive use of dreams and visions and absence of direct oracles 'thus says the Lord'. (Young claimed Daniel held the gift but not the office of prophet.) Notice 'the Prophet Daniel' in Mt. 24: 15, a title also found in a text amongst the Dead Sea Scrolls. An obvious explanation for Dan.'s place in the last part of the Hebrew Bible would be a date of composition after the canon of Prophets was closed. That is upheld by supporters of a second-century B.C. origin. The absence of Daniel from Ecclesiasticus' list of worthies (chs. 44–50) compiled about 180 B.C. is added to the argument. With equal plausibility these facts can be embodied in the proposal that a sixth century work gained final recognition with the Maccabaean successes, in the spirit of Dt. 18: 21, 22, and was then added to the existing Scriptures. Publication of Dan. at that time could have been the impetus for the apocalyptic literature that flourished during subsequent generations, moving into realms of greater fantasy as the pious patriotic expectations waned.

Interpretation

Whichever position is taken with regard to the prophecies as a whole will influence the relationship perceived between the parts, and their exegesis. Where the differences become significant the major positions are noted in the Commentary; for clarity the identities offered for the several figures are tabulated here.

	Chapter 2				Chapter 7					Chapter 8			
	Gold	Silver	Bronze	Iron	Lion	Bear	Leopard	Fourth Beast	Horns	Ram	Goat	Four Horns	Little Horn
Babylon	T M D A				T M D A								
Media		M				M				T M D A			
Persia		T D A	M			T A D	M			T M D A			
Alexander			A				A				T M D A		
Greek kings			T D	M A			T D	M A				T M D A	
Antiochus IV									M A				T M D A
Rome				T D				T D					
Anti-Christ				D					(T) D				D

T: Traditional view.   M: Maccabean view.   D: Dispensational view.   A: Alexander view.

Chapters 2, 7, and 8 each predict four future states, with ch. 7 developing another. The second-century B.C. view maintains a strict analogy between each prediction, terminating each with the reign of Antiochus IV. Essential to this view is the separation of Media and Persia as two distinct states successively ruling Babylon in order to reach the desired pattern in chs. 2 and 7. An alternative interpretation takes Medo-Persia as a unit but Alexander's rule as separate from his successors', Antiochus IV still being the culmination, here named the 'Alexander' view (see the commentary by C. Lattey).

Daniel in the New Testament

The Bible Societies' Greek New Testament lists 133 quotations from Daniel. The majority are verbal reminiscences natural to anyone as imbued with the Old Testament as the early Christian writers and dealing with related subjects (the same is true for the Dead Sea Scrolls). Some are vital to a Christian understanding of the prophecies. Chief are the citations found in the sayings of Jesus. Whatever His source for the term Son of Man to describe Himself, He identified Himself with the 'one like a son of man' of 7: 13 f. in speaking of a future when He would be vindicated and triumphant (Mt. 19: 28; 25: 31; Mk 13: 26; 14: 62). Part, at least, of that future was near (Mk 14: 62), and it is arguable that the judgment factor came to fruition at the Fall of Jerusalem in A.D. 70. If Mt. 28: 18 alludes to Dan. 7: 14, then Jesus claimed the occasion had arrived, the universal authority had been given to Him. Further, in Lk. 20: 18 it is likely He spoke of his judicial function in the guise of the stone that smashed the dream-image of 2: 34 f., 44 f. Nor did Jesus see only Himself; His disciples were the persecuted and to be glorified 'saints' of ch. 7 (cf. Mt. 10: 23 and 19: 28). Jesus utilized other verses from Dan. in His teachings. He described the time of the end with words drawn from 12: 1 (Mk 13: 19), the 'abomination that causes desolation' from 11: 31; 12: 11, and the trampling of the holy place (8: 13) being signs of the end (Mk 13: 14; Lk. 21: 24).

In Jesus' application of the 'abomination that causes desolation' lies the clue for a Christian understanding of Dan.'s visions. He knew the prophecy had had fulfilment in the desecration of 167 B.C., as recorded in 1 Mac. 1: 54, yet He could entertain a further fulfilment. Even if all the prophecies of Dan. be made to apply to the period ending in the second century B.C., a double interpretation might still be possible. S. R. Driver, who upheld the second-century view, could say 'That some of the expressions in' 9: 24 'describe what was only in fact accomplished by Christ is but natural' (*Introduction*, . . . , pp. 495-6). Lattey introduced the term 'compenetration' in this context. The NT makes very clear how far the fulfilment of OT prophecies differed from the expectations of even the most godly, like John the Baptist (Lk. 7: 19 ff.), how a fulfilment need not correspond to the original in every respect (*e.g.* Jl 2: 28-32 in Ac. 2: 17-21), and how outwardly material promises might be redeemed in a spiritual sense (*e.g.* the son of David, Lk. 1: 32). These considerations are basic in studying Daniel's prophecies.

NT prophecies of the future in 2 Th. 2 and Rev. employ Danielic phraseology without claiming fulfilment of his prophecies. Thus the four visionary beasts of ch. 7 are a single monstrous conglomerate in Rev. 13; there are ten horns but no little one in Rev. 17: 12; there

are both 'three and a half days' and three and a half years (Rev. 11: 9; 12: 6, 14—here 'a time, times and half a time'; 13: 5); one comes 'on the cloud', not 'with clouds' Rev. 14: 14. Literary allusions are more probably to be found here than fulfilments of the type Jesus claimed. See F. F. Bruce, *This is That* (Exeter, 1968); R. T. France, *Jesus and the Old Testament* (London, 1971).

Empires and Kingdoms (all dates B.C.; rulers important in Dan. in bold type)

Babylonian or Chaldaean			Ptolemaic (Egypt)		
Nabopolassar	625–605		**Ptolemy I**	323–285 (king from 305)	
Nebuchadnezzar	604–562 son		**Ptolemy II**	285–245 son	
Evil-Merodach	561–560 son		**Ptolemy III**	247–221 son	
Neriglissar	559–556		Ptolemy IV	221–203 son	
Labashi-Marduk	556 son		Ptolemy V	203–181 son, married d. of Antiochus III, Cleopatra	
Nabonidus	555–539				
(Belshazzar)	(son)		Ptolemy VI	181–145 son	
			Ptolemy VII	145	
Persian or Achaemenid			Ptolemy VIII	169–164, 145–116 brother of P. VI	
Cyrus II	538–530				
Cambyses II	529–522 son				
Smerdis	522		*Seleucid (Syria)*		
Darius I	521–486		**Seleucus I**	312–281	
Xerxes I	485–465 son		Antiochus I	281–260 son	
Artaxerxes I	464–424 son		**Antiochus II**	260–246 son, married d. of Ptolemy II, Berenice	
Darius II	423–405 son				
Artaxerxes II	404–359 son		Seleucus II	245–226 son	
Artaxerxes III	358–338 son		Seleucus III	225–223 son	
Arses	337–336 son		**Antiochus III**	227–187 brother	
Darius III	335–331		Seleucus IV	187–175 son	
			Antiochus IV	175–164 Epiphanes, brother	
Macedonian or Greek					
Alexander III	336–323		Antiochus V	164–162 son	
Philip Arrhidaeus	323–316 half-brother		Demetrius I	162–150 cousin	
Alexander IV	316–310 son of Alexander				

ANALYSIS

The Marvellous History of Daniel and His Friends (1: 1–6: 28)

I THEIR RISE IN THE COURT OF NEBUCHADNEZZAR (1: 1–21)

II NEBUCHADNEZZAR'S FORGOTTEN DREAM (2: 1–49)
   i The frustrated tyrant (2: 1–13)
   ii Daniel's wisdom (2: 14–18)
   iii Daniel's worship (2: 19–23)
   iv Daniel declares the dream (2: 24–35)
   v Daniel interprets the dream (2: 36–45)
   vi Daniel's reward (2: 46–49)

The Marvellous History of Daniel and His Friends (1: 1-6: 18)

I. THEIR RISE IN THE COURT OF NEBUCHADNEZZAR (1: 1-21)

1. In the third year of . . . Jehoiakim: Jehoiakim was placed upon the throne of Judah by Pharaoh Necho in place of his brother Jehoahaz, the people's choice, after their father Josiah had been killed at Megiddo in 609 B.C. Egypt's efforts to dominate the Levant were repulsed by Babylon in the major battle at Carchemish, 605 B.C. The very laconic Babylonian Chronicle (*DOTT*, pp. 77 ff.) and various Hebrew texts (2 Kg. 23, 24; 2 Chr. 36; Jer. 25: 1 f; 46: 2 ff.) relate the events without mentioning this siege. There are too many uncertainties about the chronology of the last twenty years of Judaean history to permit this date to be labelled erroneous; it is probably late in 605 B.C. See further *EQ*, 49 (1977), pp. 67 ff. **Nebuchadnezzar**, Babylonian *Nabukudurru-uṣur*, shows an inner-Heb. shift from *r* to *n*. **2.** A city that capitulated was not harshly treated; tribute and hostages were taken, an oath of loyalty and an annual tax imposed. Jehoiakim remained king. Dedication of some tribute to the victor's patron god was customary, so also was the adoption of high-born hostages into the royal entourage. **Shinar:** (2 mg) a name for Babylonia current in the second millennium B.C., the normal term in Heb. before the rise of Nebuchadnezzar's empire; cf. Jos. 7: 25; Isa. 11: 11. **3. Ashpenaz, chief of his court officials:** the name has not yet received satisfactory explanation. His status may be taken literally here, he was the major-domo (in other passages a general meaning 'officer' is required, notably Gen. 39: 1). **nobility** Heb. *partemîm* is the first of nineteen Old Persian loan-words in the book; for details see Kitchen in *Notes*, pp. 37 ff. **4. young men without any physical defect:** their age is not given, but their careers suggest they were twelve or thirteen years old at least, the flower of Judah's next generation. Their physical perfection was a gift from birth, its maintenance their responsibility. **Chaldaeans** (mg): Assyrian inscriptions from the ninth century B.C. onwards record wars with Chaldaeans in southern Babylonia and show them struggling for control of Babylon itself. Later in the eighth century Merodach-Baladan was a Chaldaean chief who held Babylon for a few years (cf. 2 Kg. 20: 12 ff.) and it was a descendant of his, Nebuchadnezzar's father, Nabopolassar, who finally overthrew Assyria (612 B.C.). Information about the Chaldaeans is very meagre; the name occurs rarely, for the people belonged to several tribes and were usually described thus, just as Hebrews are more often 'of the tribe of Judah' than 'the

Israelite'. They were connected with the Aramaeans and spoke the same language, or a very similar one. In Dan. the name is used less of the people (5: 30; 9: 1) than of a class amongst the wise men (see 2: 2, 4, 10, 13; 3: 27). It may be that the 'national' name was applied to particularly distinguished men, somewhat in the way of Jn 1: 47; it is not applied directly to Daniel. The Greek historian Herodotus gave Chaldaeans the specialized sense 'wise men' in his *Histories* written about 440 B.C. (i. 181 ff.) by which time any political value had faded. This need not mean the use in Dan. is anachronistic; Herodotus being our earliest known source outside Dan. does not supply an upper limit. The same author does supply a partial analogy in the Magi, a Median tribe by origin, giving its name to a caste of wise men, dream-interpreters, and priests (i. 101; vii. 37, etc.). See further *EQ*, 49, pp. 69 ff. **language and literature:** Aramaic was the common tongue (see on 2: 4), probably even in the court of Babylon but learned men and conservative scribal tradition kept the ancient Babylonian language and cuneiform script alive until the first century A.D. The young Judaeans may have learnt both in their undergraduate course; their education was intended to fit them for the royal service. That Jews should undergo such treatment may have been distasteful, but these men had no alternative, like Joseph, and duly showed how the faith could be maintained in adverse circumstances. **5. assigned them a daily amount:** Babylon's bureaucracy was highly organized; similar rations for a few foreigners in the vast court, including eastern Greeks, Persians, Egyptians, and Jehoiachin king of Judah, are listed on clay tablets surviving from the archives (*DOTT*, pp. 84 ff.), though only after years of captivity was Jehoiachin raised to eat the king's fare fed to Daniel from the first (2 Kg. 25: 27 ff.). **to enter the king's service:** cf. v. 19; the new graduates were to join the king's permanent retinue, a large body, highly privileged, but totally dependent upon the royal whim. **6. Among these:** the scene has been set for the heroes to be introduced. **Daniel:** 'God has judged', a name known from other ancient texts, but any connection with the man of Ezek. 14: 14, 20; 28: 3; Jubilees 4: 20, or much earlier texts from Ugarit is wholly speculative. **Hananiah:** 'the Lord has been gracious'. **Mishael:** 'who is what God is?' **Azariah:** 'the Lord has helped'. **7.** Re-naming avoided the inconvenience of varied foreign names, helped to unify the mixed court, and displayed Babylonian lordship (cf. Gen. 41: 45; 2 Kg. 23: 34; 24: 17). The Babylonian names stand in the stories involving Nebuchadnezzar and Belshazzar especially, otherwise the narrator prefers the Hebrew. These names have defied explanation for a century; now it can be seen they are satisfactory Babylonian forms (details in P. R. Berger, *Zeitschrift für Assyriologie* 64. (1975), pp. 224 ff., 232 f.). **Belteshazzar:** *Bēlet-sharru-uṣur* 'O Lady, protect the king', the Lady being the wife of Marduk, god of Babylon, cf. 4: 8. **Shadrach:** *Shūdurāku* 'I am very fearful (of a god)'. **Meshach:** *Mēshāku* 'I am of no account'. **Abednego:** probably an Aramaic equivalent of a Babylonian name, 'Servant of the shining one'. **8. defile himself:** by consuming food prepared regardless of the Israelite regulations, likely to include meats there declared unclean (*e.g.* pig), possibly associated with pagan rituals. Wines were named after the producing regions, and could be enriched with honey or spices. **9.** Daniel's resolve was recognized by God for its pure motive, so that his extraordinary request won a reasonable reply. **10. looking worse:** the word is that describing the pharaoh's men in Gen. 40: 6, physical state reflecting unrest. The chief eunuch could be suspected of misappropriating the king's bounty. **11. the guard:** a title, not a name as AV. Presumably this man found he could carry out the test without involving his superior. **12. vegetables:** lit. 'seeds', grains of barley, etc., boiled or roasted, AV 'pulse', with high nutritional value, still a staple of Near Eastern meals. **ten days:** effects of a rich diet would show in the skin of the face and general alertness or sluggishness of demeanour. **15.** Fatness indicates sufficiency and prosperity throughout the OT. Was Daniel inspired to venture the test? Did he simply take a risk in faith? We are left to decide for ourselves. **17.** The faithfulness of the four friends God rewarded with first class honours, fitting the men for any aspect of government. Daniel's special subject had a history reaching back to Joseph's age and beyond, for dreams were believed to be a means of supernatural communication. **20. magicians:** Heb. uses the word from Gen. 41; Exod. 7, 8, 9, that has an Egyptian origin but became domiciled in Babylonia; **enchanters** is a Babylonian word, specifically 'exorcists'. Both words denote those who trade in supposed control or knowledge of the unknown, universal and continuing, condemned by biblical law (Lev. 19: 31; 20: 6, etc.). **21. Daniel remained there until the first year of king Cyrus:** shows Daniel's career spanned the entire period of the Exile in Babylon; in fact 10: 1 tells he was active in Cyrus' third year.

II. NEBUCHADNEZZAR'S FORGOTTEN DREAM (2: 1–49)
i. The frustrated tyrant (2: 1–13)
1. second year: 603 B.C. If Daniel was deported in 605 B.C., that was counted as Nebuchadnezzar's accession year in Babylonia, so that his second year would be Daniel's third in

exile. **he could not sleep:** suddenly awakened by a vivid dream, the superstitious king demanded an immediate explanation. **2. sorcerers and astrologers:** (mg Chaldaeans) extends 1: 20; the listing of the king's academic corps underlines their prominence, revealed equally in their surviving writings. **4.** The address, and all that follows to the end of ch. 7, is written in Aramaic, not Hebrew (see Introduction, 'The Languages of Daniel'.) This change is noted by the words **in Aramaic** after 'answered the king', added, it is thought, as a warning to readers and copyists. Aramaic was written with ink on papyrus or parchment in Babylonia, substances that have rotted in the damp soil, so examples of the language from Nebuchadnezzar's capital are solely brief notes scratched on more durable surfaces. They suffice to prove the widespread use of Aramaic there. **live forever:** the common prayer for a monarch's life in the OT from David onward (1 Kg. 1: 31). **interpret:** Aram. *pešar*, implies a solution inaccessible to most; in Daniel it is often God-given, and applied to mysteries that normal skills cannot unravel, as in 2: 30; 4: 9. Later the Heb. form of the word was employed by the men of Qumran in their commentaries on Scripture, explaining it in the light of current events (see F. F. Bruce, *Biblical Exegesis in the Qumran Texts*, London, 1960). **5.** Nebuchadnezzar demanded satisfaction for the privileges enjoyed by his scholars; anything he wanted to know they should be able to tell him. He may have pretended, or he may have really forgotten the dream, only knowing he had dreamt vividly, an experience shared by many. **This is what I have firmly decided** takes an unusual word as an Old Persian loan meaning 'decided' now attested in ancient texts, hence the difference from AV. **cut into pieces . . . gifts and rewards** are the extremes typical of absolute rulers, seen again in 3: 29; 5: 7, now displaying the king's panic before his dream's menacing shadow. His impatience (8, 9) is a further sign of his fright. **10, 11.** Babylonian learning rested upon observed facts and events, so affording no means to satisfy the king since he could not, or would not, furnish the basic data. Their reply is definite, the wise men were inadequately qualified, their spells could not persuade their gods to reveal the dream. **12, 13.** The frustrated or defrauded king had no compunction; the formal order was issued for their execution forthwith. All the wise men were condemned, not only the unsuccessful ones who had faced the king.

ii. Daniel's wisdom (2: 14–18)
Daniel's demeanour saved him from instant death. Clearly a rota-system or other business allowed him and his friends to be absent from court and unaware of the crisis. As he had with the chief eunuch (1: 9), so Daniel gained the

good-will of the king's captain. By now, may it be supposed, the king had calmed his agitation, for he received Daniel and gave him the period of grace he sought. In his volatile state, Nebuchadnezzar may not have intended Daniel to be killed also. Doubtless all the wise men were reduced to prayer; Daniel and his friends were in the same extremity, but, like Elijah, they worshipped a deity they knew had set them where they were, and was able to bestow the mercy of reprieve by revealing the **mystery** (see on v. 4).

iii. Daniel's worship (2: 19–23)
The words of Daniel's hymn were apposite in every phrase. Honoured by the king for his learning, and about to be richly rewarded, he proclaims God's name to be honoured supremely as the spring of wisdom, controller of epochs, dynasties, and monarchs, omniscient, the one who supplies His own as they have need. **19. God of heaven** denotes Israel's God particularly in the post-exilic writings, sometimes with 'and of earth' added, identifying Him by His universality and transcendence, avoiding local ties that might appear to limit Him.

iv. Daniel declares the dream (2: 24–35)
24. Although he had had access to the king shortly before (v. 16), Daniel now made his approach through the captain of the guard, delaying him in his executions, and enabling the man whom the king might be expected to trust the most to introduce him for this ticklish matter. **26.** A note of desperate hope may be detected in the king's question as the brilliant parvenu stands before him. **27.** Daniel's reply is in keeping with his own attitude, and the attitude of his pagan colleagues; the problem exceeded human skill. **28. There is a God in heaven** gently leads the king to the thought of a Being different from his own gods. **what will happen in days to come:** the question every man wants answered at some time in his life was answered remarkably for the king. Why should God unroll future history for Nebuchadnezzar? His reaction, encouraging for all faithful Jews in Babylonia, was one reason. Another was provision in the written record of a prophecy that could be followed by future generations. Within **days to come** is included the future from that time until a decisive moment, *e.g.* the Assyrian conquest in Num. 24: 14–24; Israel's rebellion in Dt. 29: 39; here the establishment of the divine kingdom. **29.** In his second year, already a military victor, monarch of a large realm, Nebuchadnezzar understandably had his next years in mind, planning and scheming for the greater glory of Babylon's gods and king. The dream intruded upon a receptive mind. Daniel carefully emphasized his own human inability and assured the king he would give him the explanation for his benefit, not for his own glory. **31–35.** The dream was straightforward, but fearful. Was Nebuchadnezzar portrayed, a figure to be toppled? Was he the stone? His anxiety was natural. The image of exaggerated size is a typical dream phenomenon; no identification need be sought in an idol at Babylon. Only the **feet partly of iron and partly of baked clay** cause slight difficulty in understanding the sight. Most probably the feet were moulded in pottery (the precise meaning of **baked clay**) upon an iron core or skeleton which keyed into the legs, in the way reinforced concrete buildings are erected. As Babylonians and Hebrews alike had no concept of 'natural' events, **a rock cut out but not by human hands** would be heaven-sent. For the **chaff** cf. Ps. 1: 4, etc.

v. Daniel interprets the dream (2: 36–45)
The interpretation gives a meaning to each part, yet with notably little elaboration, individual features such as eyes, hands, are not isolated. **36. we will interpret:** Montgomery aptly compared 'Paul's "we" (*e.g.* 2 Cor. 1: 6), used with a certain humility; the present message was not Dan.'s own'. However, it was expressed by Daniel, and he chose the courtly words of v. 37, modelled on royal etiquette, substituting emphatically **the God of heaven** where pagan deities would have been named by the other wise men. **37. king of kings** continued to be the title of the Persian monarch until modern times; it was given prominence by the Achaemenid rulers, but they borrowed it from their predecessors, Assyrian and other kings bearing it centuries before. **ruler over them all** would represent Nebuchadnezzar's claim, even if not strictly correct, while the inclusion of animals and birds alludes to the supreme power of those kings so graphically illustrated in the Assyrian hunting reliefs. To Daniel there may have come the thought of Gen. 1: 28 also, cf. Jer. 27: 6; 28: 14. **38. head of gold:** looking back, Babylon appears less impressive than the following Persian Empire in territorial extent and length of life. In this context no other portrayal of the current power was possible, because Nebuchadnezzar would hardly regard himself as inferior to any previous king, nor favour hints of any successor painted brighter. If he felt flattered, Daniel taught him his great majesty came from the same God as his dream. **39. another kingdom:** no names were told to Nebuchadnezzar, leaving the field open for speculation ever since! How it would be **inferior** is unknown. **a third kingdom** is characterized by its universality, **a fourth kingdom** by its violence and its diversity, a composite state, attempting unity through intermarriage, and failing thereby. In the structure of the dream-image each section fits to the next so that historical explanations

may not assume a hiatus between one kingdom and the next. While the stages descend from greatest to least in monetary value, they ascend in strength, a factor to be weighed in interpreting the figure. Following Nebuchadnezzar's empire came the Persian (see on 5: 30 and Introduction, 'Daniel and History') which is, therefore, the second **kingdom**. Many who hold the view that all of Daniel's prophecies culminate with Antiochus Epiphanes are forced to interpose a Median state at this juncture, which cannot be substantiated (see Introduction, 'Daniel and History'). Alexander the Great's empire provides the **third kingdom**, its descendants eventually giving way to the **fourth**, Rome. This is the view traditionally held in the Christian Church. Arguing that all Daniel's prophecies have the same references, gives the **third kingdom** to Persia and the **fourth** to Alexander or the **third** to Alexander and the **fourth** to his successors. (The description of the fourth can be suited to Rome or to Alexander.) The **rock** is then 'the kingdom of God', indeterminate. On the traditional view then, as Paul said of another stone, 'the Rock was Christ' (1 C. 10: 4) whose advent introduced a new kingdom truly universal and enduring. **45.** Daniel's speech ended as it had begun with a reminder of the Author of the vision, **The great God**, and the certainty of fulfilment. There were no conditions.

vi. Daniel's reward (2: 46–49)

46. The king's reaction showed his relief, and the rightness of Daniel's understanding. If he had forgotten his dream, Daniel brought it back to mind; if he was pretending, Daniel passed the test. Nebuchadnezzar's homage to Daniel has worried commentators for the human, and pious, Daniel seems to be given divine honours. Jerome supposed the king was adoring the God whom he knew through Daniel, and Young felt certain Daniel 'would not have taken to himself honor which belonged to God alone'. Valid as these observations may be, there are indications that acts reserved for divine worship in Hebrew and Christian practice were directed to exalted persons in Babylonia and Persia. Nebuchadnezzar's relief may easily have led him to as exaggerated an attitude as his earlier fury. **47.** Daniel had told the king how powerful and exalted was his God; now Nebuchadnezzar acknowledged Him as the source of Daniel's insight. He hailed Him as greatest of the gods without becoming a monotheist. Then he rewarded Daniel as he had promised, and Daniel ensured his friends who had prayed with him shared. Governorships brought great wealth in taxes, whilst carrying responsibilities. By delegating those, Daniel could retain his influential place in the king's cabinet. **48. in charge of all its wise men** has been assailed as an impossible position for a faithful Jew, along with Daniel's title 'chief of the magicians' in 4: 9. Yet his charge need not implicate him in his subordinates' activities; his own prowess in the field had been proved. Daniel's friends appear quite naturally to share his triumph. Their presence also eases the transition to ch. 3 where they are prominent and Daniel entirely absent.

III. THE IMAGE AND THE GODLY THREE (3: 1–30)

i. Nebuchadnezzar's image (3: 1–7)

Improvement of old statues or provision of new ones was a regular feature of kingly duties. Which god was honoured by this statue is unknown, no trace of it survives outside this chapter; it is unlikely that the king was represented by it. Some have suggested that the dream of ch. 2 induced Nebuchadnezzar to erect this colossus. Contrariwise, the idea already growing in the king's intentions may have precipitated the dream. **ninety feet high and nine feet wide** (27.5 by 2.75 metres). Whatever figure was created may have stood upon a plinth raising it so far. Golden statues frequently stood within temples, ancient texts describe many. The gold was overlaid upon a core of baser material (cf. Isa. 40: 18 ff.). Nebuchadnezzar tells of the gold he lavished upon the shrines of Babylon, and Herodotus describes their rich equipment and large statues (i. 183). **Dura:** an unknown site in the flat river land of Babylonia, where the monument would be visible from afar, catching the sunlight. **2. summoned:** to display the king's achievements and ensure the loyalty of his officials. Listing titles was a part of the narrative style (cf. 2: 2) preserved in Babylonian writings also. There is a list of Nebuchadnezzar's court extant, found in Babylon (*ANET*, pp. 307 f.). Half of the eight titles are Old Persian words (satraps, advisers, treasurers, judges), two Assyrian assimilated into Aramaic (prefects, governors), two Aramaic (magistrates, officials). The sonorous list is repeated for literary effect in v. 3 and partly in 27, as the musical instruments are repeated in vv. 5, 7, 15. **4. the herald:** an indispensable member of any court before the days of mass communication. As in Est. 3: 12, etc. care was taken to convey the decree to everyone. **5.** Music was an essential for ancient temples and palaces. Singers and players were drawn from far and near, willingly or as tribute or captives. Of the six instruments in Nebuchadnezzar's orchestra, three have Greek names, zither, harp, pipes (*qîtros, psantērîn, sūmponyā*). Since Greeks were certainly present in Nebuchadnezzar's Babylon (see on 1: 5 and Introduction, 'The Languages of Daniel'), these words are not 'solid philological evidence for the reflection of Hellenic civilization in Dan.' (Montgomery). Although no example of *sūmponyā* as a musical instrument occurs in Gk. sources prior to the second century B.C., it is common earlier in other musical senses (harmony, certain groups of notes), and could be so used here (see T. C. Mitchell and R. Joyce in *Notes . . .* , and J. Rimmer and T. C. Mitchell, *Ancient Musical Instruments of Western Asia in the British Museum*, London, 1969). **6. furnace:** the punishment is known from rare references in cuneiform legal texts (cf. *ANET*³, pp. 627 f.). Between the Tigris and Euphrates around Babylon were many brickfields, some with kilns (although the majority of bricks were simply sun-baked), providing a ready mode of execution for the king's enemies.

ii. The three confident friends (3: 8–18)
8. denounced: from jealousy, a common fate for the honest, without satisfactory means of refutation for the charge was not untrue. **10. decree:** a different word from the Persian *dāt* of 2: 9 ff.; 6: 5 ff., possibly its Aram. synonym. **12. some Jews:** lit. 'men of Judah', the foreign race helps to build a picture of disaffection. **pay no attention to you:** stress is laid on the king's goodness to the three and their disloyalty as well as their religious stance; they are portrayed as rejecting Nebuchadnezzar's values. **13.** These false accusations touch the king's weak point, yet he would not punish the men unheard. If true, such defiance would be worth seeing, and its punishment a healthy public spectacle. His question concentrated on the religious aspect (neither here nor in v. 18 is the accusation 'pay no attention to you' repeated) and he still offered a chance for the accused to prove their loyalty, under duress. **Then what god** echoes the taunts of Sennacherib's Rabshakeh (2 Kg. 18: 32–35), pride that insidiously claims the highly successful. **16–18.** In answer the three friends admitted they had no defence; they trusted themselves wholly to their God. Verses 17, 18, are better rendered: 'If our God whom we serve is able to save us, he will save us . . . but if not, let it be known to you . . .' as RVmg, responding to the king's question of v. 15 (see P. W. Coxon, *VT* 26 (1976), pp. 400–409). The faith of the three would not let them **serve** the Babylonian's **gods or worship the image of gold** even if their God was not willing to intervene.

iii. Out of the flames (3: 19–30)
Determined defiance, as he saw it, inevitably goaded Nebuchadnezzar to the peak of fury. To display the tyrant's absolute power the fire was stoked to maximum heat, not a trace should be left of the insolent rebels, not even identifiable ashes. (Burning human remains was reprehensible, Am. 2: 1.) **21.** The three were bound by the strongest guards as a part of the exhibition. Apparently the friends were wearing court dress; the terms are obscure,

probably all three are Persian. **24, 25.** Neither the tyrant nor his furnace proved so powerful as he had supposed; the seemingly groundless hope expressed by the three (v. 17) was vindicated. Nebuchadnezzar could see into the furnace through a stoke-hole or vent at the side, whereas the three had been thrown in through an upper opening whence the heat shot out to kill their guards. Nebuchadnezzar alone saw the fourth figure, one of clearly supernatural form. His words **a son of the gods** do not disclose how recognition was made. If the Aram. can be taken as equivalent to the Heb. 'son(s) of god(s)', this was a member of the heavenly court (Job 1: 6, etc.), as the king's account states (28). A pre-incarnate appearance of Christ is probably not to be found here; the NT makes no attempt at such an identification (contrast Isa. 6: 1 in Jn 12: 41). **26. Most High God:** Nebuchadnezzar's perception of a personal power far above any he or his gods could show. Even as he confessed, he remained nonetheless a polytheist, cleaving to the gods he had known from infancy rather than devote himself to the One newly introduced. **27.** God's protection extended to the last hair and thread of the three, testimony to His absolute power and control of natural forces (contrast the fate of the king's men, v. 22). **28, 29.** The faith the three held so tenaciously in the teeth of the tyrant's threats has tribute from the tyrant himself. Henceforth theirs was a permitted and protected religion. So the faith of the few benefited many.

IV. NEBUCHADNEZZAR'S MADNESS (4: 1–37)
In a letter to his subjects Nebuchadnezzar explains why he had decided to worship the God of a small, conquered, deported nation (1–3). Verses 19–33 are third person narrative, contrasting with the first person of the opening and closing verses; the shift may have been designed for dramatic effect.
i. The King's Dream (4: 4–18)
When all was well another portentous dream agitated the king, he could recall this one, but his experts were baffled again. As a high officer of state, Daniel was called last, addressed under his Babylonian name by the king (also vv. 9, 18, 19); cf. 1: 7 for the proud **after the name of my god . . . spirit of the holy gods:** 'inspired'; the plural 'gods' is probably correct. **10–12.** Previously a huge image, now a great tree was central, in either case standing for the king himself. A luxuriant tree symbolized prosperity (cf. Ps. 1: 3), attracting man and beast for shelter and rest. **13. a messenger, a holy one:** v. 17 shows he was an agent of godhead, heavenly reflection of earthly kings' information services as in Zech. 1: 10; 3: 10, with power to act upon his observations. **14.**

The sentence was severe, yet not fatal, as a stump remained; cf. Isa. 6: 13. **bound** . . . evokes varied explanations. If the personific-ation of the next sentence has begun, the mental restraints of madness could be meant; if the tree continues, a protection against damage, or a device to stunt growth. No doubt of the sig-nificance was left with the following words **Let him be drenched . . .** , hence the king's alarm. **16. seven times:** Aram. for 'times' means 'a specific period', in this case undefined; nothing favours years (cf. mg.) over seasons or any other measurement. **17. that the living may know** touches the wider effect, brought about by the king deciding to circulate this account. No-one could know without a reliable interpretation.

ii. Interpretation (4: 19–27)
The hesitation now came from Daniel as he saw the alarming message of the dream. **19.** He replied to the king's courtly encouragement in approved style, hinting delicately at an un-favourable prognosis. **20, 21.** Daniel repeated the description, except for **from it every crea-ture was fed**, to give impact to his verdict. **you, O king. 22–26.** There is some conven-tional flattery in the characterization (cf. 2: 38), for Nebuchadnezzar was aware of Medes in the east and Greeks in the west outside his domain. Great as he was, the king was subject to the **decree of the Most High.** The tree was a figure; the metamorphosis of the man was to be real. **until you acknowledge . . . your kingdom will be restored:** the experience would be effective, unpleasant, but essential lest the king's pride soon revive, and carrying the promise of security afterwards. **Heaven rules** is the oldest example of this surrogate for God widely employed later, *e.g.* Lk. 15: 18. **27.** The interpretation ended with an exhortation to behave as kings were expected to do, in fact as Nebuchadnezzar claimed he did in his inscriptions. **your prosperity will continue** is best understood to refer to the time after the king recognized the Most High, with Young, rather than a repentance that might cause the decree to be rescinded. Porteous observes Ne-buchadnezzar 'has been given the main truth he has to learn without any interpretation, but a general truth has little influence until it is appropriated by the individual. Nbk. must first learn humility before he can make the general truth of God's sovereignty truly his own.'

iii. Fulfilment (4: 28–37)
29. Twelve months had seen no change of outlook. With the evidence of his power at his feet, the king spoke words reminiscent of those stamped upon thousands of bricks in his build-ings and in longer, boastful inscriptions. At the peak of his pride he was reminded of the prophecy. **31. a voice came from heaven:** there was no human intermediary. **33. what**

had been said . . . was fulfilled: the master of men preferred the posture of man's servants, the beasts; all personal care or interest was gone. The king lived in the open country away from his fellows (cf. Job 39: 5–8), suffering from an illness known to medicine as lycan-thropy, a form of schizophrenia. The Baby-lonians thought such behaviour a sign of divine anger. **34.** The malady lasted for the set time and had its intended effect, the king prayed to God and was restored to sanity, recognition of God's pre-eminence being the only path to sanity for any man. Nebuchadnezzar's praise of God enlarges upon his opening words: God's rule is not limited by death, nor His wishes thwarted by His subjects. **36.** Once he was seen to be in his right mind, improved, indeed, the nobles were eager for audience, his reputation was enhanced. **37.** All the purpose of the illness was completed with the king's final declar-ation. **the King of heaven** is unique in the OT, though a set title of Babylonian gods, the gods whose power had never been felt in such a way.

V. BELSHAZZAR'S FEAST (5: 1–31)
i. The apparition (5: 1–12)
1. King Belshazzar: see Introduction, 'Daniel and History: ii'. **a thousand of his nobles:** several ancient kings record enormous num-bers of guests on special occasions. **wine:** cf. 1: 8. Royal bounty was unstinted, when the wine was flowing Belshazzar ordered a more lavish display. The Judaean temple treasures may have excited feelings of pride: Babylon, her gods and her kings, were the victors. **3. gold goblets:** RSV has 'gold and silver' follow-ing Vulg. and one Gk. version, but this is not essential. What the king, his lords, and his women did with the plate was blasphemous in Jewish eyes, more so if there was any religious element in the banquet. *The Writing on the Wall.* Babylonian palaces had walls richly decorated with polychrome tiles or simply whitewashed. Against the latter the fingers would show sharply in the lamp-light. Any Babylonian would have been disturbed at an ominous sign; the tipsy Belshazzar was far more unnerved than Nebuchadnezzar had been and his prom-ises more exaggerated. Purple cloaks and golden necklets were long-standing signs of rank. **7. the third highest ruler:** a similar title occurs in Assyrian and Babylonian for a military functionary of no high status; the the-ory that Belshazzar could only bestow third place because he himself was second to his father Nabonidus may be correct. **8.** The wise men **could not read the writing**, that is, understand or make sense of it; the words Daniel read were ordinary Aramaic (see at v. 25). **9.** Thus the king's plight worsened; to his fevered mind so extraordinary an event must

have a significance. **10.** The queen's arrival reduced his distress. Her words, and the presence of Belshazzar's wives (vv. 2, 3), suggest she was the queen-mother (cf. mg.), a lady receiving deep respect. She carefully introduced Daniel, who had, perhaps, retired from court for a while (8: 27 shows him active a decade before). She had seen him in action, spoke of his qualities from experience. She spoke of him by his native name, maybe to avoid confusion with the king's name, maybe as an acknowledgement of his God's superiority. **King Nebuchadnezzar, your father:** see Introduction, 'Daniel and History: ii'.

ii. The Interpretation (5: 12–28)

Belshazzar greeted Daniel in a way which can be called 'gracious' (Montgomery), or 'haughty' (Young). He showed awareness of his past and concern with nothing but his present problem. Daniel replied with courtesy and courage, refusing the reward to show his integrity and place himself in a better position to denounce the king. Belshazzar should have studied the recent history of Babylon; he might have learnt how even the magnificent despot Nebuchadnezzar owed all his glory to God Most High. Verse 19 stands in contrast with 4: 34, 35. **20.** In ch. 4 the reason for Nebuchadnezzar's affliction is hinted; for Belshazzar it is plainly stated. Aware as Belshazzar was of his predecessor's suffering, he had not taken the lesson to heart, he had behaved quite perversely. The Most High is **the God who holds in his hand your life and all your ways**. Daniel's scorn for Babylon's powerless idols follows consistent OT teaching about the foolish paradox of men worshipping their own creations. **24. Therefore he sent the hand:** at the moment Belshazzar's presumption reached its self-exalting peak (cf. 4: 31). **25. this is the inscription:** Daniel read the signs as Aramaic words for units of weight or currency, 'a mina, a mina, a shekel, and fractions'. If the wise men could not read them, it may be they were abbreviations like £. s. d. (examples are extant from early times). These units Daniel interpreted by punning, a favourite device among Babylonian scholars. **28. peres** is grammatical singular of **parsin**. Note: Mede(s) always stand before Persian(s) in Dan.; cf. Introduction, 'Daniel and History: iii'.

iii. Rewards (5: 29–31)

29. Satisfied with the solution, despite the note of doom, Belshazzar repeated his promise to honour the interpreter. No time had been revealed; he was unaware he would not see the dawn. **30. That very night Belshazzar the king of the Babylonians was slain:** the verdict was final, Belshazzar's sin counted more gravely than Nebuchadnezzar's for he failed to follow the lessons he knew, and mocked the God of Jerusalem. Gk. writers tell how Persian

forces eventually captured Babylon by diverting the Euphrates and wading up its bed through the massive defences, taking the defenders by surprise as they feasted (Herodotus, i. 191). A Babylonian text gives the date October 12, 539 B.C. (Verse 31 belongs with ch. 6, of which indeed it is the first verse in the Hebrew Bible.)

VI. DANIEL IN THE LIONS' DEN (6: 1–28)

i. A New Administration (5: 31–6: 5)

5: 31. Darius the Mede remains a problematic figure, see Introduction, 'Daniel and History: iv'. Other sources name Cyrus as the conqueror of Babylon, giving his age as about **sixty-two** years. **6: 1.** The **hundred and twenty satraps** cause a problem, too, for the number given by Persian and Greek records is between twenty and thirty. Some Greek writers apply the term loosely to high officers in general, a usage some find here, comparing the 127 provinces of Est. 1: 1, and noting their place after 'prefects' in v. 7. Nothing is known of Cyrus's administration in detail. **2. three administrators:** essential to oversee so large a body. **3–5.** Daniel's association with the ousted regime was outweighed by his integrity and unusual abilities in the king's eyes, understandably arousing the jealousy of the other officers. Their only avenue of attack lay in his personal belief, called **the law of his God**, 'law' being the word discussed at v. 8.

ii. The Plot (6: 6–9)

Persian rule fostered religions within its bounds, the dynasty worshipping Ahuramazda in the way of Zoroaster (present-day descendants are the Parsees). The king had priestly functions by virtue of his office; great authority would be required to upset the norm. Therefore Daniel's enemies moved cunningly. They would flatter the king by preventing anyone from making a request except through him, causing a demonstration of his authority in every sphere; his delegates would be powerless, and all priests, the king being the only intermediary with heaven. A limit of thirty days would be time enough for the plotters, and make the proposal more acceptable to the king; a new custom was not being introduced. For that time the decree should be binding **in accordance with the laws of the Medes and Persians, which cannot be repealed**. Use of a Persian word for 'law', *dat*, may imply a new concept, perhaps this irreversible quality; it has already been used of God's law (v. 5) and Nebuchadnezzar's decree (2: 9, etc.), and is regularly employed in Ezra and Esther. Recently the term has been found in an Aramaic inscription whereby the satrap of Lycia established a new cult, giving its provisions the status of law.

iii. The Execution (6: 10–18)

Uncowed, Daniel continued his daily devotions of prayer and praise. His enemies witnessed him and made their accusation, suppressing all his good points, stressing his foreign, subject origin. Darius found them inflexible. Commentators quote the account of Darius III who sentenced a man to death: 'immediately he repented and blamed himself as having greatly erred, but it was not possible to undo what was done by royal authority' (Diodorus Siculus, *Histories* 17.30). All the king could do was hope the Object of Daniel's faith would prove worthy. **16. the lions' den:** the animals were kept for the kings to chase in their parks and kill, symbolizing their royal power. The den is likely to have been a cavern with a small opening in the roof for feeding, etc., and a trap at a lower level for the lions' egress. **A stone . . . sealed:** the king and his lords were involved so neither party could interfere.

iv. The Vindication (6: 19–28)

Darius' affection for Daniel dominated him; were he safe it could only be through the power of **the living God. 21.** Daniel's courtly reply is almost ironic: Daniel lived despite the edict because his God had intervened, only He could give the living long life! **22. I was found innocent:** he was in no way disloyal to the king, refusing obedience to a wrong order in fact served the king well. **24.** The accusers were punished in the way they had devised for Daniel. **the men** may be all or some of the 120 satraps; **along with their wives, and children** conforms with recorded Persian practice; the family is the most likely to profit from a criminal's activities, and to emulate him (cf. Est. 9: 7–10; Jos. 7: 24–26). **26, 27.** Darius's new decree echoes Nebuchadnezzar's in 4: 3, 34, 35, setting Daniel's God above all others on the basis of experience. **he endures** (Aram. *qayyām*) later became a common title for God in Jewish and Samaritan circles. Ironically, the Aram. word is related to the verb 'establish' used in vv. 8 and 15 of the royal edict that God had just overturned. **28. Darius . . . Cyrus** present a historical difficulty considered in Introduction, 'Daniel and History: iv', perhaps read with mg. 'the reign of Darius, that is, the reign of Cyrus the Persian'.

The Visions of Daniel (7: 1–12: 13)

Up to this point Daniel has been presented as the God-inspired interpreter of signs and dreams, henceforth he is the one who sees visions and needs interpretations. For Daniel the clues given in those interpretations may have been sufficient; the treatment of the book in the Christian Church shows they are far too slender for later readers to reach certainty on many points.

VII. THE FOUR BEASTS, THE JUDGMENT, AND THE KINGDOM (7: 1–28)

i. The four beasts (7: 1–8)

1. The date places this vision after the death of Nebuchadnezzar, still within the era of Babylon, about 553 B.C. **He wrote down the substance of his dream** realizing that its message would have relevance beyond his lifetime. **2. the four winds** blew from the cardinal points of the compass, setting the sea in turmoil, so rousing the **beasts** from its depths. **the great sea** need not be identified. In ancient thought the sea and many of its creatures were hostile to order, and the Hebrews regarded both as unruly yet under God's control (*e.g.* Ps. 104: 6–9; 148: 7; Job 26: 12, 13). **3. Four great beasts:** fabulous beasts were commonplace in Babylonian religious poetry and art, whence they passed to Persia (notably as relief decoration on palace walls in Babylon, Susa, and Persepolis). A sea-monster mentioned several times in the OT as Rahab was used poetically to mean Egypt (*e.g.* Ps. 87: 4; Isa. 30: 7). That use is analogous to Daniel's for v. 17 informs **The four great beasts are four kingdoms**—or kingdoms personified in their rulers—**that will arise from the earth**. They were **each different from the others** in human estimation. **4. The first** was composite and suffered a change. If this beast stands for Babylon (the **will rise** of v. 17 cannot be pressed against this view; three of the states would still be future), the change may reflect the career of Nebuchadnezzar culminating in 4: 34 ff. **5. a second beast** in the act of conquest, devouring its prey and stepping out for more, spurred by the divine command. For some the bear is Media, the Persians for others, some who share the latter view identifying the **three ribs** with the kingdoms of Lydia, Babylon, and Egypt incorporated into the Persian Empire. **6. another . . . like a leopard** with strange differences! **Four wings** for maximum speed; **four heads** for universal extent. Support can be found in various references to fit the figure for Cyrus by those who see the bear as the Medes, and equally to fit it for Alexander the Great by those who take the bear as Persia. **7.** The **fourth beast** has its own introduction and is indescribable, **different**, no comparison could be made. Its nature was clear, fierce, powerful, destructive, resulting in the **ten horns** and the ultimate blasphemy. With **iron teeth it crushed and devoured**, echoing the style of the fourth part of the statue in ch. 1. Extending from it were the **ten horns**, and an eleventh, called **little** but seeming greater than its fellows (20). Its arrogance broke far beyond the divine limits so judgment had to be pronounced upon it. Until that crisis the horn was overcoming the saints, v. 21 adds, and it was that that could not be allowed to continue.

ii. The Judgment (7: 9–14)

9, 10. From the horror of the horned beast, Daniel was turned to the solemn splendour of the heavenly court. There sat one **Ancient of Days**, venerable, entirely pure (**white**), purging and consuming wrong (**fire**). Knowing all that had passed in history, he was qualified to judge the latest upstart as He had judged others before (Assyria, Isa. 10; Babylonia, Isa. 14, etc.). Judicial authority was displayed in the **river of fire**, and the requisite power in the innumerable **thousands** at His call. Beside the Judge were various **thrones set in place** (not 'cast down' as AV) for the principal attendants, cf. 3: 25. Before this court the books recording the deeds of the accused **were opened**. (Heavenly records of human activities are alluded to by many ancient writings, cf. Ps. 56: 8; Mal. 3: 16, also Exod. 32: 32 f.). **11.** Read 'Then I was watching from the sound of the great words . . . , I was watching until the beast was slain . . .' Nothing could distract the seer until the drama ended with the presumptuous punished in the **fire** of justice. **12.** Three beasts remained, powerless, for a set **time** (as in 4: 25).

13, 14. There before me was one like a son of man: contrasting with the beasts which were inherently hostile to God stood this visionary figure, like a human being. That is the meaning of **son of man**, as in Ezek. 2: 1 etc., similar to 'son of the gods' in 3: 25. Whereas Nebuchadnezzar seemed to see a heavenly person in the setting of his earthly judgment, Daniel saw a human being in the place of God's justice. This figure, however, came **with the clouds of heaven**. In all other passages within the OT, and outside, the clouds are an accompaniment of deity, though usually ridden upon or among. There is, then, a heavenly element beside the human. Whether some earthly achievement fitted a mortal for translation to appear before **the Ancient of Days**, or whether a celestial being donned human form is still debated. The investiture that followed is unique. By its style the kingdom plainly echoes the description of God's Kingdom in 4: 3, 34, 35; 5: 26, and especially 2: 44, yet also the kingdom of the saints with which it is identified (vv. 18, 27). Many interpret the son of man figure in the light of those last verses as a symbol of God's people, a human representative. Against this view stands indisputable evidence for a recognized messianic understanding of the passage from the NT (Mt. 26: 64; Mk 14: 62—barely two centuries after the book's composition on the late dating) and from Jewish writings a little later (where 'he of the clouds' is also a messianic title). Maintenance of this view in Judaism despite its adoption

by the Christians suggests it had ancient and authoritative status.

iii. Interpretations (7: 15–29)

15. Daniel's reaction was like Nebuchadnezzar's alarm and concern for the purpose of his vision. **16.** He found an interpreter whose first terse reply contained the basic clues. **the true meaning** or 'the certainty', as in 'True, O king', 3: 24. **18.** The people of God are to possess the realm entrusted to the 'one like a son of man' in vv. 13, 14. If he is to be understood as an individual, then the saints will be his loyal subjects. **The saints** are, literally, 'the holy ones' (Aram, *qaddīš*), a term rare outside this chapter (elsewhere in the equivalent Heb. form *qāḏōš*, pl. *qᵉḏōšīm* in 8: 24; Ps. 16: 3; 34: 10); the usual Heb. word rendered 'saint' is *ḥāsīd*, but this may have been unknown in Aramaic. **19–22.** Daniel's concern required more detailed response, since the fourth beast was so malignant. His second description enlarges at some points upon the first, see on vv. 7, 8 above. In **23–27** the fuller explanation is given.

The **fourth kingdom** is to be harsher and more extensive than the three before it. **ten kings will come from this kingdom** and **another . . . different** either as an integral part of it, or as a separate stage of the kingdom's existence (so Young and the dispensational school). (The division implied in the second view results rather from interpretations of other passages than from the text itself.) If the kingdom is Alexander's and the eleventh king Antiochus Epiphanes, it is all but impossible to count ten kings without including an assassin who never reached the throne (Heliodoros, chancellor of Seleucus IV) and the rightful heir whom Antiochus displaced, but who followed him, Demetrius Soter. If the kingdom be Rome, then Julius Caesar may be reckoned first, Titus eleventh, although it was his father Vespasian who **subdued three kings**, or at least succeeded in holding the throne they had failed to secure. For those who divide kingdom from kings, Rome is the former, the ten are rulers in ensuing or yet future centuries, the eleventh is Antichrist. Blaspheming and persecuting (**appears**), the eleventh will attempt to abolish established religious observances, but his rule is to be limited (v. 25 is parallel to vv. 20, 21). **25. a time** is the word noted at 4: 16; nothing prescribes a year, a month, a decade, or a day, it is a time determined by the Most High. **times** can be dual, 'two', or plural, as understood by LXX. The formulation here, like its Heb. equivalent in 12: 5, may be indefinite and symbolic, a first period followed by one twice as long or longer, the next expected increase being cut short. For a precise period, three and a half years, to be stated so obliquely, even in a visionary interpretation of a vision, appears more obscure than the rest of the book!

Most High is the word used in vv. 18, 22, 27, a form of intensity, a superlative more forceful than the term used in the second clause and other places. **27. the kingdoms . . . will be handed over . . . to the saints . . . :** in historical interpretations this kingdom has to be treated as spiritual; by futurists it can be understood in the same way, commencing with the Second Advent, or as the 'millennial reign' of Christ and His church on earth. **28.** The vision was completed, leaving Daniel perturbed, with a deep impression that would constantly return to his mind.

VIII. THE TWO BEASTS AND THE DREADFUL HORN (8: 1–27)
i. The Two Beasts (8: 1–8)
After two years Daniel received a vision with a more precise interpretation. The time was significant: **the third year of King Belshazzar's reign**, 550–49 B.C., saw Cyrus the Persian subjugate Media. Daniel viewed this and subsequent happenings from one of the Persian capitals, **Susa**, ancient metropolis of Elam standing amid streams and canals, the chief being the **Ulai** (now Sha'ur). **3, 4. a ram with two horns:** according to v. 20 symbolic of the kings of Media and Persia, noticeably coupled. From Daniel's viewpoint the supplanting Persians appeared invincible, although Cyrus was eventually killed in battle far to the east. **4. He did as he pleased** is ever the mark of the tyrant and the reason for judgment. **5–8. the goat:** distinguished by a single large horn, portrayed the unparalleled career of Alexander the Great, cf. v. 21, from his obscure beginning in Macedon through his triumphs in Egypt, Babylon, Persia, and India, to his inglorious end drunk with power and pleasure. His **great rage . . .** attacking **furiously** (or 'embitteredly') could be understood as a reflection of Alexander's initial crusading zeal to 'liberate' and Hellenize the world, fusing Greek and Persian. He was succeeded by four of his Greek generals (**from his nation**, 22), each ruling a section of his empire: Cassander in Macedonia, Lysimachus in Thrace and Asia Minor, Seleucus in Syria, Mesopotamia and Persia, Ptolemy in Egypt. 'Notable horns' some of these were, yet they are justifiably described as **not having the same power** (22).
ii. The Little Horn (8: 9–14)
Another horn which started small came **out of one of them**, the kingdoms not the individuals, in fact the Seleucid state of Syria. This was Antiochus Epiphanes, and could refer to the fact that he was not the heir. (RSV and most commentators read 'a little horn' by a slight alteration, yielding a parallel to the Aram. expression in 7: 8). Verse 23 places his rise **in the latter part** of the four kingdoms, and, indeed, shortly after the time of Antiochus, the eastern

part of Alexander's empire reverted to local rule, Greece and Asia Minor were dominated by Rome, Syria and Egypt grew weaker and eventually fell under the same sway. **grew in power:** Antiochus campaigned with some success against Egypt, in Persia, and, most important for Daniel, against Judaea **the Beautiful** ('Land' is supplied on the basis of 11: 16, 41). His activity there is the focus of the next verses. **10. It grew . . .** finds explanation in v. 24, **He will destroy . . . the holy people**, that is, the pious of Israel. **11.** As others before, so this figure **set itself up to be as great as the Prince of the host** who is God Himself, **Prince of princes** in v. 25. The presumption displayed itself in stopping the regular offerings in the Temple, God's due. In pagan thought a god without a cult was as good as dead. **the daily sacrifice** (also 11: 31; 12: 11) was the sacrifice prescribed for every morning and evening in Exod. 29: 38–42. the **place . . . was brought low** or possibly 'despised' as implied by **trampled underfoot** in v. 13. **12.** The Hebrew here is obscure and any translation is tentative. **Because of rebellion** refers to the renegade Jews of v. 23. With **truth was thrown to the ground** (with change of Heb. vowels) or 'it was casting down truth' (without change) compare v. 25. Truth is God's absolute which no human can change, try as he may. **13. a holy one:** an angel; cf. 4: 10. What he was **speaking** was the matter of the vision; the inquirer's concern was the duration of the horror which he knew must have an end. **14.** A time was revealed 'to me' according to *MT*, 'to him' according to the versions; as it was, both wanted to know! **two thousand and three hundred evenings and mornings:** the first of Daniel's mysterious numbers, debated for two thousand years. Any who would attempt exact calculations should note major uncertainties: the year may have been lunar (354 days) or solar (364/5 days), with a month added at intervals to the lunar year to keep pace with the seasons, intervals unknown for Palestine; the exact dates of Antiochus' entry into Jerusalem or his decree. (Until 1954 his death could be placed between Spring 164 and 163 B.C., then publication of a Babylonian King-List showed it was November-December 164 B.C.) In this verse and in v. 26 the Heb 'evening morning' could mean 2300 whole days or 2300 evening and morning sacrifices, 1150 days; the phrase is unique. Gen. 1: 5 and other passages adduced by those who argue for the longer period (*e.g.* Young) specify 'day'. The context, with the twice daily offering so prominent, favours the shorter period. Neither figure fits known dates exactly, and the second is short of the 33 times of 7: 25, if they be years. Whichever period be accepted, it closed with the vindication of the sanctuary, its justification in the restored worship of the God of Israel.

iii. The interpretation (8: 15–27)

15–18. Daniel's reaction was intensified by the appearance of an angel in the form of a strong man (Heb. *geber*) named **Gabriel** 'man of God'. Only Daniel names angels in the OT, Michael being the other named (10: 13, etc.). They were chief ministers of the divine court, their names distinguishing them from the myriad others. **from the Ulai** or 'between the Ulai and another stream'. **a man's voice** involves a suppressed comparison, 'a voice like a man's'. **I was terrified:** throughout Scripture meeting of undisguised heavenly and human beings has this effect as holy meets impure, *e.g.* Jg. 6: 22, 23; Isa. 6: 5; Ezek. 1: 28; Rev. 1: 17. Daniel's swoon (v. 18), Gabriel's awakening touch and setting him upright, copy the ceremonial at entry to the king's presence, cf. Est. 5: 2. **Son of man:** i.e. human, yet one to be given knowledge men always seek and fail to gain. The time had to be made clear, the events were not all imminent. Daniel, in Belshazzar's Babylon, might have doubted their truth otherwise. **19–26.** The explanation has been partly covered in the comments on vv. 1–14. **19. the time of wrath** is God's anger against Israel for her apostasy, cf. Isa. 10: 25; 26: 20. **the appointed time of the end:** better 'for an appointed time has an end', cf. NEB. As in 4: 26; 8: 25, 26, a limit was set, God's plan was fully formed. **23.** Jews were **rebels** who adopted Hellenic manners irrespective of their own religious laws (see 1 Mac. 1: 11–15). They were ready to conform to the will of the insolent (cf. Dt. 28: 50), deceitful, and destructive **king. 24.** RSV treats as a doublet from v. 22 **but not by his own power** which *MT* has here (NEB omits without note). Young gives the hint of divine permission they contain as reason for keeping them. **25.** Many relate **when they feel secure he will destroy many** to the attack of Antiochus' tax-collector told in 1 Mac. 1: 29–36. All his wicked deeds led the king to his attack on God, and to his fall through divine intervention, dying on his sickbed with Jerusalem lost. **26.** Gabriel's explanation was completed with a declaration that **the vision** is correct, on the pattern of 2: 45, etc. Its fulfilment was to be long after the seer's day, so steps were taken to preserve the record, **seal up** means 'close'; cf. 12: 4 and Isa. 8: 16. **27.** Far distant the awful events may have been, yet their promise had a greater physical effect on Daniel than the previous dreadful vision of ch. 7, again partly because of his inability to understand it.

IX. A PRAYER AND A VISION (9: 1–27)

i. Daniel's prayer for his people (9: 1–19)

1. Darius son of Xerxes mg. Ahasuerus: see 6: 1 and Introduction, 'Daniel and History:

iv'; the name Ahasuerus appears as Xerxes in Greek. **a Mede:** better 'of Median stock'. Emphasis is laid on the date (vv. 1, 2), for a major change occurred in world history and in the fortunes of Jewry when **Darius . . . was made ruler over the Babylonian kingdom**. Whatever solution of the Darius question appeals, the date is clearly intended as 539 B.C., the date of ch. 5. Daniel, aware of God's rule in history, thought on current affairs in the light of earlier prophecy and realized Jer. 25: 11f.; 29: 10, forecasting a Babylonian term of seventy years, had almost come to fulfilment. (As often, the exactness of the figure need not be pressed.) Daniel's discovery brought him to pray that God would remember His promise of restoration, a prayer penitent and determined, involving him body and soul. Until this point, and after the prayer, God is portrayed primarily as the absolute ruler of the universe, but here, in Daniel's prayer, He is repeatedly given His name, **LORD** i.e. Yahweh, peculiar to the covenant relation with Israel. Throughout the prayer the link between God and His People founded at Sinai is in view, just as it is in Jeremiah. With the covenant-terms as his yardstick, Daniel assessed both God and Israel. So fully did God measure up to the scale, so far short fell Israel, that the prayer had to begin as a confession of sin and entirely proper punishment (vv. 4–14). In language the prayer resembles those in Ezr. 9, Neh. 1, 9, yet it is independent of them, sharing a heritage running onwards from Deuteronomy. Thus v. 4 is rooted in Dt. 7: 9, 21; v. 5 is reminiscent of Solomon's prayer, 1 Kg. 8: 47; v. 6 recalls Jer. 26: 5, etc.

God is righteous, no accusation can be brought against Him; Israel must hang her head **because of** her **unfaithfulness**. It is God who shows himself **merciful and forgiving**; Israel has nothing to forgive, can only cry for mercy, **even though we have rebelled**. **11–14** reflect the covenant-curses which threatened increasing penalties for breaches, culminating in exile from the Promised Land. The people's life in Babylon was the inevitable punishment for blatant disregard of the covenant. God had chosen His people to be an example, because of their failure, their punishment was also exemplary, **nothing has ever been done like it**. All this was predicted **in the Law of Moses**. **13. we have not sought the favor of the Lord:** Montgomery admirably rendered 'mollified'; repentance and a fresh start would have brought mitigation and a swift end to their sufferings (the idea is illustrated by Jer. 26: 19). Until repentance is real, **the disaster** will continue, the **righteous** God cannot be lax or indifferent.

15–19. Having fully admitted the depths to which he and his nation had sunk (for the state of the majority embraces the individual, just as the individual can affect the body), Daniel could put his request for national restoration. In earlier days God's reputation, His **name**, had been enhanced world-wide by the Exodus when mighty Egypt was seen powerless. Now a people forever in exile would harm that reputation (cf. Jos. 7: 9), as would the state of the **desolate sanctuary** (17) and **city that bears** His **Name** (18). Often in the past God had justified or vindicated Himself by His righteous act towards His people; Daniel had those precedents for his present plea, and hope despite the holy city and holy people having become **an object of scorn**, a laughing stock. 'Much will be required of those to whom much is given', yet Israel passed for bankrupt. There was no ground for Daniel's prayer in anything that might count to his credit, it could only rest upon his knowledge of God's character, His **great mercy**, that had been displayed so often in the past when final judgment seemed due. With that he could end in the imperatives of prayer: **listen, forgive**, prerequisite attitudes for the following tasks **hear, act, do not delay**, tempered still with the thought of God's repute. Daniel's prayer is summarized in v. 20: confession of sin, petition for God to act for His own.

ii. The Response (9: 20–27)

The response, vv. 20–27, interrupted the prayer (to be conceived as far more extended than its reported words) in the late afternoon. It was brought by the angel already known, coming urgently. The impression that the angel set out as soon as Daniel began to pray, derived by some from vv. 21, 23 is wrong. As soon as Daniel began to pray this response was issued, but Daniel had to be allowed to shed some of his burden before Gabriel came to him. (Notice there is no trace of the angel acting as intercessor on Daniel's behalf as in apocryphal and pseudepigraphical literature, *e.g.* Tob. 12: 12 ff.) **22. He instructed me and said:** Heb. is difficult but may be taken as an introductory term. As he understood Jeremiah's prophecies, Daniel was inspired to pray for Jerusalem's restoration. That knowledge which he had gained from Scripture and the use he had made of it showed him fit for more instruction in the ways of God. Daniel was counted **highly esteemed** or 'most precious' (23).

iii. The vision of the 'Seventy Weeks' (9: 24–27)

Seventy years had been in Daniel's mind since he read Jeremiah; now he received a vision that built upon the old prophet's words in answer to the prayer they had stimulated. **24. seventy 'sevens':** mg 'weeks' is an interpretative translation; Heb. gives literally 'in sevens, seventy', the word 'in sevens' being a masculine form as in verse 26, whereas the feminine normally stands for 'weeks'. The masculine recurs in 10: 2, 3, but qualified as 'in sevens, days'. To understand 'weeks' here without reserve is unwarranted, accordingly the term 'sevens' is used in these comments. Seventy literal weeks are unlikely to be intended by the expression, and, with Jeremiah at the start of the chapter, seventy 'sevens' or weeks of years are commonly understood. That this remains an interpretation bears repeating, and a few commentators, latterly Young, hold the periods to be indefinite in this verse. Within the time Israel will be rid of three defects: **transgression** will be finished (AV, RV, RSV, NIV) or 'restrained' (AVmg, RVmg, NIVmg, Young)—Heb. allows either rendering; sin will be sealed up (so AVmg, RVmg with the traditional Heb. text, *lhtm*) or brought to **an end** (AV, RV, RSV, NEB, NIV, Young, follow a very ancient variant reading that could be superior, *lhtm*); **wickedness** will be wiped away, by God. In their place three advantages will be introduced: (*a*) **everlasting righteousness**, never hidden on God's part (see vv. 7 ff.), will be plain to all and shared by all with the end of transgression; (*b*) prophetic **vision** will be needed no longer, just as sin was ended, it will be sealed, taking 'to seal' in its main OT usage; alternatively, it will be ratified, the other value of the word; (*c*) the final clause **to anoint the most holy**, corresponds to the wiping away of iniquity, the essential cleansing for consecration (*e.g.* Lev. 8), but the object here is not stated: 'a holy of holies' could be the Temple or its sanctuary, its furniture, altars, or offerings, as in other parts of the OT, and so most modern writers, like RSV, envisage the Temple or the altar, yet the references to 'an anointed one' in the next verses, and the use of a related Aram. word in 7: 18 etc., may allow the personal application (cf. NIVmg b) to the Messiah common to Jewish and Christian tradition.

Verse 25 begins a progressive analysis of the seventy sevens that defies final resolution. From the time the decision was taken **to restore . . . Jerusalem** to the time of **the Anointed One** there would elapse a period lasting either for 'seven sevens' as set by the traditional Heb. text, RSV, etc., the city then enduring 'in distress' for sixty-two 'sevens', or there would elapse a period of 'seven sevens and sixty-two sevens' as understood from the time of the Greek translators onward, cf. NIV, Young. A decision in favour of one or the other depends in part upon the interpretation of the whole passage, although the syntax is easier for the former. **trench**, or 'water-channel, conduit' is a good example of an increased knowledge of Heb. giving more precise meaning to a word than AV could ('wall'). **the Anointed One**, the **ruler** may be a secular or a sacred figure. **26.** Signalling the end of the city's the word was sure; unpublished it might be changed. Israel's guardian angel Michael (see 12: 1), unlike his charge ever loyal to God's agents, had to give aid **because I was detained there with the king of Persia**, whose own angel had been overcome or put to flight. (*MT* has 'kings', and one Gk. version differs slightly, and RSV follows it.) Verse 14 resumes the declaration of v. 12, **in the future** citing Gen. 49: 1 (see on 2: 28); here, as there, the terminal point in the deliverance of 12: 1. **For the vision concerns a time yet to come**: or 'for there is still a vision about the days'.

15–17. Even this encouragement left Daniel confused, the impact of the vision was like labour pains, as in 1 Sam. 4: 9. The speaker had first to assure him he could speak in his presence, cf. Isa. 6: 7. **10: 18–11: 1.** Finally a figure touched **and gave . . . strength to** Daniel with words of greeting, so that, at length, he was ready. **20.** His attention turned to the subject by the question promising expansion of v. 14. **Soon** introduces the subsequent words rather than linking with those before; the messenger's work is to restrain the Persians' angel, then the Greeks', that God's limits be maintained. The affairs to be unveiled to Daniel were certain, **written in the Book of Truth**, of God's decrees. The speaker was responsible for control of the coming events, with the aid only of Michael. **11: 1.** He had been striving on Israel's behalf since Babylon fell, **the first year of Darius**, supported by the speaker in turn.

ii. The History of the Latter-Days (11: 2–12: 3)

(a) Persia, Alexander and his successors (11: 2–4)

2. the truth: as contained in the book (10: 21). Persia's career needed little comment for her rule of the Jews was mainly beneficent. What Daniel needed to know was the link between the Persian era and the next, heavily involving Israel, unexpressed in ch. 8. That began with the wealthy Persian king who would **stir up everyone against the kingdom of Greece**. His identity involves **three more kings** and **a fourth** (better 'the fourth'). If all four are future at the time of the vision, they may be Cambyses, Smerdis, Darius the Great, and Xerxes; if one be Cyrus, then Smerdis (probably an imposter) can be discounted. There is wide agreement that Xerxes is the fourth king for he made the most massive and disastrous attacks on Greece (defeated at Thermopylae, Salamis, Plataea, Mycale, 480–78 B.C.). Montgomery and a few others have thought of Cyrus, Xerxes, Artaxerxes, and Darius III, 'the four Persian kings named in the Bible', believing that a second-century B.C. author had unreliable information about the Persian Empire's duration, although Darius III hardly suits the description of the fourth. That proposal removes any time gap before v. 3—**Then a mighty king shall appear**—for Alexander, indubitably portrayed here, conquered Darius III. However, a gap of almost 150 years is permissible when the time is not defined (unlike 9: 24–27); Xerxes was the great instigator of Hellenic anti-Persian feeling. Verse 4 describes Alexander's meteoric course; cf. 8: 7, 8. **his descendants**: the two children supplanted within a decade of his death by his ambitious generals who broke the empire between themselves (cf. 8: 22).

(b) The kings of south and north (11: 5–19)

Soon after Alexander died Seleucus had Babylonia as his realm, then lost it to Antigonus and found refuge in Egypt where Ptolemy made him a general. When Antigonus came against Egypt in 312 B.C., Seleucus helped Ptolemy to victory and control of Palestine, going on to recover Babylon. His rule eventually stretched from India to Anatolia. So Ptolemy is **the king of the South** in v. 5, Egypt signified by its relation to Palestine, Seleucus **one of his commanders**.

6–9. *The first conflict*. **After some years** which saw hostility between the two powers, **they** become **allies**: Antiochus II, grandson of Seleucus, and Ptolemy II, son of Ptolemy, cemented it by the marriage of the Egyptian's daughter Berenice to the Syrian in 252 B.C., displacing Antiochus's first wife Laodice. On Ptolemy II's death Berenice was divorced and Laodice re-instated. She poisoned her husband and secured the throne for their son, Seleucus II, 246 B.C. Berenice and her son were murdered, together with her retinue, as obscurely described at the end of v. 6. **7.** Berenice was avenged by her brother, Ptolemy III, **one from her family line**, who succeeded Ptolemy II (**in her place**, note *MT* has 'his place' referring back to 'the king of the south' in v. 6). He swept into Syria, took Damascus and Antioch, **his fortress**, executed Laodice, campaigned further and carried immense booty home **to Egypt**. Seleucus II made an abortive counter-attack (9) then agreed to a ten-year truce. **10–19.** *Victory and Defeats*. Antiochus II's sons Seleucus III and Antiochus III followed him, facing enemies in several regions (**prepare for war**), before an attempt to wrest southern Syria and Palestine from Egypt brought Antiochus III to the southern frontier, perhaps Gaza or Raphia, **his fortress**. The armies clashed, Antiochus's **large army** lost some 15,000 men to the peaceable Ptolemy IV (217 B.C.). If **he was filled with pride** by the victory, he failed to follow it through to secure Palestine, hence **he will not remain triumphant** (cf. NEB). Antiochus re-asserted his rule in Persia until **after several years** he re-entered Palestine (201 B.C.), Ptolemy IV having died. Some Jews felt that this was the moment of **fulfilment of the vision**, but were 'law-breakers', **violent men**, and failed. **15.** Antiochus defeated an Egyptian general, besieged and captured Gaza, then Sidon. **16.** With Egypt powerless, Antiochus entered Jerusalem to a general welcome (198 B.C.), and **power to destroy it**. But Jewish religion and privileges were re-affirmed. **17.** To insure his position Antiochus married his daughter to Ptolemy V, hoping she would work on her father's behalf in Egypt **to overthrow it**. Cleopatra I, a **daughter in marriage** (lit. 'a daughter of women,' possibly a superlative) proved loyal to her husband, even after his death, so the alliance was no **help** to Antiochus. **18, 19.** Antiochus moved to western Anatolia, **the coastlands**, where initial successes were cancelled by the Roman **commander** Scipio at Magnesia in 190 B.C. Severe peace terms turned Antiochus' **insolence back upon him**, and he was killed looting a temple near Susa to get funds for the indemnity he had to pay (187 B.C.).

(c) The first oppressor (11: 20)
Seleucus struggled to pay off the imposition through taxation. An attempt to rob Jerusalem's Temple was miraculously halted (2 Mac. 3). Seleucus' prime minister, the **tax collector**, assassinated him (175 B.C.), perhaps implied by **yet not in anger or in battle**.

(d) The desolator's rule begins (11: 21–24)
Seleucus IV's younger son Demetrius was hostage in Rome; the elder, Antiochus, was a minor; so the throne fell under the care of their uncle Antiochus. He disposed of the assassin, and later of the boy heir, seizing the throne as Antiochus IV. Inadequate knowledge of his acts leaves uncertainty over the following verses (see Mørkholm for Antiochus's history). Verse 22 could refer to the defeat of Ptolemy V recounted in vv. 25–28, despite the absence of a title, or to the deposition of the high priest Onias III; **a prince of the covenant** (or 'the . . . of a . . . .') could be Ptolemy allied by Cleopatra's marriage, or the high priest. **23.** Antiochus owed his crown to intrigue and treachery, manipulating opposing parties to his profit. His habits were notoriously prodigal, **distributing plunder . . .** , waging war, but only in God's time.

(e) The first attack on Egypt (11: 25–28)
Following Cleopatra's death in 176 B.C. the guardians of her son Ptolemy VI planned to regain Palestine and southern Syria, but Antiochus, forewarned, overwhelmed their army (170–69 B.C.). He made himself Ptolemy's protector and all but ruler of Egypt. Patriots made Ptolemy's brother king in Alexandria and Antiochus failed to capture the city and withdrew. The Egyptian brothers were reconciled. On his return to Syria Antiochus entered Jerusalem and was given much treasure

from the temple. His war was fruitless, **to no avail**.

(f) The second attack on Egypt (11: 29, 30)
Antiochus attacked again in 168 B.C. but was foiled by intervention from **the western coastlands** (mg. Kittim an old name for Cyprus, Num. 24: 24, extended west to Rome). While he was besieging Alexandria a Roman envoy brought a peremptory senate decree commanding him to leave. Antiochus was stupefied, lost **heart**, and complied (June 168 B.C.). Henceforth Rome would be the ultimate power in the Mediterranean.

(g) Attack on the people of God (11: 30–35)
Strife broke out in Judaea at news of this reverse. The high priest, who had bought his post from Antiochus, was attacked and shut up in the citadel. Syrian troops stormed the city, sold many people as slaves, and quartered themselves in the citadel. Hellenizing Jews were favoured, the orthodox persecuted (32). Worst of all, the distinctive elements of Judaism were proscribed, sacrifices halted, and the temple dedicated to Olympian Zeus, the Hellenized Baal (December, 167 B.C.). **the abomination that causes desolation:** Heb. *šiqqûṣ šōmēm* may be a derogatory word-play on *ba'al šāmēm* 'lord of heaven'. Some still remained faithful, **the people who know their God** from experience. Through their example and teaching others were heartened to endure. Relief came with the patriotic Maccabees and their adherents, some of them prudent rather than convinced (34). **35.** Persecution of the **wise** had purgative effect, refining true from false, sharpening the sense of the faithful. Again Daniel was assured; a limit was fixed for these dread events.

(h) The arrogance of the Anti-God (11: 36–39)
36. the king may most naturally be understood as the villain of the previous verses. However, that person is carefully not termed king, except perhaps in v. 27, in contrast to the ruler of vv. 5–19. Accordingly, the remainder of ch. 11 is often applied to a later figure than Antiochus IV, an historical person or the Antichrist. The passage may be read as a description taking its rise in the first and merging into the last. The phrases are as specific as before, yet less applicable to Antiochus IV, although modern knowledge is defective. The king's conduct follows the little horn's in ch. 7. Antiochus decreed uniformity of cult and law throughout his realm according to 1 Mac. 1: 41; 2 Mac. 6: 1, 2; his actions in Judaea being forwarded by apostate Jews who had his ear, for a price (39). Amid this frightful recital comes a note of assurance **until the time of wrath is completed; for what has been determined must take place** (cf. 8: 19). Verses 37, 38 do not suit Antiochus well according to current knowl-

edge. He may have been personally devoted to Olympian Zeus, yet supported other cults. **he will show no regard** conceivably alludes to the plunder of temple treasures. **the one desired by women:** apparently the popular Tammuz or Adonis; cf. Ezek. 8: 14. **but will exalt himself** could reflect Antiochus's assumption of the title 'God Manifest' (Gk. *theos epiphanēs*) imprinted on coins. He was the first of his line to do so. That he was portrayed as the god is disputed. **a god of fortresses:** obscure; the title Zeus Akraios, 'of the heights', can be related tenuously to the citadel, Akra, of Jerusalem, secured by the Syrians in 167 and held until 141 B.C. Otherwise it might be a personification of war. What the **foreign god** (39) was is unknown.

(i) **The final effort and end (11: 40–45)**
Antiochus IV's last campaign was directed to Persia where he died near Isfahan late in 164 B.C. These verses obviously do not describe that. Favouring a Maccabaean date for Daniel involves acceptance that they are a prophecy of Antiochus' end composed a year or two before it, and turning out to be wrong, the common view. A prophecy presently proved false, without any refutation, would be an unparalleled phenomenon in Scripture, and one that the pious Jews who welcomed Daniel as Scripture might have rejected, having the facts before them in 1 Mac. 6, for example. Furthermore, it is hard to imagine a contemporary of Antiochus IV expecting him to make a third attack on Egypt after the mortifying and irreversible Roman intervention. The alternative, open to proponents of either date for the book, is to read the passage as entirely shifted to a future king, or Antichrist. The language is no different, lest the image disappear; its referent is varied, just as Daniel's use of Kittim v. 30 varies from the older use. **40. the time of the end:** linked with v. 36 and 8: 17 offers a uniform expression easily related to the events of 167–64 B.C. but not limited to that moment, still having prospective value. **the king of the South . . . the king of the North:** the latter remains the villain, though it is he who is provoked to a destructive onslaught engulfing (**like a flood,** cf. 9: 26; 11: 10, etc.) Palestine, **the Beautiful Land,** and **Egypt,** the southern state (cf. v. 8). **41. Edom,** etc., ancient enemies of Israel 'shall escape' (with AV, cf. NEB, rather than RSV, NIV) the northern king's hostility. **43. Libyans and Nubians** (better Cushites, as NEB, of modern Sudan) represented extremes of Egypt. **44, 45.** While overcoming foes in the south, trouble in provinces considered secure will draw him from Egypt. On the way he will camp between the Mediterranean and Jerusalem and, presumably there at the mountain of God, **he will come to his end,** as the figures in 7: 11, 25; 8: 25; 9: 27. **his royal tents:** NEB 'his royal

pavilion', Heb. uses a Persian word describing the great audience halls of the Achaemenid kings known at Persepolis and Susa. **the seas:** Heb. has a poetic plural.

(j) **The triumph of the godly (12: 1–3)**
These verses can be read wholly or partly as a poem, cf. NEB. **1. At that time:** the time of 11: 40. With the oppressor banished from thought, attention can turn to his victims. They have an aide in **Michael the great prince,** unlike him who, at this end, had **no one** to **help him** (11: 45). For the angel see note at 10: 13; a hint at the scheme may lie in Dt. 32: 8 where LXX and a Heb. text from Qumran have 'He set the bounds of the nations according to the number of the angels of God' (cf. NIV mg). **your people —everyone whose name is found written in the book—will be delivered. Be delivered** could be rendered 'escape' as in 11: 41, NEB mg, but the present context indicates the idea of deliverance. For **the book** see at 7: 10. **multitudes who sleep** in death, a fitting figure which implies the possibility of awakening glimpsed in Ps. 13: 3; Jer. 51: 39, 57, now revealed unambiguously. Martyrdom understandably stimulated deeper thought about death so that ideas of resurrection grew stronger with the persecutions of Antiochus and later troubles, see 'Theology of the Old Testament' (pp. 73–84). **everlasting life:** the first occurrence of the phrase. **shame . . . :** the outcasts of the refuse heap, as in Isa. 66: 24. **multitudes:** those killed during the final wars, or the whole community, or the clearly good and clearly bad, the rest lingering in the shadows; see Young and Montgomery. The **wise** were shown at work in 11: 33; their achievements are spelt out in poetic parallelism. **who lead many to righteousness:** cf. Isa. 53: 11. Outstanding on earth in God's sight, they shall be outstanding in heaven.

iii. Preservation of the book (12: 4)
In 8: 26 Daniel was told to preserve his writing because its relevance was far ahead. Here it is to be closed and sealed, authenticated and protected from tampering (cf. Isa. 29: 11; Jer. 32: 9 ff.). At the end of time men will be vainly seeking to discover God's plans, as Amos foretold (8: 12), 'in order to increase knowledge'; then the only answer will lie in God's Word. (NEB 'punishment will be heavy' relies on a homonym of the Heb. word for 'knowledge' by an unsatisfactory linguistic argument.)

iv. Final words (12: 5–13)
The seer requested answers to the riddles (7: 16, 19), so did heavenly beings (8: 13), and now one of two further angels. **6.** *MT* has 'and he said', early versions **'one of them said',** 'and I said' cf. RSV; either may be correct. The Highest Authority or His special envoy alone could answer the question. **astonishing things:** NEB has well 'portents'. **7.** Solemnity

enwraps the reply. Oaths were sworn with one hand raised (Dt. 32: 40); the angel lifted two. An oath **by him who lives forever** would be especially binding because He would ever enforce it, unlike a mortal king or powerless statue. **a time . . . :** cf. 7: 25. At the close of the final half period the shattering of the power of the holy people will come to an end, and so will all the events foreseen by Daniel. **8.** Daniel's perplexity persisted, he would know the outcome. **9.** His anxiety was assuaged, although his curiosity may not have been satisfied, no more would be explained to him. **Go your way:** or simply 'Go!' meant the matter was closed. **10.** From that point, or at the time of the events, there will be saints and there will be sinners; the ways of God will be made known to the **wise**; to the wicked they will grow more obscure. Verse 11 re-iterates the relatively short span of the final outrage, given here as 1290 days or 3½ years of 360 days each, with one leap-year. That this figure can be used to define the times of v. 7 and 7: 25 is debatable. **12.** Complete triumph would follow 45 days later. **13.** Daniel was bidden turn to other affairs **till the end**, of his life, most plausibly, or of the future events, although he had been told that that was far from him. **you will rest** in the grave: his service and the burden of his visions past (8: 27, etc.), until he **will rise** at the triumphal **end**.

'With all this in mind, what are we to say?' We who have received knowledge beyond the privileges of Daniel, who know the Son of Man as the living, loving Lord, can take the words of Paul 'If God is on our side, who is against us?' and find their truth in Daniel's experience, and in his visions their promise that 'nothing in all creation can separate us from the love of God in Christ Jesus our Lord' (Rom. 8: 39).

BIBLIOGRAPHY

Commentaries

BALDWIN, J. G., *Daniel. TOTC* (Leicester, 1978).

BEVAN, A. A., *A Short Commentary on the Book of Daniel* (Cambridge, 1892).

DRIVER, S. R., *The Book of Daniel. CBSC* (Cambridge, 1900).

HAMMER, R. J., *The Book of Daniel. CBC* (Cambridge, 1976).

HARTMAN, L. F., and DI LELLA, A. A., *The Book of Daniel. AB* (Garden City, N. Y., 1978).

HEATON, E. W., *The Book of Daniel. TC* (London, 1956).

LACOCQUE, A., *The Book of Daniel*, E. T. (London, 1979).

LATTEY, C., *The Book of Daniel* (Dublin, 1948).

MONTGOMERY, J. A., *The Book of Daniel. ICC* (Edinburgh, 1927).

PORTEOUS, N. W., *Daniel. OTL* (London, [2]1979).

RUSSELL, D. S., *Daniel.* Daily Study Bible (Edinburgh, 1981).

TREGELLES, S. P., *Remarks on the Prophetic Visions of the Book of Daniel* (London, [4]1852).

YOUNG, E. J., *Daniel* (Grand Rapids, 1949; London, 1972).

Other works

BRUCE, F. F., *Israel and the Nations* (Exeter, 1969).

CASEY, M., *Son of Man: The Interpretation and Influence of Daniel 7* (London, 1979).

FRYE, R. N., *The Heritage of Persia* (London, 1962).

HENGEL, M., *Judaism and Hellenism* (London, 1974).

MØRKHOLM, O., *Antiochus IV of Syria* (Copenhagen, 1966).

ROWLEY, H. H., *Darius the Mede and the Four World Empires in the Book of Daniel* (London, 1935).

SMITH, S., *Isaiah, Chapters XL-LV* (London, 1944).

WISEMAN, D. J., MITCHELL, T. C., and JOYCE, R., MARTIN, W. J., KITCHEN, K. A., *Notes on Some Problems in the Book of Daniel* (London, 1965).

HOSEA

G. J. POLKINGHORNE

From the first verse of Hosea, we learn of its relation to the reigns of Jeroboam II of Israel and of Uzziah through to Hezekiah of Judah. Jeroboam died about 746 B.C. and six of his successors reigned in the years to Hezekiah's ascension. As there is no indication that Hosea saw the fall of Samaria in 722 B.C., it is likely that his term of activity ran from 750 to 724 B.C., though very little of his prophecy can be precisely dated. Following the prosperous years of Jeroboam, this was a stormy period for Israel. There were recurrent troubles within, evidenced by four of the kings being assassinated, and invasion or threats thereof from without. Resurgent Assyria presented the greatest of these threats, culminating in capitulation to her shortly after the end of Hosea's writing. Comparison of the turbulent circumstances of the ministry of Jeremiah, just prior to the collapse of Judah to Babylon, is suggestive.

Three other prophets were contemporary with Hosea: Amos, who began work before him, and Micah and Isaiah slightly later. The latter two were concerned with Judah; Amos spoke as a Judean in the northern kingdom; while Hosea was a native of the Israel he addressed. Again, comparison of Amos and Hosea is instructive.

Nothing is known of Hosea except what his book reveals, which is little enough considering the personal problem that formed the starting-point of his ministry. That problem lay in the unfaithfulness of his wife, Gomer. The view taken here is that, at the time of their wedding, she was a virgin, but later committed adultery and forsook him. He remained true, even to the extent of buying her back from slavery (ch. 3). Out of the agony of his own soul, he appreciated the broken heart of God over the prostitution of Israel, who followed other Gods and neglected him—a *motif* that recurs repeatedly throughout the book. While the word 'prostitution' is used figuratively in this connection, it serves to reflect the sensual and obscene nature of the Baal cult.

Israel encounted Baals when she entered Canaan. These gods were regarded as in control of the rain and the fertility of the soil. They were worshipped with sexual rites, a kind of imitative magic. Long before Hosea's time, the struggle against them began, as witness Elijah's contest on Mount Carmel (1 Kg. 18). Ultimately, the nation was banished from the land over them—cf. 2 Kg. 17: 16 ff. Meantime, the worship of Yahweh became deeply Baalized. Although radically rejecting the false cult, Hosea skilfully appropriated some of its ideas to expound the faith of Israel, with an amazing wealth of metaphor.

Along with such aberrant worship, Israel was prone to political alliances rather than trust in the Lord. The two things are connected, as treaties between nations involved mutual acceptance of national gods. Yet there are no denunciations of foreign nations such as we find in Jeremiah and Amos. What is denounced is the people's confidence in military strength (horses and chariots) and in the leadership of the non-Davidic monarchy, which is seen as a manifestation of self-reliance and a rejection of God.

G. A. Smith graphically characterizes Hosea's message as 'The Problem that Amos left', which can be summed up in the word *hesed*. The NIV variously translates this word as 'love' 'mercy' and 'unfailing love' (cf. further on 2: 19). While the Lord's *hesed* is unfailing, Israel's is as ephemeral as the morning mist (6: 4). He endures every sort of provocation from them, yet refuses to cast them off. Inevitably, the show-down must come: God will cast them off (1: 6; 3: 4; 8: 10, etc.) but will accept them back later (3: 5; 14: 4f., etc.). Hosea is always concerned with the nation as a whole. He has no concept of individual responsibility, as developed in Jeremiah or Ezekiel, nor of the Remnant, whereby Isaiah overcame the tension of the restoration of the disobedient people. Throughout, the wrath of God has as its objective the restoration of Israel to himself. Indeed, 'acknowledgement of God' is another major thrust of this prophecy. Lacking in decadent Israel (4: 1), it will be perfect in the future (2: 20).

Some modern scholars are inclined to dismiss references to Judah as the work of a later hand. It is possible, however, that Hosea ended his days south of the border and edited his book there. In any case, very few late insertions need be postulated. But the state of the text is a real problem, for Hosea seems to have suffered more corruption in transmission than any other book of the Old Testament. Brief notes on the more difficult passages are given below, but the scope of this work does not permit full discussion. The English reader can get some insight into the question by comparing the versions, especially the marginal notes, and from H. L. Ellison, *The Prophets of Israel*. The fact that Hosea is the only native of the northern kingdom whose writings have come down to us suggests that dialectical variations in vocabulary and syntax may lie behind some at least of the problems.

The first three chapters form a coherent whole, dealing with the prophet's marital misfortunes as parabolic of the national behaviour. Chapters 4–14 consist of a collection of messages, probably delivered orally at various times and brought together on no obvious plan. It is often difficult to decide the precise limits of the original spoken unit. Sometimes 'catchwords' appear to be the basis of collation, as in ch. 4, where the expression 'prostitution' is found in vv. 10, 12, 13, 14 and 18. A. Alt has shown

that the Syro-Ephraimitic war (2 Kg. 16: 5 ff.; Isa. 7: 1–16) was the background of 5: 8–6: 6, but little else can be firmly dated.

Although Isaiah is frequently called 'The Evangelical Prophet', it may be questioned whether anywhere outside the New Testament is divine grace more vividly set forth than in Hosea. Here we find the foretelling of the New Covenant one hundred years before Jeremiah (2: 14–20); a presentation of the perseverance of God's unmerited mercy (11: 8 f.) anticipating the wonder of Calvary; a graphic use of marriage as a simile of God's relationship with his people, richly developed in the concept of the church as the bride of Christ; and a story of a prodigal wife, richer in gospel truth than Luke 15. Throughout, we hear the authentic note of all scripture—the call to trust God and walk worthily of Him.

ANALYSIS

While the two broad division, chas. 1–3 (Hosea's broken marriage) and 4–14 (God's wayward people) are clear enough, there is very little logical connection in the latter section. Purely as a basis for exposition, the following outline is proposed.

I. HOSEA'S BROKEN MARRIAGE (1: 1–3: 5)

The first verse forms the heading of the book. Comparison with the opening verses of Isaiah and Micah as well as Joel, Jonah and Zephaniah suggests that an editor inserted the verse. It

shows that the prophecy brings the **word of the LORD** in the context of history. Probably Hosea had finished his ministry before Hezekiah ascended the throne but was active not only in the reign of Jeroboam II but also of his six successors, including Hoshea, whose overthrow by Assyria completed the downfall of the nation (cf. also Introduction).

i. The marriage of Hosea (1: 2–9)

This chapter gives an account in reported speech of the prophet's marriage, at the express command of the Lord, to a woman who bore him three children, each of whom is given a significant name. The relationship to this narrative to ch. 3, which describes in the first person Hosea's dealings with an unnamed woman, is disputed. The view taken here is that Hosea married Gomer (1: 2 f.) who proved unfaithful to him and left him for another man. Later (3: 1 f.), he found her deserted and up for sale as a slave. He bought her and after a period of discipline, resumed marital cohabitation. This takes the chapters as factual and concerned with Hosea and Gomer only, with the first chapter temporally prior to the third.

The principal alternative views are summarized below. (For discussion, consult the works by Ellison and Rowley in the bibliography.)

(a) The stories are not historical but entirely allegorical—a view that removes the whole foundation of Hosea's ministry.

(b) Both accounts describe the same events and derive from different times in the prophet's ministry or from different sources.

(c) The woman of ch. 3 is not Gomer, but another person. This interpretation provides two women to symbolize wayward Israel and destroys the imagery of God's abiding faithfulness.

(d) Gomer is the woman of both passages, but ch. 3 is historically prior to ch. 1, a view that throws some light on **an adulterous wife** (1: 2) but means that Hosea married a woman he knew to be an adulteress.

Whatever interpretation is preferred, it is noteworthy that ch. 1 stresses the unfaithfulness of Israel and ch. 3 the faithfulness of the Lord.

an adulterous wife (2) is difficult, as God is unlikely to direct the prophet to marry a promiscuous woman. Some scholars suggest that Gomer was a temple prostitute, which sharpens the comparison with Israel's apostasy, but does not really remove the difficulty, since Hosea was undoubtedly opposed to the practice of ritual prostitution. It is also inadequate to view her **adultery** as consisting solely in her belonging to a sinful nation. The best solution —not altogether free from objection—is that the phrase is proleptic, introducing a later appreciation of the situation (cf. Jer. 32: 8). At the time of the wedding, Gomer was a virgin but later proved unfaithful. This accords with the impression of Israel's pristine purity derived from 9: 10; 11: 1; 13: 1.

for the land is guilty of the vilest adultery in departing from the LORD brings out the purpose of the story: Hosea's domestic traged-

ies are parabolic of the Lord's disappointment with Israel. He learnt therefrom how God felt about his people's apostasies. 'As a result there seems to be no one in the Old Testament who drew nearer to an understanding of God's love' (Ellison). On **prostitution** as reflecting the Baal cult, see Introduction.

Gomer's three children indicate the progression of Hosea's suspicions about her behaviour—notice **him** after **bore** in v. 3, but no allusion to the father in vv. 6 and 8. Each name has a message for Israel (cf. Isa. 8: 3 f.). **Jezreel** foretells vengeance on the dynasty of Jehu, to which Jeroboam belonged, for the bloodshed accompanying its accession (2 Kg. 9 and 10). What is criticized is not the revolt, instigated by Elisha, but the brutal manner of its execution. Fulfilment of the forecast is described in 2 Kg. 15: 10 and may also be seen in the fall of Israel to Assyria. Cf. on 3: 5 for Hosea's view of the northern kingship. In 1: 11 and 2: 22 f. the name Jezreel is taken up positively in the light of its meaning 'God plants'. **Not loved** (6 margin) and **Not my people** (9 margin) reflect the rejection of Israel by God for her sins. The latter, coupled with language echoing Exod. 3: 14, amounts to a repudiation of the covenant —cf. 2: 2. The reference to **Judah** is often regarded as an interpolation (cf. NEB), but Ellison sees it as a reminder that the sonship of Israel continued in Judah after the extinction of the northern kingdom, which had no monopoly of the name of Israel.

ii. The reunion of Judah and Israel (1: 10–2: 1)

This is another passage frequently treated as a late insertion, but on inadequate grounds. It anticipates the reunion of the two kingdoms under a Davidic monarch and their return to the Promised Land (cf. 3: 5) in a better **day of Jezreel** (11; cf. 1: 4). The New Testament quotes 2: 1 at Rom. 9: 25 f. and I Pet. 2: 10 in a fresh sense, the calling of Gentiles into the body of Christ. Thus, what was originally a private concern of Hosea and Gomer becomes significant, first for Israel after the flesh and then for the new Israel.

What **come up out of the land** (11) means is uncertain. 'Gain ascendancy', 'grow up like plants', and 'go up to Shechem to crown a ruler' are all plausible suggestions; but the most likely is 'return to the land from exile'.

Note how the names of the three children recur in 1: 4, 6, 9; 1: 10, 11; 2: 1; and 2: 22 f., and are implicit in 2: 2, 4, 8.

iii. The Lord's plea (2: 2–13)

Sandwiched between the two narratives of Hosea's dealings with Gomer is this passage which states the Lord's complaint against Israel in terms of the analogy of marriage. **Rebuke** (Heb. *rîb*) is a legal term connoting accuse and translated 'charge' in 4: 1 and 12: 2. Compare the legal imagery found in 5: 5; 7: 10 and in Isa. 3: 13 and Mic. 6: 1 ff. God threatens to take Israel, his wife, to court not to secure a divorce but a reconciliation; cf. the succeeding portion (2: 14–23) and Hosea's own behaviour in 3: 1 ff. The portrayal fluctuates somewhat, as the children are both witnesses for the prosecution (2) and involved in the guilt (4).

In 2–5 the Lord states his case: Israel has committed prostitution for hire with the Baals. **she is not my wife** cannot be taken in this context as a formal declaration of divorce. NEB legitimately renders 'Is she not my wife?' Verse 3 is reminiscent of the treaty curses against covenant breakers in the Ancient Near East—cf. also Ezek. 11: 36 ff.

In 6–8, Israel is warned that she will be subjected to the frustration of failure to attain her desires, in the hope that it will impel her to return to God. The threefold **therefore** (6, 9, 14) consistently indicates divine reaction to the people's actions. For **go back** or return, which echoes repeatedly throughout the book, see on 3: 5. **Baal** (8) is singular here, v. 16 and 13: 1; elsewhere, plural.

Verses 9–13 reveal what happens if the warnings go unheeded: chastisement will follow—the deprivation of all prosperity and joy. Since the attribution to Baal (v. 8) of the God-given fruits of the earth cancelled Israel's whole understanding of God's role in the universe, it was the ultimate in apostasy. Hence, the gifts are removed. Similarly, as the feasts of v. 11 (cf. Gal. 4: 10) originally honoured the Lord but were diverted to celebrate Baal, they had to be stopped. But behind all the discipline is the divine *cri de coeur* of v. 13, reminding us of Rev. 2: 4, while the whole procedure reflects the principle stated in Heb. 12: 6.

declares the Lord (13) is a solemn oracle formula frequently used in the prophets to stress that a message came from God. It is used also in vv. 16 and 21 with promises of restoration and otherwise occurs only at 11: 11 in Hosea. Equally serious are the threats of doom and the forecasts of hope!

iv. The great restoration (2: 14–23)

After threats of doom come forecasts of blessing a recurrent pattern in Hosea—cf. 3: 4 f.; 5: 15; 11: 8 ff.; 14: 1–8. There is no need to posit the hand of a redactor in this, as it aptly accords with the prophet's kindness to his wife. Although the metrical style runs through from vv. 2 to 15 and there is a unifying factor in the three 'therefores' of vv. 6, 9 and 14, the passage vv. 14–23 has a unity of message which justifies our division.

14. allure might be rendered 'seduce' as in Exod. 22: 16. In context, it is a bold word, strongly reflecting the yearning of God for his people. The seduction arises because **the desert**, seemingly a place of punishment,

proves to be one of renewal of love (Ellison). **15. the Valley of Achor** picks up the story of Jos. 7 and illustrates two features of the prophet's style: his citation of place-names and his fondness of plays on words: **Achor**, literally 'trouble', becomes **hope**. **Egypt**, for Hosea along with most pre-exilic prophets, was the place of Israel's election by God—cf. 11: 1; 12: 9, 13; 13: 4—and to return there amounted to the cancellation of that choice—8: 13; 9: 3. As at the Exodus, the election was jeopardized through sin at Achor, but averted by judgment; so the present threat of rejection will be turned away as a result of the 'trouble' described in vv. 3–13, and lead on to a second honeymoon with God, marked by a change of heart by Israel (15 f.) and a renewal of favour by God (18). Note the word-play in v. 16: Baal (cf. mg) is translated 'husband' in, *e.g.*, Jer. 31: 32.

Then follows the wonderful triple betrothal, vv. 19 f., including promises that compare well with the New Covenant of Jer. 31: 31–34, more than a century later. Here we meet some of the great key-words of Hosea's theology:

love (*ḥesed*), concisely defined by Taylor as 'loyalty to one's covenant obligations and devotion to one's covenant partner', is amply displayed by God though woefully lacking in Israel. Not used by Amos, it is the main thrust of Hosea's appeal in 4: 1; 6: 6 and 12: 6.

justice (*mišpaṭ*) has a wider connotation than in English and implies all the conditions of the covenant. Its association with mercy here is reminiscent of Rom. 3: 26.

compassion translates the same word as 'my loved one' (2: 1) and so significantly reverses the verdict of 1: 6. McKeating sees in this word 'the kind of tenderness spontaneously called forth by what is small or hurt or cuddly'. Whereas love presupposes a relationship, mercy is conditioned only by the needs of the object.

faithfulness (from the same root as 'amen') is God's reliability and consistency, in contrast to the waywardness of the people.

To **acknowledge the Lord** is expected of the covenant people and fits the simile here cogently—cf. Gen. 4: 1. It includes an inner disposition towards God but also a familiarity with the deeds of God in history (cf. 13: 4 f.) and obedience to the covenant conditions as set out in the Law (cf. 4: 6).

The idea of marriage as a figure of the relationship between God and Israel is taken up in the New Testament, particularly in Eph. 5: 23 ff. and Rev. 21: 9 ff., one of many seed thoughts initiated by the first of the Minor Prophets.

Verses 21 ff. look forward to **that day** when God's purposes in discipline are accomplished and the punishment is reversed by grace. So the names of the three children recur with fresh significance.

The sexual simile is well sustained throughout the passage: courtship (14 f.) leads on to marriage (19 f.) which is consummated in fruitfulness (21 ff.)

v. The recovery of Gomer (3: 1–5)

After the excursion into the wider application of Hosea's marital difficulties, we are now given a final look at Gomer. Cf. on 1: 2–9 for the general view taken of the interrelation of the chapters.

As the Lord had commanded the marriage, so now he requires the resumption of relationship. **1. again** might be taken with **said** or **go** or **love**, with varying shades of meaning, but on the view taken here, Hosea finds his wife on sale as a slave, perhaps for debt, and buys her back. This displays the Lord's inalienable love for Israel. G. A. Smith's title for the chapter is worth quoting: 'The Story of the Prodigal Wife.'

For **loved by**, LXX has 'loving' (active), which makes better sense. **sacred raisin-cakes** were used in the worship of false deities (cf. Isa. 16: 7; Jer. 7: 18). Thus, the Lord's love is not extinguished even by the ultimate in apostasy. **I bought her** renders a verb of uncertain meaning: NEB's 'I got her back' confirms the interpretation we follow. The first **and** of v. 2 may be taken as epexegetic ('even'), indicating that the barley was worth fifteen shekels. It is attractive, however, to regard it as simple 'and', suggesting that Hosea did not possess enough silver to buy Gomer, but had to make up the deficiency in kind, thus showing that he stretched his resources to the utmost to acquire her. The period of discipline (v. 3) required before the resumption of full marital relations signifies the exile Israel had to undergo before the restoration **in the last days. 5. return** is a keyword, used 22 times in the prophecy. Israel's true happiness, like Gomer's, lay in reunion with her rightful husband. That the way back remained open was a miracle of grace. **David their king** is their rightful monarch, as **the LORD** is **their** true **God**. Hosea thus expected the northern kingdom to resume allegiance to the dynasty rejected under Jeroboam I. His objection is not to kingship as such, but to the northern monarchy, as in rebellion to the man God chose: cf. also 8: 4; 9: 9; 10: 3, 9 f.; and 13: 10 f.

Some scholars would excise v. 5 as an addition of a Judean redactor; but this is unjustified.

GOD'S WAYWARD PEOPLE (4: 1–14: 9)

At 4: 1 we find the only indisputable division of the prophecy, except perhaps 14: 1. The other sub-divisions are given herein for con-

venience but are somewhat arbitrary. Gomer and her dealings with Hosea are not further mentioned though they remain the background for a treatment of the Lord's relations with Israel.

II. GOD'S CHARGE AND THE OUTCOME (4: 1–8: 14)
i. God's charge (4: 1–5: 7)

The proclamation formula **hear**, etc., is found only at 4: 1 and 5: 1. As in 2: 2, the Lord is taking legal action (*rîb*) against Israel in general and the priesthood in particular for breach of covenant. For the terms used—**faithfulness, love** (*ḥesed*), **acknowledgement of God**— see on 2: 19. Religious apostasy (1) leads to rejection of the law of the Lord (2, which reflects a knowledge of the written Sinaitic code) and this in turn produces drought (3– **mourns**, margin 'dries up'). NEB renders the verbs of v. 3 in the future. We may compare another chain reaction described in 2: 21 ff., in the opposite direction. The Hebrew of v. 4 is obscure; see RSV for the correction adopted by many modern versions. Verse 5 is also difficult and the corrections of NEB, GNB may well be right. But the general sense of the passage (4– 10) is clear enough: because the priesthood is neglecting its proper function of teaching the true knowledge of God and his law, they and the people with them will be cast off. **6. knowledge** in each case has the article: specific knowledge, i.e., of God and his word, is meant. It is possible that behind the whole passage a dispute situation such as is reported at Am. 7: 10–17 and Jer. 20: 1–6 may have existed.

To **feed on the sins of my people** (8) indicates that the priests prefer to prosper from their share of sin offerings for wilful sin rather than act to dissuade the people from evil. God's intervention will cancel the profit (9 f.) and condemn them to futility (cf. 8: 7; 9: 12, 16; Am. 5: 11; Rom. 8: 20).

Verses 10–14 launch a full-scale attack on the Baal cult, opened and closed by what appear to be popular proverbs (11, 14b). The sole possible outcome of the stupidity and debauchery of the idol worship—drunkenness, sacred prostitution and illicit sacrifice—is ruin.

Verses 15–19 warn Judah, perhaps as a rhetorical device, not to follow Israel in this pathway nor to enter false shrines, not even 'to swear by the life of the LORD' (NEB), i.e., ostensibly to worship the Lord. Compare *DOTT* p. 131 for a similar prayer 'by the life of Baal'. **Beth Aven** is a scornful nickname for Bethel —cf. Am. 5: 5, 'Bethel shall come to nought (Heb., *'awen*)'. For **Gilgal** cf. 9: 15; 12: 11. **17. leave him alone**, although somewhat conjectural, underlines the advice to Judah to ignore Israel's example. **Ephraim** is the first of 37 occurrences in Hosea. Why it is used is uncertain. Ellison suggests that it reflects a division of rule, with Menahem and Pekahiah reigning in Samaria and Pekah in Gilead between 752 and 740 B.C. (2 Kg. 15: 17–31, cf. also Hos. 5: 5 and 7: 1). He sees also a spiritual reason in that, while the jealousy of Ephraim contributed to the split of the kingdoms under Jeroboam I, yet the northern kingdom is denied the title Israel so long as it refused allegiance to David.

The text of v. 18 is also doubtful, but the themes of drunkenness and prostitution continue.

The legal imagery continues into ch. 5: cf. **judgment** (1) and **testifies** (5), while the opening verses renew the charge against the nation's leaders, the priests, heads of houses and the royal family. **1.** The phrase rendered **this judgment is against you** could mean either 'you should execute justice' or (as NIV) 'you too will be judged'. Instead, they are the undoing of the country, as three similes from hunting show. The uncertain meaning of **the rebels are deep in slaughter** can be seen by comparing NEB, RSV. 1–18. **Tabor** and **Mizpah** may be associated with Baal worship.

The speaker in v. 3 could be Hosea or Yahweh. The effect of evil in debarring a return to God (4) foreshadows the mortal sin of Mk 3: 29, I Jn 5: 16. Hence, they find that God has withdrawn himself, so as not to receive their sacrifices (cf. 5: 15; 6: 6) as once he did (Exod. 10: 9). His withdrawal, however, is voluntary, unlike the death of God in the Baal myths. **5. Israel's arrogance** is not a name for the Lord, but a sinful attitude of the people, cf. Am. 6: 8; Isa. 28: 3, which gives evidence in court (cf. 7: 10). **7.** the mention of the new moon is difficult, so that NEB emends to 'an invader', which anticipates the following verses. But it could refer to a ritual occasion—as NIV **New Moon festivals** or signify 'within a month.'

ii. A cautionary war (5: 8–6: 11a)

The threat made in v. 7 becomes real in vv. 8 ff., in which an invader's onslaught is narrated. A. Alt has shown that the background is the Syro-Ephraimite War of 734 B.C., mentioned in 2 Kg. 15: 37; 16: 5–9 and Isa. 7: 1–16. Israel and Syria, having allied to oppose Assyria, invaded Judah to compel her to join them. Ahaz appealed for help to the Assyrians, who readily responded. What Hosea recounts is the Judean counter-attack, since the place names, **Gibeah, Ramah, Beth Aven** (Bethel), move from south to north.

The warning trumpets of v. 8 are echoed in 8: 1, cf. also Jer. 4: 5; 6: 1 and Jl 2: 1. **8. lead on, O Benjamin** is rendered 'We are with you' by NEB and 'Into battle' by GNB but, on the analogy of Jg. 5: 14, could be a war-cry: 'After you, Benjamin'. As the Judean armies advance, Ephraim is laid waste (9) and the boundary marks between the two nations are

swept away (10), which provokes the wrath of God, cf. Prov. 22: 28. But the disaster is ultimately Ephraim's own fault (11b, where GNB probably brings out the sense of a difficult clause: 'she insisted on going for help to those who had none to give'—cf. also v. 13). The real enemy of the sinful people is none other than God himself (12, 14, cf. 13: 7), to whom they ought to have turned. Instead, they went to Assyria, **the great King** (cf. 10: 6) being a correction of the Hebrew in line with Isa. 36: 13. When this happened is uncertain, though 2 Kg. 17: 3 may be the event in mind. Finally (15) the Lord withdraws from them (cf. on 5: 6), awaiting true repentance, as NIV, or (as GNB) 'until they have suffered enough for their sins' (cf. Isa. 40: 2).

Although 6: 1 builds around one of Hosea's key words 'return' (cf. on 3: 5) his intention is obscure. Is he formulating a genuine expression of penitence, or a liturgy of lament, or—as the reaction of 4ff. rather indicates—does he describe a shallow, even hypocritical, response (cf. NIV heading)? The people are confident that God's answer to their prayer will be swift— **the third day . . . as surely as the sun rises** —that he has torn and injured solely to heal and bind. **heal** is used with a redemptive sense in 7: 1; 11: 3; 14: 4. But God's reply is less enthusiastic (cf. also 8: 2). Their very **love** (ḥesed, see on 2: 19) is ephemeral and hopelessly inadequate for the business in hand. They have already been told by earlier prophets (5) that he requires a deeper response—**mercy** and **acknowledgement of God**— not mere cultic acts. See similar pleas in I Sam. 15: 22; Am. 5: 21–24; Isa. 1: 12–17 and Mt. 9: 13; 12: 7, where Jesus quotes this passage.

Verses 7–11a is taken as a sequel of the foregoing, though it could be a separate pericope. **Like Adam** is an allusion to the first man's defection in Eden. Adam, cf. Jos. 3: 16, is on the Jordan and 'as at Adam' (mg) may connote that Israel breached the covenant as soon as they set foot in the promised land (cf. GNB). NEB reads 'Admah' (cf. 11: 8) which has no known association with the covenant. The noun can also be translated 'a man', which weakens the thought to 'like men' mg. The idea of covenant is rare in the pre-exilic prophets. Here, as at 8: 1, it refers to the Sinaitic covenant of Exod. 24: 3–8, the terms of which the nation broke. The concept is implicit in much of Hosea, though explicitly mentioned only twice. 10: 4 and 12: 1 allude to covenants between men.

Gilead (8) is not elsewhere called a city and no light can be thrown on the reference. **Shechem** (9), an ancient sanctuary, was used for priestly robbery, either by rapacious greed for sacrifices (4: 8) or by raids on passing caravans of pilgrims. **10. the house of Israel** could be understood as Bethel; NEB's 'Israel's sanctuary' is tantamount to this (cf. 8: 1).

Thus, instead of penitence, all that God could find in Israel was wickedness. And (11a) **Judah** is little better (cf. 5: 5). So for both there is trouble in store.

iii. Help frustrated (6: 11b–7: 16)

The key thought of this passage is 'How do you help people like this?'—cf. 13c 'I long to redeem them but . . .' and 15, 'I trained them but . . .'.

6: 11b–7: 2 show how God's efforts to heal expose the corruption of all Israel, Ephraim and Samaria alike—cf. on 4: 17. **11b. restore the fortunes** translates *šub šebut*, signifying the great restoration, the recovery of the pristine covenant relationship, anticipated in the New Year festival. For its prominence in later eschatology, see E. Jacob, *Theology of the Old Testament*, 1958 pp. 320 f. Ac. 3: 21 also picks up the idea. For **heal** see on 6: 1.

Verses 3–7, a passage fraught with much textual uncertainty, describe a palace intrigue of a kind all too common in Hosea's times, when four of Israel's kings were assassinated in twelve years. Verse 3 shows how the conspirators 'win over' (NEB instead of **delight**) the king and other leaders. As a baker's oven (see *NBD*, p. 166 for sketch) is heated up to a required level and then left quiescent until the dough is ready, so the plotters lay their plans and await the pre-arranged moment. **On the day of the festival of our king** perhaps the enthronement festival on New Year's Day, they get everyone drunk, including the king himself. Overnight they wait, but in the morning they strike, killing the king and scattering his supporters. I Kg. 16: 9 f. gives a concrete historical instance. So it is, following the NEB of v. 7b, that 'king after king falls': cf. 13: 10f.

The imagery of the bakery continues in v. 8, **mixes** relating to oil and flour being made into a cake. But the alien elements, foreign alliances involving homage to strange gods, prove disastrous, so that Ephraim resembles a spoilt **cake**, burnt on one side, raw on the other. Like Samson, Jg. 16: 20, he is unconscious of his weakness, and **does not return to the Lord his God.** For **Israel's arrogance** see on 5: 5. There is insufficient ground in this passage for the conjecture that the prophet was a baker.

Verses 11 f. picture Ephraim in her stupid vacillations as a pigeon flapping clumsily around. 2 Kg. 17: 3 ff. describe the foreign policy criticized, playing off Egypt and Assyria (cf. also 8: 9). Instead of achieving safety, she will merely be caught like a bird in a fowler's net (cf. 5: 1).

The section ends (13–16) with a warning of final disaster (**Woe**), a return to Egypt, implying the cancellation of God's choice of Israel:

cf. 11: 1, 'Out of Egypt I called my son'; see also on 9: 3. Thrice God complains of the way he is misrepresented—**speak lies** (13), **turn away from me'** (14), **plot evil** (15). Note that **against me** occurs three times in these verses. **13. redeem** might connote the Exodus, or subsequent deliverances, or, as NIV, the Lord's frustrated intentions.

The wailing and slashing (mg) of v. 14 is a practice of Baal worshippers (I Kg. 18: 28), so that NEB well represents the sense with 'there is no sincerity in their cry to me', i.e., they are not really crying to me but to Baal. The translation of v. 16a is debatable: for **Most High**, NEB gives 'their high god' (Heb. *'al*), Ellison 'a people that cannot help' and GNB, most probably, 'gods that are useless'. J. B. Phillips gives good sense for 16b: 'their arrogant talk makes them a laughing stock in the land of Egypt'.

iv. Judgment inevitable (8: 1–14)

While details may be uncertain, the overall theme of this portion, preparing for the new section, is a condemnation of the cult and the kingship, ending in a warning of return to Egypt. The fact that the first king, Jeroboam I, initiated also the idolatrous cult adds cogency to the joint condemnation. A fresh **trumpet** (cf. 5: 8) signals the approaching danger. As the griffon vulture (not an **eagle**) is mentioned, the slaughter has already taken place, since this bird is a scavenger of carrion. But what is **the house of the LORD?** Not the Jerusalem Temple, as Hosea is concerned with the northern kingdom. Various possibilities remain: the land which the Lord has given Israel to occupy (cf. 9: 3, 15); Israel herself as the Lord's heritage (Dt. 32: 9); or a sanctuary, perhaps Bethel (house of God) (see also on 6: 10). That the people make the contradictory claim of knowing God while flouting his covenant and law arouses God's anger. The plea has already been exposed as empty in 4: 1; 5: 4; 6: 6. For **covenant** cf. on 6: 7.

Verse 4a denounces the monarchy as not approved by God—cf. on 3: 5—but as part of Israel's attempt to do without him. **set up kings** summarizes historic events back to Jeroboam I, but note the present tense, of events in progress. The **calf-idol of Samaria** is denounced in vv. 4b–6. NEB has the plural (calves) reminding us that there were two, one each at Bethel and Dan (I Kg. 12: 29). **Samaria** may mean the kingdom (I Kg. 13: 32), as there is no record of such a calf-god in Omri's city of that name (I Kg. 16: 24). As man-made things, they will be destroyed. **6. it is not God** indicates that the calf itself was worshipped, not regarded as a mere throne for the deity. The last line of v. 5 is difficult. RSV appends the first words of v. 6 to complete the sense; NEB emends to read 'What sort of God is this bull?' which makes good sense; and GNB aptly paraphrases 'How long will it be before they give up their idolatry?'

In vv. 7–10, we return to political matters, especially external alliances. Two proverbs are quoted in v. 7: 'They sow the wind and reap the whirlwind' and 'The stalk has no head, it will produce no flour', the latter being a rhymed couplet, a rarity in Hebrew: for other proverbs cf. 4: 11, 14b. A bewildering variety of metaphors is used in v. 8f to describe Israel's foreign policy—cf. also 7: 8, 11. **8. swallowed up** (same root as in, v. 7) by the potential allies; **worthless thing** failing in the divine purpose; **a wild donkey** apart from its herd; and **sold herself to lovers**, returning to the prostitution imagery of the earlier chapters, with the ironic twist that this prostitute gives rather than receives presents, perhaps the tribute of 2 Kg. 17: 3. But the result is inevitable: they will cease to be a nation. None of the attempts made to clarify v. 10b carry conviction: perhaps (GNB) they will writhe under Assyria's oppression, which is close to NIV, or (RSV, NEB) they will cease anointing kings of their own; both involve emending the text.

In vv. 11–14, Hosea reverts to the cult, with renewed threats of punishment. **altars**, properly intended to remove sin, have actually increased sin, through their misuse for Baal (cf. on 4: 8), while the **law** of God, obviously known to the prophet in a written form (cf. 4: 2; 8: 1) is treated as **something alien**. **13. They offer sacrifices** renders an obscure Hebrew phrase by inference from the context. With 8: 13 cf. 9: 9 and Jer. 14: 10: their sacrifices cannot blind the Judge to their misdeeds. The judgment foreseen includes Judah as well as Israel (14), such being the result of having **forgotten his Maker. Maker** relates to the election of Israel (Ps.100: 3; Mal. 2: 10) not its physical creation. On **return to Egypt** (13) see on 7: 13–16 and 9: 3: the forgotten God remembers the people's sin and cancels his choice.

III. THE GLORY DEPARTS: ORACLES ON THE FALL OF ISRAEL (9: 1–12: 1)

Here we have five sub-sections asserting and lamenting Israel's fall from grace. Connections between the oracles are less easy to determine.

i. Joyless festivals (9: 1–9)

The repeated allusions to cultic events (vv. 1, 4, 5, 8) suggest that Hosea delivered this oracle at the Autumn Festival of Tabernacles or Booths. He deprecates the rejoicing which accompanies the occasion, because Israel lies under the threat of deportation. GNB paraphrases v. 1b effectively: 'Stop celebrating your festivals like pagans' (cf. 7: 8 and Eph. 4: 17 NEB). Ellison points out that the Mosaic emphasis on

the historic liberation from Egypt (Lev. 23: 42 f.) had fallen into the background in the Canaanized harvest cult. Thus, the remark on prostitution on the threshing floor in v. 1 has a double meaning: not only is there sacred prostitution but also the worship of false gods. The dual reference to **Egypt** and **Assyria** (3), as in 7: 11; 11: 5, 11; 12: 1,leads to the inference that the places of punishment are figuratively meant, so that **Egypt** signifies the recall of the divine election here and in 7: 16; 8: 13. **Assyria** ultimately became the place of Israel's exile (2 Kg. 17: 6).

Verses 4 ff. underline the misery of the coming exile: there will be no festival offerings or celebrations—cf. Ps. 137: 1–6 for an example of the kind of reaction when it happened.

4. the temple of the LORD, as in 8: 1, presents a problem. It cannot refer to the Jerusalem Temple and must signify another place of worship dedicated to the Lord, although this is not likely to be permitted in exile. Verse 6 indicates that while the Israelites are dying in Egypt, their own land will be overgrown with weeds, a picture of total disaster (see also 10: 8). **Their treasures of silver will be taken over by briers** is precariously corrected by NEB to 'the sands of Syrtes shall wreck them', for which McKeating proposes 'Tahpanhes shall mourn them', which fits well with the preceding lines.

Verses 7 ff. could well be a separate oracle, and can be interpreted as a dialogue between prophet and people, which might have taken place in the festival postulated as the background of vv. 1–6. The latter part of v. 7 is then a hostile reaction to the first part, as in Am. 7: 12–17 and Jer. 20: 1–6. A listener responds to the prediction of punishment, **the prophet is . . . a fool**, etc., to which the prophet replies that, as **a watchman over Ephraim**, he has a duty to oppose the people's iniquity. Verse 8 is then a comment about the fact that hatred accrues to the servants of God in his very house. See NEB for another approach, wherein, as part of the punishment, the prophet will be made crazy, so as not to give the genuine word of the Lord. Verse 8a in NEB is incomprehensible and McKeating prefers 'The prophet is the watchman of Ephraim with my God'. In this reading, the rest of the verse shows how the prophets become agents of the impending disaster because they mislead the people and v. 9 extends the description of the prophets' activity, whereas in NIV it continues the denunciation of the people. See also Ellison (p. 134) for another approach to the translation of this difficult passage. The idea of the prophet as **watchman** is developed in Ezek. 33: 1–9. **9. the days of Gibeah** may be a reference to the appointment of Saul (1 Sam. 10) or to the shocking crime of Jg. 19: 22–30; cf. on 10: 9 f.

ii. Spoilt fruit (9: 10–10: 2)

This section contains a series of sayings retrospecting on Israel's history. Ellison sees in it a foreshadowing of the doctrine of original sin. **10. grapes** growing **in the desert** would be a fantastic boon to the finder, while **early fruit on the fig tree** spell out hopes of harvest. Such was the Lord's joy in Israel at the Exodus (cf. Jer. 2: 2 f.). But her promise collapsed at **Baal Peor**, as narrated in Num. 25: 1–5, a story of sexual aberration very much in keeping with Hosea's central accusation. An important spiritual law is enunciated in the last line of v. 10: that we become good or bad according to what we admire. The positive aspect of it is presented in Phil. 4: 8. The departure of **glory** is reminiscent of 1 Sam. 4: 21: it might mean simply a fall from honour consequent upon childlessness, but **when I turn away from them** (12) suggests that it is the glory of the Lord that is intended. **Woe** occurs only here and at 7: 13, two passages that fit well together: because Israel has strayed from the Lord, they incur the misery of his departure from them.

Verse 13a is obscure. NEB gives 'As lion-cubs emerge only to be hunted', perhaps an allusion to the Assyrian practice of lion-hunting. But the general sense of the passage is clear. When the Lord departs, fruitfulness goes also. Even if children are born, they will come to slaughter. Verse 14 could be alternatively a curse or a blessing. In view of the inevitable end of offspring, it would be a mercy not to have them, even though generally 'sons are a heritage from the LORD' (Ps. 127: 3). So the expectations of the worshippers at the festival (cf. on 9: 1) are unfulfilled: there is no vision of the glory of the Lord, nor any blessing of fertility.

The reference to **Gilgal** (15) obviously meant more to Hosea than it can to us—cf. similar cryptic place names at 6: 7 ff. and 9: 9. Probably we may link it with 4: 15 and 12: 11 as a site of false cult. NEB prefers a past tense, which points to Saul's proclamation as king and offering illegal sacrifice there (1 Sam. 11: 15; 13: 8–14); cf. also on 10: 10. But the Lord's words, **hate** and **no longer love** enforce the terrible dangers of sinning. Knight comments hereon that God hates both the sin and the sinner, since they are in the last analysis inseparable (but see 14: 4). For **my house** see on 8:1, though here it is probably figurative of the land. Maybe also Hosea's marital problems obtrude here—cf. 2: 3. So the cast off people (17) wanders barren among the nations, a prophecy fulfilled after the fall of Samaria in 722 B.C., since when Israel has lost her identity.

10: 1 f. introduces a fresh though related metaphor of the **spreading vine**. NEB renders 'rank vine', taking a different view from NIV

on the etymology of the Hebrew word. But the message is clear: prosperity led to a proliferation of false religion rather than true worship (cf. also 13: 6). And the outcome is equally unmistakable—the destruction of the shrines. **sacred stones** (cf. 3: 4) were upright stones, symbolic for Canaanite religion of the male deity, and banned by the law of God (Lev. 26:1).

iii. Useless kings and cult (10: 3–10)

This brief section predicts the abolition alike of the monarchy and the cult, because from the earliest days they have not only been useless but at the root of all the national failures.

Verses 3 f. might have been uttered after the assassination of Pekah (2 Kg. 15: 30) but could be construed as a forecast of a future situation: so GNB renders 'Soon they will be saying, etc.' (cf. 3: 4). Because the rulers made no effort to fulfil their coronation promises, annually renewed, they were **false oaths**. Therefore, **lawsuits** were debased and became **poisonous weeds** in the body politic, instead of a health-giving herb. So weakness and corruption on the throne led to increased use of the court procedures, doubtless with bribery, to pervert justice.

Verse 5 pours scorn on **the calf-idol of Beth Aven** (see on 4: 15). As a 'god' it ought to care for its worshippers; instead, they were anxious for its safety. Such **splendour** as it had will depart, as had the glory of Ephraim (9: 11). **rejoiced** and **taken from** have similar sounds in Hebrew. Eventually, the thing itself will go to Assyria, as a tribute to the **great king** (for which see on 5: 13), to the shame of Israel.

In the coming terror, the king and the sanctuaries shall be swept away and the refugees seek shelter in the hills (7 f., a prophecy taken up by Jesus in Lk. 23: 30 and by Rev. 6: 16). For **the days of Gibeah** see on 9: 9. The **double sin** might be the two events there mentioned: other possibilities are that two events unknown to us are meant; that the cult and the non-Davidic monarchy, or the rejection of the true kingship and continuation in schism are intended; or that **double** is a synonym for 'very great' (cf. GNB many sins').

iv. Wicked ploughing (10: 11–15)

Once more, Ephraim is likened to a **heifer** but now, in contrast to 4: 16, a **trained** one. At first given the attractive task of threshing (cf. Dt. 25: 4), it was later made to plough. Similarly, Ephraim in the wilderness days had light service but after entry into the Promised Land had to toil on their farms. Applied to the moral and spiritual realm (12) the yoke of the law involved the duties of righteousness, unfailing love and seeking the Lord (cf. 2: 19 f.; 4: 1; 6: 6). **unploughed** fits in with the figure of the cow having to begin hard work. **righteous-**

ness renders *ṣedeq*, which is essentially a right relationship with the Lord, which in turn led to deliverance, so that the meaning 'salvation' (RSV) was appropriate.

What Ephraim actually did, however, was far removed from the divine requirement (13a): **wickedness**, **evil**, **deception**. Trusting in their own efforts, they receive military defeat. No record of the sack of **Beth Arbel** has survived, but such cruelty as is described was not uncommon, and might be expected by defeated Ephraim. **when that day dawns** makes good sense, but cf. the NEB 'as sure as day dawns' and the GNB 'as soon as the battle begins', i.e. at break of day.

v. God—holy Father (11: 1–12: 1)

McKeating's heading for 11: 1–11 is attractive: 'The Prodigal Son'. God is presented as a Father torn between love and severity for a wayward child. **I loved him** is better rendered, with G. A. Smith, 'I began to love him', cf. 9: 15 RSV, 'I began to hate them'. So the Lord's dealings with Israel are dated, as always in Hosea, from Egypt (cf. 12: 9; 13: 4). But, as at 9: 10 and 13: 1, they fell away to the Baals, to whom they both **sacrificed** and **burnt incense**, the latter being better translated at 4: 13 by RSV as 'make offerings'.

Verses 3 f. bring the fatherhood of God vividly to life as they present the early days of Israel with God in terms of a baby learning to walk, perhaps based on Hosea's experiences with his own children after Gomer left him. NEB extensively corrects the text to sustain this analogy and gives very good sense. **Healed** is difficult in the context. It is used redemptively at 5: 13; 6: 1; 7: 1; 14: 4 but is inappropriate here. GNB 'took care of' is meaningful and the NEB 'harnessed them with leading strings' keeps the metaphor at the expense of the language.

With the whole passage compare the parable of the foundling in Ezek. 16. We may observe that the fatherhood of God here is moral and spiritual, in contrast to the physical ideas of the Baal cults, and is corporate, in contrast to the individual interpretation in the New Testament.

But (5 ff.) the behaviour of the child evokes the Father's wrath, more strongly stated than, *e.g.*, at Prov. 3: 11 f., where the sonship continues through the chastisement, whereas here the punishment is the breaking off of the relationship. Other modern versions follow the LXX in omitting **not** before **return to Egypt** (5) but NIV takes the sentence as a question. Ellison states that 'the negative belongs in a changed form to the end of the preceding verse' though Cheyne notes that 'no tenable way of fitting it in to the construction there has yet been proposed'. If, with RV, we retain the negative, we may have an anticipation of the failure of Hoshea's pro-Egyptian policy as described in 2 Kg. 17: 4 ff. In

any case, severe discipline is in store for Ephraim, military defeat and exile.

The text of 6 f. is highly problematical. NIV gives as good a rendering as can be obtained. NEB of 7b envisages the people calling on 'their high god' instead of the Lord; cf. on 7:16.

There follow three separate oracles, each of two verses. Verses 8 f. are 'the finest presentation in the Old Testament of the tension between the love and justice of God' (Ellison). Not until the cross do we see the full resolution of this tension, whereby God can be both 'just and justifier' (Rom. 3: 26). The background of 11: 1–7 may well be in Dt. 21: 18–21, which requires parents to deliver up a rebellious son for the death sentence. Now the Divine Father finds himself unable to do it. **Admah** and **Zeboiim** were near to Sodom and Gomorrah (Gen. 10: 19) and were evidently destroyed at the same time (Dt. 29: 23). Again, the Lord is unable to do such a thing to Israel. For 9b, the NEB is to be preferred: 'I will not turn round and destroy Ephraim', as we know of no previous destruction to justify the **again** of NIV. Ellison translates v. 9 in the form of questions: 'Shall I not execute my fierce anger' etc., believing that the attractive idea that God will not exact the full penalty has no place in the Old Testament, but that the penalty is exacted in history, while the restoration is eschatological.

However, the vital point is **I am God and not man**. Parents do deliver children to death and husbands divorce wives, but God will never give up his chosen people (cf. Isa. 49: 15). Thus **the Holy One** demonstrates that his behaviour ultimately transcends the best of humanity. Cf. also Isa. 31: 3; Ezek. 28: 2; Num. 23: 19. Verses 10 f. show how the divine compassion will work out its purpose, recalling the people from exile after the disasters of 5 f. Note the different use of the concept of God as a lion from that of 5: 14; 13: 7 and of Israel as birds from that of 7: 11 f. The oracle formula **declares the LORD** occurs only here and 2: 13, 16.

The next two verses conclude this section of the prophecy (9: 1–12: 1) and sum up the sin of Israel, particularly their double-dealing with Assyria and Egypt. That **Judah** should be mentioned (12c) is unexpected. Also uncertain is the intention of the passage. NIV renders it unfavourably to Judah, but a good sense is possible, cf. NIV. Again, **the Holy One** is not singular, as in v. 9, but plural, which could be a device of emphasis or, alternatively, could be rendered 'the idols he counts holy' as in NEB. Even the word for **God** (*'el*) may well point to a Canaanite deity.

IV. LESSONS FROM HISTORY (12: 2–13: 16)

Now follow four short oracles on the historical

tradition, 'a meditation on the history of Israel's relations with God' (McKeating), going back beyond the Exodus to the common ancestor of Ephraim and Judah, Jacob, which is unique in this prophecy.

i. Jacob's deceit (12: 2–9)
The legal imagery which began the second section (4: 1) recurs here: **charge** rendering the same word again Jacob's supplanting, first his brother and then God (3 ff.), is linked with Ephraim's deceitful trading practices (7).

Judah, as in 11: 12, is unexpected. While it might be attributed to an editor in the southern kingdom, Ellison suggests it might indicate that the sin under consideration is not peculiar to Israel. **Jacob**, introduced as progenitor of both nations, is treated less favourably than in Genesis and also the order of treatment of the events differs. Verse 3a alludes to Gen. 25: 26, with the verb used as in Gen. 27: 36; 3b and 4 reflect the word-play of Gen. 32: 28, but 4b reverts to Gen. 28: 11–17, unless Hosea regarded **Bethel** as the location of struggle with the angel. Verse 4 is ambiguous in the original: it could be Jacob or the angel who prevailed (cf. NEB and margin). No reference to weeping is found in the Peniel incident in Genesis. It could derive from Gen. 33: 4, 10, where Jacob on meeting Esau both **wept and begged for his favour**. If this is so, Jacob got his own way by various methods twice over his brother as well as over God. He thus appears as the arch-twister.

The tense of the verb changes at the end of v. 4 and the noun is absent, perhaps being supplied in v. 5. Ellison accordingly renders 'At Bethel He would meet us and there He would speak with us', presenting a challenge to Hosea's immediate hearers, possibly at the sanctuary at Bethel, in view of the doxology in v. 5. Verse 6 applies the message to the reader, using some of Hosea's great words—**return** (cf. on 3: 5), **love**, *hesed* (cf. on 2: 19) and **justice** (cf. also Mic. 6: 8).

True to their progenitor's trickery (7 ff.) is the business procedure of the descendants. **The merchant** translates the word 'Canaan', which is both the name of the pre-Israelite dwellers in the Promised Land and a pejorative title for a merchant. Instead of driving out the former inhabitants, Israel had sunk to their level. **Defraud** is consistent with **dishonest scales**—cf. Prov. 11: 1. In v. 8a, Ephraim makes the dubious claim that the end justifies the means, with the tacit erroneous assumption that wealth must be the final proof of divine approval. 8b could be taken, with RSV and NEB, as an observation by the prophet or, with GNB, as a continuation of the people's claim: 'No one can accuse us of getting rich dishonestly'.

Verse 9 can also be interpreted in two ways. It might be a threat to reduce this successful businessman to his original penury or, better, a reminder of first principles. As God chose Israel in Egypt, despite Jacob's known failings, so he by a new Exodus (cf. 2: 14) will bring her back to her walk with him. **the appointed feasts** include Tabernacles, which was prophetic of the return to God—cf. 9: 1.

ii. Prophetic opportunities (12: 10–14)
As there is no discernible thread of discourse in this brief section, each verse must be taken alone.

Verse 10 may hark back to the criticism of the prophet in 9: 7 f. **told parables** could be rendered 'destroyed' (cf. 6: 5), as in GNB 'Through prophets I gave my people warning'. From this and Zech. 1: 4 ff. it is evident that God sent more prophets to his people than we know about. **Gilead** and **Gilgal** have already been mentioned as sites of evil (6: 8; 9: 15). Both NEB and GNB identify the **wicked** deeds of Gilead as idolatry, which enhances the parallel with the second member. McKeating notes a play on the word *'wn* in v. 3 ('as a man'), 8 ('wealthy'), and here ('wicked'). In 8: 11 reference was made to the proliferation of altars: in these two towns, one on each side of the Jordan, they were as plentiful and as useless, or worse, as stones piled up by a farmer after ploughing a field.

The link between vv. 12 and 13 lies in the Hebrew word *šmr*, rendered successively **tended** and **cared for**. Resuming the subject of vv. 2 ff., these verses perhaps criticize the agreement made between Jacob and Laban the Syrian (Gen. 29: 15–20), which would be germane to the alliance leading to the Syro-Ephraimitic war, for which see on 5: 8 ff.. Alternatively, that he **served** for **a wife** may be paralleled with the Baalistic sex-cult. Further, whereas Jacob as a lone man did service, Israel at the call of God was served by a prophet, Moses (cf. Dt. 18: 15). Either way, the adverse attitude to Jacob is maintained.

Verse 14 gives the final verdict on Israel from the patriarchal period onwards. His severe provocation of the Lord necessitates the death penalty, which it is not proposed to waive. Only here does Hosea use the word for 'Lord', Heb. *'adonay* (as distinct from *YHWH*).

iii. Lost power (13: 1–3)
Translation and textual problems make the precise meaning of this short section difficult to ascertain. In v. 1, NIV gives a message similar to 9: 10 and 11: 1 f., that the once exalted Ephraim (cf. Gen. 48: 15–20) fell by Baal worship. **became guilty** implies, by the structure of the Hebrew, a specific momentary action, which Ellison identifies as the setting up of the calves by Jeroboam I. The variant translation offered by NEB leaves the sense obscure.

Verse 2 advances from past to present: despite the consequences of their sin, they keep at it and manufacture ever more idols. In the last two lines, RSV again gives good sense, with some assistance from NIV. The NEB does not improve the sense with its 'Those who kiss calf-images offer human sacrifice', which signifies that homage to the images is no more acceptable to God than human sacrifice. But the condemnation of v. 3 is quite unmistakable: as their love is like the morning mist (6: 4) so they themselves would be ephemeral and disappear without trace.

iv. The wrath of God (13: 4–16)

Hosea's message of doom culminates in this passage with a threat of disaster with every appearance of finality. That it can be followed in the next chapter by a call to repentance and an offer of hope demonstrates the conditional nature of all prophecy as well as the perseverance of divine grace.

Verses 4–8 illustrate Congreve's line: 'Heaven has no rage like love to hatred turned'. Staking his claim to be their God because of his choice of them in Egypt, as is usual in Hosea, God reviews their history to remind them that in the past they knew no other God or helper. Correspondingly, he **cared for** them in the **desert**. Yet on entry to the land, the very prosperity he gave caused them to forget him. Compare also 10: 1, and note the recurrence here of 'acknowledge' and its converse 'forget'. In consequence, God becomes their worst enemy and his anger is described in language of terrible violence (cf. 5: 14 and Am. 3: 2). Curses of a similar kind occur in Hittite vassal treaties of this period.

The text of vv. 9 ff. needed some correction to make sense, but NIV brings out the general sense that in the crisis ahead, the national leaders will prove useless, since the foe is not man but God, as in 2: 10 and 5: 14. Verse 11 comments on the fact that fourteen of the twenty-two non-Davidic kings of Israel had died prematurely, including all but two of the successors of Jeroboam II. (Cf. also on 3: 5 and 8: 4.) The singular **king** may indicate that a particular individual was in mind. It is interesting to reflect that Israel's punishment for asking for a king was actually the granting of the request—cf. Ps. 106: 15.

12. stored up alludes to the way that documents, such as the Qumran scrolls, were preserved by wrapping in cloth and depositing in jars. So was the record of Ephraim's sin permanently retained. In a change of metaphor, the next verse describes him as a child too foolish to be born (cf. 2 Kg. 19: 3) because he will not embrace his last chance to return to God.

The position being such that only a miraculous intervention by God could avail, we have to decide whether or not v. 14 holds out such a hope. Commentators are divided on the issue,

since it is possible to translate as NIV, AV and RV **I will ransom . . .** or as RSV and NEB 'shall I ransom . . . ?'. **where . . . are . . . is** in the following lines involves a slight correction of the Hebrew with the LXX, cf. RSV margin. As the preceding and succeeding verses unmistakably bring a threat of doom, we should probably take v. 14 so. The Lord asks whether he should act as *ga'al*, kinsman-redeemer, and pay the ransom price, but decides against it. **Death** and **Grave** are then invited to do their worst, as **compassion** is not to be exercised. Contrast 11: 8, where the opposite decision is made, but see notes thereon.

Paul quotes part of this verse in 1 C. 15: 55 and reaches a hopeful conclusion on the basis of the death and resurrection of Christ, factors yet future to Hosea, and the very miraculous intervention of God which was postulated above as the sole chance of deliverance.

In v. 15 there seems to be an echo of the blessing of Joseph in Dt. 33: 13–17, especially in the phrases **among his brothers** and **treasures**. For consistency, RSV and NEB emend so as to give the picture of Ephraim flourishing like a reed plant in a swamp, but even there the devastating **east wind** of judgment does its work, as in Jer. 4: 11 f.

Finally, doom is pronounced (v. 16). An invader will put everyone to the sword, even little children and pregnant women, as was common enough in the ghastly inhumanity of war. **Samaria**, the capital city, is named either as synecdoche for the whole country or as the centre from which the evil was organized. So ends Hosea's message relating to the immediate condition of Israel. It was to be tragically fulfilled in 722 B.C., when the Assyrians sacked Samaria, as recorded in 2 Kg. 17: 6.

V. FINAL APPEAL (14: 1–9)

After the total disaster of 13: 4–16, anything but silence could hardly be expected to follow. Yet a further chapter of blessing and hope is appended, parallel with the restoration of Gomer in ch. 3. Despite 1: 11 and 3: 5, the re-union of the two nations and the restoration of the Davidic dynasty do not figure in the portrait of final bliss. Neither is there any concept of a remnant, as is found in Isaiah, nor of individual, as opposed to corporate, reaction to God's pleas. Doubtless the principle observed in Heb. 1: 1 is here working out: Hosea's vision is partial. The revelation of God's total plan awaited future developments.

The chapter has too much in common with the rest of the book for us to accept the theory that it was not composed by Hosea. Rabbinic expositors use the passage as the basis for teaching on repentance.

Apart from the final editorial note (9), the chapter falls into two sections: vv. 1 ff., the prophet's summons to return, including a prayer of penitence; and vv. 4–8, the divine response. This is the obverse of 6: 1–6, where the people propose repentance, but God rejects it as too shallow.

On **return** (1) see 3: 5; the Heb. verb recurs in vv. 2, 4 and 7, while **waywardness** (4) has the same root, echoing **turned**, and **dwell** (7) has a similar form. The passage thus has a kind of sonata form, with **return** as the theme.

downfall occurs also at 4: 5 and 5: 5 where NIV renders 'stumble' and may be used as in Rom. 11: 11, to denote something less than a total fall. As yet the possibility of recovery remains open, hence the exhortation to realise it.

In the prayer of v. 2, **fruit** (Heb. *peri*) differs from 'bulls' of NIVmg (Heb. *parim*) in respect only of two-vowel points and a variant division between two words; it is perhaps a reflection of Hosea's distrust of animal sacrifices, as noted at 6: 6; 8: 13. If so, NEB 'cattle from our pens' mars the sense. NIV follows the LXX, as does Heb. 13: 15. Compare also Prov. 12: 14; 13: 2.

In v. 3, three false objects of trust, so often denounced in this prophecy, are explicitly denied—foreign alliances, military power and idols. GNB best brings out the significance of the last line: 'You show mercy to those who have no one else to turn to', i.e., Israel confesses its total dependence on God's grace.

That grace is beautifully expressed in God's response in vv. 4–7. The promises in 5 ff. resemble Ca. 2: 1, 3, 13; 4: 8. For **heal**, a frequent figure of divine mercy, cf. 5: 13; 6: 1; 7: 1. **7. He will flourish like the grain** is a correction for consistency with the context; RSVmg and NEB are closer to the Hebrew.

Verse 8 can be understood in a number of ways, none of them free from difficulty. As translated by NIV it might be taken as a monologue by the Lord, who virtually asks, 'How can you associate me with your idols?', or as a dialogue, with Ephraim and the Lord speaking the successive lines. NEB, GNB, follow the former alternative, taking the first clause, as NIVmg, with LXX, as 'What has Ephraim to do with idols?' Thus the prophet's work ends as he sees both full vindication for the Lord and complete restoration and blessing for Israel.

The final verse is an editorial note, advising the reader to pay careful attention to the message of the book: cf. Ps. 107: 43. So the last word of Hosea himself is echoed by the Lord Jesus in Jn 15: 5: 'He who abides in me . . . bears much fruit'.

BIBLIOGRAPHY

ANDERSEN, F. I. and FREEDMAN, D. N., *Hosea. AB* (Garden City, N.Y., 1980).

CHEYNE, T. K., *Hosea. CBSC* (Cambridge, 1892).

ELLISON, H. L., *The Prophets of Israel* (Exeter, 1969).

HARPER, W. R., *Amos and Hosea. ICC* (Edinburgh, 1905) [On the Hebrew text].

KNIGHT, G. A. F., *Hosea. TC* (London, 1960).

LINDBLOM, J., *Prophecy in Ancient Israel* (Oxford, 1973).

McKEATING, H., *The Books of Amos, Hosea and Micah. CBC* (Cambridge, 1971).

MAYS, J. L., *Hosea* (London, 1969).

ROWLEY, H. H., *Men of God* (London, 1963), ch. 3: 'The Marriage of Hosea'.

SMITH, G. A., *The Book of the Twelve Prophets. EB* (London, 1896).

TAYLOR, J. B., *The Minor Prophets* (London, 1970).

RAD, G. VON, *The Message of the Prophets* (London, 1968).

WOLFF, H. W., *A Commentary on the Book of the Prophet Hosea*, E.T. Hermeneia (Philadelphia, 1974).

JOEL

PAUL E. LEONARD

Authorship

Joel, the son of Pethuel, is a figure unknown apart from the book which bears his name. The name means 'Yahweh is God' but it is unclear whether this name was given him at birth or ascribed later in response to his ministry. He emerged without fanfare from Israel's ancient past, spoke a clear word to his generation and provided future eras with a brief but perceptive glimpse into the spiritual life of the people of God of his time. Then he vanished, leaving behind a vivid recollection, a prophetic insight recognized by successive generations of God's people as 'the word of the LORD' (Jl 1: 1).

Dating

Estimates of the period of Joel's prophetic activity vary widely, ranging from the ninth to the fourth centuries B.C. There are no specific historical details to rely upon, therefore arguments are largely based on internal evidence. Judah's enemies are identified as Edom, Egypt, Philistia and Phoenicia, opponents from pre-exilic days. Certain emphases such as the day of the Lord, the outpouring of the Spirit and the ultimate restoration of the nation are shared with prophets of the sixth (Ezekiel) and eighth (Amos) centuries B.C. If Jl 2: 32 includes a quotation from Ob. 17 we have an early sixth century *terminus a quo*. On the other hand Joel's alleged inclusion of post-exilic terms has been seen as evidence for a later date. There is no easy solution to this problem. While a slight preference might be stated for a sixth-century date, and the majority opinion is for the fifth century, the timelessness of the prophecy itself renders the need for decision relatively unimportant.

Message

A plague of locusts had invaded the productive lands of Joel's audience (1: 4–7), destroying all plant life in its path. The prophet interprets this natural calamity as a warning from God (1: 15). The loss is incalculable. Not only will there be no harvest, but the cattle and sheep, as well as people, will perish for lack of food (1: 18). Even farm buildings will deteriorate, there being no grain to store (1: 17). Eventually the nation's worship itself will suffer, since without food 'joy and gladness' is cut off 'from the house of our God' (1: 16). Joel further warns that this disaster is only a prelude to the coming apocalyptic judgement of God (2: 1 ff.). In order to avoid this far greater disaster he calls the people to a solemn assembly where they must fast (1: 14) and return to the Lord (2: 12 ff.). Yahweh is to be reminded that Israel is his people and that should they be destroyed the 'nations' will challenge the very existence of Israel's God.

Yahweh's response to the people is introduced with the words 'Then the LORD will be jealous for his land, and take pity on his people' (Jl 2: 18). The following narrative describes first the deliverance from the plague of locusts (2: 20), followed by restoration of the land and crops (2: 21–22). The people shall once more have plenty and shall know that Yahweh is in their midst, never again to put the people to shame (2: 23–27). But there is more—the prophet now looks to the future when according to Yahweh's promise there will come a great outpouring of his Spirit upon his people (2: 28–29). This promised event will presage the coming 'dreadful day of the LORD' (2: 31) to be accompanied by portents in the sky (2: 30), the salvation of everyone 'who calls on the name of the LORD' (2: 32) and the restoration of the 'fortunes of Judah and Jerusalem' (3: 1). Yahweh will then assemble those nations who have oppressed his people and will avenge the innocent (3: 2–15).

In the end, those who might have been the instrument of judgement upon the disobedient people of God, will themselves be judged for their evil (3: 19). However all who seek refuge in the Lord will be vindicated (3: 16 ff.) and the blessing of Yahweh will once and for all rest on his repentant people (3: 17–18) for 'Yahweh dwells in Zion' (3: 20–21).

Significance and Use in NT

While this is one of the briefest books in the Old Testament it is at the same time one of the most profound. Both in its grasp of the relationship between historical events and the suprahistorical expectation of the day of the Lord, and also in its impact on early Christian theology, its influence has hardly been proportionate to its size.

As a harbinger of Jewish apocalyptic, Joel shares with this literary genre (*a*) an emphasis on a pastoral motif in the description of the new age (cf. Jl 3: 17–18; Isa. 2: 1–4); (*b*) an increasing awareness that Israel is uniquely the focus of God's redemptive efforts toward mankind and that the nations represent an incarnation of evil attempting to thwart the purposes of God; and (*c*) a spiritual emphasis (2: 28–29) based on the expressed Mosaic wish that 'all the LORD's people were prophets, that the LORD would put his spirit on them' (Num. 11: 29) (see *art.* 'Joel', *IDB*).

Following the ecstatic outbursts associated with the events of Pentecost, Peter offers Jl 2: 28–29 in explanation of the apparently bizarre behaviour. It is through the Spirit of God that all present are reminded of 'the wonders of God' (Ac. 2: 5–11). And the apostle Paul, writing to the Roman church [possibly founded

by Jewish Christians who were in Jerusalem during the events of this Pentecost (Ac. 2: 10)] includes Greeks as well as Jews within the embrace of the promise of Joel that **everyone who calls on the name of the LORD will be saved** (Rom. 10: 11–13; cf. Jl 2: 26b, 32).

For other NT references probably dependent on Joel see Mk 4: 29 (Jl 3: 13); Ac. 2: 39 (Jl 2: 32); Rev. 6: 12 (Jl 2: 10, 31; 3: 15); 6: 17 (Jl 2: 11); 9: 7–9 (Jl 1: 6; 2: 4–5); 14: 15, 18 (Jl 3: 13).

ANALYSIS

I. TITLE (1: 1)
While little is known of **Joel, son of Pethuel,** the identification of his work as the **word of the LORD** is a crucial imprimatur. The authority attending his message is a divine authority. The message was entrusted to an individual, who as trustee was responsible to deliver the message to the people. In the fulfilment of this task Joel affirms his prophetic calling, declaring to the congregation the **word of the LORD.**

II. PLAGUE OF LOCUSTS: PRELUDE TO JUDGEMENT (1: 1–2: 27)
i. Devastation of the Plague (1: 2–20)
(a) **Unprecedented calamity (1: 2–3)**
Not in the recollection of the aged men (**elders**

appropriately emphasizes the leadership role of these men), nor even in that of their fathers could such an onslaught of pestilence be recalled. So traumatic was the disaster that parents are urged to recall the details to their **children** so that they might relay the report to **their children** and they in turn to the succeeding **generation.** Five generations are here encompassed, suggesting the importance of the locusts' onslaught to the prophet. Because such infestations are not uncommon in the near-east, the special significance of this one relates not only to its severity but also to the fact that it is seen as a prelude to the divine devastation the prophet envisions for the disobedient people of God and those nations which have oppressed her.

(b) Description of the Plague (1: 4–12)
The language used to describe the locust plague
reflects accurately the several growth stages and
effects of this destructive insect. Great swarms
arrive periodically from the south, the native
region of the desert locust being the Sudan
(*IDB* 3, 144 ff.). They are capable of migrating
with the wind (Exod. 10: 13) more than 1200
miles, not altering direction during a flight
which might last up to three days. Upon descent their ravenous appetite is appeased by
destruction of most plant life within reach. The
female then deposits a large number of eggs in
a hole she previously excavated in the ground.
Larvae emerge from these eggs within weeks,
capable of moving along the ground by leaps,
the **young locust** (RSV 'hopping') (4). Hopper
swarms climb and pass unhindered over rocks,
walls and hills, swimming rivers and filling
trenches with the bodies of dead over which
the rest march. Devouring great quantities of
vegetation as they go, the hoppers moult several times, finally emerging as the adult **other
locust**, able to fly and thus reach further plant
life. Apparently this second generation of locusts is unable to reproduce and so eventually
disappears from the area providing relief until
another swarm appears.

5. An immediate result of the plague is that
the grape harvest has been destroyed. There
will be no new **wine**. The annual harvest festival of ingathering (Exod. 23: 16), will be observed with weeping, rather than the usual
joyful celebration. The **drunkards**, whose
minds and spirits have been rendered insensitive are warned to **wake up**. Otherwise they
are in danger of missing the significance of the
calamity that has befallen the nation.

6. The infestation of the locusts is further
described figuratively as **a nation . . . powerful and without number** which **has invaded
my land**. Its strength is depicted as that of **the
teeth of a lion** or **fangs of a lioness. 7.** The
result of the onslaught is that the grape vines
have been ruined and the fig trees not only
ruined, but their bark **stripped off**.

The prophet now calls on the nation, including its ministers and farm workers, to mourn.
8. Like the young virgin, widowed before she
could be taken as wife by the **husband** (mg.
'betrothed') **of her youth**, they grieve their
loss. **9.** The failure of the harvest has made it
impossible to continue the daily offerings in
the **house of the LORD**. The **priests are in
mourning** because they are unable to discharge their duties of maintaining communion
with God through sacrifice on behalf of the
nation. No disaster greater than this could overtake the people of God. As part of the covenant,
daily sacrifice of two lambs was dictated (Exod.
29: 38 ff.). The lamb sacrificed in the morning
was offered alone but the evening lamb was

offered along with a 'grain offering' (Exod. 29:
41). As long as the offering continued, God's
presence with his people was assured (Exod.
29: 42–46). The inability to fulfil this obligation
as well as the impossibility of celebrating the
harvest festival, likewise a covenant requirement, put the covenant relationship itself in
jeopardy. To suspend the sacrifice was to suspend the covenant relation and thus to suspend
the relationship between God and his people.

11. The **farmers** and the **vine growers** likewise mourn because the grain and vine are
destroyed. However the locust damage extends
also to **all the trees of the field** (12) to include
the fig, pomegranate, palm and apple trees.
The devastation is complete. Every source of
food has been affected and **the joy of mankind
is withered away**.

(c) Call for repentance (1: 13–20)
A new section, formal in character, is introduced with the exhortation to the priests. **13.
Put on sackcloth . . . and mourn . . . wail,
you who minister before the altar.** Repentance is the proper response to the disaster at
hand, and it must begin with the spiritual
leaders. Their livelihood as well as their role as
representatives of the people before God is at
stake. **14.** They must appoint a fast and call a
sacred assembly. It is not enough that the
leaders repent. They must gather the elders and
all the people **to the house of the LORD** and
beseech him for mercy. At this juncture the
prophet warns that the present sadness is
merely a prelude to an even more disastrous
possibility. **15. the day of the LORD is near:**
this destruction has come from **the
Almighty**. There is a play on words in Hebrew: a *shōd* from *Shaddai* (cf. Isa. 13: 6). **17.**
The plague has been accompanied by drought
so that seed freshly sown was **shriveled beneath the clods**. Not only has term damage
already occurred to trees and rivers and the
present harvest been destroyed, but the prospect of a future harvest is dim due to insufficient
moisture to germinate the seed. Since the granaries will not be used they are falling into
disrepair and since there is insufficient pasture
the cattle and sheep suffer and face an uncertain
future (18). **19.** The prophet himself now cries
to the Lord on behalf of all the afflicted, complaining that the situation is such that **even the
wild animals pant for you; the streams of
water have dried up** (20) and wilderness pasture has been destroyed by fire (19).

**ii. Apocalyptic Judgement Threatened
(2: 1–27)**
**(a) Day of the LORD will bring destruction
(2: 1–11)**
For Joel the plague of locusts is an earnest of
the judgement to come. For him as for other
prophets the 'day of the LORD' (*yôm Yahweh*)
is always at hand. This 'day', described in Isa.

2: 12–22, is one in which God will destroy everything that has exalted itself against him. It was expected that the covenant promises of God would be fulfilled in the day of his coming, that he would 'tend his flock like a shepherd' (Isa. 40: 11) and that Jerusalem's 'hard service' would be ended (Isa. 40: 2). At the same time there would be a fearsome rooting out of evil. Since Israel was guilty of sin and indifference to justice, the Lord's coming would bring judgement instead of blessings (cf. Am. 5: 21–24; 6: 1 ff.).

1. With the locust plague in mind the judgement of God upon the nation is described with apocalyptic overtones. The **trumpet** is the *shōfār*, the ram's horn used to call the people to battle (Jg. 6: 34 ff.), to worship (Ps. 150: 3), to announce an important event (1 Kg. 1: 34) or the presence of God (Exod. 19: 16). The trumpet is here used to **sound the alarm** on Mount Zion. All the inhabitants should **tremble** realizing that the judgement of God is near. Drawing on the vivid recent impression of skies darkened by hordes of locusts the prophet describes the 'day of the Lord' as a **day of darkness and gloom**, and the invader, **a large and mighty army**, the like of which has never existed before nor will again **in ages to come** (2). They cover the mountains **like dawn** (RSV 'blackness') and are led by the Lord Himself (cf. v. 11). Their onslaught is devastating. Like a marauding fire they sweep over the land which **is like the garden of Eden before them, behind them a desert waste** (3).

In vv. 4–11 the judgement associated with the day of the Lord is depicted in metaphors more distinctly military in nature. **4.** The face of a locust reputedly resembles that of a horse and the speed of movement could likewise compare with that of a horse. **5.** The colouring of the adult locust, a bronze tint to their wings, reflects sunlight so as to resemble flames. More to the point, the assault by hordes of the creatures on grain stalks can indeed resemble a **crackling fire** racing across the land. **6.** The reaction of people to such an attack is that of pure **anguish**. Nothing can be done to slow down the advance. The organization is superb. **7. like soldiers they scale walls** and with a military-like discipline **not swerving from their course, all** marching **in line**. Through sheer force of numbers they overcome the perimeter defence weapons and move quickly to occupy the city house by house (9). In earthly terms, their triumph is complete. However the prophet further describes in apocalyptic language the result of the rampaging forces on the elements of nature. **10. Before them the earth shakes, the sky trembles:** using terms commonly used of the day of judgement, **the sun and moon are darkened** (cf. Isa. 13: 9–10; Ezek. 32: 7; Jl 2: 31; 3: 15; Mk 13: 24). In

the terror of darkness **the LORD thunders** (11), issuing commands at the head of his great army. NEB 'countless are those who do his bidding' is a better translation than the NIV text **mighty are these who obey his command** (11). His description of the terror of judgement complete, the prophet exclaims **the day of the LORD is great; it is dreadful**. In the light of the ravages of the locust and the threatened ravages of a yet far greater doom he adds, with an almost audible sigh, **who can endure it?**

(b) Call for repentance (2: 12–14)
The first part of the prophecy (1: 1–20) described the effect of the locusts on land and worship with an appeal for the appropriate response of mourning, lamenting and crying out to God. The second part (2: 1–21) dwells on the disaster as mirroring (or actually inaugurating) the impending judgement of the **day of the LORD**, stressing the effect on the people themselves.

12. The scene shifts: **'return to me with all your heart,'** says the Lord. **'Even now'** emphasizes that though judgement has already begun, it is not too late to stay God's hand: **fasting** (see *art.* 'Fasting', *NBD*), **weeping**, and **mourning** are outward accompaniments of true repentance which is a **return** to the Lord. **13.** Tearing of garments was the ordinary expression of mourning but such an outward demonstration is inadequate. It is necessary rather to **rend your heart**. The heart in Semitic thought represents the centre of the whole man with all his attributes, physical, intellectual and emotional (see *art.* 'Heart', *NBD*). To **rend your heart** represents a radical change of mind, the adoption of a different way of looking at all of life. The old patterns are to be destroyed, replaced by new attitudes suitable for those through whom God is making himself known in the world (Watts, *Joel*, etc., pp. 27 f.). The invitation to **return to the LORD** is repeated, this time followed by additional reasons the people should respond. God is **gracious** and **compassionate, slow to anger and abounding in love** (cf. Jon. 4: 2; Jas 1: 19). **14a.** While he has determined to judge the evil among his people, if they only change their wilfully evil ways he too will change his will and **relent** from the intended judgement. The character of God here portrayed is identical to that declared by the Lord himself on Sinai (Exod. 34: 6–9). As the offerings and feasts (Jl 1: 9, 13) witness to the continuing validity of the covenant relationship between God and Israel (Exod. 23: 14–19) so the gracious and steadfastly loving God who revealed himself to Moses will repeatedly forgive 'wickedness, rebellion and sin' (Exod. 34: 7) when approached by a truly repentant people. Faced with such a possibility the Ninevites were prepared to test God (Jon. 3: 6–10), but Jonah rebelled (Jon. 4: 1–3).

Lacking pity, he failed to understand that the promise of God at Sinai could be fulfilled even at Nineveh. He had railed at evil for so long he forgot that God was not only holy and pure but also merciful and prepared to forgive when people turned from their evil. Joel on the other hand *was* prepared to claim the covenant promise and hold it out as a lifeline to the people of his day.

14b. Instead of the threatened judgement, the Lord **will leave behind a blessing**, denoted by **grain offerings and drink offerings for the Lord, your God**. The effect of the locust plague will be removed, the land will be healed. There will be food once more for use by the priests in the daily offerings.

(c) Plea for deliverance (2: 15–17)
15–16a. Fulfilment of the promise is however fully dependent on the repentance of the people. Once more the command is given: **Blow the trumpet in Zion**. Instead of an alarm (2: 1), the trumpet is now intended to **call a sacred assembly**, to **declare a holy fast**, to **gather the people**, language parallel to 1: 14.

15b. The **sacred assembly** is to include all the **people**, starting with the **elders** and including not only the **children** but even **those nursing at the breast**. The **bridegroom** too and his **bride** are to leave their pre-occupation with each other to join the fasting assembly. As all are included in the judgement of evil, so must all join in the public repentance of the nation. The parallelism is striking, both between the first verses of the prophecy (Jl 1: 2–3) and this narrative, and within vs. 15 and 16 themselves (see *art.* 'Poetry', *NBD*).

17. the priests, identified as **those who minister before the Lord** (cf. 1: 13) and represent the nation before the Lord. To stand **between the temple porch and the altar** is to stand in front of the 'holy of holies', before the very presence of God. There they **weep**, pleading with the Lord, saying **'Spare your people, O Lord'**. While repentance was the attitude of the people, the priests appeal to the Lord on the grounds that to destroy Israel would make **your inheritance an object of scorn, a byword among the nations**. It is not easy to construe the precise meaning of **byword** (*māshāl*) here. However its use in Dt. 28: 36–46 is helpful. Moses not only warns Israel that one consequence of disobedience is that she will become . . . . 'an object of . . . ridicule (*māshāl*) to all the nations . . .' (v. 37) but he also warns about another consequence —locusts will destroy the harvest (vv. 38, 42)! The question put in the mouth of the nations, **'Where is their God?'** serves as additional commentary on the meaning of **byword**. The question assumes a negative answer—the God of the covenant is ineffectual, or has abandoned

his people, or worse, does not exist. With such a plea the priests rest their case. Joel contemplated the horrors of the 'day of the Lord' and then asked, **who can endure it?** (11). The people have been urged to repent and cast themselves on the mercy of a God who has promised to be merciful. **17.** The final rhetorical question is not so much a taunt in the face of God as it is a recognition that Israel has been chosen by God—it is through her that he intends to make himself known to the nations. With such knowledge the real question is not so much 'will God abandon us?' as it is 'how can we not repent?'

(d) Restoration promised (2: 18–27)
The success of Joel's appeal can be measured by the divine response. **18.** First, **the Lord will be jealous for his land**. This jealousy is that of one who has been deprived of something which rightfully belongs to him, and is under compulsion to reclaim it (cf. 1: 6 'my land'; also Exod. 20: 4–6). To have **pity on his people** is better translated 'he was moved with compassion for his people' (NEB). This compassion, responding to repentance, prompts God to reverse the damage done by the locusts. **19.** The **grain, new wine and oil** which were destroyed (10b), are soon to be replaced. No longer will Israel be **an object of scorn to the nations**, an answer to the priest's plea of v. 17.

20. Second, **the northern army** which has ravaged the land will be driven out. Both Jeremiah (4: 6 f.) and Ezekiel (38: 15 ff.) had warned of destruction from the north. When righteousness no longer prevails among the people of God, judgement in the form of an invading host overwhelms them, so 'that the nations may know me when I show myself holy through you before their eyes' (Ezek. 38: 16). Joel sees the locusts in the role of the **northern army** who comes to judge an unrepentant people. According to Ezekiel God then destroys the invader for his own evil (Ezek. 38: 18 ff.). So, following the nation's repentance, the northern invader is repulsed, driven **into a parched and barren land**. The division of the locusts into two groups, cast respectively into the seas to the west and east is reminiscent of the fate of the locusts which descended on the land of Egypt prior to Pharaoh's release of the Israelites. Following Moses' entreaty 'the Lord changed the wind into a very strong west wind, which caught up the locusts and carried them into the Red Sea. Not a locust was left anywhere in Egypt' (Exod. 10: 19). The rotting remains produce a **stench** and **smell** commensurate with the scale of evil inflicted by the invader.

In a reversal of the lament of 1: 15–20, Joel exults in a prophetic hymn of praise (see Allen, pp. 90 ff.). **21. Be not afraid, O land, be glad and rejoice**, is the appropriate response to the

LORD who **has done great things!** The heroic acts of God are ironically cast in the same language as the **great things** or 'proud deeds' (NEB) of the invader. Not only the land should rejoice in the deliverance, but likewise the **wild animals** should enter into the festive celebration because the **pastures** shall be **green** and the trees and vines shall once more produce fruit (22). And finally, the **people of Zion**, the congregated community, should **be glad . . . and rejoice in the LORD your God** (23). As in the days of old, God has provided the gifts of rain. The **autumn rain** is necessary for proper preparation of the soil for planting. The **spring rain** is that needed for full ripening of the crops for the harvest. The rain is interpreted as a visible sign of the vindication of the nation and restoration to the place of God's blessing.

The word for **autumn rain** (*mōreh*) can also mean 'teacher'. In conjunction with Hos. 10: 12, where the word is similarly associated with a word for 'righteousness', it has been understood as part of the biblical basis for the 'teacher of righteousness' of the Essene covenanters (F. F. Bruce, *Second Thoughts on the Dead Sea Scrolls*, ²1961, p. 94).

The result of the removal of the plague and replenishing of moisture to the soil is that the dark spectre of famine is banished. **24. The threshing floors will be filled with grain:** the storage **vats will overflow with new wine and oil** and in a reversal of the events of 1: 4, compensation will be made for the harvests lost to the ravages of the locusts, God's **great army, that I sent among you** (25).

Verses 25–26 outline a threefold result for the people of God. First, they shall once more **have plenty to eat, until you are full.** Second, their worship will be restored as they **praise the name of the LORD your God.** And third, the taunt of the **nations . . . 'Where is their God?'** (2: 17) shall be answered, **Never again will my people be shamed** (26). Cf. Rom. 10: 10–13. The doubt engendered by the devastation of the land is replaced by the experimental knowledge 'that I am present in Israel, and that I and no other am the LORD your God' (27, NEB).

As at Sinai (Exod. 20: 2), so here, the uniqueness of God's covenantal relationship with Israel is reaffirmed.

Through deliverance of the nation from disaster, the people are publicly declared to be **my people** by the One who claims their undivided allegiance. In view of the still forthcoming 'day of the Lord' the reaffirmation is particularly important. Evil will be judged wherever it be found but God's covenant people will be spared the destruction they remember so well, **never again** to **be shamed**. The reference is primarily to the recent locust invasion and the spectacle this presented to the surrounding nations.

However it might also allude to the destruction of Jerusalem and the exile of its people in 587 B.C. (Watts, p. 37), a dreadful event very much alive in the memory of the nation.

III. PROMISE OF THE SPIRIT: JUDGEMENT OF OPPRESSOR (2: 28–3: 21)

The **great and dreadful day of the LORD** (31) will be preceded by two startling series of events and an opportunity to avoid the consequences of the divine wrath.

i. The outpouring of the Spirit (2: 28–29)

The first of three strophes in this section represents a reversal of the pattern of Spirit indwelling in the OT and a fulfilment of the implied prophecy of Num. 11: 29. The Spirit of God was usually given to certain individuals with special tasks in mind (*e.g.* Bezalel, Exod. 31: 3; Moses and the 70 Elders, Num. 11: 17, 25; Balaam, Num. 24: 2–3; Othniel, Jg. 3: 10; Samson, Jg. 14: 6, 19; 15: 14, 19; Saul, 1 Sam. 10: 6; David, 1 Sam. 16: 13; Azariah, 2 Chr. 15: 1; Zechariah, 2 Chr. 24: 20; Isaiah, Isa. 61: 1; the Servant of the Lord, Isa. 42: 1). Now however, in line with the prophetic wish of Moses that 'all the LORD's people were prophets' (Num. 11: 29), Joel reports the promise of God that **I will pour out my Spirit on all people** (28). The balance of vv. 28–29 implies that Israel is primarily in view and that the outpouring of the Spirit would affect all members of the nation without regard to age, sex or social standing. It is true that **people** (*bāsār*) 'distinguishes man as belonging to an order of being other than that of God' (Allen, p. 98) and that **all people** could thus embrace all of humanity. This suggests the possibility of a wider point of view in which 'all people' extends beyond the provincial limitation of the covenant nation. The promise of v. 37 would support such an application and there is no doubt that in the NT this passage was used in the wider sense. See Rom. 10: 10–13 where the apostle Paul alludes to this among other texts in Joel in support of his argument that 'there is no distinction between Jew and Gentile' (Rom. 10: 12). However it is not clear that Joel understood it in this way.

The significance of these verses is twofold. First, no longer would the Spirit of God come only upon certain individuals for special purposes but would be poured out upon all, with the resultant ministry expressed as **prophecy**, **dreams** and **visions**. Dreams and visions are media by which God reveals himself to the prophet (Num. 12: 6). The terms may be synonymous here, a literary device, the point being that both **old men** and **young men** will be the recipients and ministers of the prophetic word of God. Second, servants too, **men** and

women, will receive the out-poured Spirit (29). There is no record of a slave receiving the gift of prophecy in the OT. Ancient Jewish interpreters had difficulty with this passage, interpreting the servants as belonging to God ('my servants' in LXX^pt.). However the basis of equality of believers without regard to social status is here established (cf. 1 C. 12: 12–13).

ii. Warnings and deliverance (2: 30–32)
(a) **Portents of disaster (2: 30–31)**
Joel, in the second strophe, outlines the cosmic signs which along with the outpouring of God's Spirit will herald the 'day of the LORD'. **30. wonders** represent warnings to the nations even as the outpouring of the Spirit is a sign to Israel. These warnings shall appear **in the heavens** as **the sun will be turned to darkness, and the moon to blood**—probably referring to a solar eclipse (Allen, p. 101)—and **on the earth, blood and fire and billows of smoke**—in the OT signs of theophany as at Sinai (Exod. 18: 18), but here most likely of the ravages of warfare. Both the sun and moon represent God in their constancy (cf. Ps. 72: 5, 17; 89: 36–37). Any radical change in their usual appearance would be eminently able to arouse feelings of anxious expectations regarding things that are about to happen. **31. the great and dreadful day of the LORD** is at hand.

(b) **Opportunity for deliverance (2: 32)**
To **call upon the name of the LORD** is an act of worship and an acknowledgement of dependence on God. In a test of the reality of their Gods, Elijah and the prophets of Baal agreed they would 'call on the name of' their respective Gods to send fire on their sacrifices (1 Kg. 18: 24). The prophets of Baal 'called on the name of Baal' (v. 26) but there was no answer. Elijah likewise prepared an altar, put wood and the sacrifice on it, and then 'called on the name of the LORD' as stipulated in v. 24. His words however constituted an address to the 'God of Abraham, Isaac and Jacob' with a request that God answer so 'that these people will know that you, O LORD, are God . . .' (v. 37). The divine response was to send the fire —when the people saw it, they worshipped him saying 'The LORD (Yahweh) he is God' (v. 39)! So too, Joel promises that in the time of trouble, whoever acknowledges God by calling on his name for deliverance, will be delivered. In support of this promise, the prophet, perhaps citing a known text, explains that 'on Mount Zion and in Jerusalem there shall be deliverance, as the LORD has said' (cf. Ob. 17). Then, to complete his argument he points out that the 'remnant' (NEB) who are to be saved shall be those **whom the LORD calls**. The gracious call of God complements the seeker's call on the name of the Lord. Peter, citing Jl 2: 28–32 in his Pentecost sermon (Ac. 2: 17–

21) argues that God has spoken to his people through Jesus of Nazareth (vv. 22 ff.) and that repentance and baptism are the prerequisites of the outpouring of the Spirit (Ac. 2: 38). Paul, pointing out that men cannot call on one of whom they have not heard, affirms the call of God through the preaching of the gospel (Rom. 10: 14–17).

iii. Judgement of the Nations (3: 1–16)
(a) **Trial narrative (3: 1–3)**
1. Joel now introduces a more detailed description of the judgement God is about to inflict on Israel's oppressors. **at that time** associates the destruction of the 'day of the Lord' with the restoration of **the fortunes of Judah and Jerusalem**. At the time of the outpouring of the Spirit, God will **gather all nations**. The place where judgement is to be dispensed is **the Valley of Jehoshaphat**, a name chosen because it means 'Yahweh judges'. The general charge on which judgement is based is the **nations'** abuse of **my inheritance, my people Israel** (2). Three specific charges are laid. First, the people have been **scattered** (dispersed) among the nations repeatedly by successive invaders (Assyrian—733, 721 B.C.; Babylonians—597, 587 B.C.). Moses had warned of such a dispersion (Lev. 26: 33; Dt. 28: 36 ff., cf. also Ezek. 12: 15; 22: 15). Second, **they have divided up my land** implying that God considers the people and the land as his (cf. Lev. 25: 23; Lam. 5: 2). Trespassers are violators of divine property. Third, they **cast lots for my people**, selling them into slavery. (3). To add insult to injury the price accepted for a Hebrew slave is disrespectful, trading **boys for** (the use of) 'a whore' (NEB) or **girls for wine** which is soon consumed. These are 'war crimes' and while they were repeated again under the Romans in the first century, God has promised to bring the perpetrators to justice (see Allen, p. 110).

(b) **Tyre, Sidon and Philistia (3: 4–8)**
4. Tyre and Sidon (Phoenician cities), plus **the regions of Philistia**, are singled out as representatives of Israel's abusers and in vv. 4–8 their crimes and judgement are elaborated. God is both prosecutor and judge who identifies with the accused—**are you repaying me for something?** Justice will be swift. The charges are twofold—**you took my silver and my gold** (5), probably temple treasures, and **You sold the people . . . sending them far from their homeland** (6); see Am. 1: 9., where Tyre is accused of mass deportation of God's people to Edom (cf. also Zech. 9: 3 f.). The penalty assessed against the perpetrators of these crimes is that their own **sons and daughters** will be delivered into the hands of the **people of Judah** (8) and will be sold to the Sabeans, traders of Sheba in Southwest Arabia who would funnel the slaves along the eastern

trade routes they dominated (see J. Bright, *History of Israel*, ²1972, pp. 211 f.).

(c) **Judgement narrative (3: 4–16)**
Now the prophet returns to the judgement of the nations announced in v. 2. A proclamation is issued **among the nations**, inviting them to **prepare for war** (9). In a parody of the expected messianic pacifism announced in Isa. 2: 1–4, the warriors are exhorted to **beat your ploughshares into swords, and your pruning hooks into spears** (10). The nations should gather **to the valley of Jehoshaphat** (12), for God is there preparing to judge them in a monumental trial (v. 2) by 'a holy war' (NEB). **13. the harvest is ripe . . . the winepress is full:** emphasizing the timeliness of the conflict. While the instruments of God's justice are not positively identified, v. 11b identifies as **your warriors** those who **swing the sickle** and **trample** on the grapes in **the winepress** (13).

At the hour of judgement **the sun and the moon will be darkened** (15; cf. 2: 30–31) and even the stars withdraw their light. The darkness serves Joel's purpose as a curtain dropped at the climactic moment of destruction. Omitting the lurid details, he announces the act of destruction. **16. the LORD will roar from Zion:** (cf. Am. 1: 2). As at creation God spoke and the worlds came into being, so in judgement his voice is an adequate vehicle to convey the destructive forces focused on the assembled powers of evil (cf. Isa. 55: 10–11; Ps. 33: 8–9; 105: 34). It is ironic that this judgement should occur at the very site of the earlier humiliation of God's people but the **thunder from Jerusalem** affirms it so. While the Lord speaks judgement to the nations, in words reminiscent of Ps. 46 he assures his people that he is **a refuge** and **a stronghold**.

IV. RESTORATION OF THE PEOPLE OF GOD (3: 17–21)
In observing the judgement of the oppressor, Israel **will know that I** am **the LORD your God** who once more will **dwell in Zion** and Jerusalem shall not again be violated by **foreigners** (17). Furthermore, Judah is now to enter into the messianic age where she will enjoy the richest blessings of God. In beautiful pastoral metaphors shared with Amos (9: 13) and Zechariah (14: 8) Joel describes the abundance of **new wine**, flowing **milk** and **water** (18). During the plague drought had cut off temple worship due to failure of grain and water supply (1: 8–12). Mourning was the only appropriate response (1: 13). Now, however, the temple itself would become the source of a life-giving stream. Even the 'Wadi of Acacias'

(JB) would be watered. While the location of this wadi is not identified, it suggests a dry hot gorge, so many of which run down to the Dead Sea, like the Kidron Valley, called in its lower stretch *Wadi en-Nar*, 'wadi of fire'. The water flowing from the temple of God will be sufficient for even the most remote and waterless ravine. (For the eschatological idea of a river issuing from the temple see Ezek. 47: 1–12, Ps. 46: 5 and in the NT, Rev. 22: 1 f.)

Egypt and Edom have **shed innocent blood** in the land (19): presumably a reference to the abuse of Judeans deported to their countries. For this reason they have been judged along with the other nations. With a final passing glance at their desolation Joel proceeds to his final prophetic affirmation. The result of Israel's idolatrous disobedience was devastation of her land and deportation of her people by the enemy (cf. Lev. 26: 27–33). Now however it is the enemy whose land is desolate and **Judah will be inhabited forever** (20). As for those whose lives were lost and for whom the promises are too late, God 'will avenge their blood' (21a RSV). The second phrase of this verse is obscure and may reflect an ancient gloss. The general sense however is likely parallel to that of v. 21a: 'God will not let the guilty go unpunished' (JB). Injustice will not go unrecognized. NIV, however predicts a general pardon. In the end righteousness will prevail for **the LORD dwells in Zion** (21b)—God is on his throne.

BIBLIOGRAPHY

AHLSTRÖM, G. W., *Joel and the Temple Cult of Jerusalem*, SVT 21 (1971).
ALLEN, L. C., *Joel, Obadiah, Jonah and Micah*, NICOT (Grand Rapids, 1976).
DRIVER, S. R., *The Books of Joel and Amos*. CBSC (Cambridge, 1915).
KAPELRUD, A. S., *Joel Studies* (Uppsala and Leipzig, 1948).
ROTH, C., 'The Teacher of Righteousness and the Prophecy of Joel' *VT* 13 (1963), pp.91–95.
SMITH, G. A., *The Book of the Twelve Prophets*, Vol. II (London, ²1928), pp.367–426.
THOMPSON, J. A., 'Joel's Locusts in the Light of Near Eastern Parallels' *JNES* 14 (1955), pp.52–55.
THOMPSON, J. A., 'Joel', IB, Vol. 6 (1956), pp.727–760.
WATTS, J. D. W., *Joel, Obadiah, Jonah, Nahum, Habakkuk and Zephaniah*. CBC (Cambridge, 1975).
WOLFF, H. W., *Joel and Amos* Hermeneia (E. T. Philadelphia, 1977).

AMOS

J. KEIR HOWARD

I. The Historical Background

The prophet Amos was the first of the great classical prophets whose words have been recorded in written form, and he probably ranks as the greatest of the so-called Minor Prophets. His words were delivered during the reign of Jeroboam II, the son of Jehoash, who reigned over Israel from 786 to 746 B.C. This was a time when the fortunes of the northern kingdom of Israel reached their highest point of prosperity and peace. Jeroboam's father, Jehoash (801–786 B.C.), had been a vigorous leader and during his reign Israel had been able to take advantage of the change in the balance of power throughout the Middle East. The thorn of Syria to the north had been effectively removed as a result of earlier defeats by Assyria and, as a result, both Israel and Philistia, who had been vassals of Syria, were able to take their opportunity and revolt against the rule of Syria's king. Syria was now tributary to Assyria but the Assyrian rulers had pre-occupations elsewhere and this, together with the ineptness of their rulers in this period, prevented them from following up their success. The result was that Jehoash was able to consolidate his own position, regaining the territory which had previously been lost to Syria.

By the time that Jeroboam II ascended the throne of Israel, much of the land previously lost to the Aramean dynasty of Syria had been recovered. Furthermore, there was peace with the southern kingdom of Judah after a long period of conflict and while Judah was in many respects subservient to Israel, there was now, nonetheless, a spirit of co-operation and mutual enterprise resulting in a flow of trade and commerce between the two kingdoms. The accession of Jeroboam to the throne of Israel heralded a time of prosperity and splendour that was matched by a corresponding economic advance in Judah under his contemporary Uzziah.

The military successes of his father were continued by Jeroboam himself, who pursued the war into Syria, taking advantage of the internal weakness of the country at that time and also the fact they themselves were preoccupied with the continuing struggle with the kingdom of Hamath. Jeroboam was thus able to extend his frontiers to almost those of the old Davidic kingdom, and he also pursued a vigorous expansionist policy into Transjordan

(see 2 Kg. 14: 25). The military successes of Jeroboam II were paralleled by his development of the country's economy. Phoenicia remained the dominant commercial power in the Middle East at this time and Israel had derived considerable benefit through her close relations with this country. Tolls were levied upon all the caravans passing through Israel and now that the main trade routes were effectively under her control, this brought considerable revenue into the treasury. As a result Samaria had risen from being a small capital of a second-class nation into a commercial centre of no small importance in the eastern Mediterranean area.

The increased expansion and the developing trade brought wealth into the country, but concurrently with the increased wealth there was an associated rise in those social evils which characterized the prosperity of Solomon's reign; the rich became very rich and the poor became even poorer. 'The older homogeneous economic structure of Israel gave way to the sharp distinctions of wealth and privilege' (J. L. Mays). The increase in wealth led to extensive building programmes and the simple brick buildings of earlier days gave way to buildings of hewn stone and the ivory decorations which had made Ahab's palace famous (2 Kg. 22: 39), a fashion borrowed originally from the Phoenicians and now widely copied (3: 12 f.). Excavations at Samaria and elsewhere have confirmed the splendour of this period of Israel's history yet they also emphasised the distinctions within society for, whilst in the tenth century the houses appear to have been of uniform size, in the eighth century there was an area of large expensive houses and one of small huddled structures. (See R. de Vaux, *Ancient Israel*, [2]1965, pp. 72 ff.)

Amos repeatedly attacks this division between rich and poor and in particular the luxury of the rich on the one hand and the misery of the poor on the other. He paints a graphic picture of the circumstances of the time. He notes the many fine buildings in the capital city of Samaria (3: 10) but he also points to the fact that those who own such buildings, the rich merchants and others, were men who would stop at nothing in order to increase their profits. They hated any day in which they could not do any business (8: 5). The rich enjoyed an indolent and indulgent existence, urged on by the rapacity of their wives who demanded more and more luxuries (4: 1 f.; 6: 1–6) and their houses were loaded with everything that would lead to a more opulent life of ease (3: 12; 6: 4), while on the other hand the poor were subjected to an evil economic exploitation (2: 6–8; 4: 1; 5: 10–12; 8: 4–6). The small man was forced out of business by the big monopolies and was unable to obtain any redress for his wrongs in the courts, for these were in the hands of the syndicates and, as a result, justice was perverted, witnesses were bought and judges were bribed (2: 6; 8: 5 f.; 5: 10). The justice offered to the poor was a bitter draught indeed (5: 7) for the legal processes had been totally corrupted and were used in fact as instruments of oppression. The courts had become little more than a market in which the poor man was enslaved and in which the last piece of land or produce could be wrung from him and his rights violated with impunity (2: 7).

Side by side with the decay of the social order there was the corruption of Israel's religion, a matter again ably demonstrated by Amos. The Canaanization of the worship of Yahweh had proceeded apace since the days of Solomon and the break-up of the united kingdom under Rehoboam and Jeroboam I. In Israel it would appear that the worship of Yahweh, although continuing, had become inextricably bound up with the degrading practices associated with Canaanite worship, although perhaps it is true to say that it never quite reached the same depths of apostasy as it did in Judah under the rule of Manasseh. It is interesting to note that an examination of the Samarian ostraca of this period yielded nearly half as many names compounded with Baal as with Yahweh (W. F. Albright, *Archaeology and the Religion of Israel*, 1942, p. 160). It would appear that, apart from such isolated voices as those of Amos or Hosea, even the prophets had degenerated into time-servers, blinded with the complacency of the nation. Religion certainly flourished in the nation but it was a religion that was completely divorced from reality. There was a great deal of activism and outward show with crowds thronging the shrines at the times of the great festivals (4: 4 f.; 5: 5). Ritual was elaborate (5: 21–24), but it was accompanied by those features such as sanctuary prostitution and bacchanalian orgies which were part of the fertility cults of the nations about them (2: 7 f.). There was no true life and no evidence that real spiritual values had any place and Yahweh was patronized with a presumption bordering upon arrogance (5: 14–20; 6: 3).

It was to this situation that Amos came with his word from Yahweh. It was a situation which was superficially bright and looked full of hope for the future, but Amos could see what Israel failed to see, that deliberate renunciation of the divine principles for the nation had led to the undermining of the whole foundations of society. The country was to be compared with a basket of over-ripe summer fruit, fit only to be thrown out and destroyed (8: 2).

II. The Prophet

The prophet Amos is known only from the book in which his sayings were collected and preserved. To those who compiled the prophetic books the important thing was the message rather than the man who gave it. Nonetheless, it is possible to obtain some picture of the prophet from the sparse information which is in the book. At the time in which he took up his prophetic ministry Amos was living in the desert country of southern Judah in the region of Tekoa (1: 1). This was a small mountain-top town some twelve miles from Jerusalem and some six miles south east of Bethlehem. He appears to have been a native of the southern kingdom and a citizen of Judah (1: 1; 7: 12). Tekoa was the centre of a large sheep-farming district and this is in fact the calling which Amos followed. Amos asserts that when Yahweh called him to the office of prophet he was following the flock (7: 14).

Two terms are used to describe him at that verse; **shepherd** and dresser of **sycamore fig-trees**. At 1: 1, however, a third term is used *nōqēd*, translated **shepherd**, which was used to describe the keeper of a particular kind of desert sheep that were highly prized on account of the excellence of their wool. The word is unusual, occurring elsewhere only at 2 Kg. 3: 4 in respect of Mesha, King of Moab. The inference is that the term refers to a sheep owner who had other shepherds under him and it may well have been that Amos was a substantial and respected man in his community. In no sense is he to be thought of as a simple and uncultured rustic. As E. W. Heaton has observed (*The Old Testament Prophets*, 1958, p. 19), 'His social station is peculiarly difficult to determine but so articulate a critic of the corruption of urban society could hardly have been a mere country bumpkin'.

It would appear that Amos augmented his income with a small orchard of 'sycamore fig-trees'. These were, in fact, the wild fig or fig mulberry, the fruit of which was pricked or bruised to improve the sugar content. They do not grow at Tekoa, but by the Dead Sea, to which the land around the town sloped to the east, these trees may be cultivated. It is impossible to reconstruct the career of Amos in any real sense. It appears, however, that his main activity was centred in Bethel although there is a possibility that he may also have preached in Samaria. Certainly it was in Bethel that he came into conflict with the religious establishment of the northern kingdom and many of his sayings would fit the congregation which had gathered at this important religious centre for the autumn festival (*e.g.* 2: 8; 3: 14; 4: 4; 5: 5; 6: 21–27). It is possible that his ministry did not last beyond the one year implied by the introductory verse (1: 1).

Amos emerges from his collected sayings as a man with a deep conviction of God's call and a deep conviction of the message he had to bring. 'We see in Amos a worthy successor of Elijah, a man on fire with a zeal for a revival of religion and social morality, to whom the Canaanizing practices of official Yahwism were almost as abhorrent as were specifically pagan rites' (W. F. Albright, *From the Stone Age to Christianity*, ²1957, p. 313). The call that came to him 'wrenched him out of his normal life and put him in another country crying, "woe" to its society, religion, and government in the name of God. He became solely the messenger whose life was the vehicle of the message' (J. L. Mays).

III. The Message

Amos would probably have known Israel well as he was likely to have visited its markets to sell his produce. His speeches witness to a thorough knowledge of the situation. The essential feature of the message of Amos can be summed up in the word 'righteousness', understood as what God requires. He came to a nation in which the weak, the poor, the afflicted and the innocent were suffering under various forms of injustice, being sold into slavery, being dispossessed and exploited. The prophecy of Amos is an indictment of the northern kingdom for allowing such a situation to develop. As followers of Yahweh, righteousness, in the sense of right conduct and right lives ordered according to the law of God, should have characterized the nation. The prophecy of Amos came as God's response to injustice and unrighteousness. The weak and the poor had cried to Yahweh and the reply of Yahweh came in the prophecy of Amos. It is a message of unrelieved gloom, made up entirely of judgment upon an irreligious nation.

His words were directed to three areas of the nation's life: the administration of justice in the law courts, the affluence of the wealthy and the state of worship in the various sanctuaries. In the eyes of Amos the court seemed to represent the central institution in the nation's life, for it was here that righteousness should be revealed and justice established. The courts should have defended the weak and the poor but, in fact, as Amos observed, the justice which was given to the poor was as bitter as wormwood (5: 7). The legal processes were totally corrupted and were used as an instrument of oppression. Amos also directed his attention to the affluence of the wealthy classes. It is important to recognize that he did not direct his judgment against

the wealthy because he was himself ascetic, but rather the wealth he denounced was the wealth gained by the oppression of the poor through social injustice and in turn this derived from the form of religion in the nation. It was a religion which was empty in content though full of ritual. Amos insisted that God had no time for a ritualistic religion without heart. True religion must be demonstrated in terms of action, and the action God requires is true righteousness. Such righteousness is to be shown in compassion, in mercy and in social justice. Israel was privileged, but privilege is related to responsibility and Israel had forgotten the obligations of responsibility that were bound up in the worship of Yahweh.

The behaviour of Israel was such that judgment was already at the door. Like the lion ready to spring on its prey so Yahweh was ready to bring judgment upon His people. Yahweh would no longer pass by (7: 8; 8: 2) but rather He would pass through the midst of His people with a judgment so severe that it would remove them from the face of the earth (5: 17). 'The God who gave Israel its past will give them no future as a vindication of His will against theirs. The oracles that derive from Amos offer no hope for any other future to Jeroboam's Israel' (J. L. Mays).

The message of Amos was presented in a clear vigorous style. The prophet demonstrated an able grasp of rhetorical devices, his sentences were well formed and, above all, he possessed a remarkable gift for illustrations. Most of these were culled from his own observations and experiences of country life. He used the picture of the lion making off with the sheep from the flock and the vain attempts at rescue (3: 12). He spoke of threshing implements (1: 3) and traps for wild fowl (3: 5). He referred to the activities of fishermen (4: 2) as well as such things as mildew and blight, and other aspects of country life familiar to those who were countrymen themselves. In all these pictures of natural events, most particularly those of disasters and catastrophes, he showed careful observations of the world about him. The NIV demonstrates well the fact that the great majority of the oracles which go to make up the book of Amos are in poetic form. Poetry was a medium in which the prophet was well versed and most would today agree with the words of G. A. Smith (*EB*) in his assessment of Amos as one whose mastery of the pure Hebrew style was never surpassed by any of his successors. 'The text is one of the best preserved among the prophetic books' (E. Hammershaimb). There are very few passages where the text presents serious problems and these will be noted in the commentary.

ANALYSIS

I. PROLOGUE (1: 1, 2)

The first two verses of the book form the introduction to the whole collection of oracles. Verse 1 may be viewed as the title placed at the beginning of the collection. It tells the reader that the book is composed of sayings—**words**. It tells who spoke those words, to whom and when. The dating is quite specific, **two years before the earthquake**. This event is mentioned elsewhere in OT only at Zech. 14: 5, and the impression is given that it was one of a particularly catastrophic nature. Josephus (*Ant.* ix. 10. 4) and later rabbis synchronize it with the leprous Uzziah's expulsion from the temple (2 Chr. 26: 16 ff.). Excavations at Hazor have revealed traces of an earthquake which has been dated to about 760 B.C. If this dating is correct it places the work of Amos somewhere to the end of the fourth decade of the eighth century. This is further borne out by the synchronization with the reigns of Uzziah of Judah and Jeroboam II of Israel. This synchronization is derived from an editor who may well have been from the same school as those who edited the books of Kings and some of the other prophets. The fact that the name of Uzziah precedes that of Jeroboam is suggestive that the final editing occurred in Judah.

Amos is described as **one of the shepherds of Tekoa**. Mention has already been made that the word translated **shepherd** (*nōqēd*) suggests a breeder of sheep who had a position of some note in the community. **Tekoa:** see Introduction II. The suggestion is strong that he was a Judean and Tekoa was probably his home town (note 7: 12). His mission, however, was to Israel, the northern kingdom, and it is clear that the prophetic office as seen in Amos represents part of God's total activity amongst His people and, in this context, the political boundaries which separated Judah and Israel were irrelevant. The fact that Amos **saw** the words that he was to give to Israel underlines the fact that he received his message by revelation from God. It was an expression used conventionally for the specific prophetic vision. The content of the message is contained in v. 2, a couplet summarizing the word of judgment which Amos gave. The evils which beset the nation of Israel had reached such a level that God had no option but to act in righteous judgment. The two halves of the couplet form perfectly synonymous parallels in the 3+3 rhythm. The word used for the **roar** of the Lord (*šā'ag*) denotes the lion's roar as it pounces upon its prey. It would indicate Yahweh's wrath and the imminence of His righteous judgment and its inescapability. However, it may also indicate the roar of the storm, especially in view of the parallel use of the expression **thunders** which does not indicate an articulate word of God but rather an awesome noise such as the roar of thunder (see Ps. 18: 13; 39: 3–9: Job 37: 45; 2 Sam. 22: 14; Ps. 68: 33; 46: 6, etc.). The metaphor of a thunderstorm does not fit well, however, as the judgment is described as drought. The roar comes from **Zion**, i.e. Jerusalem, the divine residence and place of God's authority, and it withers the pasture lands of Israel. The imagery of drought is one frequent in the prophetic works (Isa. 5: 6; 11: 15; Jer. 12: 4, etc.). It is particularly noteworthy that it is **the top of Carmel** that withers and becomes scorched by the drought, an area of particular fertility in the time of Amos, as indeed its name testifies (the orchard or fertile land). The whole passage indicates the seriousness of the desolation that is to come upon the land.

II. ORACLES AGAINST THE NATIONS (1: 3–2: 16)

This section consists of eight short oracles consisting of messages of judgment, initially against the nations surrounding Israel and then finally a larger and more expanded word of doom on the nation of Israel itself. Each of the oracles has a basic structure consisting of the opening 'messenger formula', **this is what the LORD says**, followed by the indictment, then the announcement of judgment and the concluding 'messenger formula', **says the LORD**. Each indictment also begins with a formula consisting of the words, **for three sins . . . and for four I will not turn back my wrath**. This type of graded numerical saying occurs in several places in the Bible (Prov. 6: 16–19; 30: 15 f., 21–23, 29–31; Job 19: 3 f.; 33: 14 f., etc.). A number of similar expressions may be found elsewhere outside biblical literature. These forms of numerical sequences are a dramatic way of providing emphasis and also devices by which a number of items may be organized into sequences for a particular thought. Amos uses the formula in order to focus attention upon the final item. He does not enumerate the first three, but moves directly to the fourth, the one which, in the context, was, as it were, the final straw that brings the judgment of Yahweh upon the nation. (On the formula see further W. M. Roth, 'Numerical Sequences X/ X+1 in the OT' *Vetus Testamentum* 12 (1962), pp. 300–311.) Judgment in these oracles is inevitable. Indeed the foundation of the entire message of Amos is the certainty that Yahweh has already initiated the punishment on those who have rebelled against him. The thought of rebellion is implicit in the word which Amos uses for **sin** (*peša'*). The NIV translation does not really bring out the true sense of this word. Transgression indicates the breaking of moral laws but the word essentially implies flouting authority and indicates rebellion and revolt. It might almost be said to be a political rather than a religious term, but at the same time it expresses what is at the heart of the biblical concept of sin. What in the human sphere is rebellion against an earthly overlord, in biblical terms becomes rebellion against the authority and sovereignty of God. What is significant about this prophecy is that Amos is extending the concept of Yahweh's rule beyond His covenant people to all nations. God is portrayed as the King of His world who judges sin and unrighteousness irrespective of where it might occur. He is ruler; all nations including His covenant people stand under His authority. This is the message that Amos brings. Yahweh is the sovereign of history and is about to bring the sinful nations under His judgment.

i. The sins of Damascus (1: 3–5)

Damascus stands as representative of Syria, the largest of the Aramean kingdoms lying to the north-east of Israel. It was one of her major adversaries throughout the incessant border wars which ran from the ninth century to the beginning of the eighth. (See for this whole period J. Bright, *A History of Israel*, ²1972, 225–263.) This particular oracle contains more historical detail than any of the others and seems to refer to a specific military campaign (3), and goes on to mention particular persons and places in the announcement of judgment (4, 5). Only one **Hazael** of Damascus is known (from Syrian and Assyrian as well as from Hebrew records); he ruled from about 842 to 800 B.C., founding the dynasty referred to here as **'the house of Hazael'**. His son who succeeded him was **Ben-Hadad** III (2 Kg. 13: 3), and he is probably the Ben-Hadad referred to in this verse. The name is almost certainly a throne name, meaning 'son of Hadad', the ancient storm god of that area. That military expedition against **Gilead** is probably the one reported at 2 Kg. 13: 3–7. The same metaphor that Amos uses (**she threshed Gilead with sledges having iron teeth**) is used in 2 Kg. 13: 7 of the inhuman way in which the Syrians treated the people of Israel. The event may be dated to about 850 B.C. Judgment on Syria would be the total destruction of its cities and the exile of its people. The Assyrians would batter down the great gate of Damascus and take its people into captivity. Events fell out as Amos predicted, when the Aramean dynasty collapsed under the onslaught of Tiglath-Pileser in answer to the request of Ahaz king of Judah, his vassal (2 Kg. 16: 5 f.).

The places mentioned in v. 5 are not easy to identify apart from Damascus itself. The **Valley of Aven** may be a revocalization of the consonants of the name On, probably to be identified with Baalbek, a city not far to the north of Damascus. **Beth Eden** has been identified with Bit-Adini an Aramean city state lying on the upper Euphrates, but this is uncertain. According to 9: 7 **Kir** was the original home of the Arameans. It is not possible to identify this exactly but it is probably a site in Mesopotamia.

ii. The sins of Philistia (1: 6–8)
The oracle begins with the standard formula, emphasizing the greatness of the crimes which the nation had committed by the time of Amos. The Philistines had virtually lost their identity as a distinct people by this time becoming amalgamated with the local inhabitants of the Palestinian coastal plain and under the partial sovereignty of Judah. The Pelethites mentioned in several places as mercenaries in David's army were probably Philistines. It seems clear, however, that the Philistine city states had been able to maintain some form of autonomy, and the measure of this may well have increased in the years following the division of the united kingdom.

The sin of the Philistines was the maintenance of the slave traffic. **Gaza**, the largest and most important of the Philistine cities, was well situated to deal in this inhuman trade for it stood at the junction of several important trade routes. The territory raided is not detailed although the probability points to Israel or Judah. Such slave raids could only be carried out when the state concerned was in a defenceless condition and, if Israel was the victim, they probably occurred in the period when Jehoahaz was oppressed by the Arameans. The slaves were sold later in the markets of **Edom** where they were possibly resold to the south (note Jl 3: 6–8). The law of Israel expressly forbad this traffic (Exod. 21: 16).

For their crime the Philistine states would be overwhelmed and destroyed. Amos mentioned by name four of the five city states. The notable omission of Gath has raised a variety of problems including the suspicion that this oracle presupposes the destruction of Gath in 711 B.C. by the armies of Sargon for its part in the rebellion against Assyria (see Isa. 20: 3). However, there are other possibilities which offer a better explanation for the absence of the name. Gath was frequently included in Judean territory and may have been under the authority of Ashdod at this period.

iii. The sins of Phoenicia (1: 9, 10)
The oracle against **Tyre**, representing the whole nation of Phoenicia, continues the standard pattern but fills out the detail slightly differently from previous sayings concerning Damascus and Gaza. The Phoenicians were perhaps the greatest trading nation of the ancient world and the buying and selling of their fellow men was probably merely one facet of their total business pursuits. **Tyre** had supplanted Sidon as the dominant city by the time of Amos and was famed throughout the Eastern Mediterranean for its far-reaching trade (see 1 Sam. 23; Ezek. 27). The offence of the Phoenicians was similar to that of the Philistines. **6. she took captive whole communities:** it is possible that 'Aram' (i.e. Syria) should be read in place of **Edom** at the end of this verse. The difference between the words in Hebrew is slight and the present reading may have resulted from the confusion with the previous oracle on the part of a scribe (so *ICC*).

Their guilt is further compounded by the fact that they did not remember **a treaty of brotherhood** (9). This refers to some treaty made between Tyre and another state. Brotherhood was an essential element of international treaties at this time because they involved mutual obligations between parties which were similar to those which belonged between the members of a family. It is likely that the covenant mentioned was that established between Solomon and Hiram (1 Kg. 5: 12; 9: 13). (On this subject see further J. Priest 'The Covenant of Brothers' *JBL* **84** (1964), pp. 400 f.) The judgment which was to fall upon Tyre was identical to that of Gaza (10). The judgment of God was again to be effected by human agency.

iv. The sins of Edom (1: 11, 12)
With the oracle against Edom the series moves to the south-east of Israel. The nation of **Edom** lay along the Arabah southward from the lower end of the Dead Sea. Throughout biblical times it was closely involved in the life of Israel and had always been considered one of her hereditary enemies. The prophet singles out **Teman**, possibly a city in the south, and **Bozrah**, an important centre in the north (perhaps the capital; see Gen. 36: 33), for particular mention, demonstrating that the judgment of God is to fall upon the whole land from north to south (12). Edom's sin was against **his brother** (11). The reference is clearly to Israel. The kinship of Jacob and Esau is underlined in the patriarchal stories and Edom is frequently referred to as the brother of Israel (Num. 20: 14; Dt. 2: 4; 23: 3–7; Ob. 10–12; Mal. 1: 2 f.). The indictment expressly states that Edom refrained from exercising compassion and **pursued his brother** relentlessly and with unremitting anger—**his fury flamed unchecked** (11). Such hostility was no doubt shown in the constant harassment by border raids.

The specific crime is the violation of the obligations of kinship and the problem arises as to the period that is in view. Edom was firmly under Judah's control from the time of David into the reign of Uzziah except for the short period of the reign of Jehoram (about 850 B.C.). It is thus difficult to fit a picture of persistent vindictive hostility into this period although Amos may well have drawn upon traditions that are at present lost in regard to Edom's conduct during the previous struggle for independence. On the other hand, there are numerous passages in the OT which relate specifically to the conduct of Edom against Judah in the immediate post-exilic period (Ob. 10, 12; Lam. 4: 21 f.). It is of interest to note that Obadiah makes precisely the same point as Amos, that Edom betrayed his kinship obligations to his brother Judah. It is likely that the other OT passages referring to Edom's enmity also come from the same period (Isa. 34: 5 f.; Jer. 49: 7; Jl 3: 19 and Ps. 137: 7). 'Edom exploited the collapse of Judah to its fullest extent, active with vindictiveness against refugees, and steadily appropriating Judean territory in the south' (J. L. Mays).

v. The sins of Ammon (1: 13–15)
The kingdom of **Ammon** lay on the east side of Jordan with Moab on the south and Gilead to the north, occupying much of what is the present kingdom of Jordan. At one period Ammon belonged to the Davidic empire but became independent with its own king soon after the death of Solomon. The reference at v. 13 appears to be to a period of border war conduc-

ted by the Ammonites in order to expand their border into the territory of **Gilead**. The particularly inhuman act of murdering pregnant women in this area (13) was sometimes a feature of warfare in those days (2 Kg. 8: 12; 15: 16; Hos. 13: 16) and indeed has not been unknown in more recent times. It was particularly frequent in border warfare where the purpose was to terrorize and also to decimate the resident population. The judgment of Yahweh is described in military terms; the enemy would sweep through **Rabbah**, the capital of the Ammonites (on the site of modern Amman) like **violent winds on a stormy day**, dissolving the city in **fire** and destroying everything that stood before it (14). The concept of tempest and whirlwind frequently combine in the prophetic pictures of those catastrophes which would herald the judgment of Yahweh (cf. Jer. 23: 19; 30: 23; Hos. 13: 15, etc). The tempest of Yahweh is the form in which His wrath against His foes will take shape, and the judgment thus takes on the form of the coming of the Day of Yahweh (see further 5: 18–20) seen here, not in eschatological terms but as a specific historical event when God brings war as catastrophic judgment over the whole area. The result would be that both the **king** and his principal **officials** would **go into exile** (15).

vi. The sins of Moab (2: 1–3)
The land of **Moab** lay to the east of the Dead Sea and the frontier with Israel was not fixed although the river Arnon was generally considered the boundary. The point of interest in the condemnation of Moab is that the crime had nothing to do with Israel in any way. They are condemned because they **burned, as if to lime, the bones of Edom's king** (1). The exact historical circumstances of this deed cannot be determined and the nature of the crime is also somewhat obscure. It seems likely, however, that the Moabites had desecrated a royal tomb in Edom (note 2 Kg. 23: 16). Grave robbing and disturbance of graves were particularly contemptible crimes, for much importance was attached to a dead man resting in the family burial place. The Moabites, on the other hand, may have captured an Edomite king and after killing him burnt his body until the bones were calcined. This appears to have been a treatment reserved only for criminals in the culture of the time (note Gen. 38: 24; Lev. 20: 14; 21: 9).

Once again the punishment to be meted out to them is total military disaster (2) and the removal of power and authority (3). It is of interest to note that the second part of v. 2 is composed of sound words, drawn from the vocabulary of battle, and the line evokes all the tumult and noise of an army in the midst of the attack including **war cries**. **The trumpet** (*šôphār*) was the ram's horn used for sounding the alarm or the attack. The **ruler** of Moab and the leaders of the people will be exterminated (3). Amos uses the word **ruler** (šōp̱eṭ) here instead of king. It may be that the word is simply a synonym for king in this context, but normally the word appears to have been reserved for civil leaders of lower rank such as the judges of the Israelite confederation, whose task was to ensure justice and settle legal disputes. It is just possible that the use of the term indicates that Moab was tributary to some other state at this time, perhaps even Israel herself (note the vague comment of 2 Kg. 14: 25).

The real importance of this section lies in the fact that Amos indicates to Israel that their God is the God of all the earth, the one who was vitally concerned with all people and would judge sin wherever it was found. He was concerned, therefore, not only with Israel and those who troubled her but also with the relationships of all states and nations to one another. The laws of conduct which were revealed to Israel were valid throughout the international realm. Yahweh was not merely a tutelary deity, interested in His own people alone, but He was the God who would have justice and righteousness among all nations, for His rule extended to all men, and in all circumstances.

vii. The sins of Judah (2: 4, 5)

This oracle moves from the periphery to the geographic centre. The circle of oracles has moved round the surrounding nations leaving now only Judah and Israel in the centre. The sin of **Judah** (4) is not as specific or concrete as the indictments in the other oracles in this series. The charge levelled against Judah is disobedience and apostasy in general; deliberate rejection of the demands of Yahweh on their life, national and individual. The verses underline the biblical concept of sin as the state of active rebellion against God demonstrated in that **they have rejected the law of the LORD**, that is, the revelation of His will. Judah's neglect of the **decrees**, the specific commandments, of Yahweh was in spite of the apparent recovery of genuine worship under Uzziah. It is apparent that there was only a recovery of the externals of worship, seen in the fact that **they have been led astray by false gods** (presumably the Baal cult) which were still being worshipped by the people as they had been in times past. It has been thought likely by a large number of scholars that this particular indictment is out of character with the other oracles of the series and represents an addition inserted by later editors of the prophecy. The genuineness of these words is well defended by Hammershaimb (pp. 45 f.).

viii. The sins of Israel (2: 6–16)

Amos has now gone full circle and has reached the actual audience to whom his message is primarily directed. The various nations surrounding Israel have been considered. In so doing he has prepared the way for his final indictment of Israel herself. The tacit agreement of his hearers with the previous judgments was in fact a self-condemnation; in condemning others they condemn themselves. Amos embarks on his indictment of the nation with a catalogue of the nation's sins. The oracle against Israel is much longer and more complex, in both structure and style, than the previous oracles against the surrounding nations. This is only to be expected as the indictment is an extended list of the sins of Israel. The announcement of judgment itself does not begin until v. 13, where the exclamation **Now then** introduces the proclamation of God's judgment against the nation.

The indictment begins with a reference to slavery (6) and a biting comment on the state of the law courts which no longer dispensed impartial justice. The situation envisaged in v. 6 may refer to the sale of an insolvent debtor to pay off his accumulated debts (note Lev. 25: 39; 2 Kg. 4: 1; Neh. 5: 5). In a land in which drought was a regular happening and blight and locusts brought frequent havoc, a major loan was often the only way in which the family farm could be kept going. Once in debt, however, it was no easy task to repay; the interest levels were exorbitant and many Israelites were forced to sell themselves in order to pay off the accumulated debts standing against them. The term **for silver** simply means money, possibly a trivial sum. The parallel term **a pair of sandals** may be an idiom for the legal transfer of land, both referring to the fact that a man was sold either for money or land. On the other hand the expressions may mean no more than that the judges in Israel could be influenced by paltry bribes.

What is clear from the indictment is that the legal processes were doing nothing to help the **righteous** (ṣaddîq). The word does not mean here the morally upright but indicates the innocent party in a lawsuit, the man that the court should have vindicated. The courts were perverse and the influential and rich were able to dominate them. The result was social injustice as the rule of the day. The honest man was **denied justice** (7) because the poor were oppressed rather than helped. The expression **trample on the heads of the poor as upon the dust of the ground** is probably a figurative expression for treading under foot the rights of the poor (cf. Isa. 3: 15).

There are two possibilities of the interpretation of the situation in v. 7b where **father and son use the same girl**. It could be a reference to sanctuary prostitution which was a regular feature of the worship of the fertility cults of the ancient world. It is clear from the other prophetic writings that Israel had adopted the practice along with other aspects of local Canaanite religion. On the other hand, it has been suggested that the maiden was a female bond-slave who was being used as a concubine by both father and son, expressly prohibited at Exod. 21: 8 (note also Dt. 22: 30). The emphasis on both father and son thus highlights the promiscuity involved in this situation. In view, however, of the relationship of these statements to v. 8 which clearly is in a cultic context, and the fact that the verb translated **use** is not the normal verb for sexual relations, it seems preferable to view the indictment as relating to the institution of cultic prostitution in the land of Israel, by which Yahweh's **holy name** is **profaned**. Verse 8 continues to underline the fact that Israel's religion had become totally divorced from morality and any thought of practical ethical behaviour. Such a divorce between religion and morality had resulted in a general corruption of society.

8. garments taken in pledge: a reference to the standard way in which a debt was secured. A debtor left his cloak with the lender as surety for the debt. However, Exod. 22: 26 lays it down that such a garment given in pledge has to be returned to him before sunset, for it was his covering and acted as the man's blanket at night. Amos thus indicates that such legal limitations were being totally disregarded. Worship had degenerated into an excuse for indulgence in various orgies; the **wine** that was drunk was paid for with the money derived from court fines, and the clothes on which they sprawled were forfeited pledges. Such behaviour was bound to have serious effects on the state of the nation. The poor were suffering under the power of the rich, who were able to use the courts to their own advantage as instruments of exploitation. Social institutions were being continuously violated and justice had been displaced by rapacity, materialism and greed.

Verses 9–12 underline the fact that Israel's behaviour was all the more heinous in view of the mighty acts which God had wrought for their salvation. The order of the themes is perhaps surprising for the Conquest (9) comes before the reference to the Exodus and the desert wanderings (10). 'This unusual order has its own logic; it emphasizes that Israel's existence in the land of the Amorites is the result of Yahweh's work' (J. L. Mays). The focus of attention is on the immense power of God and points to 'the glaring contrast between Yahweh's acts of kindness to the people and the sinfulness with which they have so shamefully repaid His kindness to them' (Hammershaimb). **9. the Amorite:** used of the various Canaanite groups rather than the specific tribe

of that name. A number of the original tribal groups of Canaan were described as having gigantic size and strength hence the reference to **cedars** and **oaks** (Num. 13: 22–33; Dt. 2: 10, 20). It is of interest to note that the Amorites were singled out as being amongst the worst offenders in regard to the religious practices of Canaan. The various fertility cults are grouped together under the single heading 'the sin of the Amorites' (Gen. 15: 16) and this brings into even greater prominence Israel's despising of Yahweh and His ways since they were now lapsing into the evil practices of the very nations the might of Yahweh had driven before them.

The action of Yahweh, however, was not limited to the Exodus and Conquest, but continued amongst His people. It was seen in the raising up of **prophets** and **Nazirites**, i.e. 'dedicated ones' (11), whose work is a continuing manifestation of the power and presence of God. Israel, however, had ignored the presence of God amongst them and scorned His servants. The ascetic Nazirite had been forced to break his vows and **drink wine** (Num. 6: 1–3); prophets had been intimidated so they dared not speak (12). God had not left His people without witnesses to His work and His word but Israel had rejected God and rejected His idealists in the Nazirites, and suppressed the truth of the prophets. It is hardly surprising that in such a situation the God of might and power, who had once overwhelmed the Amorites for the good of His people, was now the God whose power would turn salvation-history into judgment history.

Amos thus moves into a statement of judgment, occupying vv. 13–16, described in more detail than in the preceding oracles. The righteous judgment of God would vindicate Him and His own justice and in doing so the nation would be crushed as sheaves of corn on the threshing floor. The text of v. 13 is difficult, the verb occurring only in this place in OT and of doubtful meaning. The RSV suggests the effect upon the nation is as though they were crushed beneath a heavy **cart loaded with grain**, but this is based on an Aramaism which is unlikely for the time of Amos. Alternatively the verb may mean 'to cut up' and the thought would then be that the nation would be cut up as the threshing cart cut up the straw (better than **grain**) on the threshing floor. Whatever meaning is given to the verb it is clear that the ultimate effect of the action of God would be catastrophic upon the nation. The boasted military might of Israel would stand for nothing in the day of the revelation of God's wrath and judgment. There would be none who would escape (14–16). It would not matter how **fleet-footed** they were, however brave or strong, indeed the bravest of them would strip off his clothes to make good his escape

(16). The storm cloud of Assyria would sweep over the land and there would be none would who stand against it.

III. THE CORRUPT LAND
(3: 1–6: 14)

This section consists of five further well defined oracles in which the prophet shows in greater detail the depth to which Israel has fallen, and the inevitability of God's righteous judgment upon them as a result. Three of the oracles commence with the proclamation formula **Hear this word** (3: 1; 4: 1; 5: 1) and two commence with the expression **Woe** (5: 18; 6: 1). Each of the oracles is a picture of unrelieved gloom, highlighting various aspects of the evils which beset the nation.

i. The inevitability of judgment (3: 1–8)

The first two verses of this oracle underline the special relationship of Israel to Yahweh and base the coming judgment upon this relationship. Clearly the prophet is thinking in terms of the covenant between God and His people and the unique relationship of Israel to Yahweh although the expression 'covenant' is not used by Amos.

The fact that Israel had been **brought up out of Egypt** (1) forms the basis for God's claim upon and sovereignty over them. The great redemptive act of God is the basis of the exclusive relationship which Amos enunciates in v. 2: **You only have I chosen of all the families of the earth**. This is an emphatic statement and isolates Israel in the context of world history. Out of all nations in the world Israel alone is the one that Yahweh 'knows'. The problem is the strict interpretation of the verb 'to know' (*yāda‘*) (NIV **chosen**). In some texts (*e.g.* Ps. 1: 6; Nah. 1: 7; etc.) the verb simply means to care for or watch over. Elsewhere the verb is used in a sense very close to the idea of election (*e.g.* Jer. 1: 5; Dt. 9: 24; Hos. 13: 5). The context of the verses suggests that such a meaning is the one required here and we should, perhaps, interpret the verb to mean 'to recognize by covenant'. Thus because Yahweh has chosen and recognized Israel alone as His covenant partner, He will punish them for all their iniquities. The great privilege which had been conferred upon Israel carried with it equally great responsibilities, but from the beginning these had been ignored, Israel had looked upon election as merely a form of favouritism instead of a calling to special responsibilities. Thus Amos introduces the inexorable **therefore** (2), because of their special position they have a special reason to expect God's judgment upon their sin and failure. To be chosen by God is to be put under His judgment, a message which needs constant reaffirmation for our own day (Lk. 12: 48).

In these verses Amos proceeds to authenticate both his message and his calling as a prophet. The whole saying is a very skilful linkage of cause and effect. It is developed as a series of questions, each of which can only be answered by the agreement of the audience, leading up to the final statement (8) that in the same way as natural events are linked in such a causal chain so too there is a causal relationship behind his own words to Israel.

The various word pictures that Amos uses in this section are culled from the everyday life of the country, observations derived from his life as a shepherd. Furthermore, it also illustrates the expertise of Amos in handling both the materials and techniques of traditional proverbial argument. The sequence builds up in vv. 3–6; two people are not likely to be found walking on the lonely hills of Judah **unless they have agreed to do so** (3). The lion does not **roar in the thicket** (4) unless it has caught some wild animal. The verb **roar** indicates the ferocious sound of the lion seizing its prey in contrast to the contented growl given over his dead prey (4). A bird does not **fall** unless a **snare** (net) has been thrown over it, nor does a **trap spring** unless an animal has been caught in it (5). Again if the sentry's **trumpet** sounds an alarm the whole village will be thrown into confusion for it will certainly mean that brigands are approaching (6). Similarly should some misfortune such as a plague befall a town, it would be the action of God behind it (6). Verse 7 seems to be somewhat out of order in these verses and it is not impossible that it represents an editorial addition underlining the important truth that the prophet stands in the divine counsel (**plan:** *sôd*) and God reveals His message to the prophet because the prophet stands in this unique relationship to God and knows His policy and how it had been formulated and decreed. Hence his messages are true and are to be believed and acted upon.

In v. 8 the section reaches its climax. From illustrations now comes a statement of fact, **the lion has roared**, therefore judgment is imminent. **The Sovereign LORD has spoken** and Amos can do nothing else **but prophesy**. The parallel between the lion's roar and the voice of God (found also at 1: 2; Jer. 25: 30) is based upon the rolling sound of thunder. God utters His voice in the thunderstorm as He appears against His enemies. Amos has heard Yahweh's voice, the thunder is rumbling, the storm is approaching and it is upon Israel that the storm will break.

ii. The cause of judgment (3: 9–11)

In these verses Amos issues a rhetorical summons to the heralds telling them to carry the invitation to **the strongholds of Ashdod** and **Egypt**. It is certain that Assyria (9 RSV) is correct over against 'Ashdod' and the RSV has used the LXX reading in this case. They are invited in this ironic manner to view the appalling situation that exists within Israel. **great unrest:** indicating both the abandoned life of Samaria and the disintegration of the rule of law, resulting in **oppression** or acts of violence. The main indictment is simply that **they do not know how to do right** (10). The word **right** means what is straightforward and honest in contrast to what is false, and in this context Amos seems to use the word to mean what is acceptable and right in relation to court and trade practices. The main problem was that the old society had become changed. The **fortresses** (palaces) (10) had become treasuries in which the rich were able to store the profits of **plunder and loot.** Thus follows the **Therefore** (11) of moral logic; because of the state of the country and the rapacity of the principal people that nation would be destroyed. The Assyrians had already been called upon to witness the evils of the land and now, although not strictly specified, there is little doubt that Amos envisages them as the instrument of God's judgment, to become the **enemy** who will **overrun the land**. The result is that the **strongholds** will be brought down and the **fortresses** shall be **plundered**.

iii. The completeness of judgment (3: 12–15)

Verse 12 forms a parabolic type of statement in which a situation that is well known, in this case a shepherd retrieving part of a sheep from a lion, is compared with the situation that would follow the destruction of Israel by the Assyrian onslaught. Such similar parabolic comparisons are to be found elsewhere in Amos (2: 13; 5: 7, 24; 6: 12; 9: 9). The style is that of a popular proverb and our Lord Himself was an able user of this form of teaching. During his years of experience as a shepherd, Amos would have had to rescue members of his flock that had been taken by lions and the situation described at v. 12 would have been all too familiar to him. The shepherd makes his vain pursuit and finds in fact only a few scraps, **two legs, or a piece** (lobe) **of an ear** that the lion had left. In such a situation **saves** is somewhat ironic. Such, says Amos, will be the fate of Israel, the roar of the lion had already been heard and its destructive leap was near at hand.

The latter part of v. 12 introduces some textual problems. The NIV rendering **who sit . . . on the edge of their beds and on the corner of their couches** possibly conveys the sense (the AV is virtually meaningless at this point although it follows the actual Hebrew text almost literally; for details of the textual problems see the larger commentaries). The meaning may be that the few who would escape the onslaught would have nothing except an

odd piece of furniture or perhaps a piece of cloth but the interpretation of this passage is obscure. Verses 13–15 detail the way in which this judgment would come. The judgment would be both upon the religious and civil aspects of the nation's life.

The **altars of Bethel** (14) symbolize Israel's religion. Bethel was the pre-eminent shrine of the northern kingdom in the time of Jeroboam II (7: 10, 13; Jos. 4: 15; 10: 5, etc.). The sanctuary was destroyed by Josiah when he extended his reformation to what had been Israelite territory (2 Kg. 23: 15). The **horns of the altar** were small projections at each corner of the top of the altar. A fugitive could obtain sanctuary by holding on to the altar horns (1 Kg. 1: 50; 2: 28) but every form of security was going to be removed. Israel would find no sanctuary from the enemy that was coming against her, indeed the very altars themselves would be destroyed. It was not only the house of their god that would be destroyed, however, and perhaps Amos has an ironic note here in his use of Bethel, but also the houses of men. **15. the winter house along with the summer house; and the houses adorned with ivory:** these were the evidence of the luxury that had been built upon the exploitation of the poor and this was also to come under the righteous judgment of Yahweh. **houses adorned with ivory:** a reference to the mansions decorated with ivory inlay (note 1 Kg. 22: 39 and see further *NBD* under 'Ivory' and 'Samaria').

iv. The women of Samaria (4: 1–3)

The second of this group of oracles begins with a bitingly sarcastic attack on the women of Samaria who are compared to a herd of prize cattle living on the fat of the land. **1. Bashan:** recognized throughout the region for the richness of its pastures and the excellence of its cattle. The luxury and its associated evils was an offence to God but the offence 'lay not just in its stark contrast to the condition of the poor, but in the fact that the affluence was built on the suffering of the needy' (J. L. Mays). It is worth noting that for Amos to call the wives of the rich, **cows of Bashan**, was not such a dreadful insult as it would be in modern society. In the idiom of the ancient east women would not necessarily be offended at being called cows (note the expressions used as compliments in the eastern love poetry of the Song of Songs, and the personal name Eglah, lit. 'heifer', in 2 Sam. 3: 5). Amos, however, makes the reference sarcastic in comparing the sensibility of these women to an herd of cattle crushing the grass or flowers beneath its feet. In the same way they **oppress the poor and crush the needy**. They urged on their husbands to procure for them the luxuries that they required to support their lives of ease and indolence. The expression **Bring us some**

drinks means essentially 'so that we can have our parties'. The expression **the time will surely come** (2) is one of the standard formulae of what has been called 'prophetic eschatology'. It indicates the time when God will break into human affairs to set things right whether to bring judgment or to bring salvation. In Amos the coming days are to be equated with the day of Yahweh (see further 5: 18).

The text of vv. 2b and 3 presents a large number of problems. The two words which have been translated **hooks** and **fishhooks** do not appear elsewhere in the OT with this meaning. Heb. *ṣinnôt* usually means 'shields'; the second word *sîrôt* may mean 'pots'; both have a masculine form which can mean 'thorn', hence 'hook'. G. R. Driver proposed the translation 'They will lift you high in shields and your children in fish baskets'. However, it is generally assumed that the nouns refer to some form of hook used to drag away corpses or to fasten the captives to one another in the line to be marched away. The word **Harmon** is unknown. There are several variations of the text in different versions. Some ancient translations have 'the mountains of Minni', implying a part of Armenia. The LXX seems to suggest that the women would end their days as temple prostitutes or as a sacrifice to Rimmon, and this certainly makes sense. Some versions have 'Hermon' with its ironic underlying twist, since Hermon is part of the Bashan range and the cows of Bashan would end up where they belong.

It seems most likely that the picture is that, as in the days of idleness they had behaved as cattle, so in the day of judgment they would be treated in the same way, dragged out of the ruins of the city with rings through their noses like cows to the slaughterhouse, one behind the other (the likely meaning of **each go straight out**). The Assyrian illustrations depict such scenes with captives being led with hooks through their noses or mouths, and Amos was no doubt familiar with this barbaric practice.

v. The worship of Israel (4: 4, 5)
The oracle concerning the worship of Israel continues in the same vein of biting sarcasm that was employed in denouncing the self-indulgent women of Samaria. **Bethel** and **Gilgal** were ancient shrines which had been associated with the worship of the local gods long before the conquest of Canaan by the people of Israel. It was possibly on account of their long religious history that Jeroboam I had chosen them as centres of the northern cultus. The words of Amos followed the style of a priestly exhortation to join in the worship of the sanctuary or perhaps a pilgrimage song, but the words of Amos must have seemed like an irreverent blasphemy to his audience. The Israelites, who had come to establish peace with their God through sacrificial ritual and receive His blessing, were being told in effect that their piety was an offence against the God whom they had come to worship.

The list of the rituals (4, 5) to which Amos invites his hearers would appear to be the standard catalogue of normal acts of worship which would have been performed at that time. The expression **sacrifices** is the general term for any offering in which an animal is killed. The **tithes**, which had an ancient connection with the Bethel shrine (Gen. 28: 22), were the tenth of the annual yield of the land which the Israelite was to bring to the LORD for use in the festival meals (Dt. 14: 22–29). The expression **every three years** (4) is difficult. It may refer to the pilgrim's tithe being presented on the third day of his visit to the shrine (cf. mg), the sacrifice being made on the first or, it may be a somewhat vague reference to the three great annual pilgrim feasts of Passover, Pentecost and Tabernacles. **5. leavened bread:** most unlikely to be a sarcastic reference to a breach of the regulations on the part of the worshippers (see Lev. 2: 11; 7: 11, but note also the use of leavened bread at Lev. 7: 13; 23: 17). It is unlikely that the prohibition of burning leaven was in force at Bethel and the statement is simply a reference to one of the normal ritual procedures.

The picture which emerges is of a religious life of great activism, full of the pomp and ceremony of show, but having no place for the concepts of righteousness, holiness and justice which Yahweh demanded from His worshippers. Indeed the whole of this oracle from the initial ironical invitation to **sin** and **sin yet more**, down to the sarcasm of **this is what you love to do**, is a total charge that the sacrificial worship of Israel had nothing to do with the LORD their God.

vi. The wilfulness of Israel (4: 6–14)
This section consists of a recounting of historical events, but one which was very different to the usual approach to history which saw in it the action of God in bringing deliverance and salvation to His people. When Amos looked at history he saw the very opposite of blessing and salvation; he saw the disasters that had overtaken the country in which God was seeking to bring back a wilful and rebellious people to Himself. Although Amos never refers to the covenant relationship between Yahweh and Israel, such an interpretation of history can only possess significance within the covenant situation.

The prophet looks at five natural disasters which had overtaken the nation and each ends with the refrain **yet you have not returned to me** (6, 8, 9, 10, 11). Famine, pestilence and sword are the first three examples that Amos gives and are basic parts of covenant curses (note Lev. 26; Dt. 28). The catastrophe of v. 11, **as** God **overthrew Sodom and Gomorrah,** does not occur in the lists of curses that would come upon the nation through the breaking of the covenant, but the image occurs frequently throughout the OT indicating that such a judgment was considered a likely outcome of disloyalty to God. There is no indication of the cause of the famine at v. 6, but the drought (7, 8) relates to the same type of situation. The drought was not complete. One region appeared to be barren and parched while another had rain, a phenomenon characteristic of the area. The main drought took place **when the harvest was still three months away,** i.e. it would appear that it was the 'latter' or spring rains, essential for the final growth of the corn, that had failed.

As well as famine and drought there was also **blight and mildew** (9) indicating a rapidly spreading fungal disease in the crops for which no treatment would have been known. In addition there were the dreaded **locust** hordes (9) to devour and ruin what little was left. In spite of the situation Israel remained unrepentant.

A fresh disaster in the form of **plagues** overtook the nation (10). **10. as I did to Egypt:** probably a reference to the events of Exod. 5: 3 (cf. Dt. 28: 27). In the insanitary conditions of the time such plagues would quickly sweep through city and country (note the rapid spread of bubonic plague through the Philistine cities, 1 Sam. 5). The catastrophe (11) which is compared to the disaster that **overthrew Sodom and Gomorrah** could be a reference to a major earthquake or, perhaps, a serious fire that destroyed one of the cities. Memories of such disasters would be easy to recall by the audience in their own time or in the times of their fathers. Amos, however, points the moral, underlining that their cause lay in the refusal of Israel to humble herself before Yahweh and **return** to Him in repentance. Israel's misfortunes were not mere punishment but a chastisement designed to bring about their return. In view of the recalcitrance of Israel there would be ultimately a total judgment.

12. Therefore: introducing the judgment sentences **this is what I will do to you, Israel**. The actual encounter in judgment is not detailed but the reality of the judgment is underlined and Israel is called upon to **prepare to meet your God**. These are expressions which normally are related to the preparation of people for worship; here however, it is not the ceremony of worship nor even the ceremony of covenant renewal, but rather it is a ceremony of judgment to which Israel is called. The summons of Israel to meet her God is the announcement of the final judgment day of Yahweh Himself.

Verse 13 is one of the three hymnic sections in the book of Amos the others being 5: 8 and 9: 5, 6. Each stands quite distinct from its immediate context both in style and in subject matter. The style is that of the hymn and they depict the majesty of Yahweh, the One whose power can shake the world and whose sovereignty all must accept. It is possible that all three passages come from the same hymn. The concluding refrain **The LORD God Almighty is his name** occurs almost exactly in 5: 8 and 9: 6. There is nothing in the form or content to suggest that these doxologies could not date from the time of Amos, or even before, but the most likely explanation for their presence is that they were later liturgical insertions for public reading. The language is paralleled in many of the psalms. They stand as magnificent and majestic descriptions of the One who has made His appeal to Israel, the One who sustains the world with His creative power but who also will reveal that power in judgment.

vii. A lament for the nation (5: 1–3)
This short oracle is a further example of the mastery by Amos of a wide variety of traditional forms of expression and literary styles. The lament over Israel is a miniature masterpiece of the mourning song or funeral dirge (*qînāh*). The funeral dirge was the main part of a funeral ceremony in Israel. It was a poem of grief for the death of a kinsman, friend or leader, usually written, as here, in 3+2 metre. A particularly fine example is David's dirge for Saul and Jonathan (2 Sam. 1: 17–27; see also Jer. 9: 17, 19, 20–22). The use of this form is not merely for a dramatic emphasis; it also indicates the reality of the feeling of Amos himself and his grief at the desperate plight in which the nation of Israel would soon find itself. In the dirge the judgment is treated as though it had already come and the lament speaks of the irrevocable fall of the nation; **Fallen is Virgin Israel, never to rise again** (2). The hitherto unconquered land (the probable implication of the word **Virgin**) will be unable to resist the might of Assyria. The ruin would be complete and there would be **no one to lift her up** to her old status again. Only a tenth would escape the disaster and return from the battle to tell the tale. Such a decimation would spell the complete and total collapse of the country. The expressions **thousand** and **hundred** (3) are probably not arbitrary figures but relate to the way in which the military forces in Israel were apparently organized (1 Sam. 17: 18; 18: 13; 22: 7; 2 Sam. 18: 1, etc). In earlier days the military forces were drawn from tribes and clans, but now the cities and towns would have to produce levies of the correct number in times of national emergency. The remnant from the conscripted forces would leave little hope for the future and the nation faced only total disaster.

viii. An appeal to the nation (5: 4–17)

Normally the invitation to **seek the LORD** would be an exhortation to turn to the Lord and worship Him in His sanctuary, but this oracle underlines quite plainly that the two are mutually exclusive as far as Israel was concerned: **Seek me and live; do not seek Bethel** (4, 5). It is the Holy One rather than the holy place that Israel must seek. To seek Yahweh implied the observation of His commands and obedience to His will which required, not sacrifice or ritual, but morality in life (note Mic. 6: 6–8; Hos. 6: 6–10). These words of Amos, like some of the other oracles in the book, would have been as shocking and paradoxical to his hearers as the words of our Lord at a later time.

Both **Bethel** and **Gilgal** had long associations with Israel's worship and were places of great significance, hallowed by their history and associations with the early worship. The impending fate of the two sanctuaries is announced in a word-play which cannot be rendered in English. G. A. Smith suggested 'Gilgal shall taste the gall of exile'. Wellhausen produced 'Gilgal will go to the gallows'. **Bethel** will become 'āwen, a word which expressed the powers of evil as well as that which was empty or without existence (**nothing** as here). The house of God will become the house of evil. Hosea uses the same word-play (Hos. 4: 15). In the day of judgment these centres of a vain and lifeless religion would become the empty perversion that for so long they had represented. There would be no help in looking to them, only by looking in repentance to Yahweh Himself. The exhortation from v. 4 is repeated at v. 6, **Seek the LORD and live**. The way to God is the way of life if only the people of Israel would turn to it. The alternative, **he will sweep through the house of Joseph like a fire**, is a judgment from which no one will be able to rescue them. The failure of the courts to provide the justice of God is one of the continuing themes of this prophecy. The rulers of the nation had forgotten the meaning of **justice** and **righteousness**, two words which continually recur in pairs in parallel forms throughout this book (note 5: 7, 15, 24; 6: 12). For the ordinary man the courts were so full of bribery and corruption that the very thought of justice was to him **bitterness** (Heb. 'wormwood'). Wormwood (*Artemisia absinthium*) was well known as a desert plant and was used as a symbol of calamity and disaster on account of its extremely bitter taste (note Prov. 5: 4; Lam. 3: 15, 19; Jer. 9: 15; 23: 15).

The section is interrupted by one of the hymnic refrains (see note on 4: 13) which exalt the LORD, referring initially (8) to His majesty in creation and then (9) to His power upon earth as the one who will bring forth **destruction** against those whose imagined security is in their own power and strength rather than God. The lesson is clear, for all who live in God's universe are dependent upon Him and subject to His authority.

The argument of v. 7 is continued in vv. 10 f. The prophet describes the attitude of the upper classes in Israel who detest any form of true justice, and the perverters of justice who set themselves up in opposition to the proper functions of the courts. The phrase they **hate the one who reproves** (better, 'who conducts a case') **in court** refers to the one who presents the case for the poor. The **court** (Heb. 'gate') was the regular place in which the local courts in Israel's cities and towns were held. It was at the same time the market place, magistrates' court and public platform, serving something of the same functions as the Greek agora or Roman forum (Ru. 4: 1 ff.; Am. 5: 12, 15, etc). Justice was no longer in the courts of Samaria, and integrity was an unknown quality in the land of Israel.

The organization of justice in Israel was not so formally organized as in modern times. All the adult male citizens of a town, unless disqualified for some reason, were eligible to sit in the court as court assessors and anyone could testify as a witness or provide advice. It was because the proceedings of the court were conducted in this somewhat informal manner that the administration of justice depended upon the integrity of those who acted as assessors in speaking the truth and upholding justice. The decalogue (Exod. 20: 13) prohibits the false witness, as part of the words of God in establishing the foundation of the nation. Therefore to **hate** or **despise** those who advocated justice and truth was essentially to reject the whole system that God had established and therefore, to reject the God of Israel Himself.

Verse 11 gives details of the type of exploitation that existed at that time. The word is directed against those who were driving the yeoman farmer away from his independence into a form of slavery. He was no longer owner of his ground but a tenant farmer from whom the wealthy urban landlord demanded the maximum. It was a situation in which they **trample on the poor** and **force him to give you corn**. This form of exploitation did not serve to improve the economy of the nation but went to pay for the magnificent extravagance of the court and the rich. The judgment would suit the crime. They may build their fine houses but they would **not live in them**, they may plant their **lush vineyards** but they would **not drink their wine**. This section consists of at least two oracles but the exact reconstruction of the section cannot be made with certainty. It is likely that the assertion **I know** (12) is a response to the claims of innocence on the part of his audience. Amos answers by insisting that their actions are **offenses** and **sins**, in short, the nation of Israel is in rebellion against God, for such is the concept of **offense** (*peša'*). The bribery and corruption of the court made it clear that the rulers of the people were no longer shepherds of Yahweh's flock but rather wolves destroying it. They boasted in the claim that God was with them and if this was so it should have been demonstrated by a love of good and hatred of evil (14). Verse 13 may be a comment by a later editor. The line is in prose and its reference to the **prudent** suggests that the editor was one familiar with the Wisdom literature. If this is so it becomes an editorial observation that when times are evil and corrupt, wisdom lies in waiting for the day when justice will come from God rather than seeking to alter the conditions and appeal to the judgments of men. On the other hand, if original, the verse expresses an empirical truth, 'that the wordly man will know how to protect his skin and will not take up the cause of the oppressed' (Hammershaimb).

Verses 14, 15 do not appear to belong to the oracle that begins at v. 12 and is taken up again at v. 16. The sayings in vv. 14, 15 consist of exhortation followed by conditional promises indicating that there is still a chance for Israel. The repetition of **good** and **evil** in different sequences, together with the specific illustration of what good means, namely to **maintain justice in the courts**, indicates that the whole is a single rhetorical unit and is in fact cast in the style of a priestly exhortation or call to worship. The word **seek** indicates essentially 'being devoted to', 'being concerned about', and the other imperatives **hate** and **love** (15) demonstrate the emphasis on the importance of bringing into force all the resources of the individual's character to do what is right. To seek **good** rather than **evil** is to make a decision for Yahweh (note vv. 4, 6) and therefore will bring blessing, but to decide for evil is to decide against Yahweh and will bring about His judgment.

The condition is clear in v. 15, **perhaps**. There is no certainty about Israel's repentance. What is certain is the reality of judgment if Israel persists in her present behaviour. This is underlined in vv. 16 and 17, which in a sense pick up the thread from v. 12. The present course of conduct will bring inevitable ruin and God will pass through the land in judgment. Amos pictures a time when the land will be filled with funerals; such is the terrible reality of the coming judgment (note Jer. 9: 17–22; Mic. 2: 4, etc). **16. the mourners:** the persons outside the immediate family circle who were professional mourners and well versed in the funeral songs traditionally sung at such times.

The words **'cries of anguish'** render the wail of the mourners. Wailing and mourning with loud public lamentation mark the funeral rite throughout the east. They will be heard throughout the land for God **will pass through** Israel (17) rather than passing over. Once, the destroying angel had passed through Egypt, bringing death to that land, and those who would not seek the LORD that they might live would find that He would pass through them as He did through the land of Egypt of old.

ix. The Day of Yahweh (5: 18–20)
This section is perhaps one of the most famous sections of Amos and it introduces for the first time in Scripture a theme which was to recur constantly, the concept of the **day of the LORD** (18). The oracle begins with a cry of woe against those **who long for the day of the LORD**. The term appears only in the prophetic texts (*e.g.* Isa. 2: 12; 13: 6, 9; 32: 5; 34: 8; Jer. 46: 10; Ezek. 17: 13; Jl 2: 1 ff.; Zeph. 1: 7, etc.). It is clear that the idea is not the creation of Amos and the origins of the concept are unknown. By the time of Amos it was an idea which had taken deep root in the religious thought of Israel. Initially it was probably simply the battle day of Yahweh when he demonstrated His effective Lordship over all creation and it was possible that it referred originally to the new year festival of Tabernacles, in which Israel celebrated God's victory over His enemies and a renewal of prosperity for His people. Later it came to be the eschatological day of salvation when Yahweh would break into history once more for the deliverance of His people.

Amos, however, and the other prophets reverse the hopes associated with this day and proclaim the day of the LORD, not as a day of deliverance, but as a day of judgment and doom. Amos warned his hearers that to **long for the day of the LORD** is, in fact, nothing more than a longing for their own disaster, for the day of the LORD is **darkness, not light** (18, 20). This oracle may have been delivered to the crowds assembled at Bethel for the annual autumn festival, 'the day of the festival of Yahweh' as it appears to have been called in the northern kingdom (note Hos. 9: 5). The religious fervour of the crowd was raised to high expectation, but Amos dashed their hopes with his prophecy of disaster. The day would be darkness, not for their enemies but for themselves. It would be a day of **pitch-dark without out a ray of brightness** (20). They might understand the theology of the day of the LORD; what they did not understand was the nature of the LORD Himself and how He is to bring judgment upon His enemies which might even be His own people.

In taking up this theme Amos deals with one

of the fundamental concepts of Israel's religion. The events of the Exodus and the establishment first of the Davidic kingdom and then of the divided kingdom held hopes expressed in the kingship which thus far had been unrealized in Israel's experience, but that these promises would be fulfilled was essential to Israel's philosophy of history. History was a process in which God was actively present; the day of the LORD would be a day upon which the LORD would reveal Himself, in which He would work to display His power for the benefit of the chosen nation. But Amos looks beyond theology to the reality of the nature of God Himself, he knows Yahweh and he knows the decision which He has made. From the perspective of what is right and is just, the day of the LORD can only mean the coming of God's judgment upon His people.

The imagery that Amos uses here is vivid and is drawn from events of everyday life; he pictures a man who escapes from **a lion** and is met by **a bear**. In desperation he manages to reach the shelter of his house. He arrives breathless, leans his hand against the wall to catch his breath and as he does so **a snake**, hidden in some crevice, emerges to bite him (19). The death he thought he would escape awaited him at his own house. Thus it was to be for Israel, there would be no escape; the day of Yahweh would be a day of gloom and darkness in which there would be no relieving feature for the rebellious house of Israel.

x. The vain religion (5: 21–27)

This oracle must have scandalized its hearers. Each of the essential elements of Israel's worship were examined, the festivals (21), sacrifices (22) and the praise of God in song (23). In each case they are totally rejected by God. What God required was not the ritual or offerings but rather righteousness in the courts, the markets, and in every aspect of conduct, for this is the essential element of the worship of God, not the outward show.

The verbs which are used indicate 'nauseated disgust and vehement rejection' (J. L. Mays). The word **hate** (21) expressed total detestation. The LORD hated the cults of Canaan (Dt. 12: 31; 16: 22). Amos was saying in effect that the worship of Israel was on the same level as the hated worship of Canaan in the years before the exile. The word for **religious feasts** (ḥag) denotes the three major pilgrim festivals of Unleavened Bread, Pentecost (Weeks) and Tabernacles. The expression **assemblies** is a term denoting any period of festival when the people took a holiday to celebrate (Lev. 23: 36; Dt. 16: 8; Num. 29: 35). The prophet alludes to the main sacrifices, the **burnt offering**, a sacrifice in which the entire animal is consumed, and the **grain offering** (minḥāh) a wide term covering any sacrifice brought as a gift

and presented almost in the sense of a tribute. In later times it became the specialized designation for the offerings of vegetables and particularly grain, hence 'cereal offering'. The **choice fellowship offering** was a communion sacrifice (šelem) which was designed specifically to re-establish relationships between man and God.

At every point in the description of Israel's worship the prophet uses the complete negation of the normal verbs which describe God's positive pleasure with what was done. God **will not accept, will have no regard** (22) and **will not listen** (23). It is clear that the religion of Israel was full of punctilious attention to detail, with everything celebrated regularly and correctly, but it was all an empty show rather than true religion. Yahweh did not desire the slavish observance of ritual, he desired right conduct, which in itself is an act of true worship. Hence comes the magnificent couplet of v. 24 where again the great nouns **justice** and **righteousness** occur. They are to flow forever as a mighty river, not drying up like the streams that only flow in the rainy season. God required **justice** (mišpāṭ), the rightness of the social order, the protection of the weak and the poor through the processes of law. God demanded **righteousness** (ṣᵉdāqāh), that which demonstrates the fulfilment of interpersonal relationships and the responsibilities that these involved. Social justice and personal morality is the essence of the religion of Yahweh (note Jas 1: 27). Without such characteristics of life the festivals remain **your religious feasts** or **your assemblies** (21); they are not the worship of God.

Verses 25–27 continue the theme of sacrifice but the verses probably represent a separate oracle from the previous words. The main point is the denial by Amos that sacrifice is a means by which Yahweh can be satisfied. He announces that because of their reliance upon this, instead of upon the basics of true religion, the Israelites would fall into the power of foreign gods (26) and be taken into **exile** into their territory.

Verse 25 poses a number of problems. Amos appears to be denying that sacrifices had been part of the initial religion of Israel or part of the relationship established between Israel and Yahweh during the period of the Exodus. It is interesting to note that Jeremiah states something almost similar (7: 21–24). There is no easy way in which this problem can be overcome. Certainly for both Jeremiah and for Amos at least, sacrifice does not appear to have an authorized place in the constitution of Israel as the people of the LORD. The real point of the words is clear, however; the LORD, the God of Israel, demanded right conduct rather than sacrifice and the outward trappings of worship (Hos. 6: 6; Mic. 6: 6–8; Jer. 6: 20, etc). **Sakkuth** and **Kaiwan** (26 mg) are both forms of the name of the Assyrian war god Ninib, god of the planet Saturn. Their form in the text is due to the scribes adding to the consonants the vowels of the word for a detestable thing (*šiqqûs*) a common device for derogatory names of false gods. Amos makes no explicit comment on the worship of false gods in Israel, but it is clear from this verse and elsewhere that he viewed their worship of Yahweh as being no better than idolatry for it was a religion divorced from morality. The result of their behaviour would be that the God who once delivered them from bondage would send them into a new bondage **beyond Damascus** (27), to the land of the gods that she has apparently worshipped. **27. exile:** a concept of deep foreboding. To be moved from the promised land, the land in which God Himself had established His dwelling was, in fact, an excommunication, being cut off from the community.

xi. The idle rich (6: 1–7)

This oracle is directed against the self-confidence of the ruling class. It focuses attention on their pride and self-sufficiency (1–3) and on the elegant luxury in which they lived (4–6). No doubt the sense of well-being had arisen from the general prosperity and peaceful conditions that prevailed at the time. The upper classes had been lulled into a false sense of security. Both **Samaria** and **Zion** (Jerusalem) were royal cities whose history was linked directly with the monarchy in Israel. It is interesting that Amos introduces Zion here, as essentially his messages are against Israel, but the shoe fits those in Jerusalem as well as in Samaria and, although his mission was to Israel, the word which he spoke would apply to those whose lives were similar in the south. The link also underlines the real unity of the people of God.

The expression **notable men of the foremost nations** (1) is ironical rhetoric. These top people, as they imagined themselves, thought of themselves in these pompous terms. The irony continues in v. 2 where Amos puts words into the mouth of these so-called notables, which are sheer boasting. They said, in effect, that as people journey about they would observe that none of the other countries around were as large as Israel and Judah. **Calneh** and **Hamath** were city states to the north of Israel. The reference to **Gath** is somewhat difficult as in the time of Amos this city was under Judean suzerainty.

The complacent pride of Israel no doubt sprang out of the magnificence of Jeroboam's reign coupled with their belief that, as they were the people of God, no harm could come to them. In their foolish optimism they imagined **the evil day** was far away (3) and in consequence they continued to behave as though change would never come about and they pursued their ways of violence as though their deeds would never be called into question by a righteous God. The expression **evil day** indicates essentially a day of disaster and may be used as an alternative term for the day of Yahweh (note 5: 8, 20; 8: 10). The word **reign** is literally 'seat' used here in the technical sense of a throne or seat of judgment; violence reigned in the land of Israel in the days of Jeroboam II.

Verses 4–6 paint a picture of affluent decadence that marked the life of the wealthy in Israel. It was a life of self-centred luxury, marked by gluttony, drunkenness and extravagance. **4. beds inlaid with ivory:** ornamented with ivory inlay, a type of very expensive furniture. The food they demanded is rendered by Moffatt as 'fresh lamb and fatted veal'. The feasts were eaten in a reclining position (**lounge**). This is the first mention of reclining at meal in the Bible; the normal custom of Israel had been to sit on rugs or seats when eating.

The verb rendered **strum away** (5) occurs only here in the OT. The word probably means 'improvise' and the impression is thus given of extempore singing with the tunes and words made up at the time, as in the following words, **improvise on musical instruments**. The suggestion has been made that **instruments** should read 'all sorts of', or else that the word has been added under the influence of 1 Chr. 23: 5 and Neh. 12: 36, where there is particular reference to the musical instruments of David. However, the essential thought of the words is the mockery by Amos of those who imagined that their drunken attempts at singing make them appear like another **David**. The heart of the tragedy lay in the fact that they did not grieve over **the ruin of Joseph** (6). While they continued in their extravagant and self-centred lives they were totally insulated from the ruin which was coming upon the whole country. Instead of being guardians of the country's life and morals they were an example of unparalleled selfish greed, and in their self-centred lives they did not care that the whole country was fast going to ruin about them. **Therefore**, said the prophet (7), those leaders of today will be tomorrow the leaders of the pitiful columns of exiles going into captivity.

xii. Impending doom (6: 8–14)

The common theme running through these words is the wrath of God soon to be revealed against the pride of Israel. There is a variety both in the style and literary character of this section suggesting that the whole is composed of small fragments or summaries of sayings of Amos that had been brought together because of their similar subject matter. The behaviour that Amos has described would lead only to one result, which by this time should have been self-evident even to the smug citizens of Samaria. The judgment of God would not merely come upon the rich but upon the whole of the country. The expression **the Sovereign LORD has sworn** is used on three occasions by Amos (4: 2; 8: 7) to introduce the statement of the judgment that God was going to bring upon the nation; such an oath makes the decree of God final and absolute since His whole person is invested in this form of an oath in its most binding form. The **pride of Jacob** indicates the overweening self-confidence of the nation; God loathes this pride which is at the heart of the nation's rottenness. They regarded their national destiny and position as the work of their own hands and they expressed this in the indulgent luxury which ignored the desperate plight of the poor. Their pride meant that the reality of Yahweh's overlordship was forgotten or ignored.

Verses 9, 10 appear to picture some form of pestilence or plague striking a city, perhaps as a result of the warfare around and the conditions that such situations produce. The severity of the situation (9) would be common to plagues of varying forms in the insanitary conditions of the time. **10. relative:** on the father's side, an uncle or cousin. The expression **who is to burn the bodies** is difficult, as cremation was not an accepted burial practice among the Israelites, although it may have been in the circumstances of epidemics or plagues. It is possible that the word may mean a kinsman on the mother's side, the two together being those who had the responsibility for burial. When they came to perform their duties to the dead and ask if there are any left the answer is **No**.

Whole households would thus perish in the disaster and in these circumstances they **must not mention the name of the LORD**. The command for silence in these circumstances is in case the mention of the Divine Name would bring again the terrible curse that the LORD's appearance had already brought upon them. To mention the name of the LORD would only be to invite further disaster.

The message of doom continues with the reminder of the absurdity of Israel's behaviour (12). Nobody would attempt to race a horse down a precipice nor attempt to plough a furrow through the sea with his yoke of oxen, yet in effect this is exactly the sort of foolishness which characterized the behaviour of Israel. The style is characteristic of the language of folk wisdom and parables, the question posing what all would see as being both impossible and absurd; such exaggeration underlines the point and drives home the lesson that the prophet is making. The wealthy classes had turned **justice into poison** and **righteousness into bitterness**. This point had already been

made at 5: 6 where the point was underlined that the rulers had made righteousness and justice as bitter as wormwood and in so doing they had destroyed the two pillars which would have offered support for the nation in time of trial.

While they boasted in their own strength God was about to bring about their downfall (13, 14). Verse 13 is in fact a rather elaborate pun, the name **Lo Debar** (a town mentioned in 2 Sam. 9: 4; 17: 27, and located in the eastern part of Gilead) means nothing or a thing of no value. **Karnaim** literally means 'horns'; it was a city to the north-east of Israel, mentioned later in 1 Mac. 5: 43 f. (cf. also Ashteroth Karnaim, Gen. 14: 5). 'Horns' is a metaphor for strength. Amos is saying sarcastically that the leaders are rejoicing in something that is really nothing and imagined they had captured strength by their own strength. The forces of Israel might be able to capture two insignificant border towns but they would be no match for the might of Assyria. From the north (**Hamath**) to the south (**the valley of the Arabah**, 14) the whole land would lie in the hands of the conqueror and Israel would find only oppression and slavery as they came to know the sovereignty of the LORD and His judgment upon His erring subjects.

IV. VISIONS OF DOOM (7: 1–8: 3)

The material in this section is made up of five narratives, mainly in the first person singular. There are differences of style between them and there is a biographical piece inserted at 7: 10–17 giving an account of the confrontation between Amos and the priest of Bethel. The other pieces of material represent accounts of visionary experiences, each introduced with the formula **This is what the Sovereign LORD showed me**. These conclude with a dialogue between Amos and Yahweh. These conversations essentially form intercessions on the part of Amos and initially these are successful in bringing about a respite from judgment for the land of Israel, but the real burden of the visions themselves is not blessing and salvation but rather the revelation of God's wrath and judgment upon His people. Even when the disaster is averted the situation nonetheless remains ominous and threatening. It is noteworthy that the visions are of natural events that everyone could see, but Amos saw in them the activity of God. 'He turned sight into insight' (J. Marsh).

i. The locusts (7: 1–3)

In the first vision Amos is shown a plague of **locusts** being created and made ready to destroy the land, **just as the second crop was coming up** (1), i.e. spring time. The late planting or latter growth is the last growth of pasture before the long dry season of summer begins.

If it were lost there would be nothing to carry the people over into the next harvest. The word used for **locusts** is only found here and at Nah. 3: 17. It may represent one of the species or, more likely in the context, a young form. The **king's share** would seem to indicate either there was a tax levied on the first crop harvested or that the king had the claim to the first cutting of hay to feed the royal chariot-horses (note 1 Kg. 4: 7; 18: 5; 1 Sam. 8: 15, 17). A plague of locusts devouring these crops would be a disastrous occurrence in a land with an already weakened agricultural economy. As Amos reminds God, **How can Jacob survive? He is so small** (2). **2. When they had stripped:** better rendered 'when they were on the point of finishing'.

These visions are of great significance, for in the direct appeal which Amos makes, the prophet demonstrates the force of his claim to be like other prophets, in the counsels of God. Like Abraham and Moses before him Amos was able to take his case right into the presence of God and there plead his cause. There could be no greater authentication of the genuineness of his prophetic call than this ability to approach God directly and speak with Him as a man would speak with his friend. Amos pleads for forgiveness and God hears his prayer; **The LORD relented** and the disaster is averted (6). The verb relent does not imply any sense of regret or remorse about a course of action being wrong, it is simply an expression which insists upon the reality of God's personal involvement in His actions towards man and His awareness of responsibility in the consequences of His acts. It is part of the overall biblical theme that God is a personal God, one who feels and displays His emotions, not an abstract and mechanical Deity. It is also important to note that Amos did not think of God as being imprisoned in His own immutability. God was Lord of history and all that happened was according to His sovereign will, but He was a free agent, not bound by determinancy.

ii. The fire (7: 4–6)

The second vision is probably to be related to the fires of the dry summer season. Such fires spread with great rapidity, destroying grassland, trees and even villages standing in their path. There is no chance of fighting the fires as streams and watercourses are dried up. Here the fire is so intense that it had devoured the **great deep** (*tᵉhôm*), that is the primeval waters. The expression **calling for judgment** (4) indicates a court room scene in which Yahweh is prosecutor, judge and the one who carries out the sentence. The intercession of Amos is once again effective in averting the judgment of Yahweh on the land (5, 6).

iii. The plumb line (7: 7–9)

In this vision Amos does not witness a destruc-

tive force about to bring ruin to the nation, but rather the internal state of Israel about to bring about its own collapse. Amos sees Yahweh **standing by a wall . . . with a plumb line in his hand** (7). The plumb line was a lead weight attached to a line to ensure walls were perpendicular. It was not only used in building but also to test dilapidated walls to see whether they should be pulled down. The plumb line is set **among my people Israel** (8) and reveals the desperate state of the structure of Israel's society. The twin pillars of religion and a just social order which should support the nation are so far out of true that they must be pulled down. Hence **the high places** and **the sanctuaries of Israel will be ruined** and the **house of Jeroboam** (exemplifying the civil order) will be exterminated (9).

iv. Conflict with Amaziah (7: 10–17)

The sequence of visions is interrupted at this point by a biographical narrative. It is not possible to fit this into any chronological order of Amos's ministry although it may well have taken place at its end and marked the termination of his work in Israel. The expression **priest of Bethel** (10) must indicate the high priest of the sanctuary. His name, **Amaziah** (Yahweh is strong) is compounded with Yahweh and would indicate that the sanctuaries of Israel maintained the worship of Yahweh although the evidence of Amos and Hosea suggests that it had become corrupted with aspects of Canaanite worship.

The accusation that **Amos is raising a conspiracy** (10) relates to his prophecies of judgment rather than in a true prophetic conspiracy such as lay behind Jehu's revolution (1 Kg. 19: 15–18; 2 Kg. 9: 1–10). This is borne out by Amaziah's quotation (11) where the implication is that Yahweh's punishment will be carried out by a hostile power rather than an internal insurrection. Such words would, however, be viewed as a conspiracy, for words given with power were considered able to bring about the declaration and hence the presence of Amos would be viewed as a direct threat to the king's position. Thus Amaziah says, **the land cannot bear** (endure) **all his words** (10).

The response of Jeroboam to Amaziah is not given, but it must be presumed that the expulsion order (12) was given with the king's authority. The words **'You seer'** are almost certainly a sarcastic taunt. The word (*hōzeh*) might be translated 'visionary' and Amaziah treats Amos as nothing more than one of the itinerant professional fortune tellers to whom people went for advice. He tells him to **go back to the land of Judah. Earn your bread there** (12), that is, 'take yourself back to Judah and make your living there as a prophet'. He must no longer prophesy at Bethel as it is **the king's sanctuary**, a **temple of the kingdom**

(13), a clear indication of the importance of the Bethel sanctuary at this time. As the king's sanctuary it would parallel the Jerusalem temple which, as initially conceived by David and Solomon, appeared to be designed as the 'chapel royal'.

Amos replied to Amaziah denying that he has anything to do with the professional prophets (4). There appears to be no real difference between **prophet** (*nābî'*) and **seer** (*ḥōzeh*) (12) in this context. The NIV rendering **prophet's son** obscures the fact that the reference is to a member of one of the prophetic bands into which men were taken to learn the art of prophesying as a way of earning their living. Amos was thus indignantly denying an association with the prophetic schools and emphasized that his calling was not his choice but **the LORD took me . . . and said to me, 'Go, prophesy . . .'** (15). He had been taken from his sheep to fulfil the divine mandate. His status depended on the divine call, not his own choice, and it is clear that 'the convictions of Amos were as different from those of contemporary prophets as the convictions of Luther from those of contemporary monks' (R. H. Pfeiffer). (On the calling of Amos see Introduction.) The word rendered **shepherd**, implying the handling of cattle as well as sheep, only occurs here in the OT and may be a copyist's error for the word found at 1: 1. The two words could easily be confused in Hebrew. Amos finally declares God's punishment on Amaziah in person (16, 17). His wife would only be able to find a living as a **prostitute in the city**, his family would **fall by the sword**, his land would be divided up among the conquerors and he himself would end his days as an exile in **a foreign country**, that is a land of foreign gods in which he would be unable to offer the sacrifices necessary to hallow the crops and the food.

v. The summer fruit (8: 1–3)
This vision continues the sequence interrupted by the account of the encounter with Amaziah. It may be related to the period of the Autumn Festival when the harvest was presented at the Feast of Tabernacles. The point of the vision depends on a play on words in the Hebrew. The basket of ripe **fruit** (*qayis*) reminds Amos not of the joyful harvest festival but that Israel is ripe for judgment and **the time** (*qēs*) **is ripe**. In place of **songs of the temple** at the great feast, there would be **wailing in that day**. The Assyrian invasion would produce **everywhere bodies** (3). The bodies would be **flung** out in the same way as a basket of over-ripe fruit on the point of decay. **3. Silence:** the word cannot be taken as an adverb but is an interjection, a warning not to mention the name of Yahweh in the time of judgment. It is to be noted that there is no plea for mercy in this vision and this

time there is no promise of respite; judgment is now inevitable, for the message of the prophet had been manifestly rejected.

V. THE TIME HAS COME (8: 4–9: 10)
This section consists of a collection of oracles which have little connection with one another apart from the general theme of Israel's doom.
i. A corrupt land (8: 4–8)
This oracle with the opening formula, **Hear this**, and its general context, seems to belong to the collection of 3: 1–4: 3. It is directed against the wealthy merchant classes who by their dishonest and corrupt practices **trample the needy** and **do away with the poor** (4). The two regular feast days of **the New Moon** and **the Sabbath** go back to the earliest period of Israel's history. It is not clear that the new moon was originally a day in which work was forbidden, although it was a prominent festival (1 Sam. 20: 5, 24; 2 Kg. 4: 23; Isa. 1: 13, 14; Hos. 2: 11). The implication here, however, is that at this time a ban on work existed on both days and this proved extremely tiresome to the fraudulent traders who were concerned only in making money.

The grain dealers worked on the principle of short measures, overcharging and false weights too, if they could get away with it (5). **The measure** (Heb. ephah) was a measure of volume (approximately 40 litres) and the **price** (Heb. shekel) a unit of weight (approximately 11 grams). Coinage was not used at the time of Amos, but various metals were used in exchange, being weighed and their value calculated. The corn dealers were asking for larger quantities of metal than was fair, particularly as they were giving less than the correct measure in return and also selling chaff as good grain (6). The result of these unscrupulous practices was that the poor were having to sell themselves as slaves (6) in order to live.

Yahweh would not forget this treatment of the poor for He was the champion of the weak and oppressed (Ps. 9: 9; 10: 14, 18, etc.), and would execute judgment on their exploiters. The inevitability of judgment is underlined by an oath **by the Pride of Jacob** (7). This is equivalent to saying 'by Himself', but the words are not accidental for Amos wished to remind the people of what Yahweh ought to be to them. The punishment would take the form of an earthquake (8), in which the land would be tossed about like the waves of a river in flood. The cosmic nature of the judgment adds weight to the conception of the day of Israel's judgment being the day of Yahweh.
ii. A day of gloom (8: 9, 10)
These words may belong to the previous oracle, but they are generally treated as separate by most commentators. **9. in that day:** a reference to the day of Yahweh, the day of judgment

to be heralded by an eclipse of the sun that would warn of the impending calamities. The **religious feasts** (10), the great pilgrimage festivals (see 5: 21) would be turned to **mourning** and **weeping**. As a sign of mourning **sackcloth** was worn and the hair pulled out (**shave your heads**). The bitterness of the day of judgment would be like the mourning for **an only son** which marked the end of hope for the family unit.

iii. A new famine (8: 11–14)

The expression **the days are coming** (11) is essentially parallel to **that day** of the previous oracle and indicates the period of judgment. In that time Yahweh would remain silent and this is itself part of the judgment. The people will come to the source of their life but, though they may hunger and thirst for a word from God, there will be a **famine through the land** (11) **but they will not find it** (12). The people of Israel would learn too late that the source of the spiritual life was in obedience to Yahweh, not their vain and empty religious show. **12. from sea to sea:** probably from the Mediterranean to the Dead Sea (i.e. the western and eastern boundaries of the land).

The reason for this particular judgment is emphasized at v. 14. To **swear by** a god is the same as to honour and worship him. Three separate oaths are given which appear to allude to the worship of Yahweh at three different sanctuaries (Samaria, Dan and Beersheba). The expression **shame** (mg. Ashima) **of Samaria** may refer to the goddess worshipped by semi-pagan Jews at Elephantine in Egypt in the fifth century B.C. It could thus mean a goddess worshipped as Yahweh's consort, but it is probably better to retain the *MT* vocalization and translate as the 'guilt' or 'sin' (NIV **shame**) of Samaria and see here a contemptuous alteration of an oath that related to a bull image of Yahweh at Samaria (note Hos. 8: 5f.). The bull image at **Dan** is alluded to in the second oath and the third may again be a circumlocution, but it is probable that the text should be altered slightly to read 'your honour, Beer-sheba' or 'your god, Beer-sheba' (a reading preserved in LXX as NIV). In this case each oath would relate to a sanctuary where there was an image of Yahweh. Such false worship of gods of their own making underlines the reason for the judgment in which the true God would remain silent in Israel's hour of need.

iv. Yahweh over the altar (9: 1–6)

It was in the religious realm that the decay of Israel was most evident for it sprang out of a false concept of worship and a total misunderstanding of Yahweh's nature. All the other ills derived from the basic cause. In this final vision Amos declares the destruction of the whole people beginning at the centre of religious life. **1. by the altar:** better read 'upon'. The impression given is of Yahweh towering over the altar. The description of the destruction of the sanctuary is reminiscent of the old epic story of Samson (Jg. 16: 23–30). The judgment of the nation was to be pursued relentlessly, and Yahweh would track down and overtake all who escaped the initial disaster (2–4). **2. the grave**, mg. Sheol: the underworld, the land of the dead, a place of a shadowy and unreal existence. **3. the top of Carmel:** a reference probably to the thousands of limestone caves which occur in this mountainous ridge and which would normally protect a fugitive from pursuit. **the serpent:** a reference to the chaos monster defeated by Yahweh in the creation stories, referred to as Leviathan (Ps. 74: 13, 14; Isa. 27: 1) or Rahab (Isa. 51: 9; Ps. 89: 11). Nowhere in the universe would there be a hiding place for God **will fix** his **eyes upon them** (4), not to protect (**for good;** cf. Jer. 24: 6; 39: 12) but to destroy (**for evil**).

The short doxology of vv. 5, 6 may belong to the same hymn as 4: 13; 5: 8 f. (see notes on those sections).

v. God's sovereignty (9: 7–10)

These verses are a remarkable affirmation of the sovereignty of Yahweh over all the earth. Israel's election was no different in principle from the way in which God guided and directed all nations. Israel must therefore not treat her election as something unique which would confer special privilege. Israel may have been brought up **from Egypt** (7), but that would not give them an advantage or mean that they could escape judgment. 'God's purpose for Israel is not the only purpose which he has in the world, and Israel is not of herself indispensable to God, any more than is Syria or Ethiopia or Philistia' (J. Marsh).

7. Cushites refers to the dark-skinned people of what is now the Sudan. They were despised by Israel which lends point to the statement that in God's eyes there was no difference between them. **Caphtor** is the Egyptian name for Crete, but in this context is probably an inclusive name for the Aegean area from which the Philistines are believed to have come as one of the 'Sea Peoples' that threatened the eastern Mediterranean about 1200 B.C. On **Kir** see 1: 5.

It is not clear whether vv. 8–10 should be included with this oracle or be taken with the epilogue (11–15). There is a change of tone and the first hint that a remnant will escape (**I will not totally destroy**, 8). On the other hand the statements are a continuation of the prophecy of doom. The **sinful kingdom** was to be destroyed, but Amos recognized that grace and mercy were part of God's character and these could not be put to one side. Hence, as in the other prophets, judgment and mercy are strangely linked without contradiction. The result is that Israel will be passed through **a sieve** (9) in their time of exile (**among all the nations**). The word refers to the coarse sieve used to separate the corn from earth and stones. The corn passes through but not the stones: so RSV 'no pebble shall fall to the earth' cf. NEB. The wicked are thus held back and will not survive the exile.

VI. EPILOGUE—PROMISED RESTORATION (9: 11–15)

In the short epilogue to the book a bright future is depicted in which the promise is made that there will be a brilliant restoration of the house of David, now only a simple **tent** that has already **fallen** (11). The tent will be rebuilt **as it used to be**, which must refer to a restored united kingdom in view of the statement 'I will restore the fortunes of my people Israel' (14 mg.). Israel's sovereignty under a new Davidic monarchy would extend to all the nations that were once within its empire (12). **12. bear my name:** equivalent to 'take possession of', 'confirm as one's property'. The LXX (see mg.) uses an alternative and attractive reading of the text, quoted at Ac. 15: 17. The picture of abundant fertility (13) in hyperbolic imagery rounds off the promise of restoration, together with the assurance that Israel shall **never again . . . be uprooted** (15).

BIBLIOGRAPHY

Commentaries

CRIPPS, R. S., *A Critical and Exegetical Commentary on the Book of Amos* (London, 1955).
HAMMERSHAIMB, E., *The Book of Amos: A Commentary* (Oxford, 1970).
HARPER, W. R., *A Critical and Exegetical Commentary on Amos and Hosea.* ICC (Edinburgh, 1905).
HOWARD, J. K., *Amos Among the Prophets* (London, 1967).
MARSH, J., *Amos and Micah.* TC (London, 1959).
MAYS, J. L., *Amos: A Commentary.* OTL (London, 1969).
SMITH, G. A., *The Book of the Twelve Prophets*, i (London, ²1928).
WOLFF, H. W., *Joel and Amos*, E.T. Hermeneia (Philadelphia, 1977).

Short Commentaries

BUSSEY, O., 'Amos' in *NBCR* (London, 1970).
FOSBROKE, H. E. W., 'Amos' in *IB*, vol.6 (New York, 1956).

Other works

KAPELRUD, A. S., *Central Ideas in Amos* (Oslo, 1961 [=1956]).
KAPELRUD, A. S., New Ideas in Amos, *Vetus Testamentum, Suppl. 15, 1966, pp.193–206.*
WATTS, J. D. W., *Vision and Prophesy in Amos* (Leiden, 1958).

OBADIAH

W. WARD GASQUE

Historical Setting

The fourth prophecy in the Hebrew 'Book of the Twelve' (Minor Prophets) and the shortest book in the OT is directed against the Edomites, the descendants of Esau, twin-brother of Jacob, and therefore close relatives of the Israelites (cf. 'Edom, Edomites', in NBD). The date of writing is disputed among scholars since no definite historical reference is given by which we may date the prophecy with certainty. Verses 11–14 suggest the period immediately following the destruction of Jerusalem in 587/586 B.C., since it is definitely recorded that the Edomites participated in this event (Ps. 137: 7; Lam. 4: 21; Ezek. 25: 12; 35: 10; 1 Esd. 4: 45)and the picture is so very vivid, as in recent memory. Others, however, feel that vv. 16–21 reflect a mid-fifth century date. In the latter case, the account of the destruction of Jerusalem would be an adaptation of an older prophetic oracle (cf. the close similarities between vv. 1–9 and Jer. 49: 7–22).

Author

The prophet's name, meaning 'servant of Yahweh', is a very common one in the OT, being given to some twelve different individuals (cf. 'Obadiah' in NBD). He was from Judah presumably, though the Talmud says he was an Edomite proselyte. It is possible that he belonged to a circle of prophets attached to the Jerusalem temple. There is no reason to identify him with any of the other Obadiahs mentioned in the Bible. Thus we know nothing about his life or personality other than what we can infer from his brief prophecy.

Message

The heart of Obadiah's prophecy is aimed at the Edomites, who stand under the judgment of God for their inhumanity to Israel in the day of its suffering (10). Edom's crimes are listed in order of their ascending horror (11–14): the LORD will not allow what Edom has done to go unpunished. What the Edomites have done will return upon their own heads. However, Obadiah moves from the general to the particular, from God's judgment upon Edom to the 'day of the LORD', which will mean His judgment upon all nations, Israel included, and the establishment of the universal kingdom of God (cf. 'Day of the Lord', DBT, 110–11; 'Day of the Lord', NBD).

ANALYSIS

Title (1a)

Obadiah's prophecy is called a **vision** (Heb. *ḥāzôn*), a term used to speak of the revelatory nature of the prophet's insight into the meaning of particular historical events. The prophet's vision is one with the word of Yahweh (cf. 1b).

I. GOD'S JUDGMENT UPON EDOM (1b–10)

1. The title **the Sovereign LORD** (Heb. *'Adōnāi* *Yahweh*) stresses the honour and majesty of Israel's God: He alone is 'Lord (Heb. *'ādôn*) of all the earth' (Ps. 97: 5; Mic. 4: 13; Zech. 4: 14), He is the sovereign Lord of history. **about Edom:** the Edomites lived in mountainous territory to the SE of Judah, between the Dead Sea and the Gulf of Aqabah (cf. above). **We have heard:** Ob. speaks as the leader of a community of prophets. AV 'rumour' for **a message** ('news' or 'a revelation') is misleading. **an envoy** ('herald': angel?) **was sent to**

the nations to call them to war against Edom. 2–4. God's word is against a proud nation. The people who think they are so great will be brought low. **in the clefts of the rocks** (Heb. *sela'*): the Heb. echoes the name of Edom's mountain fortress of *Sela* (cf. 2 Kg. 14: 7), which dominated the basin in which the later and more famous Nabatean city of Petra was built. But Edom's self-assurance is a false one: even if it were able to **soar** high above its fortified city **like the eagle**, to the very **stars**, it would be unable to evade God's judgment. 5. The impending doom of Edom is portrayed by means of vivid images. The plunderers of Edom are compared to **thieves** who come in the night and **grape pickers**: thieves normally take only what they want, and gatherers of grapes leave a residue for the poor (Lev. 19: 10); but those who plunder Edom will leave nothing. 6–7. The prophet mourns the death of Edom as though it were already a past event. The style is that of a funeral dirge. **Esau:** note the use of the name of an individual to represent a larger group, a typically semitic way of thinking which scholars call 'corporate personality'. Cf. also the use of 'Edom' (=Esau) and 'Jacob' to personify the Edomites and Israelites throughout the book. (On this very important OT idea cf. E Jacob, *Theology of the OT*, 1958, 153–56; and esp. H. W. Robinson, *Corporate Personality in Ancient Israel*, 1964.) 8. **Mountains of Esau** represents the mountainous region inhabited by the Edomites in contrast to 'Mount Zion' (Jerusalem; cf. 17). 9. **Teman** was the chief Edomite city and was protected by the nearby fortress-city of Sela; its inhabitants were renowned for their wisdom (cf. Jer. 49: 7 and the name of one of Job's comforters, Eliphaz the Temanite). 10. **Because of the violence against your brother Jacob** introduces the reason for the sentence pronounced on Edom. This is expanded in the section which follows.

II. THE REASONS FOR EDOM'S JUDGMENT (11–14)

The style of this section is again dirge-like. Observe the repetition of phrases. 11. Edom **stood aloof** from Judah and failed to help their brothers when **strangers** (probably the armies of Nebuchadnezzar in 587/6 B.C.) sacked Jerusalem. In spite of blood-ties with Israel they behaved like the invading army of strangers. 12. The Edomites looked on with malicious satisfaction **in the day of** Israel's **misfortune.** 13. They even joined in the looting of Jerusalem. 14. Edom's treachery toward Judah reached its extremity by refusing to receive refugees from Jerusalem after its destruction.

III. THE COMING DAY OF THE LORD (15–21)

15. The judgment of God upon the Edomites is but one aspect of the approaching **day of the** LORD, which will be a day of judgment upon all nations (cf. *DBT*, 110–11). That day will be a day of great reversals: **As you have done, it will be done to you. 16.** 'The day of the LORD' also means judgment upon Israel. **Just as you drank on my holy hill:** this is probably a reference to the destruction of Jerusalem as God's judgment upon His sinful people. The image of drinking a cup filled with a stupefying wine is frequently used in the OT for the experience of God's wrath (Ps. 75: 8; Isa. 51: 17; Jer. 13: 13; 25: 15–16; Hab. 2: 15–16; Zech. 12: 2; Ezek. 23: 32–34; Lam. 4: 21). **17–18.** But a remnant of Israel will be established upon a re-consecrated **Mount Zion** (cf. Jl 3: 17); **the house of Jacob** (i.e. Judah, the southern kingdom) and **the house of Joseph** (i.e. Israel, the northern kingdom; cf. Am. 5: 6; Zech. 10: 6) will be reunited (cf. Isa. 11: 13–14; Jer. 3: 18; 23: 5–6; 31: 1; Ezek. 37: 15–27; Hos. 2: 2; Mic. 2: 12; Zech. 9: 10), and **the house of Esau** (Edom) will be destroyed. **19–20.** The restoration of Judah will involve an expansion of its territories: Israelites from **the Negev** will inherit the land of Edom (**the mountains of Esau**); Israelites of **the foothills** will occupy the coastal plain known as **the land of the Philistines:** the territory of the former northern kingdom (**Ephraim** and **Samaria**) will be re-inhabited by Israelites, as will **Gilead** in Transjordan; **exiles** will return to possess the land as far north as **Zarephath** and as far south as **the Negev.** See map for geographical locations of the places mentioned. **20.** The exact location of **Sepharad** is unknown; the most probable identification is with Sardis in Asia Minor (known to the Persians as *Sfarda*). **21.** **Deliverers:** —leaders raised up by the LORD from among the people as in the days of the judges (cf. Jg. 2: 16; 3: 9, 15, etc.)—will be established in Jerusalem to **govern** the land of Edom (and the other nations). The **kingdom** which will be established will not be simply a human kingdom, but rather **the LORD's** (cf. 'Kingdom', *DBT*, 292–93).

BIBLIOGRAPHY

ALLEN, L. C., *The Books of Joel, Obadiah, Jonah and Micah*. NICOT (Grand Rapids, 1976).

BEWER, J. A., 'Obadiah', in *A Critical and Exegetical Commentary on Micah, Zephaniah, Nahum, Obadiah and Joel*, J. M. P. Smith et al. ICC (Edinburgh and New York, 1911).

EATON, J. H., *Obadiah, Nahum, Habakkuk and Zephaniah*. TC (London, 1961).

MEYERS, J., *Hosea to Jonah*. Layman's Bible Commentary (London and Richmond, 1959).

WADE, G. W., *The Books of the Prophets Micah, Obadiah, Joel and Jonah*. WC (London, 1925).

WATTS, J. D. W., *Obadiah: A Critical Exegetical Commentary* (Grand Rapids, 1970).

JONAH

MICHAEL C. GRIFFITHS

Historical Setting

The key to understanding any Biblical book is to find the setting in which it was first written, to whom it was first addressed and especially what message it conveyed to them. 'Prophetic writing is not a stringed instrument upon which the Christian preacher is free to play any tune he pleases. The proper understanding of the prophet's message must therefore begin with the discovery of its original intentions and purpose' (J. H. Stek).

Certainly the book of Jonah conveys its message to exclusive Jews of all generations. It conveyed a message to unrepentant Jews at the time of our Lord. It has several applications to ourselves today, but we must first grasp its original message to its first hearers.

The book of Jonah is anonymous, so that we do not know who the author was or when he lived. The view that Jonah wrote the story of his own disobedience and his debate with the merciful God has not been made wholly untenable.

Our chief clues to understanding, external to the book itself, are the use made of it by the Lord Jesus (Mt. 12: 38–41; Lk. 11: 29–32) and the introductory reference to Jonah the son of Amittai, identifying Jonah with the prophet of 2 Kg. 14: 23–27. Jeroboam II 'restored the boundaries of Israel from Lebo-Hamath to the Sea of the Arabah, in accordance with the word of the LORD, the God of Israel, spoken through his servant Jonah the son of Amittai, the prophet, from Gath-hepher' (v. 25). The context is significant. 'The LORD had seen how bitterly everyone in Israel, whether slave or free, was suffering; there was no one to help them' (v. 26). Israel had been terribly harassed by the constant attacks of the Syrians on their northern border. Jonah's remarkable prophecy of the restoration of Israel to its dimensions at the time of Solomon was fulfilled during the reign of Jeroboam II, even though the context makes plain that he was not a godly ruler (v. 24). Jonah's mission does exemplify his name of 'dove' (Hebrew yônāh) in bringing rest after terrible judgment (as in Gen. 8: 8–12). Jonah must have enjoyed great popular respect as a true prophet when Syrian border raids against his native Galilee came to an end. This may explain his reluctance to accept a less popular commission, which might fail and cause him to lose substantial face.

In seeking to place the book of Jonah in a historical context, the next verse (v. 27) is enigmatic but possibly relevant. 'And since the LORD had not said he would blot out the name of Israel from under heaven, he saved them by the hand of Jeroboam the son of Joash.' When could it have been thought that the LORD *would* blot out the name of Israel, and why? Was it during the period of Syrian ascendancy over Israel? Or later when Assyria was attacking Israel and Judah? Or even later when Babylon carried Judah into captivity? What is the meaning of these explanatory notes by the writer of the book of Kings? See F. Crüsemann, 'Kritik an Amos im deuteronomistischen Geschichtswerk', *Probleme Biblischer Theologie* (G. von Rad *Festschrift*, ed. H. W. Wolff, München, 1971, pp. 57–63).

The deliberate identification by the author of the subject of the book with Jonah the son of Amittai suggests we should examine the period of Jeroboam II to see if it produces further clues. It does not follow that the book of Jonah was necessarily written or intended for the people of that period, but it remains the most obvious period to consider. (A helpful historical treatment of this period may be found in John Bright's *A History of Israel*, SCM, London, 1960.)

Syria under Hazael of Damascus and his son and successor Benhadad II had been the constant enemy of Israel, occupying all Transjordan and infiltrating down the coast as far south as Gath (2 Kg. 13: 3, 5, 22). But now Assyria under Adad-nirari III (811–783 B.C.) crushed Syria in a series of campaigns culminating in the capture of Damascus in 805 B.C.

Thus it was that Jonah appeared: 'from the death of Elisha to the prophesying of Amos, nearly forty years must have elapsed, during which the only recorded prophetic voice . . . Jonah's . . . announced beforehand the coming victories of Jeroboam II' (Ellison). In fulfilment of his prophecy the eighth century saw a dramatic reversal of fortunes which brought Israel and Judah prosperity unknown since the days of David and Solomon. This was partly because both states were blessed with able and long lived rulers, Uzziah of Judah (790–740 B.C.) and Jeroboam II of Israel (793–753 B.C.). It was also because Assyria had weakened Syria and then was herself in difficulties. While Adad-nirari III exacted tribute from Tyre, Sidon, Edom, Philistia and Israel, he was unable to follow up this success because Assyria was weakened by its own internal dissensions and menaced by the powerful mountain kingdom of Urartu (Ararat) to the north. He died childless and his successors Shalmaneser IV (783–773 B.C.), Asshurdan III (773–754 B.C.) and Asshur-nirari V (754–746 B.C.) were ineffectual rulers who scarcely maintained a foothold west of the Euphrates. By the mid-eighth century, Assyria seemed threatened with disintegration. The resurgence of Israel's fortunes and the restoration of their borders corresponded with this period of Assyrian weakness.

During this period of prosperity, first Amos began to speak *c.* 752/1 B.C. and then Hosea by 743 B.C., both prophesying judgment upon God's sinful people. Amos may have been understood to mean that the election of Israel did not guarantee her protection and that she would be blotted out (see Clements). Amos gave strong prophecies of destruction (5: 2, 18, 27; 7: 8, 9; 9: 8) (see also J. A. Motyer, *The Day of the Lion*, 1975, p. 22).

The situation and the message of the book of Jonah would seem appropriate to the situation both in Nineveh and in Israel during the middle years of the eighth century. Assyria was in a position in which anything could happen. From the closing days of Shalmaneser III (859–824 B.C.) they were increasingly involved in a struggle with Urartu to the north in which the frontier was pushed south until it was less than a hundred miles from Nineveh. If the fierce mountaineers of Urartu ventured down into the plain of the Tigris, the ensuing battle would be the end of Assyria. This would explain the readiness of Nineveh to listen to Jonah's message. '"Nineveh will be overthrown" is no longer a vague menace: for speaker and hearers alike, it meant a sudden swift and decisive attack by the northerners' (Ellison).

But the message of the book is also relevant if some thought that Amos had declared a final end. Were they lost in a hopeless end-time fatalism: a kind of apocalyptic determinism? The message of Jonah is that God's judgments, even if prophesied, can be averted by genuine repentance. Some suggest that the reference of Jesus to 'an adulterous generation which asks for a miraculous sign' (Mt. 12: 39) suggests a comparison with the generation which Hosea described as adulterous. Significantly, Amos makes no mention of Assyria in the list of foreign nations awaiting judgment, whereas Hosea mentions Assyria five times and Isaiah thirty-four times. This gives some indication of the rapid resurgence of Assyria later in the century.

From the time Tiglath-pileser III (745–727 B.C.) seized the throne of Assyria in 745 B.C., he became the rod of God's anger (Isa. 10: 5),

smiting Israel till it ceased to be a people and Judah till it was brought to the verge of destruction (Isa. 1: 9). For the first few years of his reign he engaged in campaigns against Urartu in order to secure his northern frontier. In 732 B.C., he captured Damascus, Galilee, Jezreel and Gilead (2 Kg. 15: 29). By 722 B.C., at the end of Shalmaneser V's reign (727–722 B.C.), Sargon II had captured Samaria and the following year deported 27,290 people (2 Kg. 17: 6, 23, 24; cf. *ANET*, pp. 284, 285). Sennacherib later ravaged Judah, besieged Jerusalem and then mysteriously withdrew in 701 B.C.

It seems more credible then to assign the events of the book of Jonah to the middle eighth century B.C. than to decide that Jonah is an allegory directed to post-exilic Jewish exclusivism, and to place the book much later in Jewish history long after the death of the historical Jonah son of Amittai.

It could be argued that the book was addressed to a later generation than the people of the northern kingdom in the mid-eighth century, but some sense of divinely given mission to the nations was already present (Isa. 2: 2–4, as well as the original covenant with Abraham, Gen. 12: 3, etc.). Thus the universalist or missionary message of Jonah demonstrating Yahweh's concern for the nations is relevant as early as the eighth century.

The force of the message about God's judgment upon Nineveh not being fulfilled because they repented, would be lost after 612 B.C. when Nineveh *was* finally overthrown after a two and a half months siege as foretold by the prophet Nahum. If the purpose of the prophecy is to encourage Israel to believe that if they repent, the LORD will restore them, then the story of Nineveh would carry far less force if the book of Jonah were first addressed to the people at a time when Nineveh had already been overthrown and left desolate.

(Chapter 3: 3 has been taken to mean that Nineveh was no longer standing when the book of Jonah was written, but it is more likely a synchronous tense (see text).)

Literary Form

The book is a third-person account of the mission of Jonah, the son of Amittai, to Nineveh, written in prose apart from the poetry of the Thanksgiving Psalm of chapter 2. Unlike all other books of the prophetic canon, it delivers its message through a narrative story and not through a series of oracles. 'The writer has woven his narrative very tightly' (Stek). The book is thus more akin to the first part of Daniel or the stories of Elijah and Elisha who also went to foreign nations (Elijah to Zarephath in Sidon, 1 Kg. 17: 8 ff., and Elisha to Damascus in Syria, 2 Kg. 8: 7 ff.). 'If Jonah does not actually belong to the same cycle of stories as those of Elijah and Elisha, it could well have been modelled on them' (D. W. B. Robinson). The actual message to Nineveh is only five Hebrew words and the book is more interested in Jonah than in his message. The book is unique in that it records a true prophetic message from God which was not fulfilled until a later period (612 B.C.). The inclusion of this book among the prophets is entirely appropriate for although it is not a collection of explicit prophecies, it is about prophecy, and its subject is a truly prophetic one.

It is possible to regard Jonah as transitional between the more narrative prophets like Elijah and Elisha on the one hand, and Hosea on the other whose unhappy marital experience becomes an acted parable of Israel's unfaithfulness. The experience of Hosea becomes typical of God's relationship with His adulterous people. Jonah's experience of being swallowed and disgorged may have become typical of a remedial judgment and a swallowing up in exile. Most people do not regard Hosea's experience as fictional, because it is used typically or parabolically of Israel. Because it is possible to understand Jonah's experience also as typical of Israel, this does not necessarily imply that the narrative account of Jonah's adventures is fictional merely because they include the miraculous.

The message of Jonah is that God's judgments, even when declared in prophecy, can be averted by genuine repentance. If God forgave the heathen sailors, if God forgave Jonah and if God forgave Nineveh, how much more His own people of whom Jonah may be regarded as representative? The people of the eighth century needed to know that Yahweh was the Lord of Assyria as well as of Israel and that behind all His smiting was His love.

The book seems very neatly arranged and to have an obvious didactic purpose, and we now turn to an attempt to elucidate this.

Interpretation and Application

Many possible interpretations of this book have been offered:

(a) *The Historical View*, that is, the narrative describes events which actually took place.

Arguments for the Historical View

(i) The style is simple historical narrative, mentioning specific places.

(ii) The writer chooses a historical character as its hero.

(iii) Realistic intimate details that could be known only to Jonah are included.

(iv) The Jews did not regard the book as a parable, but as a record of real historical events (cf. Tob. 14: 4; 3 Mac. 6: 8). The canonicity of the book never seems to have been questioned and the Twelve Prophets, of whom Jonah is one, are mentioned by Ben Sirach (Sir. 49: 10). Its literal truth was never ques-

tioned. Ellison suggests that Philo of Alexandria, that master of allegory, would doubtless have seized upon a symbolic or allegorical explanation had one been known to him.

(v) Our Lord Jesus Christ treats it as historical in the solemn pronouncements of Mt. 12: 41 and Lk. 11: 32 in which he assumed that the Ninevites actually repented at the preaching of Jonah.

(vi) There is a consistency between Jonah's first ministry to Israel as 'the dove', declaring the Lord's unmerited and gracious interposition of His power on behalf of his people (2 Kg. 14) and his later ministry to Nineveh which while declaring to them judgment, brought them grace. God is consistently merciful both to undeserving Israel and to Nineveh, Israel's undeserving enemy.

(vii) The linguistic arguments against an early date are weak, for we are almost totally ignorant of the Galilean dialect under the northern monarchy. It is impossible to know at what time isolated Aramaic words may have found their way into the Hebrew language, and the use of Phoenician loan words for nautical terms seems predictable. Certainly there are six words found in Jonah which are not found elsewhere, but Amos has twenty-four, Hosea twenty-five and Micah thirteen. Of the twenty-four verbal forms found in Chapter 2, every one is found in the writings of Jonah's eighth-century contemporaries.

(viii) Apart from occasional interpreters who were disposed to treat the book allegorically, from Gregory of Nazianzus (4th century) to Luther (15th century), the historical and literal view was only challenged in comparatively recent times—by some frivolously, as 'an attempt to placate incredulous scientists who found difficulty in accepting the ingestion of a man by a great fish' (R. K. Harrison), by others more seriously, on the ground that the literary *genre* of the book is best identified not as historiography but as 'that of a parable with certain allegorical features' (L. C. Allen, p. 181).

Objections to the Historical View

(i) Some would reject the book as historical because of the miraculous content. To those whose view of history rules out the miraculous by definition it may be said with D. W. B. Robinson that 'if the miraculous will not do in history, it equally will lend no conviction to parable' (*NBCR*).

(ii) The inclusion of Aramaic words alleged not to occur in Hebrew until much later in Jewish history (see above).

(iii) The size of Nineveh and the title of the king are said to display ignorance of the historical situation (see text).

(iv) The absence of any secular account of the conversion of Nineveh.

(b) *The Allegorical View.* An allegory is a story consisting of a series of incidents which are analogous to a parallel series of happenings that they are intended to illustrate. Thus the dove had for long been a symbol for Israel (Ps. 74: 19; Hos. 11: 11). The flight of Jonah symbolizes Israel's failure to fulfil its spiritual mission before the exile. Many nations (the mariners) threatened by the judgment of God (the storm) arouse Israel (Jonah) sleeping in their midst unconcerned about their fate. Jonah's disappearance in the sea in the great fish, and his ejection upon the land symbolize the exile of the Jews and their restoration to Palestine. 'Like a serpent he has swallowed me and I will punish Bel [i.e. the dragon] in Babylon and make him spew out what he has swallowed . . . Come out of her, my people' (Jer. 51: 34, 44).

The swallowing up of Jonah by the sea-monster reflects Israel being swallowed by the Babylonian 'dragon' (cf. Russian Bear, British Lion, etc.). The Jews having been swallowed and regurgitated must now resume their ministry to preach to the nations without grudging.

However, the people of the northern kingdom were not restored from captivity. To suggest that Jonah being swallowed by the sea-monster is typical of the Jews going into the Babylonian captivity, would imply that the book is much later than the time of Jonah the son of Amittai and probably after the fall of Nineveh itself. It is possible to maintain that the book is at the same time historical and intended to be understood with a typical meaning, but there are problems over this view.

(c) *The Parabolic View.* A parable is a short, pithy moral story with a didactic aim (*e.g.* Good Samaritan). Jonah was chosen because he appears in history as typical of the narrow-minded, exclusive Jew with no love for the nations beyond Israel's territories. He despises non-Jews and sees the Almighty as the God of the Jews only, with no care for the rest of his creation. The book demonstrates in a series of parabolic episodes that the Lord cares for Gentile sailors, for the Ninevites and even for cattle and plants which he has created.

The chief objection to this view is that other Old Testament parables are simple, treat of only one subject, and are always followed by an explanation of their meaning, while none is given in this book (see D. W. B. Robinson, *NBCR*). The unparalleled complexity of Jonah

as a parable, which usually make one main point, and the absence of any interpretation is against this understanding.

'First of all, as a question of general method, we must accept that the purpose of the book is straightforward, and that it lies evident within the narrative which we have. We should rule out therefore any hidden allegorical meaning which relies upon finding equivalents for the actors in the narrative, especially since there is no hint anywhere that this is required. In fact, the usual critical interpretation appears to have arisen precisely as a result of following such a view and regarding Jonah as a typical Jew and the Ninevites as typical Gentiles. Rather we must see that this is a story which should be viewed as a whole in which the action is of primary significance' (R. E. Clements).

(d) *Other suggested interpretations*

It is impossible to deny that all the above views have certain merits as well as difficulties, and some kind of synthesis of them all is possible, accepting them as a true chronicle of historical events with a typical meaning and even the possibility of parabolic interpretation, as follows:

The Lord Himself is the chief character, who speaks first and last, and acts in between. While his dealings with the sailors, with the Ninevites and the plant are all significant, it is the Lord's dealings with Jonah which are the chief subject of the book. Jonah does seem to play a representative role, as did two other prophets on occasion, Hosea (1: 2; 3: 1) and Ezekiel (chs. 4, 5; 12: 1–20; 24: 16, etc.). The man becomes a sign (Ezek. 24: 24; 12: 6, 11). The Lord says (Lk. 11: 30) that Jonah became a sign to the Ninevites. 'The book is too carefully constructed to suppose it is a mere chronicle' (Stek).

The following themes may be discerned:

1. An emphatic proclamation that the Lord's mercy extends to Gentile people for their own sake and a reminder to Israel that his election of them is with a view to their sharing their faith with the Gentile nations. It is the OT equivalent of reluctant Peter at Joppa going to Cornelius (Ac. 10, 11).

Israel had a national reluctance to fulfil its divine mission: 'Who is blind but my servant, or deaf like my messenger I send?' (Isa. 42: 19 ff.). Many Jews could only see God's kingdom being established by the overthrow of the kingdoms of the world. Jonah is the type of such people. Like them, he flees from the duty God has laid upon him. Like them, he leaves his own land, is cast for a time into a living death and like them, rescued, only to exhibit once more extreme reluctance to believe that God has any fate for the heathen except destruction. The Lord strongly rebukes, in the person of Jonah, Jews who are unwilling to see God's mercy extend beyond Israel. They were blinded by hatred, born of Gentile oppression, as well as by their scorn for heathen idolatry. This missionary outlook is not often articulate in Israelite literature except outstandingly in Isa. 40–55. That God has granted to the Gentiles also repentance unto life is nowhere else in the OT so vividly illustrated. It may not be a treatment of mission as such, but its consciousness of the prophetic responsibility of God's elect to the nations is obvious. The book is both a polemic against Israel for its reluctance to go to the heathen and a proclamation of God's pardon to all nations through the preaching of repentance.

2. The present unfaithfulness of Israel will not prevent the Lord fulfilling his historical purposes, any more than Jonah's reluctance can prevent God's gracious purpose for Nineveh. If the elect fail, God will chasten and purify the elect. The sub-episode of the ship is portrayed too neatly to be unintentional. The sailors do seem typical of the nations being used to stir up indifferent, sleeping Jonah to concern about their fate, as well as being used as instruments of God's corrective judgment on His people.

3. The repentance of Nineveh as a result of the one-sign ministry of Jonah contrasts with Israel's stubborn refusal to listen to a whole succession of prophets. The readiness of the Ninevites to change their lives after hearing one message from Yahweh declared to them was a salutary lesson to the Jews of that and succeeding generations (and Christians now), renowned for their stubbornness and lack of faith, in spite of hearing Moses and the prophets. Jesus hints that the Ninevites' response to the sign of Jonah would have an analogy in the response of the Gentiles to the sign of his resurrection. God's purpose is to demonstrate and display his grace proverbially, which is how the Lord Jesus expounds this event later. '*They* repented at the preaching of Jonah. . . .'

4. God is unchanging in His merciful character and therefore always changes his reaction when men repent. If they do not repent, he judges. If they repent, he restores. When a prophet says that a city or a people is about to be overthrown (Jon. 3: 4), it does not necessarily mean that they will actually be destroyed, because there is always the possibility that the people may repent (see Clements). Even though prophecies are expressed in absolute terms, there is a contingent element. God's action is contingent upon (not a necessary consequence of) some kind of human response. In the light of man's actions, **God may yet relent . . . of the destruction he had threatened** (Jon. 3: 9, 10). That is why Jonah is angry with God rather than with the Ninevites.

Jer. 18: 7, 8 explains the general principle which Jon. 3: 10 illustrates, namely that God's words of judgment through a prophet can be repented of and changed if the people repent; an important truth at any time in Israel's history when God's prophets are foretelling the destruction of Israel. It is also a crucial theological truth relating human repentance to escaping from anticipated judgment.

Jesus and Jonah

Jonah is the only minor prophet referred to specifically by Jesus, and the only prophet with whom he compares himself. Both came from Galilee of the Gentiles—the Pharisees were forgetting Jonah when they gibed that no prophet came out of Galilee (Jn 7: 52). Gathhepher, the modern Khirbet ez-Zurra', is only a few miles northeast of Nazareth (Jos. 19: 13). Jonah's mission to Nineveh was significant in pointing to salvation for other sheep outside the house of Israel. The Galilean disciples in responding to the great commission to make disciples of all nations, given to them in Galilee, were following Jonah's reluctant example. The early church had to be chastened by persecution before it started to reach out to the Gentiles, and Peter also had to go down to Joppa before he got the message (Ac. 9: 43). Part of the long range purpose of God was to illustrate proverbially his mercy upon repentant people and this is how the Lord Jesus used the events of this book in preaching.

The teaching of Jesus implies Jonah's historicity (Mt. 12: 38–42; 16: 4 and Lk. 11: 29–32). He considered the repentance of the people of Nineveh to have been accomplished through the preaching of Jonah. It is bad exegesis to accept the Queen of Sheba and Nineveh as historical, but Jonah and the whale as fictional. The reference to three days and three nights (Mt. 12: 40) suggests that Jesus himself gives his authority to the typical view of Jonah as pointing not only to Israel, but ultimately to himself (see D. W. B. Robinson, *NBCR*).

Significantly, Jonah is read in the Jewish synagogue lectionary as one of the readings for Yom Kippur, the day of atonement. Commenting upon this Rabbi J. H. Hertz says 'The Gentiles too are God's creatures, and worthy of pardon, if sincerely repentant'. The atonement extends to them also.

Jonah, having prophesied an event which did not take place, was bound to suffer extreme loss of face, as a false prophet. He would rather that one hundred and twenty thousand Ninevites were destroyed than that he lost face. Even this finds a contrast in the atonement accomplished for all mankind by Jesus which involved his 'face being more marred than any man's'. Jesus had claimed power and glory, but his enemies deliberately destroyed his face, and took away his credibility by the humiliating disgrace of crucifixion. Jesus is truly greater than Jonah in his willingness to lose face and to be misunderstood as a deceiver. And nothing less than the sign of the prophet Jonah, of real resurrection from death, was necessary to make him again a credible Prince and Saviour.

ANALYSIS

"Mighty salvation belongs to Yahweh" (2: 9)

I   Chapter 1   The LORD saves pagan sailors from death in the storm.

II   Chapter 2   The LORD saves disobedient Jonah from death by drowning.

III Chapter 3   The LORD saves the repentant Ninevites from judgment.

IV   Chapter 4   The LORD saves disgruntled Jonah from wrong attitudes.

Chapter 1

1. the word of the LORD came: seven of the Twelve Prophets start this way (Hosea, Joel, Jonah, Micah, Zephaniah, Haggai, Zechariah). **Jonah son of Amittai:** identifies Jonah as the historical character of 2 Kg. 14: 25 who prophesied mercy upon Israel (see v. 26) fulfilled in the reign of Jeroboam II (*c.* 793–753 B.C.). Jonah=dove; Amittai=truth. The use of the third person narrative means Jonah himself need not be the writer, though information must, assuming historicity, have come from Jonah himself. **2. Go to . . . Nineveh:** other OT prophets denounced foreign nations from a safe distance. If proclamation were merely prediction, it could have been made equally well from Galilee. The fact that Jonah had to go into the actual situation to Nineveh and announce the overthrow to the inhabitants could only mean that God wished to give them the opportunity of repentance and redemption (J. H. Hertz). **the great city:** Nineveh was situated on east bank of Tigris River near modern Mosul. Ruins are marked by the mounds called Kuyunjik and Nabi Yunus (Prophet Jonah) which are still inhabited and not yet excavated though they conceal a palace of Esarhaddon. Nineveh was one of the four cities founded by Nimrod or Ashur after leaving Babylon (the words of Gen. 10: 11, 12, 'that is the great city' are probably alluded to here). By the reign of Tiglath-pileser I (1114–1076 B.C.), it was established as an alternative palace to Ashur and Calah. Sennacherib extensively rebuilt and fortified the city as the last capital of Assyria (*c.* 705 B.C.). **3. Tarshish:** a place rich in silver, iron, tin and lead (Ezek. 27: 12; Jer. 10: 9). The term probably means 'smelting place'. Ships of Tarshish were Phoenician vessels carrying smelted metals to Phoenician ports of Joppa, Tyre, etc. Tarshish could be any Western Mediterranean Phoenician colony rich in metal deposits. Tartessus in Spain or Sardinia are possibilities. Going to Nineveh meant 500 miles northeast across the desert. Going to Tarshish meant 2,000 miles west (cf. 'in the opposite direction', GNB). **ran away:** missionaries often do feel like running away. Even Jeremiah considered silencing the word of God (Jer. 20: 9). Elijah wanted to give up (1 Kg. 19: 3–4).

Why did Jonah flee? See Jonah's reason given in 4: 2. Suggestions include:
(i) Fear of going to hostile cruel city.
(ii) The Rabbis suggested that Jonah foresaw that the repentance of Nineveh would reflect adversely upon the Israelites who in spite of many prophetic warnings had not repented. He was unwilling to see mercy brought to Israel's enemy, for a pardoned Nineveh would fall upon helpless Israel as the 'rod of God's anger' (Isa. 10: 5). 'One will have to be a Frenchman, who three times, or a Russian who twice in a lifetime has felt the might of Germany tearing its country's vitals, fully to grasp how a man like Jonah must have regarded Assyria. Three times at least, the threat had drawn near, three times the hot breath of destruction had been felt, three times the threat had spent itself on others' (Ellison).
(iii) He was afraid of loss of face, as a false prophet whose words were not fulfilled. **from the LORD:** cf. Gen. 3: 8; 4: 16; Exod. 33: 14; 2 Kg. 13: 23; 24: 20; Ps. 51: 11; 95: 2; 139: 7; Isa. 64: 1–3. The LORD may cast us out of His presence, or man, like Jonah, may try to evade it. It need not imply that Jonah thought of God's localized cultic presence only in Israel (see v. 9 and *NBCR*). The idea of God as local in influence is found (1 Kg. 20: 28; 2 Kg. 5:

17), but Jonah's contemporary, Amos, teaches the Lord's wider authority to judge the nations (Am. 1: 3, 6, 9, 11, 13). Jonah, the prophet of successful reputation for his wonderful fulfilled prophecy of restoration of the borders of Israel, now tries to abandon his call and resign his commission. Experimentally he is trying to evade the Lord (but see 2: 4), and especially running away from the dramatic stage where God is working out His purposes and judgments. **Joppa:** main Mediterranean seaport, where Peter was later commanded to go to the Gentile Cornelius (Ac. 10: 5). **found a ship . . . paying the fare:** funds in hand and a convenient ship should not necessarily be regarded as circumstantial guidance! Divine interference could have caused Jonah to have an accident, fail to find a vacant berth or be without enough money for the fare. Why does the Lord, who obstructed Balaam prophesying against Israel (Num. 22: 22 ff.), allow Jonah to walk in the pathway of disobedience? God does not force man by manipulating him like a puppet, rather he shapes Jonah's experience of life in order to bring about the consent of his will toward what God had decided. On each occasion, a man can refuse (Ellul p. 24). Jonah needed

(i) to learn the lesson of God's power and onmipresence;

(ii) to learn that the pathway of disobedience is uncomfortable, through the storm and the fish's belly;

(iii) to be swallowed by the 'fish', which was surely of significance not only in the distant future in relation to the resurrection of Jesus, but was of itself a 'sign' possibly to the Ninevites and certainly to Israel.

4. storm: LXX has *klydōn*, billow, surf. This was not a purposeless demonstration of the Lord's power over the elements, nor even just to smash inflexible Jonah, but to give him a sense of concern for the sailors and thus for Ninevites. **5. sailors:** Hebrew *mallāḥîm*, 'salts' (cf. Ezek. 27: 9, 29). **below deck:** the ship's hold (GNB). Hebrew *sephînāh* probably represents Phoenician nautical terminology but related to Hebrew verb *sāphan* to cover.

Israelites although living within distant view of the coast, were essentially inland people without much experience of the sea (maritime experience is only referred to in Jonah, Ps. 107 and Ezek. 27, which also related to Phoenician Tyre). With the howling wind and terrific green breakers, no wonder the worn-out prophet went below and was fast asleep (suffering from culture shock!). **6. the captain:** this is the only place where the captain of a ship is mentioned in the OT. As the only Galilean prophet, we might expect Jonah to use a few words which might be peculiar to the dialect of the northern kingdom. We would also ex-

pect that as the Jews were not a sea-going people, a number of more nautical and oceanographic expressions would have been borrowed from Phoenician sailors manning the ship of Tarshish with whom Jonah came into contact, and this is in fact the case. **your god . . . :** Hebrew *'elōhîm*, which accords with the common heathen word (see Kidner).

9. I am a Hebrew: the name Hebrew virtually never occurs in the OT save in narratives of the earliest period, and then chiefly in the mouth of a foreigner speaking of Israelites (Gen. 39: 14, 17; Exod. 2: 6; 1 Sam. 4: 6, 9) or of an Israelite who wishes to identify himself to foreigners (Gen. 40: 50; Exod. 3: 18; 5: 3) (Bright, *History of Israel*, p. 84). **the LORD, the God of heaven:** the Phoenicians worshipped 'the lord (*ba'al*) of heaven' and under the circumstances in which Jonah was placed, who could have made a more sensible and perspicuous response to the question of the sailors? The phrase is thus not necessarily a post-exilic title of late date (cf. Gen. 24: 3, 7; Dt. 4: 39), though it was used in Daniel in the presence of kings who worshipped other gods. Jonah believed theoretically in God's omnipresent reign, but not psychologically and experimentally as he was now discovering it. **10. 'What have you done . . . ?'** not a question but an exclamation of horror. Jonah has evidently told them before about fleeing and we shall meet later examples of the writer's economy of words in supplying necessary information earlier omitted.

12. throw me into the sea: was this suicide? Remorse at causing them suffering? Substitutionary death? Why the assurance that the storm will calm down when Jonah is thrown into the sea? On board the ship, Jonah saw 'foreigners' as persons. The prophet and his natural enemies experienced their common humanity upon the straining and breaking ship. Jonah not only feels the kinship of the heathen with himself, but their susceptibility to the knowledge of his God (G. A. Smith). All that he has fled to avoid happens before his eyes, and through his own mediation, he sees heathen turn to the fear of the Lord. **13. back to land:** ships of the ancient world hugged the coastline, keeping within sight of the shore. **did their best:** the men show their concern for Jonah's life in trying to avoid sacrificing him. The climax is reached, neither when Jonah feels his common humanity with the heathen (the Lord is teaching Jonah) nor when he discovers their awe of his God, but when in order to secure for them God's sparing mercy, he offers his own life . . . , so God still forces us to the acceptance of new light and the performance of strange duties (G. A. Smith). God 'makes concrete for him the situation of the other person. Now it is worth considering. Jonah did not want to carry salvation to

Nineveh. He must carry salvation to the men on the ship. Whether he likes it or not, he cannot escape the significance of his name. He is "the dove"' (Ellul, p. 34). **14, 15. Please do not let us . . . :** with a prayer on their lips, they throw Jonah into the sea. The men thought they were sacrificing Jonah to save themselves. Certainly one life was given for many. With Jonah's calm decision to be a scapegoat compare Moses 'blot me out of the book' (Exod. 32: 32). The sea is miraculously still (cf. Mt. 8: 23, 27). Jonah saved them humanly and materially: they will not be drowned because of his fault. He also saves them spiritually (Ellul). **16. feared the LORD. . . a sacrifice to the LORD:** this repetition of God's covenant name makes it clear that the sacrifices were not to the god of the sea but to Jonah's God, Yahweh (cf. Kidner).

17. a great fish: Hebrew *dāg gādôl*, LXX *kētos* ('sea-monster'). The Hebrews were not a sea-going people, and we cannot expect twentieth-century biological distinctions. Even modern people sometimes describe air-breathing mammals like porpoises as large fish. The absence of the word 'whale' is an accident of English translation rather than Biblical inspiration. The word *dāg* ('fish') included shellfish, crustaceans and even seals (also air-breathing mammals incidentally). In the NT, the Greek *kētos* is translated by AV, RV, and RSV as 'whale' but 'sea-monster' is zoologically less specific (NIV's 'a huge fish'). The only place under the raging waves to find a replenishable supply of oxygen is within the pharynx of an air-breathing mammal (a cetacean). Zoologically speaking, a man swallowed by a fish would drown as rapidly as in sea-water. There seems little reason to create difficulties for the sceptical, and the argument is not settled by allowing (as any Christian must) that the Lord could, if He chose, miraculously keep a man alive inside a water-breathing fish, if in fact, the words of the inspired Scripture are as equally admissible of a marine air-breathing mammal, as of a fish strictly defined. Whales come in two main groups: plankton-eaters with a small gullet, incapable of swallowing a human (Spermaceti), and the great toothed-whales (Odontoceti) which eat giant squids and large seals, and are therefore fully capable of both swallowing (and digesting) a man. Cases are occasionally cited of men recently lost overboard being recovered by whalers still alive inside their catch. However, an enquiry through Lloyds to the captain of the 'The Star of the East' has exploded the sailor's yarn told by James Bartley (*Expository Times*, xvii, 1905–1906, p. 521; xviii, 1906–1907, p. 239).

The miracle then is one of timing, so that the LORD sent the marine creature to swallow Jonah when he must otherwise have drowned at sea. While the fact of the occurrence may be questioned, there is no scientific reason for insisting that this very rare event could not possibly have taken place. However, we must not be 'so obssessed by what was going on inside the whale that we miss seeing the drama inside Jonah' (Gaebelein).

Why was Jonah swallowed by the great fish?

(i) To save him from drowning.

(ii) To discipline the prophet.

(iii) To provide a foreshadowing of the death and resurrection of the greater than Jonah who also came from Galilee.

(iv) As an acted parable (much like the sad marital experience of Hosea which became typical of the Lord's judgment of and separation from His adulterous people) of the swallowing of Israel by Babylon and its subsequent regurgitation 'Nebuchadnezzar like a serpent has swallowed us' (Hebrew *tannîn*) (Jer. 51: 34) and 'I will make him spew out what he has swallowed' (Jer. 51: 44). To accept this typical meaning does not involve denying that the miracle actually took place. It should be noted however that the word for 'serpent' in Jeremiah, is different and variously translated as 'dragon', 'sea-monster', etc. (George Cansdale, *Animals of Bible Lands*, 1970, see 'Whale', p. 137, 'Dragon', p. 252).

What was Jonah's psychological state? He was giving his life for the sailors and he expected to drown. Some argue that Jonah actually died by drowning and was subsequently resurrected. Jonah may well have blacked out and become unconscious, so without more Biblical evidence the discussion remains somewhat academic.

three days and three nights: cf. Mt. 12: 40. Jonah, disorientated in such dark confinement, would have been unable to measure the passage of time. The usage of the resurrection of Jesus shows that this could be an expression for a whole day and portions of adjacent days i.e. not more than thirty-six hours. Notice Hos. 6: 1, 2: 'Come let us return to the LORD; for he has torn us to pieces but he will heal us. . . . After two days he will revive us; on the third day he will restore us that we may live in his presence'. These words of a contemporary prophet with Jonah surely had to mean something for *his own day*, as well as finding its greater fulfilment in the death and resurrection of the Lord Jesus.

Chapter 2

While the rest of the book is in prose, this chapter is linguistically poetry, a psalm in quatrains in the elegiac measure with an additional couplet at the close. Some have therefore suggested that this chapter is a later addition to the text, but there is no textual evidence that the book ever circulated without the psalm which is found in the same form and position in our earliest Hebrew manuscript, a Dead Sea Scroll of the Twelve Prophets dating from the second century A.D., and also in the earlier LXX Greek translation probably late third or early second century B.C.

1. Jonah prayed to the LORD: parallels 4: 2, which also refers back to earlier distress experienced by Jonah (cf. Landes, whose whole paper on the Jonah psalm is worth studying). **2. I called . . . he answered . . . I called . . . you listened:** past tenses indicate that the text of the first prayer is not given (see v. 7). Our psalm is thus Jonah's second prayer. Jonah had already lamented, cried for help and expressed repentance, but this psalm now expresses Jonah's gratitude that he had escaped drowning and survived three days in the belly of the fish and most of all that he is back 'in the presence of the LORD'. This answers the objection of those who feel that the thanksgiving psalm is inappropriate to Jonah's uncomfortable predicament. The writer is deliberately not always chronological (cf. 4: 2 when Jonah explains why he did not want to go to Nineveh). **the depths of the grave:** equals 'the world of the dead' (GNB), a unique expression. **3. all your waves and breakers swept over me:** the four Hebrew words so rendered are found also in Ps. 42: 7, a Psalm of Korah: it is not clear who is quoting whom. A prophet soaked in the psalms would be prone to echo their language in his prayers. **4. banished from your sight:** helps in understanding 1: 3 as more an experimental subjective experience, than objective theological truth. Jonah expresses this as past, for having repented, he is now conscious of the Lord's presence again as he prays inside the fish.

5. waters: as for Noah in the flood, and Moses in the Red Sea, denotes swallowing up in death. **seaweed wrapped around my head** is unique, though the Hebrew *sûph* for seaweed is found elsewhere *e.g. Yām sûph* (Reed Sea). Is it possible that this vivid description *is* experimentally descriptive of the whale's viscera? **6. the earth beneath barred me in:** 'The land whose gates locked shut forever' (GNB). **7. your holy temple:** also v. 4; this is probably not the literal Jerusalem temple (Jonah came from the northern kingdom), but the heavenly temple of Isa. 6: 1 ff. **8. worthless idols:** or 'lying vanities' (AV). R. D. Wilson sees here the only other direct quotation in the psalm (from Ps. 31: 6), possibly a current cliché; similar expressions are used by Jonah's later contemporary Hosea (10: 4; 12: 11). **9. Salvation:** the Hebrew form is intensive—*mighty* salvation **comes from the LORD.** This could be taken as the theme of the whole book; a treatment of salvation, grace and repentance.

10. For helpful comparisons between Jonah's experience and that of the Lord Jesus, see D. W. B. Robinson (*NBCR*) on these verses.

Chapter 3

1–3. On the basis of Jonah's further experience first hand of 'foreigners' and the implications of 'only one God, only one gospel', the LORD now repeats his call to Jonah; LXX says 'according to the former message which I spoke'. This time Jonah obeys **the word of the LORD.** The certainty of God's call is very clear. **Now Nineveh was:** a great deal has been built on this Hebrew perfect tense. Many have argued for a later date on a basis of this verse, which seems to imply that Nineveh was no longer so, therefore it is argued the book must have been written after the fall of Nineveh (*c.* 612 B.C.). This is a crucial verse for dating.

Various replies are possible:

(i) The Hebrew perfect can be used synchronistically to mean 'has been and is', that is, Nineveh was already a great city at the time when Jonah entered it.

(ii) The sentence is introduced with an explanatory 'and' and the form of the sentence is that used for a parenthetical note, and it is possible that this is a later note interpolated into the text by an editor. Commentators who argue for a later date are prone to suggest interpolations in other passages, and it would seem unwise therefore for them to base arguments for a later date on this verse (see Wilson; also D. W. B. Robinson, *NBCR*).

(iii) Others point out that the entire story would lose its force after Nineveh had been ultimately destroyed in 612 B.C.

a very large city: to the provincial Galilean familiar with the small tightly packed Israeli towns on their tells, the wide expanse of Nineveh including even open land within its walls must have seemed enormous (Ellison). (Did Jonah suffer further culture shock?) **a visit required three days:** Remains show that historical Nineveh was less than eight miles in circumference. It is suggested that the satellite towns of Nineveh, Rehoboth-Ir, Calah and Resen are included in the measurement, and support for this view may be found in the circumstances in Genesis (10: 10–11), where the four together are called 'the great city' (J. H. Hertz). The Hebrew translation for using Nineveh in each case did not distinguish between the whole administrative district (Assyrian *ninua(ki)*) and the metropolis (Assyrian (*al*)-*ninua*; cf. Wiseman, *NBD, s.v.*, 'Nineveh'). **4. started into the city, going a day's journey:** Jonah was proclaiming his message on each street corner as he went along, and this would explain the time taken.

he proclaimed: what language did Jonah use? Isa. 36: 11 and 2 Kg. 18: 26 suggest that Aramaic was a *lingua franca* for the educated classes, understood by Jews and Assyrians alike, as the language of diplomacy. **Forty more days and**

Nineveh will be destroyed: Jonah's message is abbreviated to five Hebrew words only: the book is more interested in the prophet than the details of his message. LXX and Old Latin have 'three days' rather than 'forty days'. There were times in the eighth century of such political uncertainty with the fierce Urartu only a hundred miles from Nineveh when this would have seemed an imminent possibility. **5. believed God:** this phrase was an expression of justifying faith in Abraham (Gen. 15: 6; Rom. 4: 3) and v. 10 indicates that there was also genuine repentance (Mt. 12: 41). **sackcloth:** sackcloth is a Phoenician loan word in Hebrew (*saq*), Greek (*sakkos*) and English (according to Snaith).

According to Wiseman, there is no external evidence in known Assyrian records, so far, of such a turning to the LORD. But such a 'people's movement' is not uncommon, and every missionary knows that it is possible to labour for years without result, and then suddenly there may be a remarkable turning only explicable in terms of divine sovereignty, *e.g.* Korea or Cambodia. The fact that Jonah's mission left no mark on extant Assyrian records may indicate that its effects were not very deep or long lasting. It would be rash however to infer that there was no such turning. Jewish legend says that after forty years they departed from the path of piety, and they became more sinful than ever. Then the punishment threatened by Jonah overtook them, and they were swallowed up by the earth! (Louis Ginzberg, *The Legends of the Jews*, Philadelphia: Jewish Publication Society of America, 1913, Vol. IV, pp. 252–253.)

'As Jonah was a sign to the Ninevites' (Lk. 11: 30) are mysterious words, which some have understood to mean that Jonah's experience in the 'great fish' was made known to the Ninevites in Jonah's preaching. It would have been a sign that Jonah had had no wish to come, but the Lord had made him come. And if the Lord had mercy on Jonah when he repented, so he would on the Ninevites. But why would they believe this story? Some have related it to the fact that Nineveh was named after Nina, the earlier Sumerian name of the goddess Ishtar written with a sign depicting a fish.

Others more sensationally have suggested that Jonah's skin was bleached by the digestive juices of the sea-monster and suggested that this was how Jonah was 'a sign to the Ninevites'. 'It would be rash to deny this possibility merely by arguing from the silence of Scripture, but it is surely much rasher to make the central point of the story depend on something the Bible does not mention' (Ellison, p. 58). It is probably better to take Jonah himself and his experience as being a sign, as also

was Ezekiel's experience (Ezek. 12: 6, 11; 24: 24).

6. the king of Nineveh: he is not named; some have argued that the correct title would be 'king of Assyria', and have suggested that the author must therefore have been writing much later. Various possible answers can be given:

(i) The Hebrew word for king may mean no more than governor (see Wilson). Interestingly Isa. 10: 5–8 which speaks of Assyria as 'the rod of my anger' also says 'Are not my princes (NIV 'commanders', NEB 'officers') all kings?'

(ii) In the eighth century B.C., kings were frequently named after their capital city, *e.g.*, Ahab is called king of Samaria, not Israel (1 Kg. 21: 1) and Benhadad is called king of Damascus, not Syria (1 Chr. 24: 3). Foreigners are notoriously vague about correct titles. However Nineveh may not have been the capital of Assyria until *c.* 705 B.C.

(iii) Omission of the king's name can be paralleled in the story of Naaman (2 Kg. 5: 1, 2), and both Nahum (3: 18) and Isaiah refer to the 'king of Assyria' without mentioning his name. Between the strong kings, Adadnirari III and Tiglath-pileser III, during the period 783–745 B.C., four kings are known to have reigned in Assyria, which was in a state of almost continuous insurrection, pestilence and commotion (R. D. Wilson).

Note that Jonah did not warn the king explicitly (as Elijah did Ahab, or Nathan David), but rather the people generally.

7, 8. beasts: the idea of animals joining in mourning is not unparalleled (cf. Jdt. 4: 10). It is not that animals are in need of forgiveness, but that withholding food from beasts is an added penance and grief to their owners (J. H. Hertz). **violence:** a particular sin of the Assyrians illustrated in their bas-reliefs. The people of Nineveh knew why they might expect judgment to fall upon them. **give up their evil ways:** a common phrase occurring frequently in many prophets (Jer. 26: 3; 36: 3, 7); notice also 'repented' (Mt. 12: 41). **9. Who knows? God may yet relent and with compassion turn from his fierce anger:** i.e. perhaps Jl 2: 14a is seen as an allusion, especially in view of correspondence of Jl 2: 13 with Jon. 4:2.

10. God had compassion and did not bring upon them the destruction he had threatened: the OT has no embarrassment in God changing His mind. God Himself never changes in His essential nature, but His nature is such that when men repent and change, then He has mercy (cf. Exod. 32: 14; 2 Sam. 24: 6; Am. 7: 3, 6). There would seem to be a verbal correspondence with Jer. 18: 9, 10. Jeremiah's is a general rule demonstrated in the particular case of Nineveh. Whether the rule precedes the illustration or the actual case results in the rule is not clear.

Chapter 4

Jonah had not stopped needing to learn lessons, because he had become obedient to his call. Jonah appears not to have understood his own adventure and has already forgotten the grace lavished upon himself and seems unconscious that it should be shared with others. Jonah now behaves rather like the unforgiving servant or the older prodigal. This does not exhaust God's love and patience and he again takes this rebellious servant in hand.

Why, we ask, is 'the dove' such a hawk where Nineveh is concerned? Is this patriotic indignation lest Israel's enemies should be spared to become 'the rod of God's anger' (Isa. 10: 5) upon Israel? We notice significantly that one result of Jonah's successful mission to Nineveh is to undo all the blessing brought to Israel through Jonah's earlier prophecy. All the extended borders of Israel under Jeroboam II will be lost to the Assyrians. No wonder Jonah is angry.

2. He prayed: as he had done in the fish. Even with wrong attitudes, we maintain the outward form. **LORD:** Jonah uses the word, but disputes God's right to Lordship. 'Lord, didn't I say before I left home, that this is just what you would do?' (GNB). This gives us at last the reason for Jonah's original reluctance, for 'the dove' did not want to go on a redemptive mission of mercy to spare Israel's most dangerous enemy. **I knew:** because of his own personal experience of grace, experienced in spite of his disobedience, he knows that God is a forgiving God who will have mercy on the sinner. **you are a gracious and compassionate God slow to anger, and abounding in love, a God who relents from sending calamity:** Jonah is quoting 'the Thirteen Attributes' (Exod. 34: 6, 7), also quoted by Joel (2: 13). He may well have memorized them as a child—but he did not want to accept them. **3.** Jonah begs for death. Is he angry at the personal indignity of being made to prophesy something which both the Lord and he himself knew would not come to pass, thus making him appear a fool, and worse, a false prophet (Dt. 18: 20–22)? For the hitherto popular and successful prophet, this loss of face is too much. Why live any longer? His attitude is reminiscent of Elijah (1 Kg. 19: 4), both men having apparently risked their lives for nothing while Israel's enemies were still powerful. Both men seem close to nervous breakdown.

To reconcile God's general will to save, and his particular will that Jonah should be a prophet of destruction is not always easy. When God chose Jonah, he wanted his people (the church) to have a part in the salvation decided for Nineveh (Ellul). If Jonah receives the call, if he is truly saved, it is for others. We must be permeated by the conviction that if grace is being conferred on us, it is primarily for others. The Christian is not just the man who is saved by Christ, he is the man whom God uses for the salvation of others by Christ. **4.** It is easier to repent of open sin as the Ninevites have done, than to repent of a grudge in the heart as Jonah must. 'Such men are best treated by a caustic gentleness, a little humour, a little rallying, a leaving to nature and a taking unawares in their own confessed prejudices. All these—I dare to think, even the humour—are present in God's treatment of Jonah. This is natural and beautiful. Twice the Divine Voice speaks with a soft sarcasm: "art thou very angry?" Jonah would not answer—how lifelike is his silence here!' (G. A. Smith, *ad. loc.*).

Jonah's attitude here is surely a picture of Israel's attitude to the Gentiles. Thus the Jewish commentator, J. H. Hertz (*Pentateuch and Haftorahs*, Soncino edition, 1968) writes 'Nor can it be only the lesson that the Gentiles too are God's creatures and worthy of pardon if sincerely repentant . . . the essential teaching is that the Gentiles *should not be grudged* God's love, care and forgiveness'. The knowledge that God was infinitely gracious haunted their pride: there arose a jealous fear that He would show His grace to others than themselves. God had been so gracious and longsuffering to themselves that they could not trust Him not to show these mercies to others, even to their oppressors. In which case, what was the use of their uniqueness and privilege? (Let the Lord's elect in every age ponder that!)

5. Jonah sits and watches. Did God really speak to him? Was it just an illusion of his own senses? Could he have mistaken God's call? The remarkable way in which he first refused God's call and was then brought to see the need to accept it, meant that Jonah could not doubt his call, only accepted at the second invitation. Does he then still hope that Nineveh will be destroyed by fire and its inhabitants grilled? Has he perhaps misunderstood God's mercy?

6. the LORD God: this composite expression *Yahweh-'Elōhîm* is a feature of Genesis 2 and 3, 'possibly relevant to the miraculous provision of the sheltering plant' (Kidner). Generally, 'the LORD' is used in an Israelite context, where Jonah is involved, and 'God' in the context of the heathen sailors and the Ninevites although this pattern breaks up after this verse, and *'Elōhîm* has dealings with Jonah in vv. 7–9. **a vine:** generally reckoned to be the castor oil plant (*Ricinus communis L.*), sometimes called the *palma Christi*, because of its hand-shaped leaves, and remarkable for the rapidity of its growth. In tropical countries, plants like bamboo normally sprout very quickly indeed, and we need not necessarily regard this provision as miraculous, but rather as providential (cf. R. K. Harrison, *Introduction to the OT*, pp. 910 f.). **7. a worm:** everything but Jonah has obeyed God's direct command (1: 4; 2: 10; 4: 6, 7, 8), even an insect pest. **8. a scorching east wind:** a *sirocco* (cf. Jer. 18: 17; Hos. 13: 15), a dry, oppressively hot and dusty wind blowing off the desert, aggravating the discomfort of Jonah's vigil. The Lord's preparing of the gourd, the worm and the wind to bless Jonah one day and blight him the next is surely a demonstration of His sovereignty in His dealing with nations like Israel and Nineveh and reminds us that it is of the sovereignty of God that we receive weal or woe, health or sickness. **9, 10.** Both the plant and the Ninevites were God's handiwork and He cares for what He creates. **11. should I not be concerned?** This is the great question, for Jonah has been angry because of God's forgiveness for the repentant enemy of Israel. **one hundred and twenty-thousand people who cannot tell their right hand from their left:** a unique expression, so there are no Biblical grounds for deciding between either children who have not reached the age of accountability, or more probably the whole ignorant population. Calculations based on the dimensions of a comparable Assyrian city Nimrud in 879 B.C. with a population of 69,674 persons but geographically of only half the size (*NBD*) suggests that this figure is more likely to be that of the whole population. **many cattle:** it is entirely appropriate to this book in which a sea-monster, a worm and a plant, as well as the natural elements obeyed God's will, that He should have mercy on dumb animals also.

Thus, God has compassion and delays judgment upon Nineveh for the sake of its ignorant people and animals. The final judgment upon Nineveh was declared by Nahum and fulfilled in 612 B.C. Why did God spare Nineveh and allow them to become the 'rod of His anger' (Isa. 10: 5) upon Israel? Israel needed to know that God was *Lord* in Assyria as well, and that if now He brought judgment upon them, this did not mean that He was not sovereign. God is sovereign to give both judgment and mercy to whom He pleases.

BIBLIOGRAPHY

AALDERS, G. CH., *The Problem of the Book of Jonah* (London, 1948).

ALLEN, L. C., *The Books of Joel, Obadiah, Jonah and Micah*, *NICOT* (Grand Rapids, 1976).

BROCKINGTON, L. H., 'Jonah' in *Peake's Commentary on the Bible*, 2nd edition, edited by M. Black and H. H. Rowley (London, 1962).

CHILDS, B. S., 'Jonah: A Study in OT Hermeneutics', *SJT* 11 (1958), pp. 53–61.

CLEMENTS, R. E., 'The Purpose of the Book of Jonah', Congress Volume 1974 (*Supplement to Vetus Testamentum* XXVIII), pp. 16–28.

ELLISON, H. L., *The Prophets of Israel* (Exeter, 1969).

ELLUL, J., *The Judgment of Jonah* (Grand Rapids, 1971).

GAEBELEIN, F. E., *Four Minor Prophets* (Chicago, 1970) (incorporating earlier book, *The Servant and the Dove*, 'Our Hope' Press).

HARRISON, R. K., *Introduction to the Old Testament* (London, 1970), pp. 904–918.

HERTZ, J. H., *Pentateuch and Haftorahs* (Soncino, 1968), pp. 964 ff

JOHNSON, A. R., 'Jonah II. 3–10: A Study in Cultic Phantasy', in H. H. Rowley (ed.), *Studies in Old Testament Prophecy* (Edinburgh, 1950), pp. 82–102.

KIDNER, F. D., 'The Distribution of Divine Names in Jonah', *Tyndale Bulletin* 21 (1970), pp. 126–128.

LANDES, G. M., 'The Kerygma of the Book of Jonah' (The Contextual Interpretation of the Jonah Psalm), *Interpretation* Richmond, Virginia, Vol. XXI, No. 1 (Jan. 1967), pp. 3–31.

ROBINSON, D. W. B. 'Jonah', *New Bible Commentary Revised* (London, 1970).

SMART, J. D., *The Interpreter's Bible Vol. 6*, edited by G. A. Buttrick and others (Abingdon, 1956).

SMITH, G. A., *The Book of the Twelve Prophets²* (London, 1928).

STEK, J. H., 'The Message of the Book of Jonah', *Calvin Theological Journal*, Vol. 4, No. 1 (April, 1969), pp. 23–50.

WATTS, J. D. W., *Joel, Obadiah, Jonah, Nahum, Habakkuk and Zephaniah*. CBC (Cambridge, 1975).

WILSON, A. J., 'The Sign of the Prophet Jonah', *Princeton Theological Review*, Vol. XXV (1927). pp. 630–642.

WILSON, R. D., Two articles on 'The Authenticity of Jonah', *Princeton Theological Review*, Vol. XVI (1918), pp. 280–298, 430–456.

MICAH

DAVID J. CLARK

Authorship and Date

Of Micah himself we know no more than we are told in 1: 1. His name is a shortened form of Micaiah, as Jer. 26: 18 shows, and means 'Who is like the LORD?' He came from the township of Moresheth in the southern uplands of Judah, and as the prophecy itself makes clear, he shared the small-town attitudes of his neighbours towards the capital and its decadence. There is some difference of opinion among scholars as to whether he was a relatively well-to-do farmer, or a member of the depressed and exploited classes about whose plight he protests so vehemently.

Of the dates of his ministry, we can set outer and inner limits from 1: 1, but we have no sure means of attaining greater precision. His work began not earlier than the accession of King Jotham c. 740 B.C. and ended not later than the death of Hezekiah in 687 B.C. Some of his oracles seem definitely linked with the Assyrian invasion of 701 B.C., and it appears probable that the bulk of the recorded prophecies come from the last quarter of the eighth century.

It has been common for modern scholarship to deny to Micah various parts of the book. Such views are based largely on preconceptions about what sentiments may or may not be expected in the eighth century, and the divergence in detail among their exponents is a fair measure of the subjectivity of the approach. On the other hand, some conservative commentators have been tempted to impose on the book an artificial unity which its sometimes abrupt changes of topic can hardly sustain. In this commentary we shall attempt to steer a course that avoids both extremes. The whole book will be treated as coming from the prophet Micah, and thus as primary evidence for the prophetic insights of his era. Yet full recognition will be given to the span of years covered by Micah's prophetic activity, his freedom to speak on diverse topics, and to juxtapose the resulting oracles without further explanation. It is a mistake to impose on the text modern western ideas of chronological ordering and thematic development.

Historical background (cf. 2 Kg. 15–20; 2 Chr. 27–32; Isa. 36–39)

Like any of the prophets, Micah cannot be appreciated apart from his historical setting, and a thumbnail sketch of the period is therefore in order. The second half of the eighth century was a turbulent one for the small states of Western Asia. After the death of Jeroboam II of Israel in 746 B.C., the northern throne was occupied by a parade of worthless pretenders, all equally ineffective in countering the growing power of an Assyria that became strongly expansionist after the accession of Tiglath-Pileser III in 745 B.C. Pekah ben Remaliah of Israel (737–732 B.C.) formed an anti-Assyrian coalition, into membership of which he attempted to coerce King Jotham of Judah. The death of Jotham (735 B.C.) left his son Ahaz to deal with the situation. Despite the advice of Isaiah (Isa. 7) Ahaz appealed to the Assyrians for help (2 Kg. 16: 7). The coalition was crushed, and Pekah's assassin and successor Hoshea submitted to Assyria. Judah had escaped but at the desperate expense of becoming an Assyrian vassal herself. This meant not only heavy tribute to be paid, but also the official acknowledgement and acceptance of the suzerain's gods. Ahaz apparently cared little for this, or for the loosening of ethical standards which such syncretism always brings with it. It is in this period that much of Micah's invective against social ills is best placed.

In 727 B.C. Tiglath-Pileser III was succeeded by Shalmaneser V and, as often, a change of monarch was the signal for rebellion. Hoshea by withholding the Assyrian tribute signed Israel's death warrant. Shalmaneser invested Samaria, but did not live to see its end. Despite the surrender of Hoshea, the new Assyrian king Sargon II (722–705 B.C.) destroyed Samaria with great cruelty, and deported the survivors (721 B.C.). The significance of this event was not lost on Judah. It both vindicated the earlier prophets Amos and Hosea, and served as a grim warning of what could happen to the southern kingdom. Nevertheless both patriotic sentiment and anti-syncretistic influences put pressure on King Hezekiah to throw off the Assyrian yoke. Sargon II was occupied elsewhere with the rebellion of Merodach-Baladan that gave Babylonia a precarious independence for more than a decade. Egypt was also growing in power after the establishment of the vigorous rule of the twenty-fifth dynasty c. 715 B.C., and might be a source of support. Hezekiah proceeded with religious reforms which were already in essence an act of rebellion, though apparently he refused to join in a Philistine-led revolt that was put down in 711 B.C. But on the accession of Sennacherib to the throne of Assyria in 705 B.C., Hezekiah at last formally rebelled by withholding tribute. After dealing with revolts elsewhere in his dominions, Sennacherib turned in 701 B.C. to the west. Tyre and Philistia soon fell, but Jerusalem was delivered by a miraculous intervention (2 Kg. 19: 35 f.). This event gave rise to the dogma of the inviolability of Zion that in no small way contributed to its ultimate destruction.

ANALYSIS

I. GOD'S JUDGMENT ON HIS PEOPLE (1: 1–3: 12)

This section foresees the destruction both of Samaria (1: 6) and of Jerusalem (3: 12). The reason for this punishment is the evil conduct of God's people, especially the rich, and those in authority.

i. The superscription (1: 1)

Though Micah's message concerned both **Samaria** and **Jerusalem**, his period of activity is dated only by the reigns of **kings of Judah**, emphasizing both his origin and his main interest. His message is not merely astute political observation and comment, but is **the word of the LORD**.

ii. The fate awaiting Samaria (1: 2–9)

2–4. Micah opens with a short section that establishes two premises basic to his whole outlook. First, the Lord is sovereign; and second, the Lord's dwelling place is utterly **holy**, a reflection of His person (2). Thus all the **peoples** of earth are summoned to give attention to his accusation (2) and even the **earth** itself is pictured as trembling under His tread. In vivid figurative language the **mountains** are depicted as melting **beneath him . . . like wax before the fire** (4). The language of earthquake and thunderstorm is typically associated with the presence of the Lord (cf. Exod. 19: 16–20; Jg. 5: 4–5; Ps. 18, 29; 97: 1–5).

5–7. The reason for the Lord's coming to exercise His sovereign judgment is that His holiness has been outraged by **Jacob's transgression** and **the sins of the house of Israel**. **Jacob** stands for the northern kingdom, and **Israel**, as often in Micah, for the southern kingdom (cf. the expression 'both houses of Israel', Isa. 8: 14). This is made clear by the parallelism of the second half of v. 5, where in each case, the capital city is indicated as leading the way into sin, and thus inviting more severe punishment. In vv. 6, 7 the total devastation of Samaria is promised. Buildings will be demolished to their **foundations**, leaving the town a **heap of rubble**. The **images** and **idols**, symbols of her corrupt religion, are singled out for deliberate destruction. The sense of the rather difficult metaphor of prostitution of v. 7 is rendered in non-figurative language by GNB, 'Samaria acquired these things for its fertility rites, and now her enemies will carry them off for worship elsewhere.' That the destruction of Samaria is still future indicates that this section is to be dated before 721 B.C., though perhaps not long before.

8, 9. Despite his acknowledgement that the punishment is richly deserved, Micah, like Moses (Exod. 32: 11 ff.) and Amos (Am. 7: 2, 5), is filled with bitter sadness. To **go barefoot and naked** (divested of outer garments) was a sign of mourning (cf. Isa. 20: 2–4) to which the cries of **jackals** and **owls** would be a fit accompaniment. The moral **wound** of Samaria is not only **incurable**, but has also infected her neighbour **Judah**, and festers in **Jerusalem** itself. As so often, a bad example is easier to follow, and more popular, than a good one.

iii. The enemy approach to Jerusalem (1: 10–16)

In theme, this passage describes the advance through the towns and villages of Micah's home area of an enemy army on their way to attack Jerusalem (12). In detail, it is extremely complicated because of the exceptionally long series of word plays on the place names. Not all the places can now be identified, and some of the puns have been obscured in transmission. More important, however, than the identification of the places or the recovery of the word plays, is the appreciation of the impact of the paragraph as a whole. Whereas in modern English usage, the pun is a linguistic device reserved almost exclusively for humour, in Hebrew it was regarded as a fit vehicle for much deeper emotions (cf. Jer. 1: 11–12; Am. 8: 2). Its extensive employment here is both a measure and a reinforcement of the prophet's distress at seeing his home area invaded, and at feeling what lay in store for Jerusalem. **Tell it not in Gath** (10) is a repetition of David's lament for Saul and Jonathan (2 Sam. 1: 20). The whole passage is variously referred to the invasion of Sennacherib in 701 B.C. (JB fn.), to that of Sargon in 711 B.C. (Wolfe), or to the presence of Assyrian forces in Palestine after the fall of Samaria in 721 B.C. (Dahlberg). However, the mention of Gath as an enemy (cf. GNB) from whom the humiliation of Judah is to be concealed, makes it possible that the passage dates from the invasion of Judah by Pekah's anti-Assyrian coalition of 735 B.C., during which the Philistines attacked the Shephelah district (Bright, p. 272). Though none of the places listed as occupied in 2 Chr. 28: 17 occurs here, the general area is the name, and the reference to David's lament is more poignant if the Philistines were the invaders Micah had in mind. Such a setting for the paragraph is consistent with its present location among prophecies which must date from early in Micah's career.

Lachish (13) is singled out as the town in which **the transgressions of Israel** first flourished, that is the pagan practices which soon gained a foothold in **the Daughter of Zion** (Jerusalem). In another reference to David (15),

Micah sees **the glory of Israel**, that is, the court of Jerusalem, fleeing the city, just as David took refuge in the cave at **Adullam** (1 Sam. 22: 1). Because of this situation, the people should **shave** their **heads** in mourning (cf. Am. 8: 10), making themselves **as bald as the vulture**. The reference to **the children in whom you delight** being taken **from you into exile** arises from the policy of deporting the population of conquered territories, which was regularly employed by Tiglath-Pileser and his successors. The occurrence of such a reference here, however, is not conclusive evidence for the view that the Assyrians are the advancing enemy. Since the practice of deportation was known and feared even by those who had yet to taste it, its mention would form an effectively menacing climax.

iv. The punishment of those who exploit the poor (2: 1–13)

This chapter takes up the theme of social evil so common in the eighth century prophets (cf. Isa. 1: 16–17, 21–23; 3: 14–15; 5: 8–23; 10: 1–2; Hos. 7: 1–3; 12: 7–8; Am. 2: 6–8; 4: 1; 5: 10–13; 6: 4–6; 8: 4–6). It is perhaps to be dated in the dark days of Ahaz.

1–5. In an agricultural society, land ownership is the key to rural prosperity. In Israel, every family had its own inheritance, intended to be inalienable (cf. Lev. 25: 25–28; Num. 27: 1–11; 36: 1–12; Dt. 19: 14). As long as it remained so, a fairly homogeneous standard of living prevailed in the countryside. Under the monarchy, the tendency arose for property to pass into the hands of the (usually urban) rich. Farmers lacked the capital to cushion the effects of a series of bad harvests and could thus be compelled by circumstances to part with their patrimony. That this was a step to be taken only in extreme straits is evidenced by the story of Ahab and Naboth's vineyard (1 Kg. 21). Nevertheless, in Judah as in Israel, the rich came to seize every opportunity of acquiring other people's land, and even to manufacture opportunities. Micah speaks of them lying awake plotting at night (they **plan iniquity . . . on their beds**) and in the **morning** enjoying the evil exercise of **their power to do it** (1). They not only buy up what comes on the market but **covet fields and seize them**, thus oppressing whole families. Such behaviour is an affront to the God who is Lord of land as well as people, and against its perpetrators He in turn is **planning disaster, from which**, as Micah asserts, using the metaphor of an ox yoke (not brought out by NIV), **you cannot save yourselves**. The punishment will indeed fit the crime, for it will consist in the loss of the ill-gotten property to an enemy invader **(He assigns our fields to traitors**, 4). Far from walking **proudly**, the oppressors will in **that day** be the objects of a (proverbial) **taunt**

song of **mourning**. They will **have no one** of their own families left to represent them **in the assembly of the** LORD. **To divide the land by lot** is a reference to the original apportionment of the promised land by lot (Jos. 14: 2, etc.).

6–11. Such forthright condemnation of the abuse of wealth could not fail to make enemies for Micah. The reactions **'Do not prophesy'** (or 'rant', as NEB) and **'disgrace will not overtake us'** (6) show how firmly he and his message were rejected (cf. Am. 2: 12; 7: 10–13). In the NIV, v. 7 is taken as the prophet's response to his rejection; it seems better, however, to understand these words as a continuation of the words of the objectors, as in JB and GNB. They cannot envisage **the Spirit of the** LORD becoming **angry** with them, or doing such **things**. So complete is their moral blindness that each considers himself as one **whose ways are upright**, and to whom therefore **words** truly coming from the Lord must **do good**.

Micah immediately strips off their illusions. Walking uprightly before God is utterly incompatible with the objectors' actions: the **people** were behaving **like an enemy**, robbing those who desire only to be **without a care** and to be allowed to **pass by like men returning from battle** (8). **Women** were driven out **from their pleasant homes** and **their children** deprived **forever** of their true spiritual heritage (**my blessing**, 9). Today, there are still multitudes, who share the same desire for peace and the same frustration as their hopes are thwarted by self-seeking authorities, both of the left and of the right. Peasants are still dispossessed by the unscrupulous rich; women and children are still made refugees at the whim of an ideology or an economic policy. Micah's declarations retain a pressing relevance in a world in which such conditions continue. Now, as in his day, the Lord sees, and in His own time and way, will punish. His servants should not allow opposition or unpopularity to deter them from declaring this. Taking up again in v. 10 the thought of v. 4, Micah warns the oppressors that they will have to **get up, go away**, no longer having a **resting place** in the promised land. Their own **defilement** would be the cause of **ruin beyond all remedy** (10). The paragraph closes with a biting vignette of the prophet who, by contrast with Micah himself, would be popular with the rich —a man who would be **a liar and deceiver** and **prophesy . . . of wine and beer**. There remains today a willing audience for anyone who panders to the vices of the age under the guise of proclaiming God's truth.

12, 13. These two verses, set amid condemnation, look beyond the punishment to the restoration. **Jacob** and **Israel** stand for the whole nation, which Micah foresees as gathered again after the defeat and deportation of v. 4. The God who dispersed can **bring . . . together** and recreate a nation which is a **throng of people**, like **a flock** of **sheep** in **a pen** or **pasture** (12). The people will **break** out triumphantly from their place of captivity, under the leadership of **their king**, none other than the LORD himself, who **will pass through before them . . . at their head** (13). Since the doctrine of **the remnant** (12) is well attested in the eighth century (Isa. 4: 2–3; 10: 20–23; 11: 10–16) there is no need to follow those scholars who regard these two verses as a later insertion into the text.

v. The corruption of the leadership (3: 1–12)

In this chapter, Micah attacks Judah's leaders, political, legal, and religious. On the testimony of Jer. 26: 17–19, this passage or at least the last part of it, comes from the early years of Hezekiah's reign, and was influential in stimulating reform.

1–4. The task of rulers is to **know justice** and to put it into practice but the **leaders of Jacob** and **rulers of the house of Israel** (here synonymous terms for the leaders of Judah) do exactly the opposite. They **hate good and love evil** (cf. the warning given earlier by Amos to the Northern leaders, Am. 5: 14 f.) and treat the people, **my people**, as a butcher treats a carcase. They **tear the skin from** the people, and separate **the flesh from their bones**. They **eat . . . the flesh**, and **break their bones in pieces** as for a stew. They are in fact no better than cannibals in their dealings with the people of God.

Such conduct cannot be carried on with impunity however. Its perpetrators may attempt to preserve a veneer of religious respectability, and **cry out to the** LORD, but they have forfeited their right to an answer (4). **At that time** when their need is greatest, **he will hide his face from them**. Those who persistently **have done evil** must inevitably face the consequence of irrevocable alienation from God.

5–8. From the political leaders, Micah turns to **the prophets**, from whom better things might be expected. But their desire for a comfortable life has made them mere parasites of the rich. They **proclaim 'peace'**, that is, pronounce favourable oracles to anyone who **feeds them**, but **wage war** with avaricious threats against those too poor or too honest to do so. Desperate indeed is the state of any country in that day or this where those who claim to speak in the name of God tailor their standards to suit the current fancy of wealthy patrons (cf. 2 Tim. 4: 3, 4). But the ultimate exposure and humiliation of such venal prophets is assured. When true spiritual revelation is needed most, they will have nothing to say, because they will receive **no answer**

from God (7). It will be like the **darkness** of **night** for them. **Without** true **visions** or **divination**, they will **be ashamed**, and forced to endure **disgrace**. By contrast, the true prophet, as Micah himself, does not dilute his message to the hearer's taste. When **the Spirit of the LORD** fills a man, he receives **power** and **might** (or 'courage', GNB). His concern is not with lining his pocket, but with **justice**. Thus he is able to speak boldly and **declare** to the Lord's people their **transgression** and **sin** (8). The administration and reception of such reproof remains a test of the presence of the Spirit of the Lord, for without His aid it can neither be given in love nor received in humility.

9–12. This third paragraph repeats the summons of the first to the leaders and recapitulates the charges against them. Far from ensuring justice, they **despise . . . and distort** it. The **bloodshed** and the **wickedness** they do are compounded rather than excused by being made to serve the cause of building **Zion**. In the courts, judgment is given in favour of those who buy it rather than those who deserve it. The **priests** give instruction to those who can afford it rather than those who need it. The **prophets** speak for material reward rather than from moral compulsion. Yet all deceive themselves that their reliance is **upon the LORD**, that He is **among** them. This pathetic delusion leads them to the false hope that **'No disaster will come upon us'**. Their fatal mistake was to make, or rather remake, God in the image of their own venality and duplicity. But He is not to be manipulated, and will even reject **Zion** rather than betray His own holy nature. Micah therefore fearlessly proclaims that **Jerusalem** will share the fate of Samaria, and become **a heap of rubble** (cf. 1: 6). Even the temple **hill** (12) would be desolate and overgrown following the destruction of the temple itself. All this would come about **because of you**. Those who reject the moral claims of God on their conduct can look for no comfort from His promises. Thus Micah, with a boldness unsurpassed even by Isaiah, made clear to Hezekiah the final destination of the path Judah's leaders were treading. Though his warning could not prevent the nation's ultimate tragedy, it could, and under the guidance of a prudent monarch, did serve to postpone it. The impact of Micah's preaching was still remembered a century later in Jeremiah's day (Jer. 26: 17–19). That Judah still existed a century later is a mute testimony to its effectiveness.

II. HOPE FOR THE FUTURE (4: 1–5: 15)
Commentators often regard these chapters as exilic or post-exilic additions to Micah. However, their difference in subject matter from

chs. 1–3 is by no means conclusive evidence. Micah's career covered several decades, and there is no reason why his early visions of judgment could not be followed by mature insights of restoration and hope. Indeed, there is good reason to suppose that they would be, for a prophet who could utter the uncompromising threat of 3: 12 could not avoid asking himself how God could fulfil such a threat and still remain true to promises like those of Gen. 17: 8 and especially 2 Sam. 7: 8–16. The answer is implicit in such a passage as 1 Kg. 8: 46–53, and is here elaborated in terms of an idealized Davidic monarchy that would embody not only all that the actual dynasty should have been, but far more besides. As Jewish interpreters later understood, such a comprehensive hope could be fulfilled only in the advent of the Messiah (cf. Mt. 2: 1–6; Jn 7: 42). In terms of the history of Micah's own day, it seems quite likely that his eschatological hope would blaze most brightly at the time when outward circumstances were darkest and the destruction of Jerusalem seemed imminent. These chapters are therefore fittingly, albeit tentatively, set against the background of Sennacherib's siege of Jerusalem (cf. the view of King). This would be dated in 701 B.C., or if Bright's suggestion is followed, 688 B.C. (see Bright pp. 296–308 for a discussion of the problem). It has been a common experience of the people of God through the centuries that the assurance of the ultimate vindication of His character and purposes is strongest when it seems most fiercely challenged by the events of the day. Without the foundation of such a confidence in such a God, the nation of Israel could never have survived the trauma of the exile, much less triumphed over it.

i. The Lord's future reign (4: 1–5)
Verses 1–3 are almost identical with Isa. 2: 2–4, and commentators have debated inconclusively which, if either, is dependent upon the other. It seems most likely that the sentiments expressed here were part of the common property of eighth-century prophetic vision, and are incorporated into their oracles by both prophets in a manner similar to that in which Paul incorporated portions of hymns or catechisms into his letters (*e.g.* Phil. 2: 6–11; 1 Tim. 3: 16; 2 Tim. 2: 11–13). The passage, despite its different emphasis, is set appropriately after 3: 12, since it again speaks of **the mountain of the LORD'S temple** (1). However, the phrase **in the last days** alerts the reader to the eschatological nature of the reference. The language is symbolic in meaning: the temple site is depicted as **raised above** and **established as chief among the mountains** (1; cf. Ezek. 40: 2). Representatives of **many nations** will stream towards it, not as mere sightseers, but with a desire that **the God of Jacob** will **teach us his ways** so

that **we may walk in** them. The basis of the instruction they will receive is **the law** which has authority as **the word of the LORD**, and whose influence will radiate outwards **from Jerusalem** (2). The Lord will adjudicate among the nations and **settle disputes** for them for ever. The resulting peace is described in terms of the form it would take in an agricultural economy such as that in which Micah lived. **Swords** and **spears**, instruments of battle, will be exchanged for **ploughshares** and **pruning hooks**, instruments of rural prosperity. (Contrast Jl 3: 10.) **Every man** will enjoy the uninterrupted use of **his own vine and . . . his own fig tree**, that is, his own ancestral land. (For the formulaic nature of v. 4a, cf. its occurrence in 1 Kg. 4: 25; Zech. 3: 10.) The guarantee that these blessings will see fulfilment is the fact that they are promised by **the LORD Almighty**. Whatever the allegiance of other **nations** to their own gods (5), the prospect of future bliss for the people of Israel elicits the response that they will worship and obey **the LORD our God for ever and ever** (cf. Isa. 2: 5).

ii. The return from exile (4: 6–5: 1)
In this section the perspective oscillates beween the future restoration and the present agony. **6–8.** The LORD speaks of the people whom **I have brought to grief** (6). The realization that exile is divine retribution and not merely a quirk of a random and meaningless historical process fortifies the prophet's faith in an ultimate restoration. The Lord will **gather** and **assemble** His people. Though they may seem like sheep, **lame** and **driven away**, they will constitute **a remnant**, no longer a grim reminder of past failure and punishment, but now a spark of hope for a bright future. They will again form **a strong nation**, strong not by virtue of military power, but by having **the LORD** to **rule over them in Mount Zion**. Though the return from exile partially fulfilled this hope, the terms of permanence in which it is here announced (**from that day and forever**, 7) lend it messianic overtones.

The pastoral metaphor is reinforced in v. 8. When the nation returns, gathered like a flock, Jerusalem will be again like a **watchtower** 'where God, like a shepherd, watches over his people' (GNB). Its **former dominion** will be restored, that is, its territory will be as extensive as it was in the halcyon days of the united monarchy under David and Solomon.

9, 10. Such may be the future blessing, but the present reality is much less idyllic. Whatever glory would ultimately spring from it, the present was a time of anguish, a time for enduring the **pains** of **labor**. In a situation like that of 701 B.C., the leadership was as impotent as though it no longer existed, as though there were **no king** or **counselor**. Though the end

for Jerusalem was not to come in 701 B.C., eventually it would no longer be postponed, and the inhabitants would have to **leave the city** into exile, just as their northern neighbours had. But even in that dreadful day, they could reassure themselves that they would **be rescued**, that **the LORD** who was allowing punishment would one day **redeem** them **out of the hand of** their **enemies**.

The fact that **Babylon** is specified as the place of exile is one of a number of considerations which lead many scholars to assign to these verses an origin later than 597 B.C., when King Jehoiachin and other leaders were deported (2 Kg. 24: 8–17). The words of the previous verse **have you no king? Has your counselor perished?** (9), are adduced in support. While this is a possible view, it is scarcely a necessary one. The words in v. 9 are a question, not a statement, and may perfectly well be understood figuratively, as in the above comments. Neither is the mention of **Babylon** (10) conclusive. Some scholars reckon it as an alteration or addition by a later scribe to make the passage more relevant to his own day, though even this suggestion need not compel assent. If Micah lived through Sennacherib's siege, he saw the destruction of Jerusalem deferred, but the example of Samaria clearly showed that delay would not be permanent. If Judah walked in Israel's path, it would sooner or later share Israel's fate; whether the agency would be Assyria or another power was an issue quite secondary. A man with as much insight as Micah into the moral realities of his own country would not find it hard to see that an empire based as nakedly on military force and repression as Assyria's was, would rot from within rather than fall to an external power. The persistent disaffection of the province of Babylon throughout this period would easily have led a perceptive observer to see it as the worm in the heart of the Assyrian apple that would eventually bring about its fall. A change in the identity of the leading Mesopotamian power would not necessarily involve a change in the policy of deporting the populations of rebellious vassals, and would certainly not involve a change in divine principles of sin and retribution. It is then perfectly possible for the identification of Babylon as the site of Judah's exile to come direct from Micah himself. Cf. 2 Kg. 20: 12–18, where Isaiah makes a specific link between the diplomatic moves of Babylon against Assyria, and its destiny as the place of Judean exile. Moreover, the oracles of Isaiah include a prediction regarding Babylon (Isa. 13, 14) which does not require the preceding downfall of Assyria; Tiglath-Pileser III gloried in his status as king of Babylon quite separately from his rule over Assyria.

11–13. The scene continues to be that of

Jerusalem under attack, but attention is now focused on the contrast between the vindictive aims of the enemy and the inscrutable purpose of God. If these verses refer to Sennacherib's attack, the **many nations** would be the provincial contingents in the Assyrian army. The attackers' anticipation of victory is likened to the unwholesome eagerness of one about to commit rape, for such is the force of the expressions **'Let her be defiled, let our eyes gloat over Zion'** (11). But **the thoughts of the LORD** and **his plan** are hidden from them. It is their own downfall that He intends, for **he gathers them like sheaves to the threshing floor** (12). Rather than the heathen nations, it will be the Lord's people (the **Daughter of Zion**) who triumph. He will make them invincible, with **horns of iron** and **hoofs of bronze**; their victory, however, will not be an occasion for self-congratulation, but for giving thanks **to the Lord of all the earth** (13) to whom they will **devote** their spoils. This word probably implies total destruction, as in the days of the conquest under Joshua (cf. Jos. 6: 17 ff.). **5: 1.** This verse is rather obscure in Hebrew, and may go either with what precedes or what follows. Its position as 4: 14 in the *MT* makes the former seem more probable. The topic which continues to be the **siege . . . laid against** Jerusalem, also supports this view. The insult of being struck **with a rod . . . on the cheek** suffered by the earthly **ruler** of Israel contrasts sharply with the power and glory of the Messianic ruler of the paragraph following. The contrast may be viewed as an instance of the recurring biblical motif of exaltation after suffering (cf. Isa. 52: 13 ff.).

iii. The future ruler (5: 2–4)

In this brief section, the prophet's attention reverts to the future. Whereas in 4: 8 the emphasis was on the extent of the territory to be restored to Israel, here it turns to the ruler himself. The terms used are such as to transcend the nature or achievements of any merely human leader, and could be completely fulfilled only in the Messiah. This **ruler over Israel** will arise from the Davidic line, indeed from the same town of **Bethlehem**, which despite its obscurity (**small among the clans of Judah**) gave birth to the line's founder. The **origins** of this line **are from of old**, stretching back not merely three centuries, but as the expression **from ancient times** implies, beyond time altogether (cf. NIVmg). God may **abandon** His people to their enemies, but only temporarily, **until the time** is ripe for Him to act. The description of the woman **who is in labor** stands in the same vein of prophetic revelation as Isa. 7: 14. Here the woman is probably best understood as referring to the nation of Israel. The duration of her labour is limited, and **when she . . . gives birth**, that

is, when the labour is over, then the ruler's 'fellow countrymen who are in exile will be reunited with their own people' (v. 3, GNB). Micah himself may have seen in these words only the return from Babylon, but from our post-resurrection vantage point, we cannot but see 'great David's greater son' delivering His people from the captivity of sin. In v. 4, the ideal qualities of a Davidic king are magnified to a messianic scale. He will not only **shepherd his flock** (contrast the ravages wrought by the leaders of ch. 3), but will do so with the **strength** and **majesty** that come from **the LORD. . . God** Himself. His greatness will extend far beyond the boundaries that David's kingdom knew, and will reach **to the ends of the earth**. With no external enemies left unvanquished (cf. 1 C. 15: 25–28; Phil. 2: 9–11), His people will at last **live securely**. Most modern translations (NEB, JB, GNB) as NIV, fittingly conclude this paragraph with the first phrase of v. 5, thus understanding the Messiah himself to **be . . . peace** (cf. Isa. 9: 6–7).

iv. The nation's future characteristics (5: 5–15)

The prophet here looks into the dark tunnel of the exile to see what awaits the nation there. **5b–6.** There seems to be no special significance to the numbers **seven** and **eight**. Probably they are used in the same manner in which Amos uses three and four (Am. chs. 1 and 2), and simply indicate a number of leaders adequate to meet the exigencies of the situation **when the Assyrian invades our land**. Not only will they **deliver us from the Assyrian** invader, but they will **rule the land of Assyria** itself. **The land of Nimrod** is a parallelistic synonym for Assyria; Nimrod was the founder of its capital Nineveh in the tradition of Gen. 10: 8–12. These verses are rather difficult and admit of more than one interpretation. If referred to the background of Sennacherib's siege, they portray not merely deliverance but even military conquest of Assyria itself—**they will rule the land of Assyria with the sword**. Such a situation is so out of keeping with the historical realities that it seems preferable to view these verses either as a reference to events still future, or perhaps as a figurative description of Judean leadership coming into positions of prominence *during* the exile, and delivering the people in the sense of preventing their assimilation and disappearance as a distinct religious and ethnic group. Though this last view is by no means fully satisfying, it does attempt to keep these two verses in the same field of reference as their context.

7–9. These verses detail two complementary aspects of the relationships of the exiles with their neighbours. On the one hand the **remnant of Jacob** will have the refreshing influence of **dew** or **showers** on the **many peoples**

in whose **midst** they will find themselves. Their ability to do so comes **from the LORD** in circumstances beyond the control of mere humanity (**man . . . mankind,** 7). On the other hand the same **remnant of Jacob** will exercise irresistible power **among the nations**. As **a lion** excels the other **beasts of the forest**, so will the influence of Israel excel. As **a young lion** loose **among the flocks of sheep** destroys **and mangles,** with **no one to rescue** the defenceless animals, so will Israel triumph **over your enemies**. So it has been down the centuries. The spiritual blessings given uniquely to Israel enabled her to outlast all the persecutions of her **enemies** from Nebuchadnezzar to Hitler and Nasser and to survive after they have been **destroyed**.

10–15. Unique blessing carries unique responsibility (cf. Am. 3: 2); the nation which is to triumph over its enemies must depend wholly on God. In the military and political sphere, **horses** and **chariots** (10), **cities** and **strongholds** (11) will all be swept away. In the more fundamental religious sphere, **witchcraft** and **spells** (12), forbidden by the Mosaic Law, will be removed. **Images** and **sacred stones** (13), and **Asherah poles** (14), symbols of decadent pagan worship (see *NBD*), will be destroyed. **No longer** would God's people commit blasphemy and **bow down . . . to the work of** their own **hands**. And if such stringent measures are needed to purify Israel, how much greater the **anger and wrath** with which God **will take vengeance upon the** pagan **nations** which, though they may have been instruments of His disciplinary purpose (Isa. 10: 5), **have not obeyed** Him (cf. 1 Pet. 4: 17–18).

III. CONDEMNATION AND CONSOLATION (6: 1–7: 20)

These two chapters reflect the diverse moods of the prophet. The main burden, as in chs. 1–3, is the sin of God's people, though in the final section (7: 8–20) the hope of restoration shines brightly. Dating is difficult, but the reference to the northern kings, Omri and Ahab, in 6: 16 makes it likely that at least 6: 1–7: 7 come from the reign of Ahaz, and before the fall of Samaria. The mention of child sacrifice in 6: 7 may also reflect the conduct of Ahaz in 2 Kg. 16: 3.

i. The case against Israel (6: 1–5)

This section is cast in the form of an accusation before witnesses in a law court (cf. Ps. 50; Isa. 1: 2; Hos. 4: 1). The Lord does not simply convict out of hand, but first invites His people to **plead your case,** with **the mountains** and **hills** as witnesses (cf. 1: 2). In turn **the LORD has a case against his people,** and opens His case in vv. 3–5. Rather than bringing a series of accusations, the Lord simply asks what He

has **done to** the people to make them abandon Him. In answer to His own rhetorical question He catalogues His past actions on their behalf. He **redeemed** them and **brought** them out from the slavery **of Egypt**. He provided them with the leadership of **Moses, Aaron and Miriam** (4). He protected them from the machinations of **Balak king of Moab,** putting a blessing instead of a curse into the mouth of **Balaam the son of Beor** (Num. 22–24). He saw them safely across the Jordan **from Shittim** (the last camp on the east bank, Jos. 3: 1) **to Gilgal** (the first on the west, Jos. 4: 19). The consideration of even such a brief and selective list of the Lord's historical dealings with Israel should have been enough to sustain their allegiance to Him. The faith of Israel and the faith of the Church depend alike at rock bottom not on theological propositions but on the knowledge of **the righteous acts of the LORD**. In times of temptation for both individuals and groups, the rehearsal of the Lord's blessings already experienced remains the strongest form of prophylaxis against apostasy.

ii. The essence of true religion (6: 6–8)

This passage, the best known in the book, should be understood as the response of the contrite Israelite to the challenge of vv. 3–5, with v. 8 as the prophet's commentary upon that response. **6, 7.** The Israelite inevitably expresses his desire to bring acceptable worship to God in terms of the sacrificial system familiar to him. Can the magnification of ritual offerings win the favour of God, and make amends for past failures? The offerings envisaged steadily increase in value to reach a monstrous climax. **Burnt offerings** were a normal part of worship, but to offer the valuable **calves a year old** (6) was the prerogative of the rich. On state occasions, **thousand of rams** were offered (*e.g.* 1 Kg. 8: 63; 2 Chr. 30: 24), but for the individual to do so would be absolutely ruinous. Oil was a prescribed accompaniment to a cereal offering (*e.g.* Lev. 2); **ten thousands of rivers of oil** presuppose cereal offerings vast beyond imagination. It is as though the worshipper understands the futility of merely outward ritual before being told, for the series culminates with the frightful (and forbidden, *e.g.* in Exod. 13: 13; Lev. 18: 21) suggestion of child sacrifice. But the death of the **firstborn . . . the fruit of my body,** far from removing **my transgression . . . the sin of my soul** (7), would merely multiply it. To this dilemma of the ultimate ineffectiveness of the prescribed system of sacrificial worship (cf. Heb. 10: 4), the prophet gives an answer unsurpassed in spiritual insight anywhere in the OT. What **the LORD** requires, **he has** already **showed:** acting **justly** in dealings between man and man; the humble **walk** of a man **with . . . God;** and **mercy** (better 'steadfast love', 8, as RSVmg) as the bond between the horizontal and vertical relationships of life. Thus Micah stands in the tradition of prophetic insight stemming from Samuel (1 Sam. 15: 22), finding eloquent expression in Amos, Hosea and Isaiah, and leading towards Jesus' definitive summary of the OT (Mt. 22: 37–40).

iii. The wages of sin (6: 9–16)

These verses may perhaps be seen as a continuation of the indictment begun in vv. 3–5, though most exegetes take them as a separate entity. The theme returns to that of ch. 3, social injustice. In v. 9, **the city** may be Samaria if a date before 721 B.C. is accepted. If the date is later, then Jerusalem is the target of the paragraph. The inhabitants, are summoned to hear the Lord's charge, and reminded that **it is wisdom to fear** Him. He recounts to them their evil practices (9b–12), which affect both commerce and personal relationships. In trade, they overcharge with their **dishonest scales and . . . false weights** and give short quantity with their **short ephah** (cf. Am. 8: 5). The general prevalence of **liars** and deceit has its outcome in violence on the part of **rich men**. Their wickedness may lead to the accumulation of **treasures** at home, but the Lord will neither **forget** nor **acquit**. Indeed, He has already **begun to destroy . . . because of your sins** (13). The punishment consists partly in the inevitable failure of his ill-gotten goods to satisfy the materialistic oppressor. He may have plenty to **eat**, but will **not be satisfied** because of his inner hunger for the food which is more than bread. His attempts to **save** for the future will be frustrated (14), and even his normal agricultural round will not bring its expected reward (15). If these verses were first addressed to the leaders of Samaria during its final siege, their fulfilment was both quick and literal, for in 721 B.C., savings and harvests alike found their way into Assyrian possession. Such is the outcome of wickedness (Gal. 6: 7). Because the people followed the evil example of **Omri** (1 Kg. 16: 25) and his dynasty (**Ahab's house**), they could expect only punishment from God. Their city would be **a ruin** (cf. 1: 6) and they themselves would have to bear the **derision** and **scorn of the** heathen **nations**. So today for those who persistently refuse to heed the demands and warnings of God, there remains only 'a fearful prospect of judgment' (Heb. 10: 27).

iv. The prophet's despair and hope (7: 1–7)

Micah speaks in the first person in the opening and closing verses, and in the intervening ones describes scathingly the decadence of the society in which he lived. In v. 1 Micah shares the despair of loneliness experienced earlier by Elijah (1 Kg. 19: 10). He feels **like one who gathers summer fruit** of people faithful to

God, with not even one **cluster of grapes** nor a single **fig** left by the gleaners. Whereas Amos had earlier pictured the **godly** as few and powerless (Am. 5: 13), Micah sees them as altogether **swept from the land**, with **not one** left to offer him fellowship. Instead, his compatriots are bent on shedding **blood** (2) and **skilled in doing evil**. Among their leaders, both **the ruler** and the judge are all too ready to go into conclave with **the powerful**, and **for bribes** to **conspire together** schemes that will accomplish **what they desire**, disregarding its **evil** nature. Even today, there are many Christians who have to spend their lives in a society where this kind of abuse is all too common. In one recent *cause célèbre*, a man charged with the murder of his wife and a large number of other people by causing a plane crash was acquitted in the face of overwhelming prosecution evidence. That the acquittal left him free to collect a huge sum of insurance money makes it doubly hard to believe that the course of justice was not obstructed. In a situation like this, even **the best** and **most upright** are 'worthless as weeds' (4, GNB), though **the day God visits** them foretold by the prophets (**watchmen**) cannot be for ever delayed, and **the time of their confusion** has come. Meanwhile, a man can have **no trust** or **confidence in a friend** or **a neighbor**, or even in the closest members of **his own household**, his children and his wife (**her who lies in your embrace**). The outward prospect is truly daunting, and vv. 5–6 may reflect quarrels in Micah's own family. But notwithstanding all this, he retains his faith in **God my Savior** (cf. Hab. 3: 17–19). He will continue to **watch in hope for the LORD** in the assurance that He **will hear me** (7). No one who follows the Lord for long will fail to experience at some time a similar sense of loneliness and overpowering opposition. This was especially the lot of Jeremiah (Jer. 1: 18, 19; 11: 18–20; 15: 10–18; 18: 18; 20: 7–18). Jesus Himself was certainly not immune to it, and probably drew support from this passage which was frequently in His thoughts and teaching (Mt. 10: 21, 35–36; Mk 13: 12; Lk. 12: 53). It may be that meditation on v. 1 also influenced His symbolic action in Mk 11: 12–14.

v. The Lord's compassion for His people (7: 8–20)

In these closing words of his prophecy, Micah speaks on behalf of the nation, and in particular on behalf of Jerusalem, which will both bear the main brunt of God's punishment, and witness the chief glory of His restoration. Like other parts of the book (2: 12–13; chs. 4, 5), this section directs its spiritual thrust towards the generation that would have to undergo the anguish of the exile and discover God's mercy in adversity.

8–10. The faith expressed in these verses contains the basic understanding of God's dealings with Israel that enabled her to survive political downfall, and outlast deportation and exile. Such an experience was rendered necessary **because I have sinned against him**. The arrogant disobedience of the past would have to give place to a humble submissiveness that would contain the germ of future hope. Israel must patiently **bear the LORD's wrath**, and in so doing come to realise that it is only for a limited time, **until he pleads my case** (9). The confidence that He will eventually do this gives the assurance that the **enemy** has no right to **gloat** over the fallen nation, for it will **rise** once more. Even while enduring the **darkness** of His wrath, Israel will find that **the LORD will be** her **light** (8), and eventually **will bring** her **out to the light** (9) of restoration. This will also mean that He **establishes** her **right** against her **enemy**, who had not only defeated Israel but defied **the LORD** her **God**. The enemy will in her turn be **covered with shame** and **trampled underfoot like mire in the streets** (10), and it will be Israel's turn to **see her downfall**. The enemy is not identified, but the description of her conduct is probably related to the Assyrian message of 2 Kg. 18: 28–35.

11–13: In the day of restoration, Micah sees not only the **walls** of Jerusalem rebuilt, but a national **boundaries** that will be far extended beyond the attenuated limits of the Judah of his own day. **In that day**, the exiles will return from all directions, from the east (**Assyria**), and the west (**Egypt**), to repopulate the land. Israel will flourish, while her traditional oppressors **will become desolate** because of their evil **deeds**. **14–17.** The prophet prays for the Lord's protecting care over the restored nation, as a **shepherd** protects his **flock** when it is **by itself in a forest**. He asks for them freedom to graze even in the fertile transjordanian lands of **Bashan and Gilead**, as they had **in days long ago** (14), that is, under the united monarchy. In reply, the Lord promises intervention on behalf of his people comparable to that **in the days** of the exodus **when you came out of Egypt**. When the Lord shows **wonders** (15), the **nations** who **see** can only be **ashamed**, embarrassed (**their hands on their mouths**, 16), humbled (**they will lick the dust**) and **trembling** (17). But no display of God's power on behalf of His people is ever merely ostentatious; here its purpose is evangelistic, namely that even the nations who have defied Him (10) will **turn in fear to the LORD our God** and seek His mercy. **18–20.** This confidence in the ultimate triumph of mercy over judgment leads Micah into his final outburst of praise. God may, indeed must, punish disobedience, yet he does **not stay angry for ever**, but **will again have compassion on us**. Because of the **mercy** in which **he delights**, there will always be a **remnant** whose **sin and . . . transgression** will be pardoned. And the pardon will finally be complete, with **iniquities** totally vanquished, and **sins** removed as far beyond recall as if **hurled . . . into the depths of the sea** (19). The Lord is a true God, and the promises he has **pledged on oath to our fathers** (the patriarchs) **in days long ago** will certainly be fulfilled, whatever the vicissitudes through which their descendants must pass. This assurance given to Israel to sustain her through her darkest days retains all its potency for the Church of our day as it faces the end of the age.

Promise and covenant God surely keeps;
He watching o'er us slumbers not, nor sleeps

BIBLIOGRAPHY

Commentaries

ALLEN, L. C., *The Books of Joel, Obadiah, Jonah and Micah. NICOT* (Grand Rapids, 1976).

ARCHER, G. L., *Micah.* NBC³ (London, 1970), pp.752–761.

DAHLBERG, B. T., *The Book of Micah. The Interpreter's One-volume Commentary on the Bible* (Nashville, 1971), pp.483–490.

KING, P. J., *Micah. The Jerome Biblical Commentary* (Englewood Cliffs, 1968), pp.283–289.

MAYS, J. L., *Micah. OTL* (London, 1976).

SMITH, G. A., *The Book of the Twelve Prophets*, Vol. I. EB (New York, 1897).

SMITH, J. M. P., WARD, W. H., and BEWER, J. A., *Micah, Zephaniah, Nahum, Habakkuk, Obadiah and Joel.* ICC (Edinburgh, 1911), pp.3–156.

WOLFE, R. E., *Introduction and Exegesis of Micah.* IB6 (Nashville, 1956), pp.897–949.

General

BRIGHT, J., *A History of Israel* (2nd edition, Londn, 1972), pp.267–308.

ELLISON, H. L., *Men Spake From God* (London, 1952).

DE VAUX, R., *Ancient Israel* (New York, 1961).

NAHUM

E. M. BLAIKLOCK

The Author

In the opening verse (1: 1) of this passionate poetic prophecy the author is named as 'Nahum the Elkoshite'. Elkosh is variously placed. Jerome believed it was Elcesi in Galilee. Nestorius, with less likelihood, mentioned an alleged 'tomb of Nahum' at Alqosh north of Mosul. Beit Jibrim, between Jerusalem and Gaza, has been suggested without convincing evidence. Finally, and most likely, is Capernaum which means, almost certainly, 'the village of Nahum' (Kfar Nahum today).

The Date

Two events confine the available period of conjecture. Thebes, or No-Ammon, capital of Upper Egypt, has fallen (3: 8–10), a catastrophe dated 664/663 B.C. Nineveh, after a period of notable decline, fell in 612 B.C. In the passage quoted, the destruction of Thebes is mentioned as past, that of Nineveh as imminent, but yet to be. Some critics, who find prophecy, in the sense of 'foretelling', difficult to accept, conjecture dates later than 612 B.C. for Nahum's writing, but conservative scholars refer the book to the period defined, and, since the city is generally pictured as strong and full of her old imperial arrogance, as nearer the earlier date than the later. After the death of Ashurbanipal in 627 B.C., Assyria was obviously ripe for defeat. Even during Josiah's reign (639–609 B.C.) the Empire had lost its hold of territories to the west. Ten years after its fall, Thebes had begun to rise from its ruin and, too long postponed after the event, the reference to the horror of the sack of Thebes would lose some of its power. Hence the probability that Nahum wrote soon after the middle of the century. During this half-century, there appears to have been an inconclusive assault on Nineveh by the Mede Kyaxares about 626 B.C. It is, however, impossible to link either portent to the theme of Nahum's prophetic oracle.

Historical Background

The brutal imperialism of Assyria had cursed the lands of the Middle East for almost two centuries, when Sennacherib (705–681 B.C.) established the great capital, Nineveh. The royal palace had an area of almost 100,000 square feet, and its walls and precincts were sculptured with scenes of the king's victories, superb, cruel, realistic reliefs, which included the siege of Lachish and the payment of tribute by Judah. The city was enclosed by a wall seven

and three-quarter miles in extent, with fifteen main gates, of which eight still await excavation. Stone colossi in the shape of bulls stood guard at each. It was a garden city, with parks and even a zoo, watered and irrigated by great works of hydraulic engineering. When Jonah spoke of Nineveh as requiring 'three days' journey' to cross, he had in mind, not only the administrative heart of the city with its royal palace and noblemen's dwellings, but the associated suburbs and irrigated support areas (Jon. 3: 4). Jonah's figure of 120,000 inhabitants is quite true. In Calah, the southern Assyrian city, 69,754 people inhabited a city half the size of Nineveh.

The thread of relevant history may be picked up at the time of Sennacherib's assassination in the temple of Nisroch by his sons in 681 B.C. His younger son, Esarhaddon (681–669 B.C.), succeeded him, regained control of Nineveh, and built a palace there. It was a demonstration of his royal presence, for Esarhaddon spent much time at his major palace in Calah. Pursuing the traditional Assyrian role of imperial aggression and conquest, Esarhaddon set out to subdue Egypt. He died while marching on Egypt in 669 B.C. He was succeeded by his son (a twin), Ashurbanipal, who reigned until probably 627 B.C.

Ashurbanipal lived most of his time at Nineveh. Esarhaddon's policy against Egypt was resumed in strength. Ashurbanipal sailed up the Nile to Thebes, which surrendered and was spared (667 B.C.). Egypt, however, perhaps sensing some loosening of the Assyrian grip, rebelled again, and in 663 B.C. the Assyrian king again invaded Upper Egypt and destroyed Thebes with every horrible accompaniment of Assyrian aggression. The royal report reads '. . . That city, in its entirety, I conquered with the aid of Ashur and Ishtar . . . Silver, gold, precious stones, all the possessions of his palace, many-coloured clothing, linen, great horses, men and women attendants, two high obelisks of shining orichalcum 2,500 talents in weight. The door-posts of the temple door, I took from their bases and removed to Assyria. Heavy booty, beyond counting, I took away from Thebes. Against Musur and Kusi I let my weapons rage and showed my might. With my hands full I returned to Nineveh, my residence-city, in good health.'

The reign of Ashurbanipal was the Indian

Summer, to use Toynbee's phrase, of Imperial Assyria. The brutal people seem to have exhausted themselves, and with the king's death in 627 B.C. troubles came to a head. Sinshariskun, one of the heirs apparent, succeeded to the monarchy in 620 B.C. with the vassal states in open revolt. The Babylonians sacked the two cities of Ashur and Calah in 614 B.C. Two years later, in alliance with an invasion force of Umman-manda (possibly Scythians) the siege of Nineveh began. It lasted three months, and ended, according to the Babylonian Chronicle, by some breaching of defensive dykes, at a time when the Tigris was in high flood, with the melting snow waters of the Armenian watershed (Nah. 2: 6–8). Sinshariskun, or Sardanapalus to Latinize the Greek form of his name, died in the ruins of his palace. The somewhat fragmented account in the Chronicle runs: '(In the fourteenth year) the king of Babylonia called out his army and marched to . . . , the king of the Umman-manda and the king of Babylonia met each other in . . . Kyaxares made the king of Babylonia to cross and they marched along the Tigris river bank and pitched camp by Nineveh. From the month of Sivan to the month of Ab they (advanced?) only three . . . They made a strong attack on the citadel and in the month of Ab, (on the . . . th day the city was taken and) a great defeat inflicted on the people and (their) chiefs. On that same day Sin-shar-ishkun, the Assyrian king, (perished in the flames). They carried off much spoil from the city and temple-area and turned the city into a ruin mound and heap of debris . . . of Assyria moved off before (the final attack?) and the forces of the Babylonian king (followed them). On the twentieth of Elul, Kyaxares and his army returned to his land; the Babylonian king and his army marched as far as Nisibis. Booty and prisoners . . . and of the land of Rusapu were brought before the Babylonian king at Nineveh. In the month of (. . . Ashuruballit) sat on the throne in Harran as the king of Assyria' (*Babylonian Chronicle*: BM 21901, 38–50; *DOTT* 76).

The 'fourteenth year' of Nabopolassar, the king mentioned, is 613/612 B.C. The Umman-manda ('barbarian hordes') are either a Median confederation under Kyaxares, or Scythians from the northern hill-country . . . So, as Nahum and Zephaniah (2: 13–15) had predicted, Nineveh fell. A little after two centuries later, Xenophon the Athenian, and 'the Ten Thousand', backing out of their entanglement in Persia, passed the site without recognizing that the ruin-mound covered the rich remains of a mighty city (Xenophon, *Anabasis*, 3. 10). Beneath that barren tell lay the terraced gardens, palaces and temples of one of the most magnificent of ancient cities. The great library

of Ashurbanipal lay scattered. The splendid temple of Ishtar, east of Sennacherib's palace fell, with the goddess's statue left headless in the rubble. The temple of Nabu, south-east of Ashurbanipal's palace, where the king had recorded on stone slabs his victories over the Elamites, and his devotion to his god, lay shattered, the inscriptions ironically broken. The parks with their exotic plants, and the gardens where lions roamed were buried (Nah. 2: 11). The city was no more (Diodorus Siculus 2. 26, 27; Campbell Thompson in *Cambridge Ancient History*, 3. 206).

The Unity of the Book

Much ink has been wasted in an attempt to break up the text of Nahum into alleged basic documents, additions and redactional interpolation. Nahum was a poet, and the intrusion of what appears to be a portion of an alphabetical psalm (1: 2–10) in no way proves the insertion of alien matter into the text. In fact, to give semblance to this theory requires a quite unacceptable tampering with verse order, and emendation. Nahum did not necessarily write progressively from the first verse to the last. His psalm was a part of a major whole, and is not irrelevant to the theme. Nor can the intervening passage (1: 11–2: 2) be dismissed as an editor's insertion. The canonicity of the book has been generally accepted from early times. The taunt of the Sanhedrists (Jn 7: 52) is an angry retort, and can be used only against the identification of Capernaum as the prophet's birthplace. The text of the book is well-preserved.

The Value of the Book

Nahum's poem presents certain truths. The first is that there is a moral law woven into history which works inexorably to a certain climax. It is a reflection of the justice of God. God may seem to tarry, but inevitably his will moves to its overwhelming end. The poet's faith in this is absolute. As James Russell Lowell put it:

> Careless seems the great Avenger; history's
> pages but record
> One death-grapple in the darkness 'twixt old
> systems and the Word;
> Truth forever on the scaffold. Wrong forever on
> the throne . . .
> Yet that scaffold sways the future, and behind
> the dim unknown,
> Standeth God within the shadows, keeping
> watch upon His own.

But the nineteenth-century American had the advantage of the demonstration which Christ and Calvary gave. Nahum, six centuries before Christ's coming, had to hold faith more desperately, as he and his people watched the ebb and flow of empires, and drew from the mighty spectacle the laws and principles of history.

And today? It is sad to read the closing comments of George Adam Smith's eloquent commentary, written at the end of the Victorian Age. He sees danger only in the inroads into Britain of alien elements. Britain, creative, with colonizing genius, 'carrying everywhere the spirit which had made her strong at home', bore no resemblance, the great geographer and Old Testament scholar said, to Assyria and Babylonia, exhausted by war, betrayed by alien admixture, bound to break at the first disaster. 'If we only be true,' he concludes, 'to our ideals of righteousness and religion, if our patriotism continues moral and sincere, we shall have the power to absorb the foreign elements which throng to us in commerce, and stamp them

with our own spirit.'

About the same time Rudyard Kipling in his *Recessional* warned his fellow-countrymen, on the morrow of Victoria's diamond jubilee:

Lo! all our own pomp of yesterday
Is one with Nineveh and Tyre.
Judge of the nations, spare us yet,
Lest we forget: lest we forget!

Without comment let us lay these more recent words, three generations old, beside Nahum's small book. Like John, raising his taunt song of prophecy over persecuting Rome, many in this age have thought such scorn of fallen tyrannies. We indeed know Christ and wider wisdom, but let this book not be cast aside as dated and irrelevant.

ANALYSIS

I   EPIPHANY OF THE DIVINE AVENGER (1: 1–15)

II   NINEVEH BESIEGED, STORMED AND SACKED (2: 1–13)

III THE DOOM OF THE CITY OF BLOOD (3: 1–19)

I. EPIPHANY OF THE DIVINE AVENGER (1: 1–15)

1–9. In this vivid Psalm God is shown as the Lord of Nature and of History. His coming and His passing-by are described as a tempest sweeping east from the rocky land of Bashan to the ridge of Carmel by the sea, and drying the young foliage on Lebanon. Or else it is like the heaving of the earth, when the Lord appears, or the fervour of volcanic fires. So, when the time is ripe, a wind of fury which blows where it will, comes the tornado of an angry God on Nineveh (1–6).

But the same Lord is tender to those who wait for him, and under the shadow of the ruthless empire, the cowering peoples had waited long (7). They are safe, as the whirlwind of vengeance passes by like a flood down a wadi floor. He pursues His enemies into the darkness of the tempest (8). 'No adversaries dare oppose him twice' (9, NEB); 'Not twice will trouble arise' (George Adam Smith). There is pathos in the words. Habakkuk may have heard the choir of the Levites sing this psalm, when he was a boy. As a man, he saw the power of Babylon arise to take over the power, the destructiveness and imperialism of Nineveh.

10–15. It is easy to catch Nahum's note of exultation. One must see Assyria as her victims saw her, remember the gasping piles of living bodies, with hands cut off and eyes gouged out, left to die in agony, the nobles flayed

alive the helpless prisoners staked through the stomach, the pyramids of heads, the smoking waste of cities . . . George Adam Smith writes: 'Let us place ourselves among the people, who for so long a time had been thwarted, crushed and demoralised by the most brutal empire which was ever suffered to roll its force across the world, and we shall sympathise with the author who for the moment will feel nothing about his God, save that He is a God of vengeance. Like the grief of a bereaved man, the vengeance of an enslaved people has hours sacred to itself' (*The Book of the Twelve Prophets*; II, p. 90).

The prophet sees the world's tyrants as a flash flood, a wall of water sweeping past and away. The image is extended to cover those engulfed, afflicted for a season and rescued (12), the staff of the aggressor and the bonds of his servitude burst asunder (13). And how true the grim prophecy of the next verse. The garden city is to become a graveyard of its beauty and its greatness. Then vividly, in the closing verse of the chapter, the congregation are bidden lift their eyes to the northern skyline where the feet of the messenger, like the runner who brought the news of Marathon to Athens, will be heard, bringing the news that the tyrant is down, the terror past. Those who remember 1918 and 1945, will understand the jubilation. 'Wicked men shall never again overrun you' (NEB).

II. NINEVEH BESIEGED, STORMED AND SACKED (2: 1–13)

2. It seems likely that the first two verses are transposed and should be read in reverse order as in NEB. It does seem logical that at this point, with the news of the tyrant's fall crossing the mountains, the hope which shone at the time of Josiah's revival should find expression—that of a reunited land. Assuming that Jacob means the Northern Kingdom, and, that Israel means Judah, then this meaning emerges (Isa. 9: 8). Isaiah (ch. 5) develops the figure of the vine and this significance.

1, 3–13. With these verses, says C. V. Pilcher (*Three Hebrew Prophets*, p. 71) 'we come to the flaming centre of Nahum's book, to the powerful and vivid lyric which has earned him his immortality as a lord of language.' Verses 10 and 11 of the first chapter could in fact belong to this section, as v. 1 seems to do, and to assume some disruption of order in no way diminishes the authority of the book.

The storming and capture of Nineveh runs before the eyes in this wild poem like a film. The hammer is the battering ram, mounted against the gates (1). The chariot and cavalry screen races, shields flashing, in a wide line in the forefront of the assault (3, 4). The wall is rushed, and such towers as are shown in the Assyrians' own reliefs are thrust forward to overtop the walls and clear the battlements of the defending bowmen (5). Then comes the crowning stratagem. The Tigris, or some interconnecting system of irrigation canals is dammed, and the waters let down on the city in a swift and devastating flood (6), and 'Nineveh has become like a pool of water, like the waters round her, which are ebbing away' (8, NEB). The pitiable train of captives from queen to slave girl, go out moaning and beating their breasts. Many a wall in Nineveh had depicted such scenes where whole populations perish under the Assyrian assault, and, past their tortured dead, lines of captives are led, with arms bound agonizingly over shoulder yokes, or led by cords hooked into the nostrils. As Nineveh had done so was it done to her.

The victors leap upon the spoil, the looted treasure of Nineveh's victims (9) as the anguished remnants of the conquered watch (10). The imagery then becomes striking. Lions roamed in game parks in Nineveh, and many Assyrian sculptures show lion hunts with heavy-featured, bearded kings on chariots striking down the great beasts with arrows from powerful bows. One fresco actually shows a lioness, roaring savagely as it drags its hind quarters, its spine smashed by one arrow. Ashurbanipal is shown in another relief, in full royal dress, pouring a libation on the heads of four enormous dead lions stretched side by side before an altar. And now it is all over. Those

that take the sword perish by the sword . . .

'Assyria', wrote George Adam Smith with his usual eloquence, 'was the great Besieger of man. It is siege, siege, siege which Amos, Hosea and Isaiah tell their people they shall feel . . . It is siege, irresistible and full of fury, which Assyria records as her own glory. Miles of sculpture are covered with masses of troops marching upon some Syrian or Median fortress. Scaling ladders and enormous engines are pushed forward to the walls under cover of showers of arrows . . .' Nahum but describes what the lands of the Middle East had feared for longer than any man who was alive could remember. And now it was over, and a great poet was loose upon the theme.

III. THE DOOM OF THE CITY OF BLOOD (3: 1–19)

The vivid passage which constitutes the first half of this chapter begins with the customary prophetic cry of woe (1). Then the ghastly scene overwhelms his imagination again, and in brief staccato clauses, harsh-sounding, almost incoherent in the tumult of their imagery, come two long verses of battle sounds and sights, ending strikingly with a thrice-repeated 'corpses . . . corpses . . . corpses' (2, 3). And why? Because, like a beautiful wanton, an image John repeats of Rome in Revelation, Nineveh had lured the nations to their death. And so there comes upon her the ultimate degradation of the convicted harlot, in language almost too violent and vivid to utter (4, 5, 6). And a numbed and astonished world looks with incredulity on what had seemed for generations an impossibility. 'Nineveh is laid waste—and who shall shed a tear?' 'Nahum,' says Smith, 'gives voice to no national passions, but to the outraged conscience of mankind.' And so it was, by seeing the universal suffering which the great river-city spread through helpless nations, Nahum expressed for Israel, paradoxically, the idea of a common humanity.

BIBLIOGRAPHY

EATON, J. H., *Obadiah, Nahum, Habakkuk and Zephaniah. TC* (London, 1961).

GOSLINGA, C., *Nahum's Godsspraak tegen Ninevé* (Zutphen, 1923).

HALDAR, A., *Studies in the Book of Nahum* (Uppsala, 1947).

HAPPEL, O., *Das Buch des Propheten Nahum* (Würzburg, 1902).

HAUPT, P., 'The Book of Nahum', JBL 26 (1907), pp. 1–15, 151–164.

HUMBERT, P., 'Le problème du livre de Nahoum', *Revue d'Histoire et de philosophie Religieuses* 12 (1932), 1 f(f).

MAIER, W. A., *The Book of Nahum: A Commentary* (St. Louis, 1959).

PILCHER, CHARLES VENN, *The Three Prophets* (London, 1931).

SMITH, G. A., *The Book of the Twelve Prophets*. EB.

Volume 2 (London, 1898), revised edition (London 1928), reprinted (Grand Rapids, 1950).

WATTS, J. D. W., *Joel, Obadiah, Jonah, Nahum, Habakkuk and Zephaniah*. CBC (Cambridge, 1975).

HABAKKUK

A. G. NUTE

Introduction

Habakkuk is exceptional for the intellectual honesty and the moral and spiritual integrity with which he faces up to profound issues. He grapples with these in a way which can only be described as courageous. The conflict which erupts in his heart and mind is occasioned by an inability to reconcile the tragic realities of the historical situation with a conviction that all history is under the direct control of a sovereign, omnipotent and holy God. The inescapable facts appear flatly to contradict a fundamental and cherished belief. Habakkuk finds it impossible to ignore the problem; indeed the need to resolve it becomes, for him, imperative and urgent.

The prophecy begins in a storm of anguished question and complaint. As it proceeds its turbulence finds an answering echo in the tempestuous events of the Exodus, vividly described in poetic form in chapter 3. At length, however, the turmoil subsides and Habakkuk emerges tranquil and confident. In a memorable, triumphant ode he exclaims . . . 'yet I will rejoice in the LORD, I will be joyful in God my Savior'. This goal has been reached not in consequence of a successful unravelling of the mystery, but through response to the central revelation of ch. 2, v. 4—'the righteous will live by his faith'.

The Prophet

Whoever eavesdrops on this agonized interchange with God must feel, at length, that he 'knows' Habakkuk. And yet in other respects the prophet remains an almost complete stranger. His name has been associated with an Assyrian plant name; it is also said to derive from a Heb. root signifying 'to clasp, or embrace'. The latter would not be inappropriate for one who, Jacob-like, clings to Him with whom in desperation he has wrestled. It is doubtless this meaning that gave rise to the conjecture which identifies Habakkuk with the son of the Shunammite woman (2 Kg. 4: 16). Both this, and the further suggestion which links him with Isaiah's watchman (Isa. 21: 6; cf. Hab. 2: 1), may be discounted. On the positive side, though no reliance should be placed upon the reference in the apocryphal story 'Bel and the Dragon' to the effect that Habakkuk was 'of the tribe of Levi', nevertheless he could well have been a Levite. The musical terms which annotate his psalm (ch. 3) would suggest this. Certainly he was a poet of no mean order and possessed considerable literary skill. Some see Habakkuk as a member of a group or guild of 'Temple ministers' (Eaton, p. 81), and this seems the more likely if it can be shown that the book bears signs of being a liturgical composition. Chapter 3 certainly has this characteristic, though the theory that it was presented in dramatic form (*cantata* is the word used by Lindblom, p. 254) is far more conjectural and a number of scholars express reservations about this (see Rowley, *Worship in Ancient Israel*, p. 170).

The one clear statement about Habakkuk occurs in the heading—'Habakkuk the prophet' (1: 1; see also 3: 1). Such an introduction is relatively uncommon (cf. Hag. 1: 1 and Zech. 1: 1), but what significance is to be deduced from it, is not easy to decide. Inasmuch as Habakkuk's ministry is the reverse of the prophet's traditional role, in that he deals with God for the people rather than dealing with the people for God, it is conceivable that the title is attached as a claim to the office. Certainly he fulfils the divine criterion of the prophet as outlined by Jeremiah, for he stands 'in the council of the LORD to see or to hear his word', thereafter faithfully to transmit it (Jer. 23: 18, 22).

Historical Setting

The setting of the prophecy has been the subject of considerable debate and a number of theories have been advanced. The only certain key is to be found in the reference to the Babylonians (1: 6); even so, some have argued that this should read *Kittim* (Cypriot Greeks) rather than *Kasdim* (Babylonians mg. Chaldeans). This emendation would have the effect of placing the prophecy in the days of Alexander the Great (late 4th cent. B.C.). It is said that this would fit better the Hebrew text of ch. 1, v. 9, but as it is exceedingly difficult to establish the precise wording of this verse it seems far too precarious a ground for such a radical alteration, especially as serious misgivings are commonly felt about the change in v. 6. There is fairly general agreement that the Kasdim were the new force under the Chaldean Nabopolassar which overthrew and replaced the Assyrian empire towards the end of the 7th cent. B.C. Nineveh, capital of Assyria, fell to the Chaldeans and their allies in August 612 B.C.; thereafter the empire of the Babylonians was well and truly established.

Any attempt at dating the prophecy must face one crucial question: Is Habakkuk's description of the Chaldeans prophetic foresight or is it a straightforward reporting of facts already well-known at the time? It reads more like the latter. If this is so, it was probably uttered either just before or soon after the critical battle of Carchemish (605 B.C.) when the Chaldean forces, led by Nabopolassar's son, the crown prince Nebuchadrezzar, routed the Egyptians. The fact that the prophet is warned that he will be greatly shocked by the news about to be disclosed to him (1: 5), suggests a date before rather than after this event. After 605 B.C., Habakkuk, in common with his contemporaries, must have been well aware that the subjugation of Judah by the Chaldeans was inevitable. It could only be a matter of time.

The other point at issue is the identification of those responsible for the injustice and oppression which provoke the prophet's initial complaint (1: 2–4). The case for an external enemy such as the Assyrians inflicting these conditions upon Israel, generally relies upon a dislocation of the text. Various rearrangements of the verses have been proposed, but this seems the least satisfactory way of dealing with the difficulty. Some commentators refrain from this device and yet maintain that an external foe is in view. This makes the argument of the succeeding paragraphs less convincing than when the troubles are regarded as internal. The latter is the general interpretation, and is the one adopted here.

The untimely death of Josiah, inexplicably interfering in Pharaoh Necho's advance on the weakened Assyria (609 B.C.), brought Israel under Egyptian control. It also meant an abandonment of those reforms which Josiah had introduced. Largely ineffectual as they were, the state of affairs that followed proved infinitely worse. The people chose as king, Jehoahaz. Within a few months Pharaoh Necho deposed him, removed him in chains to Egypt and replaced him with another of Josiah's sons, Jehoiakim (2 Chr. 36: 4). Those evils that had marked the reign of Manasseh now flooded back. Corruption and cruelty were rampant, and the victims found no redress. Habakkuk's brief agonized portrayal of the situation in his day (1: 2–4) aptly corresponds to this tragic period of Judah's history.

Support for this setting of the prophecy may also be found in certain parallels between Habakkuk and Jeremiah which would indicate that they could well have been contemporaries. Jeremiah's outline of the character of the despicable Jehoiakim and the oppressive nature of his regime (Jer. 22: 13–19) answers almost precisely those conditions which Habakkuk de-

plores (1: 3, 4). In addition, their reaction is almost identical. Jeremiah, too, questions and expostulates with God as he struggles with the intractable problem of the prosperity of the wicked (Jer. 12: 1–4; see also 13: 17; 15: 10–18; 20: 7–18).

A test of the credibility of the historical situation envisaged is whether it provides a reasonable framework for the unfolding dialogue of the book; and that, preferably, without recourse to a rearrangement of the text. Against the background as outlined above the thread of the dialogue in ch. 1 would proceed as follows. Habakkuk complains bitterly at the failure of the Lord to intervene for the correction of the widespread abuses in Judah, concerning which he has been making persistent and urgent representation to Him (vv. 2–4). God's reply is to the effect that action has already been taken in this matter. Incredible as it may appear to His servant, He has selected and prepared the Babylonians to be the instrument in His hand for the chastisement of His people. Moreover, He is about to use them in this way (vv. 5–11). This calls forth an expression of horror from the prophet. He regards it as inconceivable that a holy God should be willing to employ such a proud, rapacious and idolatrous nation for the execution of His purpose (vv. 12–17). As far as chs. 2 and 3 are concerned the historical setting is not of the same importance.

For certain scholars the problem is resolved by regarding the events and Habakkuk's reaction to them as a mosaic, untrammelled by a chronological sequence. This certainly has the advantage of softening some of the more glaring difficulties which the text presents. But whichever approach is adopted, there is no need to view the prophecy as other than a coherent whole.

Value

Fortunately, the true value of the book is independent of all such considerations. Its principal lesson, as its abiding relevance, is discovered as one traces the path by which the prophet comes at length to the peace of faith. From the Qumran community (providing the earliest extant commentary on Hab.) to the present day, where men attempt to think through the age-old problem of evil and seek to relate the grim facts of history to a God of justice and power who holds all in His control, they find themselves drawn to Habakkuk. In this engrossing record they encounter an individual as he passionately attempts a theodicy. More important, they hear the word which demands, as it inculcates, the virtues of faith and patience. This, as the NT shows, is the primary and timeless challenge of the book (Rom. 1: 17; Gal. 3: 11; Heb. 10: 37, 38).

ANALYSIS

I. A DRAMATIC DIALOGUE
(1: 1–2: 20)
i. Title (1: 1)
The introduction is marked by simplicity and a sense of spiritual authority. Habakkuk's name and office are stated but attention is concentrated on the nature and origin of his message. **The oracle** indicates a divine communication received, to be transmitted as an authoritative, solemn declaration. 'Burden' (AV, RV) stresses the responsibility which devolves upon the human agent. (For a detailed examination of *maśśā'* see Zechariah, *TOTC*, pp. 162 f., *Additional Note*.) The expression **received** leaves deliberately vague the means whereby this disclosure was transmitted (cf. Am. 3: 7).
ii. Habakkuk remonstrates with God (1: 2–4)
The conditions: A spirit of anarchy is abroad and, as today, it employs as weapons **destruction and violence**. As a result of bitterness between rival factions, **there is strife, and conflict abounds**; on every hand there exists moral chaos. Not long before, under Josiah, **the law** (*torah*) had been rediscovered and reapplied to the life of the community (2 Kg. 21, 22). Now it is once again inoperative (**paralyzed**, lit. '*numb*'). Intended by God for the direction of the lives of His people in matters moral as well as ritual, it is being openly flouted and, in consequence, brought into disrepute. Everywhere might seems to be on the side of wrong, so that 'the wicked gets the better of the upright' (JB). The **righteous** look in vain for support or redress from the courts. The **justice** they are offered is but a travesty of the same for it **is perverted**. What champions of truth and purity there are find themselves mocked or ignored. The law (*torah*) is rejected and, in consequence, justice (*mišpāṭ*) is abandoned.
The effect: For Habakkuk the grimness of this tragic state of affairs is accentuated because he

sees the situation all too clearly (3a). Indeed, he virtually censures God for compelling him to gaze upon the desperate plight of his people. An escapist attitude, however desirable it may seem (cf. Ps. 55: 6, 7; Jer. 9: 2), is impossible. Sensitivity both to the wrongs and to the needs of society, arises from a relationship with God.

But the deepest problem and the root cause of his distress is that God appears both silent —**do not listen**, and inactive—**do not save** (2). This, far more than the lawlessness, injustice and oppression, occasions the prophet's perplexity. His cry is **how long?** (cf. Ps. 89: 46; Jer. 12: 4; Zech. 1: 12; Rev. 6: 10). His intercessions have been urgent and sustained, and indeed his alarm has at times erupted in an ejaculatory cry of **"Violence!"** (a one-word prayer). He is mystified and aggrieved because the God he knows and whom he addresses by His covenant name *Yahweh*—**LORD**, fails to intervene. But worse is to come: 'the enigmas of the divine guidance of history are to grow even darker' (von Rad, p. 190).
iii. God answers (1: 5–11)
Look at the nations: (cf. 'look at injustice' v. 3). Habakkuk's gaze needs a change of direction. It also requires to be focused as the imperative, **look**, implies. The answer he receives corresponds to the two-fold complaint he has made. God informs him that despite all appearances to the contrary He is not inactive—**I am going to do something in your days**. And if He has been silent it is only because of an unwillingness on the part of the prophet and the people he represents to receive the solution God is proposing—**you would not believe even if you were told** (cf. Isa. 53: 1). God was not, as Habakkuk imagined, standing back and allowing matters to proceed unchecked. He had already commenced to act, but in a manner which would prove unbelievable and wholly unacceptable. The duplication **watch —and be utterly amazed** indicates to Habak-

kuk how completely baffled he will be when confronted by the incomprehensibility of the divine plan. Preconceived ideas may well have made it more difficult for him to accept God's answer, yet his prayers cannot be reckoned as unavailing.

Note: Paul uses this verse in his synagogue sermon at Pisidian Antioch (Ac. 13: 40, 41). He quotes it from the LXX 'which lent itself better to his purpose' (F. F. Bruce, *Acts—The English Text*, p. 279) and proceeds to apply it to the amazing salvation offered in the gospel, as well as to the staggering judgment which awaits those who refuse it.

The following vv. (6–11) describe the weapon forged by the Almighty as the rod of His anger (cf. Isa. 10: 5). It is enough to make the stoutest heart quail. **I am raising up** can hardly refer to the establishment of the Babylonians as a world-power, but to their attention being turned towards Judah. Of the picture drawn in these verses of the Babylonians forces it has been said, it 'does not accord with the actual progress and character of Nabopolassar's armies after 625' (Eaton, p. 89). This, however, seems not to recognize sufficiently the poetic and dramatic nature of this portrayal of the foe.

It is likely that Habakkuk already knew of the immense military strength and the character of the Babylonians. Such was their ferocity and determination that it seemed nothing could withstand them. Driven on by selfish ambition and greed they **seize dwelling places not their own**. Threatened invasion by them leaves a population terror-stricken (7a, 9a). They recognize no codes of military conduct, they own no superior power; **a law to themselves** they **promote their own honor**. The nature of these standards, which they alone determine, may be gauged from the panic they inspire.

Powerful imagery is employed to depict the enemy's cavalry: like **leopards** for the swiftness and suddenness with which they descend upon their victims, like **wolves at dusk** for the ferocity and relentlessness with which they pursue the foe, **like a vulture swooping to devour** the prey for the unexpectedness of their attack.

Though the text of the remaining verses of this paragraph (9–11) is uncertain, the picture it conveys is not. **violence** is more accurately rendered 'plunder' (9a, JB). The following clause is regarded by the majority of translators as referring to the 'faces' of the enemy. 'A sea of faces rolls on' (NEB), 'their faces scorching like an east wind' (JB). If the latter is accepted, the figure of a sand-storm may be behind the next statement: **and gather prisoners like sand**. Wholesale deportation follows an attack. They are not intimidated by men of renown

nor deterred by the strongest fortress. **they build earthen ramps and capture them** refers to the siege mound raised against the walled city enabling the attackers to advance and storm the bastion (cf. Jer. 32: 24). The description comes to its climax with the words **they sweep past like the wind and go on**. Their career of conquest is as devastating as a hurricane. Throughout this sketch of the Babylonian forces the dominant feature is that of their swift and irresistible progress.

The principle by which they operate is one which has motivated many a despotic power before and since—'might is right' (7b). In their case, however, this evil is compounded and made more heinous by the fact that they deify and worship their invincibility—**whose own strength is their god** (11). It is this, above all else, that merits for them the verdict—**guilty men**. Little wonder then that this section needed to be prefaced with the warning, **be utterly amazed. For I am going to do something in your days that you would not believe even if you were told** (5). God speaks of this horrific prospect as a direct, personal action of His (note the repeated **I am** 5, 6). This cannot be expected to have any other effect than to plunge His servant into deep perplexity.

iv. The prophet protests (1: 12–17)

Habakkuk, about to voice his objection to the divine strategy, first steadies himself with a restatement of belief. (i) God is eternal. This he doubtless finds to be a comforting truth (cf. Dt. 33: 27; Ps. 90: 1). The corollary **we will not die** (cf. Mal. 3: 6) may well represent an emendation by an early scribe for whom the linking of 'God' and 'death' was regarded as irreverent (cf. 'who never dies' JB, 'the immortal' NEB). (ii) **LORD**—He who in covenant love binds Himself to bless His people. (iii) **God**—supreme, mighty, reliable. (iv) **Holy One**—holy in character and righteous in dealings (a conviction the prophet refuses to relinquish). (v) **Rock**—the permanent refuge of all who trust in Him. Thus, Habakkuk recites what he knows of God, and employing twice the personal and possessive pronoun **my**, takes a firm grip upon the one great reality. In addition, he confirms that he understands the plan which God has made known to him, namely, that the Babylonians are to be an instrument **to punish** (12b). This combination of faith and understanding constitutes, on the one hand, the vantage point from which he faces the crisis, and on the other, the cause of his perplexity. This perplexity he now brings out into the open.

The course proposed by God seems in flagrant contradiction of His character. How can One whose eyes must ever consume evil (Rev. 1: 14) **look on** ('countenance' NEB) the treachery of evil men? **13. treacherous:** ('faithless' RSV cf. 'faithfulness' 2: 4b mg.) Earlier Habakkuk had deplored that 'the wicked *hem in* the righteous' (4), he now faces the fact that **the wicked swallow up those more righteous than themselves**. Innocent victims are to suffer a worse fate than before, and God appears to be but a passive spectator—**silent**. Far more baffling, He is seen to be actively employing an impure agent for the execution of His purpose (12b, 14). The immediate relationship between God's actions and man's is underlined by referring to both by the same metaphor (cf. **you** of God, 14; **he/his** of Chaldeans, 15–17). With his protest in full spate one must wonder if the prophet has gone too far in his reproach of God (14), and whether an element of exaggeration has crept into the picture of the fisherman worshipping his net. The outburst comes to a head with a challenging question being thrown down for God to answer (17).

v. God replies (2: 1–5)
In expressing his resolve to resort to the watchtower there to await God's reply, Habakkuk both employs a familiar figure of speech (Isa. 21: 6, 8) and adopts the accepted approach of one who seeks a divine communication (Ps. 5: 3; Mic. 7: 7). His is a spirit of dependence and expectancy; at the same time, his language indicates an attitude which is 'bold', if not defiant. His faith is under siege and he finds it hard to imagine that any relief can be forthcoming. The problem he has posed appears insoluble; even so, he determines to wait and watch for an answer. He anticipates that exception will be taken to his **complaint** and that he will be 'called to account' (Knox). In view of this, in addition to looking to **see what he will say to me**, Habakkuk occupies himself considering 'what I shall reply when challenged' (NEB). Cf. Syr. *he will answer*, followed by JB. 'what answer he will make'.

The actual oracle is prefaced by certain instructions regarding it. **revelation** describes the mode of communication to the prophet (see note on 1: 1), as well as its nature as far as the wider audience is concerned. The command to **write down the revelation** ensures exactness in its transmission; **make it plain on tablets** guarantees its publicity. The idiom **may run with it** represents not the influence of the word but its legibility; it must be 'easily read' (JB). A further reason why the revelation must be recorded in writing could be to stress the immutability of its contents for circumstances will appear to deny its validity and apparent delay in its outworking will suggest that it has been annulled. The prophet is assured that such will not be the case (3; cf. Heb. 10: 37).

The vital truth now stated consists of 'two unchangeable things'—sin does not go unpunished, and, righteousness is always rewarded

(4). God insists that He has not abandoned the moral ordering of His world.

The author of Heb. 10: 38 appeals to the first half of v. 4 (loosely quoted from the LXX) to emphasize that lack of perseverance is equivalent to being **not upright**—a condition which ends in failure; but this he makes subordinate to the happier truth—'my righteous one will live by faith'. Paul's use of the text (Rom. 1: 17; Gal. 3: 11) concentrates upon the exercise of faith rather than, as here, upon its evidence —'He strips faithfulness to its core of faith in God' (L. C. Allen, *Vox Evangelica*, 1964, p. 8). The promise **will live** becomes 'eternal life' (Rom. 6: 22 f.) and 'righteousness' man's acceptance with God (Rom. 3: 21–26). Clearly, the revelation made to Habakkuk is the gospel in embryo.

For the prophet, if it was a solution to an intellectual difficulty that he sought, it was not granted. Instead, and far more important, the answer given relates to the practical situation and is addressed to his personal spiritual dilemma. He is assured that though all around seems to contradict the fact, the wicked who proudly deviates from God's path 'shall fail' RSV. As surely, the individual marked by loyalty to God and by integrity will 'be preserved and prosper' (Allen, *op. cit.*). The key may not unlock the dark mystery of divine providence, but it will admit its user to a realm of increased confidence in God and, therefore, of peace.

Verse 5 presents a number of textual and exegetical problems. It is probably best viewed as a link verse connecting v. 4 with the section that follows. In it the prophet portrays an inebriate whose conduct is both foolish and dangerous: doing so, he amplifies the reference to the one who **is puffed up** and summarizes the extended description contained in the rest of the chapter. (The Qumran commentary reads 'wealth' for **wine**, so also JB. If misused, wealth as wine proves a passport to catastrophe.)

vi. The song of the five woes (2: 6–19)
In uttering maledictions upon the Babylonian oppressor the prophet acts as the spokesman for many (6a). The poetic form he adopts is that of the 'taunt-song' (cf. Isa. 14: 3–23; Mic. 2: 4). Each stanza with its **Woe to him** expands the statement of v. 4a and from various standpoints illustrates the fundamental principle that sin brings its own nemesis. In the retribution that is meted out there is always an element of appropriateness; the punishment is made to fit the crime. In the main, this takes the form of retaliation on the part of the exploited and oppressed, though the dispositions of the sovereign LORD are not entirely ignored (13, 16).

Woe 1 (6–8)
Māšāl, which in this context is well translated **taunt**, has as its basic meaning 'a comparison'

(cf. Ezek. 24: 3 'allegory'), and this is not wholly absent from its use here. The reference to **extortion** and **debtors** which, by some, has been taken literally to refer to features of Jehoiakim's reign, is probably better understood in its figurative sense of the Babylonians' heartless policy of sequestration. Nothing restrains their insatiable greed, even though it involves **bloodshed and wholesale destruction**. Little wonder that the sufferers cry out **how long**? (6; cf. 1: 2—see comment). But the day of reckoning will come, 'pledges' (RSV) will be redeemed, though in a wholly unexpected fashion. The survivors from among the enemy's victims will counter-attack with devastating effect, the plunderer will be **plundered**.

Woe 2 (9–11)

Comfort and fancied security have been procured by illegitimate means—**unjust gain**. It is a case of 'the unacceptable face of capitalism'. The price paid has included the **ruin of many peoples**. The eventual cost will, in fact, be the forfeiture of **life**. The first instalment of this payment is the accusation of a guilty conscience. The very materials of the house constructed from these ill-gotten gains, find voice and testify against the owner-occupier (11; cf. Jas 5: 3). Even though he **set his nest on high** it fails to afford the anticipated protection.

Woe 3 (12–14)

Babylon is not specifically mentioned but a comparison with Isaiah's taunt song (Isa. 14: 3–23) and Jeremiah's oracle against Babylon (Jer. 50; 51, esp. 51: 58) leaves no doubt as to the identity of the city threatened with destruction. 'Futile' is the verdict uttered by **the LORD Almighty** on the achievements of the unscrupulous; their end will be emptiness and loss. In striking contrast to this bleak prospect, is the bright hope of the universal breakthrough of God's **glory** (14, refracted from Isa. 11: 9).

> These things shall vanish all;
> The city of God remaineth.   (Luther)

Woe 4 (15–17)

The Babylonians' scorched earth policy involved deforestation—**violence . . . to Lebanon**, with consequent 'havoc' (NEB) to wildlife—**destruction of animals**. (Both are a matter of divine concern, Dt. 20: 19; Jon. 4: 11.). To excessive cruelty—**man's blood** and the obliteration of whole **cities**, they added sacrilege, for the 'earth' (RSV) they devastated 'is the LORD's' (Ps. 24: 1). Such outrage carries within it the seeds of its own destruction (17). Moreover, the Lord Himself ensures that this conduct, likened to the obscenities of a drunken orgy (15), will be avenged with an unmistakable exactitude (16).

Woe 5 (18–19)

The recurrent theme of the song, that sin recoils upon the sinner, sounds once more in this final stanza. This **woe** is uttered upon the idolator.

The inexplicable folly of his practice is exposed. Effort (**a man has carved it**) and expense (**gold and silver**) are involved in the idol's construction, yet it is impotent to help or advise. But the man **who says to wood, 'Come to life!' Or to a lifeless stone, 'Wake up!'** demonstrates that idolatry is no innocuous folly; it is injurious, for it destroys man's basic intelligence. Sin, whatever its nature, does not go unpunished, and the punishment is essentially retributive.

vii. Postscript (2: 20)

Abruptly attention is diverted from the lifeless idol to **the LORD. . . in his holy temple**. The idolator in his folly is vocal before the 'dumb stone'; **all the earth** should **be silent** in the presence of the living God. At the solemn call—'Pray silence!', the heart and mind are subdued, and yet alerted to the majestic revelation which is about to be made.

II. A PSALM (3: 1–19)

It is claimed that 'a majority of critics deny this poem to the prophet Habakkuk' (J. B. Hyatt, *Peake's Commentary*, p. 639). There are, however, a number of scholars who find no difficulty in taking the heading—**A prayer of Habakkuk** literally. For some, the chapter has little or no 'direct connexion with the preceding prophecy' and its appearance here is attributed to an editor who wished to bring together all the extant work of Habakkuk' (H. L. Ellison, *Men Spake from God*, p. 76). Others, and notably Eaton, see it as the *coup de grâce* of the whole composition (*TC*, pp. 83 f., 108).

If behind the 'faithfulness' by which 'the righteous . . . live' lies 'faith' (2: 4 and mg), this chapter presents us with the object of such faith. The theophany is the ground of prayer (2), the subject of meditation (3–15), and the source of trembling joy (16–19). While the psalm is essentially personal (**I/my** 2, 16, 18, 19), the musical annotations (1, 19b, as well as the triple **Selah**) indicate that it was designed for public worship.

i. The God of judgment and salvation (3: 1–16)

Shigionoth (plural of **Shiggaion**, Ps. 7: 1) is believed to refer to the wild beat of the song, its tempo corresponding to the profound emotions it describes and is likely to engender.

The 'report' (RSV) of the LORD and His **deeds** at which the prophet confesses himself to be awestruck, doubtless covers both the revelation imparted by the pageant of sacred history (3–15), and that given by direct divine communication (1: 5 f.; 2: 2–4). In the one, God's notable dealings with Israel in the past are remembered; through the other, the crises which the future holds are glimpsed. As for the present, the familiar picturesque expression 'in the midst of the years' conveys an impression of spiritual doldrums. The need for an *evident* renewal of God's activity is acute; it is for this that Habakkuk prays. But appreciating that to pray for revival is to invite judgment, he asks that **wrath** (present turmoil and future discipline) be tempered with **mercy** (cf. Jer. 10: 24).

Initially it was God's role in human history which troubled the prophet. He now sees God's ways in history as proof of His power, both in the realm of creation and redemption (3–15). This section of the psalm is dominated by the revelation of God's might achieving the Exodus-deliverance for His people; bringing them out of bondage, through the wilderness and dispossessing their enemies before them. Echoes of earlier ascriptions of praise to God for this His work, reverberate throughout (*e.g.* the songs of Moses, Dt. 33: 2; Deborah and Barak, Jg. 5: 4 f.; David, Ps. 68: 7 f.; Asaph, Ps. 77: 16–19, and Miriam, Exod. 15: 21). The poetry is turbulent, the text is not easy to establish (see *NBC*³ on v. 9), and many of the words used are obscure. The pronouns change from third person (3–6), to first (7) and then to second (8–15). The style befits the subject which is dramatic and for Habakkuk himself literally overwhelming (16).

In his vision the prophet sees the Almighty advancing from the wilderness, 'marching in the greatness of his strength'. The word for **God**—*Ēlōah*—is found almost exclusively in the poetic scriptures (40 out of 52 occurrences in Job). **Teman**, an area to the north of Edom, and **Paran**, which lies beyond it towards Sinai, represent the territory which witnessed the birth of Israel both as a nation and as the covenant people of God. (It was to this region that the querulous Elijah resorted when granted a storm-accompanied theophany 1 Kg. 19: 8–12.) The statement in v. 3b finds a counterpart in the exultant song of the heavenly host (Lk. 2: 14) which celebrated the event which engulfed all earlier manifestations of God to man.

The imagery employed to portray the progress of the invincible Lord is that of a violent storm. Lightning flashes suddenly dispel the enveloping darkness and the night is as day (4a; 4b; cf. Job 26: 14). He is accompanied by the apocalyptic 'dogs of war'—**plague** and **pestilence** (5). His might is absolute: He does not need to move from His place to shake **the earth**, nor do other than 'look' for **the nations** to tremble; before His eternity the timeless **mountains** and **hills** depart (6). Little wonder that the frail **tents of Cushan** and the **dwellings of Midian** are 'terrified' (JB).

The rivers become raging torrents; the sea is lashed into a fury. The question arises—is there not something deeper and more significant here than the operation of natural laws? Are not the elements His servants, instruments in His hand for the execution of His glorious purpose—

your victorious chariots (8; cf. Ps. 104: 3 f.; 148: 8).

The soliloquy over, Habakkuk's description of the storm continues, though now it is merged with metaphors of battle; the clouds are war-clouds, thunderbolts and lightning flashes are **arrows** which fly from the unsheathed bow (9). All nature is in turmoil as the Lord pursues His triumphant way. Even **the deep**, which some heathen mythologies regarded as a rival to His dominion, **roared** in alarm and threw up 'its hands' (RSV) in surrender (10), whilst **the sun and moon** halt in their courses as the battle proceeds, (11a is a possible allusion to Jos. 10: 12–14). Neither **the earth** nor **the nations** can thwart His imperial progress (12; cf. 6).

Suddenly, as though a lightning flash illumines the darkness (4, 11), the divine objective in the conflict is disclosed—**You came out to deliver your people, to save your anointed one** (13a). Voluntariness and determination, grace and power, lie behind the words. Moreover the words ring with rejoicing, gratitude and confident hope. Nor is this great statement to be confined to the events of Habakkuk's day, or to the fortunes of Israel. It is satisfied only when applied to the advent of Him of whom it was said, 'you are to give him the name Jesus, because he will save his people from their sins' (Mt. 1: 21).

Verses 13b–15 continue to depict in graphic language (abounding in problems for the translator) the defeat of all who array themselves 'against the LORD and his anointed'. The pronoun (**us**, 14) creeps in as the prophet recalls the deliverance experienced when under attack. The vision ends with victory complete. As at the Exodus the **churning** of **the great waters** symbolizes the final overthrow of all the enemy's vaunted power.

To behold the glory of the Lord and to enter into His purposes is an exacting experience (Isa. 6: 1–5; Ezek. 1: 28; Jer. 23: 9; Dan. 10: 8; Mt. 26: 38). Habakkuk found it so. The apprehension he had expressed at the onset of the vision (2) proves wholly warranted for when it is over he is left in a state of collapse (16a). Knowing that it is inevitable that bitter travail must precede the birth of deliverance, the prophet resolutely composes himself to await **the day of calamity** (16b).

ii. The confidence of the godly (3: 17–19)
There is no more moving comment on the prime truth of this prophecy—'the righteous will live by his faith'—than that which is contained in these verses. The affirmation is exquisitely and nobly worded.

The faith Habakkuk professes is no blind faith, for it is exercised in clear prospect of a complete catastrophe (17). Through natural disaster or, more likely, through enemy action, crops fail, cattle are decimated, the nation's economy collapses and famine ensues. His **yet** (18) is worthy to stand alongside the 'even if . . . not' of Shadrach, Meshach and Abednego (Dan. 3: 18), and is only surpassed by Jesus' 'nevertheless' (Mt. 26: 39). It is a submissive and determined faith; better still, it is an exultant one—**I will rejoice . . . I will be joyful**. The secret is to be found in the focus of his faith; its object is **the LORD**. From the repetition of the name and titles of God we may gauge that the prophet has arrived at a renewed appreciation of the One in whom he trusts.

Salvation described in v. 13 is now experienced personally—**God my Savior**—both in adversity (17) and prosperity (19). The path of life may lead through 'the valley of deep darkness' or traverse the **heights**; it matters not to one who is assured that **GOD, the Lord** is in total control, that His goal is salvation and that He Himself is the source and secret of **strength**.

The footnote (19b) signifies that the psalm was sung at the Temple services. In various paraphrases, and notably in William Cowper's *Sometimes a light surprises*, it is sung still. This alone provides testimony to the abiding relevance of the prophecy.

BIBLIOGRAPHY

DAVIDSON, A. B., *Nahum, Habakkuk and Zephaniah*. Cambridge Bible (Cambridge University Press, 1896).

DRIVER, S. R., *The Minor Prophets*. Century Bible (Edinburgh, 1906).

EATON, J. H., *Obadiah to Zephaniah*. TC (London, 1961).

ELLISON, H. L., *Men Spake from God* (London, 1952).

EISSFELDT, O., *The Old Testament: An Introduction* (Oxford, 1965).

GAILEY, J. H., *Micah to Malachi*, Layman's Bible Commentaries (London, 1962).

HARRISON, R. K., *Introduction to the Old Testament* (London, 1970).

LINDBLOM, J., *Prophecy in Ancient Israel* (Oxford), 1962).

PUSEY, E. B., *The Minor Prophets with a Commentary* (London, reprinted 1906).

RAD, G. VON, *Old Testament Theology, Vol. 2* (Edinburgh and London, 1965).

ROWLEY, H. H., *The Faith of Israel* (London, 1956).

ROWLEY, H. H., *Worship in Ancient Israel* (London, 1967).

SMITH, G. A., *The Book of the Twelve Prophets, Vol.2* (London, revised edition 1928).

WATTS, J. D. W., *Joel, Obadiah, Jonah, Nahum, Habakkuk and Zephaniah*. CBC (Cambridge, 1975.

ZEPHANIAH

VICTOR A. S. REID

The Prophet

'Zephaniah', in its present form, means 'Yahweh has hidden', i.e. 'treasures' or 'protects'. Possible, long forgotten, derivation of the name from 'Zephon is Yahweh' (cf. *ICC*, p. 184; Watts, p. 153) involves identification of Yahweh with an important Canaanite deity. While there is evidence that names of some Canaanite deities were used to express facets of Yahweh's character, *e.g.* El Elyon (Gen. 14: 18–24), any such appropriation required stripping the title of its mythological Canaanite concepts, and its transformation into an assertion of Yahweh's sovereignty over the area of life previously claimed for the Canaanite deity. Thus, far from being syncretistic, the adoption was the expression of apologetic for Yahwism and polemic against paganism. It is usually held that Zephaniah's name indicates that he lived during the persecutions of Yahwists, by Manasseh, from which Yahweh protected him.

His genealogy is much longer than the usual prophetic pedigree (cf. *ICC* for details) and traces four generations. Suggested reasons for this are (*a*) to overcome opposition to him because of his African father, 'Cushi' meaning 'Ethiopian', though this does not tally with Dt. 23: 8. (*b*) that 'he probably belonged to a family of some importance' (Ellison). Almost unanimously, commentators identify Hezekiah with the Judaean king, the title 'king' being withheld here and retained for the contemporary monarch Josiah (K. F. Keil).

That Zephaniah may have been a Jerusalemite is indicated by his familiarity with the city (1: 4; 1: 10 ff.) and his focus on Jerusalem as the main subject of his prophecy. He contrasts sharply with Amos, the countryman, and draws no metaphor from the beauty or peace of nature. His prophecy 'is everywhere fire, smoke and darkness, drifting chaff, ruins, nettles, salt-pits, and owls and ravens looking from the windows of desolate palaces' (G. A. Smith, p. 48). His starkness of expression may relate to Zephaniah's youth; the genealogical link with Hezekiah indicating that he was a contemporary of Josiah, who commenced tentative reforms in 626 B.C. at the age of 21. This is balanced by his universalism which is as broad in salvation (3: 9 f.) as in judgment (1: 2 f.), and is based on his belief in the centrality of Israel's covenant commitment to Yahweh.

Date of Writing

The conditions of life in Judah as described by Zephaniah include syncretism and idolatry (1: 1–4), and unjust, corrupt practice among all the ruling classes (1: 8 f.; 3: 1–7). Since the Josianic reformation purged Judah of precisely these corruptions, and the prophecy makes no allusion to reforms, it seems likely to have a pre-reformation date. The ministry of Zephaniah is explicitly placed in Josiah's reign by 1: 1, but it is difficult, though not impossible, to relate the four generations to Hezekiah to such an early date (cf. *IB*). The oracles against foreign nations are perfectly understandable in this context; see commentary on text. If the book was written after tentative reforms in 626, but before the main impetus in 621, the phrase, 'every remnant of Baal' (1: 4) can be accepted as it stands in NIV rather than as 'false worship wholly' (Davidson). For arguments for a date in the reign of Jehoiakim see Hyatt.

Historical Background

The reign of Manasseh was characterized by a pro-Assyrian policy which, although necessary as a demonstration of loyalty by the vassal-king, 'went far beyond the merely perfunctory' (J. Bright, *History of Israel*, 1972, p. 311; cf. J. W. McKay, *Religion in Judah under the Assyrians*, 1973) and included the erection of altars to Assyrian deities in the Jerusalem temple, permission of pagan cults and practices, sacred prostitution, divination and magic, and the practice of human sacrifice. See 2 Kg. 21: 1–16; 23: 4–7; Zeph. 1: 4 f., 8. Judah was thus led into apostasy during the fifty-five years of Manasseh's reign under the military dominance of Assyrian general-emperors Esarhaddon (680–669) and Ashurbanipal (668–627).

Manasseh's son, Amon, was assassinated after reigning two years, and his eight-year-old son Josiah was enthroned by the 'people of the land'. Josiah's tentative reforms began in 626, a year after Ashurbanipal's death, and less than twenty years before the fall of Assyria. Discovery of 'the book of the law' in 621 gave impetus to these reforms which became effective legislation but were, as Jeremiah saw, spiritually inadequate.

The spiritual conditions which Zephaniah addressed were of outright apostasy and religious syncretism before any real effect of the Josianic reformation.

Integrity of the Text

Various scholars have denied certain verses to Zephaniah. B. Stade rejected 2: 1–3, 11; and most of ch. 3. F. Schwally (1890) doubted 2: 1–4 but tended to accept them while denying 2: 5–12 and ch. 3. K. Budde (1893) was content to reorder various verses in ch. 2 and denied ch. 3. A. B. Davidson (1896) expressed some doubt only about 3: 10, 14–20. W. W von Baudissin (1901) denied 2: 7a, 8–11 and 3: 14–20. S. R. Driver (1912) discounted 2: 7b, 11; 3: 9–10, 18–20. More recently A. Weiser (1957/61) observes 'traces of later revision' in 2: 7, 8–11 but does not thereby date 2: 4–12 late. He claims 'no uncertainty' for 3: 1–13 despite 'some later touching up' in 3: 8 ff. He regards 3: 8–19 as 'from the prophet himself' with only 3: 20 as a late addition. G. W. Anderson (1959) feels 'there is little or nothing which is inappro-priate to the period'. O. Eissfeldt (1966) regards the beginning and end of 2: 7, 8, 9, 10–11; 3: 8–10 as having undergone later elaboration, and he is dubious to the point of tending to deny 3: 14–17, 18–20. J. D. W. Watts (1975) feels that there is no reason to deny any part to Zephaniah.

The discrepancies between the views of the various scholars given above is obvious. It will be noted, however, that the earlier scholars are more pessimistic than the more recent. Their wide use of conjectural emendation is now largely rejected and we have entered a period which has more reverence for MS authority. That there are problems will be seen from the commentary, but they are of comparatively small proportions, and, for the most part, of little more than academic interest.

ANALYSIS

I INTRODUCTION (1: 1)

II WORLD DESTRUCTION: FOCUS ON JUDAH AND JERUSALEM (1: 2–6)

III ANNOUNCEMENT AND DESCRIPTION OF THE DAY OF THE LORD (1: 7–18)

IV CALL FOR JUDAH'S REPENTANCE (2: 1–4)

V ORACLES AGAINST THE NATIONS (2: 5–15)
  i The oracle against Philistia (2: 5 ff.)
  ii The oracle against Moab and Ammon (2: 8–11)
  iii The oracle against Ethiopia (2: 12)
  iv The oracle against Assyria (2: 13 ff.)
  v The oracle against Judah (3: 1–7)
  vi Summary (3: 8)

VI ANNOUNCEMENT OF RESTORATION (3: 9–20)
  i The conversion of the nations (3: 9 f.)
  ii The restoration of the remnant in Zion (3: 11–20)

I. INTRODUCTION (1: 1)

1. On Zephaniah, his genealogy and date see Introduction.

II. WORLD DESTRUCTION: FOCUS ON JUDAH AND JERUSALEM (1: 2–6)

A cosmic cataclysm, more destructive than the Noahic Flood, of **men and animals . . . birds . . . and the fish** is anticipated. In Biblical theology, man's sin is always seen as having cosmic consequences. **earth:** Heb. *'ădāmāh* here and in 1: 3. Cf. *'ereṣ*, 1: 18 (twice); 3: 8. Both terms may mean simply 'land'. But if Zephan-iah means that Israel is the prime target of wrath which includes only a few of her immediate neighbours, he is standing the eschatology of Amos (1: 3–2: 8; 5: 18 ff.) on its head, for Amos, contrary to popular belief, includes Israel with the nations under universal wrath, and not the nations with Israel. The universal interpretation makes it difficult to reconcile 1: 2–18; 3: 8 with 2: 1 ff., 6 f., 9, 14 f.; 3: 9–20. But to Zephaniah, the townsman, the reference to flocks and herds pasturing where once stood a city is as much a picture of dereliction as is 1: 2 ff. See also on 1: 18; 2: 13b–14a. In 1: 4–13 is given a general picture of evils in Judah. These include religious syncretism (4 ff.), national disloyalty (8), social plunder (9), and indifference to Yahweh (12). Alternatively these verses may describe various religious deviations (cf. Watts): worship of Baal (4) and the Assyrian deities (5), syncretism of Yahwism with Ammonite religion (5), apathy towards Yahwism (6), the worship of Melek (8), adoption of pagan cultic robes (8), sacrilege of the Holy of Holies, or participation in idol worship (9a), the introduction of pagan worship to the Jerusalem temple (9b), and the consequent materialistic scepticism among the common people (10–13). **4. every remnant of Baal** implies that reforms had begun; see Introduction: Date of Writing. Others translate: 'Baal (worship) to the very last vestige (remnant)', but NIV is more natural. A positive reappraisal of the historicity of 2 Chr. 34: 3–7, usually doubted, would help. Cf. J. Bright, p. 317; F. F. Bruce, *Israel and the Nations* (1969), p. 71. AV 'with the priests' is omitted by the best LXX texts and is metrically superfluous in *MT*. Heb. *kōhᵃnîm* has a wide range of meaning including orthodox Yahwistic priests and priests of other religions (*BDB*), but the meaning of *kᵉmārîm* is uncertain: cf. F. F. Bruce, *Israel and the Nations*, p. 80; *NBD art*. 'Chemarim'. Heb. 'im hakōhᵃnîm, 'with the priests' may be a corruption of šēm hakōhᵃnîm, an earlier marginal note to explain the rare šēm hakᵉmārîm, **the names of the idolatrous priests** in the original main text. NIV takes the two words as respectively **pagan** and **idolatrous priests. 5. the starry host:** worship of astral deities was a feature of Assyrian religion adopted by Manasseh (2 Kg. 21: 3 ff.; cf. *ICC*, pp. 188 ff.). The passage portrays the religious chaos in Judah: pagan worship (5a), syncretistic Yahwism, or, perhaps, polytheism (5b), apathy (6), disillusionment and scepticism (12). **Molech:** *MT* malkam means 'their king' i.e. their god; or Milcom, the proper name of the Ammonite deity; cf. *NBD art*. 'Malcam'. Verse 6 may refer to rejection of Yahwism for pagan cults, or syncretistic Yahwism, which so distorted the perception of the character of Yahweh that the prophets denied it to be Yahwism at all, or apathy towards Yahweh.

III. ANNOUNCEMENT OF THE DAY OF THE LORD (1: 7–18)

7. Be silent: a phrase redolent with the awe of occasion. **the day of the LORD:** see general article on the Theology of the Old Testament. **a sacrifice . . . those he has invited:** usually Judah is identified as the victim and the invading peoples as the guests sanctified, i.e. rendered ceremonially fit (cf. 1 Sam. 9: 22 ff; 16: 2–5). J. H. Gailey suggests that at such a feast the consecrated guest might be honoured,

whereas here the guests, whom he takes to be Judah, are to be slaughtered. The terminology is strikingly reminiscent of the purge under Jehu in 2 Kg. 10: 18–28; cf. Zeph. 1: 4. **8. princes:** i.e. princes, or the cultic officials of Melek. **the king's sons:** Josiah's sons were too young (2 Kg. 23: 26; 22: 1; cf. *ICC*); NEB: 'royal house'. Watts renders 'sons of Melek', the Ammonite deity, by transliterating Heb. *melek* instead of translating it as **king.** See *NBD art*. 'Molech'. **foreign clothes:** evidence of lack of national self-respect (*IB*: cf. 12b; Mt. 11: 8), or, in context, pagan cultic garments. **9. avoid stepping on** (or 'leaps over' RSV) **the threshold:** this obscure phrase may refer to (a) social injustice: the forceful deprivation of the weak by the strong without warning (Pusey); (b) burglary: avoidance of contact with protective household gods believed to reside in the threshold (*WC*); (c) adoption of a Philistine custom, cf. 1 Sam. 5: 5 with the presence of the Kerethites (see 2: 5 below) or Carites in the temple in 2 Kg. 11: 4, 19; (d) 'those who leap on the temple terrace' NEB, climbing on the Holy of Holies, or on the altar platform (cf. Exod. 20: 24 ff.), 'probably a common practice in the worship of the stars' (Watts); (e) 'who mounts the pedestal (of an idol)', Gerleman, i.e. 'who worships an idol' (Hyatt). See *ICC* for further suggestions. **the temple of their Gods:** Heb. 'their masters' house' either (a) the temple; LXX 'who fill the house of the Lord their God with falsehood and fraudulence', or Watts, 'who fill . . . with their lords (idols), false and fraudulent' (cf. 2 Kg. 21: 3–8; Jer. 7: 30; Ezek. 8: 5 ff.); or (b) the royal palace: treacherous and disreputable royal sycophants (*ICC*); or (c) houses of the nobility: fraudulent practice by sycophants of the nobility (*WC*). Of the districts of the city (10 f.) only the location of **the Fish Gate** is certain. The language is graphic and places Zephaniah with the traders in **the market district,** (mg the Mortar) NEB: 'lower town', lit. 'quarry', while the horrific sounds of defeat sweep progressively nearer from **the Fish Gate,** through the **New Quarter** to **the hills** surrounding them. In *MT* the switch to vocative in 11 indicates that this is his visionary vantage point. **merchants:** Heb. lit. 'Canaanites'. Here by innuendo it refers to Judeans who trafficked in religious deviations. **12. search . . . lamps:** Yahweh, by the hand of the invader, will purposefully and methodically bring every man to judgment. **like wine left on its dregs:** NEB paraphrases: 'sit in stupor over the dregs of their wine'. G. A. Smith, p. 54, should be consulted. As unracked wine spoils, so God's people, whose lives have been undisturbed for too long, have lost their vitality and sense of destiny. **do nothing either good or bad:** i.e. irrelevant to life because He makes no significant difference: the ultimate denial of OT revelation of the character of Yahweh as 'He who acts'; cf. J. N. Schofield, *Introducing OT Theology* (London, 1964), ch. 2. Theology is a vital element in the formation of character, attitudes and behaviour, cf. 2 C. 3: 18. Being 'transformed into the same image' is as true for worshippers of erroneous conceptions of deity as for worshippers of Yahweh Himself, Jer. 2: 5, 8, 11. Denying divine involvement with history, God's people themselves have become uncaring and uninvolved. **13f.** the alleged inconsistency between vv. 13 and 14 (*IB*) is due to a wooden literalism in interpreting the vivid presentation of different aspects of truth. The frustration of materialistic ambition (13) and the proximity of judgment (14) are not inconsistent particularly when the time-scale is the life of the nation. **the shouting . . . there:** NEB 'Swifter than a runner the day of the Lord, And speedier than a warrior'. G. A. Smith: 'A strong man—there—crying bitterly'. The better Heb. style of the NEB emendation is poor compensation for the loss of poignancy. **15. That day will be a day of wrath:** wrath, as a controlled but vigorous initiative against sin, is an anthropopathism. Purged of the notions of loss of control associated with human passions, it is a legitimate and necessary image. The effects of divine wrath are profound emotional crisis, loss of material possessions, cosmic upheaval, and the terror of invasion (15 f.). Cf. 1: 18. **17. distress . . . like blind men** describes the purposeless, directionless, stumbling state of shock at the magnitude of the calamity. **blood . . . like dust:** the signs of violent death commonplace as roadside dust. **entrails:** Heb. uncertain. Only other use Job 20: 23: possibly a euphemism for 'bowels' NEB. **filth:** parallel to **dust**; too common to evoke comment in a society using animals for transport and without a modern underground sewage system. **18. silver . . . gold . . . save them:** 'buying off' an invader was a common practice, so there is no certain link with Psammetichus of Egypt and the invading Scythians (Herodotus, *History* i, 104 f.). **jealousy . . . consumed:** despite a metrical problem, its relation to 3: 8, its tautology with the next line and the universal destruction predicted, there is no objective MS evidence for interpolation (cf. *IB*: Hyatt). Divine jealousy (see 1: 15) is a passion creative of trust and of a loving relationship between God and His people by which He will eradicate any incursion detrimental to the relationship.

a sudden end . . . in the earth: that such total destruction would preclude any possibility of the relationship it was intended to engender does not seem to trouble Zephaniah, apart from 2: 1 ff. perhaps! This alone should warn against the application of a literalistic hermeneutic. Zephaniah did not yet see the NT

revelation of a new relationship purged of all blemish and reaching fulfilment in a life hereafter (Cf. Col. 1: 21 f.; Jude 24; Rom. 8: 28 ff.; 1 C. 15: 42 ff.; Phil. 1: 23; 1 Th. 4: 13 ff., etc.).

IV. CALL FOR JUDAH'S REPENTANCE (2: 1–4)

1. Gather together . . . shameful nation: the addressee is not named. **shameful nation** is usually a gentile designation. Ch. 2: 3 is often regarded as an interpolation and 2: 4 refers to four Philistine cities. If 2: 3 is not original then 2: 1–7 is an oracle against the Philistines, but there is no MS evidence for omission. If 2: 3 is retained, 2: 4 relates more naturally to 2: 5 ff., unless 2: 3 is regarded as an aside relating to Judah in the midst of an oracle against Philistia, as indeed 2: 5 may also be. On the whole it seems best to take it that 2: 1–4 addresses Judah. In the light of pagan practices denounced in ch. 1, **shameful nation** is apt enough. Chapter 2: 3 is thus retained and 2: 4 forms a basis for the plea for repentance and a bridgehead into the oracles against surrounding nations. On the considerable difficulties of the Heb. text see *ICC*; Hyatt; Watts. In v. 2 the text is even more obscure. *MT* lit.: 'Before a decree is born, like chaff a day has passed away' (RSVmg). Possibly LXX and Syriac versions are here based on an earlier reading: 'before you become like drifting chaff'; cf. RSV; NEB. The general meaning is clear: the nation is called to repentance before God's judgment falls. **3. Seek the LORD**, a parallel to **seek righteousness** involves seeking to know the character of Yahweh as revealed in His mighty historical acts, especially the Exodus, and to bring one's life into harmony with the covenantal responsibilities implied by it. **you humble of the land:** those with no power and few rights, who do not assert themselves against God, in contrast to 'the proud'. This kind of **righteousness** has little to do with legalistic observance *per se.* **humility** is another parallel for **righteousness** here. The **humble** accept the normative implications of the character of Yahweh in covenantal dependence. Heb. *'nāwîm*, sometimes translated 'meek', denotes a strength of faith-commitment to Yahweh that spurns self-assertion: God will vindicate their cause, cf. Num. 12: 3. **who do what he commands:** i.e. those who, in contrast to 1: 4–13, fulfil the covenant relationship. **perhaps . . . sheltered:** the verbal root *str* is used in Amos and elsewhere of 'escaping God's notice' (*BDB*), especially of escaping His judgment. (The root *spn*, from which 'Zephaniah' is derived, means to hide as treasure in order to protect.) There is no question of self-concealment (cf. 1: 12; 18; 3: 6). **4. at midday:** may mean that on the day of attack all will be over by noon, or, an attack at the noon siesta will cause confusion in the unprepared city. This verse is not so much an oracle against Philistia as a reason for Judah to take heed of the one possibility of escape.

V. ORACLES AGAINST THE NATIONS (2: 5–15)
i. The oracle against Philistia (2: 5 ff.)
No specific reason is given for the inclusion of Philistia, Ethiopia and Assyria under judgment. Their wickedness may have been too vivid in the nation's mind as a memory (*e.g.* 1 Sam. 31: 5, 10) or as a present threat (Assyria), to necessitate an explicit catalogue of their offences. The alleged 'tendency on the part of the prophet to regard the enemies of his people as the enemies of God' (*IB*) is unworthy of Zephaniah's universalism; see also on 2: 8. **5. who live by the sea:** refers to the Philistines by designating their territory as the coastal plain. **Kerethite:** lit. Cretans; some of the Philistines evidently invaded Canaan from a base in Crete (see *NBD*). **Canaan, land of the Philistines:** their extension of power over Canaan after the battle of Gilboa (1 Sam. 31) was incomplete and reversed by David after his accession (2 Sam. 5: 17–25; 8: 1). Even so, they have given the land its name Palestine. This verse may be a general declaration of judgment on the whole of Canaan, including Judah, which has been inserted into the specifically Philistine oracle. If so, it is a scathing attack upon Judah, classing her with the immoral Philistines, cf. 1: 4–9 and 2: 1. But some suggest emendation *e.g.* NEB reads *'aknî'ēk*, for MT *kᵉna'an*, giving 'I will subdue you' which makes good sense and an apt parallel, the words being similar in the consonantal text. If the emendation is adopted, the verse refers to the Philistines proper and the unity of thought in the passage is preserved, but it is arguable whether the extant reading is difficult enough to justify conjectural emendation. **6. shall be a place for shepherds:** for Zephaniah, the townsman, **a place for shepherds and sheep pens** are images of dereliction. For discussion of textual emendations see *ICC, IB*. The message is plain: the entire Philistine population and culture are to be obliterated. **7. remnant . . . of Judah:** for the first time in the prophecy a positive future appears for Judah (cf. 2: 7b, 9). It develops as a major theme in 3: 11–20. Some scholars attribute all reference to hope to the work of later redactors but see Introduction: The Integrity of the Text. **there they will find pasture:** see on v.6. **In the evening:** *IB* suggests a 'slight' emendation to 'in Ekron' *ba'ereb* to *bᵉ'eqrôn*, which while providing an excellent parallel, is not so 'slight' as claimed and is without MS support. **care for . . . their fortunes:** the verb is translated 'punish' in 1:

8. Watts prefers 'when the Lord their God punishes them he shall restore their fortunes'; cf. *IB*.
ii. The oracle against Moab and Ammon (2: 8–11)
8. the insults of Moab and the taunts of the Ammonites: this is often regarded as a post-exilic addition, its historical background being believed to be the fall of Jerusalem, cf. Ezek. 25: 3, 6, 8; Jer. 48: 26, 30 also Ezek. 35: 12; Ob. 12. But the omission of Edom here would be inexplicable (Ps. 137: 7–9). The 2 Kg. 24: 2 incident in 602 B.C. is a more apt historical setting, and retains the integrity of the verses. However, it presupposes dating the book in the reign of Jehoiakim; cf. Hyatt. Tradition and history doubtless treasured many recollections of indignities and hostilities endured by Israel at the hand of her eastern neighbours. It is therefore rash to assume that the oracle must relate to an event recorded in scant and selective documents. **made threats against their land:** lit. 'made themselves great', may refer to annexation of Israel's territory by her neighbours (NEB). The translation preferred by *ICC* is 'to enlarge the mouth' (cf. RSV 'boast'). LXX 'my territory' provides a better parallel for the preceding **my people**. No idea of Yahweh as a territorial land-owning baal is to be inferred. Israel's unique representative role in 'salvation-history' (*Heilsgeschichte*) meant that to **taunt** Israel was to affront the glory of Yahweh. **9. like Sodom . . . Gomorrah:** the overthrow of these cities (Gen. 19: 24 f.) was always regarded as the epitome of judgment. The images of **weeds**, a rare and obscure Heb. word, and **salt-pits, a wasteland**, eclipse the cultural destruction of Philistia, 2: 5 ff. **the remnant . . . survivors . . . inherit their land:** see on v. 7. **11. The LORD will be awesome:** some regard this as a later addition but without MS support. LXX 'will appear against them'. To exegete rather than excise such a fundamental aspect of the character of Yahweh as His personal and vigorous reaction against all that opposes man's highest interests would enhance our understanding of God's love and save it from the sentimentality which has provided the cultural seed-bed for our weak sociology. **destroys:** Heb: *rāzāh*, better, 'makes lean' or 'wastes away' BDB; 'famishes' RSV. **all the gods:** the gods of the Sumerian/Babylonian Flood Epic were famished by the end of the period of the flood because no sacrifices had been offered. Here the image indicates figuratively that the conversion of their devotees will cause these deities to die out. **will worship him, every one in its own land:** may be translated 'they (the gods) shall bow down to him, each from his own place (from his own temple), all the demons of the nations' (Watts); cf. 1 Sam. 5: 3 f. Alternatively

(as NIV) it may imply the conversion of the Gentiles to Yahweh.

iii. The oracle against Cush (2: 12)

This oracle is so short and inexplicit that it is usually regarded as a fragment of the original. **Cushites** may be a reference to Egypt whose 25th dynasty, 712–663 B.C., had been Cushite. Since the other nations mentioned are on the west, east and north points of the compass, it seems that Cush was chosen as representing the south. **my sword:** whatever the agency of destruction the judgment is the sword of Yahweh.

iv. The oracle against Assyria (2: 13 ff.)

Hyatt's opinion that this section is so remarkably accurate that it must be 'prophecy after the event' which dates it shortly after 612 B.C., is a conclusion very much influenced by his particular presuppositions about prophecy and his view of the date of the book. The downfall of the apparently impregnable Assyria and the reduction of her capital city Nineveh to **dry as the desert** (13) highlights the insecurity of a weak, but equally perverse, Judah (cf. 1: 44 ff.; 3: 1–7). The alleged 'incongruity' between 13a and 14b (*ICC*) may be eased if *ṣiyyāh*, **dry**, is seen as a relative condition. If absolute, it 'would involve the drying up of the Tigris which ran along the south-west side of the city, and also of the Khusar which skirted the north-west side. An extensive system of canals conveyed a plentiful supply of water within the walls. Gardens and orchards accordingly flourished' (*ICC*). The incongruity recedes further if 'Flocks and herds' (14) refers to wild animals which would shelter in the ruins; cf. the rest of the context (14b f.). It may be best not to press details of the imagery since the prophet seems to use images for their force, perhaps at the expense of homogeneity or congruity, *e.g.* 1: 3 f.; cf. 2: 6, 14 f. **of every kind:** Heb. *goy*, 'nation', cannot be correct. NIV takes it as an abbreviation. NEB adopts *gaw*, an emendation omitting one letter of the consonantal text: 'of the wild'. **will roost on her columns:** defilement of the carved heads by their use as perches and nests for unclean birds and vermin (*ICC*). **desert owl:** Heb. *kōm*, an emendation of *MT qōl*, 'voice'. **screech owl:** *'ōreb*, an emendation of *MT ḥāréb*, 'desolation'. NEB emends to *hōreb*, 'bustard'. **the beams of cedar will be exposed:** *MT* is conjecturally omitted by many (*ICC*). If genuine, it refers to the stripping of the expensive cedar-wood panelling used in temples and palaces. **15. 'I am and there is none besides me':** cf. Isa. 47: 8, 10. While Nineveh's position in the world was without equal, her attitude ignored her dependence of Yahweh's sovereignty over history and was the opposite of 'humility' (cf. 2: 3). **scoff and shake their fists:** a derisive gesture expressing the intense scorn and malicious satisfaction of all who once lived under her oppression.

v. The oracle against Judah (3: 1–7)

1. the city that is **rebellious:** following the oracle against Assyria, the passage does not identify the 'target' city. One is left to assume that Assyria is still being addressed. The effect of this, probably deliberate, ambiguity is to elicit approval for the principle that rebelliousness, defilement, oppression and incorrigibility deserve and incur divine wrath; cf. Am. 1: 3– 2: 8. Such accedence is likely to be more readily given when the doomed city is thought to be Nineveh. Jerusalem, the holy city, is portrayed as if she were the corrupt capital of heathen Assyria (3: 1–4); cf. Jer. 7: 28. Her **correction** (2, 7) refers to adverse circumstances sent to chasten, but resulting only in loss of faith and fellowship with Yahweh **her God**—implying her truck with the pagan deities of her neighbours (cf. 1: 4 ff.). **3. Her officials**, either cultic, or more likely here, princely (*śārîm*; cf. 1: 8), and **her rulers**, devour their prey until nothing is left. **4. Her prophets** wantonly make extravagant prophecies to gain popular acclaim. They are **treacherous**: i.e. either full of deceit, or productive of self-originated oracles. **Her priests:** custodians of the sacred 'torah'; they commit sacrilege (cf. 1: 4 ff.) and thus **do violence** to the divine instruction. **5. The LORD:** 'Yahweh', the covenant name implying the divine covenant faithfulness. **his justice:** i.e. his consistent help of the oppressed, illustrated by the sure, daily deliverance from the oppression of darkness. **yet the unrighteous knows no shame:** omitted by *ICC* on grounds of style and context, but there may be a relation between **he does not fail**, *'awlāh*, and **the unjust**, *'awwāl*. **6. I have cut off:** 'The fall of great empires was God's doing . . . a preview of the great judgment day' (Watts). See on 2: 13 ff. **7. her dwelling would not be cut off, nor all my punishments come:** Heb. difficult. The fate of other nations made Judah complacent when it should have been heeded as a warning.

vi. Summary (3: 8)

'Therefore wait for me': the phrase, usually associated with piety, may be an oracle of irony against the wicked. If, alternatively, it is an encouragement to the godly remnant to remain steadfast during **my fierce anger** (Keil), it links with vv. 9–20 and 2: 1–4. Cf. Hab. 3: 16–19. **to testify:** LXX and Syriac presuppose *MT* emended from *lᵉ'ad*, 'to the prey', to *lᵉ'ēd*.

VI. ANNOUNCEMENT OF RESTORATION (3: 9–20)

i. The conversion of the nations (3: 9 f.)

9. purify the lips: linked with **call on the name**, indicates conversion from prayer to, and swearing by, pagan deities. If Babel (Gen. 11: 1–9) signifies that self-assertive man (cf. Gen. 3: 5 ff.) lost communion even with his fellow-beings, purified **lips** is Zephaniah's image for the dawning of a new age. Self-assertive rebellion will be purged from the earth so that **all . . . may call on the name of the LORD**. The new purified **lips**, which will come as a result of man's recognition of the moral demands of God's character, will enable men to **serve him shoulder to shoulder**. Furthermore the scattering of **my people** (Gen. 11: 8 f.) will be reversed (10). **10. From beyond the rivers of Cush:** i.e. 'the dimly recognized limits of civilization as the prophet knew them' (Watts), Yahweh's **scattered people** will acknowledge His deity and worship Him. These may be exiled Judah, or **the peoples**, in harmony with Zephaniah's universalism which is as wide in salvation as in judgment.

ii. The restoration of the remnant in Zion (3: 11–20)

In Zephaniah arrogant self-assertion is the root sin, and acknowledgement of dependence on Yahweh fundamental to relationship with Him (2: 1, 3, 8, 10, 15; 3: 3, 5). While pride is reduced to shame and demoralization by God's judgment (1: 14–17), humility issues in unspeakable joy, not only for His people (3: 14, 20), but for God himself (3: 17). Acknowledgement of the shame of sin (2: 1) issues in God-given exaltation (3: 20). Zephaniah is here in the main stream of biblical thought (cf. Gen. 3: 5 ff.; Phil. 2: 5–11). The biblical paradox is that, in order that they **will not be put to shame**, Yahweh must remove **those who rejoice their pride** and the **haughty** (11). Thus the **meek and humble**, who acknowledge their dependence and **trust in the name**, i.e. the character, **of the LORD**, so that they **do no wrong . . . speak no lies** and have no **deceit in their mouths**, these shall be provided for in security (13b) and shall . . . **rejoice with all your heart** (14). The old rebellious Jerusalem (3: 1) having been eradicated (3: 6 ff.; cf. 1: 2–2: 4), the new Zion replaces it. Undoubtedly Zephaniah thought of it as a geographical Jerusalem, but it is not its material, but its spiritual values that concern him: humility (11 f.), obedience (13a), security (13b, 15b, 17 f.), exuberant joy (14), the theocracy and presence of Yahweh (15b), confident morale (16), divine love and fellowship (17b), concern for the socially weak (19), belonging, togetherness and renown (20). **14. Sing . . . with all your heart:** Zion is called upon to enjoy exuberant gladness. In Heb. **heart** is the seat of the whole personality, especially the intellect. This rejoicing is directed away from the orgiastic and unthinking worship of Baal rites (cf. 1: 4–9) to the reverent, intelligent, but none the less enthusiastic, worship of Yahweh. Divine wrath and judg-

ment are replaced by the presence of Yahweh: **the LORD . . . is with you** and in His rightful place as **King of Israel**, thus re-establishing the theocratic ideal. (15). Zephaniah offers no criticism of Judah's kingship nor of the king despite his experience under Manasseh and Amon.

Jerusalem **never again will . . . fear any harm**; opposition and invasion by foes are diminished, so purposeful action and achievement are again possible (16). In a time of barbarous Assyrian war-techniques, the knowledge that Yahweh **is with you . . . mighty to save** (17) was possibly not so much the expression of a crass desire to thrash foes in battle as hope of national security. Yahweh's presence is one of intimate relationship. **He will take great delight in you, he will quiet you with his love:** Heb. 'be silent in his love' may mean no more talk of judgment, or love so profound that it is inexpressible in words, or his silent planning for Israel's benefit. The metrical structure is correct as *MT* or LXX stands; thus omission is excluded. Either way the future holds an intimacy of love with Yahweh. **he will rejoice over you with singing:** The Heb. text is impossible: see *ICC*, *WC*. Cf. Eph. 1: 18b. **18. The sorrows of the appointed feasts I will remove from you; they are a burden and a reproach to you:** Heb. is obscure as also LXX. The textual emendation on which NIV is based, if accepted, denotes the removal of all occasion for taunts (cf. 2: 8, 10 f.). Verse 19b is an exposition of the Heb. concept of righteousness: the putting down of **all who oppress you** and the upholding of the interests of the socially weak—**the lame** and the **scattered**. They are, in this context, the politically disabled and exiled people of Judah who will find their **shame** changed to **honor. I will deal . . .** 'is all the more terrible for its indefinite and general character' (*ICC*). Verse 20 is generally regarded as a repetitious gloss, but perhaps Zephaniah, like other preachers, found the repetition of a particularly exciting truth too tempting to avoid! God's humbled people (3: 12) will be brought to their divinely designated **home**. Scattered relatives He will **gather**. A people broken and demoralized by jibes at its national catastrophe will be acclaimed throughout the whole earth. **when I restore your fortunes:** or 'when I reverse your captivity', AV. **before your very eyes:** may emphasize the dramatic realization of the events, rather than actual fulfilment of events in their lifetime.

BIBLIOGRAPHY

Commentaries
DAVIDSON, A. B., *The Books of Nahum, Habakkuk and Zephaniah*. Cambridge Bible (Cambridge, 1896).

Zephaniah

EATON, J. H., *Obadiah, Nahum, Habakkuk and Zephaniah*. TC (London, 1961).

GAILEY, J. H., *Micah to Malachi*, Layman's Bible Commentaries (London, 1962).

HYATT, J. P., 'Zephaniah', in PCB (London, [2]1962).

SMITH, G. A., 'Zephaniah', in *The Book of the Twelve Prophets*, ii (London, [2]1928).

SMITH, J. M. P., 'The Book of Zephaniah', in *Micah, Zephaniah, Nahum, Habakkuk, Obadiah and Joel*. ICC (Edinburgh, 1912).

TAYLOR, C. L., 'The Book of Zephaniah: Introduction and Exegesis', in IB vi (New York/ Nashville, 1956).

WATTS, J. D. W., *The Books of Joel, Obadiah, Jonah, Nahum, Habakkuk and Zephaniah*. CBC (Cambridge, 1975).

Other works

HYATT, J. P., 'The Date and Background of Zephaniah', JNES 7 (1948), pp. 25–29.

McKAY, J. W., *Religion in Judah under the Assyrians 732–609 B. C.* (London, 1973).

SMITH, L. P. and LACHEMAN, E. R., 'The Authorship of the Book of Zephaniah'. JNES 9 (1950), pp. 137–142.

HAGGAI

F. ROY COAD

The short Old Testament book of Haggai, like Paul's brief letter to Philemon in the New Testament, forms a delightful little vignette of practical religion. As with Philemon, the social circumstances it assumes are far removed from those of the present day: but, again like Philemon, its practical ethical message is as fresh and living today as ever it was.

In 597 B.C., and again in 587, the calamity which had been often and urgently foretold by the prophets had overwhelmed Jerusalem and its temple, when the Babylonian empire took reprisals for the revolt of Jewish kings against its sway. With the majority of its population deported to Babylon, and its contents sacked, the land had lain waste and idle, awaiting the distant restoration prophesied by Jeremiah (Jer. 25 and 26). Then, in 539 B.C., the Medo-Persian king Cyrus, a ruler of wisdom and even broadmindedness, had finally established his hold on the world of the Middle East by taking Babylon itself, capital of the empire. On consolidating his power, one of the first actions which Cyrus took, whether from genuine respect for the religions of his subject peoples, or from a shrewd expediency, was to issue an edict *inter alia* for the rebuilding of the Jerusalem temple.

The background to Haggai's prophecy can be read in Ezr. 1: 1 to 4: 5, and 4: 24 to 6: 22 (4: 6–23 appears to be a parenthesis recording events a generation or two later during the reigns of later kings). Work had started on the temple on the issue of Cyrus's edict, in 537, only to lapse in face of the opposition of the mixed peoples who had remained in the land during the long captivity, and who feared the restoration of Jewish power. To add to the troubles of the returned Jews, Cyrus had died in battle in 530, and the armies of his tyrannical son Cambyses had marched through the land on their way to subdue Egypt. They would have laid tribute on its produce as they went, impoverishing its inhabitants yet further. At last, in 522, Cambyses himself died, and an ambitious but nobler man, Darius, an officer of his armies and himself of royal stock, seized power. It is at the beginning of his reign that Haggai prophesies: the moment of his prophecy is described in Ezr. 4: 5; 4: 24–5: 2; 6: 14.

ANALYSIS

The book contains five separate and specifically dated prophecies, with related narrative, which form a natural framework for its study. The dates can be related to the modern calendar.

I HAGGAI'S APPEAL TO RECOMMENCE THE BUILDING OF THE TEMPLE
(1: 1–11)
(Second year of Darius, sixth month, first day: August 29, 520 B.C.)

II RESPONSE, AND HAGGAI'S SHORT MESSAGE OF ENCOURAGEMENT
(1: 12–15)
(Second year of Darius, sixth month, 24th day: September 21, 520 B.C.)

III HAGGAI'S FURTHER MESSAGE OF ENCOURAGEMENT,
SET IN CONTEXT OF GOD'S UNIVERSAL PURPOSE (2: 1–9)
(Second year of Darius, seventh month, 21st day: October 17, 520 B.C.)

IV HAGGAI'S MESSAGE OF PROMISE, SET IN CONTEXT OF GOD'S
UNMERITED FAVOUR (2: 10–19)
(Second year of Darius, ninth month, 24th day: December 18, 520 B.C.)

V HAGGAI'S PERSONAL MESSAGE TO ZERUBBABEL, THE JEWISH LEADER
(2: 20–23)
(Same day as preceding prophecy)

(From Ezr. 6: 15 we learn that the temple was in fact completed about four years later.)
NOTE: Some commentators have considered that 2: 15–19 in fact belong to the second prophecy, and should follow 1: 13, having become detached in the course of transmission or editing of the manuscripts. This would require an emendation of the date in 2: 18 to read 'the sixth month'. The NEB footnote picks up and extends this thought. There are certain attractions in the idea, but it has no MS support. Further reference appears in the body of the commentary.

I. HAGGAI'S APPEAL (1: 1–11)
Aug. 29, 520.

Apart from the references in Ezr. 5: 1 and 6: 14, nothing is known of Haggai, except that which his own book indicates. He may have been a newcomer from Babylon, or a longtime resident who had watched the loss of his people's early enthusiasm, and their demoralization by opposition and the trials of natural disaster and foraging armies. He and his colleague Zechariah (Zech. 1: 1) were stirred into voice as the Spirit of God awoke them to the condition of their nation. Their messages were messages of encouragement and hope, as well as of exhortation. The cure for the peoples' ills was in the hand of their God, and their God was supreme both over nature and over the history of nations (Hag. 1: 11; 2: 6, 7): He was near at hand and accessible to the seeking heart (Hag. 2: 4, 19). The careful dating of Haggai's messages indicates the awesome importance attached to the return to the people of the authentic voice of prophecy, after long silence in the land. God had also matched the restoration of the prophetic voice by the provision of leaders worthy of the heroes of their past; in Zerubbabel, descendant of the royal house of David, and the high priest Joshua, bearer of a name significant to every Jew.

The two prophets were well matched. Haggai was simple, practical, direct. His words are in simple metrical form, appealing to the people's sense of shame and rousing them from their selfish lethargy and resignation. Zechariah was a visionary and a poet, raising their demoralized spirits by heart-warming words: 'This is what the Lord Almighty says: "I am very jealous for Jerusalem and Zion, but I am very angry with the nations that feel secure"' (Zech. 1: 14, 15); 'This is what the Lord says, "I will return to Jerusalem with mercy"' (Zech. 1: 16); and that wonderful reassurance, 'whoever touches you touches the apple of his eye' (Zech. 2: 8).

Direct and practical though Haggai was, his true prophetic insight is apparent in this opening paragraph. Two separate and apparently unrelated facts, the prevalent economic distress and the long-standing folly of the barely started temple reconstruction (by now so familiar as to be taken for granted), are fused in a sudden enlightenment. For nearly twenty years the people had withdrawn into themselves in the face of overwhelming discouragement; accepting their subject role, they had resigned themselves to making themselves as comfortable (v. 4: the word rendered **paneled** might mean no more than 'roofed'), and as unnoticeable, as possible. Haggai suddenly sees their passivity as a cause, rather than the result, of their demoralized condition; and the force to awaken them into national revival is the reawakening of their active religious commitment and zeal. The neglected temple was a patent symbol of their spiritual and moral condition (some commentators indeed see 2: 13 as a picture of the temple lying like a ritually unclean 'dead body' in their midst). Spurred into urgent action to rebuild the house of God, they would find that the cure to their other distresses also lay in their own hands. The cause of their weakness did not lie in forces beyond their control, but its remedy was in their own power (vv. 7, 8). It was a message that matched another prophet's stirring invitation in Isa. 55: 1–3 (see vv. 6, 11). Haggai's insight throws a fascinating and important light upon the function of religious faith in society: 'Seek first his kingdom and his righteousness, and all these things will be given to you as well' (Mt. 6: 33).

The section is also interesting for the indications of contemporary economic conditions and developments (vv. 6, 9, 10–11). The reference to putting wages into a bag (v. 6) may not be an indication of the use of minted coinage (see Zech. 11: 12, where wages were 'weighed out' in pieces of precious metal); though minted coinage was indeed beginning to be used at this time, and Darius is credited with introducing it into Persia from Lydia (see *NBD* article *Money*). But we are plainly in a society where a rudimentary monetary economy is beginning to replace the immemorial system of barter, in which precious metals had been but one medium of exchange. Certainly, the last clause of v. 6 reads like a vivid description of monetary inflation, possibly caused by the depredations of Cambyses' troops, as well as by the natural disasters described in this passage (and see 2: 16, 17). A modern economist may well smile at Haggai's suggestion that the diversion of productive resources into an unproductive exercise of public expenditure such as the rebuilding of the temple could remedy such an inflation: but his objection would be answered quite remarkably when within a short time Darius authorized substantial aid to the project from the Persian treasury (Ezr. 6: 8, 9): an injection of foreign aid that might well have stimulated the flagging economy.

NOTES. (*a*) **Zerubbabel** (1) appears as the great-grandson of King Jehoiakim in 1 Chr. 3: 16–19 and the nephew of Shealtiel; Haggai stresses his heirship by regarding him as the son of Shealtiel for the purposes of a formal succession. **Joshua** (1) was in the Aaronic priestly line (1 Chr. 6: 1–15, where the line finishes with his father Jehozadak). Both men had been in the first return of 537 B.C. (Ezr. 2: 2; 3: 2).

(*b*) **timber** is to be brought for the rebuilding (v. 8): not, of course, that the structure was of timber, but the stonework was readily available in the surrounding ruins, and indeed part of the original walls may have been standing.

II. RESPONSE (1: 12–15) Sep. 21, 520.

The prompt response of leaders and of people brings a brief message of encouragement through the prophet: '**I am with you,**' declares the LORD (13). As work on the rebuilding starts in earnest, the writer, true to the biblical insight into the sovereignty of God, sees the renewed zeal of the people as itself the result of divine initiative (14). The response to God's call is met by God's own response of ready encouragement (13), and by an access of faith and devotion that is itself the gift of God (14). So the New Testament gospel ever lies latent in the Old Testament (see Phil. 2: 12–13). NOTE. For comment on the suggestion that vv. 15–19 of ch. 2 should follow at this point, see introductory remarks above and also *ad loc.* below.

III. GOD'S UNIVERSAL PURPOSE (2: 1–9) Oct. 17, 520.

Almost a month later, the prophetic voice was heard again. The moment was important. Sufficient time had elapsed for the first enthusiasm to be waning, and sufficient progress had been made for a realization of their own practical problems and shortcomings to begin to depress the workers. A few old men among them might even have infant memories of the old temple, and their old men's recollections would have added a lustre to the old that was sadly lacking from the new. To all of them, the long years of tradition and hallowed associations of the old temple must have seemed pitifully absent from that which their hands were now shaping. God, as always, is near to

the doubts and weaknesses of His people.

The encouragement comes both in retrospect and in prospect. The deepest racial memories of the people are stirred by a reminder of their national roots in the great deliverance of the Exodus. What they saw happening, the work which their own hands was shaping, was not to be despised, for it was all of a piece with their long national experience of the faithfulness and lovingkindness of their God. The parallel is enforced by the message to Joshua (v. 4), which echoes the similar encouragement given to another Joshua as Israel had entered the promised land long centuries before (Jos. 1: 5, 6). That of which they were themselves a part was another example of the tangible and visible fulfilment of God's ancient promises to their race. They are promises also which foreshadow the wider promises of the gospel (Mt. 28: 20; Jn 14: 23–26).

The retrospect leads on to prospect. The LORD **Almighty** (or the Lord of hosts—a ringing name for God that was plainly a favourite of Haggai) was Lord of the earth and of the nations. As Solomon's temple had been filled with wealth from many nations, so this new building also would be filled by their treasure, until it outshone its predecessor. Were not the treasures of the earth the possession of their God? (8). NOTES. (*a*) The translation of v. 7 ('**the desired of all nations**') carries messianic overtones. Although it is a misleading translation, and probably an inaccurate reading of the overt sense of the original (see 'The Ancient Versions', p. 14), no Christian reading these verses can fail to reflect that treasure and splendour, in a sense unguessed at by Haggai's contemporaries, was indeed to grace the site on which they were working, in the person of the lowly Son of Man. In a literal sense, Darius's generous subsidies already referred to (see Ezr. 6: 8, 9) would have given the people an early sense of the fulfilment of the prophecy: further fulfilment came in later centuries in the splendid extravagances by which the egregious Herod sought to buy Jewish loyalty (see Jn 2: 20). But to Christian understanding the supreme fulfilment was surely when He visited it who was Himself without earthly treasure, and whose rejection brought about its destruction (Mt. 24: 1, 2).

(*b*) **9. peace:** the many-coloured word *shālôm*, embracing peace, righteousness and wholeness.

IV. UNMERITED FAVOUR (2: 10–19) Dec. 18, 520.

Two further months have passed, and nearly four since the first prophecy by Haggai. This next section of the book contains its major puzzle. What was the pretext and the subject matter that caused the strange ritual questioning of vv. 10–14? As we have seen, some commentators have put forward as a solution a hypothetical textual corruption, and suggest that vv. 15–19 were originally attached to the second prophecy, following v. 13 of ch. 1 (and amending the month in 2: 18). The suggestion has superficial attractions: the verses read at first sight naturally after 1: 13 (but see comments in note below), and the awkward vv. 10–14 would then stand to be interpreted on their own. On this basis, they have been referred to the Jewish returned exiles' tendency to intermarry with the surrounding mixed peoples (cf. Ezr. 9: 1–3; Neh. 13: 23–31; but on any other count this would seem an anachronism here). It is on the basis of such an interpretation that some commentators have seen Haggai as a father of Judaistic exclusiveness; one, indeed, naming the date of this prophecy as 'the birthday of Judaism' (G. Fohrer, *Introduction to the Old Testament*, p. 460).

As already remarked, however, there is no MS evidence for such a reconstruction of the book, however attractive. There is nothing explicit in the passage to relate it necessarily to the problems of racial and cultic purity, which may well have come to prominence rather later. It is equally possible, and surely in context more appropriate, to relate it to the circumstances which have hitherto been to the fore in Haggai's preaching. This would interpret the 'uncleanness' as just that lassitude and lack of moral purpose which he had already castigated in 1: 4–11. Sloth and general demoralization are as invidious and debilitating as many a more open sin. It is in this precise insight that Haggai's prophetic insight and stature show themselves. The cultic principle of the transmission of ritual uncleanness then becomes for him a practical object lesson of deep moral principle, and of the deadly contagiousness of falling morale and carelessness. If it is of doubtful validity to see him as the father of Judaistic exclusiveness, it is surely not unreasonable to credit him with a considerable part in forming a much more attractive trait of Judaism: its sense of moral purpose and direction. Haggai would have been at home with the Victorian evangelicals!

There are other insights in this passage. Pre-eminent is the consciousness of ethical order that pervades the prophet's knowledge of God. To Haggai, life is responsible, and man is answerable to a God whose prerogative is the execution of justice in the ordinary events and commerce of life. If many see no connection between moral attitudes and men's material experiences, Haggai on the contrary announces a direct link between them. But parallel with that insight is the understanding that God is also a God of mercy and of compassion, ready to reward and succour even the unclean nation, though it be unclean in every work of its hands and every offering it brings; if the nation will but respond to God's call. So he can round off this fourth prophecy with a resounding confirmation of the promise that was implicit in his first rebuke.

NOTES (a) **19. Is there yet any seed left in the barn?:** This phrase can be used in different ways. As part of a December saying it reminds the hearers that their seed is no longer in store, but already sown, latent with the promise of the harvest that God has promised: an accurate parallel with the next question asking if the fruit trees are still barren. If it had been a September saying (as the theory that this section of the book is displaced would require) it would refer to the ripe 'seed' of the harvest, standing ready for storage, and with the next question would imply another disappointing crop.

(b) **18. the day when the foundation of the LORD's temple was laid:** Ezr. 3: 10, 4: 24 would suggest that this was in 537; but it is also possible that Haggai was referring to the recommencement of the work that had just occurred. The second alternative would make the theory that this section of the book should be related back to ch. 1 a little more plausible. See Joyce G. Baldwin, *Haggai, Zechariah, Malachi. TOTC*, pp. 52 f., for a note on the ambiguity of the expression.

V. PERSONAL MESSAGE TO ZERUBBABEL (2: 20–23) Dec. 18, 520.

The fifth prophecy occurred on the same day as the fourth. Addressed personally to Zerubbabel, the Jewish leader and himself a prince of the house of David, it forms an eschatological epilogue to the book, and after the trauma of the exile it re-establishes, with messianic overtones, the ancient prophecies of God in relation to David's line.

In this prophecy we can sense the typical prophetic foreshortening. **21. I will shake . . . :** these are words typical of the establishment of a new era, a new aeon in the purpose of God, marked by the construction of the new temple. Despite the overthrow of the nations of the earth, and the collapse of the existing order into suicidal chaos, God's chosen servant will remain unshaken, secure as the ring on the hand of God Himself. He will in fact be the visible embodiment of the truth that God is the originator of the judgment, and Himself remains unshaken, a secure foundation for faith and trust amidst collapsing worlds. It is the same note as that on which Habakkuk closed his prophecy (Hab. 3: 17–19).

For the Christian reader, the endings of the

two books, one (Habakkuk) written in expected economic collapse and the other (Haggai) in political, combine to point to one man: the ultimate Chosen of God, Himself God manifest in flesh.

NOTE. The prophecy of the **signet ring** (23), the symbol of executive power, for it was the impression of the ring that sealed the royal authority on documents issued in the king's name, reverses the judgment pronounced on Zerubbabel's grandfather Jeconiah (Jer. 22: 24). The reversal is confirmed by the pronouncement that **Zerubbabel** is **my servant**, thus linking him directly with the great servant prophecies of Jewish tradition.

BIBLIOGRAPHY

ACKROYD, P. R., *Israel under Babylon and Persia.* NCB (Oxford, 1970).

BALDWIN, J. G., *Haggai, Zechariah, Malachi.* TOTC (London, 1972).

JONES, D. R., *Haggai, Zechariah and Malachi.* TC (London, 1962).

MASON, R., *The Books of Haggai, Zechariah and Malachi.* (Cambridge, 1977).

WISEMAN, D. J., 'Haggai' in NBCR (London, 1970).

ZECHARIAH

DAVID J. ELLIS

The collapse of the Babylonian Empire and the rise to power of Cyrus II, ruler of Anshan, were events which were destined to exert a formidable influence on world history in general, from 539 B.C. onwards, and on the exiled Jews in Babylon in particular. Cyrus himself regarded the decline and defeat of Babylon as a judgment against Nabonidus for his forsaking the Babylonian god, Marduk, and his removal of local idols to Babylon in the wake of the great Persian advance of 546 B.C. (Cf. *The Cyrus Cylinder* in *ANET*, pp. 315 f.; *DOTT*, pp. 92 ff.)

To the Jews in exile there was a wholly distinct aspect to the change of power. Cyrus, having conquered Astyges his Median overlord —probably aided by a mutinous army, according to the *Nabonidus Chronicle*—became heir to a double kingdom; Cyrus who was hailed as 'King of the Persians' now ruled over the Medo-Persian Empire, the greatest so far known. But this master-stroke signalled to the Jews the commencement of a restoration through the hands of one they came to regard as a divinely appointed deliverer.

Such an interpretation, however seemingly out-of-character for the people of Israel, was eventually justified by events which followed Cyrus' consolidation of his rule. Both the OT and the *Cyrus Cylinder* indicate how clearly Cyrus encouraged the exiles to return to their own land in 538 B.C. (2 Chr. 36: 23; Ezr. 1: 2 ff.). No doubt Cyrus was reversing the policies of his former Babylonian enemy, but possibly also relieving himself of further responsibility for the welfare of the exiles within his Empire.

Specific mention is made, moreover (Ezr. 1: 2), of the charge which Cyrus had received from **The LORD, the God of heaven** . . . to build him a house at Jerusalem. Some light is shed upon this by the *Cyrus Cylinder* in which the king pleads, 'May all the gods whom I have placed within their sanctuaries address a daily prayer in my favour . . .', and suggests that Cyrus' tolerant, even benevolent attitude towards the returning exiles was not entirely without self-interest. Nevertheless, the Jews were assisted in the rebuilding of the Temple, aided in part by donations of timber granted by Cyrus (Ezr. 3: 7) and supported morally by the fact that the sacred vessels confiscated by Nebuchadrezzar were restored to their rightful place. So, in the second year after the Return a celebration of thanksgiving was held for the commencement of rebuilding operations.

These immediate ambitions were not to last for long. The mixed population which had occupied Jewish territory during the absence of the exilic community endeavoured to share in the work of restoration. The repatriates, under leadership of Joshua the high priest, and Zerubbabel, were adamant in their refusal to allow these 'people of the land' any share in the work. This became the seed-bed of permanent hostility between Jews and Samaritans, and serious work on the Temple was halted until 520 B.C.

To sensitive Jews, however, the reconstruction of the house of God was of paramount importance. However nobly the Jews in exile had continued some form of worship, the Temple as the centre of Israel's religious life remained fundamental. Both Jeremiah and Ezekiel had asserted that both as a witness to the nations (Ezek. 37: 28) and as the evidence of God's continuing purpose for Israel (Jer. 7: 11), the name Zion was of unique significance. Doubtless the circumstances of the Exile had brought home to the Jews the fact that the honour of God was bound up with the existence of the Temple in Jerusalem and with the continuity of its function. Moreover, the re-emergence of the house of God in Zion would be the sign that the covenant had been renewed, and this was, as former prophets had declared, the condition on which the new messianic age depended.

This Israel who went into exile a nation was to return again in character as a church. The moral and spiritual impetus that was necessary to bring about the rebuilding of the Temple came to be provided by two great prophets who appeared when the time was ripe—Haggai and Zechariah. The effective message of the former was directed against the apathy and selfishness which had combined to hinder the progress of construction; the emphatic call of the latter was directed towards the place of God's house in a future and glorious age, when the blessing of God would be extended beyond the particular limits of his own people and reach out to the rest of the nations.

Composition

There are clear differences between the two sections of the book. The first section (chs. 1–8) contains unmistakable references to time and place, most of which are attached, by a series of three references, to Zechariah (1: 1, 7; 7: 1). In the second part (chs. 9–14) the name of Zechariah does not appear and there are no clear allusions of an historical nature—most notably an absence of any indication of the completion of the Temple as might be expected from the occupation with the Temple in the first part of the book.

A significant difference also appears in the interest which the prophet shows in the restoration of an earthly dynasty in the earlier chapters, whereas later in the book hopes seem to be pinned on a coming messianic figure, though some see an exception to this in the passage alluding to the pierced man of chap. 12. The former section (cf. Analysis) mainly comprises an anthology of visions and oracles; the latter part of the book is a collection of independent eschatological sayings.

Generally speaking, the literary styles of the two sections are distinct from each other. The earlier chapters, with the exception of two short passages (2: 6–13; 8: 1–8), are in prose. The later chapters are poetic (except 11: 4–16 and some isolated units in chs. 12–14). Differences in literary style, however, are not invariably a pointer to different authorship, and the change in the overall message of the later chapters, especially 9–11, could well account for stylistic change alone.

Critical studies in Zechariah go back at least to the seventeenth century and to the investigation of the book by Joseph Mede who was initially concerned with the quotation of Zech. 11: 13 in Mt. 27: 9 where it is attributed to Jeremiah. Mede concluded that chaps. 9–11 of Zechariah were from the hand of Jeremiah. Other critical viewpoints were soon to follow. Some earlier scholars gave chaps. 12–14 a pre-exilic date, but it was H. Corrodi (1792) who first assigned the whole of chaps 9–14 to a post-exilic date and long after Zechariah. Variations on this theme have appeared from time to time ever since. A number of notable scholars have claimed that these later chapters bear distinctive marks of the Greek period (*e.g.* J. G. Eichhorn, 1824, K. Marti, 1904, and B. Duhm, 1911). More recently others have placed them firmly in the Maccabean period (*e.g.*, W. O. E. Oesterley) while a few scholars have argued for the Greek period in general whilst dating certain sections of these chapters before and after that time.

It is worth noting, however, that no single pre-exilic or post-exilic, post-Zechariah hypothesis for the later chapters has met with universal acceptance among those scholars who divide the book. Whilst it is true that chaps. 9–14 are cast in eschatological writing and look forward to a messianic ruler, the king in the earlier chapters is messianic also (cf. 6: 12 f.), and it can justly be claimed that these messianic figures portrayed in the two sections are harmonious.

A major difficulty felt by scholars appears in the reference to '. . . your sons, O Greece.' (Heb. *yāwān*, 9: 13). It has been extravagantly asserted that this is possibly decisive evidence against unity of authorship. Greece, we are told, is characterized here as a contemporary enemy to be fought and conquered. But the usual rendering of this word in English owes as much to interpretation as it does to translation. Heb. *yāwān* refers elsewhere in the OT to distant and alien peoples (Gen. 10: 2, 4; Isa. 66: 19). E. A. Speiser regards the Genesis text as a reference to the Ionians (*Genesis*, 1962, pp. 45 f., 65 f.). The name appears to be linked with *Iawones* in Homer (*Iliad*, 13: 686; cf. Dan. 8: 21; 10: 20). E. J. Young, however, rejects this as necessarily pointing to a dating after the time of Zechariah. He argues that the passage speaks of the defeat of Greece rather than her triumph, and in any case Greece was a notable power in Zechariah's time (*An Introduction to the Old Testament*, 1966, p. 280). The words are treated as a gloss in both the NEB and the JB.

In spite of arguments to the contrary, the possibility that the book of Zechariah is a unity must not be lightly dismissed because most claims for alternative authorship of chaps. 9–14 are generally inconclusive. It has been suggested that even if the book is not from Zechariah altogether the second part may be followed the first within a short space of time. W. E. Barnes actually suggested that the book comprises the work of Zechariah the prophet, followed by the writings of 'Zechariah the disciple' (*Haggai, Zechariah and Malachi* in The Cambridge Bible, 1917). A specific designation such as this, however, is purely gratuitous. It is quite possible that these later chapters represent two out of three short prophetic collections, each beginning with the phrase **An oracle . . . the word of the LORD** (Zech. 9: 1; 12: 1; Mal. 1: 1), which, because they were fragmentary in nature, were attached to the scroll of another (known) prophet to avoid their being lost. This was a view held in rabbinical circles for a considerable time and is published in certain Talmudic writings. It is also the conclusion reached by some modern commentators (*e.g.*, H. L. Ellison, *Men Spake From God*, 1952, p. 123 f.; F. F. Bruce, 'The Book of Zechariah and the Passion Narrative' in *BJRL*, vol. 43, no. 2, 1961, p. 337 f.; cf. also *NBD*, 1962, p. 1356).

Without definitive evidence for or against the unity of the book it is therefore wiser to take and read the book as a whole. That there is an underlying unity of thought and message is undisputed. In order to understand Zechariah and appreciate what it is saying to the present-day reader no advantage can be gained by dissection. Zechariah spells out the purpose of God in the time of crisis; it re-affirms a fundamental faith in God as All-Sovereign Lord who will one day take a firm and immediate hand in world affairs, bringing his people back to

their true centre and restoring them to their proper heritage. God holds the reins of governments and nations, and even in the midst of distraction and discouragement the prophet announces that there is nothing that God cannot refashion according to his purpose.

ANALYSIS

First Section: A Prophetic Anthology
(1: 1–8: 23)

I. A CALL TO REPENTANCE (1: 1–6)
1. In the eighth month of the second year of Darius: words which firmly place this section of Zechariah in October–November 520

B.C. **The prophet Zechariah son of Berekiah, the son of Iddo:** it is unusual in the OT for a prophet to distinguish himself as such. But the use of the third person here may indicate the work of an early editor—one who was perhaps responsible for collecting various portions of the general prophetic corpus (cf. 7: 1). Some commentators see problems in the mention of

Berekiah, and either omit his name as a gloss (cf. JB) or understand the title as a conflation for two authors of the book: Zechariah the son of Iddo for chs. 1–8, and a deutero-Zechariah, a son of Berekiah, for chs. 9–14. But the preferable interpretation lies in regarding the names as father and grandfather respectively. The reference to 'Zechariah the son of Berakiah' (Mt. 23: 35) is a slip probably made by a later copyist (contrast Lk. 11: 51). The Matthew reference makes more sense if applied to Zechariah, the priestly son of Jehoiada (cf. 2 Chr. 24: 20 ff.).

2. 'The LORD was very angry . . .': cf. v. 15. The anger (Heb. *qāṣap*) of the Almighty is not so inconsistent with the NT as some suppose (cf. Rom. 1: 18–32; 2: 4; Eph. 2: 3). The word employed here describes a consistent element in God's nature as contrasted with a momentary or temporary indignation (Heb. *ḥārāh*) which is applied in the OT both to God (cf. Exod. 4: 14) and to man (cf. Jon. 4: 1, 4, 9). God is angry both with Israel (here) and with the nations (v. 15), since in different respects both had acted to obstruct the divine purpose.

3. Return to me . . . and I will return to you: the operative verb (Heb. *shûb*) is the OT counterpart to the word 'repentance' (Gk. *metanoia*) in the NT though the message of the prophet required some physical reformation (see next verse; also Mal. 3: 7). **4. the earlier prophets:** these were apparently by this time accorded some sort of 'canonical' status; Jeremiah seems to be particularly in mind (cf. Jer. 18: 11; 17: 23). His words are now authenticated by Zechariah's fresh insistence on the need for repentance. But Zechariah has hope. In referring to the forebears of his people he implies that there is still opportunity for amendment, though not without hinting at the possibility of punishment. **6.** God's words are irrevocable in their authority: **did not my words . . . overtake . . .?** (Heb. *hissîg*). That the outcome of God's unheeded warnings to Israel was certain to bring its recompense had been amply demonstrated by the Exile. **Then they repented and said . . . :** referring almost certainly to the words of the prophet's contemporaries, though some understood these words as an allusion to the 'forefathers' (v. 4). But the latter interpretation makes the sequence of thought less clear. The clause possibly introduces us to a standard confessional retained by the Jewish people during and after the Exile.

II. VISIONS AND ORACLES (1: 7–6: 8)

Whilst each symbol presented in the following eight prophetic visions must be understood independently, it is clear that the book is designed to bring home a single message overall by arranging the collection chiastically. The similarities of structure throughout this section

and a number of the visions of the Book of the Revelation, together with a degree of common symbolism is well-known (cf. A. M. Farrer, *The Book of the Revelation*, 1964; W. Hendriksen, *More Than Conquerors*, 1944; and F. F. Bruce, 'Revelation', below).

i. Four horsemen (1: 7–17)
Horses symbolize dominance and strength (cf. Rev. 6: 1–8). The 'man' (8) and the 'angel' (9) are clearly one and the same; angels appear in apocalyptic literature as those who interpret visions. This interpreter supplies the key to the successive visions imparted to the prophet (cf. 1: 8; 2: 3; 4: 1, 5; 5: 5; 6: 4). The 'angel of the LORD' (11, 12) is possibly a further figure represented as an intercessor for Jerusalem and Judah.

7. the eleventh month . . . Shebat . . . : a Babylonian month-name (January–February), used only here in the OT. The second year of Darius was 520–519 B.C.; this is the date of all the visions to the end of ch. 6. The day referred to was February 15, 519 B.C. **8. a man riding a red horse:** the horses of this passage may be patterned according to the mounted despatches used by Persia in controlling the Empire. Too much extra significance should not be read into the colours of the horses. One interesting suggestion is that these horses reflect in turn sunset, whereas in 6: 2 they represent dawn (cf. G. von Rad, *Old Testament Theology* 11, 1965, pp. 282 f.). Other suggestions, notably from G. R. Driver and W. D. McHardy, are that the text should be reconstructed on the assumption that these colours would originally have been abbreviated, though McHardy reads the same four colours here as in 6: 1–6, *viz.*, red, yellow, black, white (cf. W. D. McHardy, 'The Horses in Zechariah' in *In Memoriam Paul Kahle*, BZAW 103, 1968). What is probably more significant is that in this passage the horses, with their riders, are engaged in reconnaissance; in 6: 2–8 they draw chariots to the four compass-points of the earth as emissaries of destruction. In this manner only can Zechariah's vision be aligned to Rev. 6 and the following chapter in which four winds of judgment are restrained by four angels (Rev. 7: 1 ff.).

a ravine (Heb. *meṣûlāh*) means a depression or hollow, used only here and probably as a reference to a specific location. J. G. Baldwin (*Haggai, Zechariah, Malachi*, 1972, p. 95) thinks that the reference is to the Kidron valley, suggesting that the Lord had arrived within the precincts of Jerusalem. **11. '. . . the whole world at rest'** (Heb. *shōqāṭet*): the natural sense of this report from the four horsemen is that the enemies of Darius have been subdued and consequently peace is at last being enjoyed throughout his Empire. But the Hebrew suggests that this peace is one of subjugation and passive acceptance of injustice rather than contentment. If so, this is not what God wants (cf. vv. 14 f.) for in the midst of an uneasy quiet the Temple remains unbuilt, and the interjection of **the angel of the LORD** (12) indicates how far the present time of quiet was from serving God's purpose. **these seventy years:** whilst immediately suggesting the time of the Exile (cf. Jer. 25: 11 f.), the phrase probably also conveys a period of time long enough to assure the prophet's hearers that any hope of their seeing the rebuilding of God's house was likely to be shattered.

14. Then the angel . . . said to me, 'Proclaim this word . . .': we are not given the full message of comfort supplied in God's answer to the angel. But the substance of that answer is handed on to the prophet for him to proclaim. **I am very jealous for Jerusalem and Zion:** if Jerusalem marked the natural heart and centre of the Jewish people, then Zion signified her spiritual home. Jerusalem was the focal point of Judah's station in the ancient world; Zion was the city in which the Temple had been designed as the centre of God's purpose. The Lord's zeal for Jerusalem is more fully spelled out in 8: 1–8. But in this immediate context divine zeal is coloured with divine fury against the nations who have **added to the calamity** (15)—going beyond the limits which God will allow in chastising his people. These nations **feel secure** (cf. Am. 6: 1), enjoying a respite that is ill-gotten and ill-founded. God now comes to Jerusalem in compassion. Whereas some building work on the Temple had already been undertaken, how far it had progressed is indicated by reference to **the measuring line** (16) stretched over the boundaries of the city. This is the divine assurance given to stimulate afresh the work of rebuilding. **17. again . . . :** four times over a word of hope accompanies the prophet's message. He must also continue *his* work and **Proclaim further.** Cities shall again **overflow** (Heb. *pûs*) **with prosperity** (Heb. *ṭôb*), that is, with all that is good and derived from a spiritual harmony with the purpose of God. Judah will once more become an influence for good (Heb. *ṭôb*) among her neighbours. Comfort will again surround Zion, and God's choice of Jerusalem as dedicated to his glorious intention will again be seen.

What therefore may have appeared to be a period of rest in the world of the prophet Zechariah was not in fact furthering God's purpose among his people. The prophet was urged to proclaim God's compassion and wrath side by side, coupled with an assertion that the divine purpose would nevertheless succeed to such an extent that the moral and spiritual prosperity of God's people would overflow among the nations. This is a re-affirmation

of former prophetic messages in which God's intention for good is extended beyond the national frontiers of Israel (cf. Isa. 2: 1–4; Mic. 4: 1–4; Jer. 33: 7 ff.).

ii. Four horns and four craftsmen (1: 18–21)
In the Hebrew Bible this section marks the opening of the second chapter of the book. **18. four horns:** presumably horns of living animals, though these are not part of the vision. A horn (Heb. *qeren*) in the OT symbolizes strength (cf. 1 Kg. 22: 11). Cut off, as they may be here, they represent the spoils of victory (Ps. 75: 10) or are displayed as a victory symbol in poetic writing (Ps. 132: 17). Here, in addition, they signify specific world powers. (cf. Dan. 7: 7 ff., 20 f.; 8: 9–13; Rev. 13: 1). **19. Judah, Israel and Jerusalem** collocated here represent the totality of God's people united in a single place of worship. (Some LXX manuscripts omit 'Jerusalem'.) **20. four craftsmen:** the agents of divine intervention. **21. These . . . :** preferably rendered 'Those are the horns'.

iii. Surveying Jerusalem (2: 1–13)
This vision underlines the former promise (cf. 1: 16) by showing that God's future plans for Jerusalem will be achieved by human hands. **2.** The implication of establishing the dimensions of the 'new' Jerusalem seems to be that the expanse of the new city will surpass that of the old city (cf., however, Ezek. 40: 1–39). **4.** The **young man** who acts as surveyor in the vision needs fuller instruction in God's purpose. What would have appeared sensible and natural in providing walls as defences is not, however, in God's new plans. For the new city will be open and without either danger or fear. **5. I myself will be a wall of fire:** God emphatically announces his intention to defend the city against every possible threat in the future. The words inevitably took the prophet back to the inauguration of the nation under the leadership of Moses. Fire and glory recall Exod. 13: 21 f. Just as fire led and protected Israel then, so now fire will shield and protect her again. With no visible wall for protection God alone will be the one to whom the people will turn for their safety. **I** (emphatic) **will be its glory within:** some commentators (*e.g.,* Th. Chary, *Les Prophètes et le culte à partir de l'exil*, 1955, pp. 132 f.) believe that the (unusual) inclusion of the Hebrew verb 'to be' here is an allusion to the theophany of Exod. 3: 14.

Verses 6–13 contain two poetic oracles interspersed with comments by the prophet. J. G. Baldwin (*op. cit.*) rightly argues that these two poems are clearly distinguished in vv. 6–9 and vv. 10–13; each one gives its reason for the divine announcement—**for** (6, 10)—and the second follows on from the first in direct continuation of an overall message. **6. Come!**

Come! is an exclamation of alarm tinged with pity (cf. RSV Isa. 29: 1; 55: 1). The word is addressed to exiles remaining in Babylon, urging them to forsake the comfort of their exilic existence and to return to Jerusalem. The urgency of the announcement is heightened by the call to **Escape** (Heb. *himmāleṭî*).

8. after he has honored me and has sent me against the nations is capable of several interpretations. **after** (Heb. *'aḥar*) may either be the normal Hebrew conjunction, as in most cases in the OT, or possibly meaning 'with'; **honor** (Heb. *kābôd*) is a noun derived from a root meaning 'heaviness'. Three renderings are therefore possible; (a) 'after the Lord in his glory sent me', in which case the meaning is that, like Isaiah (cf. 6: 1 ff.), Zechariah received a vision of the glory of the Lord at the time of his commission for the prophetic ministry; (b) 'with dignity he sent me' reading 'with' for the Heb. *'aḥar*; cf. Ec. 12: 2; Ps. 73: 25, where this rendering makes better sense (for Heb. *kābôd* as 'dignity' we have a number of OT precedents: e.g., Mal. 1: 6; 2 Chr. 26: 18); or we may read (c) 'after the glorious vision the Lord sent me' (so H. G. Mitchell, *Zechariah*, ICC, 1912). In this rendering (which is followed by the RV) 'glory' is equated with 'vision', and the prophet delivers his message afterwards. The rendering offered by Chary (*op. cit.*) is unacceptable.

9. By God's hand the nation which had threatened his people will be overthrown and a reversal of the fortunes of Israel will take place. **Then you will know that the LORD Almighty has sent me** are the prophet's own words. Fulfilment of the word will endorse the authority of the messenger (cf. Ezek. 33: 33). **10. Shout and be glad** opens the second poem. The return of the Lord at last to Zion is good cause for celebration. **O Daughter of Zion:** refers to the city of Jerusalem and its populace as distinct from the Temple (cf. 2: 4 f.; 8: 3). With this promise the covenant relationship is assured as it was in former days (cf. Exod. 25: 8; 1 Kg. 6: 13) and the visible signs of God's presence will be good cause for jubilation. **11.** But this covenant will not be exclusive: . . . they **will become my people** is singularly covenant language and is applied to **many nations** who, by a positive act of will, are to **be joined with the LORD. 12. the holy land:** a phrase used only here in the Bible (but cf. Ps. 2: 6; 15: 1; 99: 9). The oracle denotes not just a holy place with sacred ordinances and special symbols, but an entire national home given over to the purpose of God.

13. Be still: there is, however, a tension in the message. The songs of joy must be tempered with awesome expectation (Heb. *has*) surrounding the movement of the Lord from his heavenly abode (cf. Hab. 2: 20). The two

poems thus end on a solemn note of anticipation. When God moves men must wait in reverential stillness (cf. Rev. 8: 1).

iv. Joshua, the High Priest (3: 1–10)
1. Then he showed me . . . : refers to the angel of the previous three visions. On this occasion the prophet is drawn aside and directed towards the substance of the vision, and together with its location (the Temple?) the vision differs from earlier visions since it more specifically portrays a celestial court scene in which **Joshua the high priest** is arraigned before the Lord as judge. **Satan** is the accuser. The fact that the text has the definite article before the name Satan (Heb. *hassāṭān*) suggests that it is principally in the role of prosecuting counsel that the adversary is seen.

This noun *sāṭān* is variously rendered in the OT: as adversary (1 Kg. 11; 1 Sam. 29: 4) and as opponent (Num. 22: 22–32). The Septuagint renders Heb. *sāṭān* as *diabolos*, i.e. informer. Probably the most complete as well as incisive reference to Satan in any single passage is found in Job (chs. 1–2). Important to note is its connection with the present passage. In Job Satan is represented as one of the 'sons of God' (Heb. *benê hā'elōhîm*). In this capacity he is a regular attender in the divine presence. The context of the Job passage is not altogether dissimilar from this either. The following chapter of Zechariah refers to 'seven eyes of the LORD' which range through the whole earth (Heb. *shûṭ*, 'run to and fro'; cf. comment *in loc.*). In Job (1: 7) Satan stands before the Almighty as one who has similarly run 'to and fro' on the earth. More fundamentally, therefore, Satan appears in conjunction with the present passage to be one of the sons of God who roams the earth to bring to God unfavourable reports of men. (There is some linguistic evidence to support the contention that the Heb. verb *shûṭ*, referred to above, has direct links with the name of Satan, since the latter may originally have been *shāṭān*—the difference being only a tiny diacritical point over the first letter of the word. Cf. N. H. Tur Sinai, *The Book of Job*, Jerusalem, 1957, pp. 38 ff.) From this it is easy to understand why ideas of 'opponent' and 'accuser' should develop.

2. Satan's accusation, whatever it may have been, is of little avail, for God says to him **'The LORD rebuke you, Satan!'** Joshua appears to stand as representative of his people, described as **a burning stick snatched from the fire** (cf. Am. 4: 11), probably recalling God's merciful deliverance from Egypt, where Israel's oppression was likened to a furnace (Dt. 4: 20). **3.** Joshua, moreover, is dressed in **filthy clothes** (Heb. *begādîm ṣô'îm*) such as would be the case of one who had escaped fire. But the dirty clothing signifies the iniquity of the people, against which Joshua is helpless. So the angel commands that the soiled clothes be exchanged for **rich garments** (4) and on the head of Joshua is placed **a clean turban** (5), that is, the priestly biretta, or mitre, indicating that Joshua and, by implication, his people with him are once more accepted in God's presence. **6.** Joshua is now reinstated. He is freshly commissioned to his work, and with this he is offered twin promises which were clearly not given to priests before him. **7. If you will walk in my ways:** an exhortation to positive obedience to God's will; at the same time it implies a total rejection of anything which would concede ground to the ways of man. Moreover, if Joshua will **keep my requirements** (Heb. *mishmeret*), that is, faithfully enact the priestly ritual (cf. Num. 3), he **will govern my house**. The Heb. verb (*dîn*) means 'to judge' and denotes that the judicial authority in all matters concerned with the Temple and its function, which in former days had been executed by the monarch (cf. 1 Kg. 2: 27; 2 Kg. 16: 10–19), is now transferred to Joshua and all who will succeed him. Moreover, whereas in the past the high priest alone had access into the Holy of Holies, Joshua is now offered the right of direct entrance into the immediate presence of God **among these standing here**. In short, Joshua is promised a spiritual privilege far greater than those of the priests of former times, when entrance into the Holy Place was a physical right signifying a unique advantage taken once annually; Joshua is now granted something far greater—a promise which could only come to true fulfilment in later days in the person and work of Jesus (Heb. 4: 14) and through him be granted to his followers (Heb. 4: 16).

8. Joshua's colleagues, who sit with him in the priestly congregation, are described as **men symbolic of things to come** (Heb. *môpēt*) in that their continuation in priestly work throughout all the vicissitudes of the Exile and before carries the divine guarantee that God is to do something greater, something better through his servant **the Branch** (cf. 6: 12 f.).

The **Branch** (Heb. *ṣemaḥ*) is more explicitly described in Jer. 23: 5 in connection with a future Davidic ruler where that prophet personalizes a more indefinite promise of an earlier prophecy (Isa. 4: 2). In a further prophetic word Jeremiah assured his hearers (cf. 33: 15) that the 'Branch' was God's way of indicating that the twin virtues of justice and righteousness would be maintained by descendants of David. These twin virtues are already confirmed in Joshua (cf. v. 7 above), but because the removal of the iniquity of the people is highlighted in this passage Joshua is promised that the very presence of his priestly friends with him is to prepare the way for a successor of messianic proportions. The 'Branch' is moreover called **my servant** (which recalls the

Servant passages of Isaiah, but especially the final poem in 52: 13–53: 12) in anticipation of a fuller statement in 6: 12 f.

9. The figure of speech now changes. **the stone . . . that one stone** (Heb. *'eben*) is almost certainly a precious stone associated with the high priest's mitre (cf. Exod. 29: 6 f.) together with the various additional priestly robes laid down for the ritual of the Day of Atonement (cf. Exod. 28: 36 ff.). Also, Exod. 28: 10–12 speaks of two stones upon which are engraved the names of the tribes of Israel. Here upon one stone with **seven eyes** will be engraved an inscription probably recording the merciful removal of the guilt of the people. Any suggestion that the stone is connected with the foundation stone of the Temple, as some commentators think, is probably to be ruled out. On the contrary, this seven-faced stone represents the complete direction of all activity from the messianic Temple. **10. In that day . . .** , a familiar futuristic phrase in the OT (Heb. *bayyôm hahû'*), men will live together in extraordinary contentment, sharing together the blessings of an age of peace.

v. The Lampstand and two Olive Trees (4: 1–14)

In a fitting continuation of the previous imagery associated with priest and Temple, Zechariah now sees **a solid gold lampstand** , obviously reminiscent of the Tabernacle (cf. Exod. 25: 31 ff.). Ten such lampstands were also provided by Solomon for his Temple (1 Kg. 7: 49). A lampstand (Heb. *mᵉnôrāh*) is distinguished from a solitary lamp (Heb. *nēr*; Gk. *lychnos*) in that it functioned on a pedestal or tripod. The lamp as such has become traditional in Judaism to this day (the Menorah), and is pictured in Titus' Arch in Rome as from the Jerusalem Temple in the time of Herod. C. H. H. Wright (*Zechariah and his Prophecies*, 1879, pp. 84 f.) attempted a reconstruction of this lampstand on the 'Titus' model, but ran into difficulties. It is certain that Zechariah's lampstand, together with its archetype, was much less refined and decorative than is usually suggested; it was possibly constructed around a single stem with a cupola (Heb. *gullāh*) at the top, branching out into **seven lights** (Heb. *nēr*) each with **seven channels** (Heb. *mûṣāqôth*) or 'pipes'. The item is therefore fairly simple to visualize and probably not unlike incense burners discovered by T. Dothan in 1958 near Accho (cf. C. H. H. Wright, *op. cit.*, pp. 84 ff.; R. North 'Zechariah's Seven-Spout Lampstand' in *Biblica*, 51, 1970; also D. J. Wiseman, *Illustrations from Biblical Archaeology*, 1958, p. 102). **3.** the **two olive trees** on either side of the lampstand provide cover. **4.** Zechariah's question is not immediately answered (cf. vv. 5, 11, 12). **6.** A more pressing word is given for Zerubbabel, the other active leader in the plans for rebuilding the Temple, which *will* be completed, but: **Not by might** (Heb. *ḥayil*, i.e., sheer force of labour), **nor by power** (Heb. *kōaḥ* i.e., ability), **but by my Spirit** (Heb. *rûaḥ*). The Spirit (or 'wind') of God which formed the earth, parted the seas, and raised the dead was no less to be the driving force for God's new work in the prophet's day. The message, indeed, is that whilst all manpower, provisions of materials, and expertise were part of the Lord's plan, over them all his Spirit would unify all that was done to bring the work to a glorious completion.

7. What are you, O mighty mountain?: what obstacles, then, can stand in the way of God's work if his Spirit empowers all those who seek to do it? Possibly the mountain was suggested by a heap of debris which bore witness to the failure of former days. But that a full-sized physical mountain is meant is no more the case than in a similar reference in Isaiah (cf. 40: 4; 41: 15). What above most things was called for at this time was the discernment of God's purpose and an authoritative interpretation of his ways. Nor can it be the case that the 'mountain' stood for some specific personal opposition to the prophet's work. Interesting examples can be cited from Rabbinic literature in which a man who shows spiritual discernment is termed 'a mountain remover' (Heb. *'ōqēr hārîm*). This alone makes proper sense of Jesus' words in Mk 11: 23 (cf. 1 C. 13: 2). **Zerubbabel . . . will bring out the capstone** (Heb. *hā'eben ha-rô'shāh*): this is the stone of chief importance in the new Temple in that it completes and unifies all the rest of the building. It will be brought out amid cries of wonder: **'God bless it! God bless it!'** (cf. Ps. 118: 22 ff.; Mt. 21: 42). **9. 'The hands of Zerubbabel have laid the foundation . . .'** and Zerubbabel will complete the work, as the text goes on to say. But, as J. G. Baldwin points out (*Haggai, Zechariah, Malachi*, 1974, pp. 52 f., 122), the translation is misleading in suggesting a relaying of foundations for the Temple. These were still in place. The confusion arises because of the absence of any proper noun for 'foundation' in the Hebrew text. As it stands, the verb (Heb. *yāsad*) can with equally good sense be read 'to build'. (This suggestion also helps to remove the difficulty encountered between the building operations carried out by Solomon, in 1 Kg. 6: 37 f., and those mentioned in Ezr. 3: 10 f.) The message is therefore one of firm assurance; Zerubbabel, who is to commence the work of rebuilding, will see its completion also. **10.** Moreover, there is encouragement for those who are doubtful. Those who have despised **the day of small things** (Heb. *qᵉṭannôth*), a cryptic phrase denoting a time of insignificant beginnings, and live to see God's word passing

into fulfilment, would have good cause to rejoice meanwhile when they **see the plumb line in the hand of Zerubbabel**. (The NEB renders this: 'the stone called Separation' to preserve a link with v. 7. There is no doubt that 'the stone' must be kept in the text. The translation offered by the RSV, in common with others, owes more to early Aramaic, Latin and Greek versions, rather than to the Hebrew *ha'eben ha-bᵉdîl*.) The AV at least offers an alternative in the margin: 'stone of tin'—which is not helpful. Heb. *bᵉdîl* is derived from a root meaning 'to separate' (as an alloy; cf. use in Isa. 1: 25). Lexicons indicate that, with the one exception of this passage, the noun usually refers to tin or dross, i.e., that which is separated. The Syriac version shows that 'separation' provides better sense here. On this assumption the passage falls into place. The people will have cause for rejoicing when, at last, they see Zerubbabel place the final stone of the new building into position. This, therefore, is not the same stone as in 3: 9. It is the final stone, set apart, separated, for the glorious completion of the house of God.

'(These seven are the eyes of the LORD . . .)': the angel now turns to the answer of Zechariah's question in v. 4. The following two trees supply the oil for the lampstand by pipes to the 'seven lamps' of v. 2. Whilst, on the one hand, the Lord's presence is in the Temple, his 'eyes' **range** (Heb. 'run to and fro') throughout the earth. **12.** The two **olive trees** carry **two branches** beside **two gold pipes that pour out golden oil:** the text here is difficult. Literally, the Hebrew reads: 'the two golden pipes which empty the gold out of themselves'. It is certain enough that the two trees supply the oil for the lampstand by means of 'pipes' (Heb. *ṣantārôth*, perhaps 'spouts'). From what follows (v. 14) it would appear that the two trees are thus symbols of Joshua and Zerubbabel. But it does not do justice to the text to suggest, as some do, that these two men are pictured as giving all of themselves, or of their best, to the Lord. The NIV and RSV are probably correct in taking 'gold' to mean 'golden oil'. Since oil is not specifically mentioned, however, the text should not be pressed to mean that the lampstand and its function are solely maintained by Joshua and Zerubabbel. Yet they are literally 'sons of oil' (14), i.e., filled with oil as two who have been clearly anointed to act as God's appointed agents.

The lampstand thus represents not the Lord, as some have suggested, but the testimony of the Temple and its people to him. The solution for the impotency of the nation lay in a reemphasis upon the fundamental character of witness which God had, through the new Temple, again called his people to undertake, and also in the provision of leadership which was obedient, responsible and active. If Zechariah's visions are read in this manner it becomes clearer that they prepare the way for a fuller adumbration of the relation between witness and leadership of which we read in the New Testament (cf. Mt. 5: 14; Rev. 1: 12).

vi. The Flying Scroll (5: 1–4)

This vision and the one which follows (vv. 5–11) deal with three evils which stand to be dealt with in the wake of spiritual renewal: theft and false witness, here, and unrighteousness in the next vision. **1. a flying scroll** is depicted thus to be seen and read by all and is an appropriate picture for post-exilic times when a renewed interest in the teaching of the Torah was to take place. Its dimensions (approximately 9 metres by 4.5 metres) correspond to those of the entrance to Solomon's Temple (cf. 1 Kg. 6: 3). The symbol is a familiar one in the OT. The difference with this scroll is that it is wide open. Some have seen an allusion here to the dimensions of the Holy Place in the Tabernacle, and have deduced that it possibly recorded the main outlines of the Torah. This is much less likely to be the case, for it clearly contains **the curse** against **every thief** and **everyone who swears falsely**. Though stealing may well be specified as the theft of property, the two evils represent damage which can be caused by a man against his neighbour. Other and more damaging forms of theft can be committed, such as the theft of a man's good name or his reputation, and this would provide a firm link with false witness. Worse still (4) is the invoking of the divine **name** in the bearing of false accusation. Those who commit such evils **will be banished** (Heb. *niqqāh*) . . . **according to what it says**. God's ancient Law will remain the standard by which the deeds and words of men will be tested; the Heb. verb suggests being purged out from the faithful congregation. God's word is sent forth and because it goes out with his authority it accomplishes the purpose for which it is given (cf. Isa. 55: 11). The curse is therefore clearly connected with the covenant (as was the case in Dt. 29: 12, 18). Any implied association between the scroll and Solomon's Temple, as suggested above, not only fits the general context of the prophecy as a whole, but the tenor of the present passage in particular, and possibly foreshadows the prophetic witness of the Seer of the Book of Revelation, whose vision of the heavenly Temple was coloured by a similar proscription against those who practise abomination and falsehood (cf. Rev. 21: 22–27). No human agency or executive appears in the vision. God's word in the day of renewal will do God's work irrespective of the judgments of others. It is a vision of a time when the word of the Lord is so unfettered that it finds its way into the homes

and the consciences—**it will remain**—of all who dare to transgress.

vii. The Lead-covered Basket (5: 5–11)

The previous vision has dealt with iniquity amongst God's people. This vision is directed against evil which is to be seen alongside those who are called to live by the moral standards of the Law. **6. 'It is a measuring basket':** the ephah was a large barrel by which, in earlier times, measures were estimated. (An ephah barrel measured approximately 15 to 18 litres; Ru. 2: 17.) But since this ephah contains a human figure it has no real bearing on the barrel as a unit of measurement. Its significance is immediately identified by the interpreting angel: **'This is the iniquity of the people . . .'** (Heb. *'êynām*). The Heb. literally reads, 'This is their eye'; NIVmg has 'This is their appearance'. The text of the RSV follows the Greek and Syriac versions which are usually good guides in cases of an indeterminate text. The sense of the RSV also harmonizes with other passages (*e.g.*, Am. 8: 5), where the ephah and shekel are symbols of injustice. The Heb. word 'eye' has a number of moral and spiritual connotations in the OT so that a definitive rendering here is not easy to make. The reading of the RSV text also depends on changing one small Heb. letter (*yōd*) into another (*wāw*), and there is abundant evidence from the manuscripts that these two letters can become confused in transmission. Such emendations, however, cannot be made by rule of thumb, and for this reason it may be preferable to accept NIVmg reading of 'appearance'. This is in fact how RSV understands Heb. *'ayin* in Num. 11: 7 and 1 Sam. 16: 7.

Taking 'appearance' here also suits what follows. 'This is the appearance (of the ephah) throughout the land' prepares for the specific mention of wickedness (8). **7.** The full significance of the basket appears when it is opened and wickedness is uncovered, personified in a woman (cf. Rev. 17: 3). **8. wickedness** (Heb. *hā-rish'āh*)**:** a portmanteau word denoting a variety of forms of evil—social, ethical and spiritual—which can only be dealt with by superior forces. **9.** God matches wickedness personified in a woman with **two women** who appear as his chosen servants who have the **wind in their wings**, possibly denoting the power of the Spirit, **wings like those of a stork** (Heb. *h°sîdāh*, possibly a heron). There is a possible association here with the steadfast love (Heb. *hesed*) of God which has already been seen in the removal of Joshua's stained garments (3: 4). In any case, the mention of 'spirit' serves to remind the prophet that this removal of wickedness was the work of God alone. **11.** The basket is summarily removed **to . . . Babylonia** (Heb. Shinar), an ancient name for Babylon which stood for lasting antagonism to God's purpose. This location was in the plain where Babel was built (cf. Gen. 11: 1–9). There will be erected **a house for it**, probably a shrine. In Isa. 11: 11 the LXX reads 'Babylon' for 'Shinar'. Thus where Judah had been exiled was a fitting place for wickedness to be worshipped, but not in the land where God had placed *his* name. The idolatry of Babylon must once and for all be separated from the worship of the God of Israel. Unlike the fourth vision in which Joshua is relieved of his filthy garments, this vision is concerned with the truth that wickedness often hidden from men so far as its real identification is concerned, is a power which must be reckoned with and never underestimated, but removed by the aid of God's immediate authority.

viii. Four chariots and horses (6: 1–8)
1. four chariots: the similarity between this vision and the first (1: 7–17) is plain. There are, however, significant differences. The mention of chariots (Heb. *merkābāh*) probably denotes little more than a trap or riding seat. The fact that they come from between the mountains suggests moreover that they were probably not military vehicles (chariots were of little value in this kind of terrain) but concerned with reconnaissance, as the context seems to show. Von Rad (in *Old Testament Theology*, ii, p. 287) and others believe that the differences in the sequence of colours between this passage and 1: 8 are accounted for most easily by assuming that the first vision was in the early evening, whilst this one was at sunrise, seen as a new day in the history of Judah. Others have suggested further significance in the different sequences of the colours of the horses, but little is gained by placing any emphasis upon them. **3. dappled** (Heb. *beruddîm 'amuṣṣîm*) means literally 'strong speckled'. P. R. Ackroyd (in *PCB*, p. 649) suggests that 'strong' (or 'steeds') is a detail possibly added to the text from the original v. 7.

5. 'These are the four spirits of heaven . . .': NIV misses the proper sense which is: 'these are the four winds (Heb. *rûḥôth*) going out (again, cf. 1: 11), having presented themselves before the LORD . . .' **6.** Since 'four spirits' are mentioned in the previous verse we would expect all four corners of earth to be mentioned here and in the following verse. But this verse is clearly broken at the beginning. JB and NEB, following a number of standard commentaries, are probably correct therefore in adding, 'the red horses go towards the east country', since red horses are not mentioned and 'east' is also missing. **the one with white horses toward the west** (Heb. reads literally 'after them'): but with the simple addition of a single *yod* the text can be made to read 'after the sea', i.e., seaward, or westward (cf. Gen. 13: 14; Num. 2: 18; 14: 4; Ps. 107: 3). **7.** With

their instructions settled the horses in the vision are champing at the bit to go about their work. But **those going toward the north country** (8)—presumably, though not definitely, Babylon—are noticeably effective, for the vision ends with the message that they **have given my Spirit rest**, lit., 'have caused my spirit to rest'. This affirmation may be understood either (*a*) as a note of finality, or (*b*) as a note of encouragement. The former is less obvious; the latter, as Ackroyd indicates (*PCB*, p. 649), makes a better link with the following, non-visionary, section. It also provides a clearer sense; God's spirit is now in operation among the exiles to equip them for the renewal of their proper spiritual activity in the service of the Lord.

III. THE EXALTATION OF JOSHUA (6: 9–15)
9. The word of the LORD came to me: an introductory formula which serves to show that this is a prophetic oracle that must be kept distinct from the preceding vision, and not, as J. G. Baldwin (*Haggai, Zechariah, Malachi, ad. loc.*) and others suggest, part of that vision. Three exiles have arrived from Babylon, presumably carrying offerings for the new Temple. The prophet is commanded to receive them and to (11) **make a crown** (Heb. *'atārôt*): the crown is singular though the noun is plural. It has been observed (*e.g.* by Edward Lipinski, in *VT* 20, 1970, pp. 25 ff.) that this is a primitive form having an antique or sacred connotation.

Zechariah is instructed to **set it on the high priest, Joshua son of Jehozadak**. Many take the view that though Joshua is mentioned, Zerubbabel is in fact meant. The main arguments for this case run thus: (1) the crown here was a royal crown and therefore unsuitable for a priestly wearer, (2) the name of Joshua appears here rather than Zerubbabel in the light of subsequent events, *viz.*, that Persian intervention prevented any such 'coronation' and so Joshua's name was inserted to counteract subsequent disillusionment on the part of the readers of the prophecy, and Zerubbabel's name disappears from the records from now on, and (3) therefore a scribal alteration became necessary to retain the general cohesion of the prophecy.

All these arguments are hazardous. As has also been observed, the crown here is not that which would be used at a royal ceremony; it betokens special dignity but not royalty. Moreover, if a scribe removed the name of Zerubbabel at this point in the text he would have needed to remove the clear allusion to him later (v. 13). To assume that the eventual disappearance of Zerubbabel lay at the root of such an excision from the text is to overlook what is essential in this passage, *viz.*, that although honour is given to Joshua, Zerubbabel is the greater of the two for in him lie the organic links with the Messiah. H. L. Ellison points out rightly (*Men Spake From God*, p. 130) that the passage, whilst not naming Zerubbabel, except by the appellation 'the Branch', is eschatological and looks forward to a specific realization in the future. (Cf. also W. Eichrodt, *Theology of the Old Testament*, ii, 1967, p. 343 and footnote.)

12. . . . **'Here is the man . . .'** (Heb. 'behold a man'): words which further indicate that *besides* Joshua there is another who is very much part of God's message—**whose name is the Branch** (Heb. *ṣemaḥ*). Cf. 3: 8, where the prophet has already prepared his hearers for the introduction of this title. Undoubtedly the absence of an explicit reference to Zerubbabel at this point means that complete and satisfactory identification of him as the 'Branch' is ultimately ruled out in the sense that the designation, though it has messianic flavour, falls short of the messianic ideal in that Joshua and Zerubbabel play a combined part in the rebuilding of the Temple. The former, as priest, prefigures an age in which priesthood will perfectly deal with the needs of the people; the latter, as king, only faintly shadows the ruler to come who was to reign for ever. Moreover, in this prophecy we have a partial presentiment of the comprehensive role of the New Testament Messiah (cf. Heb. 1: 1–9). The idea of two Messiahs was more fully expressed in Qumran literature (cf. F. F. Bruce, *Second Thoughts on the Dead Sea Scrolls*, ²1961, pp. 80 ff.). A doctrine of two Messiahs is also to be seen in the *Testaments of the Twelve Patriarchs* (cf. R. H. Charles, ed., *The Apocrypha and Pseudepigrapha of the Old Testament in English*, ii, 1963 [1913], pp. 282 ff.).

P. R. Ackroyd, however (*op. cit.*, p. 649), believes that both Joshua and Zerubbabel were crowned and that v. 13 should be read as a poem in which personal references alternate between the two. This view is possibly more acceptable if we see the poem as alternating between Joshua (in reference to the Temple) and the Branch (in reference to an eschatological priest-king), since, indeed, **and he will be a priest on** (Heb. *ʿal* can also mean 'by') **his throne** (13) is capable only of a strictly futuristic interpretation. The fact that there will be **harmony between the two** would most naturally be taken as a direct reference to Joshua and Zerubbabel, yet nevertheless looking forward to a time when kingly and priestly rule are combined in one. **14.** As a long-standing memorial to this oracle **the crown will be in the temple of the LORD**, principally for the benefit of those, who by Heldai, Tobijah and Jedaiah, sent the offerings of gold and silver. In the Heb. text *ḥēlem* 'strength' appears for the

name of Heldai, and *ḥēn* for the name of Josiah. Various suggestions have been made to remove the difficulty. It is probably best to read *ḥēlem* as an alternative name for Heldai, but to read possibly *ḥēn* in its usual connotation as 'grace', thus giving some such sense as: '. . . and (a memorial) to the grace of (Josiah) the son of Zephaniah' (NIV text reads **Hen**).

15. 'Those who are far away . . .': pushes the closing words of the oracle far into the future. The words cannot mean that exiles or dispersed Jews would have a hand in the building of the Temple. That was well on its way to completion. The words can only sensibly be understood as those which harmonize with other prophetic passages (*e.g.* Isa. 2: 2 ff.; 19: 23 ff.; cf. Zech. 2: 11; 8: 22) in which the arrival of the Messiah will extend the blessings of the covenant to men far beyond the bounds of Judaism. In that day the Temple will not be made by human hands (Rev. 21: 22; cf. Jn 2: 19 ff.) but will be formed by a living community gathered round one Lord and one God. But for Zechariah's hearers, in the meantime a glorious, albeit partial, fulfilment such as this will demand diligent obedience, as indeed did the ancient law of God (cf. Dt. 17: 12–16).

IV. VARIOUS PROPHETIC ORACLES (7: 1–8: 23)

i. Questions about fasting, and answers (7: 1–14)

This section brings the first part of the book of Zechariah to a close and is noticeably introduced by the date **the fourth year of King Darius** (1), i.e., 518–517 B.C. That the record has, however, been faithfully edited is seen in the specific mention of **the fourth day of the ninth month** (i.e. December 7, 518 B.C.) and the adding of the words **the month of Kislev** (cf. D. J. Wiseman, 'Calendar', in *NBD*, pp. 177 f.).

2. There is no general consensus of agreement with regard to the translation of this verse. The main problems lie in the mention of **Bethel . . . Sharezer and Regem-Melech**, and with the placing of the verb. The Heb. text literally reads thus: 'and sent Bethel, Sharezer, and Regem-Melech and his men'. The critical apparatus suggests that Regem-Melech is the object of the verb, though there is no positive evidence to support this contention. If this were the case we should read: 'Bethel-Sharezer sent Regem-Melech and his men . . .' The NIV and RSV paraphrase the text by inserting **the people of** before **Bethel**, but this is difficult to justify. Otherwise, a few commentators omit the words **the word of the LORD came to Zechariah** and make Darius the subject of the verb in v. 2. But this is almost certainly incorrect. The most probable solution is in making

Bethel-Sharezer a personal name (as above). There is a Babylonian counterpart to this (cf. W. F. Albright, *Archaeology and the Religion of Israel*, 1956, p. 169; cf. also J. P. Hyatt 'A Neo-Babylonian Parallel to *BETHEL-SAR-ESER*, Zech.7.2' in *JBL*, 56, 1937, pp. 387–393). Note also similar compounded names *e.g.*, in Jer. 39: 3, 13. D. J. Wiseman refers to the possibility that the name is a corruption of the Babylonian *Bel-šar-uṣur* (cf. 'Sharezer' in *NBD*, p. 1170). **Regem-Melech** is not a personal name but an official designation. Though both 'Regem' and 'Melech' are compounded in personal names elsewhere (cf. 2 Kg. 23: 11; Jer. 38: 7), the evidence of Jer. 39: 3, 13 suggests that this is a Hebrew rendering of an Assyrian title, 'Rab-Mag', denoting a diplomatic officer. The text should therefore in all probability read: 'Bethel-sharezer (the officer?) sent his men' and this calls only for the excision of a small Heb. particle *waw* ('and') as well as retaining 'his men' (after the Heb) rather than 'their men' (so RSV).

The fact that the arrival of this delegation is so carefully dated would imply a longer journey (from Babylon) rather than a shorter one (i.e., from Bethel); and the text may well also imply that the journey had taken close on four months (cf. v. 3).

These men came **to entreat the LORD** that they might participate in the sacrificial worship of the Temple (2). Yet with their worshipping spirit they brought also a solemn question to put to **the priests . . . and the prophets** (3). These two offices often go together in the OT as is evident, for example, from the prophecy of Jeremiah (cf. 23: 11; 29: 26; 35: 4). It is clear that prophets alongside priests belonged to the Temple staff (cf. Lam. 2: 20). In Chronicles, prophets are accorded Levitical status (cf. 1 Chr. 25: 1 ff.; 2 Chr. 20: 14 ff.; cf. also A. R. Johnson, *The Cultic Prophet in Ancient Israel*, 1944, pp. 51 ff.). **'Should I mourn and fast . . . ?':** the question was put representatively though with the urgency of the first person singular. The keeping of fast days was one of the observances by which the Jews in exile had been able to keep alive their collective worship though separated from the Temple in Jerusalem. Surprisingly, the NIV omits 'consecrating myself' (Heb. *hinnāzēr*), perhaps following the LXX at this point. But it should be retained; fasting and consecration (or separation) go together. **in the fifth month:** the fast to which they alluded marked the day upon which the temple was destroyed (cf. 2 Kg. 25: 8). The prophet's direct reply to this specific question is reserved for later (cf. 8: 19). The fast of the fifth month marked the ultimate tragedy of the Exile. The fast of the fourth month recalled the breaching of the city walls (cf. Jer. 39: 2); the fast of the seventh month

commemorated the assassination of Gedaliah (cf. Jer. 41: 1 f.); and the fast of the tenth month (cf. 8: 19) was for a remembrance of the siege of Jerusalem by Nebuchadrezzar (cf. Jer. 39: 1). The question which was put, then, included in principle all the causes for fasting brought about by the calamities of former days. But now, with the restoration in full view, such ritual might well have lost its original and essential meaning.

5. Though the prophet's answer does not immediately deal with the question put by the delegation, what he now says goes to the root of the spiritual teaching of which fasts were an outward expression. He asks *them*, **was it really for me that you fasted?** It was indeed possible that so great a tragedy as the destruction of the Temple, remembered in **the fifth month**, could be recalled with mechanical adherence to the calendar and without real attention to what the Temple had denoted in the purpose of God; it was indeed possible that the fasting of **the seventh month** (Tishri) had paid greater attention to Gedaliah and the sufferings of the people of his time than to the Lord himself. Ritual devoid of a necessary occupation with its proper object could become sterile. Moreover, there is the strong inference in the prophet's words (v. 6) that just as feasting was enjoyed in self-interest, so fasting could similarly be undertaken for motives other than those for which self-denial was originally designed. **7.** The **earlier prophets** had similarly observed a lack of true response in times when both cities and countryside were abundant with people and prosperity. In a word, the hallmark of Judah had become *failure*.

8. Nevertheless the word of the Lord must be repeated. So Zechariah resumes the central teaching of the notable prophets of pre-exilic times—Isaiah, Jeremiah, Hosea, Amos and Micah—with a formidable fourfold challenge. **9. Administer true justice** (Heb. *mishpāṭ*): judgment is no merely legal occupation. It involves the recovery of equity and peace when there has been injustice and discord if it is to be 'true' and godlike (cf. Ps. 76: 9; Hos. 2: 19). **show mercy** (Heb. *ḥesed*): steadfast love is the special quality which should mark all closer personal relationships within the larger community. Hosea, especially, saw the breakdown of society epitomized in the lack of *ḥesed* (4: 1) but singularly exemplified in his own tragic marital disruption. These two positive demands are followed by two warnings concerning what God's people should avoid. **10. do not oppress** (Heb. *'āshaq*) those who are, by their situation, all too open to exploitation. **In your hearts do not think** (Heb. *ḥāshab* 'devise' RSV) **evil of each other.** Evil is not only to be seen in false accusation in law (cf. 8: 16 f.) but in unseen and unspoken plans formulated in the secret thoughts. Here, then, is a concise yet comprehensive range of ethical teaching condensed into four pithy utterances. Without attention to their importance any fasting becomes a mere parade of ritualism which, as the history of Judah had shown, can lead to moral and spiritual disaster. **11.** The forefathers of Zechariah's people had failed to pay attention to the teaching of prophets in their time, but more positively had **stubbornly . . . turned ther backs** —a statement in all probability recalling the occasion of the giving of laws and statutes recorded in Deuteronomy (cf. 6: 6, 13, 17), and they had **stopped up their ears** (lit. 'made their ears heavy') by deliberately refusing to listen to the word of God. **12.** They stifled their emotions, making their hearts **as hard as flint** (Heb. *shāmîr*, 'flint'), fearful lest the words spoken by God's messengers should penetrate to their consciences (cf. Ezek. 3: 8). Since the injunctions of earlier prophets were obviously based on the Pentateuch, it is thought that **the law** (Heb. *tôrāh*) refers to this. This is not necessarily the case in this context. It is intrinsically possible that 'law' is to be taken in its more basic sense of 'teaching' (the Heb. verb from which *tôrāh* is derived means 'to throw', hence 'direction' or 'guidance').

But the prophets of former days were no less the spokesmen of the Lord. They uttered words **which the LORD. . . had sent by his Spirit**. This reference to the Spirit as the unifying influence behind the prophets' preaching is unique in the OT literature, apart from Neh. 9: 30, in that nowhere else is the idea of inspiration so clearly stated (cf. E Jacob, *Theology of the Old Testament*, 1958, pp. 121–127). **So the LORD Almighty was very angry:** the Pentateuch, especially Deuteronomy, as well as the prophetic literature, relates the wrath of God to the transgression of his revealed will in the covenant, since at the heart of that covenant lies an affirmation of God's sovereignty. Moreover, the context indicates that the catastrophe of the invasion of Judah and the subsequent exile were instruments of God's anger or indignation. So divine retribution is succinctly described. God called to his people and found no response. In their distress they cried to him and were given no answer, save that the events which followed eloquently testified to the divine displeasure as they were blown like chaff in a whirlwind, and the pleasant land promised them ages before was devastated and empty (14).

Thus, whilst Zechariah may well not have answered the original enquiry directly, he had nevertheless taken up the very essence of ritual in the heart of the worshipper, which was that the outward form of religious activity was useless and lifeless without an accompanying spirit of obedience, confession and repentance.

ii. Messianic promises (8: 1–23)

Zechariah's message was not, however, even at this juncture, designed to dwell on the past, but to prepare his hearers for renewal in the future. So the terse words concerning failure and accompanying judgment now give place to a series of ten oracles concerned with the fulfilment of God's promises and the glorious future awaiting Zion and her people.

2. I am very jealous for Zion (Heb. *qin'āh*): just as God's anger is to be understood in relation to the covenant, so, too, is his jealousy, or zeal to be understood. The Heb. word suggests a surge of feeling such as would be seen in the face of a person red with emotion. It is as though God can restrain himself no longer despite the obduracy and sin of his people. He is **burning with jealousy for her**, or better, 'with great zeal'. **3.** So great, indeed, is God's love for Zion that he announces his intention to return and dwell in Jerusalem, whose sad fortunes will be reversed as she becomes **The City of Truth**, i.e. the place where belief and good conduct go hand in hand (cf. Isa. 26: 2 f.; Jer. 3: 17) and thus distinct from all other places—a **Holy Mountain**. **4.** Fear will no longer haunt **the streets** (Heb. *rᵉḥōbôt*) or 'squares' and long life will be crowned with peace and well-being. **5. boys and girls** at play will provide the evidence of a return of new and healthy family life which will augur well for the future of the nation. **6.** Yet all this is promised for **the remnant** (Heb. *shᵉʾērîth*)— that faithful nucleus, which, without the solid assurance of the word of the Lord would have had little reason for hoping for better things. **7.** In all this, God says, **I will save** (Heb. *môshîaʿ*) **my people**: to 'save' in Heb. usually connotes deliverance from captivity or bondage. Probably two ideas are mingled here; certainly the remnant represented God's saving mercy. Yet in delivering a remnant God was in fact saving *a people—his* people—from the possibility of extinction by bringing them home from the far-flung corners of the earth to receive the renewed covenant promise (cf. Exod. 19: 5; Jer. 31: 33).

9. The prophet now turns his attention to offering encouragement for the future by drawing lessons from the past. Verses 9–17 form a two-part sermon. The first contrasts the dismal situation of the past with the glorious prosperity of the future. **'Let your hands be strong'** challenges the prophet's hearers who have listened to his preaching to grasp the opportunity and responsibility of completing the Temple structure. **prophets:** those who have been serving the spiritual and moral needs of God's people since the material work was started; it is likely that Zechariah is in fact referring to Haggai and himself, since these two are the only ones known to us who were active during this specific period of time, i.e. 520–519 B.C. (cf. Hag. 1: 6–11, esp. v. 12; 2: 15–19). Before this work was started the commercial and civic situation was desperate. Both man and beast lived below 'the bread line' and constant danger lurked for all who travelled any distance at the hands of the **enemy** (Heb. *ṣār*)—most probably a reference to the Samaritans who turned hostile when their offer of help in reconstruction was rebuffed (cf. Ezr. 4: 1–6)—and thus the whole fabric of a once peaceful and happy society crumbled as **every man** was **against his neighbor**. 11. **But now** those days are over. 12. **The seed will grow well**: this opening phrase is somewhat obscure. The RSV text over-paraphrases the Heb. The NEB seems preferable: 'They shall sow in safety' —which takes Heb. *shālôm* in a less common sense, though one which is perfectly acceptable, and which anticipates what follows: abundant vineyards and generally fruitful land. In this Zechariah is clearly recalling the testimony of Haggai who noted the crop failure due to lack of dew and rain (cf. Hag. 1: 10 f.) but who similarly promised a return of abundant crops as a signal of God's favour (cf. Hag. 2: 19). 13. So the contrast between the past and the future is now crystallized in the closing words of the oracle; Judah, once **an object of cursing** far and wide, will now become a blessing to others as a re-united people, **Judah and Israel**, and therefore there is good reason for them to turn their hands confidently to the work God had planned.

The second part of the sermon re-emphasizes the necessity for the co-operation of the people with God in bringing about a new era of blessing. 14. The calamities of past years were all part of God's overall design. 15. But to no lesser extent the better days to come have purpose also. 16. For their part the people must maintain honest dealings with one another. Civil law, administered in the **courts**, must be characterized by equity and thus establish a harmonious society. Offensive things, such as hatred and perjury, must be removed.

18f. The prophet has dealt with major ethical and spiritual principles which underlie all outward observances. From what he has said, as well as the way he has said it, it is evident that his 'digression' from the specific question put to him (cf. 7: 3) was for a good purpose. Now he turns to answer that question. The solemn fasts he has enumerated shall become **festivals** (Heb. *mô'ēd*) and therefore preparation of heart by setting a high value on **truth and peace**, exemplified by charitable relationships and the pursuit of social justice, is called for.

20. Earlier in the prophecy there is an intimation of spiritual universalism (cf. 2: 11). This is now enlarged to bring the first part of the book to its conclusion. **Many peoples . . .**

will yet come: that is, those from a variety of nationalities, saying, **'Let us go at once to** join the worship of **the LORD'** (21). The tone is urgent, for the final clause literally reads: 'let me go also'. P. R. Ackroyd suggests (*PCB*, p. 651) that this interjection may possibly reflect either the first person of 3: 5 or an enthusiastic comment of an early scribe. 22. Jerusalem is no longer viewed simply as the heart of Judaism but as the centre of God's dealings with all nations, and as a glorious realization of the ancient promise given to Abraham (cf. Gen. 12: 3). 23. **In those days** is in contrast with 'now' (15) and is probably synonymous with 'in that day' of other prophetic sayings (*e.g.* Isa. 4: 1; 17: 7; Ezek. 29: 21; Hos. 2: 16 ff.; Am. 8: 9; Hag. 2: 23). **ten men:** a figure denoting completeness (cf. Lev. 26: 26; 1 Sam. 1: 8). **from all . . . nations:** Heb. *gōy* was, and often still is, a term used by the Jew as a contemptuous reference to the non-Jew. **will take firm hold of one Jew by the edge of his robe:** the verb here (Heb. *ḥāzaq*, 'grab') occurs twice in the sentence, and denotes an impulsive but deeply sincere action, probably a plea for friendship (so J. G. Baldwin, *Haggai, Zechariah, Malachi*, p. 156; cf. 1 Sam. 17: 35), and is possibly to be equated with one similar action recorded in the NT (cf. Mt. 9: 20). The 'Jew' (singular) is mentioned as such infrequently in the OT outside Ezra and Nehemiah. The sincerity of the non-Jew is demonstrated by his confession: '. . . **God is with you.'** The evidence provided by a genuine renewal and reformation among God's people must be compelling (cf. Isa. 7: 14; 45: 14; 1 C. 14: 25; cf. Jn 14: 17). True spirituality is attractive to those who exercise genuine faith; but to others it may be a deterrent. The universalism with which the first part of the book ends is therefore not one of expediency, brought about by dialogue or conference. It is the work of God, initiated by him and mediated through his people. The glory of God will not be fully manifested until he is universally acknowledged in the fullness in which he made himself known to Israel in the first instance. But that glory will only be manifested by what he himself has done.

Second Section: Eschatological Sayings (9: 1–14: 21)

I. THE RESTORATION OF JUDAH (9: 1–11: 3)

i. Divine invasion (9: 1–8)

The outstanding differences between the first and second sections of the Book (cf. Introduction, pp. 964–5) mainly centre in a sense of immediacy about the promises of the first section, linked particularly to the theme of the reconstruction of the Temple in its latter passages, whilst in the second section there is a more pronounced apocalyptic tone and a stronger messianic flavour. Yet the two sections are obviously linked by their attention to the plan of divine deliverance. If, as the text shows, the Temple and its future is to the forefront of the prophet's mind in the first section (especially chaps. 7 and 8) the fact that different and more indefinite horizons appear to be in view in the second section, interspersed with a number of relatively short prophetic pieces having an overall difference of style, need not be taken as firm indication of difference of authorship. It goes far beyond the evidence to suggest that unity of authorship would involve 'a weird split personality' (so C. Stuhlmueller, 'Haggai, Zechariah, Malachi', in *The Jerome Biblical Commentary*, p. 395).

1. An Oracle is not, as NIV suggests, a title to be superscribed over the work, but introduces **The word of the LORD**. Although 'word' often refers to a prophetic oracle this presents no difficulty. 'Oracle' (Heb. *maśśā*) is derived from a verb *nāśā* 'to lift up' hence 'burden'. The term often appears in connection with a prophet's essential work in the OT, but in only three instances is it immediately joined with 'the word of the Lord': here, in 12: 1 and in Mal. 1: 1. It describes a burden placed upon a prophet's shoulders, a message that was far from easy to deliver, thus placing the prophet under heavy constraint.

The NIV and RSV wrongly translate **against the land of Hadrach**. The Heb. preposition here means 'in'. Hadrach is not mentioned elsewhere in the OT. It is probably to be identified with a city in northern Syria, Hatarikka, so named in Assyrian cuneiform inscriptions (cf. J. B. Pritchard, *ANET*, 1955, p. 282 f.). The word of the Lord will also **rest upon Damascus** (lit. 'and Damascus its resting place'). Damascus, the capital of Syria, was a traditional enemy of Israel. The message seems to be that the word of the Lord, having operated within Judah, now begins to influence her neighbours: **For the eyes of men are upon the LORD** is a literal translation of the text. But 'Adam' (man) in Hebrew can in textual transmission be confused with 'Aram'—a difference only of an angular Heb. *dalet (d)* and a more rounded Heb. *resh (r)*. Similarly 'eye of' (Heb. *'ēyn*) could be confused with 'cities of' (Heb. *'ārê*), though this is less probable. We must therefore endeavour to keep as near as possible to what the context appears to demand. For this reason it is possibly better to read: 'For the eye of the LORD is upon Aram (Syria) as it is upon all the tribes of Israel', which follows on naturally from the first half of the verse, as well as connecting suitably with what follows. **2. Hamath:** mentioned in Am.

6: 2 as a city of some importance. The earlier OT references show that this place, near the river Orontes, was a self-governing colony (Gen. 10: 18) which for a time was on good terms with Israel (cf. 2 Sam. 8: 9 f.; 1 Chr. 18: 9 f.). It was also the scene of Nebuchadrezzar's rout of the retreating Egyptian army after the battle of Carchemish in 605 B.C. (cf. D. J. Wiseman, *Chronicles of Chaldean Kings*, 1956, p. 69). The city remains today and is known as Hama, between Aleppo and Damascus. **Tyre** was an important and industrial city in earlier times, and was particularly remembered for its trade agreements with both David and Solomon. Later, in the eighth century, Tyre came under pressure from Assyria, and her future was gloomily portrayed by both Jeremiah and Ezekiel (cf. Jer. 27: 1–11; Ezek. 26: 1–28: 19). For an important outline of Tyrian history cf. D. J. Wiseman 'Tyre' in *NBD*, pp. 1302 f.; cf. P. K. Hitti, *History of Syria* (London, 1951).

Sidon was one of the first Phoenician cities to be founded, and was especially noted as a seaport. **though they are very skillful:** this, as J. G. Baldwin points out from RSV rendering (*Haggai, Zechariah, Malachi*, p. 159) is a mistranslation. The verb is singular—'is very wise'. The phrase should therefore be read as the commencement of the next sentence, to give 'Though she is very wise, Tyre has built herself a rampart'. Here also is a play on words; Tyre (Heb. *ṣōr*) and rampart (Heb. *māṣôr*). **heaped up silver . . . and gold:** Hiram I, king of Tyre (*c.* 979–945 B.C.), constructed a causeway linking the seaport to his fortress (2 Chr. 8: 5). This reference to gold and silver, as well as reflecting the general economic wealth of Tyre, possibly refers also to imports of gold, and silver—an operation which was undertaken with the collaboration of Solomon (cf. 1 Kg. 10: 22; 2 Chr. 9: 21). **4. the Lord will . . . destroy her power on the sea:** despite her strength and her financial resources, Tyre is destined for destruction. Her 'power' (Heb. *ḥayil*) is probably a comprehensive reference to her economic strength and her mighty defences. Certainly the Heb. noun is capable of embracing both. And what remains after the onslaught will be **consumed by fire**, just as Amos, too, had predicted (cf. Am. 1: 10). If any specific fulfilment of this oracle is to be sought in history, it is probably to be seen in the conquest of Tyre by Alexander the Great in 332 B.C. Though the city subsequently recovered to some extent under the Seleucids it never again rose to its former prominence. **5. Ashkelon will see it, and . . . be deserted:** the prophet freely adapts an earlier oracle uttered against the three Philistine cities mentioned here (cf. Am. 1: 6 ff.). Ashkelon shares the fate of Ashdod in depopulation; **Gaza** shares the loss of its king with Ashkelon; **Ek-**

ron will be judged more specifically (see v. 7). Since these Philistine cities are known to have lost their independence in the time of Nebuchadrezzar, this oracle in particular may have been taken by the prophet from a pre-exilic writer. **6. foreigners** (Heb. *mamzēr*) **will occupy Ashdod:** the Heb. noun occurs twice only in the OT (cf. Dt. 23: 2, where RSV has 'bastard'). The derivation of the noun is uncertain but seems to have some connection with an Arabic root 'to be foul'. Here the reference is most probably to a multi-racial population such as presented problems for Nehemiah (cf. Neh. 13: 24). Philistia was the territory on the south-western coast of the Holy Land and occupied by the Philistines from very early Bible times. The modern name 'Palestine' for the Holy Land is derived from this name. From the time of Joshua the Philistine people were a constant source of frustration to the Israelites, particularly throughout the reigns of Saul and David. This mention of the Philistine people is the last in the OT (cf. 'Philistines' and 'Philistia' in *NBD*, pp. 988 ff.). The pride of these people, says the prophet, will be broken; their pagan sacrificial system will be removed and Philistia shall become 'a remnant' (7), that is, incorporated into the faithful core of the people of Judah (cf. 8: 6). **Ekron will be like the Jebusites:** Ekron, one of the five principal Philistine townships, is promised a peaceful future of co-existence such as was afforded the ancient Canaanite residents of the suburbs of Jerusalem after David had captured that city. **8.** With the south-western seaboard thus controlled, the land will now be secure. The Lord now comes to defend his land and his people. His eyes (cf. 4: 10) watch over their safety so that no enemy or invader may trespass again.

ii. The Messiah-King (9: 9–10)
In order to bring the future into closer perspective the prophet now focuses attention upon the arrival of the king. This short oracle is well-known from the NT (cf. Mt. 21: 4f.; Jn 12: 14 f.) where, however, there is significant deviation from the Hebrew text and the Septuagint. **9. Rejoice greatly . . . shout:** indicating the fervour of the prophet's announcement. **Daughter of Zion:** as has frequently been noted, 'daughter' is a term which often connotes severed relationships in the OT (*e.g.* Isa. 1: 8; Jer. 4: 31; Lam. 2: 1). This passage is an exception. By contrast Jerusalem is given the news that the time of waiting is over; the arrival of her king is imminent. He is **righteous** (Heb. *ṣaddîq*) (cf. Isa. 9: 7; 11: 4 f.), that is, actively righteous in correcting the injustices and oppression of former days. He has **salvation** (Heb. *nôshā'*, lit. 'saved') in the sense that victory for him is assured. This collocation of righteousness and salvation is paralleled in the Servant passages of Isaiah. At once, therefore,

there is forged a link with the Servant of the Lord (cf. H. G. Mitchell, *Haggai and Zechariah, in loc.*; J. G. Baldwin, *Haggai, Zechariah, Malachi, in loc.*) and this fact would have provided enough essential material for the oracle to find its way into prominence in the Passion narratives of the NT. The Messiah-king is **gentle** (Heb. *'ānî*), indicating that he comes in meekness or in peace. The Heb. adjective is frequently used to denote the 'poor'. It was in consequence of poverty that people often suffered at the hands of their richer neighbours in OT days, and it is as a reflection of this that the adjective takes on the meaning of 'humble' (cf. 7: 10; 11: 7–11). The king comes **riding on a donkey**, fortifying the image of a peaceful ruler. The donkey, however, possibly links the oracle with Jacob's blessing of Judah, in which the anticipated ruler 'tethers his donkey to a choicest branch' (Gen. 49: 10 f.). The presence of two animals is the product of Heb. parallelism. Only a single animal is intended. That both animals find their way into one of the NT references to this oracle (cf. Mt. 21: 7, but contrast Jn 12: 14 f.) indicates a rigorous attachment to the literal Hebrew text on the part of the Evangelists. (For an exhaustive examination of this and other passages in the NT see F. F. Bruce 'The Book of Zechariah and the Passion Narrative' in *BJRL*, vol. 43, no. 2, March 1961, pp. 336–353.) **10.** The immediate task facing the messianic king is to act as God's agent for peace. He thus abolishes weapons of war. The joining of **Ephraim** and **Jerusalem** is a hint of the re-unification of the northern and southern kingdoms. **he will proclaim peace to the nations:** so bringing a cessation of strife not only in Israel but throughout the world. It lies in his essential authority to do this; it is a matter of his 'proclamation'. The only indication of the spoken word by him is that of 'peace' (Heb. *shālôm*; cf. Hag. 2: 9). Then the oracle closes with a free quotation from Ps. 72: 8 in which the writer gives voice to a universal longing for peace. The prophet's contribution to that longing is in his announcement that these hopes are to be realized at last in a king of God's choice.

iii. Judah's Victory (9: 11–17)
With the scene set for the coming of Israel's king and the establishment of worldwide peace, the prophet now turns to Judah's deliverance. In keeping with the promise to his people in the time of Moses God will intervene **because of the blood of my covenant** (cf. Exod. 24: 8). The original basis of God's special dealings with his own people is never forgotten. The thematic essence of the covenant was remembered daily in the services of the Tabernacle (cf. Exod. 29: 38–46) and recalled by Jeremiah (cf. Jer. 31: 31). Yet the actual words 'blood of (the) covenant' occur only here, in Exod. 24: 8

and in Mk 14: 24. In the latter reference they assume their total significance. Moreover, the words which follow—**I will free your prisoners** (Heb. perfect tense)—suggest that the prophet saw God's intervention reaching out beyond the particular circumstances of the Exile, which is nevertheless viewed as a deliverance **from the waterless pit**. This phrase has been read as a gloss by a number of scholars basically on the grounds that it does not fit in with the general tenor of the context and appears to destroy its poetic structure. The words are omitted by NEB. Yet it is questionable whether this criticism is justified. The prophet is speaking of a dramatic change in the fortunes of the people, and thus in the nature of the case he would be likely to employ highly colourful language in describing their freedom from captivity.

12. Return to your fortress (Heb. *l^ebiṣṣārôn*): though the noun is of uncertain derivation, various suggested emendations do little to improve the sense. The RSV rightly leaves the text as it stands for in a real sense Judah and Jerusalem were strongholds of divine protection in which the returning exiles could safely trust. These exiles had been **prisoners of hope**, captivated by the expectation of the day of deliverance, and fortified by the declaration that **I will restore twice as much to you**, undoubtedly implying that the despair of the captivity was to be replaced by an abundance of joy. **13.** Yet God's power still rests with his people. The north and south would share alike in God's purpose for victory just as **bow** and arrow must be used together. Furthering the figure of speech, the sons of Zion are the sword of the Almighty to be flourished **against your sons, O Greece** (Heb. *yāwān*). This line of the poem is omitted by NEB, and regarded as an explanatory gloss by a number of commentators (cf. H. G. Mitchell, *op. cit.*, pp. 279 f.). The reasons usually given are that the first two lines of the verse form a couplet and would normally be followed by a second couplet. But these words break the pattern and therefore are an addition to the text. Such an addition would, in the opinion of a number of scholars, have easily been made in Maccabean times in which a specific mention of Greece would have been a convenient means of updating the prophet's words making them more immediately intelligible in a situation which involved a struggle against Hellenism. But the Greek version retains the words and this is strong evidence that they should be retained in our text. Though Heb. *yāwān* is usually taken as 'Greece', the reference here is probably more general and applied to alien peoples (cf. Introduction, p. 965).

14. The prophet now employs distinctive apocalyptic language in depicting the decisive battle against Israel's enemies. God **will appear** (cf. Hab. 3: 3, 11), sounding the trumpet of battle as he goes forth **in the storms of the south**—probably reminiscent of his appearing to Moses, Aaron and the elders of Israel (cf. Exod. 24: 9 f., 15) and possibly also of the Song of Deborah (cf. Jg. 5: 4 ff.). **15.** With the promise of God's victorious protection there comes also the assurance of celebration to follow. Because of difficulties of translation this verse has often been misrepresented. The RSV text portrays a revolting enactment of revenge over Israel's enemies which is almost certainly false. **they will destroy** (Heb. *'ākal*, usually connoting 'to eat'): the reference to **slingers** (Heb. *'abnê qela'*) should be 'slingstones' which the victorious people kick aside in contempt. Moreover, '**they shall drink their blood like wine**' from RSV is a rendering based on the Greek version rather than the Hebrew and depends on changing Heb. *hāmû* to *dāmām*. The result is a repugnant picture of a bloodthirsty rampage and not only alien from the spirit of the prophecy in general but foreign to the present context in particular (cf. v. 11). Heb. *hāmû* is better read as the imperfect tense of the verb 'to make a noise'. The verse can then be read: 'they shall eat, and kick aside the slingstones, and they shall drink, and make a noise as though with wine'. AV in fact gives a rendering closer to the meaning of the text as does NIV. In their festivities they are **full like a bowl** that overflows as the vessels underneath the ancient altar of sacrifice overflowed (cf. Lev. 4: 7). **16.** Thus with a picture of the people restored and rejoicing without restraint in God's mighty deliverance, the prophet sees them as **jewels in a crown**, living emblems of all that the Lord has done for them. **17.** Conditions of peace will be attended by conditions of plenty in the land to be populated by youthful men and women, together signalling a happier and fruitful future for the nation.

iv. From strength to strength (10: 1–11: 3)
The picture of peace and material prosperity is associated in the prophet's mind with spiritual strength that must go hand in hand with it. The salvation of Israel will be realized when the religious needs of the nation are met. **1. rain:** referring therefore to an outpouring of divine blessing in contrast with the waterless condition of the exile (cf. 9: 11). In this sense only is the opening of the chapter to be realistically linked with what follows. **2. The idols speak deceit:** these were the household gods, notably used in the time of judges for divination (cf. Jg. 17: 5; 18: 5). Similarly **diviners** were sought to foresee the future whilst **dreamers** claimed to impart special divine messages to their hearers. The use of all these was forbidden in Israel (cf. Dt. 18: 10 ff.) for to his people God had given prophets, all anticipating '*the*

prophet' to whom, in various ways, the prophets of different ages looked forward (cf. Dt. 18: 15 ff.). Spiritual leadership is Israel's primary need. Without this God's people **wander like sheep** and suffer in consequence **for lack of a shepherd**. The prophet's words clearly allude to Ezek. 34: 6–8 (cf. 1 Kg. 22: 17) and possibly remind us even more pointedly of the crowds upon which our Lord had compassion when he saw them 'as sheep without a shepherd' (Mk 6: 34). A perpetual tragedy afflicting the people of God throughout biblical times until now has lain in their being at the mercy of 'shepherds' who are either uncalled or unqualified for leadership (or both). The 'shepherd' as a designation for 'ruler' or 'leader' was taken up in the OT from very early times, often in reference to the king (so Isa. 44: 28; Mic. 5: 4; Ezek. 34: 23 f.), but ultimately to refer to God himself (cf. Gen. 49: 24; Ps. 23: 1; Isa. 40: 11).

The high spiritual tone of this section is then set. The physical victory described in the previous section must be accompanied by a deeper and more fundamental spiritual battle. As Carroll Stuhlmueller rightly observes: 'references to shepherds . . . and warriors cast the passage in the setting of a charismatic war' ('Zechariah' in *The Jerome Biblical Commentary*, p. 395).

3. **'My anger burns against the shepherds . . .':** God now directly utters his word of judgment. The inference of these opening words is that those **shepherds** who are self-styled and uncalled to God's service are in fact responsible, however indirectly, for the continuing presence of apostasy amongst God's people. **and I will punish the leaders** (Heb. *'attûdîm*, 'he-goats'): they are thus described since they are not only uncalled but also unqualified for pastoral care. Their failure can be summed up by a lack of true concern for those in their charge. Nevertheless, **the LORD Almighty will care for** (Heb. *pāqad*) **his flock:** the verb literally means 'to visit', either in deliverance (so here) or in judgment (3a). With the benefit of God's active concern for the people of Judah, once like helpless sheep, these people are to be transformed into **a proud horse in battle**. It is not clear whether these words continue the utterance of the Lord or whether they constitute the words of the prophet as a commentary on what God has said. In either case the change of metaphor is dramatic. A new and decisive spiritual strength is to be seen in the place of helplessness.

4. From Judah . . . from him (Heb. 'out of him'): repeated three times in the verse. It is the emphasis which God uses to underline Judah's new place in God's purpose. **the cornerstone** or capstone (cf. Isa. 28: 16; Ps. 118: 22; cf. Mt. 21: 42; 1 Pet. 2: 7): the unique,

irreplaceable stone upon which an entire edifice depends for completion as well as security. The term is used in a number of OT passages to symbolize a messianic ruler. One of the more noteworthy (Ps. 118: 22) speaks of its being rejected by men—a theme to which the prophet turns in the next section (11: 4–17) and which is taken up in the NT (cf. refs. cited above). **the tent peg:** an insignificant thing in man's eyes, but symbolizes that strength which is able to withstand all those pressures that arise when true leadership is undertaken. **the battle bow** (cf. 9: 10): formerly taken out of the hands of men is now represented in the hands of God's ruler who will strike in battle as perfectly as he defends his people's cause. And from now on —**every ruler**—a tradition of leadership will be established in Judah which will accomplish God's ongoing purpose. The Targum, indeed, reads this as a positive messianic prediction.

5. Judah will be united and victorious in battle because **the LORD is with them**, enabling them to overcome the most heavy odds: infantry against cavalry.

6. The message of the prophet now moves towards God's ultimate purpose. Clearly the Exodus pattern of deliverance is uppermost in the wording. **Judah and . . . Joseph:** standing for the southern and northern kingdoms respectively. They will be brought back to that land where God originally intended they should be. Moreover, in their return they will prove that God's compassion is quite unlike the mawkish sentimentality of man and quite different from that sort of human 'compassion' which tends to hide a continuing grievance nevertheless, because **They will be as though I had not rejected them**. The time of exile and rejection must end. True compassion is never satisfied until restoration has been effected and the cause of alienation is *forgotten*. **7. The Ephraimites**, the first to collapse in the wake of Assyria, will no less than Judah attain the strength which God will supply, and no less than Judah will have cause to rejoice in what God has done (cf. 9: 15 ff.). **8. I will signal** (Heb. *'eshrᵉqāh*) **for them:** the Heb. verb means 'to whistle' as a shepherd would call his sheep. The NIV 'signal' depends on the Greek version. In mysterious furtherance of his purpose the Lord had called for Assyria to invade the land as an instrument of his judgment (cf. Isa. 5: 26). Now, as true shepherd of his flock, he calls the sheep and gathers them home. **I will redeem** (or 'ransom') **them:** already the prophet sees the essence of completion in God's work. What remains to be seen is the actualizing of Ephraim's response, and this is no small part of the promise, for **they will be as numerous as before**; that response will, indeed, be so great that the population will appear to be back to its former size

—a remarkable promise for Ephraim especially in the light of the distribution of her people throughout the Assyrian Empire which would have made so remarkable an ingathering of her people humanly impossible. **9. Though I scatter them:** the NIV makes a clear departure here from the AV, which reads the Heb. exactly as it stands, i.e., 'I will sow them'. The Heb. verb *zāra'* is the common word 'to sow'. But by exchanging the initial letter of the root the Heb. can be made to read *bāzar* 'to scatter' which is what the NIV accepts. Certainly these emendations fit the context. Yet the idea of sowing the people among the nations is not out of keeping with the context either, nor is it without parallel elsewhere in the OT (*e.g.* Hos. 2: 23). If the original wording be taken then the prophet is looking to a future time when the dispersed of Israel will achieve some definite mission within God's purpose. It should be noted that the imperfect tenses of the remaining verbs of the verse lend greater weight to the Heb. as it stands. Though in far-off lands, the people of Israel will not forget their God, and generation after generation will survive along with the expectation of a final homecoming.

10. The twin motifs of slavery and exile in **Egypt and . . . Assyria** are dominant. The returning exiles will overrun the northern and eastern frontiers of the homeland. The mention of Gilead is possibly associated with the original occupation of Transjordan under Moses. **11. They will pass through the sea of trouble:** the Heb. text reads 'he shall pass through the narrow sea' (Heb. *bayyām ṣārāh*). The alteration of this to 'Egypt' (Heb. *miṣraim*) as in RSV has no basis whatsoever even though Egypt figures in the passage so prominently. With the Heb. left unemended the deliverance theme is still clear. Whatever barriers may stand in their path the Lord will effect the salvation of his people by dramatic means similar to those of the wilderness wandering. **12.** Following the promise given to Judah (cf. v. 6), Ephraim is reassured with the words **I will strengthen them in the LORD** (Heb. *bᵉyahweh*). Just as the ineffable name was the guarantee of deliverance from Egyptian slavery under Moses, so now it stands as the name in which the people of Ephraim may have confidence. **and in his name they will walk:** the RSV prefers the Greek 'they shall glory' (from the Heb. verb *hālal*) rather than 'they shall walk' (Heb. *hālak*) which is what the text reads. The Heb. text as it stands is preferred. The departure of Israel from Egypt was made when the people were ready for the road. Likewise God's new deliverance will be attended by marching orders—'and they shall march in his name'.

11: 1 ff. This section ends with a taunt-song against Israel's enemies, Lebanon and Bashan

in particular. The pride of these two, the cedars of Lebanon and the oaks of Bashan, is to be destroyed, and possibly the mention of their trees by name symbolizes the respective strengths of these two alien powers (note especially **the dense forest** of Bashan). The two means of destruction of trees, fire and axe, are irresistible as God prepares the way for the return of his people. The imagery of the song is expanded as shepherds mourn for their flocks ravaged by lions. Even the lush thicket of the Jordan—the rich and thick undergrowth alongside the river—does not escape the terrifying arrival of the Lord in delivering judgment.

II. THE GOOD SHEPHERD AND BAD SHEPHERDS (11: 4–17)

Without doubt this passage is one of the more elusive in the OT. But whilst a number of its details are difficult to specify with any certainty, a number of main items are clear. The flock is Israel. The shepherds are the leaders of God's people, and the prophet himself is pressed into service as the shepherd of the Lord's choice. The passage is mainly allegorical; its application extends beyond the people of Israel in particular (as the passage shows) and beyond the time setting of the words themselves. There is therefore a permanent lesson in the prophet's teaching here. Certain parts of the passage are to be found repeated in the life and experience of Jesus. And, if the reader is willing, lessons, however unpalatable, are here which have relevance for those who occupy positions of pastoral leadership in the church as the new Israel, for the implications of godly leadership and the perils of bad leadership are matters which all too easily are glossed over when we are unwilling to listen.

4. 'Pasture . . .': immediately we are introduced to an autobiographical section of the prophecy (cf. vv. 7, 15) in which the prophet is commanded to take a personal hand in the welfare of **the flock marked for slaughter** (cf. v. 7). **5. Their buyers slaughter them . . . Those who sell them . . . :** the rearing of sheep for slaughter is a picture dramatically employed to demonstrate the devastating corruption to which the people were exposed. Presumably 'those who sell them' are **their own shepherds**, which brings the ultimate responsibility for this tragic state of affairs to the door of those who had set themselves up as leaders. These men are without pity and yet can say **'Praise the LORD . . .'.** There is but one thing equal to the evil of bad leadership and that is the hypocrisy which so often goes with it.

6. Judgment is therefore inevitable. Every man will be **handed over to his neighbor** (Heb. *rēʿêhû*). The RSV adopts the emendation of vowel points of the Heb. *rōʿēhû*, 'shepherd'.

The emendation is contextually understandable but not necessarily justified. The original makes good sense. Each man becomes a prey to his neighbour and every man lives in fear of the ruling power of the day. There is therefore a serious breakdown of mutual trust as well as responsibility. The prophet's message is one which could be applied to various points in the history of Israel, particularly the second century B.C. We may also think of the words of Jesus regarding the close of the age, when men will betray one another and false teachers will arise (cf. Mt. 24: 3–13). Yet despite the catastrophic picture put to him in God's words the prophet takes up the divine command and becomes the representative of the Lord in this special capacity of shepherd because of **the oppressed of the flock** (7). The text at this point literally reads 'because of Canaanites' but it is fairly certain that the consonants have been wrongly divided into two words—a division which would give us 'poor of the flock' (but cf. v. 11). At any rate the meaning is clear; the bad shepherds have been exploiting their position and have used their privileged occupation for trading in sheep for personal gain. As symbols of his unique authority the good shepherd takes two staves, **one . . . called Favor** (Heb. *nōʿam*), **the other . . . Union** (Heb. *ḥōbᵉlîm*). Tending the flock is principally concerned with the bestowing of the benefits of the favour of God which serves in turn to promote harmonious relationships among the sheep. The bad shepherds neither had divine approval nor saw their charges living in peace and safety.

8. In one month I got rid of the three shepherds. Clearly the presence of the definite article here would denote three particular persons. P. R. Ackroyd ('Zechariah', *PCB*, p. 653) may be right in suggesting that this is an interpretative comment relating the general message of the section to some particular historical situation. Only on such an assumption can any guess be hazarded with regard to the identity of the three shepherds (cf. also R. C. Dentan, 'Zechariah' in *IB*, VI, p. 1104). They were 'got rid of' (Heb. *kāḥad*, 'to hide or efface'). J. G. Baldwin (*op. cit.*, p. 181) rightly thinks that 'destroyed' is too strong a translation. Yet the force of the good shepherd's testimony must not be lost. Perhaps we should read '. . . I disposed of the three shepherds'. Beyond this it is virtually impossible to identify these shepherds with anything approaching probability. A host of attempts has been made. Of the more traditional views, that which sees the 'good' shepherd as Onias III, the high priest in Jerusalem (198–174 B.C.), and the three removed as those three who acquired office by means of bribery—Jason, Menelaus and Alcimus (cf. 2 Macc. 4: 1 ff.)—is one of the

most attractive. Another, and similar, interpretation is that the shepherd is the son of Onias III (also named Onias), but that the three bad shepherds expelled are the sons of Tobias. This view largely rests on the confusion of the two Oniases by Josephus (in the *Jewish Wars* i). More recently H. H. Rowley (*The Zadokite Fragments and the Dead Sea Scrolls*, 1952, 62 ff.) suggested that Onias III might be the Teacher of Righteousness of the Qumran community. Similarly, C. Rabin (*The Zadokite Documents*, 1956, p. 30 f.) thinks that the smitten shepherd (cf. 13: 7) might well be the Teacher of Righteousness. **I grew weary of them:** i.e. of the flock at large. **9.** So the good shepherd abandons his flock in the face of blind opposition. **10.** He breaks his staff Favor to symbolize the Lord's displeasure and the annulling of the covenant which he had made **with all the nations** though the singular 'people' is meant (cf. v. 14). **11. and the afflicted . . . knew that it was the word of the LORD:** here we should clearly read 'the poor of the flock'—the faithful few who recognize the word of the Lord, who know true authority when they see it in action.

12. With this termination of his office as shepherd, the prophet asks for his wages, yet not without appeal to the conscience of his hearers. **So they paid** (Heb. *shāqal*, 'weighed') **. . . thirty pieces of silver:** a paltry sum estimated as compensation for a slave in ancient times (cf. Exod. 21: 32). Although coinage as we know it was not in use at the time the verb probably means 'paid'. (The Gk. verb used here in LXX is reproduced in Mt. 26: 15.) **13.** The Lord then commands the prophet, **Throw it to the potter:** Heb. has *yōṣēr*, 'potter', but the Syriac version reads *'ôṣar* ('treasury') which is preferred in the RSV. But *yōṣēr* here may refer to the silver moulder, or silver melter of the Temple. F. F. Bruce ('The Book of Zechariah and the Passion Narrative' in *BJRL, op. cit.*, p. 350) suggests that this provides the real link between the potter's field (cf. Mt. 27: 3–10) and Judas's blood money. The prophet regards this payment with some contempt as a sum **at which they priced** (Heb. *yāqar* 'to be prized or appraised') **me**. The NIV catches the irony of the action. **14. Then I broke . . . Union:** for with the rejection of the Lord's chosen pastor there will be little to maintain the peace of the flock by the unity of north and south.

15. By their rejection of good leadership the people are in reality choosing an alternative **foolish shepherd**. So the prophet spells out his character and his deeds. His failure will be both positive and negative. He will neglect almost every aspect of a true shepherd's responsibility, serving rather himself and his own ends. He feeds himself on the sheep, **tearing off their hoofs:** that is, throwing away the carcasses when he is finished with them. **17.** And with a final graphic poem the oracle ends. The worthless shepherd comes in for judgment. He is paralysed and blinded; at one and the same time he is rendered incapable of defending his flock in the hour of danger as well as of watching over their day-to-day welfare.

III. FINAL SUFFERING AND FINAL DELIVERANCE (12: 1–14: 21)

i. Impregnable Jerusalem (12: 1–9)

1. An Oracle: cf. comment on 9: 1. **concerning Israel:** these final chapters make no distinction between the northern and southern kingdoms. 'Israel' here refers to the whole nation (cf. 11: 14). The cosmic tones of this introduction form a fitting prelude to the apocalyptic character of what follows. Jerusalem is now very much the focal point of the prophet's message down to the end of the book. **2.** The city is about to become **a cup that sends . . . reeling** and **an immovable rock** (3). Jerusalem is to be laid under siege. Her inhabitants will be hopelessly outnumbered. However extraordinary it may seem that the history of this city has been repeated again and again, there can be little doubt that the extremity she suffers is an indication of the fact that she is regarded as the centre of God's purpose, and in consequence she attracts the perpetual antagonism of the enemies of God. Jerusalem had once before 'drunk from the hand of the LORD . . . the goblet that makes men stagger' (Heb. *ra'al*, Isa. 51: 17). Now, however, she herself will be 'a cup that sends . . . reeling' (Heb. *sap ra'al*) that others will drink. She will be 'an immovable rock' that will cause injury to any who try to shift. **4.** Yet the reversal of Jerusalem's fortunes does not end there. The prophet reports that God has said **I will strike every horse with panic, and its rider with madness** (Heb. *shiggā'ôn*), which is reminiscent of a similar judgment, against disobedience, in earlier times (cf. Dt. 28: 28). But in contrast to the sudden blindness of the enemies' horses God will open his eyes in help and salvation during this day of judgment. **5.** This demonstration of the power of God will cause **the leaders** (Heb. *'alluph*) **of Judah** (lit. 'the clansmen of Judah') to consider their position in relation to the people of Jerusalem who have been given the victory because of God's presence among them. **6.** And following this reassessment on their part the men of Judah similarly become powerful with the Lord among them also, causing devastation among their enemies round about. **7 f.** Moreover, any vestige of alienation between Judah and Jerusalem will be overshadowed by the unmistakable evidence of God's protection. Ackroyd correctly observes that any hope of pinning this passage to some specific historical situation

is ill-founded (*PCB*, p. 654). The picture is apocalyptic, and this accounts for the prominence nevertheless given to **the house of David** where all the ideals of the future are centred. David's house shall be **like God** (Heb. *kē'lōhîm*): perhaps 'as a god' which is qualified by **like the Angel of the LORD**, the select messenger of the Almighty. This verse must be read *in toto*. God will strengthen the weakest among Israel and similarly he will honour all from the highest to the lowest. And from then on, every nation that rears its head against the holy city will meet with God's certain and destructive judgment (9).

ii. Lamentation in Jerusalem (12: 10–14)

Those, however, who are promised the blessings of the previous section are in need of renewal if those blessings are to be fulfilled to the measure of God's intention. God will supply the means for this renewal also. **10. I will pour out . . . a spirit of grace and supplication . . .:** the two operative words in Heb. are *ḥēn* ('grace') and *taḥanûnîm* ('supplication for favour'). In other words, the twin gifts from the Lord are complementary: the attitude of supplication for God's favour will be accompanied by a gracious demeanour each to the other. **when they look on me, the one they have pierced:** this clause presents various problems. The Massoretic text reads: 'when they look on *me* whom they have pierced' and this is supported by almost all the major versions, including AV and other English versions. (NEB also combines both readings: 'They shall look on me, on him whom they have pierced'; God regards as done to himself the injury done to his representative.) The reading of RSV (on *him* whom . . .) supported by a few Heb. manuscripts, the early Fathers, and especially Theodotion, with whose version agrees the use of this verse in Jn 19: 37. But John's use of the passage is more of an allusion than a direct reference. If the RSV translation be accepted, then we have either to consider the application of this to some historical figure (Onias III?) or the Servant of the final Song in Isaiah (Isa. 52: 13–53: 12). The latter interpretation is followed by most evangelicals but is almost certainly not correct. A more positive and illuminating treatment of the passage has been made by D. R. Jones (*Haggai, Zechariah, Malachi*, TC, 1962, p. 161) in which he understands the accusative particle of the clause to mean 'concerning'. This has some support from the lexicons (cf. Brown, Driver and Briggs, *Hebrew and English Lexicon of the Old Testament*, 1952, p. 85). We would then read: 'they shall look to me (God) concerning the one (or ones) whom they pierced'. At first sight this has the merit of harmonizing fairly well with the usual collective interpretation given to the Servant Song of Isaiah (cf. above). On the other hand, if 'they' refer to the enemies of Israel, as some think, then the pierced one(s) might well be the dead of Judah's battle. But perhaps more convincing than most interpretations is that of Matthias Delcor, who takes the verb rendered 'pierced' (Heb. *dāqar*) to mean 'to profane' or 'to insult', and understands the clause to mean: 'they shall look to me whom they have profaned (or insulted)', cf. 'Zacharie xii. 10' in *RB*, 58, 1951, pp. 189–199. In support of this it is interesting to note that in Ezek. 36: 16–21 a synonym for Heb. *dāqar*, viz., *ḥalal*, is taken as 'to profane'.

11. This lamentation will be **like the weeping of Hadad Rimmon in the plain of Megiddo**. Those who take Hadad Rimmon as a place name usually follow the interpretation of Jerome, referring this to a city near the plain of Megiddo, and possibly identified in modern times as Tell Mutesellim. Much more likely, however, is the suggestion that this is the name of a fertility god (cf. 2 Kg. 5: 18) whose death was mourned annually in the dry season, much in the same fashion as the weeping for Tammuz was condemned in the message of Ezekiel (cf. Ezek. 8: 14). F. F. Bruce has further suggested that this liturgical ritual may have become linked with the annual memorial for Josiah (cf. 2 Chr. 35: 25) who was slain in battle at Megiddo (cf. *This is That*, 1968, pp. 111 f.). Delcor arrives at a similar conclusion though by a different route. He believes that an examination of the Aramaic text of the passage reveals that it should be emended to: 'the lamentation of that day will be like the lamentation for the son of Amon (i.e., Josiah) in the plain of Megiddo' (cf. 'Deux passages difficiles: Zacharie 12: 11 et 11: 13' in *VT*, 3, 1953, pp. 67–73).

12 ff. That this great penitence is a product of God's gift (cf. v. 10) is endorsed by its spontaneous nature. Each family, each group weeps with remorse, though the royal and priestly houses are singled out for special mention, presumably because the people follow their genuine example.

iii. The abolition of uncleanness (13: 1–6)

1. The apocalyptic, even eschatological fervour of the message is heightened by the repetition of **On that day** (cf. vv, 2, 4; 14: 1, 4, 6, 8, 9, 20, 21). At the sign of Israel's repentance provision is made for the removal of her impurity. It is **a fountain**: probably having in mind the promise of Ezekiel (cf. 36: 25). This will deal with both **sin** (Heb. *ḥaṭṭā't*) or 'error' and **impurity** (Heb. *niddāh*, denoting ritual impurity, and probably in reference more specifically to idolatry; cf. also Ezek. 36: 17). **2. names of the idols:** indicating that a foremost place had been given to powers other than to the power of God. These must be done away with. Priority of attention, however, is given

to false prophecy collectively described as **the prophets and the spirit of impurity**. The latter phrase (Heb. *rûaḥ ha-ṭumᵉ'āh*) occurs only here in the OT. Spiritual powers are not always so easy to distinguish, and in the nature of the case any distinction between true and false must be carefully and clearly made—an emphasis found in the NT (cf. 1 C. 2: 13 ff.; 1 Jn 4: 1–6). Yet the essence of the distinction lies in severing all associations with the 'spirit of impurity' in contrast with the Spirit of God, who in the NT especially, is regularly designated 'the Holy Spirit'. **3.** In spite of the removal of false prophets the possibility of their re-emergence remains a threat. But in 'that day' the quality of renewal in Israel will be such that even those who are closest to the false prophet will have a greater regard for truth than for kinship, and they will **stab him** (cf. 12: 10). This re-occurrence of the Heb. verb *dāqar* makes it inconceivable that the prophet is actually condoning homicide. Some kind of decisive denunciation must be meant and in which case it would lend greater weight to the interpretation suggested for this verb in 12: 10.

4. The result of this total rejection of false prophecy will be that the work of the prophet will no longer be of 'professional' status. The **garment of hair** will count for little, and the words may even suggest that it will be recognized as a uniform of disgrace. Men will avoid rather than clamour for the prophetic role, saying, **I am not a prophet**: a return to that healthy diffidence seen amongst the earliest of God's spokesmen (cf. Am. 7: 14). **6.** Yet false prophets, recognizing the judgment against their kind, will make every attempt to conceal their association with false prophecy. When one of them is asked: **'What are these wounds on your body?'** (Heb. *bēn yādēkā*, lit. 'between your hands') he will attribute his injuries to some squabble among his friends rather than, as the words would seem to suggest, to the lacerations inflicted in prophetic trance (cf. 1 Kg. 18: 28). There is just the possibility, if the usual translation of Heb. *dāqar* (v. 3) is accepted, that the reply indicates that the false prophet has in fact suffered at the hands of his parents.

iv. Refining the Remnant (13: 7–9)

This is the final poem of the book. Scholars have varied in their opinions regarding its original location. But it is best to view the poem as a resumption of the shepherd theme of 11: 4–17, in which case it is not out of place following the two previous sections. The atmosphere of deep sorrow described in 12: 10–14 would be such as would make the judgment contained in the second half of the poem understandable, however difficult to accept in fact, especially if it were to lead, as the end of the poem shows, to the ultimate glory of the messianic age. It is therefore with ch. 12 that the section is to be more directly linked.

7. '**Awake, O sword, against my shepherd . . .**': who is this shepherd? Fortunately, we are left in no doubt so far as the NT is concerned. The substance of this verse fell from the lips of Jesus who clearly saw in its words a presentation of himself as the true Shepherd of Israel, and in a situation in which he foresaw the flight of the disciples in the face of danger. He said: 'You will all fall away, for it is written, "I will strike the shepherd, and the sheep will be scattered"' (Mk 14: 27). The shepherd is moreover described as **the man who is close to me** (Heb. *geber 'amîtî*). This is the king who is close to God as he to whom God has delegated divine authority to rule. The idea of striking the king is not unknown in the OT (*e.g.* Mic. 5: 1). But many see a more cogent reference here to the Servant of the Lord in Isaiah, who gives his back to those who beat him (Isa. 50: 6), and who indeed was smitten by God himself (cf. Isa. 53: 4, 10). Yet it is not only in the NT that we find a reflection on this oracle. As F. F. Bruce has pointed out, the oracle is quoted in the Damascus Document (otherwise known as the Zadokite Work), first discovered in the Cairo Genizah in 1896, and fragments of which were found at Qumran. Whether the author of the Zadokite Work had in mind a reference to a wicked ruler, in using Zechariah at this point, or whether, as Rabin has suggested, he saw in these words an adumbration of the suffering of the Teacher of Righteousness, we cannot be certain, though the latter alternative is more in keeping with Zechariah's context (cf. F. F. Bruce, *This is That*, 1968, pp. 102 f.; C. Rabin, *The Zadokite Documents*, 1956, p. 31).

8 f. The oracle, however, looks further ahead still. Two thirds of the population of the land perish, and the remainder are purified as precious metals are refined in a furnace (cf. Ezek. 5: 1–12). But the result of this cataclysmic judgment is to be seen in a people who, in consequence of the purifying intervention of the Lord, more readily and more fervently testify to their knowledge of God. They call on his name, and his answering voice re-assures them that they are indeed his people.

v. The Struggle for Jerusalem (14: 1–21)
The final drama surrounding Jerusalem and her people now comes to its high point. The city collapses and half its population is carried off into captivity. But as the situation reaches its most extreme point the Lord descends to intervene, and with vivid apocalyptic sequences the picture changes. The powerful nations are disarrayed, and from this centre of eschatological activity God begins his reign as King over all the earth, unifying all those who accept his victory and his sovereignty.

1. a day of the LORD is coming: this is perhaps not *the* day of the Lord but its antecedent. It announces the time when God commences taking a hand in human affairs *towards* that day (cf. vv. 6, 8) which marks the end of man's day and the beginning of the day of the Lord. **your plunder will be divided among you:** God's judgment is equable as well as universal. With righteousness he deals with his own people first (cf. Ezek. 9: 6; 1 Pet. 4: 17). **2.** That **all the nations** should arrive on the scene to do battle is not so unrealistic as at first sight. The eschatological nature of the prophecy must be kept in view. Thus although the accumulated strength of the nations might conjure up a fantastic picture it must be remembered that it is their collective and united ambition to capture *territory* that lies behind the events described by the prophet. Looting and rape, persistent accompaniments of war throughout human history, take place.

3. Then the LORD will go out and fight against those nations: a number of early commentators, together with a few modern writers, have understood the Heb. preposition (*be*) here to mean that in some mysterious purpose God joins battle against Jerusalem *among* the nations. This cannot be; the NIV gives the correct sense. God no longer stands aloof. He fights for his people **as in the day of battle**, as he had done in the past (cf. Exod. 14: 13 ff.). **4. On that day:** this now brings us to the day of the Lord when **his feet will stand on the Mount of Olives**, so named here for the first time. Flanking the eastern side of Jerusalem, it provides for those who surmount it a panoramic view of the city. Both David (cf. 2 Sam. 15: 30) and Jesus (cf. Lk. 19: 37–41) came here at a critical moment of their lives. It is fairly certain that the promise of the return of Jesus (cf. Ac. 1: 11) has this verse in mind. But now the mountain **will be split in two . . . forming a great valley** (cf. Hab. 3: 6) making an escape route for the panic stricken inhabitants of the city (cf. v. 5). **5.** The Heb. of this is notoriously ambiguous. The verb (Heb. *nastem*) which occurs three times here is more easily understood in this context as 'you fled'. Slightly pointing, however, could mean 'will be blocked up' (*nistam*). The RSV follows the guidance of the Aramaic text and reads 'to be stopped up' for the first verb and 'to flee' for the second and third occurrences. The LXX favours 'to be blocked up' for all three. This is accepted by Ackroyd who believes that the flight of the city's population is not harmonious with the free access to Jerusalem described in v. 2. Ackroyd also refers to Josephus (*Ant.* ix. 225) where there is an account of the **earthquake** which occurred **in the days of Uzziah king of Judah** (cf. Am. 1: 1). Josephus writes: '. . . and before the city at a place called Eroge [probably the En Rogel of 1 Kg. 1: 9] half the mountain broke off from the rest of the west, and rolled itself four furlongs'.

One of the more extraordinary reconstructions of this text is that of H. G. Mitchell (*Haggai and Zechariah*, 1912, pp. 343 ff.), who argues that the verb *nistam* in the OT invariably alludes to the stopping up of wells or springs. Since the construct case for 'valley' and Gihon are similar in Heb., Mitchell goes on to suggest that this may be a reference to the stopping up of Gihon in the Kidron valley. But this argument has not met with general assent. **Then the LORD my God will come:** Heb. reads 'my God', some Eng. versions have 'your God'. Whichever is accepted the comment of Ackroyd is apposite: '. . . it could be an interjection of confidence.' (*op. cit.*, p. 655).

6. The Heb. of this verse appears to be damaged and is very puzzling. The text appears to read. 'In that day there will be no light but cold and condensation (ice?)'. Some take the sense to be that there will be absence of both light and heat; others read the absence of extremes of temperatures. Other than such suggestions as these it is impossible to reconstruct the text satisfactorily. **7.** Night will cease. The prophet takes up the words of Isaiah (cf. 60: 19 f.) and this in turn is alluded to in Revelation (cf. 21: 25; 22: 5). **8.** But Jerusalem will be the source and supply of **living water** which will not fluctuate with the seasons but run eastward and westward to the Dead Sea and the Mediterranean. This is an even greater wonder than the promise of Ezekiel (cf. 47: 1–12) and possibly has in mind the primeval river of Eden (cf. Gen. 2: 10 ff.). Moreover, with the idea of water as a signal of God's miraculous provision the prophet may be recalling the theme of earlier prophets (*e.g.* Jl 3: 18), especially Isaiah (cf. 30: 25 f.) or taking up the idyllic poetry of the Psalmist (cf. 65: 9). And there may well be implicit in the words the restoration of Israel who formerly had rejected the Lord as 'the spring of living water' (cf. Jer. 2: 13). Very clear reference to this verse, however, is to be found in the NT in the words of Jesus concerning those who believe in Him and who will be gifted with 'streams of living water' (cf. Jn 7: 38; for a comprehensive examination of this see C. K. Barrett, *The Gospel According to St. John*, 1958, pp. 195 f., 271).

9. Then will come the time when God's worldwide kingdom will be seen and acknowledged by all. And in that day the supreme sovereignty of God will no longer be a mere credal affirmation (as in Dt. 6: 4) but a demonstrated truth to which men will give their total submission. **10.** The land will then be levelled out leaving Jerusalem exalted above the rest, **from Geba** (6 miles NE of the city) **to Rimmon** (36 miles SE). The city itself will be compacted and complete. **the Benjamin Gate:** situated at the NE corner of the city (cf. Jer. 37: 13), whilst . . . **the First Gate** and the **Corner Gate** are probably one and the same, i.e., at the NW perimeter. **the Tower of Hananel** (cf. Neh. 3: 1): situated at the NE extremity; **the royal winepresses** lay to the south. **11.** The notable allusions to the book of Nehemiah in this and the previous verse probably serve to underline the prophet's assurance that Jerusalem will now be separated and secure under God's protection.

12. From this time God will wreak vengeance by **plague** on all who take up arms against the city. The ghastly scene of internecine bloodshed (13) possibly recalls the epic of Gideon's rout of the Midianites (cf. Jg. 7: 21 f.). **14. Judah too will fight at Jerusalem:** there is some ground for the view that the text has suffered some slight dislocation at this point, since v. 15 would more naturally follow on immediately after v. 13. It is clear that the RSV has wrongly translated the opening clause of this verse. Note AV and NEB: 'Judah shall fight in (or with) Jerusalem'. And those who would have robbed the city of her treasures will themselves be despoiled of their possessions.

16. the Feast of Tabernacles: one of the most ancient of Israelite festivals, commemorating the season of harvest (cf. Lev. 23: 34; Exod. 34: 22, etc.). It had historical reference to the deliverance of Israel from Egypt and emphasized the belief that the life of the nation began, and would continue, under the redemptive care of her God, and each occasion of the feast was accompanied by the solemn reading of the Torah (cf. Neh. 8: 14–18). Its association more specifically with rain was not generally known until after the Exile (cf. Mishnah *Sukkah* 4: 9), when libations of water were brought from Siloam to Jerusalem—an added link with Jn 7: 37 (cf. note on v. 8 above). **18. The Egyptian people:** used representatively throughout this passage. They stand in this context for those nations or peoples who do not rely upon the Lord for their well-being and survival but rely upon 'natural' resources, *e.g.* the flooding of the Nile. **The LORD will bring the plague on them** (Heb. 'upon them shall *not* come the plague'): NIV avoids the obvious difficulty by omitting the offending 'not'. But perhaps the Heb. is a rhetorical question: 'shall not the plague come upon them?' The repetition of 'the nations that do not go up to celebrate the feast' (19) may be due to dittography.

20. In a situation in which nations worship the Lord together in acknowledgement of his sovereign power and his provision of man's needs there will be no place for superstition. **the bells of the horses:** used by pagan warriors to avert evil spirits, but now to be emblems of the holiness of the Lord, just as the mitre of the high priest was declared holy in days long ago (cf. Exod. 28: 36). **21.** Holiness will mark each aspect and item of daily life down to pots and pans. Whereas in former days each family kept certain cooking utensils separate for use on holy days only, such a separation will no longer be needed, for all will be sacred and fit for the service of God.

As for the Temple and its worship this will be unmarred by human error and malpractice. The provision of sacrifices in the Temple precincts will not give opportunity for racketeering at the expense of pilgrims and tourists, for **there shall no longer be a Canaanite in the house of the LORD Almighty** (cf. note on 11: 7). This final word was taken up by Jesus, probably in underlining this oracle in particular as well as the message of Zechariah in its total importance (cf. Jn 2: 16; cf. Jer. 7: 11). It is certain that our Lord insisted, as the prophet was declaring here, that true and inward holiness rendered the special provision of sacrificial animals superfluous among people who had already devoted themselves and their possessions wholly to the Lord.

JONES, D. R., *Haggai, Zechariah, Malachi.* TB (London, 1962).
KAUFMANN, Y., *The Religion of Israel* (London, 1960).
KLAUSNER, J. *The Messianic Idea in Israel* (London, 1956).
LINDBLOM, J., *Prophecy in Ancient Israel* (Oxford, 1962).
MITCHELL, H. G., *Haggai and Zechariah.* ICC Edinburgh, 1912).
MOWINCKEL, S., *He That Cometh* (Oxford, 1956).
NORTH, C. R., *The Old Testament Interpretation of History* (London, 1946).
RAD, G. VON, *Old Testament Theology*, 2 vols. (Edinburgh, 1962).
RINGGREN, H., *Israelite Religion* (London, 1966).
ROWLEY, H. H., *The Faith of Israel* (London, 1956).
ROWLEY, H. H. (ed.), *The Old Testament and Modern Study* (Oxford, 1957).
ROBINSON, H. W.(ed.), *Record and Revelation* (Oxford, 1938).
RUSSELL, D. S., *Between the Testaments* (London, 1963).
RUSSELL, D. S., *The Method and Message of Jewish Apocalyptic* (London, 1964).
SMITH, G. A., *The Book of the Twelve Prophets*, ii (London, 1898).
STUHLMUELLER, C., 'Haggai, Zechariah, Malachi' in *The Jerome Biblical Commentary* (London, 1968).
THOMAS, D. W., 'Zechariah' in IB (6th edn.) (New York), 1956).
VRIEZEN, TH. C., *The Religion of Ancient Israel* (London, 1967).
WRIGHT, C. H. H. *Zechariah and His Prophecies* (London, 1879).

BIBLIOGRAPHY

ACKROYD, P. R. 'Zechariah', in PCB (London, 1962).
ACKROYD, P. R., *Exile and Restoration* (London, 1968).
BALDWIN, J. G., *Haggai, Zechariah, Malachi.* TOTC (London, 1972).
BRIGHT, JOHN, *History of Israel* (London, 1960).
BRUCE, F. F., *Israel and the Nations* (Exeter, 1963).
CHARLES, R. H. (ed.), *The Apocrypha and Pseudepigrapha of the Old Testament*, 2 vols. (Oxford, 1913).
EISSFELDY, O., *The Old Testament: An Introduction* (Oxford, 1965).
FROST, S. B., *Old Testament Apocalyptic* (London, 1952).
HARRISON, R. K., *Introduction to the Old Testament* (London, 1970).
HARRISON, R. K., *Old Testament Times* (London, 1971).

Additional Literature
ALBRIGHT, W. F., *Archaeology and the Religion of Israel* (Baltimore, 1956).
BALY, D., *The Geography of the Bible* (London, 1957).
BRUCE, F. F., *This Is That* (Exeter, 1968).
BRUCE, F. F., 'The Book of Zechariah and the Passion Narrative' in BJRL, 43, 1960/1 pp.336–353.
CHARY, T., *Les Prophètes et le culte a partir de l'Exil* (Paris, 1955).
JONES, D. R., 'A Fresh Interpretation of Zechariah IX-XI' in VT, XII, 1962, pp.241 ff.
MAY, H. G., 'A key to the Interpretation of Zechariah's Visions' in JBL, 57, 1938, pp.173–184.
McHARDY, W. D., 'The Horses in Zechariah' in *In Memoriam Paul Kahle* (Beihefte zur Zeitschrift für die alttestamentliche Wissenschaft 103, 1968).
THOMAS, D. WINTON (ed.), *Documents from Old Testament Times* (Cambridge, 1958).

MALACHI

W. WARD GASQUE

Malachi, the last of the short books which go to make up the Hebrew 'Book of the Twelve' (Minor Prophets), concludes the second section of the Hebrew canon (cf. 'Canon of the OT' p. 48), and is closely linked with Haggai and Zechariah with which it gives us a brief glimpse into the otherwise obscure post-exilic period of Jewish history. Some have suggested that Mal. was originally simply a continuation of Zech. 9–14 (comp. the similar introductory formulas in Zech. 9: 1; 12: 1; and Mal. 1: 1), but this is uncertain. In spite of this apparent literary link and the problem of our lack of knowledge concerning the author, the book bears the imprint of a single personality and is not otherwise theologically linked with Zech. 9–14. A more certain link is with the historical period narrated by the books of Ezra and Nehemiah (see below, **Date**).

Although not the final book in the Hebrew Bible, it is in the modern Protestant canon and has always been understood as a connecting link between the two Testaments. It would not be wise to push this idea too far, in view of the difference between the Heb. and Eng. arrangements, but this does seem particularly appropriate in view of the important reference to the messianic herald in Mal. 3: 1 (applied to the ministry of John the baptist by the NT. Mk 1: 2; Mt. 11: 10) and also to the eschatological ministry of Elijah in 4: 5 (cf. 9: 11–13).

Author

We know nothing whatever concerning the author except what is revealed about his character through his book. As in the case of Obadiah and Habakkuk, the names of his parents and his home are not revealed, nor is his prophecy connected by the superscription with any particular time in Israel's history (though the internal evidence makes the approximate date clear; cf. below). Even the prophet's name is uncertain, for 'Malachi' means simply 'my messenger' (so translated in 3: 1) and, in view of its absence as a proper name elsewhere in the OT, has been regarded by some scholars as a *nom de plume* or an editor's title. This seems to be the view of the Greek translator who produced this portion of the Septuagint, which reads 'his messenger', though the Targum of Jonathan (an Aramaic paraphrase of the prophetic books dating from the fourth or fifth cent. A.D. but containing much earlier traditions) gives him (in a characteristically improbable rabbinical identification) the name of 'Ezra the scribe' (so Jerome and Calvin). The whole matter is ultimately uncertain, and perhaps unimportant; but it is possible that this otherwise unknown name, Malachi, was in fact the prophet's actual name.

Date

A general date for the book would be sometime after the return of the Judean exiles to Jerusalem, i.e. the general period of Ezra and Nehemiah. This is indicated by the mention of 'your governor' (Heb. *pehāh*) in 1: 8, the same word used by Haggai to describe Zerubbabel (1: 1) and in Neh. to indicate Nehemiah's own position (5: 14). It has been suggested that the absence of any reference to the rebuilding of the temple and the impression of a drift into rather causal attitudes regarding worship indicate that some time had passed since the rebuilding took place (cf. J. Baldwin, *Haggai, Zechariah, Malachi*, p. 213). Temple services have been resumed long enough for the priests to become weary with the regular performance of them (1: 13), and certain irregularities have crept in (1: 7–8, 12–14; 3: 8–9). Absence of any reference to the reforms of Ezra and Nehemia seems to indicate a date prior to their arrival, perhaps even preparing the way for the success of their important ministries. This would give a date of c. 470–65 B.C. or (if Ezr. is to be dated after Neh., cf. pp. 524 f.) c. 445–4, but these are at best only approximate.

Structure

The fundamental literary characteris of the book is the use of the disputation method, which introduces each main section. Thus there is usually an opening statement (.'"I have loved you," says the LORD,' 1: 2) followed by a question, often an objection or response put into the mouth of the hearers. But you ask, "How have you loved us?"'), which in turn is followed by an enlargement of the theme and driving home of the point (cp. Isa. 40: 27–28; Jer. 2: 23–37; Ezek. 12: 28; Mic. 2: 6–11). The words put into mouth of the LORD's opponents are not necessarily to be regarded as actual statements of the hearers but rather represent the attitude and actions of the people as the prophet understands them. In this way he makes clear to them their true selves, their rebellion against and their need of repentance.

The style of Malachi is that of the *spoken*

word. The book is very much like the letter of James in the NT and resembles a collection of loosely connected oracles rather than a carefully organized literary work, though some have found it in a logical progression of thought. The six oracles (1: 2–5; 1: 6–2: 9; 2: 10–16; 2: 17–3: 5; 3: 6–12; 3: 13–4: 3) are introduced by a heading or title (1: 1) and concluded by an epilogue (4: 4–6). The last three verses may be an editorial addition, intended to draw the Book of the Prophets to a conclusion, though the style is in keeping with the rest of the book and could well have come from the prophet himself.

Message

The literary form which Mal. uses, the dialogue or disputation, reflects his prophetic life-style. He is not content merely to speak the word of God in a mechanical way to his own disciples; rather, he wishes to take God's message into the marketplace, confronting men and women in their neglect of God and His ways, or in their open rebellion against His law. Thus he is concerned to debate with those who call into question the LORD's goodness and justice whether by word or by life—rather than to avoid the unpleasantness of forthright confrontation.

Malachi's message centres in the faithfulness of God in contrast to the unfaithfulness of His people. He has entered into a father-son relationship with Israel (1: 6; 3: 17) and desires the very best for his children (3: 10–12). But Israel has constantly spurned this relationship and has utterly failed to live up to the terms of Yahweh's covenant. Both priests (2: 8) and people (2: 10) have broken the covenant. Rather than responding gladly to Yahweh's goodness, they have been unfaithful to Him and have failed to give Him the best, as the law prescribed, in their worship (1: 13–14); and they have not kept the commandment concerning the presentation of their tithes and offerings (3: 8). In effect, they have despised the LORD (1: 16). And having failed in their covenant relationship with Yahweh, they have also failed in human relationships. A supreme example of their failure of relationship is in the prevalence of divorce (2: 14–16), the breaking of the most important human covenant.

The prophet thus calls the people to repentance (3: 7, 10, etc.), to turn from their sin to their God, who is longing to bless them. The LORD is a loving father to Israel; but He is also Master and King (1: 6, 14), a God of justice (2: 17). And His judgment is certain. The day of His justice is coming, and it will then become clear to all that loyalty and justice are not forgotten by the LORD, and a new order of righteousness will prevail (3: 1–5, 16–18, etc.). A concrete illustration of the fact that God is still in control of history, loves His people and will not allow unfaithfulness to go unpunished is the recent fate of the Edomites (1: 2–4). The present troubles being experienced by the people are also tokens of this future judgment (1: 6–2: 9; 3: 7–12); but the worst—and the best—is yet to come.

Malachi also gives us a beautiful description of the ideal priest (3: 5–7), portrays for us the blessings of obedience (3: 10–12, 16–17; 4: 2–3), and adds to the OT concept of the day of the LORD the figure of an appointed forerunner (3: 1–4; 4: 5–6).

ANALYSIS

Title (1: 1)
Oracle (Heb. *massā'*) is used some sixty times in the OT. The idea is that of a 'burden' imposed by a master, a ruler, or a deity on his subjects. It can apply to a position of leadership among God's people, to a religious duty, or to the judgment of God. Here it emphasizes the prophet's sense of constraint and responsibility in giving the message which has been entrusted to him. He would not necessarily have chosen to say such a thing, but the choice is not his: the burden has been placed upon him by the LORD, and he simply has to accept it and discharge his duty. The message of the prophet is not one which he has invented, nor does he speak because he likes to hear the sound of his voice or to feel that he has an influence on men. Rather, it is a message which has been laid on his heart as a 'burden'; and it is meant to weigh also on the consciences of his hearers. It is **the word of the LORD**, a revelation from God, **to Israel**, His people returned from exile who were beginning to forget Him, **through Malachi** (cf. Introduction).

I. THE LORD'S LOVE FOR ISRAEL (1: 2–5)
Malachi introduces his word from God by reminding the people of Yahweh's great love for his people, a central theme of the OT prophets (cf. Hos. 11: 1–4; Jer. 31: 1–3; Isa. 43: 1–4; Zeph. 3: 17; and esp. Dt. 7: 8, 13; 10: 15, etc.). The lack of human love in the community, illustrated by such things as divorce and marital unfaithfulness (2: 13–16), has undermined their confidence in the divine love; and what God did in bringing them back from exile to re-establish the city of Jerusalem and rebuild the temple has apparently been forgotten. Therefore, the people are faced with the essential presupposition of their existence: the covenant love of Yahweh (cf. 'Love', *EBT* II, pp. 518–42; 'Love', *NBD*). **2–3.** The demonstration of God's love for His people is seen in the case of **Jacob** and **Esau**, twin sons of Isaac and Rebekah who had equal opportunities: both were sons of Isaac and therefore heirs of the promise, yet one was chosen and the other rejected. Jacob was the one especially favoured by God. The OT nowhere says that Jacob was more worthy of God's love or more 'loveable' than Esau; but God's electing and redeeming love was manifest toward him (cf. H. H. Rowley, *The Biblical Doctrine of Election*, 1950, pp. 44–68). Verses 2–3 have been a problem to many Christians. They seem to make the love of God an arbitrary matter. Three comments may help to clear the confusion a little. (i) Hebrew tends to make use of the literary device of hyperbole or exaggeration to make a point: thus **Esau I have hated** does not mean that God literally 'hated' Esau but rather is a vivid

way of contrasting God's special love for Jacob (cf. Gen. 29: 30–31; Prov. 13: 24; and Jesus' statement about 'hating' one's father and mother, Lk. 14: 26 // Mt. 10: 37) with His relation to Esau, whom He did not choose in the same way. (ii) Hebrew also makes frequent use of what scholars have called 'corporate personality', i.e. a manner of thinking in which individuals represent groups of people or nations (cf. E. Jacob, *Theology of the OT*, 1958, pp. 153–56; and esp. H. W. Robinson, *Corporate Personality in Ancient Israel*, 1964): thus the references to Jacob and Esau refer not merely to the two sons of Isaac but also to their descendants, the Israelites and the Edomites. (iii) Malachi's message from the LORD comes at a time in history when the identification of the Edomites against Yahweh and His people was a fact of history: the Edomites (the descendants of Esau) had sided with the destroying armies of Babylon in the destruction of Jerusalem and the plundering of Judah (see on Ob. 10–14). On this passage see Rom. 9: 13; Isa. 34; 63: 1–6; Jer. 49: 7–22; Ezek. 25: 12–14; Ob. 2–3. The phrase **the LORD Almighty** (*Yahweh ṣeḇā'ôt*) recurs like a refrain throughout the prophecy of Malachi (24 times); it indicates Yahweh's role as Saviour, Protector and Judge of His people (cf. Ps. 46: 7, 11). **4–5.** God's judgment on **Edom** is sure. Edom can seek to be a great nation again, but it will not happen: God will not allow it. However, Israel must not be proud or feel self-righteous. God's hand of judgment will be on her too, as the prophet will point out later.

II. AN INDICTMENT OF THE PRIESTS (1: 6–2: 9)
People like to think of God's judgment as being directed to other people; but the message of the Hebrew prophets is that it includes Israel as well as the nations, the servants of Yahweh as well as the people: judgment always begins in God's own house (Am. 3: 2; Jer. 25: 29–30; Ezek. 9: 6; 1 Pet. 4: 17). Thus Malachi first presents Yahweh's indictment against the priests (1: 6–29) and then against the people as a whole (2: 10–17). **6.** The prophet speaks in terms of ordinary human relationships which are familiar to his hearers—**father**-son and **master**-servant—which demand honour and respect (Exod. 20: 12; Prov. 30: 11). But if honour and respect are due in human relationships how much more is this true in the relationship which exists between Yahweh and His people! By their actions the **priests** have shown that at heart they really **despise** Yahweh's **name** (i.e. God Himself; cf. *IDB*, *s.v.* 'Name', *NBD*, *s.v.* 'Name'); cf. also 1: 11, 14; 2: 2, 5; 3: 16; 4: 2. **7–8.** The priests have despised Yahweh by **placing defiled** (ritually unclean) **food upon** His **altar**. The fundamen-

tal problem, however, was not mere ritual but heart-attitude, though this attitude of mind led to carelessness in matters of prescribed ritual (*e.g.* the offering of **blind, crippled** or **diseased** animals for sacrifice; *contra* Exod. 12: 5; Lev. 1: 3, 10; 22: 18–25; Dt. 15: 21; etc.). The expression **the LORD's table** (vv. 7 and 12) is used in the OT only by Malachi (but cf. Ps. 23: 5; Ezek. 44: 16); the primary reference is probably to the tables provided in the inner temple court for the slaughtering of sacrifices. The proof of the priests' basic alienation from Yahweh lay in the fact that they failed to give Him the very best, i.e. they attempted to offer to God what was of no value to man. **9.** This verse expresses irony. The purpose of a gift in the ANE was not only to acknowledge kindness received but to secure favour for the future. Here **God** is implored **to be gracious** by offering to Him decidedly inferior gifts. **10.** 'Stop being hypocritical!' says the prophet; 'It would be better to bar the doors of the temple than to continue to profane God's altar in this manner.' Cf. Isa. 1: 13; Am. 5: 21–24. **11.** This is sometimes taken as an endorsement of pagan worship, i.e. to mean that in contrast to Judah's corrupt practices the Gentiles—by their good works, by the cult of the 'God of heaven' which was widespread in the Persian empire, or simply by the sincerity of their religious devotion—worship the one true God. But the reference is more likely to the perfect sacrifice of the messianic age, when God's name will be **great among the nations**, i.e. when Gentiles come to know God and worship Him outside the narrow confines of the land of Palestine and Israelite religious ritual (cf. J. Baldwin, *op. cit.*, pp. 227–230). **12.** By way of contrast, Malachi turns back to the priests: the **you** is emphatic. He goes behind the external ritual to the real thoughts and intentions of the heart: you say **of the LORD's table, 'It is defiled'** (better: 'may be despised', NEB), **and of its food, 'It is contemptible.' 13a. you sniff at it:** JB 'you sniff disdainfully at me'. **13b–14.** Once again Malachi stresses that God is unwilling to accept anything but the best. **injured . . . animals:** cf. Exod. 22: 31; Lev. 22: 20, 25. The reference in v. 14 is to a voluntary offering, vowed to God in time of trouble as a thanksgiving if deliverance is granted; the temptation was to offer a worthless substitute. But the man who attempts to cheat God will not go unpunished: he will find out that God is **a great King** as well as father and master (1: 6).

2: 1. The final v. of ch. 1 might be understood as extending beyond the priesthood, but here Mal. focuses once again on the sins of the **priests. This admonition** (Heb. *miṣwāh*) indicates that what follows is not simply the prophet's message but a self-fulfilling word from Yahweh. **2. I will send a curse upon you:** cf. *DBT*, *s.v.* 'Curse'; *NBD*, *s.v.* 'Curse'. **I will curse your blessings** could mean 'I will cause your material resources to become, in effect, curses'; or 'I will cause the words of blessing you pronounce as priests to have the effect of curses.' **3. I will rebuke your descendants** (lit. 'seed'): NIV understands this phrase to refer to the descendants of the priests (i.e. the effects of your sin will be felt by subsequent generations), while AV and RV take the 'seed' literally as referring to poor harvests which result in decreased tithes and offerings. JB and NEB give different vowels to the Heb. word and translate respectively: 'I am going to paralyse your arm' and 'I will cut off your arm', i.e. render you incapable of officiating as priests (1 Sam. 2: 31; Ps. 10: 15). **I will spread on your faces the offal of your festival sacrifices:** 'The offal of sacrificial animals was to be removed from the sanctuary and burnt (Exod. 29: 14; Lev. 4: 11; etc.), but so revolting to God were those who offered to Him sacrifices of no value that they and their offerings were to end up on the dung-heap, excluded from God's presence' (J. Baldwin, *op. cit.*, p. 233). **4–5b.** The priests are reminded of God's **covenant with Levi**—another example of the Heb. concept of 'corporate personality': Levi represents the 'tribe of Levi' of the Levites (Num. 3: 45; 18: 21–24; Dt. 33: 8–11)—which is described as **a covenant of life and peace**, an expression occurring only here in the Bible. To enter into covenant relationship with Yahweh is to find the door to fulness of life (cf. *NBD s.v.* 'Life') and peace (*shālôm*: wholeness, prosperity, health, salvation; cf. *IDB*, *s.v.* 'Peace in the OT'). **this called for reverence:** the covenant brings with it not only blessing but responsibility. To reverence God is to respect His authority, obey His commands, and to forsake evil (on the 'fear of God' in the Bible, cf. *DBT*, *s.v.* 'Fear'). **5c–6.** Levi is presented as the model priest: (i) he **revered** Yahweh, standing in **awe** at His **name**; (ii) **true instruction** (Heb. *tōrāh*) **was in his mouth:** He taught the word of God faithfully (on the Heb. concept of *tōrāh*, cf. *NBD*, *s.v.* 'Law'; *DBT*, *s.v.* 'Law'); (iii) **nothing false was found on his lips** (cf. Ps. 15: 2, 3; Prov. 12: 17–19, 22; Mt. 12: 33–37; Lk. 6: 45; Jas 1: 26; 3: 2–12); (iv) **he walked with** God **in peace and uprightness**, indicating continuous and close communion with God, both enjoying and keeping His covenant; and (v) his ministry was such that it **turned many from sin:** he was an influence for good among the people (cf. 4: 6). To the Christian believer this will naturally call to mind the Lord Jesus Christ, our great high priest (Heb. 4: 14–10; 18) who left an example for His servants to follow (1 Pet. 2: 21). **7.** Thus the ideal priest should be sought out by men because of his personal **knowledge** of God and his law (**instruction: Heb. *tōrāh*), **because he is the messenger of the LORD Almighty** (Lev. 10: 11; Dt. 21: 5). **8.** By way of contrast, the priests of Malachi's day have **turned from** their high calling and **have caused many to stumble** by teaching a false *tōrāh*, thus violating **the covenant of Levi. 9.** The result of their having despised God's law and name is that they themselves will be despised **before all the people** (cf. Mic. 3: 9–12; Mt. 23: 1–36).

III. ISRAEL'S FAITHLESSNESS IN WORSHIP AND IN MARRIAGE (2: 10–16)

Here the prophet focuses on the nation as a family. Not only has the covenant between Yahweh and His people been profaned but also the covenant relationship which should exist in the community (2: 10, 14). **10.** The unity of the people is found in their relation to their God, who is both father and creator (cf. Dt. 32: 6; Isa. 63: 16). Yet the people have been **breaking faith with one another**, thus contradicting this relationship. **11. detestable thing** (Heb. *tōʻēbāh*) is a very strong word connected with the worst sort of heathen practices (2 Kg. 16: 3; Dt. 18: 9–14), but it is also applied to the offering of sacrifices in the wrong spirit (Prov. 15: 8; Isa. 1: 13) and unethical behaviour (Prov. 12: 22; 20: 23). **marrying the daughter of a foreign god:** the problem was not simply one of mixed marriages but rather the relaxing of the requirements of conversion to Yahweh and formal incorporation into the covenant community. **12.** The prophet prays that the LORD will not allow the wicked to have children to remember him and to perpetuate his sin in the next generation. **13–14.** Worship and life are intimately connected. God does not accept worship, no matter how apparently earnest, from those whose lives are a contradiction to their profession. **the LORD is acting as the witness between you and the wife of your youth:** marriage is not simply an individual matter, or even a social institution; rather, it is a divine ordinance: the LORD Himself is the chief 'witness' at the wedding ceremony! Cf. Gen. 2: 24; Ezek. 16: 8; Hos. 2: 19; Mk 10: 2–9; Eph. 5: 21–33. **15.** The Heb. text is corrupt here; cf. J. Baldwin, *op. cit.*, pp. 240–241. Only when parents remain faithful to their marriage vows will God's desire for **godly** children be fulfilled. **16. covering himself with violence:** their **divorce** is compared to a great injustice, which, like the blood of a murdered victim, leaves its mark for all to see.

IV. THE DAY OF THE LORD'S JUSTICE (2: 17–3: 5)

The Jews of Malachi's day were faced with a problem with which the OT wrestles time and again; the apparent prosperity of the wicked (cf. Job 21: 7–16; Hab. 1: 2–4, 13). **17.** The people were cynical and had stopped taking right and wrong seriously. practically, if not theoretically, they doubted the justice of God. **3: 1. See:** lit. 'Behold me', 'See what I am about to do.' **my messenger:** the Heb. is the same as the name of the prophet, but it is doubtful that this is intended to refer to Malachi himself. The reference is more likely to a future prophet who would be a forerunner **to prepare the way** for the coming day of the LORD (see 4: 5). The NT sees this role as being fulfilled by John the Baptist (Isa. 40: 3; Mt. 11: 10–12; Mk 1: 2; Lk. 1: 17, 76; 7: 27). The identification of **the messenger of the covenant** is also difficult. Jewish interpretation understands it as a reference to the (an) angel of the LORD, or to Elijah. It seems better to understand it as a reference to Messiah, or even the LORD Himself. **2–4. like a refiner's fire or a launderer's soap:** the purpose of Yahweh's judgment is the purification of character (cf. *NBD, s.v.* 'Refiner, Refining'). lit. **offerings in righteousness**. When a moral transformation of the priests has taken place offerings which are acceptable to the LORD will once more be offered in the temple. **5.** But what is a refining process for some will be punishment for others. Those who are responsible for social injustice do not merely sin against their neighbours but also against the LORD: by their behaviour they demonstrate that they **do not fear** Him. God Himself will be the chief witness against them in the day of judgment (cf. Zeph. 1: 14–18; 3: 1–8; Mk 13: 14–37; 2 Th.2: 1–12).

V. TITHING AND THE LORD'S BLESSING (3: 6–12)

The prophet calls the people to genuine repentance, *viz.* repentance which demonstrates its reality by costly action. God's response to such repentance will be equally open to human observation. **6–7a.** Because Yahweh is steadfast in His character and is faithful to His promise (cf. Num. 23: 19; Heb. 13: 8; Jas 1: 17) His people **are not destroyed**, in spite of their faithlessness and rebellion. **7b.** The call to repentance goes unheeded by the people because there is no apparent consciousness of sin. **8–9.** The appointed **tithes and offerings** required by the law (Lev. 27: 30; Num. 18: 21–24) were being withheld; therefore the curse of crop failure (cf. 3: 11). **10.** Cf. Dt. 28: 2–12; Ezek. 34: 25–31. **Test me in this:** let those who doubt the goodness and justice of God discover His desire to shower down **so much blessing** by seeking to honour Him with their substance. The **storehouse** was the repository for the tithes attached to the temple and presided over by the Levites (1 Chr. 9: 26, 29). **11.** An authentic turning to God will have ecological ramifications in the land: the OT sees a close connection between physical and spiritual blessing. **12. Then all nations will call you blessed:** cf. Gen. 12: 2–3; 18: 18; Ps. 72: 16–17; Isa. 61: 6–9; Jer. 4: 1–2; 33: 7–9; Ezek. 34: 29–31.

VI. THE VINDICATION OF THE RIGHTEOUS IN THE DAY OF THE LORD) (3: 13–4: 3)

The prophet returns to the subject of judgment. **13. You have said harsh things against me:** again, actions speak louder than words. **14.** To paraphrase, 'It is not worth the sacrifice demanded to serve God in times like these' (cf. Job 21: 15). The Levites would be especially hard-hit by the failure of the people to render the tithes. **15.** Cf. Ps. 73. **16.** In contrast to the 'arrogant' (v. 15) there is a faithful remnant who truly reverence the LORD, encourage one another through regular fellowship, and meditate often concerning His character. Because they remembered Yahweh, He has remembered them. **a scroll of remembrance:** cf. Exod. 32: 32–34; Ps. 69: 28; 87: 6; Isa. 4: 3; 65: 6; Dan. 7: 10; 12: 1; Rev. 20: 12; the 'book of chronicles' at the Persian Court (Est. 6: 1) may provide an analogy here. **17.** The faithful remnant is very precious to Yahweh: **my treasured possession** (cf. Exod. 19: 5–6; Dt. 7: 6; 14: 2, 21; 26: 18; Ps. 135: 4; Tit. 2: 14; 1 Pet. 2: 9). **18.** The day of judgment will make clear the difference between the **righteous** (= **those who serve God**) and **the wicked** (=**those do not**). Therefore, it *does* make sense to serve God even in a day when it seems that the majority have forsaken Him! **4: 1.** 4: 1–6=3: 19–24 in the Heb. text. **burn like a furnace:** the day of the LORD will not only be a day of purification (3: 2) and blessing (3: 17), but also a day of destruction (cf. Mt. 3: 12; 13: 30). **2. But for you who revere my name** that day will be a day of salvation; **the sun of** God's **righteousness** will bring health and healing (cf. 2 Sam. 23: 4; Ps. 84: 11; Isa. 60: 1–3). The early church fathers interpreted the expression 'the sun of righteousness' as a messianic title; it seems more likely, however, that the reference is to God Himself. **leap like**

calves: there is great rejoicing in an agricultural society over the new offspring of cattle. **3.** There will be a turning of the tables in the day of judgment: no longer will the righteous be the down-trodden of the earth.

Appendix (4: 4–6)

The final verses conclude not only the prophecy of Malachi but the 'Book of the Twelve'. It is uncertain whether they were a part of the original prophecy or are an editorial addition. In any event, they form a fitting conclusion to both Malachi and the Hebrew prophets.

4. The **law** (Heb. *tōrāh*) is summed up in this verse as **the decrees** (Heb. *huqqîm:* categorical law) and **laws** (Heb. *mishpāṭîm:* case law) that Yahweh ordered through Moses for the benefit of **all Israel**. Horeb=Mt Sinai (cf. Exod. 3: 1). **5–6.** Having looked backward to the giving of the law at Sinai, Malachi now looks forward to the coming of a future prophet who will fulfil the role of **Elijah** and call the nation to repentance before **the great and dreadful day of the LORD** (an expression occurring also in Jl 2: 31). The forerunner's ministry is described as a bridging of the generation gap. The NT sees John the Baptist as fulfilling this role (Lk. 1: 17; Mt. 11: 10, 13–14; 17: 10–13); it is interesting that his message bears a striking similarity to that of Malachi (cf. Mt. 3: 11–12).

BIBLIOGRAPHY

BALDWIN, J., *Haggai, Zechariah, Malachi*. TOTC (London and Grand Rapids, 1972).

HAILET, H., *Commentary on the Minor Prophets* (Grand Rapids, 1972).

JONES, D. R., *Haggai, Zechariah and Malachi*. TC (London, 1962).

LAETSCH, T., *The Minor Prophets* (St. Louis, 1956).

MASON, R., *The Books of Haggai, Zachariah and Malachi*. (Cambridge, 1977).

SMITH, G. A., *The Book of the Twelve Prophets*, vol.2. EB (London and New York, revised edition 1928).

SMITH, J. M. P., *et al.*, *Haggai, Zechariah, Malachi and Jonah*. ICC (Edinburgh and New York, 1912).

PART THREE

GENERAL ARTICLES—THE NEW TESTAMENT

THE AUTHORITY OF
THE NEW TESTAMENT

G. C. D. HOWLEY

'The Christian community was in essence not "bookish": it had been called into existence by a series of events well remembered; it lived under the continued personal guidance, as it believed, of the central figure of those events; and the time would not be long, so it imagined, before he would return to sight. Its authority was "the Lord and the Apostles".' These words of C. F. D. Moule[1] draw attention to an interesting fact concerning the early Christians. The churches were for the most part composed of people who were not 'bookish', and the community as a whole partook largely of that nature. Yet Christians have always been 'people of the Book', and in this matter they claim a spiritual ancestry reaching right back to the first generation of the Church.

What were the books to which they turned? How did they originate? What did they accomplish? Their holy books were those which had been fulfilled in the great facts centred in their Founder and Head, Jesus Christ. Their spiritual life was centred in Him, and their witness was always pointing to Him. They looked back to the history of the people of God before Christ's advent, and realized their continuity with them. As Moule further says of the early Church: 'The only book it needed was the collection of scriptures already recognized by the Jews, in which the Christians now found explanation and confirmation of their own convictions, while conversely, they found the scriptures explained and confirmed in an entirely new way by the recent events'.[2]

If the early Christians inherited the sacred books of the Hebrews, it was because they found them to be introductory to the period in which they lived. The vital link between the two periods was their acknowledgment of Jesus as their Messiah. 'It is exactly the concept of messiahship which demands both continuity with the old order and its fulfillment. Messiahship is essentially unintelligible apart from the presupposition of the old covenant and it remains unrealized unless it ushers in the new covenant. . . . The divine messiahship of Jesus is then the basic fact behind the formation of the New Testament.'[3] This messianic awareness was something that characterized the Old Testament writings; and within the life of the early Church the same awareness marked their faith. They had learned from the Old Testament something of the ways of God in redeeming His people, and the promises bound up in the prophets concerning the Coming One who should deliver His people.

In Jesus the first Christians had found the reality to which the Old Testament shadows led on. They found themselves living in the age of fulfilment, and looked back to the earlier centuries as those of promise. They believed that in the fulness of the time God had sent forth His Son . . . to redeem. H. Cunliffe-Jones expresses the fact excellently: 'If Jesus Christ does not make plain the meaning of the Old Testament revelation, then His mission is false and the claims Christians have made for Him are mistaken. But in fact the Christian theologian, acknowledging the authority of the Bible in its witness to the revelation of God, must both acknowledge the faith of the Old Testament as the revelation of the one God of Christian worship and also treat the Old Testament as something inherently incomplete, with the key to its own understanding not given in itself, so that its real meaning is only made plain in Jesus Christ'.[4]

If these Christians believed that Jesus had brought to them the fulfilment of God's ancient promises, it is plain also that they recognized the importance of His teaching, through which He had brought them God's message. At all costs they desired to preserve a faithful record of His words and works. Harnack once said that 'the earliest motive force, one that had been at work from the beginning of the Apostolic Age, was the supreme reverence in which the words and teaching of Christ Jesus were held'. If Judaism had reverenced the writing of Moses, it is not surprising that Christians should hold the words of One infinitely greater than Moses as supreme in importance; nor that, when His words had been written down, they should give high place to those records. In Jesus Christ God had spoken to men, and His great redemptive purposes had been and were being worked out in Him: this was the good news the Church existed to proclaim. In a very real sense, then, the words and works of Jesus Christ lie directly behind the writing of the

New Testament books. The oral message led on quite naturally, and inevitably, to the written record of that message.

The function of the writers in apostolic times was to witness to Christ. This they did as men who had enjoyed a personal experience of Him. Some of the writers had known Him during His earthly ministry, while others had come to know Him at some time subsequent to His death and resurrection. They had a diversity of spiritual experience but in each case it was something that rang true in the minds of those who encountered either them or their writings. There was a certain boldness about those new writings. One of the earliest letters of Paul closes with the solemn charge, 'I charge you before the Lord to have this letter read to all the brothers' (1 Th. 5: 27). The expectation that his letters would be read publicly in the assemblies for worship and instruction indicated that the apostle rated their importance highly. And that this custom was not confined to Thessalonica is seen from the injunction to interchange two of his other letters so that each church might benefit from what had been written primarily to another community (Col. 4: 16). Nor was there anything out of place in this assumption of authority. They were the apostles of Christ, commissioned by Him and acting on His behalf, having derived their authority directly from Him. Small wonder, then, that they expected their writings to be read in the public assemblies of the churches, even if this tended to give those letters equal prominence to the Old Testament scriptures which would habitually be read on such occasions. Justin Martyr, writing in the mid-second century, may be regarded as acquainted with Christian custom over a wide area; in his *Apology* (I. 67) he says: 'On the day called Sunday all those who live in the towns or in the country meet together; and the memoirs of the apostles and the writings of the prophets are read, as long as time allows. Then, when the reader has ended, the president addresses words of instruction and exhortation to imitate these good things'. The fact to note is that Justin assumes equal authority for the apostolic and the prophetic writings; and it is fair to assume that this recognition was general in the churches of his generation.

There were many writings in circulation among the early Christians, but only a proportion of them received general acceptance in the churches as possessing apostolic authority. C. H. Dodd sums up the situation thus: 'The Church read as Scripture those writings which it felt to be most vitally related to the spiritual impulse that created it. . . . So far as we are able to compare the writings of the original Canon with their competitors, especially with those which were ultimately excluded, there

can be no doubt that as a whole they stand, spiritually, intellectually, and aesthetically, on an altogether higher plane'.[5] The books that were recognized among the churches received this acknowledgment by their own merit. As for the rest, they lacked the direct and immediate note of inherent authority and, as has many times been said, nobody excluded them from the body of New Testament writings: they excluded themselves.

We are now in a position to see why the term, 'The New Testament', is used of the second part of the Biblical literature. A. H. McNeile rightly says that 'This title, as applied to the collection of sacred Christian writings, is often used with no clear understanding of its meaning'.[6] The word 'Testament' comes into our English Bible from the Latin *testamentum* which means 'covenant' or 'testament', while the Greek *diathēkē* carries the same meanings. As McNeile further says: 'There were two eras in the world's history, in which there were two *diathēkai*, the one involving slavery, the other freedom. . . . What we call the Old and the New Testaments are two collections of writings containing the divine message, which belong respectively to the two dispensations'.[7] If we replace the word 'Testament' with 'Covenant' we see at once that these books bring us into the atmosphere of the new era which was inaugurated by the coming of Christ into the world. Here we breathe the pure air of primitive Christian faith and thought.

The facts to which the Christians' books bore witness were not merely connected with life on a temporal plane, though they were deeply involved in life's problems. The writings in question contained the record of a divine revelation to men. Herein also lay part of their continuity with the Old Testament, for the earlier books recorded God's revelation to His people. Judaism received the older writings as from God; and the Church regarded the apostolic books similarly as the record of His full and final revelation in Christ. The Bible affirms that at certain points in history God disclosed Himself to men, this revelation being therefore both historic and personal. It was not, however, merely a revelation in deed but also in the necessary word to explain the deed, or, as Dodd puts it, 'events plus interpretation'. We fall from the level of apostolic thought if we think of this revelation as only given in divine action. Surely God must reveal the meaning of His acts? On this point B. B. Warfield commented acutely: 'It is easy to talk of revelation by deed. But how little is capable of being revealed by even the mightiest deed unaccompanied by the explanatory word?'[8] If we regard the divine revelation as only in action, are we not in danger of mere subjectivism when we turn to examine the writings that contain that revelation?

There is a pattern discernible throughout scripture in which we perceive the hand of God at work in the salvation of men. In the Old Testament it is shown in the event of the Exodus, with all that sprang from it in the subsequent history of Israel. It has been said that 'the saving character of God is the thread, and that election is the instrument employed to effect the saving purpose of God', as seen throughout the Old Testament. The last and greatest act, however, takes us beyond that period, to the point where we see God the Saviour at work, now to redeem and deliver, not from Egypt or Babylon, but from Satan, sin and death. 'His deeds bear the stamp of salvation, and their doer the character of a saviour.'[9] It may be well while on this point, to consider a wider assessment of this principle. 'As the divine saving pattern is the link between prophecy and fulfilment, and insight into this pattern constitutes the ground of prophecy, so it is this same pattern that constitutes the ground and criterion for legitimate typology'.[10]

How is this divine revelation to be received? The simple answer is, by faith. There have been many who have demanded that we bring the Bible to the bar of human reason, but (to quote some wise words of Pascal here) there are 'two forms of excess: to exclude reason, and not to admit anything but reason'; and again, 'Reason's last step is the recognition that there are an infinite number of things which are beyond it; it is merely feeble if it does not go so far as to grasp that. If natural things are beyond it, what are we to say about supernatural?'[11] Such words may check an excess of enthusiasm in applying human reason to the Bible beyond a certain point. It is in this very matter, we judge, that some have missed the way in handling the Bible. It is true that God addresses man as a rational and moral being, and also, as Alan Richardson expresses it, 'we must use our reason and common sense when we seek to find God's message for us in the Bible'.[12] But he well adds the following: 'we must remember that its message for us can be understood only by means of a "diviner light". Biblical faith . . . is uncompromisingly opposed to all forms of rationalism—the view that the human reason is, in virtue of its own inherent perfection, a competent and impartial judge of truth and falsehood in all matters, whether secular or religious'.[13] This is a necessary balance. To that witness we add that of R. R. Williams: 'The revelation in the Bible is not to be tested and verified by the reason, but appropriated by the heart and conscience. When that is done the reason can be given its fullest play, with complete assurance'.[14]

Space does not allow a detailed survey of the views of scholars and theologians of the past hundred years or so, but mention needs to be made of some of those trends. The modern debate embraces the Liberalism of the nineteenth century and beyond which was marked by a strong vein of subjectivism. T. W. Manson summed Liberalism up in words that cannot be misunderstood: 'The upshot is that Liberalism was predisposed against a God who intervenes in the world, or in history, whether by deed or word; and predisposed in favour of an interpretation of religion which would make it no more than an element in human civilization, the sum of man's deepest and gradually achieved convictions about ultimate Reality and absolute values'.[15] Man's thought about God took the place of God's revelation of Himself, and such views contain within themselves the seeds of their own destruction.

What of the post-Liberal era? This has been marked by the development of the theology associated with the names of Karl Barth, Emil Brunner and other scholars. From the stream of neo-orthodoxy flow many of the elements in contemporary theology. In discussing the relationship of the new theology to the intellectual climate of today, Francis A. Schaeffer comments upon the passing of the older Liberalism: 'So it was not so much neo-orthodoxy which destroyed the older form of liberalism, even though Karl Barth's teaching might have been the final earthquake which shook down the tottering edifice; rather it had already been destroyed from within'.[16] There is a danger that, in thinking of the Bible as merely the earthen vessel in which is to be found the treasure of God's revelation as He makes Himself known in personal encounter—as is the case with neo-orthodoxy—insufficient serious attention may be given to Holy Scripture itself. Can we afford to regard as unimportant the framework through which God has been pleased to communicate His revelation? The standpoint of this volume is that both form and content are important. The words of S. T. Coleridge have sometimes been quoted as a guide in discovering or hearing the Word of God, 'Whatever finds me bears witness for itself that it has proceeded from a Holy Spirit'.[17] What is this but making the test of what is or is not of the Holy Spirit within ourselves? It is but another form of bringing the Word of God to the bar of the human mind, and we have already considered the weakness of this approach.

A new form of Liberalism has arisen in recent years associated with the names of theologians such as Rudolf Bultmann and Paul Tillich. Though their approaches differ, they affirm that the Christian message needs translating into terms modern man can understand. We are told that in the form in which it is found in the New Testament it is mythological, and the mythological draperies must be removed before we can perceive the real meaning of Christianity. This element of myth is found in the image of God, the virgin birth, the resurrection and ascension of Jesus. The Bible history of redemption must be 'demythologized'; we will then be left with the real Christian faith. Tillich tells us that we must forget everything traditional that we have learned about God. It is admitted by many that there is a great deal of confused language in some of these modern views; are we wrong in assuming some confusion of thought also? Certainly such views depart from the historic faith at various points, besides tending to bewilder many persons.

'There is a measure of continuity in Christian thought', writes Bernard Ramm, contending that it is important to take the history of theology seriously because it possesses manifestations of the teaching ministry of the Holy Spirit. He gives three reasons why the interpreter must pay due regard to the history of theology: (*a*) the Holy Spirit is the Teacher of the Church; (*b*) the present Church is the inheritor of all the great scholarship of the past; (*c*) theological and ecclesiastical crises drive men to think deeper and clearer than they do in ordinary circumstances.[18] So long as Christian thought has been based on Holy Scripture it has been within the scope of the ministry of the Holy Spirit, of whom Christ said, '(He) will teach you all things, and will remind you of everything I have said to you' (Jn 14: 26). The Lord had brought the Word of God to men during His ministry, and He promised that this ministry would be continued by the Holy Spirit. The apostolic age saw the fulfilment of this promise, as the Christian writings came into being, meeting the needs of the young churches. Then came the Patristic period, during which Christianity became established. In the doctrinal disputes of the period, appeal to the authority of the Bible was sufficient; while during the long period of the Middle Ages, even though the Bible was not in the hands of ordinary people, we are told that in their preaching, the friars chose and announced their texts with care. 'The handbooks for preachers insist on this: the text must be from the authentic canonical scripture . . . no word is to be added, no tense or number changed, nor an unfamiliar translation employed.'[19]

The allegorizing of scripture was common. Master Rypon of Durham declares that 'Holy Scripture is not merely to be understood according to its literal or grammatical sense, but with equal truth according to the mystical or moral sense'. Stephen Langton tells us that 'Jerusalem can mean four things: the city overlooking the valley of Cedron in Palestine (that is the literal and historical place), allegorically the Church Militant, anagogically the Church Triumphant, and tropologically the faithful soul'.[20] This varied interpretation of scripture may have run wild at times, but bound up with it was a recognition of the Bible as the revelation of God. The Church of the Middle Ages had many faults, some of them glaring evils, but even though the Bible was overloaded with the interpretations of the Church, it was always regarded as the Word of God.

To the fact of divine revelation we must add that of the illumination which marks those who receive the Word of God by faith. (This is indicated by such passages as 1 C. 2: 6–16; 2 C. 3: 12–4: 6, and 1 Jn 2: 20, 27.) Psalm 36: 9 shows the relationship of revelation to illumination: 'For with you is the fountain of life; in your light we see light'—the light of illumination flowing from the light of the revelation. The objective revelation of God needs to be supplemented by an internal work of the Holy Spirit, bringing the experience of illumination. The natural man is a stranger to this experience, as Paul clearly states: 'The man without the Spirit does not accept the things that come from the Spirit of God, for they are foolishness to him and he cannot understand them because they are spiritually discerned' (1 C. 2: 14).

It may be asked, how can we tell when the revelation of God came to an end? Or does it continue today in the same way as in Biblical times? The New Testament is the primary witness to the events associated with the supreme revelation of God in the person of His Son Jesus Christ. It is this event that effects the redemption of the world, therefore the apostolic witness is the final word of objective revelation. 'To ask for more revelation than this is to misunderstand the entire philosophy of special revelation. Special revelation is the knowledge–correlate of divine redemption. When redemption reaches its climax, special revelation reaches its climax. With the end of the events of redemption comes the end of special revelation. Hence the word of the apostles in witness to Jesus Christ, the climax of redemption and special revelation, is the end of revelation . . . The New Testament written by the apostles is the delegated authority of the Lord Jesus'.[21] This expresses quite clearly what we believe to be the truth of the matter. When the need for special revelation ceased, then the revelation found completeness.

What made these books unique was their quality of inspiration. By this we do not refer to anything parallel to the masterpieces of literature that have been given to the world through the centuries. Their writers were 'inspired' in another sense, but not in the strict

Biblical meaning of the term. 'The prophets have the timeliness which belongs to genius' one writer states: and while this is true, it is not the whole truth. They had something more, 'the burden of the word of the Lord'. 'Inspiration may be regarded in one aspect as the correlative of revelation', wrote B. F. Westcott in 1851; 'Both operations imply a supernatural extension of the field of man's spiritual vision, but in different ways.' Inspiration was a direct intelligible communication of God's will to chosen messengers. The word *theopneustos* (2 Tim. 3: 16), means 'God-breathed', in Warfield's definition 'produced by the creative breath of the Ahnighty'.[22] If this definition is correct, it indicates that inspiration does not merely attach to the men, but to the product of their work, the inspired books. The reasonableness of this view may be seen when we consider the purpose of the writings, to bring the knowledge of God to man.

Does this, then, imply a form of mechanical dictation which would make the writers of the Biblical books mere 'typewriters'? So far from this being the case, all the evidence goes to show that the men who wrote the sacred books were in full possession of their faculties at the time of writing. The different personalities of the writers shine out in all they write. Each man writes according to his distinctive experience of God; his style is his own entirely, and strong differences mark the literary talents of the different authors: he uses his own vocabulary and emphasis, so that one writer will use words and phrases that are seldom found in the other books. So far from the personalities of the writers being suppressed at the time they were engaged in their tasks, we may rather conceive that their powers would be heightened as they were under the control of the Holy Spirit.

The testimony of 2 Peter is equally plain, and, we may add (because of the non-Petrine viewpoint on authorship which is held by many scholars), whatever the authorship or date of this letter, it exhibits a high view of the doctrine of inspiration. 'Above all, you must understand that no prophecy of Scripture came about by the prophet's own interpretation. The prophecy never had its origin in the will of man, but men spoke from God as they were carried along by the Holy Spirit' (2 Pet. 1: 20 f.). The New English Bible renders v. 21: 'men they were, but, impelled by the Holy Spirit, they spoke the words of God'. The prophetic word did not originate in mere human thought or intuition, it was not created by human initiative, for the men who wrote became at that time the divine spokesmen, they were 'carried along by the Holy Spirit'. There was a combination of divine and human elements at work in the writing of the books of the Bible—God and man: the moving power and the living instrument. As Westcott said: 'We have a Bible competent to calm our doubts, and able to speak to our weakness. . . . It is authoritative, for it is the voice of God; it is intelligible, for it is in the language of men'. Inspiration is, thus, dynamical and not mechanical. Even in God's hand, man does not become a mere machine. The mysterious interpenetration of the divine and the human elements in Holy Scripture resulted in a unity which is rightly called the Word of God.

The testimony of these scriptures is in harmony with the general viewpoint of the New Testament writers. They do not appear to regard inspiration as attaching only to the religious teachings of the Bible, or merely to its ideas or truths, but also to the form in which they were presented. The remarkable assurance that characterizes Paul's account of his own ministry (cf. 1 C. 2: 6–16) pervades the whole body of literature. If those men of God were borne along by the Holy Spirit, then the Spirit of God is in a sense the Author of scripture, and also (to borrow some words of F. F. Bruce), 'in Abraham Kuyper's phrase, the Perpetual Author, continually speaking through the Word to the believing reader and unfolding fresh meaning from it'.[23] The Spirit and the Word are essentially conjoined, the scriptures functioning through the ministry of the Holy Spirit, while the Spirit functions through the medium of the Word. This was without doubt the belief of the Reformers. In emerging from the shackles of the Pre-Reformation era they rediscovered for themselves the living character of scripture. While in some details their views differed, in regard to the Bible they appear to have stood close together.

Divine inspiration does not entail holding rigid ideas that could not face up to the evidence. For example, our Lord spoke in Aramaic, but the record of His words is preserved in the Gospels, written in Greek. The many differences between the Hebrew text of the Old Testament and the Septuagint are to some extent reflected in the quotations from that version in the New Testament. As D. W. Gooding says: 'The Septuagint is not an original composition but a translation, and a translation that has often been revised in order to make it represent the original Hebrew more faithfully'. And further: 'The wide differences between the Greek and the Massoretic texts obviously date from times earlier than all our extant Greek evidence'.[24] The speeches recorded in The Acts of the Apostles are without doubt given in summary form, as Luke himself indicates following his report of Peter's sermon at Pentecost, 'with many other words he warned them; and he pleaded with them, "Save yourselves from this corrupt generation"' (Ac. 2: 40). What has been recorded contains every essential element for faith, and for the written record of God's revelation. In this connection, Philip E. Hughes said, in a valuable address on 'The Reformers' View of Inspiration', given at the Oxford Conference of Evangelical Churchmen in 1960: 'Of course the words of Holy Scripture are of vital importance. They are the units of meaning and the means of communication. But they are significant only in combination. Words isolated from their context have lost their significance and are not sacrosanct. What is essential is the truth which the words unitedly reveal'.

'The question of authority . . . in its religious form, is the first and last issue of life', wrote P. T. Forsyth. 'As soon as the problem of authority really lifts its head, all others fall to the rear.'[25] The problem of the seat of authority in religion is a perennial one, for while one person may find what he is seeking, another will be wandering in spirit, looking for safe anchorage. The historic answers to this question point variously to the Church, to Reason, or to the Bible, the latter being the anchorage found by the Reformers. It has sometimes been suggested that they elevated the Bible to the place of final authority because they looked for something to replace the authority of the Church. In other words, they found a substitute to fill the vacuum created by the abandonment of the authority of the Papacy. Perhaps another view of the situation might be that what they did was to re-establish in its rightful place that which had always been regarded with some degree of reverence, the Bible itself. In this they did justice to Holy Scripture, while, as a secondary issue, man's need for authoritative guidance was met.

This recognition of the authority of scripture was fundamental in the moulding of the Reformed Churches, and it is necessary to affirm this truth in the face of modern pessimism and a general reaction against authority in many spheres of life. We must recognize and retain the authority of the scriptures because they are for us the normative account of the beginnings of Christianity; further, the written documents act as a check on the many vagaries, both of doctrine and of conduct, that otherwise could choke spiritual life; but also because God does speak to men in every age through scripture. We have already seen that this Biblical insight marked the teaching of the Reformers. In a recent symposium on Biblical authority for today, representatives of widely different churches contributed chapters on fundamental considerations. In each case (with one exception which was for reasons of the more limited scope of the article) the writers emphasized the internal witness of the Holy Spirit as a prominent element in their overall conception of scripture. In this they are on common ground with the Reformers.

In his *Prologue to the Book of Genesis* Tyndale wrote: 'The Scripture is the touchstone that trieth all doctrines, and by that we know the false from the true'. Cranmer said that even in regard to 'learned and godly-minded' persons, they were to be believed 'no further than they can show their doctrine and exhortation to be agreeable with the true Word of God written. For that is the very touchstone which must, yea, and also will, try all doctrine or learning, whatsoever it be, whether it be good or evil, true or false'. This was the general standpoint of the great leaders of the Reformation. But in no sense did they look upon the scriptures as something static, rather they perceived them to be living oracles, the oracles of God. It was the ministry of the Holy Spirit on which they depended, in His testimony within their hearts and lives. A modern scholar draws the same lesson: 'The proof of its authority lies in its continued power to speak, and the limits of the literary history cannot limit God's power to make use of what true word He will, in speaking to the soul of man'.[26]

There is an instinct of authority in the Biblical writers, and in the books they produced. This authority characterized the writings from the moment of their origin, as will be seen from the necessity for immediate attention that marks, for example, the New Testament letters. The idea of authority is rooted in the fact of divine revelation, and because the readers of those books believed them to convey God's message, they were brought into the obedience of Christ as they received and acted upon that message. This submission to the Word of God was in no way hostile to freedom. On the contrary, it was the way through which Christians found that His service is perfect freedom. The same passage that affirms Holy Scripture as being 'God-breathed' goes on to show the essentially pragmatic nature of scripture, as profitable for several eminently practical reasons (2 Tim. 3: 16 f.), bringing Christian people to maturity of life and experience. Every part of life is affected by the penetration of God's Word, as was the case in the first days of Christianity when the apostolic letters dealt with the plainest and most matter-of-fact everyday things from the standpoint of the will of God for His people. Not that the New Testament writings brought men and women into legalistic bondage, or hedged them around with commands and prohibitions. Those documents were never intended to be regarded merely as a collection of precedents, to be followed blindly, but rather as providing guiding-lines for daily life in their outlining of spiritual principles.

God has expressed His authority by divine self-revelation; and this revelation has found its supreme manifestation in the person of the Lord Jesus Christ, the Son of God. His whole life bore the stamp of divine authority. It was seen in the moral perfection of His life, for (to quote again from C. H. Dodd), 'the effect He produced upon men with whom He came in contact—the effect indeed which He still produces upon men—is such that we cannot think He had any unresolved discords in His own soul'.[27] Throughout His earthly ministry the Lord showed an awareness of His unique relationship to God, and of His own authority. In contrast to the teachers of that age, He affirmed with assurance of the truth of His words, and His right to say them, 'I say unto you . . .'. The living Word Christ brought to men was itself the revelation of God, and in His life, death and resurrection He spoke that Word and demonstrated that it was a Word of salvation for men. It is to Christ risen and ascended to heaven that we look as the One in Whom all authority is vested by God. He is, therefore, the ultimate and final authority for all believers.

From these facts, therefore, we find the authority of the New Testament. It bears the stamp of apostolic authority in its witness to Christ. This witness of the apostles is made good to men today by the internal witness of the Holy Spirit, of whose function Jesus said, 'He will bring glory to me by taking from what is mine and making it known to you' (Jn 16: 14). It is in the fellowship of the church that Christians can enter into much of the reality of this inner testimony of the Spirit, as they come under the Word of God within the sphere where Christ, crucified and risen, is worshipped. Yet not only in relation to church life, but also as individuals, believers are brought into the power of a personal relationship and communion with Christ, as they respond by faith to the Holy Spirit's witness to their spirits (cf. Rom. 8: 16).

In the final chapter of his book, *The Authority of Scripture*, J. K. S. Reid says that the authority with which the Bible is credited needs to be carefully defined: 'It will have, for one thing, to rest on something other than internal but trivial characteristics or impressive but external guarantee'. He suggests it will have to be permanent, simple, universal, categorical and acceptable. The response Christians will give is, of course, that all of these things mark the authority of the New Testament (with which we are particularly concerned). It is permanent, covering all life and not patchy or fragmentary in its bearing; it is simple, open to all people and to be understood by all; it is universal, for its teaching fits into every kind of human life (even as every kind of person finds that he can fit into its framework); it is categorical, straightforward in its instruction and its challenge and brooking no evasion; and it is accept-

able, in that it can secure the assent of those who feel its impact. God's will is 'good, acceptable, and perfect', writes Paul to the Romans, and the New Testament, as the medium whereby He communicates to us the knowledge of His will, can bring us into a rich spiritual experience in which we stand 'mature and fully assured' in all the will of God (Col. 4: 12).

The events recorded in and attested by the New Testament writings are unique. The life that is associated with the Christian gospel is also unique in its ideal expression, seen first in Jesus Christ, and then, by the Holy Spirit, in those who believe on Him and are members of His Body, the Church. To this end the apostles bore their witness; and to this end the Holy Spirit witnesses in the hearts of believers everywhere, through the instrumentality of the written Word of God, to bring them into the fullness of the knowledge of God. 'Thus for the New Testament, as for the Old', wrote John Baillie, 'God is One who is directly known in His approach to the human soul. He is not an inference but a Presence. He is Presence at once urgent and gracious. By all whom He seeks He is known as a Claimant; by all whom He finds, and who in Christ find Him, He is known as a Giver. The knowledge of God of which the New Testament speaks is a knowledge for which the best argument were but a sorry substitute and to which it were but a superfluous addition. "He that hath seen me hath seen the Father; and how sayest thou then, Shew us the Father?"'[28]

REFERENCES

1. *The Birth of the New Testament* (London, 1981), p. 238.
2. *op. cit.*, p. 239.
3. N. B. Stonehouse: 'The Authority of the New Testament', *The Infallible Word* (London, 1946), p. 108.
4. *The Authority of the Biblical Revelation* (London, 1954), p. 48.
5. *The Authority of the Bible* (London, 1928), p. 196.
6. *An Introduction to the Study of the New Testament* (Oxford, 2nd edition, 1953), p. 1.
7. *op. cit.*, p. 2.
8. *Biblical and Theological Studies* (London, 1952 edition), p. 17.
9. J. K. S. Reid: *The Authority of Scripture* (London, 1957), p. 249.
10. *op. cit.*, p. 251.
11. *Pensées*, IV. 267.
12. *Christian Apologetics* (London, 1947), p. 222.
13. *op. cit.*, p. 223.
14. *Authority in the Apostolic Age* (London, 1950), p. 122.
15. 'The Failure of Liberalism to Interpret the Bible as the Word of God', *The Interpretation of the Bible* (London, 1944), p. 95.
16. *The God Who is There* (London, 1968), p. 52.

17. *Confessions of an Enquiring Spirit*, Letter I.
18. *The Pattern of Authority* (Grand Rapids, 1957), pp. 57 ff.
19. C. Pepler, 'The Faith of the Middle Ages', *The Interpretation of the Bible* (London, 1944), pp. 26 f.
20. *op. cit.*, pp. 35 f.
21. Ramm, *op. cit.*, pp. 54 f.
22. *The Inspiration and Authority of the Bible* (London, 1951), p. 296.
23. 'The Scriptures', *The Faith—A Symposium* (London 1952), p. 18.
24. *The Account of the Tabernacle* (Cambridge, 1959), pp. 1 f.
25. *The Principle of Authority* (London, 1913), p. 1.
26. H. Wheeler Robinson: *The Bible in its Ancient and English Versions* (Oxford, 1940), p. 299.
27. *The Authority of the Bible* (London, 1928), p. 240.
28. *Our Knowledge of God* (Oxford, 1939), p. 126.

BIBLIOGRAPHY

ABBA, R., *The Nature and Authority of the Bible* (London, 1958).

DODD, C. H., *The Bible To-day* (Cambridge, 1946); *According to the Scriptures* (London, 1952).

DUGMORE, C. W. (ed.), *The Interpretation of the Bible* (London, 1944).

GELDENHUYS, NORVAL, *Supreme Authority* (London, 1953).

HENRY, C. F. H. (ed.), *Revelation and the Bible* (London 1959).

JAMES, M. R., *The Apocryphal New Testament* (Oxford, 1924).

McKIM, D. (ed.), *The Authoritative Word* (Grand Rapids, 1983).

MOULE, C. F. D., *The Birth of the New Testament* (London, 1967).

MOULE, C. F. D., *The Phenomenon of the New Testament* (London 1967).

REID, J. K. S., *The Authority of Scripture* (London, 1957).

RICHARDSON, A. and SCHWEITZER, W. (ed.), *Biblical Authority for Today* (London, 1951).

ROBINSON, H. W. (ed.), *The Bible in its Ancient and English Versions* (Oxford, 1940; New (revised) edition, 1954).

ROGERS, J. (ed.), *Biblical Authority* (Waco, Texas, 1977).

ROGERS, J., and McKIM, D. (ed.), *The Authority and Interpretation of the Bible* (New York, 1979).

ROWLEY, H. H., *The Unity of the Bible* (London, 1953).

SMALLEY, BERYL, *The Study of the Bible in the Early Middle Ages* (Oxford, 1941; New (revised) edition, 1952).

STONEHOUSE, N. B. and WOOLLEY, PAUL (ed.), *The Infallible Word* (London, 1946).

WARFIELD, B. B., *The Inspiration and Authority of the Bible* (London, 1951).

WILSON, R. McL. (ed.), *New Testament Apocrypha*, E.T., 2 vols. (London, 1963–4).

THE TEXT AND CANON OF
THE NEW TESTAMENT

DAVID F. PAYNE

I. CANON

Introduction

Orthodox Christians everywhere today take it for granted that Holy Scripture consists of two parts or Testaments, between them containing 66 books. We should be disconcerted, to say the least, if on purchasing a new Bible we found that it omitted any of these 66 or included any extra books. Some Bibles, to be sure, include the Old Testament Apocrypha, but those that do so normally indicate the fact clearly on the outside cover. But the New Testament, which is here our concern, is never added to. It is probable that the percentage of Christians who have any acquaintance with New Testament apocryphal books is very small indeed.

We possess, then, a New Testament of 27 books, which in the ordinary English Bible always appear in the same order. This is the Canon of the New Testament; we find in it 5 narrative books, 21 letters, and a single book of quite a different character, aptly called The Apocalypse or Revelation; and in them we acknowledge the supreme and complete guide for Christian doctrine and faith.

But the apostles themselves had no such written rule of faith and conduct. Their Bible, and that of the Jews to this day, consisted of the Old Testament; this was the Canon of Holy Writ accepted by Jesus Himself, and referred to simply as 'the scriptures' throughout the New Testament writings. It was not until the year A.D. 393 that a church council first listed the 27 New Testament books now universally recognized. There was thus a period of about 350 years during which the New Testament Canon was in process of being formed. It is our purpose here to trace the developments of those years.

The Canon and Authority

The Greek word *kanōn*, as used by the early church fathers, had a number of meanings and uses, two of which are relevant to this study. From a basic sense of a ruler or measuring rod, with its markings, there derived the metaphorical meanings 'list' and 'rule' (i.e. 'standard'). It is important to note that the first sense is that intended in the phrase 'Canon of Scripture'. The New Testament Canon is simply the list of books contained in the New Testament; the books on this list are 'canonical', all others are 'uncanonical'. But the second meaning is easily confused with the first, since the canonical books are those which alone we find authoritative, presenting the 'rule' of faith and conduct. The Canon and the authority of the New Testament are thus closely related topics; but it is misleading to equate the terms 'canonical' and 'authoritative', because the Canon is not an authoritative list of books, but a list of authoritative books. Each book of the New Testament was authoritative from the beginning; but none of them could be called canonical until collections and lists of such books were made. The only authority the Canon wields is that of its component parts.

The New Testament Documents

The great majority of the New Testament books were penned between A.D. 50 and 100. The writers were apostles and their associates, and were men specially fitted and commissioned to convey to mankind the Word of God as revealed in the acts and the teachings of the Lord Jesus. They both spoke and wrote with authority, adapting the message of Christ to the needs of the hearers and readers. It seems that some apostolic writings had only temporary or local value, and were not therefore preserved; one letter (at least) written by Paul to the church at Corinth has disappeared (cf. 1 C. 5: 9), and possibly a letter by him to Laodicea too (unless the reference in Col. 4: 16 is to what we know as the Letter to the Ephesians). Nor was all the oral ministry of the apostles put into written form and preserved. John explicitly states his principles of selection of material worth recording (Jn 20: 30 f.); and we may conclude that our New Testament is the authoritative apostolic message suited to the needs of posterity. It is highly probable that apocryphal works do contain, here and there, genuine additional information about Jesus and the apostles; but in the canonical books we have all we need to know for salvation and instruction in righteousness.

The First Collections

Some of the New Testament books were expressly addressed to individuals, some to churches or groups of churches; and even those which reveal nothing about the intended recipients, and seem to have been meant for more general use, must have circulated in a very limited area in the first place. But the self-evident authority and value of them all quickly made them prized possessions, and they were copied and re-copied for an ever widening public. The earliest 'canon' was that possessed by the church at Thessalonica soon after A.D. 50, and consisted of two letters, both by Paul; but we may surmise that in due course a copy of his letter to neighbouring Philippi was added to their 'canon', while doubtless copies of their own two prized letters were sent to the Philippian church. Paul himself gave the initial impetus for such a practice in Asia Minor (cf. Col. 4: 16).

By about the year 90, many churches possessed a collection of Paul's letters, and early in the second century the four Gospels were brought together (conceivably from original 'homes' in Syria, Italy, Greece and Asia Minor respectively). It is generally agreed that Luke's two books, the third Gospel and Acts, were originally two parts of a single work; the incorporation of the first part of his history in the fourfold Gospel left the second part to fend for itself, but it was well able to stand on its own merits, and besides it served admirably as an introduction to the collection of Paul's letters. The second century churches, then, had two collections of inspired and authoritative books, above and beyond the Old Testament Scriptures, 'the Gospel' and 'the Apostle'. Acts was also recognized, and the other New Testament books too, although they were not all known and used so widely. (The Syriac speaking churches, for instance, ignored 2 Pet., 2 and 3 Jn, Jude and Rev. until the sixth century.) By now some Christian writings which do not figure in our New Testament were in existence, and enjoyed a certain popularity, usually purely local; we may instance the Epistle of Clement and the *Shepherd* of Hermas. The former is a genuine letter of one of the apostolic fathers, and like all such bowed to the authority of the apostles and their writings. Such works neither demanded nor received true canonical status, even though they might be reckoned among a church's literary treasures. The *Shepherd* was an allegorical work, which has often been compared with Bunyan's *Pilgrim's Progress*; it enjoyed a similar popularity in the early church. We should remember that books were rare and expensive, and few individuals in the early church can have afforded a Christian library; hence Christian writings of any value, canonical or not, were owned by the local church and publicly read there. But we need not doubt that it was clearly recognized which books were truly inspired and authoritative, and which were of lesser value.

The Influence of Heresies

Another category of Christian literature sprang up in the second century, and to it belong most of the books in the New Testament Apocrypha. It consists mainly of religious fiction, and the majority of such works were penned under false names; Gospels, Acts, Letters and Apocalypses were written and attached to a variety of apostolic names, notably Peter's. As a rule the spuriousness of such documents is immediately evident, and few of them can have misled the majority of church leaders and congregations. But not all were simply essays in fiction; some were deliberately promulgated in the endeavour to support with apostolic authority heretical teachings. Such works constituted a real danger to simple Christians, and it is not surprising that church leaders began to feel it necessary to define the New Testament Canon, in order to ensure that such insidious propaganda should not be read in church.

One outstanding heretical teacher of the mid-second century, however, sought to limit the Canon, rather than add to it. This was Marcion, a native of Asia Minor who challenged the orthodox churchmen in Rome from about A.D. 140. He rejected the Old Testament, since he considered the God revealed in it to be a much inferior deity to the God about Whom Jesus had taught. Everything in the New Testament that smacked of the Old, or appeared to support its concepts and theology, was therefore anathema to Marcion. Small wonder, then, that he limited his canon to writings of Paul, the Apostle to the Gentiles, and Luke, the only Gentile among the Biblical writers (so far as we know). His Bible consisted of Luke's Gospel, and the Pauline Letters with the exception of those to Timothy, Titus, and the Hebrews. He excluded Acts, since it told of some activities of apostles other than Paul; to Marcion, all the other apostles were Judaizers who had adulterated the truth of the Gospel. But even the eleven books he did accept required expurgation, he felt, and he revised them in the light of his own theological views.

Orthodox church leaders, sensible to the dangers of such heretical doctrines, found themselves with a twin responsibility; they must ensure that nothing contrary to God's revealed will should be read or taught in the churches, and at the same time they must take care not to exclude any writings that bore the impress of divine inspiration. So from this time onwards Christian writings were subjected to a close scrutiny. It was only natural that some individuals and churches and groups of churches should err on the side of excessive caution, while others proved not cautious enough; but the degree of unanimity churchmen exhibited over the next century or two is remarkable. In the event, the Canon of the

New Testament, as we know it, was defined not by church council, still less by papal decree, but by the consensus of Christian opinion everywhere. In this we may well see the hand of God—He who inspired the Biblical writers in the first place, guided those responsible for its safe keeping and transmission as well. Another important reason for the unanimity was that to Christians everywhere the New Testament books plainly exhibited their divine authority. The church never *gave* the New Testament writings any authority; it merely acknowledged the authority they already possessed.

After Marcion

Orthodox churchmen realized that the apostles had written with particular authority, for they had accompanied the Lord Jesus and heard His instruction at first hand. Marcion's claim that Paul was the only true apostle was accordingly rejected out of hand. *All* the apostles had spoken and written with authority. So apostolic authorship became an important criterion, though by no means the only one, or the Gospels of Mark and Luke would never have ranked with those of Matthew and John. Some care was taken to detect forgeries. The fragmentary Muratorian Canon testifies to these two interests; emanating from Rome towards the end of the second century, it gives a list of New Testament books, and says something about their origins and authenticity. It explicitly excludes several works bearing Paul's name which were recognized as Marcionite and other gnostic forgeries. It contains fully 22 of our 27 New Testament books; its only surprise inclusions are the apocryphal Wisdom of Solomon and Apocalypse of Peter, although it admits that the latter was disputed. The *Shepherd of Hermas* is mentioned as wholesome but not authoritative.

From much the same date, we have the testimony of Irenaeus. His views are of special interest, because he was widely travelled, and was acquainted with the views of church leaders in more than one region. In his writings, he refers to and quotes from all our New Testament books except five shorter ones. It is quite possible that he knew and recognized at least some of these five as well; the lack of reference to them could well be accidental. Irenaeus made use of the Letter to the Hebrews, but he considered it of lesser worth and standing than the rest of the New Testament books known to him. Many writers of the early Christian centuries were dubious about this letter; its place in the Canon was not assured until it became universally held to be Paul's work. But it is an exaggeration to state that Hebrews was accepted for no better reason than that Paul's name became attached to it; it was rather the intrinsic value of the book that ensured its ultimate acceptance everywhere.

From the first half of the third century we have the testimony of Tertullian (of Carthage and Rome) and Origen (of Alexandria and Caesarea). Both of them accepted Hebrews as canonical, though neither writer attributed it to Paul; Tertullian claimed that the author was Barnabas, while Origen thought that some disciple of Paul must have written it. As for the rest of the New Testament (and incidentally it was Tertullian who first used this title for the Christian Canon), it is clear that by now all the books we know, with the exception of James and 2 Peter, were accepted nearly everywhere. There was no unanimity regarding these two letters as yet; but Eusebius, early in the fourth century, could say that while some still disputed the canonicity of one or two of the smaller letters, the majority of Christians accepted them. In A.D. 367, the bishop of Alexandria, Athanasius, in a letter announcing the date of Easter, listed exactly the 27 books with which we are familiar. Thirty years later the Synod of Carthage ratified this list.

Some areas, mostly of rather heterodox views, were slow to fall into line with other Christians; the Syriac church, in particular, held aloof till the sixth century (see above). But since then all branches of the Christian church have recognized the same New Testaruent Canon, not because of any decree, but because of the unmistakable authority and inspiration of these 27 books.

We may conclude that it seems reasonable to suppose that He who inspired the New Testament writers also overruled in the transmission of the text and in the formation of the Canon. And thus we may confidently believe that we have in our hands the Word of God, complete and unadulterated.

II. TEXT

Introduction

Marcion's challenge to his contemporaries is still a fair one: have we the New Testament books exactly, word for word, as they were penned by their authors? This is obviously a vital question; yet at first sight there seem grounds for pessimism about it, since we do not possess the autograph of any New Testament book, and although we have between four and five thousand Greek MSS of the New Testament (in whole or part), no two of them agree exactly. It is the task of textual criticism to examine these many copies and to decide which of the many variant readings are original. It is clearly an immense task, and one which can never be fully completed, if only because of the fact that new MSS keep coming to light. Textual criticism calls for critical and subjective judgments; on the other hand, it is an objective discipline to the extent that in nearly all cases of variant readings the original wording must be represented somewhere in the MSS available. There is evidence in abundance, in fact; the chief problem is that of weighing it accurately.

The problems faced by the New Testament textual critic might be compared with those that would confront someone who set about reconstructing the original wording of English hymns simply by examining a number of current hymnbooks. The compilers of some hymnbooks (notably *Songs of Praise* and the *Little Flock* collection, despite their very different character) have pursued a thorough policy of revision, and the investigator would soon discover that such books would need to be used very cautiously. It is interesting to note that some similar principles of revision were adopted by early copyists of New Testament documents and by compilers of English hymns more recently. Both groups wanted to 'improve' their material in various respects. (See below, *Variant Readings*.) It would be a serious mistake to suppose that the more accurate hymnbooks presented a completely unrevised text of every hymn. And it would be an equally serious error to imagine that the earlier the date of publication the more accurate the hymnbook. These two rather natural assumptions must be avoided by every textual critic.

The Evidence

(a) The Greek Manuscripts. The witnesses, in view of their numbers, have to be marshalled into some sort of order. They have been classified in various ways. The age of the MSS is one important aspect; hand-written copies known to us date from the early second century down to and well into the age of printing. It is clear that the earlier they are, the less corrupt the text ought to be, since generations of copyists would inevitably add error to error, alteration to alteration. (But it should be noted that some early MSS were carelessly transcribed, while some very later MSS were copied directly from early and excellent witnesses.) Some MSS were dated by those who copied them; but in any case various tests, especially the study of ancient hand-writing (palaeography), can establish the approximate age of any ancient Greek document; till the ninth century it was invariably the custom to use capital letters only, each letter separate and distinct, but thereafter a flowing script was gradually introduced. MSS using the former method are known as 'uncials', those in flowing script as 'cursives' or 'minuscules'. From the fourth century onwards, the common form of MS was the parchment (vellum) codex, the precursor of the modern book. Till then, codices made of papyrus were the norm. The original New Testament documents were probably written on papyrus scrolls; but scrolls had to be unrolled for reading purposes, and would have been too cumbersome for documents longer than Luke's Gospel, so in the papyrus scroll era the New Testament could never circulate as a whole.

The MSS of the New Testament in Greek can usefully be classed in three categories, then, papyri, uncials and cursives. Late papyri are however less important than early uncials, and in turn, some cursives of good pedigree are more valuable than some late uncials; the value of a MS depends on the value of that from which it was copied.

(b) Lectionaries. Besides Greek MSS of the New Testament or its component parts, there are three other sources of evidence. The first of these are the lectionaries—MSS containing New Testament passages arranged in accordance with the church calendar, to be read publicly at services. Of the four types of witness, this has been the least studied to date.

(c) Versions. From very early Christian days it has been the practice to translate the New Testament into other languages, and the early versions of the New Testament are therefore important witnesses to the Greek text. The most valuable versions are those in Latin, Syriac and the Coptic dialects; before A.D. 500 the New Testament had been translated into Armenian, Georgian and Ethiopic as well. But the value of this type of evidence is limited by two considerations: first, a translation can bear witness only to the *meaning* of the original, not to its exact words; and secondly, these versions in turn have a textual history, which requires detailed examination. There are extant far more MSS of the Latin than the Greek New Testament. Indeed, in the fourth century, there were so many variations in the Old Latin versions that Pope Damasus commissioned Jerome to make a careful revision, which we know as the Vulgate; but the history of variant readings in the Latin New Testament did not cease with its publication—in fact, the Vulgate was afterwards 'corrupted' by intrusions from the Old Latin texts it was intended to supersede.

The Syriac equivalent of the Vulgate, the Peshitta, was published at much the same time. Behind it lay the Old Syriac versions. Earlier still, the four Gospels had been woven into a harmony called the Diatessaron by a man called Tatian (c. A.D. 180). Unfortunately no copy of it remains, except in translation, but it seems to have affected the later text of the Syriac Gospels, and perhaps the Gospels text in other languages too.

(d) Patristic Quotations. The early church fathers quoted scripture very freely, and bear witness to the text they knew. But a new problem faces us here; we have no way of telling when they were quoting accurately, when they were quoting (perhaps inaccurately) from memory, or when they were themselves 'improving' the text. Furthermore, these writings too have their own textual history, as they were copied and recopied; and since not all the fathers wrote in Greek, the factor of translation is again a problem. The special value of patristic evidence is that we know exactly when and where the fathers lived; as we shall see, knowledge of locale as well as date can be useful.

Variant Readings

It may fairly be asked why there should be so much variation in the MSS. The first reason is simply that until printing was invented, a number of variations from one MS to another were bound to occur, however careful the scribes. All ancient documents which passed down from hand to hand demonstrate the difficulties of such transmission. Such accidental changes (mis-spellings, mis-readings, omissions and repetitions) can usually be readily identified and corrected by the expert.

But in the New Testament far more variations were deliberately introduced, by scribes who thought (not always without justification) that they should 'correct' what they found written in front of them. Such alterations were intended to improve the grammar, sense, or the theology. Another type of 'improvement', sometimes unconsciously done, was the assimilation of similar or parallel passages; thus a copyist thoroughly familiar with Matthew's Gospel would frequently introduce 'Mattheanisms' into Mark's Gospel.

Sometimes scribes made considerable additions to the text, on the basis of extra material known to them; this happens particularly in the Gospels and Acts. Two such additional passages amount to twelve verses each in length (see Appendix A).

It will be seen that the textual critic has not only to attempt to reconstruct the original readings, but also to explain the reasons for the alterations.

Criteria

How is the investigator to decide which readings are original? There are certain basic principles which may be applied. First, it is the case that the true text is usually shorter than its 'improvements', since scribes tended to expand the text in an effort to clarify it. Secondly, it is often true that the original reading is the one that seems at first sight least probable, for difficult and 'improbable' statements were precisely those that needed altering and amending. Copyists rarely made easy sentences difficult! Thirdly, the expert can employ linguistic, stylistic, and doctrinal analysis; the New Testament writers have clearly recognizable characteristics. Finally, the textual critic must be guided by the best MSS available.

On the negative side there are certain errors to be avoided. It must not be thought that the true reading can be elicited by taking the majority verdict of the MSS; on the contrary, it is now certain that the majority of MSS belong to the least reliable textual 'type'. But the mistake to be avoided at all costs is that of reconstructing the text according to one's own theological presuppositions. The authenticity of a verse must never be defended simply because it happens to be a useful peg to hang a doctrine on.

History of the Text

We can only guess at the history of New Testament transmission in the first two or three centuries A.D., in the light of later phenomena. It seems that the majority of variant readings crept into the text during this period. Among the early Christians there were probably few trained scribes, so mistakes in copying will have been plentiful; and it was only in the earliest period that there were 'floating' traditions about Jesus and the apostles, which could be inserted in the texts.

In due course there emerged a number of distinct textual families, which scholars have come to associate with several great centres of early Christianity. (The MSS in any one family are not exact replicas of one another, but they tend to show similar characteristics, recognizable to experts.) It seems that at these centres a careful revision of the text was made at one time or another, in an early effort to get rid of the multiplicity of variant readings, and to impose a standard text. Thus a measure of uniformity resulted, as MSS were copied and recopied from these basic standard texts. The families generally recognized today are commonly called Alexandrian, Western, Caesarean, Syriac and Byzantine. The Byzantine was the latest of these, and the one which eventually became standard throughout Christendom. Naturally enough, it was used for the earliest printed Greek New Testaments. Erasmus prepared the first Greek New Testament for the press (1516); in a revision of it by Stephanus published in 1633, the printing house (Elzevir) could claim that the Greek text used was accepted by everyone—the much publicized 'Received Text'. But gradually more and more MSS of great age have come to light, and by the nineteenth century it became apparent that the Received Text must be set aside, and attempts made to reconstruct the original text. Several scholars made their contributions to the new science, but the outstanding names are those of B. F. Westcott and F. J. A. Hort, whose text (1881) and whose principles of action have remained fundamental for more recent researches.

The Families

Setting aside the Byzantine text, Westcott and Hort had to choose between the Alexandrian and Western families (the Caesarean and Syriac families were not viewed as distinct from the Western until the present century). The Western MSS are characterized by frequent additions and interpolations, which Westcott and Hort decided could rarely be original; and so they treated the Alexandrian MSS (especially Codices Vaticanus and Sinaiticus, both dating from the early fourth century) as the superior text. They dubbed this text 'neutral'; but it is now clear that it was as much a revised text as any other. Papyri found since 1930 antedate the revisions (probably none of which was made much before A.D. 300) which resulted in the various families, and their affinities are clearly mixed. Today, therefore, textual experts do not lean too heavily on any one family, but use the best individual MSS available and apply all suitable criteria to each individual variant reading; sometimes even Byzantine readings have been accepted as original after all.

Conclusion

A great deal of intensive research yet remains to be done in the field of New Testament textual criticism; considerable uncertainty about the exact wording often remains, although the vast majority of variant readings have no appreciable effect on the meaning, especially in translation. It is to be noted that all the research of the last 150 years has not presented us with a radically different Bible; not one article of the Christian creed has been overthrown by newly accepted readings. We may perhaps lose favourite verses, such as 'all things work together for good . . .' (Rom. 8: 28, AV), but usually the same thought can be found elsewhere in Scripture. (Many of us feel happier to think that 'God'—cf. NIV or NEB— rather than 'things' is at work.) But on the other hand, views and doctrines based on single verses and more particularly on single words, are always liable to be upset by textual criticism.

Those who value the Word of God must be grateful to those scholars who so painstakingly strive to know and show the exact words of Scripture as originally written; and we must always be willing to accept the facts they elicit and set before us, often by the medium of up-to-date translations of the Bible.

Appendix A

Some examples of variant readings, comparing AV with NIV.

(a) Mt. 6: 13; Lk. 11: 4. The final sentence of the Lord's Prayer (as we know it), derived from 1 Chr. 29: 11, was obviously a liturgical addition in Matthew; it can command only Caesarean and Byzantine support. Luke's version originally finished at the word 'temptation', but some Western and the Caesarean MSS harmonized it with Matthew's.

(b) Mk 16: 9–20. This section is omitted by the principal Alexandrian authorities, included by the Caesarean, while the Syriac and Western MSS are divided. The style is not that of Mark; and there is no reason why if genuine it should have been omitted by so many MSS. It must have been a very early, and indeed valuable, independent summary of resurrection appearances, subsequently added to Mark's record.

(c) Jn 5: 4. This verse is omitted by the Bodmer Papyrus, the Alexandrian MSS, and the leading Western MS. It is clearly an interpolation, designed to lay a foundation for the paralytic's remarks in verse 7. Whether the additional sentence records fact or superstition is a question outside the scope of textual criticism.

(d) Jn 7: 53–8: 11. The story of the woman taken in adultery is left out, or placed elsewhere (even in Luke's Gospel!), by all but Western and many late MSS. While the story may well be true, stylistic analysis indicates that John was not the writer.

(e) Eph. 1: 1. There are some grounds for thinking that this Letter was originally intended to circulate; this view is perhaps supported by the fact that the words 'in Ephesus' are omitted by the Chester Beatty Biblical Papyrus II (P46) and the leading Alexandrian MSS.

(f) 1 Jn 5: 7 (AV). The most spurious verse in the AV! The sentence has not even the support of the Byzantine family—it is found in just a few very late MSS. Erasmus included it in his printed text only with reluctance and under pressure. It must have been interpolated to give an explicit Biblical expression of a Trinitarian formula.

Appendix B

Some famous manuscripts.

(a) A fragment of papyrus (P52), now in the John Rylands Library, Manchester, containing a few verses from Jn 18, is the earliest extant New Testament MS; it dates from A.D. 100–150.

(b) A very valuable papyrus (Bodmer II; P66), now at Geneva, was only published in 1956–58. It contains John's Gospel, though with gaps.

(c) The Chester Beatty Biblical Papyri I, II and III (P45, P46, P47), housed mainly in Dublin, date from the third century, and cover most of the New Testament, though with gaps. The text of Mark is of the Caesarean family.

(d) The fourth century Codex Sinaiticus (ℵ), in the British Museum, includes the whole New Testament. Its text is Alexandrian.

(e) The fourth century Codex Vaticanus (B), in the Vatican City, has all the New Testament except the Pastoral Epistles, Philemon and Revelation. Its text is Alexandrian.

(f) The early fifth century Codex Alexandrinus (A), in the British Museum, includes the whole New Testament, with some gaps. It seems to be a precursor of the Byzantine textual family.

(g) Codex Bezae (D), in Cambridge University

Library, the chief witness to the Western text, dates from the fifth or sixth century. It contains the Gospels and Acts, in both Greek and Latin, with some gaps.

BIBLIOGRAPHY

On the Canon:
BLACKMAN, E. C., *Marcion and his influence* (London, 1948).
CAMPENHAUSEN, H. von, *The Formation of the Christian Bible*, E.T. (London, 1972).
FILSON, F. V., *Which Books belong in the Bible?* (Philadelphia, 1957).
GRANT, R. M., *The Formation of the New Testament* (London, 1965).

On the Text:
FOX, A., *Meet the Greek Testament* (London, 1952).
KENYON, F. G., *The Text of the Greek Bible* (rev.edn., London, 1949).

METZGER, B. M., *The Early Versions of the New Testament* (Oxford, 1977).
METZGER, B. M., *Manuscripts of the Greek Bible* (Oxford, 1981).
METZGER, B. M., *The Text of the New Testament* (2nd edn. Oxford, 1968).
ROBERTSON, A. T., *Studies in the Text of the New Testament* (New York, 1926).
TAYLOR, V., *The Text of the New Testament* (London, 1961).
TWILLEY, L. D., *The Origin and Transmission of the New Testament* (Edinburgh, 1957).

On both:
BRUCE, F. F., *The Books and the Parchments* (Basingstoke 3rd edn., 1984).
MCNEILE, A. H., *Introduction to the Study of the New Testament* (London, 1953).
SOUTER, A., *The Text and Canon of the New Testament* (2nd edn., London, 1954).
See also relevant articles in *The New Bible Dictionary* (ed. J. D. DOUGLAS, Leicester 2nd edn., 1982) and *Peake's Commentary on the Bible* (rev. ed., M. BLACK and H. H. ROWLEY, London, 1962).

THE LANGUAGE OF
THE NEW TESTAMENT

DAVID J. A. CLINES

The language of the NT writings, at least in their present form, is Greek. But Greek has been for more than three thousand years a living language, and subject throughout this period to a multitude of changes, so that the Greek of each century is recognizably different from that of the previous one. The NT, belonging as it does to the first century A.D., is written in the Greek of that period, known as 'Koinē' or Common Greek.

DEVELOPMENT OF THE KOINĒ

The dominating trends in the development of the Greek language were largely dictated by the political history of the Greek people. In the pre-classical period of Greek, Greece consisted of geographically isolated, politically autonomous city-states; the variety of the Greek dialects was merely an expression of this insularity.

The first movement towards a common dialect for all the Greeks was made by one such city-state, Athens. Its founding, early in the fifth century B.C., of a Greek naval confederacy spread the influence of Attic, its own dialect, far beyond the walls of the city: the administration of the league, as well as the transactions of Athenian merchants throughout the Aegean, was conducted in Attic, which gained thereby considerable status as a *lingua franca*. Athens' political supremacy was short-lived, but the fifth century was also witnessing in Athens an unparalleled flowering of culture which earned for it, far more permanently than did its fleet, the title of 'the Greece of Greece'. By the end of the century, Attic could boast of being the paramount dialect of Greece; was it not the language of Sophocles, Aristophanes, Thucydides, to name but three representative giants?

It was in this role as purveyor of culture and literature that Attic was adopted into the court of the Macedonian kings. And it was one of their number, Alexander the Great (356–323 B.C.), who made Greek an imperial language, first by imposing a unity upon the Greeks which they had never been able to achieve by their own efforts, and secondly by his remarkable eastern conquests which carried him, and Greek language and civilization, as far as India.

Not only was Greek the administrative language of this now enormous empire, which encompassed Asia Minor, Syria, Palestine, Mesopotamia, and the lands to the east as far as the Indus, as well as Egypt and Greece itself, but also his garrisons and colonies throughout the empire were natural centres for the dissemination of the language. By the time of Roman expansion outside Italy and the eventual incorporation of the greater part of Alexander's empire into the Roman Empire, Greek was firmly entrenched as the official, and often as the vernacular, language everywhere in the Near East.

Not all, by any means, of Alexander's soldiers and settlers were Attic-speakers, and though Attic enjoyed the sanction of the Macedonian court, in the mêlée of Greek dialects that was to be heard in the empire, some of Attic's idiosyncrasies, which sounded strange to the ears of most Greeks, were eliminated in favour of features more characteristic of the other dialects. The resultant idiom was in fact a compromise between the strongest (Attic) and the majority.

Besides this blending of the Greek dialects, there were other forces at work towards establishing a new set of distinctive characteristics for the common language. By the time of the NT, most of the speakers of the Koinē were non-Greeks, and to many of them Greek was a second language; hence inevitably a certain diminution of the precision and elegance of the classical Attic tongue.

What would have appeared the most startling change to the ears of a fifth-century Athenian could he have been confronted with a Greek-speaker of the first century A.D. would have been that from a tonic accent to a stress accent; traces of a tendency towards a stress accent are discernible in Greek of pre-Koinē times, but the difficulties of non-Greeks with an unaccustomed tonal system must have hastened the process (an Englishman used to a stress accent in English finds the tone system of Chinese equally difficult).

Other changes in the vocabulary and grammar of Greek, often significant for the interpretation of the NT, had taken place; the following examples illustrate how inaccurate a reading of the NT solely in the light of classical Greek must be. There is a general tendency toward the weakening of meaning: *trōgō*, which meant 'gnaw' in Attic, means simply 'eat' in colloquial Koinē; *ekballō* 'cast out' can mean 'lead forth' in Koinē (*e.g.* Mk 1: 12; NIV 'sent him out' may be too strong). Compound verbs replace simple ones: *peripateō* 'walk' is now used where simple *pateō* once sufficed. There is increasing failure to draw the precise distinctions so characteristic of the classical language. Thus partially synonymous words tend to become confused, so that, for instance, no firm line can be drawn in the NT between *kalos* and *agathos* 'good', or between *phileō* and *agapaō* 'to love'. Superlative is at times used for comparative, and diminutives without special diminutive force. The meaning of particles, prepositions, and conjunctions, and the classical distinction between the tenses of the verb have all become blurred. Partly in reaction to these confusions, and partly perhaps in response to the needs of non-Greeks, there is an emphasis on clarity which a Greek of classical times would feel to be otiose: personal pronouns are inserted to make subject and object of a verb explicit, though in classical Greek they are regularly omitted when they may be understood from the context; the use of certain prepositions (*eis*, *en*, *ek*) has been greatly increased to make everywhere explicit prepositional notions which in classical Greek were felt to be implicit in the verb. Simplicity is everywhere a dominant motif, most noticeably perhaps in the sentence-structure of Koinē writings; it is a far cry from the complexity of the Thucydidean or Demosthenic period to the simple sentences of the Gospel of Mark. But the same tendency has been at work less obtrusively in the virtual disappearance of the optative mood, and in the elimination of many anomalous nouns and verbs, difficult to non-Greeks because not regularly declined or conjugated. Thus the normal word for 'ship', *naus*, occurs but once in the NT (in Acts), for its place has been taken by the regularly declined *ploion*; difficult verbs of the type of *histēmi* 'set up' are being replaced by new formations like *histanō*, which conforms to a more regular pattern.

It remains to remark that the foregoing tendencies appear for the most part further worked out in modern Greek. The synonymity of *kalos* and *agathos*, for instance, has resulted in the virtual elimination of *agathos* as superfluous; the increasing use of the prepositions has made the dative case unnecessary, and except in a few stereotyped expressions it no longer survives.

RELATIONSHIP OF NT GREEK TO KOINĒ

It must be observed that the term Koinē covers a wide variety of strata of language, both spoken and written. Of course, it is impossible for us to be informed of the exact nature of the spoken language, yet extant letters and other documents composed unreflectingly by people of little literary training approximate closely enough to the spoken language. At the other end of the spectrum from popular language is the formalized literary Koinē of writers like the historians Polybius, Diodorus Siculus, Plutarch, and Josephus. (The works of other authors of the period, such as Dionysius of Halicarnassus and Lucian, who wrote in an artificial Atticizing style, are useless for the study of the Koinē, except in so far as they unwittingly betray traces of the current vernacular in spite of their intended adherence to archaic models.) At what point in the gradation from literary Koinē to the language of the common man the NT stands is a disputed matter; but it is generally agreed that, along with the *Discourses* of the philosopher Epictetus, the NT has most in common with the popular language of the non-literary papyri. A more precise setting of the NT as a whole cannot be made, for there is a considerable range within the NT itself from the most literary parts (Hebrews, parts of Luke-Acts) to the least (Revelation).

Semitisms

The language of the NT, although basically the non-literary Koinē of the first century A.D., is set apart from it to some extent by distinctive features, most of which it shares with other examples of 'biblical Greek' (principally the Septuagint version of the OT [the LXX]; also the pseudepigrapha). These features, termed Semitisms, were introduced into the NT in two ways: (I) as quotations from the LXX or adaptations to its style (ii) as direct translation from a Semitic original.

(i) Most Jews of the first century A.D. read their Bible in Greek (i.e. the LXX), for Hebrew and Aramaic were little used outside Palestine. (The letter to the Hebrews was written in Greek!) Hence Jewish Christians especially would naturally find their vocabulary and style when speaking of religious subjects to be largely fashioned by the familiar phrases of the LXX. But the LXX is not always a model of good Greek style; some portions are, for reverential reasons, scrupulously literal renderings of the Hebrew, and hence far from idiomatic Greek. Thus there are taken into the NT expressions that are really Hebrew idiom in Greek clothing.

It was even possible for a writer who knew neither Hebrew nor Aramaic to adapt his style to that of the LXX and thus write a Semiticizing Greek. Such appears to have been the case with Luke, the opening chapters of whose Gospel in particular abound with Semitisms. These are perhaps due to a Semitic source which he is translating, but there appear to be other instances where Luke, uninfluenced by Semitic sources, has yet written in Septuagintal style. (Similarly John Bunyan could write in Authorized Version English, which is full of Hebraisms, without knowing any Hebrew himself.)

(ii) It is plain that the sayings of Jesus recorded in Greek in the Gospels were originally uttered in Aramaic (or perhaps in Hebrew), and that therefore there has been translation from one to the other at some stage in their transmission. So it is not surprising that above all other parts of the NT the words of Jesus display evidence of their Aramaic originals. Thus a passage like Mt. 11: 28–30, when retranslated into Palestinian Aramaic, exhibits not only poetical structure, but also alliteration and even rhyme, and shows incidentally that the model our Lord chose for His addresses was the poetical 'sermon' of the Hebrew prophets.

More, however, than the sayings-material in the Gospels shows traces of its Semitic origin. Some scholars have postulated Aramaic documents behind all the Gospels and Acts, but the evidence does not compel us to go so far, and is fully satisfied if we see in Matthew, Mark, and John men who thought in Semitic and wrote in Greek, and in Luke a Greek writing in the familiar style of the LXX, with reference to Aramaic sources as occasion demanded. A good case can be made out that parts at least of Revelation have been translated from Hebrew, or perhaps from Aramaic. Of the rest of the NT writers it may be said that their Greek, though generally idiomatic, often bears a Semitic colouring.

It should be remarked that an expression in the NT may be a Semitism even although it can be paralleled in extra-Biblical Greek. In some cases an expression, while not foreign to the idiom of the Greek language, but rarely attested, has become in the NT a living expression, under the influence of a Semitic idiom. Thus the Semitic nature of the expression lies not in its existence, but in the frequency of its occurrence.

It is often not easy to distinguish between a Hebraism and an Aramaism; for first, the two languages have many idioms in common; and secondly, the Aramaic of the period is best known from targums (explanatory translations of the OT), so that what appears to be an Aramaic expression may be only a literal translation of a Hebrew one. So no attempt is made here to unravel the intricate evidence; rather, various Semitisms are grouped together to illustrate the effect of its Semitic background on the NT.

(a) *Parataxis* (the use of co-ordinate, rather than subordinate, clauses). This stylistic characteristic is common to Hebrew and Aramaic, and is especially frequent in Mark. For example,

whereas Luke says, using a participle, 'Having left our homes we have followed you' (18: 28), Mark writes, 'we have left everything and followed you' (10: 28). (In the English of the NIV, the syntax is the same in both sentences.) But simplicity of style is a general characteristic also of Koinē; the Semitic element lies probably in the frequency of its use.

(b) *Parallelism*, well-known in Heb. poetry, is found in many sayings of Jesus, *e.g.* Mt. 5: 45; Lk. 12: 48.

(c) *Adjectival Genitive*. Hebrew, being poor in adjectives, often expressed an adjectival notion by appending a noun in a genitival relation; thus 'a man of wealth' means 'a wealthy man', and 'the hill of my holiness' means 'my holy hill'. In NT some clear cases are: 'the son of his love' for 'his beloved son, the son he loves' (Col. 1: 13), 'the strength of his might' for 'his mighty strength' (Eph. 1: 19), 'the mammon of unrighteousness' for 'unrighteous mammon' (Lk. 16: 9; NIV less precisely 'worldly wealth'), 'the body of this death' for 'this mortal body' (Rom. 7: 24; NIV 'this body of death'), 'men of (God's) good-will' for '(God's) chosen people' (Lk. 2: 14; NIV 'men on whom his favour rests'). But it is not always easy to decide whether the Semitic idiom is being used; does 'the riches of his glory' mean 'his glorious riches' (Eph. 3: 16)?

(d) The '*Infinitive Absolute*' construction. The 'absolute' form of the Heb. infinitive is used with a finite form of the same verb to express emphasis or duration, *e.g. môt tāmût* 'dying (infin.) you will die'='you will surely die' (Gen. 2: 17). This idiom occurs in NT in quotations from LXX (*e.g.* 'blessing I will bless you', Heb. 6: 14), and also a few times in Luke: 'with desire I have desired' (*epithymiā epethymēsa*) = 'I have eagerly desired' (Lk. 22: 15); 'with a commandment we commanded' (*parangeliā parēngeilamen*)='we gave you strict orders' (Ac. 5: 28). Cf. also Ac. 4: 17 (*v.l.*); 23: 14; Jn 3: 29. The idiom can be paralleled from classical sources, but seems to be a Septuagintalism in Luke.

(e) *Indefinite Third Person Plural*. Where in English we might use the passive or 'one' when the subject of the verb is indefinite (cf. French *on*, German *man*), Heb. and Aram. tend to use a third person plural verb (like English 'they say'='indefinite persons *or* people in general say'). Thus in Jn 15: 6, 'they pick them (the branches) up and throw them into the fire', we do not need to ask who 'they' are; it merely means 'such branches are picked up, thrown into the fire'. Cf. also Lk. 12: 20 'this night they (indefinite) demand your life'; 6: 38 (where both passive and third person plural are used); Mk 10: 13; Mt. 5: 15. In classical Gk. this construction is used mostly with verbs of saying (so also in modern Gk.), but under the influence of Aram., which avoids the passive, its use is extended in NT.

(*f*) '*And it came to pass that . . .*' Perhaps the most conspicuous Semitism in the NT, it has a similar connotation in the Gospel narratives as it does if used today: it is a direct reminiscence of Biblical language. It is not idiomatic Gk., but a literal translation of the common Heb. phrase *way**hî w* (lit. 'and it befell and . . .').

(*g*) '*Not all*'='*none*'. In place of the usual Gk. word for 'none, no one', we sometimes find 'not all', formed on the model of a Heb. idiom (*e.g.* 'all shrubs of the field were not as yet'= '—not one shrub was yet', Gen. 2: 5). Similarly *ou pas* in NT: 'all flesh would not be saved' = 'no flesh would be saved, NIV 'no-one would survive' (Mt. 24: 22). So also Rom. 3: 20; 1 C. 1: 29; Ac. 10: 14; 2 Pet. 1: 20. But not every instance of 'not all' requires this interpretation; 'not everyone who says to me, "Lord, Lord"' (Mt. 7: 21) means exactly what it means in English, 'some, but not all'.

(*h*) '*Answered and said*'. Various tautological formulas for introducing discourse are modelled on the Heb. idiom which prefixes direct speech with 'saying'. Hence in NT we find the types 'he answered and said' (*e.g.* Jn 1: 48) (often in Jn, seldom in Mk and Lk., never in Mt.), 'he answered, saying' (Lk. 3: 16), 'answering, he said' (Mt. 3: 15) (not common in Jn). On the same pattern 'saying' is used with other verbs, such as 'testify' (Ac. 13: 22), and 'write' (Lk. 1: 63).

(*i*) *Various pleonasms.* Heb. is given to describing activity with a wealth of detail we find unnecessary, though perhaps picturesque, *e.g.* 'he opened his mouth and spoke', 'he arose and went', 'he lifted up his eyes and saw'. The influence of this manner of speech is seen in the following examples: 'a mustard seed, which a man took and planted' (Mt. 13: 31), 'I shall arise and go' (Lk. 15: 18; NIV 'set out and go back'); cf. Mt. 13: 33, 46; 25: 16; Ac. 5: 17. Very frequently 'begin' is used pleonastically, especially in Mark (*e.g.* 1: 45; 5: 17; 6: 7), but it is not pleonastic in *e.g.* Ac. 1: 1 (Acts continues what Jesus *began* to do and to teach).

The Semitic background of the NT is also claimed to appear in certain places where the putative Semitic original explains a difficulty in the present Greek text. Much ingenuity has been employed in the study of such passages, but in the absence of the originals it is a hazardous task, and there is hardly a proposed solution that commands general agreement. Some examples are:

(*a*) Lk. 1: 39 (*eis polin Iouda*) seems to mean 'into the town Judah', which is curious because Judah is a province, not a town. It is suggested that *polin* 'town' represents the Aram. *m**dînah* which had meant 'province', but in the 1st cent.

A.D. was coming to mean 'town'. Hence the word was ambiguous, and it is suggested that the translator (Luke or his source) chose the wrong sense. But it is easier to suppose that *eis polin Iouda* means 'into *a* town of Judah'.

(*b*) Lk. 12: 49b should mean 'How I wish it were already kindled!' But the introductory word *ti* means 'what', which is almost unintelligible (RV 'what will I, if it is already kindled?'). However, the Aram. *mā* can mean both 'what' and 'how', and it is possible that the ambiguity there is the source of the error in translation. Yet *ti* can mean 'how' in modern Gk., and it may be that it can bear this meaning in the NT also.

(*c*) Mt. 7: 6 reads 'Do not give dogs what is sacred; do not throw your pearls to pigs'. It is suggested that 'sacred' is a misunderstanding of the original Aram. *q**dāšā* 'ring' as *qudšā* 'sacred' (the two words would be written identically in Aram., viz. *qdš*, but pronounced differently). 'Ring' would then be in parallelism with 'pearls': 'Do not give a ring to dogs, and do not throw your pearls before swine'. This is an attractive restoration of the original form of the saying; it may be noted, however, that many would prefer to speak not of a 'misunderstanding' by the evangelist, but of his 'interpretation' of the meaning of 'ring' as 'what is sacred.'

The most obvious influence of a Semitic background on the NT, namely, Hebrew and Aramaic words transliterated into Greek, must also be mentioned. From Hebrew we have: *allēlouia*, *amēn*, *batos* 'bath' (a Heb. 8–9 gallon measure), *geenna*, *korban* 'gift', *koros* 'kor' (a Heb. 10–12 bushel measure), *manna*, *pascha* 'passover', *sabaōth*, *sabbaton* 'sabbath', *satanas*, *hyssōpos*. From Aramaic (though some of these originally were Hebrew): *abba* 'father', *eloi* 'my God', *ephphatha* 'be opened', *korbanas* 'temple treasury', *lama sabachthani* 'why have you forsaken me', *mammōnas* 'mammon', *maran atha* 'our Lord has come' or *marana tha* 'our Lord, come!', *rabbi* 'my master', *rabbouni* 'my lord', *raka* 'fool, empty-head', *saton* 'measure' (a Heb. 1½ peck measure of grain), *sikera* 'strong drink', *talitha koum(i)* 'little girl, get up!' Most of the Heb. terms survive in English, being technical terms of religion; the Aram. phrases and words from the Gospels are preserved as such, being the *ipsissima verba* of our Lord.

THE LANGUAGE OF INDIVIDUAL WRITERS

Reference has already been made to the wide variety of styles and levels of Koinē Greek in which the NT is written, and we come now to examine the styles of the individual writers in more detail.

Mark writes in a simple, straightforward style which is equally evident in Greek and in English translation. The abundant use of parataxis (*e.g.* 1: 9–13) is typical of unsophisticated writing in any language, but in the case of Mark it may also be a reflection of the Semitic speech of his reputed informant, Peter. The historic present tense (*e.g.* 2: 15, 17, 18), an element in Mark's well-known vivid style (it occurs usually at or near the beginning of a paragraph when a new scene is introduced), can be paralleled from Gk. of all times, but again may be influenced by the use in Aram. of the participial sentence. Other Semitic traces are to be found in his common use of the periphrastic present tense ('he is eating' instead of usual Gk. 'he eats'), which was just possible in Gk., but frequent in Aram. (Only Luke has a higher proportion of periphrastic presents; his are in imitation of LXX style, Mark's are through mental translation from Aram.) The word-order in Mark's sentences frequently reflects the Semitic style: while it is possible (and common with verbs of saying) to put the verb first in normal Gk., in Semitic the verb regularly comes first; so often in NT, and especially in Mark. Mark's Greek also contains a number of Latin loanwords: *e.g.*, from military and official terminology: *praitōrion* 'praetorium', *legiōn* 'legion', *kentyriōn* 'centurion', *Kaisar* 'Caesar', *phragelloō* 'to whip' (from vulgar Lat. *fragellum* 'whip'=*flagellum*), *spekoulatōr* 'spy, scout, executioner'; from commercial terminology: *modios* 'peck-measure', *dēnarion* 'denarius', *kodrantēs* 'quadrans' (the smallest Roman coin, one sixty-fourth of a denarius); and a Latin idiom, *to hikanon poiein* (15: 15) literally = Lat. *satisfacere* 'to satisfy'. The deduction to be made from Mark's use of these Latinisms is not, as some have suggested, that Mark is translated from a Latin original, but that he reproduces faithfully the vernacular of the Roman Empire.

Luke writes at times in an elevated and elegant style (*e.g.* the polished opening period of the Gospel, 1: 1–4; also the well-phrased sentence, Ac. 15: 24–26), at others in imitation of the LXX or in a very ordinary Koinē (*e.g.* Lk. 1: 5 plunges immediately into Septuagintal style; the more Semitic passages appear to be either where he is dependent on an Aram. source or where he feels a Septuagintal style to be appropriate). But in general he is more conscious of style than most of the NT writers; thus in his use of Mark's material he often makes corrections and improvements in the language. Various connective particles (*te, de, oun*) and asyndeton are employed in place of Mark's ubiquitous and sometimes wearying *kai* 'and' (*e.g.* Lk. 8: 34–39; Mk 5: 14–20). He appears to go out of his way to choose a Gk. equivalent for Mark's Latin loanword, no doubt regarding the native Gk. word as more literary than the vernacular loanword. For

example, *hekatontarchēs* 'centurion' (23: 47) for Mark's *kentyriōn* (15: 39), *phoros* 'taxes' (20: 22) for Mark's *kēnsos* (Mk 12: 14; also Mt. 22: 17); cf. also *epigraphē* 'title, written notice' (23: 38) instead of John's *titlos* (19: 19). Other instances of his substitutes for Mark's more colloquial vocabulary: *pais* (8: 54) 'child' for Mark's *korasion* (5: 41) 'little girl', post-classical diminutive of *korē* 'girl'; *limnē* (5: 1) 'lake' for Mark's *thalassa* (1: 16) 'sea' in classical Gk. but also 'inland lake' in Koinē; *agō* (4: 1) 'to lead' for Mark's *ekballō* (1: 12) 'to cast forth' in classical Gk. but also 'to lead out' in 1st cent. Koinē, though still colloquial. Luke uses *esthiō* exclusively for 'to eat', while Matthew (sometimes) and John (always) use the more colloquial *trōgō* ('to gnaw' in classical Gk.). Almost half of the NT occurrences of the obsolescent optative mood are found in Luke; he also perpetuates the use of the future infinitive and the future participle of purpose, which are rare elsewhere in Koinē. He keeps the classical word *heteros* 'other of two' along with *allos* 'other' which in Koinē is usurping the meaning of *heteros* (Mark never uses *heteros* [it occurs in the non-Markan ending, Mk 16: 12], and John only once); but he does not always observe the classical distinction between the two, and in *e.g.* Lk. 8: 6 he writes incorrectly *heteros*, though Mark had already used the correct *allos* (4: 5).

Matthew employs 'a correct if rather colourless Greek which avoids the vulgar forms without displaying a mastery of the literary syntax' (J. H. Moulton). While with Mark he uses the less formal words *korasion* 'little girl' and *ekballō* 'to take out', he shows little sign in his language of his Semitic origin, and avoids in fact not a few of Luke's deliberate Hebraisms (*e.g.* *enōpion* 'before the face of'= Heb. *lipnê*; the periphrastic present, common in Luke and Mark, is rare in Matthew). He alone of all NT writers distinguishes correctly between *eis* 'into' and *en* 'in' (Mk 1: 39, for instance, has 'preaching into (*eis*) the synagogues'; in modern Gk. *eis* has absorbed the functions of *en*, and the process is already at work in Koinē).

John's Greek is, even more than Mark's, the most colloquial in the NT, and also the furthest advanced in the direction of modern Gk. For example, Attic *piezō* 'squeeze, press down' is only in Lk. 6: 38, but the Doric equivalent *piazō* is colloquial for 'seize' (8 times in John, 4 in the rest of the NT), and hence modern Gk. *pianō* 'seize'; *opsarion* and *prosphagion*, which meant in classical Gk. 'relish, tidbit' (*i.e.* cooked food eaten with a meal), mean in colloquial Koinē 'fish' (both words only in John), and modern Gk. for 'fish' is *psari*, from *opsarion*. John's simple and repetitive style is *de l'homme même*, and is not indicative of any difficulty with the language, in which he finds himself completely at home.

Revelation is the work of an author, according to C. F. D. Moule, 'who writes like a person who, nurtured in a Semitic speech, is only just learning to write in Greek. He is capable of horrifying grammatical blunders and patently Semitic idioms, but is not thereby prevented from achieving extraordinary power and sometimes a quite unearthly beauty'. So striking, indeed, is the difference between the Greek of Revelation and the Greek of John's Gospel and Letters, that many have found it difficult to believe that both styles of Greek are from the pen of one writer; but the difficulty may be overcome by assuming that John's original Aramaic (or Hebrew) has been translated into Greek by a scribe with very meagre knowledge of (or respect for) grammar. The most patent solecisms of Revelation are failures to observe grammatical concord, e.g. 'from Jesus Christ (genitive case), the faithful and true witness (nominative case)' (the latter phrase should also have been in the genitive); 'saying' is often used without regard to the case or person with which it should agree (very possibly on the model of the indeclinable Heb. *lē'mōr* 'saying'). The use of prepositions is interesting: instrumental *en* = 'by' (like Heb. *b^e*) is particularly frequent; so also *enōpion* 'before' (= Heb. *lipnê*); *syn* 'with' (frequent only in Luke and Paul) has yielded to *meta* 'with' (which, in the form *me*, alone survives in modern Gk.); the classical *hypo* with the accusative case for 'under' has been replaced by the compound adverb *hypokatō* (a formation typical of Koinē). Not all instances, however, of grammatical anomalies are to be attributed to the author's Semitic background, for many may be paralleled in the least literary of the papyri from Egypt; lack of grammatical concord, especially with participles, can be observed in mediaeval Greek, and perhaps the author of Revelation is, in this instance, but an early witness to a long history of confusion which culminated in the indeclinable participle of modern Greek (*blepontas* is 'seeing', in whatever case, person, or gender).

Paul is capable of a lively and forceful idiomatic Greek. His style is often tortuous and cumbrous, but equally often rhythmic and natural. A few examples will suffice to show that he writes an educated Greek: the well-known classical idiom of a neuter adjective for an abstract noun appears in the NT almost exclusively in Paul (e.g. *to chrēston* 'the good, kind thing'='goodness, kindness', Rom. 2: 4; *to mōron*='foolishness', 1 C. 1: 25); he uses the optative mood more frequently than any other NT author. Semitisms of grammar are virtually non-existent in his writings (though see 'not all = none' and 'adjectival genitive' above); but on every page there may be found many words which reveal their Semitic content by

forcing their interpreter to turn to his LXX rather than his classical lexicon for a correct understanding of them (e.g. *eirēnē* 'peace', *diathēkē* 'covenant', *euangelion* 'gospel', *epistrephō* 'convert', *eidōlon* 'idol', *peripateō* 'walk' (in the moral sense)).

Hebrews is the most literary of the books of the NT; Origen recognized it as 'more Greek' than any of Paul's letters. An instructive example of the author's adherence to classical models is his avoidance of hiatus (in some circles it was considered inelegant to use a word beginning with a vowel if the previous word ended in a vowel, certain unavoidable words excepted). Other instances of his careful grammar are: use of neuter adjective for abstract noun (e.g. *to asthenes* 'weakness', 7: 18); future infinitive and future participle (both only in Acts and Hebrews in NT); the conjunction *hina* is used only in its classical sense 'in order that', although Koinē was introducing *hina* clauses in various functions, notably to replace the infinitive, a process well nigh complete in modern Gk. The more formal classical particles like *men . . . de* 'on the one hand . . . on the other hand' are rare in the NT, but Hebrews, together with Acts and some Pauline letters, has examples of this combination; the only NT occurrence of the classical and literary *dēpou* 'surely, as you know' is in Heb. 2: 16; *hothen* 'whence' (='for which reason') occurs 6 times in Hebrews and elsewhere in the NT only in Acts and Matthew (once each); Attic *kathaper* 'as' appears only in Hebrews and Paul. The author of Hebrews is very evidently steeped in the language of the LXX, but its Greek does little harm to his; some Semitic touches are: 'spoken by, or, through (*en*, lit. 'in', like Heb. *b^e*) the prophets' (1: 1), 'evil heart of unbelief' (3: 12) (adjectival genitive, translated 'unbelieving heart' by NIV).

James is not unaware of classical style; witness the classical locutions *age nyn* 'come now!', now listen!' (4: 13; 5: 1) (nowhere else in NT), *chrē* 'it is necessary' (replaced in the rest of NT by *dei*), *eoika* 'seem' (only here in NT), and *tis* 'a certain' in the classical sense of 'a kind of' (1: 18) (thus only elsewhere in Luke and Hebrews). His unhesitating and vivid choice of words declares him an expert in the Greek tongue, and few traces of Semitism can be detected. His fondness for *idou* 'behold' has been thought reminiscent of the omnipresent *hinnēh* in the OT; there is an imitation of the 'infinitive absolute' in a description of Elijah (5: 17): 'with prayer he prayed' (*proseuchē prosēuxato*) (a deliberate Septuagintalism?). 'A hearer of forgetfulness' (1: 25) for 'a forgetful hearer' likewise cannot but be Semitic.

Peter is not the ignorant fisherman sometimes imagined—'unschooled' (*agrammatos* 'without letters') in Ac. 4: 13 does not mean 'illiterate', but 'without formal theological training'. The Greek of I Peter is not necessarily therefore due to Silvanus, but rather implies Peter's long familiarity with the language (his brother Andrew had a Greek name!). That he had been brought up on the LXX is evident from his numerous quotations from it and reminiscences of its language. But apart from these direct influences of the LXX on his writing, few Semitisms can be traced; 'children of obedience' (1: 14), and perhaps the participle used as an imperative (*e.g.* 3: 7 ff.) (also in Paul) may be cited. 2 Peter has been described as Atticizing and bookish, and it is striking that it contains no quotations from the LXX, only a handful of allusions to it, and barely one Semitism (*en empaigmonē empaiktai* 'mockers with mocking' [3: 3] may be an 'infinitive absolute' construction).

Jude similarly shows himself familiar with the Koinē, and shares with 2 Peter a predilection for the long and sonorous word. He appears equally innocent of Semitisms.

BIBLIOGRAPHY

Dictionaries
ARNDT, W. F., and GINGRICH, F. W., *A Greek-English Lexicon of the New Testament and other Early Christian Literature* (Chicago/Cambridge, 1957) (the best for general use).

MOULTON, J. H., and MILLIGAN, G., *The Vocabulary of the Greek Testament illustrated from the papyri and other non-literary sources* (London, 1930) (not a NT dictionary proper, but illuminates the NT from Koine usage).

KITTEL, G., and FRIEDRICH, G. (ed.), *Theological Dictionary of the New Testament* E.T., 10 vols. (Grand Rapids, 1964–75).

SOUTER, A., *A Pocket Lexicon to the Greek New Testament* (Oxford, 1916).

Grammars
FUNK, R. W., *A Greek Grammar of the New Testament and other Early Christian Literature: a revision of F. Blass and A. Debrunner, 'Grammatik des neutestamentlichen Griechisch'* (Cambridge, 1961) (an excellent grammar, convenient to use).

MOULTON, J. H., *A Grammar of New Testament Greek* (4 vols., Edinburgh, 1906, 1919—29, 1963, 1976, (vol. 3 on syntax and vol. 4 on style being by N. Turner)).

MOULE, C. F. D., *An Idiom Book of New Testament Greek* (2nd edn., Cambridge, 1959).

WENHAM, J., *The Elements of New Testament Greek* (Cambridge, 1965). Replacing H. P. V. Nunn's Grammar, this is probably the best grammar for beginners; it includes exercises and vocabulary.

Other works
BARCLAY, W., *A New Testament Wordbook* (London, 1955).

BARCLAY, W., *More New Testament Words* (London, 1958).

BARR, J., *The Semantics of Biblical Language* (Oxford, 1961).

BLACK, M., *An Aramaic Approach to the Gospels and Acts* (3rd edn., Oxford, 1968).

HILL D., *Greek Words and Hebrew Meanings* (Cambridge, 1967).

TURNER, N., *Grammatical Insights into the New Testament* (Edinburgh, 1965).

WILCOX, M., *The Semitisms of Acts* (Oxford, 1965).

ARCHAEOLOGICAL DISCOVERIES
AND THE NEW TESTAMENT

A. R. MILLARD

The NT, being based upon events which took place in history, can be associated with historical information from other sources. These may be employed to supplement data in the NT and to verify it. Too often they are used by Christians attempting to 'prove' Scriptural statements, or by sceptics to discredit them. A balanced approach will remember that the NT is also an ancient document, deserving as much respect as any other writing surviving from antiquity. Of course, its particular nature will be taken into account, as will that of any text, but this does not permit one to jettison every awkward passage, any more than it allows uncritical acceptance of every word. While we are not saying that the NT is to be read solely as an historical work, our attention is directed to this general aspect in the present study.

Less value is attached by most people to archaeological discoveries relating to the NT than to those relating to the OT, because so much written information has survived from the era of Roman world rule. Moreover, the NT contains a smaller amount of narrative which might be associated with monumental remains. Thus it is not surprising that NT archaeology is frequently concerned with details, at first sight of small worth.

Documents

One category of those details is the precise meaning of words, idioms, and figures of speech. For centuries the NT stood isolated; while it could be understood with much greater surety than the Hebrew of the OT, through comparison with other Greek books, no works were known composed in quite the same form of Greek. Then, about a century ago, documents written in ink on *papyrus* (ancient equivalent of paper) desiccated in the desert sand, and others written on less perishable potsherds (*ostraca*), were unearthed in Egypt. At first they came in a trickle, the chance treasure troves of peasants and looters all over the land, then in a flood from official excavations in the rubbish heaps of several towns that flourished in the millennium 300 B.C. to A.D. 700. They were tax returns, census records, and other humdrum remnants of imperial bureaucracy, and the papers of citizens, their letters and accounts, wills and legal deeds, and some of the books they used to read. So many were obtained that a vast quantity remain unpublished; those available in catalogues need intensive further study.

Isolated examples may be amusing, pathetic, amazingly up-to-date, or may impart historically valuable information. The material as a whole is vitally important, for its language is virtually identical with New Testament Greek, that is, it reveals the language of the NT to be, basically, the language of daily life, of commerce and of government. (See 'The Language of the New Testament', pp. 1076 ff.) One result is the clarification of many passages in AV by exhibition of rare words in new contexts. So legal use perhaps delimits the 'substance of things hoped for' of Heb. 11: 1 as 'the title-deeds of things hoped for', and the expression rendered 'I have all and abound' (Phil. 4: 18) and 'they have their reward' (Mt. 6: 2, 5, 16) is revealed as the formula for quitting a claim, paying in full. (On the meaning of *hypostasis* in Heb. 11: 1, see also F. F. Bruce: *The Epistle to the Hebrews*, 1964, p. 278.) The 'earnest' of Eph. 1: 14 (AV) is seen to be a payment in advance, deposit, or first instalment, of a sum due later. In a contract of apprenticeship is a penalty clause in case of slackness or truancy, and the term for that is the 'disorderly' (AV) of 2 Th. 3: 6 ff. (RSV 'idleness'). That same letter and others speak of the Lord's coming, the *parousia*. Orders from senior officers to municipal bodies require them to make elaborate preparations for the coming of the emperor (like the medieval 'royal progress'), employing *parousia* for the state visit. In Lk. 17: 21 stands the enigmatic clause 'the kingdom of God is within you'. Study of the papyri and of other examples of Greek literature has demonstrated that 'to hand, within reach' was the everyday meaning. A doctor wrote asking for a woollen jacket to be sent to him 'so that I may have it with me' in a letter of *c.* A.D. 270. In Luke this produces a sense which is arguably more in agreement with the tenor of other NT passages.

The papyri yield many further linguistic secrets, and, more than these, they offer a vast number of facts on many aspects of life. While the Egyptian context should be remembered, much can be transferred to the Palestinian scene, or to any other province of Rome in the east Mediterranean region. In the sphere of government light is thrown on the census procedure and the problems concerning the date of the Lord's birth (see below, p. 1086). A notice of A.D. 104 ordering persons to register in their home districts has survived, such as caused Joseph and Mary to go to Bethlehem, their ancestral home, and there are several actual census returns. Evidence is plentiful, also, of the resentment aroused by the oppressive taxes levied by Rome and the system of farming out the collections to grasping 'publicans' like Zaccheus. Important official letters, written by clerks, amanuenses, from dictation, or transcribed from shorthand notes (several systems of shorthand are attested, and some manuals have been recovered), were authenticated by the high-ranking sender adding the words of greeting in his own handwriting. Paul took this action when he felt a need to assert his apostolic authority and the genuineness of his words (*e.g.* Gal. 6: 11; 2 Th. 3: 17). Seals were impressed upon the outside of rolled-up letters and documents and upon consignments of goods as a guarantee against falsification or tampering.

More personal correspondence abounds. In one letter a 'prodigal son' begged for his mother's pardon, he was ashamed to return home because of his ragged clothing, and admitted that his condition was his own fault. In different vein, an absent husband wrote to his wife affectionately, urging her to care for their child, yet instructing her to expose (to death) a girl baby should she give birth to one. Christianity offered a quite opposite ethic, demanding a very real conversion. Other social customs repugnant to Christians (and to others nowadays through their influence) appear in the papyri beside allusions to diverse religious beliefs, Egyptian, Greek, Jewish, Roman, and mystery cults, all rivals and enemies of the new faith. (See 'The Religious Background, Pagan', p. 1113.)

Official and legal papers normally bear a date, following one or two of the several systems in use, so from careful scrutiny of their handwriting and other characteristics, charts can be drawn to show the changing styles of script over the centuries. From them the undated texts can be allocated approximate dates by minute comparison. The value of this exercise is proved when copies of NT books are disinterred, since their worth in textual criticism largely depends upon their age. Works of literature rarely bear a date themselves.

Several pieces of NT books (and some of the OT in Greek) were found in the rubbish heaps, the oldest being a fragment of John's Gospel said to date from the decades prior to A.D. 150 (now in the Rylands Library, Manchester).

More complete copies, parts of small libraries, found elsewhere in Egypt, comprise one or more books copied in the years around A.D. 200 and during the subsequent centuries (the Chester Beatty Collection, Dublin, and the Bodmer Collection, Geneva, are two major groups). To date nearly fifty Greek NT papyri are known as old as, or older than, the famous Sinai and Vatican codices (*c.* A.D. 350). Some of them enable us to read many parts of the text as it was copied little more than a century after the last books were composed. (See 'Text and Canon, II: Text', pp. 1071.) An interesting sidelight is the suggestion that our current book form was brought into general use for literary works by the early Christians; hitherto it had been a secondary form, used only for notes and technical handbooks, the usual scroll being too cumbersome for speedy reference. The multiplicity of NT manuscripts testifies to the centrality of the written word in early Christian life.

The other major collection of ancient 'papers' is the Dead Sea discovery. Aspects of language and society arise here; the theological value is discussed later (p. 1087). They are by far the oldest Jewish books of their kind, showing just how the OT appeared in the Gospel period, and how one sect of religious zealots treated it. Like the papyri they provide a contemporary source for elucidating the meanings of words, especially words with ritual or legal Jewish undertones. Hebrew, Aramaic, Nabataean and Greek are the languages represented in the texts from Qumran and the slightly later ones from caves farther down the coast (*c.* A.D. 130). Hebrew was in use more extensively than suspected before, perhaps partly in patriotic fervour. The impression that many Palestinians were bilingual or trilingual which the NT conveys receives support. The very number of the Biblical scrolls (many score, and dozens of copies of certain books), some obviously used heavily, may presuppose a highly literate society (notice that a country carpenter could read, according to Lk. 4: 16). A potsherd unearthed in the ruins of the communal building at Qumran, where the Scrolls' owners evidently met, carries a student's exercise in writing the Hebrew alphabet. The same ruin contained smashed remnants of writing-benches for the scribes, and their inkwells. Undoubtedly schools existed in many other areas, apart from special centres like Qumran. Various mundane activities were carried out in the building, making it a good fount for knowledge of daily work. Thus we learn about the smithy and the potter's workshop, about a fuller's plant, a tannery (primarily, maybe, for preparing the vellum to be made into scrolls) and, in a separate place, a complete farm.

Sites

No question has ever arisen over the sites of the major cities in the NT stories. Jerusalem, Damascus, Rome stand to this day. Numerous smaller towns are difficult to locate, despite traditional identities, or sometimes because of them, for a lost town or monument can be 'found' for the pious by the more mercenary! Here the study of texts joins with ground survey and excavation to establish the terrain and occupancy of one or another site, balancing each segment of evidence in reaching a conclusion. Often the two former researches may be ambiguous, but the actual digging decisive.

Emmaus has had three candidates for its name, each of different merit, but only one agreeing in its distance from Jerusalem with the sixty furlongs given by the majority of good manuscripts of Lk. 24: 13 (other manuscripts have one hundred and sixty furlongs, the distance of the Emmaus mentioned in 1 Mac. 3: 40; 4: 1 ff.). This site, el-Qubeibeh, produced relics of the New Testament period when excavated; the traditional site at Amwas did not.

The remote town of Derbe in Anatolia (Ac. 14: 21, etc.) was an out-of-the-way backwater in Paul's day, and no one had known its exact whereabouts for centuries before 1956. In that year an inscription was deciphered relating to the citizens of Derbe in A.D. 157, and, in 1958, another was found bearing the name of a bishop of Derbe. From these stones the town can be identified with their place of origin, near Kerti Hüyük, lying about thirty miles farther east than had been surmised for the site of Derbe. Now maps of Paul's journeys may be drawn more accurately.

Cities are seldom forgotten, scenes of brief events often. In Palestine the first generation Christians did not concern themselves with the places of the gospel story, although they could say where they were if necessary; their interest lay in the fact of the story. Forty years after the Crucifixion the Roman military occupation would have hindered the sanctification of sites, and the key Jerusalem church was scattered. Not until late in the second century are there signs of a special aura attached to a scene of Christian history, and that is Peter's tomb beneath the Church of St. Peter in Rome. During the fourth century, following Constantine's 'conversion', pilgrims began flocking to the Holy Land, and undoubtedly there were dozens of such holy places to be seen then.

Chief among the sacred sites was the Holy Sepulchre in Jerusalem, more appropriately called the Church of the Resurrection in those days. The authenticity of the spot ornamented by Constantine's great church (now mostly rebuilt and altered) has been disputed by many people. However, its claim is strengthened by recent excavations in Jerusalem and the hints they give of the route of the city wall. Proof will never be found for that particular tomb, yet it is clear now that that area lay within a Jewish cemetery beyond the line of the city wall. (The 'Garden Tomb' is an increasingly implausible rival; the skull formation of the adjacent rock cannot be so old.)

Excavated remains coupled with a text from the Dead Sea Scrolls assure the position of the Bethesda Pool north of the Temple area, and also solve the problem of its name, obscured by scribal variants from a very early date. The widely used spelling Bethesda is nearest the Aramaic, which means 'place of flowing water', and is written with a grammatical termination showing that there were two pools as the excavation found.

Parts of the substructure of Herod's Temple remain and have recently been cleared down to street level. The huge, finely cut stones show something of the magnificence which so impressed the disciples (Mk. 13: 1) and can still be seen in the shrine Herod built for Abraham's tomb at Hebron. His masons were responsible for the greater portion of the fine outer wall still standing there.

A vivid relic of Herod's Temple is the 'Stone of Forbidding', a block inscribed in Greek with a warning that any Gentile who passed it would be responsible for his resulting death. The precinct wall of the inner courts contained several notices like this; a complete one is in a museum in Istanbul, part of a second is preserved in Jerusalem. That wall Paul and Trophimus were supposed to have penetrated (Ac. 21: 28 f.), but it no longer had any real significance, as Paul hinted later (Eph. 2: 14).

In the Holy City it is natural to endeavour to connect every discovery with the Scriptures, so archaeology can raise more questions and give rise to opposing theories. Many scholars adjudge the broad stone pavement laid bare beneath the Convent of the Sisters of Zion in Old Jerusalem as authentically Gabbatha, the courtyard upon which Pilate condemned Jesus (Jn 19: 13). The massive stones laid before A.D. 70, and the soldiers' games scratched upon them impress every visitor. Yet there is no proof that the Fortress of Antonia, to which the paving apparently belonged, served as Pilate's praetorium on the occasion of Jesus' trial. Herod's palace on the opposite, west, side of the city (now the Citadel), is an equally reasonable site. Excavations have not yielded a solution.

Finally, we notice that several allusions in the Letters to the Seven Churches (Rev. 2: 3) have been illumined by archaeological exploration. Local landmarks and characteristics metaphorically conveyed the Lord's message to each church. Laodicea's rebuke was couched in terms of her water supply. As no main source arose in the city, the water was drawn from hot springs at a distance and conveyed through stone pipes, arriving tepid, 'neither hot nor cold', suitable only as an emetic.

People

'Not many were influential, not many were of noble birth . . .' (1 C. 1: 26): Paul's survey of Church society reveals the reason why few NT figures are known from extant remains. Inevitably rulers are attested by monuments and coins, yet the name of Pontius Pilate exists on no more than a single inscribed stone, from Caesarea. The pomp of Herod the Great. re-echoes in dedications to pagan deities found in Greece, as well as in the fashionable temples he built in the non-Jewish parts of his kingdom. Similarly, memorials from other provinces contain the names of Roman officials, and their manifold titles are seen to correspond appropriately with the various ranks given them by the author of Acts. Thus the authorities at Thessalonica were *politarchs* (Ac. 17: 6), a title confirmed by a number of inscriptions concerning that city, while Publius was called 'chief man' (lit. 'first man') in Malta (Ac. 28: 7), which texts show to be his correct designation in Greek and Latin. A firm date in Paul's career is provided by an imperial decree engraved at Delphi early in A.D. 52 during the year of office exercised by the proconsul Gallio, the period when the apostle was in Corinth (Ac. 18: 11–17). Perhaps we may recognize in Paul's friend Erastus the city-treasurer of Corinth (Rom. 16: 23) the Erastus who gave a pavement to the city, a munificence recorded in Latin on stones now uncovered.

Two prominent persons named by Luke receive meagre external testimony to their existence. Sergius Paulus, proconsul of Cyprus (Ac. 13: 7), is attested in the date-formula, alone, of a stone from Paphos of A.D. 55, and Lysanias, tetrarch of Abilene (Lk. 3: 1), was not otherwise known until attention was turned to a dedication by one of his freedmen dated *c.* A.D. 20 which had been found at Abila, north of Damascus, and to one mentioning his rule as contemporary with Tiberius (A.D. 14–37). Previously Luke had been accused of error, since the only Lysanias of Abilene then known was executed by Antony and Cleopatra in 36 B.C.

When instances like these can be cited favouring Luke's historical accuracy, his unsupported statements become more creditable. To discount the record of the census held at the time of Jesus' birth, while Quirinius was governor of Syria (Lk. 2: 2) is to discard an ancient source for which no other can be substituted. In fact, a recent study (L. Dupraz: *De l'Association de Tibère au Principat à la Naissance du Christ*, 1966) reinterprets related documents widely believed to invalidate Lk. 2: 2 with the result that a governorship of Quirinius between 7 and 5 B.C. becomes feasible, although Luke's remark is the most explicit evidence. (See also 'Historical and Political Background, Chronology', pp. 1108 f.)

Archaeology can often inform on the mundane matters of life. Statuary helps to envisage appearance and modes of dress, and some representations of women exhibit the elaborate coiffure disliked by the apostles. Humble household artefacts, the pots and pans that comprise the bulk of an archaeologist's material evidence, have their place in building up a general picture of daily life. Occasionally they have a special relevance, like the common pottery oil-lamp illustrating metaphors and parables. Long-necked perfume bottles are unexciting finds in themselves, but they lend colour to one incident. The woman at Simon's banquet (Mk 14: 3) apparently had one of these (AV 'box' is misleading). In her haste to honour the Lord she did not trouble to open the sealed mouth, but snapped the neck, releasing the unguent and rendering the container useless. Attempts at polishing ancient metal mirrors explain Paul's comparison with our present understanding of Christ (1 C. 13: 12), because their surfaces could never give a clear reflection.

The tombs of the dead form a profitable source of information. Many Jewish cemeteries of the years prior to A.D. 70 have been explored in the neighbourhood of Jerusalem. One type of rock-cut tomb agrees with that described in the resurrection narratives in its construction. Examples can be seen to-day, one of the best being the 'Tomb of the Kings' in northern Jerusalem. There the low entrance conforms to Jn 20: 5 (many tombs have rather larger entries); the stone cover lies to one side, in a slot cut to allow for rolling it across. Inside these tombs the body was laid on a rock-cut shelf, above floor level. After decomposition, the bones were normally gathered into stone chests (ossuaries) for their final rest. Names written on the chests found in such tombs include some also met in the NT, among them Elizabeth, Mary, Sapphira, Lazarus, Jesus son of Joseph—none, of course, necessarily identifiable with the Biblical figures. There is a possibility that two chests of *c.* A.D. 50 bear brief prayers addressed to the risen Jesus.

In this connection may be included the 'Nazareth Decree'. On a marble slab, said to originate in Nazareth, is a Greek inscription ordaining that tombs remain undisturbed, and that anybody found guilty of demolishing one, moving the remains, or breaking the seals should be executed. No date or name is given, but the heading 'ordinance of Caesar' displays its imperial warranty. The question is, which Caesar. Palaeographical study points to a date between 50 B.C. and A.D. 50, other arguments favour Claudius (A.D. 41–54) who was concerned at Jewish-Christian disputes according to the biographer Suetonius. Were the text pre-resurrection in date it would underline the heinousness of the offence of which the Temple authorities attempted to accuse the disciples; were it later it would seem to emphasize the spread of the resurrection faith, and of efforts to quench it.

Another possible witness to early Christianity is the famous word-square:

```
R O T A S
O P E R A
T E N E T
A R E P O
S A T O R
```

Specimens are listed from a late second century site at Manchester, from a third or fourth century A.D. structure at Cirencester, from a third century town on the Euphrates (Dura), and from Pompeii, destroyed by Vesuvius' eruption in A.D. 79. A case can be made for a Jewish origin in translating portions of Ezekiel 1 and 10 into Latin. More convincing is the unravelling of the letters around the central N to form the initial words of the Lord's Prayer in Latin, with the Latin equivalents of Alpha and Omega (observe the cruciform TENET, too):

The preceding paragraphs summarize a few examples of archaeological discoveries in the realms of material culture and history. Matters of faith and doctrine cannot be subject to inquiry on the same level by reason of their character. However, two great finds made since the Second World War do impinge upon the study of religious thought in the background of the NT. These are the Dead Sea Scrolls, writings of a Jewish sect flourishing from the second century B.C. until *c.* A.D. 68 in the Judaean wilderness, and the Nag Hammadi Texts, thirteen volumes of Gnostic origin found in Egypt, copied about A.D. 400 and after. As neither group of manuscripts is

published in entirety all discussion should retain an element of caution; new evidence can so swiftly upturn fashionable theories. In the case of the Dead Sea Scrolls this point is particularly valid because the more exciting documents have naturally attracted wide attention. Taking one or two texts and making sensational claims for them is an abuse of a wonderful treasure.

Among the non-Biblical scrolls are long-forgotten books which enlarge our knowledge of Jewish thought and beliefs in the Gospel period. In general it can be said that they serve to re-emphasize the OT foundation of Judaism and Christianity, weakening theories of extensive Persian and Greek influence on them. Peculiar practices and doctrines (asceticism, celibacy, frequent baptism, the priestly line, calendar, eschatology, exclusivism) marked off the sect from the main stream of Judaism, nevertheless it remained essentially Jewish, looking for the coming of the Messiah (or Messiahs), performing punctiliously rites of purification and worship. (See 'Religious Background, the Jewish Religious Parties', p. 1121.) In their psalms and their Biblical exegesis these men approach the sentiment of some NT passages, and while they also believed that 'salvation' was available to their followers and none beside, in their exclusivism they went further, almost severing themselves from the world at large. Unlike the Christians, their missionary activity appears to have been minimal; applications from prospective members were awaited rather than invited. Despite that, their society continued for about two centuries at Qumran and probably in other centres. Parallels drawn between Christian organization and the hierarchical structure laid down in the Scrolls have their appeal for those who seek the origins of the Church. No proof of borrowing can be adduced; the parallels turn out to be superficial when viewed against the contradictory motives and beliefs underlying the institutions. So little does survive from that age in Judaea that it is sensible to extract every morsel of information from whatever is found, and improbable theories spring fast from the field.

The Jewish flavour of Mt. 5—Christ's enunciation of the Law in the light of His advent—is enhanced by linguistic echoes in the Scrolls. 'Poor in spirit', to take a single phrase, clearly meant 'the spiritually loyal', those who held faithfully to the covenant. A different product is a text with Nero Caesar spelt in Hebrew letters which, if given numerical values, have a sum of 666 (cf. Rev. 13: 17 f., with note *ad loc.*). It is as Jewish writings two centuries earlier than the compilation of the main rabbinic traditions (the Mishnah) that the Scrolls give their richest contribution to the vari-coloured world of the NT. It is instructive to read these records of a movement that failed beside those of a faith still flourishing.

Gnosticism has also been gleaned in the search for seminal concepts that flowered as Christianity, even although its early history has been extremely obscure. The Nag Hammadi books are translations into Coptic of Greek works written between A.D. 150 and 300, and include major compositions from various Gnostic parties. They indicate, by quotation, that the NT books were mostly recognized as canonical by A.D. 150 or thereabouts, and that Gnostics borrowed extensively from them. More important, they contradict the contentions that Paul's and John's writings adopt Gnostic ideas in formulating or explaining their doctrine (as members of the Bultmann school have argued), ideas which, it is said, require to be purged away before pristine Christianity can be seen. They illustrate the perversion of the Christian faith into one of the earliest heresies. Gnosticism claimed a monopoly of divine revelation, and the attainment of this knowledge (*gnosis*) was the aim of the Gnostic. For him matter was evil; release therefrom could be gained by following Jesus who broke the power of the physical realm and showed the way to the spiritual. (See 'The Religious Background, Pagan', pp. 1115 f.) Some of the writings imitate NT forms to propound new doctrines. 'The Gospel of Thomas' is a string of sayings purportedly delivered by Jesus to Thomas Didymus. Some rephrase familiar texts; others are utterly strange; a few may be authentic. Other books speak of the state of the world, the strata of celestial society, the resurrection, sometimes cast in letter-form. Here is an ancient example of the common tendency to exalt man and to add his ideas to the revelation once given.

By the unearthing of these two libraries of ancient writings NT studies have been given a new impetus. Along with the other archaeological evidence, they have brought in a phase in which old theories are being critically reviewed, and in which a more serious consideration is being given to the words of the gospel and their truth.

BIBLIOGRAPHY

This material is very scattered. Many relevant articles appear in *The Biblical Archaeologist*, published quarterly since 1938 by the American Schools of Oriental Research, 4243 Spruce Street, Philadelphia, PA. 19104. See also relevant articles in NBD.

BARRETT, C. K., *The New Testament Background* (London, 1957).

BLAIKLOCK, E. M., *Out of the Earth* (London, 1957).

BRUCE, F. F., *Second Thoughts on the Dead Sea Scrolls*[3] (Exeter, 1966).

DEISSMANN, A., *Light from the Ancient East*[4], E.T. (London, 1927).

FINEGAN, J., *Light from the Ancient Past*[2] (Princeton and Oxford, 1959).

FINEGAN, J., *The Archaeology of the New Testament*, 2 vols. (Princeton, 1969; Boulder, Colorado, 1981).

GRANT, R. M. and FREEDMAN, D. N., *The Secret Sayings of Jesus* (London, 1960).

HARRISON, R. K., *Archaeology of the New Testament.* Teach Yourself Books (London, 1963).

HELMBOLD, A. K., *The Nag Hammadi Gnostic Texts and the Bible* (Grand Rapids, 1967).

KIRSCHBAUM, E., *The Tombs of St. Peter and St. Paul*, E.T. (London, 1959).

METZGER, H., *St. Paul's Journeys in the Greek Orient*, E.T. (London, 1955).

MILLIGAN, G., *Here and There among the Papyri* (London, 1922).

MOULTON, J. H., *From Egyptian Rubbish Heaps* (London, 1916).

PARROT, A., *Golgotha and the Church of the Holy Sepulchre*, E.T. (London, 1957).

PARROT, A., *The Temple of Jerusalem*, E.T. (London, 1957).

PFEIFFER, C. F. (ed.), *The Biblical World* (London, 1967), especially articles 'Bethesda', 'Emmaus', 'Nag Hammadi Gnostic Texts', 'Oxyrhynchus Papyri', 'Pontius Pilate'.

RAMSAY, W. M., *The Bearing of Recent Discovery on the Trustworthiness of the New Testament* (London, 1915).

THOMPSON, J. A., *The Bible and Archaeology* (Grand Rapids and Exeter, 1962).

UNGER, M. F., *Archaeology and the New Testament* (Grand Rapids, 1962).

VAN UNNIK, W. C., *Newly Discovered Gnostic Writings*, E.T. (London, 1958).

YAMAUCHI, E. M., *The Archaeology of New Testament Cities in Western Asia Minor* (Grand Rapids, 1980).

AN ENVIRONMENTAL BACKGROUND TO THE NEW TESTAMENT

J. M. HOUSTON

Four miles to the east of Naples lie the excavated ruins of Herculaneum, perhaps the most perfectly preserved of the Roman towns. On the upper floor of one of the largest houses there is a modest apartment that was rented possibly by some craftsman or merchant. There, on a white stuccoed panel, is imprinted a large cross.[1] If associated with a Christian family, it demonstrates the existence of the Christian faith in this small town of 4–5,000 inhabitants before it was engulfed in mud-flows from the eruption of Vesuvius in A.D. 79. More vivid still is the *graffito* on the wall of a house in the Palatine district of Rome. Here the representation of the Crucifixion is a blasphemy (fig. 1). Christ is depicted with an ass's head, suspended on a cross. Alongside it, there reads in illiterate scrawl with contemptuous scorn: 'Alexamenos worships God'.[2] Perhaps a slave, Alexamenos was certainly the butt of his fellows for being a Christian. At opposite ends of the Roman world there is also evidence of the spread of Christianity. At the Roman

Fig. 1

fort of Dura Europos built on the Euphrates a house-church has been excavated. A room, later enlarged with two more to hold possibly a hundred people, together with baptistery and murals of Biblical scenes, has been unearthed, dating from the third century.[3] At Lullingstone villa near Eynsford in Kent, England, one small room clearly used as a chapel has on the wall a monogram with the letters 'Alpha and Omega'. It dates from the fourth century.[4]

Here, then, is archaeological evidence of the rapid spread of Christianity. While the abundant testimony to personal faith can be read in the thousands of epigrams in the Roman catacombs, the essential simplicity of the primitive church may be inferred from the meagre evidence of these house-churches. It is not until the age of Constantine and the acceptance of Christianity as the official religion of the state, that ecclesiastical architecture is developed and archaeological finds become abundant.

The simple atmosphere of these household meetings is vividly recaptured in Ac. 20: 7–8 when the Apostle Paul visited Troas. Biblical discourse, before the Breaking of Bread, harked back probably to the synagogue with its ministry of the Word. Christian life, however, centred around a novelty, the celebration of the Lord's Supper, as described in 1 C. 11: 23–26. Originally in Jerusalem, the Christian Jews used a communal meal as the setting for the Breaking of Bread, or Eucharist. It was the Lord's Supper.

Even when the Christians formed only a small minority in the local community, they were scattered in the town and they did not form ghettoes. In the second century, Tertullian objected to the accusation that the Christians were anti-social and a caste apart. 'How is it that we are called a burden to the community, we who live with you, who eat the same food, wear the same clothing, have the same furniture and other necessities of life? We are not Brahmans or Indian yogis, dwellers in the woods, and exiles from civil life . . . We live in this world with you, making use of your forum, meat market, baths, inns, shops, farms, markets, and every other commercial venture. We sail, serve in the army, go on vacations and trade with you. We mix with you and even publish our works for you to use'.[5]

The inscriptions of the catacombs testify clearly to this.[6] Christians occupied all walks of life, all grades of society and diverse cultures. This is itself legitimate reason for having some background to the geographical, political, social and religious environments of Primitive Christianity. There is also the challenge of Polybius that has been taken up now by many generations of classical scholars. 'Can anyone be so indifferent or idle', he asked, 'as not to care to know by what means and under what kind of polity, almost the whole inhabited world was conquered and brought under the dominion of the single city of Rome, and that too within a period of not quite fifty-three years?' That is not quite our challenge, but rather the quest of how a small community of Jesus' disciples in Jerusalem could scatter and multiply in this Roman world. What facilities did they have? What problems did they face in their society? What differences of environment, of culture, of modes of life, did they have? These are immense questions and no one can be a professional in attempting to answer them all. Nor are we sure that in the criticism of evidence due weight is attached correctly. We never can think exactly as those in the past were influenced to think.

THE CLASSICAL WORLD

It was probably the pagans at Antioch who first called the followers of Christ 'Christian'. It was the Emperor Nero who first made membership of this group a crime, distinguished Christians from Jews and proclaimed their faith to be illicit. It was Pliny the Younger, in his report to the Emperor Trajan, who first produced an imperial edict concerning the treatment of all Christians. Thus it was in, and by, the conflict with Rome that Christianity became more formalized until eventually hostility was changed to public favour and acceptance in A.D. 312. The rise of the Catholic Church was thus the first world-wide religious organization to be accepted officially within the Roman Empire.[8] However, the indirect contribution made by Rome to the spread of Christianity was much more important. It presented Christian missionary enterprise with the gifts of justice, good roads, a uniform coinage and a common language. Never before or since have such gifts been provided more opportunely. It was as the Apostles realized, 'the fulness of the times'.[9]

i. Pax Romana

The concept of a world empire was not new in 31 B.C. when the Roman Republic was finally transformed into an imperial dictatorship.

Much earlier, the great hydraulic societies of the Near East had developed the massive organization of technical co-division of labour, efficient transport and despotism, in the irrigated plains of Egypt and Mesopotamia. Then arose the Persian Empire with its proud symbol of a highway between Susa and Ephesus 1,800 miles away. Alexander the Great bridged the Dardanelles to link Greece with an Asiatic empire that stretched to the Himalayas and the Gobi desert. It was left, however, to the Romans to be first to convert the Mediterranean Sea and its surrounding lands into one empire. This waterway gave cohesion to a vast domain, forming the axis of an ellipse that stretched 2,300 miles from the Straits of Gibraltar to the Syrian coast. Wherever possible, the borders were geographical: the transition between the deciduous and coniferous forest zones of the Rhine and upper Danube; the desert border of the Sahara; and the Euphrates in the east.

After two centuries of uncertainty, the Augustan era was heralded as a new age of peace. It was a peace guarded by an army of less than three hundred thousand men, but the Roman roads enabled its twenty-seven legions to be concentrated at trouble spots.[10] Travel by Roman roads was indeed better organized in the time of Paul's missionary work than in Wesley's tour of England eighteen hundred years later. Not until modern times was there the same security from pirates on the high seas.[11] Thus political unity was achieved through good communications. The letters of Paul give us some idea of how thought could travel throughout the Empire, even by men who were not wealthy by Roman standards. True, Roman peace may be exaggerated as Paul's own encounter with robbers would attest. Moreover, imperial propaganda through the coinage did not give the missionaries all the free hand they might have wished. 'Whose is this image and superscription? And they said unto Him, Caesar's'.[12] Likewise the events of Paul's life in Syria were to be re-examined and judged 1,500 miles away in Rome.

ii. Citizenship

For the government of his empire, Augustus wisely refrained from hastening a unified legislation. He combined a strong central government with many forms of local independence. This is seen vividly in the Gospels in the administration of Judaea; a governor directly responsible to the Emperor in Judaea proper and Samaria; a native ruler like Herod the tetrarch in Galilee and Transjordan. There were cities which possessed the full Roman franchise; *coloniae* that had been settled by Roman citizens and *municipia* where citizenship had been given to a previously autonomous community.[13] The spread of Roman citizenship was restricted to those who could genuinely represent the Roman way of life. At its apogee there were 5,627 civic bodies in the Empire, each a 'package' arrangement containing those physical facilities of forum, baths, theatres, stadium, library, shops, etc., that were required to Romanize the populace.[14] Thus Paul was proud to be both a citizen of Tarsus—'no mean city'—and of Rome.

iii. Commerce

Roman law and roads, together, laid the foundation for much mercantile enterprise. Rome came to depend on the import of some 180,000–190,000 tons of wheat each year, employing a fleet of up to 2,000 vessels.[15] Much of the grain was brought from Sicily and Egypt. The eighth hill of Rome, Monte Testaccio, is eloquent testimony of the oil trade with Andalusia, for it was the rubbish heap built up of broken *amphorae*. The silver mines of Cartagena enriched the coinage. The finest pottery came from Southern Gaul. During the first two centuries, Roman enterprise linked the commerce of the Indian Ocean with that of the Mediterranean.[16] The Nile delta became a conservatory, where exotics like rice, bananas, sugar cane, citrus fruits, etc., could be first cultivated away from their native hearth of south-east Asia. The range of commodities traded, notably by Greek and Syrian merchants, is catalogued in Revelation: 'cargoes of gold and silver, jewels and pearls, cloths of purple and scarlet, silks and fine linen, all kinds of scented woods, bronze, iron and marble, cinnamon and spice, incense, perfumes and frankincense, wine, oil, flour and wheat, sheep

and cattle, horses, chariots, slaves, and the lives of men. The fruit you longed for'.[17]

With such commerce we also meet Christian traders such as Lydia in Philippi, three hundred miles away from her native city. Among Christian travellers, apart from Paul and his companions, we meet Phoebe journeying to Rome from Corinth; Epaphroditus travelling from Rome to Philippi; Aquila and Priscilla are recorded at Rome, Ephesus, Corinth and again in Ephesus.[18]

Roman coinage had a political propaganda value rather like the varied issues of postage stamps today. But a common coinage was of inestimable value. It facilitated in the Primitive Church the ready assistance of charity between the Greek churches and Judaea, recorded in 2 Corinthians.[19] With its mixed government and at the threshold of varied cultures, the Palestine of the Gospels, however, reflects a mixed lot: the Roman *as*,[20] *quadrans*,[21] and *denarii*;[22] Greek *talents*,[23] *didrachma*, *drachmas*[24] and *stater*;[25] *lepta* and *mina*.[26] No wonder money-changers are mentioned in Jerusalem. The impact of a decree from Caesar Augustus that all the world should be enrolled in A.D. 6 had not yet standardized the Palestine 'hoards' of the period.

iv. A Common Language

The Lord's rule to the disciples: 'Go into all the world', was also facilitated by the use of a common language. All the documents of the NT were written in Greek and even the Gospel tradition, formed in the first instance in Aramaic, has been transmitted in a Greek dress.[27] This was called by the grammarians the 'Com-

The major roads in Roman times.

mon Dialect' to distinguish it from regional dialects of Greek. It was the *lingua franca* of the common people, only a few of whom were Greeks.[28] The name 'Greek' was no longer a national but a cultural term, as for example in Mk 7: 26: 'A Greek woman, Syro-Phoenician by race'.

The importance of Greek, circulated with Hellenistic culture in the Mediterranean world, was more than the convenience of a common language. With the balanced, humanistic ideal of the development of the whole man, Greek had a richer vocabulary than Latin. As Lucretius acknowledged: 'It is a hard task to set clearly in the light the dark discoveries of the Greeks, above all when many things must be treated in new words because of the poverty of our tongue and the newness of the themes'.[29] For in every branch of knowledge Hellenistic scholars had reached new conclusions by the application of reason.

It was this living, universal language that had already contributed to the rebirth of the Hebrew Scriptures in the Septuagint. After the Greek translation of the OT in Alexandria had begun in the third century B.C., the diffusion of the Scriptures in the vernacular was not dissimilar to the impact made by Wyclif in the fourteenth and Coverdale in the sixteenth century. From an appeal to the Scriptures, Paul was able to demonstrate that Christ is the real content of them.[30] The apostolic appeal to the Septuagint is itself evidence of its knowledge by Hellenized Jews.

v. The Diaspora

Wherever the pioneer Christian missionaries went, they had a ready-made audience among the scattered colonies of Hellenized Jews. Their number is only an intelligent series of guesses, such as Philo made in Egypt. Perhaps 7 per cent of the total population of the Roman world, or some 4–4.5 million Jews, existed in the reign of Tiberius.[31] There were about a million of them in Egypt, rather more in Syria and perhaps less than 700,000 in Palestine. There were at least 10,000 in Rome, with other large colonies in the great mercantile cities of Greece and Asia Minor. Beyond the Empire, they were also massed in Mesopotamia and Media. As Josephus observed: 'There is not a community in the entire world which does not have a portion of our people'.[32] During the struggles for power, Julius Caesar had received the support of the Jews, and his decrees on their behalf have been called their Magna Carta.[33] For three more centuries they enjoyed special privileges, including the full freedom of worship.

As a revealed religion, Judaism took itself seriously. The unique importance of the Law was emphasized, in whose observance a Jew had no ulterior motive but the love of God

and obedience to His Word. Moral purity was stressed. For the first time in its history, Judaism had begun to blossom out from being a national faith to a world religion. Proudly the Jew felt he had something to proclaim to the whole world.[34] As Harnack has indicated, the Christian was indebted to the Jews for six reasons: A field tilled all over the Empire; religious communities already formed in the towns; the background of the Holy Scriptures and liturgy; the habit of regular worship and the control of private life; impressive apologetics on behalf of monotheism, ethics and God's purposes in history; and the feeling that witness was a duty.[35] So great was the debt, as Paul well appreciated (Rom. 9: 1–5; 10), that at first Christianity appeared to be no more than a sect of Judaism. But in the uproar that followed, the division became sharper and bitterer, until John the Apostle could speak vehemently of 'those who say that they are Jews, and are not, but are a synagogue of Satan'.[36] We have the reference in Suetonius's biography of Claudius that the Emperor 'expelled from Rome the Jews who persisted in rioting at the instigation of Chrestus', perhaps between A.D. 41 and 49.[37] Among those driven out were Aquila and Priscilla (Ac. 18: 2).

CHRISTIANITY IN PAGAN SOCIETY

Another and even more menacing conflict was that between Christianity and pagan society. This was largely fought out in the field of private life. The ordinary pagans thought of the Christian as essentially anti-social, and on this basis their relations must often have been very strained.

i. Social Life

Roman society was divided fairly rigidly into social classes. All free-born were separate from slaves who originally had no legal rights or even personality. Many were treated like brute-beasts. The aristocracy of senators and knights had legal protection that favoured the miscreant much more than in the lower classes. As a fellowship of brotherly love, where in Christ there was neither slave nor free, the freedom of spirit and personal dignity realized would appreciably affect pagan households. Already Jewish slaves were unpopular as they insisted on the observance of the seventh day and refused to eat pagan food. Their ready redemption by fellow Jews was often accepted with alacrity. Similar trends might well have developed with Christian slaves, although Paul's letter to Philemon clearly indicates the Christian leaders had no intention of deliberately upsetting the *status quo*.

Slavery degraded marriage, for it introduced concubinage into family life. Not the slightest stigma was attached to it by public opinion, and the average Roman lacked any ideal to counter this practice. Seneca reveals the state of affairs: 'No woman need blush to break off her marriage since the most illustrious ladies have adopted the practice of reckoning the year not by the names of the consuls but by those of their husbands. They divorce in order to remarry. They marry in order to divorce'.[38] Another cause of this laxity was the diminution of the stern discipline of the *pater familias* since the days of the Republic. Women were in many cases as emancipated as they are now, and such feminism tended to emulate man's vices. Children tended to be spoilt. At the same time infanticide was common, an unwanted baby being 'exposed', often left on the rubbish heap to die of hunger, cold or be devoured by the dogs. Paul's picture of pagan society in Romans chapter one is no exaggeration of its morals.

The boredom and leisure of the populace could be dangerous to the state. It was in the political interest, therefore, that the chariot races of the circus diverted the passions of the masses with their thrills and gambling. In the theatre, slices of pagan life were served up, hot and spicy, nearing the limit of even Roman conventions. The amphitheatre with its gladiatorial spectacle of human slaughter was foul and debased.[39] The baths where the citizens took their daily afternoon wash were the most innocent of daily pleasures, but even here the social life and the opportunities for promiscuity made them feared by the Christians.[40] The one main meal of the day, in the evening, was the occasion of much drunkenness and gluttony. Clubs were an important feature of Roman life where further licence was found. Faced by all these features of daily life, the Christians had to reject a great deal. No wonder they were viewed as killjoys, whose negativism did so much to stir the wrath of the pagans. When the Christians were thrown to the lions it would cause pagan satisfaction that they were both forced to attend the very amphitheatre they had denounced and also provided a Roman holiday at their martyrdom.

ii. Economic Life
The Augustan peace had fostered trade immensely. The spirit of materialism dominated life in the cities. Private enterprise was open and individual fortunes were amassed. The blatant display of luxuries and the waste of money by the rich, caused blind discontent among the masses.[41] Sycophancy was ostentatious and beggary rapacious. The paying of homage to patrons and superiors involved each day a merry-go-round of salaams. Trade was split into a multitude of specialist lines, and Rome alone had over 150 corporations, which Augustus co-ordinated by careful legislation.

Living in such a hostile environment, the collective forbearance of the Christians could readily touch the pockets of the pagan tradesmen until it hurt them.[43] At Philippi and Ephesus, Paul was attacked by the men whose business had suffered by the preaching of the gospel. When the meat market with its sales of cheaper meat that had been offered to the idols was boycotted, the effect would be felt in poorer Christian homes. Many Christians, however, must have found it very difficult to decide how far to compromise with pagan society. Between Paul's advice on the eating of sacrificial meat and John's denunciation of the Nicolaitans, there must have existed many fine and difficult decisions to make.

iii. Religion
The materialism of Roman life contributed to the decay of pagan religion. Priesthood could not be held with a secular office, and as every man of good family had business in the provinces, few would be attracted. Many temples in the Augustan era fell into neglect.[44] Moreover, the old gods of the household, under the Republic, had been associated originally with the spirits of nature and of the needs of agriculture. Their relevance to city life was less obvious. Roman religion had little to offer in the way of emotional appeal, and of the explanation of life and its immediate problems. The Roman stood on the narrow base of 'right and duty', of observance of traditional cults, rather than with a concern for personal belief.[45] The thoughtful who viewed the gods as mere superstitions, had nothing to replace them, and as the practice of ceremonial cults was all that society demanded, their inner thoughts might never be revealed.

As the migration of peoples intensified with the expansion of the Empire, mystic cults of the East—of Osiris, Mithras and numerous lesser superstitions—were introduced.[46] The intellectual muddle of 'gods many, lords many' could not be overcome, despite some efforts at syncretism. The only questions asked concerning their adoption by the State were three: Would they upset the existing cults? Were they politically unsafe? Were they morally undesirable?[47] As grossly immoral rites were associated with the Eastern cults, especially that of Isis, their worship on occasion was stopped, but never permanently. Added to the amalgam were demonology, astrology, magic and mystery religions.

From the time of Augustus onwards, there appeared also the worship of the Emperor. In the Provinces of the Eastern Mediterranean, the cult had a spontaneous growth, and their peoples readily accepted godhead in their rulers. In Italy, however, the idea of ascribing divinity in any sense to a man was repugnant.[48] There, the 'deification' of the Emperor meant little more than a certain sacrosanctity to the office and the observance of loyalty, flattery and whatever sycophancy would be tolerated.

iv. Persecution of the Christians

It is well attested that the first Roman persecution of the Christians occurred after the Fire of Rome in A.D. 64. Nero might well have chosen the Jews as a scapegoat for the event, had not the Empress Poppaea Sabina been particularly sympathetic to the Jews. Instead, he used the Christians. From then until the Decian persecution of A.D. 250-1, the persecution went on automatically, if sporadically. It is fallacious to distinguish between 'good' and 'bad' Emperors, according to their treatment of the Christians. Until the third century, it was the provincial governor who played the more significant rôle. As Pilate had yielded Jesus to the cries of the Jews, so too later governors were often influenced by public outcry against the Christians.[49] At Ephesus and elsewhere the apostle Paul had seen how the mob could be whipped up into a frenzy, and after Nero's persecution the Christians were a conspicuous sally for public discontent, wherever there was a disaster. As Tertullian said: 'If the Tiber overflows or the Nile doesn't, if there is a drought or an earthquake, a famine or a pestilence, at once the cry goes up, "The Christians to the lions"'.[50] The monotheistic exclusiveness of the Christians was believed to alienate the gods, and in the closely-knit structure of Roman life this was considered a danger to all—state and individuals.

The Jews were recognized to be different. They were atheists on licence, because their customs were venerable with age and could be overlooked because of their antiquity. But the Christians had actually departed from their ancestral rites. The negative attitude towards the pagan way of life created deepest resentment, and for those who wished to stir up trouble for the Christians it only needed to be pointed out that their practices were treasonable.[51] They worshipped a man who had been condemned to death in Judaea for a treasonable offence. Their loyalty to the state was doubtful because they refused to swear an oath by the Emperor's Genius. They were always talking about the end of the world. One of their writers had spoken in bitter hatred of Rome, prophesying its doom in the thin disguise of Babylon. As Trajan instructed Pliny, governor of Bithynia, procedure was simple. Whoever acknowledged that he belonged to Christ and recanted not the Name, could be punished with death. Perhaps at Pergamum some had been put to death for refusal even to worship the Emperor,[55] but normally this test was not applied. The Name they bore was usually the sole charge. Yet it was this intense idealism of the Early Church to die for their faith, that gave them such dynamic power. As Tertullian exclaimed: 'The blood of the Christians is seed',[54] seed that flourished with an increasing missionary harvest.

v. Philosophy

There was, finally, the encounter the Christians constantly faced with philosophy. Its emphasis on man's needs was more pragmatic than much modern philosophy, and it was popularized by open-air preachers. On Paul's visit to Athens we read that certain philosophers of the Epicureans and of the Stoics encountered him[55] in a city where the founders of both movements had taught.

The serious followers of Epicurus are misrepresented in associating them with desire only for physical pleasures;[56] rather peace of mind was their quest. Like some modern psychiatrists, the Epicureans considered religion was the chief enemy to eradicate, for it only stirred up fears of the mind and what we would term today 'guilt-complexes'. They denied the existence of life after death so there could be no substance for fear in hell or the after-life. The universe merely consisted of the chance association of atoms and void. Happiness, which was the great good for man to attain, could be achieved through the cultivation of the quiet mind and of friendships. Evil was avoided by justice. Thus Epicureanism was a gospel of escape, of ignoring the problems, and not facing them.

Much more important in the Western Mediterranean was Stoicism, which suited the Roman temperament and dominated Rome for three centuries.[57] Zeno had diagnosed desire as the fundamental sickness of man, of which other evils were symptoms. An earlier philosopher, Heraclitus, had discovered Reason to be both in the centre of human life and in the Universe. By allowing personal reason to be in harmony with cosmic Reason, or Nature, man could be self-sufficient and defy evil. Such a faith could put steel into disillusioned Romans but it gave scope only for the mind, not the emotions. It gave support to the cosmopolitanism of Roman law, for if the Greek was the genius of beauty, the Jew the genius of righteousness, the Roman was the genius of law. Hence Stoicism had great power in the Roman world, and it was advocated by some of its finest men.

However, the abnormal opportunities for self-indulgence in the period brought decay to even the noblest system of thought. Epicureanism popularized turned to vice. Stoicism's elastic ability to come to terms with the gods gave popular superstitions a spurious respectability. Moreover it tended to widen the gulf between state morals and individual immorality. Christianity succeeded for the masses in its unique capacity to meet the social needs of the age.[58] That God should be righteous, yet still love the sinner, must have been a potent attraction.

Ideas were put into practice and not simply discussed. Hospitality to the stranger, the warm and friendly fellowship of house-churches,[59] the consistent practice of ethical ideals in family life, must all have met the social needs of many a convert.

REGIONAL ENVIRONMENTAL FEATURES

In the physical and social environments of Primitive Christianity that both repelled and fostered the growth of its communities, there were also nuances and even marked differences. After all, the territory of the Roman Empire was vast and its habitats, peoples and cultures of varied character. Four regional contexts may be distinguished: Judaea, Syria, Asia Minor and the cities of Greece and Rome. Egypt, with its great Jewish community in Alexandria, might be a fifth, but little is known of it in the first century and it is not a relevant NT background.[60]

i. Judaea

A fundamental distinction in Mediterranean environments that has lasted since classical times is that of town and country, the former progressive and commercial, the latter conservative and agricultural. Now the scenery of the Gospels is essentially rural despite reference to our Lord's ministry at Jerusalem, notably during the Passion Week. The rural world of the Gospels is also of limited extent, involving journeys on foot of no more than three days from west to east, and perhaps a week from

THE PALESTINE OF THE GOSPELS

(Places mentioned in the New Testament are underlined)

——— Provincial frontiers
----- Main roads

0 5 10   20   30 Miles

north to south. Its so-called 'towns', many of ancient origin, have been for long no more than rural centres fostering the agricultural needs of a district. It was only Hellenistic influence that grafted on rural Palestine 'towns' in the Roman sense; such were Caesarea, founded in 22 B.C., and Tiberias, c. A.D. 18. The Hellenistic 'cities' of the Decapolis on the east side of Palestine remained small throughout the first century.

With its higher rainfall and deeper soils, Galilee was particularly well populated. Some of its numerous villages according to Josephus had 15,000 inhabitants or more. Of the 47 synagogues known to have existed in Roman Palestine, about 33 were in Galilee. Mark describes accurately the custom of these larger centres with their synagogues administering a district or toparchy;[61] its officials are alluded to in the parable of the talents. This hierarchical system of village administration is very ancient, and there are comparable allusions to it in Vedic literature, in India.[62] Judges rather than city magistrates are referred to, and the court life of petty, rural monarchs is described. There is the example of a single village defying the authority of such a 'king'. Scenes from the countryside are frequent in the parables and other sayings of our Lord. As Sherwin-White has noted: 'The absence of Graeco-Roman colouring is a convincing feature of the Galilean narrative and parables. Rightly, it is only where the scene changes to Jerusalem that the Roman administrative machine manifests itself, in all three accounts, with the procurator and his troops and tribunal, and the machinery of taxation'.[63]

Judaean Christians must at first have been largely country-folk, to whom were added Hellenistic town-dwellers, notably in Jerusalem. Their distinct outlook led to a cleavage and the appointment of seven guardians of the poor, all having Greek names. Chief among them was Stephen, stoned as the first martyr because of his implication that the cultus of the Temple no longer mattered. This view was also shared by some of the Diaspora who were not Christians. Like Huss, Stephen died for an issue he could not foresee. It is likely that the Jewish Christians, still orthodox in their observance of the Law, were left alone by the authorities. There were already various parties within the commonwealth of Israel, such as the Pharisees, Sadducees, Zealots and Essenes. In the minds of orthodox Jews, the Nazarenes were admitted probably as yet another group, whose absurd claim to know the Messiah personally was largely undermined by His crucifixion. Their only danger was a political one, for in an age of threatened revolt the Nazarenes' daily prayer for a 'kingdom' and their expectation of the return of their Messiah could be conflagratory propaganda for hotheads. Perhaps it was for this reason that in A.D. 62, in the interregnum between the Roman procurators Festus and Albinus, the high priest caused James, leader of the Jerusalem community, and others to be stoned. Four years later, extremists took over the city and Jerusalem was destroyed by the Romans in A.D. 70.

Meanwhile, at the Council of Jerusalem in *c.* A.D. 49, the distinction between Gentile Christians and Jewish Christians had been faced and settled somewhat vaguely. Philip's mission in Samaria, and Peter at Caesarea, had involved the Nazarenes in this difficult problem of Jewish-Gentile relations. Paul's own activities caused greatest embarrassment to the orthodox. By A.D. 64 Rome, however, had clearly distinguished between Jews and Christians, and by A.D. 70 they had diverged in Palestine. Those engaged in missionary enterprise and a universal church now looked north to Syria and west to the Mediterranean world. Those orthodox, anxious to conserve their Jewish roots, migrated to Pella in Transjordan after the death of James.[64] There, they are lost sight of, although traces of them are found down to the Muslim conquest.

ii. Syria
Much more Hellenized was Syria to the north. Great highways from Damascus south to Arabia, and from Antioch east to Mesopotamia, laid it open to much cultural influence from the Orient. It traded with the Mediterranean and beyond, through its Phoenician ports. It boasted some of the greatest cities of classical times, Antioch 'the Vienna of the Near East', Damascus rich in irrigated lands.[65] It was to this cosmopolitan, city life that the first missionaries came from Jerusalem, Barnabas the Cypriot, Simeon Niger, Lucius of Cyrene, Manaen and Paul.[66] At Antioch, the third city of the Empire, there was the first Gentile community of Christians. So distinct were they from the Jews that their pagan opponents nicknamed them 'Christians'.[67] Antioch was also the point of departure for the first mission to the Gentiles and a base of operations for men like Barnabas, Paul and Silas. Possibly, too, it was from Antioch that the gospel was first taken to Rome, for through its seaport of Seleucia there was constant communication with the west.

The Judaism of Syria appears to have been different from that of Palestine.[68] It is no wonder that in its mixed communities questions like circumcision were ignored until delegates from Jerusalem, three hundred miles away, disturbed the peace. In this area of diverse cultures and easy ways, syncretistic tendencies were encouraged. We have the example of false prophets like Simon Magus. Together with Samaria and Alexandria, this was a great spawning ground of Gnosticism. It is a tradition that Luke was a native of Antioch. Some think Matthew's Gospel was written in Syria and that perhaps James wrote his letter for the benefit of Syrian believers. Geographically and theologically, Syria proved to be a bridgehead between Judaea and Asia Minor.

Asia Minor.

iii. Asia Minor

The task of evangelism in Asia Minor might have seemed much more formidable. Its great size of 200,000 square miles, its remote high interior and the illiterate paganism of its country folk were all major obstacles.[69] There is, however, clear evidence that the apostolic missions were carefully and strategically planned. Paul's Syrian base of Antioch, his Cilician birthplace of Tarsus where he had lived for some years after his conversion, his Roman citizenship and, above all, his clear understanding of the call to evangelize the Gentile world, placed him in a strong position to penetrate Asia Minor.[70] This he did by use of both sea-routes and the highways of the interior. The road net-work was the legacy of Persian, Seleucid and Roman engineering, and he kept to the major highways.[71] Also, he and his companions concentrated attention on the major cities with the Graeco-Roman culture, and it was not until later that the country districts were evangelized.

Along the south coast was the province of Cilicia, with poor communications. Here the Taurus range narrows the coastal plain and is a formidable obstacle, best traversed through the Cilician Gates north of Tarsus. As in Cyprus, Cilicia had early received contact from Christian missionaries, but there is little subsequent reference to it. To the east, Cappadocia was more isolated and scarcely reached with the Gospel. The central districts of Pamphylia, south Galatia and Lycaonia were contacted in the mission of Paul and Barnabas. Although the synagogues were first visited, the Gentile church of Pisidian-Antioch was one of the earliest successes in the pagan world. The northern province of Bithynia was later to become one of the strongholds of Christianity as Pliny's concern attests. Paul was guided, however, to turn his footsteps westwards. The province of Asia was the wealthiest and most urbanized of Asia Minor, stretching along the west coast where the great overland routes terminated. Ephesus, the richest city and chief seaport, was also the great missionary headquarters of the apostle. Within easy reach there were twelve churches established, seven of which are enumerated in John's letters to the churches.

The documents of these churches, Ephesians, Colossians, 1 Peter and the Johannine writings—especially the rich allusions of Revelation[72]—clearly demonstrate specific dangers that faced these communities. Judaizing teachers that dogged Paul's footsteps are alluded to frequently, notably in the letter to the Galatians and most harshly later still in John's Apocalypse. Converts who reverted to paganism or compromised with pagan ways are recognized, perhaps in the guise of the 'Nicolaitans'.[73] Later, Pliny refers to those who had renounced their Christian faith some twenty years previously.[74] The worship of the Emperor, traditional to the Asians, was a severe test of some communities, notably at Pergamum, a royal city and seat of the Proconsul.[75] Syncretism, and the spread of Gnosticism were recognized, especially in 1 John, as a growing threat.[76] The affluent society, in rich trading centres, was also a cause of spiritual decadence,

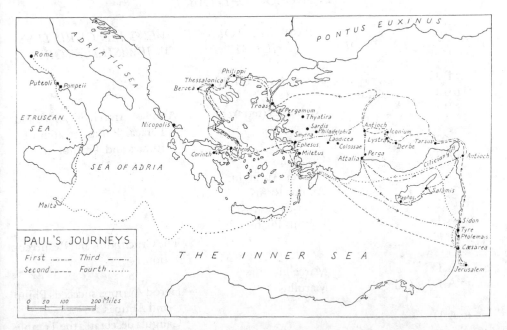

PAUL'S JOURNEYS

First .... Third _.._.._.

Second ____ Fourth ....

0   50   100   200 Miles

in Ephesus and notably so in Laodicea. Thus in the apostolic age, the very environment where Christianity had been most successfully established, was also most in peril.

iv. The European Churches

In Asia Minor Christianity, although introduced first into the cities, spread by the end of the first century into the villages of the countryside. Village churches became an important feature of Phrygia; and Bithynia has already been mentioned.[77] However, in Europe the Christian communities remained for much longer concentrated in cities. Probably Paul may have founded three churches in the province of Macedonia: Philippi, a Roman military colony; Thessalonica, now Salonica, the seat of the proconsul and chief seaport; and Berea, a regional centre. From their inception they had been in touch with Asia Minor. Consequently the same perils, notably Gnosticism, that endangered Antioch and Asia also affected Philippi. In Achaia, Paul had laboured longer, with scant results in Athens, but with some success in Corinth, then the greatest city of Greece, and at its seaport of Cenchreae. The First Epistle of Clement, sent to it c. A.D. 96, indicates that it had become a very large church, but affected by schism.[78] Many foreign Christians visited it, so that news of discord travelled quickly. Perhaps from it the gospel had been taken to Crete.[79] But the cause of the disunity which gave such bad testimony to the Church Universal was conflict between officialdom and the Spirit.

In the Western Mediterranean, Rome is the only church of which we have any data, although there was also a community at the Neapolitan seaport of Puteoli before Paul's arrival. The beginnings of Christianity in Gaul and North Africa may have taken place also in the first century. The church at Rome was started through unknown missionaries. There, at the end of his life, Paul worked for several years unhindered, if not free. Some converts had been made in the imperial household, but as the Emperor had some 20,000 slaves alone, it is clear that many might not have been freedmen. Tradition also maintains that Peter came and died in Rome; as John indicates in his Gospel, he was crucified.[80] The persecution of the Roman Christians in A.D. 64 is briefly mentioned by Suetonius[81] and at length by Tacitus.[82] It was then, perhaps, that both apostles were martyred.

If the Roman church was particularly vulnerable to persecution, the imperial household was also open to influence by Christianity through its servants. There is thus evidence that in Domitian's reign, relatives of the Emperor were themselves accused and condemned for being Christians. But this church served non-Latin, that is Greek-speaking, peoples whose cosmopolitan character enabled it to maintain a universal rather than parochial character, and in the break-down of paganism Christianity was to offer a new hope for the World.

CHRONOLOGICAL TABLE

DATE	EMPERORS	PROCURATORS OF JUDAEA	EVENTS IN CHRISTIAN OR JEWISH HISTORY
37 B.C.		Herod the Great (King)	
31 B.C.	Augustus		
4 B.C.		Archelaus (tetrarch)	Antipas tetrarch of Galilee and Peraea. Philip tetrarch of Ituraea and Trachonitis
6 A.D.		Coponius	
?		Marcus Ambivius	
?		Annius Rufus	
14 A.D.	Tiberius	Valerius Gratus	
26 A.D.		Pontius Pilate	
c. 29–30 A.D.			The Crucifixion and Resurrection
36 A.D.		Marcellus	
37 A.D.	Caligula	Marullus	Herod Agrippa succeeds Philip and Antipas
40 A.D.			Caligula desecrates the Temple

41 A.D.	Claudius	Herod Agrippa (King)	Death of James, son of Zebedee. Death of Herod. Paul's missionary journeys, 41–54
45 A.D.		Cuspius Fadus	
46 A.D.		Tiberius Alexander	Famine
48 A.D.		Ventidius Cumanus	
49 A.D.			The Apostolic Council
51–52 A.D.			Gallio, proconsul of Achaea
52 A.D.		Felix	
54 A.D.	Nero		
59 A.D.?		Porcius Festus	
61 A.D.?		Albinus	Death of James, the Lord's brother
64 A.D.		Gessius Florus	Fire of Rome and persecution of Christians
66 A.D.			The Jewish Revolt
69 A.D.	Vespasian		
70 A.D.			Destruction of Jerusalem
79 A.D.	Titus		
81 A.D.	Domitian		Further persecution of Christians
96 A.D.	Nerva		
98–117 A.D.	Trajan		

REFERENCES

1. Istituto Geografico de Agostini, *Herculaneum and the villa of the Papyri*, 1963, pp. 25–26.
2. Gough, M., *The Early Christians*, London, 1961, p. 83.
3. Rostovtzeff, M. I., *Excavations at Dura Europos, Preliminary Report on fifth season of work*, Oxford 1934.
4. Meates, G. W., *Lullingstone Roman Villa*, London, 1955.
5. Tertullian, *Apologeticus*, 42, 1–3.
6. Hertling, L. and Kirschbaum, E., *The Roman Catacombs*, London, 1960, pp. 177–195.
7. Quoted by F. R. Cowell, *Cicero and the Roman Republic*, London, 1961, p. xi.
8. Ehrhardt, A., 'The adoption of Christianity in the Roman Empire', *Bull. John Rylands Library*, 45, 1962, pp. 97–114.
9. Gal. 4:4.
10. Mattingly, H., *Roman Imperial Civilization*, London, 1957, pp. 137–160.
11. See Charlesworth, M. P., *Trade-Routes and Commerce of the Roman Empire*, Cambridge, 1924.
12. Mt. 22:20.
13. Caird, G. B., *The Apostolic Age*, London, 1955, p. 9.
14. Houston, J. M., *The Western Mediterranean World*, London, 1964, p. 110.
15. Cowell, *op.cit., p. 117*
16. See Warmington, E. H., *The Commerce between the Roman Empire and India*, Cambridge, 1928.
17. Rev. 18:12–14, NEB.
18. The travels of Aquila and Priscilla may be traced as follows:—Rome, Ac. 18:2; Corinth, Ac. 18:2; Ephesus, Ac. 18: 19; 1 C. 16: 19; Rome, Rom. 16: 3 f.; Ephesus again, 2 Tim. 4:19.
19. 2 C. 8–9.
20. Mt. 10:29.
21. Mk 12:42; 14:5.
22. Mk 6:37.
23. Mt. 18:23–34.
24. Lk. 7:41;10:35;12:6;15:8.
25. Mt. 10:29;17:24–27.
26. Lk. 19:12–20;21:2.
27. See Beare, F. W., 'New Testament Christianity and the Hellenistic World' in *The Communication of the Gospel in New Testament Times*, A. Farrer et alii, London, 1961, pp. 57–73.
28. Lietzmann, H., *A History of the Early Church*, translated by B. L. Woolf, London, 1961, p. 89.
29. Lucretius, *De rerum natura* i. 136–139.
30. Rom. 1:2 f.
31. Harnack, A., *The Mission and Expansion of Christianity in the first three centuries*, translated by J. Moffatt, new edit., New York, 1962, pp. I–II.
32. Josephus, *Bell.* ii. 16,4.
33. Leon, H. J., *The Jews of Ancient Rome*, Philadelphia, 1960, pp. 9–10.
34. Rom. 2:19 f.
35. Harnack, *op. cit.*, p. 15.
36. Rev. 2:9;3:9.
37. Leon, *op. cit.*, p. 25.
38. Seneca, *De Beneficiis*, iii. 16,2.
39. See Carcopino, J., *Daily Life in Ancient Rome*, translated by E. O. Lorimer, London, 1962, pp. 223–270.
40. Mattingly, *op. cit.*, p. 176.

41 Cowell, *op.cit.*, pp.326–340.
42. Ac. 16:19;19:19,25.
43. See Blaiklock, E. M., *The Christian in Pagan Society*, London, 1951.
44. Fowler, W. Warde, *Social Life in Rome in the age of Cicero*, London, new edit., 1963, pp.319–352.
45. Halliday, *op.cit.*, pp.171–182.
46. See Halliday, W. R., *The Pagan Background of Early Christianity*, London, 1952.
47. Barrow, R. H., *The Romans*, London, 1949, p. 144.
48. Ibid., p. 145.
49. Ste. Croix, G. E. M.de, 'Why were the early Christians Persecuted?', *Past and Present*, 26, 1963, pp. 6–31.
50. Tertullian, *Apologeticus*, 40.1–2.
51. Frank, Tenney, *Aspects of Social Behaviour in Ancient Rome*, Cambridge, Mass., vol.2, 1932, p. 115.
52. Pliny, *Epistles* x,96 and 97.
53. Rev. 2:13.
54. Tertullian, *Apologeticus*, 50.
55. Ac.17:18.
56. Festugière, A. J., *Epicurus and his Gods*, translated by C. W. Chilton, London, 1955.
57. Bailey, C., *Phases in the Religion of Ancient Rome*, London, 1933, Ch.7.
58. See excellent study of A.D.Nock, *Early Gentile Christianity and its Hellenistic Background*, London, Torchbook edit., 1964.
59. Judge, E. A., *The Social Pattern of Christian Groups in the first century A. D.*, London, 1960.
60. Lietzmann, H., *A History of the Early Church*, translated by B. L. Woolf, London, 1953, p. 275.
61. Mk 8: 26–27.
62. Desai, A. (edit.), *Rural Sociology in India*, 1960, p. 160.
63. Sherwin-White, A. N., *Roman Society and Roman Law in the New Testament*, Oxford, 1963, pp. 127 ff.
64. See Bruce, F. F., *The Spreading Flame*, London, 1958, p. 70.
65. Jones, A. H. M., *Cities of the Eastern Roman Provinces*, Oxford, 1937.
66. Ac. 11:19 f.; 13:1.
67. Ac. 11:26.
68. Weiss, J., *Earliest Christianity*, translated by F. C. Grant, New York, 1959, vol.2, pp.756–766.
69. See Sir Wm. M. Ramsay, *St. Paul the Traveller and Roman Citizen*, London, 1896.
71. Metzger, H., *St. Paul's Journeys in the Greek Orient*, translated by Prof. S. H. Hooke, London, 1955, p. 13.
72. See Sir Wm. M. Ramsay, *The Letters to the Seven Churches*, London, 1904.
73. Blaiklock, E. M., *The Christian in Pagan Society*, *op.cit.* (n.43).
74. Pliny, *Epistles*, *loc. cit*.
75. Case, S. J., *The Evolution of Early Christianity*, London, 1914, pp.195–238.
76. See Grant, R. M., *Gnosticism and Early Christianity*, London, 1959.
77. Weiss, *op.cit.*, vol.2, pp.780–782.
78. For convenient English translation see Lake K., *The Apostolic Fathers*, 1, 9–121.
79. Tit.1:5 f.
80. Jn 21:18.
81. Suetonius, Nero, 16.
82. Tacitus, *Annals*, 15.44.

BIBLIOGRAPHY

Atlases

Atlas of the Classical World, edit. by A. A. M. Van der Heyden and H. H. Scullard (London, 1959).

Atlas of the Early Christian World, F. van der Meer and C. Mohrmann, translated and edited by M. F. Hedlund and H. H. Rowley (London, 1959).

New Atlas of the Bible, ed. J. H. Negenman, E.T. (London, 1969).

Bibliography

BAYNES, N. H., *The Early Church and Social Life*, *Hist. Assoc.* 1927, 16 pp.

TENNEY, M. C., *New Testament Survey* (London 1961). pp.433–453.

General Works

BLAIKLOCK, E. M., *The Christian in Pagan Society* (London, 1951).

BLAIKLOCK, E. M., *Rome in the New Testament* (London, 1959).

BRUCE, F. F., *The Spreading Flame* (London, 1958).

CADOUX, C. J., *The Early Church and the World* (Edinburgh, 1925).

CAIRD, G. B., *The Apostolic Age* (London, 1955).

CARY, M., *The Geographic Background of Greek and Roman History* (Oxford, 1949).

GLOVER, T. R., *The Conflict of Religions in the Early Roman Empire* (London, 1909).

GUIGNEBERT, C., *The Jewish World in the Time of Jesus*, tr. S. H. Hooke (London, 1939).

HALLIDAY, W. R., *The Pagan Background of Early Christianity* (Liverpool, 1925).

HARNACK, A., *The Mission and Expansion of Christianity*, tr. J. Moffatt (London, 1908).

LAKE, K., and CADBURY, H. J., *The Beginnings of Christianity*, vol. V.(London, 1933).

MALHERBE, A. J., *Social Aspects of Early Christianity* (Baton Rouge, 1977).

MATTINGLY, H., *Christianity in the Roman Empire* (London, 1955).

MEEKS, W. A., *The First Urban Christians* (New Haven, 1983).

MOMIGLIANO, A. (edit.), *Paganism and Christianity in the Fourth Century* (Oxford, 1963); see especially article by A. H. M. Jones, 'The Social Background of Christianity'.

MOORE, G. F., *Judaism in the First Centuries of the Christian Era* (Cambridge, Mass., 1927).

NOCK, A.D., *Early Gentile Christianity against its Hellenistic Background* (New York, 1928).

NOCK, A.D., *Conversion* (Oxford, 1933).

OAKLEY, H. CAREY, 'The Greek and Roman Background of the New Testament', *Vox Evangelica* No.1, 1962, pp.2–3.

THEISSEN, G., *The First Followers of Jesus*, E.T. (London, 1978).

THEISSEN, G., *The Social Setting of Pauline Christianity*, E.T. (Edinburgh, 1982).

WORKMAN, H. B., *Persecution in the Early Church* (London, 1906; new edit., 1960).

WRIGHT, G. E., *An Introduction to Biblical Archaeology, pp.147–198 (London, 1959).*

THE HISTORICAL AND POLITICAL BACKGROUND AND CHRONOLOGY OF THE NEW TESTAMENT

HAROLD H. ROWDON

The Historical and Political Background

Though a glance at an atlas of the world shows that the Roman Empire covered only a fraction of the inhabited earth, yet in the first century A.D. it was regarded—with justice—as a world empire of a new order. Rome, a city situated on the western side of the Italian peninsula, had gained control not only of Italy, Gaul, Spain, and North Africa in the west, but also of all the lands bordering the eastern coasts of the Mediterranean Sea. That sea had become a Roman lake, the security of which required further expansion to the river-boundaries of the Rhine, Danube and Euphrates. Not even far-off Britain was omitted.

Palestine was situated in the extreme east of the Roman world, in the large area stretching from Greece to Egypt where Greek culture and the common dialect of the Greek language had spread as a result of trade and colonization even before Alexander the Great had swept all before him in military triumph. There, too, Rome had established her sway. Already in control of Greece and the west of Asia Minor by the end of the second century B.C., Rome waged war for a quarter of a century against Mithridates of Pontus and his allies until, at the end of 64 B.C., Pompey, who had already achieved fame by clearing the Mediterranean of the pirates who infested it, brought peace to the eastern hinterland of that sea by establishing the Roman province of Syria. Among the client kingdoms where native dynasties were entrusted with control and made responsible for peace, order and the prompt payment of taxes was Judaea, which was part of Herod the Great's kingdom where Jesus was born at Bethlehem.

For centuries Rome had been organized as a republic. The Roman senate, largely composed of former magistrates who had been elected to office by the people, though theoretically only an advisory body, had become the real ruler of the empire in the second and third centuries B.C. and had acted as a conservative force against political development. During the last century of the republic, its supremacy had been challenged again and again by military commanders, the greatest of whom, Julius Caesar, defeated the senatorial forces in civil war and became dictator. His autocratic rule deeply offended the Roman nobility and led to his assassination in 44 B.C. Caesar's nephew, Octavian, employed greater diplomacy and while professing to restore the republic in 27 B.C. actually transformed it into an empire, and was later granted the honorific title of 'Augustus'.

The theory of Roman government rested on the concept of *imperium*, the authority to command obedience. This was given to the emperor whose direct authority extended to most of the provinces where troops were stationed. The senate was entrusted with the government of the rest of the empire, with the exception of a few client-kingdoms, mainly in the east. The emperor's powers were nominally limited in time and required renewal, and there was no guarantee that Octavian would have successors. Nevertheless, the arrangement proved to be more than a delicately balanced constitution of limited duration.

Since the emperor was responsible for the frontiers and the more disturbed areas, whereas the senate administered internal and settled provinces, the emperor was empowered to act as *imperator*, commander-in-chief of the armed forces. His authority ran in senatorial provinces as well as his own. His tribunician powers eventually gave him powers of legal veto and appellate jurisdiction (Ac. 25: 11 may be explicable on other grounds, but shows the line of development by which, eventually, 'appeal to Caesar' replaced the traditional 'appeal to the people'). His *auctoritas* gave immense prestige to his pronouncements so that soon imperial instructions by edict, mandate or rescript came to acquire the force of law. Octavian's family name was Caesar; he was given the title of honour, Augustus, which signifies something set apart for the service of the gods; and the term, *Princeps*, by which he was designated, though it defined him merely as first citizen, came to elevate him above all others. The fact that he normally resided at Rome, and the gradual steps taken to dignify his person and office—later to culminate in the cult of emperor worship—underlined and enforced his supremacy. The long reign of Caesar Augustus —he lived until A.D. 14—also served to establish the new order which was able to survive a succession of somewhat second-rate or sinister emperors.

Augustus's elderly stepson, Tiberius, who reigned from A.D. 14–37, lacked the tact and prestige of Augustus. Gaius Caligula succeeded. He was a megalomaniac who was assassinated in A.D. 41. Claudius (A.D. 41–54) was not without ability, but suffered from a physical defect which may have been the result of Parkinson's disease or a spastic condition (Blaiklock). A letter of Claudius, written in A.D. 41 to the people of Alexandria, forbade the Jews there 'to admit Jews who come down from Syria or Egypt. . . . Otherwise I will by all means take vengeance on them as fomentors of what is a general plague infecting the whole world'. In A.D. 49, Claudius expelled the Jews from Rome (Ac. 18: 2) because of the disorders arising 'at the instigation of one Chrestus' (Suetonius). These may be uncertain allusions to Christianity, but there is no doubt that Claudius's adopted son, the infamous Nero who became emperor in A.D. 54, inflicted savage punishments on Christians in Rome, Peter and Paul probably among them. Nero, who had a passion for Greek art and culture, was dissolute and irresponsible and alienated almost every section of the community. His act of suicide in A.D. 68 was followed by a period of bitter civil strife, mainly in A.D. 69, the 'year of the four emperors'.

Vespasian emerged, an able and competent administrator who brought order out of chaos (A.D. 69–79). The new Flavian dynasty continued with Titus, son of Vespasian and conqueror of Jerusalem, who reigned A.D. 79–81, and ended with Domitian, the younger brother of Titus, who was emperor A.D. 81–96. Roman writers, such as Tacitus, portray Domitian as suspicious, sinister and cruel. Christian traditions single him out as the next great persecutor of the Church after Nero. The Apocalypse was doubtless written under the shadow of Domitian as well as with memories of Nero.

The Roman Empire comprised some 40 provinces at the end of the first century A.D. Senatorial provinces were ruled by proconsuls who were responsible to the senate by whom they were appointed. Their appointment was normally for one year, though this might be renewed. In Paul's day, Sergius Paulus was proconsul of Cyprus (Ac. 13: 7) and Gallio proconsul of Achaia (Ac. 18: 12). Imperial provinces were governed by senatorial legates appointed by the emperor with the title of propraetor, or by *equites* with the title of prefect or procurator: all these were responsible directly to the emperor and held office at his pleasure.

A number of Roman provinces figure in the New Testament. Spain (Rom. 15: 24) and, possibly, Gaul (2 Tim. 4: 10) receive a brief mention, but the action of the New Testament took place almost entirely in the eastern part of the empire. Illyricum (Rom. 15: 19), now western Yugoslavia, was subdued largely by Augustus and was subsequently enlarged and divided into Pannonia and Dalmatia (2 Tim. 4: 10). Augustus formed Greece into two provinces: Macedonia (Ac. 16: 9) with its capital at Thessalonica, and Achaia (Rom. 15: 26) where Corinth was the chief city. Colonies of veteran soldiers were established at numerous places, such as Philippi, and several Greek cities, including Athens, remained free cities with treaty rights.

In Asia Minor there were only three provinces in 27 B.C. Asia (Ac. 20: 4) contained many Greek cities. Roman jurisdiction was exercised through nine or more assizes (Ac. 19: 38) presided over by the proconsul. Bithynia (Ac. 16: 7) was administered with Pontus (1 Pet. 1: 1) as a single province. Cilicia, as a separate province, disappeared during the early empire and was administered with Syria (Gal. 1: 21) until A.D. 72 when it was reconstituted. In 25 B.C. Galatia became an imperial province, embracing not only the old ethnic kingdom of Galatia but also parts of Pontus, Phrygia, Lycaonia, Pisidia, Paphlagonia and Isauria (Gal. 1: 2). Cappadocia (1 Pet. 1: 1) was constituted a province by Tiberius in A.D. 17. Pamphylia (Ac. 13: 13) and Lycia (Ac. 27: 5) were organized as a joint-province by Claudius in A.D. 43. The island of Cyprus had been a Roman province since 58 B.C. It became a senatorial province in 27 B.C. and was therefore ruled by a proconsul in New Testament times (Ac. 13: 7).

Syria (Gal. 1: 21) was the eastern province most important for the security of the empire since it lay adjacent to the Euphrates frontier. Four legions were regularly stationed in the province and the governor, always a man of experience, was responsible for the safety of nearby provinces. Needless to say, Augustus classed Syria as imperial. Antioch became one of the chief cities of the whole empire, and the bastion of the east.

The kingdom of Judaea (Mt. 2: 1) bordered on Syria. When the east was settled by Pompey, Galilee, Samaria, Judaea and Peraea east of the Jordan were entrusted to Hyrcanus II as high priest and ethnarch, and the cities of the northeast were incorporated into the administration of the Syrian province. Subsequently, Herod, son of Antipater, Hyrcanus's minister, journeyed to Rome, ingratiated himself with the future Augustus, and was granted by the Roman senate the dignity of King of Judaea. He had to fight for his position, for he was bitterly opposed in Judaea, not only by reason of his Roman patronage, but also because he was of Idumaean, non-Jewish blood. By 37 B.C. he was able to enter Jerusalem and commence his rule. His marriage to Mariamne, the heiress of the Jewish priestly house, was a bid to win the favour of the Jews.

Herod retained the favour of Augustus and secured some extension of his rule. During a vigorous reign of some 33 years he suppressed the old aristocracy and established a new nobility of royal officials, fostering the party of the Herodians who may have viewed him in a messianic light (Mt. 22: 16; Mk 3: 6; 12: 13). Herod was a great builder who (c. 20 B.C.) commenced the reconstruction of the Temple at Jerusalem (Jn 2: 20). This was intended as a sop to the Jews, but Herod also constructed the port of Caesarea in token of his affection for Rome. Ruthless and cruel, Herod sustained his policies with the aid of astute diplomacy and armed force backed by the power of Rome.

When Herod the Great died in 4 B.C. his kingdom was parcelled out to three of his sons who survived his murderous intrigues. Philip received the remote territories north-east of the Sea of Galilee where he reigned in peace for over 30 years. Herod Antipas received Galilee together with Peraea east of Jordan and the minor title of tetrarch. He built Tiberias, named in honour of the emperor, but lived as a professing Jew and entertained a certain respect for John the Baptist (Mk 6: 20). Though married to the daughter of Aretas, King of Nabataea, Herod Antipas succumbed to the attractions of Herodias, daughter of one of his half-brothers and wife of another. This liaison involved Herod Antipas in war with Nabataea. During the course of this war he celebrated his birthday in the stronghold of Machaerus (according to Josephus) where Salome, Herodias's daughter, danced and brought John the Baptist to his death (Mt. 14: 6–12; Mk 6: 21–29). Antipas was defeated and had to appeal to Rome for help. On the death of the emperor, Tiberius, who had trusted him to the extent of using him as a mediator between Rome and Parthia, Antipas, urged on by Herodias, petitioned Gaius Caligula for the title of king. Instead, he was banished to Gaul as the result

of a charge of treasonable conduct brought against him by his nephew, Herod Agrippa I, who was given his territories as a reward (A.D. 39).

The major part of Herod the Great's kingdom—Judaea and Samaria—was bequeathed to his son, Archelaus. He became so unpopular as to provoke numerous uprisings which eventually necessitated the intervention of the Governor of Syria, Varus (cf. Mt. 2: 22). It became necessary for Archelaus to journey to Rome in order to defend his position against the counter-claims of relatives, such as Herod Antipas, and the representations of the Jewish people (cf. Lk. 19: 11–27). Strangely, Archelaus was confirmed in power by Augustus, though without the royal title. He proved an incompetent ruler and a deputation of Jews and Samaritans secured his banishment in A.D. 6.

Judaea was then placed under a Roman procurator who was loosely subordinate to the Syrian legate but directly responsible to the emperor. The procurator's headquarters were in Caesarea, though in times of unsettled conditions, such as the Jewish feasts, he might reside in Jerusalem. He had a small force of 3,000 men, raised in Palestine from the non-Jewish section of the population. One cohort was stationed in Jerusalem in the castle of Antonia overlooking the Temple. The procurator was responsible for law and order and taxation, but otherwise the internal government and legal administration of the land was largely in the hands of the Jews. Yet Judaea seethed with discontent. In A.D. 6–7, the 'census' almost produced general rebellion, and men like Judas of Galilee (Ac. 5: 37) led 'underground' movements which fostered hatred and bloodshed.

The early procurators of Judaea are of little importance for the background to the New Testament apart from the appointments they made to the office of high priest. When Quirinius reorganized the province of Judaea in A.D. 6 he deposed the high priest who had been nominated by Archelaus and appointed Annas, the son of Seth (Jn 18: 13, 24; Ac. 4: 6). Annas remained high priest during the procuratorships of Coponius (A.D. 6–9), Marcus Ambivius (A.D. 9–12) and Annius Rufus (A.D. 12–15).

When Valerius Gratus became procurator in A.D. 15 he deposed Annas in favour of Ishmael, the son of Phobi. Ishmael was followed in quick succession by Eleazar, son of Annas, Simon, the son of Kami, and Joseph Caiaphas who was son-in-law to Annas. Caiaphas remained high priest for 18 years, including the ten years of Pilate's procuratorship, until Vitellius, legate of Syria, deposed him in A.D. 36. He was followed by two sons of Annas: first Jonathan, and then, after a year, Theophilus. It was costly in bribes both to secure office and to retain it, and only wealthy families such as that of Annas could afford the luxury.

Pontius Pilate held the office of procurator from A.D. 26–36. Time and again he provoked Jewish hostility, almost to breaking point. He issued copper coinage bearing heathen symbols to the great scandal of the Jews, but withdrew it from A.D. 31. He ordered the Roman standards with their representations of the Emperor to be taken into Jerusalem under cover of darkness, but eventually removed them. He hung votive shields dedicated to the Emperor in Herod's palace in Jerusalem, but withdrew them on orders from Rome. He financed the building of an aqueduct to bring water into Jerusalem from the sacred Corban fund, and quelled by treachery the tumult that resulted. The same mixture of truculence, cowardice and subtlety may be discerned in Pilate's dealings with Christ. The unhappy man was recalled to Rome in A.D. 36 after a massacre of Samaritans had taken place (cf. Lk. 13: 1).

Marcellus (A.D. 37) and Marullus (A.D. 37–41) followed Pilate, and then for a few years the whole of the territory which had formed the kingdom of Herod the Great was ruled by Herod Agrippa I, his grandson. Agrippa, who was high in the favour of the mad emperor, Caligula (he was able to dissuade him from setting up a statue of himself in the Temple of Jerusalem), was granted in A.D. 37 the northeastern territories which had been ruled by Philip. Two years later, when Herod Antipas was exiled at Agrippa's instigation, the latter was given Galilee and Peraea. Upon the accession of the Emperor Claudius in A.D. 41, Agrippa received virtually all the territory that his grandfather had ruled. King Agrippa I ingratiated himself with the orthodox Jews and persecuted the Christian Church (Ac. 12: 1–19). His ambitions were cut short in A.D. 44 by a sudden disease, described by Josephus in terms similar to those of Ac. 12: 23, and authority over the whole land passed to another succession of Roman procurators.

The first to be appointed was Cuspius Fadus (A.D. 44–46). He claimed the right to appoint high priests which had recently been exercised by Agrippa and which was a source of income as well as influence. In response to Jewish representation the Emperor ruled that it should go to Agrippa's brother, Herod, king of Chalcis. After his death in A.D. 48 it was given to Agrippa's son, Herod Agrippa II, who retained it until the outbreak of the Jewish War in A.D. 66. Soon after Fadus became procurator one, Theudas (not to be confused with the Theudas of Ac. 5: 36), laid claim to miraculous powers and raised one of the messianic followings which were soon to become a feature of the times.

Tiberius Julius Alexander became procurator in A.D. 46 at a time of famine (Ac. 11: 28). As an apostate Jew—his uncle was the famous Jewish philosopher, Philo—his action in crushing a Jewish rising led by two sons of Judas of Galilee was especially unpopular. Other risings followed during the procuratorship of Cumanus (A.D. 48–52).

Antonius Felix who became procurator, probably in A.D. 52, was a man of humble origin. He had once been a slave in the household of Claudius's mother, Antonia. Nevertheless he married well and his third wife was Drusilla, the daughter of Herod Agrippa I. Felix tried to deal with the problem of disorder in Judaea, but this did not endear him to large sections of the people who regarded insurgents as patriots.

Among the rebel leaders of the time was an Egyptian who claimed to be a prophet and led a following of about 4,000 to the Mount of Olives, promising them that at a signal the walls of the city would fall flat and enable them to march in and seize the city. Instead, he and his followers were scattered by Felix's troops. A few years later, Paul was mistaken for this Egyptian (Ac. 21: 38). Some of the extremist Jews began to practise assassination, stabbing their victims with daggers which they carried concealed in their cloaks. They became known as *sicarii* (dagger-men), a word which is translated 'Assassins' in Ac. 21: 38.

One of the notorious high priests of this period was Ananias, the son of Nedebaeus (A.D. 47–58). His greed was such that he seized and sold those parts of the temple sacrifices which were the perquisites of the ordinary priests who, in consequence, were brought to the point of starvation. Ananias presided over the scandalous meeting of the Sanhedrin that examined Paul (Ac. 23: 1–9).

Felix, whom Tacitus described as 'a master of cruelty and lust' (cf. Ac. 24: 25) was recalled by Nero about A.D. 59 and was succeeded by Porcius Festus, a worthier representative of Rome (Ac. 25).

Festus consulted the remaining member of the Herodian house who figures in the New Testament. Agrippa, son of Herod Agrippa I, was considered too young to succeed his father. Later he was made king of Chalcis, a Lebanese territory. In A.D. 53 he exchanged Chalcis for the territory north-east of the Sea of Galilee over which his father had ruled. Nero granted him further accessions of territory, including the cities of Tiberias and Bethsaida Julias. In gratitude, he changed the name of his capital from Caesarea Philippi to Neronias. Herod Agrippa II was 'a Herod of the better sort' (Blaiklock) who was consulted by Festus regarding the charges brought against Paul (Ac. 25: 13–26: 32). He strove, though without success, to avert the catastrophe of the great rebellion against Rome, A.D. 66–70.

Festus died in office, c. A.D. 62, and a three months' interval elapsed before his successor, Albinus, arrived. This enabled the high priest, Annas II, to put a number of his enemies to death. The most notable of these was James the Just, leader of the Christian Church in Jerusalem. This apparently shocked many in Jerusalem who revered James for his asceticism and piety and who later said that the fall of Jerusalem was not unconnected with the judicial murder of James.

Albinus was followed by Gessius Florus (A.D. 65–66). Discontent had been increasing for some time and non-payment of taxes had become chronic. In A.D. 66 Gessius Florus appropriated a large sum from the funds of the Temple. His ruthless crushing of the riots that followed led to a revolt in which the mob gained virtual control of Jerusalem. The Roman garrison had to be withdrawn from the city. The rebels stormed the Dead Sea fortress of Masada and the revolt soon became nationwide.

The Jewish forces in Galilee, where the full pressure of the Roman punitive expedition might be expected, were put under the command of a young priest, Joseph. In February A.D. 67 Nero appointed Vespasian to reduce Palestine to obedience, and Joseph was unable to withstand the Roman forces. Instead, he surrendered to the enemy and later ingratiated himself with the future emperor, becoming his friend and secretary. As Flavius Josephus, he found time to write his famous volumes on Jewish history. By June A.D. 68 only a few strongholds, including Jerusalem, remained in Jewish hands.

Jerusalem gained an unexpected respite as a result of Nero's suicide in that month. Little could be done in the year of the four emperors to reduce Palestine to full obedience. Meanwhile zealots of several factions, bitterly opposed to each other, crowded into Jerusalem to their mutual discomfort. Remembering her Master's warning (Mt. 24: 16), the Christian community fled to Pella, a Greek city of the Decapolis.

When Vespasian became emperor he made his son, Titus, commander in Palestine. By the spring of A.D. 70 Jerusalem was invested. At the cost of fearful bloodshed, the city was reduced to the accompaniment of bitter strife among the defenders themselves. City and Temple were destroyed. Other Jewish strongholds were taken one by one, the last being Masada, the Dead Sea fortress which held out until April A.D. 73.

Judaea remained a separate province with its procurator directly responsible to the legate commanding the tenth legion which was stationed at Jerusalem. The Sanhedrin, high priesthood and temple worship were abolished and the tax formerly payable by Jews to the Temple funds was diverted to the temple of Jupiter.

Though the province was the normal unit of administration in the Roman Empire, the most vital element in governmental, social and economic affairs was undoubtedly the city. Rome itself, the hub of empire, was a city and city life was fostered throughout the empire as a matter of policy. In the East this was no innovation, for the Greeks who equated city life with civilized life had established a large number of colonies, such as the cities of the Decapolis east of Jordan.

Rome recognized the right of cities to municipal self-government. The citizens, met in lawful assembly (Ac. 19: 39) or in less official ways, were often a force to be reckoned with, but power resided in the magistrates who were increasingly drawn from the ranks of the well-to-do. The Roman law which they administered served as one of the most vital unifying factors in the empire (Ac. 19: 38–40).

Cities served as centres of culture and refinement as well as of entertainment provided through the varied facilities of baths and theatres. Their strategic importance for commerce is perhaps linked with the fact that every city of significance came to have its Jewish community. They served as foci for the surrounding countryside, providing not only market facilities in their splendid *fora* but also stimulus to religion in their costly temples and protection from enemies behind their ample walls. The common Greek which was the language of commerce made intercourse easy, even between men of different races. Small wonder that Paul made the cities the centre of his missionary endeavours!

Social life in the cities posed severe problems for Christians. In addition to the immorality which was commonplace and often hallowed by association with religion, the ubiquitous guilds produced situations fraught with dilemma. These 'voluntary associations of people with common interests' (Oakley) were of many kinds: guilds of artisans and traders, burial clubs and social clubs of all descriptions may be mentioned. The banquets held by such associations in heathen temples and the civic feasts produced acute dilemmas for conscientious Christians (1 C. 8: 10; 10: 19–22).

Cities were of different kinds. *Coloniae* were cities settled by Roman citizens, often veterans from the army who received the franchise on discharge. *Municipia* were cities that had been autonomous communities and, under Roman rule, were given the freedom of Rome. Municipal office might carry with it Roman citizenship which was also given to individuals in recognition of outstanding services to the empire.

Under certain circumstances, Roman citizenship might apparently be purchased (Ac. 22: 28). It was granted sparingly until A.D. 212. It conferred both financial (cf. Mt. 17: 25, 26) and legal (Ac. 16: 37) immunities and was regarded as a high honour (Ac. 16: 21, 38; 22: 28). Citizenship of any city, especially if it possessed some claim to fame, was a source of pride (Ac. 21: 39).

Cities which remained independent were allowed to issue their own coinage, an important concession since, apart from other considerations, coinage was universally regarded as an instrument of propaganda. In general, imperial coinage was in use throughout the empire, though the Jews were allowed to mint their own coinage for the Temple tax and also for the use of strict Jews who would not touch a coin bearing the imperial image and superscription (cf. Mt. 22: 15–22). Taxation was an ever-present reminder of the claims of Rome. It was partly in the hands of *publicani* who were regarded in fiery Judaea as collaborators with the hated occupying power as well as financial exactors who unscrupulously lined their own pockets.

Slavery was a universal institution. Legally, the slave had no rights and was regarded as the chattel of his master. Under the influence of Stoicism a more generous attitude began to appear. In the guilds, slaves were allowed to associate on an equal footing with free men, and it became possible for a slave to buy his freedom with the savings which his master allowed him to accumulate (cf. Gal. 3: 28; Col. 3: 11; Phm. 16).

The provinces and cities of the empire were linked together by a magnificent transport system. Roads radiated from Rome, built originally for military purposes and maintained by military labour. The central government assumed major responsibility for the upkeep of roads and for the maintenance of the *cursus publicus*, a system of communications for official purposes. Rest houses were provided at intervals of 25 miles and changes of horses more frequently, though only for the use of imperial couriers. Brigandage was ruthlessly suppressed, though it was not unknown (Lk. 10: 30; 2 C. 11: 26). Travel by sea was made relatively easy after Pompey had cleared the Mediterranean of pirates. A corn fleet sailed at regular intervals to convey corn from Alexandria to Rome (Ac. 27: 6, 38), but sailing was dangerous in autumn and almost impossible in winter (Ac. 27: 9). Goods, persons and ideas travelled freely in the Roman world, as is abundantly clear from the pages of the New Testament.

The Chronology of the New Testament

To an age in which historical research has become a highly specialized study that has developed in a distinctive direction, the New Testament is disconcertingly bare of information which would enable us to turn its historical data into the form of history with which we are familiar. In New Testament times there was no fixed point of reference similar to our dating scheme of B.C.-A.D. Indeed, historians of those days were not unduly concerned to provide a closely-knit narrative of events linked together in chronological sequence. Moreover, the Biblical writers were more concerned to show the relation of the events they recorded to the eternal purposes of God than they were to write historical narratives in the form to which we are accustomed.

This is not to say that the accuracy of the historical data of the New Testament is in question. There is every reason for confidence in the reliability of the sacred record, and the instances where cavil is possible are few. But the task of trying to transpose the New Testament into another form from that in which it was written is a difficult task. It is well worth attempting because of the very great help which it gives to the endeavour which the attentive reader ought to make to see the sacred story as an integrated whole, set in the history of the first century A.D.

The starting-point is naturally the birth of Jesus. This took place during the reign of Herod the Great (Mt. 2: 1), that is, before 4 B.C. Luke tells us that the great event occurred at the time when a census was being taken at the behest of Caesar Augustus and when Quirinius (Cyrenius) was governor of Syria (Lk. 2: 1, 2). We know that Quirinius was governor of Syria in A.D. 6–7 when a census that was being taken in Palestine provoked the revolt of Judas of Galilee (Josephus; Ac. 5: 37). Some scholars have therefore concluded that Luke has made a mistake.

Among the possible explanations, the most likely is the one elaborated by Stauffer. He argues that there is a certain amount of evidence which suggests that Quirinius served as a kind of commander-in-chief in the east for most of the period 12 B.C. to A.D. 16. In this respect he would be in the tradition of men like Pompey and Marcus Antonius. During part of the period Quirinius acted as governor of Syria but at other times an imperial procurator served under him as governor of the province. Stauffer further argues that the census that Quirinius made was not an ordinary census but a *descriptio prima* taken as a basis for the levying of taxation. The first stage would take the form of a registration of all taxable persons and objects and (like the English Doomsday Book) would involve a lengthy process and much opposition. Eventually it would be possible for the final assessment to be made. According to Stauffer, the census of A.D. 7 was such an assessment, made on the basis of the registration which had been commenced some long time earlier.

When was it commenced? Mt.2: 2 shows that it was at the time when an astronomical phenomenon was observed. Stauffer has drawn attention to two ancient records, one forecasting the conjunction of the planets Jupiter and Saturn in the constellation of the Fishes for 7 B.C., the other declaring that this would signify that 'there will appear in Palestine in this year the ruler of the last days'. Contemporary evidence and astronomical calculations suggest that this conjunction did occur in the year forecast. It is therefore possible to suggest that the birth of Christ during the opening stages of the census procedure took place in the year 7 B.C. (A difficulty to this view is the fact that the word used in Mt. 2: 2 is that for a single star.)

The baptism of Jesus took place when He was about thirty years of age, but this is clearly a round figure (Lk. 3: 23). This event took place after the beginning of the ministry of John the Baptist, though it is not clear whether there was any appreciable interval. This is unfortunate for our present purpose since Luke plainly states that John's ministry began in the fifteenth year of the reign of Tiberius (Lk. 3: 1, 2). Yet even this clear statement is capable of different interpretations. Tiberius's reign used to be reckoned from the beginning of his co-regency with Augustus, but it is now thought that it should be reckoned from the death of Augustus which took place on 19 August A.D. 14. If so, then John the Baptist commenced his ministry in A.D. 28 or 29 and Jesus was baptized soon after.

A month or two later, after the call of the first disciples, the marriage in Cana and a short stay in Capernaum (Jn 1: 35–2: 12), Jesus went to Jerusalem for the first passover of His ministry (Jn 2: 13). This was probably the passover of A.D. 30. The remark made by the Jews on this occasion that the Temple had taken forty-six years to build (Jn 2: 20) does not fix the date with precision. We know that Herod began to 'build' the Temple *c*. 20 B.C., but some time may have been spent in preparation before the actual work of building commenced. Furthermore, the remark recorded in Jn 2: 20 need not imply that the work had recently been completed. All that it tells us with certainty is that Jesus visited Jerusalem for the first passover of His ministry at least 46 years after 20 B.C.

The length of Jesus's ministry is another open question, though it seems likely that it extended for just over three years. It has been suggested that the length was no more than a single year. This view was originally put forward on the ground that Lk. 4: 19 (Isa. 61: 2) refers to the acceptable 'year' of the Lord. The evidence of the synoptic gospels does not ex-

plicitly exclude this view, though the amount of activity they record could hardly have been fitted into a single year. The fourth gospel flatly contradicts it. Some maintain that the ministry covered two years as John's gospel suggests at first sight by its allusions to three passovers (Jn 2: 13; 6: 4; 11: 55). But it is more likely that the ministry of Jesus lasted for three years.

It is true that there is no direct mention of a fourth passover or of any other fact to compel such a view, but the indirect evidence of both the fourth and the synoptic gospels suggests that the interval between the two passovers of Jn 2: 13 and Jn 6: 4 was more than a single year. Jesus and His disciples spent some time in Judaea after the first passover (Jn 4: 1–3). Indeed, it appears that they did not return to Galilee until the following winter, four months before harvest time (Jn 4: 35; it is unlikely that this was a proverbial saying since the interval between sowing and reaping was six months). Jn 5: 1 implies some further lapse of time before Jesus returned to Jerusalem for a feast, the name of which is not given. It is unlikely that this was the feast of Purim which was observed in February/March. It may have been the passover of March/April or even a later feast, such as Pentecost or Tabernacles. If so, the passover of Jn 6: 4 would be that of the following year. That this was the case is confirmed by the amount of activity recorded in the synoptic gospels as taking place between the commencement of our Lord's Galilean ministry and the passover observed about the time of the feeding of the five thousand, which is that of Jn 6: 4. No fewer than three evangelistic tours, as well as that of the Twelve and sundry other activities, are recorded (Mt. 4: 12–14: 13; Mk 1: 16–6: 32; Lk. 4: 31–9: 10).

The ministry of Jesus ended, as it had begun, under the procuratorship of Pontius Pilate. Pilate was procurator A.D. 26–36. The death of Jesus did not take place near the beginning of this period, for independently of the above discussion of the dating of His ministry, the events referred to in Lk. 13: 1 and 23: 12 seem to require that Pilate had been procurator for some time. True there are traditions going back to Tertullian that date the crucifixion A.D. 29, but there are difficulties to this dating, even if we were to push back the period of the ministry.

It seems clear that Jesus died on a Friday at the time of the paschal full moon, and the tradition of Tertullian and others places that Friday on 25 March. But astronomical calculations indicate fairly decisively that the paschal full moon of A.D. 29 was in April.

The gospels require that the Friday in question was either 14 or 15 Nisan. Since the date of the month Nisan was fixed by the full moon, astronomers have been able to calculate that 15

Nisan was a Friday in A.D. 27 and 14 Nisan was a Friday in A.D. 30 and 33. In view of the evidence already adduced to suggest that the ministry of Jesus extended from A.D. 30 to 33, we may conclude that it is at least likely that the crucifixion took place in A.D. 33.

There is no reason to think that the period between Pentecost and the conversion of Paul was unduly protracted, though the precise length of the interval is unknown. It has been asserted that the stoning of Stephen could not have taken place while Pilate was procurator and must therefore be dated after A.D. 36. But fanaticism is unpredictable and may be unloosed at any time, regardless of consequences.

A tradition was preserved by Irenaeus to the effect that the interval between Pentecost and the conversion of Paul was 18 months, and this may not be very wide of the mark. A clue is given in the New Testament where Paul stated that three years after his conversion he left Damascus (Gal. 1: 18), presumably on the occasion when the governor under King Aretas attempted to seize him (2 C. 11: 32 f.). Damascus was in Roman hands, certainly until A.D. 33 and probably until 37. Since Aretas died in A.D. 40 he probably gained possession of Damascus between A.D. 37 and 40. During this time, therefore, and probably nearer the beginning than the end, Paul escaped from Damascus. Since this was three years after his conversion, this must have taken place soon after A.D. 34, if not in that year.

After his departure from Damascus in precipitous haste Paul spent 15 days in Jerusalem (Gal. 1: 18) before retiring to Syria and Cilicia (Gal. 1: 21) where he remained in obscurity for an unspecified period until Barnabas went to seek him out (Ac. 11: 25). Barnabas brought him to Antioch where he remained a year (Ac. 11: 26). The two men were then deputed by the church at Antioch to carry aid to the brethren in Judaea who had been stricken by famine. This took place at an unspecified time during the reign of Claudius (Ac. 11: 27–30). A.D. 45 was a year of disastrous harvests in the eastern Mediterranean area, as we learn from Egyptian papyri, and it is therefore likely that this famine-visit, as it has been called, was made by Paul and Barnabas late in A.D. 45 or early in 46. That this was so is confirmed by the fact that Luke interrupts his narrative at the point of the visit in order to relate the persecution of the Church by Herod Agrippa I and the death of the king (Ac. 12: 1–23) which took place 'about that time' (Ac. 12: 1). Herod died in A.D. 44.

Paul's first missionary journey probably took place during A.D. 46 and 47. There is nothing in the narrative to suggest a protracted stay at any of the numerous places visited (Ac. 13: 4–14: 26). It is stated, however, that the missionaries stayed a long time at Antioch after their return (Ac. 14: 28).

The so-called Council of Jerusalem took place after the end of the first missionary journey and before the beginning of the second (Ac. 15). Since the commencement of the second journey can be dated with some certainty late A.D. 49 or early 50 at the latest (see next paragraphs), it seems clear that the Council took place in A.D. 49. If, as is reasonable, this Council is to be identified with that of Gal. 2: 1–10, and if the statement in Gal. 2: 1 is taken to mean that this took place 14 years after Paul's conversion, the conclusion that the Council of Jerusalem took place in A.D. 49 is strengthened.

The view that Paul's second missionary journey lasted from late A.D. 49 or early 50 to the autumn of A.D. 51 rests upon the following data. The journey began not long after the Council had ended (Ac. 15: 33–36). After spending an unspecified time visiting the churches in Syria and Cilicia and the newly-founded churches of Asia Minor, Paul and his companions 'went through' the region of Phrygia and Galatia. If the churches addressed in the letter to the Galatians were churches in the ethnic region of Galatia (according to the North Galatian theory) rather than the churches of southern Asia Minor in the Roman province of Galatia (according to the South Galatian theory), then the brief statement in Ac. 16: 6 must be taken to mean a period of evangelistic activity. Paul then crossed to Europe and, after short stays in Philippi, Thessalonica, Beroea and a short visit to Athens he remained in Corinth for rather more than 18 months (Ac. 18: 11, 18).

It was towards the end of this period that there occurred the Gallio incident, the dating of which can be set with some precision. The Jews in Corinth brought their accusations against Paul to Gallio, undoubtedly soon after he became proconsul of Achaia (Ac. 18: 12). An inscription at Delphi shows that Gallio's year of office began in midsummer of either A.D. 51 or 52. If, as seems likely, it was the former, Paul must have arrived in Corinth early in A.D. 50 and remained there until the summer of 51, when he returned to Antioch via Ephesus and Jerusalem before the onset of winter made sea travel impossible.

This timing is confirmed by the fact that when he arrived in Corinth Paul met Aquila and Priscilla who had recently been forced to leave Rome in consequence of Claudius's edict expelling Jews from Rome (Ac. 18: 2). Since it was probably in A.D. 49 that the edict was issued, it is most likely that Aquila and Priscilla would have reached Corinth early in A.D. 50, not long before Paul arrived.

Paul's third missionary journey was his longest. It followed soon after the conclusion of the second and probably commenced in A.D. 52. After an unspecified period spent in ministering to the churches of Galatia and Phrygia (Ac. 18: 23; cf. 19: 1), Paul spent the greater part of three years at Ephesus (Ac. 19: 8, 10, 21 f.; 20: 31); visited Macedonia and stayed three months in Achaia (Ac. 20: 1–3); and may have journeyed as far as Illyricum (Rom. 15: 19). One of his great concerns on this journey was to gather an offering from the Gentile churches for the poor saints at Jerusalem.

He was anxious to be at Jerusalem by Pentecost (Ac. 20: 16); the year was A.D. 56 or 57. There he was apprehended. He was subsequently examined by Felix (Ac. 24). Two years later, probably in A.D. 59, Festus succeeded Felix (Ac. 24: 27). Arraigned before Festus, Paul made his appeal to Caesar (Ac. 25: 10), and after the hearing before Herod Agrippa II (Ac. 26) Paul sailed for Rome in the autumn (Ac. 27: 9).

For two years, A.D. 60 and 61, Paul remained a prisoner in Rome (Ac. 28: 20). Subsequent events are shrouded in uncertainty. Possibly the case against Paul went by default, or, more likely, insufficient evidence was brought against him, and he was released. The Pastoral Letters indicate that Paul undertook fresh missionary work before his death which probably took place at Rome before the death of Nero in A.D. 68, and possibly in A.D. 64 at the time of the Neronian persecution.

Peter was miraculously released from prison prior to the death of Herod Agrippa I in A.D. 44 (Ac. 12: 3–19). He left Jerusalem for a time (Ac. 12: 17), but subsequently returned and was present at the Council of Jerusalem (Ac. 15: 7). He visited Antioch (Gal. 2: 11) and may have been at Corinth (1 C. 1: 12). He probably paid at least one visit to Rome. Tradition is strong to the effect that he, as well as Paul, suffered death in Rome. The significance of 1 Pet. 5: 13 is debatable, though Peter may well have used 'Babylon' as an 'apocalyptic' designation for Rome. Almost certainly he fell a victim to Nero's cruelty.

James, the Lord's brother, who became the outstanding Christian leader in Jerusalem (Ac. 12: 17; 15: 13) was stoned to death, probably in A.D. 62. The death of John which, according to tradition, occurred about A.D. 100 marks the close of the apostolic age.

RULERS OF JUDAEA

Herod the Great (King)	37–4 B.C.
Archelaus (Tetrarch)	4 B.C.–A.D.6

Procurators

Coponius	A.D.6–9
Marcus Ambivius	9–12
Annius Rufus	12–15
Valerius Gratus	15–26
Pontius Pilate	26–36
Marcellus	37
Marullus	37–41

King

Herod Agrippa I	41–44

Procurators

Cuspius Fadus	44–46
Tiberius Julius Alexander	46–48
Ventidius Cumanus	48–52
Antonius Felix	52–59
Porcius Festus	59–62
Albinus	62–65
Gessius Florus	65–66

ROMAN EMPERORS

Augustus	27 B.C.–A.D. 14
Tiberius	A.D. 14–37
Gaius (Caligula)	37–41
Claudius	41–54
Nero	54–68
Galba	68–69
Otho	69
Vitellius	69
Vespasian	69–79
Titus	79–81
Domitian	81–96

A SUGGESTED CHRONOLOGY OF THE NEW TESTAMENT

The Birth of Jesus	7 B.C.
The Baptism of Jesus	A.D. 29 or 30
The Death and Resurrection	33
The Conversion of Paul	34 or 35
Paul's First Missionary Journey	46–47
The Council of Jerusalem	49
Paul's Second Missionary Journey	49–51
Paul's Third Missionary Journey	52–56 or 57
Paul's First Imprisonment in Rome	59–61
The Death of James	62?
The Death of Peter	64?
The Death of Paul	64?
The Death of John	c. 100?

THE FAMILY OF HEROD

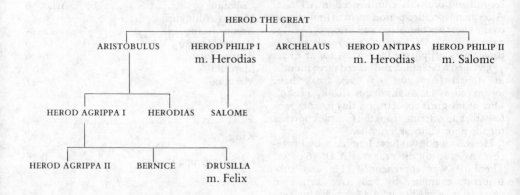

BIBLIOGRAPHY

BLAIKLOCK, E. M., *The Century of the New Testament* (London, 1962).

BLAIKLOCK, E. M., *Cities of the New Testament* (London, 1965).

BRUCE, F. F., *New Testament History* (Basingstoke, 1982).

CHARLESWORTH, M. P., *The Roman Empire* (London, 1951).

GLOVER, T. R., *The World of the New Testament* (Cambridge, 1933).

GRANT, M., *The Jews in the Roman World* (London, 1973).

JEWETT, R., *Dating Paul's Life* (London, 1979).

JUDGE, E. A., *The Social Pattern of Christian Groups in the First Century* (London, 1960).

MATTINGLY, H., *Roman Imperial Civilisation* (London, 1957).

OAKLEY, H. C., 'The Greek and Roman Background of the New Testament', *Vox Evangelica* (London, 1962).

OGG, G., *Chronology of the Public Ministry of Jesus* (Cambridge, 1940).

OGG, G., *Chronology of the Life of St. Paul* (London, 1968).

SCHÜRER. E., *The History of the Jewish People in the Age of Jesus Christ*, new edn., 3 vols. (Edinburgh, 1973–).

SHERWIN-WHITE, A. N., *Roman Society and Roman Law in the New Testament* (Oxford, 1963).

SMALLWOOD, E. M., *The Jews under Roman Rule* (Leiden, 1976).

WELLS, J. and BARROW, R. H., *A Short History of the Roman Empire* (London, 1950).

THE RELIGIOUS BACKGROUND OF THE NEW TESTAMENT (PAGAN)

HAROLD H. ROWDON

The century of the New Testament was an age of faith. True, the old forms of religion were effete, being more appropriate to city states or at most a small empire than to the world empire that had been created by Rome. Nevertheless at the local level religious fervour found expression in the practice of magic and the veneration of traditional deities who could be equated with, or at least related to, the great gods of Greece and Rome.

Religion was used as a device of government —Augustus restored no fewer than 82 temples in Rome—while emperor worship, which began as a spontaneous movement, was fostered as a means of creating a sentiment of loyalty to the empire as well as to the emperor. New forms of religious life, of which the mystery religions of the East are a well-known example, spread throughout the empire. Philosophical faiths, both old and new, won devotees.

The religions of the first century A.D. shared, to a greater or lesser extent, numerous common features. Usually there was an underlying belief in some form of religious dualism. Though pagan religions were often amoral, if not immoral, there was frequently a strong sense of the conflict between good and evil, or at least between forces benevolent and malevolent to man. Again there was usually an unquestioned acceptance of the possibility of magical control over things and persons. This appears not only in the practice of magic but also in the belief that the punctilious observance of the appropriate religious rites avails to secure the favour of the god in question. At the same time there was usually belief in the activity of Chance or Fortune operating through Fate or Destiny which was in the control of gods, demons or men. The assumption was almost unquestioned that human destiny was ultimately fixed by the stars to which, with the sun, personal existence was ascribed. Needless to say, the reality of the miraculous was generally taken for granted, and unbounded confidence was reposed in sacred writings especially if these were ancient mysterious or cryptic.

The world of the New Testament was the Roman world which, although restricted to the area surrounding the Mediterranean Sea, was virtually co-extensive with civilization. It is therefore appropriate to conduct a brief survey of public religion from the standpoint of Rome.

Roman state religion, like that of Greece with which it was associated, was polytheistic in character and was largely concerned with the maintenance of right relationship with the gods. The deities of the Roman pantheon included Jupiter, often lauded as 'greatest and best'; Mars, legendary parent of the Roman people, and mighty in war; Minerva, goddess of all who worked with brain or hand; and Vesta, goddess of the undying hearth fire, and symbol of home-life and the family.

The worship of these gods was largely formal and was associated with temple, altar and image. It was also basically civic, particularly on the great festal days when all were expected to take part in the rites. In view of the fact that the family was the basic unit in Roman society, it is not surprising that religion was more strongly entrenched there than in the context of civic worship which was often formal to a degree. *Lares* and *Penates*, symbolic of hearth and home, drew forth the religious devotion of the family.

In the countryside, where religion was more conservative, rustic shrines were erected wherever there was some special sense of the presence of life and power and mystery (the divine *numen*), whether it were a spring, a grove of venerable trees or a range of lofty mountain peaks. To these shrines offerings of milk, cheese, grain or even a few flowers would be brought: the nymphs who inhabited such places must be honoured, and along with them, Faunus god of woodlands, Sylvanus god of unconquered nature, and the like. There were also Terminus who protected fields and boundaries, and the various deities who protected crafts and trades.

The gods who must be approached by the way of sacrifice might also communicate with their devotees by means of dreams, oracles and the answering of prayers. Indeed, if the gods failed to respond to propitiation by answering prayer not only would the promised tribute be withheld but the worshipper might react in disillusionment and turn away to other deities.

An important characteristic of first-century religion was its capacity for syncretism. The way for this had been prepared by the striking development of the Greek Empire and the tendency within Hellenistic religion to identify the deities of different peoples and to fuse their cults. Indeed, the religion of the Hellenistic age has been described by F. C. Grant as being like a chain of lakes with many tributaries. Rome likewise, as she conquered the world, followed the same policy of bringing together the religions as well as the nations under her presidency.

As a result Jupiter and the gods of Rome were equated with Zeus and the gods of Greece. The process may have gone further, for it is likely that when the men of Lystra hailed Barnabas and Paul as Zeus and Hermes (Ac. 14: 11–13) they had in mind not the great deities of Rome but local deities whom they had equated with them. It was not always a question of conquered peoples desiring to acquire the benefits in the power of the gods of their conquerors. The victorious Romans felt it necessary for the gods of a country they had subdued to be honoured since they might be 'Roman gods in native dress' (Charlesworth) and in any case, if they were gods, they must wield some power in their own domains at least. 'Always call on the gods for aid', said a second-century Roman emperor of a philosophical turn of mind (Marcus Aurelius).

During the course of the first century a fresh religious sentiment was fostered in an endeavour to further the unity and well-being of the Roman world. Yet emperor-worship was scarcely a novelty. It was not unknown in the Middle East; Alexander the Great had been given divine honours; and, in any case, since some of the gods of the pagan world were thought to have been men before they became gods and might appear again in human guise, the line between the human and the divine was thin in certain places.

Emperor-worship underwent gradual development, especially in the West where it was eventually fostered for political purposes. At first the emperor was regarded as the representative, if not the incarnation of, the *genius* or presiding spirit of his dynasty; and as *princeps* he represented Rome itself. He was the guardian of the state, the defender of peace and order, the preserver of the empire, its *soter* or saviour. As such it was an easy step for highly revered emperors, such as Augustus and Vespasian, to be included in the roll of those whom the state worshipped as *divus* or divine. For an emperor to demand worship during his lifetime was long regarded as an aberration worthy only of a Caligula or a Domitian.

Yet the increasing pomp and ceremony with which Roman emperors were surrounded made them appear more and more removed from the ranks of ordinary mortals. Men came to worship or take oaths by the *genius* or spirit of living emperors, though emperor-worship was restricted to acts or words of reverence or praise and did not extend to the addressing of prayer or receiving advice in dreams. Especially in the provinces, emperor-worship served as a unifying factor, a sentiment of loyalty to the *status quo*. Joint dedications to a local god and the emperor were frequent, and worship of the emperor was often coupled with that of Rome. The acute embarrassment which this came to present to the Christian may be seen reflected in the pages of the Apocalypse.

One of the most powerful solvents of established religion was provided by the development of philosophical thought. True, Greek religion had declined for other reasons also—disillusionment with the standards of divine conduct, the dissolution of the Greek city-states with which Greek religion had been so closely linked, and the attendant growth of individualism on the one hand and a world-view of things on the other. Yet all this was connected with the rise of philosophical schools of thought which discredited not only Greek religion but also that of Rome.

There was a certain amount of genuine Platonism in the first century: the rise of Neo-Platonism did not come in force until the third century. Platonism 'stood for a view of reality as spiritual, ideal, invisible: the external visible objects in the universe being only copies or shadows of the invisible realities' (F. C. Grant). Such a view produced an attitude of renunciation and asceticism, for the body came to be looked upon as little more than the temporary abiding place of the soul. An interior type of piety was developed which sought to lessen the attachment of the soul to the body, and eventually in Neo-Platonism rigorous asceticism was advocated as a means of releasing the soul from the down-drag of the body.

Attention has been drawn to the contrast between earthly shadows and heavenly realities which is a theme in the Letter to the Hebrews (cf. 2 C. 4: 18) and to passages such as 2 C. 5: 1–8. But the similarities are superficial: the richness and quality of the Biblical thought make it altogether distinctive.

The Epicurean philosophy taught that pleasure should be the object of life. Though in common parlance the Epicurean view gave rise to the motto, 'Let us eat and drink, for tomorrow we die', yet the pleasure that was sought was not necessarily or even characteristically that which is the product of bodily sensations. The pleasure that was sought was happiness. This, it was maintained, depended on peace of mind. Since religion tended to undermine such happiness with its fear of the supernatural and its bogy of punishment after death the Epicurean was anti-religious. For him the universe consisted of atoms and space. Chance ruled everything and there was no providential oversight by Fate or the gods. At death the soul disintegrated, so there need be nothing to fear thereafter. The existence of pain was not denied but Epicurus declared in a famous phrase that if sharp it is short and if long it is light. Pain, he declared, can always be offset by the memory of past happiness.

The disciples of Epicurus formed scattered groups which followed a common life under careful regulation. There they practised, though only among themselves, their prime virtue of friendship. Paul met Epicureans at Athens (Ac. 17: 18). Though they had gods of their own—beings of supernatural beauty and power living in paradises somehow protected from the general decay—the Epicureans were generally classed, with Christians, as atheists since they denied the existence of the traditional deities.

Cynicism—even more than Epicureanism a household word in the twentieth century—was an attitude held quite widely in the first century. The Cynic affected a lofty disregard for everything external to himself. True nobility, he held, lay in man's mind and not in external trappings. The great aim in life should be to prove that a man can do without things and yet be happy, healthy and wise. Cynicism easily led to contempt for authority and morality as well as religion. Yet the Cynics were never sufficiently numerous to be dangerous, and Vespasian dismissed them as 'barking curs'.

The most important philosophical attitude of the time was undoubtedly that of Stoicism. According to Wendland the hallmark of the Hellenistic age, Stoicism, was the one product of Greek intellectual enquiry to assume significant proportions in the western part of the Roman world. Cicero, Seneca and, in the second century, Marcus Aurelius, the philosopher-emperor, were among those who propagated it.

The problems to which Stoicism addressed itself were those which traditional religion had failed to solve and which other philosophies were grappling with. They have been well defined as 'how to behave in a world that had grown so large, and where man seemed so small and unattached, how to meet the onset of fortune (whether good or bad) without

flinching, how to face death and bereavement, how to remain master of your soul' (Charlesworth).

The answers which Stoicism provided to these questions stemmed from a view of the universe which may be defined as 'pantheistic materialism'. 'God is Nature, is Fate, is Fortune, is the Universe, is the all-pervading Mind' (Seneca). The fiery ether which was regarded as the divine and basic substance of the universe was identified with that reason or intelligence which constitutes man as man whoever he may be. The ethical ideal of Stoicism was a life in which a man does what is appropriate to his nature. This 'law of nature' is known to all men everywhere. What is needed is for men to be men by living according to that reason which is the law of their being. If they do, they will not give way to passion, unreasonable grief or cowardice, or any display of emotion: they will be free, within the fortress of their own minds, to follow the law of their being and thus to achieve the goal of 'self-sufficiency' by the twin way of 'apathy' and 'self-discipline'. Such was the logic of Stoicism. Though highly critical of traditional religion, Stoicism was able to come to terms with it by means of an allegorical interpretation of the old offensive religious myths.

The use by Paul of ideas such as conformity to nature, sufficiency, things being 'not convenient', and the like, have caused some to argue that he was influenced by Stoicism. Certainly Paul was not averse to using terms in current use: but he invariably filled them with new meaning. The vastly different presuppositions of Christianity and Stoicism (monotheism in contrast with pantheism, for example) require that Paul's thought should run in a direction far removed from that of Seneca. 'In many cases, where the parallels are most close, the theory of a direct historical connection is impossible; in many others it can be shown to be quite unnecessary; while in not a few instances the resemblance, however striking, must be condemned as illusory and fallacious' (Lightfoot). It is not really surprising that Marcus Aurelius, despite his lofty sentiments, should have despised Christians and countenanced their persecution.

A good deal of uncertainty still exists over the precise nature of Gnosticism and its rôle in the first century. It is certain that it constituted a serious threat to the Christian Church in the second century. Nor is there much doubt that it did not exist in the first century in a developed form. But the precise nature of Gnosticism is still a matter for scholarly debate. It seems to have been essentially eclectic, drawing its ideas from many sources. Whether Greek, oriental or Jewish ideas predominated in the final amalgam, it seems clear that many of the notions which contributed to it were common coin in the first century.

Among such ideas were the following: the dualistic basis of approach; the idea of intermediaries between a transcendent deity and a world which, being material, must needs be evil; the emphasis on the redemption of the spiritual element in man from the material body and world in which it has become imprisoned; the claim that initiation into *gnosis* (knowledge) is the way of freedom and release; the ascetic way of life which some gnostic sects required and the antinomianism which others permitted or even advocated. These were ideas current in the first century, some of them in systems of thought which have been summarized above.

Paul had occasion to warn against these very things. Dualism stands condemned in 1 Tim. 4: 1–5. The worship of angelic intermediaries is reproved in Col. 2: 18 and indirectly in Col. 1: 15–17. Over-emphasis on knowledge is deprecated in Col. 2: 8 and 1 C. 8: 1–3, and undue asceticism in Col. 2: 20–23. The incipient Gnosticism opposed by Paul seems to have been associated with Judaism (Col. 2: 16 f.).

The various schools of philosophy had their popularizers in wandering philosophers who peddled their wares just as religious teachers often did. Paul found it necessary to distinguish himself and his companions from such (1 Th. 2: 3–6).

Traditionally there was ample place in the Greek and Roman worlds for the practice of private religion. This normally supplemented the official religion, though if a suppliant were disappointed he might turn to private religion as a virtual substitute for the public cult which henceforth would be for him a purely perfunctory duty. With the increasing failure of the imperial cult to satisfy their spiritual aspirations men turned to new or developed forms of private religion.

Private religion might take the form of magical practices. In these, spiritual aspirations mingled with the grossest requests for material and physical satisfaction. There was no clearcut line of demarcation between magic and religion: divination, for example, was a recognized element in the latter. Magical papyri containing prayers and hymns might be utilized (Ac. 19: 19) and magical curses and imprecations uttered. The use of astrology and grossly superstitious practices figured in popular religion, especially among the lower classes of society.

Minor deities, less remote than the Olympians and the gods of the Pantheon, might be approached in private devotions. Asclepius, god of healing, was a universal favourite. Diana of the Ephesians (Artemis) enjoyed a widespread appeal (Ac. 19: 27). Sometimes fasts and purifications were employed in the hope of attaining to the vision of a god.

Perhaps the most remarkable feature of first-century religion, apart from the spread of Christianity, was the proliferation of new cults from the East, and particularly the growing popularity of the Mystery Religions. These new cults spread largely because of the failure of traditional religion to satisfy the growing religious consciousness of an age which was one not only of world empire but also of widespread individualism.

The Mystery Religions offered salvation on the basis of a divine revelation and the assurance of divine aid to redeem individuals from this life through 'rebirth for eternity'. Symbolic purifications and sacramental meals provided initiation into the 'mystery' and lent colour and some degree of plausibility. There was usually a monotheistic slant, the god of the cult being either the supreme deity or his son, consort or loyal friend. The appeal was individualistic, addressed to the soul in its solitariness, even if the individual was brought into a religious fellowship with social implications. There might be ethical implications also, often in the direction of ascetic renunciation.

The Mystery Religion was no innovation. The worship of Demeter at Eleusis had constituted a local religion of this kind in the days of ancient Greece. Several of the best-known Mystery Religions were introduced to Rome before the beginning of the Christian era, though the first century saw their widespread dissemination.

There were striking differences as well as common features in the various Mystery Religions. That of the Egyptian Isis was 'widespread, genteel, mystical and very feminine' (F. C. Grant). Isis, not alone, claimed that the names of other deities were titles that were rightly hers and that their functions really belonged to her. She was the great mother goddess of the world. The sacred mystery of her cult was the dismemberment of her consort, Osiris, by his enemy, Set; the search for the scattered limbs undertaken by the faithful Isis; and their restoration. The dignified processions; the services in her temples with lustrations and offerings of incense instead of bloody sacrifices; the open shrine; the hymns and sacred liturgy: all were capable of inspiring both excitement and devotion. Mattingly has described Isis as in many ways a prototype of the Virgin Mary.

The worship of Cybele, the great mother of Anatolia, and her young consort, Attis, was of a very different sort. It had originated in Phrygia where, in mad hypnotic dances, its devotees had mutilated themselves in honour of Cybele and her divine lover. It spread far and wide. In Rome, the temples of Cybele with their eunuch priests eventually gained acceptance, despite the sacrament of the *taurobolium* in which the initiate was apparently promised rebirth through drenching in the blood of a bull.

Mithraism, though it became the most popular of the mystery religions with a special attraction for soldiers, was not widespread until the second and third centuries. Of Persian origin, Mithraism was based on the myth of the cosmic struggle between Ahura-Mazda, the force of truth and light, and Ahriman, the force of falsehood and darkness. Mithras, champion of truth and light, had slain the great bull for the salvation of the world, and a bas-relief at the far end of the cave, real or artificial, in which meetings of his cult were held, depicted his exploits. Mithraism offered a fellowship in which members were pledged by initiation ceremonies and common meals to loyalty towards each other. Initiates could rise through various grades and were given the promise of a blessed life in the hereafter.

The similarities between the Mystery Religions and Christianity are obvious: the differences are more significant. In particular, the Mystery Religions did not posit an historical figure as saviour. There is no proof of any influence exerted by the ideas of the Mystery Religions upon Christianity. Indeed it has been asserted that one might as easily argue that there was influence in the opposite direction.

In the Roman world, religion came within the scope of state control: it was not regarded as merely a matter of personal conviction. Both religious and political considerations demanded this. On the one hand, the favour of the gods was thought to depend on the faithful observance of the cult by all subjects; on the other, the integrity of the empire was thought to be safeguarded by the universal observance of the imperial religion. But Rome was remarkably tolerant. Provided a man performed his duty in regard to the official *religio* he was free to choose his own *superstitio*, provided that it was neither antagonistic to the official cult, politically subversive nor offensively immoral. Unofficial religions which offended on any of these counts were likely to be proscribed, like Druidism in Gaul and Britain.

The extent to which Roman toleration might go is seen in the case of Judaism. Here was a religion that was uncompromisingly monotheistic and characterized by nationalistic fervour and proselytizing zeal. Yet it secured a *modus vivendi*. This was partly due to the face-saving consideration that the Jews offered sacrifice to their deity on behalf of the emperor. More significant, perhaps, was the fact that the Jews were of vital importance for the commercial prosperity of the empire. Above all, the Jews were a closely-knit community established throughout the empire, and to prohibit their worship would have caused widespread trouble of a kind that the Romans were always reluctant to provoke. The toleration granted to Judaism was somewhat uneasy, however, and might be forfeited by Jewish rebellions or by popular outcries against the Jews (cf. Ac. 18: 2).

At first Christianity shared the toleration granted to Judaism. Thus at Corinth Gallio regarded Christianity as a sect of that religion and would take no cognizance of it (Ac. 18: 12–17), and neither Festus (Ac. 25: 25) nor Agrippa (Ac. 26: 31, 32) regarded Paul's beliefs as reprehensible. But the Jews themselves were not slow to accuse Christians of political or religious subversion (Ac. 17: 6, 7; 18: 13), and Gentiles whose material interests were injured by the growth of Christianity (Ac. 16: 19–22; 19: 23–28) drew attention to the religious anomalies of Christianity.

Before the end of the New Testament period Christianity, which had become more and more distinct from Judaism, was regarded by those who had no intimate knowledge of its adherents as undesirable on political, religious, social and even moral grounds. Its attitude to pagan religion was sufficiently appreciated and its political and moral outlook was sufficiently misunderstood to render it the object of mingled fear and scorn. The crazed emperor, Nero, who was widely suspected of having wantonly set fire to Rome, was able to divert attention to the Christians by means of the persecution of A.D. 64.

In his first letter, Peter warned the Christians of Asia Minor of the sufferings that they must expect (1 Pet. 2: 12, 19 ff.; 3: 14; 4: 12 ff.) and urged them to silence by their display of good works the ignorance of their enemies who shared that ignorance, it may be noted, with celebrated Roman authors. (Tacitus described Christianity as a 'pernicious superstition', and Suetonius called it 'a novel and mischievous superstition'.)

Towards the end of the first century further persecution broke out at Rome as the result of the malevolence of Domitian. In other parts of the empire, and at all times, Christians were exposed to the hazard of persecution (Rev. 2: 13). Christianity was without legal sanction, and there were precedents for persecution. Moreover a hostile individual or mob might force the hand of a reluctant magistrate by creating a situation of public disorder, as at Ephesus in the time of Paul (Ac. 19).

BIBLIOGRAPHY

Angus, S., *The Mystery Religions and Christianity* (London, 1925).

Barrett, C. K., *The New Testament Background: Selected Documents* (London, 1956).

The Religious Background (Pagan)

GRANT, F. C., *Hellenistic Religions* (New York, 1953).

HINNELLS, J. R. (ed.), *Mithraic Studies*, 2 vols. (Manchester, 1975).

KEE, H. C., *Miracle in the Early Christian World* (New Haven, 1983).

LIGHTFOOT, J. B., *Saint Paul's Epistle to the Philippians*, pp. 270–328 (London, 1903). First published, 1868).

RUDOLPH, K., *Gnosis*. E.T. (Edinburgh, 1983).

WALLS, A. F., 'Gnosticism', NBD.

YAMAUCHI, E. M., *Pre-Christian Gnosticism*, 2nd edn. (Grand Rapids, 1983).

THE RELIGIOUS BACKGROUND OF THE NEW TESTAMENT (JEWISH)

H. L. ELLISON

In NT times Jewry was divided into three fairly distinct sections:

(a) those in Palestine and inland Syria;

(b) those in Mesopotamia and Persia—at the time they were outside the Roman empire;

(c) those in Mediterranean countries generally.

The second group does not enter the NT story directly (but cf. Ac. 2: 9). Hence it will not be mentioned further. The third group is dealt with partly in the article in passing, partly in a special section at the end.

THE EFFECTS OF THE BABYLONIAN EXILE

To understand the Jewish religious world in the NT period, we must look back to the return from the Babylonian exile in 538 B.C. and to certain outstanding events in the Inter-Testamental Period.

The return from exile and the years immediately following involved the Jews in a number of disappointments, the greatest of which was that political independence was not restored and the house of David did not regain the throne. Förster may be correct in maintaining that the pious had realized even in exile that return would not bring national independence with it, but if that is so, they formed a minority of the exiles, and most will have thought that the rebuilding of the Temple in 519 B.C., at the insistence of Haggai and Zechariah, would be followed by political freedom, but nothing happened to justify even the smallest hopes. The nature of the Persian empire was such that revolts might lead to a change of ruler but not to local independence.

Some 70 years later an event happened which vitally affected Judaism down to the present day. It seems clear that under the Monarchy the Law of Moses was largely the possession and concern of the priests and ruling classes. The ordinary man knew as much of it as was recited at the pilgrim feasts or as he was commanded to keep. In approximately 440 B.C. Ezra, aided by Nehemiah, presented the Law

to the people as something which it was each individual's responsibility to keep; the tears of Neh. 8: 9 were mainly tears of joy. Though this is not definitely stated, the theory behind Ezra's action was undoubtedly that the exile and subsequent lack of independence had been caused primarily by neglect of the Law, and that if all Israel (not merely its priests and elders) kept the Law as it should be kept, the fulness of God's blessing would come on His people.

Ezra's reformation meant that from that time on the religious life of the Jew changed very gradually from a temple ritual to an ordered system of life, which increasingly embraced all its aspects. It was very soon assumed that though the Law did not contain specific commandments covering every possible aspect of life, yet principles could be deduced from it on which the necessary new commandments could be based. The revelation at Sinai was *torah* (instruction), not merely a law-book.

This enabled the majority who had remained in Babylonia and who came only rarely to Jerusalem to follow the same pattern of life as was becoming standard in Palestine. That Ezra should have come expressly from Babylonia to introduce the new pattern into Palestine shows how conscious the Eastern dispersion was that it was only the keeping of the Law that really stood between them and assimilation to their pagan surroundings.

Just over a century later the conquests of Alexander the Great made Palestine part of the Greek world. This did not bring political independence with it, but it caused the spread of a large number of Jews into the Greek cities, old and new, of the eastern Mediterranean, especially Alexandria. This new dispersion, which very rapidly adopted Greek as its language, was kept from assimilation only by its observance of the Law and by its continuance of the pattern of life observed in Palestine.

The Greek civilization carried by Alexander into Asia and Egypt is usually called Hellenism (its adjective is Hellenistic); the form of Gk.

used by it, which differed considerably from classical Attic Gk., we call *Koinē*. Hellenism, like all Gk. culture, was based on cities, and so was slow to influence the countryside. In addition, it presupposed a leisured, slave-owning class of citizens. For that reason the Jews of Palestine, who were mostly poor farmers, were slow to be influenced, even though a number of pagan, Hellenistic cities were founded in the country. For all that the influence of Hellenism on the Jews was far-reaching, both positively and negatively.

SOME INFLUENCES OF HELLENISM
There was no real division felt between the Jews of the East and those of Palestine and Syria, apart from those living in Hellenistic cities like Syrian Antioch. They all spoke Aramaic, a Semitic language akin to Hebrew; they all formed part of the traditional Asiatic world that had changed little down the centuries; they were mostly farmers or artisans. In the Hellenistic world the typical Jew spoke Greek; Paul was an exception; he was 'a Hebrew of Hebrews' (Phil. 3: 5), i.e. although he knew Greek his home language was Aramaic. Further he was with few exceptions a city dweller —here Paul conformed to the pattern—and tended to be far more of an individualist than the Palestinian Jew, though not to the degree we are so familiar with today.

While the Law was read in Hebrew in the synagogues of the Western dispersion—fragments of MSS with the Hebrew written in Greek letters are still in existence; cf. also the second column of Origen's Hexapla (cf. *NBD* p. 1,260a)—it had to be followed by a translation into Greek. By 50 B.C. the whole OT had been translated in a rendering traditionally called the Septuagint (LXX). The first Greek translations of the Law go back in all probability to before 200 B.C., though the traditional story found in *The Letter of Aristeas* is merely pious propaganda. The recasting of Hebrew religious thought into Greek meant subtle changes in outlook, which were hardly felt when Hebrew had to be turned into Aramaic; these also laid them the more open to the influence of Hellenism.

The greatest fascination of Hellenism for the Asiatic was its apparent freeing of man's mind. In the old systems the whole of human activity moved in a totalitarian religious setting. Hellenism freed large areas of thought from the control of the gods. Even before Palestinian Jewry was brought into full contact with it, its influence may be seen at work.

This may best be seen by comparing *Proverbs* with *Ecclesiastes*, which we must date not too long before 200 B.C., and even more with *The Wisdom of Jesus ben Sira* (*Ecclesiasticus*), which in its Hebrew original dates from *c*. 180 B.C.

The strain of intellectual rationalism in the latter is the more remarkable, as Ben Sira seems to have been an outspoken enemy of Hellenistic thought. At this period there entered Judaism a strain of rationalism it has never lost. One sign of it is the introduction of 'all your mind' (Lk. 10: 27; Mk 12: 30) into the quotation from Dt. 6: 5. Cf. p. 1143.

Among Hellenistic Jews this led to clearer and sharper thought. It was no chance that in Palestine and the East Christianity was able to remain within Jewry until after A.D. 90, and even then the breach was more political and national than theological. But in the Mediterranean world it seems to have been a clear-cut either-or from the first. There was the added factor that in the Greek dispersion the Jew felt the keeping of the Law far more a matter of spiritual life or death than did the Palestinian Jew, for whom it was rather the highest religious privilege.

There is no saying how much Judaism might have been penetrated and corrupted by Hellenism had it not been for another of its facets. Hellenism looked on itself as a system given by the gods to unite and revive a fragmented and weary world. To accomplish this it adopted a system we call syncretism. Instead of decrying and seeking to abolish the Asiatic gods and goddesses, it identified them with the Greek gods of Olympus. A city would continue to worship its old deities but under new names and with a Greek slant. For a short time new life really seemed to flow into the outworn systems. We must note two results, one minor, one major, for Jewry.

In the first century B.C. there entered the Mediterranean lands from further east dualistic systems, which were as much philosophies as religions. In the syncretistic society already described they were made welcome, the more so as they did not try to displace the accepted cults but, as was explained, sought to give them deeper meaning. Just because of their appeal to reason and special, esoteric knowledge, these *Gnostic* systems, as we call them, made a great appeal to some Hellenistic Jews, and even to some in Palestine. They felt they could follow them without any disloyalty to the religion of Moses. Most of the incipient Gnosticism combated in the Pauline letters is to be attributed to Jewish sources.

THE STRUGGLE AGAINST HELLENIST DOMINANCE
Among the heirs of Alexander the Great the most powerful was Seleucus I, who ruled (312–281 B.C.) from Syria to India. This wide-stretching empire was already showing signs of collapse, when Antiochus the Great (223–187 B.C.) was defeated by the Romans at Magnesia (190 B.C.) and had to accept crippling

peace conditions. When Antiochus Epiphanes (175–163 B.C.) came to the throne, it was clear that a major effort had to be made to unify his kingdom, or it would crumble away in his hands. He considered himself to be an incarnate manifestation (the force of Epiphanes) of Olympian Zeus and so decided to use Hellenistic religion as the unifying mortar for his kingdom.

His policy coincided with the rise to power in Jerusalem of a small group of rich men, mainly from the more important priests, who wanted to turn Jerusalem into a Hellenistic city. The outcome was that in 167 the Temple was rededicated to Olympian Zeus, with whom Antiochus, after the normal syncretistic fashion, identified Yahweh. An attempt was made to ensure that all Jews sacrificed to Zeus. Circumcision and the possession of portions of the OT Scriptures were made capital offences. One test used was to make Jews eat pork.

It it useless speculating about the motives of those Jews that supported his policy. Probably he went very much further than they had expected, but having once started, they could not draw back. More important is to realize to what extent Hellenism had affected some Jewish circles.

The policy of Antiochus led to vigorous armed resistance. Three years later (164 B.C.) the Temple was cleansed and in 142 B.C. Judaea became independent for the first time since Josiah. Though freedom was won by desperate courage and sordid intrigue, it was gained more through the break-up of the Seleucid empire than through Judaea's own strength. So when Rome appeared on the scene in 63 B.C., the independence of the Jewish state quickly ended, not to be renewed until our own days. An understanding of the effects of the century from Antiochus Epiphanes to Rome is vital for the background to the NT.

Every conscious approximation to Greek thought was made impossible. Whatever the reasons found for refusing social contacts with Gentiles (cf. Ac. 10: 28; 11: 3), probably the main motive lay in a deep fear of dangerous influences.

THE JEWISH RELIGIOUS PARTIES

The Sadducees probably had considerable sympathy for the ideological position of the rich Jewish Hellenists in the time of Antiochus Epiphanes; certainly they were in some ways their successors. But they never ventured to go outside the framework of the Law, even if their interpretation of it was often other than that of the Pharisees. They were drawn mainly from the richer landed aristocracy and the leading priestly families, so never found sympathy among the masses. (It should be remembered that none of their writings have come down to us, so we are dependent for our knowledge of them mainly on statements by the Pharisees, their deadly enemies; so dogmatism in judging them is out of place.)

The lamentable failure of the Hasmonean priest-kings, both morally and politically, so disgusted the better elements of the population that they abandoned all thought of political independence until God Himself should intervene. They were known at first as the *Hasidim* (probably God's loyal ones), but comparatively early in this period they split into at least two parties.

The more radical section we know as the Essenes, and our main information about them is gleaned from the Qumran discoveries. They denied the right of Simon the Hasmonean (143–134 B.C.) to the high-priesthood, which they considered belonged to the descendants of Onias III, deposed by Antiochus Epiphanes. When John Hyrcanus and especially Alexander Jannai added moral unworthiness to the lack of hereditary right, the Qumran group despaired of reformation, decided they were in the last days, turned their backs on the Temple and people and withdrew to the wilderness to await the final struggle between good and evil. They were essentially a secret society, which is one reason why they are not mentioned in the NT, and had little direct influence on the people. The very fact of their protest and existence must, however, have had wide-reaching effects. Their special form of Biblical interpretation was in some way a preparation for that of the NT. Their very existence as an influential, dissident sect within Jewry made it easier for the early Church to be tolerated for a time. After A.D. 70, when their movement dissolved with all its dreams shattered, many of them joined the Church with disastrous theological results for the Hebrew Christians, most of whom were not strong enough to resist the fanatical concepts for which the Essenes stood.

In some relationship to the Essenes stood the writers of apocalyptic and pseudonymous literature, the best known of which is the collection found in *The Book of Enoch*. We know virtually nothing about them; though they shared much of the Essene outlook, it is unlikely that they are to be identified with them. Their theories of fixed times and seasons, of cosmic conflicts centred on this earth and of a mighty struggle between good and evil soon to be ended with the triumph of God, did much to create the fanaticism that was the chief cause of the fall of the Jewish commonwealth and Temple; they left their lasting mark also on popular Christianity.

The other section of the *Hasidim* came to be known as the Pharisees. They were normally utterly rigorous with themselves, but were prepared to compromise where the common man was concerned, for they had not completely given up hope of national reformation. The Essenes looked down on them and called them 'Seekers after smooth things'. This was unfair. Their meticulous tithing policy, which largely cut them off from those whose tithing methods they suspected, and often caused them serious financial loss, showed that they had not chosen an easy way or one that brought them personal gain. What they did was to base themselves on statements like '*Be careful to follow every command I am giving you today, so that you may live and increase . . .*' (Dt. 8: 1) and insist that the Law must be so interpreted that the ordinary poorer citizen could keep it. This was one of the main reasons why they had the support of the majority in the time of Christ. Josephus gives their numbers in the time of Herod the Great as 6,000; the other groups mentioned will have been smaller still.

John Hyrcanus (134–104 B.C.) reconquered the south of Judaea. It had been settled by Edomites during and immediately after the Babylonian exile and was in consequence called Idumaea. He gave the inhabitants the choice of exile or Judaism; most preferred the latter. Aristobulus I (104–103 B.C.) did the same to Galilee, where most were probably descended from the northern tribes. In each case there was produced a population more fanatical than pious. The Idumaeans played an important part in the revolt against Rome. In Galilee there was armed resistance to Roman nominees after the fall of the Hasmonean house (63 B.C.). Herod, while still only procurator of Galilee (*c.* 47 B.C.) had major trouble in his province, and when he was made King of the Jews by the Romans much of the main opposition was again in Galilee. By his death these men, under the name of Zealots or Cananaeans (cf. Mk 3: 18—Cananaean is the Aramaic equivalent of Zealot) had become a major influence in Palestine and, at least in Galilee, soon became more popular than the Pharisees. This is easy to understand. Fighting Romans, killing tax-collectors, robbing foreign caravans and making Jewish merchants contribute to their war chest was more satisfying than just keeping the Law and waiting for God's time for salvation. Another reason for the increasing popularity of the Zealots was that they were comparable with the Levellers and Fifth-Monarchy men of the Commonwealth in England. They sought not merely freedom from foreign rule but also a social revolution which would give the poor their rights.

It was mainly they who wished to make Jesus king by force (Jn 6: 15) and who hailed Him as Messiah on the first Palm Sunday (Mk 11: 9, 10). The question about the tribute money (Mk 12: 14) was intended to discredit Him in their eyes, unless He answered in a way that would make Him appear dangerous to the Romans. It was they who precipitated the revolt against Rome and made any compromise solution impossible. They even hastened the destruction of Jerusalem by destroying the stocks of food in it (Jos. *War*, V. i. 4) probably believing that God *was bound* to intervene at the eleventh hour, and so the sooner the crisis came the better.

It is clear there were also a number of other smaller sects, many of them in the lower Jordan valley and Transjordan. Josephus (*Life* 2) tells of one Banus, who lived 'in the wilderness, wearing clothes from trees, and frequently bathing himself with cold water by day and night for purification'. He was doubtless typical of many others.

When we remember that there were also communities from the Greek diaspora in Jerusalem, who maintained their separate language and identity (cf. Ac. 6: 1, 9), it should be clear to us that no really unitary Jewish religious background to the NT existed.

THE SYNAGOGUE AND THE STUDY OF THE LAW

The Pharisees did not go as far as the Essenes and turn their backs on the Temple, but they were deeply disgusted by the venal and corrupt priests who controlled it—this is no judgment on the priests in general but on a few families who held all the real power and were able to pocket most of the revenue. Their answer was to build up the influence of the Synagogue. Its roots go back possibly to the Babylonian exile, but there is no evidence that it was influential in Palestine until near the beginning of the first century B.C. It began by offering the possibility of the study of the Law by the ordinary man, and—little though that was the original purpose—it laid the foundations of a service for the worship of God virtually divorced from the sacrificial ritual of the Temple.

The Pharisees quickly recognized the possibilities offered by the Synagogue for spreading their own concepts and for decreasing the power of the priestly Sadducees. Thanks to their efforts there was probably by 50 B.C. a synagogue in every Palestinian village with a Jewish population of any size. Attached to the synagogue was a school, where the boys learned to read. It was not there to encourage literacy—girls were seldom taught—but to ensure that each man could read the Law.

The original purpose of the Synagogue was expressed by the reading of the Law (to which was later added a prophetic passage) on the Sabbath, and also on Mondays and Thursdays, the regular market days. If there was one present capable of doing it, the passage read could be expounded. Soon there was added to the reading a simple service of praise and prayer.

Its heart consisted of the *Shema* (Dt. 6: 4, very early expanded to Dt. 6: 4–9; 11: 13–1; Num. 15: 37–41), the Ten Commandments (dropped about A.D. 100, when Christians stressed them to the exclusion of the remainder of the Law) and the *Amidah*, or *Shemoneh Esreh* ('Eighteen Benedictions'), a great complex of praise, petition and thanksgiving (cf. *NBD* p. 1,228b). Various factors soon led to daily services in larger communities, but they could be held only if there were ten males over thirteen years old present.

It should be noted that the officers of the Synagogue were only administrative. There were one or three elders and a *hazzan*, who was responsible for order, acted as attendant (Lk. 4: 20), and was normally the schoolmaster. Anyone who had the knowledge and piety could lead the congregation in worship.

The Rabbi was an expert in the Law, to whom all difficult cases were brought and who tried to guide others in their studies of it. The only privilege of the priests in the Synagogue was in the public reading of the Law and the pronouncing of the Benediction (Num. 6: 24–26). This helps to explain why the apostolic church knows no sacerdotal caste.

Very few Palestinian Jews living at any distance from Jerusalem will have attended the Temple services, except at the three great feasts of Passover, Pentecost and Tabernacles, and it is not likely that the poorer will have attended all three—there is no mention of Christ's having been in Jerusalem for Pentecost. Those who lived in the Dispersion could often manage only one or two visits in a lifetime. So of necessity the Synagogue had largely displaced the Temple for the ordinary man, even before the latter's destruction.

Though most knew the Psalter off by heart, the main purpose of Bible study was to discover the demands of the Law on the individual and community. Not long after Ezra it was agreed that it contained 613 commandments, 365 of them negative and 248 positive. The *Hasidim* then made a hedge about these commandments, i.e. they made new laws, not a few based on old traditions, the keeping of which would guarantee the keeping of the original commandments. Though at first they were unable to enforce these new laws, increasingly after the struggle with Hellenism they were accepted by the bulk of the people. They represent 'the traditions of the elders' attacked by Christ.

Even with the traditions these basic commandments did not cover the whole of life. So from *c*. 100 B.C. a complete code of law was slowly developed, based on the principles of the Torah, as they were understood by the Pharisees. Their full formulation is found in the Talmud. Since many of the new demands

ran counter to the traditional legislation administered by the Sadducees, they could not be enforced until after A.D. 70. It is often impossible for us to know what the actual law in force in the time of Christ was. Until recently commentaries took for granted that the trial of Jesus offended not only against natural justice but also against specific Jewish law. It is now known that these Talmudic laws were not in force, and indeed some may never have been more than theoretical. The complete Pharisaic system was not accepted by the common people until *c*. A.D. 150 and that after a most bitter struggle.

SOME SPECIAL PROBLEMS OF THE DISPERSION

Julius Caesar had granted the Jews freedom to observe the Sabbath and to gather in synagogues, exemption from military service and the right to live according to their own laws. In addition, provided a non-Jew or a Roman citizen was not involved, they could judge their law suits before their own courts both in Palestine and in the Dispersion generally.

In Palestine such rights could be taken more or less for granted, but in the Dispersion they were exceptional and precious; indeed without them it might have been almost impossible to live openly as Jews. The Roman world did not welcome Sabbath keeping, and was strongly opposed to any faith that would release its adherents from military service or the more onerous municipal or state offices. So while no effort was made to reduce Jewish privileges, it was expected that they would not increase their numbers by proselytizing. Hence in Acts we meet far more 'God-fearers' (NIV 'God-fearing Gentiles', *e.g.* Ac. 13: 26), people who had accepted Jewish principles without becoming Jews, than proselytes, who ranked as full Jews. Quite apart from their attitude to his teaching, the Hellenistic Jews considered that Paul was endangering their privileges by attracting too many non-Jews into what was still regarded as a Jewish sect.

It should be obvious that it was not possible for the average Hellenistic Jew to keep the finer points of the Law in the way a Pharisee would in Palestine. This rendered him the more zealous about those points which he could keep, and the more bitter about anyone who would seek to abrogate them.

Mention was made earlier of those Hellenistic Jews who were influenced by Gnostic speculation. There were others who deliberately adopted various heathen superstitions, going at times as far as a real syncretistic worship. Examples of these tendencies may be found in Ac. 13: 6–11; 19: 13–16 and 19: 19, to which may be added Simon, a Samaritan (8: 9, 10).

THE TENSION OF THE TIME

During the time of Christ's ministry the Jewish people were coming to the end of their tether. The century of political independence under the Hasmonean priest-kings had ended by their being more firmly under the heel of Rome than they had ever been under their Persian or Greek rulers. The collapse of the Hasmonean house had brought terrible suffering with it. Klausner (*Jesus of Nazareth*, p. 144) estimates that in the thirty years from the death of Queen Shalom-Zion (Salome Alexandra) in 67 B.C. till Herod the Great was fully in power as king in 37 B.C. 'far more than a hundred thousand Jews were killed. And these were the pick of the nation, the healthiest, mainly the young men, and the most enthusiastic, who had refused to suffer the foreign yoke'. In 31 B.C. an earthquake killed about 30,000 (Josephus, *Ant.* XV. v. 2, *Wars* I. xix. 3); there were famine and pestilence in 25 and 24 B.C. (Josephus, *Ant.* XV. ix. 1). After Herod's death thousands more perished in a vain attempt to get rid of his house. Herod bled the land white to pay for his grandiose building schemes in Jerusalem, Sebaste (Samaria), Caesarea, his great fortresses like Machaerus and Masada and even outside his borders in Tyre and Sidon, Rhodes, Athens, Pergamon and other cities. There is no evidence that taxation grew less after his death, though the money was squandered on even less profitable schemes. F. C. Grant (*The Economic Background of the Gospels*, 1926) reckons that the Romans and the Temple together accounted for thirty to forty per cent., and possibly more, in income tax on the people.

In addition to what the Jew suffered from his rulers must be reckoned the whips of his own countrymen. There is ample evidence that the bulk of the land and commerce was in the hands of a relatively small section of the population, and that they normally used their position with scant humanity (cf. Jas 2: 6; 5: 1–6).

Consequently something had to happen. The folly of a Roman procurator loosed the whirlwind of the revolt against Rome (A.D. 66–73). This swept away Sadducees and Zealots, Qumran Essenes and apocalyptists alike. Jewry had to choose between the infant Church with its message of a crucified and risen Messiah and the Pharisees with their cult of the Law. For a short time it seemed that the Church might triumph, but for the Hebrew Christian the Law was normally too precious to be let go. So the zeal of the Pharisee triumphed over a divided loyalty to the Messiah Jesus. By A.D. 90 the Hebrew Christian found himself being squeezed out of the community of Jewry, whatever his attitude to the Law.

BIBLIOGRAPHY

(Simpler works are marked ★)

General
★BRUCE, F. F., *Israel and the Nations* (Exeter, 1973).
★ELLISON, H. L., *From Babylon to Bethlehem* (Exeter, 1976).
FÖRSTER, W., *Palestinian Judaism in New Testament Times* (Edinburgh, 1964).
KLAUSNER, J., *Jesus of Nazareth* (London, 1929).
★PEROWNE, S., *The Life and Times of Herod the Great* (London, 1956).
PFEIFFER, R. H., *History of New Testament Times* (New York, 1949).
SCHÜRER, E., *History of the Jewish People in the Age of Jesus Christ*, 3 vols. (Edinburgh, 1973–).

Religion
★EDERSHEIM, A., *The Temple: Its Ministry and Service as they were at the Time of Christ* (London, 1847; reprinted 1960).
MOORE, G. F., *Judaism* (Cambridge, Mass., 1927–30).
NEUSNER, J., *The Rabbinic Traditions about the Pharisees before 70 A.D.*, 3 vols. (Leiden, 1971).
PARKES, J., *The Foundations of Judaism and Christianity* (London, 1960).
SAFRAI, S., and STERN, M. (ed.), *The Jewish People in the First Century*, 2 vols. (Assen, 1974–76).
SANDERS, E. P. (ed.), *Jewish and Christian Self-Definition*, 3 vols. (London, 1980–84).

Qumran
BLACK, M., *The Scrolls and Christain Origins* (London, 1969).
★BRUCE, F. F., *Second Thoughts on the Dead Sea Scrolls* (London, 1966).
BURROWS, M., *The Dead Sea Scrolls* (London, 1955).
BURROWS, M., *More Light on the Dead Sea Scrolls* (London, 1958).
★VERMES, G., *The Dead Sea Scrolls in English* (Harmondsworth, 1962).

Reference may be made to articles in NBD and other Bible Dictionaries. Further authorities will be found mentioned in the works cited. Certain older works are not mentioned as not being any longer reliable.

THE DEVELOPMENT
OF DOCTRINE
IN THE NEW TESTAMENT

WALTER L. LIEFELD

To read the NT is to take an exciting journey of discovery. The point of departure is, in the words of Mark, 'the beginning of the gospel about Jesus Christ, the Son of God' (Mk 1: 1). Journey's end is a vantage point from which the Christian looks ahead exclaiming 'Come, Lord Jesus!' (Rev. 22: 20). The journey is taken in the confidence that after centuries of fragmentary communication, God has spoken with finality in His Son (Heb. 1: 1 f.). This word by and about the Lord Jesus Christ needs to be interpreted as the growing church is increasingly able to comprehend its significance (Jn 16: 12–15). The history of redemption has reached its climax in Christ who 'offered for all time one sacrifice for sins' (Heb. 10: 12). Yet the message of the cross not only has to be carried across the world, but needs to be understood in all its implications and applied to Christian life. The central event of history lies not in the future but in the past (Heb. 9: 28), but instead of living in a new world with enemies conquered and sin restrained (a popular Messianic expectation), the Christian is now a citizen of two worlds, an inhabitant of two ages, daily awaiting the future consummation.

The actual writing of the NT took place in but a fraction of the time spanned by the OT. Yet the doctrinal progress, against a changing background of circumstances, is remarkable. The Gospel of John (which itself reveals new dimensions of Christology unseen in the Synoptics) relates a promise of the Lord Jesus regarding this development of doctrine: 'I have much more things to say to you, more than you can now bear. When the Spirit of truth comes, He will guide you into all truth' (Jn 16: 12 f.). In saying that His disciples could not yet 'bear' this further truth, Jesus probably had reference in part to the fact that they needed the strengthening experience of witnessing His resurrection after the sorrowful experience of the cross. They also needed to receive the Holy Spirit at Pentecost, who would bring into their experience the reality of the truth He would teach them. It is certainly also true that the significance of this further revelation could be understood only as the disciples experienced the opportunities and problems of the first Christian decades. Also one must bear in mind that revelation was given in accordance with God's orderly plan.

The NT, then, like the OT, contains a progressive revelation given by God in various contexts of experiences. Some of the most important doctrinal statements are introduced in response to questions, such as Jn 14: 5–9, or problems, as Phil. 2: 1–13. The growing church itself was full of questions, and provided both the occasion and the context of a developing theology.

In taking this fact into consideration, however, one must avoid some prevalent misconceptions. We cannot say, for example, that the church *created* the teachings of Jesus, as is sometimes claimed on the basis of form-critical studies. A study of the environment within which the Gospels were formed helps us to understand the selection and form of the teachings of Jesus, but this is quite a different thing from asserting that the early church formulated material to meet their own needs and then read it back into Jesus' life.

Likewise, one must not assume that the progress of doctrine in the NT is the same thing as an evolutionary development. Attempts have sometimes been made to place NT materials on a linear scale extending from the 'simple beginnings' of the teachings of Jesus in the Synoptics to the 'higher theology' of John or the later Letters. Certainly there was a maturing of thought. Yet recent studies have emphasized both the depth of the theology of the early Jerusalem church and the early date of much NT material. A simple linear development is also ruled out by the fact that various aspects of divine truth were being unfolded simultaneously in many different places and circumstances. The questions posed by the pagans at Ephesus, the new Christians at Corinth, and the Jews in Jerusalem required different formulations of the Christian message.

Recognition of these varying matrices, however, has occasioned other unsatisfactory hypotheses. The postulations of the 'Tübingen school' regarding an antithesis between Peter and Paul have still not been completely abandoned. The idea that Paul was significantly influenced by Hellenistic thought and the mystery religions is also still being circulated, in spite of the fact that research has demonstrated the exaggeration and anachronisms inherent in some of the suggested comparisons. The Gentile churches did not develop in isolation from the Jerusalem church and its influence. Also the differences between Palestinian and Diaspora Judaism are now acknowledged to have been much smaller than formerly thought, especially in light of the extensive Hellenization of Palestine. Still it must also be noted that the very success of the Christian mission in penetrating by stages beyond Palestinian Judaism into the Diaspora and then into the pagan world called for reformulations of the message.

A realistic reconstruction of the process of development will therefore take into account both the unity and diversity of the NT life and thought. Theologians have long sought for a unifying theme in the NT as, for example, love or the kingdom. Recent stress has been put on 'salvation-history'. Understood rightly as the redemptive acts of God in history and their interpretation in the Scriptures, this is not just a theme but the historical reality in which the church was actually taking part. Our Lord Jesus Christ Himself is certainly the focal point of all the NT. The early church was called on to explain the implication of their message not only regarding the person of Christ, and His death, resurrection and ascension, but also their own very existence as a church: their identity, mission, and destiny.

THE NATURE OF THE DEVELOPMENT

How may we trace the stages of development of NT doctrine? One way, obviously, is to study the successive books in their canonical order. This is the method followed in the famous Bampton lectures given a hundred years ago by Thomas Dehany Bernard, entitled in their published form, *The Progress of Doctrine in the New Testament*. He chose this approach, as his preface explains, in preference to a survey of the development of specific doctrines. He begins by contrasting the Gospels with the rest of the NT, asserting that in the former Christ is the source of doctrine, in the latter He is the subject. The Gospels, he suggests, create a sense of need, give a pledge of revelation to come, provide an initial deposit of material to be drawn on, and provide a safeguard to the later development. This approach has value in

that it honours the canonical order and provides helpful thoughts for the person who reads the NT books consecutively. Doctrine can thus be studied book by book and by authors to see their individual theological contributions. The following brief summary will suffice to illustrate this.

Starting with the Gospels, we find that each of them is a distinctive theological composition, a fact stressed again by recent scholarships after long neglect by those who saw the Gospels mainly as editorial rearrangements of the traditions about Jesus. Matthew, in presenting Him as the promised Messiah, draws not only on specific OT predictions, but employs a method of interpretation then common, to show that in Christ the full significance of OT history (especially the Exodus) is realized. Even the order in which he presents the teachings of Jesus reflects his orientation to Jewish methods of teaching. He shows the Lord Jesus as giving final meaning to the law and as introducing the Kingdom.

Mark's shorter (and probably earlier) work is a gospel of action. The Son of Man performs healings, trying to avoid public identification with the inadequate popular concept of the Messiah. His death for sinners is clearly predicted several times, and a major part of the book describes the event. Luke, both in his Gospel and in the book of Acts, enlarges on the sovereign acts of God in Christ, through the Holy Spirit, toward the accomplishment of His will in the spread of the gospel by the church. John, the beloved disciple, combines an emphasis on the divine Sonship of Christ, to whom many 'signs' or confirmatory miracles clearly point, with a stress on His true humanity. He is the sent One, who has both descended to earth and ascended again, whose power and love are now being realized among men by the Spirit. These themes are found in the Letters as well as in the Gospel of John.

Among the doctrines developed in the Pauline Letters are those of God as Creator, just and merciful; of Christ as Son and Redeemer; of the Holy Spirit as a motivating and powerful force in the believer's life; of the gospel of grace; of the church; and of the place of the Jews and their heritage. Hebrews deals further with the Jewish religion and the superiority of Christ and His work over all that had been said and done in the days of the law and the prophets. James reaffirms the Biblical doctrine of God, His Word and human responsibility, and shows that a professed faith unsubstantiated by deeds proves itself to be no faith at all. Peter, writing under the stress and unbelief of the times, displays what is really of value in this life: Christ Himself, His death, His example, His Word and His promises. The later writings of the NT emphasize the importance of sound doctrine, holy life and steadfast hope in the promised return of Christ.

This development of doctrine in the NT is founded on the teachings of Jesus, along guidelines He laid down during His ministry and, perhaps especially, in His private instruction of the disciples between His resurrection and ascension. One must keep in mind, however, that while the Gospels preserve these foundational words of the Lord Jesus, they were not the first NT books to be composed. Nor are the rest of the books in chronological order. Therefore a consecutive reading of the NT does not convey the doctrinal development as it actually took place in the early church. A survey of the books in order is therefore not completely adequate for a study of the development of doctrine. An alternate approach is the consideration of individual doctrines. Yet it is immediately apparent that the NT does not present a systematic treatment of doctrine, nor can individual doctrines be isolated from each other or from the life and developing needs of the early church.

In recent years much attention has been given to the context of the growing church as providing an understanding of its maturing theology. This context includes not only the church itself but its environment. The Jewish sects, the successive cultures penetrated by the gospel, the various heresies which challenged orthodoxy are all a part. Knowledge of this background is continually being increased from such discoveries as the Dead Sea Scrolls and the Nag Hammadi documents. Much of the NT can be understood better when seen as a response, engendered and guided by the Holy Spirit, to the questions asked of and by the Christian community. The most important of these questions centred about the person and work of Christ. The resurrection had implications which could not humanly have been anticipated before it took place. If Christ and His work were to be proclaimed, they must first be understood. The missionary task of the church necessitated the marshalling of facts and meaning of the gospel in terminology understandable by each successive audience. The cross had to be explained as well as preached, and this doctrine is constantly being augmented throughout the NT. The gospel preaching did not, however, always find a favourable response. The adverse reaction of many Jewish people raised significant questions: What would become of those who did not accept their Messiah? Were they still the people of God? What was the relationship of the Christian to the Jewish community, to the OT law, the temple, the priesthood? What support for the answers could be found in the OT? If God was now carrying on His purposes through the church instead of through Israel, what was the relationship of Jewish and Gentile believers? What was the nature and destiny of the church? How was it to worship, to serve, to be governed? What place did the church have in salvation-history? The Messiah had come, but had clearly left some important prophecies unfulfilled. He had promised to return, but time was passing with no sign of this taking place. How were Christians to live while waiting for their Lord? In what ways were converts from paganism to change their former way of life? What should be done about the increasing opposition felt from pagans, Jews and heretical Christians? These are a few of the issues that called for further revelation. Some of them will be discussed further below.

The doctrinal answers to these questions were not independently conceived, but went back, as we have suggested, to the teaching of the Lord Jesus Himself. Scholars have been concerned not only to go back to the Gospels, but to ascertain what were the earliest formulations of doctrine in the preaching and teaching of the early church. C. H. Dodd is generally recognized as the one who gave impetus to this study with his reconstruction of the early *kērygma*, or preaching.

The *kērygma* is the essential message of the gospel. It is expressed, for example, in 1 C. 15: 3 ff., and includes the fact of the death of Jesus the Messiah in accordance with OT prophecies, his burial and resurrection, and the fact that his death was an offering given for our sins in voluntary obedience to God. It also included a brief summary of the earthly ministry of the Lord Jesus, and an explanation, based on OT texts, of the reason why the Messiah had to suffer, His vindication by the resurrection, and His future glory. This message is found in the early chapters of Acts, in Peter's message to Cornelius in Ac. 10: 34–43 and in Paul's preaching to the Thessalonians in Ac. 17: 1–3.

Another early doctrinal element was the confession, the personal affirmation that a new convert made to his faith in Christ and his loyalty to Him. It was not only a testimony to conversion but a doctrinal predication regarding Christ. Such a confession is probably seen in Rom. 10: 9. The confession here is 'Jesus is Lord'. In Mk 8: 29 and parallels the apostles confess that Jesus is the Christ. The Gospel of John was written to demonstrate that Jesus was the Christ, the Son of God (Jn 20: 31). These confessions form a basis for later Christological teaching.

There are also fuller credal statements which are now acknowledged by many scholars to be among the earliest strands of the NT. They may appear in a hymnic style. Some find in the use of the relative pronoun, 'who', a key to the credal statements. So Phil. 2: 6–11, which relates the humiliation and exaltation of Christ begins, 'who being in the very nature of God . . .', and Col. 1: 13 ff., 'For he (lit. 'who') has rescued us . . . in whom we have redemption . . . He (lit. 'who') is the image of the invisible God . . .' etc. 1 Tim. 3: 16 may well be another example of an early credal statement. The best manuscripts have the word 'who' instead of the word 'God', and the creed therefore began evidently, 'who was manifest in flesh . . .' (NIV 'He appeared in a body . . .'). See also Heb. 1: 1–4 and 1 Pet. 2: 22 ff.

Another early element may well have been a collection of moral and ethical exhortations given to new converts. This suggestion is based on a comparison of passages containing such similar expressions as 'put off' ('rid yourselves'), 'put on' ('clothe yourselves'), 'submit', 'be watchful' and 'resist' (e.g. Col. 3: 5–4: 5; Eph. 4: 17–6: 9; 1 Pet. 2: 11–3: 9). A study of these passages and others shows that there is a great similarity in the content of the injunctions. In each case there is some reference to new life in Christ, and attention is given to the relationship of Christians to each other, in their families, to the government, between servants and masters, between husbands and wives, and parents and children.

Such elements of early Christian teaching as have been summarized above undoubtedly form part of what is known in the NT as the 'tradition'. This word (sometimes also used in a bad sense) is a frequent one in the writings of the apostle Paul (e.g. 2 Th. 2: 15; 3: 6; 1 C. 11: 2; Col. 2: 6; 1 Tim. 6: 20; 2 Tim. 1: 14). There is little ground for the idea that Paul superimposed his own complex theological system, different in spirit and content, upon the simple teaching of the Lord Jesus. Instead, he speaks of doctrines and practices which he had 'received' (1 C. 11: 23; 15: 3), and one can find in Paul's writings echoes of the words of the Lord Jesus (cf. e.g. Rom. 12: 14, 17, 21 with Mt. 5: 38 ff.; Rom. 13: 7–10 with Mt. 22: 15–22, 34–40; Rom. 14: 10 with Mt. 7: 1; Rom. 14: 13 with Mt. 18: 7; Rom. 14: 14 with Mt. 15: 11). There is therefore a continuity in the doctrinal development, from the teachings of Christ through the initial affirmations of the early church and the theological contribution of Paul and others, to the final corpus of doctrine in the NT. We shall now briefly survey a few representative themes.

THE PERSON AND WORK OF CHRIST

The most urgent need of the early church was a better understanding of the person and work of the Lord Jesus. Some questions were answered by the very fact of His death, resurrection and ascension, but many others were raised. Since belief in Christ was the *sine qua non* of Christianity, the confession, 'Jesus is the Christ' or 'Jesus is Lord' was, as we have seen, an early and basic doctrinal affirmation. Further evidence of the early identification of Jesus as divine Lord is found in 1 C. 16: 22. Here the transliteration of the Aramaic *maranatha* (which, according to the way the word is divided, may mean either 'may the Lord come' or 'the Lord is coming') testifies to the early belief of the young Aramaic-speaking church at Jerusalem. The Aramaic expression was evidently in such common use that Paul transliterated it rather than use a translation. It testifies to their belief both in the Lord and in His return. The word 'Lord', though common in the Gospels, was evidently not often used as a title during His earthly ministry. However He is so designated in Mk 11: 3, and in Mk 12: 36 the word occurs in a quotation from Ps. 110: 1.

The early chapters of Acts tell us that shortly after His resurrection the Christians declared that Jesus had been exalted by God and designated both 'Lord' and 'Christ' (Ac. 2: 33–36). He is also declared to be the Prince of Life (Ac. 3: 15; 5: 31) and the prophet predicted by Moses (Ac. 3: 22; 7: 37). The apostle Paul began his Christian career by seeking to persuade his Jewish associates that Jesus was the Christ, the Son of God (Ac. 9: 20–22).

The original preaching of the church regarding Jesus, according to the book of Acts, laid stress on His rôle as the suffering Servant of Isaiah. Although this was not the major theme of the Gospels, Mt. 12: 17 ff. applies Isa. 42: 1–3 to Jesus. The thought is also certainly present in the saying of the Lord Jesus that the Son of Man came to serve and give His life a ransom for many (Mk 10: 45). The preaching of Peter, who stands behind Mark's Gospel and who represents the early Palestinian missionary effort, stresses Jesus' rôle as servant. This is evident not only from his writings (1 Pet. 2: 21–25) but also from his preaching (Ac. 3: 13, 26; cf. Ac. 4: 27, 30).

It is clear then that as the doctrine concerning the Lord Jesus developed, stress was first of all laid upon His exaltation as Lord and Messiah, and on His suffering in obedience to the will of God. The allusions in 1 Peter to Isaiah 53 undoubtedly reflect the common use of that passage by Jewish Christians.

In the great Letter to the Romans Paul begins with the affirmation that Jesus is the royal Messiah, the Lord, and the Son of God, as demonstrated by His resurrection (Rom. 1: 3 f.). From these essentials, the doctrine of Christ is expanded as the Holy Spirit leads Paul to a fuller realization of their implication. So Paul strongly declares the pre-existence of Christ. This is done not only in such typological references as 1 C. 10: 4 ('the rock was Christ') and in passages where His pre-existence is implied (Gal. 4: 4; Rom. 8: 3), but also in definite statements such as 2 C. 8: 9, 'though he was rich, yet for your sakes he became poor', and 1 C. 15: 47 'the second man is from heaven'. The pre-existence of Christ is also stressed in the Christological summaries of Col. 1: 15–20; Phil. 2: 5–11. Furthermore the Lord Jesus is now in heaven where He intercedes for the believers (Rom. 8: 34), and where those who have been raised spiritually with Him should focus their attention (Eph. 1: 3; Col. 3: 1).

Not only did the Lord Jesus come from and return to heaven, but he has a universal cosmic rôle as creator of all things and rightful head of the universe (Col. 1: 13–18; Eph. 1: 10; Phil. 2: 10). The Letter to the Colossians was written to combat a heresy which lowered the dignity of Christ and therefore it is especially this Letter which expresses His pre-eminence (1: 18).

As these doctrines are stressed, expressions multiply which clearly associate Christ with God Himself (Rom. 1: 7; 1 Th. 1: 11; 2 C. 13: 14). OT passages which refer to God are applied to Christ. Thus Rom. 10: 11 may be compared with Isa. 28: 16; Rom. 10: 13 with Jl 2: 32; 1 C. 2: 16 with Isa. 40: 13; and Phil. 2: 10 with Isa. 45: 23. It also becomes apparent that the concept of Christ as the Son of God is not merely an 'official' or functional Messianic expression, but that it has a more intimate meaning. Thus God sends 'his own Son' (Rom. 8: 3) and permits 'his own Son' to die (Rom. 8: 31). Although other interpretations are possible, Rom. 9: 5 would seem to make the identification complete.

In the Pauline writings the rôle of Christ as the second Adam is also developed. It is He who undoes the evil brought about through the failure of the first Adam and who is the representative of the believer (Rom. 5: 12–21; 8: 29; 1 C. 15: 45–47). In the Pastoral Letters the Lord Jesus is described as our Saviour, Mediator and Ransom (1 Tim. 2: 3–6), and as the giver of eternal life (2 Tim. 1: 10). His Messiahship and resurrection are unassailable truths which are to give encouragement to the Lord's servants (2 Tim. 2: 8). The Greek of Tit. 2: 13 suggests the identification of Christ as God (cf. 2 Pet. 1: 1).

During the period in which the various Letters were being written, the Holy Spirit was leading in the formation of the four Gospels. The need for written records of the life and teachings of Jesus increased as the gospel was carried across the Empire and as converts needed instruction. The church has traditionally, and correctly, seen in them four portraits of the Lord Jesus carefully drawn for different audiences. Although the Gospels do not always make theology explicit, the core of Christology is here, expressed in such terms as Messiah, Son of Man, Lord and Son of God. By presenting vivid descriptions of the gracious deeds of Jesus, they provide far more than would have been given in mere doctrinal affirmations. They portray Him who was possessed of true humanity, and yet spoke with absolute authority, laying claim to Deity and Lordship over men. He is seen as unequalled in the glory of His personal character, not only with respect to the absence of sin, but, positively with respect to the presence of all moral virtues in perfect balance. His passion and resurrection form a major part of each book.

The Gospel of John concentrates on fewer discourses and miracles of Christ, but through these expands our concept of Him. We realize that He is the 'Word', who has eternally existed in the divine relationship, Creator of all things, who came as the full and perfect expression of the truth and grace of God. In the Johannine Letters stress is laid not only on Jesus as the Son of God but on His true manhood, in opposition to the heresy which denied this fact (1 Jn 1: 3, 7; 3: 23; 4: 2 f.; 5: 1, 5, 10, 13; 2 Jn 7, 9). In the book of Revelation the future vindication and glory of Christ are described. In that apocalyptic work we are told of the future great conflict and the ultimate victory of the Lord Jesus Christ. Against the backdrop of the cosmic events of the last times, He whose personal history encompasses all else from beginning to end appears from heaven as final victor.

THE MEANING OF THE CROSS

We have seen how the basic Christological affirmations of the early confessions and *kērygma* were expanded in the NT writings. Just as the implications of the facts regarding the nature of Christ were spelled out, so were those of the fact of His death. We have seen that a basic statement is found in 1 C. 15: 1 ff. Here Paul speaks of the fact of Jesus' death and of its connection with our salvation. The early Christian preaching as found in the book of Acts does not explicitly state the place of the cross in the realization of our salvation. Yet although the theology of the cross is not developed, its centrality is affirmed. The death of Christ is seen as completely within the foreknowledge and plan of God (Ac. 2: 23). This fact can be stated with confidence because of the resurrection. Just as Christ Himself was vindicated through the resurrection so the place of the cross in God's plan is established. Jesus is therefore exalted as Saviour (Ac. 5: 31). The Christian message reflected in Acts stresses first of all repentance (2: 38; 3: 19). The unrepentant are to be judged by the very one whom they have rejected, the risen Christ (Ac. 10: 42; 17: 31). Forgiveness is only through His name, the efficacy of which is demonstrated by a miracle of healing (Ac. 3: 12 ff.; 4: 10 ff.; cf. 10: 43 and 16: 30).

Before considering the way in which the

doctrine of salvation is developed in the Letters we should take note of the foundation which was laid in the teaching of Jesus. It is noteworthy that John the Baptist, Jesus Himself, and His disciples all began their public ministry with a call to repentance (Mt. 3: 1 f.; 4: 17; Mk 6: 12). Jesus followed His call to repentance with an exhortation to 'believe the good news' (Mk 1: 15). These books which contain the teachings of Jesus are themselves properly called 'Gospels'. They contain the essentials of the message not only by but about Christ. The need of man for salvation is frequently stressed in the sayings of Jesus. The Sermon on the Mount expresses throughout the culpable failure of man and the consequences of his evil. Although self-righteous Pharisees are singled out for censure, the guilt of all men is made clear. Even fathers who give good gifts to their children are by nature 'evil' (Mt. 7: 11). External righteousness cannot hide internal sin.

Equally stressed, however, is the forgiveness which Christ seeks to bestow upon men. His authority in this respect is challenged and defended (Mk 2: 5–12). Not only is Jesus' authority to forgive mentioned, but also the means by which He was to actualize the promise. The confession at Caesarea Philippi was followed by the first of a series of passion predictions (Mt. 16: 21 and parallels). Other hints of His approaching death are given. Among these is the statement in Mk 10: 45 (cf. Mt. 20: 28) that the Son of Man would give His life a ransom for, or in place of, many. The institution of the Lord's Supper provides the most significant setting for a further explanation of His death, as Jesus makes it clear that His blood was to be shed for the forgiveness of sin (Mt. 26: 28).

As the apostle Paul repeated the essential elements of the gospel in his missionary preaching, his inquiring mind began to penetrate further implications of the death and resurrection of Christ. As questions and objections were raised by his hearers, he prayerfully went to the OT Scriptures, and at the same time sought out contemporary modes of expression to explain the significance of the gospel. In the Letter to the Romans Paul carefully forged out the implications of the gospel message. Although the theme of Christ's vindication and victory, and the fact of reconciliation and redemption through the cross of Christ, are prominent in Paul's writings, it is the concept of justification by grace through faith which is Paul's most notable contribution. Rom. 3: 21–26 is a summary of this doctrine, culminating in the statement that through the cross of Christ God was able to maintain His own righteousness while yet declaring the believer in Jesus free from guilt. The holiness and justice of God are vindicated. Human guilt makes self-effort useless, and salvation is solely through the

death of Christ, appropriated by faith. The theme of the death of Christ, signified in verse 25 by the word 'blood', is repeated elsewhere. Christ was delivered up for our trespasses (Rom. 4: 25). He died for the ungodly and for sinners (Rom. 5: 6, 8). He was made sin for us (2 C. 5: 21). We are justified (Rom. 5: 9), redeemed (Eph. 1: 7) and reconciled to God through His blood (Rom. 5: 9; Eph. 1: 7; 2: 13; Col. 1: 20). Christ gave Himself for our sins (Gal. 1: 4) and even incurred the curse of the law for us (Gal. 3: 13).

Since God, who had concluded all men under sin, has judged sin in the person of His own Son on the cross (Rom.), brought the law to fulfilment with the death of Christ (Gal.), and reconciled Jew and Gentile together by the gracious act of the cross (Eph.), His great salvation is available through one means only: faith. The doctrine of faith is by no means new with Paul, for it was stressed by Jesus. However it is now emphasized as the sole essential for salvation (Rom. 3: 28; Eph. 2: 8).

The saving work of Christ is further expressed in the Pastorals in His designation, noted above, as Mediator (1 Tim. 2: 5), Ransom (1 Tim. 2: 6), and Saviour (2 Tim. 1: 10; Tit. 2: 13 f.; 3: 6). In Tit. the gospel of the saving grace of God is urged as a motivating force toward purity of life.

The early Christian *kērygma* is amplified also in the writings of Peter. The word for 'gospel' itself is found in 1 Pet. 1: 12; 4: 6, 7. Peter's recollection of the cross is still fresh, as is seen by his reference to the blood of Christ (1 Pet. 1: 2, 19). Writing sometime after the event and during the period of some stress, Peter has made assessments of relative value (as people in distress often do). The word 'precious' and its cognates appear several times in his writings and the blood of Christ is so designated. The death of Christ is seen as substitutionary, as He 'bore our sins in his body on the tree' and 'died for sins once for all, the righteous for the unrighteous', and also as an example of patient endurance of wrong (1 Pet. 2: 21–24; 3: 18). The suffering of Christ is thus seen to bear upon the Christian's moral life (1 Pet. 4: 1 ff.). The Christian must learn to draw upon the benefits of the cross as he lives in the lengthening period between the first coming of Christ and His return, which will bring the consummation of salvation (1 Pet. 1: 6 ff.).

The writer of the Letter to the Hebrews stresses the rôle of Christ as both priest and sacrifice. The death of Christ not only satisfies the typology of the OT sacrifice, but signals its end. The finality of the sacrifice of Christ is emphasized in chapters 9 and 10. The readers are urged on this basis, and in the view of the fact that God has established a new covenant which supersedes the old, to rely completely on Jesus as the 'pioneer and perfecter of our faith' (12: 2).

The completed work of Christ upon the cross is augmented by His present intercession in heaven. This further revelation is given by the writer of Heb. (7: 23–25), by Paul (Rom. 8: 34) and by John (1 Jn 2: 1). The latter passage refers to Christ as an 'advocate' (the same word applied in the Gospel of Jn 14: 16, 26 to the Holy Spirit) and goes on to speak of Him as the 'propitiation' for our sins. These two concepts in conjunction stress the need of a Saviour to avert the just wrath of a holy God. (It is important to remember here that such language is not intended to represent God as being petulantly angry with His creatures in the pagan sense and requiring to be placated, but as Himself in love providing the atonement for the removal of their guilt and of the retribution which it attracts. The RSV renders the word 'expiation'.)

The book of Revelation provides us with vivid reminders of the cross. Christ 'has freed us from our sins by his blood' (1: 5). The symbol of the Lamb is prominent in the book both as representative of a sacrificial victim (5: 6 ff.) and, unexpectedly, as a victorious conqueror (6: 1; 7: 9 ff.; 8: 1; 14: 1 ff.; 19: 7 ff.; 21: 9 ff.). This new rôle of the Lamb is expressed most dramatically in the expression 'the wrath of the Lamb' (6: 16). Judgment falls on all whose names are not in the Lamb's book of life (20: 15; 21: 27). The Apocalypse concludes with a description of the Holy City, in which the Lamb is both temple and light (21: 22 f.).

THE NEW PEOPLE OF GOD

In presenting their case to the Jewish people, it was not enough for the Christians simply to state the claim of Jesus of Nazareth to be the Messiah. They also had to overcome objections to this claim, objections which were largely focused on the cross. In short they had to explain why God allowed His own Son, the Messiah, to die. The problem was compounded by the fact that His execution was by the worst conceivable method, the cross, which, as a form of hanging, incurred the OT curse (Dt. 21: 23), and by the fact that the alleged Messiah was rejected by the covenant people and betrayed by one of His own circle.

The Christians approached this problem by a selective use of OT passages which proved that the Messiah first had to suffer (Ac. 17: 3). Paul, however, went even further than this by using the curse of hanging as a strong element in his presentation of the gospel in Gal. Quoting Dt. 27: 26, he shows that those who choose to live under the law but fail to keep it are under a curse. By becoming a curse Himself,

Christ bore that curse which was due to us (Gal. 3: 10–14). Furthermore he adds a point not calculated to win Jewish approval, that this vicarious acceptance of the curse by Christ brings the blessing promised in the OT to Gentiles (Gal. 3: 14).

Another problem which faced the Christians at the very beginning of their missionary effort was the place of the Jewish temple and ritual. The issue had already been raised by a misinterpretation of the remarks of Jesus regarding the destruction of the 'temple' (meaning His body), remarks which were introduced into Jesus' trial (Mt. 26: 61). The Jerusalem believers, according to Ac. 2: 46; 3: 1, attended the temple. Soon, however, opposition crystallized. Stephen was accused of detrimental comments against it, and made it an issue in his defence (Ac. 6: 12 ff.; 7: 44–50). The suggestion that there existed links between Stephen, the 'Hellenists' of Acts and the Essenes may have inadequate support, but the issue of the temple was indeed widespread. Hebrews, as we have seen, takes the position that the OT temple rites fulfilled their purpose. It finds the value of the building in its usefulness as a type of the real sanctuary into which Christ has entered (Heb. 9). John sees a substitute for the temple in the person of Jesus Himself, noting that the 'Word' was present among us in the 'tabernacle' of the body of Jesus (1: 14). Paul states that God's present temple is the Church both as a corporate group and as individuals (Eph. 2: 19–22; 1 C. 3: 16 f.; 2 C. 6: 19 f.).

Likewise the sacrifices of the OT era and the services of the priesthood had no intrinsic value apart from their foreshadowing of the perfect work of Christ, whereby He was both priest and victim (Heb. 8–10). Continuation of the temple cult was therefore futile (Heb. 10: 18). In fact not only had individual provisions of the old covenant been rendered obsolete, but the entire covenant had been superseded by a new one. This was, the writer hastens to affirm, already envisioned in the OT (Heb. 10: 16 f.), but it is new, not only as a covenant but (in the other sense of the Greek word *diathēkē*) as a testament or will. As such it necessitated the death of the 'testator', a further reason for the death of Christ (9: 15 ff.).

What is now the relationship of the Christian to the OT law? The answer to this has its roots in the teaching of the Lord Jesus Himself. In the Sermon on the Mount He makes it clear that He did not come to destroy the law (Mt. 5: 17 ff.), but at the same time He affirms His own authority with respect to its interpretation. It is quite clear that Jesus intended the moral imperative of the law to be obeyed. This is echoed in the Letter of James which contains many allusions to the Sermon on the Mount. Paul said, 'love is the fulfilling of the law'

(Rom. 13: 10), a statement in keeping with Jesus' teaching (Mt. 22: 34–40 and parallels). The Gospels show Jesus as fulfilling the law in His teaching, and in His life He also fulfilled the prophecies of the OT, especially with respect to His death (Lk. 4: 21; Mt. 26: 54). Jesus' charge against the Pharisees was not that they observed it too punctiliously, but that they did not obey it consistently and contradicted its spirit (Mt. 5: 20; 23: 23 ff.).

However, the law involved more than the moral aspect, and it seems clear that the Jewish people did not make a firm distinction between this and the so-called 'ceremonial' injunctions. Therefore it was necessary that eventually within the NT there should be a clear statement regarding the place of the whole law in the New Covenant. This definitive statement was made by Paul. He showed that the law could never bring righteousness, and that Christ was the end of the law in this respect, offering that righteousness which comes by faith in Him (Rom. 10. 1–13). Paul's own experience, like that of all men who consciously face the demands of the law, is that it at best brings the knowledge of sin (Rom. 7: 13). The law served its purpose up to the time of Christ when He, having fulfilled it Himself, bore the curse it brought upon sinful mankind and thereby annulled it for those who would believe in Him (Gal. 3: 21–26; Eph. 2: 14–16). The kind of life the law required is now produced not by an external code but by the indwelling Spirit (Gal. 5: 16–25; Rom. 8: 4).

All these issues lead to a basic question: Who now are the people of God? Initially, of course, the Christian believers were Jews who had found the fulfilment of their ancient faith in the person of their Messiah Jesus. It might have been supposed that they could continue as a Jewish sect. According to the early chapters of Acts, as we have noted, the Christians continued in their temple worship. Their teaching, however, occasioned not only disagreement but opposition. The Synoptic Gospels indicate that Jesus had enjoyed, for the most part, the support of the 'common people' with opposition stemming mainly from the Pharisees and the Sadducees. Likewise Acts describes the early opposition as coming from the Sadducean chief priests (Ac. 4: 1–6), while the Christians enjoyed a good reputation among the Jewish people as a whole (Ac. 2: 47). As the missionary enterprise moves forward, however, Luke notes increasing resistance. In the synagogue at Antioch Paul speaks of the unbelief of 'those who live in Jerusalem and their rulers'. As the narrative of Acts continues, antagonism to the gospel comes from the 'Jews' as a group (Ac. 13: 50). The situation is described in the same terms in the Gospel of John where in 7: 1, for example, the threat to Jesus' life comes not from the Pharisees or Sadducees but from 'the Jews' in Judaea.

Thus it became necessary to deal with the fact that the Christians were a people apart. Even though the author of Acts is careful to point out the Jewish origin of Christianity (and may in part be seeking to demonstrate that as a daughter religion Christianity should enjoy the rights granted the Jews), it is clear even in this work that the division is decisive. The book closes with Paul applying Isa. 6 to contemporary Jews, 'this people's heart has become calloused . . .' followed by the concluding statement 'therefore I want you to know that God's salvation has been sent to the Gentiles and they will listen' (Ac. 28: 25–29).

Under these conditions several problems presented themselves. Paul expresses one of them in Rom. 11: 1, 'Did God reject his people?' In his reply he does not minimize the seriousness of the unbelief of Israel, but describing Israel as branches broken off from an olive tree, he affirms his belief that God is able to replace the branches (Rom. 11: 23–32). Paul makes it very clear, however, that during the present time it is the Christian church which constitutes the people of God; all Christians are spiritually heirs of Abraham. 'There is neither Jew nor Greek . . . you are all one in Christ Jesus.' And 'if you belong to Christ, then you are Abraham's seed, and heirs according to the promise' (Gal. 3:28 f.).

Also significant is the fact that Peter applies the description of Israel in Exod. 23: 22 to the Christians: 'But you are a chosen people, a royal priesthood, a holy nation, a people belonging to God' (1 Pet. 2: 9). The words of Hos. 2: 23 are now fulfilled: 'Once you were not a people but now you are the people of God' (1 Pet. 2: 10).

The Letter to the Ephesians provides further revelation to guide the Christians in their quest for self-understanding and for an articulate expression of their identity over against both Judaism and paganism. Here Paul describes a 'mystery' (divine truth unknowable except by revelation, but now openly proclaimed). Through the cross God not only reconciled men to Himself, but He also united Jew and Gentile in a 'new man' (Eph. 2: 15). This is part of God's eternal plan to exalt Christ as head of the universe (1: 10). The Church then takes its place as part of a plan of God 'who accomplishes all things according to the counsel of His will'. In view of the sovereign work of God in history and through the cross it is clear that salvation is to be viewed as connected with God's workmanship, i.e., of grace and not of our own works (2: 8–10).

The Church is therefore an organic union of all believers (Eph. 3 and 4). This union must be expressed, whatever personal sacrifice is necessary, in the practical unity of Christians (4: 1 f.). Christians share a common life in Christ. They are spiritually united to each other because they are vitally united to Him. This intimate relationship is frequently described by Paul as being 'in Christ' (an expression which borders on, but does not pass over into, mysticism). Jesus had taught His disciples that He would build His Church, that He would be spiritually present, and that believers would be united in divine love (Mt. 16: 18; 18: 20; Jn 17: 20–26). Paul shows that the unity of the Church with its Lord is so unique that it may be described as that of a living body and its head (Eph. 4: 11–16; 1 C. 12: 12–27). Other descriptions of the Church illuminate its varied functions: flock (Lk. 12: 32; Ac. 20: 28), the planting (1 C. 3: 19), the household (Eph. 2: 19 f.), the temple (1 C. 3: 16), the bride (Eph. 5: 25 ff.), and, when deviation from Christian doctrine was becoming more overt, 'the household of God . . . the pillar and foundation of the truth' (1 Tim. 3: 15).

ACCORDING TO THE SCRIPTURES

As the young church sought to gain self-understanding and to meet the challenges put to it, the OT was diligently searched. It yielded substantiation for their Messianic affirmations, the gospel message, their stance toward Judaism, and their eschatological hope. Their use of the Scriptures derives from the example and teaching of the Lord Jesus. According to the Gospels Jesus made frequent use of the Scriptures not only in His teaching but in His personal experience of temptation (Mt. 4: 1–11) and in controversies with Jewish leaders. At one point His rejoinder was 'is not this why you are wrong, that you know neither the Scriptures nor the power of God?' (Mk 12: 24). In this same controversy passage Jesus is seen referring to a Messianic Psalm (Ps. 110: 1). In the fourth Gospel He not only bases a reply on the OT, but He adds the words 'Scripture cannot be broken' (Jn 10: 35). Our Lord clearly stated that He was purposefully acting to fulfil the Scriptures (Lk. 4: 16–21; Mt. 26: 54, 56). The Scriptures are found not only on the lips of Jesus but in the comments of the writers. This is particularly true of Matthew. His use of OT verses to illumine events in the life of Jesus may occasionally seem strained to the modern reader. Several things must be borne in mind, however. The type of exegesis by which some NT writers applied OT Scriptures to contemporary events is similar to a known type (called Midrash *pesher*) and has parallels in the Qumran literature. Second, the Gospel of Matthew was undoubtedly written after the Christians already had some experience in the use of the OT Scriptures in debate with Jews. Like other NT writers, Matthew felt the cre-

ative liberty of the Spirit in adapting the Scriptures to the recent events which provided their greatest fulfilment. In doing this, he, as well as the other NT authors, had the precedence and the instruction of the Lord Jesus on the road to Emmaus (Lk. 24: 25–27) and perhaps during the period between His resurrection and ascension, when He 'interpreted to them in all the Scriptures the things concerning himself'. We have already seen how an appeal was made to the Scriptures to substantiate the claim that Jesus was the Messiah and to explain His seemingly paradoxical death. Paul had recourse to the Scriptures to explain the gospel and such a crucial matter as the Christian attitude to the law. The Letter to the Hebrews draws heavily on the Biblical descriptions of the institutions of priesthood and sacrifice. The early Jerusalem church drew heavily on the Scriptures, as is seen in Acts, James and 1 and 2 Peter.

There are several ways in which the OT Scriptures were used. One is the use of proof texts. This is seen in the reference to different verses which mention a stone: Ps. 118: 22; Isa. 28: 16; 8: 14; Dan. 2: 34 f. They appear singly and in combination in Mk 12: 10 f.; Lk. 20: 17 f.; Ac. 4: 11; Rom. 9: 33; 1 Pet. 2: 6 ff. These instances suggest that such verses were in common use by the Christians. Some have even postulated the existence of a collection of such verses or *testimonia*. This hypothesis has been aided, but certainly not proved, by the similar use of the Scriptures by later Christian apologists; it may also be illustrated by the collections of *testimonia* among the Qumran texts in the previous century.

Other ways in which the Scriptures were used may be described under the general term 'typology'. There are instances where a one-to-one comparison is made as, for example, in 1 C. 5: 7 where Jesus is described as our 'passover', 1 C. 10: 1 ff. where the supernatural rock in the wilderness is identified with Christ, and Heb. 7, which compares Christ directly with Melchizedek. Beyond these specific instances there is also the underlying assumption of the NT writers that the experiences of Christ were foreshadowed in that of Israel and of individual OT saints. In Matthew one may discern the 'Exodus motif'. Israel came forth from Egypt; so did Christ, and therefore it is said 'out of Egypt have I called My Son' (Mt. 2: 15). Moses and Christ both had a wilderness experience, gave a Law, and so forth. It is, of course, all too easy to read far more typology into the Bible than is intended. The whole subject has been receiving some renewed attention lately in theological works.

THE NEW AGE

At the beginning of His ministry, the Lord Jesus illustrated the newness of His gospel by reminding His audience that men do not put new wine in old wineskins (Mk 2: 22). According to John, His first miracle was the changing of water into wine, followed by the cleansing of the temple and the teaching of the new birth (Jn 2: 1–3: 14). By these words and actions the new age is introduced. This was anticipated in the infancy narratives of Matthew and Luke, as the expectations of believing Jews were finally realized in the birth of their Saviour–Messiah. It is taught expressly in the words of the Lord Jesus that 'the law and the prophets were proclaimed until John; since that time the good news of the kingdom of God is being preached' (Lk. 16: 16). So the Lord Jesus, when He began His ministry in Galilee, declared, 'The time has come, and the kingdom of God is near; Repent, and believe the good news' (Mk 1: 14).

The nearness and power of the kingdom were seen in the mighty works of Christ, primarily in His exorcisms. Then, as the claims of the King were pressed, and the initial surge of response changed into varied attitudes of misunderstanding or unbelief, Jesus withdrew from the Galilean crowds, eventually to confirm in the minds of the disciples His divine nature and mission. At the confession 'You are the Christ, the Son of the living God', He proceeded to reveal His intention to establish the Church, following His death and resurrection (Mt. 16: 13–23). The Church is mentioned only one other time in the Gospels, this also in Matthew (18: 17). As we have just seen, the doctrine of the Church is elaborated in the Letters. In contrast, the kingdom, which is a major theme of the teaching of Jesus in the Synoptics, receives little emphasis in the Letters. This is understandable in view of the fact that the kingdom was announced and 'inaugurated' as the reign of Christ over His people, but that it will not have its eschatological consummation until the future appearing of Christ. Some Scriptures, such as Mt. 8: 11 f.; 19: 28; 26: 29; the Olivet discourse of Mt. 24 and parallels, and the parables of Mt. 13 and 25, along with the parable of the nobleman in Lk. 19: 11–27, indicate unmistakably that a full future expression of the kingdom must be awaited. Other verses, as Mt. 12: 28 (cf. Lk. 11: 20); Mt. 11: 12 (cf. Lk. 16: 16), and those that speak of people receiving and entering the kingdom, suggest that in a real sense the kingdom is present. The apostles preached the kingdom (so Paul in Ac. 20: 25) and believers knew that they were now in 'the kingdom of the Son he loves' (Col. 1: 13). A connection (but not identification) clearly exists between the kingdom and the Church, as is indicated in the relationship of the words 'Christ' (or Messiah), 'church', and 'kingdom' in Mt. 16: 16–20. It was also clear that they were living in an eschatological tension 'between the times'.

God was not only going to *break into* history (in the sense common to the apocalyptic writers), but He was also doing something *now in* history (in the sense of the prophetic tradition). This is the period of God's activity, not just an interlude between acts.

The consummation lay in the future. The book of Revelation provides graphic descriptions of this, and 1 C. 15: 24 ff. gives a hint of the state of things under the ultimate rule of God. The early believers were sure both that the central event of history had already occurred, and that their Lord would 'appear a second time, not to bear sin but to bring salvation to those who are waiting for him' (Heb. 9: 28). However, they were left without certainty as to the time of His return. Their attention was to be given to His work now (Lk. 19: 13), which consisted mainly of witnessing for Him (Ac. 1: 8). They were to maintain an attitude of alertness in the expectation of His return (Mt. 25: 1–13; 1 Th. 5: 1–11). The evil world was still about them, but they could now live a victorious life based on Christ's own triumph over evil (Col. 2: 15; 2 C. 2: 14).

As the years passed, Christians probably became more aware that the time before the return of Christ was of indefinite duration. Such events as Caligula's impudent attempt to have his image set up in the holy place in Jerusalem (A.D. 40) and the destruction of the Temple (A.D. 70) must have stirred speculation and drawn attention to the Olivet discourse. Much discussion has centred about the question as to whether Paul initially expected the return of Christ during his lifetime and then, adapting his thinking to the possibility that he would die before the second advent, changed his doctrinal stance in this regard. 1 Th. 4 glows with the expectation of the return of Christ. 2 Thessalonians introduces more eschatological detail. In the Corinthian correspondence Paul includes himself among those who may not live to Christ's return (1 C. 6: 14; 2 C. 4: 14; 5: 1–9). Philippians shows the author's readiness to die, along with his hope of Christ's return (1: 21 ff.; 3: 20 f.). Such a change in attitude is, of course, partly explained by the practical fact that imminent death was a frequent possibility in Paul's experience. More important is the fact that a change in Paul's personal outlook does not necessarily constitute a modification of doctrine. The evangelical view of inspiration differentiates between an author's personal attitude and the infallible doctrine which he is led to express in the Scriptures. (Paul makes this explicit himself in another connection in 1 C. 7: 25.)

The increasing span of time from the resurrection event was, of course, a major problem to some. This is seen in one of the later books of the Bible, 2 Peter, which challenges those who scoff saying 'where is this "coming" he promised?' (2 Pet. 3: 1–13). The Christian, however, is to live in view of the coming of his Lord, conducting himself in a godly way (2 Pet. 3: 11 ff.; Tit. 2: 11 ff.), aware that whether he lives until the Lord's return or whether his earthly home is dissolved, he has a heavenly dwelling, will be with his Saviour, and will have his present life evaluated by the Lord (2 C. 5: 1–10).

Meanwhile, pending the consummation, converts were being won who needed instruction in the business of daily Christian living. A body of ethical teaching, built on a doctrinal foundation, was developed. Mention has been made of the form of instruction which was evidently common among Christians. This teaching involved the Christian's moral life, his relationship to unbelievers, and his relationship to other Christians (Eph. 4: 17 ff.; 5: 21 ff.; Col. 3: 5 ff.; 1 Pet. 2: 11 ff.; 5: 5). Paul reminds his Thessalonian congregation that he had given them ethical 'instruction' before, and urges them on to personal consecration. The believer is not to live without restraint, even though he is not under the Mosaic Law, for the 'law of love' now controls him (Rom. 13: 8–10; Jas 1: 22–25; 2: 8–13). He lives under the influence of the Holy Spirit, who accomplishes in his life what the law, hindered by the flesh, could not produce (Rom. 8: 2 ff.; Gal. 5: 13–26). The 'old man' came to his end at conversion; his deeds are to be forsaken and the flesh considered crucified with Christ (Rom. 6: 1–11; Eph. 4: 22–24; Col. 3: 5–10). Thus the intent of the OT law, expounded by Christ, could now be realized. So the believer is to live during this present age as a child of the new age, a son of the light, a son of the day (1 Th. 5: 5).

THE PATTERN OF SOUND WORDS

Among the factors which stimulated the development of doctrine in the NT were the adverse circumstances faced by the early Christians. We have already seen that the unbelief and opposition of the Jewish people called for both a defensive apologetic and a positive formulation of doctrine by the Christians. The same was true with regard to resistance to the gospel on the part of Gentiles. This is seen in the book of Acts where Paul turned demonstrations of pagan unbelief into opportunities for a declaration of the creative and saving activity of God (Ac. 14: 11–18; 17: 16–34). The latter of these is the well known address by Paul on the Areopagus. Their erroneous ideas about God are refuted by summaries of the Biblical doctrine of God, culminating in an appeal to repentance based on the responsibility men now have to the resurrected One who has the authority of judgment.

It has long been recognized that not only the speeches of Acts but the entire book itself is an apologetic directed to the Roman mind, if not to the Roman government itself. Luke is careful to show, as he did with respect to the trial of Jesus, that whenever Christianity confronted a judicial representative of Rome it was acquitted. In another apologetic, this time in opposition to the many fraudulent peddlers of religion who were travelling from city to city, begging for money and practising immorality in the name of their religion, Luke is concerned to set in contrast the irreproachable ministry of Paul. This is naturally also the concern of the apostle himself, and he occasionally writes in vindication of his methods. Thus we find him working honestly at his trade (Ac. 18: 3), not accepting financial support from those to whom he preached the gospel (1 C. 9: 15–23), and giving himself totally to those whom he sought to win (1 Th. 2: 1–12). It may seem strange to some that NT writers seem to attack the morals of their opponents as well as their doctrine (*e.g.* Phil. 3: 17–19). It is simply a fact of the ancient world, however, that itinerant preachers in general had a poor reputation and also that arguments between sects commonly included charges of hypocrisy and immorality. It is to this fact that we are indebted for some of the examples and exhortations in the NT on behalf of purity in the life of God's servants.

In Paul's address to the Ephesian elders in Ac. 20 he warns against false teachers who would actually invade the church itself. This was the concern of the Christians for many decades. The struggle against doctrinal perversion and heresy produced some of the clearest expressions of doctrine in the NT. Among the most troublesome antagonists were those who opposed seeking Gentile converts and accepting them fully without their submitting to certain Jewish customs. These Judaizing legalists, against whom Paul wrote Galatians, evoked from him a summary of the purpose of the law and his declaration of Christian liberty, to which we have already alluded.

Against another developing system of thought later known as Gnosticism, a higher knowledge, deprecating the created world, and lowering Christ to an inferior position in a world of intermediary beings, Paul presented a lucid and powerful Christology. So we were given the Colossian Letter. Employing the heretics' own vocabulary, he demonstrated that Christ embodies the fulness of God and is due the place of pre-eminence, and that God's creation is for our proper use and pleasure.

Those Letters which were apparently the last to be written reflect the growing problem posed by false teachers. The repetition in 2 Peter of the charge of immorality against these heretics serves to underscore the fact that similar charges by Paul were not an expression of personal vindictiveness but were justified by the facts. We are the beneficiaries of the controversy, for in 2 Peter some significant expressions of doctrine have been called forth by the conflict. First is the exhortation to Christian maturity and holiness (1: 3–11). Second is the invaluable passage regarding the inspiration and historical validity of the Scriptures. 'We did not follow cleverly invented stories . . . We have the word of the prophets made more certain . . . Men spoke from God as they were carried along by the Holy Spirit' (2 Pet. 1: 16–21). Next is a revelation of the judgment which will be brought against the opponents of the truth (2: 1–22). Finally, the scoffing of those who used the delay of the *parousia* as an occasion for denying the truth of God's promise occasions further revelation concerning the consummation of God's purposes in earth and heaven: '. . . that day will bring about the destruction of the heavens by fire and the elements will melt in the heat. But in keeping with his promise we are looking forward to a new heaven and a new earth, the home of righteousness' (3: 11–13). Encouragement is also given on the basis of God's patient grace, 'not wanting anyone to perish but everyone to come to repentance' (3: 9, cf. v. 15). The conclusion of the book includes a valuable reference to the writings of Paul, in which they are classed with 'the other scriptures' (3: 16).

The Johannine Letters contain strong warnings against a heresy which came to be known as docetism. This was a denial that the Son of God actually lived in a real body, a proposition based on the wrong assumption that the body, being material, is evil. Therefore, these Letters stress the fact that Christ actually, and not only in appearance, lived and died in a material body. 'That which was from the beginning, which we have heard, which we have seen with our eyes, which we have looked at and our hands have touched, . . . we proclaim to you ' (1 Jn 1: 1, 3). 'This is how you can recognize the Spirit of God: every spirit that acknowledges that Jesus Christ has come in the flesh is from God, every spirit that does not acknowledge Jesus is not from God' (4: 2 f.; cf. 2 Jn 7). Stress is also laid, as we have seen already, on the deity of Christ. These Letters breathe the air of the latter days of the NT period when 'many deceivers have gone out into the world' (2 Jn 7).

Not only is further doctrine unveiled in response to such heresies, but the claim is increasingly pressed that there was a body of doctrine already revealed which could not be altered. This is highly important as it sets a limit upon the revelation of new truth, and affirms the existence of a commonly recognized corpus of doctrinal propositions. The very fact that some were charged with deviation testifies to the existence of a body of truth from which deviation was possible. Jude, whose Letter is in many ways similar to 2 Peter, writes against those who indulged the flesh, and set themselves against the very person of Christ (Jude 4). In his attack on these dangerous persons he appeals to his hearers to 'contend for the faith which was once for all entrusted to the saints' (Jude 3). The finality of the revelation in Christ is thus affirmed. A similar position is taken in 2 Peter who reminds the Christians 'of these things, even though you know them and are firmly established in the truth you now have' (2 Pet. 1: 12). Apostates were guilty of having turned from 'the sacred commandment' (2 Pet. 2: 21).

There is a significant sequence of verses in the Pastoral Letters. Instruction is given to Timothy so that he 'may know how one ought to behave in the household of God, which is the church of the living God, the pillar and foundation of the truth' (1 Tim. 3: 15). This is followed by the Christological creed: 'He appeared in a body, was vindicated by the Spirit, was seen by angels, was preached among the nations, was believed on in the world, was taken up in glory' (1 Tim. 3: 16). Immediately after this is the statement that 'the Spirit expressly says that in later times some will depart from the faith by giving heed to deceitful spirits and doctrines of demons' (1 Pet. 4: 1). The 'truth' and the 'faith' have thus come to signify the body of revealed doctrine (cf. 2 Tim. 2: 15; 1 Pet. 1: 22).

In 2 Timothy, Paul likewise encourages fidelity to the revelation already given: 'Do your best to present yourself to God as one approved, a workman who does not need to be ashamed, and who correctly handles the word of truth' (2 Tim. 2: 15). In the face of opposition Timothy is urged to follow the example of the apostle Paul as regards behaviour (3: 10–13), and to hold to the inspired Scripture which he had learned from childhood (3: 14–17). Paul urges him to 'preach the word' (4: 2), and asserts that he himself has 'kept the faith' (4: 7). This latter statement exhibits the use of the word 'faith' in the sense of a body of doctrine which was seen in Jude 3. This doctrine he had passed on to Timothy, who was to 'What you heard from me, keep as the pattern of sound teaching . . . Guard the good deposit that was entrusted to you . . .' (1: 13 f.). The word here translated 'pattern' is used in the sense of a standard, and is a cognate of the word translated 'standard' in Rom. 6: 17: 'the standard of teaching to which you were committed'. Paul had also insisted on fidelity to 'the traditions which you were taught by us' in the earlier Thessalonian correspondence (2 Th. 2: 15).

We have seen that there was a continuum of

teaching which had its origin in the very words of the Lord Jesus and which was transmitted through the earliest generations of Christians including Paul himself. This was to be considered a 'standard' and an unalterable 'faith' to which Christians were to adhere, and for which they were to contend. No liberty could be taken after the Canon was completed to supplement or modify the standard of accepted truths.

BIBLIOGRAPHY

BERNARD, T. D., *The Progress of Doctrine in the New Testament* (London, 1864); reprinted, Grand Rapids, 1949).

BRUCE, F. F., *New Testament History* (London, 1969).

BRUCE, F. F., *Paul: Apostle of the Heart Set Free* (Exeter, 1977).

BUCK, C. H., Jr. and TAYLOR, G., *Saint Paul* (New York, 1969).

CULLMANN, O., *The Early Church.* Eng. trans. (London, 1956), pp. 59–140.

CULLMANN, O., *Salvation in History.* Eng. trans. (London, 1967).

DODD, C. H., *The Apostolic Preaching and Its Developments* (London, 1936; rev. ed. 1944).

DODD, C. H., *According to the Scriptures* (London, 1952).

DUNN, J. D. G., *Unity and Diversity in the New Testament* (Philadelphia, 1977).

FULLER, R. H., *The Foundations of New Testament Christology* (London, 1965).

GUTHRIE, D., *New Testament Theology* (Leicester, 1981).

HUNTER, A. M., *Paul and His Predecessors* (London, 1961).

JEREMIAS, J., *New Testament Theology: The Proclamation of Jesus* (New York, 1971).

KÜMMEL, W. G., *The Theology of the New Testament.* E.T. (London, 1973).

LADD, G. E., *A Theology of the New Testament* (Grand Rapids, 1974).

MARSHALL, I. H., ed., *New Testament Interpretation* (Exeter, 1977).

MARSHALL, I. H., *The Origins of New Testament Christology* (London, 1976).

MARTIN, R. P., *Worship in the Early Church* (London, 1964).

MORRIS, L., *The Cross in the New Testament* (Exeter, 1965).

MOULE, C. F. D., *The Birth of the New Testament* (London, ³1981).

MOULE, C. F. D., *The Origin of Christology* (Cambridge, 1977).

MOUNCE, R. H., *The Essential Nature of New Testament Preaching* (Grand Rapids, 1960).

NEUFELD, V. H., *The Earliest Christian Confessions* (Grand Rapids, 1963).

THE FOURFOLD GOSPEL

F. F. BRUCE

The Gospel and the Gospels

We talk familiarly about the four gospels, the apocryphal gospels, and so forth, using the word 'gospels' quite freely in the plural. But this usage would not have been understood in the church of apostolic days, nor yet for nearly a century after the apostolic age. The first known occurrences of the word 'gospels' in the plural in this later sense come in the second half of the second century—in Justin Martyr, Claudius Apollinaris, Clement of Alexandria, Irenaeus, and the Muratorian Canon. Justin (*First Apology* 66. 3) speaks of the memoirs of the apostles 'which are called gospels' (Gk. *euangelia*), while elsewhere (*Dialogue with Trypho* 10.2; 100.1) he speaks comprehensively of the 'gospel' (*euangelion*). Clement (*Stromata* iii. 13) refers to 'the four gospels (*euangelia*) which have been handed down to us'. Irenaeus (*Heresies* ii. 11. 8) speaks not only of 'the fourfold gospel' (*euangelion*) but also of the 'gospels' (*euangelia*). Similarly the Muratorian Canon, while it calls Luke's record 'the third book of the gospel' (singular), refers to John's as 'the fourth of the gospels' (plural). From the way in which some of these writers oscillate between the singular and the plural, it may be inferred that the plural 'gospels' was just coming into use. Earlier writers use the singular, whether they refer to a single gospel-writing or to a collection of such writings. And the use of the comprehensive singular to denote the fourfold record continued for long after the earlier attested occurrences of the plural. To the early Christians there was only one gospel, 'the gospel of God concerning his Son' (Rom. 1: 1–3), variously recorded by Matthew, Mark and the others. The overall caption for the fourfold account was the singular *Euangelion*; the four writings included under that caption were particularized as 'according to Matthew', 'according to Mark', and so on. Even outside the canonical four, such a document as *The Gospel according to the Hebrews* was regarded by those who acknowledged it as the self-same gospel of Christ, in the form in which it was recorded among the 'Hebrews'.

It is noteworthy that none of our four canonical gospel-writings calls itself a 'gospel', and that all four are, strictly speaking, anonymous. In both respects they differ from a number of uncanonical writings of the second and later centuries, which style themselves 'gospels' and claim the authorship of an apostle or other leading light of the first Christian generation. The authorship of the canonical four must be determined, as far as is possible, by internal and external evidence; more important than individual authorship is the truth of the gospel to which all four evangelists bear witness.

In the New Testament the gospel is, first, the proclamation by Jesus that the kingdom of God has drawn near, and, second, the subsequent proclamation by the disciples that in the humiliation and exaltation of Jesus the kingdom of God has been inaugurated, and that forgiveness and life eternal have been secured by Him for all believers. The second phase of the gospel arises inevitably out of the first; indeed, Jesus Himself distinguished the two phases. There was a limited phase in which the presence of the kingdom of God was manifested by His casting out of demons and similar mighty works (cf. Lk. 11: 20; 17: 20 f.); but the present limitations would be removed when the kingdom of God came 'with power' before the eyes of some of His hearers (Mk 9: 1). The passion and triumph of Jesus, which formed the basic subject-matter of the apostolic witness, crowned His ministry and embodied and confirmed all that He had taught about the kingdom of God.

The background of the noun *euangelion* and its related verb *euangelizomai* ('bring good news'), as used in the New Testament, must be sought in the second part of the book of Isaiah—in Isa. 40: 9; 52: 7; 60: 6 and 61: 1. The good news of Zion's liberation, celebrated in Isa. 40: 9 ('O thou that tellest good tidings to Zion . . .'), is interpreted in the New Testament as adumbrating the good news of a greater liberation, just as the voice of Isa. 40: 3 calling for the preparation of a way across the desert for the God of Israel to lead His exiles home is interpreted of another voice which, on the eve of the ministry of Jesus, called for repentance in preparation for the advent of the Coming One (Mk 1: 3). The words of Isa. 52: 7 ('How beautiful on the mountains are the feet of those who bring good news . . .') are to the same effect as those of Isa. 40: 9, and are applied by Paul in Rom. 10: 15 to the preachers of the gospel of Christ.

But more important still for New Testament usage is Isa. 61: 1, where an unnamed speaker (identified in the New Testament with the Servant of the LORD in preceding chapters of Isaiah) introduces himself by saying: 'The Spirit of the Sovereign Lord is on me, because the LORD has anointed me (made me Messiah) to preach good news to the poor.' In Lk. 4: 17–21 Jesus is depicted as reading this scripture in the Nazareth synagogue and applying it to Himself, and the narrative of Jesus' reply to John the Baptist's message from prison records how He emphasized as the conclusive argument for His being indeed the Coming One of whom John had previously spoken the fact that 'the good news is preached to the poor' (Mt. 11: 5; Lk. 7: 22).

The Oral Gospel

For the first thirty years or so after the death and resurrection of Christ, the necessity for a written account of His ministry was not greatly felt. So long as eyewitnesses of the saving events were alive who could speak with confidence of what they had seen and heard, the living voice sufficed by way of testimony. Even when the good news was told by men and women who had not had direct contact with Christ in the days of His flesh, they could always appeal to the authority of those who spoke with first-hand knowledge. And this attitude of mind was long in dying out. As late as A.D. 130 Papias, bishop of Hierapolis in Phrygia, tells us how eagerly he used to interview those who knew the apostles and their associates and ask them what the apostles really said, for he felt that in this way he was in much closer touch with the original gospel facts than he could ever be by reading a written record.

We are not thrown back on our imagination when it comes to envisaging the forms in which the material later written down in our gospels was preserved and transmitted orally during the first generation after the death and resurrection of Jesus. Certain lines of evidence are available to us.

(a) **The Words of Jesus.** When Jesus first 'came into Galilee, preaching the gospel of God', the burden of His message was that the appointed time had now arrived and the kingdom of God had drawn near; He urged His hearers to repent and believe the good news (Mk 1: 14 f.). His preaching was no bolt from the blue; it was the fulfilment of the promise of God communicated in earlier days through the prophets. Now at length God had visited His people; this was the burden not only of Jesus' preaching but of His mighty works (Lk. 7: 16), which were signs that the domain of evil was crumbling before the onset of the kingdom of God (Mt. 12: 22–29; Lk. 11: 14–22). The same theme runs through the parables of Jesus, which call His hearers to decision and watchfulness in view of the advent of the kingdom.

In addition to His public ministry, Jesus took care to give His disciples systematic instruction

in a form that they could easily commit to memory. His debates with the Pharisees and other opponents, too, led to pronouncements which, once heard, would not be readily forgotten, and which in fact stood His disciples in good stead later on when they were confronted with controversial issues in which it was helpful to recall their Master's ruling.

(b) **The Apostolic Tradition.** There are several references in the New Testament letters to the 'tradition' (Gk. *paradosis*) received by the apostles from their Lord and delivered by them in turn to their converts. This tradition, in the fullest sense, compnses the apostles' witness to 'all that Jesus began to do and to teach, until the day he was taken up' (Ac. 1: 1 f.). Their witness was borne and perpetuated in many ways—especially in missionary preaching, in the instruction of converts, and in Christian worship.

i. Missionary Preaching

Some idea of the outline of the early Christian preaching (*kērygma*) can be gathered from the Pauline and other letters and from the speeches in Acts.

The Pauline letters were written to people who were already familiar with the *kērygma*; any reference to the *kērygma* in them, therefore, will be incidental and reminiscent. In 1 C. 15: 3 ff., for example, Paul reminds his readers of the most important features of the message which had brought them salvation on his first visit to Corinth: 'that Christ died for our sins according to Scriptures, that he was buried, that he was raised on the third day according to the Scriptures, and that he appeared to Peter, and then to the Twelve. After that he appeared to more than five hundred of the brothers at the same time, most of whom are still living, though some have fallen asleep. Then he appeared to James, then to all the apostles. . . .'

The message thus summarized Paul says that he himself had 'received' from others (*parelabon*) before he 'passed it on' in turn (*paredōka*) to the Corinthians. The others from whom Paul 'received' this outline were probably the two individuals mentioned in it by name, Peter and James, whom he met when he paid a short visit to Jerusalem in the third year after his conversion (Gal. 1: 18 f.). Brief as it is, it contains more than a recital of the bare facts that a certain person died, was buried, rose from the dead and appeared thereafter to a number of people who knew him. These facts are interpreted: the person referred to was the Christ, i.e. the expected Messiah of Israel; his death was in some sense endured for the sins of others; and his death and resurrection alike took place in accordance with the prophetic writings of the Old Testament. From incidental references in the same letter we learn that the death of Christ was inflicted by crucifixion, a fact which scandalized many who heard the gospel story: the very idea of a crucified Messiah was a 'stumbling-block to Jews and foolishness to Gentiles' (1 C. 1: 23). From other letters of Paul we learn that Jesus was born a Jew and lived under the Jewish law (Gal. 4: 4), that He was not only a descendant of Abraham but also a member of the royal house of David (Rom. 1: 3), that while He died the Roman death by crucifixion, yet some responsibility for His death rested with Jews (1 Th. 2: 15). If we are allowed to regard 1 Tim. 6: 13 as Pauline, we learn there that He appeared before one Pontius Pilate and witnessed a good confession, although (according to 2 Tim. 4: 1) He Himself was the divinely appointed judge of living and dead. Having been raised from the dead, He was now exalted at God's right hand (Rom. 8: 34; Eph. 1: 20; Col. 3: 1). Before His tribunal, says Paul, 'we must all appear' (2 C. 5: 10). This judgment is linked with His future appearance, an event to be accompanied by the resurrection of the dead and the receiving of immortality by those then living (1 C. 15: 52 f.; 1 Th. 4: 16). That Paul's *kērygma* contained some account of this consummation of the divine redemption at the advent of Christ is evident, *e.g.*, when he writes to his Thessalonian converts, reminding them how, at their conversion, they 'turned to God from idols, to serve the living and true God, and to wait for his Son from heaven, whom he raised from the dead—Jesus, who rescues us from the coming wrath' (1 Th. 1:9 f.).

Paul insisted (1 C. 15: 11) that his gospel was basically the same as that preached by the other apostles. It is not surprising, therefore, to find in 1 Peter the same facts presented as the foundation of the *kērygma*: the death and resurrection of Messiah (1 Pet. 1: 3), His exaltation to God's right hand (3: 22), His glory yet to be revealed (5: 1)—all presented as the fulfilment of Old Testament prophecy and as basic for the bestowal of God's salvation.

The writer claims to be a witness of Christ's sufferings, and describes the saving events, especially Christ's patient endurance of undeserved ill-treatment and death, so vividly that (in C. H. Dodd's words): 'That in general its thought follows the apostolic preaching is clear, and we could easily believe that in places its very language is echoed. . . . We shall not be so ready as some critics have been to put all this down to "Pauline influence". It is a clear echo of the preaching which lies behind Paul and the whole New Testament' (*The Apostolic Preaching and its Developments*, 1936, pp. 97 f.).

The same general pattern of redemptive events is the underlying premiss of other New Testament letters, notably Hebrews and 1 John, and also of the Apocalypse. In the primitive message, then, to which these various documents bear witness, the following elements can be distinguished: (1) God has visited and redeemed His people by sending the promised Messiah, at the time of the fulfilment of the divine purpose revealed in Old Testament scripture. (2) The Messiah came, as was prophesied, of Israel's race, of Judah's tribe, of David's royal seed, in the person of Jesus of Nazareth. (3) As the prophets had foretold, He died for men's sins upon a cross, was buried, and (4) rose again the third day, as many eyewitnesses could testify. (5) He has been exalted in glory at the right hand of God, while (6) His Holy Spirit has been sent to those who believe in Him, and (7) Christ Himself is to return to earth to judge the living and the dead and to consummate the work of redemption, both for His people and, through them, for all creation. (8) On the basis of these facts remission of sins and the life of the age to come are offered to all who repent and believe the good news; those who repent and believe are further baptized into Christ's name and incorporated into a new community, the church of Christ.

The speeches ascribed to Peter and Paul in the first half of Acts are probably not the free invention of the historian, but reliable summaries of the early apostolic preaching. Of these speeches the most important are those delivered by Peter in Jerusalem on the day of Pentecost (Ac. 2: 22–36) and in Caesarea in the house of Cornelius (10: 36–43), and that delivered by Paul some years later in the synagogue of Pisidian Antioch (13: 17–41). Further fragments of the *kērygma* can be traced in 3: 13–26; 4: 10–12; 5: 30–32 and 8: 32–35. In all these we find the same message as is reflected in the Pauline and other letters. The message itself is called the good news; it is announced as the fulfilment of Old Testament prophecy; its subject is Jesus of Nazareth, a descendant of David, whose public life began during the ministry of His forerunner, John the Baptist, and whose mission was divinely attested by His works of mercy and power. He was betrayed to His enemies, handed over to the Romans by the Jewish rulers, and consequently crucified (this is referred to more than once in language reminiscent of Dt. 21: 23: 'anyone who is hung on a tree is under God's curse'). He was then taken down from the cross and buried, but raised by God the third day, the apostles constantly emphasizing their eyewitness testimony to His resurrection. The resurrection, they claimed, declared Him to be Lord and Messiah, exalted to God's right hand, whence He had sent forth His Spirit upon his followers. He was to return to assume His divinely given office as judge of quick and dead; meanwhile the call to those who heard the gospel was to repent, believe, be baptized and receive the remission of sins and the gift of the Holy Spirit.

Acts and the letters tell us the same story. The message was essentially the same no matter who the preacher was. Stereotyped religious teaching was the regular practice throughout the world in those days and the gospel formed no exception.

A similar outline of the *kērygma* has been discerned as the framework on which the body of Mark's Gospel has been built, or (one might say) the thread on which Mark has strung his several units of gospel material. It is noteworthy that Mark begins where the outlines of the *kērygma* begin, with the activity of John the Baptist, and that it ends with an account of the passion and resurrection of Christ which (as in the other Gospels) receives what might appear from a purely biographical point of view to be a disproportionate amount of space. But this is a prominent feature of the *kērygma* in all the forms in which we can trace it.

ii. Early Christian Teaching

Some occasional samples of the instruction of converts appear in the letters, from which it is plain that the basis of this teaching was what Jesus Himself had taught. Thus in giving instruction about marriage Paul quotes Jesus' commandment forbidding divorce (1 C. 7: 10); he similarly quotes His ruling about the maintenance of gospel preachers (1 C. 9: 14). But there is evidence of more systematic instruction by the catechetical method; and as the number of converts increased, especially in the course of the Gentile mission, 'schools' for the training of instructors would have become almost a necessity, and digests of the teaching of Jesus would inevitably have been drawn up, orally if not in writing. We may envisage such a life-setting for the 'sayings collection' on which Mt. and Lk. drew, and at a later date the Matthaean gospel itself has been viewed as taking shape in such a school.

iii. Early Christian Worship

In worship too the works and words of Jesus were bound to be recalled. In the earliest days of the faith those who had known Jesus could scarcely avoid saying to one another, when they met informally or at the stated occasions of fellowship and worship, 'Do you remember how our Master . . . ?' In particular, the Lord's Supper provided a regular opportunity for retelling the story of His death, with the events immediately preceding and following it (1 C. 11: 26). The institution of the Lord's Supper, incidentally, like the outline of the redemptive events in 1 C. 15: 3 ff., is narrated by Paul as something which he 'received' (by a tradition stemming from the Lord Himself) before he 'passed it on' to his converts (1 C. 11: 23 ff.). Not only did the Supper bring the Lord to remembrance; each occasion on which Christians ate the bread and drank the cup was an anticipation of His coming again.

The passion narrative, indeed, being told and retold both in Christian worship and in missionary preaching (cf. 1 C. 2: 2; Gal. 3: 1), took shape as a connected whole at an early date—a conclusion which is otherwise established by the form-criticism of our existing Gospels. By the form-critical method an attempt is made to isolate and classify the various self-contained units which have been brought together in the written Gospels and to envisage the living situations in which they originated and were preserved in the oral stage of transmission. The value of the form-critical method is greatest when what was originally one and the same unit of teaching or narrative can be shown to have come down along two separate lines in two different 'forms'—a situation which appears repeatedly when one compares a Synoptic account with its Johannine parallel. We are thus helped to envisage the material of such a unit as it was before it began to be transmitted.

The Written Gospels

The beginning of gospel writing, as we might expect, coincides with the end of the first Christian generation. As 'those who from the first were eyewitnesses and servants of the word' (Lk. 1: 2) were removed by death, the necessity of a permanent written record of their witness would be more acutely felt than before. It is just at this point that second-century tradition places the beginnings of gospel writing, and rightly so: all four of our canonical Gospels are probably to be dated within the four decades A.D. 60–100. We need not suppose that the transmission of the apostolic witness had been exclusively oral before A.D. 60—some at least of the 'many' who, according to Lk. 1: 1, had undertaken to draw up an orderly account of the evangelic events may have done so in writing before A.D. 60—but no document of an earlier date has survived except in so far as it has been incorporated in our written Gospels.

Several strands of tradition can be distinguished in the four Gospels. In this respect, as in some others, John stands apart from the other Gospels and is best considered independently. The other three Gospels are interrelated to the point where they lend themselves excellently to 'synoptic' study—*e.g.*, as when their text is arranged in three parallel columns, so that their coincidences and divergences can be conveniently examined. For this reason they are commonly known as the 'Synoptic Gospels'—a designation first apparently given to them by J. J. Griesbach in 1774.

(a) **The Synoptic Gospels.** A comparative study of Mt., Mk and Lk. leads to the recognition that there is a considerable body of material common to all three, or to two out of the three. The substance of 606 out of the 661 verses of Mk (Mk 16: 9–20 being left out of the reckoning) reappears in abridged form in Mt.; some 380 of the 661 verses of Mk reappear in Lk. This may be stated otherwise by saying that, out of the 1,068 verses of Mt., about 500 contain the substance of 606 verses of Mk, while out of the 1,149 verses of Lk., some 380 are paralleled in Mk. Only 31 verses of Mk have no parallel in either Mt. or Lk. Mt. and Lk. have each up to 250 verses containing common material not paralleled in Mk; sometimes this common material appears in Mt. and Lk. in practically identical language, while sometimes the verbal divergence is considerable. About 300 verses of Mt. have no parallel in any of the other gospels; the same is true of about 520 verses in Lk.

There is no short cut to a satisfactory account of this distribution of common and special material in the Synoptic Gospels. There is no *a priori* reason for holding one gospel to be earlier and another later, for holding one to be a source of another and the latter to be dependent on the former. Nor will the objectivity of statistical analysis guarantee a solution. A solution can be obtained only by the exercise of critical judgment after all the relevant data have been marshalled and the alternative possibilities assessed. If unanimity has not been reached after a century and a half of intensive synoptic study, it may be because the data are insufficient for the purpose, or because the field of enquiry has been unduly restricted. Yet certain findings command a much greater area of agreement than others.

One of these is the priority of Mk, and its use as a principal source by the other two Synoptic evangelists. This finding, which may be said to have been placed on a stable basis by Carl Lachmann in 1835, depends not merely on the formal evidence that Mt. and Mk sometimes agree in order against Lk., Mk and Lk. more frequently against Mt., but Mt. and Lk. never against Mk (which could be explained otherwise), but rather on the detailed comparative examination of the way in which common material is reproduced in the three Gospels, section by section. In the overwhelming majority of sections, the situation can best be understood if Mk's account was used as a source by one or both of the others. Few have ever considered Lk. as a possible source of the other two, but the view that Mk is an abridgement of Mt. was held for a long time, largely through the influence of Augustine. But Mt. and Mk have material in common, Mk is fuller than Mt., and by no means an abridgement; and time after time the two parallel accounts can be much better explained by supposing that Mt. condenses Mk than by supposing that Mk amplifies Mt. While Mt. and Lk. never agree in order against Mk, they do occasionally exhibit verbal agreement against Mk, but such instances mainly represent grammatical or stylistic improvements of Mk, and are neither numerous nor significant enough to be offset against the general weight of the evidence for the priority of Mk.

The common Markan element in the Synoptic tradition is the more important because of the close relation between the framework of Mk and the apostolic preaching. It is interesting, too, to recall in this connection the tradition which points to Peter as the authority behind Mark's account. The earliest witness to this tradition is Papias, who records it on the authority of someone whom he calls 'the elder': 'Mark, the interpreter of Peter, wrote down accurately all the words or deeds of the Lord of which he [Peter] made mention, but not in order . . .' (quoted by Eusebius, *Ecclesiastical History* iii. 39. 15). This tradition is corroborated by internal evidence in some parts of Mk's narrative. One of the most interesting pieces of evidence in this regard is presented by what has been called 'Turner's mark' (a feature of Mark's usage the significance of which was pointed out in a series of studies by C. H. Turner). 'Time after time a sentence commences with the plural, for it is an experience which is being related, and passes into the singular, for the experience is that of discipleship to a Master' (C. H. Turner, *The Gospel according to St. Mark*, 1930, p. 9). One example comes in Mk 1: 21, '*they* went into Capernaum; and immediately on the sabbath *he* entered the synagogue and taught.' Where the other Synoptic evangelists reproduce such passages, they tend to replace the initial plural 'they' by the singular 'he' (cf. Lk. 4: 31, '*he* went down to Capernaum . . . *he* was teaching them on the sabbath'). If the reader will now take one step further and put back Mk's third person plural into the first person plural of the narrator, he will receive a vivid impression of the testimony that lies behind the Gospel: thus in 1: 29, 'we came into our house with James and John: and my wife's mother was ill in bed with a fever, and at once we tell him about her' (*ibid.*). In a study of the contexts in which this feature appears, T. W. Manson suggested that the following sections of Mk may reasonably be recognized as Petrine: Mk 1: 16–39; 2: 1–14; 3: 13–19; 4: 35–5: 43; 6: 7–13, 30–56; 8: 14–9: 48; 10: 32–52; 11: 1–33; 13: 3–4, 32–37; 14: 17–50, 53–54, 66–72 (*Studies in the Gospels and Epistles*, 1962, p. 42). This excludes, for example, the ministry and death of John the Baptist (1: 1 ff.; 6: 17–29) and the greater part of the passion and resurrection narrative (14: 55–65; 15: 1–16: 8), for which other sources of information were accessible.

The material common to Mk and one or both of the other Synoptic gospels consists mainly of narrative. (The principal exceptions to this are the parables of Mk 4 and the eschatological discourse of Mk 13.) On the other hand, the non-Markan material common to Mt. and Lk. consists mainly of sayings of Jesus. One might also say that the Markan material relates what Jesus did; the non-Markan material, what Jesus taught. We have here a distinction comparable to that commonly made (albeit to an exaggerated degree) between apostolic 'preaching' (*kērygma*) and 'teaching' (*didachē*). The non-Markan material common to Mt. and Lk. is conventionally and conveniently labelled 'Q'. In the commentaries on the separate gospels in this volume the label 'Q' is used as a shorthand designation for this material.

This body of material, extending to between 200 and 250 verses, might have been derived by the one evangelist from the other, or by both from a common source. Few, if any, can be found to suggest that Mt. derived it from Lk., although theoretically it might be easier to sustain this thesis than that Lk. derived it from Mt. This latter supposition continues to receive diminishing support in some quarters where tradition counts for much, but it is specially vulnerable because it implies that Lk. reduced to relative disorder the orderly arrangement in which the 'Q' material appears in Mt., without giving any plausible reason why this should have been done.

The supposition that the 'Q' material was derived from a common source by Mt. and Lk. involves fewer difficulties than any alternative supposition.

When we attempt to reconstruct this postulated common source, we must beware of thinking that we can do so in anything like a complete form. Yet what we can reconstruct of it reminds us forcibly of the general pattern of the prophetical books of the Old Testament. These books commonly contain an account of the prophet's call, with a record of his oracles set in a narrative framework, but with no mention of his death. So the 'Q' material appears to have come from a compilation which began with an account of Jesus' baptism by John and His wilderness temptations; this forms the prelude to His ministry, and is followed by groups of His sayings set in a minimum of narrative framework; but there is no trace of a passion narrative. There are four main groups of teaching, which may be entitled (i) Jesus and John the Baptist; (ii) Jesus and His disciples; (iii) Jesus and His opponents; (iv) Jesus and the future.

Since our only means of reconstructing this source is provided by the non-Markan material common to Mt. and Lk., the question whether Mk also made some use of it cannot be satisfactorily answered. That it is earlier than Mk is probable; it may well have been used for catechetical purposes in the Gentile mission

based on Antioch. The fact that some of the 'Q' material in Mt. and Lk. is almost verbally identical, while elsewhere there are divergences of language, has sometimes been explained in terms of there being two distinct strands of tradition in 'Q', but a much more probable account is that 'Q' was translated more than once into Greek from Aramaic and that Mt. and Lk. sometimes use the same translation and sometimes different ones. In this regard it is apposite to recall the statement of Papias (quoted by Eusebius, *Hist. Eccl.* iii. 39. 16) that 'Matthew compiled the *logia* in the Hebrew (Aramaic) speech, and everyone translated them as best he could.' *Logia* ('oracles') would be a specially appropriate term for the contents of such a compilation as we have tried to recognize behind the 'Q' material.

What other sources were utilized by Mt. and Lk. is an even more uncertain question than the reconstruction of the 'Q' source. Mt. appears to have incorporated material from another sayings-collection, parallel to 'Q', but preserved in Judaea rather than in Antioch—the collection conveniently labelled 'M'. To this material may be assigned certain sections in the Sermon on the Mount (Mt. 5: 17–24, 27 f., 33–39; 6: 1–8, 16–18; 7: 6); the parables of the tares (13: 24–30, 36–43), of the hidden treasure (13: 44), of the pearl of great price (13: 45 f.), and of the dragnet (13: 47–50), of the unforgiving servant (18: 23–35), of the labourers in the vineyard (20: 1–16), of the obedient and disobedient sons (21: 28–32), of the marriage feast (22: 1–14), of the ten virgins (25: 1–13) and of the sheep and the goats (25: 31–46); the two 'church' sayings, with their references to binding and loosing (16: 17–19; 18: 15–20); and parts of the lament over the scribes and Pharisees in ch. 23 (verses 2 f., 5–10, 15–22). This and other special material is interwoven by Mt. with the Markan and 'Q' material so as to yield a well-arranged document, comprising both narrative and teaching, in which incidents and sayings dealing with the same general subjects are for the most part found together. In consequence, to anyone who keeps the general structure of this Gospel in mind it is usually easy to decide where a saying of Jesus on a particular subject is most likely to appear. The sayings are grouped together in the five great discourses which form the most conspicuous feature of the structure of Mt.; each of the discourses is introduced by an appropriate narrative section, mostly, but not entirely, derived and abridged from Mk. The greater part of Mk 1: 2–6: 13 is thus embodied in Mt. 3: 1–13: 58, but the sequence of this part of Mk has been completely rearranged in Mt., possibly in order that each section of narrative in Mt. may provide a suitable introduction to the discourse that follows it. The remainder of the Markan account (Mk 6: 14 ff.) is reproduced in Mt. 14: 1 ff. without such rearrangement.

How far Mt. has rearranged the sequence in which he found his 'Q' material is naturally much more difficult to decide. It is noteworthy, however, that the best parallel arrangement of the 'Q' and 'M' material is to set 'Q' in Luke's order alongside 'M' in Matthew's order (which, of course, is the only order in which 'M' is available to us).

The arrangement of sources in Lk. is quite different from that in Mt. Whereas each section of Mt. presents an interweaving of material from all the sources, Lk. arranges Markan and non-Markan material in alternate blocks. Thus we have Lk. 3 narrating the ministry of John the Baptist in alternate non-Markan and Markan sections; this is followed by Lk. 4: 2–30 (non-Markan); 4: 31–44 (Markan); 5: 1–11 (non-Markan); 5: 12–6: 19 (Markan); 6: 20–8: 3 (non-Markan); 8: 4–9: 50 (Markan); 9: 51–18: 14 (non-Markan); 18: 15–43 (Markan); 19: 1–27 (non-Markan); 19: 28–38 (Markan); 19: 39–44 (non-Markan); 19: 45–22: 23 (largely, but not entirely, Markan). Then comes the passion narrative, parallel to that in Mk, but plainly drawing upon other sources of information peculiar to Luke among the evangelists: we may think of the words of Jesus to Peter and the other disciples in Lk. 22: 27–38; the angel and the bloody sweat in Gethsemane (22: 43 f.); the appearance before Herod Antipas (23: 5–16); the weeping women on the way to the cross (23: 27–31); the prayer for forgiveness (23: 34), and the incident of the penitent robber (23: 39–43). The resurrection narrative, after the women's discovery of the empty tomb (24: 1–8), is also peculiar to Luke (24: 9–53).

Luke has been pictured as inserting blocks of Markan material into a narrative (sometimes called 'Proto-Luke') which he had already drawn up. Whether this earlier and shorter draft had been published by itself is almost impossible to determine. One of the most striking features of his use of Mk is his omission of the contents of Mk 6: 45–8: 26. The point in Lk. where we might have expected to find his parallels to this Markan section is between verses 17 and 18 of Lk. 9; but we find none. This is commonly referred to as Luke's 'great omission'. This section of Mk appears to reproduce, on largely Gentile territory, a sequence of events similar to that found in the preceding section, Mk 4: 35–6: 44 (cf. Lk. 8: 22–9: 17, except that Lk. does not reproduce the narrative of Mk 6: 14–29), where the setting is distinctively Jewish. The earlier of these two Markan sections includes the feeding of the five thousand (Mk 6: 31–44); the other includes the feeding of the four thousand (Mk 8: 1–10). Augustine distinguished these two feedings as signifying our Lord's communication of Him-

self to the Jews and to the Gentiles respectively; and to some extent the same kind of distinction may be recognized between the two Markan sections in which these feeding narratives appear. (Early in the second of these two Markan sections comes our Lord's abrogation of the food-laws and other ceremonial ordinances which constituted such a barrier between Jews and Gentiles.) But why should the Gentile Luke, with his interest in the Gentile mission, omit this section if this is its significance? Perhaps because he was deliberately reserving the theme (as distinct from the detailed contents) of this section for his second treatise, where (from Ac. 10 onwards) the communication of Christ to the Gentiles is his main subject.

The non-Markan material in Luke's account of the ministry may best be described as 'Q' amplified by material peculiar to Lk. (which we can conveniently label 'L'). Luke, as he traced the course of events accurately from the beginning (cf. Lk. 1: 3), perhaps took around with him a copy of the sayings-collection which underlies 'Q' and enlarged it by means of information which he was able to acquire from the household of Philip in Caesarea and from many other quarters, thus compiling the preliminary draft which was later expanded further by the insertion of Markan blocks.

Some of the most memorable elements in the Synoptic accounts belong to Luke's special material. They include the Baptist's advice to his hearers, including tax-collectors and soldiers (Lk. 3: 10–14); Jesus' sermon at Nazareth (4: 16–30); the miraculous draught of fishes (5: 1–11; cf. Jn 21: 1–11 for a post-resurrection parallel); the raising of the widow's son at Nain (7: 11–17); the incident of the penitent woman and the parable of the two debtors (7: 36–50); the parable of the good Samaritan (10: 30–37); the visit to Martha and Mary (10: 38–42); the parables of the friend at midnight (11: 5–8), of the rich fool (12: 13–21), of the great supper (14: 16–24), of the lost coin (15: 8–10), of the prodigal son (15: 11–32), of the unjust steward (16: 1–12), of Dives and Lazarus (16: 19–31), of the importunate widow (18: 1–8) and of the Pharisee and the tax-collector (18: 9–14); the healing of the ten lepers (17: 11–19), and the story of Zacchaeus (19: 1–10), in addition to the peculiarly Lukan features of the passion and resurrection narratives already mentioned. When we consider how poor we should have been without all this, we may have some idea of our indebtedness to this evangelist for his labour of love in collecting and recording the material for his Gospel.

Luke is a literary artist with a sense of historical setting; he is also keenly interested in the broad humanitarian aspects of Jesus' teaching and action. While even his record cannot be called a biography in the modern sense, he shows more interest in biographical touches for their own sake than the other evangelists do. His Gospel therefore is often felt to be the most readable and appealing of the four for men and women today.

The nativity narratives which introduce Mt. and Lk. lie outside the general scheme of Synoptic criticism; with regard to them some dependence on Semitic documents cannot be excluded. Each of the two is independent of the other.

It must be emphasized that, fascinating and instructive as gospel source-criticism is, the gospels themselves are much more important than their putative sources. It is interesting to consider what sources the evangelists may have used; it is better to consider what use they made of their sources. Each of the Synoptic gospels is an independent whole, no mere scissors-and-paste compilation; each has its own view of Jesus and His ministry, and each has its special contribution to make to the full-orbed picture of Jesus with which the New Testament presents us.

(b) **The Fourth Gospel.** One of the last survivors of Jesus' closest associates continued to think long and deeply about the meaning of all that he had seen and heard. Much that had once been obscure became clearer to his mind with the passage of time.

What first were guessed as points, I now knew stars,
And named them in the Gospel I have writ.

—Browning, *A Death in the Desert*

He himself experienced the fulfilment of the promises recorded in his gospel, that the Holy Spirit would bring the teaching of Jesus to the disciples' remembrance, make its significance plain to them, and guide them into all the truth. In his old age he realized more than ever that, although the conditions of life in Palestine which had formed the setting for Jesus' ministry before A.D. 30 had passed away beyond recall, that ministry itself was charged with eternal validity. In the life of Jesus all the truth of God which had ever been communicated to men was summed up and made perfect; in Him the eternal Word or self-expression of God had come home to the world in a real human life. But if this was so, the life and work of Jesus could have no merely local, national or temporary relevance. So, towards the end of the first century, he set himself to tell the gospel story in such a way that its abiding truth might be presented to men and women who were quite unfamiliar with the original setting of the saving events. The Hellenistic world of his old age required to be told the regenerating message in such a way that, whether Jews or Gentiles, they might be brought to faith in Jesus as the Messiah and Son of God, and thus receive eternal life through Him. Yet he would

not yield to any temptation to restate Christianity in terms of contemporary thought in such a way as to rob it of its essential uniqueness. The gospel is eternally true, but it is the story of events which happened in history once for all; John does not divorce the story from its Palestinian context in order to bring out its universal application, and at the heart of his record the original apostolic preaching is faithfully preserved.

The content of Jn represents a good primitive tradition which was preserved independently of the Synoptic lines of tradition, not only in the memory of the beloved disciple but in a living Christian community, quite probably in the milieu from which at a rather later date came the Christian hymnbook called the *Odes of Solomon*. (This collection of over forty poems belongs probably to the second century and is the oldest surviving Christian hymnbook; it has been preserved in a Syriac version. The hymns, many of which seem to have a baptismal reference, breathe high spiritual devotion and poetical genius; in a number of respects, and especially in their doctrine of the Logos, they present affinities with this gospel.) The large area of common background which Jn shares with the Qumran texts is but one among recent discoveries which have helped to impress upon us that the Johannine tradition has its roots in Jewish Palestine, however much the requirements of a wider Hellenistic audience were borne in mind when this gospel was given its literary form at the end of the first Christian century.

As for the feeling sometimes expressed that there is an essential difference between the Christ who speaks and acts in the fourth gospel and the Christ who speaks and acts in the Synoptics, it is relevant to reflect that many have testified that John leads them into an even deeper and more intimate appreciation of the mind of Christ than do the other three. The members of the Christian Industrial League, an organization which carries on a gospel witness among the tough characters of Skidrow, in the heart of Chicago's 'Loop' area, say 'that in their work they have found that St. John's gospel is the best for dealing with these tough, hard men. Its straight, unequivocal words about sin and salvation somehow go home and carry conviction to the most abandoned, while its direct invitation wins a response that nothing else does' (A. M. Chirgwin, *The Bible in World Evangelism*, 1954, p. 113). Or we may listen to a testimony from a very different source, the late Archbishop William Temple, theologian, philosopher and statesman: 'The Synoptists may give us something more like the perfect photograph; St. John gives us the more perfect portrait . . . the mind of Jesus Himself was what the Fourth Gospel disclosed, but . . . the disciples were at first unable to enter into this, partly because of its novelty, and partly because of the associations attaching to the terminology in which it was necessary that the Lord should express Himself. Let the Synoptists repeat for us as closely as they can the very words He spoke; but let St. John tune our ears to hear them' (*Readings in St. John's Gospel*, 1940, pp. xvi, xxxii).

When we read one of the earlier gospels, we sometimes get the impression that in the story which we are reading there is more than meets the eye, something beneath the surface, which if we only could grasp it would give fuller meaning to the record. This is specially true of Mark's gospel. But when we come to John's record, he brings this deeper truth to the surface, so that what was formerly implicit now becomes explicit: the ministry of Jesus was the activity of the eternal Word of God, who had become incarnate as man for the world's salvation. The mighty works of Jesus were 'signs' through which those who had eyes to see might behold the glory of God dwelling among men in the person of His Son. In Him every other revelation which God had ever given of Himself reached its fulfilment and culmination: to see Christ was to see the Father; He was the way, the truth and the life, apart from whom none could come to God. John thus supplies the key to the understanding of the gospel story as told by the other evangelists.

John's aim in presenting this record has been realized, not only among Jewish and Gentile readers of the Hellenistic world at the end of the first century A.D., but throughout successive generations to our own day. As he introduces us to Jesus as the perfect revealer of God, as love incarnate, as the embodiment of that life which has ever been the light of men, his record still comes home with the self-authenticating testimony which characterizes eternal truth, as it constrains twentieth-century readers to endorse the statement of those men who first gave the evangelist's words to the public: 'we know that his witness is true.'

The Gospel Collection

The gospels of Mark, Matthew and John appear to have been associated at first with three early centres of Christian witness—Rome, Antioch and Ephesus. Luke's twofold work was not originally written for church use but as a work of apologetic for the more unprejudiced members of the Roman official and middle classes. But at an early date after the publication of the fourth Gospel, the four canonical gospels began to circulate as a collection and have continued to do so ever since. Who first gathered them together to form a fourfold corpus we do not know, and it is quite uncertain where the fourfold corpus first became known—claims have been made for both Ephesus and Rome. Cath-

olic and Gnostic writers alike show not only acquaintance with the fourfold gospel, but recognition of its authority. The Valentinian *Gospel of Truth* (*c.* A.D. 140–150), recently brought to light among the Gnostic writings from Chenoboskion in Egypt, was not intended to supplement or supersede the canonical four, whose authority it presupposes; it is rather a series of meditations on the 'true gospel' which is enshrined in the four (and in other New Testament books). Marcion (*c.* A.D. 144) stands out as an exception in his repudiation of Mt., Mk and Jn, and his promulgation of Lk. (edited by himself) as the only authentic *euangelion*. The documents of the anti-Marcionite reaction (*e.g.* the anti-Marcionite prologues to the gospels and, later, the Muratorian canon) do not introduce the fourfold gospel as something new but reaffirm its authority in reply to Marcion's criticisms.

In the half-century following A.D. 95 Theodor Zahn could find only four gospel citations in surviving Christian literature which demonstrably do not come from the canonical four. That the 'memoirs of the apostles' which Justin says were read in church along with the writings of the prophets were the four gospels is rendered the more probable by the fact that such traces of gospel material in his works as may come from the pseudonymous gospels of Peter or Thomas are slight indeed compared with traces of the canonical four.

The situation is clearer when we come to Justin's disciple Tatian, whose gospel harmony or *Diatessaron* (compiled *c.* A.D. 170)—a rearrangement of the fourfold record so as to form one continuous narrative—remained for long the favourite (if not the 'authorized') edition of the gospels in the Assyrian church. Apart from a small fragment of a Greek edition of the *Diatessaron* discovered at Dura-Europos on the Euphrates and published in 1935, our knowledge of the work has until recently been indirect, being based on translations (some of them secondary or tertiary) from the Syriac text. But in 1957 a considerable portion of the Syriac original of Ephrem's commentary on the *Diatessaron* (written about the middle of the fourth century) was identified in a parchment manuscript in Sir A. Chester Beatty's collection; further study of this text promises to throw valuable light on the early history of the *Diatessaron*.

Tatian began his compilation with Jn 1: 1–5, and perhaps ended it with Jn 21: 25. It was the fourfold gospel that supplied him with the material for his harmony; such occasional intrusions of extra-canonical material as can be detected (possibly from the *Gospel according to the Hebrews*) do not affect this basic fact any more than do the occasional modifications of the gospel wording which reflect the vegetarian dogma of Tatian's Encratite group.

The supremacy of the fourfold gospel which Tatian's work attests is confirmed a decade or so later by Irenaeus. To him the fourfold character of the gospel is one of the accepted facts of Christianity, as axiomatic as the four quarters of the world or the four winds of heaven (*Heresies* iii. 11. 8). His contemporary Clement of Alexandria is careful to distingnish 'the four gospels which have been handed down to us' from uncanonical writings on which he draws from time to time, such as the *Gospel according to the Egyptians (Stromata* iii. 13). Tertullian (*c.* A.D. 200) does not even draw upon such uncanonical writings, restricting himself to the canonical four, to which he accords unique authority because their authors were either apostles or men in close association with apostles. (Like other western Christian writers, he arranges the four so as to make the two 'apostolic' gospels, Mt. and Jn, precede Lk. and Mk.) Origen (*c.* A.D. 230) sums up the long-established catholic attitude when he speaks of 'the four gospels, which alone are undisputed in the Church of God beneath the whole heaven' (*Comm. on Mt.*, quoted by Eusebius, *Hist. Eccl.* vi. 25. 4). (Origen, like Irenaeus before him, arranges the four in the order with which we are familiar today.)

The four evangelists, writing from their distinct points of view, concur in presenting us with a comprehensive, sufficient and heart-compelling portrayal of Jesus as Messiah of Israel and Saviour of the world, Servant of the LORD and Friend of sinners, Son of God and Son of man. Their fourfold record coincides in its character and purpose with the mission of the church in the world; the explicit aim of the fourth gospel is equally applicable to the other three: 'these are written that you may believe that Jesus is the Christ, the Son of God, and that believing you may have life in his name' (Jn 20: 31).

BIBLIOGRAPHY

ALAND, K., and others, *The Gospels Reconsidered* (Oxford, 1960).

BAIRD, J. A., *Audience Criticism and the Historical Jesus* (Philadelphia, 1969).

DODD, C. H., *The Apostolic Teaching and its Developments* (London, 1936).

DODD, C. H., *History and the Gospel* (London, 1938).

DODD, C. H., *The Interpretation of the Fourth Gospel* (Cambridge, 1963).

FRANCE, R. T., and WENHAM, D., *Gospel Perspectives*, 6 vols. (Sheffield, 1980–).

GUTHRIE, D., *New Testament Introduction: The Gospels and Acts* (London, 1965).

HIGGINS, A. J. B., *The Reliability of the Gospels* (London, 1952).

HIGGINS, A. J. B., *The Historicity of the fourth Gospel* (London, 1960).

KELLY, W., *Lectures Introductory to the Study of the Gospels* (London, 1874).

LÉON-DUFOUR, X., *The Gospels and the Jesus of History* (London, 1968).

MANSON, T. W., *The Teaching of Jesus* (Cambridge, 1935).

MANSON, T. W., *The Sayings of Jesus* (London, 1949).

MANSON, T. W., *Studies in the Gospels and Epistles* (London, 1961).

ROHDE, J., *Rediscovering the Teaching of the Evangelists* (London, 1968).

STREETER, B. H., *The Four Gospels* (London, 1924).

TAYLOR, V., *The Formation of the Gospel Tradition* (London, 1933).

THE APOSTOLIC CHURCH

F. ROY COAD

The Christian Church was born out of historical happenings: happenings in which it is conscious of a unique intervention of God in the history of mankind.

That fact justifies yet another examination of those events. Because God revealed Himself to real men in an historical situation, the story of the apostolic church can never lose its relevance. Nor can it ever lose its interest, so long as men seek to discover what it was, in everyday terms, to have known the earthly presence of Christ or the ardour of the first days of His Church.

The Paradox of the Church

For a basic conception of the Church we turn naturally to the teaching of our Lord Jesus Christ: yet we do so only to be confronted by the startling fact that the Church seems almost wholly absent from His teaching. Instead, He speaks much of the Kingdom of God—a kingdom which is no organized body, but something to be received, and received 'like a child' (Lk. 18: 17; Mt. 18: 3, 4). This Kingdom presents a twofold aspect. It is something imminent and inward, to be received in the present in quiet humility; but it is also to appear in the future as a culminating event of supernatural glory. These two aspects of the Kingdom, present and final, are united in a short parable which is recorded only in Mark's Gospel (Mk 4: 26–29).

Yet, as Jesus taught, He consciously gathered around Himself a community of disciples, who later formed the nucleus of the apostolic church. That community He related directly to the central theme of the Kingdom: 'Do not be afraid, little flock, for your Father has been pleased to give you the Kingdom' (Lk. 12: 32). The promise contrasts with a judgment pronounced on the leaders of Israel: 'The kingdom of God will be taken away from you and given to a people who will produce its fruit' (Mt. 21: 43).

The Lord Jesus identified the community, then, with the flock of the Lord, the faithful remnant of the covenant people of God (Jer. 23 and 31; Ezek. 34): and yet He placed it in marked contrast to the existing expression of that covenant people. Second, the little flock is to be the recipient of the Kingdom, and thus shares from the start that twofold nature which we have noticed: it is *eschatological*, that is, stamped with the character of the end things,

and yet it is of immediate and present import. This dual character is confirmed by the whole context of Lk. 12: 22–56. Third, Jesus's words imply a tension between the community and its environment: a fear, which is set against a new and intimate relation with its Father-God.

These features are developed in the classic passage of Mt. 16: 13–28, the only passage recorded from the mouth of our Lord which unambiguously names the Church, but before tracing them we must notice in that passage another reference back to Old Testament thought, in the question 'Who do people say the Son of man is?' There, Jesus adopts the representative identity of the Son of man of Dan. 7, the regal personage who in Himself incorporates the whole *people of the saints of the Most High* (Dan. 7: 13, 14, 27) (see K. L. Schmidt, *The Church*, pp. 39–41 and notes; and Cullmann, *The Early Church*, pp. 128, 130). He is the representative head, awaiting the body; the king awaiting his people. Peter's confession, 'You are the Christ, the Son of the living God', appears as the counterpart to this identification, and therefore expresses the characteristic feature of that people of the Most High. Over against the representative Son of man, there stands the representative confessor of Christ, chosen of the Father ('this was not revealed to you by man, but by my Father in heaven'): the pattern of all who should exercise a like response to Christ. It is of such, men who are called, chosen and faithful, that the people of the Most High will consist. That Peter appears in representative rather than in personal capacity is confirmed by his rejection in verse 23, demonstrating that Peter in himself was nothing—a rejection which was to have a later parallel at Antioch (Gal. 2: 11) (even if Peter is considered to appear in personal capacity, it remains that the whole Church is Peter's successor; see E. Schweizer, *Church Order in the NT*, pp. 4 f.). Peter's representative position is analogous to that which is occupied by Abraham, the father of the faithful, and a parallel to Abraham may well be hidden in the reference to Peter as the rock, a reference echoing Isa. 51: 1, 2. (Despite the many alternative explanations, the author feels compelled by the plain sense of the passage to understand Peter as the rock. See article *Peter* in *NBD*.)

We now trace those features already noticed in Lk. 12: 32. Behind the word 'church' used in Mt. 16: 18, there lies a word already familiar to Jewish thought as the designation of the congregation of Israel. So Jesus, in this passage also, identifies His Church with that community, and yet distinguishes it; for this is 'my church', and the building is in the future and is to be His own activity, its membership deriving from the same personal response and confession of Himself which Peter had shown.

Here also, the Church is related directly to the Kingdom. By an act of deliberate divine renunciation, in the committal of the keys, the Church (Peter again being representative; see Mt. 18: 18) is marked as the main earthly instrument of the Kingdom (E. Schweizer, *op.* and *loc. cit.*, has a very different and less robust interpretation). The twofold nature of the Kingdom appears in the Church. The present binding and loosing on earth is to be consummated in the binding and loosing in heaven (see also Jn 20: 23). The revelation of the Son of man in His kingdom is imminent for the chosen (28), and yet it is also future, hidden from the world (20) and awaiting the ultimate unveiling (27). The Church is a final thing, impregnable to the powers of death (18).

In this passage also the Church is seen in tension with its environment. If the keys of the Kingdom are committed to it, it is not for earthly glory, but at the cost of that same renunciation and suffering which the Son of man himself must endure (vv. 21–24; cf. 17: 22; 20: 22 f.; Lk. 17: 22–25; etc.).

The Church thus envisaged is, then, a community founded upon a personal confession of Christ, and sharing the elusive dual quality of the Kingdom: it is, in fact, the instrument of that Kingdom on earth, and exists in consequence in constant tension with its environment. This community is a *little flock* and an *ekklēsia*, as was the chosen people of Israel, and is thus a continuity of the congregation of the people of God, but it is also distinct and of the future ('my church' and 'I will build'). In it the last things of God find an anticipatory fulfilment.

It is after we have traced our Lord's intentions for the community that we recognize that His teaching contains provisions for its continuity which are in character with its nature. There is the presence of the Paraclete for the continual support and increase of its life, and the new foundation commandment of mutual love (Jn 13–16). There are provisions for the self-discipline of the community (Mt. 18: 15–22), and paradoxical rules of an anti-hierarchy (Mt. 20: 25–28). There are also ordinances expressive of its unity: the fellowship of the Last Supper and of the new covenant which it enshrines; and, at the very end, the command to baptize, significantly embodying a trinitarian formula (Mt. 28: 19).

Here, then, is a basic conception of the Church. Its existence lies in its relationship to the Father, a relationship established by personal response to and confession of Christ. Provision for its continuity is not in an organizational structure, but in the abiding of the Holy Spirit, while the relations of its members to each other are the paradoxical reverse of institutional. Its rites emphasize not office, but fellowship and identification. It is the fulfilment of the ideal of the old covenant, and yet a new thing. Its nature is essentially eschatological: it is the anticipatory fulfilment of God's final act, in the present world the holder of the keys of the Kingdom, but, like the Kingdom, the seed springing up in token of the reaping to come. For this reason it is in perpetual tension with its environment: it is in the world, but it is of the world to come.

[Note: In connection with the treatment of the Kingdom here, it may be noted that Cullmann, *op. cit.*, pp. 109–120, distinguishes on the basis of 1 C. 15: 24 between the 'regnum Christi' (the present era) and the 'kingdom of God' ('purely future'). Cullmann nevertheless emphasizes the tension between present and future in the Church.]

Growth to Self-Awareness

After the shattering events of passion week and its sequel, the community of disciples eventually collected in Jerusalem. One central motive united them: a consciousness of a commission to testify to the acts of God which they had witnessed. Those who later recorded that consciousness realized that from the earliest times it held latent a potential which extended far beyond the traditional boundaries of Judaism (Mt. 28: 19; Ac. 1: 8). Yet this wide calling was sensed but uncertainly as yet. Until the outburst of Pentecost, the seed lay dormant, the little community's only development being the filling of the vacancy in the apostolate left by Judas's suicide; a careful completion of the number of the twelve which was essentially Jewish in its inspiration (see Lk. 22: 28–30).

This Jewish atmosphere persists after Pentecost, in the early addresses of Peter. That which has happened is the crisis of Judaism. Although response requires an act of repentance and of renunciation of their generation, with which the act of baptism is associated (Ac. 2: 38–40), yet that renunciation is not a rejection of their whole background. The converts devote themselves to the apostles' teaching and fellowship, but they do so while still attending the temple together (Ac. 2: 42–46). The promise is 'for you and your children and for all who are far off—for all whom the Lord our God will call', but the precise scope of those words remains uncertain. This could be only a reform within Judaism; but an infinitely wider vision is dawning. In Ac. 3, Jesus is 'the Christ appointed *for you*' (20), and the proclamation is strictly within the national ideal: yet the promise quoted from Gen. 22: 18 hints at wider horizons. Jesus has been sent 'first to you': this implies others to follow (25, 26).

In Ac. 4: 12 there appears the exclusive claim to salvation in Christ alone. Then, in the context of the solemn act of judgment of Ac. 5, the community is first named a 'church' with all that implies in realization of a separate ethos (11). (The AV of Ac. 2: 47 arises from a variant reading now usually rejected.) The second appearance of the word is on the occasion of the great persecution, by Jews, which followed the death of Stephen (Ac. 8: 1). So the fires of judgment and persecution forged the Church's realization of its separate destiny, and compelled it to its world-wide mission. How slow this process was is apparent from Ac. 24: 14, where, in Jerusalem itself, 'the Way' is still, a quarter of a century later, regarded as a Jewish sect.

Here then is no carefully constructed society, shaped according to the constitutional pattern of a founder, but rather a growing and developing organism growing out of its circumstances and being shaped by the reaction of its own inherent life to its environment (see Eph. 4: 16; 1 Pet. 2: 5). So it continues throughout the Church's later expansion. A matter as vital as that of the acceptance of Gentiles to equal membership is resolved only by broadening experience and by painful controversy. The situation as to the assimilation of Gentiles differs from church to church at any one time. It is the same with forms of government. Officers are appointed, and their functions determined, as need arises, and the structure of authority differs from place to place.

Most interesting of all are the indications of differing views on the polity of the Church itself. Around Jerusalem a sense of unity grew in a church which was necessarily fragmented by sheer numbers and lack of meeting places, and the result is that the Church over a considerable district is regarded as a unity (Ac. 9: 31, not AV). Paul, on the other hand, writes with the experience of smaller churches in scattered towns, and his outlook is in consequence more nearly congregational, even when applied to those same Judean congregations (Gal. 1: 22, and see v. 2, but note v. 13). (Hort, *The Christian Ecclesia*, pp. 144–149, emphasizes that the concept of the universal church appears in Pauline teaching only at a later date, in Eph. and Col.)

These facts suffice to illustrate important factors for guiding study of the apostolic church. We cannot look for any single prescribed pattern of church order or government, nor is there any suggestion that we should do

so. Indeed, such a model would be contrary to the very nature of the Church. We do find two important features. The first is that of an obvious growth and development within the period of the New Testament itself, and the second is that of diversity at any one time between different churches.

[Note: These are of course the two theses of Streeter, *The Primitive Church*, ix. But they are much older than Streeter, as witness the two following quotations from Henry Craik of Bristol (*NT Church Order*, 1863): 'A more fully developed church organization and official position were introduced as occasion called for them. . . . We hear nothing at first of Presbyters or Overseers, and the office of the Deaconship appears to have been suggested by the pressure of urgent necessity . . . the possession of spiritual gifts led to the development of rulers, teachers and evangelists, during the apostolic period' (p. 24).

'It appears to me that the early Churches were not, in all places, similarly constituted' (p. 4).]

New Life in Christ

Those who composed the Church stood in a new and profoundly different relationship to God from any that had previously been known. True, they could trace their kinship with the faithful of preceding ages, and their covenant of faith to Abraham himself; but their own relationship to God was based on two radically new experiences. These experiences were individually realized, but they were essentially corporate in their nature. There was the new experience of union with God in and through Christ; a union which had sharply separated those who knew it from 'the world' which did not, while at the same time uniting them indissolubly among themselves. This first experience received its highest devotional expression in the writings of John and its profoundest theological exposition in the letter to the Ephesians. The second experience bore more particularly on the practical outworking of their faith. It was that experience of the indwelling Spirit of God which is such a marked feature of the history recorded in the Acts of the Apostles, and which forms the experiential foundation of the note of assurance in the letters of Paul. These two experiences transcended all known divisions of society. By one Spirit they had all been baptized into one body—Jews and Greeks, slaves and free—and had all been made to drink of one Spirit (1 C. 12: 13).

In the letters to the Ephesians and Colossians these two experiences blend with the early insights concerning the eschatological nature of the Church, and mature into a vision which transcends the temporal world. In an earlier writing of the New Testament, the transcendence of God had been stressed—'to whom be glory *eis tous aiōnas tōn aiōnōn*' (Gal. 1: 5). Much later, in the second letter to Timothy, the calling in Christ is portrayed as a product of this transcendence: part of the age-old purpose of God *pro chronōn aiōniōn*, and is related to the revelation of life and immortality: but it is set in the immediate context of the here-and-now of witness and suffering (2 Tim. 1: 8–12). In the Ephesian letter, however, the here-and-now itself has receded from sight in the greater shining of the glory of eternity. The Church is there a central feature of the divine plan for all created things and for the fullness of time. This purpose centres in Christ, but in Christ as 'head over everything for the church, which is his body, the fullness of him who fills everything in every way' (Eph. 1: 3–23). The relationship of Church to Christ is as that of wife to husband (Eph. 5: 22–33). The witness of the here-and-now is emphatically present, but it is immeasurably broadened and enlarged, for 'the unsearchable riches of Christ' include this, 'that through the church, the manifold wisdom of God should be made known to the rulers and authorities in the heavenly realms' (Eph. 3: 7–12).

Yet those two experiences, of unity and of the Spirit, were no visionary distractions, but they were basic to a new dimension of practical living. John's experience of union with Christ was expressed in vivid terms, intimately related to the present as well as to eternity. The experience is an eating and drinking of Christ, a believing in Him which brings the gift of eternal life and the resurrection at the last day: and yet that bread of which men eat is 'he who comes down from heaven, and gives life to the world' (Jn 6: 33), and the result of believing is that one should be a present source of 'streams of living water' (Jn 7: 38). The life in Christ is a present experienced indwelling of the Godhead (ch. 14), a union of the branches with the vine (ch. 15). That indwelling implies the present enlightenment of the Spirit (14: 26), an enlightenment which has a direct relevance to sin and righteousness and judgment in this present world (16: 4–15); and the union of the branches with the vine is for the immediate purpose of present fruitfulness. Such fruitfulness is in fact the proof of true discipleship (15: 8). Union with God in Christ might provoke the hostility of the world, but it brought with it a new and direct responsibility within and toward the world. Its effects are expressed in varying practical outworkings: in witness, in enlightenment, in effective prayer and in conduct towards fellow men. 'I have set you an example that you should do as I have done for you' (Jn 13: 15). Above all, the union with God in Christ was to issue in a visible unity among those who shared it. Jesus had come to die, 'for

the scattered children of God, to bring them together and make them one' (Jn 11: 51, 52), and that unity was to be the supreme witness to the world (Jn 17: 23).

[Note: In passing, the following extract from Robinson's *Guide to Tottenham* (1840 edition) is of interest, as giving the view of the early Brethren assembly then meeting at Brook Street: 'They consider that Christ appointed that all His disciples should form *one visible church* . . .']

The letter to the Hebrews gives this experience of union with Christ a new and heart-warming aspect. Not only is human life lifted to a transcendent fellowship with the Father and His Son Jesus Christ, as John emphasized in his first letter, but in the incarnation the Son has shared in humanity and partaken of the same nature: 'So Jesus is not ashamed to call them brothers' (Heb. 2: 11–18). In the Church, not only do men share the things of God—but God partakes in the things of humanity.

In a similar manner, the second experience, that of the Spirit, was seen as directed to the future consummation—'a deposit guaranteeing our inheritance until the redemption' (Eph. 1: 14): but essentially the experience was of immediate and practical import. 'You will receive power when the Holy Spirit comes on you; and you will be my witnesses . . .' (Ac. 1: 8). It is to the evident practical working of that Spirit—the 'miracles' worked among the Galatians—that Paul can point in justification of the gospel which he preached: and those *dynameis* included the practical virtues of love, joy, peace, patience, kindness, goodness, faithfulness, gentleness and self-control (Gal. 3: 5; 5: 22,23).

The intensity of the early Church's realization of these two aspects of its relation to the Godhead, cannot be illustrated more effectively than by two quotations which are the more striking for their incidental character. The first, the union with Christ, is contained in the words addressed to Saul, the persecutor of the Church: 'I am Jesus, whom you are persecuting' (Ac. 9: 5). Persecution of the Church was persecution of Jesus Himself. The second, the experience of the Spirit, appears in the letter which contained the findings of the Council of Jerusalem: 'It seemed good to the Holy Spirit and to us . . .' (Ac. 15: 28). The desires of the Spirit and of the Church were one.

The Fellowship of the Common Life

When a convert joined himself to a community of the early church, he entered upon a profoundly new type of human relationship. The fellowship of the local congregation entered into every aspect of his life. 'If one part suffers, every part suffers with it; if one part is honored, every part rejoices with it. Now you are the body of Christ and each one of you is a part of it' (1 C. 12: 26, 27).

This sense of community and of mutual responsibility made the genuine unity of the congregation a matter of supreme importance (Eph. 4: 1–7). Unity demanded mutual forbearance and a tolerance strong enough to overcome the inevitable differences among members (Rom. 15: 5; 1 C. 1: 10–13; Phil. 2: 1–5, etc.). It was to be demonstrated in a genuine sharing of burdens and problems (Rom. 15: 1; Gal. 6: 2); in a fellowship of witness and a sympathetic participation in the sufferings and dangers of one another (Phil. 1: 27–30; Rev. 1: 9). Nor was this sense of unity confined to the local congregation. The churches from the beginning maintained a lively interest in the progress of other Christian communities, and were encouraged to a sense of solidarity, which was turned to the practical relief of the necessities of other churches (Ac. 11: 22–30; 15: 3; 1 Th. 2: 14; Rom. 15: 25–27; 1 C. 16: 1–4; 2 C. 8; etc.). Letters were shared among the churches (Col. 4: 16), and teachers were supported while they were working among other communities (2 C. 11: 8; Phil. 4: 16). A warm hospitality was shown to visiting Christians, a brotherly hospitality often experienced by Paul and his companions during the journeyings recorded in the Acts, and forming a regular and important feature of the life of local congregations (see Rom. 16: 23; Heb. 13: 2; 3 Jn 5–8).

The cement of this unity was love—the 'royal law' of Christ (Jas 2: 8). In one of the latest of the writings of the New Testament, when

> *What first were guessed as points, I now knew*
> *stars,*
> *And named them in the Gospel I have writ.*

—(Browning, *A Death in the Desert*), it was these two elements, unity and love, which were brought out as the basic principles of our Lord's testament for the community which would arise from those He was leaving behind Him (Jn 13–17).

Unity and love were cultivated by ungrudging hospitality, by the holding of possessions not for selfish ends, but with a sense of personal stewardship for one another (1 Jn 3: 16, 17; 1 Pet. 4: 8–10). All barriers between individuals, of nationality, sex, or social class, were to be overridden in the new loyalty of Christ (Gal. 3: 28; Col. 3: 11; Jas 2: 1–4).

It was a radical new ethos, and in an attempt at its expression the early Jerusalem church turned to a not unfamiliar pattern within its own society, the pattern of community of goods (Ac. 4: 32–37). But the ideals and the vision of the faith of Christ could never remain confined within the inevitably narrowed horizons of such a community. The failure of

the idealistic attempt was inevitable. Its chief result, after the first deceptive well-being of the participants (Ac. 4: 34), may have been that chronic impoverishment of the Jerusalem church which haunts the later pages of the New Testament (see F. F. Bruce, *The Book of the Acts*, p. 109 note).

After this first failure, the Church approached this problem also in a pragmatic fashion. In Thessalonica an early misunderstanding of Christian ideals again led to social ills, against which Paul felt obliged to intervene in language of severity (1 Th. 4: 9–12 with 2 Th. 3: 6–15). By the time of the first letter to Timothy, some at least of the churches had worked out the social expression of Christian love into a code which was capable of enduring expression. We are given a picture of a community carefully organized to provide for the needs of its poor, and quietly working out the new ideals of brotherhood, in the manner of the Kingdom, from within the existing framework of society (1 Tim. 5: 1–6: 10).

Community life implies the need for discipline also. If each member bore responsibility for the welfare of the others, then that obligation brought with it the need for a personal self-discipline extending to the most elementary actions of life. 'If your brother is distressed because of what you eat, you are no longer acting in love' (Rom. 14: 15, and see 1 C. 8: 12, 13). Yet even this principle was not to be applied in such a way as to pander to the bigot (1 C. 10: 25–30, although different versions indicate the ambiguity of this passage). Discipline must also require open repudiation of the flagrant evil-doer (1 C. 5: 11–13), and it called also for adequate and just machinery within the community itself for the settlement of grievances (1 C. 6: 1–8).

It is a fascinating task to trace the scattered references which show us the early churches in their gatherings for worship and the service of God. The sharing of the common life was of the essence of the community, and from the day of Pentecost this *koinōnia* had been the distinctive feature of the Church: 'they devoted themselves to the apostles' teaching and to the fellowship, to the breaking of bread and to prayer . . . All the believers were together and had everything in common . . . Every day they continued to meet together in the temple courts. They broke bread in their homes and ate together with glad and sincere hearts, praising God and enjoying the favour of all the people' (Ac. 2: 42–47). For their meeting places, the temple courts, private homes, a hired schoolroom, an upper chamber, were all put to service as need arose. The Jewish tradition of religious community life, the synagogues of the dispersion, possibly aspects of Gentile organization, were all available to be drawn upon. The

Church took tribute from each, but shaped what it took to the purposes of its own destiny, transforming the conception of office by its new law of humility.

In Ac. 12 a group of disciples, at a moment of crisis, engages in prayer in the house of Mark's mother: a type of cottage meeting which must have been a common feature of the life of the unwieldy and scattered church in Jerusalem. By contrast, Ac. 15 introduces us to a formal conclave on a matter of deep importance. In Ac. 20 a group of disciples is found gathering for the breaking of bread on the first day of the week: apparently a regular gathering, for Paul seems to have prolonged his stay in Troas in order to attend. At it the visiting apostle is expected to, and does, preach at length. In contrast, in Ephesus, Paul holds daily sessions of discussion and teaching through a period of two years (Ac. 19: 9, 10), and in so doing builds up a powerful church.

The regular gathering together of Christians for their mutual fellowship and edification, for public reading of Scripture and for preaching and teaching, often under the guidance of a visiting teacher or apostle (1 Tim. 4: 13), was early seen as one of the vital features of the life of a local church. So, from a different tradition, there comes the exhortation not to neglect their meeting together (Heb. 10: 25), and this aspect of the *koinōnia* is surely not lacking from the exhortation of ch. 13: 16 of the same book (see Gk.).

It is in the first letter to the Corinthians that we are given the most detailed insight into early church meetings: and, disorderly as much of the conduct at Corinth may have been, Paul gives no indication that the general tenor of their activities was not typical: in fact his opening words, although ambiguous, indicate that what he had to say would be widely relevant among the churches. In many of the gatherings of that church each member was expected and encouraged to make a personal contribution to the worship: 'when you come together, everyone has a hymn, or a word of instruction, a revelation, a tongue or an interpretation' (1 C. 14: 26—it should be added that the interpretation which reads this verse as a rebuke to the Corinthians is, in view of the context, a little odd!). The apostle was concerned to remedy the abuses which this freedom engendered, but his exhortations were directed to the exercise of a proper self-control, rather than to the restriction of vocal activity to a handful of members. The regulatory principles are to be edification (26) and order (40): the latter in a sense which may indicate some pre-arrangement (*kata taxin*).

In Corinth, we find that the celebration of the Lord's Supper had become a regular and frequent feature of the gatherings of the church.

It is possible indeed that it formed a part of every gathering (11: 17–21), and thus had become sadly interwoven with the merely social (not to say convivial) incidents of their meeting together. The apostle's exhortations are directed to emphasizing the solemnity of the occasion, rather than to restricting the frequency of the observance.

There were yet more sombre occasions of meeting, when the church found it necessary to exercise its discipline. In 1 C. 5 we are shown the church assembled for this purpose—'when you are assembled in the name of our Lord Jesus and I am with you in spirit, and the power of our Lord Jesus is present, hand this man over to Satan, so that the sinful nature may be destroyed and his spirit saved on the day of the Lord'. The ardent unity of the early Church, and its intense sense of the indwelling Spirit, laid upon such an act of excommunication an awful significance.

It would appear that women were accustomed to taking a prominent part in activities of the early Church. This is a notoriously controversial subject, and what follows represents a personal interpretation of the NT evidence. Paul's early and emphatic denial of sex distinctions in Christ (Gal. 3: 28) would have encouraged feminine gifts, as would the frequent and important contribution made by influential women as the Church expanded (Ac. 1: 14; 9: 36 ff.; 12: 12; 16: 13–15; 17: 4, 12; 18: 2, 26). Their contributions were not confined to the exercise of guidance behind the scenes. At a late date we find no hint of disapproval when Paul found the daughters of Philip prophesying (Ac. 21: 8, 9): a fact of the greater interest when his earlier instructions to the Corinthian church are remembered. Differences of function in the churches arose in principle only from the gift bestowed on the individual, and not from distinctions of rank or of sex (cf. 1 C. 12).

Yet, in the licentious centres of Gentile civilization liberty could deteriorate into licence. Certainly the results in Corinth were unhappy. Once again, the church was forced under God to adapt its order to the circumstances of the society in which it moved. Although the participation of women in prayer and prophecy was still contemplated (1 C. 11: 5), it became necessary to restrict their liberty, both in matters of dress (1 C. 11: 4–16) and in public worship (1 C. 14: 33–35). In other aspects of service in the churches, women continued to take prominent part (see Rom. 16: 1; Phil. 4: 3; 1 Tim. 3: 11; 5: 10; Tit. 2: 3 ff.).

By the date of the first letter to Timothy, this aspect also of the churches' life had found a stable form of regulation. That female participation in public prayer was still contemplated may well be indicated. The contrary has been deduced from the use of the word 'males' in the Gk. of 1 Tim. 2: 8: yet surely this is a contrast to the 'women' of v. 9. The passage, taken as a whole, implies that as men were to adorn their prayers with holy characters, so women should adorn theirs with modesty in dress and in conduct. Female participation in teaching or in authoritative rule was forbidden (1 Tim. 2: 11–15). That these rules were not universally applied, and equally that in the first century they were often highly desirable, was demonstrated by the unsavoury happenings a generation later in Thyatira (Rev. 2: 20; see page 1603).

[Note: It may be held, with Lightfoot, that the 'Jezebel' reference is symbolic; but the question would still remain as to how such a symbol came to be used if such female activity was completely unknown.]

It is the Apocalypse which introduces a novel element into any discussion of the worship of the early church. For, contrary to all that we would expect from the other records of the New Testament, the visions of the seer introduce an element of magnificence and imaginative form that startles and entrances (Rev. 4: 7–5: 14; 7: 9–12; 19: 1–8). As the music of the calls to worship and of the thunderous responses dies away, we are left to wonder about the experiences and forms of worship which had shaped the prophet's vision. What experiences of public worship had led him to illustrate the ultimate in human worship in forms such as these? To that question, the remainder of the New Testament affords us no answer.

Government and Gifts

To one who knew only the New Testament, it would be astonishing that discussion of the Church should so often be preoccupied with conceptions of the ministry. Still less could it seem possible that the very term 'the Church' should become confined to its officers, or that conceptions of the Church itself should turn upon this doctrine.

Yet perhaps some such development was inevitable. As the Church grew, its whole environment demanded a strong and coherent structure of authority to meet the pressures of persecution, the pretences of upstart demagogues, speculation and false doctrine, and the requirements of discipline. The very structure of authority so developed would ultimately generate pressures and interests which would lead to its perpetuation for its own sake. Later, when persecution had ended, doctrine would too easily follow the desires for power which are endemic in human nature. It would be for the Church to experience in its own being the paradox that in saving life, life would be lost, and that in losing life it would be saved.

Amongst the earliest believers, the twelve apostles held an especial position. They were 'the apostles He had chosen' (Ac. 1: 2): those who had been with Jesus and were the especial witnesses of their Lord's resurrection and the recipients of His teaching (Mk 3: 14; Ac. 1: 3, 21, 22). In this respect at least their position was unique and unrepeatable (for a discussion of the uniqueness of the apostolate, see Cullmann, *op. cit.*, pp. 75–87).

Upon these twelve, then, there probably fell the brunt of the early leadership. The sudden expansion of the Church after Pentecost made their task impossible, and to meet the problem special administrators were appointed (Ac. 6: 1–6). The subsequent development of this office is lost in oblivion (although it is still a distinguishing mark a generation later—Ac. 21: 8), but at least two of them soon progressed to become active in the Word of God.

Side by side with the administrative tasks for which men could be chosen and appointed, other gifts were forcing themselves to the fore. Some of these were natural gifts of leadership and eloquence, of intellect and personality. Enhanced by the energies of the Spirit, such gifts were of supreme importance to the Church. But there were other gifts also, more sensational and more obviously inspirational, gifts of tongues and prophecies and healings. In them was seen a palpable evidence of the working of the Spirit, and those who exercised them would attract a measure of deference which was often unhealthy, and which led to Paul's words of correction at Corinth (1 C. 12: 27–13: 3).

It was likely therefore that the authoritative structure of the Church would develop along two lines. On the one hand, gifts of leadership and intellect would produce ordered systems, which would make use of natural administrative abilities. These systems would differ in accordance with local circumstances. On the other hand, inspirational gifts would be unpredictable and erratic, not easily subjected to control, and impatient of regulation.

In Jerusalem development was from the beginning of the more ordered type. It is true that inspirational gifts were prominent. Ecstatic utterances were known, and recognized as basically similar to the experience of Pentecost, even if not identical in character (Ac. 10: 44–47; also cf. Ac. 2: 8–11 with 1 C. 14: 6–13). The evangelization of Samaria produced 'great signs and miracles' (Ac. 8: 13), while the gift of prophecy was also prominent (Ac. 11: 27).

Nevertheless, these gifts were exercised in an ordered context. When the twelve were scattered, a settled authority was needed to replace them, and accordingly we find that elders appear at Jerusalem during the period of years covered by Ac. 11, where previously there had been 'apostles and brothers' (Ac. 11: 1, 30). It is to be noted that in the letter of James, deriving from Jerusalem, the only reference to a possibly miraculous gift sees that gift as exercised strictly within the authority of the body of elders (Jas 5: 13–15). No indication is given of the circumstances or manner of appointment of these elders in Jerusalem. On the analogy of Ac. 6, we might suppose that they were chosen by popular election, ratified by the apostles: a mode which was different from that later adopted by Paul and Barnabas in the South Galatian churches (Ac. 14: 23; cf. Tit. 1: 5).

These elders at Jerusalem soon received considerable authority within the church, acting equally with the apostles (Ac. 15). Beyond their authority, James the Lord's brother also assumed a personal prominence. He was already in a prominent position in Ac. 12: 17 and Gal. 1: 19, although this was not yet a solitary position (Gal. 2: 9). In Ac. 15 his voice is decisive in discussion. In Ac. 21, some seven years later, he appears in a position of primacy similar to that which tradition assigns to him. Yet despite these developments, it is plain from the letter of James that the position of teacher was still open to all whose gifts qualified for it and who understood its solemnity (Jas 3: 1).

Developments among the churches influenced by Paul were of a different character. At Antioch the only leadership of which we know was that of prophets and teachers (Ac. 13: 1). By contrast, the churches in South Galatia were furnished with elders at an early stage of their history (Ac. 14: 23). Yet the letter to Galatia which followed soon afterwards makes no reference to those elders, in a matter of doctrine where we might have expected an appeal to them, and it is possible (though unlikely) that their functions were mainly administrative. At Corinth it would appear that the appointment of elders was at first omitted: if elders did exist there, it is remarkable that a letter dealing with disciplinary matters as closely as First Corinthians should make no reference to them, and it is difficult to reconcile the exhortation of 1 C. 16: 15, 16 with the existence of previously appointed elders. Perhaps the appearance of gifts in that church, as they had appeared in the other great city of Antioch, led the apostles to rely on the example of that church at the first. At Thessalonica, there were 'those who work hard among you, who are over you in the Lord and who admonish you' (1 Th. 5: 12). Considerable emphasis is placed on the eldership at Ephesus (Ac. 20: 17–38): it is interesting to recall that the first letter to Corinth was written towards the end of Paul's long stay in Ephesus (Ac. 19), and we might speculate whether the emphasis on the eldership at Ephesus derived something from the unhappy experiences of an elder-less Corinth. For the Ephesian elders were certainly not mere administrators: they were *episkopoi* ('bishops') and

shepherds and guardians of the flock.

[Note: For the identity of 'bishops' and 'elders' in the NT see J. B. Lightfoot, *Philippians*, pp. 95–99. On the non-appointment of elders by Paul see E. Schweizer, *op. cit.*, 7k.]

The letter to the Philippians indicates a still more formal structure. There *episkopoi* are accompanied by *diakonoi* (Phil. 1: 1), a structure which probably provides separately for the functions of administration and of spiritual oversight. If the Philippian letter dates from Paul's Roman imprisonment, this further development would arise naturally from the tendencies already noted. If, as some think, the letter was written from an earlier imprisonment in Ephesus, it would be contemporary with the first letter to Corinth, and the developed church order in Philippi would be a remarkable contrast to Corinth. It is probable that Paul had left Luke to care for the church at Philippi (as the 'we' passages in Acts indicate): might we connect the two things? For it is Luke whose writings evince an interest in the practical matters of church administration that is largely absent from the earlier Pauline letters, until the Corinthian troubles arose. Was it the orderly mind of the historian of the primitive church which influenced the later structure of the Pauline churches?

[Note: With this cf. E. Schweizer, who places Luke's view of the Church firmly within the historical and hence tending to the hierarchical view, over against Paul. (*Op. cit.*, 5.7d.20d.)]

The Ephesian and Philippian structures proved to be durable. By the time of the Pastoral Letters, the ordering of the churches, like so many other aspects of their life, had developed in places a stable and formalized character, basically similar to that of the earlier letter to Philippi. In 1 Timothy, the Ephesian church now has both *episkopoi* and *diakonoi*, and the *diakonoi* must serve a probationary period (1 Tim. 3: 10). The Pastorals add one further interesting feature, for they contemplate that a teacher might reside in a district (the residence here being temporary) and during that residence might appoint elders (and, where they are needed, deacons), and also exercise a considerable personal authority. In the examples of Timothy and Titus, this authority derived directly from that of the founder-apostle. It should also be noted that it is implied that the absence of elders is a definite defect, to be remedied (Tit. 1: 5).

The remaining books of the New Testament add to the general picture. Hebrews knows of 'leaders . . . who spoke the word of God to you' who are to be obeyed for 'They keep watch over you as men who must give an account' (Heb. 13: 7, 17). It might be that the early teachers are here the *de facto* leaders, as in early Antioch. 1 Peter has 'elders' who are responsible shepherds with a definite charge, although the context is completely open, and the persons concerned might be at any point from that of older men exercising authority simply as such, to that of monarchical elders of individual churches (1 Pet. 5: 1–5).

It is the third letter of John, however, which adds two fresh facets to our knowledge. From it we learn of the existence of travelling preachers (5–8), who are also referred to by Jude (3, 4), the latter indicating vividly some of the dangers to which the system gave rise. John's letter also indicates, in the person of Diotrephes, the growth of autocratic rule over the churches; and this evokes a reaction which is still more interesting in its claim to a more than local authority on the part of John 'the elder'. It must be noticed therefore that John does not denounce the monarchic position as such, but that he might even hint, in Demetrius, at a suitable replacement for the obdurate Diotrephes (3 Jn 9–12) (see R. W. Orr, 'Diotrephes: The First Gnostic Bishop?', in *Evangelical Quarterly*, 33, 1961, p. 172).

Thus, alongside the settled and more ordered service of elders and deacons, largely but not exclusively local, there appears to have arisen another ministry, not localized, and consisting of travelling teachers as well as of men claiming to exercise the more inspirational gifts of prophecy. It is possible that these are the 'apostles' of Rev. 2: 2, where the title was claimed with little regard to the spiritual realities, and conceivably of Rom. 16: 7 (see also 2 C. 8: 23; Phil. 2: 25 and Hort, *op. cit.*, pp. 64 f.). It was a system that gave ample freedom to the charlatan, and yet in 3 John such teachers are specifically upheld against a domineering local leader.

We are thus brought closer to the world of the immediately post-apostolic era; the world of the Didache, with its travelling teachers honoured above the local officers, and of the letters of Ignatius, with the single 'bishop' presiding in each Asian church, and their elders and deacons. The trends in development are thus confirmed by those writings, but we have little need of extra-Biblical evidence in tracing the clouds which were already gathering over the Church. The opening chapters of Revelation indicate the corruptions which developed in both streams of ministry: while elsewhere hints of speculation and wild imaginings (*e.g.* Col. 2; 1 Tim. 1: 3–5; and see 1 C. 11: 18, 19), foreshadow the need which would arise for strong hands to take hold of the churches when Jerusalem and the apostles had gone for ever.

How and when this occurred remains unknown, but by the middle of the second century the order of many churches had been systematized and transformed. Bishop Light-

foot considered that there are good grounds for believing that developments in the direction of monarchical government within individual churches had taken place within the lifetime and with the knowledge of the apostle John ('The Christian Ministry', in *Philippians*, pp. 206, 228, 234). It may well be so; but the impressions which we derive from the writings of the first century will probably always depend upon the background from which we approach them, and it is dangerous to assume that our knowledge of some of the churches is characteristic of all (cf. 'When there were some eight hundred bishops in the Province of Africa in the fifth century they must have been a great deal more like Presbyterian ministers than Anglican metropolitans.' [John Oman on 'The Presbyterian Churches' in *Evangelical Christianity, Its History and Witness*, 1911, p. 67]).

It remains to consider the indications of a degree of centralization in the early Church, which some have deduced from the account of the council of Jerusalem in Ac. 15. It is possible that much of Paul's letter to the Galatians is a protest against just such claims to a central authority. Be that as it may, the evidence of Ac. 15 and 16 must remain inconclusive. On the one hand, there is clear recognition of an especial value residing in the judgment of the apostles and elders of Jerusalem on the points in question, and with that judgment there is linked not only the remainder of the church there, but also the authority of the Holy Spirit Himself. On the other hand, it is plain that Jerusalem was being asked to pronounce on a dispute which had been raised by teachers coming from within its own ranks, as the judgment itself recognizes. It is therefore unsafe to base any firm inferences on the incident. The careful self-limitation of the judgment in its claims to authority is of especial significance.

To this survey of the practices of the New Testament church, it is necessary to add some general observations.

First, it is misleading to distinguish too sharply between the inspirational and the more natural gifts, as though only the former were truly charismatic. Both alike are *charismata* (Rom. 12: 6–8), gifts of bounty, as free as the new life of God itself (Rom. 6: 23). (In view of Rom. 12, where *diakonia* is one of the *charismata*, it is surely correct to read the threefold *charismatōn, . . . diakoniōn . . . energēmatōn* of 1 C. 12: 4–6 as parallel descriptions of the whole range of gifts, rather than as a division into classes. See Schweizer, *op. cit.*, 22b, c, d.) All gifts are the direct provision by God for the nourishment of the Church's life, traced at times to the operation of the Head of the Church Himself, and at others to the direct working within the Church of the Holy Spirit (Rom. 12: 4–8; 1 C. 12; Eph. 3: 5; 4: 7–12).

(J. B. Lightfoot, *op. cit.*, p. 185; Hort, *op. cit.*, p. 145 and ch. 10.)

Second, there is no idea of a limited priesthood. All believers alike were priests before God (1 Pet. 2: 5; Rev. 1: 6; 5: 10). The teaching of Hebrews is relevant here. (See J. B. Lightfoot, *Philippians*, p. 119, on *leitourgia*. The universal priesthood is 'the fundamental idea of the Christian Church'.)

Third, there is no limitation of the exercise of spiritual gifts, or of the administration of the sacraments, to those with governmental authority. True, elders are responsible for guarding and feeding the flock (Ac. 20: 28; 1 Pet. 5: 2), and the *episkopos* is to be an apt teacher (1 Tim. 3: 2 and see 1 Tim. 5: 17) and to provide for a proper succession to his teaching (2 Tim. 2: 2): but governments are among the gifts, not conditions precedent to their exercise (1 C. 12: 28). Perhaps the example of Corinth (1 C. 14: 26) is too invidious to provide a safe foundation, but there are other passages which are equally explicit. Paul is satisfied that the Romans are 'competent to instruct one another' (Rom. 15: 14). Grace was given to each according to the measure of Christ's gift (Eph. 4: 7). Each had received a gift, and was to employ it for the benefit of one another, as good stewards of God's varied grace (1 Pet. 4: 10). Indeed, it was the gifts which determined the authority: both governmental and otherwise, they were recognized as carrying with them an authority which demanded respect and obedience (1 C. 16: 16; 2 C. 10: 8; 1 Tim. 1: 20; 5: 19; Heb. 13: 17; 1 Th. 2: 6; 5: 12, 13), and which was capable of severe disciplinary action, particularly over false teachers (1 C. 5: 3–5; 3 Jn 9–10; Tit. 1: 13).

Fourth, the gifts are not poured out on men without regard to natural talent: rather, the Holy Spirit takes up and enlarges a gift which is already there. It is the men themselves, within whom the gift is operative, who are seen as the gifts to the Church in Eph. 4: 11. The natural corollary is that each man must soberly estimate his own gift: while he might earnestly desire the best, the welfare of the Church demands that there should be a proper self-assessment, and a proper self-control and a decent order (Rom. 12: 3; 1 C. 13: 1–3; ch. 14). The impulse of the moment was not the indispensable sign of the movement of the Spirit.

For this reason, it was often the custom of the churches to recognize the possession of gift formally and with solemnity. The laying on of hands was at times associated with the dedication of an experienced leader to a special task (Ac. 13: 3; cf. 6: 6), but there is also an indication in the letter to Timothy of the direct association of the laying on of hands with the gift itself (1 Tim. 4: 14; 2 Tim. 1: 6). The context shows that this bestowing of gift through the laying on of hands was a formal recognition of a gift which already existed, for it had been pointed out by prophetic utterance (1 Tim. 1: 18) (whose utterance, is not clear).

Fifth, the use of a gift brought with it a right to the pecuniary support of the church (1 C. 9: 14; 1 Tim. 5: 17, 18). As yet, there were no possibilities of complete maintenance, and Paul himself worked regularly for his own and others' support (Ac. 20: 34; 1 Th. 2: 9; 2 Th. 3: 8); but the right was inherent in the service of God. To demand scriptural precedent for the regular payment of a spiritual teacher, or for the endowment of his support, is to demand an anachronism; but of the principle itself the relevant passages leave not a shadow of doubt.

It is inevitable that an element of hindsight should enter into discussion of the gifts and government of the New Testament Church. We are liable to read into the record the systems with which we are familiar, or to react against them and to see only their denial. Both attitudes are essentially wrong. The New Testament Church was a living, vigorous community, inhibited from no order or arrangement which ministered to its life, but bound by no bonds of administration where these would restrict or restrain it. No system is in itself necessarily wrong, but equally no system can claim for itself an exclusive validity. The Church could rejoice over its gifts, as the earliest disciples had rejoiced on the first glad day of Pentecost: He 'has poured out what you now see and hear' (Ac. 2: 33; see Heb. 2: 4). A ministry, whatever authority it may claim, which no longer bears the fruits of that grace of Christ is a valid ministry no longer.

Conclusion

'God's household, which is the church of the living God, the pillar and foundation of the truth' (1 Tim. 3: 15). 'It is time for judgment to begin with the family of God; and if it begins with us, what will the outcome be for those who do not obey the gospel of God?' (1 Pet. 4: 17). In those two verses, the paradox of the Church presents itself again. On the one hand, we have the chosen Church, the Church which is the bearer of the keys of the Kingdom and the sharer of the new life of God: on the other, the Church which lies under the judgment of God, even as all the world must lie.

Lord, when we cry Thee far and near
And thunder through all lands unknown
The gospel into every ear,
Lord, let us not forget our own.
—(Chesterton, *Hymn for the Church Militant*).

Yet—and here is the Church's hope and its glory, and its final difference from that world —even while it lies under that judgment, the Church is the body of Christ. It is crucified with Christ, and dead to the law through the body of Christ (Gal. 2: 20; Rom. 7: 4). The judgment of God must fall, time and again, in temporal manner: but the Church's ultimate judgment is suffered and accomplished and displayed for ever in the eternal awful Act at Golgotha. Both the verses last quoted appear primarily in the context of individual experience: and, just because of that individual experience of entering and enduring the terror of judgment in Christ, so those who have shared it are knit for ever to Him and to each other. The experience of that dying they express in individual baptism: their continuing identification with it in the corporate Supper.

The Church is part of God's final act. For that reason, we shall never reach the ultimate truth concerning its being, as we shall never reach the final truth concerning God Himself. Even our experience of the truth in our own existence is partial: we are too close to our own experience, and too distant from that of our predecessors. So every attempt at understanding the Church is inadequate. The classic distinction between the visible and the invisible church is probably misleading. (Brunner, *The Misunderstanding of the Church*, ch. 1, and see K. L. Schmidt, *The Church*, pp. 65 f. Compare with this J. N. Darby: 'To escape from this anomaly, believers have sought to shelter themselves under a distinction between a visible and an invisible church; but I read in scripture—"Ye are the light of the world." Of what use is an invisible light?' [*Reflections on the Ruined Condition of the Church* (1841), p. 5].) Even the distinction between the local and the universal church does not do full justice to the Biblical usage (K. L. Schmidt, *op. cit.*, pp. 68 f.). Adaptable as any work of God, the *ekklēsia* is apparent where two or three are gathered, no less (although in a different manner) than in the universal Church. Again, the Church in Scripture (as E. Schweizer has shown) appears both as a heavenly body, taken out of time and history, in timeless union with God: and also as a body in history, part of God's continuous working. We picture it yet again from the standpoint of the individual, to whom this world is but a passing thing: and we picture it as the church militant, in the world as long as the world endures, and with no *raison d'être* except in relation to the world. We call it 'an extension of the incarnation'; yet, if we use that to justify a priestly succession, we are reminded that God incarnate was a layman.

These things are not irrelevant to the present situation. For no unity can be true unity of the Spirit which fails to recognize that the wind blows where it wills. Those Christian bodies which have been called out of organized church history, as an expression of the total independence of the Spirit from any regulation en-

trusted to man, can never express the fulness of truth, for their very calling denies them that. But that which they have is of vital importance to the continued life of the Church of God: any movement or union which ignores or despises them, does so at its peril. Meanwhile, we must continually return to the Scriptures and to the Act of God which they record: for there alone can be our final authority for understanding in our own situation that which is needful to us concerning the life and fellowship of the Church of God.

> There shall always be the Church and the
>   World
> And the Heart of Man
> Shivering and fluttering between them,
>   choosing and chosen,
> Valiant, ignoble, dark, and full of light
> Swinging between Hell Gate and Heaven
>   Gate.
> And the Gates of Hell shall not prevail.
> Darkness now, then
> Light.   —(T. S. Eliot, *The Rock*.)

APPENDIX

(The author is grateful to Mr. H. L. Ellison for suggesting that an alternative view of the development of the eldership in the apostolic church should be mentioned. Mr. Ellison puts forward the following as arguable propositions:

1. In Palestine, Christian services from the first were an adaptation of the Synagogue pattern (this can hardly be denied when we remember the strong synagogue influence we find in the Christian pattern in the third and following centuries—it must have come in from the first).
2. The influence of the *presbyteros*, i.e. *senex*, older man of worthy character, is basic in the synagogue set up.
3. Therefore we may assume the influence of *presbyteroi* in both the Palestinian churches and in every *diaspora* church where there were numerous Jewish Christians from the first. If they had been brought in at a given moment, it is hard to believe that Luke would not have mentioned this.
4. The actual importance of the *presbyteroi* will depend on the amount of charismatic gift present. This would explain why they are not mentioned in Jerusalem until the scattering of the apostles, in Antioch in a matter which depended on revelation, and in Corinth where the charismatics seem to have taken the bit between their teeth.
5. A view is held by many that while every *episkopos* was a *presbyteros*, not every *presbyteros* was an *episkopos*. In other words, *episkopoi* were *presbyteroi* with special administrative duties. This would go a long way to explain the rapid rise of the monarchical episcopate.
6. Incidentally, Clement of Rome was almost

certainly a disciple of Paul's, and when he wrote to Corinth on behalf of the Roman church rebuking them for removing their elders, he had no idea that Corinth was ever elderless at the beginning.)

BIBLIOGRAPHY

BANNERMAN, D. D., *The Scripture Doctrine of the Church* (Edinburgh, 1887).

BARTLET, J. V., *Church-Life and Church-Order during the First Four Centuries* (Oxford, 1943).

BRUNNER, E., *The Misunderstanding of the Church* (London, 1952).

CRAIK, H., *New Testament Church Order* (London and Bristol, 1863).

CULLMANN, O., *The Early Church* (London, 1956).

HORT, F. J. A., *The Christian Ecclesia* (London, 1897).(1898 edn.quoted.)

KIRK, K. E. (ed.) *The Apostolic Ministry* (London, 1946).

LANG, G. H., *The Churches of God* (London, 1959).

LIGHTFOOT, J. B., Dissertation on 'The Christian Ministry' in *Philippians* (London, 1868). (1908 edn.quoted.)

MANSON, T. W., *The Church's Ministry* (London, 1948).

MANSON, T. W., *Ministry and Priesthood: Christ's and Ours* (London, 1958).

MORRIS, L., *Ministers of God* (London, 1964).

NEWBIGIN, L., *The Household of God* (London, 1953).

SCHLATTER, A., *The Church in the New Testament Period* (1926, Eng. trans., London, 1955).

SCHMIDT, K. L., *The Church* (1938, Eng.trans., London, 1950).

SCHWEIZER, E., *Church Order in the New Testament* (1959, Eng.trans., London, 1961).

STIBBS, A. M., *The Church Universal and Local* (London, 1948).

STREETER, B. H., *The Primitive Church* (London, 1929).

General:

BRUCE, F. F., *The Spreading Flame* (London, 1958).

LATOURETTE, K. S., *A History of Christianity* (London, 1954).

LIGHTFOOT, J. B., ed., *The Apostolic Fathers* (London, 1891).

THE LETTERS OF PAUL

G. C. D. HOWLEY

PAUL THE MAN

A passage in a second-century document, *The Acts of Paul and Thecla*, is fascinating in that it is the origin of the only tradition we possess concerning the physical appearance of the apostle Paul. It reads: '. . . And he saw Paul coming, a man little of stature, thin-haired upon the head, crooked in the legs, of good state of body, with eyebrows joining, and nose somewhat hooked, full of grace: for sometimes he appeared like a man, and sometimes he had the face of an angel'.[1] It is impossible to judge the accuracy of this description—it may be a legend—nor does it really matter. Whatever the likeness of Paul may have been, the New Testament is stamped with evidences of his personality and work. His likeness is there in a more important sense. 'Apart from Jesus Christ, St. Paul is the greatest figure in the history of Christianity', said A. H. McNeile;[2] to which we may add a further comment by the same writer: 'The Christianity of today is broadly speaking the Christianity of St. Paul'.[3] This conclusion is undoubtedly correct, for it was the ministry of Paul, under God, that made Christianity of universal importance.

What was it that brought about this vital change, as compared with the limited outlook that marked the Jerusalem apostles at the first? To answer this we must consider something of the life, history and development of the person whose first mention in the New Testament is, 'A young man named Saul' (Ac. 7: 58). Saul was a native of Tarsus, one of the three university cities of that age (the others were Alexandria and Athens). A Jew by birth, and proud of his pure-blooded Jewish ancestry, he was possibly educated in Tarsus in early years, though Ac. 22: 3 suggests that he might have been sent to Jerusalem for education when quite young. He would have an understanding of his background in the Hellenistic environment of Tarsus, realizing what it had imparted to him; but his Jewish heritage was the paramount element in shaping his outlook. He was born to Roman citizenship, a fact of which he was justly proud; and this gave him certain privileges in life from the first, as well as influencing his attitudes in certain situations, as some events in his life make clear. Paul was, as has been said, a citizen of the world of that time, blending elements in his person of Hebrew, Greek and Roman life. He was the right kind of person for the immense task God planned for him, and we can therefore understand the import of the words spoken by the Lord to Ananias: 'This man is my chosen instrument to carry my name before the Gentiles and their kings and before the people of Israel' (Ac. 9: 15).

The name Paul is used for the first time in Ac. 13: 9 ('Saul, who was also called Paul'), and from that time his Jewish name gave place to his Roman *cognomen* Paul, the environment of his service being largely in the Roman world. The subsequent history of his ministry makes clear how fully he accomplished the divine plan for his life. W. M. Ramsay used to speak of 'the charm of Paul', and this charm must have shown itself from his youth. Our first glimpse of him is as a young man, and yet one already prominent and trusted in Jewish circles in Jerusalem. His assignment to root out the disciples, 'on the authority of the chief priests' (Ac. 26: 10) gives evidence of the extent to which the religious leaders reposed trust in him. He was without doubt regarded as one of the coming men, a certain leader for Judaism within the next few years. Yet all this was to fail of realization. God had something far greater in store for Paul.

Saul's encounter with the risen Christ on the road to Damascus was the crisis that completely altered the course of his life. The angry young man had systematically persecuted the believers in Jerusalem and Judea, and he was on his way to carry on the same savage work in Damascus when 'a light from heaven flashed about him'. This light was that of the glory of Christ Himself, and it was destined to penetrate to the very depths of Saul's personality, leaving him a new man. He saw the Lord, he heard Christ's voice, and from the moment of his question, 'Who are you, Lord?' and the receiving of the answer, 'I am Jesus, . . .', his whole outlook was changed. From that time, the one presiding element in his life was the love of Christ. It was this that controlled him henceforth. His whole life developed from this fresh centre, the reality of the risen Lord Jesus Christ. Describing his conversion years afterwards he spoke of God's outworking purpose: '. . . God, who set me apart from birth and called me by his grace, was pleased to reveal his Son to me . . .' (Gal. 1: 15). The divine intervention and the revealing of Christ to Saul was to prove a crucial moment in the early days of Christianity.

From the first the new disciple began to serve the Lord, preaching and witnessing boldly amongst those who looked with wonder at this erstwhile proud Pharisee. His early witnessing was to grow into a full-blooded, reasoned declaration of the faith, a mingling of proclamation of the truth coupled with clear and brilliant teaching of all that Christianity meant for mankind. It has been said that Paul spent the rest of his life interpreting to others the significance of his pivotal experience on the Damascus road; and there is truth in this statement. Christ's appearance to him was to mean that he would spend his life expounding the deeper meanings of the resurrection, not just as a fact of history but even more as an essential element in understanding the meaning of the Christian life. Paul's personal relationship with Jesus Christ was the one thing that mattered henceforth. As he said in later years: 'to me to live is Christ' (Phil. 1: 21). This demonstrated itself in many ways, one of which was his description of himself as a 'servant' (*doulos*, slave) of Christ Jesus (Rom. 1: 1; Phil. 1: 1, etc.). He who had been so self-confident now rejoiced in being the willing subject, the slave, of Christ. Life was now to be worked out in terms of obedience to his heavenly Master. Paul's period of retreat in Arabia (not defined as to its length) will have given him time to adjust his mind to his new life; and the longer time spent later in Tarsus must have given him the preparation he needed for his great life work.

THE LETTERS

Letter-writing was common in the Apostolic Age. There is little need for us to explore this realm here, and readers should refer to the article on 'Archaeology and the New Testament'. The question, 'Epistles or Letters?' has intrigued scholars during the past century. Perhaps it would be true to say that some of Paul's letters fall into the category of letters, pure and simple, while others are more in the style of 'epistles', pastoral or encyclical letters intended for wide circulation. To take extremes, Philemon falls into the former class, Romans perhaps into the latter. Of Paul and the other New Testament letter writers Stephen Neill wrote: 'They do not write exactly as Plato or Demosthenes wrote; but they knew what they wanted to say, and went straight to their object with that directness and economy of words which is the indispensable condition of great writing. There is an immense difference between the vigour and general correctness of the New Testament writers, and the halting, broken jargon of so many writers of the papyri'.[4]

There are thirteen letters in the New Testament that bear Paul's signature. They could be viewed as merely a bundle of old letters; but old letters age in more ways than appearance. They cease to be relevant; their writers and their original readers are past and gone. The messages they carried no longer apply. How different is the case, however, when we begin to examine this bundle of letters! Without particularizing for the moment, they scintillate with life; they speak to the heart; they penetrate to the conscience; they possess an ageless quality that makes them always up-to-date. Even now that the immediate circumstances that brought them into being have become ancient history, the abiding principles of their teaching give them importance. It has been well said: 'We should not find in these letters such a living reflection of their writer if they were not, in the main, real letters, sent to definite persons under actual circumstances, evoked by particular needs, and representing, as a true letter always does, what the writer would have wished to say by word of mouth, if absence had not prevented him from doing so (II Cor. x, 11)'.[5] Indeed, the reflection of the personality and essential experience of the author provided by the letters gives us all that we need of insight into the heart of this great man of God. A famous missionary of two generations ago, Dan Crawford, used to speak of 'the Pauline gleam'. We can discern that gleam throughout this collection of letters.

The arrangement of the letters of Paul in the New Testament is in general that of their length. When we rearrange them into their chronological order, fitting them as far as possible into their life-setting within the record of the Acts of the Apostles, they begin to yield up more of their treasures; they become self-explanatory, to a greater extent than when this background is ignored. The letters can be divided into four groups, and this is perhaps the more usual way of considering them. The criteria for this are their subject-matter and style. If we accept this division, we would arrange them in this fashion:

Eschatological. 1 and 2 Thessalonians.
Evangelical. 1 and 2 Corinthians, Galatians, Romans.
Captivity. Ephesians, Colossians, Philemon, Philippians.
Pastoral. 1 Timothy, Titus, 2 Timothy.

(G. G. Findlay, in discussing Paul's earlier letters, made this comment: 'The Thessalonian letters contain very little that bears directly on what we are accustomed to call *the doctrines of salvation* . . . In the second group of St. Paul's writings, . . . the case is entirely altered. Here the cross meets us at every turn. . . . Christ's atonement forms their central and dominant theme, as His second advent that of the epistles to the Thessalonians. For this reason we entitle them collectively *the evangelical epistles . . .*'.

The Epistles of Paul the Apostle, pp. 54 f.)

A difficulty arises, however, if we place Galatians as the first of Paul's extant letters; for plainly it is related much more closely to Romans than to the Thessalonian letters. We shall probably find a clearer and easier approach to the letters if we regard them as dividing into three rather than four groups. Viewed stylistically they undoubtedly fall into four groups, but this grouping loses something of its strength immediately Galatians is removed from its traditional place. If we take the letters, then, as three groups, and place the first six letters in one group, they may be described in the words of F. B. Clogg, 'the Epistles of Paul the Traveller',[6] or with A. D. Nock, 'the letters written on journeys'—'The Travel Letters'.[7]

The Travel Letters. These letters are essentially missionary letters, filled with the spirit of love and understanding towards those recently converted to the Christian faith, and marked by strong concern where they seem to be in any danger, either through conduct unworthy of disciples of Christ, or teaching calculated to turn them aside from the purity of the apostolic faith. Paul's letters normally open with thanksgiving and prayer for his readers, and his feeling of affection and regard for them is plainly seen in his constancy of spirit in prayerful remembrance of them. It was indeed from this deep desire for their welfare that his letters sprang.

It is fascinating to observe the differences of place, people and experience that are reflected in these missionary letters, as also the variation in the mood of the writer from time to time. We note the fickle Galatians, the sturdy loyalty of the Macedonians, the pride of the Corinthians; and see Paul's anxiety, indignation or satisfaction as he faced and sought to meet their varying needs. Much has been written about Paul's style, and it may be well to bear in mind that a man's style may differ as he encounters different circumstances. In ordinary modern life we would expect this, why not, therefore, in the writings of the Apostolic Age? Paul can be persuasive, controversial, logical, contemplative, ecstatic, as the mood or the need takes him. His use of the thought-forms of his age, that were familiar to his readers, made his letters *real*, they 'rang a bell' in the minds of his readers. Here was nobody who beat the air: he had a purpose in writing, objectives to attain, and he used every means within his not inconsiderable powers of literary ability to bring his readers to a right frame of mind, so that they would submit to the teaching given them and accept his apostolic direction. Paul was a preacher of the great truths of Christianity. He did not—like some moderns—occupy his time with secondary matters except as they impinged upon the vital matters being expounded. If we survey the main themes dealt

with in this group of travel letters, these are typical of his teaching: the Cross in Christian experience (Galatians), conversion and the Christian hope (Thessalonians), the common life of the body of Christ (1 Corinthians), the apostolic ministry (2 Corinthians), the gospel of God (Romans). Our author is never lost for words, but his words are always profitable. His exposition of the scope of the gospel lifts his Roman letter to the heights; while we discern his deep feelings of love and concern for the Galatian, Thessalonian and Corinthian Christians, even though at times he has to chide some of them sharply. Further, the apostle never fails to make clear all that is involved in Christian discipleship. His plain-spoken words to the Thessalonians, and the Corinthians, give evidence of his original preaching of the gospel among them as always being shot through with explanation of what it would mean to become a Christian in the society of that age.

The Captivity Letters. Luke is an exact writer; he is also at times a tantalizing one! Never do his readers feel more frustrated than when he rings down the curtain with Paul's arrival in Rome, followed by his two-year sojourn there 'in his own rented house' (Ac. 28: 30). What happened after the termination of this period? All kinds of questions arise in our minds when we reach that point in our reading. We assume in this article that the answer lies in what is revealed in the 'Prison Letters'. Space hardly permits an investigation of the place of origin of the four letters usually set at this point of time, but we assume just now that they emanated from Paul's Roman captivity. The ultimate spiritual value of the letters of the captivity does not depend upon their place of origin; they are like an overflowing well of light and truth, leading ever closer to what Paul calls 'the fulness of Christ'.

Some may discern certain differences of style or emphasis in this group of letters, as compared with those of Paul's active missionary journeys. This could be exaggerated, but it is true that with his altered situation, Paul applied himself to using his captivity for the furtherance of the cause of Christ. And this he did most successfully. A century ago J. B. Lightfoot believed that Philippians was written first, of the four captivity letters, with Ephesians, Colossians and Philemon being written later. Nowadays many scholars believe that the group of three, Ephesians, Colossians and Philemon preceded Philippians, which, they think, was written towards the end of the two years in Rome. There are many scholars today who do not believe that Philippians was written in Rome. This is referred to briefly in the Introduction to the commentary on the letter. If there are grounds for regarding Paul as a mystic, they are based upon these letters.

Though a prisoner, he displays a profound penetration into the deep things of God. Not for nothing does the writer speak of his ministry to make known the 'unsearchable riches of Christ' (Eph. 3: 8). If anything, Paul knows his Master better and expounds Him more richly in this period of his life. There are other developments too: for not only does he bring us a rich teaching about Christ, but this is closely related to the new life of Christians, life 'in Christ'.

Albert Schweitzer has an interesting passage concerning Paul's mystical doctrine of Christ: 'Of what precise kind then is the mysticism of Paul? It occupies a unique position between primitive and intellectual mysticism. The religious conceptions of the Apostle stand high above those of primitive mysticism. This being so, it might have been expected that his mysticism would have to do with the unity of man with God as the ultimate ground of being. But this is not the case. Paul never speaks of being one with God or being in God. He does indeed assert the divine sonship of believers. But, strangely enough, he does not conceive of sonship to God as an immediate mystical relation to God, but as mediated and effected by means of the mystical union with Christ. . . . In Paul there is no God-mysticism; only a Christ-mysticism by means of which man comes into relation to God. . . . This "being-in-Christ" is the prime enigma of the Pauline teaching: once grasped it gives the clue to the whole'. (Schweitzer added elsewhere that while this was true of Paul, he was the only Christian thinker who knew only Christ-mysticism, unaccompanied by God-mysticism: 'In the Johannine theology both appear alongside of one another and intermingled with each other'.)[8]

In these letters, not only is Christ viewed as risen and glorified; the Christian shares in His resurrection and triumph. He is 'in Christ'. A. M. Hunter expresses it thus: 'When a man was baptized "into Christ", he passed into His possession, became "in him". Whatever else it means, "in Christ" must mean "in communion with Christ". This experience was basic to Paul's Christianity, as it still is to any Christianity worthy of the name. . . . The Christian, we may say, lives in a Christ atmosphere. . . . Yet this, while true, is but half the truth. . . . We have to say then that the phrase means not only "in communion with Christ" but also "in the community of Christ". It implies membership in the Church, which is Christ's Body'.[9] Deissmann regards the phrase as describing 'the most intimate fellowship imaginable of the Christian with the living spiritual Christ'.[10] To refer to yet another witness, W. D. Davies says: 'The formula which Paul most frequently used to describe the nature of the Christian man was that he was "in Christ". We have

already seen that by this Paul meant that the individual who accepted Christ was part of a new humanity of which He was the head; that he was being ingathered into the true Israel of God. It agrees with this that there are passages where to be "in Christ" is clearly to be in the Church. In short *en Christō* is a social concept, to be *en Christō* is to have discovered the true community.[11]

If the earlier letters reveal Paul as the ardent pioneer missionary, the captivity group show us not only the theologian but the pastor-teacher at work, or, as F. W. Beare sums up this important aspect of his work, 'his work as Spiritual Director'.[12] We find Paul at work in this way throughout his life, and through all his letters; this ministry cannot be confined to any one group of letters. Yet the depth of his teaching at this time, when seen in combination with his down-to-earth application of truth, brings us face to face with a great master in pastoral care. Here is no ponderous autocrat at work, trying to pressure people into certain avenues of thought or life; neither, on the other hand, do we find any suggestion of practical talk without sufficient substance behind it to strengthen his words. There is, as always, a remarkable balance in the messages Paul delivers to churches or to individuals. If we link the captivity letters with Luke's reference to this period in Ac. 28: 30 f., they give us Paul's own explanation of how he set about preaching the kingdom of God and teaching about the Lord Jesus Christ—and what fruitful service it was!

The Pastoral Letters. In this final group of letters traditionally attributed to Paul, we meet the veteran, serving in conjunction with his younger but trusted colleagues Timothy and Titus. It is evident that, as Paul drew near to the close of his ministry, he was concerned to provide for a continuance of the apostolic teaching through men who would share in such a succession. Timothy and Titus were in that succession; but it would not end with them. It was to continue into the next generation, as he made clear by his instructions to Timothy: '. . . the things you have heard me say in the presence of many witnesses entrust to reliable men who will also be qualified to teach others' (2 Tim. 2: 2). The two men were very different types of persons: Titus appears to have been strong, able to cope with complex situations; Timothy was more diffident, perhaps holding back at times from the full thrust of his ministry. Something of this order seems hinted at by the way in which Paul seeks to encourage him in his service (cf. 1 Tim. 4: 14; 2 Tim. 1: 6).

It is not easy to fit the Pastoral letters into the framework of Luke's narrative in the Acts. The view that has held the field until comparatively recent years is that after the two years in Rome, Paul was released, and travelled for some time, seeking—ever watchful as he was —to strengthen and consolidate the churches against the time to come. He himself was well aware that his period of service was limited, and his concern was for the churches, that they should hold their own, and make advance, after his departure. Further, his affection for his co-workers made him desirous of strengthening their hands, so that later, without his support, they would continue the work of the earlier years, and Christianity would continue to expand. The present writer regards these letters as the proper climax of Paul's life. Here, it is true, Paul does not engage in a rich instruction in truth as in the letters of his captivity. But what matters that? His task is different; and while the letters may not contain long passages of teaching, they are filled with allusions to the doctrine that had characterized his ministry over the years. Allusions they may be, but nonetheless significant.

A further consideration is that the tasks before Timothy and Titus were of an administrative nature, so of necessity, Paul has much to say of detailed instruction, even if at times it seems pedestrian in character. Dealing with simple, everyday matters can be pedestrian in modern church life, yet it has to be done, so that provision is made for the many diverse needs of the persons concerned. With reference to the affirmation of some scholars that the letters contain a 'lowered theology, shorn of the watchwords of the apostle's previous teaching', E. K. Simpson refutes this by replying: 'These criticisms are altogether wide of the mark. For doctrinal edification lies outside the immediate scope of the Pastorals; they comprise executive counsels blended with the ethical. Moreover, no chasm yawns between Christian doctrine and Christian practice'.[13]

The second letter to Timothy is an affectionate call to fidelity, as the apostle sees that his end is near. The tenderness of the bond between the two men is evidenced throughout the letter, and Paul's references to his own earlier service is intended to encourage the younger man. If the two earlier letters of this group were written during Paul's period of freedom, this was composed during his last imprisonment, when his status and condition were very different from the time of his honourable confinement in a hired apartment. Now he is 'suffering even to the point of being chained like a criminal' (2 Tim. 2: 9). His exact whereabouts had to be ascertained by Onesiphorus—'he searched hard for me until he found me'—his mind is now set on his departure; he is ready; his work is done. And so Paul writes the finale to his life-story.

Chronological Outline
The following chronological outline may be accepted as a working arrangement (even for those letters whose location in the course of Paul's ministry is reasonably certain there is a margin of doubt of a year or two on either side of the dates suggested).

THE TRAVEL LETTERS
Galatians	Written from Antioch in Syria, A.D. 48.
1 Thessalonians	Written from Corinth, A.D. 50.
2 Thessalonians	Written from Corinth, A.D. 50.
1 Corinthians	Written from Ephesus, A.D. 54–55.
2 Corinthians	Written from Macedonia, A.D. 55–56.
Romans	Written from Corinth, early A.D. 57.

THE CAPTIVITY LETTERS
Colossians	Written from Rome, A.D. 60–61.
Ephesians	Written from Rome, A.D. 60–61.
Philemon	Written from Rome, A.D. 60–61.
Philippians	Written from Rome, A.D. 61–62.

THE PASTORAL LETTERS
Titus	Written from Ephesus, after A.D. 62.
1 Timothy	Written from Macedonia, after A.D. 62.
2 Timothy	Written from Rome, A.D. 64–65.

PROBLEMS
We are well aware that the foregoing survey of the thirteen letters traditionally attributed to Paul has been anything but complete. Its very brevity has demanded that many matters of interest and importance have had to be omitted from our consideration. Certain problems, however, have been deliberately ignored, so that they could be looked at separately at this point.

Galatians. Two matters that have engaged the attention of scholars with regard to this letter are the identity of its recipients, and the time when it was written. The two problems are closely related. Earlier scholarship believed that Paul wrote to churches in North Galatia, and that this region is referred to in Ac. 16: 6 and 18: 23. The travel and researches of Sir William Ramsay convinced him that Paul wrote to the churches founded during his first missionary journey, i.e., Pisidian Antioch, Iconium, Lystra, and Derbe, cities which were all within the Roman province of Galatia. Ramsay further affirmed that the references in Acts should read 'the Phrygio-Galatic region' (16: 6), the part of Phrygia that was in the province of Galatia; and 'the Galatic region and Phrygia' (18: 23), where 'the Galatic region' is Lycaonia Galatica.[14] There is no record in Acts of any missionary activity in the north of the province. The matter is fully discussed by Guthrie,[15] while an objective account is also given by R. A. Cole.[16] Suffice it to say that this volume contains both viewpoints, the writer on Acts accepting the northern theory, while the commentary on Galatians regards the southern theory as the correct one.

If the letter was addressed to the churches of Paul's first journey, it follows that it might well have been written shortly after the conclusion of that journey. It could have been produced at a time between the return of the travellers to Antioch in Syria, and the Council of Jerusalem, that is, during the interval in time between Ac. 14: 28 and 15: 1. There are reasons for believing this may have been the case. Cole says: 'If we follow the Southern theory concerning its destination, then we could place the Epistle very early indeed'.[17] The conclusion that we may legitimately reach, but suggest without dogmacy, is that this is the first of the extant letters of Paul, written not long before the Jerusalem conference, in A.D. 48 or 49.

2 Corinthians. Was this letter written as we find it now in our Bibles, or is it composite, being actually made up of three letters or fragments of letters? An article by R. V. G. Tasker in the *Expository Times* for November 1935 entitled 'The Unity of 2 Corinthians' defended the unity of the letter. During the intervening years we have not found any sufficient reason for moving from that position. Tasker developed this theme in his Introduction to his commentary on the letter.[18] Allan Menzies in his excellent commentary on the letter also defends its integrity, and in the course of a thorough discussion of the matter says, 'If we take the Epistle as it lies before us, we find it not unintelligible'.[19] A powerful supporter of the unity of the letter is found in the Danish scholar Johannes Munck, who roundly affirms, with reference to the 'fragmentary' theory that 'this assumption will not hold water'.[20] Munck provides a learned and lengthy chapter on the subject (chapter 6) to which interested readers may refer. The matter is also dealt with in the Introduction to the commentary in this volume, so that we may leave further discussion at this point. We do not pretend to have done justice to both sides of the argument, but for ourselves accept the unity of the letter, believing that it makes sense as it stands. (For further study, see Guthrie, *op. cit.*)

The whole subject of the Corinthian correspondence is both fascinating and complex. There were a number of letters that passed

between Paul and the church in Corinth, and the two letters preserved in the New Testament are but a part of all that was written. It should be said, however, that we believe that what was preserved was all that was essential for the Christian Church, and that any lost letters were allowed to go into oblivion because they contained nothing that was not already found in other apostolic letters, nothing therefore that added anything to the content of the Christian faith. One letter preceded 1 Corinthians (cf. 5: 9); then, after a letter (and possibly a delegation) being received by Paul from Corinth (cf. 7: 1), came 1 Corinthians. Paul seems to have paid a visit to Corinth some time after this was written (cf. 2 C. 1: 23–2: 1; see also 12: 14; 13: 1). It was of a painful character, and was followed later by a severe letter (cf. 2 C. 2: 4). When Titus came to him with encouraging news from Corinth, Paul wrote 2 Corinthians. This brief summary oversimplifies a situation that was at the time not at all simple, but it may be regarded as a short sketch, however inadequate, of the events associated with our two letters to Corinth.

The Pastoral Letters. The Introduction to the commentary includes a survey of some aspects of the problem of the authorship of these letters. We do not propose, therefore, to go over the ground, except on a few matters. Firstly, we discount theories that suggest that any writer used Paul's name falsely, even to spread the teachings of the apostle more widely. There is a reference to a hoped-for visit Paul wanted to make to Timothy in Ephesus (1 Tim. 3: 14; 4: 13). And 2 Timothy includes a request for Timothy to come to Paul in Rome. What possible point would such references have were the letters written long years after the death of Paul? We concur with the judgment of C. F. D. Moule when he says: 'Some may say that this is an obvious device to lend verisimilitude, and I know that judgments of this sort are difficult to assess objectively. I can only say that to me it seems a piece of gratuitous irony and in bad taste'.[21] In his Manson Memorial Lecture here quoted, Professor Moule put forward a new theory towards a solution of the problem of the Pastorals. The lecture, delivered in Manchester in November 1964, offered the suggestion that these letters were written, in fact, in the lifetime of Paul and with his express sanction. 'My suggestion is, then, that Luke wrote all three Pastoral epistles. But he wrote them during Paul's lifetime, at Paul's behest, and, in part (but only in part), at Paul's dictation.'[22] He accepts the view that Paul was released at the end of his two years in Rome. Following some comments about the general situation thus envisaged, he adds: 'This means a thoroughgoing reinstatement of the old-fashioned theory of a journey to Crete and perhaps to Spain and all the rest of it. But why not? Objections are fashionable, but not, I think, cogent'.[23] The interest in such a theory is that it associates the letter firmly with Paul's life and affairs, and accepts it as genuinely Pauline in character. For ourselves, we accept the Pauline authorship of the letters. The problems touched upon in this section are merely a few of those that have a continuing interest for New Testament scholars. We hope that it may be enough to stimulate fresh enquiry and to establish faith.

DISTINCTIVE ELEMENTS IN PAUL'S THEOLOGY

There is a notable phrase in Philippians where Paul expresses one object in Christian witness as being the defence and confirmation of the gospel (1: 7). It can be said that his letters all had this objective, whatever their immediate cause. The truths the apostle proclaimed were held close to his heart, and his constant desire was to further their acceptance among men. As we survey his letters, certain elements of truth stand out as being prominent in his thinking. Paul was a man of affairs, able to grasp and sum up varying situations. He observed the needs of men, in relation to mankind as a whole, and in relation to God. He believed that his gospel provided the solution to world problems of the day. There was separation between God and man—but his message of justification met this need. He saw all around him the evidence that peace between man and man was non-existent—his doctrine of the Body of Christ met this lack. At every point Paul's teaching was related to life—life as it then was, but so wisely presented was his teaching that it relates immediately to life in any or every generation. Such considerations will save us from ever regarding Pauline theology as merely academic. With this in mind, we may turn our attention to some of the salient features of his doctrine.

Justification. Paul was brought up to understand the gravity of sin, and its universal character. The revelation of God in the Old Testament would impress upon him the reality of the wrath and the judgment of God. The age-old problem of how men could be just with God found its solution in his own reconciliation to God through Christ. He realized the guilt of man, including his own people the Jews. But he had met with Christ, and his outlook was changed. 'He had to urge that their painful efforts to win merit in God's sight were rendered needless by the wondrous exhibition of the very meaning of God in the cross of His Son. So that his central doctrine of Justification by faith is not a scholastic abstraction, formulated to round off an artificial theory.'[24] The answer to man's plight was found in the divine

provision in Christ. His atoning work provided the means whereby the sin of man could be forgiven—a note that stood to the front of all Paul's preaching. Further, this message was in sharp contrast to the mould of thought that shaped the minds of multitudes of Jews under the old covenant. 'For God has done what the law, weakened by the flesh, could not do: sending his own Son in the likeness of sinful flesh and for sin, he condemned sin in the flesh . . .' (Rom. 8: 3). This teaching was not original to Paul. 'Jesus himself taught a doctrine of justification of sinners by the outgoing righteousness of God. . . . It is implicit in his conception of himself as the instrument of God's salvation for penitent sinners: "I came not to call the righteous, but sinners" . . .'.[25] As to the faith that marks the justified, this is beautifully described by C. K. Barrett: 'The hearing of faith (which is certainly not an attitude that man is able of himself freely to adopt, but is a gift from God, made possible in the Holy Spirit) is itself a reversal of the rebellious dissatisfaction of Adam, who was not content to accept the place God assigned him, but set out to secure a better place for himself. . . . It is not that faith is in Pauline or any other proper usage a shibboleth, or an "Open Sesame" which operates as a magic formula. It is not even that faith is an indispensable agent or instrument which by itself effects justification or salvation. It is simply that faith is a description (from the human side) of the relationship with God for which God created man, in which man lets God truly be God, and lets himself truly be man, that is, the obedient creature of the loving God'.[26]

The Body of Christ. Paul used several images to express the truth of the Church, the community of Christians. His conception of the Church as the Body of Christ gave a touch of life and reality to this doctrine. There is a noticeable development in the apostle's teaching on this subject. 'In 1 Cor. the head, so far from being superior to the other members, is not distinguished from them: it is merely one organ among many'[27]—whereas in the captivity letters Christ is named as 'the head of the body, the church' (Col. 1: 18). There is no conflict between these two conceptions; the difference lies in the language, the essential truth conveyed by the metaphor of the Body of Christ is communicated in both cases. From the first days of Christianity the oneness among believers created by the Holy Spirit showed itself in many ways. The early chapters of Acts stress this as a joyful reality in the church in Jerusalem (Ac. 2: 44, etc.). What was true all the time from Pentecost onward found a distinctive interpretation in the Pauline doctrine of Christ's Body. They were indeed one, sharing a common life, making their contribution to the community, exercising their spiritual gifts for the edification of others, and in a thousand ways manifesting the bond that united them in Christ. In the face of all the separating factors in first-century society, Paul affirms that Christ had broken down the dividing wall of hostility (Eph. 2: 14), bringing men together who once had been apart, even at enmity.

The Holy Spirit. In pre-Pauline Christianity the outpouring of the Holy Spirit at Pentecost was recognized as the sign of the Age of Fulfilment. It is the teaching of Paul, however, that gives colour to the whole outlook of the New Testament on the Spirit of God. In his witness to the truth of the gospel certain distinctive insights concerning the Holy Spirit characterized his doctrine. He taught that it is by the Spirit the ministry of the risen Christ is communicated to believers, in particular because it is through the Holy Spirit that Christians are incorporated into the Body of Christ. He revealed the way in which our present experience is linked up with the life that is to be, because the Holy Spirit is the earnest, the guarantee of glory yet to come. His frequent need to guide the converts along avenues proper to discipleship took him again and again to the basic fact that by the Spirit's indwelling and abiding presence with them, the believers possessed a resource whereby they could live for the glory of God and produce spiritual fruit in Christian character.

The Person of Christ. In three passages (Rom. 5: 12–21; 1 C. 15: 20–23, 45–50) Paul draws certain parallels and contrasts between Adam and Christ, 'the last Adam'. He shows the baneful effects of the one act of disobedience of Adam, contrasting it with the beneficial effects of the one act of obedience of Christ, in His obedience unto death. Man's relationship with Adam condemns him to death; but the link the renewed man has with Christ gives him the promise of life eternal. As now men bear the stamp of Adam, so Christians will ultimately 'bear the likeness of the man from heaven' (1 C. 15: 49). In Christ, the last Adam, man is recovered from the effects of the Fall, and given the pledge of his final entry into the presence of God. And what is the pledge? It is that Jesus Christ is risen, and we shall rise again in Him. Yet another phase of Paul's doctrine of Christ is his teaching concerning Christ and the universe. The cosmic significance of Jesus Christ means that, while Christians may rejoice in a personal knowledge and experience of Him, His influence stretches far beyond any one individual life, beyond His place in the whole Church: it is universal in its scope. In reply to the false teachers who gave Christ a lesser place than God, Paul revealed His place

in the universe, declaring that, in view of the place of the Son in relation to the Father, His creative activity and the fact that 'in him all things hold together', His glory is established beyond all argument; as Paul sums up, 'that in everything he might have the supremacy' (Col. 1: 18 f.). In refuting the error that unsettled the Colossian Christians, Paul expounded the nature of Christ, 'to show that he completely overshadows all the angelic powers that could be imagined, and that they can have nothing to offer men which is not already secured to them in Christ'.[28] It is plain that Paul envisaged a conflict continuing in the invisible, planetary world. There were 'authorities, . . . powers, spiritual forces of evil in the heavenly realms' (Eph. 6: 12) engaging in a ceaseless warfare against God and His hosts. Christ is superior to them all, Paul affirms; further, He has defeated them by His Cross. His cosmic rôle is brought into the open; His supremacy is established beyond all cavil. From this flows the teaching that calls upon Christ's people to show by their behaviour the new life in Christ they enjoy.

Bound up with the fact of Christ's assured triumph is the promise of a full deliverance for the whole creation—to be reconciled to God by the Cross—and its freedom from its age-old 'groaning in travail'. The existing world order is to give place to a new order, from which the marks of sin will be eliminated. 'The final Judgement—"the day of wrath and revelation of the righteous judgement of God"—remains still in the future; the concluding act of the great world-drama has yet to take place; and there are "enemies" still to be subdued . . .'[29] The apostle declares that in the final summing-up of all things, evil will be judged and Christ's glory will be manifested. The Christian will figure with his Lord in the great events of the end-time: 'When Christ who is your life appears, then you also will appear with him in glory' (Col. 3: 4). The hope of resurrection for the believer in Christ is no vague, uncertain thing, but already pledged to him in the fact of Christ's resurrection from the dead. The ultimate for all who belong to Christ is the fulfilment of God's purpose, the realization of their destiny, for they have been 'predestined to be conformed to the likeness of his Son' (Rom. 8: 29). Attaining to perfect likeness to Christ is the glorious hope of the believer in Him.

Some General Observations. We have noted some of the settled ideas that characterize the ministry of Paul, and the fact that in some realms of thought a development is traceable. We have seen also how doctrine and experience are so intertwined that Paul is never like a person evolving theories that have no relation to life and everyday affairs. His balanced thought is everywhere in evidence. Many years ago an important contribution to the study of the apostle Paul was written by C. A. Anderson Scott, *Christianity According to St. Paul*. In this book he stated: 'St. Paul's conception of Christianity can best be studied under the aspect of Salvation'.[30] The term 'Salvation' was considered to be 'the most comprehensive term for what the Apostle found in Christ'.[31] Salvation or deliverance is found in one form or another in most religions. But how it is attained or experienced is often an uncertain thing, lost in obscure doctrines. Christianity, on the other hand, came into the open with its offer of forgiveness in Christ. Paul was recognized as its leading exponent in his day, teaching the reality of salvation in Christ. He viewed it as a fact of the past, as a progressive experience, with its consummation in the future. Scott's book was first published in 1927. In 1954 A. M. Hunter published *Interpreting Paul's Gospel*, and in its Preface said: 'To unlock the wards of Paul's theology, I have unashamedly borrowed the key (the word "salvation") which Anderson Scott, a quarter of a century ago, so successfully employed in his *Christianity According to St. Paul*, in many ways still the best book on Paul's theology we have'.[32] The weight thus laid upon the term salvation is surely right. The concept of salvation, deliverance, lights up the whole of Scripture, linking Old and New Testaments as the developing 'Salvation-Story', and finding its full interpretation in Christ. The great apostle was the privileged 'chosen instrument' of God to make it known universally.

PAUL'S PERMANENT INFLUENCE

There is no doubt about the remarkable originality of the mind of Paul. Ronald Knox well said: 'And St. Paul's was no ordinary mind; sensitive, yet fearless, logical, yet poetic, infinitely tender with the scruples of others, yet unflinching in its honesty. A delicate instrument, it will interpret the melody of Christian thought in its own way. We must listen patiently, allowing him his own choice of language, not trying to fix on his words a meaning which has since become technical, not allowing our minds to be disturbed by the echoes of later controversies. You must come to St. Paul with fresh eyes if you are to feel his magic.'[33] In giving thought to the abiding influence of Paul upon Christianity, we may first bear in mind that, despite his great originality, his debt to his predecessors was a real one. The Christian message did not originate in Paul; he shared it in common with the rest of the apostles. He drew upon some words of the Lord to enforce his teaching at various points (*e.g.* Ac. 20: 35; 1 C. 7: 10; 9: 14; 11: 23; 1 Tim. 5: 18). He used the Old Testament as pointing to the truth of the apostolic gospel

(Rom. 1: 2; 1 C. 15: 3, etc.). 'The apostle's conception of Christ obviously owed much to the Christology of those who preceded him as Christians, as did also his doctrine of the Spirit.'[34]

In his own day he was a bulwark for the truth of God. Even another apostle has to be corrected if the vital principles of the gospel are at stake (Gal. 2: 11). While gladly admitting Paul's debt to others, as we have done above, we must not fall into the mistake of 'cutting him down to size', of losing the greatness of the man. This is exactly what H. J. Schoeps thinks happened in the early Church. Paul's letters, though devoutly read, 'seldom found understanding'. 'No other apostle had such a vividly marked theology, a personality of such sharp outline. . . . The church was not in a position to digest such a towering figure.'[35] Today this is no longer the case: Christians of all persuasions and throughout the world have come to see his permanent significance. Throughout the centuries of Church history Paul's teaching has proved formative, at many of the main turning-points in Christian history, and in some of the principal exponents of its truths. Whether we think of Augustine, Luther, Wesley or Karl Barth, Paul's voice has been heard throughout the years. We cannot do better in concluding this study than draw upon some words written a few years ago by Donald Coggan, former Archbishop of Canterbury: 'I would say that whenever there has been a renewed grasp of the truths at the heart of St. Paul's gospel, then there has been a revival of true religion. . . . And if you ask me why I believed that history pointed this lesson so clearly, my reply would be that I believe St. Paul was the greatest exponent of the mind of Christ who ever lived. His language differed very greatly from that of his Master, but his great doctrines were derived from Him. There lay his secret, and there it still lies for you to rediscover, if you will.'[36]

REFERENCES

1 M. R. James, *The Apocryphal New Testament* (Oxford, 1924), p. 273.
2 *St. Paul: His Life, Letters and Christian Doctrine* (Cambridge, 1932), p. ix.
3 *op. cit.*, p.v.
4 *The Interpretation of the New Testament* 1861–1961 (Oxford, 1966), p. 150.
5 H. N. Bate, *A Guide to the Epistles of Saint Paul* (London, 1926), p. 5.
6 *An Introduction to the New Testament* (London, 1937), p. ix.
7 *St. Paul* (London, 1938), p. 145.
8 *The Mysticism of Paul the Apostle* (London, 1931), pp. 3, 5.

9 *Interpreting Paul's Gospel* (London, 1954), pp. 37 f.
10 *Paul: A Study in Social and Religious History* (London, 1926), p. 140.
11 *Paul and Rabbinic Judaism* (London, 1962), p. 86.
12 *St. Paul and His Letters* (London, 1962), p. 134.
13 *The Pastoral Epistles* (London, 1954), p. 12.
14 W. M. Ramsay, *St. Paul the Traveller and the Roman Citizen* (London, 1895), p. 104.
15 *New Testament Introduction: the Pauline Epistles* (London, 1961), pp. 72–88.
16 *The Epistle of Paul to the Galatians (TNTC)* (London, 1965), pp. 15–23.
17 *op. cit.*, p. 21.
18 *The Second Epistle of Paul to the Corinthians (TNTC)* (London, 1958), pp. 23–35.
19 *The Second Epistle of the Apostle Paul to the Corinthians* (London, 1912), p. xxxvii.
20 *Paul and the Salvation of Mankind* (London, 1959), p. 170.
21 *The Problem of the Pastoral Epistles: A Reappraisal* (Reprinted from the Bulletin of the John Rylands Library, Vol. 47, No. 2, March 1965), p. 447.
22 *op. cit.*, p. 434.
23 *op. cit.*, p. 451.
24 H. A. A. Kennedy, *The Theology of the Epistles* (London, 1919), p. 63.
25 Alan Richardson, *An Introduction to the Theology of the New Testament* (London, 1958), pp. 81 f.
26 *From First Adam to Last* (London, 1962), p. 103.
27 D. E. H. Whiteley, *The Theology of St. Paul* (Oxford, 1964), pp. 191 f.
28 F. W. Beare, *St. Paul and His Letters* (London, 1962), p. 109.
29 A. E. J. Rawlinson, *The New Testament Doctrine of the Christ* (London, 1926), p. 147.
30 *Christianity According to St. Paul* (Cambridge, 1927), p. 16.
31 *op. cit.*, p. 17.
32 *Interpreting Paul's Gospel* (London, 1954), p. 9.
33 *Saint Paul's Gospel* (London, 1953), p. 9.
34 A. M. Hunter, *Paul and His Predecessors* (London, 1961), p. 150.
35 H. J. Schoeps, *Paul* (London, 1961), p. 273.
36 *Five Makers of the New Testament* (London, 1962), pp. 21 f.

BIBLIOGRAPHY

BARRETT, C. K., *From First Adam to Last* (London, 1962).
BATE, H. N., *A Guide to the Epistles of Saint Paul* (London, 1926).
BRUCE, F. F., *Paul: Apostle of the Free Spirit* (Exeter, 1977).
DAVIES, W. D., *Paul and Rabbinic Judaism* (London, 1962).
DEISSMANN, A., *Paul: A Study in Social and Religious History* E.T. (London, 1912; 2nd edition, 1926).
DODD, C. H., *The Meaning of Paul for Today* (London, 1920; Fontana edition, 1958).
ELLIOTT-BINNS, L. E., *Galilean Christianity* (London, 1956).
HUNTER, A. M., *Interpreting Paul's Gospel* (London, 1954); revised as *The Gospel According to St. Paul* (London, 1966).
HUNTER, A. M., *Paul and His Predecessors* (London, 1961).
KENNEDY, H. A. A., *The Theology of the Epistles* (London, 1919).
KIM, S., *The Origin of Paul's Gospel* (Grand Rapids, 2nd 1984).
LIGHTFOOT, J. B., *Biblical Essays* (London, 1893).
LIGHTFOOT, J. B., *Dissertations on the Apostolic Age* (London, 1892).
LIGHTFOOT, J. B., *Notes on Epistles of St. Paul* (London, 1895).
McNEILE, A. H., *St. Paul: His Life, Letters and Christian Doctrine* (Cambridge, 1932).
MUNCK, J. *Paul and the Salvation of Mankind*, E.T. (London, 1959).
NOCK, A.D., *St Paul* (London, 1938).
RAMSAY, W. M., *St. Paul the Traveller and the Roman Citizen*, 14th edn. (London, 1920).
RAMSAY, W. M., *The Teaching of Paul in Terms of the Present Day* (London, 1913).
RIDDERBOS, H. N., *Paul: An Outline of his Theology* E.T. (Grand Rapids, 1975).
SANDERS, E. P., *Paul and Palestinian Judaism* (London, 1977).
SCHOEPS, H. J., *Paul: The Theology of the Apostle in the Light of Jewish Religious History*, E.T. (London, 1961).
SCOTT, C. A. A., *Footnotes to St. Paul* (Cambridge, 1935).
WHITELEY, D. E. H., *The Theology of St. Paul* (Oxford, 1964).

THE GENERAL LETTERS

F. F. BRUCE

Their Designation and Canonicity

In the Authorized Version as earlier in the Geneva Bible of 1560, five letters have the word 'general' included in their titles—'The General Epistle of James', 'The First Epistle General of Peter', 'The Second Epistle General of Peter', 'The First Epistle General of John' and 'The General Epistle of Jude'. This distinctive adjective is translated from Gk. *katholikē* (Lat. *catholica*), whence in the Rheims New Testament of 1582 (following Jerome's Vulgate) two of these letters have the word 'catholic' included in their titles—'The Catholic Epistle of James the Apostle' and 'The Catholic Epistle of Jude the Apostle' (in R. A. Knox's version these are entitled respectively 'The Universal Epistle of the Blessed Apostle James' and 'The Universal Epistle of the Blessed Apostle Jude').

Whether the rendering 'catholic', 'general' or 'universal' be used, its significance in the titles of these letters is plain enough: unlike other letters which are addressed to specific churches or persons, these are addressed to a wider and more indefinite circle ('the twelve tribes in the Dispersion', 'the exiles of the Dispersion' in several Roman provinces, 'those who have obtained a faith of equal standing with ours' or 'those who are called, beloved in God the Father and kept for Jesus Christ'), and one of them (1 Jn) has no formal address whatsoever.

This is not the only meaning, however, which the word has borne in this context. At one time seven 'catholic letters' in all were listed, including 2 and 3 Jn as well as 1 Jn. But if 2 and 3 Jn were called catholic letters, it could not be on account of any indefiniteness in their addresses, for 2 Jn is addressed 'to the chosen lady and her children' and 3 Jn 'to my dear friend Gaius'. At an early date the word 'catholic' as applied to these letters appears to have been understood not only as 'addressed to the Church Catholic' but also, occasionally at least, as 'acknowledged by the Church Catholic'. Sometimes one of these meanings was uppermost, sometimes the other.

Eusebius (*Hist. Eccl.* ii. 23, 25) mentions that the Letter of James was reckoned 'the first of the letters called catholic. But we should observe [he goes on] that some regard it as spurious, since not many of the ancients have made mention of it; the same is true of the letter called Jude's, which is also one of the

seven called catholic. Nevertheless we know that these letters have been used publicly along with the rest in most churches.' Eusebius's personal estimate of the canonicity of certain New Testament books was more conservative than that of the church at large in his day (*c.* A.D. 325). But he seems to connect the epithet 'catholic' as used of these seven letters with their being publicly accepted in most churches.

The first person known to us who used this epithet of any of these letters was one Apollonius, towards the end of the second century. In a treatise against the Montanists he accuses Themison, one of their number, of having 'dared, in imitation of the apostle, to compose a catholic letter for the instruction of those whose faith was better than his own' (Eusebius, *Hist. Eccl.* v. 18. 5). (In imitation of which apostle? Of Peter, perhaps, since 2 Pet. is addressed 'to those who have received a faith as precious as ours', whereas Themison, according to Apollonius, wrote for those who had received a faith *more* precious than his. If this surmise is sound, this would be our earliest external evidence for 2 Pet.) About the same time (*c.* A.D. 190) the Muratorian list of New Testament books, drawn up at Rome, mentions the Letter of Jude and two of John's as being in *catholica*, meaning presumably that they were accepted in the Catholic Church. Clement of Alexandria, who also wrote late in the second century, is said by Eusebius (*Hist. Eccl.* vi. 14. 1) to have given, in his *Hypotyposeis*, 'concise accounts of all the canonical scriptures [of the New Testament], not omitting even those that are disputed—I mean the Letter of Jude and the rest of the catholic letters, and the Letter of Barnabas and the Apocalypse ascribed to Peter.' It is a natural, if not certain, inference from Eusebius that Clement expounded all seven of the catholic letters. Clement may well have called them 'catholic' himself; indeed, in another of his works he applies the epithet to the apostolic letter of Ac. 15: 23–29 (*Stromata* iv. 15).

In the generation after Clement, Origen applies the epithet 'catholic' to 1 Pet. and 1 Jn (and possibly to Jude), and also to the Letter of Barnabas. His disciple, Dionysius of Alexandria, also speaks of 1 Jn as John's 'catholic letter' —perhaps in contrast to 2 Jn and 3 Jn which name particular addressees (Eusebius, *Hist. Eccl.* vii. 25. 7).

After Eusebius we find the Council of Laodicea (A.D. 363?) and Athanasius of Alexandria (A.D. 367) explicitly including the 'seven catholic letters' in their lists of New Testament books. Among the Latin Fathers, from Jerome (347–420) onwards, the Greek adjective was sometimes transliterated (thus Jerome speaks of the Letter of James as being *de septem catholicis* 'one of the seven catholic letters') but it was sometimes rendered by the adjective *canonicus*, also of Greek origin (thus Jerome in another place speaks of 'the seven letters which are called "canonical"'). Several later Latin writers adopted the practice of referring to the seven *canonical* letters rather than the seven catholic letters. This was an awkward designation for them, as all the New Testament letters could be called canonical; in so far as the term was applied distinctively to the seven, it marked them out as canonical not in contrast to the other letters but in addition to the others.

These seven are all the New Testament letters not included in the Pauline corpus. (Hebrews, although not a Pauline letter, was included in the Pauline corpus in the east from the second century onwards, in the west from the fourth century onwards.) The Pauline letters received canonical recognition earlier than the others; hence, when the others are called 'catholic' in the sense of canonical (acknowledged by the Church Catholic), they are so called because they, as well as the Pauline letters, are entitled to this designation.

A powerful stimulus to the church's definition of the authoritative writings of the new covenant was provided *c.* A.D. 140 by Marcion's publication of his twofold Christian canon—the *Euangelion* (his edition of Lk.) and the *Apostolikon* (his edition of ten Pauline letters —all those bearing Paul's name except the three Pastorals.) The publication of this canon made it urgently necessary for the leaders of the apostolic churches to say precisely what the true Christian canon was, since they condemned Marcion's as false. In general they replied that (unlike Marcion) they did not reject the Old Testament, but retained it, acknowledging alongside it, as its proper fulfilment, the New Testament; that they acknowledged the fourfold Gospel, not a single mutilated gospel-writing (as Marcion did); that they acknowledged the Acts of the Apostles, which provided independent testimony both for Paul's apostleship (which Marcion accepted) and for that of the Twelve (which Marcion refused); that they acknowledged thirteen Pauline letters, not ten only; and that, in addition to the Pauline letters, they acknowledged the letters of other apostles and 'apostolic men' (men who were either disciples of the apostles or otherwise closely associated with them). It is these other letters that came to be called the

'catholic letters'. Not that they lacked canonical recognition before Marcion's time; two of them at any rate, 1 Pet. and 1 Jn, were quoted as authoritative documents by Polycarp of Smyrna earlier in the same century. But from now on their status as a well-defined group within the New Testament writings was assured. Some of them took longer to win general acceptance than any other New Testament books, but they were all acknowledged in the Greek and Latin churches by the end of the fourth century; the Syriac churches were slower in following suit.

Before it became the practice to include the whole New Testament (or the whole Bible) in a single codex, it was quite common to include Acts and the Catholic Letters in one codex—a companion codex to the Gospel-codex, the Pauline codex and the Apocalypse codex. Even after the whole New Testament (or the whole Bible) was included in a single codex, the Catholic Letters commonly continued to follow immediately after Acts. Thus in the *Codex Sinaiticus* the Gospels are followed by the Pauline corpus, which is followed in turn by Acts and the Catholic Letters; in the *Codex Vaticanus* Acts and the Catholic Letters come after the Gospels and before the Pauline Letters. It is this last order which is followed in Westcott and Hort's edition of the Greek New Testament, as in earlier critical editions of the nineteenth century. The arrangement with which we are most familiar, where the Catholic Letters come between Hebrews and Revelation, is that of the Latin Bible.

Their Teaching

What distinctive contribution do these seven letters make to the New Testament scriptures? With all their differences of viewpoint and content one from another, they give us a valuable picture of non-Pauline Christianity. Outside the Gospels, Paul dominates the New Testament. Thirteen of the twenty-one letters bear his name, and more than half of Acts is taken up with his apostolic career. The Catholic Letters (with Hebrews), set alongside the letters of Paul, enable us to get a stereoscopic view of first-century Christianity.

For all the individuality of his personality and his ministry, Paul insists that the gospel which he and the Twelve proclaimed was basically one and the same: 'Whether then it was I or they, this is what we preach, and this is what you believed' (1 C. 15: 11). He knew that others were giving currency to a message which they called the gospel, but it was so different from the true gospel that he refused to recognize it as a gospel at all (Gal. 1: 6 ff.; cf. 2 C. 11: 4). When the true gospel was proclaimed from unworthy motives—out of a desire, for example, to rub salt into his wounds when he was in prison and unable to engage freely in apostolic activity—he could thank God, because the unworthiness of the motives or the messengers could not detract from the glory of the message (Phil. 1: 15–18). But the most exalted messenger could not make a false message the true gospel, not even if he were an angel from heaven (Gal. 1: 8).

Can we accept Paul's claim that the gospel preached by James the Lord's brother, and by Peter and the rest of the Twelve, was fundamentally the same as he himself preached? The evidence of the Catholic Letters encourages us to believe that we can. It is, of course, open to those who wish to emphasize the difference between Paul and those others to say that Pauline influence can be traced in some of the Catholic Letters, especially in 1 Pet. But in fact there is not nearly so much Pauline influence in them as has often been maintained. What has frequently been called Pauline influence should in most cases be regarded as derived from that common fund of primitive preaching and teaching which Paul shared with the Twelve and others who were in Christ before him. This is particularly true in 1 Pet., where 'the reader is aware of an atmosphere which seems in some respects nearer to that of the primitive Church, as we divine it behind the early chapters of Acts, than anything else in the New Testament' (C. H. Dodd, *The Apostolic Preaching and its Developments*, 1936, p. 97).

1 Peter

There is some reason to think that a good part of 1 Pet., from 1: 3 to 4: 11, is a baptismal address in literary form, intended for 'newborn babes' in the spiritual sense who require to be taught what their manner of life in a pagan environment must henceforth be. Their Lord must be their supreme example, not least when they are called upon to suffer unjustly or challenged to defend their Christian hope. 'Therefore, since Christ suffered in his body, arm yourselves also with the same attitude, because he who has suffered in his body is done with sin' (1 Pet. 4: 1). The language is different, but the sense is much the same as Paul's when he urges his readers to reckon themselves 'dead to sin but alive to God in Christ Jesus', since 'anyone who has died has been freed from sin' (Rom. 6: 11, 7). Only, when Peter speaks of the sufferings of Christ we catch the note of an eyewitness (1 Pet. 5: 1) as we do not in Paul's writings.

The situation in 1 Pet. is two or three years later than what we find in Paul's last letters to churches. As Paul enjoins obedience to the powers that be since 'rulers hold no terror for those who do right, but for those who do wrong' (Rom. 13: 3), so Peter enjoins submission to the emperor and governors appointed by him: 'who is going to harm you', he asks, 'if you are eager to do good?' (1 Pet.

2: 13 ff.; 3: 13). But the situation in this letter is changing before our eyes. In 1 Pet. 3: 14 suffering for righteousness' sake is a remote possibility; in 4: 12 ff. suffering for the name of Christ has become an imminent certainty. Imperial law, which in the fifties of the first century had indirectly protected a Christian missionary like Paul through its benevolent neutrality, as in the outstanding case of Gallio (Ac. 18: 12–17), was now turning hostile, so that in effect Christians had to suffer for the very fact that they professed the Christian name (and it would make little practical difference if lawyers said that they were suffering not for the name itself but for crimes invariably associated with the name). In this turn of affairs Peter sees a token of the impending judgment of the end-time; as in Ezekiel's day (Ezek. 9: 6), so now, it is the house of God that experiences His judgment first. Such suffering as Christians are now compelled to endure must, however, be accepted by them as a sharing in the suffering of Christ, and a harbinger of their sharing in His glory on the day of revelation (4: 13 f.; 5: 1).

James

The Letter of James reflects a phase of first-century Christianity more detached from imperial policy than 1 Pet. It is addressed to the twelve tribes in the Dispersion, i.e. to Christians, and more particularly Christians of Jewish birth, throughout the world; but its background is Palestinian. The people addressed acknowledge 'our Lord Jesus Christ' as 'glorious', i.e. the incarnate manifestation of the glory of God (Jas 2: 1; the thought is not unlike that of Jn 1: 14); the name of Jesus is the 'noble name' by which they have been called (2: 7). They must beware of the temptation to think that orthodoxy of doctrine will compensate for the lack of works of mercy and faith (2: 14 ff.). (We may compare Paul's description of justifying faith in Gal. 5: 6 as 'faith expressing itself through love'.) They must beware, too, of a quarrelsome spirit (4: 1 ff.). If the letter is to be dated in the period preceding A.D. 62, when the Zealots were increasing their hold on popular sympathy in Palestine, many of the Palestinian believers must have been in danger of embracing the Zealot outlook, in place of the self-effacing charity inculcated by Jesus. The dominant attitude to the law in their environment was that of the 'all or nothing' school of Shammai, according to which a 99 per cent. success in law-keeping was really a failure: 'whoever keeps the whole law but fails in one point has become guilty of all of it' (2: 10). After A.D. 70 the milder school of Hillel became dominant, especially under Rabbi Aqiba (d. 135), whose interpretation implied in practice that a 51 per cent. righteousness would suffice to open the way to paradise: 'a man who is more than half good is not half bad' (I. Zangwill). The people addressed do not belong for the most part to the wealthy land-owning classes, although they have to be warned against showing deference to a wealthy man just because he is wealthy. It is the wealthy land-owners who oppress and prosecute them, and speak ill of the name of Jesus (2: 6 f.). But a fearful fate lies in store for these wealthy oppressors; the blistering attack on them in 5: 1 ff. is well up to the standard of the great prophets of Israel, and the prediction of wretchedness and ruin for them was amply fulfilled in the years following the revolt against Rome in A.D. 66. The party of the Sadducees, who are principally in view in James's attack on the rich, disappeared for good in those years. But as in 1 Pet. 4: 17 ff., so for James the present distress and impending disasters are signs of the last days: let humble believers wait patiently for the coming of the Lord, for 'the Judge is standing at the door' (5: 3, 7 ff.).

While in English James's letter reads like a series of extracts from OT prophecy, in Greek it reminds one of the moral disquisitions of a philosopher with a feeling for good style. The Greek of the letter may be the result of careful literary revision. The letter passes suddenly from one subject to another, sometimes returning later to one which has already been touched upon. But the opening verses provide something like an index of contents to the main divisions of the letter: the reference to trials in 1: 2 is amplified in 1: 12–17; the words about steadfastness and all-round completeness in 1: 3 f. anticipate the general teaching of chapter 2; what is said about true wisdom in 1: 5–8 is expanded in chapters 3 and 4, and the encouragement to the lowly and warning to the rich in 1: 9–11 are taken up and applied in chapter 5.

The Johannine Letters

The other catholic letters make us aware of a number of the doctrinal and ethical currents and cross-currents in the church's life in the later decades of the first century and beginning of the second.

The Johannine letters probably come from the province of Asia—the western part of the region to which 1 Pet. was sent. From 1 Jn we gather that there had been a considerable secession from the churches in that area in favour of a new and attractive form of teaching which its champions presented as an advance on what had been taught already. What were the criteria by which it might be known for certain whether this new teaching was right or wrong?

If, as is practically certain, the author of 1 Jn is 'the elder' by whom 2 Jn and 3 Jn were composed, he was in a position to be specially helpful to younger friends who were perplexed by the new teaching and recent secession. For he was known as 'the elder' probably not in any official sense but because he was a survivor from the first Christian generation—he belonged to those who had witnessed the saving events and followed Jesus during His Palestinian ministry. He could therefore give a well-informed answer to the question: Is this new teaching a faithful interpretation of the original gospel? No, said the elder, it is not. The original gospel—'that which was from the beginning' —is the message in which you were brought up, not this new teaching which some are finding so attractive. I know, because I was there; and I am writing to share with you what I saw and heard, together with my companions, in those early days when 'the eternal life which was with the Father . . . has appeared to us' (1 Jn 1: 2). So, 'see that what you have heard from the beginning remains in you' (2: 24). (The message which John says was 'from the beginning' is manifestly the same in essence as that proclaimed by Paul.)

That was one criterion; another was something which they could judge for themselves. The new teachers claimed to have reached an advanced stage in spiritual experience where they were beyond good and evil; they maintained that they had no sin, not in the sense that they had attained moral perfection but in the sense that what might be sin for those in a less mature stage of inward development was no longer sin for the perfectly spiritual man: for him ethical considerations had ceased to be relevant. To this the elder replies that ethical considerations can never cease to be relevant to the gospel. Since God is light, those who have fellowship with Him must live in the light; their character must be marked by goodness and truth—this is the Johannine counterpart to the injunction of 1 Pet. 1: 15, 'as he who called you is holy, so be holy in all you do'. Since Christ was pure and righteous, those who name His name must be pure and righteous too, and above all else they must love one another, in accordance with His commandment and example. The new teachers were not outstanding for love; on the contrary, they limited their illumination to an élite minority of specially gifted souls. But in the gospel the true illumination is for all believers without distinction: 'you, no less than they, are among the initiated; this is the gift of the Holy One, and by it you all have knowledge' (1 Jn 2: 20, NEB).

Moreover, these new teachers' interpretation of the gospel was so false that it had no right to be called Christian: they denied the incarnation, denied that Jesus Christ had come in a real human body. Whether this was maintained by argument or imparted by prophetic utterance, no matter; it must be refused. Prophetic utterance need not come from the Spirit of God;

it might come from some other spirit. Such utterances must be tested by their witness about Christ; if they refused to confess His true incarnation, then they proceeded manifestly from 'the spirit of the antichrist' (1 Jn 4: 3).

In this new teaching we can recognize adumbrations of second-century Gnosticism, which manifested itself in a rich variety of forms, but consistently maintained a sharp dualistic opposition between spirit and matter which menaced the Christian doctrines of creation, incarnation and resurrection. One of the forms it took was Docetism, which taught that the humanity (and therefore also the death) of Christ was only apparent, not real. Towards the end of the first century Cerinthus (traditionally the heresiarch whom 'the elder' more particularly opposed) taught that the Christ-spirit came upon the man Jesus at His baptism and left Him just before His death on the cross. This may explain the insistence in 1 Jn 5: 6 that Jesus Christ came 'by water and blood, . . . not . . . by water only, but by water and blood' (i.e. the Christ who was baptized is the Christ who truly died).

In 2 Jn the elder urges the church to which he is writing to give no countenance or hospitality to people who come with this subversive teaching; in 3 Jn he has to complain that in one of the churches over which he exercises spiritual authority his own messengers have been refused hospitality—although this may have been for reasons of personal rivalry rather than of doctrinal divergence. But in respect of church administration and theological debate alike we find ourselves in these letters on the eve of well-known second-century developments.

Jude and 2 Peter
The remaining catholic letters, Jude and 2 Pet., attack a form of incipient Gnosticism which, regarding matter as morally neutral, refused all ethical restraint on bodily actions. Jude describes those who take this line as 'ungodly persons who pervert the grace of our God into licentiousness' (Jude 4); in 2 Pet. they are condemned as misinterpreters of the gospel of free grace who argued, in terms earlier reprobated by Paul, that they should 'go on sinning so that grace may increase' (Rom. 6: 1), as 'ignorant and unstable' persons who 'distort to their own destruction' the writings of 'our dear brother Paul' (2 Pet. 3: 15 f.). Their antinomian excesses may be inferred from the fact that the judgment in store for them is viewed as being foreshadowed by the fall of the angels who were captivated by the daughters of men and by the destruction which overtook the cities of the plain (Jude 6 f.; 2 Pet. 2: 4 ff.)

These libertines called themselves 'spiritual' (Gk. *pneumatikoi*), but their lives showed them to be 'devoid of the Spirit' (Jude 19). When

Jude says that they 'set up divisions' (19), he probably has in mind their classification of mankind into the 'spiritual' (themselves), the 'psychic' (those whom they hoped to win to their way of thinking) and the 'carnal' (the rank outsiders, including all who were incurably wedded to the apostolic gospel). In fact, says Jude, it is they themselves who are 'psychic' ('who follow more natural instincts' NIV)—but he uses the word, as Paul does in 1 C. 2: 14, of 'the man without the Spirit' (RV 'the natural man') who 'does not accept the things that come from the Spirit of God, for they are foolishness to him, and he cannot understand them because they are spiritually discerned.' Just as the false teachers in 1 Jn are called 'antichrists' so here the libertines are called boasters (Jude 16), mouthing 'empty boastful words' (2 Pet. 2: 18), in language which echoes Daniel's description of the little horn with 'a mouth that spoke boastfully' (Dan. 7: 8) and of the wilful king who is to 'say unheard of things against the God of gods' (Dan. 11: 36) —OT figures on which the NT antichrist is modelled.

While 2 Pet. incorporates the substance of Jude, it adds further teaching of its own for the stabilizing of Christians who were in danger of being shaken from their foundations by current winds of change: in particular, it deals with the problem posed for some by the deferment of the parousia by reminding them that God does not reckon time as men do, and that if the day of the Lord is postponed, it is to provide men with a further opportunity for repentance: had not Paul himself said that God's kindness is meant to lead you to repentance (Rom. 2: 4)? But this divine kindness must not be abused: the day of the Lord will certainly come, with the dissolution of the present world-order and the introduction of 'a new heaven and a new earth, the house of righteousness' (2 Pet. 3: 13). And those who look for such a consummation must live lives of righteousness and peace here and now. The catholic letters are at one with the Pauline letters, and with the whole New Testament, in their emphasis on the ethical implications of the gospel.

BIBLIOGRAPHY

Brown, R. E., *The Community of the Beloved Disciple* (London, 1979).

Brown, R. E., *The Epistles of John* AB (Garden City, N.Y., 1982).

Bruce, F. F., *Men and Movements in the Primitive Church* (Exeter, 1979).

Bultmann, R., *The Johannine Epistles*, E.T. (Philadelphia, 1973)

Ehrhardt, A. A. T., 'Christianity before the

Apostles' Creed', *Harvard Theological Review* 55 (1962), pp.73–120, reprinted in *The Framework of the NT Stories* (Manchester, 1963). pp.151–199.

ELLIOTT-BINNS, L. E., *Galilean Christianity* (London, 1956).

FOERSTER, W., *Gnosis: A Selection of Gnostic Texts*, 2 vols. (Oxford, 1972–4).

GRANT, R. M., *Gnosticism and Early Christianity* (New York, 1959).

GRANT, R. M., *Gnosticism: An Anthology* (London, 1961).

GUTHRIE, D., *New Testament Introduction: Hebrews to Revelation* (London, 1962).

JONAS, H., *The Gnostic Religion* (Boston, 1958).

KELLY, J. N. D., *A Commentary on the Epistles of Peter and of Jude*, BNTC (London, 1969).

LOGAN, A. H. B., and WEDDERBURN, A. J. M. (ed.), *The New Testament and Gnosis: Essays in Honour of R. McL. Wilson* (Edinburgh, 1983).

MARSHALL, I. H., *The Epistles of John*. NICNT (Grand Rapids, 1978).

MOFFATT, J., *The General Epistles*. MNT (London, 1928).

REICKE, B., *The Epistles of James, Peter and Jude*. AB (Garden City, N. Y., 1964).

RUDOLPH, K., *Gnosis*, E.T. (Edinburgh, 1983).

STREETER, B. H., *The Primitive Church* (London, 1929).

WILSON, R. McL., *The Gnostic Problem* (London, 1958).

WILSON, R. McL., *Gnosis and the NT* (Oxford, 1968).

YAMAUCHI, E., *Pre-Christian Gnosticism* (Grand Rapids/London, 1973).

See also bibliographies appended to commentaries on the various General Letters in this volume.

THE NEW TESTAMENT USE OF THE OLD TESTAMENT

DAVID J. ELLIS

AN AUTHORITATIVE COURT OF APPEAL

The fact that the New Testament refers constantly to the Old Testament, both directly and indirectly, is clear from a casual reading of the Bible. Even the traditional system of marginal references, in spite of its obvious limitations, shows how frequently the NT writers made the scriptures of the OT their authoritative court of appeal.

It is axiomatic that the NT depends on the OT largely for its proper understanding, and that the books of the OT look to those of the NT for their ultimate fulfilment, not only in the prescribed realm of prophecy, but also in their entire mission and message. H. H. Rowley has said that 'it [NT] gathers up the Old Testament into the unity of the Christian Bible, but to illumine the Old with its own light. For the New Testament must be finally normative for the Christian understanding of the Old' (*The Re-discovery of the OT*, 1945, p. 11).

Of the one thousand or more direct references to or quotations of the OT in the NT, the greater majority seem to have been taken from the Septuagint. B. F. C. Atkinson ('The Textual Background of the Use of the OT by the New', *Journal of Transactions of the Victoria Institute*, 79, 1947, pp. 39–60) puts the figure at six out of every seven, and others would not vary widely in their judgment on the matter. Besides these direct references, however, there are many *allusions* to the OT in the NT which may be nothing more than a rhetorical device employed by some writer of the NT to give liveliness to a certain argument or train of thought. This literary method was common enough in Bible times, and can still be used effectively today. Nor should we be surprised that such a method was employed by NT writers, because both they and the characters of their pages would be men and women whose minds were usually soaked in the language of Scripture. Luke, for example, records the words addressed to Mary by aged Simeon (Lk. 2: 35) where it seems that when he said 'and a sword will pierce your own soul too' he had nothing else than the wording of Ps. 37: 15 running through his mind. It does not seem that an explicit reference to this scripture has

any vital part to play in the story; in fact, the original context of the psalm is retributive and has nothing whatever to do with the circumstances described in the nativity passage.

The NT writers apparently relied much upon memory. This fact must be taken into account when surveying their use of the OT. But the greater number of their references, even allusions, are fairly recognizable, though with varying degrees of accuracy and inaccuracy. It is one of the chief merits of the treatment of this subject by R. V. G. Tasker (*The OT in the NT*, 2nd edn., 1954) that he has helped us to recognize these references, scarcely apparent at times, and here and there nothing more than a mere phrase. But their identity, nonetheless, becomes clearer on examination of their texts and contexts. Atkinson (*op. cit.*, p. 40) has pointed out that this factor does not lend to much classification of OT quotations, except that the Psalms, in general, seem to have been more accurately quoted than most other parts of the OT. The reason for that fact would not be far to seek. Here, perhaps, it should be mentioned that there are clearly many quotations, which, in spite of their variations from one NT book to another, would appear to have been obtained from a prior collection of quotations, on account of their frequent usage in certain contexts. This question will be examined later.

In making reference to the OT, the NT writers clearly regarded it as their authority. The full consensus of the attitude taken by NT writers shows that they regarded the OT as the Word of God without question or reserve (Heb. 4: 12 f.). So Paul, for example, claims that 'the Scripture says . . .' (Rom. 10: 11; cf. Isa. 28: 16) and uses his reference as an authority for making an unassailable premiss, backed up by further appeal to the OT (Rom. 10: 13; cf. Jl 2: 32). This use of the OT by running together several passages is quite common in Paul, for as E. Earle Ellis has put it, 'the Scripture is adduced as a final authority and one divinely planned whole, whose significance is bound up inseparably with the New Testament Covenant Community of Christians' (*Paul's Use of the OT*, 1957, p. 25; cf. also F. F. Bruce, 'Promise and Fulfilment in Paul's Presentation of Jesus' in *Promise and Fulfilment*, essays presented to S. H. Hooke, 1963, pp. 36–50). This 'high' view of the Scriptures is reinforced in the NT by categorical statements concerning the nature of inspiration which it was believed the OT carried. So 2 Pet. 1: 20 is in no doubt about the matter. 'Above all, you must understand that no prophecy of Scripture came about by the prophet's own interpretation . . . For prophecy never had its origin in the will of man but men spoke from God as they were carried along by the Holy Spirit.' We may find the diffident attitude expressed by C. F. D. Moule on this statement (*The Birth of the NT*, ³1981, p. 81) one with which it is difficult to concur. For the juxtaposition of ideas seems clear enough. Our author seems to be saying that just because OT prophets and writers transmitted their messages under the direct influence of the Holy Spirit, it follows that their words can only be properly interpreted by the enlightening help of that same Spirit. And there can hardly be the thought in the writer's mind here that one's own interpretation might be set against the collective authority of the Church.

More than this, however, the fact of inspiration in the OT is made clear by the *mode of reference* which NT writers often employ. It seems evident here that they were following the example set by our Lord Himself in His view of the OT scriptures. Jesus (Mk 12: 36, cf. Mt. 22: 43) speaks of David (Ps. 110: 1) as 'speaking by the Holy Spirit'. In the earliest Christian preaching, Peter designates the utterances of David in the same manner as that 'which the Holy Spirit spoke . . .' (Ac. 1: 16–20; cf. Ps. 69: 25; 109: 8). Paul preaches in the same strain, and warns his congregation (Ac. 28: 25 ff.) that their refusal to heed the voice of the Scripture is indeed something foretold by Isaiah the prophet *in the Holy Spirit* (cf. Isa. 6: 9 f.). Such references as these, therefore, serve to underline that authority with which the NT brings its message out from the OT.

PRINCIPLES OF INTERPRETATION

These questions, however, raise the important matter with regard to the precise way in which the NT writers understood the OT, and how, in consequence, they adduced their references from the OT for the matter in hand. Is their use of the OT uniform, or was each one free to follow his own predilections? Did they inherit any formally accepted principle of Biblical interpretation, or did they bring some fresh, inspired understanding of the OT to light within their message? Moule has shown (*op. cit.*, pp. 68 ff.) that to understand the earliest Christian use of the OT three decisive factors have to be borne in mind. (i) Pre-Christian Judaism had certain stereotyped methods of exegesis. (ii) Jesus Himself inherited some of

these, it is plain, though He turned them inside out with perfect originality. (iii) And on to His controlling attitude towards the OT the early Church placed its conviction that 'the Spirit of Christ' who had inspired and guided the prophets of old, was now freshly active in Christ's people, awakening their minds to a vitally new understanding of the Scriptures.

Jewish exegetes believed that the very text of their Scriptures was inspired. Either that text was to be correctly understood through the channel of rabbinical schools of interpretation, or else, as was freely claimed by others, the individual reader could, by leaning solely upon the help of God, derive a perfect understanding of the meaning of Scripture. 2 Pet. 1: 20 f., indeed, may well have been addressed to such a situation. The basic presupposition all the way through, however, was that the revelation of God in the OT was final and complete. (The Targums, however, were by their nature interpretative translations of the Hebrew text, developed from certain oral traditions. Their influence is probably to be seen, here and there, in the NT interpretation of the OT, a notable example being Mk 4: 11 f. [cf. Mt. 13: 13]; cf. Isa. 6: 9 f., where we may possibly read 'that they may ever be seeing but never perceiving . . .' instead of Mark's that they may be ever seeing but never focussing or instead of Matthew's 'though seeing they do not see . . .'. Similar influences may lie behind Lk. 4: 18 f. [Isa. 61: 1 f.] and Eph. 4: 8 [cf. Ps. 68: 1]. For the importance of the Targums, cf. F. F. Bruce, *The Books and the Parchments*, 3rd edn., 1963, pp. 133 ff.)

But finality and completion do not rule out the possibility of fulfilment. If one thing marked the use of the OT by the Lord Jesus it was a profound sense of consummation. So, at Nazareth, when in the synagogue he declares 'Today this scripture is fulfilled in your hearing' (Lk. 4: 17–21), and the early Christians were not slow to follow up this dramatic appeal to the OT. J. A. Fitzmyer ('The Use of Explicit Old Testament Quotations in Qumran Literature and the New Testament', *New Testament Studies*, 7, 1961, pp. 297 ff.) has demonstrated how these early Christians believed that they were living in the last days, and how, accordingly, they were bound to understand the OT in eschatological terms. Peter, for example, on the day of Pentecost maintains that it 'was spoken by the prophet Joel: "in the last days, God says . . ."' and apparently alters the Septuagint reading, unless he is conflating a small phrase from Isa. 2: 2. But whatever it is, it is clear that he has quoted this prophecy concerning the outpouring of the Spirit in order to set the events of Pentecost, as a turning point in the purpose of God, at the dawn of the age of the Messiah. This also means that Peter saw the Pentecost events as revelatory, which therefore could rightly be understood only by appeal to OT scriptures. But such apocalyptic tendencies were by no means confined to early Christians. The use of the OT made by the Qumran sect goes along similar lines, but with significant differences which leave the NT use of the OT still unique. It was characteristic of the Qumran commentators to provide a running commentary (Heb. *pesher*) along with the text they were citing. Something approaching this can be detected here and there in the NT (*e.g.*, Mt. 26: 31; cf. Mk 14: 27; Lk. 4: 21; Jn 13: 18; Ac. 2: 16, etc.). Generally speaking the men of Qumran saw in a given passage a number of ideas which were germane to their own preferences of interpretation, and for which they consequently sought a contemporary application and justification. The *Habakkuk Commentary* is a classic example of this.

But in contrast NT commentators usually appeal to a passage in its entirety, seeking to understand and underline its fundamental message. So in Ac. 15: 15 ff. James, referring to Am. 9: 11 f., sees in the resurrection and exaltation of the Lord the fulfilment of that prophet's oracle concerning the restoration of the Davidic house. Some attention to the matter of contextual considerations on the part of the NT has been given by S. L. Edgar ('Respect for Context in Quotations from the OT', *New Testament Studies*, 9, 1962, pp. 55–62). He concludes, having allowed for factors in translation, that in many of such quotations there seems to be little point, or else, at best, the quotation has been made in the interests of pushing home some basic religious tenet. Among a number of instances of this Edgar draws our attention, for example, to the use made by Paul of Isa. 28: 16 in Rom. 10: 11, *viz.*, 'Everyone who trusts in him will never be put to shame'. We may put aside the question of Paul's rendering of the Isaiah passage at this point, except to point out Paul's addition of 'all' (Gk. *pas*) to indicate the universality of salvation. Or, again, Paul's use of Isa. 52: 5 (in Rom. 2: 24) Edgar maintains has been freely adduced to show the effects upon the heathen of the helplessness of God's people. This may be true of the original context of the Isaiah passage, but, as Lindars and others have shown, there is a shift of application in perfect accord with the change of circumstances. Says Lindars (*New Testament Apologetic*, 1961, p. 22): 'It is the Jews' failure to keep the Law which [now] causes the scandal, rather than God's failure to act'.

The difference in exegetical method between Qumran and the NT is seen even more clearly in the attitude which each adopts towards the old Israel in relation to the new situation. For the men of Qumran the old order, after a temporary period of substitutionary offerings and the like, would be restored in a purified form, and their community life, indeed, was built around the expectation of establishing a ritualistic system without delay when the new age dawned. But with the NT it is different. The Church is the new Israel (Gal. 6: 16). Its members constitute a 'chosen people, a royal priesthood . . .' (1 Pet. 2: 9). Just as the Passover and Exodus had heralded the birth of a chosen race in the OT, so now the exodus of the Christ (Lk. 9: 31) and His paschal death (1 C. 5: 7) have brought into existence this new nation in the purpose of God. No longer can it be imagined, affirms the NT, that the old order is to be revived, purified and re-established. The new order is, indeed, linked with the old in God's purpose, in that the promise given to Abraham (Rom. 4) is fulfilled in all, Jews and Gentiles alike, who are now united to Christ by faith. And to this the prophets of the OT give their witness. It is not surprising, therefore, that the difference between Qumran exegesis and NT exegesis of the OT should finally be crystallized in certain messianic passages. F. F. Bruce shows (*Biblical Exegesis in the Qumran Texts*, 1960, pp. 75 f.) that both the men of Qumran and the earliest Christians saw that the OT pointed forward to the coming of a great prophet, a prominent priest, and a majestic king. The difference of interpretation, however, between the two is clearly that in Qumran the three figures are kept distinct till the end of the age, whereas in the NT they are all three clearly seen as perfectly fulfilled in the Lord Jesus (Heb. 1: 1 ff., 8 f.). 'Here, then, is the key to that distinctive interpretation of the Old Testament which we find in the New Testament. Jesus has fulfilled the ancient promises, and in fulfilling them He has given them a new meaning . . . more comprehensive and far-reaching than was foreseen before He came' (Bruce, *op. cit.*, p. 77).

Our Lord's use of the OT is marked by frequent appeal to certain well-known prophetic passages which were also employed by others in the NT. Possibly the most distinctive of these are His references to the Son of Man. A. J. B. Higgins (*Jesus and the Son of Man*, 1964, pp. 185 ff.) has recently tabulated three categories in Jesus' sayings concerning this figure. There are those which concern his earthly activity (*e.g.* Mk. 2: 10; Lk. 9: 58 [Mt. 8: 20]; 19: 10), others which speak of his sufferings (*e.g.*, Mk 8: 31; Lk. 24: 7), and others which announce his forthcoming glorification (*e.g.*, Mk 8: 38; Lk. 12: 40 [Mt. 24: 44]; 21: 36; Mt. 24: 30). In spite of many different views on these quotations it seems clear that the historical-eschatological figure of Dan. 7: 13 is in mind, and that other possible literary sources do not fit the various NT contexts so well.

'Who is this "Son of man"?' (Jn 12: 34) asked Jesus' hearers on one occasion. To them, the twin ideas of the eternity of the Messiah, and the suffering of the Son of man, to which Jesus had plainly referred, were mutually exclusive. But the Lord teaches that it is by way of death that His 'lifting up' must take place. The coming of the Danielic Son of man is made actual at His crucifixion, as, indeed, Jesus also indicated, the world would also stand judged (Jn 12: 31). However much the symbol in Dan. 7 may primarily refer to a faithful group within Israel, Jesus clearly applied the symbol to Himself as the Representative of that people, humiliated for the moment, but later to be glorified. And in view of this it is difficult to accept Higgins's statement that 'Jesus said nothing whatever about himself as the Son of man. He referred to him as if to a future advocate, witness or judge. He also spoke of His own mission . . . But in his teaching on these matters the idea of the Son of man played no part' (*op. cit.*, pp. 199 f.).

THE USE OF 'TESTIMONIES'

Similar unravelling of prophetic passages can be seen in Jesus' great saying concerning 'the stone which the builders rejected . . .' (Mk 12: 10; Mt. 21: 42; Lk. 20: 17 f.; cf. Ps. 118: 22 f.). Jesus' claim to be the Messiah is well-founded by the fact that the religious experts, to whom 'builders' refers, instead of recognizing Him for what He was, rejected Him, who was that stone most vital for the erecting of a new edifice. It was the presence of such 'stone passages' which primarily led Rendel Harris (*Testimonies*, 1916–1920), largely following E. Hatch (*Essays in Biblical Greek*, 1889) to postulate books of *Testimonies* from which he believed NT writers probably adduced their authority for the message of Jesus as the Messiah. Such books of *Testimonies* are known to have been used by Cyprian of Carthage and others of the early Fathers, and Harris believed that at least one such may underlie the OT quotations in the NT. It is clear, of course, that there are certain passages which recur with significant variations or connections with other OT texts. The 'stone passages' are one example. Whatever may be said with regard to the recurrence of these quotations, it is clear that their usage in different parts of the NT was for different expositional purposes, and that, indeed, the various contexts show how differing doctrinal emphases are underlined by their presence.

We have already seen that our Lord's use of a 'stone passage' (Ps. 118: 22) is purely for the purpose of confounding the claim of religious leaders who rejected His authority. Peter, however, uses the same reference (Ac. 4: 11 f.) to show that the resurrection was an event at one with the mood of the Psalm. Another important use of the same reference is in 1 Pet. 2: 1–10 where it is conflated with Isa. 8: 14 and 28: 16. The two latter 'stone passages' are employed as a commentary on the first. Christ, writes Peter, was the 'stone' rejected by men but exalted by God. Yet the significance of the events in His life is that He was (and is) 'chosen and precious' (1 Pet. 2: 6) and therefore worthy of trust. But to unbelievers He becomes 'a stone that will cause men to stumble . . .' (1 Pet. 2: 8). And here, it may be added, the stone seems to be even more firmly and closely identified with the Person of our Lord, as against the possible analogical use of the text by Jesus Himself.

Barnabas Lindars argues that, by their text forms and functions in their NT contexts, such 'testimonies' reflect a final 'atomistic' stage of selection, in which they are detached from their original setting, and by this means he seeks to add greater weight to the *Testimonies* theory (*op. cit.*, pp. 272 ff.; cf. also L. Morris, *The New Testament and the Jewish Lectionaries*, 1964, pp. 53–63). But such selection might not be so arbitrary as might at first appear. Even the 'formula quotations' suggested by K. Stendahl (*The School of St. Matthew*, 1954, pp. 162 f.) in his examination of the use of the OT made by Matthew and John, could be accounted for as a compilation of texts, sometimes combined with others, to form their own commentary, as we have already said. It can certainly be shown that a *proof text* has been commonly abbreviated by a number of NT writers, as in the case of the use made by Matthew, John and Revelation, of Zech. 12 (Mt. 24: 30; Jn 19: 37; Rev. 1: 7; cf. Zech. 12: 10–14). Lindars examined this example thoroughly (*op. cit.*, pp. 122–127). He sees, apart from an initial desire on the part of the NT to free the required text from its original context, certain differences of application. So, Matthew restricts himself to the apocalyptic suddenness of Christ's appearing in triumph, causing the unbelieving Jews to wail. Thus he separates Zechariah from the Passion story as such. John, on the other hand, retains the Passion significance entirely, and with the additional evidence of Ps. 34: 20 sees in the OT a prediction of the wounding of the Saviour's side with the spear (not as Matthew who uses the same text to refer to the wailing at the appearance of the 'sign of the Son of man'). And in Revelation we have almost a total occupation with the return of Christ and the grief shared by humanity at the sight of His wounds—not like Matthew, again, who warns a somewhat smaller body who might feel responsibility for the actual crucifying of Jesus.

Zechariah, indeed, figures prominently in the Passion Narrative, and its place among the *Testimonies* might well be all-important. What is important, clearly, regarding its place in the

Gospels is, as F. F. Bruce has said that 'the Evangelists saw such a clear correspondence between the prophetic *testimonia* and the events to which the apostles and their colleagues testified . . .' ('The Book of Zechariah and the Passion Narrative', *Bulletin of the John Rylands Library*, 43, 1960–61, p. 353).

The Lord also referred to popular expectations concerning Elijah *redivivus*, and applied them to the person and mission of John the Baptist (Mk 9: 13; Mt. 17: 12; cf. Mal. 4: 5) and related them also to His own forthcoming sufferings at the hands of the elders, chief priests and scribes. But more than this, Jesus may well have implied that what the prophet had had to say concerning the coming Day of the Lord was to be inaugurated through His Passion.

That Jesus used certain well-known OT passages is clear. It would not be surprising, therefore, to find that the writers of the NT followed His example in this. Does it follow, however, that these facts are only explicable by positing the existence of books of *Testimonies*? Rendel Harris concluded that they were only understandable on some such hypothesis, since many of these recurring quotations, often in forms differing from the Septuagint, were grouped together in sequences, and even cited, occasionally, as having come from a single OT author (*e.g.*, Mt. 27: 9 f. cited as 'Jeremiah'; but cf. Zech. 11: 12 f.; Jer. 32: 6–15) so as to suggest that they were once contained in a single collection. Harris's case has been somewhat supported by the Qumran discoveries in that the Scrolls from the Dead Sea have brought to light certain messianic collections (4Q *Testimonia*) and certain other expository or homiletic collections (*midrashim*) besides specifically selected collections of texts with pesher commentary (4Q *Florilegium*), which would show that such collections did exist among some pre-Christian communities. (Lindars, however, would not see anything in these Qumran documents comparable to Harris's *Testimonia* because it is not certain whether they were for public use or were only private collections of *memoranda*.)

C. H. Dodd has examined the use of OT quotations in the NT very closely, and in his valuable work on the subject (*According to the Scriptures*, 1952) he has indicated some of the difficulties lying behind Harris's suggestions, not least the mystery that, if such *Testimonia* collections did exist and were used by the early Christians in the formation of the NT, they have apparently disappeared. And Harris's attention to the non-Septuagintal quotations is not quite so fundamental as might appear since these are not so numerous, either where *one* agrees with the Septuagint, or where *both disagree*. On the contrary, Dodd has shown that there are obviously some books, or parts of

books, of the OT which are very frequently laid under quotation in the NT. These quotations are usually quite short, however, and rarely do we find that some passage is quoted at length. But closer examination will show that there are also large tracts of OT territory which hardly, if ever, appear in the NT. And again, a particular cluster of quotations may all be used by a single NT writer, *e.g.*, Exodus and Leviticus will be seen again and again in the Letter to the Hebrews. This fact may, of course, be accounted for by the predilections of the author of Hebrews, but where, in other circumstances, references begin to accumulate from a variety of NT books it would suggest that certain parts of the OT were of special interest to the writers of the NT. Dodd has clearly shown, too, that there is, in fact, a fairly large body of lengthy quotations which suggests that, from a very early date, Christians appealed to a body of *Scripture* for the preaching of their message.

PATTERNS OF FULFILMENT

A striking and obvious example of lengthy or detailed quotation is that of the use made by NT writers of Isa. 53. There are some twelve verses in our text of this chapter, and one only of these possibly does not appear in the NT either by direct reference or indirect allusion. No one author quotes Isa. 53 very extensively, and it is rare for more than a single writer in the NT to quote the same verse. Philip (Ac. 8: 32 f.) uses two verses, but in a situation which indicates that he had the entire chapter before him. The rest of Isa. 53 appears, or is alluded to, in all four Gospels, Romans, Philippians, Hebrews, and 1 Peter. Dodd claims that, in fact, if all of the original text of Isa. 53 had been lost it would not necessarily have been irretrievable, but possible to restore almost the whole chapter in Greek translation. This shows that however the NT writers might seem, on the face of it, to have selected their material for shortened quotations very carefully, yet this chapter *considered as a whole* had outstanding significance for the understanding and presentation of the Christian message on the part of its first preachers.

Moreover it is apparent that the NT use of Isa. 53 is coloured by an interpretation which sees in that passage a 'plot', to use Dodd's own word, which is repeated substantially, yet with minor variations, in most of the OT passages quoted *in extenso* by the NT. In general this plan marks out the submission and suffering of one person, or group of persons, clearly intended to portray the Servant of the Lord. This Servant submits to insults and suffering, and finally, death, or, if the picture be of a nation, extinction. But this loving obedience is rewarded with triumphant exaltation through the grace of God.

There are at least two other passages, apart from Dan. 7, which speak of the Son of Man, and which reveal the same basic pattern. Ps. 80 vividly describes, with the aid of colourful imagery, the experiences of the people of God in prosperity and adversity. The vine which formerly flourished is ravaged by wild beasts, until the poet exclaims 'Return to us, O God Almighty! Look down from heaven and see! Watch over this vine . . .' (Ps. 80: 14). But after this the picture changes, and the prayer becomes 'Let your hand rest on the man at your right hand, the son of man you have raised up for yourself' (v. 17). The psalm is never expressly quoted, yet we can see how, and where, it has supplied some of the standing imagery of the NT. The same expression occurs in Ps. 8: 4, a passage several times quoted directly in the NT (cf. Mt. 21: 16; 1 C. 15: 27; Eph. 1: 22), yet only extensively in one place (Heb. 2: 6 ff.). There 'son of man' stands for humanity, and the writer sees the crown of glory, which God destines man to wear, as having already been awarded to Jesus Christ.

Joel is fairly often quoted in the NT, particularly ch. 2–3. The Day of the Lord is heralded by the emergence of a renovated people of God, possibly seen as the Son of man, or Servant in another guise.

Already we have seen that the Book of Zechariah is extensively quoted in the narrative of events towards the close of our Lord's earthly life. In particular the two oracles (Zech. 9–11; 12–14), whose interrelation is not certain, essentially constitute an apocalyptic message concerning the Day of the Lord. First there is the kingly figure who enters Zion, meek and riding upon an ass (Mt. 21: 4 f.; cf. Mk 11: 1–10; Jn 12: 14 f.), and then the scene closes with all the nations coming up to worship at Jerusalem in honour of God their King. In the middle, however, there is a wealth of material much used by the Evangelists for corroboration of events during Passion Week. Basically, in the prophecy's original setting there is the picture of Israel, as the flock of God, passing through several stages of rebellion against God, incurring the punishment she richly deserves, in the course of which the shepherd is smitten and the flock scattered. So in spite of suffering which is deserved there is a glimpse of a leader who is humiliated, but who comes through in triumph. Lindars (*op. cit.*, pp. 110–134) has given close attention to the passage and has shown that the Evangelist sifted his material in order to demonstrate that the very details of Passion Week—the triumphal Entry (cf. Zech. 9: 9), the treachery of Judas (cf. 11: 12 f.) and the scattering of the sheep (13: 7)—indicate that the messianic claim of Jesus is built into the twin patterns of atonement and the wrath of God. The text of Zechariah is abbreviated to draw attention solely to the point at issue in the Passion story, namely, that each event in that story was decisive, and played a vital part in the final drama in which the 'blood of the covenant' (Zech. 9: 11; Mt. 26: 28) preceded the inauguration of the kingdom (Mt. 26: 29; Zech. 9: 10).

Each of these scriptures mentioned is a record or commentary on events which happened in the course of the history of Israel. Moreover the way that these prophets, of different periods, interpret the history of their own times, and forecast the future in its light, shows that they understood that the entire course of that history demonstrated certain fundamental principles upon which God worked His plan for the nation. The Day of the Lord was to be the culmination of vision to which they appealed. And it is from Acts 2 onwards that we see how the early Church recognized that the Day of the Lord had dawned in fact, in the events of the humiliation, death and resurrection of Christ (cf. Peter's quotation and application of Jl 2: 31 on the day of Pentecost). So to make clear this conviction, and to justify it, the NT writers appealed, in their turn, to prophetic passages which spoke both of the Day of the Lord and of the events which led up to it. The hope and fears of the prophets were at last realized and consummated in Christ. So, Peter, in bringing the message of Christ to Cornelius, announced that Christ is 'the one whom God appointed as judge of the living and dead. All the prophets testify about him' (Ac. 10: 42 f.). Dodd concludes, therefore, that the whole body of prophetic passages as adduced by NT writers, Luke, Acts, John, Paul, the author of Hebrews, and 1 Peter, provided the 'substructure' of their theology, which they believed underlined the fact that the events of history, which took place under Pontius Pilate, nevertheless could be seen also as a demonstration of 'God's set purpose and foreknowledge' (Ac. 2: 23).

ALLEGORY AND TYPE

Mention must be made, however, of two uses to which the OT was distinctively put by NT writers which have so far been omitted from this discussion. In the world of the NT there was a widely accepted method of interpreting ancient literature, which, though regarded as authoritative, presented certain problems for the commentator. This was the allegorical method of interpretation. It was employed by Jewish exegetes, largely under the leadership of Philo of Alexandria. Its purpose was not so much to give the would-be expositor a freedom which was best served by a very fruitful imagination, but to avoid certain difficulties which the traditional text presented to the Greek mind, and also to give some weight to philosophical ideas with which, of course, the original authors of the text can hardly have been acquainted. Perhaps it is surprising, at first sight, that such a method is not more frequently found in the NT than appears to be the case. Paul's treatment of the episode of Hagar and Ishmael (Gal. 4: 21–31) is, as the apostle expressly states, allegorical (Gal. 4: 24, Gk. *hatina estin allēgoroumena*). Hagar stands for Sinai, the mountain of the law, and Ishmael, her son, for the Jews as the sons of the law. Isaac, the promised child, resembles the Church, afflicted under suffering, and the whole argument of Galatians up to this point in the letter, *viz.*, the antipathy of faith and the law, is thus pictured. Then Paul, as we have already seen, runs together other passages (*e.g.*, Isa. 54: 1) to serve as a commentary on the whole section.

In the allegory it is not the original historical context (Gen. 16 and 21) or the original intention of its author that is expounded (see p. 453). This means that the OT supplies certain imagery which alone is sufficient for the later re-inforcement of some NT idea. But the idea itself is not derived *from* the OT. Paul, it may well be, is answering certain objections from Jewish circles which had presumably employed some allegorical method against his own mode of exegesis, so that he turns round the argument by the very means used by his opponents. This alone should be sufficient warning for the modern exegete with regard to a dangerous form of biblical interpretation.

Moreover, the fact that such examples of true allegory are uncommon in the NT makes it fairly evident that another method of OT exegesis used by NT writers, similar to it, should, however, be kept distinct. This is the *typological* method. E. Earle Ellis (*op. cit.*, p. 126) rightly says of Paul's employment of this method that '"type" used as an exegetical method has . . . a much more restricted meaning than *typos* would suggest . . .'. We may disagree, however, with Ellis's designation of the Hagar-Ishmael episode as typological. There a number of other figures would have served Paul's argument, and in any case, as we have already suggested, he does not take much of the original historical situation into account. But with restricted typology it is different. Adam, in a unique setting, becomes a type of which Christ is the antitype (Rom. 5); that Christ is a new and better 'Adam' is what he has in mind to say, and that Christ's saving work is extended in its effects to all men, just as Adam's sin extended in its effects beyond him. Thus, Adam 'was a pattern of the one to come' (Rom. 5: 14). (There is the further correlation between Adam and Christ in that

both stand at the head of a course of events: Adam, at the beginning of history; Christ, at the beginning of salvation-history. In the same way, in 1 C. 15: 20 ff., to be 'in Adam' is to belong to the natural order. To be 'in Christ' [cf. Rom. 5: 17] is to receive all the blessings of the new age. Cf. J. Munck, *Paul and the Salvation of Mankind*, 1959.)

Again, the Paschal Lamb (Exod. 12) is yet another type of Christ 'our Passover lamb' (1 C. 5: 7) in that historical events associated with that sacred meal both have their counterpart, as well as direct fulfilment, in Christ. Further (1 C. 10), Paul uses the word 'type' to denote an association between the OT and the Christian message. Twice over he uses it in 1 C. 10: 'Now these are examples (Gk. *typoi*) for us . . .' (1 C. 10: 6), and 'These things happened to them as examples . . .' (v. 11, Gk. *typikōs*). E. E. Ellis (*op. cit.*, p. 126) associates this passage with other strict typological exegesis in Paul and elsewhere. But the sense of Paul's words in this passage, brought out well by the RSV, would suggest that he was comparing Israel's sin with that kind of sin which seems to beset God's people in every age, so that just as Israel fell by the wayside in the desert by reason of her unbelief and disobedience, so also today, Christian people, for the selfsame reason, are tempted to fall on one side from the path of holy and obedient living in accordance with the will of God. This means no more than that Paul is saying that Israel's trouble turns out, on reflection, to be a *typical* trouble, and that there is no further significance than this for his use of the term *typos*, which, elsewhere, however, might have a much more technical connotation.

There is an important example of explicit typology in Hebrews. Apart from some cases of imprecise typology (*e.g.*, Moses, ch. 3; Aaron, ch. 5, etc.) it is with the figure of Melchizedek (ch. 7) that the writer works out his thesis with some care. As is his custom, the author first quotes a psalm—in this case the much-quoted Ps. 110—and then enlightens this quotation by reference to OT narrative, here Gen. 14. First in significance for Hebrews is the name *Malki-ṣedeq* 'king of righteousness' and 'king of peace', the latter being treated as another rendering for the original 'Salem' for Jerusalem (Gen. 14: 18). F. F. Bruce ('Hebrews' in *Peake's Commentary*, 1962, p. 1,013) suggests also that 'the collocation of righteousness and peace is naturally found suggestive' (cf. Isa. 32: 17) to the writer (cf. also F. C. Synge, *Hebrews and the Scriptures*, 1959). Further, however, Melchizedek is a priest for ever, another typological factor, and the indication that the circumstances of his birth and death are not mentioned in the OT combines to make this mysterious OT priest a most fitting type of

Christ, whose priesthood knows no end, and the suggestion of the author of Hebrews is reinforced in his exposition by appeal to yet another strange fact that Levi, who 'was in the body of his ancestor' (Heb. 7: 10) paid Melchizedek tithes in the person of Abraham, thus suggesting that the priesthood which Melchizedek typified is greater even than that of Levi.

In the NT there are two instances of the use of the term 'antitype' as a definitive expression (Heb. 9: 24; 1 Pet. 3: 21). The first of these presents little difficulty to the modern commentator. Christ, says the writer, has not entered into an earthly sanctuary, 'a copy of the true one' (Gk. *antitypa tōn alēthinōn*) but into heaven itself. The antitype here is substantive. Both the earthly sanctuary and the heavenly counterpart represent the same spiritual original, namely, entrance into the holy presence of God.

But the type-antitype relationship in 1 Pet. 3: 21 is not so clear, though E. G. Selwyn (*The First Epistle of Peter*, 2nd edn., 1961, pp. 298 f.) has made out a good case for taking baptism 'which corresponds to this' (so RSV), i.e. the flood water, to mean that the Flood only faintly indicated that perfect salvation which is dramatized in baptism.

It will be seen, therefore, that with typological interpretation in the NT there was a certain amount of flexibility. Yet throughout we may discern a number of basic principles underlying typological exegesis. The type always has its own place and meaning independently of what it may prefigure. Thus the Flood brought disaster to mankind in Gen. 7 but salvation to those who found refuge in the Ark. Or, the paschal lamb of Exod. 12 brought to fulfilment the promise of deliverance to the captive people of Israel, even apart from the greater sacrifice which it came to symbolize. Thus the NT writers never destroyed the historical sense of OT scripture in order to establish some spiritual lesson from its pages. Nor did they find some intricate hidden meaning in the original text before them, but a plain and straightforward meaning. And they seem to have confined the typological method to discover prophetic indications of fundamental doctrines affecting the Person of Christ, or the life and practice of the NT Church. The value of such basic 'rules' will be apparent to the modern commentator.

In spite of Dodd's wish to limit the texts from which the primitive preachers may be thought to have preached and reasoned, he would not, of course, limit their acquaintance with the general substance of the OT. Indeed, examination of typological interpretation in Paul's writings and elsewhere shows how the minds of the NT writers could range over a vast area of the OT. And this fact, whilst assuring us of their knowledge of the OT, also serves as a brake against finding unnecessary typological material where it was not originally intended. It is quite possible, even in modern times, for a writer to have an idea or an image in his mind effectively enough to shape what he says without his being aware of it at all. Whether or not, for example, our Lord's words 'I will give you the keys of the kingdom of heaven' (Mt. 16: 19) is a deliberate allusion, as Tasker (*The Old Testament in the New Testament*, 2nd edn., 1954) would suggest, to Isa. 22: 22, it is certain that the one text has contributed to the formation of the other. (More explicit reference to the Isaiah text, however, is made in Rev. 3: 7.)

THE 'AMEN' TO GOD'S PURPOSES

What is clear in the NT use of the OT is that, from a multiplicity of OT quotations, the NT writers brought their message to bear upon a certain series of undisputed facts comprising the gospel story. The diversity and richness of their use of the OT scriptures, woven together into a single strand, enabled them to affirm with confidence that these scriptures demonstrated 'God's set purpose and foreknowledge' (Ac. 2: 23) and its consequent fulfilment. Climactically, the NT writers saw fulfilled in Christ the involved and very diverse prophecies concerning the Servant of the Lord and the Son of man. If the former figure be understood as basically the nation of Israel in its entirety, then Christ is the true Israel, and all who are 'in Christ' are heirs to the promises, though we should, possibly, hesitate to go further, as L. C. Allen does ('The Old Testament in Romans I-VIII', *Vox Evangelica* III, 1964, p. 23), to project the image so as to include Paul as a special emissary of the gospel. The Son of man figure, whether he be taken as an individual representing the whole people or not, is clearly understood in the NT as a prophetic prefiguring of Christ, who, as Man, would by suffering, death and exaltation achieve all that God designed for humanity.

For the NT writers the Passion of our Lord was decisive for any proper understanding of the prophetic adumbration of the NT message. Indeed, there are a number of passages which speak of Christ's pre-existent activity in such a manner as makes Him both subject and object of OT prophecy. Paul identifies the rock (Exod. 17: 6) with Christ (1 C. 10: 4). And the prophets, writes Peter, who foretold of the grace which should be shown us, were moved by 'the Spirit of Christ in them was pointing when he predicted the sufferings of Christ and the glories that would follow' (1 Pet. 1: 11).

The great stream of the scriptures, therefore, broadens with the emergence of the NT. But it is an extension of that former revelation, and at the same time, the guarantee which authenticates its normative importance (2 Tim. 3: 14–17). And of course, the divine inspiration given to the writers of the NT was such that, as C. F. D. Moule puts it, 'they came to scripture from an already given experience, and had only to read in its main contours and its living story the confirmation that what they had experienced was not alien, though so new; it was the climax, the culmination, the "Amen" to all God's purposes (2 C. 1: 20)' (*The Birth of the New Testament*, 1981, p. 90). And there can, after all, be no greater authority for the preaching of the Christian message, in any age, than that Christ's saving work was completed 'according to the Scriptures' (1 C. 15: 3 f.).

BIBLIOGRAPHY

ALLEN, L. C., 'The Old Testament in Romans I–VIII' (*Vox Evangelica* III, 1964).

BRUCE, F. F., *The Books and the Parchments* (London, 1950; 3rd edition, 1963).

BRUCE, F. F., *This is That: The New Testament Development of Some Old Testament Themes* (Exeter, 1968).

BRUCE, F. F., *The Time is Fulfilled* (Exeter, 1978).

BRUCE, F. F., *Biblical Exegesis in the Qumran Texts* (London, 1960).

DODD, C. H., *According to the Scriptures* (London, 1952).

ELLIS, E. E., *Paul's Use of the Old Testament* (Edinburgh, 1957).

FREED, E. D., *Old Testament Quotations in the Gospel of John* (Leiden, 1965).

GOPPELT, L., *Typos: The Typological Interpretation of the Old Testament in the New*, E.T. (Grand Rapids, 1982).

GUILDING, A., *The Fourth Gospel and Jewish Worship* (Oxford, 1960).

HARRIS, J. R., *Testimonies*, i,ii (Cambridge 1916, 1920).

HANSON, A. T., *Jesus Christ in the Old Testament* (London, 1965).

HANSON, A. T., *The Living Utterances of God* (London, 1983).

HEBERT, A. G., *The Authority of the Old Testament* (London, 1947).

LINDARS, B., *New Testament Apologetic* (London, 1961).

LONGENECKER, R. N., *Biblical Exegesis in the Apostolic Period* (Grand Rapids, 1975).

McNEILE, A. H., *The Old Testament in the Christian Church* (London, 1913).

MANSON, T. W., *The Servant-Messiah* (Cambridge, 1953; reprinted 1961).

MANSON, T. W., *The Teaching of Jesus*, 2nd edition (Cambridge, 1935; reprinted 1963).

MORRIS, L., *The New Testament and the Jewish Lectionaries* (London, 1964).

MOULE, C. F. D., *The Birth of the New Testament* (London, ³1981).

MOWINCKEL, S., *He That Cometh*, Eng. trans. by G. W. Anderson (Oxford, 1956).

ROBINSON, H. W., *The Cross in the Old Testament* (London, 1955).

STAUFFER, E., *New Testament Theology*, Eng. trans. by John Marsh (London, 1955)

STENDAHL, K., *The School of St. Matthew* (Uppsala, 1954).

SUNDBERG, A. C., *The Old Testament of the Early Church* (Oxford, 1964).

TASKER, R. V. G., *The Old Testament in the New Testament*, 2nd edition (London, 1954).

WENHAM, J. W., *Our Lord's View of the Old Testament* (London, 1958).

PART FOUR
THE NEW TESTAMENT

MATTHEW

H. L. ELLISON

Preliminary Remarks

Mt. raises so many wider problems, to which must be added others affecting all four gospels, that the exegesis has had to be kept as short as possible. Wherever practicable the reader is referred to the treatment of parallels in other gospels. Writers are cited by name only; the title of the work will be found in the Bibliography. All points of Jewish practice and teaching have been checked with Strack & Billerbeck (cited as *SB*); hence citations are rarely necessary.

Authorship

The reader should turn first to the essay on *The Fourfold Gospel*. Mt. is strictly anonymous, i.e. we derive the name from early Christian tradition and usage, not from any hints in the gospel (for 9: 10 cf. comment *ad loc.*). This tradition is of doubtful value, for though it was firmly established by the time of Irenaeus (*c.* 180), it seems in every case to go back to Papias (*c.* 130). He affirms, 'Matthew compiled the oracles (*ta logia*) in Heb. and everyone translated them as best he could'. 'Oracles' is not a normal name for a gospel, and the present Gk. text of Mt. is certainly no ordinary translation. If Matthew had re-written his gospel in Gk., Papias would surely have said so.

If we accept the view that the writer of Mt. used Mk, it becomes virtually impossible to see our Mt. in Papias's tradition. It seems preferable to assume that the anonymous writer combined Mk with other material, mainly Matthew's 'oracles', which will have contained chiefly teaching; thus Matthew's name has been linked with the gospel as a whole.

This view is supported by Tasker, pp. 11–17. Stonehouse, in a thoroughly conservative study, though he supports Matthew as author, agrees that he used Mk (ch. 2) and denies the gospel is a translation (ch. 3). Guthrie (pp. 31–42, 126–132) reaches similar conclusions, after giving most of the rival views.

Date and Purpose

Except where Mt. is considered the earliest gospel it is normally dated between 75 and 80, but cf. Robinson. Its author, who could have known Matthew, if he was not the apostle, was a member of a church, possibly that of Antioch, where Jewish Christians were numerous, but he did not write exclusively for them. The gospel was intended to serve the church as a teaching manual. This explains its exceptional fivefold structure (see below).

This fivefold division gave rise recently to the view that we have here a Christian Pentateuch, with the Sermon on the Mount taking the place of the Law-giving at Sinai. It is now realized that Mt. breaks the fetters of any such artificial categories, including the older ones of Jewish Gospel, Royal Gospel, etc. Rather, to the Church, to whom the privileges of Israel have been extended, is presented a rounded picture of its King.

Already Papias commented on the lack of chronological order in Mk, and Cole, p. 35, shows convincingly that this derives from Peter's purposes as a teacher. What Mk did for the narrative, Mt. carried further and did to the teaching as well, adding extra illustrative material to the great centres of teaching. All the teaching is Christ's, but we must not assume that it was necessarily all given in the context in which we now find it.

ANALYSIS

Prologue: Birth and Infancy (1: 1–2: 23)

I   i   Narrative: Proclamation and Appearance of the Messiah (3: 1–4: 25)
    ii   Teaching: The Sermon on the Mount (5: 1–7: 29)

II   i   Narrative: Miracles in Galilee (8: 1–9: 34)
    ii   Teaching: The Mission of the Twelve (9: 35–11: 1)

III   i   Narrative: Growing Hostility (11: 2–12: 50)
    ii   Teaching: The Kingdom of Heaven (13: 1–52)

PROLOGUE: BIRTH AND INFANCY (1: 1–2: 23)

The Genealogy (1: 1–17)

Cf. Lk. 3: 23–38. It may be taken for granted that both genealogies are of Joseph, that in Mt. showing his legal claim to the throne, that in Lk. giving his actual descent. The view that Lk. gives Mary's genealogy conflicts with the language, seems to have been unknown in the early Church and first achieved prominence *c.* 1490 (*HDB*, II, p. 138b). For the reconciliation of the genealogies cf. *NBD*, p. 459; Machen, pp. 202–209.

The main purpose of the genealogy is probably less to prove Jesus' legal claim to the Davidic throne, and more to show that he was not merely a revealer of divine truth but far more the climax of a divinely guided historical process. The mention of the four women (3, 5, 6), all of them unattractive by orthodox Jewish standards, will have been to counter discreditable rumours about Jesus' birth circulating in Jewish circles.

The device of breaking up the genealogy into three groups of 14 names stresses the natural divisions of the history, gives an aid to memory, and stamps the name of David on each, for the value of the letters of his name in Heb. adds up to 14. The omission of three names in v. 8 is for the sake of the pattern and quite consistent with Jewish practice (cf. Williams, I, p. 16). In the last section there are strictly only thirteen names, for Jechoniah belongs to the second. It is probable that in the Heb. original of the genealogy Jehoiakim was misread as Jehoiachin in v. 11 (so Schniewind).

The Birth of Jesus (1: 18–25)

Humanly speaking Jesus' claim to the Davidic throne depended on the willingness of Joseph, the legal heir, to accept Him as his son. Hence Mt. gives only Joseph's version of the story. For a brief discussion on the Virgin Birth cf. comments on Lk. 1: 26–38; see also Machen. Here let us note that apart from the divine activity in conception, Christ's birth was completely normal. He was not conceived until Mary was married; betrothal was legally marriage (24, **he . . . took Mary home as his wife**). Joseph was His father in every way except procreation. Long-distance foretelling of names is exceptional in prophecy. **23. Immanuel** is intended to give the significance of the child's birth, not his name. Except for those who approach it with minds made up, **but he had no union with her until she gave birth to a son** (25) seems incompatible with the doctrine of the perpetual virginity of Mary.

A Harmony of the Nativity Stories. The popular interpretation of the story of the wise men, bringing them hard on the heels of the shepherds, makes it impossible to harmonize Lk. and Mt. When we follow the clue of 2: 16 and realize that Jesus was born anything from a year to two before their visit, there is not much difficulty.

Joseph was a citizen of Bethlehem, possibly owning a small piece of ground there; that is why he went there for the census (Lk. 2: 4), that and his knowledge that the Messiah must be born there. After the presentation in the Temple, they returned to Nazareth (Lk. 2: 39). Joseph will have sold up there and returned to Bethlehem, believing that the Messiah must grow up in David's town. After they had settled down the wise men came, and then the story unfolded as in Mt.

The Visit of the Wise Men (2: 1–12)

The **Magi** (*magoi*) were astrologers, who believed that the movements of the heavenly bodies and the destinies of men were linked. They 'observed the rising of his star' (2, NEB) and connected it with the birth of the expected Jewish king. Too little is told us to allow us to decide what sort of a star it was and why they linked it with the birth of the Messiah. There is no suggestion that **the star . . . went ahead of them** (9) until the final stretch of the journey, nor are we told how it could do so.

The story is prophetic of what was to happen. 'This time Magi forestalled Israel, who possessed the clear prophetic word' (Schlatter). They must have heard of Israel's hope through Jews, but they had to tell Israel that it had been fulfilled.

It was God's will that His Son, who is prophetically called Israel (Isa. 49: 3), should recapitulate the history of Israel (2: 15), so He had to go to Egypt. For this the gifts of the Magi were divinely provided. The **gold** paid the cost of the journey, the **incense and myrrh**, easily carried and fetching very high prices in Egypt, provided for their first needs there.

The Road to Nazareth (2: 13–23)

We do not know how long they stayed in Egypt, for we do not know how long before Herod's death (4 B.C.) Christ was born. The quotation from Hos. 11: 1 causes no difficulty, when we realize that Mt. is saying that Jesus was recapitulating the history of His people, but what are we to say of v. 18 with its quotation of Jer. 31: 15? This stands shortly before the joy of the promise of the New Covenant (Jer. 31: 31–34). Even so, when the Maker of the Covenant came, He had to be preceded by sorrow. **22. Archelaus:** Son of Herod: cf. *The Historical Background*, p. 1039.

Nazareth is mentioned in an inscription found at Caesarea in 1962 and in a synagogue poem of the seventh century based on much older material, but it has no place among the hundreds of Galilean place names in both Josephus and the rabbinic writings. Built a little higher up the hill than most of the modern town it stood near the junction of three secondary roads, but it was little more than a village, overshadowed by its neighbours (cf. Dalman, ch. III).

23. 'He will be called a Nazarene' is not really a direct OT quotation. It serves three purposes. (i) It links with Isa. 11: 1, *'from his roots a Branch (nēṣer) will bear fruit'* and through it with all passages indicating the humble origin of the Messiah. (ii) Through the humbleness of Nazareth it reminds us of passages like the Servant Songs in Isa. 40–55. (iii) In his spelling of Nazareth Mt. intends to remind us of the Nazirite (Num. 6: 1–21) and hence of Jesus' single-minded devotion to God. For the prophecies in this ch. as a whole cf. *The New Testament Use of the Old Testament* (pp. 1110 ff).

I. i. THE PROCLAMATION AND APPEARANCE OF THE MESSIAH (3: 1–4: 25)

The Ministry of John the Baptist (3: 1–12)

See comments on Lk. 3: 1–18. The fierceness of the attack on the Pharisees and Sadducees (7 cf. *The Religious Background*, pp. 1055 f.) was because as religious leaders they should have been familiar with the heart of John's message even before he began to preach.

The Baptism of Jesus (3: 13–17)

See comments on Mk 1: 9–11. Jesus was 'born under law' (Gal. 4: 4); since John was God's messenger, He had to **fulfill all righteousness** (15) by accepting his baptism, though he did not need it.

The Testing (4: 1–11)

See comments on Mk 1: 12 f.; Lk. 4: 1–13. It should be noted that *peirazō* (to tempt) and *peirasmos* (temptation) mean in secular Gk. to test and testing. It is only our fallen nature that turns our necessary testing into temptation. Hence we should use the popular rendering only when the context makes it unavoidable. There is no obvious lesson to be deduced from the different order of testings in Mt. and Lk.

The First Message in Galilee (4: 12–17)

See comments on Mk 1: 14 f.

Note on 'The Kingdom of Heaven' (17). In this period the pious Aram. speaking Jew avoided not only the revealed name of Yahweh (Jehovah), by substituting *Adonai* (Lord), but also *Elohim* (God), for which he used especially *ha-shem* (the Name), *maqom* (Space) and *sha-mayim* (heaven). The last of these is found especially in the expression *malkuth shamayim* (the kingdom of heaven).

The attempt to find some difference in meaning between the kingdom of God and the kingdom of heaven is one of the less profitable exercises in NT exegesis we have inherited. The repeated parallelisms between the kingdom of heaven in Mt. and the kingdom of God in Mk and Lk. should in themselves have shown that they were identical; the rabbinic use proves it. Jesus will normally have used 'kingdom of heaven'; Mt. preserved it, with the exception of 12: 28; 19: 24; 21: 31, because his readers will have been familiar with it. Mk and Lk. felt it necessary to substitute 'kingdom of God' so as to be certain of being understood.

Kingdom (*malkuth*, *basileia*) is primarily 'sovereignty', kingly rule and power. It is something which has always existed, but in its fulness it is yet future. It entered the world in a new way with the coming of the King (Mk 1: 15) and will be experienced in all its fulness, when at the name of Jesus every knee shall bow (Phil. 2: 10).

There are a few passages where it is used more in our sense of the sphere in which God's sovereignty is exercised. Even here, however, the stress on God's sovereignty is normally prominent.

The Call of the First Disciples (4: 18–22)

See comments on Mk 1: 16–20.

A Summary of Early Activity in Galilee (4: 23–25)

Since this is a summary, there are no exact parallels, but cf. Mk 1: 39; 3: 7 f.; Lk. 4: 44; 6: 17 ff.

I. ii. THE SERMON ON THE MOUNT (5: 1–7: 29)

For over a century an intensive comparison has been made between Christ's teaching and that of the earlier rabbis. It has been conclusively shown that there is very little in the Sermon which cannot be in measure paralleled from rabbinic writings, and the discussion has often degenerated into a question of priority, as though the rabbis would have borrowed consciously from Jesus. The similarities are due to both basing their teaching on the OT. But while the rabbinic parallels are obtained by sifting hundreds of thousands of words, the brief compass of the Sermon stands unique in its power to shake those who are prepared to expose themselves to its concentrated shock.

No attempt is made here to discuss the relationship of these chapters with 'the Sermon on the Plain' (Lk. 6: 17–49). There are no grounds for assuming that all recorded here by Mt. must have been spoken on one occasion, or that Jesus did not repeat Himself, sometimes with considerable variations.

The Beatitudes (5: 3–12)
Cf. Lk. 6: 20–23. The contrast between the Sermon and the Law-giving at Sinai is at its greatest here. The latter begins with the Ten Commandments, which give the fundamental laws governing the behaviour of those that would be in covenant relationship with God. The Beatitudes are addressed to those who show by their lives that they have achieved what the Decalogue demands. So far from being a new law, as some 'dispensationalists' believe, the Sermon describes the life of those who by grace have passed beyond law.

For v. 3 cf. Isa. 11: 4; 57: 15; 61: 1; for v. 4 Isa. 61: 1; for v. 5 Ps. 37: 11; for v. 6 Isa. 55: 1 f.; for v. 8 Ps. 24: 3 f.

Salt and Light (5: 13–16)
Cf. Lk. 11: 33; 14: 34 f. The stress continues on character rather than works. Salt and light function in virtue of what they are, not what they do. It is probably the preservative rather than the seasoning value of salt which is here being stressed. **13. if the salt loses its saltiness:** This is usually explained by the salt being the outside layer of rock salt, where the salinity has been lost by the action of sun and rain (*NBD*, p. 1125b), or that it had been adulterated (M'Neile; Filson suggests both). Neither really suits the context. Rather the physically impossible (Schniewind) shows that the disciple without a salty effect has never been a true one. Note that our **light** (16) is not our **good deeds**, but the means by which people see that they are good.

Jesus and the Law (5: 17–20)
Jesus then turned to His relationship to the already extant revelation of God. The threefold division of Scripture (Lk. 24: 44) had not yet become general (*SB*), so here the **Prophets** (17) mean all the books of the OT apart from the **Law**. He had come to fulfil (*plēroo*) all of them, but since His great conflict with the Pharisees would be about the law, He confined His remarks to it. The law was a revelation of God's will and would therefore stand **until heaven and earth disappear** (=**until everything is accomplished**, 18). To relax a commandment (19) is to claim authority over God.

20. The **righteousness . . . of the Pharisees and the teachers of the law** was inadequate because, with all its zeal, it represented a merely human interpretation of God's demands through the law. Jesus' interpretation, so far from destroying, fulfilled. First He really kept the law (and this righteousness is imputed to us); second He revealed 'the full depth of meaning that it was intended to hold' (M'Neile). When His Spirit indwells us, we have His interpretation written on our hearts.

On Murder (5: 21–26)
Cf. 12: 57 ff. The principle that anger and scorn are in God's sight as evil as the murder they can easily lead to was recognized by the rabbis, but Jesus supplied a new note of seriousness. His words are not easy to follow. **Judgment** must bear the same meaning in vv. 21, 22; it will refer to the local Jewish courts of 23 members. Then **the Sanhedrin** (22) will be the 71 member Sanhedrin in Jerusalem, the supreme court. **22. Anyone who says to his brother, 'Raca':** *Raca*, an Aram. word, means 'empty head,' and is often mentioned in rabbinic writings as a common term of abuse; *mōre* (**you fool!**) is not Gk. here but Aram. and equivalent to 'godless fellow'. Jesus means that the local court *should* try anger as much as murder, while the denial of a man's self-respect *should* concern the supreme court. To deny a man's moral standing before God is so serious that only the Heavenly Court is competent to deal with it. Of course, human courts seldom deal with these matters, but that will not prevent the Heavenly Court from doing its duty. To give another a just charge against us is so serious that putting the matter right is more important than worship (23). To say that vv. 25 f. refer to a man's relationship to God is an example of perverse allegorical ingenuity.

22. the fire of hell (*geenna*) In the OT the place of the dead, both good and bad, is called Sheol, rendered Hades in the NT. With the growth of belief in the resurrection during the Inter-Testamental period, we find in the Bk. of Enoch (*c.* 150–100 B.C.) the concept of a 'hell' for sinners after the final judgment. This was soon universally called Ge-Hinnom, short for Ge-ben-Hinnom, the Valley of (the son of)Hinnom—in Gk. *ge(h)enna*. Literally this was the valley south of Jerusalem, where child sacrifices had been offered under Ahaz and Manasseh, which from the time of Josiah became the place where the rubbish of Jerusalem was tipped and burnt. In the later first century A.D. a group of Pharisees considered that Gehenna had a purifying rôle for lesser sinners consigned there; in the second century it was expanded to mean also a sort of purgatory before the final judgment. These latter uses are not found in the NT.

On Adultery and Divorce (5: 27–32)
Cf. 19: 9; Mk 10: 11 f.; Lk. 16: 18. For the OT fornication and adultery are not two stages of one sin but different types of sin. The former

is expressly condemned only in its more aggravated forms, though it is always regarded with disfavour. The latter was a fundamental sin against the family, and so against society, and carried the death penalty with it (Lev. 20: 10; Dt. 22: 22). The pious Jew regarded all sexual sin, whether of act or thought, with abhorrence. If Jesus concentrated on the more serious offence, He was not in any way condoning the lesser.

The popular opinion that the rabbis were very lax about divorce comes from an ignorance of their exegetical methods. The disciples of Shammai (1st cent. A.D.) rendered Dt. 24: 1 as in RSV; their rivals, the disciples of Hillel, understood it as 'anything offensive'. On the basis of this they said that burning her husband's food would be ground enough for divorce, or if he saw someone more beautiful (Aqiba, died 135). But this was only expounding the law as they understood it. In fact they deprecated divorce, and there is no evidence that it was common.

Jesus' use of **adultery** (28) implies that the man and woman were debarred from being married. Presumably *gynē* (**woman**) bears here, as so often, the meaning 'wife' (so *Arndt*). The sin, even in thought, is so serious that it would be worth while to cripple oneself to avoid it. This would seem to answer in anticipation the modern argument that adultery and fornication are, under certain circumstances, natural and necessary for fulness of life.

Christ's saying on **divorce** has caused so much controversy, that we must confine ourselves to a statement of facts. (*a*) Jesus was addressing people whose characters are depicted in 5: 3–10. He was not placing the unregenerate Gentile under greater restriction than had aleady been laid on the Jew (Dt. 24: 1–4). (*b*) Since the Gospels did not circulate in one *codex* until the 2nd century, we must not read into **except for marital unfaithfulness** (*porneia*) a meaning so important that those possessing only Mk or Lk. would seriously misunderstand Christ's words. (*c*) *Porneia* is never used in LXX or NT of simple adultery. The Orthodox Church has understood it to mean here repeated acts of adultery, which make the wife no better than a harlot. (*d*) From the fact that it carried the death penalty, it may be argued that adultery automatically ends a marriage, but this cannot be inferred from this passage. (*e*) Only three, not mutually exclusive, meanings of the exceptive clause seem to have claims to consideration: (i) that of the Orthodox Church, which should know the meaning of the Gk.; (ii) that unconfessed pre-marital sin is indicated, i.e. the marriage was entered on under false pretences; (iii) that marriage within the prohibited degrees is intended, as in Ac. 15: 20, 29—the idea that the early Gentile Christians were given

to sexual promiscuity is foolish and uncharitable. **32. causes her to commit adultery:** Under the social conditions of the time it was almost impossible for a younger woman to live an independent single life.

On Swearing (5: 33–37)
23: 16–22 is considered here also. The telling of the complete truth at all times is so fraught with danger, that it is possible only to the one who trusts completely in God. Once my word is not regarded as reliable, I shall try to establish my veracity by the use of oaths; but these tend rapidly to become mechanical and virtually meaningless. The rabbis tried to counter this by laying down oaths which could be relied on. Jesus is concerned here, not with the demands of authority that under certain circumstances an oath be taken, but with that perfect honesty which will make oaths unnecessary. I, as a Christian, am entitled to expect that those who know me will accept my word, if I am invariably truthful. Why should a judge, or other authorized person, who does not know me, accept my uncorroborated statement that I am a Christian and release me from an oath, or affirmation, which is an oath under another name? Jewish jurisprudence, in any case, did not know our evidence given on oath. The only cases where one was required were like Exod. 22: 10 f.

In an oath I call on God, or someone or something else, to bear witness to the truth of my statement and, if necessary, bring disaster on me. But I cannot control **heaven, earth, Jerusalem**, or even my **head**. It is still worse when I make a distinction between oath and oath (23: 16–22). I may deceive the man unversed in these subtleties and so profane holy things. These differences are not found in second-century rabbinic writings. It is probable that this is one of the cases where Jesus' rebuke was taken to heart; cf. comment on 15: 4 f.

On True Love (5: 38–48)
Cf. Lk. 6: 27–36. Any and every effort to explain these verses in terms of law is bound to fail. We are simply given a picture of how the regenerate will behave, if they respond to their new nature. We should render v. 48, 'Ye therefore shall be perfect, as your heavenly Father is perfect' (RV). This is merely a variant of Lev. 19: 2, '*Be holy because I, the LORD your God, am holy*'. Buber says on this (p. 128), 'more in the form of a promise than in the form of a demand'. Experience has shown that it is not difficult for a Christian to carry out this section spontaneously, but it is almost impossible as the result of deliberate action.

The law, **eye for eye, and tooth for tooth** (38; Exod. 21: 24; Lev. 24: 20; Dt. 19: 21), does not command revenge, but moderation in revenge, which should not exceed the damage done. While the high-priestly party among the

Sadducees still applied the law literally at this time, most Pharisees insisted on the monetary equivalent's being paid. The context shows that **Do not resist an evil person** (39) means that one should not seek justice for *oneself*. There is no suggestion that by inaction or silence we should encourage injustice to others. Nor is it implied that we should not lay our case in the Divine Judge's hands. Four practical cases are envisaged. (i) Positive injustice: 'If someone slaps you on the right cheek' (39, NEB). Injured honour as well as physical pain are involved. Not passive but active acceptance is advocated. (ii) Possible injustice: **if someone wants to sue you** (40). His action, though apparently unjust, might prove to be well founded. The **tunic** (*chitōn*) is the long inner shirt, the **cloak** (*himation*) the much more valuable outer garment, which by law could not be taken (Exod. 22: 26 f.). (iii) Official burdens: 'If a man in authority makes you go one mile' (41, NEB). *Angareuō* is the Persian, possibly Babylonian, loanword (*Arndt*) for the age-old system of unpaid service that those in official service were entitled to demand. It was looked on as slave-service, and therefore degrading. To go a second mile would relieve another from the burden. (iv) Unreasonable claims: the context suggests that the beggar and borrower would deprive one of what one needs oneself. What of it, if the other is really in need? Ac. 3: 6 illustrates one way of carrying out this precept.

43. Love your neighbor and hate your enemy: It is normally assumed that Jesus was placing beside narrow Jewish national love for their own people (**your neighbor**) a wider love embracing the Gentiles (**your enemy**) as well, but this is improbable. It is true that the rabbis always interpreted Lev. 19: 18 as referring to fellow-Jews, as indeed it does. Controversy only concerned which classes of Jews might legitimately be excluded from its scope (cf. Lk. 10: 29). But nowhere do we find in their writings the suggestion that all Gentiles were enemies and to be hated. The nearest to it is the exceptional passage in *Sifra* (89b), which says, commenting on Lev. 19: 18a, 'Against others you may be revengeful or bear a grudge'. By **hate your enemy** Jesus was putting into words the ordinary accepted attitude towards all regarded as enemies, whether Jews or Gentiles. Here, as so often in the NT, the emotional side of love is not under consideration. The parable of the Good Samaritan is the classic example of what Jesus meant by loving one's enemy, and here even a greeting is seen as an example of it (47).

The very illustration of the Father's love (45) is an indication of the type of being **perfect** (48) that Jesus was teaching. If they were holy (see above) and mature sons of the Father, they would, as sharers of His Spirit, partake in His impartial love of men. The NT does not suggest that we receive more from God, but what we receive can be rightly applied and used (cf. Rom. 8: 28). The perfection is not sinlessness, but a complete control by God's Spirit.

On True Religion (6: 1–18)
The character described in ch. 5 will express itself in outward actions, which collectively we call 'religion' (Jas 1: 26 f.) or **'acts of righteousness'** (1, *dikaiosynē*, lit. righteousness). The quality of these actions does not depend on whether men see them, but on whether men are intended to see them; those whom Jesus was rebuking undoubtedly did them for God also.

Rewards (1). For many today the chief difficulty created by the Sermon on the Mount is its stress on rewards, which are mentioned nine times. But this is an element found throughout the NT, *e.g.* Mt. 10: 41 f.; Jn 4: 36; 1 C. 3: 8, 14; 9: 17 f.; Heb. 11: 6; 2 Jn 8; Rev. 11: 18; 22: 12. Some do respond to grace more readily than others, and 'God is not unjust; he will not forget your work and the love you have shown him as you have helped his people and continue to help them' (Heb. 6: 10). Even though Judaism had tended to work out a mathematical relationship between works and rewards, yet it realized that the latter were essentially an expression of God's grace (*SB* IV, pp. 487 ff.). For the nature of the reward see next section.

Alms (2 ff.). Almsgiving was considered by Judaism to be the foremost act of piety. The need was created by the large number of those physically and psychically incapable of work. There were also many landless men, who could not hope to maintain their families by their casual labour (cf. Mt. 20: 1–16, and also Jas 2: 14 ff.; 1 Jn 3: 17). In our modern setting it is our time rather than our money they need.

Most charity was exercised by the Synagogue as representing the community. This made begging less necessary and helped to preserve the anonymity of the poor. So the ostentation condemned is not in the giving to individuals but in the public proclamation of the amounts given to the community for the purpose (**trumpets** is vivid hyperbole). For **hypocrites** see additional note at end of the chapter; there is no suggestion that here (or vv. 5, 16; 7: 5) scribes and Pharisees are particularly under attack; the practices were not peculiar to them. **Their reward** was the praise of men, so God's reward, which they forfeited, is God's praise, His 'Well done'. **left hand . . . right hand:** a vivid expression implying absolute secrecy. Judaism insisted on charity being kept secret so as not to shame the poor; it should be so secret that we ourselves should forget we helped the poor man, when we meet him again.

Prayer (5–8). Neither community prayer, which Jesus never condemned, nor the secret outpourings of the heart, which need no guidance, is under consideration, but the then usual, though not compulsory, association of the individual, wherever he might be, with the national morning and evening prayer in the Temple (cf. Ac. 3: 1; 10: 3, 30). It was easy to arrange to be in a prominent place at the time. It was normal **to pray standing**. The use of 'empty phrases' (RSV) is noted as a Gentile weakness, though the Jewish Prayer Book provides some examples. Prayer is not intended as a memory-jogger for God (8), but as a means by which the Christian's desires are brought under God's scrutiny, and the one who prays is reminded of the character, will and purposes of God.

The Pattern Prayer (9–13). Cf. Lk. 11: 2–4. When the community, and the individual conscious of his unity with the community, are praying, some guidance as to the scope of their prayer is needed (completely private prayer is not under consideration). The shortened and slightly variant form of words in Lk. 11, the omission of any confession of sin beforehand and of any doxology at the end (the familiar one in AV is very early but indubitably not original) all suggest that we have a guide and framework for our petitions rather than a fixed formula.

I am a member of a community, so I say **our**; I have been made a son, so I say **Father. in heaven** reminds me that there is neither inability to give nor folly in giving. I pray first that God may have His rightful place among men. The nearest approach to the meaning permitted by modern Eng. idiom is probably 'may your name be honoured' (Phillips), or 'may thy name be held in reverence' (Filson); **name** 'means God as he has made himself known' (Filson). The prayer for the coming of the **kingdom** (cf. note on 4: 17) is not merely for the Second Coming of Christ but also for subjection to His will in society and the individual. The **kingdom** implies submission, but God's **will** can be done even against their own will by those that rebel. **On earth as it is in heaven** applies to all three introductory petitions.

Daily (*epiousios*) has been found only once in non-Christian writings, so its meaning is uncertain; this is reflected in the varying early Christian interpretations. It may well mean 'daily ration' (cf. *Arndt*, pp. 296 f.), or 'bread for the immediate future' (Tasker). There is no justification for the Eng. Prayer Book rendering, 'our trespasses . . . those that trespass . . .', Trespass in the Bible has the connotation of rebellion, and any such sin would have to be confessed before a man could even think of normal prayer. At the most our

falling short ('sin', Lk. 11: 4) and our failure to give God due honour are intended by **debts**, just as **we also have forgiven** (*aphēkamen*, an aorist and so a fact) those that have slighted our self-esteem. 'And do not bring us to the test' (NEB, cf. Jas 1: 2 f. and note on 4: 1–11): temptations are mainly our fault (Jas 1: 13 f.); testing is a divine necessity to reveal the reality of our faith and protestations. We should shrink from it, but when the time comes that we must pass through it, we ask for deliverance in it. **from evil** (mg): So also Phillips; RSVmg., RV, NEB and most commentaries 'from the evil one'. The Gk. is ambiguous, but on the whole the personal rendering is better, for God uses Satan as the tester. It may well be that the original Aram. was equally ambiguous.

A Necessary Preliminary to Prayer (14, 15). Cf. 18: 23–35; Mk 11: 25. Some seared consciences unavailingly try to avoid the force of this warning by pleading that it does not apply to Christians. Others try to make out that their circumstances are so peculiar that they override Scripture. Should the regenerate man refuse to forgive the wrong done to him, he effectively cuts himself off from fellowship with God, who is the Forgiver, until he forgives. If the allegedly regenerate man is marked out by an unforgiving spirit, it is the truest sign that he has never been born again (1 Jn 3: 10, 14, 15).

Fasting (16–18). A person under strong emotional stress tends to shun normal food. Hence fasting, without any recorded command from God, became a natural way for the penitent, and for all who felt themselves under divine wrath, to approach God. In the Law fasting is commanded only for the Day of Atonement (Lev. 16: 29, 31; Num. 29: 7), where it is called *to afflict the soul* (RV), which suggests the essentially dual nature of true fasting; it must not be a matter of the body alone. Fasting is frequently mentioned elsewhere in OT, and indeed it is taken for granted. In NT it is nowhere commanded or even positively commended—the verses quoted in its support, *e.g.* Mt. 17: 21; Mk 9: 29; 1 C. 7: 5; Ac. 10: 30, are taken from inferior MSS corrupted by the Church's growing asceticism. Christ mentions fasting as something that will happen (*e.g.* 9: 15, cf. Ac. 13: 2 f.) and regulates its practice. In addition, by fasting in the wilderness (4: 2) He showed that it could have major spiritual importance.

Plainly Jesus is not calling the believer to disassociate himself from the fasts of the community, but is speaking of voluntary fasting (see note on 9: 14), whether regular or occasional (this is borne out by the Gk. syntax). Such a fast is the concern only of the faster and God. **17. put oil on your head:** Self-anointing with olive oil was a regular custom, omitted only in times of mourning and fasting. Jesus did not tell His disciples that they should put on an appearance of joy, but that they should behave normally. The head is specially mentioned as the only part of the body where the anointing would be obvious. In addition the faster or mourner often put ashes on his head (cf. 2 Sam. 13: 19).

On Trust in God (6: 19–34)
In NT times, and indeed down to our own, the local Jewish community in measure fulfilled the functions of the modern welfare state, but its finances were normally precarious, and those helped by it had little status in it. This section is concerned with both the individual's security and status.

True Treasure (19–21). Cf. Lk. 12: 33 f. Oriental treasure normally consisted of silver and gold and also costly clothing (cf. Gen. 45: 22; 2 Kg. 5: 23). Here **on earth moth and** 'worm' (mg, lit. 'eating') would see to the latter and **thieves** to the former. That one could transfer one's treasure to **heaven** by charitable acts is often found in contemporary Jewish thought. With Jesus the motivation is not reward in heaven as with the rabbis, though this is not denied, but the transference of the affections.

The Sound Eye (22, 23). Cf. Lk. 11: 34 ff. The Mishnah says, 'These are things whose fruit a man enjoys in this world while the capital is laid up for him in the world to come: honouring father and mother, deeds of loving-kindness, making peace between a man and his fellow; and the study of the Law is equal to them all' (*Peah* 1: 1). Jesus was speaking less to earth-bound men and more to those who thought in terms of 'both . . . and'. So He gives them the parable of the 'single eye' (RV). The exact meaning of *haplous* is hard to fix. From single we move to sincere, sound, and finally generous. The man who fixes his eyes on God (heaven), will give generously without second thought. The man who tries to look at God and the world at the same time will see neither clearly; in fact he will not see at all.

The Slave with Two Masters (24). Cf. Lk. 16: 13. *SB* and Schniewind stress that it was possible at the time for a slave to be shared by two owners. In spite of the Rabbinic evidence it seems clear that Jesus is speaking of the impossible in practice. 'Men can work for two employers, but no slave can be the property of two owners' (M'Neile). Mammon, a word of uncertain etymology, was used in the language of the time to mean property generally. It is not the name of a heathen god, but the Aram. word is probably kept to suggest that property can become a master and even a god.

Anxiety (25–34). Cf. Lk. 12: 22–31. Few of the numerous mistranslations in AV have been more unfortunate than its rendering 'take

no thought' in this passage; it has provided both the fanatic and the sceptic with overmuch ammunition. *Merimnaō* means to be anxious, worried, careful; its use in Lk. 10: 41 illustrates its force. **25. Therefore:** vv. 19–24 have shown that there can be no satisfaction or profit from a 'both . . . and' attitude, therefore we must decide on an 'either . . . or'. **life** (*psychē*) . . . **body:** Jesus is here using OT words and is speaking, not of the fact of life, but of man's personality (generally and misleadingly rendered soul) and of the body by which it knows the world and makes itself known to it. The former needs food for its preservation, the latter clothing for its protection and honour (Schlatter). But personality (**life**) and **body** are God's gift, so will He not give the lesser as well? Commentators divide fairly evenly between the text and margin in v. 27, but both the context and the normal use of *hēlikia* favour 'span of life'. In fact, few things shorten life more than worry. Man is better than **birds** and 'wild flowers' (Phillips—whatever flower was meant by *krinon*, it would not be called a lily today) by the order of creation. The behaviour of bird and flower is that allotted them in creation. Man is not intended to imitate them, but to fulfil his role in creation (cf. v. 33); if he does this, he can be assured of God's care. The **pagans** (32) are mentioned not in condemnation but because they do not know God's order of creation. Those who know God's revelation behave unnaturally, if they do what those ignorant of it practise naturally; they then become men **of little faith** (30).

Up to this point Jesus has been speaking of the known problems that make men worry. In v. 34 He passes to those as yet unknown. When the morrow brings knowledge of them, it will also bring the answer to them.

Note on 'Hypocrite'. Hypocrite, which is merely a Gk. word written in English letters, is found in NT only in the Synoptic gospels and always on the lips of Jesus. We find it 13 times in Mt. (6: 2, 5, 16; 7: 5; 15: 7; 22: 18; 23: 13, 15, 23, 25, 27, 29; 24: 51), once only in Mk and three times in Lk. In Mt. it is used generally five times and in the remaining eight specifically of 'the scribes and Pharisees'.

In NT times the word had a wide range of meaning, but that of a bad man deliberately pretending to be good was not one of them. It is probable that the meaning 'actor' will satisfy all the NT passages; it certainly does in the Sermon on the Mount. Even when it is applied to the scribes and Pharisees we get the impression that they had so persuaded themselves of the rightness of their position and actions that they were oblivious of their wrongness.

The fact that the word is used only by Jesus, with His unique knowledge of human character and motivation, should make us reticent in judging those whom He so castigated. See further *NBD*, article 'Hypocrite', and the literature there mentioned.

On Criticism (7: 1–6)

Cf. Lk. 6: 37 f., 41 f. The chapter division coincides with a real break in thought. The obligation of judgment is laid on a limited number of people only. The context makes it clear that they are not under consideration but it is those who arrogate the right of judgment to themselves. Phillips' rendering 'Don't criticize people' would be idiomatically preferable, were it not clear that contemporary Jewish idiom implies that **you will be judged**, 'it shall be measured unto you' (RV) refers to God's action (*SB*, Schniewind, Filson, Schlatter).

5. You hypocrite: Less because a man, whose vision was so impaired, could hardly see to remove **the speck**, and more because he was behaving as though he saw perfectly.

Schlatter is probably correct in linking v. 6 closely with vv. 1–5. The judgment Jesus is particularly condemning is our efforts to make all conform to our own standards of perfection. Quite apart from our own failure to conform, we are liable to find those we judge spiritually unprepared. We have to distinguish between our proclamation of Christ and our own understanding of His standards.

On Our Treatment of Others (7: 7–12)

Cf. Lk. 11: 9–13; 6: 31. The usual treatment of this passage makes vv. 7–11 an additional exhortation to prayer (but why does it not stand after 6: 15?) and regards v. 12 as an isolated saying, 'The Golden Rule'. It is quite possible that Mt. and Lk. are both dealing with a contextless passage on prayer. The Gk. prefaces v. 12 with 'therefore', which indicates that we are to understand the whole passage in the context of this verse. God behaves to us, as we would expect an earthly father to behave, only better, for earthly fathers are **evil** (11). We would wish men to behave thus to us, so we should behave thus to them.

'The Golden Rule' is found in Tob. 4: 15, in its negative form which is also attributed to Hillel and Philo. It is unlikely that much difference of meaning should be read into the difference between the positive and negative forms, the more so as a number of Talmudic sayings virtually assume the former. So it should not be regarded as the mountain peak of Christian ethics.

It is very doubtful whether **ask . . . seek . . . knock** should be regarded as three stages in prayer. Rather we have the one separated from God who knocks, the one who has strayed who seeks, and the child at home who asks; all receive equally. **Evil** (*ponēroi*) stresses not men's positive wickedness, but their worthlessness when placed in God's light. Note Lk.'s 'Holy Spirit' in place of **good gifts. 12. the**

Law and the Prophets: Here the whole OT, cf. 5: 17. Jesus means, 'This is what the OT teaches', not 'this is the essence of the OT', as it is so often understood.

Three Contrasts (7: 13–27)

Jesus ends His address with a call to action and self-judgment.

The Two Ways (13, 14). Cf. Lk. 13: 23 f. The contrast between the two ways was common in Jewish thought (cf. Jer. 21: 8), but there are no real parallels in it to the two gates. Behind this is the teaching of both John the Baptist and Jesus, which demanded a step of decision, which for the moment left the man making it a single entity dealing with God purely as an individual.

Judaism does not really know this position. Lk. 13: 23 f. shows that we have no right to interpret v. 13 except of Jesus' own time, though the consensus of Christian opinion is that it has been true of many other periods too.

True Fruit (15–23). Cf. 12: 33 ff.; Lk. 6: 43–46; 13: 26 f. **False prophets** are more likely, at the first at any rate, to be self-deceived than deceivers. It is its hunger, not its malignity, that gives the wolf its reputation. So it is with the man that would serve both God and mammon (6: 24). He serves God provided he can have mammon too. Only those actions that reveal character are a valid test with such men. Preaching and even miracles are no necessary indication of genuineness. Rev. 13: 3, 12 suggests (we are not entitled to say more) that even the resurrection of Christ may be counterfeited in the end time. The evidential character of all miracle is to be decided by the character of him who performs it.

The True Response (24–27). Cf. Lk. 6: 47 ff. **and puts them into practice:** The Gk. tense implies that not an isolated act but a lifetime of doing is implied. While the storm (25) undoubtedly refers to the final judgment, yet, as with the OT phrase *the day of the Lord*, any earlier catastrophe, which seriously foreshadows the final judgment, is included. Lk. 6: 49 shows that we are to understand light soil rather than literal **sand** (26). As the picture of any hill village in Galilee will show us, to build on **sand** implies building in the valley bottom, where the flood waters are bound to come. It would be an act of extreme folly and improvidence.

The Effect of the Sermon (7: 28, 29)

Cf. Mk 1: 22; Lk. 4: 32. This astonishment is generally interpreted by the rabbinic custom, wherever possible, of citing an earlier teacher for the opinion or ruling given. This is inadequate, for frequently a rabbi had to give an independent judgment resting on no true precedent. The rabbis considered that they and the prophets before them were merely authoritative expounders of the Mosaic law. The authority was vested in this law and nowhere else. But Jesus repeatedly taught on His own authority. This explains the questions about authority (21: 23), the demands for signs (12: 38; 16: 1) and the controversy about tradition (9: 14; 12: 2; 15: 1 f.). This was bound to awaken the hostility of the religious leaders. The mass of the people **were amazed** but unprepared to abandon those who had been their guides for so long.

II. i. MIRACLES IN GALILEE (8: 1–9: 34)

The choice of incidents in this section is in every case to bring out Jesus' authority in action. It is difficult, however, to explain the order of events, where this differs from that in Mk. There are no grounds for suggesting that Mt. is trying to correct Mk's order.

The Healing of a Leper (8: 1–4)

See comments on Mk 1: 40–45 (Lk. 5: 12–16). Lk. 5: 12 makes it clear the healing was done in a town. In NT times the impurity caused by a leper was strongly insisted on but the regulations of Lev. 13 had been relaxed in one important detail. Except in walled towns the leper was allowed to live among his fellowmen, provided he had a house to himself (*SB* IV, pp. 751–7; Edersheim I, p. 492). Josephus is often quoted against this, but in *Ant.* III xi. 3, *War* V. v. 6 he means Jerusalem by 'the city'; in *Contra Apion.* I. 31 he may be referring to the original enforcement of this command. R. G. Cochrane, *Biblical Leprosy*, has shown that Lev. 13 is not describing typical cases of leprosy (Hansen's disease), and it is not certain that leprosy in the modern sense was known in Palestine in OT times, though it was in NT. There is no evidence that the Messiah was expected to heal lepers (Edersheim I, p. 495).

The Healing of the Centurion's Servant (8: 5–13)

See comments on Lk. 7: 1–10. There seems to be no reason for trying to harmonize the two accounts. In dealing with the centurion's representatives Jesus was dealing with him. For mainly Gentile readers Lk. stresses the winning of Jews by a Gentile's love; for mainly Jewish readers Mt. stresses the acceptance of faith wherever found. There are no grounds for identifying the earlier healing of Jn 4: 46–54 with this miracle; it may, however, have given the centurion hope and boldness to approach Jesus.

The Healing of Peter's Mother-in-Law (8: 14, 15)

See comments on Mk 1: 29–31 (Lk. 4: 38 f.).

The Healing of the Crowds at Sunset (8: 16, 17)

See comments on Mk 1: 32–34 (Lk. 4: 40 f.). The quotation from Isa. 53: 4 is probably intended to make clear that Jesus' miracles of healing were not done merely by a word of power, but rather by an act of self-identification with the diseased. The passage, incidentally, is an answer to the claim that the Christian can demand physical healing of right as part of the work of Christ on the cross.

True Discipleship (8: 18–22)

Cf. Lk. 9: 57–60. This section is placed here to indicate that already early in Christ's ministry there was little reality on the part of many who followed Him. **Foxes have holes . . . :** This does not imply that Jesus had to 'sleep rough' most nights (oriental hospitality would normally take care of that), but that He had nothing, however mean, to which He could retire at need. (This is not contradicted by Mk 2: 1; the house at Capernaum had doubtless been obtained for His mother.) The very fact that **another disciple** (21) was with Him is sufficient proof that his father was not yet dead. He did not want to be too far away when death came, perhaps because he wanted to make sure of the inheritance.

22. The dead means, as sometimes in rabbinic writings, the spiritually dead. For **the Son of Man** see additional note at the end of the chapter.

The Storm on the Lake (8: 23–27)

See the comments on Mk 4: 35–41 (Lk. 8: 22–25).

The Gadarene Demoniacs (8: 28–34)

See the comments on Mk 5: 1–20 (Lk. 8: 26–39). Mt. gives a much briefer account, but mentions a second demoniac (28), who is not mentioned in the other two gospels, since he played no major part in the story. There can be little doubt that the correct name of the district is 'the country of the Gergesenes', though it is not given by the best combination of MSS in any of the Synoptic Gospels. For a full discussion see Dalman, pp. 176–180.

Additional Note on The Son of Man. The title 'The Son of Man' (*ho hyios tou anthrōpou*) is found 31 times in Mt., 14 in Mk,. 25 in Lk., 13 in Jn and once in Ac. 7: 56 (there are also three cases without the article, meaning a man). Except in the last case it is always used by Jesus Himself. This suggests that it was meant to veil the exact claims of Jesus, and that the apostles ceased to use it, once His death and resurrection made it no longer necessary.

It seems to have two main uses, both with some parallels in Jewish usage, though these are never brought together. Jesus is *the* man, the ideal heavenly man (1 C. 15: 45, 47), the Servant of Jehovah; cf. 8: 20; 9: 6; 20: 28; Mk 8: 31. Then He is the heavenly man who will come with the clouds of heaven as the judge (Dan. 7: 13; Enoch; 2 Esd.), cf. 16: 28; 19: 28; 24: 27, 37–44; 25: 31–46; 26: 64; Mk 8: 38; Lk. 17: 22 ff.; Jn 5: 27. The title was an obvious claim to special status, but it veiled its exact nature until the time had come for disclosure. In both its senses it stressed the links between Jesus and those He had come to save and rule. Cf. Moule, pp. 11–22.

The Healing of the Paralysed Man (9: 1–8)
See comments on Mk 2: 1–12 (Lk. 5: 17–26). It is insufficiently realized that it is equally easy to say **Your sins are forgiven** and **Get up and walk**, but both are equally futile in the mouth of the ordinary man.

1. his own town: Obviously Capernaum. The phrase implies that He had had a home there for at least a year.

The Call of Matthew (9: 9–13)
See comments on Mk 2: 13–17 (Lk. 5: 27–32). There can be no doubt that Matthew and Levi (Mk 2: 14; Lk. 5: 27) are the same person. The idiom in v. 10 (*en tē oikia*) is the same as in Mk 2: 1, where it is translated 'at home'. But now we are in Matthew's house (Lk. 5: 29); hence it is argued (*NBC*, p. 771) that this must have been penned by Matthew. If the argument is valid, it proves no more than that the author used material from Matthew. **10. sinners:** This was used as a general term covering persons who were not allowed to act as judges or witnesses because of their moral unreliability. The Talmud enumerates them as dice players, pigeon racers, usurers, dealers in produce from the Sabbatical year, robbers and other violent criminals, herdsmen, customs officials and tax collectors.

The Discussion about Fasting (9: 14–17)
See comments on Mk 2: 18–22 (Lk. 5: 33–39). **your disciples do not fast:** See notes on 6: 16 ff. Fasting was prohibited to the bride and bridegroom and the wedding guests. Jewish fasts were (i) official, *viz.* the Day of Atonement, 9th of Ab (commemorating the destruction of the Temple by Nebuchadnezzar, and later also of the Second Temple by Titus) and on special occasions of drought, famine and pestilence; (ii) occasional private fasts due to special grief, etc. (cf. Tob. 12: 8; Jdt. 8: 6; Lk. 2: 37), which might become the normal feature of a person's life; (iii) regular private fasts. It is clear that some at least of the Pharisees had adopted the custom of fasting twice a week (Lk. 18: 12), *viz.* on Mondays and Thursdays, and John the Baptist had evidently taken over the custom. This seems to have been due to the prevalence of sin, *scil.* non-observance of the Law according to their standards. How attractive such a custom can become is seen in the *Didache* (early 2nd cent. A.D.), where Christians are exhorted, 'And you must not fast as the hypocrites do, for they fast on Monday and Thursday; you must observe your fast on Wednesday and Friday'!

The 'days of the Messiah' were compared to a marriage feast, so in v. 15 Jesus was not merely giving the first intimation of His death but also of His Messiahship.

Jairus' Daughter and the Woman with a Haemorrhage (9: 18–26)
See comments on Mk 5: 21–43 (Lk. 8: 40–56). In Jewish areas each synagogue was managed by a committee of seven, in Gentile areas of three. In addition there was 'the ruler of the synagogue' (Lk. 8: 41), normally the most respected member of the community, who could but need not be a member of the committee of management. His chief task was the supervision of the services. Cf. p. 1057.

20. the edge (fringe) **of his cloak:** See note on 23: 5. A special holiness was supposed to attach to the fringes because they were demanded in the Law (Num. 15: 38 ff.; Dt. 22: 12). The woman showed that faith and superstition can go hand in hand.

Acceptance and Rejection (9: 27–34)
We have here two miracles of healing peculiar to Mt. Though there are strong similarities between vv. 27–31 and 20: 29–34, they are probably accidental. The whole point of the story is the exceptional faith shown by the blind men. The fact that they received their sight proved that they believed (28 f.). This is the only case where healing is made entirely conditional on the faith of the person healed.

Son of David: See 12: 23. It is quite possible that vv. 32–34 are a preview of 12: 22–24. Mt. ends the section of evidential miracles by an example of outstanding faith and equally outstanding rejection.

II. ii. THE MISSION OF THE TWELVE (9: 35–11: 1)
This section has no real parallel in the other Synoptic gospels. While there is little in it that is peculiar to Mt., much of it is found in other settings in Mk and Lk. Mt. has placed the choice of the Twelve somewhat later in Jesus' ministry in order to combine it with their being sent out in twos. To the instruction then given he has added other appropriate teaching. It seems that Mt. was not so much concerned with the Twelve as to give comprehensive teaching in Christ's words for those who should continue their work.

He had compassion on them (9: 35–36) The need was not the motive for the choice of the Twelve, but for sending them out (9: 35–10: 1); this was true of the Seventy as well (Lk. 10: 1 f.).

The Choice of the Twelve (10: 2–4)
See comments on Mk 3: 13–19 (Lk. 6: 12–16). The language makes it clear that Mt. is recalling a choice which had been made earlier.

The Charge to the Twelve (10: 5–16)
Cf. Mk 6: 8–11; Lk. 9: 1–5; 10: 2–12. They were **disciples** (1), for they were learning, but when He sent them out they were **apostles**

(2). This term meant that they were the valid representatives of Him who had sent them. As such they were given the same message as Jesus' (7; cf. 4: 17) and His authority over disease and demons (1, 8). Since they were Jesus' representatives, they were under the same limitations as their Master. Hence they were not to go to **Gentiles** or **Samaritans** (5). This prohibition is the counterpart of the restriction laid on Jesus by the Father, 'I was sent only to the lost sheep of the house of Israel' (15: 24, *q.v.*). It is not mentioned in the parallel passages, for there is not the same stress on apostleship there.

It is likely that vv. 8–15 have been responsible for more fanaticism than any comparable passage of Scripture. That we are dealing with principles, not rules, is made clear by Paul's practice (though he was an apostle!). He took care to have a travelling companion of equal status (cf. Mk 6: 7), but, at least in Corinth, he made a point of not accepting the hospitality of any (1 C. 9: 12; 2 C. 11: 9; 12: 13) and of earning his own living. Again his taking first of Mark and later of Timothy is hardly to be explained by the disparity in age between him and the apostles at the first (cf. note on 17: 24–27). Quite simply, conditions varied so much between Palestine and the Gentile world, and even within the latter—contrast Ac. 16: 15 with the position in Corinth—that principles had to be differently applied. To this we must add that the apostles were coming as heralds of the king to His allegedly loyal subjects; the mission to the Gentiles was to men, who, if they knew their king at all, were in open rebellion against Him.

They were to go in haste and hence unburdened with baggage. As heralds they were to make no charge (8b), and they were to expect hospitality from the king's subjects (10). For most the **belt** served as a purse. **extra tunic:** The tunic (*chitōn*) was the long wool or linen undergarment next to the skin; two could be worn (Mk 6: 9). Jesus was forbidding unnecessary comfort; a change of undergarment could be expected from those that received them. **or sandals** (so Lk. 10: 4, but note 'carry' (ASV)): But Mk 6: 9 expressly commands them. Since going barefoot on journeys was unknown, it is probable that we are to apply the **extra tunic** to the **sandals** as well and see a prohibition against a spare pair. There is a similar contradiction in **or a staff** (so Lk. 9: 3), expressly permitted by Mk 6: 8. Since there is no suggestion that it was for defence (cf. Lk. 22: 36), it probably means that the next best stick would suffice.

The apparent haphazardness of Mk 6: 10; Lk. 9: 4 is corrected by v. 11. The king's heralds go to the king's subjects. The opinion of others is not always reliable, so vv. 12, 13 give the test of the suggested host. 'Will come . . . will

return (13, Phillips) is preferable. The shaking off of **the dust** (14) is probably explained by the mention of Sodom and Gomorrah; everything connected with the place carried a curse. Jesus knew that Israel's allegiance to God was in fact largely nominal (16a). The second half of the verse seems to have been a proverbial expression.

Predictions of Persecution (10: 17–25)
Cf. Mk 13: 9–13; Lk. 21: 12–17, 19. Since, apart from v. 16a, there is no suggestion of persecution in the ministry of this period, it seems wisest to see this section transferred from the eschatological discourse of ch. 24. The honour of apostleship includes suffering, even as the Master has suffered, but His spirit is with them. The promise of vv. 19 f. is not intended to be a lazy man's excuse for lack of thought and preparation in a position that has been foreknown and freely chosen. The disrupting influence of the unadulterated Christian message in society (21 f.), whether pagan, nonreligious or nominally Christian, is one of the main charges those who proclaim it have to face. Western 'Christian' society has been created largely by the silencing of those who would not accept compromise (cf. also vv. 34–36).

17. Be on your guard against men: 'Men' is frequently used in the Gospels of men without God. **22. he who stands firm to the end will be saved:** Cf. Rev. 2: 7, 11, 17, 26; 3: 5, 12, 21; 20: 4, etc. There are many passages in NT which stress the necessity of endurance and overcoming, and their theological interpretation is a matter of controversy. Their general setting and use suggest special status and honour in the kingdom rather than salvation from the second death. **23. you will not finish going through the cities of Israel . . . :** It is purposeless to enumerate the many strange interpretations of this verse. Firstly it is a warning that the accomplishment of Christ's purposes will not be carried through by us, whether in the mission of the Twelve, or in the Church's mission to Israel (Rom. 9–11), or even in the wider field of missionary enterprise (though this is not directly envisaged). The apostle is his Master's representative, not His replacement. Secondly it is only the Master who must die; His representatives are not to court unneeded martyrdom. **25. Beelzeboul** (mg): See note on 12: 24.

The Apostles' Security (10: 26–33)
Cf. Lk. 12: 2–9. Our lack of fear is due to Christ's victory through death. The revelation of the **hidden** is God's work, to whom it is already **known**. A great deal of Jesus' teaching was given in private but was intended ultimately to be made public. There is no room for the esoteric in Christianity. Verse 28 draws a contrast between men and God.

The Disunity Produced by the Gospel (10: 34–36)

Cf. Lk. 12: 51–53. See note on 10: 21. This passage is based on Mic. 7: 6. Very often in the Bible the inescapable result of an action is expressed as its purpose (34).

Conditions of Apostleship (10: 37–39)

Cf. 16: 24 f.; Mk 8: 34 f.; Lk. 9: 23 f.; 14: 26 f. The difference of expression here and in Lk. 14: 26 f. is explained by the hearers here already being disciples. **is not worthy of me:** The sense is given by Phillips, 'does not deserve to be mine'. **anyone who does not take his cross:** So far as is known the expression is one of Jesus' own coining. It means taking up the position of a condemned criminal.

Conclusion of Discourse (10: 40–11: 1)

Cf. 18: 5; Mk 9: 37, 41; Lk. 9: 48; 10: 16. We are finally reminded of the intimate relationship between the apostolic representative and the Master whom he represents. The rabbis repeatedly stressed, 'A man's representative is as the man himself'.

III. i. GROWING HOSTILITY (11: 2–12: 50)

This section runs from the doubts felt by John the Baptist to Jesus' turning from earthly relationships.

John and Jesus (11: 2–19)

Cf. Lk. 7: 18–35. It is most unlikely that John shared the popular views on the Messiah, but he had preached him as the Judge (3: 10–12); Jesus was apparently merely functioning as the agent of mercy. Jesus' answer was an oblique quotation of Isa. 29: 18 f.; 35: 5 f.; 61: 1—a direct one would have involved a public claim He was not yet ready to make. Lk. 7: 21 does not imply that all these miracles took place in the presence of the messengers; popular report will have guaranteed some of them.

3. the one who was to come: This was not an official title of the Messiah. John knew that Jesus would understand its implications.

6. Blessed is the man who does not fall away on account of me: It is less what Jesus did and said that makes Him a stumbling block for many; it is rather that He does not conform to what we think He ought to have done and said. **7. A reed swayed by the wind:** There was nothing private about John's delegation. Though the crowd will not have been sure of John's meaning, they grasped that he was disappointed in some way in Jesus. Jesus defended him against the possible charge of fickleness. He was only being true to the message that had been entrusted to him. **10. This the one about whom it is written:** By applying Mal. 3: 1 to John Jesus confirmed the claims that John had made for himself. By calling him Elijah (14, cf. Mal. 4: 5) He implicitly denied the popular, literalistic interpretation of the passage—not dead in some Christian circles to this day—and thereby also the dominant messianic concepts of the time. **11. there has not risen anyone greater than John the Baptist:** Greatness may be the expression of greatness of spirit, but the Bible does not anticipate the judgment of God on a man, or it may be a greatness created by position. Of all who had heralded the king John was the greatest, for he was nearest to Him. But the least who would experience the full power of the king would be greater than he—in position, but not necessarily in character or final reward.

Schniewind's exegesis of the difficult v. 12 (cf. Lk. 16: 16) has much to commend it. The Pharisees spoke of bringing in the end of the age by force through fasting, study of the Law, etc. Jesus accepted the thought but transformed it. **Forcefully advancing** is the whole-hearted acceptance of the preaching of John and Jesus (**until now**), which involved, as foreshadowed in John's baptism, a dying to self and to the past and the new life of the new age. This is more likely than 'God's power is at work through Jesus to establish his reign, but his kingdom is suffering violence; violent men are trying to seize or snatch away this blessing and keep men from accepting God's rule' (Filson). Most of their contemporaries stood aloof from both John and Jesus, like children refusing to join either a mock marriage or a mock funeral in the market place. For them John was too mad, Jesus too vulgar. For **sinners** see note on 9: 10. **But wisdom is proved right by her actions:** Though the MSS support for this reading is superior, most think that Lk. 7: 35 is correct. In any case **wisdom** is Jesus (and John), 'children' are those who accept Him.

Rejection and Acceptance (11: 20–30)

Cf. Lk. 10: 13 ff., 21 f. The deliberate incompleteness of the Gospels is shown by there being no other mention of Korazin, except in the parallel, Lk. 10: 13. The failure of the cities to repent was due to their being **wise and learned** (25), thinking they knew how God should do His work. Contrary to M'Neile and Tasker we should see thanksgiving not merely for the revelation to **little children** but also for the hiding from **the wise and learned**. An essential part of the gospel is that human advantages, including intelligence and knowledge, do not help a man to salvation (cf. 18: 3 f.).

Knowledge of God is by revelation, but there is no revelation that will enable us to grasp the inner mystery of the Son, the God-man. There is nothing in Jn that goes beyond the saying of v. 27, a fact we should remember when the teaching of the Fourth Gospel is challenged as incompatible with the Synoptics.

The **little children** are those **who are weary and burdened**. While the evangelistic application to those under the weight of sin is not illegitimate, the call refers primarily to those who are not 'wise' enough to ease their way from under the burdens of life and of the Law (cf. 23: 4). **29. my yoke:** The yoke was a common symbol of submission and service. The Rabbis spoke of the yoke of the Law (cf. Ac. 15: 10) and of the Kingdom of Heaven. **rest** (*anapausis*): In LXX *anapausis* is used as a regular equivalent of *shabbat* (Sabbath). It was the true Sabbath-rest Jesus was offering, a desisting from their own work to do the work of God (Heb. 4: 9 f.—AV is inadequate here). That this is the meaning is borne out by the next two incidents, which deal with the true use of the Sabbath. **your souls:** Not merely the inner man but the whole man is intended.

The Plucking of the Ears of Corn (12: 1–8)
See comments on Mk 2: 23–28 (Lk. 6: 1–5). Mt. adds vv. 5 ff., in which Jesus mentions the templework of the priests on the sabbath. We can be as pedantic as the scribes in the question of Sunday observance. Jesus' argument is that those who are doing the work of **the Lord of the Sabbath** are not under sabbath laws. **one greater than the temple** (6, cf. 12: 41, 42): i.e. the Kingdom of God. The quotation of Hos. 6: 6 (7) is the denial of the right of judgment until the motives behind an act are known. It may be added that the hunger of the disciples shows that the customary sabbath hospitality had not been offered to Jesus and His disciples.

The Healing of the Man with the Withered Hand (12: 9–14)
See comments on Mk 3: 1–6 (Lk. 6: 6–11). **Therefore it is lawful to do good on the Sabbath:** To do the work of Christ is to do good; this is the principle that cuts through all human legalism and sophistry. It should be added that on the human plane the Pharisaic attitude towards using a doctor on the sabbath was eminently sensible. If life was in danger, all that was necessary should be done. If it was not, why trouble the doctor? It was this incident that showed the Pharisees that the point at issue between them and Jesus was not varying interpretations of the Law but a fundamentally different approach to it; hence the decision to **kill Jesus**.

The Healing of the Multitudes (12: 15–21)
See comments on Mk 3: 7–12 (Lk. 6: 17–19). Mt. by quoting Isa. 42: 1–4 wishes to make it clear that Jesus did not resist deliberate opposition. Once someone had made up his mind about Him, he was left to it. It is not to be inferred, however, that there was an enthusiastic acceptance by the common people. They were drawn by His reputation as a healer, which had now reached its climax (15).

The Beelzeboul Accusation (12: 22–37)
See comments on Mk 3: 22–30 (Lk. 11: 14–23)

and note on Mt. 9: 32 ff. The very surprise of the people at the healing shows how little real faith there was. It was probably the man's instantaneous ability to speak and see that influenced them most. **23. the Son of David** (cf. 9: 27; 15: 22; 20: 30 f.; 21: 9, 15): We need not doubt that the title is used Messianically. If there were Roman spies around it was a safer expression to use. **24. Beelzeboul** (mg): There is probably no connection with Beelzebub. It means 'lord of dung (*zebul*)', i.e. of heathen sacrifices. Others prefer 'lord of the high place'. **27. your people:** Your fellow Jews. Quite apart from the exceptional case in Ac. 19: 13–16, we know of a number of prominent rabbis who acted as exorcists. A baseless charge against Jesus would involve them equally. **31, 32. blasphemy against the Spirit:** Jesus does not imply that any sin is so great that it cannot be dealt with by the atonement. A man who deliberately calls good evil and evil good is so warped that he will not want forgiveness, a prerequisite for being forgiven. For v. 33 cf. 7: 16–20. **36. every careless word:** This is to be understood in the light of v. 35 (cf. 15: 11, 18, 19). A man's premeditated words are seldom a safe guide to character, the unpremeditated are.

The Demand for a Sign (12: 38–42)
See comments on Lk. 11: 29–32. For the Jewish religious leaders a request for a sign seemed reasonable. God had given Moses signs for his people (Exod. 3: 12; 4: 1–9); why should not Jesus, who came with a new authority, give them also? The signs given to Moses were of two types: (*a*) for unbelief (Exod. 4: 1–9)— these were adequately represented by His miracles of healing; (*b*) for faith (Exod. 3: 12)— this took place *after* the Exodus, even so **the sign of the prophet Jonah** would come at the end of His ministry.

40. three days and three nights: The period given in Jewish tradition. Problems raised by this phrase with regard to the day of the crucifixion are baseless (see Additional Note to ch. 27). In Biblical and Rabbinic time-reckoning part of a period is reckoned as a whole period. 'Rabbi Elazar (*c.* A.D. 100) said, "A day and a night make an '*onah* (i.e. 24 hour period) and the portion of an '*onah* is reckoned as an '*onah*".' **41, 42. one greater:** See note on 12: 6. They might be excused for not recognizing His person, but not for their failure to accept His person and work.

The Peril of the Empty Man (12: 43–45)
See comments on Lk. 11: 24 ff. Though these verses are a literal statement of fact, they also form a parable. They are not a warning to the Jews in general (so M'Neile, Filson, Tasker, Schniewind) but are addressed to the scribes and Pharisees (Schlatter). Parabolically understood they refer to the work of the Law, which

could prepare Israel for the Messiah but could not 'fill' it.

Jesus' True Relations (12: 46–50)
See comments on Mk 3: 19b–21, 31–35 (Lk. 8: 19–21). The interruption of Jesus' teaching was a personal insult and a rejection of its divine authority. On the other hand the incident makes 'it clear that not the whole of Jesus' generation was evil' (Tasker).

III. ii. THE KINGDOM OF HEAVEN (13: 1–52)

The Problem of the Parables. The rabbis often used parables, so the surprise of the disciples (10) cannot have been at the fact that Jesus used them. The rabbinic parable, when it went beyond a simile, was generally a brief semi-allegorical story, the meaning of which was normally obvious. Jesus' parables can be divided into two types. Some arise out of a stated background and effectively give God's answer to it. The majority, in spite of their variety, fall into this class, and we ignore their setting to our loss; it is not recorded that they caused any surprise. Then there are those grouped in this chapter, which are complete in themselves. No background is suggested beyond their general setting in Jesus' ministry. It is this purely parabolic teaching that caused the surprise. Modern efforts to supply them with suitable backgrounds as a basis for interpretation have carried little conviction.

The Interpretation of the Parables. The traditional exegesis of the Church saw in the parables masterpieces of allegory in which every detail had a meaning. Dodd (pp. 11 f.) reproduces Augustine's treatment of the parable of the Good Samaritan as an example. The method is far from dead but has been abandoned by almost all responsible expositors.

The dominant modern view, expressed especially by Dodd and Jeremias, swings to the other extreme. It has been described by Dodd (pp. 18 f.): 'The typical parable, whether it be a simple metaphor, or a more elaborate similitude, or a full-length story, presents one point of comparison. The details are not intended to have an independent significance. In an allegory, on the other hand, each detail is a separate metaphor, with a significance of its own . . . In the parable of the Sower the wayside and the birds, the thorns and the stony ground are not, as Mark supposed, cryptograms for persecution, the deceitfulness of riches, and so forth. They are there to conjure up a picture of the vast amount of wasted labour which the farmer must face, and so bring into relief the satisfaction that the harvest gives, in spite of all.'

In spite of valuable light thrown on the par-ables and the removal of much dead wood in exegesis, this method has often been singularly unsatisfying. It demands a seriously distorted picture of the apostolic Church and places the skill of the modern scholar in the place of the understanding of the first disciples and of the guidance of the Holy Spirit.

The truth seems to lie between the extremes. A parable has only one message, but many of the details are semi-allegorical contributions towards it. Where the setting indicates the meaning, it is comparatively simple to distinguish between the heart of the story and the necessary 'scenery' that has no bearing on the application. In the collection of ch. 13 there is no setting, and therefore interpretation becomes much more difficult; we have to be very careful what we dismiss as 'scenery'.

The Problem of Hardening (13: 10–17)
Cf. Mk 4: 10 ff. (Lk. 8: 9 f.). The outstanding simplicity of many of the parables, *when interpreted in their setting*, has made this explanation for parabolic teaching a major difficulty in exegesis. Once it is grasped that it refers to this collection of the Parables of the Kingdom, *and to them alone*, much of the difficulty vanishes.

It is illegitimate to concentrate on **though seeing they do not see** (13) and to ignore 'so that they may indeed see but not understand' (Mk 4: 12). The use of Isa. 6: 9 f. (cf. Jn 12: 39 f.; Ac. 28: 25 ff.; Rom. 11: 8) shows that we are concerned with something more than voluntary obtuseness. It is still more illegitimate to attribute this thought to the early Church and not to Jesus (Dodd, pp. 13 ff.). Far more acceptable is Jeremias's view. He separates Mk 4: 11 f. from these parables; on the basis of the presumed underlying Aramaic he renders Mk 4: 12 'unless they turn and God will forgive them'. But once again there is the driving of a wedge between Jesus and the early Church.

We cannot reasonably escape the conclusion that the teaching of this section of parables, but of them alone, was judicial in form, part of God's mysterious dealing with Israel. If the interpretation of these parables given below is accepted, it will be seen that every one to a greater or less extent cuts across standard rabbinic teaching, and indeed many commonly accepted ideas in the Church. Therefore they will not have been understood by many of the hearers, just as they are often misunderstood today.

11. the secrets (*ta mystēria*) **of the kingdom of heaven:** This must be interpreted as an enlargement of Mk 4: 11, 'to you has been given the secret (*to mystērion*) of the kingdom of God'. This secret is Jesus Himself, so **the secrets** are the effects of His message and ministry. To say this is not to agree with the *Scofield*

Bible that these seven parables 'taken together, describe the result of the presence of the Gospel in the world during the present age, that is, the time of seed-sowing which began with our Lord's personal ministry, and ends with the harvest'. As elaborated there this view demands a consistent and minute allegorization and implicitly assumes that we are dealing with a block of consecutive teaching, Mt. not having carried out its normal practice of grouping teaching.

The Parable of the Sower (13: 1–23)

See comments on Mk 4: 1–20 (Lk. 8: 4–15). The stress on the site of the parable (1 f.; Mk 4: 1) suggests that the parable was based on what Jesus could see from the boat. It also explains the use of the definite article with sower, rightly rendered in English idiom **a farmer**. All this suggests it is unwise to lay heavy stress on sowing. The apparent wastefulness of the sower in sowing in unsuitable places is explained by the fact that he was followed by the ploughman (Jeremias); he had no means of judging what lay under the unbroken earth, or even where **the path** would run.

The explanation (18–23) shows that it is a parable of soils rather than of the sower. No suggestion is made why some soil is suitable, some not; there is not even a suggestion that the soil is to blame. It is really an affirmation of Isa. 6: 9 f. in practice. It has special relevance to Israel (Rom. 11: 25) but is true of all nations. Judaism has never had any understanding for the prophetic teaching of the remnant; the parable is a reaffirmation of it in equally ununderstood words.

The Parable of the Weeds (13: 24–30)

The kingdom of heaven is like . . . : This and similar expressions (31, 33, 44, 45, 47) do not compare the exercise of God's sovereignty with some person or thing in the parable, but with the picture given by the parable as a whole. NEB renders well, 'The kingdom of Heaven is like this'. For **kingdom of heaven** see note on 4: 17. **weeds** (*zizania*): So also Phillips. The rendering 'darnel' (RVmg, NEB) is preferable, for *Arndt* and *SB* show a specific plant is intended (Heb. *zûn*), i.e. darnel, which the rabbis believed to be corrupt wheat. Schniewind throws cold water on interpretations that stress the similarity between wheat and darnel, at first at any rate, or the poisonous nature of ripe darnel seeds, because these points are not mentioned. Would it have been necessary for those who knew the properties of darnel or the use it could be put to?

29. you may root up the wheat: Both the difficulty of distinction and the tendency of darnel to root itself more firmly than wheat are suggested.

38. the field is the world: Possibly 'mankind'; it is less the planting of men and more the implanting of divine or diabolical principles that is being stressed. In any case all possibility of exact allegory breaks down. It is not stated that at any given moment all men are either wheat or darnel, though we may perhaps infer that at the last they will be one or the other. It is generally taken as a 'church' allegory, but in fact it is the divine prohibition against any (including angels) making a final separation before the end. In addition we learn that the devil can transform men as effectively as the gospel. Considerable dissension has been caused by the allegorists who maintain that since the darnel is collected first, there must be a rapture of the wicked before that of the just.

The Parables of the Mustard Seed and Leaven (13: 31–33)

For the former see comments on Mk 4: 30 ff.; for the latter cf. Lk. 13: 20 f. Though the former tells of the exceptional and the latter of the commonplace, the two parables obviously belong together. While the mustard seldom exceeds four feet, under exceptionally suitable circumstances it can reach even 15 feet (*HDB* III, p. 463; *NBD*, p. 1006). The **three satas** (mg) **of flour** represent the OT *ephah*, or about a bushel (56 lbs.). Passages like Gen. 18: 6; Jg. 6: 19, show that it was a not-uncommon quantity for a batch of baking. The **yeast** was generally a piece of dough from the previous batch of baking, which had been allowed to ferment.

The usual interpretation sees the rapid spread and all penetrating influence of the Kingdom through the Church for good in these parables. The consistent allegorist insists, 'Leaven is the principle of corruption working subtly; it is invariably used in a bad sense, and is defined by our Lord as evil doctrine (Mt. 16: 11 f.; Mk 8: 15)' (*Scofield Bible*). This forces him to give a bad sense to the parable of the Mustard Seed as well. Lev. 7: 13; 23: 17 cast doubt on the universally evil symbolic meaning of leaven (the notes *ad loc.* in the *Scofield Bible* are not convincing). It seems more likely that leaven is symbolically neutral, referring to the hidden forces the human spirit can release. Since man by nature is evil, these forces are normally evil also, but as the symbolism of Lev. 7: 13; 23: 17 shows, they can be transformed to good by fellowship with God.

It seems wisest, therefore, to regard these parables as neutral. They proclaim the fact of growth and influence, but their quality is left in question. The mustard 'tree' is a most insecure growth that will in any case die down with the coming of winter; no Christian advance has of necessity any guarantee of permanence. Historically not every 'christian' influence has been spiritually welcome, and some are undoubtedly helping forward the coming of the final apostasy.

The Parables of the Hidden Treasure and the Pearl (13: 44–46)

Once again the two parables belong together. The difference between them is that in one case the action is the result of an accident (the man was probably a hired labourer), in the other it is the result of deliberate search. Both result in the finder's selling all, a term we have no right to water down. There is no suggestion of purchasing salvation, but that coming under the sovereignty of God means the complete denial of self (cf. 10: 38 f.; 16: 25; Jn 12: 25).

The Parable of the Net (13: 47–50)

The parable of the Weeds revealed that this world of men is the visible expression of invisible forces. Here it is rather the visible activity of the Kingdom through the Church that is under consideration; note that it is not the leaders of the Church but the angels that make the separation, as with the weeds. **the bad:** Probably, when used of the fish, the ritually impure, cf. Lev. 11: 9–12; Dt. 14: 9 f.

Conclusion of the Parables (13: 51, 52)

A **teacher of the law** (scribe), in its NT sense, was one who so knew the OT that he could be trusted to copy and expound it—the normal connection with the Pharisees was in one way accidental; there were scribes of the Sadducees, and there were probably some linked with no party. Jesus wanted those who would undergo the discipline of knowing the Kingdom. They would be able to expound both the revelation of the OT (**old treasures**) and that of the NT (**new treasures**).

IV. i. THE SHADOW OF THE CROSS (13: 53–17: 23)

The Rejection of Jesus at Nazareth (13: 53–58)

See comments on Mk 6: 1–6; Lk. 4: 16–30.

It should be clear that the rejection here described (and in Mk) is a second one, subsequent to that in Lk. The details are quite different. If we take the tense of **he began teaching the people** (*edidasken*, imperfect) strictly, it may mean that Jesus was there some little time—Mk 'he began to teach' is compatible with this. They had to show more respect to an established teacher with a number of disciples than they had at the beginning of His ministry.

The Death of John the Baptist (14: 1–12)

See comments on Mk 6: 14–29. Mt. saw in John's death a foreshadowing of the death of Jesus.

The Feeding of the Five Thousand (14: 13–21)

See comments on Mk 6: 31–44; Lk. 9: 10–17; Jn 6: 1–13. Dalman (pp. 172–176) makes it clear that the 'Bethsaida' of Lk. 9: 10 must be taken as an approximation, and that the miracle

must have taken place much nearer the middle of the eastern shore, a little north of Hippos (the modern Ein Gev).

The Walking on the Water (14: 22–33)

See comments on Mk 6: 45–52 and Jn 6: 15–21 for vv. 22–27. The disciples' journey was to be to the other side in the general direction of (*pros*) Bethsaida, which was only just east of the Jordan (Mk 6: 45). There is no evidence for a Bethsaida west of Jordan (Dalman, pp. 161–166). That they landed further west (14: 34) will have been due to the storm.

Peter is often blamed for trying to walk on the water, but he had Jesus' permission. He walked a little distance with the wind in his back. **He saw the wind** by the spray whipped off the waves. He had virtually reached Jesus when he grew fearful, and he and Jesus will have walked back to the boat together in the teeth of the gale.

Healings at Gennesaret (14: 34–36)

See comments on Mk 6: 53–56.

36. the edge of his cloak: See note on 9: 20.

Washing of Hands and Defilement (15: 1–20)

See comments on Mk 7: 1–23. The washing of hands before and after a meal was a purely ritualistic action with little thought of bodily cleanliness. It was recognized that it was not based on the Law but on rabbinic authority. It may have been an old custom, but it had not yet been generally enforced in the time of Jesus.

5. Whatever help you might otherwise have received from me is a gift devoted to God is usually interpreted to mean that the man refused to help his parents because he claimed his property had been dedicated to God, yet he continued using it for his own profit. Such an action would have been impossible then and probably at any time in Israel's history. *SB*, on the basis of Rabbinic sources, translate, 'As a sacrifice be what you might have gained from me'. No one could profit from a sacrifice, and this was a formula, not dedicating anything to God, but declaring that his parents must so look on it. It was putting under a solemn curse anything his parents might try to get from him. The Talmud makes it clear that this was not so uncommon, and that many rabbis were far from happy about the custom; they were probably influenced by Jesus' criticism.

Jesus was not advocating the abolition of the dietary laws (17, Mk 7: 19) but was stressing that they had nothing to do with pure and impure, but as Mk makes clear the abolition was the logical outcome.

The Syrophoenician Woman (15: 21–28)

See comments on Mk 7: 24–30. **22. Son of David:** See note on 12: 23. It is doubtful whether the woman knew the meaning of what she was saying; if she did, she was really under obligation to become a proselyte.

24. I was sent only to the lost sheep of Israel: See note on 10: 5. This is less heartless than it sounds, for the way was always open for the woman to become an Israelite. As soon as the woman ceased to use empty words, which were perhaps intended to appeal to Jesus' vanity, and based herself on need she was heard.

Many Healings (15: 29–31)

See comments on Mk 7: 31–37. Mk concentrates on an individual, Mt. stresses the large numbers involved. As Mk makes clear, Jesus was moving in the region NE of the lake, largely Jewish but outside the jurisdiction both of Herod Antipas and of the religious authorities in Jerusalem. Since this area had seen little of Him, it explains the large number flocking to Him for healing.

The Feeding of the Four Thousand (15: 32–39)

See comments on Mk 8: 1–10. It is doubtful whether any positive distinction can be drawn between this miracle and that of the feeding of the five thousand (14: 13–21). Probably the site will have been much the same. We cannot even lay much stress on the different terms used for the baskets. 'The *spyris* (15: 37), cf. Ac. 9: 25, did not differ from the *kophinos* (14: 20) in size, but in material, and to a certain extent in use' (M'Neile). The power, which Jesus would not use for Himself (4: 3 f.), was freely available for the needs of others. Indeed, this section warns us against attributing any uniqueness to the feeding of the five thousand. Dalman (p. 128) considers that **Magadan** is a corruption of Magdal (=Magdala) and Dalmanutha (Mk 8: 10) of Magdal Nuna (=Magdal Nunaiya, i.e. Magdal of fish).

A Request for a Sign (16: 1–4)

See comments on Mk 8: 11–13 and Mt. 12: 38–42. NEB with the best MSS omits vv. 2b, 3, cf. Mk; for them cf. Lk. 12: 54 ff. Possibly the sign **from heaven** asked for was the voice from heaven (*bat qol*) met with occasionally in rabbinic stories.

The Disciples' Shortage of Bread (16: 5–12)

See comments on Mk 8: 14–21. The disciples took Jesus' saying literally, because they had just left Jewish territory (15: 39) for a semi-Gentile one (16: 13; Mk 8: 22), where they might find it hard to find a Jewish baker. Jesus used the term **yeast** (6) of the teaching of the religious leaders because, though very few Galileans were attracted by it (cf. Ac. 15: 10), they were being subconsciously won over to it, as the religious developments after the destruction of Jerusalem were to show.

The Confession at Caesarea Philippi (16: 13–20)

See comments on Mk 8: 27–33 (Lk. 9: 18–22) for vv. 13–16, 20. The fact that Mk and Lk. omit **the Son of the living God** suggests that Jesus pronounced His blessing on Peter because he had recognized Him as Messiah, not because he had realized His divine nature. The early acknowledgment of Jesus as Messiah (Jn 1: 41, 45, 49) had been an act of enthusiasm; Peter's confession expressed mature conviction created by divine revelation. **17. Son of Jonah** (*Yona*), presumably is an unusual abbreviation of *Yochanan*, i.e. John (Jn 21: 15). **18. you are Peter** (*petros*) **and on this rock** (*petra*) **I will build my church:** Until it was demonstrated in the last decade of the 19th century that Jesus must normally have taught in Aramaic, the popular Protestant exegesis of this verse contrasted *petros*, a stone, with *petra*, a rock, thus seeking to rule out the thought that Peter was in any sense the foundation of the church. Already earlier, once the true nature of *koinē* Gk. began to be known, some were unhappy about a word play that suited classical Gk. better than *koinē*. Once it was grasped that the name bestowed was the Aram. *Kepha* (Gk. *Kēphas*, Eng. Cephas), it was clear that the alleged pun had to be abandoned, for it was impossible in Aram. That Kepha was the name given is shown by Paul's using it eight times to the twice he employs Peter (Gal. 2: 7 f.). It seems clear then that the much attacked rendering of NEB (and Phillips) is justified, 'You are Peter, the Rock, and on this rock . . .' Fortunately the truth or falsity of Roman Catholic claims about the authority of the Papacy is not to a decided by the exposition of a doubtful pun. Unless, against the clear suggestion of the text, we picture Jesus as turning from Peter to the others, **this rock** cannot be Peter himself but is contrasted with him, i.e. it must be his confession. The greatness and leadership of Peter may be seen in Ac. 1: 15; 2: 14; 5: 3, 8, 15; 8: 14; 10: 46 f. On the other hand Mt. 18: 1; 19: 27; 20: 21; Lk. 22: 24; Ac. 11: 2; Gal. 2: 11, etc. show no sign that Peter or the others had any conception that an absolute primacy had been conferred on him. **my church** (*ekklēsia*): The word used by Jesus must have been *qahal* (Heb.), often rendered *ekklēsia* by LXX. In seeking to fix its meaning we must look away from connotations Paul's Gentile converts may have read into it. *Qahal* (Heb.) or *kenishta* (Aram.) was used for the whole congregation of Israel, i.e. Israel as a whole acting as the people of God; it was used also of the smaller local units, which ideally represented the whole. It is the wider sense that is used here, the narrower in 18: 17. 'The powers of death' (RSV): A good rendering of **the gates of Hades**. It is not a question of Satanic powers, but of death, which Jesus was to conquer in His resurrection. **19. the keys of the kingdom of**

heaven are to be understood in the light of Isa. 22: 22; and the authority to bind and loose is not of admission and exclusion, but deciding what is and what is not the Lord's will. This latter promise is in 18: 18 extended not merely to the other disciples, but by inference to all spiritual Christians.

The First Prediction of the Passion (16: 21–23)
See comments on Mk 8: 31–33.

The Cost of Discipleship (16: 24–28)
See comments on Mk 8: 34–9: 1 (Lk. 9: 23–27). In reading the careful note on Mk 9: 1 we should bear three points in mind. (*a*) The usual modern view that Jesus was anticipating an early second coming is ruled out, quite apart from the attribution of fallibility to Him, by His emphatic statement, not so long afterwards, of His ignorance on the subject (24: 36, Mk 13: 32). (*b*) Interpretations involving transfiguration, resurrection and the pouring out of the Holy Spirit all stumble over the time factor, for none of His hearers need have died by then. (*c*) The destruction of Jerusalem, though satisfying the time factor, does not possess the aura of glory implied, cf. Jesus' weeping over the city. The only interpretation that seems to do justice to all these factors sees no one incident foretold; rather the whole of the opening period of the Church's existence from the resurrection onwards is foreseen (the transfiguration was a foreshadowing of the resurrection). This in many ways found its close in the destruction of Jerusalem.

The Transfiguration (17: 1–8)
See comments on Mk 9: 2–8; Lk. 9: 28–36. Scripture does not interpret this incident, which was obviously a major happening in the Ministry (cf. 2 Pet. 1: 16 ff.; Jn 1: 14). Both Jn 17: 5 and 2 Pet. 1: 17 lead us to see in the transfiguration an act of the Father's. It seems more probable that it was the glory of the manhood rather than of the Deity of Christ that was revealed. By perfect obedience He had reached the goal that Adam should have attained, and death had no more claim on Him. Presumably He could have ascended to the Father then and there, but the conversation about His departure (Lk. 9: 31) marked His voluntary going forward to the cross. Was this perhaps the point suggested by Heb. 2: 10, 18; 5: 8, 9, which must have come before the perfected high priest offered up the perfect sacrifice? Note that it was the divine voice (17: 5 f.) and the cloud (Lk. 9: 34) that made the disciples afraid, not Jesus' glory.

The Discussion about Elijah (17: 9–13) See comments on Mk 9: 9–13.

The Healing of the Demon-possessed Boy (17: 14–21)
See comments on Mk 9: 14–29. The evidence

of MSS for omission of v. 21 cannot be questioned; cf. mg and Mk 9: 29.

20. you can say to this mountain: Rabbinic parallels suggest that moving mountains was a proverbial expression at the time for doing the impossible.

The Second Prediction of the Passion (17: 22, 23)
See comments on Mk 9: 30–32.

IV. ii. THE CHURCH (17: 24–18: 35)
The Temple Tax (17: 24–27)
In its setting this historical incident becomes virtually a parable of the disciple's relationship to other communities that claim his allegiance.

Exod. 30: 11–16 tells of a special half-shekel census tax given to the Tabernacle. After the exile a voluntary cultic tax of a third of a shekel was adopted (Neh. 10: 32 f.). Before the time of Jesus this had been changed to a compulsory half-shekel tax payable annually by every free male of twenty and over, whether he lived in Palestine or the diaspora. Refusal to pay would have been regarded as an act of apostasy. After the destruction of the Temple in A.D. 70 the tax had to be paid to the temple of Jupiter Capitolinus in Rome as a punishment for the rebellion.

25. From their own sons: i.e. members of the royal family. Jesus claimed exemption in virtue of His sonship, and extended it through Peter to the other disciples. The miracle was not a gratuitous act of divine power, but a demonstration that those who do not insist on their religious rights can experience God's blessing in His provision. There is no suggestion that Jesus did not have the money available. The 'St. Peter's fish' found in the Lake of Galilee today is quite capable of holding a shekel coin in its mouth. Since there is no ground for disassociating Peter from the other disciples in the matter of temple-tax, it is hard to resist the conclusion that he was the only member of the Twelve over twenty (cf. note on 20: 20).

The Dispute about Greatness (18: 1–5)
See comments on Mk 9: 33–37 and 10: 15. From outside claims we turn to the church community itself. In a well-ordered society and family a little child, with all its faults, will not be concerned with any scale of greatness. God is so great, that any differences of rank in His kingdom must pale into insignificance, when seen in His light. In addition His scale of values is so different from man's that for Him the reception of a child can be ranked as the reception of Jesus (5).

4. Whoever humbles himself like this child: 'The sense is not humbles himself as this little child humbles himself but humbles himself until he is like this little child' (Tasker).

The Importance of the Little One (18: 6–14)

In this section vv. 8, 9 interrupt the connection between vv. 6, 7 and 10–14. They are a repetition of 5: 29 f., intended to point the reader back to that passage and would be best placed in brackets. They serve to underline the awfulness of sin and temptation. The change from 'child' to **little ones** suggests that we are dealing both with children and those that have become childlike (3 f.). **Causes one of these little ones . . . to sin** is not an adequate translation of the Gk. Knox is better with, 'hurts the conscience of'. Modern psychology has demonstrated that failure to meet a child's standards can cause lasting psychic and spiritual damage; the same is true of many recent converts. There are those who have never come to faith because of the unfaithful conduct of the 'faithful', and there are many spiritual cripples thanks to their early impressions of a church. **7. Woe to the world because of the things that cause people to sin:** Knox, 'Woe to the world for the hurt done to consciences!'

The fact that we are repelled by sentimental pictures of children's guardian angels is no reason for rejecting the literal meaning of **their angels in heaven always see the face of my Father . . .** It is, of course, true that 'The angel, therefore, symbolizes the believer's relation to God' (M'Neile), but in view of the almost universal, contemporary, Jewish belief in guardian angels, it seems impossible not to see a confirmation of the concept by Jesus, though not of many fanciful embroideries of it. So we have no ground for saying, 'Their angels are their counterparts, or their spiritual doubles, who have access at all times to the Father's presence' (Tasker). This seems to be an invalid deduction from some rabbinic sayings.

For vv. 12, 13 see comments on Lk. 15: 1–7. The use of the parable here shows that we are to include repentant 'tax collectors and sinners' among the little ones. The evidence of MSS is clearly against the insertion of v. 11 here (cf. Lk. 19: 10). **14. that any of these little ones should be lost:** 'One' is neuter, looking back to the sheep, i.e. this is the conclusion of the parable, showing that it is the Father (MS evidence is about equally divided between my and **your**) who goes out after the lost, through the Son, of course. So long as there is hope He will do all that can be done without depriving a man of his personality.

The Church's Dealing with the Sinner (18: 15–20)

This section should always be read in the light of vv. 10–14. We are dealing with the human counterpart of divine love in action.

15. If your brother sins against you: The evidence of the MSS is unclear, but it is probably best to omit 'against you' (NEB). The

words may well have been inserted to discourage the idea that Jesus was giving a charter to the busy-body. Should anyone enjoy carrying out this task, it is clear evidence that he is not suited to it. Since all sin damages, the Christian should not be indifferent to a brother's sin. A personal approach should rouse a minimum of ill-feeling and gives least publicity to the sin. The **two or three witnesses** (cf. Dt. 19: 15) are not merely to report on the offender's attitude, if he does not listen to them, but also to check on the validity of the accusation—the accuser is not always right. If he refuses to hear the local church, he is clearly a poisonous influence and must be excluded. In the mouth of Jesus **a pagan or a tax collector** clearly implies that the one excluded is there to be won back. It would not avail the offender to appeal to the court of heaven, for if Jesus' teaching has been sincerely and lovingly followed, God will endorse the church's decision (18; cf. 16: 19).

In their original setting vv. 19, 20 show the two or three of v. 16 preparing for their task —only when they have been ignored, does the whole church come into consideration. **Agree** (*symphōneō*) implies a harmony that can be created only by much prayer and detailed study of the case. Those so engaged can be certain of Christ's presence with them. **20. come together in my name:** The rendering 'unto my name' (J. N. Darby) is more literal but hardly intelligible. *eis to onoma* in the papyri means 'to the account of', 'into the possession of', i.e they meet as the conscious possession of Jesus. While v. 20 may be rightly used as a word of encouragement to those that meet in small companies for conscience' sake, it offers no support to those who think that by using a verbal formula they have become God's favourites.

Forgiveness (18: 21–35)

Peter evidently realized that if an erring disciple was to be reconciled to God, he had to be reconciled to his fellow-disciples as well. **Up to seven times:** The idea found in some older commentaries that the rabbis fixed the number of times a man had to be forgiven at three, is based on a misunderstanding of the rule that if the offender asked three times in the presence of witnesses for forgiveness, he had to receive it. Peter was probably choosing seven as the perfect but limited number. Jesus answer reversed the proud boast of Lamech (Gen. 4: 24).

The parable that illustrates the point is placed at the court of some oriental potentate, where gold flows like water and the courtiers are called **servants** (*douloi*), i.e. slaves. **28. a hundred denarii:** No trifle, for it represented a hundred days' wages for a labourer (cf. 20: 2). It is not the actual sums involved but the disparity between them that is the point of the parable. Tasker suggests two or three million pounds and two or three hundred pounds. M'Neile suggests a disparity of 600,000 to one. Jesus did not suggest that the debts owed us by men's sins might not be grievous—they often are—but compared with our debts to God they are virtually nothing. For v. 35 cf. 6: 15.

V. i. THE WAY TO JERUSALEM
(19: 1–23: 39)

Most of this section is found in Mk and also very much in Lk.

Jesus' Teaching on Marriage and Divorce (19: 1–12)

See notes on 5: 31 f. and comments on Mk 10: 1–12. A frequent weakness in exposition springs from the idea that the Pharisees were a closely knit and unitary body. There are no grounds for thinking that the Pharisees involved in this incident were any more hostile than the one of 22: 35, or Lk. 10: 25. The question **Is it lawful for a man to divorce his wife for any and every reason?** shows that the questioners belonged to one of the rival groups of Hillel or Shammai and hoped to be able to quote Jesus in their favour.

The disciples felt, like so many moderns, that Jesus' answer was inhuman. He made it clear that He was not a new legislator but was holding up an ideal for the spiritual. For some men and women their physical make-up is such, that marriage is at best a social convenience for them. Others do not marry, because they have been castrated, or because they have been placed in circumstances, *e.g.* slavery, where marriage is impossible. Yet others will be lifted above the material and physical urge to marriage. Should they marry, they will not find Jesus' ideal impossible or even difficult. It is insufficiently realized by the Church that many, perhaps the majority of marriages between Christians are entered on a mainly physical level. For these the strict enforcement of Jesus' teaching may be very difficult.

Jesus' Blessing of the Children (19: 13–15)

See comments on Mk 10: 13–16; Lk. 18: 15–17. The story is so placed as to dispel any idea that in vv. 11 f. Jesus was attributing any special merit to celibacy. What motivated the parents (there is no suggestion that only mothers were involved) remains unknown, for there are no parallels in Jewish custom. The linking of the passage with infant baptism is a curiosity in Christian thought.

The Rich Young Ruler (19: 16–30)

See comments on Mk 10: 17–31; Lk. 18: 18–30. **Teacher, what good thing must I do to get eternal life?:** In all legalistic systems there is the temptation to think that there must be some act so outstanding as to ensure eternal life (cf. Lk. 10: 25). In His answer Jesus said, **Obey**

the commandments; the tense in Gk. implies not a single action but a continued process.

Mk and Lk. concentrate on the title 'good' given to Jesus and the rejection of it as unseemly, Mt. on the **good thing** and the rebuke that we are concerned with the Good One and not with a good principle. **If you want to be perfect** is sufficiently explained by 'You lack one thing' (Mk and Lk.). The giving up of his possessions was not a universal law of perfection, as it was taken by Francis of Assisi to be, but the decisive challenge to a particular man. **24. a camel to go through the eye of a needle:** A rabbinic equivalent is an elephant to go through the eye of a needle. The popular interpretation in certain circles that the eye of a needle is a small door within a city gate is baseless. Salvation is obtained by complete trust in God; riches of any kind, including natural talents, make such trust virtually impossible. **26. with God** (*para theō*) **all things are possible:** This does not mean 'everything is possible for God' (NEB). It is hard to conceive of any Jewish teacher's making such a trite remark. We should render, 'In God's presence all things are possible', i.e. the man who turns from men to God will find there the power to overcome the otherwise unovercomable. **28. at the renewal of all things** (*palingenesia*): Better 'in the world renewal' (Filson), which would be brought in by the Messiah. A transference of the concept from earth to heaven does violence to the sense. **The twelve tribes of Israel** in such a setting is equivalent to 'all Israel' (Rom. 11: 26).

Parable of the Labourers in the Vineyard (20: 1–16)

This parable was told to explain the warning of 19: 30. Being a parable it does not set out to give the whole truth, and it has to be supplemented by 25: 14–30. Its stress is that God owes no man anything (cf. Lk. 17: 7–10), and so every reward is essentially an act of grace. If the last are first, it is only in the eyes of those that expect more (the few minutes difference in order of payment is not under consideration). It is their disappointment that makes it seem that the others had preferential treatment. In a time of underemployment they should have been thankful that they had had a full day's work. Tob. 5: 14 and various rabbinic passages show that **a denarius for the day** was a good day's wages; many earned less.

The Third Prediction of the Passion (20: 17–19)

See comments on Mk 10: 32–34.

The Request of James and John (20: 20–28)

See comments on Mk 10: 35–45; for vv. 25–28 cf. also Lk. 22: 24–27. The making of the request shows how little 16: 18 f. was looked on as giving a primacy to Peter. That James' and John's mother, Salome (cf. 27: 56 with Mk

15: 40), was involved is very strong support for the suggestion about their youth; cf. the note on 17: 24–27.

The Healing of Bartimaeus (20: 29–34)

See comments on Mk 10: 46–52; Lk. 18: 35–43. **30. two blind men:** See note on 8: 28–34. The exceptional fact that the name Bartimaeus (Mk: 10: 46) has been preserved suggests that he became a well-known member of the Jerusalem church. Hence the other blind man recedes into the background in Mk and Lk.
Son of David: See note on 12: 23.

The Entry into Jerusalem (21: 19)

See comments on Mk 11: 1–10; Lk. 19: 28–40; Jn 12: 12–19. **Bethphage:** Mk and Lk. have 'Bethphage and Bethany'. Since Dalman (pp. 252 ff.) has shown conclusively that Bethphage lay nearer Jerusalem than did Bethany, it seems likely that the donkey was fetched from the latter. In view of His links with the village, Jesus had probably made quiet advance preparations (cf. note on 26: 18). **5. a donkey . . . a colt:** 'Two animals in Mt. only. Probably "Matthew" or his source thought of two animals because of Zech. 9: 9. In this poetic verse the prophet speaks in parallel lines of the animal the king will ride; both lines refer to the same animal. But the double reference seems to have led to the prosaic assumption that there were two animals' (Filson). This is a typical example of modern statements on the passage; the facts are correct, the conclusions most doubtful. An unbroken donkey's colt would be steadied by the presence of its mother. **7. on them:** There is adequate MS evidence for reading 'on it' with Lk. (M'Neile, Tasker). Jn 12: 16 makes it highly improbable that it was the riding on the donkey that moved the crowd to enthusiasm. It was probably a prearranged demonstration by the Galileans who had formerly tried to make Jesus king (Jn 6: 15) and were now trying to force His hand. Many of them had already reached Jerusalem and came out to meet Him (Jn 12: 12 f.).

Jesus in the Temple (21: 10–17)

See comments on Mk 11: 15–19; Lk. 19: 45–48; for vv. 10, 11 cf. Jn. 12: 19. It is clear that Mt. places the cleansing of the Temple on the Sunday, Mk on the Monday; Lk. is too brief for us to draw any certain conclusions. The story of the fig tree makes much easier sense, if we accept Mk's order. We shall be wise, therefore, to see in Mt.'s order one of his deliberate inversions to bring out that the King of Israel is Lord of the Temple. The nearest picture we can get of what was happening is to imagine a cattle-market in a cathedral close. It had been permitted because those who sold had undoubtedly to pay space rent to the priests. **13. a den of robbers:** The sacred surroundings had doubtless no influence on the commercial morals of the dealers, and a pilgrim who had not brought his sacrificial animals with him was very much at their mercy. It is frequently urged that Jn 2: 13–20 must represent the same incident, having been misplaced by design or accident. There are, however, sufficient differences for us to take it as a separate incident. If it were not, it seems incredible that Mt. and Mk should not have recorded Jn 2: 19 as a preparation for 26: 61; Mk 14: 58. **16. Do you hear what these children are saying?:** The authorities could not discipline the mob of children excited by the arrival of the pilgrims and the events of the day, but they expected Jesus to disassociate Himself from them. In signifying His approval by quoting Ps. 8: 2 He implicitly claimed to be the Messiah.

The Cursing of the Fig Tree (21: 18–22)

See comments on Mk 11: 12–14, 20–24. The view that Mt. has compressed incidents from two days into one has been given in the last section. We need not press **immediately** (19 f.) to mean that the tree became visibly dead while they stood and watched it. The facts about the fig tree and its fruit can be best found in *HDB* II, pp. 5 f., or *NBD*, p. 422. 'To see if he could find anything on it' (Mk 11: 13) shows that in the ordinary affairs of life Jesus did not exercise a supernatural knowledge. What He hoped to find were a few figs left over from the autumn; at the height of Jerusalem, even under the most favourable circumstances, no fig tree could have had early ripe figs on it at Passover time. He did not find any left-overs on it, for which the tree was not blamed, but there was also no promise of any for the coming crop. The cursing of the fig tree was undoubtedly parabolic. Profession without fruit is an abomination. In spite of views to the contrary, the fig tree is not 'a picture of Israel', and so the parable is a general one, though applied in the first place to 'His own'. The fact that the acted parable is applied as a sign of the power of faith—for v. 21 see note on 17: 20—seems to support the general meaning suggested.

The Question concerning Jesus' Authority (21: 23–27)

See comments on Mk 11: 27–33; Lk. 20: 1–8. Jesus was not merely dodging a question by catching out His questioners. By confessing that they were not able to judge John the Baptist's authority, they confessed themselves incompetent, though representing the Sanhedrin, to judge the claims of one who was acclaimed by John as being so much greater than he (3: 11).

The Parable of the Two Sons (21: 28–32)

This is the first of three parables teaching the unworthiness of the religious leaders; they must not be transferred from them to the Jews generally. There are two difficulties in the text. There is good evidence for placing first the son who said 'Yes' and did not go. This puts the representative of the leaders where he belongs, i.e. first of all (NEB, Phillips, M'Neile, Schlatter, Nestle, B. & F. B. S. Diglot). Then, a small but significant group of MSS, which follow the NIV order, have in v. 31 'the second'. This is so absurd and cynical that it is probably correct (Schniewind). We can picture a man like Caiaphas giving such an answer as a refusal to be heckled by a Galilean artisan. When the authorities rejected John the Baptist, they confirmed an attitude taken up long before. For the outcasts John's invitation was the first indication that their rejection of God's will could be reversed.

The Parable of the Wicked Husbandmen (21: 33–46)

See comments on Mk 12: 1–12; Lk. 20: 9–19. The cynical response to the previous parable made Jesus turn to the people (Lk. 20: 9), though the representatives of the Sanhedrin continued to listen (45). Theological mountains have been built on v. 43. Without it British-Israel theory would lose one of its main foundation stones. It is also a main prop for the traditional view, whether in its Patristic or Calvinistic form, that the Church is Israel, or the new Israel, or true Israel, or has taken over the functions of Israel. If it were a momentous declaration of the end of Israel's rôle, one would expect that it would appear in the other Synoptics, at the very least. Such interpretations ignore the point of the parable and equate the husbandmen, instead of the vineyard (Isa. 5: 7), with Israel; they are the higher priesthood and other religious leaders. In fact, as Filson says, 'The Kingdom will be taken from the disobedient Jewish leaders; their rejection of the prophets and the Son makes them liable to judgment'. The destruction of Jerusalem meant the sweeping away of the whole ruling religious caste in Jewry. Even the *Nasi*, the representative recognized by the Romans after A.D. 70, was of the family of Hillel, a humble commoner, though of Davidic origin. Whatever the truth of the theological views mentioned, they must seek their justification elsewhere.

The Parable of the Marriage-Feast (22: 1–14)

Cf. Lk. 14: 16–24. The force of this, the third parable, is often lost by a wrong comparison with Lk.'s parable of a private banquet. Unlike the invitation of a private individual the royal one was virtually compulsory—hence Mt. gives no excuses. The refusal to attend the marriage of the king's son implied disloyalty to the royal house as well. Those envisaged in vv. 2–6 are the religious leaders of Jerusalem, and v. 7 foretells their destruction with that of Jerusalem (**their city**, singular). The arguments of M'Neile, Filson and Tasker that the

verse is out of place forgets the unchronological element so often found in OT stories—obviously the destruction took place after the feast.

Jesus then turned to the crowd, which was enjoying the impotent fury of the representatives of the Sanhedrin, and stressed in vv. 11–14 that they had a responsibility as well. There are no grounds for thinking that Gentiles are here envisaged (Tasker), though in fact they were to reap the benefits of the rejection of the Jewish leaders (Rom. 11: 11, 12, 15).

A wrong use of Lk.'s parable has led to a misunderstanding of v. 9 in terms of Lk. 14: 21 ff. This has led to the question how **wedding clothes** could reasonably be expected from such people and how would they have had time to get one. Hence many, *e.g.* M'Neile, Filson, Tasker, Dodd, Jeremias, but not Schlatter or Schniewind, see in these verses another parable, the beginning of which has been lost. This criticism ignores the more leisured pace of the East and overlooks that the element of hurry is not present in Mt. Judging by similar rabbinic parables, the man had simply continued about his own business until it was too late to go home and change. The view often met with that the wedding garment is the king's gift (cf. *NBC ad loc.*), though at least as old as Augustine, has no evidence to support it. In other words, the wedding garment has no allegorical meaning such as Christ's righteousness. The earlier guests insulted the king by their refusal, this latter one by his unwillingness to turn from his own affairs to prepare himself. **12. Friend:** The king assumes that he has a good excuse. **13. outside . . . the darkness:** 'The dark outside' (Phillips); cf. note on 25: 30.

The Question about the Poll-tax (22: 15–22)

See comments on Mk 12: 13–17; Lk. 20: 20–26. **19. Show me the coin used for paying the tax:** For this tax and this tax alone the Romans had coined special silver coins with the emperor's figure and name, and only they might be used in payment (cf. *HDB* III, p. 428a; *NBD*, p. 841a).

The Question about the Resurrection (22: 23–33)

See comments on Mk 12: 18–27; Lk. 20: 27–40.

The Question about the Greatest Commandment (22: 34–40)

See comments on Mk 12: 28–34. Lk. 10: 27 shows clearly that we do not have original teaching by Jesus here. **Expert in the law** (*nomikos*), though common in Lk., is found only here in Mt. It is probable that a scribe (Mk 12: 28) whose speciality was *halakah*, i.e. the detailed application of the Mosaic Law, is intended. There is no obvious reason why in the quotation of Dt. 6: 5 Mt. omits 'strength' (cf. Mk 12: 30, Lk. 10: 27). The NT does not really introduce a fourth element into Dt. 6: 5. MSS of LXX vary in their rendering of Heb. *lebab* between *kardia* (heart) and *dianoia* (mind). The former is more literal, the latter gives the sense better, because the intellect and will predominate over the emotions in Heb. *lebab*.

About David's Son (22: 41–46)

See comments on Mk 12: 35–37; Lk. 20: 41–44.

Woes against the Scribes and Pharisees (23: 1–36)

Cf. Mk 12: 38–40, Lk. 11: 39–52; 20: 45 ff. For **teachers of the law** see note on 13: 52, for **Pharisees** see *The Religious Background*, p. 1121, and articles *Judaism* and *Pharisees* in *NBD*, for **hypocrites** see note at end of ch. 6. The reader of this chapter must never forget that the bulk of the people approved of the Pharisees, even though they tried to avoid the more onerous points of their legislation, legislation they were not able to enforce in full until after A.D. 70. Hence Jesus must be speaking of the deeper things of the spirit, where only His eye could penetrate. We have in this section seven woes (13–31) with an introduction and conclusion.

Introduction (1–12). Jesus was not attacking their teaching in general but the way they applied it in their own lives (3). By saying they **sit in Moses' seat** (2) He acknowledged the general correctness of it. If one is to keep the Law of Moses, one is virtually compelled to accept the approach of the scribes. Sitting was the position of the teacher (cf. Lk. 4: 20). In the fourth century A.D. there were special synagogue chairs called Moses' seat for rabbis, but it is doubtful whether they existed in the first century; the sense is that they were official expounders of the Law.

The modern Jew considers vv. 3 f. a major insult, and so they are, if we take them purely at their face value. No Pharisee would have maintained his place in the brotherhood for long, if it had been obvious that he preached but did not practise. In the rabbinic expansion of the Law much was man-made commandment intended to guarantee the keeping of the divinely given laws. The learned man might be trusted to ignore or circumvent much of this man-made legislation in ways that the ordinary man knew nothing of. On a deeper level Jesus was condemning, not lawlessness on the part of those who preached law, but rather a strictness, especially among the disciples of Shammai, which was bearable for the richer and more leisured, but almost impossible for the poor. There has been all too much of this in the Church.

With vv. 5–7 cf. 6: 1–8, 16–18; it is the condemnation of all behaviour and ritual, even the anti-ritual of the extremer Protestant, which, professing to address itself to God,

keeps one eye at least on man. **5. phylacteries:** See *NBD*, p. 995. In the first century A.D. their use had not yet become obligatory, so the pious were under very strong temptation to rebuke the non-observant by wearing them as large as possible. **tassels** (or 'fringes'): (Dt. 22: 12; Num. 15: 38 f. and cf. 9: 20; 14: 36): see *HDB* II, pp. 68 ff. They were almost universally worn at the time; they were intended as a reminder to the wearer (Num. 15: 39), not as a proclamation to others. Leading rabbis repeatedly insisted that the learned should not use their knowledge of the Law for personal profit, but they took a very poor view of those who did not show them honour; they would have certainly subscribed to the modern adage that the soldier salutes not the man but his rank. This type of carnal honour is all too prevalent in the Church.

For vv. 8–12 cf. 20: 24–28. Titles which express a fact or are merely conventional often make communication easier and are normally unexceptional. Others are flattery and often worse. **Rabbi . . . master:** Jn 13: 13 gives the usual titles of respect for the Jewish teacher, 'You call me Teacher (*rabbi*) and Lord (*mari*)'. Jesus was so uniquely Lord, that there was no room for a man to be so called in the Church. Teacher lived on (Ac. 13: 1; Jas 3: 1; 1 C. 12: 28; Eph. 4: 11) but there is no evidence for its being used as a title of respect. Even *kyrios* (lord), which to the Gk. speaker meant no more than Sir in secular contexts, is found after the resurrection in the NT only in Rev. 7: 14 as a title of address to others than Christ, on Christian lips that is to say. **9. do not call anyone on earth 'father':** Jesus is not suspending the fifth commandment. The rabbis disliked using the title 'father' except for the Patriarchs, but they were prepared to use it for an outstanding rabbi. We need a greater sensitivity to these things, not just criticism, in the Church today.

The First Woe (13). The meaning of this verse is sharply limited by v. 15. The fact that they had rejected both John the Baptist and Jesus showed that they had not submitted themselves to the sovereignty of God. Their teaching, if accepted in the sense it had for them, made it impossible for others to submit either. After the destruction of Jerusalem it was the greatest single human factor that made the Jews as a people reject Christ.

Widows' Houses (14) (cf. Mk 12: 40; Lk. 20: 47). The MSS are overwhelmingly in favour of the exclusion of this verse; Edersheim's argument (II, p. 410) that the eight Woes balance the eight Beatitudes seems a trifle far-fetched. Any interpretation involving deliberate knavery is grievously to misunderstand the Pharisees, even though they had their black sheep, some of whose acts are recorded in the Talmud.

The insistence on fulfilment of vows and the encouragement of giving, where this was out of place, is a sufficient interpretation.

The Second Woe (15). Both Roman emperors and later a triumphant Church were to punish Jewish proselytizing by death, but the activity was wide-spread at this time. The Synagogue attracted many sympathizers, the *sebomenoi* or *phoboumenoi ton theon*, which NIV renders 'devout' (Ac. 10: 2), 'God-fearing' (Ac. 10: 22; 13: 50), 'you . . . who worship God' (Ac. 13: 16), 'a worshipper of God' (Ac. 16: 14). The readiness of many of them to listen to Paul shows that the teaching they had received was very often for good. To become a full proselyte (*ger ṣedeq*) involved adopting all the legal minutiae of the Pharisees. It is noteworthy that only one, possibly two, of the latter class are expressly mentioned as becoming Christians, *viz.* Nicolaus of Antioch (Ac. 6: 5) and perhaps the Ethiopian eunuch (Ac. 8: 27). This principle holds also for the person more concerned to win a convert for a denomination than for Christ.

The Third Woe (16–22). See note on 5: 33–37. **blind guides:** It is their teaching rather than their practice which is here condemned. **You blind fools** (*mōroi*): Jesus the judge permits Himself language forbidden to His followers (5: 22). *Mōroi* here, as in the Sermon on the Mount, is a reproduction of the Aram. word.

The Fourth Woe (23, 24). It is one matter if I am very strict with myself because of the witness of the Spirit within me. If, on the other hand, I decide I must hold whatever I find in Scripture strictly, however small it is, experience shows that I shall become increasingly legalistic in my demands on others and increasingly blind to the real demands God is making on me.

The Fifth Woe (25, 26). This is a widening and intensification of the fourth woe. Had the Pharisees behaved literally in the way suggested by v. 25, they would never have been looked up to by the people. But their estimate of the character of others was normally based on the measure in which they observed externals. The acceptance of an invitation to a meal would depend mainly on the measure in which the laws of tithing and purity were observed there. Their attitude may be compared with our judgement of fellow-Christians by their outward orthodoxy. **26. Blind Pharisee:** The singular is probably due to the underlying Aram., which could be taken as singular or plural. 'Give . . . to the poor' (Lk. 11: 41): if my cup and plate are full of extortion and rapacity, I shall be too; my willingness to give up what I have includes the giving of myself. This seems to be the meaning of the extremely difficult sentence in Lk.

The Sixth Woe (27, 28). This is the culmination of the two previous woes. In Adar (March), after the heavy rains, graves were whitewashed to prevent those going to the Temple, especially priests, from being defiled by contact with the dead. The graves were made resplendent just because they were graves. The Pharisees marked themselves out by their piousness and legalism just because they were sinners. Had they not been, they would not have felt compelled to act as they did. In their failure to realize this lay their play acting.

The Seventh Woe (29–31). Just as Christians are all too ready to make excuses for the many crimes committed down the centuries in the name of Christ (the Church's treatment of the Jews probably being the worst), so the rabbis could seldom bring themselves to a whole-hearted denunciation of the sins of their ancestors. They were virtually saying, 'It could not happen here'. The rejection of Jesus by the religious leaders shows the justice of His words.

Concluding Condemnation (32–36). The **prophets, wise men and teachers** are Christians (cf. Eph. 2: 20; Mt. 13: 52). The persecution of Jewish Christians here foretold (not many Gentile Christians were involved) fell into two parts, a lighter period before A.D. 70 and a more serious one culminating in the rebellion of Bar Cochba (132–135). Similarly, for Jewry the bloody defeat of Bar Cochba was probably a heavier blow than even the destruction of Jerusalem. We have no right to extend this woe beyond 135; it is also a warning against a too rigid interpretation of **generation. 35. Zechariah son of Berakiah:** Jesus was giving the equivalent of our 'from Genesis to Revelation', for the Heb. Bible ends with 2 Chr. (not Mal.!), and the last righteous man mentioned by name in 2 Chr. to be murdered is Zechariah (2 Chr. 24: 20 f.). He was the son of Jehoiada, Berakiah being the father of the prophet Zechariah (Zech. 1: 1). Lk. 11: 51 does not contain 'the son of Barachiah'. It is possible that Mt. has added these words as a pointer to perhaps the worst of the judicial murders in the final days of Jerusalem (Jos. *War*, IV. v. 4). For a full discussion cf. Williams, II, pp. 45–48.

The Lament over Jerusalem (23: 37–39) Cf. Lk. 13: 34, 35. That these words fit magnificently in their present position is obvious. The condemnation of the scribes and Pharisees has shown that there is nothing more to hope for. Only the way to the cross remains. It could have been said twice; more likely Lk. moved it, for he does not have this context in his gospel. **Jerusalem:** From the time the ark was brought there by David and Solomon built his temple, Jerusalem became the expression of Israel in a unique way. **under her wings:** Cf.

Ru. 2: 12. The fulfilment of v. 39 and also Lk. 13: 35 is at the Second Coming.

V. ii. ESCHATOLOGY (24: 1–25: 46)
The Eschatological Discourse (24: 1–36)
Cf. Mk 13: 1–32; Lk. 21: 5–33; 17: 23, 24, 37.

Owing to lack of space it is impossible to deal with this section as it merits. The reader is therefore requested to read the careful contribution on Mk 13: 1–37 first—a somewhat less extreme presentation of the same view is given by Tasker. This will probably convince most readers that the view that would push the whole chapter to 'the Great Tribulation' and the Second Coming is unsatisfactory. After all a comparison of v. 3 with Mk 13: 4; Lk. 21: 7 show that the destruction of the Temple was uppermost in the disciples' minds; any interpretation that makes it secondary must be mistaken.

Having read this we must go on to ask whether with all its correctness it has not exaggerated. For those who know Gk., Beasley-Murray will be specially useful.

This is an 'apocalyptic' discourse, and just as in Rev. we should hesitate to interpret the terms too sharply. **This generation** (34) undoubtedly normally refers to Jesus' contemporaries, but it can also mean 'this nation' (*Arndt*, Schniewind), and we cannot exclude Lang's explanation (pp. 70, 387) of the generation of the fulfilment. A reference to M'Neile *ad loc.* will make it clear that all three interpretations have had support in the past. In any case, even if we feel compelled with Filson and Beasley-Murray to accept the first interpretation, it does not force us to limit the scope of the prophecy. This tension between soon and not yet is found in much of the NT's teaching on the Second Coming.

Take Heed (4–8). Cf. Mk 13: 5–8; Lk. 21: 8–11: i.e. things would not develop as they expected. The period from A.D. 33 to 70 was not particularly marked out by wars and natural disasters, and the first serious claimant to be Messiah was Bar Cochba (132–135). **birth pains:** The birth pangs of the Messiah, i.e. the sufferings that would precede the setting up of the Messianic kingdom. It was a technical term at the time. **the end is still to come:** 'Christ does not come with war' (Schlatter).

The Tribulation (9–14). Cf. 10: 17–23 and Mk 13: 9–13; Lk. 21: 12–19. Mk 13: 9–12; Lk. 21: 12 are represented by 10: 17–21, which was doubtlessly deliberately moved from here to its present place (see comment *ad loc.*). As already said on 23: 34 ff., it is difficult to restrict this to the period before A.D. 70. **You will be hated by all nations** (9) clearly looks beyond A.D. 70, unless we take the desperate step of making 'nations' an insertion by Mt. The same

conclusion must be drawn from **this gospel of the kingdom will be preached in the whole world** (14). So it should be clear that the first two sections place the destruction of Jerusalem within a larger context (so also Tasker).

The Destruction of Jerusalem (15–22). Cf. Mk 13: 14–20; Lk. 21: 20–24. Some may allow themselves a double reference here both to A.D. 70 and the Antichrist. It is often forgotten that this is bound up with a questionable interpretation of a number of OT prophecies. Furthermore, if this double interpretation was intended, it is hard to see why Jesus did not give some hint of the fact. **The abomination that causes desolation**, or 'abomination of desolation' (so Phillips and NEB), a conscious quotation of Dan. 9: 27; 11: 31; 12: 11, but 'the appalling abomination' (Beasley-Murray, Tasker) is better. This almost certainly means the Roman army; cf. the paraphrase in Lk. 21: 20.

The Climax (23–31). Cf. Mk 13: 21–27; Lk. 21: 25–28. Already in the previous section there were touches which surpassed reality, *e.g.* 'never will be' (21), 'no human being' (22). Tasker's exposition shows that this section can be pressed into the straitjacket of the fall of Jerusalem. It is easier to say that it includes the fall but looks on to a greater climax. **The coming** is world wide (27). In A.D. 70 the vultures of judgment (28) gathered at Jerusalem, now they will be everywhere (30). While v. 29, based on passages like Isa. 13: 10; 34: 4 suggests that the Coming has cosmic significance, it also points to the destruction of all earthly powers. We cannot interpret v. 29 merely of judgment; cf. Dan. 7: 13 f. For **the sign of the Son of Man** (30) cf. Isa. 11: 10; probably it is the light of v. 27. The **loud trumpet call** (31) links with 1 Th. 4: 15 f. To see in v. 31 merely the Church liberated by the fall of Jerusalem for its true task of evangelism (Tasker) shows merely the extremes to which the straitjacket of a theory will bring one.

The Time of the Coming (32–36). Cf. Mk 13: 28–32; Lk. 21: 29–33. The time of the Coming is unknown, except to the Father, but there will be clear signs before it. It is not permissible to equate the fig tree with the Jews; it is never so used elsewhere. It is chosen because it stands out in the Palestinian winter more than other trees in its bareness, and the coming of leaves is a sure sign of spring. For the watcher the signs of the Coming will be equally clear, when they are given. There is no doubt of the textual authenticity of **nor the Son** in v. 36; Mk 13: 32. It is as irreverent to suggest that Jesus was making Himself temporarily ignorant for convenience as it is to deduce whatever other form of ignorance happens to suit the reader.

It is hard to avoid the conclusion that we are moving in the OT phenomenon of the Day of the Lord. There the Day is a final climax of judgment and blessing, yet there are repeated events which so foreshadow it, that they may be called the Day. So it would seem to be with the Coming. Ever and again it has seemed to be at the doors, and the greatest of these events was the fall of Jerusalem and the destruction of the Temple. It does not matter just how much of the discourse we apply to this event, so long as we realize that we must look beyond it. Even the events of A.D. 70 were means to a greater end.

Be Alert! (37–41). At this point the Synoptics go their separate ways, so it is wisest to see in 24: 36 the solemn end of the discourse and in 24: 37–25: 46 separate teaching intended to drive home its lessons. It may be possible to incorporate these sections into a complete outline of the Coming, but their original purpose was practical rather than theological and their hearers were not at the time able to give them a systematic interpretation. These comments confine themselves to Christ's original purpose. It should be considered also that though the actual 'apocalypse' has ended, 'apocalyptic' language continues; i.e. it is dangerous to make the picture language too literal.

The Coming is decisive and final. Neither people nor things can ever be the same again. One must decide one's attitude to it and to Christ before it happens, because afterwards it is too late. If the comparison above with the OT teaching on the Day of the Lord is correct, it means that men are constantly being faced with the possibility of minor events being equally decisive at the time. Jewish Christians for the most part did not grasp the decisiveness of the events of A.D. 70, and so the majority drifted into Ebionite heresy. The Gentile Christians did not understand the implications of the sack of Rome in 410, and so the Church became largely paganized. Those who did not accept the Reformation did not have another chance, and the religious boundaries drawn then have remained relatively fixed to this day. Each reader may wish to add other examples. The call to watch (*grēgoreō*), implying spiritual alertness, is not only in view of the Coming, but also of those judgments in the world, which by their decisiveness foreshadow the Coming.

There was ample warning of Noah's flood, but that did not make it any less sudden, when it came. Then the division was made by God's hand that shut to the Ark (Gen. 7: 16); at the Coming it is the action of the angels (31). There follow four parables illustrating various aspects of the Coming.

The Watchful Householder (24: 42–44)
Cf. Lk. 12: 39 f. The picture of Christ's coming as a thief in the night is found also in 1 Th. 5: 2; 2 Pet. 3: 10; Rev. 3: 3; 16: 15. The main stress is on the unpredictability of the time, but there is also a threat of loss, which is never expounded, the nearest being Rev. 16: 15.

The Faithful and Wise Steward (24: 45–51)
Cf. Lk. 12: 42–46. The Church is not a democratic assembly but 'the household of God' (Eph. 2: 19). To some of its members Christ delegates authority. Forgetfulness of the Coming, which is the present goal set for the Church, leads to the belief that they have inherent right to authority and that in turn to its abuse.

The Parable of the Ten Maidens (25: 1–13)
From the head servants Jesus turned to those of 'the household' of no particular standing. At a Jewish wedding the bridegroom, surrounded by his friends, went, generally after sunset, to the home of the bride to fetch her. The bride, dressed in her best, was carried in a litter to the bridegroom's house, a procession being formed by her and the bridegroom's friends. Light was provided by lamps on poles. When the bridegroom's home was reached the wedding supper was eaten.

Our interpretation of the parable must partly depend on whether we read **to meet the bridegroom** (Tasker) or 'the bridegroom and the bride' (Schniewind, M'Neile)—the MS evidence is fairly evenly balanced. Our decision should not be influenced by the non-mention of the bride in v. 6; etiquette would not permit it. The shutting of the door (10) strongly suggests the latter reading, for M'Neile is wrong in suggesting that the feast was at the bride's house. Tasker says, 'It is most probable that it is *this* (the bringing home of the bride) procession that the ten girls in the story are pictured as going to meet, though whether as official bridesmaids, servants of the bridegroom, or children of friends and neighbours we have no means of knowing.' Official bridesmaids are ruled out, for as honoured guests the bride's parents would be responsible for all they needed. Either or both the other explanations, including servants of the bride, are equally possible. They are persons who have received no invitation but who will be welcomed in, if they form part of the procession, the more so if they honour the bridal pair with lights.
Lamps (*lampas*) is not the word used in contexts like 5: 15; 6: 22; Lk. 15: 8. It means a torch, which could be fed with oil. They kept their torches on because no Oriental likes to be in the dark. Seen from the angle of an everyday wedding, where the details in the story are fixed by what actually happened, it should be clear that the parable is refractory to any allegorical treatment (cf. introduction to ch. 13). The two features are that the girls had no claim to be guests, which is entirely secondary,

and that their getting in depended on their being awake and ready at the right moment. **13. Therefore keep watch:** It is mental rather than physical alertness that is meant. This is no story of eternal destiny decided by the Coming. The foolish have lost something but need not be lost themselves.

The Parable of the Talents (25: 14–30)
Cf. Lk. 19: 12–27. It seems impossible to find any essential difference between the parable of the talents and that of the pounds (Lk. 19: 12–27). The difference in the size of the amounts entrusted—a talent was worth about fifty 'pounds'—is probably due to the latter's having been told to a wider audience, the former to the Twelve with their very much greater responsibilities, not this time in the Church but rather in the world. The difference between this and the previous parable is that there it was lack of serious thought that caused the trouble, here the lack of good will. There is no suggestion of the eternal fate of the third servant; like the foolish maidens he has lost something. **that worthless** (achreios) **servant:** 'useless' (NEB, Phillips). **outside, into the darkness** (to skotos to exōteron): 'the darkness outside' (Phillips), 'the darkness' (NEB); no special kind of darkness is meant—the reckoning takes place after nightfall. In Lk. it is not even mentioned. If we wish to continue the story, we shall find that the morning will come, and the slave is still his master's slave, only he has irreparably lost something. The often heard remark that no Christian could speak or think as the servant does in v. 24 comes from living in a monastery without walls.

The Judgment (25: 31–46)
This is not a parable but a description in apocalyptic language with a simile in v. 32. Since **the people** (32) is masculine and **nations** (ethnē) is neuter, the correct translation is 'He will separate men into two groups' (NEB, similarly Phillips). We are witnessing the judgment of the individuals who make up the nations. The exact when and who is not important, for God's principles of judgment are immutable. **40. one of the least of these brothers of mine:** That 'the Jewish Remnant' is meant could never have suggested itself to the hearers, who had 12: 46–50 as a key to the interpretation. Anyone who befriends those whom Jesus is prepared to call **brothers of mine** in the hour of their need and persecution would do the same to their Master, if he had the chance. This passage is no complete answer to the problem of those who have never heard the gospel, or have heard it inadequately. It does reveal, however, the type of criterion that will be used, and it is intended to be a warning to us. Since from His **brothers** He will expect more, not less, this can serve as a check on the reality of our profession.

EPILOGUE: PASSION, DEATH AND RESURRECTION (26: 1–28: 20)
The Plot to Arrest Jesus (26: 1–5)
See comments on Mk 14: 1, 2; Lk. 22: 1, 2; cf. Jn 11: 47–53.

The Anointing of Jesus' Head (26: 6–13)
See comments on Mk 14: 3–9. The differences between this incident and Jn 12: 1–8 make it difficult to believe that the same woman is involved. It was usual to offer a guest at a meal oil to anoint his head with, but there is no evidence from Palestine for such an anointing of an honoured guest's head. It was obviously a completely spontaneous action, though possibly prompted by Mary's action (Jn 12: 3).

The Betrayal Agreement (26: 14–16)
See comments on Mk 14: 10, 11; Lk. 22: 3–6. The complex character of Judas has always defied analysis. The NT does not try to motivate his action, but see 27: 3.

Preparation for the Passover (26: 17–19)
See comments on Mk 14: 12–16; Lk. 22: 7–13. The secrecy in the arrangements was to prevent Judas acting too early. If some prefer to see prior arrangement here and in 21: 2 f., it is not to depreciate Jesus' powers, but because the actions of the others involved suggest pre-arrangement. It would have been virtually impossible to find accommodation of the type described in Mk 14: 15 on 14 Nisan without prior arrangement, owing to the vast crowds of pilgrims that had to be accommodated in Jerusalem.

The Last Supper (26: 20–29)
See comments on Mk 14: 17–25; Lk. 22: 14–38; 1 C. 11: 23 ff. The supper demands the background of the Passover meal for its understanding. The rabbis distinguished between the Egyptian and the Palestinian Passover. One main difference was that the former had to be eaten standing and in haste (Exod. 12: 11), the latter reclining (Jn 13: 23, 25) and at leisure. Here **Jesus was reclining at the table** (anakeimai). A necessary part of the meal was four cups of red wine. The second cup, that of Lk. 22: 17, was drunk after the 'proclamation' of the story of the Exodus. The 'morsel' given to Judas (Jn 13: 26) was during the meal that followed, i.e. Judas was at the Passover meal, but not at the institution of the Lord's Supper —following Jn 13: 30 rather than Lk. 22: 21; the former gives the impression of fixing the time. After the meal a half matzah (unleavened bread) that had been hidden away was brought out and eaten. This will have been the **bread** of v. 26. Earlier Jesus will have said, as He showed the unleavened bread, 'This is the bread of affliction which our fathers ate in the land of Egypt'; His disciples must have understood **this is my body** in the same way. Though not so clearly, the red wine is used as a picture of the blood shed in Egypt. 'The cup of blessing'

(1 C. 10: 16) was the third cup, which still bears this name. It precedes the second part of the Hallel (Pss. 115–118, possibly then 114–118), cf. **when they had sung a hymn** (30). The only part of the picture missing is the fourth cup, but this is explained by v. 29. Jesus deliberately did not close the ritual, because the fulness of the salvation He was bringing would not be realized until the fulness of His Father's rule (**kingdom**) was revealed at His Coming.

Owing to the constant liturgical use of the words of institution later MSS show considerable corruption and assimilation to one another. There is little doubt that **Take, (eat); this is my body** is the original wording for the bread; 'which is (given) for you' is a liturgical development—'broken for you' has no real claim to consideration. In fact the bread points to the life of Christ rather than to His death. Jeremias has made out a very strong case— some would call it absolutely convincing— when he argues for the authenticity of Lk. 22: 19b, 20 against the majority of modern scholars. The omission of 'new' in v. 28 (Mk 14: 24) need not detain us. **The covenant** needed no explanation for the Twelve, but 'new' had to be added as a liturgical explanation for Gentile believers. Here too Mk 14: 24 gives the most primitive version. The form of the words in Lk. 22: 19 f.; 1 C. 11: 24 f. represents the liturgical form used c. A.D. 50. The fullest modern discussion may be found in Jeremias.

for many: This, as in 20: 28, represents a Heb. idiom meaning, 'All, who will be very many', cf. Isa. 53: 12.

This linking of the Lord's Supper with the Passover is not merely of antiquarian interest. The Passover lamb in the Palestinian Passover had no atoning or saving power. The service was merely a symbolic re-enactment of the Egyptian Passover. Similarly the Lord's Supper can be only a symbolic re-enactment of the all-saving sacrifice of the Cross. The first Supper looked forward to it, all others have looked back.

Additional Note on the Date of the Last Supper. The Passover lambs were always killed in the Temple on 14 Nisan, and they were eaten on 15 Nisan—the Jewish day began at sunset. The above exegesis was based on the assumption that the Last Supper was a Passover meal, it having been prepared on 14 Nisan (26: 17) and eaten soon after dark on 15 Nisan. No other view is possible, if we confine ourselves to the Synoptics. But Jn clearly identifies Christ as the antitype of the Passover lamb (19: 36) and implies, though it is not stated, that Jesus died at the time the lambs were being sacrificed. In addition he indicates that the priests on the Friday morning had not yet eaten the Passover (18: 28). It seems that for him the supper was on 14 Nisan as was the crucifixion. In addition

superficial reading will find nothing in Jn 13– 17 to suggest the Passover. To this basic fact have been added a number of further objections, which, so it is claimed, prove that the Supper cannot have been the Passover. The ten most important are listed and answered by Jeremias.

Earlier efforts at a solution of the problem either tried to minimize the impression created by Jn, interpreting 18: 28 to mean the *Chagigah*, or special festival offering (Num. 28: 18–22— cf. Edersheim II, pp. 566 ff.), or suggested that Jesus, knowing that He would die on 14 Nisan, anticipated the Passover, eating it twenty-four hours before others. The former is possible but runs counter to the general impression created by Jn; the latter is impossible, no priest would have sacrificed the lamb before the time, and it is contradicted by Mt. 26: 17; Mk 14: 12; Lk. 22: 7, all of which can refer only to 14 Nisan. Many scholars today reject the testimony either of the Synoptics or Jn, mainly of the former. Quite apart from inspiration, this is impossible; people's memories do not play them tricks in this kind of thing.

We must assume, therefore, that it was possible for the Passover to be eaten *officially* on two nights in that year. Two possible ways have been suggested. (i) SB II, pp. 812–853, argues from the known fact that the beginning of the month was fixed by visual observance of the new moon and that at least once there was deliberate fraud in the claim to have seen it. It maintains that in their ritual controversy with the Pharisees the Sadducean priests would have gained by 14 Nisan's falling on a Friday. The Pharisees, suspecting that in the year of the crucifixion Nisan had started a day late, insisted on keeping Passover on what they maintained was the evening of 15 Nisan, but the Sadducees 14 Nisan. Hence in this particular year it was possible for Jesus to eat the Passover with those that followed the Pharisees and yet die with the official Passover lambs on the official 14 Nisan. The theory is entirely possible but unprovable. (ii) More recently it has been claimed that according to the *Book of Jubilees* and the Essenes of Qumran the correct calendar was not a lunar but a solar one. According to this 14 Nisan would have been a Tuesday. Jesus ate the Passover at the same time as these people, was arrested on the Tuesday night, but was not crucified until the Friday. It has yet to be proved that the Sadducean priests were prepared to make concessions to a calendar they did not follow, something which is highly improbable. In addition, unless it is maintained that Jesus was crucified on a Wednesday (see Additional Note at end of ch. 27), it means that He was held under arrest for forty-eight hours, something contrary to the whole spirit of the Gospel account. Unless more evidence can be adduced, this view must be regarded with extreme suspicion, the more so as no Gentile reader would have guessed that two calendars existed among the Jews.

The Way to Gethsemane (26: 30–35)
See comments on Mk 14: 26–31; Lk. 22: 31–34, 39; Jn 13: 36–38; 18: 1.

The Agony in the Garden (26: 36–46)
See comments on Mk 14: 32–42; Lk. 22: 40–46. In our reconstruction of the scene we have to allow for a late hour of the night. The Passover never ends early, and we have to allow ample time for Jn 14–17. The failure of the Twelve to stop Judas shows that even then they had not really taken in what was to happen —was it due to a deep-rooted belief that when it came to the point Jesus would use His supernatural power to save Himself?—and so their sleep can easily be understood. The account of the agony must, at least in part, have come from Jesus after the resurrection. **39. cup:** Cf. 20: 22. It was a common OT term expressing the fate, good or bad but more often the latter, of a man or nation.

The Arrest (26: 47–56)
See comments on Mk 14: 43–52; Lk. 22: 47–53; Jn 18: 2–12. **49. and kissed him:** An act of insolence. There was not nearly as much kissing practised by the Jews as is often thought. A rabbi might kiss a pupil as a reward for special wisdom, but we do not find the pupils kissing their rabbis.

The Jewish Trial. Though the Jewish trial bears its unfairness on its face, we must not suggest that it broke the Jewish rules of jurisprudence. Older works, and some modern ones too, base themselves on the information contained in the *Mishna*. This took its present shape c. A.D. 200, and the Talmud itself bears witness that these rules were not in force at the time of Jesus' condemnation. He was tried according to Sadducean rules, of which we know nothing.

The trial before the Sanhedrin falls into three parts. (i) A preliminary investigation before Annas (Jn 18: 13, 19–24). This was presumably to save time, while Caiaphas was making arrangements with Pilate for a quick trial in the morning (see note on 27: 11). (ii) A hearing before as many of the Sanhedrin as could be collected in a hurry (26: 57–68). (iii) The confirmation of its verdict by a full Sanhedrin at dawn (Lk. 22: 66–71). Only the last was really official.

A very strong case has been made out recently that the Jews did in fact have the right to inflict the death penalty, especially in matters involving their religion. If this is correct, Jn 18: 31 must be interpreted to mean that once they had brought a political charge against Jesus (Lk. 23: 2), the case had passed out of their competence. The Sanhedrin was probably shirking the opprobrium they would have aroused by putting Him to death as a blasphemer.

The Second Stage of the Jewish Trial (26: 57–68)
See comments on Mk 14: 53–65; Lk. 22: 54, 63–65 (Jn 18: 13, 14, 19–24). **63. I charge you under oath by the living God:** Under the later legislation of the *Mishna* such an adjuration could be addressed only to a limited class of witnesses, who had to answer that justice might be done; it could not be addressed to the accused. It is improbable that it was legal under the Sadducees either.

64. It is as you say: In some settings this could mean no more than a polite refusal to answer a question. Here, however, it must mean, 'I am' (Mk 14: 62). **in the future** (*ap' arti*): We must render 'from now on' (NEB, Arndt). Jesus is not referring to the eschatological vision of Rev. 1: 7, but to the religious leaders' growing realization that all their efforts have been in vain, and that the prisoner is their King and Judge. **Mighty One:** Another way of avoiding 'God' (see note on 4: 17). As in His use of 'heaven', Jesus conformed as far as possible to the practices of His time. **65. the high priest tore his clothes:** An action expressive of grief that was obligatory on hearing blasphemy.

Peter's Denial (26: 69–75)
See comments on Mk 14: 66–72; Lk. 22: 55–62; Jn 18: 15–18, 25–27.

The Third Stage of the Jewish Trial (27: 1 f.)
See comments on Mk 15: 1; Lk. 22: 66–71. For legality's sake the verdict of the night council had to be rubber-stamped by the whole Sanhedrin. Time was saved by repeating the decisive question. When the same answer was given, the verdict of blasphemy was adopted.

It is often urged, especially in Jewish circles, that the whole story of the trial must be unhistorical, because none of the Twelve can have been present at it. (i) This is an implicit denial of the resurrection; otherwise the information could have come from Jesus Himself. (ii) It forgets that such trials were not held *in camera*, especially disciples of the rabbis were expected to attend to gain experience in legal matters. Some of them may well have been converted later (cf. Ac. 6: 7; 15: 5). (iii) Joseph of Arimathea (Lk. 23: 50 f.) was evidently present and could have given all the information needed. Cf. Bammel.

The Death of Judas (27: 3–10)
Cf. Ac. 1: 18, 19. Judas had been admitted into the court room or was waiting in a nearby room. It seems that he had expected that Jesus would at the last use His miraculous power to save Himself and to confound His enemies, though it is hard to believe that this was the

real motive of the betrayal. At any rate the reality caused a violent revulsion of feeling. **5. into the temple** (*eis ton naon*): There are no adequate reasons for doubting that Mt. is observing the usual distinction between *hieron*, the whole range of the temple area, usually rendered 'temple', and *naos*, the sanctuary itself and the court immediately around it, where only priests and Levites could go. Judas, in his desperation, seems to have hurled the coins into the court of the priests; some of the money could even have reached the temple porch. The perverse scrupulosity of the priests, for which there is also Talmudic evidence, forced them to regard the coins as 'holy' because they had landed in the sacred area, but they could not be put into one of the regular accounts. In vv. 9 f. we have a rather free quotation of Zech. 11: 12 f., apparently attributed to **Jeremiah the prophet**. The difference in the text of the quotation is not due, as so often in NT, to LXX, but may be a free citing from memory. Some have suggested, therefore, that Jeremiah is a slip. This is unlikely. The only explanation with some measure of probability is that at that time the 'Latter Prophets' were headed by Jeremiah, not Isaiah as now, so it would mean no more than 'in the prophetic books'. There is a full discussion in Williams II, pp. 50–55.

The Roman Trial. The Roman trial also fell into three parts. (i) The first hearing by Pilate is found in 27: 2, 11–14; Mk 15: 1–5; Lk. 23: 1–7; Jn 18: 28–19: 10—though some of the order here is different. The fullest account is in Jn, the Synoptics being less interested in what was essentially a preliminary hearing. (ii) The hearing by Herod. This is recorded only in Lk. 23: 8–12, because it was essentially an interlude. (iii) The second hearing by Pilate is found in 27: 15–26; Mk 15: 6–15; Lk. 23: 13–25; Jn 18: 39, 40; 19: 4–6, 12–16 (as said above, Jn's order cannot always be reconciled with that of the Synoptics). It should be noted that with the exception of Lk. 23: 4 only the chief priests, the elders and the scribes are mentioned in the first two hearings. It was a desperate gamble by the Jewish authorities to get the case out of the way before there could be any public reaction. The multitude gathered in order to demand the release of a popular prisoner (Mk 15: 8), and it is doubtful whether they would have called for Jesus' death, had it not been presented to them as a choice between Jesus and Barabbas. Pilate really held the whip hand, until he virtually stepped down from his judgment seat and suggested that popular acclaim should settle the matter.

The First Hearing before Pilate (27: 11–14) See comments on Mk 15: 2–5; Lk. 23: 2–5; Jn 18: 28–19: 10. **11. the governor asked him, 'Are you the king of the Jews?'** This could not possibly be the beginning of the hearing,

which had to start with a charge. The first step is given by Jn 18: 29 f. There was no love lost between Pilate and the Jewish leaders, so the insolence of v. 30 can only mean that some prior arrangement had been reached between Caiaphas and Pilate, which the latter chose to ignore. Then came the charge (Lk. 23: 2), which by its profuseness suggests that it was thought up on the spur of the moment. Pilate tried to push Jesus back on the Sanhedrin (Jn 18: 31). Only then did he turn to Jesus. In judging Pilate's attitude we must not forget that his spies must have brought him fairly full reports of the doings and teaching of Jesus, and especially since the triumphal entry a fairly full dossier must have been compiled. Pilate knew that he was dealing with an innocent man.

The Second Hearing before Pilate (27: 15–26) See comments on Mk 15: 6–15; Lk. 23: 17–25; Jn 18: 39, 40; 19: 4–6, 12–16. There is no evidence outside the NT for Pilate's power to pardon a prisoner, and indeed it was an exceptional privilege, for pardon was normally a prerogative of the emperor.

16, 17. Barabbas: A small but influential group of MSS have 'Jesus Barabbas', which is accepted by NEB, B. & F. B. S. Diglot, Schniewind and considered probable by M'Neile, Filson and Tasker. It is difficult to explain its existence, if it were not original. Pilate's offer of the choice of Barabbas or Jesus seemed most shrewd. He knew of the tumultuous welcome of the triumphal entry and that the common people, especially the nationalists, loathed the Sadducean priests. He had no means of gauging how bitterly Jesus had disappointed the activists by His passivity since the Sunday of the Entry. In addition a Messiah who owed his life to Roman clemency would have been a blow to Jewish pride (Schlatter). **19. his wife sent him this message:** Christian tradition knows much about Pilate's wife, but secular history knows nothing! So there is no point in speculating about her action. That she even knew of the trial may be some support for the suggestion that Caiaphas had gone round to Pilate's house the night before to arrange the trial. **22. Crucify him!:** Jn 19: 6 shows that the horrid suggestion came first from the chief priests. They knew that this punishment would put Jesus' memory under a curse (cf. Gal. 3: 13; Dt. 21: 23). To many Jews He is still *talui*, the hanged one. **25. Let his blood be on us and on our children:** Few things in the Church's history are more shocking than its use of this cry. Just as little as Pilate could remove his guilt by washing his hands could the people pass on their guilt to their descendants for a hundred generations. At the most we could speak of the third and fourth generation, but surely the curse was outweighed by the prayer of Lk. 23: 34. **24. he took water and washed his hands:** A Jewish custom (Dt. 21: 6); Pilate had been long enough in the country to have seen it. **26. he had Jesus flogged:** Scourging was part of the punishment of crucifixion; by weakening the victim, it probably accelerated death.

The Mockery of the Soldiers (27: 27–31)

See comments on Mk 15: 16–20; cf. Jn 19: 2 f. **29. Hail, king of the Jews:** In the insult to the people the penalty of rejection already begins to work itself out.

The Road to Golgotha (27: 32)

See comments on Mk. 15: 21; Lk. 23: 26–32.

The Crucifixion (27: 33–44)

See comments on Mk 15: 22–32; Lk. 23: 33–43; Jn 19: 17–24. **Golgotha:** Those interested in the topography are referred to Dalman, ch. XXI, or Parrot. Dame Kathleen Kenyon's recent excavations have shown that the traditional site will have been outside the city wall at the time. 'Calvary' is taken from the Latin. It means the same as Golgotha, but is, strictly speaking, not a Biblical name.

In the older MSS followed by NIV no reference is made to Ps. 22: 18 in v. 35. This was first done in Jn 19: 24. This helps to show the falsity of the sceptical view that the details of the passion were invented from alleged prophecies in the OT.

There is no real contradiction between v. 44 (Mk 15: 32) and Lk. 23: 39–43. Jesus' behaviour on the cross convinced one of the robbers, who had been mocking Him, that this was no false Messiah, who had broken down in the moment of crisis, but the true King.

The Death of Jesus (27: 45–56)

See comments on Mk 15: 33–41; Lk. 23: 44–49; Jn 19: 25–37. The evangelists, not being scientists, make no suggestions about the cause of the darkness (45). All that can be profitably said is that it was not an eclipse; quite apart from its duration the moon was full. There is no reason to think that it extended beyond Judea.

46. Eloi, Eloi, lama sabachthani: Cf. Mk 15: 34. There are considerable variations in the older MSS due to Aram. being unknown to most Christian copyists. It seems clear, however, that Jesus was not quoting the Heb. of Ps. 22: 1 (*Eli, Eli, lamah 'azabtani*), which is the more remarkable as the Heb. Psalter was normally learnt off by heart by the pious. No explanation of this cry is offered in NT, and we do well not to try to explain the unexplained. The following points may, however, be worth consideration. The assumption that Jesus was associating Himself with Ps. 22 is made questionable by His use of the Aram. Then, while the Aram. (like the Heb.) is ambiguous, being translatable 'Why hast thou' or 'Why didst thou', the Gk. can only legitimately bear the meaning, 'Why didst thou forsake me?' (so RVmg). This combined with the loud voice suggests a forsaking ended and the shout of the victor rather than a cry of present dereliction. After all, the victor's shout of 'It is finished' (Jn 19: 30) shows that Jesus knew the victory won before he gave up His spirit.

Do we render **the Son of God** (54) or 'a son of God' with mg and first edition of RSV? Lk's version, 'Certainly this man was innocent' clearly favours the latter.

51. from top to bottom: Stresses the supernatural nature of the event. The curtain could be either the one between the holy and most holy place, or the one that prevented the worshippers from seeing into the holy place when the temple doors were open. On theological grounds the former seems more likely.

52. the bodies of many holy people who had died were raised: This section of Mt. stands unique in the NT and we have no other Scripture to help us understand it. There are no references to it in Jewish tradition either. It was the earthquake that opened the tombs, Christ's resurrection that made the rising of the saints possible. Mt.'s own reticence suggests that he himself had no clear understanding of what happened

Additional Note on the Seven Words from the Cross. We have not been given a four-fold gospel so that we should create a single gospel from it. Therefore there can never be certainty about our reconstructions. The fact that the scheme suggested contains an inner harmony does not guarantee its accuracy.

The most likely order of the seven words seems to be:—1. The prayer of Lk 23: 34. 2. The promise to the penitent robber (Lk 23: 43). 3. The words to Mary and John (Jn 19: 26 f). 4. The cry of dereliction (Mt 27: 46; Mk 15: 34). 5. 'I thirst' (Jn 19: 28). 6. 'It is finished' (Jn 19: 30; Mt 27: 50). 7. The final prayer (Lk 23: 46).

The Burial of Jesus (27: 57–61)

See comments on Mk 15: 42–47; Lk 23: 50–56; Jn 19: 38–42. **60. he rolled a big stone in front of the entrance to the tomb:** This is usually taken as a description of the mill-stone type of tomb-closer sometimes used for Jewish graves (not as often as imagined). The language suggests, however, that the tomb was not entirely finished and that it was a large boulder that was rolled up; this would have been much more difficult for the women to tackle.

The Guarding of the Tomb (27: 62–66)

Preparation Day (*paraskeuē*) was Friday (see Additional Note at end of ch.). The religious authorities would do no work on the sabbath, which was for them also 15 Nisan, but that did not prevent their having an interview with Pilate. They had to obtain permission for a guard, not because they had no soldiers of their own—there were the Temple police—but because the corpse of the crucified 'criminal' was Roman property entrusted to Joseph. Pilate's answer may be translated, 'You have a guard' or **Take a guard**. The former permitted them to use the Temple police, the latter granted them a squad of Roman soldiers; most modern translations (except NEB) favour the former, most commentators the latter. But why should Pilate, feeling sore about the day before, grant them this favour of the use of Roman soldiers? In addition there were few more serious charges against a Roman soldier than to be asleep on duty. Is it credible that they would have put their heads in a noose by accepting the priests' proposal (28: 13 ff.)? Even a temple policeman on special duty was in some danger, but so long as the Captain of the Temple was satisfied the governor would hardly intervene.

It may well be that we should change the punctuation and end the chapter with the first words of the next, i.e. 'posting the guard after the Sabbath' (*opse de sabbatōn*). The negotiation was carried out on the Sabbath, the work of sealing and setting the guard as soon as darkness had come.

Additional Note on the Day of the Crucifixion. Though the Church as a whole has shown remarkable unanimity in its acceptance of Friday as the day of the crucifixion, the view is too frequently met today that it must have been a Wednesday. The main motivation is avowedly to allow a complete fulfilment in terms of three 24 hour days for Mt. 12: 40. One senses too a frequent anti-traditional note among some of its supporters. The great weakness of the view was that it involved a denial that the Last Supper was a Passover meal. It has now taken on new significance and possibility in the light of the suggestion that the Supper took place as a Passover on the Tuesday evening (see Additional Note on the Date of the Last Supper).

A crucifixion on a Wednesday would answer the objection that the gospels know nothing of a 48 hour imprisonment. There are, however, three passages that seem an insuperable barrier, to the acceptance of the theory, plus, of course, consistent church tradition.

(i) Lk. 24: 21, 'it is now the third day' seems irreconcilable with it; cf. also Mt. 16: 21; 17: 23; 20: 19; Lk. 9: 22; 24: 7, though these latter passages would be easier to explain.

(ii) 'the next day, the one after Preparation Day (*paraskeuē*)' (Mt. 27: 62): *paraskeuē* without qualification had become a technical term for Friday, more especially Friday afternoon. Even if we could disassociate this from its context, it seems incredible that the priests would have waited until the Saturday after a Wednesday

crucifixion before taking effective action to guard the tomb.

(iii) We have *paraskeuē* a number of times in Jn 19. In v. 14 it is qualified by 'of Passover week' and bears a non-technical sense; we would say 'Passover Eve'. In v. 31 we have 'Now it was the *paraskeuē* . . . and the next day was to be a special Sabbath'. Here we have the technical sense of Sabbath Eve again. Though 15 Nisan, along with similar feast days, was kept as a sabbath, the Jews use the term sabbath only for the Day of Atonement, in addition to the weekly sabbath. Obviously, if 15 Nisan and the sabbath coincided, it would be a 'special Sabbath'. Finally in v. 42 we have 'because it was the Jewish' *paraskeuē* where once more the meaning of Friday must be found.

In the light of all these passages it seems impossible to deny that the crucifixion took place on a Friday.

The Resurrection (28: 1–10)
Many efforts, none of them entirely convincing, have been made to bring together all the resurrection stories into one completely harmonious whole. It seems clear that, while the apostles soon realized the need for a fairly standardized account of the life and teaching of Christ, the impact of His death and above all resurrection was so immense that no attempt was made to weave the eye-witness accounts together.

It is clear enough that this passage corresponds to Mk 16: 1–8; Lk. 24: 1–11; Jn 20: 1, 11–18; an exact harmony eludes us. We are clearly intended to let Mt.'s story carry its own message without check and counter-check.

It has been urged that the two Marys in Mt. come only to look at the tomb, because the guard would prevent their doing more (*e.g.* Schniewind, Tasker). They were most unlikely to know about the guard, since it was set late the evening before—irrespective of whether the suggestion on 27: 66 (*q.v.*) is adopted. B. & F. B. S. Diglot is indubitably correct in translating v. 2, 'Now there had been a great earthquake' (so essentially Tasker)—there is good Hebrew-style story telling behind the narrative. We cannot otherwise imagine the women not sharing in the paralyzing terror of the guards. The rolling away of the stone was to let the women into the grave, not to let Jesus out. Resurrection life transcends grave-clothes, a sealed tomb and armed men.

Jesus did appear to the Eleven in and near Jerusalem, because He knew their need. Ideally, however, the meeting place was to be in Galilee (7, 10; 26: 32; Mk 14: 28), so Mt. omits all the Jerusalem appearances, except the one that attested His resurrection—even there Jesus probably appeared to the women because of their fear (8). The fact that the risen King was to show Himself in Galilee is a prophecy of the separation of His Church from the old symbolized by Jerusalem.

The opening words are a bit of clumsy writing. **after the Sabbath** (*opse sabbatōn*) means after the sabbath had come to an end. **at dawn** (*epiphōskō*) **on the first day of the week:** *epiphōskō* means to dawn in a literal sense; Mt. is not speaking of the drawing on of the first day, i.e. nightfall on Saturday evening, but of the first signs of dawn on Sunday, cf. Mk 16: 2; Lk. 24: 1; Jn 20: 1. **9. Greetings** (*chairete*): Lit. 'rejoice'. This had become a standard greeting with its original sense more or less lost and had been taken up as a loan-word in Aram. *Arndt* suggests 'good morning'; NEB is probably wise with its 'He gave them his greeting'. Phillips 'Peace be with you' has no justification.

The Bribing of the Guards (28: 11–15)

Filson remarks, 'The weakness of this story is, first, that it assumes that the Jewish leaders had advance notice of the resurrection, and second that in it the guard consented to the circulation of a story which made them liable to the death-penalty.' The second difficulty, as pointed out earlier, has been created by the expositor himself. There is no evidence that they were Roman soldiers. The former overlooks a common psychological phenomenon. The more I am personally committed in a matter, the less likely I am to notice anything that runs contrary to my preconceived notions. The thought of Jesus' death was impossible to the disciples, so the promises of resurrection passed almost unheard and entirely unheeded. The religious leaders had their minds fixed on Jesus' death, and so the rumour of resurrection—cf. the use of Jn 2: 19 at the trial—must have jarred horribly. While they will not have understood exactly what had happened, they never doubted that the empty tomb was a fact, and Mt. 26: 64 will have come ringing in the ears of those who had heard the words. One of the minor confirmations of the priestly fears is found in Ac. 6: 7.

The Commissioning of the Apostles (28: 16–20)

If, as we surely should, we take 'brothers' (10) in a wider sense than the Eleven, then there were more than the Apostles on the mountain, and we can identify the appearance with some probability with that of 1 C. 15: 6. Mt., however, ignores the others. Here was the consummation of the apostles' first appointment. Then He had given them a limited commission (10: 5 f.) because His own commission was limited (15: 24). Now His authority was world-wide and absolute, so their commission was also world-wide. The commission was given to the Eleven as the representatives of the Church to be. This is not a command to each individual (more are called to stay at home than to go)

but to the Church as a whole. There may be good reasons why this individual or that should not go, but there are never good reasons for the Church's failing to reach out and go.

We need not be surprised at the first hesitant steps of the apostolic church. Far more important, as we learn from Ac., is that whenever it became clear that a new step forward was of God the leaders, at any rate, accepted it without hesitation.

19. baptizing them in (*eis*) **the name of the Father . . . :** More literally 'into the name', i.e. as the possession of, cf. note on 18: 20. There is no suggestion that men are made disciples by being baptized. NEB is nearer the sense with 'make all nations my disciples; baptize men everywhere in the name . . .'

The Ascension is not mentioned. Once the Commission had been given, it mattered not how the Lord of the Church moved to the right hand of the Father, where He waits until His enemies be made His footstool.

BIBLIOGRAPHY

Commentaries, etc.

B.& F. B. S. Diglot: Greek Text and English Translation of Matthew for Bible Translators (London, 1959).

BEARE, F. W., *The Gospel according to Matthew* (San Francisco, 1981).

BEASLEY-MURRAY, G. R., *A Commentary on Mark Thirteen* (London, 1957).

COLE, R. A., *The Gospel according to Mark*. TNTC (London, 1961)

FILSON, F. V., *The Gospel according to St. Matthew. BNTC (London, 1960)*.

GUNDRY, R. H. *Matthew: A Commentary on his Literary and Theological Art* (Grand Rapids, 1982).

HILL, D., *The Gospel of Matthew*. NCentB (London, 1972).

LANG, G. H., *The Revelation of Jesus Christ* (London, 1945).

M'NEILE, A. H., *The Gospel according to St. Matthew. [On the Greek text.]* (London, 1915).

S, A., *Das Evangelium nach Matthäus* (Stuttgart, 1929; 1963). Spiritual and scholarly.

SCHNIEWIND, J., *Das Evangelium nach Matthäus*. Das Neue Testament Deutsch (Göttingen, 1938).

SCHWEIZER, E., *The Good News according to Matthew*, E. T. (London, 1975).

TASKER, R. V. G., *The Gospel according to St. Matthew*. TNTC (London, 1961).

General

BAMMEL, E. (ed.), *The Trial of Jesus* (London, 1970).

BORNKAMM, G., BARTH, G., and HELD, H. J., *Tradition and Interpretation in Matthew* (Eng.trans. London, 1963).

BUBER, M., *The Prophetic Faith* (London, 1949).

DALMAN, G., *Sacred Sites and Ways* (London, 1935).

DAVIES, W. D., *The Setting of the Sermon on the Mount* (Cambridge, 1964).

DODD, C. H., *The Parables of the Kingdom* (London, 1935).

EDERSHEIM, A., *The Life and Times of Jesus the Messiah* (4th edn. 2 vols. London, 1886).

GUTHRIE, D., *New Testament Introduction: Gospels and Acts* (London, 1965).

JEREMIAS, J., *The Parables of Jesus* (2nd edn. Eng.trans. London, 1963).

JEREMIAS, J., *The Eucharistic Words of Jesus* (2nd edn. Eng. trans. Oxford, 1955).

JEREMIAS, J., *Jerusalem in the time of Jesus* (Eng. translation, London, 1969).

MACHEN, J. G., *The Virgin Birth of Christ* (2nd edn. New York, 1932).

MOULE, C. F. D., *The Origin of Christology* (Cambridge, 1977).

PARROT, A., *Golgotha and the Church of the Holy Sepulchre* (Eng. trans. London, 1957).

ROBINSON, J. A. T., *Redating the New Testament* (London, 1976).

STENDAHL, K., *The School of St. Matthew* (Uppsala, 1954).

STONEHOUSE, N. B., *Origins of the Synoptic Gospels* (Grand Rapids, 1963).

STRACK, H. L. and BILLERBECK, P., *Kommentar zum Neuen Testament aus Talmud und Midrasch* (6 vols. Munich, 1922–1961).

WILLIAMS, A. L., *Christian Evidences for Jewish People* (2 vols. Cambridge, 1911, London, 1919).

MARK

STEPHEN S. SHORT

Authorship and Destination

This Gospel, like the other three in the New Testament Canon, is written anonymously. That its author was John Mark, however, is attested by such second-century church writers as Papias, Irenaeus, Clement of Alexandria, etc. John Mark lived in Jerusalem with Mary his mother during the early church period, his home being an early Christian meeting-place (Ac. 12: 12), and perhaps the main meeting-place of the church at Jerusalem. Possibly it was the venue of Jesus' 'Last Supper', and of the Easter Sunday evening resurrection-appearance. Mark accompanied Paul and Barnabas on the first stage of their first missionary journey (Ac. 13: 4–13). Later on he served with Barnabas in Cyprus (Ac. 15: 39), and later still he was at Rome (Col. 4: 10; Phm. 24; 2 Tim. 4: 11; also 1 Pet. 5: 13, where 'Babylon', as in Rev. 14: 8, seems to be used as a code-word for 'Rome').

That it was while Mark was at Rome that he wrote this Gospel is attested by Irenaeus, Clement of Alexandria, Origen, Eusebius and Jerome. Evidence of this adduced from the Gospel itself is to be found in the considerable number of Latin terms which Mark uses, preferring these to their Greek equivalents, e.g. his words for 'executioner' (6: 27), 'kettles' (7: 4), 'taxes' (12: 14), 'penny' (12: 42), 'flogged' (15: 15), 'praetorium' (15: 16), 'centurion' (15: 39). A further, though decidedly equivocal indication of Mark's Gospel having been written primarily for Christians in Rome, where he produced it, consists in the mention of 'Rufus' in 15: 21, with whom, inferentially, the original readers were well acquainted, and his possible identification with the Christian who lived at Rome named 'Rufus', mentioned in Rom. 16: 13 (assuming that Rom. 16 was addressed to Christians in Rome; see notes ad loc.). Further evidence in the same direction may be adduced from the phrase in 6: 48, 'the fourth watch of the night', on which see notes.

Whether or not Mark's Gospel was written for Christians in Rome, it was certainly written principally for Gentiles. This is indicated (a) by the way in which Jewish customs and terms are carefully explained (e.g. 7: 2 ff.; 12: 42; 14: 12; 15: 42); and (b) by the way in which the Aramaic words and sentences Mark introduces periodically are regularly translated thereupon into Greek (e.g. 3: 17; 5: 41; 7: 11, 34; 14: 36; 15: 22, 34).

Sources

There is no evidence of Mark's having been an eye-witness of most of the events in Jesus' life which he describes in this Gospel. Some have submitted, however, that the 'young man' mentioned in 14: 51–52 is the author's anonymous allusion to himself (for evidence regarding this, see notes ad loc.); in which event Mark would have been a witness of the sequel to Jesus' arrest.

There is no positive proof that the author used an earlier written narrative as a source of his Gospel, though some have claimed that he used such a narrative (now lost) of the Passion story. Augustine regarded Mark as having produced his Gospel by abridging the more extended record of Matthew, and this was the normal view till the nineteenth century. It is now held almost universally that Mark's was the earliest Gospel, and that it was used as a source for the writing of the Gospels according to Matthew and Luke. Evidence for this is found in the excision by Matthew and Luke of words and phrases from Mark's descriptions such as they seem to have regarded as superfluous, in order to make room for the large sections of additional material they were wishing to record. Further such evidence is that Matthew and Luke tend to improve on Mark's style when reporting the same incidents, and either to omit altogether statements by Mark which might offend or perplex, or else to present these in a less provocative form (e.g. 4: 38b; 5: 26; 10: 17, 35–37; 14: 33, 37, 71; 15: 34). See also pp. 1075 ff.

That Mark's main source for the writing of his Gospel was the preaching and instruction of the Apostle Peter is attested by Papias, Justin Martyr, the Anti-Marcionitic Prologue to Mark's Gospel, Irenaeus, and Clement of Alexandria, all of the second century. The testimony of Papias (bishop of Hierapolis c. A.D. 140) reflects Christian opinion on the matter at the very start of the century, for his statement is in fact a quotation from an anonymous 'Elder', who was dead when Papias wrote. Evidence from the Gospel itself of Peter's having influenced Mark in his narration of events is as follows:—(a) The prominence of Peter in the story, including allusions to him which none but himself would probably have recalled (*e.g.* 16: 7); (*b*) The fact that at almost all the scenes described, Peter was present (NB 1 Pet. 5: 1 implies that he witnessed Jesus' crucifixion); and that at some of them (*e.g.* 5: 37; 9: 2; 14: 33, 66–72, etc.), he was one of the very few who were present; (*c*) The inclusion of such details in the record as suggest that the descriptions in question originated in an eye-witness (*e.g.* 1: 19; 4: 38; 6: 39; and such mentions of Jesus' acts and gestures as are related in 3: 5; 7: 33; 8: 23; 10: 16, etc.).

Date

Peter's martyrdom by crucifixion was predicted by Jesus (Jn 21: 18–19; 2 Pet. 1: 14). There are early Church writers who affirm that this occurred at Rome, in connection with the Neronian persecution of the Church in A.D. 64. But such writers express differing opinions as to whether Peter was alive or dead when Mark wrote this Gospel. Clement of Alexandria and Origen believed that Peter was still living, whereas Irenaeus and the writer of the anti-Marcionitic prologue to Mark's Gospel believed that he was dead. It could be inferred that such was also the belief of Papias, though he does not state this categorically. This is the most commonly held view today, with the consequence that Mark's Gospel is usually regarded as having been written *c.* A.D. 65. It was the opinion of Harnack, however, that this Gospel was written 'during the sixth decade of the first century, at the latest' (*Date of the Acts and of the Synoptic Gospels*, 1911, p. 133), for he did not regard it as incontestable that Peter was dead before Mark wrote. Harnack considered it self-evident that the book of Acts, in view of how it closes, was written prior to Paul's death, and in A.D. 62, or thereabouts, in which event, Luke's 'first book' (Ac. 1: 1), *viz.* his Gospel, would have been written shortly before this, and the Gospel by Mark, consequently (fairly evidently, a source of Luke's Gospel), would have been written earlier still. It is difficult to see any really compelling reasons why Harnack's argument must be abandoned. Referring to Mark's record, T. W. Manson stated: 'The composition of the Gospel may be put several years earlier than the date commonly accepted' (*Studies in the Gospels and Epistles*, p. 45), suggesting between A.D. 58 and 65 (*ibid.*, p. 5).

Characteristics

Mark's Gospel is the shortest of those in the Canon. It is terse and full of action, a feature which would appeal to the practically minded Romans for whom, evidently, it was primarily written. The proportion of it which is devoted to recording Jesus' deeds, rather than His words, is greater in Mark's Gospel than in the others. Eighteen miracles are related, as against only four full-scale parables. An unusually large number of instances of Jesus' exorcizing of demons is noted (1: 23–27, 32–34; 3: 11, 22–27; 5: 1–20; 7: 25–30; 9: 17–29). Little is provided by way of comment on these happenings, the actions being left usually to speak for themselves.

Unlike standard biographies, Mark's Gospel states nothing about Jesus' birth, upbringing and appearance; and it specifies neither the length of His public ministry, nor His age at the time of His crucifixion. About a third of the record is devoted to a description of the eight days between Jesus' entry into Jerusalem on the colt, and His resurrection.

Theme

The thesis of this Gospel is that Jesus Christ is the Son of God. This is stated in the book's prologue (1: 1). As the story unfolds, Mark shows Jesus to have been proclaimed 'Son of God' by His heavenly Father (1: 11; 9: 7), by demons, who possessed supernatural knowledge (3: 11; 5: 7), and by Himself (12: 6; 14: 61 f.). The story's climax is that of a man of Roman nationality making this proclamation (15: 39), the author's intention, clearly, being that his action in this regard might be copied by those of Roman nationality for whom he wrote who read his book.

ANALYSIS

I. INTRODUCTORY EVENTS
(1: 1–13)
The ministry of John the Baptist (1: 1–8).
(Parallels: Mt. 3: 1–12; Lk. 3: 1–20; Jn 1: 19–37.)

Mark informs his readers that the Old Testament had predicted that the arrival of the Messiah would be preceded by the coming of a forerunner, quoting to this end Mal. 3: 1 and Isa. 40: 3. He identifies this fore-runner with John the Baptist, by indicating that John preached in the **desert** (4, cf. Isa. 40: 3), and by recalling that John's clothing (6) was reminiscent of that of Elijah (2 Kg. 1: 8), who, in Mal. 4: 5, is equated with the **messenger** of Mal. 3: 1. John's message was twofold: (a) He called men to repentance, adding that if they did so, his cleansing of their bodies in baptism would symbolize God's cleansing of their souls from sin (4); (b) He announced his Successor, who would baptize people with the Spirit (7, 8). This Jesus did on the day of Pentecost (Ac. 1: 5).

The baptism of Jesus (1: 9–11).
(Parallels: Mt. 3: 13–17; Lk. 3: 21–22.)
Jesus received baptism from John (9) by way of identifying Himself with sinners in anticipation of His doing so to even greater purpose in His crucifixion. Both the Spirit (10) and the Father (11) bore witness to Jesus as being the Messianic Son of God, the Spirit in the form of a dove, and the Father in words echoing Ps. 2: 7 and Isa. 42: 1. Mark, in contrast to the later evangelists, only mentions the vision of the dove and the words from heaven as having been perceived by Jesus Himself.

The temptation of Jesus (1: 12–13).
(Parallels: Mt. 4: 1–11; Lk. 4: 1–13.)
In Jesus' temptation, He was being urged by Satan to turn aside from His divinely appointed pathway of service and ultimate suffering. For a fuller treatment of this, see notes on Luke ad loc. Mark alone of the evangelists mentions the presence of the **wild animals** during Jesus' temptation. It is more likely that their mention is to emphasize the awfulness of the experience than to depict them as friendly and subject to Jesus.

II. THE GALILEAN MINISTRY
(1: 14–7: 23)
Christ's initial preaching in Galilee (1: 14–15).
(Parallels: Mt. 4: 12–17; Lk. 4: 14–30; Jn 4: 43–45.)
Prior to Jesus' journey to Galilee (14), He had carried out His early Judaean ministry as described in Jn 1: 29—4: 43. The occasion of His proceeding to Galilee was the arrest by Herod Antipas of John the Baptist (14), for the reason stated in 6: 17 f. The theme of Jesus' preaching in Galilee was to the effect that God's appointed period of waiting had now been completed, and His kingdom was at hand; and that in view of this, men were to **repent** (i.e. turn from their sin to God), and **believe** the good news (15). The implication of this announcement is that Jesus' conception of the divine kingdom was not the popular one of a cataclysmic outward triumph over all that was evil, but was the rule of God in people's hearts. Because of His advent and mission, Jesus showed this to be a present reality (Mt. 12: 28; Lk. 17: 21), though it would have a future consummation (Mt. 6: 10; Lk. 22: 18).

The calling of the first disciples (1: 16–20).
(Parallel: Mt. 4: 18–22.)
The record assumes these fishermen to have had a previous knowledge of Jesus, which fact is confirmed in Jn 1: 35–42, where it is shown that they already believed Jesus to be Israel's Messiah. In asserting thus His right to people's whole-hearted allegiance to Him, Jesus displayed His consciousness of His personal authority. Jesus' command to them to **follow** Him (17) involved not only that they should accompany Him on His journeys, but that they should accept a disciple-Rabbi relationship in His regard. His promise to make them **fishers of men** related to their winning of others to His cause. Peter recalled to Jesus his sacrificing of his livelihood for His sake in 10: 28.

The exorcism in the synagogue (1: 21–28).
(Parallel: Lk. 4: 31–37.)
In Capernaum, situated on the north-west shore on the sea of Galilee, as well as elsewhere in Galilee, Jesus was frequently given opportunities for teaching in the synagogue on the sabbath day. On the occasion here described, His presentation of His theme (15) was characterized by an authoritativeness which amazed the hearers, and forced them to contrast Him with the teachers to whom they were accustomed (22). This authoritativeness was also displayed in His exorcizing a demon from one of the congregation. The demon, in contrast to the onlookers, penetrated the mystery of Jesus' person, and so knew the explanation of Jesus' authority. The demon's cry: '**What do you want with us?**' means 'Why are you interfering with us?' for the demons knew that the establishing by Jesus of the kingdom of God necessarily involved their own destruction (24). The effect of Jesus' words and deeds in the synagogue that day on the people as a whole was to excite wonder, but not to evoke faith; and thus it was throughout Galilee (28).

The healing of Peter's mother-in-law (1: 29–31).
(Parallels: Mt. 8: 14–15; Lk. 4: 38–39.)
This story shows Jesus' power in the healing of a different type of malady, viz. fever. And His method of healing was different, the grasp of His hand being here noted rather than some vocal utterance. The speed and completeness of the woman's cure is shown by her serving

the company at table immediately afterwards. Although both this and the previous healing were performed on the sabbath day, no opposition to them is mentioned, since these cases were urgent, and the latter, additionally, was wrought in a private house.

The healing of the crowds at sunset (1: 32–34). (Parallels: Mt. 8: 16–17; Lk. 4: 40–41.)
The populace of Capernaum, aware now of Jesus' healing powers, desirous of securing from Him the restoration of their sick friends, **brought** (32) (lit. 'carried') them to Jesus at **the door** of Peter's house, awaiting **sunset** before so doing, when, with the sabbath over, this 'work' of carrying them was lawful. Jesus healed **many** (34), which, according to Semitic idiom, means 'all who were brought'. Although the demons discerned the nature of Jesus' person, Jesus deemed it unfitting that this should be announced by such minions of Satan (34).

Travelling and preaching throughout Galilee (1: 35–39). (Parallel: Lk. 4: 42–44.)
Jesus' praying during this retreat of His (34) (which, uncharacteristically, is not mentioned by Luke), reveals His communion with, and dependence on, His heavenly Father. It may have been occasioned, in part, by disappointment on the part of Christ that His miracles were only evoking a response of amazement, not of committal to Him. Determined not to be interrupted in His preaching ministry through having acquired fame as a healer, Jesus proceeded to other Galilean towns instead of returning to Capernaum.

The healing of the leper (1: 40–45). (Parallels: Mt. 8: 2–4; Lk. 5: 12–15.)
Though Jesus was resolved not deliberately to seek out sick people so as to heal them, He was prepared to cure such as this leper who happened to cross His path while He was engaged in more vital tasks. Leprosy, as described in the Bible, is probably not to be identified with the current disease of that name, though it was certainly a grave malady, and was regarded by the Rabbis as humanly incurable, a belief endorsed by Christ (Lk. 4: 27). Yet the Jews believed that the Messiah, when he came, would be able to cure lepers (Mt. 11: 5); and this leper was convinced Jesus could heal him (40). Having cleansed him, Jesus forbade the man to talk about his cure, for Jesus did not wish people to come to Him merely to receive physical benefits; but the man disobeyed, not being able to repress his joy. Jesus also told him to go to the priest at Jerusalem so as to comply with the regulations of Lev. 14, **as a testimony to them**, meaning perhaps, 'so that they may appreciate that I do not disregard the ceremonial law wantonly, but only where this conflicts with the law of love'. An instance of the ceremonial law being over-ruled by the law of love had been furnished by Jesus' touching the leper.

The healing of the paralysed man (2: 1–12). (Parallels: Mt. 9: 1–8; Lk. 5: 17–26.)
Jesus' temporary withdrawal from Capernaum (1: 38) having now served its purpose, He returned there, and found people who would gather around Him to hear His preaching (2) rather than to be healed, though this story shows the latter category of folk still to be existing. The roof of the house where Jesus was teaching would probably have consisted in matting, covered with earth and twigs, suspended over rafters, and would be reached by an outside staircase. Dealing first with the greater need of the paralysed man whom his friends had let down through the roof, Jesus conferred on him the forgiveness of his sins, announcing this to him publicly. The scribes who were present were electrified at the proclamation, and drew the only conclusion which, to those failing to appreciate Jesus' Deity, is open, namely that He was blaspheming. Though they did not express this charge vocally, Jesus knew it to be in their minds. To prove, therefore, the reality of His possessing authority to confer forgiveness and of His having exercised it in this instance, Jesus provided a visible sign, healing the man's paralysis.

The calling of Levi (2: 13–14). (Parallels: Mt. 9: 9; Lk. 5: 27–28.)
Capernaum was a customs post. Levi, identified in Mt. 9: 9 with Matthew, a customs official in the service of Herod Antipas, immediately obeyed Jesus' call to him to become one of His disciples, from which it is to be inferred that Levi already knew of Jesus, and possibly already believed Him to be Israel's Messiah.

The feast in Levi's house (2: 15–17). (Parallels: Mt. 9: 10–13; Lk. 5: 29–32.)
Shortly after having become a follower of Jesus, Levi gave a reception in his home to some of his former business colleagues, and to other associates of his, for the purpose of giving them an opportunity to meet his new Master. It is probable that the **sinners** (15) whom Levi invited were so called, not on the ground of their being notoriously bad characters (though in verse 17 Jesus took up the word in a moral sense), but on the strength of their not being in the habit of studying and practising 'the tradition of the elders' (for which see notes on 7: 3), on which account they were depised by the Pharisees (Jn 7: 49). Tax collectors also were despised, both because ultimately it was for the Romans that they were collecting money, and also because they commonly enriched themselves by making unjust and extortionate demands from people. To consort with such, and particularly to share meals with them, was regarded by the Pharisees as a mark

of gross impiety. On Jesus being criticized for doing this, He replied that it was only by establishing contact with them that He could fulfil His mission of imparting to them salvation.

The discussion about fasting (2: 18–22). (Parallels: Mt. 9: 14–17; Lk. 5: 33–39.) Jesus incurred further criticism on the grounds of His disciples not joining in with other pious Jews who were observing a fast (though not one prescribed in the law of Moses, which only ordained fasting on the Day of Atonement). Jesus' reply was that His presence among His people was as much an occasion for rejoicing as was that of a bridegroom among the guests at his wedding. The conduct appropriate to it, consequently, was as incompatible with the practices of contemporary Judaism (with their fasts, etc.), as was (i) a new patch on an old garment, which, as it shrank, would pull away the adjacent threads from the old garment, (ii) new wine in wineskins brittle with age, which, as it fermented, would cause the skins to burst. Jesus added, however, that the day would come when for His disciples to fast would be fitting indeed, namely when He died (Jn 16: 20), a statement proving that Jesus foresaw His death from this early stage of His public ministry.

The plucking of the ears of corn (2: 23–28). (Parallels: Mt. 12: 1–8; Lk. 6: 1–5.) The Mosaic Law permitted a hungry traveller to pluck and eat corn from another person's field, so long as he only used his hands for the purpose, not a sickle (Dt. 23: 25). Since, however, the scribes, somewhat pedantically, regarded this as technically being 'reaping', they forbade the practice on the Sabbath, on which day reaping was divinely disallowed (Exod. 34: 21). On Jesus incurring criticism once again, this time on the grounds of His disciples having infringed this regulation, He referred His critics to the story 'in the passage about Abiathar the high priest', recounted in I Sam. 21: 1–6. This suggested rendering, which is parallel to the NIV's rendering of the equivalent Greek phrase in 12: 26 ('in the account of the bush'), seems preferable to the rendering in the text here, **in the days of Abiathar the high priest**, (feasible as that also is as a translation), in that it does not require that Abiathar was high priest when the event occurred, which was, actually, during the high priesthood of Abiathar's father Ahimelech. Jesus reminded the Pharisees that when, like the disciples, David on this occasion was hungry, what was a breach of the letter of the ceremonial law (Lev. 24: 9) was committed by himself; and the fact that Scripture does not condemn him for it shows that in cases where a human need existed, God allowed that regulations concerned merely with ritual matters might be waived. Since, furthermore, the Sabbath was ordained for the well-being of humanity, rather than as an end in itself (which was how the Pharisees tended to conceive of it), Jesus contended that humanity's Lord and Representative was authorized to be the official arbiter as to how the Sabbath should be observed (27, 28).

The healing of the man with the withered hand (3: 1–6). (Parallels: Mt. 12: 9–14; Lk. 6: 6–11.) Jesus' statement of 2: 28 suggested to the Pharisees that His infringements of the Sabbath regulations which had been imposed by the elders on the Law of Moses were being undertaken deliberately, which inference they decided now to put to the test. The Pharisees in the synagogue fully recognized that Christ had the ability to heal the man with the withered hand; their solitary interest lay in whether He would do so (which, to their way of thinking, was to perform 'work'), on the Sabbath. Jesus bade them, therefore, consider thoughtfully what would be involved if He refrained from healing him. Indicating to them in His question of verse 4 the two alternative courses lying before Him, He claimed that to refuse to heal the man would technically be a 'work' just as much as to cure him, and an evil one at that, **to do evil**, in its essential nature, indeed, **to kill**. This, however, the Pharisees failed to appreciate, their great fault being that they had **stubborn hearts** (5), meaning not callousness, but unteachableness. So, on Jesus having healed the man, they resolved to have Jesus put to death, consorting to this end with the Herodians (6), the supporters of Herod Antipas, who feared that political unrest might result from Jesus' actions.

Jesus' acceptance with the common people (3: 7–12). (Parallel: Mt. 12: 14–21.) The opposition to Jesus of the Jewish leaders was more than offset by His acclamation by the common people, who gathered to Him both from the south and from the north (8). Many of these were healed of their illnesses by simply touching Him, apart, apparently, from any direct action on His part (10). As in 1: 34, Jesus refused to accept testimony to the nature of His person from demons (12).

The choosing of the apostles (3: 13–19a). (Parallels: Mt. 10: 1, 2; Lk. 6: 12–16.) Of the crowds who were flocking to Him, Jesus selected twelve men to be constantly with Him, so that they might receive from Him a more intensive spiritual training, and later (6: 7 ff.; 16: 15) be dispatched by Him to preach and heal. It is unlikely that James and John were called by Jesus **Sons of Thunder** because of their being quick-tempered, divinely given names always being bestowed with reference to some commendable characteristic. Perhaps

the name related to their energy. A **Zealot**
(18), was a member of a strongly nationalistic
Jewish group who was bitterly opposed to their
Roman overlords. **Iscariot** probably means
'from Kerioth'; Kerioth Hezron (Jos. 15: 25)
was twelve miles south of Hebron. For comments on the variation in the apostles' names
as given in the different lists, see notes on Mt.
ad loc.

**The protest by Jesus' family (3: 19b–21, 31–
35).** (Parallels: Mt. 12: 46–50; Lk. 8: 19–21).
Jesus, having returned **home** to Capernaum
(19), was hindered from taking proper meals
through pressure of work (20). **His family**
(21), i.e. **his mother and his brothers** (31),
regarded this as madness, and so set out from
Nazareth to try to restrain Him from continuing His ministry. Jesus' brothers were unbelieving (Jn 7: 5) till after His resurrection (Ac. 1:
14), and even His mother misunderstood Him
(Lk. 2: 49; Jn 2: 4). As to the identity of Jesus'
brothers, see notes on 6: 3. The fact of Joseph
not being mentioned here is presumptive evidence that he was now dead. This event gave
Jesus an opportunity to teach that His closest
affinities were with such as obeyed God's message through Him (cf. Lk. 11: 27 f.; Heb. 2: 11),
rather than with such as were physically related
to Him (35).

The Beelzebub accusation (3: 22–30). (Parallels: Mt. 12: 24–32; Lk. 11: 15–22; 12: 10.)
It seems apparent that the religious authorities
in Jerusalem, having heard of the stir created
by Jesus' ministry, sent this deputation of
scribes to Galilee to investigate the situation.
They alleged that Jesus was possessed by **Beelzebub**, and that it was by Beelzebub's power
that Jesus exorcized demons (22). In the Greek
text this name is given as 'Beelzeboul' (see mg),
which means 'lord of the house' or 'lord of the
high place'. 2 Kg. 1: 3 shows that a god of this
name was worshipped at Ekron in the territory
formerly occupied by Philistines. The styling
of him as 'Beelzebub' ('lord of flies') was probably a mocking pun on his proper name. Beelzebul, being denoted here **the prince of demons**, is to be identified in this controversy
with Satan. By way of reply, Jesus asked these
scribes (23) as to why Satan, who was the cause
of demon-possession, should be concerned to
terminate the condition. It would indicate that
Satan's kingdom was involved in pursuing two
opposite policies, in which event it would destroy itself through civil war (24–26). Jesus
informed His critics thereupon of the correct
explanation of His exorcisms, which was that
He Himself, being endued with the power of
God, was stronger than Satan, and that having
bound Satan, He was able now to **rob his
house** (28). Jesus added that since the Holy
Spirit was God's Agent in effecting these exorcisms, to attribute them to Satan was to **blas-

pheme against the Holy Spirit** (29), which
was **an eternal sin**, in that it carried eternal
consequences. By **blaspheme** here, is denoted
not bad language, but defiant hostility.

The parable of the sower (4: 1–20). (Parallels: Mt. 13: 1–23; Lk. 8: 4–15.)
This parable shows that the reason why Jesus
was opposed by the religious leaders and
others, and misunderstood even by His own
relations (3: 19b–35), was the spiritual condition of their hearts. In addressing this parable
to the crowds by the lakeside, Jesus wanted
them to give careful consideration to the nature
of their own hearts. Some hearers of His teaching, He pointed out, never grasped His message
at all; others were discouraged through difficulties, and others again were seduced through
prosperity, so that only a limited proportion
became lastingly committed to it.

Prior to explaining the parable to His disciples, Jesus answered their question as to why
He employed parables (10–12). The essence of
His reply seems to be that He did so in order to
test the spiritual responsiveness of His hearers.
Those who were provoked by them into intensive reflection could proceed thereupon to obtain enlightenment concerning them (*e.g.* by
asking Jesus their meaning, as did the disciples
in this instance); whereas those who omitted
to reflect on them would **be ever seeing but
never perceiving** (quoting Isa. 6: 9 f.), i.e.
understand the literal meaning of the words,
but not the parables' deeper signification.

**The aim of Jesus' parables, cntd (4: 21–25,
33–34).** (Parallels: Mt. 5: 15; 10: 26; 11: 15; 7:
2; 13: 34; Lk. 8: 17f.; 12: 2; 6: 38.)
Just as a lamp is only useful when placed on a
stand (21), the ultimate purpose of Jesus' parables was to reveal truth rather than to hide it
(22), though they might express the truth in a
somewhat mystifying manner initially. **Consider carefully what you hear**, said Jesus
(24), i.e.: 'Do not regard these parables as being
mere stories, but penetrate to the message
which they are intended to impart'. **The
measure you use** (of attention to the parables),
will be that with which **it will be measured
to you** (of spiritual profit from the parables).
For **whoever has** (by way of application of
heart) **will be given more** (by way of divine
blessing), whereas casual hearers will only land
themselves in a state of ever-increasing confusion (25). By speaking in parables Jesus suited
His teaching to the degree of receptivity of His
hearers (33), hoping that through the parables
His hearers might not only apprehend the
truth, but be drawn to Himself, the discloser
of the truth (34).

**The parable of the seed growing secretly
(4: 26–29).**
In this brief parable, peculiar to Mark's Gospel,
Jesus taught that the kingdom of God would

certainly attain its consummation, even though initially nothing very dramatic was observable. By Jesus' ministry of preaching, the seed had been sown, and nothing could now prevent the harvest which would ultimately result from it. Rather than be fretful, therefore, one should show calm patience and confident expectation.

The parable of the mustard seed (4: 30–32). (Parallels: Mt. 13: 31–32; Lk. 13: 18–19.)
This further parable Jesus told testified to the mighty future destined for the kingdom of God despite the meagre company who up till then had been born into it. Mustard seed, proverbially the tiniest of seeds, within but a few weeks could develop into a shrub of over ten feet in height, furnishing an apt picture of the phenomenally rapid spread of Christianity during the apostolic era. **The birds of the air**, which rested in the shade of the shrub, were probably intended to depict the inclusion within God's kingdom of people from gentile nations (cf. Ezek. 17: 23; 31: 6; Dan. 4: 21 f.).

The storm on the lake (4:35–41). (Parallels: Mt. 8: 23–27; Lk. 8: 22–25.)
From 4: 35 to 5: 43 are related three acts of divine power wrought by Jesus in a situation of human helplessness and despair (the last of these acts being a double one). The first of them was that of His stilling of one of the violent storms which not infrequently descended with great suddenness on the Galilean lake. Weary at the close of a day of teaching, Jesus was rowed eastwards across the lake by His disciples. Upon the boat's cushion (provided for the guest of honour, and placed at the stern, away from the splashing of the waves), Jesus rested His head, and fell asleep. On the storm arising, the disciples aroused Jesus, suggesting to Him that He was indifferent to their peril. His calming of the waters, however, caused them to be awe-struck before Him (41).

The healing of the man with many demons (5: 1–20). (Parallels: Mt. 8: 28–34; Lk. 8: 26–39.)
Having given peace to people who were troubled by the world outside (4: 35–41), Jesus now gave peace to someone who was troubled by that which was within him. The probable location of the incident was at Kersa, a small town of that period on the east coast of the sea of Galilee. The name Kersa later became confused with Gerasa, a town over thirty miles south-east of the lake, which confusion explains how the corruption **the region of the Gerasenes** (1) has occurred. Most of the inhabitants of the area were Gentiles, which explains (a) why the farmers among them kept **pigs** (11), which creatures were 'unclean' to the Jews (Lev. 11: 7); (b) why Jesus commanded the man, when healed, to proclaim his cure

throughout the district (19). Contrast with this the injunction Jesus gave to the healed leper (1: 44), in view of the misunderstanding and dangerous enthusiasm Jesus foresaw resulting, had undue publicity been given to the leper's cure in Jewish circles. **The Decapolis** (20), however (meaning 'the ten cities'), where the cured demoniac promulgated his deliverance, was predominantly Gentile in population, being a group of towns, most of which were east of Jordan, and which were governed somewhat independently of the rest of Palestine.

The **tombs** (3) in which this demon-possessed man lived would have been caves. People's attempts to control him by binding him with chains had been in vain (4); yet the demons were exorcized by Jesus on the utterance of a single command (8). Jesus' purpose in asking the man his name (9) was probably so as to recall to his consciousness the awful plight in which he stood. As in 1: 24, the demons knew that their encounter with Jesus would result in their destruction (7). A likely reason for Jesus permitting the expelled demons to enter the swine (13) was so that the healed man, seeing the demon-occupied swine rushing madly into the lake, might be reassured as to the reality of his deliverance. The loss of the swine sustained by the local farmers, together with their fear of Jesus' miraculous powers (15), impelled them to request Jesus to leave their district (17). This He did; and there is no record that He ever returned to it.

The raising of the daughter of Jairus (5: 21–24, 35–43). (Parallels: Mt. 9: 1, 18–19, 23–26; Lk. 8: 40–42, 49–56.)
Although the Jewish religious leaders, for the most part, were hostile to Jesus, Jairus, the supervisor of the synagogue probably of Capernaum, to which city Jesus had just sailed from the east of the lake (21, Mt. 9: 1), was prepared to beg Jesus' help when his daughter was ill. Jesus responded to his entreaty, but the interruption that occurred, as recorded in 25–34, must have been most frustrating for Jairus, and meanwhile his daughter died. On reaching Jairus's home at length, Jesus announced that the child was merely **asleep** (39), by which He meant that the period of her being dead was only going to be as short as a sleep. But the mourners (probably professional mourners, hired by the family, cf. Mt. 9: 23), understanding Jesus' words in a literal sense, ridiculed Him. Jesus only allowed His raising of the girl to be witnessed by such as truly believed in Him, besides the girl's parents (37, 40), so that the act might be rightly understood and reported; but to obviate His being thronged again (24) by the people, He did not wish the reporting of the miracle to be immediate (43), though, obviously, the deed could not have been kept secret for long.

The healing of the woman with the haemorrhage (5: 25–34). (Parallels: Mt. 9: 18–22; Lk. 8: 43–48.)
The continuous uterine bleeding from which, presumably, this woman suffered would have rendered her ceremonially unclean (Lev. 15: 25–30), with the consequence that law-abiding Jews would tend to shun her. This fact, together with her natural modesty, and the embarrassment she felt on account of the nature of her malady, made her anxious to secure the healing which she believed Jesus could impart to her without the publicity which was normally inevitable in the event of such healings. Such was her faith in Jesus that she believed He could cure her apart from a personal interview, and by her merely touching His clothes (28; cf. 3: 10; 6: 56), this, despite the failure to help her of the many physicians she had consulted (26). This faith of hers, on being put to the test, was fully vindicated (29), and on her being healed, she endeavoured to disappear unnoticed into the crowd. Jesus, however, conscious of a release from Him of supernatural power, and aware of how this had occurred, demanded that the person responsible should come forward. Though fearful of Jesus' anger, and dreading now being exposed, the woman presented herself before His face and explained to Him her action, whereupon Jesus commended her for her faith, and assured her of the completeness of her cure.

The rejection of Jesus at Nazareth (6: 1–6). (Parallel: Mt. 13: 53–58; cf. Lk. 4: 16–30.)
From Capernaum, Jesus proceeded twenty miles west-south-west to Nazareth, **hometown** (1), where previously He had been living, and He preached there in the synagogue (2; see note on 1: 21). His townsfolk admitted the wisdom displayed in His preaching, and also the power displayed in His miracles; but they were at a loss to explain these things. Had He visibly descended on to this earth out of heaven (as many believed the Messiah would do), all would have been comprehensible. But He was merely the local **carpenter** (NB though the word *tektōn* could apply also to workers in stone or in metal, probably a worker in wood is here denoted); and His mother, brothers and sisters were all well known to them (3). The root of their perplexity about Jesus was their **lack of faith** (6); and Jesus marvelled at it. Only at the unbelief of His townsfolk and, by contrast, at the faith of a foreigner (Lk. 7: 9), do the Gospels represent Jesus as marvelling. As in 3: 31, Joseph is not mentioned here in 6: 3, which suggests again that he was now dead. The 'brothers' of Jesus (3) were probably sons of Joseph and Mary subsequent to the birth from Mary of Jesus. The suggestions that they were either half-brothers of Jesus (i.e. children of Joseph by a former marriage), or else cousins of Jesus, are not natural interpretations of this passage, and arose when the state of virginity came to be regarded as 'holier' than that of marriage, and, as a consequence, belief in the idea of Mary's perpetual virginity was becoming popular. As to Jesus' being rejected by those among whom He had lived, He commented that this was what prophets generally had experienced (4). Because of the unbelief of the people of Nazareth, Jesus was unable, consistently with the principles on which He acted, to do miracles among them, apart from His healing **a few sick people**, who, presumably, did display a modicum of faith in Him (5).

The mission of the twelve apostles (6: 7–13). (Parallels: Mt. 9: 36–11: 1; Lk. 9: 1–6.)
The purpose of this mission was twofold. It was partly to give the apostles some practical training in missionary work by way of preparing them for their later responsibilities as envoys to the world (see on 3: 14), and it was designed also to bring without delay to as many Galileans as possible the call to repentance. The reason for the urgency of the need for these to repent is not stated here in Mk, but Mt. 10: 7 shows this to have been in view of the near arrival of God's kingdom. Because of the haste with which the disciples would be required to act, they were to travel as light as possible. For the supply of their material needs they were to trust in God's care for them rather than in resources of their own providing (8). Should they discover, having been in some house for a day or two, a more congenial habitation near by, they were not to transfer themselves to it (10). On leaving villages which had proved unreceptive, they were to **shake the dust off** their feet, as a token that their personal responsibility to them had been discharged, and that the inhabitants would now have to answer for themselves (11; cf. Ac. 18: 6). Having received their commission, the disciples travelled throughout Galilee preaching and healing (12, 13), and thus proclaiming the kingdom in the way that Jesus did Himself.

The death of John the Baptist (6: 14–29). (Parallels: Mt. 14: 1–12; Lk. 3: 19 f.; 9: 7–9).
Jesus, because of the miracles He wrought, was becoming regarded by many as a supernatural person, *e.g.* as a reappearance of **one of the prophets of long ago** (15), such as Elijah. The allusion here is not to the culminating Prophet foretold in Dt. 18: 15 f., and there is no mention at this point of Jesus being regarded as the promised Messiah. Another view which was prevalent, however, was that Jesus was the resurrected embodiment of John the Baptist (14), for though John wrought no miracles in his mortal life (Jn 10: 41), he would be quite expected to do so if he rose from the dead. This latter view was held by Herod Antipas (16),

tetrarch of Galilee (Lk. 3: 1) and Perea from 4 B.C. till A.D. 39, who had been responsible for John's execution; and the circumstances of that execution are now related (17–29). John the Baptist had protested, presumably on the grounds of Lev. 18: 16 and 20: 21, against Herod's marriage to **Herodias, his brother Philip's wife** (17), Herodias having divorced Philip in order to marry Herod. 'Brother' here means 'half-brother'; and the 'Philip' here mentioned was not the tetrarch of Iturea and Trachonitis (Lk. 3: 1), but Herod Antipas' half-brother in Rome, so Josephus affirms (*Ant.* XVIII. v. 4). For making this protest Herod had imprisoned John (17), Josephus stating that the site of the imprisonment was Machaerus, a frontier fortress in the south of Perea, and east of the Dead Sea (*Ant.* XVIII. v. 2). Herodias, however, was not satisfied with John's merely being imprisoned, and schemed to have him killed (19). Her opportunity came on the occasion of Herod's birthday. Herod spread a banquet for his leading officials (21), at which, at the instigation, no doubt, of Herodias, her daughter performed a dance (22). This won Herod's favour, who promised her thereupon anything she cared to ask (23). Acting on her mother's instructions (24), she demanded the head of John the Baptist (25), who was incarcerated in the prison below; whereupon, with bitter regret (26), Herod ordered John to be executed and his head to be brought (27).

The feeding of the five thousand (6: 30–44). (Parallels: Mt. 14: 13–21; Lk. 9: 11–17; Jn 6: 1–14.)

On the twelve apostles returning from their mission (30), the continual presence around them of the crowds (31; cf. 3: 20) induced Jesus to propose that they should journey with Him by boat to an isolated region on the lake's north-east shore in the vicinity of Bethsaida Julias (Lk. 9: 10). The fact that the crowds, who noticed their departure and proceeded to the apostles' destination by foot, arrived there first (33), suggests that the wind on the lake was unfavourable to the boat's quick progress. On disembarking Jesus' impression of the crowd was that they were **like sheep without a shepherd**, i.e. bewildered and helpless. He attended at once therefore to their primary need, and preached to them (34). When it was evening however, instead of agreeing to the apostles' perfectly reasonable suggestion of dismissing the crowds so that they could obtain food from the neighbouring villages (36), He Himself attended now to their physical need by multiplying and having distributed the five loaves and two fishes, which was all the food that was there available. The fact that twelve baskets of fragments were collected afterwards (43) suggests that each apostle carried one basket. This miracle was not only an expression of Jesus' compassion towards the hungry crowds, 6: 52 and 8: 16–19 showing that it was intended to teach the disciples some deeper truth. The state of the righteous in the life to come was pictured by the Jews as a great banquet presided over by their Messiah (cf. Isa. 25: 6 ff.; Lk. 13: 29; 14: 15; 22: 16, 30, etc.), and Jesus may perhaps have desired this 'feast' to be envisaged as an anticipation of that banquet. The significance attached to the miracle in John's Gospel, however, is that of Jesus Christ, depicted as the Bread of Life, offering Himself as 'food' to the famished world to which He had descended from heaven.

The walking by Jesus on the water (6: 45–52). (Parallels: Mt. 14: 22–33; Jn 6: 15–21.) (On the section Mk 6: 45–8: 26 see p. 1078.) The urgency with which Jesus pressed His disciples to embark into the ship is shown by Jn 6: 15 to have been due to the intention of the crowd regarding Jesus, to 'take Him by force to make Him king'. While Jesus was departing by Himself to pray on the hills (46), His disciples crossed the lake, travelling probably from the region of Bethsaida Julias (see note on 31) to 'Bethsaida in Galilee' (45; Jn 12: 21), on the north-west shore of the lake. Their journey, however, proved difficult, though not on account of a sudden storm (as in 4: 37), but because of a strong headwind (48) (the wind during the previous few hours having changed direction, if the suggestion contained in the note on verse 33 is correct). From the hillside Jesus saw the disciples in distress, presumably by the light of the moon, and between 3.0 and 6.0 a.m. (**the fourth watch of the night**, adopting, as in 13: 35, the Roman reckoning; for in the Jewish reckoning the night was divided into three watches only), Jesus walked towards them across the surface of the water. **He was about to pass them** (48), probably in order that they might make a personal appeal to Him for help (cf. Lk. 24: 29). Though the cry (49) of the disciples on seeing Him was a shriek of fear rather than an appeal for help, Jesus responded to it and calmed their spirits (50), whereupon He entered the boat and the wind ceased (51). Their astonishment, though natural, is stated by Mark to have been blameworthy, in that having just previously witnessed Jesus' multiplication of the loaves (52), they should have been more conscious of the divine power with which He was endued.

The healings by Jesus at Gennesaret (6: 53–56). (Parallel: Mt. 14: 34–36.)

Gennesaret, where the disciples landed (53), was presumably a village on the small but heavily populated plain of Gennesaret just south of Capernaum. In this neighbourhood

Jesus healed at this time many invalids. Like other male Jews who were loyal to the law, on each corner of Jesus' outer garment was a blue tassel (see Num. 15: 37 f.; Dt. 22: 12), and many obtained healing through expressing their faith in Him by the act of their touching such a tassel (56).

The discussion concerning purification (7: 1–23). (Parallel: Mt. 15: 1–20.)

The enthusiasm in relation to Jesus of those featuring in the story of 6: 54–56 stood in sharp contrast with the criticism of Him by most of the Jewish leaders. In 7: 1, as earlier in 3: 22, a deputation of scribes from Jerusalem journeyed northwards to Galilee to join issue with Him. Their objection to Him on this occasion had to do with the behaviour of His disciples (cf. 2: 18, 24), and was to the effect that they ate their meals without previously submitting their hands to a ritual cleansing (2), infringing thus one of the regulations contained in **the tradition of the elders** (5). The 'tradition of the elders' was a body of legislation which had been formulated by the rabbis, and to which the Pharisees attached great importance, in which were prescribed detailed applications of the Law of Moses to particular situations. Jesus, however, as also the Sadducees, rejected this supplementary legislation (though the Sadducees had their own tradition, which in many points coincided). He stressed to this end its human origin, styling it not 'the tradition of the elders' as did these scribes, but **the tradition of men** (8), which stood in antithesis to **the commands of God**. Quoting against those who upheld it Isa. 29: 13 (6, 7), He contended that although it may have been propounded with the aim of helping people to observe the Mosaic Law, in **many** cases (13b) it led people to disobey that law, and of this He provided an example. The Law of Moses enjoined that children had a responsibility to support their parents financially, and Jesus cited in this regard Exod. 20: 21 and 21: 17 (10). But some of the Jews evaded this obligation by taking upon themselves an oath to the effect that such resources of theirs which might otherwise have been available for the upkeep of their parents had been promised instead for the upkeep of the temple (11, 12). This sort of conduct constituted those practising it **hypocrites** (6), for despite the outward appearance of piety on their part to which it gave rise, in reality their behaviour was in complete variance with the will of God. Reverting thereupon to the subject of purification, Jesus urged that it was not consuming meals without a prior ritual cleansing that defiled a person, nor was it even the eating of particular kinds of food (18, 19), but that what did so was the state of that person's heart, which indeed was the root cause of every manifestation of moral evil (20–23).

III. THE NORTHERN JOURNEY (7: 24–8: 26).

The healing of the daughter of the Syrophoenician woman (7: 24–30). (Parallel: Mt. 15: 21–28.)

Apart from what is recorded in 8: 10–13 and 9: 30, Jesus' ministry in Galilee was now concluded. His declaration of His freedom from many of the regulations of Judaism with which that ministry terminated (7: 1–23) forms an appropriate prelude to this record of a second journey He undertook (cf. 5: 1) into Gentile territory. This time He proceeded not eastwards, but northwards, **to the vicinity of Tyre** (24). No reason for this journey is stated, but it may well have been undertaken with the aim of freeing Himself from the crowds so as to gain an opportunity of concentrating His attention more than had been possible previously on training and instructing His apostles.

Whilst in a certain house in this district, Jesus was approached by a **Greek** (i.e. Gentile) woman who was **born in Syrian Phoenicia** (26), who begged Jesus to exorcize a demon from her daughter. This, however, Jesus declined at first to do, telling her that it was among the Jews, not among the Gentiles, that His appointed ministry lay. The figure of speech Jesus used in stating that fact was that in which the Jews were represented as **children**, the Gentiles as **dogs** (the diminutive Greek noun *kynarion* suggesting 'that the reference is to the little dogs that were kept as pets, and not to the dogs of the courtyard and the street'; Cranfield, *ad loc.*), and the benefits of Jesus' ministry as **the children's bread** (27). The woman accepted the truth Jesus here affirmed; but pressing somewhat further the analogy He had employed, she pointed out that when children were given their food, the dogs received some slight benefit through the crumbs which the children dropped on the ground (28). While thus she did not wish to diminish the Jews' privileges, she did nevertheless crave to obtain from Jesus, as it were, an incidental mercy. And she received it, Jesus healing her daughter (29) without even setting eyes on the child (as also in Mt. 8: 5 ff., and Jn 4: 46 ff.).

The healing of the man who was deaf and dumb (7: 31–37).

In the **Decapolis** (31; see notes on 5: 20), which was the area where the man who had been indwelt with many demons had witnessed to his cure, Jesus was requested to heal a deaf and dumb man who was brought to Him (32). The man in question, though living in a Gentile district, was probably Jewish, for Jesus addressed him when healing him in Aramaic. But it was not by a mere word that Jesus healed Him, though so to heal was His normal custom. As in the stories of Mk 8: 22 ff. and Jn 9: 1 ff., He used saliva (33) doing so, probably (and touching also his ears and tongue), in order to awaken in the man faith by encouraging him to expect healing. Because, being deaf, the man would not have been able to hear a vocal prayer on his behalf, Jesus indicated to him that He was praying in that He **looked up to heaven** (34). The fact that Jesus emitted **a deep sigh** demonstrated the spiritual wrestling in which He was engaged. Jesus then commanded the man's ears to **be opened**. He did not command also that his tongue be released, realizing that his difficulty in speaking was simply a secondary consequence of his inability to hear. The outcome therefore of Jesus' command to the man's ears to be opened was that both his auditory and vocal defects were remedied (35), Jesus fulfilling thus, in part, the prophecy of Isa. 35: 5, 6.

The feeding of the four thousand (8: 1–10).
(Parallel: Mt. 15: 32–39.)
Similar in many respects as is this narrative to that of Christ's feeding of the five thousand (6: 30–44), there are, nevertheless, some arresting differences between the two accounts. This miracle was wrought in Gentile territory, *viz.* in 'the region of the Decapolis' (7: 31), southeast of the sea of Galilee; and it has been plausibly suggested therefore that whereas in His feeding of the five thousand, Jesus was symbolizing His ability to impart the bread of life to the Jews, in His feeding of the four thousand, He was symbolizing His ability to impart the bread of life to the Gentiles (see p. 1078). The type of basket used for the gathering of the fragments seems to have been different in the case of the two miracles, for in the first of them this is denoted by the Greek noun *kophinos* (6: 43), whereas in the second of them this is denoted by the Greek noun *spyris* (8), this being (according to some authorities), a larger sort of basket than the former, and big enough for an adult human being to sit in (Ac. 9: 25). **The region of Dalmanutha** (10) to which Jesus departed after performing the miracle has not been identified, and Matthew has replaced this phrase by 'the vicinity of Magadan' (Mt. 15: 39). See p. 1138.

The request by the Pharisees for a sign (8: 11–13). (Parallel: Mt. 16: 1–4.)
Although Jesus, in His healings and exorcisms, had furnished many signs to the effect that the power of God's kingdom was being exercised at last in the overthrow of the domain of Satan (Mt. 12: 28), the Pharisees now demanded **a sign from heaven**, meaning probably some apocalyptic vision. Jesus refused their demand, however, realizing that were such a spectacle granted, men's allegiance to Him would virtually be compelled, and the need for the exercise of faith on their part, which He knew to be so vital, would be precluded.

The disciples' shortage of bread (8: 14–21).
(Parallel: Mt. 16: 5–12.)
While in the ship (13) crossing from Dalmanutha (10) to Bethsaida (22), Jesus warned His disciples against **the yeast of the Pharisees** (*viz.* false religion), and **that of Herod** (*viz.* irreligion) (15). The disciples, supposing that Jesus was speaking about literal leaven, instead of using the word metaphorically to denote moral evil of a corrupting nature, assumed that Jesus was complaining at their not having brought with them sufficient bread for their communal needs on this journey they were making (16). Jesus was vexed with His disciples in consequence, but not so much for their having misunderstood His figure of speech, but for their having imagined that a shortage of food could be a worry to Him. Reminding them of how, with but the most paltry provision, He had twice fed great multitudes (19, 20), He reprimanded them for having their **hearts hardened** (17; see note on 3: 5), and applied to them the words of Isa. 6: 9 ff., which in 4: 12 He had applied to 'those outside' the Kingdom of God.

The healing of the blind man at Bethsaida (8: 22–26).
As with the healing of the person who was deaf and dumb (7: 31–37), in order to awaken faith in this blind man, Jesus used saliva, and applied His hands to the functionless organ (23). But on account, perhaps, of the weakness of the man's faith, he did not at first attain full clarity of vision as a result of Jesus' dealings with him (24). Jesus would not, however, leave the man only half-cured, and the outcome of His placing His hands on the man's eyes a second time was that the restoration of his sight became complete (25). Desirous, probably, that the man's relations should know of his cure before other people, Jesus told him to go home, rather than to the near-by village (26).

IV. THE JOURNEY TO JERUSALEM (8: 27–10: 52)

Peter's acknowledgement of Jesus' Messiahship (8: 27–30). (Parallels: Mt. 16: 13–20; Lk. 9: 18–21.)
The main task Jesus had to undertake on the course of this journey of His from the north of Palestine to Jerusalem was to prepare His disciples for His ensuing crucifixion at the capital city. His initial need to this end was to ascertain whether the disciples, despite how He had been acting, remained as convinced that He was Israel's Messiah as they had been convinced of it when first they met Him (Jn 1: 41, 45, etc.), and when, a little later, they sacrificed their homes and livelihood so as to live in His company (Mk 1: 16–20; 2: 14). Resolved to enquire from them concerning this, Jesus con-

ducted them to **the villages around Caesarea Philippi** (27), i.e. the countryside around this town which was situated on the lower slopes of Mount Hermon, near the source of the river Jordan. Paneas was its original name; but on its being rebuilt by Philip the tetrarch, it was re-named 'Caesarea', in honour of the Roman Emperor; but to distinguish it from the city of that name on the Mediterranean coastline, its full name became 'Caesarea Philippi', in recognition also of its founder. Jesus introduced this enquiry of His by asking the disciples as to what was the opinion of men generally concerning Himself. Their reply (28) was similar to that recorded in 6: 14, 15 (see notes *ad loc.*). On testing the disciples themselves regarding this, however, Peter, as the spokesman, no doubt, of the entire group, answered: **'You are the Christ'** (29), meaning: 'You are the Messiah, God's appointed Saviour of His people, whose advent has been foretold in our sacred Scriptures'. The reason for Jesus enjoining them thereupon to refrain from promulgating this truth (30), was that He did not want people to integrate this identification into the 'political' concept of Messiahship which so many of them entertained, and imagine, in consequence, that Jesus was destined to expel the Roman legions from Palestine.

The first prediction of the Passion (8: 31–33). (Parallels: Mt. 16: 21–23; Lk. 9: 22.) With the disciples unitedly convinced now that Jesus was the Messiah, He was able at last to give them explicit teaching about His forthcoming death (though incidental allusions to it had been made previously, *e.g.* 2: 20). **The Son of man must suffer**, He told them (31), the cause of the necessity being regarded by Him, doubtless, as the will of God, as that will was expressed in such Scriptures as Isa. 53. Peter, however, though convinced of Jesus' Messianic status, was appalled at the thought of its carrying such implications, and he contested Jesus' assertion concerning His future to His face (32). This protest of Peter's was seen by Jesus as a repetition of the devil's temptation of Him in the wilderness to seek popular acclaim rather than pursue the pathway of service and suffering to which His Father had appointed Him. He rejoined to Peter here therefore, as He had rejoined to the devil there (Mt. 4: 10), **'Get behind me, Satan'** (33).

Jesus' teaching on the cost of discipleship (8: 34–9: 1). (Parallels: Mt. 16: 24–28; Lk. 9: 23–27.) Jesus, having indicated what Messiahship would mean for Him, proceeded to explain now what discipleship would mean for the apostles and His other hearers. The person who enlisted in His cause, He taught, would need to **deny himself** (34), i.e. abandon the attitude of self-centredness, **and take up his cross**, i.e. be prepared to face martyrdom, with the indignity of being made to carry the transverse beam of his cross to the place of execution, which was the practice under the Romans (Jn 19: 17). He would have thus to be willing to lose his mortal life; and all this, for Christ's sake **and for the gospel** (35), i.e. for the sake of spreading abroad the good news of the kingdom of God; for only in this way would he attain the true life, that of the age to come. He, by contrast, who aimed to **save his** (mortal) **life**, especially such as sought to enrich themselves, and **gain the whole world** (36), would be spiritually destitute in the eternal order, Christ Himself manifesting towards them then His utmost displeasure (38). The coming of the kingdom of God **with power** (9: 1), moreover, would not be long delayed, for certain of those then listening to Him would still be alive when this occurred. That God's kingdom was a present reality in the ministry of Jesus, and yet would have a future consummation, is indicated in the notes on 1: 15. Various suggestions have been made as to what might be denoted here by **the kingdom of God come with power**, *e.g.* Jesus' transfiguration, His crucifixion and resurrection, the descent on the apostles of the Holy Spirit, 'a visible manifestation of the Rule of God displayed in the life of an elect community' (Vincent Taylor, *ad loc.*), the spread of Christianity throughout the Roman empire, etc. Since the natural implication of the words **some who are standing here**, etc. is that although most of those there standing would then be dead, a minority nevertheless would still be living (suggesting the elapsing of some thirty or forty years), the identification of the event with the destruction of Jerusalem by the Romans in A.D. 70 and its glorious sequel for the Christian Church has been proposed by some; and this suggestion is developed further in the notes on 13: 24–27.

The transfiguration of Jesus (9: 2–10). (Parallels: Mt. 17: 1–9; Lk. 9: 28–36.) According to ancient tradition the **high mountain** (2) on which Jesus was transfigured was Mount Tabor, ten miles south-west of the sea of Galilee. The objections to this identification are (*a*) that it is less than two thousand feet high; (*b*) that at this time a fortress stood on its summit; and (*c*) that since, in 8: 27, Jesus was near Caesarea Philippi, and in 9: 33 He was at Capernaum, a site north of Capernaum would have been more natural. Perhaps, therefore, the transfiguration occurred on a spur of Mount Hermon (9,000 ft.), though this was in Gentile territory, and it would therefore be somewhat remarkable to have found **teachers of the law** at its foot (14); or perhaps it occurred on Jebel Jermaq (3,962 ft.), north of Merom, in the north of Palestine. To display to Peter, James and John yet further truth concerning Himself,

Jesus re-assumed before them His pre-incarnate glory (Jn 17: 5). The appearance with Him of Moses and Elijah was doubtless so that the disciples might see the giver of the law and a representative of the prophets both testifying to Jesus as being the one to whom they had pointed forwards (4). Peter, however, misunderstood the sight, his proposal of making **shelters** of inter-twined branches of trees for Jesus, Moses and Elijah (5), implying that he viewed them as all three being on an equality. God's answer to this suggestion was to remove Moses and Elijah (8), and to proclaim concerning Jesus: **'This is my Son, whom I love; listen to him'** (7). The first part of this announcement had been made by the Father previously, at the time of Jesus' baptism, though as recorded in 1: 11 (on which see notes), it was addressed solely to Jesus Himself. The second part of the announcement identified Jesus with the prophet whose coming was foretold in Dt. 18: 15–19. The reason why Jesus forbade Peter, James and John to disclose what they had seen to others till after His resurrection (9), was, presumably, that only as from then would they really have grasped its proper significance, and so be in a position rightly to propound it.

The discussion concerning Elijah (9: 11–13). (Parallel: Mt. 17: 10–13.)

The beholding by Peter, James and John of Elijah, as it were, in vision, prompted them to enquire of Jesus as to how it was that His own coming had not been preceded, as the scribes had deduced and taught from Mal. 4: 5, by a coming of Elijah in person (11). Jesus replied, alluding to John the Baptist, who had exercised his ministry 'in the spirit and power of Elijah' (Lk. 1: 17), that already Elijah had come amongst them (13), adding that though indeed his coming was, in a certain sense, to restore **all things** (12), there were, nevertheless, definite limitations as to how such restoration was to be conceived; for the Scripture did not thereupon predict that so spiritually minded would the people then be that his successor the Messiah would be received by them with acclamation, but rather that he **must suffer much and be rejected**.

The healing of the demon-possessed boy (9: 14–29). (Parallels: Mt. 17: 14–20; Lk. 9: 37–43.)

A distracted father, endeavouring to make contact with Jesus so as to obtain from Him healing for his demon-possessed son, had found nine of the disciples, but not Jesus Himself. He requested these, therefore to exorcize the demon. This they attempted to do, but without effect. Their failure gave rise to an argument between certain scribes in a crowd which had now assembled, and the disciples (14). Suddenly Jesus appeared on the scene, having descended from the mount of His glorious transfiguration to this scene of tragedy, frustration and helplessness. The amazement of the crowd on seeing Jesus (15) may have been due to His 'unexpected and opportune arrival' (so Cranfield), or possibly, as others have suggested, to some of the glory of His transfiguration still lingering on His face (cf. Exod. 34: 29, 30). On the boy's father having outlined to Jesus his predicament (17, 18), Jesus exclaimed: **'O unbelieving generation'** (19). It was probably the nine disciples, rather than the crowd or the scribes or the boy's father, to whom He was here referring, for the reason Jesus gave as to why the disciples could not exorcize the demon as stated in Mt. 17: 20 was: 'Because of your little faith'. The corresponding explanation as stated here in Mk 9 is: **'This kind can come out only by prayer'** (29). It is decidedly likely that this does not relate so much to the actual procedure of making requests from God, as to the attitude of moment-by-moment dependence on God which is the source and basis of prayer. Mk 6: 7 describes how Jesus gave His disciples 'authority over the evil spirits', and 6: 13 relates how they exercised this. Their being castigated now as 'unbelieving', was not, as the word might have suggested, on account of any lack of expectation of success on their part, for their failure quite astonished them (28), but because their adequacy to cope with the situation now confronting them, was something which, in the light of their previous experiences, they were taking for granted. In contrast to the disciples who were 'unbelieving', the boy's father possessed faith, though a faith which he knew to be imperfect (24). Jesus informed him that a person who had faith should not say to Him: **'If you can'** (22), but should set no limit to His divine ability (23). This ability was displayed thereupon in the healing of the boy (25–27).

The second prediction of the Passion (9: 30–32). (Parallels: Mt. 17: 22, 23; Lk. 9: 43b–45.)

The desire of Jesus that this journey of His through Galilee should be kept private (30) was due to His desire to forewarn His disciples regarding His forthcoming rejection without being interrupted (31). The piece of information additional to that mentioned in 8: 31 which Jesus disclosed here was that He would be **betrayed into the hands of men**, conveying a hint of His being betrayed. The failure of the disciples to understand from Jesus' words here that He would shortly be put to death (32) was due to the infatuation of their minds with the popular notions as to the course which the Messiah was destined to follow. It was to avoid these conceptions of theirs being disturbed that they **were afraid to ask him** further concerning the matter.

The discussion concerning greatness (9: 33–37). (Parallels: Mt. 18: 1–5; Lk. 9: 46–48.)
Jesus evidently had been walking in front of His disciples as they proceeded towards Capernaum (as in 10: 32); but He knew what they had been discussing among themselves on the journey (Lk. 9: 47), namely **who was the greatest** among them (34), and on their arrival at Capernaum, He asked them to confess it (33). On their refusal to do this, He told them that the essence of greatness lay in performing acts of service for other people (35; also 10: 43, 44), even though the people concerned were as insignificant as the child He proceeded then to take up in His arms before them (36). His plea, thereupon, that they should receive such a child as that in His Name (37), meant that they were to act towards such children in kindly ways, because in a certain sense they represented Him. For their encouragement to that end He added that this service in their regard would be divinely evaluated as though done to Jesus Himself, even as service done to Jesus would be divinely evaluated as though done to God the Father.

The independent exorcist (9: 38–40). (Parallel: Lk. 9: 49–50.)
It was not only Jesus and His followers who succeeded in casting out demons, as is shown by Mt. 12: 27. Ac. 19: 13 ff. confirms this, telling of certain non-Christian Jews who did so, though in the Name of Jesus. A Jewish exorcist who was engaged in casting out demons in Jesus' Name, though not himself a follower of Jesus, was seen by the apostle John, who, offended at the apparent inconsistency of such conduct, endeavoured to prevent him from continuing this practice of his (38). Jesus, however, criticized John's action in this matter, pointing out that the man in question was **not against** them (40), and that it was highly unlikely that he would follow up working a miracle in His name by publicly reviling Him (39).

Jesus' final teaching in Galilee (9: 41–50).
Jesus taught that even a very small act of service done to another would be divinely rewarded (41), whereas inducing young believers in Him to sin was an outrage that incurred such a punishment, that it would be highly advantageous were a person who was contemplating such a course to be drowned in the sea prior to implementing his intention, so that the punishment attendant on that atrocity might be averted (42). Not only, however, was it wrong to cause sin in other people; it was wrong also to cause sin in oneself; and if temptation assailed one through such organs as one's hand, one's foot, or one's eye, precious as these organs were, it would be better, nevertheless, to remove them altogether, than, through retaining them, **to go into hell** (43–47). The Greek

word translated here 'hell' is 'Gehenna'. 'Gehenna' is a transliteration into Greek of the Hebrew phrase 'valley of Hinnom', which lay to the west and south of Jerusalem. Here, at one time, children were consumed by fire in sacrifice to the heathen god Molech (Jer. 7: 31; 32: 35). After this practice had been stamped out by King Josiah (2 Kg. 23: 10), the valley became Jerusalem's refuse dump. Fires were always kept smouldering there so as to burn up the garbage, and maggots bred there in abundance, feeding themselves on the offal lying around. Because of the place's vile associations, the Jews, in due course, came to denote the place of future torment for the wicked by the name 'Gehenna', picturing that place in consequence as a domain **where their worm does not die, and the fire is not quenched** (48, echoing Isa. 66: 24). Developing further the thought of 'fire', Jesus then said: **Every one will be salted with fire** (49), meaning that every disciple of His, in order to be spiritually purified and made like salt, would need to undergo a fiery ordeal of suffering. Developing thereupon the thought of 'salt', Jesus said that the disciples were like salt, for they exercised the valuable functions of seasoning and purifying the world, and this was **good** (50). He cautioned them, however, against losing that which they had received from Him which was what had conferred on them their goodness. If, consequently, instead of arguing with each other as to which of them was the greatest (34), they were to **be at peace with each other**, what they would need for this purpose would be to have in themselves 'salt', i.e. love for their neighbours, and a readiness to serve them, and make sacrifices for their sakes.

Jesus' teaching on divorce (10: 1–12). (Parallel: Mt. 19: 1–12.)
Jesus, having now reached Perea, in the south of the country, and to the east of the river Jordan, resumed His ministry to the general public (1; and see notes on 7: 24). The question He was there asked by the Pharisees, **'Is it lawful for a man to divorce his wife?'** was put to Him in order to test him (2), i.e. to try to induce Him to incriminate Himself by contradicting the Mosaic Law. Jesus elicited from His questioners that Dt. 24: 1–4 allowed a man to divorce his wife, provided that the man safe-guarded his wife's interests by writing out and giving to her **a certificate of divorce** (4), which would enable the woman to establish, as and when necessary, that her divorce had been formal and official, and that she was perfectly free, in consequence, to marry someone else. Jesus' comment on this Deuteronomic injunction, however, was that it did not represent God's absolute will, but something rather which, on account of the perversity of the human heart, He permitted,

in order that the consequences of that perversity might be kept in restraint (5). He indicated, thereupon, that God's original intentions with regard to marriage were stated in Gen. 1: 27 (6), and in Gen. 2: 24 (7, 8a), statements which depict the marriage bond as indissoluble. A married couple, Jesus therefore deduced, were **one** (8b). The margin states that the Greek here means 'one flesh', involving that the relationship between the pair was just as unbreakable as was a blood-relationship, such as that between a father and a son. His conclusion, consequently, was that **man** (i.e. the male member of the partnership, rather than some legal body), has no right to sever his matrimonial union (9). It is a fair assumption that divorce on the ground of adultery, being so obviously permissible, was not within the scope of what Jesus and the Pharisees were here discussing. Those committing adultery, indeed, were required to be put to death (Lev. 20: 10; Jn 8: 5), which would sunder the nuptial bond without the need of having recourse to divorce proceedings. Speaking privately to His disciples only (10), Jesus developed the teaching He had given to the Pharisees. Already He had shown that for a man to divorce his wife was a sin; but what He affirmed now was that if, additionally, that man married another woman, he made himself an adulterer (11). The adulterous union described in verse 12 was that which Herodias perpetrated, who, availing herself of the provisions of Roman law, had severed her union with Philip, and had married subsequently Herod Antipas (see notes on 6: 17).

Jesus' blessing of the children (10: 13–16). (Parallels: Mt. 19: 13–15; Lk. 18: 15–17.) The disciples felt it to be an unwarrantable intrusion on their Master's time to have children brought to Him **to have him touch them** (13). Their rebuking those who conducted them to Jesus for this purpose earned a rebuke from Jesus for themselves; for He not only received the children, but went beyond that which was asked of Him, taking the children in His arms and blessing them (16). In saying: **'for the kingdom of God belongs to such as these'** (14), Jesus' meaning, probably, was that the kingdom or God belonged to people who, though not literally children, were embued with such characteristics of children as trust and receptiveness. This truth is developed in verse 15. Children allow people to give them things apart from any thought of merit or desert on their part; and it is only by adopting such a childlike attitude that people can appropriate the blessedness of the kingdom of God.

The rich young ruler (10: 17–31). (Parallels: Mt. 19: 16–30; Lk. 18: 18–30.) As a complementary emphasis to the truth of verse 15, where salvation is depicted as a free gift, the story narrated here indicates the immense costliness of salvation for certain people. A wealthy man (22b), despite his having observed the Mosaic law as best he knew (20), was spiritually dissatisfied notwithstanding, and so asked Jesus what he needed to do **to inherit eternal life** (17). His approach to Jesus, however, was unbecomingly obsequious, for, in contravention of normal Jewish custom, he addressed Him as **'Good teacher'**. Jesus rebuked him for this, reminding him that **'good'** was a designation which was normally reserved for God, only God being good without qualification (18). Jesus was not hereby disclaiming being either 'God' or 'good', but was merely criticizing His being addressed thus by someone who clearly was completely unaware of His divine nature. In reply to the man's enquiry Jesus tried to deepen in the man a consciousness of sin by quoting to him the commands of the so-called 'Second Table of the Decalogue' (19) (the injunction 'Do not covet' being interpreted here as **'Do not defraud'**). The implication to be derived from the man's retort that he had obeyed these laws from his youth (20), is that he had no understanding as to all that these requirements involved. There were qualities about this man, however, which caused Jesus greatly to love him (21a). But the way in which He expressed towards him that love was not by lowering His demands with regard to him in order the more easily to win him into the company of His followers, but by laying His finger with utter frankness on what it was that was impeding his quest for eternal life, namely his wealth. Telling him, therefore, that he lacked but a single thing (which, presumably, was an unreserved dedication to God's cause and kingdom), He bade him sell his possessions, giving the proceeds to the poor, and become then one of His disciples (21). But he could not bring himself to do this, and in contrast to the eagerness with which he **ran up** to Jesus (17), he went away sorrowful (22) (cf. Mt. 13: 45, 46). Commenting on the man's decision, Jesus told His disciples that by nature it was impossible for a rich man to receive salvation, as impossible indeed as for a camel, the largest animal in Palestine at that time, **to go through the eye of a needle** (25) (quoting here a current proverb which was memorable on account of its very grotesqueness). He hastened, however, to allay the disciples' amazement at this assertion of His by reminding them that **all things are possible with God** (27). To the rejoinder of Peter that what that rich man had failed to do had been performed by his companions and himself (28), Jesus answered that such would receive a **hundred times as much in this present age**, though **persecutions** would constantly befall them, **and in the age to come, eternal life** (30). But He warned them against being self-satisfied at what they had done, informing them that many disciples of His, prominent now because of their manifest piety, would find themselves in the life to come rated much less highly than certain far less conspicuous of His devotees, who nevertheless were of greater worth in the sight of God (31).

The third prediction of the Passion (10: 32–34). (Parallels: Mt. 20: 17–19; Lk. 18: 31–34.) The reason why the disciples were **astonished** as they walked behind Jesus on the road to Jerusalem (32), was probably because of the look of determination on their Master's face as He proceeded onwards (Lk. 9: 51). This third prediction of His approaching Passion which He thereupon made to them was fuller than the earlier ones, and included the additional facts that the Jewish leaders would cause His death to be at the hand of **the Gentiles** (33), who, prior to executing Him, would **mock him, and spit upon him**, and **flog him** (34).

The request of James and John (10: 35–45). (Parallel: Mt. 20: 20–28.) That the disciples no more comprehended their Master's third prediction of His Passion than they did His earlier ones (8: 32; 9: 32), is proved, not only by the explicit statement of Lk. 18: 44, but also by this request to Him from James and John to be allowed to sit on His either side in His **glory** (37), meaning in the Messianic kingdom (Mt. 20: 21) He was about to set up, as they envisaged this. Jesus refused their request, explaining that the matter in question did not come within the scope of His personal jurisdiction (40). He indicated by implication, nevertheless, that the issue would be dependent, at least in part, on the willingness of His followers to suffer for His sake. Such suffering He described metaphorically as drinking from His cup and being baptized with His baptism, figures of speech which, although suggestive of suffering to the point of death, and involving this in the instance of Jesus Himself, did not involve this necessarily in the case of other people (cf. Isa. 51: 17; 43: 2). Jesus asked James and John, therefore, whether they were prepared to undergo this ordeal (38), and on their replying to Him in the affirmative, He told them that such in fact would be their experience (39), a prediction which was fulfilled in James being killed 'with the sword' (Ac. 12: 2), and in John being exiled to the island of Patmos (Rev. 1: 9). The sufferings of these, however, were comparable with those of Jesus only in a limited respect, for they were not, of course, atoning sufferings.

The disreputable request of James and John was succeeded by the equally disreputable reaction to it of their fellow-apostles (41). Addressing them all twelve, therefore, Jesus explained to them (as in 9: 35–37, on which see notes) wherein spiritual greatness really consisted. He showed them that whereas in the kingdoms of men the test of greatness lay in the number of people one could control (42), in His kingdom it lay in the number of people one could help (43, 44). He emphasized that the highest honour to which a man could aspire consisted not in occupying a kingdom's chief seats, but in serving other people. As an example of this attitude, He cited Himself, who came **to serve** (45). It is quite likely that He made the claim here, by inference, of fulfilling the rôle of God's 'Servant' foretold in Isa. 52: 13–53: 12, of whom the prophet declared: '*He poured out his life to death*', and '*He bore the sin of many*' (Isa. 53: 12); for He depicted His supreme act of service on behalf of men as His giving **his life as a ransom for many**. The word 'ransom' implies deliverance from bondage by the payment of a price. The word 'for' (Gk. *anti*) normally bears a substitionary sense (as in Mt. 2: 22). With regard to the word 'many', see notes on 1: 34.

The healing of Bartimaeus (10: 46–52). (Parallels: Mt. 20: 30–34; Lk. 18: 35–43.) The **Jericho** of New Testament times which Jesus now entered (46) had been built by Herod the Great and his son Archelaus (Mt. 2: 22), and stood somewhat to the south of the OT city of that name, and to the west of the present one. Bartimaeus, the blind beggar who lived there, was among the first of those, outside the ranks of the apostles, who are recorded as having proclaimed Jesus to be the Messiah (though cf. Jn 4: 29, 42); for **'Son of David'** (47), the title by which he addressed Jesus, was one which was specifically Messianic, as is shown by its occurrence in the seventeenth of the pre-Christian 'Psalms of Solomon' (cf. also Mk 12: 35). The reason for Bartimaeus's conviction that Jesus could cure his blindness may have been his knowledge that Isa. 61: 1 (LXX) (cf. Mt. 11: 5) foretold that the Messiah would enable the blind to see (see notes on 1: 40). On his appealing for Jesus' help, he was rebuked by those around for making a nuisance of himself (48; cf. 10: 13). Jesus' cure of him (52) is the last healing miracle recorded in Mark's Gospel (cf. Lk. 22: 51). It is to be observed that Jesus did not command him to refrain from proclaiming His Messiahship, as He had done to the demons (cf. 1: 34, on which see notes).

V. THE JERUSALEM MINISTRY (11: 1–13: 37).

The entry into Jerusalem (11: 1–11). (Parallels: Mt. 21: 1–11; Lk. 19: 28–44; Jn 13: 12–19.) Jesus, approaching Jerusalem from Jericho, reached **Bethany** (known now as El Azariyeh), on the east side of the **Mount of Olives** (1). Deeming that the time was now ripe for Him publicly to confess His Messiahship (cf. 10: 47, on which see notes), He decided to do so by an act which constituted a claim that the prophecy of Zech. 9: 9 related to Himself. Instead, therefore, of entering Jerusalem on foot, as was customary in the case of pilgrims, He resolved to enter it mounted on a **colt** (2), and one, furthermore, which had never previously been ridden, in accordance with the prophet's description of such a creature as 'a new colt' (LXX). Mt. 21: 2 and Jn 12: 14 indicate that the colt in question was that of a donkey, and Jesus' use of this was a witness that, despite popular opinion, it was not as a warrior that He would fulfil His Messianic office (in which event a more appropriate beast on which to ride would have been a horse), but in great meekness and lowliness. Jesus told two of His disciples, accordingly, to fetch such a colt from the village opposite them, which perhaps was **Bethphage**. Whilst it is possible that Jesus' knowledge of the location of the colt, and of how people would respond to its being untethered (3), was due to an arrangement He had previously made with its owner, it is more likely that Jesus was exercising here His supernatural knowledge (cf. 1 Sam. 10: 2–7). On the colt being brought to Jesus, an improvised saddle was laid on it (7), on which Jesus sat. As a token of homage to Jesus, **cloaks** (cf. 2 Kg. 9: 13) and leafy **branches** were spread on the road before Him (8). The word **'Hosanna'** (9), which the crowds cried out, is derived from the Hebrew exclamation 'Save now', as recorded in Ps. 118: 25. It may have been an appeal to God to save the Israelite people now that the Messiah had appeared among them. **'Hosanna in the highest'** (10b) may mean: 'Save now (O Thou that dwellest) in the highest' (Cranfield). **'Blessed is he who comes in the name of the Lord'** (9b) (quoted from Ps. 118: 26) are probably best understood Messianically, for 'He who comes' was a standard title by which the Messiah was denoted (see Mt. 11: 3). The crowds, rightly, identified the coming of the promised **kingdom** with the coming of the promised King (10). It is probable that the lodging-place at **Bethany** to which Jesus retired for the night (11) was the home of Martha, Mary and Lazarus (Jn 12: 1, 2).

The cleansing of the temple (11: 15–19). (Parallels: Mt. 21: 12–17; Lk. 19: 45–46; and cf. Jn 2: 13–22.)
One of the actions predicted of the Messiah in the OT was His cleansing of the temple worship (Mal. 3: 1–3), and to this He now attended. In the temple's outer court (the 'court of the Gentiles'), He found that the Jewish authorities had erected trading-booths, where wine, oil, salt, and various animals were being sold, all of which were needed for the sacrifical ritual. **doves** (15) were used for such ceremonies as that described in Lk. 2: 22–24. It

is implied that the merchants were guilty of profiteering in conducting these transactions (17b). The **moneychangers** changed the Greek and Roman coinage of the Jewish pilgrims from the Dispersion into Tyrian currency, to enable them to pay the temple tax of half a shekel a year which was required from every male Jew (Exod. 30: 11 ff.; Mt. 17: 24), and which had to be paid in Tyrian currency. A further abuse to which the temple's outer court was put was that of people laden with baggage, instead of walking around the outside of these holy precincts, making a short cut by walking through them (16). All these activities Jesus stopped, quoting against those who engaged in them Isa. 56: 7 and Jer. 7: 11 (17). Mark alone, of the evangelists, relates Jesus to have continued the quotation from Isaiah so as to bring out the prophet's point that in the Messianic age the Gentiles equally with the Jews would be permitted to use the Jerusalem temple. The desire of Jesus, evidently, was to remove that which hindered the Gentiles being able quietly and reverently to worship God in what was intended as **a house of prayer for all the nations**.

The cursing of the fig-tree (11: 12–14, 20–25). (Parallel: Mt. 21: 18–22.)
The leaves of the fig-tree in Palestine appear in March, and are accompanied by a crop of small edible knobs called *taksh* which drop off before the true figs form, which ripen in June. An absence of *taksh* indicates that the tree in question will bear no figs. It was therefore, entirely reasonable for Jesus, shortly before Passovertime in mid-April, to go up to a fig-tree **to find out if it had any fruit** (13), and then to condemn the tree on discovering on it **nothing but leaves**. This action of His was a piece of prophetic symbolism of a type with which the Jews had been made familiar through such acts as those recorded in 2 Chr. 18: 10, and also Jer. 27: 2, together with 28: 10 ff. Jesus was proclaiming hereby that just as that fig-tree bore leaves but not fruit, the Jews, by means of their numerous ritual observances, made a fine show of religion, but had failed to produce those spiritual qualities which God most wanted from them, and for which indeed He had brought them into being. He was compelled, therefore, to pronounce over them, as over the fig-tree, a sentence of doom (13: 2). On the fig-tree having, by the following morning, withered away (20), instead of Jesus impressing on His disciples, from this, the certainty of the doom which was to befall their nation, He used the incident as a practical demonstration of the power of faith (22), which could effect, so He informed them, not merely the withering of a tree, but the removal of a mountain (23), by which hyperbole He meant that by the exercise of faith in God, people can

do what humanly appears utterly impossible. It follows from this, accordingly, that when engaged in the activity of prayer, given an attitude of faith in God (24), and forgiveness towards one's fellow men (25), the petitions which are made (assuming that these are not contrary to the will of God) will assuredly be granted.

The question concerning Jesus' authority (11: 27–33). (Parallels: Mt. 21: 23–27; Lk. 20: 1–8.)

It is to be presumed that **the chief priests, the teachers of the law and the elders** (27) who now approached Jesus were a delegation from the Jewish Sanhedrin, to whom the temple police were ultimately responsible. They enquired from Him, accordingly, who had authorized Him to perform such deeds as His cleansing of the temple (28), desirous, no doubt, of forcing Him to admit that He had, in fact, no authority for so acting. In reply, Jesus recalled to their minds the case of John the Baptist, and He asked them whether John had ministered by divine appointment, or whether, by contrast, he had been commissioned for this by the Jewish authorities (30). This question they refused to face honestly on account of the perplexing consequences in which they saw they would, through facing it, become involved. To have admitted that John had been divinely authorized for his ministry would have been to have invited from Jesus the rejoinder as to what they made of the fact that He Himself had been identified by John as the One, greater than he, who was to succeed him (31), whereas to have alleged John to have acted purely from some private whim would have incurred for them the wrath of the people generally, who had always believed John to have been a prophet (32), and the more so latterly, now that he had been martyred. Impaled thus on the horns of a dilemma, they declined, through cowardice, to answer Jesus' question, whereupon Jesus declined to answer theirs (33), though He did so indirectly in the parable which He thereupon addressed to them.

The parable of the wicked husbandmen (12: 1–12). (Parallels: Mt. 21: 33–45; Lk. 20: 9–19.)

There were many estates at this time in Galilee which were owned by foreign landlords, and farmed by Galilean peasants, who, not unnaturally, felt highly disgruntled by the status they occupied. This situation may form the background to this parable which Jesus told, and which was designed not only to indicate that His authority, about which He was being questioned (11: 28), was even higher than that of the prophets (in that a prophet was a **servant** of God, whereas He Himself was God's **Son**), but additionally to warn those to whom He was speaking, and who were plotting His death, both of the heinousness of their proposed crime, and of the dreadfulness of its inevitable sequel. The parable's opening words **'A man planted a vineyard'** (1) must immediately have recalled to the hearers' memories the parable recorded in Isa. 5: 1–7 (with its provided interpretation), and indicated to them that it referred to the relationship of Almighty God to the nation of Israel. In accordance with contemporary custom, the landlord is described as having **rented the vineyard to some farmers** (representing here the Jewish leaders), in return for an agreed proportion of the vineyard's produce. The servants, however, whom the landlord sent to claim this rent which was owing to him, were abused and wounded (2–4), and some were even killed (5). On sending them finally his son, he too was killed (6–8). The consequence of this, as was hardly surprising, was the coming of the landlord, with government authorization no doubt, to **kill those tenants and give the vineyard to others** (9), a clear prediction of the destruction of Jerusalem in A.D. 70. Jesus reminded His audience, at that point, of the statement contained in Ps. 118: 22–23, deducing from it that although within but a few days the Jewish leaders would reject Him decisively and finally, He would subsequently be exalted, nevertheless, to the most honoured place of all.

The question about the poll-tax (12: 13–17). (Parallels: Mt. 22: 15–22; Lk. 20: 20–26.)

Despite Jesus' warning to the Jewish religious leaders as given in the foregoing parable, they continued their campaign against Him. Some of the **Herodians** (13; see notes on 3: 6), who had come down from Galilee to celebrate the Passover, joined with **some of the Pharisees** in asking Jesus a question out of **hypocrisy** (15), i.e. not to discover the truth, but **to catch him in his words**. The question was as to whether it was in accordance with the law of God to pay to Caesar the poll-tax (14), which had been demanded as from A.D. 6 from all provincial Jews. This particular tax was exceptionally unpopular, being the token of the Jews' subject status. The questioners felt that for Jesus to insist on its payment would alienate the people from Him, whereas for Him to deny the legitimacy of the tax would be something for which He could conveniently be reported to the Romans as a rebel against their authority. Jesus' reply was to the effect that since the money they possessed, having embossed on it the image of the Emperor Tiberius, was, according to the contemporary viewpoint, Caesar's property, it was implied hereby that they acknowledged their subservience to him, so that they should pay to him the poll-tax. What Jesus thereupon added, however, implied that should, at any time, Caesar demand something which properly belonged to God, Caesar's demand then would need to be refused (17).

The question about the resurrection (12: 18–27). (Parallels: Mt. 22: 23–33; Lk. 20: 27–40.)

Whereas the former question had been aimed to place Jesus in a political diificulty, this next one was aimed to place Him in a theological difficulty. It was addressed to Him by members of the priestly and aristocratic Sadducean party, who endeavoured now to make the doctrine of the resurrection, in which they disbelieved, look ridiculous. Their contention, ultimately, was that it was incompatible with the law of levirate marriage, as laid down in Dt. 25: 5–10, which they quoted loosely to Jesus (19). Jesus in effect denied that this was so, provided that the resurrection-life was correctly conceived; and He hinted that the reason why the Sadducees found difficulty with the doctrine of the resurrection was because of their prior rejection of the existence of angels (Ac. 23: 6–8); for just as angels, being immortal, did not need to marry, nor did human beings in their resurrection state (25). Turning His attention, thereupon, from the issue as to the manner of the resurrection to that of its fact, Jesus demonstrated that belief in the resurrection was logically implied right back in the Pentateuch. He pointed out that in Exod. 3: 6, God described Himself as being, during the life-time of Moses, the God of men who, according to the flesh, were no longer alive (26), the inference being that God was still caring for them then, and that at the last, necessarily, He would raise up their bodies, so that they might become sharers together in the final blessedness. The fault, therefore, with the Sadducees was that they did not **know the Scriptures** which taught the resurrection, **or the power of God** which could effect the resurrection (24).

The question about the greatest commandment (12: 28–34). (Parallel: Mt. 22: 34–40.)

In the question submitted to Jesus now, as contrasted with those submitted earlier, there seems to have been no spirit of hostility, which, seeing that its propounder was **one of the teachers of the law** (28), was unusual (cf. verses 38–40). On being asked as to which was the most important of all the commandments, Jesus replied by quoting the *Shema* (Dt. 6: 4, 5), which pious Jews recited daily, but He added, as did the lawyer in Lk. 10: 27, to what was stated in the Old Testament that God was to be loved with the **mind** as well as with the other human faculties (28, 29). Although Jesus had not been asked also as to which was the next most important of the commandments, so inseparable, in His eyes, were the first and the second (cf. 1 Jn 4: 21), that He expressed Himself further about that too, quoting, to this end, Lev. 19: 18 (31). It should be appreciated that there is a great deal more involved in 'loving God' and 'loving one's neighbour' than might superficially be imagined, the implications of the latter of these duties having been expanded by Jesus earlier, in His parable of the Good Samaritan (Lk. 10: 30–37). The scribe concurred with Jesus' answer (32), and, without in any way belittling the importance of offering sacrifices, commented that to love God was a higher duty still (33; cf. 1 Sam. 15: 22; Ps. 69: 30–31; Hos. 6: 6). While, however, the scribe had been appraising Jesus, Jesus had been appraising the scribe; and His final rejoinder to him was that he came quite near to possessing the necessary characteristics qualifying a man to enter **the kingdom of God** (34). Whether, by personal committal to Jesus, he was ever actually born into that kingdom is not stated.

Jesus' question about David's Son (12: 35–37). (Parallels: Mt. 22: 41–46; Lk. 20: 41–44.)

The initiative in the discussion was now claimed by Jesus, who asked those around Him a question, the purport of which was to show that the Messianic title **'Son of David'** (35; and see notes on 10: 47), used so commonly by **the teachers of the law**, accurate though it was, did not however convey the total truth regarding the Messiah's person. Proof of this fact, as Jesus pointed out, was that when David himself wrote concerning the Messiah in Ps. 110: 1, he characterized the Messiah, not, as might have been anticipated, as 'my son', but rather as **'my Lord'** (36), with the implication that the Messiah possessed not only a human nature (as David's son), but a divine one too. Jesus raised this point, clearly, with the hope that His hearers might be induced to relate it to Himself.

Jesus' condemnation of the scribes (12: 38–40). (Parallels: Mt. 23: 1–39; Lk. 20: 45–47.)

Having criticized what the scribes said (35), Jesus criticized now what the scribes did. As to their liking **to go about in flowing robes** (38a), these were the garments which characteristically were worn by men of learning. In a variety of situations they expected the utmost deference to be paid to them (38b, 39). From needy widows they extorted unreasonable sums of money; and they endeavoured to win the esteem of men by engaging themselves in prolonged acts of prayer (40a). The reason why Jesus said they would be **punished most severely** than others (40b) was because the evil practices they committed were craftily carried out under the guise of religion.

The widow's gift (12: 41–44). (Parallel: Lk. 21: 1–4.)

Having spoken of the avarice of the scribes (40), Jesus spoke now about a woman whom He noticed who surrendered for the work of God **everything** she had (44). Next within the temple's 'court of the Gentiles' (see notes on

11: 15), was the 'court of the women', around the walls of which, according to the *Mishnah*, were placed thirteen trumpet-shaped offering-receptacles. In contrast with certain **rich people** whom Jesus saw deposit into them **large amounts** (41), this widow, as unobtrusively as possible, no doubt, dropped into one of them **two very small copper coins**, the smallest coins in circulation (42). The reason why Jesus proclaimed this to have been a greater gift than the offerings of the rich (43), was that it was a sacrificial gift, and left her with nothing for herself, whereas the rich retained plenty for themselves.

The eschatological discourse (13: 1–37).
(Parallels: Mt. 24: 1–50; Lk. 21: 5–36.)
'Mark 13 is the biggest problem in the Gospel' wrote A. M. Hunter; and he was right. The exposition of it presented hereunder, therefore, is submitted quite tentatively, and with due deference to the different way in which the discourse is treated in the notes on the parallel passages in the Gospels by Matthew and Luke.
(*a*) *The circumstances of the discourse* (1–4).
Having concluded a day of teaching in the temple (His entry into which is noted in 11: 27), Jesus emerged from it and, while so doing, had His attention directed **by one of his disciples** to the magnificence of its **stones** and **buildings** (1). Jesus' response was to predict the temple's complete destruction and devastation (2). Jesus spent the nights, at this time, on the Mount of Olives (Lk. 21: 37). When, therefore, He and His disciples had crossed the Kedron valley and had ascended this hill (from the slopes of which they would have obtained a magnificent view of the city and its temple), the four senior disciples asked Jesus when the temple's destruction would occur, and what sign would indicate the imminence of this (3, 4). It is to be observed that the record here in Mark, as well as that in Luke (Lk. 21: 7), makes no mention of the disciples asking Jesus concerning any other matter than that. Necessarily, therefore, this was the dominant topic of which, in His reply to their enquiry, Jesus treated. Reference, however, to the record in Matthew's Gospel (Mt. 24: 3), shows that the disciples asked Jesus additionally: 'What will be the sign of your coming, and of the close of the age?' It is highly probable that the reason why they submitted to Jesus this supplementary question was because of the misapprehension under which they laboured to the effect that the return of Jesus and the close of the age were destined to coincide as regards time with the temple's destruction. Seeing, therefore, that some information about Jesus' second advent came, incidentally, within the scope of the disciples' enquiry, Jesus did, in His reply, say something about it, but only secondarily, and at the close of His answer to their basic ques-

tion, as will be demonstrated in the notes which follow.
(*b*) *The discourse itself* (5–37).
It is here submitted that the key to the understanding of this discourse lies in Jesus' affirmation of verse 30: '**I tell you the truth, this generation will certainly not pass away until all these things have happened**', which He thereupon endorsed by means of the intensely solemn assertion of verse 31, stating (with the use of a Hebraic idiom), that even though heaven and earth should pass away, His words (and this utterance, presumably, in particular), would never do so. Everything, therefore, which Jesus predicted up to that point in His discourse, He declared would be fulfilled within the ensuing forty years (understanding the word 'generation' in its normal and natural sense); and fulfilled it was. The teaching in this discourse on Jesus' second advent is confined to the statements of verses 32–37, and the change of topic is indicated by the word '**these**' in verses 29 and 30 being replaced in verse 32 by the adversative demonstrative adjective '**that**'. In verses 5–14, Jesus foretold the occurrence of various happenings which, despite how some might deign to interpret them, were not to be regarded as the immediate precursors of the destruction of the temple. All of them in fact took place during the succeeding forty years. The nature of the sign indicating the imminence of the temple's destruction (and which was that, consequently, concerning which the disciples had enquired in verse 4), Jesus described in verse 14a as '**the abomination that causes desolation**' standing **where it does not belong**, which, in the corresponding statement in Luke's Gospel (Lk. 21: 20), is characterized as 'Jerusalem surrounded by armies'. When, therefore, the Christians in Jerusalem saw the Roman legions investing their city, any notion that God might intervene miraculously to preserve it, as He did in the days of Hezekiah, was to be ejected from their minds, since precisely this was the divine sign of the proximity of the time when both city and temple would be razed to the ground. The Christians' resort, rather, on witnessing the commencement of this investment taking place, was, without delay, to **flee to the mountains** (14b); and this, in the event, the Christians at Jerusalem, because of Jesus' words here, did, hastening away just in time to the town of Pella, on the east side of the river Jordan. In verse 28, Jesus explained that just as one can foretell the approach of summer when one sees that the **leaves** of **the fig tree . . . come out**, the Christians in Jerusalem would be able to foretell the time of the sacking of their city, and the dawning of the glorious era beyond, when they saw **these things happening** (29). That the statements in verses 24–

27 could conceivably furnish an apocalyptic description of the Fall of Jerusalem and its sequel, will, of course, by very many, be hotly contested; but there is considerable evidence, nevertheless, that this is so. The apocalyptic language of verses 24 and 25 is remarkably similar to that used (i) in Isa. 13: 10, to describe the judgment of God upon Babylon, (ii) in Isa. 34: 4, to describe the judgment of God upon Edom, (iii) in Ezek. 32: 7, to describe the judgment of God upon Egypt, and (iv) in Jl 2: 10, to describe the judgment of God upon Israel. **'The Son of man coming in clouds'** (26), a description, so it is here maintained, of His acting in judgment against Jerusalem, is closely parallel to that provided in Isa. 19: 1 of God's acting in judgment against Egypt. It is to be recalled that Jesus had denoted the destruction of the Jewish State as a divine 'coming' earlier that same day, in His statement of Mk 12: 9. The assertion of verse 27 may relate to the increased impetus of world-wide evangelism which would follow the events of A.D. 70 (cf. the language of Ps. 22: 27 and Isa. 45: 22). This would harmonize with Jesus' affirmation of Mk 9: 1 (on which see notes). Verses 32 to 37 relate to Jesus' second advent. Because the date when this would occur was undisclosed (32), the paramount necessity for Christians with regard to it was to be watchful (35). To **watch**, therefore, was the injunction Jesus gave, not only to Peter, James, John and Andrew, but to Christians universally (37).

VI. THE PASSION (14: 1–15: 47)
The plot to arrest Jesus (14: 1–2). (Parallels: Mt. 26: 3–5; Lk. 22: 1–2.)
Previous attempts by the Jewish religious leaders to have Jesus arrested and killed have been noted in this Gospel in 3: 6 and 12: 12. Now they made their final attempt (1), resolving nevertheless that this should not occur **during the Feast** (2), lest this might provoke violent opposition on the part of supporters of Jesus who would be coming to Jerusalem from Galilee to observe the Passover.
The anointing of Jesus' head (14: 3–9). (Parallel: Mt. 26: 6–13; cf. Jn 12: 1–7.)
Simon the Leper (3), who was entertaining Jesus on this occasion, must have been a healed leper, and quite probably it was Jesus who had healed Him. The woman who anointed Jesus' head did so as a spontaneous expression of her conception of the honour which was due to Jesus. **Nard** was an **expensive** unguent made from a rare Indian plant; and the **jar** in which it was contained was probably a globular perfume-flask without handles. The woman snapped off the flask's neck, and poured, evidently, its whole contents over Jesus' head. On her being criticized for her action (4), Jesus replied that she was not to be blamed, for

she had seized a unique opportunity of doing honour to Him (7), adding a cryptic remark (8), which may, possibly, have been to the effect that if it was not going to be wasteful for costly spices to be lavished on Him when, so shortly, He was to be buried, neither was it wasteful for this woman to have thus anointed Him now.
The betrayal agreement (14: 10–11). (Parallels: Mt. 26: 14–16; Lk. 22: 3–6.)
Judas's motive in betraying Jesus to the authorities was, in part, avarice (Mt. 26: 15), though it may also have been due to his having become embittered at the failure of Jesus to implement His consciousness of being the Messiah in a political manner. Ultimately, however, the act was inspired by Satan himself (Lk. 22: 3; Jn 13: 2, 27). The offer which Judas made to the chief priests (10) was that he would give them information as to when an opportunity would present itself for them to arrest Jesus in the absence of a crowd of people.
The preparation for the Last Supper (14: 12–16). (Parallels: Mt. 26: 17–19; Lk. 22: 7–13.)
It was more probably by means of Jesus' supernatural knowledge than on account of a prior arrangement that Jesus was able to tell His disciples that, on entering Jerusalem, **a man carrying a jar of water** would meet them (13; cf. 11: 2, on which see notes). The man would be readily identifiable because whilst men in the east carried wine-skins commonly, it was unusual for them to carry water-jars, this being regarded as a woman's work. Tradition has it that the room where the Last Supper was eaten was in the home of John Mark, in which event **the owner of the house** (14) may well have been Mark's father, who, nevertheless, seems to have died prior to the occurrence of the events of Ac. 12: 12. The two disciples, having **prepared the Passover** (16) (i.e. the lamb, the wine, the bitter herbs, etc.), returned to Jesus.
The partaking of the Last Supper (14: 17–21). (Parallels: Mt. 26: 20–25; Lk. 22: 14–18; Jn 13: 21–30.)
As proof that Judas' treachery did not take Jesus by surprise, Jesus announced, during their participation of this meal, that one of the apostles would betray Him (18). Mark's record, however, does not describe Jesus' method of identifying the traitor to any of the others, but merely relates Jesus' statement to the effect that it was one of those who was dipping bread with Him into the common bowl placed centrally on the table, and containing a kind of fruit purée, known as the *harōseth* (20). Jesus added that although the traitor's treachery was foretold in the OT (verse 18 contains an echo of Ps. 41: 9, which in Jn 13: 18 is directly quoted), the traitor was not thereby absolved from personal responsibility for his deed (21).

The institution of the Lord's Supper (14: 22–25). (Parallels: Mt. 26: 26–29; Lk. 22: 19; 1 C. 11: 23–26.)
During the meal's course, Jesus gave thanks to God for a loaf of bread, and then broke off from it a piece for each of the disciples, and handed it to them, telling them that this represented the fact that, so shortly, His body would be broken (22). He then took a common cup containing wine, and passed it round the company, bidding them each drink from it (23), and telling them that it represented the blood which, on the morrow, He would shed in order to inaugurate the **covenant** of Jer. 31: 31–34, promising to those participating in it divine forgiveness and fellowship with God, just as the covenant of Exod. 24: 8 had been ratified by sacrificial blood (24). This, Jesus added, would be the last occasion of His drinking wine before doing so during the Messianic banquet of the future age (25; and see notes on 6: 30–44).

The walk to Gethsemane (14: 26–31).
(Parallels: Mt. 26: 30–35; Lk. 22: 39; Jn 18: 1.)
After the company had sung a hymn (26) (i.e. the second part of the Hallel, consisting of Pss. 115–118), Jesus led out the disciples to the Mount of Olives where He had been spending the previous nights (Lk. 21: 37). Quoting to them on the way the words of Zech. 13: 7, He told them that they were about to become like a scattered flock of sheep, because of the slaughter of Himself their Shepherd (27), but that after His resurrection they would find Him in Galilee and would all be re-united (28). On Peter protesting his fidelity to Jesus (29), Jesus predicted to him his threefold denial of Him (30).

The agony in the garden (14: 32–42). (Parallels: Mt. 26: 36–46; Lk. 22: 40–46.)
The 'Mount of Olives' was so called because of the groves of olive trees on its slopes. **Gethsemane** (32), which means 'an oil press', was evidently the site where the oil was crushed out of the olives. Jesus brought here His disciples and in the hearing of Peter, James and John (33), He prayed that if it was consistent with the fulfilment of God's purposes, the suffering awaiting Him (denoted here symbolically as 'this cup'; cf. notes on 10: 38) might be averted (35, 36). But soon the disciples fell asleep (37), sleeping in the presence of Jesus' agony, as they had slept in the presence of His glory (Lk. 9: 32). Having found them sleeping three times (40, 41), waking them up finally, Jesus said to them: **'Enough!'** i.e. 'Enough of this!' and seeing then the approach of Judas and those who had hired him, He said: 'Let us advance to meet them' (42; NIV: **'Let us go!'**).

The arrest of Jesus (14: 43–52). (Parallels: Mt. 26: 47–56; Lk. 22: 47–53; Jn 18: 2–12.)
Judas, who had left the room of the Last Supper earlier than the rest (Jn 13: 30), and had established contact thereupon with the servants of the chief priests, in order now to guard against the possibility of their arresting the wrong man in the darkness, had told them that the person to be arrested was the one whom would **kiss** (44). For a disciple to greet his teacher as **'Rabbi'** (45), and kiss him, was a common practice; but Judas, despicably, used these tokens of love as an instrument of betrayal. Further information as to what happened at this juncture is given in Jn 18: 4–9. On Jesus being **seized** (46), one of His disciples (*viz.* Peter, Jn 18: 10, who must have been bearing one of the 'two swords' mentioned in Lk. 22: 38), endeavouring with his sword to cleave the skull of one of Judas' rabble succeeded in severing his ear (47) (which Luke alone records Jesus to have subsequently restored to him). Jesus drew His captors' attention to their failure to try to arrest Him while He was peaceably engaged in teaching people in the Temple (48, 49), desiring them to realize that it was their cowardice (verse 2) which had impelled them to act in this way. The disciples then fled (50; cf. verse 27). No hint is given of the identity of the **young man** mentioned in verses 51 and 52. Because of that, and of the fact that this appears on the surface such a trivial and pointless episode to relate in the middle of such a solemn story, it has been plausibly suggested that Mark is here placing on record how he personally figured in this scene. If this was so, it may have been the case that when Jesus and His disciples had left his house (see notes on verse 14), Mark removed his outer garment and retired for sleep, but was aroused shortly afterwards by a messenger who acquainted him of the treachery of Judas. Without delaying to put on his outer garment Mark rushed to Gethsemane to try to warn Jesus of this situation, but arrived after the arrest had occurred. On catching up with Jesus and His captors he was himself assaulted, but escaped, though with the loss of his solitary piece of clothing.

The examination of Jesus by Caiaphas (14: 53–65). (Parallels: Mt. 26: 57–68; Lk. 22: 54, 63–71; Jn 18: 24.)
Jesus was led by His captors to the palace of the **high priest** (53), Caiaphas, who held office from A.D. 18 till A.D. 36. Here He was arraigned before the **Sanhedrin** which was the supreme judicial authority in Israel, and consisted of seventy-one members, and was presided over by the high priest, though it is possible that at this night session, only a proportion of them were present. Sorely as these men thirsted for Jesus' death, they were unwilling to assassinate Him, for such an action, inevitably, would have resulted in a riot, followed by repressive measures by the Romans. Their lust to have Jesus killed, therefore, they

had to endeavour to gratify by means of the machinery of the law. But they could not, of themselves, inflict on Him capital punishment, having been deprived of this power by their Roman overlords (Jn 18: 31). They were allowed, nevertheless, to carry out a preliminary examination of those they detained by way of preparing the way for such to be formally tried before the Roman procurator. In this instance, however, the Sanhedrin found great difficulty in framing against their prisoner a valid charge, owing to the conflicting evidence presented by the witnesses (36). Even the recollection of Jesus' statement of Jn 2: 19 (58), proved unavailing (which assertion, clearly, was intended to be understood not literally, but as a prediction of His own death and resurrection). Ultimately the high priest, knowing of Jesus' claim to be the Messiah, asked Him outright: **'Are you the Christ?'** (61). Jesus replied in the affirmative, and, applying to Himself the words of Ps. 110: 1 and Dan. 7: 13, asserted in effect that though He was now being judged by them, the day would arrive when they would be judged by Him. Caiaphas was not concerned to test the truth of Jesus' claim to be the Messiah. Sufficient was it for him that a charge had now been established which could be represented to the procurator in a political form, namely as a claim on Jesus' part to be the king (in opposition to Caesar) of the Jewish people (cf. 15: 2, 32; Lk. 23: 2). Jesus' affirmation, therefore, was pronounced **'blasphemy'** (64), and He was unanimously deemed deserving of the death sentence. He was subjected thereupon to gross physical abuse and buffoonery (65).

Peter's denial of Jesus (14: 66–72). (Parallels: Mt. 26: 69–75; Lk. 22: 55–62; Jn 18: 15–18, 25–27.)

The high priest's palace was built around a **courtyard** (54, 66). The reason why Peter was enabled to enter it is stated in Jn 18: 15, 16. **One of the servant girls of the high priest** had previously seen Peter in Jesus' company; but Peter denied both to her and then twice to **those standing around** (69, 70) that he had ever been associated with Jesus, deigning on the final occasion to **call down curses on himself** (71) should his statement be untrue. Peter's lapse was followed by his utmost penitence (72).

The trial of Jesus by Pilate (15: 1–15). (Parallels: Mt. 27: 1–2, 11–26; Lk. 23: 1–25; Jn 18: 28–19: 16.)

Early the following morning the Sanhedrin met a second time (1) to confirm their decision of the previous evening (14: 64). Thereupon they arraigned Jesus before Pilate, who was the fifth Roman procurator of Judea, and held office from A.D. 26 till A.D. 36. Pilate had come to Jerusalem from his normal residence in Caesarea, so as to endeavour to keep order during the Passover period. Knowing that Pilate would only concern himself with charges against people of a political nature (see notes on 14: 61), the Jewish authorities accused Jesus before him of claiming to be **'king of the Jews'** (2). Jesus' reply to this charge is given more fully in Jn 18: 34–37. When, furthermore, Jesus was accused **of many things** (3; Lk. 23: 2), He made no reply (5; Isa. 53: 7). But Pilate well knew that the real reason why the Jewish leaders had arraigned Jesus before him was their jealousy of His popularity and influence (10).

Barabbas, probably, was a Jewish nationalist who had been involved in a brush with the Romans in which fatalities had occurred (7). His supporters begged Pilate to release him (8) in accordance with his custom of releasing at Passover-time a prisoner of their own choice (6). The desire of Pilate was to release Jesus; but the priests inflamed the Jews who were present (who must have been the Jerusalem mob rather than the pilgrims from Galilee who were loyal to Jesus), to cry for Jesus' crucifixion (11). The consequence was that although Pilate believed Jesus to be innocent (14), in order to ingratiate himself with the Jews (15), he sentenced Jesus to crucifixion, ordering this to be preceded, as was usual, by the punishment of scourging. **The mockery of Jesus by the soldiers (15: 16–20).** (Parallels: Mt. 27: 27–31; Jn 19: 2, 3.) A cruel pastime in which the Roman soldiers would engage themselves periodically, was 'the game of the king'. The form which this took was that somebody would be chosen as 'king' (or should there be a condemned criminal available, he would be used for the purpose). He would be loaded with ludicrous honours—a mock crown, a mock sceptre, a mock robe of office, etc. and finally he would be put to death. This treatment was now accorded to Jesus inside **the palace (that is, the praetorium)** (16), i.e. on the courtyard around which the Antonia castle was built where the troops were stationed, which treatment must have seemed to the soldiers more apt than usual in the case of Jesus, seeing that it was for His alleged claim to be 'king of the Jews' that He had been condemned by Pilate.

The crucifixion of Jesus (15: 21–41). (Parallels: Mt. 27: 32–56; Lk. 23: 26–49; Jn 19: 17–37.)

In the North African town of **Cyrene** (21) there was a considerable community of Jews (Ac. 2: 10), so many, indeed, that they had established in Jerusalem their own synagogue (Ac. 6: 9) where they could assemble together when attending the Jewish feasts. **Simon,** presumably, had come from his home-town of Cyrene to visit Jerusalem for the Passover. Because, evidently, the scourging Jesus had received had greatly weakened him, and had rendered Him unable, as was customary, to carry to the place of execution the transverse beam of the cross (see notes on 8: 34), the Romans conscripted Simon (in accordance with their law referred to in Mt. 5: 41), to carry the beam for Jesus. Jesus, together with **two robbers** (27), who had been sentenced previously, was brought to **Golgotha** (22). Here the victims were offered drugged wine, in order to dull their sensibilities, by the women of Jerusalem, who acted thus routinely out of regard for the words of Prov. 31: 6. Jesus, however, refused the opiate (23), both in view of His assertion of 14: 25, and also because of His determination to avoid nothing of the suffering His Father had assigned to Him. The victims would then be stripped, laid on the ground, nailed through their hands to the transverse beam, this being thereupon fastened to the upright stake which would be permanently in position, and to which the victims' feet would then be nailed. To each cross, a **written notice of the charge** against the victim was fastened, that which Pilate had ordered for Jesus reading: 'The king of the Jews' (26), a statement which, very naturally, much offended the Jewish leaders (Jn 19: 21–22). As Jesus suffered, He was taunted by those passing along the near-by road with two of the charges made against Him the previous night, that of threatening the existence of the temple (29; 14: 58), and that of claiming to be the Messiah (32; 14: 62). This mockery of the passers-by, as also Jesus' being stripped of His garments, the piercing of His hands and feet, and His association in His death with malefactors, all occurred in fulfilment of prophecy (Ps. 22: 6–8, 18, 16; Isa. 53: 12). Jesus had been crucified at 9.0 a.m. (25). From noon till 3.0 p. m., the sky became darkened (33), which portent symbolized God's displeasure at what men were doing to His Son. Jesus, aware that His Father had 'made Him to be sin' (2 C. 5: 21), and realizing that His Father, being holy, had been compelled on this account to withdraw from Him His presence while He suffered, cried to Him, in the words of Ps. 22: 1 **'My God, my God, why have you forsaken me?'** (34). Experiencing thirst, furthermore (Jn 19: 28), He was offered by the soldiers some of the **wine vinegar** ('sour wine' NEB) with which they commonly refreshed themselves (36). To the surprise, then, of all who were watching, Jesus, although seemingly so exhausted, uttered a **loud cry** (37), which Jn 19: 30 relates to have been 'It is finished', whereupon He expired. The tearing at that moment of **the curtain of the temple** (38; Exod. 26: 31–33), separating the holy place from the holy of holies, signified both that God had at last fully revealed Himself in the death of Christ, and also that the barrier of sin separating man from God had now been removed, and that the way, therefore, of man's

entry into God's presence had been opened up (Heb. 10: 19–22). **The centurion** (39), who was the non-commissioned officer in charge of the execution squad, confessed that Jesus was **the Son of God**, and presumably became a Christian. As mentioned in the margin, there are some translations (such as the 1946 and 1952 editions of RSV, but not the 1962 edition) which prefer the *indefinite* article before **Son**. It is conceivable that a pagan, in order to express his feeling that Jesus was other than merely man, might refer to Him as 'a son of God', though the rendering in the text is much to be preferred, in that the confession of Jesus as **the Son of God** by a Roman was intended, no doubt, as the climax of this Gospel which was written, evidently, for the benefit of Romans in order to substantiate this very truth (1: 1). The women who beheld the crucifixion (40) were those who had accompanied Jesus and His disciples in **Galilee** (41), and had been 'helping to support them out of their own means' (Lk. 8: 3). They included **Mary Magdalene**, who came from Magdala, on the west side of the Sea of Galilee, **Mary the mother of James the younger** (who may have been James the son of Alphaeus, 3: 18), **and Salome**, who, evidently, was 'the mother of Zebedee's sons' (Mt. 27: 56).

The burial of Jesus (15: 42–47). (Parallels: Mt. 27: 57–66; Lk. 23: 50–56; Jn 19: 38–42.) The normal custom among the Romans was that the dead bodies of those whom they crucified were left to hang on their crosses till they decayed. It required boldness (43), therefore, on the part of Joseph of Arimathea to ask from Pilate **Jesus' body**. This, however, he did that same **evening** (42), and indeed prior to sunset, for there was still time for him to purchase **some linen cloth** (46) for a shroud before the sabbath began. Arimathea may perhaps be the same as Ramathaim-zophim (1 Sam. 1: 1), the birthplace of Samuel, the exact location of which is uncertain, though situated to the north of Jerusalem. Traditionally, however, it is identified with Ramleh, a town near the modern Tel Aviv. Joseph was **a prominent member of the Council** (i.e. the Sanhedrin), co-operating with whom in the burial of Jesus was another councillor, Nicodemus (Jn 3: 1; 19: 39). Joseph was **waiting for the kingdom of God** (i.e. anticipating the fulfilment of Israel's Messianic hopes), and his being called in Jn 19: 38 'a disciple of Jesus' shows that he had been regarding Jesus as the Messiah. His effecting Jesus' burial, doubtless, was undertaken as much on account of his personal loyalty to Jesus, as out of consideration of the law of Dt. 21: 23, which required that those who had been hanged should be buried before nightfall, so as to prevent the defilement of the land. Joseph, who obviously had no inkling that Jesus would rise again, wrapped Jesus' body in the linen shroud, into the folds of which aromatic spices had been inserted (Jn 19: 39–40), and he placed it in a niche within an artificial cave which he had excavated for his own burial (Mt. 26: 60). A stone was rolled into position to form the tomb's door.

VII. THE RESURRECTION (16: 1–20)
The women's visit to the sepulchre (16: 1–8). (Parallels: Mt. 28: 1–8; Lk. 24: 1–12; Jn 20: 1–10.)
Despite the way in which womenfolk tended to be belittled in contemporary Jewish thought, in the story of Jesus' resurrection they figured very prominently. That Jesus' body had been anointed by Nicodemus immediately after His death is stated in Jn 19: 39–40. But **Mary Magdalene, Mary the mother of James, and Salome** (1) desired to share in this anointing; and so **when the sabbath was over** (i.e. after sunset on the Saturday evening), they purchased the necessary spices, and then early on the Sunday morning they proceeded to the tomb (2). The purpose of their visit shows how completely they disbelieved that Jesus would rise again. Their question, furthermore, as to who would roll away the stone from the tomb's entrance (3) demonstrates their ignorance of the tomb having been sealed and guarded (Mt. 27: 62–66). The **young man** (5) whom, in the event, they saw in the tomb was clearly an angel, and he told the women to notify the **disciples and Peter** that, in accordance with the instructions given to them three days previously (14: 28), they were to proceed to Galilee, where the risen Jesus would meet them. Evidently Jesus wanted to show Himself as risen again to as many of those who had believed in Him as was possible, and since most of these were in Galilee where the major part of Jesus' ministry had been carried out, that was where He planned that the great manifestation of Himself should occur (see Mt. 28: 16–17; 1 C. 15: 6). Jesus' specific mention of Peter was in order to reassure him that despite his denial of Him, he had not been cast off as a renegade. This encounter with the angel startled the women, and they fled from the tomb, and temporarily said nothing to anyone (8), though Mt. 28: 8 and Lk. 24: 9 indicate that they conveyed the message to the eleven subsequently.
Jesus' post-resurrection appearances and ascension (16: 9–20). (Parallels: Mt. 28: 9–20; Lk. 24: 13–53; Jn 20: 11–29; Ac. 1: 9.)
From the fact that verses 9–20 are relegated in the RSV to the margin, it is not to be deduced that they are no part of the inspired Word of God. The reason for their being relegated to the margin is that it is unlikely that they were written by Mark himself, the evidence for this

inference being their considerable dissimilarity from the rest of this Gospel both as regards vocabulary and style, and especially their absence from the oldest and best extant manuscripts of the Gospel. It is unlikely, however, that Mark could have intended terminating his work with the banal anti-climax of the statement of verse 8. The likelihood, therefore, is either that Mark was prevented through death from consummating his story, or else that he finished it, but that the concluding column of his scroll (which would form the scroll's outer covering), was accidentally destroyed before ever it had been copied. It would not be unreasonable to suppose that such a final column contained (i) the story of an appearance of the risen Jesus to the frightened women mentioned in verse 8, which calmed their fears, and enabled them to go with confidence to the disciples and proclaim to them the fact of Jesus' resurrection; (ii) such a story as that of Jn 21, in which, when the disciples were in Galilee (14: 28), Jesus appeared to them, restoring to Peter (16: 7) his faith and status among the apostles.

Taking the place of this, however, there has been attached to the end of Mark's record a brief account written by a Christian author, perhaps of the early second century, providing a brief summary of what took place subsequent to Jesus' resurrection. Another early Christian writer provided an even briefer summary still of these events, and this, included also in the RSV margin, was originally written as an appendix to the Gospel. The longer of these summaries describes (i) an appearance of Jesus to Mary Magdalene (9–11; cf. Jn 20: 11–16); (ii) an appearance of Jesus to the two travellers on the way to Emmaus (12, 13; cf. Lk. 24: 11–35); (iii) an appearance of Jesus to the apostles (14; cf. Lk. 24: 36–49; Jn 20: 19–29). Emphasis is laid on the disciples' disbelief in Jesus' resurrection despite repeated eye-witness testimony to its having occurred (11, 13, 14). Jesus commissioned the disciples to preach the gospel to people of all nations (15; contrast Mt. 10: 5, 6); and He ordained that such as had believed the gospel should be baptized (16). He listed a variety of signs by which the gospel would be attested (17, 18); but 'whether or not such evidential manifestations were intended to be continuous in the life of the Church must be considered in the light of the rest of the New Testament' (Cole).

Jesus' ascension to heaven is then described and His session thereupon at God's right hand (19; cf. Ps. 110: 1). But the final emphasis of the book is on the Lord Jesus still being spiritually present with His apostles, and confirming as authentic the message they preached by the effecting of such signs as those mentioned in verses 17 and 18 (20; cf. Heb. 2: 3, 4).

BIBLIOGRAPHY

On the Greek Text
CRANFIELD, C. E. B., *The Gospel according to St. Mark* CGT (Cambridge, 1959; 2nd. edn. 1963).

TAYLOR, V., *The Gospel according to St. Mark* Macmillan New Testament Commentaries (London, 1952).

On the English Text
COLE, R. A., *The Gospel according to St. Mark*. TNTC (London, 1961).

LANE, W. L., *The Gospel according to Mark. NICNT* (Grand Rapids, 1974).

MARTIN, R. P., *Mark: Evangelist and Theologian* (Exeter, 1972).

MOULE, C. F. D., *The Gospel according to Mark. CBC* (Cambridge, 1965).

HUNTER, A. M., *The Gospel according to St. Mark*, Torch Commentaries (London, 1948)..

NINEHAM, D. E., *St. Mark*. Pelican Gospel Commentaries (Harmondsworth, 1963).

General
HENGEL, M., *Studies in the Gospel of Mark,* E.T. (London, 1985).

LUKE

LAURENCE E. PORTER

Authorship

All the Gospels are anonymous in the form we have, but ancient traditions have attributed authors to them. In the case of Luke this ascription goes back to the second century; and only a negligible minority of modern scholars would deny the common authorship of the third Gospel and Acts. The two prefaces to Theophilus state the fact, the general similarity of style and outlook supports it. From Eusebius in the early fourth century to the most recent writings of NT scholarship, identity of authorship and the unity of the work have been assumed as a settled matter. So C. K. Barrett (*Luke the Historian in Recent Study*, 1961, p. 8 n.), speaking of 'Luke-Acts', says: 'the term is inelegant, but I shall use it . . . because it emphasizes that the Gospel and Acts are together one book'.

Though there is perhaps not quite such unanimity as to the identity of the author of this double work, it seems reasonable to accept the evidence of the 'we-passages' in Acts. These are identical in style with the rest of Acts, whose author therefore must have been one of Paul's travelling companions, and a process of elimination among those mentioned in Acts and in the salutations of the Letters leaves a very small group of names, of whom Luke, designated by tradition, is the only one who will fit. Finally a strong point in favour of the Lucan tradition is that he was so unimportant a person in the early Church that it is difficult to see why his name should have become attached to it except for the reason that he actually wrote it.

If the ascription is correct, who was this Luke? He is the 'our dear friend Luke the doctor' of Col. 4: 14; one of Paul's most faithful followers (2 Tim. 4: 11). Many doctors in his day were slaves who had succeeded in obtaining their liberty; one interesting suggestion is that were Luke one he might well have found it easier to earn a living as a ship's doctor than as the first-century equivalent of a general practitioner. (This view does not, however, find favour among scholars in general.) Further than this it is difficult to go, except that everything points to his being a Gentile. Eusebius, following the second-century author of the anti-Marcionite prologue to this Gospel, says that he was a native of Antioch in Syria; the prologue also says that the Gospel was written in 'Achaea'. What is clear from the Acts record is that he had connections with Philippi. Sir William Ramsay (*St. Paul the Traveller and the Roman Citizen*) suggested that Luke was the 'man of Macedonia' of Ac. 16: 9; though he modified this view in the 14th edn. (1920), p. xxxviii.

Date

The date is much more difficult to determine. There are three main views. The one probably most widely held today is that Lk. was written about A.D. 80–85. The keystone of the argument in its support is that it must have been written after the Fall of Jerusalem in A.D. 70, since Luke changes Mark's prediction: 'when you see the abomination that causes desolation standing where it does not belong' (Mk 13: 14) to 'when you see Jerusalem surrounded by armies' (Lk. 21: 20). The 'abomination that causes desolation' is a vague term with little meaning except what it derives from the imagery of the book of Daniel. Armies are actually what was seen, therefore Luke must have written after the event. So B. H. Streeter says: 'Seeing that in A.D. 70 the appearance of Antichrist did *not* take place, but the things that Luke mentions *did*, the alteration is most reasonably explained as due to the author's knowledge of these facts' (*The Four Gospels*, 1924, p. 540).

But this takes no account of the possibility that Jesus did in fact refer to the coming Fall of Jerusalem in both these ways. If the Marcan version recalls Daniel, the Lucan echoes Zech. 14: 2, while the reference to armies is so vague and general that it is hardly necessary to see in it the description of an event that had occurred.

Others have tried to put the date as late as somewhere around A.D. 100, because of the mention of some events recorded also by Josephus in his *Antiquities* (A.D. 93–94). But Luke's historical data differ from Josephus's, a difficulty which Streeter (p. 557) meets by the suggestion that Luke had heard Josephus lecture, and was writing from lecture notes rather than from actual reading.

A third view is that the Gospel was actually written before A.D. 70. Acts ends with Paul still alive, and if this is because Luke stopped when he had brought the story up to date, Acts must have been written before about 65–66, and Luke (the 'first book' of Ac. 1:1) earlier still. Furthermore there is little sign in Luke or Acts of the influence of the Pauline letters, a pointer to an early date before they had gained general currency.

It is clear that Luke knew and used Mark, which it must therefore postdate, but a date about A.D. 60 is quite possible for the third Gospel. In short, a date in the first half of the 60s of the first century wonld fit in with the evidence as well as the more generally accepted A.D. 80, and indeed with much of the evidence, better.

Sources and Structure

Twentieth-century NT scholarship has examined closely the sources of information on which the evangelists drew (see the article on *The Fourfold Gospel*). Both oral and written traditions lie behind the texts as we have them; of the latter suffice it here to say that there is general agreement that in the case of Lk. there are three main groups of sources:

1. The Gospel of Mark.
2. Certain material not included in Mk, which Lk. has in common with Mt., and called 'Q' by modern scholars.
3. Other material used by neither Mt. nor Mk; this group includes much of the oral teaching, as well as nativity and childhood stories.

There are various opinions as to how these three strands came to be woven together. Streeter, for instance, thought that the second and third had already been written up to form a Gospel ('Proto-Luke') before Luke came across Mk and incorporated it to give us the third Gospel. Not all scholars would agree with this interpretation of the evidence, but the subject, interesting as it is, lies outside the scope of this essay.

What is important for our purpose is that Mk provides for Lk. not merely a great deal of information, but also *a framework*. Beginning where Jesus' public ministry began, Mark devotes roughly the first half of his Gospel to His going about doing good and preaching the kingdom, and then in his second half shows Him under the shadow of the Cross, then dying and rising again. Luke prefaces to this two chapters of infancy stories, and adds a chapter of post-resurrection appearances and the Ascension (mentioned neither by Mt., Jn, nor the 'short ending' of Mk). Luke's account of the Passion also includes a considerable amount of matter used by him alone. Between the two halves of the Marcan narrative, he also places a long section of about ten chapters where he sets out in the form of a travel account (see below, pp. 1202 f.) a great number of incidents, sayings and especially parables most of which neither Mt. nor Mk records. Included are such familiar parables as the Good Samaritan, the Prodigal Son, and the Pharisee and Tax collector.

Characteristics

The three synoptic Gospels tell substantially the same story, and yet each is quite distinguishable from the others by the way in which the author's own personality is seen in his telling of it. There are several characteristics which give the third Gospel especially an individuality of its own.

1. *It is the universal Gospel.* Says Balmforth (p. 17): 'What begins as a mission to Jews soon includes Samaritans and Gentiles as well'. Luke, a Gentile himself (he is expressly excluded from the 'men of the circumcision' in Col. 4: 11, 14), looks beyond the narrow limits of contemporary Jewish nationalism and prejudice. Christ's family tree is taken back beyond Abraham, the father of the nation, to Adam, the father of the race; and He is a 'light for revelation to the Gentiles' (Lk. 2: 32). A Gentile centurion is commended for faith unmatched in Israel itself (7: 9) and a Samaritan for thanksgiving when cured, alone of ten lepers, the others presumably Jews (17: 16). Most striking of all, a despised Samaritan is the hero of one of the noblest of all the parables (10: 30–35). Luke omits the story of the Syro-Phoenician (Mk 7: 24–30; Mt. 15: 21–28) possibly because it might give offence to Gentile readers (though it should be mentioned also that it is part of the block of 'omitted' material).

2. *It is the Gospel of rejoicing.* 'There is gladness at its beginning—"I bring you good news of great joy"—there is gladness in its middle (chap. 15); and there is gladness at its ending when the disciples "returned to Jerusalem with great joy"' (A. M. Hunter, *Introducing the NT*, 1957, p. 53). There is sadness and sternness in plenty, but cheerfulness keeps breaking in.

3. *It is the Gospel for the 'down and out'.* 'Why do you eat and drink with tax-gatherers and sinners?' (5: 30) ask the Pharisees, and the whole Gospel might serve as the answer of the Son of Man who 'came to seek and to save what was lost' (19: 10), fallen women, hated tax collectors and even a dying thief. The tax collectors were not poor, of course, but socially they were despised and shunned. Jesus was born of poor parents, and it is the visit of humble shepherds rather than of oriental sages that captured Luke's imagination. The couplet from Mary's song:

He has filled the hungry with good things,
but has sent the rich away empty,

finds its echo in numerous stories of Jesus' concern for the needy, and in parables like the rich fool and Lazarus and the rich man.

4. *It is the woman's Gospel.* One of the chief features of Luke's presentation of the Gospel is his respect and reverence for womanhood. The stories of the pregnancy of Elizabeth and of Mary, so difficult to tell, are related with a grace and delicacy that invest them with a singular atmosphere of purity. The glory of motherhood is here depicted with as much in

sight as is the tragedy of motherhood seen in the widow of Nain. Luke also delights to tell of the women who cared for Jesus (8: 1–3) and were faithful right to the end (23: 25).

5. *It is the Gospel of the supernatural*. It is true that all the Gospels have a large supernatural element; indeed they must have since their theme, the incarnation, is a supernatural event. But in two ways, Luke shows a particular interest. First, there is his interest in angels. Mt. and Mk record the appearance of angels after the temptations and accompanying the resurrection; Luke in addition has a series of such appearances in his first two chapters. Secondly he often shows a professional interest in the *details* of the miracles of healing. It is of interest that of the miracles recorded only in one of the Gospels, Lk. has more than any other.

6. *It is* par excellence *the Gospel of prayer*. As J. G. S. S. Thomson says (*The Praying Christ*, 1959, p. 11): 'of the four evangelists, Luke is the one who places greatest emphasis on prayer

. . . the main lesson he is concerned to teach is the necessity for the soul's communion with God. He enforces that lesson by showing Christ as the believer's example in prayer. For instance, he shows how our Lord turned to the Father in prayer at all the great crises of His life —at His baptism, before the call of the Twelve, before Peter's confession, at the Transfiguration, and the Crucifixion. It is also Luke who supplies us with the parables of the importunate Friend and the Pharisee and the Publican, and with a treatise on prayer which accompanies them'.

Finally, in addition to these special interests of Luke it must be pointed out that he is a literary genius of the first order. He writes in language whose grace survives translation; he has the eye of the artist for detail and the gift of evoking in a few words a whole world of meaning. Ernest Renan was not a believer yet he judged the third Gospel 'the most beautiful book in the world'—*C'est le plus beau livre qu'il y ait.*

ANALYSIS

I. THE PREFACE (1: 1-4)

The third Gospel begins with a formal prefatory address, balanced in form and classical in idiom, to a certain Theophilus. It is composed of one continuous sentence with six main clauses, the first three balancing the second three: **many have undertaken** (1a) with **it seemed good also to me** (3a); **to draw up an account** (1b) with **to write an orderly account** (3b); **as they were handed down to us** (2) with **that you may know** (4).

The four verses stand in marked contrast with the rest of the Gospel, whose Gk. has a strong Semitic flavour. There he is dependent on his sources, all Semitic in origin; here he is using no source, but probably a literary model; such prefaces are often found in Gk. literature, especially historical writing.

3. from the beginning (EVV: 'from the very beginning'): *anōthen*, which in Gk. often means 'from above', is clearly used here in a temporal sense. **most excellent Theophilus:** Theophilus's identity is unknown; he may have been (*a*) an individual of this name; (*b*) a public official addressed pseudonymously; (*c*) a purely symbolic figure, 'Dear to God'. This third is the most unlikely of the three. The designation **most excellent** suggests a high official of perhaps equestrian status; it corresponds to our 'His Excellency'.

The contents of this epistle dedicatory furnish a clue to Luke's purpose in writing. Theophilus has a general knowledge of the faith, but Lk. wants him also to have **an orderly account**, a systematic knowledge, and a written account now that the day of eye-witnesses is passing. He claims that he has himself a sound knowledge of the events; that where his knowledge was limited he has done some research, and that what he is writing will serve as a corrective to some current traditions. His claim is moderate, but as Plummer (*ICC*, p. 2) points out, this is evidence for his honesty. 'A forger would have claimed to be an eye-witness, and would have made no apology for writing.'

II. PARENTAGE AND INFANCY (1: 5-2: 52)

Mt. and Lk. alone of the four Gospels record the infancy of our Lord. Mk and Jn introduce Him at the outset of His public ministry, Jn prefacing his story with a proclamation of His eternal deity and pre-existence. Mt. and Lk. narrate the events leading up to the nativity and the nativity itself, though with significant differences. Lk., for example, sets the birth of Jesus and the events preceding it in parallel with John the Baptist's; Mt. makes no mention of John until his mission begins (3: 1). The experiences and utterances of Mary are also given in considerable detail in Lk.; while Joseph is the main focus of interest from this point of view in Mt.

But perhaps the greatest difference between the two is that, as N. B. Stonehouse points out (*The Witness of Luke to Christ*, 1951, pp. 48 ff.), whereas Mt. relates the story to the OT prophets, 'the revelational message reported by Lk. is a *contemporary* prophetic message'. To herald Messiah's coming, the long silent voice of prophecy speaks again. Stonehouse lists no less than eleven prophetic utterances: (*a*) announcement of the birth of John, 1: 13-17, 19-20. (*b*) announcement of the birth of Jesus, 1: 28-35. (*c*) Elizabeth's salutation to Mary, 1: 42-45. (*d*) Mary's response, the *Magnificat*, 1: 46-55. (*e*) the prophecy of Zechariah, 1: 68-75. (*f*) the angel's proclamation to the shepherds, 2: 10-11. (*g*) the praise of the heavenly host, 2: 14. (*h*) the oracle to Simeon that he would **not die before he had seen the Lord's Christ**, 2: 26. (*i*) Simeon's prophecy (*Nunc dimittis*), 2: 29-35. (*j*) Anna's prophecy (reported but not quoted), 2: 38. (*k*) our Lord's declaration that He **had to be in my Father's house**, 2: 49.

i. The birth of John the Baptist announced (1: 5-25)

Zechariah, an aged priest, is ministering in the Temple when he is interrupted by the appearance of the angel Gabriel bringing the news that his wife, the elderly Elizabeth, will bear him a son. This son will be a prophet in the OT tradition; more, he will be Messiah's forerunner. So astonished is Zechariah that be cannot believe the news; for his incredulity he is stricken dumb until the promise is fulfilled.

5. in the time of Herod: An indication of date. Herod ('the Great') ruled Palestine and part of Transjordan as king of the Jews from 37 to 4 B.C. **Zechariah . . . Elizabeth.** Nothing is known about John's parents except what Lk. tells us. Both were of Aaronic lineage; Zechariah was **of the priestly division of Abijah:** These divisions dated from the division by David of the Aaronic families into twenty-four groups, the descendants of Abijah forming the eighth (1 Chr. 24: 10). Each division did duty in the Temple in rotation twice a year, each period of duty lasting one week.

In a godless age the couple lived lives of exemplary piety, yet were denied the blessing without which pious Jews were regarded as under the disapproval of God—they were childless (see Lev. 20: 20-21; Jer. 22: 30).

9. He was chosen by lot . . . burn incense: The privilege of burning incense was permitted only once in the lifetime of any priest (cf. A. Edersheim, *The Temple: Its Ministry and Service*, 1874, p. 129); it was accorded, like all priestly activities, by lot. Zechariah was doubtless deeply impressed; at a given signal he had to offer the incense; as its smoke rose the whole concourse of worshippers prostrated themselves in private prayer. He now became conscious of the angelic presence standing **at the right side of the altar of incense** (11), i.e., in the place of authority. It was Gabriel, besides Michael the only named angel in the Bible (cf. Dan. 8: 16; 9: 21).

13–17. The angel's message: (*a*) Zechariah's prayer has been heard and will be answered. We are not told that he had been praying for a son; such a hope he may have given up long since. His prayer was probably more general, for 'the consolation of Israel' (in the accomplishment of which, had he but known it, his son would play a preparatory part). The child's name is to be **John:** 'Jehovah has been gracious'. (*b*) The promised son will be **great in the sight of the Lord**, and will be a perpetual Nazirite, set apart for the service of God. (*c*) He is moreover to be **filled with the Holy Spirit.** In Lk., apart from the nativity stories (John, 1: 15; Mary, 1: 35; Elizabeth, 1: 41; Zechariah, 1: 67; Simeon, 2: 25 f.), only our Lord Himself is so described (4: 1). (*d*) He will call men to repentance, as foretold in Mal. 4: 5 f. Messiah is not mentioned, so John's function as His forerunner is implied rather than explicit.

ii. The birth of Jesus announced (1: 26–38)
Six months later Gabriel visits Mary, a young countrywoman of Nazareth, betrothed but not yet married to Joseph, an artisan of Davidic descent. She, he says, will conceive; her Son will be the long-awaited Messiah. To her puzzled enquiry, Gabriel replies that conception will be brought about by the supernatural operation of the Holy Spirit. Mary expresses her acceptance of this divine mission. The annunciations to Zechariah and to Mary are very similar. Gabriel greets both (1: 19, 26), both are distressed (1: 12, 29) and reassured by the words **'Do not be afraid'** and the promise of a son (1: 13, 30). Both ask questions (1: 18, 34) and receive answers (1: 19, 34 f.), but while Zechariah hesitates, Mary believes.

26. Nazareth 'lies high on a sharp slope in the Galilean hills. Its altitude is about 1,150 feet. From the summit above the village one looks south across the extensive plain of Esdraelon, west to Mount Carmel on the Mediterranean coast, east to nearby Mount Tabor, and north to snow-capped Mount Hermon (Ps. 89: 12)' (J. Finegan, *Light from the Ancient Past*, 1959, p. 298).

28–37. The angel's message: Mary's Son was to be infinitely greater than John. (*a*) His name was to be **Jesus**, 'Jehovah is salvation' (31). (*b*) He would be **great** (32), a title which, unqualified, is usually reserved for God Himself. (*c*) As heir to David's throne He will reign over God's people (33). (*d*) His kingdom will be eternal (33). (See 1 Sam. 7: 16; Dan. 2: 44; 7: 14; etc.)

34, 35. Note on the Virgin Birth. The validity of the tradition of the Virgin Birth is often assailed, mainly along three lines of attack:
(*a*) *Textual*. It is alleged that the NT references are later interpolations not found in the original text.
(*b*) *Historical*. It is denied that the belief was generally held in the Early Church, even if Mt. and Lk. *did* teach it.
(*c*) *Philosophical and scientific*. Such an event is held to be contrary to the laws of nature, and therefore impossible.

The subject is fully examined in most commentaries. Geldenhuys deals with it briefly from a conservative point of view (pp. 107 ff.). Balmforth (pp. 111–118) gives a careful and fair-minded exposition of the evidence. A fuller treatment is found in J. G. Machen, *The Virgin Birth of Christ* (New York, 1932).

There can be no doubt that the Virgin Birth is one of the cardinal doctrines of Christian theology, and these objections are completely answerable.

(*a*) *Textual*. This is not the place for detailed linguistic study, but it can be stated that claims that the text is unsound are not supported by a scrap of evidence. It is significant that a scholar like Dr. Vincent Taylor, who is no conservative in this matter, says that to explain away the difficulties by textual emendation raises more problems than it solves (see Balmforth, pp. 112 f.).
(*b*) *Historical*. While other NT writers do not mention the Virgin Birth, neither Mk nor Paul had any reasons for mentioning it. Then, as A. E. J. Rawlinson points out (*Christ in the Gospels*, 1944, p. 23), the considerable differences between Mt. and Lk. suggest that the belief 'must go back to a period earlier than that at which the traditions lying behind the two narratives diverged'. Thirdly, it has been suggested that the idea was borrowed from pagan mythology. Legends of virgin births do exist in antiquity, but the strong Jewish colouring of the NT accounts rules out the likelihood of such borrowing.
(*c*) *Philosophical and scientific*. Our attitude to the scientific possibility of such an event will depend on our general views on revelation, the NT, and the miraculous. If we believe in the deity of Christ and in scripture miracles, we shall no doubt agree with James Denney (*Studies in Theology*, 1910, p. 64): 'Jesus came from God, all the Apostles declare, in a sense in which no other came. Does it not follow that, as two of our evangelists declare, He came in a way in which no other came?'

iii. Mary's visit to Elizabeth (1: 39–56)
As soon as she hears that her elderly kinswoman is pregnant, Mary goes to stay at her home for three months. Elizabeth greets the

mother of my Lord (43) with clear spiritual insight and complete lack of any jealousy—a trait that foreshadows her son (Jn 3: 30). Mary responds with the hymn of praise beloved in Christian devotion as the *Magnificat*.

A textual point first; some commentators give considerable weight to the reading 'Elizabeth said' for **Mary said** in v. 46, a reading mentioned by NEB in a footnote. The grounds for this support are mainly subjective; AV, RV and RSV do not even mention it in their margins. It is found only in a few Old Latin authorities.

The *Magnificat* is in form a beautiful lyrical poem uttered by a Jewish peasant girl whose cultural background was the OT writings, which supply the very expressions she uses. The main source on which she draws is the song of Hannah (1 Sam. 2: 1–10) to which her canticle corresponds in general outline as well as in various details, though there are echoes of other OT passages, as Leah's utterance (Gen. 30: 13; cf. v. 48) and some psalms (see the references in RSV, RV, etc.). The hymn falls into four stanzas:

(a) vv. 46–48.Mary praises God for His goodness to her.
(b) vv. 49–50.And to all those who fear Him.
(c) vv. 51–53.He succours the oppressed against the oppressor.
(d) vv. 54–55.In the final verses the song of praise ends in peaceful tranquillity.

'This beautiful lyric', says Plummer (p. 30), 'is neither a reply to Elizabeth nor an address to God. It is rather a meditation; an expression of personal emotions and experiences'. It is lyrical in tone not only because it is what Wordsworth declared all lyric poetry to be—the 'spontaneous overflow of powerful feeling'—but also because Mary knew the OT thoroughly, and many portions, especially the more lyrical ones, by heart. Their language became the natural vehicle of her praises.

Her emotion was evoked first of all because the unbelievable had come to pass: she was to be the mother of the Messiah, an honour which Jewesses longed for, but surely scarce dared to hope for. Mary could give no reason why she was chosen to be the recipient of such an honour, but the honour itself is the reason for her rejoicing: **my spirit rejoices in God my Savior, for he has been mindful of the humble estate of his servant** (47, 48).

This great mercy bestowed on her is the manifestation of His might and His holiness not only to her, but **his mercy extends to those who fear him from generation to generation** (50). The days of the oppressors are numbered: **he has scattered those who are proud in their inmost thoughts. He has brought down rulers from their thrones** (51–52): This is especially true for His people

Israel; what He has promised to Mary, in short, is a pattern of His purpose for His people. 'Perhaps Luke is . . . regarding Mary as the mouthpiece of Israel; through her the chosen people makes thanksgiving . . . God has looked on the humiliation of Mary (who is Sion) and now she is exalted' (Browning, pp. 41–42). Whether or not we agree with typology of this kind, it is clear that Mary saw in her experience the earnest of the fulfilment of God's promises also to His own whose land was in the occupation of alien overlords and who groaned as well under the burdens laid on them by religious leaders with their weight of tradition. Black as things might look, the great Light was about to appear bringing deliverance **to Abraham and his descendants forever** (55).

iv. The birth and circumcision of John (1: 57–80)

Elizabeth's baby is born soon after Mary's departure. A week later he is circumcised amidst the rejoicing of neighbours and kinsfolk. Elizabeth announces that his name is to be John; the father, giving signs of assent, receives again the power of speech. Local interest is intense (65–66) and Zechariah gives utterance to his canticle, the *Benedictus* (67–79).

60, 63. 'His name is John': The name was common in NT days; the neighbours' surprise was due to pious parents choosing a name that was unknown in Zechariah's family.

67–69. The song of Zechariah. The spontaneous inspired utterance of the old man, like that of Mary, is full of the language of Scripture, no doubt the reflection of his long silent meditations on the words of Gabriel in the Temple months before. It is a gathering together of many OT strands, but whereas the *Magnificat* 'breathes a regal spirit . . . the Benedictus breathes a sacerdotal one' (Geldenhuys, p. 92). Many of the OT quotations are naturally from the Psalms, though there are also echoes of the prophets: v. 69, 'the house of His servant David'; v. 76 recalls the prophecy of the forerunner in Mal. 4: 5–6; vv. 78–79 evoke the prophetic picture (Isa. 9: 2; Mal. 4: 2) of the darkest hour before the Messianic dawn.

The last two verses of the *Benedictus*, in fact, set the scene for the advent of Messiah in the next chapter, as the last few verses in Mal. set the scene for His coming recorded in Mt.

80. He lived in the desert: An ascetic life for John is already foretold in v. 15. It has been suggested that he was associated with the Qumran community of the Dead Sea Scrolls, but this is pure conjecture (see Leaney, *St. Luke*, p. 91; also F. F. Bruce, *Second Thoughts on the Dead Sea Scrolls*, 1956, pp. 128 f.).

v. The birth of Jesus Christ (2: 1–7)

An imperial order that all citizens should report

at their own home town for census purposes brings Mary and Joseph from Nazareth to Bethlehem. Mary's Baby is almost due, and is actually born at Bethlehem itself. The impossibility of finding accommodation results in a feeding-trough having to do duty for a cot.

1–5. Caesar Augustus issued a decree that a census should be taken of the entire Roman world: This census raises historical difficulties. It is said to be impossible that a *Roman* census was held in the territory of Herod, an allied king, though it is admitted that there is evidence of a census some years later in Egypt, a similar case. **Quirinius was governor of Syria** in A.D. 6, when he held the census of Ac. 5: 37; whether he had already served in this capacity several years earlier is debatable. But Luke probably means: 'This enrolment was held before Quirinius was governor of Syria'. Again the visit to Joseph's ancestral home town for registration is unusual, though attested for Egypt; Roman censuses were based on residence. Finally, the complete silence of the Roman records on this census is adduced by some as a ground for scepticism. But several authorities of weight (as Plummer, p. 48; Balmforth, p. 125; Finegan, *LAP*, pp. 258 if.) are prepared to regard the account as historical, while conservative commentators like Geldenhuys (pp. 104–106) argue strongly in favour of it. (See also article, 'The Historical Background'.)

6–7. The details that Luke gives concerning the birth of Jesus build up an impression of poverty. Joseph and Mary appear to be in no position to secure suitable accommodation; they lack so everyday a necessity as a cradle. Later, Joseph will offer the poor man's offering at the Temple presentation (see note on 2: 24).

The date of the nativity. The time of year is not known; December 25 was chosen to establish a Christian festival as an alternative to a pagan festival of the sun at the winter solstice. Balmforth (p. 128) says that nothing as to the time of the year can be inferred from the narrative; Browning, however (p. 45), says that sheep were kept out in the Judaean pastures from March to November. As for the year, this too is uncertain: a *terminus ad quem* is provided by Herod's death in 4 B.C.

vi. The angels (2: 8–20)
Meanwhile, shepherds guarding their flocks in pastures not far away learn from an angelic visitor that Messiah has been born. They hasten to pay their respects, having heard the message confirmed by a great company of the angelic host. When they have seen the Baby, they broadcast the great news.

14. '. . . **and on earth peace to men on whom his favor rests':** The exact meaning of this verse has been much discussed. The AV (and RSVmg) 'good will among men' is based

on a variant *eudokia* (nominative) which textually is not so strongly supported as *eudokias* (genitive), 'of good will'. So 'to men of good will' is preferable to 'good will among men'. But who are these 'men of good will'? The important point is that the NT usage indicates that the good will originates from God and not from men. It is 'men of His good pleasure', the objects and recipients of His good will.

15, 17. Note the missionary interest of Luke in the spread of the gospel, **this thing . . . , which the Lord has told us about** (15).

17. they spread the word: To a group of simple men God's presence was manifested. They saw His glory shining around them, as Moses had seen His glory in the burning bush, and they were given, as he had been, a message to proclaim.

vii. The circumcision and presentation (2: 21–39)
Joseph and Mary are careful that the requirements of the law should be carried out; circumcision apparently in Bethlehem and purification for which they have to travel to the Temple at Jerusalem. Here they are greeted by two remarkable people, the aged and devout Simeon and Anna, who make prophetic utterance concerning the Child.

21. it was time to circumcise him: The Mosaic law laid down (Lev. 12: 3) that boys should be circumcised at the age of eight days. Nothing is said by Luke of the doctrinal significance of the rite, but as in the case of John it was made the occasion of publicly obeying God in the bestowal of the name He had indicated. **22–24. the time of their purification:** In addition to circumcision, Lev. 12: 4–8 prescribed a service of purification 33 days after. The central feature was the offering of a lamb (see also Exod. 13: 2, here quoted in v. 23), or if this were beyond the means of the parents, a pair of turtledoves might be substituted. That this constituted Joseph's offering (v. 24) is further evidence of the family's reduced circumstances. **25. a man in Jerusalem, called Simeon:** All we know of Simeon is what Luke tells here. He was righteous as to the Law, and devout as to his religion; his heart was set upon the Messianic hopes and **the Holy Spirit was upon him**. He had already received a promise that he personally would live to see Messiah's coming; here he is conscious that the hour of fulfilment has come. Simeon and Anna provide evidence that in the last decade B.C. there were still in the Jewish nation men and women in the highest OT tradition.

29–32. *Nunc dimittis.* The old man likens himself to a slave whose duty it has been to scan the horizon for a long-awaited visitor. Now he reports to the slave-master (the Gk. is our word 'despot') that his trust has been fulfilled, and he claims the privilege, his long watch being over, of going off duty.

This canticle, like those of Mary and of Zechariah, is full of OT associations. **your salvation** (30) is personalized for Simeon in the little Child in his arms: 'The very presence in the world of this babe of Bethlehem, well before his public ministry could be discharged in terms of words and deeds, was acknowledged as the manifestation of the divine action of salvation' (Stonehouse, p. 54). This salvation, set within the context of OT prophetic expectation, was to be universal, **a light for revelation to the Gentiles** (32a; cf. Isa. 49: 6), as well as **for glory to your people Israel** (32b).

34, 35. Simeon's words to Mary. The prophet then addresses the Babe's mother, telling her that the great honour which was hers would entail suffering also, a warning of whose truth she was already aware, and an indication of the way by which salvation would be accomplished.

36. there was also a prophetess, Anna, the daughter of Phanuel: Anna occupies a position in the narrative corresponding to that of Simeon, but while his actual words are recorded, in her case only the fact that she prophesied is reported. **of the tribe of Asher:** Some members at least of the ten tribes were not lost! **she was very old:** The question of Anna's age is somewhat obscure. AV suggests that she had been 84 years a widow, RSV that she was 84 years old. The *BFBS Diglot* says: 'The Gk. may mean either 84 years old, or a widow for 84 years' (p. 9 n.).

39. they returned into Galilee, to their own town of Nazareth: It is not easy at first to harmonize Luke's account of the immediate post-infancy events with Mt.'s, but it is not impossible. A discussion of the problem will be found in the parallel section in Mt.

viii. Childhood and visit to Jerusalem (2: 40–50)

After the extraordinary events accompanying His infancy, our Lord's boyhood and young manhood are passed in obscurity. Only two things are recorded, His visit to the Temple at twelve, and His physical and spiritual growth (vv. 40, 52).

41. Every year his parents went to Jerusalem for the Feast of the Passover: The Jew was enjoined (Exod. 23: 17; Dt. 16: 16) to journey to Jerusalem for each of the great feasts (Passover, Pentecost, Tabernacles), but it seems clear that by the first century, even for Palestinian Jews, custom had often reduced the observance to one annual journey. **42. twelve years old:** The Jewish boy became a 'son of the commandment' at thirteen. According to Edersheim (*The Life and Times of Jesus the Messiah*, 1883, i. 235 and note) the legal age was customarily anticipated by one or even two

years in the matter of going up to the Temple. Jesus simply accompanied Mary and Joseph. **46, 47.** Temporarily lost sight of, Jesus was found in the Temple, engaged in questioning the assembled rabbis about the law. At festival times rabbis found appreciative audiences for their instruction in the Temple courts, as at a later date Jesus Himself did (19: 47). On this occasion He was found sitting at the feet of such rabbis. **48–50.** When the boy was found, His mother with gentle reproof asked why He had caused them all this anxiety. His reply indicates that He was conscious already of the divine mission that lay before Him: **I had to be in my Father's house.** 'He was the Son of the Father', comments J. N. Darby, 'though abiding God's time for showing it'.

ix. The silent years (2: 51–52)

After this remarkable revelation of intellectual alertness and spiritual awareness at so early an age, a veil is again drawn over the life of our Lord in His family at Nazareth until the beginning, eighteen years later, of His public ministry.

52. The general summary of v. 40 is repeated, with the additional information that other people recognized His character; in v. 40 **the grace of God was upon him;** in v. 52 He **grew . . . in favor with God and man**.

III. PREPARATORY ACTION (3: 1–4: 13)

With chapter 3 begins the narrative of the ministry of Jesus at the point where Mark begins his Gospel—the preaching of John the Baptist and the baptism of our Lord.

i. The Ministry of John (3: 1–20)

At a carefully specified point in history (3: 1–2), John startles his countrymen by his preaching, full of the fire and the faithfulness of the oracles of the OT prophets. He calls on them to repent and to make open acknowledgment of their repentance by being baptized, and he gives concrete examples of the sort of effect that should be visible in their manner of living.

1, 2. The six-fold synchronization dates, but only approximately, the ministry of the Baptist (see article, *The Historical Background*, p. 1043).

3–20. Luke gives the fullest account of the ministry of John found in the Synoptics (see notes on Mk 1: 2–8). Mk quotes from Mal. 3: 1 and Isa. 40: 3, and then tells that John, clad in garb reminiscent of Elijah's (2 Kg. 1: 8), baptized in the wilderness, that he preached a 'baptism of repentance for the forgiveness of sins' and predicted the coming of One much greater than himself. Mt. (3: 3–12) omits the Mal. quotation (he includes it at a later point, Mt. 11: 10), but adds a note of urgency in John's preaching: 'the kingdom of heaven is **near**' (3: 2); he also records more than does Mk of John's warnings to his hearers: (*a*) Addressing them as the offspring of vipers, he urges them that if they wish to escape coming judgment, repentance evidenced by changed conduct will avail more than the mere fact of their privileged position as sons of Abraham, members of God's chosen people. In Mt. 3: 7 it is the Pharisees and Sadducees who are so addressed.

(*b*) This prophetic message calling for personal righteousness is reinforced by an apocalyptic note of urgency. Time is short; 'the axe is already at the root of the trees' (Mt. 3: 10; cf. Lk. 3: 9).

Luke, drawing, it would seem, on the source which he has in common with Mt., makes all these same additions except that he lengthens the quotation from Isa. 40 to include vv. 4–5 as well as v. 3, and that he omits the saying about the nearness of the kingdom and the fact (Mt. 3: 7) that scribes and Pharisees were among the crowd.

On the other hand he adds an interesting passage not found in Mt. or Mk, reporting John's practical suggestions for the implementation of genuine repentance. The people generally (**the crowd**, 10) were told of the responsibility laid upon them to share with less fortunate neighbours their superfluity of food or clothing. Tax-collectors, universally despised and detested as unpatriotic tools, willingly placing themselves at the service of the Roman overlords or Jewish tetrarchs and as unscrupulous and dishonest extortioners lining their own pockets, were commanded to carry out their duties with scrupulous fairness and honesty. Swaggering and bullying soldiers were to refrain from summary appropriation of the goods of others, and from glib perjury to cover their tracks. It is interesting that there is nothing revolutionary in all this; even the tax-collectors are not ordered to give up their jobs. This is an 'interim ethic'—as it is sometimes called—a code of conduct whilst awaiting the day of the full revelation of the kingdom, when Roman taxes and much else beside will be swept away. A small point worthy of notice is that whereas we assume from the general tone of Mt.'s account (and Mk's also) that John's ministry was centred on one spot, Luke hints at a peripatetic ministry covering a wider area (3). The Fourth Gospel says that John was baptizing at Bethany beyond Jordan (1: 28) and represents him as active later in a district of Samaria (3: 23).

Baptism. The rite of baptism was no new thing. Water is often a symbol of cleansing in the OT, and by this time baptism may have become the mode whereby proselytes to Judaism were ceremonially admitted to their new faith. T. W. Manson (*The Servant-Messiah*, 1953, pp. 44 f.) suggests that John was inviting Jews to confess that by their sins they had forfeited the right to the status of sons of Abraham, and must make a fresh start just like Gentile proselytes.

19, 20. Luke here records the arrest of John by Herod, not mentioned by Mt. or Mk until they record his execution (see note on 9: 7–9).

ii. The Baptism of Jesus (3: 21–22)
Jesus Himself joins the throng awaiting baptism, and is Himself baptized, whereupon the Holy Spirit comes down and rests upon Him **like a dove**, and a voice is heard from heaven. (See notes on Mk 1: 9–11.)

21. One of the places where Luke alone of the Synoptics records that Jesus **was praying** (see Introduction, Characteristics, 6, p. 1184).

22. Luke adds the phrase **in bodily form** to describe the appearance of the dove. Plummer rightly comments: 'Nothing is gained by admitting something visible and rejecting the dove. Comp. the symbolical visions of Jehovah granted to Moses and other Prophets. We dare not assert that the Spirit cannot reveal Himself to human sight, or that in so doing He cannot employ the form of a dove or of tongues of fire' (p. 99). Further, it is intelligible that the Holy Spirit should be manifested in the form of a dove. It accords with the whole testimony of Scripture concerning Him.

iii. The genealogy of Jesus (3: 23–38)
The differences between the two genealogies of our Lord given in the gospels raise a number of important points. See notes on Mt. 1: 2–17.

iv. The Temptation (4: 1–13)
The experience of the Baptism, confirming the mission and Messiahship of Jesus, is followed immediately by the wilderness experience of the Temptation. Impelled into the deserts by the Holy Spirit for a considerable period He there fasts and wrestles with the suggestions of Satan: (*a*) to use His supernatural powers for the satisfaction of His purely material needs by turning stones into bread; (*b*) to attain the mastery of men's hearts by compromising, doing a deal with the Adversary; (*c*) to test the power and willingness of God to protect Him by engaging in a foolhardy escapade, plunging from '**the highest point** of the Temple'. Resisted with words of Scripture, Satan gives up the contest for a time and withdraws.

Some scholars have seen in the three temptations a reference to contemporary political views. The first temptation is paralleled in the policy of the Herodians, who would keep the people quiescent by doles of food, *panem et circenses*. The aristocratic Sadducees were willing to co-operate with the Roman authorities in order to maintain their own position; the Pharisees pinned their hopes for the fulfilment of their nationalist aspirations on a miraculous intervention of God Himself.

Mk tells the story very briefly, and without specifying the three individual forms the temptations took. His introductory description of the ordeal is more forceful than either Mt.'s or Luke's: 'At once the Spirit sent him out into the desert'—Mt. and Luke both use the milder verb, **led**.

Mt. and Luke both give a detailed account of the actual temptations, but in a different order (Mt.'s second and third are Luke's third and second respectively). This need not be regarded as a contradiction. It is an intensely spiritual experience that is being described, lasting over a period of six weeks, and it seems reasonable to suggest that the three lines of attack were pursued by the enemy throughout the whole period. Furthermore, while Mt. 4: 2 suggests that the temptations followed the fasting, Mk and Luke both give the impression that fasting and temptation were simultaneous. What is important is to see how, when our Lord's physical resources had been taxed to the full by his fasting and His spiritual wrestling, Satan suggested easier ways to win men's hearts and to fulfil His mission than the way of the Cross that lay before Him.

Whence did the disciples and the evangelists derive their knowledge of this experience? Obviously, it would seem, from the Lord Himself. 'After the Baptism', says A. M. Hunter (*The Work and Words of Jesus*, 1950, p. 38), 'there follows, with psychological fitness, the Temptation. . . . How do we know anything about it? For "forty days"—an oriental round number—He was quite alone. Obviously, the story of the Temptation is a piece of spiritual autobiography told to the disciples by Jesus Himself, told with utter simplicity as a Jewish mother might have told it to a Jewish child. We may be sure that no later Christian would have invented such a story.'

2. for forty days: Maybe an 'oriental round number', as Hunter suggests, but it is interesting that the same expression is used in connection with Moses and Elijah, who both fasted 40 days (Dt. 9: 9; 1 Kg. 19: 8).

3. 'If you are the Son of God, tell this stone to become bread': The devil's approach is very subtle. He challenges Jesus not only to satisfy His hunger but to substantiate also His claim to be God's Son. Wm. Manson (p. 37) shows further that to feed His people was one of the signs expected of the Messiah: in Isa. 49: 10 the promise 'they shall not hunger nor thirst' enters into the divine plan of salvation, while in Jn 6: 30 ff. He is challenged to prove His Messiahship by providing bread from heaven as Moses had done. **4. Man does not live on bread alone:** Quoted from Dt. 8: 3. **5. all the kingdoms of the world . . . :** Although the ruler of this world (Jn 14: 30) may have been in temporary occupation, the **authority** and the **splendor** that he offered had already been promised to Messiah and were His for the

asking: *Ask of me, and I will make the nations your heritage, the ends of the earth your possession* (Ps. 2: 8). This promise must have been much in the mind of Jesus since the baptismal Voice had quoted the preceding words: 'You are my Son, whom I love' (Lk. 3: 21; cf. Ps. 2: 7). That which was God's to give, He would not accept from another. **8. Worship the Lord your God, and serve him only:** Quoted from Dt. 6: 13. No created being might demand or receive what belonged exclusively to God. AV includes the words, 'Get thee behind me, Satan', but these are omitted from the more recent versions because of lack of textual support in the MSS. It is not a question of whether Jesus actually uttered the words or not; we know from Mt. 4: 10 that He did. They are omitted from RV, RSV, etc., because the evidence that they formed part of Luke's original text is negligible. A later scribe inserted them to make the account harmonize with Mt.'s. **9. the highest point of the temple:** An interesting modern view says: 'Most probably at the S-E angle of the court of the Gentiles. This point overlooked the Kidron Valley some 100 yards below, and Josephus states that anyone standing there would become dizzy. Thus the words of Satan are particularly relevant: cast Thyself down, for it is written: "He will give His angels charge concerning Thee; they will hold Thee on their hands, for fear that Thy foot shall be crushed against a stone"' (A. Parrot, *The Temple of Jerusalem*, ET, 1957, p. 86). But this view involves difficulties: the only point of throwing Himself down would be to gain adherents, which He would not do by throwing Himself down *outside* the Temple area.

9–11. In his third attack, Satan not only returned to the taunt **if you are the Son of God** (cf. v. 3); but reinforced his suggestion also by an OT allusion (to Ps. 91: 11–12). But it is noticeable that he omits frrom his quotation the words 'in all your ways', thus changing a general rule of life to one particular expediency, and that quite clearly contrary to God's will. **12.** Again our Lord's reply is from Dt., here 6: 16. It is striking that all three of His replies to the tempter should be drawn from a context so much concerned with Israel's being tested by God (Dt. 8: 2) and putting God to the test (Dt. 6: 16) in the wilderness. The Father's acknowledgment of Him as His Son was sufficient for this true Israelite: He would not **put God to the test** by compelling Him to show by a miracle that He meant what He said.

IV. THE RETURN TO GALILEE (4: 14–8: 56)

The account of the Galilean ministry in general follows the framework of Mk, though there are a few non-Marcan passages. The following table shows how the two accounts compare with each other:

Luke	Mark, and other material
4: 14–30	Mk 6: 1–6a—omits the details of the synagogue service, and puts the rejection at Nazareth later than does Luke.
4: 31–6: 19	Mk 1: 21–3: 19—but Mk omits Luke's story of the miraculous draught of fish (Lk. 5: 1–11).
6: 20–49	Not in Mk, but in greater length in Mt.—the 'Sermon on the Mount'.
7: 1–8: 3	Not in Mk, but part in Mt. 8 and 11.
8: 4–18	Mk 4: 1–25.
8: 19–56	Mk 3: 31–35; 4: 35–5: 43.

In short, the contents of Lk. 4: 14–8: 56 fall into four parts:

Non-Marcan—(a) 4: 14–30. (c) 6: 20–8: 3.
Mainly Marcan—(b) 4: 31–6: 19. (d) 8: 4–56.

Luke omits a lengthy passage from Mk after the Feeding of the Five Thousand (Mk 6: 45–8: 26), so the third Gospel does not include the walking on the water, the very important anti-Pharisee 'defilement' passage of Mk 7: 1–23, nor the story of the Syro-Phoenician woman. Scholars have discussed the omission at great length. Some have seen reasons why Luke should prefer not to include some or all of the passages; others (more improbably, perhaps) have thought that Luke's source was a mutilated copy of Mk from which this part was lacking. If, on the other hand, Streeter's view that the material from Mark was added to Proto-Luke (see article on The Four-fold Gospel, p. 98) is correct, Luke will have know how much of Mk he could use and still permit his gospel to fit into a standard papyrus roll.

i. The Arrival in Galilee (4: 14–15)

See notes on Mk 1: 14–15 *ad loc.*

ii. The Synagogue at Nazareth (4: 16–30)

Jesus comes to Nazareth and on the Sabbath attends the synagogue worship. In accordance with custom he is invited to read and comment on the day's lection from the Prophets. He announces that the Messianic promise has now become present fulfilment; it is clear that His hearers are deeply impressed. But when He goes on to say that the Gentiles are to share in the blessing, as they in fact did even in OT times, mob violence broke out and a unsuccessful attempt was made to murder Him.

This episode, since the time of Augustine, has been assumed to be the same as that recorded in Mk 6: 1–6/Mt. 13: 53–58. If this be so the question is asked, why did Luke put it at a different stage of the record from the other Synoptists? The whole problem is very carefully discussed by N. B. Stonehouse, *The Witness of Luke to Christ*, pp. 70–76, to which the student is referred. Suffice it here to point out that Luke does not suggest that this incident was the inauguration of the Galilee ministry; on the contrary he mentions (v. 23) that news has already come to Nazareth of what He had done at Capernaum. Stonehouse's summing-up is that 'the activity in Nazareth and in Capernaum are presented as *illustrative* of the preaching and healing ministry of Jesus as a whole'. Geldenhuys (p. 170) comments: 'Because it fits in so well with Luke's scheme, he placed it first, without pretending that it was also chronologically first'.

The scene in the synagogue: An interesting account of the synagogue and its worship is given in Edersheim, *The Life and Times of Jesus the Messiah*, i, pp. 430–450. After an introductory liturgy comprising a series of prayers and 'blessings' (eulogies), there followed a number of set readings from the OT according to a regular lectionary. Readers were designated for the various portions; if there were present a visiting Rabbi or person of distinction, courtesy required that he should be invited to read, perhaps from the *Haphtarah*, the reading from the Prophets, and to give a discourse traditionally ending at times with some reference to the Messianic hopes of Israel.

The Sermon in the Synagogue and its effect: The scene recorded in the Nazareth synagogue follows this pattern. Jesus had been brought up in the town (16) and was already being spoken of as a preacher in Capernaum (23). He was accordingly asked to read the *Haphtarah*. He turned to the opening verses of Isa. 61.

Expounding the passage, He proclaimed that the Messianic prophecy therein was even now being visibly fulfilled. His hearers were deeply impressed, and it seems not unfavourably; they **were amazed at the gracious words that came from his lips** (22), though there is a note also of incredulous astonishment: **'Isn't this Joseph's son?'** (22). But His discourse developed in a way which they did not foresee; when they heard it they were resentful. He said that if they could not believe He was a prophet it was because **no prophet is accepted in his hometown** (24), and that was why Elijah and Elisha had performed miracles for aliens, though many Jews of the day no doubt had the same needs as Naaman and the woman of Zarephath (25 ff.).

This turn of the message aroused their wrath; One whom they were prepared to listen to as their own equal was making out lepers and Gentiles as superior to them. In their fury the congregation tried to execute summary justice by lynch law. Jesus barely escaped with His life. Anyone else would probably have been killed then and there by this fierce and angry mob. But His hour was not yet come. . . . One day He won't "pass through the midst of them" any more. The angry crowds will press in upon Him to do Him to death' (Moorman, *The Path to Glory*, 1960, p. 47).

20. the attendant: Or chazzan, 'a sort of verger in the Jewish synagogue', who had custody of the sacred books' (*NBD*). He also acted as schoolmaster to the younger children, and during actual worship had the responsibility of seeing that the scrolls were ready at the correct place for the readings. **22. gracious words:** Literally 'words of grace', as RV; not words of favour or mercy so much, but suggestive rather of an attractive and beautiful personality. **23. this proverb:** So also AV; RV has 'parable', Gk. *parabolē*, from a verb meaning to put things side by side, a comparison. In the NT it is used both for a short descriptive story or, as in this case, a simple proverb that 'enlightens the hearer by presenting him with interesting illustrations, from which he can draw out for himself moral and religious truth' (*NBD*). **what we have heard that you did:** The allusion is clearly to miracles, of which reports were circulating. The Gospel miracles are regarded not merely as the compassionate acts of the Great Physician, but as the visible signs that the messianic age has dawned. The kingdom of God is not just a reformed moral order realized by human co-operation but a divine intervention. In the OT prophets, signs and miracles are to accompany the coming of the kingdom (*e.g.* Isa. 35: 5–6; Mal. 4: 2, etc.). 'The healing ministry of Jesus as well as the preaching of the kingdom of God', says A. Richardson, discussing this passage, 'is here set forth as the manifestation of the activity of the Spirit, which was to take place at the fulfilment of the time, in the acceptable year of the Lord' (*The Miracle-Stories of the Gospels*, 1941, p. 40). **25, 26.** For **Elijah** and the **widow** of **Zarephath** see 1 Kg. 17: 9 ff. **27.** For the cleansing of **Naaman the Syrian** from leprosy **in the time of the prophet Elisha** see 2 Kg. 5. **30. he . . . went on his way:** None of the Gospels records any subsequent visit by our Lord to Nazareth.

iii. A Day of Work (4: 31–41)

After the account of the scene at Nazareth, Luke, following Mk's framework, records our Lord's activity on one Sabbath day at Capernaum, which He appears now to have made His headquarters. In one single Sabbath He teaches in the synagogue, heals a demon-possessed man there, visits Peter's home and cures his mother-in-law, and then after sunset, the Sabbath being over and men entitled to rest after the worship and the necessary labours of the day, He devotes Himself to the healing of the sick and the demon-possessed of the neighbourhood. If His activity be such on the day of rest and even during the hours of rest, what will He not accomplish on a normal 'working' day?

Mk, who omits the Nazareth incident (though there is a possible reference to it later, Mk 6: 1–6), begins his account of the ministry with a series of five incidents where Jesus makes claims to authority which must bring down upon Him the wrath of the vested religious interests; not surprisingly these five stories are followed by five 'conflict' stories, where His authority is challenged. Mark's 'authority' stories are:

(*a*) 1: 16–20 *Discipleship*: Jesus claims authority to call men to give up their ordinary work to follow Him.

(*b*) 1: 21–22 *Teaching*: He teaches with His authority, not—like the scribes—with an authority derived from precedent. 'We see the final outcome of this servile secondhandedness in the dreary minutiae of the Talmud' (F. W. Farrar, *Luke, CBSC*, p. 107).

(*c*) 1: 23–28 *Unclean Spirits*: He uses the authority to exorcize demons.

(*d*) 1: 29–34 *Disease*: He exercises His authority over sickness and disease, both individual (Peter's mother-in-law) and the general healings after sunset.

(*e*) 1: 39–45 *Leprosy*: He reveals that His authority extends even to the dreaded leprosy, the seemingly incurable scourge of His day.

Luke omits the first of these episodes, presumably because he is going to deal with the call of the disciples more fully in connection with his story, unrecorded by Mk, of the miraculous draught of fishes (5: 1–11), but the others he relates in terms so similar to Mk's that it seems clear that here Mk was his source. Accordingly, the reader is referred to the notes on Mk 1 for more detailed commentary. The fifth of Mk's stories is found in Lk. 5; those in the present chapter are:

Teaching in the synagogue: Lk. 4: 31–32; Mk 1: 21–22.

Healing in the synagogue: Lk. 4: 33–37; Mk 1: 23–27.

Peter's mother-in-law: Lk. 4: 38–39; Mk 1: 29–31.

General healings after sunset: Lk. 4: 40–41; Mk 1: 32–34.

iv. Travelling and Preaching (4: 42–44)

A brief note tells us that despite an appeal from the inhabitants of Capernaum to stay (how different from the attitude of the people of Nazareth!) Jesus moves further afield and preaches in the synagogues of other towns. See notes on Mk 1: 35–38.

42. An interesting example of the impossibility of fitting the Gospels into schematic pigeonholes! Luke, as has been already mentioned in the introductory notes, gives us more glimpses of the praying Christ than any of the others, yet here he omits Mk's emphatic point that He went to the wilderness to pray. **44. the synagogues of Judea:** The best MS evidence supports this reading, so also RVmg. But AV and RV following the *textus receptus* read 'of Galilee' which on the surface seems more reasonable. This looks like the attempt of a scribe to correct what he thought an error in what he was copying. In fact, 'Judea' was often used to mean the land of the Jews in a general way, and not merely the province of the name.

v. Miracles and Discourses (5: 1–6: 11)
The outstanding feature of this section is the growing hostility of the Pharisees, consequent upon Jesus' forthright assertions and the success attending His preaching. His authority over nature itself, seen in the miraculous draught of fish, seems to be the final factor that brings Simon and the sons of Zebedee to discipleship; the news of the healing of a leper brings great crowds to hear Him and to be healed. It is at this point that **Pharisees and teachers of the law** appear from **every village of Galilee and from Judea and Jerusalem** (5: 17), apparently to find out exactly what is going on. They find plenty of which to complain: He actually declares a man's sins forgiven, He consorts with tax-gatherers and harlots, He does not enjoin fasting upon His disciples nor does He rebuke them for plucking ears of corn on the Sabbath. He even Himself heals on the Sabbath. All these things constitute offences against the edifice of observances and regulations they have superimposed on the Law of God.

(*a*) **The miraculous draught of fish (5: 1–11)**
This story, as has already been noted, replaces Mark's simple account of the call of the disciples. It is quite clear that Simon was already a friend of Jesus, who visited his home (4: 38) and preached from his boat (5: 3); in fact Jn 1: 37–42 tells of a meeting during the mission of the Baptist. The call to Simon is described in the Gospels in three successive stages: (i) the original meeting with Jesus (Jn 1: 41) where he received a new name: 'You shall be called Cephas (which means Peter)'; (ii) the call to forsake all and become a disciple (Mk 1: 16–18; Lk. 5: 11): **From now on you will catch men**; (iii) the call to apostleship (see below, on Lk. 6: 14).

1. the lake of Gennesaret: The Sea of Galilee (OT, Sea of Chinnereth, NT, Lake of Gennesaret or Sea of Tiberias). The small inland sea through which the Jordan passes in its northern reaches, a centre of the fishing industry in the first century, and surrounded in those times by an almost continuous series of villages and towns like Bethsaida and Capernaum. Today only Tiberias remains, and a few ruins marking the sites of some of the others. 'Changed patterns of commerce have robbed the lake of its focal importance in the life of the region' (*NBD*). **2, 3.** Peter, with the sons of Zebedee (10) were partners in a fishing business with two boats. Jesus sat in Peter's boat to teach the people. This is the first open-air preaching of our Lord that Luke records; hitherto He has preached in the synagogues. **4–7.** A very similar incident is described in Jn 21: 5–11; but the differences in detail are sufficiently noticeable to make it clear that there were two separate incidents. 'There is nothing improbable in two miracles of a similar kind, one granted to emphasize and illustrate the call, the other the recall, of the chief Apostle' (Plummer, p. 147). There is no need to see two differing traditions concerning the same incident. Here, Jesus is in the boat; in Jn He is on the shore; here He tells them to move out into deeper water, there they are simply to fish from the other side of the boat. In Luke's account the net was broken, in the fourth gospel we are specifically told the opposite. **8–10.** Like James and John, Peter was **astonished** at what had happened, but unlike them he was brought by the manifestation of divine power to an acute consciousness of his own unworthiness (cf. Isa. 6: 5; Job 40: 4; etc.). 'The story appears to presuppose a particular intensity in Peter's consciousness of sin' (O. Cullmann, *Peter*, ET, 1953, p. 68). **10. 'Do not be afraid, from now on you will catch men':** Jesus speaks words of peace to the anguished Peter, words which re-echo Jer. 16: 16. **11. they . . . left everything and followed him:** To gather around oneself a band of disciples was the prerogative of the great rabbis; this claim to authority to do the same must have further incensed the Pharisees.

(*b*) **A leper healed (5: 12–16)**
The last of the series of 'authority' stories: Jesus not only claims but exercises authority over the dreaded leprosy, to men of His day as widely-feared as is cancer in ours. See notes on Mk 1: 40–45 *ad loc.* Luke's account follows Mk's, but is briefer. Both tell how Jesus commanded the healed man to carry out the requirements of the Levitical law (esp. Lev. 13) reporting to the priest for a certificate of cleansing; but even this care to comply with the law did not lessen, in the eyes of our Lord's opponents, the enormity of His offence on the occasions when He healed on the Sabbath.

(*c*) **Stories of conflict (5: 17–6: 11)**
Luke, drawing on Mk, now records five episodes in each of which the Pharisees and scribes react violently to His claims:
(*i*) **Concerning the forgiveness of sins** (5: 17–26; cf. Mk 2: 1–12). Four men bring a paralytic friend for healing and, finding it impossible to get near to Jesus otherwise, they let him down through the roof. Recognizing the sick man's spiritual malaise as his most urgent problem, Jesus assures him of forgiveness, only to be accused of blasphemy for so doing. Luke makes two interesting changes of vocabulary: Mk uses the ordinary word for roof (Gk. *stegē*,

from a verb meaning 'to cover'), Luke speaks of **tiles**, Gr. *keramos*, cognate with the word for a potter. Some see here a contradiction, but no doubt both words are used in a general sense for the roof. Then for the bed, Mk uses a word meaning a truckle bed usually of wickerwork or light wood carried by beggars, Luke's word simply implies something on which one lies down. Apart from these two words there is little difference between the Lucan account and the Marcan. In v. 24, Luke for the first time refers to Jesus as **Son of Man**.

(*ii*) **Concerning social conventions** (5: 27–32; cf. Mk 2: 13–17). Jesus, having called Levi (=Matthew, see Mt. 9: 9) to be a disciple, accepted an invitation His new follower gave for his former colleagues. To the Pharisees' strictures concerning the company He kept He replies that as **a doctor** sought the sick for his ministrations, so His place was with the sinners He had come to save, despite artificial conventions.

(*iii*) **Concerning fasting** (5: 33–39; cf. Mk 2: 18–22). Fasting, Jesus taught when challenged as to why His disciples did not fast, had its place, but not at the wedding breakfast when the bridegroom was present. Mt. (9: 14–17) and Mk follow this saying with two short parables, the patched garment and the new wine in old wineskins; Luke also adds a third: **no one after drinking old wine wants new, for he says, 'The old is better'** (5: 39).

(*iv*) **Concerning the Law** (6: 1–5; cf. Mk 2: 23–28). Walking through a field on the Sabbath, the disciples pluck and eat ears of corn. To the objections of the Pharisees Jesus replies by quoting an OT case where the letter of the law had yielded place to the spirit of the law in an urgent necessity (1 Sam. 21: 1–6), and by asserting His own claim as Lord of the Sabbath to interpret its law afresh without reference to Talmudic tradition.

(*v*) **Concerning the Sabbath** (6: 6–11; cf. Mk 3: 1–6). In the story of the man with a withered hand Jesus shows again how the law of love must override ritual observances like the Sabbath, as indeed His opponents would override the law if it were a matter of saving a beast belonging to themselves.

Verse 11 summarizes the result of this series of conflicts: **They were furious and began to discuss with one another what they might do to Jesus.**

For fuller comment on this section (5: 17–6: 11) see notes on Mk 2: 1–3: 6 *ad loc.*

vi. The Appointment of the Twelve (6: 12–16)

Events are now quite definitely leading to action by the scribes and Pharisees, and Jesus must now prepare His followers to continue His work when He is no longer with them. So from among those who have followed Him as disciples He selects and commissions twelve for the greater responsibility of apostleship. Mark gives at fuller length an account of Jesus' purpose in choosing this inner circle from among the number of His followers; Luke omits this, but characteristically prefaces a note that He spent a whole night in prayer before taking the step and making the choice.

13. apostles: From a Greek verb meaning 'to send'. Cf. the English word 'missionary', from a Latin verb with the same meaning. Apostles are men who are sent forth, i.e. commissioned for a particular errand. **14–16.** The list is interesting especially when compared with those given in Mk 3: 16–19; Mt. 10: 2–4; Ac. 1: 13. The order of the names differs slightly in the four lists, but each divides into three quartets, each beginning in all the lists with the same name. The names are:

(*a*) Peter, with Andrew, James and John.

(*b*) Philip, with Thomas, Bartholomew and Matthew.

(*c*) James the son of Alphaeus, with Simon the Zealot, Judas the brother of James, and Judas Iscariot (who is last in all the lists). **16. Judas son** (RSVmg, 'brother') **of James** (cf. 'Judas not Iscariot' in Jn 14: 22) does not appear in Mt. or Mk; but Thaddaeus (Mk and Mt.) is usually presumed to be the same person. For an interesting study of what information we have on the Twelve, see Wm. Barclay, *The Master's Men* (1959).

vii. The Great Sermon (6: 17–49; cf. Mt. 5–7)

Having come down from the upland retreat where the Twelve have been chosen, Jesus is met in the plain by the customary large concourse of people, come from quite distant places, awaiting healing and relief. Again He graciously restores sick bodies and exorcizes evil spirits, and then expounds the laws of His kingdom, addressing primarily His disciples (6: 20; though 6: 17 ff. suggests that the crowds are still present). In Mt. 5: 1 the audience seems to be just the disciples up till 7: 12.

The relation between the Sermon on the Mount recorded in Mt. 5–7 and the 'Sermon on the Plain' given here has frequently occupied the attention of students. The similarities are clear enough to show that a common tradition lies behind the two accounts, yet there are significant differences which constitute a problem. Matthew's version is much fuller than Luke's, and there are considerable divergences also in actual detail. It is not, of course, impossible or even improbable that our Lord gave the Sermon to different audiences on different occasions, and that we have here independent accounts of two such discourses.

20–26. Both versions begin with a series of utterances, usually called the Beatitudes, definitions of true blessedness, which form as it were the text which the rest of the Sermon expounds. Matthew has a series of nine; of these Luke selects only the first, fourth, second and ninth; but adds to them four antithetical woes, which recall the prophetic language of the OT. Furthermore, whereas all Matthew's Beatitudes except the last are in the third person, Luke's are in the second.

27–1. The law of love, paralleled in Mt. 5: 44, 39, 40 and 42; and finishing with what is often called the 'Golden Rule' (31; cf. Mt. 7: 12).

32–36. The sayings of Mt. 5: 44–48, in a slightly different order.

37–38. An expanded form of Mt. 7: 1–2, a saying on the theme that whatsoever a man sows, the same shall he also reap. Luke adds a description of the reaping, suggesting in varying terms that it will be abundant.

39–49. A short collection of parables rounds off Luke's version as well as Matthew's. They are introduced by two sayings found also in Mt., but in different contexts. The relation between the two versions is as follows:

Lk. 6: 39. The blind led by the blind into a pit. Mt. 15: 14.

Lk. 6: 40. The disciple and his master. Mt. 10: 24–25.

Lk. 6: 41–42. The speck and the log (mote and beam). Mt. 7: 3–5.

Lk. 6: 43–45. Trees and their fruit. Mt. 7: 16–20; also 12: 33–35.

Lk. 6: 46–49. The two houses. Mt. 7: 21–27.

viii. Various Incidents (7: 1–8: 3)

The section 7: 1–8: 3 records four incidents not related by Mark; the healing of the centurion's servant, the raising of the widow's son, the answer to John the Baptist's perplexities and the anointing of Jesus. G. B. Caird gives them the felicitous titles of 'Love in action—the Gentile; the widow; the prisoner; the penitent'. The first and the third are found also in Mt., and so presumably came from Q; the second and fourth appear nowhere but in Luke.

(*a*) **The Centurion's servant (7: 1–10)** A centurion sends a message by a number of responsible Jews, asking Jesus to come and heal his slave. The Jews speak highly of this Gentile and his generosity towards them; Jesus sets out to accede to his request. On the way He is met by a second deputation who bring the suggestion that He need not even visit the house; a word from Him, the centurion believes, will effect the desired cure even at a distance. The centurion expresses his consciousness of his unworthiness to trouble the Lord, for he knows his place as a Gentile, and has a keen sense of hierarchical propriety and of discipline. Jesus not only speaks the word of healing, but highly commends the petitioner also: **I have not found such great faith even in Israel** (9).

This is the only narrative, absent from Mk, that Mt. and Luke have in common; the rest of the Q material contains exclusively teaching. In this incident, the dialogue in the two versions is practically identical, while the two narratives differ considerably, indicating it is suggested, that the Q version contained dialogue only.

The miracle has several features in common with the healing of the Syro-Phoenician woman's daughter (Mk 7: 24–30; Mt. 15: 21–28) which Luke does not record. In both the petitioner is a Gentile, parent or guardian of the patient, in both cases an apt saying procures a cure in the absence of the patient.

2. a centurion: A senior non-commissioned officer, probably in the forces of Herod Antipas. **a . . . servant, whom his master valued highly:** In Mt. 8: 5–13 the patient is called *pais*, which, like the English *boy*, could indicate a slave or a son. In Luke he is a slave, though in v. 7 he is again *pais*. John has a similar story, where the lad is **son** (Jn 4: 46) without qualification. The expression **valued highly** means 'precious', either beloved like a son, or 'valuable' (RSVmg) like a slave. The evidence is not conclusive, but whether son or slave the picture is of one to whom the centurion was completely devoted. **5. he loves our nation, and has built our synagogue:** Attempts have been made to identify this synagogue with that at Tell-Hum, the reputed site of Capernaum. Much archaeological work has been done on the site over the last hundred years, and the results have been fully described, *e.g.*, in the first of E. L. Sukenik's 1930 Schweich Lectures, *Ancient Synagogues in Palestine and Greece* (1934). Though it cannot be said with certainty that this particular synagogue was erected sufficiently early to be the one provided by the centurion, E. M. Blaiklock says, 'the synagogue excavated there [i.e., at Tell-Hum] by the Germans in 1905 [is] probably the meeting place mentioned by Luke' (*Out of the Earth*, 1957, p. 20). The more general view, however, is that it belongs to the second century, although it may well have been built on the site of the synagogue known to our Lord.

(*b*) **The Widow's Son (7: 11–17)**

Going on to Nain followed by a great crowd, our Lord is met at the gates of the town by a funeral procession. The grief of the widowed mother of the young man who had died arouses His compassion, as it has clearly awakened that of many of the townsfolk. He stops the procession and restores the son to her who mourns him. He is saluted as a great prophet: **God has come to help his people!**

This is one of three miracles of resurrection effected by Jesus in the Gospels, the others being the raising of Jairus's daughter and that of Lazarus. It is remarkable that in works where the miraculous is so important an element the number of resurrections should be so small; this restraint is surely a very telling testimony to the reliability of the record. Raising the dead to life was one of the Messianic signs to which our Lord drew attention as having been accomplished (7: 22).

The story naturally recalls the restoration of sons to their mothers by Elijah (1 Kg. 17) and Elisha (2 Kg. 4). Indeed the language in which the story is told is in places actually quoted from the OT (*e.g.*, v. 15; cf. 1 Kg. 17: 23). When the people acclaimed Jesus as **a great prophet** (16), they no doubt meant that here was a new Elijah. W. R. F. Browning (p. 84) says: 'Jesus, meeting the cortege, is moved with compassion. There is no mention here of faith, but the incident recalls similar miracles recorded in the OT of Elisha and Elijah. Nain, in fact, was near the scene of one of them (Shunem)'.

13. Luke for the first time in his narrative speaks of Jesus as **the Lord**, particularly fitting in this context where He exercises power over death itself.

(c) The enquiry of John the Baptist (7: 18–35)

John the Baptist from the prison where he is incarcerated sends messengers to ask Jesus outright a question which perplexes him: is Jesus indeed the Messiah? In reply, Jesus makes no actual assertion but points to His miracles, which are Messianic signs foretold in the OT; He goes on to pay tribute to the greatness of John.

29–30. These two verses do not occur in Mt. at this point, though the sentiment they express is paralleled in Mt. 21: 31. In NIV, though not in AV or RV, they are placed in parenthesis. **All the people, even the tax collectors, when they heard Jesus' words, acknowledged that God's way was right. the Pharisees and experts in the law rejected God's purpose:** They 'frustrated' (AVmg) God's purpose. These contrasted attitudes are linked by Luke with John's baptism; in 3: 12 he records the concern and baptism of the tax collectors, but he makes no mention of Pharisees. Cf. Mt. 3: 7. For commentary on this very important section, see notes on Mt. 11: 2–19.

(d) The anointing of Jesus (7: 36–50)

Jesus accepts the invitation of one Simon, a Pharisee, to a meal, during which a woman of the streets comes in and demonstrates her gratitude to Jesus by wetting His feet with her tears and wiping them with her hair, and anointing them with the ointment from a costly flask she has brought. His host is rather surprised that Jesus should tolerate this show of emotion from so tainted a source; Jesus, by means of a parable concerning two debtors, shows that in the depths of her love and devo-

tion she has shown herself considerably superior to Simon.

Attempts have often been made to identify this incident with the anointing by Mary of Bethany during the Passion week (Mt. 26: 6; Mk 14: 3; Jn 12: 3), but it is difficult to see in this unnamed penitent the Mary with whose character Luke was in fact well acquainted (Lk. 10: 39, 42). It seems quite clear that there are indeed two such incidents; there are many differences between the story of Luke on the one hand, and the other three Gospels on the other. Balmforth sets them out thus (*Clarendon Bible*, p. 173);

	Luke	Mark/Matthew	John
Person	a sinner	a woman	Mary of Bethany
Place	Capernaum (?) at the house of Simon the Pharisee	Bethany, at the house of Simon the Leper	Bethany, apparently at Lazarus' house
Time	during the Galilean ministry	Holy week	six days before the Passover
Objection	not a real prophet	waste of money	waste of money
Made by	Simon	some of those present	Judas Iscariot

It will be seen that the accounts of Matthew/Mark and of John agree in many details against Luke. In fact, the only important point where one of the others sides with Luke is in the name of the host; Luke and Matthew/Mark call him **Simon**. But Simon was such a very common name that nothing can really be made out of its double appearance here.

37. a woman who had lived a sinful life in that town: She is unnamed, either because of the tactful delicacy of Luke, or simply because he did not know her name. **39.** Simon is the typical Pharisee, absolutely sure what the Law demands of him, and completely incapable of discerning that there are circumstances where the law of love—'Thou shalt love thy neighbour as thyself'—transcends the minutiae of prescribed observances and regulations. So he attributes Jesus' failure to denounce the woman for what she is to a defect in His spiritual insight. The important point of the parable of the two debtors is that the woman's action does not earn forgiveness for her; it is rather the spontaneous devotion of one who is conscious of being forgiven already (47). As Geldenhuys (p. 236) says, the parable teaches that 'remission of debt produces great love, and not *vice versa*'.

(e) Another preaching tour (8: 1–3)

From now onward, Jesus is constantly on the move, preaching the gospel of the kingdom from village to village and from town to town.

He is accompanied not only by the Twelve but also by a small group of women who show their gratitude for blessings received through Him by putting their means at His disposal for Him and His followers.

2. Mary called Magdalene: Mentioned again among the band of faithful women who stayed near Jesus to the end, and were found at His tomb on the first Easter morning; cf. Mk 15: 40, 47; 16: 1; Lk. 24: 10; Mt. 27: 56, 61; 28: 1. **3. Joanna** is mentioned also in Lk. 24: 10, but nowhere else; **Susanna** not at all. Guesses have been made as to the identity of **Cuza**, but they remain guesses; what is interesting is that Luke had some information regarding Herod's court (cf. also Manaen, Ac. 13: 1).

ix. Parables (8: 4–18)
The preaching tour begins with a new kind of teaching—teaching by parables. A great crowd of people gather together and He instructs them in spiritual truth by comparisons with familiar everyday things, like the sower putting down his seed, and the ordinary household lamp. The picture of the sower makes its impression on all who hear it, but Jesus takes aside His disciples in order to explain to them its spiritual import.

It is true that Jesus had spoken in parables before this, but there are at least two points which mark a difference. First, the parable now becomes the main vehicle of instruction. The succeeding chapters of this Gospel contain the great parables which are the most characteristic and the most familiar feature of our Lord's teaching. Secondly, parables are found in various forms, ranging from the simplest of comparisons, short similitudes and even proverbs, to the full length narrative parable. Hitherto in Luke, the former have predominated, from now on it is the great parable stories that are given.

5–8. The parable of the sower. Luke's version is briefer than that of the other synoptics; for example, he omits the circumstance, recorded by both Matthew and Mark, that it was delivered from a boat to an audience on the shore. The parable itself also is shortened; *e.g.*, the rocky ground of Mt./Mk becomes **rock**, an expression that does not, of course, preclude the idea of some covering of earth for the seed to germinate. Matthew collects together with this parable a series of others all dealing with the kingdom of heaven; for notes on these parables of the kingdom, see commentary on Mt. 13. For commentary on the parable of the sower, see notes on Mk 4: 1–9.

9–15. The use of parables; The meaning of the parable of the sower. Matthew and Mark tell us that the disciples asked a question about parables in general ('The disciples came and said to him, why do you speak to them in parables?' Mt. 13: 10; 'asked him concerning the parables', Mk 4: 10). Luke, on the other hand, says that they **asked him what this parable meant** (9). Jesus replied to both questions; first concerning the purpose of parabolic teaching, He linked His answer with Isa. 6: 9–10. Matthew gives this answer, which is far from easy to understand, at considerable length (Mt. 13: 10–15); Mark abbreviates it fairly drastically (Mk 4: 10–12); Luke even more so. Secondly, Jesus went on to explain the meaning of the parable of the sower. The three synoptics all report the explanation, and their versions differ little from each other. It is sometimes suggested that because (among other things) the explanation is somewhat allegorical in method it must come from the early Church rather than from Jesus itself. But while agreeing that the teaching of most of the parables is found in the story as a whole rather than in its details taken one by one, there are a few parables, like the wicked husbandmen in the vineyard (Lk. 20: 9–18) for instance, that clearly are allegorical. The sower seems just such a parable.

16–18. The parable of the lamp. A short similitude which Matthew places in the Sermon on the Mount (Mt. 5: 15) and which Luke himself repeats in 11: 33. The verses which follow the similitude are also repeated elsewhere by Luke; cf. 8: 17 with 12: 2, and 8: 18 with 19: 26. The light shines, and it is the Church's responsibility not to let it be hidden (16), but there is a responsibility also on the hearer as to how he hears (18).

x. The Protest of the Family (8: 19–21)
As the fame of Jesus grows, stories circulate concerning Him which give His relations the impression that He has become mentally unbalanced, and so they visit Him in the hope of persuading Him to return home. But He refuses to submit even to the dearest of earthly bonds, and speaks of the much greater circle of those who are His kinsfolk by faith and obedience. See notes on Mk 3: 31–35.

NOTE: The question of the identity of **Jesus' brothers** (19, 20) is often raised. Who were they? Roman Catholic theologians, in their desire to safeguard the (non-scriptural) doctrine of Mary's perpetual virginity, regard them either as offspring of a former marriage of Joseph, or as cousins of Jesus. But there seems to be no reason for not taking the words in their natural sense, as did Tertullian, and assuming that they were subsequently-born children of Joseph and Mary.

xi. Miracles (8: 22–56)
For detailed commentary on this section, see notes on Mk 4: 35–5: 43.

The next events that Luke records are four outstanding miracles: The stilling of the storm (22–25), the deliverance of the demoniac and the destruction of the swine (26–39), the raising of Jairus's daughter (40–42, 49–56) and the healing of the woman with a flow of blood (43–48).

The Lord and His disciples get into a boat to cross the sea of Galilee, and for the first and only time in the Gospels we see Jesus asleep. Exhausted by His labours, His sleep is too deep to be disturbed by a tremendous tempest which breaks out. The terrified disciples awaken Him, and to their amazement the storm is stilled at His word of command.

Arriving on the other shore in the **region of the Gerasenes**, Jesus has no sooner disembarked than He is met by the strange figure, naked and dishevelled, of a demoniac who lives among the tombs. The indwelling demon is exorcized and allowed by Jesus to go and possess a herd of grazing pigs, which immediately stampede into the sea. The herdmen see the wonderful sight of the demoniac now **dressed and in his right mind** but, partly through terror and partly because of loss of gain from their pigs, implore Jesus to go elsewhere. The cured man desires to follow Jesus as a disciple, but he is told that he can do a much more valuable service by remaining to testify in his own town.

The ungracious welcome to Jesus and unceremonious hustling out contrast strongly with the welcome He receives when He returns whence He came. Here another suppliant meets Him, not the patient this time, for she is but a young girl of twelve, but her father, Jairus, a ruler of the synagogue. He entreats Jesus to come and heal the child.

The Lord, however, interrupts His journey to the house of Jairus to heal a woman, twelve years a victim of haemorrhages, who has struggled through the crowd to touch the fringe of His robe, believing that she will thereby be healed.

The result of this delay is the arrival of fresh messengers from Jairus saying that the child is now dead. Jesus nevertheless continues on His journey, and finds the house of Jairus in the possession of the professional mourners, but since 'He does not desire to make a theatrical, spectacular business of the raising of the dead' (Geldenhuys, p. 262), He excludes all but the little girl's parents and His three own most intimate disciples, and entering the death chamber with them, He performs a second miracle of resurrection, restoring the daughter to her astonished parents.

V. A THIRD TOUR (9: 1–50)

The ministry of our Lord is now approaching one of its great crises. Mark's narrative, which hitherto Luke has followed fairly faithfully, seems to fall into two portions, the first telling of the Son of man who 'did not come to be served but to serve' (Mk 10: 45a); the second telling of Him who came 'to give His life as a ransom for many' (Mk 10: 45b). So we have already seen how Jesus' claims to authority (chaps. 4–5) led to direct conflict with the Jews (chaps. 5–6); and how He prepared against His departure by appointing and training apostles (chap. 6) and by teaching the people in parables not easy to be forgotten (chap. 8).

Throughout the time He had been with them Jesus had been teaching His followers. Now Peter arrives at the point to which He has been leading them, and in a God-given moment of insight he realizes that Jesus is the Messiah. From now on the teaching becomes more sombre in tone, for they must learn what kind of Messiah He is to be, namely a suffering Messiah like the Servant of Jehovah in Isaiah chaps. 42–53, '*a man of sorrows and acquainted with grief*'. So from the moment of Peter's confession at Caesarea Philippi, Jesus began to impress upon the disciples what lay ahead of Him (v. 22). (For a different viewpoint on the Lord's challenge and Peter's confession, see notes on Mk 8: 27–30.)

The material in this section is for the most part paralleled in Mk, which was probably Luke's source. Apart from Peter's confession three important events are recorded, all bearing directly on 'the sufferings of Christ and the glories that would follow' (1 Pet. 1: 11):

(*a*) He mentions the death of John the Baptist. If the forerunner must die, this points to Him who must follow the same path.

(*b*) The feeding of the five thousand would remind the reader not only of manna in the wilderness, but also of the promised Messianic banquet to which He looked ahead.

(*c*) The Transfiguration links together the glory of the transfigured Christ and the Exodus which He must accomplish.

i. The Tour of the Twelve (9: 1–6, 10)

Jesus sends out the Twelve on a preaching tour. Mark's version is similar (6: 7–13); Mt. 10: 5–42 is longer and includes some material that Luke puts in the charge to the Seventy (see notes on Lk. 10: 1–20) and some from elsewhere. (See notes on Mt. 10: 5–42.)

ii. The death of John (9: 7–9)

The three Synoptics mention the death of John the Baptist at this point without committing themselves as to exactly when it occurred. Mt. and Mk describe the event at length, the Third Gospel merely mentions it, though its account of the Baptism is followed by a note (3: 19–20) that Herod had imprisoned John. (For detailed comment, see notes on Mk 6: 14–29.)

iii. The Feeding of the Five Thousand (9: 10–17)

This is the only miracle recorded in all four Gospels (Mk 6: 30–43; Mt. 14: 13–21; Jn 6: 1–13); Mk and Mt. have also a second miraculous feeding of four thousand (Mk 8: 1–10; Mt. 15: 32–39). Mark tells how Jesus takes the Twelve on their return to 'a quiet place' for a period of retreat (Mt. suggests that it followed receipt of news of John's death). But 'some rest' proves impossible, for crowds gather and, seeing the group sailing across the lake, hasten round the shore to meet them on their arrival on the further shore (a detail that Luke omits). So Jesus preaches to them, and when the day has worn on, challenges the disciples as to what they are going to do about feeding them. John tells how Andrew and Philip, who are local men, make enquiries and report the presence of a boy with five loaves and two small fishes. The Synoptics mention this total of available food, but not the lad. Such as it is, the Lord takes it, gives thanks, and having seen that the multitude are seated in orderly fashion, feeds them all miraculously from it, and enough is left over to fill the twelve baskets or hampers that the disciples, as pious Jews, carry in order that they shall not need to depend on the generosity of Gentiles. (For notes on details, see section on Mk 6: 30–44.)

iv. The Revelation of His Person and first prediction of suffering (9: 18–27)
The great confession of Peter at Caesarea Philippi that Jesus is indeed the long awaited Messiah is the watershed of the Gospel narrative; henceforward the shadow of the Cross dominates the whole story. Jesus has set His face to go to Jerusalem, there to suffer. Detailed notes will be found in the commentary on Mk 8: 27–38 and Mt. 16: 13–27. Luke makes several interesting contributions of his own. He omits Peter's rebuke to Jesus after the prediction of the Passion, and Jesus' reply. 'The omission is no doubt deliberate to avoid an incident which might seem to reflect unfavourably on the Apostle' (Creed, p. 130). He omits also the reference to Caesarea Philippi, but on the other hand he characteristically begins his account with Jesus at prayer (18).

v. The Transfiguration (9: 28–36)
The Transfiguration (see Mk 9: 2–8; Mt. 17: 1–8) is the natural sequel to the previous incident, with its prediction of suffering. God speaks His approval from heaven as He did when at His baptism Jesus deliberately embraced His mission with all He knew it would entail. It was not until Jesus had told the disciples what He was facing that they saw His true glory.

Some days after the confession He takes Peter, James and John up a mountain for prayer. His appearance is transfigured with glory, and two celestial visitors, Moses and Elijah, converse with Him concerning His coming sufferings. Peter wants to make the experience permanent by building three tabernacles, thus offering equal honours to Moses and Elijah and to Jesus. God from heaven proclaims the uniqueness of His Son. Then Moses and Elijah are no longer seen; Jesus alone remains.

28. he . . . went up onto a mountain: It was on a mountain that Moses had asked to see God's glory, and though this was not granted, his face so shone that he had to veil himself for the protection of the people (Exod. 33: 12–23; 34: 29–35). On a mountain also Elijah, who was to see God's glory without dying, saw the manifestation of His power (1 Kg. 18). **29. as he was praying:** A peculiarly Lucan touch! **31. his departure:** The Gk. word is our 'exodus'. Moses, who had led the people to deliverance from Egypt in the first Exodus, speaks with Him whose own Exodus will bring deliverance from sin. **34. a cloud appeared and enveloped them:** The overshadowing cloud is a familiar symbol of the divine Presence in the OT (cf. Exod. 40: 34; Lev. 16: 2; 2 Chr. 5: 13; etc.). **35.** To the message at the baptism quoted from Ps. 2: 7 and Isa. 42: 1 the voice adds a further clause, **listen to him** (Dt. 18: 15). **36. Jesus was alone:** The Law and the Prophets have served their turn and pass away; He who is the fulfilment of both alone remains.

vi. The Healing of the demoniac (9: 37–43)
The mountain top experience is followed as so often is the case by a devastating return to everyday things. Down in the valley once more they are faced by the spectacle of the helplessness of their brother disciples to exorcize a demon. See notes on Mk 9: 14–29.

vii. Second prediction of suffering: last ministry in Galilee (9: 44–50)
The closing verses of the first section of Luke's account of the ministry of Christ include:

44–45. The second prediction of suffering (Luke's version is very short, not specifically mentioning either the crucifixion or the resurrection).

46–48. Calling a child to His side, Jesus rebukes the disciples for their desire for pre-eminence. For a fuller account of the incident, see Mt. 18: 1–5.

49–50. A warning against the uncharitableness of exclusiveness. More detailed comment on this last section will be found in the notes on Mark's fuller version (Mk 9: 31–41).

VI. THE LATER JUDAEAN MINISTRY (9: 51–19: 27)
The long section 9: 51–18: 14 is, together with the first two chapters and the last, Luke's most distinctive contribution to the Gospel tradition. It appears on the surface to be simply the account of the last great journey that our Lord made, after the final stages of His Galilean ministry, to Jerusalem and His Passion. Various names have been suggested for the section, but B. H. Streeter (*The Four Gospels*, ch. viii)

said that most were unsatisfactory as taking something for granted. To call it the 'Peraean Section' overlooks the fact that part, at any rate, of the journey was west and not east of Jordan. The 'Travel Narrative' or the 'Travel Document' imply the existence of a document which Luke incorporated into his Gospel; of the existence of such a document no proof exists. Streeter himself proposes the 'Central Section', which begs no questions; others the 'Great Interpolation', seeing that it is interpolated whole into the Marcan framework. But whatever name be given to it, Reicke is not exaggerating when he calls it 'the central enigma of this Gospel' (*The Gospels Reconsidered*, ed. Aland, 1960, p. 107).

The question at issue is whether these chapters describe 'the great journey' from Galilee to Jerusalem as it actually took place, with the incidents recorded occurring just where Luke puts them; or whether on the other hand he uses the framework of the journey (which obviously must have taken place since the events of the last week in Jerusalem follow a ministry squarely placed in the north) as a convenient form for assembling various unrelated incidents and sayings.

It would be fair to say that the majority of academic critics favour the second view. 'The Lucan itinerary', says T. W. Manson, 'is difficult to follow . . . Whatever else Lk. 9: 51–18: 14 may be, it does not appear to be a chronicle' (*The Sayings of Jesus*, 1949, pp. 255 f.). The essay by Reicke already mentioned is probably the most recent serious examination of the question. He suggests that, finding in his sources only the briefest references to the transition from Galilee to Judaea (cf. Mk 10: 1; Mt. 19: 1), Luke filled what he considered a gap in his information with '(1) instruction of the apostles regarded (*a*) as leaders and teachers of the Christians, i.e. as ministers, and (*b*) as missionaries; and (2) discussion with adversaries and opponents' (p. 111).

N. B. Stonehouse, on the other hand, while admitting that there are difficulties, argues that the section gives an intelligible account of a journey that actually took place. Jerusalem, he says, is always in view; it is never lost sight of as the ultimate destination (*The Witness of Luke to Christ*, pp. 114 ff.). His case is well argued, and will repay careful study. Moreover, though Stonehouse represents a minority view, he is by no means alone; Plummer (pp. 60 f.), while not arguing the historicity of the journey, appears to assume it.

i. The Journey to Jerusalem via Samaria (9: 51–12: 59)
(a) Samaritan unfriendliness and would-be disciples (9: 51–62)
Our Lord's final resolve is made; the time has now arrived for the accomplishment of that for which He had become flesh. His disciples do not understand; they want to call down fire from heaven upon the unmannerly Samaritans who have refused them hospitality. Meanwhile, other would-be disciples seek to attach themselves to Him, but they show no awareness of the totalitarian claims that discipleship makes upon men.

One of the strangest features of the Gospel story is the frequent insensitiveness of the disciples, especially at times of crisis. In Mk 10: 32–36, for instance, our Lord's third and clearest prediction of His sufferings elicits from John and James merely jockeying for personal position in the kingdom. Here, as He sets out on the final stage of the pathway to the Cross, the disciples are concerned only with spectacular vengeance on the churlish Samaritans who had outraged their feelings. That this obtuseness should be recorded is an impressive testimony to the trustworthiness of the record—it would surely never have been invented.

The Samaritans were a particular thorn in the flesh to the Jews. They were descended from the miscellaneous tribes with whom Sargon II of Assyria and his successors repeopled Samaria after the fall of the Kingdom of Israel in 722–1 B.C. (2 Kg. 17: 24–34, see also F. F. Bruce, *Israel and the Nations*, 1963, p. 66) and as such were not really Jews by race. But they adopted Jewish forms of worship and read the Jewish Torah, and when, on their return from exile, the Jews refused Samaritan help in the rebuilding of the ruins, the animosity was much increased. The ill-feeling persisted, Jewish disdain for these pseudo-Jews calling forth Samaritan resentment, which is very visible in the NT narrative. In this incident, Samaritan rudeness roused the anger of the sons of thunder, who wanted to be allowed to return it with interest.

51. Jesus resolutely set out for Jerusalem: An echo perhaps of the third of the Servant Songs: '*therefore I have set my face like flint*' (Isa. 50: 7). **53.** The Samaritans refused Him hospitality because He was going to **Jerusalem** to perform His religious obligations, bypassing their shrine on Gerizim which they judged in no way inferior to Jerusalem itself. **54.** The text of Luke has come down in various slightly differing forms; in this passage the readings supported by the main weight of textual evidence are shorter than the *textus receptus* of which the AV is a translation. Here the longer text (AV, RVmg, RSVmg) associates the desire for vengeance with an incident in the life of Elijah (2 Kg. 1: 9 ff.). This reference is omitted in RV and RSV. **55, 56.** The shorter version (RV, RSV) omits the words: 'You do not know what manner of spirit you are of, for the Son of man came not to destroy men's lives but to save them'. Despite the textual uncertainty the meaning of the incident is quite clear: evil is overcome not with evil but with good.

57, 58. The first would-be disciple. a man (Mt. says 'a scribe') wanted to join Jesus, who made His reply about the birds and the foxes. T. W. Manson, dismissing the suggestion that the saying was simply a current proverb, refers it to contemporary conditions in Palestine. Birds in the Bible are often an apocalyptic symbol of the Gentile nations (Dan. 4: 12; Mt. 13: 32; etc.); foxes in Jewish literature are those akin but hostile to God's people, in Lk. 13: 32 the fox being Herod. So everyone is at home in Israel's land, Roman overlords (birds) and Edomite interloper (Herod), except the true Israel. 'The true Israel is disinherited by them, and if you cast your lot with me and mine you join the ranks of the dispossessed' (*Sayings*, pp. 72 f.). See, however, the commentary on Mt. 8: 20.

59, 60. The second would-be disciple. Another candidate wishes to postpone taking up discipleship until he has performed the most sacred of filial duties, the burial of his father. Yet there is no hint that the father has already died. The claims of the kingdom are paramount: **Let the dead bury their own dead.** This saying, which has been much discussed, is followed in Luke by the command **go and proclaim the kingdom of God**; in Mt. (8: 22) it is simply 'Follow me'.

61, 62. The third would-be disciple (Luke only). The excuse for delay is here less valid, being simply a matter of family farewells. The 'ploughman' answer of Jesus recalls that it was while ploughing that Elisha heard God's call (1 Kg. 19: 19 ff.).

(b) **The Mission of the Seventy (10: 1–24)** Seventy disciples, mentioned only by Luke, are sent out with a commission in very similar terms to that of the Twelve in 9: 1–10 (see note *ad loc.*). They return and report enthusiastically on the success of their mission; Jesus warns them against the danger of pride entering their hearts. There follows the record of a prayer of the Son to the Father, almost Johannine in its language.

1. seventy-two: Manuscript evidence is divided between 70 and 72. The latter would suggest six from each tribe, like the translators of the Septuagint. On the other hand, there were traditionally seventy nations (Gen. 10), seventy elders were appointed by Moses (Num. 11: 16 f.) and seventy members of the Sanhedrin. **two by two:** A. R. C. Leaney (p. 176) suggests that this may be an illustration of the witness principle of Dt. 19: 15. **2, 3. The harvest is plentiful . . . :** Two short similitudes introduce Jesus' charge to the Seventy; the plenteous harvest and the lambs among wolves. In Mt., both are attached to the sending out of the Twelve (9: 37–38; 10: 16).

4–12. Instructions for the journey. Their marching orders resemble closely those given to the Twelve (9: 3 ff.; cf. Mk 6: 8–11; Mt. 10: 9–14), with the addition of (a) an injunction not to salute any man by the way (4); like Gehazi's (2 Kg. 4: 29), theirs is an errand of life and death, there is no time to waste on social exchanges. (b) a denunciation of the cities of Galilee, Korazin, Bethsaida, and Capernaum, for their deafness to God's call to repent. **Korazin** is not mentioned elsewhere in the Bible or in Josephus but its ruins are visible about 2½ miles north of Capernaum; the denunciation of **Capernaum** is in terms reminiscent of the 'taunt song' against the King of Babylon in Isa. 14: 13–15.

16. They are given the authority which belongs to Him who sent them. A more forceful version of Mt. 10: 40.

17–20. The return of the Seventy. On their return they were full of enthusiasm at the wonderful things that they had been empowered to accomplish: **even the demons submit to us in your name.** This was even more than they had anticipated, for they had been commissioned only to heal the sick and to proclaim the Kingdom (v. 9). In His reply the Lord warned them against pride: **I saw Satan fall like lightning from heaven** (18). The verb **I saw** is in the imperfect tense ('I was watching'); the participle **fall** is aorist ('fallen'). Because this saying recalls Isa. 14: 12–'*How you have fallen from heaven, O morning Star, son of the dawn!*', it has been interpreted throughout Christian history as a reference to a cosmic fall of Satan in the remote past; so, for instance, Gregory the Great as early as the sixth century. But Plummer (p. 278) says: 'The aorist indicates the coincidence between the success of the Seventy and Christ's vision of Satan's overthrow'. The kingdom has come, 'the success of the disciples is regarded as a symbol and earnest of the complete overthrow of Satan' (*ibid.*; see also note on Rev. 12: 9). Whichever of these two interpretations is accepted, it is quite evident that Jesus taught unambiguously that there is a personal power of evil.

The renewed promise of power (19) recalls Ps. 91: 13 and Dt. 8: 15; but the true ground for rejoicing is that their names are written in the register of God's kingdom (cf. Exod. 32: 32 f.; Ps. 87: 6; Heb. 12: 23; Rev. 3: 5; 17: 8; etc.).

21, 22. Cf. Mt. 11: 25–27. In these two verses we are transported from the Synoptic air right into the atmosphere of the Fourth Gospel; they have been described as 'this thunderbolt from the Johannine sky'. And yet, as Plummer says (p. 282), 'it is impossible upon any principles of criticism to question its genuineness, or its right to be regarded as among the earliest materials made use of by the evangelists'.

Jesus **full of joy through the Holy Spirit**, Luke's own phrase, which does not appear in Mt.'s version, but is reminiscent of the language of Luke's first two chapters. In v. 21, He delights that His Father has chosen babes; in v. 22 He rejoices in the perfect intimacy which He and the Father enjoy one with the other. The thought of v. 21 is developed by Paul in the opening chapter of 1 Corinthians.

23, 24. A beatitude given also by Mt. (13: 16–17), emphasizing that Jesus was speaking to the Twelve and not to His followers in general. To the apostles were given the gracious unfoldings of truth that marked the Lord's teaching to His intimates: they witnessed the fulfilment of things to which the prophets had looked forward with eager longing (cf. Heb. 11: 13; 1 Pet. 1: 12).

(c) The Parable of the Good Samaritan (10: 25–37)
The most remarkable feature of the Lucan account of the great journey is the series of parables, including several of the most memorable recorded in the NT, which are preserved in none of the other Gospels. Of these, the Good Samaritan stands first. A lawyer asks the Lord what are the great commandments, and is perhaps rather surprised to be told no new-fangled doctrine, but a restatement of the honoured laws of the Torah concerning love for God and one's neighbour. The lawyer asks who is his neighbour, a question that elicits this parable by way of reply, and the exhortation with it, **Go and do likewise** (37).

The introductory dialogue is often regarded as a parallel to Mk 12: 28–31, 34, but in reality the only connection is the linking together of Dt. 6: 5 and Lev. 19: 18, and, if Wm. Manson (p. 131) is right, it is possible that 'this synthesis of precepts accredited to the lawyer suggests that contemporary preachers, in attempting to summarize the Law in one or two brief sentences, had reached agreement upon this formula'. The two contexts are quite different, and the attitudes of the two questioners also. In Mk the scribe's question is purely academic; here there is at any rate a practical element.

25. an expert in the law: The Gk. word *nomikos* is used by Luke alone of the Synoptics, except for Mt. 22: 35, where the word is omitted in several manuscripts. Luke probably uses the word in preference to 'scribe' (Gk. *grammateus*) as being more intelligible to his Gentile readers. **stood up to test Jesus:** Was the lawyer's intention to enquire or to entrap? Leaney (p. 182) suggests 'trying Him out' to convey the exact meaning of the verb. The question, says Plummer (p. 284) was not 'calculated to place Jesus in a difficulty, but rather to test His ability as a teacher'; it 'does not imply a sinister attempt to entrap Him'. Moorman (p. 126), on the other hand, holds that 'by asking an awkward question, he wanted Jesus to stumble over it so that he could then turn to the crowd and point out that matters of this kind were much better left to lawyers and trained expositors'. Wm. Manson, Browning, and others, take a similar view. **29. wanted to justify himself:** i.e., wishing to regain some of the 'face' he had lost. **30. A man was going down from Jerusalem to Jericho:** The question is often asked whether the narrative parables are records of events that actually took place, or imaginative stories. Concerning the present story it has even been suggested that Jesus was recounting an otherwise unrecorded incident from His own experience; this is, of course, pure conjecture. But the story has the ring of the factual, robbers have infested the Jericho road from that day to this. H. V. Morton says that when he told a friend that he intended to run down to the Dead Sea for a day he was warned: 'Well, be careful to get back before dark' and was given grisly details of Abu Jildah, an armed gangster who even in 1934 was terrorizing travellers on that very road (*In the Steps of the Master*, 1934, p. 85). Another suggestion is that the parable is based on a historical event related in 2 Chr. 28: 15. **down . . . to Jericho:** Jericho had a long history in the OT; it lay about 900 feet below sea level; Jerusalem stands about 2,300 feet above sea level; hence **down. 31. a priest . . . when he saw the man . . . passed by on the other side:** The priest was **going down the same road**; he also had come from Jerusalem. If, as seems likely, he was coming from the exercise of his priestly duties, he would naturally wish to avoid contact with a possible corpse for fear of incurring ceremonial uncleanness (Num. 19: 11–19). But ordinary human compassion is a higher law than the observance of any ritual obligations (cf. 1 Sam. 15: 22; Isa. 1: 11–17; Am. 5: 21–24; Mk 2: 25–26, etc.). **32. So too, a Levite . . . came to the place . . . and saw him:** A lesser official of the Temple, the Levite seems to have been as callous as his superior, for he also approached, saw, and passed on. It is possible of course that both were cowardly rather than callous: 'it was quite a common thing for bandits to use decoys. . . . When some unsuspecting traveller came by and stopped over the apparently wounded victim, the rest of the band would suddenly rush from their concealment and catch the traveller at every disadvantage' (W. Barclay, *And Jesus said*, 1953, p. 95). **33. a Samaritan:** A surprising *dénouement* to the story; 'the hearers would assume that the villain of the piece had arrived upon the scene' (*ibid.*). The priest and the Levite had neglected their plain duty to their neighbour; the despised Samaritan did what none could have reasonably expected him to do—a salutary lesson for John and James! **35. two silver coins:** Mt. 20: 2 tells us that this was the daily wage of an agricultural labourer, so the 'seventeen pence' of the RSVmg is not realistic as to the purchasing power of the coin, which nowadays would be at least two pounds.

36, 37. The meaning of the parable. Fanciful allegorizing interpretations like those of Origen and Augustine (see A. M. Hunter, *Interpreting the Parables*, 1960, pp. 24 f., and C. H. Dodd, *Parables of the Kingdom*, 1935, pp. 11 ff.) pay so much attention to the leaves that the tree itself is obscured. The important thing is not to identify each tiny detail in the story, but to see how Jesus, as well as drawing a superb picture of neighbourliness, or love, in action, brought home to the lawyer the challenge of the Law, in which he was an expert, to his own heart, to condition his thinking and to inspire and regulate his doing.

(d) **Mary and Martha (10: 38–42)**
The parable of the Good Samaritan emphasizes the need for practical application of God's word; the little scene in Martha's house shows that meditation has its place as well. While Martha attends to the household chores, her sister Mary sits as a learner at Jesus' feet. The overburdened Martha complains; Jesus gently suggests that she might have done the same instead of making such a labour of the housework. This incident is particularly interesting in that Martha and Mary, well-known in the pages of John, appear here only in the Synoptics.

38. a village: Luke does not name this village, which must have been Bethany, though some find that this view raises geographical difficulties. If the incident occurred during Jesus' visit to Jerusalem for the Feast of Tabernacles (Jn 7), it would explain His presence in Bethany at this time. **40. Martha was distracted:** So distracted indeed that not only did she resent her sister's apparent idleness, but even scolded Jesus for not sending Mary to help. **41, 42.** Jesus answers gently; the double vocative **Martha, Martha,** is a kindly mode of address. He points out that if she is overworked it is she herself who has created the toil. **one thing is needed:** One simple dish would have sufficed, Martha has gone to endless unnecessary trouble to prepare a banquet, forgetting Prov. 15: 16–17! **Mary has chosen what is better:** Notice with what tact the Lord, while commending Mary for her sense of values, does not condemn Martha by comparison; Mary has chosen the **good** portion, not the *better*.

(e) **The Lord's Prayer (11: 1–13)**
The sight of our Lord at prayer leads the disciples to ask Him to teach them to pray. He replies by teaching them what has come to be known as the Lord's Prayer, telling them the parable of the importunate friend at midnight,

and by enunciating some general principles regarding prayer. This section is of outstanding interest since Luke, of all the evangelists, portrays most often the praying Christ (see Introductory notes, p. 1251).

J. M. Creed (p. 155) says 'there is no close connection between this and the preceding paragraph'; yet it is noticeable that the encouragement to ask our heavenly Father for a day's rations at a time is the natural corrective to Martha's anxiety about many things. The Lord's Prayer is found here in a totally different setting from Mt.'s version, which comes much earlier as part of the Sermon on the Mount. Here the disciples seem to feel that they lack something. 'It was customary', says C. G. Montefiore, 'for a famous Rabbi to compose a special prayer': John the Baptist appears to have done so for his disciples (1).

The prayer that Jesus gave them on this occasion is much shorter than in Mt.; and Luke's version is much shorter still in the newer versions (RSV, NEB, etc.) than in the *textus receptus* and the AV. The main differences between Mt.'s and Luke's shorter versions are:

1. The address to God: 'Our Father in Heaven' becomes simply **Father** (Jesus' characteristic 'Abba'; cf. Mk 14: 36).
2. The third petition: 'Your will be done', and the condition: 'on earth as in heaven', are omitted.
3. Mt.'s 'Give us today . . .' becomes: **Give us each day** in Luke.
4. 'debts' in Mt. becomes **sins** in Luke; the completed fact recorded by Mt.: 'we have forgiven' is a continual performance in Luke.
5. 'Deliver us from the evil one', Mt.'s last petition, is omitted in Luke, as also is the concluding doxology (which is absent from the original text of Mt.).

For comments on the contents of the prayer, see notes on Mt. 6: 9–13.

5–8. The parable of the friend at midnight. The pattern prayer is followed by a parable teaching the importance of persistence in prayer. A man has nothing to set before an unexpected guest; the lateness of the hour precludes the possibility of purchasing bread. He therefore wakes a friend to beg him to lend. Not unnaturally, he is not received cordially, but he persists in his request and because of his very persistence (Gk. *anaideia* means 'shamelessness'; see NEB), the friend capitulates, gets up and gives him what he wants just to get rid of him.

It is clearly impossible to press the details in interpreting this parable; the point is that real prayer, effective prayer, must be in real earnest (cf. Jas 5: 16) and that if a human friend will even grudgingly satisfy the needs of one who is becoming a nuisance, how much more will a loving God answer the prayers which He delights to hear, and that not grudgingly.

9–13. A collection of sayings on prayer. This appendix corresponds roughly to the **Go and do likewise** of the previous parable, and is paralleled in Mt. 7: 7–11 (see notes *ad loc.*).

(f) **Controversy with the Pharisees (11: 14–54)**
An exorcism leads to the accusation that Jesus can do these things simply because He is in league with the prince of demons. He shows the absurdity of such a charge, for Satan is not divided against himself. The Jews want a sign, yet the signs are there clear enough in the OT, if they will but see them; they have the light but are wilfully obscuring it. A Pharisee invites Him to a meal; attacked by the Pharisees present for not observing social and ceremonial etiquette, He turns the tables by showing how far in their regard for the minutiae they have departed from the true law of God and even murdered God's servants. The result of this clash is, not unnaturally, a hardening of the determination of His enemies to accomplish His downfall.

14–26. The Beelzebul controversy. See also notes on Mk 3: 22–27; Mt. 12: 22–30. Mk omits the fact that it was an exorcism which started off this controversy; Mt. tells us that the dumb man was blind as well. Communication with the poor fellow must have been difficult; yet the cure was immediate and complete (Mt. 12: 22). The onlookers were amazed. Some attributed His power to demoniac powers; others wanted a sign, tangible evidence that He was not in league with the powers of darkness (14–16).

Jesus replied that if Satan were the source of His power then Satan's kingdom must be so divided that it would collapse (17–18). Taking the war into the enemy's camp He pointed out that His hearers' **followers** (probably, their disciples) also exorcized demons; did they also do it by the powers of darkness? (19). No—His power was **the finger of God** (20), an expression used in Exod. 8: 19 (Mt. 12: 28 has the Spirit of God').

Then follow two short parables, the strong man spoiled (21, 22) and the unclean spirit returning to the empty house (24–26); and between them the assertion that in this warfare no man can be neutral: **He who is not with me is against me, and he who does not gather with me scatters** (23).

27, 28. Blessed is the mother who gave you birth. Only in Luke, who was interested in women's place in the gospel tradition. Though rebuked for flattery in words recalling 8: 21 and 10: 20, this woman stands in Luke's record with those of 8: 1–3 and 23: 27.

29–32. Cf. Mt. 12: 38–42. Two OT references, the 'sign of Jonah' and the Queen of Sheba's journey, are adduced as evidence of the seriousness with which even Gentiles had treated the coming judgement.

33–36. See also under Mk. 4: 21 ff.; Mt. 5: 15; 10: 26. Mk and Mt. place this saying in other contexts. Here the hearers' spiritual blindness leads naturally to the subject of **light** (33).

37–44. Luke alone tells us that Jesus accepted the invitation of a Pharisee to dinner (probably a midday meal) and, apparently deliberately, refrained from using the water brought to each guest for handwashing before the meal. That in appropriate circumstances Jesus conformed in such matters is clear from 7: 44 and from Jn 13: 4–10; but here He has another lesson to teach. The ablution that was a welcome refreshment when offered as a courtesy became a burden when imposed as an inescapable obligation. At all events, His abstention caused astonishment and gave Him the opportunity of contrasting the care the Pharisees gave to the pots and pans with their lack of care about what was put into them (39 ff.). Then He uttered His three 'Woes' against the Pharisees (see notes on Mt. 23: 23–28). They are greedy—**full of greed and wickedness** (39); they are insincere —punctilious in little things while neglectful of larger obligations (42); they are arrogant— **you love the most important seats in the synagogue and greetings in the marketplaces** (43). In fact they are unrecognized for what they are, dead men's graves without life towards God, but spreading uncleanness among men (Num. 19: 16).

45–52. See also Mt. 23: 4, 29–36, and notes *ad loc.* While the Pharisees withdrew to lick their wounds and to prepare further mischief, **one of the experts in the law**, as ready to speak as his colleague in the previous chapter, complained: **Teacher, when you say these things you insult us also.** Three more 'Woes' follow, this time directed at the lawyers (in Mt. 23 all the woes are addressed to the 'scribes and Pharisees'). They are censured because they lay down rules for others that they do not obey themselves (46): because the only prophets they honour are dead prophets, for whose deaths they must share the responsibility (47–51); and because, ignorant themselves, they withhold knowledge from those who would learn God's law (52). **51.** **Zechariah** was probably the prophet whose death is recorded in 2 Chr. 24: 20–22. 2 Chr. was the last book in the Hebrew OT so **Abel to . . . Zechariah** would include all the martyrs of the OT.

53, 54. Their enmity all the stronger because of His words, they crowd round Him with question after question, hoping to trap Him into saying something for which He might be brought to trial or excommunicated.

(g) **Public Teachings (12: 1–59)**
The solemn note of the controversy with the Pharisees is continued throughout the twelfth

chapter, where our Lord turns to His followers and utters a series of warnings they must heed. First He bids them be prepared for the persecution that surely lies ahead of them (1–12). Then He warns them against covetousness, a too high regard for material possessions, and reinforces the warning with the solemn parable of the Rich Fool (13–21). A section follows, placed in Mt. in the Sermon on the Mount, where the disciples are shown the needlessness and folly of anxiety about temporal necessities (22–34). Finally, almost the whole of the second half of the chapter (35–59) is eschatological in outlook, warning of the crisis which looms undoubtedly before them.

(*i*) **Warning of coming persecution (12: 1–12)**

The scene is vividly portrayed, one of Luke's masterpieces of simple yet telling narrative so often seen to advantage in his descriptions of the bustle and changing moods of a street crowd. Jesus left the Pharisees with whom He had been disputing, but they would not let Him go so easily; they **began to oppose him fiercely and to besiege him with questions, waiting to catch him in something he might say** (11: 53–54). But as on other occasions, especially at His crucifixion, it is He not they, the lonely figure and not the leaders of the establishment, who is clearly in command of events. **a crowd of many thousands had gathered** (12: 1) to hear Him. Not a whit daunted by the forces hostile to Him, He returns to the attack: **'Be on your guard against the yeast of the Pharisees, which is hypocrisy'**. This expression is interesting, since it occurs in Mk 8: 15 in another context, immediately before the Great Confession at Caesarea Philippi. Many, in fact, of the expressions in this chapter are paralleled, usually in different settings in Mt. or Mk; in Mt. mainly in the Sermon on the Mount (chaps. 5–7), the appointment of the Twelve (chap. 10) or the eschatological discourse of chap. 24.

1. His fearlessness has nothing in it of mere blind defiance. His eyes are wide open, and He knows full well that the Pharisees will return to the attack, and that if His disciples range themselves alongside Him, persecution will be their lot as it must assuredly be His. **2, 3.** One day, all will be revealed; but in the meantime, awaiting this Last Day, 'the halting and timid confessions of the disciples must become triumphant and public, even though they will bring persecution' (Browning, p. 119). **4, 5.** The only time in the Synoptics that Jesus calls His disciples **friends** (though see Jn 15: 14 f.). Human persecution is less to be feared than God's judgment on apostasy. **Hell:** Gehenna is the valley of the sons of Hinnom, running along outside a long stretch of the walls on the west and south of Jerusalem. Children had been

sacrificed there to Moloch (Jer. 7: 31, 32); in our Lord's days it was the perpetually smouldering and vermin-infested incinerator for the refuse and sewage of the city. Its horrible associations and abominable condition made it an apt symbol of the sufferings of the lost. **6, 7.** But the Judge who is to be feared is also a Father to be trusted. He cares for the sparrows, nay, for each hair upon our heads; how much more will He not care for His own children? **8–12.** Loyalty to God can never remain an abstract idea: Jesus is Himself the object of it. From this follow three corollaries:

(*a*) A promise that if we confess Him now, He will confess us before His Father, and a warning that the converse is also true (this is given by Mk 8: 38 as a sort of pendant to the Caesarea Philippi scene).

(*b*) The very difficult warning about blasphemy against the Holy Spirit: **And everyone who speaks a word against the Son of Man will be forgiven; but anyone who blasphemes against the Holy Spirit will not be forgiven** (10; cf. Mk 3: 28 f.; Mt. 12: 31 f.). Both Mt. and Mk place the saying in the context of the Beelzebul controversy (above, 11: 14–26). For comment, see note on parallels in Mt. and Mk.

(*c*) The promise that in persecution they will be sustained and empowered by the Holy Spirit Himself (11, 12; see Mt. 10: 19, 20; Mk 13: 11; also in the Lucan apocalyptic discourse, 21: 14, 15). Luke especially shows great interest in this promise, whose fulfilment he was later to describe in many incidents in Acts.

(*ii*) **Warning against covetousness: the Parable of the Rich Fool (12: 13–21)**

This discourse was brusquely interrupted by **Someone in the crowd** (13), who asked Jesus to intervene in a family dispute over the sharing out of an estate. The Greater than Solomon (11: 31) is asked to give judgment on the division, not of a baby but of an inheritance, and at that not even to act as an independent arbitrator, but to carry out the wishes of one party to the dispute: **Teacher, tell my brother to divide the inheritance with me** (14). But He has not come to do that which Moses got into trouble for doing (14; cf. Exod. 2: 14); His mission was not to settle the differences which brothers, joint-heirs moreover of the covenant, ought easily to have composed themselves. Great rabbis were often asked so to act, but Jesus would not act as a great rabbi.

Instead of the reply he expected, the questioner heard the story of the Rich Fool (16–20). Jeremiah had said of the treasures of the rich that '*when his life is half gone, they will desert him, and in the end he will prove to be a fool*' (Jer. 17: 11); here is an eloquent comment on the text. A prosperous farmer is so well satisfied with the produce of his fields that he proposes to retire and lead an easier life, when he has dealt with his one outstanding problem, that of storage. But 'man proposes, God disposes', and that night not all his wealth can keep the angel of death from his door. He hears God Himself label him with Jeremiah's epithet: **Fool!** (20). He must leave his riches behind him; whose shall they be? These are questions that frequently occupied the thoughts of the OT writers; see, for instance, Job 27: 8; Ps. 39: 6; etc. Verse 21 provides the 'moral', the clue to understanding the parable.

(*iii*) **Warning against anxiety and worldly care (12: 22–34)**
Cf. Mt. 6: 25–34. These verses are almost entirely in close verbal agreement with Matthew's version in the Sermon on the Mount (see notes *ad loc.*) except for a few small additions: **32.** The **little flock** are only lambs sent forth among wolves, but the good will of the Father who gives them the kingdom will surely not let them lack any protection of which they stand in need. **33. Sell your possessions and give alms to the poor:** Luke, ever practical, suggests how they can start to lay up treasure in heaven. **34.** If we know that we have treasure in heaven, the necessity to hoard earthly treasure disappears.

(*iv*) **Warning of Crisis ahead (12: 35–59)**
The rest of the chapter is taken up with Luke's first great eschatological passage; men are warned to repent while there is still time. The emphasis is on the suddenness of the crisis and the consequent call for watchfulness. Furthermore, the present time is a time of crisis, overshadowing the disciples, the Lord Himself, and the nation of Israel.

(*a*) **The Crisis and the disciples (12: 35–48)**
35–40. They are slaves who must ever be alert, both for the unheralded return of their Lord, and for the possible intrusion of thieves. There is no exact parallel in Mt., though the Parable of the Maidens in Mt. 25: 1–13 elaborates a similar theme. The insistence is on watchfulness: **Be dressed ready for service and keep your lamps burning, like men waiting for their master to return from a wedding banquet, so that when he comes and knocks they can immediately open the door for him** (35, 36). The time their services will be called for is uncertain; they will not see their lord return. The first indication that he is back will be a knock on the door.

37. The idea of the master serving the slave is quite revolutionary; such an act would be quite unexpected (see 17: 7–10). But Jesus girded Himself to serve them (Jn 13: 4); some (*e.g.* Balmforth, p. 222) see a reference also to the Messianic Banquet. **39, 40.** Cf. Mt. 24: 43, 44.
41–48. These slaves, moreover, have each their appointed task to perform (cf. Mt. 24: 45–51). Verse 41 is missing from Mt.'s parallel

which is otherwise very similar. Peter's question whether Jesus is speaking to the crowd or the disciples leads to special emphasis on the thought that superior privilege brings with it greater responsibility. Verses 47, 48 make a clear distinction between folly and rebellion. The slave who knows what is expected of him and fails to do it will be far more severely punished than the one who is merely careless in a general way. It is the Twelve whom Jesus has been carefully instructing since their call, and who therefore ought to know His will. The lesson of the parable of the Faithful Steward (42) is that **From everyone who has been given much, much will be demanded; and from the one who has been entrusted with much, much more will be asked** (48).

(*b*) **The Crisis and our Lord (12: 49–53)**
In these few verses of deep insight, the evangelist shows that the agony in Gethsemane was but the culmination of a long experience of facing the dark things that lay before Him; cf. Jn 12: 27.

50. The baptism here referred to is of course that which John and James so readily claimed they were capable of sharing (Mk 10: 38, 39). **51–53.** The divisive effects of Christ's challenge within the family, the misunderstandings and alienation of nearest and dearest, He Himself had been the first to suffer (8: 19–21, and even 2: 49), this having been predicted in the OT (Mic. 7: 6).

(*c*) **The Crisis and Israel (12: 54–59)**
Verses 54–56 have no parallel in Mt. George Adam Smith comments on the geographical exactness of the saying in vv. 54, 55 (*The Historical Geography of the Holy Land*, 1931, p. 66). Weather study is of vital importance to the farmer that he might be prepared for what is coming; why is this same perspicacity not also shown in spiritual matters?

56. hypocrites: A name used of the Pharisees in Luke only here and in 13: 15; but at least a dozen times in Mt. A hypocrite is originally a play-actor, someone pretending to be what he is not. At first, the word had no derogatory sense at all in Gk., though it had already come to have one in LXX. For the meaning of the word, see Wm. Barclay, *A New Testament Wordbook* (1955), pp. 56 ff.; for the Pharisees, H. L. Ellison, *art.* 'Pharisees' in *NBD.*

57–59. The Parable of the Lawsuit. In Mt. (5: 25, 26) this parable is found in the Sermon on the Mount. See note *ad loc.*

ii. The Peraean Ministry (13: 1–17: 10)
This title, commonly given to this section of the Gospel, is here used for the sake of convenience. It presupposes that the journey to Jerusalem took a longer route, east of the Jordan, presumably to avoid Samaritan unpleasantness. Mk 10: 1 says that Jesus 'went

into the region of Judea and across the Jordan', and it is suggested that Luke is here giving details to fill in the summary. This reading of the geographical indications, however, is by no means universally accepted. N. B. Stonehouse (pp. 116 f.), discussing the problem, concludes: 'It appears then that it is plainly a misnomer to speak of this section as concerned with the "Peraean Ministry"'. He says that 17: 11 indicates that our Lord is still only as far on His journey as the Samaria–Judaea frontier, so that most of the events of 13: 1–17: 10 must be placed in Galilee. But whatever the location, our Lord's face is always towards Jerusalem (13: 22, 33).

(a) **Warnings (13: 1–5)**
Jesus takes two items of topical interest to point the moral of the urgent need for repentance.

1–3. News is brought to Him of a group of Galilean pilgrims, in Jerusalem for one of the feasts, who had run foul of the Roman procurator, Pontius Pilate. He ordered their execution and their blood flowed with that of their sacrificial beasts. His hearers seem to have regarded this as evidence of the exceptional wickedness of men on whom God allowed such a catastrophe to fall, as did Job's friends and even Jesus' disciples (Jn 9: 2). But Jesus does not subscribe to this view; He does not even condemn Pilate's action, but warns His audience of their own need for repentance: **unless you repent, you too will all perish** (3). T. W. Manson (*Sayings*, p. 273) thinks that the messengers brought the news in the hope of tricking Jesus into some imprudent comment on Pilate; Plummer (p. 338) does not agree.

4, 5. A second catastrophe is mentioned, the collapse of the Siloam tower, unknown, like the previous incident, except in this passage. Eighteen persons lost their lives in an accident during building operations undertaken probably to strengthen Jerusalem's water-supply. Jesus draws the same lesson again.

(b) **Parables and a Miracle (13: 6–21)**
Jesus' stern note of warning that what has happened to others could happen to His hearers and that prudence therefore counselled repentance is followed in the Lucan account by the Parable of the Barren Fig Tree doomed to destruction, the miracle of the healing of the deformed woman, and the parables of the Mustard Seed and Leaven.

(i) **The Parable of the Barren Fig Tree (13: 6–9)**
The owner of a vineyard orders his gardener to cut down an unproductive fig tree growing there because it is occupying valuable space, but yields to the gardener's entreaties for one more chance.

This parable does not occur in Mt. or Mk, and since Luke makes no mention of the withering of the fig tree (Mt. 21: 19–22; Mk 11: 12–14, 20–22), many have assumed that Luke's parable is a 'softened-down' form of the act, others that it is the basis of Mark's story of the cursing. 'This is no more than a guess' says Balmforth (p. 225); Plummer (p. 339) says that the suggestion is arbitrary. At all events, the two passages are totally different in their emphasis. Luke's parable, following the teaching about the disasters, puts its stress on repentance, the other two synoptists on the inevitability of judgment.

6. his vineyard: Where the fig tree is growing; recalls the vineyard of Jehovah in Isa. 5. **7. For three years now:** Long enough for a reasonable expectation of fruit when once the tree had reached maturity. The tree surely will bear after another year if it is ever going to. It is doubtful if we should see in the three years a reference to the duration of our Lord's ministry, or to the number of His visits to Jerusalem. **cut it down:** Cf. 3: 9.

(ii) **The Sabbath Healing of an infirm woman (13: 10–17)**
Having cured a badly crippled woman in the synagogue on a Sabbath day, Jesus is rebuked by the ruler of the synagogue for having broken the Sabbath. He replies by defending the need to succour a neighbour in distress against mere traditionalist interpretations of the Law.

10. one of the synagogues: This is the last time Jesus is reported as teaching in a synagogue. **11. crippled by a spirit:** Cf. 11: 14 where a dumb demon means 'a demon that causes dumbness'. **13.** This is the only exorcism in the Gospels accompanied by the laying on of hands. **14.** Plummer justly draws attention (p. 341) to the 'pomposity of the ruler of the synagogue, with his hard and fast rules about propriety', and sees in such lifelike details that 'all this is plainly drawn from life'. Rather than take on directly so redoubtable an opponent as Jesus, he addresses his observations to the congregation in general. That he should use his position of authority to condemn an act of mercy because it was done on the Sabbath gives point to our Lord's teaching on the urgent need for repentance. **15, 16.** Jesus answers, first (15) that they would all attend to their beasts on the Sabbath, so how much more important that human need should be succoured; secondly (16) that the Sabbath day of rest is eminently suitable for the crippled woman to obtain rest from Satan's 18 years of bondage. **17.** The adversaries retired crestfallen; the common people, as on other occasions, received Him gladly.

(iii) **Two parables of the kingdom (13: 18–21)**
Luke places here the parables of the grain of mustard seed (Mt. 13: 31, 32) and the leaven hidden in three measures of meal (Mt. 13: 33).

Matthew puts both in his collection of parables of the kingdom in chap. 13.

For detailed comment, see notes on Mt. 13: 31–33.

(c) Further Warnings (13: 22–30)
On the move again with Jerusalem as the goal, Jesus is asked whether it is true that few only will be saved. He replies, not by satisfying curiosity, but by counselling effort to **enter through the narrow door**, otherwise there will be danger of being refused admission to the kingdom of God, the more galling as the Gentile nations will be seen entering in their place with the Patriarchs. Men's expectations will be turned upside down.

23. Nothing is known of the identity of the questioner nor of the motive for his question, if indeed it was prompted by anything more than mere curiosity. **24. make every effort:** The Gk. word is cognate with the English *agonize*, and is a favourite with Paul; *e.g.* 1 C. 9: 25; Col. 1: 29; 4: 12; also 1 Tim. 6: 11 and 2 Tim. 4: 7, in both of which it occurs both as verb and as noun, 'fight the fight'. It is connected with athletic contest, where the competitors go all out for victory. **the narrow door . . . many . . . will try to enter and will not be able:** An echo of Mt. 7: 13 f., but not an actual parallel; there, there are two ways, here, one door only. **25.** The householder's refusal to open the door to admit those he professes not to know recalls the parable of the maidens in Mt. 25: 10–12. **26, 27.** These verses recall generally Mt. 7: 22 f. **28, 29.** Matthew appends a similar saying (8: 11, 12) to his account of the centurion at Capernaum (Mt. 8: 5–13; cf. Lk. 7: 1–10). Conditions are described on both sides of the closed door. Inside, patriarchs and prophets sit down with repentant Gentiles at the great messianic banquet; outside is despair for those who have depended on favouritism ('We have Abraham as our father', Lk. 3: 8) rather than on repentance for salvation. Their punishment is the worse for the realization of what might have been. **30.** A short summary of the section; the last day will reveal many reversals of human values.

(d) The Message to Herod and the Lament over Jerusalem (13: 31–35)
The progress of our Lord towards Jerusalem is interrupted by a message brought by Pharisee emissaries from Herod suggesting that He should get out of the way to avoid the death Herod intends for Him. He replies that He is not concerned with Herod's plans, but with the path laid down for Him towards Jerusalem. Fully aware of what awaits Him when He reaches the city, His concern is for her, and not for Himself.

The Herod referred to is Herod Antipas, tetrarch of Galilee (cf. 3: 1, 19; 9: 7 ff.), son of Herod the Great; he is the Herod of our Lord's

trial (23: 7–12). It is debated whether Luke understands the Pharisees' warning as a friendly gesture or is rightly interpreted (*e.g.*) by N. B. Stonehouse as implying that 'they were virtually associated with Herod in wishing that He might be killed' (*The Witness of Luke to Christ*, p. 120). **32.** Jesus replies first that He will go when it suits Him, not Herod; and secondly that Herod's word cannot be trusted; like the fox he is contemptible and crooked, not great nor even straight. **33.** Jesus knows that He will die, but He will die in the appointed place, Jerusalem; and at the appointed time, not today, nor even tomorrow, but the third day. This of course is not a literal indication of time, but 'since the period is measured in terms of days, Jesus appears to be intimating that the consummation is not far distant' (Stonehouse, p. 122). **34, 35.** Matthew places the lament after Palm Sunday, Jesus is already in Jerusalem (23: 27). In putting Him to death, Jerusalem is living up to her ancient character of prophet-slayer (Jer. 26: 20–23; cf. Lk. 20: 10–12; Ac. 7: 52). **Jerusalem, Jerusalem:** The double vocative is a sign of affection and concern; cf. 10: 41; 22: 31. **as a hen gathers her chicks:** A familiar figure in the OT, *e.g.*, Dt. 32: 11; Ps. 17: 8; 36: 7. **35.** The inevitable outcome of Jerusalem's ways will be utter ruin. When will they say **Blessed is he who comes in the name of the Lord?** To see Palm Sunday as its fulfilment is too limited; it is rather whenever, throughout time, a Jew repents and is converted (see Plummer, p. 353), and especially, perhaps, refers to Christ's welcome from the Jews at His second coming.

(e) Dinner with a Pharisee (14: 1–24)
Still moving on, Jesus has accepted an invitation to a Pharisee's house for a meal on the Sabbath day. After incurring the disapproval of His host by healing a man suffering from dropsy on the day of rest, He speaks of the principles of true hospitality and courtesy. His discourse includes the parables of the choice of places at table, and of the great supper.

(i) The man with dropsy (14: 1–6)
This is the last of the five Sabbath miracles of mercy recorded in the Synoptics—Luke records them all (4: 31; 4: 38; 6: 6; 13: 14 and the present incident). John adds two more (5: 10; 9: 14).

1. Jesus had previously accepted the invitations of Pharisees even though they were constantly engaging in controversy with Him; in fact, we never hear of His refusing such an invitation. **he was being carefully watched:** This invitation appears to have had its ulterior motive. **2.** The man may have been brought in to trap Jesus, but it would not have been impossible, nor even unusual, for the uninvited to gain admittance to a private house (cf. 7:

37). In fact, the **sent him away** of v. 4 rather suggests that he had come to be cured, not as a guest. **3.** Jesus answered their question before it was asked; cf. 18: 22 f. **5. If one of you has a son or an ox . . .** (of the word **son**, 'other ancient authorities read *an ass*'). Whichever is the correct reading, in both cases their act of mercy, unlike His on this occasion, would really be for their own benefit. Contrast this verse with 13: 15; there it is a matter of routine watering of stock; here it is a case of accident.

(ii) **Places at table (14: 7–14)**
See Prov. 25: 6, 7. The healing of the dropsical man seems to have taken place while the guests were assembling. When it is done and he has departed, the guests begin to take their places, some making for the seats of honour. Jesus proceeds to draw a lesson for the guests on the true humility that befits His followers, and then addresses to His host the counsel that he should invite to his feasts social inferiors in no position to return his hospitality rather than social equals who might.

11. This verse re-echoes the words of the *Magnificat* (1: 52), repeated again as a pendant to the parable of the Pharisee and the tax collector (18: 14) and in one of His disputes with the Pharisees (Mt. 23: 12).

(iii) **The Parable of the Great Supper (14: 15–24)**
The relation between this parable and that of the marriage of the King's son (Mt. 22: 1–10) is the subject of perennial discussion. The similarities are marked enough to invite comparison, the differences are sufficiently great to make it clear that the two parables are entirely distinct. Their contexts are totally different; the Lucan story is evoked by the comment of one of the guests: **Blessed is the man who will eat at the feast in the kingdom of God!** (15); the Matthaean follows the parable of the vineyard, and is in the setting of controversy with the Pharisees. In Luke **a certain man was preparing a great banquet** (16); in Matthew a king sends invitations to a 'marriage feast for his son'. The guests in Luke's parable simply turn down the invitation (18–20); in Matthew's they ridicule the invitation and maltreat the servants. In both parables the invitations are amended and addressed to outcasts and the afflicted, but in Matthew's story this takes place only after a punitive military campaign against the murderers of the messengers.

15. The guest's ejaculation may have been insincere or merely superficial. 'Jesus questions, not the sentiment, which is unimpeachable, but the sincerity of the speaker, saying, in effect, "You talk beautifully about the kingdom of God but you do not mean a word of it. If you had the opportunity for which you profess to crave, you would unhesitatingly reject it"' (T. W. Manson, *Sayings*, p. 129). **16,**

17. The second invitation. 'It was a recognized custom to send a servant to repeat the invitation at the appointed time; cf. Est. 6: 14' (Creed, p. 191). Edersheim (ii, p. 427) quotes the Midrash (rabbinical commentary) on Lam. 4: 2 as authority for the Jerusalem custom of not going to a feast unless the invitation was repeated. **18–20.** The three excuses quoted all mean the same thing—'I've better things to do'. The discourtesy and the inadmissibility of the excuses lies in the fact that the men must have had these plans in mind at least when they received the original invitations, which they ought not to have accepted. A man's marriage, it is true, entitled him to a year's rest from social and military obligations (Dt. 24: 3); but courtesy should have prevented him from acceptance at the first. **21.** The original recipients of invitations, as well as the second group, lived in the city; this probably means that they are all Jews. The first group were the well-to-do, the elite of the nation, who were not interested, so now the outcasts and the despised, the publicans and sinners, are brought in. **23.** The highways and hedges could be outside the city, though, according to *Arndt* (under *phragmos*), 'Vagabonds and beggars frequent the hedges and fences around houses'. The Gentiles are now included in the invitation. **make them** (RSV, also AV; rather with RV, *constrain*): Force is not used, but the greatest efforts of persuasion. Creed suggests 'urge' or 'press'; NEB translates 'make them come in'; Ronald Knox: 'Give them no choice but to come in'. **24.** The punishment of those who had despised the invitation was complete exclusion from the feast. Matthew's parable ends much more sternly; those who have abused the messenger are destroyed and their city burned; while even at the wedding feast a guest who does not wear the robe provided is 'cast into outer darkness' (Mt. 22: 13). But then, in Mt. it is a king's invitation that is spurned, in Luke one from a private individual.

(f) **Challenge to the Multitude (14: 25–35)**
The scene now changes from the Pharisee's house; Jesus is walking along accompanied by a great multitude. He turns to them and discourses of discipleship, its cost and the disciple's need for intelligent thought and wholehearted devotion.

(i) **Discipleship calls for sacrifice (14: 26, 27)**
Kinsfolk and life itself must yield to Him first place in the disciple's affections (26; cf. Mt. 10: 37, 38). **hate** must be considered in the light of OT usage: it frequently occurs together with 'love' in contexts where it clearly means to 'love less' (Gen. 29: 31 ff.; Dt. 21: 15 ff., etc.). It is not that a man must detest his family, but that they must take second place to the Lord in his affections.

27. Cf. Mk 8: 34. A criminal bearing his

cross to the place of execution was no unfamiliar sight; what is really startling in this saying is the relation between this gibbet and the claims of the Messiah.

(ii) Discipleship may not be entered upon lightly (14: 28–33)
He who would follow Jesus must count the cost. 'The *parable of the "Tower"-builder, and of the king contemplating a Campaign*, is a call to self-testing. . . . By the lesser example of the farmer whose unfinished farm-buildings [alternative meaning of Gk. *pyrgos*, 'tower'] make him an object of ridicule, and the more important case of the king who, in planning a campaign, has underestimated the strength of his enemy, and must therefore submit to his terms of peace, Jesus drives home the exhortation: Do not act without mature consideration' (J. Jeremias, *The Parables of Jesus*, ET, 1963, p. 196).

(iii) Discipleship must be whole-hearted (14: 34, 35)
Half-hearted, it will be as insipid as stale salt. 'The true disciple is as salt; the half-hearted disciple, like tasteless salt, is useless' (Creed, p. 193). Matthew puts this similitude in the Sermon on the Mount. See note on Mt. 5: 13.

(g) Teaching Publicans and Sinners (15: 1–32)
The audience to whom these last sayings were addressed consisted of **large crowds** (14: 25); tax-collectors and sinners join in with the throng, and for the third time Luke tells us that Jesus' willingness to consort with such people draws down upon Him the censure of the Pharisees (see 5: 30; 7: 39); the question will arise again when He accepts the hospitality of Zacchaeus (19: 7). It is this criticism which evokes from Jesus the three parables recorded in this chapter, of the lost sheep, of the lost coin and of the prodigal and his brother.

The three parables all concern lost things or creatures; each in its way presents God as seeking the lost, yet each has its own emphasis. The inanimate object in the second parable is simply lost. The animal in the first has gone astray through sheer stupidity. The son in the third has deliberately gone off by a headstrong act of self-will. So in turn the uselessness, the peril, and the misery of the lost life is demonstrated. Then again in each there is an element of repentance, in the first two in the refrain only; in the third underlying the whole parable. The woman who has lost something of value makes a very thorough search; the shepherd tends the creature he has retrieved; the father extends to the son the whole gamut of forgiveness and reconciliation. In each case there is infinite trouble taken to find what is lost; and, as G. B. Caird (p. 181) points out: 'To call a man lost is to pay him a high compliment, for it means that he is precious in the sight of God'.

1, 2. The scribes and Pharisees see Jesus as debasing Himself by the company He keeps, even to the extent of engaging in the significant fellowship of a shared meal with them; they cannot accept His view that it is God Himself who wills that the outcasts should be gathered in.

(i) The Lost Sheep (15: 3–7)
Matthew records this parable (18: 12–14), but in a different setting, and with a different ending: 'In the same way your Father in heaven is not willing that any of these little ones should be lost' (Mt. 18: 14).

A sheep has gone astray; normally the whole flock follows the wanderer, but here our creature has managed to detach himself from the main company. He wanders off through the wilderness (Gk. *erēmos*, a word that in the Bible includes not only the sand dunes or rocks that colour the popular imagination of a desert, but also scrub or rough pasture land; cf. Mk 6: 34 with 39; see *art*. 'Wilderness' in *NBD*); he nibbles on at what grass he finds. When he realizes he is alone he cannot, with his limited faculties, find his way back to the rest. If no one finds him he will stay where he is, or wander yet farther away, and starve. So the shepherd seeks until he finds him, and gently laying his burden across his shoulders, carries him back to the flock, **joyfully**, and calls together his friends and neighbours to celebrate with him.

7. In the comparison between the shepherd's rejoicing and the joy in heaven over a repentant sinner, it is to be noticed that the emphasis is on the rejoicing rather than on the repentance, for the sheep clearly did not consciously repent. 'Neither the sheep nor the coin can repent; this may suggest that the sinner's repentance may be a gift of God, consequent on his being found, not the condition of his being found' (G. W. H. Lampe, in *Peake*[2], p. 836).

(ii) The Lost Coin (15: 8–10)
A woman has lost a silver coin, a drachma, the Greek equivalent of the Roman *denarius* of Mt. 20: 2, where it is the day's pay for an agricultural labourer. The total amount, ten drachmae, suggests a poor woman's savings rather than just the housekeeping money (T. W. Manson, *Sayings*, p. 284), or it may be, as Jeremias (pp. 134 f.) suggests, part of her headdress—and her dowry. Whichever it was, the small amount suggests poverty rather than opulence.

8. Does she not light a lamp, because the homes of the poor in Palestine are not well-lit, having but the smallest of windows. She turns the house upside-down, and takes no rest until the coin is found. **9.** Like the previous story, it ends in rejoicing with friends and neighbours. **10.** 'God, we are to understand, is not less persistent than men and women in seeking what he has lost, nor less jubilant when his search is successful' (G. B. Caird, p. 180).

(iii) **The Prodigal Son (15: 11–32)**
The third parable is probably the best known and loved of all our Lord uttered. Continuing the theme of the first two, it goes far beyond them in several ways: (a) The lost one on this occasion is a person, a wilful and rebellious son. (b) It follows therefore that the part of the seeker is much larger; he not only seeks, but forgives and reconciles as well. (c) While there is rejoicing over the penitent scapegrace, there is also the churlish conduct of his elder brother. It is a parable with two main points.

11. There was a man who had two sons: The designation of the parable as the 'prodigal son' is hallowed by long usage, but it is really inadequate, for attention is drawn to all three of the main characters, not only the younger son. His arrant folly and his father's surpassing love and noble generosity make the first part of the story unforgettable, it is true; but it is the episode of the elder son that says to the listening Pharisees and scribes: 'Thou art the man'. **12. Father, give me my share of the estate:** 'The younger son wanted an overdraft, the elder a current account'. There were two ways in which a Jewish father might pass on his property to his sons; by a will effective on his death; or by a deed of gift during his own lifetime. In the latter case, the property was legally vested in the son when the deed was executed, but the father enjoyed a life interest in the revenue (see, for instance, Jeremias, *Parables*, pp. 128 f.; T. W. Manson, *Sayings*, pp. 286 f.). Here it is clear that the father had gone well beyond his minimum legal obligations, placing capital at his younger son's disposal so that he might enjoy it forthwith instead of waiting for his father to die. **13. got together all he had:** i.e., he realized all his assets. **15.** His fair-weather friends having deserted him, he must now live by what means he can; he is forced to descend to the most degrading employment a Jew could imagine, tending swine. **16.** Hunger follows humiliation, he even envies his charges the carob pods on which they feed. Some have called carob pods 'St. John's bread', because they believed that John the Baptist ate these in the Jordan wilderness. 'To be compelled to eat St. John's bread was synonymous with the bitterest poverty and need' (Strack-Billerbeck, quoted by Geldenhuys, p. 411). **17–19.** Brought up with a jerk, the foolish young man comes to his senses and resolves to return to his father, to confess that he has abdicated any claim to sonship, but to beg for employment. **20. while he was still a long way off, his father saw him . . . ran . . . and threw his arms around him:** At first, the emphasis, as in the two preceding parables, is entirely on the father's joy. Scan-

ning the distant horizon, he sees the object of so many prayers. Such is his delight that he runs, scarcely a dignified procedure for an elderly oriental, and cuts short the son's well rehearsed speech. So the request for a slave's employment remains unuttered, but the father divines what is in his son's heart. The son, indeed, ought to have known his father better; he is greeted as a beloved son. The servants are ordered to invest the son with the best robe, fitting for the guest of honour; to give to him the ring of authority and the shoes of freedom (slaves wore no shoes), and to slay the fatted calf that all may share in the father's gladness. **24.** So the son is restored to his former position. Some have said that this parable is not in line with the general teaching of Jesus in the NT, in that it has forgiveness without sacrifice, or even that we have here the Lord's original teaching before it became overlaid with theories of atonement (see Creed, p. 197). Such a view, however, assumes that each parable is a complete compendium of theology, a view that cannot be substantiated. Generally, a parable takes one point and drives it home, or very occasionally (as in this case) two points. The first part of this parable underlines the truth that genuine repentance must precede forgiveness; the father does not wait to listen to what his son has to say, for he can discern in his whole demeanour a changed attitude. The young man who had left home demanding 'give me' (12) comes back begging 'make me'.

25–32. With supreme artistry, Luke changes the whole atmosphere. **They began to celebrate. Meanwhile the older son was in the field:** The elder brother hears the sound of celebration, and frigidly stands outside while he enquires what it is all about. During his brother's absence he has lived under his father's roof, and yet has been in spirit as far away from the father as the prodigal himself. The contrast between the two sons is as great as that between the brothers in Mt. 21: 28–31.

The elder brother's hostility explodes; to the narrator's reproach that his brother has been culpably extravagant he adds, no doubt from his own jaundiced imagination, the accusation that he had frequented harlots (30). His ungracious manners contrast strikingly with his father's courtesy: **His father went out and pleaded with him** (28), and spoke to him of **this brother of yours**; the elder son had spoken churlishly of **this son of yours**.

By his whole attitude the elder son reveals his kinship with the Pharisee of Lk. 18: 11, 12. The whole parable points sternly at the Pharisees in Jesus' audience who, far from rejoicing that outcasts were finding blessing, **murmured, saying, 'This man welcomes sinners, and eats with them'** (v. 2).

(h) Teaching the Disciples (16: 1–17: 10)
The crowd appears to have been melting away, though the Pharisees were still listening (14); Jesus now addresses His teachings to the disciples. His teaching ranges over various topics, and includes two of the major parables, the dishonest steward and Lazarus and the rich man.

(i) The parable of the dishonest manager (16: 1–9)
At first reading this parable comes with something of a shock since it appears to hold up a thorough scoundrel as a model to be imitated, which of course completely misses the point. Jeremias (p. 182) suggests that 'Jesus is apparently dealing with an actual case which had been indignantly related to Him'; but however that may be, the story bristles with difficulties, though many of these have arisen from treating the story as an allegory and attempting to see a meaning in each detail.

The central figure is called **the dishonest manager** (8), and there are varying views as to wherein he is dishonest. Some have suggested that his dishonesty had already been detected when the story opens and had led to his dismissal. According to this view the narrative tells of his efforts to put right the damage done. G. B. Caird (pp. 186 f.) gives an interesting account of this way of looking at the story, and suggests that the reduction of the outstanding debt may be simply the cancellation of the interest, bringing the steward's conduct more in line with OT teaching on usury; hence the commendation. There is little probability in J. N. Darby's dispensational interpretation: 'Israel was God's steward, put into God's Vineyard . . . but in all, Israel was found to have wasted His goods' (*The Gospel of Luke*, pp. 139 f.). Nor is the view too convincing that the steward's dishonesty lay in his cynical efforts to insure against the impending disaster by buying the protection of his master's debtors at the expense of the master himself. More probably the key to the parable is that a landowner on this scale will have given the stewardship to the man who promised him the highest income and whose payment would be the extra he could obtain. The steward's dishonesty consisted in **wasting his possessions** by forcing too much out of the estate. What the steward deleted was the extra he hoped to get for himself. Only so can he be regarded as using his own money wisely; according to this view, only on the premise that he was giving away what was his can we make sense of it. Then, who was it that **commended the dishonest manager** (v. 8)? Was it the **master** within the parable, or the Lord who told the parable? That it was the rich man seems the natural view; but while it is generally accepted doubts are sometimes expressed as to why one

who had suffered by his servant's dishonesty should praise him. The solution surely is in the words of v. 8: **The master commended the dishonest manager because he acted shrewdly**. Faced by ruin, he took energetic action to ward it off; it is his foresight and resourcefulness which are commended, not his dishonesty. His planning and his efforts for his own personal ends put to shame the awareness and the perseverance of many of the sons of light who ought to recognize the things that lie ahead of them. 'It is all very well for you to be indignant', Jeremias (p. 182) paraphrases the words of Jesus: 'but you should apply the lesson to yourselves. You are in the same position as this steward who saw the imminent disaster threatening him with ruin, but the crisis which threatens you, in which, indeed, you are already involved, is incomparably more terrible'.

9. The parable ends with a piece of advice for His hearers: **Use worldly wealth to gain friends for yourselves, so that when it is gone you will be welcomed into eternal dwellings:** Money, tainted as it is, should be used in such a way that **when it is gone**—that is, at death, when it can no longer avail—spiritual enrichment will be ensured in contrast with that of this transitory life. The message is clear; in our stewardship for God let us be at least as whole-hearted and energetic as was the steward in prosecuting his own interests.

(ii) Sayings about riches and pride (16: 10–15)
Any doubts one might entertain about the meaning of the parable must be dispelled by the sayings that follow, underlining the paramount importance of integrity. Honesty must be seen in the minute details if it is to be manifested in the major affairs of life (10). If we are not faithful in material things, how can we be trusted in spiritual matters? (11) and if we cannot be trusted with what belongs to others, how can we be expected to be faithful in regard to our own? (12) To serve God is full-time employment; as with slaves, all our time and all our effort belongs to our Master (13). Finally, when the money-loving Pharisees scoff at Him (14), He warns them that though they may impress men, they cannot deceive God, who loathes their pride (15).

13. This verse is paralleled in Mt. 6: 24, in the setting of the Sermon on the Mount; the remainder is peculiar to Luke.

(iii) Sayings concerning the new order (16: 16–18)
Three short sayings concerning the kingdom, the law, and divorce. The first two occur in Mt. also, and so probably belong to Q, the third is found in all the Synoptics. For v. 16, see notes on Mt. 11: 12, 13; for v. 17, notes on

Mt. 5: 18, and for v. 18, notes on Mk 10: 4, 11, 12 and Mt. 5: 31 f.

(*iv*) **The Parable of Lazarus and the Rich Man (16: 19–31)**

A rich man, enjoying every luxury of dress and of food, dies at about the same time as Lazarus, a poor wretch who sits at his door and begs, and whom he scarce deigns to notice. In the afterworld, their rôles are reversed; the beggar enjoys the felicity of **Abraham's side**, while the rich man is **in Hell, where he was in torment**. In this plight, he still wants to command menial service from Lazarus, but Abraham points out that he has already had more than his fair share of the good things; and apart from this, traffic between the two sides is quite impossible. Having failed to get some concession for himself, the rich man begs that Lazarus might be sent to his five brothers in order to warn them. But this request also is refused, since they have all the warning they need in the scriptures.

This parable is different from all the others in that the central character is named; some have, for this reason, held that it is to be regarded as historical narrative rather than parable. But this view, entirely apart from the fact that all the narrative parables probably tell of events that actually happened, ignores the element of symbolism that is quite apparent in the story. 'Abraham's side', the 'great chasm', and 'this fire' obviously ought not to be pressed into too materialistically literal a meaning, and it would be rash to attempt a description of the after-life from the details given here. As Alan Richardson justly says, 'the aim of the parable is not to acquaint us with details of the life to come, but to confront us with our duty in this life' (*A Theological Word Book of the Bible*, 1950, p. 107).

Certain truths concerning the life to come are, however, inescapably insisted on in the parable. First, there is the finality of death as far as human destiny is concerned; the state of the individual soul after death is irrevocably settled during his lifetime. Secondly, whatever is figured by the symbolic language, the parable clearly teaches that the lot of the righteous is infinite happiness, and of the ungodly indescribable distress. Both the happiness and the distress are conscious, and what is more, the memory of this life with its lost opportunities subsists in the Beyond. Thirdly, in addition to this insistence on the reality of differing conditions after death, there is an equal insistence on the truth that there is for all men a sufficient guide to heaven in the scriptures.

19. There was a rich man: His name is not given; *Dives* is merely the Latin for a rich man. Whoever he was, he seems to fit the description of a Sadducee; he is wealthy, wearing dress befitting high rank. A thorough-going materi-

alist whose philosophy seems to be 'let us eat and drink, for tomorrow we die', he is a rationalist also who does not believe in an after-life any more than do the brothers he wants, too late, to awaken to the truth. But this does not justify the assumption of T. W. Manson (*Sayings*, p. 295) and others that Luke is mistaken in mentioning Pharisees in v. 14, where he should have written 'Sadducees'; indeed, despite what has just been said, the parable has been regarded by some as an amplification of 16: 14 f., in which case the rich man would be a Pharisee after all. **20. Lazarus:** the only named character in a parable. It is the Gk. form of the OT name Eleazar, 'God is his help', and a sufficiently common name in NT days to make it unprofitable to speculate on the identity of this particular Lazarus. **22.** 'The image is derived from the custom of reclining on couches at meals. "The disciple whom Jesus loved" reclined in Jesus' bosom at the last supper (Jn 13: 23)' (Balmforth, p. 244). **23. Hell:** In general usage Gk. *Haidēs* was roughly equivalent to Heb. *She'ol*, the grave, the abode of the departed whether good or bad, but later it came to be used almost exclusively for the place of the wicked dead. **25.** A statement of a circumstance of the present narrative, not the enunciation of the doctrine that in the after-life there is a mere reversal of the fortunes of this life. **31. they will not be convinced even if someone rises from the dead:** A saying abundantly fulfilled shortly afterwards. The majority of Jews refused to be convinced when Jesus Himself rose from the dead.

(*v*) **Four more sayings (17: 1–10)**

There now follows a short series of sayings, apparently quite miscellaneous, and yet, as Geldenhuys (p. 531) says: 'It appears to us that there is a unity between the various pronouncements and that (although Luke does not expressly say so) they were uttered on one and the same occasion'. Their general theme is the responsibility of the disciple towards others, warning them of the sinfulness of leading weaker ones astray, the need for a forgiving spirit and for real, practical faith, and the danger of trusting in the mere fulfilment of obligations to obtain merit.

1, 2. Occurs in Mt. 18: 6, 7 and Mk 9: 42. Who are the **little ones** in verse 2? There is no indication of children present on this occasion; most of the commentators take the phrase as referring to the weaker brethren among the disciples. Such a reading is suggested by the Marcan parallel; Mt. however puts the saying in the context of one of his child-passages (18: 1–5). There is, of course, no reason why both should not be in view. **3, 4.** One of the marks of a disciple is willingness to forgive. Sin is not to be overlooked, nor lightly passed over; the wrongdoer must be rebuked, his sin must be discussed to his face and not behind his back. Repentance must precede forgiveness. But subject to these conditions there is no limit to the number of times forgiveness ought to be extended. In Mt. the passage is fuller and in the reply to a question of Peter's, it is followed by the parable of the unforgiving creditor (18: 15–35).

5, 6. The magnitude of the responsibility that these sayings impose awoke in the disciples a sense of their inadequacy; they **said to the Lord, 'Increase our faith!'** With oriental hyperbole Jesus gives them an insight into unsuspected possibilities. The sycamine is a tree of the mulberry family, its roots were regarded by the ancients as particularly strong. Strack-Billerbeck (quoted by Geldenhuys, p. 434) say: 'it was supposed that the tree could stand in the earth for 600 years'. To uproot it would be a virtual impossibility, to replant it in the ocean bed even more so, but faith in God surmounts impossibilities. Mk 11: 23/Mt. 21: 21 has a similar saying in the context of the withering of the fig-tree; here it is a mountain that is to be cast into the sea.

7–10. A parable of service. From speaking of faith, Jesus goes on to talk of works, inadequate because the very best that we can do is nothing more than our duty (see note on 12: 37). **unworthy servants** does not suggest the servants have been remiss or done less than their duty, but that they had simply done what their master had a right to expect.

iii. The Last Journey to Jerusalem (17: 11–19: 27)

The last stage of the Journey has now arrived: **on his way to Jerusalem Jesus travelled along the border between Samaria and Galilee.** Throughout this long journeying with which so much of Luke is concerned, Jerusalem, with the dark events that are to take place there, is constantly in view.

(a) Ministry in Samaria and Galilee (17: 11–18: 14)

(i) Ten lepers healed (17: 11–19)

At the entrance of a village, ten lepers stand at a respectful distance because of their disease and beg Jesus to have mercy on them. He sends them to the priest to certify the cleansing that He has bestowed. One only, and he a Samaritan, has the courtesy to return and thank his benefactor, who remarks on the fact that it should be a Samaritan who does so.

14. The actual healing is not described but assumed as a fact. In 5: 12–16 'Jesus reached out his hand and touched the man', not fearing the contagion of the disease. **16.** The thanks of the Samaritan was evidence of fact for those who saw in the parable of the Good Samaritan a mere fable.

(ii) The sudden coming of the kingdom (17: 20–37)

Some Pharisees approach the Lord with questions about the time of the coming of the kingdom of God. He replies that though this question is on the minds of many, the important thing that they should know is that the coming will be unheralded, and that before the coming the Son of man will be rejected and suffer at the hands of sinners. In the days of Noah and Lot people lived entirely unconcerned, not suspecting that the Flood and the destruction of Sodom impended. It will be the same with the coming of the Son of man. The kingdom will be upon men before they know, its manifestation will be quite unmistakeable, and it will cut across all human relationship of class or kinship. No answer is vouchsafed to those who enquire about the details.

Luke has three main sections concerned with the last things: (*a*) 12: 34–59. The imminent crisis, about to fall, nay, upon them already; cf. Mt. 24: 43–51. (*b*) 17: 20–37. The unheralded coming of the 'day of the Son of man'; cf. Mt. 24: 23–28; 37–41. (*c*) 21: 5–36. The parousia of the Son of man, Luke's version in the main of Mark's apocalyptic chapter 13. The 'Little Apocalypse', as Mk 13 is sometimes called, appears almost complete in Mt. and Luke; the material in Lk. 17 appears woven by Mt. in to his version of Mk 13.

20, 21. These verses have no parallel in Mt., and are not easy to understand, since the expression **within you** is rather ambiguous; the Gk. *entos* is not the usual word that Luke uses for 'in the midst of' (in fact it is found nowhere else in the Gospel). So the phrase is variously interpreted as 'among you', i.e. the King Himself is actually in your midst, or 'within you', the spiritual kingdom in the hearts of men. It is difficult to see how the latter can be the meaning here, since the words are addressed to Pharisees (20). Other possible renderings are 'within your possession' and 'within your reach'. **22, 23.** See notes on Mk 13: 21 (Mt. 24: 23). **24.** See note on Mt. 24: 27. **25.** A third prediction of the Passion (Luke only). **26–30.** See notes on Mt. 24: 37–39. **31.** See note on Mt. 24: 17, 18. **32.** A warning peculiar to Luke, evoked by the words **no one . . . should go back for anything** (31). **33.** Mk 8: 35 and Mt. 16: 25 have this saying in the context of the warnings of Jesus after Peter's confession. **34, 35.** See notes on Mt. 24: 40, 41. **37.** Cf. Mt. 24: 28. In v. 20, the Pharisees ask 'When?' now they ask **Where?** but Jesus refuses to satisfy the curiosity of 'date-fixers' and the like.

(iii) The parable of the Unjust Judge (18: 1–8)

Jesus now tells another parable, whose purpose is clearly stated: **they should always pray and not give up.** It is the story of a cynical and unprincipled judge who is unmoved by a widow's plea for justice, but finally settles her case merely because her constant requests are becoming a nuisance to him.

This is an excellent example of the rule of interpretation that the lesson of a parable must be sought in its main point, and not in its details, for a judge who ignores the two great commandments and neither fears God nor regards man can surely hardly teach us anything about the character of God. The point of the parable is in an *a fortiori* argument; if an earthly judge, devoid of all sentiment of justice, yields to the importunity of the widow from sheer weariness, how much more will not God, who loves to hear His children's prayers, delight to answer them when, as in this case, the cause is just.

8–10. An apocalyptic note is introduced; the truths of the previous chapter seem still to be occupying His mind.

(*iv*) **The parable of the tax-collector and the Pharisee (18: 9–14)**
Again a parable is introduced by an indication of its interpretation; it is told to **some who were confident of their own righteousness and looked down on everybody else**. A Pharisee at prayer is contrasted with one of the hated tax-collectors. The former takes up his position and gives thanks to God that unlike other men he performs all that the law demands and more besides. The tax-collector on the other hand, clearly distressed and agitated by his sense of his own unworthiness, pleads humbly with God for mercy. **This man**, says Jesus, **rather than the other, went home justified before God**.

11. The Pharisee does not really pray at all. He asks God for nothing, and his thanksgiving is merely a form. 'He glances at God, but contemplates himself' (Plummer, p. 417). 'He thanks God for what *he is*, not for what God is' (J. N. Darby, p. 152). **12. I fast twice a week, I give a tenth of all I get:** Pious Jews made a point of fasting on Mondays and Thursdays; Pharisees gave tithes not only of their crops, as the law required (Dt. 24: 22 f.), but even of their garden herbs (Mt. 23: 23). **13.** The tax-collector's distress is seen in that he beats his breast; cf. 23: 48. His only plea is his great need; cf. Dan. 9: 19.

(*b*) **Teaching on children (18: 15–17)**
Cf. Mk 10: 13–16; Mt. 19: 13–15. These two parables occur only in Luke, but for the account of the rest of the journey Luke again follows Mk. In this episode the disciples, seeking no doubt to spare their Master from added strain, turn away children who have been brought to Him to be blessed. Jesus countermands their order and calls the children to Him, **for the kingdom of God belongs to such as these**.

For more detailed treatment, see notes on Mk 10: 13–16.

(*c*) **The Rich Young Ruler (18: 18–30)**

Cf. Mk 10: 17–31; Mt. 19: 16–30. A ruler asks Jesus about eternal life and how it may be obtained. Jesus' answer suggests that the question is superfluous, since the rules are there for all to read in the Ten Commandments. The man claims that he has always obeyed these, but still feels his need of something more. The Lord then says that possessions are the barrier in his case; he must dispose of them and distribute to the poor. The correctness of the diagnosis is proved by the attitude of the enquirer; he is saddened by the Lord's words, because he was **a man of great wealth** (23). There follow sayings on the barrier erected by riches between their possessor and true spiritual life, and on the reward of those who for God's sake make sacrifice of riches.

18. a ruler: All the synoptics say he was rich, Luke only calls him a ruler, Matthew only says that he was young. **22.** Mark adds that 'Jesus, looked at him and loved him'. His possessions must be disposed of not because wealth is evil in itself, but because in his case it keeps him from spiritual blessing. **25. a camel:** It is not necessary to read this as 'rope', nor to see the needle's eye as a postern gate. Hyperbole is a frequently used figure of speech in our Lord's teaching; cf. 17: 6; 6: 41; also Mt. 23: 24, etc. **28, 29.** In Jesus' reply to Peter's comment about what they, the disciples, have given up, Luke omits 'sisters' and 'lands', but adds **wife** to the Matthew/Mark account. Matthew follows the incident by the parable of the Workers in the Vineyard (20: 1–16). See also notes on Mk 10: 17–31.

(*d*) **The third prediction of His death (18: 31–34)**
The third of the three predictions of the Passion recorded by all the Synoptics is uttered at this point (Luke himself has another: 17: 25). Luke omits the account of the ambition of James and John to occupy the highest places in the kingdom associated with the prediction in Mt. and Mk. This prediction is the first to link the suffering specifically with Jerusalem; Luke furthermore mentions that the sufferings are in fulfilment of OT prophecy. For comments, see notes on Mk 10: 32–34.

(*e*) **The Approach to Jerusalem (18: 35–19: 27)**

(*i*) **Healing a blind beggar (18: 35–43)**
Cf. Mk 10: 46–52; Mt. 20: 29–34. At last the long journey is almost over and they come to Jericho. At the gates of the city our Lord performs a miracle of restoration of sight. A beggar calls on Him, crying for mercy. Mark identifies the beggar as Bartimaeus; Matthew says there were two beggars. He addresses Jesus by His messianic title **son of David**, Jesus stops and asks him what he wants. He asks that his sight might be restored; his prayer is answered with Jesus' comment, **your faith has**

healed you. The result of this miracle is that not only the healed man but the onlookers also give praise to God.

(*ii*) **Zacchaeus the Tax-collector entertains Jesus (19: 1–10)**
The story of Zacchaeus, **a chief tax-collector, and was very wealthy**, is told only by Luke. He wanted to see this Jesus of whom he had heard so much, but he was so short that the crowd made it impossible for him to see anything. Accordingly, he climbed up into the branches of a tree on the route along which the party would pass. Jesus saw him in the tree and called him down, asking him for hospitality. The usual murmurs are heard that Jesus should eat with a tax-collector (cf. 5: 29, 30).

T. W. Manson calls the incident 'a fitting pendant to the parable of the Pharisee and the publican. In the parable He pillories the Pharisaic attitude towards these outcasts; in the case of Zacchaeus He shows by His own example a more excellent way' (*Sayings*, p. 312).

1. He . . . was passing through: They are now actually inside the city of Jericho. **2. a chief tax collector:** 'The title occurs nowhere else in extant Greek literature, so that its precise meaning is in doubt. He may have been a contractor who bought the local taxation rights from the Roman government' (Caird, p. 207). **3, 4.** There is no suggestion that he was trying to hide; he was quite open in his efforts to see Jesus. When Jesus spoke to him, he came down **and welcomed him gladly** (6). **8.** The profession of Zacchaeus seems to have been evoked by the ungracious comments in v. 7. There is all the difference between him and the Pharisee in the parable who gave his catalogue of good deeds from motives of pure self-congratulation. With Zacchaeus it was not so, the almsgiving and restitution of which he speaks start now as a token of the change wrought in him by his meeting with Jesus; 'not to be regarded as in the parable in self-justification, but as a statement of what he intends to do henceforth. "*Here and now I give half of my possessions to the poor*"—it is an act done there and then' (Plummer, p. 435). **10. the Son of man came to seek and to save what was lost:** The criterion in God's dealings with men is not man's merit but his need.

(*iii*) **The parable of the Pounds (19: 11–27)**
Jerusalem is at last in sight, and because the general expectation is that the prophecies concerning the kingdom will be fulfilled once they arrive within the city, Jesus tells them another parable.

A nobleman, going to a distant capital to **have himself appointed king**, leaves with various servants a pound each that they may trade until his return. He is not popular, and the citizens send a deputation in an unsuccessful attempt to secure the rejection of his claim. On his return with the desired royal dignity he calls the servants to give account of their stewardship; the successful ones are rewarded according to their success. One who confesses he has made no effort is rebuked and his pound taken from him; the rebels who have tried to throw off their master's rule are slain.

Matthew has a parable (the talents, 25: 14–30) which has striking similarities, but the differences are so marked that there is no possibility that the two are records of the same parable.

It is sometimes said that Luke's story is so mixed up that it cannot be genuine, that into Matthew's straightforward story he has worked the 'sub-plot' of the rebellious citizens. This, it is alleged, makes the story unbalanced and inconsequential. But these criticisms are without validity if, as seems likely, Jesus was relating an actual event, for real life is not always symmetrical! Josephus tells how Herod's will divided his territories after his death among his family, and how, before its bequests became valid, they had to be confirmed by the Roman Emperor. Herod's son Archelaus went to Rome for confirmation in his post, and was in fact followed by an embassy of protesting Jews. In the event, Augustus sided with Archelaus.

12. The nobleman going to receive kingly power becomes in Mt. 25: 14 'a man going on a journey'. **13.** Each servant receives a **mina**, worth, according to RSVmg, about $20 or £8. In Mt. 25: 15 different amounts—5, 2 or 1 talent—are given according to the recipient's ability. The talent was worth about $1,000 or £400, but its purchasing power was much more than that. **16, 18.** The successful servants have made profits of 1,000% and 500%; in Mt. 25: 16 f. each has made just 100%. **17–19** shows different rewards from those in Mt. 25: 22 f.

VII. THE PASSION WEEK (19: 28–22: 13)

i. The Triumphal Entry (19: 28–40)
Cf. Mk 11: 1–10; Mt. 21: 1–9. Now they enter the city, as the prophet Zechariah (9: 9) had long ago foretold, with their King welcomed by the plaudits of the people as He comes not as a military conqueror on a charger, but meek and lowly, seated on an ass, as befits the Ambassador of peace. With true majesty the Son of David moves on towards His Passion. He had made arrangements for the ass that Zechariah's prophecy might be fulfilled; He will be equally careful to see that all the other prophecies are fulfilled, even though it be His own death that is prophesied.

39, 40. It is Luke only who records the request of the Pharisees to Jesus to silence the crowds who acclaim Him as the Messiah; and His reply that if they were silenced the very stones would cry out.

For notes on details, see comments on Mk 11: 1–10.

ii. Jesus' view of the City (19: 41–44)
Cf. Mk 11: 11; Mt. 21: 10, 11. Jesus sees before Him now what earlier was but the distant goal (13: 34–38). His heart is saddened again, and He weeps over the city. Had His followers not sung His praises, the stones would have cried out. Those very stones are now witnesses to the people's blindness and obstinacy; soon their enemies **will not leave one stone on another**. Zechariah the priest (1: 67) had praised God who had visited His people; **you**, says Jesus to the people of Jerusalem, **you did not recognise the time of God's coming to you**.

iii. The Cleansing of the Temple (19: 45–48)
(Cf. Mk 11: 15–19; Mt. 21: 12, 13. For the relation of the Synoptic record of the Temple cleansing, dated early in Holy Week, to John's, which is placed at the outset of the ministry, see notes on Jn 2: 13–17.) Jesus expels from the Temple those who are turning God's house into a mere place of self-enrichment; who like robbers on the Jericho road have a sanctuary into which they can withdraw with their spoils after an attack. The Temple cleansed, Jesus spends the last few days of His freedom teaching the people there. See notes on Mk 11: 15–19.

iv. Controversy (20: 1–44)
Cf. Mk 11: 27–12: 37; Mt. 21: 23–22: 46. **every day he was teaching at the temple** (19: 47) describes His activity during the opening days of the week which is to see His crucifixion. **1. he was teaching the people in the temple courts and preaching the gospel:** Proclaiming the good news under the very shadow of the Cross. The Jewish leaders would love to silence Him, but various reasons make it unwise from their point of view. First, it is clear that the upsurge of popularity which greeted His arrival on Palm Sunday is not yet spent: **all the people hung on his words** (19: 48). Then, His action in protesting against the commercialization of the Temple worship is no doubt approved by many who could by no means be reckoned amongst His followers. Thirdly, while He is in the Temple He is under their eyes, and might possibly be caught out in something He says.

They have certainly not given up. The wheel has come full circle; our Lord's public ministry which began with conflict with the Pharisees because of His claims to unique authority closes in a further series of conflicts on the same subject.

1–8. So the attack begins. They come with an apparently guileless request for a statement from Him on the source of His authority for what He does. Instead of a direct reply He puts a question to them: **John's baptism—was it from heaven, or from men?** (4). Caught in the dilemma between admitting that they have refused the messenger of heaven or provoking popular anger by denigrating John, who by now has become a popular hero, they retire temporarily from the fray.

9–19. Jesus pursues His attack in His parable of the wicked husbandmen. The scene is the vineyard of Isa. 5: 1–7; the tenants refuse to pay their dues to the owner, and maltreat his messengers. Finally he sends his son and heir, whom the tenants murder in order themselves to seize the inheritance. The owner of the vineyard exacts retribution upon the murderers; the prophecy of Ps. 118: 22, 23 is fulfilled when the stone regarded by the builders as unfit for use becomes the chief cornerstone of the building. This stone, furthermore, brings disaster on every adversary. There is no difficulty in interpreting the parable; Isaiah tells the identity of the vineyard, its owner and its husbandmen; the Pharisees **knew he had spoken this parable against them** (19). Their determination to silence Him increases.

20–26. Spies and *agents-provocateurs* are set to watch Him, and if possible trap Him into compromising words. Luke does not mention the co-operation of the Herodians which, Mark and Matthew tell us, the Pharisees have enlisted, but he rewrites this introductory verse to make their intentions crystal clear. They open the question of tribute to Caesar, inviting Jesus to say either that it was unlawful, which would embroil Him with the Romans; or lawful, which might alienate His own followers. Replying, He shows that by using coins bearing the effigy of Caesar they are tacitly admitting the Roman claims; and, as J. M. Creed says: 'The answer of Jesus carries the implications (1) that man's relationship to God is established in its own right, and (2) that this relationship does not justify a repudiation of Caesar in his own sphere'.

27–40. This assault having failed, the Sadducees take a hand. For details of the Sadducees and their beliefs, see *NBD*. Their outlook was quite different from that of the Pharisees, whose oral tradition they rejected; they accepted nothing but the books of Moses, rejecting the existence of angels and the truth of life after death which had to be proved from the Prophets or the Writings. They pose a question which will, they hope, show that personal survival in after-life is at variance with the Mosaic teaching. According to Dt. 25: 5–10, if a man dies without an heir, any unmarried brother of his has an obligation to marry his brother's widow. The Sadducees propound the case of a woman who under this law in turn weds seven brothers; of which is she the wife in the life to come? Jesus replies, first that there is no marriage in heaven, since immortal beings have no need of procreation; and secondly that the very Pentateuch from which they have quoted bears strong testimony to the truth of life after death, for He who says (Exod. 3: 6) **I am the God of Abraham, the God of Isaac, and the God of Jacob** is the God not of the dead, but of the living! So another attempt to score a debating point has not only failed but recoiled on them to show the hollowness of their teaching. **37. in the account of the bush:** the Hebrew way of referring to Exod. 3.

41–44. In Mt. and Mk, the victory over the Sadducees is followed by a question concerning the great commandment which Luke places not here but as a preface to the parable of the Good Samaritan (10: 25–28). Jesus now puts His own question to His adversaries; it is reported by all three Synoptics: How can Messiah be David's Son if in Ps. 110: 1 David calls Messiah **Lord?** Luke, eloquently silent, records no reaction to this question. Mt. 22: 46 tells us that the Jews are completely silenced; Mk 12: 37 says that 'the large crowd listened to him with delight'. For detailed comments on Lk. 20: 1–44, see notes on Mk 11: 27–12: 37.

v. Condemnation of the scribes and Pharisees (20: 45–47)
Recorded also by Mark, and by Matthew at greater length (Mt. 23: 1–10). The long conflict of words is over; Jesus now utters a final scathing denunciation of the scribes (and Pharisees, Mt. 23: 2). See notes on Mk 12: 38–40, which Luke has almost verbatim.

vi. Jesus' observation of the widow (21: 1–4)
Cf. Mk 12: 41–44. With the spurious piety of the Pharisees and scribes, Jesus contrasts the sacrificial giving of a poor widow who casts into the treasury a mere two mites, while the rich make their lordlier donations. But it is not the amount given that is the measure of the sacrifice; it is the amount the giver has left when he has given. This widow has kept nothing back for herself. See notes on Mk 12: 41–44.

vii. The Apocalyptic Discourse (21: 5–38)
Cf. Mk 13: 1–37; Mt. 24; 25. The three Synoptics all place between the close of Jesus' public ministry and the events of the last few hours a long apocalyptic discourse, frequently referred to as the 'Little Apocalypse'. This discourse has been the subject of much discussion.

First, many who do not take kindly to the idea of predictive prophecy at all claim that Jesus did not foretell future events, and that passages which claim that He did are merely the early Church's ideas on the Last Things or her *ex post facto* 'prophecies' concerning incidents like the Fall of Jerusalem which had already taken place at the time of writing. In reply to such criticism it can confidently be said that for many years now there has been an increasing recognition of the essential part that apocalyptic and eschatology have in the teaching of Jesus; He *did* speak of things which had not yet come to pass.

Others accept this view, but see in the discourse a composite sermon composed of sayings of Jesus cognate to the subject, some or all of them authentic, but uttered at varying times and different occasions during His ministry.

Thirdly, the discourse according to Mt. 24: 3 was occasioned by two questions the disciples asked: when would the fall of Jerusalem be? and what would be the sign of His coming and of the close of the age? The result is that the two events, the impending and the remote, are in view, and it is not always easy to distinguish between them in the chapter.

Fourthly, there is the question of the relationship of the accounts of the discourse to each other. T. W. Manson (*Sayings*, p. 323) analyses Luke's version and finds that about half of its contents derives from Mk, another fifth is definitely non-Marcan (i.e. from Luke's own source), the remainder cannot be assigned with certainty to either. He interprets this as giving two possible alternatives: either that Luke had Mark's account before him and rewrote it freely (which for various reasons Manson deems unlikely) or that what we have is Luke's own source supplemented by passages from Mk. The discussion is interesting, but perhaps insufficient weight is given to the possibility that Mark and Luke each had an accurate summary of a discourse actually given on this specific occasion. Such summaries might have been independent of each other, and yet have verbal coincidences especially at important points. Even identical wording need not demand the explanation that one was dependent on the other.

Matthew, as has already been noted (see notes on Lk. 17: 30–37) includes in his version not only the material from Mk 13, but also that from Lk. 17; he also follows the discourse with a series of apocalyptic parables (chap. 25) which neither Luke nor Mark records. Notes on Mk 13 should be consulted for detailed commentary, the present notes will particularize only when Luke and Mk differ.

5–7. Cf. Mk 13: 1–4. In the opening verses Luke omits indications of place and people that Mk and Mt. give. The saying of vv. 5, 6 Mark places 'as he came out of the temple'. His companions are 'disciples'. Luke omits the place altogether and says merely that **some** spoke of the temple. V. 7 is placed by Mark 'on the mount of Olives, opposite the temple', and Peter, James, John and Andrew are with Jesus; here simply **"Teacher," they asked**. The discourse starts with reference to the stones of the Temple, a recurrence of the *motif* of 19: 40 and 20: 17, 18.

8–11. The signs of the coming judgment are going to be the rise of false Messiahs and the break-up of both the social and the natural orders with wars, disturbances, earthquakes, famines and pestilences. **8.** Luke adds to Mark's verse: **Do not follow them**.

12–19. The disciples themselves will know severe persecution from the authorities and even from their kinsfolk and friends. **12.** Here there is no reference to floggings, which Mk foretells (13: 9); Luke was later to describe in Acts some of the floggings the disciples endured. **14, 15.** This passage diverges from Mk 13: 11, to which however a close parallel is found in Lk. 12: 11, 12. **18.** The promise that **not a hair of your head will perish** is lacking in Mk. It is the experience of Daniel's three companions in the fiery furnace (Dan 3: 27). Cf. Ac. 27: 34.

20–24. Cf. Mk 13: 14–20. This passage, which tells of the catastrophes attending the fall of Jerusalem, differs at two important points from Mk's parallel: (*a*) The reference in Mk 13: 14 and Mt. 24: 15 to 'the desolating sacrilege set up where it ought not to be' (Dan. 9: 27; 11: 31; 12: 11) becomes in Luke **Jerusalem being surrounded by armies**. Many critics adduce this fact as evidence to date Luke after the fall of Jerusalem, but this very general reference to armies surrounding the city does not imply detailed knowledge of the events of A.D. 70. More likely is the suggestion of Geldenhuys (p. 532) that 'Luke is writing for Greek readers who would not understand what Jesus meant by the Jewish expression, and so paraphrases it'. (*b*) Luke omits the saying in Mt. and Mk (13: 20) about 'If the Lord had not cut short those days, no one would survive', replacing it by the statement that **Jerusalem will be trampled on by the Gentiles until the times of the Gentiles are fulfilled** (24). This refers probably to the end of the present world order.

25–28. The Great Consummation (Mk 13: 24–27). Before this section, Mk and Mt. introduce a passage which Luke has at 17: 20–23; Mt. also inserts the Lucan saying (Lk. 17: 24) about the day of the Son of man. Luke's description of the actual consummation shows two differences from Mk's: (*a*) after the prediction of signs in sun, moon and stars, he says there will be parallel calamities on earth: **anguish and perplexity at the roaring and tossing of the sea. Men will faint from terror, apprehensive of what is coming on the world** (25, 26); the sea is frequently a figure for the troubled world in the OT (cf. Ps. 107:

26–28; Isa. 57: 20, etc.); and (*b*) Mk, followed by Mt., places immediately after the actual appearing of the Son of man in glory the sending of the angel to gather in the elect from the four winds. Luke says instead: **stand up and lift up your heads, because your redemption is drawing near**.

29–31. The parable of the fig-tree (Mk 13: 28, 29). A short parable on discerning the signs of the times; very similar in all three Synoptics except that to Mk's fig-tree Luke adds **all the trees** (29).

32–36. Closing sayings. All three Gospels tell how these things (presumably those associated with the fall of Jerusalem) will take place in the present generation. Mk, however, gives no fixed time limit for the final parousia. God's word is surer, outlasting heaven and earth, but He has not revealed the precise date at which these events will occur, neither to the angels nor even to the Son (Mk 13: 32). Instead of this forthright declaration, Luke has a warning against a life of pleasure and indulgence blinding the eyes to the coming crisis, and a general exhortation to watchfulness. It is in this final section that Mt. inserts the warnings of Lk. 17: 26–30.

37, 38. Luke adds as a sort of footnote to the discourse a statement similar to that of 19: 47, 48 that Jesus preached daily in the Temple to large congregations, adding that he spent His nights on the mount of Olives.

viii. The conspiracy of the priests and of Judas (22: 1–6)
Luke follows Mk 14 closely, but omits the story of the anointing at Bethany, probably because he has already described the similar scene of 7: 36–50.

The **scribes** have not been idle since they dropped the conflicts of words in the Temple, and in Judas's approach to **the chief priests and the officers of the temple guard** they have had, from their point of view, a stroke of rare good fortune. As one of the Twelve, he is in a position to enable them to arrest Jesus in some quiet place without publicity and possible demonstrations. The crowds who saluted His triumphal entry, and those who have thronged daily to hear Him in the Temple, show that He enjoys a considerable measure of public support.

The betrayal by Judas is the definite act of Satan himself (3). But how is it possible that one who has enjoyed the daily companionship of Jesus can commit such an outrage? Did he see things going wrong, and turn 'king's evidence' to save his own skin? Was he disillusioned when Jesus did not seize the lead of some nationalistic rising, like the Messiahs of popular imagination? Was it just that he was a bad character? (John implies that he was certainly that, 12: 6.) Whatever it be, the ultimate reason for so black a deed remains an insoluble and horrible mystery.

ix. Preparations for the Passover (22: 7–13)

As with His mount for His entry into the city a few days before, Jesus has made secret arrangements for the use of an upper room where, before He suffers, He may enjoy the last hour of intimate fellowship with His disciples. Peter and John are sent on ahead to make necessary preparations for the celebration of the Passover; their guide will be easily identifiable by the water jar he is carrying. Few men care to be seen in public doing woman's work such as this!

VIII. THE LAST HOURS (22: 14–23: 56)

i. The Last Supper (22: 14–38)

I have eagerly desired to eat this Passover with you before I suffer: Like one leaving his family and first desiring a farewell meeting. 'When we see the divine glory in the person of Christ, we find the human affections shining out' (J. N. Darby, p. 171). The preparations have been made, **the hour came**, not only for the feast but also 'his hour . . . to leave this world' (Jn 13: 1); Jesus sits down with the Twelve and tells them clearly that it is the last time before He suffers. He gives them wine and bread, warning them that one of their company is the betrayer. Even such solemn circumstances do not prevent them from squabbling about their relative importance, perhaps with an eye to the succession when their Leader is gone. He recalls them to reality by reminding them of the glorious future ahead, but before that, severe testing, especially for Peter.

Two problems arising from this passage call for mention: (*a*) the differences between Luke's account and the others, and (*b*) the question whether the Passover itself was actually eaten or not.

(*a*) Luke's account of the Supper is extant in two versions, the longer one as in AV and NIV, and the shorter as in RSV, omitting vv. 19b, 20. There is good textual support for both readings, perhaps slightly more for the shorter. Taking the shorter text as a basis of comparison, there are outstanding differences between Mk and Luke:
(i) In Luke the cup precedes the bread (in the longer reading a second cup follows the bread).
(ii) The prophecy of Judas's treachery follows the institution, instead of preceding it as in Mk. (iii) Luke adds a number of sayings not recorded at the Supper by Mark.

Theologically, the most important of these differences is certainly the omission of the reference to the 'blood of the covenant', more remarkable still when linked with the fact that Luke does not include the 'ransom passage' of Mk 10: 45/Mt. 20: 28. Some claim this as evidence that Luke has no doctrine of a substitutionary atonement. It should not be overlooked however that even in the shorter version the covenant is not entirely absent, for in v. 29 the verb twice translated **confer** is etymologically cognate with 'covenant'. The longer text (19b) adds to the Mt./Mk version the injunction to perpetuate the rite: 'Do this in remembrance of me' (cf. 1 C. 11: 24).

(*b*) In v. 7 Luke specifies that it was the day **on which the Passover lamb had to be sacrificed**. In v. 15 Jesus says **I have eagerly desired to eat this Passover with you**.

Some argue that the second statement implies that the meal to which they sat down was actually the Passover; others that the first statement means that they met together on the Passover eve in preparation for the feast-day itself, and that they ate a fellowship meal; for such gatherings there were set rituals, some of which have survived. There is probably insufficient evidence to make a final decision. G. Dix, in *The Shape of the Liturgy* (1945), gives an interesting account of the ritual of the fellowship meal, and argues that the supper followed this. J. Jeremias puts the case cogently for regarding the meal as the Passover in *The Eucharistic Words of Jesus* (1955), pp. 14 ff. Balmforth also discusses the question exhaustively (pp. 261–265).

It is worthy of note that in none of the accounts in the NT (Synoptics, Jn, 1 C. 11) is there any mention of a lamb being slain. If the crucifixion itself took place on the Passover eve (see Jn 19: 14), then Jesus was on the cross at the very time the Passover lambs were being slaughtered, giving thus rich meaning to 1 C. 5: 7, 'for Christ, our Passover lamb, has been sacrificed'. There is some evidence for the observance of different religious calendars in Judea at this time: any group that chose to keep Passover by another calendar from that followed in the Temple would have to dispense with the lamb. (The reader should also note the discussion of the parallel passage in Mt.)

17. If, as has been suggested, this cup is the final cup of the preceding meal, it does not help to decide the point, since both Passover and fellowship rituals included several cups. **24–26.** Mk has a similar passage (10: 35–45), rather longer, and associated with the third prediction of the Passion. **25. Benefactors** (Gk. *euergetēs*): A favourite title adopted by Hellenistic kings. **27.** A parabolic saying that recalls Mk 10: 45. **31–33.** Peter is exhorted to stand fast, for Satan has made a similar application concerning him to that he made concerning Job (Job 1: 9–12). **35–38.** When He first sent them out to preach they were welcome everywhere. He now ironically suggests they should sell their cloaks to buy swords—they will need them! They do not detect the irony; Peter takes Him literally to the extent of using his sword.

ii. In the Garden (22: 39–46)

The scene changes from the upper room to the garden; at the supreme crisis of His life Luke once more shows us our Lord at prayer. He makes no reference to the special position of Peter, James and John, the attention being centred on Jesus Himself; and though only one prayer and not three is mentioned, the intensity of His agony is seen in the blood-like sweat and the sustaining angel, peculiar to the Lucan account.

39. The name Gethsemane does not occur here. As on the preceding days, Jesus goes to the mount of Olives (cf. 21: 37), though this means that Judas will know where to find Him. **43, 44.** Omitted in some ancient MSS, but retained in RSV.

iii. Betrayal and Arrest (22: 47–53)

Events move swiftly. Judas arrives with his new-found allies, and makes to salute the Lord with the traitor's kiss. Jesus reminds him that it is the Son of man whom he thus betrays. Peter, itching to do something, smites off with his sword the ear of the high priest's slave; Jesus' last miracle of healing is the curing of this wound. Unresisting and majestic, Jesus asks why they bring this armed rabble, when at any time they could have arrested Him in the Temple. Luke knew the answer to this question; he has already given it in 22: 2, 'they were afraid of the people'.

48. Luke does not record the fact that the kiss was a pre-arranged sign, as do Mt. and Mk. **52.** Luke only mentions that the rulers were present in person.

iv. Jesus in custody (22: 54–65)

(a) Peter's denial (22: 54–62)

Jesus is unceremoniously bundled along to the high priest's house to await His trial. Peter follows, **at a distance** it is true, but he has at least the courage to follow. Arrived at the palace he sits down among a crowd warming themselves at the fire. In this atmosphere his resolution weakens, and almost without realizing he thrice denies any knowledge of Jesus. The cock-crow reminds him of Jesus' warning. The act is done; too late he repents with bitter tears.

(b) The soldiers' horseplay (22: 63–65)

The boasted fairness of Roman justice and Jewish law is reduced to farce by the coarse buffoonery of the soldiers as they while away the hours of their guard-room duty.

v. The Trials (22: 66–23: 25)

Luke gives the completest account of the trials in the Synoptics; he alone tells of the hearing before Herod and of the fact that there were two sessions before Pilate.

(a) The Trial before Caiaphas and the Sanhedrin (22: 66–11)

As soon as morning breaks, Jesus is interrogated by the Sanhedrin, and they seek to extract from Him a claim to Messiahship. He gives them the answer they desire, and says also that He is Son of God (an answer they think they have cleverly tricked Him into giving, vv. 69, 70), but He warns them that they will have dealings with Messiah again, on a very different footing.

Matthew and Mark place the denial after this preliminary trial, Luke before. There is probably no contradiction. A trial at night, and before the comparatively small number of members of the Sanhedrin who could be mustered at once, could claim no shred of legality. An informal examination as soon as he had the prisoner in his hands was most likely made by Caiaphas and the rulers available, to be confirmed by a formal trial in full session when daybreak made the proceedings legal. Note that Luke does not refer to the suborned and yet inconsistent witnesses mentioned by Matthew and Mark.

(b) The first trial before Pilate (23: 1–7)

Having no power themselves to carry out the capital sentence, the Sanhedrin commit the accused to the court of Pontius Pilate, the Procurator, senior representative of the Roman power in Judea. They know that blasphemy will not be regarded by the occupying power as sufficient ground for the death sentence; so three trumped-up charges are formulated: (i) perverting the people by stirring up disaffection and rebellion, (ii) forbidding the people to pay tribute to Caesar, and (iii) Himself claiming to be a king. It is clear that Pilate is not impressed, yet he is loth to anger the Jews by acquitting Jesus. A very convenient way out appears to present itself when Pilate discovers that Jesus is a Galilean and therefore subject to the jurisdiction of Herod, who happens to be in Jerusalem (see article *The Historical Background*, p. 1039).

(c) The trial before Herod (23: 8–12)

The personality of our Lord seems to have exercised a curious fascination over Herod Antipas (see notes on 13: 31–33); now he **was greatly pleased, because for a long time he had been wanting to see him, he hoped to see him perform some miracle**. But it is at once clear that Jesus has no intention of satisfying his curiosity, and the 'trial' degenerates into mere horseplay. The prisoner is returned to Pilate, and the only positive result of the incident is the reconciliation of Pilate and Herod (cf. Ac. 4: 27).

(d) The second trial before Pilate (23: 13–25)

The final decision now rests squarely with Pilate, and even in Luke's brief account can be perceived the weak and vacillating character that John in his longer account portrays so clearly. 'Pilate', says Helmut Gollwitzer (pp. 46, 49), 'has power, but not freedom. . . . Pilate represents those people who *would like to* act rightly, but do not decide to do so'.

In his desire to evade his responsibilities, Pilate clutches at two straws. First he suggests to the Jews that Jesus does not deserve the death penalty, but a flogging might teach Him not to stir up the people. This does not satisfy His pursuers, so Pilate brings out his second suggestion. An annual custom permits an amnesty for one prisoner. Let Jesus be the one set free. No, say the Jewish leaders, **release Barabbas to us**—a man lying under sentence of death for acts of the very kind of which Jesus was falsely accused.

Pilate capitulates: **And their shouts prevailed** (23) . . . **surrendered Jesus to their will** (25).

vi. The Way to Calvary (23: 26–32)

In accordance with Roman custom the execution is carried out without delay. Mark (15: 15) tells us that Jesus was first flogged, a most brutal treatment as inflicted by the Romans. This, together with all He has gone through since He left the upper room, has weakened Him to such an extent that His custodians, fearing that His premature collapse might rob the gallows of its victim and them of their sport, press into service Simon of Cyrene (either a Cyrenian on a visit to the city for the feast perhaps, or a member of the Jerusalem synagogue of the Cyrenians) to relieve Him of the load of the heavy burden of the cross-bar of the gibbet which is proving too much for Him.

27–31. An incident recorded by Luke alone. A sympathetic group of women follow Him with the death wail of funeral mourners. He tells them that it will soon be they who will need comfort, for Jerusalem's doom is at hand (cf. 13: 34, 35; 19: 41–44, etc.). **29.** What dreadful calamities our Lord describes, that Jewish women should count barrenness a blessing! **30.** Quoted from Hos. 10: 8. **31.** A proverb: green wood does not normally burn, nor are innocent men executed. But if these things *do* happen now, how much worse will it be for dry wood and evil men?

vii. The Crucifixion (23: 33–49)

With two condemned criminals, Jesus is taken to a place called **The Skull**, and there the three are crucified, with Jesus on the middle cross. He prays for His murderers, and this prayer evokes curiously different reactions in His hearers. The execution squad are too intent on their gambling to heed what was taking place. The rulers scoff at such an inglorious end to one who claimed to be a king. The soldiers, parrot-wise, repeat the sneers of the rulers. A placard mocking His claims is nailed above His head. One of the criminals hanging at His side

vents all his bitterness on the one who claims to be the Messiah. One person, and one alone, seems to see any further, the other criminal, who begs and receives forgiveness and peace from the dying Lord Jesus. Then, committing Himself to His Father, Jesus dies, and the manner of His dying opens many eyes. The centurion in charge of the execution exclaims **'Surely this was a righteous man'**. The multitudes depart beating their breasts.

In all four Gospels two things above all impress in the account of the actual crucifixion. First, there is the amazing restraint with which the most brutal and dastardly crime of all history is described. To cite but one instance, none of the four tells of the nails driven through hands and feet; we know of them only through the mention of the wounds (cf. Jn 20: 25).

The full horror of the scene stands out more clearly because there is no attempt to harrow the feelings, no detailed insistence on the physical sufferings. Secondly there is the unmistakable impression that throughout the dreadful scenes it is in reality He who controls the course of events.

'Luke's picture of the crucifixion of Jesus', says Creed (p. 284), 'is based upon Mark, but his treatment, which is highly characteristic, has given a different tone to the scene. Jesus' love for the sinner, powerful in death as during life, and His unconquered trust in the Father's providential care, lighten the unrelieved gloom of the Marcan narrative'. Certain it is that Luke's picture is coloured by the three 'words from the cross' that he, and he alone, records. The general prayer for forgiveness for His persecutors, together with the personal assurance of forgiveness for the repentant malefactor reveal especially clearly that He who is God Himself is also perfect Man, still showing in the hours of bitter agony the same compassion and loving kindness as in the days of His active ministry. And the last word that Luke records as falling from His lips is the culmination of His life of constant communion with the Father in prayer, so frequently insisted on in the third Gospel: **Father, into your hands I commit my spirit!** 'He says: Father', says Gollwitzer (p. 81). 'This one word "Father", uttered by His Son in the extreme torture and agony of death, expresses more than any other word could convey of willing consent, of the inmost, heartfelt union of His will with the will of Him who permits Him to be put to death'.

33. The Skull: So-called because of the shape of the ground. Mt., Mk and Jn give the Aramaic form Golgotha, but Luke contents himself with its Gk. equivalent. In this verse, AV, following the Latin Vulgate, translates 'Calvary', the only occurrence of this Latin form in our English Bible. **34.** The prayer for His enemies is omitted in some MSS (see

RSVmg), but the textual evidence for its retention is extremely strong. For the prayer itself, see Lk. 6: 20, 35, etc. **They divided up his clothes by casting lots:** Cf. Ps. 22: 18. **35. the rulers even sneered:** Mt. 27: 46 and Mk 15: 34 quote also Ps. 22: 1 as a saying of Jesus from the Cross. **36. offered him wine vinegar:** Cf. Ps. 69: 21. **38.** AV includes a note that the superscription was in Hebrew, Greek and Latin (cf. Jn 19: 20), omitted on textual grounds by NIV as by RSV. **43. Paradise:** A word of Persian origin meaning an enclosed park or garden; used in LXX for the Garden of Eden. Notice how the prayer for mercy **when you come into your kingdom** is answered by the assurance of blessing today. **45. the curtain of the temple was torn in two:** This was the veil which separated the holy place from the holy of holies. It kept sinful man at a distance from the presence of God's glory, for only the high priest, on the annual Day of Atonement and bearing the blood of sacrifice, might enter (Lev. 16; Heb. 9: 7; 10: 19 f.). Now that the perfect sacrifice has been slain, the barrier is removed: God is fully revealed to man, and man has unimpeded access to God. **46. Into your hands . . . :** Quoted from Ps. 31: 5. **47. 'Surely this was a righteous man':** Luke rightly interprets the intention of the centurion's exclamation in Mk 15: 39, 'Truly this man was the Son of God!' (so RSV of 1962 and subsequent editions, in agreement with AV and NIV, as against 'a son of God', RSV of 1946 and 1952). Mark discerns in the exclamation a more profound significance, confirming his own emphasis (Mk 1: 1). **48. beat their breasts:** In token of deep grief (cf. 18: 13).

viii. The burial (23: 50–56)
Joseph of Arimathaea 'was a disciple of Jesus but secretly, for fear of the Jews' (Jn 19: 38). Now he comes out openly and requests Pilate's permission to inter the body of Jesus in his own tomb, newly rock-hewn. Hereby he not only fulfils the requirements of Dt. 21: 22, 23, but he also dissociates himself from the deed of the Sanhedrin to which he belongs. The request is granted, the women take note where the tomb is, so that they can return later to embalm the precious remains.

IX. RESURRECTION AND ASCENSION (24: 1–52)
i. The Empty Tomb (24: 1–12)
(For comparison with notes on this chapter, read notes on Ac. 1: 1–14, a summary of this chapter.)

The enforced rest of the Sabbath over, the women return **early in the morning** next day to the tomb, only to find that the great stone which sealed its mouth is **rolled away** and the tomb empty. As they are wondering what has happened, angelic visitors tell them that Jesus

has risen from the dead as He has said He would. The women go back to the apostles to report what has happened, but their story is received with incredulous scepticism.

Luke's story is in general outline very much like Mark's, but there are considerable differences in detail.

(*a*) Mark has one young man at the sepulchre, Luke has **two men**. (Matthew incidentally has an angel, John has two angels.) These are not necessarily contradictions. The **clothes that gleamed like lightning** of Luke suggests supernatural beings (cf. 9: 29). The difference between one angel or two may be due to nothing more than the fact that two were present, but that one only engaged in speech. At all events, the descriptions that we have are expressions in human words of a phenomenon that far transcended human experience.

But the truth of the story of the empty tomb does not depend on our ability to devise a satisfactory scheme of harmonization, but in the tremendous effect that the event had on the disciples, and on subsequent history.

(*b*) The lists of women's names in the two Gospels are slightly different. But neither of them is necessarily complete.

(*c*) Luke omits the message reported by Mark that Peter and the disciples are to meet Jesus in Galilee. The post-resurrection appearances recorded by Luke are all in Judea, but the disciples are reminded of teaching He gave them in Galilee.

(*d*) In Mark, the women were so startled by the events at the tomb that they found themselves unable to give the message to the disciples. In Luke, on the other hand, they go and report to the disciples all that has happened, though of course there is no message of a rendezvous in Galilee for them to convey.

The fact of the resurrection is one of the best historically attested facts of ancient history. For a clear and concise survey of the evidence, see J. N. D. Anderson, *The Evidence for the Resurrection* (London, 1950).

4. behold, two men: Cf. the Transfiguration (Lk. 9: 30) and the Ascension (Ac. 1: 10).
ii. The Walk to Emmaus (24: 13–25)
Later the same day two disciples are walking towards Emmaus, talking sadly over the events of the last few days when an unrecognized stranger overtakes them and joins in their conversation. He begins by seeking information, but before long they are hearing from His lips a thorough exposition of the messianic prophecies, with special emphasis on the theme of the necessity of Christ's sufferings. Arriving at their journey's end they invite Him to accept their hospitality. Soon again the rôles are reversed, their Guest seems to become their Host, for, presiding at their table, He breaks bread as they have seen Him do it before, perhaps when

He fed the five thousand. A flash of recognition, and He is gone. They return at once to Jerusalem and there the disciples tell them that Peter also has seen Him.

The Emmaus discourse is one of the most important in the NT, for in it our Lord taught how His life and mission, His death and resurrection had to be viewed in the context of God's self-revelation in the OT scriptures. It thus forms the vital connecting link between the OT promises and the apostolic exposition of their fulfilment in Jesus of Nazareth.

The OT is a book of unsatisfied longings and unfulfilled promises, which found their fulfilment when Christ came. The tragedy of the Jews was that their own presuppositions blinded them to much of what the Scriptures teach concerning the Messiah. Various strains of prophecy and promise blend in the figure of the Messiah, God's Anointed, whom He will send into the world. At times, He is the Shepherd of Israel, gently leading His sheep and caring for them. At others He is the coming King of glory and King of righteousness, who will rule the nations with a rod of iron and scatter the enemies of His people.

But there is another character, the Suffering Servant of Jehovah, the Man of sorrows, acquainted with grief, despised and rejected of men, nay even, in the hour of dereliction, forsaken by God Himself. To the Jews He was the personification of their own suffering nation, or perhaps one of the great martyr-heroes of their history. But Jesus leads the Emmaus couple to the truth that the Messiah and the Suffering Servant were one: **Did not the Christ have to suffer these things . . .?** It was only when the Scriptures had been opened to them thus (32), that their eyes could be opened also (31).

13. two of them: The masculine pronouns used of the couple and even the **foolish** (25) of EVV do not preclude the idea of man and wife, sometimes suggested to have been the case here. **Emmaus:** About 7 miles from Jerusalem. Its direction and actual location are not definitely known. **18. Cleopas** may be the same one mentioned in Jn 19: 25, but the name was quite common and there can be no certainty. Indeed Cleopas and Clopas may be quite different names, Clopas being perhaps a graecized form of the Aramaic name otherwise graecized as Alphaeus.

iii. In the Upper Room (24: 36–49)
While they are exchanging these wonderful experiences, He again appears. Despite these wonderful things they are paralysed with fear, for it seems they have been taken off their guard: **they were startled and frightened, thinking they saw a ghost**. He invites them to touch Him, He eats in their presence of the very food they are eating. He repeats briefly the

lesson of the Emmaus road, and commissions them to preach **repentance and forgiveness of sins . . . in his name to all nations**.

iv. The Ascension (24: 50–52)
The story has reached its conclusion. Six weeks after the resurrection (it is Luke himself who gives us the length of the interval, Ac. 1: 3), Jesus takes His disciples out to Bethany, where, lifting His hands in blessing, He is parted from them. The mode of departure does not seem to be recorded in Luke; the words **and was taken up into heaven** (NIV) have not very strong textual support. Again, for the details we must go to Luke's other book: Ac. 1: 9 tells us 'a cloud took Him out of their sight', the cloud that is the symbol of God's presence, the cloud out of which God had spoken in the mount of transfiguration.

What Luke does insist on is that, robbed again of their beloved Master within a few short weeks of His reappearance in resurrection life, this time they are neither depressed nor dispirited, but superlatively happy: **they worshipped him and returned to Jerusalem with great joy. And they stayed continually at the temple, praising God.**

BIBLIOGRAPHY

BALMFORTH, H., *St. Luke*. Clarendon Bible (Oxford, 1930; school edition, 1935).

BARRETT, C. K., *Luke the Historian in Recent Study* (London, 1961).

BROWNING, W. R. F., *St. Luke*. Torch Commentaries (London, 1960).

CAIRD, G. B., *St. Luke*. Pelican Gospel Commentaries (Harmondsworth, 1963).

CREED, J. M., *The Gospel according to St. Luke* (London, 1930). [on the Greek text.]

DARBY, J. N., *The Gospel of Luke* (London, 1859).

ELLIS, E. E., *The Gospel of Luke*. NCentB (London, ³1974).

FITZMYER, J. A., *The Gospel according to Luke*, 2 vols. Anchor Bible. (Garden City, N. Y., 1981–).

GELDENHUYS, J. N., *Commentary on the Gospel of Luke*. NLC (London, 1950).

GODET, F., *The Gospel according to St. Luke* (Edinburgh, 1879).

GOLLWITZER, H., *The Dying and Living Lord* (London, 1960).

LAMPE, G. W. H., 'Luke', in *Peake's Commentary on the Bible*² (London, 1962), pp. 820–843.

LEANEY, A. R. C., *The Gospel according to St. Luke*. BNTC (London, 1958).

LUCE, H. K., *St. Luke*. CGT (Cambridge, 1933). [on the Greek text.]

MANSON, T. W., *The Sayings of Jesus* (London, 1949).

MANSON, W., *The Gospel of Luke*. MNT (London, 1930).

MARSHALL, I. H., *Luke: Historian and Theologian* (Exeter, 1970).

MARSHALL, I. H., *The Gospel of Luke*. New International Greek Testament Commentary (Exeter, 1978).

MOORMAN, J. R. H., *The Path to Glory* (London, 1960).

MORRIS, L., *The Gospel according to St. Luke. TNTC* (London, 1974).

PLUMMER, A., *The Gospel according to St. Luke. ICC* (Edinburgh, 1896). [on the Greek text.]

SCHWEIZER, E., *The Good News according to Luke* (London 1984).

STONEHOUSE, N. B., *The Witness of Luke to Christ* (London, 1951).

JOHN

DAVID J. ELLIS

The late Archbishop William Temple wrote: '. . . the point of vital importance is the utterance of the Divine Word to the soul, the self-communication of the Father to His children. The Fourth Gospel is written with full consciousness of that truth . . .' Here, indeed, is the distinctiveness of the Fourth Gospel. For here the Word of God is living and active. It is Jesus Christ.

It is possible, however mistaken, to come away from the Synoptic Gospels with the impression that the essence of Christianity lies in trying to obey Christ's moral commands and in emulating His unselfish life. In the same way one may read Paul blinded to the definite personality of the Christ he worshipped. But no one dare come away from the Fourth Gospel without having seen that the writer utterly believed in the possibility of daily communion with the exalted Lord since He is the selfsame Person as the actual Man of flesh and blood who worked and taught in Palestine.

It is certain that the Gospel of John was regarded by its earliest readers as an authoritative exposition of the Church's life, in so far as this is represented by the union of every member with the risen Christ. The universality of its membership may well be pictured in Jesus' preaching to the Samaritans and the presence of Greeks at the Feast of the Passover. Its teaching on the spiritual nature of worship is reflected in the conversation between the Saviour and the woman of Samaria, and perhaps in Jesus' acted parable in the purging of the Temple. The Christian ordinances are symbolized in the Lord's discourse on 'water and spirit', and their effectual working in the life of the believer by His teaching on the Bread of Life. Here especially, John sees the dangers which attend any inordinate emphasis upon the outward sign above the inward grace which it symbolizes. John does not record the institution of the Lord's Supper. Instead he dramatically records the lesson in humility which Jesus taught His 'friends', showing them the necessity of being knit into one by their mutual love and warning them of the fatal possibility of eating 'his bread' whilst acting in treachery towards His kingdom. The allegory of the real vine in John is possibly the fullest expression in Jesus' teaching of what it means to be a disciple—a member of the Church, of Him.

There is in John a remarkable underlying agreement with distinctive Pauline teaching. Both John and Paul show that Christ is the express image of God, that creation subsists in Him, and that by adoption through Christ men are made the sons of God. Yet none of these doctrines is explicit in the recorded apostolic preaching in the Book of Acts. In that, emphasis was laid upon the Messiahship of Jesus, His death, resurrection and exaltation, with the added hope of His return to consummate the kingdom of God. Meanwhile God had provided the presence and guidance of the Holy Ghost for all those who repented and were baptized. Yet, John's experience is complementary to that of Paul. The latter constantly rejoiced in freedom from sin and the yoke of the law through the death and resurrection of Christ. This he enjoyed as a prelude to the ultimate manifestation of all the sons of God in glory. John, however, does not ignore sin. But he sees the tabernacle of God with men in Jesus Christ as the means by which men may enjoy positive communion with God here and now. Eternal life is already a fact. 'Whoever lives in love lives in God, and God in him' (1 Jn 4: 16).

John is markedly distinct from the first three Gospels. In a number of instances, however, the writer may have fallen back upon the Synoptic narratives. The feeding of the five thousand, and his references to 'the Twelve' seem to assume that the reader is familiar with the Synoptic record. There is no simple parabolic method in Jesus' teaching as recorded here. Rather is there a collection of discourses in which the relation of the Father to the Son is worked out with theological precision. In the Synoptics there is no formal recognition of Jesus' Messiahship—apart from those uttered when Jesus afterward enjoined silence upon some who would have confessed Him openly —until late in the ministry (cf. Mk 8: 29). But in John there are those, who with the Baptist recognize early on that Jesus is the Messiah at the moment of their first meeting with Him. Yet this is only what we should expect from the nature of those special manifestations which, as John records, Jesus made to the Baptist and his disciples.

The distinctiveness of John's presentation of Jesus' teaching is compared by W. F. Howard and others with the Targumic principle of translating the Hebrew scriptures with a running commentary. Here and there in the Fourth Gospel it is clear that we have the inspired comment of the Evangelist alongside the words or actions of Jesus Himself. The Gospel is the work of reflection as well as recollection. No clearer statement concerning its purpose could be made than in the closing words of the penultimate chapter: '. . . these are written that you may believe that Jesus is the Christ, the Son of God, and that by believing you may have life in His name' (20: 31). The miracles of Jesus here, then, are signposts (Gk. *sēmeia*) towards the grounds for belief in Jesus. This is just why the Jews have special mention in the Gospel. John regards the unbelief of the Jews as one of the prominent tragedies of the earliest Christian years.

More positive reactions to the Christian message, however, came from Docetics, whose name comes from the Greek verb *dokein* 'to appear' or 'to seem'. These were semi-Christian teachers, who, in slightly varying ways according to a variety of different schools of thought, taught that if Christ were God then He could not be truly human. A later development of Docetism emphasized that God is impassible, that is, He is incapable of change such as human flesh permits in mankind, or as human emotions display in human beings. To them deity was by necessity totally removed from any kind of human contact, and therefore, as one of their leading exponents declared, when commenting on the Passion of Christ, 'he only seemed to suffer'. John combated these ideas by special emphasis upon the humanity of Jesus (cf. 2: 24; 4: 6 f.; 6: 51; 11: 35), which reaches its climax in the Gospel with the solemn declaration by Pilate, 'Here is the man!' (19: 5) and the physical details surroundings Jesus' final moments of suffering on the cross (cf. 19: 28, 34 f.).

'"Jesus", writes F. F. Bruce, "came . . . by the water *and* the blood"; that is to say, Jesus was manifested as Messiah and Son of God not at His baptism only but on the cross as well; the one who died was as truly the Incarnate Word as the one who was baptized' (*The Spreading Flame*, 1958, p. 246).

F. von Hügel pointed out that this Gospel is history from the eternal point of view (*Encyclopaedia Britannica*, 1962, vol. 13, p. 99). So the facts so often plainly elaborated in the Synoptics are interpreted in John. Some scholars have even seen the relation of John to the Synoptics as a juxtaposition of history and theology. The Synoptics, they claim, are presenting theology from a historical point of view, whilst John writes history from a theological standpoint. When we read of Jesus' word to the disciples, '. . . I have called you friends . . .' (15: 15) we know He is the supreme Friend who drew the children to Him (cf. Mt. 19: 13 ff.) and who

spoke of them as they played at weddings (and funerals!) in the market-place (Mt. 11: 16 f.). He is the Friend who told of the compassionate Samaritan and the long-suffering Father (Lk. 10: 29–37; 15: 11–32). And conversely when we read in the Synoptics of Jesus' authority to forgive sins, it is in John that we learn whence such authority is derived in eternity and how it is exercised in full co-operation with the Father.

No arguments regarding the authorship of this Gospel can be concluded without all the facts, external and internal, in mind. It is generally held that the writer was a Jew, living in Ephesus towards the end of the first century, though some scholars have advanced a date somewhat later than this. It has been held by some that three minds have contributed to the final result—the witness (cf. 19: 35; 21: 24), the Evangelist, and a redactor. In spite of this view, however, there has been little agreement by the main proponents of this theoretical trio as to the part played by each member in the composition of the finished Gospel. Some argue that the special chronological arrangement of John is due to the redactor, while others, notably Bernard, believe that he was responsible for the placing of a few minor notes.

It has been cogently argued that the Gospel was first written in Aramaic, and that though the writer was widely influenced by Greek thought he was more interested in the background of Jewish thought as a prelude to the message of Christ. Indeed, it is probable that the supposed influence of Greek ideas in John is an idea which has been taken too far by some modern commentators. Any special usage of Greek words and ideas in the Gospel may merely reflect that there were terms in current use at the time when the Gospel was written which were specially valuable for depicting the Person and Work of Christ in the way which is germane to the Fourth Gospel.

A distinction has been made between the Elder John, and the Apostle of the same name. Eusebius assigned Revelation to the Elder and the Gospel to John the Apostle. Modern scholars have, from time to time, reversed this order and assigned the Gospel to the Elder and the Revelation to the Apostle. Whatever may be the difficulties regarding the author of the Apocalypse, he was certainly identified as the Apostle John by Justin Martyr (*c.* A.D. 140). It is clear that the theological outlook of the two books is strikingly similar, so that we can say with certainty at least that the *milieu* of the two works seems to be identical. None of the usual arguments set forth in order to distinguish 'the beloved disciple' from John the Apostle is finally convincing. That he should have been known in this manner is quite in keeping with the various ways in which this disciple is portrayed in the Gospel. Indeed, the statement of Papias recorded by Eusebius (*HE* III. xxxix 4), which has been widely used to keep John the Apostle distinct from 'the elder John' can be read to mean that the Elder and the Apostle are one and the same.

The Letters of John are almost certainly from the Evangelist. The First Letter applies the Gospel to the problems of the primitive Church. It is less concerned with the hostility of the Jews, however, and more with the dangers of Gnosticism. Westcott has said that the burden of the Gospel is 'Jesus is the Christ', of the Letter that 'the Christ is Jesus' (p. lxxxviii). (See pp. 1652 ff.).

ANALYSIS

PART ONE—INTRODUCTORY (1: 1–2: 11)

I THE WORD MADE FLESH AND MANIFESTED (1: 1–2: 11)

i Prologue (1: 1–18)
ii The witness of John (1: 19–34)
iii Jesus' first followers (1: 35–2: 11)

PART TWO—THE PUBLIC MINISTRY (2: 12–12: 50)

I CHRIST'S PREACHING OF HIS MESSAGE (2: 12–4: 42)

i The cleansing of the Temple (2: 12–25)
ii Jesus and Nicodemus (3: 1–21)
iii The Baptist's final testimony (3: 22–36)
iv The Samaritan woman (4: 1–42)

II REVELATION BY DEEDS AND WORDS (4: 43–6: 71)

i The official's son (4: 43–54)
ii The cripple of Bethesda (5: 1–47)
iii Feeding the masses (6: 1–15)
iv A storm at sea (6: 16–21)
v Living Bread (6: 22–59)
vi Disciples' faith and unbelief (6: 60–71)

III JESUS, THE SOURCE OF ALL TRUE BLESSINGS (7: 1–10: 39)

i Controversy at the Feast of Tabernacles (7: 1–52)
ii The true Light and its implications (8: 12–59)
iii The man blind from birth (9: 1–41)
iv The Good Shepherd (10: 1–21)
v Final encounter with the Jews (10: 22–42)
vi Lazarus' resurrection and its sequel (11: 1–57)

IV THE LAST SCENE OF CONFLICT (12: 1–50)

i The supper at Bethany (12: 1–11)
ii The Messianic Entry (12: 12–19)
iii The Greeks' request and Jews' rejection (12: 20–43)
iv Christ's summary of His message (12: 44–50)

PART THREE—FINAL DISCOURSES AND EVENTS (13: 1–21: 25)

I THE UPPER ROOM MINISTRY (13: 1–21: 25)

i Practice and precept in humility (13: 1–17)
ii The traitor (13: 18–35)
iii Comfort for the disciples in distress (13: 36–14: 31)

PART ONE—INTRODUCTORY

(1: 1–2: 11)

I. THE WORD MADE FLESH AND MANIFESTED (1: 1–2: 11)
i. Prologue (1: 1–18)

There is probably no other place in the NT where so much is said, as here, with such economy of words. Here is set forth the uniqueness of Christ and the great consequences which follow from His self-sacrifice embodied in the Incarnation. In this Prologue John announces his main theme, which is the glory of Jesus Christ shown by all which He both said and did. **1. In the beginning was the Word:** Unlike the Synoptic writers, the fourth Evangelist begins the story in eternity; and it is from here that he understands the significance of the work of Christ. **In the beginning** (cf. Gen. 1: 1) pushes back our conception of the purpose of God beyond even Creation so that the Word, as the second Person of the Trinity, existed in His own right. The **Word** (Gk. *ho logos*) was supposedly employed by the writer for reasons of making the Gospel relevant to his first readers. Yet the conception of *ho logos* is of supreme importance for the Evangelist's doctrine of Christ apart from any other special reason for which he used the term. [See Additional Note 1. see p. 1263]. **and the Word was with God** (Gk. *kai ho logos ēn pros ton theon*): That is, from eternity there has ever been a distinction within the Godhead. It does not help us much to understand this as the Word existing 'over against' the Absolute God. The simpler sense suggested here seems to be endorsed elsewhere where prepositions are similarly used (cf. Mk 6: 3; cf. also Mk 10: 27). **and the Word was God** (Gk. *kai theos ēn ho logos*): The fulness of the Godhead and the Word are identified. The active Word immanent in the world is no less God than the transcendent God beyond all time and space. The absence of the definite article in front of

'God', taken by some to mean that the Word possessed something less than full deity, implies, however, that other persons exist outside the second Person of the Trinity. **2. He was with God in the beginning:** Both the Word and His relationship to the Eternal are eternal. There was never part of His pre-existence which found Him to be separated in any sense from the Godhead. So the deity of Christ is set forth without yet any specific personal qualities being ascribed to Him as the second Person of the Trinity. C. K. Barrett aptly comments: 'The deeds and words of Jesus are the deeds and words of God; if this be not true the book is blasphemous' (p. 130). **3. Through him all things were made** (Gk. *di' autou*): The Word, coming forth from God, was the Agent in Creation, which, unlike Him, is not eternal, and yet, **nothing was made that has been made** (cf. Prov. 8: 30). There is not, as some Gnostic thinkers were disposed to believe, any other means of creation than God Himself. There is a possible alternative reading here, *viz.*, 'without him was not anything made. That which has been made was life in Him.' The usual reading is preferable, however. John tells his readers that in Christ there is a visible link between God and the material world. This world rightly belongs to God, who made it (cf. Heb. 1: 2; 11: 3). It is generally agreed that Gnosticism was never far from the mind of the writer of the Gospel. The Gnostics taught that only spirit can be good and matter is essentially evil. But John, in common with Paul (cf. Col. 1: 16) maintains by his doctrine of creation by the Word of God, and the Incarnation of that Word, that this world of matter is indeed the handiwork of the Almighty, who has entered into it in Jesus Christ. It is not *essentially* evil, though man by sin has wrought misery within it (cf. Gen. 1: 10, 12, 18, 21, 25). **4. In him was life:** The universe, made by the Word of God, and immersed in His living active will, shows in itself the organic, active property of life. And this principle in the created world shows itself again in Christ, who has come to bestow life by the Incarnation (cf. 10: 10). This life becomes the **light of men**. It is the living, developing element in the universe that shows God to man (cf. Rom. 1: 20); it is the basis and truth of revealed religion. **5. The light shines . . . :** This is the burden of the Fourth Gospel, namely, that God is revealed absolutely in Jesus Christ. All that men may expect by way of revelation and salvation is to be seen in Him. Yet God has provided man with continuous revelation, for the light shines **in the darkness**, which describes man's distance from God, and showing that God has always revealed Himself to man in some way. The Incarnation, however, has revealed God with unique clarity, such that, in the nature of the case, **the darkness has not understood it**.

'Life' and 'light' are two words especially associated with John in the NT. Later in the Gospel Jesus asserts that He is both the Life (cf. 11: 25; 14: 6) and the Light (cf. 8: 12; 9: 5). In the Prologue, however, these claims are put in to their essential setting. What Jesus claims to be *in* the world He is *always*. This is characteristic of God in the OT. Divine activity has created life and sustains it. God is, thereby, the source of man's illumination (cf. Ps. 36: 9 f.). In the Gospel, moreover, 'life' carries distinct overtones of salvation, deliverance. In so far as it is brought into the world by Christ (cf. 2 Tim. 1: 10), it denotes His particular work on behalf of mankind, the most responsible section of the created world. 'Light' in John implies revelation which leads men towards 'life', which places men under solemn responsibility, and by this brings them into judgment if they refuse it (cf. 3: 19). The presence of darkness is usually taken for granted where 'light' is mentioned. And when there is no response to the true Light, then, whatever 'light' men may profess to have, in reality they have no light at all (cf. 9: 41).

6. There came a man . . . : Now the theme distinctively breaks in upon human history. John the Baptist is mentioned here first since he acted as a **witness to testify concerning that light** by being a 'burning and shining lamp' (cf. 5: 35) so that through his work **all men might believe**. **9.** The meaning here has been obscured by the AV. It is best preserved by rendering (as RSV and NIV) **coming into the world** and attaching the phrase to **the true light**, not to **every man**. He, distinct from John, is **the true light**, Gk. *to phōs to alēthinon*, meaning real or genuine light (not true as distinct from false, which would be expressed by *alēthēs*). In what sense can He be said to enlighten every man? Only in the sense that 'light' brings judgment (cf. v. 5 and 3: 19–21). Christ's coming has shed light on the darkness of the human situation and continues to do so

in the life of every man. **10. the world was made through him . . . :** This applies to that part of creation (cf. v. 3) which is capable of making sensible response. The **world** (Gk. *kosmos*) is the world of people, especially those who, in this Gospel, are confronted with the truth in Christ. (Often in the Gospel, however, it is described as 'this world', which refers to *our* world over against the world above from which Christ came; cf. 8: 23.) Both uses of the term imply the antagonism which was shown to Christ. **the world did not recognise him:** This use of the verb 'to know' (Gk. *ginōskō*) means 'to recognize'. It is noteworthy that the Evangelist never uses the corresponding noun 'knowledge' (Gk. *gnōsis*); he is at pains to avoid that form of Gnosticism which taught salvation by knowledge for an intelligent élite. Since 'knowing' in John implies observation, obedience and trust, it is not surprising that 'knowing' and 'believing' are almost synonymous (cf. 17: 3; 6: 69). **11. He came to that which was his own, but his own** is a paraphrastic translation of Gk. *ta idia*, though it aptly expresses what the writer intended in referring to that particular area—Palestine—which within the world occupied a special position in God's favour (cf. 19: 27). But **his own** (*hoi idioi*) **did not receive him**, though from 13: 1 onwards the title *hoi idioi* is restricted to those who did receive him. This at once summarizes the rejection of Christ and the reasons, humanly speaking, for His suffering. To such, however, who received Him by faith in His name **he gave** (Gk. *edōken*) **the right to become children of God**. This is God's gift. Men have no natural claim to be the children of God. Only Christ gives men the power (Gk. *exousia*— 'right') to become such. **Children born** since life in Christ commences by birth, i.e., by the distinct activity of God as the Source of all. This birth contains no human element at all; nor does it lie within the scope of human achievement, **nor of human decision**, nor is it mediated by reason of maturity—**a husband's will** (Gk. *ek thelēmatos andros*). **14. The Word became flesh:** There is no suggestion in these words that at the Incarnation the Word became a Person. Personality had always been His possession. 'Flesh' (Gk. *sarx*) denotes the human realm compared with the heavenly (cf. 3: 6; 6: 63). Here, then, is the great inexplicable part of the doctrine of Christ, that the Eternal Word entered into human life. Nor did He surrender His identity in flesh, for while He dwelt among men—a fact to which the Gospel essentially turns—there were those who had **seen his glory**, i.e., the visible manifestation of God, whose nature was, as men had understood in the past, **full of grace**, denoting the initiative taken by God when He bestows favours upon men, **and truth** as the final and perfect embodiment of divine revelation. The grace of God and the truth of God are alike enshrined in the Christian message. God in Christ calls men to trust Him and adore Him. And the perfect balance of grace and truth, demonstrated in the unfailing equanimity exercised by Jesus on earth, is shown in the succeeding chapters. Often He took the initiative in coming to men when they needed Him; and He embodied the truth in His own Person (cf. Exod. 34: 6; Jn 14: 6), as **the one and only who came from the Father**, that is, uniquely Son of God. His eternity precludes any notion that His being was derived from the Father, but, as the words suggest, His existence and work were never independent of the Father—a fact to which Jesus Himself bore testimony (cf. 10: 25, 30). John leaves the doctrine of the Logos at this point, and now concentrates upon the relationship between the Father and the Son. **16. from the fullness of his grace we have all received:** The doctrine of Christ and of God which opens this Gospel is never to be regarded as a mere credal affirmation. The **fullness** of grace and truth is something which is mediated to men via experience. And the Evangelist is not alone in this. 'We have received it', he writes, perhaps linking the testimony of other believers at Ephesus in his day, or joining in spirit with all who subsequently to his own testimony would have faith in Christ. Moreover, the combined testimony of the people of God concluded that the Christian life was **one blessing after another**, as every experience of His loving help led on to a fuller experience of God's goodness. **17. For the law was given through Moses:** God's gift of salvation to His ancient people was through the external compulsive power of law. Now, in Christ, men are constrained to love God by the compelling power shown in Jesus Christ. **18. No one has ever seen God:** This is a basic assumption of the OT. Even where it might be suggested that something of God had been seen by men (*e.g.* Exod. 33: 22 f.; Isa. 6: 1; Ezek. 1: 1), the Aramaic Targums, which were paraphrases of certain parts of the OT, tended to use circumlocutions for the divine name, and would have rendered it by some such term as *memra*, i.e. 'the word'. But the importance of this for understanding the background of John has been over-emphasized by some commentators. God is now seen in the incarnate Word, **the One and Only Son**. There is a variant reading here, *viz.*, 'God only-begotten', which is supported by a number of important MSS, and by some of the earliest patristic commentaries. It would be quite in accordance with what John elsewhere records concerning the deity of Christ (cf. 20: 28; 1 Jn 5: 20). Yet acceptance of the usual reading seems preferable since this also accords well with John's writing (cf. 3: 16, 18; 1 Jn 4: 9). Christ **is at the Father's side**, an expression denoting a relationship of love and perfect understanding.

ii. The witness of John (1: 19–34)
The Evangelist now turns to John the Baptist in order to spotlight the person of Jesus through his ministry. The philosophical language of the Prologue is dropped and we pass to a chronological record of some six days (not seven as some infer from v. 41) taking us eventually to 2: 11.

19. the Jews have special mention throughout the Gospel. Here they seem to be the leaders of the people in Judea, and are the strongest opponents of the Lord. Possibly John wishes to portray the tragedy of those who fail to recognize Jesus as the Messiah, or His coming as the advent of the kingdom. **Levites** were members of the Temple staff who attended to its material care and acted as its guards. **20. I am not the Christ:** John's answer to the first question shows how dramatic must have been his appearance in Judea as the Baptizer. Few could escape noticing him. **21. Are you Elijah?:** John disclaims any connection whatever with Messianic fulfilment (cf. Mk 9: 13; Mal. 4: 5 f.). **Are you the Prophet?:** The prophet like Moses (Dt. 18: 15 ff.) who in these days was widely expected to arise on the eve of the messianic age (cf. 6: 14; 7: 40). **No:** So John's threefold denial in self-abnegation is complete. The three answers which he gives ring true as those which would naturally succeed each other in heated conversation. When pressed, however, the Baptist admits that he is **the voice. . . .** (23). He claims no dignity save that which is conferred upon him as a preacher of the Word (cf. Isa. 40: 3). **the way for the Lord:** Stauffer has shown that this conception lies at the heart of the earliest records of the ministry of Jesus (*NTT*, pp. 25–29). **24. some Pharisees** (cf. *NBD*, pp. 981 f.) apparently had a special interest in the authority which lay behind John's baptismal practice. **26. I baptize with water . . . :** John makes no reference here to Christ's baptism with the Holy Spirit. This was not understood, we may presume, until he had seen that Spirit descending upon Jesus at His baptism. But he does point out that there is someone close to hand who is unexpected. Their acquaintance with baptismal practice is clear (cf. v. 25). But Christ will exceed their understanding of what forms true religion. For John this is based on pure faith; he will not even be presumptuous enough to call himself His slave (27). **28. Bethany** is not the Bethany of Mary and Martha (cf. 11: 1; Mk 14: 3–9). Some texts read 'Bethabara'. But though its precise location is uncertain by the third century, ch. 11 indicates a careful distinction between two such places known by the same name (cf. 10: 40 with 11: 18), and the reference there to 'the place where John at first baptized' is significant. **29. Look, the Lamb of God:** Here an amalgamation of OT metaphors seems to present itself. We may recall the Paschal lamb (Exod. 12) or the divinely given offering of Abraham (Gen. 22: 8), where the force of the Heb. text might be that 'God will *see* . . . a lamb . . .' Or we may think of the expiatory sacrifices in general Jewish liturgical practice (cf. Lev. 23: 12 ff.). There appears to be an obvious link with Isa. 53: 7, where, in the LXX, Gk. *amnos* 'lamb' renders Heb. *raḥel* (cf. Ac. 8: 32). Here the sin-bearing function is implicit more than explicit. Yet it is not unlikely that the daily Jewish offerings were in John's mind. The greatest OT passage is that which depicts the goat for Azazel which carried away Israel's sin (cf. Lev. 16: 21) into a solitary land. Barrett sees John's reference as twofold: the Paschal lamb of Exod. 12, together with the victim who vicariously bears away Israel's sin in Lev. 16. It is altogether unlikely, as Dodd suggests, that the title is purely Messianic, and synonymous with the titles of 1: 49, and the lamb (Gk. *arnion*) of the Apocalypse (cf. Rev. 14: 1), who leads His people in victory. Yet it is significant that it *is* only here and in Revelation that Christ is described as the Lamb of God (cf. note on 19: 36). Burney has suggested that some confusion has arisen here between Aramaic 'servant' and 'lamb' (*talya*; cf. *AOFG*, pp. 104–109), but this rests entirely on the validity of Burney's general thesis that John was originally an Aramaic work. **the sin of the world:** John saw by faith that Christ was able to bear away the totality of sin, which idea, indeed, will have been close to his mind if he were thinking of the Isaianic prophecy (cf. Isa. 53: 11). This then is the principle upon which life in the new age begins, that Christ is the universal Saviour. **32. I saw the Spirit come down . . . :** John's work was to show men the way to Christ. So, too, from the beginning, the Spirit singles out Christ. He descends upon Him, and in so doing makes His unique witness that Jesus is Son of God (cf. v. 34). And the imparting of the Spirit which the Lord Himself makes is likewise for a witness to Himself (cf. 16: 14). Note the fact that in the Synoptics (cf. Mt. 3: 16) it is Jesus who sees the Spirit coming down, whilst here He is observed by the Baptist. This makes the whole incident clearly one which was shared by Christ and His forerunner, and not a private experience known only to the one or the other. **34. . . . the Son of God** (cf. Mk. 1: 11): The close connection between John's recognition and the manifestation of the Spirit must be noted. Only by the Spirit can a true confession of Christ be made (cf. 16: 8–11; 1 C. 12: 3). Some early authorities read here 'the chosen

One of God'. But this reading is probably an assimilation to Lk. 9: 35 (cf. Ps. 2: 7; Isa. 42: 1).

iii. Jesus' first followers (1: 35–2: 11)
John's renewed confession now induces two of his disciples to go after Jesus (cf. Mt. 11: 2–6; Lk. 7: 18–23). **37. followed:** No doubt lay in the minds of those who understood John's message. **38. Rabbi:** The term occurs frequently in John (cf. 1: 49; 3: 2; 4: 31; 6: 25, *et alia*). It is a title given to a teacher. There were many in NT times (cf. *NBD*, p. 1072). **39. about the tenth hour:** i.e., about 4 p. m. The following verses, 40–42, are an appendix to the event just described in vv. 35–39. **40. Simon Peter** is the double name usually employed in John. **41. the Messiah:** Only John uses this transliteration of the Heb. *māshīaḥ*. The mention of the title is in no way conflicts with the 'messianic secret' of Mark. Here it is a personal and private testimony, and in its context it accords well with the apostolic preaching (cf. Ac. 10: 38). Moreover the sequence of events just enacted would be such that would inevitably lead some to recognise in Jesus the embodiment of OT ideals and expectation (cf. Dan. 9: 25; on the term in OT generally see *NBD*, pp. 811–818). **42. Cephas** (cf. Mk 3: 16): The word is Aramaic. There is no suggestion at present regarding the purpose for which Simon was given this name. **45. We have found the one Moses wrote about:** Barrett suggests that this refers to rabbinic interpretation of a number of Pentateuchal passages. (But cf. 3: 14; see also Gen. 49: 10; Dt. 18: 15; Ac. 3: 22; 7: 37.) Yet Philip makes Jesus known by terms which would have been commonly understood— . . . **the son of Joseph. 46. Come and see:** Nathanael reflects the general wariness of the Jews in NT times, and retorts that no recognition of the Messiah could be expected until he were seen. So Philip's answer invites Nathanael to see for himself. **47. Here is a true Israelite, in whom there is nothing false:** Unlike Simon, Nathanael is given no second name. Jesus' omniscience is seen by his reference to **the fig tree** (48). There is no allegorical significance here. **49. the Son of God:** On Nathanael's lips this may mean little more than 'Messiah' (cf. Ps. 2: 7); to the Evangelist it means much more. **the King of Israel:** The definite article is omitted in the Greek text. Nathanael's confession was spontaneous and all-embracing. This is a messianic confession. The true Israelite acknowledges his true King. **50. You believe:** Perhaps Nathanael's acclamation, however, was restricted to this messianic and nationalistic sense (cf. 2 Sam. 7; 13 f.). If this is so, Nathanael will indeed see **greater things. 51. You shall see heaven open** (Gk. *aneōgota*): Perhaps this is an eschatological picture (cf. Mt. 26: 64; but see also Mk 1: 10, where the verb used means 'torn apart', echoing Isa. 64: 1). **the angels of God**

ascending and descending: An undoubted reference to Jacob again (cf. Gen. 28: 10–17). Westcott understands this of prayers taken to God through Christ, and the answers sent in Him, seeing that He is ever present (cf. Mt. 28: 20). But Jesus' words are more likely to have been coloured by Jewish theology and apocalyptic (cf. Dt. 33: 2 f.; Zech. 14: 5 f.; Dan. 7: 13 f.). **on the Son of Man:** The Heb. text of Gen. 28: 12 is grammatically ambiguous. Some rabbis interpreted 'on it' (Heb. *bō*) to refer actually to Jacob himself, and saw in the event an interaction of the heavenly and earthly man. More probably we should understand this picture as denoting the embodiment, in Jesus, of a heavenly fellowship between God and man, brought about by the death of Jesus, which John sees as one with His glorification, and which would be underlined by his usage of 'Son of man'. In the Synoptics the idea is founded not on Ps. 8, but on Dan. 7. The Son of man is a heavenly figure who enters the earthly realm, yet whose real abode is ever in heaven (cf. 3: 13; 6: 62; Mk 13: 26; 14: 62). His appearance on earth is but part of a journey which ultimately will take him back into heaven (cf. 6: 27; 8: 28; Rev. 1: 14). Probably Jesus' teaching was not static on this matter, but comprehended a wide range of connotation. Whatever the disciples understood by the term as it was used by Him it needed some re-interpretation (cf. Mk 8: 31). T. W. Manson suggested that the idea of *corporate personality* was used by our Lord, based upon the remnant interpretation of passages in Isaiah referring to the Servant of the Lord, but with Himself as the starting point and centre, 'the Proper Man, whom God Himself hath bidden'. Whatever else may be thought, Jesus used the term whilst speaking of Himself as the pre-existent, heavenly Man, who had entered the world to achieve the purpose of God (cf. S. Mowinckel, *He That Cometh*, 1956; J. Klausner, *The Messianic Idea in Israel*, 1956). **2: 1. Cana in Galilee:** Not definitely located, though Dalman (*Sacred Sites and Ways*, 1935) would identify it at Khirbet Qana. (Cf. also J. A. Thompson, *The Bible and Archaeology*, 1962, p. 359.) It is interesting to note that Nathanael belonged here (cf. 21: 2). The link with Nathanael seems to be implied by **on the third day**, i.e. after Jesus' interview with him formerly. **Jesus' mother was there:** She is never named in John, presumably because of the special care which the beloved disciple had for her (cf. 19: 25 ff.; also 2: 12; 6: 42). **his disciples** probably means the Twelve, though no 'call' is recorded in this Gospel, apart from the 'Come and see' and 'Follow me' of 1: 39, 43. **3. When the wine was gone** (Gk. *hysterēsantos oinou*): There are a couple of later glosses to the first half of this verse, both attempts to clarify the situation. The mother of Jesus reported the matter to Him presumably knowing that He could save the situation. **4. Dear woman, why do you involve me?** (Gk. *ti emoi kai soi*): This is a translation of an idiom, both in classical Greek and Hebrew, meaning 'leave me to follow my own course'. No one has any *right* of access to the Lord in this manner (cf. Mk 1: 24; Mt. 8: 29). **My time has not yet come:** Some commentators would restrict the meaning of 'the hour' to the moment of the death or exaltation of Jesus. The term, however, must include some thought which connects His Passion and exaltation with the general pattern of works which He is already performing, as here (cf. v. 11). There is divine constraint upon the Person of Jesus so He performs His works only as He receives direction from the Father (cf. Mk 14: 41; Mt. 26: 18; see also Lk. 13: 31 f.; 22: 53; Jn 7: 30). But our Lord's mother is a woman of faith, and she understands enough to prepare the servants at the wedding for Jesus' intervention. **6. ceremonial washing:** Ritual purification was usually observed by Jews before and after meals. John, however, seems to make the reference capable of spiritual interpretation also. We may summarily reject any significance in the fact that there were six jars. The inadequacy of the old covenant was to be superseded by the cleansing and satisfying new covenant. **8. Now draw some out** (Gk. *antlēsate*): This verb often denotes the drawing of water from a well (cf. *antlēma*, something to draw with, in 4: 11). When the jars were filled, more water was drawn from the well and taken to the feast. Others, notably Hoskyns and Davey, suggest that the saying teaches that Christ is the well of living water. **9. the master of the banquet** was the person to whom the running of such festivities was entrusted. **10.** The serving of a poorer wine at the end of the banquet was not necessarily to be expected. The emphasis is all upon the excellence of what the Lord provided. So, to take the former spiritual lesson a stage further, the sign points to the superiority of the new order over the old. **11. signs** (Gk. *semēia*): The miracles of Jesus in John are so called to draw attention away from the miracles *per se* and point to their significance. 'Signs and wonders' alone provide no basis for true faith (cf. 4: 48). The whole life of Jesus is, indeed, an acted sign (cf. 12: 33; 18: 32), but each of His signs in particular shows that they are the 'works of God' (cf. 10: 37; 14: 10, and especially 6: 25–30) and faith is the only faculty which can rightly apprehend them (cf. 4: 54; 6: 14; 12: 18). The overall importance in John's use of this term, therefore, lies in the visible representation of invisible and eternal reality which Jesus' miracles make. Their purpose is to encourage belief; and Jesus' disciples did in fact believe at this point (cf. 20: 31).

PART TWO—THE PUBLIC
MINISTRY (2: 12–12: 50)

1. CHRIST'S PREACHING OF HIS MESSAGE (2: 12–4: 42)
i. The Cleansing of the Temple (2: 12–25)

This incident, coming where it does in John, raises the question of the relationship between the Fourth Gospel and the Synoptics (see Introduction). The event is placed near the end of the ministry in the first three Gospels (cf. Mk 11: 15–19; Mt. 21: 12–17; Lk. 19: 45–47). Scholars are divided as to whether there was only one cleansing of the temple or two; while those who consider only one to have taken place are again not agreed as to whether this was at the beginning of the Lord's ministry (as in John's Gospel) or during Passion Week (as recorded by the other three Gospels). C. K. Barrett maintains in his commentary (pp. 162 f.) that there was only one such incident in the life of the Lord. William Temple gives reasons for accepting 'the Johannine narrative as correct' so far as chronological order is concerned (*Readings*, p. 170); while R. H. Lightfoot thinks that the cleansing during Passion Week 'is more likely to be historically correct' (*St. John's Gospel*, p. 112).

It should be said, however, that the older view of there being two cleansings has much to support it. Westcott says, 'a comparison of the two narratives is against the identification' (*The Gospel according to St. John*. Greek Text, Vol. 1, p. 96), and he gives various reasons to support his view. The *Commentary on the Gospel of St. John*, by W. Milligan and W. F. Moulton (1898), old but still valuable, asks: 'But is it really at all improbable that two cleansings should have taken place, separated by such an interval of time as the Gospel narrative presupposes?' (p. 27), and lends further support to this view. Among recent writers, R. V. G. Tasker holds to the view of two cleansings (*The Gospel according to St. John, TNTC*, p. 61).

Whatever may be the case, what seems uppermost in the mind of John is, as R. H. Lightfoot observes: 'to represent the judgment or discrimination effected by the presence and work of the Lord among men as in operation from the outset of His activity'. The temple incident calls attention to this aspect of His work (p. 112, *op. cit.*). That its significance is fundamental to John may perhaps be attested by the fact that he records that the animals were driven out of the temple. In Christ sacrificing Judaism is brought to an end. Here, notes Barrett, John 'begins to develop the main theme, that in Jesus the eternal purposes of God find their fulfilment' (p. 163). (See note on v. 21. For *Passover*, see article 'The Religious

Background of the NT'.) **14. men selling:** That is, for the purpose of sacrifice. This was a service provided especially for worshippers who travelled long distances to Jerusalem. Those **exchanging money** sat in the Temple precincts mainly on business of exchanging currency for the payment of Temple tax which was exacted from all adult male Jews, including those from the Dispersion. This exchange was used as a commercial enterprise, and profits were made, mainly because the high priests had insisted that all such dues should be paid in Tyrian currency. **15. and drove all from the temple area:** The wording of this verse would imply that the main object of Jesus' anger were the moneychangers. But the **sheep and cattle** were driven out *with them*. This may lead us to suppose that the marketing of the animals here was not altogether objectionable, though this, too, may have been abused (cf. next verse), since the normal place for this cattle market was on the Mount of Olives. **16. . . . a market** (cf. Zech. 14: 21, '*there shall no longer be a trader . . .*'): John does not record the stronger language reminiscent of Jer. 7: 11 as do the Synoptists. This is probably because his emphasis is different. John sees deeper implications in Jesus' action, which involve (cf. vv. 18–22) the end of the temple cultus. **17. Zeal for your house will consume me:** Cf. Ps. 69: 9 (the words immediately following are applied to Christ in Rom. 15: 3). The future tense seems to provide the more acceptable reading. This gives the psalm a messianic flavour. **18. What miraculous sign can you show us:** Here is an example of a wrongful request for a sign. The parallels in the Synoptics (cf. Mk 11: 28) show that it was proof of Christ's authority which the Jews sought. Jesus does not explicity answer their request, but for such an answer see on 7: 17. Yet in His answer here, Jesus provides a sign for those who will heed what He says. Even the disciples, however, failed to understand what He meant until after the resurrection. **19. Destroy this temple:** As, indeed, the Jews would virtually do in their folly not many years hence. **20. It has taken forty-six years to build:** The Temple was begun in 20 B.C. by Herod the Great. This saying, then, might seem to imply that the structure was complete in A.D. 27, that is, just within the span of the Lord's ministry. But we know that the Temple was by no means completed until A.D. 64. There is, however, no problem. The clue to the seeming difficulty may lie in John's use of Gk. *naos* for 'temple' which is normally distinguished from Gk. *hieron* (also translated 'temple'; cf. v. 14). In this case, the meaning is either (*a*) 'the inner sanctuary has taken forty-six years to build . . .' or (*b*) 'the whole work has taken forty-six years, *so far*'. The latter is probably the better explanation of the words. **21. the temple . . . his body:** The body of Christ is a regular Pauline metaphor for the Church (cf. Eph. 2: 21 f.). Further, just as in a parallel passage (Mk 11: 17) the true house of God is a 'house of prayer for all nations' so through the Holy Spirit the same will be true in Christ's Body—the Church. **24. Jesus would not entrust himself to them** (Gk. *ouk episteuen hauton autois*): Jesus' knowledge of men was absolute and sympathetic by virtue of the Incarnation. He knew men, indeed, with the knowledge of God. Presumably He saw the imperfections of their belief (v. 23).

ii. Jesus and Nicodemus (3: 1–21)
The link here with what has preceded seems to be that our Lord now demonstrates that divine understanding of men by His interview with Nicodemus. But the message which Jesus brings to him, though spoken for his personal good, has a universal application. The Evangelist's comments (vv. 16–21), which set the work of Christ in its universal setting, are intended as a sequel to that challenge presented to the individual. **1. a man of the Pharisees** (see article 'Religious Background of the NT', and *NBD*, pp. 549b; 981f.): Pharisees were represented on the Sanhedrin. They were not as a whole so hypocritical as people think, since many of them had preserved much that was best in Judaism from Maccabean times onwards. **2. at night:** That this was for reasons of secrecy is almost beyond doubt. This is recalled later (cf. 19: 39) when Nicodemus embalms the Lord's body. And his cautious remarks in the Sanhedrin (cf. 7: 50 ff.) are worthy of note. **Rabbi:** Cf. 1: 49. **we know** seems to refer to those who had seen Jesus' 'signs' (cf. 2: 23). Nicodemus, therefore, represents Jews who are confronted by the inescapable uniqueness of Jesus' ministry. **a teacher who has come from God:** Nicodemus at least believes that Jesus' preaching is of divine origin. **if God were not with him:** Though true, this is inadequate as an expression of faith (cf. Ac. 10: 38; Exod. 3: 12). **3. I tell you the truth:** This formula, often repeated by Jesus (cf. 1: 51; 3: 5, 11; 5: 19, 24, 25; 6: 26, 32, 47, 53; 8: 34, 51, 58; 10: 1, 7; 12: 24; 13: 16, 20, 21, 38; 14: 12; 16: 20, 23; 21: 18) is a form of the Heb. *amēn, amēn*, from a verb root meaning 'to be sure, or founded'. The *double* Amen on the lips of Jesus is peculiar to John. It therefore adds some poignancy to the words which follow in each case; though it should also be noted that Jesus uses these words in reference to something which has gone before, suggesting, 'In truth there is a much deeper meaning in this than you think'. **born again** or, 'born from above' (Gk. *gennēthē anōthen*): Christian experience commences with birth, for it is a *new* existence —a new creation (cf. 2 C. 5: 17; 1 Pet. 2: 2).

But the act of begetting belongs to God. It is, says R. V. G. Tasker, to be 'likened to physical birth, for it is an emergence from darkness to light, when the restricted and confined is at last set free' (p. 67). The word *anōthen* can be rendered 'again' or 'from above', though 'anew' is better since it makes clearer that second birth is, indeed, *new* birth in quality as well as essence. **he cannot see:** No very clear distinction should be made between this statement and the similar one **he cannot enter** (v. 5). To 'see' might imply enjoyment, and 'enter' possibly denotes becoming a citizen. The Lord's statement, however, corrects the idea in Judaism that national ties alone were sufficient for entry into the kingdom, and that this **kingdom of God**, mentioned here only by John, though it is one of the leading ideas in the Synoptics, is concerned with the material world, *viz.*, for the Jews primarily the overthrow of the Roman army of occupation. The kingdom of God is the reign of God, where His will is supreme, whether in the individual heart or in the community of His people in this life or in the life hereafter. Only God's children understand what His will is—and there is the connection between the 'new life' and the kingdom of God. **4. he cannot enter . . . to be born:** Nicodemus presumably understood only one side of the Lord's reference to new birth (cf. v. 3). **5. water and the Spirit:** This is linked immediately with new birth. There is not much to commend the view that 'water' refers to physical birth, and 'the Spirit' to spiritual regeneration, though John's baptism and/ or proselyte baptism might well have provided a background of thought, particularly John's prediction concerning the relation between water and the Spirit in 1: 33 f. It seems best to apply the primary meaning of Ezek. 36: 25 ff., where water and Spirit denote cleansing and regeneration respectively. One application of 'water' may, indeed, be the act of John's baptism to repentance; though the idea of Christian baptism is not entirely unconnected, since in the NT it is closely linked with the imparting of the Spirit to the individual (cf. Ac. 2: 38). **6. flesh . . . spirit:** There is a gulf between what is basic to all human nature, flesh, and what is specifically divine in its origin, spirit. Both flesh and spirit bring about their respective fruits (cf. 6: 52–55). **7. You must be born again:** Jesus' reply, addressed now not to one but to many, embraces all who need new birth. **8. The wind** (Gk. *pneuma*) **blows wherever it pleases:** Jesus intends to refer to both wind and spirit. Just as the wind is unpredictable, so in the spiritual realm man cannot foresee the working of the Spirit. **its sound** might also refer both to 'noise' and 'voice', thus pressing the analogy further. **11. we speak of what we know:** Nicodemus, although a representative of the learned and pious in Israel, had failed to grasp the meaning of the work of God. Jesus now identifies Himself with all those (whether Jews at large, or His disciples) who had in some way comprehended the working of the Spirit. They had *seen* it, that is, had by experience mediated through faith. And the plural again reflects Jesus' kindliness as He spoke, through Nicodemus, to all those Jews, who, for whatever reason so far, had rejected His ministry. **12. earthly things . . . heavenly things:** The former (Gk. *ta epigeia*) means Christ's teaching on earth about the new birth. Earthly things are therefore those which, in fact, originate in God yet have their place on the earth, sometimes understood by human analogy. 'Heavenly things' (Gk. *ta epourania*) have no earthly analogy which will help us to understand them. They concern the supreme revelation of God in Christ, and in this the mystery of the Son's relationship to the Father. This is expanded in the following verse. **13. No-one has ever gone into heaven except the one who came from heaven:** The Son of man (cf. 1: 51) is the link between heaven and earth. By the Incarnation are shown heavenly things. This, however, in only part of the story. He has yet to ascend in exaltation and power, though this (cf. next verse) will be by way of suffering. [**who is in heaven** (margin) though omitted by a number of early MSS should probably be left in the text. Jesus revealed the life of God, which exists in heaven, whilst He was upon earth. His permanent dwelling-place is there; He only 'dwelt among us . . .' (cf. 1: 14).] **14. Just as Moses lifted up the snake:** Cf. 8: 28; 12: 32, 34. In these references to 'lifting up', with the possible exception of 8: 28, two ideas are combined: first is the Lord's death on the Cross uplifted; but then in John, the Son of Man returns to the Father to be uplifted in exaltation when He will attract all men to Himself (cf. next verse). The lifting up is all one great drama; it is the work of the Father when from the moment of the lifting up on the Cross He receives the Son back to Himself. **15. eternal life:** Cf. 3: 16, 36; 4: 14, 36; 5: 24, 39; 6: 27, 40, 47, 54, 68; 10: 28; 12: 25, 50; 17: 2 f. This life bears the quality of the new age of God (cf. Dan. 12: 2); but it is a present gift from God. Duration is not the main idea though that is present. Christ is Himself both the personification and guarantee of this life (cf. 1 Jn 5: 12), and the Father, by raising the Son, bestows upon Him the authority to grant this life to others (cf. 5: 26 f.; 17: 2 f.). **16. For God so loved the world:** We now pass to the inspired comment of the writer of the Gospel (so RSV punctuates, rightly). The work of Christ finds its origin in the Father's love; this is the only 'reason' behind His self-revelation. Love is not merely a continuous

attitude of God. He has acted. In Christ He gave His unique Son, the very image of Himself. His love is reciprocal. Only those may enjoy it who respond by receiving God's gift in Christ. And when they receive Him, their response is inevitably one of giving back their love to God (cf. 14: 21, 24 f.). This is new in Jewish ears. Their particularistic ideas of God's special favour for Israel now give way to His revealed love for all mankind. **his One and Only Son:** Cf. 1: 18. **shall not perish** (Gk. *mē apolētai*): Another characteristic word in John (cf. 6: 12, 27, 39; 10: 28; 11: 50). Here the verb is used intransitively, in the middle voice, to mean 'to be lost' or 'to suffer destruction'. This is the only alternative to life eternal, for it is separation from Christ and God. There is no active sense of judgment yet (cf. next verse). That follows *ipso facto*, for condemnation passes upon all who refuse life in Christ (cf. v. 18). **17. God did not send his Son . . . to condemn:** Cf. 5: 27; 9: 39 ff. Our text wisely renders Gk. *krinō* as 'condemn' (cf. 12: 47 f.). **19.** Christ as the world's true Light shows men what they essentially are. **21. whoever lives by the truth** knows that there can be no goodness apart from the Source of all good. Faith must be accompanied by a new quality in living which only can give credence to belief (cf. Jas 2: 14, 17, 24).

iii. The Baptist's final testimony (3: 22–36)
22. the Judean countryside: The words occur nowhere else in the NT. **23. John also was baptizing** might appear to conflict with the Synoptic tradition (cf. Mk 1: 14). But John makes it clear (v. 24) that the Baptist was not yet in prison, whereas Mark (1: 14) shows that Jesus did not begin His *Galilean* ministry until after John's arrest. The Evangelist is here recording an earlier, Judean and Samaritan ministry of Jesus, between His baptism and appearance in Galilee, of which the Synoptists have nothing to say. **Aenon** and **Salim** were in Samaritan territory (cf. W. F. Albright, *Archaeology of Palestine*, 1960, p. 247; *NBD* p. 1125). At this stage John and Jesus work together. The setting serves to bring out the force of v. 30. **25. an argument . . . over the matter of ceremonial washing:** This is (intentionally) unspecified. The passage leads up to the displacement of John as the forerunner of Jesus and as the last representative of expectant Judaism. **27. A man can receive only what is given him:** There is not a trace of bitterness at the news of Jesus' success. That such authority is divinely given, John believes in self-evident. **29. the friend who attends the bridegroom:** A graphic parable showing the central place to be occupied by Christ, and yet the unique position afforded to John the Baptist as 'best man', as His close friend. 'The bride' may refer to Israel (cf. Isa. 62: 4; Ezek. 16: 8;

Hos. 2: 19 f.) and to the Church as the new Israel (2 C. 11: 2; Eph. 5: 25 ff.; Rev. 21: 2; 22: 17), but this should not be pressed. There could be some allusion here to the marriage at Cana (cf. v. 25; 2: 1–11). **That joy is mine, and it is now complete:** Fulfilment is linked with joy several times in John (cf. 15: 11; 16: 24; 17: 13). The Baptist's joy is that which comes at the completion of one's task. **30. He must become greater; I must become less:** The significance of John's ministry lasts only in so far as he opened up the way for the fuller and eternal work of Christ. Vv. 31–36 were almost certainly not uttered by the Baptist (see RSV quotation-marks). The theme of the Nicodemus interview and the Baptist's confession are welded into one by the Evangelist to sum up the truth manifested so far in Jesus. **31. The one who comes from above** (Gk. *anōthen*) is a designation of Christ which confirms the nature of His work (cf. 13: 1). In the Synoptics, 'he who comes' (cf. Mk 11: 9; Mt. 11: 3, etc.) is a messianic title. **34. without limit:** The fulness of the Spirit marked the Lord's ministry on earth, whereas the prophets of OT times were given the Spirit by measure. **36. God's wrath:** In the NT for the most part the wrath of God is spoken of in eschatological terms. Here only in John, like eternal life, it is set in the present as men stand to be judged here and now according to their relationship with Christ, and so, as in Rom. 1: 18, are placed in an eschatological position.

iv. The Samaritan woman (4: 1–42)

Samaritans are not infrequently mentioned in the Gospels (cf. Lk. 9: 51–56; 10: 29–37; 17: 15 f.; and *NBD*, pp. 1131 f.). **1. Jesus:** V. 2 is an editorial comment correcting false rumours. **4. He had to go through Samaria:** In John, Jesus is shown as working in close association with His Father, even in the events leading up to the final 'hour'. But here it is probably no more than a geographical necessity which is meant. **5. Sychar:** Usually identified with the modern Askar, not far distant from the traditional 'Jacob's Well' to be seen today, though W. F. Albright (*Archaeol. Pal.*, p. 247) favours the Old Syriac reading 'Sychem', that is, Shechem (cf. Ac. 7: 16). **near the plot of ground Jacob had given to his son Joseph:** That this was near to Shechem is fairly clear (cf. Gen. 48: 22 'mountain slope', Heb. *shechem*, also Gen. 33: 19; Jos. 24: 32). **6. tired as he was** (Gk. *kekopiakōs*) is one of a number of intentional emphases in the Gospel (cf. Introduction) to underline the humanity of our Lord. **the sixth hour:** i.e. twelve noon. **9. Jews do not associate with Samaritans:** This antagonism goes back to the late sixth and fifth centuries B.C. when exiled Jews returned to Judah from Babylon, who regarded this mixed populace as unclean. The rift was widened by the erection of the rival Temple on Mt. Gerizim. In rabbinical literature specific prohibitions exclude virtually all contact between the two parties. Such regulations may lie behind John's statement here (Gk. *synchraomai* means 'use together with', *e.g.* pots and pans). Accordingly NEB renders: 'Jews and Samaritans, it should be noted, do not use vessels in common'. **10. If you knew the gift of God:** Only this gift of God can ever close such breaches between man and man, as they learn to share everything given by the Father through Christ. But the Son is Himself also the Gift (cf. 3: 16). **living water:** Primarily flowing water. In the OT, however, the picture was used for divine activity in giving life to men (cf. Jer. 2: 13; Zech. 14: 8; Ezek. 47: 9, etc.). **14. whoever drinks** (Gk. *hos d' an piē*): Barrett rightly would translate 'whoever shall drink', i.e. once for all, contrasted with the day-to-day necessity for water. **a spring of water** (Gk. *pēgē hydatos*): Jacob's well is described by the same word (v. 6). It was supplied by running water. But the RSV wisely makes the distinction between v. 6 and v. 14. (The Gk. word *phrear* is used in v. 11 f.) Both words are employed because this *phrear* is also fed by an underground *pēgē*. The spring of which Jesus speaks comes from outside the man, thus ensuring an unfailing supply. **15.** The woman, however, does not see that Jesus is speaking of a spiritual counterpart to the well which she used continually. **16. call your husband:** This is a startling approach in the light of eastern social reserve with such matters. **17. I have no husband:** Her reply was both a pitiful defence and a truthful confession. And Jesus observes the honesty of the statement though it may not have been seen by the woman who made it. But He will go further than accept what is right in order to expose the whole truth. Tasker comments: 'because she has spoken the truth, the truth makes her free —free to receive the gift that Jesus can give her' (p. 76). **19. a prophet:** There is alarm in these words. The Samaritans however, did not accept the authority of the prophets after Moses. But if Jesus is a prophet He must be *the* prophet of Dt. 18: 15 ff., the prophet like Moses, the *Taheb* of Samaritan expectation. **20. Our fathers worshiped on this mountain:** i.e. Gerizim, which was sacred to the Samaritans. This was the place where, according to the Samaritan text of Dt. 12: 5, God 'has chosen', not 'will choose' to put His name. Surely someone with prophetic insight can now solve the age-old problem? But the question is irrelevant here. Worship will, henceforward, be offered to God in every place (Mal. 1: 11) through Christ. **22. salvation is from the Jews:** In spite of the evidence of this woman's unsatisfactory life, Samaritans tended to be stricter than the Jews. But the election of the latter was for the spreading of the saving power of God to the 'uttermost part of the earth' (cf. Isa. 49: 5 f.). **23. in spirit and truth:** That is, in virtue of new birth, and in the light of the revelation of truth in Christ. 'Spirit' is vague enough here to denote both that supernatural essence of Christian life, and the means, *viz.*, the Holy Spirit, through whom it is imparted. There can be no separation of the two; the former follows acceptance of the latter. **24. God is spirit** (Gk. *pneuma ho theos*) is more a question of describing sovereign freedom which God has in contrast to men, enclosed in a material world, than it is a definition of His nature. Men must therefore worship Him in spirit by which alone they can commune with Him. **25. Messiah (called Christ) is coming:** The Lord's words concerning the essential mode of worship cause her to respond. She believes at least that God will ultimately reveal His purpose. **26. I who speak to you am he:** Lit. 'I am (he) who speaks to you'. This self-disclosure makes the Lord's immediate purpose complete (cf. v. 19). 'I am' occurs many times in John (cf. 6: 35, 51; 8: 12, 18; 10: 7, 9, 11, 14; 11: 25; 14: 6; 15: 1, 5). Its strong resemblance to the OT Yahweh ('I will be what I will be') has been often noted. But the idea is not necessarily inherent in all these references as they stand, though certain implications may have suggested themselves to John and his earliest readers. This is the first self-confession of Jesus in the Gospel. **28. Leaving her water jar:** This is no allegorical reference. At this poignant moment the woman may, indeed, have set down her jar for Jesus' use. She tentatively asks: **Could this be the Christ? 32. I have food to eat:** Just as the woman did not perceive the meaning of Jesus' references to living water, so the disciples apparently misunderstand Jesus' saying here about food (cf. Ps. 119: 103) by which He refers to His mission in life, **to do the will of Him who sent me** (34) in His works and words (cf. 9: 4; 10: 25,37 f.; 14: 10 f.; 17: 4; also 7: 17; Dt. 8: 3). **and to finish his work:** Jesus' obedience to the Father was full and perfect (cf. 17: 4). **35. Do you not say:** i.e. 'is it not a common fact?' There is probably no proverb here. Barrett links this with the supposedly seasonal accuracy by which first fruits were offered to God on 16 Nisan (cf. *art.* 'Environmental Background to the NT'). **look at the fields! They are ripe for harvest:** That is evidenced by the dealings with Nicodemus and the woman of Samaria. **36. the sower and the reaper may be glad together:** Jesus has both sown the seed and reaped an early harvest. **38. I sent you to reap:** Probably a reference to the baptismal activity of the disciples in which they had truly entered into the labours of others, like John the Baptist (cf. 3: 23; 4: 2). **42. the Savior of the world:** What ultimately transpired during Jesus' two

days' stay in Samaria we shall probably never know; they may provide a background to Philip's Samaritan mission of Ac. 8: 5 ff. But we do know that certain Samaritans were convinced beyond all doubt that Jesus was God's provision for universal salvation.

II. REVELATION BY DEEDS AND WORDS (4: 43–6: 71)

i. The official's son (4: 43–54)

There is one similarity between this miracle and that of the healing of the centurion's slave (cf. Mt. 8: 5–13; Lk. 7: 1–10). It lies in the fact that both cures were effected from some distance. **44. his own country** (*patris*) must mean here not Nazareth in Galilee, as it usually does in the Synoptics (cf. Mk 6: 4, etc.), but, in view of the messianic context, Jerusalem in Judea, regarded by all Jews as their proper home. **48.** The signs which Jesus performs are only intended as sign-posts to the compassion of God. To use them alone as a basis for belief is not enough. **50. The man took Jesus at his word:** Even so, his faith was not yet *saving* faith. It was only as yet assurance that Jesus was genuine (cf. v. 53). **52. the seventh hour:** i.e. about 1 p. m. **53. So he and all his household believed:** This was now absolute faith which gave value to his earlier belief without seeing (cf. 20: 29). **54. the second miraculous sign:** Cf. 2: 11.

ii. The cripple of Bethesda (5: 1–47)

This has some similarities with a cure recorded by the Synoptists (cf. Mk 2: 1–12; Mt. 9: 2–8; Lk. 5: 18–26). Both incidents give rise to controversy. In Mark the connection between the man's condition and Jesus' power to forgive sins is emphasized, whereas here the man's sins are mentioned almost in passing (cf. v. 14). It is interesting to note how at festival times Jesus severely indicted the unbelief of the Jews (cf. v. 29; 11: 55 ff.; 7: 2–9) in a way which finally hastened the climax of His ministry. **1. a feast:** The absence of a definite article leaves this unspecified, though some (among them R. H. Lightfoot and J. Rendel Harris) have suggested that this may have been New Year. **2. Bethesda:** Both the MS evidence for the name and its precise meanings are uncertain. 'Beth-zatha' (or perhaps 'Bezatha') has much to commend it, being known to Josephus. On the other hand many scholars still prefer the rendering 'Bethesda' (lit. 'house of mercy') possibly because of its suitability as a place where Jesus performed a miracle. Beth-'eshda ('house of outpouring'), preferred by Calvin, seems to be confirmed by the copper scroll from Qumran Cave 3. [Vv. 3b and 4 are rightly omitted from the text. They are clearly a later addition to the story, and find no strong manuscript support. They probably preserve some tradition which accounted for the moving of the water. The

narrative reads perfectly well without them.] 6.
Do you want to get well?: Not a superfluous
question. It seems that our Lord addressed the
most needy case there and accordingly wished
to evoke some faith from this man. 7. **when
the water is stirred:** The phenomenon is interpreted in the verses omitted as an angelic intervention. Westcott comments: 'The healing
properties of the pool may have been due to its
mineral elements'. Excavations at the Pool of
St. Anna have revealed five porticos (cf. *NBD*,
pp. 143 f.). 9. **a Sabbath:** In a terse statement
the Evangelist prepares for the discourse which
now follows. 10. **the law forbids:** The Jews
treat what they see in terms of law. Rabbinic
writings made careful distinctions regarding
the removal of furniture on the sabbath. A bed
may not be carried, though to carry a patient
lying on a bed was permissible. 13. **the man
. . . had no idea who it was:** This seems
strange to us, but the oriental mind learned
to accept the supernatural, often forgetting to
trouble itself with the means of its operation.
In any case, **Jesus had slipped away** to avoid
the curiosity of the crowd. 14. **Stop sinning:**
This implies that Jesus saw some connection,
however indirect, between this case of suffering
and some sin of which the man was guilty (cf.
9: 23). Forgiveness has not been mentioned,
though 'no more' suggests that sin so far in the
man's life was forgiven. 17. **My Father is
always at his work to this very day, and I,
too, am working:** The rest of the discourse
flows from this statement. God rested on the
seventh day, according to the scriptures (cf.
Gen. 2: 2 f.). Yet sabbath observance was not
intended as a rest of inactivity, but rest which
comes from spiritual communion with God,
who is ceaselessly active as Creator and Sustainer of the universe. 18. **he was even calling
God his own Father** (Gk. *patera idion*): This,
above all else so far, incited the Jews to murderous hatred of Jesus, together with His avowal
that He acted in direct communion with the
Father, saying, **'the Son can do nothing by
himself'** (19). Jesus' relationship with the
Father is unique, so that He does not work
independently of the Father. **the Son also
does:** Jesus' range of activity is coextensive
with the Father's. 20. **greater things than
these:** That is, greater than the healing of this
cripple. These will compel the attention of the
Jews, *e.g.* the raising of Lazarus (cf. 11: 45). 21.
as the Father raises the dead: Most Jews
believed that the raising of the dead was reserved for a coming age (cf. Ezek. 37: 13) and
would be realized in the Messiah. V. 22 is a
statement later explained in v. 27. Meanwhile
one clear purpose for this delegation of authority to Christ is **that all may honor the Son**
(23), recognizing His equality in authority and
action. 24. **whoever hears my word and**

believes: The construction here shows that
both hearing and believing are to be taken
together. Hearing is not a passive activity only.
The great *Shema*ʿ ('Hear, O Israel . . .') of the
OT (Dt. 6: 4–9) presupposed faith by works.
So here the word of Christ evokes a response
(cf. 6: 63, 68; 15: 3), and he who makes it **has
eternal life and will not be condemned**—
by faith he now anticipates and enjoys final
acquittal and the life of the resurrection age.
25. **a time is coming and has now come:**
Cf. 4: 23. The 'dead' here are the spiritually
dead. The Son of man has already awakened
them by His word. That those who hear will
live is based upon OT expectation (cf. Isa. 55:
11). So Christ's word bringing life separates
man from man, thereby bringing some into
judgment (cf. v. 27). 26. **he has granted the
Son . . . to have life:** It is part of the Son's
essential nature, shared with the Father, that
He is capable of being a source of life to others
(cf. 1: 4). 27. **because he is the Son of Man**
(Gk. *hoti hyios anthrōpou esti*): The Danielic Son
of man (cf. Dan. 7: 13 f.) is never far from the
minds of the Evangelists. Here, clearly, His
humanity is uppermost in thought. Because He
fully shares humanity, and in virtue of the
supreme authority conferred on Him by the
Father, He can dispense judgment. 28. **all who
are in their graves:** Cf. v. 25. Both good and
bad are included (cf. next verse). The resurrection of those physically dead is something to
come later in the divine programme. Jesus'
voice will be heard in final judgment, though
there is no embroidering of the details (cf. Dan.
12: 2). 30. **I seek not to please myself:** This
puts the judgment spoken of by Christ beyond
all question. In Him there is no suggestion of
self-aggrandisement (cf. vv. 41–44). 31. Jesus'
saying here might seem to contradict what
He says later (cf. 8: 13 f.). But there is no
contradiction. Here, He is referring to those
claims which He might have made by self-
assertion. But His testimony is at one with the
Father's, so He trusts Him (cf. v. 32). 34. **I
mention it that you may be saved:** So great
is Jesus' concern for the Jews that He will draw
their attention to the work of John the Baptist
if that will lead them to Him. 35. **John was
a lamp that burned and gave light** (Gk.
lychnos): John's testimony, at the best, was
secondary (cf. 1: 8, 33; 8: 14). He bore witness
as a *lamp* through which the true light shone in
the measure of the oil given him. **you chose
for a time to enjoy his light:** Religious fervour, perhaps, led many Jews to interest themselves in John's preaching, since it was concerned with the proclamation of the kingdom.
37. **the Father . . . has himself testified concerning me:** This presumably refers to the
baptism of Jesus. They did not hear His voice
(cf. Mk 1: 11) nor did they see His form (Gk.

eidos, external form; cf. Lk. 3: 22)—in the dove which descended (1: 32): **38. nor does his word dwell in you:** Here Jesus' charge against the Jews comes to its climax. If the Word of God had a real place in them they would have recognized both the authority of Christ and the Baptist. **39. You diligently study the scriptures:** The verb may be either imperative or indicative. The latter gives the better sense. Jews believed the scriptures to be life-giving, but they failed to understand them as a witness to Christ (cf. v. 21; Lk. 24: 25 ff., 44 ff.) in that they did not find their way to Him. **42. you do not have the love of God in your hearts:** Their devotion to God was not genuine, else they would have received Christ's testimony. Yet they are further condemned in that they are ready to receive some self-styled teacher (v. 43). **45. Your accuser is Moses:** They need not think that Moses is their advocate; he is their prosecutor, and judgment lies in the authority of the Word (12: 47). **47. how are you going to believe what I say?:** Belief in the OT sees it as incomplete, ever pointing forward to fulfilment (cf. Dt. 18: 15 f.). This argument addresses the Jewish religious mind. If they do not believe the scriptures it is hardly likely that they will accept the teaching of this Rabbi upon them.

iii. Feeding the masses (6: 1–15)

1. After this: Some feel that this chapter should precede chap. 5 in chronological sequence, on the ground that 7: 1 follows more naturally on chap. 5 (see especially 5: 18). But the idea is insufficiently grounded to make it satisfactory (see note on 7: 15). **the Sea of Tiberias:** So named after the city, founded by Herod Antipas in A.D. 26 in honour of Tiberius Caesar. John may have used the up-to-date name for the benefit of non-Jews (cf. 21: 1). **4. the Jewish Passover Feast was near:** This Passover is probably a year later than that of chap. 2 because on the earlier occasion the Baptist had not yet been imprisoned; and according to Mark he was not only imprisoned but executed by the time of feeding of the 5,000. The Passover was near enough, perhaps, to allow John to insert a chronological note, which gives point to the later discourse (vv. 22–59) in the light of the Paschal feast (cf. 1 C. 5: 7; Mt. 15: 29–39). **5. a great crowd coming toward him:** Having walked round to the NE corner of the Lake, Jesus is moved with pity upon them (cf. Mk 6: 33 f.). **Philip:** In the Synoptics it is the disciples who express concern for the crowd. Here, complementarily, Jesus puts one of them to the test. **9. how far will they go among so many:** Andrew's problem is recorded to show how meagre are man's resources in proportion to his needs. **11. Jesus . . . gave thanks** (Gk. *eucharistēsas*): That John records this at length, whilst he does not record

the Last Supper in detail, is surely significant. Thanksgiving is, however, only what we should have expected Jesus to make, and John's word for this may carry a technical meaning which would *immediately* associate this event with the Holy Communion. The primary lesson here seems to be that Jesus was acting in dependence upon the Father, so that eucharistic associations should not, in any case, be pressed too far. **12. Gather the pieces that are left over:** Any thought-projection on the part of the Evangelist here to the completeness of the Body of Christ symbolized at the Communion table is quite unlikely. Rather is it plain evidence of the fact that Jesus cared about wastage, and intended to bring back the disciples to the reality of human need far from the world of the miraculous. **14. Surely this is the Prophet:** The recent murder of John the Baptist had increased the desire to find a popular Messiah. Their acclamation hailed Jesus as the prophet like Moses (Dt. 18: 15 ff.) who had formerly fed his people in like manner (cf. 1 C. 10: 1–5). **15. they intended to come and make him king:** The multitude 'like sheep without a shepherd' (Mk 6: 34) was an army looking for a captain to lead them against the Romans. **Jesus . . . withdrew:** Mark tells us that it was for prayer (cf. Mk 6: 46). This was a critical moment. Worldly kingship was far from the mind of Jesus (cf. 18: 33 f.) as the temptations had already shown (cf. Mt. 4: 1–11).

iv. A storm at sea (6: 16–21)

The disciples now return to the western side of the sea of Galilee. **19. they had rowed three or three and a half miles:** The Gk. *stadion* was equal to about 606 feet or 185 metres, rather less than an English furlong so 'five and twenty or thirty furlongs' (AV). **walking on the water** (Gk. *epi tēs thalassēs*): The precise meaning of the Gk. phrase has been disputed. Some claim that it means 'by the sea' (i.e., 'on the shore'), as in 21: 1, so withdrawing miraculous meaning from the words, and supporting their claim with the contention that the gladness of the disciples to receive Jesus into the boat did not lead to their *actually* receiving Him thus, because **immediately the boat reached the shore**. But their arrival at the shore need not be so speedy as these words suggest, for their distance (v. 19) would suggest that, when they saw the Lord, they were about half way across. And the text is difficult to understand unless they did actually take Jesus with them into the boat.

v. Living Bread (6: 22–59)

25. Rabbi, when did you get here?: The question of the crowd opens up the whole discourse. Their question was one involving both time and manner, for their curiosity in the miraculous was not easily lost. So Jesus says, **you are looking for me . . . because you ate the loaves and had your fill** (26). But what kind of interest was it? They only came to Him for the satisfaction of the moment, and not for **the food that endures** and which, here and now, nourishes eternal life in those who take it. **27. on him God . . . has placed his seal:** The sign of the loaves and fish are the divine authentication of the words of Jesus. **29. 'The work of God is this: to believe in the one he has sent':** Their grasp of the main idea of Jesus' words is still limited. But Jesus says that faith in Him will bear fruit naturally, not as a labour of duty. The tense denotes continuation rather than a single act. **30. What miraculous sign then will you give:** Their unbelief is scarcely credible. The miraculous feeding has apparently produced no inward effect. Jesus refuses their allusion to Moses because their understanding of that miracle (cf. Exod. 16: 15; Neh. 9: 5) was defective. **32. my Father . . . gives you the true bread:** The manna of Moses was not 'the real bread', and in any case, it was not given by Moses but God. The real bread **gives life to the world** (33). The people begin to appreciate the distinction which Jesus is making between the manna and the spiritual sustenance of which the manna is a type, so they answer with more respect but still with incomplete understanding, **Sir, . . . from now on give us this bread** (34), like the Samaritan women's 'give me this water' (4: 15). Therefore Jesus makes the nature of the true bread plainer still. **35. I am the bread of life:** Hitherto in the discourse this bread is given by the Son of man (v. 27) as the Father's agent (v. 32); now He identifies it with Himself, thus calling forth the sharpest criticism yet. **he who comes to me will never go hungry:** Total commitment to Him will result in total salvation. Just as there is nothing partial in God's giving of life, so there can be no partiality in receiving Christ. **37. All that the Father gives me will come to me:** Is this *so* arbitrary? Temple adds, 'To realise that my not "coming" is itself due to the will of the Father, who has not yet drawn me, and to accept this, is one beginning of trust in Him, one sign that in fact He is really drawing me to come' (Vol. i, p. 88). **38. the will of him who sent me:** Cf. vv. 39 f. The will of God is the kernel of the work of Christ in salvation. And Christ's doing of that will is perfect so that He should **lose none of all** (39). Eternal life is the gift which God wills to give to men. **40. I will raise him up:** Westcott has aptly commented that the doctrine of eternal life makes the necessity of resurrection obvious. John always thinks of eternal life as a possession here and now, though **the last day** shows he does also include the idea of judgment. **42. Is this not Jesus, the son of Joseph?:** Jesus' elaboration of the Bread

of Life sayings undoubtedly led some of His hearers to accept what He was saying as true (cf. v. 34). Now, however, it is not so much the Bread of Life which they query, but that these claims should be made by One of such humble origins. **44. No one can come to me unless the Father . . . draws him:** The Jews' incredulity does not help the matter. The initiative in saving men always is taken by the Father, so the solving of theological riddles will bring no ultimate advantage, for **they will all be taught by God** (45; cf. Isa. 54: 12 f.). God teaches men in that He alone can utter His word. All who hear and respond worthily to that word inevitably will turn to Christ. The test is plain (cf. vv. 45 f.). **51. This bread is my flesh which I will give:** In summing up, Jesus again reminds the hearers that the manna was only a type of the real bread of God (cf. vv. 49 f.). *He* is the true Bread of Life. It is *His* life which will be given. This is Jesus' sacrifice of Himself, for he could hardly give His flesh and blood (cf. v. 56) apart from death. **53. unless you eat the flesh . . . and drink his blood:** The question concerning the relationship of this saying to the Lord's Supper, in which those who partake do so by faith (1 C. 10: 16) is inescapable. In the Synoptics the Lord's Supper is recorded primarily as that which the Lord Himself instituted. Here, however, we may see the teaching of the Lord Jesus which can only be fully understood in the light of the feast which He inaugurated, and which, without referring directly to that Supper, conveys truth which should give the Lord's Supper deep meaning for the believer. The language is vividly metaphorical, denoting the appropriation of Christ by faith. 'It is a figure', says Augustine, 'bidding us communicate in our Lord's passion, and secretly and profitably store up in our memories that for our sakes He was crucified and slain' (*On Christian Doctrine* 3. 16). Bernard explains the words **whoever eats my flesh and drinks my blood** (54) to mean: 'He who reflects upon my death, and after my example mortifies his members which are upon earth, has eternal life—in other words, "If you suffer with me, you will also reign with me"' (*On Loving God* 4. 11). It should be noted that 'flesh' here corresponds to 'body' in the Synoptics and in 1 Cor. 10: 16; 11: 24, 27, 29. If there is any distinction to be made between the two it would be that 'flesh' stresses the utter humanity of Christ, whilst 'body' would signify His person as an organic entity, and the fact that John had docetic teachers very much in his mind should not be overlooked in this connection. 'My body' and 'my flesh' would alike represent Aram. *bisri*. **58. This is the bread that came down from heaven:** The contrast between Christ and the Law, between the living Bread and the manna, is now complete. As the Lord Jesus is fully identified with the Bread of God, so only he who partakes of Him will know what life from God really means.

vi. Disciples' faith and unbelief (6: 60–71) Jesus now concentrates upon the disciples when opposition hardens elsewhere. **60. This is a hard teaching:** It is hardly surprising that the disciples should be filled with consternation, knowing so little about the future for Jesus as they did. **62. What if you see the Son of Man ascend:** He came down to give life. The time is coming when He will return to the Father in power and glory. If they have seen Him in the flesh, which He is to give for the world, and are amazed, what then will be their reaction when He goes away in a blaze of glory? **63. The Spirit gives life, the flesh counts for nothing:** Cf. vv. 53, 55. The words of Jesus must be understood in a spiritual, not in a carnal sense. His flesh is the vehicle of the Spirit, and therefore can impart life. But, as He said to Nicodemus, nothing basic in human nature can help man in his need. **64. some of you . . . do not believe:** Jesus has accepted the Passion, and knows already who they are who will not believe. Further, this is His first reference to the traitor, and coincides exactly with the Synoptics' first references to the Passion. Jesus insists (v. 65) that some will inevitably turn back, and turn back they did (v. 66) at that precise moment. **68. You have the words of eternal life:** Cf. Mk 8: 29. The first impulsive faith of the disciples now gives way to rational conviction based on experience. Jesus' words may be hard to understand, yet their claims and genuineness are all too clear. They believe now, but they were chosen already (v. 70), though one of them, instead of going back, remains within the Twelve, a disloyal member, perhaps seeking to distort the kingdom to his own pattern. He was the son of **Simon Iscariot** (71; cf. 13: 2, 26). His name indicates that he came either from Kerioth Hezron, or (less probably) that he was linked with the *sicarii* (cf. Ac. 21: 37 f. and *NBD*, pp. 673 f.).

III. JESUS, THE SOURCE OF ALL TRUE BLESSING (7: 1–10: 39)
i. Controversy at the Feast of Tabernacles (7: 1–52)
2. Feast of Tabernacles: Otherwise known as 'Booths', an autumnal festival, lasting eight days from 15th to 22nd Tishri inclusive (Lev. 23: 33–36), the last day of which was sabbatical. Jerusalem would be thronged with pilgrims celebrating harvest-home, and God's historic care in the wilderness wandering; and many erected their own shelters near the Holy City for the occasion (cf. Lev. 23: 42). **3. Jesus' brothers:** There is no good reason to suppose

that they were not the children of Mary and Joseph. They urged our Lord to make an open show of His power, and in v. 5 the Evangelist indicates that their request grew out of their unbelief. Some MSS insert 'then', presumably to reconcile this with other passages such as Ac. 1: 14. But the fact that they were unbelievers *as yet* enables us to see partly why Jesus committed the care of His Mother to another disciple (cf. 19: 25 ff.). **6. The right time** (Gk. *ho kairos ho emos*): Not the Johannine 'hour' (Gk *hōra*). There may be some little distinction. 'Time' here speaks of opportunity, whereas 'hour' elsewhere (cf. 7: 30; 8: 20; 12: 23; 13: 1; 17: 1) speaks of His appointed death and exaltation. **7.** For most pilgrims one visit to Jerusalem for Tabernacles might have little to distinguish it from others. But for Jesus it means that His presence, awakening sin in others, stands to evoke their hatred. **8. I am not yet going up:** Jesus' movement towards Jerusalem will only be, as Stauffer puts it, when 'The Father had given the sign!' (p. 27). **10. he went also, not publicly, but in secret:** John records a number of visits by Jesus to Jerusalem (cf. 2: 13; 5: 1; 12: 12), but this one accords clearly with the Synoptic writers (cf. Mk 9: 30), where Jesus' secrecy is a prelude to the final drama which leads to the Arrest, Trial and Crucifixion. And because of His private entry, Jews in the city were asking where He was (v. 11). They were not kept waiting long (v. 14). This is John's first notice of public preaching by Jesus in Jerusalem as distinct from answering questions. **15. learning** (Gk. *grammata*, lit. 'letters'): Those who contend that chap. 6 is displaced refer, among other things, to the fact that this question seems to follow on from the saying about Moses' 'writings' (*grammata*) in 5: 47. This cannot be pressed. The words **without having studied** mean that Jesus was not trained in the rabbinical schools. With the present question we may compare the Jewish leaders' later observation that Peter and John were 'uneducated (*agrammatoi*), common men' (Ac. 4: 13); their ability to expound scripture was explained by their having 'been with Jesus'. **17. If anyone chooses to do God's will, he will find out:** There can be no greater authority than this which can be put to the test. Elsewhere, our Lord was similarly questioned (cf. Mt. 21: 23; Jn 6: 30) and He gave always the same answer in principle. **19. not one of you keeps the law:** If these men really sought to do the will of God (v. 17), then the law of Moses would be their supreme guide in all matters. But they deny Jesus' authority, and their threat to kill Him enabled Jesus to turn round the argument. They had accused Him of openly breaking the Sabbath (cf. 5: 1–9). **22. Moses gave you circumcision:** Although this was practised by the patriarchs, Moses regular-

ized it within the Law (cf. Lev. 12: 3). And it
is certain that rabbinic interpretation of the
Leviticus passage made circumcision on the
Sabbath supreme over the Sabbath itself. **24.
make a right judgment:** Jesus' teaching here
on circumcision adds to the general Sabbath
controversy as we have it recorded in the Synoptics. Jesus is concerned with making men
whole, and not merely with bringing a more
liberal interpretation to bear upon Levitical
regulations. **28. you know where I am from:**
Jesus' openness was a source of astonishment.
Surely the authorities had not capitulated? But
no; the Christ will have no known origin, that
is, the time and manner of His appearing were
expected to be a mystery. **29. I know him . . .
he sent me:** Jesus claims both divine knowledge and authority. It seems that John almost
suggests (v. 30) that the Jews were physically
incapable of laying hands on Him before 'the
hour' struck. **33. I go to the one who sent
me:** The verb 'I go' (Gk. *hypagō*) in John denotes particularly our Lord's return to where
He belongs (cf. 8: 14; 13: 33, 36; 14: 4 f., 28;
16: 5, 17, etc.). His death would not be the end
of His work. It would be, as Luke puts it, only
an 'exodus' (Lk. 9: 31) to the Father. **34. where
I am:** Cf. 14: 3; 17: 24; also 8: 21; 13: 33. Christ
is essentially with the Father always, in spirit.
But shortly He will return there bodily. In
some of these passages a more precise historical
separation is in view. 'Where I am' could be
accentuated to mean 'where I am about to be'.
But in all separation remains a hard fact—**you
cannot come**. The Jews sought Him now in
anger. The time is coming when they will seek
Him in anguish. **35. scattered:** Diaspora was
a collective name for Jews in foreign lands (cf.
Jas 1: 1; 1 Pet. 1: 1). To go to them was bad
enough, but they ironically add **and teach the
Greeks?** The real irony, of course, lay in the
fact that they were speaking the truth and did
not foresee Christ's mission to the Gentiles in
the Body of His Church. So now Christ openly
makes a universal invitation on the eighth **the
last and greatest day of the Feast** (37). **let
him come to me and drink:** Probably the
ritual libations of water offered on certain days
during the Feast of Tabernacles were fresh in
the Lord's mind. These reminded Jews of the
seasonal faithfulness of God (cf. Zech. 14: 7 f.).
The idea of spiritual nourishment has, however, been elaborated already (cf. 4: 14; 5: 26;
6: 53 ff.). Here we are explicitly told that
**Streams of living water will flow from
within him** (38), meaning that others may
slake their thirst at the overflowing bounty of
life in the believer. A general collocation of
references is in mind (cf. Isa. 44: 3; 55: 1; 58:
11; Zech. 13: 1; 14: 8). The reference is to the
Spirit who would come in all His cleansing
and refreshing power after Jesus was glorified

through death and exaltation (1 C. 12: 13). **40.
Surely this man is the Prophet:** As Moses
had drawn water from the rock, so now Jesus
promises His people water to drink (cf. 6: 14;
1 C. 10: 4). **43. the people were divided:**
The people seem to have adopted a three-fold
standpoint. Some remained convinced that
Jesus was an impostor, probably linking His
Galilean origin with their doubts. Others believed that He could be the prophetic forerunner of the Messiah. And others accepted His
claims in their entirety. **47. he has deceived
you also:** The officers who returned helpless
to the chief priests need make no specific confession. Their amazement eloquently testified
to their reaction to Jesus. But the Pharisees
retort, 'none of the *spiritual* leaders have been
so misled'. If the others had been beguiled by
this Jesus, so much the worse for them. But
were they *all* adamant? No, one of them, Nicodemus, showed tactful impartiality, for he had,
indeed, given Him a hearing (v. 51). **a prophet
does not come out of Galilee:** Lit., 'out of
Galilee a prophet does not arise'; but Papyrus
66, the oldest extant manuscript of Jn, has the
singular reading 'the prophet' (cf. v. 40) for 'a
prophet' of our other authorities. (The reading
with the article had been conjectured by Rudolf
Bultmann before it turned up in P. 66.) **[The
woman taken in adultery (7: 53–8: 11)** is
treated in Additional Note 2; see p. 1333.]

**ii. The true Light and its implications
(8: 12–59)**
In this section we come to the second great
self-disclosure of the Lord which is brought to
a climax by the ensuing discussion. **12. I am
the light of the world:** The division among
the Jews (cf. 7: 43) was due to blindness. Jesus
declares that He is the Light of which Life is
the source and which shines on the way to a
fuller experience of God. In the beginning God
manifested Himself by the bringing of Light
(cf. Gen. 1: 2). The Feast of Tabernacles, moreover, brought to remembrance God's heavenly
guidance of Israel by the fiery pillar and a
ceremony of lights was performed which provided illumination throughout the Temple.
Darkness is where God is unknown. He who
follows Jesus emerges from chaotic darkness
like the world at the beginning. **15. I pass
judgment on no one:** Though He has authority to execute judgment as Son of man (cf. 5:
27), Jesus withholds it (cf. 17: 2). The statement
probably accounted for the insertion of the
adultery passage preceding this. Significantly
too, that deals with a capital offence which was
only chargeable on the testimony of several
witnesses (cf. Dt. 17: 6; also v. 13 above). **16.
But if I do judge . . . because I am not
alone:** Jewish law required evidence from at
least two witnesses (Dt. 19: 15). But though
Jesus' witness is irrefutable, they answer that

God's evidence cannot be asked for corroboration as if He were an earthly witness (cf. v. 19). **20. the place where the offerings were put:** The area containing offering-chests, probably in the Court of Women (cf. Mk 12: 41) close by the Sanhedrin chamber. **his time:** Cf. 7: 30. **21. I am going away:** Cf. 7: 33. Now Jesus explains that His departure to the Father will have dire consequences for some (cf. 16: 8–11). **22. Will he kill himself:** A gross misunderstanding of Jesus' words. Yet they are unconsciously ironical for He would, indeed, lay down His life (cf. 10: 17). **23. You are from below:** Both realms, 'above' and 'below', meet on earth, the scene, indeed, of their conflict. The terminology may be that of a three-decker universe, but it is used in an ethical sense to distinguish the realms of good and evil. **25. Just what I have been claiming all along:** Gk. *ho ti kai lalō hymin* could be rendered with the opening words 'Why do I speak to you at all'? (so NEB) which would fit in with the general sense of the passage. **28. When you have lifted up the Son of Man:** Though the 'lifting up' idea is usually fraught with theological implications (see note on 3: 14), here it is less so. Jesus refers to the act of the crucifixion by men, which would, nevertheless, bring about His exaltation. His death will demonstrate His obedience. His exaltation will endorse His messianic claims. So forthright were Jesus' words here that **many put their faith in him** (30). **31. If you hold to my teaching:** Some Jews had believed in Him (Gk. *pepisteukotas autō*) in a manner which formally accepted His teaching. Others (cf. v. 30, Gk. *episteusan eis auton*) had exercised dynamic faith in Him. **32. the truth will set you free:** Only by setting aside all preconceptions, tradition and self-will can a man see the whole truth, especially the truth about himself. **33. We . . . have never been slaves of anyone:** These Jews were not denying the plain facts of their history. Rather they were asserting that religious freedom had always been granted to them in some way. **35. a slave has no permanent place in the family:** Jesus speaks, however, of serfdom under sin (cf. Rom. 6: 17). A son is always free; a slave cannot free himself (cf. Gen. 21: 9–14). Isaac remained in his father's house, whereas Ishmael, son of Hagar, was put out. **36. So if the Son sets you free:** John reserves the noun *hyios* in relation to God for Christ alone. **39. If you were Abraham's children:** There are several variant readings suggested for this. The main alternative reads, 'If you *are* Abraham's children, then do Abraham's works.' (But cf. v. 42) which would suit the former reading better.) 'Children' implies blood relationship (cf. 1: 12), though John uses the plural *tekna* rather than *hyioi* regardless of finer implications. **40. Abraham did not do such**

things: Perhaps Jesus is thinking of the welcome given by Abraham to God's messengers (cf. Gen. 18). **42. If God were your Father:** Cf. v. 39. Jesus denies the Jews' ultimate right to claim descent from Abraham spiritually. Yet more, if any nation could claim the right to address God as Father, it was Israel (cf. Hos. 11: 1; Mal. 2: 10). But Jesus refuses to acknowledge even this right, since these Jews have rejected the unique Son of God. Now follow two sharp unanswerable questions. **43. Why is my language not clear to you?:** It is because they cannot listen to His message. Their difficulty is a moral one, not intellectual. So the Jews' silence evokes some of the sternest ever of Jesus' rebukes (v. 44). **46. Can any of you prove me guilty** (Gk. *elenchei*) **of sin:** None! Then He *does* speak the truth, and the burden of guilt lies hard on their side by what He has said. Indeed, the Spirit will later convict *them* of sin (cf. 16: 8). But their ears are dull because they **do not belong to God** (47). **48. you are a Samaritan:** Their hot repudiation of Jesus' words led them to suggest that His denial of their kinship with Abraham was founded on Samaritan prejudice, and it may well be that Jesus' words had reminded them of the terminology of Samaritan theologians. The term 'Samaritan', however, is more probably a simple means of abuse (cf. v. 41). **51. he will never see death:** Here is madness indeed! for **Abraham died** (52). Jesus, however, speaks of death as the final and irrevocable separation from God. **56. Abraham rejoiced at the thought of seeing** (Gk. *ēgalliasato hina*) **my day:** Abraham anticipated the fulfilment of the initial promise of God (cf. Gen. 12: 3), especially at times of trial (cf. Gen. 22: 18). **he saw it and was glad:** Some ancient commentators believed this to be Abraham's vision (cf. Gen. 15: 17–21) of the extent of his posterity. Philo interpreted the laughter of Abraham (cf. Gen. 17: 17) as rejoicing rather than incredulity. Others have suggested that Abraham saw Christ's work from Paradise. Surely it rather refers to that penetration into the purpose of God, by which Abraham rejoiced in the Word of God, who was now made flesh for men to see. But how, ask the Jews, can He know so much about Abraham? **58. before Abraham was born, I am:** This is a clear claim to eternity of being. What correspondence with the Ineffable Name was intended in Jesus' use of the expression **I am** must be open to question. It must be remembered that Jesus is primarily answering the Jews' cavil concerning the length of His life. But that they saw blasphemous implications in what He said is clear (v. 59); perhaps they discerned an echo of 'I am he' in Isa. 41: 4, etc. So the conclusion to which the argument has led is that the time of special privileges for the physical descendants of Abraham has passed away (cf. Mt. 3: 9). The eternal Word has come in flesh to found a new community. The chosen people is now made up of Christ's followers, and the prerogatives of Abraham's seed have passed to them.

iii. The man blind from birth (9: 1–41)

In this section there is a perfect illustration of the fact that what Jesus does is inseparable from what He says. The next note of time occurs in 10: 22. There the passage follows on closely from chap. 9. So possibly the controversies in chap. 8 should be regarded as summing up discussions between Tabernacles and Dedication. **2. who sinned, this man or his parents:** They assume the old explanation of suffering so hotly challenged by Job. Moreover, the suggestion that the man himself might have been at fault seems to rest on Jewish speculation with regard to transmission of guilt or something carried over from Rabbinic Judaism, where, for example, in Midrash Rabbah on Dt. 31: 14, a pregnant woman who sins makes her unborn child to sin (cf. N. P. Williams, *Ideas of the Fall and Original Sin*, 1927, p. 98). Jesus repudiates any notion that there is a direct causal connection between his blindness and some sin. **but this happened so that the work of God might be displayed in his life:** The right attitude is to see in suffering not a reason for imputing guilt, but an occasion for the revealing of God's glory in the way it is dealt with. [There is a further possible rendering by an alteration of punctuation, *viz.*, 'It was not that this man sinned, nor his parents. But that God's work may be shown in him, I must do His works who sent me while it is day'.] **5. While I am in the world, I am the light of the world:** So long as Jesus remains, performing the work for which He was sent, there remains the inescapable revelation of the character of God. **7. Go . . . wash in the Pool of Siloam** (modern Silwan): Cf. Isa. 8: 6. This pool lies at the southern end of the Tunnel of Hezekiah from the Virgin's Fountain, at the southern extremity of the Tyropoeon valley. John explains its meaning, doubtless seeing a significance in the light of Jesus as sent from God. **14. the day on which Jesus had made the mud . . . was a Sabbath:** Here is the strongest reason for the Pharisees' rejection of the sign. Mishnaic rules for healing and the use of saliva on the Sabbath were complicated; but Jesus had made clay, and so had done work. So they triumphantly claim that Jesus **is not from God** (16) if He can openly break the Sabbath. **17. He is a prophet:** There is no theological significance in this. The man simply realized that Jesus possessed extraordinary powers. **18. The Jews still did not believe:** Either the whole story is a fabrication, they say, or else the man has confused the day on which he received his sight. His parents are

dumbfounded, too, and they **were afraid of the Jews** (22). The fear of excommunication held them. This could operate in two ways. The less severe, meant here, involved separation from the privileges of the synagogue for a period up to thirty days, though actual attendance at the synagogue was required as a disciplinary measure. This could virtually be enforced by anyone—even a woman. The more severe form involved flogging and exclusion from all social contact, except within the family, though it was seldom enforced. In Jesus' days the severe ban could only be inflicted by the Sanhedrin, but by the time of John's writing local synagogues could enforce both forms— and did so against the Christians. **24. Give glory to God:** A colloquialism meaning 'admit the truth' (cf. Jos. 7: 19). **we know this man is a sinner:** This is where they condemn themselves (cf. 3: 18). **25. one thing I do know:** Stubbornly, the man refuses to be coerced away from the plain fact. They may know their theology; he knows his cure. Which is ultimately more acceptable? The coming of sight has not solved all his problems, but his new life is beyond question. So their cross-examination cannot shake him. **27. Do you** (of all people) **. . . want to become his disciples:** No, indeed they do not. **28. we are disciples of Moses:** Their taunt against the man as **Jesus' disciple** and themselves as those who adhered to the law foreshadows the inevitable cleavage which was to take place between Christians and Jews in early NT times. **33. If this man were not from God he could do nothing:** Now the man comes towards the climax of his faith. Jesus, he believes, must be sent from God. And the Pharisees' rejection of so open a sign astonishes him. **34. You were steeped in sin at birth:** Their insinuation of the man's moral legacy, and their anger at his resistance, causes them to cast him out, and in principle cast out the Saviour with him. **35. Do you believe in the Son of Man?:** [Some MSS, followed by AV and RV text, read 'Son of God' here.] Barrett is probably right in saying that, as yet, the man's faith was imperfect. Perhaps the question should be phrased, 'You believe in the Son of man, do you not?' In the light of ch. 10, we may see Jesus, the Shepherd, taking care (v. 35) of a sheep lately sent away from the fold of Jewish legalism. **37. You have now seen him:** The primary meaning is that the man, with his eyesight restored, had seen the Son of Man without realizing who He was. Elsewhere in the Gospels seeing the Son of Man is reserved for the future (cf. Mk 14: 62). But by the eye of faith the future sight of Him can be enjoyed here and now. **39. For judgment I have come . . . that . . . those who see will become blind:** Cf. Isa. 29: 18; 35: 5; 42: 7, 18. Here there is an interchange between physical and spiritual sight. Jesus is more concerned with the latter, though the man just cured had received both. Those Jews who rejected Jesus had become wilfully blind to the truth (12: 40; cf. Isa. 6: 9 f.). Jesus had come to give spiritual sight to those who knew they were blind, but also to correct the defect of those who were satisfied with the 'sight' which they already possessed, so that they could now move forward on a new basis of faith. **41.** The Pharisees understand that Jesus is speaking of spiritual sight, and take their stand on their knowledge of the scriptures. Jesus now shows them that their sin lies nevertheless in their possession of the truth without understanding it, whereas ignorance from blindness is teachable. And the fact that they insist that they can 'see' makes their sin wilful.

iv. The Good Shepherd (10: 1–21)

This section is an elaboration of matters raised in ch. 9. The shepherds in Israel had failed; now the Good Shepherd takes over. The passage is a lengthy parable (Gk. *paroimia*, v. 6) and the alternation between symbolism and reality has to be followed carefully by the reader. **2. The man who enters by the gate is the shepherd:** Here is a straightforward reference to what most Jews would have seen day by day; but later both the door (v. 7) and the shepherd (vv. 10, 14, etc.) symbolize different aspects of Jesus Himself. The wording suggests that the gatekeeper was someone paid by a number of shepherds collectively to keep their sheep in one fold since Jesus refers to several shepherds by inference (v. 16) and repeats **his own sheep** on a number of occasions (vv. 3, 4, 12, 14). **6. figure** (Gk. *paroimia*) is used alone by John among the Gospel writers (cf. 2 Pet. 2: 22 and Prov. 1: 1, LXX) and seems to mean 'a veiled utterance' as distinct from forthright speech (cf. 16: 25, 29). **7. I am the gate for the sheep:** He does not say 'of the fold' for it is the sheep who concern Him, so perhaps, 'I am the door *for* the sheep'. **8. All who ever came before me:** Jesus does not refer here to the OT prophets. He means self-appointed leaders in Israel. **9. He will come in and go out:** The emphasis here is different from that in v. 7. Christ is the only Way into the security of the fold of God. But once entered the sheep enjoy complete freedom. **11. I am the good shepherd:** God is depicted as the Shepherd of Israel in the OT (cf. Ps. 23: 1; Isa. 40: 11; Jer. 31: 9; Ezek. 34; *et alia*). Gk. *kalos* here suggests the beauty of perfect competence as well as of moral goodness. True care of the sheep comes about through ownership. Those who have no right over the sheep flee when there is danger, but Jesus, in virtue of that relationship He has with the Father (cf. v. 15) lays down His life for the sheep. **16. other sheep:** These are the Gentiles. They are already

His sheep, though He has yet to bring them to join the others; thus they will constitute **one flock**—not 'one fold' (AV)—in virtue of their attachment to the **one shepherd**. These verses have an obvious bearing on the methods of seeking Christian unity (cf. Eph. 2: 11–22; Ezek. 34: 23); as in 11: 52, it is Christ Himself who 'gathers into one the children of God who are scattered abroad'. **17. The reason my Father loves me:** The perfect conformity of will between Son and Father is shown, says Jesus, by His laying down of His life. **Only to take it up again:** The resurrection of Christ in the NT is consistently spoken of as an act of God. Here, however, Jesus shows that it is something in which He will participate in action (Gk. *labō*), receiving it again. **18. I have authority . . . I have authority:** That is, supreme freedom is the prerogative of Jesus in His Incarnation. But He lays down His life by virtue of the command of the Father, which speaks as much of the Father's authority as it does of the Son's ability to know what the will of the Father is. Vv. 19–21 follow very suitably after 9: 41, and some scholars transfer them to that position, but as there is no textual evidence for this the justification for it is insufficient.

v. Final Encounter with the Jews (10: 22–42)

22. the Feast of Dedication (Heb. *ḥanukkah*): This feast celebrated the re-dedication of the Temple in 164 B.C. by Judas Maccabeus after its defilement by Antiochus Epiphanes. A prominent feature of the feast was the illuminations provided by the lighting of lamps in the Temple, and in houses round about. **24. If you are the Christ, tell us plainly:** This was no desire really to know, but a question asked in annoyance by the Jews who had so far been incapable of catching Jesus in His own argument. But Jesus cannot tell them plainly, for with their wrong views either 'yes' or 'no' would have been equally misleading. Either He must show messianic signs according to the scriptures, or else He must make Himself the kind of Messiah that they wanted. **26. you do not believe, because you are not my sheep:** The sheep recognize their shepherd for what He does. But the very fact that these Jews had asked such a question put them well and truly outside the flock of God. **27.** Indeed, their following Him and His knowing them are mutual. **30. I and the Father are one** (Gk. *hen*): The neuter gender rules out any thought of meaning 'one Person'. This is not a comment on the nature of the Godhead. Rather, having spoken of the sheep's security in both Himself and the Father, Jesus underlines what He has said by indicating that in action the Father and He can be regarded as a single entity, because their wills are one. **33. blasphemy:** Jewish legal tradition, supported by the Mishnah and other rabbinic literature, made blasphemous any statement in which a man uttered the Ineffable Name. But their charge is a tragic consequence of their blindness. Jesus is indeed both Man and God. **34. Is it not written . . . 'I have said, you are gods'?:** This answer, with its appeal to Ps. 82: 6, is a typical rabbinic argument. It seems to imply 'I have given you the truth in allegorical form. You cannot accept that. Very well, I will now meet you with the kind of argument you do appreciate' (cf. 7: 15–24; Mk 12: 35 ff.). The psalm refers to Israel's judges—sometimes called 'princes'—who, even though they failed, were designated 'gods' because they administered justice as part of their divine commission. How then can they charge Jesus with blasphemy if He is evidently sent from God (36)? **38. the Father is in me and I am in the Father:** These words will occur once more in the Lord's great prayer (cf. 17: 21) and will be considered there. **40.** Jesus returns to the place where His ministry began. Associations with John the Baptist are strong here, and as Temple suggests. Jesus may have gone over the whole story of His emergence into public again. John, indeed, spoke the truth. That is evident. And upon this evidence many believe in Him (42).

vi. Lazarus' resurrection and its sequel (11: 1–57)
Jesus' earlier self-disclosure (cf. 5: 18) had incited the Jews to murderous hatred. But Jesus had added to that the claim that His was the power to bestow life (cf. 5: 21). The subsequent story shows how a demonstration of this power set the Jews in their final determination to put Him to death (cf. vv. 46, 53). The sign has a number of counterparts in the Synoptics (cf. Mk 5: 21–43; Lk. 7: 11–16 and parallels). **1. Lazarus . . . from Bethany:** This was close to Jerusalem (cf. v. 18) and is carefully distinguished by the Evangelist from Bethany of Transjordan (cf. 1: 28) where, most probably, Jesus was when the news of Lazarus' sickness reached him. **2. Mary . . . who poured perfume on the Lord:** This identification precedes the incident recorded later (cf. 12: 1–8). There is no persuasive reason, apart from verbal resemblance, to identify her with the woman of Lk. 7: 36–50. **4. This sickness . . . it is for God's glory:** At once Jesus suggests that He intends doing something, as well as implying that He knew how near to death Lazarus was, in fact. And John assures us that Jesus loved the family (5). **6. he stayed where he was two more days:** Jesus so moved in perfect accordance with the divine plan that not even His love for Lazarus' sisters moved him to go to Bethany a moment early. Indeed, the messenger must have reached Jesus about the time that Lazarus died. Jesus waited because He knew it was better, although He knew that

it would add to the temporary grief of the sisters. His tears of sympathy (cf. v. 35) were perfectly natural. Nor is it true to say that Jesus waited in order to perform a greater miracle, and thereby evoke greater wonder from the bystanders, by adding to the restoring of breath to the body the greater wonder of restoring the already decomposing flesh (cf. v. 39). This is inconsistent with all that we know about Him. The extra hours of sorrow were more than compensated for the sisters; and who can measure the effect upon Jesus himself? **9. Are there not twelve hours of daylight?:** So long as time remains for Him to work, Jesus is assured that no harm will befall Him. 'Hour' here is not used in the Johannine technical sense. **11. Lazarus has fallen asleep:** Jesus' knowledge of the circumstances is clearly supernatural. Yet to Him physical death is like sleep (cf. Mk 5: 39) and He will awaken Lazarus again. 'Sleep' became the favourite metaphor to denote the state of death in which early Christians awaited the parousia (cf. Ac. 7: 60; 1 Th. 4: 13 f.; 1 C. 15: 20, 51 et alia). **15. I am glad I was not there:** Here is the perfect sympathy of the Lord. He knows that greater *faith* will be aroused both in the sisters and the disciples than if He had been there to prevent Lazarus from dying. Yet the desire to comfort the sisters is not far from Jesus' mind. He says, **Let us go to him. 16. Thomas** is one of the most consistent characters in the NT. Though only mentioned by name four times in John (cf. 14: 5; 20: 24 ff.; 21: 2) he is most clearly depicted. He asks for hard facts, and, however unpalatable they may be, he will accept them for he is loyal to what he believes. **25. I am the resurrection and the life:** Martha cannot think much beyond the traditional belief concerning resurrection, taught by the Pharisees and indeed endorsed, so far as it went, by the Lord Himself (cf. 5: 28 f.; 6: 39 f., 44, 54). But Jesus shows that in Him eschatological hope becomes actual and present. Death is only the moment when eternal life passes from activity and experience in the material world. The life which Jesus promises is immortal. So in response to this revelation Martha heaps up all the messianic terms she can muster to express her faith in Christ. **28. The Teacher is here:** Jesus' friends will habitually have referred to Him as 'the Rabbi' (Gk. *ho didaskalos*); cf. 13: 13 f.; 20: 16; Mk 14: 14. **33. Jesus . . . was deeply moved** (Gk. *enebrimēsato*) **in spirit and troubled** (Gk. *etaraxen heauton*): These two Greek phrases speak of indignation and sorrow respectively. Temple aptly renders the second as 'shuddered'. It is certain that Jesus was moved with sorrow for Lazarus—so close a friend. But the sight of the professional mourners may account for the first expression. It is likely, also, that Jesus already contemplated the violent reaction which this miracle would ultimately produce. *Enebrimēsato* also occurs in the Synoptics (cf. Mt. 9: 30; Mk 1: 43), and probably suggests there the physical and spiritual energy involved in working wonders. **35. Jesus wept** (Gk. *edakrysen*): The Jews' weeping was not unlike the loud organized mourning of the East. Jesus shed tears. He groans again as He contemplates the great encounter with the arch-enemy of man—death. **40. Did I not tell you that . . . you would see** (Gk. *opsei*) **the glory of God:** Perhaps we are meant to understand by this that Jesus promised Martha that she would have a vision (suggested by the word for 'see') of the glory of God over and above the physical event to be witnessed by the others. (For *opsei* as used by John in this sense, cf. 1: 51; 3: 36; 11: 40.) **41.** So, as the stone is removed, Jesus faces the challenge of all challenges so far in His ministry. But He meets it with prayer, given moreover to help others to see that He is acting in communion with the Father. **43. Lazarus, come out:** In this momentous event others are allowed to share. They lift the stone, but only Jesus can bring the dead man out. They free him from the grave cloths, but only after Jesus has imparted life to him. The astounding facts are recorded in rapid succession.

Some of the bystanders believed. Others **went to the Pharisees** (46). This is a turning point in the Saviour's ministry. In the Synoptics the same crucial moment seems to come at the cleansing of the Temple. **48. the Romans will come and take away both our place and our nation:** This is a typical Sadducean reaction. So far the priestly party have shown little interest. Now they are alarmed for their privileged position. So Caiaphas now takes the lead. He was high-priest that fateful year. (The expression **that year** does not imply that John regarded the Jewish high priesthood as an annual office; Caiaphas in fact occupied it from A.D. 18 to 36.) It is, he says, **better for you that one man die** (50), so that all Jews do not otherwise perish. His pronouncement was prophetic. As John shows, he could not have spoken more eloquently of the vicarious death of the Lord Jesus. But his words are tinged with bitter irony as well. Not many years hence the Jewish nation will suffer bitterly under Rome. **54. Ephraim** was some fifteen miles NE of Jerusalem. Jesus remained there until Passover. The final paragraph shows how many there must have been who were watching the mounting tide of events with intense interest.

IV. THE LAST SCENE OF CONFLICT (12: 1–50)
i. The supper at Bethany (12: 1–11)
1. Six days before the Passover: A chronological difficulty arises here from the uncertainty with regard to the day of the Crucifixion. Westcott suggests that this took place on 14 Nisan, and that therefore, the visit to Bethany was made on 8 Nisan. If the Crucifixion took place on a Friday then this visit was made the preceding Friday, the intervening Sabbath being left out of the reckoning as a *dies non*. **3. an expensive perfume** (Gk. *nardos pistikē*) was probably liquid perfume. This anointing may be compared with other accounts (cf. Mk 14: 3–9; Mt. 26: 6–13), where the mention of the house of Simon may be explained by the fact that Jesus stayed in and near Bethany for a time (cf. 'two days', Mk 14: 1). (It has even been suggested that Simon was the father of Martha, Mary and Lazarus.) The reference to Mary's wiping Jesus' feet with her hair is the only parallel with another Synoptic story (cf. Lk. 7: 36–50), where, however, the situation is quite different. **6. he was a thief:** This is the only clear reference to Judas's tendencies apart from the blood-money which he gained from the chief priests (cf. Lk. 22: 5). **7. she should save this perfume for the day of my burial:** The sense here is not absolutely clear without reference to the Markan account (cf. Mk. 14: 8). The ointment could hardly be kept if it were used at that moment. But Jesus seems to say that Mary has anticipated His burial, even though she may have reserved the perfume for some charitable purpose elsewhere. **10. the chief priests made plans to kill Lazarus as well:** In endeavouring to suppress the news of Lazarus' resurrection they are already finding that their policy of expedient death must be extended further than one person.

ii. The Messianic Entry (12: 12–19)
John alone records the reason for the glad acclamation of the crowd at this juncture (cf. Mk 11: 7–10; Mt. 21: 4–9; Lk. 19: 35–38). **13. Hosanna:** They took up the antiphonal chant of the last of the Hallel psalms (Heb. *hoshi'a nā*, lit. 'save us now'; cf. Ps. 118: 25). Jesus' action was designed to stir the faith of the onlookers, which, at least among the disciples, was not understood until later (v. 16) as a fulfilment of scripture (cf. Zech. 9: 9). The act was intended as a sign of peace; Zechariah goes on to say (cf. Zech. 9: 10), 'he shall command peace to the nations'. And Jesus clearly intended *that* significance to underlie His announcement of the kingdom (cf. F. F. Bruce: 'The Book of Zechariah and the Passion Narrative'; *Bulletin of the John Rylands Library, Manchester*, 43, 1960–61, pp. 336–353). **19. the whole world has gone after him:** An idiom simply meaning 'everyone'. But to the Evangelist this may well have suggested the universal appeal of the gospel (cf. v. 32).

iii. The Greeks' request and the Jews' rejection (12: 20–43)
The presence of these 'God-fearing' *Hellenes*,

viz., Greek-speaking foreigners who had adopted Jewish worship, but not the law in its entirety, is mentioned only by John. Yet the discourse which follows seems to echo a number of Synoptic passages (cf. Mk 4: 1–9; 8: 34; 9: 1, etc.). They may have come to Philip being attracted by his name. Philip's possible hesitancy suggested by his consulting Andrew before they both tell Jesus about the visitors, is possibly to be accounted for by the remembrance of Jesus' former words about Gentiles (cf. Mt. 10: 15; 15: 24). **23. The hour has come:** Jesus sees that events now point directly to His approaching Passion. Yet He will be glorified as the Heavenly Man since the Incarnation spells out His humiliation. **24. unless a kernel of wheat falls . . . and dies:** The Synoptic parable of the seed depicts the kingdom (cf. Mk 4: 1–20; Mt. 13: 1–9; 18–25; Lk. 8: 4–15); in John a similar metaphor is used to denote the King. He teaches that what becomes true of Himself is a principle in all nature. So Paul (cf. 1 C. 15: 36 ff.). **25. The man who loves his life will lose it:** The saying about life through death (v. 24) is capable of general application, and Jesus here applies it to His followers (cf. Mk 8: 35; Mt. 10: 39; Lk. 17: 33) in their sufferings with Him. To hate (Gk. *miseō*) one's life means to turn one's back on it as of secondary importance compared with the cause that matters most. **26. where I am, my servant also will be:** Jesus is not promising some happy issue out of suffering, *viz.*, in future glory. He is saying that the experience which is about to befall Him may be expected by His faithful disciple. But just as that servant may expect to share Christ's suffering, so also, of course, he can expect to enter into glory with Him (Ac. 14: 22; Rom. 8: 17; 1 Tim. 2: 11 ff.). **27. Now my heart is troubled:** Jesus now faces the call to His personal endurance. He expresses the same feelings in the Garden of Gethsemane later (cf. Mk 14: 32–42; Mt. 26: 36–46; Lk. 22: 40–46), so we learn from this that He felt this agony of spirit at other times than the Thursday night before His death. **what shall I say? 'Father, save me from** (Gk. *ek*) **this hour':** Did these words form an actual prayer, or were the words only contemplated? Jesus was certainly not thinking of avoiding the Cross. The preposition *ek* ('out of') implies that He committed Himself into the Father's hands as death drew near. In any case it is clear (v. 28) that He came to this moment for the Father's glory. **30. This voice was for your benefit:** Yet the sound was unintelligible to some, and misunderstood by others. God had glorified His name once (cf. 11: 40) and now in the Passion He would glorify it again. **31. Now is the time for judgment on this world:** The world stands judged before the prospect of the Cross, both for its part in crucifying the Prince of Life, and for the fact that its moment of victory will, by the resurrection, come to be the moment of its utter defeat. **32. I, when I am lifted up . . . will draw all men:** Until then He was subject to restriction in the range of His mission (cf. Lk. 12: 50); after that, His saving grace would be equally available to Greeks (like the present inquirers) and Jews. Whatever broad meaning may attach to 'lifting up' (see note on 3: 14), the crowd is shrewd enough to detect what Jesus has in mind at this moment, and they can connect it with Jesus' earlier words (cf. vv. 34, 23). No special passage suits what they say they **have heard from the law** (34), though we may think of Isa. 9: 6 f.; Ps. 110: 4, etc. **34. Who is this Son of Man?:** But Jesus cannot explain by word only (cf. 8: 25). Their only hope of understanding is to **put your trust in the light** (36), that is, to try to understand Him as He is. For a few hours yet the Light is still shining in the world, and with this the special privilege given them of becoming 'enlightened men' by believing what they see (cf. 20: 29).

With these words Jesus departs. His last utterances (cf. Mk 13: 35 f.) urged His hearers to take that final opportunity of putting faith in Him, yet, **they still would not believe in him** (37), thus bringing to pass a prophecy of Isaiah. This prophecy did not become meaningful only through the event; the event fulfilled the prophecy in so far as the word of Isaiah declared the will of God (cf. Isa. 53: 1). Neither Jesus' words, the 'report', nor His works, the 'arm of the Lord', had convinced them. **39. they could not believe:** The consequence of unbelief was bound to follow. As Temple has aptly put it: 'God does not cause sin, but He does cause its appropriate consequence to result from it by the law of the order of creation' (*Readings*, p. 202). **40. He has blinded their eyes:** Cf. Isa. 6: 10. The blindness of the Jews is part of the divine plan, therefore; though they are not thereby absolved from guilt, for they 'hated the light' (cf. 3: 20) and so brought into bondage the freedom of their wills. But out of their unbelief arises the mystery of that Sacrifice which is to redeem the world. (Isa. 6: 10 is similarly applied in Mk 4: 12 and parallels and in Ac. 28: 26 f.) **41. Isaiah . . . saw Jesus' glory:** Cf. Isa. 6: 1. John seems to base his reference on a Targumic paraphrase of the prophet's words, which originally omitted any personal description of the Almighty. His glory was manifested in the Incarnation, and was thus seen again by mortal men (cf. 1: 14). **42. many even among the leaders believed in him** (Gk. *episteusan eis auton*): It is surprising that John uses this phrase meaning full belief when they obviously, because of their position on the Sanhedrin, avoided embarrassment by remaining secret disciples (but cf. the use of the phrase in 2: 23). Nicodemus and Joseph of Arimathea were examples among them.

iv. Christ's summary of His message (12: 44–50)

In view of the finality of Jesus' words in v. 36a and His subsequent departure from the Jews (36b), coupled with the decisive nature of the quotations of v. 37, some scholars have suggested that vv. 44–50 are displaced, and should probably follow v. 36a. Whether this is so or not, we may reasonably conclude that the Evangelist chose to end the present section of the Gospel by bringing together some of the Saviour's most pregnant sayings containing the leading ideas in His self-revelation, i.e. on Light, His authority from the Father, the nature of judgment, the Father's command to the Son in His preaching, and the Life which issues from His words (cf. comments on 5: 24–29; 7: 17; 8: 12). **46. I have come into the world as a light:** Jesus sheds light on the way to God. The man who believes in Him in fact puts his trust in God. His trust is not based on the limited temporal life of Jesus 'in the days of his flesh', but in the eternal Life of God which was made known in Christ. And because God wills the salvation of men He gave Christ the commandment for His message.

PART THREE—FINAL DISCOURSES AND EVENTS
(13: 1–21: 25)

1. THE UPPER ROOM MINISTRY (13: 1–17: 26)
i. Practice and precept in humility (13: 1–17)

John does not record the details of the supper itself. But he does preserve certain actions and words which were lasting symbols of Christ's nature, and which He wished the disciples ever to remember. **1. before the Passover Feast:** It is held by some that John's chronology differs from that of the Synoptics in placing the Last Supper earlier in Passion Week, **before** the Passover, whereas the Synoptists represent it as a Passover meal (cf. Mk 14: 1–26). The apparent discrepancy of one day could, however, be overcome if it could be clearly shown that the Pharisees and other groups in Israel commemorated Passover a day earlier than the Sadducees. Some support for two distinct calendars has been provided by the Dead Sea Scrolls. R. V. G. Tasker has suggested that this whole verse might be separated from the adjoining passage and understood as an introduction to it. (For further indications of time, cf. 18: 28; 19: 14, 31, 42.) **2. The evening meal was being served** (Gk. *deipnou ginomenou*):

For *ginomenou* (present) there is a well-attested variant *genomenou* (aorist), whence AV, 'supper being ended'. C. H. Dodd (*Interpretation of the Fourth Gospel*, 1953, p. 401) points out the significance of this phrase, indicating that the following action has its setting within the Lord's Supper with its theme of remembrance. If this were the Passover meal we should have expected John to be much more explicit. Further, the **already** of this verse, referring to Judas, implies that the moment of his defection during Passover had not actually arrived. **4. took off his outer clothing:** By this act Jesus pictures the humiliation which, in its fullest expression, meant for Him the laying down of His life. There can be no further allegorical significance than this, and to look for it is to overlook v. 15 which plainly states that the act was primarily an exemplary one. Jesus took the slave's posture, when He took the towel, which indeed He adopted supremely as the Servant of the Lord. **8. Unless I wash you, you have no part with me:** Both AV and RV also render 'with me' which is, in fact, much nearer to what Jesus actually said. Jesus' words again enforce the point that what He is doing is an enacted parable. If Peter, therefore, will be associated with his Lord he must let Him do what He wishes. Men must not only have the desire to serve Christ, but to accept His service for them. And that some cleansing is typified here seems reasonable, though we should not press the picture further. **10. needs only to wash his feet:** C. K. Barrett rightly suggests that the textual problem of these words, whether or not they should be omitted (as some MSS), cannot be decided on textual grounds alone but also on interpretation, for the shorter reading makes it impossible to suppose that what Jesus had done was not of supreme importance. **14. you also should wash one another's feet:** Jesus has spoken of that fundamental cleansing which He brings by way of His life and death. Now those who are cleansed by Him must work out their cleansing by loving and humble service each for the other. **17. you will be blessed if you do them:** The lesson must appeal to their wills as well as to their intellects. And he who puts into practice what he knows finds true happiness.

ii. The Traitor (13: 18–35)

18. I know those I have chosen: In spite of Judas, Jesus can say that his knowledge of them all has been full from the beginning. But Judas's action only shows how fully the scriptures (*e.g.* Ps. 41: 9) are fulfilled in Him (cf. 17: 12). **lifted up his heel against me:** It is in compassion that Jesus does not disclose the details of the traitor's act. 'Heel' (Gk. *pterna*) is a NT *hapax legomenon* (occurring once only in the NT). E. F. F. Bishop tells how this saying, especially among Arabs (and the Heb. 'heel' *'aqeb* [cf.

Jacob], is cognate with the Arabic term), implies a dastardly insult on the part of a close friend. **23. One of them, the disciple whom Jesus loved:** Some have thought that this was the 'ideal' disciple who did not figure in real life, who perfectly responds to Jesus' teaching. This, however, may be dismissed. According to 21: 24 he was 'the witness' on whose evidence this Gospel is founded, and by whom it was written (cf. also 19: 26; 20: 2). This witness was known to the Jerusalem authorities and provided first-hand testimony of the Crucifixion (cf. 18: 15; 19: 35). For a fuller discussion see *Introduction*. **25. Lord, who is it?:** This question, put by John, accords well with the general impression which we have of him throughout the NT. Elsewhere (cf. Mk 14: 17 ff.; Mt. 26: 20 ff.) each of the disciples asks in astonishment if he himself is the traitor. But this man, with clearer conscience, asks Jesus for direct nomination. **26. It is the one to whom I will give this piece of bread:** At Eastern meals it was a common gesture of special friendship for the host to offer a morsel to one of the diners. Jesus' action, then, seems to say to Judas that in spite of his intention, the Saviour's love remains unchanged. **30. he went out:** Judas' intention now becomes a settled purpose. He goes out from the light and companionship of Jesus' and His friends into the night (cf. 6: 64). The lesson here for all time is surely that even with the love of God upon him, man is free to choose evil rather than good. **31. Now is the Son of Man glorified:** Cf. 17: 1. Jesus, in the perfection of human character, accepts Judas's decision. But this does not go unnoticed. **32. God will glorify the Son in himself:** The dignity with which Jesus as Man accepts the desperate resolve of Judas is counterpart to the dignity with which God will invest Him through the work upon which He now embarks. **34. love one another:** With what emotion these words were uttered at this moment we cannot tell. Judas had displayed the evil born of self-centredness. Jesus was about to show to them His undiluted love for the Father in obedience to His will. He is to leave them physically—they cannot follow—and the only bond which will keep them together is love, fostered within them by the Spirit (cf. 14: 15 ff.).

iii. Comfort for the disciples in distress (13: 36–14: 31)
36. you will follow later: It is here that the stark truth of what Jesus says begins to dawn upon Peter. But he is undaunted. He thinks more of Christ's companionship than of his own life, whatever failure he may have suffered later in the story. But he does not yet understand that Jesus promises him that he will follow, indeed. It will be to death, and after death to vindication. The thought of separation is

hard enough. But the thought of failure at the moment of separation is far worse. So Jesus comforts the disciples by urging them to look into the future joy of re-union. **14: 1. Trust in God; trust also in me:** Currency in English has undoubtedly weakened the force of this statement. The words are capable of three renderings: (*a*) 'you trust in God, (so) trust also in me'; (*b*) 'you trust in God and you trust in me'; and (*c*) 'trust in God and trust in me' (as above). On the whole, the last of the three is preferable. Jesus is concerned to strengthen their faith in the face of the trials soon to begin. As Jews they profess to have faith in God. Now they must learn what it is to renew that faith in Christ. **2. many rooms:** Jesus has been rejected by the stewards of the house of God on earth (cf. 2: 16), so He returns to the eternal counterpart in heaven. But these disciples must not think that they are left behind because of any lack of the Father's hospitality. **3. I will come back:** The final thought here is certainly an eschatological one—the second advent of Christ. But that by no means exhausts what Jesus is saying. Jesus will come again in the Spirit (cf. vv. 18, 21, 23). There is no vacuum between the days of His flesh and the final arrival in the Father's house, even for these (cf. 20: 22, where see note), however much arresting delay there is before the completion of the work. **6. I am the way, and the truth, and the life:** Not, 'I *show* the way . . .'. Christ is *Himself* the vital link between heaven and earth (cf. 1: 51) so apart from His teaching (the truth) and His work (to bring life) there is no salvation. What Jesus *is* cannot be separated from what He *does*. **7. If you really knew me:** The pluperfect tense here (Gk. *egnōkeite*) is puzzling. The readings of other MSS, notably Sinaiticus, D (*Codex Bezae*, Cambridge) and P. 66, seem to imply 'if you have known me, you will come to know the Father as well'. The second half of the verse would support this. So, the verse could tell us that when these men come to find that Jesus is indeed the Way, they will date their vision of the Father from that revelation. **8.** The instances in which Philip appears in the Gospel are noteworthy (cf. 1: 45 f.; 6: 5 ff.; 12: 21 ff.; 14: 8). His question here is evidence to the slowness with which he had developed spiritually. **9.** But there is nothing in the ministry of Jesus which should not lead men to the Father, for He is uniquely the image of God (cf. Col. 1: 15; Heb. 1: 3). And as Jesus has already indicated (cf. 10: 25), the evidence of His works is a lower path to faith in God (cf. 20: 29). **12. greater things than these:** The works performed by the Christian are done in communion with the living Saviour. But they are greater in their sphere of influence. Jesus' works were limited to the days of His flesh and the land in which He lived. But the

Church which is His body has a worldwide influence in winning men for Him. **16. another Counselor** (Gk. *paraklētos*): The word is borrowed from legal usage. There it denotes an advocate or defending counsel, although this specifically seems to be secondary in John—except perhaps 16: 8–11 where He is the *prosecuting* Counsel! It is derived from Gk. *parakaleō*, 'to call alongside', thus 'a helper'. Elsewhere in the NT *parakaleō* frequently denotes a memorable utterance encouraging or hortatory in character (cf. Ac. 2: 40). Barrett shows that it is just a combination of these two functions which seems to lie behind the statement here. The Holy Spirit speaks of 'things to come' (cf. 16: 13) and thereby, whilst bringing conviction to the consciences of men, strengthens the believers (here, and cf. 16: 7–15; 1 C. 14: 3 ff.). For His intercessory ministry, another essential aspect of His work as Paraclete, cf. Rom. 8: 26. **17. the Spirit of truth:** This qualification is always employed in conjunction with the Paraclete in John (cf. 15: 26; 16: 13; 1 Jn 4: 6). **The world cannot accept him:** By very definition the world and the Spirit are contrasted. The world is materialistic and thereby basically hostile to anything which does not conform to the nature of matter. In 14: 16 f. we have the first of five 'Paraclete Sayings' in the upper room discourse, the other four being 14: 25 f.; 15: 26 f.; 16: 5–11 and 16: 12–15. Together, these five sayings present a doctrine of the Holy Spirit in advance of any references to Him elsewhere in the Gospels, but bearing a remarkable affinity with the portrayal of His presence and ministry in Acts. **18. I will come to you:** Cf. v. 3. Jesus probably refers to the post-resurrection appearances and the Spirit's advent as well as to the great day of His coming. **19. because I live, you also will live:** A fresh thought appears to enter the narrative at this point. But it is probably preferable to link these words with the previous clause, i.e., 'but you will see me. Because I live; you also will live!' **20. you will realize that I am in my Father:** The resurrection appearances would be unearthly visitations of Jesus after His resurrection, tangibly demonstrating to them His divine incursion into their affairs. The real basis of their union with Him will not be His appearances to them, but their love for Him by which their vision will constantly keep Him in view. And the verification of their love must ever be in their keeping of His commands. **21. I too will . . . show myself to Him:** That Jesus combines the beatific vision and His eschatological appearance seems evident from Judas's question (cf. v. 22). The very word (Gk. *emphanizō*) seems to carry overtones of OT theophany (cf. Exod. 33: 18). But Jesus assures Judas that this will be no mere passing visitation. The Father and He together will make

our home with him (23). **27. Peace I leave with you:** This is more than the conventional greeting or farewell. It is *His* peace, not like the world's estimate of tranquillity, but bringing comfort and strength in the midst of distress. **28. the Father is greater than I:** These words need lend no support to a lowered doctrine of Christ. The Father is 'greater' in that the Incarnate Son derives His being from Him. And Christ could especially utter this as the *Word* Incarnate. Moreover, the 'greaterness' of the Father means that the revelation of Him manifested in Jesus is full so far as was possible in a human person. The world of creation and history, in which the Word is immanent, is what it is because God is what He is. But His nature is not dependent upon its manifestation. **31. Come now; let us leave** (Gk. *egeiresthe agōmen enteuthen*): Did Jesus leave the room at this precise moment? Were the discourses of chaps. 15–16 spoken *en route* to Gethsemane? C. H. Dodd (*Historical Tradition in the Fourth Gospel*, p. 72) has shed some helpful light upon this point: *egeiresthe* can be taken to mean 'bestir yourselves'; similarly *agōmen enteuthen* may be taken as 'Let us encounter the enemy' in which case the link with the preceding verse would be exceptionally strong. As R. V. G. Tasker puts it: 'Jesus is here giving expression to his *spiritual* determination to meet the prince of this world' (p. 170). No physical movement from the upper room need therefore be understood at this point. And, as Dr. Dodd has pointed out, 'rise', though referring to sleep in Mk 14: 42, is frequently used of stirring oneself from a state of lethargy. Westcott aptly comments that though similar words occur in Mark, they are 'such as would naturally be repeated under like circumstances' (p. 211).

iv. Union with Christ and its consequences (15: 1–27)

1. I am the true vine: Some would place the following discourse in the Temple precincts by the door to the Holy Place where was a golden vine, symbol of the life of Israel (cf. Isa. 5: 1–7; Jer. 2: 21; Ps. 80: 8–16). But it has already been suggested that there are grounds also for supposing that Jesus was continuing His ministry in the upper room (cf. 14: 31). All that Israel was destined to be, but failed to be, Jesus was —the true (ideal) vine, producing acceptable fruit for God in His personal life and in the lives of His disciples, united to Him by faith. There may be a connection between these words and those spoken by the Lord during the Last Supper concerning the fruit of the vine with its implications concerning His blood by which all disciples are made sharers with Him in the new Israel (cf. Mk 14: 25). **my Father is the gardener:** He has charge of the whole (cf. Mk 12: 1–12). **2. He cuts off every branch . . . that bears no fruit:** The absence of fruit in the branch of the vine casts grave doubt upon its real union with the central stem, however otherwise it may appear. Such useless members must be cut off; perhaps Judas is the outstanding example. **every branch that does bear fruit he prunes** (Gk. *kathairei*): The word means literally to cleanse, the inference being the cutting away of dead wood which is a complete antithesis of the life evidenced by fruit. **3. You are already clean:** By the total effect of the Lord's teaching the disciples had been cleansed and prepared for the continuance of His work. **4. Remain in me, and I will remain in you:** The two parts of this statement must be taken as they stand without understanding their inter-dependence in any conditional sense. The revelation of which Jesus has just spoken cannot sustain life. Life in Christ must be identified with union with Him. **5. I am the vine, you are the branches:** Each member of Christ enjoys equality of status with all others. Yet Christ does not describe Himself as the central stem. He *is* the vine. Every branch is incorporate. **7. ask whatever you will and it shall be done for you:** Union with Christ is the basis of prayer. This prayer, moreover, will be effective. What the member wills will be one with His will since their union is complete. Yet the branch, in the nature of the case, depends upon the vine, for its prayer is a sign of that dependence. **8. showing yourselves to be my disciples:** This saying is no anti-climax. It rather describes all that is involved in full discipleship. **9. so have I loved you:** The aorist here (Gk. *ēgapēsa*) denotes a completed action. There is no restraint with Christ's love. In the reality of the Incarnation lies the totality of His love which He has lavished freely upon these men. **16. I chose you and appointed** (Gk. *ethēka*) **you:** He chose them to be His friends. That is, His choice was first motivated by the desire to *have* them (cf. Mk 3: 14), and then to send them out as His missionaries. His sending them forth is grounded in His confidence in them as His friends, and this conversely (same verse) is their ground of confidence in prayer. **18. the world . . . hated me first:** There are no middle feelings which may make the disciple's lot bearable in this world. Jesus warns them that the love within the Church will find a strong contrast outside. **20. Remember . . . I spoke to you . . . 'No servant is greater than his master':** Cf. 13: 16; there it was a lesson in humble service; here it becomes a lesson in endurance. But their work, like His, will reap positive fruits as well as negative. If there were those who kept Christ's word, so they may expect to find similar sympathy with their message here and there. But the basis of the world's hostility (v. 21) will be lack of the knowledge of God. **22. Now however, they have no excuse for their sin:** Jesus' work

constituted evidence of God's intervention in the world. Here, as in 14: 11, is the appeal to a lower form of evidence. But, nevertheless, true righteousness has been manifested in Christ. Men have seen the right way to live in Him. But they still do not believe (cf. 20: 29). **25. They hated me without reason:** Cf. Ps. 35: 19; 69: 4. This is the witness of *their* law, says Jesus pointedly. But though they may reject Him, and remain blind to the witness of their scriptures, the Holy Spirit will yet bear witness. **27. you also must testify:** Their insight into the truth which communion with Christ brings arises out of the divine nature of that truth itself. But it is the Incarnation that gives it its impetus. And when it is received it carries with it the conviction of the deity of Christ. So the witness of the Incarnation becomes united with the testimony of Christ's disciples. With the conjoining of the witness of the Spirit and the disciples in vv. 26 f. cf. Ac. 5: 32, 'we are witnesses . . . and so is the Holy Spirit'.

v. The disciples, the world, and the Advocate (16: 1–33)

1. so that you will not go astray: The treatment which the infant Church was to receive was destined to provide the strongest cause of apostasy, as the early history of the Church showed. **2. They will put you out of the synagogue:** Cf. comment on 9: 22. The plural, as in AV and RSV, implies that each case of excommunication will be a direct act of antagonism, in their experience, against Christ, (cf. 9: 22). **4. the time:** Cf. Lk. 22: 53. The hour of the world will be when men wreak their vengeance upon the Church unrestrainedly. **5. none of you asks me, 'Where are you going?':** Both Peter (cf. 13: 36) and Thomas (cf. 14: 5) had in fact asked this question verbally already. But then it was because of their dismay rather than because of a real desire to know Jesus' destiny (cf. 14: 6). **7. It is for your good that I am going away:** There is a twofold point in these words. First, the departure of Christ in the body is both the necessary condition and cause of future individual union. Then each member of His spiritual Body will become a veritable shrine of deity (cf. 1 C. 3: 16; 6: 19). Second, it will be to the disciples' advantage that the Spirit, when He is imparted, will empower the Church's ministry, convicting the world (cf. v. 8) in respect of its state before God. **8. in regard to sin, and righteousness, and judgment:** The supreme sin lies in unbelief (v. 9). Jesus' return to the Father will mark the vindication of His righteous life here below and since His return to the Father is by way of death and resurrection, He pronounces judgment over the prince of the world whose domain is clearest of all in death. In this sentence is prophesied the

Church's spiritual power within and over the world. **13. he will guide you into all the truth:** There will not be one permanent or fundamental principle which is overlooked in the Spirit's ministry to the Church. **what he hears** signifies that His ministry will ever be direct from the Father. **what is yet to come:** Prophecy is one function of the Spirit. This is not merely prediction of the future, near or far (cf. Rev. 1: 1, 19), but an aspect of the Spirit's ministry as the earnest of what is yet to be. There are three functions of the Spirit mentioned in this discourse (cf. 14: 26; 16: 13) in which the three phases of the NT message seem to be summarized, *viz.*, history, doctrine, and eschatology. **14. He will bring glory to me:** The Spirit does not usurp the authority of the Son. But since the Son shares the authority of the Father in revelation, the triune God is here depicted in perfect harmony of operation. **16. after a little while, you will see me:** Both the 'little while's' of this verse may be understood as one and the same. There is less justification for understanding the second as referring to the parousia of Jesus. If anything were to distinguish the two phrases (Gk. *mikron*) it would be that John uses a different verb 'to see' in each half of the verse. The first is his normal Gk. *theorein*, whilst the second is his more suggestive Gk. *opsesthai* with its inference of beatific vision (cf. 1: 51; 3: 36 and esp. 11: 40). The whole statement makes better sense when understood as a reference to the passing of Jesus from physical sight, and His subsequent resurrection appearances. We are certainly right in omitting the first occasion of the words 'because I go to the Father', found in AV (cf. v. 17). In v. 17 the disciples are remembering the statement of vv. 5 and 10. But when Christ reappears their sorrow will indeed **turn to joy** (20; cf. 20: 20). **22. no one will take away your joy:** Just as the new life given in childbirth fills the mother with mystical joy, overcoming all the former anguish, so the joy of the resurrection, for all the world's persecution, will become the dominant factor in Christian experience. **23. In that day you will no longer ask me anything:** 'Ask' here seems to be used synonymously with 'ask' in v. 24, in which case the statement refers to the direct approach to God which believers may make in the light of the exaltation of the Son. If, on the other hand, there be some subtle difference of meaning, the former statement will refer to the anxious questions which were heaped up in chaps. 13–16, as distinct from prayerful supplication which they will make henceforth in Jesus' name. The second half of the next verse could be used to endorse either interpretation of v. 23. **25. figuratively** (Gk. *en paroimiais*): The RSV text would suggest that Jesus is making reference to the discourses of the immediate

past. But the wording might well mean that He speaks of the parabolic method which He employed as a whole. Their understanding of the same message will, in a day to come, be enlarged by the richness of experience. **27. the Father himself loves you:** Cf. 15: 12–17. No greater impetus for prayer could be given than in these words. In this unique way, the Father makes Himself known. **28. I came from the Father and entered the world; now I am leaving the world: I came from the Father** suggests that v. 28a should be linked closely with v. 27b, continuing to state what the disciples **have believed**. This would then mean that the disciples had accepted the divine mission of Jesus in all its implications. If, however, v. 28 be taken quite separately from v. 27, it becomes a crystallization of the Christian message. In either case the words show just how plainly Jesus was now speaking to the disciples. **33. I have told you these things, so that in me you may have peace:** Jesus is not only concerned to prevent their distress when they see the tragic events a few hours hence. Rather the whole Paschal discourse, and especially that of the present chapter (cf. 16: 1), has been specifically designed to calm these timorous disciples in the face of provocation. The world, as the great outer ring of human experience, will move this way and that; but at the centre—**in me**—is the stable compass directing their way into the peace of God. And because the will of the world had already exposed itself, Jesus could consider it defeated in principle already. There only remains His love which He will pour out in prayer for His friends and the world which He came to redeem.

vi. The great prayer of Jesus (17: 1–26)
This prayer, as the text shows, covers three distinct matters. Jesus consecrates Himself for the work which He is about to undertake (vv. 1–5). He then prays specifically for the disciples (vv. 6–19), and finally for the whole Church (vv. 20–26). Consecration, indeed, is the key thought which pervades the whole. In attempting to analyse the meaning of individual phrases we inevitably lose the majesty of the prayer as it stands, and the spontaneity with which the Saviour passes from one phase to the next. After a study of the details it should be read without interruption.

1. Jesus said this: From chapter 13 to 16 Jesus has unfolded the meaning of His departure. His teaching ends with the words, 'I have overcome the world' (cf. 16: 33), meaning that ultimately it could be said that, in Him, the purpose of God had been, and will be achieved. So with His eyes lifted towards heaven, Jesus terminates His work as a prophet on earth, and contemplates His work as a Priest, entering, in spirit, the Holy Place. This prayer, accordingly, has often been called His 'high-priestly' prayer—first, apparently, by David Chytraeus (16th century). **glorify your Son:** The departure of Judas had signified the arrival of the 'hour' in which Jesus committed Himself to His death (cf. 13: 31), yet the glorification of the Son has already been manifested by His words and works (cf. 1: 14; 2: 11). **2. you granted him authority:** Already Jesus claimed to have power in the exercise of judgment (cf. 5: 27) and forgiveness (cf. Mk 2: 10). Already He has said that He judges no man (cf. 8: 15) and now He sees His power to be in the authority to 'give eternal life' (cf. 1: 4, 12). **3. Now this is eternal life: that they may know you:** The knowledge of the Father must be linked now with the apprehension of the Son, since the revelation of God in Christ cannot be transcended. This is not intellectual understanding, but the perfection of personal, moral trust. **Jesus Christ, whom you have sent:** Literally, as in RV, 'him whom thou didst send, *even* Jesus Christ'; it may be that '*even* Jesus Christ' is an explanatory addition by the Evangelist (cf. 1: 17). **4. I have brought you glory on earth:** The glory of God was paramount in the life of Jesus. He could only pray with this fact established by a life of submission to the Father. The tense denotes a completed action in the past. **5. glorify me in your presence:** This is no selfish request *for* recognition. Rather it is a prayer which already recognizes that the historic lifegiving work of Christ may truly reveal the eternal nature of the Godhead, and the relation of the Word, immanent and active in creation and salvation, to the eternal and unchanging transcendent God. **6. They were yours:** Jesus ever recognizes the priority of the purpose of God. But His part in that purpose was to reveal the name of God, i.e. His nature. The divine revelation was by words. Jesus imparted these to the disciples (cf. v. 8). Now they **accepted them. They knew with certainty** (8), an intellectual conviction borne of the evidence they have seen in Jesus, that He had come forth from the Father, **and they believed**, that is, put their moral trust in the fact that Jesus was *sent*, coming not on His own authority alone, but with the full authority of the Godhead. **11. Holy Father, protect** (Gk. *tērēson*) **them:** That is, separate from the profanity of the world, **by the power of your name**. Their holiness will be achieved only by relationship with the Father (cf. Lev. 11: 44 f.), whose name has, in principle, already been given to the Son (cf. Phil. 2: 9), **that they may be one**. Union can be perfectly expressed by a loving relationship (cf. 5: 42 f.; 14: 9–15) and is a reflection of that eternal union enjoyed by the three Persons within one substance, the Trinity. **12. none has been lost except the one doomed to destruction:** The defection of Judas was the one tragic exception which proved the rule. The fulfilment of scripture in his case (cf. Ps. 41: 9; Jn 13: 18, 31) indicates that Judas was destroyed only by his own qualities, which might have been turned to good account but were perverted to an evil end. **16. the evil one:** Whilst it is clear that Jesus believed in and taught the personality of Satan, the words here might convey the sense that He wished the disciples to be guarded from that personal *power* of evil which had shown itself in Judas (cf. 1 Jn 5: 18 f.). **17. Sanctify them by the truth:** This is not a prayer for purification. They are already clean (cf. 15: 3). But it is the truth, the revelation of eternal values, that can both keep them unstained in the world, and provide the burden of their message. This truth is the Word of God (cf. Ps. 119: 142), which can bring deliverance (cf. 8: 32). **19. I sanctify myself:** He is to become a 'high priest for ever' in virtue of His vicarious death. And the truth is related to Christ's death, so far as disciples are concerned, in that their ministry will only be relevant if it is coloured by the implications of that death (cf. Heb. 7: 26 ff.; 1 C. 1: 23).

Now the Lord turns to pray for the entire Church. Because His prayer is effectual the work of evangelism will go forward. So unity must be worldwide. **21. that all of them may be one . . . that the world may believe:** That first miracle of unity which was to mark the earliest disciples Christ sees as the vital character of the Church in all ages. Nothing less than organic unity will satisfy the prayer of the Saviour. It is **Father, just as you are in me:** and this unity is for a specific purpose that the world may learn that He is, indeed, the Word Incarnate, bringing to men the knowledge and love of God (cf. v. 23). **24. I want those . . . to be with me:** That companionship which had begun a few years earlier the Lord wishes to take into eternity. Historically they would not follow Him immediately (cf. 13: 33); yet Peter would eventually follow Him through suffering (cf. 13: 36). But now with His work finished, with His will perfectly expressed as being one with the Father, Jesus makes this one personal request. Yet he will derive the greatest joy from knowing that they will behold His glory, so completing their apprehension of Him. Their vision of the Father will also be satisfied. **25. the world does not know you:** This clause is essentially, if not grammatically, subordinate to what follows: **though the world does not know you, I know you, and they** (the disciples) **know that you have sent me**. The Saviour thus declares this intention to manifest the name of God again in the crucial act of the Cross. But this is the darkness before dawn, after which the Saviour will reveal the love of God realistically and effectively within each of His own. Thus, in His exaltation He will continue to teach them.

II. THE BETRAYAL, ARREST AND EXECUTION (18: 1—19: 42)

i. The arrest. Peter's denial (18: 1–27)

1. the Kidron Valley: This lies between the Temple hill and the Mount of Olives. On the further side Jesus entered Gethsemane. John does not record the agony of the Garden (cf. Mk 14: 32–42; Mt. 26: 36–46; Lk. 22: 40–48) but He does record a similar agony to which the Saviour gave expression (cf. 12: 27–33). Jesus clearly understood all that was to happen as being part of the divine plan. **5. I am he** (Gk. *egō eimi*): With this majestic answer (cf. 8: 58), Jesus forestalled the plan arranged between Judas and the armed officers (cf. 8: 24, 28; 13: 19). The Synoptists tell us of the deadly kiss. Here, however, we have a picture of the Saviour taking the initiative at every stage (cf. v. 11 below). The falling to the ground of His captors was not necessarily miraculous, but possibly their falling over each other in confusion at Jesus' calm. **9. This happened so that the words he had spoken would be fulfilled:** Here is an inspired commentary which takes the words of Jesus' prayer (cf. 17: 12) quite literally. Jesus was therefore willing and able to enter into the implications of His prayer life. **10. a sword:** The meaning of this dramatic act is that Simon Peter was not going to accept such a tame release as was suggested by Jesus' appeal to the officers. **Malchus:** Only John names the injured officer, as only Luke records his being healed again (cf. Lk. 22: 51). **11. Shall I not drink the cup:** This is John's counterpart to the Gethsemane utterance 'not what I will, but what thou wilt' recorded by the other evangelists (cf. Mk 14: 36–40; Mt. 26: 39–42; Lk. 22: 42). He announces that His desire is to take the cup, for that, indeed, is the Father's will for Him. **13. Annas:** Matthew alone (cf. Mt. 26: 57) mentions Caiaphas's house; the other evangelists simply refer to the chief priests (cf. Mk 14: 53; Lk. 22: 54) and Luke gives no account of the Jewish hearing. Annas was former high priest (A.D. 6–15). In Hebrew law, the high-priesthood was an office held for life. But under the Romans it was frequently changed. Annas had been deposed in A.D. 15, but was succeeded by other members of the family, besides Caiaphas, who was high priest from A.D. 18 to A.D. 36. Yet even after his deposition, Annas remained an elder statesman of Judaism. **15. another disciple:** He is probably, though not certainly, the beloved disciple (cf. 13: 23; 19: 26; 20: 2; 21: 20). He was known to the high priest, and apparently knew the Sanhedrin members and their households fairly well (cf. Malchus's

name, v. 10). His entry into the audience chamber illustrates the truth that he who remains close to Christ is the more likely to resist temptation to deny Him. **17. You are not** (Gk. *mē kai sy*) **one of this man's disciples, are you?** The form of the question would normally expect a negative answer, though 'Yes' may have been the reply expected. This question favourably reflects the position of the other disciple. **19. The high priest questioned Jesus:** This is almost certainly Annas. Attempts have been made to prove that it was Caiaphas by placing v. 24 after v. 13, *e.g.*, by the Sinaitic Syriac, by the minuscule 225, and by Luther. But most commentators adopt the usual order of the text to whichever of the two men they believe this reference to apply; the suggestion that an early copyist placed v. 24 where we have it, after accidentally dropping it out after v. 13, while possible, is unconvincing. Annas continued to be known as high priest long after his deposition (cf. Ac. 4: 6). **22. one of the officials . . . struck him:** This blow may well have been an indication of the loyalty which many of the Jews continued to feel towards Annas, whom they regarded as the rightful high priest, though he was forcibly living in retirement. Jesus' reply makes it clear that nothing hurts more than the truth in the ears of those who have already made up their minds against it. **24. Annas sent him, still bound, to Caiaphas the high priest:** Caiaphas's name here seems to support earlier comments on v. 19. Caiaphas has not yet figured in the trial (cf. Mk 14: 53–65; Mt. 26; 57 f.; Lk. 22: 63–71), although AV attempts to represent him as having done so by the mistranslation: 'Now Annas had sent him bound unto Caiaphas . . .'.

The scene now returns to Simon Peter. **26. Didn't I see you with him in the olive grove?:** The final question may well have been put out of fellow-feeling for Malchus, the injured officer. John omits any reference to the oaths and curses with which Peter consummated his denial. Nor does he explain, as does Mark (cf. Mk 14: 72), how remorse swept into the man's heart. It was presumably on the way to Caiaphas that Jesus turned to look upon Peter (cf. Lk. 22: 61).

ii. Pilate's judgment (18: 28–19: 16)

This part of the proceedings was enacted in order to get the death sentence confirmed (cf. Mk 15: 2–20; Mt. 27: 11–31; Lk. 23: 1–25). **28. the palace** was the official residence of a procurator. He would have normally resided at Caesarea, on the coast, and come to Jerusalem at festival times to preside over law and order. The Jews did not enter here in accordance with custom that no Jew should enter Gentile houses where there was always the possibility of defilement; to incur such defilement at present would make them unfit to eat the Passover (see note on 13: 1). **31. but we have no right to execute anyone:** Power of life and death had apparently not been exercised by the Sanhedrin since the time of Herod the Great, though opinions differ on this point. **32. the words Jesus had spoken:** How far Jesus' earlier words about being 'lifted up' (cf. 3: 14; 12: 32) had been understood is difficult to say. But the evangelist clearly sees their fulfilment in the Passion. **33. Are you the king of the Jews?:** The English text misses what might possibly have been a note of scorn here: 'You! Are you king of the Jews?' Pilate implies that the prisoner did not look much like a revolutionary leader who had caused so much disturbance by calling himself king (cf. Lk. 23: 2). The religious charge had been replaced by a political one to carry more weight with Pilate. Jesus' answer challenges Pilate's conscience (v. 35), but he brushes it aside. Nevertheless, Pilate is puzzled that such a claim should have evoked the Jews' hostility (v. 35b). **36. My kingdom:** Jesus refers to His place in the divine purpose. If that kingship were earthly His servants would resist Pilate and his men (cf. Mt. 26: 53). **37. Everyone on the side of truth listens to me:** Jesus' reply to Pilate's question is again non-committal, in so far as He refuses Pilate's terms of reference. But He *is* king, though not in the sense in which Pilate would understand the word. **38. What is truth?** At the best this was a quasi-philosophical question. Yet by asking it Pilate is demonstrably not 'of the truth'. **39.** Pilate's fears are now twofold. He is aware of the pressure of Jewish custom at Passover, and he is further moved by his wife's fears (Mt. 27: 19). **40. Barabbas** was an insurgent (cf. Mk 15: 7) and therefore, like Jesus, a 'political' prisoner. Their renewed cries show that the Jews' former outburst began with Jesus' earlier appearance (cf. Mt. 27: 13 f.). **19: 1. Pilate took Jesus and had him flogged:** Elsewhere (cf. Mk 15: 15) Jesus is scourged after sentence is passed (though John does not say expressly when the sentence was passed, its passing is implied in 19: 13–16). The implication of John's account is that Pilate hoped either to satisfy the Jews short of capital punishment, or else to obtain direct evidence from Jesus under torture. **3. went up to him** (Gk. *ērchonto pros auton*): The words seem to tell us that the soldiers did some mocking obeisance. That this was all part of a 'game of the king' is evidenced in Jerusalem today where a tableau is marked on stones close to Gabbatha (cf. v. 13). Their mockery is possibly directed as much against the Jews generally as against Jesus personally. Whether these Roman soldiers understood the implications of the trial is hard to say. **5. Here is the man!** The most poignant moment so far. Pilate's appeal to the Jews' finer feelings goes unheeded. John, moreover, records this as part of the Christian message; here in Jesus is the perfection of humanity tragically portrayed at the point of His self-sacrifice. Perhaps, also, the Evangelist's anti-Docetic purpose is in mind. **6. You take him:** Pilate is determined to exasperate the Jews as far as possible. He knows that they have no authority to crucify; yet by demanding crucifixion they have handed Jesus over to the Romans for their decision. **7. We have a law . . . he must die:** Cf. Lev. 24: 16. The Jews now return to the religious charge on the seeming failure of the political charge. **9. Where do you come from?** Pilate is afraid. His question is interpreted on two levels by John. Jesus gives no reply (cf. Mk 15: 5; 14: 60 f.; Lk. 23: 9), since Pilate is not now likely to be moved by any answer He gives him, even if he understood anything about the divine origin of Jesus' mission. **11. You would have no power . . . if it were not given to you from above:** Jesus means that Pilate is an instrument under divine control (cf. Rom. 13: 1 ff.). So, too, was Caiaphas. But Caiaphas's failure brought the whole drama into operation, so he **is guilty of a greater sin**. **12.** The Jews' answer to Pilate now virtually forces his hand. So he brings Jesus before the seat of judgment (Gk. *bēma*, 'tribunal', v. 13; cf. Rom. 14: 10; 2 C. 5: 10), from which alone sentence could be pronounced. **13. sat down . . . at a place known as The Stone Pavement:** The precise location is not certain, though we have reason to believe that part of the Pavement (Gk. *lithostrōtos*) is still visible beneath the Ecce Homo Arch (cf. *NBD*, p. 445). In spite of suggestions to the contrary, we must understand that Pilate himself sat down here, though the verb (Gk. *ekathisen*), used transitively, might mean 'he caused (Jesus) to sit down'. The Docetic 'Gospel of Peter' (late 2nd century) takes it in this latter sense. The procurator's action at this moment is not likely to have been in a light-hearted vein, but the idea that the verb is ambiguously used to suggest that, in fact, Jesus *was* sitting in judgment on His accusers, is worthy of attention. **14. Preparation of Passover Week:** Cf. 18: 28; 19: 31; i.e., Passover Eve, Friday of Passover Week. **15. We have no king but Caesar** are words which form the greatest Jewish apostasy of all time. Thus 'Israel abdicated its own unique position under the immediate sovereignty of God' (C. K. Barrett, p. 454; cf. 1 Sam. 8: 7). **16. Finally Pilate handed him over** (Gk. *paredōken auton*): Put in this way, Pilate's action, in the eyes of the Evangelist, carries the overtones of the divine plan: though Jesus died at the hands of Roman soldiers, the Jews were primarily responsible for His death.

iii. The Crucifixion and Burial of Jesus (19: 17–42)

17. Carrying his own cross: Cf. Mk 15: 21.

The Evangelist may be drawing some special attention to the fact that, in contrast to others, Jesus bore His own cross. M. Black has pointed out that the Greek (literally rendered in RV, 'bearing the cross for himself') may be the translation of the ethic dative in Aramaic (pp. 75 f.), the reference being to that part of the gallows (the *patibulum*) which was carried by Jesus. **Golgotha** has not been identified with certainty. There are two sites which make claims to be the place of the skull (cf. A. Parrot, *Golgotha*, 1957). According to an early tradition the place was so named because Adam's skull lay buried here. This tradition is preserved inside the Church of the Holy Sepulchre. **19. a notice** (Gk. *titlos*): This was usually a statement of the charge placed over the criminal's head. The Jews at once disputed the wording, but Pilate was determined to have the final word. To the Jews the title, as it stood, was a blasphemous insult (cf. Dt. 21: 23; Gal. 3: 13). **23. this garment was seamless:** There is no reason to suppose that Jesus wore this garment with intended significance; but John's seeing some connection with the high priest's robe may be another matter (cf. Exod. 38: 31 f.). The soldiers' dividing of His clothing was customary, though John saw the scriptures fulfilled here (cf. Ps. 22: 18). In the psalm the two clauses represent the parallel structure of the Hebrew poetry. **26 f. Dear woman, here is your son . . . Here is your mother:** Such was the love of Jesus that He should make provision for His mother at the last moment. Jesus hands her into the care of the 'beloved disciple' until such time as His brothers will accept their responsibility toward her as true followers of Him. And it may be added that the brothers did, quite soon, accept this responsibility, for Mary is later seen in their company, whereas John seems to be grouped quite distinctly from them (cf. Ac. 1: 14). The two passages might suggest that deeper fellowship which begins at the foot of the Cross and is maintained in prayer. **28. I am thirsty:** Jesus prepares to utter the final words from the Cross, bringing scriptures to fulfilment as He does so (cf. Ps. 69: 21). And that the Evangelist sees anti-Docetic material in this detail is certain. NEB has suggested that instead of 'hyssop' here we might read 'javelin'. The reading in the text could be accounted for by accidental dittography—Gk. *hyssōpos* for *hyssos*; though G. D. Kilpatrick has notably maintained 'hyssop' in the text in his edition of the Greek Testament and his Gk.-Eng. Diglot (BFBS). See also his 'The Transmission of the NT and its Reliability' in *Journ. Trans. Vict. Inst.* 89 (1957), p. 99. **30. It is finished** (Gk. *tetelestai*): This is the moment at which Jesus has fully entered into every phase of human existence from birth to death. So His work is completed

—the work which the Father gave Him to do. More than this, He dismisses His spirit through which He consciously and willingly offered Himself spotless to God (cf. Heb. 9: 14). **31. Preparation:** Cf. notes on vv. 14, 41; 18: 28. **Special Sabbath:** Because it coincided with Passover in the Temple calendar. **34. blood and water:** In view of the Evangelist's comments upon this (cf. next verse), we may take his record of these details as part of his scheme to set forth the absolute humanity of the Saviour. Jesus' speedy death was remarkable (cf. Mk 15: 44). Various commentators have shown how medically accurate this tradition is. Yet physical details can never outweigh the theological implications here. The blood is clearly a symbol of the means of salvation offered to all through the death of Christ, for apart from this there is no means for removing sin (cf. Heb. 9: 22). The water may be understood in an equally symbolic manner with other allusions in the Gospel (cf. 4: 14; 7: 38 f.; 1 Jn 5: 6). By the death of Jesus sinners may be forgiven and receive the life of God imparted through the Spirit. These things, writes John (v. 35), are themselves sufficient to bring men into conscious communion with the living God. And for Jews particularly, the ideal Lamb of God perfectly accorded with the ancient sacrificial regulations of the Passover (cf. Exod. 12: 45; Num. 9: 12; Dt. 21: 23; see also Ps. 34: 20). **37. They will look on the one they have pierced:** Cf. Zech. 12: 10. The conditions which obtain in Zechariah appear to be very different from those at the crucifixion, in so far as there was no apparent grief among the Jews (see, however, the further application of the oracle in Mt. 24: 30; Rev. 1: 7). But, as F. F. Bruce puts it: 'it is the event that has suggested the *testimonium*, and not the other way about' though there are clear links with the later oracle of Zech. 13: 7 concerning the stricken shepherd of Israel (cf. F. F. Bruce, 'The Book of Zechariah and the Passion Narrative', *BJRL* 43, 1960–61, pp. 350 f.). **38. Joseph of Arimathea:** Like Nicodemus, he was a member of the Sanhedrin (cf. Mk 15: 43). Joseph may well have been one of the secret disciples mentioned earlier (cf. 12: 42). Together with Nicodemus he brought **about seventy five pounds** of spices, and gave the Lord's body a royal burial (39, 40). Their action not only showed their devotion to Jesus, but prevented possible mutilation after burial. **41. a new tomb:** Here, because also of the difficulty of moving the body far on Sabbath Eve (cf. Lk. 23: 54), they laid Jesus.

III. RESURRECTION APPEARANCES (20: 1–31)

1. Early on the first day . . . Mary Magdalene went to the tomb: Cf. 19: 25; Lk. 23: 56. i.e., on Sunday morning. **2. They have**

taken the Lord: Her fears were aroused since body-snatchers might have been at work. The **we** is reminiscent of the Synoptic narrative (cf. Mk 16: 1–8; Mt. 28: 1–8; Lk. 24: 1–12), where we are told that several women visitors came to the tomb. **4. the other disciple outran Peter:** Cf. v. 2; 13: 23; 19: 26; 21: 20. This is a natural touch, showing how vividly the beloved disciple, probably the younger of the two men, recalled the event. **6. Simon Peter . . . went into the tomb:** That impulsiveness which marked Simon through the years of Jesus' ministry is still there. And what he saw (cf. next verse) seems to describe what the burial cloths would look like if Jesus had left the tomb without disturbing them. **8. Then the other disciple . . . saw and believed:** The appearance of the cloths was enough for him. Yet he needed this much evidence for as yet neither of the two men understood the scriptures with regard to the resurrection (cf. Ps. 16: 10; Ac. 2: 29–32), that the same divine necessity which determined Jesus' death also determined His rising from the dead. **10.** Apparently the faith of the beloved disciple was enough to kindle faith in Peter, so that they both left the tomb.

Mary, however, had followed the others to the tomb and now arrived, waiting outside weeping (v. 11). **16. Mary:** Hearing her name was sufficient to tell her who it was who spoke to her. It was the same powerful voice which had lifted this woman from her earlier demon-possessed life (Lk. 8: 2). **She turned towards him and cried out in Aramaic, 'Rabboni!':** There is some evidence, especially from a consideration of the possible Aramaic background to the Gospel, that **turned** here means 'recognized'; this is supported by the Sinaitic Syriac, and suggested also by M. Black. (Aramaic—a closely related language to Hebrew which employs the same script; cf, *NBD*, pp. 712 f.) **17. Do not hold on to me:** The 'touch me not' of the AV is weak. The attitude expressed in Mary's emotion would be such as would prevent Jesus, if not from entering into His glory, at least from imparting that vital manifestation of which He had spoken to His disciples (cf. 14: 15 ff.). Says Jesus rather: **I am returning.** Jesus' appearance to Mary now is to assure her that He is returning to the Father. John does not present the ascension as a physical event which happened after forty days' interval from the resurrection, but as something which was already taking place. In John Christ's death is His exaltation—His 'lifting up'. Never before has Jesus spoken of **my brothers:** yet even now He distinguishes His sonship from theirs by saying **to my Father and your Father**.

19. fear of the Jews: Each of the resurrection appearances of Jesus fulfilled a special purpose. For Peter and the beloved disciple it was the proclamation of victory; for Mary it was the satisfaction of love; now for the rest of the disciples it is the calming of fear. **20. he showed them his hands and side:** No substitution had taken place; He was the same Jesus. How He could pass through closed doors is a mystery to us, though in the light of what is known about the nature of matter such 'unnatural' phenomena are by no means so inconceivable as they once were. **22. Receive the Holy Spirit:** The breath of God is a regular metaphor in the scriptures for the Holy Spirit (cf. Gen. 2: 7; Ezek. 37: 9 f.). The first effusion of the breath of God made man a living being. Here, the breath of the risen Christ makes the timorous disciples into new men. There is no reason for assuming that the Holy Spirit was not fully imparted at this moment. A comparison with the Lukan account (cf. Lk. 24: 33) would suggest that others besides the ten disciples were present here. What is later described in the Acts (cf. Ac. 2: 1–4) was an outpouring of the Spirit especially understood in the light of the apostles' international ministry on the Day of Pentecost. That they were quickened here is beyond question. (But see H. B. Swete, *The Holy Spirit in the NT* [London, 1909], pp. 164–168.) **23. If you forgive anyone his sins:** These words, properly understood, refer to the disciples as the first nucleus of the Spirit-filled society. Its ministry in the gospel will be effectual. Some will be forgiven; others will reject its message and be hardened. If we are inclined to doubt the power of the Church to fulfil such a responsibility, it is because we know (as the apostles knew) that the 'spirit of the world' still plays its part in the lives of its members. But when the Church functions as the true Body of Christ she can pronounce on sin with the same assurance as Jesus when He gave this command. **25. Unless I see . . . I will not believe it:** Thomas (cf. 11: 6) in fact demanded the basic evidence for resurrection, i.e., the identity of that Body which he had known before Jesus died, and with it the evidence of continuity. The production of that evidence here is therefore fundamental to the cumulative nature of the resurrection passages, and Thomas can do little else than cry, **My Lord and my God!** (28). So to that disciple who most firmly demanded factual evidence was given the honour of making the first confession of faith in the completeness of the revelation summed up in the resurrection of Jesus Christ. **29. Blessed are those who have not seen and yet have believed:** We are probably mistaken if we understand these words as a rebuke. Others may count themselves happy (though not happier) to believe with less palpable evidence. The Lord embraces all those who had come to faith prior to His death without any such compelling evidence of His deity with all those who subsequently would believe on the evidence of the Word written and spoken. But the faith of all will be equal in status. **31. these are written that you may believe:** Our textual authorities vary between the aorist tense (implying the dawn of faith) and the present (implying the persistence of faith). Not all the facts of the life of Jesus are recorded. The Gospels are not biographies. They are *Gospels*, which, writes C. H. Dodd, 'declare the glory of God by revealing what He has done'. To comment on this last sentence would mean re-reading or re-expounding the Gospel. To give ground for faith and the possession of **life** has been the Evangelist's object throughout. **that Jesus is the Christ, the Son of God: Christ** is not restricted to the Jewish conception of the Messiah, but is to be understood in the sense of **the Son of God** presented in this Gospel as the Revealer of the Father.

IV. APPENDIX (21: 1–25)

The last two verses of chap. 20 probably constituted the original ending of the Gospel. The present chapter was probably added as an appendix, to clear up a misunderstanding that had arisen regarding Jesus' words concerning the future of the beloved disciple (vv. 20–23), and to record the restoration of Simon Peter to a position of unique responsibility within the Church (vv. 15–19).

3. I'm going out to fish (Gk. *hypagō alyein*): The construction would imply a return to one's former occupation. Since each of the resurrection appearances conveyed some spiritual truth (cf. note on 20: 19), so here the risen Lord makes His power known in daily occupations. That the men had no catch is not surprising since they had been away from fishing for years! **5. Friends** (Gk. *paidia*): A colloquialism (so NEB). **6. Throw your net on the right side:** Whatever may be the further implications of this command, the primary lesson is one of complete obedience to the Master. **7. It is the Lord!** This alone would suggest that the event occurred after the earlier appearances, and would further imply that the resurrection appearances of 20: 19 ff. are not necessarily to be placed before the ascension of 20: 17. **Peter . . . jumped into the water:** This distinguishes the incident from the miraculous catch of Lk. 5: 1–11. There Peter is painfully conscious of his sin; here, with impetuous joy, perhaps tinged with remorse, he rushes to the Saviour. The quick intuition of the one disciple and the quick action of the other are typical. **11. 153:** The number is significant enough to have been recorded. It was a large catch, and would therefore naturally have been counted. That 153 symbolizes one of each kind (Jerome) or refers to the sum of the numerals in 10 and 7—the commandments and the gifts of the

Spirit (Augustine)—is highly conjectural, involves an unnecessary allegorizing of other details in the chapter, and is therefore clearly unwarranted. **15. do you truly love me:** In these verses two different words are used for 'to love' (Gk. *agapaō* and *phileō* respectively) but John probably uses them quite synonymously (compare 3: 35, *agapaō*, with 5: 20, *phileō*). **more than these?** (Gk. *pleion toutōn*): Either masculine or neuter may be understood. Masculine is clearly intended, however; Peter had readily assumed that his loyalty could be counted on. Now Jesus asks: 'Do you love me more than these (disciples)?' **18. you will stretch out your hands:** Cf. 13: 36 f. This ultimately points to death, though it may speak of Peter's lot in the meanwhile of being at the mercy of others as a messenger of the gospel. But then another will gird him, carrying him to his martyrdom. **19. Follow me!:** It is to loyalty true enough to suffer death that Jesus bids His followers. **23.** That the question of the Lord's second advent was much in the minds of people at the time is evidently true from the fact that they imagined it possible that one of His disciples should remain alive until He came again. But Jesus discountenances such a thought. **24. This is the disciple who testifies:** The beloved disciple remains to bear out the truth of Jesus' words, whether we understand **these things** to refer only to the last few verses or to the whole Gospel. **we know** is either an undefined collective (cf. 1: 14) or possibly a joint statement from the elders of the church from which John originally wrote (cf. 3 Jn 12). **25. I suppose:** The use of 'I' seems strange after the former 'we'. But there is a little evidence that this verse was added some time after the writing of the Gospel (the first scribe who copied *Codex Sinaiticus* originally omitted it, but added it later); it could be an inspired comment by one of the earliest collectors of the four Gospels into a single volume. The words are a common enough hyperbole, but behind them lies the truth that, as T. R. Glover whimsically suggested, there are not four Gospels but 'ten thousand times ten thousand, and thousands of thousands, and the end of every one says, "Lo, I am with you always even unto the end of the world"'.

ADDITIONAL NOTE I.

The Word (Gk. *ho logos*). John's doctrine of the Word has been shaped by two influences. The Word is conceived as distinctly related to the Word of the OT. And the conception here is also coloured by contemporary Greek thought as it was preserved in the late first century.

Christianity was cradled in Judaism. But the Evangelist recognizes that Gentile missions necessitated a presentation of Christ in terms which would be understood by both Jew and Greek. The 'word' for the Jew *did* things. He conceived language as something vitally active. How much more so this would then be true of the Word of God! It was by the Word that God brought the earth and heavens into being (cf. Ps. 33: 6–9) so that the earliest writers of the OT could unhesitatingly speak of the utterance of God in the act of bringing forth (cf. Gen. 1: 3, 9, 11, 14, 20, 24, 26). Moreover, the Word of God never returned to Him as an unfaithful echo, but ever fulfilled that purpose for which it had been spoken (Isa. 55: 11), pre-eminently as a life-giving power (Isa. 55: 3) and as a constraint upon His messengers (Jer. 23: 29). This is a basic assumption of the OT. Where, however, certain passages of the OT implied that something of God could be seen by men (*e.g.*, Exod. 33: 22 f.; Isa. 6: 1; Ezek. 1: 1; Isa. 48: 13, etc.), or that He possessed human parts, the later Aramaic Targums removed such references, inserting circumlocutions instead, usually *memra*, 'the word', which may lie behind John's employment of *logos*. God has now been seen in the Word made flesh. It should be remembered, too, that the Book of Proverbs, with other Wisdom Literature, personifies Wisdom and represents her as associated with God in the creation of the world (cf. Prov. 8: 22–31).

To the Greek mind *logos* was similarly a significant term. From Heraclitus onwards, when thinkers began to formulate a doctrine of the creative control inherent in the universe, the *logos* came to be a technical term among philosophers, particularly the Stoics (as well as Philo).

This authority, writes John, revealing the very nature of the Godhead and His wisdom in creation and salvation is made known in Christ. He wields eternal power by reason of His deity. But His acts are rational and therefore revelatory. He is God. He is Christ. He is Lord. Therefore He can alike make unparalleled claims and give unequalled promises (cf. Heb. 1: 1; Col. 1: 16 ff.). It is mainly this idea of God, active and immanent in the created world and revealed in the events of history, that is implied in John's use of 'the Word'. But no doubt he recognizes the Greek conception as conveying rationality of the universe which implies a thinking purposive mind. John adds distinct personality to the two ideas, even though there may be hints at personality in the Proverbs passage. Though the Word is not specifically mentioned in the Gospel after the Prologue, the fact that Jesus is the Eternal Word Incarnate should never be lost sight of wherever He speaks or acts. And with the testimony of Revelation (cf. Rev. 19: 13) to this Word, John would have his readers remember that his is no theological treatise alone, but a testimony to

Christ as the One who alone is worthy to receive glory and honour. '"Worship God"! The testimony of Jesus is the Spirit of prophecy' (Rev. 19: 10).

ADDITIONAL NOTE II.
The Woman Taken in Adultery (7: 53—8: 11). It is certain that these verses are a later insertion into the original work. They are omitted by the best authorities for the text, though one group of MSS places them after Lk. 21: 38. They completely break the thread of chapters 7 and 8, and the adjoining verses read perfectly well without the passage in question. They may well have been inserted to give an illustration of Jesus' words, 'You judge according to the flesh, I judge no one' (8: 15). But the story has an authentic air about it, and adequately describes the perfect balance which Jesus ever kept between truth on the one side, by which He condemns the woman's sin, and grace on the other, with which He withholds condemnation from the woman herself.

The dilemma of the situation in which the scribes and Pharisees brought this woman to Jesus lay in the fact that if Jesus said she should not be stoned, He then would be open to a charge of withstanding the authority of the Jewish Law; but if He said she could be, He could be accused under Roman law of incitement to murder, since capital jurisdiction was withheld from the Jewish authorities. Jesus' action in writing on the ground with His finger was intended to take their callous eyes off the woman, and to give them an opportunity to withdraw. His reply, **'If anyone of you is without sin, let him be the first to throw a stone at her'**, raises the whole issue from a legal plane to a moral level.

Jesus then turns to the woman, and refuses to pass judgment on her, even though He has the right to do so. For an essential condition of His treatment of this woman is the certainty of His own sinlessness.

BIBLIOGRAPHY
BARRETT, C. K., *The Gospel According to St. John* [on the Greek text] (London, 1962).

BERNARD, J. H., *A Critical and Exegetical Commentary on the Gospel According to St. John* [on the Greek text], *ICC* (London, 1928).

BERNARD, T. D., *The Central Teaching of Jesus Christ* (London, 1900).

BLACK, M., *An Aramaic Approach to the Gospels and Acts*[3] (Oxford, 1967).

BROWN, R. E., *The Gospel according to John*, AB (2 vols., Garden City, N. Y., 1966, 1970).

BRUCE, F. F., *The Gospel of John* (Basingstoke, 1983).

BULTMANN, R., *The Gospel of John*, E.T. (Oxford, 1971).

BURNEY, C. F., *The Aramaic Origin of the Fourth Gospel* (Oxford, 1922).

DODD, C. H., *The Interpretation of the Fourth Gospel* (Cambridge, 1953).

DODD, C. H., *Historical Tradition in the Fourth Gospel* (Cambridge, 1963).

HOSKYNS, E. C. (ed. F. N. Davey), *The Fourth Gospel* (London, 1947).

HOWARD, W. F., *The Fourth Gospel in Recent Criticism and Interpretation* (London, 1935).

HOWARD, W. F., *Christianity According to St. John* (London, 1943).

HUNTER, A. M., *According to John* (London, 1968).

LIGHTFOOT, J. B., *Biblical Essays* (ed. J. R. Harmet) (London, 1893).

LIGHTFOOT, R. H., *St. John's Gospel* (Oxford, 1961).

LINDARS, B., *The Gospel of John*, NCentB (London, 1972).

MORRIS, L., *Studies in the Fourth Gospel* (Exeter, 1969).

MORRIS, L., *Commentary on the Gospel of John*, NIC (Grand Rapids, 1971).

NUNN, H. P. V., *The Authorship of the Fourth Gospel* (Eton, 1952).

SCHNACKENBURG, R., *The Gospel according to St. John*, E.T., 3 vols. (London, 1968, ;80, '82).

STRACHAN, R. H., *The Fourth Gospel, its Significance and Environment* (London, 1941).

TASKER, R. V. G., *The Gospel According to St. John. TNTC* (London, 1960).

TEMPLE, W., *Readings in St. John's Gospel*, 1st and 2nd series (London, 1959).

WESTCOTT, B. F., *The Gospel According to St. John* [on the Greek text] (London, 1908).

WESTCOTT, B. F., *The Gospel According to St. John.* Speaker's Commentary (London, 1880, reprinted 1958).

Other main references:-

The Gospels Reconsidered (Oxford 1960).

DODD, C. H., *The Bible and the Greeks* (London, 1954).

EDERSHEIM, A., *The Life and Time of Jesus the Messiah* (London, reprinted, 1959).

KLAUSNER, J., *Jesus of Nazareth*, E.T. (London, 1950).

RAWLINSON, A. E. J., *The New Testament Doctrine of the Christ* (London, 1949).

SMALLEY, S. S., *John: Evangelist and Interpreter* (Exeter, 1978).

STAUFFER, E., *New Testament Theology*, E.T. (London, 1955).

ACTS

E. H. TRENCHARD

Authorship and Date

That Luke is the author of the dual documents Luke-Acts is a fact so well established that a brief summary of the evidence is sufficient here. (1) *The Anti-Marcionite Prologue* (c. 160), names Luke as the author and all other external evidence is consistent with this statement. (2) Luke is named as a companion and fellow-worker of Paul's in Col. 4: 14; Phm. 24: 2; Tim. 4: 11. (3) The link between the two documents is found in the address to Theophilus (Lk. 1: 3; Ac. 1: 1), in a style common to both, in an approach to persons and incidents which is consistent with a common authorship. (4) The author of the Acts reveals his presence as a participant in Paul's labours by using the pronoun 'we' in 16: 10–18; 20: 6–21: 17; 27: 1–28: 16. If the ascription of the *Anti-Marcionite Prologue* is correct, then the modest author is Luke, and he is 'our dear friend, Luke, the doctor' who was with Paul in Rome.

Luke's purpose. Luke's stately introduction to the Gospel (1: 1–4), important from many points of view, clearly defines his purpose of presenting the 'most excellent Theophilus' with a carefully compiled account of the facts of the beginnings of Christianity. The reference to 'my former book' in Ac. 1: 1 has the effect of including the dual work under the same introduction and general purpose, though the second work has naturally to continue the ministry begun by Christ in the Gospel, describing how He effects it through the power of the Holy Spirit in the apostles as the gospel is preached first in Jerusalem, and then world-wide.

Behind Theophilus we may imagine a group of interested readers of some culture and position who are beginning to take an interest in the strange happenings which took place in Palestine and the Near East from A.D. 27 onward. God chose a man of culture, with a wide interest in contemporary history, master of an excellent Hellenistic Greek, a fine story-teller and an exact historian, to write a wonderfully selective account of the great happening from the birth of John the Baptist until Paul's first imprisonment in Rome (c. 62).

Luke's methods. Luke makes no idle claim when he states that he 'carefully investigated everything' (Lk. 1: 3) with a view to compiling an orderly account of what had taken place. For parts of Paul's ministry he had his own memory and notes. For the rest, he sought out reliable eyewitnesses and previous documents (Lk. 1: 1, 2), using them conscientiously. He is so sensitive to atmosphere, and so faithful to his sources, that the early chapters of both Gospel and Acts are Hebraic in setting and style, despite the fact that he is a Greek, writing in Hellenistic Greek. Sir William Ramsay's classic researches, which found expression in works such as *The Church in the Roman Empire* and *St. Paul, the Traveller and the Roman Citizen*, showed once and for all the accuracy of Luke as an historian. The extensive journeys through a variety of provinces described in Acts necessitated numerous references to provinces, cities, institutions, native and Roman officers of different grades, customs, etc., in relation to which a careless story-teller would be bound to fall into endless traps. Luke, however, falls into none and his work is taken as reliable evidence in all matters he touches on.

The date of writing. Some critics have attempted to prove a late date for Acts, quoting mainly the author's supposed dependence on Josephus for the account of the death of Herod Agrippa I. As Josephus wrote his *Antiquities* in 93, this would give a date near the end of the first century. Actually Luke's account, while consistent with that of Josephus, is independent of it and we are more impressed by the fact that the story closes abruptly when Paul had spent two years as a prisoner in Rome (probably in 62), without giving a clear account of the result of the appeal to Caesar, noting also that the emphasis on the general protection afforded to Christians by Roman officials would have been out of place and anachronistic after the Neronian persecution of A.D. 64/5. It is very probable indeed that Luke used the two years of Paul's Caesarean captivity to gather his material for Luke and early Acts from eye-witnesses and documents in Palestine. Adding this to his own notes and information from Paul himself he could have had all his material at hand during the two years in Rome and could then have given shape, in two stages, to his great work. Writing is one thing and circulation another, but Luke intended his work to be read in times when it seemed possible that Christianity might attain official recognition, i.e. before A.D. 64.

The place of Acts in the NT. If Luke wrote a two-part account of the beginnings of

Christianity for the benefit of Theophilus and his friends—as well as for all men everywhere in the course of the centuries—why is Luke separated from Acts in the NT? The answer is found in God's providential care of the canon of the NT, working through the spiritual perception of discerning Christians during the early years of the second century, when four presentations of the Gospel were recognized as especially authoritative and gathered together as 'The Gospel', subdivided into the sections 'according to Matthew', etc. John was seen to be the spiritual consummation of the series, and Luke was given the third place. About the same time the Letters of Paul were gathered together under the title of 'The Apostle', and before long it was seen that Acts was the divinely provided link between 'The Gospel' and 'The Apostle', welding two fundamental series into a library already comprising the greater part of our NT. The importance of this history of the beginnings of the Church and the spread of the gospel from Jerusalem to Rome was further appreciated during the anti-Marcionite debate which straddled the middle of the second century.

God's providence thus provided the ideal bridge between the ministry of our Lord and that of the apostles contained in the Letters, which answers numberless questions arising from the study of the Letters which would have presented insoluble problems apart from the second section of Luke's masterpiece.

Purpose and Plan

The need of a history of the early years.

We have already seen that Luke wished to give an accurate selection of the facts of the origins of Christianity to Theophilus and the 'reading' class he represented. All other purposes must be subordinated to this primary one, remembering that he was inspired thereto by the Holy Spirit. Luke saw the Lord's mission, the descent of the Holy Spirit which gave birth to the Church, and the apostolic labours which extended the gospel world-wide, as one great happening. The 'former book' (1: 1) therefore demanded the writing of its supplement and complement, which is the book we are studying.

The plan of 1: 8.

Our Lord's command in 1: 8 has been rightly considered to be the ground plan of Acts: (a) a Jerusalem ministry, chs. 1–7; (b) a Palestine ministry—reaching out to Syria in the end, chs. 8–12; (c) a world-wide ministry, chs. 13–28. Luke is obviously very much concerned with establishing for his readers Paul's apostolic call and special ministry, but this did not and could not be seen in perspective apart from a clear account of the early years of the church, during which Peter's apostolic ministry is especially prominent. Hence the parallelism between the 'Acts of Peter' (chs. 1–12) and the 'Acts of Paul' (chs. 13–28), in which many analogous features have been discerned.

Luke's writing is 'apologetic'. In the real sense of the word it was so in various ways. (a) He presents the origins of Christianity to cultured readers of the Graeco-Roman world, showing that the disturbances associated therewith as a rule owed nothing to its essential nature, but were stirred up by Jews who rejected their Messiah. (b) Many of the speeches of Acts present the Christian message to Jewish audiences, showing the historic foundations and prophetic predictions which manifested Jesus of Nazareth as the Messiah. (c) In Paul's Jerusalem and Caesarean speeches the Christian message of hope and resurrection is shown to be the heart of the OT revelation. It is not therefore a heresy, but the true continuation and fulfilment of the former revelation. (d) Before both ignorant and cultured Gentiles, Christ the Lord is shown to be God's messenger over against the multiplicity of the 'lords many' of the contemporary pagan scene (14: 14–18; 17: 22–31). (e) Luke establishes Paul's apostleship by the threefold account of his conversion and the gradual manifestation of the signs of his special ministry, until God's works through him were recognized by all except the Judaizers. The opposition of the latter, though a diminishing force within the Church, explains Luke's insistence, which links naturally and closely with Paul's own defence of his apostleship in Galatians, 2 Corinthians, etc.

The developments of a transitional period. Much confused comment has been made on Acts because writers have failed to take into account that the story covers thirty years of development during which God's special witness on earth passed from the hands of the godly remnant of Israel—representing the ideal nation—to those of the church, composed at first entirely of Jewish believers, but latterly of believers who were probably mainly Gentile in origin. It was essential that the risen Messiah should be first presented to Israel in Jerusalem, according to the well-established principle 'to the Jew first'. It is also clear that the universal nature of the church, as superseding Israel's witness, was not forced upon the understanding of the apostles until they were able to bear it. Hence the descent of the Holy Spirit on Gentile believers—extending to them the blessings of Pentecost—did not take place until some years had passed, when it was also plain that official Israel had rejected the risen Messiah as finally as it had rejected the Palestine ministry of Jesus of Nazareth. The instruments who received light in order to guide the church through these stages were themselves Jews by birth and not bound to throw over their national and religious 'customs'. To this must be added the transition seen in Paul's ministry, who was first called as it were in secret. Afterwards he worked alone in Cilicia—in silence as far as the record is concerned—before becoming Barnabas's helper in Antioch. Luke denotes this period by the use of the terms 'Barnabas and Saul', but eventually he was revealed as God's apostle to the Gentiles in the course of the first journey. The phrase 'Paul and his companions' in 13: 13 marks the moment of public acknowledgment. In the writer's view the discussions and the strong claims—then and there acknowledged —of Gal. 2: 1–10 cannot be fitted into the period of subordinate ministry indicated by the term 'Barnabas and Saul' without overriding this principle of historic development. It belongs to the moment of Paul's apostolic plenitude, both in the revelation of doctrine and in the working out of missionary strategy. Notes in the Commentary will indicate points in which the factor of constant growth from Jewish beginnings to the fulness of the apostolic presentation of 'the faith that was once for all entrusted to the saints' must be borne in mind in order to avoid doubtful exegesis. The movement is not wholly contained within the historical period of Acts, but closes with the Letter to the Hebrews in the Canon, and with the verdict of history when the Temple was destroyed by Titus. After that distinctively Jewish

elements are gradually eliminated from the testimony of the church.

Chronological Table

Luke is vague in recording the passage of time, and extra-biblical data only help on three occasions: the death of Herod Agrippa I (A.D. 44), the proconsulship of Gallio in Achaia (A.D. 51–52), and the beginning of the procuratorship of Festus in A.D. 59. Other dates are necessarily approximate and the suggestions of scholars differ considerably. This tentative scheme is meant only as a general guide.

A.D.

30	Pentecost.
33 or 34	Conversion of Saul.
42 or 43	Barnabas co-opts Saul in his labours in Antioch.
44 (fixed)	Herodian persecution and visit of Barnabas and Saul to Jerusalem.
45–47	First journey.
47–48	Period in Antioch and visit to Jerusalem on circumcision question (chap. 15) (14 years after Saul's conversion).
48–52	Second missionary journey (end fixed by Gallio's proconsulship).
52–57	Third missionary journey.
57	Paul arrested in Jerusalem.
57–59	Paul a prisoner in Caesarea.
60–62	Paul a prisoner in Rome.
62	Probably freed.
65 (?)	Martyrdom in Rome

ANALYSIS

I. THE LINK WITH THE GOSPEL (1: 1–26)

i. Theophilus and the 'Former Book' (1: 1)
Theophilus: The title 'most excellent' given to Theophilus (='friend of God') in Lk. 1: 3 marks him out as a high official in the service of Rome, or a member of the equestrian order. It also confirms our impression that he was a real person, already a believer, maybe, or at least greatly interested in Christ and His message. Luke doubtless hoped to reach a wide circle through his correspondent. The absence of the title in 1: 1 may indicate that the relations were less formal and more brotherly than when

the 'former book' was written, although dates are probably close (see Introduction, pp. 1266 f.). The dedication to Theophilus indicates that the gospel was beginning to spread among cultured persons of the Graeco-Roman world.

The continuance of a divine work (1: 1). Luke would have been in hearty sympathy with the brief *résumé* of apostolic ministry in Mk 16: 20: 'The disciples went out and preached everywhere, and the Lord worked with them . . .'. The same Lord who **began to do and to teach** as recorded in the Gospel, continued His mighty works by the Spirit through the apostles in the period following the consummation of the cross and the resurrection. The whole process is continuous throughout all the historical phases and the centre is the great Servant who declares: 'My Father works hitherto and I work'. The work takes priority over the teaching which is based on it.

ii. The commandment given to the Apostles (1: 2–5)

The need of teaching. The Lord's redemptive work was consummated, so that nothing divided His person from heavenly spheres. He nevertheless spent a clear, historical period of forty days with the apostles before **the day he was taken up**. Phrases here and in the epilogues of the Gospels indicate that the period was of the greatest importance to apostolic witness for His servants needed a continuance of their training *after* the tremendous fact of the crucifixion, in the light of the resurrection and under the personal guidance of the same Master. The mention of the Holy Spirit in relation to these commandments does not, of course, weaken the authority of the Master, but stresses once more that the whole work was a 'combined operation' of the Triune God. 'The Spirit of the Lord is on me because He has anointed me to preach . . .' (Lk. 4: 18; cf. Isa. 61: 1, 2) was as true after the resurrection as before.

The apostles. The Twelve were the accredited and commissioned witnesses both to the person and work of Christ, the depositories of the truth related to the great event of God's intervention in history, in the person of His Son, for the redemption of men. So much depended on the accuracy of their ministry that the risen Lord continued to instruct them until His ascension. In 1: 21, 22 we shall return to the characteristics of the ministry of the Twelve in contrast to that of Paul, but note here the importance of the joint witness of the Holy Spirit and the apostles (Jn 14: 26; 15: 26, 27; Ac. 5: 32). These men were not self-appointed babblers, but **the apostles he had chosen** speaking in words which were inspired and confirmed by the Holy Spirit.

The substance of the commandment (1: 3, 4, 8). The 'commandment' mentioned perhaps included the various aspects of the Great Commision detailed in Mt. 28: 19, 20; Lk. 24: 44–49; Jn 20: 21; 21: 15–17. In our context the Lord speaks of the **kingdom of God**, by which we may understand all the spheres which acknowledge God's sovereignty, with special reference here to believers who should enter the kingdom through the worldwide preaching of the gospel. The 'kingdom' and the 'church' should not be set in opposition, but the latter should be understood as the central province of the kingdom because of its most intimate relation with the King. (For a balanced presentation of this great theme, see G. E. Ladd, *The Gospel of the Kingdom*, London, 1959.) The

command to await **the gift my Father promised** in Jerusalem (4) links back to John the Baptist's prophecy (5; cf. Mt. 3: 11) and further back still to the promises of the outpouring of the Holy Spirit by OT prophets (Jl 2: 28, 29; Isa. 32: 15; etc.). The Father's counsels direct the different phases of the work of redemption, so that **the gift my Father promised** is a phrase which aptly describes the gift of the Holy Spirit, the necessary complement of the Incarnation and Atonement.

iii. The Times and Seasons (1: 6, 7)

The disciples' question (1: 6). Is this question yet another proof of the slowness of the apostles in comprehending the spiritual nature of the kingdom, or can it be understood with reference to the particular point at which they had arrived in their instruction by the Master? Let us note the following factors: (*a*) The apostles were steeped in OT prophecies in which the constantly repeated theme is the restoration of Israel to the heart of a universal kingdom on earth. All pious Israelites meditated on this theme (Lk. 1: 33, 55, 68–75). The fierce and unspiritual nationalism of the majority of Jews did not annul these prophecies, though it did distort them. (*b*) The risen Christ taught His disciples that it behoved the Messiah to suffer and then 'enter his glory' (Lk. 24: 26, 27), opening their minds to understand prophetic Scripture concerning His sufferings and resurrection (Lk. 24: 44–46). (*c*) The disciples, having understood the meaning of Isa. 53, naturally meditated on the possibility of the manifestation of the kingdom, as nothing had been revealed which would annul the predictions.

The answer (1: 7). There is no rebuke expressed or implied in the Master's answer, which reiterates that there are 'times and seasons' but remits the order of their manifestation to the Father's authority (cf. 1 Th. 5: 1). In the meantime they had a task to perform in the power of the Holy Spirit and must await further light on the time of the messianic kingdom (1: 7, 8). The 'times' are *chronoi* and the 'dates' *kairoi*; although the meaning of these terms overlaps, *chronoi* lays more stress on the duration of the period and *kairoi* on the crises which mark their consummation.

iv. The Apostolic Witness (1: 8)

Its power. You will receive power when the Holy Spirit comes on you, for the new age was to be that of the Holy Spirit who alone could empower the witness and complement the external and historic work of the Son by those internal and subjective energies which would regenerate and sanctify all true believers (cf. 1 C. 2: 4, 5).

The witnesses. In the first place we must understand the apostolic witnesses who were to speak of Christ and His work as the chosen depositories of the truth (cf. note on 1: 2), declaring what they had seen and heard as good eye-witnesses should do (1 Jn 1: 1–3). But while, in that sense, the apostles could have no successors, all true Christians feel—or should feel—the personal obligation placed on them by the command: **you will be my witnesses.**

The sphere. In Jerusalem, and in all Judea and Samaria, and to the ends of the earth denotes a universal sphere of witness to be reached by stages. It seemed impossible to begin **in Jerusalem**, where the Lord Himself had been rejected and crucified, but such was the command and chs. 2–7 reveal the means by which it was implemented. The next stage was **all Judea**, which, with Samaria mentioned and Galilee implied, coincided with Palestine. Chs. 8–12 narrate the fulfilment of this commission. Peter was to open the door of the world-wide Gentile sphere, and Paul was to be its apostle. Luke tells the story of this last stage in chs. 13–28. We have here, therefore, the programme of the early stages of world evangelism and the main structure of Luke's history.

v. The Ascension (1: 9–11)
The fact and the purpose. It was the Lord's good pleasure to provide a definite and visible end to His ministry on earth in fulfilment of Jn 16: 28: 'I came from the Father and entered the world; now, I am leaving the world and going back to the Father'. Lk. 24: 50 and Ac. 1: 12 fix the place as being the Mount of Olives, in 'the vicinity of Bethany'—a place hallowed by many memories. Our Lord's resurrection body was visibly **taken up** before the disciples until a cloud—presumably a celestial phenomenon, the cloud which enfolds the divine presence (cf. Lk. 9: 34 f.)—received Him out of their sight. Besides marking the end of Christ's earthly ministry, the ascension inaugurated His session at God's right hand (Ac. 2: 36; 5: 31; Rom. 8: 34; Heb. 1: 3; 1 Pet. 3: 22, etc.), and coincides with the 'glorification' without which the Holy Spirit could not be given (Jn 7: 39; cf. Jn 15: 26; Lk. 24: 49). Both Father and Son are spoken of as sending the Holy Spirit.

The Ascension and the Coming (1: 10, 11). The **men . . . in white** were certainly angelic messengers sent to warn the disciples against a sentimental longing for the wonderful days of fellowship with the Master on earth and to cheer them by the prediction of our Lord's personal and visible return **in the same way you have seen him go into heaven**. The period of witness led to a definite goal.

The return to Jerusalem (1: 12). Lk. 24: 52, 53 speaks of the disciples' 'great joy' on returning to the upper room, which indicates a complete understanding of their Lord's last instructions and of the angelic message. They awaited the coming of the **power** with eager expectation, expressed in prayer and supplication. **A Sabbath day's walk** was about six furlongs and was the distance a pious Jew might travel without breaking the rest of the seventh day. The term does not indicate that the ascension took place on the sabbath.

vi. Waiting for the Promise (1: 12–14)
Zahn and others suggest the probability that the disciples returned to that same upper room which had been placed at the Lord's disposal for the celebration of the Passover (Lk. 22: 7–13).

The Eleven (1: 13). It is natural that there should be a 'roll-call' of the apostles before the new stage of the work was inaugurated. The names are given as in Lk. 6: 14 ff. For considerations on the differences between this list and that of Matthew and Mark, see F. F. Bruce, *The Acts of the Apostles*, p. 43. The important fact to be noted in this context is that one member of the original apostolic body, Judas Iscariot, was missing, which leads directly to the appointment of Matthias.

The waiting company (1: 14, 15). As many as 120 persons could be accommodated in a large upper room. Eleven were apostles, and the rest faithful disciples. Mary's presence is noted before she disappears from the pages of Holy Writ, and it is fitting that she should have shared in the experience of the birth of the spiritual body of Christ. The phrase **and with his brothers** reveals the secret of the conversion of these formerly antagonistic men (Jn 7: 5). Every line prepares us in some way for the great event, and expectancy was naturally expressed by a spirit of prayer which identified the yearnings of the company with God's declared purpose.

vii. The Appointment of Matthias (1: 15–26)
The twelfth apostle. The oft repeated idea that the Eleven should have waited for the Lord to make it clear that Paul was to be the twelfth apostle fails to take into account the following considerations: (*a*) The election of Matthias is given by Luke as a part of the introduction to Pentecost; twelve witnesses, representatives of the true Israel, were to stand together that day (2: 14). (*b*) Peter could not be wrong in his understanding of the situation and yet inspired in the quotations from the Psalms and in his estimate of Judas. (*c*) The Twelve were apostolic witnesses to the ministry, death and resurrection of Christ (1: 21, 22), and that Paul could never be. He underlines their specific ministry in 13: 31. His ministry was to the risen Lord as Head of the Church (Eph. 3: 1–12; Col. 1: 24–29, etc.).

Peter's speech (1: 16–22). We must note that 1: 18, 19 constitutes an explanatory parenthesis given by Luke for the benefit of his readers, which sums up the recollection of the end of Judas in Jerusalem when the author gathered up his evidence in (say) A.D. 57–59.

For the rest, the speech has two movements: (*a*) Peter sees in Ahithophel the type of the arch-traitor, Judas, and applies the 'traitor' psalms to the latter (2 Sam. 17: 23; Ps. 69: 25; 109: 8). Judas had really been **one of our number**, great though the mystery is, and his vacant office must be filled. (*b*) The remaining movement (21, 22) is of great importance since it shows that the Twelve had necessarily to be eye-witnesses of the whole of Christ's earthly ministry so as to be reliable witnesses to the great fact of the resurrection.

The election. The Eleven could discern no difference in eligibility according to the given conditions between Joseph Barsabbas and Matthias, and so had recourse to the system of lots (as between two alternatives) sanctioned in the OT. The Urim and Thummim seem to have been used in similar circumstances. The moment was unique for the Master was not there in person to appoint His witness, and the Holy Spirit was not yet given in the special way of Pentecost. The Eleven would remember Prov. 16: 33 and acted accordingly. The silence of Scripture as to the future ministry of Matthias is no more significant than that which surrounds the work of the majority of the apostles.

II. PENTECOST AND THE PREACHING (2: 1–47)
i. The Descent of the Holy Spirit (2: 1–13)
The Event (2: 1–4). The company was gathered in normal assembly (*epi to auto*), in the **house** previously referred to (2: 2; cf. 1: 14, 15). The **blowing of a violent wind** revealed the event and an appearance of **tongues of fire** was seen on each Spirit-filled disciple. It is probable that the company speedily left the house and proceeded to the Temple, where the **sound** (perhaps a 'solemn declaration') drew the crowds together. The **wind** as a symbol of the Spirit was known through Ezekiel's prophecy (Ezek. 37: 9–14) and was used by the Lord (Jn 3: 8). The **fire** represents the outworking of divine energies.

The meaning of the Descent. (*a*) The coming of the Spirit closes the series of happenings which together constitute God's intervention in human history for the salvation of man, and cannot be separated from the incarnation and earthly ministry of Christ, His atoning death and triumphant resurrection. His exaltation made possible the outpouring (1: 33; Jn 7: 39). (*b*) John the Baptist's prophecy and Christ's reference back to it in 1: 5 show that this baptism was the culmination of the work of the Messiah. The cross removed the obstacle of sin so that believers could again live in full communion with God. (*c*) The baptism with the Spirit is thus a 'once for all' event with continuous results, its benefits being extended to Gentile believers in Caesarea (10: 44–48; 1

C. 12: 13). (*d*) Everything indicates the tremendous novelty of the great event, and fulfils the Lord's purpose (future when He spoke): 'on this rock I will build my church' (Mt. 16: 18).

Speaking with tongues (2: 4–13). This is a 'sign', a happening outside the usual course of nature and the workings of human intelligence, which gave evidence of the presence and power of the Holy Spirit. There are further cases as the benefits of Pentecost are extended in 10: 46 and 19: 6, but apart from these references tongues are mentioned only in Mk 16: 17 (in the longer appendix to Mk) and in 1 C. 14: 13, where 'speaking with tongues' becomes an internal matter for the local church, ecstatic and unintelligible unless interpreted. On the day of Pentecost the tongues were intelligible to a number of hearers from different countries, and it is impossible to say how these two manifestations are related.

The reactions of the multitude (2: 5–13). The many devout Jews of the Dispersion who had gone to Jerusalem for the feast are selected for special mention—perhaps an early emphasis on universality. Many of them had lost the use of Aramaic and would normally depend on Greek as a *lingua franca*. The proclamation of **the wonders of God** (11) in the languages of the countries of their adoption would naturally excite their keen interest, followed by amazement as it was found that *all* understood what was being said—presumably by one or other of the speakers. It was a *teras* (a wonder) which became a *sēmeion* (a sign) that God desired to make Himself known despite the Babel-confusion of human tongues. Here was a remarkable story to take back to countries spreading from Persia to Rome and over the North of Africa (8–11)! We must remember, however, that all the hearers belonged to the commonwealth of Israel.

Apart from the amazement and perplexity of the pilgrims, we know nothing of other immediate reactions except that of the 'smart' people who produced the easy formula: 'These men are drunk'! Their theory was soon deflated by Peter.

ii. Peter's Speech (2: 14–36)
The kerygma for Jews. Now filled with the Spirit, Peter could begin to 'proclaim as a herald' the great fact of redemption, lifting up his voice, as he stood **with the eleven**, to give solemn utterance to the inspired message (2: 14). Before Jews, the 'herald's message' (Gk. *kerygma*) generally includes the following features: (*a*) the guilt of the people who crucified their Messiah; (*b*) God's reversal of their verdict in the resurrection and exaltation of Jesus; (*c*) the evidence of Christ's well-known ministry of grace and power; (*d*) appeals to OT texts; (*e*) the continuing possibility of blessing for Israelites who would repent and believe.

Introduction (2: 14, 15). It's only nine in the morning, when Jews would not normally have had a meal, much less have taken wine. 'This is not drunkenness', says Peter, in effect, 'but inspiration.'

Joel's prophecy (2: 16–21). NT writers quote from the OT in a variety of ways, more often on the basis of analogy of principle than on that of direct fulfilment. In the writer's view, a special use made of an OT prophecy does not annul its meaning as fixed by the original context. In Jl 2: 28–32 the prophet speaks of the outpouring of the Spirit on *everybody* as the climax of the blessings God will bestow on restored Israel. This is preceded by the usual portents of judgment in the last days and by a promise of salvation to all who call on the name of the Lord. The terrible portents of 2: 19, 20 were not fulfilled by the darkening of the sun on the day of the crucifixion and are constantly associated with the Day of Jehovah (Isa. 13: 9–11; Ezek. 32: 5–8; Jl 2: 10; 3: 15; Hab. 3: 11; Mt. 24: 29 and parallels; Rev. 6: 12; 8: 12). The Holy Spirit descended on a limited company, and has still not filled all persons, old and young, of all social categories. The conditions for quotations from the OT in the NT are fulfilled if we understand that elements of Joel's prophecy were seen in the happening of Pentecost, and that the cross and resurrection had opened a new age which would culminate in universal spiritual blessing. (See article 'The New Testament Use of the Old Testament', pp. 1111 ff.)

Christ and Israel (2: 22–24). Peter appealed to the personal knowledge of the Palestinian Jews when he spoke of the ministry of Jesus of Nazareth, whose mighty works showed that he was attested by God as His messenger to Israel (22). The terrible responsibility for the rejection of such a Man fell squarely on the shoulders of the inhabitants of Jerusalem: **this man . . . you, with the help of wicked men put . . . to death by nailing him to the cross.** But their unreasoning hatred became the instrument for the fulfilment of the divine plan established in the foreknowledge of God.

The Resurrection (2: 24–32). The apostles were above all 'witnesses to the resurrection' (1: 22) and Peter states: **God raised him**, for the Prince of life could not be held down by the pangs of death (24). The shameful verdict of the Sanhedrin was reversed by Omnipotence.

Both Peter and Paul (13: 35) appeal to Ps. 16 as a prophecy of the Resurrection. Much of the psalm expressed David's own experiences, but certain elements—as in all the messianic psalms—could only be fulfilled in his greater Son. Note especially the phrase: **nor will you let your Holy One see decay** (27, 29). As a prophet David saw that the resurrection life of his descendant would be the means of fulfilling the covenant (29–31; cf. 2 Sam. 7: 12–17; Ps. 89: 3, 4, 26–37; 132: 11–18).

The exaltation of Christ (2: 33–35). The verb **raised** of 2: 32 refers to the resurrection to which the apostles bore witness, but it leads directly to the exaltation of the Messiah as prophesied in Ps. 110: 1. Peter has not forgotten the original theme, and relates the outpouring of power witnessed by the multitude that day to the fact of Christ's exaltation. David did not rise from the dead, nor did he ascend into heaven to be exalted to a throne of glory, so that Ps. 110: 1 must refer to another. **Sit at my right hand, until I make your enemies a footstool for your feet** presupposed a completed task and then a period of waiting—not divorced from activity—until the final triumph over the enemy is achieved.

The appeal (2: 36). Prophecy and contemporary facts had been welded into a strong argument which was the basis of a direct appeal to **all Israel**. God had constituted Jesus, the crucified one, both Lord and Messiah for His people, despite their tragic rebellion.

iii. The First Christian Church (2: 37–47)

Repentance and baptism (2: 37–41). They (37) refers to those who received the word, crying, **what shall we do?** Peter's answer is cogent and clear in the light of other Scriptures, for repentance, 'a change of mind and attitude', is the negative aspect of that faith in Christ which is clearly implied. Baptism in itself could not procure the forgiveness of sins and the reception of the Holy Spirit, but was the outward sign of a new attitude which abjured the crime of the great rejection and placed the confessors on the side of the Messiah. **In the name of Jesus Christ** (38) shows that the converts confessed Jesus as Messiah and participated in the fulness of their Lord and Saviour.

By the phrase **for all who are far off** (39) Peter understood the dispersed as well as Palestinian Jews, and the promise was for the humble-minded who escaped from the **corrupt generation** of rebellious Israel, forming a faithful remnant of witnesses.

The foundation of the church (2: 41). Peter could have used Paul's description of his church building: 'I laid a foundation as an expert builder . . . for no one can lay any foundation other than the one already laid, which is Jesus Christ' (1 C. 3: 10, 11). The word was faithfully preached and received by a large number of believers who were then baptized and added to the church. It has been objected that 3,000 people could not have been baptized by immersion in Jerusalem. Nothing, however, is said about the time taken or the number of persons employed in the task. Around the city there were plenty of places for ceremonial ablutions, and there were also many irrigation pools.

The practices of the church (2: 42). This verse sums up succinctly the main elements of the life and activity of the Jerusalem church: (a) **Perseverance in the apostles' teaching.** The apostles were called upon not only to witness to the world but also to teach the Christian family. At this stage the teaching would be mainly the reiteration of the facts of the ministry, death and resurrection of Christ seen in the light of OT prophecy. We must think of the large company divided into groups for such instruction by the apostles and their helpers. This 'oral tradition'—in the right sense —was to give rise to the written material we find in the Gospels and opened the way for the further revelations of the Letters. (b) **Fellowship** (*koinōnia*) indicates an openhearted sharing in which each believer gave to others what he had himself received, whether of spiritual or material blessings (see its basis in 1 Jn 1: 1–4). (c) **The breaking of bread** in this context is equivalent to the Lord's Supper (taken as part of a common meal), as only a fundamental activity of the church would be put alongside **teaching** and **prayer**. The solemnity of our Lord's charge, 'Do this in memory of me', in the shadow of the cross would lead to speedy obedience once the church was formed. (d) **Prayer.** The emphasis is on collective prayer, for in times of the plenitude of the Spirit there is always a glad recognition of the spiritual profit and blessing flowing from joint praises and petitions. A church lacking these features is in danger of spiritual decay.

Outward influence and spiritual unity (2: 43–47). The outward influence of the church was seen in a widespread awe, in the performance of miracles and in the addition to the company of those whom God was saving (43, 47). The great features of the inner life of the church were joy in the Lord, the community of goods, fellowship, and meetings in the temple courts (44–46). Believers were so near the cross and the resurrection and so filled with the Spirit, that for a while selfishness was swallowed up in love. It was thus easy to sell possessions and think of the good of all. In this way arose the 'church-community' of Jerusalem, which, considered as an experiment, was of a temporary nature; it lent itself only to a peculiar set of circumstances which did not persist and were not reproduced elsewhere. In later years the church in Jerusalem was chronically poor, and the difficulties of distribution are illustrated in 6: 1. Considered as an example of love, however, the community has much to teach us. The increase (47) was the natural result of the spiritual state of the church.

III. THE NAME OF THE LORD JESUS IN JERUSALEM (3: 1–5: 42)
i. The Power of the Name (3: 1–10)

The first stage of the plan—the evangelization of Jerusalem—was quite hopeless if the Twelve had to measure themselves against the Sanhedrin and the dominant high-priestly party, backed in a last resort by Rome. But their Master had promised that they should do 'greater works' in His name because He went to the throne of God to administer a completed mission, and His name is His own authority manifested through His servants (Jn 14: 12–26). They spoke and prayed in the name, but in this section it is very important to note that they performed miracles in the name, as this power provided them with both credentials and protection until the rebellious capital had been filled with the message of the crucified and risen Messiah. Over against the carnal power of the Jewish rulers, God appointed another 'power' through the name which turned the weakness of the apostles into spiritual strength and dignity.

The healing of the lame man (3: 1–10). Three in the afternoon was the hour of national prayer associated with the evening sacrifice. Peter and John worshipped as Israelites with no sense of a need to break away from the temple.

The details of the healing stress the hopeless lameness of the temple beggar and the material poverty of the apostles. But the name was there, and by its power the man's feet and ankles were strengthened so that he could enter the Temple courtyard leaping and praising God. (For details of the setting see *NBD, art.* 'Temple'.)

Despite the fact that Palestinian Jews had been very familiar with our Lord's healing work, the worshippers in the temple were **filled with wonder and amazement** (10). The wonder-worker had been crucified, but a similar power to his was still working in Jerusalem!

ii. Peter's Second Speech (3: 11–26)
The setting. The audience was entirely Jewish and was found in the temple courts—the visible centre of their religious life. The Christology is messianic, with close links with the OT, as is natural at this stage.

The source of the power (3: 12, 13). Peter passes at once from the people's astonishment to the beginnings of the race—Abraham's call and God's covenant with him—for power through the name of Jesus was directly related to the purposes of the God of Abraham.

The titles of the Messiah. The Christology of the period is especially revealed by the names applied to the Saviour in this speech and in the following verses. **Servant** (or 'Child') in 3: 13, 26; 4: 27, translates *pais* and links with the 'Servant Songs' of Isa. 42–53. The **Holy** One (14) links with 4: 27 and was known even to demons (Mk 1: 24). The **Righteous One** (14) is used by Stephen (7: 52), by Ananias (22: 14) and by John (1 Jn 2: 1), expressing one important aspect of the person and work of the Messiah. **The author of life** (15) is in striking contrast with the Jerusalemites' choice of **a murderer** (see also Heb. 2: 10; 12: 2). **A prophet** (22) fulfils Moses' prophecy in Dt. 18: 15, 16. A little later the apostles were to speak of 'the Lord's Anointed' (4: 26). Each title focused messianic prophecy fully on the person of Jesus of Nazareth. At this stage there is no reference to the pre-incarnation Son and Creator as in Phil. 2: 6–11; Col. 1: 15–20; Jn 1: 1–3; Heb. 1: 1–3.

The Jews' verdict and God's verdict (3: 13–15). The glorious titles of the Messiah emphasize the guilt of those who rejected Him. God's work in resurrection, witnessed to by the Twelve, reversed the shameful verdict of the Sanhedrin.

Healing by 'faith in the name' (3: 16). However awkwardly the best Greek text reads here, it certainly emphasizes the saving interrelations between the name and the faith of the healed man who was the 'living text' of this discourse.

Repent! (3: 17–21). Although Peter seems to allow some excuse for ignorance, yet only sincere repentance could blot out the crime of rejecting the Messiah and make possible His return in blessing. The phrases of 19–21 must be interpreted in the light of the many prophecies of blessings on Israel and the nations in the coming kingdom. It would be absurdly anachronistic to suppose that Peter was applying them to the church by a spiritualizing method!

The prophets and the Prophet (3: 22–26). Moses' prophecy of Dt. 18: 15, 16 may be interpreted as God's raising up of true prophets in general, but some Jews (especially the Qumran community) certainly considered it as in some sense messianic (cf. Jn 1: 21b; 6: 14) and the same concept is underlined in Heb. 1: 1. **Samuel** is important as inaugurating a prophetic period in which 'schools' of the prophets maintained a witness in Israel. The Jews were **heirs of the prophets and of the covenant** (25) in the Hebrew sense of having a close participation in the covenant and prophecy leading to messianic blessings (26). But their portion might either be lost by incredulity or confirmed if they received the Servant God had raised up—as He had previously raised up Moses. **God . . . sent him first to you, to bless you by turning each of you from your wicked ways.** It was a national question, for Christ was sent to the chosen people. It was a moral question, needing repentance. It was a personal question for each one needed to receive the personal Saviour.

iii. The First Collision with Official Judaism (4: 1–22)

Peter and John arrested (4: 1–4). The temple area was controlled by the priests, and the dignity of the captain of the temple (the *sagan*) was second only to that of the high priest. Pending trial, those who **were . . . proclaiming in Jesus the resurrection of the dead** were put into custody in the lock-up under the control of the *sagan*. The dominant party was Sadducean in doctrine, hating the idea of resurrection. In the meantime two thousand more souls had been added to the church, making a total of 5,000 (4).

The trial (4: 5–22). Here we have the first post-pentecostal collision of the two 'powers': that of the Jewish 'establishment' and that of the name of the risen Lord. (For the constitution of the Sanhedrin see *NBD*, art. 'Sanhedrin'.) Peter and John stood where their Master had stood, being accused—presumably on the basis of Dt. 13: 1–5—of having employed unauthorized methods of healing, invoking the name of one recently convicted of 'blasphemy'. The accusation gave Peter a wonderful opening for witness before the authorities, which he used to the full in the power of the Holy Spirit. The healed man was present as a living text proclaiming the essential goodness of the work performed (9, 21, 22). The power was well known, for it was that of Jesus of Nazareth, crucified by those judges but raised by God's power. The judges were the foolish builders of Ps. 118: 22 and all salvation was through **the name** (8–12).

Men from the school of Jesus (4: 13). The rulers' estimate of Peter and John as 'uneducated laymen' reflects the spiritual pride of the professionals in theology, but does not mean what many readers of the av suppose. The skill and power of Peter's defence were admitted, but as the apostles had not been trained in rabbinical schools, their obvious capacity was due to their training in the 'unofficial school' of Jesus.

The Sanhedrin's decree (4: 14–18, 21, 22). The hands of the rulers were tied by the 'evidence' of the healed man and by the enthusiasm of the multitude. In secret session they decided that it was unwise to condemn the apostles to flogging or death, but they did decide that speaking and teaching in the name of Jesus was to be prohibited. The seriousness of the decree must not be underestimated, as any future preaching became an act of defiance against the supreme Jewish tribunal. War was declared between the earthly authority of the Sanhedrin and the divine authority of the Name.

Peter declares a basic principle (4: 19–22). The rabbis themselves justified civil disobedience in certain circumstances if a superior divine command could be proved. Peter appealed to such a command to justify the declaration of what they had seen and heard.

iv. God's Plan and the Disciples' Prayer (4: 23–31)

The apostles and the Christian family (4: 23). The apostles returned to the Christian family and their information, seen in the light of the prophetic word, became the basis of intelligent and powerful prayer (cf. 1: 14).

Characteristics and results of the prayer (4: 24–31). This is a wonderful model for prayer in times of persecution, being unanimous and empowered by the Spirit. It was appropriately addressed to the **Sovereign Lord** for He was able to suppress the wrath of the Jerusalem rulers and carry out His plan until final triumph was achieved. Ps. 2 is a 'key' portion of prophecy showing that God will establish the kingdom in the hands of His Anointed despite the confederated wrath of peoples and rulers. The disciples saw the crisis of the cross as a 'sample' both of the great rebellion against God's **holy servant Jesus** and of the way in which God caused the rebels **to do whatever thy hand and thy plan had predestined to take place** (28). With such confidence in God's providence they only needed to present the threats of the Sanhedrin before their Sovereign Lord to make a twofold plea: (*a*) for boldness in witness; (*b*) for renewed manifestations of power **through the name** (29, 30).

The experience of v. 31 was not another 'baptism of the Spirit', but a renewed manifestation of His power among believers entirely surrendered to God's will. The prayer was answered, as is noted here and in the succeeding passages.

v. Unanimity and Grace (4: 32–37)

The Christian community described in these verses would appear to the Jews as a special sect of Judaism, rather like that of Qumran, except that it had its centre in the heart of Jerusalem and gave an aggressive testimony, in marked contrast to the passive separation of the Essenes. For the 'church-community' see notes on 2: 43–47. In 4: 32 Luke underlines the inwardness of the fellowship which sprang from being **one in heart and mind**—that of the closely knit spiritual body in Jerusalem.

Barnabas. Much grace was upon them all, and no one laid claim to his own possessions (4: 32, 33). Every general movement is better understood by a concrete example, so Barnabas is mentioned. He also stands out in dramatic contrast to Ananias and Sapphira and his name prepares the way for further developments in the future (11: 22 ff.). The apostolic testimony was especially to the fact of the resurrection (4: 33).

vi. Power for Judgment: Ananias and Sapphira (5: 1–11)

The historic moment. Very many Christians, nominal or otherwise, have committed Ananias's sin and have not fallen down dead, but let us remember: (*a*) That he and his wife sinned against the bright light of the almost perfect testimony of the early Church; (*b*) that God often shows His disapproval openly when sins besmirch the beginnings of a new stage of His witness in the world, so that all who follow may, at least, know His mind on the matter (see Achan, Jos. 7; Nadab and Abihu, Lev. 10: 1–7).

The voluntary nature of giving. Peter's statement in 5: 4 shows clearly that no pressure was brought to bear on believers to induce them to sell their properties or to bring the sale price to the common fund. Presumably the couple could have stated that they wished to keep back a part of the price, when the other part would have been accepted.

The nature of the sin. Whether Ananias and Sapphira were carnal Christians or 'mere professors' cannot be determined and does not affect the case. They wanted to stand before the church as equal to Barnabas in faith and generosity, and such seekers after human glory fall under the Lord's strong condemnation (Jn 5: 44). Not only so, but they were prepared deliberately to plan means whereby they could keep their financial reserves in secret and still acquire the reputation they craved. This meant an acted lie, which Sapphira, at least, was prepared to back up by a deliberate untruth (5: 8). Let no one marvel that divine disapproval should have been manifested by immediate judgment in days of the plenitude of the Spirit of holiness. The lie was to God (and to the Holy Spirit, who is God) although they wished to act their part before men. The agreeing together to tempt the Spirit of the Lord was especially heinous, as the sin links back to that of rebellious Israel in the wilderness—the sin of 'seeing how far a man can go' with his cravings and desires in opposition to God and in His very presence (Mt. 4: 7; Exod. 17: 2; Dt. 6: 16).

The judgment and its effects (5: 5, 6, 10, 11). From the point of view of the Christian company the death of Ananias and Sapphira was a drastic example of 1 C. 5: 7—an act of discipline in order that the 'fresh dough' of the early church might yet continue unleavened. It must not be deduced that sickness and death among the Lord's people are always directly related to some special sin, as discipline through trials may be the special experience of those who follow the way of holiness (Heb. 12: 4–11). In exceptional cases there are such visitations for the health of the local church (1 C. 11: 30).

The name was shown to be powerful, not only for witness and healing, but also for judgment, and the fear which came upon the church and others was entirely salutary.

vii. A Climax of Blessing Through the Name (5: 12–16)

A period of many miracles (5: 12, 15, 16). The prayer of 4: 30 was abundantly answered, and the scenes in Jerusalem in this climax of apostolic witness remind us of the heyday of our Lord's ministry in Galilee and of Paul's ministry by works and word in Ephesus, at a later date (19: 11). Peter's shadow and Paul's handkerchiefs were unimportant in themselves, but served as a medium for faith, analogous to the mud with which Jesus anointed the eyes of the blind man (Jn 9: 6, 7). The blessing was shared by neighbouring towns (16).

No one else dared join them (13). This difficult phrase may well be understood in relation to the normal meetings of the believers in Solomon's Portico. Read as NEB: 'They used to meet by common consent in Solomon's cloister, no one from outside their number venturing to join them.' That is, worshippers passing by kept away from the Nazarene throng unless they were of those being added to the church.

viii. The Second Clash with the Sanhedrin (5: 17–42)

An impossible situation (17, 18, 22). The power of the name, manifested in many works of healing, preserved the apostles and gave them tremendous popularity and prestige in Jerusalem. The situation was similar to that following the resuscitation of Lazarus (Jn 11: 47–53) when the rulers had either to believe —which they would not do—or decide on desperate measures of violence, despite the danger from the mob. All the apostles seem to have been thrown into **the public jail**—presumably by the *sagan* (see 4: 1).

Deliverance for witness (19–26). The deliverance effected by the angel was for further witness, not for escape to safety, as is made clear by the command of v. 20—the message of life must be proclaimed, and in the temple itself, centre of the enemies' territory! This surprising intervention adds greatly to the guilt of the judges who were **puzzled** but continued to sin against so clear a light (21–26).

The accusation (27, 28). The apostles were accused of rebellious defiance of an official decree (4: 18), with the addendum—clearly reflecting the uneasy consciences and hidden fears of those who dared sentence Jesus Christ —that they were plotting to avenge the death of their Master. Notice how the high priest— with mingled scorn and fear—speaks of **this man's blood**.

The defence and witness of the apostles (29–32). Peter speaks with and for the Twelve, and his brief discourse is a marvel of cogency

and clarity. **'We must obey God rather than men'** links back to Peter's words at the end of the former trial (4: 19, 20). Then, as in all trials before that tribunal, the accused became the accusers of the guilty judges. Two great facts were first asserted: God **raised** up **Jesus** in fulfilment of His promises, but the rulers had hanged Him upon the shameful **tree** (*xylon*). Two sublime titles, **Prince and Saviour**, belong to Jesus in this messianic exaltation (31) (cf. Dan. 7: 13, 14; Ps. 110: 1). A double gift comes from the hands of the exalted Messiah for Israel—**repentance and forgiveness of sins**. Naturally, what was given potentially needed to be received subjectively. Two witnesses guaranteed the historic facts of God's work through Jesus whom He had raised up, for the **Holy Spirit** confirmed the witness of the apostles (32). The speech concludes with a reference to Pentecost—God **has given** the Holy Spirit **to those who obey him** by submitting to His Son.

Luke probably gives only the main points of Peter's witness, but even so it is a model for public utterance. Its very cogency aroused the homicidal rage of the Sanhedrin judges in general (33) but God willed a gracious extension of opportunity to Jerusalem.

Gamaliel's counsel (34–39). Gamaliel, the teacher of Saul of Tarsus, was the leader of the more liberal sector of the Pharisees, and his learning was so appreciated that he received the honourable appellation of the 'Rabban', 'our teacher'. In private session he makes a plea for moderation in typically Pharisaic terms. In support of this he adduces two examples of self-appointed 'messiahs' whose factions were destroyed by the Romans (not mentioned by name) and who were slain. The **Theudas** of 5: 36 cannot be the false messiah of the same name mentioned by Josephus as his rising took place at a date later than that of this trial. The name was common, and there must have been a former rebel called Theudas. **Judas the Galilean** led a dangerous revolt in A.D. 6 opposing a census ordered by Quirinius, governor of Syria. (This is not the census mentioned in Lk. 2: 1.) The Zealot movement, ready to oppose Rome by violence, sprang from Judas's rebellion. In 5: 38, 39, Gamaliel draws the moral from these incidents: leave the Nazarenes alone, for if the movement is of man **it will fail**; should it be of God the Sanhedrin could not overthrow it, and might be found 'fighting against God'.

The moderation of Gamaliel stands out pleasantly against the unreasoning hate of his colleagues, but his arguments are weak and his position untenable. How much more evidence did the leaders of the nation need in order to determine if Christ and His work were of God or the devil? We are reminded of the Lord's challenge to the Pharisees in Mt. 21: 23–27. It was no moment for halting between two opinions, and blindness is evidenced not only by aggressive opposition to the truth, but also by failure to act on it when it is revealed.

Suffering and witness (5: 40–42). With tremendous inconsistency the Sanhedrin accepted Gamaliel's advice but proceeded to have the apostles beaten, reiterating the prohibition to speak in the name. The beating would be the Jewish 'forty strokes save one' (Dt. 25: 3).

The disciples did not resign themselves to suffering, but rejoiced **to be counted worthy of suffering disgrace for the Name** in the place where their Lord had been condemned (cf. Phil. 1: 29). At the same time they continued to obey the higher authority, and **never stopped teaching and proclaiming . . . Jesus is the Christ.**

IV. TIMES OF TRANSITION AND STEPHEN'S WITNESS (6: 1–8: 1a)
i. An Administrative Problem Solved (6: 1–7)
General considerations. The appointment of the Seven has been traditionally understood as the establishment of a permanent 'order of deacons' in the church, devoted to its material needs. Doubtless the incident before us coloured popular ideas about the diaconate at a later date, but we must remember: (*a*) the need arose in the Jerusalem church-community which was not to be the model for future local churches; (*b*) although the verb *diakoneō* appears, the Seven are not called deacons; (*c*) the only two administrators of whom we read anything apart from their names and functions in this section—Stephen and Philip—became known for ministries different from their function here. We get the impression of a situation arising from the temporary communal life of the Jerusalem church, the problem of the Hellenistic widows being dealt with in a practical and spiritual fashion. General lessons of corporate living and service stand out clearly, but no fixed model is imposed on future local churches. The atmosphere is Jewish, and this must modify deductions based on this passage as to the election of church officers; the modern democratic principle of 'one man, one vote' would be entirely anachronistic in this setting. In the OT, apart from the priestly function, determined by descent, God Himself chose His servants, often by the means of others already tried and proved. Elders were men of experience and judgment and no decisions were cast back on a mere number of 'members'. The **brothers** addressed in v. 3 were perhaps outstanding men who could discern the spirituality and capacity of their companions, presenting suitable men to the apostles. The **whole group** could approve, but not direct (5). The apostles took the final responsibility and identified themselves with the Seven by the laying on of hands.

The **Grecian Jews** (Greek-speaking Jews) in the church come into prominence here, as they will be God's instruments for initiating the second and third stages of the programme of evangelization.

Differing ministries (6: 1–6). The language difficulty—some of the disciples were Aramaic-speaking and some Greek-speaking —must have caused real difficulties of administration and the needs of the Hellenistic widows had been overlooked. Up to that time the Twelve had received all the voluntary offerings and had been responsible for their distribution among thousands of believers. The complaint showed that a devolution of ministries was necessary. It was not right that the specific ministry of the Twelve should be subordinated to administrative work (2, 4) and so help was needed. But administration was a delicate matter affecting the well-being of the whole church, so that this humble service required a good reputation, wisdom, and, above all, a manifestation of spiritual power (3). The brethren who helped in the selection of suitable men (3, 5) would naturally bear these conditions in mind, and also, very wisely, thought of presenting Hellenistic helpers, as is shown by the names of the Seven. There could thus be no further thought of favouritism in favour of the **Aramaic-speaking community**. Stephen is especially noted as a **man full of faith and of the Holy Spirit** (5) and the wise and practical proceedings were accompanied by prayer (6).

The climax of testimony in Jerusalem (6: 7). Luke again interrupts his story for a moment to sum up the results of past witness; indeed, v. 7 denotes both the zenith and the end of the 'prosperous' period of the evangelization of Jerusalem and we may suppose that everyone in the city had had an opportunity of hearing and believing the message. The word increased, the number of disciples was multiplied and even **a large number of priests became obedient to the faith**. The future testimony of these priests is not revealed, and it must be remembered that no one had been taught that Christians must give up their Jewish customs.

ii. Stephen's Witness Determines a Crisis (6: 8–7: 1)
Transition and crisis. As the implications of the Christian *kerygma* became increasingly apparent, and as the multitude grew accustomed to miracles, a reaction against the disciples was bound to come. It actually centred round Stephen and originated among the Hellenistic Jews who had returned to Jerusalem, meeting in their own synagogues.

Stephen and his message (6: 8–15).

Stephen was full of the Spirit, of wisdom, **grace and power**, being empowered by God to work miracles among the people (3, 5, 8). As a Hellenist, he found his sphere of witness in the Greek-speaking synagogues, with special mention of that **of the Freedmen**. This may have included the Cyrenians, Alexandrians and Cilicians (9). Saul of Tarsus would possibly attend the same synagogue, although indeed he was no Hellenist but a 'Hebrew of Hebrews' (Phil. 3: 5).

Stephen's ministry was so powerful that his opponents despaired of victory in discussion and resorted to plots and violence. What was his message? It doubtless included the elements common to the *kerygma* presented to Jews but the accusations levelled against him, with the terms of his own defence (6: 11, 13 with ch. 7), make it probable that his preaching emphasized the new life of the gospel in a way which clashed with official Judaism. The accusations, as such, were false, yet the instigators would take care that they bore some resemblance to the truth. The similarity of these charges to those adduced in the trial of Jesus is striking. Stephen was said to have used **words of blasphemy against Moses and against God**; before the Sanhedrin he was alleged to have stated that Jesus of Nazareth would **destroy** the temple and **change the customs** attributed to Moses (11, 14). We may gather that he stressed the tremendous 'novelty' of the new creation founded on the death and resurrection of Christ, with the relative unimportance of the material types which foreshadowed the great reality.

Stephen's trial (6: 12 ff.). The Hellenistic fanatics were successful in getting the high priest to convoke the Sanhedrin once more. Whether the Roman governor was absent from his province (as some have thought) or not, the political position was favourable to the high-priestly caste, who would note a change of attitude in the multitude. Perhaps Caiaphas saw in the incident the possibility of a flanking attack against the Nazarene sect which did not directly involve the redoubtable apostles. Stephen went much farther than they did in emphasizing the clean break with the old order implied by the work of Christ. The official accusation would reflect the false witness already noted, and then Stephen, his face shining with celestial light (15), was allowed to speak in his own defence (7: 1).

iii. Stephen's Defence (7: 2–53)

Stephen's method. At first sight a long extract from Israel's history seems a strange means of 'defence' against the charges noted in 6: 11, 14, but (a) it assured a hearing for the message, as the judges could not cut short a summary of their sacred history; (b) it appealed to the valid Hebrew concept that God reveals Himself by what He does in history and not only by what He proclaims through the prophets. Stephen's hearers were to understand the diversity of God's self-revelation as **the God of glory** (2) and to see their own crime prefigured in the behaviour of national leaders who had repeatedly rejected both divine revelation and the men God had raised up to further His purposes.

The experience of Abraham (2–8). The title **the God of glory** links on to the vision granted to Stephen before his martyrdom (55, 56). It is significant that Abraham knew God and submitted to His commands in distant lands, first in Ur and afterwards in Haran. The land was promised, but God's providential purposes were variously fulfilled before it was occupied by the Israelites.

The experience of Joseph (9–16). God revealed some of His purposes to faithful Joseph, but the patriarchs, moved by jealousy, resisted them, though God turned their evil into good. The point is that Joseph, rejected by his brethren and exalted by pagan Pharaoh, became the means of his family's salvation in time of famine. As a result the nation was multiplied outside Palestine. The parallel with the rejected Messiah is complete. The reference to **seventy-five souls** (14) differs from the computation of Gen. 46: 27 and Exod. 1: 5, but agrees with the LXX, the reading of which appears in an early Hebrew manuscript of Exodus from Qumran. The exact number would depend on the inclusion or exclusion of Joseph's family and on the number of his children. The reference to the burial place of the Hebrew fathers (16) presents a difficulty, as Jacob was buried at Hebron, in the cave of Machpelah which Abraham bought from Ephron the Hittite (Gen. 23: 16 with 49: 29 ff.), while Joseph was buried in Shechem, in the property bought by Jacob **from the sons of Hamor. Their bodies were brought back** generalizes the situation and we have an obvious conflation of the two purchases, one carried out by Abraham directly and the other mediately through his descendant Jacob. We must remember the strong sense of racial solidarity among the Hebrews, and that Stephen is speaking extempore.

The experience of Moses in Egypt (17–29). The theme is still God's purposes and the blindness of Israel. Despite the apparent failure of the promises during the Egyptian captivity, God saved Moses from death and had him trained in the Egyptian court. Moses' spiritual experiences are summed up in Heb. 11: 24–26, but here we glimpse his plan for delivering his people, perhaps by using his position and influence. His overtures were scornfully rejected by the Hebrews. The man who thrust him aside represents the many rejectors, down to the time of Caiaphas himself.

The experience of Moses as the leader of the people (30–41). The theme of the self-revelation of the God of glory is very clear in the reference to the **flames of a burning bush** (30), which turned Horeb into **holy ground** (33). The Israelites had said: **Who made you ruler . . . ?** but after forty years God said to Moses: **now come, I will send you.** The **angel** is practically identified with Jehovah, as in Exod. 3: 2 ff.

The whole of the Exodus is summed up in v. 36, and a further criminal rejection of God's instrument is noted in 39–41 when the people set up the golden calf at the foot of the mount where God manifested His presence.

The 'Prophet' prediction of Dt. 18: 15–18 (cf. Ac. 3: 22 f.) throws the consummation of God's purpose forward, beyond Moses and the system he was led to establish, and is a partial answer to the accusation of 6: 11. Moses, as God's mouthpiece, proclaimed the **living words**, which were broken by the sinning people. Were their descendants any more obedient to the witness of Moses? Was it Stephen who spoke blasphemous words against him, or did the Sanhedrin deny him by their acts as their fathers had done?

The temple theme (42–50). Amos's strong denunciation of apostates went back to the seemingly ideal conditions of the tabernacle worship in the wilderness (Am. 5: 25–27). The **tabernacle of Testimony** (44) was made according to the pattern, but what was the internal spiritual condition of the people? **The book of the prophets** (42) means the Twelve Minor Prophets; Stephen quotes from the LXX, except that 'beyond Damascus' becomes **beyond Babylon**, in the light of the Babylonian exile.

The 'sanctuary' story is summed up in 44–50, and is related to the accusation of 'speaking words against this holy place' (6: 13). Stephen recognizes the divine origin of the tabernacle and of the temple which replaced it, but in line with the highest OT revelation, he sees the material 'dwelling' as a figure and promise of a final spiritual reality. The witness of the throne and temple in the reigns of David and Solomon was effective and widespread according to the terms of Solomon's inaugural prayer, which evidences a clear vision both of the infinitude of the Creator and of the universal significance of the house (2 Chr. 6: 12–33). But the generation which rejected the Christ had become carnally proud of its privileges and particularist in its outlook. For them the quotation from Isa. 66: 1, 2 was especially fitting.

Stephen accuses his judges (51–53). Perhaps Stephen had something more to say about the revelation of the glory 'in the face of Jesus Christ', but signs of impatience among the judges may have warned him to get quickly to his peroration. Realizing that he would not be granted a fair trial, he was led by the Spirit to pronounce a solemn 'woe' on the leaders who had rejected both the Christ Himself and the loving invitation to repentance given by the risen Christ through the apostles. Their 'circumcision' was meaningless, for it did not affect heart or ear (cf. Dt. 10: 16; Jer. 4: 4; etc.); they had resisted the strivings of the Holy Spirit even more persistently than their fathers, for their predecessors had martyred the prophets, and they had betrayed and murdered **the Righteous One** (cf. 3: 14; 22: 14), theme of prophetic promises. Claiming to be the guardians of the law, they were really chief among its transgressors. On this note the widespread testimony in Jerusalem was brought to a close, and the lament over the city was heard once more (Lk. 13: 34, 35; 19: 41–44).

iv. Stephen's Martyrdom (7: 54–8: 1a)
The rage of the judges (54). RV 'they were cut to the heart' is more expressive than NIV **they were furious** and preserves the metaphor behind *diapriō*. Stephen's words had revealed their fanaticism, rebellion and hypocrisy, and as they would not repent they raged against him with a vehemence more suited to a lynching than to proceedings before a court of law (57, 58). Some remnants of respect for procedure are seen in that the witnesses throw the first stones (cf. Lev. 24: 14) and Saul seems to have presided over the lapidation (58).

Stephen's vision (55, 56). The glory had departed from Jerusalem and was centred **at the right hand of God** where Stephen saw **the Son of Man standing** to receive him (cf. Lk. 12: 8). The relation between the vision and the theme of the speech must not be missed. Cf. Christ's own testimony before the same tribunal based on Dan. 7: 13, 14 (Mt. 26: 64–66).

Stephen's prayers and death (59, 60). Pilate was probably in Caesarea and faced with so many problems that Caiaphas and his associates felt it safe to take matters into their own hands, having Stephen stoned with no appeal for Rome's confirmation. Death by stoning was a dreadful proceeding but less shameful than crucifixion. Stephen's first prayer was analogous to his Master's last: **Lord Jesus, receive my spirit**, with obvious reference to the vision, which may have persisted to the end. His final prayer was like Christ's first petition from the cross: **Lord, do not hold this sin against them.** The leaders were perpetrating one more heinous crime, but Stephen longed for the blessing of the nation, despite this (cf. Rom. 9: 1–5).

Luke's simple and telling phrases stress the dramatic contrast between the cruel violence of the stoning and the inner peace and joy of the martyr and intercessor who **fell asleep** on earth in order to join his Lord in heaven.

Saul of Tarsus is named (7: 58; 8: 1a). The mention of Saul as presiding over the lapidation links the martyrdom to the first general persecution of the church, and, indirectly, to the subsequent phase of evangelization led by the former persecutor. He appears as an enemy, but 'the kicking against the goads' of conscience doubtless began as he listened to Stephen's testimony and saw his triumphal end. Saul was already a leader of Pharisaic Judaism (8: 1; 9: 1, 2; 22: 5; 26: 10; Gal. 1: 14), and, as he voted death sentences against the Nazarenes, he may have been a member of the Sanhedrin, despite his relative youth.

V. PERSECUTION AND EXPANSION (8: 1b–9: 43)
i. The Second Stage of Christian Witness (8: 1b–25)
The anonymous evangelists (8: 1b–4). Jerusalem had been thoroughly evangelized under the protection of the name, but Palestine was to hear the word by the lips of those who were scattered throughout its area by the fierce persecution raging in Jerusalem. Thus 'God fulfils Himself in many ways' and brings His purposes to pass through the wrath of men. We reach the second stage of the programme of 1: 8—'all Judea and Samaria'.

It is impossible to overstate the importance of individual witness in the spread of the gospel. Philip is mentioned later as God's messenger to Samaria, but **those who had been scattered preached the word wherever they went** (4). Hundreds of anonymous evangelists were preaching the gospel to thousands of souls, and the message became known over the whole area. When the preaching of the word is 'professionalized', a large part of the vitality of Christian witness is lost.

A severe persecution (8: 1b–4). The persecution probably affected the Hellenistic Christians much more than the Aramaic-speaking disciples, faithful to all the 'customs'. The apostles were respected, probably because some of their aura of popularity as workers of miracles persisted. The sweeping statement **all . . . were scattered** (1b) would probably be modified if one could see the picture in the writer's mind. The Twelve would scarcely have remained had there been no flock at all to care for, and many Hebrew Christians were found in Jerusalem later on.

Saul **began to destroy the church** (3) with the fierce energy of a devastating army. The details of 8: 1, 3 should be supplemented by Paul's future statements which revealed a conscience for his crimes which his future service never entirely stilled: 22: 4; 26: 9–11; 1 C. 15: 9; Gal. 1: 13; Eph. 3: 8; 1 Tim. 1: 13.

The **godly men** (2) who buried Stephen's body were probably pious Jews who could appreciate the power of the martyr's life and witness.

Philip in Samaria (8: 5–8, 12, 13). Different Greek texts give 'the city of Samaria' (AV, RV) or **a city in Samaria** (RSV; 'a city of Samaria'). A smaller city and its surrounding area fits the picture better than the busy, Hellenized capital, then called Sebaste. Good seed had been sown thereabouts by the Master Himself, and some must have flourished (Jn 4: 39–42). Although a Jew, Philip was well received, being helped by the 'credentials' of his miracles (6–8). His message is beautifully described (12) as **the good news of the kingdom of God and the name of Jesus**, which links the saving work of Christ with God's overall purpose in the kingdom. Believers were baptized, but no manifest evidence of the Spirit's power was granted them at first. This does not mean that they were not regenerate.

Simon Magus (9–11, 13). Simon seems to have had special knowledge and maybe demon help, which enabled him to work certain wonders and claim to be **the divine power known as the Great Power**. The Samaritans worshipped Jehovah, but probably thought of Simon as a special agent of Deity: 'God's grand vizier' as someone has suggested. He was impressed by Philip's spontaneous miracles, recognizing powers superior to his own, and so **believed.** Peter's stern denunciation in 20–23 shows that he never was regenerate. His baptism is the classic example of the outward sign wrongly applied to one whose profession of faith was not genuine.

The visit of Peter and John (14–25). Why did the Spirit not 'fall upon' the Samaritan believers as He did later on the Gentiles who received the word in Caesarea (10: 44–48)? It must be remembered that the Samaritans had maintained a Jehovistic worship for centuries, divorced from Jewish witness, God's channel of salvation (Jn 4: 22). The believers 'in the name' might have desired to run their own show, carrying the schism over to the church. For that reason Peter and John—who came from the hated Jerusalem, but were Christ's commissioned apostles—arrived to inspect the work in Samaria, and, recognizing the hand of the Lord, became the means of conveying the fulness of the Spirit by prayer and an act of identification, the 'laying on of hands'. The church was thus seen to be one, and Samaritans were blessed through the only channel of Christian testimony. The normative experience was clearly the reception of the Holy Spirit when men and women believed (10: 44; 19: 2; Eph. 1: 13; 1 C. 12: 13) and nothing is elsewhere known of any apostolic 'gift' by which the Spirit was bestowed. This is the exception, and must be explained as such. (We may note, also, that it must have been just as hard for the church in Jerusalem to recognize the Samaritans, as vice versa; cf. also Peter, Ac. 10: 14.)

Simon's errors (14–24). To Simon's unregenerate eyes, the manifestation of a new power in the believers sprang from a 'magic touch'. If he had *that* in his repertoire it would produce a wonderful effect on the multitudes! According to his standards, everything had its price, so that he offered to buy **the gift!** Hence the word 'simony' to describe the purchase of ecclesiastical offices. As Peter clearly saw, such a fundamental error meant that Simon was entirely foreign to the way of life. **Repent . . . pray . . . ,** said Peter, but Simon replies in effect: 'You pray for me to save me from the punishment!' (22–24), which shows that he still thought in terms of magic powers and of 'influence', having no desire to draw near to God personally as a repentant sinner. An anti-Christian sect called the Simonians existed in the second century, but the traditions which connect it with this Simon are unreliable.

ii. Philip Preaches to the Ethiopian (8: 26–40)
The minister of state (26–28). Ancient Ethiopia is not Abyssinia but ancient Nubia, south of Aswan, which was a highly developed area in antiquity. The king was considered as a god and retired from public view, so that active government devolved on the queen mother, who always bore the title of **Candace** (27). Her ministers would be eunuchs and among them the Chancellor of the Exchequer would be one of the most important. Jews penetrated into all lands which offered possibilities for commerce, so that the official may have heard of Jehovah, the God of Israel, through them. The long and arduous journey to Jerusalem was undertaken for **worship**, which indicates that the eunuch was at least a God-fearer. The story illustrates the great principle: 'He that seeketh findeth'. We imagine that the Ethiopian may have been disappointed in the temple ritual, but the only certain thing is that he acquired a roll of the prophet Isaiah which he eagerly read as he returned home (27, 28). The reading, the Spirit's command to Philip, the meeting between the seeker and the Lord's servant, illustrate very clearly God's providential workings (28, 29).

Reading and understanding (29–35). The meaning of Scripture is not always self-evident, even to the earnest seeker, and God provides those, who, having been taught themselves, are able to guide others (30, 31). The portion could not have been more suited to the Ethiopian's needs, but he echoed an ancient enquiry (34)—who was the Sufferer who overcame? The Jewish rabbis (especially of later date) sometimes thought in terms of suffering Israel;

the eunuch wondered if it could be Isaiah. The sublime prediction goes far beyond the experiences of a nation or a prophet, and the Lord Himself emphatically declared that the Suffering Servant of Jehovah of Isa. 42–53 was also the triumphant Messiah (Lk. 24: 25–27, 44–47). The apostles repeatedly underscored the lesson they had learnt from the Master (2 C. 5: 21; 1 Pet. 2:. 21–23; Phil. 2: 6–11). The quotation in vv. 32, 33 is from the LXX and the passage presents textual problems even in the MT. We can be sure that Philip included Isa. 53: 4–6 when he preached **the good news about Jesus** from this scripture. The lesson may have lasted for hours as the chariot was driven slowly on, and brought full conviction to the heart of the Nubian potentate. Jesus Christ was the Messiah, the Lamb of God, the Sinbearer!

The baptism of the Ethiopian (36–39). The sight of water—the road to Gaza crosses several river beds or wadis—suggested baptism to the new convert (37), for Philip had been faithful to the commission of Mt. 28: 19. The Ethiopian says in effect: 'Is there any requisite other than faith for baptism?' V. 37 of the AV is not in any good Greek text, but according to F. F. Bruce, the early insertion in the Western text 'certainly reflects primitive Christian practice' and constitutes the earliest known baptismal creed: 'I believe that Jesus Christ is the Son of God'. This baptism followed profession of faith. The joint descent into the water (38, 39) certainly suggests immersion.

Separation, joy and service (39, 40). This important case of conversion did not deflect Philip from his work as an evangelist which seems to have centred thenceforth on Caesarea, with special reference to the coastal area (40; cf. 21: 8). The new convert did not mourn the loss of his teacher, but rejoiced in his Saviour (39). The story is parenthetical in that it does not advance the story of the spread of the gospel westward, but shows how the good news was spread in all kinds of unlikely places during the early years. We can take it for granted that the eunuch witnessed in Nubia.

iii. Saul's Conversion and Call (9: 1–30)
Saul and his call. The Christian message was spreading over all Palestine, and before long Peter was to preach the gospel to a Gentile household, opening the door of the Kingdom to the uncircumcised. At this moment the Lord lays His hand on the Chief Inquisitor, who, in God's counsels, was to be the apostle to the Gentiles. Years were to pass before Barnabas and Saul set out on what is called the 'first missionary journey', but God commissioned his servant betimes so that he might be trained in secret before being recognized as the apostle who would complement the work of the Twelve in the Gentile world.

Long afterwards Paul spoke of God's providential workings in him from his very birth (Gal. 1: 15) for, born a Hebrew, son of Hebrew parents, trained in the best tradition of Judaism and yet a citizen of Tarsus and of the Empire, thoroughly conversant also with Hellenistic culture, he was ideally fitted to bridge East and West, bearing the message prepared and nurtured in Israel to the ends of the earth. His rare intellectual endowment was energized by a strong temperament which knew nothing of half-measures. As persecutor he was terrible, but once he had yielded obedience to Jesus the Christ, his loyalty was absolute and his service unstinting. This was God's chosen vessel, the great teaching apostle, commissioned by the glorified Lord to mark out the lines of missionary strategy and to be the principal 'steward of the mystery' of Christ and His church (Eph. 2; 3; Col. 1: 24–2: 7; 1 Tim. 1: 12–17; 2 Tim. 1: 8–12; Ac. 26: 16–20).

The conversion narratives. Luke emphasizes Paul's apostleship by giving the story of his conversion and commission three times in Acts: here, as a part of the general history; in 22: 3–16 as Paul's testimony before the Jews; in 26: 9–19 as the main element in his defence before Agrippa II. Differing purposes determine the slight differences of detail, mainly due to the degree of condensation.

A proposed extension of the persecution (1, 2). Saul breathed out threatenings against the Nazarenes after the supposed manner of fire-breathing dragons (1) and saw the danger of the spread of the 'disease' among the Jews of the Dispersion, where the Sanhedrin's influence was weaker. This body had certain extra-territorial powers over synagogues abroad, and the extradition of Jews for trial was not unknown. In Damascus some ten thousand Jews met in several synagogues, and news of the presence of Nazarenes among them had been received in Jerusalem.

Saul's rage was the more deeply inflamed by the thrusts of an uneasy conscience, which is the only explanation of his 'kicking against the goads' (26: 14). Conversions such as this are not produced in a psychological vacuum. For other references to the Christian faith as **the Way** see 18: 26; 19: 9; 22: 4; 24: 14, 22.

The encounter (3–6). The lightning-swift light (so the verb), brighter than Syria's noon-day sun, could only be the *shekinah* glory, indicative of the divine presence. From this glory came the amazing question: **Saul, Saul, why do you persecute me?** Who was the person who spoke thus? The voice from the glory could only be the voice of God; hence **Lord** in Paul's question, **Who are you, Lord?** (5), is meant as a divine title, not as a mere courtesy 'Sir'. **I am Jesus, whom you are persecuting** was the answer—a revelation

which meant that, in one tremendous moment of time, Saul had to identify the Lord Jehovah of the OT whom he zealously sought to serve, with Jesus of Nazareth whom he ferociously persecuted in the person of His saints. The shock to his innermost soul was tremendous and showed itself physically in the loss of sight; but once the identification had been made Saul had no doubts or reserves, and from that time forward could truthfully say: 'For to me, to live is Christ' (Phil. 1: 21). NIV preserves the true text of this narrative, but the added details of the later narratives should be noted. Paul's companions 'felt' the celestial presence but did not see the Lord; they heard Saul's voice, but not that of the Lord (7; 22: 9).

Ananias and Saul (7–19). Perhaps the three days' rest was necessary so that Saul might recover from the shock and meditate on the meaning of the celestial encounter before receiving further messages. The fact that Saul really *saw* the Lord (cf. 26: 16) is important from the point of view of his special apostleship (1 C. 9: 1; 15: 8).

Why was Ananias of Damascus chosen to convey Saul's commission (cf. 22: 14–16) instead of the apostles in Jerusalem? (*a*) As a Jewish Christian, who adhered to the 'customs' of Judaism, Ananias was an unimpeachable witness to the truth of Saul's call and apostleship. (*b*) It was fitting that Saul, the leading persecutor of the disciples, should be received into the fellowship by one of the despised Nazarenes in Damascus whom he had meant to seize. (*c*) An ecclesiastical reason becomes clear as we read Gal. 1: 15–2: 10, for it had to be made quite clear that Paul's apostleship was not received from men, but directly from the Lord. The intervention of Ananias supports the view that, in NT times, there was no idea of any special succcssion of grace flowing from the apostles. Ananias acted in a prophetic capacity, and his remonstrance (13) is not that of a stubborn servant, but is rather a sign of holy familiarity with his Lord. The directions were clear, and he learnt that the ex-persecutor was praying, having received a further preparatory vision.

Once his doubts were removed, Ananias thoroughly identified himself with the Lord's purpose: **Brother Saul**, he said, **the Lord— Jesus who appeared to you on the road . . . has sent me.** Again the placing of hands meant identification, for Saul now belonged to the people he had formerly persecuted. The scales fell from his eyes—something of symbolic import—and he received the fulness of the Spirit and was baptized (see note on 22: 16).

The terms of the commission (15, 16). For fuller detail of the commission see 26: 16–18. Even in this abbreviated account the following fundamental points stand out clearly: (*a*)

Saul was a 'chosen vessel' especially set aside by the Lord Himself (15). (*b*) He was to be the Lord's standard-bearer among **the Gentiles** (cf. Rom. 11: 13)—a special 'grace' finally recognized by all (Gal. 2: 7–9). (*c*) He was to witness before **kings** (men in high places) which is the theme of chs. 21–28. (*d*) A ministry to **the people of Israel** was not excluded, though it was to be largely rejected (22: 18). (*e*) He who had caused many to suffer was to be made an example of suffering for Christ's sake (16).

Witness in Damascus (19–25). Damascus was the scene of Saul's first fellowship with Christians and of his first service for the Lord, and Christological depth marked his earliest messages for he heralded Jesus as **Christ** and **Son of God** (20, 22). The Jews soon perceived the danger of the witness of an outstanding theologian turned renegade, and persecution was the natural result.

The visit to Arabia (Gal. 1: 17). Paul's own story of these days (Gal. 1: 13–20) is important, and he stressed the fact that he did not receive his authority from those who were apostles before him. The visit to Arabia is mentioned in relation to that theme, and its significance is limited by it. 'Arabia' (the Nabatean kingdom) was a large, ill-defined area cast of Syria and Palestine, reaching northwards from the Gulf of Akaba nearly to Damascus itself; any quiet spot where meditation was possible and revelations could continue would have suited his purpose, although the hostility of the Nabatean authorities (2 C. 11: 32) suggests that he also engaged in more active witness there. See pp. 1484 f., 1492.

The first visit to Jerusalem (26–30; cf. Gal. 1: 18, 19). Paul refers to this visit for the purpose already noted, while Luke is interested in it from the point of view of the spread of the gospel. Hence the difference in detail and emphasis. Saul's escape from Damascus was dramatic and humiliating (cf. 2 C. 11: 32 f.) and his reception by the saints in Jerusalem more than cool. Was the conversion story true, or was Saul's approach the action of an *agent provocateur*? Fortunately Barnabas had full knowledge of the facts, and was able to present Saul as one who had seen the Lord and witnessed in Damascus (27). Saul's hope that his witness to his old companions of the Hellenistic synagogues would be effective was not realized (cf. 22: 17–21) and a plot was soon laid to take his life. The journey to Tarsus initiates the hidden period of Saul's life during which he was probably disowned by his family and suffered the 'loss of all things' (Phil. 3: 8). It may be highly probable that he witnessed in the synagogues of Cilicia and that certain sufferings listed in 2 C. 11: 21–28 belong to this period. We do not meet him again until Barnabas

sought him as a co-worker in Antioch (11: 25, 26).

iv. Peter's Apostolic Labours (9: 31–43)
Peace and prosperity (31). This *résumé* sums up the situation following Saul's conversion, when the saints in Palestine enjoyed a period of peace and prosperity. The mainspring of the persecution had been broken, while the Jews had other matters to think about, especially when Caligula insisted that his image should be set up in the temple. The danger of rebellion was only averted by the assassination of the emperor in A.D. 41. Believers, however, walking in the fear of the Lord, were multiplied. The expression **the church throughout Judea . . .** is quite special, for everywhere else in the NT 'church' in the singular is either the whole company of the redeemed, or else a certain local church—never a federation of local churches. The exception is due to Luke's sensitiveness to historical development, for, at that moment, believers throughout Palestine still felt themselves to be members of the original Jerusalem community.

Peter's journey (32). This verse emphasizes the wide range of Peter's apostolic labours. The groups formed by anonymous witness were not left to fend for themselves but received pastoral and teaching visits from Peter, and, most probably, from other apostles and missionaries as well.

The healing of Aeneas (33–35). Lydda was on the route from Jerusalem to Joppa, where the foothills merge into the Plain of Sharon—a likely place to have received early Christian witness. Once again a miracle was God's megaphone, directing attention to a powerful and saving word. The form of address from the apostle to the sick man is very direct: **Aeneas . . . Jesus Christ heals you**. Peter spoke, but the Lord was present in healing power, and the man gave proof of his faith as he arose and rolled up his pallet. **All those who lived in Lydda** may be a relative term—all whose hearts were opened by the sign to receive the saving word. Quite probably, however, we are intended to envisage a mass-movement.

The raising of Tabitha (36–43). This story takes us back in spirit to the simplicity and power of the Gospel narratives of healing. We do not know exactly what the brethren of Joppa hoped for when they sent for Peter, but they knew that his presence would be a help in a moment of deep sorrow and distress. Tabitha ('Gazelle') had beautified herself by good works and her departure was much lamented (39). On his arrival Peter needed to be alone with the 'God who raises the dead', in the presence of the corpse, in order to discern His will. His prayer as he knelt reminds us of the spiritual struggles of Elijah and Elisha in similar circumstances. Peter received the assurance he sought and turned to the body with the simple command: **Tabitha, get up.** What a moment when the greathearted sister was presented again to the believers—alive! (41). The high value of Tabitha's previous testimony underlined the powerful message of the miracle and **many people believed in the Lord**. By these means Peter had been led of God to the place where he was to receive new and strange marching orders, constituting one of the greatest landmarks in the history of redemption (43).

VI. GENTILES ENTER THE KINGDOM (10: 1–11: 18)

i. The Meaning of Caesarea

A crucial moment. The commission of Mt. 28: 19 includes all nations but the ultimate goal was reached by the stages we have noted already. The apostle to the Gentiles was converted and commissioned while the gospel was preached in the whole of Palestine. Peter, prepared by various experiences for the great new lesson he was to learn and teach, was now to open the door of the kingdom to the Gentiles by the only possible 'key'—the Word preached in the power of the Holy Spirit (Mt. 16: 19).

Caesarea, an extension of Pentecost. Peter expressly associates the event in Cornelius's house with that of Pentecost and with the Lord's purpose to baptize His own by the Holy Spirit, so that in Caesarea the one fundamental provision was made available to Gentile believers, as it is to each believer united by faith to the one body (1 C. 12: 12, 13).

No Jew imagined that Gentiles could not be saved, but—quite logically as far as God had then revealed His thoughts—all were convinced that Gentiles must become Jewish proselytes if they were to share in messianic blessings. God's working and revelation in this crisis made it clear to submissive hearts that the cross opened the door of salvation to all mankind on equal terms, for *all* must repent and believe in order to be saved. Jews were thus put on a level with the 'sinners of the Gentiles' (Gal. 2: 14–17).

ii. Divine Messages and an Encounter (10: 1–33)

Cornelius and his vision (1–8). An **Italian Regiment** is known to have served in Syria in A.D. 69. Cornelius was in command of 100 men, part of the Caesarean garrison. Centurions had the responsibilities of captains but were non-commissioned officers. Cornelius must have had some private fortune as he maintained a large establishment and gave alms generously. He was obviously a 'God-fearer', a Gentile who attended the synagogue services and modified his way of life so as not to scandalize the Jews. Above all, he is a classic example of the type of Gentile, who, in patient well-doing, sought 'for glory, honour, incorruption

and eternal life' (Rom. 2: 7, 10). His prayers and alms did not gain him salvation, but were the outward signs of an attitude of soul which God could bless.

A **vision** is 'something seen' not normal to human sight, and one was granted to Cornelius as he gave himself to prayer at **about three in the afternoon** (cf. 3: 1). His fright was natural but he accepted the situation at once and listened carefully to the good news given by the angel. There is no sensationalism in the narrative; the exact instruction of the angel reads like an address on an envelope: Mr. Simon Peter, c/o Mr. Simon, The Tannery, Sea Road, Joppa. With military promptness Cornelius obeyed the instructions received from heaven (3–8).

Peter's vision and its confirmation (9–23). By special providences God prepared his servant Peter for the visit of Cornelius' emissaries. Peter's hunger was an element of revelation, and one may imagine that he was gazing at the elongated lateen sail of a boat entering the harbour as he waited for his food. In his trance the unclean animals he was commanded to kill and eat were gathered up in a sail-like object lowered from the sky. The command seemed all wrong, for a Jew had not only to reject the unclean animals listed in Lev. 11, but also to refuse all meat not prepared in the *kosher* manner. His protest was very 'Peter-like', but the voice repeated the command three times, with the epoch-making explanation: **'Do not call anything impure that God has made clean'** (15; cf. Mk 7: 19). Voices in the street below were enquiring for Peter and at that very moment the message of the vision was confirmed by a command given by the Lord the Spirit: 'Go with these men; **I have sent them**.' Further resistance would have been rebellion. The pieces of the jig-saw puzzle were falling into place as the apostle learnt that God had made possible the cleansing of all men (cf. 28).

The journey and the reception (24–33). Next day Peter set out northward with witnesses from Joppa and the messengers from Cornelius. The distance was about 30 miles. The reception was warm, for a company of hungry souls were waiting for God's messenger. The verb for 'reverence' (25) is *proskyneō*, which can mean a man's reverence for a superior, and the sight of a Roman centurion at the feet of a Galilean fisherman was remarkable evidence of the revolutionary changes wrought within the sphere of the kingdom. The mutual explanations (27–33) are quite clear and the well-known v. 33 shows that never did a preacher have before him a better prepared audience.

iii. Peter's Message to Gentiles (10: 34–43)

Introduction (34, 35). The general features of

the early *kerygma* are all present, but adapted to a company of Gentiles. As many were God-fearers, some reference to the prophets was possible (43), but the emphasis falls mainly on the life, death and resurrection of Jesus Christ as a historical reality witnessed to by the Twelve. In his introduction Peter shows that he had learnt the lesson of the house-top vision (34, 35).

Phases of the main message (36–43). *God's word to Israel in Christ Jesus* (36–38). The partially known facts of our Lord's earthly ministry were authoritatively interpreted for these Gentiles. Jesus Christ was **Lord of all**, the Preacher of **peace**, God's Anointed for a ministry of healing, restoration and spiritual liberty.

The apostolic witness (39–42). The apostles were **witnesses of everything he did** in Jerusalem and Palestine (=**the country of the Jews**). The tremendous significance of the death and resurrection of Christ demanded the best of proofs of the fact itself, and these were supplied by men chosen to accompany the risen Lord. The mention of the central fact of the cross is brief and undoctrinal (39), but the typical *kerygma* declaration follows: **but God raised him . . . on the third day and caused him to be seen**—not publicly, but to the body of **witnesses** to which Peter belonged.

The prophetic and apostolic messages (42, 43). Peter joined the prophetic witness of the OT with the historic witness of the Twelve in order to show that Christ was ordained by God not only as final Judge of all, but also as the Saviour who gives **forgiveness of sins** to all believers. There was much more to say, but the saving facts had been announced, and were immediately received by faith.

iv. The Holy Spirit Falls on Gentile Believers (10: 44–48)

The gift of the Holy Spirit (44–46). The 'hearing' was the submission of faith which united these souls to the Lord in whom they believed. The power of the Holy Spirit fell on the believers at once, investing them with celestial energies and gifts by which they spoke with tongues and glorified God (45, 46; cf. 2: 3, 4, 11). The Pentecostal baptism was extended to Gentile believers on the sole ground of repentance and faith in Christ.

Baptism in the Name (47, 48). Peter's question (47) is a kind of challenge, addressed especially to the Jewish Christians brought from Joppa. Despite the absence of circumcision, the Gentile believers had received the Holy Spirit just as the Jewish believers had received Him in the upper room. Who could **keep** them from the **water** of baptism? By that symbolic act they passed visibly to the sphere of the name, having been transferred from the realm of darkness to the kingdom of God's beloved Son (Col. 1: 13), apart from any prior link with Israel. The repercussions from Peter's decision would be felt throughout the world and for all time.

v. Reactions in Jerusalem (11: 1–18)

An inevitable question (1–3). It was natural that the **apostles and the brothers throughout Judea** would want to know the meaning of the extraordinary happenings in Caesarea. 'They that were of the circumcision' (RV) is an alternative to **the circumcised believers**. Such a party was formed only following these discussions. These men asked why Peter had broken the rules of ordinary Jewish living (2, 3).

Peter's defence (4–17). Peter, backed by the witnesses from Joppa, defended his action in the only way possible—by telling the story of God's dealings with him and Cornelius. The connection between Caesarea and Pentecost comes out clearly (15): **the Holy Spirit came on them as he had come on us at the beginning**, and this is linked with the Master's promise based on the Baptist's prophecy (16; 1: 4, 5). All must submit to what God had clearly revealed, strange though the lesson might be.

The consequences (18). The spiritual leaders of the churches in Judea accepted the new revelation and glorified God. Many Jewish Christians, however, might hear only partial accounts of the event, which seemed to them quite insufficient to demolish the apparently inexpugnable position of Israel as presented in the OT 'Let the message be preached to the Gentiles', they said, 'but on believing they must be circumcised and placed on the basis of the Jewish covenant.' These conservative Jewish Christians became known as the Judaizers. We shall meet them again in ch. 15 and the Letter to the Galatians is the inspired answer to their pleas, which would have reduced Christianity to the dimensions of a Jewish sect.

VII. ANTIOCH, A NEW CENTRE OF MISSIONARY ACTIVITY (11: 19–30)

An extended witness (19–21). Years had passed since the dispersion noted in 8: 1, 4, but waves of blessing still resulted from the original impetus. Jews had been reached by Hellenistic Christians in Phoenicia, Cyprus and Antioch —the great Syrian capital which bridged East and West. It may be assumed that Jewish Christians in Antioch soon heard of the great happening in Caesarea, and would thus be emboldened to preach Jesus as Lord to the Gentiles, many of whom were heartily sick of the 'gods many and lords many' of paganism. Using a Hebrew idiom, Luke tells us that **the Lord's hand was with** the anonymous witnesses so that **a great number** of Gentiles turned to the Lord (20, 21).

Barnabas in Antioch (22–24). On hearing the news of a mass movement among the Gentiles, the Jerusalem Church neither sought to impose the authority of the 'mother church' nor did it wash its hands of an important happening. Instead the brethren sent Barnabas, the man of grace and wisdom, to see if the work was of God, and to act accordingly. He greatly helped this new church, composed of believers from Jews and Gentiles, contributing what was needed in line with the Spirit's operations.

Barnabas and Saul in Antioch (25, 26). Barnabas was humble enough to recognize his need of help in teaching, so sought and found Saul in Tarsus. A wonderful partnership in service was established, by which the church was built up. The emphasis during a year's labour was on the teaching of the word (26). So many people were now talking about Christ in Antioch that their presence was felt by the populace, who coined the nick-name **Christians**, i.e. 'Christ's men'. In early times this name was mainly used by outsiders or by enemies (26: 28; 1 Pet. 4: 16).

Barnabas and Saul in Jerusalem (27–30). Extra-biblical history mentions periods of scarcity during the reign of Claudius (A.D. 41–54), one of which especially affected Judea (28). The prophecy of Agabus stirred up loving generosity among the saints in Antioch, who knew that the Judean brethren would be the chief sufferers, so that each gave according to his ability—a principle afterwards to be established on a wider scale in 2 C. 8: 9. Barnabas and Saul were the bearers of the gift to the elders in Jerusalem.

The date of Saul's second visit to Jerusalem as a Christian is fixed in general terms as being that of the Herodian persecution (12: 1, 25) and in the writer's view cannot be made to coincide with that of Gal. 2: 1–10. The following factors should be considered: (*a*) Dates may not be changed in order to fit an *a priori* hypothesis, and that of this visit is A.D. 44. (*b*) The circumcision question did not become acute until after the great blessings of the first missionary journey (15: 1, 2). (*c*) Luke still uses the term **Barnabas and Saul** which marks the period prior to the general recognition of Paul's apostolic 'grace', which was manifested by the Spirit's working through him during the first journey. As a helper of Barnabas, he could not have defended his apostleship in the terms of Gal. 2: 1–10. The turning point is found in 13: 13. (*d*) The recommendation to 'remember the poor' of Gal. 2: 10 would sound strangely when Barnabas and Saul were in Jerusalem for the express purpose of passing on the Antiochene gift to the Judean poor. (For another view than that propounded here see notes on Gal. 2: 1–10, pp. 1419 ff.)

VIII. HEROD'S ATTACK ON THE CHURCH (12: 1–25)
i. Herod, the Apostles and the Church (12: 1–17)
Herod Agrippa I. This monarch was the son of Aristobulus, fruit of Herod the Great's marriage with the Hasmonean princess, Mariamne. He was clever, charming, ambitious and unscrupulous. He was utterly loyal to Rome, having been helped by both Caligula and Claudius to wide authority in Palestine, but knew the importance of gaining the sympathy of the Jewish leaders in order to consolidate a kingdom practically co-terminous with that of Herod the Great, over which he ruled from A.D. 41 to 44. A persecution of the Nazarene sect was an easy way to ingratiate himself with the Jews, and he saw the importance of striking down the leaders (1, 2).

The Lord and His servants (1–5). Why did the Lord allow James to be beheaded while He intervened miraculously to deliver Peter? The answer is found in the mystery itself, for we cannot possibly investigate the reasons which determine the lifespan of God's servants on earth, but we can be sure that God was glorified both in the martyrdom of James—the first martyr among the apostles—and in the deliverance of Peter (cf. Mt. 20: 20–23).

The praying church (5, 12). Many foolish remarks have been made about the Church which prayed and was surprised at the answer. This church was a company of potential martyrs, skilled in the ways of the Lord, and assured that any one of them might glorify God either by life or by death (cf. Phil. 1: 19–24). As real, human people, they *were* surprised at the *manner* of Peter's deliverance—should not we have been?—but the Jerusalem church is a model of constant prayer and faith on a sublime level.

The deliverance (6–11). Agrippa wanted to make quite sure that his important prisoner should not escape (6)! Peter had denied his Lord at that very time of the year, but in this case he slept soundly on what seemed to be his last night on earth (cf. 1 Pet. 5: 7). God had His plan for Peter, the need was urgent, and man could do nothing about the problem, which explains angelic intervention. All the phrases and circumstances indicate a *heavenly* messenger who limited his help to what Peter could not do for himself (7, 8, 10). As soon as the apostle was free, he had to 'come to' and think for himself (11).

Peter and the Christian company (12–17). Peter supposed that believers would be gathered for prayer in Mary's house, so presented himself there. The story of his knocking at the outside door, of Rhoda's surprise and confusion, with the reactions of the believers, stands out clearly in Luke's graphic style. The psychological reasonableness of every point convinces us of its truth—an invention in the style of later martyrologies would have been very different! The disciples' supposition that it was **his angel** must be read with Mt. 18: 10. 'The angel is here conceived of as a man's spiritual counterpart, capable of assuming his appearance and being mistaken for him' (F. F. Bruce). The good news was to be given **to James and the brothers**, which indicates that James, the brother of our Lord, was in Jerusalem at the time, but not any other apostle. The **brothers** would include the elders of the church (17, cf. 15: 4, 22). Peter **left for another place**—probably one of the many convenient hiding places in the Judean hills. The regular meeting-places of the church would be the first to be raided when Herod's search-parties set to work. There was no bravado, and no assumption that miraculous deliverances would be repeated.

ii. The End of Herod Agrippa I (12: 18–25)
The dramatic contrast between the apostle's deliverance by an angel and the end of the proud, persecuting monarch, smitten by an angel in the moment of being acclaimed as a god, is obvious to all. Josephus speaks of a feast in honour of the emperor in Caesarea, while Luke notes the end of a crisis between Herod and Phoenicia, but this information is complementary and not contradictory. It must be remembered that Herod was a professing Israelite and as a monotheist, claiming to sit on David's throne, could not accept the king-god concept so common in the East. The crowd's adulation: **'The voice of a god, not of a man!'** (22) was the climax of a life of tortured ambitions changed by the God he defied into a death sentence. Herod's dream was thwarted for ever. **But the word of God continued to increase and spread** (24).

IX. THE SYSTEMATIC EVANGELIZATION OF THE GENTILES: PAUL'S FIRST MISSIONARY JOURNEY (13: 1–14: 28)
i. Paul's Missionary Strategy
The first missionary journey is the beginning of a systematic apostolic work among the nations, which determines the fulfilment of the last stage of the over-all plan. The outstanding figure is Paul, for during this journey Barnabas's colleague was shown to be God's chosen vessel as apostle to the Gentiles. Not only did Paul receive revelations regarding the nature and constitution of the church (Eph. 2: 11–3: 11; Col. 1: 25, 26) but he was also the great missionary strategist, to whom God commended His plan for heralding the *kerygma* to the Gentiles. He saw the need of establishing centres of witness in busy ports and other centres of communication, counting on the gifts that the Holy Spirit would raise up in the new churches—not only for the edification of the believers, but also for the extension of the gospel in surrounding areas. The early visits to local synagogues did more than comply with the established order 'to the Jew first', for they also provided a nucleus of pious converts in each place, already instructed in the OT scriptures. The help of various colleagues made it possible to confirm new churches by visits, and Paul's Letters were also written with this end in view. But Paul never settled permanently in any one area, understanding that God had commissioned him as a spiritual pioneer. By such means a vast area was evangelized, stretching from Palestine to the Adriatic, in little more than a decade, *c.* A.D. 45–57. See Rom. 15: 17–21.

ii. Barnabas and Saul Separated for Special Service (13: 1–4a)
The prophets and teachers in Antioch (1, 2). It is important to note that God's purpose was made known to certain **prophets and teachers**, experienced in the ways of God, and willing to wait on Him by worship, prayer and fasting. It was such men—and not the Antiochene church as such—who received the message providing for the systematic evangelization of the Gentiles, and we may believe that they were praying under the sense of this very need. The command **Set apart for me Barnabas and Saul . . .** probably came by means of a prophetic message.

The separation (2–4). This is no ordination, for Saul was an apostle with long years of service behind him, and Barnabas was a spiritual father to the Antiochene church, devoted to the Lord's work for many years. When the Holy Spirit indicated that these two outstanding workers were to lead the next forward movement, their colleagues bowed to the Lord's will and identified themselves with Barnabas and Saul by the act of laying on of hands. The church was doubtless present at the final act (14: 26). The sending by the brethren was merely an act of fellowship, for they being **sent on their way by the Holy Spirit, went down to Seleucia** (4).

iii. Witness in Cyprus (13: 4b–13)
The route (4–6). Seleucia was Antioch's port, and the missionaries sailed from there to Cyprus, Barnabas's native island, taking with them John Mark, cousin to Barnabas. Personal links would be helpful, but the first steps of this stage of the journey look rather like a 'family concern'. The typical work of evangelizing the Gentiles did not really get under way until the party arrived at the mainland under Paul's leadership. In Salamis **they proclaimed the word of God in the Jewish synagogues** (5) and then seem to have passed rapidly

through the island westward until they reached the capital, Paphos.

Sergius Paulus (6–12). The missionaries presumably preached to Jews and Gentiles in Paphos, but Luke focuses our attention on an incident which brought Paul into prominence as the God-appointed leader of the expedition. Sergius Paulus was senatorial proconsul of Cyprus, and, like many thoughtful men of his day, interested in the mysticism of the East. Hence Elymas ('the learned one') attracted his attention. Probably Bar-Jesus was the man's Jewish name and 'Elymas' his professional title. When Sergius Paulus heard of Barnabas and Saul and summoned them to his presence, the jealous ire of the false prophet was roused, and he probably denounced the Nazarene 'heresy' (8). Then **Saul, who was also called Paul** (9) **filled with the Holy Spirit**, openly declared the deceit and villainy of Elymas, pronouncing a doom of temporary blindness upon him—a punishment fitted to the crime of making a living by deepening the spiritual blindness of his dupes (9–11). There is every reason to think that the proconsul really believed, being interested in the word rather than the sign (see phrases in 7, 8, 12); Sir William Ramsay found indications that some members of the family later became prominent in Christian circles in Asia Minor (*The Bearing of Recent Discovery on the Trustworthiness of the NT*, 1915, pp. 150 ff.).

The name Paul. Saul was the apostle's Jewish name, and **Paul** would be his cognomen as a Roman citizen. The latter was more fitted for the leader of an evangelistic mission to the Gentiles, and Luke does not drop into using it casually, but notes thereby that the Paphos incident brought to a head the wide recognition of the 'signs' of Paul's apostleship, which publicly confirmed the secret call on the Damascus road. The expression 'Barnabas and Saul' is dropped as belonging to a transitional stage which had now been superseded, and it was **Paul and his companions** who set sail to Pamphylia (13). (As a Roman citizen Paul was in a special class, but for the custom—at least as early as the second century B.C.—of Jews' having a Gentile as well as a Jewish name cf. Ac. 12: 12, 'John, also called Mark'.)

On to Pisidian Antioch (13: 13–16). John Mark's defection in Perga may have been due to his dislike of the change of leadership by which Paul seemed to displace his revered cousin. Tragic indirect results would follow later. There is not the slightest hint in Luke's story that Paul fell sick in Perga and decided to get to the healthier climate of the interior, which is Ramsay's supposition in support of the 'South Galatian' theory of the destination of the Letter to the Galatians, according to which the 'churches' of Gal. 1: 2 were those

planted during the present journey (*St. Paul the Traveller*, pp. 95 ff.). The crossing of the Taurus mountains would have been a difficult undertaking for a sick man. Gal. 4: 13 attributes the evangelization of the Galatians to a sudden change of plan due to serious illness, whereas it is precisely at this point in the Acts narrative that Paul comes to the fore as leader and decides to get to Pisidian Antioch because it was an important road junction. Luke details the synagogue message and general procedure in Pisidian Antioch as typical of Paul's strategy, and as a model for future operations. Pisidian Antioch was not actually in Pisidia, but in Phrygia, part of which was temporarily included in the Roman province of Galatia—a fact which did not affect ethnic and linguistic factors. (A judicious statement of the cases for and against the 'South Galatian' and 'North Galatian' views respectively is given by D. Guthrie in his *NT Introduction: The Pauline Epistles*, 1961, pp. 72 ff.)

iv. Paul's Kerygma to the Jews (13: 14–41) Paul and Barnabas in the synagogue (14–16). The importance of beginning the witness in new territory in the local synagogue has already been noted. Division and persecution were bound to follow the preaching, but meanwhile the Messiah had been presented to the Jews, according to God's plan, and the first converts were either Jews or God-fearers—i.e. men nurtured in the Scriptures, of a high moral standing and completely free from the degrading influences of paganism. The importance of such a nucleus in the local churches can scarcely be overestimated and accounts for the stability of the witness in the early years. The order of service in the synagogue, and the function of the rulers are sufficiently indicated in v. 15. (See also *NBD, art.* Synagogue.)

The general theme. Paul's presentation of the *kerygma* to the Jews of the Dispersion should be compared with Peter's when he faced the Jews in Jerusalem (2: 14–36; 3: 12–26; etc.). The main points will be seen to be identical, but adapted to an audience far from the scene of the cross and resurrection. Paul, like Stephen, reviews Israel's history, but his purpose is to show God at work until the promises are fulfilled in Jesus the Messiah, rejected by the Jerusalem leaders, but divinely approved by the mighty act of resurrection. The pivotal point is the raising up of David, who links on to the Son of David.

God's dealings with Israel until the time of David (17–21). Israel was chosen by God, and therefore delivered from Egypt and introduced into Canaan. The times of the judges and of Saul were of relative failure, but God had prepared His king who would do all His will. The **450 years** (19) may extend from the patriarchs to the beginning of the judges, as the period in which God ordered the giving of the land.

David's Son and John's witness (23–25). David was a man who fulfilled God's will **in his own generation** (36, 37) but whose Son was to be the Messiah. This would strike a sympathetic chord in the hearts of Jewish hearers, but they would be amazed when they heard: **From this man's descendants God has brought to Israel the Savior Jesus, as he promised** (23). The introduction of John the Baptist's testimony before an audience of the Dispersion was telling, as he was widely believed to have been a prophet (24, 25).

The happenings in Jerusalem (26–31). The Jews of Antioch, would, of course, have heard garbled reports about the crucifixion and it was a delicate matter to report on the great rejection. Paul insists on the message of salvation in Jesus (26) and attributes the rejection to (a) the leaders' lack of recognition of their Messiah; and (b) their lack of a true understanding of the messianic prophecies relating to the sufferings of Jehovah's Servant (27–29). As in Peter's preachings, there is a strong emphasis here on the resurrection as God's act which negated the leaders' verdict and made possible the preaching of the good news; the incredible is made credible by the reliable witness of the early apostles (30, 31).

Paul's message (32–41). On the basis of God's manifest work of salvation Paul can say: **we tell you the good news . . .** (32). The basic fact of the resurrection of Jesus is proved, as with Peter, by references to the Psalms and Isaiah (see also 30, 31). God's purposes of blessing through the Son (linked with David) were announced in Ps. 2: 7 and Isa. 55: 3, and the Messiah who saw no corruption was prophesied in Ps. 16: 10 (cf. 2: 25–31). **Therefore, my brothers, I want you to know . . .** introduces Paul's application of God's great saving work to the needs of the Jews of Antioch; vv. 38 and 39 are characteristically Pauline. Paul's great verb *dikaioō* is obscured in RSV. Read as in RV: 'Through this man is proclaimed unto you remission of sins; and by him everyone that believeth is justified from all things, from which ye could not be justified by the law of Moses.' (See also vv. 38, 39 in NEB.) Both the context here and the sum of Paul's teaching in Romans and Galatians give the meaning that the law cannot justify the 'worker' from anything, since all his works are stained with sin, so that only the believer who establishes vital contact with the Saviour who died and rose again is 'justified' from all things. The remission of sins had often been stressed in Peter's *kerygma*, but here we have a preview of Paul's doctrine of justification by faith. The warning (41) is taken from Hab. 1: 5. In the prophecy wilful sinners would be overwhelmed by the judgments which were to fall on Judah during the Babylonian invasion. Here the **scoffers** (perhaps Paul saw some already in the congregation) were in danger of a final judgment on unbelief.

v. Typical Reactions to the Message (13: 42–52)
First converts (42, 43). Paul's message had an immediate effect on a number of Jews and pious Gentile God-fearers whose new-found faith caused them to follow the missionaries for further instruction.

Opposition and division (44–48). The news that a powerful new message was being preached in the synagogue by visitors from Palestine brought a great crowd together on the following Sabbath, but this widespread interest had the effect of stirring up the jealous opposition of unbelieving Jewish leaders. Obviously they created such tensions in the synagogue that Paul and Barnabas had to withdraw with their converts, but not before they had pointed out the necessity of a first message to Israelites, the rejection of which opened the way for a full testimony to the Gentiles. The Christ-rejectors showed by their attitude that they were **not . . . worthy of eternal life** and Isa. 49: 6 was quoted as evidence that the Messiah-Servant, proclaimed by His messengers, was to be a means of **salvation to the ends of the earth** (46, 47). We must not deduce any change of policy from v. 46, for Paul returned again and again to the Jews of the synagogues after this date. We can well imagine the joy of the Gentiles as they entered the kingdom through faith in Christ, knowing that they, too, as believers, showed that they were on heaven's list of citizens (**appointed** is *tetagmenoi*, enrolled or inscribed, 48).

Extension and expulsion (49–52). Hundreds of converts became God's witnesses to the surrounding area, and this factor will be assumed in future instances. In the meantime hostile Jews succeeded in enlisting the help of God-fearing women of social standing who could influence their relatives in high places. Thus the resulting persecution and mob pressure was directed from above; or, at least, was carried through with the connivance of the authorities. As the missionaries' commission was to preach everywhere, and contacts in Antioch were being made difficult or impossible, their purpose was better forwarded by flight to Iconium, but not before they had pronounced a typical symbolic judgment on the Christ-rejectors (51; cf. Mt. 10: 14 and parallels). The disciples left in Antioch depended on the Lord, and so **were filled with joy and with the Holy Spirit** despite their tribulations and the loss of their spiritual leaders (52).

vi. Witness in Phrygia and Lycaonia (14: 1–20)

Work in Iconium (1–5). This city lay to the east of Antioch, and was also a centre of communications and a garrison town. The missionaries' experiences in Antioch were repeated in large measure in their next centre of witness. Undeterred by former sufferings, they went together to the synagogue and **a great number of Jews and Gentiles believed**. There soon came a first reaction against the message and the messengers (2) which did not hinder a prolonged stay in the town, during which Paul and Barnabas exhibited their apostolic credentials of **signs and wonders**. The good effect produced by the miracles doubtless enabled them to resist pressure longer than in Antioch, but possible outside influences (cf. 19) finally provoked a violent persecution supported by the rulers. Stoning was talked of, and the Lord's servants once more followed the divinely indicated strategy in such cases (6; cf. Mt. 10: 14, 23). We may suppose the same joy and power in the newly formed church, as was evident in Antioch. Iconium was on the borders of Phrygia and Lycaonia, and the escape route led to Lystra, due south, in the heart of Lycaonia.

Ministry and a miracle (8–13). The healing of the lame man was not the first happening in Lystra. The missionaries had preached in the surrounding country, and doubtless had given their usual testimony in the synagogue, and we may deduce that Timothy was converted at that time (6, 7; cf. 16: 1, 2). Luke has no need to detail a type of work already well known, and goes on to something which reveals Paul's methods in an area on the margin of the Hellenistic world. The story of the miracle is similar to that of the healing of the lame man at the temple gate by Peter (3: 1–8), although the reactions of a Gentile crowd are very different. Paul had doubtless preached in the open air in such a way that the lame man was attracted to the message and **had faith to be healed**. The command is forthright, and the leaping up and walking instantaneous (9, 10). The ignorant crowd was impressed, but Paul could not speak to them of the power of the God of Abraham, as Peter had done to the Jews. The excited shouting went on in the Lycaonian speech, not in Greek, so that the apostles seem not to have been aware that the priest of Zeus was taking advantage of the miracle to prepare sacrifices and garlands. That gods should have come down to perform works of mercy seemed the more probable in Lystra as a local legend preserved the story of the hospitality which a pious couple dispensed to Zeus and Hermes, unaware of the quality of their guests. That a miracle can be a godsend to a local shrine has been obvious throughout the history of world religions.

The message proclaimed to ignorant pagans (17, 18). The great interest of this section lies in the way Paul sought to gain entrance for at least a minimum of light in the understandings of uncultured pagans; his fundamental approach is analogous to the one he used to the learned pagans of the Areopagus, though the terms are so different. The missionaries first used 'sign language' by avoiding any raised dais and rushing among the people, tearing their clothes in token of their horror. Paul was probably the speaker and proclaimed that they were merely men, albeit 'men with a message', which was aimed precisely at turning deceived human beings from the worship of hollow vanities to that of the living Creator God, whose handiwork all could see. Generations had passed with no special revelation in pagan lands, though God's goodness in providing for **crops in their seasons** for the satisfaction and gladness of men had been a constant witness to His being and to His providence (15–17). This was doubtless intended as an introduction to a more concrete presentation of Christ and His saving work, and we suppose that some doubtless were led to seek fuller light. The rest, however, were disappointed with the 'gods' who refused to function, and their disillusionment made them the more ready to receive a very different impression when the Jews from Antioch arrived.

'Given up to death for Jesus' sake' (19, 20: cf. 2 C. 4: 11). There is no need for Luke to stress the fickleness, cruelty and violence of men living under demon-controlled systems of idolatry. The simple statements of two verses reveal both the hatred of religious enemies of the gospel and the crazy reactions of the Lystra mob, who stoned the 'god' of yesterday and **dragged him outside the city**, leaving him for dead. But Paul considered himself as under constant sentence of death, and trusted God who raises the dead (Rom. 4: 17; 2 C. 1: 9, 10; 4: 7–14). He was not dead, as many supposed, but was miraculously helped to overcome utter prostration and dangerous wounds so as to set out on his journey to Derbe next day. Timothy was a witness of what it cost to serve the living God in spheres under the sway of heathendom (2 Tim. 3: 10–13).

vii. The Return Journey to Syrian Antioch (14: 21–28)

Derbe, end of the outward journey (20, 21). In Derbe, south-east of Lystra, near the border of the Galatian province, a strong church was founded. Over the other side of the Taurus range was Paul's native town of Tarsus, but he and his company turned back from Derbe along the route of their triumphs and sufferings.

Confirming the churches (22, 23). The dangerous return journey well illustrates Paul's set purpose of strengthening the churches he left so quickly after their foundation. Although the Lycaonian and Phrygian churches showed no sign of spiritual fluctuation, Paul exhorted them to constancy in the inevitable tribulation. He was also able to discern what the Holy Spirit had done in his absence, for a number of brethren in each church had given proof of having received the pastoral gift, and these were appointed as elders. The special prayer and fasting of v. 23 seems to be related to the act of committing these leaders to the Lord, for much would depend on their faithfulness and zeal. Ac. 20: 17–35 beautifully illustrates the relationship which existed between the apostles and the elders of the different churches, as also between the latter and the flocks they shepherded. It is widely agreed that during the apostolic age, elder=bishop (overseer)=pastor (cf. 20: 17, 28), and that there was a plurality of these in each local church, forming the 'presbytery' (1 Tim. 4: 14).

A welcome in Syrian Antioch (24–28). After preaching the word in Perga, Paul and his company sailed to Syrian Antioch from Attalia. The whole church of the home base is more in evidence in the return of the missionaries than in their departure, and they were able to report on a work fulfilled, since God had widely opened the door of faith to the Gentiles. The chronology of the first journey and of the subsequent stay in Syrian Antioch is complicated by Luke's vague phrases: 'a long time', 'no little time', etc. Some two years would be a reasonable guess for the first journey, from 45/46 to 47/48.

X. AGREEMENT ON THE POSITION OF THE GENTILE BELIEVERS
(15: 1–35)
i. The Circumcision Question (15: 1–5)
Discussions in Antioch (1, 2). As more and more uncircumcised believers entered the church, the fears of Judaizing Christians increased, for the kingdom, rejected by the majority of the Jews, was fast being peopled by converted Gentiles. This seemed contrary to the special promises and covenants of the OT and Judaizers believed that the only remedy was to campaign for the circumcision of all Gentile converts, so that they might belong to the assembly of Israel. On the other hand, Paul and Barnabas were assured by God's revelations in a new age that the church was universal and spiritual and in no wise to be subjected to the legalistic requirements of Judaism. Men from Judea were teaching in Syrian Antioch that circumcision was necessary to salvation and the resultant distress was acute. The leaders thought it necessary to act quickly in order to avoid a division which would cut the church into two branches.

The embassy sent to Jerusalem (1–5). The name 'council of Jerusalem' is quite inappropriate to the discussions between the Antiochene leaders and the apostles and elders in Jerusalem on the position of Gentile believers. Leaders of the two large churches involved discussed the matter fully and made recommendations for their area, which is rather different from the modern concept of an ecumenical council. The Antiochene embassy was formed by Paul, Barnabas 'and some others', doubtless leading brethren in the church.

Private discussions (6). Luke describes the public occasion for he is interested in the advance of the history of the kingdom, although v. 6 allows a place for private discussions. These probably included the recognition of the apostolic 'grace' granted to Paul and of the evangelistic mission of Paul and Barnabas. This is the aspect of the talks which Paul is keen to put on record in Gal. 2: 1–10. We have put forward reasons for thinking that the brief visit of 11: 30; 12: 25 could not coincide with the tremendous occasion detailed here, but find the following reasons for a coincidence between Gal. 2 and this passage: (*a*) The question of circumcision is the same; (*b*) the place is the same; (*c*) the *dramatis personae* are the same; (*d*) following the marvels of the first journey, the time is ripe for the full recognition of Paul's apostleship; (*e*) time is allowed for the 'fourteen years' of Gal. 2: 1. We shall see later that there was no reason why the letter of 15: 23–29 should have been produced in the Galatian controversy. The smooth flow of discussion and resolution in 15: 7–29 would have been very difficult apart from a prior understanding between Peter, James, John on the one hand and Paul and Barnabas on the other, which is precisely what is indicated in Gal. 2. (For another interpretation see notes on Gal. 2: 1–10, pp. 1419 ff.)

ii. Public Discussion (15: 6–21)
Persons involved (6, 12, 22). The people most concerned with this matter are the apostles present in Jerusalem, the elders of the church, and the visiting embassy, but vv. 12 and 22 seem to indicate the presence of the whole church. Full debate was permitted, and then Peter, Paul and Barnabas brought the discussion to a head so that James (who seems to have presided) might propose a solution.

Peter's speech (7–11). Peter's remarks are a marvel of simplicity, humility and of spiritual logic. Never has 'freedom from the law' been better expressed. The Caesarea experience showed clearly that God gave the Holy Spirit to uncircumcised Gentile believers just as he had done to the 120 disciples on the day of Pentecost. Why put such people under the yoke of the law that Israelites had never been able to bear? In his final phrase he places both Jew and

Gentile on an equality, saying: **'We believe it is through the grace of our Lord Jesus that we** (Jews) **are saved, just as they** (Gentiles) **are.'**

The witness of Barnabas and Paul (12). The principle God had established in Cornelius's house, had been confirmed by the abundant and victorious experiences of the first journey. The church must recognize the further revelations God was giving through inspired messages confirmed by mighty works.

James' summing up and proposal (13–21). Symeon's (i.e. Peter's) experience, says James, shows that God's purpose in this age is to take **from the Gentiles a people for himself**. The divine purpose is supported, in the usual way, by a quotation from the OT (Am. 9: 11–12). The point was that God had announced universal blessings for the Gentiles in the end times, so that the calling out of a people to His name in this age finds its place in the general perspective of prophecy. Fulfilment of the prophecy is partial and analogical rather than literal, as in the case of 2: 16–21. Unless the promises given through the prophets to Israel are interpreted with reference to the same people and in the same sense in which they were originally given, the exegesis of prophecy becomes a guessing game controlled only by the predilections of the expositors.

The main conclusion is the confirmation of the liberty of the Gentiles already revealed: **'It is my judgment therefore, that we should not make it difficult for the Gentiles who are turning to God'** (19). The question of principle was clear, but practical difficulties remained: (*a*) How were converts from Judaism and the nations to live together? (*b*) What would be the effect of Gentile Christian liberties on the progress of the gospel where there were synagogues? James's mention of the Jews of the Dispersion in v. 21 is very important to a correct exegesis. The answer is that Gentile believers in the area most affected (Cilicia and Syria) were to be asked to abstain from practices which were repugnant and scandalous to the Jews because of the constant reading of such legal prohibitions as those of Lev. 11 and 17. Such wise restraint would go far to diminish friction between brethren and would remove obstacles to the spread of the gospel. The exegetical difficulty is to explain why the fundamental sin of fornication should have been included in this list of stumbling blocks to Jews. The Gk. word is *porneia*, normal for fornication, and it is difficult to see why it should be confined here to 'marriage within the prohibited degrees' (cf. 1 C. 5: 1). We must remember that sexual purity was extraordinarily rare among pagans, but at the same time abstinence from sexual sin could never have

been treated as voluntary or optional as the other restraints later were (cf. 1 C. 5; 6: 12 ff.). The debate on this problem is still open.

iii. The Letter (15: 22–29)
Its value and limitations. The letter expresses in writing the agreement reached. It is important to note the following points: (*a*) It was written in the name of **the apostles and elders, your brothers** (23). (*b*) It was not a rescript binding on the whole church for ever, but a communication from the persons named **to the Gentile believers in Antioch, Syria and Cilicia** (23). It constituted a strong recommendation, but must not be considered an obstacle to future normal revelations through the apostles, with special reference to the authority of Paul as apostle to the Gentiles. For spheres further afield the production of the letter would not be helpful for Paul's apostolic authority had to be defended against any idea of a subordinated authority derived from Jerusalem or from earlier apostles (Gal. 1 and 2). (*c*) The collaboration of the witness of the Holy Spirit and the apostles was normal to the epoch and refers to the recommendation about **requirements** or 'convenient' things at that time of transition. When the church spread widely over Gentile lands and the Jewish element became a small minority, the question ceased to have validity. In regard to 'doubtful things' we can learn all that is necessary from Paul's writings, especially 1 C. 8 and 10, with Rom. 14.

iv. Rejoicing and Ministry in Antioch (15: 30–35)
When Barnabbas and Silas read the letter and confirmed it personally a great cloud was lifted from the minds and hearts of the believers in Antioch, and this relief opened the way for renewed labours in which many gifted brethren taught and preached the word (35). The risen Lord was conferring abundant and varied gifts on His church (Eph. 4: 7–13).

XI. THE GOSPEL REACHES MACEDONIA: THE SECOND MISSIONARY JOURNEY (15: 36–18: 23a)
i. A Tragic Separation (15: 36–39)
The purpose of the journey (15: 36). The second journey, under the guidance of the Holy Spirit, was to open vast new areas to the gospel, mainly in Macedonia and Greece; but the original purpose was that of revisiting the churches already formed so that they might be strengthened in the faith (cf. notes on 14: 21–23).

A sharp conflict of opinions (15: 37–39). We can only guess at possible deep psychological motives behind the sharp discussion between Paul and Barnabas, arising from the change which led to Paul's acknowledged leadership. The blood-relationship between Mark and Barnabas may have played its part. In the matter at issue both distinguished leaders were right from different points of view. Barnabas had a shepherd's heart, and probably had personal reasons for knowing better than Paul the depth and sincerity of John Mark's repentance. On the other hand, Paul—also a spiritual shepherd—was concerned with the spiritual success of the second journey in which much depended on the help they might receive from younger men. These must be tried and proved in a public fashion, and it could not be said that John Mark had been so tested since his defection. It is a kind of sad consolation to know that outstanding and spiritually minded leaders can hold irreconcilable opinions at times, when the wise thing is for each to get on with the work in different spheres. The passages showing that Mark 'made good', later on, even in the eyes of Paul, are well known: Col. 4: 10; Phm. 23; 2 Tim. 4: 11.

ii. New Companions (15: 40–16: 5)

Silas had been one of the bearers of the Jerusalem letter, and we must understand that he had first returned to Jerusalem and then been led again to Antioch (33, 40). Silas is identical with Silvanus (2 C. 1: 19; 1 Th. 1: 1; 2 Th. 1: 1; 1 Pet. 5: 12), and seems to have been a cultured Roman citizen. He replaces Barnabas as an intimate companion of Paul, while Timothy was soon to be the junior helper. The Antioch church gave the two men an official send-off on their important mission, the first stage of which consisted in the confirmation of churches in the united province of Syria and Cilicia (40, 41).

Timothy chosen as a younger helper (1–5). Paul and Silas must have crossed the Taurus range by the Cilician Gates and struck the end of the former route in Derbe. Lystra linked Derbe and Iconium, and there Paul found that his convert, Timothy, had grown in spiritual stature, being well reported of by the churches in the district. Paul took the initiative in choosing the new helper, but Timothy's own sense of a call to a new kind of labour must be understood, and the Pastoral Letters throw light on the part played by the presbytery and prophets in the call and preparation of the young worker. This is an occasion in apostolic missionary history in which the mind of the Spirit is manifested not only to the candidate, but also to the spiritual leader on the field and to the elders of the local churches (1 Tim. 1: 18; 4: 14; 2 Tim. 1: 6; 2: 2).

Timothy's circumcision (16: 3). Paul would on no account allow the Gentile Titus to be circumcised, even in Jerusalem (Gal. 2: 3–5), but he himself caused Timothy to be circumcised. The seeming inconsistency arises from the fact that Timothy's **mother was a Jewess and a believer**, and he would be brought up in Hebrew piety. He could exercise a ministry among Jews and Gentiles so long as his racial position was clear and his circumcision would facilitate such a service. Titus was a Gentile born, converted and active in the gospel before visiting Jerusalem, so that his circumcision would have indicated that something was lacking in his spiritual life which could be supplied by the Jewish rite. In this case Paul's arguments in Galatians apply in their entirety.

A note on progress in the area of the first journey (4, 5). The churches of the Lycaonian and Phrygian portions of the Galatian province were near enough to the centre of the dispute on circumcision (Syrian Antioch) to make it advisable for them to receive the Jerusalem letter (4). In v. 5 we have one of Luke's summaries of progress which follows the confirmation of the churches founded during the first journey and settlement in the East of the circumcision dispute. From this optimistic summary onwards he deals with new ground opened during the second journey.

iii. New Ground (16: 6–10)

The region of Phrygia and Galatia (6). As the Lycaonian and Phrygian churches in the province of Galatia have already been visited, the area called **Phrygia** here must be the ethnic region of that name attached to Asia. **Galatia** would then be the real ethnic 'Galatia' of the north, the former kingdom of the Galatians (Celts). Numerous details in the Letters show that Luke passed rapidly over considerable periods of Paul's ministry when a full story would not forward his general purpose, so that there is nothing impossible in J. B. Lightfoot's theory that the period of uncertainty noted in v. 6 saw the founding of the North Galatian churches because Paul was held up by an illness (Gal. 4: 13), which, as has been said, fits badly into the story at the point noted in 13: 13, 14. (For a defence of the 'South Galatian' destination of the Letter to the Galatians see pp. 1415 f. Since 1897 it has been widely accepted in Britain, although the 'North Galatian' view is held by probably the majority of scholars in the United States and the continent of Europe.)

Negative and positive guidance (6–10). Maps must be consulted in order to trace Paul's probable movements at this time. His labours in Asian Phrygia and Galatia (we may think of Pessinus) left him on the NW borders of the province of Asia (another ethnic amalgam). He naturally thought of the great possibilities of Asia, and could easily have descended from the highlands to the coast. The time was not yet ripe, however, and the missionaries were forbidden by the Spirit to evangelize Asia then. Should they turn N and NW to the prosperous provinces of Bithynia and Pontus? Again the attempt was vetoed by **the Spirit of Jesus**, presumably by means of a prophetic message or a vision. **Mysia** would be the high land at the junction of the three great provinces of Galatia, Bithynia and Asia, Mysia being included in the last of these. From whichever part of Galatia they came, the fact that they were forbidden to evangelize Asia or Bithynia meant that they were compelled to come out at the coast in the direction of the port of Troas, at some distance from the ancient city of Troy. There Paul, in a night vision, saw the Macedonian who appealed for help. This positive guidance cast light on the past vetoes, and they rightly concluded that they were to cross the northern part of the Aegean Sea to Macedonia. Luke had his share in the decision, and the beginning of a **we** passage (10) shows that he joined the apostolic band at that point as a fellow-labourer.

iv. Peaceful Advance in Philippi (16: 11–15)
The journey and the city (11, 12). After a quick voyage the missionaries landed in Neapolis, a port at the eastern end of the Egnatian Way, but proceeded at once to Philippi, converted into a Roman colony following the defeat of Brutus and Cassius in that area in 42 B.C. Why a declining city, peopled mainly by Roman citizens and without a synagogue, should have been chosen as the first base for missionary work on the continent subsequently to be known as Europe, has puzzled scholars, and must be attributed to direct guidance.

The place of prayer (13–15). Jews had not been attracted to Philippi, so that no synagogue had been established. But the apostles found a meeting place for prayer, used by Jewish (or proselyte) women, on the banks of the river Gangites. The beginnings in Macedonia could not have been humbler, but as the missionaries told their story to the women, Lydia at least was converted and placed herself and her house at the disposal of the Lord's servants. V. 40 seems to indicate that the church met in her house, which was likely to be commodious as her business was important (14). Before the interruption (16), we must suppose a period of successful witness both at the place of prayer, in Lydia's house and perhaps by public preachings, as a church had been founded and brethren could be visited after the release of Paul and Silas.

v. Progress Through Persecution (16: 16–24)
The healing of the slave girl (16–18). The slave had a 'Python spirit'; F. F. Bruce remarks: '"Pythons" were inspired by Apollo, the Pythian god, who was regarded as embodied in a snake (the Python) at Delphi (also called Pytho).' Why an evil spirit should have given the testimony to the apostles (17) is a mystery, but is analogous to expressions used in the presence

of the Master (Mk 5: 7) with the same use of **the Most High God**. We should correct **the way to be saved** in NIV to '*a* way of salvation' (RVmg, NEB), so that the testimony is really a subtle distortion of the truth of the *one* way identified with the Lord Jesus Christ. In any case, demonic witness was never accepted either by the Lord or by His servants so that, despite obvious dangers, Paul exorcized the pythonic spirit in the name of Jesus Christ.

Roman justice goes wrong (19–24). The slave girl would no longer bring revenues to her owners by her divinations, so that these, quite foreign to the spiritual issues involved, turned on the men responsible for changing a valuable medium into a mere working girl. The account is abridged, for the accusation presented to the two collegiate chief magistrates was so cleverly worded that it could not have been drawn up in the midst of turmoil. The citizens of Philippi were Romans, but the leaders of the apostolic band were Jews, so that the accusation questioned the legitimacy of the proclamation of new teachings and practices in a Roman colony, as there was nothing to show that the new religion was a *religio licita*, one authorized by imperial law. According to the accusation, such teachings had produced the present disturbances. The magistrates would have been justified in examining such an accusation, appealing, perhaps, to the proconsul of Macedonia for a ruling; but, instead of such a judicial and judicious procedure, they yielded at once to mob pressure, ordering Paul and Silas to be beaten violently in their presence, giving them no chance to speak in self-defence or to allege their Roman citizenship. On their strict charge (23) the governor of the prison took all possible measures against the escape of the accused (23, 24).

vi. God Speaks by the Earthquake and by His Word (16: 25–40)
God's intervention (25, 26). God's voice was first heard in Philippi in quiet conversations by a flowing stream. Afterwards the city had been filled with the word of apostolic witness. Then God's powerful word effected a miraculous healing, and was afterwards heard through the triumphant songs and prayers of the suffering prisoners (25). Now, exceptionally, God spoke through an earthquake (cf. 1 Kg. 19: 11, 12) which shook the foundations of the prison, opened all doors, and broke the bonds of all the prisoners. The atmosphere is tense with mystery and emotion, but the Lord's servant is in absolute control of the situation, even to the point of seeing that the prisoners should not take advantage of the opportunity to escape (cf. 25). The governor of the prison might have been an old army officer, for whom suicide would be the only honourable solution to the problem of the loss of his prisoners. Paul could

probably see the man silhouetted against the opening of the door, and cried out in time to save his life (27, 28). How could the officer get to the point of asking about spiritual salvation in such a brief space of time (30, 32)? Or was he only anxious about his professional standing? If the latter, why did he fall down in supplication before Paul and Silas, or why did Paul advance a spiritual answer? We should remember the following factors: (*a*) The governor of the prison may have known a good deal about the apostles' witness prior to this event. (*b*) He would certainly have noted the remarkable demeanour of the prisoners, and may have heard their songs and prayers. (*c*) The moment is one charged with intense emotion, as God is working by extraordinary means, so that the personal danger of the officer and the sense of a spiritual crisis might well have coalesced in his thoughts and reactions. (*d*) The conversion of the officer and of the members of his household was not only due to the great declaration, **Believe in the Lord Jesus, and you will be saved**, but also to **the word** which was fully preached both to the man and his household (32). Measures would have been taken to restore the security of the prison, as the Western text says explicitly, but Luke concentrates on the joy with which the officer and his household received the word, showing their faith by their kindly care of the Lord's servants whom they had treated so brutally before (33, 34). The officer's household would probably be composed of his wife and family, servants and attendants. It is mere surmise that small children were present and were therefore baptized, as the whole household rejoiced in their new-found faith (34).

Paul's stand before the magistrates (35–40). The magistrates (*stratēgoi* = 'praetors' because Philippi was a Roman colony) considered that the two unwelcome visitors had been taught a lesson, so better get them out of the city now without more ado. To their surprise, the men returned a message claiming their rights as Roman citizens, and demanding that the magistrates themselves should lead them out of the prison as an acknowledgment of illegal violence. Was it arrogance and lack of faith? Was Paul deeply attached to his Roman citizenship and Greek culture as Ramsay thought? The fact seems to be that Paul never claimed his rights unless he found himself in an extremity (22: 25–29) or when such a claim might help in the spread of the gospel (see notes on 25: 10–12). His stand in this case would be a definite help to the Christian flock which he had to leave at a moment when popular feeling had been stirred up against it. Wrong had been done, but as it was publicly acknowledged some measure of protection was assured to the budding work. The Macedonian Christians in general were a great cheer to Paul's heart, and the letter to the Philippians makes it clear that a well-ordered, zealous and self-sacrificing community was born, first in peace and then in affliction.

vii. The Foundation of the Thessalonian Church (17: 1–9)

Thessalonica (Salonika) is still an important port, but was relatively more important during the first century as it handled much of the east-west trade passing from the East through Macedonia, and so to Rome along the Egnatian Way. It is typical of the kind of city Paul sought for as a centre for his message, and in this case the word rapidly spread from the Christian church to all the surrounding area (1 Th. 1: 8). Luke rightly calls the civic authorities 'politarchs' (6), a designation attested on inscriptions for the chief magistrates of several Macedonian cities.

Beginnings in the synagogue (1–4). Testimony in the synagogue often took the form of discussions, and vv. 2, 3 give an admirable summary of Paul's arguments when dealing with Jews: (*a*) Prophetic scriptures showed that the Messiah was to suffer and rise from the dead. (*b*) Those scriptures had been fulfilled in Jesus, whom Paul presented to his fellow-countrymen as their Messiah. A full example of his presentation of the *kerygma* in such cases has already been given in 13: 16–41. Paul's cogent reasoning convinced some Jews and many God-fearers and highly-placed ladies (4). The **three Sabbath days** (2) must refer to the first three sabbaths of unhindered testimony in the synagogue, which were followed by an indefinite period of preaching in the house of Jason, his host, before the riot and Paul's flight. A sufficient time for the founding of a church fully acquainted with the main Christian doctrines is demanded by the contents of the two letters to the Thessalonians.

Opposition and flight (5–9). Perhaps the strange methods adopted by the jealous and antagonistic Jews were due to the fact that believing ladies in high places would influence authority in favour of the Christian church rather than against it. It seems as if the Jews could only get a hearing by producing a riot, of which the politarchs had to take cognizance (6, 7). The accusation is different from that of the Philippian citizens, but is equally subtle: (*a*) the missionaries were notorious disturbers of the peace (6); (*b*) their propaganda was contrary to the decrees of Caesar; (*c*) they proclaimed **'another king, one called Jesus'** (7). It was well that Paul had been hidden and was not there to answer in person for even the breath of suspicion of any subversive propaganda against the Emperor could be fatal. It was such an accusation which affected Pilate so strongly (Lk. 23: 2; Jn 19: 12). Jason would probably be a well-known Jewish citizen who could not be tried on the grounds of Paul's message, but could be made responsible for public order, and the security would be **bail** to a considerable amount. He may have had to promise that Paul would keep away from Thessalonica, which would explain the persistent obstacle to his revisiting the city during the following months (1 Th. 2: 17, 18).

viii. A Church in Berea (17: 10–15)
Flight and encouragement. Again we note the method of leaving the continuance of the work to less conspicuous brethren while Paul repeated his methods in another city. Berea was about 60 miles from Thessalonica, but somewhat off the main routes, which might have been an advantage at the moment. The 'nobility' of the Berean Jews consisted in their open-mindedness, for as the visiting preachers appealed to the OT scriptures, they were very willing to examine them again in the light of the message **to see if what Paul said was true**. It is thus easy to understand that **many** soon **believed**, and that the blessing rapidly spread to the Greeks, among whom were more ladies of high society (11, 12). The Thessalonian Jews, who were such bitter enemies of the Gospel (see their character in 1 Th. 2: 14–16), were not long in getting wind of the work and repeated their technique of stirring up the mob (13). After an uncertain period, the brethren hurried Paul away in the direction of Athens by the sea-route (14) while Silas and Timothy stayed to strengthen the nascent church. Paul, meditating on the possibilities of Achaia, sent back the urgent message of v. 15. Besides the churches founded in Philippi, Thessalonica and Berea, we must suppose the up-surge of a number of satellite churches in the Macedonian area, due to the labour of various workers and the testimony of a host of anonymous witnesses (Rom. 15: 19; 1 Th. 1: 8; 2 C. 8: 1).

ix. Paul in Athens (17: 16–34)
A varied witness (16–21). Perhaps Paul thought of Athens as a place in which he could pray about future strategy, remote from the usual conflicts; but he could not see the noble city—the 'mother' of western civilization—**full of** foolish **idols** without being passionately stirred to immediate witness in the synagogue, and in the market place, speaking to all who would listen in a city notorious for its liking for 'intellectual chat' (21). What a change from the days of Socrates and Plato! The Epicureans formed a philosophical school which thought of pleasure as the greatest good, though their pleasure might be presented as refined and tranquil; the rival school of the Stoics was pantheistic, but especially stressed the superiority of a reasoning will over the passions of men, putting a high value on human self-sufficiency. Paul's preaching of Jesus and the resurrection

(*anastasis*) was thought to be the presentation of **foreign gods** and as questions of religion and morals were the province of the learned body, the Court of the Areopagus (so called because it had formerly met on the Areopagus, the 'Mars' hill' of AV), an opportunity was unexpectedly provided for a Christian witness before the intellectual *élite* of the day.

The speech (22–31). This first encounter between the Christian message and Greek philosophy has always aroused an almost excited interest. On the surface the results do not seem very striking (33, 34), but there is no ground for imagining, on the basis of a superficial interpretation of 1 C. 2: 1–5, that Paul was mistaken in his methods, correcting them when he went to Corinth. Luke was divinely led to give a summary of the speech for our learning and we must think of it as an introduction to Christian doctrine which would have led to the full message of the cross had the learned men of Athens been prepared to listen. Scores of interesting questions arise from the speech, which has been analysed in many learned writings (see, *e.g.* N. B. Stonehouse, *The Areopagus Address*, 1951), but our space only allows us to note the main movements: (*a*) A striking introduction was provided by the altar dedicated **'To an unknown god'**—one which might have been overlooked, despite the crowd of 'divinities' honoured by so many temples and altars. The Athenians, then, were **very religious**, since they feared such an omission. Paul changes the stress, underlining their ignorance of the true God (22, 23). (*b*) God the Creator is proclaimed, who is **Lord of heaven and earth**, not needing men's poor temples for a dwelling place. This is the language of Isaiah and of all the OT prophets. The Creator is also the Lifegiver (24, 25; cf. Isa. 66: 1, 2). Many of the scholarly hearers would assent to the strong monotheism of these phrases. (*c*) God's dealings with His creatures, or God in His providence, is the next step in the argument. Instead of the 'gods many' who help their favourites and devotees within narrow territorial limits, Paul proclaims the God who caused the race to spring from one man, providentially ordering man's boundaries of space and time so that they might seek and find God within a relatively ordered life (cf. the Noachian covenant, Gen. 9: 1–17). Paul quotes lines from Epimenides and Aratus in which Zeus is considered as the source of all life, and these quotations would help to maintain the interest of the councillors (26–28). (*d*) Humanity's great crisis is emphasized (29–31), for a true understanding of man's relationship with a Creator God would obviate the folly of idolatry, which tries to represent divinity by means of material and man-made objects. Centuries of **ignorance** had gone by, **overlooked** by

God—which does not annul human responsibility during the period—but times had changed, and God had intervened by fixing a day of judgment and by appointing the Judge who had been approved in the sight of men by the fact of his resurrection **from the dead**. Now men must **repent** and turn to God.

Paul had prepared his hearers as well as he could by stressing the highest moral and spiritual levels their thoughts could rise to, and at least some were impressed by the proclamation of human responsibility before their Creator God. But the concepts of v. 31 were strongly opposed to their ideas about the 'soul of the universe' moving in endless cycles, as also to the reabsorption of the human soul into that of the universe. A kind of future existence might well have been admitted, but **the resurrection of the dead** required a complete change of outlook, only possible if hungry and submissive souls turned to the Lord for light and salvation. The mockers made it impossible for Paul to continue, but a wonderful body of truth had been expressed, essential to our thinking about God and His providence.

Reactions and results (32–34). Luke certainly shows that the world of Hellenistic culture was not likely to receive the gospel with open arms, but there is no 'failure' as far as the proclamation is concerned, since **a few . . . believed**, among them distinguished figures like Dionysius and Damaris, so that a church was founded which was a temple to the only true God amid the many shrines of Athens. The mockers would reap what they sowed; the procrastinators never heard Paul again as far as we know; but the vital nucleus of believers would continue to preach the wonders of divine wisdom in the centre of Greek civilization.

x. Corinth (18: 1–18a)

The city. While Athens was the cultural capital of Greece—as also of the whole area of Hellenistic civilization—Corinth was the commercial centre. Destroyed in Rome's wars of conquest, it had been rebuilt as a Roman colony by Julius Caesar in 46 B.C. on the narrow isthmus which separates the Greek mainland from the large peninsula of Peloponnesus, having Cenchreae and Lechaeum as its ports on the East and West respectively. The great temple of Aphrodite made it a centre of idolatrous worship on the lowest possible moral level. This low level of sexual morality must be borne in mind when reading the Corinthian Letters. Politically, Corinth was the capital of the Roman province of Achaia.

Paul's arrival (1–4). Paul's state of mind when he arrived at Corinth is revealed in 1 C. 2: 1–5. There may have been other preoccupations as well as the relatively meagre result of the great witness in Athens. He was comforted by meeting Aquila and Priscilla, lately expelled from Rome by the Claudian edict against the Jews (2), who were probably Christians already. Their common trade helped to cement a wonderful friendship and fellowship in service which was to last for many years. See especially Rom. 16: 3, 4. Work in the synagogue seems to have begun on a minor key until the arrival of Silas and Timothy (4).

A mighty work (5–11). Paul was cheered by the good news that the Macedonian churches were constant, faithful and generous in the midst of persecution. During the following months the Thessalonian Letters were written. A stronger testimony in the synagogue accelerated the inevitable reaction of the Jews who refused the message of Jesus the Messiah, but not before **Crispus, the synagogue ruler**, had been converted, with **Titius Justus**, a god-fearing Gentile, whose house became the centre of the work. He may be 'Gaius, mine host' of Rom. 16: 23, in which case his full name would be Gaius Titius Justus. For reminiscences of these early days in Corinth, see 1 C. 1: 14–16. The **many** Corinthians converted (8) would have been won mainly from paganism, so that the proportion of well-taught and disciplined converts from the synagogue would be less than elsewhere; a fact which accounts for a certain instability of the work in Corinth. A tremendous attack by influential Jews was to be expected, but Paul was prepared for it by the vision of vv. 9, 10, in which the Lord encouraged His servant to continue to speak in Corinth in view of the **many people** to be won. Paul was assured that he would not be forced to leave the work hastily to begin again elsewhere as in so many other cities.

Gallio ignores the Jews (12–17). Gallio was brother to Nero's tutor, Seneca, the Stoic philosopher, and as his proconsulship most probably began in July 51, we have here an approximate date for the Corinthian ministry. The Jews were not so clever in formulating their accusation as in Thessalonica for they wished to prove that Paul's doctrines were not genuinely Jewish, and therefore not protected by the concessions made by Rome to Israel. To Gallio, however, that looked like an internal squabble between Jewish sects, so he scornfully referred the matter back to their own religious tribunals. Jews were not popular, so that he did not interfere when his sentence gave rise to some Jew-baiting. The victim, Sosthenes, must have been the ruler of the synagogue who replaced Crispus. This ruling was probably of considerable importance for the spread of the gospel during the following years, for Achaia was a major province, and Gallio an outstanding figure, so that his ruling, implying that Christians were covered by the special authorization given to the Jews, would influence minor authorities in the whole of the Aegean area. Thus was the Lord's promise (10) fulfilled and Paul himself was able to guide the early stages of a difficult work.

xi. The Journey to Syria (18: 18b–23)
Paul's vow (18b). Paul was to visit Jerusalem and Antioch again before entering new fields. The discussion about his vow can be simplified by the consideration that, during this period of transition, Jewish believers did not generally forsake the customs of their people, so that Paul was completely free to take a vow, shave his head, or to offer sacrifices, according to his own leading, fulfilling also the principle of 1 C. 9: 20. Let us remember that his plan of service still led him to the synagogues where these were found. Gentile colleagues were entirely and necessarily exempt from all such things, and one day the transition period would end. See note below on 21: 23–26.

Ephesus (19–21). Paul was received in a friendly fashion when he visited the synagogue in Ephesus, but he had not planned for a long stay then. Aquila and Priscilla remained as able witnesses, while Paul promised to return.

The end of the second journey (22, 23a). It is implied that the **church** visited following the landing at Caesarea was Jerusalem, after which the apostle spent some time in the well-loved church of Antioch in Syria. The new territories which had been evangelized since he was last in Antioch were Macedonia and Achaia (practically the whole of modern Greece), and probably an area in ethnic Galatia; the approximate dates were A.D. 48–53.

XII. THE EVANGELIZATION OF ASIA: THE THIRD MISSIONARY JOURNEY (18: 23b–21: 16)
i. A Ministry of Confirmation (18: 23b)
In a few words Luke sums up many months of confirmatory labours in which Paul goes **from place to place** where churches had been founded in Phrygia and Galatia. If he employs the ethnic terms for the areas visited, **Phrygia** would mean Galatian and Asian Phrygia and **Galatia** the ethnic Galatia in the north. A second visit to the Galatians in which he 'told them the truth' is implied in Gal. 4: 16 (see p. 1498).

ii. Apollos Appears (18: 24–28)
Apollos the man (24, 25). Alexandria was famous for its school of philosophy, literature and rhetoric, which influenced the large Jewish minority. Apollos was obviously the product of Alexandrian Judaism, but in some way he had heard of Jesus apart from the main apostolic stream of witness. Christian witnesses may well have preached in Alexandria before the great consummation of Pentecost. Apollos's courage was equal to his eloquence, for he at once preached in the synagogue in Ephesus on his arrival there.

Instruction and blessing (26–28). Paul's friends, Aquila and Priscilla, realized that Apollos's message was incomplete, so they invited him home for further instruction. Thus God raised up an outstanding witness to the truth in those years, who was to be made a special blessing in Corinth. The fact that **the brothers . . . wrote** an introductory letter on Apollos's behalf to the Christians in Achaia (mainly Corinth) shows that a Christian church already functioned in Ephesus, though it seems to have been Jewish in composition. For Apollos, see 1 C. 1: 12; 3: 5, 6; 4: 6; 16: 12.

iii. The Twelve Disciples (19: 1–7)
Paul in the 'upper country' (1). See notes on 18: 23 and 16: 6–8. The term fits in well with the assumption that churches had been founded in the highlands of Galatia. How much we should like to know of these busy months which Luke dismisses in a few words!

The group in Ephesus (1–7). The twelve disciples could not have been in contact with Aquila, Priscilla and the 'brethren' in Ephesus, or the conditions described would not have obtained. As in the case of Apollos, the men had heard of Jesus, had been baptized with John's **baptism of repentance**, but had not been informed of the 'consummation' in Jerusalem. A separate and early stream of witness probably stemmed from Galilee. Paul's question: **'Did you receive the Holy Spirit when you believed?'** (properly translated in NIV), shows that he expected disciples to receive the Spirit as soon as they believed. The reply (2) does not indicate that the disciples knew nothing about the Holy Spirit (clearly presented in the OT and in the Baptist's teaching), but that they had not heard of the giving of the Holy Spirit through the Messiah as promised by John. The significance of the 'laying on of hands' corresponds closely to that of 8: 17 and, according to its fundamental meaning of identification, denotes the closing of the breach between an incomplete position, bringing it into line with apostolic authority.

iv. The Evangelization of Asia (19: 8–20)
The province. Asia was one of the major Roman provinces, including the whole of the prosperous and thickly populated Ionian coast from the Hellespont to Lycia, with a deep spread inland to the heart of Asia Minor. During its evangelization **all the Jews and Greeks who lived in the province of Asia heard the word of the Lord** (10). The great centre was Ephesus, situated at the mouth of the Cayster River. Later on its importance declined because of the silting up of the harbour, but in the first century it was the metropolis of a vast area, important both for its commercial links and its religious significance. The temple of Ephesian Artemis—'Diana of the Ephesians' in AV—was counted as one of the seven wonders

of the world, and brought worshippers from all over the world. Originally a nature cult, the worship of the 'mother goddess' had been assimilated to that of the Greek Artemis.

The hall of Tyrannus (8–10). Paul made his usual beginning in the synagogue, stressing the theme of the kingdom of God (8), and he was soon beset by the stubborn unbelievers among the Jews who reviled **the Way**. He withdrew the disciples when further testimony in the synagogue became impossible, and found a preaching centre in the **hall of Tyrannus**. It has been deduced from the habits of the Ephesians that Paul worked at his trade in the mornings (cf. 20: 34) while the normal activities were carried on by Tyrannus in his **hall** (which might be compared to a lecture hall with a gymnasium, where leisure was spent); Paul then gave his 'lectures' during the siesta time after 11.00 a.m. He afterwards reminded the Ephesian elders of this public ministry which was complemented by visits 'from house to house' (20: 20). Distinguished visitors seem to have listened to the preaching in Tyrannus's hall, since Paul won friends even among **the officials of the province** (the principal citizens of Asia, 31). Despite the many plots of the Jews, and the sharp suffering of that period, Paul was enabled to continue in Ephesus for a period covering from two to three years (10, 20, 31 with 20: 19; 1 C. 15: 32), and his ministry provides the most perfect example of the strategy which selected important centres from which the gospel could be widely spread throughout the whole area by his colleagues and converts. During this time Epaphras evangelized the towns of the Lycus valley (Col. 1: 7). At some point during Paul's Ephesian ministry he paid his 'painful visit' to Corinth (2 C. 2: 1; see p. 1389).

The 'Name' in Ephesus (11–20). In chs. 4–6 Luke described the power of the name over against the strength of Judaism. Here the same name is shown to have prevailed against both the superstitious worship of Artemis of the Ephesians and the false 'names' of the prevalent magic. Once more a servant of Christ was accredited by means of miracles which drew attention to the word. The hellenistic world respected the occult powers associated with the East, so that it would not be difficult for the Sceva family to 'work up a connection', claiming, perhaps to know the sacred name of the God of Israel. F. F. Bruce suggests that we should read **chief** (or high) **priest** 'in inverted commas', as something which the head of the house claimed to be in Gentile lands, where little was known of the priestly hierarchy in Jerusalem. The misguided exorcists thought that they could put the names of **Jesus** and **Paul** into their bag of tricks (cf. 8: 19) and use them for casting out demons. The first attempt

was so disastrous that their ridiculous failure was widely commented on, creating a wave of interest in **the name of the Lord Jesus** as preached by Paul and his associates (13–17). The significance of the event was especially clear to the professionals of magic arts, who burnt their satanic literature, despite the high market price at that time (19). But again and again the emphasis is placed not on the miracles, but on the name and the **word** which spread and **grew in power** (20).

v. Future Plans (19: 21, 22)
Paul and the future (21, 22). These verses are important as they open up perspectives leading to a wider and different ministry which was to follow the three missionary journeys. RSV is doubtless right in adding the words 'in the Spirit' with a capital in v. 21, as Paul was divinely led to plan a tour of confirmation in Macedonia and Greece, and then to go to Jerusalem (it is the period of the collection for the poor saints in Judea) after which he understood that his mission as apostle to the Gentiles must take him to Rome. His thoughts are clearly expressed in Rom. 15: 15–29, written a few months later, when his vision already included Spain.

vi. The Riot in Ephesus (19: 23–41)
The reason for the narrative. We have seen how Luke sometimes condenses the description of months of important ministry into a few words, but here we have a long section on an event which does not advance the annals of world evangelization. It seems that he was led to select typical incidents which illustrate the impact of the *kerygma* on different sectors of the hellenistic world. Here superstition—as is always the case—is entwined with material interests resulting from local cults. The number of converts was so considerable that Demetrius (president of the silversmiths' guild) realized that the business of the shrine-makers was on the decline. At the same time, it was still possible to inflame the masses into violent opposition to the men who were thought to have brought discredit to their goddess, of whose shrine the city of Ephesus prided itself on being **the guardian of the temple** (35).

Demetrius and the guild (23–28). Demetrius's speech is a marvel of carnal ingenuity, for he plays alternately on the theme of possible financial loss and on that of despite done to the goddess. He could thus excite the company but could not lead his men to any practical suggestion or conclusion, though maybe the enraged shouts (28) were designed to arouse the masses.

The gathering in the theatre (28–41). This theatre has been excavated by archaeologists who calculate that there was seating capacity for more than 25,000 people. It was a natural gathering place, but the meeting was extraordinary, unofficial, uncontrolled and confused (32). Paul's Macedonian colleagues were dragged there, but escaped with their lives. Paul himself was persuaded by Christians, and by friendly officials of the province of Asia, not to present an 'apologia' in the theatre, as the temper of the mob was dangerous, and he might well have been lynched. We do not know what Alexander the Jew was supposed to do (33), but, in any case, he could not get a hearing. The senseless reiteration of the cry **Great is Artemis of the Ephesians**—especially in its AV form with 'Diana' instead of **Artemis**—has become proverbial as an illustration of frenzied and ignorant local fanaticism.

The city clerk's speech (35–41). The **city clerk** was the principal local official, directly responsible to the proconsul for public order. He probably waited for the mob to shout itself hoarse before attempting to control it. Then he made his masterly speech: (a) The honoured position of Ephesus as 'doorkeeper' or warden to the goddess was universally known and indisputable—a wise sop to their exacerbated local pride and superstition (35, 36). (b) They had brought Gaius and Aristarchus there, but these men could not be accused of sacrilege or of blasphemy. This shows that Paul did not attack local superstitions directly, but outflanked them by a clear preaching of the gospel (37). (c) Concrete complaints could be dealt with by the usual procedure before the **proconsuls** of Asia (the generalizing plural is perhaps used because at the moment the proconsulship was vacant). (d) Larger issues could be decided in lawful assembly. (e) The commotion was dangerous in view of Roman concern in all matters relating to public order (40). The speech was like a cold shower on a feverish head, and the official **dismissed the assembly** (41).

vii. From Ephesus to Achaia (20: 1, 2)
Departure from Ephesus (1). Paul's work in Ephesus was done, and the officials would probably advise his leaving the city. Luke's account of the evangelization of Asia is very brief, and should be supplemented by studying Paul's address to the Ephesian elders (17–35), as well as the passing references to this ministry in the Letters to the Corinthians, written from Ephesus. The apostle was often in danger from Jewish plots, and under a constant strain. Could some of the imprisonments mentioned in 2 C. 11: 23 be fitted into the Ephesian ministry? Some scholars have thought so, but this cannot be roundly affirmed. Besides this suffering, he carried the tremendous burden of the attitude of an anti-Pauline party in the Corinthian church which caused him much anguish of spirit, while he felt the constant pressure of anxiety for all the churches he had been led to

found (2 C. 11: 28, 29). The Ephesian period is a great success story, but the hero was also a martyr (2 C. 1: 8–11).

Macedonia and Greece (2, 3). Paul's aim was to encourage the believers, but behind the vague phrase **he travelled through that area** may lie a journey to Illyricum, on the Adriatic coast (Rom. 15: 19). **Greece** here means Achaia, and the background of the journey is supplied by 2 C. 1: 15–2: 16. We gather that the three months' visit to Corinth (implicit in vv. 2, 3) was a happy one, thanks to Titus's good work and the effect of the letters. In Gaius's hospitable home Paul was able to dictate his great letter to the Romans, inspired by his plans for proceeding thither after his proposed visit to Jerusalem (Rom. 15: 16). At the same time he completed his plans for conveying the help of the Gentile churches to the poor 'saints' in Jerusalem (1 C. 16: 1–3; 2 C. 8; 9; Rom. 15: 25–28).

viii. From Corinth to Miletus (20: 3–16)
A plot and a change of plan (3–6). Paul had thought to embark in Corinth for Syria, but, on learning of a plot against him, he changed his route, undertaking the long détour around the Aegean Sea. He was thus in Macedonia again, and celebrated the Passover in his beloved Philippi (3, 6). We can better understand the list of the names of his companions, with a mention of the districts they came from, if we remember that the main purpose of the journey was to convey a considerable sum to Jerusalem, and that these men were not only colleagues, but representatives of the churches in their districts (4; with 1 C. 16: 3 f.; 2 C. 8: 16–23). The meeting place was to be Troas, and the pronoun **we** (6) shows that Luke joined the apostle again in Philippi (where the previous 'we' section ended in ch. 16).

Events in Troas (7–12). We understand v. 7 to indicate that the Breaking of Bread on the first day of the week was customary during the apostolic period. Pliny the Younger's communication to Trajan (c. A.D. 112) indicates that 'a sacred meeting' was held early on a fixed day, doubtless Sunday, among the Christians in Bithynia. Luke seems to be 'seeing' the crowded upper room with its many lights as he pens v. 8 (he was there at the time). The lesson to be deduced from the story of Paul's extended ministry and of the accident to Eutychus, is not that preachers should not go on too long, but that in days of the plenitude of the Spirit everything was subordinated to the word. Paul embraced the corpse and recalled back the departed spirit, returning to the upper room, not to comment on the accident or the miracle, but to continue the ministry of the word until the day dawned. It might be the last opportunity to build up the believers in Troas, and that was the overriding consideration. At the same time the Christians were not dead to natural affection, and the members of the family who took Eutychus home alive **were greatly comforted** (12).

Paul's lonely walk (13–17). While the ship slowly coasted the SW promontory of Mysia, Paul walked across the headland to Assos, doubtless seeking solitude and communion with his Master. The names which Luke lovingly transcribes—Assos, Mitylene, Chios, Miletus—are redolent of mythical and historical lore, prized by a classical scholar such as he was. At Miletus, birthplace of western philosophy, Paul had summoned the elders of the Ephesian church to meet him, avoiding the delay which would have been inevitable had he made a halt in Ephesus.

ix. The Address to the Ephesian Elders (20: 17–38)

The leaders of the church (17, 18). This section throws clear light on church government and ministry in the orbit of Paul's labours, and demands a more thorough analysis than we can give here. When Paul wished to counsel the leaders of the church, a definite number of men set out to meet him. Not one, nor the whole church, but a group obviously recognized by all as the **elders** were invited. In v. 28 these men are called *episkopoi*, translated 'guardians' in RSV, but usually 'bishops' or **overseers**. That they were also the 'shepherds' or 'pastors' is clear from the same v. 28. Here, as elsewhere (cf. 14: 23) the identity of 'elders' ='overseers' ('bishops')='pastors' is established, each term defining a particular aspect of the qualifications and mission of the leaders of the local church. The message is not so much an exhortation from an apostle to elders, but rather the presentation of a great example of pastoral service, and Paul might have said with Peter: 'To the elders among you, I appeal as a fellow elder' (1 Pet. 5: 1).

The first movement of the address: an example of service (18–21). Paul can confidently appeal to his own example of service **from the first day.** (*a*) Personal experiences predominate in v. 19, such as humble service, **tears** and **tested.** (*b*) Varied ministry is stressed in vv. 20, 21, for nothing **helpful** was withheld, either in public or private teaching and preaching, while the 'proclamation' to Jew and Gentile called for **repentance and . . . faith in our Lord Jesus**.

Second movement: the future course (22–27). Paul goes on to speak of his future course, which provides both example and warning. (*a*) The journey to Jerusalem (22–24). This journey was not a 'mistake', since a Spirit-empowered apostle had received instructions from his Lord about the matter, while the messages through the prophets rightly stressed the danger involved. This is what **compelled**

by the Spirit must mean so that the **prison and hardships** predicted could not turn him from his course which must be accomplished, irrespective of personal considerations, since his life was not precious to himself but only as a means of serving the Lord (23, 24). (*b*) The **task** is defined as testifying to **the gospel of God's grace** which is identified with the proclamation of **the kingdom** (24, 25). (*c*) **the whole will of God:** Paul's conscience was clear with regard to his service in Ephesus, for he had proclaimed, not a part of a divine message, but **the whole will of God** revealed in the OT and completed by the NT revelations (25–27).

Third movement: warnings for the elders (28–31). (*a*) The **Holy Spirit** had fitted the overseers for their labours in relation to the flock for which Christ died, so that their responsibility was very great. (*b*) First they must take care of their own testimony, so as to be able worthily to care for the flock. The strange phrase **which he bought with his own blood** may indicate the oneness of essence between Father and Son manifested even in the work of redemption (cf. 2 C. 5: 19), but another translation is possible: 'with the blood of His own', with 'Son' or 'Servant' understood. (*c*) Perils would arise from within and without, and v. 30 reminds us of the many warnings of the Pastoral Letters. (*d*) The warning was emphasized by memories of Paul's own constant admonitions (31).

Fourth movement: commendation to the Lord and the Word (32). Paul will no longer be with them, but he commends them into the mighty hand of his Lord and to the enlightenment and power of the word, which is able to build them up with a view to the great **inheritance** of the **sanctified.**

Fifth movement: the example of generous giving (33–35). The epilogue underlines the fact that love delights to give, and is thus fully blessed. Paul was especially careful that he should not be classified with religious leaders who turned their sacred mission into a motive of personal aggrandisement or material profit. The elders must follow this example. The quotation at the end of v. 35 shows that collections of 'Sayings of Jesus' circulated which have not been incorporated into the canonical Gospels.

The farewell (36–38). We are thankful for this glimpse of the 'family relations' of the believers, and for the manifestation of love and gratitude from the taught to the teacher.

x. From Miletus to Jerusalem (21: 1–16)

The Christian family in Tyre. From Patara the apostle and his company were on the route of the wheat trade from Egypt to Rome. Tyre was the great merchant city of the Phoenicians in ancient times, but lost a good deal of its importance after its savage destruction by Alexander the Great in 332 B.C. The existence of a Christian church in the city shows how the gospel had spread throughout Palestine and neighbouring countries by the year 57. The command (doubtless through a prophet) that Paul should not go up to Jerusalem has puzzled many, but in view of 20: 22–24 must be considered as a prediction of trouble ahead, which was overridden by a revelation given to Paul himself. The idea that Paul obstinately pressed on against the prohibitions of the Holy Spirit must be rejected. The farewell and prayer meeting on the beach is especially revealing, and more so as these believers—unlike the elders of Ephesus—had had but little personal contact with the apostle (5, 6). If circles of local churches lose the sense of their oneness as a spiritual family, the mere preservation of sound doctrines and right practices will mean but little.

Paul in Caesarea (7–14). There were **brothers** to be **greeted** in **Ptolemais** on the way to Caesarea, the natural port for Jerusalem. We should like to know more about the constitution of the church into which Gentile believers were first introduced on equal terms with the Jews (ch. 10), but we are only given a glimpse of **Philip the evangelist, one of the Seven** (cf. 6: 5), and his **daughters**, hosts of the apostolic company. Philip had continued to exercise the special gift of an **evangelist** from the dispersion onward (ch. 8). The fact that his daughters **prophesied** throws interesting light on the ministry of gifted women, as prophecy is, by definition, a public ministry. 1 C. 11: 5 supports the view that such gifted women had more than a merely domestic ministry in apostolic times.

The **symbolic and vocal prophecy of Agabus (11)** is very much in the style of OT prophetic ministry, and gave rise to renewed appeals that Paul should spare himself bonds and imprisonment. But his witness before governors and kings must needs be fulfilled, and when Paul persisted in his willingness to suffer all things **for the name of the Lord Jesus**, all submitted to what was recognized as **the Lord's will** (12–14).

The important third journey had lasted from approximately A.D. 53 to 57; the three great expeditions had together opened up vast areas to the gospel, stretching from Antioch to Illyricum. Apart from our Lord's own ministry on earth, no such period of time has had anything like the significance of the twelve years A.D. 45–57. From now until the end of Luke's story, Paul will be Christ's 'ambassador in bonds' (Eph. 6: 20).

XIII. THE AMBASSADOR IN BONDS: PART ONE: IN JERUSALEM (21: 17–23: 35)

i. Contact with the Jerusalem Church (21: 17–26)

Difficulties real and imaginary. The description of Paul's arrival at Jerusalem, his contacts with the brethren, and their advice calculated to conjure the perils which might arise from the opposition of the Jewish-Christian multitude, certainly involve exegetical difficulties, but these have been exaggerated by the failure to take into account the transitional nature of the period. This failure in perspective leads expositors to judge the situation as if the Jerusalem church were a local church in Gentile lands after the testimony had passed to the great majority of Christians of Gentile birth. When the Jerusalem elders said to Paul: **you yourself are living in obedience to the law** (24; cf. 1 C. 9: 20) they recalled the well-known fact that Paul, in Jewish circles, observed the customs so as to be able to continue his ministry among Jews to the end. When this is understood, there is no need for excuses on one hand or for condemning a compromise on the other. It is of interest to note that, apart from a passing reference in 24: 17, Luke does not mention the primary purpose of the visit to Jerusalem: the handing over of the funds resulting from the offerings of the Gentiles, which occupied so much of Paul's thoughts at that time (see note on 20: 3–6; Rom. 15: 25–28; 2 C. 8; 9). What he does record is that Paul and his company were well received by James and the elders, and given ample opportunity to detail what God had done among the Gentiles, which motivated sincere praise.

The **problem and a proposed solution (20–26).** Obviously the great majority of believers in Jerusalem (after the dispersion of 8: 4) accepted Jesus as their Messiah, thinking of themselves as the 'faithful remnant', without understanding the universal nature of the church and its freedom from the shadows of the old regime. They were pious Jews confessing Christ (20) and still practising the customs they had received. The enemy Jews had taken care to represent Paul's labours among the Gentiles as the sabotage of an apostate who taught Jews **to turn away from Moses, telling them not to circumcise their children or live according to our customs**. This was not true, but the elders of Jerusalem were concerned with the fact that it was largely believed in their own community. They did not go back on their letter of 15: 23–29 (25) but suggested that Paul should show by something visible and concrete that he, as a Jew among Jews, observed the customs. Previously he had purified himself after a vow of his own (18: 18b); now he is to undertake the expenses for four men, who, at the end of the period of a Nazirite vow, had to offer the prescribed sacrifices. This was a recognized act of piety among the Jews. It is not often noted that the solution was probably successful with reference to the multitude of Jewish Christians, and the generous offerings of Gentile believers would have helped towards mutual understanding and fellowship. The danger arose unexpectedly, not from the legalistic section of the Jerusalem church, but from unbelieving **Jews from . . . Asia**, who, visiting Jerusalem, recognized Paul and Trophimus. (For a Nazirite vow see 18: 18b with Num. 6: 2 ff. In NT times the vow usually lasted 30 days.)

ii. The Riot in the Temple Area (21: 27–40)
Paul in danger of a violent death (27–31). The prophecies as to perils in Jerusalem were fulfilled, but Paul was delivered from the hands of fanatical Jews in order to fulfil his ministry as an ambassador of Christ in bonds. The plan proposed by the elders went forward normally, with Paul's full co-operation (26). Despite the NIV translation of v. 27, the time reference in 24: 11 makes it probable that the violent interruption took place early in the proceedings: 'when the seven days were going to be fulfilled' (F. F. Bruce, *Acts, Gk. text*, p. 394). The Asian Jews had seen the Gentile, Trophimus, with Paul in the city, and then, finding the apostle with the Nazirites within the sacred precincts, near the chambers assigned to the purification rites in question, supposed—no proof was ever forthcoming—that he had introduced a Gentile beyond the outer court: an offence punishable by death and one which would have defiled the temple (27–29). The Asian Jews denounced the supposed crime to the worshippers in the temple, and the news spread like a train of gunpowder to the multitudes in the city. Paul was seized and dragged out to the Court of the Gentiles, while the temple attendants shut the gates of the inner court. This picture of the excitable mob, so easily induced to an act of lynching by a false report, is in entire agreement with the atmosphere of the times—the years preceding the great rebellion.

The intervention of the Romans (31–42). The Roman garrison had its barracks in the tower of Antonia, a fortress overlooking the Temple area at its NW angle, which accounts for the rapid appearance of troops under the leadership of the military tribune (colonel in charge of a cohort and senior Roman official in Jerusalem at the time) who would be fearful of riots on feast days. The officer could get no clear charge from the mob and formed his own conclusion that this was a renewal of trouble by the *sicarii* or **terrorists** (38), chaining Paul

and having him borne towards the fortress steps.

Paul managed to get the ear of the tribune, who, struck by his good Greek and citizenship of Tarsus, rather surprisingly admitted his request to address the multitude (37–40). Josephus mentions an Egyptian who claimed to be a prophet and led a multitude into the desert in A.D. 54, where his followers were either killed or dispersed. Lysias confuses them with the *sicarii*, the dagger men employed by fanatical anti-Roman Jews.

iii. Paul's Defence before the Multitude (22: 1–30)
Paul and his fellow countrymen (1, 2). Luke is concerned to present the apostle over against representative persons or companies, typical of his age. The speech from the steps of the tower of Antonia underlines the Jewish rejection of his person and message in the very heart of Judaism. Miraculously the seething mob quietened at the sound of a polite address in Aramaic, and thus received one more opportunity to respond to the Christian message.

Paul's history as a Jewish leader (3–5). A younger generation of Palestine Jews would know little or nothing of Saul of Tarsus, though Paul could appeal to the memories of the high priest and the Sanhedrin (5). There is an obvious fitness in stressing his former complete identification with zealous and fanatical Judaism, his training in Gamaliel's school, and his leadership of the persecution of the Christian **Way**. No one could understand better than he the religious passions now aroused in opposition to himself and his message.

The renewed story of his conversion (6–16: cf. 9: 1–19; 26: 12–20). If Paul was formerly what the Jews continued to be, they could become as he was now if only they could understand the significance of Christ's appearance on the Damascus road. Hence the story of his conversion, which tallies with Luke's account in ch. 9, with the addition of Saul's question: **What shall I do, Lord?** (10). The bystanders may have heard Saul's voice, but not the Lord's (9). It is natural that Ananias's intervention should be stressed here and not in 26: 12–20, as the witness of a pious Jew would be valuable as a means of gaining the ear of the Jerusalem crowd, but useless before Agrippa and an audience of Palestinian and Roman officials. Ananias's message is here couched in OT terms, with the use of **the Righteous One** (14) as a messianic title (cf. 3: 14; 7: 52). Emphasis falls on the reception of a messianic message to be delivered **to all men** (15).

The middle voice imperative of v. 16 means: 'Get yourself baptized and your sins washed away', and must be understood in the light of NT teaching on forgiveness of sins and baptism (see notes on 2: 38; 8: 12 ff.; 8: 36 ff.; 10: 47). Saul had been closely associated with crimes against Christ and His church, and his baptism was a public dissociation from those sins, and thus a 'cleansing'.

The vision in the Temple (17–21). The vision in the temple must belong to Paul's first visit to Jerusalem following his conversion (9: 26–30). It is difficult to understand why Paul introduced an incident, which, although it explains his mission to the Gentiles, was bound to raise the ire of the mob by the very mention of a command to leave Jerusalem to go far away to the nations (18–21). The point is to be found presumably in his own intercession (19, 20), which reveals Paul's long-held conviction that his former record as a persecutor would serve to convince the Jews that some special and divine communication had caused him to preach the message he had formerly so violently rejected. In this he was mistaken and was so informed by his Master from the beginning, for Jerusalem was to reject him as it had the Lord Himself, the Twelve and Stephen.

Reactions to the witness (22, 23). The spell was broken, and frantic protests followed the story of the vision in the temple. The Jews again pronounced their sentence against the followers of the Crucified: **'Rid the earth of him! He's not fit to live!'**

Paul claims his Roman citizenship and Lysias convokes the Sanhedrin (24–30). In commenting on 16: 35–40 we have already expressed the opinion that Paul, as a Hebrew descended from Hebrews, took no natural pride in Hellenistic culture or in Roman citizenship. If he had wished to boast in fleshly matters they would have related entirely to his race and religion (Phil. 3: 4–7; cf. Rom. 9: 1–5). He knew the Graeco-Roman world well, and would use his knowledge of it and his Roman citizenship if thereby he could further the kingdom of God. There was no further attachment. The terrible Roman scourging, so lightly proposed by Lysias, would have killed him or maimed him for life. Such a crisis elicited the fact of his Roman citizenship—how proved we do not know—which exempted him from scourging (24, 25). The attitude of Lysias changed at once. He himself had bought the precious privilege, but his prisoner had been born to it (28) and as a privileged Roman must be protected and given the opportunity of a fair trial. Paul's future witness to governors and kings hinges on the privileges of Roman citizenship, with the probability that he was able, at that time, to bear the financial burdens of the trials and the eventual appeal to Caesar. Unable to get information by torture, Lysias decided to convoke the Sanhedrin and place Paul before this supreme council. This blood-guilty tribunal thus heard a renewed witness,

though in circumstances not of its own choosing.

iv. Paul before the Sanhedrin (23: 1–11)
The circumstances. Paul's presence in this session of the Sanhedrin completed his witness in Jerusalem. His attitude and his statements have been criticized, but we must remember that it would have been fatal if the session convoked by Lysias for the investigation of charges against Paul had been converted into a trial by a court invested with full authority over Jews in religious matters. The situation was delicate and the atmosphere tense, and Paul owed his life—under God's providences—to the protection afforded by Rome to a citizen as yet uncondemned by its tribunals. The Sanhedrin was the continuation of the tribunal guilty of the blood of Christ, of Stephen and of other Christian witnesses. Internal dissensions, as well as methods both corrupt and violent, had robbed it of much of its ancient prestige, and it was soon to reap the utter ruin it had sown. The president was the vile Ananias, whose unscrupulous intrigues maintained him in power from A.D. 47 to 58, despite many accusations against him. He was assassinated by Zealots in A.D. 66. Paul's methods must be judged against this background, and we must also remember that Luke's account is necessarily abbreviated. Unlike Peter and John (4: 5–20), Paul was a recognized rabbi who 'spoke the language' of his judges, being utterly familiar with the machinery and proceedings of the Sanhedrin.

Paul and Ananias (1–5). The session had probably been opened in the normal way, so that Paul's declaration: **'I have fulfilled my duty to God in all good conscience'** (1) would be the opening phrase of his defence. For his concern in doing nothing against his conscience, see 1 C. 4: 4; 1 Tim. 1: 5, 19; 3: 9; 2 Tim. 1: 3.

Ananias broke the law in spirit and in letter when he ordered his underlings to smite Paul **on the mouth** and the apostle's angry retort had in it something of the old prophetic witness against iniquity in high places, and may even be taken as a prediction of Ananias's violent end (3). Our Lord 'opened not His mouth' in similar circumstances, but different times demand different types of witness within the framework of divine truth. The stern denunciations of Mt. 23 exemplify Christ's condemnation of religious iniquity. However, though apt and prophetic, Paul's stern rebuke was contrary to the letter of Exod. 22: 28, and he at once admitted it. The president was a criminal, but the 'seat' was sacred. **I did not realise that he was the high priest** possibly means: 'I did not recognize his high priesthood (in my rebuke).' (Cf. 1 Th. 5: 12 for this use of the same verb.)

The Hope and the Resurrection (6–9).
Paul's declaration (6) looks like a tactical move in order to divide the council and thwart any possibility of an adverse sentence. Such a move just then was legitimate and necessary, but could Paul, in good conscience, at that stage, declare: **'I am a Pharisee, the son of a Pharisee'**? The term has an unpleasant sound in many ears because of the opposition of the sect to the Master's person and ministry, but before judging Paul we must bear in mind: (*a*) The Pharisees held fundamental doctrines based on the OT, which the Sadducees utterly refused. The faithful remnant, who looked for the hope of Israel, were all Pharisees doctrinally, and did not have to unlearn the Biblical truths they possessed, but only to apply them to Jesus as the Christ and to reject legalism. A Sadducee would have to cease to be one on becoming a Christian, but not a Pharisee. (*b*) The **hope in the resurrection of the dead** was not a theological sophism but the essence of the gospel. Paul stirred into life something real in some of his old companions when he reminded them that their most treasured possession was the messianic hope and the doctrine of the resurrection. This was true OT succession, and not the sterile formalism of the Sadducees and the legalists (cf. 26: 57, 23). The effect was striking as some scribes of the Pharisees were, momentarily at least, prepared to advocate an absolutory sentence and admit the possibility of a special revelation given to Paul—with reference, presumably, to his encounter with the risen Christ near Damascus (9). We can hope for blessing in the hearts of some of these—the Nicodemuses and the Josephs of Arimathea of their day.

The sequel (10, 11). The strife between Sadducees and Pharisees in the council was such that the pagan Lysias had to rescue his prisoner by armed force (10). Paul must have felt both physically and spiritually battered and worn that night, and so received special cheer from his Lord (11). Notice there is not a whisper of reproach but: (*a*) encouragement from the Lord of all comfort; (*b*) the ratification of the witness in Jerusalem, despite all the turbulence; (*c*) the confirmation of the purpose that Paul should witness in Rome, with equal fidelity and efficacy.

v. From Jerusalem to Caesarea (23: 12–35)
A renewed deliverance (12–24). Illegal and violent solutions of inter-party problems were becoming frequent in Jerusalem, as the time of the 'dry tree' approached (Lk. 23: 31), and the plot of the forty fanatical assassins is typical of the times. They could count on the co-operation of at least a 'rump' of the Sanhedrin (12–15). This time God's deliverance was effected, not by angel intervention as in 12: 6–10, but by means of Paul's nephew. The apostle's witness had been blessed to some of his relatives (Rom. 16: 7), despite the probable rupture with the family (Phil. 3: 8) and we would like to think that his sister was a Christian (16). The puzzle is how the young man could have got to know of the plot were he suspected of Christian sympathies, or why he should have taken the risk of warning his uncle if he was associated with fanatical Jews. The secret is not revealed and God ordered the circumstances in His providence. The story of vv. 16–22 is detailed and graphic, revealing Luke's presence and observation, although he does not name himself. The nephew's witness confirmed Lysias's conviction that the presence of Paul in Jerusalem would be a source of continued disturbance and that it would be difficult to preserve the life of this Roman citizen outside the fortress. His decision was to transfer him to Caesarea to be tried by the procurator, Felix. His estimate of the violent courage of the Jews is revealed by the size of the escort as far as Antipatris: 200 heavily armed soldiers, 200 light armed men and 70 horsemen (23)! The **mounts** (in the plural) for Paul suggest the presence of friends; perhaps Luke was one (24).

Lysias's letter (25–30). The clever way in which the events referring to Paul's arrest are summarized—with a twist of the facts in favour of the tribune (27)—is obvious. The psychological fitness of the communication is evidence that the historian had first-hand knowledge of it, though how, we do not know. Luke had a good eye for relevant documents!

Caesarea (31–35). Caesarea was the capital of the province and owed much to Herod the Great's planning and building. Antipatris was 25 miles from Caesarea, and beyond the sphere of action of the fanatical mob in Jerusalem so that the foot soldiers returned, leaving the cavalry to escort the prisoner to the capital. Felix took cognizance of Lysias's letter and of the arrival of Paul, ordering his accommodation in Herod's praetorium until the accusers could come down from Jerusalem. Paul's status as a Roman citizen was respected.

Antonius Felix was not a good example of a Roman procurator; he owed his position to the influence of his brother Pallas, a favourite of Claudius and a freedman of the emperor's mother, Antonia. He had dealt severely with bandits, but had stirred up widespread opposition by his violence and venality. Tacitus remarks that he 'exercised the power of a prince with the mentality of a slave'. His third wife, Drusilla, was a daughter of Herod Agrippa I.

XIV. THE AMBASSADOR IN BONDS:
PART TWO: IN CAESAREA (24: 1–26: 32)
i. Paul before Felix (24: 1–27)

A time of testimony before rulers. During the two years spent as a prisoner in Caesarea, Paul was to witness before Felix, Drusilla, Festus, Herod Agrippa II, Bernice, and also before a varying number of high officials, thus fulfilling the Lord's purpose announced in 9: 15.

The accusation (1–9). In order to exercise the maximum pressure on the governor, the high priest, Ananias, attended the trial in person, accompanied by some councillors. Tertullus was perhaps a Hellenistic Jew, trained in Roman legal procedure, and to him was committed the presentation of the accusation. (*a*) The exordium (2–4) was hypocritically flattering, for Felix's record was bad and the Jews hated him. (*b*) To call Paul **a troublemaker** was insulting and the description of his activities too vague for legal purposes (5). (*c*) Tertullus could bring no evidence to prove that the main charge—that of profaning the temple—was a fact (6). (*d*) Verses 6b–8a (RSVmg; cf. also AV) are from the Western Text, and though lacking in support in the best texts, seem to reflect an attempt to twist Lysias's action in arresting Paul—compare Lysias's own manipulation of the evidence in the opposite direction (23: 27). **The Jews** made Tertullus's unsatisfactory accusation their own (9).

The defence (10–21). (*a*) The necessary exordium (10) was brief, but courteous, with a mention of the only true fact in Felix' favour—the length of his governorship made him well acquainted with Jewish matters. (*b*) In the second phase Paul shows the absence of proof of any particular offence against public order or Jewish customs during the few days he was in Jerusalem (11–13). (*c*) The third phase turns one point of the accusation into a testimony: he did follow **the Way**, but this was in perfect accord with the law and the prophets. The resurrection hope was also that of many of the Jews, so that Paul, in his activities, maintained a **conscience clear before God** and man (14–16). (*d*) The fourth phase marks a return to the accusation, noting the pious and patriotic purpose of his visit, stressing his worship according to the laws of purification, and putting his finger on the weakest point of a weak case—why were the Asian Jews, who accused him of defiling the temple, not there to substantiate the charge which gave rise to the riot? (17–19). (*e*) The closing phase made it clear that the Sanhedrin had been unable to formulate any charge against him, as the belief in the resurrection would also condemn the Pharisees (21).

Paul was not so much concerned with clearing himself—although his defence was a very able one—as with proving the Christian faith to be a legitimate interpretation of the OT, the sacred book of the Jews, and indeed its due fulfilment. Christians, therefore, should share in the privileges of the *religio licita* granted to the Jews. The wise and effective testimony is apparent to all.

Felix' decision (22). The high priest's charges had collapsed through lack of proof, and Felix should have set his prisoner at liberty. The delay—the excuses were paltry—means that he wished to use Paul as a pawn in the game of his intrigues with the Jews, thinking also that the prisoner might be a possible source of illegal income (22, 26).

The two years' imprisonment (23–27). Felix was interested in his unusual prisoner and heard him speak of his faith in Christ Jesus when his wife Drusilla was in Caesarea. Paul emphasized the great principles of justice and self-control—so obviously lacking in his judge—showing that there was a future crisis of judgment. Felix was terrified, but put off the day of consideration and decision—which never arrived. Tradition has it that Drusilla influenced him against the truth, and this is psychologically probable as Felix had induced her to leave her husband Azizus, king of Emesa, in order to 'marry' him. The acceptance of the stern and wholesome teaching of v. 25 would have meant breaking with the life personified by Drusilla. Paul was in *custodia libera*, chained by one wrist to a soldier, but otherwise able to order his own life (23), so that prayers, letters, counsels to visitors continued. Luke probably used this time for gathering up material for both Luke and Acts.

ii. Paul before Festus (25: 1–12)

Festus and the Sanhedrin (1–5). We can only judge Festus's character by brief references in the writings of Luke and Josephus, and he strikes us as a worthy but limited official of the equestrian class, out of his depth when confronted with the complicated and explosive situation in Judea, rendered even more dangerous by the impact of nascent Christianity. He could not avoid an official visit to Jerusalem almost immediately after taking up his governorship, and was at once beset by Jewish leaders who claimed Paul as a 'religious' prisoner, though behind the façade of legality they planned to have him ambushed and killed (2, 3). Festus, who would know of Paul's Roman citizenship, insisted on a trial in Caesarea.

The trial before Festus (6–9). After the period noted in v. 6, Festus sat on the tribunal (Gk. *bēma*)—symbol of Roman judicial authority—and heard the confused and malicious **shouting** of the Jewish plaintiffs (v. 24). The substance of the charges can be gathered from Paul's brief defence: he had neither committed an offence against **the law** (the OT Scriptures) nor against **the temple**, nor against **Caesar** (8; cf. 24: 10–21). As in the trial before Felix, the vague charges were not substantiated by any evidence valid before a Roman tribunal (cf. 17–

19). Festus was concerned not to provoke the fierce Jewish leaders and asked Paul if he would agree to be referred back to the Sanhedrin, certainly unaware of the plot to kill him.

The appeal to Caesar (10–12). Paul found himself in a worse position than when Lysias had remitted him to Caesarea, and realized that the strong and persistent pressure of the Jewish leaders would hinder his release from any Palestinian prison. Hence his dramatic **appeal to Caesar** (11) in which he reaffirmed his rights as a Roman citizen. As the Jews had urged a political offence, Paul could quite firmly declare that he ought to be tried by Roman justice. He may have been moved by two other considerations pondered over during his imprisonment: (*a*) He was assured that he must minister in Rome, and his appeal would take him thither (19: 21; 23: 11). (*b*) A favourable verdict before Caesar's tribunal would establish a precedent, practically equivalent to declaring Christianity a *religio licita*, which was greatly to be desired, since the gap between Judaism and Christianity was becoming increasingly apparent. An appeal to Caesar was a long and expensive matter, but the die was cast.

iii. Agrippa and Bernice in Caesarea (25: 13–26: 1)

The king and his sister (13). Herod Agrippa II of our portion was the son of Herod Agrippa I of ch. 12 but had not been able to obtain from Rome the wide domains of his father and had to be content with Chalcis, a small kingdom in the Lebanon mountains, later exchanged for Trachonitis and associated territories to the NE of Galilee. He was granted the privilege of appointing the high priests in Jerusalem. He was, of course, subordinate to Rome, but represented a house which had frequently served the Empire well and was useful to Rome in dealing with the Jews. Bernice, a younger sister, was the widow of another Herod (her father's brother) who had also been king of Chalcis! Her close association with her brother was suspect. Both strove unsuccessfully to ward off the great rebellion, and both were finally driven by Jewish fanaticism to throw in their lot with Rome. These were the last members of the Herod family to influence Jewish history or to cross the triumphant path of Christian testimony. Herod Agrippa II does not seem to have inherited the anti-Christian policy of his father. It was convenient both for the king and the governor to maintain good relations, which explains the early and prolonged diplomatic visit to Caesarea (13, 14).

Festus's problem (14–21). Festus could make no sense of the Jewish charges against Paul, yet had not released him and had admitted his appeal to Rome. Hence his problem—how was he to word the official charge (26)? The wording was also, of course, of great import-

ance to the prisoner as a favourable report would give a good start to the proceedings in Rome. Festus realized that his royal visitor —Jew by religion and thoroughly versed in Palestinian politics—was the man to solve his problem. At the same time the audience for the investigation could be turned into an act of homage to his guests, and into a convenient display of his own authority and resources as Rome's representative.

In general the private explanation given by Festus in 14–21 is a fair summary of the situation, with some trimming in his own favour (16, 17), but the main interest centres on v. 19 where the reaction of a reasonably honest and cultured Roman to the Christian message is revealed. The phrase **their own religion** (of the Jews) is not necessarily derogatory, for the meanings of 'superstition' and 'religion' meet in *deisidaimonia*, the word used. But all that Festus had perceived in Paul's witness was that it was **about a dead man named Jesus who Paul claimed was alive.** The tremendous meaning of the resurrection was lost on this well-meaning pagan.

The public explanation given to the distinguished gathering (24–27) was naturally more formal, and stressed the need for Agrippa's examination in order to formulate a charge on remitting the prisoner to the Emperor. Agrippa would already know a good deal about the Christian 'Way' and was probably familiar with the name of Paul. Hence his interest in conducting the examination (22). Providentially, therefore, the cream of Palestinian aristocracy, with high-ranking Roman officials, were arrayed to hear the witness of the 'ambassador in bonds', and, owing to the special circumstances, no one was in a hurry (23). We reach the zenith of this special ministry as far as Palestine is concerned. After the introduction by Festus, Agrippa took charge, and at once gave Paul permission to speak in his own defence (26: 1).

iv. Paul's Defence before Agrippa and Festus (26: 2–23)

The substance and style of the defence. This speech is not an improvised defence and testimony as was his message to the multitude in ch. 22, for Paul had had ample time for preparation and realized the importance of the occasion. For this reason the speech is so rich in doctrinal, historical and apologetic interest, and therefore very difficult to summarize in limited space. Some scholars inform us that Paul remembered his lessons in rhetoric learnt in the schools of Tarsus, as he gives unusual attention to style on this occasion, though the language is, of course, hellenistic and not classical Greek. Others, however, regard it as extremely doubtful that Paul ever attended Greek school in Tarsus, interpreting Ac. 22: 3 to mean that Jerusalem was the city of his boyhood.

The exordium (2, 3). The exordium was obligatory in such 'apologies' before distinguished judges, and again Paul knew how to combine courtesy and truth, being indeed **fortunate** to be able to marshal his arguments before a potentate thoroughly versed in Jewish questions, and not ignorant of the beginnings of Christianity.

Saul the Pharisee (4, 5). Paul is desirous that his conversion and Christian ministry should be seen against the background of his early history as an orthodox Jew, adherent of the strictest party, that of the Pharisees. Although he was a native of Gentile Tarsus, his life was lived among those of his own nation, though this does not exclude Greek influences.

Paul adhered to the Hope of Israel (6–8). He was no dangerous deviationist, but held firmly to the hope which sprang from the fundamental promises given to the nation (Gen. 12–15) and which found their consummation in the resurrection; for from the beginning Abraham had learnt to trust in the God who gives life to the dead (Rom. 4: 16–25). The ideal nation of the twelve tribes (actually represented by the faithful remnant) had never given up this hope in the course of their divine worship, and the resurrection of the dead is incredible only to those who do not know God.

Saul the persecutor (9–11). Paul goes back to his history and shows that not only was he a Pharisee, but also the outstanding leader of the first general persecution of the church in Jerusalem. We may note the graphic details of that tragic period and Saul's **obsession against them.** It is difficult to understand the reluctance of some scholars to admit that the statement **when they were put to death, I cast my vote against them** means that Saul, despite his youth, was a member of the Sanhedrin, for lesser courts could not bring in death sentences.

Saul's conversion (12–15). For the third time we are presented with this vital narrative (cf. 9: 1–19; 22: 6–16). Its importance as an explanation of Paul's ministry is obvious, and Agrippa would see the force of an experience analogous to that of prophets in the OT when called to divine service, noting the *shekinah* glory (the **light from heaven, brighter than the sun**), the prostration, the command: **get up and stand upon your feet.** (Cf. Exod. 3: 1–15; Isa. 6: 1–9; Ezek. 1: 1–3: 4; Dan. 10: 7–11.) Ananias's part in the event is naturally omitted here, and the terms of the commission are given as if they were fully announced on the road to Damascus. In the best texts the important reference to Saul's 'kicking **against the goads**' is given only here (14). Saul the Pharisee became Paul the apostle because he

saw Jesus as the Lord of glory and could not be disobedient to the heavenly vision (19).

Paul's commission (16–18). The messages from the Lord to His apostle were to be continuous (16) and he thus received the deposit of divine truth—also called the 'mystery'—which he was so careful to administer (1 C. 4: 1–6; Eph. 3: 1–13; Col. 1: 26–2: 6; 1 Tim. 1: 12–14; 2 Tim. 1: 11–14; etc.). In his labours he was promised deliverance (17; cf. Jer. 1: 18) and his summary of our Lord's communication includes such vital themes as spiritual illumination, the conversion of believers **from darkness to light**, their translation from Satan's **power** to God's, the **forgiveness of** their **sins** and their standing among the **sanctified** (17, 18; cf. Col. 1: 12–14 for an almost identical summary). How strangely such terms would fall on the ears of the distinguished audience in the hall of Herod's palace!

Paul's preaching (19–23). Paul has described his commission and now passes on to the way in which he fulfilled it, as obedient **to the vision from heaven.** (*a*) The sphere of service (20) includes Damascus, Jerusalem, the country of Judea and the vast Gentile lands. The third item offers some difficulty as we have no other mention of labours in Judea as a province. Perhaps Palestine in general is meant, and Paul would not cease to preach wherever possible as he travelled to and from Jerusalem. (*b*) The main themes were repentance from sin, conversion to **God** and **deeds** which would prove the reality of conversion (20). (*c*) The link with the OT is provided in vv. 22, 23. The Jews tried to kill him, not because he had abandoned the OT revelation, but because he proclaimed **to small and great** the prophetic content of the OT as fulfilled in the sufferings and resurrection of Jesus the Messiah, who would, through His servants, spread spiritual **light both to his own people** (Israel) **and to the Gentiles** (cf. 13: 47). This emphasis links back to the preliminary mention of the resurrection theme in vv. 6–8.

v. The Effects of the Message (26: 24–32)

Festus's exclamation (24, 25). The blasé audience expected to be mildly interested in the defence of a man so well known because of his effective propaganda and so well hated by the Jews; but as Paul developed his thesis and told his thrilling story in refined and skilful language, the interest must have increased and the tension mounted. Some must have come to the unexpected conclusion that the message of the Jewish rabbi had something to do with them! The tension is clear from Festus's loud exclamation when Paul came to a pause—perhaps before a final peroration which he was not permitted to give. Festus, sensing the tension but unable to follow the meaning, abbreviated the proceedings by his shout which admitted

Paul's learning, but put his testimony down to a divine madness—the expression was not necessarily insulting. Paul rejects all idea of 'madness'—even of the oracular sort—and insists that what he is saying **is true and reasonable**, turning at once to Agrippa who could recognize the terms of his address.

Paul and Agrippa (26–29). Paul's appeal to Agrippa takes for granted, not only his knowledge of the OT scriptures, but also his acquaintance with the origins of Christianity which held the attention of Palestinians over many vital years (26). The challenge to Agrippa's belief in the prophets (27) suggested a belief also in their fulfilment in Jesus Christ—hence the king's reply: 'In short you are trying to make me act the Christian!' (trans. F. F. Bruce). The 'almost thou persuadest me' of the AV must be abandoned on textual and exegetical grounds. Paul took up the king's slightly cynical evasion, with a word play on *en oligō* ('in short') and turned it into a most telling testimony: **'Short time or long—I pray God that not only you but all who are listening to me today may become what I am, except these chains'**. How much wealthier was he, in Christ, than the wealthiest listener! How much happier than the happiest! Luke tells us nothing of spiritual fruit, but by such means the gospel was introduced into the highest spheres of the Empire in these and in succeeding years.

Drafting the report for Caesar (30–32). The king, the procurator and their advisors withdrew for consultation, and the general opinion was that Paul was innocent, but that Festus must needs send him to Rome since he had appealed. It was not mentioned that on those same grounds, Felix and Festus should have released him long ago! It is a natural deduction from vv. 31, 32 that the report drawn up for Caesar's tribunal was favourable to the prisoner.

XV. THE AMBASSADOR IN BONDS: PART THREE: ON THE JOURNEY TO ROME (27: 1–28: 15)

i. A Detailed Report

At first sight Luke's narrative of the hazardous journey to Rome seems disproportionately long when compared with his brief summaries of periods and circumstances which would throw much more light on apostolic ministry and on the function and testimony of local churches. Perhaps Paul's Master would have us know what His servant was like when he shared the vicissitudes and dangers of life with his fellow men, and that the work of service and ministry must not be estimated merely by sermons and writings. Paul, as God's man (23), became the real leader of a heterogeneous

company of people on board a ship drifting toward wreckage, and was the means of their temporal salvation. Luke's narration is acclaimed as one of the masterpieces of 'shipwreck' literature—it reads well in NEB—but we are concerned, not so much with the dramatic incidents, as with the witness of an apostle who was in the counsels of God just as much in the perils of the sea as when he received those special revelations which did so much to complete the NT scriptures.

ii. From Caesarea to Fair Havens (27: 1–12)

Paul and his companions (1, 2). Julius, a **centurion who belonged to the Imperial Regiment** and possibly an officer-courier in the Emperor's service, was about to leave Caesarea with soldiers and prisoners, so that Paul was handed over to his custody. He was accompanied by Aristarchus of Thessalonica, who afterwards laboured with the apostle in Rome (Col. 4: 10; Phm. 24), it being probable therefore that he volunteered to serve him (cf. 20: 4). Luke's presence is indicated by the pronoun **we**. A coasting vessel en route to Asian ports served for the first stage of the journey, until Julius could transfer his company to a wheat vessel going to Rome.

From Caesarea to Myra (3–6). In Sidon there were **friends** (doubtless a local church) to care for Paul, who was treated with courtesy and kindness by the centurion. The journey was slow from the start, and the ship from Adramyttium worked with difficulty round the east end of Cyprus, coasting Cilicia and Pamphylia before getting to the harbour of Myra in Lycia. There Julius transferred his company to an Alexandrian wheat ship bound for Rome. It was probably under government contract, and Julius would be senior officer on board.

Myra to Fair Havens (7–12). Large sailing vessels of the period could tack to a certain extent, but persistent head winds made progress difficult as they left Cnidus (extreme SW of Asia Minor) and sought the shelter of the eastern and southern coasts of Crete. The delays were a serious matter as the period 15th October to 10th November was considered dangerous for navigation and ships were then laid up until after February. The **Fast** (9) was that of the day of Atonement which fell late in the year 59—an indirect confirmation of the estimated date of this journey.

It was now clear to the owner, to the captain and to Julius that it would be impossible to get to Rome before winter, so that the consultations (9–12) were to decide whether to winter in Fair Havens, or to try to push on to Phoenix, further along the south coast of Crete, which was thought to provide a better harbour for their purpose. Modern Phineka is largely silted up, but there is no reason to suppose another port, and it does face SW and NW (follow RSVmg here). Paul could proffer advice as a respected Roman citizen, brought up in the area, although he was a prisoner on a vague, non-criminal charge; but the centurion naturally followed the advice of the experts.

iii. Paul's Witness in the Storm and Wreck (27: 13–44)

The storm (13–20). A south wind seemed to promise an easy passage to Phoenix, less than 100 miles to the west, but Paul's prediction of disaster found early fulfilment when a violent NE wind from off Crete struck the ship with such force that the only solution was to run before the gale with a minimum of sail. The **lifeboat** (16) was the dinghy, normally towed behind. The undergirding (17) of the hull with ropes, to brace the timbers against the impact of the waves, was a well-known operation. As no land or sky was visible, navigation was impossible, though the westward course (when driven by a NE wind) seems to indicate some steering to avoid the dreaded Syrtis shoals off the North African coast. The operation noted in verses 18–20 tended to relieve strain by throwing overboard all unnecessary rigging and to lighten the ship. The situation was desperate and the conditions for the 276 people aboard distressing in the extreme (20).

Paul's moral leadership (21–26). No maritime skill was of any avail, but God's servant received a message not only for himself but also for the frightened crowd on board. Addressing them, he reminded them of his rejected advice in Fair Havens. There was nothing wrong in this according to Paul's straightforward thinking and it enhanced his authority as he gave them a message full of cheer. There was a supreme God, whom he worshipped and served, and to whom he belonged. His God had sent an angel to confirm His purposes for His servant, saying: **Do not be afraid, Paul. You must stand trial before Caesar; and God has graciously given you the lives of all who sail with you** (24). Paul accepted God's message with unreserved faith, knowing that things would turn out exactly as he had been informed. As something clear to his own prophetic spirit, he added that they would **run aground on some island**. Being perfectly confident himself, he was doubtless able to instil some cheer into men and women who had hitherto felt that pagan Fate had doomed them to perish in the raging sea. We deduce that Paul had interceded for his fellow passengers, for it is said that God granted them to him as a gift (*kecharistai*, v. 24).

Approaching Malta (27–38). Fourteen days from Fair Havens to Malta seems a long time, but experts calculate a drift of only 26 miles a day in such circumstances (F. F. Bruce, *The Book of the Acts*, ad loc.). Perhaps the noise

of breakers on the Malta coast warned the mariners of the proximity of land and led them to check the situation by soundings (27, 28). The anchors were cast from the stern and not from the bow, as the vessel needed to be held —by a minimum of sail—in the direction of the wind and ready for beaching when morning came. These precautions taken, they **prayed for daylight**. How long the hours must have seemed from midnight to dawn! Paul again intervened for the general good when he perceived that the sailors intended to steal a march on the rest by getting to shore in the dinghy. Their skilled help was needed for the dangerous manoeuvre of beaching, so, on Paul's warning, the soldiers cut the ropes and let the dinghy drift—a swift Roman reaction which lost them the boat! Before daybreak Paul nerved the company for their forthcoming ordeal by very practical advice and example. He renewed his divinely-given assurance of protection for their lives, but reminded them of the need of food after the prolonged fast, for physical energies would be necessary. He himself took bread, and ate it, but not without the striking testimony of giving thanks to God before them all (33–35). The rest plucked up courage and 'took food themselves' (NEB) before throwing the rest of the wheat into the sea in order to lighten the ship as much as possible for beaching.

The wreck (39–44). The light of day revealed an unknown coast, but a bay and beach offered them the possibility of running the ship ashore. Anchors were cast off, the oars which served as rudders loosed, and the foresail carried the ship forward. Verse 41 seems to indicate that, before striking the beach, they were caught in a cross current caused by the island of Salmonetta and that the bow of the ship got fixed on a shoal. The waves were breaking up the stern, but the bow served as a diving board for swimmers, while the rest helped themselves over the remaining distance by planks. According to Paul's prediction, no life was lost. It is strange that Paul's own life should have been endangered by the rigidity of Roman discipline at the very moment when others were saved thanks to his prayers and counsels. Prisoners —who might or might not be guilty—must not be allowed to escape (we remember the Philippian jailer's reactions, 16: 27) and so should be killed. Julius, however, intervened against his subordinates' advice in order to save Paul, in whom he now had a personal interest. Despite the absence of a beach, it seems to be sufficiently established that St. Paul's Bay, as it is now called, was the opening on the N coast of Malta where the wreck took place.

iv. Blessing in Malta (28: 1–10)

Malta and its inhabitants (1, 2). The island of Malta had been used as a trading centre by the Phoenicians and Carthaginians, and had been visited by a variety of peoples; the harbour of Valletta was well known. The **islanders** were 'barbarians', not because they were uncivilized, but because they did not speak Greek. They spoke a language derived from Phoenician, and were little affected by the Graeco-Roman culture. Their kind reception of the victims of the wreck contrasts well with practices on the Cornish coast as late as the eighteenth century.

Was Paul a criminal or a god (3–6)? Paul's practical and humble helpfulness is spotlighted in v. 3, but seemed badly rewarded by the viper's bite. His shaking the torpid creature **into the fire** and remaining unharmed may be reflected in Mk 16: 18 (in the later appendix to the Gospel). The reactions of the natives were natural in the circumstances—here is a prisoner who escapes death in a shipwreck, but is bitten by a serpent. The Fates got the criminal after all! But when Paul continued his homely tasks unharmed, they decided **he was a god**. Better that way round than in the contrasting case in Lystra (14: 8–20).

A ministry of healing (7–10). The chief magistrate, called Publius, possessed lands near the site of the wreck and shared in the hospitality. In that way Paul learned that Publius's father was suffering from dysentery and was led to pray for him, laying his hands on the sick man who was healed. The laying-on of hands is only rarely associated with healings in the NT, but see Lk. 4: 40 and Ac. 9: 17 (with Mk 16: 18). Others were naturally desirous of receiving similar blessings and brought their sick to be healed. Luke does not mention preachings and conversions, but the analogy of the Ephesian ministry—and all Biblical precedents—suggests that miracles always open the way for the word. We should like to think of a number of disciples among the grateful people who brought their gifts to the apostolic party as they boarded the 'Castor and Pollux'.

v. Paul reaches Rome (28: 11–15)
The journey renewed (11–14). Suitable weather about mid-February encouraged Julius to embark his company on another Alexandrian ship (probably belonging to the wheat fleet) and to continue the journey so dramatically interrupted. Syracuse, the great Sicilian harbour, and Rhegium on the Italian side of the Straits of Messina, had figured largely in Greek and Roman history. Of greater interest to us is the fact that brethren were found in Puteoli—another evidence of the wide spread of the Gospel by A.D. 60. As Paul was invited to stay with them, his ministry in Italy began there. It seems as if Julius decided to travel by road from Puteoli, so that a seven days' stay there would enable him to equip himself and his men—after the loss of nearly everything in the wreck—

before entering Rome. The believers would have helped Paul and his company.

An official welcome to Rome (15). Luke anticipates the longed-for goal: **And so we went to Rome** (14), but adds an important note with reference to welcoming companies of brethren from the church in Rome, some of whom got as far as **the Three Taverns**, 33 miles along the Appian Way, and others 10 miles further on to **the Forum of Appius** (15). The wait in Puteoli would allow time for messengers to announce the coming of the apostle. Paul had prepared the church for his coming years before by writing his Letter to the Romans, and had perhaps received favourable news by letter. But now brethren—including elders, doubtless—press along the Appian Way to give him an official reception (*ēlthon eis apantēsin hēmin*). This was the long-awaited sign of a friendly reception. **At the sight of these men Paul thanked God and was encouraged.**

XVI. THE AMBASSADOR IN BONDS:
PART FOUR: PAUL'S MINISTRY IN ROME (28: 16–31)
i. Paul's Witness to the Jews in Rome (28: 16–28)
Paul in 'free custody' in Rome (16). The best Greek texts make no reference to the way in which Paul was handed over to Roman authorities, but the relative comfort of his captivity is emphasized (16). He was able to provide for his own lodging, but was fastened to his soldier guard by a light chain. He had to be available when his case was tried, but was quite free to receive visits, to preach and to write in the meantime. Finance did not seem to be a problem at that time.

Paul's explanations to local Jewish leaders (17–22). The first three days in Rome were probably devoted to contacts with Christian leaders, but Paul was not likely to forget his debt to the Jew first (Rom. 1: 14–16). Not only must he fulfil his mission to the people, but it was necessary to find out whether local Jews were to act as his accusers at the instance of the Sanhedrin. Paul could not go to the synagogues, but the Jewish elders responded to his invitation and met him in his lodging. The explanation of the appeal to Rome (17–20) is brief but exact, and Paul is careful to show that there was no hostility on his part to the Jewish nation. The **hope of Israel** was the messianic hope, incarnate in Christ Jesus and brought to a climax by the resurrection (cf. notes on 23: 6; 24: 15; 26: 6–8, 22, 23).

Strangely enough, the Jewish leaders in Rome had received no specific information from Jerusalem about Paul and therefore no instructions to present the case for the accusers.

The high priest and his colleagues must have realized the hopelessness of seeking an adverse sentence in Rome when they had failed in Caesarea. The elders, however, were desirous of hearing the truth about the Nazarene sect, which **people** were **everywhere . . . talking against**, from the lips of such a well-known leader. Because of the slow growth of the Christian church in Rome over the years, and the frequent decrees of expulsion against the Jews, there was probably little contact either way between the two communities in Rome.

Discussions with the Jews and a last warning (23–28). Great numbers of Jews came for information and discussion to Paul's lodging, which was obviously commodious. Paul's presentation of the gospel to the Jews has been considered in notes on 13: 16 ff.; 17: 2, 3; etc., and his method is unchanged in Rome, for the exposition would necessarily be based on OT scriptures fulfilled in the ministry, death and resurrection of Jesus, proclaimed as the Messiah. This constituted a solemn testimony to the kingdom of God which depended on the recognition of the rightful King (23). The long session **from morning till evening** would include the discussions common to Jewish debate. As always, the word divided the company into those who were persuaded of its truth, and the rest who were incredulous. Before the guests departed, arguing now among themselves, Paul couched his last recorded warning to his own people in the well-known words associated with Isaiah's call (Isa. 6: 9, 10). The heart of Israel—seat of desires, affections and will in Scripture—had grown dull, or gross, and this inner evil of wrongly directed desire closed the people's ear to the message and shut their eyes to the glory of God in the face of Jesus Christ (26, 27).

ii. Paul's wide Ministry in Rome (28: 30, 31)
Luke's abrupt ending (30, 31). It seems extraordinary that Luke should not give us clear information about the result of the appeal to Caesar, so dramatically presented in chs. 25 and 26. It can be deduced from the tendencies noted above, and from these verses, that the case went by default because the accusation was not followed up. The **two whole years** (the aorist tense of **stayed** denotes something completed) would give time to wind up the legal proceedings. Believing Paul to be the direct author of the Pastoral Letters, we follow conservative scholars in thinking that from 62 to 65 Paul was a free man, visiting Crete and points round the Aegean Sea (Tit. 1: 5; 2 Tim. 4: 13, 20) and *possibly* fulfilling his desire to visit Spain. When Nero turned against the Christians he was arrested again and wrote 2 Timothy as a farewell message to his younger colleague. Paul is the hero of the Acts from

ch. 13 onwards, but we must remember that Luke's purpose was to trace the spread of the gospel from Jerusalem to the ends of the earth (1: 8). This vast movement reached its climax when Paul, the apostle to the Gentiles, exercised a wide ministry in the metropolis of the Empire, so that the abrupt end is far from being an anti-climax, for the author's task was completed.

The nature of Paul's ministry (30, 31). In the first place, Paul received all who came to him. These would be men like Epaphras, who linked the apostle with the churches of the Lycus valley in the province of Asia, and gave occasion for the Letter to the Colossians (Col. 1: 7, 8). Other visitors would share his vision for the evangelization of the West (Rom. 15: 17–29) and would go from his lodging to Gaul and Spain. His intercessions, teachings and counsels linked him with the whole westward movement of the kingdom. As for Rome, he proclaimed **the kingdom of God** to varying companies of people, with results such as those mentioned in Phil. 1: 12–18. By his teaching **about the Lord Jesus Christ** he handed on his deposit of Christian doctrine according to his own principle expressed in 2 Tim. 2: 2.

It is still much more probable that Philippians, Colossians and Ephesians were written during the two years in Rome than during a supposed, but unrecorded, imprisonment in Ephesus, in which case we owe the deep and full Christology of these sublime writings—the climax and crown of his special revelation—to his meditations and inspiration during the time when he could not travel, but was therefore freer to receive and express the truth of Christ and His church, the centre of God's plan throughout the ages. God's 'ambassador in bonds' fulfilled his ministry both before the highest tribunal of the Empire (cf. 2 Tim. 4: 17) and in the deepest recesses of the sanctuary, giving glory to 'him who is able to do immeasurably more than all we ask or imagine, according to his power that is at work within us, to him be glory in the church and in Christ Jesus throughout all generations, for ever and ever! Amen' (Eph 3: 20, 21).

BIBLIOGRAPHY

Commentaries
BRUCE, F. F., *The Acts of the Apostles*[2] [on the Greek text] (London, 1952).
BRUCE, F. F., *The Book of the Acts*. NICNT (Grand Rapids, 1954).
HAENCHEN, E., *The Acts of the Apostles*, E.T. (Oxford, 1971).
HANSON, R. P. C., *The Acts of the Apostles*. NCB (Oxford, 1967).

KELLY, W., *The Acts of the Apostles*² (London, 1914).

KNOWLING, R. J., *The Acts of the Apostles*. EGT [on the Greek text] (London, 1900).

LAKE, K., and CADBURY, H. J., *The Acts of the Apostles* [Vol. IV of *The Beginnings of Christianity*] (London, 1933).

MARSHALL, I. H., *The Acts of the Apostles. TNTC* (Leicester, 1980).

MUNCK, J., *The Acts of the Apostles. AB* (New York, 1967).

NEIL, W., *The Acts of the Apostles. NCentB* (London, 1973).

PACKER, J. W., *The Acts of the Apostles*. CBC (Cambridge, 1966).

PAGE, T. E., *The Acts of the Apostles* [on the Greek text] (London, 1886).

RACKHAM, R. B., *The Acts of the Apostles*⁶. WC (London, 1912).

WILLIAMS, C. S. C., *The Acts of the Apostles. BNTC* (London, 1957).

WILLIAMS, R. R., *The Acts of the Apostles*. Torch Commentaries (London, 1953).

General Works

CADBURY, H. J., *The Book of Acts in History* (New York, 1955).

CADBURY, H. J., *The Making of Luke-Acts* (New York, 1927).

DIBELIUS, M., *Studies in the Acts of the Apostles*, E.T. (London, 1956).

DUPONT, J., *Études sur les Actes des Apôtres* (Paris, 1967).

DUPONT, J., *The Sources of Acts*, E.T. (London, 1964).

GASQUE, W. W., *A History of the Criticism of the Acts of the Apostles* (Grand Rapids, 1975).

HENGEL, M., *Acts and the History of Earliest Christianity*, E.T. (London, 1979).

JACKSON, F. J. F., and LAKE, K. (editors), *The Beginnings of Christianity*. Part I: *The Acts of the Apostles*. Vols. I-V (London, 1920-33).

KNOX, W. L., *The Acts of the Apostles* (Cambridge, 1948).

O'NEILL, J. C., *The Theology of Acts in its Historical Setting* (London, ²1970).

RAMSAY, W. M., *The Church in the Roman Empire*⁴ (London, 1895).

RAMSAY, W. M., *St. Paul the Traveller and the Roman Citizen*¹⁴ (London, 1920)

SIMON, M., *St. Stephen and the Hellenists in the Jerusalem Church* (London, 1958).

SMITH, J., *The Voyage and Shipwreck of St. Paul*⁴ (London, ⁴1880).

WILCOX, M., *The Semitisms of Acts* (Oxford, 1965).

ROMANS

LESLIE C. ALLEN

It was probably during the winter of A.D. 56–7 that the apostle Paul in a house in Corinth wrote his letter to the Romans. His third missionary journey was drawing to a close, and for three months he was the guest of Gaius (cf. Ac. 20: 3). He could look back upon twenty years of Christian life and service. He had toured the chief cities of most of the eastern provinces of the Roman Empire, preaching Christ, establishing young communities of Christians and building them up into holiness and harmony. His previous letters had all been concerned with the problems and needs of local churches; now out of his missionary experience he dictates to Tertius his mature thoughts about God's gospel for the world and its place in history and in society.

This is the end of an epoch for Paul. He has canvassed the eastern Mediterranean for Christ's sake, and now he looks further afield. From Corinth he will go back to Jerusalem; from Jerusalem he, the apostle to the Gentiles, hopes to cross the sea to Rome, the capital of the Gentile world. But it is to be only a stepping stone. He intends to set out from there and lead a Spanish campaign. For this new venture he will need the backing of the household churches at Rome for prayer, personnel, finance and initial contacts. He had not founded the Christian community at Rome, and has never been there. This letter is to be his letter of introduction to people who for the most part had only heard about him, and heard perhaps conflicting reports. He writes ahead, informing of his visit and mentioning his plans. To help win their support he carefully explains the content of his missionary preaching and its relation both to God's past and future plans for the world and to contemporary society. The first eight chapters, after an opening greeting, expound the doctrinal basis of the gospel. *'The righteous-by-faith shall live'* is its theme-text. It serves as a pointer both to the sin and death that characterize the religious and pagan world, and to God's universal offer of justification and eternal life in Christ through His Spirit. In chapters 9 to 11 Paul reasons out from Scripture and his missionary experience God's present and future plans for Jew and Gentile. In the rest of the letter he discusses the outworking and implications of the gospel in the Christian community and in pagan society.

ANALYSIS

I   GREETINGS AND PRAYER (1: 1–15)

II THEME AND TEXT OF THE GOSPEL (1: 16–18a)

III THE GOSPEL FOR THE WORLD: '*THE RIGHTEOUS-BY-FAITH SHALL LIVE*' (1: 18b–8: 39)

   i *The righteous-by-faith* . . . (1: 18b–5: 11)
    a) The failure of the world (1: 18b–3: 20)
    b) Faith-righteousness (3: 21–4: 25)
    c) The joys of faith-righteousness (5: 1–11)
   ii . . . *Shall live* (5: 12–8: 39)
    a) Life in Christ (5: 12–7: 6)
    b) Life in the Spirit (7: 7–8: 30)
    c) Triumphant life (8: 31–39)

IV THE GOSPEL FOR THE WORLD IN GOD'S PLAN (9: 1–11: 36)
   i The Jews' tragic rejection of Christ (9: 1–5)
   ii God's present plan for Jew and Gentile (9: 6–10: 21)
   iii God's future plan for Jew and Gentile (11: 1–32)
   iv Praise of God's wisdom (11: 33–36)

I. GREETINGS AND PRAYER (1: 1–15)

1–7. Paul formally introduces himself to the churches at Rome, for this is the first direct contact he has had with them. He gives his credentials and shows the centrality of Jesus Christ in God's gospel for the world. **1.** He works not in his own right but as a **servant** at the disposal of his King and Lord. **Servant** (literally 'slave') has OT associations of a royal minister of state (*e.g.* 2 Kg. 22: 12) and of devotion to the worship and service of God (*e.g.* Ps. 113: 1). Paul's apostolic task is not a career of his own choosing but his response to the summons of God, who has singled him out like Jeremiah to be His herald (cf. Gal. 1: 15; Jer. 1: 5). **2–4.** That **the gospel** is **of God** is proved in that it was no new-fangled human idea but His own OT promises come true. God's 'mighty act' (NEB for **power**) in raising Jesus from the dead also authenticated the gospel. These verses echo an early confession of faith to which Paul also referred in his sermon at Pisidian Antioch (Ac. 13: 23, 32 f.). The subject of the gospel is God's eternal **Son, Jesus Christ our Lord**, the incarnate Saviour and promised King who binds His subjects to Himself and to each other. He is the properly accredited Messiah, 'born' (RV) of David's line in His earthly life (**as to his human nature**) (lit. 'flesh') and so qualified to be King of God's people. As great David's greater Son He had inherited the coronation promise and divine decree of Ps. 2: 7: *You are my son, today I have become your Father.* For **declared** probably read 'decreed' to capture the allusion. The resurrection was God's pronouncement officially installing Him as His Messianic King (cf. Ac. 13: 33) in fulfilment of the ancient decree. **Son of God** may partly be used as a title of the Messiah (cf. Ac. 9: 20 with Ac. 9: 22). Christ fulfilled His sonship in officially taking up His kingship. **Through the Spirit of holiness** means 'in the realm of the Holy Spirit', denoting Christ's post-resurrection life (cf. 1 Pet. 3: 18). In rabbinic thought the age to come was to be the era of the Spirit: for the Church it had dawned with the resurrection of Christ. **5.** Ps. 2 had promised the Messiah not only royal honours but royal dominion to the ends of the earth (cf. 10: 12 n.). Accordingly God had commissioned Paul (**we** is like the editorial 'we') to work throughout the world to win allegiance to Christ's name, and had equipped him with enabling **grace** that fitted him for his task (cf. Eph. 4: 7 f.). The object was the **obedience** that flows from **faith**, to make Gentiles first trust, then obey (cf. NEB). **6.** This world-wide commission explains Paul's interest in and authority over the Romans themselves. NIV interprets correctly AV's literal 'the called of Jesus Christ'; it is God the Father who calls (8: 30). When God issues His summons He claims a man as Christ's possession and appoints him to a destiny of salvation (cf. Isa. 42: 6; 43: 1). **7.** Like God's people in the OT they have been set inside the intimate circle of God's love. **Called to be saints** (Gk. *klētois hagiois*) or 'saints by calling' (J. N. Darby) echoes a term used of Israel—'*sacred assembly*' (Gk. *klētē hagia*: Exod. 12: 16; Lev. 23; Num. 28: 25). An ordinary letter in the 1st century A.D. began 'A. to B. greetings' (Gk. *chairein*). Christians gave this conventional opening a subtle spiritual turn by substituting **grace** (Gk. *charis*). To this Gentile-based greeting Paul adds the Jewish salutation of **peace** (Heb. *shālōm*). This beautiful invocation of divine blessing may be an echo of the Aaronic benediction of Num. 6: 24 ff. 'Note how this born-and-bred monotheist can set Jesus unequivocally on that side of reality which we call divine' (A. M. Hunter).

8–15. After that official introduction Paul, on a more personal note, confides his prayers. It was usual in a letter to follow the opening greeting with a prayer to a god (cf. C. H. Dodd's commentary for examples). In a Christian letter the true God, reached through Jesus Christ, took over where other gods generally held sway. Paul's praying was marked by thanksgiving, persistence, acknowledgment of God's sovereignty and a desire to be a channel of grace to others. **8.** News of the existence of believers at Rome had spread to every church in the Roman Empire. **9 f.** As part of the Christian work which expressed Paul's spiritual worship of God (**serve** is Gk. *latreuō:* cf. Gk. *latreiā*, 'worship', in 12: 1), he longed to visit them (cf. 15: 23 n.), but so far God had kept him elsewhere (Ac. 19: 21). Arrest, trial, two years' languishing in prison and shipwreck were to intervene before his prayer was answered. **12.** 'In the same breath he takes the low place with them' (Darby) in gracious humility. Paul tactfully corrects himself to make it clear that he will not come to lord it over them but to receive as well as give (cf. 2 C. 1: 24). This verse came true for Paul: see Ac. 28: 15. **14 f.** At Rome Paul hoped to engage in evangelism as well as in ministry to the churches. His apostolic commission had endowed him with a sense of world-wide missionary obligation (cf. 1 C. 9: 16 f.; Ac. 9: 15) which, as it transcended all types of civilization and degrees of culture, naturally extended to cosmopolitan **Rome**, where representatives of all these types could be found. **Greeks** are those who had adopted the international Hellenistic civilization, as distinct from **non-Greeks**, who kept up their national language and culture. On the other hand, in v. 16 a religious term **Gentile** is used. **Wise** and **foolish** are educated and uneducated people.

II. THEME AND TEXT OF THE GOSPEL (1: 16–18a)

16. Paul must have paused here and pondered. **Rome**—what thoughts of grandeur, power and even pride the word must have evoked in Paul the Roman citizen! But **the gospel** of Christ not only equalled but eclipsed the achievements of Rome. It too was something to be proud of, for it was God's own means—as dynamic as the resurrection (cf. v. 4)—of saving any one in the world who entrusts himself to Him (see note on faith at 3: 22), an offer made **first** in time to **the Jew**, then to **the Gentile**. The gospel knows no frontiers save the frontier of faith. **17. A righteousness from God . . . revealed** continuously in gospel-preaching, is a complex term (see note below). In brief it is God's righteous way of putting men right with Himself. On man's side it is 'based on faith and addressed to faith' (NEBmg. Lit. 'from faith to faith' as NIV margin: cf. 3: 22). Paul takes Hab. 2: 4 as his theme-text: 'The righteous-by-faith shall live' (cf. RSV, NEB). In its primary meaning the text was an assurance that despite threat of invasion and upheaval the man whose life was in line with God's will would be preserved and prosper under God's good hand on account of his firm loyalty to God. In the new fulfilment in the era of Christ the issues are lifted to another plane. There is a divine warfare against sin. Faithfulness is stripped to its core of faith and linked closely with 'righteous'. The promised life is the very life of the risen Christ. **18.** The gospel

not only reveals God's **righteousness**. Also 'the death of Jesus Christ on the Cross is the revelation of God's wrath from heaven' (Karl Barth). The **wrath** of God is generally taken as the outworking of God's judgment in human history. But the parallelism of **is revealed** in vv. 17 f. suggests a double reference to the contents of the gospel, and accordingly some have explained **wrath** in terms of the proclamation of judgment to come in the apostolic gospel. But 3: 25 and 8: 3 demonstrate a close connection between the Cross and God's **wrath** or condemnation of sin. In the OT 'righteousness' and 'wrath' are found as two sides of one coin. When 'righteousness' is God's intervention on behalf of His oppressed people, 'wrath' is a complementary aspect of the same process, the same intervention as experienced by the enemy oppressors (Isa. 59: 16–18; 63: 1–6). If righteousness is directed towards the restoration of man, it is directed against sin (see note at end of ch. 5)—**all the godlessness and wickedness**—and takes the form of **wrath**. In so far as sin is a force that controls a man's life, **wrath** must be directed against that man until he is rescued from its power. At the Cross God intervened **from heaven** and 'condemned' or defeated 'sin' by the death of His incarnate Son (8: 3). Apart from Christ **men** are doomed to meet God's **wrath** at the judgment day (2: 5), for it is their own **wickedness** that sets them in opposition to God and prevents His spiritual and moral **truth** from influencing their lives. But in advance 'the fire of wrath was kindled on Golgotha' (Barth). The last judgment was anticipated at Calvary. Sin was judged and deliverance was made available for the believer. He is shielded from God's **wrath** by the propitiatory power of the Crucified (3: 25).

NOTE ON RIGHTEOUSNESS

Righteousness has been defined by William Manson as 'a way of salvation which does justice to the moral reality of God's relations with men, while at the same time enabling men's restoration to right relations with God'. This definition of the word is far from what would be found in an English dictionary. This is because its roots lie deep in the Hebrew Scriptures, the seed-bed of the NT revelation. In the OT 'righteous' is primarily a term used in a court of law meaning 'in the clear', 'in the right'. It refers to the verdict of a judge upon a man on trial. Jer. 3: 11 reports God's verdict: 'Israel hath justified herself more than Judah' (AV) means that Israel 'is more righteous' (NIV). 'Righteousness' could also be applied to a judge. The rôle of a judge in Hebrew lawsuits was often to champion the oppressed against their oppressors, to protect and vindicate against wrong treatment. He was 'righteous' in so far as he came to the aid of the victimized.

In Lk. 18: 6 it is the judge's reluctance to try the case of the wronged widow that earns him the epithet 'unrighteous'.

The term 'righteous' came in due course to have a wider range of application than the law court. It developed also a moral significance: presumably the acquitted man helped by the judge against his adversaries received this verdict because he had previously acted in a morally right way. But the legal and moral uses of the word are not synonymous. When a judge acquitted a man and made him legally 'righteous' he did not thereby make him morally righteous.

As the reference to Jer. 3: 11 has shown, the idea of 'righteousness' came to be applied to the relations between God and man. God has as it were a law court to condemn wrongdoing and a court of appeal to reverse the verdict of corrupt judges of His people. God's righteousness is both His moral holiness and His saving activity on behalf of Israel. 'Righteous' became part of the vocabulary of the covenant between God and His people. In Gen. 15: 6 'righteousness' is Abraham's right relationship to God based upon his approval. The patriarch was not only 'in the right' before God his Judge but also 'right with' his covenant-God. He had a favourable standing of acceptance with God. The covenant relationship meant that Israelites could appeal to God for help, just as in an ancient treaty a vassal-king could appeal to his overlord if he was attacked. When foreigners invaded, Israel could appeal to the supreme Judge for aid. This appeal was made even when Israel had broken her side of the covenant and was strictly no longer eligible to claim God's 'righteousness'—but God did intervene to champion His unworthy people! The way was being paved for the NT where God reveals 'righteousness' to those completely outside a covenant-relationship in fulfilment of His own gracious promises. In Jg. 5: 11 God's activity in defending Israel against the Canaanites is called His 'righteousnesses' or 'righteous acts' (AV, NIV; RSV 'triumphs'). His 'righteousness' in this sense is His intervention in warfare. The Judge executes His judgment as a Warrior; the law court is the very field of battle. In Romans 'righteousness' is God's saving victory over sin, man's enemy, as well as a moral attribute of God and man, and man's acceptance by God. In the Cross and resurrection of Jesus Christ God has acted in moral and saving righteousness; He has offered to man the gift of the righteousness of acceptance with the intent that man may go on to live a life of moral righteousness.

III. THE GOSPEL FOR THE WORLD: 'The righteous-by-faith shall live' (1: 18b–8: 39)

Paul explains the doctrine of his gospel in terms of Hab. 2: 4, unfolding its relevance for the new Christian era. God by the death of Christ has set men right with Himself, if they will but put themselves by faith into His hands. The faith-righteous man shares the life of the risen and exalted Christ now in part and hereafter fully.

i. 'The righteous-by-faith . . .' (1: 18b–5: 11)

The apostle brings out the Christian significance of the first half of the text. Words associated with righteousness occur 36 times in this section and words associated with faith occur 29 times. The passage is pervaded with a law-court atmosphere. Men are guilty in God's court but by the good offices of God in Christ a favourable verdict is secured. The force of the forensic language is that men who were estranged from God, victims of their own sin, are reconciled to God by God in Christ and liberated from sin's fatal consequences.

(a) **The failure of the world (1: 18b–3: 20)** God's salvation is enhanced by first erecting a dark backcloth of human failure and then setting against it the splendour of divine grace. Paul proves why at the day of judgment God's wrath must fall upon the world of Jew and Gentile before he presents the alternative of faith-righteousness in Christ.

The failure of the pagan world (1: 18b–32) Paul is first speaking of mankind in general in v. 18, but as he goes on he has Gentiles specifically in view. He weighs up the Hellenistic society of his day and finds it wanting. Everywhere is chaos. Animals have become gods, man has become woman, wrong has become right. Nature without the true God has become unnatural. The Creator has been rejected and creation is in chaos: for the apostle these two facts are cause and effect. **19 f.** The absence of truth is not God's fault: it has been deliberately suppressed. 'There is no possible defence' (NEB) for the non-Jew. God has shown enough of Himself in the natural world for men to be unable to plead ignorance. The natural world is a window through which God has shown part of Himself to man, through which thinking man may 'see' His unseen **power** and 'divineness' (Knox. The NEB brings out the paradoxical play on words).

The rest of the chapter is made up of three parallel sections grouped round the phrase **God gave them over**, which is solemnly hammered out in vv. 24, 26, 28. **21–24.** Because they did not **glorify** Him, their fate was the sexual **degrading** of their bodies. Rejecting the evidence before them (cf. Ac. 14: 17), men substituted irrational ideas about God for a right use of reason (cf. v. 20). Paul is echoing the LXX of Jer. 2: 5; 10: 14, where **futile** and **fools** are applied to idolaters. They degraded

God to the level of created things. Ps. 106: 20 is in the apostle's mind at the beginning of v. 23. This is Israel all over again. The Gentile world too did not consider His works (Ps. 106: 7, 13). They too lapsed into idolatry, worshipping a lot of dummies. As God *handed Israel over to the nations* (Ps. 106: 41, LXX *paredōken*), so **God gave over** (Gk. *paredōken*) the Gentiles to their fate. Israel's experience had been mirrored and magnified in the Gentile world. Wrong behaviour was not merely the consequence of wrong worship, but a divine chastisement for it, although it was not the full punishment for their sin (cf. 3: 25), the final separation from God which is 'death' (v. 32, cf. 6: 23) or God's wrath at the judgment day (2: 5, 8). God made them harvest the crops they themselves had sown. **25–27.** Because they **exchanged** the real God for false gods, by way of temporary punishment they **exchanged natural** sexual intercourse for homosexuality. **25.** Paul breaks out of the foul atmosphere of vice and idolatry into the fresh air of a doxology. **27. Perversion** is their idolatry: Gk. *planē* (lit. 'wandering') is often so used in the LXX. **Penalty** is more literally 'corresponding penalty' or 'fitting wage' (NEB): the punishment fitted the crime. **28.** Because they did not **think it worthwhile** (Gk. *edokimasan*) to acknowledge God, their fate was an unfit (Gk. *adokimon*) mind. The price they paid for rejecting God was to become moral rejects. **29–31.** A haphazard catalogue of sins of personality and of personal relationships. **32.** This is the climax of sin. To assent coldly and objectively to others' sins is worse than to succumb to temptation oneself in the heat of the moment. Gentiles had inexcusably stifled their conscience (cf. 2: 15) so that evil was accepted as if it were good. All such must expect sentence of death at the judgment day.

The failure of the Jews (2: 1–3: 20)
Paul subtly turns to prove the Jews defenceless too, first in veiled language, later openly with 'a "Thou art the man", somewhat after the manner of Nathan's parable to David' (Sanday and Headlam). **1 f.** The Jew 'stood in his own estimate on a higher elevation than that of mankind at large. But the words "O man" were intended to disallow that claim' (B. W. Newton). The would-be judge is himself put in the dock—and condemned—on the same charge as the Gentiles. There is the same pattern of experience: knowledge and wilful ignoring. The Jews, including Paul who has previously felt this shock of failure himself, **know** of God's judgment of wrongdoers from the law, 'the embodiment of knowledge' (v. 20). **3.** The Jew's attempt to cover up his own sin with tut-tutting will not avert his punishment. At the end of the verse **you** is emphatic: 'you, any more than they' (NEB). **4 f.** God's **kindness** in deferring judgment has been abused: it has not

coaxed the Jew into **repentance**, but served to provoke blatant presumption. Wealth of grace, when thus slighted, turns into wealth of **wrath** ('treasure up' is better with AV, RV), which will be paid out at the **day** of **judgment. 6.** The Jew cannot escape the evidence of his own Scriptures. That the verdict will be based upon actual behaviour and not upon high ideals or theoretical superiority God's Word has already made clear (Ps. 62: 12; Prov. 24: 12 are echoed). **7. Eternal life**—life in the age to come which follows the day of judgment (5: 9 f., cf. Gal. 6: 8)—will be given only to those who prepare for it with consistent good living which aims at **glory**, or enjoying the radiant presence of God (cf. 5: 2), and **honor**, God's 'well done' (cf. Jn 12: 26; 1 Pet. 1: 7) and **immortality**, which Christ makes possible (2 Tim. 1: 10; 1 C. 15: 53). Paul's usage of this vocabulary elsewhere makes it clear that this blessing is for the faith-righteous man. 'Oh, it is a living, creative, active, mighty thing this faith! So it is impossible for it to fail to produce good works steadily' (Luther). 'It is faith alone which justifies, but the faith which justifies can never be alone' (Calvin). The Christian is not exempt from a trial of works (14: 10 ff.; 2 C. 5: 10; Jn 5: 29). 'The righteous will be rewarded not on account of but according to their works. Good works are to them the evidence of their belonging to that class to whom for Christ's sake eternal life is graciously awarded' (C. Hodge). Cf. 8: 13 n. **8.** Those who 'suppress the truth by their wickedness' (1: 18) will encounter God's **wrath.** NEB has 'governed by selfish ambition' for **self-seeking:** Gk. *eritheia* is 'the ambition which has no conception of service and whose only aims are profit and power' (W. Barclay, *A NT Wordbook*, p. 40). **9–11.** It is perhaps significant that the Gk. words for **trouble** and **distress** occur three times in the LXX of Dt. 28: 53 ff. in a curse on those who break the covenant-law. Paul is reminding **the Jew** of what he already knew but liked to forget. If the Jews' ancient priority of privilege counted for anything, it meant priority of responsibility (cf. Am. 3: 2). The principles of God's judgment are the same for all. Ultimately, 'God has no favourites' (NEB). Gk. *prosōpolēmpsia* (**favoritism**) is only found in Christian writings. It is based on the LXX translation of a Hebrew phrase 'lift up the face'. Originally it was used of accepting with favour a prostrate suppliant by raising his chin with the hand. Later the expression for favour became an idiom for favouritism. **12–16.** V. 11 is expanded: Jew and Gentile stand on an equal footing. The **law** is not a charm which can guarantee the Jew immunity but the very plumbline of his own judgment. Paul is attacking his fellow-Jews on their own ground, countering one popular tenet of Judaism with another. The principle of doing the works of the law, carried to its logical conclusion, cancels out the privilege derived from possessing the law. It also amounts to a criterion by which both Jew and Gentile will be judged together. For the Jew merely to listen to the law being read out in the synagogue Sabbath by Sabbath does him no good. And although Gentiles were not blessed with a revelation of the law, like Israel at Sinai, yet they do at times show a natural awareness of its standards. 'When the heathen honours his parents, he does something that is good and in keeping with the law. At another time he violates the law, but that is not Paul's point' (Anders Nygren). **15. Conscience** is here a man's moral consciousness by which after a deed is done he pronounces it right or wrong. It is 'a juridical faculty after action, not a legislative faculty before' (R. H. Fuller). Thus besides the Gentile's instinctive behaviour there is another witness to the fact that he knows God's standards, albeit imperfectly. The last clause is apparently a further definition of the activity of **conscience**. Man

> *ever bears about*
> *A silent court of justice in his breast*
> *Himself the judge and jury, and himself*
> *The prisoner at the bar.* (Tennyson, *Sea Dreams*)

16. On the **day** of judgment God will bring **secrets** out into the open, both the mental accusations of Gentile consciences and the reality behind Jewish claims. Part of Paul's gospel was that judgment to come would be in the hands of Jesus Christ acting as judge for God (Ac. 17: 31). The verse does not dovetail smoothly into the preceding one; probably it goes with v. 13, and vv. 14 f. are in parenthesis. **17–24.** The law, their boast, has been broken. The so-called Jew had a superior air about him, which Paul could describe easily because it had once been his own. **17.** He complacently 'leaned' on the **law** (cf. Mic. 3: 11). His **relationship to God** made him cocksure. **18–20.** He knew it all. He expected the rest of the world to kowtow to him. They had to come to him to get the benefit of his moral discernment and learning. They were **blind**, 'benighted' (NEB), **foolish, infants**, but not he, because he had the law. The phrases in vv. 19 f. 'may have been phrases used by the "Foreign Mission Committee" of Pharisaic Judaism' (A. M. Hunter). **21 f.** A deliberate anticlimax. Paul cites the Jews' flagrant breaches of the law, which were obviously well known. They did not live up to their own ideals, and therefore had no cause for smug self-satisfaction. **23.** The very people who shook their heads over the Gentiles' dishonouring God were doing the same. **24.** Isa. 52: 5, as it appears in the LXX, sums up the situation.

25–29. Circumcision is no security. To the average Jew the sign of circumcision, his distinguishing mark, exempted from judgment as surely as the sign of the rainbow. But Paul points out its uselessness unless the covenantal obligations inherent in the rite are kept. 'If you flout the law, you are to all intents and purposes uncircumcising yourself' (J. B. Phillips). 'The hearers of God without God may be compared to a traveller who remains standing under the signpost instead of moving in the direction to which it directs him. The signpost has become meaningless' (Barth). **26.** Reversing the argument, Paul contends that an uncircumcised Gentile who does keep these obligations is virtually circumcised, a member of the Israel of God (Gal. 6: 16), and will be treated as such at the day of judgment. The apostle has Gentile Christians in mind, as comparison with 8: 4 shows (see RV). **27.** Cf. Mt. 12: 41 for the thought. **28, 29.** Being a 'Jew' depends not upon rite, race or **written code**, but upon an attitude of **heart**. Paul is reiterating a lesson the OT itself often taught (*e.g.* Dt. 10: 16; Jer. 4: 4). Was this also Stephen's words (Ac. 7: 51) still ringing in Paul's ears? A true Jew is one who lives up to the meaning of his name by pleasing God and winning His **praise**, not his neighbour's (cf. Mt. 6: 1; Jn 12: 43). **Jew** (Gk. *Ioudaios*) comes from 'Judah', which is linked with *hōdāh* 'praise' in Gen. 29: 35; 49: 8.

3: 1–8. Jewish protests are silenced. On his missionary travels Paul must have met many Jewish hecklers in synagogue and market-square. From his experiences he here replies to some Jewish reactions to his gospel. **1.** Does not this condemnation of the Jews deny that they have any racial privileges? **2.** Indeed not: in a non-saving sense they have many, such as being trustees of God's OT promises. Paul intended to go on to mention other privileges, such as the ones listed in 9: 4 f., but the first diverts him to another objection. **3.** According to Paul some of the Jews (most in fact, but Paul is being charitable; cf. 11: 17) have been bad trustees and have let God down. Does not this mean that there is no future for God's people and that He will be forced to abandon them and let them down? **4.** Paul shudders at the blasphemy. God will ultimately keep His promises to them, he will argue in ch. 11. Instead of God's faithfulness being nullified, may the opposite happen: may God make His word come true and at the same time may the statement wrung out of the Psalmist by bitter experience (Ps. 116: 11) be verified—may **every man** break his word because God's faithfulness would thereby be enhanced. Paul quotes Ps. 51: 4 in support. He has the whole verse in mind (cf. 11: 26 n.): *Against you, you only, have I sinned . . . , in order that you may be proved right. . . .* God used David's murder and adultery to glorify Himself. By divine intent 'man's sin brings out into a clearer light the justice and holiness of God' (A. F. Kirkpatrick, *The Psalms, ad loc.*). **5.** But, it may be objected, if human wrong shows up the rightness of God in greater relief (Gk. *synistēsin*: cf. 5: 8 n.), if the worst in man brings out the best in God, man's sin surely serves a useful purpose in God's plan. Then what room is there for human responsibility and liability? Ought not God in fairness to recognize this service and give man credit for it instead of condemning him in **wrath** at the day of judgment (2: 5, 8)? Gk. *epipherōn* should probably be translated not **bringing** but 'pronouncing': cf. its forensic use in Jude 9. Paul apologizes for even quoting this implication that God is unfair and fallible. **Using a human argument** means 'arguing as if God were a man'. **6.** That God would **judge the world** was common ground for Paul and his Jewish critic. Paul tries to checkmate his opponent with a clear implication of that fact: such a God must give 'righteous judgment' (2: 5). *Will not the Judge of all the earth do right?* (Gen. 18: 25) may have been at the back of Paul's mind. **7.** The objector—and perhaps Paul himself—is not satisfied, and presses his point. What right has God to judge him **as a sinner** if he lies? For the logical conclusion of Paul's contention is that a man can lie to the **glory** of God, seeing that God uses his lie to throw His own truth into sharper relief. **8.** He goes on, 'since the end—God's glory—is good, does not that justify the means, which in this case is my sin?' (F. F. Bruce). Paul has been accused of implying this by his teaching about God's grace. Does he not say 'Where sin increased, grace increased all the more' (5: 20)? And did he not suppose a crucifixion to be the means of salvation? Paul faces up to this objection that his gospel breeds immorality in ch. 6, a more appropriate point in his train of argument. At the moment he merely snaps a retort in disgust.

9–20. The OT confirms Jewish failure. Paul's accusations have been universal in scope. Jew and Gentile alike are **under** the thumb of **sin**. Despite their historic privileges the Jews cannot claim exemption from the workings of God's moral law. **10–18.** This indictment has the authority of Scripture behind it. The OT affirms the sin of God's people as well as promises of their salvation (2). Paul may be using an existing collection of OT texts originally compiled to show that the whole being of man has shared in evil (**throat, tongues, lips, mouth, feet, eyes**). A string of verses from the Psalms and Isaiah show not merely what man can be like but what a Jew can be like, since the Jew who is meant to read the OT cannot with a good conscience shrug off these verses as referring only to 'Gentile sinners'. **19. The law** in its first occurrence means the OT,

as in 1 C. 14: 21. A longer title is used in v. 21. Now not only the Gentiles but the Jews also have been put on trial in God's court and shown to be defenceless. This condemnation was in line with God's purposes of ultimate grace (cf. 11: 32). **20.** Ps. 143: 2, here quoted, is a permanent principle. No one will be able to pass God's scrutiny on the day of judgment who supposes that his behaviour conforms to God's standards revealed in **the law**. On the contrary, in Paul's experience, as he will explain in 7: 7–25, to know God's standards is to realize one's own hopeless inadequacy. 'It is the straight edge of the law that shows us how crooked we are' (Phillips).

(b) Faith-righteousness (3: 21–4: 25)
God's gift of faith-righteousness (3: 21–31)
The analysis of mankind has revealed signs of desperate failure. The verdict of the day of judgment is a foregone conclusion. Is there then no hope? David in Ps. 143 knew the only possibility: to throw himself, unrighteous as he was, upon God's promises of salvation. Before pleading with God not to enter into judgment with him he had appealed: *In your faithfulness and righteousness come to my relief.* To this hope Paul now turns in v. 21, after quoting Ps. 143: 2 in v. 20. The appeal has been answered for mankind. **A righteousness from God . . . has been made known.** He has personally undertaken to set men right with Him (see 1: 17 n.). It has happened **now**, wiping out the past and inaugurating a new age with new prospects. For Paul and for every believer all the preceding exposure of failure and of coming wrath is only a 'then', something that lies behind him. In the rest of this paragraph Paul goes on to define the new **righteousness** as to its channel, warrant, scope, cost, basis, divine consequences and human implications. As to its *channel*, saving **righteousness** comes to man **apart from law**. It does not depend on doing one's best to keep up to the standards of God's moral law, as Judaism taught. The *warrant* for it is in the OT (see v. 19 n.). Although it cuts across the tenets of Judaism, the contemporary heir of the OT, yet there is clear evidence in the Scriptures that this is really and solely how God works, as ch. 4 will show. **22 f.** Its only *channel* is **faith in Jesus Christ**. **Faith** is the opposite of self-reliance. It is 'an act which is the negation of all activity' (C. H. Dodd), an act of life-committal, entrusting oneself to **Jesus Christ**, the spearhead of God's saving work. The *scope* is universal, impartially embracing any Jew or Gentile who commits himself in trust. A universal offer of salvation matches the already proved universality of sin. The **glory of God** here refers to the reflection of God's radiant being in man, the moral and spiritual kinship to Him with which Adam was created as the

image of God. The image is sadly disfigured in fallen man. It is only in Christ, the Second Man and the greater Image of God, that the work of restoring the image can begin (2 C. 3: 18; cf. 5: 2 n.; 8: 30 n.). **24.** As to the *cost*, getting right with God costs man nothing but was very costly to God. God Himself in His **grace** or generous, undeserved love has by Christ's work of 'ransom' (Moffatt) bought the believer out of sin's slave-market (cf. 6: 6, 17; 7: 14). **Redemption** also hints at the Exodus of God's people in Christ (cf. 9: 17 n.; Dt. 7: 8; Isa. 51: 11). The logical subject of **are justified** is 'all who believe' in v. 22; the intervening words are best taken as a parenthesis. **25 f.** The divine *basis* of setting men right is the sacrifice of Christ. God proffered Him as the antidote to human sin. But He was more: He became not only **a sacrifice of atonement** but 'the means of propitiation' (Moffatt; cf. AV, RV) or 'place of propitiation'. While expiation (cf. RSV) deals with human sin, propitiation deals also with wrath, the divine reaction to sin. Up to now the threat of God's wrath has been hanging over men's heads, ready to fall like the sword of Damocles. In Christ the threat vanishes, for it descended upon Him (1: 18). Here is a 'a theological comment on the meaning of the Markan cry from the cross: "My God, my God, why has thou forsaken me?"' (R. H. Fuller). In Christ the God of love (5: 8) Himself provided the means of inflicting His wrath upon man's sin in such a way that man is saved. The underlying Gk. word *hilastērion* means 'mercy seat', the cover of the ark and the place of propitiation, in Heb. 9: 5. Probably here too a ceremonial reference is intended and Paul has in mind the rites of the Day of Atonement (Lev. 16), which culminated in the sprinkling of the mercy-seat with the blood of sacrifice. Christ is our mercy-seat and Christ the sacrificial victim. Subjectively propitiation is brought about through the medium of **faith** (cf. RV), whereby the individual claims it for himself. Objectively it is achieved by virtue of Christ's **blood** poured out in a sacrificial death. The *divine consequence* of God's setting men right in this way is that He upholds His **justice**. Paul is now highlighting a specific facet of righteousness, God's moral justice. He must often have heard his gospel criticized in Jewish circles on the ground that it made a mockery of God's **justice**. Some of this criticism that the Christian view of God is immoral has been reflected earlier in this chapter. The notions of Christians that a moral God (*a*) had made an accursed execution the means of blessed life (Gal. 3: 13) and (*b*) accepted sinners, were clearly preposterous, argued the Jew. Paul replies that (*a*) the OT and Judaism do not go far enough. Taken as the full and final revelation of God they, and not the Cross, are a scandal.

It is only the God of the Cross who clarifies His **justice**. In seeming complacency God had leniently **left the sins committed beforehand unpunished** of Jew (2: 4) and Gentile (1: 24 n.; Ac. 17: 30), but He had only done so because His eye was on the Cross. Now He had acted according to character and rent the heavens (1: 18) in a display of His abhorrence to, and punishment of, sin. It is only the Christian view of God and sin that makes sense. (*b*) God may now for the first time receive back the repentant sinner without prejudice to His moral justice because acceptance depends on **faith in Jesus**. Translate: 'He is righteous *even while justifying* . . .' (H. C. G. Moule. The Gk. *kai*—and—is here adverbial). 'By appropriating to himself the homage rendered to the majesty of God by the Crucified One, the believer is himself crucified as it were in the eyes of God: moral order is established and judgment can take end by an act of absolution' (F. Godet). **27–31.** The *human implications* of God's justifying activity are three-fold. (*a*) Self-sufficient claims are invalidated by the principle of self-effacing **faith**. 'The whole matter is now on a different plane—believing instead of achieving' (Phillips). 'Self-contained, self-sufficient, self-justifying goodness cannot be real goodness because its effect is to set up man's moral independence of God; it is thus the expression of man's egoism, and is in its very nature a rebellion against the source of all good' (G. O. Griffith). (*b*) Now therefore the human race is put on a common level: Jew and Gentile meet at the Cross (cf. Eph. 2: 11 ff.). **There is only one God** is part of the *Shema* or Jewish creed, based upon Dt. 6: 4 ff. From an article of the Jewish faith Paul deduces that as God of all He will treat all on the same principle on the day of judgment. **By** (Gk. *ek* as in v. 26 and 1: 17) and **through** (Gk. *dia* as in vv. 22, 25) are variations due to style. (*c*) **The law** is placed 'on a firmer footing' (NEB). Despite Paul's attitude to the law in vv. 21, 28 its moral obligations are ultimately met in the Christian life, as chs. 6, 8 explain.

Faith-righteousness a divine principle (4: 1–25)

This chapter enlarges the claim made in 3: 21 that faith-righteousness has Scriptural warrant, and explains the assertions made in 3: 29 ff. that God accepts both Jew and Gentile, but only on the ground of faith. Paul took it for granted that God would never be false to the basic principles of His OT revelation. God stays the same and His Word is ever contemporary (cf. v. 23 f.). There must be an essential unity between the old and the new revelations of God. Faith-righteousness is in fact nothing new, but the ground on which God met with the very founder of Israel. The apostle is incidentally striking at the roots of Judaism's national and spiritual pride. He takes as his text Gen. 15: 6, which puts in a nutshell the relationship between God and Abraham in the Genesis stories. This whole chapter is a careful analysis of that text and its implications. In the light of it Paul gives four answers to the question of v. 1. (*a*) Abraham became right with God by faith, not by works. That the text itself makes clear (2–8). (*b*) He became right with God by faith, not by circumcision. So teaches the position of the text, coming as it does before Gen. 17 (9–12). (*c*) He became right with God by faith, not by the law. This again is evident from the position of the text, which comes much earlier in the Pentateuch than the account in Exodus of the giving of the law (13–17a). (*d*) The context of Gen. 15: 6 defines Abraham's faith as confidence in God's promise of life (17b–25). In the course of each answer Paul shows that there is a principle at stake which is relevant to the gospel

1–8. Abraham had faith-righteousness. In his mind Paul is arguing with fellow Jews. As later Jews did, they probably cited Gen. 26: 5 to support their claim that it was Abraham's obedience to the law that made him acceptable to God. **3.** But Scripture gives a different answer. **Righteousness** here and in Gen. 15: 6 is 'a right relationship to God conferred by a divine sense of approval' (J. Skinner, *Genesis*). Isa. 41: 8 sums it up in the word *friend*, as James saw when he connected the two verses (Jas 2: 23). **Credited** has other OT roots apart from the text quoted. It is used to describe the judgment or estimate of the priests as representatives of God whereby they approved or rejected an Israelite's offering (*e.g.* Lev. 8: 18; 17: 4). Thus here and in Genesis it refers to a divine evaluation, which although it may conflict with a human assessment is in no way fictitious (cf. 2: 26). The word was also a current commercial term for crediting something to one's account. It is not out of generosity that an employer credits his staff with their salaries: they have a claim to remuneration. **5.** But the relationship between man and God does not fall into the category of **work** and wage-claims. Empty hands outstretched in **faith** are all that man has to show to God. A right relationship based on grace is paid into the believer's account, as it were: he is accepted, **wicked** though he has been. **6–8.** God accepts the ungodly? Yes, Paul can prove it. Using a rabbinic comparative principle of interpretation, he defines Gen. 15: 6 in terms of Ps. 32: 1 f., where the idea occurs again: crediting-righteousness means not-crediting-sin. 'The only thing of my very own which I can contribute to my redemption is the sin from which I need to be redeemed' (William Temple).

9–12. Faith justifies, not circumcision. Having established that disregarding sin in for-

giveness is the same as regarding as righteous, Paul can now apply *blessed* of Ps. 32 to the man regarded as righteous. But is the Gentile excluded from this category? In reply Paul again takes Abraham's experience as the pattern of God's dealings with man. Gen. 15 comes before Gen. 17: his acceptance on the basis of faith preceded his **circumcision**. The order is important: it implies that **circumcision** was never meant to be exploited as an automatic rite which could predispose God to accept a man. In **circumcision** God was merely confirming and adding His signature to His earlier pronouncement, which was based on Abraham's personal confidence in Himself. Abraham was a virtual Gentile in Gen. 15. His spiritual successors are therefore (*a*) Gentiles who trust as Abraham did and (*b*) only those Jews who **walk in the footsteps** of Abraham's **faith.**

13–17a. Faith justifies, not the law. The **promise** of Gen. 17: 4 ff. to the faith-righteous Abraham, that his posterity would be found the world over significantly antedated the giving of the law. **Law** is a shorthand expression loaded with deep psychological content. Here as often one must know the man before one can know the meaning of his words. Paul's attitude towards the law is coloured by his own experience inside Judaism. What had originally been founded upon God's gracious act of redemption (Exod. 20: 2) had eventually become by and large the basis of human claims upon God. Added 'explanations' turned it into a burden that crippled a conscientious Jew like Paul, a burden made all the heavier by loss of spontaneity, of joy and of a sense of God's gracious initiative. Paul attacks the law for the legalism with which it had become synonymous. The Jews had dragged it down and perverted it into an organ of human achievement. To such God's **promise** could not come. The law is 'a heap of clinkers marking a fiery miracle which has taken place, a burnt-out crater disclosing the place where God has spoken, . . . a dry canal which in a past generation and under different conditions had been filled with the living water of faith and of clear perception' (Barth). **15.** The law cannot bless, only condemn: see 3: 20 n.; 5: 13 n. **16.** The **promise** was a matter of **grace** on God's side and of **faith** on man's. It was thus independent of the law. God was in advance making it clear that his heirs would not be confined to Jews (cf. Gal. 3: 8). **17.** Indeed, God **made** him **father of many** Gentiles, as Gen. 17: 5 declares (Gk. *ethnē* means 'Gentiles' as well as **nations**). Abraham was 'assigned the rôle of a mediator of blessing in God's saving plan for *all the families of the earth*' (G. von Rad, *Genesis*, on Gen. 12: 3).

17b–25. Abraham's faith is compared with

Christian faith. The promise of v. 17a was given to Abraham as he stood **in the sight** of God. The context of Gen. 15: 6 links Abraham's faith with God's promise of Isaac. His wife's and his own sexual deadness (19; Gen. 18: 11 ff.) ruled out confidence in himself and directed him to God, who can both renew life and issue His creative call (cf. Isa. 41: 4 and *Let . . . in* Gen. 1). **18.** His **hope** based upon believing God's promise cut right across the grain of natural expectation. 'We are able to hear his "Yes", whilst the world above and below him cries out to him "No"' (Barth). **So** directed Abraham's gaze up to the stars studding the night sky. **19.** NIV rightly follows RV in omitting 'not', which some ancient MSS added to the text (as in AV, 'he considered not his own body'). 'Faith does not mean to close one's eyes to the facts. Faith has no kinship with optimistic self-deception' (Nygren). There was a rabbinic saying that a centenarian is 'as though he were dead and gone'. **20.** Paul disregards Abraham's temporary lapses from faith in Gen. 16: 2; 17: 17 either because his thoughts are centred upon Gen. 15 or because Abraham's doubts were short-lived. **21 f.** It was Abraham's throwing himself upon God's promise and His power to keep it that underlay God's accepting him as right with Himself. **23 f.** And it is the same today! Christian faith is Abraham's faith all over again, faith in the same Giver of miraculous life, who has now demonstrated His power in the miracle of the resurrection. **25.** The verse reads like a line of Semitic poetry. **Jesus our Lord. He . . .** is probably a quotation from a confession of faith used in the worship of the Palestinian churches. The first half echoes Isa. 53. Paul uses the quotation to round off and support his comparison of Abraham's and the Christian's faith because it links **justification** with Jesus' risen life. His resurrection is the basis of the believer's justification. The resurrection justified Christ (1 Tim. 3: 16; cf. Rom. 1: 4 n.), proving Him not personally subject to God's wrath, and this condition is shared by those who are in Him.

(*c*) **The joys of faith-righteousness (5: 1–11)**
The righteous-by-faith . . . has been expounded. Before going on to the Christian force of *. . . Shall live*, and in the process of transition to it, Paul lifts up his heart in an outburst of joy and thanksgiving for the implications of faith-righteousness (cf. 8: 31 ff.; 11: 33 ff.). Justification is for him not merely a doctrine to define and defend: he has found it a cup of blessing that runs over into his whole life. **1.** There is strong support for 'let us have' in manuscripts and versions. But a statement of assured fact reads more naturally here than an appeal. The fact that the two verbal forms were pronounced in the same way in Hellenistic and later Greek explains the textual variation. **Peace** is here

not an inward feeling but the relationship of reconciliation with God. The Christian is no longer in the enemy camp. Through Christ's atoning death God now deals with him as a friend (cf. vv. 10 f.). **2.** Christ has put us on a new footing with God, setting our feet firmly on the rock of **grace**. There is the prospect of one day enjoying the fullness of God's presence. **Glory** is the radiant brightness of God's presence, His Shekinah-glory. Christians are already privileged to share the restoration (cf. 3: 23) of this radiant glow in standing (8: 30) and in progressive growth (2 C. 3: 18), but the consummation of the process is yet to come (Phil. 3: 21; 1 Jn 3: 2). **3 f.** These blessings are realities which do not belong merely to a detached spiritual world, but are relevant to the concrete world of human affairs. The joy of being right with God enables a man to take in his stride **suffering** borne for Christ's sake (cf. Hab. 3: 17 f.). Indeed he finds it helps him on his way. God has designed it to produce by a chain reaction the qualities of constancy, sterling **character** (Gk. *dokimē*—something tested) and convinced **hope**. 'We are weaned from the world, and become better able to perceive and appreciate what is heavenly. So the hope which is already in us becomes clearer and brighter' (J. N. Darby). **5.** Scripture attests the certain fruition of hope in God: allusion is made to the LXX of Ps. 22: 5. The ultimate basis of the Christian's hope lies not in his reaction to persecution, although that may strengthen it, but in God Himself as a God who has proved His **love**. The chief blessing **poured out** with His Spirit (an echo of Jl 2: 28) is a sense of His love (cf. 15: 30). When once the Spirit has made His Calvary-love overwhelmingly real to a man in inward experience, he is bound to think evermore: if God loves me as much as that, He will love me to the end. **6–8.** The extent of God's **love** is shown in that there was nothing admirable or lovely about man which could have evoked it. Human self-sacrifice demands intrinsic worth in its object, whether scrupulous fairness or kindly goodness. God's love, revealed in Christ's death, wonderfully makes no prior demands at all. God has proved how well He loves us, His love is confirmed and enhanced (Gk. *synistēsin:* cf. 3: 5 n.) in that it was shown to weaklings, to impious **sinners**, when He broke into history at the crucial moment, His appointed **time** for inaugurating a new era of grace. **9 f.** Since God has already done so much, He can be trusted to put the finishing touches to His work (cf. Phil. 1: 6). The past guarantees the future. Acceptance through Christ's death (cf. 3: 25) carries with it an assurance that He will finally save from the **wrath** of the day of judgment when sinners are punished (cf. 2: 5 ff.; 1 Th. 5: 9). Reconciliation assures us of the future bliss of eternal life. Christ's risen and exalted life is an extra guarantee: 'His life is a pledge and security for the life of all His people' (C. Hodge). Cf. 6: 8; Jn 14: 19. '"Jesus died, and Jesus lives"—these are the truths that contain everything for us. All that a dying and a living Saviour can do is ours' (A. Bonar). **11.** Paul again brings his readers back to earth (cf. v. 3 AV, RV). The fruits of justification do not all lie in the future by any means. Christ in establishing friendly relations with God has given something which makes us **rejoice** here and now **in God** Himself.

ii. '. . . Shall live' (5: 12–8: 39)

Paul now turns to the second half of his theme text. The promise of life is shown to find its fulfilment in Christ and in the Spirit. 'Life' and 'live' occur 25 times in this section and only three times in the preceding one. 'Die', 'death', etc. occur 37 times here and only six times before (five in 5: 6 ff.).

(a) Life in Christ (5: 12–7: 6)

First Paul expounds the principle of life in Christ and then he makes a threefold demand for the practical outworking of what it implies.

Solidarity in Christ (5: 12–21)

Just as the first main section contrasted the hopelessness of man with God's gift of faith-righteousness, so now life in Christ is set over against death in Adam. Adam was a **pattern**, foreshadowing his future Counterpart: both are heads and inclusive representatives of the human creation, Adam of the old and Christ of the new (1 C. 15: 45 ff., 2 C. 5: 17). But Christ is viewed not only as the Second Man, but also as the Servant. V. 19 is a direct allusion to Isa. 53: 11. The whole section can be regarded as a linking up of Gen. 3 and Isa. 53: 11 with Hab. 2: 4. The ideas of **righteousness, justification, many** and **obedience** come from Isa. 53: 11 (see v. 19 n.). The thought of **life** comes from Hab. 2: 4. The opposite themes of **sin, trespass, condemnation, disobedience** and **death** are suggested not only by contrast with the positive concepts, but also by the story in Gen. 3 of Adam's eating the forbidden fruit in spite of God's threat of death. These are the key ideas of this section. Paul has reflected upon his OT sources and woven them together with the unifying thread of the work of Christ. The work of the Servant-Man who by His obedience brought righteousness and life to the new humanity in Him is enhanced by setting it against the dark background of Adam's failure and its fatal results for Adam's race.

> When all was sin and shame,
> A second Adam to the fight
> And to the rescue came.

One must therefore not expect to find in these verses a clear-cut comprehensive doctrine of original sin. The purpose is to stress God's work of renewal in Christ, and all else is subordinate to that purpose. There is much mystery concerning the nature and extent of our corporate relationship with Adam, which systematic theologians have variously attempted to explain. G. O. Griffith has helpfully compared 'the psychological notion of a general "racial unconscious mind" which each individual coming into life inherits, with its race-memories, urges, inhibitions and sense of guilt. From this inheritance he cannot dissociate himself—cannot achieve a self-contained selfhood; he is bound up with the race and the race with him.' Since the entry of sin 'each man who is born into the world . . . finds a compromised situation confronting him. . . . Each generation and each individual act in such a way that the inner strength of rising individuals and generations is enfeebled, deflected and at times destroyed' (F. J. Leenhardt). **12.** The sentence is left unfinished. It should logically have continued 'so through one Man righteousness came into the world and through righteousness life'. But Paul breaks off the comparative construction and does not return to his main thought till vv. 18 f. Adam opened the door to sin and let it loose in the world of men. His sin marked the invasion from outside of an evil force. Once it had ignited a fatal spark in **one man** it spread like wildfire through the human race. **Sinned** refers to actual sins (cf. 3: 23) viewed as an individual expression and endorsement of Adam's representative act. 'The individual sins are, as it were, only the eruptions of this sin for ever bubbling in the deep' (Emil Brunner). **Death** is not merely physical but the sign of the extinction of man's spiritual life. In order to make the main thought clear vv. 18 f. will be considered before the parenthetical vv. 13–17. **18.** The verse is a summarized formula without verbs in the Greek (notice AV's italics). God's two-part plan for the old era in Adam and for the new era in Christ had means, scope and result in both cases. The *means* was (a) **one trespass**—almost 'fall' since Gk. *paraptōma* is literally a 'fall sideways'—and (b) **one act of righteousness**. Over against Adam's wrong act towers the Cross where Christ fully accomplished the will of God. The *scope* was and is **all men**. The limiting phrase in v. 17 suggests that in the second case it is restricted to those who actually accept God's offer of salvation. To suppose that Paul taught the universal salvation of all individuals is to ignore the realism which years of missionary experience must have inculcated in him. 'All in Adam', 'all in Christ' is meant. The *result* of God's double plan, was (a) **condemnation** and (b) 'justification of life' (AV), a favourable verdict which leads to eternal life. **19.** The second half is a quotation of Isa. 53: 11 with the verb put into the passive because underlying the whole passage is the thought of God's execution of His plan rather than of the Son's accomplishments by themselves. The future tense refers to the day of judgment which heralds the consummation of the new era in Christ (cf. 6: 5 n.). The new humanity in Christ will be constituted **righteous**, in the right, 'acceptable to God' (Knox). **The many** (Gk. *hoi polloi*) is a Hebrew idiom for the mass of men. Paul had in v. 18 translated it into Greek idiom as **all**. **Obedience** is probably a paraphrase of the Hebrew word underlying *knowledge* in Isa. 53: 11. Modern Hebrew study suggests that it really meant 'humiliation', 'submission'. Phil. 2: 8 also stresses Christ's obedience in His rôle of Servant. **13 f.** Paul is side-tracked by **all sinned**. To speak of sin after Adam and before Moses raises a problem. If sin is defined as the conscious breaking of God's moral standard, how could what God regards as sin qualify for the death-penalty when that standard was not known in the period between Adam and Moses? Paul is using the OT representation of mankind's history. He leaves his theological difficulty unanswered (cf. 2: 12 ff. where he answers it in terms of natural law). The fact is that men did die before the Mosaic law was given, although their sins were not like Adam's, who deliberately broke a known rule. **15–17. Pattern** implies likeness, and Paul must carefully point out that there is contrast in the character and result of Adam's and Christ's influence. Christ's work is a glorious power for good, the opposite of the wretched mass-murder which arose from Adam's sin. God has intervened to check the expanding process of sin. In Adam **one sin** had a condemning effect; in Christ **many trespasses** are forgiven. Instead of being subjects of King Death, men's prospect is to live like kings. They may share in the Messianic Kingdom, if only they accept God's **gift of righteousness. 20.** Paul is speaking from personal experience (cf. 4: 13 n.). He had found that the law, introduced in the old era of Adam, had an effect in keeping with its era; it made one realize one's sin and actually triggered off a reaction of sin, as 7: 7 ff. explains. 'The law is not simply a reagent by which the presence of sin may be detected; it is a catalyst which aids or even initiates the action of sin upon man' (C. K. Barrett). It 'came in on the side' (Gk. *pareisēlthen*) with the subordinate rôle of an accessory working on fallen Adam's side. The law was God's way of bringing sin to a head (1 C. 15: 56) before He broke its virulence with strong grace. **21.** King Sin has been deposed along with **death**, the instrument of his tyranny. Grace is now on the throne and will dispense the life of the age to come to those made right with God by Christ's work.

NOTE ON SIN

Paul did not conceive of sin merely as an action or attitude contrary to God's will. A study of the vocabulary used in association with it clearly shows that he personified it. Sin is a king (5: 21; 6: 12), a slave-owner (*e.g.* 6: 6), is dead or alive (7: 8 f.). Sin is an external power alien to man's true nature as God intended it. It is an enemy that has invaded man, has occupied his 'flesh', and holds him captive (7: 23). The world apart from Christ is under sin's control (3: 9). Christ's work was to attack sin on its own ground and defeat it (8: 3). The man in Christ enters into this victory and is delivered from sin's tyranny (6: 18; 7: 24). But it is obvious from Paul's arguments in chs. 6–8 that the Christian is not made morally perfect at conversion. Christ's work of personal deliverance is a reality for the Christian, but it is on a different plane of reality from the moral issues of everyday living. Yet it must find its counterpart in the Christian's life. Paul argues that because sin *has been* once and for all deposed on one plane of reality, it *should* not reign on the moral plane of human thought and behaviour. In this life sin is ever trying to re-assert its old authority, but Christians are urged to shut their doors against it, for it has no right to come in again.

Living out life in Christ (6: 1–7: 6)

The faith-righteous man has been brought within the circle of the new humanity headed by, and summed up in, Jesus Christ. Union with Christ is for Paul 'the sheet-anchor of his ethics' (J. S. Stewart). For the move is no mere formality, but implicitly demands a corresponding moral change. Paul explains why as he counter-attacks a mistaken conclusion from his teaching on divine grace (cf. 3: 8), drawn both by Jewish legalists and by antinomian Christians. God is certainly magnanimous in His grace (5: 20), but to conclude from this that sin no longer matters and that His grace may be exploited for evil ends is a travesty of the truth. Union with Christ calls for a new moral life. Paul hammers this home with three heavy blows. (*a*) The Christian is one with Christ—in death to sin (6: 1–14). (*b*) In Christ Christians are God's righteous servants (6: 15–23). (*c*) The Church is committed to Christ in a new marriage-union (7: 1–6).

1–14. Christians have become one with Christ in His relation to sin. So Paul argues in a series of deductive and inductive arguments which now overlap, now attack the problem from a new angle and now reveal earlier presuppositions. It will be easier to consider the passage as a whole rather than verse by verse. As ever, the starting point is the Cross. Christ **died** in relation **to sin**: He passed out of sin's environment. His death removed the possibility of His ever meeting it again, for it was

once for all, a clean break. His resurrection by His Father's majestic power (4, **glory**: cf. Dt. 5: 24) marks His permanent freedom from sin's instrument of tyranny (cf. 5: 21 n.). All this is personally relevant to the Christian, for he is **in Christ Jesus**, who has represented His people and included them within Himself (cf. the concept of the body of Christ). For a man to be in Christ implies that he was there at Golgotha and in the garden-tomb. What is true of Christ is true of the Christian. For him personally Christ's death marked the end of the old era, and His resurrection the inauguration of the new era. God transcends time and at conversion takes a man back to A.D. 33. When he is incorporated into Christ on profession of faith, he is given a personal share in the great events of Christ's work and transferred from his old existence to a new plane of life. In the early Church when baptism generally followed hard on the heels of a man's accepting the gospel, baptism and the divine renewal behind faith could naturally be regarded as the outside and inside of the same thing. Baptism by immersion is a dramatic mime of what God has done with a man. It is to this enacted parable of salvation that Paul appeals. Let us look back, he says, and see what God has done in our lives. Our baptism was the outward evidence that He incorporated us believers into Christ. Our being plunged into water means that He associated us with Him in His **death**. Therefore we too **died** as far as sin is concerned, moving out of and beyond the old era. How then can we—dead and buried men—go back to the old life—'breathe its air again' (Knox, v. 2) by carrying on sinning? It would be a contradiction in terms. God made to share in Christ's crucifixion our Adam, ourselves as we were in Adam (6, **old self**, lit. 'old man'): from our new standpoint 'the man we once were' (NEB) is relegated to a bygone age. In Christ's death we were 'justified' (7, **freed**), from sin, released from its prosecution. God's intention was to change our behaviour (v. 6: cf. v. 4; 8: 4 for other practical clauses of purpose), to put out of action **the body of sin**, the body in so far as it has become enemy-occupied territory. The body at work expresses the personality, and so it comes to mean the personality in action (there are close links with Heb. psychology here). Paul might have gone on to say that we were raised with Christ in baptism (Col. 2: 12; cf. Eph. 2: 6), but he deliberately breaks the parallelism in order to stress that the new life is not merely a *fait accompli* but a continual endeavour. Instead he speaks about the future. Just as Christ's death and burial were the precursors of His resurrection, so our vital share in the former events guarantees our coming resurrection (cf. 2 C. 4: 14; Phil. 3: 21). The new era in its fulness lies in the future, and

the old is still running its course; on another plane the new era has been projected forward and the old already finished. For the Christian the two eras overlap. His past participation in the end of the old era, and his future participation in the beginning of the new are both pointers to his present obligation to behave in keeping with the new era and not the old (4, **live** lit. 'walk' is a Biblical idiom for behaviour). **11.** The man **in Christ** must take account of the fact that he has shared in His clear-cut break with sin in His death and God-directed risen life, and conduct himself accordingly. **12 f.** The Christian's behaviour must not be characteristic of sin's old régime (5: 21). His personality had for long been enemy-occupied territory, and indeed is not only doomed to suffer the fatal consequences of its occupation before resurrection (8: 11), but continues to have in it subversive elements which urge rebellion. But God has set His flag flying over the body and claimed it as His own territory. Let not then the Christian fight to keep sin in power. Let him not go on as of old (Gk. *paristanete:* present imperative) making his faculties available to sin as weapons (so the Gk. *hopla* signifies elsewhere, not **instruments**) of wickedness. Rather let him turn them into weapons of right living and make a fresh start (Gk. *parastēsate:* an ingressive aorist) by putting himself and them at God's disposal. **14.** Sin's mastery is broken for good because the era in which law was in active control promoting sin (5: 20) is over, and now **grace** is in control (5: 21).

15–23. A new Master has replaced sin. Union with Christ has made the Church God's righteous servant. Paul still has in his mind the thought of Christ as the righteous and obedient Servant of God. Men in Christ move in a new atmosphere of obedience and righteousness (5: 18 f.) and are themselves God's servants. Accordingly 'servants' is better than **slaves** throughout this passage (Gk. *douloi:* cf. *doulos* of Christ as the suffering Servant, Phil. 2: 7). It is these concepts that belong to grace in the new era (cf. 5: 15 ff.) and are safeguards against its being interpreted in terms of indifference to moral laxity, as its contrast with the law might at first suggest. Sin was a master in the old era of Adam and demanded shameful living which it promised to repay with death. The righteousness of Christ that leads to eternal life (cf. 5: 19, 21) calls forth from Christians right living as its corollary. The whole passage is the application of 5: 12 ff. to the Christian's moral life. **15.** Paul is going to tackle the same question (cf. v. 1) from a different angle. **16.** Man's freedom is limited. Either he puts himself at sin's disposal and becomes its servant, and eventually dies; or else he devotes himself to Christ-like **obedience** to God with the result that he—not only enters into life but also—does what is morally right. **17 f.** For Christians the first possibility has been ruled out, ever since their voluntary submission to a new authority, the **form** or 'pattern' (Gk. *typos*) of obedience, Christian moral teaching (cf. Tit. 2: 1 ff.). Paul will give details of that teaching in chs. 12 ff. There has been a change of ownership. **19.** An apology for describing the relationship between God and a Christian in such crude, human terms (cf. 8: 15). Lack of moral sensitiveness demands that its moral implications be shown to be so compelling and inexorable. The time is past when their faculties could be put at the disposal of dirty and uncontrolled habits which lead to 'moral anarchy' (NEB). Now, in the new era of Christ, they are to be devoted to right hving that is the basis of saintliness. **20 f.** The readers' consciences support the writer's argument, for now they blush at the immorality of their old lives when **righteousness** had no jurisdiction over them. And how unprofitable it was, leading only to **death. 22.** Christians' lives are to reflect the change of ownership. They are to produce moral behaviour that makes for saintliness and prepares for life in the age to come. **23.** Sinners can only expect to die—that is the fair **wages** which sin pays its servants. God's servants have the sure prospect of **life** because they are **in Christ**; yet they·cannot earn it but only receive it as a gratuity.

7: 1–6. A new Husband has replaced the law. The Church has been united to Christ in marriage. The third appeal to Christians to become what they are in Christ revolves around a new metaphor, that of a fruitful marriage-union. Christians constitute a widow who has married again. The first, unhappy marriage, with its offspring of bad living, has been brought to an end. The new marriage demands suitable progeny—good living. Marriage, in which two become 'one flesh', is a natural illustration of incorporation into Christ and is used elsewhere in the NT (*e.g.* 1 C. 6: 16; Eph. 5: 29 f.). It has its roots in the OT where God's people, bound to their Lord by covenant, are represented as His wife (*e.g.* Hos. 2; Jer. 2). Marriage is regarded as the wife's subjection to the husband as master. The first husband was the law—a picture drawn from the state of being 'under (the control of) the law' in the old era (6: 14). In Christ Paul had escaped his involvement with the law and so with sin, whose unwitting accomplice the law was. The fact carries with it strong moral obligations. **1. The law** is probably not the general concept of law but the moral and social law revealed in the OT which the Church had taken over. **2 f.** Death releases from the marriage-law: a widow is perfectly free to re-marry. **4.** In a new sense death has released Christians

from the law. The illustration of the marriage-law is a parable (not a detailed allegory) of their relationship to the law. A death has taken place, and so the ties which bind men in subjection to the law have been broken. The death is that of the crucified **body of Christ** in which they were represented. Their consequent oneness with their risen Lord is a figurative new marriage-union with Him which calls for offspring dedicated **to God. 5.** In the era of **the sinful nature** (mg. 'flesh') the law had been the means of evoking sinful feelings and impulses which operated in human faculties and produced deadly offspring. Flesh in the OT is often man in his weakness over against the omnipotent God; in the NT it is often human nature whose weakness is shown in its constant and inevitable succumbing to sin. Here it refers to the pre-Christian life (cf. 8: 9 n.). **6. By dying** to the tyranny of the law, Christians have a new sphere of service—**the new way of the Spirit**. The last two phrases are virtually a heading to the next section.

(*b*) **Life in the Spirit (7: 7–8: 30)**
With the headline at the end of 7: 6 Paul reaches the second application of . . . *Shall live* (Hab. 2: 4) to the Christian life. As in the section on *The righteous-by-faith*, he first discusses the opposite of his intended point in order to highlight the necessity and the glory of God's gift of the Holy Spirit.

The letter kills (7: 7–25)
Paul analyses from a Christian standpoint his own past experience of the law, as an objective standard which he knew to be right but which he could not reach, however hard he tried. Intention went one way, action went another. Some have found difficulty in squaring this account of failure with Phil. 3: 6. But there Paul is testing his life against certain prescribed standards of outward conduct held by his Judaizing critics and challenges them to point out any failure of his to carry them out. Here he probes into the inner failures of which only God and he were aware, failures that were now heightened by his present Christian knowledge. 'The true meaning of sin was not discovered at the feet of Gamaliel but at the foot of the Cross' (E. K. Lee). **7.** Having made disparaging references to the law, Paul now makes clear that it is not on a par with sin. But it had introduced him to sin by provoking him to taste the sweetness of forbidden fruit. 'Law says, *Don't* walk on the grass: sin says at once, *Shall* walk on the grass, if I like' (G. T. Thomson). **Known** in its first occurrence refers to involvement and experience rather than awareness. Significantly the one commandment that defeated Paul was the tenth, the one that concerns an inner attitude and not externals with which it is by comparison easy to conform. **Coveting** in Greek is a wide word covering

all kinds of wrong desire. **8.** Sin used **the commandment** as a starting-point from which to launch its attack upon him. The law brought responsibility for wrong-doing and gave sin an active power (cf. 4: 15; 5: 13). **9.** Paul had enjoyed a blissful, carefree childhood, unrestricted by the law and so by sin. Relatively speaking, this was life. 'But all of a sudden I met Moses, carrying in his hand the law of God'—Spurgeon's boyhood experience was apparently Paul's too. At the age of thirteen he followed Jewish practice and became a *bar mitswāh*, lit. 'son of commandment'. He was received into the community and regarded from then on as morally responsible. Then it was that sin sprang to life, inactive no longer. A sensitive teenager, Paul found that the inner tensions of growing manhood and the new responsibilities which the law laid upon him from without tragically combined. He was filled with misery and felt estranged from God. **10.** In his experience the intended guide to **life** (Lev. 18: 5) led him fatally astray (cf. NEB). **11. Deceived** is an allusion to Gen. 3: sin had the same rôle as the tempter in Eden (cf. 2 C. 11: 3) and tricked him by using for its own ends the law, of all things. The law did not prove the remedy for evil, as the rabbis taught, but an irritant from which a fatal allergy developed. **12 f.** Paul must again insist that the law is of divine origin and the revealed standard of morality. It was not this good thing that Paul found fatal, but sin, which the law exposed in its true colours. **14.** From here to the end of the chapter Paul uses the present tense, emotionally re-living his life as Saul the Pharisee. There is no need to assume that the crisis of conversion has intervened between 13 and 14. The verse begins with 'for' (AV, RV), giving the reason for the good law's bad effect upon him. The reason lay within: he had been **sold** like a slave into sin's control (cf. 6: 17 f.) because he was made of weak 'flesh' (**unspiritual:** Gk. *sarkinos*) which had succumbed to sin (see v. 5 n.; 8: 3). **15–20.** He lived a Jekyll and Hyde existence, with Mr. Hyde as the dominant self. He gave full theoretical assent to the law, but was forced to act against his better judgment by sin which was 'squatting' (Hunter) in his flesh. In his case it was not merely that he knew God's will and approved what is excellent, yet did not do it (2: 17 ff.). He knew and approved and intended to do it, but *could* not. In so far as he regards himself as his better self, he had since adolescence (**no longer:** cf. 9 n.) become mere putty in the hands of sin which controlled him completely. In so far as his identity was that of his lower self, he was bad through and through. **21–23.** Paul had known the distress of bitter conflict which racked him and tore him apart. In his unintegrated life there were two laws or governing principles at war. His faculties and powers were enemy-occupied territory. Sin had invaded them and was fighting to stamp out every attempt at resistance—and succeeding again and again. **24.** Vividly recalling his emotions, as in a nightmare, Paul desperately shrieks for help from any source. His sin-dominated personality (cf. 6: 6) is enduring a living death (cf. vv. 9 ff.). **25.** Another cry from the heart, this time of relief and triumph. He knows that his appeal has been answered, and thanks the One who came to his rescue, **God** who has given the victory through **Jesus Christ** (cf. 1 C. 15: 57). Then, his emotions exhausted, Paul dispassionately sums up his divided life under the law. Without the aid of Christ (**I myself**, Moffatt 'left to myself'), his better self made sincere efforts to comply with the law, but his **sinful nature** dragged him down to surrender to sin. 8: 1 will give a corresponding counterpart to his cry of relief.

The Spirit makes alive (8: 1–30)
Judaism taught that the Holy Spirit had been withdrawn and would only be restored when the age to come began: then Jl 2: 28 would be fulfilled. The Church knew that it had been fulfilled: the awaited age to come had been inaugurated. It is true that in its full splendour it still lies in the future, but in the outpoured Spirit the power and life of the full age to come are anticipated. He is pledge and foretaste of the future and puts within the Church's grasp a new potential of which they not only may but must avail themselves.

1–4. The basis of the Spirit's work is the Cross. There is not so clear-cut a break as the chapter division and our own section heading suggest. The calm contrast of 7: 25b and 8: 1 is a double deduction from the emotional contrast of 7: 24 and 7: 25a. Both 7: 25b and 8: 1 begin with Gk. *ara* (**so, therefore**); **then** in 7: 25 (Gk. *oun*) indicates a transition (see Arndt and Gingrich, *Greek Lexicon, s.v.*, *ara*). **I myself** is matched by **those who are in Christ Jesus**. God took it upon Himself to end in principle the constant mastery of sin over man. God in Christ subdued sin, doing what the law was powerless to do because it had such poor material to work on—**the sinful nature** (mg. the flesh). Human nature had let the law down by falling under sin's spell. The pre-existent (so **sending** implies) Son became man and conquered man's enemy on its own ground. **The likeness of sinful man** (Gk. 'flesh') does not deny the real humanity of Christ; it affirms His personal sinlessness. 'Flesh' could not be used here by itself (contrast 1: 3) because it had been used in the context in an immoral sense. God made Him a **sin-offering**. There may well be a reference to Isa. 53: 10, where the same phrase is used in the LXX: He was the suffering Servant who became an atoning sacrifice. On the Cross Jesus absorbed the worst that sin could do and drained it of its power. God thereby executed a sentence of condemnation against the enemy and overcame sin (see note appended to 1: 17). Now, in the new era inaugurated by God's mighty act, sin has lost its control over the man in Christ (cf. 6: 7 n.; 7: 25b). Slavery to **sin and death** was a mark of the old era of Adam to which he belonged before. **In Christ** he finds himself released and put under a new authority, that of **the Spirit of life** (see note on sin at the end of ch. 5). God's aim was the meeting of the law's **righteous requirements** in behaviour that fits the new realm of **the Spirit** and not the old régime of **the sinful nature**. Paul's quarrel was not with the law as morality (cf. 7: 12, 14) but with its degraded form as legality. 'Paul as a Jew had thought that men should keep the law in order that they might be saved. As a Christian he saw that men must be saved in order that they might keep the law' (C. A. Anderson Scott).

5–13. The Spirit is contrasted with the flesh. (See Gal. 5: 19–23 for further exposition of this contrast.) Men in the new era must live differently from those in the old. **5–8. The mind** on each occasion represents Gk. *phronēma* which, far from being contrasted with action, is an underlying attitude to life that determines behaviour. The outlook dictated by **sinful man** separates from God in a living **death** because it fights against the God of life in inevitable disobedience to His law, as ch. 7 has described. The Spirit prompts to new interests and aims, which are the secret of true **life** and harmony with God. **9 f.** Christians must not fall in with the suggestions of **the sinful nature** because they have left its era behind and are now in the era of **the Spirit** The decisive test of belonging to Christ is possession of the Spirit which is demonstrable (cf. Ac. 10: 45 f.), being outwardly verified by evidence of His gifts (cf. 1 C. 12: 4–11) and/or of His fruit. **Spirit of God, Spirit of Christ** and **Christ** are used interchangeably: the Spirit is the Father's agent in making the Son real to the Christian. The Spirit (read 'the Spirit is life' in 10) gives **life** to the justified (cf. 5: 21), although sin has made it inevitable that the bodies which express their personalities will one day die. **Dead** is a vivid expression for 'doomed to die'. **11.** But Jesus' resurrection is a guarantee of the future resurrection of the Christian's body. The Spirit will then bring His reviving process to completion. **12 f.** The Christian is obliged to resist the tendencies of **the sinful nature**, which lead to ultimate death. If any man accepted in good faith into a church persists in a low level of living, Paul categorically denies that such a man really belongs to Christ or will attain to eternal life (cf. v. 9 n.; 2: 7 n.). Life in the consummated age

to come is a prospect only for those who kill off the (immoral) actions of their personalities which are so used to the bad old ways (cf. 6: 6n.).

14–17. The Spirit assures of sonship. Cf. Gal. 4: 4–7. **14.** Practical God-likeness, which comes of willing response to the control of His Spirit, is proof of being **sons of God**. 'Like Father, like son' is the thought, as in Mt. 5: 45. **15 f.** The **Spirit of sonship** is the Spirit of the Son (Gal. 4: 6) transferred to the Christian: He enables him to look at God with Christ's eyes and makes in him the Son's own filial response to the Father (cf. Mk 14: 36). **Abba** is 'Father' in Aramaic; **Father** represents the Gk. equivalent. The cry passed bilingually into the worshipping vocabulary of the Church, and it is here regarded as evidence that the Spirit is at work. The Christian's own conviction of sonship is supported by the Spirit's evoking this cry in the worship of the church (cf. Gal. 4: 6; 1 C. 12: 3). The Spirit is not one who maintains the frightening, servile conditions of the old era, but gives the confidence that God is a personal Father. In referring to **sonship** Paul is not alluding only to the Hellenistic custom of adoption, but no doubt has OT parallels in mind (cf. 9: 4; Gen. 15: 2 f.; Exod. 2: 10; 1 Chr. 28: 6; Isa. 1: 2). 'Son' or 'sons' was a title of the OT people of God; it passed to Christ who summed up their destiny in Himself (Hos. 11: 1; Mt. 2: 15), and thus it passed to the Church in Him. **17. Children** have the prospect of an inheritance: so it is with Christians. They, like Christ and with Christ, are **heirs of God** (cf. Mt. 21: 38; 25: 34). But before sharing His glory they must be prepared first to live out His sufferings (cf. 2 Tim. 2: 11 f.). Identification with the crucified Christ by faith (6: 3) is no substitute for identification on the level of practical experience (cf. 2 C. 1: 5; 4: 10; Phil. 3: 10 f.). Viewed in this light, the adversities of the present life do not contradict but rather confirm the prospect of glory in the consummated age to come.

18–25. The Spirit assures of future glory. **18.** Cf. 2 C. 4: 17. Present adversity did not make Paul stumble but faded into comparative insignificance—so real to him was the unseen age to come. **19–23.** It was possession of the Spirit that made it real, for He is its **firstfruits**, a specimen sheaf cut and brought as sure evidence that a whole field of such sheaves is waiting to be harvested. When the new age fully comes it will reveal the Church in their true light as **sons of God**, in all respects like the exalted Son (cf. Col. 3: 4; 1 Jn 3: 2). It will also transform the world of nature, fulfilling the OT Messianic promises of a renewed earth (*e.g.* Isa. 35). At the Fall God enslaved nature to **frustration** and **decay** (**frustration** echoes the refrain of *Ecclesiastes*), but such was not to be its permanent state, for God even then envisaged its emancipation. As willy-nilly the rest of creation was dragged down with man (Gen. 3: 17), its leader (Ps. 8: 6), so it will rise with him. Nature is dependent upon God's glorification of the Church. In poetic idiom it cranes its neck (**eager expectations:** Gk. *apokaradokiā*, Phillips 'is on tiptoe'), waiting for this signal of its own restoration; it is in labour for the birth of the new creation. 'It is nothing short of a universal law that suffering marks the road to glory' (Sanday and Headlam). The Church in so far as they are physically part of the material world share nature's many pains, but they too look forward to release from infirmity, to the renewing of their bodies so that they are like that of the risen and exalted Son (cf. Phil. 3: 21). **24 f.** 'We were saved with this hope in view' (Moffatt). The salvation given at conversion had implicit in it promises which have yet to be fulfilled. Contrary experience may now bombard the believer's senses, but it cannot reasonably invalidate his glorious **hope** because its fulfilment essentially lies in the future (cf. 2 C. 4: 18). We must bide God's time.

26–27. The Spirit intercedes. **26. In the same way** links 'groan' (Gk. *stenazomen*) of v. 23 with **groans** (Gk. *stenagmois*). The Spirit does not despise such expressions of frailty, but makes them the means of His pleading the Church's interests before God; thus He turns the **groans** to good account. Inarticulate feelings of inadequacy and vaguely conceived yearnings may at times be the nearest one can get to expressing oneself aright to God because 'we cannot tell what is really best for us' (Hodge) and the needs we do express in prayer are often lesser needs. But the **groans** become the very voice of the Spirit in intercession (cf. v. 15 f.). **27.** God, scrutinizing the whole conscious and unconscious make-up of every man (an OT thought; cf. 1 Sam. 16: 7; 1 Kg. 8: 39; Ps. 139: 1 f.; Jer. 17: 10), understands what the Spirit means by His dumb sighs deep within because it is His own purpose for His own people that the Spirit is pleading to be realized.

28–30. The Spirit carries out God's plan. The Spirit is active not only via the unconscious or semi-conscious mind but throughout the whole range of life's experiences. He is co-operating with the Christian **in all things** to bring about a **good** end. V. 29 explains the good end (**to be conformed . . .**) and 5: 3 f. the general thought. Read '*in everything he works for good*' (RSVmg). The text has followed some ancient authorities which add **God** as the subject of the verb, but in the Greek *ho theos* (**God**) reads unnaturally after *ton theon*, the same noun in another case. But the addition is evidence that the verb was regarded as having a personal subject. The theme of the section suggests that the Spirit is the implicit subject (so NEB). **Those who love him** is an OT expression for God's followers who throw themselves wholeheartedly into His service and identify themselves with His aims (*e.g.* Exod. 20: 6; Jg. 5: 31; Dan. 9: 4). The Spirit co-operates with such because they have been summoned by God and assigned a rôle in His redemptive purposes (cf. 1: 6 n.). God's eternal plan was to create for Himself a family modelled upon His unique Son. Before the world began (Eph. 1: 4) He intended this destiny for those whom He had made the objects of His personal care and concern (**foreknew:** cf. Gen. 18: 19; Jer. 1: 5; Am. 3: 2). The Spirit is responsible for the gradual moral transformation which they are now undergoing on earth. **30.** All the steps in God's purposes that are now accomplished have been leading up to the end expressed in v. 29. Having decided long ago whom He would appoint for this destiny, He summoned them, made them right with Himself and illumined them with His glory (cf. 2 C. 3: 18; 4: 6). Paul may be echoing the LXX of Isa. 45: 25, where 'justify' and 'glory' occur together describing a single activity.

(*c*) **Triumphant life (8: 31–39)**
In a grand climax inspired by God's outworking of His purposes Paul lifts up his heart in a lyrical assertion of security and triumph. The passage is parallel with 5: 1–11. Both are encouraging deductions from earlier doctrinal truth. Both stress the love of God in allowing His Son to die, the death and risen and exalted life of Christ, God's being on our side, the Christian attitude to adversity, and the past being a guarantee of the future. **31.** The Christian's reaction to all the foregoing truths is first a sense of complete security. *The Lord is with me; I will not be afraid* (Ps. 118: 6) is in Paul's mind. **32.** An allusion to the LXX of Gen. 22: 16. The apostle regards Abraham's unhesitating but painful surrender of Isaac as an illustration of what it meant to God to give up **his own Son** to death. The greatest gift carries a promise of all smaller gifts: He is 'all other gifts in one'. **32 f.** Does not sin threaten? No, God's chosen need have no fear of any accusing finger at the judgment day, since God has dealt with their sin. Isa. 50: 7–9 is a promise that Paul claims for the Church. The Judge Himself, **Christ Jesus** (cf. 2: 16), will not **condemn**, seeing that it is He who carried through the mighty saving acts of death and resurrection, who now sits triumphant as His people's King (Ps. 110: 1). The exalted Servant there continues His work of intercession (Isa. 53: 12). **35.** Is not adversity a threat? No, His **love** will never let go of His own, whatever strains and pressures are brought to bear on them. Paul writes out of experience as one who has himself known the firm, unyielding grip of Christ's

love in these very crises (2 C. 11: 23 ff.). **36.** Indeed, they are not obstacles to God's purposes, but His appointed way for His people, as Scripture makes clear in Ps. 44: 22. Note the contrast between the original context of despairing complaint and the apostle's tones of exultant triumph: Christ and hope of heaven transformed the attitude of God's servants towards a hostile environment. **37.** Far from being victims of circumstances, Paul and all who stand with him are given 'overwhelming victory' (Phillips, NEB) **through** Christ whose love is 'strong as death' (Gk. *agapēsantos*—an aorist—points to the Cross). **38. Death** cannot **separate** because it is 'swallowed up in victory' (1 C. 15: 54) nor **life** because, for all its infirmity and decay, it is yet the scene of Christian service (Phil. 1: 20 ff.). The loving Lord guards and guides through all the unknown contingencies of the present and future. **Angels** and **demons**, and **powers** too, the hostile or potentially hostile forces behind the material universe, have been stripped of their power to harm by Christ's victory (Col. 2: 14; 1 Pet. 3: 22). **Height** and **depth** in Hellenistic Greek were astrological terms for the highest and lowest points reached by a star. It was a widespread contemporary belief that men's lives were fated by the positions of the stars as spirit-powers. Paul asserts that all such fears are groundless for the Christian. **Creation** has implicit in it the comfort that there is no factor or force in the universe that is not under the control of the God who made it—and He is for us. The truth that God is creator of all gives added assurance to the redeemed (cf. Isa. 40: 28 ff.; 42: 6 f.; 44: 24).

IV. THE GOSPEL FOR THE WORLD IN GOD'S PLAN (9: 1–11: 36)

The cry of triumph of 8: 31 ff. has died away and in the ensuing silence another shadow falls across Paul's mind, requiring like the rest to be dispelled by the light of God in Christ. Why had the Jews not come flocking into His kingdom? Why had Christ's own people not welcomed Him when He came home (Jn 1: 11)? Why had the Christian mission to the Jews sagged so miserably? In the OT it appeared that Israel was to be the missionary body evangelizing the world. In present experience the Jewish response to their Messiah was a miserable parody of what had been promised. It was a bitter disappointment, but it was more: it opened the door to all sorts of doubts. 'Will their lack of faith nullify God's faithfulness?' (3: 3). If God let Israel down like that. . . . 'Not at all' (3: 4): Paul could not admit that premise, let alone draw the conclusion that He might let the Church down. But it was a problem that had been burning deep in Paul's mind for years, especially as it sprang directly out of his missionary experience. He had seen the synagogue reject the gospel time and time again. But the problem was larger than that: since all was under God's control, Paul himself had been personally involved in bringing about God's rejection of the Jews. What was the strategy behind God's tactics? After enquiring into the OT where God had revealed some of His plans, Paul arrives at the convictions of chs. 9–11, convictions based both on reflections upon his missionary experience and on his knowledge of the OT. These chapters are the product not of a systematic theologian but of a mature missionary thinking aloud and interpreting the facts by Biblical principles. Paul meant 11: 33 f. to be taken seriously. He did not claim to know the complete answer from A to Z. But he did claim to have found important clues which were enough for man to know of God's unfathomable designs. It is important to understand the angle from which Paul was writing. He had no intention of answering those who queried, or were curious about, the truths of divine sovereignty and election and human responsibility and their compatibility. Rather, he is interpreting the first-century missionary situation in terms which he shared with both his Christian and Jewish contemporaries. He with them had taken over the viewpoint of the OT and it did not occur to him to question it. His Jewish critics demurred only at his application of OT doctrines, and not at the doctrines themselves.

Paul found three different clues that helped to solve his problem. The first is a number of OT precedents and promises of divine control over the history of God's people for His appointed ends. He stressed God's sovereignty in order to hit out at the cocksure Jewish notion that God *had* to save them, bound by the bonds of the law, circumcision and good works. Paul insists strongly that God is free and gracious. Side by side with the first clue he places a second one without attempting to square the two. The Jews have refused to go God's way, and, as long as they do not believe, put themselves out of God's saving reach. The third clue, again unco-ordinated with the earlier ones, is God's faithfulness. The One who never breaks a promise can be trusted to bring Israel to salvation. God's present tactics may be pro-Gentile and anti-Jew, but His overall strategy is for the ultimate benefit of the Jews and the enrichment of the Church.

i. The Jews' tragic rejection of Christ (9: 1–5)

1 f. Paul is heart-broken that the bulk of his fellow-Jews still stand outside God's kingdom. He solemnly expresses the sincerity of his sorrow. **3.** His words here are 'white-hot with love and wild with all regret' (J. S. Stewart). So strong are his feelings that, were it feasible, he would become *anathema* (Gk. for **cursed:** cf. Dt. 7: 26) and have his union with Christ severed if his beloved people could take his place. The servant here reveals how deeply he has imbibed the self-sacrificing spirit of his Servant-Lord (cf. 1 Jn 3: 16). **4 f.** What an anticlimax to so glorious a heritage is the Jews' present hostile reaction to God's purposes! With **adoption as sons** compare 8: 15 n.; Exod. 4: 22. **Glory** is the Shekinah-glory, God's localizing His presence in a unique way within Israel (cf. Exod. 24: 16; 29: 43). **The covenants** (cf. Eph. 2: 12) are the basic covenant made with Abraham and its later amplifications and confirmations in Israel's history. **The worship** is the elaborate ritual of tabernacle and temple. With **the promises** cf. 1: 2; 3: 2; 4: 13. At the end of 5 the text is a more natural rendering of the Gk. from the point of view of syntax than the margins. In face of the general Jewish denial that Jesus was the Messiah, Paul is driven in reaction to avow his own recognition of Him in terms stronger than he tends to use elsewhere. See further A. W. Wainwright, *The Trinity in the New Testament,* 1962, pp. 54 ff.

ii. God's present plan for Jew and Gentile (9: 6–10: 21)

God's purposes have been revealed (9: 6–29)

6–13. The OT gives evidence of a preliminary narrowing process in God's purposes, and it is in this light that the present situation is to be explained. The rejection of Christ by most of the Jews does not come as a surprise to God, and on second thoughts need not to the Church, since it is in line with a divine principle. God is indeed *fulfilling* His **word.** As in the early history of Israel His habit was to select only one branch of the family tree for His special purposes, so it has been designed that at first the Church should contain only a certain number of Jews. Neither blood nor behaviour qualifies a Jew for divine acceptance. **6–9.** Paul argues again (cf. 2: 25 ff.) that the Jews' view of themselves as automatically a chosen nation is a fallacy. Their slogan of assurance 'We have Abraham as our father' (Lk. 3: 8; Jn 8: 33, 39) is historically unsound, since the chosen line bypassed his son Ishmael according to Gen. 21: 12. God's choice depends not upon a hereditary process but upon His personal **promise,** as Gen. 18: 10 proves. In Paul's mind **promise** is antithetic to adhering to the law (4: 13 ff.). **10–13.** Nor on the other hand can God's choice rest upon works, upon any supposed claim with which man may arrogantly demand a place in God's redemptive purposes. God did not wait to see how Jacob and Esau would turn out before He selected one of them (Gen. 25: 23; Mal. 1: 2 f.). His own call was the decisive issue, irrespective of individual merit or demerit. Paul is returning to his attack on Ju-

daism's justification by works (chs. 2, 3).

14–29. The non-Christian Jew cannot dictate to God on this issue. Paul vetoes the possibility that one may accuse God of unfairness and think to compel Him to do otherwise. He gives three reasons. (*a*) Scripture reveals the principle of God's free will (15–18). (*b*) It would be tantamount to claiming to be God's equal instead of God's creature (19–24). (*c*) Scripture reveals the promise of the very things which have taken place—God's limitation of His people to a Jewish remnant and the extension of His people to include Gentiles (25–29). (*a*) **15–18.** God is free. **15 f.** Exod. 33: 19 implies that God's grace cannot be forced into a groove of man's making. When God condescended to reveal Himself to Moses it was not because even Moses had any claim upon God by his service. This was meant as a principle for the future (**will**) as well as for Moses. **17.** Exod. 9: 16 shows that God is free too to employ instruments which apparently oppose His purposes but whose use will lead to His ultimate glory and to world-wide blessing. As Paul later makes clear (vv. 22 f.; 11: 7), he sees contemporary Jewry in the rôle of Pharaoh. The Exodus has been re-enacted in Christian history with Israel playing Pharaoh's part. Their opposition and persecution have only served to promote God's ends (cf. 11: 12; Ac. 8: 1, 4). **18.** The Jews may not glibly hold Gentiles to be outside the pale and themselves to have an incontrovertible claim upon God's grace. Just as God had permitted Pharaoh to be hardened against His word (cf. Exod. 8: 32; 9: 12), so He had the Jews. (*b*) **19–24.** Man is God's creature. **19–21.** Paul has ringing in his ears a conclusion drawn in actual discussion by a Jewish objector, as by Job in Job 9, 10: God's ways are then simply immoral fatalism (cf. 3: 5, 7). This conclusion Paul rejects, but he waits until ch. 10 to answer it (cf. 3: 8 n.). But, like Zophar in Job 11: 7 ff., he is shocked at his opponent's thus shrugging his shoulders at the transcendent God and attempting to 'bandy words' (Knox) with Him. Paul protests in OT language: man is nothing but the product of the Potter's hands. So the OT stresses again and again, *e.g.* in Gen. 2: 7 where *formed* (Heb. *yātsur*) is the activity of a potter (Heb. *yôtsēr*). There is a clear echo of Isa. 29: 16 in 20 and of Jer. 18: 6 in 21. The divine Craftsman could put His **lump** of humanity to any providential use for which there is a need, without first asking man's permission. **22–24.** God had demonstrated His **power** by cutting off the unbelieving Jews from their inheritance, and He had declared a sentence of condemnation against them (cf. Mt. 10: 14 f.; Ac. 13: 46, 51). **Choosing** must mean 'because He chose' not 'although . . .' in view of the comparison with Pharaoh (cf. v. 17). They had shown themselves 'fit only for destruction' (Knox), 'ripe and ready to be destroyed' (Moffatt), yet God had not destroyed them but put up with their hardness of heart so that they might be object-lessons of His **wrath** (contrast 2: 4 f., where His patience is attributed to His kindness: the two ideas are complementary). Alongside this severe judgment, and enhanced by it, was God's glorious dealings of grace with the Church. 10: 1 and ch. 11 show that latent in Paul's mind is the hope that **the objects** (Gk. 'vessels') **of wrath** (a phrase borrowed from the LXX of Jer. 50: 25) would eventually be re-shaped when God's present purposes were fulfilled (cf. Jer. 18: 4, 8; 2 Tim. 2: 20 f.). (*c*) **25–29.** This is prophecy come true. **25 f.** Paul cites Hos. 2: 23; 1: 10 as adumbrations that the Church, the elect instrument of God's purposes, would largely be made up of Gentiles. The OT reveals God's plan that the Gentiles were to become His **people**, His **loved one**, His **sons.** Cf. Ps. 87; Isa. 19: 25. **Place** means for Paul the whole Gentile world. **27–29.** Secondly, Isaiah's teaching on **the remnant** in Isa. 10: 22 f.; 1: 9 pointed forward to the present situation, when a Jewish minority formed the nucleus of the Church. It was not that anything had gone amiss in the execution of God's plan: of that the OT gives assurance.

The Jewish and Gentile reactions to the gospel (9: 30–10: 21)

God's plan is centred in a universal gospel of faith-righteousness (cf. 1: 16 f., 3: 21 ff.). Gentiles are in the Church simply because they have accepted that gospel. The bulk of the Jews are at the moment outside the Church simply because they have refused it. Reference to the OT proves the validity of this assessment. Earlier Paul has been analysing the contemporary situation in terms of God's overall control. Now he paradoxically but unhesitatingly affirms the responsibility of man's choice when confronted with the gospel. 'If we are dealing with two measurable categorical contraries, both of them on the same plane, we must reject the contradiction, since a definitive assertion and its definitive negation cannot both be true; but the case stands otherwise when we are dealing with the intersphering mysteries of the human and the divine. Conscience affirms the freedom of man, and faith the freedom of God: the Scriptures affirm both; and Paul rests his case on the Scriptures' (G. O. Griffith). First Paul briefly gives the human explanation of the situation in 30–33; then in ch. 10 he develops his thesis at greater length.

30–33. The Jews' position is their own fault. It is sadly ironic that the goal which the Jews missed the **Gentiles** have reached without trying. The Jews had been going the wrong way about it. They sought to get right with God by their **works**, basing their hope of salvation

upon the **law**, which they could not keep. The Gentiles now in the Church had made no such attempt but accepted the ready-made faith-righteousness offered by God through the work of the Cross. To the Jews a crucified Messiah was a stumbling-block (1 C. 1: 23), but to those who read the OT with Christian eyes this comes as no surprise since Isa. 8: 14 envisages this very situation. Christ is the Stone, as He Himself claimed (Mt. 21: 42; cf. Ac. 4: 11). Isa. 28: 16, quoted from the LXX, presents positive teaching about the Stone: God will certainly save the man who makes Him the object of his faith. Paul is quoting from a collection of OT quotations current in the early Church (cf. 1 Pet. 2: 6 ff.).

10: 1–4. The Jewish rejection of faith-righteousness is a tragedy. Paul reaffirms (cf. 9: 1 ff.) his longing that not ruin (9: 22) but salvation may be the Jews' lot. Their obvious sincerity is misguided. ('Behind these verses it is not hard to discern Paul's own struggle to find salvation'—A. M. Hunter.) They cannot grasp that Christ has inaugurated faith-righteousness, which spells the termination of attempting to get right with God via the law (Gal. 3: 23 ff.).

5–13. The gospel of faith-righteousness is easily attained and universally available. **5.** Law-righteousness demands life-long success in the moral struggle as its prerequisite for eternal life (Lev. 18: 5: Paul implicitly contrasts with it Hab. 2: 4, as Gal. 3: 11 f. shows). **6–8.** But the OT also witnesses to the gospel of faith-righteousness. Dt. 30: 12 ff., with its emphasis upon the initiative of divine grace and upon humble reception of God's proffered word, may be applied to the gospel. The change to **descend into the deep** is influenced by Ps. 107: 26: Gk. *abyssos* can refer to both the sea and Hades. The gospel of faith-righteousness is not something to strive and strain after with superhuman efforts, but is **near** at hand, ready for a man to take in his **mouth** and into his **heart**. It is news of something already done by Christ: He has taken the initiative and come to man; He has conquered sin and death, and risen triumphant. **9 f.** Man has only to **believe** and **confess** to be saved. **Confess** comes before **believe** to conform to the order **mouth . . . heart** in the quotation. The next verse has the logical order. Salvation depends upon outward profession matched by inner conviction. **Jesus is Lord** was the earliest confession of faith (cf. v. 13 n.; 1 C. 12: 3); this may well refer to its use in baptism. To believe in the resurrection (cf. 4: 24) is no mere intellectual assent, but involves the shattering realization that God has miraculously intervened and inaugurated the Messianic reign (cf. 1: 4 n.; 6: 11 n.). After such a realization no man can ever be the same as he was before. **11–13.** Isa. 28:

16 is quoted again to confirm that the believer's salvation is guaranteed. Paul now borrows 'anyone' (Gk. *pās*) from Jl 2: 32 (quoted in 13) and adds it here (cf. AV, RV 'whosoever') to bring out the implications. If keeping the law were the condition for salvation, salvation would be merely a Jewish concern; since faith is the criterion it is available to any, Jew or Gentile (cf. 3: 22). The risen **Lord** has been given universal dominion, and 'he has enough and to spare' (Knox) for any who appeal to Him for salvation (cf. Eph. 4: 8). Now that the Spirit has inaugurated Christ's kingdom upon earth (cf. Jl 2: 28 ff.) the universal offer of Jl 2: 32 is operative. In the OT text **the Lord** represents Yahweh or Jehovah, the Heb. name for God. Here as often in the NT it is re-interpreted of Christ (cf. 1 C. 1: 2; Ac. 3: 21, 36) since God had conferred upon Him His own name, 'the name which is above every name' (Phil. 2: 9).

14–21. God has given the Jews every opportunity. He has done everything possible to get the gospel across to them, but they have not responded with faith. **14 f.** The gap between God's gospel and a man's appropriation of it must be covered by a chain whose four links are the apostles, preaching, hearing and faith. God **sent** (Gk. *apostalōsin*) the apostles to them. Isa. 52: 7 is quoted as the divine authorization of their mission. **16.** An adjacent verse, Isa. 53: 1, is put on the apostles' lips as their report that their making the message heard—about the suffering Servant—has met with little response of faith from their fellow-Jews who heard it. The Jews broke the last link in the chain. **18.** But if they did not believe, that is not because they did not have the opportunity to hear it. It is underlined that the fault is not on God's side: He has let the Jews hear the gospel. Ps. 19: 4 is true of the apostolic testimony: it has penetrated every corner of the earth (Paul is thinking of the then known world). **19–21.** Moses and Isaiah have the answer why the Jews did not accept the gospel. Dt. 32: 21 revealed that Gentiles with **no understanding** (cf. 2: 20), a non-nation (cf. 9: 25), would understand. So difficulty in understanding was not the problem. Isa. 65: 1 f. discloses the real obstacle to be the Jews' obstinate disobedience in the face of God's repeated appeals, so that God had to turn to the Gentiles instead (cf. Lk. 14: 16–24).

iii. God's future plan for Jew and Gentile (11: 1–32)

The present state of affairs was not to be permanent. Paul took seriously God's election of the Jews and His OT promises to them and could not entertain the idea that they were to be by and large excluded from attaining those promises. When the 'full number' of the Gentiles had been incorporated into the Church, then, and only then, it would be the turn of the Jews as a whole—not a mere handful as now—to acknowledge Jesus as Lord and thus reveal their now hidden character as God's elect. Their prejudiced, closed minds would be opened to the truth of the gospel, just as once his own had been, and then the final outworking of the 'one new man' in Christ (Eph. 2: 15) would be realized. This hope was the driving force behind Paul's world-wide evangelism, for ultimately it would redound to the Jews' advantage. The full evangelism of the Gentiles would usher in the salvation of Israel. It is significant that Paul did not assert, as the manner of some is, that the OT promises to Israel had automatically passed *en bloc* to the largely Gentile Church, because such a view would make mockery of God's election. Nor, however, did he dissociate the Church from Israel's promises: that would deny the unity of the 'olive tree' and ignore the continuity of the OT people of God with the Church, which for Paul was ultimately to comprise the 'full number' of the Gentiles *plus* the bulk of the Jews. Until then the Church would be lop-sided and incomplete and the purposes of God among men not yet fulfilled. To prove that God has not abandoned Israel, Paul argues that their rejection is both partial and provisional. For the time being a remnant is being saved (1–10). Eventually God will save the rest when He has finished gathering Gentile Christians (11–32).

1–10. Now a remnant of Israel is being saved. **1–5.** Scripture echoes and re-echoes with the sure principle which Paul is quoting: **God did not reject his people** after having lavished such care and concern upon them (Ps. 94: 14; 1 Sam. 12: 22; Jer. 31: 37; 33: 24 ff.). 10: 20 f. cannot be God's last word, for He is not fickle. His faithfulness to covenant-promises may not be exploited by arrogant presumption, but it is a dependable source of security to the humble believer. Paul regards himself as a token of God's faithfulness to His people. If Israel were rejected, he himself would not have been saved. But Paul is not a lone survivor. He finds a historical parallel in 1 Kg. 19 where Elijah was reassured that he was not left alone despite the opposition of so many Israelites to the true faith. As then God had preserved 7,000 followers, a fraction of the nation, so now there is a Jewish-Christian **remnant, chosen by grace** (cf. 9: 6, 27–29). **6.** **Grace** by its very definition is the opposite of **works:** the self-made Jew is automatically debarred from the faithful few. **7. Israel** as a whole has not achieved salvation, but out of it has been saved the **elect** minority, while the majority have been made insensitive to the gospel for the time being (cf. 9: 18 n.). **8.** Scripture is finding a fresh application. God has sent most of the Jews into a paralysing **stupor,** according to Isa. 29: 10. Their present state is that of blind, deaf men, as Israel of old were described in Dt. 29: 4. **9 f.** The Psalmist's curse has come true (Ps. 69: 23 f. LXX). Their very religious observances, as a substitute for Christ, only lead the Jews astray. 'The picture of a blind, decrepit old man, bowed down in age and infirmity . . . is a very pathetic representation of a people in a state of religious senility' (E. K. Lee).

11–32. Eventually Israel as a whole will be saved after the full quota of Gentile Christians has been made up. **11–15.** Israel has only **stumbled** over the Stone (9: 32 f.), not collapsed altogether. God has not dropped them. The unbelief of most of the Jews has been God's temporary means to the end that the gospel should come to the Gentiles. The Gk. for **transgression** may be translated 'lapse' (Weymouth, Moffatt) or 'false step' (Knox). The Gentiles' acceptance of the gospel made the Jews **envious** (cf. Ac. 13: 44 ff.)—and designedly so. The reason why Paul made much of his Gentile **ministry** was that it fulfilled God's revealed purpose (Dt. 32: 21 quoted in 10: 19), which was to provoke his **own people** not merely to jealous indignation, but in the case of **some** to emulation, to a positive desire to share the blessings accruing to Gentile Christians. His Gentile missionary work was not only for the Gentiles' sake, Paul assures them in anticipation of his later attack on their cocksureness and contempt for Jews. His Gentile apostleship was but a round-about way of reaching the Jews. Arguing from the greater to the less as in 5: 9 f., Paul contends that if Israel's falling away has resulted in so much good, **how much greater riches** can be expected when they are restored! Their return to God's favour will mean the influx of new, blue blood into the Church from virtual **dead** bones (cf. Ezek. 37: 1–10). **16.** What guarantee is there that the Jews will play so glorious a rôle? The answer lies in Israel's ancient religious history. There is a natural sanctity in Israel, endowed by God. In so signally revealing Himself to their forefathers (cf. v. 28) in His mighty acts and promises, God had set a pattern to which Israel would again conform in due course. 'When the first loaf is consecrated, the whole batch is consecrated with it' (Knox), and Israel's patriarchs were like the first loaf. Paul has Num. 15: 20 f. in mind. Israel's ancestors have left to their descendants a legacy of spiritual wealth which they will one day claim and use. In a sense the rabbis were right about Israel's election: they went wrong in holding a doctrine of works and in failing to submit to God's will by recognizing Jesus as the Messiah, the only avenue of God's blessing.

17–24. The illustration of root and branches in v. 16 is developed into a horticultural allegory describing God's plan for present and future. The idea comes from Jer. 11: 16 where Israel is compared with an *olive tree*, once having *fruit beautiful in form*, but now spoilt by sin and due for punishment: *its branches will be broken*. Paul finds the current situation explained in this verse. The tree is the people of God. Its branches are living Jews. Now **some of the branches**, unbelieving Jews, have been pruned away and the only natural branches left are the believing remnant of Israel. But the divine Gardener has replenished the tree with a **wild olive shoot**. Gentile converts to Christianity comprise a cutting from an oleaster shrub inserted into the stock of the cultivated olive tree. There is evidence in ancient horticultural books that occasionally this strange practice was followed in the belief that an oleaster scion would invigorate an old tree (see Leenhardt's commentary; W. M. Ramsay, *Pauline and Other Studies*, pp. 219 ff.). But the normal practice was to use a good quality olive scion. The very unusualness is no doubt an intended part of the allegory. God has acted in grace that transcends human custom and expectation. But the Gardener has not finished His work yet. The **natural branches** that have been removed will one day be **grafted in again**, as soon as they cease to **persist in unbelief**. Now there are only a few Jewish branches left (cf. v. 17) in company with a large wild shoot taken from the Gentile world: they are all there because of their common faith, faith in God who has revealed Himself through Jesus Christ. One day the Jewish and Gentile Christians will be joined on the tree by the mass of renegade Jews, who will come to share their faith and be restored as active members of the people of God.

Paul gives this explanation in the context of a warning, at which he has already hinted in vv. 13 f. There was evidently an anti-Jewish bias among Gentile converts. Gentiles were learning to shout down Judaism's proud claims with even louder counter-claims of their own privileges and the Jews' deprivation. In their eyes it was no doubt a shameful thing to be a Jew, a member of the race that had rejected their Messiah. They deserved all the kicks they got. God had had to come to the Gentiles before He could get any satisfaction (cf. 10: 20 f. n.). Paul deplores this unhealthy attitude of contempt: it was the mentality of the worst type of Jew all over again. He reminds them of their debt to the Jewish heritage. 'In a sense the converted Jew is the only normal human being in the world. To him, in the first instance, the promises were made, and he has availed himself of them. He calls Abraham his father by hereditary right as well as by divine courtesy. He has taken the whole syllabus in order, as it was set. . . . Every one else is, from one point of view, a special case, dealt with under emergency conditions' (C. S. Lewis). Paul warns the Gentile Christians that the Jews' fate could be theirs unless they **continue in** God's **kindness** (cf. 2: 4 ff.; 8: 13 n.; 1 C. 10: 12). God can thin out the branches again. The Jews' fate should arouse in Gentile Christians not arrogance but humble faith and respect for a God who is not to be trifled with. Woe to the Christian 'for whom grace is no longer grace on the hundredth or the thousandth day as it was on the first' (Godet).

25–32. God's plan is in two stages. **25.** The first stage is the rejection of most of the Jews in order that God may make up the **full number**, which only He knows, of Gentile Christians. **26.** The second stage, which He will put into operation as soon as the first is completed, is a **mystery**, a secret design of God which human minds would not have hit upon apart from revelation. **All Israel will be saved**, brought into the Christian blessings into which now only a remnant of the Jews have entered. **All Israel** means the Jews as a collective whole, not the arithmetical sum of all individual Jews. The phrase is obviously contrasted with **part** of Israel, and **Israel** consistently refers to the Jews in chs. 9–11. **So** signifies 'by such means' described in v. 25b. **Saved** is to be taken in the same spiritual sense as in vv. 11, 14. (The question of a political future for converted Israel does not arise here, but hangs upon the interpretation of other Scriptures.) In Scriptural support of this astounding statement, Paul cites Isa. 59: 20 f., mainly from the LXX. 'To Zion' of the Heb. text became 'for Zion's sake' in the LXX; here it is changed to **from Zion** under the influence of Ps. 14: 7. God had pledged Himself to Israel for ever (the unquoted continuation of the OT passage is no doubt also in Paul's mind: cf. 3: 4 n.). His plan was that Jesus, the **deliverer** (cf. 1 Th. 1: 10), would first set out with His witnesses from Jerusalem to the end of the earth (cf. Ac. 1: 8; Mt. 28: 19 f.) and then eventually go back to His own people and turn their unbelief to faith. The concluding words are from Isa. 27: 9: God had promised so to do. He would freely forgive the Jews' rejection of Christ. **28 f.** At present the mass of unbelieving Jews have a dual character in God's eyes. They are the temporary objects of His displeasure, having opposed and rejected **the gospel**. This was intended for the benefit of the Gentiles so that they might have the opportunity of receiving it (cf. v. 11). But simultaneously they are the objects of His election-love as heirs of the glorious Israel of old (cf. v. 16 n.), since the never-changing God does not take back a gift or cancel a summons. **30 f.** Now the Gentile Christian had passed from rebellion to pardon; so would the Jew one day. As for the Gentile the present is a reversal of the past, so for the Jew the future will be a reversal of the present. Now the Jew is serving the Gentile as the means of God's pardoning the latter; the Gentile is to serve the Jew as the means of pardoning the Jew. **32.** God gave up one class of man, the Gentiles, to rebellion as a preliminary to pardoning him now; so God is now treating the other class, the Jews, in preparation for granting them pardon later on.

iv. Praise of God's wisdom (11: 33–36)
Paul's discussion dissolves into worship, for 'theology is doxology or it is nothing at all' (E. Stauffer). The interpreter of God's purposes to man is forced to break out in spontaneous praise to God: 'How great Thou art!' He has seen God's purposes of lavish grace (**riches**) and **wisdom** stretching from horizon to horizon, but clearly there is yet a vast universe of the divine will beneath and beyond, out of human sight. Isa. 40: 13 and Job 41: 11 are testimonies to God's transcendence and gracious initiative. How futile is any attempt on the part of little man, Jew or even Gentile, to think that He regards men as His consultants to tell Him what to do, or that they can ever earn acceptance with God by merit. For God is 'Source, Guide and Goal of all that is' (NEB).

V. THE GOSPEL IN ACTION (12: 1–15: 13)
'The gospel has two sides—a believing side and a behaving side', as A. M. Hunter quotes. It is to the second side that Paul now turns. Previously in chs. 6–8 he had laid down the general principle of the 'newness of life' required of the Christian. Here he analyses God's requirement into a series of duties that range over most of life and also present by analogy principles to cover every situation.

i. Behaviour in the church and in the world (12: 1–21)
A new life of self-dedication (12: 1–2)
1. The worship of 11: 33 ff. turns into an appeal for worship in the widest sense as a response to **God's mercy**. Divine initiative and human response is the pattern in both OT and NT. The OT ritual laid down as the medium of part of Israel's obedience to the God who had redeemed them must find a counterpart in the Church. Their personalities in all their manifestations (cf. 6: 6 n.) must be sacrificed alive as a whole-offering which satisfies God's moral requirements. **Living** has all the associations of the resurrection life that is life indeed, which was expounded in chs. 5–8. **Spiritual** (Gk. *logikēn*) is derived from 'word' (Gk. *logos*) and so here means 'figurative, metaphorical' as distinct from the material **worship** of OT ritual. NEB has 'the worship offered by mind and heart'. **2.** The old 'age' (Gk. *aiōn*, NIV **world**) is still running its course in one sense, but in another sense it has already passed away (cf. 6:

4, 5, 8 n.). The rabbis used to contrast 'this age' with the 'coming age'. For the Christian who has entered the age to come the old conventions and habits in vogue around him are out of date. Instead his whole attitude to life must be renewed (cf. 6: 4), re-modelled on the lines of his new status, and orientated towards God. His aim must be to exercise sound spiritual judgment at every turn, in every situation to find out **God's will**. This rather high-sounding phrase resolves itself in practice into what is good for God and for one's neighbour, what is personally pleasing to God, and what is the ideal response to a situation (cf. Eph. 5: 9 f.).

Co-ordination in the church (3–8)
Paul ventures by virtue of his apostolic authority to develop co-operation and harmony in the local church. A this-worldly spirit of self-seeking and competition must not rear its ugly head. An exaggerated view of one's own importance must give way to a sensible estimate of one's position. Christians' **faith**, or the gospel which they believe (cf. v. 6) is the standard by which to measure themselves. 'They then and only then achieve a sober and sensible estimate of themselves as, equally with their fellows, both sinners revealed in their true colours by the judgment of the Cross and also the objects of God's undeserved and triumphant mercy in Jesus Christ' (C. E. B. Cranfield). From that source the Christian learns too that he is **in Christ**, a phrase which implies corporate solidarity: he is in the **body** of Christ. Consequently, like a limb he is responsible for making a specific contribution to the well-being of the whole church, and must neither neglect his own function, as if he was superfluous, nor usurp others' functions, as if he was meant to do everything (cf. 1 C. 12: 12 ff.). God has allocated different functions to different spiritual limbs in Christ's body, and Paul stresses that the credit belongs to the Giver and not to the gifted. He proceeds to enumerate some of those functions (cf. a different list in 1 C. 12: 4 ff.) and the way in which they are to be carried out. The wide range of the list 'shows clearly that Paul made no such hard and fast distinction between clerical and lay ministries as later emerged in the Church' (C. H. Dodd). The prophet, 'the eye of the Church to receive new revelations' (F. Godet), must check what he says against the Christian **faith** to see that they agree (cf. 1 C. 14: 29; 1 Jn 4: 1). A man equipped for practical **serving** (cf. 1 Pet. 4: 11) or a teacher or a preacher must each confine himself to his own work and not think he can do another's task and/or neglect his own. When one gives to Christian funds, that is a spiritual work to be done whole-heartedly, not reluctantly or in a niggardly way. A supporter of a Christian project (**leadership:** Gk. *proista-*

menos, which Arndt and Gingrich define here as 'be concerned about, care for, give aid'; 'help' in 16: 2 is Gk. *prostatis*, a cognate noun) should not tail off into indifference. The 'sick visitor' (Moffatt) must make himself affable or his visit will be wasted. In fine Paul's advice is: do your own job, and mean what you do.

Love in action (9–21)
Turning to broader questions of personal attitudes and relationships in the church and outside, the apostle counsels **sincere love** that takes its cue from God's love in Christ and is out for the very best for other people. It is to be guided not by sentiment or indulgence but by the highest moral standards. Its manifold implications include touches of affectionate tenderness and mutual rivalry in showing respect. **11.** The Christian's consistent attitude must be one of enthusiasm, a warm fervour which the Spirit promotes (cf. Ac. 18: 25; Rev. 3: 15), and the dedication of every activity to Christ as **Lord** (cf. Col. 3: 23 f.). **12.** The church must be marked by a confident tone inspired not by wishful thinking but by the solid reality of the Christian hope. This will result in a dogged refusal to give in to adverse pressures. But how is it maintained? By persistent praying that keeps regularly in touch with God. **13.** Further outworkings of love towards other Christians are the relief of material **need** and the opening of the home to Christian visitors to the locality (cf. Ac. 16: 15; 1 Pet. 4: 9). **14.** The early Church obviously treasured the Sermon on the Mount: Paul here echoes his Master's words (Mt. 5: 44; Lk. 6: 28). A natural reaction to persecutors is to be transcended by invoking a blessing upon them: this is the new way of love. **15.** One's natural mood must give way to a ready sympathy with the experiences of others. **16.** Read with NEB: 'Have equal regard for one another'. This being 'actuated by a common and well-understood feeling of mutual allowance and kindness' (Alford) rules out any caste system and calls for a willingness to mix unselfconsciously with slaves and others low on the social ladder (cf. Phm. 16). Prov. 3: 7, here quoted, warns against the vanity that is the basis of snobbery. **17–21.** Paul uses an adjacent precept (Prov. 3: 4, quoted from the LXX) to urge Christians not to provide their pagan neighbours with just cause for criticism. One way is non-retaliation, and this principle the apostle now elaborates. The early Church, set as they were in naturally suspicious or hostile communities, needed wise and cool heads. It takes two to keep the peace, but the Christian must not be responsible for breaking it. It is the natural reaction to retaliate, a reaction based partly at least on an instinct for fair play. But it can safely be left to God eventually to get justice done, on the day of judgment (cf. 2: 5, 8). Dt. 32: 35 claims vengeance as God's right

and so not man's. But there is one positive way in which the Christian may react. Scripture lays it down with vivid irony (Prov. 25: 21 f.). Tit-for-tat would only aggravate the situation and set up a vicious circle, but there is a real possibility that repaying the other party's hostility with unexpected kindness and 'treating him as someone in need' (Barth) will make him burn with pangs of guilt and remorse and realize the error of his ways; and so the breach will be healed and 'vengeance be transformed into the victory of love' (H. C. G. Moule).

ii. Church and state (13: 1–7)

As part of the 'living sacrifices' which the Christian is to offer (12: 1) Paul lays down what his general attitude should be towards the state. The apostle 'shares to a certain extent the thankful attitude of the provinces which recognized in the empire the guardian of peace, the principle of order versus chaos, the bulwark of order and justice' (J. Weiss). **1 f.** The Christian view is conditioned by the relationship between God and the state. God is no merely 'religious' God: in His providential care are included the control of nations and the maintenance of civil order within them. The OT had taught Paul that it is God who sets up civil rulers and that their authority is delegated from Him (*e.g.* Jer. 27: 5 f.; Dan. 2: 21, 37 f.; 4: 17). God is as much the God of Nero as He was the power behind Cyrus (Isa. 45: 1 ff.). From this truth of divine sovereignty stems the individual Christian's obligation of civil obedience. Generally speaking, to subject oneself to the civil authorities is but an indirect way of obeying God Himself. At bottom the issue is in a sense not 'either God or state' nor 'both God and state' but 'God via the state'. This is a general and basic principle; it is not lightly to be laid aside, but it may be complicated by specific circumstances which create a conflict of loyalties, as Ac. 4: 19 f.; 5: 29; Rev. 13 acknowledge. Over every man hangs the sobering prospect that he will be answerable to God for his civil behaviour and will be punished by Him for civil misdemeanours. **3 f.** A second reason for civil obedience (**for** is parallel with **for** in v. 1) is the general axiom that the state upholds moral standards (to a certain level at least). In that respect the Christian should instinctively view the government not as an enemy but as an ally and helper towards his own moral endeavours. In fact the civil power is God's **servant**, doing God's work positively and negatively by encouraging virtue and discouraging vice. With **to do you good** cf. 8: 28 f.: this is one of the providential ways by which God accomplishes His purpose for the Christian. The civil ruler is empowered to inflict retribution upon **the wrongdoer**, as is shown by his right to use **the sword** for the maintenance of civil order. It is implied that the state has a God-given

power, albeit capable of abuse, of life and death over its subjects. 'Through the state there takes place a partial, anticipatory, provisional manifestation of God's wrath against sin' (C. E. B. Cranfield). **5.** The motive for civil obedience comes **not only** from a desire to avoid God's wrath, either in its provisional (v. 4) or final (cf. v. 2) form, **but also** from the consciousness the Christian has of the subordination of the state to God. **6 f.** Moreover it is this consciousness that justifies the Christian's paying taxes to the authorities: 'it is as God's servants (and therefore as those whose claim must not be rejected or evaded) that they busy themselves earnestly with this very thing, namely the matter of tribute' (Cranfield). There is no doubt a reference here to the saying of our Lord (Mk 12: 17). 'The Christian is under obligation to pay his dues to the state because, as a beneficiary of it, he owes it some payment in return for the protection and amenities it provides, and because no state can function without resources and therefore a fundamental refusal to pay taxes would be a fundamental "No" to the state as such' (Cranfield). **Taxes** are direct taxes, the 'tribute' of the Gospels, while **revenue** is an indirect tax on goods. It should be remembered that Paul is here laying down the political obligations of the Christian in an authoritarian state. His obligations in a democracy, where every citizen has a responsible, albeit small share in government, are not necessarily confined to the obligations enumerated in this passage.

iii. Motives for Christian behaviour (13: 8–14)

Paul adduces two motives for goodness. The first is love, and the second is the consummation of the new age. The two are implicitly linked. Love for Paul is the supreme blessing of the Spirit who is poured out in the last days in anticipation of the Messianic age in its fulness (cf. 5: 5 n.). **8–10.** The Christian's political, economic dues (v. 7: Gk. *opheilas*) lead on to his social dues (**debt** is Gk. *opheilete*). He has one such obligation—**love**. 'The debt of love is permanent, and we never get out of it; for we pay it daily and yet always owe it' (Origen). Paul echoes his Master's approval of Lev. 19: 18 as the summary of the law (Lk. 10: 26 ff.; cf. Mt. 22: 40) as far as human duties are concerned. Love aims at the very best for others. He who loves another will shrink from harming him in any way, and thus from breaking those of the ten commandments that refer to treatment of one's **neighbour**. It is love that keeps the law; and the law is the yardstick of love. This love is no feigned emotion but an active, continual attitude fostered by the Spirit, by which the love of God in Christ, having once been poured out in the Christian's heart, proceeds through his whole life and beyond him to every man he meets. **11–14.** The age to come begins with 'the day of the Lord' (1 Th. 5: 2); accordingly this age (cf. 12: 2 n.) may be regarded as the preceding **night**. Day and night are also natural picture-words for right and wrong. Paul alludes to the baptismal hymn he quotes in Eph. 5: 14 and urges Christians to rub the sleep out of their eyes, to live now in the light of the coming day, to be up and doing —good works (cf. Jn 3: 19 ff.; 1 Jn 1: 7; 2: 8 ff.). **Salvation** is the fulfilment of the promise implicit in initial salvation (8: 24 n.). The attitude of the early Church was to expect Christ's return in their lifetime; indeed, only thus can the Christian hope exert any moral stimulus (cf. Lk. 12: 36). Light and darkness also carried associations of war in the contemporary Jewish world. One of the scrolls of the Dead Sea sect describes the war between 'the sons of light' and 'the sons of darkness'. Paul here makes use of this mixed imagery that was 'in the air', as he did also in 1 Th. 5: 8. **Night** is the time for **orgies**, etc. and is a cover for any shameful act; but now the night is over for the Christian who lives in the **day** of Christ's resurrection (cf. Eph. 5: 8: 'Lord' is a resurrection title) which sets a new pattern of moral propriety. The thought of putting on Christ is a baptismal one (cf. Gal. 3: 27). Indeed, these verses ring out as loudly as 6: 1 ff. with the call to live out the implications of baptism. The new convert who strips off his clothes before baptism and dresses himself again afterwards is enacting a symbolic demand upon himself to don new habits that express Christ: 'Put on the character of the Lord Jesus Christ' (Moffatt). The OT had prepared the way in likening a new status and a new kind of life to a new garment (Isa. 59: 17; 61: 10; Zech. 3: 4). Gal. 5: 16–24 is Paul's own commentary on the last two clauses.

iv. Corporate harmony and personal convictions (14: 1–15: 13)

Paul turns from general moral exhortation to advice in handling specific situations that arise from human diversity. Nowhere is his level-headed insight into problems of personal relationships displayed more than here. Every individual carries within him a set of convictions born of past experience and the influence of other personalities upon his own. He is apt to consider his opinions sacrosanct and rationalize principles out of them. A desire for self-justification may prompt him to regard with scorn those who do not conform to his views, and write them off as unreasonable and intolerable. Even a group of individuals with similar backgrounds and interests is liable to be broken up by this kind of reaction. The danger lurks constantly at the door of a church: there the basis of union is not similarity of interests nor mutual attraction but an individual response to God's offer of salvation made to men

of all types (1: 14). Petty differences can soon be blown up into major issues under these circumstances. To prevent such a situation developing the apostle here gives advice both to critics and criticized. He appears not to have in mind problems besetting the Roman churches, but to write from earlier experience of trouble in other fellowships, in order to warn the Romans of dangers that are likely to arise. First, when a Christian thinks another at fault in a practice not covered clearly by the moral traditions passed on to the Church by the apostles (1 Th. 4: 1 ff.) he must stifle his impulse to interfere, and be tolerant (14: 1–12). Secondly, when a Christian is considered by others to be thus at fault, his desire must be not to injure them; he should be prepared to make concessions rather than be the cause of trouble in the church (14: 13–15: 6). Thirdly, Paul adduces broader incentives to unity (15: 7–13).

1–12. An individual Christian is responsible to the Lord alone. In Corinth, where Paul was writing from, he had had to deal with the issue of eating meat, and it is to this very situation that he most probably refers here to illustrate his teaching. Read 1 C. 8–11 for the background of the problem and a fuller discussion. The problem arose from the fact that the slaughter of animals in the Hellenistic world was connected closely with religious ritualism, as it was in Judaism (cf. Lev. 17). The chances were that a joint bought in the market had been consecrated to pagan gods. Some Christians with tender consciences preferred to be vegetarians; others reasoned the matter out and concluded that there was nothing wrong in eating meat. Paul himself shared fully the conclusions of the latter group (cf. Col. 2: 20 ff.; Paul is there condemning not an individual's right to follow his conscience but an attempt to compel a company of Christians to conform —or else). But his heart went out to the others in sympathetic understanding. The mixture of Jews and Gentiles in a church provided another problem. It was one which the apostle had met in Galatia (Gal. 4: 10), but in the much more acute form of an attempt to secure a human claim upon salvation. The Christian-Jew or proselyte had been in the habit of regarding certain days as holy, such as the weekly Sabbath and the annual Day of Atonement. It was ingrained in his conscience that not to observe them was wrong. On the other hand, an ex-pagan could make out a foolproof case to prove that such practices were no longer necessary (cf. Col. 2: 16 ff.).

In all such differences of opinion the natural reaction is to seek to bring about uniformity —to one's own opinion! Paul condemns this attitude and lays down directions for the Christian who thinks another is in the wrong. In the scrupulous man, background and psychological make-up have combined to produce a reaction of emotional abhorrence to behaviour that other Christians find unobjectionable. Such a man is certainly **weak** and has not grasped the full implications of his **faith**. But any quick forceful attempt to 'educate' him would end in disaster, Paul wisely realized. Accordingly, he does not take the logical step of ordering conformity. Instead he counsels: let the other man be. The principle he adduces is the Christian's personal responsibility to his Lord and Master. He is God's, for it is God who **has accepted** him into fellowship with Him; and so others are obliged to **accept** him too, not give him the cold shoulder. He is Christ's **servant** (cf. v. 9) and responsible to Him. It is nothing less than usurping Christ's sovereign authority over a fellow-Christian for one to criticize him over a difference of opinion: for the less scrupulous to **look down on** the more scrupulous, and for the more scrupulous to **judge** the less scrupulous. Christian fellowship does not imply a right to run other people's lives for them: only Christ can—and will—discharge such a right. The temptation to criticize some one else must be resisted. Instead one must re-examine one's own views, in case they are based upon selfish expediency and personal profit, and in an exercise of spiritual judgment come to as informed and responsible a conviction as one is psychologically capable of. Whichever conclusion one comes to, one must consecrate it and its outworking to the Lord, for the whole of life is to be devoted to Him as 'a living sacrifice' (12: 1). Whatever a Christian does is to be his personal act of worship to Christ and of thanksgiving to God. 'You are not your own' (1 C. 6: 19). The doctrine that the risen Christ is Lord and Judge of all (Ac. 17: 31) finds an application here. Christ confronts the Christian at every turn, in life and also in death; he is His for good and all. Accordingly, the Christian's duty is not to find fault with his neighbour's behaviour where a difference of opinion is concerned—such a judgment unconsciously has the effect of approving his own behaviour as praiseworthy—but to leave the verdict to God who will judge all men at His 'tribunal' (Moffatt) and receive all the praise Himself. Cf. 2 C. 5: 10 where the **judgment seat** is Christ's. In 2: 16 God is said to judge through Christ or to delegate judgment to Him. Paul oscillates easily between God and Christ: there are several instances in this very passage. In the free quotation from the LXX of Isa. 45: 23 the apostle may well be interpreting **Lord** as referring to Christ (cf. Phil. 2: 10; compare **live** with **returned to life** in v. 9 and the contrast of **Lord** and **God** in v. 6).

14: 13–15: 6. Paul now changes sides, and advises not the critics, but the criticized. Before, he was addressing both the 'strong' and the 'weak', but now he singles out the non-scrupulous person with whom the scrupulous Christian finds fault. Two points are made: (*a*) the sanctity of conscience and (*b*) the responsibility not to impede another's Christian progress. The apostle's considered standpoint 'as a Christian' (NEB) is that of the non-scrupulous, in line with Christ's own teaching in Mk 7: 14 ff., but he can appreciate the problem the other side has and urges sympathy for them. If the scrupulous are wrong from an objective, absolute point of view, they are subjectively right —and that is more important than the 'strong' realize. The 'weak' have a conscience about whatever it is, and one's duty is always to obey one's conscience even if others regard it a superstitious qualm over a trifle. **Faith** in 23 is subjective: a strong 'conviction' (NEB) of what is right and God's will for oneself. One must respect one's own personal convictions; to act despite a troubled conscience amounts to sinning against God. 'If in doubt, don't' is not merely a safe principle to follow, but a vital principle in matters of conscience. C. H. Dodd helpfully compares the saying attributed to our Lord in one MS of Lk. 6: 4: 'On the same day, seeing some one working on the Sabbath, He said to him "Man, if you know what you are doing, blessed are you; but if you do not know, cursed are you and a breaker of the law".' The second point for the 'strong' to bear in mind when they feel inclined to resent and ignore the criticisms of the 'weak' is the consequences of their enlightened behaviour. Love takes precedence over knowledge. If the 'strong' do not care about the sensitivities of the 'weak' but openly fly in the face of them, what will the result be? Will the 'weak' be **distressed**, ruined, for example by their being led to act against their consciences? Will they be put off and made to backslide as a result of the example of the 'strong', which to them is sin? If so, the overall loss is surely far, far greater than the net gain. It is not worth division and disharmony in the church. Paul urges: consider the long-term results of thoughtlessly pursuing what is good to you. On occasions (C. K. Barrett points out that **eat, drink** are aorist infinitives referring to particular occasions) a policy of vegetarianism, teetotalism and any other abstention one may personally think unnecessary is better than causing some one else in the fellowship a spiritual set-back. Such callousness is far from the spirit of Christ's dying love. 'Those who meet at the foot of the Cross find that they are spiritual blood brothers and must act as such' (A. M. Hunter). It is a question of priorities: the things of value in **the kingdom of God** are spiritual things, and the 'strong' are exalting **eating and drinking** above them if they eat and drink to the spiritual detriment of some of their fellow-Christians and so ultimately of the

Christian community as a whole. Paul is most probably alluding once more (cf. 12: 14 n.) to the Sermon on the Mount (Mt. 6: 31 ff.) **15: 1 f.** The Christian is no self-contained unit: his actions may well have repercussions on his **neighbor**. He must therefore be motivated by **his good** so that he may grow and progress. 'To please my neighbour is not weakly to comply with his desires but to act with a view to his lasting benefit' (W. E. Vine). The **weak** are psychologically incapable of making concessions, but the **strong** can and ought. **3.** 'Why should I?'—Paul anticipates the question by pointing to the example of Christ. He fulfilled Ps. 69: 9 in its deepest possible sense as the epitome of the righteous sufferer. The text is as it were His voice speaking to His Father. If making God's enemies His own enemies took Him to the Cross, should not the Christian put himself out a little for his spiritual kith and kin by helping them carry their burdens? **4.** Paul breaks off to urge his readers ever to be alert to the personal message of the OT, since it is expressly meant for them. Reading it will keep the Christian's hope undimmed and bright, and confirm the reality of the divine unseen. It is from the Scriptures that he will derive **encouragement** and remain true. **5.** A closing prayer for **unity** in the church. The OT encourages and sustains because behind it is God, the source of these very qualities. May the self-denying example of Christ be followed so that, secondary matters not obtruding, a harmonious setting may be procured for the church's concerted worship of God.

15: 7–13. Paul puts his appeal for unity on a broader basis. Underlying much of the friction in the early churches must have been the presence of both Jews and Gentiles together. The Jewish Christian would have to fight hard against the temptation of religious snobbery. The Gentile Christians would tend to regard the Jew and his traditions as a hangover from the obsolete past (cf. 11: 18, 25 n.). Over against these natural reactions Paul again makes Christ's example the Christian criterion. To spurn a fellow-Christian is to be out of step with Christ, who has **accepted** him as well as oneself. The Gentile in the Church who looks down upon the Jew as a back-number must remember that Christ Himself submitted to becoming a Jew (Gal. 4: 4) and received the Jewish heritage of the Messianic promises (cf. 9: 4). The Jew in the church who despises his Gentile fellow-believer as an interloper and a second-rate Christian must remember that Christ came also for the very purpose of bringing Gentiles into the Church. In both these purposes God was showing His **truth** in making His word come true. Lest doubts linger in the Jew's mind, Paul reminds him that the admission of the Gentiles is in line with his own traditions and was envisaged in the OT, the source-book of God's plans. Ps. 18: 49 is taken as the words of the pre-incarnate Christ to His Father (cf. Heb. 2: 11 ff.), promising that He will lead Gentiles' praises to God. The invitations of Dt. 32: 43 (LXX) and of Ps. 117: 1 and the Messianic promise of Isa. 11: 10 (LXX) all look forward to the Gentiles' participation in the worship of the Church (cf. v. 6) and in possessing the Christian hope as validly as Jewish Christians. Behind this **hope** is the one God who inspires it equally in Jew and Gentile. Paul's prayer is for right perspectives; he harks back to the vocabulary of 14: 17. May spiritual qualities be exalted in the Christian community in place of discord over material and human matters. If **hope, joy, peace**, a continual attitude of faith and **the power of the Holy Spirit** fill the vision of God's people and direct their judgment, then secondary matters will fall into their proper place and be viewed aright.

VI. PAUL'S MISSIONARY PLANS (15: 14–33)

14–16. Paul first tactfully apologizes for his letter (cf. 1: 12 n.) and then justifies it. He regrets if he has appeared to be taking liberties **on some points** (*e.g.* 6: 19; 11: 25; 14: 4). He is fully aware of the mature balance—the firm grasp of doctrinal truth and its warm-hearted outworking—to be found in the Roman churches. But he has written to refresh their memory. And he claims the right to instruct them by virtue of his apostleship (cf. 1: 6 f.; 12: 3). He is nothing less than Christ's agent to the Gentile world, and even God's priest to offer to Him a sacrifice consisting of Gentile converts won to the gospel and nurtured in the faith (cf. Phil. 2: 17). This is a specific application of the priesthood of all believers, whereby all Christian work is viewed as a sacrifice. **17–21.** Paul reviews his past missionary work and policy. The phrases he has used may be high-sounding, but they are fully justified by the results. He does not want to take any credit for other people's work, like some 'superlative apostles' he has come across (2 C. 10: 13 ff.; 11: 4 ff.). The past record of his own work is the testimonial of his apostolic commission. But it is not his personal achievement but Christ's work **through** him. His preaching and teaching, his travelling and feats of endurance (cf. 2 C. 11: 23 ff.), his miracles (cf. Ac. 14: 8 ff.; 2 C. 12: 12), his effectiveness brought about by the Holy Spirit—all these confirm his apostolic claims, should the Romans have any qualms or reservations about him. His area of missionary work has been vast: the eastern provinces of the Roman Empire from **Jerusalem** to the province of **Illyricum**, on the east coast of the Adriatic. The latter limit refers to his most recent journey recorded in Ac. 20: 2: behind Luke's vague description apparently lies work done further west than Macedonia. Paul had evangelized half the Roman world by his method of visiting the main centres and leaving converts to preach the gospel in the surrounding regions. There were areas he had not visited but this was because they were already covered by other pioneer missionaries. Isa. 52: 15 (LXX) represents a principle in the proclamation of the gospel of the Servant which governs Paul's policy (2 C. 10: 13 ff.): his task is to open up virgin territory.

22–32. The apostle outlines his future plans. Now he is free to visit Rome, an ambition he has had **for many years.** Ac. 19: 21 and 2 C. 10: 16 are evidence that he already had a western mission in mind two years or so before. It may well have been Priscilla and Aquila who had suggested it to him about seven years previously (Ac. 18: 2). His idea was to do pioneer work in Spain, as there were already Christians in Italy. But he would call at Rome on the way, and indeed sought their commendation and backing in the Spanish mission. Such is the force of **to have you assist me on my journey:** cf. the use of the verb in Ac. 15: 3; Tit. 3: 13; 3 Jn 6. Rome was to be his base of operations. He apparently hoped that the Roman churches would contribute to expenses, provide assistants and generally support his western campaign. This may partly explain why Paul so carefully defines his missionary preaching in this letter, as C. H. Dodd suggests. Before setting out for the west the apostle had an errand: he must first take to Jerusalem the proceeds of a collection for the poor in the church there. James, Peter and John had asked Paul to 'remember the poor' in this way in return for their recognizing his missionary work among the Gentiles (Gal. 2: 10). Since then Paul's relations with the churches of Judaea had deteriorated, but nevertheless he had encouraged the churches of Greece, which was divided into the two Roman provinces of **Macedonia** and **Achaia,** to contribute to a relief fund. Actually the churches of Asia and Galatia also contributed, as Ac. 20: 4; 1 C. 16: 1 make clear. They had willingly complied with his fervent appeals (1 C. 16: 1 ff.; 2 C. 8: 9). Indeed, it was only fair that they should repay with **material** aid those who had given them **spiritual blessings**. When the business of the fund had been signed and settled (so perhaps 'sealed' (28, Gk.) means), Paul was intending to visit Rome on his way to Spain. He is sure that he will bring to Rome a special **blessing** from Christ (cf. 1: 11). But Paul cannot get his coming visit to Jerusalem off his mind, and he must return to it. The strong terms in which he craves the Romans' prayers show how worried he is about it. **The love of**

the Spirit is 'the love which the Spirit inspires' (Moffatt, cf. Weymouth). This uncovering of Paul's inner thoughts casts much light upon the narrative of Ac. 20 f. Even before the journey he is very conscious that he is walking into a den of lions. Stephen's fate was printed indelibly on Paul's mind. He knew, no doubt, that distressed synagogue officials had reported the harm the cause of Judaism had suffered at Paul's hands (Ac. 21: 28). Now Paul was to visit the headquarters and the Jews would have a unique chance to get their hands on him. But he had another worry: would the Jerusalem church accept his gesture of unity and fellowship? In their eyes Paul had let down the Christian cause badly by unscriptural policies (Ac. 21: 20 ff.). Could they have fellowship with such a brother? Was not the money he brought a bribe to get them to condone his misdemeanours? Poor as they were, ought they not to stand firm for the truth and avoid the temptation? Such might be their reactions. In fact they accepted the money, but demanded proof of Paul's orthodoxy. James in embarrassment had to give way to the pressure of 'myriads' (so literally Ac. 21: 20) and make Paul submit to a test of soundness. Amid all these thoughts of danger and disunity Paul turns to the God of peace and as he commits his readers to Him no doubt he also casts himself upon Him in a silent prayer.

VII. CLOSING MESSAGES (16: 1–27)

1–2. Paul introduces a lady who was presumably the bearer of the letter, and commends her to the Romans' Christian care. **Phoebe** belonged to the church at the port of Corinth, **Cenchreae.** It is uncertain whether Gk. *diakonos* is an official term, deaconess, (cf. mg.) or a more general one, **servant.** Too little is known of the constitution of the early churches for a final decision (cf. Phil. 1: 1 n.; 1 Tim. 3: 11 n.).

3–16. The apostle sends his affectionate greetings to those he knows in Rome. Most of them are not mentioned elsewhere in the NT, but behind the mention of the names obviously lies a wealth of personality, service and warm fellowship. **3. Prisca** (Gk. a more formal variant of Priscilla) **and Aquila** were partners not only in marriage but also in the leather business (see Ac. 18: 3 n.). After Claudius's edict had expelled the Jews from Rome in A.D. 49, they had come to Corinth (Ac. 18: 2). From there they had moved to Ephesus (Ac. 18: 18 ff.) and in fact toured extensively combining business with Christian service (cf. **all the churches**). Now, the edict apparently having become a dead-letter, they had returned to the imperial capital. **4.** No details are known of this occasion: it may have been that of Ac. 19: 23 ff. **5.** They opened their **house** for Christian meetings. The **church** here mentioned was obviously only a part of the total number of Christians in Rome. Vv. 14 f. seem to refer to two other household churches in Rome. Apparently there were at least three churches there, and probably more. **7. Andronicus** and **Junias** (or perhaps Junia, a lady, as in AV) must have belonged to the same group of Hellenistic Jews in the Jerusalem church as Stephen (Ac. 6: 1 ff.). They had done distinguished work as commissioned missionaries: **apostles** is used in a wider sense than the Twelve, as in Ac. 14: 4, 14; 1 C. 15: 5 ff. **8. Ampliatus** was a common Roman slave name. In the Catacombs there is a tomb ornately inscribed with this name in the cemetery of Domitilla, the cousin of Domitian, a later emperor. If it refers to the person here mentioned, it probably reflects the high esteem in which he was held by his fellow-Christians. **10, 11. In household** the reference is to a staff of slaves or ex-slaves. **Narcissus** may well be the famous freedman who was a counsellor of the Emperor Claudius and played a large part in the political intrigues of his day. He had committed suicide shortly before this letter was written, and his household of slaves would pass to the emperor, probably with the distinguishing name of *Narcissiani*. Lightfoot suggested that these *Narcissiani* were among the 'saints of Caesar's household' in Phil. 4: 22. **12. Tryphena and Tryphosa** are generally supposed to have been sisters. Is there subtle wit here? Both names are connected with the Gk. word *tryphaō* 'live luxuriously, live a life of ease'. Paul is perhaps playing on the derivation: these certainly did not live up to their names! **13. Rufus** was very likely a son of Simon of Cyrene who carried the cross (Mk 15: 21), especially if Mark's Gospel was written from Rome as tradition strongly suggests. Was it at the difficult time of Ac. 9: 28 that Paul was made welcome at Rufus' home and looked after by **his mother**, before the family moved to Rome? **16.** Paul may have been authorized to pass on the greetings of **all the churches** by their representatives, if they were now at Corinth waiting to set off to Jerusalem with the fund (cf. Ac. 20: 4). The **holy kiss** was apparently a feature of Christian communal fellowship; in this case it would be given partly in Paul's name.

17–20. Paul rather jerkily inserts into his greetings a warning against disturbers of the peace (cf. Gal. 6: 11–16; 1 C. 16: 22). Are they antinomians or Judaizers? The terms Paul uses suit either, but more probably he had Judaizers in his mind. He was very likely still brooding over his forthcoming visit to the Jerusalem church and his mind passed on to the havoc that their ilk had already caused in his circles. He complains not of Hellenistic Jews found in churches in company with Gentiles, but of outsiders from Judaea who had followed him around to Antioch (Ac. 15: 1), Galatia and Corinth (2 C. 11) in an attempt to counteract his 'looseness' (cf. Gal. 2: 4). They might well turn up in Rome. Phil. 1: 17 probably means that they were there a few years later. **18. Their own appetites** is literally 'their own belly' and may refer either to their obsession with clean and unclean food or to their working for their own ends (**appetites**). They presented an attractive, plausible case which might well convince the unwary. **19.** Paul urges the Romans to live up to their reputation of **obedience** by developing their moral judgment so as to be able to cope with this new attack. He appears to be deliberately quoting our Lord's own warning (Mt. 10: 16). **20.** If they are diligent in this way, the trouble will soon be settled. The Judaizers are working for Satan (2 C. 11: 15). But God Himself will work through the Romans' efforts and quickly restore the **peace** which characterizes Him and which He imparts to His own. There appears to be an allusion to Gen. 3: 15.

21–23. After the closing verses at the end of v. 20 the remaining verses are a postscript. **21.** Was **Jason** Paul's host in Thessalonica (Ac. 17: 5 ff.)? **Sosipater** looks like a longer form of Sopater, the Berean who was about to travel to Jerusalem with Paul (Ac. 20: 4). **22.** Paul must courteously have said to his amanuensis: 'Add your own greetings, Tertius.' **23. Gaius** is presumably the Gaius of 1 C. 1: 14, whom Paul had baptized. Paul was staying with him, and indeed his door was ever open to any Christian traveller. **Erastus** had an influential post as an important municipal official. His name has been found on a pavement which he donated to Corinth. V. 24 is rightly omitted as not original.

25–27. Paul closes with a long doxology, summing up the main thoughts of the letter. God had long kept to Himself His plan of salvation, but now He had acted at last, and disclosed it in the work of **Jesus Christ**. Paul had been commissioned with this **gospel** by God Himself and instructed to make the divine plan known throughout the world, commanding men to trust and obey (cf. 1: 5 n.) the one and only God. Supporting him in this work were the OT Scriptures (cf. 3: 21), now unlocked by the key of Jesus Christ and seen to be the manifesto of the **wise** God's plan. For the Church the present is the point upon which all eternity impinges. The planning of *eternal* ages past (**long:** Gk. *aiōniois*) has burst out into time, the present time. The **eternal** God (Gk. *aiōnion*) reveals Himself to men through the living Christ. It is the Church's privilege to share in God's *eternal* praise (Gk. *eis tous aiōnas tōn aiōnōn:* 'for ages and ages').

[Note: This doxology appears in the Byzantine text after ch. 14 and in papyrus 46 after ch. 15; this probably points to the early circulation of shorter editions of the Letter. On this subject, as also on the question whether the greetings of ch. 16 belonged to a copy intended for the church of Ephesus (which has been inferred from verses 3–5 in particular), see F. F. Bruce, *The Epistle of Paul to the Romans*, pp. 25 ff., 266 ff.]

BIBLIOGRAPHY

Commentaries:
BARRETT, C. K., *The Epistle to the Roman. BNTC* (London, 1957).
BARTH, K., *The Epistle to the Romans*, E.T. (Oxford, 1933).
BLACK, M., *Romans. NCentB* (London, 1973).
BRUCE, F. F., *The Epistle of Paul to the Romans. TNTC* (London, ²1985).
CRANFIELD, C. E. B., *The Epistle to the Romans*, 2 vols *ICC* [on the Greek text] (Edinburgh, 1975–79).
DODD, C. H., *The Epistle of Paul to the Romans. MNT* (London, 1932).
GODET, F., *The Epistle to the Romans* (Edinburgh, 1880).
HODGE, C., *The Epistle to the Romans* (Edinburgh, 1835).
HUNTER, A. M., *The Epistle to the Romans.* TC (London, 1955).
KÄSEMANN, E., *Commentary on Romans*, E.T. (Grand Rapids, 1980).
LEENHARDT, F. J., *The Epistle to the Romans* (London, 1961).
MOULE, H. C. G., *The Epistle to the Romans. EB* (London, 1893).
MURRAY, J., *The Epistle to the Romans, NICNT* (Grand Rapids, 1959–65).
NYGREN, A., *A Commentary on Romans*, E.T. (London, 1952).
SANDAY, W. and HEADLAM, A. C., *Romans. ICC* [on the Greek Text] (Edinburgh, 1902).

Books on Paul important for Romans:
HUNTER, A. M., *Interpreting Paul's Gospel* (London, 1954).
SCOTT, C. A. A., *Christianity according to St. Paul* (Cambridge, 1927).
STEWART, J. S., *A Man in Christ* (London, 1935).

1 CORINTHIANS

PAUL W. MARSH

Corinth

Situated in southern Greece on an isthmus dividing the Corinthian Gulf from the Saronic Gulf, Corinth became a natural centre for trade and a convenient halting-place for travellers moving east and west.

Although destroyed by the Romans in 146 B.C., it was reformed as a Roman colony under Julius Caesar a century later. The new city was at first peopled by Caesar's veterans and freed-men, but gradually Greeks returned, hellenizing the Italians and giving their language to the colony. However, its geographical position on the trade routes of the Middle East transformed it into the most cosmopolitan of cities, influenced by the life and habits of all the nations of the Mediterranean seaboard. From 27 B.C. onwards it was the seat of administration of the Roman province of Achaia.

Corinth was depraved. Going beyond the licentiousness of other trading cities and ports it lent its own name as the symbol of debauchery and corruption. As Robertson and Plummer state, 'The name of Corinth had been a byword for the grossest profligacy, especially in connection with the worship of Aphrodite Pandemos (1 *Corinthians*, *ICC*, p. xii). This monstrosity—sexual perversion in the name of religion—overshadowed the life of the city as a mushroom cloud of moral destruction.

Paul and Corinth

It was not, however, the great evil of this city which probably urged Paul to work there, but rather the strategic position it occupied. Its trading community ensured that anything preached in Corinth would soon reach far beyond the province of Achaia.

Paul first came to Corinth during his second missionary journey (Ac. 18: 1–18), and remained for eighteen months. Initially alone, he was subsequently joined by Silas and Timothy. Discouragement experienced during his earlier activities in Greece expressed itself in his 'weakness and fear', as he walked the streets of Corinth and argued in the synagogue (1 C. 2: 3). Threatened and reviled by the Jewish community, Paul received God's personal promise in a much needed vision of preservation from the mob and of fruitful service (Ac. 18: 10). The Jews, further inflamed by the conversion of Crispus and his household, launched a united attack on Paul before Gallio, the proconsul of Achaia. This hostility may well have continued unabated, for it would seem from the subject matter of the Corinthian letters that by far the majority of the converts came from the pagan community of that city.

After eighteen months Paul moved from Corinth together with Priscilla and Aquila. Leaving them in Ephesus he continued his travels in Syria. At the same time, Apollos, contacted in Ephesus by Priscilla and Aquila and brought to a full knowledge of Christ, went on to Corinth to consolidate and extend the activities of the church.

Paul's Letters and Subsequent Visits to Corinth

From the Acts and Paul's letters to Corinth we understand that three visits were paid and four letters written.

The first visit resulted in the founding of the church and is recorded in Ac. 18, to which Paul refers in 1 C. 2: 1–5.

Then came the first letter, which Paul mentions in 1 C. 5: 9. He had written telling the believers 'not to associate with sexually immoral people' meaning not the 'immoral of this world', but the immoral who bore 'the name of brother'. Because they had misconstrued his meaning, Paul explains the issues involved more fully when writing for the second time, i.e. in 1 Corinthians as it appears in our NT.

Nothing more is known of this 'first letter'. Some scholars suggest that part of it might be identified with 2 C. 6: 14–7: 1. This seems improbable but is widely accepted. For a fuller discussion of the subject, consult D. Guthrie, *NT Introduction: The Pauline Epistles*. We assume therefore that this first letter has not survived. As Dr. Leon Morris states, 'This need cause no surprise. Paul's reference to it in 1 C. 5: 9 shows that it had been misunderstood. He mentioned it only to clear up a misconception as to what it meant. Thus the newer letter superseded the older, and accordingly there was no point in preserving it' (1 *Corinthians*, *TNTC*, p. 21).

Now to the second letter, 1 Corinthians. The situation in Corinth had deteriorated. Dissensions and factions developed. The rhetoric of Apollos, coupled possibly with an allegorical method of preaching, contrasted sharply with the lack of eloquence and studied simplicity of Paul. Comparisons made by the congregation hardened into cliques.

Paul, now living in Ephesus, undoubtedly received frequent reports, for except during the winter months regular contact between the two cities was maintained. Knowledge of one such report has been preserved, that of 'Chloe's household' (1 C. 1: 11). So disturbing was this news that Paul despatched Timothy (1 C. 4: 17) and wrote immediately, dealing at the same time with a letter received from the Corinthian converts themselves concerning problems about which they required guidance (1 C. 7: 1).

For the purpose of this introduction it is assumed that Paul's second visit to Corinth now took place. This is the 'painful visit' referred to in 2 C. 2: 1. For a full discussion of this visit the reader should consult Robertson and Plummer's Commentary on 1 *Corinthians* (*ICC*). It is sufficient to record here that Paul's words, 'Now I am ready to visit you for the third time' (2 C. 12: 14), 'This will be my third visit to you' (2 C. 13: 1), and '. . . when I was with you the second time' (2 C. 13: 2), indicate very clearly a second visit before the writing of 2 Corinthians. (See pp. 1462, 1466.)

It is therefore suggested that Paul's second letter (1 Corinthians) failed in its attempt to correct and conciliate the warring factions, but that the situation deteriorated still further. A personal visit from Ephesus, painful in the extreme, therefore became necessary. This second visit is nowhere recorded in the Acts, possibly because of its brevity—a brief absence from Ephesus during Paul's three years' ministry—and its painful character.

Returning to Ephesus Paul wrote again. References to the third letter in 2 C. 2: 4 and 7: 8 indicate its extremely serious and censuring tone, so much so that Paul temporarily regretted its despatch. Had this letter failed in its purpose the situation might have deteriorated far beyond Paul's power to retrieve it. As it is, 2 C. 7: 9 records the measure of his joy at their repentance—'I am happy, not because you were made sorry, but because your sorrow led you to repentance'.

Did this third letter, like the first, fail to survive? While further discussion of this problem belongs properly to the introduction to 2 Corinthians, it may be observed for the sake of completeness, that not a few scholars, and notably Strachan, argue strongly that the 'severe letter' is preserved in part in 2 C. 10–13. The change in tone from commendation (chapters 1–9), to censure (10–13) is explained by this hypothesis. Upholders of the unity of 2 Corinthians explain this abrupt change by suggesting that in 1–9 Paul is addressing the reconciled majority, while in 10–13 he returns to the recalcitrant minority (see pp. 1462 f., 1479 f.).

Worried as to the effect of the 'severe letter',

Paul proceeded to Troas hoping to find Titus who had presumably taken it to Corinth. Great was his relief and joy on finally locating his colleague in Macedonia, to find that his fears were groundless and that the church was restored (2 C. 2: 12 ff.; 7: 6 ff.).

To express his thankfulness to God Paul's fourth letter (2 Corinthians) was written, to be followed shortly afterwards by his third visit.

Paul's three visits and four letters may therefore be set out as follows in their chronological order:

1. The church founded; first visit.
2. The first letter (referred to in 1 C. 5: 9).
3. The second letter: 1 Corinthians.
4. The painful visit.
5. The third letter: severe in tone (2 C. 2: 4; 7: 8).
6. The fourth letter: 2 Corinthians.
7. The third visit.

Authenticity

Robertson and Plummer remark 'that those who attempt to show that the Apostle was not the writer succeed chiefly in proving their own incompetence as critics' (1 *Corinthians*, *ICC*, p. xvi). Internal and external evidence for the Pauline authorship is exceedingly strong.

It is the first letter in the NT to be referred to in early Christian literature. Clement of Rome writing to Corinth about A.D. 95 quoted it by name and called it the 'letter of the blessed Paul, the Apostle'. The writings of Ignatius echo the epistle as do those of Polycarp. No NT book is more quoted by the early church Fathers; among them, Justin Martyr, Irenaeus and Tertullian. It heads the list of Paul's letters in the Muratorian Fragment and is included in Marcion's Canon.

Internally, the character, style and language of the letter are all consistent with what we know of the apostle and his writings, while historically it conforms with the demands of the Acts narrative.

Occasion of Writing

Two factors prompted Paul to write 1 Corinthians: (i) reports of dissensions received from Chloe's people and (ii) a letter received from the believers in Corinth seeking guidance on a variety of questions. While seeking in this letter to restore the unity these factions threatened to destroy and to answer the problems which concerned them, Paul took the opportunity of introducing detailed teaching on the resurrection.

Date

While it is impossible to date the letter with certainty, it was clearly written from Ephesus (1 C. 16: 8) on Paul's third missionary journey, probably around A.D. 55.

1 C. 16: 8 indicates that Paul planned to remain in Ephesus until Pentecost and then

leave. This could not refer to his very brief visit to Ephesus immediately after leaving Corinth for the first time (Ac. 18: 19). Allowing time for the ministry of Apollos, the writing of the first letter (1 C. 5: 9), and the development of party rivalries, we find Paul back in Ephesus toward the end of his three years' ministry there.

Ac. 18: 12 reveals that Gallio, the proconsul of Achaia, was in Corinth during Paul's stay. An inscription found at Delphi, recording certain privileges granted to the city by the Emperor Claudius, mentions the name of Gallio and is also dated. From this we therefore learn that Gallio was proconsul of Achaia in early A.D. 52. From the Acts narrative it is reasonable to deduce that Paul left Corinth during that year. Ac. 18: 18 indicates that while he did not leave immediately, no great time elapsed before his departure. The NIV rendering of this verse is good; 'Paul stayed on in Corinth for some time. Then he left . . .' Allowing for the completion of the second missionary journey and of most of Paul's three years in Ephesus, we are brought to the mid-fifties before 1 Corinthians could be written.

ANALYSIS

I. INTRODUCTION (1: 1–9)

i. Salutation (1: 1–3)

Paul's salutation follows the pattern of most first-century Greek letters, having three parts; the writer's name (1), the addressee (2), and a greeting (3).

1. called . . . an apostle: Two facts concerning himself. The situation in Corinth demands the full use of his God-given office and authority. **Sosthenes** is unknown unless he be identified with the Corinthian Jew of Ac. 18: 17, although this would pre-suppose his conversion and removal from Corinth to Ephesus. **2. the church of God:** One church in spite of its divisions; God's church, not Apollos's, or Cephas's, or Paul's. **sanctified . . . holy:** Two words derived from the same root, emphasizing the high moral standard which is to characterize God's church. They are set apart (*hēgiasmenois*; a perf. part. implying a fixed state) in spite of their blatant imperfections. **call on the name:** A phrase by which Christians were identified in the early church; cf. Ac. 9: 14, 21; 22: 16; Rom. 10: 12. **3. grace . . . peace:** A characteristically Pauline greeting, bringing together both Greek and Hebrew salutations.

ii. Thanksgiving (1: 4–9)

Dissensions there may be, not to mention gross immorality and a host of other evils flowing from the carnality that had captured the church; yet Paul gives thanks! Assailed by Satan as they are, their spiritual life is evident. They are Christ's, and in a missionary situation surrounded by pagan depravity, this is abundant cause for praise.

4. his grace given . . . in him you have been enriched (5) **. . . our testimony . . . was confirmed** (6). The three verbs are aorists, a tense demonstrating the historical finality of their position. **grace . . . given:** God's loving favour, which frequently expresses His empowering for life and service. For its use with this verb see 3: 10; Rom. 12: 3, 6; 2 C. 6: 1; Eph. 4: 7. **5. enriched:** Cf. 2 C. 6: 10; 9: 11 and the cognate verb in 1 C. 4: 8. **all your speaking** and **all your knowledge:** The high-lights of their spiritual enrichment, stressing their grasp of truth and their ability to express it; qualities particularly prized by Corinthians and indeed by Greeks in general. Paul deals with the carnal abuse of these very qualities in the first three chapters of this letter. **6. confirmed:** To establish durably, make real with the deepest conviction; a technical term in Greek commercial law, meaning to warrant, guarantee a title to. Their gifts were adequate evidence of Christ's work in them. See NIV; cf. Rom. 15: 8; Heb. 2: 3, 4. **7, 8. spiritual gift** (*charisma*): The church was deficient in none; evidence that gifts can co-exist with the grossest evil. The matter is dealt with fully in 12: 1–14: 40. **as you wait:** The expectation of the coming of Christ is constantly with the apostle; it is the one hope which characterizes every local church in a persecuting pagan society; cf. 16: 22; 1 Th. 1: 10. **to be revealed** (cf. Rom. 8: 19; 1 Pet. 1: 7, 13; 1 Jn 3: 2) and **the day** are synonymous for that one great cataclysmic event, **the end,** the second coming of Jesus Christ, until which He Himself will **keep you strong blameless:** Unimpeachable—although not sinless, no charge can be preferred against them (cf. Rom. 8: 33; Col. 1: 22, 28). **9. God . . . is faithful:** What He has begun He will complete (Phil. 1: 6), for He has **called** them just as He called Paul (1: 1), and that **into fellowship with his Son,** the very antithesis of division. The nine verses of this introduction record nine occurrences of the name of the Lord Jesus Christ. In all Paul's thinking, He is of cardinal importance and whether it be the problem of division, moral failure, or doctrinal error, Christ is the answer and Paul has cause to give thanks.

II. DIVISIONS IN THE CHURCH (1: 10–4: 21)

i. The fact of division (1: 10–17)

In flagrant disregard for the fellowship of Christ into which they had been called (10), dissensions abound. The facts are painfully obvious, for through Chloe's people the petty, yet bitter quarrelling has been reported (11). Personalities, methods of preaching and, probably, aspects of doctrinal emphasis become rallying points for division. That this is not the will of Paul, or Christ, the apostle makes abundantly clear (13–17).

10. I appeal . . . brothers: No matter how deep the divisions, he insists on the unity of the family of God; his **brothers.** Note the frequent use of this word. The instrument of appeal is **the name of our Lord Jesus Christ,** one who cannot be divided; cf. v. 13. **that all of you agree:** Literally, speak the same thing; an expression taken from Greek political life which might be paraphrased, 'Drop party cries'. **divisions** (*schismata*—cliques, not schisms) can result only in **quarrels** (11), an expression of the works of the flesh, and evidence of the carnality of the Corinthian church, cf. *eris* in Gal. 5: 20, 'strife'; also Rom. 1: 29–31; 2 C. 12: 20; 1 Tim. 6: 4. **Quarrels** are never right and are nowhere condoned or excused. **12. I belong to Paul:** A loyal clinging to their father in Christ, which overlooked his limitations of speech and appearance. **to Apollos:** Drawn by the rhetoric and possibly, the more allegorical approach of Paul's successor. **to Cephas:** The man who walked with Christ, the leader of the Twelve; an appeal to the traditionalist. **to Christ:** Possibly the ultra-libertarians, who stressed their complete liberty in Christ, formed the Christ party and either coined for themselves the watchword 'All things are lawful', or else perverted Paul's use of it to excuse their own excesses (see 6: 12 ff.; traces of the same attitude are found in chapter 8). All are wrong, and each alike receives Paul's condemnation. **13. Is Christ divided:** Or, 'Is Christ parcelled out among you?': the property of one small section of the church. Westcott and Hort, with Lightfoot, make the phrase affirmative, but this breaks up the homogeneity of the three-fold interrogative. Paul reduces the situation to basic principles; other leaders cannot take the place of Christ. **Was Paul crucified . . . :** The thought is ludicrous. His persistent teaching must demonstrate irrefutably the fallacy of factions; cf. 1: 23; 2: 2. **baptized into the name of Paul:** The Son, with Father and Holy Spirit, was the **name** designated by Christ, according to Mt. 28: 19. That the trinitarian formula was used at this stage by Paul or his associates is not clear. The Acts record rather suggests that the name of Christ alone was used. However, Paul's point is clear; none could accuse him of making personal proselytes. **14–16. I did not baptize any of you except:** Almost certainly to avoid making personal disciples (15). Those whom he did baptize were the very first converts. For **Stephanas,** see 16: 15; **Crispus,** Ac. 18: 8; and **Gaius,** possibly Rom. 16: 23 (perhaps also to be identified with the Titius Justus of Ac. 18: 7). The administration of ordinances then passed into the hands of local leaders; a most important missionary principle. **17. not . . .**

to baptize but. . . .: The apostle is not speaking in absolute terms, but is underlining the priority of his calling, **to preach the gospel. human wisdom:** Such wisdom, '*sophia logou* —cultivating expression at the expense of matter (17)—is the gift of the mere rhetorician, courting the applause of the ordinary Greek audience' (Robertson and Plummer). Paul determined that such 'language of worldly wisdom' (NEB) should not make the **cross of Christ be emptied of its power.** For other uses of *kenoō* (**emptied,** vain, fruitless) see 9: 15; Rom. 4: 14; 2 C. 9: 3; Gal. 2: 2; Phil. 2: 7, 16.

ii. False wisdom and the gospel (1: 18–2: 5)
(a) The message of the cross (1: 18–25)
Worldly wisdom, that expression of carnality among the Corinthian believers, is the very antithesis of the wisdom of God revealed in the cross of Christ. This section abounds in contrasts as Paul demonstrates the total alienation of thought between that worldly wisdom so prized by the Corinthians and the wisdom of God. The gospel, the word of the cross, is folly to the wise man of this age, but God will reveal their falsity, showing His foolishness as superior to their wisdom! **18.** Men react differently to the one message—**the message of the cross**—according to their condition. To **those who are perishing,** in the process of, or on the way to perish (*apollymenois* is a pres. part.), it is 'sheer folly' (NEB); whereas to those 'on the way to salvation' (NEB) it is **the power of God.** Again the pres. part. is used, implying not uncertainty but the final issue. It is not just the wisdom of God, but **power,** God's wisdom in action.

19. Paul maintains and elaborates this contrast. The worldly man with his wisdom will be destroyed in all his scepticism of God's ways. **it is written:** A very free rendering of the LXX translation of Isa. 29: 14, where 'the prophet, referring to the failure of worldly statesmanship in Judah in the face of the judgment of the Assyrian invasion, states a principle that the wisdom of man is no match for the power of God. Paul seizes the principle and applies it' (Robertson and Plummer).

20. Where . . . where . . . where: The challenge to produce the **wise man, scholar,** or **philosopher** who can stand before God reflects the scene of Isa. 33: 18 when all sign of the apparently invincible Assyrian conqueror has been swept away by the power of Jehovah. The exact designation of **wise, scholar, philosopher** (perhaps Gentile, Jew, Greek) is not clear. Most probably, Paul is making no specific reference to Jew or Greek, but his terms refer to all those champions of worldly wisdom, whom God is determined not merely to outclass, but to prove utterly foolish. **21. God was pleased:** Indicating the sovereignty of His choice, to save men through faith in the message of the cross and through no other means. **those who believe:** A pres. part. indicating habitual faith. See v. 18 for the same usage. **22, 23. Jews . . . signs . . . Greeks . . . wisdom:** The national characteristics of Jews and Greeks only increase their difficulties in accepting what is preached—**Christ crucified.** Jewish demands of Christ for a **sign** indicated the pattern of their thought; cf. Mt. 12: 38; 16: 1, 4; Mk 8: 11 ff.; Jn 6: 30. The sign of Jonah proved the greatest stumbling block of all. Greek speculation could not accept a doctrine of salvation based on the **foolishness** of the crucified Nazarene. The acceptance of **Christ crucified,** 'Christ nailed to a cross' (NEB), called for the abandonment of all their cherished concepts. As in 2: 2 (see note) the perfect tense indicates that the Christ cannot be separated from the cross. **24. Christ the power of God:** As demonstrated in the miracles of incarnation, death and resurrection; cf. Rom. 1: 4. **the wisdom of God:** True wisdom, for it brings salvation, the point at which Greek thinking failed. Christ Himself is the personification of wisdom (30). **called:** Having an effectual calling, as in Rom. 8: 30; 9: 11, 24, etc. **25. foolishness of God:** The cross in all its **weakness** and **foolishness** when measured by human standards is presented by God as His power and wisdom, both infinitely greater in saving capacity than all man's mightiest efforts can produce.

(b) **The messengers of the cross (1: 26–31)**
Further, not only is the message of the cross folly (18–25), but to present that message, God takes men commonly considered to be foolish, weak and of no consequence and through them vindicates the superiority of His own wisdom as seen in the gospel of Jesus Christ (26–31). **26. Think of what you were . . .:** The circumstances of the Corinthian church illustrate Paul's point. **you were called:** A reference to their conversion, not vocation, which came to them for the most part as people not **wise, influential,** or **noble** by worldly standards. **not many:** Some were in fact gifted, influential and cultured. Crispus was ruler of the synagogue (Ac. 18: 8) and Erastus, the city treasurer (Rom. 16: 23). **27. God chose:** Poor and weak, but objects of God's sovereign choice through whom He has purposed to shame the **wise** and **strong.** Repeated three times, this verb points ahead with unerring certainty to the accomplishment of His purpose, not only **to nullify the things that are** (the wise, etc.), so excluding all human boasting, but to His complete and absolute exaltation in Christ as the fount of all true wisdom and salvation (30, 31). To this end, as media of the revelation of His power and wisdom, He uses **the lowly things of this world and the despised . . . and the things that are not**—the

nonentities of this life—'mere nothings' (NEB). **to nullify** (*katargeō*): To reduce to ineffectiveness, render inoperative. The verb has considerable breadth of meaning (cf. 2: 6; 6: 13; 13: 8, 10, 11; 15: 24, 26). **30, 31. It is because of him . . . :** From the meanness of man Paul turns to the greatness of the Godhead. 'You are in Christ Jesus by God's act' (NEB). Christ is revealed as the embodiment of God's **wisdom . . . that is, our righteousness, holiness and redemption.** While AV, RV, and RSV translate these last three qualities as co-ordinates, it is possible, with RVmg and NIV, to regard them as definitive of wisdom. In either case, Christ is all of these, which eliminates the possibility of all human boasting—except **in the Lord.** The quotation is from Jer. 9: 23, an example of a passage which in the OT refers to Jehovah, being applied to Christ; cf. 2: 16.

(c) **The preaching of the cross (2: 1–5)**
So convinced was Paul of the superiority of the word of the cross over the wisdom of the world and of God's purpose to use human nonentities for the revelation of His wisdom in Christ, that he resolved when preaching in Corinth to do so with all the simplicity and weakness of ungarnished, trembling speech, that the dynamic of the cross of Christ alone might be experienced. This was to achieve the one objective, that their faith should rest not in the wisdom of men, but in the power of God.

1. the testimony (*martyrion*) **of God:** As a mere witness himself Paul had no need of lofty speech. He was concerned with relating facts. **2. Christ crucified:** A perf. part., signifying the enduring efficacy and effects of the death of Christ; cf. 1: 23.

3. in weakness: 'weak . . . nervous and shaking with fear' (NEB); a reference perhaps to his unimpressive bodily presence (cf. 2 C. 10: 10); his initial loneliness and discouragement after his experience in Athens (cf. Ac. 17); anxiety for the Thessalonian Christians; the overwhelming wickedness of Corinth; and possibly, sickness (cf. Gal. 4: 13). **4. with a demonstration of the Spirit's power:** As opposed to the plausible, persuasive words of wisdom, which Paul so strictly avoids. **demonstration** (*apodeixis*): Found only here in NT; it indicates stringent proof leading to absolute certainty. The power of **the Spirit,** not worldly wisdom, demonstrated Paul's message to be true, and on this their faith could rest (5).

iii. **True wisdom and the Spirit (2: 6–16)**
(a) **The impartation of wisdom (2: 6–13)**
In showing the total inadequacy of the wisdom of the world and the complete sufficiency of God's wisdom in accomplishing man's salvation, Paul has aimed blow after blow at the cause of dissension in Corinth. Worldly wisdom will devastate a church.

Yet the church is not without wisdom. To

those who are called, Christ the wisdom of God (1: 24) is made our wisdom (1: 30) and is increasingly comprehended as maturity develops. This true wisdom, hidden in past ages and unrecognized by men of worldly power and intellect, has now been revealed through the Spirit. Just as a man alone knows his own thoughts, so the Spirit comes from the being of God himself to give understanding of His mind to those who have received Him. This is the wisdom Paul himself imparts as taught by the Spirit of God.

6. among the mature (*teleioi*): Does not here mean 'perfect'. While the word was common in the mystery religions, this in no way coloured Paul's usage. As a pioneer, in common with modern missionaries, he took the language of his day and invested it with Christian content. Note the terminology which Paul consistently employs: *teleioi* are the mature Christians; cf. 14: 20; Phil. 3: 15; Eph. 4: 13. In the same class are the *pneumatikoi*—'the spiritual' (used synonymously in 2: 13–3: 1). In contrast to these are the *nēpioi*, 'infants' (cf. 3: 1), who are identified as *sarkinoi*, 'men of the flesh', 'worldly', or 'those made of flesh' (3: 1); also *psychikoi*, 'man without the Spirit', 'natural' (2: 14), and at an even lower level, *sarkikoi*, 'of the flesh', 'fleshly', or 'characterized by flesh' (3: 3, 4, see note). *Teleioi* and *pneumatikoi* signify ideal Christians, those dominated by the Spirit. A growth to this maturity is envisaged, when they will be able to understand the wisdom Paul imparts. **rulers of this age:** Possibly spiritual world-rulers (cf. Lk. 22: 53; Eph. 2: 2; Col. 2: 15) who have usurped control of the world, but who are **coming to nothing** (cf. 15: 25), also, possibly, those who crucified Christ: Pilate, representing the ruling world power, in league with the rulers of the Jews, especially in view of v. 8. See also Ac. 3: 17. The 'hour—when darkness reigns' (Lk. 22: 53) operates through human agencies.

7. secret wisdom, a wisdom that has been hidden (*mystērion*, 'secret'): Not unintelligible, or difficult to understand, but a secret hidden in the counsels of God, now made known by His Spirit; here, that age-long purpose of redemption, reconciliation and restoration through Christ, kept secret, but now revealed (cf. Rom. 16: 25, 26; Eph. 3: 3–10). However, this wisdom of God still remains hidden in a very real sense to those who are perishing (1: 18). **destined . . . before time began:** God's redemptive plan is no afterthought (cf. Eph. 1: 4). **for our glory:** I.e., for the attainment of our complete salvation; cf. Rom. 8: 18–23. **8. Lord of glory:** Perhaps the most exalted title given to Christ; cf. Jas 2: 1. It associates Him in dignity and majesty with the Father; cf. Eph. 1: 17; Ac. 7: 2; Ps. 24: 7. **9. as it is written:** Paul regularly uses this phrase when quoting from canonical Scriptures, yet this question agrees exactly with not one OT text. Origen and others suggest a quotation from the Apocalypse of Elias, or the Ascension of Isaiah, but it may well be that they were quoting Paul. Possibly the saying was in circulation as a floating logion in Paul's day; the Gospel of Thomas includes it as one of the 'secret' sayings of Jesus. Alternatively, we may assume that Paul is 'quoting' very freely and from memory, and probably from the LXX translation of Isa. 64: 4 with reminiscences of Isa. 65: 17. Clement of Rome in the earliest extant quotation of 1 C. 2: 9 goes back to the LXX of Isa. 64: 4, indicating his opinion as to its original source. The verse itself clinches Paul's argument that the natural man through his physical senses is not able to understand God's wisdom in the cross of Christ. **10. God has revealed:** Demonstrates the superiority of the divine disclosure to man (**to us**, i.e. to things that are not) over the strugglings of human wisdom. The verb is aorist, indicating a definite time for the revelation; the secret now made known. **the Spirit searches:** God's medium of revelation, the Spirit, fathoms the depth of God's being. The activity is not indicative of ignorance, but of accurate knowledge. The depths are plumbed. **the deep things of God** (*ta bathē*): Some Gnostics recognized a divine essence as 'the deep', 'the unknowable', but the Spirit knows all. **11.** Two Greek words are commonly translated 'to know'. Both occur in this verse; **who among men knows . . .** (*oida*) and **no one knows . . .** (*ginōskō*). *oida* is to know by reflection based on intuition or information supplied (rendered 'understand' in v. 12). *ginōskō* is to know by observation and experience; to know, recognize, comprehend. *ginōskō* here seems to put the things of God a degree more out of reach than does *oida* the things of man. **12. received:** Aorist, indicating a definite time. **The spirit of the world** may mean Satan (cf. Jn 12: 31; 2 C. 4: 4; Eph. 2: 2; 6: 11, 12; 1 Jn 4: 3; 5: 19), although in the NT **world** (*kosmos*) is not regarded as inherently evil. More probably it means 'the temper of the world', the spirit of human wisdom, as alienated from God, and would be equivalent to human wisdom in v. 13. **what God has freely given us:** 'all that God of his own grace gives us' (NEB), the content of Christian revelation and experience, made comprehensible by the Spirit. **13. expressing spiritual truths in spiritual words:** The Greek is ambiguous and is capable of the alternative translations. See the NIV and RSV footnotes. The problem arises from (i) the different meanings which *synkrinontes* may have, i.e., **expressing** or interpreting (LXX usage); combining (classical usage); comparing (the obvious meaning in 2 C. 10: 12), and (ii) the gender of *pneumatikois* (**spiritual**), which may be masculine or neuter. Phillips and NEB support RSV text, which makes good sense in that at the end of this paragraph Paul returns full circle to v. 6 ('among the mature we impart wisdom', i.e., to those who possess the Spirit). In addition, the transition of thought is achieved in the new paragraph, from v. 14, where by comparison, the unspiritual man is brought under discussion. For a detailed study of v. 13, see Robertson and Plummer.

(*b*) **The recipients of wisdom (2: 14–16)**
The unspiritual, natural man lacks spiritual discernment. To him the things of the Spirit just do not make sense. By contrast, the spiritual man, without fear of refutation, can make mature judgments in everything, knowing that he has the mind of Christ.

14. The man without the spirit (*psychikos*): The unrenewed natural man, as distinct from one who is actuated by the Spirit; cf. Jas 3: 15; Jude 19, 'worldly people'. **does not accept:** i.e., rejects, 'refuses' (NEB). **15. The spiritual man makes judgments . . . :** The verb, *anakrinō*, is used three times in vv. 14, 15, and is translated, **discerned**, and **judgment.** Basically the word means to examine well, search out, sift. The spiritual man can therefore scrutinize and sift since he has the faculty to do it, but the unspiritual man finds the spiritual man and spiritual truths beyond his scrutiny; cf. v. 14. **is not subject to any man's judgment:** Presumably by no unspiritual person. **16.** A quotation from the LXX of Isa. 40: 13, which uses '*mind*' for spirit, which in God are identical, and seals Paul's argument concerning the inscrutability of spiritual things except to those who **have the mind of Christ. we have the mind of Christ:** Because we have His Spirit; cf. 2 Pet. 1: 4.

iv. Carnal misunderstanding concerning God's servants (3: 1–9)
(*a*) **Carnality and its effects (3: 1–4)**
Paul's exposition of the spiritual and unspiritual brings him to another fundamental cause of the dissensions which threaten to wreck the Corinthian church: gross carnality. Yet even as he prepares to castigate his readers, the rebuke is softened by that recurring term of affection, **brothers.** The Corinthians at conversion had been babes in Christ, and for that there is no censure. However, the passage of time had seen no growth, but rather, a fleshly attitude dominated the believers, expressing itself in jealousy and strife, as they lived on the 'purely human level of your lower nature' (NEB). **1. I . . . could not address you:** Refers to Paul's initial visit when the church was founded. Then they were not **spiritual**, i.e., the mature of 2: 6, but understandably **infants** (*nēpioi*), **worldly** (*sarkinoi*), and therefore received **milk.** See note on 2: 6. **2. you are still**

not ready: Describes a wholly inexcusable condition. By now they should have grown up. **3. still worldly:** Not *sarkinoi* of v. 1, which was excusable at that stage of their development, but *sarkikoi* (used twice in this verse), indicative not just of their state, but of their attitude, fleshly, and wholly inexcusable; cf. Heb. 5: 11–14. Here, **flesh** for Paul has a moral and ethical significance; cf. Rom. 7: 5, 14; 13: 14; Gal. 5: 13. Its usage in the NT is varied; (i) material flesh (15: 39); (ii) the body itself (1 Pet. 4: 1); (iii) medium of relationship (Mk 10: 8); (iv) human nature, with special relation to its frailty (Jn 1: 14); (v) seat of sin; Paul's characteristic usage for man's evil nature, as opposed to the higher one. Sin is not inherent in flesh, as the Gnostics held, but its power is manifest in the flesh. **jealousy and quarreling:** Both works of the flesh (cf. Gal. 5: 20); and the latter, flowing from the former, creates the parties to which Paul again refers. **like mere men** (*anthrōpoi*): Repeated in v. 4, and is used as the equivalent of *sarkinoi*.

(*b*) **The true function of the apostles (3: 5–9)**
Carnality has obscured entirely their understanding of the true function of God's servants, so Paul explains the real relation between himself and Apollos. Far from establishing varying schools of thought and conflicting loyalties, they as God's servants, insignificant fellow-workers, were called so to labour according to His direction that their complementary activities might result in a divinely given growth. They are nothing, God is all.

5. What, after all, is Apollos . . . Paul?: The neuter **what**, instead of 'who' focuses attention on their activities rather than their personalities. **servants** (*diakonoi*): A word denoting active service. **as the Lord has assigned to each:** May refer to the faith granted to each believer, or the ministry granted to each of His servants. The context suggests the latter. **6. I planted the seed, Apollos watered it, but God made it grow:** The first two verbs are aorists summing up the specific tasks which Paul and Apollos completed (cf. Ac. 18: 1–18 and 18: 24–19: 1 respectively), but an imperfect expresses the continuous God-given **growth** through it all.

8. have one purpose: Literally, are one thing (neuter), 'on the same level' (Moffatt); this gives the lie to any accusation of opposing factions that Paul and Apollos were at variance. It is well expressed by NEB, 'they work as a team.' Yet, each is individually answerable to God (cf. vv. 10 ff.). **9. God's fellow workers:** A phrase occurring only here. Two meanings are possible; 'fellow workers with one another in God's service', or 'fellow workers with God', as AV. While the force of the Greek may favour the latter, the context suggests the former, i.e., the unity of Paul and Apollos in the work for God. **God's field, God's building:** The emphasis is on the process which results in the tilled field and final edifice. The former looks back to vv. 6–9, and the latter ahead to vv. 10 ff.

v. True conception of the local church (3: 10–23)
(*a*) **The builders: their responsibility and reward (3: 10–15)**
It is about the building process that Paul is concerned. While he has laid a good foundation —'Jesus Christ and him crucified'—the local believers in Corinth have the responsibility for raising the structure. For good or bad they will incorporate the equivalents of gold, silver, etc., according to the lives they individually live. The final Day of reckoning will come, involving not the salvation of those who built, but the gain or loss of wages as the work is tested.

10. grace: *charis*, here involves an enduement of divine power (cf. 15: 10). **an expert builder** (*sophos*): Literally 'wise': used of skilled craftsmen who built the tabernacle; cf. LXX of Exod. 35: 10; 36: 1, 4, 8. **I laid a foundation:** The aorist refers to his eighteen months' stay, as do 2: 1; 3: 1, 6. **Someone else is building:** Not a reference to Apollos, but indicates the termination of Paul's contribution. **But each one should be careful:** Stresses the personal responsibility of **each** one taking part. It is not merely the doctrinal structure of the church that is here in view, but all aspects of its corporate life. **12. gold, silver,** etc. cannot be pressed into representing specific details in the building. Rather, that which is valuable, true and enduring is contrasted with the worthless, shallow and inferior qualities of Christian conduct and service. **13. the Day will bring it to light:** The day of judgment; cf. 1 Th. 5: 4; Heb. 10: 25. **it will be revealed with fire:** The Day itself will be so revealed; cf. 2 Th. 1: 7, 8; 2: 8; Dan. 7: 9 ff.; Mal. 4: 1. **14, 15. a reward:** Might be translated 'wage', as in v. 8. As Paul and Apollos will receive wages according to their work, so will the one who builds, according to what survives the testing fire. Similarly, he whose work is burned suffers the **loss** of wages, though not of salvation. **as one escaping through the flames:** It is the fire of judgment (13), not purgatory.
(*b*) **God's concern for His church (3: 16, 17)**
The imagery changes as Paul moves from the builders and their process of building, to the picture of God's temple, the sanctuary of His presence; the church at Corinth. If anyone through dissension and strife would mar this holy shrine, God will mar him.

16. God's temple (*naos*): Comprising the holy place and holy of holies, rather than *hieron*, which comprised the whole temple area. Here the local church is referred to, but see 6: 19 for its application to the individual believer.

17. If anyone destroys . . . destroy him: The verb has two meanings: (i) to defile, corrupt, (ii) to destroy. To rend a church with division is to reduce it to ruin and in exactly the same terms God will deal with those responsible. This verb (*phtheirō*), chosen no doubt for its double meaning, does not convey the thought of annihilation or eternal torment, but leaves one in doubt as to the exact nature of the divine retribution. The enormity of the sin of dissension in God's sight is clear.

(*c*) **The need for true wisdom (3: 18–23)**
The situation is urgent and in the face of impending judgment Paul appeals again to those who cling so foolishly to the wisdom of this world, which, as he has already shown and the Scriptures themselves declare, God will bring to nothing. From the vain boasting of men he turns them to the immeasurable greatness of their possessions in Christ. They are not to be gripped within the narrow confines of a party, for all teachers are theirs, the world itself with all its contrary currents; and they are Christ's and He is God's. All culminates in that unity of the being of God in which they are all partakers. To understand this is true wisdom.

18. he should become a 'fool': By accepting God's wisdom which the world calls folly, already expounded in 1: 18–20; 2: 14. **19. it is written:** A quotation from Job 5: 13, not from the LXX, but possibly Paul's own rendering of the Hebrew. **He catches:** In Greek a participle, indicating the strong grip God has on the slippery cleverness of the wicked (cf. 1: 20). **20.** is typical of the freedom with which Paul quotes from the LXX (Ps. 94: 11). However, **wise,** which he introduces in the place of 'man', is found in the context which is contrasting the designs of men with those of God. **21, 22. All things are yours . . . :** Paul and the 'party leaders' do not possess the Corinthians, rather, the Corinthians possess these servants of God and not only so, but **all things** (neuter)—all God's creatures without limit (cf. Rom. 8: 32). **the world** (*kosmos*): The universe we inhabit. **life or death:** Viewed physically, but over which Christ has given victory (cf. Phil. 1: 21; 1 C. 15: 55–57), involving all circumstances whether in **the present** or **the future. 23. you are of Christ:** Possessing 'all things' they do not possess themselves (6: 20; 7: 23). Yet no one can say that his possession of, or in, Christ is greater than another's (1: 13). All individually and equally are members of Christ's body (12: 27; see also 12: 14–26). **Christ is of God:** A statement of the relation of Christ to God which in no way detracts from His deity. His essential nature and equality (Phil. 2: 6) with God are not under discussion, but His subordination for man's salvation; cf. 11: 3; 15: 24ff.; Jn 14: 28; 20: 17.

vi. Correct attitude to the servants of God (4: 1–21)

(a) Do not sit in judgment (4: 1–5)

Paul returns to the question of 3: 5. Whereas in 3: 5–8 he had demonstrated that, far from being party leaders, he and Apollos were mere servants accountable to God, as they were themselves (3: 10–17), now he outlines the correct attitude they should adopt toward the apostles. It is not for the believers in Corinth to sit in judgment on the respective merits of Paul, Apollos and Cephas. Paul is not concerned that he should receive a favourable report or party backing from Corinth, or any other human court. His judge is his Master, Christ, and his hope, divine commendation. Therefore, abandon party preferences, for Christ at His coming will deal with true values, not the estimates of carnal Corinthian minds.

1. as servants (*hypēretēs*): A word used only once by Paul (it originally denoted an underrower in a trireme) and used by Luke for those who minister the word (cf. Lk. 1: 2; 4: 20). **as those entrusted** ('stewards', AV, RSV): The *oikonomos* was a house manager with responsibility for the stores; a slave in relation to his master, but an overseer in relation to the other servants (cf. Lk. 12: 42; 16: 1). For Paul's 'stores', the mysteries of God, see 2: 7. **3. am judged by you:** The same verb as in 2: 14, 15 (see note), used 3 times in vv. 3, 4. The verb implies nothing as to the verdict; only the process of sifting evidence. **human court:** Literally, 'human day', in contrast to the Lord's day of judgment; cf. 3: 13. **I do not even judge myself:** That the use of conscience and self-criticism are essential is not denied, for Paul has a clear conscience (cf. v. 4), yet in the context of stewardship, Paul is no more competent than the Corinthians to pass judgment on his life and service. His assessment can only be subjective. **5. judge nothing before the appointed time:** The negative *mē* with the present imper. could be rendered, 'stop pronouncing judgment'. **wait till the Lord comes:** Or until . . . ; *heōs an* with the subjunctive, giving a sense of uncertainty, not of the coming, but of the time. **what is hidden in darkness:** Darkness may have an ethical significance as 'things morally bad', or perhaps, things either good or bad of which one is ignorant. **praise from God:** Has an undoubted connection with the wages, or reward, of 3: 8, 14. **from** (*apo*) indicates the finality of the award from which there is no appeal.

(b) Learn from the example of Paul and Apollos (4: 6, 7)

Using Apollos and himself as an example, or illustration, Paul has endeavoured to teach the Corinthians the true function and character of God's servants, both toward each other as

equals (3: 8), in relation to the church and before God Himself. And for this one purpose only: that they might learn to **not go beyond what is written.** For them, it is the necessity of learning the subordinate place of man and the exalted position of God; human wisdom abandoned for God's, human leaders abandoned for Christ. This is the cure for factions —the puffed up pride that would 'patronize one and flout the other' (NEB)—and for their conceited boasting, which mistook God's gifts for their own achievements.

6. applied these things to myself and Apollos: The verb *metaschēmatizō* means literally, 'to change the form of ', 'alter the arrangement of '. Therefore, 'Paul implies that while speaking of himself and of Apollos he had others in view. If the congregation understands that it is forbidden to judge Paul and Apollos, she will more easily concede that all judging is forbidden' (Grosheide, 1 *Cor.*, p. 102). **these things:** The preceding 5 verses. **take pride:** the Greek verb (*physioō*) is used by Paul 6 times in this letter (4: 6, 18, 19; 5: 2; 8: 1; 13: 4) and only once outside it (Col. 2: 18), indicating the extent to which the sin of pride had gripped the Corinthian church. **7. makes you different from anyone else:** The verb *diakrinō* has various meanings, but here suggests, 'to distinguish favourably from others', and is well rendered by NEB, 'Who makes you, my friend, so important?' Pride's bubble is pricked.

(c) Corinthian pride and the apostles' trials (4: 8–13)

So pernicious is their pride, Paul can no longer restrain his pent-up passion. With biting irony he assails their carnal conceit, contrasting their imagined exaltation and attainments with the utter degradation, poverty and distress which were the apostles' daily lot. If they should learn from the illustration of Paul and Apollos in vv. 1–5, how much more from the selfless conduct of these apostles who for Christ's sake (10) are reckoned fools, dishonoured and destitute— yet toiling with their hands lest they be a burden to the church—suffering every indignity, considered 'the scum of the earth' (NEB). While Corinthians cavort as kings, rending the church they wish to rule, the apostles turn the other cheek, try to conciliate and teach the lesson of true humility.

8. you have all you want: Used of food, 'to be satiated', 'fed full'. **become rich . . . become kings:** Both verbs are aorists and the latter might well be translated, 'you have begun to reign!' All three verbs are suggestive of the fulfilling of all the blessings of the Messianic kingdom; cf. Lk. 22: 29–30; I Th. 2: 12; 2 Tim. 2: 12. Their own little millennium was already launched! **without us:** The 'without' of exclusion; 'and left us out' (NEB). **9.** bears the stamp of the arena; doomed men on show. **spectacle** (*theatron*): From which we derive 'theatre'. The verb is used in Heb. 10: 33. **to the whole universe, to angels as well as to men: angels** and **men** are probably descriptive of **universe.** Concerning the presence of angels in the world, see 11: 10; Gal. 3: 19; Heb. 1: 14. **10. wise:** Not the word Paul has used in previous chapters. *phronimoi* may be translated, 'sensible', 'prudent'; 'sensible Christians' (NEB). Paul's irony is continued. **11.** Note the contrast with v. 8. It is as **servants** (slaves) of Christ and God that Paul and the apostles suffer; cf. 4: 1. See also 2 C. 6: 4–10; 11: 23–29. Their experiences were Christ's; **hungry** (Lk. 4: 2), **thirsty** (Jn 19: 28), **brutally treated** (Mk 14: 65), **homeless** (Lk. 9: 58), **cursed** (1 Pet. 2: 23), **persecuted** (Jn 15: 20). **12. we work hard** (*kopiōmen*): Indicates toil involving weariness and fatigue, an attitude he inculcated in others; cf. 1 Th. 1: 3. He spent himself that he might not be a burden (cf. 9: 6; 2 C. 11: 7; 1 Th. 2: 9; 2 Th. 3: 8; Ac. 18: 3; 20: 34), but note his reaction to gifts from Philippi (Phil. 4: 10–18). **we bless:** Their action conformed with Christ's command; cf. Lk. 6: 28. **13. scum of the earth:** While the word has two meanings, 'rubbish' or 'sweepings from a thorough cleaning', and 'scapegoat', it is more probable that the former is intended here. **refuse:** Approximates to the previous noun in both its meanings and signifies the scrapings of a plate.

(*d*) **A personal appeal for reconciliation (4: 14–21)**
With a change of tone so characteristic in Paul's letters, the apostle moves to conciliation in his final appeal to the divided church. To induce a sense of **shame** on the level of human comparison would not be difficult, but he would rather plead from the uniqueness of his position as their **father through the gospel,** that they copy him. **Timothy,** his own child in Christ (as they themselves were), had already been sent to remedy if possible the deteriorating situation. Paul himself would shortly arrive to deal with those whose haughty, arrogant speech served only to reveal their poverty of power. Yet while the **whip** is ready, how much better that he should come **with a gentle spirit,** the situation already resolved.

14. to warn: Used only by Paul in the NT, reflecting the duty of a parent; cf. Eph. 6: 4. It carries a note of sternness. **my dear children:** No matter how dire the distress, Paul will not disown his relationship. At the point of sharpest censure, he uses the term of deepest endearment. **15. ten thousand guardians:** Tutors or guides, servants who escorted the children to school (*paidagōgos,* as in Gal. 3: 24). A position of great responsibility and trust, but not of fatherhood. As there was one planting, one foundation, so one spiritual father. **16.**

urge you to imitate me: On the basis of his special relationship, Paul calls for a family likeness, particularly in the terms of vv. 10–13; cf. 11: 1; Phil. 3: 17; 1 Th. 1: 6. **17. I am sending to you Timothy:** Timothy had probably already left Ephesus, although the letter may well have arrived before him; cf. 16: 10, 11; Ac. 19: 22. **18. Some of you have become arrogant:** A conspicuous failing in the Corinthian church; a concomitant of the stress on worldly wisdom (vv. 6, 19; 5: 2; 8: 1), leading them to suppose that Timothy's arrival indicates Paul's fear to come himself. **19. if the Lord is willing:** Paul is not his own master; cf. 16: 7; Jas 4: 15. **not a matter of talk . . . but of power:** These two—*logos* and *dynamis*—are contrasted. Paul has no time for the former. Note the contrast in 1: 17 and 1: 24; 2: 1 and 2: 4. **20. kingdom of God:** Characterized by spiritual power. In this context the phrase signifies the inward reign of Christ over the hearts and lives of the believers (Rom. 14: 17; see also 1 C. 15: 24 note), and is in contrast to the shallowness of the church's experience, cf. v. 8. **21. with a whip** (i.e., to chastise and rebuke) . . . **or in love . . . :** Yet the two attitudes are not mutually exclusive, for as a father Paul knows the significance of the lesson taught in Heb. 12: 4–11.

III. MORAL DISORDERS IN THE CHURCH (5: 1–6: 20)
Carnality continued to take its devastating toll of spiritual life in Corinth. Whether it was their emphasis on worldly wisdom, resulting in division, or the conceit of self-satisfaction which expressed itself in a blatant disregard for the basic concepts of Christian morality (chapters 5, 6) all stemmed from the fact that although 'in Christ', they were still very much 'of the flesh, and behaving like ordinary men'.

i. The case of immorality (5:1–13)

(*a*) **The offence and its implications in the church (5: 1–8)**
Corinth was a by-word for immorality, yet with all the debased, licentious habits of the Greeks, there was no relationship commonly known among them to compare with the depravity to which one of the Christians had sunk, living with **his father's wife.** Condemning their continued arrogance Paul calls for the immediate excommunication of the offender, for the purity of the whole church is in peril; an evil which if discreetly concealed can only lead to the utter pollution of the whole body. The sacrifice of Christ, the Passover **lamb,** demands conformity with those standards of purity typified in the diligent rooting out of all **leaven** in the ancient Jewish festival.

1. does not occur even among pagans: Although such cases of immorality can actually be quoted, they were most uncommon and certainly not countenanced, as in the Corinthian church. **A man has his father's wife:** while not necessarily suggesting formal marriage, most certainly indicates a permanent relationship. **his father's wife:** Not the offender's mother, but a stepmother, probably divorced from the father. The latter may even have been dead. **2. you are proud: you** is emphatic, stressing the incongruity of their attitude. **grief:** Often used of mourning for the dead (cf. Mk 16: 10); it may reflect Paul's attitude to the loss of this church member. See Moffatt. Mourning should result in the offender's removal. **3. I am with you in spirit: I** is emphatic; Paul does what they should have done. He maintains spiritual contact although physically removed (cf. Col. 2: 5). **I have already passed judgment:** The verb is perfect and indicates finality. Note Paul's disciplinary authority, a reflection of 4: 21.

See also 2 C. 13: 2, 10. The construction of vv. 3–5 is not easy. There are several possibilities:

(i) Take **in the name** with **assembled** and **the power** with **hand over**, as AV, or

(ii) Take **in the name** and **the power** with **assembled**, as NIV, NEB and many Greek commentators, or

(iii) Take **in the name** and **the power** with **hand over**, or

(iv) Take **in the name** with **hand over** and **the power** with **assembled**, as Robertson and Plummer and Leon Morris, or

(v) Take **in the name** with **I have already passed judgment**, as RSV, Moffatt and CGT. The sense of this last construction is good, for here Paul's solemn judgment bears the authority of the name of Christ as will the assembled church bear the stamp of His power. **5. to hand over this man to Satan:** The expression occurs elsewhere only in 1 Tim. 1: 20. It implies formal excommunication where one is removed from the sphere of the church to that of Satan, the world, a 'dominion of darkness'; cf. Eph. 2: 11, 12; Col. 1: 13; 1 Jn 5: 19. **sinful nature may be destroyed:** Two views are possible and both may be true: (i) **sinful nature** may be understood as the seat of sin. He is to be handed over for the mortification of the flesh—the destruction of sinful lusts—to learn again the terror of Satan's power. For Paul's characteristic usage, see 3: 3 note; Rom. 8: 6–9, 12, 13; Col. 3: 5. (ii) **sinful nature** may be physical. **destroyed** (*olethros*) is a strong word implying physical suffering and destruction. Such is involved in God's punishments and in Satan's attacks; cf. 11: 30; Ac. 5: 1 ff.; Lk. 13: 16; Heb. 2: 14; 2 C. 12: 7. **his spirit saved:** Punishment is plainly remedial. At the judgment day, **the day of the Lord** , he will be with the Lord's people (cf.

1: 8; 3: 13; 4: 5). **6. boasting:** The outcome of their arrogance (2), and wholly out of place. **a little yeast. . . :** A common illustration carries home the point. One such immoral man could utterly corrupt the church. Paul had seen the principle at work among the Judaizers in Galatia; cf. Gal. 5: 9. **7. Get rid of the old yeast:** Symbolized the removal of moral impurity and recalled the practice of Israel in preparation for the Jewish Passover (Exod. 12: 15 ff.) A custom developed when with candles the smallest crumbs of leavened bread were searched out in every corner of the house (cf. Zeph. 1: 12). **without yeast—as you really are:** So they were in Christ. Paul urges them to be in character—'bread of a new baking' (NEB)—what they were in theory. **For . . .** (*kai gar*): Introduces an additional urgent reason for purging: **Christ, our Passover lamb** is already slain and the house is not yet cleansed (cf. Dt. 16: 4–6). **8. Let us . . . keep the Festival:** The verb is present subjunctive, suggesting continuity. Godet remarks, 'Our festival is not for a week, but for a life-time'. **malice and wickedness:** In direct contrast with **sincerity and truth.** The old and new life are mutually exclusive. Note Paul's contrast in this letter between worldly wisdom and divine wisdom, the fleshly and the spiritual, the old and the new. The Christian is not a patched up pagan, but **a new** person (cf. Eph. 2: 1–5). **sincerity** (*eilikrinia*): Probably derived from *eilē*—the sun's rays, or heat—suggesting transparent purity of purpose and character.

(b) A misunderstanding rectified (5: 9–13) There follows in vv. 9–13 what appears to be a digression from the immediate subject, although connected with the theme of immorality. Paul is perhaps reminded by the unmixedness of *eilikrinia* (8) of what he had written in a previous letter, and so proceeds to clarify the issue about mixing with fornicators. The Corinthians had misunderstood Paul, thinking he had forbidden them to associate with immoral pagans. Concerning such Paul has no brief; to avoid them is impossible. His concern is with Christians, and with those who return to the immoral and sinful practices of pagan society, no association is possible.

9. I have written: Not an epistolary aorist, but a letter, apparently well known to the Corinthians, now lost. See Introduction, p. 1419. **not to associate:** Literally, 'not to mix yourselves up together with'. The verb occurs elsewhere in the NT only in 2 Th. 3: 14. It implies a close relationship. **10.** summarizes the three vices characteristic of the non-Christian world; moral laxity, greed (**greedy** and **swindlers** are brought into one class by a single def. art. coupling both nouns) and superstition. **11. anyone who calls himself a brother:** A profession denied by conduct, but not necessarily implying an unregenerate state. A pagan environment continues to exert tremendous power over those newly born again. **idolater:** Note the ease with which a man might be influenced by previous practices; cf. 8: 10; 10: 7, 8, 14 ff. **slanderer** and **drunkard:** Added to the list of v. 10, reflecting again the social background from which the converts were drawn. **With such a man do not even eat:** Mirrors the life of Asia throughout the centuries; the shared meal demonstrates friendship, its prohibition, utter separation; cf. Lk. 15: 2; Gal. 2: 12. Its secondary result was to bar the offender from the Lord's Table. **13. God will judge those outside:** The church must set its own house in order; God deals with the world. The tense of the verb is best regarded as present, indicating the normal attribute of God. **Expel:** Possibly a quotation from Dt. 17: 7.

ii. Lawsuits and heathen courts (6: 1–11)
The mention of judgment in 5: 12, 13 brings the apostle to another matter for censure. Grievances between Christians had apparently been taken to the civil courts for settlement. If believers are destined to **judge the world** and **angels**, the settlement of trivial temporal disagreements should surely not be beyond the capabilities of the local church (1–6). **Lawsuits** between Christians are wrong; better by far to suffer injustice than to fight (7, 8). Let them reflect (9–11). They were **washed, sanctified, justified**, and yet have begun to act with that unrighteousness so characteristic of those destined to be excluded from the kingdom of God. Such conduct is blatantly wrong.

1. dispute (*pragma*): In its legal sense, a cause for trial, a case. **take it before the ungodly for judgment:** The verb is in the middle voice, i.e., they were seeking judgment in their own interests. **the ungodly:** Does not suggest that the court judges were unjust, but indicates their relationship to God in contrast to that of the saints. Rabbis taught the Jews never to take a case before the Gentiles. **2. the saints will judge the world:** Anticipates Christ's return and the final judgment. This goes beyond our Lord's teaching to the Twelve in Mt. 19: 28; Lk. 22: 28 ff. (see also Dan. 7: 22), in terms of both the judges and the judged. It is possible to understand **judge** in the Hebraic sense of 'reign', a function incorporating judgment, and basic to NT eschatology; cf. Rom. 8: 17; 2 Tim. 2: 12; Rev. 2: 26, 27; 3: 21; 20: 4. **cases** (*kritērion*): Has various uses—means or rules of judging; the place of trial, the tribunal (RVmg and Robertson and Plummer); persons that judicate; the cases before the court (AV, RV, RSV, NEB). **3. judge angels:** Some angels are reserved for judgment; cf. Mt. 25: 41; 2 Pet. 2: 4; Jude 6. **4. appoint**(*kathizete*) **as judges . . . :** Three renderings are possible; *kathizete* may be imperative, as rendered by

NIV, AV, or indicative and affirmative, or indicative and interrogative as in RV, RSV, and NEB. The third rendering is generally preferred. **men of little account:** A strong expression, rendered 'despised' in 1: 28. Identified in the terms of RSV text, such judges, whatever status they may have in the world, have as such no status in the church. Pagan judges are of little significance compared with those who will judge the world. Settling differences between Christians before heathen courts is utterly shameful.

5. nobody among you wise enough: Illustrates the poverty of true wisdom in Corinth in contrast to their apparent regard for worldly wisdom. Note the progression of thought in vv. 4–6; to have cases is bad, that they should be between brethren is worse, but that they should be brought before unbelievers is scandalous. **7. defeated already:** A default, defect and so in this context, a defeat. It refers not to the legal outcome, but to the spiritual issues involved. Origen notes that a legal victory may be a spiritual defeat. Nowhere in this section does Paul seek to discredit civil justice. **Among you** is the key to his thinking and the basis of his censure. Lawsuits may be forced on a believer, or become inescapable in his dealings with unbelievers. Paul's teaching and conduct revealed his respect for the law as appointed by God; cf. Rom. 13: 1–7; Ac. 18: 12 ff.; 25: 16. **Why not rather be wronged . . . be cheated?:** Reflects the law of Christ; cf. Mt. 5: 39–41. **8. you . . . cheat and do wrong:** Their cases against each other were not based even on just grievances. Rather than **suffer wrong**, they would inflict it. **9.** No English version conveys the significant connection between vv. 8 and 9: **you . . . do wrong** (*adikeite*) (8), but wrong doers, **wicked** (*adikoi*) **will not inherit** (9). Such Corinthians must re-examine their standing in Christ. Paul thus moves from the particular to the principle involved; cf. Eph. 5: 5, 6. It is a warning against antinomianism. **idolaters:** Grouped with those guilty of sexual sins, illustrating the immoral character of Greek religion with its temple prostitutes. **10. kingdom of God:** Referred to in its future aspect, while in 4: 20 it has a present significance; cf. 15: 24. **11. But** (*alla*): Preceding each of the three verbs in the Greek text, it serves to contrast forcefully their present state with that from which they came. **you were washed:** The middle voice—you had yourselves washed, emphasizing the voluntary character of their action. Nothing in the context identifies this act with baptism, although the same word has this association in Ac. 22: 16. Washing is indicative of regeneration (Eph. 5: 26; Tit. 3: 5) of which baptism is the visible confession. The use of the aorist as in **sanctified** and **justified** is suggestive of one definite act. **justified** coming last (*edikai-*

ōthēte, declared righteous) brings Paul's thought to a climax, contrasting their present condition with the **wicked** (*adikoi*) of v. 9. **in the name:** Qualifies all three verbs and emphasizes the divine origin and execution of salvation.

iii. Fornication and purity (6: 12–20)

Paul returns to the subject of immorality, now to deal with it not as a particular issue, as in chapter 5, but as a general principle. Fornication, condoned by the average Greek and Roman alike, and indeed being an almost integral part of pagan religion in Corinth, became a snare to test the moral discipline of the local church to the hilt. To those 'declared righteous' (11) came the temptation born of past licentious living to substitute licence for liberty. Paul's doctrines were easily perverted (Rom. 5: 20; 6: 14) and the seed of antinomianism sown. The lesson, **'Everything is permissible for me' —but not everything is beneficial** (12) had yet to be learned. Vv. 12–14 demonstrate the true use of Christian liberty in fulfilling God's purpose for the **body**, while the remaining verses (15–20) apply this to the problem of the **prostitute** and the consequent desecration of the **temple of the Holy Spirit.** The lesson is summarized in the final verse, a principle to govern all conduct: **honour God with your body.**

12. 'Everything is permissible for me' . . . : Possibly a phrase previously used by the apostle now misused by the Corinthian Christians to excuse their excesses. However, see note on 1: 12 where it is suggested that the phrase may have been a watchword of the libertarian party. In either case, this twice repeated maxim is now qualified (**but . . . but** . . .) to prove that **everything** is not an unrestricted absolute. There are moral bounds; **not everything is beneficial,** some things enslave. **13, 14. 'Food for the stomach . . .':** Probably another current saying, suggesting to the Corinthians that as one indulges an appetite for food, that being the function of the stomach, so should the physical urge for sexual indulgence be gratified. Paul refutes the argument: **stomach** and **food** are purely temporal. Not so the body; cf. 15: 35–50. **The body is not meant for sexual immorality . . . :** If **stomach** answers to **food**, the **body** answers, not to **immorality**, but to **the Lord.** Each is fitted for the other; cf. vv. 15a, 17, 19; Eph. 3: 16, 17; 2 C. 6: 16. **14. God raised . . . :** The body is meant for immortality; cf. 15: 20; Rom. 8: 11. Note the contrast; the **stomach** and **food** God destroys, the **Lord** and the **body** God raises. **15. members of Christ:** In the sense of limbs, as NEB, 'limbs and organs of Christ'. His possession of us is physical as well as spiritual. Hence the horror of using parts of His body for fornication. **16. Do you not know . . . :**

Paul appeals to the obvious, to common knowledge, as whenever he uses this phrase (3: 16; 5: 6; 6: 2, 3, 9, 15, 16, 19). It is the choice of being **one with her in body** (16), or **one with him in spirit** (17).

17. unites: Literally 'to glue', signifying the closest of ties, which here results in complete union, or fusion. The one verb expresses union with Christ and the union with a prostitute (see 'joins himself . . .' in v. 16). **18. Flee . . . immorality:** Some things are too powerful to be opposed and safety comes only in flight. See 10: 14; 1 Tim. 6: 10, 11; 2 Tim. 2: 22. **All other sins . . . are outside his body:** Literally, 'All sin . . .' Every sin has an outward aspect and effect, including immorality (16), but the unique difference for the fornicator, who **sins against his own body,** is that his sin is against the very nature and purpose of the human body. Other sins too which Paul has mentioned affect the body, *e.g.,* drunkenness, but fornication uniquely so. Its appetite stems wholly from within and demands the gratification of personal lust, the acme of self-violation. **19. your body is a temple:** Brings into sharp contrast the Christian concept of holiness with that of pagan Corinth, where in the temple of Aphrodite prostitutes were priestesses, intercourse with whom counted as consecration. **temple** (*naos*): See note on 3: 16. There the reference is to the church, here to the individual Christian. **of the Holy Spirit:** Cf. Rom. 8: 11; 2 C. 6: 16; 2 Tim. 1: 14. **20. bought with a price:** Carrying the seal of God's purchase; the Holy Spirit (Eph. 1: 13, 14). **bought:** Suggestive of the whole redemptive act, having the imagery of the slave-market and the consequent change of ownership. See 1 Pet. 1: 18, 19. **Therefore honour God with your body:** A positive injunction balancing the negative of v. 18. **Therefore** (*dē*): Strengthens the imperative; 'Be sure to . . .'

IV. DIFFICULTIES IN SOCIAL LIFE (7: 1–11: 1)

i. Marriage (7: 1–40)

(*a*) General background (7: 1–7)

Paul now deals with a variety of subjects mentioned by the Corinthians in their letter to him, the first of which is marriage. That Paul favoured celibacy is clear (1, 7, 8, 9, 27b, 38b) and for this he presents his reasons: the prevailing circumstances (26, 29), undivided devotion to Christ (32, 34, 35), and freedom from physical necessity (37). Recognizing its practical necessity, Paul countenances marriage (2), stipulating the mutual responsibilities of husband and wife and the relation of these to their spiritual lives (5). To understand Paul's teaching, two facts must be remembered: (i) Ascetic practices were highly esteemed, demanding among other things a celibate life.

This probably prompted some such question in their letter to the apostle as, 'Is marriage to be permitted?' Paul replies, recognizing many advantages of celibacy, but maintaining too the virtue of marriage (2, 9, 28, 36, 38a). (ii) Conditions at that particular time suggested that marriage might be unwise (26, 29). Paul is therefore not writing a treatise on marriage, but is answering their question within the context of current attitudes and the circumstances of the day. A balanced picture of the Christian concept of marriage is therefore to be gained from a study of the NT teaching as a whole; cf. Jn 2: 1–11; Eph. 5: 21–33; 1 Tim. 5: 14; Heb. 13: 4; 1 Pet. 3: 1–7.

1. It is good for a man not to marry is probably quoted from the Corinthians' letter; an ascetic party in the church may have taken this stand by way of reaction from the laxity of the environment. 'So far as I am concerned', Paul comments in effect, 'that would suit me very well, *but . . .*' Note his repeated use of **it is well** (commendable, but not *morally*, or intrinsically, better), in this connection in vv. 8, 26, 38. **2. But since there is so much immorality:** Reflects not a low view of marriage, but the moral conditions of Corinth. Paul is a realist, not a mere theorist. His attitude is defined in Eph. 5: 21–33. **each man . . . each woman . . . :** A clear statement of monogamy. **3. marital duty:** Literally 'debt' (*opheilē*). These are jointly shared by husband and wife. **give** (*apodidotō*): A present imperative, indicating the normal condition, the mutual paying of a debt. A wife is no mere chattel. The relationship is clarified further in v. 4, where the same statement is predicated separately of both husband and wife, demonstrating their equality. **4. does not belong** (*ouk exousiazei*): They have not the right to use their own bodies just as they will. **5. Do not deprive each other:** May be translated, 'Stop defrauding one another', to bring out the force of the pres. imper. with the neg. *mē*. It suggests that married couples in Corinth were refraining from intercourse on the grounds of mistaken asceticism. Only a limited period of abstinence by agreement, for special devotions, is permissible. Clearly then, procreation is not the sole purpose of intercourse. **Come together again** is suggestive of something far more frequent, regular and intimate. **6. I say this:** Refers back to the preceding 5 verses. Marriage is permitted by concession, but is not a command for all. **7. each has his own gift** (*charisma*): Marriage, just as celibacy, is a special gift from God. The same word is used for gifts of the Spirit in 12: 4–11.

(b) The unmarried and widows (7: 8, 9)
Specific classes are now dealt with; here those without marriage ties. The guidance is a restatement of vv. 1 and 2.

8. the unmarried (*tois agamois*): Probably refers to men—bachelors and widowers. The case of virgins is discussed in vv. 25–38. However, Leon Morris maintains that the term includes all not bound by the married state. **stay unmarried, as I am:** The verb, an aorist, suggests a permanent and final decision. The suggestion that Paul was a member of the Sanhedrin and therefore must have been married, is hard to substantiate. It is by no means certain that he was a member, nor is it certain that every member of the Sanhedrin in the period before A.D. 70 had to be married. But if Paul had once been married, he could now have been a widower, or his wife may have left him at his conversion (she would then be included in the 'all things' of Phil. 3: 8). **9. burn with passion:** A verb in the present tense (as is **cannot control themselves**) and indicative of a continual struggle such as would make spiritual growth impossible. Such a man has not the gift of celibacy.

(c) The married (7: 10, 11)
Here both partners are Christians (the case of mixed marriages comes next), and for such divorce is not permitted. If, however, it does take place another marriage is out of the question. The mention of the woman first and the note in parenthesis referring only to her leaving her husband, suggests that Paul had an actual case in mind.

10. I give this command: A military word. There is now no question of concession (6). **not I but the Lord:** Not merely Paul's command, but Christ's; cf. Mk 10: 9; Lk. 16: 18. Christ's allowance for fornication is not mentioned (cf. Mt. 5: 32; 19: 9).

(d) Mixed marriages (7: 12–16)
Some had married before their conversion and Paul now speaks to them. The Christian partner should not divorce the unbeliever who consents to continue the marriage relationship. The union is **sanctified** and the children undefiled. If however, the unconverted partner desires a divorce, the Christian is free to permit it.

12. I say this (I, not the Lord): That is, in this instance Paul cannot refer to any direct command of Christ, as he could for the previous case (10, 11). Yet his words carry the full weight of inspiration and apostolic authority. **14. the unbelieving husband has been sanctified through his wife:** This meets the fear of the Christian partner that the believer is going to be defiled in terms of 6: 15. But there is nothing unholy in such a marriage where the unbeliever elects to stay with the Christian partner. Such consecration has nothing to do with personal consecration as understood in terms of conversion and salvation, but of **sanctification** of the unbeliever for the purpose of the marriage union. On the analogy of *whatever* touches the altar shall be holy (Exod. 29: 37; Lev. 6: 18), so the unbelieving husband, in becoming one flesh with his believing partner, is sanctified in the wife for the purpose of marriage. On this basis the **children** of such a marriage are not **unclean** (*akatharta*), a word used for ceremonial impurity, but the very reverse; as far as the marriage is concerned, **they are holy**, that is, clean. Therefore the believer is required to separate from neither the unbelieving partner nor the children. **15. is not bound:** Seems to imply freedom to remarry. The unbeliever having 'taken himself off ', which is the force of the middle voice of **leaves**, no further compulsion to preserve the marriage remains on the believer. **God has called us to peace:** This encompasses the whole problem of mixed marriages. The believer is to become involved neither in the turmoil of seeking to terminate such a partnership, nor in the conflict of seeking to preserve it against the will of the unbeliever. Here submission issues in **peace** (Rom. 8: 28).

16. how do you know: Expresses the uncertainty of the believing partner being able to save the other by clinging to the marriage in spite of the partner's determination to end it. An exactly opposite view is, however, taken by Lightfoot and Findlay, expressing the hope of salvation, 'How do you know that you will not save your husband?' (so also NEB). The NIV rendering is probably to be preferred.

(*e*) **The life the Lord assigns (7: 17–24)**
V. 17 sums up the apostle's teaching on mixed marriages and at the same time introduces a general principle which must govern the actions of those converted to the Christian faith. This is defined in v. 20, **Each one should remain in the situation which he was in when God called him**, and restated in v. 24. Just as a believing partner in a mixed marriage is not to seek dissolution of the union, so with Jewish and Gentile converts, and indeed with the slave. While their conversion to Christ will produce a fundamental moral and spiritual change, yet their social status will not be altered. In that environment they are to live for Christ. Undoubtedly exceptions will be found, as when a pagan partner contracts out of marriage, or a slave is offered his freedom. Nevertheless, the principle is valid, **each man . . . should remain in the situation God called him to** (24).

17. retain the place in life (*peripateitō*): A pres. imper. with the force of 'continue walking'. There is a social continuity with the past. Christianity is not intended to bring a violent revolution from without, but to be a sanctifying influence within society. The position in life when **called**, is the one **the Lord assigned. This is the rule:** Strong apostolic authority. For the same usage see 11: 34; Tit. 1: 5; Ac. 24: 23. **all** is emphatic. **18, 19. he**

should not become uncircumcised. They should remain within Jewish society. To remove such a sign as a Jew, or to seek it as a converted Gentile was pointless; the rite 'counts for nothing' (Moffatt) in the Christian code; cf. Gal. 5: 2, 3; Ac. 15: 1, 5, 19, 24, 28. Converted Jews and Gentiles were both needed within their social groups. Paul never ceased to be a Jew; cf. 9: 20. **God's commands:** The moral law, understood in terms of Gal. 5: 6; 6: 15. **20. remain:** A pres. imper. with the same force as **retain the place in life** in v. 17. **21** is capable of two interpretations: **if you can gain your freedom, do so** literally 'rather use', refers either to the opportunity to become free, or to the opportunity to use one's vocation as a slave, i.e., to continue as a slave and so fulfil the general principle to remain in the state in which one was called. NIV, RSV, Moffatt, Phillips and NEB take the former view, which is the more probable from the use of the aorist imper. which is suggestive of availing oneself of a new opportunity as opposed to the pres. imper. of vv. 17, 20, 24. **22. The Lord's freedman . . . Christ's slave:** What matters is not one's temporal state, but one's spiritual standing and relationship. This was Paul's boast; cf. Rom. 1: 1; Phil. 1: 1; Tit. 1: 1. **23. You were bought:** See note on 6: 20. **do not become slaves of men:** Refers not to physical slavery—no such injunction would be needed—but probably to the temptation of yielding to social and religious pressures, which would be incompatible with their being slaves of Christ.

24. each: As in vv. 17, 20 it is emphatic, stressing the duty of the individual.
(*f*) **The advantages of remaining single (7: 25–38)**
Having dealt with marriage in relation to widows, unmarried men and those already married, Paul now turns to the **unmarried** women—virgins. What he writes is in response to questions on the subject from Corinth and without the knowledge of those questions and the identity of the virgins, the exact translation of this passage, especially vv. 36–38, must remain a matter of conjecture. Paul's opinion concerning these young women is influenced considerably by **the present crisis** (26), which he further defines by saying that **the time is short** (29). See also v. 31. Of this situation we have no precise knowledge, although to some extent it seems in Paul's mind to be associated with events leading up to the Second Coming. So critical and precarious are the circumstances, that before dealing with the particular case of the virgins, the apostle urges that marriage and all aspects of life be conducted with the utmost caution and solemnity (26–31).

In these circumstances the advantages of remaining single are obvious. The man or woman without other responsibilities is able to be concerned wholly in the **the Lord's affairs**, while those who are married become engrossed in each other. **Undivided devotion to the Lord** is the apostle's aim (32–35).

Having established the principle involved, Paul returns to the particular case of the young woman he has in mind (36–38). The problems of interpretation are considerable. While the translators of AV and RV had a father and daughter in mind, NIV and RSV view them as an engaged couple (see note on v. 36). Although the precise identity of the individuals must remain in doubt, Paul's conclusion is clear. If the young man marries he **does right**, but he who remains single **does even better**. So the principle enunciated in 7: 1, 2 is carried through; in the present circumstances it is better not to marry, although for most marriage must be the norm.

25. Now about virgins (*parthenoi*): normally applying to women only, although in Rev. 14: 4 it refers to men (see p. 1700). Thus RSV translates it loosely to cover unmarried men and women and NEB renders it 'celibacy'. Most translations and commentators restrict the meaning here to unmarried women. **I have no command from the Lord:** Indicates as in v. 12 that Christ gave no specific instruction. **I give a judgment:** Not that Paul is not sure of his facts (cf. v. 40). The situation does not call for a command, as opposed to v. 10, for the individuals involved must decide for themselves between the possible alternatives; cf. vv. 27, 28, 35, 36–38. Paul presents principles for guidance. **26. the present crisis:** May be rendered 'present distress', or 'necessity'. The word is a strong one and is used in Lk. 21: 23. Paul's usage has been variously interpreted as (i) a reference to events preceding the Second Coming (and so vv. 29, 31), (ii) general opposition to Christian profession, although the language is too strong for this, (iii) particularly difficult circumstances through which the Christians in Corinth were then passing. Combined influences of all three might be involved. **28. you have not sinned:** Marriage may be unwise because of the **present crisis**, but not sinful (cf. v. 36). **many troubles:** Literally, 'affliction in the flesh', an experience normally balanced by compensating blessings and joys. Yet the worry and distress resulting from family responsibilities in times of violence and persecution are immeasurably increased. **29. the time is short . . . :** As with vv. 26 and 31 it may be understood in terms of the Second Advent, although the apostle nowhere else suggests that its anticipation should lead to the abandonment of basic human relationships. Rather, he uses it as a stimulus to holiness (1 Th. 5: 1–10). A local crisis of extreme gravity more probably existed and Paul's allusions to it were readily understood in Corinth. See Phil-

lips's translation. **from now on:** I.e., during the emergency, not merely the unmarried, but all in the church, the married, the mourners, the joyous, the traders, all must live in measure as detached from their experiences. **31. as if not engrossed:** The compound form of the verb intensifies its meaning, i.e., 'not using to the full'. Phillips is excellent, 'Every contact with the world should be as light as possible'. **this world in its present form** (*schēma*): Literally, 'the outward appearance'. All is transitory, explaining why contact with it should be light. **32. free from concern:** I.e., the **many troubles** of v. 28. Note their effect in Mk 4: 19; Lk. 21: 34. Yet there is a proper anxiety which Paul proceeds to employ, to demonstrate the advantage of remaining single; **an unmarried man is concerned . . . how he can please the Lord.** This was Paul's own great desire; cf. 2 C. 5: 9; Gal. 1: 10; 1 Th. 2: 4; 4: 1; 2 Tim. 2: 4. However, the equally right anxiety in the realm of family life—**affairs of this world**—to please one's partner, introduces a potential conflict of loyalties which becomes apparent under conditions of stress and crisis (33)—**interests are divided** (34). A case in point: single men and women invariably remain in missionary work, while married men and women frequently abandon the task for 'family reasons'.

34. his interests are divided (*memeristai*): This clause involves a problem of punctuation and therefore translation. Should *memeristai* (**divided**) be taken with v. 33, or with v. 34? While AV and RV take it with v. 34, NIV, together with Moffatt, RSV and NEB, link *memeristai* with the preceding sentence. There are also a number of textual variations which complicate the issue. A decision is difficult, but Paul's general sense is clear. **devoted to the Lord in both body and spirit:** Refers to consecration, not ethical attainment. The single woman is unhindered by such responsibilities as characterize a married woman. **35. restraint:** Literally 'halter' or 'lasso'. See NEB: 'keep you on a tight rein'.

36. Yet even in the present circumstances Paul sees the possible necessity for some to marry. The verse obviously answers a question raised by the Corinthian believers. **the virgin** (*parthenos*) **he is engaged to:** has been interpreted in three ways; (i) the father and his virgin daughter (AV, RV), (ii) a couple involved in a 'spiritual marriage' while remaining celibate (Moffatt and NEB), (iii) a young man and his fiancée (NIV, RSV). According to (i), the father was responsible for his daughter's marriage. Yet if he felt that 'he behaveth himself unseemly' (RV), i.e., was treating her unjustly in failing to arrange a marriage, and 'if she be past the flower of her age' (so RV renders *hyperakmos*), i.e., of marriageable age with the bloom of youth commencing to fade, then he may arrange a marriage; 'he sinneth not' (RV), i.e., she has not the gift of continence (cf. v. 7). On the other hand, if he is aware of no such 'necessity' (RV) then he may keep her as his own virgin daughter. If (ii) the 'spiritual marriage' is correct, vv. 36, 37 are translated as in RSV except that *parthenos* becomes 'spiritual, or celibate bride'. This practice existed in the 2nd century and was condemned by Cyprian in the 3rd century, but there is no evidence that it existed in Paul's day. The third suggestion (RSV) translates *parthenos* as **the virgin he is engaged to** or 'betrothed' and *hyperakmos* as **if she is getting along in years** or 'If his passions are strong'. This interpretation is probably the most attractive. In the lower social classes from which most of the members of the Corinthian church were drawn the contracting of marriages would often be left to the young people concerned and would not be viewed as the responsibility of the parents.

(g) **Widows (7: 39, 40)**
Remarriage is permissible **but he must belong to the Lord,** i.e. let her marry a Christian, but, as in v. 8, the apostle considers **she is happier** if she remains single.

39. A woman is bound to her husband: Christian marriage is indissoluble till death. **40. I have the Spirit of God:** Cf. v. 25. Paul's **judgment** is Spirit-led. Robertson and Plummer conclude, 'The preference given to celibacy is tentative and exceptional, to meet exceptional conditions.'

ii. Food offered to idols (8: 1–11: 1)
(a) **Idols are nothing (8: 1–6)**
Food and **idols:** The problem loomed large in Corinth for the two were inextricably linked. Undoubtedly much of the meat available to the shops had been originally offered in pagan rites and later disposed of by the priests as surplus to their needs. But that was not all; normal social functions involving a meal were often held in temples, creating situations where Christians would almost inevitably be present and participate. On such occasions sacrifices to the idols would be made. What should the Christian do? That was their problem and the substance of the question to Paul. While one scorns the very existence of idols and eats with impunity, another, weak in the faith, is stumbled and destroyed; for him the idol is a living reality. The conclusion? Avoid anything that would cause your brother to fall (13). In vv. 1–6 Paul states the principle that our **knowledge** of the absolute nonentity of idols must be balanced by **love.**

1. Now about: Paul's phrase for introducing the subjects on which the Corinthians have sought guidance; cf. 7: 1, 25; 12: 1; 16: 1. **We all possess knowledge:** Possibly a statement from their own letter, and on this assumption

RSV adds quotation marks. See also NIV footnote. As with wisdom, the Corinthians had a typically Greek regard for **knowledge.** Alone, it engenders pride; **puffs up** (see note on 4: 6). **Love builds up:** A word used of building construction, cf. v. 10; 10: 23; 14: 4, 17 for *oikodomeō* in this letter. Note the contrast; hollowness and solidity. **2. thinks he knows:** 'thinks'—is used with similar effect concerning wisdom in 3: 18. True knowledge should lead to humility, the recognition of ignorance. Love aids this attitude (cf. 13: 12b). **3. is known by God:** The divine response to human **love.** To obtain His recognition is all important. One who truly loves is better equipped to solve the problem of food offered to idols than one who merely knows. **4. we know:** Appears to introduce more quotations from the Corinthian inquiry. Note the RSV quotation marks. Paul accepts their assertions, **'an idol is nothing at all'** and **'there is no God but one'**, but reserves his treatment of the underlying implications of idolatry to 10: 14–22 (cf. Gal. 4: 8). **5. in heaven or on earth:** The abode of the gods of Greek mythology. **many 'gods' and many 'lords':** Pagan terms of address. Lord (*kyrios*) is a title frequently given to gods in Greek inscriptions. **6. one God . . . one Lord:** As opposed to many, affirms strongly the positive Christian position. The prepositions are instructive; of **God: from whom** (*ek*—out of), the source of creation; **for whom** (*eis* —into), the flow-back of redeemed creation, suggesting the direction of our lives—we live for Him (cf. Rom. 11: 36; Eph. 4: 6); of **Christ: through whom** (*dia*—by means of), the medium of creation; **through whom we . . . ,** the medium of the new creation (cf. 2 C. 5: 17; Col. 1: 15–20).

(b) **The weak brother (8: 7–13)**
While one scorned the very existence of idols and ate freely, another weak in the faith is encouraged to do what he feels to be wrong. He eats and for him the idol once again becomes a living reality. He stumbles, wounded, a spiritual wreck. For Paul his duty is clear; **I will never eat meat again, so that I will not cause him to fall.**

7. not everyone knows this: Literally, 'this knowledge is not in all'. There is a difference between knowing theoretically (*oida*, vv. 1, 4) and having that knowledge in one as an activating reality. **accustomed to idols:** Suggests force of habit (note that the AV is based on an incorrect variant). Even though they are now Christian, habits formed over years of idol worship reawaken in their conscience old associations and sensations of the idol's power. **8, 9. Food does not bring us near to God . . . :** The future tense looks to the judgment. Food is amoral and of itself will bring neither approbation nor condemnation.

What will be of consequence will be the misuse of their **freedom** (*exousia*, 'authority', 'right'). See Rom. 14: 13–20.

10. in an idol's temple: May refer to the occasion of some official function or festival. **emboldened:** Literally, 'built up', i.e., the weak man's conscience is built up to participate, to its own downfall. Note the ironical contrast with v. 1. They sought to build up with *knowledge; love* would build differently. **11. is destroyed** (*apollytai*): The present tense; his ultimate condition is not being discussed. 'spiritual disaster' (Phillips), 'ruined' (Moffatt), give the sense. Goudge comments, 'Every word helps to bring out the heinousness of the enlightened Christian's conduct. The weakness of the person injured, the greatness of the injury . . . his relation to the injured, the love of Christ for him, the means by which the injury is inflicted, all make the guilt greater.' Cf. Mt. 18: 6, 7. Many a Muslim and Hindu has trod this path. **2. sin . . . wound . . . sin against Christ:** The enormity of the sin is revealed. His brother was Christ's (cf. Mt. 25: 40, 45). **wound:** The only metaphorical use of the verb in the NT. Note the three metaphors used concerning the **weak conscience: defiled** (7), **stumbling-block (9), wound (12). 13.** Paul's principle—avoid the cause of stumbling—is based on love, not knowledge. The two words stressed in this passage, **weak** (5 times) and **brother** (3 times), reveal a condition and relationship which should have evoked tenderness and love, but which received only the callous disregard of a misguided knowledge. See Rom. 14 for a fuller treatment of the subject.

(c) **Paul's example (9: 1–27)**
This chapter is not a digression written in self-defence, nor as some conclude, an insertion from some other letter. It is an illustration of the apostle's privileges as a freedman in Christ; privileges he did not use. The typical man of knowledge in Corinth insists on the full exercise of these rights (liberty—8:9), riding rough-shod over the susceptibilities of the weak. Paul shows a better way, and the principle he enunciates in 8: 13 he demonstrates in daily conduct, a life which shows by its refusal to claim its rights, the exercise of the highest right of all—to **become all things to all men . . . save some (22).**

(i) **Paul's rights as an apostle (9: 1–14)**
These rights were all the more reasonable in connection with the Corinthian church because of his special relationship with them (1, 2). He had a **right** to be supported by the local churches among whom he worked; the **right** to **food and drink** (4), the **right** to take around **a wife** (5), the right to refrain from secular work (6). These rights based not on mere expediency or personal desire, but on the prac-tice of **other apostles** (5); on the analogies of human experience—the soldier, the farmer, the shepherd (7, 10); on the clear commands of the Mosaic Law (8, 9); on the recognized rights of the Levites in the Temple (13), and finally, on the explicit decree of Christ himself (14). God's servants called to full-time service, whoever or wherever they may be, are therefore the direct responsibility of God's churches. Every apostle was not called to be a Paul.

1. Am I not free?: 'Not here as in Rom. 6: 18, 22, but from all external law of all kinds as in Gal. 4: 22–31; 5: 1; 1 Pet. 2: 16' (Parry). The thought is resumed in v. 19. **Have I not seen Jesus . . . ?:** A claim made all the more emphatic by the use of *ouchi* (**not**) in preference to the ordinary negative (*ouk*) of the preceding questions. The reference is primarily to the Damascus road experience (Ac. 9: 3, 17, 27; 22: 14), but see also Ac. 22: 17, 18 and Ac. 18: 9, where 'vision' is the same word as is used of the transfiguration in Mt. 17: 9. His ability to testify to the resurrection of Christ fulfilled in part the requirements for apostleship laid down in Ac. 1: 21, 22. **result of my work** refers back to 3: 5–7, but it was **in the Lord**, for God gave the grace and the growth (3: 7b–9). **2. the seal of my apostleship:** Among other things the seal was the mark of authenticity. Their existence as a living church vindicated Paul's claim. **3.** may be taken with either the preceding or the following verses. If **defense** (*apologia*—a legal word as is **sit in judgment**) refers to the authenticity of his apostleship, it should be taken with vv. 1, 2. Most commentators take this view, as also Phillips and NEB. If however **defense** has to do with his contention concerning rights and freedom—the theme of the chapter—then it may legitimately commence a new paragraph as in the NIV and RSV. **4. the right to food and drink:** Maintenance from those he serves. In using the plural Paul may be associating Barnabas with himself, cf. v. 6.

5. wife: Undoubtedly the correct translation of *adelphēn gynaika*; cf. NEB. The churches would be responsible for the support of the woman as well as the man. **the Lord's brothers:** Most probably the sons of Mary and Joseph (cf. Jn 7: 5; Ac. 1: 14; Gal. 1: 19), although the phrase could include a wider circle of relatives. The view that they were first cousins has been held by some Protestant expositors on grounds other than the Roman Catholic dogma of Mary's perpetual virginity. **6. only I and Barnabas: only** is singular (*monos*) referring to Paul, while **Barnabas** seems to be added as an afterthought; 'only I —and Barnabas . . .' The inference is that all other apostles refrained from working for a living. Paul's practice of working with his hands would offend the Greek mind; cf. 4: 12;

Ac. 18: 3; 1 Th. 4: 11; 2 Th. 3: 8–12. **7.** Each with his different status, the soldier—a wage-earner, the vine planter—an owner, the shepherd—probably a slave, had one thing in common: they derived their living from their occupation, a right Paul relinquished. **8. human point of view:** Refers to v. 7, which Paul has argued from human analogies, but the law vindicates his claim. The quotation is from Dt. 25: 4. **9. Is it about oxen that God is concerned?:** Calls for a negative answer (10). The suggestion that God is not concerned for the welfare of oxen is more apparent than real. God in His general providence cares for all creation, cattle, birds and even the grass of the field (cf. Ps. 145: 9; Mt. 6: 26, 30), yet the animal creation exists for man's benefit (cf. Gen. 1: 28). Paul considers that the allegorical significance of the text in Dt. 25: 4 completely outweighs its literal meaning. The verse is similarly applied in 1 Tim. 5: 18. **10. Surely he says this for us:** May be rendered, 'doubtless, or clearly for our sake' (so RVmg, Knox and NEB). God's care for the oxen is not altogether excluded. **12. others:** May refer to Apollos, or Peter (5), or even suggest that there were resident teachers in Corinth supported by the church. Their claim was rightful and his even more so, cf. v. 2. **we did not use this right:** Anticipates Paul's arguments of vv. 15–23. **we put up with anything** (*stegomen*): A verb expressive of Paul's character and used only by him in the NT. He would bear up under all pressures for the sake of others, cf. 13: 7 note; 1 Th. 3: 1, 5. **hinder** (*enkopē*): Literally 'an incision', a word, notes Findlay, which became a military term in later Greek for breaking up a road to hinder the advance of an army. There must be no such obstacle in the way of the gospel. **13. Don't you know . . . :** Cf. 6: 15 note. The provision for **those who work in the temple** is outlined in Lev. 7: 6, 8–10, 14, 28–36; Num. 18: 8–20; Dt. 18: 1–4. The Levite was supported by the things of the altar. He had his rights through which he lived. By the tithes of the people the work of God was supported—and when these were withheld the Levites were forced to till their fields (Neh. 13: 10). In response to Malachi's call to the people, the tithes were brought and the Temple service resumed, with consequent blessing for all. **14. In the same way:** Reveals the continuity which exists between OT and NT orders. **the Lord has commanded:** Paul's final authority; cf. Mt. 10: 10; Lk. 10: 7. The case is proved; the care of God's servants is His people's concern.

(ii) **Paul's rights assessed in relation to the needs of others (9: 15–23)**
Having justified his claims, the apostle forthwith abandons them! All his carefully planned arguments in vv. 3–14 lead to the final declaration, **But I have not used any of these**

rights (15). The underlying reason for Paul's statements must be borne in mind, that the Corinthians should learn through his example to be prepared to surrender their right to eat food offered to idols, in order that weaker brethren might not be stumbled. His abandonment of personal rights is for one purpose only; that the gospel may be presented freely (18). This is a right to claim and one of which to boast, the right to refuse all remuneration lest it blunt the edge of his message, causing misunderstandings among those he sought to reach (15–18).

That Paul was not paid for his work gave him independence, freedom of thought and action. Yet it was not a liberty to be selfishly employed, but rather a means to **win as many as possible** (19). Whatever the condition of men, wherever he might find them, whether Jew or Gentile, he was free to identify himself with them in their need and so win them for Christ (19–23). Throughout these two paragraphs the overriding consideration with the apostle is: How can I best preach the gospel? How can I best bring others to Christ? He had learned the true relation of personal rights to Christian responsibility.

15. I would rather: Weakens the Greek. Paul is saying it were good (*kalon*), i.e., better for him to die than accept remuneration. **boast:** In making the gospel free of charge (18), not in his personal ability to do so, for he received support from other churches in order to make it free in Corinth; cf. 2 C. 11: 7–10. There is no contradiction with Gal. 6: 13, 14 where Paul is refusing to boast of circumcision. See Rom. 5: 3; 1 C 1: 31; 2 C 11: 30; 12: 5, 9; 2 Th. 1: 4 for subjects in which Paul boasts. He never boasts on his own behalf; cf. 2 C. 12: 5. **16. I am compelled to preach:** Paul *had* to preach; cf. Rom. 1: 14; Ac. 9: 15, 16; 26: 19. That was nothing to boast of. He was called to do so (2 Tim. 1: 11). He was a slave to obey (Gal. 1: 10 —written in connection with preaching the gospel). **Woe to me:** The impulse of a quickened conscience, the knowledge of future judgment and the constraint of the love of Christ.

17 is rather obscure. **If I preach voluntarily:** Could refer to ordinary teachers, not conscious of a particular call, but preaching because they wished to. Such would receive wages (*misthos*—**reward**). **if not voluntarily** would then refer to one such as Paul who acted, not on the basis of his own volition, but as **discharging the trust.** As such, his **reward** (wages) was not in the form of money, but the privilege of presenting the gospel freely (18). Perhaps it is better to understand both parts of the verse as referring to the slave **compelled** to serve (16); he may preach willingly and receive the **reward** of v. 18, or even if unwilling, he is still not excused from his duty. Willing or unwilling, Paul could not escape his responsibility. **trust** (*oikonomia*): Stewardship. See 4: 1–4 in connection with stewards (*oikonomoi*). **18. I may offer it free of charge:** Paul's regular practice to which he frequently refers; cf. 1 Th. 2: 9; 2 Th. 3: 8; Ac. 20: 33–35; 2 C. 11: 7–12. This last reference explains.

19. to win as many as possible: Paul's guiding principle, motivated by love. Nothing less could enable one who was **free** (see v. 1—not only in matters of support, but in all aspects of Christian experience) to make himself a **slave to everyone.** Here Paul returns in thought to 8: 1–3. His love which surrendered all rights would save, where their knowledge tenaciously defended would destroy. **20. I became like a Jew:** Illustrated by his circumcision of Timothy to avoid needless offence (cf. Ac. 16: 3; also 18: 18; 21: 18–26), but where Judaism conflicted with Christian revelation Paul was adamant (cf. Gal. 2: 4, 5). **those under the law:** As distinguished from the Jews, all who had accepted the Jewish religion, even Judaizing Christians who considered themselves bound by the Mosaic law. **I myself am not under the law:** Although conformity is permitted where principles are not compromised, Paul is careful to emphasize his freedom from the law (*nomos*), which here undoubtedly means the Mosaic law as a whole; cf. Rom. 7: 4; Gal. 2: 19; 5: 18; Eph. 2: 15; Col.2: 14. **21. To those not having the law:** The heathen. Peter similarly accommodated himself; cf. Gal. 2: 11–14. See also Ac. 17: 22–28 where Paul uses illustrations readily understood by the heathen mind. Yet Paul is **not free from God's law.** He is not lawless. **Christ's law** governs his conduct; cf. Rom. 8: 2–8; Gal. 6: 2; see also Jas 1: 25; 2: 12; Gal. 5: 13, 14.

22. To the weak I became weak: Reveals the extent of Paul's identification; he drops the *as* used of the other groups. The **weak** are undoubtedly included as a separate group in view of the theme of Paul's argument (8: 7–13). **all things to all men:** Never involved the abandonment of principle, but demonstrated the ability to enter the lives of others with the acutest understanding and sympathy. **have become:** Perfect tense, an accomplished fact still continuing to govern his life. **23. that I may share** (*synkoinōnos*): The noun expresses the experience of being a co-partner, the emphasis being not on getting, but *sharing* with others in the **blessings** of the gospel.

(iii) The result (9: 24–27)
To share in blessings is one thing, but to receive a **prize** is quite another. If the abandonment of personal rights and the identification of oneself with others for their spiritual blessing were desirable, then the Corinthians were sadly lacking. Not only would they fail to share with

others in the blessing of the gospel to the extent that the apostle desired, but in the Christian race they were lagging far behind. As a stimulus to renewed consecration and effort, Paul gives yet another illustration. He makes two points; the motive for competing—to gain the prize, and the means employed—self control.

24. in a race: Paul draws on the Corinthians' knowledge of the Isthmian Games which were held every fifth year close by their city. He frequently has this metaphor of the athlete in mind; cf. Ac. 20: 24; Phil. 3: 12–14. **Run in such a way:** Run to win; why be an also-ran? Note Paul's example in 2 Tim. 4: 7. **25. strict training:** A basic requirement. Ten months of rigorous training preceded the Games. A thorough knowledge of the rules was demanded (2 Tim. 2: 5). If such discipline at best could yield a **crown that will not last**, how much more worthy of discipline is the **crown that will last forever**? Cf. 2 Tim. 4: 8; Jas 1: 12; 1 Pet. 5: 4; Rev. 2: 10; 3: 11. **26. I do not run . . . aimlessly . . . beating the air:** The athlete keeps his eye on the track, the boxer on his opponent. Every stride must be purposeful, every blow must count; cf. Phil. 3: 14; Heb. 12: 1, 2. **27. I beat my body . . . :** Paul's greatest problem in the contest is himself. Distractions and hindrances arise chiefly from within. **body** (*sōma*): Here synonymous with bodily desires, the flesh, through which Satan so easily strikes; cf. Rom. 6: 6; 8: 3. Paul overcomes this, not through asceticism (Col. 2: 23), but by utter dedication in training, the constant employment of himself in the service of Christ. His approach is positive; cf. Gal. 5: 16; Phil. 1: 20–22. **disqualified** (*adokimos*): Paul's concern is lest he should lose, not his salvation, but the victor's wreath, the prize for which he has exhorted others to run.

(d) Dangers of indulgence (10: 1–22)
In using himself as an example Paul has demonstrated to the Corinthians the superiority of love over knowledge, the better course of relinquishing one's rights in order to help those in spiritual need. On these grounds alone it is better to refrain from eating meat offered to idols and so save the weak from stumbling. Yet a further and most cogent reason exists for abstaining from the meat of heathen sacrifices. The situation is such that eating food in idols' temples constitutes an unjustifiable temptation to become deeply involved in all the implications of pagan worship, which is the very antithesis of the Lord's Supper.

(i) The example of Israel (10: 1–13)
In spite of the great redemption of the Exodus and the miraculous deliverances and provisions of the wilderness wanderings, many Israelites perished (5). Lacking in self-control they fell into sin, of which Paul enumerates four instances: they became **idolaters** (7), indulged in

immorality (8), tested the Lord (9), grumbled and **were killed** (10). From this solemn lesson Corinth must learn (6, 11). Scornfully to reject the existence of idols and on the basis of this superior knowledge to eat sacrificial meat in the very temples where evil, corruption and immorality reign, is to court disaster (12). Undoubtedly, they will be invited and tempted to attend. Better by far to refuse, and see God make a way of escape for them (13).

1. RSV ignores 'for' (*gar*) with which the chapter commences, linking it with 9: 27. What the athlete won by discipline, the Israelites lost by indulgence. **our forefathers:** The spiritual ancestors of all Christians, whether Jews or Gentiles. Note the emphasis on **all:** it occurs four times in these verses. Although the privileges extended to all, the majority abused them. **the cloud:** Cf. Exod. 13: 21, 22; 14: 19, 20; 40: 34–38; Num. 9: 15–23; 14: 14; Dt. 1: 33; Ps. 78: 14; 105: 39. **the sea:** Associated with the cloud in Exod. 13: 21; 14: 20. **2. baptized into Moses:** Passing through the cloud and sea they were united with their human leader and deliverer, Moses. This becomes a type of Christian baptism, figurative of our union with Christ; cf. Rom. 6: 3; Gal. 3: 27. The aorist middle may suggest the voluntary character of that baptism (cf. Ac. 22: 16). **3. spiritual food:** i.e., manna (Exod. 16: 4, 16 ff.), of heavenly origin. **spiritual drink:** The water from the rock. **4. spiritual Rock:** Cf. Exod. 17: 6; Num. 20: 7 ff., identified as Christ. The whole history is spiritualized. The manna, the water and the rock, truly material, become subjects of divine miraculous provision. Paul's usage goes beyond a mere typological reference— **that Rock was Christ,** not 'is', or, 'is a type of '—and is a clear statement of the pre-existence of Christ. **accompanied:** Christ the Rock was constantly with His people, the true source of every provision. Note the use of 'Rock' as a divine name in the OT (Dt. 32: 4, 15, 18, 30, 31, 37; Ps. 18: 2, 31; Isa. 30: 29, etc.). **5. with most of them:** Contrasts strongly with the repeated 'all'. Only two who saw the Exodus survived. 'What a spectacle for the eyes of the self-satisfied Corinthians; all these bodies full-fed with miraculous nourishment, strewing the soil of the desert!' (Godet). **6. examples, to keep us from:** Paul applies the lessons of history. *typoi* (**examples** or warnings) is capable of various meanings; the mark of a blow (Jn 20: 25); the stamp of a die; a standard (Rom. 6: 17); a type (Rom. 5: 14); as here, an example for imitation or warning (Phil. 3: 17; 1 Th. 1: 7). **7. Do not be idolaters:** A quotation from Exod. 32: 6 in connection with the worship of the golden calf. Such idolatrous festivals commonly included dancing and singing. In view of the trouble at Corinth (chapter 8), the

warning is of primary importance. **8. immorality:** A temptation already assailing the church, associated as it was with Corinthian temple worship (chapters 5 and 6). Israel succumbed in similar conditions to idolatrous fornication; cf. Num. 25: 1–9. The tone of Paul's warning is softened by the use of the first person: **We should not commit** (indulge). **9. We should not test the Lord:** Could fit a variety of circumstances, *e.g.*, the misuse of the Christian liberty in attending pagan feasts (14–22). **test** (*ekpeirazein*): Has a primary and secondary meaning; (i) to prove, as Abraham was tested (Heb. 11: 17); (ii) to test with the purpose of causing failure, hence to tempt. In the incident referred to (Num. 21: 5 ff.), God was put to the test, tried beyond measure, by the persistent ingratitude of His rebellious people.

10. do not grumble: Almost certainly refers to the incident of Korah (Num. 16: 41 ff.), where violent retribution ensued. **the destroying angel,** though not mentioned in the Numbers passage, is viewed by Paul as the agent of God's wrath, as in Exod. 12: 23. Findlay suggests that Paul had in mind the murmurings of jealous partisans and unworthy teachers in Corinth (cf. 1: 11, 12; 4: 6, 18 ff.). **11. on whom the fulfillment of the ages has come:** Paul probably means that the end of 'this age' and the inauguration of 'the age to come' are being experienced by their generation; between the saving work of Christ and His parousia the two ages overlap (cf. Heb. 9:26; Mt. 13:39, 40, 49; 28:20).

12. So: The application is plain: **if you think you are standing firm**—the wise (3: 18), the rich (4: 8), the man of knowledge (8: 10)—**be careful. 13. no temptation** (*peirasmos*): Consolation after warning. It can be understood in the more general sense of 'trial' as in NEB. The trials besetting the Corinthian church were indeed temptations to sin. Paul may have in mind the plea of some that they were forced to attend the temple feasts. Nevertheless, whatever the temptation—to idolatry, fornication, or any other—it is **common to man.** Theirs is no special case; the Israelites had it long before them. **God is faithful:** He can be trusted; cf. 1: 9; 1 Th. 5: 24; 2 Th. 3: 3; 2 Tim. 2: 13; 1 Pet. 4: 19. **beyond what you can bear:** As Christians; cf. 2 C. 12: 9, 10. **a way out** (*ekbasis*): Note the def. art.—every trial has its own particular God-given way of escape. **can stand up under it:** Ability to endure is given **when you are tempted,** not apart from it. The word is characteristic of the apostle's attitude to all forms of trial; cf. 2 Tim. 3: 10, 11.

(ii) The implications of the Lord's Supper (10: 14–22)

Paul has already conceded the point, at least academically, that an idol as such has no existence (8: 4). Idols as deities do not exist. He agrees with the Corinthians that indeed **there is no God but one.** This position he still maintains (10: 19), but clarifies the issue; sacrifices offered by pagans are not to deity, but **to demons.** Therefore, stipulates the apostle, it is better to keep away from pagan temple festivals. Think of the meal in which you share there and recall too the remembrance meal of the Lord's Supper. Just as we, by partaking of the bread and wine, identify ourselves with all that the death of Christ means, so by partaking in a temple meal you become partners with demons. The implication of eating meat at a heathen feast is analogous with the practice of Israel. They, eating the sacrifices, communed with God. To share in an idol sacrifice is to commune with demons. The two are incompatible. Is not this the very sin of putting God to the test (22)? Keep away from idols.

14. Therefore: Links the verse closely with v. 13 and suggests that idol feasts are the primary temptation Paul has in mind. **my dear friends:** Cf. 4: 14; 15: 58; 2 C7: 1. His commands flow from deep affection. **flee from idolatry:** As with immorality (6: 18), flight is the only sure way of escape. The phrase clearly refers to idol feasts. **15. sensible people** is void of all sarcasm. They could well appreciate Paul's arguments and understand the validity of his conclusion. **16. The cup of thanksgiving:** A Hebraism, the name given to the third cup of the Passover feast over which a prayer of thanks giving was pronounced. **thanksgiving** (*eulogia*) therefore refers not to the cup but to the prayer over it. This is made clear by **for which we give thanks** (*eulogoumen*), cf. Mt.26:26,27; Mk 14: 22, 23; 1 C. 11: 23 ff. **participation** (*koinōnia*): Variously rendered, 'communion', 'partnership', or 'fellowship'. It is used to express our relationships on a human level(cf. 2 C. 1: 7; 8: 4; Heb. 10: 33; 1 Jn 1:7), as well as the divine (cf. 1: 9; Phil. 3: 10; 2 Pet. 1: 4; 1 Jn 1: 3). Participation on both levels may be expressed in terms of identification, or association of oneself with the object defined. Their very act of participation in the cup declared their association with the sacrificial death of Christ.

17. Because there is one loaf . . . : Paul's concept of the unity of the body of Christ is clearly expressed through the analogy of the one loaf, a symbol preserved by many churches at the Lord's Supper. **many:** In diversity there is unity. This is developed in 12: 12–31; Eph. 4: 1–16; cf. 1 Jn 1: 7.

18. Israel: Literally, 'Israel after the flesh'. The Israel of history is distinguished from the spiritual Israel of God; cf. Gal. 6: 16, also Phil. 3: 3. **participate in the altar:** The Jews in eating sacrifices from the altar associate themselves with all that the altar signifies. Eating at pagan

sacrificial feasts was analogous with this (20, 21). **20. to demons, not to God:** Possibly a quotation from Dt. 32: 17. Robertson and Plummer and also Grosheide suggest that as in Dt. 32: 17 **God** should be rendered 'god', *ou theō* having the force of 'to a no-god'; cf. Dt. 32: 21. This improves the sense. **demons:** The real force behind all pagan religion; attested not only by the OT and NT, but by missionary experience. Idolatry is a medium through which satanic power is particularly manifest; cf. 1 Jn 5: 19, 21. **21. You cannot drink:** Not the physical impossibility, but the moral and spiritual incompatibility of participation in the **the Lord's table and the table of demons.** The respective hosts are clearly demonstrated by these genitives. To partake of both the Lord's Supper and heathen feasts (21) must inevitably **arouse the Lord's jealousy.** This phrase is reminiscent of Dt. 32: 21, referred to in v. 20. **the Lord:** Almost certainly a reference to Christ, to preserve the continuity of thought from the previous verse—another instance of the freedom with which the apostle applies to the Lord Jesus OT references to Jehovah; cf. 1: 31; 2: 16. **Are we stronger than he?:** Israel could not stand before the might of Jehovah (6–10). The Corinthians have still to learn their essential weakness; cf. v. 12.

(e) **Practical guidance (10: 23–11: 1)**
Paul brings together the threads of his arguments on the subject of eating meat offered to idols. Three canons of conduct emerge, each applicable to differing circumstances. (i) Eating at heathen festivals involves idolatry and is unconditionally condemned (14–22). (ii) Eating whatever is sold in the market, regardless of its origin, is unreservedly permitted (25). (iii) Eating in a pagan friend's house is similarly sanctioned, except when the sacrificial origin of the meat is pointed out. This conditional prohibition is not on the grounds of involvement in idolatry, but merely out of consideration for the informant (27–29). The controlling motive is twofold; a desire for the glory of God, and the blessing of men (31–33).

23. 'Everything is permissible': See 6: 12 note. **not everything is constructive:** Recalls the basic principle enunciated at the commencement of this section; cf. 8: 1. **24. the good of others:** Recalls the command of Christ; cf. Mt. 22: 39; Lk. 10: 27–37. It is the fundamental guide for social conduct in both the OT and NT. **25–27** are directed against overscrupulousness. When shopping in the **meat market,** or eating in the home of **some unbeliever,** no question should be asked. **For 'the earth is the Lord's . . .':** A quotation from Ps. 24: 1 and Paul's justification for the advice just given, agreeing with our Lord's pronouncement in Mk 7: 14–19; cf. Ac. 10: 15; 1 Tim. 4: 4. **28. But if anyone:** Possibly the heathen host, but more probably a fellow-guest —a weaker brother, as it is his conscience which is the more likely to suffer. The inform- ant uses the regular pagan word for **offered in sacrifice** (*hierothyton*), either out of respect for the host, or as one recently converted, who still thinks in terms of his old life.

28, 29. do not eat it . . . for conscience sake — the other man's conscience I mean, not yours: Exemplifies the principle of v. 24. Vv. 29b and 30 seem to be out of sympathy with Paul's preceding statement. To avoid this RSV has placed vv. 28, 29a in brackets, making 29b refer to v. 27. Little is gained by such a reconstruction. The meaning of Paul's state- ment depends on the translation of *hina ti gar*, **For why . . . ?** *hina ti* never means 'by what right' but 'for what purpose'. Accordingly, Findlay translates, For what purpose is my liberty judged by another conscience?' i.e., 'What good end will be served by my eating under these circumstances, and exposing my freedom to the censure of an unsympathetic conscience?' Similarly, the second rhetorical question, **If I take part . . .** (30), is rendered, 'Why incur blame for food for which I give thanks . . . ?' (Robertson and Plummer). In asking these two questions Paul puts himself in the place of the strong brother who must recognize the futility of insisting on his liberty and giving thanks, when his action can only result in offence and denunciation by the weaker brother. NEB and Phillips treat the two questions as objections raised by the strong Christian, the answer to these objections being supplied in vv. 31 ff. Undoubtedly, Rom. 14: 16 is the key to the correct understanding of these verses. **with thankfulness:** Literally, by grace. If the AV and RV reading is followed, it suggests that the strong partake only by the enabling grace of God. Modern versions follow the NIV and RSV. Both translations are legitimate and make good sense. **31. the glory of God:** The overriding consideration. This extends be- yond the immediate subject to **whatever you do**; cf. 6: 20. **32. Do not cause anyone to stumble:** Literally, cause of stumbling; cf. 8: 9. It summarizes Paul's attitude to unconverted Jews and Greeks; cf. 9: 19–22. **the church of God:** The sing. noun may refer to those in the local congregation at Corinth (1: 2), but is probably used in its widest significance, as in 11: 22; 15: 9. **33. to please everybody:** Not to be understood as currying favour (cf. Gal. 1: 10) but in terms of his sympathetic under- standing of others' needs as in 9: 19–22, with the consequent abandoning of his own rights and privileges, i.e., **not seeking my own good. 11: 1. Follow my example:** In that attitude of self-sacrifice for the salvation of others (10: 33) which characterized Paul and Christ. **my example:** Cf. 4: 16; Phil. 3: 17; 1

Th. 1: 6. **example of Christ:** The supreme example; cf. Rom. 15: 2, 3; 2 C. 8: 7–9; Eph. 5: 2; Phil. 2: 4–7.

V. DISORDERS IN PUBLIC WORSHIP (11: 2–34)
i. Veiling of women (11: 2–16)

Paul now deals with the subject of public worship. The first matter requiring attention, that of the veiling of women, reflects a situation commonly misunderstood in western culture. Underlying Paul's reasoning is the principle of subjection. Woman's subjection to man is understood not in the sense of inequality, or inferiority, but in terms of Christ's relation to God. This position of subjection was expressed by the veil and the long hair worn by women; a custom consistently followed in much of Asia and the Middle East from the dawn of history to the present day. To break with such a con- vention is deemed **a disgrace**, being a revolt against the dictates of nature and accepted con- duct. The problem which exists for those who seek to interpret the text lies in determining to what extent the apostle is teaching conformity with local concepts of subordination and pro- priety and the degree to which Christians today should conform to the letter of these instruc- tions. One thing is certain; within the context of our contemporary culture, the modern west- ern hat—decorative, attractive and often ob- structive—cannot be said to compare with the veil, either in appearance, function, or purpose. At best it is a token veil. Its significance when taught in the church is valuable, but in common thought the hat is no longer the local means of expressing subordination. To what extent must local churches modify their traditional modes of worship in the light of a changing culture? Western culture has no readily recognisable means of expressing woman's subordination, having largely abandoned the concept. Although this particular symbol has lost its meaning, the truth of a woman's divinely ap- pointed status need by no means be lost; it finds its natural and proper place in the normal course of biblical exposition. Truth is not dependent on cultural forms.

2. I praise you: There is no contradiction with v. 17. In general, the traditions—the de- livered instructions (cf. 11: 23; 15: 3; 2 Th. 2: 15; 3: 6)—had been faithfully kept. That they wrote to Paul concerning their problems indi- cates their desire to conform with his instruc- tions. **3. head:** Symbolic of authority, su- premacy. **man:** Male, not mankind. **the head of every man is Christ:** Cf. Eph. 1: 22; 4: 15; 5: 21–33; Col. 1: 18; 2: 19. **the head of the woman is man:** Cf. Col. 3: 18; 1 Pet. 3: 1. **the head of Christ is God:** Cf. Jn 14: 28; 1 C. 3: 23; 15: 27, 28. These three statements express partnership as clearly as subordination (cf. v.

11). NEB legitimately translates, 'While every man has Christ for his Head, woman's head is man as Christ's Head is God.' It is subordination among partners; man is to woman as God is to Christ, but not as Christ is to man. **4. with his head covered:** In corporate worship the male has no visible superior. Therefore a head covering would be improper. It is not suggested that men were acting in this way; the statement gives point to the censure on women who were acting like men. **dishonors his head:** Almost certainly a reference to his own physical head, but an allusion to Christ cannot altogether be excluded. The uncovered head was contrary to Jewish custom, although, in fact, it was an optional matter at the time. For Paul, the head covering of the Jewish male possibly symbolized his continuance in spiritual darkness from which the Christian had been liberated. Now in worship he need not be veiled (the woman remains veiled only as a sign of her subordination to man). Logically therefore, a Jew or Muslim attending Christian worship should not be required to remove his headwear for 'the veil remains unlifted' (2 C. 3: 13 f.). **prophesies:** Cf. 12: 10. **5. every woman who prays or prophesies . . . :** Suggests that women took part in public worship in Corinth. Paul makes no comment concerning the practice; he is dealing with the veil, not the ministry of women (cf. 14: 34; 1 Tim. 2: 12). There is nothing in the text to indicate that they took part only in informal meetings, in sisters' meetings, or in family prayers and not in the general meetings of the church. Feeling the compulsion to pray or prophesy, the women would find it easier to take part without the encumbrance of a veil and might be tempted to throw it aside. **dishonors her head:** Either shames her own head, or dishonours her husband. In either case she abandons that expression of subjection which contemporary custom demands of her. Ordinarily, in any public place a woman was veiled. In an immoral society like Corinth any act of impropriety must be sternly checked. **shaved:** Literally, *the* shaven. The def. art. denotes the class to which such a woman would belong. This may refer to her putting herself in the same category as a male, or, as David Smith renders it, being 'the same thing as the shaved adulteress'. **6. she should have her hair cut off** (middle voice): If she discards her veil like a man, she should crop her head like one too! Paul makes his point in the strongest terms. **7. man ought not** (*ouk opheilei*) **to cover his head:** He is under moral obligation to be bare-headed, as is the woman to be veiled (*opheilei*, v. 10). **glory:** Man as the crown of God's creation honours and magnifies Him (cf. Ps. 8: 5, 6; Gen. 1: 26, 28). In the OT the reference is to

mankind, i.e., men and women (Heb. '*adam*, Gk *anthrōpos*), that is, the crown of God's creation. Here, Paul using *anēr* refers only to the male, not with the intention of degrading the woman, but with the purpose of defining her relationship to man—she is **the glory of man.** This he further clarifies in vv. 8 and 9. **woman is the glory of man:** Being formed from him (cf. v. 8; Gen. 2: 22, 23). **9.** vv. 8 and 9 are parenthetical, as indicated by RSV. The creation of **woman for man** is clearly stated in Gen. 2: 18. God's purpose, not only in Christ (3), and social custom (5b, 6), but also in creation itself is to give woman a position of subjection.

10 presents two major problems of translation and interpretation: (i) the meaning of 'veil'. The word here is *exousia*, authority. While the context might suggest that this be interpreted as 'a sign of being under authority', i.e., 'a veil', the word itself suggests that it is rather 'a sign of her own authority'. A study of life among veiled women in Asia reveals that both aspects of the word are true and that in experience no contradiction exists.

The concept fundamental to all cultures utilizing the veil, is the subjection of woman to man.

Yet within the realm of subjection, the woman has a place of authority, dignity, respect and security. This is provided by the veil itself which preserves her dignity in contrast to the unveiled woman whose bare face is the evidence of loose morals, or the general shamelessness of western habits. Many Muslim women confess to a feeling of utter nakedness and shame on being seen without a veil; the veil is their greatest right and security. Paul argues from a somewhat similar background. For a Corinthian woman to throw off her veil in church was not only to deny her subjection, but to abandon her dignity. (ii) **because of the angels:** A phrase variously interpreted—(*a*) that the angels are present in worship and will observe their conduct and be offended. That they do observe human conduct, see Lk. 15: 7, 10. (*b*) because they might tempt the angels (cf. Gen. 6: 1, 2). (*c*) because the angels do so, i.e. veil themselves, as in Isa. 6: 2. This is an attractive interpretation. **11, 12** are parenthetical, but preserve the balance of Paul's argument, proving that woman is not inferior to man. Throughout, the apostle is reasoning not on the basis of her inferiority, but of her partnership with man. Neither is **independent** of the other and as Christians—**in the Lord**—this relationship is enhanced. In Christ the submissive wife is not despicable. **everything comes from God:** Woman was made from man, but now he is born of her—and God makes both. **13, 14. Judge for yourselves:** A final appeal based on humanity's sense of propriety instilled by **the nature of things. is**

it proper: Ie., becoming, natural. **long hair . . . is a disgrace to him:** Paul argues within the limits of his location and period. Differing cultures have had differing concepts as to what is fitting, but as a generalization the statement is still true. Most men, whether eastern or western, wear their hair short in contrast to their womenfolk. **15. if a woman has long hair, it is her glory:** Still true in general. Asian women usually regard the length of their hair with pride. Even within a western culture a woman's hair is usually kept longer than a man's. Yet the limitation too of such generalizations must be recognized. The average African woman is singularly bereft of this source of pride; this is neither the physical nor cultural pattern by which she can demonstrate, through this natural **covering**, the principle of subjection.

16. we have no other practice: Adds finality to the argument. Any deviation from the apostle's ruling could only be interpreted as an exhibition of brazen disregard for the accepted codes of conduct by the women of his day. The principle endures; women should show clearly their subjection. The means of expression will vary according to the race and culture in which the church is planted.

ii. The Lord's Supper (11: 17–34)
(a) **Its abuse (11: 17–22)**
However well the traditions had been maintained in other aspects of their corporate life, their assembling as a church for the Lord's Supper had been sadly marred by their deepseated factions which revealed themselves in the formation of cliques or parties. The fellowship meal, itself designed to be a demonstration of unity in Christ (10: 16, 17), degenerated into an unholy free-for-all, in which the memory of their Lord became blurred beyond all recollection before the poverty of one and the gluttony of another. The prosperous ignored the poor; the practice of fellowship was forgotten. Such humiliation of the needy could only increase their divisions, while their despicable disregard for the church of God inevitably earned divine retribution. The love feast was dead.

17. I have no praise for you: In v. 2 they could be praised, but here where basic Christian instincts should have sufficed, Paul could not commend. **your meetings:** Literally, 'when you come together'. Their corporate worship is marred. The verb is used three times; see vv. 18, 20. **do more harm:** Defined in vv. 18–21 by the terms **divisions, differences, each of you goes ahead**, etc.: the very antithesis of corporate fellowship. **18. there are divisions** (*schismata*): They had developed (see 1: 10–13) far beyond cliques confined to private homes, a mere undercurrent of unrest. The church was visibly rent (21). Note Robertson and Plum-

mer's rendering, 'I continually hear (present tense) that dissensions among you prevail' (*hyparchein*, not simply the verb 'to be'). **19. there have to be** (*dei*): '*dei* affirms a necessity lying in the moral conditions of the case' (Findlay). Corinth being what it was, Paul acknowledges the inevitability of this. See NEB. **differences** (*haireseis*): Basically, a wilful choosing of one's own line independent of other authorities; cf. Tit. 3: 10. *hairesis* differs little from *schisma*, but perhaps signifies the attitude of mind which produces it. The self-willed by their **differences** reveal those who are **genuine** (*dokimoi*) —those who have been tried and have stood the test). Compare *adokimos*, 9: 27—'disqualified.' **20. not the Lord's supper:** Rather, their own. The disorders make it a travesty of the true. **21. each of you goes ahead . . . :** Indicates clearly that an actual meal was envisaged. The early church observed this practice of the common meal, known as the *agapē*, or 'love-feast'; cf. 2 Pet. 2: 13, RSVmg; Jude 12. **One remains hungry, another gets drunk:** The division of poor and rich. There was no sharing of food, contrary to the custom of the common meal. **drunk:** Must be given its usual meaning of intoxication; cf. Mt. 24: 49; Jn 2: 10; Ac. 2: 15; 1 Th. 5: 7. **22. Don't you have homes . . . ?:** i.e., if the purposes of the love-feast are abandoned—the expression of mutual love through the shared out food, culminating in the remembrance of Christ's great act of love—then it is better to eat at home.

(b) **Its institution (11: 23–26)**
In marked contrast to the deplorable display of personal greed and humiliation at the common meal, Paul reminds his readers of the solemn simplicity with which the Lord Jesus had ordained this act of remembrance. This record is the earliest extant written account of our Lord's institution of the ordinance.

23. I received from the Lord . . . I . . . passed . . . : A direct revelation to Paul is not implied. The two verbs *paralambanō* and *paradidōmi* are not words used for receiving and communicating a direct revelation, but for transmission in a chain from one to another. The tradition stems from the words of Jesus Christ himself in the upper room; that is what is meant by **from the Lord.** Leon Morris seeks to demonstrate the possibility of a direct revelation from the use of the preposition *apo* (**from**), citing Col. 1: 7; 3: 24 and 1 Jn 1: 5. It is, however, the particular verbs used, rather than the preposition, which determine the interpretation. There was no need for a supernatural communication; the facts were readily available to Paul. More important, Paul had already **passed on** this communication to the Corinthians. They had no excuse. **24. given thanks:** Used by Luke, while Matthew and Mark have 'blessed'. Both words refer to the same prayer of thanksgiving. **'This is my body'** has become the main support for Roman and Lutheran views of transubstantiation and consubstantiation, views rendered vulnerable by the fact that the Supper preceded the Passion. Christ himself was physically present. His words were symbolical and a similar usage of **is** may be found in Jn 8: 12; 10:9,etc. See the note on Mt.26:26. **Do this:** A present imperative conveying the idea of continuity. Just as the Passover had been a memorial of Israel's deliverance from Egypt, so the Supper is to be an act of remembrance. 25. **the new covenant** (*hē kainē diathēkē*): Found only once in the LXX in Jer. 31: 31; Christ probably had this reference in mind. While *diathēkē* is used regularly in Greek for a will (cf. Heb. 9: 15–18, RSV), LXX uses it consistently for 'covenant.' The choice of *diathēkē* rather than *synthēkē* is significant. The latter is a covenant in which the parties contract on equal terms, whereas in the former one party only lays down all the conditions (hence its use also for a will). This is the relation between God and man. There is no **new covenant** without the **blood**. Hebrews expounds the association; cf. Heb. 9 and 10. (Consult the exposition of Heb. 9: 15 ff. for a fuller treatment of the subject.) **my:** Emphatic. 26. **Whenever:** Gives no directive as to how often, though a frequent remembrance is implied. In Ac. 20: 7 it was arranged for Sunday evening. The first day of the week may well have been the convenient and regular time for its observance. **you proclaim** (pres. indic.): The breaking of bread is a continual proclamation of the Lord's death; not an act of mourning, but an occasion of living hope **until he comes.**

(c) **Warnings and instructions (11: 27–34)**
The apostle warns his readers. While the Supper may be a fitting climax to the spiritual fellowship of the *agapē*, it is not to be the culmination of a carousal. Neither may its celebration be marred by divisions, whether expressed in the contempt of the rich for the poor, or in party spirit. **whenever** may be too often for the man or woman who with that contempt born of undue familiarity ceases to **examine** his own spiritual condition.

Such conduct can only court **judgment** and to some in Corinth retribution has already come.

Sober self-examination preserves from condemnation.

27. **an unworthy manner:** Caused through the lack of love, factious spirit, greed and contempt which Paul has been rebuking so strongly. **guilty of sinning against . . . :** The guilt is not primarily against fellow-believers, great as that is, but against the person of Christ symbolized in the elements (cf. Ps. 51: 4). 28. **examine:** i.e., let a man test himself. It calls

for a minute scrutiny of heart and motives to ascertain one's moral and spiritual condition before partaking. Note its usage in 2 C. 13: 5; Gal. 6: 4. 29. **without recognizing the body: the body** is held by some commentators to refer to the church (so also Moffatt and NEB). Others understand it in terms of the Lord's Supper as in v. 27. Both interpretations make good sense. **of the Lord**, added in NIV, is not the Greek text. *diakrinein* (to discern or **recognize**) is rendered **judged** rightly, in v. 31. It seems to carry this basic idea in v. 29. One who judges rightly will distinguish, discriminate. Therefore, depending on the significance given to **the body**, one who participates without due self-examination does not distinguish between the Lord's Supper (the body) and an ordinary meal, or alternatively, does not discern the true character of the Body, the Church. **judgment:** Not final condemnation (cf. v. 32), but a very definite punishment according to the measure of guilt (30). 30. **That is why . . . :** A direct connection exists between their sickness and death, and the judgment of the previous verse. 31. **if we judged ourselves truly:** An unfulfilled condition. The verb is used almost synonymously with **examine** in v. 28. Absence of self judgment necessitates divine judgment. **ourselves:** Emphatic. 32. **we are being disciplined:** Implies discipline for the purpose of improvement. God's judgment of His children is remedial (cf. Ps. 94: 12; Prov. 3: 11, 12; Heb. 12: 5–11; see also 1 C. 5: 3–5), even though it involves sickness and death. **the world** (*kosmos*): Here, all that is at enmity with God, destined to be condemned; cf. 1 Jn 5: 19. 33, 34. The practical remedy lies with them. **wait for each other:** Satisfy your hunger **at home:** these are correctives to vv. 21, 22, which, together with the self-examination already demanded, will create a proper atmosphere for the Lord's Supper. **further directions:** probably in connection with questions from the Corinthians' letter which were still outstanding, in addition to less important details concerning love-feasts and the remembrance service.

VI. SPIRITUAL GIFTS (12: 1–14: 40)
The background of rivalry, envy and division in Corinth must be constantly borne in mind. In conditions where the base qualities of party spirit were apparent, where moral standards were disregarded, where women emulated men and the rich despised the poor, the apostle could write, **you do not lack any spiritual gift** (1: 7). In this also their rivalry and envy were evident. The possession of spiritual gifts and the attainment of moral stature were not yet related in experience. To remedy this inconsistency is Paul's main purpose in these three

chapters. In chapters 12 and 13 he lays down the general principles involved—the place of gifts and the power of love—while in chapter 14 he deals with specific details.

i. Varieties of gifts (12: 1–11)

Moving forward from his introductory statement that genuine expressions of spiritual gifts may be discerned by the loyalty of the utterance to Jesus Christ (1–3), the apostle establishes that the gifts in all their variety emanate from the one **Spirit of God.** He overrules, and in granting these experiences individually to whomsoever He wishes, removes the ground for envying and aping another's experience.

1. Now about: Probably another matter raised in the Corinthians' letter; cf. 7: 1, 25; 8: 1; 16: 1. **I do not want you to be ignorant:** A phrase regularly introducing an important subject in Paul's writings; cf. 10: 1; Rom. 1: 13; 11: 25; 2 C. 1: 8; 1 Th. 4: 13. **2. led astray** (*apagomenoi*): Has the sense of leading away by force; cf. Mt. 26: 57; 27: 2, 31. The agent is not specified. As with **somehow or other you were influenced,** the suggestion is that of the domination of the power of evil. **3.** In sharp contrast to v. 2, the motivating influence here is the **Spirit of God. 'Jesus be cursed!'** (*anathema*): The word itself was the equivalent of the Hebrew *ḥerem*, signifying anything that was devoted to God for destruction as under His curse (as Achan in Joshua's camp). The expression would most likely come from a Jew and in all probability had been frequently used by Paul himself in his unregenerate state (cf. 1 Tim. 1: 13). Possibly, he and other Jews had sought to give scriptural authority to these words by appealing to Dt. 21: 23. The blasphemy he tried to make believers utter (Ac. 26: 11) may have been 'Jesus is anathema'. It is not necessary to assume that someone at Corinth in ecstatic utterance had spoken these words, although the matter is put forward so specifically that this might well have occurred. In either case, Paul is assuring the believers that the controlling **Spirit** will not lead men into blasphemy. Similarly, **'Jesus is Lord'** is a real confession, clearly distinguishing the Christian from the Jews and pagans around him. As a confession this is frequently used in the NT; cf. Rom. 10: 9; 2 C. 4: 5; Phil. 2: 11. **4. different kinds** (*diaireseis*): Occurs nowhere else in the NT. Here it is possibly used in the sense of apportionings, or distributions, as suggested by the use of the verb in v. 11. In the LXX it is regularly used for the 'courses' of the priests. **gifts** (*charismata*): A typically Pauline word (used only once by any other NT writer, 1 Pet. 4: 10), signifying special endowments of the Spirit to men. A 'grace-gift', it is taken from the same root as *charis*—grace. For a full discussion, see Sanday and Headlam, *Romans, ICC,* pp. 358 f. **5. service** (*diakonia*): The use

of the gift. The word, cognate with *diakonos*, 'servant', is used frequently of the work of the apostles and other believers; cf. Eph. 4: 12; Rom. 11: 13; Col. 4: 17; 2 C 4: 1; Rom. 15: 31; 1 C. 16: 15. Note the strong trinitarian emphasis in connection with the distribution of spiritual gifts in the church: **the same Spirit** (4) . . . **Lord** (5) . . . **God** (6). Distinctions between the functions of the Godhead, in **gifts, service** and **working,** must not be pressed. Just as these are complementary ideas expressing one complete experience, so **Spirit, Lord** and **God** emphasize unity of function; cf. 2 C. 13: 14; Eph. 4: 3–6.

6. working (*energēmatōn*): The energizing of the gift, it conveys the idea of power, cf. v. 10. **7. To each:** Spiritual gifts are not to the select few. **the manifestation of the Spirit:** May mean, 'that which the Spirit makes manifest', or 'that which manifests the Spirit' (as NEB), depending on whether the genitive is taken as objective or subjective. Both refer to the spiritual gift; one as producing it, the other revealing Him through it. The **common good** is in view, not the advantage or self-glorification of the gifted individual. Vv. 8–11 enumerate the gifts for the **common good. 8. message of wisdom:** Not easily distinguished from **message of knowledge.** While the latter indicates an intelligent grasp of Christian principles and facts, the former expresses an understanding of their application, a spiritual insight into the principles. **9. to another faith:** Not a reference to saving faith possessed by all Christians, but to the special gift of 'mountain-moving' faith that defies the 'impossible'; cf. 13:2; Mt. 17:20; 21: 21. As in one sense all have knowledge (8: 1), so all have faith, but not of the order of *charismata*. **gifts of healing:** Frequently evident in the NT period and used by Paul himself; cf. Ac. 19: 11, 12; 20: 9–12. Both nouns are plural, suggesting possibly gifts for a variety of healings demanded by different diseases. **10. miraculous powers:** See note on **working** (6). Accordingly, **miracles** were most evidently acts of power. Such instances are recorded in Ac. 5: 1–11; 13: 11.

prophecy: Primarily not foretelling, but telling forth the Word of God with power to meet a specific need (cf. 14: 1; Rom. 12: 6; 1 Th. 5: 20; 1 Tim. 1: 18; 4: 14). This was the function of both OT and NT prophets. However, the element of prediction must not be excluded.

to distinguish between spirits: An attitude demanded of all believers (1 Th. 5: 20, 21; 1 Jn 4: 1), but a gift granted only to some. **different kinds of tongues** and **the interpretation of tongues:** These come at the end of Paul's list although their use was probably the most prized in the Corinthian church. As one of the *charismata* the gift of tongues was supernatural and therefore does not refer to human languages, which could be learned and interpreted without divine aid, but rather to an ecstatic experience granted to some, not all.

This is a miraculous spiritual language for communion with God. The plural **kinds** points to considerable variation within this experience. While some speakers could also interpret (14: 5, 13), to others it was a separate gift (14: 27, 28). The subject is also dealt with in chapter 14. **11. one and the same Spirit:** Responsible for all these gifts. Paul's constant repetition in vv. 4, 5, 6, 8, 9 of their single divine source suggests that their attainment should not be the subject of rivalry or jealousy, for the divine distribution is **as he determines**, Note that the personality of the Spirit is implied here.

ii. Unity in diversity (12: 12–31)
Just as the gifts are many, but the Giver one, so the recipients, varied and dissimilar in quality and function, form one organic whole. This Paul states briefly (12, 13), and demonstrates through the illustration of the human body (14–26). The apostle argues (i) no one can opt out of the body on the ground of dissatisfaction, or jealousy for a 'higher' gift. The body's constitution demands their God-given function (14–20), (ii) there is mutual dependence throughout the body (21, 22), (iii) there must be mutual respect and care. Sympathetic understanding produces true harmony (23–26). The remaining verses (27–31) apply the illustration to the church, the varieties of gift being restated, with a series of rhetorical questions indicating the chaotic condition which would result from all the believers exercising the same gift. Unity in diversity creates a balanced body. This analogy is used frequently by the apostle (cf. Rom. 12: 4, 5; Eph. 4: 16;5: 30; Col. 2: 19).

12. so it is with Christ: As in the human body, members of Christ are indissolubly associated with Him. They are a new creation (2 C. 5: 17; Eph. 4: 22–24), His life is theirs (Gal. 2: 20), they constitute His body (Eph. 1: 23). The same truth was taught by Christ in the figure of the vine (Jn 15: 1–8). **13. for we were all baptized by one Spirit . . . : by** (*en*) is rendered in the RV and NEB as 'in', indicating the sphere in which baptism takes place (the same prep. *en* is similarly used in Mt. 3: 11 and is translated 'with water' and 'with the Holy Spirit', i.e., they are to be immersed in the Spirit as in water). **baptized:** May refer not to the rite, but to the act of regeneration in the Spirit to which the ordinance bears witness. **given the one Spirit to drink:** A parallel statement, in purely figurative language, symbolic of the indwelling of the Spirit at the new birth; cf. 3: 16; Eph. 1: 13. **to drink:** Conveys the idea of being saturated or imbued with one Spirit; an 'irrigation' of one's inner life by the Spirit of God. **all:** Constantly contrasted with

one; the extreme diversity of background, character and gift at Corinth find absolute unity in the Church—the body. **14.** In the body diversity is not a problem to be overcome, but is essential for its existence. **15, 16.** The **foot** envying the **hand** and the **ear** the **eye**, probably reflect the condition of the weaker members in the Corinthian church envying the apparently higher and more responsible members with their spectacular gifts. **17.** A **body** all **eye** or **ear** not only eliminates other necessary functions, but ceases to be a body: the conclusion arrived at in v. 19. **18. God arranged the parts in the body . . . as he wanted them to be:** The aorists are preserved in RSV and NIV, pointing to God's design of the human frame in creation. The believer's particular function in the church is the result of divine planning. Discontent can only result in deformity. **each one:** No believer, however lowly, lacks a God-given gift. **21. 'I don't need you':** The attitude of those possessing the apparently superior or more spectacular gifts, in contrast to the lowly members of vv. 15–20. The **head** cannot afford to look down on the **feet**, for without them she is rapidly reduced to the same lowly level; the body crippled. Independence cannot exist in the body of Christ. **22. parts . . . that seem to be weaker:** Only **seem to be** so. Their intrinsic worth, purely as part of the body, makes them **indispensable.** This applies with even greater force to **that we think** in v. 23. These members are not specified and indeed would vary in different cultures. **23. we treat with special honor:** Probably refers to clothing, with which parts considered **less honorable** and **unpresentable** were covered. The verb **treat** is used of clothing in Mt. 27: 28. **24. presentable:** Literally, wellformed, not needing the adornment of clothes. **God has has combined the members of the body:** His sovereign choice (18) is matched by His tender care, an attitude to be emulated in Corinth. **25. so that:** Introduces a *hina* clause denoting the purpose for which God has balanced the body, giving **greater honor to the parts that lacked it.** It is to eliminate **discord** and to inculcate mutual **care:** the two great needs of the believers in Corinth. **division** (*schisma*): Immediately recalls the primary problem broached in 1: 10 (see also 11: 18). A humble acceptance of God's appointments in the body (27–31) will restore harmony. **equal concern for each other:** Might be rendered more strongly 'anxiety', 'thoughtful trouble'. **26** expresses an organic necessity. Pain cannot be isolated; sensations transmitted to the brain affect in measure the whole being. Whether expressed in terms of suffering or rejoicing, this is the Christian law of sympathy—to 'feel with' another. **27. you are the body of Christ: you** is emphatic. The divided Corinthians in spite of their shortcomings are undeniably 'Christ's body' (NEB), for they were 'all baptized into' it (13), and **each one of you is a part of it**. The objective now is a balanced body (28–31) and its attainment depends on their individual response to the Spirit's choice for them (11). **28. God has appointed:** Note the divine sovereignty (18, 24). The verb is middle, indicating His own purpose. **the church:** Clearly the Church Universal. **first . . . second . . . third:** The ranking of gifts in order of honour, an order maintained in Eph. 4: 11; see also Rom. 12: 6–8; Eph. 2: 20; 3: 5. **apostles:** Not restricted to the Twelve, but including Barnabas, James the Lord's brother (Gal. 1: 19), Paul and lesser known figures (Rom. 16: 7); cf. 1 C. 15: 5, 7 indicating a wider group than the Twelve. While **prophets** and **teachers** were not necessarily apostles, apostles were both prophets and teachers, cf. 4: 17; 14: 6; Col. 1: 28; 1 Tim. 1: 11. **teachers:** Closely linked with pastors (Eph. 4: 11) and would bear considerable responsibility on the local level for building up the church through the exposition of the Word of God. **workers of miracles . . . those having gifts of healing:** See note on vv. 9, 10. **those able to help others:** The noun is found nowhere else in the NT, but occurrences of the verb (Ac. 20: 35; Rom. 8: 26) suggest helping particularly the weak and needy. Deacons may also have had a part in this responsibility. **those with the gift of administration:** Derived from the idea of piloting a boat. Steersmanship in the local church was a gift demanded of elders. Note that these verses deal with gifts, not offices. The officer in the church officiated by reason of his gifts. **tongues:** See v. 10 and chapter 14. **29, 30** enforce the argument in typically Pauline style, stressing the necessity for diversity. All the questions demand negative replies. **31. eagerly desire the greater gifts:** Not in the evil sense of the verb ('envy', 13: 4). This they had done (cf. 3: 3). Rather, they were to desire the higher gifts from higher motives, being anxiously careful for one another (25). **the most excellent way:** Either the way in which to seek the higher gifts—through the controlling influence of love—or love viewed as an end in itself, surpassing all *charismata*, which invests life with a moral quality without which spiritual gifts in themselves become objects for dissension.

13: 1–3 and 14: 1 underline this latter view. **iii. The supremacy of love (13: 1–13)** It is hardly correct to refer to this chapter as a digression, providing as it does that cardinal Christian quality without which all the *charismata* are worthless. Moreover, the theme of 'gifts' as it is continued in chapter 14 proceeds to unravel its many practical problems under the all prevailing plea, **Make love your aim.** It is the essential link between the principle

expounded in chapter 12 and the practice explained in chapter 14.

Love is a specifically Christian revelation. The Greek language with all its richness, incapable of expressing this deep reality, provided an obscure word to be invested with an entirely new connotation by the NT writers. While Greeks praise wisdom and Romans power, Paul pens a psalm in praise of love which stands alone, bypassed or ignored in a world of hate.

The three paragraphs of this chapter are its natural divisions: (i) the absence of love can be compensated by no other quality however spectacular, be it spiritual gifts or religious zeal (1–3), (ii) its characteristics, reminiscent of the character of Christ and the fruit of the Spirit (4–7), demand (iii) an eternal continuance when the earth-bound qualities of the church have forever ceased (8–13).

The apostle's sensitivity to the nature of love is perhaps most adequately perceived when, by the substitution of the name of Jesus for love, a simple, yet perfect picture of the incarnate Christ stands out.

1. tongues of men and of angels: While including the gift of tongues (12: 30), it extends beyond this to include all ecstatic utterance, in languages known and unknown, earthly or heavenly. None can compensate for a lack of love. **love** (*agapē*): Found in LXX, Philo, and other Jewish Greek literature, but thus far attested only once unambiguously in pagan Greek. In classical Greek its verbal and adjectival forms are used of contentment or affection, but to the exclusion of all sense of sexual passion (although both noun and verb are capable of such a meaning in LXX, *e.g.* 2 Sam. 13: 15).

Taken up and invested in NT Greek with a new meaning and spiritual fervour it gained an exclusively Christian connotation. **resounding gong** (literally, copper or bronze) is preferable to trumpet as suggested by some commentators (as Phillips). The **gong** and **cymbal** were associated with pagan worship. **2. gift of prophecy . . . all mysteries . . . all knowledge:** Paul moves from the ecstatic gifts to those of instruction. **mysteries:** The revelation of God's deep purposes by the Spirit; cf. Mt. 13: 11; Eph. 3: 3 ff. **knowledge:** Cf. 12: 8. **faith:** As in 12: 9. **that can move mountains:** A common proverbial phrase used of great difficulties; cf. Mk 11: 22, 23. **3. give all . . . :** Literally, to feed with small mouthfuls. The verb is aorist; in one act all is given away, doled out to the poor. **surrender my body to the flames:** The ultimate self-sacrifice in a most painful form.

There may be an echo here of Dan. 3: 28, or possibly a reference to an Indian who burned himself alive in Athens (Lightfoot). Such burn-ings are not uncommon in pagan religion today. Westcott and Hort argue strongly for the variant 'that I may glory' (see NIV and RSV footnotes) which only differs by one letter in the Greek. However, most commentators support the NIV reading.

Paul has cited all four classes of spiritual gifts: the ecstatic (tongues), the instructive (prophecy), the wonder-working (faith), the helps (giving). Without love three results ensue: I convey nothing (1), **I am nothing** (2), **I gain nothing** (3). **4. Patient and kind:** Cf. 2 C. 6: 6; Gal. 5: 22; Col. 3: 12. **patient** (*makrothymeō*): Not a limp, unresisting acquiescence, rather patient perseverance in the face of injury received. It is a divine quality; cf. Rom. 2: 4; 1 Pet. 3: 20; 2 Pet. 3: 9; 1 Tim. 1: 16. **kind:** The active complement of patience. **does not envy** (*zēloō*): Here used in its bad sense in contrast to 12: 31, 'earnestly desire'; cf. Ac. 7: 9; 17: 5; Jas 4: 2. **does not boast:** Nowhere else in the NT, but used by later Greek writers for intellectual pride and rhetorical display—a Corinthian failing. **5. not rude:** Used in 7: 36 and seems to suggest unseemly or unmannerly conduct, such as the behaviour of the women in 11: 5, 6, or the rich at the Lord's Supper in 11: 21. **is not self-seeking:** Cf. 10: 24, 33. The principle applies to lawsuits in 6: 1 ff. **not easily angered:** 'not quick to take offence' (NEB). In Ac. 15: 39 the noun is rendered 'sharp contention'. **keeps no record of wrongs:** Love does not bear a grudge. Literally, 'does not reckon up', a word from accountancy. See NEB and Phillips. Cf. Rom. 4: 8; 2 C. 5: 19; 2 Tim. 4: 16. **6. evil:** i.e., others' wrong-doing; cf. Rom. 1: 32; 2 Th. 2: 12. **rejoices with the truth:** Literally, 'with the truth'. Love and truth unite to rejoice in its triumph over wrong; cf. 2 C. 13: 7, 8; Jas 3: 14. Christ is the truth (Jn 14: 6); the Spirit also (1 Jn 5: 7). **7. It always protects** (*stegō*): From the basic meaning, to cover, or roof over, two usages emerge, (i) to protect that which is covered and in so doing (ii) to bear or endure what descends upon it. The latter meaning is the more usual as in 9: 12; 1 Th. 3: 1, 5. **always trusts:** While love learns spiritual discernment, it maintains its faith in others. Far better to be deceived in a doubtful case and suffer hurt, than as a sceptic to hurt another who should have been believed. In this spirit it **hopes** looking for the ultimate triumph of truth and **persevered**, steadfast in all things; cf. Rom. 8: 25; 2 Tim. 2: 10. Endurance is more active than patience. **8. prophecies . . . tongues . . . knowledge . . . will pass away:** The contrast is with unending love. These three principal gifts are taken as illustrative of all the *charismata* which are purely temporary and transitory, given for building up the body of Christ (Eph. 4: 11–16), a process to be completed at the consummation **when**

perfection comes (10). In God's immediate presence, prophets, ecstatic speech and limited understanding are alike rendered redundant. Note the force of *katargēthēsontai*, 'will pass away'—to render useless, inoperative (cf. 1: 28 note). **9. imperfect:** Present **knowledge** and **prophecy** are only 'fragmentary'. **10. when perfection comes:** Anticipates the Parousia, the culmination of this age. To suggest that perfection refers to the completion of the Canon of Scripture fails to find any support in the biblical usage of 'perfect', or in any of its cognate forms. Such an interpretation exists only by virtue of the need to explain the absence of certain *charismata* in many churches today. **11, 12** are an illustration of the ultimate condition of **perfection** (*to teleion*) in contrast to the present **imperfect**. The tenses employed give force to the illustration; three imperfects **—talked, thought, reasoned**—denoting habitual action in the past, followed by a perfect **—when I became a man** ('now that I am become a man', as in RV, is better), giving the sense of completeness. **put childish ways behind** (*katērgēka*): Is the fourth occurrence of the verb *katargeō* in vv. 8–11, previously rendered by the passive **will pass away**, underlining again the transitory nature of all the gifts, and by implication, the enduring character of love which will crown the final Day. **12. but a poor reflection:** Corinthian mirrors of polished metal were famous, yet at best they reflected a somewhat blurred and distorted image. **dimly:** Literally the phrase means in a riddle, or enigma, and is rendered by Moffatt, 'baffling reflections'. The sense is clear. Our knowledge only fragmentary, our reasoning sometimes faulty, deduces often a distorted image of divine reality. At His coming we shall see and know with an immediacy as yet unknown. **face to face:** Cf. Num. 12: 8; Job 19: 26, 27; 1 Jn 3: 3; Rev. 22: 4. **I know in part; then I shall know fully:** The knowledge common to all believers and not the *charisma* of v. 8, which will pass away. **13. And now:** In its logical rather than temporal sense. **Faith, hope** and **love** in contrast to the transitory gifts **remain**, even at the coming of the Lord. **remain:** The Greek verb is singular, although the subject is plural, indicating the indissoluble unity of these virtues. **the greatest of these is love:** 'Love is the root of the other two; "Love believeth all things, hopeth all things." Faith and hope are purely human; Love is Divine' (Robertson and Plummer).

iv. Prophesying and tongues (14: 1–40)

The apostle now proceeds to apply the principles which he has so clearly laid down. The variety of spiritual gifts within the fundamental oneness of the body of Christ (chapter 12) may be kept in perfect balance only by the exercise of love, in whose light the true value and function of all *charismata* are readily assessed (chapter 13). There are higher gifts, earnestly to be sought (12: 31), not with the greed and envy so characteristic of Corinth, but in the spirit of love. Chapter 14 deals with this discernment. The gift of prophecy is to be desired more than tongues (1–25), yet the exercise of each has its proper place and both must be carefully controlled to avoid abuse (26–33a). Any participation by women in the church must be similarly regulated, that their subordination may be evident (33b–36). In summarizing his instructions, the apostle presents them as divine directives (37–40).

(a) **Prophecy is superior to tongues (14: 1–25)**
The Corinthian believers, carried away by the mysteriousness and extreme ecstasy associated with tongues, gave to this experience an importance in relation to the other *charismata* which was quite out of keeping with its God-given function. While recognizing the place of tongues in personal worship (2), Paul sees the great need of the church for inspired preaching, the prophetic word, through which it may be built up (3, 5). Illustrations strengthen his argument; (i) their own experience of Paul as a teacher (6), (ii) the meaningful sounds of inanimate instruments (7, 8), (iii) the sounds of human language (10, 11). Just as the well known bugle call galvanizes the army into action, so a language understood by the hearer will produce positive results. Conversely, while one may worship in deepest harmony with the spirit in a tongue, the uninitiated in the church, bereft of gifts, is in no position to endorse what is said (13–19). Finally, while tongues may be a sign to the unbeliever of impending doom, it is through the gift of prophecy that he will be led to salvation (20–25).

1. Follow the way of love: Literally, pursue love—a characteristic Pauline verb for spiritual endeavour; cf. Rom. 9: 30, 31; 12: 13; Phil. 3: 12 ff.; 1 Th. 5: 15; 1 Tim. 6: 11; 2 Tim. 2: 22. The verse summarizes chapters 12 and 13, and sets the tone for what follows. Note the repeated phrase, **eagerly desire . . . prophesy** (12: 31; 14: 39). **2. a tongue:** One of the *charismata*, understood only by God unless accompanied by the gift of interpretation. It is not merely a foreign language, for no one understands it, and it is addressed to God. **with his spirit:** While interpreted by the RSV (also Moffatt, and NEB, inspired') as a reference to the Holy Spirit, it can equally refer to the spirit of man, as distinct from his mind and is translated by NIV. **mysteries:** See note on 13: 2. **3. everyone who prophesies:** The gift of inspired preaching, perceiving the will of God and speaking to the specific needs of the congregation. See note on 12: 10. **strengthening:**

Paul's dominant desire for the Corinthian church. It lies behind chapter 3: cf. 8: 1; 10: 23; 14: 4, 5, 12, 17, 26. See also 2 C. 12: 19; Eph. 4: 29; Rom. 14: 19; 15: 2. This metaphorical usage is peculiar to Paul in the NT **4.** The contrast is between the edification of one individual through a tongue and of the whole congregation through prophesying. **5. I would rather have you prophesy:** Places the balance where it ought to be without deprecating the gift of tongues. **unless he interprets:** Reintroduces the possibility of tongues being used in meetings of the church; cf. vv. 13, 26, 27. **6. if I come . . . what good will I be to you . . . :** The criterion is still their edification, profit. Uninterpreted tongues give nothing. **revelation . . . knowledge . . . prophecy . . . word of instruction:** These demand intelligent speech and build up. The former pair imply an inward endowment, the latter their outward expression. **Revelation** precedes **prophecy** as does **knowledge** the **teaching. 7, 8. lifeless things . . . flute . . . harp . . . bugle:** Each has its particular function, the first two being associated with feasts, funerals and religious functions, the last with fighting. Yet the instrument's tune and rhythm, its call must be clear, interpreting the occasion of festivity or mourning, the need to charge or retreat. **9. So it is with you:** What is achieved by the inanimate is demanded of the human tongue. For edification the word must be intelligently expressed. **10, 11. all sorts of languages . . . yet none of them is without meaning:** But all are valueless if ignorance of the language prevents communication. **12. So it is with you:** Be articulate in the language that builds up the church. **eager to have spiritual gifts:** Commendable, but the motive is crucial; not puffing up the self, but by love building up the church. Paul's words may be tinged with irony. **13. that he may interpret:** May be granted to the man who already has the gift of tongues. That gifts are given in answer to prayer clearly demonstrates the possibility of a developing ministry in keeping with spiritual growth and the needs of the local situation. The *charismata* are not given in a 'package deal'. **14. my mind is unfruitful:** May mean, 'my mind is not profited'—it gains no fruit, as NEB, or 'my mind produces nothing for the benefit of others', as Moffatt. **15. I will pray with my spirit but I will also pray with my mind:** For Paul **mind** is intelligence. He therefore uses a means of communication intelligible to mind and spirit, both his and the congregation's. Here Moffatt translates *pneuma* as 'Spirit'. **16. If you are praising God with your spirit:** I.e., in a tongue. As an expression of ecstatic utterance Paul uses a variety of terms; **speaks** (13), **pray** (14), **sing** (15), **praising, thanksgiving** (16)—all aspects of a corporate act of worship in which the believers took part as they were led; cf. v. 26. Yet the presence of **one . . . among those who do not understand** demands that every part of the worship be intelligible to him, either in the language of the worshippers, or if a tongue, through interpretation. **those who do not understand** (*idiōtēs*) suggests not laity, for no such distinction then existed, but rather, the unlearned, or inexperienced believer, or as RVmg suggests, one that is without gifts. The word occurs in Ac. 4: 13 and 2 C. 11: 6. **'Amen'**: A colloquial expression for associating oneself with the prayers, etc., offered in congregational worship. The practice of the synagogue was adopted in Christian churches. Cf. Ps. 106: 48; Neh. 5: 13; 8: 6. **17. you may be giving thanks well enough:** The tongue itself is not despised, but the ungifted is not edified. Hence it fails to meet the test. **18, 19. I speak in tongues more than all of you. But in the church . . . :** The gift in which Paul excelled was not paraded in church to impress, but in private, personal worship expressed in untrammelled joy the deep devotion of his ransomed spirit. **20. stop thinking like children . . . be adults:** A preference for tongues over intelligent speech was childish, immature. Yet **in regard to evil**—comprehensive of all evil dispositions—a child-like innocence was commendable. Mature thinking, intelligibly expressed, is essential if unbelievers are to be converted; cf. vv. 23–25. **21, 22. In the Law it is written . . . :** Isa. 28: 11 ff. is quoted. God speaks to the rebellious, unbelieving, in an unintelligible tongue, as He spoke to the scoffing Israelites through the Assyrian foes. The illustration shows nothing more than that, spectacular as tongues may be, they are ineffective in bringing unbelievers to salvation.

They are however **a sign . . . for unbelievers** of their own impending doom, as was the Assyrian tongue to the unbelieving Jews of Isaiah's day; not a saving sign, but a judicial sign of condemnation: a sign to be rejected confirming them in their unbelief; cf. v. 23. It seems that on occasion our Lord's use of parables was somewhat similar; cf. Mt. 13: 10–15. On the other hand, **prophecy . . . is for believers, not for unbelievers**, in that it creates those who believe, bringing them to faith. **23. the whole church:** Suggests a general gathering for worship as opposed to the more limited and informal groups which might meet in various parts of the city. **everyone speaks in tongues:** I.e. all who take part, as in v. 24. For the sake of his argument Paul is probably stating an extreme case. Undoubtedly some would normally take part in an intelligible tongue. **you are out of you mind:** A conclusion drawn not only by **unbelievers** (*apistoi*) but by those who as yet are unlearned—those

who do not understand. See v. 16 note. **24. by all:** Suggestive of the cumulative effect of the inspired word presented by speaker after speaker. The gender may be neuter or masculine; by everything, or everyone. **convinced:** Has considerable breadth of meaning; cf. 'convict', Jn 16: 8; 'expose', Eph. 5: 11; 'rebuke', 1 Tim. 5: 20. **judged by all** (*anakrinetai*): Used of judicial examination. See note on 2: 14, 15; also 4: 3; 9: 3. **25. the secrets of his heart will be laid bare:** Being the direct result of the examination. This verb and the preceding two in v. 24 reveal varying aspects of the one experience, involving convincing, convicting, exposing, sifting, revealing; the product of prophecy, the invasion of man's soul by the Spirit of God. The inward rebuke of the Spirit results in the outward response of the sinner; **he will fall down and worship God, exclaiming 'God is really among you!'** If to him tongues suggest that the church is mad, prophecy proves that God is present.

(b) **Tongues and prophesying in the local church (14: 26–33a)**
The apostle having concluded his arguments on the respective merits of tongues and prophesying, issues directives. His conclusions summarize the previous 25 verses. (i) Of first importance, all must be for **for the strengthening of the church** (26). The church must be built up; cf. vv. 3, 4, 5, 6, 12, 17, 19. (ii) If there are tongues, they must be accompanied by interpretation (27, 28); cf. vv. 2, 5. (iii) The **prophets** are to participate (29). (iv) Decorum and order must be maintained (30–33).

26 presents graphically the composition and manner of worship of a congregation in the early church. **everyone:** Not that everyone present would of necessity take part; rather it indicates the general distribution of gifts throughout the local church. **has a hymn, a word of instruction . . . :** The verb 'to have' is repeated with each gift in the Greek text and is possibly suggestive of the individual possession of specific gifts. Each comes prepared to contribute, yet equally ready to remain silent as the need becomes evident; cf. v. 32. **27. If anyone speaks in a tongue:** If implies the possibility of no such individual being present. This is the more significant in view of Paul's grammar where, in this particular constmction, *eite* ('if') should normally be followed by another *eite*, so completing a distributive sentence. This second part could have commenced at v. 29, but the idea of the presence of prophets being in doubt is so unacceptable to Paul that he abandons the construction and inserts an imperative: **Two or three prophets should speak . . .** It matters little if tongues are not present, but prophets there must be. **one at a time:** Ensured the preservation of order, as did **someone must interpret**, rendering it impossible for several to break out in ecstatic utterance together. **28. If there is no interpreter the speaker should keep quiet:** As with all other *charismata*, the exercise of tongues must be under the immediate control of the speaker. **29. two or three prophets:** As with tongues, the number that could profitably be heard in one meeting. **and the others should weigh carefully what is said:** While it could refer to the whole congregation, **others** were most probably the remaining prophets, or others in the church who had the gift of discernment; cf. 12: 10, 'the ability to distinguish . . .' The advice was sound, for false prophets early infiltrated the churches; cf. 2 Pet. 2: 1; 1 Jn 4: 1. **30. If a revelation comes to someone who is sitting:** The guidance of the Holy Spirit throughout is clearly anticipated. **31. you can all prophesy in turn:** Not all in one meeting, for the limit of two or three is set, but an opportunity will eventually come to all so gifted. **so that everyone may be instructed:** Suggests that the varying needs of all the believers will be met through a variety of speakers; some by one, some by another. This in no way invalidates a sustained Bible-teaching ministry such as Paul, Apollos, Timothy and others undoubtedly pursued. **32. the spirits of prophets . . . :** Reads almost as a maxim and makes explicit the statements of vv. 28 and 30, that under the superintendence of the Spirit the recipients of gifts are in full control and are responsible for their use. **33. For God . . . :** The order so achieved reflects the character of the Giver of gifts. **not a God of disorder but of peace:** The very antithesis of the chaos and commotion that currently reigned in the church at Corinth; see 11: 17-22.

(c) Women in church (14: 33b-36)

The guiding principle in Paul's teaching concerning the place of women in the life of the church is subordination, submission. What constitutes subordination? Here again the principles of Scripture must be worked out within the framework of contemporary society. That the problem is complex is clear, not only from the reference to their participation in 11: 5, but also from what was obviously known to the apostle: the ministry of women in the OT and also within his own life-time in the Church (cf. Ac. 21: 9). While on the one hand one must recognize that almost all the heretical sects of Christendom number women among their leaders, yet it is also beyond dispute that God has vindicated the ministry of women, consecrated, holy women, whose lives have been humbly sacrificed in the service of Christ in the missionary world. Understood within the context of the NT it is hard to accept that all spoken ministry is denied to women.

33b. As in all the congregations of the saints . . . : Taken by NIV, RSV and NEB with the following verses and is probably the reading to be preferred. Following NIV, the basis of Paul's appeal is the general conduct of the churches. This accords with v. 36. **34. the women should remain silent:** This is the third call to be **silent**. See v. 28 for tongues without interpretation and v. 30 for one prophet giving way to another. As tongues and prophecy are subject to limitations, so is the speaking of women. This may be understood in two ways: (i) if 11: 5 is taken as giving permission to women to pray and prophesy, then this prohibition must refer to the abuses of such freedom; a departure from the subordinate attitude which the law and society demand, the calling out, and asking of questions which disrupts the orderly state of the meeting on which Paul is insisting (see vv. 33, 40); (ii) the limitation may refer to the occasion: **in the churches.** It may be held, although it is nowhere suggested in the text, that the apostle is referring to the more informal meetings of Christians in 11: 5, in contrast to the formal gatherings of the whole church which he undoubtedly has in mind in 14: 1-40, cf. especially v. 23. The phrase **they are not allowed to speak** does not clarify the issue. The verb *lalein* (to speak) is too general to refer to any particular kind of speaking. It is used of tongues (27) and also prophecy (29) and refers equally to the questions with which the women might interrupt a discourse. So general is the word that the suggestion that Paul is merely referring here to irregular talking, be it chattering, calling to children, soothing or more often rebuking babies, or interjecting a remark or query, cannot be ruled out. At church services in Asia the rebuke is frequently heard, 'Sisters, be silent; don't talk in church'. And the verb used is the general equivalent of *lalein*. Few things are so conducive to confusion and disruptive of peace as the noise which emanates from the women's section of the congregation—the sexes are segregated—in an Asian worship service. They **must be in submission:** this is the crux of the matter; not only to their husbands (11: 3-9; 14: 35), but in questions of conduct, submitting in all things for the good order and decent arrangement of the service (40). It is on the same grounds of submissiveness that Paul states categorically that a woman shall not teach (cf. 1 Tim. 2: 11, 12). **as the Law says:** A reference to Gen. 3: 16. **35. they should ask their own husbands at home:** To have asked one's husband in church would have involved calling across the room, creating disorder. Paul has, as in chapter 11, married women in mind. The unmarried could ask through their own families. **shameful:** Scandalous; a strong word, found elsewhere in the

NT only in 11: 6; Eph. 5: 12; Tit. 1: 11. Such is Paul's estimate of one who ignores the limits of subordination and disrupts the order of holy worship. **36. Did the word of God originate with you . . . ?:** Is Corinth the fount of revelation, the sole repository of truth? Corinth was obviously at variance with **all the churches**; gross disorder reigned (chapter 11), the reflection of their arrogant self-esteem (4: 8, 19).

(d) **Conclusion (14: 37–40)**
The verses are reminiscent of 11: 16, but now his source of authority transcends the ruling of the apostles and the practice of the churches; it is the command of Christ. The test of their spirituality is their acceptance of his claim. The balance assiduously sought throughout is finally summarized; the priority of prophecy, the legitimacy of tongues, and well-ordered worship.

37. a prophet or spiritually gifted: The second is the wider term including all who have spiritual gifts, although here it could refer specifically to one who spoke with tongues, the gift Corinthians considered to carry the hallmark of spirituality. **let him acknowledge:** The pres. imperative, literally, let him *ever* acknowledge, or recognize. The same verb is used in 16: 18; 2 C. 1: 13. **the Lord's command:** The stamp of apostleship, the conviction of inspiration. The point is, those who have spiritual gifts are not to act as a law to themselves, but are to conform to the law of Christ revealed through the directives of the apostle. **38. If anyone does not recognize this:** Sometimes, as here, the verb (*agnoei*) implies wilful ignorance or disregard. **he himself will be ignored:** The whole verse is cryptically and concisely expressed in five Greek words. Such opposition is dismissed with suitable brevity.

This implication of wilful ignorance in *agnoei* perhaps gives force to the variant reading 'let him be ignorant' (RV), especially as it is supported by papyrus 46, our oldest Pauline manuscript. **39. be eager:** Cf. 12: 31; 14: 1. Prophecy is of paramount importance in edifying the church. Nevertheless, tongues have a God-given function (5). **do not forbid:** No spiritual gift is to be despised. **40** expands the thought of v. 33. **decently** (*euschēmonōs*): Cognate forms are found in 7: 35; 12: 23, 24 with the underlying concept of comeliness and beauty. Worship should be attractive. **in order** (*kata taxin*): 'Everything in its proper place and sequence', expressing the precision with which a well-ordered army moves.

VII. THE RESURRECTION (15: 1–58)
Although there is no suggestion that the Corinthians had written about the subject, the apostle had undoubtedly heard reports of misconcep-

tions gaining ground in the church. By some even the possibility of a resurrection was being denied (12). It is not altogether surprising that such a problem should exist, for nothing in the Greek background of the Gentile converts suggested the plausibility of a physical resurrection (cf. Ac. 17: 18, 32). The Jewish minority in the congregation, while probably accepting the doctrine in view of their OT background, would be in no position to influence the Gentile majority. Paul's answer, the product of uncompromising conviction and lucid reasoning, demonstrates the position of fundamental importance that this doctrine holds in the Christian faith. Based on the historical resurrection of Christ (3–11), its denial not only relegates the Messiah to a martyr's grave, but renders faith futile, sin triumphant and the hope of glory a pitiful myth (12–19). In terms of positive truth, Christ risen from the dead gives assurance of human resurrection, the conquest of death, the subjugation of evil and daily empowering for Christian service (20–34). Yet how are the dead raised? Anticipating inevitable queries, the apostle, from nature, OT history and Christian revelation, describes the body that is yet to be (35–58).

i. The resurrection of Christ (15: 1–11)
A risen Christ was fundamental to Paul's gospel (1–4); it was historically attested (5–8) and uniformly preached by all the apostles (9–11).

1, 2. I want to remind you: So also RSV and NEB. However, many commentators prefer the 'declare', or 'make known' of AV and RV, suggesting that this is not a mere reminder, but an emphatic declaration of the message originally given. Note the usage in Gal. 1: 11, 'I would have you know'. **preached . . . received:** Both aorists recalling the specific time of their belief. **your stand:** A perfect, signifying their stand already taken, the results of which continue into the present. **you are saved:** A continuous present tense, stresses the progressive nature of their salvation; cf. 1: 18; 2 C. 2: 15. **if you hold firmly:** To deny the resurrection was to relinquish their hold on what Paul had taught, for without the resurrection, they would have believed in vain. **in vain** (*eikē*): Without grounds. If their understanding of the gospel did not commit them to belief in the resurrection, theirs was no saving faith. **3. For what I received I passed on to you:** See notes on 11: 23. The essential point is that the message was not of Paul's creation; he merely transmitted the truth, facts committed to him.

Christ died: An atoning death, **for our sins:** cf. 2 C. 5: 21; Gal. 1: 4; Heb. 9: 28; 10: 12; 1 Pet. 2: 24; 3: 18, etc. **according to the Scriptures:** A fact the disciples originally found hard to accept; cf. Lk. 24: 26 ff.; see Ac. 3: 18; Isa. 53. **4. he was buried:** The evidence of His death. Outside the Gospels, Paul is the only NT writer to refer to it; cf. Ac. 13: 29; Rom. 6: 4; Col. 2: 12. **he was raised:** Literally, 'has been raised'. Paul changes from the aorists to the perfect, signifying the continued life after the resurrection; cf. Rom. 6: 9. For similar uses of the perfect in this chapter see vv. 12, 13, 14, 16, 17, 20. **according to the Scriptures:** Isa. 53: 10–12; Ps. 16: 10. See also Lk. 24: 46. **5–7** give a limited list of the resurrection appearances. **Peter:** Lk. 24: 34. **the twelve:** A general term for the apostles, Judas excepted. **five hundred of the brothers:** Not recorded in the Gospels, but that most were still alive at the time of writing provided incontrovertible proof. **James:** Probably the brother of our Lord. **all the apostles:** As a reference to the twelve follows Cephas, so the **apostles** following **James** (assuming him to be the brother of the Lord) refers to a somewhat wider circle of Christ's followers. Paul's use of 'apostle' is of wide application; cf. 12: 28 note. So far as Cephas and James are concerned, Paul's information was probably acquired during his visit to Jerusalem described in Gal. 1: 18 f. **8. Last of all . . . to me also:** 'even to me' (NEB); a reference to his Damascus road experience, the vividness of which never faded in his memory; cf. Ac. 22: 6–11; 26: 12–18. **one abnormally born:** It could point to the dramatic suddenness of his spiritual birth and the extraordinary manner in which he joined the apostolic group, or, in keeping with v. 9, be a term of abuse hurled by his enemies—a miscarriage of an apostle—a charge he did not endeavour to deny. Yet another suggestion is that Paul's conversion (from violent opposition to Christ) is an anticipation of the day when Israel shall see him, but happening before the due time. **9. least of the apostles and do not deserve . . . : least,** not in the character of his apostleship (cf. 9: 1, 2; 2 C. 11: 5; 12: 11, 12), but because he **persecuted the church:** cf. 1 Tim. 1: 15; Eph. 3: 8. This too he never forgot; cf. Gal. 1: 13; 1 Tim. 1: 12–14; Ac. 26: 9–11. **10. But by the grace of God:** Paul's unworthiness serves only to enhance sovereign grace. **not without effect** (*kenos*): Empty, fruitless. **I worked harder than all of them . . . :** Signifies the character of the grace given; a divine enduement of power; cf. 3: 10; 2 C 9: 8; 12: 9; Eph. 3: 7; 2 Tim. 2: 1 for examples of this usage in Paul's letters.

It was not Paul but **grace** that **worked.** **11. I or they:** Whatever their comparative importance, or intensity of activity, all the apostles **preach** (continuous present) the same gospel of which the resurrection is an inalienable part. This the Corinthians had **believed** (aorist). Not only the resurrection of Christ, but their belief in it was an historical fact.

ii. The consequences of denying the resurrection (15: 12–19)
The denial of a resurrection of the dead must inevitably involve a denial of Christ's resurrection, which in turn demands an admission that the preachers are false, faith is vain, sin remains and the Christian dead have perished. There is no hope.

12. some of you: Probably Gentile believers who while accepting the Greek concept of the immortality of the soul could not accept a physical resurrection. If the resurrection of Christ is a proven fact, which none of them denied, it is illogical to say **there is no resurrection of the dead. 13. Christ has not been raised:** Since they had never questioned the resurrection of Christ, Paul's reasoning reveals the inconsistency of their assertion. **14. our preaching** (*kērygma*) **is useless:** *kērygma* refers not to the act of preaching, but to the content; cf. 1: 21; 2: 4. The message is **useless** (*kenos*, as in v. 10): without meaning, and inevitably, their **faith** in that message. **15. We are then found** (*heuriskometha*): Often used in moral judgments when detecting the true character of an individual or matter; so 'we are even discovered to be' (Amplified Bible). **testified about God:** Here *kata tou theou* (of God) could be translated, 'against God' (its more usual meaning), i.e. accusing God of doing something that He did not do. However, it is probably better to render it simply as 'about God', in keeping with the previous phrase, **false witness about God. 17. faith is futile:** Surely so if sin remains unatoned. *mataios* (**futile**) differs little from *kenos* (v. 14), except that it is concerned more with lack of result, and *kenos* with lack of reality.

in your sins: Deliverance depends on Christ being raised from the dead; cf. Rom. 4: 24, 25; 6: 1–11; Eph. 2: 1, 5. **18.** While denying the possibility of a resurrection for humanity, the Corinthians fully expected those who were **asleep in Christ** to be saved, being united with Him in an after-life state. The apostle therefore demonstrates that no salvation is possible if there is no resurrection. **those . . . are lost** (*apōlonto*): Experiencing total ruin, not extinction, but total loss of the salvation for which they hoped **in Christ**, for it is those who are not **in Christ** and die who perish; cf. 1: 18; 2 C. 2: 15; 4: 3.

19. only: Emphatic and qualifies either **hope** (as RSV, RVmg), or **For this life** (as NIV, AV, RV, NEB), or the whole clause, i.e., 'If in this life we are hopers in Christ and have nothing beyond.' This last is favoured by many commentators. **have hope:** The perf. part. with the verb 'to be', expresses not what we do, but what we are: we are hopers. Hope seeks fulfilment (cf. Rom. 5: 1–5; 8: 24, 25; 1 Th. 4: 13, 14), yet if the resurrection is denied and nothing lies beyond, **we are to be pitied** (pitiable) **more than all men.**

iii. The consequences of Christ's resurrection (15: 20–28)

Turning from the terrible conclusions which must accompany any doctrine of no resurrection, the apostle now enumerates the glorious consequences of Christ's being risen from the dead. Man will surely rise, as surely as all must die. It is a matter of order, Christ first, then when He comes again, those who are His. As first fruits He had vanquished death; but now as Sovereign He subdues every evil beneath His feet and death the last great foe can terrify no more. Paul contemplates the last majestic scene; earth's history ends as the Son delivers up the kingdom to the Father, and God is all in all.

20. But Christ has indeed . . . : The argument of the previous paragraph, based on a false premise (13, 14), ended in tragedy. Paul now reasons from fact, a fact the Corinthians accept. **first fruits:** Reminiscent of the first sheaf from the field brought to the Temple in thanksgiving and offered to the Lord (cf. Lev. 23: 10 if.), a promise of the full harvest yet to be. Others had been raised from the dead, only to die again. Christ is uniquely the first fruits in that He died, rose and is alive for evermore (Rev. 1: 18; Rom. 6: 9) in anticipation of believers who have fallen asleep, but will be raised to be with Him for ever; cf. 1 Th. 4: 16, 17. **21. For since death came through a man . . . through a man:** Developing from the concept of first fruits the thought implies unity of species. This theme of the last Adam is worked out more fully in Rom. 5: 12–21. **death:** The penalty of sin resulting from Adam's rebellion. **22. all die . . . all will be made alive:** The implication of all is governed by the context. It is often argued that since **all** who are **in Adam**, i.e., all humanity, **die**, so **all** who are **in Christ**, i.e., all the redeemed, are **made alive.** However, in this passage Paul is thinking primarily of those who **have** fallen asleep in Christ (18), to which also v. 20 probably refers. The unbelieving dead are not under review. Therefore **all** may refer to believers in both clauses: **all** believers **die** because they are **in Adam**, and **all** such will **be made alive** because they are **in Christ.** This is further supported by v. 23 where the order of resurrection is stated—**each in his own turn**; first Christ, then those who are His. The apostle would not deny the resurrection of the lost, but they are not mentioned in the order here, for they just do not form part of Paul's present subject.

23. in his own turn (*tagma*): A cognate form of *taxis* (14: 40), a military metaphor, suggesting companies appearing in their proper order and position. **when he comes** (*parousia*): The second advent. The word itself is of general application to any individual's arrival or presence as in 16: 17; Phil. 2: 12; 2 Pet. 1: 16. Used of Christ's second coming it often suggests not merely arrival, but His continued presence; cf. Mt. 24:3,37; 1 Th. 4: 15ff.; 5:23; 2 Th. 2: 1, 8; Jas 5: 7, 8; 2 Pet. 3: 4. **24. Then the end** (*telos*) **will come:** The absolute end—the termination of world history—rather than a third order implying the resurrection of the lost; cf. Mt. 24: 6, 14; Mk 13: 7; Lk. 21: 9; 1 Pet. 4: 7. **Then** permits an interval between Christ's coming and the final consummation; a period for destroying all opposing powers; a period which culminates in His delivering the kingdom to God; cf. 2 Th. 1: 7–10. **when** (*hotan*): Denotes indefiniteness of time. **the kingdom** (*basileia*): Note the initial preaching of Jesus and His purpose to establish that reign, or sovereignty; a spiritual realm (Col. 1: 13) not merely in the lives of His people (Lk. 17: 21) but also visible, a kingdom yet future; cf. Lk. 19: 11 ff.; 21: 10 ff., espec. v. 31. See also 2 Tim. 4: 1. This sovereignty, a commission granted to the Son, will be fulfilled **when he hands over the kingdom to God** the Father. **destroyed** (*katargeō*): See 1: 28; 13: 8—render inoperative—opposition is liquidated. **rule, authority and power:** Words not evil in themselves; their content is determined by the context. They are declared **enemies** in v. 25.

25. he must reign until . . . : Strong necessity, both the prophetic word (Ps. 110: 1) and the divine commission of the kingdom demand it. **until he . . . :** Until God has put all Christ's enemies beneath Christ's feet, in accordance with Ps. 110: 1. **26. The last enemy . . . death:** Resurrection terminates death's power for those who are Christ's; cf. Lk. 20: 35, 36. The state of the unbelieving dead is not mentioned as Paul is concerned only with conditions as they affect believers. **27. 'For he . . .':** A reference to Ps. 8: 6, which refers to man's position of dominion over all creation. Christ as the last Adam, the perfect man, fulfils God's purpose in the highest possible sense. Heb. 2: 5–9 makes a similar exposition. **it says** (as also RSV and NEB—'Scripture says') probably gives the best rendering. Others render, 'he says', meaning either the psalmist speaking to God, or Christ speaking in the psalmist, i.e., announcing the subjugation of all things. **28. the Son himself will be made subject . . . :** The question here is one of function. Just as the incarnate Son was subject, or subordinate to the Father to effect eternal redemption at His first advent (cf. Jn 5: 19; 8: 42; 14: 28), and to that extent owned Him as greater, so coming again the second time for the final accomplishment of that commission the same relationship continues. The task completed, the Redeemer, man's Mediator, surrenders the kingdom to Him who sent Him. Their essential equality and unity remain; cf. 3: 23 note. **God . . . all in all:** The Son's mediatorial function completed, God now reigns not through Christ, but as 'immediate sovereign of the universe' (Hodge).

iv. Arguments from Christian activities (15: 29–34)

Paul with typical abruptness terminates his reasoned arguments and turns with obvious passion to the reality of daily experience, as if frustrated by the Corinthians' failure to comprehend the resurrection hope that lay behind his every word of witness and mode of life. To risk one's life for Christ were utter folly if the dead are never to be raised. Their rejection of the truth is a sin which threatens to undermine their whole Christian experience.

29. baptized for the dead: One of the most difficult phrases in Scripture. Of the many interpretations offered the most plausible is perhaps that which views the practice as an irregular type of baptism, possibly by proxy (so Moffatt) for those who died unbaptized.

This is what the text appears to say, as **for**, 'on behalf of' is the natural translation of *hyper*.

However, no such baptisms are recorded before Tertullian's time. The obvious futility of such a practice, if the dead are not raised, would greatly strengthen Paul's argument. Would he reason from so heretical a practice without condemning it? He might. That he does not identify himself with the practice is clear from the pronoun **those**, whereas in the next verse he reverts to **us** (RSV 'I'). Others view it as regular Christian baptism and translate as, 'with an interest in the resurrection of the dead', i.e., expecting to be raised. The Greek text does not mean this. Still others suggest a baptism of suffering or death, as in Lk. 12: 50. Apart from the difficulty of making the Greek mean such a thing, Corinth was not a persecuted church. Grosheide offers an interpretation which renders *hyper* as 'above', suggesting that Christians in Corinth were baptized over the graves of the dead believers, thus expressing their unity in Christ with them. While it is an historical phenomenon, there is nothing to connect the practice with Corinth. Chrysostom's view that baptism was in any case for the dead, i.e., for oneself as dead in sin, illustrates how from the earliest centuries of the Church this verse has posed a constant problem. **30. Why do we endanger ourselves:** An appeal to the manner of life of Paul and his colleagues. If there is no resurrection their conduct is senseless. Why throw one's life away? Cf. Rom. 8: 36; 2 C. 4: 11; 11: 23 ff. **31. just as surely as I glory over you:** An assurance that he is speaking the absolute truth, i.e., 'As surely as I am proud of you, I die daily'. See Moffatt and NEB. In spite of their failings in vile Corinth, Paul saw much in them for which to give thanks; cf. 1: 4–9; also 2 C. 7: 14. **I die every day:** Cf. 2 C. 1:

8–10; 4: 7–12; 11: 23b. **32. beasts in Ephesus:** Refers almost certainly, not to any encounter in the arena—such would surely have been recorded in the Acts, or 2 C. 11—but to the fierce struggles with Jews and Gentiles in that city when his life was gravely threatened. 2 C. 1: 8, 9 may refer to this. **'Let us eat . . .':** A quotation from Isa. 22: 13 and a reasonable philosophy if there is no resurrection. Man is then no better than the beasts that perish (cf. Ec. 2: 24; 3: 21). **33. Do not be misled:** The negative *mē* with the pres. imper. probably suggests, 'Stop being deceived . . .', i.e., by this pernicious doctrine. **'Bad company . . .':** Keeping company with men who reject the resurrection will corrupt Christian character. The quotation is a line from Menander's *Thais*, c. 320 B.C., although it may by Paul's time have been a common Greek proverb. **34. stop sinning:** The category in which their attitude really belongs. Their doctrinal error has moral implications; they had missed the mark. **ignorant** (*agnōsia*): The emphatic position of the noun is expressed by Robertson and Plummer, 'For utter ignorance of God is what some have got'. *agnōsia* denotes failure to take knowledge, not merely that lack of it.

v. The nature of the resurrection (15: 35–49)

Paul is in no mood for foolish questions, yet accepting their anticipated queries, he turns them to the world in which they live, to things that they can see and understand. The resurrection body? It is like the seed which dies before it sprouts and grows. Then it appears in another form, a different form for every kind of seed (35–38). This differentiation is discernible throughout the entire animal kingdom (39) and is perceived in the infinite variety of the stars (40, 41). The principle, obvious in nature, is illustrative of the resurrection body. Man, the seed, is sown perishable, inglorious, weak, physical, but is raised a transformed being. The earthy likeness will be transformed into a heavenly one (42–49).

35. 'How . . . what kind of body . . . ?': Paul deals with the latter question first and in detail, while the former is only answered by implication, for it is an act of God to be accepted by faith. **36. How foolish!** (*aphrōn*): Implies lack of understanding. 'A senseless question!' (NEB). They should know better; the resurrection is well illustrated in the things with which they are most familiar. This is emphasized by the emphatic **you** in **you sow. come to life:** A passive verb. The quickening, germinating process is of God and is contingent on the death of the grain—**it dies.** Both are fundamental to the resurrection. **37, 38. the body that will be:** While in appearance different, it is in essence the same, for **wheat yields wheat—to each kind of seed he gives its own body—**

suggesting continuity of essential character or identity. **God gives** this body. Note the implicit answer to the **how** of v. 35. **39, 40, 41** explain **each . . . its own body.** Diversity abounds in God's creation, not haphazard, but God-given. Further, while there is a differentiation of species—**men, animals, birds, fish, stars**—yet within each class there are multitudinous differences distinguishing one individual creation from another, for **star differs from star in splendour.** If therefore in the present universe these personal characteristics are evident within the various categories of creation, God is well able at Christ's coming to invest each individual believer with a new resurrection body which will be in perfect harmony with his own essential being (see 42a). **heavenly bodies:** While some suggest that this refers to heavenly beings, as opposed to earthly beings (**earthly bodies**), the weight of opinion seems to favour interpreting the phrase in terms of v. 41—the **sun, moon** and **stars.** This involves a dual meaning of **bodies** (*sōmata*), for **earthly bodies** undoubtedly denotes the living organisms on earth.

42, 43, 44. So will it be: On the basis of the preceding principle, the nature of the resurrection body is now more clearly defined. **the dead:** Believers, as throughout the chapter. Using again the figure of the seed, the concepts of the **perishable, dishonor, weakness** are introduced, all characteristics of the **natural body** (*psychikos*), the body fitted for this present transient life. **perishable:** Cf. Rom. 8: 21; Gal. 6: 8; 2 Pet. 1: 4; 2: 12, 19.

dishonor: Rendered 'disgrace' in 11: 14 and 'shameful' in Rom. 1: 26; 'humiliation' (NEB) gives this sense (cf. Phil. 3: 21). In sharp antithesis **imperishable, glory, power** portray the **spiritual body** that is to be; qualities that make it perfectly adapted to the new life to be lived. **glory** translates *doxa*, rendered 'splendour' in vv. 40, 41.

Two facts emerge; (i) God can bring life out of death, and (ii) the new body, while identical in essence with the first, is as different from it as the plant from the seed. **natural** (*psychikos*): Natural, signifies that which pertains to the soul or life of man, i.e., what he is in Adam. See 2: 14 note. **spiritual** (*pneumatikos*): Denotes that which pertains to the spirit, generated and controlled by the Spirit of God. See 2: 13, 15; 3: 1; 14: 37. **45. So it is written:** Only the first clause refers to Gen. 2: 7 (note NIV quotation marks). The second part is Paul's comment. **first** and **Adam** are the apostle's insertion, to give the correct sense in this context. The contrast is between the first and the last Adam. The first Adam became a life-possessing soul; the last Adam a life-imparting spirit. Adam and therefore humanity are on the natural level, subject to decay; Christ on the spiritual level

—**life-giving. the last Adam:** In the first, man finds his genesis; in the last, he gains his goal. **46. the natural . . . after that the spiritual:** A general law—seedtime precedes harvest, the physical is preparatory to the spiritual. **47, 48, 49.** As the physical and spiritual bodies were contrasted (42–44), so now Adam and those in him are compared with Christ. On the one hand are the **man of the dust** and all humanity in his **likeness**, on the other the **man from heaven** and we in His **likeness** at the resurrection. **of the earth** defines man's origin, as **from heaven** denotes Christ's. The **first man** stands at the head of the old creation, the **second man** at the head of the new. **we have borne:** An aorist, probably viewing this in its entirety. Literally, 'we did put on', the verb is commonly used of wearing clothes. **so shall we bear:** The weight of textual evidence supports the subjunctive *phoresōmen* ('let us bear'), but the context demands the future *phoresomen* ('we shall bear'). There would be hardly any distinction in pronunciation between these two forms by the first century A.D. It refers to the day of resurrection. Note the similar thought in v. 53. We shall have **the likeness** of Christ; cf. Rom. 8: 29; 2 C. 3: 18; Phil. 3: 21; Col. 3: 10; 1 Jn 3:2.

vi. The result of the resurrection (15: 50–58)
Whether we are living or dead at the coming of Christ, this wonderful transformation will take place; the resurrection day will have come and the final victory of Christ will be proclaimed.

50 serves better as an introduction to the new (as in NIV, RV, NEB), than as a conclusion to the preceding argument (RSV). **the perishable:** That is, the physical man (**flesh and blood**) as he is in this world needs a transformation; without it he inherits nothing. It is not this present physical body that will find its possession in **the kingdom. inherit:** Here understood in the broader sense of taking final possession at the coming of Christ. **51. a mystery:** Cf. 2: 7; 4: 1; 13: 2; 14: 2; here, the fact that the living as well as the dead will experience immediate physical transformation at Christ's advent, to possess **the kingdom** and all that the **imperishable** conveys; cf. vv. 50 and 53. **We will not all sleep:** Paul was prepared for an imminent return of Christ, but equally so for death; cf. 2 C. 4: 14; 5: 1–10; Phil. 1: 21–24. One should be in a constant state of readiness; cf. Mk 13: 32, 33, 37; Ac. 1: 7; 1 Th. 4: 13 ff.; Phil. 4: 5; Rom. 13: 11, 12; 1 C. 7: 29–31; 16: 22.

52. the last trumpet: The final manifestation of God to man in his earthly condition. It heralded the Lord's descent at Sinai; cf. Exod. 19: 16; Heb. 12: 19. See also Mt. 24: 31; 1 Th. 4: 16; Rev. 11: 15. **53** applies the principle of

v. 50. **perishable** and **mortal** are used synony-mously, although the latter is a more compre-hensive word. **put on:** An aorist indicating the momentary character of the change, cf. v. 52. The verb (*endyō*) 'implies that there is a perma-nent element continuing under the new con-ditions' (Robertson and Plummer). See 2 C. 5: 4. **54.** The reference is to Isa. 25: 8. **'Death has been swallowed up . . .':** The moment of Christ's appearing, when death is utterly de-stroyed (cf. v. 26). **'. . . in victory':** Paul's own rendering of the Hebrew expression ('for ever' in English versions), differing from that of LXX—although LXX repeatedly renders the expression thus elsewhere, and Paul's choice of the rendering here provides a link with **victory** in Hos. 13: 14, quoted in the next verse. **55.** **'O death . . .':** From Hos. 13: 14. **your vic-tory:** It reigned from Adam; cf. Rom. 5: 14. **your sting:** Portrays death as venomous. Sa-tan's fangs are drawn.

(AV 'O grave' in place of the second **O death** reflects the inferior reading (*hadēs*) of the 'Re-ceived Text'.) **56. The sting of death is sin:** Sin causes death; cf. Rom. 5: 12, 13, 21, etc.

the power of sin is the law: Paul expounds this in Rom. 7: 4–20. **57. victory through . . . Christ:** He is the end of the law (Rom. 10: 4); free from sin (1 Pet. 2: 22); conqueror of death (Ac. 2: 24); redeemer of His people (Heb. 9: 28). **gives:** The pres. part. not only signifies that it is characteristic of God to give **the victory**, but that victory may be continually experienced. **58. stand firm, let nothing move you:** Cf. 7: 37; 16: 13; Col. 1: 23; a firm grip of the fact of the resurrection will strengthen their stand and give added incentive for service; cf. 3: 13 ff.; 15: 10; 2 C. 9: 8. Note AV, RV, RSV rendering 'be steadfast . . .'; literally, 'become' what they had not fully been before.

VIII. CONCLUSION (16: 1–24)
Paul brings his letter to a close, dealing briefly with a variety of matters which still require his attention.

i. The collection (16: 1–4)
Believers in the church at Jerusalem were in need; it was the Corinthians' privilege to help them. Instructions are given concerning the proper procedure for collecting the offerings, which in due course the apostle will send, or himself take to their destination.

1. the collection for God's people: Cf. Rom. 15: 26; 2 C. 8: 1 ff.; 9: 1 ff. Presumably the Corinthians already knew of the proposed contribution (there is no mention of Jerusalem until v. 3) and may have asked for further instructions in their letter. **2. the first day of every week:** Suggests that Christians regu-larly met on Sundays, the first indication of the practice; cf. Jn 20: 19, 26; Ac. 20: 7; Rev. 1: 10.

Note the guidance given; it should be regular and systematic, involving every member, each giving according to his means. **saving it up:** The inference being that the gifts are to be put by at home week by week. **3. letters of introduction to the men you approve:** The money was theirs, not Paul's, and he carefully avoided personal contact with it. Baseless alle-gations could too easily be made; cf. 2 C. 8: 20–22; also 2 C. 12: 14–18. RSV follows the RV reading, but most translators (Moffatt, Phil-lips, NEB, NIV) adopt the RVmg alternative, that Paul would write a letter of commendation to be taken by those men whom they themselves should select. **4. If . . . for me to go:** Then no letter would be necessary.

ii. Personal matters (16: 5–18)
Paul's plans are fluid. He would like to spend time with them, not merely to call while pass-ing through. However, the opportunities in Ephesus prevent him from cutting short his ministry there. Timothy will see them on his way back to Ephesus; they are to look after him well. Apollos may come later. In the meantime there are local men to whom they do well to listen.

5. Ac. 20: 1, 2 suggests that Paul finally carried through this plan, although 2 C. 1: 15, 16 indicates that alternatives were later suggested. See also 2 C. 1: 23. In addition a brief 'painful visit' probably took place from Ephesus, preceding that of Ac. 20. See Intro-duction, p. 1420. **6. I will stay with you:** you is emphatic and is repeated three times in vv. 6. 7, emphasizing that it was particularly with them that he wanted to spend time. A passing visit would not permit him to accomplish all that he hoped to do. This letter left several matters still unresolved; cf. 11: 34. He finally spent three months in Greece (cf. Ac. 20: 3). **wherever I go and if the Lord permits** reveal the uncertainty of his plans. Either this was written before the occasion of Ac. 19: 21, 22, or Paul was not yet in a position to confirm his intentions. **8. Ephesus:** The place from which Paul writes. **Pentecost:** Gives a general guide as to time, for by then the ships would again be sailing. **10, 11. If Timothy comes:** Cf. 4: 17; Ac. 19: 22. **see . . . he has nothing to fear** (literally, 'without fear') and **No one, then, should refuse to accept him**, recall phrases in Paul's letters to him long after; cf. 1 Tim. 4: 12; 2 Tim. 1: 7. His temperament and, at this time, extreme youth, made it easy for people to underestimate his true worth. **carry-ing on the work of the Lord, just as I am:** Cf. 1 Th. 3: 2; Phil. 2: 20–22. **12. Now about . . . :** The same usage as in 7: 1, 25; 8: 1; 12: 1; 16: 1, which suggests that they had written asking about **Apollos**, hoping he would come to them. **the brothers:** Probably those of v. 11 who may have taken Paul's letter to Corinth.

He was quite unwilling: Most commentators and versions prefer 'his will', i.e., Apollos himself was adamantly opposed to going. He may well have felt that the situation in Corinth was too critical for him to handle. However, there is sufficient evidence for the absolute use of *thelēma* ('will') in Jewish Greek to mean 'God's will' to lend support to the RSV rendering here. **13, 14.** The apostle inserts his final brief exhortation. The first four imperatives call for militant action, the last for **love.** The first pair are defensive, the second offensive. **be on your guard:** A call to alertness, often associated with the second coming; cf. Mk 13:35,37; 1Th.5:6; Col.4:2. **stand firm:** Be stable, a quality hitherto lacking; cf. Rom. 11: 20; Gal. 5: 1; Phil. 4: 1; 2 Th. 2: 15. **be men of courage:** Literally, 'act like men'. LXX usage suggests courage for the fight as in Jos. 1: 6, 7, etc. **be strong:** Cf. Eph. 3: 16; sometimes linked with **courage** in the LXX as in Ps. 27: 14. **love:** Recalls chapter 13, a quality which must dominate even in the fight. **15, 16. household of Stephanas:** Cf. 1: 16. **first converts:** Literally, first fruits. See note on 15: 20. As there were conversions in Athens (also in the Roman province of Achaia) before Paul's Corinthian visit this refers either to their being the first *family* to be converted, or indicates that they came to Christ elsewhere before Paul arrived in the city. **submit to such:** The service of others characterized such men as Stephanas, and now the others were to be subject to them, so creating an endless circle of mutual care and esteem; a certain remedy for division (cf. Phil. 2: 3). Those who serve, work and labour gain Paul's respect. The last verb (*kopiaō*) suggests toil involving fatigue; those who spent themselves for Christ and His people; cf. 4: 12 note; 1 Th. 1: 3. **17, 18. Stephanas, Fortunatus and Achaicus** possibly brought the Corinthians' letter to Paul and would return with his reply. Their presence had a twofold effect; **they have supplied . . . :** brought Paul a breath of Corinth; **they refreshed my spirit . . . :** their presence alone proved to the apostle that such men of sterling character, as servants of the Corinthian church, were God's own guarantee of its ultimate stability and growth.

iii. Final greetings (16: 19–24)
19. The churches in the province of Asia: The Roman province of Asia—Ephesus and its neighbouring cities. **Aquila and Priscilla** had intimate associations with Corinth, where their home had been the base for Paul's activities (Ac. 18: 2 f.). Now in Ephesus the church met **at their house,** as it was later to do in Rome (cf. Rom. 16: 5). **20. a holy kiss:** The customary greeting of Paul's day; cf. Rom. 16: 16; 2 C. 13: 12; 1 Th. 5: 26. **21. in my own hand:** Having dictated the letter up to this point the apostle pens the concluding sentences himself

as a token of its genuineness; cf. 2 Th. 3: 17; Col. 4: 18. **22. a curse be on him** (*anathema*): Absence of **love** for **the Lord** could have but one result; cf. 12: 3; Gal. 1: 8, 9. **love:** The use of *phileō* instead of *agapaō* may suggest, 'If one does not have even affection for the Lord'. Note John's use in Jn 21: 15–18. **Come, O Lord!** (*Marana tha*): A transliteration of the Aramaic. While the verb has been rendered by past, present and future tenses, it is probably best to understand it as an imperative; a prayer not only characteristic of the time (see Rev. 22: 20), but well fitted to the context. According to the *Didachē* (10: 6), an early second-century manual of church order, it was used as an invocation at the Lord's Supper. **23. The grace . . . :** A phrase with which all Paul's letters begin and end, not as a mere convention, but in the conviction of its sure supply and all sufficient power. **24. My love** embracing **all of you in Christ**, ties into one the diverse strands of Paul's deeply stirred emotions. Rebuke, exhort, praise, counsel, scourge, encourage; do what he must—or they their worst—he will **love** them to the end.

BIBLIOGRAPHY

BARRETT, C. K., *The First Epistle to the Corinthians.* BNTC (London, 1968).

BRUCE, F. F., *1 and 2 Corinthians.* NCentB (London, 1971).

CONZELMANN, H., *1 Corinthians*, E.T. Hermeneia (Philadelphia, 1979).

FINDLAY, G. G., *The First Epistle of Paul to the Corinthians.* EGT (London, 1900).

GODET, F., *The First Epistle to the Corinthians* (2 vols. Edinburgh, 1886; reprinted Grand Rapids, 1957).

GOUDGE, H. L., *The First Epistle to the Corinthians.* WC (London, 1903).

GROSHEIDE, F. W., *Commentary on the First Epistle to the Corinthians, NIC NT* (Grand Rapids and London, 1953).

GUTHRIE, D., *NT Introduction: The Pauline Epistles.* (London, 1961).

HÉRING, J., *The First Epistle of Saint Paul to the Corinthians.* (London, 1962).

HODGE, C., *An Exposition of the First Epistle to the Corinthians* (Edinburgh, 1957; reprinted, London, 1958).

HURD, J. C., *The Origin of 1 Corinthians* (London, 1965).

KELLY, W., *Notes on the First Epistle to the Corinthians* (London, 1878).

MOFFATT, J., *The First Epistle of Paul to the Corinthians.* MNT (London, 1938).

MORRIS, L., *The First Epistle of Paul to the Corinthians.* TNTC (London, 1958).

ORR, W. F., and WALTHER, J. A., *1 Corinthians.* Anchor Bible (Garden City, N. Y., 1976).

PARRY, R. St. J., *The First Epistle of Paul the Apostle to the Corinthians.* CGT (Cambridge, 1916).

ROBERTSON, A. and PLUMMER, A., *A Critical and Exegetical Commentary on the First Epistle to the Corinthians.* ICC (Edinburgh, 1911).

SMITH, D., *The Life and Letters of St. Paul* (London, 1919).

THRALL, M. E., *I and II Corinthians.* CBC (Cambridge, 1965).

VINE, W. E., *First Corinthians* (London, 1951).

2 CORINTHIANS

DAVID J. A. CLINES

Historical Background

The following is a suggested outline of events between the writing of First and Second Corinthians.

(i) About the time of his dispatching 1 Corinthians, Paul sent Timothy to Corinth (1 C. 4: 17; 16: 10). He was to travel via Macedonia with Erastus (Ac. 19: 22). We know nothing of the specific purpose of his visit, nor indeed can we be sure that he ever reached Corinth; we next hear of him with Paul in Macedonia (2 C. 1: 1).

(ii) Paul made a hurried visit from Ephesus to Corinth. The purpose of this visit is not known (perhaps it was because 1 Corinthians had not been well received, or else because Paul had heard that his apostolic authority was being challenged); it is clear, however, that it ended disastrously and with great humiliation for Paul (cf. on 2 C. 12: 21). He refers to it later as a 'painful' visit (2: 1).

(iii) In order to rectify the situation he wrote a letter 'out of great distress and anguish' (2 C. 2: 4), known as the 'severe' letter (7: 8). It was taken to Corinth by Titus, who was to return to Ephesus via Macedonia and Troas.

(iv) Impatient for news of how his letter had been received, Paul travelled to Troas to meet Titus (2 C. 2: 12; Ac. 20: 1). When he did not find him there, he was too anxious to settle down to preaching, so he crossed to Macedonia (2 C. 2: 13).

(v) In Macedonia he met Titus, who brought good news from Corinth. In his joy and relief, Paul wrote 2 Corinthians (the fourth of his letters to Corinth known to us). It is clear from the letter that he now commanded the general support of the church, but there was apparently still a dissentient minority as well as glaring moral errors in the lives of church members.

The 'Previous' Letter

It is sometimes argued that the previous letter referred to in 1 C. 5: 9 is to be found embedded in 2 C. 6: 14–7: 1. There is no doubt that the passage in question breaks the train of thought very sharply, and also that it could easily have been misunderstood in the way the 'previous' letter had been. If the passage is omitted from its present position in 2 Corinthians, 7: 2 appears to read very naturally directly after 6: 13.

The main objection to this theory is that it is extremely difficult to imagine how this fragment of the 'previous' letter (it is surely not the whole letter) became interpolated at this point in 2 Corinthians. It is improbable that part of another manuscript was accidentally copied into 2 Corinthians, and even more improbable that an editor of Paul's letters inserted this section in what appears to be a most unsuitable place. It is more likely that Paul himself digressed from his theme (a habit in which he indulges quite frequently); in 7: 3 ('I have said before that you have . . . a place in our hearts') he resumes the subject from which he knows he has digressed.

The 'Severe' Letter

The 'severe' letter referred to in 2 C. 2: 3 f. and 7: 8 ff. has been traditionally understood to be 1 Corinthians, but it is recognized by most modern interpreters that the terms in which Paul speaks of the letter are inapplicable to 1 Corinthians.

A suggestion which has been accepted by many scholars is that the 'severe' letter has been partly preserved in 2 C. 10–13. Several features in these chapters correspond to what we know of the 'severe' letter, although the principal subject of that letter, the 'offender' of 2 C. 2: 5–11, does not find a place there.

The marked *change of tone* at the beginning of 2 C. 10 from expressions of joy and confidence to indignant self-defence and condemnation of his opponents is easily explained by the hypothesis that the final portion of the 'severe' letter begins here. If 2 Corinthians is a unity it may well seem rather tactless of Paul to append these harsh and sarcastic words to his delicate appeal for contributions to the collection (ch. 8, 9). On the other hand, it has appeared even from ch. 1–9 that there is still some resentment against Paul at Corinth (cf. 1: 13, 17; 5: 12 f.; 6: 12 f.); it would not be unlike Paul to begin his letter with praise of his converts and thanksgiving to God for their progress in the faith (cf. 1 C. 1: 4–9; Phil. 1: 3–11; 1 Th. 1: 2–10), and to leave to the end his criticisms and his vindication of himself (cf. Gal. 6: 12–17; Phil. 3: 2–4: 3; 2 Tim. 4: 14–18). There is some truth also in R. A. Knox's view that the severity of ch. 10–13 is less out of keeping with the rest of the letter than the confidence and approval of ch. 7–9.

Certain *references to a visit* are intelligible if 2 C. 10–13 is part of the 'severe' letter and therefore earlier than 2 C. 1–9. Thus 1: 23 'It was . . . to spare you that I did not return to Corinth' may be understood in the light of 13: 2 'On my return I will not spare'; 2: 3 'I wrote as I did so that when I came I should not be distressed' could refer to 13: 10 'I write these things when I am absent, that when I come I may not have to be harsh'. But these references are equally explicable if 2 Corinthians is a unity: 1: 23 explains why he has not come when he said he would, 13: 2 points out that he cannot postpone his visit indefinitely; 2: 3 explains why he wrote the 'severe' letter, 13: 10 why he writes the severe parts of this letter.

It is also argued that between the 'severe' letter and 2 Corinthians Paul's *attitude to self – commendation* has changed: in ch. 10–13 Paul commends himself (11: 5, 18, 22–29; 12: 1, 12), but in the later letter, ch. 1–9, he says that he will not commend himself 'again' (3: 1; 5: 12). It becomes apparent, however, when all his references to self-commendation are taken into account, that his attitude is this: he will not commend himself as the false apostles do, with words unsubstantiated by actions (3: 1 ff.), nor according to worldly standards (5: 12, 16) (though he feels compelled at one point to prove that he can outstrip his opponents even if he is judged by such standards [11: 18–29]), nor beyond the bounds of truth (10: 13), but by his honest life (1: 12 ff.), his faithful preaching of the gospel (4: 2), and the testimony of his converts (3: 2). These credentials are not his own achievements, but are due to the grace of God (1: 12; 4: 1), so that it is the Lord, not he himself, who gives him his commendation (cf. 10: 18).

Thus, although the hypothesis that 2 C. 10–13 is part of the 'severe' letter cannot be disproved, it does not appear necessary; its greatest weakness is the absence of any reference in 2 C. 10–13 to the person who was the occasion of the 'severe' letter (cf. on 7: 12), and it is 'better to assume that the whole of the "sorrowful letter" is now lost than to assume that its most important part is no longer extant' (D. Guthrie).

ANALYSIS

I. GREETINGS (1: 1–2)

1. an apostle of Christ Jesus by the will of God: Cf. 1 C. 1: 1. The presence of **Timothy** in the superscription does not mean that he is co-author of the letter, but only that he was present when it was written. **Achaia:** The Roman province comprising all Greece south of Macedonia. The most important church in Achaia appears to have been that in Corinth, the capital of the province, though we know of others, in Cenchreae (Rom. 16: 1) and Athens (Ac. 17: 34). It is the greeting, presumably, rather than the letter itself, which is addressed to **all the saints throughout Achaia**. **2. Grace and peace to you:** Cf. Rom. 1: 1.

II. THANKSGIVING FOR GOD'S COMFORTING (1: 3–11)

i. His Comforting in all Afflictions (1: 3–7)

3–7. 'I thank God that He strengthens me in my trials—not for my sake alone, but so that I may share my strength with others (3, 4). (This is all through Christ, in whose sufferings and strength I have a share [5].) Thus *my* trials and *my* strengthening bring *you* strength in your affliction (6), and so I have every hope that you will be strengthened too (7).'

3. Father of compassion: A Semitic turn of phrase for 'merciful Father'. **comfort:** I.e. 'encouragement' and 'consolation', with the overtone of 'strengthening' (present by derivation also in the English 'comfort'). **4.** God's comforting is more than enough for Paul himself, and overflows into comfort for others. **us:**

'We', 'us', and 'our' in 2 Corinthians is often to be understood of Paul alone, as is shown clearly by *e.g.* 7: 5 ff. But sometimes of course it includes his fellow-missionaries (*e.g.* 4: 6) or the Corinthian church (*e.g.* 2: 11). **5. the sufferings of Christ flow over into our lives:** Because he is a follower of Christ, he suffers affliction and persecution as Christ did, and so shares in the 'fellowship of his sufferings' (Phil. 3: 10 RV; cf. 2 C. 4: 10 f.; Col. 1: 24). **6. for your comfort and salvation:** His afflictions, like all the rest of his life, are for their sake (cf. on 4: 15 'all . . . for your benefit'). The close bonds between Paul and the Corinthians mean that they suffer when he suffers, and likewise share in his strengthening. This at least is the ideal, and though lately they have not enjoyed this reciprocity, Paul has every confidence that when they hear of God's strengthening of him in his recent affliction (8 ff.) they will find it to be to their strengthening also.

ii. His Comforting in a Recent Trial (1: 8–11)

8. That he does not speak more precisely of his **hardships** suggests that the Corinthians must have known the nature of them, though they were apparently unaware of their intensity. A severe illness would suit his language (and would explain why he felt he had the 'sentence of death *within*' himself [9 RVmg]), as would also an outbreak of persecution or mob violence, or a flogging such as he refers to in 11: 23 ff. The riot in Ephesus (Ac. 19: 23–41) might well be thought to be the occasion referred to, except that Luke does not hint that Paul was in any personal danger at that time. **Asia** is the Roman province of that name; Ephesus was its most important city. He **despaired ... of life**, but he never despairs of God's ultimate deliverance of him (4: 8).

9. He was so close to death (he felt God's **sentence of death** had been passed on him) that he could turn only to the **God who raises the dead** (cf. Rom. 4: 17; 2 C. 4: 14), a title of God with which he was familiar from the Jewish prayer, the Eighteen Benedictions: 'Blessed art thou, O Lord, for thou makest the dead to live.' **that we might not rely on ourselves:** Cf. 2: 16b; 3: 5 f.; 4: 1, 7; 13: 4. **10. he will continue to deliver:** Cf. 2 Tim. 4: 17 f. **11.** They must **help** him by their **prayers** in his future trials, so that when God has answered their prayers by delivering Paul, **many**, not only Paul, may **give thanks** to God on his behalf.

III. EXPLANATION OF HIS ALTERATION OF PLANS (1: 12–2: 13)

i. His Conduct has Always been Honest (1: 12–14)

12–14. 'I dare to ask for your prayers because my conscience assures me that I have always acted honestly, especially where you are concerned (12). I am sincere in all I write; I hope you will give me credit for this (13)—you have to a certain extent done so already—and realize that there is nothing in my conduct you need be ashamed of. By God's grace I will be able to be just as proud of you at Christ's judgment seat' (14).

12. holiness and sincerity: He had been accused of dishonesty (cf. on 12: 16; 8: 20 f.) and equivocation (1: 17; cf. 2: 17; 4: 2). **worldly wisdom** (cf. 1 C. 1: 17; 2: 4, 13): His detractors had said he lived like a worldly man (1: 17; 10: 2; cf. 5: 16). **God's grace**, expressed in the love of Christ (5: 14), is the dominant ethical force in his life. **13, 14.** It had apparently been said in Corinth that he was insincere and lacking in candour in his letters, writing one thing and meaning another. His critics had fastened on his failure to carry out his expressed intention of visiting Corinth, and Paul deals with their criticism in the following verses. He is thinking also of a more general complaint, that the Paul of the letters is a different person from the Paul they know in the flesh (cf. 10: 1, 10). His reply is that his letters mean just what their recipients read and understand by them; he hopes that they will not only understand his letters but also fully understand or realize that they can be proud of his integrity. They have already shown their partial understanding of this by their punishment of the offender (2: 9) and their reception of Titus (7: 7, 11, 15). But he is concerned not only to justify himself (cf. 13:

7), but also to be able to reciprocate their pride in him (**as we will boast of you in the day of the Lord Jesus** [cf. 1 C. 1: 8]). On that **day** of Christ's appearing and of His judgment seat (cf. 5: 10), the value of the Corinthians' lives and of Paul's work as an apostle will be tested (cf. also 1 C. 3: 12 f.; Phil. 2: 16; 1 Th. 2: 19 f.).

ii. He is not Fickle in Changing his Plans (1: 15–22)

15–22. 'I was so sure of your approval of me that I wanted to revise my plans and visit you twice, once going to Macedonia, and a second time returning from Macedonia (15, 16). This change of plan, however, has been dubbed by my opponents "vacillation", and worse, "unspirituality" (17). I have my reasons for changing my plans (15b, 23), but let me first assure you that I am no will-o'-the-wisp, neither in my plans (17) nor in my preaching (18). Nor is Jesus Christ, the subject of our preaching (19); so far from being unreliable, He is the very fulfilment of all God's promises (20). It is His reliability that we acknowledge whenever we say the Amen in His name. This confession also honours God's faithfulness (20b), and it is this faithful God who gives us the gift of steadfastness (21), and has certified me and my fellow-workers as reliable' (22).

15. Paul's *first* plan (in his mind when he wrote 1 Corinthians) was to visit Corinth after Macedonia and continue to Jerusalem if he judged it opportune (1 C. 16: 4–7). His *second* plan (presumably intimated to the Corinthians by Titus) was to travel Ephesus—Corinth—Macedonia—Corinth—Jerusalem (16). The change of plan brought against him a charge of fickleness, which he is at pains to refute (1: 17–2: 3). His opponents will have even more ground for criticism when they read this letter, for he has changed his mind again, and his *third* itinerary is in fact Ephesus—Troas—Macedonia—Corinth. Nevertheless, there was never any question of a total change of plan; he would still be coming to Corinth in order to receive their contribution for Jerusalem. His revised plan would have given them the double (lit. 'second') **benefit** of two visits of the apostle. **16. send me on my way:** The word (*propempō*) may mean that they would not only make travel arrangements for him and accompany him to the ship, but also provide from their number travelling-companions (cf. 1 C. 16: 3). **17. do it lightly:** The use of the article before the noun 'vacillation' suggests that he is replying to a charge ('*the* fickleness of which I am accused'). **in a worldly manner:** Lit. 'according to the flesh' (cf. 5: 16; 10: 2 f.). **in the same breath ... "Yes, yes" and "No, no":** I.e. 'changeable' rather than 'double-tongued'. There is no connection with the similar phrases in Mt. 5: 37 and Jas 5: 12.

18. Our message probably means 'all communication of mine to you', preaching as well as announcement of travel plans. **as surely as God is faithful:** An oath, like 'God is witness' (Rom. 1: 9, etc.), elliptical for 'As God is faithful to His promises that He will punish the deceiver, I swear . . .'. Less probably, the phrase means that God's providential faithfulness will ensure that His apostle is free of duplicity. **19. in him it has always been "Yes":** This is not a strictly logical development of his argument. There is no objection to being yes *or* no, only to being yes *and* no. But Paul seizes on the word 'Yes', and says Christ is 'Yes *and not* No'. This striking phrase is elucidated by the next verse. **20. no matter how many promises God has made:** Phrased emphatically. Specifically, they are the OT promises of a Saviour, *e.g.* Ac. 13: 23; Gal. 3: 14; Ac. 2: 39. **they are "Yes":** They will be executed and fulfilled, so proving God to be reliable. **Amen:** 'Truly, surely', is a Heb. equivalent for Gk. *nai* 'yes' (they occur together in Rev. 1: 7). The train of thought is: 'Christ is God's Yes; that is why it is in Christ's name that we say Amen (=Yes) at the end of our prayers'. **21. makes . . . us . . . stand firm** continues the word-play on 'Amen' with another reference to the meaning of the Heb. verb *āmēn* 'to make firm' (a similar play on the words 'sustain' and 'faithful' in 1 C. 1: 8 f.). **anointed:** with the Holy Spirit for service. **us:** He is not thinking of the anointing common to all Christians (cf. 1 Jn 2: 20), but of the appointment of Silas, Timothy, and himself (probably himself primarily) to the Christian ministry. **21, 22. anointed . . . set his seal . . . put:** These three terms refer to the same event, Paul's conversion and calling to the apostleship. **Set his seal . . . on us** virtually means 'endued us with power from heaven' (cf. Jn 6: 27). Perhaps, however, the metaphor of the seal is from the commercial world, where a seal attests or validates a document. **Spirit . . . as a deposit:** The Spirit *is* the 'guarantee' (RSV), the 'deposit', or 'first instalment' of salvation (so also in Rom. 8: 23; Eph. 1: 14). Paul's argument is: 'If God has put His mark of approval upon me, how can I be an unreliable, fickle kind of person?'

iii. Why he has Not Visited Them (1: 23–2: 4)

1: 23–2: 4. 'No, it was not from fickleness that I changed my plans, but out of consideration for you, to avoid the pain and mutual embarrassment of another visit like the last (2: 1). My "severe" letter likewise was for this purpose, to clear up our differences before I arrived' (3, 4). **23. to spare you:** Cf. on 13: 2. **I did not return:** That is, 'I did not come any more' after the two previous visits. **24.** On reflection,

he realizes that the word 'spare' has unfortunate connotations. If he can *spare*, he could also have been overbearing, so he hastens to add, 'Not that we lord it . . .'. The verse is better punctuated: 'Not that we lord it over your faith (we work *with* you for your joy), for you stand firm in your faith'. He does not tyrannize over their Christian life, for first, he is merely a *fellow*-worker, and secondly, they are strong enough to stand on their own feet. **2: 1. another painful visit:** Lit. 'not come again to you with sorrow'. The Gk. could mean 'that my second visit should not be a painful one', but this is not his second visit (12: 14). **2. If I hurt you, who will be left to gladden me but sad people? A great comfort that will be!' Cf. Knox: 'Was I to make you sorry? It meant bringing sorrow on those who are my own best source of comfort'. **3. I wrote:** The 'sorrowful' or 'severe' letter, his third letter to the Corinthians (cf. 7: 8; 10: 10; Introduction). **as I did:** Reprovingly, as parts of this letter also are written (13: 10). Better a severe letter than a visit which would hurt everyone. **4. not to grieve you:** He did hurt, and knew he would, but his intention was not to produce pain, but repentance leading to joy (cf. 7: 8–12).

iv. Punishment and Forgiveness of the Offender (2: 5–11)

5–11. The 'severe' letter has had at least one salutary effect: the leader of the opposition to Paul has been punished by the church, and has repented of his rebellion. Paul therefore forgives him, and asks the church also to forgive him.

The person in question here has been traditionally identified with the incestuous man of 1 C. 5; this view is necessary only so long as the existence of an intermediate letter is not recognized, and is now generally abandoned for the following reasons. (i) The Corinthians' attitude to this offender is a matter of obedience to Paul (9); the case of the incestuous man was a matter of ethics. (ii) Here, the church discipline has been sufficient punishment, and the offender is to be restored (6, 7); in 1 C. 5 the wrong-doer has been delivered to Satan for the destruction of the flesh (5). (iii) It puts it too mildly to say that the incestuous man caused pain to the church only 'in some measure' (2 C. 2: 5).

5. anyone: Tactfully, he speaks indefinitely, but he refers to a definite individual ('him' [7, 8]). **Not so much . . . me** only, or mainly (cf. 7: 12). The fact that one man has opposed Paul is far less important than that he has carried the church with him into rebellion against Paul's God-given authority. **6. The majority** need not imply any minority but the offender himself; it would be better translated 'community, church'. The nature of **the punishment** is unknown. **8. Reaffirm** means 'decide in favour of love, or 'confirm, validate' your love for him by public announcement of his forgiveness.

9. I wrote: Cf. on v. 3. They have proved themselves **obedient** in this matter, but they have yet to prove that they unanimously accept Paul's authority (cf. 10: 6). **11.** 'Some Satan destroys through sin, others through the unmeasured sorrow following on repentance for it. To take by sin is his proper work; by repentance, however, is more than his due, for that weapon is ours, not his' (Chrysostom). **Outwit us** probably means 'you and me'; Satan would have gained the advantage over them if he had been able to keep Paul and his converts estranged.

v. How he Met Titus in Macedonia (2: 12–13)

12–13. Paul reverts to the account of his travels (1: 15 f.), only to embark almost immediately on a digression which lasts until 7: 4.

13. He **had no peace of mind** because of anxiety over how his severe letter had been received in Corinth (cf. 7: 5 'fears within'). **them:** His converts, later mentioned as a church (Ac. 20: 6 ff.).

IV. THE APOSTOLIC MINISTRY (2: 14–5: 21)

i. His Apostolic Travels Ordained by God (2: 14–17)

14–17. 'I thank God that all my travels are steps in the triumphant progress of the gospel (14); in fact, through my preaching I am God's travelling dispenser of life and death (16). This task has immense responsibilities, but I am able to discharge them because I am no mere travelling salesman, but a man commissioned by God' (17).

14. thanks: The mention of 'Macedonia' brings the sudden memory of his joyful reunion with Titus there (7: 6 f.), and he interrupts the account of his travels with gratitude for God's guidance of his affairs. **leads us in triumphal procession:** The picture is of a victorious Roman general leading his captives in triumphal procession. Paul thinks of himself as one of Christ's captives: if he stays in Troas or leaves for Macedonia, if he goes to Corinth or remains in Ephesus, it is not according to his own desire, but at the direction of Christ. For the picture of the triumph, cf. Col. 2: 15 where the captives are the defeated evil powers, and 1 C. 4: 9 where the apostles form the rear of the procession, the position assigned to those who were to die in the arena. **fragrance of the knowledge:** It is possible that the metaphor of the Roman triumph is here continued by reference to a custom of burning incense along the route of the procession; to the victors it would be a 'fragrance of life', but to the de-

feated a reminder of their imminent execution, a 'smell of death' (16). **15. aroma of Christ:** In v. 14 the fragrance (Gk. *osmē*) is the knowledge of God, in v. 15 the aroma (Gk. *euōdia*) is Paul, who spreads that knowledge. It is not necessary to attempt to harmonize the two uses of the metaphor; having taken up a metaphor, Paul often uses it in more than one sense (cf. 'letter' [3: 2 f.], and 'veil' [3: 13 ff.]). **16. the smell of death:** Perhaps a reminiscence of the Jewish doctrine concerning the Torah, that if a man uses it in the right way it becomes for him a medicine of life; if not, a deadly poison (TB, *Yoma*, 72b). **death:** Paul's view of the 'deadly' effect of the gospel has the Lord's authority (cf. Mt. 18: 18; Jn 9: 39), yet 'it is always necessary to make a distinction between the proper and natural office of the gospel, and that which it has by accident, which is to be imputed to the perversity of men' (Calvin). **who is equal to:** I.e. capable of bearing such responsibility, as a dispenser of life and death, unless qualified by God? (cf. 3: 6). **17.** Paul's reply is that he is 'equal to such a task', but only because he has been **sent from God** (cf. 3: 5; 1: 9). 'Peddlers' are hucksters or retail tradesmen (ill-famed in antiquity), especially wine-merchants, who sell shoddy goods, adulterate good wine by mixing it with water, or have an eye to their own profit rather than the customer's benefit. Which of these malpractices Paul ascribes to the **many** (cf. 11: 13, 20) is hard to tell (probably the last); they are all eschewed by men **with sincerity** (cf. on 1: 12).

ii. This is not Self-praise, for he Needs None (3: 1–3)

1–3. 'My remarks about myself (2: 17) might sound like self-praise, but I really need none (1), for you Corinthians are sufficient letter of recommendation to commend me both to yourselves and to the world (2). You prove, by the work of the Spirit in your lives, that I indeed brought Christ to you—and that not in word only' (3). The metaphor of letter is exploited in several ways, which cannot be completely harmonized.

1. Self-advertisement is one of Paul's failings, according to his opponents. Their criticism doubtless stemmed from expressions of his authority in the 'severe' letter, and such passages as 1 C. 2: 16; 4: 16; 11: 1; 14: 18; Paul is at pains to deny this misrepresentation (cf. 2 C. 4: 5; 5: 12; 10: 13). He had nothing against **letters of recommendation** in themselves. What else was 8: 16–24 or the letter to Philemon? (Cf. also Rom. 16: 1; 1 C. 16: 10.) But self-commendatory letters and 'spiritual bills of clearance' (Hughes) are alike unnecessary for Paul, though *de rigueur* for **some people** (a favourite term of his for his opponents [cf. 10: 2; Gal. 1: 7; 1 Tim. 1: 3]). **2.** Because Paul has played such an intimate part in the conversion and the Christian life of the Corinthians, his credentials are **written on** their **hearts**, a more permanent and more convincing commendation than those written merely with ink on paper. But what is written on their hearts must be expressed in their lives (cf. Mt. 12: 34), and so Paul's commendation is **known and read by all men**. 'Your' (RSV), though weakly supported by MSS, is probably preferable to **our** (NIV, NEB); the two words are frequently confused in MSS of the NT because they were coming to be pronounced identically. **3.** Paul uses his metaphor somewhat differently: the Corinthians are not only his letter of recommendation, but also a **letter from Christ** (their lives bear the mark of His authorship), **the result of our ministry**. This last word (lit. 'ministered') is chosen because Paul is already thinking of the law/gospel contrast (6 ff.), where 'ministration' figures prominently. **tablets of human hearts:** Lit. 'tablets of flesh, that is, hearts'. **With the Spirit of God** and 'tablets of flesh' are characteristics of the nature of the New Covenant (Jer. 31: 33; Ezek. 11: 19; 36: 26).

iii. All his Ability is from God (3: 4–6)
4–6. His reflections on the contrast 'tablets of stone'/'hearts of flesh' lead (by way of Jer. 31: 33) to a profound and moving study of the contrast Old/New Covenants. But first he will answer his question of 2: 16; what sufficiency he has does not come from himself, but from God.

4. His **confidence** is in his own integrity, corroborated by what the Corinthians know of him (1–3), and guaranteed to him **through Christ**. **5.** He does not depend upon the qualification of himself or other Christians (cf. 10: 12), but on that of **God**; so he had learned in Asia (1: 9b). **6. ministers of a new covenant:** Paul (together with all preachers of the gospel, of course) plays a similar rôle in the New Covenant to that of Moses in the Old: just as the law was given 'through Moses' (Jn 1: 14), so the knowledge of Christ is spread abroad 'through us' (2 C. 2: 14). (For the law as given by the mediation of *angels*, cf. Heb. 2: 2; and for *Christ* as Moses' counterpart, cf. Heb. 8: 6; 12: 24.) **the letter . . . Spirit:** The contrast is between the Old and New Covenants (Jer. 31: 33 is still very much in Paul's mind; and cf. Rom. 7: 6). There is no suggestion here of 'the letter of the law' versus 'the spirit of the law'; this distinction is proper elsewhere, though it is noteworthy that Christ (contrary to modern use of the phrase) regards the 'spirit' as more stringent than the 'letter' (Mt. 6: 20 ff.). **the Spirit:** It is not certain that there is a direct reference to the Holy Spirit; the contrast may be that between the external and the internal (cf. Rom. 2: 29; outwardly'/'inwardly' = 'in the letter'/'in the spirit').

iv. The Superiority of the New Covenant (3: 7–18)
(a) Its Superior Glory (3: 7–11)
7–11. The New Covenant is more glorious than the Old because (i) it comes from the Spirit, and does not lead to death (7, 8); (ii) it brings acquittal, not condemnation (9, 10); (iii) it is permanent, not transitory (11).

Though 2: 14–3: 6 is inspired by a polemical motive, Paul seems now, in turning to the superiority of Christianity over Judaism, not to be assailing hypothetical Judaizers at Corinth (cf. introduction to ch. 10), but merely developing the high point of 2: 14 and 'making much of his ministry' (Rom. 11: 13).

7. ministry: I.e. administration, set of arrangements **that brought death:** In effect, not intention. Cf. Rom. 7: 10 and Midrash Rabba, *Exodus*, 41: 1: 'While Israel were standing below engraving idols to provoke their Creator to anger . . . God sat on high engraving for them tablets which would give them life'. **glory:** Paul fastens on the fact that Moses' face shone (Gk. *dedoxastai*, Exod. 34: 29, 35 LXX) as symbolizing the glory (Gk. *doxa*) of the Old Covenant. *Doxa* does duty both in an abstract sense ('splendour, majesty, glory') and in a physical one ('brightness, rays of light'); for Paul, the spiritual can be well expressed by the physical. **could not look steadily at Moses' face:** Exod. 34: 30 says merely that because of the brightness *they were afraid to come near him.* Paul here apparently reproduces a current Jewish view (*e.g.* Philo, *Life of Moses*, 2: 70), which is not incompatible with the Exodus narrative. **Fading though it was** is to be elaborated in v. 11. Here it means 'for all its impermanence the splendour was none the less bright'. **8. the ministry of the Spirit:** 'The administration of the New Covenant which is symbolized by the Spirit (or, by spirit)'. **9.** 'If splendour accompanied the dispensation under which we are condemned, how much richer in splendour must be that one under which we are acquitted!' (NEB). **10.** In comparison with the New, the splendour of the Old Covenant hardly seems to be splendour at all, like the light of the moon and stars before the brightness of the sun (Calvin).

(b) Its Superior 'Openness' (3: 12–18)
12–18. The New Covenant is moreover 'open'; Paul's ministry of the New Covenant has the same 'openness' or frankness as the Covenant itself (cf. 2: 17; 4: 2 ff.).

12. Since he has **such a hope** that the New Covenant will prove to be glorious (7 f.), justificatory (9 f.), and permanent (11), he can speak frankly in the most exalted terms of his vocation, even though to his opponents this reeks of self-commendation (1). **very bold:** Better, 'frank and open' (Moffatt). NIV fails to bring out the contrast between Paul's openness and

Moses' veil. **13.** It is not said in Exod. 34 that
the glory on Moses' face was fading, but Paul
deduces reasonably enough from *his face was
radiant because he had spoken with the* LORD
(Exod. 34: 30) and *when*(ever) *he came out Moses'
face was radiant* (34: 34 f.) that when he was
not talking to God, the glory was fading. To
conceal **the radiance . . . fading** was not
necessarily Moses' own motive for covering
his face; Paul is probably thinking that it was
God's providence that the Israelites never saw
that the glory was fading. **while the radiance
was fading away:** lit. 'to the end of what
was ceasing'. Older commentators, translating
'could not steadfastly look to the end of that
which is abolished' (AV), thought of Christ as
the End (cf. Rom. 10: 4, 'the End of the law');
but why should Moses have desired to hide
Christ from them? Paul's meaning probably is:
If the Israelites had ever seen the glory on
Moses' face altogether faded, they might have
thought that the glorious law was abrogated.
14. made dull: More appropriately, 'blinded'.
the old covenant in v. 6 meant 'the old
régime', here 'the *terms* of the old covenant',
i.e. the Pentateuch or the whole OT. Paul rings
the changes on **the same veil** (as he does on
'letter' [1 ff.], and 'limit' [10: 13 ff.]): in v. 13
it is the veil over Moses' face; in v. 14 the
(metaphorical) veil over the Jews' hearts. **It
has not been removed** so long as they find
permanence in the Old Covenant. (A less likely
punctuation gives the sense: 'The same veil
remains, it not being revealed that in Christ it
is taken away'). **16. whenever anyone turns:**
The Gk. is ambiguous: 'when he (Moses)/it
(Israel)/one (anyone) turns'. Certainly Paul is
thinking of Moses and Exod. 34: 34, and most
probably is saying that any Israelite can, like
Moses, have the veil removed if he **turns** (i.e.
is converted) **to the Lord** (in this case, Christ).
There is a play on the literal and spiritual meaning of the word 'turn'. **17. the Lord is the
Spirit:** Either he means that the Lord (Christ)
is the 'spirit' which is characteristic of the New
Covenant (6) (cf. 1 C. 15: 45, 'The last Adam
(became) a life-giving *spirit*'); or that He is *one
with* the Spirit (for Christ and the Spirit as
identical *in experience*, cf. Rom. 8: 9 ff.). Whichever interpretation is adopted, it is clear that
Paul's thought has come full-circle again to v.
6. The spiritual **freedom** is freedom from the
'law of sin and death' (Rom. 8: 2; cf. Gal. 5:
1). **18. we . . . all:** All Christians, not just one
man, Moses. **unveiled:** Once for all (perfect
participle), unlike Moses' repeated veilings and
unveilings. **we . . . reflect:** The word is a
present participle, signifying a constant action,
not one that is temporary and occasional, as
Moses' was. **reflect:** The word meant in classical Gk. 'to look at oneself in a mirror', but
that requires steady looking when mirrors are

metal, and so the word has probably come
to mean simply 'to gaze steadily' cf. NIV mg
'contemplate'. 'Beholding as in a (dull) mirror'
(RVmg, cf. AV) is out of place here (it is the
excellence of Christian vision that occupies
Paul, not its present imperfection as in 1 C. 13:
12). NIV's translation, **reflect** is attractive (also
RSVmg, NEB), as if to say that 'every Christian
has become a Moses' (J. Héring), and Num.
11: 29 is fulfilled! But it seems rather that Paul
is contrasting Christians with Moses in the
presence of God, not Moses before the people.
into his likeness: Man is already created in the
likeness of God (Gen. 1: 27; 1 C. 11: 7; Jas
3: 9), but this is not incompatible with the
Christian's growth in likeness to Christ (cf.
Rom. 8: 29; Eph. 4: 24; Col. 3: 10) and his
eventual perfect similarity to Him (1 Jn 3: 2).
with ever-increasing glory: Cf. on 2: 16
'from death to death'.
**v. His Ministry of Light Against Darkness
(4: 1–6)**
1–6. Paul returns (1) to the subject of his apostolic ministry (cf. 3: 6), expanding his theme
of the 'openness' of his gospel (2). 'It is true
that to unbelievers it is not "open" (3), but that
is because they (like the Jews, 3: 14) are blinded
by Satan to the glory of Christ (4), who is the
theme of my preaching, now that God Himself
has enlightened me' (6).
1. This ministry is that of the New Covenant (3:6), which he says he has received
through God's mercy, thus excluding self-
esteem (cf. 3: 1) and self-sufficiency (cf. 3: 4).
we do not lose heart: The responsibilities are
God-given; so is the energy for their fulfilment.
2. Denney's warning is sound, that we must
not read Paul 'as if he had been expressly accused of everything which he says he does not
do, and as if he deliberately retorted on his
opponents every charge he denied'. But 12: 16
shows he had been accused of craftiness, and
2: 17 refers undoubtedly to his opponents' insincerity.
2. setting forth the truth plainly: He is
accused not so much of obscurity as of lack of
candour (cf. 2: 17 f.). **3.** 'But how do you
explain the fact that the gospel is not equally
plain to all?', someone might ask. This is due,
replies Paul, not to obscurity in the gospel, but
to the blindness of unbelievers. **4. the god
of this age:** A unique expression for Satan,
though reminiscent of Christ's 'the prince of
this world (*kosmos*)' (Jn 12: 31). **this age** (*aiōn*),
rather than 'world' (RSV), is the present age,
which is in process of being superseded (and in
some senses has been superseded [5: 17; Gal. 1:
4; Heb. 6: 5]) by the age to come, otherwise
called the last days, the kingdom of God, etc.
(1 C. 2: 6; Ac. 2: 17; Mt. 12: 28; 1 Jn
8). Satan's authority, even over this age, is
usurped, and only partial, for God Himself is

king of the ages (1 Tim. 1: 17). **The image of God** describes Christ not only as 'very God' (cf. Heb. 1: 3), but also as 'the proper man', fulfilling the purposes for which man was created in God's image (cf. on 3: 18). **5.** Paul underlines 'Christ' in v. 4, and exclaims, 'It is not myself I preach! No, it is Christ as Lord. I am no lord (1: 24); I am your slave! (cf. 1 C. 3: 5).' **for Jesus' sake:** He deliberately uses the name that recalls Christ as servant (cf. 10, 11; Phil. 2: 10). **6.** The connection with what precedes is unclear. Either, **for** introduces a reason why Paul cannot preach himself: because he knows he owes everything to God. Or, v. 5 is a parenthesis and the sense is: 'In *their* case, the god of this age has blinded their minds. (It is not so with me) for the God who created light has shone in my heart'. **For God, who said, 'Let light shine':** 'Then indeed He said, Let it be, and it was; but now He said nothing, but Himself became our light' (Chrysostom). **made his light shine in our hearts:** Paul is thinking probably of his own conversion in particular (cf. the great light from heaven, Ac. 26: 13), but he associates his fellow-missionaries with himself.

vi. Paul the Unlikely Apostle (4: 7–12)

7–12. Paul is recalled from his reflections on the glory of his ministry by the sobering thought of his own natural insufficiency. But this paradox of a frail mortal as God's spokesman is in fact designed by God to instil in him an aversion to 'confidence in the flesh' (cf. 1: 9; 12: 9). Possibly Paul's apparent unsuitability as God's messenger had been ridiculed by his opponents; if so, he is making capital out of their criticism.

7. this treasure: The light of the knowledge of Christ, or possibly, what springs from that, 'this ministry' (1). It is entrusted to **jars of clay**, the bodies of His apostles. The inappropriateness of the vessel to the treasure it contained did not prompt Paul to doubt his vocation; rather, it illustrated the truth that *salvation comes from the Lord* (Jon. 2: 9; cf. 2 C. 4: 13) (Denney). **8. hard pressed . . . not crushed:** More accurately 'harried . . . not hemmed in' (Moffatt). There is a play on the words **perplexed . . . not in despair**, which Hughes reproduces with some success as 'confused but not confounded'. **10, 11.** He compares his own constant experience of persecution and suffering with that of **Jesus**, the name reminiscent of the suffering servant (as in v. 5). Vv. 10, 11 are equivalent, except that in v. 10 his life is a dying life, *like* Jesus', in v. 11 a dying life **for Jesus' sake. carry around:** in his missionary travels. The **life of Jesus** is the life that Jesus lives now, His resurrection life (cf. Rom. 6: 4; Phil. 3: 10 f.). **12.** His physical sufferings (little dyings which will eventually lead to death, 1: 8 f.) are the means

by which spiritual life becomes operative in the Corinthians.

vii. The Christian Hope is his Encouragement (4: 13–18)

13–18. 'But my life is not unrelieved gloomy suffering. I share with you a hope of future bliss (14, 17), and so I speak out with assurance (13). The present suffering is but temporary, and will be swallowed up in eternal glory' (17, 18).

13. It is written: in Ps. 116, a hymn of thanksgiving for deliverance from death. Not just this verse (10), but the whole psalm fits the experience of Paul admirably, and was doubtless in his mind. Ps. 116: 6 is reminiscent of the theme of 2 C. 1: 9 and 4: 7; v. 5 is magnificently illustrated by 4: 10–12; v. 9 has its Christian counterpart in 4: 16–5: 5. (The Heb. of Ps. 116: 10 is obscure [cf. RSV], but Paul quotes LXX.) **we also believe:** I.e. have our trust in God. **we speak:** The sense is, 'We speak out confidently' (cf. 3: 12). **14.** Though in 1 Th. 4: 17 and 1 C. 15: 51 he has spoken of the Second Coming as imminent, here he contemplates, for the moment, his own death. His views on the Coming have not changed (as some maintain), but his life-expectation has diminished because of recent experiences (1: 9; 4: 8 ff.); and in any case he has not abandoned hope of being alive at the Coming (5: 2 f.). **With Jesus** does not mean 'to be with Jesus', but expresses the Christian's togetherness with Christ in His resurrection: just as *without* Christ there is no resurrection (1 C. 15: 14), so the believer's resurrection is *with* Christ. **15. All:** I.e. all my sufferings, are for your sake. They are 'for Jesus' sake' in that he suffers because he preaches Christ's gospel (4: 11), they are for his converts' sake in that they benefit (1: 6), and ultimately they are for God's sake in that He is more greatly glorified. 'All for your sake' is a minor theme of the letter (cf. 1: 6; 5: 13–15). **16. Therefore we do not lose heart** looks back to v. 1, and sums up the chapter. In turning his attention, in what follows, from the present to the future, the same conviction remains unshaken. **outwardly** (AV: 'our outward man') =jars of clay (7), bodies (10), mortal body (11). His 'inner nature' is his whole personality, which is undismayed and undespairing (8); his body is beaten and decaying, but his spirit is daily reinvigorated. **17. light and momentary troubles:** It is only by comparison with the eternal glory that it seems insignificant (Hodge). **glory that . . . outweighs:** In Heb. the same root means 'to be heavy' and 'to be glorious'; hence the striking image of glory 'outweighing' troubles (usually we think of troubles, not glory, as heavy). **Glory** is the *leit-motiv* of the world of the resurrection (Héring).

viii. But will Death Intervene before the Advent? (5: 1–10)

1–10. The prospect of death is exceedingly unpleasant, because it involves a bodiless 'nakedness' (3). But he is not afraid, for his attention is concentrated on the resurrection body that awaits him (1). Better, of course, than being clothed with this new body *after* death would be to put it on while still living, i.e. at the Parousia (2–4). Yet death, mitigated as it is by hope of immediate reunion with Christ (8), is preferable to this bodily life of 'absence' from Him (6–8). Whether he will be dead or alive at the Parousia, however, he cannot tell; the fixed point on his horizon is the judgment seat of Christ, and his present concern must be to fit himself for that by pleasing Christ (9, 10).

1. we know: He deduces from the familiar saying of Jesus (Mk 14: 58) that by virtue of his union with Christ the Christian too will have a new body **not built by human hands**. The contrast between the tent (the mortal body) and the **building** recalls that between the temporary tabernacle and the permanent temple. **destroyed:** I.e. dismantled. **We have need** not imply that our resurrection bodies are already prepared, but that we are assured of them (cf. 1 Jn 5: 15). **2.** Changing the metaphor for the resurrection body from 'house' to 'garment' (though retaining the word **dwelling**), Paul expresses his longing to **be clothed with** the new body over the old, as one puts one garment on over another, i.e. to be 'further clothed' (4) at the Parousia with the new body while he is still alive. **3.** If this occurs, he will not even momentarily be **naked**, divested of a body. **4.** He would willingly be out of this body, not because disembodiment is desirable, but because of the resurrection body which will inevitably follow death. He expressly disassociates himself from Platonists, Pythagoreans, and Gnostics, who thought of the body as a prison for the soul, and were only too glad to be free of it. **We groan**, not to be rid of the body, but to have the new one superimposed. **5.** God is the one who has designed **this very purpose**, the clothing with the new body. The Christian hope is already partly actualized by the work of Christ; God has **given us the Spirit as a guarantee** of its complete realization (cf. 1: 21 f.). **6. Therefore** refers back to 5: 1 and 4: 16, but perhaps also to the Spirit as guarantee (5). **confident:** In the face of death. But confidence to face death is for him a confidence to face life. Death is the worst that life can bring, so all other hazards and afflictions he can take in his stride. **7.** The sense in which we are away from the Lord (6) is here clarified: the presence of Christ by **faith** is known (cf. Eph. 3: 17), but not the 'face to face' **sight** of Him (cf. 1 C. 13: 12). **8.** Paul must indeed be

confident to be able to say he would **prefer to be away from the body** or 'unclothed'; this is an evil, but a lesser evil than being absent from the Lord. 'Do you see how, concealing what was painful, the words "death" and "the end", he has employed instead of them such as provoke great longing, calling them presence with God; and leaving aside those things that are accounted to be sweet, the things of life, he has expressed them with painful names, calling the life here an absence from the Lord?' (Chrysostom). **9.** It is not for him to make the decision whether he will be **at home** in the body or **away** from it when the Lord returns, but he can decide to make his life pleasing to Christ. It is possible that **at home** means 'at home with the Lord', and **away** 'in the body'. Paul's endeavour then is to please Him, whether called before His judgment seat (10), or preaching the gospel (11). **10. we . . . all:** All Christians, not all men (as in Rom. 2: 6 ff.). The judgment seat of God (Rom. 14: 10) is here called **the judgment seat** (Gk. *bēma*, lit. 'tribunal' or 'platform' on which the seat is placed) **of Christ**, who is the judge (cf. 2 Tim. 4: 1; Ac. 17: 31). The judgments dispensed are evaluations of the worth of individual Christian lives, varying from 'Well done, good and faithful servant' (Mt. 25: 23) to a total rejection of a life as worthless (**bad**, Gk. *phaulos*, strictly 'mean, worthless') (cf. 1 C. 3: 12–15). In accordance with this assessment the good or bad character of a Christian's life is recompensed by reward or loss of reward (the word for **receive** [Gk. *komizomai*] means 'to receive what is one's own or one's due', and thus emphasizes the strict impartiality and justice of the judgment). The believer's salvation is of course not called in question here; it is **the things done while in the body** that are judged.

ix. His Motives in his Ministry (5: 11–15)

11–15. 'It is in the light of the judgment seat of Christ that I conduct my ministry. God is witness to my integrity, and so you may be too (11, 12). There is no self-interest in my ministry—it is all for your sakes (13). And that is because my life is shaped by the self-giving love of Christ, who died for the sake of others (14), that their lives in turn might be free of self-interest' (15).

11. Paul's critics had very possibly claimed that he used dishonest methods of persuasion (cf. Gal. 1: 10; 1 Th. 2: 3 ff.). He replies by acknowledging that he **persuades** men, but he does so with a good conscience, in the **fear** of **the Lord**, for his motives are **plain to God**, and will be revealed at the judgment seat. He does not mean that it is because he knows how terrifying the judgments of God upon unbelievers are that he persuades men to accept the gospel. **12.** Again, as in 3: 1, Paul realizes that protestations of his integrity will be read as self-commendation. Far from commending himself, he says, he is simply giving the church weapons to employ in his defence, in which he hints, perhaps with gentle irony, they are already eager to engage themselves. **13.** They may well defend him, for he has never lived for himself, but only for God and his converts. If he was ever beside himself, lost in spiritual ecstasy (had his critics also said that he was quite crazy? cf. 11: 16), that was for God's sake; if he was in his **right mind**, that was for the Corinthians' sake. **14. Christ's love**, expressed pre-eminently by His giving Himself for others, **compels** Paul, i.e. dictates Paul's motives in life, restraining him from a life of self-interest. The love of Christ, however, has this effect not only on Paul, but also on all those for whom Christ died. In the death of Christ, **all** who are 'in Christ' also died to the old life of self-interest (cf. Rom. 6: 3 ff.). (Note that it is not 'then were all dead' [AV], but 'all [believers] died' in union with Christ.) **15.** And further, His death was in order to create in those who died with Him a life-for-others, that they **should no longer live for themselves**. The idea of life-for-others runs like a ground bass throughout the paragraph (cf. 4: 15; 10: 8).

x. The Theme of his Ministry (5: 16–21)

16–21. 'Because what motivates me now is Christ's love for others, external appearance and distinctions do not enter into my estimate of others, not even of Christ (16). This radically altered view of people is a revolution the New Order brings about (17), this New Order which is both God's doing and characteristic of God Himself. He is the one who in His love for others was reconciling the world to Himself (18a, 19a), and who has ordained the proclamation of this reconciliation through us His messengers (18b, 19b, 20). He Himself has put an end to the estrangement caused by sin by giving Christ as an atonement for sin'.

16. from now on: Ever since he discovered the meaning of Christ's death as self-giving love for others. To 'know no man after the flesh' (AV) is rightly understood by NIV as to **regard no one from a worldly**, or purely human, **point of view**. He does not mean that he once knew the earthly Jesus, and now knows Him no longer as such; still less is he making a distinction between the Jesus of history and the Christ of faith, or declaring that knowledge of the historical Jesus is valueless. **17. he is a new creation:** Better, 'there is (an instance of) the New Creation'; in his case at least **the old** order **has gone** and **the new** order **has come**, i.e. there is a partial realization of the hope of new heavens and new earth ('there is a new world' [NEB]; cf. 2 Pet. 3: 13; Isa. 65: 17; Rev. 21: 1, 4 f.). In this context, **the new** is specifically seen in the changed outlook on people

(16), and the change from self-interest to life-for-others (15). **18.** As in the old creation, everything was created by God through His word, so in the new **all . . . is from God** through Christ. God Himself brings about the reconciliation; the idea of a loving Jesus winning over a stubborn and wrathful God is foreign to Paul's gospel.

19. God was reconciling the world . . . in Christ: The wording may mean 'God was in Christ, reconciling' (AV, cf. RSV), or 'in (=by, through) Christ God was reconciling' (RSVmg, NIV). The context does not call for a special emphasis on the fact that God was in Christ, and indeed the phrase sounds Johannine (cf. Jn 10: 38) rather than Pauline, so the latter translation (parallel to v. 18) is to be preferred. **God was reconciling:** Paul's use of the imperfect instead of the simple past tense (as in v. 18) perhaps indicates his hesitation to say that the world has been reconciled in the same sense as 'we' have; in the case of the believer, the reconciliation is effective in both parties, while in the case of the world the reconciliation means that 'He was disposing of everything that on His part made peace impossible' (Denney). But the reconciliation is of cosmic effect; it is not merely the church, but the world, the universe (cf. Col. 1: 20), that is the object of God's reconciliation. His reconciliation is evidenced, first, by His **not counting men's sins against them**, but by putting them to the account of their substitute (21), and secondly, by His entrusting to His apostles **the message of reconciliation**, that God has made peace with the world. 'At bottom, the Gospel is not good advice, but good news. All the good advice it gives is summed up in this—Receive the good news' (Denney).

20. Paul emphasizes the dignity of his office by calling himself an **ambassador**, the technical term for a legate of Caesar, who speaks not only 'on behalf of' but also 'in the place of' (AV) his master. Cf. the plenipotentiary status of Paul in 2: 14–16. But he does not simply stand on his dignity; he beseeches men. **We implore you:** 'You' is lacking in the Gk. He is not addressing his converts who have already been reconciled (18), but giving the substance of his message: 'We implore (men), saying, Be reconciled to God, accept His offered friendship'.

21. V. 20 expands 'committed to us the message of reconciliation' (19), v. 21 develops 'not counting men's sins against them'. **Made** is devoid of any idea of compulsion; Christ's sacrifice was freely willed (Jn 10: 8). **made him . . . to be sin:** The Heb. word for 'sin' (*ḥaṭṭā't*) and consequently the LXX *hamartia* 'sin', Paul's word here, are occasionally used for 'sin-offering' (*e.g.* Lev. 4: 24), and it is probable that this is Paul's meaning here (so

NIVmg). Christ's death is frequently spoken of as a sin-offering (e.g. Rom. 8: 3; Heb. 7: 27; 9: 12; Jn 1: 29; Isa. 53: 6, 10), and all legitimate inferences from other interpretations of 'made him to be sin' (e.g. He stood in the place of sinners, He accepted the penalty of sin) are embraced by the concept of Him as a sin-offering. Paul is careful to avoid any suggestion that Christ became sinful or a sinner (though a too strict parallelism with 'we become righteousness' as an equivalent of 'we become righteous' might suggest this), and explicitly asserts that He **had no sin. We . . . become the righteousness of God** means 'we become righteous before God', with the added nuance that it is *God's* righteousness that is imparted to us.

V. RENEWAL OF BONDS BETWEEN PAUL AND THE CORINTHIANS (6: 1–7: 16)

i. An Appeal for the Corinthians to be Reconciled to Paul (6: 1–10)

1–10. 'Do not let God's gift of reconciliation lie idle in your lives (1)—for this is the Day of Salvation when old hostilities are broken down (2). I for my part have gone out of my way not to provoke opposition (3), but have rather striven to prove my good faith by enduring hardships for the sake of the gospel (4, 5), and by manifesting the fruits of the Spirit (6, 7), no matter what my reputation or outward appearance might be' (8–10).

1. Paul is **God's fellow-worker** in that God's work is the reconciliation, Paul's the proclamation of it. Although the word **God's** is not in the text, it is supplied more naturally than references to other Christian workers (cf. 1 C. 3: 9), or the Corinthians themselves as collaborators. **We** throughout chaps. 6 and 7 plainly means Paul himself. **God's grace** appears to be in particular the gift of reconciliation. The Corinthians will **receive** it **in vain** if they do not allow it to operate in their lives, i.e. if they will not be reconciled to Paul. Thus it is likely that 6: 1 begins his plea for full restoration of friendly relations, a plea which becomes explicit in 6: 11–13 and 7: 2. **2.** He quotes Isa. 49: 8 in order to show that the promised age of salvation has now arrived and that therefore it is for Christians to live in accord with its principles. **now is the time of God's favor:** He does not primarily mean, 'Today is the acceptable time, tomorrow may be too late', but 'Today we are living in the new age, when salvation and reconciliation are present realities'.

3–10. The theme of the apostolic ministry, first introduced in 2: 14, is now briefly recapitulated, with the reappearance of many motifs from his earlier treatment (e.g. endurance in affliction [4: 16]; sincerity [2: 17; 4: 2]; outward appearance and inward reality [4: 7 ff.]). His intention is to remove all grounds of suspicion and criticism, which have only made for strained relations. **4, 5.** His hardships ('a blizzard of troubles' [Chrysostom]) are arranged in three groups of three, preceded by the keyword **endurance**, his attitude in them all. The first group, **troubles** (pressure of a physical and mental kind), **hardships** (inescapable difficulties, 'necessities', AV), **distresses** (frustrating situations) are general trials imposed on him by circumstances or his opponents. The second group are particular sufferings inflicted on him by men: for **beatings**, cf. on 11: 24, for **imprisonments**, cf. on 11: 23, and for **riots**, see Ac. 13: 50; 14: 19; 16: 19; 19: 29; 21: 30. The third group of hardships are those he imposed on himself for the sake of the gospel: **hard work** as an evangelist and a leather-worker (1 C. 4: 12), **sleepless nights** (Ac. 20: 31; 1 Th. 3: 10; 2 Th. 3: 8), **hunger**, 'fastings' (RV), probably through poverty (Phil. 4: 12), and imprisonment. **6.** A different kind of proof of his integrity commences here, his God-given qualities of character (the first of which is perhaps endurance, v. 4). **Understanding** may seem out of place here, but spiritual wisdom is a gift of God (1 C. 2: 6 f., 12 f.). **7.** The first two items, **truthful speech** and **the power of God** are probably to be taken as continuing the list of personal qualities. **Weapons . . . in the right hand** are offensive weapons (e.g. sword) and **in the left** are defensive (shield). Cf. Eph. 6: 16 f. By **weapons of righteousness** (a phrase from Isa. 59: 17) he means that he uses only upright methods of self-defence and attack on his critics. **8–10.** The contrasts here are not only between his reputation and his real character (e.g. impostor/true), but also between his 'outer' and 'inner' nature (4: 16) (e.g. having nothing/possessing everything); in the latter case he would regard both aspects as true, though from different viewpoints. **9.** It is not clear whether he means that he is unjustly **regarded as unknown**, a nobody, or that he really is **unknown** to men, yet well **known** to God (cf. 1 C. 13: 12, where the same verb 'to know fully' is used). **Beaten** is 'chastened' (RV) or, 'disciplined by suffering' (NEB); he agrees that he is chastised by God's affliction, but has not been given over to death (cf. Ps. 118: 18). **10. sorrowful:** I.e. full of pains, griefs. His experiences bear a striking resemblance to those of the Servant of Isa. 53. **poor, yet making many rich:** Cf. 8: 9.

ii. They Should Return Paul's Affection (6: 11–13)

11–13. 'I have spoken without reserve to you, my friends, and my love for you is equally unreserved (11). It is you, not I, who are holding something back in your affection (12). Play fair (if I may use a children's phrase), and return my love!' (13). **11.** His address of them by name, **Corinthians**, is a mark of affection (elsewhere only Gal. 3: 1; Phil. 4: 15). **opened wide our hearts** ('enlarged', RV): 'Just as what is heated expands, so the work of love is to enlarge' (Chrysostom). The phrase is reminiscent of Ps. 119: 32 (AV), 'Thou hast enlarged my heart', but there the meaning is 'Thou hast increased my understanding' (cf. RSV). **12. you are withholding yours from us:** 'Any stiffness between us must be on your side' (J. B. Phillips). **13. As a fair exchange:** For the moment he uses playground language, 'fair's fair', appealing to them as to children, who have a strong sense of fair-play. Perhaps, however, he means, 'I address you as (my) children'.

iii. A Warning against Association with Pagans (6: 14–7: 1)
6: 14–7: 1. In his first letter to the Corinthians, the 'previous' letter (cf. on 1 C. 5: 9), Paul had warned them not to associate with 'immoral men'. Some misunderstanding of his meaning had prompted him to write in 1 C. 5: 9 that he had referred only to such within the church, and he went on, in chaps. 8–10, to deal with the legitimacy of a Christian's occasional participation in social activities with pagans. Perhaps because of further misunderstanding he now insists that *permanent* association with unbelievers is to be eschewed.

For the hypothesis that this section was originally part of the 'previous' letter, see Introduction. There can be little doubt that the passage is logically connected neither with what precedes nor with what follows; the view that the Corinthians' association with unbelievers was an obstacle to the full restoration of friendly relations between them and Paul, and thus follows 6: 11–13 appropriately (A. Menzies), has not met with general acceptance. Perhaps some connection may be discerned thus: having assured the Corinthians of his unconditional love for them, Paul is emboldened to admonish them, yet with love (7: 1), not censoriously. **14. Do not be yoked together** (RV 'unequally yoked', RSV 'mismated') **with unbelievers:** A spiritual application of the law *Do not plow with an ox and a donkey yoked together* (Dt. 22: 10). He is speaking generally of permanent association with unbelievers; but not all associations are yokes. He does not exhort them to abandon any such ties they may have contracted (cf. his instructions to the Christian husband of an unbelieving wife [1 C. 7: 12 ff.]), but warns them not to continue forming them. **15. Belial:** Originally 'the place of swallowing up', the underworld (cf. Ps. 18: 4), from Heb. *balaʿ* 'to swallow up', but later re-interpreted as a compound noun from *bʿli* 'without' and *yaʿal* 'profit', i.e. 'worthlessness'. Hence 'sons of Belial' (*e.g.* Dt. 13: 13) are 'worthless fellows',

and Belial comes to be a proper name meaning 'worthless one'. It is first used as a term for Satan in intertestamental literature, and appears only here in NT.

16–18. These verses are a catena of OT quotations (cited from LXX), the applicability of which is founded on the assumption of the fundamental similarity, if not identity, of the old Israel and the new.

16. The temple of God is not the individual believer (as in 1 C. 6: 19), but the whole body of believers (as in Eph. 2: 21). **I will . . . walk among them . . . my people** is from Lev. 26: 12. **I will live with them** is suggested by Ezek. 37: 27, *My dwelling place will be with them*; perhaps Paul deliberately substitutes 'live' or 'dwell' to emphasize the permanence of God's dwelling among His people under the new covenant.

17. The first three lines of this verse were originally a call to the exiles to leave Babylon (Isa. 52: 11). The return from exile, constantly compared with the exodus (*e.g.* Isa. 43: 16–19), is here contrasted with it: the Egyptians were spoiled (Exod. 12: 35 f.), the Babylonians left with their 'unclean' possessions (but cf. Ezr. 1: 4). **Come out from them** must be understood with the qualification of 1 C. 5: 10. **And I will receive you** is from Ezek. 20: 34, also in reference to the return from exile as a new exodus (cf. v. 36). **18.** 2 Sam. 7: 14, *I will be his father, and he* (Solomon) *will be my son* is conflated with Isa. 43: 6, *Bring my sons from afar and my daughters from the ends of the earth* (at the return from exile). **7: 1. These** is emphasized: 'Since these are the promises we have'. **let us purify ourselves:** By including himself with them, and call them **dear friends**, lit. 'beloved' (a word of which he is not prodigal), he softens the severity of his warning.

iv. His Confidence in Them (7: 2–4)
2–4. 'Take me back into your hearts. I have done nothing to cause you to keep me out (2). But I am not saying "Welcome me back" in order to complain that you haven't done so already; that kind of meanness finds no place in the undying affection I have for you (3). Yes, I have the greatest confidence and pride in you now that you have responded to me so loyally' (4).

2. Make room for us in your hearts: He resumes the appeal begun in 6: 11–13. **we have corrupted no one**, etc.: Probably a denial of charges made against him. **exploited no one:** Cf. 12: 17 f. Alternatively, he implies that these are the practices of his opponents. **3.** The tone changes from exhortation to rejoicing as he recalls his meeting with Titus (6 ff.; cf. 2: 13 f.). **I do not say this to condemn you:** Exhortations contain implicit reproofs, but does not say this by way of reproof, but in order to complete the reconciliation, that he may be as much in their hearts as they are in his. **I have said before** probably refers to 6: 11–13, and so indicates he is aware that he has digressed in 6: 14–7: 1 (see Introduction). But he did not use precisely these words in 6: 11–13 (though 'open wide your hearts also' [13] implies them), so some think he is referring to 3: 2, 'You . . . are . . . written on our hearts' (but see on 3: 2). **We would live or die with you** simply means that they have a sure place in his heart no matter what happens to him, 'come death, come life' (F. F. Bruce). In the Greek **live** follows **die** not because he is thinking of the after-life, but because life seems a less likely possibility to him than death (cf. 4: 11).

v. Reflections on the Severe Letter and its Consequences (7: 5–13a)

5–13a. Paul resumes from 2: 14 his narrative of his journey to Macedonia, and describes first his relief at the arrival of Titus with good news from Corinth (5–7), and secondly, his reflections on the severe letter and its salutary consequences (8–13a). **5. came into Macedonia:** Ac. 20: 1. **this body of ours:** Rather, 'my body'. The Gk. is singular (lit. 'our flesh'), and he is plainly speaking of himself alone. Both mind (cf. 2: 13) and body must have been affected by nervous tension. What the **conflicts on the outside** were we do not know (perhaps persecution; the Macedonian Jews would not have welcomed him back); the **fears within** were doubtless over the situation at Corinth. **6. the coming of Titus:** From Corinth with news of the church's acceptance of the severe letter. **who comforts the downcast:** A reminiscence of Isa. 49: 13. **7. Longing** to see Paul again, or to be reconciled to him, **deep sorrow** for their past behaviour to him, **ardent concern** for him revealed by their obedience in punishing the evil-doer, and in defending him against his critics. 'previously the longing, lamentation, and eagerness had been St. Paul's, and it was a delight to his emissary to find similar feelings in the Corinthians' (Plummer). Hence the repeated emphasized **your. my joy was greater than ever:** I.e. his joy at their response was doubled when he saw how glad they had made Titus.

8. if I caused you sorrow: I.e. 'If I hurt you', not 'If I caused you to repent' (as RSV 'if I made you sorry' might suggest). **my letter:** The 'severe' letter (cf. 2: 3 f.). **I see that my letter hurt you** is explanatory of **I caused you sorrow by my letter**, not of course of **I do not regret it**. Knox's version is clearer than NIV: 'Yes, even if I caused you pain by my letter, I am not sorry for it. Perhaps I was tempted to feel sorry, when I saw how my letter had caused you even momentary pain, but now I am glad; not glad of the pain, but glad of the repentance the pain brought with

it'. **9.** He would not like them to think that he is rejoicing over their humiliation, so he carefully explains why he felt such joy: it was not their sorrow but the fruit of their sorrow that gave him joy. They did not receive the letter with natural human irritation or self-justification but with **godly sorrow**, in this case sorrow for sin. **10. worldly sorrow** is not only a regret for sin in which there is no place for repentance (cf. Heb. 12: 17), for 'all sorrow, whether it be due to disappointment, affliction, bereavement, or sin, is deadly in its operation so long as it remains unsanctified' (Tasker). It is the repentance, not the salvation (RVmg), that **leaves no regret**. Paul is perhaps quoting an aphorism found in fuller form in the Jewish *Testament of Gad* (late 2nd or 1st cent. B.C.), 5: 7, 'True repentance after a godly sort driveth away the darkness, and enlighteneth the eyes, and giveth knowledge to the soul, and leadeth the mind to salvation'. **11.** The Corinthians themselves are the proof of this statement. See how their repentance has led to salvation, i.e. to salutary results. It has produced **earnestness** to set matters right, **eagerness to clear** themselves of Paul's accusations by correcting their behaviour, **indignation** at the shame brought on the church, or at the trouble-maker (2: 3) or the false apostles (11: 13), **alarm** (lit. 'fear') at God's wrath, or perhaps at Paul's anger (cf. 15; 1 C. 4: 21), **longing** for his favour and his return, **concern** for Paul and against his opponents, **justice done** upon the offender(s). In **every point** they have **proved** themselves **innocent**, or 'clear', now (not that they *were* guiltless, but Paul does not want to cloud his joy by thinking of their rebellion), by disassociating themselves from, and punishing, those who had defied Paul's authority. **this matter:** He uses this neutral term to avoid specifying the unpleasant subject (cf. 'any one', 2: 5). **12.** By saying that he wrote the severe letter **not on account of the one who did the wrong** (2: 5 ff.) nor on account **of the injured party** (himself) he cannot mean that the contention between his opponent and himself was not the occasion of the letter, but 'it was not so much for his sake and mine as for the sake of us all. My main object was to bring you to realize your real attitude to me, and to realize that the bonds between us are too strong to be quickly shaken off'.

vi. The Joy of Titus (7: 13b–16)

13b. Paul now returns to the thought of v. 7, and describes in detail the joy of Titus. The fact that he speaks of Titus' mind being **refreshed by all of you**, together with 'you were all obedient' (15), and 'complete confidence' (16), has been used by some as evidence that the church was now completely reconciled to Paul, and that therefore chaps. 10–13, which plainly depict a hostile minority, cannot be part of this letter (cf. Introduction). But we may surely allow Paul, in the relief and enthusiasm of the moment, now that the offender has been punished and the church has expressed its loyalty to him, more optimistic expressions than later reflection will warrant; moreover there are indications even within chaps. 1–9 that all was not well at Corinth (cf. 5: 12; 6: 12). **14. I had boasted to him about you:** (cf. 9: 4). It is plain that Paul had spoken proudly to Titus of the Corinthians' loyalty (hoping against hope, it may be), and Titus was no doubt anxious for Paul lest his confidence in them should be rudely disappointed. **I had boasted:** 'His love had enabled him to see deeper than the rebellious attitude of the moment' (F. V. Filson). **you have not embarrassed me:** By proving him wrong. **just as everything we said** (i.e. have ever said) **to you was true:** A passing reference to his truthfulness (cf. 1: 15 ff.).

15. fear and trembling: Not panic, but 'an anxious scrupulous desire not . . . to do less than one ought to do' (Denney). **16.** His **complete confidence** is not simply 'perfect reconciliation', but also confidence for the future. So these words pave the way for the next topic, the collection for the Jerusalem poor (chs. 8, 9).

VI. THE COLLECTION FOR THE JERUSALEM POOR (8: 1–9: 15)

Paul was organizing a collection from his Gentile churches for the poor in the Jerusalem church, and he had already broached the subject with the Corinthians (1 C. 16: 1–4). The breakdown in relations between Paul and the Corinthian church had very probably brought about also an interruption of preparations in Corinth for making a contribution, and Paul must naturally have felt unable to continue his exhortations to them on this subject so long as the breach between them remained unhealed. The loyalty to himself which the Corinthians had evinced by their reception of Titus encouraged him now to re-open the subject; a reference to the collection a few months later (Rom. 15: 26 f.) indicates that the Corinthians had responded well to the exhortations of these chapters.

The motive for this collection was doubtless originally Paul's undertaking to 'remember the poor' (Gal. 2: 10), given upon a previous occasion when he had been involved in a famine relief fund (Ac. 11: 27–30; Gal. 2: 1–10). But he saw also spiritual significance in the 'offering for the saints': it was a way for Gentile Christians to express their gratitude to the Jews for the spiritual blessings they had received through them (Rom. 15: 27; cf. Rom. 11: 11; Jn 4: 22). He regarded it as the visible token of his 'priestly duty' which would result in the Gentiles becoming 'an offering acceptable to God' (Rom. 15: 16), and as such set great value on it, even endangering his liberty and life (Ac. 21: 10 ff.) in order to deliver the gift personally (Ac. 24: 17).

Although he does not say so specifically, it is more than likely that he also looked upon the gift as a bond that would draw Jewish and Gentile Christians closer together, and would prove, by removing Jewish suspicions of his Gentile mission, that the 'dividing wall of hostility' (Eph. 2: 14) had indeed been broken down. Hence his request for the Roman Christians' prayers that the gift might prove acceptable to the Jerusalem saints (Rom. 15: 30 f.), that is, that they might accept not only the money, but also the spiritual implications of the gift.

He encourages the Corinthians to give by appealing to the example of the Macedonian churches (8: 1–7), to the example of Christ Himself (8: 9), and to the eagerness they themselves had previously shown (8: 10 f.; 9: 1–5); he further makes arrangements for the visit of Titus (8: 16–24), and expounds the principles of Christian giving (8: 12–15; 9: 6–15).

i. The Example of the Macedonians (8: 1–7)

1–7. 'Let me tell you of the great liberality of the Macedonian churches (1, 2). Though they were so poor, they gave to the fund more than could have been expected (3) (as though I was doing them a favour to allow them to contribute! [4]), for they gave more than their money to the Lord's work—they gave themselves! (5). Encouraged by *their* response, I have asked Titus to visit *you* and make final arrangements for your contribution (6). May Corinthian generosity match Corinthian excellence in other spiritual gifts!' (7).

1. The generosity of the Macedonians and their joy amid afflictions are the **grace that God has given**. The **Macedonian churches** known to us by name are Philippi, Thessalonica, and Berea. The Philippians are praised for their generosity in Phil. 4: 15. **2.** Their **joy** combined with their **poverty** has **welled up in rich generosity**, not perhaps a great amount of money (the amount is never mentioned), for it is their spirit of generosity that Paul is urging the Corinthians to emulate. For the Macedonians' joy in affliction, cf. 1 Th. 1: 6; 5: 16; and for Paul's, 2 C. 7: 4. The **extreme** (lit. 'abysmal') **poverty** of the Macedonians is illustrated by the fact that Paul never finds it necessary in his letters to Thessalonica and Philippi to warn these Christians against the dangers of wealth or to address an exhortation to the rich (cf. 1 Tim. 6: 9 f., 17 ff.). **3. beyond their ability:** More literally, 'contrary to'; their gift was so generous that it was almost in contradiction to their poverty. **4.** 'It was they, not Paul, who did the begging' (Chrysostom); perhaps Paul had been reticent about asking them because of their poverty. The **saints** here are the church at Jerusalem (so also 9: 1; 1 C. 16: 1). Rom. 15: 26 speaks of the collection more specifically as for 'the poor among the saints in Jerusalem'. **5. not . . . as we expected:** I.e. 'They have done more than I expected' (Moffatt), in that **first** and foremost they **gave themselves** (not just their money) **to the Lord and then to us**, i.e. put themselves at the Lord's disposal and so at Paul's, by offering to send some of their number to accompany him (8: 18 f., 9: 4). Reflection on their action may well have inspired Rom. 12: 1 f., written a few months later.

6. Titus had **earlier made a beginning** of organizing the collection, perhaps when he carried 1 Corinthians to Corinth (if indeed he was the bearer), or more probably even earlier, for the abrupt introduction of 'the collection for God's people' in 1 C. 16: 1 suggests that the Corinthians already knew about it (cf. 12: 18).

ii. The Example of Christ, and Principles of Christian Giving (8: 8–15)

8–15. 'I do not mention the Macedonians in order to but pressure on you to equal them, but just to show you how genuine self-giving love acts (8). (And of this the greatest example is, as you know, the Lord Himself [9].) So I am not commanding, but I do advise you to complete the collection you began so enthusiastically last year (10, 11). The enthusiasm is the important thing—not the amount, for that is dictated by your income (12). I am not asking you to enable the Jerusalem Christians to live in luxury at your expense (13), but to ensure an equitable distribution of goods (it may prove beneficial to you one day!) (14), which after all is a biblical principle' (15).

8. He is not commanding them, for love and liberality, which is an expression of love, must be spontaneous, but he is giving them the example of **the earnestness of others** (the Macedonians) as a touchstone to test their **love** to him; if their expressions of love are as genuine as the Macedonians', they will give as generously as they. **9.** This sentence, though formally a parenthesis, provides the finest example of self-giving love (he says **grace**, the same word [*charis*] as is translated 'gracious work' in vv. 6 f.)—that of **our Lord Jesus Christ**, the full title adding to the impressiveness of the appeal (Plummer). **For your sakes** is placed in an emphatic position (cf. 5: 15). **He became poor** by becoming man (cf. Phil. 2: 5 ff.). His earthly poverty is not directly in view here. In what way Christ became poor Paul does not specify, for he is interested here not in the theology but in the ethics of the incarnation. **10.** 'I do not command (8), but I give my advice, which is the suitable way of approach-

ing people like you (**best for you** is more literally 'suitable for you'), who have already proved that you need no commanding.' **Last year:** (as in 9: 2), i.e. any time between 9 and 21 months ago (Hughes). **not only to give but to have the desire:** Desire is in the climactic position because the desire to give (the spirit of liberality) is greater than the gift itself. This does not commit Paul to the doctrine that the only thing necessary is a good will. A more prosaic interpretation is: 'since it was you who led the way, not only in giving, but in proposing to act, as early as last year' (Knox), i.e. 'you began the preparations for the collection earlier than the Macedonians'. **11. according to your means:** I.e. 'in proportion to your means', 'according to what a man has' (12) (cf. 1 C. 16: 2). He does not oblige them to match the Macedonians' giving 'beyond their means' (3). **13. that there might be equality** does not mean a doctrinaire equalization of property. Scripture avoids 'on the one hand the injustice and destructive evils of agrarian communism, by recognizing the right of property and making all almsgiving optional; and on the other the heartless disregard of the poor by inculcating the universal brotherhood of believers' (A. P. Stanley). **14. your plenty:** Though mainly from the lower classes (1 C. 1: 26–28), the Corinthian Christians appear to have been better off than the Macedonians, even though these numbered among themselves (at least in Thessalonica) 'not a few' of the upper classes (Ac. 17: 4). **their plenty will supply what you need:** If necessary in the future. **15.** Paul quotes Exod. 16: 18 to illustrate God's intention that *all* His people should have enough for their needs. The OT narrative appears to indicate that no matter how much manna anyone had gathered, when it was measured it was found to be (miraculously) the exact amount sufficient for his needs, an omer per day.

iii. Forthcoming Visit of Titus (8: 16–24)

16. Paul is sending Titus, as he began to say in v. 6, to supervise the final stages of the collection. He is not coming himself, partly to avoid any criticism that some of the collection will go into his pocket (cf. 20 f.), and partly because he wants the collection to be ready when he arrives with friends from Macedonia (9: 3–5). **The same concern . . . for you:** The enthusiasm of Paul and Titus is not simply for the Jerusalem Christians, but **for you**, the Corinthians. **17. our appeal:** The 'urging' of v. 6. **he is coming:** With this letter. **18. the brother who is praised . . . for his service to the gospel:** Possibly Luke. Several pieces of evidence connect Luke with Philippi (*e.g.* Ac. 16: 11 f. 'we' and 17: 1 'they'; 20: 3 'he' and 20: 6 'we'), and make it possible that he was the representative of the Philippian church who accompanied Paul to Jerusalem (no Philippian is mentioned in Ac. 20: 4, but Luke was certainly with them [5]). So he could be the one 'chosen by the churches (of Macedonia) to accompany us' (19). **20. We** (='I') **want** by sending not only my own colleague Titus, but also a man of repute, chosen by the Macedonian churches independently of me, and another trusted brother (22), to give no occasion for any **criticism of the way we administer this liberal gift**. It is bound to be a large sum; all the more reason why the handling of it should be above suspicion. **21.** He quotes Prov. 3: 4 (LXX), *Provide things honest in the sight of the Lord and men.* Justice has to *appear* to be done. **22. Our brother** is unidentifiable. **23.** 'In short, to forestall any criticism, let me set down their qualifications.' Titus is Paul's own representative, his 'minister for Corinthian affairs' (**fellow worker among you**); the other two are **representatives** (Gk. 'apostles', i.e. officially appointed delegates) **of the churches** of Macedonia. They are **an honor to Christ**, i.e. they bring credit on Christ by their life. Less likely is the interpretation that they reflect to others something of the splendour of Christ. **24. so that the churches can see it:** What the representatives of the churches see and hear will be reported to their home churches.

iv. Why Titus is being Sent (9: 1–5)

1–5. He explains why, instead of coming himself, he is sending Titus and the two other brethren: to make sure that the collection is finalized by the time he himself arrives.

1. It is unnecessary for him to go on writing, partly because his envoys will be arriving, and partly because he has already given instructions (1 C. 16: 1–4). **2.** Their **eagerness** is their 'desire' of 8: 10 f. They are not fully ready (4), i.e. the collection is not completed. **Achaia** primarily means Corinth (cf. on 1: 1). **most of them:** He does not mean that some are still unwilling to give, but that it is the Corinthians' zeal that has been for most of them the greatest incentive to contribute. **3.** His **boasting** about them would **prove hollow**, if, after boasting to the Macedonians that the Corinthians were more than keen, he should find that this zeal had not been directed into finishing the collection. **4.** If, as seems likely, Titus' two companions were Macedonians, then two Macedonians at least would know very soon that the Corinthians were not quite ready. This would not be so serious because the deadline had not yet been reached, but if Paul were to arrive in Corinth on his way to Jerusalem, accompanied by Macedonian delegates, and were to find the collection still incomplete, it would be a humiliation both to him and the Corinthians. **If any Macedonians come** is not hypothetical, but = 'when' (cf. 13: 2). **we . . . would be ashamed:** The disgrace would really be the Corinthians', but Paul so much identifies

himself with his converts that he feels the disgrace to be his. **5.** If he arrives while the collection is still incomplete, the contributions which will be made then will be more like **one grudgingly given** (the Corinthians would feel under an obligation to give) than a **gracious**, or rather 'willing', **gift**; the time for spontaneous giving will have passed.

v. The Nature of Christian Giving (9: 6–15)

6–15. 'Giving is like sowing: you reap in proportion to what you sow (6). Giving must be methodical and cheerful (7). If you give in that way, God will make sure you have enough for your own needs and enough to give away (8), as the psalmist says (9). Yes, if you sow benevolence, God will keep on increasing the amount you have to sow (10). And your enrichment, spiritual as well as material, will result in greater generosity, and also in much thanksgiving to God from those who receive your gift (11), for giving does not only bring help to the saints, but causes God to be glorified by them (12). And it is not only they who will glorify God—you too, by your giving, will prove your obedience to Christ, and so glorify God (13). What an expression of fellowship, with giver and getter joined by their prayers for one another! (14). But what is the origin of giving? God, who put giving into our hearts by the gift of His Son. Thanks be to Him!' (15).

6. Prov. 11: 24 f. and 19: 17 are echoed here (cf. also Lk. 6: 38). In itself, this is not a very exalted motive for giving, but it is Paul's purpose to expound the whole nature of giving, and in any case 'it is right to present to men the divinely ordained consequences of their actions as motives to control their conduct' (Hodge). **7. what he has decided in his heart:** The giving is not to be casual, but planned. There will be a certain moral **compulsion** to give if Paul arrives before the collection is complete. **God loves a cheerful giver:** More exactly 'It is the cheerful giver that God loves', a quotation from Prov. 22: 8 (LXX). **8.** There is no risk in generous giving, for God will always recompense the giver with **all that you need** for his own needs and enough to give to **every good work. 9.** He reinforces the thought of v. 8 by quoting Ps. 112: 9, which says of the liberal man who **has scattered abroad** (i.e. does not sow sparingly) that his almsgiving **endures for ever**, i.e. he will never run short of money for giving. **Righteousness** is used here in the sense of 'almsgiving' (RSVmg, NEB; cf. Mt. 6: 1). **10. seed to the sower and bread for food:** A quotation from Isa. 55: 10 (LXX). **Your store of seed** is 'what you have to sow with', and the **harvest** (lit. 'the fruits') **of your righteousness** (the wording borrowed from Hos. 10: 12 [LXX]) is the reward for benevolence. **11.** The reward of their benevolence will be that they **will be made rich in every way**, spiritually as well as materially, and this will have two results: first, they will be able to **be generous on every occasion** and secondly, **through us** (Paul) and our delivery of the collection for the saints, a great volume of **thanksgiving to God** will be produced. **12. is . . . supplying:** More literally, 'helps to supply'; the Corinthians were not the only contributors. **13.** Benevolence is to be the test of the Corinthians' sincerity, as affliction was that of the Macedonians (8: 2). **men will praise God:** rather than '*you* will glorify God' (as RSV). 'They (the Jerusalem Christians) will glorify God' for this proof of Gentile loyalty and obedience to Christ, of which they had been highly suspicious. **and with everyone else:** A gift to a part of the Church is a gift to the whole Church (1 C. 12: 26); or perhaps Paul is expressing a hope that this will not be the last gift the Corinthians will make to needy Christians. **14. their hearts will go out to you:** The Jerusalem Christians will recognize that this generous gift owes its origin to the surpassing grace of God in the Corinthians, just as in the Macedonians (8: 1). **15.** In reflecting on the grace of generosity to be given by God to the Corinthians, Paul is led to think of Christ, God's inexpressibly generous gift.

VII. PAUL'S SELF-DEFENCE AGAINST THE 'FALSE APOSTLES' (10: 1–13: 10)

In spite of Paul's general satisfaction with the church at Corinth, there was apparently still a group which disputed his apostolic authority, and professed themselves followers of certain leaders whom Paul refers to as 'false apostles' (11: 13). Their activities and teaching are to us far from clear, though this is not of course due to any intention on Paul's part to make only obscure references to them, but to the fact that they were only too well known both to the Corinthians and to Paul.

Certain facts about the 'false apostles', however, are plain. They were Jewish Christians (11: 22 f.), visitors from outside Corinth (cf. 11: 4), who came armed with letters of commendation (3: 1) claiming for them a higher authority than Paul's (10: 7). Their method of gaining adherents was to assert their own authority, no doubt with some eloquence (cf. 10: 10; 11: 6) and a great deal of mutual admiration (10: 12), and to denigrate Paul before his converts (10: 1 f., 10; 11: 7, etc.). They were evidently not averse to receiving financial support from the church (11: 12, 20), yet behaved in a high-handed and insolent way toward it (11: 20), and boasted of the Corinthians as though they were their own converts (cf. 10: 5). It is attractive to suppose, in view of their

claim to be 'Christ's' (10: 7), that they based their authority on their having seen Christ in the flesh (could not, for example, the Seventy [Lk. 10: 1 ff.] have regarded their commissioning from Christ as of a higher order than Paul's, who presumably had never seen Christ in the flesh?). Support for this view from 5: 16, however, where Paul says he knows no man any longer after the flesh, can only be gained by an erroneous interpretation of that statement.

Virtually nothing is known of their teaching. Many have seen them as judaizers, but Jewish Christians do not necessarily judaize, and if they were in fact requiring the Corinthians to keep the law, it would be very strange that Paul does not attack their doctrine (as he does in Galatians). It is not likely that Paul's exposition of the superiority of the New Covenant to the Old (3: 7–18) is dictated by polemical motives, nor should we see in 'servants of righteousness' (11: 15) an allusion to judaizers who insisted on law-works.

Yet Paul calls them 'false apostles' (11: 13). He enters into no dispute about their authority or about their teaching, but on the ground of their unchristian behaviour both to the Corinthians (*e.g.* 11: 20) and to himself (cf. *e.g.* 10: 13–15), he feels justified in saying that they are doing the devil's work.

i. Paul, 'Humble' by Preference, 'Bold' if Necessary (10: 1–6)

1–6. 'I am accused of being inconfident when I am in Corinth, and overbearing when I am away. I prefer the gentle approach (1), and I hope I shall not have to be "bold" against my opponents when I come. But I will if they continue to accuse me of unspirituality (2); my activities are not worldly—nor are my weapons; they are spiritual, and therefore strong enough to crush all opposition and disobedience (3–5), and I am prepared to use them against my critics if necessary' (6).

1. 'In the very sentence in which he puts himself and his dignity forward with uncompromising firmness, he recalls to his own and his readers' hearts the characteristic temper of the Lord' (Denney). **Meekness** is an inward virtue, the acceptance of God's discipline and will, **gentleness** is 'consideration' (Moffatt) for others. These are the qualities of Christ Paul would prefer to imitate. **I . . . who am 'timid':** He reproduces his critics' charge that he displayed cowardice when present, bravado when absent (cf. v. 10). Probably they referred to the failure of his 'painful' visit (cf. on 2: 1) and the subsequent severe letter (cf. on 2: 3). **'timid':** 'A Uriah Heep, very humble and cringing and artful' (Plummer). **2. expect, think:** suspect: The same verb in both cases. **Think** is too weak; better, 'who have made up their minds that I move on the low level of the flesh' (Moffatt). **Some people**, the false apostles and their partisans (cf. on 3: 1), have by their remarks about Paul implied (they may not have spoken so plainly themselves) that he was acting **by the standards of this world**. The criticism is too general for us to infer the particular charges, but cf. 1: 17; 2: 17; 4: 2; 5: 11, 16; 7: 2; 8: 20 f. **3.** A more literal translation: '. . . who reckon that we walk according to the flesh (2). For though we walk *in* the flesh, we carry on a war not *according to* the flesh (3)'. To live *in the flesh* is to be a human being (cf. Gal. 2: 20; a different meaning in Rom. 8: 9); to live *according to the flesh* is to be at the mercy of the impulses of the sinful nature. His humility (1) is not worldly cowardice or craftiness, nor is his boldness self-assertion. Cowardice is the last thing to accuse him of; his whole life is a **war** against opposition to the truth of the gospel (cf. 6: 7; 1 Th. 5: 8; Eph. 6: 11–17). **4.** Because his **weapons** are not **of the world** but spiritual, they **have divine power**. For the concept of spirit as powerful, and stronger than flesh, cf. *e.g.* Zech. 4: 6; Isa. 31: 3. **5.** There is a destructive element in his apostolic work (cf. v. 8), directed against the **arguments** or sophistries of men, and, to use the widest terms of reference, **every pretension**, lit. 'high thing' or 'rampart' (Moffatt); the military metaphor is continued. **take captive every thought:** 'Thought' probably means 'plot, design'. An alternative interpretation is that his goal is not simply outward submission, but inward obedience (in **thought** or 'mind') to Christ. But there is no suggestion of an assault on reason or a 'sacrifice of the intellect'. **6. ready to punish:** As Christ's apostle, he has the authority to pass sentence (Mt. 16: 19). **every . . . disobedience:** I.e. anyone who is still recalcitrant when the church as a whole reaffirms its allegiance to Christ and to Paul. Moffatt suggests that the military metaphor is still being used: 'I am prepared to court-martial anyone who remains insubordinate, when your submission is complete'.

ii. Paul's Authority not Inferior to the False Apostles' (10: 7–11)

7–11. 'Face the facts! Are my opponents sent by Christ? so am I (7). I could say more, but forbear for the moment (8)—any expression of my authority would only give fresh grounds for complaint about my severe letters (9). Bold as brass his letters are, they say, but he has no strength of character (10). Such critics had better realize that I am capable of acting in the spirit of my letters' (11).

7. You are only looking on the surface of things: Other possible translations are: 'Look at what is before you eyes' (RSV); 'Do you look . . . ?' (AV, RVmg). RSV means: 'Face the facts! As much as they do'. The claim to be **Christ**'s does not appear to have any connection with the 'Christ-party'

of 1 C. 1: 12, but is a claim to special authority given by Christ (see introduction to this chapter). The mere assertion of superior authority by Paul will not settle the issue, so he simply says that his commissioning is at least not inferior to theirs. **8.** 'Though were I to claim higher authority than theirs, I would not be exaggerating'. He takes the word **boast** from his opponents' mouths; they doubtless labelled all his claims to apostolic authority as 'boasting'. **Somewhat freely:** RSV 'a little too much' perhaps gives the wrong nuance to a word which may also mean 'a little more' than he has done (in v. 7, perhaps in vv. 3–6), or than he usually does. The proper work of **authority** is to build up (so also 12: 19; 13: 10), and this has been the effect of Paul's work in Corinth. It is only the rebellious (not **you**, he hopes) who suffer its destructive work (cf. v. 5). Perhaps he also alludes to the 'false apostles', whose authority has been used only for destruction. **will not be ashamed of it:** By being proved to have exaggerated. **9.** 'But I will say no more about my *authority*, for that would be "frightening" you!' **10. His letters are weighty and forceful:** A valuable contemporary estimate of his writings by witnesses not prejudiced in his favour! **in person:** Not only his physical appearance, but also the way he acts when present. **speaking amounts to nothing:** Devoid of rhetorical artifice (cf. 1 C. 1: 17; 2: 1–5). He appears to admit the charge (11: 6). **11.** He does not retort that when he comes he will *speak* well, but he will *act*. **what we are in our letters:** He particularly refers to being severe (cf. vv. 2, 6).

iii. His Motto is 'Nothing beyond the Limit' (10: 12–18)

12–18. 'Of course, I would not dare to class myself with these men who boast without limit (How foolish self-commendation is! It has no external standards of reference) (12). I will keep within my limits—and my "limits" include you (13), for I was the first to preach the gospel in Corinth, and so I have staked out a claim to you (14). I do not boast beyond my "limits"— of work done in territory other than my own; and I hope this will remain my policy when I move on to other countries (15, 16). But all this talk about boasting in work done or not done is beside the point; we should glory in the Lord, not our work (17). And it is His commendation we need, not our own' (18).

12. In v. 11 he has affirmed his readiness to use his strength against his opponents, but now in mock humility and cowardice he says that of course he would not **dare** to put himself in the same **class** or even to **compare** himself with these authoritarian 'apostles' (cf. 11: 20). By their commendation of one another, they show themselves to be **not wise** because they do not see that their judgments are purely relative. **13.** He plays on the word **limit**. If he is to boast at all, he **will not boast beyond proper limits**, i.e. he will limit himself to the truth (unlike the false apostles, whose conceit knew no bounds). But the **limits** within which he will keep will be, in another sense, *geographical* limits, the provinces which **God has assigned** to him as apostle to the Gentiles (Gal. 2: 9). Unlike his opponents, he will not encroach on other men's territory (cf. Rom. 15: 20) and steal their converts. **14.** 'It is not **we** (=Paul) who **are going too far**, stepping outside the agreed boundaries, **as . . . if we had not come to you**, "as if you lay beyond my sphere" (Moffatt). No, I **did get as far as you with the gospel** (cf. 1 C. 3: 6–10; 4: 15), and so you are within my province.' **15. Beyond our limits** does not mean 'excessively' (as in v. 13), but 'beyond the limit of my commission' (cf. NEB), and thus is equivalent to **in another man's testimony**. When the Corinthians' **faith continues to grow** and makes his presence there no longer necessary, he will be able to turn his attention to lands beyond them (cf. Rom. 15: 23–29). Instead of **our area of activity among you** we should translate: 'that . . . our field may be greatly enlarged *by* you', i.e. they can open up new fields for him if they will acknowledge his authority at Corinth and so let him get on with his work elsewhere. **16. to boast about work already done:** His personal principle of not building on another man's foundation (Rom. 15: 20) both avoided friction with other missionaries and ensured the rapid spread of the gospel over a wide area. He did not object to others doing 'follow-up' work, provided they built in accordance with the foundation already laid (1 C. 3: 10 ff.), and did not take the credit for another's work to themselves. **17.** A Christian worker should not boast of work he has not done, nor even of work he *has* done, but only of **the Lord**. Paul here condenses Jer. 9: 24.

iv. Paul Expresses his Intention to Boast (11: 1–21a)

(a) Why he must boast (11: 1–6)

1–6. 'If I go on to boast about myself, do be patient with me! (1). (It is only because I am driven to it by my concern for you [2] and my fear that unless I boast of my credentials you will lose, together with your respect for me, your respect for the gospel I preach [3]. Yes, I do believe that if some one were to come with an utterly different gospel, you would accept him [4]). I am entitled to boast, I think, because I am in no way inferior to these "apostles" (5); perhaps I am ineloquent, but I do at least know what I am talking about, as you can bear witness' (6).

1. The **little foolishness** is the boasting of vv. 21 ff. He knows it is foolish (cf. 10: 17), but he feels it is necessary for the sake of the Corinthians. They have accepted the false apostles on the strength of their credentials, and since higher appeals have not been totally successful, Paul must appeal on this low level also. **You are already doing that** may alternatively be taken as an imperative 'Do put up with me!', or ironically, 'Yes, I know, you have to do a lot of putting up with me!' **2.** He feels the **jealousy** for the Corinthian church that a father feels for his daughter (cf. 1 C. 4: 15), that is, for her honour. It is a **godly** jealousy (lit. 'the jealousy of God') because God too feels it. Paul has **promised** the church **to Christ, to present** it **as a pure virgin** to Him, at the Parousia. (For the universal Church as Christ's bride, cf. Eph. 5: 27 ff.; Rev. 19: 7 f.) **3.** But he fears that the bride-to-be, instead of being a pure bride presented to her one husband, will be seduced by the false apostles. **4.** Paul is so fearful for the stability of the Corinthians that he can even imagine them being carried away by some utterly different gospel. The whole sentence must be regarded as hypothetical: 'If some one were to come . . . you would submit' (an alternative MS reading makes this interpretation explicit). It is improbable that he refers to the false apostles; if they had preached another Jesus, would he have simply defended his own authority and not said one word in refutation of their heresy?

5. those 'super-apostles': A sarcastic reference to the Jewish Christians who had come to Corinth (see Introduction to chap. 10). The original twelve apostles are not in mind (as in AV, RV).

6. not . . . a trained speaker: Without formal rhetorical training. His **knowledge** of the truth has been given him by God (4: 6). It is either this knowledge of the truth that he has always **made . . . clear** (cf. 4: 2), or else the fact that he possesses it.

(b) Has he wronged the Corinthians? (11: 7–11)

7–11. 'Why then do you regard me as inferior to these "apostles"? Have I wronged you in some way? Was my sin to have preached to you without demanding wages? (7). It was at the expense of other churches that you heard the gospel (8), and why? because I would not impose on you by taking money (9a). And this will always be my policy (9b, 10). Does this prove I don't love you? Of course not!' (11).

7. The false apostles, in their campaign of vilification against Paul, had apparently claimed that his financial independence of the Corinthians (cf. 1 C. 9) betokened a lack of intimacy with them; perhaps also that it was most undignified for the apostle to the Corinthians to support himself by manual labour, it being the custom in Greece for orators and preachers to be paid by their adherents. The earlier insinuation of some that his refusal to accept maintenance betrayed a bad conscience about his apostolic claims (1 C. 9: 1–15) does not appear to have been revived. It is arguable that these extremely perverse criticisms were not actually made, but are ironically imagined by Paul in order to introduce the contrast between his and the false apostles' attitudes to financial support (12 ff.). **8.** He **robbed other churches** (he is thinking especially of the Macedonians, cf. v. 9) by accepting their gifts which they could ill afford. It was not fair (therefore 'robbery') that they should have had to support Paul when the Corinthians could have done so. **9. was not a burden:** More exactly, 'did not put pressure on anyone', or 'sponged on no one' (NEB). **the brothers . . . from Macedonia** (Silas and Timothy) **supplied what I needed** (Ac. 18: 5): Previously he had had to spend some of his time in manual labour, but now with the Macedonian gift he could 'devote himself entirely to preaching' (Ac. 18: 5 NEB). **10.** We do not know whether the Corinthians had ever offered him support, but in any case he has now spoken to them so plainly about their failure to provide for him that it would be too embarrassing on both sides for him ever to receive anything from them. **As the truth of Christ is in me:** An oath (cf. 1: 18). **nobody in the regions of Achaia will stop this boasting of mine:** I.e. 'I will never accept money from the church of Corinth' (cf. 1 C. 9: 15). **Achaia:** Cf. on 9: 2.

(c) **The false apostles (11: 12–15)**
12–15. 'My policy of not accepting support will be one way at least of showing my superiority to these "apostles" (12)—false apostles they really are, doing Satan's work (13). No wonder that his servants disguise themselves as true apostles (15), seeing that he himself disguises himself as an angel of light' (14).

12. what I am doing: I.e. his policy on not accepting support (10). Though the false apostles sneer at Paul's refusal of maintenance, they admit to themselves that it is a powerful proof of his integrity, and they would gladly drag him down to their own level and boast that in all respects they **are equal . . . in the things they boast about. 13.** They are **false apostles** (not so much 'false teachers'), for they claim Christ's authority when they have none but their own; and **deceitful workmen** because they are serving not Christ but themselves (perhaps also because they are doing destructive work [cf. 10: 8]). **14.** The belief that **Satan himself masquerades as an angel of light** is not explicit in OT (though he appears among the 'angels' in Job 1: 6, but not in disguise), and it is suggested that Paul may be alluding to a Jewish legend that Satan appeared to Eve in the form of an angel and sang hymns like the angels (*Life of Adam and Eve* [2nd-4th cent. A.D.], 9: 1 [R. H. Charles, *The Apocrypha*

and Pseudepigrapha of the Old Testament, vol. ii., p. 136]). But it is equally possible that Paul is referring to the habitual conduct of the devil as the deceiver (cf. 2: 11; Eph. 6: 11; 1 Tim. 3: 7), rather than to a particular incident. **15.** They are **servants** of Satan in that the work of destruction and vilification they are doing is Satan's work. But in v. 23 Paul seems to admit that they are servants of Christ. Similarly, Peter, a servant of Christ, could do Satan's work (Mk 8: 33). **Their end will be what their actions deserve:** A Biblical principle applicable to all men, whether Christian or not (Prov. 24: 12; Rom. 2: 6: 2 C. 5: 10; 1 Pet. 1: 17).

(d) **The folly of boasting (11: 16–21a)**
16–21a. 'Before I begin to boast according to the flesh (21b–29), I repeat (cf. 1) that I recognize that it is a foolish thing to do (16), and sub-Christian (17), but I am driven to it (18). You tolerate fools so easily that you should have no difficulty in putting up with me! (19). Oh, yes, you can tolerate far worse things than folly—even personal injury and abuse (20). I must confess, I have been too weak to inflict that on you!' (21a).

16. 'I repeat (cf. v. 1), I know boasting is a fool's game, and I would not like anyone to **take me for a fool**, for, to be honest, it goes very much against the grain for me to play the fool. But even if you will not pay me the compliment of realizing that I speak with tongue in cheek, pay me the attention you would a fool (**receive me . . . as you would a fool**), **so that I** too (remember, I didn't start it!) **may do a little boasting** for the sake of the record'. **17.** He cannot claim **the Lord**'s authority for boasting, for to boast is not in accord with the character of Christ. Yet boasting, i.e. producing his credentials, seems to be the only way of re-establishing his authority. 'By itself indeed it is not "after the Lord", but by its intention it becomes so. And therefore he said, "that which I speak", not accusing the motive, but the words; since his aim is so admirable as to dignify the words also' (Chrysostom). **18. the way the world does:** Lit. 'according to the flesh'. Paul will for a time boast on the same low level (21b–29), but his true boast is in his weakness (30) and the power of Christ (12: 9).

19. The Corinthians are so sure of their own wisdom (cf. 1 C. 4: 8–10) that it gives them a certain pleasure to indulge **fools. 20.** They can easily bear with *folly*, for they put up with far worse things than that, tyranny, oppression, violence, insult (all of which, he implies, have been practised by the false apostles). **enslaves:** Contrast Paul's attitude (1: 24; 4: 5). **exploits you:** Lit. 'devours' by exacting money (cf. Mk 12: 40). **takes advantage** (cf. 12: 17): Or possibly, 'catches you, like birds in a trap'. **21a.**

Paul ironically reproaches himself for having proved weaker than the domineering false apostles, and implicitly rebukes the Corinthians for preferring their tyranny to his gentleness.

v. Boasting 'According to the Flesh' (11: 21b–29)
21b–29. 'Here are my credentials. I am a pure-blooded Jew (22), and a servant of Christ, as is proved by all I have suffered for the gospel's sake (23), at the hands of officials (24, 25a) and mobs, and through natural calamities (25b); often in danger on my frequent journeys (26), suffering bodily privations (27) and mental distress' (28, 29). **22.** There is little difference between the terms **Hebrews, Israelites**, and **Abraham's descendants**. **Hebrews** perhaps refers to the fact that they spoke Aramaic as well as Greek (cf. Ac. 6: 1), though 'a Hebrew of Hebrews' (Phil. 3: 5) refers to pure descent, 'a Hebrew born of Hebrew parents'. **23. Servants of Christ** is their own description of themselves, and Paul will not argue about their standing before God, plain though it is that they are doing Satan's work in Corinth (13). His reply to their claim to superiority as apostles of Christ is that for him the signs of a true apostle are his sufferings in the service of Christ. He is **more** a servant of Christ because he has suffered, while they have not. He does not mean, by speaking of his working **much harder** and being **in prison more frequently** to contrast the number of his sufferings with theirs, but simply to contrast his real sufferings with their mere claims. **I am out of my mind to talk like this:** He winces at the thought of where this self-praise is leading. **in prison . . . frequently:** Luke informs us of only one imprisonment before this time, at Philippi (Ac. 16: 23), but we know of four later: in Jerusalem and Caesarea, and two in Rome. Very probably he had been imprisoned in Ephesus during the two-year visit of Ac. 19. Clement of Rome (*Epistle to the Corinthians* [A.D. 96], 5: 6) says that Paul was imprisoned seven times. **exposed to death again and again:** Cf. 'I die daily' (1 C. 15: 31) and 2 C. 1: 9; 4: 10 f. **24.** Only two of the thirteen incidents in vv. 24, 25 are recorded elsewhere in the NT, and even this list must be selective (cf. 'besides everything else', v. 28). **forty lashes minus one:** The law (Dt. 25: 1 ff.) allowed 40 stripes, but to prevent an infringement of the law through miscalculation, Jewish custom had 'built a hedge around the Torah' by limiting the number to 39. The punishment, to which half a tractate of the Mishnah is devoted (*Makkoth*), was inflicted in the synagogue (cf. Mt. 10: 17) by the minister (or servant), who gave 13 stripes on the chest and 26 on the shoulders (*Makkoth*, 3: 12). **25. beaten with rods:** By Roman lictors. Only one instance of this punishment is recorded in

Acts (16: 22 f., 37; cf. 1 Th. 2: 2; for an attempt to beat him, cf. Ac. 22: 24 ff.). It was contrary to Roman law that a Roman citizen (as Paul was) should be beaten, but cases were not unknown. **stoned:** At Lystra (Ac. 14: 19). Being **shipwrecked** is not mentioned by Luke. A later one is described in Ac. 27. **27.** Privations he has suffered (cf. on 6: 4 f.). **labored and toiled:** The same phrase as in 1 Th. 2: 9; 2 Th. 3: 8. **28. all the churches:** Perhaps he means 'not only those founded by me'. **29. weak:** Not only weak in conscience (1 C. 8: 7) (cf. Knox: 'Does anyone feel a scruple? I share it'), but weak in all other ways too. **Who is led into sin:** He is no doubt thinking particularly of the Corinthians, who have been 'led into sin' by the false apostles.

vi. Boasting in Weakness (11: 30–12: 10)
The word 'weak' (29) has led him to reflect on the subject of weakness. I would far rather boast of my weaknesses, he thinks, than of my strengths, because it is in my weaknesses that *God's* power has been evidenced. He illustrates the theme of his weakness by the story of his escape from Damascus (11: 32–33), and by the account of his vision of the third heaven and the subsequent thorn in his flesh (12: 1–10).

(a) **His escape from Damascus (11: 30–33)**
30–33. 'No, I will boast no more "according to the flesh". If I must boast, it will be of unheroic things, my weaknesses (30). God knows I would rather boast of them (31). One such inglorious episode, in which I glory nevertheless, was my escape from Damascus' (32, 33). **30.** 'The true apostle, . . . far from being able to boast of honour and power . . . is, like Jesus, a suffering and dying figure, whose work and power and victory arise from his weakness and infirmity and defeat' (J. Munck). **31.** A solemn asseveration of his preference for reflection on God's strength in his weakness, rather than on what *he* has achieved. Some think, less probably, that he is binding himself with an oath that all the details of vv. 32 f. (or 24–27) are correct. **32, 33.** This rather humiliating incident (Ac. 9: 23 ff.), which a boaster 'according to the flesh' would keep well hidden (and perhaps Paul had been called a coward because of this escape), is Paul's first illustration of 'strength made perfect in weakness' (12: 9); it is an admirable foil to the episode of the third heaven (though the contrast between 'lowered' [11: 33] and 'caught up' [12: 2] may be only fortuitous). Many, however, feel these verses to be strangely placed here, and regard them, since they describe a 'suffering' of Paul's, as an afterthought (cf. 1 C. 1: 16) to the catalogue of vv. 24–27. Opinions differ on the function of the **governor** (lit. 'ethnarch') under **King Aretas** IV of the Nabataeans (his capital was Petra); he may have been the viceroy of Aretas, or (if the Romans were at this period in pos-

session of Damascus) merely head of the Nabataean colony there, or a (Jewish) ethnarch responsible for the Jewish community in the city. Paul's stay of three years in (Nabataean) Arabia (Gal. 1: 17) and Damascus (Ac. 9: 22) had apparently provoked both Nabataeans and Jews against him; it seems to have been at the instigation of the Jews that the ethnarch had the city gates watched in order to seize Paul.

(b) The third heaven and the 'thorn in the flesh' (12: 1–10)

1–10. The visionary experience is not related for its own sake, but as a preface to the lesson of the 'thorn in the flesh'. His physical weakness, which gives an opportunity for the power of Christ to be displayed, is a more agreeable subject of boasting than his experiences of the sublime, about which he is noticeably reticent.

1. I must go on boasting: He is impelled by the situation (cf. 11: 1, 16 ff., 21, 23), but he knows that **there is nothing to be gained** from it—it is not edifying (cf. 10: 8). **2.** He refers to himself as **a man in Christ** because the man who underwent such experiences seems to be almost a different person from the Paul of everyday life. His specification of the date, **fourteen years ago**, is reminiscent of the dating of their visions by OT prophets (*e.g.* Am. 1: 1; Hag. 1: 1; 2: 1, 10, 20). If A.D. 56 is accepted as the date of 2 Corinthians, Paul would have had the vision while he was in Tarsus (cf. Ac. 11: 25); others reckon it a couple of years later, while he was in Antioch (cf. Ac. 11: 26). **The third heaven** was apparently regarded by Paul as the highest heaven; the concept of three heavens may have been deduced from the expression 'the heavens, even the highest heaven' (1 Kg. 8: 27). Later the view that there were seven heavens became dominant in Judaism (cf. TB, *Hagigah*, 12b). **whether in the body or apart from the body I do not know:** Paul recognized the possibility of a corporeal ascension (like Elijah's or Christ's; cf. 1 Th. 4: 15 ff.) as well as of an incorporeal rapture, in which the soul was separated from the body (cf. 5: 1 ff.). During his vision he was not conscious of his body, and so now he cannot say whether it was a corporeal ascension or not. **4. paradise** (originally a Persian word meaning 'park, pleasure-garden') was used in LXX of the garden of Eden, and hence in later Jewish literature and NT (Lk. 23: 43; Rev. 2: 7) of the abode of the blessed after death. V. 2 and v. 3 refer to the same vision, and 'paradise' merely describes the character of the third heaven. **4. inexpressible things:** Either because they cannot be put into words (cf. Rom. 8: 26), or because they are specially sacred (cf. NEB). **5.** He continues to speak of **a man like that** (lit. 'such a man') as if he were not himself. Such experiences may well be boasted of, but because they are *given*,

and are not his own achievement, they reveal nothing of his own character. **6.** He could go on to boast of his experiences without exaggerating (cf. 10: 8), but he wants no one to judge him on his unverifiable statements about himself, only on the evidence before their eyes. **7. these surpassingly great revelations:** Either means 'the abundance of things revealed' during the one rapture of vv. 2 f., or should be translated 'the excellence of the revelations'. **a thorn . . . in the flesh:** The word for 'thorn' (*skolops*) meant in classical Gk. a 'stake', but the meaning 'thorn' was apparently more common in Hellenistic times. In spite of views that the thorn in the flesh was suffering in persecution (was this a thorn only for Paul?), or doubts or temptations to evil (if so, why should the Lord tell him not to pray for its removal?), the most natural interpretation is that it is a physical ailment. If it is the same thing as the 'illness' of Gal. 4: 13 f. (as seems probable, but cannot be proved), we can define the malady as being of a repulsive nature (cf. 'you did not despise me', lit. 'did not spit me out'), as well as acute ('thorn') and recurrent ('three times', 'harass'). The most probable conjectures are ophthalmia (cf. Gal. 4: 15; 6: 11; Ac. 23: 5) and malarial fever (perhaps contracted at Perga [Ac. 13: 13], and the cause of his journey to the healthier climate of Galatia [Gal. 4: 13]). The **messenger of Satan** is the thorn in the flesh, not a personal enemy. Like Job's calamities, the thorn was inflicted by Satan, though permitted by God. **torment:** Lit. 'buffet', a frequently recurring action. **9. he said:** The perfect tense is used with its proper significance, 'He *has* said (and His answer still holds good)'. **My grace is sufficient:** The 'summit of the epistle' (Hughes). Christ's promise has had a marked effect on Paul's attitude to life (cf. 3: 5; 4: 7, etc.). **Grace** is not just a vague benignity, but indicates 'power' as well as 'favour' (Strachan). **my power is made perfect in weakness:** 'My strength finds its full scope in thy weakness' (Knox). It is **Christ's power**, not freedom from the pain, that is indispensable to him. **may rest on me:** Lit. 'may tabernacle upon me', the word (*skēnoō*) being reminiscent of the shekinah glory which filled the tabernacle (Exod. 40: 34). **10.** He **delights**, or rather, is 'well content' (NEB), with weaknesses, not because they are desirable in themselves, but because it is in them that the power of Christ becomes conspicuous. 'Weakness' means more to Paul than physical weakness; whenever the proud natural man that is in him sees his dignity, reputation, finances, comfort, or liberty suffer, he feels his own weakness, and Christ's strength.

vii. Paul not Inferior to the False Apostles (12: 11–13)

11–13. 'There now, I have been a fool and done

my boasting! But it is your fault that it was necessary; had you been loyal you would have sprung to my defence unbidden. With good reason you could have commended me, for though I am nothing in my own right, I am not all inferior to your precious "apostles" (11); all the signs of a true apostle I performed among you (12). Are you thinking that I made *you* inferior, because I didn't sponge on you? I'm so sorry!' (13). **11. I am not in the least inferior:** Better, 'I was not inferior', when in Corinth. **the 'super-apostles':** Cf. on 11: 5. **12. The things that mark an apostle:** A comprehensive term for all the proofs that he has been sent by God (cf. 1: 12; 4: 2; 6: 4; 1 Th. 1: 5). **perseverance**, or 'endurance', may be intended as one of these signs (it has a wide range; cf. on 6: 4); or perhaps he means that despite all opposition he patiently and consistently exhibited the marks of a true apostle. **signs, wonders**, and **miracles** are three terms for miracles, expressing three aspects of the nature of miracle (the same phrase in Ac. 2: 22; Heb. 2: 4; cf. 2 Th. 2: 9). They are another instance of the signs (marks) of a true apostle. **13.** His meaning appears to be: '*I* was not inferior, so that could not have been why you would not defend me. Did I make *you* inferior, by favouring you less than the other churches?' **burden:** Cf. on 11: 9.

viii. In Anticipation of his Third Visit (12: 14–13: 10)

(a) Why he will not 'burden' them (12: 14–18)

14–18. 'On my forthcoming visit I will continue my policy of financial independence; I claim a bigger salary than your money—yourselves! It is I who should be supporting you, not you me (14). I will gladly spend all I have for you; and will you let your love diminish as mine increases? (15) Is there a suggestion abroad that some of the collection for Jerusalem will go into my pocket? (16) Answer me this: have I ever taken advantage of you through my delegates (17), Titus or the other brother? The honesty of Titus is beyond suspicion; am I not one with him in character and action?' (18)

14. the third time: His first visit was on his second missionary journey (Ac. 18: 1 ff.), his second the 'painful' visit (2 C. 2: 1; see Introduction), the third will be to collect the gift for Jerusalem (Ac. 20: 2). **children should not have to save up for their parents:** An appeal to an obvious fact of human life. One does not expect little children to put money aside for their parents' future; rather the other way around. **15.** He will not only put by a little something for his children in the faith; he will gladly **spend** all he has and **expend** himself completely for their sake. **16.** His opponents are bound to grant that Paul himself never

received money from Corinth, but they insinuate (Paul probably speaks more plainly than they did) that Paul will take his own share out of the collection for the Jerusalem poor. **crafty fellow that I am:** RSV inserts 'you say' (better, 'they say'), which is not in the Gk., but is rightly supplied to indicate that this is a charge brought against Paul—not an admission he makes! **caught you by trickery:** Lit. 'trapped' (cf. 11: 20).

18. I urged Titus to go: This probably refers to Titus' original visit (cf. on 8: 6), not his visit with the severe letter (2: 13; 7: 13 ff.). It is just possible that 'I urged Titus' and 'sent the brother' are epistolary aorists, and should be translated 'I am urging Titus and sending the brother' (=8: 17 f.), in which case Paul's meaning is: 'Are you going to complain because I am sending my fellow-workers? Have they ever wronged you in the past?' **Did we** (=I) **not act in the same spirit:** Titus is above reproach (cf. 7: 13 ff.). Could Paul, therefore, being in such harmony of spirit with Titus, be guilty of duplicity?

(b) Fears for what he will find in Corinth (12: 19–21)

19–21. 'You must not think that I have been speaking simply in order to defend myself. It has really been for your upbuilding (19). I am afraid that when I come I will find disharmony and opposition (20), and the morals of pagans among members of the church (21). I want to prevent this by dealing with the critical and the disobedient now.'

19. Since 10: 1 he has not just been defending himself, but clearing away misconceptions and negative attitudes for the sake of the **strengthening** of the church (cf. 10: 18; 13: 10). And it has not simply been a defence **to you**, but **in the sight of God**, to whom alone he is answerable. **20. For:** I.e. 'there is *need* of upbuilding for . . .'. **you may not find me as you want me**, but stern and ready to punish (13: 1 ff.). Paul's fears for the state of the church have been thought incompatible with his satisfaction expressed in chap. 7. But here it is a question of order and morality (21) within the church, in chap. 7 a question of their submission to his authority. There was still much room for improvement within the church, but Paul could not begin to restore order and impose punishments on offenders until his apostolic authority was generally upheld in Corinth. **21. God may humble me before you:** He will be humiliated if he finds his converts still living like pagans. **Again** is to be taken with **humble**, a reference to his previous humiliation on the 'painful' visit. **be grieved** perhaps means 'mourn as over the dead', with the implication that the offenders will have to be excluded from the church.

(c) **He can be severe if necessary (13: 1–4)**
1–4. 'If you have accusations to bring against your brethren, make sure that they are fully substantiated when I arrive (1), and I will punish all wrong-doers with appropriate severity (2); that should convince you all that I have Christ's authority (3). Weak I may be in myself, but when I come to judging evil you will find that Christ has given me enough vigour for that' (4).

1. This will be my third visit: Cf. on 12: 14. He introduces the prescription of Dt. 19: 15, *a matter must be established by the testimony of two or three witnesses*, apparently meaning that if on his *third* visit he finds them still in sin, his three visits will be *three* sets of evidence (**witnesses**) against them, and so he will be quite entitled to punish. (This view explains why he emphasizes 'here for the *third* time I am coming'; the number of his visits is otherwise unimportant.) An alternative interpretation is that when he comes, he will set up a full judicial enquiry, if it is necessary, and all discipline will be imposed after a just trial with sufficient witnesses. **A matter:** An accusation of Corinthian against Corinthian, not, apparently, against Paul. **2. those who sinned earlier:** Cf. 12: 21. **the others:** Either those who may have fallen into sin since his second visit, or the rest of the church who have tolerated the sinners. **I will not spare:** He has delayed visiting them in order to spare them (1: 23) by giving them time to rearrange their affairs, but he cannot put off his visit indefinitely, for the gift for Jerusalem is a pressing matter; so he warns them to be prepared. **3.** He will demonstrate his apostolic authority, which they have doubted, by exercizing his power, given him by Christ, who is **powerful among you** (cf. *e.g.* the 'signs and wonders and mighty works' [12: 12]). **4. To be sure,** Christ was **crucified in weakness,** and sceptics might think that that is all that can be said of Him (cf. 1 C. 1: 23), but believers know that He **lives by God's power** evidenced in His resurrection (Rom. 1: 4; 6: 4; 1 C. 6: 14; 15: 43). And as Christ, His apostle: Paul is **weak,** lacking in self-assertion and self-assurance, **in him,** i.e. by virtue of his union with the Christ who did not His own will; but like Christ, he will display the power of a resurrection life (**we** [=I] **will live with him**) when it comes to dealing with the Corinthians.

(d) **Punishment can be avoided if they will examine themselves (13: 5–10)**
5–10. 'It is yourselves, not me, you should be testing for marks of genuineness. Can you say that Christ is living in you? You should be able to, unless perhaps you were never converted (5). What I hope is that you will discover by yourselves, without needing me to inflict punishment, that I do indeed have Christ's auth-

ority (6). I would prefer that, even though it may mean that I will have no opportunity to prove my apostleship (7), for my own good name is secondary to the interests of the gospel (8). Yes, when you are living the life of faith and are "strong" so that I do not need to assert my authority (and so am "weak"), I am glad (9). All these warnings I give now so that when I come I may be able to use my apostolic authority not for punishment, but for its proper work, your edification' (10).

5. Examine yourselves: 'Yourselves' is emphatic and implies 'Don't examine me'. **in the faith:** Not fidelity to doctrine, but the vitality of the faith which works (Allo). 'Are you living the life of faith?' (NEB). **6. We have not failed** the test of genuineness. **7.** 'I could prove to you *my* genuineness (as an apostle of Christ) by meeting your sin with the severity of my authority. But I would far rather you did not sin (**not do . . . wrong**) than that I should be proved a true apostle; yes, I would rather you did **what is right**, even though that may mean that I appear not to be a true apostle (through lack of opportunity to assert myself)'. **8. the truth:** Roughly equivalent to 'what is right' (7). He means that 'he cannot desire that they should be found to be doing wrong, in order that he may be proved to be right' (Plummer). Some interpret **the truth** as 'the gospel', which gives a similar sense: He cannot allow himself to further his own interests (even to clear his name), if this would hinder the work of the gospel in men's lives. The verse should not be taken as a general principle, that no one can successfully oppose the truth (however valid this principle may be). **9. perfection:** Or, 'perfecting' (RV), i.e. full restoration to health. He is not content only that they should do no evil (7) but desires that they should be perfected in holiness (cf. 1 Th. 3: 11 ff.). **10.** At the conclusion of the section 10: 1–13: 10 he admits the charge he refers to in 10: 1, that he is severe while absent and humble when present, for he has now explained why he behaves thus. **authority . . . for building you up:** Cf. 10: 8; 12: 19.

VII. FINAL EXHORTATIONS AND BENEDICTION (13: 11–14)

11. good-bye: Or perhaps 'rejoice' (as Phil. 4: 4). **Aim for perfection:** More literally 'be perfected' (the same word as in v. 9). **12. a holy kiss:** Paul encourages them to put Christian significance (a *holy* kiss) into a customary mode of greeting. Judaism knew of a 'kiss of reconciliation'; there was also the customary kiss of greeting exchanged before or after a synagogue service. The Christian 'holy kiss' apparently soon became incorporated into the liturgy (cf. Justin Martyr, *First Apology*, 65). **14.** This benediction, the fullest in Paul's letters, is couched in trinitarian form; as a witness to the primitive Christian belief in the trinity it is all the more impressive because it is a spontaneous and not a consciously formulated expression of it. **The fellowship of the Holy Spirit** seems to mean the sense of unity within the church which the Holy Spirit bestows.

BIBLIOGRAPHY

Commentaries on the English Text:

BARRETT, C. K., *The Second Epistle to the Corinthians. BNTC* (London, 1973).

BRUCE, F. F., *1 and 2 Corinthians. NCentB* (London, 1971).

DENNEY, J., *The Second Epistle to the Corinthians. EB* (London, 1849).

HODGE, C., *An Exposition of the Second Epistle to the Corinthians* (New York, 1860; reprinted Grand Rapids, 1950).

HUGHES, P. E., *Paul's Second Epistle to the Corinthians. NICNT* (London, 1962).

KELLY, W., *Notes on the Second Epistle to the Corinthians* (London, 1882).

STRACHAN. R. H., *The Second Epistle of Paul to the Corinthians. MNT* (London, 1935).

TASKER, R. V. G., *The Second Epistle of Paul to the Corinthians. TNTC* (London, 1958).

THRALL, M. E., *I and II Corinthians. CBC* (Cambridge, 1965).

Commentaries on the Greek Text:

HÉRING, J., *The Second Epistle of Saint Paul to the Corinthians*, E.T. (London, 1967).

MENZIES, A., *The Second Epistle of the Apostle Paul to the Corinthians* (London, 1912).

PLUMMER, A., *A Critical and Exegetical Commentary on the Second Epistle of St. Paul to the Corinthians. ICC* (Edinburgh, 1915).

GALATIANS

F. ROY COAD

The letter to the Galatians is happily free from critical problems concerning authorship, scholars having been virtually unanimous in endorsing it as a genuine work of the apostle Paul. The problems which do exist relate to the date of composition of the letter, and to the location of the churches to which it was addressed.

In the middle of the first century, the Roman province of Galatia covered a great tract of central Asia Minor. The north-eastern part of the province, centred upon the three tribal capitals of Pessinus, Ancyra and Tavium, was controlled by a people of Celtic or Gallic descent (hence the name *Galatia*—cf. *Gaul* and *Galicia*), who had entered the land some three hundred years before and established dominance over the earlier inhabitants. Their lands lay away from the main trade and travel routes of that time, although they were to come brilliantly into their own in later centuries, after Constantinople had become the centre of imperial rule, and the main highways passed through Ancyra (modern Ankara).

In contrast, the south western part of the province was based on the Roman *coloniae* of Pisidian Antioch and Lystra (a third of its cities, Iconium, also became a *colonia* at a later date). Through it ran the highly important roads to Syria and the East from the Greek towns of the western seaboard of Asia Minor, and the native inhabitants (Phrygian around Antioch and Lycaonian around Lystra) had come strongly under the influence of foreign manners: of the Greeks who had followed Alexander, of the Jews who had been settled there by the Seleucid kings, and then of the Roman conquerors.

Debates concerning the destination and the date of the letter are closely involved with this division of the country. We may distinguish three main views.

i. That it was written to churches supposedly founded by Paul in the northern part of Galatia. This is the oldest view, but it has lost much ground since the researches of Sir W. M. Ramsay, in the late years of the nineteenth century, into the history and peoples of Asia Minor in classical times (see pp. 1360, 1365).

ii. That it was written to the churches which were undeniably founded by Paul in Southern Galatia during his first missionary journey, but that the letter was written at some time after one of his later visits to those churches.

iii. That it was written to those same churches, but immediately after the first missionary journey, and before the apostolic council of Acts 15.

The third view is that adopted in this commentary, and an explanation of this view is desirable at this point.

The destination of the letter

Acts names *Galatia* (or, more accurately, *Galatic territory*) twice in its accounts of Paul's journeys: once in 16: 6, on the outward stage of the second missionary journey, and again in 18: 23, on the outward stage of the third missionary journey. Until the end of the nineteenth century this *Galatia* was commonly held to be the northern region of the Roman province of that name, the only part in which dwelt persons strictly by race *Galatian*. The southern part of the province had later been severed from Galatia, and thus the fact that it was part of Galatia in the apostle's day tended to be overlooked. Thus, on each of these journeys, Paul was held to have deviated from the direct westerly and north westerly route across Asia Minor to visit this region. He certainly did not visit North Galatia on his first journey. The churches which he established in this northern part of Galatia, it was held, were those to whom this letter was written.

This view presented three major difficulties. *First*, there are no other known indications that Paul established churches in North Galatia, which lay well away from the Aegean centres of his work, and from the roads to them. Such foundations also seem out of keeping with what we know of Paul's missionary strategy. *Second*, if the letter was not written until the later journeys of the apostle, it must have been written considerably after the council of Ac. 15, when the very question at issue in the letter was deliberated upon in Jerusalem. On that occasion an agreed and authoritative statement had been issued by that church, under the authority of James, the apostles and the elders. In such circumstances, it is inconceivable that this letter should make no reference to that decision, even while it is arguing the whole issue out afresh. (It is no answer to point out that no reference is made to the council's decisions in 1 C. 8 or 10. The question there discussed, that of food sacrificed to idols, was indeed covered in the findings of the Jerusalem council, but it was peripheral to the debate: nor were the

Jerusalem findings on the whole relevant to the issues at Corinth. On the other hand, the letter to the Galatians deals with the whole issue of the Jewish obedience, which was precisely the crux of the Jerusalem council.)

Third, this view is normally associated with the identification of the visit of Paul to Jerusalem described in Gal. 2 with that of Ac. 15: a view which leads almost inevitably to the conclusion that one or other of the accounts is inaccurate (see commentary on Gal. 2: 1–10 below).

As against this view, then, many commentators look for the destination of this letter to the churches established by Paul on his first missionary journey in the southern part of the Roman province of Galatia. Although Luke does not use the term in his account of that journey in Ac. 13 and 14, they lay within *Galatic territory*. The work of Sir W. M. Ramsay at the end of last century established convincing reasons, based on a profound knowledge of the political and social conditions in Asia Minor in the first century, for believing that the letter was addressed to those churches. Such a view accords convincingly with other Biblical data and has been widely adopted by British and American scholars.

The date of the letter

Even if this second view as to the recipients of the letter is accepted, its date must still be determined. Many commentators, impressed by the similarity of the thought and style of the letter to that to the Romans, consider that it must have been written at much the same time, probably during the third missionary journey. Others see it as written just before that journey (this was Ramsay's original view, but he later dated it before the Council of Ac. 15). (See also Hogg and Vine, p. 7.) But this view still leaves us with the second of the difficulties referred to above, and normally with the third as well.

An attempt to explain the second difficulty, the lack of reference to the Jerusalem decrees of Ac. 15, is made by suggesting that Paul's own actions relating to those decrees, described in Ac. 16, had themselves lent colour to the allegations of his opponents. He had taken care to deliver the decrees to the South Galatian churches, thus causing the churches to conclude that his apostolic authority was subject to that of the Jerusalem leaders. He had also circumcised Timothy, and thus strengthened the circumcision party. Thus, on this view, we account for the expression 'even if we' in Gal. 1: 8, and for the allegation that he himself preached circumcision (referred to in Gal. 5: 11). These two matters, Paul's authority and the teachings of the circumcision party, are the two main themes of the letter.

Yet such a view surely renders the lack of direct reference to the very decrees which had given rise to the misunderstanding, still more inexplicable: particularly when the non-circumcision of Titus is specifically discussed (2: 3 ff.). A reference to the incident concerning Timothy would have been inevitable, on this hypothesis.

Both difficulties are removed by the belief that the letter was written before the events of Ac. 15 had taken place. It is of interest that Calvin came to this conclusion purely on the internal evidences (see his commentary on 2: 1–5), although he did not follow through the implications as to the destination of the letter.

The situation then becomes plain. Paul, returning from his first missionary journey to Antioch, finds himself in controversy with the Judaizing teachers from Jerusalem who, we know from Ac. 15: 1, visited the city at that time (see also Gal. 2: 12). While he is engaged in this very controversy, news reaches him that similar teachers, following hot-foot in his steps, have visited the newly founded churches of his first journey (Ac. 13 and 14), and are succeeding in betraying his work. The result is this letter written white-hot with urgency, and under great emotional stress. The issues which it raises were, a few weeks later, to produce the Council of Jerusalem.

If this third view is adopted, it has important results for NT chronology, and for the understanding of the progress of doctrine within the Testament. Galatians becomes the first of the writings of the NT, written in A.D. 48 or 49, less than twenty years after the crucifixion. Following the data in the letter itself, we must then place Paul's conversion in approximately A.D. 33. The view has other far-reaching results, which cannot be discussed here: one notable difficulty, concerning Paul's Damascus visit, is referred to in the commentary on 1: 18–24.

ANALYSIS

III THE AUTHORITY OF PAUL AND OF THE GOSPEL HE PREACHED
(largely biographical) (1: 10–2: 21)

IV THE GOSPEL EXPLAINED AND EXEMPLIFIED (largely doctrinal) (3: 1–4: 31)

V THE OUTWORKING OF THE GOSPEL (largely practical) (5: 1–6: 10)

VI CONCLUSION (6: 11–18)

I. INTRODUCTION (1: 1–5)

1, 2a. From the profound mystery of Deity, the Word had spoken. Such was the certainty which had gripped and inspired the soul of Saul of Tarsus. Within that wonder, lay another: the knowledge that he himself was an instrument of that divine Word. In Jesus, God had appeared: the resurrection had established that fact beyond doubt. Now Saul of Tarsus was the bond-servant and the deputed legate of the Lord Jesus Christ: **Paul an apostle**, by direct divine appointment.

There were men who did not understand it so. They, too, professed the name of Christ —but to them the message which Paul was preaching was a betrayal of the ancient ways of God. Nurtured in the tradition of the ancient covenants, and gripped by the Jewish Law, as the divinely appointed way of life, they could not easily adapt themselves to the thought that these things were now to be laid aside. Moreover, they could claim proud, if strictly unsanctioned, authority: the credentials of Jerusalem, the church of the apostles and of James the brother of the Lord. To them Paul was but an upstart from Antioch of Syria, and they did not hesitate to emphasize it.

So Paul takes pains, as he opens his letter, to assert the basis of his authority. Did his opponents claim the authority of men of note? His authority needed no such mediation, but came directly from the God who had spoken decisively in Christ, raising Him from the dead. Yet, even among men, he was not alone. With him were the devoted companions the Galatians knew.

[Note: **from men** and **by man**: the prepositions imply respectively the primary source and the intermediary source of authority.]

2b. Who, then, were these **churches in Galatia**?

The answer to that question has been discussed in the introduction: this commentary takes them to be the churches founded in South Galatia by Paul on his first missionary journey (Ac. 13 and 14).

3–5. In challenging Paul's authority the Jewish teachers had an ulterior motive: to discredit the gospel which he preached. So, in his salutation, Paul re-affirms the essentials of the gospel. It was a self-giving for our sins and a deliberate movement of the will of God: a free act of divine grace, unquestionable by man, to which it is an impious presumption to add any further requirement. To emphasize this the transcendence of God is stressed. The will of Him whose glory extends to the aeons of the aeons (**for ever and ever**) has moved to deliver us from this single evil aeon (**the present evil age**). The deliverance is His act in which He delighted; a deliverance, as it were, for Himself (on the significance of the use of the middle voice see Vine, *Expository Dictionary of NT Words*, '*Deliver*' 8). If Christ **gave Himself**, dare we add a further requirement?

We must not overlook the importance of this passage at this extremely early stage of Christian teaching. The name of **the Lord Jesus Christ** is already coupled in equality with that of **God our Father**: a fact the more striking in view of the intense Jewish feeling which surrounded the whole subject matter of this letter. Moreover, His self-giving is **for our sins**: the redemptive purpose of the death of Christ is already established as the basis of the Gospel in this very early surviving formulation. Here, then, we have the earliest and most essential elements of Christian preaching.

II. THE OCCASION OF THE LETTER (1: 6–9)

Something of the teaching which was brought by the Judaizing teachers to Galatia can be learned from later references in the letter. It accepted the Messiahship of Jesus, but added another requirement to that of faith in Christ: acceptance of the Jewish obedience, particularly as symbolized in circumcision and the keeping of the ethical and ceremonial law (Ac. 15: 1; Gal. 3: 2, 10; 4: 10, 21; 5: 2; 6: 12, 13).

To Paul also it was axiomatic that faith in Christ exercised a radical effect upon conduct (5: 19–24). But the place which the Judaizers gave to the law was not, for him, only a different emphasis. It perverted his message, was **a different gospel**, and **other than the one we preached to you**: a reversal (*metastrepsai*, v. 7) of the gospel.

The reasons for that antagonism are worked out in detail in the letter. The new teaching was retrograde, a return to bondage (5: 1; see Ac. 15: 10). Behind it all lay yet a deeper reason. To surrender to the Judaizers was to reduce the way of Christ to merely another of the quarrelling Jewish sects, and inevitably to throttle at birth the universal message of Christ. Paul himself must have realized this: but it was a vision far beyond the horizons of the narrow sectaries of Jerusalem, concerned as they were with the minutiae of observance and with the fear of the only persecution which the Church had yet known (6: 12;). The apostle keeps his counsel, but his realization burns in the passion of his words. Here, if ever, was an issue where to hasten slowly, to be insufficiently radical, was to defeat the purposes of God: was to **desert the one who called you**.

[Notes: i. **8. eternally condemned:** *anathema*.

ii. **6, 7. a different gospel—which is really no gospel at all:** There are different views on the precise sense here, which are reflected in different versions. Was Paul implying that the Judaizers' message was no gospel at all; or that it was not a different message, but merely a perversion of the true? The difference arises from contrary views of the force of the Greek words *heteros* and *allos* taken *e.g.*, by Lightfoot and Ramsay. (The NIV takes the first option.)

iii. **8. even if we:** Paul's own divine authority is valid only while his message remains authentic. Cf. Peter (Gal. 2: 11).

iv. Notice the change from a remote possibility, **if we . . . should preach** (8) to a contingency only too really present, **if anybody is preaching** (9).]

III. THE AUTHORITY OF PAUL AND OF THE GOSPEL HE PREACHED (1: 10–2: 21)

1: 10. The AV translated the first question literally: 'For do I now persuade men, or God?' By the sheer incongruity of any other reply, this demands the answer 'men': but it is felt that this does not conform with the context, and most other translations follow the course of the RSV and translate the Greek word *peithō* (persuade) by **win the approval of** or a similar expression (see Ac. 12: 20). The question is thus parallel to that which follows: **am I trying to please men?** The whole verse takes a sideglance at the charge that Paul was watering down his message to win men over—the very charge which he later brings against his opponents (6: 12). This rendering of *peithō* is accurate and well attested.

Yet the AV rendering may express a deliberate ambiguity in the original. Paul, reared an ardent Pharisee, had bowed before the unanswerable act of God. What was his opponents' case? Faced with God's unquestionable act, they were virtually insisting that God could work

in their way, and in no other. So, ironically, Paul may be asking—does he, like his opponents, seek to persuade God to bow to his ideas, or men to bow to God's? The obvious answer is that suggested by the AV—'men'. The renderings of most other translations, of course, require the answer 'God'. See 2 C. 5: 11; cf. Ac. 17: 4. The emphatic 'now' would suit this interpretation. Paul, the persecutor, had now bowed to the irresistible act of God (notice also the 'still' in the latter part of the verse).

[Note: The Gk. places an article ('the') before 'God', but not before 'men'. On this Lightfoot draws attention to a similar construction in 4: 31 ('not of *a* bondwoman', i.e. of *any* bondwoman, 'but of *the* freewoman', i.e. of the *only* lawful spouse), suggesting a similar sense in this passage.]

11–17. Paul now commences the first section of his argument, and develops it until the end of ch. 2. It concerns the basis of his own authority, and therefore that of his message. He sets out to demonstrate his direct dependence upon God for the gospel which he preached: an approach which requires him to avoid both horns of a dilemma. On the one hand, he must show that his teaching was not derived from any human agency: on the other, that it was no idiosyncrasy, but had been acknowledged and recognized by his fellow-apostles.

His conversion was the first and most telling evidence in his favour. He can offer the only convincing explanation for that dramatic reversal of the whole tenor of his life: an unveiling (*apokalypsis*) of Jesus Christ. He emphasises that there was no question of human influence at the sensitive stage immediately following this revelation: he **did not consult any man**, but retired (into solitude?) to Arabia. This information adds to the knowledge we derive from Ac. 9. The precise time that he was in Arabia is not known, for the three years of v. 18 include the considerable activity in Damascus of which Ac. 9 informs us.

What was the revelation by which Paul received the gospel (12)? The other revelation, of v. 16, was centred upon the dramatic experience on the Damascus road (see note ii), but the growth of understanding of the gospel was not necessarily of a supernatural nature. Paul's own concern is to avoid the allegation of mere human speculation. The careful argument of this letter is evidence enough of the source of the revelation in Paul's meditations upon the OT. We can deduce some of the passages which were most formative: the story of Abraham, Habakkuk, and the latter part of Isaiah were obviously prominent. Behind and confirming his convictions lay the consciousness of a divine overruling and shaping of his life (15; cf. Jer. 1: 5 and Isa. 49: 1).

[Notes: i. With v. 12 cf. 1 C. 11: 23; Eph. 3: 2–12; Col. 1: 25–29. Contrast 1 C. 15: 3 and see Gal. 1: 18. There is no contradiction. See Cullmann *The Early Church*, 1956, art. *The Tradition*, pp. 59 ff.

ii. **16. to reveal his Son in me** (*en emoi*): Other renderings prefer 'through me' (i.e. by Paul's preaching; as Lightfoot), or 'in my case' (i.e. in distinction from others; as Hogg and Vine), or 'to me' (RSV).]

18–24. The visit to Jerusalem referred to here is also recorded in Ac. 9: 23–30. From there we learn that Paul's introduction to Peter was not easily accomplished, until Barnabas befriended him. Paul adds the following information to that which we gather from Ac.:—

i. At Jerusalem 'the apostles' to whom Barnabas introduced him (Ac. 9: 27) were two in number only (James, although not one of the twelve, fulfilled the requirements of apostleship) (v. 19).

ii. Paul indicates that a meeting and consultation (*historēsai*) with Peter was a definite purpose of his visit to Jerusalem; a purpose on the part of the disciple of Gamaliel which pays eloquent tribute to the intellectual and spiritual capacity of the Galilean fisherman (v. 18).

iii. Although Paul 'went in and out among them at Jerusalem' (Ac. 9: 28), he had not been able to visit the Judean churches (v. 22).

iv. Some allege a discrepancy between the **fifteen days** of v. 18 and the apparently longer period implied by Ac.: but the former period relates explicitly only to the duration of Paul's actual residence with Peter.

In 2 C. 11: 32 Paul tells us that his escape from Damascus took place while that city was guarded by a governor of Aretas, king of the Nabateans. On the chronology discussed above, the date of Paul's escape would be A.D. 35 or 36 (the inclusive mode of reckoning must be borne in mind). For the problems associated with this see the *NBD* articles *Aretas, Chronology of the NT* and *Paul*.

Ac. also refers to the retirement **to Syria and Cilicia**, with the more specific information that Paul returned to his native Tarsus (Ac. 9: 29, 30). The name Syria and Cilicia is that of the combined Roman political division, and does not necessarily imply that Paul visited Syria itself, although that is possible. Compare also Ac. 22: 17–21, where we learn that the urgency of Paul's brethren was confirmed in a personal vision.

Paul then disappears from the account in Ac. for a period of some ten years, until Barnabas brought him from Tarsus in Cilicia to Antioch in Syria (Ac. 11: 25, 26). That they were not years of idleness is shown by references in the other letters. Many of the experiences which Paul describes in 2 C. 11: 23–27 may be dated to this period, including the beatific vision of

2 C. 12: 2–4. Paul's evangelization of his home district during this period, clearly implied in Gal. 2: 2, would also account for his avoidance of Cilicia on his first missionary journey, when the missionaries travelled to the mainland by way of Barnabas's native island of Cyprus.

Paul's anxiety to affirm the accuracy of his account (v. 20), indicates how important these facts are to his argument. He is still laying stress on his isolation from influence, other than that of Peter and James. The tacitly suggested unity with those two leaders, on the other hand, could only add strength to his case.

[Note: **23. the faith:** The use of 'faith' as a synonym for the gospel is of course in line with the whole exposition contained in this letter. See Lightfoot *in loco*.]

2: 1–10. With this section we reach a question which is crucial to the understanding of the place of this letter in the NT story. On which of Paul's visits to Jerusalem did these incidents take place?

The second visit recorded in Ac. appears at Ac. 11: 30 and 12: 25. The story of Paul's contacts with Jerusalem and his fellow-apostles is essential to his argument, and we should not therefore expect him to omit any of his visits to Jerusalem. On the face of it, therefore, we have described here incidents of the famine visit of Ac. 11: 30 and 12: 25. Calvin, indeed, says in his commentary on these verses that 'on any other supposition, the statements of Paul and Luke cannot be reconciled'.

Two difficulties, however, appear.

i. First and foremost is the difficulty of chronology. A casual reading of Ac. 12 suggests that the famine visit took place before the death of Herod Agrippa I in A.D. 44. The NIV rendering of Gal. 2: 1 suggests that fourteen years elapsed from the first visit of Gal. 1: 18: and that was three years after Paul's conversion. No probable system of chronology could justify this, as Lightfoot saw (*Commentary*, p. 124) (although it has been suggested that 'fourteen' could be a copyist's error for 'four').

ii. There are certain apparent similarities between Ac. 15 and this chapter, which have led to a traditional identification of the visit of Gal. 2 with that of Ac. 15 (see p. 1363).

Is this dilemma as serious as it appears? Further study suggests that the dilemma does not in fact exist, and that the visit of Gal. 2 is after all the famine visit of Ac. 11: 30 and 12: 25.

i. It is known from Josephus (*Antiquities* xx. 5. 2) that the famine recorded in Ac. 11: 28–30 took place during Roman governorships later than the death of Herod, and the most probable date for the famine visit is A.D. 46. The account of the persecution and of Herod's death in Ac. 12 is in fact a flashback, picking up the account of what had been happening in Jerusalem while the events of Ac. 11: 19–26 were taking place. (See F. F. Bruce, *The Book of the Acts*, pp. 257 f.) Moreover, the fourteen years of Gal. 2: 1 are not necessarily dated from the previous visit at all—it is just as likely that both periods (the three years of 1: 18 and the fourteen of 2: 1) are dated from the same starting point—Paul's conversion.

Now fourteen years back from A.D. 46 on the old inclusive reckoning would bring us to A.D. 33, a date for Paul's conversion which is not at all out of the question.

ii. The apparent similarities between this account and Ac. 15 tend to disappear on closer examination, and it is the discrepancies which become more obvious. Calvin's suggestion of irreconcilability was not frivolous.

Further support for the identification with the earlier famine visit is afforded by such hint as the passage contains of the situation within the Jerusalem church. By Ac. 15 the eldership had assumed a much more prominent position in the councils of the church than is implied here—a development accounted for by Peter's (and possibly John's) travels from Jerusalem in the interval (see v. 11 below).

If Gal. 2 does in fact describe events during the visit of Ac. 15 we could not of course maintain that the letter was written before that visit, and the difficulties already described on any other hypothesis would again arise (see introduction). If, on the other hand, we identify Gal. 2: 1–10 with the famine visit, all the pieces of the puzzle fall convincingly into place. Indeed, the **revelation** of v. 2 could be Agabus's prophecy of Ac. 11: 28, although this is not altogether in harmony with the tone of the passage in Gal. It is easier to assume that a personal revelation to Paul, coinciding with Agabus's prophecy, led him to accept a delegation to a city which he had every reason to avoid. (See a similar combination of events in Ac. 9: 30 and 22: 18.)

We can now return to the main theme of the letter. On this visit two events important to Paul's argument occurred. First, he laid before the leaders of the church the gospel which he was preaching, **for fear that I was running or had run my race in vain**. It is uncertain whether this phrase implies a desire to ensure himself at length of the full fellowship of the Jerusalem leaders in the message committed to him, now that it had been thoroughly tested in practical evangelism in his native province (see Lightfoot *in loco*); or whether he wished to forestall the undoing of his work by a faction from Jerusalem. In either event, the result for his present argument was similar. Hitherto he had been dealing with one horn of the dilemma, and had emphasized his freedom from human influence. Now he was able to show that his gospel had been acknowledged and recognized

by his fellow-apostles.

The second event of the visit was unplanned. One of Paul's companions on his visit was Titus, a Greek, who thus appears as one of the earliest, as he was to be one of the latest, of Paul's fellow-workers. The question of Titus's circumcision had been raised, apparently by a group described as **false brothers** (4). It would seem that the leaders, 'the men of repute' (6) (F. F. Bruce—there is nothing necessarily derogatory in the phrase) may have wavered. Paul, who was ready on appropriate occasion to become as a Jew in order to win Jews (1 C. 9: 20), and who would himself later circumcise Timothy, son of a Jewish mother and therefore, in Jewish eyes, himself Jewish (Ac. 16: 3), and would himself submit to requirements of Jewish ritual (Ac. 21: 20–26), realized that in this demand applied to a Gentile lay the crucial question of the future of the gospel (see commentary on 1: 6–9). Adamantly he had stood his ground, and with the indisputable facts of his own work to support him (7, 8), he had won his point. The very confusion, almost incoherence, of his language in this passage (a phenomenon which recurs in the letter) is evidence of what that struggle had cost him, and of how deeply it stirred him to find himself fighting the same battle yet again. Today, looking back at the long history of the Church, we can realize something of the immensity of the issues for which he contended, and can admire again the largeness and penetration of his vision.

For the purpose of his present argument, Paul has said enough. One unanswerable fact faced any doubters: **the grace given to me**. With that evidence of God's approval Paul, directly authorized by God, had also received **the right hand of fellowship** from the Jerusalem leaders. From that freedom given by the Jerusalem leaders what great things were to spring!

How carefully Paul fulfilled the other part of the agreement, **to remember the poor**, is apparent from his other letters: was it not indeed the very purpose of this visit to Jerusalem (Ac. 11: 29, 30)?

[Note: The poorly attested variant reading of v. 5, which omits the negative, is surely incredible. It would require the emphasis in v. 3 to be placed on 'compelled': suggesting that Titus *was* circumcised, but voluntarily as a concession to the weaker consciences.]

11–21. Into the claims of the Judaizers the name of Peter was entering: Peter, who had himself suffered from the antagonism of **the circumcision group**, and whose experiences at Joppa and Cæsarea had made him a natural sympathiser with Paul. What lay behind this? That the incident described in these verses took place some two or three years after the meeting of the preceding verses is probable. Peter had visited Antioch, apparently about the time of the return of Paul and Barnabas from their first missionary journey, only to be followed there by the circumcision party, suspicious of him as ever (see Ac. 15: 1). These Judaizers claimed the authority of James (Gal. 2: 12), but apparently without justification (Ac. 15: 24). The brief unhappy incident which followed rings true to the experience of all who have seen the fruits of the jealous carping scrutiny of men warped by party spirit. Both Peter and Barnabas evoke our sympathy, for an excessive attachment to dogmatic strife on the part of lesser men will always batten upon the more honourable. If malice could drive such as these into prevarication, it behoves us to recognize the spirit of the heresy hunter and to shun it for the plague it is, however orthodox its trimmings. Ac. 15: 2 indicates that Barnabas was soon rallied by his stronger companion, while Peter himself took well to heart the comments which Paul had made, taking them up and applying them decisively in Jerusalem soon after (cf. v. 14 with Ac. 15: 10).

The tenor of Paul's reference to Barnabas indicates that the latter was known to the Galatian churches—a further indication that they were the churches of the first missionary journey.

The historical survey is over, and Paul is able to turn to more congenial matter. Whether the closing verses of the chapter represent the gist of his discussion with Peter, or whether they are added for the purposes of the letter, is of little importance. In them Paul is able to restate the basic gospel, not in terms of the theological exposition which is to follow, but in terms of personal experience.

It is clear that Paul's opponents shared the common position of justification by faith, but the force of the repetition in v. 16 suggests that **observing the law** (not merely its ceremonial aspects) was added as an additional agent of justification. So Paul repeats his own experience. **16. we, too, have put our faith in Christ Jesus, that . . . :** The Greek aorist corresponds to that in 3: 6. It was a deliberate and permanent act, arising consciously and from reasoned knowledge: a personal committal to Christ, *eis Christon Iēsoun*, not a mere mental assent (and can therefore exist in company with a great deal of mental bewilderment or doubt). The third repetition, which closes v. 16, glances back to Ps. 143: 2. The expression **Gentile sinners** in v. 15 ironically picks up the standard Jewish terminology.

The verses which follow are confused and have been treated in very different manner by different versions. **Sinners** (17) appears to refer back to the same word in v. 15. If the gospel made empty the Jews' privilege of the law,

reducing them to the status of Gentiles without the law, was not Christ the agent of their reduction to the status of sinners? Paul was to answer this question in Rom. 3, at a later date, with the bold assertion that 'there is no distinction'. Here he answers in a manner similar to that in which he will answer the charge of antinomianism (see commentary on 5: 1). To attempt to justify myself by the law is to rebuild the very standard of judgment which I by my sin have destroyed, and which itself condemns me (18). In fact, I have received the sentence of death from the law itself: and by that very sentence the law has removed me from its jurisdiction (19). For the sentence of death has been executed—but executed in the body of Christ on the cross (cf. Rom. 7: 4). Therefore, if I live now, it can only be by right of Christ, and in freedom from the condemnation of the law. My life can now be nothing but the life of Christ, maintained by the continuation of that once-for-all act of faith in Him (20).

Have we here the beginning of that development of Paul's thought on identification with the body of Christ which later leads to the doctrine of the Church as the body of Christ? Compare the link with the death of Christ as it is expressed in the Lord's Supper (1 C. 10: 15–17).

To close the section, Paul turns his opponents' argument against themselves. They had suggested that his gospel emptied the law of meaning. He shows that their doctrine, retaining the law but adding to it faith in Christ, simply emptied the cross of meaning. Wherein had the death of Christ changed the situation? On this basis the cross was a pointless excrescence on the scheme of salvation (21).

[Note: Calvin's commentary on vv. 17–20 is of particular importance and should be consulted.]

IV. THE GOSPEL EXPLAINED AND EXEMPLIFIED (3: 1–4: 31)

3: 1–5. The proof of his authority and that of his message is complete, and Paul turns to the positive task of expounding the gospel. The exposition proceeds by the following stages.

3: 1–5.	An appeal to the Galatians' experience.
3: 6–14.	An appeal to Scripture.
3: 15–24.	The relationship of law and the promise worked out.
3: 25–29.	The full achievement of the gospel.
4: 1–7.	Recapitulating with a history of redemption.

The argument from experience is simple and effective. The gospel had *worked:* their own senses saw its evidence (hence the 'senseless' Galatians and the 'bewitchment' of v. 1). The Holy Spirit was an obvious possession of the new converts, without the outward tokens of the law. It is the same argument that had carried the day for Peter after Cornelius's conversion (Ac. 11: 17), and which he was to use as effectively at Jerusalem (Ac. 15: 8, 9). In passing, we might acknowledge the insight which this argument gives into the life of those churches, and ask ourselves whether it would be as effective in our own churches today.

The **miracles** (5) would probably have included those supernatural evidences of the Spirit which were common in the early churches (see Ac. 14 in relation to the S. Galatian churches). Yet no stress is laid upon such manifestations elsewhere in this letter: rather the working of the Spirit is seen in moral qualities (5: 16–24), and the word here undoubtedly includes the patent moral transformation of many of the converts. Calvin applies it to 'the grace of regeneration, which is common to all believers'.

The gift of the Spirit is the continuous work of the Head of the Church: the Greek implies liberality (v. 5).

[Note: **1. clearly portrayed:** The sense is 'placarded up, as on a public poster'.]

6–9. For his argument from Scripture, Paul goes directly to a verse which had unlocked for him a new understanding of the OT. In following the apostle's exposition here and in Rom., a sympathetic mind can picture the OT blazing with a new light to him: there is little wonder that he spoke of that vision as a revelation from God, or that it has brought to birth a similar light in many a later soul.

Yet the quotation in v. 6 was not unfamiliar in current Jewish exegesis. It is taken from a passage in Genesis (15: 6) where, interestingly enough, Abraham's faith was at a low ebb (Gen. 15: 2, 3). At such a moment, God had seen the movement of faith in Abraham's soul, and treasured it the more for the weakness from which it sprang. Abraham, in his weakness, became 'the model man of justification by faith' (Principal D. Brown): heir to a promise embracing all nations.

The promise to Abraham had been threefold: a promise of descendants, of blessing to all nations, and of the land for an inheritance. In the second aspect, germane to the apostle's immediate purpose, he sees the essence of the gospel (8). The blessing carried within it the promise of the Christ; but its scope made baseless the Judaizers' attempt to limit it. The aspect of the seed is taken up in startling manner later in this same chapter, as in the parallel passage in Rom. 4: 16–25, and the promise of the Christ is found yet more explicitly in that aspect. The aspect of the land is merely hinted at in v. 18 of this chapter, but appears in Rom. 4: 13. To Paul and his Christian contemporaries its meaning could only be spiritual, a point made

explicit by the writer to the Hebrews (Heb. 11: 8–10, 16). The land was the temporal and material background to the mighty acts of redemption of which the whole promise spoke: but in Rom. 4: 13 it becomes 'the world', while in the vision of the Apocalypse 'a new heaven and a new earth' is seen as an essential part of the ultimate state (Rev. 21: 1). For, in man's redemption, the redemption of man's environment also is comprised (Rom. 8: 19–23): while even in his redemption, man remains man, not aspiring to godhead, but limited still to appointed bounds (cf. Ac. 17: 26) and maintained by the free grace of God.

10–14. The previous section contained the positive testimony of scripture to faith: this section contains the negative testimony to the law. First, the law on its principle of strict recompense cannot in the nature of things bless, but only curse. Second, Habakkuk had spoken of living on the principle of faith (Hab. 2: 4— the original Hebrew had the sense of faithful endurance, but the context includes the Pauline sense, cf. Hab. 3: 17–19): a principle which clearly excluded the legal principle of strict recompense.

Then, by a daring use of the Deuteronomic curse on the hanged man (Dt. 21: 23)—a curse much quoted by those Jews who rejected Christ —Paul reverts again to the thought of 2: 20. There, the capital condemnation of the law on the sinner had been executed, but executed in the body of Christ. Here it is the curse on the sinner which is taken and absorbed on the cross. There the sinner, dead to the law, was alive to God: here, free from the curse, he is open to the promised blessing. That blessing is identified with the experience of the Spirit to which Paul has already appealed.

[Note: It is of interest to notice that Paul also quoted from Habakkuk in his address at Pisidian Antioch, Ac. 13: 41.]

15–18. At the next stage of his exposition, Paul turns to consider the true relationship between law and the promise. In an argument similar to that of Rom. 4, but with a significant difference, he argues from the priority of the promise. It is unthinkable that God should qualify a free promise by a condition imposed unilaterally, centuries later: still less is it possible that the condition should be such as virtually to nullify the promise, changing a free gift into something to be 'earned' by conformity to a law beyond man's capacity. The reference to the **inheritance** (18) picks up the fact that the solemn ratification of the promise (see v. 17) in Gen. 15 related particularly to that aspect of the promise which concerned the land.

In some versions **covenant** (v. 15) is rendered 'will', which causes an unnecessary difficulty by importing inappropriate associations with death (as Heb. 9: 16, 17). The most helpful modern equivalent is that suggested by F. F. Bruce; a settlement of property (the purist would prefer *an irrevocable settlement*). Ramsay explains the passage by reference to Greek law by which members of a family only might inherit: to benefit a stranger in blood it was therefore necessary to adopt him into the family, the act of adoption itself being both irrevocable and constituting the title to the inheritance.

Verse 16 is a parenthesis, but contains an important thought. The word 'seed' obscures the force of the original, for the original was a collective noun which would have been inappropriate in the plural. The argument is directed not so much to the distinction between singular and plural, as to emphasizing that a collective noun might equally have a purely singular meaning: in effect, that God deliberately used a word not normally used in the plural. Hence the word, apparently comprising the whole nation, is seen to have a deeper meaning referring to the single seed—Christ. The NEB reproduces the sense ingeniously by using the word 'issue' (RSV 'offspring'). There also lies behind the verse the thought of the one seed chosen out of many as the true seed: Calvin pointing out the narrowing of the line of promise from the first generation of Abraham's descendants. We have here, then, another pointer to that corporate capacity of our Lord which was implicit in His own use of the title *Son of Man*, and is related so closely to the doctrine of the Church as the body of Christ.

[Note: **17. 430 years:** From the LXX of Exod. 12: 40.]

19–22. The argument from priority was particularly powerful to the Jewish mind (cf. Jn 1: 30), but it raised an important question. **What, then, was the purpose of the law?:** The answer given is that the fulfilment of the promise would be dangerous until man has learned his own sinnership, and is prepared thus to welcome the Saviour-seed, in whom alone the promise is secure and mankind can find wholeness and unity (Col. 2: 10); the offspring in whom the whole offspring would be one. **because of transgressions** thus has the sense of 'to reveal' rather than 'to curb' transgressions (see 1. Tim. 1: 8–11).

Verse 20 has attracted a vast number of interpretations: it is probable that the meaning is that the law, needing a mediator (which implies the existence of two parties), cannot be stronger than the weaker of those two parties, namely man. The promise, however, rests upon God alone and is unbreakable.

It may be possible, however, that Paul is answering an objection unknown to us, so that the full significance of the words is lost. V. 21 reads as if intended to be a part of the argument,

while the interpretation just given reads it as a fresh start in the argument. The opposition might have argued on these lines: the law was the product of mediation, implying a conflict. God was one; a gift implies no conflict. Was the conflict then between the promise on the one hand and the law, the righteousness of God, on the other? For then it was the law which was manifestly triumphant, and Paul's argument from priority is turned back on himself.

Whatever lies behind vv. 20 and 21, Paul's reply is the same. If the law had been triumphant, then the cross of Christ would have been unnecessary: **righteousness would certainly have come by the law** (21). As this was manifestly not so, then the law was a stage in God's purposes, preparatory to the full promise through **faith in Jesus Christ** (22). (For **the Scripture** see Rom. 3: 10–18.)

23–29. So Paul triumphantly sums up the full achievement of the gospel. The law was the essential forerunner to faith: now, in Christ, the full freedom of the gospel's achievement stands revealed. Here is a new relationship to God and man, transforming every possible social relationship.

Verse 27 is important (and cf. Rom. 13: 14). Baptism is a 'putting on' of Christ, a 'clothing oneself' with Christ (the middle voice implying a conscious and responsible act). The sign is spoken of as comprising the underlying reality which it symbolizes (cf. Gal. 2: 20 with Rom. 6: 3–11). Because it is a self-clothing with the one Christ, it is also a becoming-one-in-Christ on the part of all who share the experience. Thus it is a symbol of the miracle by which the single offspring can resume its collective sense. **If you belong to Christ, then you are Abraham's seed, and heirs according to the promise.**

[Note: **24, 25. put in charge** (*paidagōgos*): Not 'teacher' ('schoolmaster' as AV), but rather 'supervisor and moral trainer'.]

4: 1–7. In this section the story of the gospel is recapitulated in terms of simple soul-experience, and thus the eyes of the Galatians are turned (in preparation for the appeals which follow) from doctrinal disputation to their fulness in Christ. We may prefer to see the individual's experience in this description; or (with Calvin) the generic experience under the old and new covenants. Both are valid applications.

Verse 3 presents a difficulty (**the basic principles of the world**). The RSV translation 'the elemental spirits of the universe' introduces a Colossian nuance which is foreign to the atmosphere of this letter. The argument has previously remained entirely within a Jewish and OT context, and it is startling to assume that Paul equates these with the demonic powers of the stars which were then prominent in popular superstition, and are implied in the RSV rendering. The same problem arises in v. 9. Possibly the expression is deliberately ambiguous, hinting at the bondage of a materialistic Jewish rite, at current superstitions, and also at the persistent survivals of the ancient Anatolian religion, corruptly harnessing the most elemental instincts of life, which the Galatians would know so well. In contrast, see the grace of God in Christ!—**born of a woman** (but what a contrast to the corrupt religion of the goddess-mother), **born under law** (but He who came to deliver us from the slavery of the law). Here the Son of God comes to stand where we stand, that He might shoulder our curse, and raise us from out of it to **the full rights of sons**.

[Notes: i. **4. sent** (*exapesteilen*): 'Sent forth from out of'. Precisely the same word is used in v. 6 of the Spirit.

ii. **5. full rights:** See commentary on 3: 15 above.

iii. Note the transition: v. 5 'we', v. 6 'you' (plural), v. 7 'you' (singular).]

8–11. The doctrinal explanation of the gospel is now followed by a number of appeals to the Galatians. The first appeal is to the contrast between their old standing and their new. The passage again hints at the mixed Jewish and Gentile background of the Galatians (see commentary on v. 3), and harmonizes well with the account in Ac. 13 and 14 of the S. Galatian churches. That account also demonstrates that the detailed argument of the letter from the OT scriptures would not be unfamiliar ground even to the Gentile converts among them: it was precisely that familiarity which had smoothed the path of the Judaizers.

Notice the careful correction in v. 9, pointing again to Paul's intense consciousness of the sovereign act of God in the Gospel, and illuminating his sense of the impious nature of the Judaizers' rejection of that act.

[Note: **9. over again:** *Anōthen* (as Jn 3: 3).]

12–20. The second appeal is personal, and presents us with an insight into the warm heart of the apostle, and his intense self-identification with those whom he sought (cf. 1 C. 9: 19–23).

Ac. does not mention the ailment which had led to Paul's first visit to Galatia (vv. 13–15): v. 15 might suggest a disfiguring ailment of the eyes, but this is mere speculation, and not a necessary meaning of the verse. Why should this incident have so impressed the Galatians? Did Paul make for the Roman *colonia* of Antioch to seek medical attention for his complaint? It is tempting to allow speculation to run on. There was one of Paul's later companions whose knowledge of that district was so intimate as to suggest a resident's acquaintance, and that companion was Luke, 'our dear friend

the doctor' (Col. 4: 14) (see Ramsay, *Historical Commentary on the Galatians*, pp. 205 f., 209, 215 ff., *Bearing of Recent Discovery on the Trustworthiness of the NT*, ch. 3). It was Luke who could give such a detailed account of Paul's first visit to Pisidian Antioch (Ac. 13), and who joined Paul's party on the second missionary journey at Troas, not long after he had passed through the same district (see the 'we' in Ac. 16: 6–11). The self-effacing spirit of the author of Acts would then be sufficient explanation for the absence of reference to the illness in that narrative. But fancy is an unprofitable guide: moreover, tradition makes Luke a citizen of the Syrian Antioch, and Ramsay had yet another theory.

Verses 17 and 18 are obscure, but suggest that the Judaizers had used both flattery and threats of excommunication in their discussions with the Galatians (but see F. F. Bruce 'they simply want to cut you off from any contact with me . . .').

The closing verses of the paragraph are remarkable for the expression **until Christ is formed in you**, carrying still further the intense sense of the union of the risen Christ with His own which we have already remarked in the letter. What an indication they also give of Paul's personal involvement with the spiritual struggles of his converts!

[Notes: i. **13. first:** The Gk. might suggest that there had been two visits to the Galatians (see Ac. 14: 21). This is not essential in *koinē* usage (see NEB text and footnote).

ii. **14.** Lit. 'your affliction in my flesh'.]

21–31. The third appeal is made by way of allegory. This type of argument is uncongenial to the modern mind, but Paul is meeting on its own ground the method of debate which was urged against him by his opponents. Lest any might be tempted to slip too easily into this mode of *eisegesis*, it is well to observe that the apostle makes use of allegory only in relation to doctrine which he has already established by careful *exegesis*! 'Imagination and ingenuity are poor substitutes for apostolic authority' (Hogg and Vine, p. 220).

The passage contains two points of importance, in addition to its obvious teaching. First, the apparently incidental quotation from Isa. 54: 1 (v. 27) is another sign of the influence exercised upon the formation of Paul's understanding of the gospel by the latter part of that prophecy. This type of quotation is often of more significance in establishing such influence than the quotation of an obvious 'proof text'.

Second, this allegory marks a transition in the thought of the letter. Hitherto the contrast has been between law on the one hand and faith and the promise on the other. The letter now passes over into the contrast which had been hinted at in 3: 2, 3, between flesh and the Spirit.

Lightfoot remarked that Paul's confident application of Scripture in v. 30 is a striking tribute to his prophetic insight: at that time it was, to human eyes, far from certain that the old Jewish system would be cast out from its inheritance.

V. THE OUTWORKING OF THE GOSPEL (5: 1–6: 10)

5: 1. This verse stands equally as the conclusion of what has gone before (some in fact attach part of it to the previous sentence), or as the commencement of the practical application which follows. It strikes the keynote of the letter. 'The controversy relates to the liberty of conscience, when placed before the tribunal of God' (Calvin).

As Paul turns to the practical outworking of the doctrine he has expounded, he faces the worst misunderstanding of all: that of antinomianism, the idea that freedom from the law was freedom to disregard its precepts, and therefore to sin at will.

Paul's answer is bound up with two important features of his previous teaching.

First, the new life of the believer is not his own life at all, but rather the life of Christ in him. So Paul had earlier replied to those who accused him of making Christ **promote sin** (2: 17): far from reducing Jews to the status of **Gentile sinners**, Christ had lifted both Jew and Gentile alike to an entirely new plane. Both alike had died with Him and now lived in His new life (see 2: 20 and 4: 19). Developing this thought, he now shows that the freedom of Christ is not freedom for wilful thoughts and desires: paradoxically, that is the worst bondage of all, bondage to the flesh (the 'sinful nature'). Rather, it is the holy freedom of Christ Himself becoming my own freedom. **It is for freedom that Christ has set us free.** (It is noticeable that the verse contains no definite article before **yoke**: it is a yoke of slavery, and thus as applicable to the slavery of the flesh as to the bondage of Mount Sinai).

Second, the result of faith is the enduement of the Spirit and the Spirit is the antithesis of the flesh (3: 2, 3). The result of faith is not a theoretical or forensic change in its subject, but rather the practical and continuing ministration of the Spirit from the Source of all life (3: 5). Where the Spirit reigns, the flesh cannot have the pre-eminence. This is developed in vv. 16–25 below.

2–12. First, there must be a warning. There could, at this point in history, be no compromise with those who would strangle the gospel of Christ in its cradle: nor, for its part, could the law demand other than total obedience. In evaluating vv. 2–5 we must remember this, and also that Paul himself circumcised Timothy (Ac. 16: 3). It is not circumcision as an act which is in view (as v. 6 shows), but rather circumcision entered into as a deliberate commitment to the Jewish rite, or as relying on its efficacy for salvation.

Verse 6 contains an equation which is of profound importance. It is the reality which matters, not the form; and faith, when worked out into practical and tangible reality, equals love. The parallel passage in 1 C. 7: 18, 19 substitutes for **faith expressing itself through love** the words 'keeping the commandments of God'. Is this to contradict the teaching of Galatians, and to reinstate the law upon its throne? Far from it, for Paul is to claim in v. 14 of this chapter also that the entire law is summed up in love (see commentary below). Rather, it is the first sign of a remarkable turn in the argument, which we will find made explicit in the next section of this chapter, and which finds the law and faith ranged on the same side in this new battle against the flesh and the antinomian heresy which is its fruit. Both passages must be read in the light of Rom. 13: 8–10 and of 1 C. 13 (where the trinity of faith, hope and love which is contained in vv. 5, 6 of this chapter is developed in classic form).

The confused and staccato conclusion to the paragraph, from v. 7, betrays the intense emotion under which the apostle wrote: small wonder, when even his own words were twisted against him (11)! Yet his touching confidence in his converts (10), and his sense of tragedy in their lapse (7), both reveal the warmth of his heart and explain the roughness of his denunciation of the false teacher or teachers. The passage ends with a mocking reference to circumcision (cf. Phil. 3: 2) (but a reference to excommunication might be implied—see F. F. Bruce and W. M. Ramsay *in loco*) and the NIV hints at the play on words between the Gk. for **cut in on you** (*enkoptō*) (7) and **emasculate** (*apokoptō*) (12). Hogg and Vine link the verse with 4: 17 'they want to shut you out', but a different Gk. word (*ekkleiō*) is used there.

[Note: **11. the offense of the cross:** The Gk. for 'offense' is *skandalon*, as 1 C. 1: 23, and hence the phrase 'the scandal of the cross'.]

13–15. Paul now turns to the first part of his reply to the antinomians (see commentary at 5: 1). Paradox as that first reply was, it finds its expression in two further paradoxes, both products of the alchemy of love. True freedom finds its fulfilment in slavery—the slavery of love (13). **Serve one another** stands in emphatic contrast to the **yoke of slavery** of v. 1: cf. Mt. 20: 26–28. Second, the equation of faith with love is further developed, as we anticipated in v. 6; and in love, the outworking of faith, the law finds its complete fulfilment (14). So, by a turn in the argument which is the achievement of inspired genius, faith and the law are seen no longer as antagonists, but as allies. It is a turn of thought for which the transition from the opposition of faith and law to that of flesh and Spirit had cleared the way (see commentary on 4: 21–31).

Something of a calmer frame asserts itself in the mind of the apostle, evidenced by the hint of wry humour in v. 15.

[Note: **13. indulge:** *Aphormē*, a base of operations in war.]

16–25. The second part of the answer to the antinomian perversion of Paul's teaching is now developed. The answer lies in the place of the Spirit in justification by faith. The reception of the Spirit had been seen in 3: 1–5 as the proof of the truth of Paul's teaching. Now it is seen as its ultimate justification in experience.

Hence there is a leap in his thought. The flesh (**the sinful nature**) appears in an altogether grosser sense than hitherto, while the conflict between faith and the law which has been resolved in the preceding section can be dismissed with a side glance (18). 'Works' are now seen as an essential part of the gospel of faith, but they are works expressing themselves as the inevitable fruit of salvation and of the reception of the Spirit, not works as forming a painful pathway to a salvation which it is beyond man's power to win. Hence the apostle does not in fact use the word 'works' specifically: there are evil **acts** of the flesh (19), but the virtues are **fruit** of the Spirit (22). Where such works exist, the Law is irrelevant: **against such things there is no law**.

Thus there appears in embryo a theme which is later to be developed in the Roman letter: the conflict between flesh and the Spirit (Rom. 7). In this letter there is no scope for argument as to whether the conflict exists in pre- or post-conversion experience, and debate over the passage in Rom. would have been avoided if more attention had been paid to its germ in this letter. It may be theologically inconvenient to be told that the convert is still liable to fulfil the desires of the flesh (or 'sinful nature') (v. 16 and 6: 1), and in the same context that **those who live like this will not inherit the kingdom of God**, but it happens to accord with experience. (For **the kingdom of God** see also Rom. 14: 17.)

It is noteworthy that the essential fruits and signs of the Spirit recorded in vv. 22, 23 include none of the ecstatic *charismata* with which they are so often identified (see commentary on 3: 5). Beyond this, comment on these verses is superfluous. They stand with their peers in Christian ideal: Phil. 4: 8; Jas 3: 17; 2 Pet. 1: 5–7; Rom. 5: 3–5. (The evil list of vv. 19–21 also has its parallels: Rom. 1: 29–31; 3: 10–18; 1 C. 6: 9–10; 2 C. 12: 20.)

Verses 24, 25 indicate respectively profession and practice.

[Notes: i. **17. so that you do not do what you want:** This could be read in two ways:—

(*a*) 'to prevent you from doing the evil things which you would otherwise wish to do', or

(*b*) 'to prevent you from doing the good things which your conscience prompts you to do'. Hogg and Vine prefer the former, placing the words **they are in conflict with each other** in parentheses. The majority of opinion is, however, against them, as surely is the context.

ii. **18. not under law:** Calvin distinguishes between the *directing capacity* of the law and the *penalty* of the law. Its directing capacity remains, but grace frees us from the penalty.

iii. **24. crucified the sinful nature:** Compare and contrast the similar metaphors in 2: 20 ('I have been crucified with Christ') and 6: 14 ('the world has been crucified to me').]

5: 26–6: 10. These verses are their own commentary, in their essential simplicity and practicality. We might be in a different world from the stormy atmosphere of conflict which had provoked the letter. As in all his letters, Paul the pastor asserts himself over every other capacity.

Here are the gentle and humane rules which are to regulate inter-personal relations. The absence of self-centredness, of pre-occupation with my own dignity and standing, is to be balanced by that true concern which places myself in the position of another, and acts to that other as I would then wish others to act towards myself (5: 26–6: 2). Yet this forgetfulness of self, this unselfconscious thought for others, can be expected only of one who has learned to live with himself; to accept his own abilities and calling, and the niche in which his own inherent gifts must place him. Only in this way can a man attain the quiet assurance and confidence of a responsibility taken and conscientiously fulfilled (6: 3–5).

Finally, there is the emphasis on generosity and unselfish stewardship of material possessions. Ranging from the needs of teachers (6) (not only visiting teachers, such as the apostles, but where necessary and appropriate the needs of local teachers such as the elders of Ac. 14: 23 in these same churches), Christian concern is to reach to the whole **family of believers**, and then to **all people** (10). It is significant that the exhortation on sowing and reaping appears in the centre of this passage, flanked on both sides by instructions of practical kindness and well doing towards our needy fellows. We cannot limit its significance to this one aspect of Christian living, but, set as it is, it binds the 'sowing to the Spirit' inseparably and for ever with the practical expression of Christian mercy and kindliness. In this context, then, the expression **his sinful nature** (8) is doubly significant: this is not merely 'flesh' in the general sense, but also in the specific sense of self-indulgence in the face of others' needs.

[Notes: i. The warmth of the **brothers** in v. 1 is particularly pertinent to the letter. Cf. 4: 12–20; 5: 7–12.

ii. **1. you who are spiritual** (*hymeis hoi pneumatikoi*) refers not to any special order of 'spiritual men' ('pneumatics'), but potentially to any believer who is fulfilling 5: 25.

iii. **2. the law of Christ:** See commentary on 5: 13–15, and cf. Jas 2: 8.

iv. The AV introduces an unnecessary difficulty in vv. 2, 5, by translating two different Gk. words by **burden** (the NIV has **burden** and **load** respectively). The verses have in mind, respectively, oppressive trials or difficulties (v. 2), and due responsibilities (v. 5).

v. **7. mocked:** A striking word meaning 'to turn up the nose at': vividly, 'to cock a snook'.]

VI. CONCLUSION (6: 11–18)

The argument is over, and the apostle takes the pen from his amanuensis to add a few final paragraphs in his own **large letters** (were these for emphasis, or because of impaired eyesight, see 4: 12–15, or is it simply a humorous reference to an idiosyncrasy?). Something of the pain of the conflict creeps back into his mind (12–13) only to provoke an inspired outburst of loyalty which will live for ever in Christian hymn (14). Paul closes by reverting again to that irresistible and sovereign act of God which had transformed his life, and the life of a world beside: **neither circumcision nor uncircumcision means anything; what counts is a new creation.**

What is **the Israel of God** (16)? That it is only a faithful remnant of the natural Israel is surely out of harmony with the letter: although it might be a generalized and non-exclusive reference to those Hebrews who, like Paul himself, had obeyed the truth in Christ. Is it, then, the Church? Potentially, perhaps. Yet the concept of the universal Church, however it arose in the churches at large, is as yet future in Paul's own thought, to be developed from germs of thought such as those which we have traced in this letter, and not to reach full maturity until the Ephesian and Colossian letters

of the closing years of his life (see Hort, *The Christian Ecclesia*, chs. 7–9, esp. p. 148). Nor does Paul use the term elsewhere of the Church.

Who, then, constitute the Israel of God? The apostle himself supplies the answer—**all who follow this rule:** those who, by sharing the faith of Abraham, have become the sons of Abraham. We can have no closer definition. So we leave the apostle with the only glory he desired: on his body the *stigmata* (brandmarks) of Jesus. The debt which, under God, we and human history owe to him for his almost solitary vision we can only begin to understand.

BIBLIOGRAPHY

BARRETT, C. K., *Freedom and Obligation* (London, 1985).

BETZ, H. D., *Galatians*. Hermeneia (Philadelphia, 1979).

BRUCE, F. F., *The Epistle of Paul to the Galatians*. New International Greek Testament Commentary (Exeter, 1982).

BURTON, E. D., *The Epistle to the Galatians*. ICC (Edinburgh, 1921).

CALVIN, J., *Commentary on the Epistle of Paul to the Galatians* (Pringle's translation, Edinburgh, 1854).

COLE, R. A., *The Epistle of Paul to the Galatians*. TNTC (London, 1965).

DUNCAN, G. S., *The Epistle of Paul to the Galatians*. MNT (London, 1934).

GUTHRIE, D., *Galatians*. NCentB (London, 1969).

HOGG, C. F., and VINE, W. E., *The Epistle of Paul the Apostle to the Galatians* (London, 1922).

HUNTER, A. M., *Galatians*. Laymen's Bible Commentaries (London, 1959).

LAKE, K., *The Earlier Epistles of St. Paul* (London, 1911).

LIGHTFOOT, J. B., *Saint Paul's Epistle to the Galatians* (London, 1865; 1896 edn. quoted).

LUTHER, M., *Commentary on Saint Paul's Epistle to the Galatians* (Middleton's edition, repr. London, 1953).

RAMSAY, W. M., *A Historical Commentary on St. Paul's Epistle to the Galatians* (London, 1899).

RIDDERBOS, H., *St Paul's Epistle to the Churches of Galatia*. NICNT (Grand Rapids, 1953).

ROPES, J. H., *The Singular Problem of the Epistle to the Galatians* (Cambridge, Mass., 1929).

STOTT, J. R. W., *The Message of Galatians* (London, 1968).

EPHESIANS

GEORGE E. HARPUR

This letter forms a fitting crown to the extant writings of Paul the apostle of the Gentiles. In it his teaching is brought to an integrated wholeness and finality. Doctrines which are presented piecemeal elsewhere are here gathered in impressive harmony, each in its place in the whole concept of salvation. Doctrines which are given extensive exposition in earlier letters, such as justification in Romans, are here condensed and embedded in the outline of the eternal purpose, in proportion to the rest of the faith. The unity pressed in I Corinthians to combat their divisions is now found in its dispensational and cosmic settings (1: 10; 4: 13). The second advent is disentangled from the emotional comfort and intellectual curiosity which surround it in Thessalonians and given its brief but important place as the ripening of the eternal plan at a strategic time (4: 13, 30). The Jew-Gentile relationship which tormented the Galatian area appears as part of a cosmic unifying process (2: 15). Paul himself no longer needs to press his claims to apostleship, but can show the significance of the office in revealing the plan of God at the right moment (3: 1–5). The Christology set out in Colossians against Gnostic belittlement is assumed now as beyond question, and crucially connected with the purpose of God for men (1: 22, 23; 2: 6). The Ephesian letter is a fitting climax and *raison d' être* for all Paul's activities and doctrine. It is a statement of what God is doing in the whole business of creation and salvation.

Authorship

The letter presents such a perfect co-ordination of Paul's teaching that it is not surprising that its authorship did not come into question from Marcion's time, if not Ignatius's (Ign. *Eph.* 12: 2) until comparatively recent years, and this very fittingness is a factor in the attack upon its Pauline origin. The suggestion of E. J. Goodspeed is that the letter was written as an introduction to the issue of a collection of Paul's letters, made by a sympathetic follower in the latter part of the first century. He maintains that it bears the marks of literary dependence upon the other letters rather than originality (*The Meaning of Ephesians*, 1933, and *The Key to Ephesians*, 1956). As to the first point, there is no documentary evidence for supposing the letter was ever placed in any introductory, or even final position in the collection. Even if

there were, such a covering letter could as well be Paul's as anyone else's. On the other score the issue is brought down to earth by the examination of the facts of the case. This has been carried out exhaustively by C. L. Mitton (*The Epistle to the Ephesians*, 1951) in a comparison of Ephesians with admittedly Pauline letters (he excludes the Pastorals) but chiefly with Colossians. The difficulties are set out by E. J. Goodspeed in his book, *The Key to Ephesians*, in twenty-one points. His first point is that 'Ephesians reflects no definite, localized, historical situation which it is intended to meet' but this would be a valid objection only if it could be shown that Paul was unable or unwilling to write a circular letter. See under 'Destination and Occasion' (below). Next he thinks that the high value put upon Paul's activities (3: 2–4), could not have come from his own pen. But we find in Gal. 1: 11–2: 11 and 2 C. 11: 23–12: 11 that Paul could assess his position and worth as an apostle in the highest of terms. The statement here in Eph. 3: 2–4 is qualified straight away in 5 where he brackets other apostles and even prophets with himself; and in 8 he sets his own value down as the least of all the saints. Many other of the points are inconclusive, open to other interpretations, or hardly count in this matter. For example: number four, that 'Church' in Ephesians is always universal—but does he have to mention the local church in a letter which is agreed to be a circular, partly on the ground that it does not deal with any local matters? The use of *ekklēsia* in its local sense would be out of place in the theme of the letter. Number nine is that the principalities and powers which the Colossians were tempted to worship have in Ephesians become enemies to be fought. But why not? Paul would fight anything that displaced the worship of Christ. Did he not attack these powers of darkness in I C. 10: 20 f.? Number seventeen is that Eph. 6: 4 is hardly like Paul when all he had to say in Col. was 'do not irritate your children'. Paul was far too clever, and too much a Jew, to fail to see the value of home training in religion. Can we really believe that such an idea never occurred to him? It is certainly granted that there are minor discrepancies of word usage and viewpoint but such things can never be conclusive. Paul, of all people, had the least stereotyped kind of mind, and his adaptability of conception and fluidity of language can be seen in all his letters. Development of thought and variation of expression merely underline Pauline authorship or at the very least are as valuable in support as in opposition. The concept and teaching of Ephesians as a whole forbid the view that it is a mere patchwork of words and phrases culled from his other writings, its coherence too complete and individual. It raises considerable difficulties if we take 'Paul' to be a pseudonym, or view the personal references (1: 1, 15; 3: 1–4, 7, 8, 13; 4: 1; 6: 19–22) as manufactured and artificial. First, the alleged follower must have been a spiritual giant to be capable of co-ordinating the various doctrines of Paul's letters into what is admittedly a work of magnificent unity, from which the apostle himself could have learned a great deal. How could such a man be hidden, or why should he try to hide himself? Anonymous documents could find acceptance, *e.g.* Hebrews. Second, if he were an opponent of Paul, and therefore afraid to use his own name, why did he issue an edition of Paul's letters? And how would he evade the many still alive who knew what Paul had written, and who would certainly dispute a letter emerging years after Paul had died? Third, Paul's own warnings about letters purporting to come from him, would have raised suspicions in such circumstances, and of such suspicions there is no evidence whatever. There is a brief summary of the pros and cons of Pauline authorship in articles included in the *Studies in Ephesians* edited by F. L. Cross in 1956; cf. also the article on 'Ephesians' by F. Foulkes in *NBD*.

Ephesians and Colossians
A comparison of vocabularies shows clearly what has always been known, that these two letters have much in common. Indeed they have, though they have some fundamental differences also.

(a) Words
The evidence of word-lists shows that the letters are close together as to date, and that there is an overlapping of related themes. The result is that one often throws light upon the other. It is instructive to compare Eph. 1: 4 with Col. 1: 22, 23, 28; 1: 17 with 1: 9; 1: 20 ff. with 2: 10; 2: 5 f. with 3: 3; 3: 1–5 with 1: 26; 3: 16–19 with 1: 27; 4: 13–16 with 2: 19; 4: 20–24 with 3: 10; 5: 3–7 with 3: 5–8; 5: 5–17 with 4: 5; 5: 18 f. with 3: 16; 5: 22–24 with 3: 18; 5: 25–27 with 1: 28; 6: 21 f. with 4: 7 f. For almost identical phraseology compare Eph. 1: 7 with Col. 1: 14; 2: 5 with 2: 13; 3: 2 with 1: 25; 4: 16 with 2: 19; 4: 22–24 with 3: 8–10; 4: 32 with 3: 13; 5: 19 f. with 3: 16 f. Three words common to these letters will repay closer study, i.e. *oikonomia*, plan or stewardship: *plērōma*, fulness; and *mystērion*, mystery. That they are used

with different meanings is hard to substantiate satisfactorily, for context determines precise meanings, and many words in any case have a degree of ambiguity and some range of meaning.

(b) Style
There are slight differences of style. For example, a fulness of expression in Eph. which is unusual: 3: 5 'his holy apostles and prophets'; and a tendency to hyperbole: 1: 19; 3: 8, 20. A softer, heavier style which may be attributed to the fact that in Col. Paul is in battle with opponents whilst in Eph. he is not dealing with any pressing situation and he may well have relaxed his rule to eschew any 'excellency of speech' (1 C. 2: 1, 4). Mixing of metaphors, abrupt transitions and large parentheses are typical of Paul's style, and can scarcely be hidden, nor indeed convincingly copied.

(c) Contents
Col. is aimed at a particular local need and therefore contains what is absent from Eph.: personal greetings (4: 9–17); doctrinal warnings (2: 6–9); arguments against error (2: 16–23); a developed Christology (1: 15–20), Eph. being concerned with ecclesiology. Col. 4: 18 is something which would necessarily be omitted from a circular.

(d) Viewpoint
The only important question of divergence in a matter common to both letters concerns the headship of Christ. It is pointed out that this is ecclesiastical in Eph. 5: 23, but cosmic in Col. 2: 10. But Eph. contains 1: 22; and Col. contains 1: 18 and 2: 19. The headship of Our Lord is in fact universal, and within this is His headship of the Church which is organic rather than organizational.

Destination and Occasion
The following things have to be taken into account in any satisfactory explanation of this. i. Early MSS and writers witness to the omission of 'in Ephesus' at 1: 1. ii. All MSS nevertheless refer to the letter as *To Ephesians*. iii. Marcion calls it the epistle to the Laodiceans. iv. There are no personal greetings. v. The letter does not deal with any local questions, nor is it polemic in character. vi. Tychicus, of the province of Asia (Ac. 20: 4), accompanied the letter to a definite circle of brethren. vii. Paul wrote from prison (3: 1; 4: 1), probably from Rome (6: 20). viii. Eph. 3: 2 might be considered rhetorical, but not 1: 15. Paul envisaged a circle large enough to include some with whom he was unacquainted.

Epaphras had brought somewhat disturbing news about the churches in the area of Colossae (Col. 1: 7, 8; 4: 12, 13), necessitating a letter attacking error. Having dealt with that Paul might well consider the time opportune for a positive constructive summary of his teaching without having to turn aside to deal with controverted points. The Gnostics were developing their doctrines into a philosophical scheme. While Tychicus waited for some turning point in events at court to carry news to Asia (Eph. 6: 21; Col. 4: 7, 8) Paul would have time to lay out with precision an encyclical letter, which would inevitably be coloured by the recent composition of Colossians, and also have connections with all his other letters of any importance. With the issue of his trial soon to be reached a clear statement of the inspired basis and significance of the believing Jews' and Gentiles' union in the Church was now needed for the Church at large, together with a clarification of this in the light of the divine purpose in history. Ephesians is just such a letter. It would certainly be sent to an important and strategic centre whence a truly Pauline church could circulate it widely. Either the original had a blank space for the destination to be filled in, and the different handwriting then set the contemporary textual critics questioning it, or, perhaps more likely, the address to Ephesus was deleted from the circulated copies. Marcion probably saw one with Laodicea entered therein. Local matters and personal greetings would obviously be omitted, and the verbal instructions to Tychicus could cover all that Paul wanted to say to churches he knew personally. See 6: 21 where the 'you also' perhaps envisages a larger circle of recipient churches. The date and the identification of the imprisonment are dealt with in the article on The Pauline Letters.

Ephesus

This famous city was not only a strategic place in the missionary plans of Paul (for three years it was his centre of operations; see *St. Paul's Ephesian Ministry*, by G. S. Duncan, 1929), it also figures largely in the literary scene of early Christianity. It is traditionally viewed as the place in which John wrote his contributions to the NT, and it takes first place in the seven letters of the Apocalypse. The letters to Timothy are connected with the city, and later on Ignatius wrote to the church there from Smyrna. The city was a first-class trading centre ranking with Alexandria and Antioch. A religious metropolis of great importance in the world-famous cult of Artemis, its downfall was due to the silting up of the Cayster. Many of its remains, including in particular the site of the temple of Artemis, were recovered to modern readers by J. T. Wood in his *Modern Discoveries on the site of Ancient Ephesus* (1890).

Theme

The great spiritual blessings brought to individuals now by the promised Spirit (1: 3–2: 10), and the inclusion of the Gentiles with the Jews (2: 11–3: 13), the movement of spiritual growth of these as Christ's body (3: 14–4: 16), in manifesting the new moral standards (4: 17–6: 9) are all unfolded as having been eternally planned, and now in this age in actual achievement through the living union forged in Christ. Though this presently entails a spiritual conflict (6: 10–20), it will reach its perfect culmination in the age to come.

ANALYSIS

I   GREETINGS (1: 1 f.)

II   THANKSGIVING AND PRAYER (1: 3–19)
   i The blessings bestowed in Christ (1: 3–10)
   ii Shared by Jew and Gentile (1: 11–14)
   iii Prayer for spiritual enlightenment (1: 15–19)

III   THE NEW LIFE IN CHRIST (1: 20–3: 21)
   i The resurrection life of Christ (1: 20–23)
   ii The resurrection life of believers (2: 1–10)
   iii Jew and Gentile united in the Church (2: 11–22)
   iv This mystery was formerly a secret (3: 1–6)
   v The significance of Paul's apostleship (3: 7–13)
   vi Prayer for spiritual enduement (3: 14–21)

IV   UNITY AND DIVERSITY (4: 1–16)
   i Maintenance and basis of Christian unity (4: 1–6)
   ii The gifts that develop this corporate life (4: 7–16)

V   MARKS OF THE NEW LIFE (4: 17–6: 20)

   i In personal character (4: 17–24)
  ii In the Christian community (4: 25–5: 2)
 iii A challenge to pagan evil (5: 3–20)
  iv Between wives and husbands (5: 21–33)
   v Between children and parents (6: 1–4)
  vi Between servants and masters (6: 5–9)
 vii The heavenly warfare (6: 10–20)

VI   FINAL GREETINGS (6: 21–24)

I. GREETINGS (1: 1 f.)

The greetings follow the normal contemporary letter formula of writer, recipients and greeting. **apostle . . . by the will of God** marks the authority of the document. Many printed editions of the Greek text insert **in Ephesus** in brackets, a reading which the RSV relegates to the margin, but which gives a better rendering. See above under the paragraph 'Destination'. The phrase **in Christ Jesus** and its equivalents occurs over thirty times in Eph., a watermark of Paul's style. It implies not only personal identification with Him, but in some contexts it indicates relationship in the 'corporate' Christ. See 1 C. 12: 12. Grace and peace are regular elements in benedictions traceable back to the oldest in Num. 6: 25, 26.

II. THANKSGIVING AND PRAYER (1: 3–19)

i. The blessings bestowed in Christ (1: 3–10)

The unlimited blessings which prompt this doxology are those spiritual benefits first promised to Abraham and later confirmed by prophets (Jl 2: 28) and the Baptist (Mk 1: 8), and finally bestowed by the baptism of the Spirit at Pentecost as indicated by our Lord (Jn 7: 39; Ac. 1: 5), hence verse 13 **the promised Holy Spirit**. They reach from eternity past to the fulness of time. The cross section of them which occupies verses 4–11 traces them from before the foundation of the world, through the experience of salvation and apostolic enlightenment on to the consummation in the fulness of time. The whole complicated sentence (3–14, RV) is perhaps over-simplified in the RSV which breaks it up into several sentences. The four periods of blessing referred to above, each rounded off with a clause which begins with the words 'according to' (5, 7, 9, 11) should be read in the RV too. **3.** Paul plays on the word 'bless' which basically means to speak well of. We bless God by declaring Him to be blessed; He blesses us by actual enrichment. **heavenly realms:** The realm of heavenly things; the word occurs only in Eph., five times in all. **4–5.** God's election antedates

creation, and the selection is made in Christ. The objection to taking this to mean 'chosen to be in Christ' is that the purpose of the election is is clearly stated — **to be holy and blameless**. Positive sanctification and negative blamelessness begin now, but are not fully achieved until we are **in his sight**. The twin ideas of being holy and blameless should be consulted in the parallel in Col. 1: 22, 23, and in 1 Th. 3: 13; 5: 23. **in love** usually connects with the preceding words but is here probably best taken with 5 (see 3: 17; 4: 2, 15, 16; 5: 2). The destination fixed for the believer is sonship, a purpose of divine love so great it could not have been foreseen (1 C. 2: 9 f.). The full meaning of this lies ahead (Rom. 8: 23, 29) but the earnest is already given (14; Rom. 8: 15; Gal. 4: 4 f.). **through Jesus Christ:** As in Jn 1: 12. **6–8. the One he loves:** Which emphasizes the love already referred to in the previous verse. Redemption concerns the person; pardon has to do with our offensive activities. By such brevity does the Apostle condense the great doctrines of atonement and justification. **9–10.** Parts of the text of both 8 and 10 are taken into the scope of 9. The RV should be carefully compared. *Mystērion* is a secret which is now revealed, 'his hidden purpose', NEB. It is a pagan word, used for secret rites. It occurs often in the NT and in contemporary Jewish literature, and is found in the LXX of Dan. 2 for secret things. It does not necessarily imply anything very difficult; see the article in *NBD*. Here it is the hitherto hidden purpose of God, now made known by inspired men (Eph. 3: 5). The **wisdom and understanding** is ours, not God's; compare the prayer in Col. 1: 9. **the times . . . fulfilment:** An arrangement or administration to be carried out when the appointed period has been completed and the time is ripe. God's purpose is not limited to man's salvation, it is a cosmic intention **to bring all things . . . together** in heaven and earth under the control of Christ (cf. Heb. 2: 5–8).

ii. Shared by Jew and Gentile (1: 11–14)

who works out everything: The omnipotence and wisdom of God will secure His sovereign will whatever militates against it. **having been predestined**, an abbreviated version expanded in the NEB to 'we have been given our share in the heritage, as was decreed'. Note the parallel in Col. 1: 12. **we who were the first to hope** and **you also . . . when you heard** can be taken to indicate older Christians through whom the gospel came to Asia and the newer ones, but the reference to **the praise of his glory** (12, repeated in 14), together with the sections from 2: 11 to 3: 13, in which he deals with the union of Jew and Gentile in one body in Christ, show that the reference is to those in Israel whose hope in the Messiah anteceded that of the Gentiles. This would appear to demand that all the previous section, with its first person plural pronouns, speaks of Jewish believers. This is no real difficulty, for, if so, Paul only states the Jewish remnant's inheritance of blessing in order to bracket with them in the next sentence all the Gentile believers. Paul is not suggesting that the churches he was addressing contained only Gentiles. His pronouns move from **we** (Jews) to **you** (Gentiles) and on to a larger **our** (14) which includes both Jews and Gentiles. When the Gospel broke out of the swaddling clothes of Judaism the Gentiles also came to trust in Christ, so 13 AV, but the construction is better if we understand that they too 'were made a heritage', the verb being supplied from the Gk. of 11. The clause **whom also and** v. 13, makes clear that the Gentiles also shared the sealing of the Holy Spirit. The baptism of the Spirit came upon the first Gentile converts exactly as it did on the Jews at Pentecost (Ac. 11: 15–18). With this they inevitably received all the spiritual blessings in Christ. The argument is set out in Galatians. This teaching of the equal status of the Jew and Gentile in Christ is prominent throughout the whole doctrinal section of Eph. Though Paul was still in prison on this account (it was the root of the Judaizers' opposition) the battle for it was virtually over. He can calmly state the doctrinal position which he envisaged as apostle of the nations, and for which he fought and suffered so much. The participle rendered **having believed** makes the time of sealing coincident with the time of believing, a point left doubtful in the AV both in this verse and in Ac. 19: 2. The seal of the New Covenant is spiritual and inward (Jer. 31: 33); the reality, of which the circumcision was the outward sign, wrought by the Spirit in the heart. The guarantee points back in authenticating, and forward promising completion, as a part payment made in advance. **until the redemption:** There is a time fixed for the redemption of the pledge (4: 30, and 1 Th. 4: 16 f.). The **praise of His glory** is a thought frequently expressed from 4 onwards, stressing the intention never far from Paul's mind, that

everything about the saint should bring glory to God.

iii. Prayer for spiritual enlightenment (1: 15–19)

Their personal faith in Christ and their attitude to other believers gave evidence that they were in fact endowed with the afore-mentioned blessings, and therefore he prays that they may have an insight into three things: (*a*) the hope, the eternally planned consummation of all this blessing; (*b*) the value of the contents from God's standpoint; (*c*) the power by which it is to be achieved. **17. the glorious Father** is something more than just 'the glorious Father'; He intends to endow His people with a share in His glory (Rom. 8: 17; 2 Th. 1: 10). **The Spirit of wisdom:** No article, therefore perhaps a manifestation or work of the Spirit whom they had already received. What they needed was His active illumination in their hearts, wisdom to grasp, and revelation, the unveiling of the secrets involved. Mere intellectual information is not enough, it is the enlightening of the eyes of the heart, the inner man's vision of Christ. **19.** The power is at work **for us who believe** as in 3: 20 and Phil. 2: 13. To convince them of the immensity of this dynamic power Paul uses a battery of words: surpassing, greatness, power, energy, strength and might. The three things which Paul wants them to grasp are dealt with, in reverse order, in the following sections. When he has shown them what the power is and what it does, he works his way to the riches of the glory (3: 16), and finally to the first point of his prayer, the hope of the calling, in 4: 1, 4. The way in which his thought and exposition develop without any big grammatical break from his prayer can also be seen in Col. 1: 9 ff.

III. THE NEW LIFE IN CHRIST (1: 20–3: 21)

i. The resurrection life of Christ (1: 20–23)

The power which the Christian is to get from acquaintance with Christ is the force which has accomplished the most tremendous event in history, even exceeding that of the act of the original creation. Out **from** among **the dead**, the phraseology which first confused the disciples in Mk 9: 9, 10, and refers to the bodily resurrection of Christ, the firstborn from the dead (Col. 1: 18). Other men had been raised only to die again, but Christ is in an order of His own, He could not die any more. **at his right hand:** One of many NT echoes of this most-quoted OT verse, Ps. 110: 1. The four terms used in 21 are from the terminology of Jewish and Gnostic speculation, but Paul is not necessarily endorsing this analysis of the heavenly hierarchies, but see 6: 12. Whatever rule there is, Christ is far above it in authority, whether named as in opposition now or as reigning with Him in the age to come (Zech. 14: 9; Dan. 7: 27). Then will Ps. 8: 6 here quoted be seen to be fulfilled (cf. 1 C. 15: 24–28; Heb. 2: 5–10). The destiny of the Church is linked with Christ as He fulfils the destiny of man. He holds two headships, one over the universe achieved by His death and exaltation (Phil. 2: 9–10), and the other over the Church by its formation into a body at Pentecost (1 C. 12: 13). The Church is related to Christ in an organic way, as the body is to its head. Paul has previously used the body as a figure for the Church, without considering Christ to be its head (1 C. 12: 21), but here the figure is developed and the head is viewed as distinct from the members. Paul has extended the view of the Church functioning in a coherent fashion to that of its functioning as an expression of its head, i.e. Christ **23. fulness:** *Plērōma* could be referred to Christ, in which case the whole expression is equivalent to Col. 2: 9, but more likely it refers to the Church, in which case the Church is seen as either (a) *that without which He is incomplete*—not personally incomplete, but that He cannot reach His destiny alone, He must have His partner (5: 32)—or (b) *that in which He completely expresses Himself*—that is, He fills it, which is the teaching of 3: 17–19 and 4: 13–16. The NEB renders 'and as such holds within it the fulness of him who himself receives the entire fulness of God', cf. NEB marginal alternatives. The last clause in the chapter adds to the grammatical problem. The English versions construe the verb as middle voice, so denoting Christ's omnipresence, but some older versions take it as passive—*Him who all in all is being fulfilled*. This is an awkward phrase, indicating the progressive way in which Christ is being fulfilled in the Church (4: 13), or that the fulness of the Godhead is permanently resident in Christ (Col. 1: 19). This is the first mention of the Church in this letter, and it is immediately defined as that which is His body: not any group of Christians, or of churches, nor even Christendom, but the aggregate of those who are in Christ by the baptism of the Spirit (1 C. 12: 13).

ii. The resurrection life of believers (2: 1–10)
The power by which God's eternal purpose will be carried out has already delivered them from their old life, and lifted them into the heavenly realm in identification with Christ, and set them on the road to fulfilment. Paul is continuing his theme from 1: 20 and the flow of his mind will be caught if we read 'raising Him from the dead . . . and you who were dead'. Their spiritual death is described on three planes: (a) The personal level. Their condition was due to breaches of the will of God, but also to sins in the more general sense, including omissions and inward failures. (b)

The racial level. They followed the men of this age, as opposed to the standards of the world to come. (c) The supernatural level. Satan was at work in them. His realm is what might be called the lower heavenlies (6: 12). 'Of the spirit' (RV) is better; Satan is the fount of the spirit of the age. **3–6. All of us.** A transition from the second to the first person to show that the Jews are in the same position of need as the Gentiles. **we lived:** We conducted ourselves, as in 1 Tim. 3: 15, caring only for wishes that were carnal, led away by the commands that spring from the nature and thoughts of an unregenerated life. We were in ourselves objects of wrath, divine wrath (5: 6), as all men are. **4–6.** God is exact in judgment but **rich in mercy.** His love springs from Himself, not being called forth by anything in us, for He loved us in our spiritual ruin. The new life He gives us is not a thing apart, it is a participation in Christ's life. **alive with:** See Col. 3: 4. The believer's new life is a share in Christ's risen life and also in His reign in the heavenlies. (Rom. 5: 17). **7–10. the coming ages:** Both the millennial period and the eternal state will exhibit the infinite kindness of God demonstrated to redeemed sinners, especially in their manifestation as sons, and in their glory. By 'the grace', the article indicates the grace mentioned before at 5, and bracketed with mercy, love and kindness. **you have been saved:** The perfect tense, you have been and you are now saved. Grace is bestowed upon those who accept it. This is done by faith, but faith does not possess salvation meritoriously as if faith were any credit. **this** is neuter, not referring to either grace or faith, which are feminine, but to the scheme of salvation itself, and therefore translated **this is not from yourselves.** No human activity can result in salvation, it is God's gift. The Christian glories in nothing but Christ. **workmanship** means a creative product. In Christ a new creation begins (2 C. 5: 17), one with a moral intention, not for levitical ritual, or mere outward ceremonies, but a manner of life laid out in advance (1 Pet. 2: 21).

iii. Jew and Gentile united in the Church (2: 11–22)
In passing from the effect of the resurrection on individuals to its collective effect, he proceeds in each case in the same fashion: from the past (1–3; 11–12) to the present (4–6; 13–20) and on to the future (7–10; 21–22). The alienated Jew and Gentile are now reconciled in Christ and formed into a home for God. **11–12.** Their deficiencies as Gentiles are marked in three pairs of statements. *Physically* they lacked the ancient sign of the covenant, and family links with the promised Messiah. *Politically* they had no part in Israel's national or religious life. *Spiritually* they had no prospect or knowledge of the true God.

13–18. But all that had been changed by the death of Christ, which was for all men without distinction. Through this new way God is as accessible to the Gentile as to the Jew. The two parties had become one, not only by Christ, but in Christ. The wall of hostility alludes to the balustrade which surrounded the Temple proper in Jerusalem, barring the entrance of Gentiles (Ac. 21: 28 f.). The blood of Christ also abolished (made null and void) the law of Moses, its moral intentions having been otherwise secured (Rom. 8: 4). **the law with its commandments and regulations** (the latter meaning decrees—Lk. 2: 1 etc.—not ceremonies as such): The code of law embodied in decrees or enactments, i.e. the whole Jewish legal system. The **new man** is in place of the two; new in status, privilege and relationship, but its core was the elect remnant of Israel at that time. The death of Christ not only took away the barrier between Jew and Gentile, but also the barrier between them both and God. Isa. 52: 7 and 57: 19 are brought in to show from the prophetic scriptures that this was indeed planned. The reconciliation does not take place on Jewish ground, for He rent the veil as He broke down the fence. Both are elevated to God by a real, not ritualistic access.

19–22. Consequently summarizes 13–18 and goes on to show what has taken the place of the situation in 11 f. **aliens:** Resident foreigners who though physically present have no actual citizen rights. Gentile believers now share citizen rights in the heavenly Jerusalem, being householders with family rights. From the metaphor of a body Paul has passed quickly through that of a city and a family and now presents that of a building. In 1 C. 3: 10, 11 where the same metaphor is used the Lord is the foundation, but here He is the corner-stone, the primary foundation stone which sets the bearings for the entire building. **the apostles and prophets**, the NT ones, constitute the first layer, in which Peter was the first stone, *Petros*. Being keyed into Christ as they are added, the many stones are added to each other, to complete the shrine. A parallel picture of the growth of a body can be seen in 4: 13–16. **joined together** denotes a process of compaction and is used again at 4: 16. By **you too** Paul reiterates the Gentiles' place in all this. The concept of God taking men for an abode was not new, and no doubt ultimately derived from Lev. 26: 11 f. See 2 C. 6: 16.

iv. This mystery was formerly a secret (3: 1–6)

Having shown what is the greatness of God's power in raising Christ, and in constituting the Church His body, he now begins to expound something of the riches of the glory of this inheritance. He starts to express it in prayer, but in typical fashion is deflected by his own words . . . **prisoner for the sake of you Gentiles** and only returns to his prayer in 15.

Paul was not Caesar's prisoner, it was the will of Christ which held him captive (4: 1). It was because of his battle for Gentile liberty from the law that he got enmeshed with Rome. This was his stewardship (cf. Col. 1: 24, 25); to reveal and explain God's arrangements for the incorporation of the Gentiles in the Church, without law or circumcision. This had brought him into conflict with the Judaizers (who were 'zealous for the law') and ultimately with Rome (2 Tim. 2: 9; 4: 16 f.). For if Gentile believers were stated to be non-Jewish then they came under Roman laws about illegal religions. So long as they were regarded as a Jewish sect (Ac. 28: 22) they were immune from this law and its death penalty. What he had **written briefly**, summarily (in 1: 9 or 1: 3–14), showed his comprehensive insight into the secret purpose of God, hidden from previous dispensations, but now made known to a group of inspired men. V. 6 is a restatement in threefold form of that part of the secret which concerns the Gentiles. That the Gentiles should be blessed was clearly revealed in the OT but that they should be blessed without having to become Jews was unforeseen, as also was the fact that God would introduce a new thing, the body of Christ. They now share the inheritance, are equally members of Christ's body the Church, and the promise is now extended to them also (Gal. 3: 29).

v. The significance of Paul's apostleship (3: 7–13)

Of the good news which announces this unveiled secret Paul was a special messenger, sent to make God's purpose clear to the Gentiles, to demonstrate it before all men and the entire cosmos.

Paul traces the gift which enabled him to be a minister to the same resurrection power mentioned previously, 1: 19; and see Gal. 2: 8. He uses a comparative-superlative, **less than the least**, to express his utter unfitness for the work. He (*a*) evangelizes the Gentiles, (*b*) enlightens all men, (*c*) in order to inform the whole supernatural world. The evangel he describes as the untrackable wealth of the Christ. The enlightenment is the plan, secret in all previous ages (Col. 1: 25–27), but inherent in the creation of the universe. The information is laid out in the Church, where all heavenly intelligences may view the many-hued wisdom of God. Angels baffled by the amazing liberties allowed to Satan and men can now justify God, as they behold the clear deliberate purpose of God in the ages now unfolded in the Messiah, both Himself personally and His members corporately. **12.** Faith in Christ gives us free and confident **approach** to God, because of sonship (1: 5) based on redemption. In view of all this

(2–12, Paul's privilege, the wonderful plan, and the nearness to God Himself) they should not lose heart over Paul's trial and imprisonment. These were a joy (Col. 1: 24) to him and should be considered by them as something to glory in. Many thought otherwise, because they did not see the situation as he did, or else, like the Judaizers, they saw it all too clearly.

vi. Prayer for spiritual enduement (3: 14–21)

Resuming from 3: 1 he prays that the power (1: 19) which has altered their whole status before God (2: 1–22) might now work increasingly in them until God's full intention is realized.

In deepest reverence Paul offers this particular prayer to **the Father**, *patēr*, from whom **all fatherhood** (mg.)—every *patria*—group descended from a common ancestor—is derived. The Church is a family in a unique sense, as sharing His very life and nature. He uses the phraseology of his original prayer, 1: 18, 19, both as to the riches and to the power, and now applies these to the inner man (2 C. 4: 16), by the work of the Spirit. The alteration to their status had been instantaneous, but their moral change is progressive, in five ways: (*a*) by the strengthening of their inward spiritual life. (*b*) by the dwelling of Christ in their hearts. K. S. Wuest expands the word to 'settle down and feel completely at home in'. Cf. Gal. 4: 19. (*c*) by this firm foundation in love which provides power for comprehension. 'To lay hold of', not mere mental apprehension but the actual acquiring. It is the grasping of that fulness which is the goal for the Church (1: 23; 3: 19; 4: 13). This is only attained communally, **with all the saints**, for each individual has only his own finite measure. (*d*) by experiencing the love of Christ. Knowing what is beyond knowledge is a paradox that envisages an ever-expanding experience. (*e*) by being **filled to the measure of all the fulness of God**, a conclusion expounding Jn 17: 20–23, i.e. the Church revealing Christ in all His divine fulness. If the sea were filled with empty containers, the containers would be filled with the fulness of the sea. That God should have such an incredible purpose for man calls for a doxology indeed (20 f.). In it Paul stresses again the limitless power at work in the saints to achieve this goal, which is infinitely more than man could ask for himself or even imagine. There will then be endless glory for God through the Church, inasmuch as it will be a vehicle for the display of all the glories of Christ.

IV. UNITY AND DIVERSITY (4: 1–16)
i. Maintenance and basis of Christian unity (4: 1–6)

The high ecclesiastical doctrine of the previous sections calls for a manner of life which exhibits the transformation envisaged in it, and because of its nature this must be shown in the Christian community (4: 1–16), amongst men in general (4: 17–5: 20) and in the particular relationships of Christian men and women (5: 21–6: 9).

2, 3 describe the frame of mind which accompanies the actions of the walk, being the new spirit of 23. Twin virtues of the renewed mind are lowliness (now for the first time presented as a virtue) and meekness (being not weakness but the eliminating of self-assertion). The next pair shows how they receive others' actions directed against them. By all these four tempers they are to show an eagerness to forge a bond made of peace by which spiritual unity is safeguarded. The seven unities are a list, being introduced without a verb. Every expression of unity is based on these. **one body:** The new body of 2: 15, 16. **one Spirit:** Given alike to Jew and Gentile, 1: 13. **one hope:** As previously expounded there are no second-class Christians in God's plan. **one Lord:** Even Christ the source of all unity. **one faith:** Either the common faith given to all the saints (Jude 3), or, possibly, the subjective faith each believer puts in Christ. **one baptism:** Usually taken to refer to baptism in water, but it may reasonably refer to the baptism of the Spirit. These seven unities can be compared with the four unities which Paul sets out in 1 C. 12: 4–13, where he deals at length with the unity produced by the baptism of the Spirit. The four unities there shown are one Spirit (4, 9, 11), one Lord (5), one God working in all (6) and one body (12 f.). It would be strange to omit all reference to the Lord's supper, which is so clearly connected with the unity of the body (1 C. 10: 17), and insert baptism in water which is an unsafe basis of unity (Ac. 8: 13, 20–23). In the other items in this list, 'one' seems to mean 'one only' not 'one sort of' ('one faith' is doubtful), and is best so taken here. The seven items are so arranged that the first is set against the last, the second against the sixth, the third against the fifth, so connecting hope with faith, and Spirit with baptism. The 'one Lord' stands appropriately central to all. **one God:** He is the Father of all in Christ in the most real sense. He is over all the members, and manifested through all because working in all. Paul uses the abstract word for unity, strictly 'oneness', both here in 3, and later in 13. He is dealing with something spiritual, not a concrete, organized entity, for the NT churches were self-governing, and devoid of any central ecclesiastical bureau of control.

ii. The gifts that develop this corporate life (4: 7–16)

The unity is accompanied by diversity, like the unity of the natural body; and using this figure Paul shows that the various members each contribute to the whole until the organism reaches maturity. In the case of Christ's body, this maturity is His fulness, as outlined in 3: 18,19.

Here again Paul is elaborating a conception found in 1 C. 12, this time from vv. 24 f. Each several member has received a gift and the proportionate grace for its exercise. He takes his illustration from Ps. 68: 18, which he loosely quotes, using a text found partly in the LXX but mainly in the Targum and Syriac Peshitta. The triumphant warrior is elevated to his throne as he returns with hosts of prisoners, receiving gifts from the conquered peoples, and issuing gifts to his followers. Of the three things found in his text Paul ignores the host of captives, and substitutes instead a Descent. (a) The Ascension is the elevation of Christ far above all the heavens, where He is to fill all in all, as dealt with in 1: 20–23. (b) The implied Descent may well be more than the incarnation, the descent to Hades is the real parallel to His being lifted up **higher than all the heavens**. (c) He does not explain the captivity, but from this context of the descent to Hades it has been taken to refer to the deliverance thence of those who had in previous ages believed; but the idea is certainly wider than that, spiritual powers being included as His captives (Col. 2: 15; 1 Pet. 3: 22) and of course, all the redeemed (2 C. 2: 14 f.). An early hymn, probably Gnostic, runs:

'and to lead captive a good captivity for freedom.
'I was strengthened and made mighty and took
    the world captive . . .
'and the Gentiles were gathered together who
    had been scattered abroad.'

                    (Odes of Solomon 10: 3–5).
Consult also the additional note on the Odes of Solomon by F. F. Bruce in 'The Fourfold Gospel' (p. 1079). (d) The gifts (11) come from the ascended Christ, and are part of the promise of the Spirit. Paul ignores some gifts he has elsewhere listed, and gives those most directly related to the building up of the Church. First **apostles**, in the narrower sense of 2: 20, the permanent authority. **prophets:** Inspired men who revealed the truth of God. **evangelists:** Preaching missionaries, through whom men became followers of Christ. **pastors and teachers:** Elsewhere called elders or bishops, who cared for the converts and their growth. All pastors in a local church should be able to teach (some privately and others publicly) as well as to shepherd (see 1 Tim. 5: 17); but there were also teachers in the Church who had a more roving commission than administrators (Rom. 12: 7; 1 C. 12: 27). The three purposes of these gifts are, to prepare people, who will do service, which will build the church. The third and ultimate intention is a recurrent theme of the letter (1: 23; 2: 21; 3:

19; 4: 13–16; 5: 27). All this activity is to go on until the Church reaches the measure of the fulness of Christ. It is an attained unity, whilst the unity of 4: 3–6 is a unity already existent. The integrated oneness of the baby is real enough, but it is not the conscious oneness of the mature man. The unity towards which the Church moves is one of personal knowledge of the Son of God. The faith is more what we usually mean by knowledge, i.e. full acquaintance with the mind of Christ. **14. then:** The final clause—as the Church moves towards this final maturity it graduates from infancy and the instability that is due to inadequate doctrine and inadequate experience of Christ. The spiritual novice is wide open to false doctrine and to false men. **cunning** suggests the clever handling of dice. **scheming** recurs in 6: 11, traced to the ultimate source. **15. speaking the truth in love:** Maintaining the true doctrine in a compatible spirit and manner of life, not as a weapon for fighting but to secure a balanced growth in Christ (Col. 3: 16). This will produce a mature expression of the Head in every member of the body. **16. joined:** An architectural metaphor indicating harmony. **held:** As a body is by ligaments and joints, indicates solidity. When the parts are each working properly the head will see by its overall control that the whole body develops aright.

V. MARKS OF THE NEW LIFE (4: 17– 6: 20)

i. In personal character (4: 17–24)

17–19. As always, Paul proceeds from the dogmatic to the pragmatic, for the fulness of Christ can only at present be seen to operate in the Church in the spheres of character and service. These latter are actuated by the operation of the mind, and the moral breakdown of the Gentile world is rooted **in the futility of their thinking**. They are empty of the real values of God and eternity. This vanity, Paul teaches, originates in an inner cause, a darkened intellect: and in an outer cause, separation from God. Man is in the dark without God, for God is man's true sunlight. Both these causes spring from the **ignorance** of God **that is in**, or among, **them**, and this ignorance in turn arises from the hardness or obduracy of heart by which men repel God's revelation of Himself. Rom. 1: 18–21 unfolds this further, and both sections should be studied, together with Eph. 2: 2, 3, for a true understanding of the unbeliever's condition. **19. lost all sensitivity:** i.e. ceased to care. The soul, when deprived of spiritual resources, turns for satisfaction to the body, and even the high tides of philosophical culture break eventually on this barren shore. **20–24.** To **know Christ** is both to hear Him (hear about Him is inadequate) and to be taught in Him. The latter is initiated by the oral instruction of the new convert. This consisted of that outline of Our Lord's life and teaching which is the core of the synoptic Gospels (Lk. 1: 3, 4), and was enjoined upon all (Mt. 28: 19 f.); teaching which it is perilous to ignore (1 Tim. 6: 3 f.). **the truth that is in Jesus:** Absolute truth, not an aspect of it, as if He were to be compared with Confucius. Christ is the truth (Jn 14: 6), therefore to learn Christ is to learn truth. The discarding of the old man and the wearing of the new are two halves of one action. The moment by moment repetition of this decision is the secret of the Christian's changed life (Rom. 6: 13 f.). Note the contrast between **deceitful** and **true**. Human nature cannot be reformed (Rom. 8: 7), it must be regenerated. The new (*kainos*, new in kind) creation, which replaces the old of Gen. 1: 27, restores the likeness of God, and the renewal takes place in the innermost being, in the spirit of the mind. **righteousness** is right conduct towards God, and **holiness**, here, is right conduct towards men.

ii. In the Christian community (4: 25–5: 2)
In this section and the following one Paul deals with eight evils and the virtues which are their opposite numbers, so contrasting the walk of the Gentiles and the walk of the Christian. It is an early exposition of the theme of the Two Ways, prominent in the *Didache* and the *Epistle of Barnabas*. The sections that follow are Paul's application of 22–24.

(a)	4: 25	falsehood	v. truth
(b)	4: 26, 27	resentment	v. self-control
(c)	4: 28	stealing	v. generosity
(d)	4: 29, 30	evil speech	v. edification
(e)	4: 31–5: 2	malice	v. love
(f)	5: 3–14	impurity	v. chastity
(g)	5: 15–17	imprudence	v. wisdom
(h)	5: 18–20	debauchery	v. joy

25. put off: Remove, the same word as put off in 22. The command is quoted from Zech. 8: 16, and the next verse is from Ps. 4: 4 LXX. It is interesting to see how Paul interprets the second half of the verse from the Psalm, and to compare Mt. 5: 22–24 with the following clause in 27. Quick action takes opportunity out of the hands of the devil (*diabolos* could indicate slanderer). The anger in 26 is the feeling of provocation not just the expression of it. **29. according to their needs:** Grasping the appropriate chance of imparting grace. **30.** For **the day of redemption** see Rom. 8: 23: the believer looks forward to a resurrection body in a liberated creation at the return of Christ. Bitterness, wrath and malice are three emotional states, the other three items are the outward manifestations of these. The Christian emotions of kindness and tenderness reveal themselves in forgiveness and self-sacrifice (5: 2). Given the nature of children, God's loved

children have the ability and the opportunity of imitating their Father. All virtue is fully revealed in Christ crucified (see 1 Pet. 2: 21–24). The levitical language (reproducing Ps. 40: 6, as does Heb. 10: 5) indicates the typology of the OT sacrifices.

iii. A challenge to pagan evil (5: 3–20)
The sixth of his points, regarding impurity, is greatly extended because of the pressing ubiquity of the problem in contemporary society. **But** and **not be even a hint** both stress the seriousness of this kind of evil, which prevents a church from treating such people as Christians, as in vv. 5 ff. where the same three things are specifically mentioned. The same viewpoint is taken in 1 C. 5: 11–13. Covetousness is placed in very disreputable company; it is the antithesis of Christianity (Ac. 20: 35). Paul urges (4) that even in word they should refrain from smut, from speech on the level of morons, and from double-meaning jokes. Some people's lives make it clear that they are not in the kingdom of God at all, but that does not mean that they are beyond salvation (see 1 C. 6: 9–11). What to do with professing Christians who behave like this is made clear in 1 C. 5: 4–5. Paul's teaching on separation should be carefully examined in 1 C. 5: 9–13. By walking in the light they would be able to apply a test and so discover the will of God (9 is a parenthesis). Verses 13 f. should be set against the background of Jn 3: 19–21: that which comes to, responds to, the light becomes light itself. The quotation is not from the OT, but probably from a Christian hymn based on the language of Isa. 60: 1. **15–17.** By so coming to understand the will of the Lord they can step out of the imprudent and short-sighted policies of most men. Wisdom can turn evil days to good account. **18.** The stimulus for effective living does not come from wine, but from allowing the Holy Spirit full possession of the heart, an echo of the prayer of 3: 16, 17. **be filled with the Spirit:** The fulness of the Spirit is the subject of a command, in contrast with the baptism of the Spirit. The latter is not something to be sought for, it is part of that initial experience of every Christian (even weak ones like the Corinthians, 1 C. 12: 12, 13) by which they are incorporated into Christ. The fulness of the Spirit describes an experience or condition which could be lost or repeated (Ac. 4: 31; 6: 5; 7: 55; 9: 17; 11: 24). Being filled with the Spirit is here, as in Acts, connected with joy, courage, spirituality and character. Miraculous gifts do not necessarily prove that those who possess them are even Christians (Mt. 7: 21–23). **19–20.** 'The music that flows' is in contrast with that which follows drunkenness. **psalms** are those of the OT, or suchlike (1 C. 14: 26 Gk.). **hymns and spiritual songs** are not easy to distinguish, but praise is promi-

nent in the former word, while the latter is general.

iv. Between wives and husbands (5: 21–33)

21. The injunctions that follow are particular examples of the command concerning subjection. The division into marital, filial and occupational categories, though temporary (Gal. 3: 28), is to be accepted as the present providence of God. 5: 22–6: 9 should be compared with the condensed equivalent in Col. 3: 18–4: 1, and with 1 Pet. 2: 18–3: 7. The apostles seem to have used formally-arranged instruction in dealing with these matters, judging from the pattern observable in these cases. The threefold division of society is, however, a natural one, and universally applicable, and apart from the close parallels of Eph. 6: 5–9 and Col. 3: 22–4: 1 the treatment is independent in each case. The submission of the wife is to be matched by the Christ-like love and consideration of the husband, and similarly in the other groups. Failure on the part of one does not justify it on the part of the other, though it necessarily makes success more difficult. Paul intermingles three different facts, each of which he transfers in a figure to Christ and His Church. (*a*) The husband–wife relationship itself. The Church is a bride espoused to Christ. (*b*) A man's headship makes his wife to be his body. The Church is Christ's body. (*c*) Physical union makes man and wife one flesh. Christ and His Church are one (cf. 1 C. 6: 15–17). As to the first, the relationship springs (25) from the love and sacrifice of Christ. He uses the figure of the bride's preparation in 26 and her presentation in marriage in 27. **the washing with water** is figurative, like the wedding (Rev. 19: 7, 8). The laver, like other equipment in the Tabernacle, was typical, and spoke of that renewal brought about by regeneration (Tit. 3: 5). **make her holy, cleansing her:** That is, the sanctification is the result of the cleansing. Both words are used by the Lord when He deals with the matter in Jn 15: 3; 17: 17 (there are quite a few points of contact between this letter and the Gospel of John). It is, as He indicates, the spoken word that does the cleansing. Our 'presentation' is a frequent thought in Paul's writings, *e.g.* 2 C. 11: 2; Col. 1: 22; and in Jude 24 similarly. As to the second (23), the head of a body is its preserver, ruling and protecting it. So is Christ the Saviour of His body. The third point is illustrated from the creation of man. Eve was one with Adam both in her origin and in her union (Gen. 2: 21–24). In this way the creation of man carried a secret mystery, a hint of the purpose of God which no one would have guessed (3: 9). The AV text seems to have picked up a gloss from the context of the quotation in v. 31. The final words of the chapter echo the LXX of Est. 1: 20, a book not otherwise quoted in the NT.

v. Between children and parents (6: 1–4)

Obedience to parents is to be **in the Lord**, not limiting it to Christian parents, but making it a religious obligation to Christ. 2. It is objected that the second commandment, Exod. 20: 4, contains a promise and therefore the fifth cannot be described as the first **with a promise**. But it is the first in the table of duty towards our neighbours. The promise is generally true, notwithstanding that in some cases God's providence orders otherwise. It is easier to be severe or indulgent, but children need discipline and admonition when combined with a gentle understanding of their needs and limitations.

vi. Between servants and masters (6: 5–9)

The apostles did not consider it to be any part of their mission to alter the structure of human society (on the contrary, 1 Pet. 2: 13, 14; Rom. 13: 1, 2) by any direct activity. Christian standards of behaviour would, and do, profoundly affect society in the course of time. Paul did not imply that slaves should for ever remain slaves any more than that children should remain minors for ever (1 C. 7: 21). **slaves** (v. 6): Paul uses the same word as he uses to open the paragraph, so teaching them to regard their slavery as he regarded his imprisonment (3: 1). **from your heart** might be better attached to the following verse, as in Col. 3: 23. The master was not to treat his slaves on the ground of his legal rights but on the basis of his own treatment by his Master, Christ. V. 9 echoes Deut. 10: 17.

vii. The heavenly warfare (6: 10–20)

The command of 10 is derived from 1: 19; 3: 16. **Put on the full armor:** The Christian's new wardrobe (4: 24) includes a warsuit! The cosmic purpose of God embroils the believers with the spiritual hierarchy of the unseen world organized under the power of Satan. It is an obscure world, hinted at in Job 1 and Dan. 10, but the saint's defence and attack are not obscure. He fights in no worldly fashion (1 C. 10: 2 ff.). His armoury is figuratively described; a notion based on Isa. 59: 17, and also used by Paul in 1 Th. 5: 8, though the detailed treatment varies throughout. The use of the whole outfit enables the Christian to overcome the enemy in a day of fierce conflict, whereupon he is **to stand**, taking up his position in readiness for the renewing of the battle with a relentless foe. The instructions for such preparation are explicit. He is to tighten his belt with sincerity, truth in the objective sense being used below in 17 for the sword. He cannot afford to be slack in his dealings with God or with himself. Personal integrity will be linked with that moral rectitude, **righteousness**, Rom. 6: 13, which guards the heart as a breastplate, for vital parts are exposed by sin. God's soldier is equipped with the gospel of peace for sandals, suggesting that his movements are dictated by the needs of gospel witness. With all this a shield is required and this is provided by personal trust, 1 Jn 5: 4 f. Salvation, the helmet, is a gift provided by the Lord; 'take' here meaning receive, a different word from that in 16. His offensive weapon is the spoken word of God (see on 5: 26, and also at Heb. 4: 12). But he has an auxiliary weapon, not in the allegorical picture, viz, prayer, his vital communication with headquarters (18, 19). The need for it is plain, if adverse pressure might close even the mouth of an apostle (19). The ambassador of Christ's kingdom was at earth's highest court, but ignominiously treated to chains, contrary to international usage, but his ultimatum must be boldly delivered.

VI. FINAL GREETINGS (6: 21–24)

That Tychicus was a messenger of Paul's is clear from Tit. 3: 12. He was from the province of Asia (Ac. 20: 4), and certainly visited Ephesus later on (2 Tim. 4: 12), and appears to have taken this letter and the Colossian one with him on this journey, accompanying the distribution of the circular with verbal information. The closing greeting is, quite appropriately in a circular, couched in the third person. The unusual qualification appended to the end may reflect his awareness of the fact that there were in the Church those whose teaching and influence were inimical to the glory of Christ. But it also notes that devotion to the Lord which will endure imperishably for ever.

BIBLIOGRAPHY

ABBOTT, T. K., *The Epistles to the Ephesians and to the Colossians. ICC* (Edinburgh, 1897).

BARTH, M., *Ephesians*, 2 vols. *AB* (Garden City, N. Y., 1974).

BARTH, M., *The Broken Wall* (London, 1960).

BRUCE, F. F., *The Epistle to the Ephesians* (Glasgow, 1961).

CROSS, F. L., (ed.), *Studies in Ephesians* (London, 1956).

DUNCAN, G. S., *St. Paul's Ephesian Ministry* (London, 1929).

FOULKES, F., *The Epistle of Paul to the Ephesians. TNTC* (London, 1963).

GOODSPEED, E. J., *The Meaning of Ephesians* (Chicago, 1933).

GOODSPEED, E. J., *The Key to Ephesians* (Chicago, 1956).

HODGE, C., *The Epistle to the Ephesians* (London, 1856).

MITTON, C. L., *Epistle to the Ephesians* (London, 1951).

ROBINSON, J. A., *The Epistle to the Ephesians* (London, 1904). [on the Greek text].

WESTCOTT, B. F., *St. Paul's Epistle to the Ephesians* (London, 1906). [on the Greek text]).

WOOD, J. T., *Modern Discoveries on the site of Ancient Ephesus* (London, 1890).

PHILIPPIANS

H. C. HEWLETT

Philippi and the Church

The obedience of Paul to the Macedonian vision (Ac. 16: 9 f.) provided not only a notable landmark in his own travels and service but a turning point of apostolic history. Departing from Roman Asia, and entering Macedonia with the gospel of Christ, he planted in Philippi the first church in that province. That others were converted there besides the few expressly referred to is obvious from the reference to 'the brothers' in Ac. 16: 40. On two later occasions Paul revisited Philippi (Ac. 20: 2, 6), and the letter itself bears witness to his happy bond with the Philippian Christians.

Philippi itself was a city about ten miles inland from Neapolis, and was strategically placed on the Egnatian Way, the great Roman road running some five hundred miles from the Adriatic Sea through Thrace to the Bosphorus, and one of those roads which in the overruling of God were of the utmost use of the messengers of the gospel. Named after Philip, father of Alexander the Great, the city was refounded in 42 B.C. by Antony and Octavian (later the emperor Augustus) as a Roman colony. Its life and constitution were accordingly patterned on those of Rome, and its citizens enjoyed Roman citizenship.

The Purpose of the Letter

The apostle has been greatly cheered by the coming of Epaphroditus from Philippi bearing the gifts of the church. Grateful for the further fellowship from them and yet concerned both by the severe illness of their messenger, and by a divisive tendency among the Philippians themselves, he decides to send Epaphroditus back to them, and with him the letter. He takes occasion to express his thanks for the gift, and to give them fresh tidings of his circumstances, especially in regard to his imprisonment. He seeks for Epaphroditus the honourable welcome due to him, and thereby ensures that it is free from any misunderstanding of that good man's position. Grieved by their lack of harmony, he pleads with the Philippians to be marked by the mind of Christ and thus to be brought to a new and happy oneness of interest and character. This pleading begins early in the letter, and skilfully prepares the way for the direct, personal entreaty to two believers named in 4: 2. Finally, his long experience of the perils besetting the churches moves him to warn trenchantly against any Judaizers on the one hand or libertines on the other who may appear on the scene.

The Place and Time of Writing

It was believed anciently that the letter was written from Rome during the years mentioned in Ac. 28: 30, but this has been challenged in modern times in favour of Caesarea or Ephesus. Against Caesarea is the weighty fact that, far from expecting release there, Paul appealed to Caesar, and hence awaited the long journey to Rome. Against Ephesus is the fact that there is no express record in Scripture of an Ephesian imprisonment of Paul—although one if not more of the frequent imprisonments of 2 C. 11: 23 might be assigned to the period of his Ephesian ministry, during which, as we know from 1 C. 15: 32 and 2 C. 1: 8, he was exposed to grave dangers of which nothing is said in Ac. 19. On the whole, however, the arguments for Rome appear strongly to confirm the traditional belief. We note (a) that there is no mention of an appeal from his present situation to Caesar, and hence it is likely that Caesar was trying the case, (b) that the terms 'palace guard' (praetorium) and 'Caesar's household', while of use in the provinces, apply more naturally to Rome, (c) that the time needed for the happenings of 2: 25–30 is not incompatible with the Roman imprisonment. J. B. Lightfoot has shown that the Roman dating was feasible even if the letter were written in the early part of Paul's time in Rome, especially as the Egnatian Way would greatly facilitate travel between Philippi and Rome. This would be even more true if the letter were dated toward the end of the imprisonment. (d) It has been objected in favour of Ephesus that when Paul wrote to the Romans he regarded his work in the east as completed (Rom. 15: 25). But the intervening years would give ample opportunity for the modification of his plan for the west, particularly as the overruling of God had permitted lengthy imprisonment in Caesarea and in Rome. It was just such an overruling of his purposes that had brought him to Philippi in the first place.

The following considerations point to a date late in Paul's detention in Rome: (a) Paul expected an early decision on his case. (b) This would permit the widespread appreciation of the reason of his bonds mentioned in 1: 13, and the reaction of the brethren in more active witness in 1: 14–17.

The Unity of the Letter

This has been disputed by some because of the sudden change of tone in 3: 2, but the long autobiographical passage that follows is entirely in keeping with the compact statement of Paul's outlook in 1: 21, 'To me, to live is Christ'. Concerning the change of tone, Lightfoot has suggested that Paul was interrupted, and resumed his writing with a new burden on his heart. But it is to be noted that Paul's review of his life in ch. 3 follows naturally on ch. 2. As to the Judaizers, they had been so inveterate in their antagonism to Paul's preaching, and so persistent in seeking to subvert the churches he had planted, that they must have been very often in his thoughts, so that in giving his counsels to the Philippians he might well turn quickly to words of warning against these enemies. The sharpness of 3: 2 accords with the fact that the tactics of the Judaizers were not new, and the years had fully exposed the evil of their ways.

It is ever to be remembered that Paul is writing not a formal treatise, but a warm and loving letter, and that a rapid change of topic is in accord with the nature of a letter. Paul himself was a 'chosen vessel', suited to such a task spiritually, intellectually and emotionally, and the quick changes in emphasis and tone in his letters find their source, on the human side, in the wealth and power of his thinking and feeling. It may be concluded therefore that the letter is a single document, given from the eager heart of a man with many burdens for the churches he so truly loved.

Special Features

The phrases 'in Christ' or 'in Christ Jesus' and 'in the Lord' or 'in the Lord Jesus' are frequently used by Paul in relation to the believers' life and activities. In this letter they point not only to their standing before God in view of union with the Risen One as fellow-members of His body, but also to their finding in Christ the very sphere of their spiritual life, and that a life vigorous and joyous. Thus, though the issue of his imprisonment is still undecided, Paul writes with a joy triumphant over all his circumstances and bids his readers rejoice in the Lord and thus share his joy as they share his conflict. In the first pair of phrases the emphasis is on the wonder of such a personal relationship with Him, and hence the personal name is used; in the second pair, the use of the title 'Lord' emphasizes His authority and power, and therefore the believers' responsibility of submission and of dignity, behaviour and service.

The majestic passage in 2: 6–11 reminds one of 2 C. 8: 9 in that in both the self-humbling of Christ is presented as supreme stimulus to that self-abnegation, that spending of oneself for others which must ever be the distinctive glory of Christian character. That the Son of God has loved him and given Himself for him is an ever-present and ever-dominant note in the apostle's consciousness.

ANALYSIS

I   GREETINGS (1: 1–2)

II   PAUL AND THE PHILIPPIAN CHURCH (1: 3–26)
  i   Thanksgiving, confidence and prayer (1: 3–11)
  ii   Paul's immediate circumstances (1: 12–20)
  iii   Paul and his prospects (1: 21–26)

III   EXHORTATION AND EXAMPLES (1: 27–2: 30)
  i   Exhortation to courage (1: 27–30)
  ii   Plea for unity (2: 1–4)
  iii   The mind of Christ: humiliation and exaltation (2: 5–11)
  iv   Manifesting the mind of Christ (2: 12–30)

IV   WARNING DIGRESSION (3: 1–21)
  i   Warning against Judaizers (3: 1–3)
  ii   Paul: past and present (3: 4–17)
  iii   Warning against libertines (3: 18, 19)
  iv   The Christian's true home and hope (3: 20, 21)

V ENCOURAGEMENT, GRATITUDE AND FINAL GREETINGS (4: 1–23)

I. GREETINGS (1: 1–2)

1. Paul and Timothy: Paul links Timothy with himself both as a dear colleague and as one who shares his burden of love for them, and whom he will therefore send to them (2: 1–9). They are **servants** (*douloi*, 'slaves') **of Christ Jesus**, those who freely acknowledge His dominion over them, with its twofold right of complete ownership and of disposal of them at His pleasure. Here, as often in Paul's writings, the order is 'Christ Jesus'. This sets Him forth as pre-existent yet condescending to humiliation on earth. 'Jesus Christ' views Him as despised and yet subsequently glorified (see 2: 11; Ac. 2: 36). The former is peculiarly fitting in this letter where Paul presses the example of the mind of Christ in His self-humbling. See also 2: 5. (Cf. W. E. Vine, *Expository Dictionary*, p. 275.)

Paul addresses three classes, **saints** (*hagioi*), **overseers** (*episkopoi*), and **deacons** (*diakonoi*, 'ministers', those who attend to the well-being of others). Here in very simple form is the constitution of a local church. **Saints** refers to the whole body of Christians as the holy people of God, set apart for Him in Christ. The **overseers** (identified with elders in Ac. 20: 17, 28 and Tit. 1: 5, 7) are a recognizable group within the church. This is not surprising, for as early as Ac. 14: 23 we find Paul and Barnabas appointing elders in the churches of Asia Minor. The **deacons** are likewise a recognizable group, and according to NT usage include those who minister in spiritual things (cf. 1 C. 3: 5) and in temporal things (cf. Ac. 6: 3). The order is striking, in that the **saints** are addressed first. The **bishops and deacons** exist for **the saints**, not the saints for them. (See article on 'The Apostolic Church' pp. 1082 ff.) The expression **grace and peace** (2) brings together well known Greek and Hebrew greetings; their treasure is for all believers.

II. PAUL AND THE PHILIPPIAN CHURCH (1: 3–26)

i. Thanksgiving, Confidence and Prayer (1: 3–11)

So glad is Paul at every mark of the work of God in His people that thanksgiving characterizes all his letters save that to Galatia. Here he thanks God **every time** he remembers them, and even in memory of stripes and prison (Ac. 16: 23). He makes with joy every prayer of his

for them, for from his first dealings with them their fellowship has been a cheer to him. The words **all of you** (4) occur seven times in the letter: he recognizes no factions, actual or threatening: all the people of God are dear to him. Their fellowship, their partnership, has been marked by their special interest in him (4: 15, 'you only'), by their gifts, by their prayer (1: 19), by their conflict (1: 30), and all has been a **partnership in the gospel** (5), a partnership of **grace** (7).

6. Being confident: His confidence is strong that God will bring to completion His good work in them, to be seen in the day of Christ, at His return, for he knows that his yearning over them is borne of Christ's yearning: **I long for all of you with the affection of Christ Jesus** (8). Moreover they have shared with him **in defending and confirming the gospel** (7), in that courageous witness in the court of law or before men generally which confirms that the gospel is true. How pure is Paul's motive is shown by his claim, **God can testify** (8). Loving, he prays that their love **may abound more and more**, not irresponsibly but guarded and guided **in knowledge and depth of insight** (9). Thus sensitive in appreciation of moral issues, they **may . . . discern what is best** (10), distinguishing wherein one thing differs from another and so able to choose what is of superior quality. Their love will then be keen-sighted for each other's good. Moreover they will be **pure and blameless** (10), in singleness of motive before God, and without cause of stumbling to themselves or to others unto the day of Christ. Finally, they will be **filled with the fruit** (*karpos*, singular) **of righteousness** (11). Does this mean that righteousness bears the fruit, or that righteousness itself is the fruit? Both thoughts seem to be present here. Only that 'righteousness from God that depends on faith' (3: 9) can be adequate to produce rectitude of conduct. We are made righteous that we may become righteous. But this fruit is **through Jesus Christ**. In Him alone we are righteous, and by Him alone can the life be beautiful. All this is **to the glory and praise of God**, that the life of the Philippians may serve that supreme purpose which is the goal of Christ Himself (see 2: 11).

ii. Paul's immediate circumstances (1: 12–20)

A note of triumph pervades this section. Paul

rejoices in the overruling of God that turns to good things that might well discourage. He seeks that the cheer he has received may be shared by them in their conflict. All his mingled experience **has really served to advance the gospel** (12). Remembering that Paul's hours in the dungeon at Philippi had led to the conversion of the jailor, the Philippians would readily appreciate this. The gospel has made progress both in his testimony amongst his guards, and in the stimulus given to other Christians to more zeal in preaching Christ: **it has become clear throughout the whole palace guard** (13). The praetorians were the imperial bodyguard, those powerful and sometimes turbulent troops of whom the emperor was praetor, or commander-in-chief. What a mission field Paul has had among these guards! And his testimony has gone beyond them **everyone else**, to all others who have heard of this prisoner. (If Paul is writing from some other place than Rome, then Gk. *praitōrion* here means 'Government House', as in Mk 15: 16; Jn 18: 28; Ac. 23: 35; the NEB rendering, 'to all at headquarters here', covers all the possibilities.)

The impact of Paul's witness has been widespread among the Christians of Rome; **most of the brothers** (14) have been emboldened **in the Lord**, in their witness to Christ. Yet the apostle notes two classes among them. Some are moved by **envy and rivalry** (15); their preaching is **out of selfish ambition . . . supposing that they can stir up trouble for me** (17). Jealousy of Paul impels them to attempt to steal a march upon him, and thus to distress him. Others are moved by their love for him and their appreciation of his lonely stand as one set by God **for the defense of the gospel** (16). In both cases he finds cause for rejoicing in that **Christ is preached** (18).

19. I know that . . . will turn out for my deliverance: On the lips of such a man as Paul this means far more than deliverance from bonds. The latter are incidental; his **deliverance** is related to the great purpose of his life, and consists in being preserved from any failure to honour Christ. This will be achieved **through your prayers and the help given by the Spirit of Jesus Christ.** In answer to their prayer the supply (*epichorēgia*, 'rich provision', 'support') of the Spirit, His abundant blessing, will be poured by God into Paul's life. His eager expectation **and hope** (20) picture to us this battle-scarred veteran with head outstretched with longing that now as always **Christ will be exalted in my body** (20). His concern is not whether it means life or death, but only that through his Christ may be glorified before men and seen in His true greatness.

iii. Paul and his prospects (1: 21–26)
As for himself, the outlook is only bright. Life

for Paul finds all its meaning and coherence in **Christ** (21). This is life indeed. Death is gain, for then the momentary, the vision of the Damascus road, will become the abiding. If he lives on, he says, **this will mean fruitful labor,** literally 'fruit of work', i.e., the more work the more fruit. His dilemma is between two good things. He is **torn between the two** (23). His joy, his heart's longing, is to **depart** (*analyō*, to break camp, to set out on his last journey) **and be with Christ, which is better by far** than the richest experience on earth. Death, for the Christian, is to be 'away from the body and at home with the Lord' (2 C. 5: 8). In this disembodied state, his condition is one of consciousness, of freedom from sin and of completeness in holiness, and moreover of the joy to which earth has no equal, that of beholding Christ directly and of dwelling in His presence. For Paul death has no fear, but only gladness. On the other hand their joy, their good, lies in his remaining for their help. His joy, or their joy? This is the issue, and to state it is to know the answer. He will remain. The result on their part will be **joy in Christ Jesus** (26) for His goodness in sparing Paul to them.

III. EXHORTATION AND EXAMPLES (1: 27–2: 30)
i. Exhortation to courage (1: 27–30)
His unselfish choice seeks from them a fitting response: **Conduct yourselves** (*politeuomai*, lit. 'to behave as a citizen', hence 'to conduct oneself publicly') **worthy of the gospel of Christ** (27). The gospel is radiant with the dignity of its heavenliness; so must be the lives of those possessing citizenship of heaven (3: 20). Nor is this in any sense unpractical, for it will manifest itself in their courageous oneness in witness in the gospel and in their constancy amid persecution. **27. that you stand firm in one spirit, contending as one man:** One in spirit and one in soul, united in their perception of the right as even in their choice of it. As he later points out, their tendency is to strive among themselves; they must strive **for the faith of the gospel.** According to Lightfoot and others, the **faith** is here objective, that which is believed, the content of the gospel message, as in Jude 3, 'to contend for the faith': if so, it may be the earliest NT instance of this use of the word.

28. Without being frightened . . . by those you oppose you: The persecutors ranged against them and their message. To these adversaries the believers' fearlessness is **a sign** (*endeixis*, 'evidence', 'demonstration') **that they will be destroyed** (*apōleia*, perdition, as in 3: 19). On the other hand it will be an evidence of the believers' possession of salvation, here again spiritual and eternal, and not merely deliverance from foes. This evidence is God-given; He alone can impart such reality.

29. it has been granted (*charizomai*, to give as a favour, or mark of approval, as in 2: 9) **to you** (emphatic by position) as a boon, that which from heaven's viewpoint is an added privilege. Their belief in Christ is consummated in suffering for His sake. Their conflict is akin to Paul's. His deep encouragement in Christ is therefore to be their experience also (30).

ii. Plea for unity (2: 1–4)
The oneness which Paul craves to see in the life and service of the Philippians demands a true humility and a setting aside of all self-interest. To move their hearts, he alludes to their spiritual wealth, and to their warm regard for him personally. **1, 2. If you have any encouragement . . . with Christ**, including His responsive joy in their sufferings, **any comfort from his love**, their love inciting them to grant Paul's desire, any **fellowship with the Spirit**, any sharing with each other of which the Spirit is both secret and power (cf. 2 C. 13: 14), **any tenderness and compassion**, and well he knew the Philippians had such for him, **make my joy complete**. In 1: 4 he has spoken of his joy in them. Now he pleads that only one ingredient is needed to fill his cup. This they will grant by being one in thought, one in love, one in desire, and one in singleness of thought.

3. Selfish ambition or vain conceit will only feed their incipient dissension. Their positive steps to unity are first, **in humility consider others better than yourselves**. Humility is the recognition of our true littleness as those dependent utterly on God. Counting others better than ourselves is vividly illustrated in 1: 25 in Paul's preference of their joy to his joy. Secondly, **each of you should look not only to your own interests, but also to the interests of others** (4). Looking to the interests of others rather than to one's own is entirely opposed to the spirit of the world, so truly described in Ps. 49: 18, *a man gets praise when he does well for himself*.

iii. The mind of Christ: humiliation and exaltation (2: 5–11)
The apostle now shows that the supreme example of this mind, this looking on the interests of others, is the self-humbling of Christ. In doing so he gives a sublime unfolding of the tremendous fact of the incarnation, and does so in what has come to be widely recognized as an early Christian hymn on the humiliation and exaltation of Christ (6–11). This interpretation of the passage is based, among other considerations, on its poetical structure and Semitic linguistic substratum; it may have existed in Aramaic before it became current in a Greek version. This does not exclude the

possibility that Paul was its author; if so, he has, for purposes of his present argument, incorporated an earlier composition of his own at this point. In any case, the hymn may well be the earliest extant statement of the threefold division of Christ's career: pre-existence, life on earth, subsequent exaltation. So far as the second and third phases are concerned, the hymn appears to be based on the fourth Isaianic Servant Song (Isa. 52: 13–53: 12), where the Servant's exaltation following his humiliation is most clearly celebrated. The very wording of the Song is echoed here and there throughout the hymn.

There are in vv. 6–8 three main actions:

(*a*) **being in very nature God:** The participle *hyparchōn* ('subsisting', *though he was*) indicates that He was already in existence. 'Its tense (imperfect) contrasted with the following aorists points to indefinite continuance of being' (Gwynn). **in very nature God** (*morphē*, the essential form) is the very way in which Deity necessarily exists. Hence 'it includes the whole nature and essence of Deity, and is inseparable from them, since they could have no actual existence without it . . . The Son of God could not possibly divest Himself of the form of God at His incarnation without thereby ceasing to be God' (E. H. Gifford, *The Incarnation*, p. 35). **did not consider equality with God something to be grasped:** This **equality with God** (*to einai isa theō*, the neuter plural *isa* being adverbial) was not that of nature but of 'state and circumstances' (Gifford). 'The expression refers to rights which it was an act of condescension to waive' (Lightfoot). **a thing to be grasped:** Gk. *harpagmos*. The passive sense (cf. RV 'prize') is more appropriate to the context than the active 'robbery' of AV. 'He did not regard His being on equal conditions of glory and majesty with God as a prize and treasure to be held fast' (Gifford, *The Incarnation*, p. 71); or as a dignity to be coveted and seized, as did the first Adam (Gen. 3: 5 ff.) and Lucifer (Isa. 14: 13 f.); or (better still) as something to be exploited to His own advantage.

(*b*) **made himself nothing:** This use of *kenoō* with the reflexive object indicates a true and complete self-surrender, variously interpreted by commentators: He 'stripped Himself of the insignia of majesty' (Lightfoot); it was 'a laying aside of the mode of divine existence' (B. F. Westcott on Jn 1: 14); He divested Himself of this equality of state and thus 'made himself of no reputation' (AV); 'emptied himself of all but love' (C. Wesley). These and other attempts have been made to paraphrase Paul's concise affirmation, but it is best illuminated when we recognize that **made himself nothing . . . to death** (7, 8) is a literal rendering of the statement in Isa. 53: 12, that the

Servant *poured out his soul to death*. Utter self-denial is indicated, not any such metaphysical relinquishment of divine attributes as the once popular 'kenosis' theory, based on this passage, envisaged. (This 'kenosis' theory was invoked to explain how Christ on earth could make statements, *e.g.* with regard to OT authors or events, which were thought to imply on His part ignorance if not downright error. Paul's language gives no countenance to such a theory, and is in fact incompatible with it. Rather, in H. C. G. Moule's words *ad loc.*, 'a perfect Bondservice . . . will mean . . . a perfect conveyance of the Supreme Master's mind in the delivery of His message'.) Christ's possession of the fulness of the Godhead was not impaired by His self-emptying. Nor, when He emptied Himself by **taking the very nature** (*morphē* again) **of a servant**, did He exist any the less 'in the form of God', although the divine glory was veiled except to those who had eyes to discern it (Jn 1: 14). Never was 'the very nature of God' more fully manifested on earth than in Him who wore the servant's form. Jn 13: 4 f. (cf. Lk. 22: 27) is a graphic commentary on these words, especially in the light of Jn 13: 3. For the general attitude of Christ see Mk 10: 45; though there *diakoneō* ('serve') is used as against *doulos* ('slave') here, both words reflect the Heb. *'ebed* of Isa. 42: 1; 52: 13; etc. 'The form of a servant, man by nature; therefore the form of God, God by nature' (Chrysostom in Gifford). He took the servant's form by **being found in appearance as a man**. The expression does not detract from His true manhood, but guards the essential fact that He was thenceforth not only man but God. The plural 'men' relates Him to the race. Both this phrase and that immediately following echo Daniel's description of *one like a son of man* (Dan. 7: 13) to whom universal and everlasting dominion is given.

(*c*) **being found in appearance as a man:** This (*schēma*) refers to the outward appearance, that which strikes the senses. In appearance, dress, toil, and kindred matters, as well as in the essential inwardness of His incarnation, He shared sinless human experience. **he humbled himself:** Again a voluntary act. This He did in that he **became obedient to death, even death on a cross**. His obedience to God, like that of the Isaianic Servant, extended to death itself, and that the death of supremest shame, of 'being made a curse' (Gal. 3: 13).

The three actions set forth above found full response on the part of God. In vv. 6–8, all is of Christ; in vv. 9–11, all is of God. In the symmetry of the passage—

(*a*) 'He humbled himself' finds its response in **God exalted him** (cf. Lk. 18: 14). He was taken from the fathomless depths of Calvary's woe up to the right hand of God, to be 'higher than the heavens', and this in His holy manhood. The language here echoes the announcement of the Servant's high exaltation in Isa. 52: 13.

(*b*) 'He emptied himself' finds its response in **God . . . gave him the name that is above every name**. For 'bestowed' (*charizomai*) cf. 1: 29. Here is reputation indeed for the one who was made 'of no reputation' (AV). The name is the ineffable name of the God of Israel, spelt with the consonants YHWH. He who once said, *I am the LORD (YHWH), that is my name; my glory I give to no other* (Isa. 43: 8), now bestows that name on His Servant, and enhances His own glory thereby.

(*c*) 'He did not count equality with God a thing to be grasped' finds its response in **that at the name of Jesus** (or the name Jesus, since Gk. *Iēsou* may be either genitive or appositional dative) **every knee should bow . . . and every tongue confess . . .** Here is honour that may be paid to God alone (Isa. 45: 23); here is homage rendered by those **in heaven** (*epouranioi*, all intelligences in heaven whence He descended), **on earth** (*epigeioi*, all intelligences on earth where He suffered), **and under the earth** (*katachthonioi*, all intelligences in the realm of death which He conquered). To Him every creature shall confess, either by choice or by compulsion, **that Jesus Christ is Lord**, making full acknowledgment of His divine supremacy, **to the glory of God the Father**, whose pleasure it is 'that all may honour the Son, even as they honour the Father' (Jn 5: 23). God's glory is the goal of the work of Christ.

iv. Manifesting the mind of Christ (2: 12–30)
This section of the letter begins with Paul's urging the Philippians to obedience to his plea that the mind of Christ be in them, and then we may see (but this undesigned by Paul!) three men in whom that mind has been made manifest: himself, Timothy and Epaphroditus. In vv. 12–16 is a two-fold bidding, the first referring to deliverance from the dishonour of dissension, and the second to beauty of life and witness. The apostle reminds them of their past obedience, itself a trait of the mind of Christ, and seeks it still. **12. work out your salvation** (cf. 'my deliverance' in 1: 19): This salvation is a present one, and not so much individual as collective. The church at Philippi is in peril from inward strife, and the marring of the unity in which alone the true purpose of the church will be realized. **Work out** (*katergazomai*, the compound verb indicating achievement or bringing to a conclusion) **. . . with fear and trembling** lest they fail in this and so dishonour Christ. The phrase **with fear and trembling** occurs three times elsewhere in Paul's letters, *viz.*, 1 C. 2: 5; 2 C. 7: 15; Eph. 6: 5, and is charged with distrust of self and its

resources and abilities. This achievement he seeks will be possible because God is working in them **to will and to act** (13), touching both desire and activity, and moulding their will in order to mould their ways, **to his good purpose**, the purpose of His heart for the honour of His Son, in Him and in His people.

As to life and witness their actions must be **without complaining or arguing** (14). Lightfoot comments that the one is 'the moral and the other the intellectual rebellion against God'. They are the fruit of pride concerning oneself and of resentment concerning others. Free from these stains they will be **blameless and pure** (*akeraios*, 'unmixed', 'unadulterated', and therefore free from guile), **children of God**, displaying a character befitting the family of God. Thus even though they live in an age with a moral bias against God, they will bring no reproach on Christ and will shine as lights in the world. **Stars** (*phōstēres*, 'luminaries', used of stars in Gen. 1: 14–16, LXX, and only elsewhere in the NT in Rev. 21: 11) suggests the heavenly radiance of their witness in a world of spiritual darkness (15). This witness is to **hold out the word of life** (RV 'holding forth'). As a result Paul himself will exult when Christ comes that his toil has not been in vain (16). They will be his rejoicing then (cf. 4: 1; 1 Th. 2: 19 f.).

Vv. 17–18 provide an impressive glimpse of the mind of Christ in Paul. Very humbly, he compares his own possible death to a drink-offering, in which he will be **poured out like a drink offering on the sacrifice and service coming from your faith** (as in 2 Tim. 4: 6), upon their presentation of themselves to God as a burnt-offering, as in Rom. 12: 1. As the drink-offering was complementary to the burnt-offering (see Num. 15: 10; 28: 7), so Paul accords the greater honour to them, willing to have his supreme sacrifice reckoned to their credit, not his own. To him this will be only joy, and he bids them accept it with like joy.

In Timothy is afforded a second example of the mind of Christ (19–24). In revealing his purpose to send him to them, that he may be **cheered** and encouraged by the news Timothy will bring back, Paul pays warm tribute to his colleague. **20. I have no one else like him:** Other possible interpretations of *isopsychos* (lit. 'equal-souled') are that Paul has no one else so like-minded with himself, or (in the light of the following words, **who takes a genuine interest in your welfare**) like-minded with the Philippians. The NIV rendering implies that in the limited circle of those available at the time there is no one else who has Timothy's outlook of genuine concern for their welfare. Instead, **everyone looks out for his own interests, not those of Jesus Christ** and hence of His people. Timothy has proved his worth,

as the Philippians already **know**, in serving with Paul in moral and spiritual kinship. But, while sending Timothy, Paul longs to follow later himself. His confidence is strong that he will be set free, and that for their sakes.

The third of these noble characters is Epaphroditus. He has been the bearer of gifts sent by the Philippian church to Paul, and this service has almost cost him his life. Whether his illness was contracted on the journey or after arrival at Rome, it has been so severe that tidings of it have caused concern at Philippi. Then when Epaphroditus has learned in Rome of their knowledge of his sickness, far from being comforted, not to say elated, by the attention drawn to him, he is distressed all the more that they have this care. So for their sakes Paul sends him back to them, the bearer of this priceless letter. He calls him **my brother**, of the one family of God, and **fellow worker**, in toil for the one Lord, **and fellow soldier**, in the one conflict for the faith, **and your messenger** and minister (*leitourgos*, primarily a public servant, but used of service Godward and manward, and here as conveying the thought of a task not so much personal as representative). In these titles for Epaphroditus Paul expresses his real appreciation of his coming and of his ministry to him, and also commends him to them on his return. Paul's longing for them in 1: 8 (*epipotheō*, as in 2: 26, to yearn, especially for one who is absent) is matched by that of Epaphroditus. Again, the latter **is distressed** (*adēmoneō*, to be in great distress or anguish, cf. Mt. 26: 37). The mercy of God in sparing Epaphroditus has been a mercy to Paul also, lest he should be over-tried in seeing the Philippians deprived by death of the messenger they have sent for his sake. They are to accord Epaphroditus a glad welcome, as befits his bond with them and his sufferings, and to value highly such men, because for the apostle's sake and theirs he risked **his life** (*paraboleuomai*, 'playing the gambler with his life', H. C. G. Moule). The length of his absence from home and the fact that he carries a letter dealing, *inter alia*, with dissension in the church both add to the wisdom of this commendation.

IV. WARNING DIGRESSION (3: 1–21)

This chapter is of special importance because of its revealing of the motives which have dominated Paul's life. While warning trenchantly against false teachers who lead their followers astray, he pictures himself in the figure of an athlete in a race, running with his eyes fixed on the goal. A comparison of chapters 2 and 3 provides confirmation of the integrity of the letter as being one document and that Pauline. The one deals with Christ's downward descent, and the other with the upward call;

the one shows how Christ laid aside heavenly glory to win such as Paul, and the other how Paul has laid aside earthly glory to win Christ; the one shows Christ taking the form of a servant, being made in the likeness of men, and the other how the believer's body will be conformed to the body of His glory.

i. Warning against Judaizers (3: 1–3)

1. Finally, my brothers, rejoice in the Lord: As to all other matters (*to loipon*), he bids them meet such in the strength which only the joy of the Lord can give (see Neh. 8: 10). This prepares for the stern counsel of v. 2. '"Rejoice in the Lord" is evidently put here emphatically, with direct reference to the warning that follows' (Alford, *Gk. Test. in loc.*). **To write the same things**, to keep pressing the same lesson of joy in the Lord, so basic to this letter, finds no reluctance in Paul, and is for their safety, again a preparation for v. 2. The three terms of contempt, **dogs . . . who do evil . . . mutilators of the flesh** (2) refer to one and the same class of person, the Judaizers, who have so relentlessly followed where Paul has been, and sought to pervert the gospel of Christ (Gal. 1: 7). **Dogs**, the epithet for Gentiles, is turned back on these false teachers, as indeed being scavengers. They are **men who do evil**, in motive, in doctrine and in results, for all is evil which denies the entire sufficiency of the work of Christ. They are the concision (*katatomē*, 'mutilation', i.e., the mutilators, in scornful contrast to *peritomē*, the true circumcision as in v. 3), for they know nothing of that circumcision which is of the heart (Rom. 2: 29). For the strength of the terms used, cf. Mt. 3: 7; 23: 27. Far from dishonouring circumcision, they alone fulfil its true meaning who **worship by the Spirit of God and who glory in Christ Jesus** (cf. 1: 26; Rom. 5: 11; 1 C. 1: 31; 2 C. 10: 17; Gal. 6: 14), **and who put no confidence in the flesh**, the self-life. They do indeed have confidence, but only in Christ.

ii. Paul: past and present (3: 4–17)

But Paul does not write as one who despises what he has never known. On the contrary, he could excel all his critics both in privileges of birth and upbringing, and in behaviour. **Circumcised on the eighth day**, therefore no proselyte; **of the people of Israel**, the covenant people; **of the tribe of Benjamin** (cf. Rom. 11: 2), whence perhaps his name Saul (cf. Ac. 13: 21), of a tribe which remained true to David's line when ten tribes seceded; **a Hebrew of Hebrews**, the Aramaic-speaking son of Aramaic-speaking parents, and no Hellenist (cf. 2 C. 11: 22); **in regard to the law a Pharisee**, member of a strictly observant sect (cf. Ac. 26: 5); **as for zeal persecuting the church**, showing zeal of God though mistaken (Rom. 10: 2; Gal. 1: 13 f.); **as for legalistic righteousness, faultless**, without reproach

from men (cf. Ac. 23: 1; Mk 10: 20). All these gains (7, note plural, as if in those early days he had feasted his eyes on each in turn) he has counted **loss** (*zēmia*, singular, all being massed together, not just valueless, but actual damage), seeing their true nature in the fact that with such a past he had been a hater of Christ. **I consider**, i.e. I still count, after all the experience of the years, **everything a loss** (8). This has been for Christ's sake, **compared to the surpassing greatness of knowing Christ Jesus my Lord**, henceforth Paul's dearest ambition (cf. v. 10).

Indeed, these past gains he now counts as **rubbish** (*skybalon*, 'dung'). **8. that I may gain Christ:** It was his choice at his conversion; it is his choice still. Christ is his true gain here and hereafter (cf. 1: 21). **9. and be found in him:** In his faith-union with Christ, in his constant experience and enjoyment of this union, and (finally and especially) in the day of Christ. This means having no self-righteousness from law-keeping, but **the righteousness that comes from God and is by faith. 10. I want to know Christ:** Personally, in constantly enriched experience, until the day when he knows as he himself is known (1 C. 13: 12; cf. Exod. 33: 13, *that I may know thee*). Christ is Paul's supreme attraction, and to know Him he must know also **the power of his resurrection**, 'the power of the risen life of the Saviour realized in Paul's daily life and service' (F. Davidson, *NBC*, p. 1,034), **sharing in his sufferings**, that sacred fellowship which Paul in his own afflictions for the gospel's sake experienced with the suffering Christ cf. Col. 1: 24), **becoming like him in his death**, in an identification with Him in His death that adjusts all things to its claims (cf. 2 C. 4: 10 f.). Moreover, as this conformity (*symmorphizomenos*) concerns the *morphē*, the essential form as in 2: 6, he counts it not strange but true to his life and standing in Christ. **11. so, somehow, to attain to the resurrection from the dead:** This relates not simply to Christ's coming again, and the physical resurrection, for Paul's share in the blessedness of that is a matter not of attainment but of grace. The coming again and its consequences for the body are alluded to in 3: 21. V. 11 brings to a climax the longings of v. 10, all of which relate to present experience. As the logical and only satisfying consequence of partnership with Christ's sufferings and conformity to His death, he seeks now, even in the present body, to live as a victorious, risen man. The thought is like to that of 2 C. 4: 10, 'that the life of Jesus may also be manifested in our bodies'.

Such is his desire, but he humbly owns that he has not reached the goal in present experience, much less in consummation in glory. **12. Not that I . . . have already been made**

perfect, or 'perfected', the result in his character of obtaining what he aims at: he presses on to lay hold of that for which he was laid hold of by Christ Jesus. At his conversion Christ had placed him in the heavenward race for the very purpose of winning its prize. This is not yet in his grasp. **13. one thing I do**, with utter singleness of purpose, **forgetting what is behind**, not elated by victory or cast down by failure, **and straining toward what is ahead**, as the athlete urges every energy into the one task, **I press on** (*diōkō*, as in v. 6, the zeal once given to persecution now transformed and moving him to nobler deed) **toward the goal**, the end of the race where Christ waits to reward, for **the prize** of the upward call (14). In the light of the context, it is difficult to suppose that this prize can be anything less than Christ Himself (cf. v. 8). **15. all of us . . . who are mature** in appreciation of Christ's purposes are to be thus minded, in striving still onward. If any do not realize the need for still pressing on he is confident that God will show it to them. **16. Let us live up to**, or, let us walk in the same path (*stoicheō*, to be drawn up in line, i.e. shoulder to shoulder). In this race there is no selfish individualism. No one wins at another's expense, to another's loss. Paul's love urges his readers to run with him, and with him to receive the garland of victory.

iii. Warning against libertines (3: 18, 19)
It will be well for the Philippians to keep their eye on the example of such as Paul, for tearfully he warns that **many live as enemies of the cross of Christ** (18). Here it is not false teaching, as in v. 2, but evil living; libertines, not Judaizers, are now in view. These enemies claim the benefits of the cross, but deny its power in their life. **Their destiny is destruction**, eternal doom, as in 1: 28. They worship their sensual appetites and glory in the gross indulgence which they deem liberty but which is actually a thing of shame (cf. Rom. 16: 18). Far from having the mind of Christ, their **minds** are **on earthly things**. Pretending to the skies they grovel in earth's corruption.

iv. The Christian's true home and hope (3: 20, 21)
In sharp contrast the believer looks to the unseen and eternal, and sets his mind on things that are above, not on things which are on earth (Col. 3: 2). **20. But our citizenship** (*politeuma*, the sphere of our citizenship, our 'city home', H. C. G. Moule) **is in heaven:** A form of words which would be specially appreciated by the Philippians in view of their city's status as a Roman colony (cf. Moffatt's rendering, 'we are a colony of heaven'). From heaven we **eagerly await a Savior**, or, we expect as Saviour, whose coming again is our continuing hope, to bring us the final phase of salvation, **the Lord Jesus Christ**. Far from indulging or

even despising the body, we are to respect it, even in its present humiliation, for He **will transform our lowly bodies so that they will be like** (*symmorphos*, conformed to, as in v. 10, and no mere outward fashion) **his glorious body:** RV, 'the body of his glory' (cf. the Hebrew idiom 'the body of his flesh', rendered literally into Greek with reference to Christ in Col. 1: 27), here in contrast to 'the body of our humiliation' (RV). This is the very climax of all Paul's desire, and it will be realized through Christ's power **to bring everything under his control**, and thus to bring the universe into complete harmony with His holy and loving purposes. Then all limitation and all failure will be past, and in the glorified body Paul will rejoice in the liberty of a capacity to know Christ surpassing the highest yearnings of the path here.

V. ENCOURAGEMENT, GRATITUDE AND FINAL GREETINGS (4: 1–23)
i. The secret of harmony (4: 1–5)
1. Therefore . . . stand firm in the Lord: The words look back to the prospect unfolded in 3: 20–21, and in the certainty of that final triumph encourage to an unfaltering perseverance; **in the Lord**, as encompassed by His power and controlled by His authority. Most affectionately Paul repeats the longing and the love of 1: 8 and 2: 12, and tells of what the Philippians will be to him at the coming again of the Lord. They are his **joy** now, especially if they heed his plea in 2: 2, but will be so then in full measure, and his very **crown** (*stephanos*, the wreath of victory in the games, or of worth or of festal gladness, cf. 1 Th. 2: 19, 'crown of boasting'). Then before touching a sore spot in their affairs, he assures by using the phrase **dear friends** that their well-being is vital to him. Euodia and Syntyche, both ladies, **these women** in the following verse, are entreated **to agree . . . in the Lord** (2). That each is separately entreated indicates that both require such counsel. That they have been outstanding in their labours makes their disagreement the more sad and hurtful to others. Each is reminded of her true sphere **in the Lord**, and that all strife ends in submission to His will. This is the secret of harmony. It is well for others to help and not hinder the coming together of the erring ones. The identity of the **loyal yokefellow** (3) is not revealed. Of conjectures made that to be preferred as being the most obvious is that it alludes to Epaphroditus (so Lightfoot), in which case the term **loyal yokefellow** will aptly sum up the titles of 2: 25. If the Ephesian provenance of the letter could be sustained, the **yokefellow** (*syzygos*) might well be Luke; another possibility is that *Syzygos* is a personal name. **who have con-**

tended at my side (*synathleō*, as in 1: 27): They have shared the toil and trial of Paul's work in the gospel. As he looks back over this he thinks of one Clement and of others who have likewise shared his work with him, but he cannot stop to recount their names but rests on the fact that all are recorded in the **book of life** (cf. Isa. 4: 3; Mal. 3: 16; Lk. 10: 20; Ac. 13: 48). In that family register of heaven they are known and valued (see note on Rev. 3: 5). Three things will help to maintain harmony, *viz.*, rejoicing in the Lord, showing **gentleness** to all, and remembering the Lord's presence (4 f.). **gentleness**: Gk. *epieikes*, 'yieldingness', or 'sweet reasonableness' (so Matthew Arnold). **5. The Lord is near:** This could refer to His coming again, but seems here to indicate His present nearness, as calming and encouraging.

ii. The secret of peace (4: 6–9)
The way of peace is to **not be anxious about anything** (6), not being careless but free from the strain which turns so easily to distrust, and to bring every request to God, **by prayer** (*proseuchē*, prayer in its devotion) **and petition** (*deēsis*, prayer in its personal detail) **with thanksgiving**, for appreciation of past mercies stimulates to trust for future ones. Paul's own prayer life alluded to in 1: 3–5 is excellent example here. *The garrison of peace* is afforded by **the peace of God**, which He gives to us and which **transcends all understanding**, transcending all our mental capacity to grasp and to appreciate (7). This **will guard** (*phroureō*, to stand guard, to protect) **your hearts and your minds in Christ Jesus**, as in the very abode of peace. *The discipline of peace* follows naturally from the thought of the garrison. **Finally**, concerning every occupation of the mind comes the reminder that inward peace is not preserved by feeding the thoughts upon the unwholesome. **Whatever is true, . . . noble** (worthy of respect) **. . . right . . . pure . . . lovely** (winsome) **. . . admirably** (in good repute), and in the widest range, whatever is **excellent** (morally) and **praiseworthy**, this and this alone is suited to their minds (8). Disciplined minds will find the path of daily life set forth in the teaching and practice of Paul himself, and in this path they will prove the reality of the presence of the God from whom all peace comes. Thus both the first and second sections of this chapter close with the wonder of the divine companionship.

iii. The secret of contentment (4: 10–20)
Having poured out his heart concerning their spiritual need, particularly with regard to their lack of oneness, he is free at last to express his unfeigned gratitude for the gifts brought by Epaphroditus. He has reserved this to the end so that the closing part of his letter may deal with the bond between them which has been confirmed so truly by their generosity. **10. I**

rejoice greatly in the Lord, not for selfish interests, but tracing His goodness in that **you have renewed your concern for me**. (*anathallō*, to sprout or flourish again as a tree): Their thought for him had been unchanging but it required suitable opportunity, as the tree the coming of spring. He makes no complaint of financial want. Indeed, there is no instance in the Scripture records of apostolic days of any servant of Christ making known his own material needs to any but his Lord. **I** (emphatic, speaking from the schooling of long experience) **have learned to be content whatever the circumstances** (*autarkēs*, independent of external circumstances, used, *e.g.*, of a city needing no imports and therefore self-sufficient). This is no stoical indifference to prosperity or adversity, but the confidence given by the secret of contentment he is now to disclose. He knows **what it is to be in need**, to be brought low in the humiliation of want, and **what it is to have plenty**, having more than present requirements (12). The repeated **I know** indicates that the years have been ample in their lessons in both directions, and more, he not only knows these experiences but how to triumph in them, as is evident in respect of want in the words of 2 C. 6: 10. **12. I have learned the secret:** *myeō*, here only in the NT, is the technical term for initiation into the Greek mysteries, hence more generally to let into a secret. What is hidden, a mystery, to the natural man lies open to faith in the power of Christ. He is ready for **any and every situation**, not being their victim but their victor. And the secret is just this: **I can do everything through him who gives me strength** (13). Dwelling in Christ, whose enabling power put forth in transforming His own at His coming again has been seen in 3: 21, he finds in Him the enabling for triumph in all present circumstances. Even if it be in abasement, in being brought low, he is strengthened by One who has known abasement, having humbled Himself (cf. *tapeinoō* in 2: 8 and 4: 12). His sufficiency in Christ in no wise detracts from their kindness, and he speaks of their gifts as a sharing of his trouble (14). This is the true viewpoint which should characterize all such giving, not a meeting of need, but a partnership of service, and here actually in his sufferings. Very gratefully he reminds them that in **the early days of your acquaintance with the gospel**, when first they had heard and been blessed by it, and he had left their province, they alone of the churches had shown him such response (15). Indeed, before he left their province, while he was still in Thessalonica (cf. Ac. 17: 1–9), they had twice sent him much help (16). And the value he sees in the gift is far more than its benefit to him. It is **what may be credited to your account** (17), 'the harvest of blessing which is accumulating to your account' (A. S. Way, *The Letters of St. Paul, in loc.*). On his side his account is settled, for he says, **I have received full payment** (*apechō*, in constant use in the papyri in the sense of 'I have received' as a technical expression in the drawing up of a receipt). But the greatest value of their gifts has been that which they have meant to God, **a fragrant offering, an acceptable sacrifice, pleasing** (18), true response to the love of Christ in giving Himself for them 'a fragrant offering and sacrifice to God' (Eph. 5: 2). Because they have honoured God in meeting His servant's need God will honour them by meeting all their need.

19. my God: A phrase seven times used by Paul, see 1: 3, the God whose faithfulness and power he has proved so truly, **will meet all your needs**, and this on magnificent scale, **according to his glorious riches in Christ Jesus**. Thus not to them, not to him, but to their **God and Father** the **glory** must be eternally (20).

iv. Farewell (4: 21-23)

And now their faces rise before him, dear because of their fellowship, but dearer still because they are all **in Christ Jesus**, and he sends to everyone his greetings and those of the brethren with him (21). These latter are unnamed, but with full heart Epaphroditus will be able to speak of them all. Then he passes on the greetings of all the believers, i.e. in Rome, and **especially those who belong to Caesar's household** (22)—a term including members of the imperial civil service whether in Rome or in the provinces. One last word follows, seeking for them **the grace of the Lord Jesus Christ** (23), the grace manifested so wonderfully in 2: 5-8, the grace of the One who

though He was rich for their sakes became poor.

BIBLIOGRAPHY

BARTH, K., *The Epistle to the Philippians* (London, 1962, translation of German edition of 1927).

BEARE, F. W., *A Commentary on the Epistle to the Philippians.* BNTC (London, 1959).

BRUCE, F. F., *Philippians.* Good News Commentary (San Francisco, 1983; Basingstoke, 1984).

GWYNN, J., *The Epistle to the Philippians.* Speaker's Commentary (London, 1881).

HENDRIKSEN, W., *A Commentary on the Epistles to the Philippians* (Grand Rapids, 1962).

KENNEDY, H. A. A., *The Epistle to the Philippians.* EGT (London, 1903).

LIGHTFOOT, J. B., *Saint Paul's Epistle to the Philippians* (London, 1881). [on the Greek text]

MARTIN, R. P., *Philippians,* NCentB (London, 1976).

MARTIN, R. P., *The Epistle of Paul to the Philippians.* TNTC (London, 1959).

MICHAEL, J. H., *The Epistle of Paul to the Philippians.* MNT (London, 1928).

MOULE, H. C. G., *Philippian Studies* (London, 1897).

SCOTT, E. F., *The Epistle to the Philippians.* IB (New York, 1955).

VINCENT, M. R., *The Epistles to the philippians and Philemon,* ICC (Edinburgh, 1897). [On the Greek text].

Monographs on Phil. 2: 6-11

GIFFORD, E. H., *The Incarnation* (London, 1911, reprinted from *The Expositor,* 1896).

MARTIN, R. P., *An Early Christian Confession* (London 1960).

MARTIN, R. P., *Carmen Christi* (Cambridge, 1967).

ROBINSON, H. W., *The Cross of the Servant* (London, 1926), reprinted in *The Cross in the Old Testament* (London, 1955), pp. 55-114.

COLOSSIANS

ERNEST G. ASHBY

Colossae, set in beautiful surroundings in the valley of the Lycus, a tributary of the Maeander, was in Paul's day a city of little importance. Herodotus (c. 484–425 B.C.) and Xenophon (c. 430–354 B.C.) in their accounts of Xerxes and Cyrus respectively testified to its past greatness, but even by Strabo's time (c. 60 B.C.-A.D. 20) it had declined, being overshadowed by the neighbouring cities of Laodicea and Hierapolis.

It seems clear (1: 4; 2: 1) that Paul was personally unknown to the Colossians, having approached Ephesus from the upper country and not by the regular trade route down the Lycus valley. Epaphras had been their evangelist, acting on Paul's behalf (1: 7) and doubtless the other churches in the vicinity, and perhaps all the churches in Asia mentioned in the Revelation were the result of the Ephesian mission (cf. Ac. 19: 10).

It is assumed that Paul is writing from Rome, both in his letter to the Colossians and to Philemon. Few now favour Caesarea as an alternative, and the reasons once quoted to support this view are now used in favour of the Ephesian theory. Certainly Paul's expectation of a speedy release, followed by a visit to Colossae does not fit Caesarea, and it is strange that amongst his companions he does not mention Philip the evangelist. Much more can be said for Ephesus. 2 C. 11: 23 implies numerous imprisonments and Paul suffered some great affliction in Asia (2 C. 1: 8) which some explain by a literal interpretation of 1 C. 15: 32 and think this the occasion when Paul's friends risked their lives for him (Rom. 16: 3, 4). But such an interpretation is by no means certain, and later traditions also employed to point to the same conclusion are of doubtful value. But even granting an Ephesian imprisonment, which is quite possible, it still does not fit the facts so well. Distant Rome seems a safer hiding place for a runaway slave than local Ephesus. Acts does confirm the presence of Luke at Rome, but does not suggest that he was at Ephesus. Aristarchus was seized, but not necessarily officially imprisoned at Ephesus, and as he accompanied Paul to Rome he may well have shared his imprisonment there. Ephesus rather suggests a short, sharp crisis, whereas the contents of Colossians seem to require an imprisonment of some duration to provide for leisured thought, and the development of doctrine in this letter might imply a later rather than an earlier date. But Paul's request to Philemon for a lodging does favour an Ephesian rather than a Roman origin, for after Rome Paul hoped to go westwards, though there is considerable uncertainty concerning his later movements. In St. Paul's Ephesian Ministry G. S. Duncan argues in favour of Ephesus, for he thinks that Paul is writing to a church of comparatively recent origin, and that he would almost certainly visit it before leaving the province of Asia. An adequate discussion of the whole subject may be found in D. Guthrie's New Testament Introduction: The Pauline Epistles pp. 92–98 and 171–174.

Such discussion is interesting but has little bearing upon the exegesis of the letter save to affect its date.

Far more important is the purpose of the letter. It demonstrates the apostle's sense of responsibility towards all Christians everywhere, even those he had not met, and lays tremendous emphasis upon the need of correct doctrine and right belief. The Colossians had been well taught but were now assailed by false teaching stigmatized as 'hollow and deceptive philosphy', which he regarded as dangerous. It is difficult to identify the heresy in the absence of precise formulation, but certain ideas are refuted. References to circumcision, food regulations, the Sabbath and other legal enactments indicate that fundamentally it was Jewish, but not the Judaism which had troubled the Galatians. This was a syncretistic doctrine, fused with some elementary form of gnosticism, not surprising in a country where cosmological speculations and mysterious theosophy so readily found a home and where Jewish orthodoxy was suspect. Gnosticism, later to develop into a variety of forms, was a false intellectualism strongly tinged with mysticism. One of its fundamental tenets was the inherent evil of matter, thus denying any direct agency of God in the work of creation, and interposing a whole series of emanations and intermediary powers who must be placated and worshipped, and also destroying any true belief in the Incarnation. The material body, they taught, was evil, man's prison, and the way of release was by superior knowledge (gnōsis) granted to the initiated, leading to perfection (teleiōsis).

There were two ways of approach: either to suppress the body by rigid asceticism (as here) or to ignore it as unimportant, thus leading to grave licence (a thought not found in this letter, but it may explain 1 C. 5, 6). Here Paul has only to deal with the initial stages, but there was the danger that Christians seeking a deeper experience might try to accommodate themselves to current religious or philosophical ideas. As Paul confronted this error he doubtless meditated deeply under the guidance of the Spirit, and the result is one of his greatest christological passages. Here we see not merely the individual but cosmic significance of Christ: He is not only personal Saviour but Lord of creation and Head of the Church. Hence all such intermediaries are unnecessary; in fact any such attempt to worship these serves but to detract from the unique glory of Christ and is thus a false theosophy. The great glory of the letter is that it points to the sole sufficiency of Christ. Far from being progressive, the Jewish elements in this teaching were retrogressive, a return to the mere shadow, while the Gnostic elements were in direct opposition to the very fundamentals of the Christian faith. Certainly there *is* progress in the Christian experience, a maturity which Paul seeks for *all* these converts, and the fullness (*plērōma*) is to be found in Christ alone. Through Him deliverance comes, not by asceticism and suppression but by identification with Him in His death and risen life, and this is worked out in a number of personal relationships.

Critics have put forward two main arguments against Pauline authorship. The first is that the Gnostic heresy which Paul attacked belonged to the second century A.D., but as he was dealing with a tendency and not with the fully developed system, as was later true of Irenaeus, the criticism is largely irrelevant. The second argument that the development of thought or change of vocabulary and style apparent in the letter militates against Pauline authorship is an unwarrantable criticism of his ability or versatility, to say nothing of the fact that such stylistic criteria are no very firm grounds of critical proof in any circumstances. Here Paul merely develops his earlier thought (cf. 1 C. 8: 6; 2: 8, 10) and changes in vocabulary are explained partly by change of topic and also by the fact that at times he is adopting the very catch-words of his opponents. The letter to Philemon is clearly Pauline, and this has so many close ties with Colossians that it helps to confirm the traditional view of the authenticity of this also. A fuller discussion of its authenticity may be found in Guthrie *op. cit.* pp. 167–171. Some comment on its affinities with Ephesians will be found in the Introduction to that letter. To Paul was granted some vision of the ultimate purposes of God: here the emphasis is on the glory of Christ in relation to His Church, His resources being at their disposal; in the Ephesian letter the emphasis is on the destiny of the Church which is to be for the praise of His glory.

ANALYSIS

I. INTRODUCTION: SALUTATION (1: 1, 2)

In his opening greeting Paul links Timothy with himself, an association too frequent to be of use in identifying the provenance of the letter. Introducing himself as an apostle **by the will of God** he acknowledges his call as an act of unmerited divine grace. If he does stress his authority here it is not because it has been challenged as in Galatia, but because he is presenting his credentials to Christians unknown to him personally, and he is endorsing the message of Epaphras. **Timothy**, lacking the direct commission of the risen Christ, is described as **our brother** (but cf. 1 Th. 2: 6). While earlier letters are addressed to churches, later ones, as here, are addressed rather to the individual members. It is to the **holy and faithful brothers** or dedicated men in pagan Colossae that he writes, **holy** as set apart for God, **brothers** in their mutual love and fellowship. In view of the wording of Eph. 1: 1 it is unlikely that any stress is to be laid on the title **faithful** as indicating those not carried away by false teaching. He employs his usual greeting, the Hebrew and Greek salutation adapted to a Christian message.

2. The NIV following the reading of many of the best MSS omits 'and from Christ Jesus our Lord' which renders this form of greeting unique and somewhat surprising in view of the emphasis in this letter on the position of Christ. But its very uniqueness suggests that it may well be the correct reading.

II. CHRIST'S PERSON AND WORK (1: 3–2: 7)

i. Thanksgiving (1: 3–8)

Though Paul's rendering of thanks to God, here described as **the Father of our Lord Jesus Christ**, does follow the pattern of contemporary non-Christian letters giving thanks to their deities, it was no merely conventional opening. Its omission from Galatians and 2 Corinthians indicates that it was included only when the progress of converts was a real cause for thanksgiving, as in every prayer for the Colossians. Such rejoicing sprang from no first hand knowledge but from the report of Epaphras on their faith, hope and love. This trilogy appears also in 1 Th. 1 in the order of practical experience and in 1 C. 13 in the order of spiritual value. Here faith in Christ, the heavenly relationship, and love to the saints its

earthly manifestation are made dependent upon hope. Christ is the sphere in which this faith works rather than its object; in other words faith derives its significance from their position 'in Christ', and being not self-centred it opens out into a wider perspective embracing all those who share this common faith. The hope which maintains this faith and love is not so much the hopeful attitude as the object hoped for, even Christ Himself (cf. 1: 27). But hope of necessity involves some future element, and while 'realized eschatology' rightly stresses the present enjoyment of spiritual experience, the creation still waits with eager longing for the consummation at the parousia (Rom. 8: 19). If, as A. M. Hunter thinks [*Paul and his Predecessors*, pp. 33–35 and *Exp T.* xlix (1937–38) p. 428 f.], this idea of a triad of graces was pre-Pauline, this could be Paul's interpretation of it. This hope had reached them through the gospel (cf. Eph. 1: 13) and quite unlike the false philosophies of which Paul is soon to speak, which are but local, this message demonstrates its truth by its universal character and its capacity for fruitfulness and development wherever it has gone. At Colossae it had been received not merely with intellectual assent but thoroughly grasped and appreciated 'in its genuine simplicity, without adulteration' as Lightfoot happily renders it. As the better MSS in v. 7 show, reading **on our behalf** instead of 'for you', Epaphras their preacher was Paul's representative, a beloved colleague, and at some time perhaps a sharer in Paul's imprisonment (Phm. 23), discharging his Christian service with faithfulness. Through him Paul received a favourable report of their love engendered by the Holy Spirit, as well as other less pleasing details tactfully omitted from his thanksgiving.

6. All over the world is not to be taken as hyperbole: he had visited many provinces and worked in large representative centres from which the message could spread, and as Johannes Munck shows, Paul thought in terms of nations [J. Munck: *Paul and the Salvation of Mankind*, p. 52. The reference here is to his work in the East].

8. This is the only explicit reference to the Holy Spirit in the letter, but there is abundant evidence of His power at work.

ii. Prayer (1: 9–14)

Paul employs this report as the occasion for continued prayer for their further progress in the spiritual realm. As C. F. D. Moule states, 'the whole Christian vocabulary of knowledge is very closely connected with obedience', so different from the outcome of what was falsely brought before them as 'deeper knowledge'. True knowledge is practical, growing out of the fear of the Lord (Prov. 1: 7), and right conduct is both the aim and hallmark of right knowledge. Clearly the apostle has no desire for elementary standards nor time for superficial knowledge. To him a knowledge of the will of God is the indispensable prerequisite of a life pleasing to Him. In the divine therapy a mental transformation is the means used to achieve an ethical renewal (Rom. 12: 1, 2). Using some of the catchwords of those seeking to lead them astray, he prays for their full development in knowledge and apprehension of the will of God, **through all spiritual wisdom and understanding:** that is to say, he prays for a mind instructed in spiritual truth which also grasps the application of principles to the problems of life, with a view to worthy daily conduct which shall please the Lord in every way. Thus after evangelization comes pastoral care and he prays for the deepening of their character, to take effect in fruitful activity, in good works of every kind as they grow by (or in) the knowledge of God. But this is no human wisdom to inflate their pride as had been the Corinthian danger. This deepened character and increased strength of achievement is by the power of God's **glorious might**, not calculated to exalt the flesh but to promote humility. The aim is not the stolid impassivity of the Stoic but patient endurance in a spirit of joy.

There is progressive thought here: knowledge promotes service (9, 10), service is repaid by strength (11), and all is crowned by thanksgiving (12). Thanksgiving is due to the Father for making men, Gentiles such as were some of these Colossians, competent to share the inheritance of the saints in the realm of light, this no doubt after the analogy of the allotment of territory to Israel in Canaan. Not only is there deliverance from the authority and jurisdiction of darkness, those powers under whom the Lord suffered when it was their 'hour' (Lk. 22: 53), but He has transported believers, a thought reminiscent of OT captivity, not into the kingdom of angels or principalities, to whom the false teachers would urge them to pay homage, but into **the kingdom of the Son he loves** (13). Here the picture is varied slightly: it is deliverance, not now by the exercise of might and power but by a gracious payment of the ransom, resulting in **the forgiveness of sins**. Eph. 1: 7 states the price paid, the shedding of His blood, which is not explicitly mentioned in the best MSS here. This **redemption**, the apostle makes clear, is a present experience, for His kingdom is in operation having broken into the world of

time, though its fullness is still in the future reserved for hope.

12, 13. Light and **darkness** are terms used in various religions, and in the Dead Sea Scrolls. Christ's kingdom is contrasted with this present evil age.

13. Deliverance once for all effected by Christ on the Cross is received by individuals as they come into union with him.

iii. Christ and Creation (1: 15-17)
The thought of the kingdom naturally leads on to the king, and this great Christological passage is comparable with Jn 1: 1–4 and Heb. 1: 2–4, and in line with the Lord's own teaching in John's Gospel and with the Wisdom literature of the OT. Christ is the visible likeness of God the invisible, for while no man has seen God, the Son not merely made him but could claim, 'anyone who has seen Me has seen the Father'. He is, in fact, the effulgence of the glory of God, the very stamp of His nature, the light which shines into men's hearts (Heb. 1: 3; 2 C. 4: 6). He is **the first-born over all creation**, a phrase which the Arians made to mean that Christ was a created being and not co-eternal with the Father, but the context rules this out completely. The title here given emphasizes the thoughts of priority and superiority, declaring, as Lightfoot states, 'the absolute pre-existence of the Son'. The reference here is to His deity rather than His humanity, to the Son in His eternal being rather than the incarnate Son.

Two significant phrases are employed, **by him . . . and for him** (16): 'By Him' conveys a wealth of meaning far deeper than Philo's Logos which was virtually the Idea or the Ideal. Here is no abstraction but a divine person: Christ is the source of life as He is also the agent of all creation including the heavenly and invisible, and those very powers whom they were being urged to placate. Christ is outside creation, prior to it, distinct from it, and He is sovereign to it all, for it was created by Him and indeed for Him. In Him the purpose of the universe is found, in Him is its principle of coherence, and it is He that 'impresses upon creation that unity and solidarity which makes it a cosmos instead of a chaos' (Lightfoot).

16. The NT seems to mention five types of angel-ruler: four of them here (also 'powers' in Eph. 1: 21 and Rom. 8: 38), but no definite hierarchy can be deduced from these.

iv. Christ and the Church (1: 18)
After dealing with the cosmic significance of the Son in His eternal being, Paul now passes to the subject of the incarnate Son in His historical mission and revelation. The Church is described not as the body of Christians but as the Body of Christ, so vital a union that to persecute the members on earth is to persecute the Head in heaven. Here Paul seems to go

further than the metaphor of earlier letters (1 C. 12: 12 ff.; Rom. 12: 4, 5), dealing with the functions of individual members, and this is distinctively a Pauline revelation. As in Ephesians, Christ alone is the Head. The Sovereign of the universe is also Head of the Church, that in all things **he might have the supremacy:** this is His right for He is the beginning, presumably here with reference to the new creation, and the firstborn from the dead, as in v. 15 He was the firstborn of creation.

the body, the church: The figure chosen aptly illustrates how close is the relationship and vital the link between Christ and His Church. It exists only by His indwelling Spirit, operates by His power, and functions as His representative. But it is surely unscriptural to think of it as an extension of Christ's Incarnation, for His Incarnation was unique and He was sinless, which in experience the Church is not.

v. Christ and Reconciliation (1: 19–23)

Here again the pre-eminence of Christ is affirmed. **Fullness** is a thought not uncommon in both OT and NT, but if the heretical teachers were already employing this as a technical term to denote the totality of divine emanations, under whose power men were supposed to be living, it is peculiarly fitting that Paul should thus describe the Saviour. It is God's pleasure that all fullness, the full essence of deity, should reside in Christ, thus undermining their whole argument. Furthermore His purpose reached out to effect reconciliation, to end disrupted harmony and establish for sinful men peace with God, by the Saviour's sacrifice upon the Cross. Realizing as he does the extent of this cosmic discord (Rom. 8: 22) Paul sees that this reconciliation is far-reaching enough in its scope to embrace **all things**, though this must not be pressed to mean universal reconciliation irrespective of the will of man to accept God's offer. Of this reconciliation the Colossians have been a particular example, showing how great truths must be personally applied. Once they operated in an orbit of evil works resulting from their hostile attitude when they were estranged from God, but Christ's death has effected their reconciliation. Perhaps it was necessary to stress the reality of His Incarnation and its vital connection with atonement to correct the Colossian heresy. Christ did actually enter into the life of man and wrought out redemption as a historic fact in His body, and His purpose was to **present** them at the parousia **holy in his sight, without blemish and free from accusation**, in fact 'justified by faith'. But this involves the present responsibility of holding fast, not being drawn away by false teaching. The certainty of the divine promise offers no grounds for human complacency: they are the genuine believers who persevere to the end, and their faith is a universal one.

vi. Paul's Ministry (1: 24–2: 7)

At the time of Paul's conversion a double truth was revealed: he was a 'chosen instrument' to evangelize the Gentiles, and this would involve suffering for his Master. The apostle here takes up both these thoughts. Perhaps to strengthen the link between himself and these unknown Christians he rejoices in his sufferings for the sake of the Lord's work and in measure for them. The sufferings of Christ involved in His expiatory death are not here in view, for that work was complete and peculiar to the Lord Himself. But in the proclamation of the gospel the Church must suffer, and their sufferings are His also (Ac. 9: 4). Paul gladly has a share in this, a **commission of God** in the economy of God, that he may preach to the full to unfold the mystery now revealed, that Gentiles with Jews may share in the wealth of this glorious manifestation, that Christ should dwell in their hearts; and this is a pledge of future glory also. He continues the work of instruction even after their conversion, for his object is their spiritual maturity. By repeated emphasis that this is for all, for **everyone**, Paul refutes the gnostic claim of superior knowledge for the few, the initiates, though probably he looks to the parousia as the time of its realization. To this end he strives, as active as an athlete in the arena, but gladly acknowledging that it is the Lord's strength working within him.

26. the mystery: There is no reason to suppose that Paul borrows this term from the Greek mystery-religions, but rather from the OT (*e.g.* Dan. 2: 18 ff.). A mystery is not something which must be kept secret, but rather a concealed truth which God is pleased to unveil when the time is ripe. Thus the mysteries (NIV secrets) of the kingdom were revealed to the disciples, but not to the prophets preceding them (Mt. 13: 11–17). While the OT revealed something of God's blessing for Gentiles as well as Israelites, the method by which this would be accomplished was a mystery first revealed to Paul. In Colossians he shows that Christ indwells Gentile and Jewish hearts; in Ephesians is revealed the fact that in Christ Gentile believers are fellow-heirs with Jewish Christians.

2: 1–7. The apostle who at Miletus urged the Ephesian elders to watch over the church in their care shows his own deep concern for these converts unknown to him personally. Error is divisive, but his objective in prayer is their encouragement and harmony, for brotherly love is an indispensable condition for spiritual development (cf. Eph. 3: 18, 19; 4: 16). In this way they may be brought into the wealth of a full grasp of divine wisdom, a larger knowledge of God's revealed mystery, even of

Christ Himself in whom divine wisdom is enshrined. This is the purpose of his letter, to prevent their being deceived by plausible arguments. Even in writing to strangers Paul can feel spiritually present with them, delighting in the solidity of their Christ-centred faith, a happier association than when with the Corinthian church he dealt with the disciplining of a defaulter (1 C. 5). He urges them, therefore, that as it was no mere tradition of words they received, but Christ Himself, so they must walk and live, their way of life and thought conforming to the way of Christ and centred in Him. With rapid change of metaphor he likens them to a tree rooted in Christ once for all, then to a building being erected on Him as foundation and consolidated in the faith. So doing they would remain true to the teaching of Epaphras and this should be done with thanksgiving.

2. the mystery of God, namely, Christ: Probably this is the correct reading, having **Christ** in apposition to **the mystery of God**, and the many variations (discussed in Lightfoot, p. 252 f.) are explanations or modifications of this. In 1: 27 the mystery is Christ, **the hope of glory** indwelling Gentile hearts, here it is Christ as the incarnation of divine wisdom.

5. how orderly you are and how firm your faith in Christ is: As a military metaphor depicting their order and close phalanx resisting Gnostic infiltration this makes good sense (so Lightfoot and C. F. D. Moule). But the former term may describe national or domestic organization (cf. Abbott and also 1 C. 14: 40) while the latter may re-echo a Gnostic term denoting the barrier between the upper and lower realm (so F. F. Bruce, quoting H. Chadwick). It is also found in the LXX for the 'firmament'.

7. in the faith: Lightfoot prefers 'by their faith' in which case it would mean 'trust' rather than 'convictions'.

III. SAFEGUARDS AGAINST ERROR (2: 8–3: 4)

i. The Fullness of Christ (2: 8–10)

Here in vivid picture language Paul warns them against allowing anyone to carry them off as captives through specious, make-believe philosophy. Clearly the apostle condemns *false* philosophy, though surely he would have condemned any teaching relying upon inadequate human reason as the source of spiritual truth. His message was not 'man's gospel' (Gal. 1: 11), but theirs depended on human tradition which was their measure instead of Christ. It was according to the elemental spirits of the universe and not according to Christ, and this was fatal to it, for in Him resides all the fullness of deity and as such He must be the source and meaning of truth. In Christ they had **fullness**, an obvious correction of false teaching involv-

ing degrees of initiation or the need of ritual or mediating powers to share the *plērōma*. Christ is the head, not merely the sovereign but source of all power and authority, not merely preceding other powers (1: 17) but their conqueror (2: 15) and this must invalidate any claim of subjection to them.

8. basic principles of this world: The word *stoicheia* originally meant things in a series, *e.g.*, the alphabet, and so the rudiments of knowledge (*e.g.* the A B C) and is so used in Heb. 5: 12. Then it came to mean 'the elements of the world' in the LXX and 2 Pet. 3: 10, and finally in Hellenistic syncretism 'cosmic spirits'. It occurs here, 2: 20 and Gal. 4: 3, 9. It seems possible from a reference to days and seasons (Gal. 4: 10) that they may have been regulating their religious life by observing the movements of the stars, with which they associated certain angelic powers, hence the interpretation accepted above, but C. F. D. Moule prefers 'elementary teaching' as the other meaning is later except for these possible NT references. If Gal. 4 is interpreted to mean merely Jewish holy days, then a relapse to elementary teaching makes good sense. For fuller detail see Hendriksen pp. 135–7 which accepts Moule's view.

9. bodily form: Lightfoot seems to have grammatical support for his interpretation 'bodily' i.e. referring to the Incarnation, and the present tense 'lives' need present no difficulty in its application also to His glorified body (Phil. 3: 21). Other interpretations include 'corporately' rather than 'corporeally' or 'in totality', the complete embodiment in contrast to the supposed distribution among the intermediaries (C. H. Dodd and F. F. Bruce), or 'in reality' as opposed to the shadow (Arndt-Gingrich). Perhaps a double meaning is intended. But see Lightfoot p. 182, Moule pp. 92–4, Hendriksen p. 112.

ii. Spiritual Circumcision (2: 11–12)

The theme of the remainder of the chapter is that of reality contrasted with the shadow. To the Jew circumcision was the outward sign of union, the entering into the covenant, though Paul (Rom. 2: 28, 29) is in line with the OT when he stresses that real circumcision is inward, that of the heart. So in the death of Christ, His real 'circumcision' (as it was also a 'baptism', Mk 10: 38) of which the literal circumcision had been a 'token-anticipation' (Bruce) the Christian, too, has a share. He is thus circumcised, that is to say there is the **putting off of the sinful nature** or 'the old man', his old nature in its unregenerate state of rebellion against God. This 'circumcision' then is internal not external, of the whole not the part. As in Rom. 6, baptism is depicted as illustrating a burial to the old life with Christ and thus a sharing in His resurrection but it is through faith that this new life is imparted.

iii. Christ's Victory (2: 13–15)

Paul now passes on to results. Though previously dead, devoid of the principle of spiritual life through sin, and outside the covenant, believers are made spiritually alive, sharing Christ's life and completely forgiven. This is possible because of His cross where Christ dealt with the IOU, the legal bond of ordinances to which the Jew had agreed and to which even the Gentile's conscience had in some degree given assent (Rom. 2: 14, 15). This bond Christ took and cancelled by His death, nailing it to His cross as a challenge to the principalities and powers whom He had defeated and led in triumph, thus preventing their using this broken bond to intimidate the conscience.

13. made you alive: Regeneration is a new moral and spiritual life now and it continues through death, so it is both present and future.

14. nailing: There seems no evidence for the custom often referred to in this context that bonds were cancelled by being pierced by a nail. As there is no obvious change of subject from 'God' to 'Christ', it is understood that God in Christ was acting. The verb *apekdysamenos* could mean 'stripped Himself' of hostile powers assailing Him (so the Greek Fathers and Lightfoot) or 'stripped off' His body at the Cross (so the Latin Fathers and some modern writers) or simply **disarmed** or 'despoiled', the middle voice implying His interest in this action, and this seems most suited to the context.

iv. Christian freedom (2: 16–19)

Here Paul briefly gives some indication of the beliefs and practices of the false teachers. Discussing first food and festivals he denies the necessity of asceticism. The Levitical law did prohibit certain foods, but not beverages, and the observance of certain times was obligatory. But Christ by His death has abrogated these legal demands, and to look to these is to prefer the shadow to the substance which is Christ Himself. The Letter to the Hebrews is in fact a detailed commentary on this verse (17). The second rebuke is directed against the **worship of angels**, mediating powers, which means that respect was paid to the inferior instead of to the Head. Christians are not to be condemned for not observing ritualistic rules by those who insist on subjection to angels on the strength of their alleged visions to which they pay an unduly high regard. For all their officious parade of humility, a humility in which one takes delight is but excessive pride arising from their unspiritual nature. In acting thus they fail to adhere to the Head who is Christ, and thus they promote disintegration instead of unity (cf. Eph. 4: 16). In such unity there is divine growth, as each in love plays its part.

18. In spite of the attractive idea of **disqual-**ify, *katabrabeuetō* should probably be taken to mean 'condemn' or 'decide against'. The AV negative must be omitted as in NIV. *embateuōn*, **goes into great detail about what he has seen**. The translation 'taking his stand on (or upon)' as RSV, RVmg, though doubted by C. F. D. Moule, does seem admissible (cf. F. F. Bruce quoting Sir William Ramsay).

v. Our Death with Christ (2: 20–23)

If indeed these Colossians are dead with Christ their lives should no longer be conditioned by interests in this world, restricted by what is after all only in 'the category of the perishable' (Lightfoot). Here religious prohibition has reached its climax: these believers have been told they must not handle, taste nor even touch certain things, rules of human origin, of the kind more appropriate for the development of children than the conduct of free men. Superficially this may appear to have a form of wisdom in its apparent humility, though human traditions may mean the heart is far from God (Isa. 29: 13). In fact such asceticism far from being of any value serves only to indulge the flesh, the old unregenerate nature.

23. In this difficult verse *logos* has been taken to mean 'show' or **appearance** of wisdom, *pros* to mean 'against', i.e. to counteract or combat the fleshly desires.

vi. Our Life with Christ (3: 1–4)

The apostle now develops his ethical teaching, erecting, as is his custom, his moral superstructure upon a solid doctrinal foundation. The theme of the rest of the letter is a simple challenge to them to become experimentally what by God's grace they are: 'You are', he argues, 'raised with Christ, then let your thoughts and aspirations rise to the same level, your aims finding their end in Christ, your conduct characterized by heavenly wisdom. Sharing in His death, you also share His resurrection with a new life whose eternal perspective is something the world cannot understand. Because your life is bound up with Christ, His future manifestation will be yours also'. Paul writes in somewhat similar strain in Phil. 3: 19–20: there it is to rebuke sensuality, here asceticism.

IV. CHRISTIAN LIFE IN ACTION (3: 5–4: 6)

i. Discard the Old (3: 5–11)

5. Put to death: Paul's argument continues as follows: 'In spite of your heavenly life you are now living on earth, and so are in some degree of tension. There is indeed a place for Christian asceticism, but this is internal, not external, the renouncing of propensities belonging to the old life'. Five of these are named, immorality and impurity in deed, as well as in thought and desire, reaching their climax in greed equated with idolatry. Here Paul adopts the same pattern as the Sermon on the Mount, proceeding from outward deed to inner motive, culminating in the spirit of acquisitiveness making a god of gain. These are not dealt with by human striving but by death, a result of that incorporation with Christ described in vv. 1–4, and becoming experimental by faith (cf. Rom. 6: 6, 11). Failing that, continuance in evil practices characteristic of the old life of disobedience necessitates judgment, **the wrath of God**, no impulsive passion, but also no mere impersonal moral principle. It is God who acts in judgment (cf. Rom. 1: 18; Eph. 5: 6) against disobedience, a condition once true of them. Now they must put off the sins mentioned, like a discarded cloak, the previous list (5) laying emphasis on sensuality, this one on uncharitableness which is quite out of keeping with the new life. Paul specially deals with the tongue (cf. Jas 3: 2–10) but he makes it clear it is not merely conduct or habits which have been put off: it goes deeper, it is the very self, **your old self**, and they **have put on the new self**, being renewed in the likeness of God as was the original intention (cf. Gen. 1: 27; 1 C. 15: 45; Gal. 3: 27). This renewal in mind and spirit results from incorporation with Christ: here all barriers go, whether racial, religious, cultural or social. The gospel removes all distinctions, so visibly symbolized by the dividing wall in the Temple (Eph. 2: 14).

5 ff. 'taken off', 'put on', 'be subject', 'watch and pray' are among the catchwords thought to have been used to sum up some early Christian teaching.

ii. Put on the New (3: 12–17)
As they have been chosen to be holy they must put on the garments of salvation, the new robe of character whose texture is sympathy, kindness, humility, meekness, patience, for they are the new Israel. These are the qualities to prevent friction and will help to settle their quarrels if any exist, their forgiveness being prompted by Christ's forgiveness to them, as is expected of them (Mt. 5: 9; Lk. 6: 36; Mt. 18: 33). Above all they must **put on love**, not an additional garment but the girdle to hold the others in place, **in perfect unity** (*teleiotēs*). The apostle then refers to **peace**, which in the Ephesian letter has the function of the girdle here represented by love. These partial resemblances reveal not a different writer but the working of the apostle's mind along similar but not identical lines. Here peace, which in Phil. 4: 7 is to garrison the heart, is to arbitrate, to umpire, to discipline the mind to a decision where there is a conflict of motives or impulses, to promote a unity of purpose in a spirit of thankfulness.

16. They are also to allow **the word of Christ** to **dwell** in them, or more probably among them as a community, though of necessity it must dwell in the heart of each

individual. In this way they will **with all wisdom** teach each other by means of **psalms, hymns and spiritual songs** having a didactic value (Eph. 5: 19). The new convert can easily imbibe some theology from carefully chosen hymns, and there are not lacking indications of such woven into the text of the NT. But this must be no mere external song of praise but accompanied by inward emotion, a matter of the heart.

17. Paul deals now with motives: whether in action or speech everything must be done in the name of Christ, in an attitude of thanksgiving to the Father. Mature Christians do not need codes of rules, merely this basic principle applied to various relationships, and these applications are thought to be part of a fairly well-defined body of catechesis (cf. also Eph. 5: 22).

iii. Social Relationships (3: 18–4: 1)
The subjection of wives to husbands is indicative of a divine hierarchy (cf. also 1 Pet. 2: 18–3: 7) and what makes it remarkable is its stress on reciprocal duties, all stemming from the fundamental relationship to the Saviour, for they must do what is fitting **in the Lord**. Children also and parents have mutual responsibilities, one of obedience, the other of forbearance. Perhaps because he has Onesimus in mind Paul deals with the obligations of slavery in more detail. Acknowledging the human distinctions of master and slave, he calls for no superficial service merely to catch the eye to win human favour, but urges undivided service from the heart done as unto Christ, for while in this world the slave-master relationship survives, to members of the Church there is a higher relationship embracing all under one Master from whom the reward will be received. Whatever their human standing all are sons to share the divine inheritance. While Eph. 6 expands the thought of reward, here a note of warning is emphasized, and there must be fair dealings for there will be no divine favouritism either for unfaithful slave or unjust master.

iv. Prayer and Wisdom (4: 2–6)
Paul stresses the need of constancy in prayer, showing that a careful watch on past mercies will promote thanksgiving and a prayerful spirit (cf. Rom. 12: 12). Perhaps this call to vigilance was a recollection of the disciples' experience at the Transfiguration or their failure in Gethsemane. In their prayers Paul seeks a place for himself and his friends, for a **door for our message**, a door of opportunity, that he may with all needed courage and ability preach **the mystery of Christ**, which is indeed the cause of his imprisonment. Had he been content with a Jewish gospel, not embracing the Gentiles as part of the one Body, he might still have been free.

5 f. Here as in Eph. 5 there is the exhortation

to redeem the time by buying up their opportunities. There the reference is primarily to Christian prudence, here to the need to display a discreet sanctified conduct to silence any wrong impression among non-Christians. To this end their **conversation** must not be vapid and insipid but **full of grace**, wholesome and Christlike, since **salt** may signify either its preserving power or its flavour. It should, in fact, fit the person and the occasion.

V. CONCLUSION: PERSONAL GREETINGS AND CHARGES (4: 7–18)

The concluding greetings are more detailed than in Ephesians. Tychicus, a native of proconsular Asia and perhaps of Ephesus (cf. Ac. 20: 4; 2 Tim. 4: 12), a faithful friend and colleague, accompanied Paul eastwards on his third missionary journey, probably as a church representative in connection with Paul's collection for the poor in Jerusalem (Ac. 20: 4). Here he acts as Paul's messenger: later he is to be Paul's representative in Crete and Ephesus (Tit. 3: 12; 2 Tim. 4: 12). Here his purpose is to inform the Colossians concerning Paul's circumstances and to encourage them. With Tychicus he also sends Onesimus, now **a dear brother, a faithful minister** (see Introduction to Philemon): it is a wonderful illustration of the power of the gospel to cut across social barriers that he calls a slave **one of you**. There follow greetings from six of Paul's companions, three Jewish, three Gentiles. Aristarchus the Thessalonian would be well known from his previous visits to Asia (Ac. 19: 29; 20: 4; 27: 2) though he may not have met the Colossians personally. Lightfoot prefers to interpret the title **fellow prisoner** as meaning spiritually a captive, as there are no known facts to explain it literally, and he thinks Aristarchus left Paul at Myra. If so, he must have rejoined him later. Instructions have already been given concerning the welcome of **Mark the cousin of Barnabas**, so clearly any misunderstanding arising from the second missionary journey has been removed. **11. Jesus . . . Justus** makes his sole appearance here, as one of those standing by the apostle in his present circumstances. These three were the only Jews present to assist Paul in the work, and this line of demarcation furnishes the chief evidence that Luke was a Gentile. **12. Epaphras** comes next, one of their own number, a bondslave of Christ and hard worker, for praying is working. He wrestles in the intensity of his prayer for these three local churches, seeking their maturity of character and full dedication to the will of God. **14. Luke** is called **the doctor** and a **dear friend**, possibly a grateful acknowledgment of help received from his medical skill. Of **Demas** who has not yet defaulted little is known, but

the absence of any word of praise may be an anticipatory hint of the cooling off of his enthusiasm. Greetings are also sent to the Christians in Laodicea and to **Nympha** in whose house the local church met, a state of affairs often true of NT churches, though these may have been smaller units within the larger fellowship of believers in any city. A charge is then given that after reading this letter at Colossae it is to be read at Laodicea and conversely their letter is to be read to the Colossians. In thus giving to writings primarily local in their significance a wider, and ultimately a universal range may be seen the germinal idea of Scripture, as a body of authoritative writings. Finally there is a charge to **Archippus** (cf. Phm. 2): if passed on by a public reading of the letter in church it would no doubt gain in significance and solemnity, though it may well have caused some embarrassment, which was perhaps intended. Paul concludes his greeting in his own hand, which would prevent any thought of forgery. Pleading for a kindly remembrance in his imprisonment he leaves them a blessing, **Grace be with you.**

16. the letter from Laodicea: Presumably now lost, though some have identified it with Ephesians which we assume to have been written later, others with Philemon. There is also an apocryphal Laodicean letter.

BIBLIOGRAPHY

Abbott, T. K., *The Epistles to the Ephesians and to the Colossians.* ICC (Edinburgh, 1897).

Bruce, F. F., *The Epistles to the Colossians, to Philemon and the Ephesians,* NICNT (Grand Rapids, 1984).

Carson, H. M., *The Epistles to the Colossians and Philemon.* TNTC (London, 1960).

Griffith Thomas, W. H., *Christ Pre-eminent, Studies in the Epistle to the Colossians* (Chicago, 1923).

Hendriksen, W., NTC *Colossians* (Edinburgh, 1971).

Lightfoot, J. B., *The Epistles to the Colossians and to Philemon* [on the Greek text] (London, 1875).

Lohse, E., *Colossians and Philemon,* E.T. Hermeneia (Philadelphia, 1971). Martin, R. P., *Colossians: The Church's Lord and the Christian's Liberty* (Exeter, 1972).

Martin, R. P., *Colossians and Philemon,* NCentB (London, 1974).

Moule, C. F. D., *The Epistles to the Colossians and Philemon* [on the Greek text]. CGT (Cambridge, 1957).

Moule, H. C. G., *Colossian and Philemon Studies* (London, 1898).

O'Brien, P. T., *Colossians, Philemon.* Word Biblical Commentary (Waco, 1982).

Radford, L. B., *The Epistles to the Colossians and Philemon.* WC (London, 1931).

Schweizer, E., *The Letter to the Colossians,* E.T. (Minneapolis, 1982).

1 THESSALONIANS

PETER E. COUSINS

It was probably the winter of A.D. 49/50 when Paul and Silas, accompanied by Timothy, arrived in Thessalonica. Paul was making his second missionary journey, but in spite of his previous experience he had been badly shaken by his rough handling at Philippi (1 Th. 2: 2). Now the missionaries nerved themselves to face the challenge of Thessalonica. An important centre of communications and commerce, it had a Jewish community in which, as usual, the missionaries began their work. Three weeks passed, and Paul's preaching of a crucified Messiah whom he identified with Jesus bore fruit in the formation of a church containing some Jews and a larger proportion of Gentiles and women who had been regular worshippers at the synagogue. Angry at this blow to their own missionary work, some of the Jews instigated a riot during which an attack was made on the house where the missionaries were staying, and the owner, Jason, together with some of the converts, was taken before the authorities and made responsible for seeing that the trouble did not recur. In the circumstances it seemed wise to save the church from further trouble and the missionaries from danger, so all three moved on to Berea. Following similar riots there, Paul separated from the other two, continuing to Athens and Corinth (Ac. 17: 1–15; 18: 1).

In Athens he was joined by Timothy, but not for long. Already Paul had tried to revisit Thessalonica, but had been hindered (1 Th. 2: 18). Now he sent Timothy to the young church, himself facing the loneliness of Athens because he felt the Thessalonians needed Timothy's help. From Athens to Corinth—and here Timothy rejoined him with news from Macedonia. On the whole, it was good (1 Th. 3: 6). So remarkable was the tone of this church that the news had spread to other areas of the evangelization of Thessalonica and the spiritual growth of the converts (1 Th. 1: 6–8; 3: 6; 4: 1, 9, 10). Yet the hostility that had driven the missionaries from the city continued, and Paul wished he could give encouragement personally, for some of the converts were easily depressed (1 Th. 4: 13–18; 5: 14). In addition, they were concerned about friends who had died and about the delay in the Lord's return. Paul's absence was being pointed to as a sign of a lack of concern for the Thessalonian church, and he and the other missionaries were the objects of a whispering campaign intended to show that they were no better than the normal run of magico-philosophical charlatans (1 Th. 2: 3–12, 17–20). Certain undesirable tendencies were developing. The Gentiles had not made a clean break with their formerly low sexual standards (1 Th. 4: 3–8). Some believers, presumably in response to the eschatological element in the apostolic preaching, had given up their jobs (1 Th. 4: 11 f.; 5: 14). It may have been the reaction of others to this group that had produced disunity (1 Th. 5: 13b). Certainly there was a tendency to give the elders of the church less respect than they deserved (1 Th. 5: 12 f.).

Such were the circumstances in which Paul wrote 1 Thessalonians. It was for a long time believed to be the first of his letters, but today many scholars, particularly in Britain, are inclined to award this position to Galatians. Its sole doctrinal distinguishing feature is its stress on eschatology, and more particularly its description of the translation from earth of believers at the *parousia* (see note on this word at 1 Th. 2: 19), which is unparalleled in the NT. Otherwise the letter shows signs of its early date (*e.g.* the vagueness of reference to church office-bearers in 5: 12) though by no means of an undeveloped theology. Indeed, the Thessalonians are assumed to have become familiar during Paul's stay with a surprising variety of doctrines. These babes in Christ were well fed! Paul's companions are repeatedly associated with him in the letter (cf. the frequent use of 'we'); another prominent feature of the letter is the insight provided, especially in chapter 2, into the motives of an ideal missionary team and their relationship with their converts. It is plain that one secret of Paul's success was his personal concern for the individuals among whom he worked. In this, as in other respects, this primitive document, a relic of the earliest days of the Church, speaks to and challenges us today.

ANALYSIS

I. GREETING (1: 1)

For **Paul, Silas and Timothy** see above. (Silvanus was the Latin form of Silas's name.) Morris points out that Paul's happy relationship with the Thessalonian church enables him to dispense with any such title as 'apostle'. The description of the church as **of the Thessalonians** and **in God the Father and the Lord Jesus** is unique, perhaps a sign that the apostle had not yet formed his style. Hogg and Vine comment, 'The first part marks the assembly at Thessalonica as non-heathen, the second as non-Jewish'. Whereas 'in Christ' is commonly used to show the complete union of the believer with his Saviour, **in God** is rare (Col. 3: 3). Its use here is a powerful incidental witness to the faith of the primitive Church in the full deity of the Son.

II. THANKSGIVING FOR THE THESSALONIAN CHURCH (1: 2–10)

2. The difficulties he was experiencing at Corinth would increase Paul's joy in the strong faith of the Thessalonian converts. **continually** (3): May qualify **mentioning** or **remember**. It probably refers to both. **3. faith . . . love . . . hope:** Frequently linked in the apostolic Church (5: 8; Rom. 5: 2–5; 1 C. 13: 13; Gal. 5: 5 f.; Col. 1: 4 f.; Heb. 6: 10–12; 10: 22–24; 1 Pet. 1: 21 f.). Here the **work** is probably less that of believing than the works resulting from faith (Jas 2: 14–26). **labor:** The word implies toilsome effort; love is costly. **endurance:** Active, whereas patience (AV) is passive. It results from the Christian's certain **hope** in Christ (Col. 1: 26). **before . . . Father** is more naturally taken (with the Greek) at the end of this verse.

4–10. The Thessalonians' initial response to the gospel. 4 f. The free preaching of the gospel reveals those who are **chosen** by God. Here as elsewhere election derives from God's love. Election to damnation (the 'double decree') is not found in the NT, however 'logical' it may appear to be. Rom. 9: 21 ff. is hypothetical; Paul significantly fails to state the doctrine. **our gospel:** 'the gospel we preach'. The **power** experienced resulted neither from eloquence (1 C. 1: 17), personality (2 C. 10: 10), nor evil spirits, but from **the Holy Spirit**. **deep conviction:** The same word (*plērophoria*) occurs in Col. 2: 2; Heb. 6: 11; 10: 22. Here it refers to the freedom felt by the preachers. **5b** looks forward to 2: 3–12. **6. You became imitators:** Cf. 1 C. 4: 16; 11: 1. The aorist indicates a decisive moment, while the emphatic *you* stresses that the election of the Thessalonians was shown in their experience as well as in that of the preachers. **the message:** Here, as most often in the NT, the gospel. **suffering:** Cf. Ac. 17: 1–10; 14: 22. **joy:** Part of the harvest of the Spirit (Gal. 5: 22), who enables believers to rejoice in spite of, even because of hardship (Jn 16: 22; Rom. 5: 3–5; 1 Pet. 4: 13). **7. model:** *Typos* originally means an imprint (Jn 20: 25), then an image (Ac. 7: 43), and so a pattern (Heb. 8: 5). **Macedonia and Achaia:** These two provinces comprised the whole of Greece. **8–10.** The gospel has **rung out** (perfect, indicating that the process continues) from them, throughout Greece, aided no doubt by Thessalonica's strategic position. Paul need never tell of their heroic faith (2: 14) for the story of the mission to Thessalonica is on the lips of Christians everywhere. (Prisca and Aquila had recently arrived in Corinth from Rome cf. Ac. 18: 2.) Morris suggests that the absence of Pauline vocabulary in vv. 9 f. shows that Paul is using the common terminology of the apostolic Church. **turned:** 'Conversion is always the voluntary act of the individual in response to the presentation of truth' (Hogg and Vine). **from idols:** They were largely Gentiles. Cf. Paul's preaching at Lystra (Ac. 14: 15 ff.). **to serve:** As slaves, in total devotion. **the living God:** An OT term contrasting Jehovah with idols who can do nothing (Isa. 41: 23 f.). **true:** Not *alēthēs* (truthful) but *alēthinos* (genuine) as in Jn 1: 9, etc. Again Paul refers to the Christian hope, which is rooted in the resurrection of Jesus Christ. **rescues:** A timeless participle equivalent to 'The Deliverer' (cf. Rom. 11: 26). **coming:** A present participle stressing the inevitability of the wrath. In the light of the general NT reference of **wrath** to God's total antagonism to sin, it seems unduly limiting to interpret it here of anything less than final judgment.

III. THE EVANGELIZATION OF THESSALONICA (2: 1–16)

1–6a. The Motives of the Missionaries. The ancient world was full of wandering 'philosophers' and 'holy men' who were greedy and unscrupulous. Some of Paul's enemies suggested that he was one of these, but he denies the charge. **1. a failure:** May mean 'fruitless', or 'devoid of purpose'. Paul insists that he and his fellows had a definite object in view, and attained it. **2.** Paul remembers both the physical pain of the flogging at Philippi and the insult offered him as a Roman citizen (Ac. 16). **dared:** This verb is always used in the NT of the proclamation of the gospel and denotes freedom from stress (see Ac. 9: 27, etc.; Eph. 6: 20). **opposition:** *Agōn* is a term from athletics meaning 'a contest'; it implies strenuous activity. **3.** Paul rebuts three charges: (*a*) that the gospel was based on error, being a fallible human philosophy; (*b*) that it encouraged sexual immorality (this was true of much contemporary religion and was a common accusation against Christians); (*c*) that the methods used were underhand. **4.** Positively, he asserts the gospel is from God (so not erroneous); its ministers are not unclean but divinely attested; the methods used must withstand God's scrutiny. The words approved and **tests** are related. The root idea is of approving after carrying out tests. God has thus tried and attested the preachers. As Jer. 11: 20 says, they must reckon with a God who does scrutinize men; thus their responsibility is to 'please' (or serve) Him rather than men. **hearts:** As always in the Bible, not the emotions but the innermost life. **5.** He appeals to what the Thessalonians know of their methods and what God knows of their motives. **Flattery** here means any insincere use of words. Literally, Paul says that they have not 'come to be (and continue) in a word of flattery'. He is speaking of a settled policy of deception about the true meaning of the

message, designed, presumably, to gain adherents by false pretences. **greed** is *pleonexia*, lit. 'a desire to have more', 'insatiableness'. In the NT and elsewhere it is thought of as one of the worst of vices, and in Col. 3: 5 is called 'idolatry'. Had the missionaries been like many 'philosophers' of the day, their teaching would have been a mere pretext to conceal their greed. **6a.** Paul denies that his motive was to gain esteem and respect. He demonstrates this by referring to the missionaries' behaviour. The verse thus marks a transition to what follows.

6b–9. The Missionaries Supported Themselves. An apostle was a fully accredited representative. The Lord chose His apostles primarily to preach (Mk 3: 14). Paul asserts the privileges of apostleship but is more conscious of its responsibilities. **7. gentle:** Many MSS have 'babes' (*nēpioi* for *ēpioi*). The second part of the verse strikingly illustrates the missionaries' pastoral care. **8. We loved you:** An unusual verb of uncertain origin. It expresses 'yearning love' (NEB) as of a mother–nurse, over the converts. **we were delighted to share:** Preaching the gospel involves giving the whole personality away. **9.** All Jewish boys learned a trade; no rabbi might earn his living by teaching the Law. Paul had trained as a tentmaker (Ac. 18: 3) and often supported himself thus. The Church is now rediscovering (what some Christians have never forgotten) the value of the presentation of the gospel by men who do not earn their living by it, as well as by those whose whole time must necessarily be devoted to that task. **toil and hardship:** The first word implies wearying work, the second, the difficulty of the job. **10.** Again Paul appeals to the experience of the Thessalonians in order to refute slanders. **holy . . . righteous . . . blameless:** The first word possibly refers to goodness as seen by God, the second by man, and the third to its giving no cause for reproach ('devout, just and blameless' NEB).

11 f. The Missionaries' Behaviour was Blameless. Their ministry is described as directed in love to individual needs. Again Paul stresses the love shown to the converts. Two types of exhortation are mentioned; some needed encouragement (cf. Jn 11: 19, 31) and others stern warning. **12.** The preachers' aim was Christian living. The present continuous force of **calls** is important. Paul speaks less often than the synoptic gospels of the kingdom of God (but cf. Ac. 20: 25; 28: 31; Rom. 14: 17; 1 C. 4: 20; 6: 9, 10; 15: 50; Gal. 5: 21; Eph. 5: 5; Col. 4: 11; 2 Th. 1: 5). It is not static, but God's rule over man, in action. Present in the world now, it will one day appear to all men and its glory be made plain.

13. The Missionaries' Message was from God. Though delivered by human agency the gospel comes from God. It is to be both **heard**

and also **accepted**—the word is used of welcoming a guest. Such a welcome results in its becoming an active power that 'goes on working' in those who 'go on believing' (two timeless present tenses; cf. 1: 5).

14–16. Persecution. As Paul looks back on his experience and that of the church at the hands of his Jewish brethren, he sees that their present hostility is of a piece with their attitude throughout their history (cf. Stephen's speech in Ac. 7). His bitterness suggests that the persecution at Thessalonica, though carried on by Gentiles, was instigated by Jews (cf. Ac. 17: 5–9). They cannot escape God's judgment. Paul uses the OT metaphor of the cup of the wrath of God (Ps. 11: 6; cf. Gen. 15: 16). The inevitability of judgment is seen in his use of the aorist. The fall of Jerusalem both expresses and symbolizes this judgment, which awaits all who thus **displease God**.

IV. PAUL AND THE THESSALONIAN CHURCH (2: 17–3: 13)

17–20. Paul's Intended Visit. A new section begins here, extending to 3: 13, in which Paul speaks of his relationship to the Thessalonians. He begins by explaining that in spite of what enemies were suggesting, his failure to return was involuntary. **17. torn away:** Lit. 'made orphans'. Paul is ready to mix metaphors in expressing his love for the Thessalonians (cf. vv. 7, 10). They were out of sight but not out of mind. **made every effort:** The word 'combines the ideas of speed and diligence' (Morris). Calvin comments: 'Our feeling of attachment must be strong when we find it difficult to wait even a very short time'. **longing:** The word (*epithymia*) usually indicates intense and evil passion. **18.** The first use in this letter of the first person singular emphasizes the depth of the apostle's emotion. It is useless to speculate on the nature of the repeated difficulties that hindered the visit. They were no doubt explicable by natural causes, but Paul does not take them as 'the Lord's will', rather seeing behind them the 'prince of this world'. **19 f.** Paul explains his desire to visit them by the fact that these converts are to be his pride at the **coming** (*parousia*). Although the word means simply 'presence' (2 C. 10: 10), yet presence implies 'coming' and this is the general NT meaning, with special reference to the second coming of the Lord. In some documents it is used of the 'coming of a hidden divinity' in his cult, and of an official visit by a king or emperor. **crown:** *stephanos* is usually (not always) applied to the laurel wreath worn at a banquet or by the victor at the games.

3: 1–5. Timothy's Mission. Ac. 17: 14–18: 5 suggests that Paul was alone from the time when he left Thessalonica until Silas and Timothy joined him at Corinth. These verses show that Timothy (at least) met him in Athens, then left for Thessalonica, rejoining Paul in Corinth. The words **by ourselves** in v. 1 and the parallel between **we sent** in v. 2 and **I sent** in v. 5 suggest that the plural here is not to be taken literally. **1.** Apparently the atmosphere of Athens preyed upon Paul (cf. Ac. 17: 16a) so that only his great affection for the Thessalonians made him choose to be **left . . . by ourselves** (lit. as if abandoned or by a dead friend; cf. Gen. 42: 38 LXX). **2.** The importance of Timothy's mission is stressed by his being described as **God's fellow-worker** (this is a better MS reading). He was to **strengthen** (lit. buttress) and **encourage** (*parakaleō*) them in order to strengthen their faith. **3.** Apparently their enemies were suggesting that their suffering proved the gospel to be false. Ac. 14: 22 explains why the Thessalonian converts knew better. **unsettled:** The Gk. may mean 'disturbed' or 'beguiled' (i.e. seduced away from the faith by those who were apparently showing sympathy). **4. we kept telling you:** The continuous tense shows that the subject had been repeatedly mentioned. **5. I sent:** Paul's enemies had suggested that his failure to return showed lack of concern, hence he uses the singular and emphatic pronoun. **tempter:** Again Paul traces events to Satanic influence. The thought of temptation as testing is prominent here. It is significant that **might have tempted** is indicative in the Greek—Paul knows this is likely. In contrast, **might have been useless** is subjunctive, for he does not expect the converts to give in.

6–8. Timothy's Report. Paul's joy at hearing of the steadfast faith of the Thessalonians, their love, and their longing for him, has caused him to write immediately. **6. good news:** The word normally refers to preaching the gospel —so great was Paul's joy at what he heard. **7.** Paul is suffering physical hardship (**distress**) and persecution but is strengthened (cf. v. 2) by Timothy's news. **8. we usually live:** 'a breath of life to us' (Phillips, NEB). This passionate concern for his spiritual children is typical of Paul; it both demonstrates and explains his success as evangelist and pastor.

9 f. Paul's Satisfaction. His joy does not lead to self-satisfaction, but to thanksgiving ('What sufficient thanks can we repay?'— Lightfoot) and a realization that the converts' faith is not yet perfect.

11–13. Paul's Prayer. He seeks a blessing for himself (11) and for them (12) with the advent in mind. **11. clear** is a singular verb, for the Father and the Lord Jesus are one. A typical example of the way in which the doctrine of the Trinity is found 'in solution' throughout the NT, however rarely it may crystallize and become visible. **12. you** is emphatic, implying 'whatever happens to us'. **increase** goes with **love** which may not be confined to Christians. **13. holy:** The word used here implies a state rather than a process; though referring mainly to separation to God it connects with v. 12. The **holy ones** at the *parousia* are either angels (Dan. 8: 13; Mk 8: 38) or departed believers (Eph. 3: 18; 1 Th. 4: 16 f.); probably both are intended.

V. ETHICAL INJUNCTIONS (4: 1–12)

1 f. Introductory Exhortation. As usual, Paul devotes the last section of his letter to practical problems of Christian living. Timothy had doubtless described the needs of the Thessalonian church. **1. Finally** marks the opening of the closing section. Paul carefully avoids suggesting that the Thessalonians are at fault. But 'life is marked by either growth or decay' (Hogg and Vine). **2. instructions:** A military metaphor stressing their authoritative nature as coming **by . . . the Lord Jesus** (cf. 1 C. 7: 10). **3–8. Sexual Purity.** Unlike the Jews, the Greeks had low standards of sexual morality: even religion was tainted by prostitution. Hence even so healthy a church as that at Thessalonica needed this exhortation, which Paul grounds in the revealed will of God, who both helps by the gift of the Spirit and judges those who despise this gift. **3. be sanctified:** All who believe are 'sanctified' or set apart for God because He has chosen them for Himself. But this has implications for conduct. We must become what we are, and 'make every effort to be holy' (Heb. 12: 14). Paul now brings out the implications for sexual relationships. **4. to take a wife:** Both words present difficulties. *Skeuos* ('vessel') is translated by RSV as 'wife'. This agrees with the use of the verb *ktaomai* ('take') in Ru. 4: 10; Sir. 36: 24 for marriage. And in rabbinical literature 'vessel' can mean 'woman' (1 Pet. 3: 7 is not a parallel). This, however, implies a low view of marriage, and it is better to follow Phillips, NIV and NEB in rendering *skeuos* as 'body'. (cf. 2 C. 4: 7; *Ep. Barn.* 7: 3; 11: 9). Papyri show that *ktaomai* can mean simply 'to have', but here the sense may be 'to gain control'. 'Each of you must learn to control his own body' (F. F. Bruce, *An Expanded Paraphrase of The Epistles of Paul*). **5.** Christian behaviour is contrasted with that of the heathen (Jer. 10: 25; Ps. 79: 6; cf. Rom. 1: 18–25). This is marked by **passionate** (a word implying desire suffered by helpless man) **lust** (*epithymia*; cf. 2: 17) which is, by contrast, active and violent. **6.** 'All sexual looseness represents an act of injustice to someone other than the two parties concerned. Adultery is an obvious violation of the rights of another, but the same principle applies to pre-marital promiscuity. For the impure person cannot bring to the marriage that virginity which is the other's

due' (Morris, *TNTC*). **wrong** may be intransitive or it may have **brother** as object and mean not overstepping his rights (Darby, *A New Translation*). **take advantage of:** To defraud covetously. Three reasons are given for purity. First is the divine judgment, seen both now and at the Last Day (2 C. 5: 10, etc.). This truth had been part of Paul's mission preaching. **7.** The second reason is that God's purpose in effectually calling man is a moral one. **8.** Thirdly, impurity contemptuously ignores the indwelling Spirit of God whom God continually gives (timeless present) to the believer.

9, 10a. Brotherly Love. This section is linked with the previous one by the thought of the Spirit's indwelling. Paul has already commended the Thessalonians for their love (1: 3; 3: 6). Here he uses a word, *philadelphia*, which outside the NT refers to love of the brother by birth. Its existence within God's family is a sign of divine paternity (Jn 13: 34 f.). **taught by God:** Cf. Jn 6: 45; Isa. 54: 13, thus fulfilled. **10a.** Love within a church inevitably expresses itself in a wider context.

10b–12. Honest Work. 2 Th. 3: 6–13 shows that some people, encouraged by the generosity of others, had given up work. One motive may have been the supposed nearness of the *parousia* and the need to proclaim it, but they had become idle busybodies, ignoring the truth that we show love for our fellow-men by serving them in daily work. **11. make it your ambition:** Paul's advice is still relevant. 'If we cannot be holy at our work, it is not worth taking trouble to be holy at any other times' (Denney). Manual labour was despised by the Greeks, as by many (including some of the Carpenter's disciples) today. **12.** Two reasons are given for Paul's advice. Non-christians were being disgusted by these adventist busybodies and layabouts; also they were parasites on the church. **anybody** may be masculine (as NIV) or neuter: 'have need of nothing'.

VI. THE PAROUSIA (4: 13–5: 11)

13–18. The Dead in Christ. Although the mission preaching at Thessalonica had included a good deal about the *parousia* (cf. 2 Th. 2: 5), some questions had naturally remained unanswered. In particular the church (disturbed no doubt by recent deaths) wondered whether the glories of the great day were reserved for the living. Paul explains that dead Christians will share in the triumph, as in the resurrection of their Lord. Premillennialists of whatever school will tend to interpret **grieve** (13) as arising from a fear that the dead may not be raised until the second resurrection at the end of the millennium. Thus in v. 15 Paul explains that the blessing of the living will not **precede** that of the dead in Christ. Postmillennialists and amillennialists, however, point to **like the rest of men, who have no hope** in v. 13, saying that this implies a definitely pagan type of grief, i.e. the Thessalonians doubted whether their dead would be raised at all (cf. the error of the Corinthian church). V. 14 is explained as agreeing with this, for Paul points to the fact that Jesus both **died and rose again**. V. 17, it should be noted, speaks simply of being always **with the Lord** but does not specify whether the saints return to the earth with Him immediately, or after an interval, or whether the 'new heavens and earth' follow at once. **13.** The resurrection gave new force to the Jewish custom (1 Kg. 2: 10, etc.; Dan. 12: 2) of referring to death as 'sleep'. Phil. 1: 23 warns against arguing from the metaphor that the dead are unconscious. Pagan literature and the words of unbelievers today show an absence of the sure hope that characterizes Christian experience. Christians may **grieve** for their own loss, but not for the departed. **14.** The unspoken assumption is that believers, alive or dead, are 'in Christ' and thus share His glory. It is through Jesus that death has become sleep to His people. **15.** Paul refers to an otherwise unrecorded saying of Jesus, or possibly to a prophetic revelation. He classes himself with those who **are left** alive until the *parousia*. But this is less of an intellectual judgment concerning the nearness of Christ's return than a spiritual attitude of expectancy. **16.** Far from being at a disadvantage, the Christian dead will rise first. The Gk. suggests that either the three signals are one or at least that the **voice of the archangel** is identical with **the trumpet call of God. loud comand:** Often a military term (cf. Prov. 30: 27; Jn 5: 28). **voice of the archangel:** anarthrous, perhaps 'as of an archangel'. **trumpet call of God:** Lightfoot points to Zech. 9: 14 as a warning against a literal interpretation. Among relevant OT references are Exod. 19: 16; Jl 2: 1 ff. (cf. v. 11); Isa. 27: 13. **17.** It is trivial to pander to curiosity by interpreting this verse in a materialistic manner. The Lord comes, and His people meet Him **in the clouds** (Mk 13: 26; cf. Dan. 7: 13), not as a vehicle but as a sign of glory and divine majesty. The air was thought of as the realm of demons, but their power has now been broken (Col. 2: 15). **to meet** is used in the papyri of the official reception given to a visiting governor, whom his citizens escort into the city from which they have come to meet him. The fact, not the location, of the Church's being with her Lord is stressed. **18.** The purpose of this teaching is practical, not the satisfying of idle speculation. Christians need not **grieve** (13) for they have God-given words of consolation, far transcending any human comfort.

5: 1–3. The Time is Uncertain. Paul now reassures those who feared they might not be ready for the *parousia*. He had already told them it would be unexpected and now simply repeats this, pointing out that unbelievers will be overwhelmed by it. **1. times and dates** refer respectively to the length of time that will pass (*chronoi*) and the special character of the divinely appointed moments (*kairoi*) when God acts. **2. the day of the Lord** is an OT term for any occasion when God acts in a striking way to overthrow His enemies (cf. Isa. 2: 12) and for the final overthrow (cf. Jl 2: 31). It is the day of the Lord, as opposed to man, or the nations. The prophets insisted on its ethical implications (Am. 5: 18 ff.). In view of the fact that Jesus is called Lord throughout the NT it is unnecessary to distinguish between 'the day of the Lord' and 'the day of (our Lord Jesus) Christ' (1 C. 1: 8, etc.). **like a thief:** Cf. Mt. 24: 43. **3. labor pains** is often used in rabbinical writings (and *e.g.* Mt. 24: 8) of the sufferings preceding the establishment of the messianic age. Here the thought is of suddenness, or perhaps inevitability.

4–11. The Need to Watch. The word **night** leads to the thought of the moral darkness of the unbeliever. The believer must be ready to receive the salvation that the day of the Lord will bring to him. **5. sons of the light:** This use of 'son' to indicate close connection or resemblance is a Heb. idiom (cf. sons of the prophets . . . of Belial . . . of perdition) and the Qumran community applied this title to themselves. **sons of the day** extends the thought; the believer's sphere is the age to come. **6, 7.** As **asleep, alert,** and **self-controlled** are figurative, so presumably is **drunk.** From the literal nocturnal activities of 'sons of darkness' Paul draws the lesson that believers must be alert and self-controlled. **8.** As in Rom. 13: 12 f., Paul passes for no obvious reason to a military metaphor. The difference between these verses and Eph. 6: 13–17 (cf. Isa. 59: 17) warns against emphasizing details in applying the passage; Calvin comments (quoted by Morris in *NLC*): 'The man that is provided with faith, love and hope will be found in no department unarmed'. **9, 10.** Those who fear are reminded that the wrath is not for the believer. Salvation here (as in v. 8) includes all the believer's benefits in Christ. Its root in election is pointed by **appoint,** and man's response by **to receive.** V. 10 is the only plain statement in the two letters of the truth that Christ died for us; it also teaches that He shares His risen life and power with His people. **awake or asleep** is figurative for 'live or die'. The thought in this passage connects with 4: 13–18 rather than 5: 6. The apostle is not encouraging moral slackness. **11.** As in 4: 18, Paul expects practical use to be made of the truth; we notice his tactful conclusion.

VII. FINAL EXHORTATIONS
(5: 12–22)

12 f. Attitude to Elders. It is plain from Ac. 14: 23 that Paul selected elders to guide the churches he founded, and so in Thessalonica. Inexperienced as they were, they may not have dealt tactfully with some of the problems mentioned. Here Paul's appeal to respect them is based, not on their formal office but on the service they render. He speaks gently—**we ask** —and reminds believers that an elder's duty of leading and counselling (NEB) involves hard work. They are to be respected (lit. 'known' —perhaps 'acknowledged') and lovingly esteemed, not because of personal charm, but for the work they do. The injunction to **live in peace** is primarily, though not exclusively, addressed to the rank and file. **12. in the Lord:** The sole ground and limiting extent of authority in the church. **13. in the highest regard:** Cf. 3: 10 where (almost) the same rare word is translated 'most earnestly'.

14 f. Mutual Responsibilities. Paul begins by thinking of the duties of elders, but imperceptibly is drawn to speak of the relationship between all believers. **14. idle:** Cf. 4: 11; 2 Th. 3: 6 f., 10 ff. The word *ataktos* and its cognates are used in the NT only in these places. Originally a military term, 'out of order', 'undisciplined', it came to be used of 'idle and careless habits' (Milligan). **timid:** Cf. 4: 13; 5: 4, 9. **help:** The word implies standing by another and is used in Mt. 6: 24. **15. try to be kind:** The stress is not on a moral ideal but on strenuously pursuing (*diōkō*) what benefits others. cf. Rom. 12: 21.

5: 16–22. Prayer and Spiritual Matters. Paul now gives advice about the Christian's personal relationship to God and to problems in the church and daily life. **16.** The Christian must rejoice even when persecuted (cf. v. 15). **17.** Unceasing prayer is the secret of continual joy. **18.** Thanksgiving will result from the realization gained in prayer that God's purpose is behind all circumstances. Although **this** is singular, it must refer to all three, prayer, rejoicing and thanksgiving. God's will is not remote or impersonal but is revealed **in Christ Jesus. 19.** To **put out the Spirit's fire** might be to discourage the exercise of spiritual gifts, but it seems unlikely that such a tendency should exist in so young a church. At Corinth the opposite danger existed. Probably the emphasis is ethical, a warning against conduct which might stifle the Spirit's operation (cf. Eph. 4: 30). **20. prophecies:** 'the impassioned and inspired utterance of the deep things of

God' (Lightfoot). Regarded at Corinth as inferior to speaking with tongues, prophesying may have been in danger of being undervalued at Thessalonica because of its abuse by second advent enthusiasts. **21. Test everything:** The Christian must not uncritically accept—or reject—spiritual teaching but must be careful in all matters to distinguish the good and hold on to it. He will thus avoid 'evil in any form' (Phillips).

VIII. CONCLUSION (5: 23–28)

Only God Himself can give the strength necessary to obey the apostolic injunctions. Having prayed for this, Paul closes with three requests and a typical benediction. **23.** Although there is a reference to v. 13, the OT meaning of **peace** as prosperity and security is more prominent. Sanctification implies both separation for God, and its ethical result. A tri-partite nature of man is not necessarily implied here, for **be kept** and **blameless** are singular. **blameless** has sacrificial associations in the OT (Dt. 27: 6; Jos. 8: 31) and more explicitly in Philo. **24.** The fact that the Thessalonians have experienced the calling of God guarantees their final sanctification (Rom. 8: 29 f.). He is trustworthy. **25.** Paul never forgot his dependence on the prayers of others (cf. Rom. 15: 30; Eph. 6: 19; Phil. 1: 19). **26.** Kissing was a normal mode of greeting friends and became a sign of the mutual affection within the Christian brotherhood (cf. Rom. 16: 16; 1 Pet. 5: 14). Later it continued (to the present day in some liturgies) as a ritual observance. In the West today, even the most conservative are content to substitute the handshake as a rule—an interesting example of how it is legitimate to reinterpret apostolic injunctions in the light of later conditions. The point in this verse, however, is that individual members of the church are to be kissed as a greeting from Paul. **27.** It is difficult to explain the severity (unparalleled in the NT) of Paul's language without knowing more of the circumstances. Did he fear that the elders might withhold the contents of his letter from some? Or (as seems more likely) is he ensuring that his words reach even the idlers and the downhearted referred to in v. 14? **28.** Paul ends his letters, normally written by an amanuensis, with a few words in his own hand; here the first person singular of v. 27 may mark the point. As usual, he replaces the conventional 'Farewell' of his day with a prayer for grace, thought of as fully expressed in the Lord Jesus.

2 THESSALONIANS

While few critics have doubted the authenticity of 1 Thessalonians, rather more have found difficulties in the Second Letter. Many of these are subjective, or disappear when the circumstances of the letter's writing are understood.

Thus it is said that the style of 2 Thessalonians is formal, that it makes a greater use of the OT, that it is inconceivable that the same author should in so short a period write two letters showing such dissimilarity. These arguments are no more convincing than the suggestions that 2 Thessalonians was written first (but see 2: 2, 15; 3: 17), or that it was intended for the Jewish and 1 Thessalonians for the Greek half of the church (in spite of Paul's insistence on the unity in Christ of Jew and Gentile).

There is more force in the objection that the eschatology of the letters is inconsistent. Ultimately it results from a misunderstanding, but a misunderstanding that has not been without its effect on theology. It is pointed out that the apocalyptic section, 2 Th. 2: 3–12, is without parallel in Paul's letters, not only because of its affinities with other apocalypses, but because it teaches that the second coming is to be preceded by signs. Elsewhere Paul speaks of the suddenness of the Lord's return; some scholars conclude that 2 Thessalonians is not Pauline. One way out of the difficulty has been to distinguish between a 'coming for the saints' at any moment and without preceding signs, and a 'coming with the saints' some years later, after the 'tribulation', which will be preceded by the signs listed in 2 Th. 2. If it is true, then Paul's handling of the situation at Thessalonica was surprising. The answer to those who believed that the day of the Lord had begun would, on this view, be simple.

Paul had only to point out that the saints would all have been raptured before the onset of the day of the Lord. Instead, he lists events that must precede it, without a hint that the Thessalonians would not be in the least affected by them. We are thus led to conclude that Paul saw no conflict between saying that the *parousia* was at hand, and that certain events must nevertheless precede it.

It is relevant to point out that Joel, centuries earlier, had said that the day of the Lord was *at hand* (1: 15; 2: 1; 3: 14.) When God leads men to think earnestly about the last things, He gives a sense of urgency to their thoughts. This will have been true of Paul. But secondly, as F. F. Bruce says (*NBC*, p. 1058), 'A distinction should be made between suddenness and immediacy'. Paul's insistence in 1 Thessalonians 'on the suddenness of the *parousia* had been understood to mean its immediacy'. Hence there was some agitation, and a continued refusal by a small group to work for their living. In these circumstances, it is plain why Paul wrote again within a few weeks (for he is still accompanied by Silas and Timothy) repeating so much that he had already said, but going into greater detail about the *parousia*, and showing that it could not have already begun, because the 'man of lawlessness' had not yet appeared. A greater number of OT references is inevitable, as the teaching given has its roots ultimately in the OT. On this view the resemblances and the differences between the two letters are simply explained, as is the apostle's insistence in 3: 17 on the genuineness of the letter as opposed to the falsity of others in circulation (2: 2) that contained different teaching.

ANALYSIS

IX CHURCH DISCIPLINE (3: 14 f.)

X CONCLUSION (3: 16–18)

I. GREETING (1: 1 f.)

These verses are identical with those beginning the First Letter (*q.v.*) with two exceptions. One is the description of God as **our Father** in v. 1. The other is the addition of the words following **peace** in v. 2. This formula is found in every Pauline letter except Col. and 1 Th. The equality of Father and Son is taken for granted.

II. PRAYER AND ENCOURAGEMENT (1: 3–12)

It seems likely that some at least of the Thessalonians had felt unworthy of Paul's commendation in the First Letter for he repeats this in emphatic terms. He encourages those who were faint-hearted in face of continued persecution, pointing out its purifying effect (5) and that it seals the doom of the enemies of God's people. The day of the Lord will mean judgment for these, but all (without exception) who have believed will then be glorified and enjoy rest. He prays they may then be found worthy, being strengthened by God's grace. **3, 4.** The Thessalonians' faith and love are singled out (cf. 1 Th. 1: 3) for commendation; their courage in facing persecution even leads Paul to boast of them. **ought:** As a duty to God. **rightly so:** In fairness to the Thessalonians. **4. we boast:** Emphatic; as founders of the church, they would have kept silent had not the behaviour of the Thessalonians been so remarkable. **faith:** Probably religious (the cause of the **perseverance**) rather than moral (synonymous with it). **are enduring:** Note the present tense. **5–10.** Their steadfastness in suffering witnessed to the truth of the gospel, which includes the vindication of right and the overthrow of evil. There will be rest for the saints when the Lord Jesus Himself is revealed in a dual role, as the judge of the ungodly and the source of the glory which will then be seen in believers. The premillennialist sees in these verses a description of the final judgment that will follow the rebellion at the end of the millennium. Some would make what is perhaps a rather over-elaborate distinction between the 'day of Christ' or *parousia*, understood as primarily concerning the Church (the 'coming for the saints') and the day of the Lord, or revelation of the Lord Jesus, understood as primarily concerning the world (the 'coming with the saints'). The postmillennialist and amillennialist, however, interpret them of the single crisis of the *parousia* and judgment. V. 7 seems to link the **relief** for afflicted believers with the revelation (*apoka-*

lypsis) in wrath of the Lord Jesus. Premillennialists, who separate these by the millennium, regard the words from **and to . . . troubled** as parenthetical. **5.** Their steadfastness, itself a result of God's grace, shows they are truly his, and are suffering **for** (on behalf of) His kingdom, as are the missionaries. (The Gk. places 'also' before **are suffering**.) **6.** God's justice is seen, not only in his vindication of the righteous, but in retribution on their enemies. **7. to us as well:** A gentle reminder by the apostle of the missionaries' sufferings. **when . . . revealed:** Lit. 'in the revelation (*apokalypsis*)'. This word applied to the Lord's return stresses the unveiling of his glory and greatness. The phrase refers back to v. 6 (**repay back trouble**) as well as v. 7. Both are part of the *apokalypsis*, which is described in three ways, being **from heaven** (the unseen place of divine glory where the Lord is now enthroned); **with his powerful angels**, or better, 'with the angelic ministers of His power'; **in blazing fire**, a sign in the OT of God's majesty. The whole passage is reminiscent of the OT (cf. the RV references) and Paul does not hesitate to apply to Jesus words used in the OT of Yahweh. **8.** Divine vengeance is free from personal spite; the word here used is cognate with 'justice'. Two signs are mentioned: wilful ignorance of God (cf. Rom. 1: 18, 28), seen in all men; and disobedience to the gospel, here described with great dignity as **of our Lord Jesus. 9.** The **punishment** (lit. 'a just penalty') is said to be **everlasting**, which means unending, what ever further meaning it may have. 1 C. 5: 5 and 1 Tim. 6: 9 show that **destruction** (Gk. *olethros*) is not annihilation but (as in NEB) 'ruin'. NIV adds **shut out** (not in the Gk.) to bring out the meaning of the phrase **from . . . power**. To see the Lord's face and the glory of His might is here thought of as a privilege, whose loss is the chief punishment of unbelievers. But cf. Isa. 2: 10, 19, 21. **10.** The day of the Lord brings glory to Him by displaying the glory of His people (cf. Jn 17: 10; Rom. 8: 18 f.). **marveled at:** By faith, believers have already seen Jesus glorified by the Father; but as faith gives place to sight they are 'lost in wonder, love and praise'. **because . . . believed:** A reminder that the Thessalonians will be included. **11. With this in mind** refers in general to the salvation the apostle has spoken of, or else to **counted worthy** (5). Paul is praying that the Thessalonians will, by God's power, live a life that will deserve a favourable verdict. **12.** Cf. Isa. 66: 5 (LXX); Mt. 5: 16; Jn 17: 10, 22. **the grace:** 'the source whence all glorification springs' (Lightfoot). As a frequent title, the word **Lord** is best taken with **Jesus Christ**, not co-ordinate with **God**.

III. EVENTS PRECEDING THE PAROUSIA (2: 1–12)

1 f. The End is not Yet. Paul warns his hearers against teaching ascribed to him that the day of the Lord has begun. It is interesting to note that these verses associate **our being gathered to him** with **the day of the Lord. 1. Concerning:** *hyper* here combines the meanings 'about' and 'in the interests of'. **coming:** *parousia*. **being gathered:** The word is used in *e.g.* Mt. 24: 31; Heb. 10: 25. **2.** Two words are used to describe the unsettling effect of the teaching. It drives men 'from their sober sense like a ship from its moorings' (Frame, ref. **unsettled**) and also produces a lasting state of disturbance. Paul, who is not quite sure what has happened, refers to three possible ways in which the false teaching may have reached Thessalonica. All are governed by **supposed to have come from us:** They are (*a*) a reported divine revelation, (*b*) spoken teaching ascribed to the apostle, and (*c*) a letter, either forged or mistakenly attributed to him. It was being said that the series of events constituting the day of the Lord had begun to take place.

3–12. The Great Apostasy. Paul now outlines the events that must precede the day of the Lord—a widespread rebellion against God, directed by **the man of lawlessness**. He is supplementing teaching already given to the Thessalonians (5), which we do not possess. Hence 'this passage is probably the most obscure and difficult in the whole of the Pauline correspondence and the many gaps in our knowledge have given rise to the most extravagant speculations. It will be well . . . to maintain some reserve in our interpretations' (Morris, *NLC*). The **man of lawlessness** (as the better MSS read) is identical with the one spoken of by the early Church as 'antichrist' and regarded (in spite of 1 Jn 2: 18) as an individual to appear in the days immediately before the *parousia*. We need look no further for the origin of the idea than the book of Daniel (see 7: 25; 8: 9 ff.; 11: 36 ff.). These passages refer primarily to Antiochus Epiphanes, who in 167 B.C. installed in the Temple at Jerusalem the cult of Zeus, whose representative he claimed to be. That there is to be a further fulfilment is shown by the way in which the Lord takes the words of Daniel and applies them in Mk 13: 14 to the end-time. (His words are not exhausted either by Caligula's attempt to place his statue in the Temple or by the siege of Jerusalem.) This figure is placed in the general context of **the rebellion**, which is also spoken of in the eschatological discourse of Mk 13 as occurring in the last days. The word, *apostasia*, was used in secular Greek of a political revolt and in the LXX (cf. Jos. 22: 22) of rebellion against God. It is not stated whether **the rebellion** occurs among Jews, in the church, or is a general refusal by men to acknowledge the Creator's authority. Some interpreters understand these references to the man of lawlessness and the persecution elsewhere associated with him as phenomena existing throughout the whole of the Church's history (cf. 1 Jn 2: 18). Others expect an individual and specific fulfilment in the last days. Among these, some expect the 'translation' of the Church to take place before the appearance of the antichrist and consequent persecution, while others believe that the Church will be on earth throughout this period. **3. is revealed:** Emphatic by position, and contrasted with the *apokalypsis* of the Lord in 1: 7. **man doomed to destruction:** A Hebrew idiom, applied also to Judas Iscariot (Jn 17: 12). **4.** The 'lawless one' opposes Christ, rather than presenting himself as a false messiah, for he acknowledges no other authority than his own, whereas the Messiah is by definition subordinate to God. **God's temple:** History shows this is not the temple of Herod. But Paul may have had in mind Gaius's attempt ten years previously to have his image set up in the Jerusalem temple. See Mt. 24: 15; Mk 13: 14. The Letter to the Hebrews appears to rule out the idea of a future temple with sacrificial worship. Some interpreters, however, understand this verse literally of a revived Jerusalem cultus taken over by antichrist, in which case the worshippers are said to be the people of Israel, and Gentiles converted by Jewish preaching. Although the term may mean the Church (cf. 1 C. 3: 16 f.) yet, as Morris (*NLC*) says, 'Would not the Church by that very fact (sc. its being dominated by the man of lawlessness) cease to be the *Christian* church?' It is probably best understood as a vigorous description of his claim to divine authority, the temple being the very centre and expression of God's sovereignty and presence among men. **5.** The continuous tense shows that Paul repeatedly gave instruction on this subject (cf. Ac. 17: 7). The Thessalonians should not need this recapitulation. **6 f.** Already present in the world is a secret lawless influence (cf. 1 Jn 2: 18) which will finally issue in the rebellion of the last days. But there existed also in the apostle's day a restraining power (well understood by his hearers, though not by us) which would prevent the revelation of antichrist so long as it continued to operate. This power is referred to in v. 6 as neuter and in v. 7 as masculine. It might grammatically be the Holy Spirit, but this idea is 'without support in other parts of the NT' (Hogg and Vine).

Nor does this theory account for the apostle's mysterious way of referring to the subject. This objection also applies to the idea that the restraining power is an angelic being (cf. Dan. 10). Many understand the reference of a Roman emperor, seen as an individual (masc.) or as a personification of the empire (neuter). The best (though by no means certain) interpretation sees the Roman empire as symbolizing the God-given authority of government (Rom. 13: 1–6), which acts as a barrier against such un-bounded claims as those made by the man of lawlessness. Paul dare not refer openly to the disappearance of the empire; hence his veiled language. **holding back:** The word may mean (*a*) to hold fast (1 Th. 5: 21); (*b*) to restrain (Lk. 4: 42); (*c*) to rule. **now** may indicate time (as RSV) or logical connection (NIV). **time:** *kairos* (see 1 Th. 5: 1). **7. secret power:** A secret too deep for human ingenuity (*Arndt*), often with the implication that it has been revealed by God. The forces of lawlessness, although op-erating beneath the surface of affairs, would not be revealed until the restraint of law and order disappeared. Then they would appear, embodied in the man of lawlessness. Lightfoot points out the contrast with 1 Tim. 3: 16. **he is taken out of the way:** Lit. 'he comes out of the midst'. Arndt-Gingrich show this is simply an idiom, meaning 'is removed'; cf. Kelly's note *in loco*. **8.** Paul passes over the career of the man of lawlessness, and gives no timetable of events, confining himself to asserting the great spiritual truth of the ultimate triumph of Christ. Again he speaks of the revelation (cf. vv. 3, 6) of antichrist, but if he is revealed, so too will the Lord Jesus shine forth (*epiphaneia*) when he comes (*parousia*). 'The radiance of his coming' (Phillips, NEB) will break the power of **the lawless one. over-throw . . . mouth:** Cf. Isa. 11: 4; Ps. 33: 6. No battle takes place. Morris aptly quotes Luther: 'A word shall quickly slay him'. **9, 10a.** Paul summarizes the 'ministry' of the anti-christ, again bringing out the parallels with that of the Lord. First he stresses the principle behind it—the active power (*energeia*) of Satan. Then he describes the accompanying miracles. Three words are used, all applied elsewhere to the miracles of Christ. **All** points to their variety. As **miracles** they reveal superhuman might; as **signs** they teach some truth; as **won-ders** they amaze men. **Counterfeit** in no way impugns the genuineness of the miracles; rather does it mean 'false', for the teaching of the 'signs' is a falsehood. Finally, the accompany-ing effects on men. The faint-hearted at Thessa-lonica are reassured—only those on the road to ruin (1 C. 1: 8) will be deceived. **10b–12.** In all this the justice and sovereignty of God are vindicated. Behind these verses lies the charac-teristic OT insight that all events, even the

activities of the powers of evil, are ultimately in God's control (cf. *e.g.* 1 Chr. 21: 1; 2 Sam. 24: 1; 1 Kg. 22: 23). Men are doomed because they **refused to love the truth,** not even desiring it. Such moral delinquency exposes them to God's judgment. As in Rom. 1 God 'gives them over', so here in His sovereignty He allows them to be deceived, and they believe (lit.) **the lie** as opposed to **the truth.** This has a moral as well as an intellectual reference (cf. 1 Jn 1: 6) so that their ultimate condemnation is not on intellectual grounds; not to **believe the truth** inevitably results in having **de-lighted in wickedness** (cf. Rom. 1: 32). A similar process may be seen in the OT when Pharaoh's heart is hardened first by himself, finally by the Lord. **sends:** The present tense both indicates the certainty of the prediction (prophetic present) and points to the present operation of this principle.

IV. THANKSGIVING AND EXHORTATION (2: 13–15)

The emphatic **we** seems to imply a return to the theme of 1: 3 f., as Paul encourages the faint-hearted: 'Now we, for our part, ought to . . .' The same Lord who will destroy the law-less one loves the Thessalonian believers.

Their salvation is assured, because God Him-self has both chosen them in eternity, and in due time **called** them **through** the **gospel.** It is logical, then, that they live accordingly. **13. from the beginning:** *ap' archēs,* to interpret this of the 'beginning' of the apostolic mission is not suitable in the context (cf. Rom. 8: 29 f., 1 Pet. 1: 2, both parallels to this passage as a whole). Nor does the variant reading 'first-fruits' (*aparchēn*) make such good sense, though equally well attested. **sanctifying work . . . and belief:** God's purpose includes both the Spirit's total activity and man's response. **14. to this:** i.e. salvation, further defined in the rest of the verse. **15.** Believers, secure in the purpose of God, should not be disturbed in either their beliefs or their behaviour as were some at Thessalonica. The present imperative of **stand firm** implies a continuous action; the word **hold** suggests a firm grasp. The verse reminds us that the Christian faith is derived from Christ Himself (tradition, *paradosis,* meaning something handed down; cf. 1 Tim. 6: 20; 2 Tim. 1: 12, 14) and not a subjective construction. At first it was passed on **by word of mouth,** but by the time of this letter was already being committed to writing (**by let-ter**). Today we possess the *paradosis* in the pages of the NT. No other tradition, oral or written, is binding on the Church.

V. PRAYER FOR THE BELIEVERS (2: 16 f.)

The structure of the Second Letter resembles

that of the First (cf. 1 Th. 3: 11–4: 1). Paul realizes the power of evil, hence this prayer. The singular aorist participles (**who loved . . . gave . . .**) associate Father and Son in the crucifixion and Pentecost, which are the foundation of true Christian hope, the gracious gift of God. In Christian experience they bring **encouragement** and confidence (cf. 1 Th. 3: 2) which affect every aspect of life.

VI. A REQUEST FOR PRAYER (3: 1 f.)
The closing section (cf. 1 Th. 4: 1) opens with a request for prayer that the preaching at Corinth may prosper as it had at Thessalonica, both advancing (cf. Ps. 147: 15) and being approved of for its effect on men. Also for deliverance from a body of perverse and evil men. **faith:** Probably saving faith, rather than a body of belief.

VII. THE FAITHFULNESS OF GOD (3: 3–5)
The word **faith** speaks to Paul of the Saviour's reliability (3) so that he trustfully relies (4) on the converts' continued obedience (anticipating the requests of vv. 6–15). An awareness of God's love and the endurance of the Lord Jesus will **strengthen** them (cf. 1 Th. 3: 2).

VIII. HOW TO TREAT THE IDLERS (3: 6–13)
The problem hinted at in 1 Th. 5: 14 has become serious. Paul refers to the missionaries' example (7–9) and teaching (6b, 10) to reinforce his injunction that the work-shy minority (11) be disciplined (6) until they obey the apostolic demand (12). **6–9.** Paul's insistence on the need to imitate him is a challenge to all preachers. For his reminder of the missionaries' behaviour see 1 Th. 1: 5 f.; 2: 5–12, and for his insistence on the apostolic right to support cf. 1 C. 9: 3–14. For **in idleness** and **idle** see 1 Th. 5: 14. **6.** We notice the appeal to the Lord's authority here and in v. 12. **keep away:** *stellō*, to furl a sail, retreat into oneself. But the offender is still a **brother** and the purpose of the withdrawal is his restoration to the shared life of the church when he ceases to sin against the brotherhood (cf. v. 13 and 2 C. 2: 7). **8.** Cf. 1 Th. 2: 9; Ac. 18: 3. **9. model:** Cf. 1 Th. 1: 7. **10.** This habitual (continuous tense) teaching agrees with that of the rabbis, who insisted that even a scholar must learn a trade, and not live by his shady of the Law. The origin of the saying is unknown. **will not:** A deliberate refusal—those who *cannot* work must be helped. **11.** By a play on words Paul points out how the lack of occupation has demoralized the fanatics. Morris (*NLC*) drily conjectures: 'We may conjecture that they were trying to do one or both of two incompatible things, namely, to get their living from others, and to persuade others to share their point of view about the second advent, and so persuade them to stop working also'. **12.** Tactfully Paul (*a*) speaks of the layabouts in general terms (*b*) does not merely **command** but adds **and urge**, and not 'by' but **in . . . Christ. 13.** This exhortation to the rest of the church **never tire of doing what is right** may refer to the need to maintain a sympathetic attitude to the others or (taking it with vv. 14 f.) to take a firm line with them.

IX. CHURCH DISCIPLINE (3: 14 f.)
Those who had ignored the admonition of the elders (1 Th. 5: 14) must, if they now disobey the apostle's written word (as binding as if spoken) be taken note of in some unspecified manner. They must not be associated with. The same word is used in 1 C. 5: 9, 11, but there a more severe discipline is in view—'not even to eat' with the offender. Nor are the disobedient one whit less the people of God, but still 'of the family' (NEB).

X. CONCLUSION (3: 16–18)
Paul prays that all, including the idlers, may know God's peace (cf. 1 Th. 1: 1) and presence. He ends the letter, as was his practice (1 C. 16: 21; Gal. 6: 11; Col. 4: 18, explicitly and **in all my letters**) by taking the pen from the amanuensis and writing a few words himself to prove the genuineness of the document (cf. 2: 2). The benediction (18) is identical with that of 1 Th. apart from the word **all**. Even here we may see Paul's care for those he had censured.

BIBLIOGRAPHY

BEST, E., *First & Second Epistles to the Thessalonians*. *BNTC* (London, 1972).

BRUCE, F. F., *1 and 2 Thessalonians*. Word Biblical Commentary, (Waco, 1982).

DENNEY, J., *The Epistles to the Thessalonians*. EB (London, 1892).

FRAME, J. E., *The Epistles to the Thessalonians*. ICC [on the Greek text] (Edinburgh, 1912).

HOGG, C. F., and VINE, W. E., *The Epistles to the Thessalonians* (London, 1914).

KELLY, W., *The Epistles to the Thessalonians* (London, 1893).

MARSHALL, I. H., *1 and 2 Thessalonians*. NCentB (London, 1983).

MILLIGAN, G., *The Epistles to the Thessalonians*. [on the Greek text] (London, 1908).

MORRIS, L., *The First and Second Epistles to the Thessalonians*. TNTC (London, 1956).

MORRIS, L., *The First and Second Epistles to the Thessalonians*. NLC (London, 1959).

NEIL, W., *The Epistles to the Thessalonians*. MNT (London, 1950).

VOS, G., *The Pauline Eschatology* (Grand Rapids, 1930).

WHITELEY, D. E. H., *Thessalonians*. NCB (Oxford, 1969).

THE PASTORAL LETTERS

ALAN G. NUTE

Despite the fact that it was only in the 18th century that the letters to Timothy and Titus began to be known generally as The Pastoral Epistles, it was actually in 1274 that Thomas Aquinas, referring to 1 Timothy, wrote, 'this letter is, as it were, a pastoral rule which the Apostle delivered to Timothy'. The term, though not technically accurate, does suffice to indicate that in these letters attention is directed to the care of the flock of God, to the administration of the church and to behaviour within it. Although the letters are addressed to Timothy and Titus and contain personal injunctions, they are clearly written for the benefit of the churches concerned.

Authorship

Doubt about the Pauline authorship of this group of letters was probably first expressed during the opening years of the last century. Particularly since the publication of P. N. Harrison's *The Problem of the Pastoral Epistles* (1921) debate on the subject has been greatly intensified.

In the main, the arguments against Pauline authorship rest on the historical situation, the type of false teaching condemned, the stage of church organization described, and the vocabulary and style.

It is readily agreed that the historical allusions (*e.g.* 1 Tim. 1: 3; 2 Tim. 1: 16, 17; 4: 13, 20; Tit. 1: 5; 3: 12) cannot be fitted into the framework of the Acts. Even allowing for the selective nature of Luke's record of Paul's activities, any attempt to find room there for the happenings described in the passages listed is futile. The well-known theory that a period of liberty followed the imprisonment with which the Acts concludes would accommodate these events and, in the light of the evidence available, appears not unreasonable. Certainly Paul was expecting release (Phil. 1: 25; 2: 23, 24; Phm. 22), and the atmosphere of the final paragraphs of Acts points that way rather than towards execution. Tradition supports the idea of a temporary period of freedom during which Paul engaged in further missionary labours and which was cut short only by his final imprisonment in Rome (1 Clement 5: 7; Eusebius, *Ecclesiastical History* ii. 22. 1 f.). Some modern scholars also subscribe to this reconstruction of events (W. M. Ramsay, *St. Paul the Traveller and Roman Citizen*, 1920, pp. 360 ff.; R. St. J. Parry, *The Pastoral Epistles*, pp. xv ff.; D.

Guthrie, *NT Introduction: The Pauline Epistles*, p. 212). As a theory it has as much likelihood as the one which makes Paul's activity, if not his life, terminate with the last chapter of Acts.

Considerable effort has been expended in an attempt to prove that the false teaching referred to in the Pastorals reflects 2nd century Gnosticism. On the other hand, many deny this, pointing out that Gnosticism must have had its origins in the 1st century, and that what is here condemned is much closer to incipient Gnosticism than to the fully-developed form of that heresy. Indeed, it is not easy to discern any essential difference between the errors reproved in these letters, and an amalgam of the Gnosticism refuted in Colossians and the Judaism combated in Galatians. The approach adopted is admittedly different, refutation is replaced by denunciation, to which is added guidance on the practical handling of the situation. This may well be explained by the fact that the letters are not addressed to churches but to apostolic representatives well acquainted with Paul's answers to these heresies, though still needing his advice about the way they should deal with them.

Further objection is made on the ground that the organization of the early Church could hardly have developed during the apostolic age to the degree here described. The position accorded to Timothy and Titus, as well as Paul's use of the term 'bishop', is said to reflect a monarchical episcopate, which it is known did not arise until the beginning of the 2nd century. It is obvious that Timothy and Titus exercised a larger authority than that of the normal New Testament elder, but this was clearly as representatives of the apostle rather than as monarchical bishops. Where the singular of the word 'bishop' occurs, it is undoubtedly used in a generic sense. Far from suggesting that one bishop should be appointed in each church, Paul emphasizes the plurality of 'elders in every town'. The argument that the church government described in the Pastorals is post-apostolic loses much of its weight when the teaching of these letters with regard to bishops and elders is compared with the references to such in Ac. 14: 23; 20: 17, 28; Phil. 1: 1; 1 Th. 5: 12, 13. Of particular interest is Paul's address to the Ephesian elders (*episkopoi*) inasmuch as they were actively responsible in that church prior to Timothy's assignment there. Finally, in connection with church organization, it will be well to compare the advice given in 1 Tim. 5 regarding widows, with Ac. 6: 1; 9: 39, 41.

Probably, however, the weightiest objection to Pauline authorship stems from the clearly discernible differences between the language and style of the Pastorals and that of other letters accepted as Paul's. This argument is set out forcibly in P. N. Harrison's work. He points out that a large number of words occurring in this group of letters have not made an earlier appearance in Paul's writings, and that some, indeed, are not found elsewhere in the NT. Moreover, some that have been used previously now bear a different meaning. For example, whilst the word 'faith' had earlier borne the meaning of 'trust', here it is used to describe 'the body of doctrine'. But the most outstanding stylistic deviation from the earlier Pauline letters is in the use of particles, those words in which individual style is so largely involved and which seem not subject to the same degree of change as a writer's vocabulary and general style. The difference between Paul's other letters in this regard is less than the difference between them all and the Pastorals. In addition, there is a conspicuous absence of certain prepositions and pronouns which characterize Paul's acknowledged writings. At first sight the argument arising from statistical analyses of the words used is impressive, but its force is diminished when other factors are taken into consideration. Full weight must be given to the not inconsiderable variation of vocabulary and style which occurs in his other letters. Change of both vocabulary and style can also be attributed to some extent to the purpose in the mind of the writer. He is dealing with situations essentially different from those tackled in earlier letters. Nor should the age of the writer be ignored, or the fact that he is addressing individuals and not churches.

The method of writing which was adopted must also be borne in mind. It seems probable that the author employed an amanuensis who was permitted a measure of latitude in the actual phrasing of the material dictated to him, the letter being subsequently scrutinized by the author, and on occasion, concluded and signed with his own hand (1 C. 16: 21; Col. 4: 18; 2 Th. 3: 17; Gal. 6: 11; cf. Rom. 16: 22 where the amanuensis adds his own signature). Indeed it is likely that with increasing years and the effect on health of the rigours of his service the apostle would depend more largely than ever before on the help an amanuensis would be able to give. This so-called 'editor-secretary theory' might well account in part for the different selection of words used. It might also supply a solution to the neat, somewhat pedestrian style which replaces the more familiar

Pauline one where parentheses and anacolutha, like a series of explosions, shatter orthodox grammatical construction. Quite apart from these explanations it is probable that too great a reliance has been placed on linguistic arguments for the determining of authenticity, especially where these are based on statistical analysis.

It remains only to notice the hypothesis which suggests that fragments of genuine Pauline material were woven into the letters as we now have them by a close follower of his and were then issued under Paul's name. This is for some an attractive solution, but for many it is hardly satisfactory. They prefer to accept the *prima facie* claim which the letters make, to have been written by Paul. Again, despite all the attacks, there remains a complete absence of any positive external evidence against Pauline authorship, while, on the other hand, the numerous personal references in the letters possess a distinctively genuine ring. For a more detailed examination of these matters the student is referred to D. Guthrie, *NT Introduction: The Pauline Epistles* and the *Tyndale Commentary on the Pastorals*, J. N. D. Kelly, *The Pastoral Epistles* (A. & C. Black, 1963), and to articles by B. M. Metzger and E. Earle Ellis (see Bibliography, p. 1576).

Purpose

It is clear that here the apostle is giving his two friends and trainees help and encouragement in connection with their responsibilities in the churches to which they have been sent. In the case of the letter to Titus he is obviously confirming in writing instruction already given orally (1: 5). This is probably true also with regard to the letters to Timothy. Paul is anxious for the preservation and communication of 'sound doctrine', and for the maintenance of proper order and becoming behaviour in the local churches. This is made the more pressing by the increasing opposition of false teachers and the uncertainty of his own future. He here makes wise provision for the day when the voice of apostolic authority will be silent. Timothy, in particular, receives exhortation to self-discipline and the cultivation of other personal qualities.

The atmosphere of 2 Timothy contrasts strongly with that of 1 Timothy and Titus. Martyrdom, now, seems imminent, and the apostle is anxious that Timothy should come to him as quickly as possible. He asks him to bring Mark with him, and also bids him fetch the cloak left at Troas together with the books and the parchments. Church organization and administration receive no mention, and matters of doctrine are barely touched upon. The personal note is dominant and Paul passes on to his young friend encouragement, advice and a solemn charge. This brief letter is permeated by a spirit of warm affection, and bears a clearly discernible note of urgency.

Value

The present-day relevance of these letters is anticipated by the writer when he refers to the characteristics of the 'last days'. He contends that the development of evil will demand from the people of God a determination to submit obediently to the Scriptures, which, he asserts, are adequate for every situation which may confront them. 'Foolish and stupid arguments' must be avoided, and error must be opposed with a positive presentation of the truth. Such truth Paul here enshrines in terse statements, some designated as 'trustworthy sayings' and affirmed to be 'deserving of full acceptance'. In this way the mischievous teaching of the legalists and others who upset the believers is reproved, and the principles upon which they are to be dealt with are set forth. Not least important in this connection is the guidance given for the ordering of church life; with the appointment of elders and deacons, and the provision of an adequate ministry of the Word of God. That it may prove difficult to implement these directions should not deter. Rather should the difficulty presented by the contemporary situation be regarded as a chief reason for endeavouring to follow out these things which the Spirit through the apostle has set down for all ages. The emphasis upon the deposit of truth, namely the faith contained in the gospel and in Scripture, indicates its continuing authority.

There may also be detected throughout, a constant demand for godliness of character and the prosecution of good works. Since a harmony is shown to exist between the foundation truths of the faith, proper order in the church, and piety of life, evidence of all three is declared essential for the maintenance of an effective witness.

1 TIMOTHY

ANALYSIS

I. GREETINGS (1: 1, 2)

As he has done on a number of earlier occasions, Paul opens this letter with an assertion of his apostleship, and, in this way, justifies the note of authority frequently sounded in the letter. This apostleship, so the writer claims, is his by divine command, its dual source being **God our Savior** and **Christ Jesus our hope**.

The repeated occurrence of the former expression in the Pastorals, is in marked contrast to its almost complete absence elsewhere. Its use in these letters may well arise from a desire to encourage Timothy and Titus, for they face, on the one hand, strong opposition, and have to deal, on the other, with those in whose lives spiritual progress is slow. The reference to **Christ Jesus our hope** might also imply a further cause why they should be confident.

Timothy is affectionately addressed as one, who, in addition to having been brought to faith through Paul's instrumentality, gives proof of being a **true**, a 'genuine', **son**. Upon him is pronounced the threefold blessing of **grace, mercy and peace**, and this is invoked from the Father and the Son conjointly. The bracketing of Christ Jesus with the Father twice in these opening verses is not without significance especially in the light of subsequent teaching in the letter concerning Christ as mediator (2: 5).

II. PAUL AND TIMOTHY (1: 3–20)

i. A reminder of the charge given (1: 3–11)

The commission previously given is here reaffirmed, for the task is one of great difficulty and is not lessened by Timothy's natural reticence. The apostle's representative in Ephesus obviously needs to be nerved for the fulfilment of his responsibilities. He will find, too, that critics will not be lacking, and the opportunity to appeal to such a charge, given him by Paul, might well prove useful.

The persons needing to be reproved were mistakenly concentrating on **myths and endless genealogies**, probably of Jewish origin. **Myths** conveys the notion that these ideas were of their own inventing, lacking completely any foundation in the Scriptures of truth. **Genealogies** is used in a wider sense than that customarily accorded it, and describes fatuous and extravagant interpretations of OT history, possibly mingled with certain Gnostic philosophical notions. These are said to be **endless**, for those who wander along these strange by-paths find themselves in an interminable labyrinth, leading nowhere.

This state of affairs had arisen, it seems, from an ambition on the part of these men to be teachers. Lacking, however, the necessary understanding of the truth, as well as the ability to communicate it, they had turned aside to **controversies** and **meaningless talk**.

Paul recommends two tests by which the hollowness of such false doctrine may be exposed. (a) *All teaching must be judged by what it produces.* In contrast to the irrelevance and fruitlessness of the speculative and vain, the true ministry, here designated **God's work—which is by faith** will issue in the noble quality of love. The steps by which it will reach this goal are here traced for us. Not being mere sentiment, nor unrelated to ethical standards, the love spoken of finds birth in a heart that is pure. This, in turn, results from **a good conscience**, which is itself the product of **a sincere faith** (5). These virtues vindicate the character of the true teaching. The 'wilderness of words' (v. 6 NEB) to which the other teaching tends is its obvious condemnation. (b) **Sound doctrine**, a term confined to the Pastorals, is *the standard by which all teaching is to be tested.* Healthy, and healthful in its influence, this doctrine was, by this time, well defined; its essential features being crystallized in **the glorious gospel of the blessed God** (11). **False doctrines** (3) would immediately stand out in contrast with the true doctrine, which consisted not in theological dogma but in apostolic teaching.

Against these standards Paul measures the false teaching of these whom Timothy must reprove. In ignorance they were expatiating on the law. Mingling it with fable and fanciful interpretation they misconstrued its true purpose. **We know** (v. 8 contrasts strongly with their confident assertions of v. 7) introduces a declaration of the nature as well as the proper function of the law. 'It is good', says Paul, in a phrase reminiscent of Romans 7. Inapplicable to **the righteous**, its primary purpose is to expose and condemn sin. Paul appends a catalogue of some of the glaring vices prohibited by the Mosaic law. So to preach the law as to make men aware of their sinfulness is to use the law aright: it is a use which accords with **the glorious gospel**. This he claims is no human invention, but the truth divinely **entrusted** to him as an apostle.

ii. Paul's experience of divine grace (1: 12–17)

The mention of the entrustment to him of the message of the gospel gives rise to a paragraph of praise. It commences with the simple—**I thank Christ Jesus our Lord** (12) and reaches its climax in the noble doxology of v. 17.

Thanksgiving is first for inward strength to discharge the task allotted him. This Paul proceeds to relate to his commissioning. It was an appointment based on the divine foreknowledge that he would prove faithful, both as an apostle and a steward of the gospel. This exhibition of God's grace toward him is heightened, as he points out, by the fact that it was displayed to one who previously was **a**

blasphemer and a persecutor and a violent man. This spite, vented against the church, was nevertheless directed against the Christ Himself (Ac. 9: 4); even so, he records, **I was shown mercy.** The word suggests that this sovereign act of pity was utterly undeserved, and the phrase that follows does not negate this. Deeds of ignorance arising from blind unbelief afforded Paul no ground for claiming the mercy of God, but did place him within its range. His ignorance was culpable but not deliberate, and as such it called forth the divine compassion (cf. Lk. 23: 34; Ac. 3: 17). Where mercy is found, grace is not far distant, and here Paul tells of this grace which brought him, through incorporation into Christ Jesus, both faith and love.

The whole experience recalls to Paul's mind a **trustworthy saying** (15). Five of these occur in the Pastorals (1 Tim. 1: 15; 3: 1; 4: 9; 2 Tim. 2: 11; Tit. 3: 8), the formula not appearing elsewhere in the NT. Epigrammatic in form, these axiomatic truths of the Christian faith would be easily memorized. Being frequently repeated they soon became almost proverbial in the early Church. The saying Paul here quotes presents, in language matched only by Jn 3: 16, the central fact of the gospel. It **deserves full acceptance.** He further magnifies the grace of God in declaring that it was lavished upon him, **the worst of sinners.** The language appears extravagant, but here is neither rhetorical hyperbole nor sentimental self-depreciation. In deep humility Paul remembers his bitter opposition to Christ and His Church, and conscious of the enormity of his sin describes himself by this phrase (cf. 1 C. 15: 9; Eph. 3: 8). The exercise of mercy towards such a one as himself, Paul sees as a dramatic and convincing example of Christ's **unlimited patience.** None need despair, either for themselves or for others. All who **believe on him** (this is an unusual construction conveying the thought of reposing faith in Christ the firm foundation) are brought into the life eternal.

The contemplation of these things calls forth the doxology of v. 17. It is ascribed to **the King eternal**, as the One who, in His sovereignty, is working out His redemptive purposes through all the ages. **Immortal, invisible, the only God:** He is not as man—mortal. He is not even visible to human gaze, neither can He be compared with 'gods many' for He is **the only God.**

iii. The charge reiterated (1: 18–20)
The subject introduced in v. 3 is resumed. Timothy is affectionately addressed as **my son**, and Paul reminds him that the fulfilment of the mandate given him is but the proper outcome of his initial call. The origin of that call is suggested by the phrase **the prophecies once made about you** ('led the way to thee', RVmg). This may refer to a spiritual premonition granted to Paul as he approached Lystra on his second missionary journey, that Timothy, converted on an earlier visit, should share with him the burdens of his work for God. This was confirmed by prophetic utterances, possibly by some of Paul's company or, more probably, by the presbyters who, after conference with Paul, shared in Timothy's commissioning (4: 14). The recollection of such a call is calculated to inspire Timothy as he continues to **fight . . . the good fight.** For this fray it is imperative that he be 'armed with faith and a good conscience' (19 NEB). The emphasis is on the necessity of matching a firm faith with moral integrity (cf. 1: 5; 3: 9). This contrasts with such as Hymenaeus and Alexander, who rejecting **faith and a good conscience . . . have shipwrecked their faith.** The order is significant. Where a consciousness of sin fails to lead to repentance and forgiveness, it produces an inconsistency in life which is destructive of faith. Such conduct Paul castigates as blasphemy.

Hymenaeus (2 Tim. 2: 17) and Alexander were blatant examples of those who sought to divorce belief and behaviour. The stern disciplinary action exercised in their case was remedial in intention, as indeed such discipline must ever be. The expression **whom I have handed over to Satan** might suggest adversities supernaturally inflicted (cf. 1 C. 5: 5; 11: 30; Ac. 5: 1–11), or simply excommunication. The phrase would then describe the removal of the person from the sphere where God rules, to that where Satan has sway.

III. THE CHURCH AT PRAYER (2: 1–15)
i. Subjects for prayer (2: 1–7)
Paul now proceeds to the particular items of the charge which he has just laid upon Timothy. **First of all** stresses the primary importance of public prayer, an importance further emphasized by the use of **I urge**, and also by the mustering of what are virtually synonyms to describe this exercise. It is more likely to be for the purpose of emphasis, than to provide a four-fold classification of prayer. These words do, however, suggest different aspects of prayer. **requests**—arising from specific and urgent need. **Prayers** is a more general term. **Intercession** combines the thought of a petition offered to a superior with the intimacy of the child/father relationship. It does not necessarily include the representing of the needs of others. **Thanksgiving** find their place here for expressed gratitude must ever be mingled with our prayers.

for everyone: Prayer must never be parochial. The sectional interests of the heretical teachers must not be reflected in the prayer-life of the church. Instead, in its universal range will be included all who are **in authority** (cf. Rom. 13: 1–7; 1 Pet. 2: 13–17). The object stated is that life being lived under settled conditions, Christians shall discharge their daily duties and their Christian service with simple dignity and true piety. The prayer and its fulfilment are linked with the realization of God's gracious purpose in man's salvation (3, 4). This would obviously be furthered through the conduct described in v. 2 and the service listed in v. 7; both being assisted by conditions of peace and security.

V. 4 must not be pressed to support a numerical universalism. The expression **all men** tells us that salvation is for all, even as in v. 1 the phrase indicates that prayer must be made for all, that is, *without distinction*. On God's part is 'desire', on man's 'responsibility', the latter thought being conveyed by the phrase **come to a knowledge of the truth**. This divine desire for man's salvation has found concrete expression, and the means for it has been provided as vv. 5 and 6 declare. The universality of the gospel is the concept which underlies these verses. **there is one God and one mediator:** Strait is the gate by which all must enter. **a ransom for all:** The work He accomplishes is of infinite value. As a mediator, the Saviour answers the need poignantly expressed in Job's wistful cry for *someone to arbitrate between us, to lay his hand upon us both* (Job 9: 33). The Saviour's incarnation was His qualification for the task—'himself man' (RV). As a ransom (*antilytron*) Christ fulfils the declared purpose of His incarnation—'The Son of man came . . . to give his life a ransom' (*lytron*) (Mt. 20: 28). The addition of the prefix *anti* extends the meaning from 'a price' to 'a corresponding price'. This is further illumined by the use of the preposition *hyper*, the effect of which is to underline the vicarious nature of Christ's sacrifice.

This is the testimony borne by Christ to God's desire that all men be saved, and Paul rejoices in being himself appointed a herald, an apostle and a teacher of this glorious truth.

ii. Engaging in prayer (2: 8–15)
Turning again to the matter of prayer Paul gives direction as to the spiritual qualities to be seen in those who draw near to God. Mention is made first of all of **men**, as distinct from the women referred to in v. 9. 'Apparently all male members of the church had an equal right to offer prayer, and were expected to use this right' (C. K. Barrett, *The Pastoral Epistles*, p. 54). The prerequisite of holiness is not related to place, for prayer may be made **everywhere**, but to the character of the one who prays. The standard of conduct demanded of such is conveyed by the phrase **holy hands**, and the disposition of the heart by a freedom from

anger and inward argument (cf. Ps. 24: 3, 4; Jn 4: 21, 23.).

The adverb which introduces v. 9 *hōsautōs* seems somewhat inadequately rendered **also**. By the use of 'similarly' (Kelly) or 'so, too' (Knox) the demeanour of the women, as the integrity of the men (8), is related to the prayer-meeting. The responsibility placed upon women is that they be free from ostentation and display in matters of dress. Instead, those who would be known as Christian women should concentrate upon the apparel of **good deeds** (1 Pet. 3: 3, 4) and in this way 'adorn the doctrine'. But gradually the apostle leaves the subject of prayer to advise concerning the rôle of women in the church in general. The word **silent** can hardly be intended in an absolute sense. In all probability the RV is the more accurate when it renders *hēsychia* 'in quietness' in both v. 11 and v. 12 (cf. v. 2 of this chapter where the adjective *hēsychios* is appropriately translated 'quiet'). There is no question here of a ban of silence being imposed upon women, either in public prayer or in the gathering for instruction, where active dialogue would feature prominently. The intention is rather to forbid a self-assertive attitude, and to require that women be marked by restraint and a readiness to display the qualities of 'quietness' and **full submission**.

When, however, it comes to the matter of teaching, Paul's tone becomes more authoritative. In addition to repeating his exhortation regarding 'quietness', he declares categorically, **I do not permit a woman to teach or to have authority over a man**. This prohibition in no way contradicts Tit. 2: 2, 3 (see note). It relates to teaching in the church in the presence of men and to the fact that authority in matters concerning the church is not committed to women. The apostle's argument is founded on the initial relationship of man and woman (13, 14). The reason supplied by v. 13 is similar to that given by Paul in 1 C. 11: 8, in which passage the subject of the relationship of the sexes in the Christian church is developed in greater detail. A further plea for a submissive spirit is based on the fact that the woman in succumbing to deception revealed a tendency which disqualifies for leadership. It was when Eve acted in independence and took the initiative, refusing to remain but a help-meet for Adam, that sin entered.

The meaning of v. 15 has been oft debated. Clearly it suggests to the woman that she is not to think that her contribution is of negligible worth. The realization of her noblest instincts lies in the realm of motherhood (NEB), in which, provided **they continue in faith, love and holiness with propriety** she will know that salvation which is 'achievement' in its highest sense. Her greatest work will be ever in the home, and her profoundest influence in the moulding of the children she bears. This verse can hardly be interpreted as a mystical allusion to the incarnation which appears to be the nuance of 'the child-bearing' (RV) and especially where Gal. 4: 4 is given as a cross-reference.

IV. RESPONSIBILITY IN THE CHURCH (3: 1–16)
i. The overseer (3: 1–7)
Having enjoined upon Timothy the responsibility of ensuring that the prayer-life of the church is ordered aright and that public worship is conducted with propriety, Paul proceeds to advise him concerning those upon whom responsible office in the church will devolve. Another 'trustworthy saying' introduces this section, though some early expositors attach it to the statement which precedes it (see NEB footnote).

In the light of the fact that the common, present-day meaning of the word 'bishop' bears no relation to the position Paul envisages when he refers to *episkopoi*, it seems regrettable that not only the RSV but also the majority of other recent translations have adhered to it. The NIV gives more accurately **overseer**, but even this is not without certain ecclesiastical overtones. The idea underlying the word is that of a guardian, superintendent or leader. Instead of **being an overseer** a stricter translation might provide us with the expression 'overseership' or with such a phrase as 'spiritual supervision and leadership'. Even so, the interpretation based on the omission of the word office should not be so weighted as to imply that it is the task which is all-important, and that formal recognition and acknowledged leadership may be ignored. That such were officially appointed, known, respected and obeyed is clear from such passages as 5: 17; 1 Th. 5: 12, 13; Heb. 13: 17; Ac. 20: 17. Quite obviously Paul is not commending an aspirant guilty of unworthy self-seeking, but rather one who is moved by a true desire for the welfare of God's people. The thought in mind is surely that one who desires to serve in this capacity, sets his heart upon **a noble task**. The responsibility involved is onerous, but its fulfilment highly satisfying.

The rest of the paragraph (vv. 2–7) is concerned with standards of character and conduct which should mark the overseer; any lack of these would disqualify for leadership in the church. It is clear that his life in the church cannot be considered as independent of his personal and domestic life. He must be known to be pure in conduct, disciplined in habits, balanced in outlook, and free from those sins that mark the society and the age in which he lives. It is improbable that Paul had polygamy in mind in using the expression **the husband of but one wife**. Perhaps he deemed it advis-

able to recommend to men responsible for setting an example of strict personal discipline, that they refrain from remarriage on the death of a partner. For today, the phrase might be allowed a wider application, against a precipitate or injudicious remarriage. Further, if the elder enjoys the privilege of parenthood then his home life should have provided him with a training ground for the exercise of that fatherly care which he will be required to show towards the believers. Recent converts are deemed unsuitable for this task; it has its perils for which they would be ill-equipped. His reputation must stand high with **outsiders**; otherwise he will prove an easy prey to Satan's subtlety. The mention of **disgrace** possibly suggests that failure in this respect might occasion slander on the part of the 'slanderer' (RSVmg.) Thus Paul gives a picture of the true leader. These verses must not be turned into a hard, uncompromising list of legal requirements; they are those spiritual and moral standards which God sets before any who would take up service for Him.

ii. The deacon (3: 8–13)
The word *diakonos*, found some thirty times in the NT, is customarily translated either *servant* or *minister*, and denotes one engaged in rendering some particular service. It is used to describe domestic servants, civil rulers, preachers and teachers, and in a general way to denote Christians engaged in work for their Lord or for each other. This has led many to the conclusion that Paul is not alluding to a specific group within the church, but to all who are active in Christian service of one form or another. On the other hand, the fact that the paragraph follows immediately the one relating to overseers certainly implies that the cases are parallel and that these **deacons** have recognized functions. Support for this view might also be adduced from Phil. 1: 1 where Paul sends greetings to 'all the saints in Christ Jesus at Philippi, with the overseers and deacons', which, apart from the passage under consideration, is the only place where the NIV translates *diakonos* by 'deacons', though it should be noted that in Rom. 16: 1 mg Phoebe is described as 'a deaconess of the church in Cenchreae'. Somewhat surprisingly the seven appointed 'to serve tables' (Ac. 6) are not designated by this term.

The very vagueness which obtains in connection with this matter may be taken as indicative of the latitude to be enjoyed, and accorded to others, in the ordering of church life. Whether the deacons be taken as a distinct class upon which devolves the responsibility of attending to those matters, administrative and financial, delegated to them or as those who in a general way serve Christ and His Church, the requirements outlined in these verses are equally apposite. In addition to the demand for moral and spiritual qualities similar to those set down for elders, Paul adds three things: (a) the desirability of submitting the deacon to a period of probation (10); (b) the need for the women who contribute to the service of the church to measure up to certain standards of character and behaviour (11); (c) the beneficial results accruing to the one who faithfully discharges his tasks as a deacon. This anticipates the possibility that some not called to leadership might view the work of a deacon with disdain (13).

iii. Behaviour and belief—purpose in writing (3: 14–16)

Paul having expressed the hope that he might soon visit Timothy, goes on to explain his object in **writing . . . these instructions**. It is that he might provide apostolic guidance for the ordering of their church life. He employs three expressions to describe the church. (a) **God's household** (*oikos*): It is the same word as is used in vv. 4, 5 and 12, and the thought is clearly that of the members of a family group. In this the NIV is more accurate than the AV and RV—*house*. (b) **the church of the living God:** If the previous phrase conveys the thought of intimacy, this one emphasizes dignity. Paul might have had in mind the lifeless idol revered at Ephesus in contrast to which the God whose *ecclesia* they are is the living God. The temple devoted to 'Diana of the Ephesians' was renowned for its massive pillars; they as a company of God's people constitute (c) **the pillar and foundation of the truth:** Paul has discharged his responsibility as a custodian of the truth (2 Tim. 1: 12; 4: 7), Timothy must guard it too (6: 20; 2 Tim. 1: 14), but it must also be the task of the whole church.

There follows a summary of the truth enshrined in what was undoubtedly part of an ancient Christian hymn. This truth the writer readily concedes is a **mystery**, that is, it was hitherto both unknown and unknowable, but has now been revealed. 'Great . . . is the mystery', it has been suggested, echoes the cry of Ac. 19: 28, 34.

By the pronoun **He** with which the hymn opens, is to be understood, Christ. The Greek reading which underlies the AV translation 'God' is almost certainly wrong. Three couplets of contrasts direct attention to the Saviour. The opening phrase tells of His incarnation. The pre-existent One **appeared in a body** (cf. Jn 1: 14). In apposition to this is the statement —**vindicated by the Spirit**. Spelling the word **Spirit** with a capital letter the NIV denotes the Holy Spirit as the agent of Christ's vindication. If this is the case, then the mind is naturally directed to the climax of this vindicating work, namely the resurrection. If, however, the word should refer to His own human spirit, then we have the thought that throughout His whole

career the Saviour knew an inner vindication; that His conscience gave a positive approval of every thought, word and deed. **A body** would seem more likely to have in apposition to it the human spirit, whereas when 'flesh' is used metaphorically, its natural antithesis is the divine Spirit.

The next couplet declares the extent of His renown. It is not easy to know what is intended by the phrase **seen by angels**. If the second line applies to the resurrection, then it would be best to follow a chronological sequence and see this as a reference to the angelic witnesses of His ascension, but it could be interpreted in a much wider sense. It will be remembered that in His birth, temptation, agony in the garden, resurrection and ascension He was 'seen of angels'. There follows the statement that He has been **preached among the nations**. Far beyond the narrow limits of Jewry has Christ been heralded. For Paul the universalism of the gospel had special appeal (cf. 2: 4 f.).

The final lines tell of His acceptance on earth and in heaven. **Believed on in the world** speaks of the triumph of His work in the hearts of men; **taken up in glory**, refers to the enthronement which was heaven's verdict in relation to Him and His accomplished mission.

Viewed entirely, the hymn arches from Bethlehem to the heights of heavenly majesty; the Saviour is seen as the object of angelic contemplation and the subject of apostolic preaching; and He is acclaimed as the One vindicated not only in His spirit, but also in the hearts of all who believe in Him.

V. DANGERS TO THE CHURCH (4: 1–16)

i. The apostasy described (4: 1–5)

As a 'bulwark of the truth' (RSV) the church must be aware of the evils which will array themselves against it. Paul claims that the consistent witness of the Spirit is that the situation will deteriorate. He may have had in mind OT prophecy, the teaching of Christ (*e.g.* Mt. 24: 11), or the illumination granted by the Spirit to NT prophets. By **later times** Paul is possibly referring to that period indicated by the phrase 'after I leave' which he uses in his address to the Ephesian elders (Ac. 20: 29 f.), though the expression could equally well be extended to cover all the days from Pentecost until the end of the age (cf. 2 Tim. 3: 1). The period will be characterized by apostasy. The underlying cause of this is traced to **deceiving spirits**. These contrast strongly with 'the Spirit of truth', the author of that 'sound doctrine' to which frequent reference is made in these letters. They introduce their **teachings** through men described by Paul as **hypocritical liars**. Such may well have made claim to inspiration. **Whose consciences have been seared** means either that their consciences have become insensitive, having been cauterized by persistent submission to evil influences, or that they bear the brand-mark of Satanic ownership. The particular form of error into which they lead their dupes is a false asceticism. Probably it reflects the Gnostic heresy which regarded matter as intrinsically evil, and which found specific expression in recommending avoidance of marriage and abstinence from certain foods. Paul's answer relates particularly to **foods**, but the principles which govern it could easily be applied to the question of marriage. He gives it in three propositions: (*a*) That the divine intention in creation is not to deny these things to man, but to bestow them upon him. They are to be **received with thanksgiving** (3). This is true for all men, but is here applied specifically to **those who believe and who know the truth**. (*b*) That everything God has created **is good**. This strikes at the root of the heresy (cf. Mk 7: 19; Ac. 10: 15). (*c*) That things are legitimately enjoyed by the Christian when they are **received with thanksgiving** (4). Guthrie points out that the word *apoblētos* (to be refused) occurs only here in the NT, and that it is used in the sense conveyed by Moffatt's translation: 'nothing is to be "tabooed" provided it is eaten with thanksgiving'. The ability to render sincere thanks to God for the gift received is the determining factor. The phrase **it is consecrated by the word of God and prayer** must not be taken to mean that the food itself is affected, but rather that thanksgiving to God for it, and enjoyment at meal-times of conversation on the Scriptures, imparts a sanctity to the occasion.

ii. Timothy's rôle (4: 6–16)
Having set before Timothy the difficulties likely to be encountered, Paul now advises him regarding his personal life and spiritual responsibilities. He must endeavour to counteract the heresies, but this must be done in a spirit of gentleness and humility. Later, Paul bids him speak with authority (11), but **point these things out to the brothers** is a phrase which suggests the offering of advice rather than the peremptory laying down of the law.

For himself, it is essential that he should be **brought up** (metaphorically 'nourished') **in the truths of the faith**. Considerable prominence is given in the Pastorals to the Word as God's agent in conversion, and the controlling factor in life and service. Here the use of the present participle reminds Timothy that though he has indeed **followed** them in the past, he needs still to feed his soul constantly upon **the truths the faith and of the good teaching**. He must studiously avoid being sidetracked from these centralities. Heretics concentrate on **godless myths and old wives' tales** and Paul, recognizing a perennial danger,

warns the servant of God lest he become immersed in teachings which, lacking an adequate basis, prove futile in their outworking. Instead, says the apostle, continuing on a positive note, **train yourself to be godly**. A favourite metaphor is introduced. The rigours of athletic training are contrasted with the self-discipline required of one who makes godliness his goal, so is the transient value of **physical training** with the far more extensive and enduring benefits accruing from godliness. Its effects for good permeate every realm and are experienced both here and hereafter.

Authorities appear to be almost equally divided as to whether the familiar 'trustworthy saying' formula of v. 9 refers backward to v. 8 or forward to v. 10. One or other must have been in the mind of the apostle, but as it is well-nigh impossible to discern which, it seems not unreasonable to point out that it can be suitably applied to either, and particularly to the climax of each verse.

Once again Paul takes up the metaphor of the preceding section. **labor and strive** tells of weariness endured and intense effort expended. The secret of perseverance of this tenacious quality is found in a **hope** which is **in the living God**. He is the Creator and Preserver of **all men**, indeed He provides and offers *life* through His saving work to all. But by **those who believe**, these things are known and experienced in a special way.

The final paragraph of the chapter (11–16) assumes a more personal character. If, in answering the heretics, Timothy must adopt a quiet modest approach, in teaching the truths just enunciated he must **command**. By nature diffident, not overstrong physically, he needs to be encouraged to teach with authority. His comparative youth (probably he was in his late thirties) may lead some to treat him with a measure of suspicion, if not disdain. He must not allow himself to be intimidated. But as C. K. Barrett points out, 'a minister secures respect, not by the arbitrary use of authority but by becoming an example' (*op. cit.*, p. 71). Criticism is adequately silenced only by conduct, and true authority in the spiritual realm springs not merely from advancing years, but from a genuine piety. This must reveal itself in **speech** and **in life** both being governed by 'love, fidelity and purity' (NEB). These are the three great qualities required in the **minister of Christ Jesus**. V. 13 recommends three activities to which Timothy should give himself. The first is **the public reading of Scripture**. This had been an essential part of synagogue worship (Lk. 4: 16; Ac. 13: 15, 27; 15: 21), it was to form an equally important constituent in the worship of Christians. Out of it would flow the **preaching** (*paraklēsis*) and **teaching** (*didaskalia*). The ministry would consist in practical exhortation as well as doctrinal instruction. For the exercise of these responsibilities due preparation must be made—**devote yourself to**, but for their proper discharge nothing less than a divinely bestowed **gift** would avail. Such a gift Timothy had received. Its reception would ever be linked in his mind with the solemn occasion when the apostle and the elders of his home church had publicly attested their fellowship with him in his going forth with Paul to the work to which God had called him. This step had been the subject of **a prophetic message** (cf. 1: 18) and it was undoubtedly this that gave them confidence in identifying themselves with Timothy by the laying on of hands. Paul had probably taken the lead in this act (2 Tim. 1: 6). In addition to the action signifying identification, it appears that it was the moment of the impartation of a **gift**. The references to the imposition of hands in the OT, the Gospels and the Acts seem frequently to combine the two ideas of identification and transference, though it need hardly be said that it is nowhere inferred that it lies within human power to *effect* the transference, whether of sins or of blessing. The laying on of hands was accompanied by prayer (Ac. 6: 6; 8: 15 ff.; 13: 3). In this case the blessing sought and subsequently bestowed by God, was a gift adequate to the task requiring to be performed. Reminding Timothy of this event, Paul exhorts him **do not neglect your gift**. It must be developed (cf. 2 Tim. 1: 6), and this will demand that he **be diligent in these matters**. In fact, adds the apostle, **give yourself wholly to them**. Such concentrated effort will result in an obvious progress. V. 16 is in the nature of a summary. Timothy is reminded that he must keep under careful and constant scrutiny both what he is in himself, and what he teaches. Only thus will God's saving purpose be realized in his own life, and only thus will he bring to the same joy others also.

VI. REGARDING RELATIONSHIPS (5: 1–6: 21)
i. Seniors and juniors (5: 1–2)
In this chapter, the apostle turns to a new theme, that of personal relationships. The opening verses introduce the topic with words of general advice. The recommendations are addressed directly to Timothy, but are of wider application both to his day and ours. The word *presbyteros* is here rightly translated **older man**. Where the necessity of speaking straightly to such arises, care must be taken that there be no lack of courtesy. The **older man** must be treated with the deference accorded **a father**. **Older women** are to be regarded with that respect and affection which a mother has the right to expect from her children. With his male contemporaries Timothy is to enjoy that sense of freedom and friendship which exists between **brothers**. To the recommendation that he should regard the **younger women as sisters**, Paul adds the common-sense caveat that in this there should not be the slightest hint of impropriety.

ii. Widows (5: 3–16)
The plight of the widow in the 1st century can be gauged from the various references to widows in the Gospels and the Acts. By the time this letter was penned the Church had recognized its obligations and relief was being administered (Ac. 6: 1). The need had now arisen, however, to lay down certain principles regulating this whole question of the distribution of the Church's largesse to widows. It seems that certain widows may have been trading on their widowhood. Instead of supporting themselves from their own resources, or looking to their Christian relations for help, they were relying on the church for their support. Guidance is given to Timothy as to the way he should deal with this delicate situation.

First, Paul distinguishes between widows and **those widows who are really in need** (3, 5). She is in the latter category who is left with no living relatives who can help her, whose faith reposes in God and expresses itself in diligent prayer. **Give proper recognition**, which includes the thought of support, is to be accorded the one who is a widow 'in the full sense' (NEB); she is to be assisted financially (16).

Where the widow has believing relatives they should feel it incumbent upon them to minister to her need. The primary religious duty of a widow's **children or grandchildren** would be to find in this an opportunity of making some recompense to her. The final phrase of v. 4 echoes the fifth commandment. Paul states the truth negatively, and yet more emphatically in v. 8. Failure to make provision for **relatives, and especially for his immediate family** is equivalent to a denial of **the faith**. Indeed, inasmuch as pagans discharge their duties in this matter, to neglect this basic responsibility is to be **worse than an unbeliever**. A widow, however, may have means of her own. To use these in self-indulgence is to die to true life (v. 6; cf. Rom. 8: 6), and must exclude her from the church's aid. Timothy must give corrective ministry along this line (7).

The same subject continues in the paragraph which follows. Paul here recommends that certain of the widows receiving support be **enlisted** for specific work in the church. It would seem, as already inferred, that this was not so much a qualification for receiving relief, but was a condition for the discharge of certain tasks. The stipulations are that the widow must be over sixty, must not have remarried, and must have a reputation for **good deeds**. Her good works must have included the **bringing up** of **children**, for she may be required to act as foster-parent, and **hospitality**, for she may well be asked to engage in this service for the church. And altogether her life must have been marked by the humility that serves, though the task be menial, and by the devotion which seeks to relieve distress of every kind.

The advice not to enlist **younger widows** (11) suggests that these qualified for assistance, but were not suitable candidates for the recognized ministry accorded the older women. Apparently, the acceptance of a widow for service on behalf of the church implied that she would not remarry. It would be unfair to restrict a younger widow thus. In the early days of her widowhood she might impulsively desire to give herself wholly to Christian work, but in the event of an opportunity of remarrying she might regret the step taken. Then to renounce her 'calling' would be to stand self-condemned, her **first pledge** having been **broken** (12). Another reason is given. The tasks given the widow to perform might carry with them an inherent temptation, especially when it involved visiting other people's homes. This could easily lead to idleness, and produce mischievous results as spiritual conversation degenerated into gossip and as one desiring to help ended by becoming an interfering busy-body. The older widow is presumed to have learned sufficient wisdom not to fall a victim to this peril. As for the **younger widows**, Paul recommends that the better course for them would be to remarry, and to take up again the responsibilities of family and home. In this way would the critic, human or Satanic, be silenced. Tragically enough, some of these younger widows had already 'taken the wrong turning and gone to the devil' (15, NEB). These verses should have been noted by subsequent un-Pauline advocates of celibacy. With v. 16 Paul harks back to vv. 4 and 8.

iii. Elders, and Timothy himself (5: 17–25)
Having set down the qualifications of the overseer (3: 1–7), Paul now turns to the responsible attitude which should be adopted towards him. He uses the synonymous term **elder**, and though the word is the same as that translated **older man** in v. 1, it is clear that here it bears its technical meaning. The apostle's first recommendation is that there should be a realistic appreciation of the elder's personal needs. **Double honor** contains the two elements of respect and remuneration. 'That financial, or at any rate material, rewards are primarily intended cannot be evaded' (J. N. D. Kelly). As the assistance given to the widows was dependent on their meeting certain conditions, so those elders deserve not only respect but a suitable remuneration who are engaged

in the demanding tasks of leadership (*proistēmi* —'rule', lit. 'to stand before'), **preaching and teaching**. This injunction is underlined by two quotations, one from Dt. 25: 4 and the other from words spoken by the Saviour (Lk. 10: 7). Paul may possibly have learned the latter from Luke himself, who in all probability had by this time completed his Gospel.

Next, the apostle advises Timothy to be wary of listening to **an accusation** brought **against an elder**, 'for none are more liable to slanders and calumnies than godly teachers' (Calvin). He must insist on there being present two or three witnesses to corroborate the allegation (cf. Dt. 19: 15). Obviously this would prove an effective deterrent on the irresponsible gossip or the malevolent person. But where the **accusation** is proven and the elder remains unrepentant, in that he persists in **sin**, the matter is sufficiently grave to warrant a public rebuke (20). It has been argued that this verse applies not only to elders, but to all who sin. The context would suggest that it is the elder who is in view. The sin of one holding the position of a leader is the more reprehensible, its effects the more serious, and if these effects are to be counteracted, public censure would seem to be the only course.

Timothy is now solemnly counselled to act with complete impartiality in the implementing of **these instructions** (21). This will require moral courage and Paul seeks to impart this by expressing himself strongly on this question of being entirely free from biased judgment or prejudiced action.

Another peril of which Timothy is apprised by his mentor, is that of making rash appointments to office within the church. The advice, **do not be hasty in the laying on of hands**, immediately following the counsel regarding elders, suggests that Paul is warning Timothy against impulsively associating those with himself who would subsequently prove unsuitable. **The sins of some men are obvious:** He is not likely to be misled by such, **the sins of others trail behind them** (24). To have made a wrong choice might mean that Timothy would find himself involved in a measure of liability for the man's sins. He must exercise the greatest care. In his responsible position at Ephesus he, above others, must **keep** himself **pure**. His own life must be absolutely beyond reproach.

The obligations which have been placed upon Timothy are heavy, they have taken their toll of his health, which, in any case, had never been of the best. Paul inserts some words of kindly advice (23). They provide a salutary reminder that the servant of the Lord does not automatically enjoy a special immunity from common ills, nor can he expect to break the laws governing health with impunity. It is clear, too, that the command **keep yourself pure**, does not depend on a complete teetotalism for its fulfilment. Paul indicates the medicinal value of **a little wine**. Normal means to maintain physical fitness must be taken. Such an 'aside' as this also bears witness to the authenticity of the letter.

The admonition which follows, as already noted, is related to v. 22. Still the thought persists of Timothy's duty in connection with the appointment of elders. It would be inexcusable to incorporate in the leadership of the church one whose **sins** are **obvious**, whilst another, renowned for **good deeds**, would be a natural choice. But great discernment will be required where the true character of the individual is not so obvious. Some will only after a time reveal disqualifying traits. Others, in danger of being turned down, may subsequently show that they possessed in good measure the qualities of a first-class elder. Timothy must beware of making a rapid assessment, and arriving at a superficial judgment. First impressions are not always accurate. Where uncertainty exists caution will clearly be the wisest course. And yet Paul encourages his colleague; **good deeds**, though not always immediately discernible, 'cannot be concealed for ever' (NEB).

iv. Slaves (6: 1–2)

Quite a high proportion of the earliest communities of Christians were slaves. This accounts for the frequent exhortations directed to them in the NT letters. As has frequently been observed, nowhere do these exhortations assume political significance, and yet if fulfilled they must ultimately sound the death knell of this deplorable institution. Here Paul admonishes those slaves who have pagan masters to **consider** them as **worthy of full respect**. Failure to show such deference would have the effect of bringing the name and truth of God into contempt and ridicule. Should the slave be fortunate enough to have for a master a Christian, he must not take advantage of this situation. The very fact that they are brothers in Christ should call forth increased respect. As far as **service** is concerned, it should be regarded as a privilege, and be in quality **even better**, since **those who benefit** thereby **are believers, and dear to them**.

v. False teachers (6: 3–10)

Having been bidden to **teach and urge** these things, Timothy is now warned of those who will contradict him. Two tests will reveal them as heterodox. (*a*) **the sound instruction of our Lord Jesus Christ:** It is improbable that this means precise sayings of the Saviour, but rather the healthful words which originate and centre in Christ. (*b*) **godly teaching**; namely the instruction which aims at promoting godliness. The character of these teachers is next

exposed. They are to be distinguished by three things, conceit, contention and covetousness. Though he is **conceited**, such a man is written off with a curt phrase—**he . . . understands nothing**. According to the NEB he is 'a pompous ignoramus'. Contentious, he wrangles over words. This arises from **an unhealthy interest in controversies**. Unhealthy (*noseō*), 'ailing', contrasts designedly with the **sound** or 'healthful' **instruction** of v. 3. This spirit of contention produces a host of evil things (4*b*). Such individuals are **corrupt** in moral judgment and are **robbed of the truth**. They have only a commercial interest in the faith, and so add covetousness to their other sins.

This leads to a homily on the Christian's attitude to wealth. Taking up the phrase **godliness is a means to financial gain** as though it were their slogan, Paul concedes its truth, but only where it is utterly free of covetousness. **Contentment** (*autarkeia*) for the Stoic philosopher carried the sense of an independence of, and indifference to circumstances. For the Christian it bears a deeper meaning, a *satisfaction* with the situation ordained of God. The only other NT occurrence of the word is in 2 C. 9: 8 where the RSV renders it 'enough of everything' (cf. Phil. 4: 10–13). Reasons for contentment follow. The first, in the nature of a proverb (7), is reminiscent of Job 1: 21; Ec. 5: 15, and the parable of Lk. 12: 16–21. It emphasizes the futility of concentrating on that which is of a temporal nature only. Secondly, contentment requires the minimum for its sustenance, only **food and clothing**. Both are the subject of the Saviour's assurances (Mt. 6: 25–33). Thirdly, covetousness has tragic results. A. S. Way translates vv. 9 and 10: 'But they that crave to be rich fall into temptation's snare, and into many witless and baneful desires which whelm men in pits of ruin and destruction; for love of money is a root whence spring all evils. Some have clutched thereat, have gone astray from the faith, and have impaled themselves on anguish manifold.' He then adds the interesting footnote: 'The metaphor . . . may be taken from the wild beast which, leaping at the bait hung over a pit, falls in, and is impaled on the stake below.' The determination **to get rich**, whatever the excuse offered to the soul, cannot but prove spiritually disastrous, and Paul thinks sadly of **some** who, through the **love of money**, have **wandered from the faith**.

vi. The 'man of God' (6: 11–16)

The choice of this expression with its reminder of the OT prophet as God's man for the hour, would convey to Timothy both encouragement and challenge. Not content merely to **flee** the evils which Paul has been exposing, he must positively **pursue** those virtues in which the Christian's true wealth consists. It seems probable that with v. 12 Paul takes up again the metaphor from the games (cf. 4: 7–10). The contestant engages in the noble contest and is upheld and impelled by **faith**. To succeed he must **take hold of the eternal life**. Faith translates this future boon into a present blessing, it possesses its possessions. It is to this that Timothy was **called**. The occasion to which v. 12b makes reference has been variously suggested to be his baptism, his setting apart for the work of God, or perhaps his arraignment on some charge. Whichever is correct the appeal is that Timothy should live up to God's calling and his own public **confession**. To be faithful will be costly, and so Paul's appeal assumes the nature of a **charge**. The wording of v. 13 adds to its solemnity, but at the same time ministers encouragement. It is uttered in **the sight of God . . . and of Christ Jesus**, but it is God **who gives life**, and it is Jesus who did not deviate, for **while testifying before Pontius Pilate** He **made the good confession**, though fully aware of its inevitable consequences.

There follows the substance of the **charge** (14). **The command** might apply specifically to vv. 11 and 12, or more generally to the injunctions laid upon him at his calling and by this letter, but is preferably to be taken in the widest sense as synonymous with 'the faith'. **Without spot or blame** describes the condition in which **the commandment** must be kept, though the adjectives could refer to Timothy himself in the manner and motive of his execution of this duty. And all must be carried out in prospect of **the appearing of our Lord Jesus Christ**. In this reminder is cheer, for it hints at Christ's triumph; challenge is here too, for that day will be one of examination and testing. The thought of this glorious event **which God will bring about in his own time** (cf. Mt. 24: 36; Ac. 1: 7), immediately occasions the most majestic doxology. Its theme is the incomparable glory of God. He is the **only Ruler**, His control over time and affairs is absolute. He is unique in His supremacy, **King** over all **kings**, **Lord** over all **lords**. **Alone** in possessing inherent immortality (cf. Jn 5: 26), He is also transcendent in holiness dwelling **in unapproachable light**— 'too bright for mortal eye' (C. K. Barrett). To this One, **whom no man has seen or can see** (cf. Exod. 33: 17–23; Jn 1: 18) is ascribed **honor**

and might forever a climax well suited to the theme of the doxology.

vii. The wealthy (6: 17–19)

It is as though the writer fears that his strong words regarding wealth in vv. 7–10 might be construed to imply that it is impossible for a man to be a Christian and **rich in this present world**. This is automatically corrected by the advice given in these verses. Negatively, they are **not to be arrogant**, ever a subtle temptation for the wealthy. Nor must they rely on **uncertain wealth** (cf. Prov. 23: 4, 5). Instead, though affluent, they must **put their hope in the God** who with lavish hand **richly provides us with everything for our enjoyment**. The contrast with the ascetic's view of God is obvious. Positively, Paul views these riches which could so easily ensnare, as a means of doing **good**. The very possession of wealth will enable them to engage in **good deeds**, to be **generous and willing to share**. With a rapid change of metaphor the apostle pictures this right use of money as treasuring up **a firm foundation** for the day to come; thoughts which may well have their origin in the Saviour's Sermon on the Mount teaching. The final phrase of v. 19, which corresponds closely to **take hold of the eternal life** of v. 12, might well express a present blessing enjoyed by those who follow these injunctions.

viii. A final appeal (6: 20–21)

Paul seems almost reluctant to bring the letter to a close. The personal note in his appeal might indicate that he wrote these sentences with his own hand. Timothy is bidden to **guard** what has been **entrusted** to him. The deposit (*parathēkē*) of which he is the custodian is the Christian faith (see also 2 Tim. 1: 12, 14; cf. 2 Tim. 2: 2). In order rightly to execute this trusteeship he will need to **turn away from** those teachings which despite the extravagant and arrogant claims made for them are empty and profane. The warning is further emphasized by the sad observation that by professing the false teaching **some have . . . wandered from the faith**.

The letter concludes with a brief benediction which, as the plural pronoun **you** indicates, was addressed not to Timothy alone, but to all in the church at Ephesus and beyond who require divine grace for obedience to the truths declared herein.

2 TIMOTHY

ANALYSIS

I. GREETINGS (1: 1–2)

In accordance with the custom of the day, and in common with the majority of NT letters, the letter opens with the name of the writer, that of the recipient, and a greeting. Concerning himself Paul makes reference to his apostleship, for it is the basis of the authority he exercises. He hastens to add, however, that this apostleship is **by the will of God**. He was not self-appointed to this position, nor was he elected to it by others, nor was it his by hereditary right. In addition to looking back to his appointment as an apostle, he also declares the object of it to be **the promise of life that is in Christ Jesus**.

Timothy is affectionately addressed as **my dear son**. This arises from the fact that he was brought to faith through Paul's instrumentality; furthermore the years have forged a deep bond of friendship between the two men, which has been further strengthened by extensive fellowship in the work of God. The greeting Paul sends is identical with 1 Tim. 1: 2.

II. ENCOURAGEMENT TO TIMOTHY (1: 5–18)

i. To rekindle the gift (1: 3–7)

It seems likely that age and the knowledge that death cannot be far off combine to evoke in Paul's mind thoughts of the past, though memory, for him, is no mere nostalgic indulgence. It is made the cause for thanksgiving and the occasion of prayer. His own heritage is reason for gratitude to God, and he finds a parallel to it in Timothy's experience. For Paul the past contributed the example of his forebears who served God **with a clear conscience**; for Timothy the background was that of a godly **mother** and **grandmother** in whose lives there shone forth a **sincere faith**. Paul does not despise the religious life of his antecedents. Not as enlightened as he, yet they were true to the light they had, and that light was as the first streaks of dawn heralding the rising sun of righteousness which had now illumined the world. Similarly the **faith** of **Lois** and **Eunice** may initially have been Jewish rather than Christian, but had proved the foundation, for them, as for Timothy later, of that which makes 'wise for salvation' (3: 15). The constant prayer for Timothy to which the apostle gives himself, has added fervency as he recollects the **tears** his colleague shed when last they parted. These tears reflect to some degree the more demonstrative and uninhibited emotion of the day. But they also portray a personality, sensitive and affectionate. A reunion with Timothy would bring nothing but joy, and so Paul longs and prays for it **night and day** (cf. 4: 9, 21).

Another memory is of the time when Timothy had been commissioned to the work of God (see note on 1 Tim. 1: 18; 4: 14). It was on that occasion that Paul had publicly indicated his oneness with Timothy in the latter's dedication to the call of God, by the **laying on of . . . hands**. In response to this action God had imparted to Timothy a gift (*charisma*), a spiritual endowment. 'God never commissions anyone to a task without imparting a special gift appropriate to it' (Guthrie). Now he is exhorted to **fan** it **into flame**. The basic gift had been bestowed, but it needs to be developed. Indifference or fear might lead to its burning low, and so he is reminded that **God did not give . . . a spirit of timidity**. In these words Paul delicately administers the mildest of reproofs, softened still further by his choice of the plural pronoun **us**. Instead, he continues, the **spirit** is one of **power**, strength to discharge the task allotted; of **love**, without which all service is valueless; and of **self-discipline**, an essential in all who would influence others for God.

ii. To share in suffering (1: 8–14)
Timidity might easily degenerate into cowardice revealing itself in a reluctance to testify or suffer for the gospel's sake, or to be identified with the imprisoned apostle. The phrase **to testify about our Lord** emphasizes the testimony borne, 'the testimony of our Lord' (RV) —the message itself. To be **ashamed** of the message would lead to a failure in testimony, but he may count ever upon inward strengthening through **the power of God**. In the verses which follow, reasons are given why none need ever feel ashamed of this gospel (9, 10). Paul himself has not done so (11, 12), and Timothy must not (13, 14).

9, 10. Their own experience of the gospel and the power of God had meant salvation (cf. Rom. 1: 16), a salvation which both delivered them from the past, and introduced them to a new life of holiness, for its calling is **to a holy life**. These are blessings which arise not from self-effort, but from the gracious **purpose** of God which centred **in Christ Jesus** 'before times eternal' (RV, cf. Eph. 1: 4). This purpose of grace, he asserts, has been revealed, and ultimately realized **through the appearing of our Savior, Christ Jesus**. It was through His manifestation (*epiphaneia*) in the incarnation that the work could be wrought which, at once, **destroyed death and . . . brought life and immortality to light**. His death has annulled for the believer the power and sting of death (cf. Heb. 2: 14, 15; 1 C. 15: 56, 57), and will finally annihilate it completely (1 C. 15: 26). His resurrection has not only brought from the realm of obscurity the truth of **life and immortality** (cf. the somewhat nebulous ideas found in the OT on this subject), but is itself the ground of admission to this life. Paul's exalted view of the gospel, its origin, outworking and achievements, lends strong support to his plea—**do not be ashamed then to testify**.

11, 12. He himself has been unashamed of this gospel. For its promulgation he was appointed a **herald**, to sound it forth, an **apostle**, to declare it authoritatively, a **teacher**, to instruct in its doctrines (see note on 1 Tim. 2: 7). Though this had entailed suffering, there is no sense of regret or repining, but only a joyous confidence in the One whom he has come to know intimately and trust implicitly. **I am convinced**, he cries, **that he is able to guard. For that day** refers to the day of assessment and reward (cf. 1 C. 3: 13). Support for the alternative renderings **what I have entrusted to him** and 'what has been entrusted to me' (RSV) is fairly equally divided. The other occurrences of *parathēkē*, in 1 Tim. 6: 20 (see note), and in v. 14 of the present chapter, suggest the latter to be the case. Either would be legitimate; taken together they represent both sides of one transaction. The truth and the propagation of it, together with the requisite gift divinely bestowed, comprise what God had entrusted to Paul; for their safe-keeping he entrusts them to God. Paul's exhortation (8) has been reinforced, first by his concept of the gospel, and now by his own example.

13, 14. In declaring the message Timothy must have before him Paul's teaching. He need not repeat it parrot-fashion nor slavishly imitate his mode of presentation, but while expressing it in his own idiom, he must adhere to the content of **sound teaching** (cf. 4: 3; 1 Tim. 1: 10; 6: 3; Tit. 1: 9; 2: 1). **pattern** (*hypotypōsis*): 'rough draft' (J. N. D. Kelly). This forms the 'deposit' of truth, it must be guarded by the power of the indwelling **Holy Spirit**. But its foes are not merely external, for any lack of **faith and love** on his part would leave him open to a charge of hypocrisy. Truth communicated other than **with faith and love in Christ Jesus** remains unacceptable.

iii. To heed examples, bad and good (1: 15–18)
Timothy, in addition to being unashamed **to testify about our Lord**, must also be unashamed **of me his prisoner**. A spirit of fear is not infrequently manifested in an unwillingness to associate with the people of God, though few of them could be as *persona non grata* as was Paul with the authorities of his day. Two examples are given, the first, of those who failed in this matter. The words **deserted me** suggest that the defection was from Paul personally, and it would be unfair to imagine a wholesale apostasy. Maybe the apostle's difficulties led him to take the rather sombre view that **everyone** had acted thus, and he appears particularly upset that **Phygelus and Hermogenes** were among them. Perhaps he had expected better treatment from them.

In contrast he places the loyalty of **Onesiphorus**. Paul and Timothy had probably both benefited from the ministrations of Onesiphorus **in Ephesus** (18b), but it had been one thing for him to assist them there, and wholly another for him to be identified with Paul at Rome. Having no illusion as to the very real danger involved, he yet acted with courage. It appears that it was not without difficulty that he tracked Paul down (17), but he was determined to find him, and having done so he showed himself entirely unashamed of Paul's **chains**. **He often refreshed me** is the veteran apostle's tribute to this unknown traveller. Present **mercy** upon his family (16), and **mercy** upon Onesiphorus **on that day** (18, cf. 12) is Paul's ejaculatory prayer-wish. The references to his **household** in v. 16 and 4: 19, and to **mercy . . . on that day**, have led some to conjecture that Onesiphorus was dead when this letter was written, whilst others have gone to the extent of constructing upon this flimsy foundation arguments for prayers for the dead. But the point is that the memory of his courageous friendship moves Paul still, and provides just the example he needs to illustrate his appeal to Timothy.

III. DIRECTIONS TO TIMOTHY (2: 1–26)

i. A call to endurance (2: 1–13)

With the expression **you then**, the pronoun being emphatic, Paul again addresses his appeal to Timothy. He must **be strong** (cf. 4: 17; 1 Tim. 1: 12) and this will be possible only as he draws upon the source of all inspiration and strength—'the grace of God which is ours in Christ Jesus' (NEB). The immediate duty for which strength is required is that of teaching the truth. Reference to this responsibility runs through the whole chapter, and recurs again and again in the letter. The sacred deposit of truth is only properly guarded when communicated to others. Timothy has Paul's example of this (1: 11–14; 2: 2a) and he in turn must select suitable men to whom the faith can be transmitted, faithful men capable of passing it on to yet others. The **many witnesses** may refer to those present on the occasion of his call (cf. 1: 6 *et alia*), but owing to the length of time which would have been required for full recital of Christian doctrine, it seems more likely that reference is being made to truths in general acceptance by the Church (cf. 3: 14).

Paul returns to his call for endurance, and three illustrations supply challenging standards for those engaged in Christian service. All three are popular metaphors with the apostle, and have appeared together before (1 C. 9: 7, 10, 24). *The soldier.* (*a*) He is willing to endure the rigours of arduous campaigns; v. 3 applies this. (*b*) He recognizes the impossibility of engaging in military service and maintaining a civilian occupation. So must God's servant place priority on his calling, and refuse to allow business or home to become a hampering entanglement. (*c*) His ambition is **to please** his commander.

Loyalty and devotion must be pre-eminently to the person of Christ. *The athlete* (5). The contest was subject to stringent rules which governed the training of the athlete as well as his participation in the games. No less must Timothy subject himself to personal disciplines, some of which may be alluded to in vv. 24 and 25, if his efforts are to be rewarded by the heavenly adjudicator. *The farmer* (6). The word **hard-working** (*kopiaō*) describes the **farmer**. For his patient efforts he is ultimately compensated by the joy of benefiting personally from the harvest. This could have an immediate and financial application (cf. 1 C. 9: 11), or a future and spiritual one (cf. 1 Th. 2: 19, 20). Without making too close an application of these matters Paul suggests that Timothy thinks them over, for he is confident that where there is careful meditation upon spiritual truth, there too is known divine illumination (7).

8. Remember Jesus Christ: Here is the great incentive of Christian service, and the central subject of the Christian message. Paul directs attention to two great facts concerning Him. He is the living, victorious Christ, **raised from the dead**, and He remains, what in time He became, the Man Christ Jesus **descended from David**. The only other occurrence of this phrase in Paul's writings is in Rom. 1: 3. It is possible that in both places he is quoting from a commonly used summary of gospel facts. These truths were certainly central to Paul's preaching and for them he was prepared to suffer. Indeed he was **suffering**, as a fettered **criminal** (*kakourgos*; cf. Lk. 23: 32, 39), incidentally, a description ill-suited to the situation portrayed by the closing chapter of Acts. He rejoices that, whatever his condition, men cannot fetter divine truth, which is always free.

Next, Paul tells of the object which inspires his endurance. No hardship is considered too great when the blessing of those who are the chosen of God is involved. The goal before him is that **the elect** should **obtain the salvation** which belongs to those who are **in Christ Jesus**, a salvation which is itself the promise of **eternal glory**.

The section concludes with a quotation of an early Christian hymn, which Paul introduces with the 'trustworthy saying' formula. He uses these lines to emphasize still further his call to endurance. This may well have been an extract from a hymn sung at baptismal services, and if so it would remind Timothy of those basic principles of Christian life and service which the rite signifies. Behind v. 11 lies the teaching of Rom. 6; with v. 12a cf. Rom. 8: 17; and with v. 12b cf. Mt. 10: 33. The final line, possibly added by Paul, assures that **if we are faithless, he will remain faithful** (cf. Rom. 3: 3). No action of His will ever conflict with His character, for **he cannot disown himself.**

ii. A call to concentration on essentials (2: 14–26)

Timothy must constantly set these truths before the believers at Ephesus, and at the same time **warn them . . . against quarreling** over matters of little or no consequence. The danger was that the consideration of basic doctrine (*e.g.* vv. 8, 11–13, 19) might be replaced by **words** (14), **godless chatter** (16) and destructive **teaching** (17). This sort of thing says Paul, **is of no value**, it provides no food for the soul; instead it **only ruins those who listen**, for it unsettles and turns men away from the truth. Further, it results in progress in the wrong direction—**become more and more ungodly** (16). The persistent discussion of non-essentials is likened to a gangrenous condition where increasing areas of otherwise healthy tissue are insidiously eaten away. **Hymenaeus** (see note on 1 Tim. 1: 20) **and Philetus** are cited as glaring examples. In their philosophical disputings they had missed the way on a fundamental matter; **they say that the resurrection has already taken place**, in consequence **they destroy the faith of some** (cf. 1 C. 15).

The situation was serious, and so in the centre of his description of this state of affairs Paul inserts positive advice to Timothy (15). A personal responsibility to **do your best to present yourself to God as one approved** is laid upon him. He must be determined to enjoy a constant sense of divine acceptance, both of himself and of his work. In particular, he must know this in his handling of **the word of truth**. The AV translation of this phrase has been used to warrant a treatment of Scripture quite other than that which Paul intended. The picture in his mind might have been a straight-cut furrow or road, or possibly a stone-mason achieving a perfect symmetry in his work. Both may lie behind this appeal for a straightforward, balanced exegesis of holy Scripture. This is the only answer to the empty and impious talk here condemned, and is the sole corrective to those heretical beliefs to which such talk leads.

Faced with these difficulties Timothy is given an encouraging reminder that **God's solid foundation stands firm.** The foundation can be read as the unassailable truth, or the work of God in the souls of genuine believers—members of that Church against which the powers of death shall not prevail (Mt. 16: 18). Paul wants Timothy to remember the twofold truth which stands as a permanent inscription upon this foundation. It tells that God alone possesses infallible discernment when it comes to knowing **who are his**, and that he who claims to be Christ's must give evidence of it by turning **away from wickedness.** The story of Korah clearly lies behind these quotations, although the parallels be-

tween that mutiny and the heretical activity of Hymenaeus and Philetus must not be pressed too far. The first inscription is a direct quotation of Num. 16: 5. The second is a typical Pauline loose rendering. Here he changes the emphasis from separation from the wicked (Num. 16: 26) to 'forsake wickedness' (NEB).

The illustration that follows contains this thought of separation from evil. It is akin to 1 C. 3: 10–15 and, as there, the thought is that of personal responsibility. Paul is still concerned that Timothy shall be **approved, a workman** unashamed. That departure **from wickedness** rather than separation from individuals, is Paul's intended meaning is plain, because household utensils could hardly 'cleanse' themselves from other utensils, and in any case all such prove useful in the house, even though some are for less noble purposes. God's servant must follow such advice as is contained in vv. 22–24 and in this way purify himself so that he becomes **an instrument . . . made holy**, set apart as **useful to the Master and prepared to do any good work**. To equate the **large house** with 'christendom' is entirely arbitrary and wholly fails to regard the personal nature of the exhortation.

From illustration Paul turns to precise instruction. Negatively, Timothy must **flee the evil desires of youth**. Included in these will be not only sensual desire, but proneness to intolerance, arrogance and so on, the very antitheses of the qualities Paul proceeds to recommend. To **righteousness, faith** and **love** (cf. 1 Tim. 6: 11) Timothy must add **peace**, and all these virtues are to be known and enjoyed in the company of true fellow-Christians. Again the apostle counsels him not to be drawn into pointless debates which only result in **quarrels**. Instead of being quarrelsome the **Lord's servant** must be **kind to everyone**: the picture presented bears a striking resemblance to that portrayed by Isaiah in the Servant passages. As a teacher he must be show tolerance and patience with the difficult, and where these **oppose him** he must correct them, though always in a spirit of gentleness. At the same time he will remember that greater forces are at work. **The devil** setting his **trap** intends to capture men for his fell designs, but God is working too. Through His servants He calls men to repentance and 'the acknowledging of the truth' (AV). This is the true knowledge (cf. 1 Tim. 2: 4; 2 Tim. 3: 7; Tit. 1: 1). It is extremely difficult to decide on the person or persons indicated by the phrase **who has taken them captive to do his will.** Above, they have both been made to apply to the devil. The alternative interpretation is that those ensnared by the devil, exchange that state for a new captivity 'unto the will of God', to which blessed servitude they are led 'by the Lord's servant' (see RV).

IV. THE LAST DAYS (3: 1–17)
i. Their characteristics (3: 1–9)

In proceeding to describe the conditions which will obtain in the world of **the last days** (cf. 1 Tim. 4: 1) the writer obviously has in mind the days which will end this present era, days immediately preceding the second advent of Christ. In a broader sense Peter, quoting Joel's prophecy, could announce at Pentecost that 'the last days' had begun (Ac. 2: 17). The features here depicted can be said then, to apply not only to 'the final age of this world' (NEB) but to Paul's day, to Timothy's and to every succeeding period of the Church's history (cf. 1 Jn 2: 18). The expression **terrible times** contains within it the thought 'of threat, of menace, of danger' (Wm. Barclay, *The Daily Study Bible*, p. 209). The nature of the evils catalogued are certainly those which would produce such conditions for the Christian. They are **terrible times** inasmuch as their influence is adverse to spiritual life and occasion innumerable dangers for the child of God. The life of the ungodly is frequently corrupt, and the pressures exerted upon the believer are as a floodtide which runs strongly against him. There follows in vv. 2–5 a list of vices which constitutes a frightful picture of a world which has turned its back upon God. In a sense the first two, **lovers of themselves** and **lovers of money**, are the parent sins from which all the rest of the wretched brood are begotten. The first, the most 'natural' of sins, when persisted in and linked to the second, banishes God from the life. Where 'me and mine' is the principle which obtains, there remains little to restrain the evils here 'set out in a ghastly series' (Wm. Barclay, *op. cit.*, p. 211). The description is sufficiently plain not to require amplification. It culminates in a warning that these things may be found in the orthodox, religious person —**having a form of godliness but denying its power** (5). Where religious life consists in externals only, knowing no spiritual dynamic, the door is wide open to the entrance of such sins as these. The plain advice Paul gives to Timothy is condensed in the brief warning— **Have nothing to do with them**.

The apostle next envisages a situation which might easily arise. Not being allowed in the church, some of those already described, anxious to peddle their false religious wares, **worm their way into homes (6)**. Once in, they try to exert an influence on impressionable women, particularly by playing on their sensitive awareness of sin and spiritual shortcoming. The promises they hold out of a deeper knowledge of the truth beguile their dupes, who instead of realizing this knowledge, come ever

more and more under the sway of these unscrupulous men (cf. Tit. 1: 11).

A historical analogy is found in the story of the Egyptian magicians who **opposed Moses**. No direct reference to these individuals is found in Scripture, though ancient Jewish legends, well known to Timothy, surrounded the events described in Exod. 7: 8–12. The parallel is not pressed, though it provides a useful illustration. They are **men of depraved minds** and counterfeit **faith**. Their understanding is warped, and in consequence, the faith they hold is false. As Pharaoh's magicians were exposed to public ridicule, so these teachers must soon be revealed as impostors, their career will be short-lived (see *art.* 'Jannes and Jambres', *NBD*).

ii. The safeguards (3: 10–17)

It seems from the emphatic **you, however** that it is with a measure of relief that Paul turns from this gloomy recital to address himself to his friend. Once again Timothy is reminded of that life and career to which he is no stranger. It provides an obvious example for him to copy. Paul first lists the principles which have governed his life (10). He has given himself to **teaching**. The apostle's clear setting-forth of Christian doctrine constituted his chief contribution to the life of the Church. **My way of life**, he claims, without immodesty, has testified to the truth taught. **My purpose** will remind of that singlemindedness which dominated Paul's whole life. The heavenly vision had never been forgotten or disobeyed. **Faith, patience, love, endurance** continue to delineate the character which is set before Timothy as a model. As a craftsman demonstrates the perfect technique to his apprentice, and bids him observe and imitate, and yet is never thought guilty of egotism, so is Paul free from all trace of this fault as he reminds Timothy of these essentials.

The list of qualities in v. 10 continues in v. 11 with **persecutions, sufferings**, and in one sense these can be regarded as just as much the result of personal purpose as the rest. The example he has given consists in his determination to continue his work for God despite the afflictions which this must inevitably bring. Paul selects for mention those occasions which occurred immediately prior to Timothy's conversion, and which probably profoundly influenced him at the time. Paul rejoices to add **Yet the Lord rescued me from all of them**. On the one hand he encourages Timothy with this word, and on the other proceeds to warn him that every one who is determined **to live a godly life** must anticipate persecution (cf. Ac. 14: 22; 1 Th. 3: 4). This will be so because **evil men and impostors** (cf. v. 8) **will go from bad to worse**, the whole situation deteriorating as men are carried along, and carry others along in a progressive course of deception.

The safeguard for the servant of God is to adhere staunchly to the truth imparted by trustworthy friends and founded upon the Scriptures. The opening words of v. 14 pair up with those of v. 10 and Paul now calls upon Timothy to continue ('abide', RV) **in what you have learned and have become convinced of**. Convictions must not be lightly jettisoned, for two reasons. First, because of the persons who taught him these truths; were they not reliable guides, people of spiritual stature and holy living? The appeal is probably primarily to Lois, Eunice and Paul himself; he would be ill-advised to forsake such mentors to follow the latest religious quack. Secondly, because such truths rest squarely upon the solid foundation of the Scriptures. From his earliest years Timothy has **known the holy Scriptures** (15). Lois and Eunice had attended to that. These Scriptures, says Paul, are the source of all spiritual intelligence, and lead to **salvation** as **Christ Jesus**, the subject of them, is received by **faith**. The oblique reminder of his personal experience is intended to stimulate Timothy's confidence in the trustworthiness of the Scriptural message.

The section concludes with a statement concerning the nature and value of the Scriptures. The apostle is concerned alone with the OT, but the principle he enunciates has its obvious application to the whole of Holy Writ. Considerable debate has centred around the opening phrase of v. 16, whether it should be rendered **All Scripture is God-breathed** or 'Every inspired scripture has its use' (NEB, similarly RSVmg and RV). The difficulty arises from the absence of 'is' in the Greek text. If the word **Scripture** is given its more restricted sense of Holy Scripture, which is the general meaning accorded it in the NT and that which fits well the preceding verses, then the first alone adequately expresses the truth. If *graphē* is taken to mean writings in general, then not only is the wording of the second translation accurate but necessary, and given this meaning the first would be palpably false. Space forbids extensive examination of this exegetical problem. The matter is carefully weighed by J. N. D. Kelly, D. Guthrie and others in their commentaries; cf. also B. B. Warfield, *Biblical Foundations* (Tyndale Press), chap. 2. As for the expression **God-breathed** (*theopneustos*) the thought conveyed is that the writings under consideration are 'the product of the creative breath of God' (see *art.* 'Inspiration', *ISBE*).

The point Paul appears to be making is that Timothy, confident of Scripture's inspired nature, can rely upon it to be 'profitable'. This profit lies first in the fact that it is the source of **teaching** ('doctrine', AV). It is the basis and test of true Christian belief. **Rebuking**

suggests that it not only points out error, but is also the agent to be used in refuting it. Following refutation, comes the necessity for indicating the right path—**correcting**. Moreover, it is able also to hold a man steady in this path—**training in righteousness**. The end product is **that the man of God** (cf. 1 Tim. 6: 11) **may be thoroughly equipped** ('efficient', NEB), **for every good work**, equal to any opportunity which may arise for engaging in good works.

V. FINAL INSTRUCTIONS (4: 1–22)
i. A solemn charge (4: 1–5)
Paul has some final words of exhortation to give to Timothy. The very fact that they are addressed by one anticipating martyrdom to a younger colleague upon whom heavy responsibilities will soon devolve gives them an air of gravity. Their solemnity is further stressed by the manner of their introduction—**I give you this charge** (*diamartyromai*, cf. 1 Tim. 5: 21). It is not an expression Paul takes lightly upon his lips, he utters it **in the presence of God and of Christ Jesus**. He speaks as one answerable for his words, and makes reference to the judgment. Timothy, too, must recognize that they are commands made with heaven's authority, and that an account will be required of him by **Christ Jesus who will judge the living and the dead** as to his discharging of these obligations. Paul still further strengthens his appeal by reminding Timothy of the Saviour's **appearing and his kingdom** which it will consummate. Life must be lived and service rendered in the prospect of these glorious events.

Of the fivefold duty which is Timothy's, conveyed to him in crisp imperatives, **preach** or herald **the Word** is basic. So essential is this that he must regard no occasion as inopportune. He must adopt a varied approach—**correct, rebuke and encourage**; thus, as has frequently been suggested, addressing himself to reason, conscience and will. Men might be slow to learn, provocative in their refusal of the message; he must show **great patience**, nor must his preaching be divorced from **careful instruction**.

The situation envisaged by the apostle (3, 4) makes fulfilment of these directions doubly important. **Sound doctrine** will be rejected, its demands being too great. Instead, **men** with **itching ears**, desiring merely to be entertained, **will gather around them a great number of teachers** who will tell them only what they want to hear. **The truth** will still be taught, but they will **turn their ears away** from it, preferring to **turn aside to myths** (cf. 1 Tim. 1: 4; 4: 7; Tit. 1: 4).

Returning to Timothy (5a; cf. 3: 10, 14), Paul bids him not to be carried away by this state of affairs; rather he must stand his ground, willing to suffer if needs be. His responsibility is to **do the work of an evangelist**. Whilst the wording may imply that **evangelist** is not being used of the specific gift as listed in Eph. 4: 11 yet the exhortation consists in more than the duty resting upon every Christian to spread the gospel. A brief but comprehensive command, **discharge all the duties of your ministry**, concludes the paragraph.

ii. Paul's circumstances and prospects (4: 6–18)

Again, Paul's appeal to Timothy is reinforced by his example, but here the gravity of his position, vividly depicted, gives it increased point and power. Morbid thoughts or distressing fears are entirely absent as Paul confidently speaks of his death using imagery both glad and triumphant. Of the phrases chosen to describe the death which is regarded as imminent, the first is a **drink-offering** (cf. Phil. 2: 17). He states that his life is about to be **poured out** as a libation on an altar of sacrifice. The second, **the time . . . for my departure**, is not unrelated to the picture of a ship about to weigh anchor, or a soldier preparing to strike camp (cf. Phil. 1: 23).

Reviewing his life for God the apostle can claim to have fulfilled his ministry. **The good fight** is frequently thought to represent the wrestling match, with **the race** continuing the metaphor of the athletic contest. **I have kept the faith** may well correspond to the earlier references to guarding the deposit (cf. 1 Tim. 6: 20; 2 Tim. 1: 12, 14). The perfect tense used in each case carries the sense of completion. For Paul, the end of life brings a quiet confidence that with the long struggle over, the course stayed to the end, the stewardship worthily discharged, **there is in store . . . the crown of righteousness**.

> *'Tis no poor withering wreath of earth,*
> *Man's prize in mortal strife,*

but **the crown of righteousness**. The crown can hardly describe a reward consisting of righteousness inasmuch as righteousness is granted in response to faith alone, although the expression could mean the crown which is the reward of righteousness. Maybe, in view is a righteous crown, namely a reward consistent and just. It is more probable that the expression **the crown of righteousness** describes the anticipated righteousness, once imputed, soon to be known in reality. It will be received from **the Lord, the righteous Judge**. No justice can be hoped for from his earthly judge; but on **that day** of final assessment at Christ's appearing, says Paul, I shall not be alone in receiving a reward. A crown will be the lot of all whose lives have been controlled by the prospect of **his appearing** (cf. v. 1).

With v. 9 the apostle turns to personal requests. Earlier in the letter (1: 4) he had expressed his longing to see Timothy again, and now this is crystallized into a specific and urgent request, one which is repeated in v. 21. Much of what Paul has written was obviously put in writing in case his death should intervene before Timothy could complete the journey to Rome, but it does not make the visit unnecessary. Paul is lonely. Several factors have contributed to his solitariness. **Demas . . . deserted me:** Though previously a 'fellow-worker' (Col. 4: 14; Phm. 24) Demas had found the pull of **this world** too great, especially when compared with the dangers and privations of life with Paul. The use of the verb **loved** (v. 10) suggests a deliberate contrast between Demas and all who 'have loved his appearing' (v. 8 RV), and between this present age (RVmg) and the day of His appearing. Without reading too much into this act of Demas, it is clear that Paul felt his defection keenly. **Crescens** and **Titus** Paul has, in all probability, selflessly dispatched on missionary work, the former **to Galatia**, sometimes considered Gaul, and the latter **to Dalmatia**. As a result **only Luke is with me** (11). The last of the band of faithful men who had accompanied Paul on his extensive journeys, he still loyally ministers to the aged apostle. **Mark** had 'made good' (Col. 4: 10), and Paul besides refusing to hold past failure against him, magnanimously writes of him as **helpful to me in my ministry** and requests Timothy to 'pick up Mark and bring him with you' (NEB). Continuing the names of those dispatched elsewhere, Paul says that **Tychicus**, a trustworthy companion, and a frequent bearer of letters, has been **sent to Ephesus**. He could possibly have been the carrier of the present letter (*apesteila* being an epistolary aorist), as well as the person intended to relieve Timothy from his post for his visit to Rome. Lonely, and in prison, with winter drawing on (cf. v. 21), Paul remembers **the cloak**, a large, heavy cape-like garment which had been **left with Carpus at Troas** (13). He probably feels the need also of the mental and spiritual stimulus that the **scrolls** and **the parchments** would provide. These personal requests attest the authenticity of the letter, and many critics of Pauline authorship, outstanding among them P. N. Harrison, have felt it necessary to ascribe them to fragments of genuine material incorporated by an unknown writer. The possibility of the survival of such a fragment, and the decision to incorporate it, would seem highly unlikely.

Rapidly moving from one matter to the next, Paul warns Timothy of **Alexander the metalworker** (14). Either at his trial as a prosecution witness, or on some earlier occasion as one who had opposed the truth Paul proclaimed, Alexander had done the apostle **a great deal of**

harm. Not personally vindictive, Paul leaves it
to **the Lord** to **repay him** (Ps. 62: 12; cf. Rom.
12: 19), but promptly adds a common-sense
warning to Timothy to keep out of his way. It
is not possible to identify this Alexander with
either of the men of that name referred to
in Ac. 19: 33, 34 and 1 Tim. 1: 20, though
interesting theories have been constructed by
various commentators.

My first defence has been regarded by some
as descriptive of an earlier trial. This enables
the central phrases of v. 17 to be interpreted
as referring to further missionary activity. It
seems far more likely, however, that the 'first
defence' relates to the preliminary hearing with
which Paul's trial had opened. **No one** had
come forward on this occasion to **support** him.
Disappointment but not bitterness is discernible as he recalls the experience. Reminiscent
of Christ's prayer (Lk. 23: 34) and Stephen's
(Ac. 7: 60) are Paul's words—**may it not be
held against them**. Their failure throws into
relief the divine loyalty exultantly conveyed in
the words, **But the Lord stood at my side**.
This had resulted in an inner strengthening, so
that the occasion proved an opportunity to
proclaim **the message . . . fully**. It seems as
if Paul looked back on this experience as the
climax of his public heralding of the gospel,
and if the terms in which he describes it are
somewhat extravagant, this is understandable
if they in fact refer 'to witness borne when on
trial before the ruler of the whole pagan world'

(C. K. Barrett). The reference to being **delivered from the lion's mouth** describes
Paul's delight at the favourable outcome of the
preliminary hearing of his case. He is aware,
however, that martyrdom is not far away (6–
8), and so in v. 18 his thoughts turn to spiritual
preservation and to the **heavenly kingdom**.
He asserts his confidence in the Lord, and
breaks into a doxology ascribing to Christ
glory for ever and ever. **iii. Concluding
salutations (4: 19–22)**
Paul adds greetings to his friends and staunch
associates **Priscilla and Aquila**, and to **the
household of Onesiphorus** (see note on 1:
16, 18). Timothy is informed of the fact that
Erastus, a mutual friend, **stayed in Corinth**,
and that the illness of **Trophimus** had necessitated his being **left** behind **in Miletus**. (This
interestingly enough, happened despite the
presence of a doctor and an apostle in the
company!) But it all adds up to loneliness for
Paul, and so he repeats his request, **Do your
best to get here before winter**, the added
reference to approaching winter making his
plea yet more urgent.

Paul conveys a few further personal greetings
in which **all the brothers** join, and then concludes with a prayer for Timothy, **The Lord
be with your spirit**. The latter part of the
benediction is identical with the one which
ends the first letter, the plural pronoun being
used there also. It may be appropriated by all
who read the letter—**Grace be with you**.

TITUS

ANALYSIS

I. GREETINGS (1: 1–4)

Introduced among the many practical matters with which the writer deals in this letter are three short, but most valuable doctrinal statements. They happen to fall one in each chapter, the first being combined with the opening salutation.

Paul's designation of himself—**a servant of God** is unique, though he does refer to himself elsewhere as the 'bondslave of Jesus Christ'. A freeman, and proud of it, he nevertheless glories in his bondage to his heavenly Master. Again, he makes mention of his apostleship.

The phrase 'according to' (AV and RV) has occasioned some difficulty. It is probably intended to convey the thought—'in the interests of', 'to promote' or 'to secure', in which case it is aptly translated by the RSV as 'to further'. The object before him is described, therefore, as the promotion of **the faith of God's elect** and may cover both the bringing to faith of those chosen of God, and the development of faith in those already His people. It also includes the leading of these to a recognition and apprehension of **the truth**. This knowledge, related to and producing piety, stands in marked contrast to v. 16. The ultimate goal for them and for him, is the **hope of eternal life**. This undoubtedly acts as a powerful incentive in his work, for it is a hope not vague or uncertain, but firmly grounded in the abiding purposes of the **God, who does not lie**. An antithesis to the lying Cretans is possibly intended (12).

The message which Paul bears had its origin 'before times eternal' (RV), but was declared **at his appointed season**, in the incarnation and the divine self-revelation which was then introduced. The truth was unveiled, and its declaration was entrusted to the apostle. In each of the Pastorals he rejoices in this privilege (1 Tim. 1: 11; 2 Tim. 1: 11), and here he ascribes it, as in 1 Tim. 1: 1, to the direct **command of God**.

The opening paragraph forms, then, no mere apostolic salutation, but a majestic survey of the great purpose which spans the ages, which Paul as **a servant of God and an apostle of Jesus Christ** was called to advance.

The address to Titus in v. 4 tells that he had been brought to faith through Paul (cf. 1 Tim. 1: 2). It might also imply that he was displaying those spiritual traits which mark him as a true successor of the apostle. The several references to Titus in 2 Corinthians portray him as indeed a **true son in our common faith**. The NIV, in common with the RV, rightly omits 'mercy' from the prayer Paul utters for his colleague. The change from the title 'Christ Jesus our Lord' which occurs in parallel passages elsewhere, to **Christ Jesus our Savior**, accords with the emphasis this letter places upon God's Saviourhood. Used of the Father and the Son,

the expression may have been chosen with the intention of encouraging Titus as he faces an extraordinarily difficult situation in Crete.

II. ELDERS (1: 5–16)

i. Their appointment, qualifications and responsibilities (1: 5–9)

The impression created by the phrase **I left you in Crete** is that Paul and Titus had been labouring together on the island when the apostle felt it necessary to press on with his journeys. It is impossible to fit this into the brief call at Crete reported in Ac. 27: 7, 8, so it is assumed that this visit was made after release from the first Roman imprisonment (see Introd., p. 1472). Affairs in the churches in Crete were far from satisfactory, but Paul could stay no longer. He gave Titus advice with regard to the ordering of church life, and, having left him, now writes to confirm his oral instructions and to provide Titus with an authoritative word for the execution of these duties. Churches without properly appointed **elders**, Paul regards as 'defective' (RSV). Two things, however, should be observed: (*a*) that elders are not necessary for the *existence* of churches, and (*b*) that in keeping with advice he had given elsewhere (1 Tim. 3: 6; 5: 22) Paul refrained from acting prematurely in making appointments. Titus must now select and **appoint elders in every town**. The apostle specifies the need for a plurality of elders, and the definite appointment of them. He then proceeds to list the qualities required (see notes on 1 Tim. 3: 2–7). In his family-life the elder must show loyalty to his wife, and exercise spiritual discipline over his children. 'Faithful children' (AV, cf. similar idiom 1 C. 4: 17) may well represent the text with greater accuracy than the more restricted **whose children believe**. In this realm he must be **blameless**, as also in the church where, as **an overseer** he **is entrusted with** the stewardship of **God's work**. The five negative requirements which follow (7), list the faults which might easily have persisted in the Cretan Christians who, as yet, had not overcome the temperamental weaknesses of their race, a danger which exists in every age. Paul continues in v. 8 to enumerate the qualities which should have replaced the vices just listed. He specifies also, that the overseer **must hold firmly to the trustworthy message**, and in this insists that he is required to have not only a tenacious grip of the faith, but also a firm adherence to it in conduct. This equips and qualifies him to instruct in **sound doctrine** (see note on 1 Tim. 1: 10), and also to deal with **those who oppose it**.

ii. Their call to check false teaching (1: 10–16)

The necessity for the high standards demanded of elders is now seen in proper perspective as Paul describes the characters, activities and teachings of those who oppose the work of God (10–16). In the main these opponents appear to be church members, for Titus is required to silence them (11), and Paul expresses the hope that being rebuked **sharply . . . they will be sound in the faith** (13). Behind them, however, were teachers propagating **Jewish myths**, men **who reject the truth** (14). The members of the former group who are described as **rebellious people**, flout the authority of God's word and His appointed teachers. They talk freely but to no profit (cf. 1 Tim. 1: 6; 2 Tim. 2: 16) for they are **deceivers**. Jewish Christians form the more active section of these dissidents, perhaps because their national heritage produced in them a sense of superiority, or because of the freedom they had learnt in the synagogue in such matters. It is probable that the technique of these men was akin to that described in 2 Tim. 3: 6, that is, the private circulation of heresy. Certainly the disruptive effect of their teaching was particularly apparent amongst Christian families. Detecting that they subordinate truth to finance, Paul castigates their motives as mercenary and writes off their message as **things they ought not to teach**. He goes on to add that being Cretans they are but revealing national characteristics. In order to describe these, Paul tactfully quotes **one of their own prophets**. These lines, attributed to Epimenides (in a context from which another quotation is taken in Ac. 17: 28a), express a verdict with which Paul fully concurs. His statement implies an opinion based on a personal, and not too happy, experience. The purpose of the treatment of these men which the apostle now recommends, is a positive one, namely their recovery to spiritual health.

The dual source of the false teaching is said to be **Jewish myths** (cf. 1 Tim. 1: 4), and **commands of those who reject the truth** (cf. Col. 2: 21, 22). It was probably this amalgam of Jewish regulations and Gnostic asceticism that led Paul to quote the principle enunciated by Jesus (15a, cf. Lk. 11: 41). The inference here is that moral purity is unaffected by questions of ceremonial. J. N. D. Kelly makes the valuable observation that 'when modern people quote the apothegm, they usually take the word exclusively in the moral sense and deduce that the man who is himself pure need not fear contamination by anything impure. This is a dangerous half-truth, and far from Paul's meaning'. From this point Paul proceeds in phrases of strong condemnation to describe those responsible for these heresies. **Nothing is pure** for them, for the springs of thought and action are **corrupted**. They are corrupt in life, because unbelieving in heart. Their pretentious claim to **know God**, an expression which

implies a semi-Jewish, semi-Gnostic origin, lacks any foundation for **by their actions they deny him**. Paul rounds off his description of them with three stinging epithets, **detestable, disobedient**, useless (**unfit for doing anything good**, cf. 2 Tim. 2: 21; 3: 17).

III. CHRISTIAN BEHAVIOUR
(2: 1–3: 11)
i. Sundry groups (2: 1–10)
Cretans may be **liars**, and some of the believers **mere talkers, but you**, writes Paul to Titus, **must teach what is in accord with sound doctrine**. This is a recurring demand in the Pastorals (*e.g.* 1: 9; 1 Tim. 1: 10), but the emphasis that Paul makes here is that Titus should instruct them in the behaviour which accords with belief. Paul recommends that in doing this Titus should address himself separately to various groups.

Older men (2) because of the maturity expected of them, should be marked by restraint, seriousness of outlook and self-control. **Self-controlled** (*sōphrōn*) occurs in 1: 8 regarding the overseer and this quality is also demanded of three of the groups which follow, and of all in v. 12. The prominence of this requirement in this letter, and in those to Timothy (1 Tim. 2: 9, 15; 3: 2; 2 Tim. 1: 7), indicates the importance which the apostle attached to it. It is the 'soberminded' (vv. 2, 5, 6, RV) who are **self-controlled** (2, 5, 6), so that with thoughts and passions held in check their resultant conduct is 'sensible' (2, 5 RSV). To these general virtues, Paul adds the Christian qualities of **faith, love** and **endurance**, and these should not have degenerated with the passing years, but be **sound** still. **Endurance** is not so much a replacement for 'hope' in the triad, but is that aspect of hope required of the elderly.

Older women (3) are to be **reverent** in deportment, not only in the church, but generally; their behaviour revealing that they regard every part of life as holy. The negative commands may imply a connection between the devastating sin of slander and the tongue-loosening effect of **wine**. Thoughtless gossip indulged in on social occasions remains a prevalent evil. The danger should be overcome by occupation with private instruction in **what is good** and by the recognition of their duty to **train the younger women** both by word and example.

Younger women (4, 5), in character, must be **self-controlled** (see note on v. 2) **and pure**. Paul's main recommendations for them relate to their home responsibilities. They are to be devoted to **their husbands and children**, to be **busy at home** in that they recognize the home as their main sphere, and **kind**. Granted a new dignity by the ennobling influence of the gospel, they must not abuse their liberty but remain **subject to their husbands** (cf. Eph. 5: 22; Col. 3: 18). Any failure in these matters would expose **the word of God** to contempt by the world.

Young men (6), Titus must **encourage** ('admonish' rather than 'request') **to be self-controlled** (*sōphronein*, cf. v. 2 note). Again personal mastery of self is considered to be an essential quality.

There follows advice to Titus himself (7, 8), but the advice given has its relevance for all leaders and teachers in the Church. For his work to be effective it must be supported by a life which is **an example**. In addition, his teaching must be imparted with **integrity**. It is essential that there be no tainted motive, such as personal gain (cf. 1: 11), nor underhand method (cf. 2 C. 4: 2). The teacher must also be characterized by **seriousness**. This attitude towards his task must spring from the conscious dignity of his calling, and yet be free from affectation. If to these standards he adds **speech** which is sound, one which leaves no possible loop-hole for censure, then any opponent will be shamed into silence (cf. Ac. 4: 13, 14).

Slaves (9, 10) constitute a special class regarding which the apostle advises Titus (cf. 1 Tim. 6: 1). The submission they are enjoined to show must be demonstrated by a sincere attempt 'to give satisfaction all round' (Moffatt). This must arise from a spirit of co-operation, for **they are not to talk back**. Paul envisages the slave in his situation indulging in specious rationalizing of petty larceny, and therefore adds the words—**not to steal**. Instead, absolute fidelity must be his standard. To the negative reasons in vv. 5b, 8b which support his previous exhortations, the apostle now adds a positive one (10b). If these slaves are obedient to his counsel 'they will add lustre to the doctrine of God our Saviour' (NEB). There can be no loftier aim than this.

ii. An appeal to the grace of God (2: 11–15) Having described 'the things which befit the sound doctrine' (RV), Paul now turns to the doctrine which makes the demand. There can be no divorce between the two, and this second of the three great doctrinal passages of the letter is given as the impulse and reason for all practical godliness.

The writer first refers to that most impelling of all motives—**the grace of God**. This spontaneous loving intervention of God in history has procured **salvation** for **all men**. **Grace** seen as a tutor **teaching us**, demands, negatively, that we renounce **ungodliness and worldly passions**, that we have done with all 'godless ways' (NEB) and those desires which are dominant in the world that knows not God. Positively, it requires that the Christian's conduct **in this present age** should be marked by personal self-control (cf. v. 2 note), uprightness relative to others, and godliness.

The **grace** which has **appeared** will find its consummation in **the glorious appearing**. Both alike are powerful incentives to true Christian living, for the first promotes a response of gratitude while the second stimulates the sense of expectancy, denoted by the participle 'awaiting' (RSV). The text declaring the true **hope** of the believer to be **the glorious appearing of our great God and Savior, Jesus Christ** bears attractive testimony to the deity of Christ. The presence of only one definite article has the effect of binding together the two titles. In addition, nowhere in the NT is there any hint of separate appearances of the Father and the Son. Nor is the adjective **great** used of the Father. As Christ was the grace of God revealed (11), so will He be the manifestation of the glory of God.

A final appeal is made, this time to the redeeming act of Christ. **who gave himself for us:** These words of utter simplicity yet unfathomable profundity, tell of the price involved in ransoming men (cf. 1 Tim. 2: 6). The work was voluntary, substitutionary and infinitely costly. Its stated purpose must be regarded as having a dual aspect, namely Christ's achievement, and the Christian's obligation. (*a*) **to redeem: from** must be given the full meaning of 'right away from', and **all wickedness** must also be given its widest significance. (*b*) **to purify:** A sanctification which is complete in its formal sense (Heb. 10: 10, 14), and progressive in its ethical (Eph. 5: 25–27) is the goal of the Redeemer's work. *Saints* thereby become a people essentially His, who may be identified by their zeal **to do what is good**.

The command of v. 1 which inspired the detail of the succeeding verses, is reiterated (15), and is amplified by the additional stipulation that Titus **encourage and rebuke** (cf. 2 Tim. 4: 2). His ministry must be exercised **with all authority**, and Titus must not allow anyone to **despise** him (cf. 1 Tim. 4: 12). Whilst the letter itself would add to it, true authority would only derive from obedience to the exhortation of v. 7.

iii. In society (3: 1–2) Paul proceeds to develop the theme of the Christian's obligation to be **ready to do whatever is good** and bids Titus **remind** them of this responsibility, particularly in relation to society. It would have been easy for the Cretan Christians to be restive under the Roman yoke, they must therefore be reminded of the need **to be subject** and **obedient** to civil authorities (cf. Rom. 13: 1–7; 1 Pet. 2: 13–17). The final phrase of the verse recommends that they should be public-spirited, willing to co-operate in any effort for the common good. Paul continues in v. 2 to sketch the Christian character, which, if reproduced, will stand out like a beacon against the dark background of a pagan society.

iv. A further appeal to the grace of God (3: 3–7)

The appeal is made the more powerful by a portrayal of life as it was lived before the transformation wrought by the saving activity of the triune God. The description is general and Paul does not hold himself aloof from it. In listing seven vices he shows man at his worst, lacking spiritual intelligence, flouting God's law, deluded, enslaved by inner 'urges' and outward **pleasures**, malicious, envious and hateful. But man's depravity proves no obstacle to God. As **God our Savior** He penetrated the darkness (cf. 2: 11) and shed upon mankind the light of His **kindness and love** (*chrēstotēs*—goodness of heart, benignity; *philanthrōpia*—love for man). The consequence, as Paul exultantly declares it, was that **he saved us**. This has been well defined as 'the inward application to particular men of the universal act of redemption' (C. K. Barrett). This, he continues, arose not as a result of **righteous things we had done**, but rather **because of his mercy**. The total lack of desert serves only to heighten the spontaneity of God's saving grace. The phrases Paul uses to describe the means by which this grace is mediated to the soul, follow closely Christ's teaching to Nicodemus (Jn 3: 3–8). It is possible that both found a common origin in Ezek. 36: 25–27. It has been suggested that the conjunction **and** (*kai*) which links the expressions **through the washing of rebirth and renewal by the Holy Spirit**, could bear the meaning 'even', the second clause thus becoming explanatory of the first (see C. F. Hogg, *What saith the Scripture?* p. 145 on Jn 3: 5; cf. W. E. Vine, *Expos. Dic. of N. T. Words*, *s.v.* 'Regeneration'). Whether or not it is taken thus, **the washing** and the **renewal** are obviously closely connected. Both the writers referred to above, associate **washing** with the Word of God, although this seems to lack any clear Scriptural support. If the assumption of a common source in Ezekiel is correct, then it is better to understand **the washing of rebirth** as signifying simply the cleansing wrought at new birth, though it may well include the thought of baptism as the outward symbol of that inward cleansing. Guthrie points out that 'the whole passage is designed to exhibit the grandeur of the grace of God and many details, such as faith-appropriation' (and, we might add, the Scriptures and baptism) 'are omitted to serve that end'. The word **renewal**, especially, is forward-looking, linking the momentous event of **rebirth** with the consequent continuous operation of the indwelling Spirit (cf. Rom. 12: 2). **Washing** may be said to describe a change of condition, **rebirth** a change in status, and **renewal** a change of disposition. Each is attested by baptism, though none is conferred by it. Together they are the work of the **Holy Spirit . . . poured out** at Pentecost as a consequence of the Saviour's glorification (cf. Jn 16: 7; Ac. 2: 33). Using the pronoun **us** in the clause **poured out on us** the apostle declares his belief in a present identification with the past phenomenon of Pentecost (cf. 1 C. 12: 13). The object of this tremendous work wrought in the sinner is that he is **justified**, and the motivating force is summed up in the phrase **by his grace**. To the ideas of salvation, cleansing, justification, Paul adds, finally, that of **eternal life**. Already **heirs** and, in part, possessors of the inheritance, believers yet look forward in **hope** to its full enjoyment. Although the trustworthy saying would not be inappropriate to what follows, the NIV, in appending it to this paragraph, is most probably correct.

v. Final advice (3: 8–11)

The preceding declaration of God's grace in salvation has been given as an incentive to good works, and Titus is required to give emphatic teaching concerning these basic truths, so that believers may be stirred up to **devote themselves to doing what is good**. The alternative translation 'enter honourable occupations' (RSVmg) might represent the technical meaning of the Greek verb used, but the general meaning of 'good deeds' seems preferable. Presumably it is the truths taught that are **excellent and profitable**, for they are in clear contrast to the heretical teaching which is **unprofitable and useless** (9). The character of the false teaching which Titus must **avoid**, is presented in summary form and bears resemblance to that described in ch. 1 as well as elsewhere in the Pastorals (1 Tim. 1 and 6; 2 Tim. 2). Titus next receives counsel with regard to the **divisive person**, the one who is an adherent and propagator of his 'self-chosen and divergent form of religious belief or practice' (Alford). As a schismatic he must be cautioned, but if after the second warning he remains unrepentant there must be no further contact with him (cf. Mt. 18: 15–17). One who is unmoved by such treatment reveals himself to be completely **warped and sinful** and stands **self-condemned**.

IV. PERSONAL MESSAGES AND GREETINGS (3: 12–15)

Paul is aware that the Cretan Christians are still immature, and he knows well enough that churches cannot become indigenous overnight. He, therefore, proposes to **send** either **Artemas or Tychicus** to relieve Titus. This casual note of uncertainty leaves an imprint of genuineness upon the letter. The **Nicopolis** referred to was probably a town in Epirus which Paul regarded as a suitable rendezvous, and a strategic centre for evangelism during the coming **winter**. A further movement into Dalmatia (see 2 Tim. 4: 10) would be straightforward from Nicopolis.

Of **Zenas the lawyer** we know nothing, though **Apollos** is well known. Generous hospitality must be shown them as they journey through Crete. The apostle adds a final word about **doing what is good** (cf. v. 8 note), and possibly suggests that in this matter of hospitality, Titus should not shoulder the whole burden, for the **people must learn to devote themselves** to it too. Thus they will **not live unproductive lives**.

From the expression **Everyone with me** it may be concluded that Paul was not at a place where there was a local church, but that he is journeying and these are his travelling companions. Alternatively, if he is with a church it suggests that Titus is unknown to its members. Greetings are sent to **those who love us in the faith**, which could mean either that their love is founded upon a sharing in the common faith, or that their love is sincere and loyal. There may be here a hint of coolness towards the dissident members. But if this is the case, the apostle concludes with a prayer which embraces all the Christians in Crete. He not only uses the plural pronoun which signifies that the letter is intended for other readers apart from the one to whom it is addressed (cf. 1 Tim. 6: 21; 2 Tim. 4: 22), but he adds the word **all**. On the qualities and achievements of **grace** Paul has in this letter written panegyrics unsurpassed in all his writings; his longing for Titus and the saints in Crete he now compresses in this concluding word—**Grace be with you all**.

BIBLIOGRAPHY

Commentaries

BARRETT, C. K., *The Pastoral Epistles*. New Clarendon Bible (Oxford, 1963).

CALVIN, J., *The Second Epistle of Paul to the Corinthians; The Epistles of Paul to Timothy, Titus and Philemon*. Translated by T. A. SMAIL (Edinburgh, 1964).

DIBELIUS, M. and CONZELMANN, H., *The Pastoral Epistles*, E.T. Hermeneia (Philadelphia, 1972).

EASTON, B. S., *The Pastoral Epistles* (London, 1948).

GUTHRIE, D., *The Pastrol Epistles*. TNTC (London, 1957).

HANSON, A. T., *The Pastoral Epistles*. NCentB (London, 1982).

HENDRIKSEN, W., *NT Commentary: Exposition of the Pastoral Epistles* (Grand Rapids, 1957; reprinted in 'Banner of Truth' series, London, 1959).

KELLY, J. N. D., *A Commentary on the Pastoral Epistles*. BNTC (London, 1963).

LEANEY, A. R. C., *The Epistles to Timothy, Titus and Philemon*. Torch Commentaries (London, 1960).

LOCK, W., *The Pastoral Epistles*. ICC [on the Greek text] (Edinburgh, 1924).

PARRY, R. ST. J., *The Pastoral Epistles*. [on the Greek text] (Cambridge, 1920).

SCOTT, E. F., *The Pastoral Epistles*. MNT (London, 1936).

SIMPSON, E. K., *The Pastoral Epistles*. [on the Greek text] (London, 1954).

SPICQ, C., *Saint Paul: Les Épitres Pastorales*. Études Bibliques [on the Greek text] (Paris, 1947).

Other Studies

HANSON, A. T., *Studies in the Pastoral Epistles* (London, 1968).

HARRISON, P. N., *Paulines and Pastorals* (London, 1964).

HARRISON, P. N., *The Problem of the Pastoral Epistles* (Oxford, 1921).

HARRISON, P. N., 'Important Hypotheses Reconsidered: III. The Authorship of the Pastoral Epistles', *Expository Times* 67 (1955–56), pp. 77–81.

GUTHRIE, D., *The Pastoral Epistles and the Mind of Paul* (London, 1956).

METZGER, B. M., 'A Reconsideration of Certain Arguments against the Pauline Authorship of the Pastoral Epistles', *Expository Times* 70 (1958–59), pp. 91–94.

GRAYSTON, K. and HERDAN, G., 'The Authorship of the Pastorals in the Light of Statistical Linguistics', *New Testament Studies* 6 (1959–60), pp. 1–15.

ELLIS, E. E., 'The Authorship of the Pastorals: A Résumé and Assessment of Current Trends', *Evangelical Quarterly* 32 (1960), pp. 151–161, reprinted in *Paul and his Recent Interpreters* (Grand Rapids, 1961), pp. 49–57.

PHILEMON

ERNEST G. ASHBY

Onesimus, a slave of Philemon in Colossae, fled to Rome, re-imbursing himself at his master's expense. There meeting Paul, whether by deliberate choice in seeking help, or by apparent 'accident', he was converted, and sent back with this most sympathetic letter to ease his return. Such is the traditional and apparently correct view of the situation. But J. Knox has in brilliant style sought to re-interpret this, for he thinks the whole of Colossians is more or less overshadowed by Paul's concern about Onesimus. To him Archippus is the owner of Onesimus and the ministry he is to fulfil is to send him back to Paul. The letter comes via Philemon of Laodicea to Archippus at Colossae in whose house the church met, and this letter is therefore that mentioned in Col. 4: 16. The facts as we have them in our letter seem to rule out this interesting theory, but Prof. Knox is inclined to identify Onesimus with the Bishop of the church at Ephesus, also of the same name, to whom Ignatius wrote, and to think that he had a share in collecting the Pauline letters (J. Knox: *Philemon among the letters of Paul*, pp. 30, 38–47, 49–61, 82, 88).

It is a model handling of a delicate situation, neither infringing the rights of others nor compromising his own convictions. That there is no frontal attack on slavery was not due to fear of opposition, but such a method might well have had prejudicial results then for the slaves themselves. More important still he demonstrates that the best way to prevent evil is to apply a positive principle, and brotherly love must, and ultimately did undermine slavery.

ANALYSIS

I. GREETINGS (1–3)
In this letter of entreaty Paul introduces himself not as an apostle but as **a prisoner of Christ Jesus**, and **Timothy** is included surely as a personal acquaintance of **Philemon** rather than, as some think, a witness in view of the somewhat legal nature of this correspondence. No doubt Philemon qualified for the title of **fellow worker** by his activities in the gospel during Paul's stay in Ephesus. It is generally assumed that **Apphia** was Philemon's wife, and perhaps **Archippus** was their son. To this household church Paul sends a message of grace and peace.

II. THANKSGIVING (4–7)
Every remembrance of Philemon in prayer moves Paul to thanksgiving for his practical Christianity shown in his faith in the Lord and his love to all his fellow Christians. He prays that Philemon's **sharing** of his faith, so described because faith is the root from which such beneficence springs, may be effective in promoting a full knowledge of all the blessings which through the gospel are the possession of Christians in their Lord. The help and relief thus ministered by Philemon have brought joy and encouragement to Paul.

5. Heb. 6: 10 does indicate that love to God is displayed in love to His people, but this verse is best explained as a chiasmus. This pairs off the internal and external terms of the sentence. Though the original speaks of love and faith . . . toward the Lord Jesus and all the saints, it would then mean **your faith in the Lord Jesus and your love for all the saints**. **6. understanding:** Possibly Philemon's, or those who share in his beneficence.

Philemon

III. THE APPEAL (8–22)

Paul is indeed gracious in preferring a request to a command, in refusing to take what he desires without Philemon's **consent**, and in undertaking to make good the deficiencies of Onesimus. Waiving his right to make demands on Philemon, as the ambassador and prisoner of Christ he prefers entreaty, appealing as a father for his own **son** whom with consummate tact he now mentions for the first time. Doubtless **Onesimus** was doubly dear to him, his son in the faith over whom he had travailed (Gal. 4: 19; 1. C. 4: 15) and the child of his imprisonment thereby confirming the overruling providence of God. The apostle has begotten him as Onesimus (i.e. useful)—for so the case of the word may imply—a punning reference to his name indicating that now for the first time he was true to it. **now he has become useful** both to his master and to Paul but the latter sends him back, though it is like giving up part of his very self. The apostle admits his own inclination: he could have wished to have kept him, but decided against such arbitrary action, and perhaps **take your place** (13) is a hint that he assumes Philemon would wish that he should keep him. But he sends him back so that Philemon's hand may not be forced, and sees that perhaps in the providential ordering of God his friend suffered a temporary loss to experience the permanent gain of a brother beloved. This goes beyond the mystery religions where a slave was treated as a fellow man: to receive him **as a dear brother** was bound to create problems when slavery was part of the very social structure of the day (cf. 1 Tim. 6: 2). Paul now makes his great appeal and offer. If Philemon regards him as an intimate friend, he is asked to forget all the misdemeanours of Onesimus and **welcome him** with the same welcome as he would give to the apostle himself. An implied reason for such action has been given in recounting God's hand at work in the life of the slave, but Paul also approaches it in business-like fashion. 'Debit me', he writes in the wording of business papyri, 'if there are debts'. In such gracious words he avoids actual reference to theft, though doubtless aware of it, and refers to his own autograph here, though this need not necessarily indicate he penned the whole letter. It is a legally signed IOU, but more of a gentleman's solemn assurance than meant to be a legally cognizable bond, for the reminder that Philemon owed his conversion to Paul would surely rule out any resort to law. But the offer is sincerely made and may imply Paul still had possession of some private property or could rely on Christian gifts to meet any need arising. In the light of the next statement, that it is really for a favour to **benefit** himself that he is pleading (20) there is virtually a certainty that Philemon will freely assent, and this Paul assumes (21). In fact the preservation of the letter confirms this: had the request been disregarded the letter would have been destroyed.

9. 'ambassador' (*presbeutēs*): Though MS evidence favours **'old man'** (*presbytēs*), by that time the two words were virtually interchangeable, and the first fits the context well (cf. Eph. 6: 20). **12. sending him back:** In other contexts this means 'refer back' i.e. to some other tribunal. Paul is referring the matter back to Philemon for his decision. **22.** Paul's hope of meeting Philemon may be a further inducement to comply with his request. If written from Rome it also indicates a change of plans as he had hoped to go on to Spain.

IV. CONCLUSION (23–25)

Epaphras their own evangelist is naturally singled out from the rest, and to call him **fellow prisoner** may only mean he is voluntarily sharing Paul's imprisonment. Concluding greetings come from the same friends as in Colossians, except for Jesus Justus who may have been, as Lightfoot suggests, a Roman Christian and included in the Colossian letter for his personal devotion to Paul. The letter concludes with a benediction.

BIBLIOGRAPHY

See Bibliography on Colossians

KNOX, J., *Philemon Among the Letters of Paul* (New York, 1959: London, 1960).

HEBREWS

GERALD F. HAWTHORNE

In language and learning the letter to the Hebrews ranks first among NT writings. Its argument is as brilliant as its theme is exalted. From first to last the author skilfully weaves his rich vocabulary into two basic themes— that of admonition and doctrine, and he does so via a style of Greek which approaches that of the very best literature of the Koine period (330 B.C.-A.D. 330). Yet in spite of Hebrews' own intrinsic brilliance there is that about it which is still dark and mysterious—well-nigh inexplicable. Who wrote it? To whom was it written? When and why was it written? These are questions which still perplex today, and for which there yet seem to be no final answers. Nevertheless, they are important to consider because whatever answers are given to them will influence one's interpretation of the letter.

Authorship

The AV, following a tradition going back to the late second century, answers the question of authorship with its informative title, 'The Epistle of Paul the Apostle to the Hebrews'. But did Paul really write Hebrews? The evidence is not sufficiently conclusive to answer the question unhesitatingly. Nowhere within the body of the letter does the author identify himself—a fact which is most unusual if indeed Paul is its author. For every other letter of his not only bears his name but contains personal greetings to his readers, and includes a complimentary paragraph about them. Hebrews, however, contains none of these characteristic Pauline features. Nor do any of the oldest Greek manuscripts in existence today contain a title for the letter other than the simple unadorned caption, 'To Hebrews', and even this brief title may not have been part of the original draft, since none of these manuscripts go back beyond the second century A.D. All longer titles which identify the author and include historical statements concerning him are late additions and hence, without authority or value.

When it comes to the testimony of the early Church Fathers the matter is not so simple or so certain. The Western wing of the Church did not recognize Paul as the author of Hebrews nor Hebrews as canonical until late in the fourth century. But on the other hand, as early as A.D. 185 the Eastern Church (particularly that located in the great centre of learning at Alexandria) knew of a tradition which attributed the letter to Paul. Although some of these Alexandrian scholars questioned the reliability of this tradition, they did not, however, deny it.

The style of the writer of Hebrews is unique in the NT, and exhibits none of those peculiarities characteristic of Paul's letters. There are none of Paul's hebraisms in Hebrews, none of his anacolutha (sentences which begin in one type of grammatical construction and end in another which is not consonant with the first, or simply tail off without any end at all), none of that rapid change, none of that same fiery passion which drove Paul on to the second topic before he had finished the first, none of the characteristic Pauline formulae for introducing OT quotations. Rather the style of Hebrews is that of a studied scholar who works with a rich and varied vocabulary, choosing words with accuracy and care so as to produce the proper rhythmical cadences for his composition. The sentences are carefully formed and finished, each blending into the other with a delightful smoothness of transition reminiscent of the Greek rhetoricians. Yet with all of its precision the letter is not without its depth of feeling. There is the exulting spirit, the fiery oratory, the glowing doxology. But unlike the Pauline letters emotion never dictates the manner of expression. Hebrews has a style which reflects the purest Greek in the NT. Thus style, too, seems to point away from Paul as the author of Hebrews. Some early fathers of the Church recognized this fact but explained the difference in style by saying that it was because Paul wrote the letter in Hebrew and Luke translated it into Greek, or again, that the thoughts were the thoughts of Paul but another, perhaps one of his students, later put it in written form.

Strangely, however, even the thought of Hebrews seems unlike that of Paul. Some of the most frequently used words in Hebrews, words like 'priest', 'high priest', 'tabernacle' (Gk. *skēnē*), 'offer', do not occur even one time in any of Paul's letters, while on the other hand many of the concepts stressed by Paul in the letters bearing his name find little or no emphasis in Hebrews. Only once is specific reference made in Hebrews to the resurrection of Christ (13: 10). Rarely does the author speak of 'righteousness'. Never does he use the word 'gospel'. But who can argue conclusively from this that Paul was indeed not the author? Does not subject matter dictate the themes for emphasis? And if Paul did have it in mind to cast the Lord Jesus in the role of priest, might he not have done it in just this very way? And the suppression of his name—could it not be, as Clement of Alexandria suggested, due to Paul's modesty, 'both for the sake of the honour of the Lord, "who being the Apostle of the Almighty was sent to Hebrews", "and because it was a work of supererogation for him to write to Hebrews, since he was herald and apostle of the Gentiles"'? (A. H. McNeile, *An Introduction to the Study of the New Testament*, 2nd rev. ed., 1953, pp. 236 f.).

Nevertheless, how the author says he learned the gospel seems to be a very strong argument against Pauline authorship. Could the same person who told the Galatians so vehemently that the gospel which he preached had not been communicated to him by any man—only by revelation from Jesus Christ—ever have written to the Hebrews that he had had it confirmed to him by those who heard the Lord Jesus (2: 3), that is, that he learned it second hand?

Who then wrote Hebrews? If not Paul, could it have been Barnabas? Barnabas was a levite (Ac. 4: 36) and thoroughly familiar with the priestly services. He was known as the 'son of encouragement' (Ac. 4: 36; cf. Heb. 13: 22). He was a companion of Paul (Ac. 13: 1 ff.), and there is very ancient tradition (Tertullian, who died after A.D. 220) which says that he was indeed its author. In more recent years, however, other names have been suggested. Luke, Priscilla, Silvanus are some of these. Apollos was Luther's intelligent guess. He was a Jew and an Alexandrian. He was eloquent and mighty in the Scriptures—'a gifted teacher and an ingenious exegete' (Ac. 18: 24). He was no doubt acquainted with Paul and possibly also with Timothy. His training (and especially the place where he had received it) would certainly have enabled him to write in the style and employ the thought-forms found in Hebrews.

Nevertheless, in the final analysis it is really necessary to confess humbly one's ignorance and say in the words of Origen, 'who wrote the epistle, in truth, God alone knows'. The question of authorship, however, is not really as important now as it was in the early years of Hebrews' existence, for then authorship and canonicity were closely associated. Then Hebrews ran the risk of being excluded from the canon because there were real questions about who wrote it. Though the influence of the Eastern Church, claiming Pauline authorship for Hebrews, did help give the letter standing, yet in the final analysis its own intrinsic worth won for it the place it holds in the canon.

Audience

The second problem is very like the first in that it too is difficult to solve. To whom was Hebrews written? This question is complicated by the fact that there is no epistolary introduction which names the recipients. And although it does possess a letter-like conclusion in which the author expresses his hope of being restored to his readers (13: 19), and though it names a certain Timothy (13: 23) and sends along the greetings of those from Italy (13: 24) there is still insufficient evidence for saying positively who these readers were.

The classical answer to this question has been that they were a specific group of Jewish Christians living in Palestine, or Rome, or Alexandria, or possibly Ephesus, who had renounced their ancient religion with its elaborate external ceremony to embrace Christianity with its contrasting de-emphasis of the externals, and who now found the transition to be very difficult psychologically. They were wavering in their faith because of persecution and were in danger of abandoning Christianity in order to beat a retreat back to Judaism. One is encouraged to adopt this view by the fact that the letter bears the title 'To Hebrews', makes prolific use of the OT, refers to the 'seed of Abraham', alludes frequently to the fathers of the Hebrew religion —Moses, Aaron, Joshua—and discusses in considerable detail the Jewish sacrificial system. The force of this argument is considerably weakened, however, when one recalls the possibility of the title not being original, but rather a later addition to make this letter conform to the pattern set by other letters—'To the Romans', 'To the Galatians', etc., and when one is made aware of the possibility that the title, if original, may have been simply a symbolic designation denoting the Church as 'the pilgrim-people of God' (cf. 1 Pet. 1: 17). At least once in the OT the expression 'The Hebrew' (Gen. 14: 13 NIV), is translated by the Greek word *peratēs* meaning 'wanderer'. Perhaps then, 'To Hebrews' may have meant not necessarily 'To Jewish Christians' but 'to the wandering people of God', whoever they may be—an idea which the author develops throughout his letter but especially in 3: 7–4: 13 where he parallels 'the Christian Church with Israel on its wandering toward the promised land'. This idea reaches its climax in the stirring words 'Here we have no lasting city, but we seek the city which is to come' (13: 14; cf. E. Käsemann, *Das Wandernde Gottesvolk*, 1939). The argument for a Jewish audience exclusively, is further weakened by recalling that the OT was as much the Bible of Christians as it was of Jews. Thus its authority would be just as great for Christians as for Jews. Thus also the great leaders of the past would belong to the Gentile Church quite as much as to the Jewish. All these things coupled with the fact that Paul himself calls Christians the true seed of Abraham (Rom. 4: 16; Gal. 3: 29) tend to cancel out the arguments in favour of the letter's recipients being Jewish Christians only and should caution one against being too sure of his ability to identify them.

Others have suggested that the recipients of this letter were Jewish Christians influenced by a type of gnosticism similar to that which Paul encountered in Colossae—a gnosticism which taught that matter was evil, that there were emanations from the ultimate reality—angels —the lowest of which produced and controlled the material universe, and that asceticism (sometimes the very opposite—immorality) was the best course to follow if one wished to overcome the evil material world in which he found himself. This theory is based on such passages as Heb. 9: 10 and 13: 9, on the lengthy discussion of Christ's superiority to the angels, and on the author's insistence that matter is not evil—it was created by the Son of God (1: 2), who Himself partook of blood and flesh in the incarnation (2: 14).

More recent interpreters have turned aside from all such identification of its recipients as being Jewish to suggest that they might have been Gentile Christians or simply Christians without reference to whether they were Gentiles or Jews, whose problem was not one of wishing to return to Judaism but of drifting away from the living God (2: 1 with 3: 12). There is no mention of Judaism as such within the letter, and no trace of any tension existing between Gentile and Jew as often was the case in Paul's letters. The OT, used so frequently in Hebrews, was always the Greek translation, known as the Septuagint (LXX). Never did the author quote from the Hebrew text nor does he show any knowledge of it. This coupled with the fact that Hebrews, in spite of its many OT quotations, is the least Hebraic writing in the NT, even using religious vocabulary not derived from the LXX, certainly tells something about the audience as well as the author. Such expressions as 'repentance from acts that lead to death, and of faith in God' (6: 1), and 'cleanse our consciences from acts that lead to death, so that we may serve the living God!' (9: 14) seem certainly to indicate that they were not wholly Jewish, for in spite of his many failures the Jew did render service to and have faith in the living God. One notices, too, that the exhortations given in Hebrews are not warnings against relapsing into Judaism but are general exhortations to lead a life of faith (A. Wikenhauser, *Introduction to the New Testament*, 1958, p. 464). It is also significant that all the writer's references are to the *Tabernacle* services, not to the *Temple* activities of his day.

William Manson recently sought a fresh integration of Hebrews into the historical development of early Christian thought and life. He rejected the view that Hebrews was written to Gentile Christians, but at the same time he attempted to relate it to the Hellenistic movement within the early Church—a movement which, though Jewish in its backgrounds, had grasped the more-than-Jewish sense in which the office and significance of Jesus in history were to be understood. These Hellenists had 'perceived the universal range and bearing of the Christ-event' and had understood the full implications of being called by Christ. Hence, they were willing to accept the consequences of this call in terms of *world-wide evangelization* and were desirous of exhorting others to do the same. Manson's hypothesis is suggested by the similarities between the letter of Hebrews and the Sermon of Stephen who was the chief spokesman for the Hellenists (Ac. 6–7). He concludes, therefore, that the letter issued forth from the Hellenistic wing of the Church and was directed toward Christians of Jewish extraction who were still clinging to the Jewish ordinances and were 'hanging back from accepting the full consequences of their calling' (W. Manson, *The Epistle to the Hebrews*, 1951, ch. 1). Such a view as this accounts for the emphasis of Hebrews on Jewish ordinances, the Greek style of the letter, the absence of any specific warning against lapsing back into Judaism, and the strong urging to go on to perfection. It should be noted, however, that one serious objection to Manson's thesis is that for the Hellenistic Hebrew Christian, dietary and similar laws would have had more significance than the cultic ones used by the writer of Hebrews.

More recently some have suggested the possibility that the audience of Hebrews was a group of Jews who had formerly belonged to the Dead Sea Sect at Qumran. Perhaps they were priests of Qumran for 'only priests would have had sufficient intelligence and taste for this theology of sacrifice so that one could write an entire epistle dedicated exclusively to this theme' (C. Spicq, *L'Épître aux Hébreux*, 1953, I. p. 266). They had been converted to Christianity and had carried with them—to their own spiritual disadvantage—some of their former beliefs: (1) in two messiahs—one a priest, the other a king, with the priestly messiah superior to the kingly; (2) in the necessity for a temporary cessation of sacrifices, but also in the future restoration of these when the eschatological war would leave the elect of God triumphant (cf. F. F. Bruce, 'Qumran and Early Christianity', *NTS* 2 (1956), p. 187); (3) in the tremendous importance of angels whom they conceived to be the first-creatures of God —perhaps even 'sons of God'—the transmitters of the law, and those who in the final war would bring salvation to God's elect (see note on 1: 4; cf. also H. Kosmala, *Hebräer-Essener-Christen*, 1959).

No doubt there are other possibilities, but the variety of opinions displayed here is sufficient to show the difficulty of deciding who really did receive this letter originally. Perhaps it is not at all important to know who they were. For if Adolf Deissmann (*Light from the Ancient East*, chs. 2–3) is correct in saying that Hebrews is *not a letter* (defined by Deissmann as a non-literary composition designed only for a particular group without any thought of publication) but an *epistle*, that is, an artistic piece of literature carefully worked out in form as well as in content so as to present something literarily worthy of wide distribution, then the many hypotheses about the 'addressees' may be unnecessary—perhaps even misleading. Were it not for chapter 13 with its epistolary conclusion and the occasional reference to the readers (5: 11–6: 12; 10: 32–34; etc.), one would not at all suspect that Hebrews was a letter. It seems more like a written-down sermon intended for wide distribution, for the rhetoric is more that of pulpit oratory than prose composition and the author presents himself as a speaker rather than as a writer (Spicq, *Comm.* I, p. 18; see Heb. 2: 5; 6: 9; 8: 1; 9: 5; 11: 32). He himself terms his brilliant work a '*sermon of exhortation*' (Gk. *logos paraklēseōs*, 13: 22). Thus, if it is necessary to assume that the author wrote originally to a particular group, it can be inferred that he did so only while seeing the whole Church. He wrote with ecumenical vision!

Destination and Date

The place where these recipients resided is, of course, connected with who they were and to some extent with who wrote to them. If they were Gentile Christians, or even Jewish Christians for that matter, they well might have resided in any of the cities of the Mediterranean area. Even Jews were found in almost every important centre of the world. If they were Jewish Christians beset by a gnostic heresy, some place in Asia Minor, perhaps Ephesus, would be a possibility. If they were priests from Qumran, then Antioch in Syria could have been the place. Alexandria also has been suggested because of the philosophic nature of the letter. Rome, however, has the strongest arguments in its favour. Here Hebrews was first quoted, perhaps as early as A.D. 95 by Clement of Rome in his letter to the Corinthian church. Hebrews also includes the expression 'those from Italy send you their greetings' (13: 24), which, though ambiguous, at least links the readers with Italy in some positive way.

As to when the author wrote to his friends, this too is as uncertain as who the author was and who they were to whom he wrote. The only certain thing about the date of Hebrews is that it must have been written sometime before Clement's letter (see above), which is customarily dated about A.D. 95–96 (some date it as late as A.D. 120). Thus, A.D. 95–96 (or possibly A.D. 120) becomes the latest possible date for Hebrews. But how early could it have been written? Because Hebrews makes no mention of the destruction of the temple in Jerusalem—an event which the writer might well have capitalized upon in his emphasis on the end of the old dispensation and the dawn of the new—it is assumed by some that it must have been written before A.D. 70. Manson wishes to supplement this evidence for an early date by arguing that the letter's 'reiterated emphasis on the "forty years" of Israel's probation in the desert in chapters 3–4 makes transparent the date of the epistle to the Hebrews. Hebrews was written at a time when the fortieth anniversary of the dawning of salvation in Jesus (2: 3) was already at hand . . . therefore in the sixties of the first Christian century' (*op. cit.*, pp. 55–56). There is also the fact that Timothy was still living (13: 23) though this in itself is no certain argument for an early date, since it is not known that this Timothy was Paul's companion by that name. This much, however, seems to be clear, namely, that the letter was written not to recent converts but to those who had been Christians for some time, who, for the length of time since their conversion, should have been teachers (5: 12), who could be called upon to remember the former days, and the conduct of their leaders now deceased (13: 7). In addition, 2: 3 indicates that the author and his readers were second generation Christians at least in the sense that they had not received the message originally from the Saviour. Thus it is possible to date Hebrews only loosely as having been written sometime between the middle of the first century and the time when I Clement was written—A.D. 95–96 (no later than 120).

Aim

The writer of Hebrews himself discloses the nature and purpose of his letter when he calls it a word of exhortation (13: 22). This means that the many paragraphs of warning and admonition interspersed throughout the work are not to be considered parenthetical but primary. The theological sections surrounding them are important only because they furnish the basis for these exhortations. The writer believes in the possibility of his readers being deceived by sin (3: 13), of drifting away from the message delivered by the Saviour (2: 1), of falling from their Christian profession (3: 12; 6: 4–6; 10: 26 ff.) and his concern knows no bounds. For to turn from Christ is to turn from the living God and to renounce Christianity is to renounce the ultimate in divine revelation. There is nothing left but a fearful prospect of judgment (10: 27). From such a tragedy the writer wishes to preserve his readers, whoever they may be, whether they be persons careless of their heritage (2: 3), underdeveloped because of slothfulness (5: 11), indifferent to the importance of the Christian assembly (10: 25), pressured to give in by the dullness of daily life (10: 32–36), weary from the struggle—perhaps simply morally lax (12: 12), or influenced by diverse and strange teachings (13: 9). His course of action is simple and direct. It is to 'prove' that Christianity is the final and absolute revelation of God to man and that it alone discloses the only way of worshipful access to God (10: 19–22).

The writer does this by starting with the basic presuppositions, first, that the religion of the OT was the highest and best of all religions, because the one true God had revealed Himself to the Jews as He had to no other people, and second, that the OT constituted the inspired Scriptures containing this divine revelation. From such a basis he can prove that Christianity has superseded the OT religion simply by showing that this supersession was predicted in the Scriptures themselves. Thus it is that he uses many OT proof-texts to proclaim the surpassing excellence of the 'Son' to angels, Moses, Joshua, and Aaron, thereby asserting the transcendent character of Christ's revelation to that transmitted through angels, of His priestly ministry to that inaugurated by Aaron, of the 'rest' He provides to that offered by Joshua, and of the new covenant established by Him to that mediated through Moses.

It is this understanding that keeps prompting the writer to use the adjective 'better', as well as many other comparative words, in describing Christianity over against Judaism. His descriptive vocabulary also includes such words as 'perfect', 'stable', 'genuine', 'eternal', when commenting on the new revelation in Christ in contrast to such words as 'fragmentary', 'shadowy', 'shakeable', etc., to describe the old. But at the same time the writer is careful to show that there is no discontinuity between the two revelations. The same God who spoke long ago is the One who has spoken in these last days. The promises made in the past are the very ones being fulfilled today. The old covenant, though a shadow, was nevertheless a true shadow of the real substance now here.

This then is his argument aimed at preventing professing Christians from turning away from God's revelation in Christ. For if Judaism, the highest and best of all religions, has now given way to Christianity, as promise must give way to fulfilment, then no other approach to God is worth considering. Surely then his readers will hold fast to their Christian confession if only they can be made to grasp this great truth!

One thing more needs to be said: The writer of Hebrews approaches the subject of salvation from what might be called the 'phenomenal' approach. He understands that it is entirely possible for any group of confessing Christians to be made up of a mixed-multitude—those with and those without genuine faith. The only objective test to prove the reality of one's own commitment to the Lord Jesus, or the commitment of anyone else for that matter, is the test of perseverance—faith *made visible* by a loyalty which continues throughout life. That a vast multitude left Egypt under Moses proved nothing about the faith of that group. That only two men entered Canaan at the end of the journey did. So the warnings of Hebrews are real warnings intended to point up this possibility of a mixed-multitude existing and to point out the tragic and ultimate consequences of defection, not at all like the consequences of those who defected in the wilderness. But the encouragement offered in Hebrews is just as real: You may show to yourself and to the world that your confession was a real one by holding firm to it until the very end of life, and you may be sure of divine help in this determination to endure (4: 16).

ANALYSIS

I. GOD'S FINAL REVELATION
(1: 1–14)
i. Prologue (1: 1–4)

The first four verses of Hebrews comprise one long majestic sentence in the Greek, which befittingly serves to set forth the writer's grand theme—the transcendence of Christ as Revealer and Redeemer. The beauty and balance of it are sufficient proofs that there was no original epistolary beginning now lost.

The letter begins in such a way as to throw the nature of the earlier revelation into sharp contrast with that of the new. By stating that God spoke of old **at many times and in various ways** (1), the writer indicates that not only was the OT varied, and full and inspired, but also that it lacked finality, that at no one time in the past and through no one person, prophet or psalmist, nor through all of them together, did God fully disclose His will; whereas by the expression, **in these last days he has spoken** (lit. 'spoke', carrying with it the idea of 'once and for all'), he emphasizes the completeness and perfection of that revelation which now has come in this final stage of God's

plan of redemption (cf. Isa. 2: 2; Dan. 10: 14). And there is good reason for drawing such a sharp contrast between the two revelations as the writer now makes clear: the old came **through** (lit. 'in') **the prophets**, but the new **by** ('in') **his Son** (1–2). In the first instance the prophets were mere human instruments of revelation, nothing more; in the second, one who is Himself God's Son, possessing His same nature, is the means by which that message comes. Thus the superiority of God's revelation in Christ is due not merely to the fact that it came last and at the end of an era, but to the 'transcendent character of the person, the rank, the status, and the authority of Him through whom and in whom it comes' (Manson, *op. cit.*, p. 89). Two things should be observed from these opening remarks. First, the writer stresses the unity and continuity of the two revelations, which in essence are not two but one which culminates in Christ. The same God speaks **in these last days** as spoke **in the past**. And secondly, he implies that whenever God does disclose Himself to man it is chiefly through man that He does it. 'In the prophets' and 'in his Son' are expressions which reiterate the principle that God communicates His truth through the human personality.

But it is not just in one who is son among many that God offers His final revelation. The expression, **by his Son** (2), therefore, inadequately conveys the writer's intent at this point. It is true that the Greek lacks both definite article and possessive pronoun, but this omission is due either to the rhythmic demands of the sentence or to the writer's desire to stress the quality of this ultimate word of His. The context demands that it be translated 'His Son', 'one who is Son' (B. F. Westcott, *The Epistle to the Hebrews*, 1889, p. 7), or 'the Son', for He must be thought of as Son 'incomparable and unique'. That this is so is demonstrated by the several expressions which immediately follow. They describe the Son as (*a*) author and goal of creation, in that He is **heir of all things** and the efficient cause of their creation, and as (*b*) Himself divine, in that **The Son is the radiance of God's glory and the exact representation of his being** (3).

The word 'radiance' translates the Greek *apaugasma* which also has an active meaning of 'radiates' (cf. the translation of the NEB, 'The Son who is the *effulgence* of God's splendour'. Cf. also Wis. 7: 24 ff. where this word is used with the meanings 'reflect' and 'radiate' combined. The writer of Hebrews was no doubt familiar with this passage). By means of this word the writer shows the divine origin of the Son, His resemblance to the Father and at the same time His personal independence (cf. Spicq, *Comm.* II. p. 7)—He reflects or radiates 'the Glory'. [Note: 'of God' is not in the Gk. Since 'the Glory' was particularly associated with God in the LXX, the expression came to be a surrogate for God (cf. 2 Pet. 1: 17). Perhaps it is used that way here—'the Son reflects (radiates) God'.] The expression, **the exact representation of his being**, adds no new idea but enlarges upon the former, further defining the relationship existing between the Son and the Father. He is the 'exact representation of God's real being', and all the essential characteristics of God are brought into clear focus in Him: he that has seen the Son, has seen the Father also (cf. Jn 14: 9). This, together with the former statement, comprises one of the strongest claims for the deity of Christ found anywhere in the NT (cf. also Jn 1: 1–3; Col. 1: 15). It is strengthened by the assertion that He is **sustaining all things by his powerful word** (3). One must not, however, picture the Son as an Atlas supporting in stationary fashion the weight of the world on His shoulders, for there is within the word 'sustain' (lit. 'bear', Gk. *pherein*) not only the idea of 'maintenance', but also of 'movement toward'. Thus the Son is described as one who both maintains 'the

All' and who bears it forward to its final goal.

In the latter part of v. 3 there is a brief reference to that idea which really constitutes the main theme of the letter: the priest who made **purification for sins**. The writer of Hebrews understands the priestly service to be the essential activity of the Son, and the real reason for His coming to earth. This is reflected even in the form of the verb he uses to describe His work although the translation obscures it. When he talks about the beginning of the aeons he says that the Son **made** (Gk. *epoiēsen*) them. When he approaches the subject of purification for sins he employs the same verb but gives it a different form—a form which implies greater interest or involvement in the action on the part of the subject (*poiēsamenos*). This idea is correctly reflected in the translation of the AV: 'when he had *by himself* purged our sins . . .'

Along with the basic themes of redemption and resurrection, that of the exaltation of Christ to the right hand of God was an essential element in apostolic preaching and teaching (Ac. 2: 34; Eph. 1: 20; Rev. 3: 21). When the writer of Hebrews states that the Son **sat down at the right hand of the majesty in heaven** (3), he shows that he is in accord with this traditional emphasis. But at the same time he uses this statement to stress the finality of the Son's work (cf. the note on 10: 12), and to show that the Son is at the same time the promised Messiah. [Note: this expression concerning the Son's exaltation to the right hand is a quotation taken from a messianic psalm (Ps. 110).]

It is just possible that verse 4 was occasioned by angel worship on the part of the audience, but not necessarily so. In the OT as well as in many apocryphal books angels played a very important role. They were looked upon as creatures in closest proximity to God (Isa. 6: ff.), possibly even called 'sons of God' (cf. Gen. 6: 2 with Job 1: 6; 2: 1. Cf. also E. L. Sukenik, *The Dead Sea Scrolls of the Hebrew University*, pl. 53, fragment 2, 1. 3). They were also considered to be the mediators of the law (Ac. 7: 53; Gal. 3: 19; Heb. 2: 2). In any case, as the writer points out, the Son is superior to angels because, quite apart from His 'eternal nature', in His human rôle He earned by experience (this is the force of the expression **became**) what was already His by personality—a **name . . . superior to theirs** (cf. Phil. 2: 5–11).

ii. Proofs for the Statements in the Prologue (1: 5–14)

In a fashion typical of this writer, the OT is now called upon to give validity to the statements he has made. For him the OT is inspired by God and wholly authoritative. Its pronouncement is final, no further argument is required. For him, too, there is a deeper meaning to the OT than the historical. It is the

Christological. The Son, who is the Christ, is the key unlocking the true treasures of the ancient Scriptures. Thus, he feels free, in fact compelled, to apply to Christ the exalted language of the OT although it originally may have been spoken of another. By such an exegetical method it is quite an easy matter to establish the validity of his statements concerning Christ.

He begins the proof for his statement concerning Christ's superiority to angels with a quotation from Ps. 2: **'You are my Son; today I have become your Father'** (5). Historically this may have been sung to an Israelite monarch on the day of his coronation (cf. H. H. Rowley, ed., *The Old Testament and Modern Study*, 1951, p. 167). Later it was interpreted messianically (cf. Ac. 4: 25 f.; 13: 33). It is in this Christological sense that the writer of Hebrews uses it to establish by it the fact that the Son was always Son (the 'You *are*' describing an essential and continuing relationship with the Father), that He nevertheless earned this title of Son at some moment in history (the '*Today* I have become your Father' implying a particular 'time when'. Cf. Lk. 3: 22 (RSVmg); 9: 35; Rom. 1: 4 for possibilities as to when this was), and that He is infinitely superior to angels, **for to which of the angels did God ever say** such a thing (5)?

The writer continues piling up proof by adding a quotation from 2 Sam. 7: 14: **'I will be his father'** (5). These words were addressed originally by God to David and they concerned his son. But if the words were ever true of Solomon they are surpassingly more true of Christ. In fact, to the writer of Hebrews they find their ultimate fulfilment in Him. This passage was never applied messianically in rabbinic literature, but there is now evidence from the Dead Sea Scrolls that some Jewish communities did so interpret it. The writer of Hebrews, however, never refers to Christ as the Son of David.

He continues his proof by combining Ps. 97: 7 with the Septuagint reading of Dt. 32: 43. [Note: The Septuagint (LXX) is the Greek translation of the Hebrew OT, and at Deut. 32: 43 it has a longer reading than that found in the Massoretic Text of the Hebrew. Because it is not in the Hebrew it is not in the English translations based upon them. Now, however, for the first time there is support for the longer reading in a pre-Massoretic Hebrew text found in the Dead Sea community of Qumran (cf. F. M. Cross, *The Ancient Library of Qumran*, 1958, pp. 182 f.).] His combination of these two passages results in a command for **all God's angels** to **worship him** (6). The interesting thing about this exhortation is that in both the Psalm and the Deuteronomy passage the 'Him' refers to God Himself. But because the writer

has already made clear the community of nature that exists between the Father and the Son, he has no misgivings whatsoever in applying to the **first-born** what was said originally of the Father. The expression 'first-born' is a technical term which when here applied to Christ may mean that to the writer of Hebrews Christ is prior to and sovereign over all creation (cf. Lightfoot's note on Col. 1: 15), or it may mean that he simply intended it to be understood of Christ in His relationship to men who also are called 'sons of God' (2: 10; cf. also Rom. 8: 29).

The final proof of Christ's superiority to angels comes from Ps. 104: 4. By describing the angels as **winds** and **flames of fire** (7), the writer calls attention to their 'mutability, materiality and transitoriness' (Westcott, *Comm.*, p. 25), in contrast to the enduring qualities of the Son whose throne **will last for ever and ever** (8). 2 Esd. 8: 21 f. shows by synonymous parallelism that this interpretation of the nature of angels is correct: 'Before whom the hosts of angels stand with trembling: at whose bidding they are changed to wind and fire'.

The second set of quotations is designed to substantiate the writer's statement concerning the Son as the radiance and stamp of deity (8–9). He begins with a quotation from Ps. 45 stating that the words of this Psalm were addressed in reference to the Son: **'Your throne, O God, will last for ever and ever'** (8). Historically, this Psalm probably was composed for and sung at the wedding of an Israelite king. As was common, the king, because of his intimate relationship to God as God's representative on earth, was on occasion made the recipient of such hyperbolic attributions as '*Elohim*, 'God' (cf. Ps. 82: 6 with Jn 10: 34; cf. also Rowley, *op. cit.*, pp. 167 f.). What was symbolically true of the ancient Hebrew monarch only by virtue of his office, the writer of Hebrews see to be wholly true of Christ by virtue of His nature. The first part of this quotation is ambiguous in the Greek so that some translators are inclined to translate it 'God is your throne' (cf. the RSV mg), yet it is clear both from the context of Ps. 45 and that of Heb. 1 that the vocative of address is intended —'Your throne, O God'. There is the same ambiguity of construction in v. 9 so that the expression, **'God, your God . . . by anointing you,** may also be translated 'O God, Thy God, has anointed Thee' (cf. Aquila's translation of the Hebrew psalm; so also NEB). This anointing came originally as a reward for righteousness and justice (9). Because the writer of Hebrews now applies this psalm to Christ and because he understands the life of Christ to have been a period of 'moral probation' (2: 18; 5: 8; etc.), it is most likely that he equates the anointing of Christ with His exaltation—a reward, no less, for the successful accomplishment of His mission on earth (cf. 2: 9). **Above your companions** (9) means beyond all those who have received the royal unction before and since.

Finally, the writer establishes the truth of his statement concerning the creative activity of the Son by an extended quotation from Ps. 102: 25–27 (10–13). Originally it outlined the creative power of God—**'In the beginning, O Lord, you laid the foundations of the earth, and the heavens are the work of your hands'** (10), and His eternal qualities over against the creation's transient ones—**'they will perish, but you remain'** (11). Now, however, it is applied to the Son. The writer found this application an easy one to make because in the LXX, which he uses continuously, there was the insertion of the word 'Lord' into the text—'Thou, *Lord*, didst found the earth . . .'—which does not appear in the Hebrew. 'Lord', of course, was the title the apostolic age most frequently gave to Jesus Christ.

The author climaxes his catena of OT quotations by again referring to Ps. 110 (cf. 1: 3). With it he describes God as entering the conflict to fight the enemies of His Anointed: **'Sit . . . until I make your enemies a footstool for your feet'** (13). This quotation is not designed to show that the Son is impotent and unable to fight His own battles, but to make clear the identity of will that exists between Father and Son, and the respect the Father has for the Son (Spicq, *Comm.*, II, p. 2). Never could this be said of angels for they are mere **ministering spirits sent to serve those who will inherit salvation** (14). With this mention of 'salvation' the author closes his discussion concerning the cosmic dimensions of the Son and moves on to a new topic—the rôle of Jesus in redemption on the plane of historical events.

II. GOD'S PROGRAMME FOR SALVATION (2: 1–18)

i. Warning and Exhortation (2 1–4)

Before developing the theme of salvation the writer feels compelled to stop and issue a warning based upon the implications of his exegetical theology. This is in keeping with his method of interweaving exhortation with theology. Such 'digressions' are not to be thought of as the writer stepping aside from his main purpose. Rather he is laying bare his main purpose by means of them (cf. 13: 22)

The warning here may be the key to the understanding of the difficulty faced by those who first received the letter to the Hebrews. It seems to be a warning against neglect and indifference to the new revelation, against failure to appreciate it and to go on into its full benefits, against the possibility that we might

drift away (1). The solution to the problem is moral exercise: **pay more careful attention . . . to what we have heard** (1), which implies individual responsibility in the application of one's mind to the new revelation in such an extraordinary fashion that he obeys it with abandon.

The reason for this exhortation is to be found in the nature of this new revelation. The earlier **message** was **spoken by angels** (2) and every sin of commission and omission (**violation and disobedience**) was properly punished. But the new message of salvation **was announced . . . by the Lord** (3), who has been shown to be incomparably superior to angels. His message, therefore, is equally superior to that mediated by them, and neglect of it that much more culpable. It was never stated explicitly in the OT that the law was transmitted through angels, only implied (cf. Dt. 33: 2, LXX, and Ps. 68: 17, LXX), but it was nevertheless an axiom of Judaism (see Josephus, *Ant.* 15, 5. 3), and a belief of the Church (cf. Ac. 7: 53 and Gal. 3: 19).

Because the new revelation brought by the Son **was confirmed to us by those who heard him** (3) we have the certainty of a faithful tradition in which we can have the utmost confidence. The expression, 'was confirmed', translates the Greek *bebaioō* meaning 'make firm', 'establish', 'confirm'. Goodspeed thus more clearly expresses the idea contained here when he translates it: 'was guaranteed'. Here also is the hint that the author reckoned himself among those who received his 'authentic tradition' second hand from those who had actually heard the Saviour.

Verse 4 serves two purposes: (*a*) to show the place and purpose of miracles, namely to establish the authenticity of the NT message (God 'added His testimony' in miracle to show it had divine sanction) and (*b*) 'to emphasize the awful authority of "the things that were heard"' (F. D. V. Narborough, *The Epistle to the Hebrews*, 1930, p. 86). Not only was this message spoken by the Lord, it was visibly approved by God, and by charismatic gifts of the Holy Spirit. Father, Son, and Holy Spirit thus co-operated to produce this revelation of salvation. To drift from it or to treat it with indifference is the height of folly.

ii. The Outline of Salvation (2: 5–18)

This first section (5–9), which outlines the need for salvation and the means by which it is accomplished, becomes more intelligible if it is connected with 1: 14. Angels are **sent to serve those who will inherit salvation** (1: 14), **it is not to angels that he has subjected the world to come** (2: 5). In these words the writer is saying that in spite of what may have been a temporary policy [Note: angels were believed to rule people (Dt. 32: 8, LXX; Dan.

10: 13; 12: 1) as well as stars and planets (1 Enoch 60: 15–21; 18: 13–16; Jubilees 2: 2)], it was not God's purpose to give angels sovereignty over His 'moral, organized system' (Gk. *oikoumenē*, Westcott, *Comm.* p. 42). This sovereignty He reserved solely for man as the writer's use of Ps. 8 shows so clearly (note the casual way in which he introduces this quotation: lit., 'someone testified somewhere', implying that to the writer of Hebrews the instrument is insignificant; it is really God who has spoken): **'You crowned him** (man, the son of man) **with glory and honor, and put everything under his feet'** (7b f.). This then is the divine ideal (cf. Gen. 1: 26–28): man is to rule; the son of man who was made only a 'little less than God' (Ps. 8: 5, RSV) is destined to be sovereign, and nothing is to be left **that is not subject to him** (8). It is at this point, however, that the need for salvation becomes crystal clear, for **we do not see everything subject** to man (8b). God's goal for man is not now being realized.

Yet divine purposes cannot be frustrated. Verse 9 reveals that God has provided a means of salvation. He has found a way to restore man to his place of sovereignty: **Jesus, who was made a little lower than the angels**, is now **crowned with glory and honor**. [Note: Here for the first time is the mention of the name 'Jesus'. It is a favourite designation, used by the writer of Hebrews thirteen times in his letter.]

In the present argument of the writer, the expression 'made lower than the angels', probably means little more than that the Eternal became human, for it is to be noted that this expression is borrowed from Ps. 8 (quoted above), and is the only one that says anything at all about the nature of man. Therefore, when the writer of Hebrews states that Jesus was made lower than the angels, he is simply saying, by means of scriptural phraseology, that the Son of God became incarnate as a man, that He assumed man's position. But this is a tremendously important statement, nevertheless, for in his thinking it was only in this act of self-identification with the human race that **by the grace of God** He was enabled to **taste death for everyone** (9).

The prevalent idea of 'corporate solidarity' no doubt was in the writer's mind when he penned the foregoing statement: the redeemed together with the Redeemer 'constitute a unity and this unity is conceived in terms of substance: they and he belong to one body . . . What happens to the Redeemer, or happened while he tarried in human form on earth, happens to his whole body, i.e., not to him alone but to all who belong to that body. So if he suffered death, the same is true of them (2 C. 5: 14). If he was raised from the dead the same is true of

them (1 C. 15: 20–22)' (cf. Rom. 5: 12, 18 f.; 1 C. 15: 45 f.; R. Bultmann, *Theology of the New Testament*, 1951, I, p. 299).

From this it now becomes clear that when the writer proceeds to say that Jesus was **crowned with glory and honor** (9) he understands this event to be far more extensive than the exaltation of Jesus' single self. For if it is true that Jesus has been exalted to the place of sovereignty, it is also true that they who are bound up with Him in one body likewise share in this exaltation. Thus it is that salvation is made complete, for what man had not been able to realize, namely his divinely appointed destiny of being sovereign, Jesus has, and man through Him.

Mention should be made of two other things: First, whether the Greek expression *brachy ti* be translated to show degree, i.e., 'a little lower than the angels' (NIV), or to show time, i.e., 'a little while' (RSV, for which there is general support today), makes little difference, for it adds nothing at all to the writer's main argument. He seems to have included it primarily because it was part of a quotation he needed to show that Christ became what man was. Second, it is worth calling special attention to the fact that for the writer the exaltation (including that of man as well) came about only because of the suffering and death of Jesus. Nothing is said of His teaching as a means of human salvation. This, of course, is in keeping with the writer's emphasis upon the priesthood of Christ, and His self-sacrifice by which atonement was made (cf. 9: 14).

This next section (10–18) reiterates the great concept of the divine identifying with the human, and seeks to offer reasons why such a method of salvation was used by God. The first reason is suggested without the customary proof from Scripture, namely, that this particular method, which necessarily involved the perfecting of the Saviour **through suffering** (and death), **was fitting** to the one **for whom and through whom everything exists** (10). And not only is such a plan of redemption fully in keeping with the nature of God, but this description of Him as the final and efficient cause *of all things* lays bare two more essential truths pertaining to salvation: (*a*) that the suffering of the Redeemer was not accidental, but in accordance with the general plan of divine providence (Spicq, *Comm.*, I, *ad loc.*), and (*b*) that God Himself is the grand initiator of this redemptive process; it is He who has set all things in motion who has determined to bring **many sons to glory** (this being the key phrase, denoting the essence of salvation, cf. 7b and 9b) by perfecting their Saviour through suffering. The verb 'to perfect' (Gk. *teleioun*) means 'to complete a process', and by its use the writer has shown that Jesus became fully qualified to be the pioneer of man's salvation through the process of human suffering.

In v. 11 emphasis is again placed upon the self-identification of the Son with those He came to redeem, its completeness, and its *raison d'être*: **the one who makes men holy and those who are made holy are of the same family**, i.e., are inextricably bound up together. Hence, since suffering and death are so very much a part of humanity, it was impossible for it to have been otherwise with the Son who had graciously taken to Himself this same humanity. In making use of the verb 'made holy' the author is not commenting on the moral character of its subjects, for it is primarily a technical term meaning simply 'to set apart'. It was often used of Israel (cf. Exod. 19: 14) who, by their sanctification, were set apart as the special people of God. Now those who have been redeemed by the death of Christ are given the same designation used of ancient Israel—a fact which may signify that the writer understands Christians to be the new people of God.

Now the writer turns to the Scriptures for proof (12–13). The identification of the Son with humanity was no afterthought of God. He had announced it through the prophetic voice of psalmist and seer: **I will proclaim your name to my brothers . . .**, and, **I will put my trust in him**, and finally, **I, and the children God has given me**. How complete then was this identification? The scriptural answer given to this question is that it was as complete as that which exists between brothers, or that which exists between father and child. It was as complete as 'community of nature' could make it. The first of these OT quotations comes from Ps. 22, a Psalm which earlier had been used by the Lord of Himself while He was on the cross (cf. Mt. 27: 46). Thus it was an easy matter for the writer to apply another part of that same Psalm to Him here. The last two quotations are from Isa. 8: 17 f. (LXX), and their words originally gave expression to that prophet's personal faith in God and his conviction that he and his sons symbolized the believing remnant of Israel. When applied to Christ they reveal that in assuming humanity to Himself He was required to live within those limitations in complete dependence upon God (cf. the note on 12: 2), and that He and His 'children' comprise the new community of God's believing people.

Not only was salvation by identification consonant with the nature of God, it was also necessary (14–18). For **since the children have flesh and blood** (the word order in the Greek, however, is 'blood and flesh'), that is to say, since they are human, the Son also in just the same way (Gk. *paraplēsiōs*, 'in absolutely identical fashion') had to share **in their hu-**

manity (14) if He was to get at their real problem—death. [Note: The two verbs, **have** and **shared**, reflect two different verbs in the Greek, the first 'marks the common nature shared among men as long as the race lasts'; the second 'expresses the unique fact of the incarnation as a voluntary acceptance of humanity' (Westcott, *Comm.*, p. 53).] By becoming human the Eternal Son made Himself susceptible to death. But the great paradox is that by death He destroyed (lit. 'rendered powerless') the devil **who holds the power of death** (cf. Wis. 2: 24), and released once-and-for-all **all those who through fear of death were subject to lifelong bondage** (14, 15). The author does not here make clear how the death of Christ actually destroyed the power of the devil and released men from the fear he held them in, but he does so later on. Then he shows that Christ's death was of such a nature that it freed men from the guilt of their sin and their consciences from the dread of its consequences (cf. 9: 14; 10: 22).

Verse 16 is a summary. It shows that this salvation is intended for men not angels. The expression **helps** translates the Greek verb *epilambanesthai* which means 'to take hold of', or 'grasp'. The idea is that God graciously laid hold of **Abraham's descendants**, that is, all who like Abraham have faith in God (cf. Gal. 3: 29) in order to lead them from death to glory (cf. Jer. 31: 32 (38: 22, LXX); Isa. 41: 8 f. LXX). He has not done this for angels.

The method God designed for accomplishing this salvation is the priestly, for it was as **a merciful and faithful high priest** that Christ was to **make atonement for the sins of the people** (17). 'To make atonement' translates the Greek verb *hilaskesthai* which also carries the idea of 'to satisfy', 'appease', 'propitiate'. Here, however, with 'sins' as its object (cf. the Gk.) it most likely means 'wipe out', 'remove' rather than 'appease'. But, and again the writer returns to a much emphasized concept, the Son can be effective as a priest only by identification with those whom He is to represent. Therefore **he had to be made like his brothers in every way** (17).

III. EXHORTATION AND WARNING (3: 1–4: 13)

i. Exhortation to Consider Christ as Superior to Moses (3: 1–6a)

The previous section ends with a description of Jesus as a **merciful and faithful high priest**. This now becomes the theme for the new discussion. But in reverse fashion the author treats first the faithfulness of Jesus and secondly His mercy (4: 14 ff.).

From the vantage point of theological truth, the author makes his appeal to **holy brothers,**

who share in the heavenly call (1). The word 'holy' has the same root meaning as that of 'sanctify', and refers, therefore, to those set apart by God and for God, i.e., Christians (cf. note on 2: 11; Lev. 20: 26; I Pet. 2: 9). These Christians whose call or invitation is *'from heaven . . . and to heaven'* are now addressed directly for the first time. They are urged to **fix** their **thoughts on Jesus, the apostle and high priest**, the subject of their open confession, as being **faithful to the one who appointed him** (1–2). And yet it is not that Christians are to fasten their attention upon Jesus as faithful merely, for **Moses**, who himself was looked upon as apostle (cf. Exod. 3: 10) and priest (Exod. 24: 6–8; cf. also Philo, *On the Life of Moses*, 2. 2–5), **was faithful** (2; cf. Num. 12: 7). But they are to give careful and prolonged attention to the person and work of Christ because, by His very nature, He is completely 'other' and far greater than Moses. Moses was a faithful servant in God's house (2)—a mere witness, through the moral and ceremonial laws he established, to the gospel which **would be said in the future** (5). But Jesus is God's Son set over that house, the 'creative agent' by whom it was built, who is Himself the gospel anticipated by Moses and the One by whom it was first declared (3, 5 f.; cf. also 1: 2; 2: 3). Verse 4 is difficult, and its difficulty is only slightly eased by the RSV putting it in parenthesis, for it is not wholly parenthetical. It has some connection with the reference to Jesus as builder in v. 3. Perhaps its meaning is that **every house is built by someone, but God is the builder of everything**, whose 'creative agent' is Christ. Or possibly its meaning may best be understood by translating the word 'God' as 'divine' since in the Greek the definite article is omitted: 'the builder (i.e., Christ) of all things is divine'.

It is worth noting that the expression **God's house** ('his house', AV) refers to the 'household' or 'family' of God and apparently describes the believing people of God in the OT and also in the NT, for the 'house' is the same in both. Moses was a servant in God's house, a house which Christ founded, over which He presides, and to which Christians belong—**we are his house!** (6). This passage argues strongly for a continuity between ancient Israel and the new 'Israel of God' (cf. Gal. 6: 16).

ii. Warning against Missing God's Promised Rest (3: 6b–4: 11)
6. We are his house, if we hold on to our courage and the hope of which we boast: This warning is directed to those who have 'confessed themselves Christians. It is intended to show that true Christianity is proved by endurance, by continued confidence in and loyalty to Christ who is our hope (cf. Col. 1: 27). He does not belong to God's house who merely

professes to do so. He belongs who continues believing 'to the end' (6 RSVmg, a reading which, though parallel to 3: 14, is probably genuine here in light of its wide textual attestation). Ps. 95, which is now quoted as the voice of the Spirit still speaking to Christians today (7–11), is intended by the writer to show that Israel's tragic loss was due to rebellion or unbelief—a failure to maintain an attitude of confidence and obedience throughout their journey from Egypt to Canaan—and as a warning to professing Christians not to make the same mistake. It thus serves to illustrate the principle already laid down, namely, that perseverance is indeed the proof of faith. Israel's initial exit, their 'baptism unto Moses', their participation in the spiritual food (cf. 1 C. 10: 1 f.), i.e., their observation of divine works (9), did not guarantee their entrance into Canaan. Some continued to believe God and entered Canaan but some rebelled and never experienced God's rest (11, cf. 16–19). The journey decided the vitality of their faith.

Therefore, since the Holy Spirit is still speaking and saying **'Today'** (7, 13, 15), **See to it, brothers, that none of you has a sinful, unbelieving heart that turns away from the living God** (12). The gravity of the situation is thus heightened by three things: (*a*) by the writer calling attention to the fact that it is God speaking and not man—**the Holy Spirit says** (7); (*b*) by his pointing out that this departure is from the **living God**, a favourite designation for God in Hebrews (9: 14; 10: 31; 12: 22; cf. also 4: 12; 11: 6), which pictures God as 'all alive, active in making Himself known to men, able to keep His promises and determined to execute His oaths' (note: the warning against departing from the 'living God' does not sound like a warning against relapsing into Judaism), and (*c*) by his repeated use of the imperative (3: 12, 13; 4: 1, 11). The preventive for such a condition is to **encourage one another** (Gk. 'yourselves' stressing the 'unity of the Christian body') **daily** (13). This requires both individual and corporate responsibility. The expression **sin's deceitfulness** (13) describes sin as a seducer, and may be an allusion to that first sin when Eve was seduced by the serpent (Gen. 3: 13; cf. I Tim. 2: 14).

Verses 12 and 13 together describe that process which happens deep within a man when there is not the constant strengthening of mutual exhortation—a process which initially is invisible to any observer. First the germ of unbelief is allowed to sprout, then evil and God-defying thoughts begin to spread. These gradually dominate the entire attitude, until the whole character is changed. A new tendency is in control of the person involved. His basic response to God is NO. There is now no longer the YES of submission which he professed at his baptism (J. Schneider, *The Letter to the Hebrews*, 1957, pp. 31–32).

The writer reiterates in a more forceful fashion what he has said already (14), namely, that there is one simple test by which we can know whether or not we **share in Christ**, whether we are 'partakers of' or 'partners with' Him (Gk. *metochoi tou christou*, which itself has an ambiguity of meaning): Do **we hold firmly till the end the confidence we had at first**? [Note: the Gk. for 'confidence' is *hypostasis*, that firm support on which 'a man bases himself as he confronts the future' (J. Moffatt, *The Epistle to the Hebrews, ad loc.*, p. 48). Here it is the persuasion with which the Christian life began that God has spoken His ultimate word in Jesus Christ.] The desert experience of Israel (16–19) proves that 'this total-life picture is *the* criterion' by which one can tell objectively the reality of his faith. What is faith for the writer of Hebrews? Chapter 11 is his full discussion of the subject, but by comparing v. 18 here with v. 19 it is clear that he understands faith to be something closely akin to obedience or loyalty.

Chapter 4 continues the same warning against the possibility of failing to enter God's rest which was begun in 3: 6b. That there is such a rest the author proves in his typical exegetical fashion by a quotation from Gen. 2: 2: **'And on the seventh day God rested from all his work'** (4). That God wishes to share this rest and that the promise of entering this rest still holds good is proved by two other passages, both from Ps. 95. The first quotes God as saying that **'They shall never enter my rest'** (5). This is a concise statement compressing several ideas into one brief remark. God, who never desires a thing in vain, must have wanted to share His rest, else He would never have extended an invitation to men to join Him in it. But since He did, and since those whom He first invited **did not go in because of their disobedience** (6), and since God's purposes cannot be frustrated, the offer to enter into the enjoyment of His rest must still hold good. The writer then proceeds to use another part of Ps. 95 to prove this conclusion. God is still extending His invitation to men to join Him in His repose: **'Today, if you hear his voice, do not harden your hearts'** (7). By this 'Today' the writer understands that God again is setting **a certain day** (7), defining 'a new period in which the rest is to be open and accessible'. **There remains, then, a Sabbath-rest for the people of God** (9). From this it is learned that the 'rest of God' must not be equated with Canaan for God's second and continued invitation has come through David who lived long after Joshua (Jesus, AV) had led Israel into the promised land (8). [Note: This attribution of Ps. 95 to David

is found only in the LXX; it is not in the Hebrew text.] **Had** Joshua **given them rest, God would not** have spoken **about another day** (8). Thus the tragedy of unbelieving Israel is seen to be far greater than appeared on the surface. The greatness of their failure lay not merely in that they could not enter Canaan, but in that they also were irrevocably excluded from the eternal rest of God.

It is against this background—the possibility of an eternal rest and also of the possibility of failing to achieve it—that the writer makes his appeal: **since the promise of entering his rest still stands, let us be careful that none of you be found to have fallen short** (1). Here there is both severity and tender concern —severity, in the need for fear; tender concern in the 'cautious and delicate way' the writer expresses the possibility of failure: 'Lest any of you should seem to come short of it' (AV, in preference to the NIV or more specifically, 'should seem to have come short of it *in the judgment of others*'). Failure, the author goes on to explain, ever lies in unbelief. Mere hearing the good news is not enough. The gospel must meet with faith in the hearers (2, but cf. RSVmg for an alternate translation). When it does it becomes effective, for **we who have believed enter that rest** (3). Notice that the tense of the verb is present—'enter'. Thus God's rest is not wholly some future goal to be attained, but is a present reality to be enjoyed. The author coins a word to describe it and calls it **a Sabbath-rest** (9, Gk. *sabbatismos*), **for anyone who enters God's rest also rests from his own work, just as God did from his** on the sabbath, i.e., the seventh day (10, cf. 4).

What is meant by 'rests from his work as God did from His'? Since it is impossible to conceive of God as resting from good works, the idea of God resting must mean that God worked without hindrance or tension with energy flowing from Him with calm steadiness (cf. Jn 5: 17; cf. also A. C. Purdy, 'Hebrews', *The Interpreter's Bible*, XI, p. 631). If this was in the writer's mind then 'rests from his work' describes that cessation from futile activity done in resistance to God, that is, from dead works (cf. 9: 14), to find rest in a life of complete dependence upon Him—much like Paul's 'contrast of the life of faith in Christ and the life of performing the works of the law' (Narborough, *Comm.*, p. 95). Though it is true that God cannot rest from good works, yet the Hebrew verb (*shābath*, from which 'sabbath' comes) does mean 'to cease, desist, rest'. 'God rested', then, must mean that God desisted from what He had been doing, i.e., His creative activity. And when a man enters into God's sabbath-rest he too must desist from what he has been doing, in this case, attempting to work out his own salvation. 'More positively, we are justified in filling the word with meaning derived from the writer's dominant longing for a satisfying worship of God. This **rest** is peace in the assurance of an access to God unhindered by rites that cannot touch the conscience and made possible only by Christ's "purification for sins" that pollute and prevent our reaching the final goal of worship' (Purdy, *Comm.*, p. 631). Since then this is now available **let us therefore make every effort** (lit. 'give all diligence') **to enter that rest** (11).

iii. The Impossibility of Concealing Unbelief from God (4: 12–13)

Because unbelief is a matter of the heart it often escapes the notice of man but never of God whose word **is living and active. Sharper than any double-edged sword** (12). It has the power to reach right through to the inmost parts of one's personality. It has the power to judge (Gk. *kritikos*) both the feelings and thoughts of the heart (cf. Wis. 18: 15 ff.). It is able to discern and decide on the moral value of a man. The expression 'word of God', may refer to that message of God spoken either through the prophets or by Christ and His apostles which in itself possesses a dynamic so great that when heard and retained it creates anew (cf. Rom. 1: 16), or it may simply be a circumlocution for God Himself, as was sometimes done. Notice that in v. 13 the 'word' is left behind and it is before God Himself we stand—completely exposed. What we really are now is **laid bare before the eyes of him to whom we must give account**.

With this the author concludes his lengthy warning and comes to the subject which is closest to his heart and which he has already touched upon twice before (1: 3b; 2: 17 f.)—namely the priesthood of Jesus.

IV. THE PRIESTHOOD OF JESUS INTRODUCED (4: 14–5: 10)

i. The Priest's Sufferings and their Meanings (4: 14–16)

From warning the author now turns to consolation and encouragement which he ties inseparably to the priestly work of Christ—a theme which in a very real sense constitutes the main burden of the letter. The life of faith, though difficult, is not devoid of external support: **we have a great high priest** (14) who can **help** us (16). And the greatness of this high priest is measured (*a*) by the fact that He **has gone through the heavens** into the very presence of God, as the ancient high priest passed through the veil into the holy of holies—the place of effective service for man, and (*b*) by the names assigned Him here: **Jesus the Son of God**. These tell us that He is both man and God, both 'sympathetic and powerful'. Therefore, **let us hold firmly to the faith we profess** (14). This exhortation is based upon the fact that our high priest, too, suffered and was tempted, for these experiences of the Saviour have great significance to us. They mean that there is an incentive for us to persevere, for although Jesus was tempted **in every way . . . as we are** (15), He yet remained faithful to the end. They also mean that because He suffered and was tempted He can sympathetically understand what we are going through, appreciate our weaknesses, and do something to help (15–16). Therefore, **let us** continually **approach the throne of grace . . . so that we may receive mercy and find grace to help us in our time of need** (16), and let us come **with confidence**. This is the first statement, to be repeated many times, indicating the ultimate results of Christ's priestly work—open access into God's presence for all who wish to come. The expression 'approach' or 'draw near' (used seven times in Hebrews) was a technical term employed in the LXX of the priests who alone were able to approach God in worshipful service: Now 'the right of priestly approach is extended to all Christians' (Westcott, *Comm.*, p. 108).

The writer of Hebrews emphasizes the divine character of this new high priest beginning as he does with a description of Him in His cosmic rôle as creator and Son of God, but he also stresses the reality of His humanity as does no other NT writer. He insists, for example, that the temptations of Jesus were not mock temptations—they were genuine: **in every way** like ours. How can this be, if at the same time he were the Son of God? Would not His divine nature protect Him from the possibility of sinning? This question of the possibility of Christ's sinning has been debated for centuries and is not yet resolved to everyone's satisfaction. It cannot be discussed now. Nevertheless, assuming that it was impossible for Him to sin, because of the nature of His person, yet it is also possible to assume that He did not know this was the case. Mk 13: 32 implies that the Son, in His incarnate rôle, was not omniscient —there is at least one thing recorded there which He did not know. If, then, there was one thing He did not know, ignorance of other things was also possible, even this concerning whether or not He could sin. In any case, though Hebrews says He lived His life **without sin** (15, Gk. *chōris hamartias*, lit. 'apart from sin', not meaning 'without the ability to sin' but 'without having in fact sinned'), it also makes clear that Jesus experienced temptations in just the same manner as we do and that this sinlessness was the result of 'conscious decision' on His part in the midst of intense struggle (cf. 5: 7–9). One must never suppose that His victory over temptation was 'the mere formal consequences of His divine nature'. Any interpretation of the person of Christ which in any way diminishes the force and genuineness of His temptations cannot be correct.

ii. The Priest's Qualifications (5: 1–10)

Now the writer turns to discuss the qualifications of the high priest (1–4). He sees only two of them to be significant enough to mention: (*a*) that the priest be human, **selected from among men** (1), and (*b*) that he be appointed to his post by God (4). God ordained that the priest be a man (not an angel or some other celestial being) because the priest's main function is **to represent** men **in matters related to God** (1), that is, stand 'on the Godward side' of men (A. Nairne, *The Epistle of Priesthood*, 1913, p. 146). Only man is **subject to** human **weakness** (2). Hence, only man can understand human weakness in such a way as to **deal gently with those who are ignorant and are going astray** (2). Thus only when the priest is a man can man be assured that he is fully able to sympathize with his frailty and thus represent him fairly before God. [Note: In the days of the Aaronic priesthood the priest was constantly reminded of his own moral inadequacy (not physical inadequacy for he was to be without physical defects) by the need of constantly offering sacrifice **for his own sins as well as for the sins of the people** (3). Attention is never drawn to this part of the analogy when applied to Christ, for, as the writer has already stated, He was without sin.] The verb **deal gently** (2) translates a verb (*metriopathein*) which describes the mean between indifference and hypersensitivity. Understood in this way the priest is one who must not be apathetic to nor yet too easily affected by the problems of those he represents. The verb in other contexts, however, was associated also with such ideas as magnanimity and clemency. Hence, it also possesses the meanings of condescension, indulgence and generosity, making it almost synonymous with sympathy (Gk. *sympathein*). If this meaning is accepted it rather describes the priest as compassionate, a characteristic which belongs to his very nature (Spicq, *Comm.* II, pp. 108–9). Notice that the sacrifices to be offered are for sins of ignorance and waywardness (1–2), not for wilful sins (cf. Num. 15: 22–3 1).

Not only must the priest be human but he must be ordained by God (4). This is an office so important that no man has the right to take the honour upon himself (4)—only God possesses the prerogative of priestly appointment. The precedent was set when Aaron was so established in his office.

Having called attention to the qualifications for the priesthood in general the writer now applies them specifically to Christ in a manner which shows the studied nature of his rhetorical style. He treats these priestly qualifications in reverse fashion (5–10). Firstly, he dispenses with the divine call rather hurriedly. There is simply the statement of Christ's divine appointment as high priest (5), and the proof from Scripture: the very one who earlier had said to Christ **'You are my Son'** (Ps. 2: 7, cf. Heb. 1: 5), now has said to Him **'You are a priest for ever, in the order of Melchizedek'** (Ps. 110: 4).

Secondly, the writer discusses the humanity of the priest but in far greater detail, for in his thinking it is a subject which requires special emphasis. He wishes to show most clearly that Christ was truly human, that He truly did know what it meant to suffer as a human, that He truly did learn by experience what total submission to God involved, so that as a result He can be fully aware of our problems and fully capable of sympathizing with us in them. The writer does this with language unparalleled in the NT for its intensity (7–8). **During the days of Jesus' life on earth** (7) 'should not be pressed to imply that the writer thought Jesus was no longer incarnate after his death and exaltation' (F. F. Bruce, 'Hebrews', *Peake's Commentary on the Bible*, newly revised, 1962, *ad loc.*). We are not told what Christ asked for in the **prayers and petitions** He made **with loud cries** (lit. 'shouts') **and tears** (7), but the language is suggestive of Gethsemane, or of times similar to that recorded in Jn 12: 27: 'Father save me from (lit. 'out of ') this hour!' It can be inferred, therefore, that it was a prayer for deliverance offered, nevertheless, in submission to the Father's will. And **he was heard** because of His **reverent submission** (7). The one **who could save him from** (lit. 'out of') **death** did deliver him out of death by resurrection, though it was not His purpose to save Him from dying.

Although he was a son (8) means 'although He was Son' (cf. the note on 1: 2), and by the expression, **he learned obedience from what he suffered**, the writer is saying that He, now in the sphere of humanity, must, as must all 'sons' (cf. 12: 7 ff.), learn what it means to obey God when encircled by human sufferings and temptations. If His sufferings and temptations were genuine (cf. the comment at the end of ch. 4), then His obedience could have been won only through struggle. Hence, the perfection (9) He achieved must of necessity be a moral perfection, whose benefit extends far beyond Himself to embrace in redemptive fashion **all who** in turn **obey him** (9).

From the words the writer chooses for this section, it seems clear that he intends to describe this 'Son of God' in sharp contrast to the first 'son of God' (Adam, cf. Lk. 3: 38), who, when put to the test, chose to disobey the divine demand rather than submit to it, and who, as a consequence, became the universal cause of death rather than of life (cf. Rom. 5: 18 f.; cf.

also Heb. 10: 4–10). Jesus, on the other hand, having obeyed completely **became the source of eternal salvation** (9)—a salvation mediated through His rôle as **high priest in the order of Melchizedek** (10).

V. WARNING AGAINST THE FATEFUL CONSEQUENCES OF IMMATURITY (5: 11–6: 20a)
i. Possibility of Immaturity Leading to a Final Break with Christ (5: 11–6: 8)
It is the writer's purpose now to explore deeply the meaning of Christ's priesthood. But because this part of his sermon (Gk. *logos*, 11) is **hard to explain** to those who are **slow to learn** (11), and infantile in their understanding of **teaching about righteousness** (13), he feels compelled to postpone it until first he has stirred them out of their lethargy. From this it is clear that the problem Hebrews is attempting to resolve is the problem of inactivity, of not persevering, of dullness and spiritual immaturity. It is this kind of attitude, insignificant as it may seem, which if persisted in, slowly, almost imperceptibly leads one to break finally with Christ. As the precaution against such a tragedy the writer urges them to train themselves **by constant use** so as to be able **to distinguish good from evil** (14), to engage in a moral exercises, in the development of mental habits by which they may become mature (Gk. 'perfect'), i.e., able to appreciate **solid food**—the significance of Christ's rôle as priest, for example—and no longer require **milk**—**the elementary truths of God's word** (12), or salvation's ABC's (cf. 1 C. 2: 1–3: 2).

Since, therefore, spiritual maturity (or immaturity) is largely a matter of the will, the writer urges them to **leave the elementary teachings about Christ and go on to maturity** (6: 1). It is possible that the verb translated 'let us go on' should be given a passive meaning—'let us be carried along', for there is an ambiguity in meaning arising from the form of the Greek verb (*pherōmetha*). If the passive meaning is the true one 'the thought [would not be] primarily of personal effort, but of personal surrender to an active influence. The power is working; we have only to yield ourselves to it' (Westcott, *Comm.*, p. 145; cf. 2 Pet. 1: 21). The idea of **maturity** is consonant with that use of the word in 5: 14. It means those capable of understanding, appreciating and of being affected by 'the exposition of Christian truth with its higher development'.

The writer's summary of **elementary teachings** from which Christians are to move on in the sense of building upon a foundation, falls into three groups of two each. The first is repentance and faith and has to do with the Christian's 'personal character'. This repentance is a radical reorientation of outlook which results in a turning away from **acts that lead to death** (1), that is, from all activity done in rebellion against God (cf. 9: 14). Faith, on the other hand, is both a trust set upon and an obedience rendered to God. The second group involves the 'outward ordinances' of the Christian society and is composed of (a) **instruction about baptisms** which are plural, because instruction concerning Christian baptism required that it be set off against other baptismal rites either Jew or pagan, and (b) **the laying on of hands**, which act was 'the sequel and complement of baptism', and the symbol of ordination (cf. 1 Tim. 4: 14; 2 Tim. 1: 6; cf. C. J. Vaughan, *The Epistle to the Hebrews*, 1890, p. 103). The last group is eschatological and has to do with the Christian's 'connexion with the unseen world': **resurrection of the dead and eternal judgment** (2).

And move on we will **God permitting** us to do so (3). This statement of condition implies that some will not be able to advance, for by their own decisions they will have placed themselves beyond the range of God's permission. The writer now comes to the most solemn warning thus far in his letter as he shows the tragic end which may befall a person who has made his Christian 'confession', but who has failed to advance beyond a rudimentary knowledge of the implications of this confession, or of the ultimate significance of Jesus for the forgiveness of his sins.

The things listed here by the writer to describe the 'fallen' are most certainly things which characterize all true Christians. These **have once been enlightened** (4), an expression which could mean complete inner illumination—the God-given capacity to understand and respond positively to the Christian message (cf. Eph. 1: 18; 3: 9; 2 C. 4: 4). They also are those who **tasted the heavenly gift** (4). Now if Christ is this gift from above (cf. Jn 4: 10; Rom. 5: 15; 8: 32), and if 'tasted' means to have 'experienced' or 'come to know' in the fullest sense (cf. Arndt and Gingrich, *Greek–English Lexicon*, *geuomai*; cf. Heb. 2: 9), then obviously the writer had in mind a matter of grace and divine life procured by Christ and enjoyed fully by the Christian (the middle voice, *geuesthai*, marking more forcefully the personal character of the experience; cf. C. Spicq, *Comm.*, II, p. 150). Again, they are said to **have shared in the Holy Spirit** (4). This translation points to the fact that these may have been recipients of the Holy Spirit much the same as were the disciples of Jesus when He breathed on them (Jn 20: 22), or the Samaritans when the apostles laid their hands on them (Ac. 8: 17)—recipients of the essence of the Christian life (Rom. 8: 9b). Finally they are those who **have tasted the goodness of the**

word of God and the powers of the coming age (5). They have experienced supernatural energies resulting from the work of Christ which are clear manifestations of the nearness (or the presence) of the messianic era (Ac. 2: 11 f.; cf. Spicq, *Comm.*).

Because this description of the 'apostate' indicates that he showed every sign of being a Christian, a very great many commentators have so understood him to be, i.e., a true Christian. The Shepherd of Hermas (*c.* A.D. 148) seems to have been the first to give this interpretation to Hebrews 6, though he tempers the 'no second repentance' theme, by allowing at least one more chance (Mandates, IV. 3).

It is necessary to point out, however, that these descriptive expressions are susceptible of more than one interpretation, and, in their less than 'ultimate' meaning, may be applied to 'professing' Christians as well as to 'genuine' believers. 'Enlightened' (4) is a term applied by Justin Martyr (d. *c.* A.D. 165; 1 *Apol.* 61: 12 f.) to the baptized—those who had given consent to the truth of the Christian catechism by their submission to baptism. It is just possible, therefore, that the writer of Hebrews used it in this sense also. At least the Peshitta (a fourth century Syriac translation) so understood the word, substituting, as it did, 'have gone down for baptism' for 'enlightened'. Moreover, several interpreters (cf. Spicq, *Comm.*, II, p. 150 for a list of these) understand the expression, 'tasted the heavenly gift' (4) to mean partaking of the Lord's Supper, 'the divine gift *par excellence*' (cf. Mt. 26: 26 ff., and especially Ac. 20: 11, Gk., where 'taste' is used *à propos* of eating the eucharistic bread). 'Shared in' the Holy Spirit (4) may have the less ultimate meaning of 'partners along with' the Holy Spirit (cf. 2: 14; 3: 1, 14; 12: 8). And the last two expressions (5) may mean that these have seen the creative power of the preached Gospel and have themselves performed miracles (cf. Judas Iscariot).

To sum up: the writer, in composing such a list as this, may have intended to describe one who has all the ear-marks of Christianity and who yet is not a real Christian. The *one* proof of genuineness is a continuing loyalty which keeps faith to the very end. Just as all Israel left Egypt under Moses, crossed the Red Sea, ate the heavenly manna, observed the mighty acts of God, etc., giving all appearances of a people of faith, and yet only two entered Canaan, the rest falling dead in the desert, so it is possible that within the visible Church there may be those who have experienced all the advantages of Christianity, instruction, baptism, the Lord's Supper, manifestations of the Spirit, etc. (though it should be noted carefully that there is no gift of love mentioned in this list, cf. 6:

10), and who yet are capable of renouncing it all because the basic inner attitude, of which they themselves may not be fully aware, has become one of unbelief or disobedience, of an attitude of NO toward God. The situation here, then, may be analogous to that in Mt. 7: 21 ff.

In any case, if those who have been blessed in such an extraordinary fashion **fall away** (6, lit. 'fall by the wayside', Gk., *parapesontas*, an expression perhaps occasioned by the desert experience of ancient Israel), **it is impossible** for them **to be brought back to repentance, because to their loss they are crucifying the Son of God all over again and subjecting him to public disgrace** (6). 'Repentance' here is more than grief for past wrong done; it is a change of mind or attitude—a positive, affirmative act which accompanies the beginning of a new religious experience and moral life (Arndt and Gingrich, *Greek–English Lexicon*), rather than a mere negative turning away from sin. It refers to that disposition of mind toward Christ which prevailed when the confessing Christian was baptized, but which, through lack of moral exercise (5: 14), now has been altered radically. And the truly terrible thing about this apostate attitude is that it is *humanly* (or psychologically) impossible to change it back, for it is not the result of a quick decision in a weak moment, but of a gradual hardening process within the mind which has crystallized now into a 'constant attitude of hostility towards Christ' (as the expressions 'since they crucify', etc., using the present tenses as they do, imply). Therefore all confessing Christians must stir up themselves and others lest continued immaturity in the Christian profession lead to eventual hostility toward Christ. Those who remain loyal to the end demonstrate that their confession was genuine.

Verses 7 and 8 contain a parable the interpretation of which is consistent with this emphasis of the writer upon perseverance as the real test of genuineness: the rain is to be equated with the five extraordinary blessings enumerated in vv. 4–5, and the earth with the readers of the letter. The rain is common to both good earth and bad, i.e., great spiritual blessings are common to all confessing Christians, those who truly believe and those who merely confess that they do. It is what the soils produce—the kind of lives the confessing Christians live—that makes visibly clear what their true nature is and what kind of seed is within them. And yet, as in the horticultural realm where soil which is of poor quality and poor content often cannot be distinguished immediately from the good (for after a rain even the bad ground *looks* promising with its myriads of verdant shoots), so it is within the visible Christian Church. All may have been well instructed, etc., and made their confession of faith, and given evidence of genuineness. But as time proves some soil to be bad and its produce **thorns and thistles** (8), or the reverse, so it does with those who claim to be Christians. The perseverance of the saints, on one hand, offers proof of the reality of their confession. The lack of it gives testimony to the opposite. The one receives God's blessing (7), while the other is **in danger of being cursed. In the end it will be burned** (8). 'In danger of being cursed' does not mean merely that judgment is threatening, and may be avoided by a subsequent and unexpected fertility of the land, but that it is inevitable (cf. the same construction found in 8: 13, *engys aphanismou*, where the disappearance of the old covenant means not that it is merely liable to disappear, but rather that its disappearance is certain; cf. also Mk 1: 15 with Mt. 12: 28). Nor is it proper to think only of the fruit of the land as being burned away, for the burning is actually the punishment visited upon the accursed land itself (cf. Gen. 19: 24; Dt. 29: 22). The expression 'in the end it will be burned' may be a Hebraism equivalent to our expression 'dedicated to destruction' (cf. Ps. 109: 13). It is simply the application of the principle set forth in 2 C. 11: 15: 'Their end will correspond to their deeds'—i.e., whatever happens to their fruit happens to them also (Spicq, *Comm.*, II, p. 156). In other words, the one who confesses to being a Christian and enjoys all the spiritual benefits attendant upon this confession, but who does not persist in his loyalty to Christ to the end, can only look forward to a fury of fire which will consume him in the day of judgment (10: 27); whereas the one who confesses to being a Christian and continues faithfully in this confession enjoys and will enjoy the blessing of God.

ii. Encouragement and Consolation (6: 9–20)

After the warning comes encouragement. This section begins with an assertion of the writer's confidence in his readers, whom he calls **dear friends** only here in his letter (9). It is a confidence inspired by his knowledge of the character of **God** who **is not unjust** in forgetting their **work** (10), and of their past and present life of **work** and **love** (note this important word; it is not 'labour of love' as in AV) shown for God's sake in helping **his people** (10, cf. also 10: 32–34). The encouragement continues with the writer giving his reasons for such a severe warning. It was because of his passionate concern for the welfare of each individual Christian (11). It also was given so that they might demonstrate some excitement or **diligence to the very end in order to make your hope sure** (11), and so that they might not become dull (**lazy**, 12), or so that they might be roused out of their dullness if they were that already (cf. 5: 11), and finally, so that

they might be spurred on to be imitators of those **who through faith and patience inherit what has been promised** (12, cf. ch. 11), that is, of those who through continued obedient loyalty to God have already entered into the realization of His offer. 'Once again, continuance is emphasized as the proof of reality'. Once again, also, it is evident that spiritual lethargy, the danger of 'drifting away', indifference, and the like, are the sins combated in this letter.

The appeal to perseverance is now given incentive by assuring the reader of the absolute validity of the divine promise (13–20). Originally God made a promise to Abraham. To give him incentive to believe that the promise would be fulfilled, God, accommodating Himself to such a human custom as that of a man taking an oath by something greater than himself, thereby giving added assurance of the validity of his statement, **swore by himself** (13), since there was none greater by whom He could take such an oath. **And so . . . Abraham** was given every possible assurance that if he would patiently endure he would obtain the promise (15). Abraham did in fact obtain the promise (15), but, in the thinking of the writer, the scope of that promise was not exhausted in the earthly experience of this man. God not only had said to him, **'I will surely bless you and give you many descendants'** (14, cf. Gen. 22: 17), but He also had said 'In your seed shall all the nations of the earth be blessed' (Gen. 22: 18). Now although there is here no quotation from Gen. 22: 18, nor any explicit reference to the fact that Abraham's 'seed' is Christ, yet like Paul (cf. Gal. 3: 16) the writer surely must have had it in mind for he envisions Christians as being **the heirs of what was promised** to Abraham (17). Consequently they, too, are interested in its validity. The fact that it involves **two unchangeable things**—the promise itself and the oath which rests on the very being of God—**in which it is impossible for God to lie** provides strong encouragement (18) for Christians to persevere while hoping for the ultimate fulfilment of that promise, i.e., the heavenly blessing to which even Abraham looked (cf. 11: 8–19).

This hope, is like **an anchor for the soul, firm and secure** (19) which Christ has taken and dropped securely within the harbour. Actually the writer of Hebrews mixes his metaphors at this point, for he does not say 'harbour', as one might expect with 'anchor', but rather **inner sanctuary behind the curtain** (19). This anchor of hope ties the Christian securely to the place of God's presence, the heavenly world. This unexpected change in figure of speech is a neat rhetorical device to return the readers to the subject already begun—the priesthood of Christ (ch. 5). The veil was the inner curtain separating the holy from the most holy place. Christ has penetrated that veil and has gone into the holy of holies to work **on our behalf** (20). But He has done so as a forerunner (Gk. *prodromos*, used in classical literature of a scout reconnoitring, or of a herald announcing the coming of a king)—a word which implies that others are to follow, i.e., Christians too are to be brought into that same sacred area. This was indeed a startling statement, for though the ancient high priest was his people's representative he was never their forerunner—they were never allowed to follow him within the curtain. But the key-note of Hebrews is that the new high priest guarantees to every believer the privilege of confident access into this most holy place—the very presence of the living God, and it is summed up in one carefully chosen word: 'forerunner'. Jesus has 'gone that we may follow too' (F. W. Gingrich, 'Forerunner', Hastings' *Dictionary of the Bible*, rev. ed., pp. 303–4).

VI. THE PRIESTHOOD OF CHRIST (7: 1–10: 18)

i. In the Order of Melchizedek (7: 1–28)

The writer of Hebrews has mentioned Melchizedek several times already (5: 6, 10; 6: 20). Now he begins a full-blown discussion of him and his relation to Christ. Gen. 14: 17–20 provides the historical background, and serves several purposes: (*a*) to show the moral character of Melchizedek, (*b*) to demonstrate his greatness, and (*c*) to establish the existence of another order of priesthood than that of Aaron. Insight into his moral character is gained from an etymological study of his name and that of the city he ruled. Melchizedek is a name composed of two words which when translated mean **king of righteousness** (2). The name of his city, Salem, meant 'peace'. Hence, to the writer of Hebrews, Melchizedek was a king characterized by righteousness and his rule by peace (cf. Isa. 32: 1, 17). His greatness is seen from the fact that he blessed Abraham the patriarch (i.e., the father of us all) at a time when Abraham was second to none in the land—victor over Chedorlaomer and the kings who were with him, and from the fact that **Abraham gave him a tenth of everything** (2). Proof of the existence of another order than that of Aaron and his descendants lies in the fact that Melchizedek is **without father or mother, without genealogy, without beginning of days or end of life** (3), expressions which in themselves probably mean no more than that there is no mention of father and mother, etc., in inspired Scripture. But by a principle of exegesis, that the silences of Scripture are as significant as its statements, the writer understands from such omission that Melchizedek was a solitary figure in history who possessed his priesthood in his own right, not by virtue of descent, 'who never assumed and never lost his office', hence, whose priesthood abides forever. Significantly, the writer of Hebrews does not identify Melchizedek with Christ, but says that he resembles **the Son of God** (3). Melchizedek thus was the facsimile of which Christ is the reality. Christ, therefore, is king of righteousness and peace in the fullest sense, and priest 'like', 'in the order of' Melchizedek (15), that is, priest forever!

In vv. 4–10 the writer continues to magnify the priesthood of Melchizedek. He does this by reiterating the fact that Abraham **gave him a tenth of** (the choicest of) **the plunder** (4) and in return received his priestly blessing (6). By accepting this rôle of 'tithed' and 'blessed', Abraham who 'had the promises' doubly acknowledged his inferiority to Melchizedek (7). The writer further magnifies that mysterious priesthood by first calling attention to the fact that the levitical priests are superior to all other Israelites in that they alone have a commandment in the law **to collect a tenth from the people . . . , their brothers** (5), and then by showing that even **Levi who collects the tenth, paid the tenth** to Melchizedek **through Abraham** (9). The levitical priests, then, though superior to the mass of Israel, are indeed inferior to Melchizedek, and their priesthood to his. Thus the writer's argument runs like this: The levitical priests are superior to the rest of the Israelites, because, though mortal, they, nevertheless, tithe their brethren; Levi is superior to the priests because he is their progenitor; Abraham is greater than Levi for he is father of them all; Melchizedek is greater than Abraham if for no other reason than that he both tithed and blessed Abraham; therefore, Melchizedek is greater than Abraham, Levi, the levitical priests and all Israel. The point of all this is, of course, to prove the ultimate superiority of Christ's priesthood, which by now is quite easy to do for the writer has already implied Christ's superiority to Melchizedek when he said that Melchizedek resembled the Son of God (3). Christ is greater than Melchizedek as the reality is greater than the facsimile. Therefore, Christ is greater than Abraham, Levi and all his descendants, and His priesthood, too, is greater than theirs.

Verses 11–28 deal now with this new order of priesthood and the need for it. First of all the writer points out that the new order was predicted (he returns to Ps. 110: 4), and it was predicted because **perfection** could not be **attained through the Levitical priesthood** (11). **Perfection** here means man's ability to draw near to God (cf. v. 19; 9: 9; 10: 22). The old order of priesthood could never effect such an approach, though this was the chief purpose of the priesthood, simply because it could never fully remove the sin which barred the way. Therefore, the new order was in the mind and plan of God even while the old was in full operation. This means that the old law and the old covenant (8: 7 ff.) also were provisional, and were destined to be set aside along with the priesthood, for the whole legal system 'turned upon the priesthood' since **on the basis of it the law was given to the people** (11). Thus, **when there is a change of the priesthood there must also be a change of the law** (12). 'The high priesthood is like the keystone of the whole structure of the Mosaic Law; all the other regulations fell away of their own accord when the priesthood passed over to Christ' (E. F. Scott, *Comm., ad loc.*).

The need for such a radical change was great. It is obvious that **he of whom these things are said belonged to a different tribe** (13) to which priestly privileges did not belong. The writer understands the law to forbid one from any tribe other than that of Levi to serve **at the altar** (13). But **it is clear that our Lord descended from Judah** (14) and that He nevertheless was destined to be priest, for He was the historical reality of the prediction of Ps. 110: 4—**'a priest forever'** (15-17). Thus it is even more clear that since the law allowed only the sons of Levi to be priests it had to be abrogated to make way for this one who possessed a priesthood not by virtue of legal descent, **but on the basis of the power of an indestructible life** (16). The emphasis here is upon the eternal qualities of His priesthood which are proven by the scriptural quotation in the following verse (17). Though the writer does not mention the fact that our Lord descended from David, he demonstrates, nonetheless, that Christ combines in Himself the offices of both king and priest—'of the tribe of Judah', and 'according to the order of Melchizedek'. [Contrast the concept current in the Qumran texts of *two* messiahs, one priestly, who was superior in rank, and one kingly (cf. *Manual of Discipline*, 9: 11, in the translation of A. Dupont-Sommer, *The Essene Writings from Qumran*, 1961). It is possible that Hebrews combats this idea in this careful exegesis of the meaning of Melchizedek.]

Verses 18-19 constitute a summary of the writer's argument concerning the supersession of the law. **19. the law made nothing perfect:** that is, it brought no one to God, but the 'substitution' of a **better hope** ('of forgiveness and absolution') did (see Moffatt's comment on **is introduced**, *Comm., ad loc.*). Now it is possible for us to **draw near to God** (19), to worship truly, which to the writer of Hebrews is the fundamental element in redemption. For now man's relationship to God is no longer one of external ordinances simply, but it is an inward spiritual relationship which guarantees true communion with Him.

The ultimate superiority of Christ's priesthood is made even more clear in 20-25. Firstly, attention is called to the fact that God did not underwrite the old levitical priesthood as He did the new. They **became priests without an oath** (21). This means to the writer that it was only temporary—provisional. The priest 'after the order of Melchizedek', however, was confirmed in his office by an oath from God (21), hence His priesthood is eternal. This makes **Jesus** (note the name) **the guarantee of a better covenant** (22), for since the priesthood and the covenant are inextricably bound together (cf. note on 'covenant' in ch. 8), the covenant is only as permanent as the priesthood. Secondly, the multiplicity of the former priests in contrast to the one new priest also emphasizes the superiority of the latter. Previously death kept a priest from continuing in office (cf. v. 16); it made his work incomplete. But not so with the new priest—**he has a permanent priesthood**, 'as one not to be transferred to another' (Gk. *aparabatos*), **because** he **lives for ever** (24, cf. also 13: 8). This brings the writer to the climax of this part of his priestly discourse. Because Christ's priesthood is inviolable and 'untransferable' **he is able to save completely those who come to God through him** (25). [Note: (a) 'completely' better translates the Gk. *eis to panteles* (cf. Lk. 13: 11) than does the 'for all time' of the RSV. Thus, 'He can guarantee their total and final salvation' (F. F. Bruce, *Peake, ad loc.*); (b) the meaning and tense of the verb 'come' indicate that those who *constantly* come to worship God through Jesus Christ are the ones He is able to save.] Again, because Christ's priesthood is inviolable and 'untransferable' He is able to make continual intercession for us—uninterruptedly He can take up our case before God.

The final contrasts showing the superiority of Christ's priesthood to the levitical are made, firstly, between His personal character as priest and theirs: He was one who exactly suited our need, 'altogether pure within'; they were compelled **to offer sacrifices day after day**, even for their **own sins** (27), and secondly, between the quality of His sacrifice and theirs: His was the offering up of Himself, a conscious willing victim, of such a nature that it need never be repeated, hence it was **once for all** (27); theirs was the sacrifice of unwilling, unthinking beasts whose blood could never take away sin (cf. 10: 1 ff.), hence it was a daily perpetual affair (27).

ii. Christ's Priestly Ministry and the New Covenant (8: 1-13)

From a description of the greatness of the priest the writer now turns to discuss, as the crowning part of his argument (Manson, *Epistle to the Hebrews*, p. 123), the greatness of His ministry —a greatness which is due largely to the sphere in which this ministry is carried out. The high **point of what we are saying** (1) is not simply that **we do have such a high priest** as that described in ch. 7, but that we have such a high priest **who sat down . . . in heaven** (1). For the writer of Hebrews the unseen world is the real world which faith takes with all seriousness (2, cf. 6: 20; 11: 1 f., 16; 12: 22), and the world of the phenomenal is but a copy and shadow of that reality (cf. Num. 24: 6, LXX, and Exod. 25: 9, 40). Thus when he states that Christ as high priest is in heaven, he is doing more than merely telling his readers where Jesus is now. He is telling them that His ministry is a 'real' ministry because its sphere of operation is the real world—**the sanctuary, the true tabernacle set up by the Lord, not by man** (2, cf. vv. 5 f. for the scriptural proof for the existence of the heavenly sanctuary). Thus His ministry, as His person (ch. 7), stands in distinct contrast to that of the levitical priests. Their ministry was earthbound. Hence **They serve at a sanctuary that is a copy and shadow of what is in heaven** (5). They and their service, too, are but shadows cast by the good things which were to come, and not the very realities themselves (cf. 10: 1).

To review, the writer's argument seems to go like this: Christ is a high priest established so by God (ch. 7). Since 'the one task of a high priest is to offer sacrifice in a sanctuary', He also needed **to have something to offer** (8: 3) and a sanctuary in which to do it. But because there already were priests on earth **who offer the gifts prescribed by the law** (4), and because there was no room for Christ in the earthly sanctuary by virtue of His descent from Judah (cf. 7: 13), His sphere of priestly service must of necessity be heaven if He is to carry out the purpose of His office. This, then, means that **the ministry Jesus has perceived is . . . superior** (6). And as a corollary to this, the covenant He mediates is a better covenant than the former since **it is** (legally) **founded** (Gk. *nenomothetetai*) **on better promises** (6).

The concept of 'covenant' plays an important rôle in Hebrews, used by the writer at least seventeen times. The Greek word for it is *diathēkē*, which in classical times meant 'disposition', 'testament' or 'will'. But this meaning is never given to the word in Hebrews (with the possible exception of 9: 15 f.). The writer's context for understanding *diathēkē* is not the classical world, but the world of the OT. There it was used by the LXX translators to convey the ideas contained in the Hebrew *berîth*—a word which usually meant a covenant or an agreement between two parties consenting to certain conditions set down for the purpose of

attaining some object of mutual desire. Each party, then, was under obligation to fulfill his end of the bargain. Sometimes the covenant was sealed with the blood of a slain animal (Gen. 15: 1–10; Exod. 24: 5–8), which may have symbolized the deaths of those making the covenant—deaths which put them, figuratively speaking, in a position where they could do nothing to break the agreement entered in upon. [Note: in all likelihood the Hebrew verb 'to make a covenant', *kārath*, goes back to this very ritual, for it literally means 'to cut', i.e., to cut up an animal in order to seal the contract.] In addition to the external obligations each took upon himself in entering a covenant relationship, there was also a spiritual aspect to the ancient covenant—a pledge of loyalty or community of soul—which can best be represented by the expression, 'loyal love' or 'steadfast love'.

The covenant between God and man, however, must never be thought of merely as a contract between two equal parties. Rather God is the sole initiator, who sets down the terms under which the agreement will go into effect. He then invites men to join with Him in it (cf. Heb. 8: 8–9 where God speaks and says 'I will establish' and 'I made'; cf. also Dt. 4: 13). Though God is the Senior Partner, so to speak, men, nevertheless, are free to respond, free to choose whether or not they will accept His invitation. If they do they become His worshipping people and He becomes their God (cf. Exod. 19: 5 f. with Heb. 8: 10).

There are many covenants mentioned in the OT and the covenant concept is a developing one, but the writer of Hebrews here seems to have in mind that covenant which was inaugurated at Sinai. The conditions under which it went into effect involved the keeping of the Law (cf. Exod. 24: 6–8; Dt. 4: 12 ff.; 5: 1 ff.; 1 Kg. 8: 21). The Law, however, was an external voice to the people and never really a part of them. Hence, they could not observe it without transgressing its ordinances. This was indeed a severe weakness of the old covenant but not its greatest, since within the covenant relationship the people really were not expected to be sinless. God recognized that 'to err is human' (Heb. 5: 2; 9: 7), and, therefore, provided for such human failure by inaugurating the sacrificial system for the covering of all those sins of ignorance and error done within the covenant. [Note: Wilful sins were another matter. They were basically sins against the covenant and involved wilful rebellion and unbelief. For such sins there was no sacrifice (cf. Heb. 10: 26).] It was at this point, however, that the real weakness of the old covenant became painfully obvious. Its sacrificial system, centring as it did in its high priest, could not even cope with those transgressions done within the covenant so as to give the people involved a sense of true forgiveness (Heb. 9: 15; 10: 4). Now, however, under the new covenant (though the conditions for its effectiveness are not here made explicit), there is provided a spontaneous inner correspondence to the expressed will of God by the inscription of His laws upon the human heart (Heb. 8: 10), and the complete forgiveness of sins by the priestly work of Christ. Now God's covenant people can draw near to Him with a cleansed conscience (Heb. 8: 12; 10: 21 f.). From the idea that the covenant is a relationship existing between God and His people maintained through atoning sacrifice, it is clear that the high priest becomes the central figure in it. He is the minister of atonement. The covenant relationship, therefore, is only as good as the high priest who administers it. The ministry of the ancient high priest was imperfect. Thus the old covenant also was imperfect and hence transitory (8: 13)—weaknesses which were recognized even by the old covenant itself, for from within it comes the prediction of a new one to take its place (8). But our high priest is Jesus the Son of God (4: 14), forever ordained to this office by an inviolable oath of God (7: 21), who continually ministers effectively in the unseen world of realities (8: 1 ff.). It is no wonder then, that the writer is so sure that the new covenant **is founded on better promises** (8: 6; for this discussion see A. B. Davidson, *The Epistle to the Hebrews*, 1950, pp. 162 ff.; E. D. Burton, *Galatians (ICC)*, note on 'covenant' in the Appendix; G. Vos, *The Teaching of the Epistle to the Hebrews*, 1956).

From this it is clear that in the mind of the writer of Hebrews Jeremiah's prediction of the new covenant now has found its fulfilment in the Christian era. He does not look forward to some future time when this will be true. It is true now. The laws of God are written on the Christians' hearts (cf. Rom. 7: 22; 8: 4) and Christ is the perfect priest who makes it possible for God to **forgive their wickedness**, and to forget their sin (8: 12). That this is so can be seen by comparing this passage with 10: 15 ff. where the writer again quotes this same prophecy of Jeremiah and says that the Holy Spirit is thus bearing witness to us in the statement, 'This is the covenant that I will make with *them* . . . says the Lord'. The 'house of Israel' (8: 8, 10), thus, becomes that 'Israel of God' Paul writes of in Gal. 6: 16. Verse 11, which seems not yet to have been fulfilled, can be understood as a powerful, perhaps poetic, way of expressing the idea that the Christian, as none before him, has been brought into an intimate and profound relationship with God so that his will conforms to the will of God 'by a direct personal communication of instruction and influence' (Vaughan, *Comm.*, p. 150).

iii. The Priestly Ministry of the Two Covenants Contrasted (9: 1–28)

The writer continues his contrast between the old and new covenants by a description, not of the temple at Jerusalem and its ritual service (which would have been particularly appropriate if the readers were 'Hebrews'), but of the wilderness tabernacle (cf. Exod. 25–31; 35–40) which had been the focal point of worship for the ancient 'wandering people of God'.

He refers to the tabernacle as **an earthly sanctuary** (1), which to him meant that it belonged to the imperfect world of shadows (as contrasted with the place where Christ serves, 8: 1–5). Thus at the outset the writer again calls attention to the essential and radical difference between the two covenants. The reference to the furniture within the tabernacle is, as the writer himself implies, of secondary importance to his present discussion, hence **we cannot discuss these things in detail now** (5). Suffice it to say that what seems to be a mistake with reference to the placing of the golden altar of incense (probably not 'censer' as AV), namely, behind the second curtain and in the holy of holies (3–4 contra Exod. 40: 26), may not be a mistake at all. It must be noted that the writer says there is a tent **called the Most Holy Place, which had the golden altar of incense** (3–4). He does not say 'in which is the golden altar' as he did in describing the position of the furniture mentioned above in v. 2. The substitution of 'having' for 'in which' 'itself points clearly to something different from mere position'. It was probably intended to mean that the altar properly belonged to the holy of holies. 'The ark and the altar of incense typified the two innermost conceptions of the heavenly sanctuary, the manifestation of God and the spiritual worship of man. And thus they are placed in significant connection in the Pentateuch: Exod. 30: 6; 40: 5; cf. Lev. 4: 7; 16: 12, 18 (before the Lord)' (Westcott, *Comm.*, p. 247, cf. also 1 Kg. 6: 22). One should also note that though the tables of the covenant were indeed placed within the ark (Exod. 25: 16, 21) there is no explicit statement in the OT that the pot of manna and Aaron's staff were also put inside. Rather it is stated that they were laid up 'before the testimony' (Exod. 16: 34; Num. 17: 10). Perhaps the writer here is following a tradition which placed all within the ark in order to show that interposed between these symbols of Israel's rebellion (so Chrysostom: 'the tables of the covenant because he broke the former ones, and the manna because they murmured . . . and the rod of Aaron which budded because they rebelled') and a holy God **were the cherubim of the Glory, overshadowing the place of atonement** (in NIV) (5), i.e., interposed between God and the people's sin was the place of atonement.

The author continues in vv. 6–10 to point out the symbolic nature of the ancient tabernacle, the very construction of which was the Holy Spirit's way of proclaiming that free access to God was impossible under the old covenant (8). Everyone, except the high priest (and even he but for one day in the year—the day of atonement, cf. Lev. 16), was shut out by a thick veil (and by ritual law) from the place where God visibly manifested His gracious presence—the holy of holies. According to this arrangement it is obvious, then, that the gifts and sacrifices which were offered did not perfect the conscience of the worshipper (9) for he was ever kept at a distance from God. They were wholly external **regulations** (10), and did not penetrate deeply enough into the moral realm to clear the conscience from its sense of guilt. And 'it is an axiom of the epistle that you cannot worship with a guilty conscience' (Narborough, *Comm.*, p. 115). These things, however, the tabernacle with its two tents, its symbolic furnishings and elaborate ritual, etc., were not valueless or wrong—only temporary for they were imposed (presumably by God) **until the time of the new order** (10), until the shadow should give way to reality.

That time has now come! The veil has been rent. What the ancient priesthood with its sacrifices and earthly sphere of operation could not accomplish, Christ was able to accomplish. As **high priest of the good things that are already here** (11, not 'things to come' as AV), He has entered once for all (12) into **the greater and more perfect tabernacle that is not man-made, that is to say, not a part of this creation** (11). It was a heavenly tent He went into, being enabled to do so by virtue of (the meaning of the RSV 'taking', lit. 'through') **his own blood** (12). Thus, because of the merits of His person, the quality of His sacrifice, and the sphere of His ministry, Christ has secured *by himself* (and perhaps, 'for His own interest', Gk. *heuramenos*) an **eternal redemption** for us (12). The author does not state explicitly what this redemption is from, nor does he say to whom the redemption price was paid, but this much at least may be inferred from the context: redemption means 'release' from a guilty conscience which was made possible only at great cost to the Redeemer.

The writer admits that the sacrifices belonging to the day of atonement (**the blood of goats and calves**—cf. Lev. 16) and even the oblations offered on other occasions (**the ashes of a heifer**—cf. Num. 19), did have positive value. Though wholly external they provided ceremonial cleansing so that the defiled was not cut off from the covenant relationship with God (13). But he is willing to do this only that he might show the far greater effectiveness of Christ's sacrifice which was a 'conscious and willing' self-sacrifice, offered to God without moral blemish **through the eternal Spirit** (14). This last expression is a very difficult one. Some have interpreted it as meaning that Christ offered Himself to God 'after the power of an indissoluble life' (cf. 7: 16), that is to say, by virtue of His eternal nature. Others have understood it to mean that His sacrifice was of His own free will. Still others, that His sacrifice was offered on the spiritual plane and not on the ritual. Most probably correct is the view that as the Saviour depended upon the power and direction of the Holy Spirit to accomplish the will of the Father in all of His life, so He did in death. [Note: some early scribes must have understood it in this last sense because 'holy' appears with 'spirit' instead of 'eternal' in some ancient Greek and Latin manuscripts.] The effectiveness of the **blood of Christ** (14), is seen from the fact that it purifies the conscience (14)—it realizes in personal experience what all the other blood-sacrifices merely pointed to but could not effect.

The result of this cleansed conscience is release from **acts that lead to death** (see note on 4: 10) and the ability to **serve the living God** (14). To **serve** translates the Greek word *latreuein* which always means 'to carry out *religious* duties', 'to render service within a sanctuary' (Arndt and Gingrich, *A Greek-English Lexicon*). It is used several times in Hebrews, and at one point the one who thus 'serves' is called a 'worshipper' (9: 9). Thus to **serve the living God** really means that anyone whose conscience has been cleansed now may enter the holy of holies as a priest to render worshipful service to 'a God who is all life'.

For this reason (15), that is, because forgiveness of sins truly has been effected through the blood of Christ, as the cleansing of the conscience proves, **Christ is the mediator of a new covenant**—the one capable of guaranteeing that all **who are called** will **receive the promised eternal inheritance** (15). But does 'the called' include only those believers living in the new age? What of those people of faith who lived under the old covenant (cf. 11: 8 ff., 13–16)? Are they left in their sins, since their institutions did not adequately cope with the sin-problem, removing it only ceremonially? The answer to this question is immediately forthcoming: the range of the effectiveness of Christ's death is so vast as **to set them free from the sins** (done) **under the first covenant** (15). The death of Christ is retroactive (cf. Rom. 3: 25 f.).

16. In the case of a will, it is necessary to prove the death of the one who made it. It appears to be the writer's intention to expand upon his statement concerning Christ as the mediator of the new covenant (cf. 15). He wishes to show that He is more than a mere intermediary between God and man; He is that very one whose death was required to ratify the covenant. The word 'will' (Gk. *diathēkē*) may also be translated by the word 'covenant'. It is true that *diathēkē* had as its basic idea 'will' or 'testament', but it must not be forgotten that the author of Hebrews had the meaning of this word mediated to him through the OT (the LXX), and that he never uses it in any other sense than 'covenant' anywhere else in his letter. This, coupled with the fact that v. 16 is an expansion of the idea begun in v. 15 where Christ is described as the mediator of a new covenant, makes it clear that the writer hardly intends to shift meanings with so little warning. What then do vv. 16–17 mean if the word 'covenant' is substituted wherever 'will' is found? It is important to notice that v. 16 does not say that he who makes the covenant must die, but that **it is necessary to prove** (his) **death** (Gk. *pheresthai*, meaning 'brought forward', 'presented', 'introduced upon the scene', 'set in evidence'). Traditionally this was effected through the slaying of some animal 'introduced' by those entering into the covenant (cf. note on covenant, ch. 8). 'He who makes the covenant . . . is, for the purposes of the covenant, identified with the victim by whose representative death the covenant is ordinarily ratified. In the death of the victim his death is presented symbolically' (Westcott, *Comm.*, p. 265; cf. also pp. 298 ff.). Hence, the one who made the covenant is rendered (symbolically) incapable of doing anything to alter the covenant for in figure he has died. This is made clear in v. 17: **because a will is in force only when somebody has died** (lit. 'is ratified over dead (bodies)'; cf. Gen. 15: 7–21; Jer. 34: 18 f.), **it never takes effect while the one who who made it is living**, i.e., as long as he is not symbolically dead through the death of the covenant-ratifying victim. Thus the death of Christ, which was difficult for the readers of Hebrews to understand, was made meaningful to them by means of the covenant-concept and that which was required to put it into effect. God who made the covenant rendered the terms of the covenant unalterable, as far as He was concerned, by His death, not symbolically, but really, in the person of His eternal Son become man! [It is only proper to note, however, that this interpretation is rejected by many who see the plain sense of vv. 16, 17 to require the meaning of 'will' or 'testament' for *diathēkē*, for this is the only kind of covenant or settlement which has no validity so long as he who made it remains alive. *Pheresthai*, the Gk. verb rendered, *be established* (16) is then understood in the secular sense of 'be registered' or 'be produced as evidence', i.e., in order to secure probate of the will (F. F.

Bruce; see also his remarks in *Peake's Commentary on the Bible*, rev. ed., p. 1015, where he takes note of Westcott's interpretation adopted here in this commentary, only to dismiss it. Cf. also C. Spicq, *Comm.*, *ad loc.*, who maintains that in Heb. 9: 15, 18–20 *diathēkē* means covenant in the same sense as in the OT but that the term means 'testament' in vv. 16–17). Such a change points out the twofold aspect of *diathēkē* namely as a covenant sealed in the blood of Christ and as a will or testament by which the dying Christ bequeathed to all believers the goods of salvation.]

The writer shows the correctness of this principle by a reference to what had already happened in Israel's redemptive history: **Even the first covenant was not put into effect without blood** (18). When Moses had read the book of the covenant in the hearing of the people, he **sprinkled the scroll** (not mentioned in Exod. 24: 6 ff.), **and all the people** (19), who, by the blood of the slain oxen, declared that they were now placing themselves in a position not to alter the terms of the covenant they had agreed to: *All that the Lord has spoken we will do, and we will be obedient* (Exod. 24: 7).

The meaning of blood, however, is not exhausted when explained as representing the death of those making the covenant. Blood was also required to cleanse away the sins done within the covenant relationship (cf. the note on 'covenant' in connection with ch. 8). Hence, the writer is led on by the force of the meanings of blood and of covenant to say that **the law requires that nearly everything be cleansed with blood, and without the shedding of blood there is no forgiveness** (22; for exceptions to this requirement of blood for cleansing cf. Lev. 5: 11–13; Num. 16: 46; 31: 50).

It appears strange that the writer should say that **heavenly things** had to be purified (23). It may simply be because he was compelled by his analogy to make such a statement, or perhaps he conceived the heavenly things as having incurred 'a certain defilement through contact with the sins that are absolved' in them (E. F. Scott, *Comm.*, *ad loc.*). In any case, having offered a better sacrifice than did His counterpart, **Christ did not enter a man-made sanctuary that was only a copy of the true one; he entered heaven itself, now to appear for us in God's presence** (24). His sphere of service is the true holy of holies, and He enters it by virtue of the one final sacrifice made by Him in history **at the end of the ages** (26, cf. Gal. 4: 4; Eph. 1: 10)—the sacrifice of Himself. It is an offering so complete and so ultimate as never to be repeated again (26), a substitutionary offering which was effective in bearing away **the sins of many** (28). [Note: 'many' does not necessarily mean anything less than 'all' (cf. 2: 9 and Mk 10: 45 with 1 Tim. 2: 6); it comes into the NT as 'a legacy from Isa. 53: 11 f.' 'All' may be expressed by 'many' when the largeness of the 'all' is being stressed.] Because it was made at the end of this age, nothing stands between it and the full-realization of the age-to-come which will be inaugurated when Christ **will appear a second time, not to bear sin but to bring salvation to those who are waiting for him** (28).

iv. The Finality of Christ's One Sacrifice (10: 1–18)
In emphasizing the finality of Christ's sacrifice the writer, as has been his custom, contrasts it with the lack of finality found in the OT system of law and sacrifice. **The law**, he says, **is only a shadow of the good things that are coming** (1). It does not itself possess the true form of these realities (1). Consequently, because of its very nature—shadow and copy—it was incapable of perfecting any worshipper through its sacrifices (1). That is to say, no worshipper was ever brought 'into a real and enduring fellowship with God', for none fully lost his feeling **guilty for . . . sins** (2). To the writer of Hebrews the very fact that sin-offerings were made continually, year after year (3, cf. Lev. 16) was itself proof that the institutions of the ancient order, though divinely ordained, were not final. To this argument the writer adds that even reason itself teaches that it is **impossible for the blood of bulls and goats**, the involuntary death of irrational beasts, **to take away sins** (4); at best they were only visible symbols of something better to come.

But the one sacrifice God was pleased with, as the prophetic voice of the OT stressed again and again, was that of the conscious and willing dedication of a man's total life to do the divine will. **Therefore, when Christ came into the world, he said: 'Sacrifice and offering you did not desire, but a body you prepared for me . . . For I have come** (lit. 'I am here') **to do your will, O God'** (5–7). The writer is quoting from Ps. 40: 6 f., using the LXX which differs from the Hebrew in that it says, 'a body thou didst prepare for me', instead of 'mine ears hast thou opened'. As has been his custom, he now puts these words, originally spoken by another, into the mouth of Christ, for in the thinking of this writer 'where that is written of a *man*, which no *mere* man can satisfy, there lies under it a reference to One who is not man only' (Vaughan, *Comm.*, p. 190). Here, then, the words of the psalmist become the words of the incarnate Son, overheard as they were spoken to the Father. This Psalm implies that **sacrifices** (peace offerings) **and offerings** (cereal offerings), **burnt offerings and sin offerings** (5–6)—offerings of all types, were never decreed by God. [Note: the expression, **you did not desire**, of v. 5 really means 'thou

hast not willed or purposed' such sacrifices. Cf. B. W. Bacon, *Journal of Biblical Literature*, 16 (1897) pp. 136 ff. for the meaning of 'desired', Gk. *eudokein*. It is significant in this connection, that the writer of Hebrews changes the LXX *ēitēsas* of Ps. 40: 7, 'you asked', to this verb expressing divine will or purpose—*eudokēsas*.] They were but a stop-gap measure devised as a result of man's rebellion. What God has always wanted has been absolute loyal obedience to His will. Now at last that divine desire has been realized. The pre-existent Son became incarnate in accordance with the voice of prophecy (i.e., as it was written of Him **in the scroll**, 7) and announced 'His resolution to replace' the ancient sacrifices by His own obedience. By this gracious act He voluntarily identified Himself with humanity to such an extent that His life of total obedience to the Father, even to the point of dying on the cross (cf. Phil. 2: 8), becomes the ultimate act of obedience for all who acknowledge their identification with Him. Hence, because obedience is what God has eternally willed, with sacrifices introduced only as an interim measure on account of man's disobedience, and because man has now been made obedient by virtue of his identification with Christ (or the other way around), the whole system of sacrifice, therefore, has been abolished by the realization of the true will of God (9). This is clearly stated in v. 10 where the writer says explicitly, **by that will, we have been made holy through the sacrifice of the body of Jesus Christ once for all.** This means that we have been 'set apart' ('sanctified') 'into the true condition for making our approach to God'—i.e., that of obedience —by means of the dedication of Jesus Christ to the will of God—a dedication which reached its climax in and was supremely proven by His death, the offering up of His body once for all. The Christian now stands perfected by means of the perfect obedience of Jesus Christ (cf. Rom. 5: 18 f.; Heb. 5: 8–9).

The finality of this supreme sacrifice is further heightened by other contrasts existing between Christ and the ancient priests. The latter **stands** (11), indicative of the fact that there is work still to be done; Christ on the contrary, sits **at the right hand of God** (12), signifying that His task has been accomplished. The ancient priest **again and again he offers the same sacrifices, which can never take away sins** (11); Christ, however, **offered for all time one sacrifice for sins** (12). Thus Christ **has made perfect forever those who are being made holy**, that is, He has cleared the conscience of the Christian from its sense of guilt and has brought him as a worshipper into the very presence of God (14). That this is so is proved by the Holy Spirit who witnesses through Jeremiah that the new covenant and forgiveness of sins have been promised **to us** Christians (15–17). Thus **where these have been forgiven . . . there is no longer any sacrifice for sin** (18). The basic requirements for the full enjoyment of the covenant relationship have been wholly met—forgiveness of sin and a cleansed conscience.

VII. FINAL EXHORTATIONS TO PERSEVERANCE AND FURTHER WARNINGS AGAINST INDIFFERENCE (10: 19–12: 29)
i. Exhortation to Worship (10: 19–25)
Having concluded his great theological section on the priesthood of Jesus Christ, the writer returns again to the real purpose of his homily —exhortation and warning.

The first exhortation urges the Christian to take full advantage of the privilege of worship —of drawing near (22)—which is now available to him (19–22). The reasons given by the writer for his exhortation are twofold: (a) the confidence we now have **to enter the Most Holy Place** (19), and (b) the **great priest** we have **over the house of God** (21). Here 'confidence' (Gk. *parrhēsia*, lit. 'outspokenness', 'openness') conveys the idea of an exulting boldness, a vivid sense of freedom from all fear when it comes to entering the sacred area of God's presence. This 'open access' has been provided **by the blood of Jesus** (19), **by a new and living way** of his flesh (in contrast to the RSV which identifies 'flesh' with 'curtain') **opened for us through the curtain** (20). In these words the writer is saying that every barrier to the presence of God has forever been torn down through the blood and flesh (cf. 2: 14 for this same order) of Jesus, i.e., through the true historical human experiences, including death, of the eternal Son who is the Christian's **great priest over the house of God** (21, cf. 3: 6). Not only has this one pulled aside the separating veil, but He is there personally to escort the worshipper into the sanctuary. True worship of God, therefore, is accomplished only through Jesus Christ and His atoning sacrifice (20 f.).

Having outlined the reasons for taking advantage of the Christian's right to worship, the writer now turns to describe the manner in which it is to be done: (a) The Christian is to worship with a **a sincere heart** (22), that is to say, he is to come with sincerity in his innermost being, remembering the critical capabilities of the word of God (4: 12); (b) he is to worship **in full assurance of faith** (22), 'to have done with all doubt and misgiving', reflecting continuously on the basis for his faith— the person and work of Christ; (c) he is to worship with his heart **sprinkled to cleanse . . . from a guilty conscience** (22), and (d) his body **washed with pure water** (22), that

is to say, he is to assemble for worship only after he has gained a consciousness of sins forgiven through faith in the atoning work of Christ, and only after he has participated in Christian baptism (cf. 1 Pet. 3: 21 f.). These last two requirements for worship are cast in language suggestive of the ancient ritual performed at the ordination of the levite into his priestly service (cf. Lev. 8: 30; Exod. 29: 4; 30: 20; 40: 30), and are intended to show that the Christian stands in the high place of being a priest himself ordained for worshipful service to God.

The second admonition exhorts the Christian to **hold unswervingly to the hope we profess** (23) which he made public at his baptism (cf. Justin, 1 *Apol.* 61: 1 ff.). The strong appeal for such perseverance is found to be in the great faithfulness of God who has made His promises irrevocable (cf. 6: 17; 11: 11; 13: 5 for this same concept).

Lastly, Christians are exhorted to consider how they can **spur one another on toward love and good deeds** (24). These things are of the essence of Christianity. Since their maintenance is dependent upon the mutual interaction of the Christian society, it is absolutely essential that one assemble himself with other Christians if he is to be assured of continued spiritual development. Any type of go-it-alone Christianity is unthinkable to the writer of Hebrews who deplores the fact that, in the face of the impending Day (25), there are those who neglect to meet **together** (25). Here in these exhortations are found the Pauline trinity of faith (22), hope (23), and love (24).

ii. Warning against Defection (10: 26–39)
The mention of the coming day of judgment and of the need for continuous mutual edification provides the writer with the necessary means of transition from exhortation to severe warning, very similar to that of 6: 4 ff. (26–31). Again, it appears to be a warning against the possibility of defecting from one's confession. There is no objective evidence that one who has made his Christian 'confession' and has been baptized is indeed a Christian, other than the daily perseverance in love and good works—a persistence in the very essence of what his confession implies (cf. 23–24). For the writer of Hebrews the definition of a true Christian is one who manifests 'a life-long allegiance to Christ' (cf. Jn 15: 2, 5; 10: 27; Rom. 11: 22). It *is* possible, implies the author, for one who has received **the knowledge** (Gk. *epignōsis*, 'full-knowledge') **of the truth** to keep on sinning **deliberately** (26, *hekousiōs*—a word which really means 'willingly', 'without compulsion'). It is possible for the 'baptized Christian' who has been thoroughly instructed in the truth of Christianity prior to his baptism to reach that place in his experience where

through constant sinning (Gk. *hamartanontōn*) his attitude becomes one of continued conscious resistance to all that he has been taught. Then, because he has become psychologically hardened (cf. 3: 13) to the point where he sees no redeeming value in Christ's death, treating **the blood of the covenant that sanctified him** (i.e., the confessing Christian, or perhaps Christ Himself) as a common thing (29), there is for him, therefore, no more **sacrifice for sins** (26). He has rejected the only possibility of atonement. The only thing he can look forward to is a more fearful type of judgment than that inflicted upon the man who wilfully renounced the ancient covenant (27). The greater judgment is due to the fact that the covenant he has renounced is greater, for in this act he **has trampled the Son of God** (note the title) **under foot, treated as an unholy thing the blood of the covenant . . . ,** and **insulted the Spirit of grace** (29). The writer closes this sombre warning with a reminder that **the living God** (31) does not threaten in vain: **I will repay,** says the Lord, and scripture (which cannot be broken) promises that **the Lord will judge his people** (30).

Nevertheless, in a fashion identical with 6: 9 ff. the writer brightens as he informs his readers that their past experience of perseverance in persecution is itself objective proof of the reality of their Christian confession (32–39). Wherever and whenever this persecution took place it did not result in martyrdom. It was rather the harassment of being **publicly exposed to insult and persecution** (33), the distress of imprisonment and of the loss of property (34), which, nevertheless, is often more difficult to endure than death itself. They had persevered in all such abuses because of the certainty they had of **better and lasting possessions** (34, cf. 12: 26 f.).

Having endured under persecution, they must not now let down in the hum-drum of every day activities. The normal routine of life, uninterrupted by persecution, is often the real test of genuineness of one's Christian experience, for the very absence of trials and difficulties tends to promote spiritual drifting (2: 1), moral sluggishness and lethargy (5: 11), the slow imperceptible hardening of attitude (3: 13). Into just such a situation, comes the writer's 'word of exhortation' in order to rouse them from sleep and to advise them that they **need to persevere** (or be patient) even now **so that when** they **have done the will of God** they **will receive what he has promised** (36). How long must they wait to receive the fulfilment of this promise? Not long. **For in just a very little while, He who is coming will come and will not delay** beyond the designated time (37). With these words, freely quoted from Isa. 26: 20 and Hab. 2: 3 f. LXX,

the writer guarantees them with the certainty of prophecy of the soon return of their Lord ('the coming one'), and the realization of their hope. In addition, he has changed the sequence of Hab. 2: 4 so as to accentuate the fact that the one who is made righteous by God *lives* by faith, and so as to leave until the end that part which points up the danger of failure to persevere (38) as though he were reluctant to mention it again.

iii. **Faith Defined and Illustrated (11: 1–40)** Since faith is such an important element in perseverance as the prophecy from Habakkuk shows, so much so that it constitutes the very dynamic by which the just shall live, the writer now turns his attention to a full exposition of its meaning. He begins with a description: **faith is being sure of what we hope for and certain of what we do not see** (1). Now if this translation is accepted (note AV and Westcott, *Comm.*, p. 350, for an alternate possibility), then the writer has described faith, not as itself 'the substance of things hoped for', etc., but as an attitude of mind toward the future and the unseen that is determinative for personal conduct in the present. Faith, based as it is upon the firm word of God, is not at all a 'leap in the dark'. It assures one of the reality of the invisible world, and of its superiority to the visible, and thereby enables him to make the right choice in the moment of decision. Faith, therefore, is fundamental to perseverance, for perseverance is nothing more than a series of choices for the future and the unseen over against choices for present and transient things belonging to the phenomenal world. It was thus by faith that **the ancients** received divine approval (2), for they, as the author is about to demonstrate massively, were enabled by it to 'hold fast to the unseen in spite of the illusions and temptations of this passing world' (E. F. Scott, *Comm., ad loc.*). Thus, there is seen again a continuity existing between the past and the present—a continuity of faith in the unseen which binds the two peoples together.

It is interesting to note that in illustrating his definition of faith he does so in roughly chronological fashion. He begins with the creation of the world. **By faith we understand that the universe was formed . . . that what is seen was not made out of what is visible** (3). This statement is not intended to teach creation *ex nihilo*, or to say anything at all about the character of the prior substance from which the world was made. The writer's only point is that 'no purely physical explanation of the world is possible' (Westcott, *Comm.*, p. 353). Faith looks for its answers beyond that which is seen (1).

Next the writer calls many OT saints to witness to the meaning of faith. First in order he discusses those great heroes who lived before the flood (4–7). Abel **offered God a better sacrifice than Cain did** (4). The writer does not state in what way it was 'more acceptable' except to say that it was done in faith, and to hint at the possibility of it being a 'more abundant' (Gk. *pleiona*) offering than Cain's, a fact which would have indicated a fuller sense of God's claim upon his life than that evidenced by his brother (cf. Westcott, *Comm.*, p. 354). Notice that God accepted **his offerings** (4), not offering!

Proof for Enoch's faith lies in the fact that he **pleased God** (5, cf. Gen. 5: 24, LXX, where the Hebrew text has 'walked with God'), for one cannot please God without a faith which clearly sees Him, the unseen, as a living reality, and as one who can intervene in history to reward **those who earnestly seek him** (6). The reward for Enoch's faith was translation —he **was taken from this life, so that he did not experience death** (5).

The meaning of faith as defined by the writer of Hebrews is most clearly illustrated from the life of Noah, of whom it was said that God warned him of **things not yet seen** (7). His response showed that, though the flood was still future and perhaps unheard of, certainly unseen, he nevertheless was convinced of its reality because of the divine oracle. This conviction determined his course of action—he obeyed God. Thus he **became heir of the righteousness that comes by faith** (7, a Pauline-like expression; cf. Rom. 3: 22; 4: 13; Heb. 10: 38).

Next in order as witnesses to faith were the patriarchs extending from Abraham down to Joseph (8–22). Abraham is the first and perhaps the greatest OT example of faith. To the writer of Hebrews Abraham proved his faith by his prompt response to God's call, although it was to go to a place with which he was totally unacquainted (8), and by the fact that he did not make a permanent home in this **promised land** (9) . . . **For he was looking forward to the city with foundations, whose architect and builder is God** (10). In much the same way as he did in chapters 3–4, the writer shows that the **promised land** was for Abraham only a land of temporary promise. The real 'promised land' was the heavenly, the unseen, which, when made visible by faith, caused him to live as a pilgrim in this world. Faith is 'the conviction of things not seen'. **Isaac and Jacob . . . heirs with him of the same promise** (9), also shared his outlook on life.

According to v. 11 Sarah's faith is joined with Abraham's in a co-operative venture to produce a son. But there is no record of her faith in the OT—only of her incredulity at the promise of the Lord (Gen. 18: 12 ff.). In addition, the Greek expression translated **to become a father** (*katabolē spermatos*) is regu-

larly used of the 'sowing' of the seed, of 'begetting' (Arndt and Gingrich, *Greek-English Lexicon*), rather than of 'conceiving' as in RSV. Hence, it is most likely that the Greek should be translated, 'By faith he (Abraham) received power to beget *by* Sarah herself'. This alternate translation coincides with Rom. 4: 19 where Paul, too, ignores the faith of Sarah.

In good literary fashion the author breaks up his survey of redemptive history lest it become monotonous, and pauses to summarize what he has been saying (13–16). There is a larger fulfilment to God's promises than that which can be realized on earth in the realm of the visible—**All these people were still living by faith when they died. They did not receive the things promised** (13). Thus, though Abraham did get to Canaan—the promised land—and though Isaac was born to him in his old age, and in this sense the promises of God were realized, his faith not being totally unrewarded, it is also true that he did not receive what was promised, that is to say, he did not receive *the* promises (the literal translation of the Greek). *The* promises of God cannot be fulfilled short of that **better country—a heavenly one** (16). Recall that to the writer of Hebrews, the heavenly is the real world. The phenomenal world is but its shadow. Faith, the capacity to see that unseen sphere and to understand its superiority over the seen, compels the believer to choose for the former and against the latter. Thus it was that faith made the patriarchs live as **aliens and strangers on earth** (13 f.) because they were **looking for a country of their own** beyond earth's space-time limits (14). Hence, **God is not ashamed to be called their God** (16, cf. Mk 12: 26 f.). The writer arrives at this conclusion from the fact that while residing in the promised land the patriarchs still called themselves 'sojourners', 'pilgrims' (Gen. 23: 4; 24: 37; 28: 4; 47: 9). Faith, then, is the opposite of shrinking back; it is rather a pressing forward toward goals which are real although imperfectly seen. This, of course, is the whole theme of Hebrews, and it is compressed within the limits of one concept—faith.

The writer now returns to the faith of Abraham before going on to mention that of Isaac, Jacob, and Joseph (17–22). The supreme test of Abraham's faith was God's request that he offer up Isaac (17), of whom it was said, **'It is through Isaac that your offspring will be reckoned'** (18). Abraham obeyed though 'the command of God seemed to clash with the promise of God', because he **reasoned that God could raise the dead** (19, cf. Gen. 22: 5; here is another of the very few references to the writer's belief in the resurrection). Thus Isaac's 'resurrection' was 'by way of a parable' (NIV has **figuratively speaking**, 19) and became a type of the resurrection of Christ. Isaac, Jacob and Joseph combine, each in his own way, to illustrate again that faith is the assurance of things hoped for, the conviction of things not seen (20–22). The reference to Jacob's staff (21) where the Hebrew text mentions his 'bed' (Gen. 47: 31) is further proof of the writer's use of the LXX.

Next, the faith of Moses is dealt with (23–28). His faith, beginning as it did with his parents who by it gained 'some inkling of their child's destiny' (Josephus, *Ant.*, 11, 9, 3 cited by F. F. Bruce, *Peake's Comm.*, p. 1,017), compelled him to forfeit the immediate for the future, the seen for the unseen, to choose **to be illtreated along with the people of God** (25), rather than **pleasures of sin** for a moment. **He regarded disgrace for the sake of Christ as of greater value than the treasures of Egypt** (26). This interpretation placed upon the Greek by the NIV means that Moses had 'faith in the God who would fulfil his purpose and his promise, a fulfilment which could come . . . only in the coming of Christ' (A. C. Purdy, *Comm.*, *ad loc.*; cf. 1 C. 10: 4). Literally translated, however, this verse says, Moses 'considered the reproach of the Christ to be greater riches', etc., which could mean that Moses himself was happy to suffer that reproach which belongs to any anointed envoy of God sent to a world rebelling against Him. In other words, Moses suffered as God's Christ, His anointed, for 'this reproach, which was endured in the highest degree by Christ Jesus (Rom. 15: 3), was endured also by those who in any degree prefigured or represented Him' (Westcott, *Comm.*, p. 372).

Finally, the writer briefly touches on the faith of those from the Exodus to Maccabean times (29–38), mentioning specifically the faith of 'the people' in crossing the Red Sea and conquering Jericho (29), and of Rahab the harlot (31) showing that 'strongholds tumble before faith and even the most disreputable are redeemed by it'. Then with time failing him, he summarizes the exploits of judges, prophets, kings, exiles, and martyrs, not, however, in strict chronological order, whose exploits are etched deeply in the annals of Israel's history. This is one of the most beautiful passages from the standpoint of style to be found in Hebrews; it is also the most moving. It serves magnificently to summarize the writer's concept of faith. It is that which drives one forward always, never allowing the luxury of retreat. It is 'venturesome action'. It is trust and confidence. It is obedience. It is endurance. Faith is seeing the invisible in clear focus, so that the present visible world loses its charm. One is thereby enabled to forfeit life itself, if necessary, in order to gain that better world to come (35b). It is quite likely that the background for

much of this concluding summary comes from 2 Mac. 6: 18–7: 42. The writer considers the men and women mentioned there to rank with Gideon, Barak, Samson, David, etc., in witnessing to the meaning of faith. The reference to being **sawed in two** (37) may indicate an acquaintance with a legendary work entitled the *Martyrdom of Isaiah* where Isaiah was allegedly sawn asunder with a wood saw because he prophesied the coming redemption through Christ (cf. R. H. Pfeiffer, *History of the New Testament Times with an Introduction to the Apocrypha*, 1949, pp. 73–74).

These were all commended . . . yet none of them received what had been promised (39), that is, they did not receive '*the* promise', the *messianic* promise. All of redemptive history, with its manifold partial fulfilments, moves on to its culmination in what might be called the Christ-event. That event was the capstone, the *teleiōsis* of history, therefore, the writer of Hebrews can say God has spoken ultimately in His Son, and He has done it 'in these last days' (1: 2). Thus the Christian is living in the age of fulfilment—God's promise has been realized in the coming of the Messiah. It is in this light that the words **God had planned something better for us** (40) are to be understood. How much greater, therefore, should be our faith, our loyalty to God, than that of the ancients. And yet, the expression, **that only together with us would they be made perfect** (40) implies that the men of faith in the OT and those in the Christian era alike belong to one people of God who are *together* made perfect.

iv. Application of the Faith-principle to Life (12: 1–24)
The many heroes of faith enumerated in chapter 11 become to the writer an amphitheatre of spectators cheering the Christian runner on toward the goal. Indeed they are more than spectators; they are witnesses (Gk. *martyres*) interpreting the meaning of life to him. They encourage him by their own lives, which make clear the certain success of persistent participation, to **throw off everything that hinders, and the sin that so easily entangles** (1). This latter expression translates a Greek word, *euperistatos*, which is made difficult by the fact that there is little or no clue to its meaning from an etymological study. As it is translated in the NIV it describes the hampering effects of a clinging robe which then may refer to those sins of drifting, dullness, lack of spiritual exercise, or immaturity, which could lead one to lose the race of life. The earliest known Greek manuscript of Hebrews, however, gives a different word, *euperispastos*, which means, 'easily distracting'. This word fits in well with the figure of a runner whose eyes should be fixed only on the goal. That goal is **Jesus** (2),

who participated in our human experiences. He is not only the object of faith's vision, but He is its greatest encouragement for He is its **author and perfecter** (2). As author, He himself participated in believing (cf. 2: 13). He blazed the trail of faith for Christians to follow, for his human experience, like theirs, was controlled by faith and not by sight. But He is also faith's perfecter, for all that faith hopes for finds its consummation in Him. Jesus is a further example of encouragement to faith in that the endurance of the cross was the price He willingly paid **for** (Gk. *anti*) **the joy set before him** (2, cf. v. 16, where Esau's birthright was the price he paid for (*anti*) the single meal). Thus believers are encouraged to regard their sufferings (less, in any case, than Christ's) as a small price to pay for the prize to be secured at the end of the race set before *them*. Choosing the cross, however, resulted in Christ being exalted to **the right hand of the throne of God** (2). Because of His exemplary life, therefore, which included accepting the **opposition from sinful men**, Christians are encouraged to **consider him** (3), to study carefully His life of steadfast endurance so that in their experience they may be able to decide for the same path of suffering, if loyalty to God demands that, rather than the way of easy relief (3–4). Thus they will finish the race though weariness may tempt them to give out and quit. The life of Jesus, therefore, is a call to perseverance, for the contest is 'not a short dash to glory, but a distance race calling for endurance' (A. C. Purdy, *Comm.*, p. 739).

In the next section (5–24) the writer explains the meaning of suffering and hardship as the discipline (not 'chastisement' or 'punishment') of a loving Father (cf. 6), whose purpose in it is to educate (Gk. *paideuein*) his child. Thus in the case of the Christian, suffering is God's educational process by which he is fitted to share God's holiness (10). It is a necessary element in the Father-child relationship as the writer establishes from his book of proofs—the OT (Prov. 3: 11 f.), and from the analogy of human parenthood (8–9). If you are not being educated you are not a legitimate son (8). Since this is so, the proper attitude to take toward suffering is that of submission—**submit to the Father of our spirits** (a contrasting expression to that of **human fathers** and means 'spiritual Father'), **and live** (9). Discipline, though painful, later **produces a harvest of righteousness** (11), but only to those who exercise themselves through it, that is, 'those who have by practice acquired the capacity of reacting rightly to affliction' (Narborough, *Comm.*, p. 143, cf. 5: 14). These understand that the circumstances of their lives are dictated by God who directs their destinies through His unfailing omniscience, and whose all-loving

nature actively promotes their highest welfare.

Along with the discipline of God, however, the writer urges self-discipline and the discipline which comes through 'the power of mutual influence' (12–17): **strengthen your feeble arms and weak knees. Make level paths for your feet**, etc. (12 ff.). Here again he returns to the real problem facing his audience—dullness resulting in gradual drifting away from the living God. Only now he uses the figure of enfeeblement. 'Final failure', he warns them, 'comes from continuous weakening. The moral strength is enfeebled little by little' (Westcott, *Comm.*, p. 398). The admonitions in v. 14 are to the individual and seem to be an echo of the sermon on the mount (cf. Mt. 5: 8 f.). The expression 'see the Lord' is a common OT way of describing 'acceptable worship' (cf. Isa. 6: 1 ff., Purdy, *Comm.*, p. 745).

The exhortations given in vv. 15 ff. are to the Church. The power of the corporate body is to make sure that no one of its members **misses the grace of God** (15), or to put it more correctly, that none may lack the grace of God, i.e., fall behind by 'not keeping pace with the movement of divine grace which meets and stirs the progress of the Christian' (Westcott, *Comm.*, p. 406). The Church is to guard against the growth of any **bitter root**, an expression which, coming as it does from Dt. 29: 18, probably means a person whose heart has been turned away from the Lord and who becomes 'a root bearing poisonous and bitter fruit', thereby causing trouble within the Christian community and defiling many besides himself (15). The Church is also to make sure that no second Esau arises among them, a person who is **sexually immoral** or **godless** (16), a person who does not value spiritual things (Gen. 25: 29 ff.). The writer warns that a decision like Esau's is irrevocable. **He could bring about no change of mind, though he sought the blessing with tears** (17).

Accept the discipline of God, the writer exhorts, and discipline yourselves, because as Christians you have far greater advantages than those under the old covenant, and the end of this present educational process is much more glorious than the previous. The old covenant was inaugurated at Mount Sinai, a mountain which could **be touched** (18), material and temporal. The new has been put into effect at **Mount Zion . . . the heavenly Jerusalem, the city of the living God**, the real world, spiritual and eternal (22, cf. Rev. 3: 12; 21: 2 ff.; Gal. 4: 26 f.). The former was established in an atmosphere of dread. A blazing fire raged, darkness and gloom were everywhere. There was tempest and the sound of trumpet. People begged to hear no more (19, cf. Dt. 4: 11 f.;

Exod. 20: 18; Dt. 5: 23 ff.; Exod. 19: 12 f.).
Even Moses trembled with fear (21, but cf. Dt.
9: 19 and its context). But not so the new: there
is about it an atmosphere of joy and peace and
confidence, though at the same time awe. Here
there is a festal gathering (Gk. *panēgyris*). Present at it are angels and the assemblage of saints,
**the first-born whose names are written in
heaven** (23), 'no longer separated, as at Sinai,
by signs of great terror, but united in one vast
assembly' (Westcott, *Comm.*, p. 413). **God the
judge of all men** (23) is also there, and **the
spirits of righteous men made perfect** (23).
Jesus is there, too, whose sprinkled blood
speaks a better word than the blood of Abel
(24). Abel's cried for revenge; Christ's pleads
for forgiveness. It is to this festal gathering that
Christians are invited to come (Gk. *proser-
rchesthai*, i.e., to come as a worshipper).

**v. The Final Warning Against Refusing
God (12: 25–29)**
The contrast between the old covenant (which
to the writer of Hebrews was the highest expression of all religions) and the new is as great
as the contrast between terror and grace. Thus,
if to refuse God's covenant made on earth
(through Moses) meant death (25), to refuse
God's covenant made from heaven (through
Jesus) means far greater punishment. [Note:
The refusal is not simply the refusal of a covenant, but of God who invites one to join Him
in the covenant relationship (25).] For at Sinai
his voice shook the earth (26), but according
to the prophecy of Haggai (2: 6) God now plans
to shake the entire universe (cf. Mk 13: 31; 2
Pet. 3: 7) so that only those things belonging to
an unshakeable order may remain (27, cf.
Dan. 2: 44). Christians belong to just such a
kingdom, one that cannot be shaken (28). It is,
therefore, a cause for gratitude and worship
and also for awe (28), for we must not forget
that our God is a consuming fire (29, cf. Dt. 4:
24; Isa. 33: 14), who 'destroys all transient and
temporal things in order that what is timeless
and unchanging may emerge in full glory'.

**VIII. PRACTICAL EXHORTATIONS,
PASTORAL BENEDICTION AND
PERSONAL GREETINGS (13: 1–24)**
In a manner similar to that of Paul (cf. Rom.
12: 4 ff.; Eph. 5: 21 ff., etc.) the writer concludes his letter with practical instructions. Apparently he is following a catechetical outline
which deals with Christian ethics and which
was already well established within the early
Church. His concern is that his readers exercise
brotherly love (1), which means an active
interest in the welfare of fellow-Christians, and
that they **entertain strangers** or travellers (2),
which has its own compensations (cf. Gen. 18–
19), and that they have a fellow-feeling with

those who are **in prison** and the **illtreated** (3)
so as to provide for their needs for they, too,
being human are susceptible to identical difficulties (3), and that they not only recognize the
honourableness of marriage and the sacredness
of sexual intimacy within the marriage bond,
but also the wickedness of immorality and
adultery (4), and finally, that they be content
with what they have, keeping their minds free
from avarice (5), for God is their helper and
provider. The only intelligent response then to
an understanding of such providential care is
that given by the psalmist: **I will not be afraid**
(6b).

The writer also gives his readers advice concerning the welfare of the Church. By recalling
the faith-life of their leaders and the way they
died, i.e., **the outcome of their way of life**
(Gk. *ekbasis*), they will be stimulated to emulation (7). But the greatest of all patterns to
imitate is Jesus Christ (8). 'Human leaders may
pass away, but Jesus Christ, the supreme object
and subject of their faithful teaching, remains,
and remains the same: no novel additions to
His truth are required' (J. Moffatt, *Epistle to the
Hebrews*, *ad loc.*). The writer also warns against
departing from the doctrines of their leaders,
**carried away by all kinds of strange teach-
ings** (9). What these were is not known. The
writer merely mentions **foods** (cf. Col. 2: 16
ff.) and does not elaborate. Nevertheless, the
point of his remark is to show that Christianity
in its truest form is not regulated by externals;
it is a matter of the heart **strengthened by
grace**, by spiritual influences (9).

Verses 10 ff. are most difficult to interpret.
They may mean that though Christianity is not
dependent upon external things it does not
therefore lack anything essential as one might
be led to think. In fact, Christians really partake
of the one altar which was barred to the worshippers of the old covenant. In the earlier
dispensation the priests partook of all the sacrifices offered on the altars of Israel, except that
one sacrificed on the Day of Atonement (Lev.
16: 27), for **the high priest carries the blood
of animals into the Most Holy Place as
a sin offering, but the bodies are burned
outside the camp** (11). They could not be
eaten by the priests, not even by the high priest.
We Christians, however (and here the contrast
between the old and the new is again made
great), partake of that very sacrifice of expiation—the sacrifice of the Day of Atonement
by partaking of Christ, for He is its grand
fulfilment (cf. Spicq, *Comm.*, II, p. 424). That
Christ is indeed the antitype of this great sacrifice is now made even more clear by the
writer in the words which follow: just as the
body of the sacrificial animal, slain on the Day
of Atonement, was taken **outside the camp**
and burned, so Jesus was taken **outside the**

city gate to suffer for and sanctify His people by His death (11–12).

On the other hand, these verses may mean that Christianity is not at all determined by external things such as those sacrificial celebrations so essential to the old order. To prove this the writer points out that Christianity depends upon a sacrifice of which *no one* is allowed to partake—the sacrifice of atonement. Even the high priest, as great a figure as he was, was forbidden to eat of it (cf. Lev. 16: 27), for the law said that the bodies of those sacrificial animals *had* to be taken and **burned outside the camp** (11). Now, as the writer has already shown, Jesus is the fulfilment of that to which the sacrifice on the Day of Atonement pointed and that is why He, too, **suffered outside the city gate** (12). Therefore, the service He requires 'does not consist in any kind of ritual meal. It consists rather in suffering the world's scorn and rejection along with Him' (cf. for this view Scott, *Comm., ad loc.*).

There may be other views too. But whichever one is correct it is not necessary to see in the exhortation which is based upon it, **go to him outside the camp** (13), any command to leave Judaism or any other *religio licita* (in contrast to Manson, *Epistle to the Hebrews*, p. 151). It is more positive than that, meaning simply, you must identify yourself wholly with Jesus, though to do so may mean **bearing the disgrace he bore** (13). Such abuse is to be expected and is of no consequence, since this world is not our home; we seek the eternal city which is to come (14).

Since therefore, Christianity is not a matter of external ritual, **let us continually offer to God a sacrifice of praise—the fruit of lips that confess his name** (15; cf. Hos. 14: 2; cf. also the prevalence of this concept of worship among the members of the Dead Sea Sect: *Manual of Discipline* 9: 3 ff.; 9: 26; 10: 6, 8, 14; *Hymn Scroll* 11: 5, in the translation of A. Dupont-Sommer, *The Essene Writings from Qumran*, 1961). Worship with the lips is not enough, however. It must be accompanied by good deeds (sharing, in particular, is singled out) which are also acceptable sacrifices with God (16).

In the writer's concluding words of advice there is an entreaty to be submissive to Christian leaders charged with the welfare of all souls under their care (17). There is also an exhortation to pray: **Pray for us . . . that I may be restored to you soon** (18 f.). This request for prayer may indicate that the writer is in prison, but not necessarily so.

Having made a request for their prayer, he now offers a prayer of benediction for them. It is magnificent in its style and meaning. Herein is contained the only explicit reference to the resurrection of Christ in the letter: God **through the blood of the eternal covenant brought back from the dead our Lord Jesus** (20). The phrase 'by the blood of the eternal covenant' may have been taken from Zech. 9: 11. There the blood of the victim was that which consecrated the messianic alliance. If so, the writer is saying again that Christ, by virtue of His sacrifice, is made supreme mediator of the new covenant (cf. Spicq, *Comm.*, II, pp. 435 f.). His resurrection demonstrates conclusively that His sacrifice was accepted and that the covenant has been ratified. God now stands ready to equip us **with everything good for doing His will** (21). He is ready to work within us so that we may not offer 'dead works' but **what is pleasing to him** (21). And all this is accomplished through Jesus Christ. It is uncertain to whom the doxology is addressed: to God, or to Jesus Christ (21).

A personal greeting from the writer closes this **word of exhortation**, which he says was brief (22). He mentions that a certain **Timothy has been released**, or that he has already 'set out' on his trip, and that he himself fully intends to accompany him on his journey to them (23). The word of exhortation appears to have been written to the rank and file, not the leaders (24), or else this is a tactful way of addressing a community, including its leaders, of which he is no real part. **Those from Italy** (24) is the chief clue to the riddle of who the readers were, perhaps indicating that it was sent to Rome. But since this expression is ambiguous, it may mean 'those of Italy' as well as 'those from Italy', indicating that it was written in Rome to Italians who were away from the capital city. The writer concludes with a second benediction: **Grace be with you all** (25).

BIBLIOGRAPHY

BRUCE, A. B., *The Epistle to the Hebrews* (Edinburgh, 1899).

BRUCE, F. F., 'Hebrews', *Peake's Commentary on the Bible*, newly rev. (London, 1962).

BRUCE, F. F., *The Epistle to the Hebrews*. NICNT (Grand Rapids, 1964).

DAVIDSON, A. B., *The Epistle to the Hebrews* (Edinburgh, 1882; reprinted 1950).

GUTHRIE, D., *The Letter to the Hebrews*. TNTC (Leicester, 1983).

HUGHES, P. E. *A Commentary on the Epistle to the Hebrews* (Grand Rapids, 1977).

KÄSEMANN, E., *The Wandering People of God*, E.T. (Minneapolis, 1985).

LENSKI, R. C. H., *The Interpretation of the Epistle to the Hebrews* (Minneapolis, 1956).

MANSON, W., *The Epistle to the Hebrews* (London, 1951).

MOFFATT, J., *A Critical and Exegetical Commentary on*

the Epistle to the Hebrews. *ICC* (Edinburgh, 1924). (on the Greek text).

MONTEFIORE, H. W., *The Epistle to the Hebrews. BNTC* (London, 1964).

NAIRNE, A., *The Epistle of Priesthood* (Edinburgh, 1913).

NAIRNE, A., *Epistle to the Hebrews. CGT* (Cambridge, 1917).

NARBOROUGH, F. D. V., *The Epistle to the Hebrews* (Oxford, 1930; reprinted 1946).

PURDY, A. C., 'Hebrews', *The Interpreter's Bible*, XI (New York, 1955).

ROBINSON, T. H., *The Epistle to the Hebrews. MNT* (London, 1933).

RODDY, C. S., *The Epistle to the Hebrews* (Grand Rapids, 1962).

SCHNEIDER, J., *The Letter to the Hebrews* (Grand Rapids, 1962).

SCHNEIDER, J., *The Letter to the Hebrews* (Grand Rapids, 1957).

SCOTT, E. F., 'Hebrews', *Commentary on the Bible*, ed. A. S. Peake (Edinburgh and London, 1919).

SPICQ, C., *L'Épître aux Hébreux* (Paris, 1952), in two volumes, very complete, extensive bibliography Vol. I ch. 13. [on the Greek text].

VAUGHAN, C. J., *The Epistle to the Hebrews* (London, 1890). [on the Greek text].

WESTCOTT, B. F., *The Epistle to the Hebrews* (London, 1889). [on the Greek text].

WICKHAM, E. C., *The Epistle to the Hebrews*, 2nd ed. *WC* (London, 1922).

JAMES

T. CARSON

Character and Contents

James is the first of seven letters known as 'catholic' or 'general'. See separate article (pp. 1170 ff.). Three of the principal features of the letter are: (a) the comparative lack of distinctive Christian doctrine, (b) its practical character, (c) the Jewish background. With regard to the first Martin Luther wrote: 'It teaches Christian people, and yet does not once notice the Passion, the Resurrection, the Spirit of Christ [but cf. 4: 5]. The writer names Christ a few times, but He teaches not of Him, but speaks of general faith in God'. He therefore regarded the letter as 'a right strawy epistle in comparison with the writings of Paul, Peter and John.'

Some have even suggested that it was originally a Jewish and not a Christian writing, but this judgment has not found much acceptance. It is fully discussed fully by Mayor.

But this lack of Christian doctrine is not as great as it might at first sight appear, for: (a) 'James in this one short letter reproduces more of the words spoken by Jesus Christ our Lord than are to be found in all the other letters of the NT taken together' (Liddon). (b) Twice James uses the expression 'Lord Jesus Christ' (1: 1; 2: 1). (c) He speaks of 'the noble name of him to whom you belong' (2: 7). (d) He applies to Christ the word 'glorious' (2: 1), 'which surely involves the belief in the Resurrection and Ascension and even the Divinity of Christ' (Mayor). (e) He refers to the second coming (5: 7). (f) The word 'Judge' in 5: 9 refers to Christ. (g) The regeneration of the Spirit and the divine sovereignty in our salvation are alluded to in 1: 18. (h) The elders of the church are mentioned in 5: 14. (i) His readers are not only 'brothers' but 'my dear brothers' (1: 16, 19; 2: 5).

The following points are also worthy of notice: (a) He appears to have unbelieving Jews in mind as well as believing. See below 'Readers and Place of Writing'. (b) The more distinctive teachings of Paul may never have been fully appreciated by James and certainly not at the early period when it is believed that the letter was written. See below, 'Date'. Even as late as Ac. 21: 20 the Jewish Christians were all 'zealous for the law'. (c) James is by nature a moralist rather than a theologian. He is not so much concerned with the correct verbal expression of Christian truth as with its living expression. If he makes no reference to the Christian ordinances of baptism and the Lord's Supper, he is equally silent about the rites of Judaism. 'He wished to make the Christians better Christians, to teach them a truer wisdom, a purer morality . . . and he wished to convert the Israelites into being worthier members of the commonwealth of Israel before he could win them to become heirs of the covenant of the better promise' (F. W. Farrar, *The Early Days of Christianity* [London, 1900], p. 317). The concentration upon the ethical side may also help to explain the absence of express reference to the Cross and Resurrection, though they are implied in 2: 1, 7.

The Jewish background of the letter is evident from the following features: (a) The form of address: 'To the twelve tribes scattered' (see also below, 'Readers and Place of Writing') (1: 1). (b) The emphasis on law-keeping (2: 9–11; 4: 11). (c) The reference to the basic article of the Jewish faith (2: 19). (d) James calls Abraham 'our ancestor' (2: 21). (e) Jewish forms of oaths are quoted (5: 12). (f) The anointing of the sick with oil (5: 14–15), which is not found in any other NT letter. (g) Several references to nature which 'point to Palestine as the place of composition' (Salmon). (h) James refers not only to the life of Abraham (2: 21, 23) but to Rahab (2: 25), the prophets (5: 10), Job (5: 11), and Elijah (5: 17), and it is noteworthy that in the other NT letters Rahab is mentioned only in Heb. 11: 31, Elijah in Rom. 11: 2 and Job not at all. (i) 'The sins and weaknesses which James denounces are the very ones for which Jesus scourged His countrymen, particularly the Pharisees . . . Among these are the superficial hearing of God's word . . . ; pious prattle and profession instead of the practice of what they believe . . . ; the disposition to dogmatise . . . ; the failure to fulfil the real requirements of the law while paying devotion to its letter . . . ; the getting of wealth without any thought of God, with the impossible attempt to divide their affections between God and earthly possessions . . . ; the exercise of prayer without faith in God . . . ; slandering and cursing of their neighbours . . . ; and the taking of oaths too lightly' (Th. Zahn *Introduction to NT*, Eng. tr. [Edinburgh, 1909], pp. 90 f.). On the other hand, unlike the letters addressed to Gentiles, there are no warnings against idolatry and immorality and nothing is said of the relation of masters and slaves.

It is admitted that not all the above arguments have equal cogency, but when they are taken together, and especially when one considers the small compass in which they occur, the Jewish background is unmistakable. M. Dods went so far as to say that 'the epistle is Jewish in every line' (*An Introduction to the NT*, 1891, p. 190).

Other features are: (*a*) resemblance to the OT prophets (*e.g.* in ch. 5). James has been called the 'Amos of the New Testament' and his letter 'a golden bridge between the Old and New Testaments'. (*b*) Similarity to the Book of Proverbs. Many scholars also believe that there are echoes of the books of Wisdom and Ecclesiasticus. (*c*) Points in common with Romans, Hebrews, 1 Peter, Acts 15 and especially the Sermon on the Mount. (*d*) The letter is written in 'excellent Greek with great energy' (W. Kelly). See also below, 'Authorship'. There are several references to the LXX (*cf.* 2: 11; 4: 6; 5: 4). This is not surprising considering the number of Hellenists in the church at Jerusalem (*cf.* Ac. 6: 1). Cf. also the use of the LXX by James in Ac. 15: 16–18.

Authorship

The letter is said to have been written by 'James, a servant of God and of the Lord Jesus Christ', and it is addressed to 'the twelve tribes in the Dispersion', *viz.* to all the Jews outside Palestine. See below, 'Readers and Place of Writing'.

And who was this James? Had he been one of the Twelve, it would have been natural for him to call himself an apostle when addressing the Twelve Tribes, and there is in fact little reason for identifying him with either of the apostles of that name. But in the Acts and letters there is a James who stands out prominently, a pillar of the church in Jerusalem, whose position and character exactly suit the author of the letter. Though not one of the Twelve (*cf.* Mt. 13: 55; Jn 7: 5), he was the leader of Judaic Christianity, and so the familiar James or Jacob required no further designation. (Cf. Ac. 12: 17; 15: 13; 21: 18; Gal. 2: 9, 12.) In Gal. 1: 19 he is called 'James the Lord's brother'. Though other explanations have been given, the natural meaning appears to be that he was a child of Mary and Joseph, born after Jesus. The subject is fully discussed by Mayor in his Introduction. See also the note on Mk 6: 3.

James was not a disciple during the Lord's lifetime (*cf.* Jn 7: 5), but Christ appeared to him after His resurrection (*cf.* 1 C. 15: 7). That may mark the time of his conversion.

Eusebius has preserved for us an account of the life and character of James by Hegesippus (2nd century), and while it contains manifest improbabilities, there is much in it that harmonizes with the NT references. He says that James was holy from his mother's womb, that he drank neither wine nor strong drink; he would go into the temple alone, and would be found there on his knees and asking for forgiveness for the people, so that his knees became hard and dry as a camel's. On account therefore of his exceeding justness, he was called 'Just' and 'Bulwark of the People'.

From 'the picture of James as a stern ascetic, so deeply impressed upon the memory of the early Church', and from the fact that tradition makes no mention of his descendants, Zahn inferred that he was probably unmarried. He argued that 1 C. 9: 5 could hardly include James, who was resident in Jerusalem, whereas the persons referred to were itinerant teachers. But the inference is doubtful. Though stationed in Jerusalem, James may have visited 'the twelve tribes scattered among the nations'.

Some have objected that the Greek is too good for such a man as James, but Mayor has pointed out that Galilee was studded with Greek towns, and there were ample opportunities to learn Greek, while others, *e.g.* Zahn, have shown that the Greek of the letter could not be confused with that of a classical writer. It is possible too that James may have used one of his Hellenist brethren as an amanuensis.

Readers and Place of Writing

The letter is addressed to 'the twelve tribes scattered among the nations'. Some have understood this to refer to Christians, whether Jews or Gentiles, as the 'new Israel', the Dispersion being referred to the scattering of the Christians that followed the death of Stephen (*cf.* Ac. 8: 1; 11: 19). 'But', as Hort remarked, 'this comes in very strangely at the head of a letter with no indication of a spiritual sense', (p. xxii). His objection would apply even more to the view that the expression is purely symbolical, meaning Christians who are exiles from their home in heaven.

It has been argued that, as the 'scattering' in 1 Pet. 1: 1 includes Gentiles (which is the view of many scholars, but not all) it may also include them here, but Peter does not mention the twelve tribes and he does refer to the Gentiles (4: 3).

To the present writer the Jewish background (*cf.* above, 'Character and Contents'), the absence of any reference to the Gentiles and of anything distinctively applicable to them in the warnings, the position and character of James, and the form of address, make it clear that the letter is addressed to literal Jews (*cf.* also the note on 1: 1).

But are they believing Jews only or both believing and unbelieving? In favour of the first is the fact that in most of the letter James regards his readers as Christians, *e.g.* 1: 18; 2: 1, 7; 5: 7, 14. But on the other hand in 4: 1–4 he seems to be thinking of what took place among unbelieving Jews, and that is even clearer in 5: 1–6, where he predicts the judgment of those whom he addresses, and in v. 7 contrasts them with the brethren. It is to be noted also that in 2: 19 it is the fundamental article of the Jewish creed that is quoted.

Two conclusions seem possible. Either James is writing to believing Jews only and from time to time turns aside to address the unbelieving, as an OT prophet might address Tyre, Sidon or the Gentiles, or the letter is addressed to all Jews outside Palestine; but James, knowing that the letter will be chiefly read by the Christians, directs most of his remarks to them.

The second view seems preferable, for no restriction to believers is suggested by the 'twelve tribes' such as is found in 1 Pet. 1: 1–2, and the Book of Acts indicates that among the Jews there was not to begin with the open breach between believers and unbelievers that was found among the Gentiles (cf. Ac. 2: 46, 47; 3: 1, 11; 5: 12,42; 6: 7; 17: 2; 21: 20–26). In fact as late as A.D. 80/90 in Palestine it was necessary to take special steps to bar believing Jews from the synagogue.

It has been objected that James had no authority to address all the Jews, but, if there is any truth in the account of Hegesippus, and even of Josephus, he was esteemed by all the people, and he might well have hoped that his voice would be heard beyond the bounds of the Church. One might compare the Sermon on the Mount, which was addressed firstly to the disciples, and secondly to the multitudes (cf. Mt. 5: 1–2; 7: 28–29).

While all Jews outside Palestine are included in the address, it is quite likely, as Hort suggested, that James had principally in view those of Syria beyond Palestine, and possibly Babylonia, and in Syria especially those of Antioch. Mayor thought that in contrast to Peter's letter to the western dispersion, James wrote for the eastern. The distribution of the letter may have occurred at one of the national feasts.

As to the place of writing, there can be little doubt that it was Jerusalem, the fixed residence of James, and that is in keeping with the Palestinian references in the letter.

Date

It is not easy to determine the exact date of the letter but certain limits can be set. (a) The scattering and persecution of the Christians would indicate that it was written after the martyrdom of Stephen (A.D. 36 or 37 or a little earlier according to some). (b) It was evidently written before the destruction of Jerusalem, as the oppression of the poor by the rich Sadducees ended with the war (A.D. 66–73) and James was looking forward to judgment (5: 1–5). (c) James, according to Josephus, was

martyred in A.D. 62, according to Hegesippus about A.D. 68. As the account of the latter is late and in part legendary, the first is to be preferred. (d) Many scholars have dated the letter early, between A.D. 40 and 50 according to Mayor, before the Conference at Jerusalem (Ac. 15) and before the writings of Paul, thus making it the earliest NT document. One of the chief arguments for the early date is the lack of reference to the Gentiles and their relation to the Jewish law, a topic of special interest to James (cf. Ac. 15), and of great importance to Jewish believers (cf. Ac. 21: 18–25; Gal. 2: 11 ff.).

The case for the early date is set out fully by Mayor and is strongly advocated by Alford and Zahn. Their arguments appear convincing.

On the other hand some scholars, *e.g.* Farrar and Hort, believed that the letter was written near the end of James's life, after Paul had written Romans and Galatians. It has been argued that 'the epistle implies not only a spread of Christianity among the Dispersion, but its having taken root there some time' (Hort). Farrar's arguments are answered in detail by Mayor. On the relation between Paul and James see the note on ch. 2.

Some have ascribed the letter to an unknown writer of the second century who assumed the name of the Lord's brother. Hort however wrote that the view is based 'on very slight and intangible grounds'. And would not such a person have made more of the authority of James? G. H. Rendall, whose work *The Epistle of St. James and Judaic Christianity* is an excellent defence of the genuineness of the letter, considered that the lack of systematic teaching concerning Christ was 'one of the weighty, indeed fatal, objections to assigning a late date to the epistle' (p. 88).

Canonicity

There are resemblances to the language of James in writers of the first and second centuries, as in Clement of Rome and especially Hermas, but the letter is omitted from the Old Latin Version and the Muratorian Fragment, both of the second century. The latter however also omits Hebrews and the Letters of Peter and the text is obviously corrupt.

The first known writer to quote the letter as Scripture and as written by James was Origen, the famous teacher of Alexandria (*c.* A.D. 185–254). 'From the third century the epistle begins to be . . . included in the canon, first of all in the Greek Church, then in the Latin, and finally in the Syrian Church' (Ropes, pp. 86–87). Early ignorance of the letter, especially in the west, may be explained by the fact that it was written to Jews of the Dispersion by a leader of Judaic Christianity, who spent his life in Jerusalem.

Even when it became more widely known,

doubts were held concerning its canonicity because many were uncertain of the identity and authority of the writer, who did not claim to be an apostle. These doubts may also have been accentuated by the comparative lack of Christian doctrine and the apparent inconsistency with Paul's teaching.

Eusebius, at the beginning of the fourth century, classed it among the doubtful books, though he himself does not seem to have shared the doubts. By the end of the fourth century its canonicity was universally accepted until the time of the Reformation, and that view has commended itself to Christians generally. Luther's objection to the letter was based on the mistaken assumption that there was a conflict between James and Paul. See the notes on ch. 2. For further study of the question the reader is referred to the article on the General Letters and to D. Guthrie, *New Testament Introduction: Hebrews to Revelation* (London, 1962), pp. 60–63.

ANALYSIS

I. SALUTATION (1: 1)

1. James: See above, 'Authorship'. **servant** (i.e. bondservant) **of God and of the Lord Jesus Christ** (cf. Phil. 1: 1; Jude 1): Jude adds that he is the brother of (the more prominent) James. Though James was the Lord's brother, both here and in 2: 1 he gives Him His full title (cf. 2 C. 5: 16). Such words from a strict Jew, especially as he links the service of God and of Christ, are equivalent to a confession of His deity. **To the twelve tribes:** Cf. Mt. 19: 28; Ac. 26: 7 and above, 'Readers and Place of Writing'. Only Benjamin and Judah had returned from the Captivity to any great extent. Of the other tribes individuals could be identified from the genealogies. The Twelve Tribes were no longer a religious or political unity but in the eyes of God Israel was still one (cf. Ezr. 6: 17; Jer. 3: 18; Ezek. 37: 16–17; 48: 19; Rev. 7). **scattered among the nations:** The Jews were scattered throughout the civilized world (cf. Ac. 2: 5). The three main divisions of the dispersion were the Babylonian, Syrian and Egyptian (cf. Dt. 28: 25 (LXX); Jn 7: 35; 1 Pet. 1: 1 and above 'Readers and Place of Writing'). **Greetings:** Often rendered 'hail' or 'rejoice', found elsewhere in the NT, in this form only in Ac. 15: 23, in a letter probably composed by James, and in ch. 23: 26. In other forms it is the commonest Greek word for greeting (*e.g.* Lk. 1: 28).

II. INTRODUCTION, RELIGION IN A TIME OF TRIAL (1: 2–27)

i. The Sweet Uses of Adversity (1: 2–4)

The Christian is not to court trial (cf. Mt. 6: 13), but if he meets with it (cf. Lk. 10: 30 for the same word), he is to regard it with unreserved joy. 'Joy' in v. 2 is similar to 'greeting' in v. 1. This repetition of a word is characteristic of the letter (cf. 'steadfastness' in vv. 3 and 4 and 'lack' in vv. 4 and 5). **2. my brothers:** James addresses his readers as 'brothers' fifteen times, with the addition of 'dear' three times. They were 'brothers' because they were fellow Israelites (cf. Ac. 13: 38) and also because they were fellow Christians. Women are of course included. **3. the testing of your faith develops perseverance:** 'Testing' is the word used for 'crucible' in Prov. 27: 21 (LXX). Deissmann, however, following the papyri, both here and in 1 Pet. 1: 7, explained it as 'that which is genuine in your faith', but 'testing' seems to give better sense here. The AV gives 'patience', but the thought is rather 'endurance'. **4. Perseverance must finish its work** ('perfect work' AV): Endurance produces rich fruits in the lives of those who are spiritually exercised (cf. Lk. 21: 19, RV; Rom. 5: 3–4; Heb. 10: 36; 12: 1–3, 11; 1 Pet. 1: 6–7). **mature and complete:** The first word indicates positive excellence (cf. Gen. 6: 9, LXX) and the second

absence of defect (cf. Ac. 3: 16; 1 Th. 5:23).

ii. Prayer for Wisdom (1: 5–8)

Wisdom is one of the great themes of the letter (cf. 3: 13–17). God is its source (cf. 1 Kg. 3: 9–12; Eph. 1: 17); He gives to all **generously . . . without finding fault** in them for their unworthiness (cf. Mt. 5: 45). But we must **ask** in faith, for the doubter is like the restless sea (the first of the metaphors drawn from nature). No such **double-minded man, unstable** like a drunken man or a tossing ship (cf. Prov. 23: 29–34; Isa. 57: 20; Eph. 4: 14) **will receive anything from the Lord** (cf. Mt. 6: 22–24; 21: 21; Heb. 11: 6). **the Lord:** That is 'God' (cf. v. 5). So in 4: 10, 15; 5:4, 10, 11, but in 5: 7, 14, 15 it is used of Christ. It is possible however that James may not always have sharply distinguished the Persons of the Godhead.

iii. The Rich Poor and the Poor Rich (1: 9–11)

The RV introduces v. 9 with 'but'. 'Far from being thus undecided and unsettled, the Christian should exult in his profession' (Mayor). The lowly or poor brother is to **take pride in his high position** (9) or his 'high estate' (RV) as a Christian. The rich brother is to boast **in his low position** (10), for if a rich man is to be a Christian he has to be made low (RV) (cf. Lk. 18: 25; 22: 26). He must learn the transitory nature of earthly things (cf. Ps. 49: 16–17). Some link these verses with v. 2, the meaning being that the poor brother is to rejoice in the benefits of trial, and the rich in its humbling effect, but the above interpretation is wider and deeper. Some again take the 'rich' to refer to the unbeliever, as elsewhere in the letter, but the meaning given is unsatisfactory, *e.g.* 'let the rich man, if he will, glory in his degradation', the words being ironical. For **scorching heat** (11) the RV gives 'scorching wind', which would refer to the burning wind which blew from the desert over Palestine (cf. Ezek. 17: 10; Jon. 4: 8; Lk. 12: 55). This was the view of Hort and Mayor, but Arndt and Gingrich prefer 'heat' (cf. Mt. 20: 12). **plant** here includes wild flowers (cf. Isa. 40: 6; Mt. 6: 30; 1 Pet. 1: 24).

iv. Trial and Temptation (1: 12–15)

12. the crown of life is promised to the man who **perseveres under trial**, as it is to the martyr in Rev. 2: 10. A crown or garland was given as a reward in the Greek games. It was also 'a token of public honour for distinguished service, military prowess, etc., or nuptial joy or festal gladness, especially at the parousia of kings' (W. E. Vine). The figure is also found in the OT, *e.g.* in Ps. 21: 3; 89: 39; Prov. 4: 9; Zech. 6: 11–14. As a strict Jew James was probably not thinking of the reward at the games. It seems that **life** is here the crown. Eternal life is a gift (cf. Rom. 6: 23), possessed by all believers (cf. Jn 10: 28). It is also the end or crown of the believer's walk (cf. Rom. 6: 22; Gal. 6: 8); so here the crown is not so much a reward, as in 1 C. 9: 25, as an incentive, in contrast to vv. 10–11 (cf. Rev. 2: 10–11; 1 Th. 2: 19; 2 Tim. 4: 8; 1 Pet. 5: 4). Another less likely view is that **of life** refers to the permanence of the crown. **when he has stood the test:** RV gives: 'when he hath been approved'. 'Test' is similar to 'testing' in v. 3. **God has promised to those who love him:** Some MSS give 'Lord' and others omit. It has been thought that an unrecorded saying of the Lord is here referred to (cf. Ac. 20: 35), but there may be an expansion of OT promises, *e.g.* Dt. 30: 15–20. **to those who love him:** A general description of Christians (cf. 2: 5; Rom. 8: 28; 1 C. 2: 9; Heb. 9: 28).

James then passes from the outward trial to the inward trial or temptation, 'from our holy trials to our unholy ones' (W. Kelly). The former must be endured, the latter resisted. 'Tempt' and 'test' represent the same Greek word, which strictly speaking means 'to test'. Evidently there were those who said that God was the author of all things and was therefore responsible for our temptations but God is 'untemptable of evil' (Mayor), 'untried in evil' (RVmg). Evil never finds an entrance into His heart and therefore He tempts no-one. In Gen. 22: 1 the meaning is 'to prove'. 'Satan tempts to bring out the bad; God tests to bring out the good' (W. H. Griffith Thomas). The true source of temptation is the evil heart within. First of ill there is evil desire, which has a child called 'sin', **and sin when it is full-grown gives birth to death** (15), spiritual death now and eternal death hereafter. The latter seems chiefly in view here in contrast to 'the crown of life' (v. 12). Cf. Gen. 2: 17; Ezek. 18: 4; Mt. 7: 13–14; Rom. 5: 12; 6: 21, 23; 7: 11–13; 8: 13; 1 C. 15: 56; 1 Tim. 5: 6. It has been suggested that behind the words **dragged away and enticed** (14) there is a picture of the hunter or fisherman luring his prey from its safe retreat. Others have thought that 'he probably pictured to himself the tempter desire as a harlot' (Hort). Satan is not here mentioned as a source of temptation, as in 3: 6; 4: 7, as that would only have provided the sinner with an alternative excuse.

v. God the Source of All Good Gifts (1: 16–18)

In vv. 16, 19 and 2: 5 'beloved' is added to 'brethren'. Such an address was unknown among the Jews (Knowling). The thought of 'deception' is found three times in the chapter (vv. 16, 22, 26), though the words are different in the Greek. Far from God being the author of evil, **every good and perfect gift is from above** (17). 'Perfect' and 'gift' are translations of the Greek *dosis* and *dōrēma*. Generally *dosis* is

the act of giving and *dōrēma* the thing given, but here *dosis* is mostly taken to mean the concrete gift (a meaning attested as early as Homer but apparently not found in the papyri. See *MM*). Philo, an older contemporary of James, said that *dōrēma* was much stronger and involved the idea of magnitude and fulness, applying to it the epithet 'perfect', as James does here. For *dōrēma* RV gives 'boon'. The words are poetical in form and they may be a quotation from a Greek poet or a Christian hymn. Ropes therefore regarded the difference as purely rhetorical but Hort (and also Lightfoot) strongly maintained the distinction. He said that the second word usually implied free giving. He preferred the rendering: 'Every giving (of God) is good and every gift perfect from above' (or 'from its source'). NEB gives: 'All good giving and every perfect gift . . .' **17. Father of the heavenly lights:** God is the fountain of all light in the physical, intellectual, moral and spiritual spheres (cf. Gen. 1: 3, 14; Ps. 27: 1; Jer. 31: 35). **who does not change** (cf. Gal. 3: 28 RV): The sun may change in its course but not God. **like shifting shadows:** 'shadow cast by turning' (RV). Others give 'changing shadow'. James 'may have had chiefly in view either night and day, or the monthly obscuration of the moon, or even the casual vicissitudes of light due to clouds' (Hort); cf. Mal. 3: 6. Far from giving birth to sin, **He chose to give us birth through the word of truth** (18): Cf. Jn 1: 13; Eph. 1: 5, 11; 5: 26; 1 Pet. 1: 3, 23. James is no mere moralist but is at one with the other writers of the NT concerning the gospel of the grace of God. There is an excellent note in Alford (quoted from Wiesinger) on the evangelical implications of the verse. Some have applied the words to creation rather than regeneration, but 'begetting' and the 'word of truth' are rather the language of the gospel. **a kind of firstfruits of all he created:** In 1 C. 15: 20 'firstfruits' is used of Christ, here of Christians. Later the figure became more common, but here James introduces it apologetically with 'as it were' (Knox). Perhaps a small indication of an early date. 'Firstfruits' implies both priority and consecration. A redeemed Church is a pledge of a redeemed creation. As James is looking forward to the near return of Christ (cf. 5: 8), the meaning can hardly be that the early believers were the nucleus of the Church. Cf. Lev. 23: 10, 17; Dt. 26: 2; Rom. 16: 5; 2 Th. 2: 13 (RVmg); Rev. 5: 13; 14: 4. 'The substance of John's ministry is in verses 17, 18' (C. A. Coates).

vi. The Anger of Man and the Righteousness of God (1: 19–21)

19. Take note of this: Or 'You know this' (cf. RV). The knowledge of the new birth should lead to a new life. James warns against the sins of the tongue, a theme developed in ch. 3. With **quick to listen**, cf. Isa 50: 4; **slow to speak**, Ec. 5: 1–2; **slow to become angry**, Eph. 4: 26–27. The words appear to refer primarily to anger in debate. The angry talker is not doing what is right in God's sight. Very likely his anger is but a cloak of bitterness. **20. bring about** is here 'practise' rather than 'produce' (cf. Ac. 10: 35; Heb. 11: 33). There is probably no thought here of a right standing before God, as we find in Paul's letters, *e.g.* Phil. 3: 9. Contrast Ps. 76: 10. **21. Therefore get rid of** (as a polluted garment) **all moral filth** (cf. 2 C. 7: 1) **and the evil that is so prevalent:** Mayor preferred the 'overflow of wickedness', as in the RV, the thought being that the evil within is not to be allowed to break out in hasty words or violent temper, for there is defilement in the overflow (cf. 3: 6 and Mt. 15: 18–19). The AV 'superfluity of naughtiness' is objectionable if it is taken to mean that James is advocating the lopping off of the excrescence of evil, as if a certain amount would do no harm. Some translate 'the remainder of wickedness' (cf. Mk 8: 8), but it seems less natural. As in 1 Pet. 2: 1–2, the laying aside of the sinful tendencies is to be accompanied by the reception of the **word** (cf. the Parable of the Sower, Mt. 13), **planted** (not 'engrafted') **in you, which can save you.** The soul is the living principle and it is saved from death here and hereafter by the power of the Word (cf. v. 15 and also Mt. 16: 25–26; Lk. 6: 9; Heb. 10: 39; 1 Pet. 1: 9, 23; 2: 2, RV).

vii. Doers and Hearers (1: 22–25)
If they hear God's Word and do not obey it, there will be no blessing, only self-deception. Cf. Mt. 7: 21–27; Lk. 11: 28; Jn 13: 17 and Rom. 2: 13, the only other place in the NT where 'doers' and 'hearers' are found together. **23. his face:** RVmg gives 'face of his birth'. Hort took it to mean 'the invisible face, the reflexion of God's image in humanity', but this view seems too subtle.

The contrast appears to be a simple one. On the one hand is the careless man who looks at his natural face in a mirror. 'He glances at himself' (NEB). His face may be soiled, careworn or wrinkled, but he goes away, and, becoming absorbed in other matters, soon forgets. On the other hand is the earnest man who 'looks closely' into the divine mirror, and, instead of going away 'lives in its company' (cf. Ps. 1: 2), and, instead of forgetting, 'acts upon it' (NEB). He is the man who will receive the blessing. **25. the perfect law that gives freedom:** It is the divine law, interpreted and enriched by Christ (cf. Mt. 5: 17 ff.) and is therefore perfect. It is the 'law of liberty' (cf. 2: 12), which we obey, not because we have to, but because we want to, and in obeying which we find our true freedom (cf. Jn 8: 31–

36). Any conflict between this teaching and Paul's (*e.g.* Rom. 6: 14; 7: 4) is only apparent (cf. Rom. 3: 31; 8: 4; 1 C. 9: 21). Even OT saints had an understanding of the 'law of liberty' (cf. Ps. 119: 45, 54).

viii. True Religion (1: 26–27)
26. religion, according to R. C. Trench, is 'predominantly the ceremonial service of religion', and James 'is not herein affirming, as we sometimes hear, these offices to be the sum total, nor yet the great essentials, of true religion, but declares them to be the body, the *thrēskeia*, of which godliness, or the love of God, is the informing soul' (*Synonyms of the NT*, § xlviii). **27. pure** is the positive side, **faultless** the negative. The Jews were at times more careful of ceremonial defilement than moral (cf. Mk 7: 1–13). **God our Father:** 'our God and Father' (RV). If we know God as Father we shall be concerned about His children. **to keep oneself** (cf. the similar phrase in Ac. 15: 29, which was probably drafted or composed by James): Cf. also 4: 4; Ps. 68: 5; Isa. 58; Mt. 25: 36, 43; Mk 12: 40; 1 Tim 5: 22; 1 Pet. 1: 19; 2 Pet. 2: 20.

III. SINS, SOCIAL AND SPIRITUAL (2: 1–5: 6)
i. Partiality to the Rich (2: 1–7)
1. as believers in our glorious Lord Jesus Christ, don't show favoritism: Some take this as a question: 'Do ye, in accepting persons, hold the faith, etc.?' (RVmg) but the prohibition is more in keeping with the writer's general style. Some too think that James means the faith that our Lord exemplified (cf. Heb. 12: 2), but Mk 11: 22; Ac. 3: 16; Gal. 2: 16, 20; Eph. 3: 12; Phil. 3: 9 suggest that the meaning is simply 'faith in'. For **Lord Jesus Christ** see 1: 1. 'Lord' is not repeated in the original before 'glory' and Bengel suggested that the meaning is 'our Lord Jesus Christ (who is) the glory', and that rendering has been accepted by Hort, Mayor and others (cf. Lk. 2: 32; Jn 1: 14; Rom. 9: 4; Heb. 1: 3; 9: 5; 1 Pet. 4: 14). A simple emendation would yield the attractive reading: 'the Lord Jesus Christ, our glory'. Mayor quotes evidence to show that the Shekinah, the Jewish name for the divine glory living among men, was used of God and of the Messiah, *e.g.* 'The Lord of the serving angels, the son of the Highest, yea, the Shekinah' (cf. Zech. 2: 5; 6: 13). In the synagogues the Jews worshipped according to their importance in human estimation (cf. Mt. 23: 6), but such behaviour was contrary to the example and teaching of our Lord (cf. Lk. 14: 12–14; 2 C. 8: 9; Phil. 2). **2. a gold ring:** It was not uncommon for several to be worn and it was a mark of wealth and social distinction (cf. Lk. 15: 22). **meeting:** Literally 'synagogue' (RV). It could refer to a company of Jewish Christians or to the build-

ing. The word may be another pointer to an early date, but the reference can hardly be to an ordinary Jewish synagogue, as the Christians could not be held responsible for the conduct there. It is **your meeting**. The thrice repeated **clothes** is the same word in the Greek, though different words are used in AV. So too with **fine**: AV 'goodly' and 'gay'. Ropes believed that the visitors are undoubtedly non-Christians (cf. v. 6), but it seems better, with Alford, to leave the reference general. **3. good:** Both AV and RV say 'in a good place'. It is literally 'beautifully' or 'excellently'. **4. have you not discriminated . . . ?:** This is good sense but rather obvious. 'Are ye not divided in your own mind?' (RV) is preferable. The same word as 'doubt' in 1: 6. **judges with evil thoughts:** Literally 'of evil thoughts'. Weymouth gives 'full of'. **5. poor in** ('as to' RV) **the world to be rich in faith** (cf. Lk. 12: 21; Rev. 2: 9): 'To be' is not in the Greek but is understood by RV, Hort and Mayor (cf. Eph. 1: 4). **to inherit the kingdom:** Cf. Mt. 5: 3; 1 C. 6: 9, 15, 50; Eph. 5: 5; 1 Pet. 1: 4. **he promised those who love him:** Cf. 1: 12; Dan. 7: 18; Lk. 12: 31–32. **6. are they** ('themselves' RV) **not the ones who are dragging you into court:** The reference is to the rich, unconverted Jews dragging the poor Christians to the synagogue and heathen courts (cf. Mt. 10: 17–18; Ac. 4: 1–3; 9: 2; 12: 1–2; 16: 19). The persecutions are viewed as still continuing. 'The picture here exhibited well corresponds with that which is presented by Josephus and other Jewish authorities of the conditions of Palestine in the time following the death of our Lord' (G. Salmon, *Introduction to the NT*, p. 456). **7. Are they not the ones who are slandering the noble name of him to whom you belong?:** RVmg gives the literal rendering, 'which was called upon you', and the reference may be to the invocation of the name of Christ at baptism (cf. Ac. 15: 17; Gen. 48: 16). While 'blaspheme' (slandering) could be used in reference to both God and man, 'a Jew would not be likely to associate blasphemy with any name less than a divine name' (Knowling). Cf. Lev. 24: 11; Ac. 26: 11; 1 C. 12: 3.

ii. The Royal Law (2: 8–13)
The expression **royal law** (8) has been variously interpreted: (*a*) as describing the law of love as sovereign over all others (cf. Mt. 22: 36–40; Rom. 13: 8–9; Gal. 5: 14); (*b*) as fitted for kings and not slaves (cf. vv. 5, 12); (*c*) as given by the King. The first is the commonest explanation but James may have had more than one thought in mind. 'Law' is not generally used of a single commandment, but it may be so used here because of the comprehensive nature of the command, or possibly it refers here also to the whole law of which the commandment is a part. **found in Scripture** is to be taken with what follows, not with 'fulfil'.

you are doing right: Cf. Ac. 15: 29. **If you really keep:** RV gives 'Howbeit if ye fulfil', and the meaning appears to be that James makes no objection if their attitude to the rich is one of love, but if it springs from snobbery and self-seeking it is sinful. If the RSV rendering is adopted, which was that of Hort, the reference is rather to a general claim to fulfil the law. It is plain from Dt. 1: 17 that partiality is a breach of the law, and **whoever keeps the whole law and yet stumbles at just one point is guilty of breaking all of it** (10). Augustine explained this by saying that the whole law hangs on the love of God and that every transgression is a breach of love. It is also true that the whole law expresses the divine will, and every breach is disobedience to that will.

In v. 11 the seventh commandment precedes the sixth, as in Lk. 18: 20 and Rom. 13: 9. This may have been due to LXX influence (for James and the LXX see above, 'Character and Contents'), as Mayor believed, or the order may have been simply due to the context, as Zahn held, the Jews being more particular about the seventh commandment than the sixth (cf. 4: 2; 5: 6 and cf. Mt. 19: 18–19 for an inversion involving the fifth commandment). James does not here say that the Christians were actually guilty of killing but see the note quoted from Alford on 4: 2. The commands quoted by James, which are the first two in the Decalogue relating to our duty to our neighbour, suggest that he did not have in mind the ceremonial side of the law. It has been thought that the words of Ac. 15: 24 were based on a misinterpretation of such teaching, as if James insisted on a literal observance of the whole Mosaic code. See also the comment on this passage in the article on the General Letters. **11. lawbreaker:** The expression 'a transgressor of the law' occurs in an uncanonical saying of our Lord: 'O man, if thou knowest what thou art doing, thou art blessed; but if thou knowest not, thou art accursed, and a transgressor of the law' (Lk. 6: 4 fin., western text). **12. by the law that gives freedom:** Cf. 1: 25. This will be more exacting than a merely external law, because it will judge the heart and motive. The absence of the article before 'law' ('a law', RV), emphasizes the character of the law. **13. because judgment without mercy will be shown to anyone who has not been merciful:** Cf. 2 Sam. 12: 5; Mt. 18: 21–35. **Mercy triumphs over judgment:** The absence of a connecting particle in the Greek, the use of 'mercy' instead of 'merciful man', and the change to the present tense, all indicate that a universal truth is expressed. It is true of God's mercy that it triumphed at Calvary over His judgment, though not at the expense of His justice; it is true in the conversion of the sinner (cf. Lk. 18: 12–14); and it should also be true in our relationship with one another (cf. Lk. 6: 36–37).

iii. Faith and Deeds (2: 14–26)

This is the celebrated passage which was a stumbling-block to Martin Luther. He considered it impossible to reconcile Paul and James, but the difficulties will be seen to be more apparent than real if we note the following: (*a*) To James faith is as fundamental as to Paul. He begins and ends with faith and in the middle explains its true character (1: 3, 6; 2: 1, 5; 5: 15). It is James who says 'rich in faith' (2: 5). (*b*) To Paul works are as fundamental as to James (cf. Rom. 2: 5–11; Eph. 2: 10; 2 Th. 2: 17 and especially the Pastoral Letters). He recognizes that faith in itself can be unprofitable (1 C. 13: 2) and it is Paul who says 'rich in good works' (1 Tim. 6: 18). (*c*) The three basic words 'faith', 'justify' and 'deeds' are used differently in Romans 3–4 and in verses such as 14, 17 and 26 of James 2. In Paul faith is a living trust in God but in these verses it is a dead faith, mere belief unquickened by the Spirit of God. In Paul 'justify' means 'to acquit the sinner in the sight of a holy God' (see note on v. 18); in James it means 'to vindicate', 'to show to be righteous' before God and men. Then the deeds are different. In Paul they are deeds of the law, regarded as a ground of merit; in James deeds of obedience and love. 'The works Paul speaks about are those that precede faith, those of James, those wrought in faith' (Godet). Paul says 'a man is justified not by the works of the law but by the faith of Jesus Christ. James speaks of works without any mention of law and of faith without any mention of Jesus Christ' (Salmon). Paul's words in Rom. 2: 13 and Gal. 5: 6 are exactly the teaching of James. (*d*) Apart from the question of inspiration, it is against all probability that James should be attacking the teaching of Paul, for: (1) At the Conference of Jerusalem (Ac. 15) he supported Paul and the letter mentioned 'our beloved Barnabas and Paul' (v. 25), and in Gal. 2: 9 he gave to them 'the right hand of fellowship'. (2) There is much to be said for the view that James's letter was written before the letters of Paul (see above, 'Date'). Mayor and Zahn believed that Paul had the letter of James before him and developed the thought, but others, *e.g.* Knowling, have thought that the two writers may have simply used language that was current in early Christian circles (cf. Gal. 2: 16 ff.). (3) Some have held that James wrote after the writing of Galatians and Romans and that he had these letters before him. E. H. Plumptre however questioned whether those letters would have reached Jerusalem during James's lifetime, and, even if they did, there is no opposition, for 'a real antagonist would have followed St. Paul more closely, and come definitely into collision, which St.

James never does' (Hort). Some believe that James is attacking an antinomian perversion of Paul's teaching. The main argument for this view is the language of vv. 21–26. It is pointed out that elsewhere in the NT it is only Paul who speaks of justification by faith (even Ac. 13: 39 being spoken by Paul), and there is the common reference to Abraham's faith. This however may not be conclusive, for 'justification by faith' is a natural way of expressing the truth of Gen. 15: 6. Our Lord spoke of justification (cf. Lk. 18: 14) and of being justified by words (cf. Mt. 12: 37) and of faith saving (cf. Lk. 7: 50), and Gal. 2: 16 ff. shows that justification by faith was a subject of discussion among the apostles quite early. Besides, 'the nature of faith and the special merit of Abraham's faith were subjects often discussed among the Jews' (Plummer).

And the view is not without other difficulties: (1) Jewish believers would not have been greatly influenced by Paul. (2) If, as some believe, James was also warning Gentile believers, it would surely have been fitting, especially in view of the strong language he was using, to make it clear that it was a perversion of the doctrine of the apostle of the Gentiles that he was attacking and not his true doctrine. (3) 'If v. 14 was based upon any formula at all, it must have been some such saying as the one so often used by Jesus, "Thy faith hath saved thee"' (Zahn). (4) James quotes the fundamental article of the Jewish faith, but 'the Pauline conception of justifying faith had its object, not in the unity of God, but in Christ, His death and resurrection' (Knowling, p. 59). (5) There is no mention of grace and no suggestion that those to whom James writes desire to do evil or continue in sin, as in Rom. 3: 8; 6: 1: there is simply an absence of desire for good works.

For reasons such as the above Zahn believed that 'it is a perversion of the Christian Gospel in general rather than Paul's expression of it that James has in mind'. It should be noted that not only Paul but NT writers generally protested against such abuses; *e.g.* 1 Pet. 2: 16; Jude 4; 1 Jn 1: 6.

A third possibility, which seems to have much to commend it, is that James has in view a Jewish attitude on the subject, and that view derives support from the fact that the passage speaks of faith in general and not of faith in Christ. 'It is the cold monotheism which the self-satisfied Pharisee has brought with him into the Christian Church, which he supposes will render charity and good works superfluous, that St. James is condemning' (Plummer). Cf. Jn 5: 39; Rom. 2: 17–29 (especially v. 17 'restest upon the law', RV).

(*a*) The problem introduced (2: 14–20)

In v. 14 James is not denying that the person has faith of a kind, but it is not saving faith.

Can such faith save him: RV gives 'that faith'. **15. without clothes:** Such is the force of the literal 'naked', AV and RV (cf. Mt. 25: 36, 43). **16. 'Go, I wish you well . . .':** A common Jewish farewell (cf. Gen. 26: 29; Mk 5: 34). **17. faith:** Faith by itself is as ineffective as the previous words. **18. Show:** James is concerned with the evidence of faith. It is a mistake however to think that he has in view justification before men only, as is shown by v. 14 and the illustration of Abraham (cf. Gen. 22: 12). In this verse the objector cannot be addressing James, who is commending works rather than faith. Some think he is addressing the one whom James is criticizing, but it is simpler, with Ropes, to regard 'you' and 'I' as equivalent to 'one' and 'another', a picturesque mode of indicating two imaginary persons (cf. Rom. 2: 1–5; 9: 19 ff.; 1 C. 15: 36). The meaning then is that the gifts of God are different: to one He has given faith, to another works. But James will not hear of that. The two are inseparable. So he challenges the objector to show genuine faith apart from works and he will demonstrate the reality of his faith by his works. In v. 19 James continues to address the objector. He refers to the central article of the Jewish faith, the unity of the Godhead. Godet quotes from the heretical *Clementine Homilies:* 'A monotheistic soul has the privilege above that of an idolater that even when it has lived in sin it cannot perish'. This is an extreme form of the error condemned by James. **Even the demons** (not 'devils', for there is but one devil) **believe that—and shudder:** The word 'shudder' was 'specially used of awe of a mysterious divine power, as often of the adepts in the Greek Mysteries' (Hort). In v. 20 the AV gives 'dead' but the NIV reading **useless** is to be preferred. **you foolish man:** Literally 'empty', 'empty-headed, empty-handed, empty-hearted' (Plummer). It has been compared to the 'Raca' of Mt. 5: 22 (RSVmg) and the inference drawn that such precepts of the Sermon on the Mount refer more to the attitude of the heart than the letter of the Word.

(b) **Example of Abraham (2: 21–24)**
21. Was not our ancestor Abraham considered righteous for what he did when he offered his son Isaac on the altar?: Paul deals with the same example in Rom. 4: 1–3 (cf. also Gal. 3: 6), but he denies that a man is justified by deeds. Paul however is referring to Abraham's initial justification recorded in Gen. 15: 6, James to his crowning act of obedience some thirty or more years later. James does not say that Gen. 15: 6 was contradicted or modified, but fulfilled, for **his faith and his actions were working together** (22). So it came to full fruition and the reality of his early faith was demonstrated. 'Not for faith plus works does St. James plead, *but for faith at work*, living,

acting in itself, apart from any value in its results' (Hort). **as** (RV 'for') **righteousness:** The translation of a Hebrew idiom where 'for' was equivalent to 'as' (cf. Rom. 2: 26). **23. and he was called God's friend:** Abraham is so called by the Arabs to this day (cf. Gen. 18: 17; 2 Chr. 20: 7; Isa. 41: 8; Jn 15: 15). Both the Hebrew and Greek words indicate not only companionship but love. **24. You see that** (not 'how', AV) **a person is justified by what he does and not by faith alone:** Calvin wrote that 'it is faith alone that justifies, but the faith that justifies can never be alone', and another that 'good works are such that a man is neither justified by them nor without them.'

(c) **Example of Rahab (2: 25)**
There is a marked contrast between Abraham and Rahab. 'He is the friend of God, and she of a vile heathen nation and a harlot. His great act of faith is manifest toward God, hers toward men. His is the crowning act of his spiritual development; hers is the first sign of a faith just begun to exist' (Plummer). Rahab is one of the four women in the genealogy of Mt. 1. In Heb. 11: 31 her faith is commended, and certainly faith is revealed in Jos. 2: 9–11, for the Jordan still flowed between Israel and the Land. She was so well-known in Jewish tradition that there is no need to infer any literary connection between Hebrews and James.

A critic might dismiss the work of Abraham as murder and that of Rahab as treason, but that would be to ignore the historic setting. It is as true now as then that God is greater than family or nation.

(d) **Conclusion (2: 26)**
26. As the body without the spirit is dead, so faith without deeds is dead: NEB omits 'for'. The words sum up the previous passage. If the comparison is to be pressed strictly, faith is here the body, and works the spirit, the opposite of our general conception. The thought would be that a barren orthodoxy needs obedience to give it life. Some think that James is comparing simply the co-operation of body and spirit on the one hand and faith and works on the other (cf. v. 22). Others have taken 'spirit' here to mean 'breath', which simplifies the comparison, but that is not the usual meaning in the NT (see however 2 Th. 2: 8; Rev. 13: 15). 'In v. 17 it was said that faith, if it have not works, is "dead by itself"; in v. 20 faith without works is barren; here at the end of the discussion faith without works is pronounced absolutely "dead", and so it is' (W. Kelly).

iv. Teachers and the Tongue (3: 1–12)
'Religious fluency, the lust of teaching, the rage for casuistical discussion, have in all ages been the characteristic feature of Pharisaic piety. The third chapter of the epistle is entirely devoted to attacking this fault' (Godet). Other refer-

ences to the tongue are: Ps. 52: 2; 141: 3; Prov. 10: 18–21; 12: 18; 13: 3; 14: 23; 17: 27; 21: 23; 26: 20–22; Ec. 5: 2–3; Mt. 12: 33–37; 26: 73; Lk. 4: 22; Eph. 4: 15, 29–31; Col. 4: 6; 1 Tim. 5: 13; Tit. 2: 8. **1. Not many of you should presume to be teachers:** In NT churches teaching was not confined to a single channel (cf. Ac. 13: 1; 1 C. 14; 1 Pet. 4: 10–11). **we who teach will be judged more strictly:** James links himself with those he warns (cf. 1 Jn 2: 1). The greater the light the greater the responsibility (cf. Am. 3: 2; Mk 12: 40; Lk. 20: 47). In v. 2 James turns from public speech to uncontrolled speech in general. A perfect control of the tongue would mean a perfect life. Even Moses and Paul failed here (cf. Ps. 106: 33; Ac. 23: 5). V. 4 begins with 'Behold' (NIV **Take . . . as an example**), which is found in six places in the letter, 'a common interjection in James's native tongue' (Knowling). Two illustrations are given in vv. 3 and 4. With a bit we guide horses; **by a very small rudder** we guide great ships **wherever the pilot wants to go**, 'even when' (Hort) they are driven by strong winds. **5. Likewise the tongue**, though small, **makes great boasts:** 'Boasts' suggests haughtiness (cf. Ps. 12: 3) and is used instead of 'does' to prepare for what follows; for the tongue is capable of great evil, just as **a great forest is set on fire by a small spark. 6. The tongue also is a fire:** Cf. Ps. 120: 4; Prov. 16: 27. It is **a world of evil among the parts of the body:** 'In our microcosm the tongue represents or constitutes the unrighteous world' (Mayor). **It corrupts the whole body:** Often the effect the tongue has on others is emphasized but James emphasizes its effect on the person himself (cf. Mk 7: 21–23). The mere uttering of evil is defiling. **sets the whole course of his life on fire:** These words are very difficult. The AV gives 'course of nature'; Alford 'the orb of the creation'; Plumptre 'the wheel of life from birth'. The last seems the simplest. Perhaps the tongue is compared to the axle from which a fire sets ablaze the whole course of human life. It is **set on fire by hell.** In 1: 14 James emphasizes that temptation comes from within; here he traces it back to its Satanic source. 'Hell' here is 'Gehenna', a word used elsewhere in the NT only by the Lord in the Synoptic Gospels. With vv. 7–8 cf. Gen. 1: 24; 9: 2; 1 Kg. 4: 33. The tongue is **a restless** (not 'unruly' AV) **evil, full of deadly poison** (cf. Ps. 140: 3). **tame:** In NT only elsewhere in Mk 5: 4. Here it is the tongue under Satanic control, there the whole man. Fortunately James did not say that God cannot tame the tongue. **9. Lord and Father** (so also RV) is not found elsewhere. **made in God's likeness:** Cf. Gen. 1: 26–27. While the divine image was marred it was not wholly obliterated. 'Absalom fell from his father's

favour, but still the people recognized him as the king's son' (Bengel). Cf. 1 C. 11: 7; Col. 3: 10; Eph. 4: 24. **10. praise and cursing:** The strong denunciations of our Lord (cf. Mt. 23) and of Paul (cf. Ac. 13: 10; 1 C. 16: 22; Gal. 1: 8), may seem opposed to this teaching, but they were based on truth and love, whereas the cursing James condemns springs from bitterness (v. 11, cf. Rom. 12: 14). In vv. 11 and 12 James draws two illustrations from nature to prove the inconsistency of blessing and cursing (cf. Mt. 7: 16–20; 12: 33–36). Some have thought that James is referring to the Dead Sea (called in the OT the Sea of Salt), which had both salt and fresh springs on its shores.

v. Wisdom, the False and the True (3: 13–18)

James returns to the subject of wisdom which he has already touched upon in 1: 5. He begins by pointing out that true wisdom is not intellectual only: it is shown by a **good life** (readers of the AV should remember that 'conversation', used here and elsewhere, has generally the archaic meaning of 'manner of living' or 'behaviour') and it is marked by meekness (cf. Mt. 5: 5; 11: 28), not pride. In this James is in harmony with the consistent Biblical teaching (cf. Job 28: 28; Ps. 25: 9), but he runs counter to much worldly wisdom. Wisdom and **understanding** (13) are here linked, as often in Scripture. 'The second word expresses personal acquaintance and thus experience' (Hort). The opposite of the meekness of wisdom is **bitter envy and selfish ambition** (14). Cf. Gal. 5: 19–23. If these things characterize us, though we may boast of our wisdom, our whole life is a denial of the truth revealed in Jesus (cf. Eph. 4: 21). False wisdom is **earthly, unspiritual, of the devil** (15). For 'unspiritual' RV gives 'sensual', and in the margin 'natural' or 'animal' and for 'devilish' RVmg gives 'demoniacal'. In other words it belongs to earth rather than heaven (cf. 1 C. 15: 48), to nature rather than the Spirit (cf. 1 C. 2: 14; 15: 44–46; Jude 19) and to demons rather than God (cf. 1 Tim. 4: 1). **16** gives proof of the previous statement (cf. 1 C. 14: 33). But true wisdom is heavenly in its origin, and it is **first of all pure, then peace-loving** (17). It is pure in its essence and consequently in its manifestation it is peaceable (cf. Prov. 3: 17), **considerate** ('forbearing', Hort), **submissive** ('easy to be intreated', AV and RV), **full of mercy and good fruit** (contrast 3: 8), **impartial** or **sincere.** If we take 'mercy' and 'good fruit' together we have 'Seven Pillars of Wisdom' (cf. Prov. 9: 1). **18. Peacemakers who sow in peace raise a harvest of righteousness:** The 'fruit of righteousness' is sometimes taken to mean the 'product of righteousness' (cf. Isa. 32: 17; Rom. 6: 20–22) but it seems to fit the context better if we interpret it as 'the fruit which is righteousness', and the verse is thus the complement of 1: 20. The words are an expansion of 'peaceable' and 'good fruit' in v. 17. Some link 'righteousness' and 'peace' (cf. Ps. 85: 10), and some give 'for' instead of 'by'. Cf. Prov. 11: 30; Am. 6: 12; Mt. 5: 9; Phil. 1: 11; Heb. 12: 11. Moffatt gives: 'The peacemakers who sow in peace reap righteousness'.

v. Selfishness and Worldliness (4: 1–4)
The first three verses should be linked with the closing verses of ch. 3. The causes of war and strife are not merely economic or intellectual but moral. As there were no civil wars at this time, James seems to have had primarily in mind 'private quarrels and lawsuits, social rivalries and factions and religious controversies' (Plummer); cf. Rom. 7: 23; 1 Pet. 2: 11. See too the comment in the article on the General Letters. In v. 2 Erasmus and others after him, without any MS authority, read 'envy' for **kill**, as 'killing' would rather follow than precede 'coveting'. The difficulty, however, is largely removed, if, as in RSV, a full-stop is placed after **kill**. Another difficulty is that 'kill' seems a strange word to apply to Christians. But here, as elsewhere, James appears to be looking beyond the bounds of the Church to the unbelieving Jews where assassination was not uncommon (cf. Mk 15: 7; Ac. 21: 38). Besides 'there is no saying how far the Christian portion of Jewish communities may have suffered themselves to become entangled in such quarrels and their murderous consequences' (Alford; cf. 2: 11). Some have taken the word figuratively (cf. Mt. 5: 21–22; 1 Jn 3: 15) like 'adultery' in v. 4. It is suggested that James had Sir. 34: 21, 22, in mind: 'The bread of the needy is the life of the poor; whoever deprives them of it is a man of blood. To take away a neighbour's living is to murder him; to deprive an employee of his wages is to shed blood'. Thus understood the words are an anticipation of 5: 4. The literal meaning, however, seems the more natural (cf. 2: 11; 5: 6), as the words are connected with 4: 1 rather than 5: 4, and, where a figurative sense is required, the context generally clearly indicates it. V. 3 gives us one of the hindrances to prayer, *viz.* selfishness (cf. 1: 8; Ps. 66: 18; Isa. 59: 1–2; 1 Pet. 3: 7). Worldly Christians are described as **adulterous people** (RV 'adulteresses') (4). Hort took the word literally, but the absence of the masculine and the charge of friendship with the world rather than the violation of the commandment (cf. 2: 11) point rather to a figurative meaning. James is writing in the manner of the OT prophets (cf. Isa. 57: 3–9; Ezek. 23: 27 and especially the whole of Hosea and also Mt. 12: 39). With **the world** cf. 1 Jn 2: 16. The world has been defined as 'society as it organizes itself apart from God'. Note that in v. 4 instead of 'will be' and 'is' (AV) NIV gives **chooses to be** and **becomes**.

vii. God a Jealous Lover and the Bestower of Grace (4: 5–6)
The interpretation of v. 5 is difficult. RV gives in the margin one variation for the first part and three for the second. However the following points seem clear: (*a*) The formula **Scripture says** normally introduces a quotation, but it may give the general sense rather than the exact words (cf. Jn 7: 38); (*b*) **the spirit he caused to live in us** refers naturally to the Holy Spirit (cf. Rom. 8: 11; 1 C. 3: 16); (*c*) **envies intensely** is used in a good sense, *e.g.* Phil. 1: 8; (*d*) It is true that the word used for 'envy' (*phthonos*) regularly and everywhere else in the NT has a bad sense, but as it was used of the jealous feeling of a lover towards a rival, it could understandably be used of the Spirit's desire to have us wholly for Himself. So the most satisfactory rendering appears to be the second in RVmg: 'That Spirit which he made to dwell in us yearneth for us even unto jealous envy.' This was also Mayor's view. The exact quotation has not been found. Perhaps James had in mind Dt. 32: 11, 19, which in the LXX speaks of God's yearning love and jealousy. There may be also echoes of other Scriptures (cf. Gen. 6: 3–5; Exod. 20: 5; 34: 14; Num. 35: 34; Isa. 63: 8–16; Ezek. 36: 27; Zech 1: 14; 8: 2). Some have recently found a Qumran parallel (*Manual of Discipline*, col. 4, lines 9 ff.) and it has been suggested that behind both quotations there may have been a targum or interpretative paraphrase of Gen. 6: 3. Such a high standard of devotion may seem beyond us, but God **'gives grace** (i.e. gracious help) **to the humble'** (6). The second part of v. 6 is from Prov. 3: 34 (LXX), except that **God** is used for 'the Lord' (cf. Isa. 57: 15; Job 22: 29; Lk. 1: 52–53; 14: 11; 1 Pet. 5: 5 and v. 10 of this chapter). For the use of the LXX cf. above, end of 'Character and Contents'.

viii. Exhortations to Wholehearted Devotion (4: 7–10)
The verbs in these exhortations are in the aorist tense, indicating that these things are to be done 'once for all as a settled thing for the soul' (W. Kelly). The first exhortation is to submit to God, which is a mark of true humility and a condition of successful resistance to the devil (cf. Eph. 6: 11; 1 Pet. 5: 9). **7. then:** i.e. because of God's character as explained in vv. 5 and 6. **8. Come near to God:** Cf. Exod. 19: 22; Dt. 4: 7; Ezek. 44: 13; Zech. 1: 3; Heb. 10: 22. **Wash . . . purify:** Cf. Gen. 35: 2; Exod. 30: 17–21; Lev. 10: 3; Ps. 24: 3–4; 73: 13; 1 Tim. 2: 8. **sinners** is generally used of the openly ungodly, but here it is parallel with the 'double-minded' (cf. 1: 6, 8), and appears to be addressed to professing Christians 'to startle and sting' (Ropes), though here too the unconverted may be also in view (cf. 5: 20). **9. Grieve:** AV and RV give 'Be afflicted'. Fasting

may be included. **laughter:** Cf. Lk. 6: 25. Sometimes in the Bible laughter is a desirable thing (cf. Ps. 126: 2), but sometimes it is the shallow laughter of the fool (cf. Ec. 7: 6). In the NT it is never used in a commendable sense. With v. 10 cf. v. 6.

ix. Judging One Another (4: 11–12)
In v. 11 the RV omits 'evil' (cf. Rom. 1: 30; 2 C. 12: 20; 1 Pet. 2: 1, 12; 3: 16). **or judges:** Instead of AV 'and judgeth'. 'And' is simpler, for evil-speaking and judging are not strictly alternatives, but 'or' (which is found in the most ancient MSS) may suggest that in some cases the 'uncharitable act' is more prominent, in others the 'judicial assumption'. For **the law** see 2: 8. That the reference is to the command: 'Thou shalt love thy neighbour as thyself' seems plain from the reference to the **neighbor** in v. 12 (so RV and RSV instead of AV 'another'). The verse is found in Lev. 19: 18 and in v. 16 evil speaking is forbidden. The person who judges his brother disobeys the law, thus putting himself above it and treating it with contempt (cf. Mt. 7: 1–5; Rom. 14: 4–13). The three-fold repetition of 'brother' in v. 11 is calculated to emphasize the unbrotherliness of the conduct. **12. one Lawgiver and Judge:** Though Christ is called judge in 5: 9 'one lawgiver' points rather to God (cf. Isa. 33: 22; Mt. 10: 28; Jn 19: 11; Rom. 2: 16; 3: 6; 13: 1; Heb. 12: 23; 13: 4).

x. The folly of forgetting God (4: 13–17)
This section, as 5: 1–6, is sometimes taken to refer to unbelieving Jews, but there is nothing in it inapplicable to professing Christians. The Jews bent on trade are warned not to forget God, for they are of such a nature that they **do not even know what will happen tomorrow** (14). Their life is but a passing **mist** (cf. Job 7: 6; 8: 9; 9: 25–26; 20: 8; Ps. 39: 5; 78: 39; 90: 9; Isa. 38: 12; 1 Pet. 1: 24). There is a reading adopted by some editors: 'Whereas ye know not on the morrow of what kind your life shall be' but it gives a weakened sense, as they may not be alive on the morrow. **15. 'If it is the Lord's will, we will live and do this or that':** Of course the important thing is not a formula but the dependent attitude of mind. Sometimes Paul used one, and sometimes he dispensed with it (cf. Ac. 18: 21; 19: 21; Rom. 15: 28; 1 C. 4: 19, and Prov. 27: 1). It should be noted also that 'If the Lord wills' means more than 'If the Lord does not prevent'. We should be exercised about His will. **16. you boast and brag:** 'brag' is the same as 'vainglory' in 1 Jn 2: 16 (RV). RV here gives 'vauntings' i.e. their proud speeches. NEB also says: 'You boast and brag'. The last verse is added to give point to the previous exhortations. **17. Anyone, then, who knows the good he ought to do and doesn't do it, sins:** The words may refer especially to vv. 13–16,

but they are of general application. James is not denying the possibility of a sin of ignorance, but he is emphasizing the seriousness of sinning against the light (cf. Lev. 4: 2; Lk. 12: 48; Jn 9: 41; 15: 22).

xi. The Judgment of the Rich (5: 1–6)
It seems plain that in this section James is denouncing ungodly Jews in the manner of the OT prophets (cf. Isa. 2: 7 ff.; Lk. 6: 24–25). The context (cf. v. 6) indicates that wealthy Jews rather than Gentiles are in view. There is no call to repent but an announcement of impending judgment, and v. 7 distinguishes the 'brethren' from those addressed here (see above, 'Readers and Place of Writing'). In vv. 2–3 three kinds of riches are mentioned, goods, garments and gold. Through hoarding and disuse the goods have rotted, the garments are moth-eaten and the gold is rusted (not literally, but it has become worthless) and their ruin is a picture and prophecy of the ruin of their owners (cf. Mt. 6: 19). **3. in the last days:** The last days are already upon them. The Christian is always in the last days (cf. 1 Jn 2: 18). The reference is to the last days before the Second Advent (cf. Isa. 2: 2; Hos. 3: 5; Ac. 2: 17; 2 Tim. 3: 1; 1 Pet. 1: 5), of which the destruction of Jerusalem was a partial fulfilment (cf. Mt. 24). In the war of A.D. 66–73 the wealthy (Sadducean) landowners of Judaea lost all the riches they had accumulated. **4. fields:** Cf. Isa. 5: 8. **are crying out:** Cf. Gen. 4: 10; 18: 20; 19: 13; Dt. 24: 14–15; Mal. 3: 5. **Lord Almighty:** Apart from the quotation in Rom. 9: 29, only here in the NT (In both places the Greek text retains Heb. *Sabaoth* instead of translating it; cf. AV, RV.) It occurs first of all in 1 Sam. 1: 3 and is found in the OT chiefly in the prophetic writings. It expresses God's omnipotence and supremacy. James uses it to assure the oppressed that they have a mighty protector. He may have had in mind Isa. 5: 9, where LXX retains 'Lord of Hosts' instead of translating, *e.g.* by 'the Lord All Sovereign'. (For the use of LXX see above, end of 'Character and Contents'.) **5. in a day of slaughter:** They are like animals gorging themselves on the very day of their destruction (cf. Jer. 7: 32; Isa. 34: 2, 6). The best exposition of the text is Josephus's account of the destruction of Jerusalem. The aorist tenses in vv. 5 and 6 have been regarded as indicating the viewpoint of the day of judgment. RV and RSV however do not here distinguish from the perfect. **6.** 'the righteous man' RSV is a term elsewhere applied to Christ (cf. Ac. 3: 14; 7: 52; 22: 14) and some apply it to Him here, but, in the absence of any suggestion from the context, it seems better to apply it to **innocent** (righteous) men generally (cf. Mt. 23: 35). James himself was known as 'the righteous' and his words are an unconscious prophecy of his own end. **who were not op-**

posing you: The tense adds vividness. It 'brings the action before our eyes and makes us dwell upon this, as the central point, in contrast with the accompanying circumstances' (Mayor). Some make this clause a question but the words seem a reminiscence of Mt. 5: 39 (cf. Isa. 53: 5, 7).

IV. CONCLUSION, PATIENCE AND PRAYER (5: 7–20)

i. The Need of Patience (5: 7–11)

In view of the oppressions mentioned in vv. 3–6, James exhorts Christians to be patient until the coming of the Lord and he cites the farmer, the prophets and Job. 'Patience' or 'long-suffering' is mentioned four times and 'steadfastness' ('endurance', RVmg) twice in this section. According to Trench the first expresses patience in respect of persons and the second in respect of things (cf. 1 C. 13: 4, 7). James evidently shared with the other NT writers the conviction that the coming of the Lord was near (cf. Lk. 21: 31; 1 Th. 4: 13–18; Heb. 10: 25, 37; 1 Pet. 4: 7). **7. See how the farmer waits for the land to yield its valuable crop and how patient he is for the autumn and spring rains.** The early and late rains are the rains of autumn and spring. The first germinates the seed; the second matures it. Some of the best MSS omit 'rain', and it has been thought that 'fruit' (which is found in some good MSS) should be repeated, but OT parallels (e.g. Dt. 11: 14; Jer. 5: 24; Jl 2: 23; Zech. 10: 1) favour the common rendering. The words naturally recall our Lord's comparison of the consummation of the age to a harvest (cf. Mt. 13: 39) and Joel's prophecy of the former and latter rain after God's judgment upon His enemies (2: 23), but it is unsafe to make a simple illustration the basis of prophetical interpretation. **8. Be patient and stand firm:** Cf. 2 Chr. 15: 7; 1 C. 15: 58. **9. Don't grumble** (RV 'murmur') . . . **the Judge is standing at the door:** From v. 8 it appears that the Judge here, unlike 4: 12, is Christ (cf. Mt. 7: 22–23; Jn 5: 22). **at the door:** Cf Mt. 24: 33; Mk 13: 29; Rev. 3: 20. **10. the prophets:** Cf. Mt. 23: 29–36; Ac. 7: 52; Heb. 11: 32–39. **in the name of the Lord:** i.e. as His representatives (cf. Jer. 11: 21; Mt. 7: 22 and v. 14). V. 11 is the only place in the NT where Job is referred to, though he is quoted in 1 C. 3: 19. **11. Job's perseverance** was evidently a familiar subject, perhaps in the teaching of the synagogue (cf. Job 1: 21; 2: 10; 13: 15). **what the Lord finally brought about:** i.e. the end that the Lord brought to all his trials (42: 12–17). Some have referred this to the Lord's death but the suggestion is at variance with the context and gives to 'the Lord' two different meanings in the verse. The reason why Christ is not mentioned as an example, as in 1 Pet. 2: 21, is probably because

James has unbelieving Jews as well as believing in mind. (See above, 'Readers and Place of Writing'.) Knowling suggested that the reason might be that James wished to keep before the eyes of his readers Jesus as the Lord of glory.

ii. Oaths (5: 12)

The intention of this verse is not to forbid a Christian to take an oath before a magistrate, as is plain from the example of the Lord, who made no objection when the high priest virtually put him under oath (cf. Mt. 26: 63–64), nor to forbid oaths in circumstances of special solemnity (cf. Gen. 22: 16; Isa. 45: 23; Rom. 1: 9; Gal. 1: 20), but rather to discourage the use of oaths in the ordinary relationships of life and **above all** as an expression of impatience. See also the note on Mt. 5: 33–37.

iii. Prayer (5: 13–18)

(a) **Prayer and Singing (5: 13).** The true remedy for trouble is not complaining, far less swearing, but praying, and the true outlet for joy is not worldly frivolity but the singing of **praise**.

(b) **Prayer and Anointing (5: 14–15).** The following points are submitted to help in the understanding of this difficult and important passage: (1) The elders of the church are to be called. In NT times the care of the churches, under the Chief Shepherd, was regularly in the hands of elders (cf. Ac. 11: 30; 14: 23; 15: 2; 1 Tim. 5: 17; Tit. 1: 5; 1 Pet. 5: 1). So we have here no purely Jewish instructions, though there may have been Jewish elements present. It is noteworthy that anointing with oil is not prescribed for Christians in any other letter.

(2) The initiative lay with the sick person and the ceremony was in the privacy of the home and had little in common with modern healing movements.

(3) Among the Jews the rabbis were asked to pray for the sick and they sometimes visited them; so here the elders are sent for as those who are the most spiritual and have a care for the believers. It may surprise us that the physician is not sent for, but while such advice is given in Ecclesiasticus (38: 12–15), there was no system of medical education among the Jews in Bible times, and one reason for James's exhortation may have been to keep the Christians from resorting to heathenish incantations and superstitious practices (cf. Ac. 19: 13). Very likely also James is contemplating cases that a doctor could not help (cf. v. 15, note).

(4) Some believe that we have here the exercise of the miraculous gift of healing. The absence of any mention of laying on of hands (cf. Mk 6: 13; 16: 18) may not prove the contrary, but why not send for those who had the gift of healing rather than the elders? For it is plain from 1 C. 12: 28–30 that the gifts of government and healing were distinct, and the latter was not possessed by all. Even in the

earlier period, before the conference at Jerusalem, the gift of healing was not exercised by the elders, as far as the records go, but by the Twelve, Stephen, Philip, Paul and Barnabas (cf. Ac. 2: 43; 3: 6; 5: 12–16; 6: 8; 8: 6–7; 9: 34, 38–40; 14: 3, 9, 10). Besides it is the prayer of faith that James emphasizes, and in connection with Elijah he stresses the fact that he **was a man just like us** (17).

(5) By many the oil is regarded as medicinal. It is pointed out that oil was a common remedy at the time (cf. Lk 10: 34) and that *aleiphō* ('anoint') is used only in a non-religious sense: elsewhere in the NT. It should be noted, however, that Trench's dictum that *aleiphō* is the 'mundane and profane' and *chriō* the 'sacred and religious' word cannot be accepted without reservations; '*aleiphō* is a general term used for an anointing of any kind' (W. E. Vine). It is used occasionally in the Greek OT in a sacred sense and *chriō* is found in the papyri in a mundane sense. See Moulton and Milligan. (Besides *chriō* is never used literally in the NT.) But it seems plain that the oil cannot be purely medicinal, for the Holy Spirit would not sanction the belief that oil was a remedy for all diseases, and the words 'in the name of the Lord' suggest an invocation of the divine name (unlike Col. 3: 17; and cf. Ac. 3: 6; 19: 13; 22: 16). It is significant also that oil was used in Mk 6: 13, where the healing was plainly miraculous, and the emphasis here is on the healing power of prayer rather than of the oil. Besides the sickness may have been of the soul and not of the body. See (7) below. The best view seems to be that of Plummer, that the oil was 'a channel of divine power and an aid to faith'. In some cases it would have medicinal value, in all cases it would give relief, and it would give confidence to those who attached healing virtue to it. Compare the use of clay and spittle in Jn 9: 6. Some have viewed the oil as purely symbolical, *e.g.* R. A. Torrey, who regarded it 'as symbol of the Holy Spirit in His healing power' (cf. Ac. 10: 38), and the anointing as 'an act of dedication and consecration', while Grotius viewed the oil as 'a token of that ease and joy that they should obtain from God'. There is doubtless truth in these views but, because of the common use of oil as a medicine, it seems impossible to rule out all reference to its therapeutic value.

(6) James does not contemplate failure, but the explanation appears to be found in the expression **the prayer offered in faith** (15), which is not a prayer that can be prayed at any time but only as it is granted by the Holy Spirit. It was not always granted to Paul (cf. 2 C. 12: 8; 2 Tim. 4: 20). The absolute statement of James is similar to promises made elsewhere (cf. Mk 11: 24). In all cases we must add 'if the Lord will'.

(7) Some have limited the application of the passage to cases where sickness is the result of a particular sin. Arguments for this view are: (*A*) the word used for 'sick' in v. 15 (but see note under (9)); (*B*) the mention of sins in v. 15; (*C*) the confession of sins in v. 16 (which, however, in the manner of James, is to be linked with the latter part of v. 15 rather than v. 14); (*D*) the disciplinary famine in the days of Ahab used as an illustration; (*E*) the recovery of the erring one in vv. 19–20.

It is plain that James contemplates the possibility that the trouble is primarily spiritual, and that should guard us against the view that oil here is a crude form of medicine, but, on the other hand, the use of the general term for 'sick' in v. 14 and the 'if' of v. 15 are arguments against the suggested limitation.

(8) Historically, Extreme Unction developed out of this rite, but the significance is entirely changed, for the Roman Catholic rite has death in view, not recovery.

(9) **14. pray over:** i.e. 'stretching the hands over' (Mayor). **anoint:** 'having anointed' (RV). **in the name of the Lord:** Cf. v. 10. **15. make well** is used of physical healing as in Mk 5: 23. **sick** in vv. 14 and 15 represents two different Gk words. Some take the word in v. 15 to mean 'depressed in spirit' (cf. Heb. 12: 3) but as the article in v. 15 identifies the sick man of v. 15 with the one already referred to, it is doubtful if any distinction is intended. Mayor was not prepared to make a distinction. **raise him up** may suggest a serious illness, one that has not responded to ordinary measures.

(10) Many modern examples of the efficacy of the practice have been quoted, *e.g.* in R. A. Torrey's *Divine Healing* and H. P. Barker's booklet of the same name. In the latter a letter of J. N. Darby's is quoted to the effect that 'prayers for the sick, and healing as the result of the prayer of faith, were common among the brethren at the beginning. In the Great Cholera plague of 1832 this was so effective that the doctors were in consternation' (p. 24). Cf. J. N. Darby, *Collected Writings XXVI*, p. 396; *Letters* I, pp. 2 f., III, p. 210. Similarly, F. W. Newman's recovery from fever at Aleppo in 1831 was attributed by A. N. Groves to his anointing with oil, together with his companions' prayer of faith (H. Groves, *Memoir of Lord Congleton* [London, 1884], pp. 32 f.).

(11) However we interpret this passage, there is Biblical authority elsewhere for the use of means in sickness (cf. 2 Kg. 20: 7; 1 Tim. 5: 23).

(*c*) **Prayer and Confession (5: 16). Therefore** (so also RV) links this verse with the previous one. James proceeds to give instructions to Christians generally. Even where the elders are not called, Christians should confess their sins one to another that they may be healed, whether in body as in Jn 4: 47 or in spirit as in Mt. 13: 15. **to each other** is fatal to the Roman doctrine of the confessional, which is a perversion of a wholesome practice. Nothing is said here as to the mode or place of such confessions. 'We need not suppose any reference here to a formal confession of sin, but merely to such mutual confidence as would give a right direction to the prayers offered by one for the other' (Mayor). The latter part of the verse, which is an encouragement to mutual confession, has been variously translated. The AV gives 'fervent prayer', a meaning which the word does not seem to bear, the RV 'in its working', the NIV **effective**. Perhaps the best view is that of Hort and Mayor, 'inwrought prayer', i.e. prayer prompted by the Spirit.

(d) **The Prayer of Elijah (5: 17–18).** The references to Elijah in Matthew are sufficient to indicate the place he occupied in Jewish thought (11: 14; 16: 14; 17: 3–4, 10–12; 27: 47, 49). The miracle-working Elijah might seem to belong to another world, but James assures his readers that he was **just like us** (cf. Ac. 10: 26; 14: 15; 1 Kg. 19: 4). He **prayed earnestly** (so also RV): Literally 'with prayer' (cf. Lk. 22: 15). His prayer is not actually mentioned in the OT but it is implied in 1 Kg. 17: 1 (cf. Gen. 18: 22; 19: 27; Jer. 15: 1). Here is Biblical authority for prayer for a change of weather, and in a letter which stresses the unchanging character of God (1: 17). The three and a half years are also mentioned by our Lord (Lk. 4: 25). In 1 Kg. 18: 1 it says that the rain came 'in the third year'. Some have therefore seen a discrepancy, but, as James Orr remarked, 'it is forgotten that in Palestine rain is not an everyday occurrence, as it is with us. The ground had already been dry for six months—since the previous rainy season—when Elijah stayed the rain by his word at the commencement of the new rainy season. If the cessation lasted till the third year thereafter, the total period of drought would necessarily be about three years and six months' (*The Bible Under Trial*, pp. 264–265). Cf. Dan. 12: 7; Rev. 11: 2–3; 12: 6; 13: 5. For the second prayer see 1 Kg. 18: 1, 42.

iv. Reclaiming the Wanderer (5: 19–20)
19. My brothers: It is debatable whether these verses refer to the restoration of a truly regenerate person or the conversion of an unregenerate one. **wander from the truth** may seem to favour the first view (but cf. 2 Pet. 2: 20–22), while **save him from death** and **cover over a multitude of sins** appear to favour the latter, at least to one who holds the doctrine of the security of the true believer. Some have understood 'death' as loss of communion or physical death (cf. 1 C. 11: 30), but these views scarcely satisfy the terms used (cf. 1: 15, 21), and there is no evidence that physical death was the regular punishment of backsliding. The rendering **one**

of you should be noted. Perhaps 1 Jn 2: 19 is a parallel. It seems therefore that in their fulness the words apply only to the unregenerate (as is true also of Rom. 8: 13 and 1 Tim. 5: 6) but they have an application to a backslider. **the truth** is 'the sum and substance of the Apostolic teaching and preaching' (Knowling) (cf. 1: 18; 3: 14). This use is common in John's writings. With **sinner** (20) cf. 4: 8. AV gives 'hide a multitude of sins' but RV and RSV **cover**. There is evidently an allusion to Prov. 10: 12, which is quoted more fully, but not exactly, in 1 Pet. 4: 8. Some have thought that a proverbial saying is also behind the words. In Proverbs the meaning appears to be simply that if we love a person we hide his sins from men (cf. Gen. 9: 23), but here the thought is rather of forgiveness (cf. Rom. 4: 7). Some have referred the sins to the converter rather than the sinner, as if converting a sinner is a means of securing forgiveness for one's own sins, but, though such an idea may be found in Jewish writings, it is foreign to the NT, nor is it taught in Dan. 12: 3. It has been objected that to refer it to the sinner 'makes a bad anticlimax' but cf. Ps. 116: 8. The meaning is that 'the soul is not merely saved out of death, not merely rescued from peril, but blessed, Ps. 32: 1' (Knowling).

The letter ends abruptly, without benediction, perhaps in order to make the final words ring in the ear, perhaps also because it is not strictly a letter.

BIBLIOGRAPHY

ADAMSON, J. B., *The Epistle of James*. NICNT (Grand Rapids, 1976).

ALFORD, H., *The Greek Testament*, Vol. IV, Part 1 (London, 1870).

CADOUX, A. T., *The Thought of St. James* (London, 1944).

CALVIN, J., *Commentaries on the Catholic Epistles*, E.T. tr. (Edinburgh, 1855).

DALE, R. W., *The Epistle of James* (London, 1895).

DAVIDS, P. H., *The Epistle of James*. New International Greek Testament Commentary (Exeter, 1982).

ELLIOTT-BINNS, L. E., *Galilean Christianity* (London, 1956).

GODET, F., *Studies in the New Testament*, Eng. tr. (London, 1876).

HORT, F. J. A., *The Epistle of James* (London, 1909).

KELLY, W., *The Epistle of James* (London, 1913).

KNOWLING, R. J., *The Epistle of St. James*. WC (London, 1904).

LAWS, S. S., *The Epistle of James*. BNTC (London, 1980).

MAYOR, J. B., *The Epistle of St. James* (London, 1913). [on the Greek text].

MITTON, C. L., *The Epistle of James* (London, 1966).

PARRY, R. St. J., *A Discussion of the General Epistle of St. James* (Cambridge, 1903).

PLUMMER, A., *St. James and St. Jude.* EB (London, 1891).

PLUMPTRE, E. H., *St. James.* CBSC (Cambridge, 1878).

REICKE, B., *The Epistles of James, Peter and Jude. AB* (Garden City, N. Y. 1964).

RENDALL, G. H., *The Epistle of St. James and Judaic Christianity* (Cambridge, 1927).

ROPES, J. H., *St. James. ICC* (Edinburgh, 1916). [on the Greek text]

TASKER, R. V. G., *The General Epistle of James.* TNTC (London, 1956).

1 PETER

G. J. POLKINGHORNE

1 Peter stands with 1 John as the only Catholic Letter whose authority was never doubted by the early Church. All our textual authorities contain Peter's name in the first verse. The Petrine speeches in Acts have clear parallels in thought and language. 2 Pet. 3: 1 implies the existence of a former letter, which may not, of course, be our letter (cf. notes there). Early non-canonical writings which show knowledge of 1 Peter include those of Barnabas, Clement of Rome, Hermas and Polycarp, to mention only the clearest testimony. Despite this array of support, Petrine authorship has been challenged. The main grounds are set out and briefly considered below:

1. Language. It is held that the language and style show learning and ability beyond the reach of a Galilean fisherman. While we cannot say what may be the possibilities of such a man as Peter in Christ and may also remember that he came from a bilingual area, we must concede that the excellent Greek of a literary type showing acquaintance with classical usage is not likely to have come from Peter, despite the occurrence of Semiticisms. We may recognize the truth of this objection without abandoning belief in Peter's authorship by accepting the hypothesis that Silas (cf. 5: 12) was more than postman or even amanuensis and was entrusted with considerable responsibility for the drafting and wording. Similarities with other parts of the NT in which Silas had part, such as Ac. 15: 23–29 and the Thessalonian Letters are cited in support of the suggestion.

Another facet of this problem of language is the dissimilarity in style between 1 and 2 Peter. As ancient a writer as Jerome (died A.D. 420) proffered the solution that two different amanuenses were used for the two works. Guthrie (*New Testament Introduction, Hebrews to Revelation*, p. 181), after careful consideration of the matter, concludes that 'the kind of relationship between the two Epistles does not prohibit the tradition of Petrine authorship from being maintained'.

2. Persecution. The many references to persecution, especially that in 4: 16 to suffering 'for the Name', are held to indicate a date after Peter's death when formal and official persecution of Christians for their mere profession was instituted. The answer to this is two-fold: first, that the persecution alluded to in the Letter is not necessarily formal and offi-cial, but probably only sporadic and unofficial: second, that Acts (*e.g.*, 5: 41; 11: 26) shows how early Christians were called upon to suffer for the Name alone.

3. Dependence on Paul. It is contended that the chief of the apostles would not rely so much on Paul's ideas, nor quote so extensively from his writings. We may dispute whether there is in fact quotation from Paul's writings (cf. below). Even so, the granting of common ground with Paul does not amount to conceding that this is inevitably fatal to Petrine authorship. Cannot Peter honourably accept that which God has revealed to his brother apostle? Nevertheless, some significant Pauline emphases are lacking, notably justification by faith, freedom from the Law, the New Adam, the work of the Spirit, and the concept of mystical union with Christ. Conversely, the references to the spirits in prison (3: 19) and the interpretation of the work of Christ in terms of the Isaianic Suffering Servant are non-Pauline. This is not to imply that there is divergence of doctrine, merely that there is individuality in presentation.

4. Reminiscences of the Lord Jesus. Peter, it is said, would have included far more reminiscences of the Lord Jesus than are found in this Letter. Just how many are requisite is not prescribed, but two considerations may be mentioned. First, that more allusions to the Lord's words and deeds are found here than in all Paul's letters. Second, that there may be more such allusions than we realize with only the four Gospels to guide us.

In conclusion, it may be said that the challenge to Petrine authorship is not considered strong enough to annul the plain ascription in the text. (Further information can be found in the works by Selwyn and Beare named in the Bibliography; also Guthrie, *New Testament Introduction, Hebrews to Revelation*.)

Literary Affinities

Peter quotes frequently from the OT, almost invariably from the LXX. As to the NT, besides the reminiscences of the Lord and the parallels with the Petrine speeches in Acts already mentioned, there are many similarities to the other Letters, especially Thessalonians, Romans, Ephesians, James and Hebrews. Scholars have debated, without agreed conclusions, the reasons for these latter similarities—did Peter quote from them, or they from him, or were they all quoting from other documents, *e.g.*, liturgies, hymns, catechisms, etc.?

Date

Selwyn is probably right in placing the writing of the Letter between the death of James, the Lord's brother, in A.D. 62 and the outbreak of Nero's persecution in A.D. 64. The former publicized the breach between Church and Synagogue and exposed Christians to persecution by removing them from special privileges allowed to the Jewish religion by the Roman authorities, while expectation of the latter formed the occasion of writing. Tidings of the commencement of the painful trial appear to have reached the writer before he had finished the work and prompted the exhortation in 4: 12–19.

Place of Origin

Babylon (5:13) cannot be the city on the Euphrates, which after A.D. 41 was very sparsely populated and with which Peter had no connection. Nor can a Roman garrison in Egypt be seriously considered. Rome must be meant, cf. Rev. 17 and 18, as was universally accepted until Reformation times. The symbolic designation would save trouble should the censor's eye light on the letter in transit.

Destination

The first verse lists the recipient churches, all in Northern Asia Minor, in a region for the most part not evangelized by Paul, who probably confined his activities to southern Galatia and Asia. The order is that in which the messengers bearing the letter would reach them. Some of the members may have been Jews, but many were Gentiles, as may be deduced from 1: 14, 18; 2: 9 f.; 4: 3 f. Peter addresses them now as one new man in Christ Jesus, the spiritual heirs of the promises to Israel.

Purpose of the Letter

Many scholars have regarded the work as a baptismal sermon later adapted to a letter. The baptismal address runs from 1: 3 to 4: 11, with the baptism taking place between 1: 21 and 22, while 4: 12–5: 14 is either an address to the general congregation after the ceremony or an addition at the time of compilation of the letter. Notes on 2: 2 ff.; 3: 21 and 4: 11 discuss some of the evidence usually cited. For a fuller consideration cf. *NBD* sub 1 Peter and Guthrie, *op. cit.* pp. 121–125.

To the present writer, it seems preferable to regard the references to baptism as incidental and the work as a circular letter written to Christians already enduring suffering and expected to be further tried, exhorting them to courage, hope and faithfulness and directing their hearts to the great Example of suffering meekly borne, the Lord Jesus Christ. 4: 12 f. may be taken as an epitome of the thought.

Throughout the letter, suffering is revealed as essential to Christianity. The Prophets predicted it for Christ (1: 11) whose cross was both redemptive and exemplary (1: 18 f.; 2: 21–24; 3: 18 f.): redemptive, in that the resurrection and glory that ensued for Him (1: 3, 21) spell secure salvation for His people (1: 5); exemplary, in that Christians must share both the shame and the glory (4: 13). Hence, suffering to Christians is within the will of God (4: 19) —though Satan may attempt to gain advantage by it (5: 8)—and can get glory to God (4: 16) especially by purifying their characters (1: 7); so that it must be embraced cheerfully (4: 13), the more so as it will be brief (5: 10). Therefore, they must submit, not merely to God's hand in discipline (4: 17; 5: 6) but also to human authorities (2: 13), doing right (3: 17) and viewing the endurance of persecution as a kind of spiritual sacrifice (2: 5) acceptable to God through Christ Jesus.

The development of ideas does not lend itself readily to a brief outline, but the following is proposed as a working basis for exposition.

ANALYSIS

I. THE STATUS OF THE CHRISTIAN (1: 1–2: 10)

Writing to Christians facing a 'painful trial' (4: 12), the apostle directs their minds to the unshakeable bases of their status, the eternal purpose of God the Father, the historically completed work of Christ and the outwardly verifiable work of the Spirit. This concentration on objective fact accounts for the relative paucity of teaching about the more subjective aspects of the work of the Spirit. 'The tyrant's brandished steel and the lion's gory mane' may perchance diminish Christian joy, but they are powerless to cancel the divine election and the finished work of Calvary.

i. The Derivation of this Status from God (1: 1–9)

Frequently in this Letter, the Church is presented as the New Israel of God and parallels and contrasts with the position and experience of Israel of old are developed. The Church, like her predecessor, is both 'strangers and scattered' in its earthly experience while chosen, foreknown, sanctified, obedient and sprinkled in God's mercies. She, like the Jewish dispersion (Jn 7: 35; Jas 1: 1), is scattered in the world but united in herself, yet she enjoys the fulness of divine blessing. Indeed, the entire Trinity of the Godhead is shown to be active on her behalf. The rôle of God the Father is that of 'choice according to foreknowledge'. Foreknowledge is to be understood, as in Rom. 8: 28–30 and Eph. 1: 3–6, less as a passive 'knowing in advance' than an active 'taking note of', an eternal intention to bless. V. 20 and Ac. 2: 23 demonstrate that it was conceived and executed in Christ. God the Spirit acts to make effective the choice of the Father by calling the believer into the company of the redeemed. **Sanctifying** means 'separating to the service of God' (cf. NEB 'hallowed to his service') rather than 'making Christlike', the term in scripture often having a different connotation from common theological usage. Similarly, **new birth** in v. 3 (cf. on 1: 23) is not primarily a reference to an individual's regeneration but

a description of the formation of the New Israel. It recalls the prophecies of Isa. 66: 8; Ezek. 36 and 37, taken up by the Saviour Himself in Jn 3. God the Son provides the precious covenant blood. **Obedience** and **sprinkling by his blood** refer back to the establishment of the Mosaic covenant in Exod. 24: 7 f. and describe how the New Israel is similarly brought into relationship with God. As at that time the people promised obedience to the commands of the book of the covenant and were sprinkled with the sacrificial blood, so now the believer pledges his obedience to Christ and obtains the benefit of His blood. Once more, the thought is concrete, pointing to a known time when a decision to be obedient was made and the blood was appropriated, hence the term 'sprinkling' rather than 'shedding'. The greeting in v. 2, combining the Greek 'grace' with the Hebrew 'peace', reflects the mixed character of the churches. This mixed company is welded into one new man by a process likened to a new birth by yet another fact beyond the reach of the persecutor, the resurrection of Jesus Christ. Thereby, they are brought, as were God's ancient people, into an inheritance, but into one which, because it is heavenly rather than earthly, and **can never perish, spoil or fade**, i.e., 'untouched by death, unstained by evil, unimpaired by time' (F. W. Beare).

A double security attaches to this inheritance. It itself is 'kept', the Greek perfect tense indicating a past act with abiding consequences, and 'ready' (cf. Jn 14: 2 for the Saviour's promise to make it ready), while believers are 'shielded', the present tense indicating a continuing process—'being shielded by the might of God'!

Therefore, the various trials allowed to reach them are not perilous, being designed simply to refine their characters as precious metals are refined, by fire. The **praise and glory and honor** of v. 7 may equally legitimately be taken as due to the kept Christian or the keeping God.

V. 6 anticipated the theme of joy which is

now developed. There, the phrase **in this** is of uncertain import: it may refer to a specific antecedent, whether 'God' (3) or 'the last time' (5) or the whole circumstances of vv. 3–5, when the phrase is virtually a vague resumptive expression, 'and so'. The Greek phrase reappears in 3: 19 (NIV 'through whom')—cf. note there—and 4: 4, where the NIV ignores it in translation.

What was ambiguous in v. 6 is made clear in v. 8. It is their confidence of seeing the unveiled glory of Christ that enables them to rejoice amidst their tribulations. Already their love for Christ and the sweetness of spiritual communion bring to their hearts a joy which is **inexpressible** and **glorious** (better, with Alford, 'already glorified') and which is described as **the salvation of your souls**. As such, it is preparatory for the 'salvation ready to be revealed in the last time' (5) and akin to the 'guarantee of our inheritance' of Eph. 1: 14 and perhaps to the attained resurrection of Phil. 3: 11. Cf. also on 1 Pet. 4: 1, 7, 14.

ii. The Permanence of the Christian Status in the Counsel of God (1: 10–12)
One proof that the Christian's grace is indeed the eternal counsel and purpose of God is now adduced, in that **the prophets** spoke of it. Peter does not state that he refers to OT prophets, so that some commentators have interpreted his words to mean Christian prophets. V. 11 is then taken to concern the 'sufferings of the Christward road', i.e., the sufferings of Christians, not of Christ Himself; then v. 12 deals with the unity of Jew and Gentile in the Gospel, that is, 'they were not serving their own (Jewish) race, but you Gentiles'. Much simpler sense is obtained by understanding that OT prophets were intended. Frequently the sufferings and glory of Christ are coupled as here—cf. 3: 18; 4: 13; 5: 1—and v. 12 takes the meaning 'they were not serving their own generation, but the present one'.

Thus, the Spirit of God who spoke through the preachers who proclaimed the Gospel in Asia Minor had already spoken earlier in the OT. These prophets, realizing that the Spirit signified more by their words than they themselves could appreciate, scrutinized their writings for the deeper significance. Dan. 8: 15; 9: 2 f., is one example of this process in operation, while Isa. 53, quoted in 2: 22–25, is an instance of the type of prophesying in mind. Hence, the hopes of the OT are fulfilled in Christ: and the unity of the two Testaments is shown to include the ministry of the Holy Spirit and testimony to Christ.

So Peter introduces his major theme, which he himself learnt from his Master in Mk 8: 31–38 and to which he repeatedly returns (cf. 2: 21; 3: 14–22; 4: 12–19; 5: 1, 10) that, like Christ Himself, the Christian has to suffer on earth to be glorified hereafter. Many passages in the rest of the NT might be cited as teaching the same truth—*e.g.*, Ac. 14: 22; Rom. 8: 17 f.; 2 C. 1: 7; 2 Tim. 2: 12. Suffering for righteousness' sake, accordingly, is no unscheduled disaster overtaking the Christian without the wish of God. On the contrary, it is altogether of the warp and woof of His purposes—the very route by which the Son of His love wrought His wonderful redemption, the assured pathway whereby His many sons are to be brought to the glory.

iii. The Holiness appropriate to the Christian Status (1: 13–21)
Upon the doctrinal foundation thus laid, the apostle proceeds in typical NT fashion to raise up an ethical superstructure. The Christian must not allow pressure from outside to determine his behaviour. He must act according to the light within him. Particularly, he must be holy in all things (13–21) and, within the brotherhood of faith, loving (1: 22–2: 3).

The New Israel, as the Old, must be holy. For them, holiness is encouraged by hope (13), enforced by the character of God (14–17) and reinforced by the sacrifice of Christ (18–21).

Hope is more than a vague, amorphous aspiration. It requires that the loins of the mind be girded, (NIV **prepare your minds for action**) that is, that the loose skirts of the flowing robe must be gathered into a belt for hard work or vigorous activity. Such was the condition in which the first Passover had to be eaten (Exod. 12: 11). In using the metaphor, maybe Peter recalled his Lord's words to him recorded in Jn 21: 18. Thus, abstaining from the enervating pleasures of the surrounding paganism in which they formerly indulged, they must direct their whole being to eternal matters.

No longer are they ignorant. They know the character of God. He is not merely holy, He is actually 'The Holy One' (cf. Isa. 12: 6; 41: 16), and that character they, in common with their predecessors under the Old Covenant, must reflect (Lev. 11: 44; 19: 2; 20: 7). Therefore, they must not presume that because they say 'Our Father' to God, their relationship as sons will make Him favour them in judgment. They must remember that His judgment is impartially based on deeds done. As those who must eventually render an account to Him (cf. Rom. 14: 12; 2 C. 5: 10), they must lead lives of reverence, that is, the fear of respect, not of terror.

Strangers (17) is not the same word as is so translated in 1: 1 and 2: 11 but is similar to the word rendered 'aliens' in the latter passage.

A further incentive to right behaviour is introduced in vv. 18–21—the costly sacrifice of Christ. Their old way of life which their fathers had handed down to them is described as **empty** (RV 'vain'). Often in the OT, 'vanity' refers to idols—cf. Jer. 8: 19; 10: 14 f. RV—so that evidently Peter's readers had inherited pagan ways from their ancestors, an inference confirmed by 'detestable idolatry' in 4: 3. From these pagan ways they had been redeemed by blood so precious as to make gold and silver appear as perishable things, whether they are symbols of human wealth or human religion (cf. Mt. 2: 11; Exod. 30: 11 ff.; Ezek. 7: 19). Logically, the word 'redeem' raises the question as to whom the price is paid, but in NT times, this aspect of the word is lost to view and nowhere in scripture is that question answered for the redemption provided by Christ.

The description of the Saviour as a **Lamb without blemish or defect** directs the mind to the injunctions of the Levitical law—cf. Lev. 22: 19 ff.—but what type of sacrifice was envisaged is not made plain. The Passover lamb (Exod. 12), as the sacrifice whereby Israel was delivered from bondage and separated to the Lord, is richly significant in the context. So also is the lamb of Isa. 53, the passage so largely quoted in 2: 22–25.

But the glory of the Saviour Himself now seizes the apostle's thoughts. Here is One who was eternally **chosen**, literally 'foreknown', the centre of that great electing purpose of God mentioned at 1: 1. Such an expression implies the eternal Sonship of Christ, for which see Jn 1: 1–18; Phil. 2: 1–11; Heb. 1: 1–14, *inter alia*. This One was **revealed** at Bethlehem at the appointed time (cf. Gal. 4: 4) for our benefit. Not only did He pay the ransom price in His own blood, but also He was raised from the dead and **glorified**—a reference to His ascension (cf. Ac. 1: 6–11).

The last clause of v. 21 should be read as the RV, 'so that your faith and hope *might be* in God', showing the purpose behind this mighty display of divine grace.

Peter thus links the Christian's eternal hope, the holiness of God Himself and the person and work of Christ together to enforce a strong exhortation to right conduct. Six of the thirteen NT occurrences of the word translated 'you do' (15) are in this short letter, proving how important he knew it to be. Cf. also the exhortations at 2: 9, 11 f.; 3: 16; 4: 3, 15.

iv. Love as an Expression of the Christian Status (1: 22–2: 3)
In keeping with the objective character of the teaching throughout the Letter, the love here enjoined is to be thought of as a practical virtue, a closing of the ranks under the fire of persecution. There is to be no deserting a brother who is punished, but since all are members of the family of God (cf. v. 17 above), they are to love one another earnestly and heartily. **Purified** is in the perfect tense, pointing to a past act of obedience which has enduring results.

Deeply recalls the prayers of the church for Peter in Ac. 12: 5, where the same Greek word is used, and the prayer of the Lord in Gethsemane, where Lk. 22: 44 uses a similar word. **Born again**, as 1: 3, refers primarily to the work of God in making the whole church into one new man without by any means excluding the individual experience of each member. Once more, the concrete emphasis is apparent as the Word of God is described as the formal cause of their new life. Here is something that is **imperishable** (literally, incorruptible) living and enduring, whatever the persecutor may try to do.

2: 1 shows the negative implications of the command to love—everything disruptive is to be put away. **Malice** accordingly should be taken in the modern English sense of 'malevolence' in this context. In v. 16, the same Greek word is rightly rendered 'evil'.

Newborn babies (2: 2) is taken as evidence that the readers were new converts by the supporters of the theory that the work was originally a baptismal homily (cf. Introduction), in view of their aptness to the condition of those who have just been received into the church by baptism. But **pure spiritual milk** seems to be the dominant concept, especially in the light of the concluding vv. of the preceding chapter, and 'newborn babies' adds a touch of graphic realism. The absence of the definite article in the Greek before 'pure milk' suggests that it was a popular expression, with 'spiritual' inserted to ensure that it was taken metaphorically. Rom. 12: 1 also employs the same word (*logikos*) in the phrase 'spiritual worship'. It can also mean 'rational' or 'metaphorical' or, as the AV, 'of the word', which makes good sense in the context. The figurative use of 'milk' occurs also in 1 C. 3: 1 f. and Heb. 5: 12 f., but with the suggestion, which is absent from 1 Pet., that the mature believer should outgrow it. **Salvation** bears the meaning 'full spiritual development' and connotes the process of 'growing up' to it (cf. 2 Pet. 3: 18). This involves both the continual feeding on the Word commended here and the advancement beyond first principles implied in Corinthians and Hebrews.

V. 3 continues the thought of eating, **tasted that the Lord is good** being an allusion to Ps. 34: 8. The aorist tense of 'tasted' points back to a decisive moment of appropriation of divine grace. **Come to him** (4) also may be an echo of the LXX of Ps. 34: 5, the Hebrew having 'look to him'. The same Psalm is quoted at greater length at 3: 10 ff. It is of interest that many scholars believe that Ps. 34 was used for catechetical and baptismal purposes in the early church.

v. The Priestly Status of the Christian (2: 4–10)
The richness of the Christian's status is now

drawn out under the two analogies of the Church as a Temple, with Christ as its principal stone, and as a priesthood, though without the specific presentation of Christ as High Priest which is found in Hebrews. Notice that the thought is still of the corporate entity in which individuals participate as members. The frequent OT quotations show conclusively that the practices of the Hellenistic mystery cults are not the main sources of the writer's ideas.

(a) The Church as Temple (4–8)
For clarity of exposition, let us first note the OT scriptures quoted. For **come to him** cf. above on 2: 3. The other quotations are: Isa. 28: 16 in v. 6; Ps. 118: 22 in v. 7 (also quoted by the Lord Jesus in Mk 12: 10 whence Peter probably derived the teaching, cf. Ac. 4: 11); and, lastly, Isa. 8: 14 f. in v. 8. Compare the use of the first and last of these by Paul in Rom. 9: 33. On the principle enunciated in 1: 10–12, Peter applies the passages to Christ, though doubtless they had other associations for their original writers and readers. Christ, the living Person, is the stone rejected by the builders, but chosen and precious (better, honourable) to God. Indeed, He is the chief corner stone of God's edifice. **Cornerstone** (6) (Gk. *akrogōniaios*) is derived from the LXX of Isa. 28: 16 and occurs here and in Eph. 2: 20 only in the NT. Both it and the **capstone** (7) might be either the bottom or the top stone of the corner of the building. Most probably they signify the stone at the extremity of the angle, from which the builders work both horizontally and vertically in setting and checking the walls. So is Christ the basis and standard on which God erects His building.

Into this building, Christians as living stones made alive by Christ (1: 3) are in the process of being incorporated (5), the NIV rightly translating as the indicative rather than the imperative, the Greek being ambiguous. The figure is of God at work, erecting His building, stone by stone.

The nature of the building is suggested by **house** (5). Frequently in scripture, 'house' means 'temple', cf. Hag. 2: 3 and Mt. 21: 13. So here in Peter, the Church is presented as God's Temple, based on Christ and partaking of his preciousness or honour (7). The RV and NEB of vv. 6 f. make clearer than the NIV the connection between the great worth of Christ in the Father's estimation and the believer's appreciation of and blessing in Him.

Meantime (7 f.) those builders who have refused to use this stone in their building find that as it lies on their site it encumbers their operations by tripping them up. Such is the appointed portion of those who reject Christ, as Isa. 8: 14 f. predicts, especially of Israel after the flesh, endeavouring to continue as the people of God and to do His work while refusing His Messiah. It is noteworthy that the primary significance of Ps. 118: 22 was that the nations rejected Israel in their imperial schemes, but this mattered not, as God had His plans for His people. Later, however, Israel itself despised Christ (cf. Isa. 8: 14) and this was disastrous.

(b) The Church as a Priesthood (5, 9 f.)
Side by side with the metaphor of the Church as a Temple and the believers as stones built into it, Peter works out another analogy, that of the Church as a Priesthood. V. 5 introduces the theme, describing believers as a priesthood, or, with the NEB margin, as intended to perform 'the holy work of priesthood'. In vv. 9 f., he clarifies their position and function, showing what are the 'spiritual sacrifices' of the earlier verse. They include the submissive sufferings mentioned so often in the letter, but also the kind of sacrifice extolled in Heb. 13: 15, 'the fruit of lips that confess his name'. So, they are to **declare the praises** of God (9). The word rendered 'praises' (Gk. *aretē*) can have the meaning 'moral excellence', as in 2 Pet. 1: 5, or 'manifestation of divine power', but 'praise', as in the Hebrew text of Isa. 43: 21, accords best with the governing verb 'declare', which certainly means a verbal declaration, in contrast, for example, to the silent testimony of 3: 1.

Several OT allusions enforce the exhortation and show conclusively that the author is thinking of the Church as the spiritual heir of God's ancient people. Significantly, the passages alluded to relate to important moments in the history of Israel. Exod. 19: 5 f. 'my treasured possession . . . a kingdom of priests . . . a holy nation', deals with the establishment of the Lord's covenant with the nation at Sinai; and Isa. 43: 20 f. 'my chosen people . . . proclaim my praise' relates to the re-establishment of the national testimony after the Babylonian exile. In Christ, the Church comes into the good of these scriptures.

Out of darkness suggests that Peter's readers were formerly pagans, as Philo of Alexandria uses a similar expression regarding proselytes to Judaism. Moreover, Paul in Rom. 9: 24 ff. uses the quotation from Hos. 2: 23 to illustrate the calling of the Gentiles in Christ, although the prophet himself had in mind the restoration of Israel.

II. THE SUBMISSION OF THE CHRISTIAN (2: 11–3: 12)
Peter now turns from the status of the Christian in all its security and privilege to deal with the problems of right conduct in their present circumstances. The key-word is 'submit', Gk. *hypotassō*, which occurs six times in the Letter—2: 13, 18; 3: 1, 5, 22; 5: 5, not always, of

course, in this section. (3: 22 has no reference to Christian conduct.)

i. Introductory (2: 11 f.)

As **aliens** (Gk. *paroikos*) they have no status as citizens in this world, a sombre contrast to their standing as regards heaven, Eph. 2: 19; while as **strangers** (Gk. *parepidēmos*) their stay is only transitory. Therefore, they are not to be conformed to the standards of conduct prevailing in the world, since these 'sinful desires' 'war against your soul', a statement hinting at the state of war between the prince of this age and God.

Sinful is literally 'flesh', used in an ethical sense for that which is opposed to the influence of the Spirit, a sense more common in the Pauline letters and not found elsewhere in 1 Pet. **Soul** (Gk. *psychē*) on the contrary has a distinctively non-Pauline sense of the essential inward nature of man, without the adverse implication found, *e.g.*, in 1 C. 2: 14; Jas 3: 15; Jude 19 (cf. the *NBD* articles on these two words). **Pagans** means not merely 'non-Jews' but also 'non-Christians', hence the NEB rendering of v. 12, 'Let all your behaviour be such as even pagans can recognize as good'. The word used for **see** (*epopteuō*) occurs only here and in 3: 2 in the NT. While the rendering given is legitimate, it could also be translated 'gaining insight by your good deeds'. **The day he visits us** may be the final judgment day (cf. 4: 7) or the occasion when disaster overtakes the persecutor himself, awakening him to the truth of the Christian's position, or the time of the Christian's suffering (cf. 4: 17).

ii. The Christian's Civic Submission (2: 13–17)

Every authority instituted among men, literally, 'every human creation' can be paraphrased, with Selwyn, as 'every fundamental social institution', i.e., the state (13–17), the household (18–25) and the family (3: 1–7). Wherever the Christian finds himself in relationship with other men, he must behave in accordance with his high calling.

The apostolic injunction of submission to the state probably arose from the temptation to rebellion occasioned by persecution. Such ill-treatment of well-doers was contrary to the divine intention for the state, fully set out in Rom. 13: 1–7 and briefly summarized here in the remark that the king is supreme. The preposition translated 'by' in v. 14 is literally 'through' (Gk. *dia*) and perhaps contains a hint that governors are commissioned by the king as God's vicegerent. This recognition of the source of imperial authority in no sense supports Emperor worship, but simply indicates that God as a faithful Creator provides for the proper government of His creatures. An undertone of culpability lies in the word translated 'ignorant talk' (15), so that the Christian's

right conduct should produce conviction of sin in their slanderers. In v. 16, there is a deliberate contrast between 'free men' and 'slaves', which is the literal force of the word rendered 'servants'. Many Christians were in fact slaves (cf. the next section) but in Christ Jesus they had become God's free men. Even so, they must surrender their freedom to the will of God and enter into voluntary bondage. Christian freedom is not a veil for evil behaviour but a liberty to serve God. Rom. 6: 1 shows in what sense freedom might be abused, and Gal. 5: 13 suggests its right use.

Peter reveals his OT cast of thought by describing believers as a **brotherhood** (17), a word which occurs again in 5: 9 and nowhere else in the NT. It is evidently his synonym for 'church' (Gk. *ekklēsia*), which he does not use, possibly because it signifies a local congregation, whereas he writes to a group of gatherings (cf. the *NBD* article 'Church', especially regarding Ac. 9: 31). The absence of the word for church does not justify the conclusion that the thing is not found, nor the further conclusion that 1 Pet. was concerned with Jewish believers rather than Gentile-Christian churches (cf. Introduction).

iii. The Submission of Christian Slaves (2: 18–25)

The second fundamental social institution is the household, and the exhortation is addressed to the 'household slaves'. Evidently, many of these slaves were enduring persecution at the hands of unconverted masters, whose legal authority over them was virtually absolute. Once more (cf. on 2: 13) not revolt, or even flight, but submissive acceptance of unjust punishment is required, both out of respect for the master and of conscience toward God. **Conscious** (19) is better translated 'for conscience toward' as RV and cf. 3: 16. The expression translated **it is commendable** (19) and **this is commendable** (20) is literally 'this is grace' (cf. RVmg and *Arndt* p. 885 (*b*) end of Section (*b*)). While one can hardly translate thus, the form of words suggests the thought that it is the inwrought grace of God that enables a slave to behave in this manner.

Peter does not condemn slavery in principle, not because 'the end of all things is near' (4: 7) but more probably because he expected believers to accept the sovereign will of God in whatever social position their lot is cast. This is surely the force of 'for the Lord's sake' in v. 13. The death-knell of slavery is implicit in the gospel, as events proved, and is sounded in such passages as Phm. 16 and Gal. 3: 28. In vv. 21–25, the suffering of the Lord Jesus Christ Himself is cited to drive home the point. Note that though the sin-bearing and substitutionary aspects of the Cross are mentioned, they are not the primary concern. As in 1: 18–21, the

Cross is referred to as an incentive to right conduct, so here it is shown to be exemplary. Quoting four passages from Isa. 53, Peter recognizes the Lord Jesus as the Suffering Servant of Jehovah (cf. Isa. 52: 13) and presents Him to other suffering servants as their Pattern. The word translated **example** (Gk. *hypogrammos*) means a tracing to be written over or an outline to be filled in. It was Jesus who taught this view of Himself to Peter—cf. Mk 10: 45 and Lk. 22: 37—and it forms the special insight of his presentation of the Lord. In three verses (22 ff.) all beginning with the same Greek word (*hos*, 'who', only fully represented in the AV), the comparison between the Servant and the servants is worked out.

In the first of them, the affirmation of the sinlessness of Christ (22) is significant as coming from a man who lived so closely to Him for so long and observed intimately His behaviour in times of terrible stress. It is mentioned to show that His suffering was innocent, as that of Christians must be (cf. 19 f.) if their patient endurance of punishment is to be valuable in God's sight or effective testimony before men. Similarly, the silence of the Sufferer (23) is a pattern for copying (cf. 'gentleness and respect' in 3: 15). The RV 'committed' is preferable to the NIV 'entrusted'. What is committed is left unsaid: it could be Himself, His cause or His enemies. The imperfect tenses of this verse imply an eye-witness's report, as though Peter mentally pictures the events happening and describes them in the language of Isa. 53. In the third of these verses (24), the sin-bearing of Christ has practical rather than theoretical implications. It is referred to that **we might die to sin** (NEB excellently, 'that we might cease to live for sin') and **live** for **righteousness**. The **tree** was the instrument of death for a slave and the **wounds** were the product of just such a scourging as Pilate administered to the Lord. How precious a reflection for those called upon to follow in His pathway of suffering! A further inference from v. 24 is that those slaves who are thus expected to suffer for Christ's sake are reminded that He suffered for theirs. The verse means that he bore as substitute the consequences of our sins on the cross. Weymouth conflates two translations thus: 'He carried the burden of our sins to the tree and bore it there'. Some commentators have expanded this conflation so as to teach that as Priest, Christ carried our sins up to the Cross and as victim, He bore them on the Cross, but this overloads the language. It is also doubtful how far ideas of the Levitical sacrificial system may be read into the verse, which is based on Isa. 53: 12. Certainly, it would be wrong to think of our sins as the offering made.

V. 25 shows that the purpose of Christ's suffering was accomplished and that now He superintends and protects those who live for Him, though He may call upon them to suffer for Him.

iv. Wives and Husbands (3: 1–7)

The third fundamental social institution is the family. Although six verses are devoted to the exhortation of wives and only one to husbands, we may not deduce that Peter is anti-feminist. In fact, the gospel has proved the greatest force for the liberation of women that history has known (cf. Gal. 3: 28), as may be verified by comparing their lot in countries influenced and uninfluenced by Christianity.

The situation envisaged is that of a woman who has been won for Christ after her marriage to a pagan man—rather a more difficult situation than that of a male convert whose wife refused to become a fellow-believer. She is not therefore released from the duty of obedience (cf. on 2: 13, 18) but is required to submit to her husband, even though he may be unkind to her because of her new faith. Christlike conduct rather than perpetual preaching is prescribed as the method of winning her spouse. So, with a **gentle** (better, meek) spirit, she endures whatever is inflicted and with a **quiet** spirit, she gives no cause for offence, thus silently demonstrating the superiority of Christ. This is far more important than any cosmetic devices, such as hair style, jewellery or clothing, having the advantage of being precious in God's sight, whereas the other things at best appeal only to men. Just as elsewhere Abraham is cited as the father of the faithful, here Sarah, the mother of faithful women, is brought forward to strengthen the exhortation, since she actually called her husband 'master' (Gen. 18: 12). Those who follow her example are rather her daughters than those who happen to be her physical descendants (6) —perhaps another indication that the readers of the letter were Gentiles by birth.

Do not give way to fear (6) appears to be an allusion to Prov. 3: 25. A more exact translation is 'and are not put in fear by any intimidation', the intimidation being the husband's persecution.

Husbands are not exempt from instruction, though less is said because their problems are less pressing than those of wives at the mercy of unsympathetic husbands. They are to **be considerate** (RV 'dwell according to knowledge') with their wives, three facts being taken into account. First, that the woman is the **weaker partner**, the Greek word actually meaning 'vessel', cf. 1 Th. 4: 4; 2 C. 4: 7, and hence unable to withstand his strength; second, that as God's creature she has equal right to life as the man, so that he must not make her life a misery; and third, that prayers must not be hindered. The force of this last injunction is that a man who fails to give his wife due consideration can hardly pray with her at family prayers.

In passing, it might be noted that no attention is given to the relation of parents and children as is done in Ephesians and Colossians.

v. A Final Word on Christian Submission (3: 8–12)
From the natural relationships of state, household and family, attention is now turned to the supernatural relationships within the brotherhood of faith, all the virtues listed in v. 8 being those that make for harmony in an assembly. Even if one member of the fellowship uses harsh words (9), he is to be answered in accordance with the example of the Master (2: 23) with blessing. Ps. 34 is quoted to enforce the exhortation, as also at 2: 3 (where see note). Its essential message is that the Lord uses Christians much as they use other people, so that if we wish blessing in our lives, we must speak and do right and peaceable things. This, equally with suffering (2: 21) and glory (5: 10), is the Christian's calling, cf. the Golden Rule in Mt. 7: 12 (cf. on 3: 14 below on the words for 'blessed').

III. THE SUFFERING OF THE CHRISTIAN (3: 13–4: 19)
We now reach the most significant part of the letter, wherein the apostle tackles the practical problem confronting his readers, the problem of persecution. His standpoint differs from that of Hebrews and Revelation, which handle the same question. Hebrews warns its readers of the awful consequences of apostasy, even under the pressure of persecution. In Revelation, persecution has become an organized exercise by the imperial authorities and is shown to be demonic in origin, a manifestation of the eternal opposition of Satan to God. For Peter's readers, not only is there less enticement to abandon Christ than there was for the Hebrews, but also persecution is sporadic rather than systematic. Nevertheless, it was indeed a 'painful trial' (4: 12) for them. Hence, Peter assures them of their inalienable standing in Christ as the Israel of God (1: 1–2: 10), counsels submission to every human institution (2: 11–3: 12) and, especially in the present section, points out the divine purposes of grace in their suffering. Throughout the letter, he reminds them that the Saviour Himself was called to walk the same road.

Up to 4: 12 ff., persecution is envisaged as a possibility, which may have been realized in some instances, but at that point it becomes an actuality, as Nero's policy makes itself felt from Rome to the uttermost parts of the Empire.

i. The Manner of Endurance (3: 13–17)
A note of surprise underlies v. 13. Having counselled his readers (9–12) that their calling is to peaceableness and blessing, he asks in

effect, 'Whatever makes you think that you could possibly come to harm if you are zealous for good?' This reflects the general law and order of Roman society, whose officers were commissioned to promote morality (2: 14). Should it happen, however, that they be ill-treated—and the rare optative construction in the Greek for 'even if you should suffer' shows that the event is considered to be unlikely (contrast 4: 14, where the verb 'insulted' is in the indicative)—they would inherit the beatitude of Mt. 5: 10, 'Blessed are those who are persecuted because of righteousness'. Two words are used for **blessed** in the letter. The first (*eulogētos*), found in 1: 3 (NIV 'praise'), with a cognate form in 3: 9, focuses attention on the divine source of blessing; while the second (*makarios*), used in 3: 14 and 4: 14, as also in the Sermon on the Mount, concentrates on the happy result. NEB renders 'happy' in 1 Pet. 3: 14 and 4: 14.

In view of this blessedness, reverence for God, not fear of man, should characterize them (15). A significant variation is made in the passage from Isa. 8: 12 f. alluded to here. Where Isaiah has 'the Lord Almighty', Peter substitutes 'Christ', demonstrating that for him, Christ was truly divine.

V. 15 also gives guidance as to their behaviour should they be called to account. They are not forbidden to defend themselves. **Answer** (Gk. *apologia*) might be a formal proceeding in a law court, as 2 Tim. 4: 16, or an informal self-justification, as 2 C. 7: 11. Here, the words 'always' and 'to everyone' point to the latter, as defendants would presumably be compelled to offer a defence in legal action. This suggests that the opposition was so far unofficial and supports the arguments for an early date. Two features of the method of self-defence are stressed. It must be done with **gentleness and respect** (15). Peter seems particularly anxious to restrain them from the sharp retort— cf. also 2: 23 and 3: 9. Further, their answer is to be backed by a good conscience (16), so that the accusers rather than the accused may be put to shame. The kind of slander that might be expected is evident from 4: 14. If, despite their defence and their good behaviour, they are made to suffer (17), they can be sure that it is the will of God, as it was in the case of the Lord Jesus, as the succeeding passage shows. The recurrence of the optative mood in v. 17 (cf. on v. 14) postulates a possibility of suffering rather than a probability.

ii. Christ's Righteous Suffering and Vindication (3: 18–22)
Doctrinally and linguistically, this is the most difficult and debated passage in the letter. The limits of a short commentary preclude a detailed discussion (for which see Essay I in Selwyn's Commentary, and C. E. B.

Cranfield's article, 'The Interpretation of 1 Peter 3: 19 and 4: 6', *Expository Times*, Sept. 1958). We must be content to advance a view in the text and append a brief summary of other possible interpretations.

Happily, there is no obscurity in 3: 18 which speaks of the victory of Christ's innocent and vicarious suffering. He is designated **the Righteous** (cf. 2: 22), a quotation from Isa. 53: 11, a chapter so frequently quoted by Peter both in the speeches recorded in Acts (cf. 3: 14) and this letter. Nevertheless, He **died for sins**. 'Suffered' (AV and RV), a less well-attested variant for 'died', would suit the context better, which may account for its existence (cf. also 2: 21). The line of comparison is similar to that in 2: 21–25 (see notes there) in that the emphasis is on the example of Christ, the Suffering Servant. Though righteous, yet He died 'for sins', which might be rendered 'as a sin-offering' as in Rom. 8: 3 and Heb. 10: 6, but the plural form in 1 Pet. militates against such a rendering. Further, He died **for the unrighteous** (cf. 2: 24) in which phrase the preposition *hyper* includes the idea of 'as a substitute for' as well as 'for the benefit of'.

A new note, absent from chapter 2, enters in the words **once for all**, a note of triumphant vindication implicit in the 'it is finished' from the Saviour's own lips on the Cross(Jn 19: 30). This is underlined by the statement **to bring you to God** wherein we learn that the purpose of the Father in the crucifixion was attained, the ultimate aim of all religion, accomplished only in the gospel. So, after His death, Christ is **made alive by the Spirit**. 'The Spirit' in this passage is not the Holy Spirit despite the capital, but the spiritual aspect of the Lord's personality, cf. Rom. 1: 3 f. for a similar antithesis of the Lord's natures and 4: 2, 6 for an extension of the concept to ordinary men. Alford is worth quoting here: 'His flesh was the subject, recipient, vehicle, of inflicted death; His spirit was the subject, recipient, vehicle, of restored life'. V. 22 brings the note of triumph to its crescendo in the ascension of the risen Lord and His session at the Father's right hand. The Suffering Servant who in chapter 2 appears as the patient victim of rampant evil now is shown to be gloriously victorious.

The triumph of Christ after suffering is taken as the clue to the enigmatic verses lying between 18 and 22. After His vindication, Christ went to rebellious angels in captivity and announced His victory over sin, death, and Satan. As to the words of the passage: **through whom** need not necessarily mean 'through the spirit' but may be no more than a general resumptive expression 'and so' or 'in the course of which' (cf. on 1: 6). **Went** is the same word as 'has gone' in v. 22 and in both places equally signifies a definite journey. **Preached** means

not 'evangelized' but rather 'heralded his triumph'; cf. Rev. 5: 2, where the same Greek word is translated 'proclaiming'. **The spirits in prison** are those 'sons of God' who sinned in Gen. 6: 2, i.e., angelic beings as in Job 1: 6; 2: 1; Dan. 3: 25, 28. 2 Pet. 2: 4 f. seems decisive for this interpretation, especially if the genuineness of that letter is accepted, since the imprisonment of sinning angels is immediately followed by a reference to the flood (cf. also Detached Note, below). Likewise, the mention of angels in v. 22 as subjected to Christ bears out the meaning we see in v. 19. **God waited patiently** alludes to the delay in the judgment of the flood while Noah preached (2 Pet. 2: 5).

As in the days of Noah a small minority of the faithful rode to safety in the ark, so the antitype of Noah's company, the Christians, likewise a tiny minority, are borne to safety through the waters of baptism. The inference from all this is that, as Christ was triumphant through suffering and as Noah's little group were vindicated by deliverance, so those who now suffer for righteousness' sake will finally be partakers of glory. This theme is taken up in chapter 4.

Many interpreters regard baptism as the theme of the whole letter (cf. Introduction). To these, **now** (21) indicates that baptism has just taken place. (A similar inference is drawn from the same word in 1: 12; 2: 10, 25.) This theory certainly makes the introduction of the idea of baptism at this point comprehensible. To others, it reads like a passing allusion, prompted by the mention of Noah and the waters of the flood. The essence of baptism is shown not to consist in the cleansing of the body, but in the soul's response to God. **Pledge** is not easy to translate. It probably means the clause in a contract containing a formal question to and consent of the parties contracting and thus signifies 'a pledge to God proceeding from a good conscience'. The response usually required of a candidate prior to baptism may have suggested the statement. Baptism is thus the glad and thankful confession to God that through the death, resurrection and ascension of the Lord Jesus Christ, the believer rejoices in a cleansed conscience.

Detached Note—Some other Views of 3: 19–22

For the reader's information, three other views differing from the above (which is based mainly on Selwyn) are given:—

(*a*) The Spirit of Christ through Noah (Gen. 6: 3) preached to the men of that day, who rejected the message, perished in the Flood, and are now the spirits in prison. These same men are taken to be the 'dead' of 4: 6. This view fails to give a consistent sense to 'went' in 3: 19—cf. note above.

(*b*) The spirits in prison are all who have died

without hearing the gospel, those of Noah's day being selected as representative. Between His death and resurrection, Christ went and preached the gospel to them. Once more, the 'dead' of 4: 6 are regarded as the same persons as the spirits in prison. A theory of a second chance for the unconverted after death is sometimes deduced from this view of the passage, but does not really follow from it.

(c) Calvin took the 'spirits in prison' to be Jews who had looked for Christ's appearing and the 'prison' to be the Law, despite the fact that the Flood so long preceded the giving of the Law.

iii. Holiness of Conduct required of Christians (4: 1–7)

Therefore in v. 1 resumes 3: 18, the intervening verses being in parenthesis. Peter again links doctrine with practice (cf. on 1: 13–21). The challenge is to equip ourselves with Christ's determination to do the will of God, whatever the cost (cf. 2: 21 for a similar appeal to the example of Christ). So, **he who has suffered in his body is done with sin** must be understood, on the one hand, in the light of Christ's suffering and, on the other, in view of Peter's readers' liability to persecution. Not affliction in general, but the endurance of the world's hatred of Christ is what is in mind. Thereby is the dominion of sin broken in practical experience, because the saint who has boldly stood his ground and taken punishment for it is launched on a plane of living where sin is easier to overcome and more difficult to fall into (cf. Gal. 6: 17 for the actual experience). For him, henceforth, 'to live is Christ' (Phil. 1: 21). Rom. 6: 1–14 presents a similar teaching, though Paul goes to the root of the matter while Peter rests on the effect. Comparison should also be made with 1 Pet. 1: 8 f. (where see comments) and Phil. 3: 8–11.

As Christ (3: 18) was 'put to death in the body but made alive by the Spirit', so (2) the Christian must here and now finish with human desires and live by the will of God. Specifically, all the foul practices associated with the heathen religion they once pursued must cease, however much surprise and abuse this may occasion from those with whom they once joined in these things. **Plunge with them** (4) is literally 'run together with them' and conjures up a picture of people hastening out of their homes so as not to be late, when the signal for the idol festival is given. **Flood of dissipation** (4) is a fair description of some of the rites associated with Greek deities. The kind of abuse that Christians received for their abstinence may be illustrated from Tacitus' description of them as 'haters of the human race'.

They may safely leave their detractors to God's judgment (5), as did their Saviour (2:

23). Some expositors regard the judge of this verse as Christ, but Peter throughout thinks of God in this capacity (e.g., 1: 17; 2: 23; 4: 19). No ultimate inconsistency with such passages as Jn 5: 22 arises in view of the statements there (27, 30) indicating that the Son exercises judgment under the authority of the Father.

Difference of interpretation of 4: 6 has already been mentioned. The view taken here is that 3: 19–22 are parenthetic, so that the 'spirits in prison' of 3: 19 are not identical with the **dead** of 4: 6. Moreover, whereas the **dead** of 4: 5 are all deceased persons irrespective of character, those of the next verse are deceased Christians, about whom the early church was frequently exercised—cf. 1 Th. 4: 13; 1 C. 15: 29. Their judgment 'according to men' lies both in the condemnation of v. 4 and in the fact of their death, which is the penalty of sin upon the human race (Rom. 5: 18, etc.). But, as their Lord was made alive in the spirit after death (3: 18) so they also **live in regard to the spirit** 'according to God's standards' (NIV **according to God**). The final assessment of a Christian life cannot be made with earthly data only; the facts of the after-life must be brought in to redress the balance.

This final assessment is not indefinitely remote, for **the end of all things is near** (7) and judgment has already begun at the house of God (17). Christ's incarnation marked 'these last times' (1: 20) and His crucifixion 'judgment on this world' (Jn 12: 31). Hence, NT men lived in the consciousness that 'the fulfilment of the ages has come' (1 C. 10: 11), that the new creation had arrived (2 C. 5: 17), that they were already tasting 'the powers of the coming age' (Heb. 6: 5) in the experience of the Holy Spirit (Eph. 1: 13 f.). The unveiling of Jesus Christ was eagerly awaited as the consummation of their experience and hopes (cf. on 1: 6 ff.). The proximity of the 'end' or 'goal' (Gk. *telos*) required that they lead lives which were controlled, abstemious, and prayerful (cf. v. 7, NEB: 'an ordered and sober life, given to prayer').

iv. Christian Conduct within the Brotherhood (4: 8–11)

Against the background of the abuse of godless men (4) and the imminence of Christ's appearing (7), the apostle renews his plea of 1: 22 for mutual love among Christians. Such love **covers over a multitude of sins**—probably an allusion to Prov. 10: 12. Since only love within the brotherhood is under consideration, Mt. 18: 21–35 affords the surest guide to interpretation. Because God's love in Christ has made atonement for our many sins, we also, living by His forgiveness, must be forgiving to our brethren. In the governmental dealings of God, we receive in like manner as we give —cf. on 3: 8–12.

Hospitality is particularly mentioned (9) in view of the needs of those who had suffered the loss of goods through persecution (cf. Heb. 10: 34). It is at once a way of ameliorating their suffering and a demonstration of loyalty and solidarity which might have the consequence of exposing the giver to action by the persecutor, hence the necessity of specific exhortation.

A spiritual gift (10) (Gk. *charisma*) comes from God's grace (Gk. *charis*) and must be administered as the property of Another, that is, as a steward not a proprietor. Moreover, it is given for the benefit of the whole brotherhood, not for the possessor only. Speakers, therefore, are not free to advance their own opinions, but must speak the words of God (Gk. *logion*, 'divinely authoritative communication' cf. *NBD s.v.* 'oracle'). **Serves** (Gk. *diakoneō*) included waiting at table, as in Lk. 17: 8 and perhaps Ac. 6: 1–4, but extended to all forms of help to others and came to have the technical meaning within the church of 'deacon', cf. Rom. 16: 1; Phil. 1: 1, one who performs duties complementary to those of elders or bishops (cf. 1 Tim. 3: 1–13), whom Peter exhorts in the next chapter. Since God supplies the strength for such service, He must have the glory of it.

The doxology of v. 11 reads most simply as applying to Christ, though some scholars take it as addressed to the Father, on the grounds that glory would not be simultaneously ascribed both to and through Christ. Those who consider that the letter was originally two works would terminate the first, the Baptismal Homily, at the end of v. 11 and regard the doxology as evidence in their favour. This conclusion is precarious, however, as Westcott has shown that only three of sixteen NT doxologies terminate a letter.

v. The Painful Trial (4: 12–19)

At this point, it seems that the writer received tidings of the aggravation of the situation of his readers through the flaring up of persecution (cf. on 3: 14). But the **painful trial** is sent to test them as was explained in 1: 6 f., so that the latter end would be joyous, and three reasons for rejoicing are now advanced. First, (13) **that**, literally 'in so far' (Gk. *katho*) indicates that in precise proportion as they share Christ's sufferings they will share His glory when it is revealed. No participation in the atoning work is implied in this sharing of suffering, but simply as in Col. 1: 24, the bearing of the burden of evangelism in the face of opposition. Secondly (14), they obtain the blessing and happiness (cf. on 3: 14) of the Presence of the Glory through the mediation of the Holy Spirit. 'Glory' only once in this letter (1: 24, an OT quotation) means 'honour'. Elsewhere, it refers to the divine splendour, especially at the unveiling of Jesus Christ. Here, it connotes that

peculiar manifestation of God's presence, the Shekinah Glory (cf. *NBD s.v.* 'shekinah'). Exod. 40: 35 describes the first appearance of that glory on the Tabernacle, while Jn 1: 14 connects it with the incarnation. To the suffering Christian, the Spirit makes very real the presence of the glory of God in Christ. Thirdly (15–18), the hapless lot of the non-Christian in eternity makes all suffering for Christ's sake more than worthwhile.

The list of offences to be avoided (15) is two-fold: the initial three are criminal, and the fourth is more general. Only the latter two call for comment. **Any other kind of criminal** is of uncertain meaning: the NEB 'sorcerer' is as old as Tertullian, but hardly proven. **Meddler** also cannot be certainly defined—'busybody', 'infringing the rights of others', 'concealer of stolen goods', 'spy', 'informer', or even 'agitator' are all possible. The Christian must not incur penalties for such deeds, but to suffer for the Name itself is not shameful. *Christianos*, meaning 'a partisan of Christ', occurs only twice elsewhere in the NT, Ac. 11: 26; 26: 28. These early uses of the word dispose of Ramsay's theory that the word pointed to a formal outlawing of Christians by the Emperor and hence to a late date for 1 Peter (cf. also *NBD*, p. 975). Although originally a nickname, it may be confessed to the glory of God.

The concept that **judgment begins with the family of God** derives from such passages as Am. 3: 2; Jer. 7: 8–15; 25: 29 f.; Ezek. 9: 6. It implies that the persecutions and afflictions of Christians are part of the displeasure of God at sin, but they come upon them rather to refine away the evil than to condemn (cf. 1: 6 f.). Similar teaching is found in Jn 15: 2; 1 C. 11: 31 f.; 2 Th. 1: 3–8. Because of these disciplinary acts of God, **it is hard for the righteous to be saved** i.e., the path to life is arduous, as the Saviour Himself taught, Mt. 7: 13; Mk 8: 34; Mt. 24: 9–14. Even so, God is a faithful creator, who will keep the trial within bearable limits; cf. 1 C. 10: 13. Therefore, all can be safely committed to Him. To **commit** means to deposit for safe keeping, as in Lk. 23: 46 and 2 Tim. 1: 12, a common practice before banks existed. Exod. 22: 7–9 and Lev. 6: 1–7 show how severely breach of trust was punished. If men could be relied on to guard possessions, much more can God be depended on to protect the souls of His people.

Here ends the argument proper of the Letter. Chapter 5 is a kind of prolonged salutation.

IV. FINAL EXHORTATION AND GREETINGS (5: 1–14)

No individual greetings are included, perhaps because Peter had no personal contact with the churches he addresses. But this conclusion does not necessarily follow, *e.g.*, Galatians also lacks individual greetings, yet Paul certainly knew the Galatian churches intimately. Vv. 12, 13 imply that Mark and Silas were known personally to the recipients.

i. Exhortation to the Elders and their Younger Brethren (5: 1–5)

Peter does not base his authority to address elders on his apostleship, an omission regarded by some commentators as evidence of pseudonymity. Surely, however, a forger would most certainly have stressed apostolicity otherwise there would be little purpose in using Peter's name, so that the omission is actually favourable to Petrine authorship. Three grounds of authority are in fact claimed. First, he is a fellow elder, presumably of the church from which he is writing. Nowhere else in scripture does this word fellow elder appear. Second, he has witnessed Christ's suffering. Thirdly, he expects to share in the glory yet to be revealed. In 1: 11 and 4: 13 he has already similarly linked the suffering and glory of the Lord.

Elder (Gk. *presbyteros*) is capable of many meanings. It can signify 'older' (as in Lk. 15: 25); 'men of old' (as Heb. 11: 2); a Jewish leader, whether local (Lk. 7: 3) or national (Ac. 4: 23), i.e., a member of the Sanhedrin. But here, as frequently in the NT, it must mean a 'leader of the church'. **Serving as overseers** Gk. *episkopountes*, literally 'being a bishop', provides a further instance of the NT practice of identifying the terms elder and bishop. Not all elders were older men—cf. 1 Tim. 4: 12. Their function is described as being 'shepherds of God's flock', which involves the duties of shepherding, as outlined in such scriptures as Ps. 23 and Ezek. 34 and commanded to Peter by the risen Lord in Jn 21. Three couplets of instruction are given to them. They must be volunteers (2) not pressed into service by other Christians. They must be eager or enthusiastic, not motivated by the salary offered by the church (cf. 1 Tim. 3: 3; 5: 17 f.). And they must be exemplary Christians, not lords of the flock, which is not theirs but God's. Men like this will receive a reward from the returning Lord—a crown which, unlike the laurel wreath awarded to a victor in the games or worn as a festive garland, was as unfading and immortal as the saint's inheritance (cf. 1: 4).

Younger members (5) are to be in subjection to those who are older. The latter term might mean 'your seniors in age' but is best taken in the same sense as v. 1, 'the leaders of the church'. Humility is to characterize all. The word translated **clothe yourselves** signifies 'binding firmly on and wearing constantly', and maybe Peter in using it had in mind the towel wherewith Jesus girded Himself in Jn 13: 4. Prov. 3: 34 is cited from the LXX to prove that humility is the sure route to divine blessing.

ii. A General Exhortation to Submission to God (5: 6–11)

Many times throughout the letter, exhortations to submit occur—cf. especially 2: 11–3: 12. These are now brought to their final issue, as a matter of 'accepting your humiliations' (Selwyn), since they come ultimately from the mighty hand of God. Even the adversities they have experienced are within the ambit of His sovereign will for their lives. **In due time** (6) points on to the unveiling of Jesus Christ so often mentioned and to the salvation ready to be revealed then (1: 5). If meantime they are anxious, they may take comfort from Ps. 55: 22 and cast their anxieties upon Him who is a 'faithful creator' (4: 19). The second clause of v. 7 gains force if translated impersonally: 'It matters to Him about you'. God is not indifferent about His people's misfortunes. In the present, He will bear the anxiety; in the future, He will abundantly recompense.

If worrying is needless, watchfulness is emphatically required, and Peter repeats in revised wording the injunction of 4: 7: 'Be clear minded and self-controlled.' Someone besides God has an eye on the Christian's progress. **Enemy** and **devil** both translate the Hebrew, Satan. Enemy (Gk. *antidikos*) signifies an opponent in a lawsuit, as in Zech. 3: 1, where Satan stands ready to give evidence against Joshua. Devil (Gk. *diabolos*) includes the idea of false accusation, reminding us that he is a liar and the father of lies (Jn 8: 44). Capable of masquerading as an angel of light (2 C. 11: 14), to Peter's readers he prowls around like a roaring lion, attempting through the activities of the persecutors to devour them. Consistently, the NT exhorts resistance to him—v. 9 and Jas 4: 7; Eph. 6: 11. V. 9 mentions one strengthening consideration, that the whole brotherhood in the world confronts the same problem. F. W. Beare's translation of the clause is: 'Showing yourselves able to fulfil the same meed of suffering as your brotherhood in the world'. Thus, the courage of one church confirms that of another.

But the surest source of strength is found (10) in the personal interest of God and His promise of eternal bliss. It is His purpose that the suffering shall be little, whether in duration or extent, and that the glory shall be eternal (cf. also Rom. 8: 18 and 2 C. 4: 17). The glory to which we are called is His, and He Himself (an emphatic pronoun) will **restore**, that is, 'make complete or perfect', a word used of setting a broken bone and of equipping or arranging a fleet of ships. It brings the double thought of providing all that is needful to get them through the trials and of repairing the damage received in action. Moreover, He will **make you strong**, i.e., give all needed power, **firm and steadfast**. NEB takes the last two words together 'strengthen you on a firm foundation'.

A further doxology (11, cf. 4: 11) follows, before the words of greeting.

iii. Final Salutation (5: 12–14)

We may envisage Peter now taking the pen from Silas to write a short salutation himself, as did Paul from his amanuensis at 2 Th. 3: 17 and Gal. 6: 11.

In the Introduction mention has been made of the suggestion that Silas played a large part in the composition of this Letter. **To you** (12) comes in the Greek immediately after the name of Silas, which suggests a close link between him and the recipients. Peter testifies his confidence in him as he sends him off with the letter. Probably, he is the same person who assisted Paul in 1 Th. 1: 1 and 2 Th. 1: 1. In some translations he is called not 'Silas', which appears to be a Greek form of the Hebrew name, but Silvanus, the Latinized form, more appropriate for use in Rome.

The doctrine of the letter is similarly authenticated: it is **the true grace of God** and they must **stand fast in it**. Whatever part the amanuensis may have played, the apostle takes full responsibility for the teaching.

For **Babylon** see Introduction. In thus designating Rome by the name of the city of captivity of ancient Israel, Peter reminds his readers afresh that they, as the Israel of God, are strangers in a foreign land (cf. 1: 1).

Mark, Peter's interpreter or dragoman, according to Papias, is the composer of the second Gospel. His presence with Peter enhances the likelihood that he is writing from Rome.

The **kiss of love** (14) is not promiscuous, men kissing only men and women only women. Indeed, as a token of love between the sexes it does not occur in the NT. Rather is it a kind of formal greeting, akin to the modern Western handshake, and is still so used in some countries. At one time, it was part of the ritual of public worship in churches.

Lastly comes the greeting, not, as 1: 2 'grace and peace', but simply the Hebraic **peace** signifying that fulness of well-being that only God in Christ gives.

BIBLIOGRAPHY

Commentaries:

BEARE, F. W., *The First Epistle of Peter* [on the Greek text] (Oxford, 1961).

BEST, E., *The First Epistle of Peter*. NCentB (London, 1971).

CRANFIELD, C. E. B., *I and II Peter and Jude*. TC (London, 1960).

ELLIOTT, J. H., *A Home for the Homeless* (London, 1982).

KELLY, J. N. D., *The Epistles of Peter and of Jude*. BNTC (London, 1969).

REICKE, B., *The Epistles of James, Peter and Jude*. AB (Garden City, N. Y., 1964).

SELWYN, E. G., *The First Epistle of St. Peter* [on the Greek text] (London, 1946).

STIBBS, A. M., and WALLS, A. F., *The First Epistle General of Peter*. TNTC (London, 1959).

2 PETER

DAVID F. PAYNE

2 Peter is undoubtedly one of the least read of the NT documents. And yet it purports to come from the pen of an outstanding apostle, Peter himself, whose first letter is widely prized and loved. Small wonder, perhaps, that so many commentators have denied that Peter could ever have written it. The traditional or stated authorship of many books of the NT has been challenged by some scholars; but scholarship as a whole, with few dissentient voices, has denied flatly that this letter emanated from its stated author, 'Simon Peter, a servant and apostle of Jesus Christ' (1: 1).

The fact has to be faced that the case against the apostolic authorship is strong; answers can be found to most of the arguments raised, it is true, but there is no denying that the cumulative effect of these arguments is considerable.

The chief points at issue are as follows. If Peter was the author, how is it that the style, the language, and the treatment are all so different from those of 1 Peter? Secondly, why should a writer of Peter's calibre and authority have borrowed so much from the Letter of Jude? Thirdly, if the apostle was martyred in Nero's reign (as there is good reason to believe), in the middle sixties A.D., how is it that 2 Peter presents features which point more naturally to a date no earlier than A.D. 90? There is, moreover, no certain reference to the letter in early Christian writings till Origen (early third century), and for many years afterwards there were leading churchmen who expressed doubts about the apostolic authorship. On the other hand, the fact remains that the letter was ultimately included in the NT canon, whereas a number of spurious works bearing Peter's name were firmly excluded from it.

There is no doubt that the style and diction of 2 Peter are rather different from those of the first letter, as many commentators have demonstrated; but there are also some close similarities, which must not be ignored (cf. E. M. B. Green, 2 *Peter reconsidered*, pp. 11 ff.). (Indeed, it is currently reported that a linguistic comparison of the two letters, made with a computer, reveals clear affinities of style between them.) While it is possible that some unknown author of 2 Peter borrowed much from 1 Peter, it is equally possible that the same man produced both letters, but employed a different secretary. It is widely believed that Silvanus influenced the shape of 1 Peter (cf. 1

Pet. 5: 12); he had no hand in 2 Peter. The argument about the different treatment of the two letters is even less convincing: there are again certain similarities, in any case, and the differences may well have been dictated by the very different needs of those to whom the letters were written; there is no certainty that both letters were written to the same people. Cf. Green, *op. cit.*, pp. 14–23.

The relationship with Jude is puzzling. 2 Peter 2 is so close to the Letter of Jude that nearly all scholars are agreed that one writer borrowed from the other. The probability is that Jude is the original, though there can be no certainty. But would an apostle have utilized another, lesser, man's letter? The answer is that he might have done, for all we know to the contrary; perhaps Jude's letter was widely used as a tract attacking a certain heresy, and Peter, when obliged to counter similar false teachings, found it convenient to re-echo, embody or adapt many of Jude's arguments.

The nature of the heresy, it has been argued, demands a second century date. The false teachers scoffed at any thought of the second coming of Christ; and they contended that since faith in Christ sufficed to save a man, Christians could live as profligate lives as they wished. It is true that such views had their heyday in the second century, but there is evidence that such heretical tendencies began at an earlier date (cf. 1 C. 15: 12, *e.g.*); the second element in these teachings probably began as a perversion of Paul's gospel (cf. Rom. 3: 8; 6: 1, 15). Cf. Green, *op. cit.*, pp. 25 f.

But the clearest indication of a late date, in the opinion of many, is 2 Pet. 3: 15 f., where the writer seems to know of Paul's letters as a collection, and moreover to view them as equally authoritative with OT Scripture. The available evidence suggests that Paul's letters were not brought together and circulated as a collection before *c.* A.D. 90. However, it is conceivable that the writer of these two verses was referring not to any collection of letters, but simply to all Paul's letters he himself knew of. Paul may well have written many more letters than those that were preserved in the NT. Secondly, Paul himself viewed his writings as fully authoritative; Peter may well have considered that his fellow-apostle's letters were as much God's Word as any part of the OT.

As for the patristic evidence, it cannot in the nature of the case rule out an early date for 2 Peter; arguments from silence are notoriously precarious.

These considerations by no means prove that Peter himself did write our Letter, but they serve to show that the case against apostolic authorship is not so conclusive as is often supposed. Indeed, some features of the Letter point to a relatively early date. For instance, it is noticeable that despite the mention of Paul's letters, practically no quotations from them or allusions to them occur in 1 Peter; this fact might suggest that none of Paul's writings were available to the writer, nor could he quote them from memory. Or again, the emphasis in the Letter on the imminence of the return of Christ is a frequent feature of the NT documents, but figures relatively little in second century works.

Calvin's assessment of the evidence was that the Letter was truly Peter's, 'not that he wrote it himself, but . . . one of his disciples composed by his command what the necessity of the times demanded' (J. Calvin, *The Epistle to the Hebrews and the First and Second Epistles of St. Peter*, tr. W. B. Johnston, p. 325). Some such view may appeal to many as best suiting the evidence and resolving the difficulties.

ANALYSIS

I. SALUTATION (1: 1–2)
This is a general letter, i.e. it is not addressed to any specific church or group of churches; but 3: 1 tells us that Peter had written to his readers once before, so no doubt he did have a particular church or area in mind. V. 1 may imply that the readers were Gentiles, Peter emphasizing that they had **received** (the Gk. verb *lanchanō* implies lack of any merit) **a faith as precious as ours**; under the New Covenant, Jewish birth gave a status of no special privilege (cf. Gal. 3: 28). Alternatively, he means that the faith of apostles has no more validity than that of other Christians. **Our God** seems to be a title of the Lord Jesus Christ (2). Cf. 1 Pet. 1: 2; Jude 2.

II. A CHALLENGE TO ZEAL (1: 3–15)
The message of the letter opens with a positive declaration of what God has given the Christian. Much of the phraseology of v. 3 recalls gnostic concepts and claims (for a brief account of them, cf. Green, *op. cit.*, pp. 25 f.), against which Peter puts up the basic Christian truth that **divine power**, true **knowledge** (the Gk. word *epignōsis* implies *full* knowledge), and all that stem from them, are the gifts of God, unmerited and but for His grace unattainable. It is uncertain whether **by** or 'to' (RSV) **his own glory and goodness** (or 'might'; cf. NEB) is to be understood. Either makes good sense.

5–8. In a passage very reminiscent of the teaching of James about faith (cf. Jas 2: 14–26), Peter now indicates the Christian's responsibility: God has acted, and man must cooperate. Cranfield compares Phil. 2: 12 f. It is probable that the Christian virtues Peter proceeds to list are not intended as a systematic progression, though certainly **love** is the crown of them all. The word **goodness** (the same as that rendered 'goodness' in v. 3) has here the usual sense of moral uprightness. **Godliness**, says Cranfield, 'denotes the attitude and behaviour of the man who is truly God-fearing'. All these virtues are to be possessed and fostered (see v. 8 in NEB); the words **in increasing measure** represent the verb 'abound', in Gk. a present participle, denoting constant increase. **9.** Any Christian who does not **make every effort to add to** his **faith** in these ways is described as forgetful and **nearsighted**. Peter recalls the significance of conversion (and probably baptism); **past sins** means those committed prior to conversion.

10 f. God's saving acts have future reference and relevance. Note the emphasis, once again, on God's initiative and man's response; both are essential, or the Christian may **fall** (literally, 'stumble'). Cf. Jude 24.

11 concludes this paragraph, by outlining the Christian's hope, in terms recalling Jn 3: 5. The word **kingdom** is much more common in the Gospels than elsewhere in the NT, but the concept is found throughout, as this verse testifies (cf. Ac. 20: 24 f.). It may be that the term was generally avoided outside Jewish circles, for fear that Gentiles would misinterpret it, and view Christian teaching as seditious.

12. Reminders of the truth are often salutary: cf. Jude 5. Peter has already indicated the proneness of human beings to forgetfulness (9); and he is the more concerned because of his approaching death.

13 f. The reference here is most probably to our Lord's prediction in Jn 21: 18, in which case the point of the allusion is the fact and manner of Peter's death, and not the imminence of it (which Peter could now doubtless gauge for himself). In any event, the word **soon** should perhaps be translated 'swift' (i.e. 'sudden'), as in 2: 1. Mayor and Cranfield, however, maintain that the writer is not referring to Jn 21 but to some other experience, presumably a vision. The word **body** is literally a 'tent'—a clear reminder that life is but a pilgrimage. Cf. 2 C. 5: 1–5, a passage Peter may have in mind. Death is a **departure**; the Gk. word is *exodos*, used similarly in Lk. 9: 31. Evidently the transfiguration story was in Peter's mind, as the rest of the chapter makes patent. **15.** It seems clear that Peter is alluding here to some written 'reminder' available to his readers. He may mean this Letter itself; but an attractive suggestion is that the writer means the Gospel of Mark, which early tradition tells us was the written record of much of Peter's own preaching.

III. THE CERTAINTY OF GOD'S PROMISES (1: 16–21)

Peter now moves to a consideration of the truth of the second coming; he lays a foundation for it by stressing the historical and undeniable fact of the transfiguration of our Lord. The apostolic predictions of the return of Jesus were not **stories**, i.e. 'human speculations and inventions' (Cranfield). Peter, with James and John, had had a preview of the **majesty** of Christ, on the mount of transfiguration; thus he was in a position to certify **the power and coming** (i.e., 'the coming in power'; cf. Mk 13: 26). **17. 'This is my Son, whom I love; with him I am well pleased':** The NEB is better—'This is my Son, my Beloved, on whom my favour rests'. Peter omits the additional 'listen to him!' of Mt. 17: 5, Mk 9: 7, and Lk. 9: 35.

In other respects, the wording of the heavenly saying most nearly approximates to Matthew's account of it, but there are some slight differences in the Gk. The apocryphal 'Petrine' literature chose to follow 2 Pet. 1: 17 in preference to any of the Gospels. This fact, together with the fact that 2 Peter is here independent of the Gospels, is good evidence that these verses do emanate from the apostle himself. **18**, and indeed the whole paragraph, constitutes a claim to have witnessed the transfiguration glory of Christ, a claim which can only be viewed as fraudulent unless it derives from Peter himself. **19.** The transfiguration not only gave assurance of future realities, but it also served to confirm OT predictions. Peter now draws the moral, that having such a certain hope for the future, the Christian must regard this present life as transient; he uses a new simile (cf. the metaphor in v. 13).

20 f. This passage makes it clear that certain false teachers had been guilty of misusing OT prophecy. Peter therefore stresses that just as the OT Scriptures were God-given, through the Holy Spirit, in the first place, so too their interpretation must come from God and be guided by the Holy Spirit. 1 Pet. 1: 10–12 similarly states that the OT prophets had not been independent when they wrote. The word **men** is placed in an emphatic position in the Gk. sentence, as the NEB rendering 'men they were' indicates well; the point is made that the OT, though admittedly penned by human writers, was no human production.

Much discussion has centred round the phrase 'private interpretation' (AV) in v. 20, a phrase which, isolated from its context, is capable of several meanings: it might mean that individual passages of Scripture are not to be interpreted on *their* own, but that Scripture is to be compared with Scripture; or it might mean that Scripture is not to be subjected to 'one's own interpretation', i.e. highly individualistic viewpoints. There is much truth in both of these sentiments, doubtless, but neither is what Peter says, if we consider the context: it is not to other Scriptures nor to other people that Peter would refer us, but to the Holy Spirit. Just as the biblical authors in the first place could not have written what they did but for the Holy Spirit's activity in and through them, so no reader can properly interpret the OT prophecies without the Holy Spirit's guidance. This truth might well be applied to the interpretation of any part of the Bible, but OT predictions were what Peter was specifically discussing. Thus NIV translates **by the prophet's own interpretation**.

IV. WARNING AGAINST FALSE TEACHERS (2: 1–22)

This chapter, especially the first 18 verses, is

very closely akin to the bulk of the Letter of Jude (see Introduction). The outstanding points of similarity are the denunciation and description of false teachers; the reference to Israel's rebelliousness; and the mention of fallen angels, Sodom and Gomorrah, and Balaam. It seems most probable that one of the two writers utilized the other's letter, when facing the same problem, that of the danger of heretical and vicious teachers appearing in the churches. Evidently the heresy in question was of much the same character; in vv. 2, 10–22 Peter gives us some description of the false teachers.

1. Peter indicates first that history is repeating itself; **false prophets** are a permanent danger to God's people. By **the people** he means Israel of old; cf. Dt. 13: 1–5. He re-echoes the prediction of the Lord Jesus Christ recorded in Mt. 24: 4 f., 23 f. (and cf. 2 Tim. 3: 1–9), which may explain the future tense here; the present tense in v. 13 makes it plain that the heretics were already active. Alternatively, the future tense here may imply that the present trends are bound to occur and to continue, or may give warning that the heretics already active elsewhere will soon make contact with the readers. Whatever professions the false teachers may make, in effect they are **denying the sovereign Lord who bought them**; their actions deny His work, together with His lordship and ownership. And sad to say, these men will not be altogether unsuccessful (2). **3.** One of their methods is now exposed; their **stories . . . made up** or 'sheer fabrications' (NEB), stand in sharp contrast to the Gospel truths, which apparently they perversely described as 'clearly invented stories' (to judge by 1: 16).

4–9. Like Jude (vv. 5–7), Peter uses three well-known examples of God's punishment of the wicked and presumptuous. First he recalls the **angels** who **sinned**, probably an allusion to Gen. 6: 2 (see the commentary on Jude 6). They were **sent . . . to hell** (literally, Tartarus, the Gk. name for the very lowest hell); **dungeons** represents the better MS reading, preferable to the 'chains' of the AV. Another warning example, that of **Sodom and Gomorrah** (6), is likewise utilized by Jude as well; but where Jude draws attention to the Israelites who disbelieved God in wilderness days, Peter makes use of another OT incident, the **flood**, drawn from Gen. 6–9. Evidently this was one of Peter's favourite OT passages (cf. 1 Pet. 3: 20). The description of **Noah** as **a preacher of righteousness** is derived from current Jewish thought (cf. Josephus, *Ant.* I. iii. 1; Jubilees 7: 20–39); the concept is in turn taken from Gen. 6: 9. Peter agrees fully with Jude about the punishment of the lawless and wicked, but he shows a further concern, not mentioned by Jude: he stresses the goodness of God in rescuing His own. While **the ancient world** per-

ished, God **protected Noah**; while **Sodom and Gomorrah** were **condemned, he rescued Lot, a righteous man** (who is not mentioned by Jude).

9. The moral of the preceding verses is pointed (**if . . . if . . . if . . . if this is so**). It is not clear whether in this verse Peter means **punishment** in this life or in the intermediate state (cf. Lk. 16: 19–31); but the latter is more likely, since Peter mentions **the day of judgment** rather than 'the day of their death' or some similar phrase.

10–22. In this passage the writer reverts to a consideration of the false teachers and a description of them. Two of their characteristics, in particular, link up with the OT examples he has just recalled; they are lustful and presumptuous. They **despise authority** in general, and that of Christ in particular (cf. v. 1); Jude 8 accuses such men of despising angelic authority, and Peter now proceeds to the same thought.

11. By contrast, angelic beings do not use arrogant language against **such beings**. This, in context, can only mean the heretics; but this verse epitomizes Jude 9, where it is explicitly stated that Michael the archangel did not revile Satan. Several commentators conclude, therefore, that the writer here has been over-concise, and really means that fallen angels (rather than the heretics) were not reviled. More probably, however, Peter has extended Jude's thought, and maintains that angels do not arrogantly address any of their opponents, whether angelic or human.

12. The outspoken denunciation of the heretical teachers beginning with this verse is very like Jude's. This particular verse has several verbal contacts with Jude 10 (*e.g.* the phrase **brute beasts**), but the thoughts are Peter's own. He is not discussing the time or manner of the death of the heretics when he says that **like beasts they too will perish**; his point is that just as **animals** are **born only to be caught and destroyed**, those who wilfully act like them will suffer the same natural and predictable fate.

13. The statement that the false teachers will one day find themselves **paid back with harm for the harm they have done** must mean that they will receive the same treatment from others that they have meted out to others. Cranfield suggests that the phrase might be rendered 'being cheated of the profits of their wrongdoing'; Balaam (cf. v. 15), at any rate, certainly failed to get his expected profits, perishing miserably (cf. Num. 24: 11; 31: 8). But the heretics, without a glance at the future, in the meantime delight to carouse **in broad daylight**—shamelessly turning the Christian fellowship meals into riotous drinking-parties. The word **pleasures** represents the Gk. *apatais* (literally 'lusts' or 'deceits'), and is very probably a play on words by Peter, recalling Jude's mention of *agapais*, 'love feasts' (cf. Jude 12), although his readers can scarcely have appreciated this. Numerous Gk. MSS of 2 Peter, however, read *agapais* (see NIVmg), no doubt influenced by Jude's use of the word.

14. Nor are the evil men's vices those of the table only. Sexual licence was another hallmark of their characters, as Peter declares in a phrase reminiscent of our Lord's own words recorded in Mt. 5: 28. Moreover, they are **experts in greed**; here is a striking metaphor from the gymnasium, difficult to reproduce in English, although NEB's 'past masters' gets near it. The final exclamation, **accursed brood!**, reproduces (both in Greek and English) a Semitic turn of phrase, literally 'children of cursing', and the word 'children' gives a wrong implication in English; the sense is simply, 'they are accursed', as Barclay renders it. The following verse makes it clear that the deceivers, not those duped by them, are thus described.

15 f. Peter again turns to the OT for an example, **Balaam**; see the commentary on Jude 11. Peter has selected one of three examples used by Jude, but has expanded it considerably. It is the love of gain exhibited by the heretics that Peter was most keenly aware of. The mention of the **donkey . . . without speech** is devastatingly sarcastic: not only are the false teachers on a level with brute beasts, but their own prototype had stooped so low as to be rebuked by one!

17. Cf. Jude 12 f. These men have no value, no goal, and no future.

18. Worst of all, they are not content with indulging their own **lustful desires**; they delight in seducing new converts into similar behaviour. Sexual immorality was rife in much of the world of Peter's time, and it frequently took considerable time and patience to inculcate Christian ethics in those young in the faith. To such young, unstable Christians the heretical teachers applied themselves assiduously, with foolish **boastful words** and specious promises of **freedom**.

19. This verse recalls Paul's words in Rom. 6: 16 and Gal. 5: 1, 13; an appreciation of what Christian freedom really consists of, is vital.

20–22. V. 20 recalls Mt. 12: 43 ff. It is disputed whether this final section of the chapter refers to the false teachers themselves or to those misled by them. The former view seems preferable; if so, the passage indicates that the heretics had been orthodox Christians in the first place. The strict warning implicit in these verses is thus reminiscent of several passages in Hebrews (especially 6: 4–8; 10: 26–31). **22.** Peter concludes his denunciation by remarking that the evil men 'exemplify the truth of the proverb' (Mayor) of the dog (cf. Prov. 26: 11)

and of the sow (a proverb to be found in the ancient Story of Ahikar, 8:18).

V. GOD'S FUTURE PLANS (3: 1–10)

Peter again points out that what he is saying is nothing new, but is simply a **reminder** of what the readers had been told long before; v. 1 is therefore resumptive of 1: 12 f. He is stimulating those readers to **wholesome thinking**, *i.e.* those who had not been led astray by the heretical teachings. It is natural to take the statement that this is his **second letter** as alluding to 1 Peter; this is possible, but it is more probable that Peter had written a letter to the recipients of 2 Peter of which we know nothing. Since our letter does not name his readers, there can be no certainty.

2 f. Peter insists that the doctrine of the second advent has the strongest possible support, from **prophets, apostles** and **our Lord** Jesus Himself. The phrase **your apostles** is unique in the NT (the nearest parallel is in Rom. 11: 13); Peter may well mean that his readers could and should lay claim to the apostles and their doctrines, while disowning the pseudo-Christians and their pernicious teachings. Jude too mentions the apostles in his parallel passage (Jude 17 f., *q.v.*); Peter, however, mentions prophets as well. He has spoken of them already (1: 19–21), of course, and besides, he is making the valid point that all the testimony of Scripture (*i.e.* OT Scripture) supports the orthodox Christian views. **3.** The apostolic predictions of God's purposes included the statement that **scoffers** would arise. Jude 18 mentions this, and Peter expands the thought, clarifying the actual claims of these mockers. Jesus and the early church taught the imminence of the second coming; as time passed, there were evidently some who first doubted and then scoffed at the whole idea. But it was no embarrassment to the orthodox, who (like Peter in this chapter) continued firmly to maintain its imminence (or rather its suddenness). The scoffers argued—perhaps using Ec. 1: 1–11 as scriptural support—that all things had always continued unchanged on earth, and might be expected to remain unchanging. Numerous commentators have taken the mention of **our fathers** to refer to the first generation of Christians; this interpretation would make good sense (and incidentally rule out an early date for the letter), but 'fathers' without further description is more naturally applied to the patriarchs. This latter interpretation makes equally good sense, and has the support of the allusions which immediately follow, allusions not to events of the life of Christ, but to Genesis, the creation and the flood stories.

5. Peter's first reply to the scoffers is that the world we live in has not always existed, and has not proved consistently stable. In the Gk., **God's word** is in emphatic position; God's spoken word alone had sufficed to change the whole shape of the universe (cf. Gen. 1), and logically His promise for the future must be equally effective and capable of fulfilment. The world had been created **out of water**, certainly, but it is not absolutely clear what Peter meant by **with water**. It was not an uncommon view in the ancient world that water was the first principle of the material world; but there is no need to suppose that Peter's remark has other than a biblical basis. Possibly he is recalling Ps. 24: 1 f., but the Psalmist's language is highly pictorial; more probably he has Gen. 1 still in mind, as indicating that the very dividing of the waters produced the dry land (cf. Gen. 1: 6–10).

7. Flood had once proved disastrous to mankind; **fire**, says Peter, is the world's fate in store. This concept was widely held in Jewish (and indeed some Greek) circles at the time, but this is the only NT passage to express it. OT passages such as Jl 2: 30; Zeph. 3: 8, and Mal. 4: 1 lie behind the concept, and in view of their pictorial character, one wonders whether Peter is to be taken literally here. Hell is frequently depicted in terms of fire (cf. Mt. 25: 41; Mk 9: 43; Rev. 20: 9 f.); in this respect the imagery may derive from the use of the name Gehenna, properly applied to a valley just outside Jerusalem associated with idolatrous sacrifices by fire. Cf. also Mt. 13: 40–42; Jn 15: 6. Whether or not Peter is to be taken literally, his two chief points are plain, that the world is transient and that the wicked await judgment and punishment.

8 ff. Peter proceeds to meet the possible objection, why the delay? He first cites Ps. 90: 4, paraphrasing and expanding it; it is not simply that God counts a thousand years as practically nothing, but further, that God does not view time by human standards at all. He is eternal; 'the eternal order is other than that of time' (A. McNab). So there is no 'delay' by divine standards; but if there is one to the human mind, then it has a clear purpose—and Peter suddenly makes a frontal attack on the scoffers, **The Lord . . . is patient with you** (not 'us', as the Received Text [see article 'Text and Canon'] and the AV read). This constitutes the third argument against those who mock; God is graciously giving rebellious men time for **repentance**. Finally, Peter reiterates his firm conviction, his confident certainty, that **the day of the Lord will come**; the emphasis is on its sudden and unexpected arrival rather than its imminence. The facts and imagery of v. 10 are drawn from various earlier passages of Scripture, to be found in both Testaments. By **the elements** he may mean the heavenly bodies (so RVmg), but more probably the ma-

terial elements, or the elemental substances, of this world. The loud noise will be the sound of fire; alternatively, the phrase may simply mean 'with great suddenness'. Everything on earth **will be laid bare** (Gk. *katakaēsetai*): probably a better text than NIVmg 'be burned up'. The verb (Gk. *heurethēsetai*) would normally mean 'will be found', however, and the possibility exists that a negative has dropped out of the text. To insert a negative would give excellent sense (**everything** upon earth 'will not be found', *i.e.* will disappear) and has some slight textual support. Alternatively, the variety of readings might be explained if they are replacements for an original *heuthēsetai* ('will be burned') from the rare verb *heuō*, attested in poetry with the meaning 'singe' and cognate with Lat. *urō* ('burn').

VI. PRACTICAL LESSONS AND CONCLUSION (3: 11–18)

Peter now draws his conclusions; he is not giving a blueprint as to the manner in which God will fulfil His purposes, but rather laying stress on the certainty that He will do so, on the suddenness with which He will act, and on the fact that total destruction awaits everything useless and godless. Biblical predictions consistently demand not only our belief but more particularly behaviour compatible with our creed. So Peter demands **holy and godly lives** from all Christians, who should be expectantly **looking forward** to the day when God will act, and 'waiting eagerly' (cf. NIVmg) for Him to do so. But the Gk. word Peter uses, *speudō*, should really be rendered **speeding**, in the way that both NIV and NEB understand it. (The AVmg is to be followed; AV text wrongly inserts the word 'unto', giving quite a different sense, and one which Peter never intended.) This is a striking suggestion, implying that men can in some way speed up God's plans, and it does not commend itself to all commentators; nevertheless it may well be correct, and it would link up well with v. 9: since God delays to give men time to repent, their speedy obedience will shorte the interval prior to **the day of God**. **13.** The Gk. verb here translated **looking forward** to (used three times in vv. 12–14) means 'to expect', 'to look out for'. The Christian's hopes and expectations are not, however, centred on the threat of the world's fate, but on God's **promise** of **a new heaven and a new earth** (cf. Isa. 65: 17; 66: 22; Rom. 8: 21; Rev. 21: 1). **14.** In view of the absolutely righteous character of the universe-to-be, the Christian's present duty is clear. Peter is here particularly concerned with the Christian's behaviour within the local church: all must be harmonious (**at peace**), but at the same time any spot or blemish, in the shape of the pseudo-Christians (cf. 2: 13), must be eradicated. Truth and grace must be preserved within the church in equal measure. See too the commentary on Jude 24.

15 f. The first part of v. 15 is very concise, and presents at first sight an equation, **patience=salvation**: the sense is that God's forbearance is intended as an opportunity for men to be saved. This brief sentence epitomizes Peter's statement in v. 9.

In mentioning **Paul**, Peter is presumably not thinking merely of his fellow-apostle's similar doctrine of the purpose of God's forbearance (cf. Rom. 2: 4, for instance), but of all he had said about the second coming. Such a statement by Peter is perhaps evidence that Paul wrote far more letters than were preserved for posterity in the NT. Paul himself was aware that his teaching about justification by faith could be misrepresented and abused. Since he argued that good works could not save anyone, men so minded were able to twist this doctrine to mean that good works did not matter at all. Paul emphasized several times (cf. Rom. 6: 1, 15; Gal. 5: 13) that such a view was totally improper, and a very caricature of his own doctrines. By his reference to Paul, Peter is able to claim yet further support for the views he has expressed, and to stress once again, briefly, the vital importance of a correct interpretation of Scripture (cf. 1: 20).

17 f. Peter concludes the letter with a final word of warning, a final word of exhortation, and a brief doxology. His characterization of the heretics as **lawless** shows clearly the antinomian nature of the false teaching: *i.e.* those who held it viewed themselves as under no obligation whatever to any laws, maintaining, indeed, that no laws applied to them. The true Christian, by contrast, is to **grow** (literally,

'increase') **in the grace and knowledge of our Lord**; thus Peter recalls his opening thought (cf. 1: 5-7) that the Christian life cannot be static. The only way to be sure of avoiding **the error of lawless men** is to tread single-mindedly the path of divine and Christ-like virtues.

The word **forever** is literally 'the day of eternity' (so RSV), a Hebrew or Aramaic turn of speech for 'the eternal day', which would retain the vividness of the original; but it is difficult to improve on the simplicity of the NIV: **'To him be glory both now and forever! Amen'**.

BIBLIOGRAPHY

Commentaries

BAUCKHAM, R. J., *2 Peter and Jude*. World Biblical Commentary (Waco, 1983).

BIGG, C., *St. Peter and St. Jude* [on the Greek text]. *ICC* (Edinburgh, 1902).

CRANFIELD, C. E. B., *I and II Peter and Jude*. TC (London, 1960).

GREEN, M., *2 Peter and Jude*. TNTC (London, 1968).

JAMES, M. R., *2 Peter and Jude* [on the Greek text]. *CGT* (London, 1912).

KELLY, J. N. D., *The Epistles of Peter and of Jude*. BNTC (London, 1969).

KELLY, W., *The Epistles of Peter* (London, 1923).

MAYOR, J. B., *The Epistle of Jude and the Second Epistle of Peter* [on the Greek text] (London, 1907).

REICKE, B., *The Epistles of James, Peter and Jude*. AB (Garden City, N. Y., 1964).

WEISIGER, C. N., *The Epistles of Peter* (Grand Rapids, 1962).

For a thorough defence of the apostolic authorship.

GREEN, E. M. B., *2 Peter Reconsidered* (London, 1961).

THE LETTERS OF JOHN

R. W. ORR

This commentary proceeds upon the belief, once universally held, that these letters are the work of the Apostle John, and that the Fourth Gospel and the Revelation are from the same writer. There is no definite claim within the writings that this is so: the view is based upon the ancient testimony of the Church, upon certain internal indications, and the use in the writings of a common stock of ideas, vocabulary and style, and upon biographical data concerning John drawn from Scripture and tradition, providing a reasonable framework, as they do, for such activity.

Many scholars draw a different conclusion from the evidence, attributing the work, at least in part, to a 'Johannine school'. The different views, and the evidence upon which they are based, are presented by Dr. Donald Guthrie in his *New Testament Introduction* (Tyndale Press, 1962).

A conjectural outline may be made of the last third of the life of the Apostle John, into which the Johannine literature may be fitted. At the latest, he cannot have continued to make his home in Jerusalem much longer than the commencement in A.D. 66 of the Jewish War which ended in the destruction of Jerusalem in the year 70. Before that event, James the Lord's brother and Peter—who together with John had formed the leadership of the early disciples (Gal. 2: 9)—had both met death in martyrdom, as also Paul, and John was left alone.

At that time, the church in Ephesus, founded by Paul, was being troubled with teachers bringing a Jewish form of that arid speculation and wrangling, which was beginning to make false claim to the name of *gnōsis* (that is *knowledge*, I Tim. 6: 20). To meet that emergency, Paul had put that church under a mild martial law, so to speak, with Timothy in authority over the local elders (I Tim. I: 3; 4: 11; 5: 17–22). But with Paul now dead, and Asia fast becoming the focus of two dangerous movements (Emperor-worship and gnosticism) which in fact came near to strangling the life of the Church in the next century, John took up residence in Ephesus. John would at that time be in his mid- or late sixties, and for close on thirty years, until his death about the end of the century, Ephesus remained his home. It was a convenient centre for pastoral supervision of the province, including the well-known seven churches of the Revelation. Roads joined them all, and from a point twenty miles up the hill road from Ephesus, a compass of eighty miles would take in all seven, and the island of Patmos as well.

This framework provides a setting for the whole body of John's writings, which the historian Eusebius (A.D. 265–340), following Irenaeus (c. 140–202), affirms were composed in Ephesus. The Revelation does not concern us here. The Fourth Gospel, its apparent simplicity inwrought like figured damask with subtle symmetries and patterns, is manifestly a growth of many years of meditation and teaching. The Letters draw upon the same stock of material, and there are fairly strong indications of the priority in time of the Gospel.

I JOHN

It may well be that at the time of the publication of the Fourth Gospel in written form, the First Letter was composed—though only for the churches of Asia—as an epilogue or covering pastoral letter, pointing out the practical application of the Gospel to their lives and in their circumstances. This does not rule out the possibility of a crisis in the Asian churches at that time, perhaps linked with the publication of the Gospel, determining to a great extent the contents and tone of the Letter.

C. H. Dodd (*The Johannine Epistles*, MNT, 1946) suggests that the First Letter was called forth by the crisis referred to in I Jn 2: 19 'They went out from us'. 'They' were men of influence in the churches of Asia, with prophetic and teaching ability, and had been attempting to introduce an 'enlightened' and 'advanced' doctrine of the kind which came to be known as *gnostic*. The Church, however, with her intuitive sense of what belonged and what could not belong to the gospel which she had received, had rejected the new teaching, and its prophets had no option but to leave the fellowship of the churches.

The Gnostic's pride was in his knowledge (the root *gnō-* is the parent, or at least a relative, of our English *know* and of the Scots *ken*). Ideas were the great thing, rather than historic facts upon which faith is built. The concrete actualities of the Incarnation and the Resurrection were laughed out of court as childish literalism, and the man who had been initiated knew the spiritual meaning of these 'myths'—an attitude which has prominent comtemporary exponents. This 'knowledge' was not for all, but for the select few who had been initiated. It set them in a special class far above common humanity, and emancipated them from the morality which governed the unenlightened. Concerning certain of their sects it is reported, 'They do whatever they please, as persons free, for they allege that they are saved by grace'; and again, 'The law, they say, is not written for kings' (quoted in Law, *Tests of Life*, p. 226). One leading idea was that matter is evil, and is not the creation of God. And so it was unthinkable that the Word should become flesh, and the Incarnation was denied. Cerinthus, a heretical teacher in Asia at that period, taught that 'the Christ' came upon the man Jesus at his baptism, and left him before his crucifixion. All these denials of the Gospel are firmly dealt with in the First Letter.

So also are the false claims to spirituality which those teachers made. It is worse than idle to say, as those teachers were saying, '*We are in the light*', unless sin is being confessed and put away; the claim '*We know God*' is utterly incredible unless the heart is resolutely set to obey God's commandments. John takes the Christian vocabulary which is being abused by those false teachers, 'disinfects' it, fills it with its true Christian content, and restores it to Christian use.

Such appears to have been the occasion which called forth the encyclical which we know as the First Letter, and sent it round the churches of the province of Asia.

But it has permanent value, because the crisis of that hour is always with us. Like those originally addressed, most of us are not new to Christianity, but generations of Christian profession lie behind us, with all the confusion that is found when membership of the church may be motivated by social custom rather than conviction. The clean strong winds of the Letter separate chaff from wheat, or at least show us the lines along which one may test himself, may learn from his own behaviour whether or not he is a true Christian. This very practical letter is ours today as 'the condensed moral and practical application of the Gospel' (Westcott, *The Epistles of St. John*, p. xxx). 'The Gospel gives us the theology of the Christ; the Epistle, the ethics of the Christian' (Plummer, *CGT*, p. 36).

ANALYSIS

Additional Note on Analysis:
'Probably few commentators have satisfied themselves with their own analysis of this Epistle; still fewer have satisfied other people' (A. Plummer in *CGT*).

Although there is very clear linkage between the *sections* of each part—the leading idea of one section being found in the closing words of the previous section—there is no such linkage between the different *parts*; the only exception being in the Epilogue. The connecting words are: *commands* 2: 4 and *command* 2: 7; *born of him* 2: 29 and *children of God* 3: 1; *by the Spirit* 3: 24 and *test the spirits* 4: 1; *faith* 5: 4 and *testify* 5: 7. On the literary structure, see note on *introversion* in section VI. (p. 616)

I. PROLOGUE (1: 1–4)

Does the phrase the **Word of life** refer to *the personal Logos*, as in the prologue to the Gospel (Jn 1: 1), or is it used in the sense of *the life-giving gospel* as in Phil. 2: 16 ('holding fast the word of life')? The Apostle goes on to discuss not the person of Christ but the quality of life manifested in Him and (through the indwelling of His Spirit) in His people. For this reason the second interpretation is to be preferred. 'If the Gospel speaks of the incarnation of the Eternal Word, the Epistle speaks of the manifestation of the Eternal Life' (Bruce p. 37). On the other hand Alford is emphatic that the personal Word is meant, and points justly to the difficulty of understanding the words **we touched with our hands** in the other sense.

The other word of ambiguous meaning is **from the beginning**. Does it bear the same sense as in the Gospel: 'In the beginning was the Word' (Jn 1: 1)? Stott says Yes: 'here too the beginning of all things is meant' (p. 59); even though he has denied, as we have done, identity of meaning in the *logos* of Jn 1: 1 and 1 Jn 1: 1. But the same phrase in 2: 7, virtually repeated in 2: 24, seems to fix the meaning ('the command . . . which you have had from the beginning', that is, what Christians have always held *ever since Jesus came among men*). The whole tenor of the Letter supports this. The writer is concerned to show that although the false teachers are bringing in new teaching, the apostolic doctrine has never changed. It consists of the testimony of those who were witnesses of the salvation events, and in the very nature of things its truth is unchanging. The apostolic *beginning* is 'from John's baptism' (Mk. 1: 1; Ac. 1: 22).

There are therefore four possible ways to understand the prologue. In brief: (i) Our apostolic witness concerns the Lord Jesus, that eternal One who 'was in the beginning with God', and yet is truly man; that 'Word' concerning whom we have written that 'in him was life'. (ii) Proclaiming as we do Jesus as the eternal Word, we bring you the life-giving gospel. (iii) We who have companied with the Lord Jesus from the beginning proclaim to you that He is the eternal Word of God, in whom is life. (iv) It is out of first-hand experience as those who have been with the Lord Jesus from the beginning that we give our apostolic testimony to the life-giving gospel. All of these interpretations are possible, and all are gloriously true, but the last suits best the purpose of the Letter. The following is offered as an interpretation of the prologue.

The original gospel: the words which we (the apostles of Christ) heard, the deeds which we ourselves witnessed. We observed it all; with our hands we experienced its reality. The Life—that Eternal Life which abode with the Father—was manifested to us; we bear our witness only to what we ourselves have seen. It is the authentic gospel; we saw it and heard it, and now we are announcing it to you, so that you may share our experience. Nor is it only fellowship with ourselves to which we are calling you, but fellowship with the Father and with His Son, Jesus Christ. We are writing now to you so that by your fellowship our joy may be completed.

There are many religions based on the ideas and visions of the founder. By contrast the basis of the gospel is historical, the testimony of a number of competent and credible witnesses amenable to the universal rules of evidence.

1. That which (neuter, not the masculine *Him who*): i.e. *we proclaim the things concerning our Lord's pre-existence, and* the things *which we ascertained by actual hearing, seeing and touch concerning Him*. **with our** own **eyes . . .** with **our** own **hands:** these expressions are quite emphatic, and no simple reader would seek another meaning. Those who believe that the writer was not the apostle but a later writer of the Johannine school regard the claim of first-hand observation as being made for the Church as a whole, the apostles being the eyes, ears and hands of the Church. **have heard . . . have seen:** Perfect tense—the words and deeds of Jesus, though witnessed these many years ago are still present with the writer. The tense now changes to aorist for **have looked at and . . . touched**. The change was marked in RV by omitting *have* in the second pair, but is now disguised, as in AV. The significance is that the *looking* and *touching* are not general, but refer to the occasion of the Resurrection when, in John's account, they *looked* intently to see the significance of the empty gravecloths (Jn 20: 6), the two angels (20: 12), and Jesus Himself standing (20: 14). The unusual word *touch* (with only two other NT uses) is the Lord's word in resurrection, 'Touch me and see' (Lk. 24: 39). Thus the claim to have tested the objective reality of the Incarnation extends to experience of the Risen Lord also. This is important as perhaps the only allusion to the Resurrection in the Letter. (But see also on 4: 2 f.)

2. the life appeared: In the Fourth Gospel, alluded to in the prologue as the background of the Letter, the divine life was manifest in the person of Jesus; the Letter deals with the same divine life, in the believer. If the life—eternal life—is truly present, it also will come into manifestation; and through the Incarnation, eternal life has already been manifested in understandable human terms. **the eternal life . . . was with** (pros) **the Father** (as in Jn 1: 1 2): i.e. in relation with: eternal life, wherever found, is of the nature of that fellowship.

3. We proclaim to you what we have seen and heard: Not in the Letter but in the Gospel. The habitual sense of the present tense may be understood here: we make it our business to proclaim. Readers are thus informed that this letter is supplementary to the basic witness of the Gospel. In **you also** no contrast is intended between the present readers and others, but between the apostle and all those he addresses. His aim as an evangelist is to bring his hearers into **fellowship with us**, that is, the **fellowship** which we enjoy **with the Father and with his Son**. The phrase may be taken as typical of the constantly recurring echoes of the Fourth Gospel in this letter. In the paschal discourse the Lord had declared, 'I am the way, and the truth, and the life' (Jn 14: 6). Replying to the third question from the disciples, the Lord expanded the third term of that great saying, explaining the inwardness of spiritual life as a divine-human fellowship. 'If a man love me, he will keep my word, and my Father will love him, and we will come to him and make our home with him' (Jn 14: 23). Then follows, in ch. 15, the parable of the True Vine, an illustrated expansion of the saying 'I am . . . the life'. This is a large part of the background of the Letter. In the title God's **Son, Jesus Christ** another important matter finds expression in the prologue: that the human Jesus is one and the same as the Son of God, the Christ.

4. Having completed his brief summary of the Fourth Gospel as the basis for the Letter, the apostle now declares, like another John, that the consummation of fellowship in Christ of his readers will leave him more than contented (Jn 3: 29). More than that, in language drawn from the parable of the True Vine, he will share in the very **joy** of God. 'These things I have spoken to you, that my joy may be in you, and that your joy may be full'. Joy, the fruit of abiding in Christ second only to love (Jn 15: 11; Gal. 5: 22), becomes full or **com-** plete when the life of fellowship reaches practical and conscious realization: fruit both abundant and abiding. Allusions to the Fourth Gospel recur constantly in the Letter; the reader will find study of the parallels most instructive.

II. GOD IS LIGHT (1: 5–2: 6)

The theological affirmation **God is light** was **heard from him**, from Christ in the flesh. Yet we search the gospel records in vain for these words. It can however be taken as an epigrammatic summary of the teaching of our Lord on the inner relations of the Godhead, showing the fulness of fellowship between the Persons of the Trinity. Such teaching is abundantly found in the gospels (Mt. 11: 27; cf. Lk. 10: 22); and especially in the fourth gospel; e.g. 'The Son can do nothing by himself; he can do only what he sees his Father doing' (Jn 5: 19). A trinitarian picture of God as light may be completed with the help of 1 C. 2: 10, 'The Spirit searches all things, even the deep things of God'. Within the being of God **is no darkness at all**. See note on 'God is love' (4: 8).

Light is the frequent accompaniment of God's presence. The Shekinah, the manifestation of God's presence, was seen as a blaze of glory; and when the incarnate Word dwelt among men, there was a glory as of the one and only Son (Exod. 40: 34; Jn 1: 14). The word carries a rich complex of meaning. Light is the medium of perception, and therefore of truth and of revelation (Ps. 43: 3). Light is outgoing and self-communicating, and so light is the medium of fellowship and of love. Supremely it is **he who is in the light**, the Father and the Son in eternal, loving fellowship (Jn 1: 2, 18). The 'light of life' is the salvation which Christ brings (Jn 8: 12). And light, which cannot co-exist with or yield to darkness, is the symbol of ultimate victory (Jn 1: 5). Judgment consists of 'bringing to light what is hidden in darkness' (1 C. 4: 5), whether good or evil (Mt. 10: 26). In contrast, **darkness** represents the realm of Satan, with ignorance, enmity, guilt, and the nether gloom in which the wicked await the day of judgment (Jn 3: 19). Of these meanings, it is chiefly **fellowship** which is in view here, with its dark contrast of enmity, opposition and separation. In respect of God, light will signify source rather than emanation of rays; but even so, radiance is inseparable from its source, giving aptness to the figure in its Christological relation (Heb. 1: 3). With Isa. 33: 14 f. as background and Heb. 12: 29 as a parallel, the **light** takes on the character of the Devouring Fire, much in the sense of J. S. Stewart's words 'It is possible to sing, "Jesus the very thought of Thee . . ." without having once asked ourselves if there are not things in our life and character that that holy Presence, if it once came anywhere near us, would burn to shreds' (*The Gates of New Life*, 1937, p. 25). The foundation of true ethics is in the knowledge of the character of the God to whom we are answerable.

6. The exhortation proceeds upon this revelation of God's character to expose false claims to spirituality, probably made brazenly by the heretical teachers of 2: 19, but in some degree making their appeal to all Christians. **If we claim** [direct speech with quotation marks is used in 2: 4 and 4: 20. Some such arrangement might helpfully be extended to cover all of the supposed watchwords of the heretics—1: 6, 8, 10; 2: 4, 6, 9; 4: 20—though 2: 6, 9 are in indirect speech in Greek.] **to have fellowship with him:** 'Fellowship' being the sharing of the divine life and communion of the Father and the Son (Jn 14: 23; 1 Jn 1: 3), and 'him' being here equivalent to 'God'. ['He', etc. is frequently used in the Letter by way of emphatic reference to Christ as The Person (*e.g.* 1: 5; 2: 8, 12; 4: 17, 21), but it is sometimes ambiguous whether God or Christ is meant (*e.g.* 2: 13, 25, 27; 3: 19, 24; 4: 13). This is strong testimony to John's belief in the unity of Father and Son; statements made of the one can often be used interchangeably of the other.] **yet walk in the darkness:** Our actual conduct being such that out of shame and fear we conceal our deeds, and are not living in frank and loving fellowship with fellow Christians —then we are both speaking and acting out falsehood; 'our words and our lives are a lie' (NEB).

7. The result of **walk**ing **in the light** is not stated, as one might expect from the logical progress of the sentence, to be that we have fellowship with God, but (in the manner of the Letter, the right foot, so to speak, is not simply brought level with the left, but is placed clear ahead) our fellowship with God finds expression in **fellowship with one another** which has already (1: 3) been seen to be essentially the same things as fellowship with God. **and the blood of Jesus:** The life of the Lord's Servant given up in death as an offering for sin (Isa. 53: 10). **his Son:** Jesus who died on the cross was God's Son even at that time (despite Cerinthus: see Introduction). **purifies us:** A benefit in which John includes himself. This continually repeated cleansing is distinguished in Jn 13: 10 from the initial complete 'bath' of regeneration. (See Mt. 11: 28 f., 'the two rests'; Mt. 18: 22–35, 'the two debts' for similar distinction between the abiding reality and its practical daily realization.) Yet the repeated cleansings are confirmation that the initial bath was received, as well as being its practical fulfilment. The man who feels no need to come for the 'cleansing' has never had the 'bath', and has no part in Christ. **from all sin:** From sin of every kind.

8. If we claim to be without sin: This is the second false claim (see on 1: 6): That the root principle of sin has been eradicated from our heart—another claim of the gnostic heretics—we are not simply mistaken, but **we deceive ourselves** and have only ourselves to blame for having gone astray: an even worse situation than the failure in 1: 6. Westcott, however, teaches that the false plea of v.8 is that sin does not cleave to him who commits it; it is a mere accident, and not a continuous principle.

9. If we confess: Bring into the light of God, with what that may involve in terms of fellowship with one another. **our sins:** The actual offences arising from sin the principle. **he is faithful and just and will forgive:** The RV rendering 'faithful and righteous to forgive' is perhaps better, as what is in question is not God's character, but the character of the action. God forgives, and that consistently with His own character and in righteousness (Rom. 3: 21–26).

10. If we claim we have not sinned (see on 1: 6) our course in deceit is complete; we deny the whole testimony of God's word, and the need for His redemptive activity.

2: 1. The teaching of 1: 7–10 might be open to perverse misinterpretation: 'I may as well commit sin since everyone else does. God will forgive me; what else is He for?' Hence the caution that the writer's purpose is **so that you will not sin. But if anybody does sin:** Both verbs are aorists: acts of sin rather than a sinful course of life are in view. **we have:** Logic demands 'he has', but the apostle breaks the grammatical concord to include himself in the gracious provision. **one who speaks . . . in our defense.** a good interpretation of the Gk *paraklētos*, a title of the Holy Spirit (and by implication in Jn 14: 16 of Jesus) found only here and in Jn 14-16. 'Comforter', 'Helper', and 'Advocate' rightly indicate the breadth of the spectrum of meaning. The Holy Spirit is the Counsellor, instructed by the Father and the Son, within our hearts; here the Lord Jesus is our Counsellor, representing our interests and pleading our cause before God. But the phrase is rather **to the Father**—with (*pros*, see on 1: 2) the One who sustains a relation of intimacy with our Counsellor and of grace toward us. This present ministry of the Lord Jesus is illustrated in Lk. 22: 31 f. and Jn 17; see also Rom. 8: 26 f., 34 for the intercession of the two Counsellors. Though our restoration depends upon our confession (1: 9), the ministry of the Counsellor does not.

2. Not only does He plead our cause: He is in Himself, by virtue of his life offered up in death (1: 7) **the atoning sacrifice for our sins**, which restores fellowship (see on 1: 7). The death of Christ, in a manner which was prefigured by the levitical sin offering (Lev. 4), breaks down the barrier which sin has erected between God and man. **the sins of** is not expressed, but is perhaps implied. **for . . . the whole world:** Life for the world through individual appropriation of Christ in His death is taught in Jn 6: 51. Cf. Mk 10: 45; Jn 1: 29; 3: 16; 4: 42; 11: 51 f. God loves the whole world, and Christ died for its sake; in this lies the balance to the concentration in the Letter upon love within the boundaries of the Christian brotherhood (3: 16; 5: 1). Love learnt within the boundaries will be exercised outside; in this way the love proves to be divine (Mt. 5: 44–48). The atonement is the righteous basis for God's present forbearance in respect of a rebellious world (cf. Rom. 3: 25); and in any case, all those who are about to be called are at present in 'the world' (Eph. 2: 3).

3. And by this we know: A characteristic phrase of the Letter (2: 3, 5, 29; 3: 19, 24; 4: 2, 6, 13; 5: 2) marking the intention of offering a series of tests by which the reader may discover whether or not he has eternal life (5: 13). (When the object is personal (as in 3: 19, 24), the appropriate translation is **recognize**.) The flow of the argument would call for the statement that the proof of knowing God is in not sinning; John characteristically advances beyond that to the positive **obey his commands**. The high-sounding 'fellowship with God' (1:6) has down-to-earth expression in obedience, and that to actual commandment.

4. See on 1: 6. **5.** It is difficult to decide between **God's love**, and *love for God* (RSV) as translation of the Gk. *love of God*; but perhaps a stronger case can be made for RSV here. The practical realization ('perfection', as our writer would say) of love for God is not found in transports of mystical adoration, but in obedience, in walking **as Jesus did**.

III. THE COMMAND (2: 7–17)

This new section is prepared for in 2: 3, where the matter of 'not sinning' is advanced to its positive aspect of 'obeying his commands'. In this section, the view of 'his commands' is narrowed to the supreme command which includes all others, that of love (Mt. 22: 36–40; Rom. 13: 8 ff.): love for our brother (7–11) and love for the Father (15–17). An interjected lyrical address (12–14), in terms of particular affection, celebrates the marvels of redeeming love as the basis of a call to moral earnestness. **the old command which you had from the beginning** is undoubtedly 'As I have loved you, so you must love one another' (Jn 13: 34). Recall to the original gospel, in both its doctrine of the Incarnation and the Atonement, and its commandment of love, is the apostle's method of dealing with the crisis brought by the new

teaching. The **beginning** might be the beginning of Christ's ministry (Jn 15: 27), but in view of 2: 24; 3: 11 and 2 Jn 6, more probably = the beginning of your Christian faith. (This does not necessarily fix the sense of the word in 1: 1, in a writer who is capable of using one word in three distinct senses in one sentence ['truth' in 2 Jn 1, 2,—*q.v.*].) In a wider sense, the commandment is **old**: it is found in the Old Testament (Lev. 19: 18), and indeed it is a primal law of creation. Its correlative in the physical world was formulated by Newton, 'Every body attracts every other body with a force proportional to its mass', with the other principle in impressive proximity, 'To every action there is an equal and opposite reaction'. The principles by which the physical universe coheres are thus 'figures of the True', of love, and of justice, corresponding with the two great theological affirmations which dominate the Letter, **God is love** and **God is light**—though nature shows the more austere and—so to speak—mechanical aspects: grace comes by Jesus Christ. It is nevertheless **a new command**. In Mt. 22: 37–40 the whole of the law and the prophets is declared to depend upon the two commands of love to God and love to one's neighbour. But in constituting a new Society, the Lord promulgated a new command as the principle of its order, the command of love to the brotherhood—while at the same time confirming the first two commands. The **truth** of this new **command is seen in him**, its great exemplar, **and**, in a different degree, in **you**. (For a similar distinction between the senses in which a term may be applied to Christ and to His people, see Mt. 17: 27; Jn 20: 17.) The principle of love is true in our case because into our experience Christ has come, **the true light** which enlightens every man **is already shining** in our hearts, and our **darkness is passing** away.

9. Light is the medium of perception and recognition, of understanding and fellowship; and **he who claims to be in the light** (see on 1: 6) **and hates his brother** actually knows nothing of these things: he is still in unregenerate man's native sphere (Eph. 2: 1 ff.; cf. Exod. 10: 22 f.).

10. the light in which he who **loves his brother lives** still primarily signifies fellowship, but with all that is involved in a *holy* fellowship, a fellowship which is 'with the Father and with his Son Jesus Christ'. **Whoever loves his brother** abides in the holy fellowship, and has within him no tendency to be suddenly provoked to sin, and thus to become a cause of offence. The Gospel background of 2: 9–11 is in Jn 11: 9 f. and 12: 35.

11. hates: Not simply *dislikes*: the malign, hellish contrast to divine love, actively wishing evil to its object. Such a person is in Satan's realm of **darkness** and enmity; he is incapable of discerning the true nature of his own actions or the destiny for which he is preparing himself. Psychologically and spiritually, hatred blinds its subject just as surely as love illumines. It is characteristic of John to disregard the blurred colour of a human situation, and to insist upon the stark black and white of the underlying spiritual principle. His function is not that of a judge, weighing all the factors (Prov. 21: 2), but that of a teacher elucidating the essential spirit of a matter, indeed showing things clearer than they are in actual fact. The either/or necessity of love and hate is well illustrated in Mk 3: 1–6.

12–14. Turning again to his **dear children**, the apostle breaks out into ecstatic congratulation of them upon their place in the family of God, all the more marvellous in contrast with the darkness just considered. The brief prophetic lyric consists of two stanzas each of three lines. Each of the first three lines commencing with the verb in the present tense ('I am writing'), and the last three with the verb in the aorist ('I wrote')—apparently just a device to distinguish the two stanzas. In this way the repeated sequence of **children, fathers,** and **young men** stands out significantly. The idea that the first series, introduced by 'I am writing' refers to the Letter, while the '*I wrote*' series refers to the Gospel, has nothing to commend it, and NIV probably does well to ignore the distinction. The same aorist 'I wrote' is used in 5: 13, referring to the Letter. All those whom the apostle addresses in the Letter are his **dear children** (2: 1 etc.), and so it is improbable that **fathers** and **young men** represent different age-groups; it rather belongs to Christian experience to combine the innocence (through grace) of infants with the maturity of fathers and (this being the main point) the moral earnestness of youth. The natural order of address would be children, young men, fathers; the addresses to young men, being displaced from their natural order, are emphatic; and the purpose of the section is to be found in them. Some scholars, however (with Westcott), regard the words as indicating different age groups.

12, 13. As **dear children**, Christians enjoy the primary boon of having their **sins forgiven**, and that on **account of his name** (2: 2), and of **know**ing God as **Father**.

13, 14. As **fathers**, Christians **know him who is** ('and has been', NEB) **from the beginning,** that is, the Eternal.

13, 14. The addresses to Christians as **young men**, which would come logically between the other two, but brought to the end for emphasis, declare that the middle term between simple forgiveness and mature apprehension is that high and earnest resolve which is youth's noblest trait: standing firm, giving serious heed

to the written **word of God**, and pressing on to subdue **the evil one**.

15. Divine love, the subject of the command, is always in danger of being crushed out by a rival love, **the love** of **the world**. 'Worldliness' is identified with love of the things **in the world**. Yet when we enquire what may be the 'things' which are 'worldly', we find that 'things' do not exist in this connection except as a necessity of English translation; **everything in the world** being its spirit, its tone, its values. Worldliness consists of attitudes: the three characteristic attitudes of the world being *sensuality, materialism,* and *ostentation* (C. H. Dodd).

16. The phrase **cravings of sinful man** is plain enough, signifying the notion that desires and appetites have a right to insist upon fulfilment without reference to any superior law. The **lust of** the **eyes** is the spirit of the world in putting supreme value upon things which can be seen (as opposed to the value which faith puts upon the unseen—2 C. 4: 18), and the consequent greed to obtain them. By **boasting** is meant 'ostentatious pride in the possession of worldly resources' (Plummer in *CGT*).

17. Yet death is the termination as well as the tendency of these things, and not only the individual but the world itself has the sentence of death upon it, and is already moving toward its dissolution. **but the man who does the will of God,** who obeys the commandment of divine love, shares the very life of God, and **lives forever**.

IV. THE RIVAL ANOINTINGS (2: 18–29)

It is in this section and in section VI that the crisis which may have occasioned the Letter comes into clear view (see Introduction and note on 1: 6). The falsity of the new teaching is expressed in a play of words difficult to put into English, but which we shall understand better if we keep in mind that *Christ* means *Anointed.* Jesus is the Christ; His people share his life (Jn 14: 19 f.), and are in a derived but true sense 'christs', and do his works, having a *chrisma* (**anointing,** 2: 20, 27) from Him (cf. Jn 14: 12; 20: 21 ff.). It was well known that the end of the age would be heralded by the appearance of the **antichrist**; but, says John, his spirit is already abroad in the world. These false teachers are his people and share his spirit; they are **antichrists**, and their initiation (the rival anointing—the antibaptism, one might almost say) into this new teaching is no true *chrisma*, but an *antichrisma* which blinds them (2 Th. 2: 9–12).

18. John has been widely censured for his declaration that **this is the last hour**. A moderate statement of the view is that made by Jelf, quoted in *CGT* p. 106: 'The only point on which we can certainly say that the Apostles were in error, and led others into error, is in their expectation of the immediate coming of Christ, and this is the very point which our Saviour says is known only to the Father'. But this is a superficial view, and one which shows little regard for the teaching of the Lord Himself as to the recurring nearness of the End (Mt. 10: 23; 16: 27; 24: 14, 30; 25: 13), let alone sympathy with the regular apostolic teaching (1 C. 1: 7; 1 Th. 1: 10; Jas 5: 7 f.; 1 Pet. 1: 13). John and his readers were living in an *eschatological hour*, electric with movements of the unseen principalities which might burst into sight at any time. Jerusalem had fallen, and antichristian Rome was already closing in a mortal combat with the Church. These were the days of the eighth emperor, Domitian; would he prove to be the Antichrist, 'the eighth king' of Rev. 17: 11? (See p. 1621.) Even from our point of time, John's assessment was correct. There are periods when the End draws obviously near, though in course of time the crisis subsides and recedes. The periods of the rise of Islam, the Reformation, the Napoleonic Wars, and the present age, are examples of epochs heavy with destiny. In one such 'last hour' the End will suddenly break into its irreversible course: this realization braces Christians to special preparedness at such times (*e.g.* 1 C. 7: 26). If it be asked if John had all this in view, the answer must be 'not at all likely'. Prophets speak better than they know (1 Pet. 1: 10 ff.), and John had good reason to think about his day, as we do of ours, that it is *the* last hour; though his word here is literally '*a last hour*'.

It was a regular part of Christian expectation, though for prudential reasons passed on more by way of oral teaching than of written instruction (**you have heard:** cf. 2 Th. 2: 5), that the appearance of the sinister figure of **antichrist** would herald the end (cf. 'the little horn' of Dan. 7, 'the man of lawlessness' of 2 Th. 2: 3, and the 'beasts' of Rev. 13). Exalting himself above every object of worship, he will deny that Jesus is the Son of God incarnate. But now, says the apostle, this teaching has already appeared in Christian circles; 'the rebellion' (2 Th. 2: 3) has already begun; and with the rising of **many antichrists** what hinders the appearing of Antichrist himself? It should be noted that John's reading of his contemporary situation goes no further than this, and commentators need have no fear in leaving us under his teaching. [Antichrist: one who assuming the guise of Christ opposes Christ—to be distinguished from 'false Christs' (Mt. 24: 24), i.e. messianic pretenders. Origen taught that 'all that Christ is in reality, Antichrist offers in false appearance; and so all false teaching which assumes the guise of truth, among heretics

and even among heathen, is in some sense antichrist. The Incarnation reveals the true destiny of man in his union with God through Christ; the lie of Antichrist is that man is divine apart from Christ'. Abbreviated from Westcott, pp. 69, 90.]

19. The secession of the antichristian teachers, marking their apostasy from the truth, serves however a solemn but necessary purpose. It was not only a divine providence to limit their opportunity for mischief, but it also demonstrated that **none of them belonged to us**, or, as NEB has it, 'so that it might be clear that not all in our company truly belong to it'—a salutary warning for every church. Apostasy on the part of those in formal church membership can and does occur, but only in those who never were truly Christ's.

20. you (emphatic) **have an anointing:** The suggestion being that 'they' also had their *anointing*—probably the rite of initiation into their gnostic circle, admitting them to the esoteric teaching. 'You, no less than they, are among the initiated' (NEB). The 'anointing' bestowed by Christ as **the Holy One**, is the Holy Spirit, by virtue of which **all of you know the truth**. This translation is preferable to AV, RV. The knowledge of the truth is not the privilege of a select few, but of all God's people (Jn 18: 20; Col. 1: 28; Heb. 8: 11); this is a strong attack upon the position of the heretics.

21. The appeal to the common faith of the Church is based on the convictions of v. 20: the Church knows intuitively what belongs to her historic faith (**the truth**), and will recognize and reject any foreign elements as a **lie**. Prophets will no doubt weigh the utterances of other prophets (1 C. 14: 29), but the final judgment is that of the whole congregation. **22.** The antichristian **lie** which is being countered is the denial that **Jesus is the Christ** and **the Son** of God (see Introduction).

24. This denial is incompatible with **what you have heard from the beginning**—the original gospel which is now being corrupted —and by its very nature this denial renders impossible that fellowship, that abiding in the Son and in the Father, which (**25**) is the very nature of **eternal life** (Jn 14: 23; 17: 3). **26.** 'So much for those who would mislead you' (NEB).

27. the anointing (v. 20)—the Holy Spirit, that *chrisma* which makes us *Christians*—**remains** (Jn 14: 16) and **teaches** (Jn 14: 26). It is thus an impertinence, and worse, that people should come along and **teach** new doctrine. The Christian teacher, from this point of view, simply reminds his brethren of what they already know (at least in principle), clarifies their thinking and directs it into practical channels. The Holy Spirit will teach them to recognize what belongs and what does not belong to the gospel when they hear it (Jn 10: 5). The word **remains** (27 f.) recalls again the figure of the True Vine (Jn 15: 1–11); the ambiguous reference of **him** may be defined by taking it as 'God in Christ'. The phrase **unashamed before him** is well paraphrased by RSV as 'not shrink from him in shame'. Cf. *Hamlet*: '. . . started like a guilty thing upon a fearful summons'.

29. Even before making his dramatic transition in 3: 1 to the subject of *the children of God*, John's mind has already moved to that realm of thought, and he declares by way of anticipation that God's children will be recognized by righteous conduct—the standard of conduct being the character of God Himself, and therefore expressed in obedience to *His will*. See note on 4: 7. The 'son of thunder' takes a solid piece out of the heart of his next section to hurl as a parting shot at the apostate teachers in their *self-will*.

V. THE CHILDREN OF GOD (3: 1–24)

(i) The divine nature is manifested in being like Christ (1–3); more specifically, in (a) doing right (4–10), and (b) loving our brothers (11–18). (ii) It is by such practical obedience that we may obtain reassurance and confidence (19–24). The central thought of the chapter echoes clearly the Lord's teaching in Jn 8: 39–47: 'If God were your Father you would love me . . . you want to carry out your father's desire . . . you do not believe me'—illuminating by contrast the three marks of eternal life: love, obedience and belief.

1. How great is the love the Father has lavished on us: a translation which conveys the Apostle's wonder and gratitude. The purpose of God's love is that we should become his **children** (*children* signifying the sharing of nature, with the possibility of development; as against *sons*—not used by John except in Rev. 21: 7—emphasizing privilege and likeness of character: cf. Rom. 8: 14, 16). This is already true, and is no empty title, for so **we are** in a vital sense, by regeneration (Jn 1: 12 f.). We may perhaps interpret quite strictly the declaration that **The reason . . . the world does not know** (i.e. recognize) **us** to be God's children is that **it did not** recognize **him** as God's Son. The world would then be following out the course of wilful blindness noted in Mt. 21: 23–27 and Jn 12: 35–40. But it seems better to follow the thought of Jn 8: 39–47, and to understand that **the reason** is the same in both cases: on account of radical disparity of nature, the world has not the capacity for recognizing the divine.

2. The **now** and the **not yet** are both true, and express the tension which exists between the ideal holiness and glory belonging to men who have become God's children, and their actual observable condition of failure and distress. It is not yet manifest (to the world) **what we will be**; but of course Christians know, because they have overheard their Lord praying for them (Jn 17: 24 ff.). However unlikely it seems, the dull chrysalis will yet take the air as a butterfly; and all intelligent people know that it will be so. **we shall be like him** when we see Him at His parousia (1 C. 15: 51).

3. This hope of ultimate conformity to the moral likeness of Christ is a powerful motive to diligent moral cleansing here and now, and is one channel by which the implanted divine nature achieves progressive conformity of the indwelt life with its own law of being.

4. For any one at all (**Everyone**, including those who imagine that being saved by grace they are above mere literal obedience) to commit sin is to flout the law, and therefore the will, of God.

5. But Christ is the antithesis of all sin (**he appeared so that he might take away our sins** and He personally is free from sin). That is to say, everyone who sins is a rebel against (a) God, by refusing submission to His law; (b) the work of Christ, directed as it is to the removal of sins; and (c) the character of Christ as the Holy One of God. So—and this is the intended conclusion of the reasoning—**No one who lives in him keeps on sinning**. Here the verb 'to sin' is in the present indicative, with the sense of continued or habitual action. By contrast, the two occurrences of the same verb in 2: 1 are in the aorist, signifying isolated sins. No Christian can continue in disobedience as his way of life: it is a moral impossibility. [It should be noted, however, that Law (*op cit.* p. 219) protests strongly that the point of the argument is missed when one relies, with Westcott, as we have done, upon the *habitual* sense of the verbs 'to commit sin' and 'to do righteousness' in this paragraph. While unable to follow Law here, we may yet avoid undue reliance upon the habitual sense, as though it meant that we are at liberty to make occasional excursions into sin, provided we do not become domiciled there—an unchristian position close to that of Rom. 3: 8.]

7. 'Righteous is as righteous does' (to adapt a common saying); but it is obvious that there were teachers around with a sophisticated theory of salvation which left plenty of room for illicit behaviour. John was neither the first to encounter this, nor the first to declare that such people try to **lead you astray** (1 C. 6: 9 f.; Eph. 5: 6). For (9) **No one who is born of God will continue to sin**; and if this statement, with its verb in the present tense, seems strong, it is good to note that if the verb had been aorist, it would have been even stronger. It would then have read: 'No one born of God commits a sin . . . and he cannot commit a sin, because he is born of God'. This would be manifestly contrary to experience; contrary also to the testimony of the Letter itself (1: 8, 10). The explanation of this moral necessity is couched in the form of a strong figure. The word **seed** introduces the analogy of human begetting; cf. C. H. Dodd's translation, 'A divine seed remains in him'. The reason that Christians cannot live a life of sin is that the principle of divine life has been implanted within them by God, and life develops according to that principle. God is their Father, and their true nature accords with this, the deepest truth of their personality.

8, 10. 'All mankind is God's children by creation: as regards this a creature can have no choice. But a creature endowed with free will can choose his own parent in the moral world. The Father offers him *"the right to become a child of God"* (Jn 1: 12), but he can refuse this and become a child of the devil instead. There is no third alternative' (Plummer in *CGT*, p. 128). Correspondence between spiritual parentage and moral character means that attitudes and actions betray our spiritual nature. Then at the end of the paragraph, the next subject (brotherly love) is introduced, in the Johannine manner.

11. The command that **We should love one another** goes back to Christ Himself (Jn 13: 34), to **the beginning** of the gospel. See note on 2: 7.

12. The reference to Cain, the only allusion in the Letter to the OT, is deeply significant. Adam had been warned that in the day of disobedience he would die; yet in fact it seemed that the serpent's word was true: he 'lived' a long life and became the father of humanity. He gave to his wife—was it in perverse bravado?—the name of 'Eve': the mother of all 'living'. In their first-born, Cain, was manifested the nature of that 'life'. Cain was not master but slave of passion, and his very worship was unacceptable to God. In Cain is seen the horrifying nature of hatred: **he murdered**, and that **his brother. And why did he murder him?**—'Much might be said on both sides. It takes two to make a quarrel'. The apostle has no time for this kind of moral sluggishness which refuses to see ultimate principles; and brushing aside all possible secondary and contributory causes he declares that the sin was Cain's. Cain could not bear the contrast of **his brother's righteous** actions with **his own actions** which **were evil**, and the first murder became a monument to self-love, as the cross was to become the demonstration of divine love. Not only the world is shown in the story of Cain, but in a sense the Church too. The seed of Seth was the appointed representative of the slain Abel—and if we understand the first two verses of Gen. 6 aright, the two seeds are actually called the children of God and the

children of men. Such is the background to the apostle's thought as he moves from the 'righteous brother' (with no doubt the ever-present consciousness of the Son of Man slain out of envy by the children of men—Jn 1: 11; Mt. 27: 18) to **(13) the brothers**, and from Cain to **the world** which **hates you**. See also Jn 8: 37–47.

14. Hatred is the realm of death, love the realm of life; and assurance **that we have passed from death** (The more decisive translation of the RSV *out of death into life* is to be preferred. It is no 'to and fro' movement: we have made the passage once for all: Jn 5: 24) **into life** (and—significance of perfect tense—we remain there) is conveyed by our consciousness of brotherly love. The unregenerate man **remains in death**, which is thus implied to be his native realm. Hating his brother, he is in heart **a murderer** (Mt. 5: 21 f.), and this attitude is incompatible with **eternal life**. In visiting condemned murderers, I have met despair of God's pardon because of this verse—and without cause (Mt. 12: 31 a; 1 C. 6: 9–11; 1 Jn 1: 7).

16. *'The second John three sixteen'*. We know what 'love' in its lower meanings is: physical attraction, natural affection and friendship; but we would be totally unacquainted with *agapē*, the divine **love**, were it not that *He* took frail flesh and died for our sake. That love which has made us rich has also made *debtors* of us (a rather stronger word than **we ought**) to lay down our lives, as our Lord laid down His. **to lay down** one's **life** for the sake of another is to set oneself to seek the good of that person at all cost, even at the cost of life itself. Cf. Christ's cross and the disciples' cross (Mt. 16: 21–25). One might perhaps expect that the indwelling divine love would constrain us to die *for His sake:* but what would be remarkable in our loving Him who has done us nothing but good? Divine love goes further: it is love to the undeserving, the unthankful, even the rebellious (Jn 3: 16; Mt. 5: 43–48; Rom. 5: 6–8). **our brothers**, in their foolish and sinful weakness so truly *our* brothers, are the proper objects of our self-sacrificing love. If our love cannot encompass them, how shall it prove to be that divine *agapē* which reaches out to the world?

17. Few of us are called to die for our brothers. But in smaller things we may show the same spirit, and share whatever we have of **material possessions** with a **brother in need** (Lk. 16: 11).

18. love with words may be genuine enough, but is not fulfilled **in actions**. Love with the **tongue** consists of hypocritical utterances with no **truth** in it. We are to beware lest our love stop at mere talk, or even prove downright insincere.

19. And so by love . . . with actions and in truth we may reassure our hearts in God's presence that we belong to the Lord (a matter of value to the spiritual physician as well as to the general reader). (For 'belonging to **the truth**' see Jn 18: 37.) When conscience (**our hearts**) brings its accusations, we may appeal to the higher and final tribunal of Omniscience: I love . . .' (Jn 21: 17). But it should be noted that it is a record of actual deeds of self-sacrifice done out of unfeigned love which constitutes this sign of indwelling divine life, and not simply the feeling of adoration toward the Infinite, which so easily passes for 'love of God'. Tests, to be worth anything, have to be applied on a level available to inspection and observation. **21 f. if our hearts do not condemn us:** The accusations of conscience either having not arisen or having been silenced, then we have liberty in prayer and joy in answered prayer. **23.** The **command**, which is so often summed up as 'trust and obey' (Rom. 6: 17; 16: 26) is given in the form, 'believe and love' —**believe . . . in Jesus . . . and love one another**. In both forms it is the same faith which works through love (Gal. 5: 6), for the command in which all obedience is summed up is the new command of love. For obedience, love and belief, here found in one verse, as the three manifestations of eternal life, see on 4: 7. Then, in the manner of the Letter, the section is rounded off by an anticipation of the next section: **this is how we know**—another of the series of tests as to whether or not we possess life—by the gift of the Holy **Spirit**.

VI. THE RIVAL SPIRITS (4: 1–6)

Having accomplished his central purpose of providing practical means of identifying the children of God, John begins to retrace his course of thought—the literary structure of *introversion* which enters into the pattern of the Fourth Gospel (F. Madeley, 'A New Approach to the Gospel of St. John', *EQ* July–Sept. 1961; R. W. Orr, *The Witness*, July 1962)—and of Rev. also (R. G. Moulton, *The Modern Reader's Bible*, pp. 1708 f.).

1. The **many false prophets** who **have gone out into the world** (where they really belong) are probably the same people as 'the many antichrists' who 'went out from us' (2: 18 f.). They spoke as prophets by inspiration, and that mere fact was sufficient to ensure them a large following. But Christians forgot, and still do, that we live in a whirlpool of spiritual influences, by no means all of which are holy or divine. We must **test** the utterances, and thereby **the spirits** which inspire them. Not all that appears to be supernatural is genuinely so—there is deliberate deceit and there are delusions—and even after eliminating the spurious, there must be careful discernment as to

the source of inspiration, **whether of God** or of the devil.

2 f. The test prescribed is quite comprehensive. The witness of **the Spirit of God**, and therefore of **every spirit** which is **from God**, is to **Jesus**, the historical man of Nazareth; that He is the **Christ**, the Saviour-King foretold in OT type and prophecy; that this Jesus the Messiah *came*—implying his pre-existence— **in the flesh** (Jn 1: 14): the actuality of the Incarnation; rather, that He **has come** in the flesh, and is still truly man: the permanence of the Incarnation, implying the Resurrection. The 'confession' is thus a Christian creed in brief compass. It might be better rendered as 'Every spirit which confesses Jesus as Christ come in the flesh is of God' (Law, *op. cit.*, p. 94 n.)—a tr. which leads on smoothly to the converse.

3. every spirit which does not acknowledge Jesus (as Christ come in the flesh) **is not from God**.

4–6. Beliefs and utterances which are disloyal to the person of Jesus as recorded and interpreted in the apostolic testimony are inspired, not by the **Spirit of truth** (the Holy Spirit, Jn 14: 17) but by the **spirit of falsehood**. The spirit which will animate the Antichrist is a spirit which the world finds congenial. Right belief as to the person of Jesus is based upon the apostolic testimony, and John holds the high ground of being one of the primary witnesses appointed by God. **We** (the apostles) **are from God**. He is not here contrasting the apostles with other Christians, but with the new teachers (**they** of v. 5). The apostles received the Spirit to enable them to bear their witness, basic to the very existence of the Church; other Christians are enabled by the same Spirit to believe the apostolic witness: **whoever knows God listens to us** (i.e. listens and obeys; cf. Mt. 18: 15 f.). Prophets and teachers are therefore to be judged by their doctrine; and doctrine is to be judged, not by its emotional quality and strength, but by its agreement with the apostolic testimony to Jesus.

VII. GOD IS LOVE (4: 7–5: 5)

The latter part of the Letter is dominated by the great affirmation *God is love*, as the earlier part is by *God is light* (1: 5). The practical corollary of **God is love** is that **whoever lives in love lives in God** (4: 16). 'Living in love' is the ruling thought of this section, just as 'living in the light' (2: 10) was earlier seen to be necessarily the condition of those who live in the God who is light. The section also contains the main part of two series of tests (noted by Law, *op cit.*, p. 186 n. and p. 279): they may conveniently be shown together here.

Obedience Love Belief

Tests of being children			
of God	2: 29	4: 7	5: 1
Tests of living in God	3: 24	4: 12	4:15

Considering the human mind in its three functions of intellect, emotion and will, we see that it is renewed in all its parts by the indwelling of God: the intellect is enlightened to believe, the emotions are kindled to love, and the will is turned and strengthened to obey.

7. 'Jerome tells us that during St. John's last years "Little children, love one another" was the one exhortation which, after he had become too old to preach, he never ceased to give. "It is the Lord's command", he said, "and if this be done, it is enough"' (quoted by Plummer in *CGT*, pp. 128 f.). **love comes from God:** *Agapē* whether manifested in God or in man, is of divine origin (see on v. 9), being God's own nature; **and everyone. who loves** (not of course everyone who feels the force of natural affection or physical attraction or the warmth of friendship, but he through whom courses the divine love) **is born of God:** Perfect tense: literally 'has been born of God'. The divine begetting preceded the love: love is an activity of the implanted eternal life, and is therefore a proof that the life is present. This significance of the perfect tense is important also in the other two signs given of our being children of God (2: 29; 5: 1—see table above). **and knows God:** Love, 'the eyes of the heart' is the organ of perception of God and of His counsels (Eph. 1: 18). Cf. music, which might be studied as a branch of applied mathematics, resulting in interesting and valuable insights, but is really known only through a love of music.

9 f. We would have had no notion of what *agapē* is—the love divine, all loves excelling—but for the amazing facts of the Incarnation and the Atonement. We could conceive of the Lord Almighty sitting in His heaven, contemplating with serene detachment the self-ruin and extinction of his creatures: such is a God created by man in his own image. But that God should involve Himself in man's ruin, and Himself suffer their disgrace and pain and bereavement! The **atoning sacrifice** (see on 2: 2) due to Himself, God Himself provided, and that by sending **his one and only son** (the willing suffering of the Father is as truly manifest as that of the Son; Gen. 22: 2; Rom. 8: 32), that **we**, despite all **our sins**—rebellious as well as unworthy—might receive the supreme gift of life. This is love.

11. The proper response to divine love is to show love which has something of the divine character of self-sacrifice for the unregarding: God, the giver and forgiver, cannot be loved in that way: our brother can, especially if he has not first loved us.

12. Men have seen God manifest as man (Jn 14: 9); but God as God, **no one has ever seen nor can see** (Jn 1: 18; 4: 24; 1 Tim. 6: 16); that kind of vision of God is a fruitless aim to pursue. But the gracious presence of God making His home within us is experienced when **his love is made complete in us**, that is, when the divine life expresses itself in actual deeds motivated by love, for the good of others. Here is a practical demonstration of eternal life (see table at the beginning of this section).

13. The love of God was manifest not only in sending His own Son, but also in giving **us of his own spirit** in order to quicken faith within us.

14. The primary work of the Spirit among men was to create the apostolic testimony to Jesus, teaching the apostles the meaning of what they had **seen**, and enabling them to **testify** as to the person of Jesus, that He is the **Son** of the **Father** (Jn 1: 14), and as to His work, that He is **the Savior of the world** (Jn 4: 42).

15. By the same Spirit does each believer make his confession unto salvation (1 C. 12: 3), belief in the heart and confession upon the lips being proof that God by the Spirit dwells within.

16. It is by this further gracious action of God that the Incarnation and Atonement become good to us, and **we know and rely** on the love of God.

God is love. Whoever lives in love lives in God, and God in him. This is the great affirmation in its full form, consisting of a theological statement followed by a practical corollary, comparable with Jn 4: 24 and 1 Jn 1: 5. Equally with the earlier word 'God is light', this was surely 'heard from him'; indeed both are contained in one utterance of our Lord's, 'The Father loves the Son, and shows him all he does' (Jn 5: 20). We may suppose that God might have chosen to be eternally sufficient to Himself in the infinite plenitude of His own worth: the eternal Lover, the eternal Beloved, and the eternal Spirit of love. But it pleased Him to decree that many sons be brought to glory, and so His love must be manifested. This He did in two great acts: *the incarnation*, when **he sent his one and only Son into the world** (9), and *the atonement*, when **he sent his Son as an atoning sacrifice for our sins** (10). Thus the two great distinctives of the Christian faith, symbolized in the bread and the cup of the Lord's Supper, are at the same time the supreme demonstrations of God's love for us. This is widely hailed as 'the touchstone of all theology'; yet the holiness of God is taught as emphatically as His love.

17. One great practical result (or 'completion' as our writer would say) is **confidence** for **the day of judgment**. This contains the

compressed idea of confidence *now* as we anticipate the day of judgment: a confidence which
will not forsake us when that day actually
comes. The ground of confidence is in the
fellowship of love with God and with the brethren. If **we**, here and now **in this world** are
like him—if there is evidence that the divine
nature is implanted within us, expressing itself
in loving the brethren and in a forgiving spirit
and in seeking at cost the good of the unworthy
after the pattern of His life—then there is solid
ground for confidence that it is because He has
given us eternal life. Not of course that our
love is the ground of confidence, any more
than our trust or our obedience: it is the sign
that we belong to Him who is the Saviour.
This verse should be read along with 3: 18–20.

18. perfect love, That is, love which has
been *made complete* (4: 12), love which reaches
beyond word and speech to deed and truth,
cannot provide any occasion for **fear**, because
he who loves is living in the light (2: 10), and
is therefore being cleansed by the blood of Jesus
from all sin (1: 7), and is doing what pleases
Him (3: 22). More than that, love 'with actions
and in truth' **drives out fear** which is already
present, by the confidence it gives of fellowship
with God in the life eternal. Some, however,
understand the love spoken of to be that love
which on God's side is already full, and which
we are exhorted to make our own in full
measure, thus casting out its dark negation of
slavish fear. Bengel remarks that men may pass
through diverse conditions: without either fear
or love, in fear and without love, in both fear
and love, finally reaching love without fear.
What has **fear . . . to do with punishment**?
Fear is the foretaste, the earnest, of the punishment which conscience anticipates; but the believer can appeal from the fallible interim sentence of conscience to the judgment of Him
who knows all things, on the ground of already
having been granted the spirit of love, earnest
of the fulness of eternal life.

19. We love (*him* [AV] is properly omitted:
all activity of love, whether to man or God, is
meant) because all true love comes from God,
and is His gift.

20. But **if any one says** (see on 1: 6), **'I love
God'**, imagining that his religious feelings of
adoration and gratitude are of a higher order
than 'love with actions and in truth', while at
the same time he **hates his brother**, consciously wishing him evil, **he is a liar**—he is
telling and living a lie, and would realize that
it is so if only he would stop to consider. For
the brother whom he has seen, in all his
sinful weakness, is the appointed receptacle
for the divine love which he professes to be
receiving (Mt. 25: 40).

5: 1 carries on the thought of 4: 21, that to
love God involves loving God's children, but

v. **2** carries us to new ground: that love for the
brothers is no mere indulgent kindness, but is
holy love, grounded in and regulated by **love
for God**, and obedience to **his commands**,
desiring the highest good of the beloved, and
finding (as *agapē* always does) its pattern in
Jesus. 'For them I sanctify myself, that they
too may be truly sanctified' (Jn 17: 19). **3 f.** The
apostle looks to the moral struggle required if
we would live the holy life of love, and finds the
guarantee of overcoming strength in *whatever*
(rather than **whoever**) **is born of God**. The
Gk. neuter emphasises not personal strength,
but the fact of birth from God. Then, in vv. 4
f. he anticipates the next section by introducing
the idea of **faith** or belief. He who believes is
an overcomer: his faith is a manifestation of the
life of God which must prevail. 'Belief in Christ
is at once belief in God and in man. It lays a
foundation for love and trust towards our fellow men. Thus the instinctive distrust and
selfishness which reign supreme in the world
are overcome' (*CGT, ad loc.*).

VIII. THE TESTIMONY (5: 6–12)

The apostle keeps his aim closely in view,
that his readers may be brought into conscious
enjoyment of fellowship in eternal life. We
have already seen (4: 13–16a) that even though
the objective grounds of reconciliation are prepared—the Incarnation and the Atonement—
yet the work of the Holy Spirit is required to
bring the individual into life. This section
shows the strength of the grounds for believing
in the Son of God and in the love of His
atonement, and thus sharing in the fellowship
of life.

6. This Son of God **is the one who came**
(cf. the technical title of the Messiah as 'he who
comes' or 'he who is to come': Mt. 11: 3 etc.)
by (better, through) **water**, quite literally, at
His baptism, **and blood**, almost as literally, at
His death (see *Arndt* on *dia*). The emphatic
denial and affirmation which follow, show that
some were teaching that the Christ came only
through water, and not through blood. This
was the error of Cerinthus (see Introduction),
who taught that 'the Christ' came upon Jesus
at His baptism, but left Him before His passion:
thus denying a true incarnation and atonement.
No, says the apostle, He who passed through
the water was Jesus Christ, and he who passed
through the blood was the same Jesus Christ.

For the explanation of John's reference to the
water and the blood, one turns naturally to the
emphatic recital of the miraculous issue of
blood and water from the side of the slain
Saviour (Jn 19: 34 f.). There is good reason
for understanding the flowing blood of that
narrative to signify the propitiatory power of
the death of Christ (Jn 6: 52–57), and the water
to signify the gift of the Spirit, after the manner

of the water from the smitten rock (Jn 7: 37 ff.
with Exod. 17: 6; 1 C. 10: 4). Thus, although
there is basic correspondence in the ideas involved, a direct reference from 1 Jn 5: 6 to Jn
19: 34 would not be appropriate; the passages
point to the same eternal verities rather than to
each other—similar to the relations between
the 'bread of life' discourse of Jn 6 and the
Lord's Supper. The reversal of the terms **water
and blood** rather than 'blood and water', as
well as corresponding to the historical sequence
of the baptism and the passion, may also serve
as a warning that no direct reference is meant.
In His baptism, Jesus committed Himself publicly to the path of the suffering Servant of the
Lord, and, numbered already with transgressors, he went down symbolically into the
water of death, like Jonah into the 'depths of
the grave' (Jon. 2: 2). Then in His symbolic
resurrection, He saw heaven opened and the
Spirit of God descended. In short, the *idea* of
the Passion was represented in His baptism
(Lk. 12: 50); and for the heretical teachers,
ideas were everything. The symbolism of the
baptism would suffice: they would see no need
for the grim actuality of the timber and the
nails and the blood. The water, yes; but not
the blood. So by two great actions Jesus proved
to be the Christ: at the deliberate and solemn
inauguration of His public ministry; and when,
pouring out his soul to death, he bore the sin
of many in the fulfilment of prophetic scriptures (Isa. 53: 12).

7 f. The Holy **Spirit**, who descended like a
dove upon Him, makes a third witness, completing the full number of witnesses which the
law might require (Dt. 19: 15). Their testimony
is in agreement: that Jesus is the Christ, the
Son of God. The present tense may well be
significant: **There are three that testify**, still
bearing their concurrent testimony to Jesus: the
Spirit, whose gracious ministry in teaching,
witnessing and helping is a known fact in the
Church's life; and the water of Christian baptism and the blood of the communion cup—
permanent memorials of the Lord's baptism
and of His death. And it is undoubtedly true
that the two sacraments have great evidential
value. 'The fact that from apostolic days the
Church has met to break the bread and drink
the cup is a continuing testimony to the truth
of Jesus' interpretation of the significance of
his own death as a means of ratifying a new
covenant between God and man. The eucharistic action, the fact that it has been performed
numberless times by every generation of Christians since the first, is more impressive testimony than any documentary evidence: "as
whenever you eat this bread and drink this cup,
you proclaim the Lord's death until he comes"
(1 C. 11: 26)' (A. Richardson: *An Introduction
to the Theology of the NT*, 1958, p. 365).

Textual criticism has done a service in excis-
ing 5: 7 of the AV. The *Three Heavenly Witnesses*
appear in no Gk. MS before the 15th century.
The latter part of v. 6 was moved up by the
Revisers to make the new v. 7.

9. We all **accept man's testimony**—daily
life could not go on otherwise—how much
rather **the testimony of God**?—the historic
testimony of the baptism and death of His
Son with the attestation of His Spirit, and the
continuing testimony of the Spirit and the sacraments in the Church.

10. Moreover, every believer has first-hand
experience of this threefold testimony within
himself: it is the Spirit who works within him
faith, and enables him to make the good confession that Jesus is the Son of God; he has been
baptized in the name of the Son of God; and
the pledge of life eternal through His death is
renewed within him as often as he takes the
sacramental cup. To disbelieve the historic and
continuing testimony is nothing short of blasphemy.

12. He who has the Son making His home
within him (Jn 14: 23) **has life**; while **he who
does not** is pointedly reminded that it is **the
Son of God** whom he has refused to receive;
he remains in fallen man's state of death (1 Jn
3: 14).

IX. EPILOGUE (5: 13–21)

The body of the Letter, written to enable Christians to **know** with assurance that they **have
eternal life**, has been brought to a fitting conclusion in 5: 12. How then shall the Christian
employ himself in his glad confidence?—by
bringing his brothers into the same state. With
this, and with a summing-up of the doctrinal
results of the Letter, the brief epilogue concludes the Letter.

13 ff. Comparison of the purpose of the
Letter as declared at its commencement (1: 3
f.) and at its conclusion (5: 13) shows that joyful
fellowship with the Father and the Son and
with the people of God is one and the same
thing as the assurance of eternal life; this **confidence** brings childlike frankness and assurance
in prayer.

16. What then is the will of God in accordance with which we are to pray? Nothing less
than this, that men be brought into, and abide
in, the fellowship of the divine life (Jn 1: 13; 1
Th. 4: 3; Jas 1: 18). **If** therefore **any one sees
his brother commit a sin . . .**—and it may
well be that the reading of the Letter has
sharpened the perception of sin in others as
well as in oneself—**he should pray** by way of
intercession (not an imperative: a Christian will
spontaneously do this), **and God** [The word
God is supplied by the translators instead of *he*
to simplify a sentence which (in English) has

three 3rd person pronouns in a row. It is possible to consider the person who prays as being the one who gives life, in a secondary, instrumental sense; one engaged in such a ministry being indeed a life-giving agency in respect of his brother. John's colleague James ended his Letter on just the same note (Jas 5: 19 f.)] **will give him**—will grant to the intercessor in answer to his prayer—**life** for the brother concerned.

The difficult matter of **sin that leads**—or **that does not lead**—**to death** remains to be discussed. Under the Old Covenant, sin which was deliberate and presumptuous, knowing the Lord's will and of set purpose flouting that will and reviling the Lord, was mortal: no sacrifice would avail (Num. 16: 30). Similarly, in the NT, wilful rejection of the witness of God, and open-eyed apostasy from Christ, if persisted in, will carry the offender over the line beyond which repentance and therefore forgiveness is impossible (Mt. 12: 31 f.; Heb. 6: 4–6). The difficulty in this interpretation of the matter is how to reconcile it with the offender's being called a **brother**. In answer it may be pointed out that narrowly considered the 'brother's' sin in v. 16 is *not* mortal; however, the word 'brother' may be used as involving a judgment of charity in a case of doubt, as often it must. There is something to be said for the view of this matter which finds *sin leading to death* illustrated in Ananias (Ac. 5), the immoral man of 1 C. 5: 1–5, and the 'many' of 1 C. 11: 30 who died under God's displeasure. These may all have been believers, whose 'spirit will be saved in the day of the Lord Jesus'; and it seems that even the gross offender of 1 C. 5 continued to be the object of the prayers of the congregation (2 C. 2: 5–11; but see pp. 1464 f.).

Since in this Letter *life* is considered as fellowship with God and with His people, *sin leading to death* may signify any such action as deliberately repudiates that fellowship. In some cases, such action would be apostasy, showing that the sinner never belonged to the Lord; in others it would be a serious act of rebellion on the part of a carnal Christian, removing him from the fellowship of the church and delivering him for the destruction of the sinful nature to Satan's power (1 C. 5: 5).

Even in desperate cases, prayer is not forbidden but neither is it enjoined; and there cannot be confident assurance that the request will be granted. Even in the case of 'non-mortal' sins, it is some quite serious matter which is in view; the offender is in no frame of mind to confess his own sin even though his **life**—his conscious fellowship with the Father and with his brethren—has been suspended.

The answer to such a prayer would be a conviction of his guilt sent upon the offender, and the consciousness of access to God for confession, resulting in restoration to the fellowship which is life indeed.

Stott devotes five pages to a thorough examination of this question. He affirms that 'John must here be using the word **brother** in the broader sense of "neighbour" or of a nominal Christian, a church member who professes to be a "brother". He concludes that neither he whose sin "leads to death", nor he whose sin "does not lead to death" is a Christian, possessing eternal life . . . The difference between them is that one may receive life through a Christian's intercession, while the other will die the second death.'

The godless chatter and contradictions of the self-styled gnostics, ever learning and never able to come to the knowledge of the truth (1 Tim. 6: 20; 2 Tim. 3: 7), are finally silenced by the concluding threefold shout of triumphant certitude, summing up not only the Letter, but in a sense the New Testament, of which it is the last major writing. It might be possible to regard the Three Certitudes as consisting of the gnostic false claims duly 'disinfected' and now returned to Christian use. The ideas in the gnostic watchwords (listed in the note on 2: 4) are explicitly present here, perhaps excepting 4: 20.

18. NIV succeeds in conveying clearly the probable meaning of this difficult verse: that we are not only born by God's grace, but kept by Christ's power. The sense turns upon whether **him** (RV, RSV, NIV) or 'himself' (AV, ASV) is to be read after **keeps**, the manuscript evidence being rather equally balanced. Law prefers the latter, and finds the sense, 'He that was begotten of God taketh heed to himself', but it leads him into supposing that the divine begetting might not necessarily be of continuing efficacy. The verse then means that Christians cannot live a sinful life, because God's Son guards God's children (Jn 17: 12, 15), and **the evil one** (Satan) does not lay hold of them.

19. Satan not only lays hold upon the **whole world**; it is wholly within his grasp. The world is still the world that crucified Christ, and we are decisively with Him in the fellowship of the life of God.

20. The Son of God has come (and that *to abide*—such is the force of the verb) **and has given us understanding**—spiritual intelligence and the capacity to receive divine knowledge are in the gift of the Spirit (Jn 14: 26; Col. 1: 9)—so that we may **know him who is true** —the real and living God. Even more, **we are in him**—the real and living God, as branches in the Vine, being in Christ (Jn 15: 1; see Col. 3: 3; 1 Jn 4: 16 note).

20. He is the true i.e. real and living **God.** This is one of John's ambiguities: see on 1: 6. **eternal life:** To know Christ and to be in Him, in the fellowship of the Father and the Son.

21. Dear children, keep yourselves from the **idols**—from the gods constructed out of human speculation, the gods without life, the substitutes for the truth.

THE SECOND AND THIRD LETTERS

OF JOHN

The First Letter has been thought of as an encyclical sent round a group of churches very much like, perhaps even identical with, the 'seven churches' of the Revelation (Rev. 1: 11). The Second and Third Letters, however, are true letters addressed to particular persons or groups. We have already noted the early opinion that the Letters were all written in Ephesus; the destination of the Second and Third would be somewhere (indeed anywhere, as far as the indications go) within the province of Asia, to which the aged apostle's labours were probably confined in his old age.

The Second and Third Letters are obviously a matched pair: (1) the writer calls himself 'The Elder', a usage confined entirely to these two letters; (2) the letters, of much the same length, conclude with the promise of a visit, prefaced by a remark about disinclination to rely upon mere letter-writing.

It is possible that, as is usually held, the two letters are simply examples of the apostle's pastoral correspondence, with no other connection between them; cf. Plummer's view that these last writings of the Apostle John were written respectively 'to a Christian lady and a Christian gentleman regarding their personal conduct' (*CGT*, p. 58). But the fact that they have been preserved together (or indeed at all) suggests that they are more closely related, and of more general interest, than Plummer's view indicates. We have also the interesting fact that toward the end of the second century, Irenaeus knew of only *two* letters of John. It is difficult to imagine how such slight-seeming works as these letters could have survived to gain universal recognition unless they were present in the Johannine corpus from the beginning—and that means together. A matched pair of letters could presumably be counted as one (thus making up Irenaeus's total of two letters) in the same way as in some psalters, Pss. 1 and 2, which are separate and contrasting compositions, are counted together as 'the first psalm' (Ac. 13: 33 in 'Western' MSS). If this line of reasoning is sound, we may expect to find a common purpose in the Letters. This commentary suggests a reconstruction of the situation in which the Letters were written: the reader will of course recognize the element of conjecture.

The reconstruction stands thus: In one of the Asian churches, an elder (Diotrephes) had become enamoured of the new gnostic teaching. [Note however Guthrie's sage comment (*op. cit.*, p. 220): 'Gnostic tendencies might well have fostered such an exhibition of pride as is seen in his love of the pre-eminence, but Gnostics were not the only ones addicted to arrogance, and it is not necessary to appeal to heretical views to account for a failing which is all too often the accompaniment of orthodoxy'.] He had of course to reckon with strong conservative resistance from those who held to the original gospel, headed by the Apostle John himself in Ephesus. But our Diotrephes was an able man of forceful character, and succeeded, not only in dominating his fellow-elders to the point that he became monarchical bishop with power to excommunicate his opponents, but even in throwing off the authority of the aged apostle.

John wished to appeal to the church in its peril, but the only constitutional approach left was Diotrephes himself. Would Diotrephes read the Apostle's letter to the church? At least the attempt could be made, and it might perhaps elicit a loyal response. But those were perilous times, and it would not be an unknown thing, in those days any more than ours, for a disaffected Christian to turn over an incriminating letter to the non-christian civil authorities, and to procure prosecution of the writer for provoking a disturbance. John would write, but he would avoid names and addresses: the church would be 'an elect lady', and he himself 'the Elder'—which to an uninformed reader might simply mean, in an affectionate sense, 'the Old Man'. And of course John kept a copy of the letter.

It fell out as expected, and the report was brought back that Diotrephes had suppressed the letter (or at least had denied its authority); but it was well to have made the attempt. Now John wrote to a trusted believer (Gaius) in that same church, censuring Diotrephes in terms which left no doubt as to his unsuitability as a church leader. At the same time Gaius, and with him Demetrius, is furnished with a testimonial of unreserved confidence. The Apostle hopes to visit the church, but in the meantime the church has a chance to set her own house in order. Let her take the hint, and throw off the domination of this unspiritual autocrat in favour of the joint administration of these two well-proved men. Failing this, the Apostle will be obliged on his visit to use the less satisfactory method of dealing with things by personal authority (cf. 1 C. 4: 18–21), bringing Diotrephes to book and reorganizing the church. Below is a summary of the two Letters from this point of view, the matter in italics being what may be read 'between the lines'.

Summary: 2 John

1–3. John to the church at A.

4. I am happy to learn of the good state of doctrine and behaviour of some of your number, *but I am concerned about the remainder.*

5. With this situation in mind, here is my message for you: Remember the command of the Lord Jesus, that we love one another. *In the fellowship of love, the present danger of schism will be avoided.*

6. The fellowship will be preserved only if we hold by the original gospel as our rule of life.

7. I write in this way because of the danger to the fellowship from heretical teachers: they deny the fundamental truths of the gospel.

8 f. Beware of this danger from among your own selves; beware of anyone who leaves the original gospel to go in for this 'advanced' teaching, which is definitely antichristian.

10 f. Beware too lest this heresy come to you from outside; refuse church fellowship and any appearance of approval in such cases.

12. There is more to be said than I care to put down in black and white; I hope to visit you some time.

13. Greetings from the church here.

Summary: 3 John

1–8. To Gaius, *of the church* at A. I am happy to record my unreserved approval of you as a Christian leader, particularly in your care of the travelling preachers.

9–11. I wrote a short note to the church at A. *of which I attach a copy,* but Diotrephes will have none of it. He is an evil man, that Diotrephes, especially in the way he obstructs the travelling preachers whom you help so much; and he is no example to follow. If I come, I shall bring him before the church for discipline, *though it would be better for the church to deal with him now herself.*

12. I would have entire confidence in you and Demetrius *to succeed Diotrephes jointly in the leadership of the church, if the believers see fit.*

13–15. In the meantime this letter will suffice *to let you and the church know what I wish you to do. Let me find it done when* I visit you soon.

2 JOHN

1 f. The elder: The simple and solitary dignity of the last surviving apostle of Christ. The epithet is appropriate to the purpose of the Letters, dealing as they do with church leadership (cf. 1 Pet. 5: 1). **to the chosen lady:** Better *to a chosen lady:* there are many such. In ordinary address the significance would be *eminent* (Rom. 16: 13), but the Christian reader would understand it to mean that the **lady** is *chosen by God* (Eph. 1: 4 f.). For another example of personification of a church as a **chosen lady** (also apparently for security reasons) see 1 Pet. 5: 13. (On the other view of the Letter *to the elect Kyria,* Kyria = 'Lady' being the Gk. equivalent of *Martha.*) The **children** are the members of the church (for use of an associated figure to denote constituent members, cf. 'bride' and 'guests', Rev. 19: 7, 9). **whom** is plural, denoting the lady and her children (as also the **you** etc. of vv. 6, 8, 10 and 12. The **you** of vv. 4, 5, and 13 is singular, indicating the lady alone). **truth** is used in three distinct senses in one sentence: paraphrase: **whom I love** (i) in sincerity, **and not I only, but also all who know** (ii) the gospel, **because of the** abiding presence of (iii) Christ by the Spirit. **All who know the truth** love the local church (this statement could hardly be made of an individual lady). This whole address to the church is of surpassing beauty.

6. This is love, that we walk in obedience to his commands: Once more (as in 1 Jn 5: 18) NIV chooses one of the possible meanings of an ambiguous sentence. The reader may however wish to consider a possible alternative: paraphrase: 'Love is the commandment, just as you heard from the beginning, for you to make your rule of life' (see NEB).

7. who do not acknowledge Jesus Christ as coming in the flesh: cf. 1 Jn 4: 2. But for the latter ref. with the perfect participle (see note *ad loc.*) one might think that the new teachers were simply denying the historic Incarnation. But the contrasting use here of the present participle (which, as in English, has frequently future significance: *e.g.* the 'who is to come' of Rev. 1: 8) may suggest that the heretics were taking the logical next step in denying the personal return of the Lord Jesus at the end of the age. Both beliefs stand or fall together.

8. what you have worked for: another reading *what we have worked for*, is at least possible. Paraphrase: 'By failure on your part you will throw away the results of our labour among you; but by steadfastness you will reap its full harvest' (2 C. 12: 14 f.).

9. Anyone who runs ahead: The 'advanced' teachers of v. 7, and probably Diotrephes of 3 Jn 9, contrasted with those who **continue** in the original gospel. **the teaching of Christ:** The confession of 'Jesus as Christ coming in the flesh' (7).

10. into your house on our interpretation of 'the elect lady' will mean 'into church fellowship'. Commentators have been embarrassed by the apparent churlishness of this verse in forbidding the common courtesy of hospitality

to heretics. *E.g.* Plummer: 'The greatest care will be necessary before we can venture to act upon the injunction here given to the Elect Lady' (*CGT*, p. 183). C. H. Dodd simply declines to heed the injunction. If however we understand church fellowship to be the matter in question, the difficulty disappears: the **welcome** will signify church approval or commendation. In any case, 1 C. 5: 11 is not a true parallel, as those in view there are not people with wrong beliefs (who *may* benefit from meeting people with right beliefs), but immoral men whose behaviour is in flagrant opposition to what they themselves acknowledge to be right.

11. work (lit., *works*): Better than AV 'deeds', as including doctrine, which was where the danger actually lay.

13. The **chosen sister** is the church from which John wrote, presumably Ephesus. This verse forbids that interpretation of the Letter favoured by some early commentators, in which the *elect lady* is the universal Church.

3 JOHN

1. Gaius is already known to the church as *beloved*. The apostle adds his own endorsement: '**I love** him also in sincerity'.

2. The graceful address is well rendered in NIV. The AV 'above all things', conveying the unfortunate impression that prosperity and good health are rated above everything else, is rightly contracted into **all**, and attached as subject to **may go well with you**. Do we really speak about one's **soul getting along well**? The old and the new tr. might be combined to yield *that you may prosper and enjoy good health, as indeed your soul is prospering*.

4. my children (in a pastoral relation: cf. 1 Tim. 1: 2; contrast Phm. 10) **are walking in**, as daily habit, **the truth**, the gospel and commandment of the Lord Jesus.

5. even though they are strangers: 'Yes and strangers at that': the more difficult and therefore more praiseworthy form of hospitality (Heb. 13: 2; Mt. 25: 35).

6. send them on their way: 'Help on one's journey with food, money, by arranging for companions, means of travel, etc.' (*Arndt*); cf. Rom. 15: 24; 1 C. 16: 6, 11. **In a manner worthy of God**, whose servants they are.

7. they went out: the reference being applicable to their whole course of life as well as to that particular ministry . . . **for the sake of the Name:** a phrase of reverential awe (cf. the note at 1: 6 on *he*) is preserved in NIV (Lev. 24:

11; Ac. 5: 41). The accepting of spontaneously proffered assistance from non-christians has good precedent (Ac. 28: 2, 7, 10), and we may tr. 'they went forth from the heathen taking nothing'. I.e., in becoming Christians, and more particularly preachers, they surrendered rights of ownership and of inheritance in their heathen families. They might have insisted upon their rights, but for the sake of the Name they did not (Phil. 2: 5–11)—a renunciation still called for today in non-christian countries.

8. One of the ways in which the church fulfils her calling to spread **the truth** is by supporting such. This statement prepares the way for showing the failure of Diotrephes in a serious light.

9 f. I wrote *something* (depreciatory): Just a short note: a suitable description of 2 Jn.

10. The objection has been made that Gaius cannot have belonged to the same church as Diotrephes, otherwise he would not have needed to be told about the conduct of Diotrephes. The objection would be valid only if this were a purely private letter—but there are no purely private letters in the NT. The Letter is a formal indictment of Diotrephes as well as a testimonial for Gaius and Demetrius.

12. the truth itself: The Spirit speaking through believers, probably by way of prophecy (cf. Ac. 13: 2; 1 Tim. 1: 18). Demetrius is not, any more than Gaius, simply the apostle's nominee: his worth is independently and widely recognized. Commentators have regarded Demetrius as the bearer of the letter, or as a travelling preacher being commended to the hospitality of Gaius.

14. For the promise of a visit as a spur to immediate compliance, see Phm. 21 f. **soon:** This is now added to the half-promise of 2 Jn 12: a slight indication that 3 Jn is later than 2 Jn.

15. by name: an echo of Jn 10: 5, where the Good Shepherd calls his own sheep *by name*, an example for under-shepherds, and a good closing note for The Elder's pastoral correspondence.

BIBLIOGRAPHY

BROOKE, A. E., *The Johannine Epistles. ICC* [on the Greek text] (Edinburgh, 1912).

BROWN, R. E., *The Epistles of John. AB* (Garden City, N. Y., 1982).

BRUCE, F. F., *The Epistles of John* (London, 1970).

BULTMANN, R., *The Johannine Epistles*, E.T. Hermeneia (Philadelphia, 1973).

DODD, C. H., *The Johannine Epistles. MNT* (London, 1946).

FINDLAY, G. G., *Fellowship in the Life Eternal* (London, 1909).

GRAYSTON, K., *The Johannine Episltes. NCentB* (London, 1984).

HOULDEN, J. L., *The Johannine Epistles. BNTC* (London, 1973).

HOWARD, W. F., *Christianity according to St. John* (London, 1943).

LAW, R., *The Tests of Life* (London, 1909).

MARSHALL, I. H., *The Epistles of John. NICNT* (Grand Rapids, 1978).

PLUMMER, A., *The Epistles of St. John. CGT* [on the Greek text] (Cambridge, 1886).

SMALLEY, S. S., *1, 2 and 3 John.* Word Biblical Commentary (Waco, 1984).

STOTT, J. R. W., *The Epistles of John. TNTC* (London, 1964).

WESTCOTT, B. F., *The Epistles of John* [on the Greek text]. (London, 1892; reprinted, Abingdon, 1966).

JUDE

DAVID F. PAYNE

This Letter tells us nothing about the author, save that his name was Jude (Gk. 'Judas') and that he had a brother called James. It is quite possible that both men are otherwise completely unknown to us, but there is nothing inherently improbable in the widely held and traditional view that the writer was one of the sons of Joseph and Mary, mother of our Lord (cf. Mk 6: 3; Ac. 1: 14). His brother James became the recognized leader of the Jerusalem church.

Such verses as 3 and 17 give the impression that the Letter was written at least a generation after the earliest apostolic preaching. A date as late as A.D. 70–80 is generally acceptable—Jude, if a younger brother of Jesus, could well have lived till then. If, however, it is agreed that 2 Peter was written after this Letter (and if the genuine apostolic authorship of 2 Peter is allowed), then clearly Jude's letter must have been in existence at least two or three years before Peter's martyrdom (usually considered to have taken place in the persecution by Nero, A.D. 64). A date in the early sixties A.D. is not impossible; but the evidence for the date of Peter's death is slender, and if the apostle in fact lived into the following decade, the usual dating of Jude's letter need raise no problems. The free use Jude makes of non-canonical literature points on the whole to a first century date, since thereafter various heretical teachers began to produce apocryphal and subversive works, and the church leaders gradually came to feel themselves obliged to discard books which, however wholesome, did not have full auth-

ority as Scripture. Even so, 1 Enoch retained its popularity into the third century.

If the writer was the son of Joseph and Mary, the Letter will probably have been written in Palestine; but the Letter itself gives no hint where it was penned. Nor does it mention by name the intended recipients of the letter; it is a truly 'general' letter, though no doubt sent to one particular church in the first place.

The purpose of the Letter was to counter certain heresies which were arising inside the churches. The false teachings were evidently of an antinomian character. Antinomianism was one manifestation of gnostic thought; men of this persuasion viewed all matter as evil, and everything of a spiritual nature as good. They therefore cultivated their own spiritual lives, while allowing their 'flesh' to do just as it liked, as if they had no responsibility for its misdeeds; with the result that they were guilty of blatant immorality of all kinds.

Most of this brief letter is strikingly similar to 2 Pet. 2: 1–3: 3, so much so that it is usually thought that one writer must have borrowed from the other. Probably Jude is the earlier Letter; but see the introduction to 2 Peter for further discussion.

There are possible allusions to the Letter of Jude in early second century writings, but the Muratorian Canon (late second century) gives the first mention of it by name. It was not accepted in all quarters till relatively late, no doubt because of its extreme brevity and its use of books from the OT pseudepigrapha.

ANALYSIS

I. SALUTATION (1–2)

Jude describes himself in a truly humble way, recognizing himself as **a servant** (literally, 'slave') **of Jesus Christ**, and as insignificant in comparison with his brother **James**. He does not name those to whom he wrote; he describes them as **called, loved . . . and kept**—a reference to the Christian's past, present and future. His wish for them is that God's **mercy, peace and love** may be theirs in increasing measure.

II. THE DANGER (3–4)

Jude relates his purpose in writing; **the faith** is in danger; by 'the faith' he means primarily the whole body of the truths of the Gospel. Paul outlines such a creed for us in I C. 15: 1–11. Faithful Christians must always defend these truths vigorously against dilution or perversion; **once for all** indicates that the Gospel truths are immutable—cf. Gal. 1: 6–9. The word **entrusted** means 'handed down', and is used of traditions: the only immutable traditions Christians have are the truths of the Gospel. The chief enemies of the truth, from the earliest days of the church, were men who 'wormed their way in' (NEB), though inwardly opposed to the Gospel and all it implied, men destined (**marked out** mg) for **condemnation**, not salvation. Such false brethren in Jude's time were characterized by **immorality**; Rom. 6: 1 describes the outlook of such pseudo-Christians. Jude regards such an antinomian attitude as equivalent to a denial of the Lord Jesus Christ. (It is uncertain whether **Sovereign** here refers to God the Father or to the Son; but the Gk. construction seems to favour the latter.)

III. THE DANGEROUS MEN (5–16)

Jude knows his readers **already know** of the stories recalled in vv. 5–7; he wants to **remind** them of the implications. The three groups named had all been at one time signally favoured; they had all been guilty of presumption, lack of faith, or gross immorality; and they had all paid a dreadful penalty. The first and third examples are biblical (cf. Num. 14; Gen. 19); but the second of them, that of the fallen **angels**, is drawn from non-canonical books such as I Enoch (chapters 6–10), although the basis of the apocryphal details may well have been Gen. 6: 1–4. Such apocryphal books were evidently well known and appreciated by Jude's readers, and so he could confidently appeal to them as well as to Scripture. Books of this sort might not be truly inspired nor authoritative, but their moral lessons in particular were wholesome and worth heeding. **6. Positions** renders a Gk. word which usually means 'dominion' (cf. NEB); perhaps it includes both ideas in this context, i.e. position and status, and so 'domain' would be a convenient translation of the word. **7.** The **fire** which destroyed **Sodom and Gomorrah** Jude describes as **eternal**. It had permanent effects, to be sure; but probably the fires of hell (cf. Mk 9: 43) were in the writer's mind.

Jude's contemporary false brethren ignored such signal examples, and were equally guilty of sexual immorality and presumptuous behaviour against God's own authority and that of the angels of His appointment. **8.** The phrase **these dreamers** may suggest that these men claimed that their actions were justified by certain visions they had received. Cf. Dt. 13: 1–5. With their arrogance Jude contrasts the behaviour of a very **archangel** when challenging Satan himself: **Michael** would not speak arrogantly even to **the devil**. The source of this allusion is no longer extant, but Origen (*De Princ.* iii. 2. 1) informs us that it was a work called *The Assumption of Moses*; the actual wording of the rebuke, however, derives ultimately from Zech. 3: 2.

10. Attention is again drawn to the licentious behaviour of the pseudo-Christians. Furthermore, they are typified by a general lack of spirituality (with **Cain**), by ungodly motives and avarice (like **Balaam**), and by rebellion against divine authority (like **Korah**). **Balaam's error**, too, points to immorality and false worship (cf. Num. 31: 16; Rev. 2: 14). Such men are certainly **blemishes**, perhaps dangerous 'reefs' (RSVmg); the former interpretation seems more natural, but either is possible, since the Gk. word *spilades* is ambiguous. The term **love feasts** denotes the fellowship meals of the early church, in the course of which the Lord's Supper was often celebrated (cf. I C. 11: 17–34); evidently these men had permeated to the very centre of Christian church fellowship, some of them probably gaining positions of leadership, for **feed only themselves** means literally 'shepherding themselves' (see NEB's paraphrase).

12–14. The striking metaphors that follow are largely self-explanatory. **Twice dead** probably means firstly dead in sins (cf. Eph. 2: 1), and after professing conversion, still dead to good works (cf. Jas 2: 17, 26). The final metaphor, **wandering stars**, is an allusion to the Book of Enoch, again (18: 12–16; 21: 1–6). Jude goes on (vv. 14 f.) to give a citation from I Enoch 1: 9. V. 14 may imply that Jude actually believed that the patriarch Enoch had himself written the book bearing his name; but this is not the only possibility. The phrase describing Enoch is not Jude's own, but is again drawn from the pseudepigrapha (cf. I Enoch 60: 8). It may be that Jude was simply arguing from grounds he knew to be acceptable to his readers or opponents. We might compare Paul's use of Gk. poetry when addressing an

Athenian audience (Ac. 17: 28). At any rate, the general statements drawn from the Book of Enoch, and the inferences from them, are authenticated here and elsewhere in the NT. **16.** Jude sums up his description of the false brethren by stressing their three chief characteristics; his opponents were rebellious, licentious, and motivated by their own advantages.

IV. PRACTICAL ADVICE (17–23)

True Christians in such circumstances must be very careful, obviously; but they need not be alarmed, because the presence of evil men had been foreseen and foretold (cf. Mk 13: 5 f., 21–23; Ac. 20: 29 f.; 2 Th. 2: 3–12; v. 18 is probably Jude's epitome of the apostolic teaching on this point). False Christians are bound to create factions within a local church (cf. v. 19); vv. 20–23 show the true brethren what are their responsibilities in such adverse circumstances. Note that those of wavering faith (v. 22) need kindness and help: some MSS read 'convince', others 'pity' (cf. NEB). But the true Christian must never be complacent nor instil complacency in such vital matters.

There are several textual problems in vv. 22 f.; the general sense is plain, however. The earlier mention of Sodom and Gomorrah may have reminded Jude of Am. 4: 11, of which the phrase **snatch others from the fire** is reminiscent.

V. DOXOLOGY (24–25)

Jude reminds his readers of their bright hope and present help. The phrase **without fault** may recall v. 12, although the Gk. words are not connected; it is in any case a metaphor from the OT sacrificial system (cf. Lev. 1: 3, etc.).

BIBLIOGRAPHY

Jones, R. B., *The Epistles of James, John and Jude* (Grand Rapids, 1962).

Kelly, W., *Lectures on the Epistle of Jude* (London, 1912).

Wolff, R., *A Commentary on the Epistle of Jude* (Grand Rapids, 1960).

See also the books listed at the end of the commentary on 2 Peter.

REVELATION

F. F. BRUCE

Origin, Character and Purpose

The Book of the Revelation—or, as it might well be called, the book of the triumph of Christ—was composed and sent to seven churches in the Roman province of Asia at some point between A.D. 69 and 96 to encourage them, and their fellow-Christians everywhere, with the assurance that, despite all the forces marshalled against them, victory was theirs if they remained loyal to Christ.

Whereas before A.D. 60 an apostle like Paul could count on the benevolent neutrality, if not the positive protection, of the imperial power in his evangelization of the Roman provinces, the relation between the empire and the church changed radically in the 60's, and for two and a half centuries thereafter Christianity had no right to exist in the eyes of Roman law. So long as Roman law regarded Christianity as a variety of Judaism, Christianity profited by the status which Judaism enjoyed as a permitted cult (*religio licita*); but when the distinction between the two became plain to the imperial authorities Christianity was left destitute of any legal protection. Nero's attack on the Christians of Rome in A.D. 64 may have been due to personal motives of malice and self-protection (against the popular rumours which blamed him for setting the city on fire); but later emperors maintained a more official hostility against a movement which was suspected of being subversive and anti-social in tendency and a revolutionary ferment within the body politic.

Various reactions to this change of policy on the part of the empire may be recognized in the New Testament. Luke endeavours to refute popular prejudice by writing an orderly account of the rise and progress of Christianity, dedicated to a member of the official class in Rome. Peter urges his readers to live in such a way as to 'put to silence the ignorance of foolish men' and, if called upon to suffer as Christians, to glorify God under that name (1 Pet. 2: 15; 4: 16). The author of Revelation reminds his hard-pressed readers that, long drawn out as the campaign may be in which they are engaged, the decisive battle has already been won, and final victory is therefore assured. Their only means of resisting the assaults of their enemies is by faithful confession, suffering and, if need be, death. But this is only reasonable, for it was precisely thus that their Leader won the decisive battle. Jesus, not Caesar, is the one to whom all power has been given; Jesus, not Caesar, is Lord of history; and in His sovereignty and triumph His faithful followers share already in anticipation and will share fully at His parousia.

The symbolism in which this message of hope was conveyed to Christians whose cause, by all outward reckoning, was doomed to annihilation, was easier for them to understand than it is for us. Apocalyptic was a familiar literary form to Jews and Christians in the first century A.D., however foreign it may be to readers in the twentieth. Much of it goes back to Old Testament imagery (*e.g.* the plagues of Egypt in Exodus and the visions of Ezekiel and Daniel); even if occasionally we seem to have lost the key altogether, the main outlines of the message are clear enough.

Earlier apocalyptic passages in the New Testament throw some light on Revelation—especially Mk 13 and its Synoptic parallels and 2 Th. 2: 1–12—although they lack the exuberant imagery of the seer of Patmos.

The framework of Revelation is provided largely by successive heptads (series of seven). Some commentators have seen further heptads in the book, where the number seven does not expressly appear; but their findings have not commanded general agreement. Apart from the letters to the seven churches (2: 1–3: 22), the principal heptads are the three judgment-series, the seals (6: 1–8: 5), the trumpets (8: 6–11: 19) and the bowls containing the seven last plagues (15: 1–16: 21). These heptads are parallel to some extent, the trumpets and the bowls especially so. But all of them are marked by what A. M. Farrer calls 'cancelled conclusions'; the final and irrevocable judgment, which we expect to be executed in the last member of each heptad, is regularly deferred—in confirmation of the Bible's uniform witness to God's reluctance to press His 'strange work' to a full end.

The main division of the book falls between chapters 11 and 12. The seventh trumpet announces the time for final judgment and reward; then in a series of tableaux (12: 1–20: 15) the main themes of the visions of 4: 1–11: 19 are presented afresh. In the visions of 4: 1–11: 19 and in some of the following tableaux, the seer views things on earth from the vantage-point of heaven, to which he is caught up in ecstasy in 4: 1. Here he enjoys the privilege which Christian enjoyed in the Interpreter's House, when he was led about 'to the back side of the wall, where he saw a man with a vessel of oil in his hand, of the which he did also continually cast, but secretly, into the fire'—so that it burned 'higher and hotter' for all the endeavours of the man in front of it to quench it by pouring water on it.

The seer's name was John (1: 4, 9; 22: 8); he received his visions in the Aegean island of Patmos, to which he had presumably been exiled in the course of repressive action by the authorities against the Christians in the province of Asia. His identity with any other John of the New Testament cannot be proved; as early as Justin Martyr (died A.D. 165) he was identified with the apostle of that name. Revelation certainly comes from the same environment as the other Johannine writings. Whatever differences there are between this book and the Fourth Gospel, both present one who is called 'The Word of God' and 'The Lamb of God' saying to His followers, 'In this world you have trouble. But take heart! I have overcome the world' (Jn 16: 33); whatever differences there are between it and the First Letter of John, both encourage the people of Christ with the assurance: 'This is the victory that has overcome the world, even our faith' (1 Jn 5: 4).

Revelation in the Church

In Asia Minor Rev. was accepted from the outset, so far as we can tell, as a work possessing divine authority. In Rome and the west it was also acknowledged from an early date. There are possible echoes of it in the *Shepherd of Hermas* and the *Epistle of Barnabas* (c. A.D. 100). Papias, bishop of Phrygian Hierapolis (c. A.D. 130), evidently knew and used it. Unfortunately Papias's references to it are lost, with the bulk of his *Exposition of the Dominical Oracles*; but Eusebius ascribes to him a statement about the millennium almost certainly based on Rev. 20: 1–6; Andreas of Caesarea (6th cent.) says that he bore witness to the credibility of the book; and there is reason to believe that Victorinus of Pettau (d. 303), the earliest Latin commentator on Rev., drew upon Papias. Papias interpreted the millennium of Rev. 20 as a golden age on earth, and embellished his description of it with features drawn from Jewish sources.

Fragments of exposition of Rev. appear in Justin Martyr (d. 165) and Irenaeus (c. 180); Melito of Sardis (c. 170) and Hippolytus of Rome (c. 200) wrote complete commentaries on it. It is listed in the Muratorian Canon, a Roman catalogue of NT books (c. 190). The Montanists, who arose in Phrygia c. 150, and combined adventist and pentecostal fervour, attached high value to Rev.; by way of reaction to them the Alogoi, and more particularly

Gaius of Rome (c. 200), rejected it and ascribed its authorship to the heresiarch Cerinthus. Hippolytus replied to this aberration of criticism with his *Chapters against Gaius and Defence of John's Apocalypse*. Apart from Gaius and the Alogoi, and of course Marcion and his followers, the authority of Rev. was not seriously questioned in the west.

At Alexandria Dionysius (c. 260) denied its apostolic authorship on grounds of style and language, in a reply which he wrote to another Egyptian bishop, Nepos, who had interpreted the visions of the book (especially the millennium) in a judaizing sense—perhaps following Papias. The allegorizing methods of the school of Alexandria gradually displaced the eschatological interpretation of Rev., although the latter is still maintained in the commentary of Victorinus of Pettau. The Donatist Tyconius (c. 390), who adopted these allegorizing methods, treated the millennium as the interval between the first and second advents of Christ. His interpretation was taken over by Jerome and Augustine, and became normative in the church for the next eight centuries.

Eusebius of Caesarea (c. 325) followed the lines laid down by Dionysius of Alexandria. He includes Rev. among the books generally acknowledged by the churches of his day, but makes no secret of his own antipathy to it and his personal inclination to class it among the 'spurious' works. His example no doubt influenced the churches of the east against the canonical recognition of the book. While Athanasius of Alexandria in 367 included it in his list of canonical works, it is omitted from the lists drawn up by Cyril of Jerusalem (d. 386), Gregory of Nazianzus (d. 389), the Synod of Laodicea (363) and the *Apostolic Constitutions* (c. 380). Indeed, Amphilochius of Iconium (d. 394) says that most (in Asia Minor and Syria, presumably) regarded it as spurious. The school of Antioch, too, largely ignored it in this period, and it was not included in the Syriac Bible until 508. The Armenians do not appear to have accepted it until the 12th century. By that time its canonicity was universally acknowledged except among the Nestorians, who have never accepted it.

A revival of the eschatological interpretation of Rev. set in around 1200, especially with Joachim of Floris, under whose influence many in Europe of the 13th and 14th centuries looked eagerly for the new age which would deliver them from the evils which they saw to be rampant in church and state. It is to this period that we can trace the identification of the Papacy with Antichrist, an identification which later commended itself to Luther and other Reformation leaders. Luther was one of the first to interpret Rev., from ch. 4 onwards, as a prophetic survey of church history. Calvin did not write a commentary on Rev. as he did on all the other NT books—perhaps because the grammatico-historical study which he would have produced would have been out of step with prevalent trends.

But a partial return to the exegesis of Hippolytus and Victorinus, an exegesis partly contemporary-historical and partly eschatological, appears in the sixteenth century in the works of the Reformer Theodor Bibliander and of the Jesuits Francisco Ribera and Luis de Alcazar. In many respects they differed one from another: Bibliander maintained the identification of the Papacy with Antichrist, which the Jesuits did not; Ribera's interpretation was predominantly eschatological (in a futurist sense) while Alcazar's was predominantly contemporary-historical (preterist). They also retained elements of the church-historical method in accordance with their varying points of view. Hugo Grotius (1583–1645) followed them, with two important departures of his own: he was the first Reformed exegete to give up the identification of the Papacy with Antichrist, and he held that some of the visions of Rev. reflect the period before, and others the period after, the fall of Jerusalem in A.D. 70. He may thus be regarded as the pioneer of the literary-critical approach to the book.

No important contribution to the exegesis of Rev. was made by those who concentrated on its numerics—whether J. A. Bengel in Germany or Joseph Mede, Sir Isaac Newton and William Whiston in England—eminent as these exegetes were in other fields of study. The book itself has suffered in its reputation from the extravagances of some of its interpreters, who have treated it as if it were a table of mathematical conundrums or a divinely inspired *Old Moore's Almanack*. Extravagant interpretations of Rev. have been stimulated especially by times of international tension and war, such as the French Revolution and Napoleonic Wars (1789–1815) or the two world conflicts of this century. But the book has always spoken its message most clearly to readers who were involved in the same kind of situation as those to whom it was first addressed.

Throughout the age of persecution at the hands of imperial Rome, for well over 200 years after its publication, Rev. spoke its central message unambiguously to the majority of Christians, even if they were rather vague about some of the symbolism. The identity of the beast from the abyss was not in doubt, nor was there any doubt about the victory which awaited those who were faithful unto death. With the peace of the church in the early 4th century this clear insight into the message of the book was inevitably obscured. But it has returned in other persecuting ages.

In more comfortable times Rev. may be degraded to the unworthy status of a book of puzzles, a battleground for conflicting schools of interpretation, or it may be briefly dismissed as a putrid backwater, cut off from the main stream of Christian faith and life. But 'when tribulation or persecution arises on account of the word', the book becomes once more what it really is, a living word from God, full of encouragement and strength to those who find that 'all who desire to live a godly life in Christ Jesus will be persecuted'. Christians in our own day who have to suffer for 'the word of God and the testimony of Jesus' under régimes which set themselves 'against the LORD and his anointed' have no difficulty in identifying Antichrist or in finding themselves in the company of those who 'come out of the great tribulation'. Above all, this book reminds them that He with whom and for whom they endure these things is the triumphant Lord of history, and that His victory is theirs.

ANALYSIS

Prologue (1: 1–8)

i. Preamble (1: 1–3)
1. The revelation of Jesus Christ, which God gave him: The Greek word here translated 'revelation'—*apokalypsis*—has given its name to this whole genre of literature, called 'apocalyptic'. The common feature of apocalyptic literature is an unfolding of matters generally unknown, such as the heavenly regions or the events of the future, by someone who has been granted a special revelation of these things by God, either directly or through an intermediary, such as an interpreting angel. The most outstanding example of this literature, apart from the present book, is the OT book of Daniel. But this work is unique in that the revelation is communicated by God, not to any mortal man but to Jesus Christ, risen from the dead and exalted in glory. In many apocalypses the revelation is contained in a heavenly book—the scroll of destiny already written on high, or, as it is called in Dan. 10: 21, *the Book of Truth*. That this is true of the present revelation is made plain in 5: 1 ff., where Jesus takes the book or scroll from the right hand of God. **to show his servants what must soon take place:** The subject-matter of this revelation comprises the events of the future—the near future. The argument that Gk. *en tachei* implies that the events will not take place 'soon', but will be completed speedily once they begin, cannot be sustained; it is not what the original readers of the work would have naturally understood. **He made it known by sending his angel to his servant John:** The interpreting angel appears from time to time in the book (cf. 17: 1, 7; 19: 9 f.; 21: 9 ff.; 22: 6 ff., 16), but much of the revelation recorded takes the form of visions seen by John. **2. who testifies:** A solemn affirmation of the reliability of John's record of all that he saw. **the word of God and the testimony of Jesus Christ:** Here these words sum up the subject-matter of the revelation; they recur with a somewhat different force in verse 9. **3. Blessed is the one who reads the words of this prophecy, and blessed are those who hear it, and take to heart what is written in it:** This double beatitude conveys a direction that the book should be read publicly at church meetings—primarily, but not exclusively, in the seven Asian churches named below—and that its contents should receive careful attention from the hearers and exercise a decisive influence on their way of life. **the time is near:** Reinforcing the 'soon' of verse 1.

ii. Greetings and Doxology (1: 4–7)
4. John, To the seven churches in the province of Asia: This apocalypse is not pseudonymous. Who this 'John' was we cannot be sure; he was self-evidently a prophet (cf. 19: 10; 22: 9) and gives his credentials in verse 9. He does not claim to be an apostle; Justin Martyr, towards the middle of the 2nd century, makes this claim for him (*Dialogue with Trypho*, 81), and it may well be right. The 'seven churches' are identified in verse 11. The province of Asia

was evangelized during Paul's Ephesian ministry, A.D. 52–55 (Ac. 19: 10), and all seven of John's churches may have been founded then. While the reasons for selecting these seven are the local conditions described in the seven letters (2: 1–3: 22), the symbolic use of the number seven throughout the book suggests a symbolic significance here; while the messages are primarily for the seven churches named, they are relevant also to the churches everywhere. **Grace and peace to you:** A common epistolary greeting in the NT combining Greek and Hebrew salutations. The terms which follow are trinitarian in substance, though not in form. **from him who is, and who was, and who is to come:** That is, the Eternal One; the designation is used by John as an indeclinable nominative, in whatever construction it may be found. We may regard it as John's rendering of the ineffable name Yahweh, or of the fuller expression in Exod. 3: 14, *I am who I am.* **from the seven spirits before his throne:** Formally this expression (cf. 4: 5; 5: 6) resembles 'the seven angels who stand before God' (8: 2), but actually it denotes the Holy Spirit in the plenitude of His grace and power. At an early stage in the exegesis of this book the expression was associated with the seven designations of the Spirit of the LORD in Isa. 11: 2, LXX: *the spirit of wisdom and understanding, the spirit of counsel and might, the spirit of knowledge and godliness, the spirit of the fear of God* (so Victorinus of Pettau *ad loc.*). Cf. the lines in the *Veni Creator*:

Thou the anointing Spirit art
Who dost thy sevenfold gift impart.

'Before his throne' or 'before the throne' occurs repeatedly in Rev. as an expression for the presence of God in His heavenly temple (cf. 4: 5 f., 10; 7: 9, etc.). **5. and from Jesus Christ, who is the faithful witness:** This collocation of Christ with the Eternal One and the sevenfold Spirit is noteworthy, and consistent with the portrayal of Him throughout the book. In a day when so many of His people, like John himself, were suffering because of 'the testimony of Jesus' (1: 9; cf. 12: 11), it would encourage their fidelity to be reminded that Jesus Christ was 'the faithful witness' *par excellence.* The same expression is used of Antipas (2: 13). **the firstborn from the dead, and the ruler of the kings of the earth:** An echo of Ps. 89: 27, where God appoints David (and, by implication, the son of David) *my firstborn, the most exalted of the kings of the earth.* Here the title 'the firstborn' is related to Christ's status in resurrection, as in Col. 1: 18 (cf. 1 C. 15: 20; also Rom. 8: 29). The 'crown rights of the Redeemer' on earth are twofold: He who is 'head over everything for the church, which is his body' (Eph. 1: 22 f.), is also 'the ruler of the kings of the earth'; it was good that John's

readers should be reminded that their Lord, for whose sake they were persecuted, was also Lord over Caesar, their persecutor, even if Caesar did not acknowledge Him. **To him who loves us and has freed us from our sins by his blood:** The reading 'freed' (Gk. *lysanti*) is better attested than the later 'washed' (Gk. *lousanti*). 'Washing in blood' is not a biblical image (7: 14 is an exception, but there it is robes that are washed). **6. and has made us to be a kingdom and priests to serve his God and Father:** Israel in the wilderness, after the experience of redemption from Egypt, was called to be a *kingdom of priests* to God (Exod. 19: 6; the construction **a kingdom and priests** in our present passage is apparently a literal reproduction of the Hebrew phrase there). (Cf. Isa. 61: 6, where they are called *priests of the Lord* after a later redemption.) So the NT people of God, having been freed from their sins, are similarly designated 'a kingdom and priests' (cf. 5: 10; 20: 6; 22: 5; also 1 Pet. 2: 9). The incorporating of these words in a doxology without explanation suggests that the royal priesthood of Christians was already a thoroughly familiar concept. Those who shared their Priest-King's suffering were called to share His intercession and sovereignty (cf. verse 9, also Lk. 22: 28–30; Rom. 8: 17; 2 Tim. 2: 12). **7. Look, he is coming with the clouds:** The clouds, associated with a theophany or symbolizing the divine presence, are derived from Dan. 7: 13, where *one like a son of man* (cf. verse 13 below; also 14: 14) comes *with the clouds of heaven* (cf. Mk 13: 26; 14: 62 and parallels; 1 Th. 4: 17). **every eye will see him, even those who pierced him:** Cf. 'At that time men will see . . .' in Mk. 13: 26 and parallels, and 'you will see . . .' in Mt. 26: 64 11 Mk 14: 62; but more particularly the language echoes Zech. 12: 10, applied to Christ in Jn 19: 37, *they shall look on him whom they have pierced.* **and all tribes of the earth will wail on account of him:** In Zech. 12: 10 ff. all the families of Israel mourn over the pierced one, but here (as in Mt. 24: 30) all the families of mankind mourn. The annually repeated lamentation *for Hadad-rimmon in the plain of Megiddo* (to which the OT prophet compares the mourning over the pierced one), never finished and always fruitless, has now been swallowed up by penitent tears for a victim pierced once for all, never to be struck again.

iii. The Divine Authentication (1: 8)
8. I am the Alpha and the Omega (cf. 21: 6)**:** That is, the beginning and the end, or the first and the last, 'alpha' and 'omega' being the first and the last of the 24 letters of the Greek alphabet. This assertion by the Eternal God of His names and titles, authenticating the following revelation as His, is the more striking in view of the freedom with which in the sequel

the same titles are applied to Christ (cf. verse 17; 22: 13). In this title there may also be a suggestion of the principle that 'the end shall be as the beginning', which is amply illustrated in Rev. (cf. *e.g.*, 2: 7; 22: 1–4 with Gen. 2: 8 ff.). **the Almighty:** Of the 10 NT occurrences of this divine title (Gk. *pantokratōr*), 9 are in Rev. (the remaining one is in 2 C. 6: 18). In LXX it usually represents Heb. *tseba'oth* in the title *Yahweh ('elohe) tseba'oth,* 'LORD (God) of hosts', except in Job, where it represents *Shaddai.*

First Division: Visions of Conflict and Triumph (1: 9–11: 19)

I. THE INAUGURAL VISION (1: 9–20)

9. I, John, your brother: Whether he had apostolic status or not, he lays no claim to it here, but puts himself on a level with his readers. **your . . . companion in the suffering and kingdom and patient endurance that are ours in Jesus:** The placing of 'kingdom' between 'suffering' and 'patient endurance' is eloquent of the firmness of Christian hope (see on verse 6 above), and also of the general NT insistence that 'we must go through many hardships to enter the kingdom of God' (Ac. 14: 22; cf. 6 above). **the island of Patmos:** A small island in the Aegean Sea, some 37 miles WSW of Miletus. **because of the word of God and the testimony of Jesus:** This could mean that he had gone to Patmos to receive the revelation (cf. verse 2), or to preach the gospel, but it is traditional, and much more probable, meaning is that he had been banished to Patmos because of his Christian witness—perhaps under the process called in Roman law *relegatio,* passed by the proconsul of Asia. Eusebius (*HE* iii. 20. 9) states, on the authority of 'the account given by men of old among us', that he was released from his banishment under Nerva (emperor A.D. 96–98) and took up his abode in Ephesus. **10. I was in the Spirit:** Literally 'I became in spirit', i.e. was caught up in prophetic ecstasy—the same experience as Ezekiel describes by saying *the hand of the LORD was upon me* (Ezek. 3: 22, etc.). **On the Lord's Day:** On the *kyriakē hēmera,* i.e. the day belonging to the Lord (Latinized as *dies dominica,* whence it has passed into the romance languages). This name was appropriately given to the first day of the week as the day of Christ's triumph, when he was 'declared with power to be the Son of God . . . by his resurrection from the dead' (Rom. 1: 4). The expression is also reminiscent of the OT 'day of the LORD' —the day of Yahweh's vindication of His cause and victory over all opposing forces; the day

of Christ's resurrection (and the first day of every week on which it is commemorated) may properly be called 'the day of the Lord'. It was the 'D-day'—the decisive action—which guarantees the future 'V-day', the celebration of final victory. And the supper of the Lord, specially associated with the first day of the week (so much so that it is denoted by the same adjective *kyriakos,* 1 C. 11: 20), brings together and actualizes the past and future day of the Lord. **a loud voice like a trumpet:** A fitting prelude to the appearance of the exalted conqueror (cf. Ps. 47: 5). It is not the Son of man's own voice that is so described; His voice 'was like the sound of rushing waters' (verse 15). **11. Write on a scroll what you see:** Probably indicating a roll of papyrus. **send it to the seven churches:** The order in which the seven cities are named is that in which a messenger would visit them one by one, starting at Ephesus, going north via Smyrna to Pergamum, and then turning in a southeasterly direction to visit Thyatira, Sardis, Philadelphia and Laodicea. **12. seven golden lampstands:** As verse 20 shows, these symbolize the seven churches mentioned. There is a deliberate departure here from the more familiar figure of the seven-branched lampstand of Israel's sanctuary, in order to emphasize the separate responsibility of each local church to bear its own witness to its Lord. The lamp is a natural symbol of witness-bearing (cf. Jn 5: 35; Phil. 2: 15 f.). **13. among the lampstands was someone "like a son of man":** The separateness of the lampstands is emphasized by the fact that the Lord is seen walking among them (cf. 2: 1). The expression *one like a son of man* is based on Dan. 7: 13, where it means 'one like a human being' (cf. Dan. 8: 15; 10: 18; Ezek. 1: 26) in contrast to the wild beasts seen by Daniel earlier in his vision. To Dan. 7: 13 also our Lord's use of the title 'the Son of man' is to be traced. Here the one 'like a son of man' is plainly identified with the risen and glorified Jesus, **dressed in a robe reaching down to his feet and with a golden sash around his chest:** In other words, He wears the full-length high-priestly robe for which the same Greek word *podērēs* (lit. 'reaching to the feet') is used in the LXX of Exod. 28: 4; 29: 5, together with the sash or 'girdle' for which Greek *zōnē,* as here, is used in the LXX of Exod. 28: 4, 39. Here the sash is of gold, as befits a royal priest. In these introductory verses of Rev., then, Jesus is portrayed in His threefold office as prophet, king and priest— as the recipient of God's revelation (verse 1), as 'ruler of kings of the earth' (verse 5) and as the wearer of the high-priestly vestments (verse 13). **14. His head and hair were white like wool, as white as snow:** This is also reminiscent of Dan. 7, but there it is the Ancient of Days that is so described (verse 9) while here it is the risen Christ. This wholesale transference of the divine attributes to Jesus is characteristic of Rev., but by no means peculiar to it in the NT; it attests the spontaneous recognition by the church of apostolic days of the deity of Jesus. It may be a relevant point that the older Gk. version of Dan. 7: 13 says that the *one like a son of man* came *as the Ancient of Days*; this in turn may throw light on the prompt conviction for blasphemy which followed Jesus' application of the language of Dan. 7: 13 to Himself in reply to the high priest's question at His trial (Mk 14: 61–64). **his eyes were like a blazing fire:** Like the celestial visitant of Dan. 10: 6, whose eyes were 'like flaming torches'. The figure recurs in a similar context in 19: 12. **15. his feet were like bronze glowing . . . :** Better: 'his legs' (so *podes* is rightly translated in 10: 1); cf. Dan. 10: 6, *his arms and legs like the gleam of burnished bronze* (see also Ezek. 1: 7). **his voice was like the sound of rushing waters:** This figure, suggesting the sound of a rushing torrent after heavy rain, recurs in 14: 2 and 19: 6, of the voice of the heavenly host. In Ezek. 43: 2 the sound of the coming of the glory of the Lord is so described. **16. In his right hand he held seven stars:** Without an interpretation one would naturally think of the seven planets known to the ancients (cf. Philo's and Josephus's explanation of the seven-branched lampstand); to hold them in one's hand was a symbol of dominion over heaven and earth. In the light of the whole tendency of Rev. this general interpretation is apt in the present context, for universal sovereignty certainly belongs to Christ; but the stars are given a special interpretation in verse 20. **out of his mouth came a sharp double-edged sword:** Cf. 19: 15. The sword is the word of God (cf. Heb. 4: 12; also Eph. 6: 17); for its proceeding from the mouth of the Son of man cf. Isa. 11: 4, where the Messiah *will strike the earth with the rod of his mouth, and with the breath of his lips he will slay the wicked.* The sword in the NT application is the gospel, which proclaims grace to those who repent and put their faith in God, with the corollary of judgment on the impenitent and disobedient (cf. Jn 3: 36). **his face was like the sun shining in all its brilliance:** So, on the mount of transfiguration, 'his face shone like the sun' (Mt. 17: 2). **17. When I saw him, I fell at his feet as though dead:** A vision of divine glory can be conveyed, if at all, only in symbolism. That the language of John's vision of Christ in glory is symbolical is clear enough, especially in the detail of the sword proceeding from His mouth. A notable OT parallel is the vision of God in Ezek. 1: 4 ff. John, like Ezekiel, falls on his face before the glory, and like Ezekiel is raised to his feet. It is the man who has fallen

prostrate before God and been raised to his feet by God who can henceforth look the whole world in the face as the fearless spokesman of God. Cf. Dan. 8: 17; 10: 9, 15; and the three disciples on the mount of transfiguration (Mt. 17: 6). **he placed his right hand on me:** Cf. Dan. 8: 18; 10: 10, 18. **Do not be afraid:** Another echo from Matthew's transfiguration narrative (Mt. 17: 7). Cf. also Lk. 2: 10; Mt. 28: 5; Ac. 18: 9; 27: 24. **I am the First and the Last:** Cf. 2: 8; 22: 13. The titles of the God of Israel (cf. verse 8) are also borne by Christ, who in exaltation has received from God 'the name that is above every name' (Phil. 2: 9). *I am the first and I am the last; apart from me there is no god,* says Yahweh in Isa. 44: 6 (cf. 41: 4; 48: 12); but there is no title which He does not now freely share with His crucified and glorified Son. **18. I am the Living One; I was dead, and behold, I am alive for ever and ever!:** This punctuation is preferable to that of RV and RSV, which attaches 'the living one' as a third member to 'the first and the last'. Render with NEB: 'and I am the living one; for I was dead and now I am alive for evermore'. As the one who conquered death in death's own realm He is pre-eminently 'the living one'; 'since Christ was raised from the dead, he cannot die again; death no longer has mastery over him' (Rom. 6: 9; cf. 2 Tim. 1: 10). **I hold the keys of death and Hades:** That is, His authority extends throughout the realm of death. Therefore His people, who were threatened with death for their loyalty to Him, need not fear that death will separate them from His love; He who died and came to life again is Lord of the dead as of the living: 'So, whether we live or die, we belong to the Lord' (Rom. 14: 8 f.; cf. Heb. 2: 14 f.). **19. Write . . . what you have seen, what is and what will take place later:** What John saw embraced both the situation already in existence and things which still lay in the future. The division is twofold, not threefold. One of the chief problems of exegesis in Rev. is to distinguish those elements in the visions which symbolize 'what is' from those which symbolize 'what is to be later'. See note on 4: 1. **20. the seven stars are the angels of the seven churches:** Christ, who holds these stars in His right hand, is therefore the Lord of each local church. The angels of the churches should be understood in the light of the angelology of Rev.—not as human messengers or ministers of the churches but as the celestial counterparts or personifications of the various churches, each of whom represents his church to the point where he is held responsible for its condition and behaviour. We may compare the angels of nations (Dan. 10: 13, 20; 12: 1) and of individuals (Mt. 18: 10; Ac. 12: 15). **the seven lampstands are the seven churches:** See note on verse 12 above.

II. THE LETTERS TO THE SEVEN CHURCHES (2: 1–3: 22)

The letters to the churches follow an easily recognized pattern. The risen Christ, designating Himself by one of His titles, addresses the 'angel' of the church with the words 'I know'; there follows a brief description of the condition of the church with appropriate commendation or reproof, promise or warning. Each letter ends with the exhortation 'He who has an ear, let him hear what the Spirit says to the churches' preceding or following a word of encouragement for him 'who overcomes'—i.e. the Christian who maintains his confession steadfastly, without prevarication or compromise, even (if need be) to death itself.

The letters give a vivid impression of Christian life in the province of Asia some decades after the evangelization of the province by Paul and his colleagues (A.D. 52–55). Pressure is being brought to bear on the Christians to be less unyielding in their negative attitude to such socially approved activities as emperor-worship and the like, to be less insistent on those things which distinguish their way of life so sharply from the civilization in the midst of which they live. The pressure might take the form of active persecution, as at Smyrna and Pergamum, or the more subtle and less easily resisted form of continued emphasis on the advantages of just so much conformity to paganism as to make life a little more comfortable.

i. The Letter to Ephesus (2: 1–7)

Ephesus, at the mouth of the Cayster, was an ancient Anatolian city colonized by Ionian Greeks. At this time it was the greatest commercial city of Asia Minor and capital of the province of Asia; it retained its free constitution under the Romans, with its own senate and civic assembly. It was widely renowned as the home of the cult of Ephesian Artemis (a local manifestation of the great mother-goddess of Asia Minor), whose temple there was one of the seven wonders of the world. The Ephesian church dated from Paul's three years' residence in the city (Ac. 20: 31).

John's association with Ephesus is perpetuated in the place-name *Ayasolúk*, a corruption of Gk. *hagios theologos*, 'the holy divine'.

1. the words of him who holds the seven stars in his right hand and walks among the seven golden lampstands: For these titles see 1: 16, 13. His 'walking' among the lampstands may imply an inspection of their condition, one by one. **2. I know your deeds:** Cf. verse 19; 3: 1, 8, 15. **you cannot tolerate wicked men:** Cf. the 'men who do evil' of Phil. 3: 2 (and 2 C. 11: 13); here probably they are those who would lower the Christian standard of conduct. **have tested those who claim to be apostles but are not, and have found them false:** Cf. 2 C. 11: 13: 'false apostles, . . . masquerading as apostles of Christ'—but here the false apostles are more likely to be antinomian than Judaizing. Ignatius, in his letter to the Ephesians (*c.* A.D. 115), commends them because they refused a hearing to visitors who taught evil doctrine. **4. I hold this against you:** Cf. verses 14, 20. **you have forsaken your first love:** So penetrating a diagnosis, especially of people who have just been praised for 'persevering' and not growing weary (verse 3), bespeaks uncommon spiritual insight and long and intimate acquaintance with the church addressed. For all their commendable endurance, the fervour of their original love—their 'love toward all the saints', as the longer text of Eph. 1: 15 puts it—had waned. And nothing—no amount of good works or sound doctrine—can take the place of *agapē* in a Christian community; unless there was a change of heart and a return to the original works of love, that church's days were numbered; its lampstand would be removed (verse 5). That the church of Ephesus paid heed to this warning is a fair inference from the testimony of Ignatius, who commends it for its faith and love. **6. But you have this in your favor:** This is to your credit. **you hate the practices of the Nicolaitans:** This word means 'the followers of Nicolaus'—whether Nicolaus the proselyte of Antioch (Ac. 6: 5), as was held by the Church Fathers from Irenaeus and Clement of Alexandria (*c.* A.D. 180) onwards, or some other Nicolaus, cannot be determined. They appear to have relaxed the conditions laid down by the apostolic letter of Acts 15: 20, 29. (See verses 14 f., 20.) **7. I will give the right to eat from the tree of life, which is in the paradise of God:** That is, I will give him eternal life. The origin of the imagery is recognizably Gen. 2: 8 f.; 3: 22. The tree of life in the Eden of Genesis was the terrestrial counterpart of the tree of life in the Eden above. Cf. 22: 1 f.

ii. The Letter to Smyrna (2: 8–11)

Smyrna (modern Izmir) was an ancient Greek colony, destroyed by the Lydians in 627 B.C. It was refounded by Lysimachus, one of the successors of Alexander the Great, in 290 B.C. From 195 B.C. onwards Smyrna maintained relations of firm friendship with Rome. Its tutelary deity was the 'Sipylene Mother', a local phase of Cybele. The letter to the church in Smyrna, while the shortest of the seven, is also the most warmly commendatory.

8. the First and the Last, who died and came to life: An echo of 1: 17 f. **9. those who say they are Jews and are not:** The true Jew is one whose life is praiseworthy in God's sight (cf. Rom. 2: 28 f.). The Jewish community in Smyrna, because of its slanderous attacks on the Christians, had shown itself unworthy of the name 'Jew'; they were rather, by virtue of their opposition to the gospel, **a synagogue of Satan** (cf. 3: 9). (Satan means 'adversary', as its Greek equivalent *diabolos* means 'slanderer' or 'false accuser'; cf. 12: 9 f.) Several decades later, the Jews of Smyrna played a prominent part in the attack on Polycarp, bishop of Smyrna. **10. the devil will put some of you in prison:** The devil used the imperial authorities as his instruments (cf. 13: 2, where the imperial wild beast is energized by the dragon). Imprisonment was not a punishment in itself, but a prelude to trial and sentence. **you will suffer persecution for ten days:** For a prolonged but not unlimited period. Well-known episodes in the history of the Smyrnaean church are the martyrdom of Polycarp (A.D. 156) and that of Pionius (A.D. 250). **the crown of life:** The Smyrnaean Christians' garland won for endurance and victory in the spiritual contest would be eternal life—the promise is the same as that to Ephesus in verse 7, though the imagery is different. The imagery here is suggested by 'the crown of Smyrna', the circle of colonnaded buildings on Mount Pagos, which overlooked the city. **11. the second death:** Final judgment, the alternative to eternal life (cf. 20: 14; 21: 8).

iii. The Letter to Pergamum (2: 12–17)

Pergamum means 'citadel' (Gk. *pergamos*); the city was so named from its commanding position overlooking the Caicus valley, and the name survives in modern Bergama, which lies in the valley below. It was the capital city of the Attalid dynasty whose kingdom, bequeathed to Rome in 133 B.C., became the province of Asia.

12. who has the sharp double-edged sword: For this title cf. 1: 16; it is appropriate here because of the severity of the language of verses 14–16. **13. where Satan has his throne:** Three explanations of this expression have been offered, for Pergamum boasted (*a*) a throne-like altar to Zeus on the citadel; (*b*) the temple of the healing god Asklepios, before which stood an image of the god in association with a gigantic snake, which might have reminded Christians of the serpent in Eden; (*c*) the earliest shrine of the provincial cult of Rome and Augustus, established there in 29 B.C. In view of other allusions in Rev. to the imperial cult, this is most probably the reference here. **in the days of Antipas, my faithful witness:** Cf. 1: 5; 3: 14, where Christ Himself is 'the faithful witness'. Who Antipas was, or in what circumstances he died, we do not know; evidently his death lay some considerable way back in the past. A passage like this marks the beginning of the transition of the meaning of Gk. *martys*, from 'witness' to 'martyr' (cf. Ac. 22: 20). **14. the teaching of Balaam:** A reference to the apostasy of Baal-peor (Num. 25: 3 ff.) which

was instigated by Balaam (Num. 31: 16); it involved fornication or ritual prostitution as well as idolatry. Here the Nicolaitans and their followers (verse 15) are described as holding his teaching. From this it has been thought by some that the Nicolaus after whom the latter were called (cf. verse 6) was simply Balaam, whose name (derived from Heb. *bala*', 'devour', and '*am*, 'people', so as to yield the meaning 'devourer of the people') was translated by Gk. Nicolaus ('conqueror of the people'); but this is improbable. There was evidently a tendency by this time to dismiss the requirements of Ac. 15: 20, 29, as a dead letter, including those which forbade the eating of meat sacrificed to idols and the contracting of marital unions prohibited by the law of Israel (Lev. 18) but countenanced by pagan custom. Such a relaxation would have reduced the social differences between Christians and their pagan neighbours. It is possible, however, that more than this is involved—something amounting to a token participation in pagan worship. **16. the sword of my mouth:** The self-fulfilling word of divine judgment (cf. verse 12). **17. the hidden manna:** An abundant compensation for abstention from idol-food. As the tree of life had its heavenly archetype (verse 7), so has the manna which Israel ate in the wilderness. There was among the Jews a considerable body of teaching about this manna, hidden in heaven, which would be revealed at the end time and given as food to the faithful (so, *e.g.*, 2 Bar. 29: 8). It is called *the bread of the angels* (Ps. 78: 25) or 'the bread of God' (Jn 6: 33); in the light of the teaching about the bread of life in Jn 6: 27 ff. we can recognize the 'hidden manna' as yet another expression for eternal life. **a white stone with a new name written on it:** The meaning of this gift is uncertain, but it may denote an inscribed pebble (Gk. *psēphos*) serving as a ticket of admission to the heavenly banquet. The 'new name', according to 3: 12, is Christ's (cf. 22: 4). **known only to him who receives it:** Purveyors of magical amulets knew how important it was that a name of power should be kept secret; the power of Jesus' name is not to be commanded by magic arts, but is known in the experience of His servants.

iv. The Letter to Thyatira (2: 18–29)

Thyatira was founded by Seleucus I about 300 B.C. as a garrison city. Its other NT mention is as the birth-place of Lydia, the seller of purple, Paul's first convert in Philippi (Ac. 16: 14).

18. whose eyes are like blazing fire and whose feet are like burnished bronze: From 1: 14 f.; here, as in 1: 15, 'legs' would be preferable to 'feet'. **19. you are now doing more than . . . at first:** Up to this point Thyatira's commendation exceeds that of Ephesus, whose love had waned to a point where a return to her first works was called for. **20. You tolerate that woman Jezebel, who calls herself a prophetess:** That she not only called herself a prophetess but was recognized as such by her associates (called in verse 22 'those who commit adultery with her') and followers (called in verse 23 'her children') is certain (we may recall the Montanist prophetesses who were active in the following century in Phrygia). Her name was not really Jezebel, but she is described here as 'that Jezebel of a woman' because her relaxation of the terms of the apostolic decree or further compromises with paganism (cf. verse 14) placed her in the succession of the OT Jezebel, whose Baal-cult was marked by idolatry and ritual prostitution. **21. I have given her time to repent:** Her activity had evidently gone on for some time, and previous warnings had been unheeded; now sickness and plague will fall as a judgment on her and her votaries. **23. I will strike her children dead:** Literally, 'I will kill her children with death', where 'death' may mean 'pestilence', as in the second occurrence in 6: 8. **I am he who searches hearts and minds:** Cf. Ps. 7: 9; 26: 2; Jer. 20: 12. Once again, the attributes of God are shared by Christ. **I will repay each of you according to your deeds:** The constant principle of divine judgment in Scripture; cf. 20: 12; 22: 12; also Ps. 62: 12; Mt. 16: 27; Rom. 2: 6, etc. **24. Satan's so-called deep secrets:** As there is a heavenly wisdom which explores 'the deep things of God' (1 C. 2: 10), so a counterfeit wisdom promises to open up 'deep things', as they are called—'deep things, indeed', says the speaker, 'but deep things of Satan'. The reference is probably to some form of Gnostic teaching. **I will not impose any other burden on you:**—i.e., than those imposed by the Council of Jerusalem; the very language of Ac. 15: 28 is echoed. **25. until I come:** His coming is a visitation of judgment upon the unfaithful (verses 5, 16), but of reward for the faithful. **26–27. I will give authority over the nations—He will rule them with an iron scepter:** Cf. Ps. 2: 8 f.; Messiah's dominion (cf. 12: 5; 19: 15) is shared with His victorious followers. 'Rule' is literally 'shepherd' (*poimainein*); the shepherd's staff is a protection for the sheep but a weapon of offence against their enemies. **just as I have received authority from my Father:** Cf. Ps. 2: 8; Mt. 11: 27; 28: 18; Lk. 22: 29. **28. I will give him the morning star:** This must be understood in relation to 22: 16 (*q.v.*), where Jesus calls Himself 'the bright Morning Star' —an allusion, perhaps, to the royal 'star . . . out of Jacob' foretold by Balaam in Num. 24: 17. The conquering believer, it is implied, is to share the royal rule of his conquering Lord (cf. 3: 21).

v. The Letter to Sardis (3: 1–6)

Sardis was the capital of the ancient kingdom of Lydia, overthrown by Cyrus in 546 B.C. By Roman times it had lost its former greatness, and it never recovered from a great earthquake which devastated it in A.D. 17.

1. who holds the seven spirits of God and the seven stars: Cf. 1: 4, 16. **you have a reputation of being alive, but you are dead:** The church partook of the character of the city, 'whose name was almost synonymous with pretensions unjustified, promise unfulfilled, appearance without reality, confidence which heralded ruin' (W. M. Ramsay). Quite evidently compromise with its pagan environment had so eroded the witness of the church in Sardis that it was a Christian church in name only. Revival and repentance are urgently called for; otherwise there is no future for the church. **3. if you do not wake up, I will come like a thief, and you will not know at what time I will come to you:** This language, describing the suddenness of Christ's coming in judgment, appears in several parts of the NT (cf. 16: 15; Mt. 24: 43; Lk. 12: 39; 1 Th. 5: 2; 2 Pet. 3: 10); here it is specially apt in view of the history of Sardis, which had been captured suddenly more than once when its steep citadel was scaled at points where such access was thought impossible. **4. you have a few people in Sardis:** A minority in the church had refused to follow the compromising ways of the majority; since on earth they had kept their garments 'unstained from the world' their reward will be white robes in glory, meet for the companions of their Lord (perhaps there is an allusion here to the principal trade of Sardis—the manufacture and dyeing of woollen garments). This is the incentive held out in this letter to the overcomer, together with the promise: **I will never blot out his name from the book of life, but will acknowledge his name before my Father and his angels** (5). This promise recalls Mt. 10: 32 f.; Lk. 12: 8 f. The 'book of life' appears here, but not in the other places where it is mentioned in Rev. (13: 8; 17: 8; 20: 12, 15; 21: 27) to include at first all whose names are on the membership roll of a local church on earth, but those whose membership is but nominal have their names deleted—i.e. the Lord declares that He never knew them (cf. Lk. 13: 25, 27). Elsewhere in Rev. those whose names are in the book of life are those who steadfastly resist the temptation to apostasy and who therefore stand in God's great day.

vi. The Letter to Philadelphia (3: 7–13)

Philadelphia received its name in memory of Attalus II, king of Pergamum (159–138 B.C.) who was called Philadelphus ('lover of his brother') because of his devotion to his brother and predecessor, Eumenes II. The earthquake of A.D. 17 devastated Philadelphia as it did Sardis; out of gratitude to the Emperor Tiberius for relief given after the earthquake the city renamed itself Neocaesarea, but the name Philadelphia quickly reasserted itself.

The letter to Philadelphia, like that to Smyrna, contains no word of blame. The Philadelphian church, though small and weak, has maintained its Christian allegiance in spite of the hostility of the synagogue.

7. him who is holy and true: These two titles are given to God separately in 1 Jn 2: 20 and 5: 20; and together in Rev. 6: 10. Here they are designations of Christ (cf. Mk 1: 24; Jn 6: 69; Ac. 3: 14). **who holds the key of David:** In Isa. 22: 22 *the key to the house of David* is laid on the shoulder of Eliakim, so that *what he opens no one can shut, and what he shuts no one can open.* That is to say, Eliakim is appointed chief steward or grand vizier of the royal palace in Jerusalem. Here, however, the same language is used to designate Jesus as the Davidic Messiah—not as chief steward but as Prince of the house of David (cf. Heb. 3: 2–6). **8. I have placed before you an open door:** An opportunity for witness (cf. 1 C. 16: 9; 2 C. 2: 12). **9. the synagogue of Satan:** Cf. 9, in the letter to Smyrna. **I will make them come . . . and acknowledge that I have loved you:** They will acknowledge that the despised church of Philadelphia is the true congregation of the people of God in that city. **10. my command to endure patiently:** 'My word' of verse 8 is here made more specific as Christ's command to endure patiently for His sake, an essential element in the gospel (cf. 2: 10b; Mt. 10: 22b; Mk 13: 13b; Jn 15: 18 ff.; 16: 1 ff., 33). **the hour of trial that is going to come upon the whole world to test those who live on the earth:** This is the visitation portrayed in the successive series of judgment-visions from 6: 1 onwards, which is directed against the 'earth-dwellers'—a recurrent expression in Rev. which excludes the people of God, perhaps because the latter are of heavenly citizenship, members of the New Jerusalem. Cf. Lk. 21: 35. Against this visitation the faithful servants of God, among whom the members of the Philadelphian church are plainly included, are 'sealed' (7: 2–8). In the interpretation of Rev. it is important to distinguish between the tribulation which comes by way of divine judgment on the ungodly (as here) or on unfaithful Christians (as in 2: 22) and that which comes in the form of persecution upon the faithful (as in 2: 10; 7: 14). **11. I am coming soon:** As to the Ephesians (2: 5), Pergamenes (2: 16), Thyatirans (2: 25), and Sardians (3: 3); but to the Philadelphians His coming brings unmitigated blessing, provided that the expectation of it nerves them to maintain their loyalty and not forfeit their crown (cf. 2: 10b). **Hold**

onto what you have: Cf. 2: 25, where the faithful souls in Thyatira are similarly exhorted. **12. a pillar in the temple of my God. Never again will he leave it:** The metaphor apparently undergoes a sudden change; the pillar upholding the roof or pediment becomes a worshipper or ministrant in the shrine; but the point may be that this pillar will never be moved from its base, like so many pillars in earthquake-stricken Philadelphia. **I will write on him . . . :** As overcomer he has a triple name inscribed on him—the name of God, who owns him for a son; the name of the city of God, among whose burgesses he is enrolled; the name of Christ his Lord. Cf. 2: 17; 14: 1; 22: 4. **the city of my God, the new Jerusalem . . . :** That is, the commonwealth of saints; see 21: 2 f., 9 ff., with Ps. 87 as OT background.

vii. The Letter to Laodicea (3: 14–22)
Laodicea, founded by the Seleucid king Antiochus II (261–246 B.C.) and called after his wife Laodice. The church there is mentioned in Col. 2: 1; 4: 13 ff., as one of the churches of the Lycus valley, alongside those of Colossae and Hierapolis; all three were probably planted by Epaphras during Paul's Ephesian ministry. The Laodicean church is marked neither by steadfast loyalty nor by active disloyalty, but by a comfortable self-satisfaction which made it incapable of bearing true witness to Christ.

14. the Amen: The one in whom the revelation of God finds its perfect response and fulfilment (cf. 2 C. 1: 19 f.). A connection with Heb. *'amon* in Prov. 8: 30 (RSV 'master workman') has been suggested by some interpreters because the final part of this triple title of Jesus, **the ruler of God's creation** (lit. 'the beginning of God's creation'), comes from the same context, from Prov. 8: 22 (cf. Col. 1: 15 ff.). Jesus speaks here in the rôle of Divine Wisdom. **the faithful and true witness:** Cf. 1: 5. **15. you are neither cold nor hot:** The choice of the figure of lukewarmness to characterize the Laodiceans' ineffectiveness or lack of zeal may have been suggested by their city's water supply, drawn from the hot springs at Denizli to the south, which was still tepid after flowing for five miles in stone pipes—unlike the cold water which refreshed their neighbours at Colossae or the hot water whose healing properties were valued by those of Hierapolis. Cf. M. J. S. Rudwick and E. M. B. Green, 'The Laodicean Lukewarmness', *Exp T* 69 (1957–58), p. 176. **17. I am rich; I have acquired wealth and do not need a thing:** The church of Laodicea evidently took character from the city as a whole, which was renowned for its wealth. When it was destroyed by an earthquake in A.D. 60, the citizens declined assistance from Rome and rebuilt their city from their own resources. But, however admirable this independence might be in material things, in the spiritual realm self-sufficiency means destitution; a church's true sufficiency must come from God (cf. 2 C. 3: 5), who alone supplies spiritual riches, clothing and health (verse 18). **18. white clothes:** Laodicea was famed for the manufacture of black woollen cloaks called *laodicia*; the black sheep from which the wool was obtained have survived locally to our own day. **so you can cover your shameful nakedness:** Cf. 16: 15. **salve to put on your eyes:** There was a famous medical school near Laodicea where 'Phrygian stone' was powdered to produce collyrium (Gk. *kollyrion*, here translated 'salve'), which appears to have been mixed with oil and applied to the eyes as an ointment. **19. Those whom I love, I rebuke and discipline:** From Prov. 3: 12 (cf. Heb. 12: 6). **be earnest, and repent:** This is the fifth call to repentance in these letters (cf. 2: 5, 16, 21; 3: 3); Smyrna and Philadelphia alone require no such call. Laodicea's repentance would involve the replacement of complacency by zealous concern. **20. Here I am! I stand at the door and knock:** Christ has no place in the life of the Laodicean church, and seeks admission; even if the church as a whole pays no heed to his call, those members who do will enjoy mutual fellowship with Him. The language is reminiscent of Jn 14: 23. **21. I will give the right to sit with me on my throne, just as I overcame and sat down with my Father on his throne:** Cf. Jesus' promise in Lk. 22: 28–30 to those who had 'stood by' with Him in His 'trials'. Their conquest, like His, is won by way of suffering and death (5: 5 f.; 12: 11); those who suffer with Him reign with Him (2 Tim. 2: 12). The same promise has been made in other words at the end of the letter to Thyatira (2: 26–28). Christ's being seated on His Father's throne is His exaltation to the right hand of God, of which He spoke in His reply to the high priest (Mk 14: 62) and which was from the beginning proclaimed in the apostolic preaching and in the church's confession (Ac. 2: 33 ff.; 5: 31; Rom. 8: 34; Eph. 1: 20; Col. 3: 1; Heb. 1: 3 etc.; 1 Pet. 3: 22). 'The highest place that heaven affords/Is his, is his by right'; but participation in His sovereignty is granted to His people (cf. Eph. 2: 6). **22. what the Spirit says to the churches:** To other churches than the seven, no doubt, the seven being representative of all; and, *mutatis mutandis*, to the churches of the twentieth century as plainly as to those of the first.

III. A VISION OF HEAVEN (4: 1–5: 14)

In OT prophecy only those can learn the divine purpose who are admitted to *the council of the* LORD *to see or to hear his word*; then they are in a position to proclaim confidently what He will do (Jer. 23: 18, 22). So John learns the course of coming events by being rapt in ecstasy to heaven. His description of heaven falls into two parts, characterized respectively by the hymn of praise to God as Creator (4: 11) and by that addressed to Christ as Redeemer (5: 9 f., 12, 13b).

i. The Throne-room of God (4: 1–11)
1. a door standing open: Cf. Ezek. 1: 1, *the heavens were opened and I saw visions of God.* **the voice I had first heard . . . like a trumpet:** That of 1: 10. **Come up here:** The heavenly ascent is a well-marked feature of prophetic ecstasy; cf. 2 C. 12: 2 ff. **what must take place after this:** Cf. 1: 1, 19. Chapters 4 and 5 provide the setting for the panorama of 'what must take place', portrayed from chapter 6 onwards in the parallel judgments of the seals, trumpets and bowls (see first note on 7: 1–8). **2. I was in the Spirit:** Cf. 1: 10. **there . . . was a throne:** The vision of the throne-room of God (the heavenly archetype of the holy of holies in the earthly sanctuary) has OT antecedents such as 1 Kg. 22: 19; Isa. 6: 1 ff.; Dan. 7: 9 ff.; but there are here additional features peculiar to Rev. **3. the one who sat there had the appearance of jasper and carnelian:** Cf. Exod. 24: 10; Ezek. 1: 26 ff. Words cannot describe the divine glory; those who have seen it in ecstasy, like Ezekiel and John, can give but a general impression of how it impressed them. **A rainbow, resembling an emerald:** Cf. Ezek. 1: 28; the mention of the rainbow may recall the covenant of Gen. 9: 12 ff. **4. twenty-four thrones:** Cf. the 'thrones' of Dan. 7: 9, occupied by assessors at the divine judgment (but see a closer parallel to this in 20: 4). **seated on them were twenty-four elders:** These may constitute the order of angel-princes called 'thrones' in Col. 1: 16; they are perhaps the celestial counterpart of the 24 orders of priests in 1 Chr. 24: 4 ff., since they discharge priestly functions before the throne of God (5: 8). **5. From the throne came flashes of lightning:** Cf. 8: 5; 11: 19; 16: 18. Lightning is a regular feature of OT theophanies (cf. Exod. 19: 16; Pss. 18: 8, 12 ff.; 77: 18; 97: 4; Ezek. 1: 4, 13; Hab. 3: 4). **rumblings and peals of thunder:** Cf. the 'seven thunders' of 10: 3 f. **seven lamps were blazing. These are the seven spirits of God:** Cf. 1: 4; also Ezek. 1: 13. **6. a sea of glass, clear as crystal:** This heavenly sea (cf. Gen. 1: 7; Pss. 104: 3; 148: 4) is the archetype of the 'molten sea' in Solomon's temple (1 Kg. 7: 23 ff.), which is commonly taken to represent the cosmic flood, over which God *sits . . . enthroned as king* (Ps. 29: 10). **four living creatures:** These are closely akin to the 'four living creatures' (cherubim) of Ezek. 1: 5 ff.; 10: 1 ff. (symbols of the storm-winds upbearing the chariot-throne of God in His progress through the heavens);

but they have also some of the features and functions of the seraphim of Isa. 6: 2 f. They represent the powers of creation in the service of the Creator. **covered with eyes:** Like the living wheels of the chariot-throne in Ezek. 1: 18, a token of the divine omniscience (cf. also Zech. 4: 10b). **7. the first living creature was like a lion:** Each of Ezekiel's living creatures had the four heads (more strictly 'faces') of a man, a lion, an ox and an eagle (Ezek. 1: 10); here each living creature has one head only, but between them the four symbolize the principal divisions of the animal creation. **8. Each . . . had six wings:** Like the seraphim of Isa. 6: 2. **day and night they never stop saying:** The hymn of the living creatures is the first part of the hymn of the seraphim (Isa. 6: 3), the name of God being amplified by the title of 1: 4. The hymns of Rev. are worthy of careful study (cf. 4: 11; 5: 9 f.; 7: 15–17; 11: 17 f.; 15: 3 f.; 19: 6); the context in which they appear implies that the praise of the church on earth is an echo of the liturgy of heaven. The unceasing praise of the living creatures is the voice of creation glorifying its Creator, and is accompanied by the adoring homage of the 24 angel-princes, as they too proclaim their great Creator's praise, and **lay their crowns before the throne** (10) in acknowledgment that all sovereignty is His. The hymn of praise to God for the wonders of creation echoes the language of many of the Psalms (*e.g.* Pss. 19: 1–6; 104). But all OT worship points on to Christ, in whom it meets its fulfilment; hence the vision of heaven in chapter 4 is incomplete without the scene unfolded in chapter 5.

ii. 'Worthy is the Lamb' (5: 1–14)
1. a scroll with writing on both sides: This is the scroll of destiny containing the 'revelation' of 1: 1, but its contents must remain a mystery and not a revelation until it is unsealed. The fact that it contains writing outside as well as inside may suggest the amplitude of the revelation it contains; but more probably the writing outside is a copy or summary of the writing inside. But the writing inside is the legal document, and only when it is exposed and read can its contents be validly implemented. **sealed with seven seals:** Like a will or other official instrument under Roman law, which required to be sealed by seven witnesses. The seals could be properly broken only by someone with due authority to do so. In this instance the person authorized to break the seals will be marked out by that very fact as lord of history and master of the world's destiny. **4. I wept and wept:** As well he might, for unless the seals were broken and the scroll opened and read, the divine purpose of judgment and blessing for the world must remain unfulfilled. Man in the beginning was appointed God's viceroy over the world (Gen. 1:

26, 28; Ps. 8: 6 ff.), but has proved unequal to his responsibility. Now the 'Proper Man' appears, and *the will of the* LORD *will prosper in his hand* (Isa. 53: 10). **5. one of the elders said to me:** Cf. 7: 13 for one of these angel-princes acting as a guide or interpreter to John. **the Lion of the tribe of Judah, the Root of David:** Two titles of the Davidic Messiah; the former is based on Gen. 49: 9, and the latter (cf. 22: 16) on Isa. 11: 10, where the coming prince of the house of David is called 'the Root of Jesse' (cf. Isa. 11: 1; 53: 2). **has triumphed. He is able to open the scroll:** Christ's victory on the cross, although at the time it seemed to be defeat, guaranteed the accomplishment of God's purpose in the world. **6. I saw a Lamb, looking as if it had been slain:** Paradoxically, the conqueror announced as a lion is seen as a slaughtered lamb. Only in the Johannine writings of the NT is the title 'the Lamb' applied to Jesus. In Jn 1: 29, 36 John the Baptist calls him 'the Lamb (Gk. *amnos*) of God'— primarily (in view of the paschal emphasis of the Passion narrative in Jn) with reference to the Passover victim (cf. the simile in 1 Pet. 1: 19), although an allusion to Isa. 53: 7 (and perhaps to Gen. 22: 8) may also be recognized. In Rev. the reference is primarily to the *lamb led to the slaughter* of Isa. 53: 7 (that Rev. uses Gk. *arnion* and not *amnos* is of no great consequence here). Later in Rev. 'the Lamb' becomes a permanent title of Christ with no sacrificial emphasis; thus in 7: 17 the Lamb is a shepherd and in 19: 7 ff.; 21: 9 ff. the Lamb is a bridegroom whose bride is a city. Here, however, the sacrificial connotation is essential: Christ's sacrifice *is* His victory. The moment is that of His appearance in heaven, fresh from the suffering and triumph of the cross. **Standing in the center of the throne:** Since the Lamb has not yet come up to the throne, it might be better to render with RSV 'between the throne and the four living creatures'. **He had seven horns and seven eyes:** Denoting plenitude of power and wisdom. **the seven spirits of God:** Cf. 1: 4. **sent out into all the earth:** Cf. Zech. 4: 10b. **8. Each one had a harp, and they were holding golden bowls full of incense:** This sentence refers to the elders alone. **which are the prayers of the saints:** Cf. 8: 3 f. The elders perform priestly functions in heaven. **9. And they sang a new song:** New in comparison with the ancient song of creation in 4: 11 (cf. Job 38: 7). **You are worthy . . . :** The advent motifs with which Roman emperors were acclaimed included such terms as 'Worthy art thou' and 'Worthy is he to inherit the kingdom'; but only one is worthy to exercise world sovereignty, and He has won that right by His obedience and blood. **you purchased men for God:** The elders are not the objects of redemption, as is implied by the inferior reading of AV ('hast redeemed us')—inferior in spite of its presence in *Codex Sinaiticus* (which is rather inaccurate in Rev.). So in verse 10 read (this time with the support of *Sinaiticus*): **have made them** (not 'us') **a kingdom and priests:** Cf. 1: 6. **and they will reign on the earth:** The textual evidence is fairly evenly divided between this reading and the present tense (RV: 'they reign upon the earth'). The latter reading emphasizes that believers, even while suffering persecution on earth, have already been made 'a kingdom and priests' to God, reproducing here below the eternal worship of heaven. The former reading points on to their coming reign with Christ (20: 4); hence J. N. Darby renders 'they shall reign over the earth' (i.e., from heaven). **11. thousands upon thousands, and ten thousand times ten thousand:** Cf. Dan. 7: 10. The hymn of praise to the Lamb is taken up in ever widening circles; from the elders it is taken up by all the heavenly host (verses 11 f.), and from them by all creation (verse 13; Phil. 2: 9–11), while the praise of creation to God and the Lamb is sealed by the word and adoring action of those in closest proximity to the divine throne (verse 14).

IV. THE BREAKING OF THE SEVEN SEALS (6: 1–8: 5)

As Christ takes the scroll of destiny and proceeds to break one seal after another, the 'unveiling' properly begins. His action in heaven determines events on earth. Since He is envisaged as taking the scroll in A.D. 30, it is not surprising to find a rather close correlation between the first six seals and the forecast of the immediate future to be fulfilled within a generation, presented in the eschatological discourse of the Synoptic Gospels (Mk 13: 5 ff. and parallels). Invasion, civil war, scarcity, widespread mortality, persecution and earthquake are announced: 'such things must happen, but the end is still to come' (Mk 13: 7). The seven seals, like the seven trumpets which follow them, fall into two divisions of four and three, with an interlude before the seventh. The breaking of the first four seals unleashes the four horsemen of the Apocalypse, each of whom rides into the arena at the summons of one of the living creatures. These may recall the four horsemen of Zech. 1: 8 ff.; 6: 1 ff., sent by Yahweh to patrol the earth; but their function is more sinister by far. 'The messianic games begin with the usual race in four colours. But it is not the usual race, it is the apocalyptic death-race, a frightful game in which the heavenly Imperator mocks the defiant and fearful heart of the Roman false Christ. All hopes and promises of the imperial rule are shattered; all the fears of the Roman world are realized' (E. Stauffer, *Christ and the Caesars*, p. 184). The appearance of the horsemen marks 'the

beginning of birth pains' which herald the winding up of the age (Mk 13: 8).

i. The First Seal (6: 1–2)

1. I heard one of the four living creatures say, . . . "Come!": Summoning the first horseman (cf. verses 3, 5, 7), not issuing an invitation to John (as AV 'Come and see' suggests). **2. a white horse! Its rider held a bow:** One long-established interpretation understands this of the victorious progress of the gospel, the rider on the white horse being Christ, as in 19: 11. But the analogy of the other horsemen, and the fact that this horseman is equipped with a bow (like the mounted archers of the Parthian army), suggests rather invasion from beyond the eastern frontier of the Roman Empire. **he was given a crown:** A suitable token for one who **rode out as a conquerer bent on conquest**.

ii. The Second Seal (6: 3–4)

4. fiery red (Gk. *pyrrhos*): The blood-red colour of the horse is in keeping with the mission of its rider, which is to sow strife and slaughter on earth—civil war this time rather than foreign invasion: such civil war as had recently been experienced during the 'year of the four emperors' (A.D. 68–69).

iii. The Third Seal (6: 5–6)

5. a black horse: The colour of this horse is not specially significant: it is scarcely the discoloration caused by famine (cf. Lam. 4: 8), for scarcity, high prices and rationing, rather than famine, are implied by the proclamation of verse 6. **Its rider was holding a pair of scales in his hand:** An indication that bread must be sold and eaten *by weight* (Lev. 26: 26; Ezek. 4: 10, 16). **6. A quart of wheat for a day's wages, and three quarts of barley for a day's wages:** The 'quart' is a *choinix*, a dry measure slightly greater than a litre. In the 5th century B.C. a *choinix* of grain was a fair daily ration for a Persian soldier or a Greek slave; for a Greek soldier twice as much was thought suitable. A **day's wages** is lit. a denarius (a Roman silver coin weighing 1/8 oz., rather less than a fivepenny piece or a quarter in size; cf. Mk 12: 15); according to the parable of Mt 20: 2 this was a labourer's daily wage in Palestine in A.D. 30. The announcement is thus to the effect that a man's daily wage would buy just enough wheat for one, or just enough barley for three—appreciably more than the siegerations of Ezek. 4: 10, but at a price up to ten times as high as in normal times. **but do not damage the oil and the wine:** This injunction is evidently addressed to the horseman; the olive and vine are to be spared at this stage, but they too will suffer with other trees when the winds of wrath are unleashed against them (7: 1, 3; 8: 7).

iv. The Fourth Seal (6: 7–8)

8. a pale horse: A livid, corpse-like colour is

implied (Gk. *chlōros*, usually translated 'green', as in 8: 7; 9: 4). **Its rider was named Death, and Hades was following . . . :** Death and Hades (Sheol) appear in synonymous parallelism in OT (*e.g.* Hos. 13: 14), but in Rev. they are personified as two allied but separate beings (cf. 20: 13 f.). **They were given power** ('authority' Gk. *exousia*) **over a fourth of the earth:** Four kinds of death are specified, by which a quarter of mankind is wiped out. **by sword:** In continuation of verse 4. **famine:** The scarcity of verse 6 has been intensified. **plague:** Lit. 'with death' (as, possibly, in 2: 23). Cf. Jer. 15: 2 with Ezek. 5: 12 for this restricted sense of 'death'. Plainly what is required here is a particular form of death, not death in general. **by the wild beasts of the earth:** These would multiply in territory devastated and depopulated by war, famine and plague.

v. The Fifth Seal (6: 9–11)
9. I saw under the altar: John is still in heaven 'in the Spirit'; the 'altar' is therefore the altar of incense in the heavenly temple, on which the prayers of saints are offered to God (8: 3 f.). The souls of the praying martyrs are accordingly pictured as beneath the altar from which their prayers ascend. **10. Sovereign Lord** (Gk. *despotēs*): Their prayer for vindication is addressed to God upon His throne (cf. Lk. 18: 7). **the inhabitants of the earth:** See note on 3: 10. **11. a white robe:** A token of their blessedness (cf. 7: 9, 13 f.). **wait a little longer, until the number . . . was completed:** The persecution, launched in A.D. 64, must run its course. But when the full tale of the martyrs is made up, the prayers of the saints on the altar fall in judgment on the earth (8: 5).

vi. The Sixth Seal (6: 12–17)
12. a great earthquake: A recurrent sign of divine visitation in the Bible (Exod. 19: 18; Zech. 14: 4 f.; Mt. 27: 51). **The sun turned black like sackcloth . . . the whole moon turned blood red:** For the darkening of the heavenly bodies on the day of the LORD cf. Isa. 13: 10; Ezek. 32: 7 f.; Jl 2: 10; 3: 15; but more particularly Jl 2: 31, quoted by Peter on the day of Pentecost as part of the prophecy fulfilled at that time (Ac. 2: 20). Peter's hearers could remember the preternatural darkness at noon on Good Friday, seven weeks before; whatever darkened the sun on that day may well have caused the paschal full moon to rise blood-red. That was the day of the LORD in realized eschatology, the day when this feature of apocalyptic symbolism was for once experienced in sober fact. **13. the stars in the sky fell to the earth:** Cf. Mk 13: 25: The collapse of established authority is meant. **late figs drop from a fig tree:** The simile resembles that in Isa. 34: 4, where on the day of the LORD the host of heaven is compared to *shriveled figs from the fig-tree*. The 'late figs' (Gk. *olynthos*, as in Ca.

2: 13, LXX) are the green figs which appear before the leaves, and which readily fall off when the wind blows. **14. the sky receded like a scroll, rolling up:** From Isa. 34: 4. **every mountain and island was removed from its place:** A complete convulsion of heaven and earth is implied; the use of such language to describe political upheaval is well established in biblical prophecy. Cf. the picture of chaos-come-again in Jer. 4: 23–26, where the desolation caused by foreign invaders is intended. **15. Then the kings of the earth . . . hid in caves:** We have here an echo of Isa. 2: 10, 19, where *men flee to caves in the rocks and to holes in the ground, from dread of the LORD, and the splendor of his majesty, when he rises to shake the earth.* But John elaborates the picture by enumerating the successive ranks of men, from **kings** to **every slave and every free man**, who seek refuge thus on the day of wrath. **16. They called to the mountains and the rocks, "Fall on us":** From Hos. 10: 8; but the best commentary on the present passage is found in our Lord's words to the 'daughters of Jerusalem' on the Via Dolorosa (Lk. 23: 30), where He applied Hosea's language to their plight during the forthcoming siege and destruction of their city. If the same crisis is in view here, the first six seals span the forty years up to A.D. 70. **the wrath of the Lamb:** A daring paradox, on which A. T. Hanson's book *The Wrath of the Lamb* is an extended commentary. **17. the great day of their wrath has come, and who can stand?** Cf. Jl 2: 11. This 'wrath' is the retribution which must operate in a moral universe such as God's universe is; even if we call it 'retribution' rather than 'wrath' to exclude the intemperate passion which is so rarely absent from our anger, yet it is not a principle operating independently of God, but it is the response of His holiness to persistent and impenitent wickedness. It is indeed His *strange work* (Isa. 28: 21) to which He girds Himself slowly and reluctantly, in contrast to His proper and congenial work of mercy; but where His mercy is decisively repudiated, men are left to the consequences of their freely chosen course. If here the wrath of God is also 'the wrath of the Lamb', it is because that wrath is not detached from the cross; indeed, it is best understood in the light of the cross.

Interlude before the Seventh Seal (7: 1–17)
(a) The Sealing of the Servants of God (7: 1–8)
From this point on to the end of ch. 11 John describes visions of the end, 'what will take place later', seen by prophetic perspective as the immediate sequel to his own day. **1. four angels . . . holding back the four winds of the earth:** The winds are winds of judgment for they are restrained from harming earth, sea

and trees until God's elect are sealed (verses 2, 3). **2. another angel, . . . having the seal of the living God:** The seal with which God's servants are to be sealed (cf. 9: 4) is elsewhere called His name (see notes on 14: 1; 22: 4). **3. until we put a seal on the foreheads of the servants of our God:** This sealing is based on Ezek. 9: 4, where those inhabitants of Jerusalem who deplore her abominations have a mark (the X mark of the Hebrew letter *tau*) put on their foreheads to safeguard them in the impending judgment on the city. So here the faithful are sealed against the great day of divine wrath. **4. a hundred and forty-four thousand sealed, from all the tribes of Israel:** The followers of Christ are here viewed as the true 'Israel of God'; and the number indicates the sum total of the faithful; this is emphasized by the breaking down of the number among the twelve tribes (cf. 21: 12). **5. From the tribe of Judah 12,000 were sealed:** The unusual order of the tribal names here may have a special significance; but if so, it escapes us. Judah, however, is doubtless placed first because Christ belonged to it (cf. Gen. 49: 10; Heb. 7: 14). **6. from the tribe of Manasseh 12,000:** It is strange to find Manasseh listed separately, since the **tribe of Joseph** (embracing Ephraim and Manasseh) is listed in verse 7. On the other hand, the tribe of Dan is omitted. It may be thought that Dan originally stood where Manasseh now stands, but such a conjecture is unsupported by any evidence. It was held by many early expositors from Irenaeus onwards that Dan is omitted because Antichrist is to come from that tribe—a belief based by Irenaeus on the LXX version of Jer. 8: 16. But this roll-call of the tribes is schematic; we are not dealing with a census tribe by tribe as in Num. 1: 20 ff.; 26: 5 ff., and need not be over-concerned about the inclusion of Manasseh or the exclusion of Dan.

(b) **The Triumph of the Martyrs (7: 9–17)**
9. a great multitude that no one could count: The Christian Clement of Rome and the pagan Tacitus both describe the victims of Nero's persecution as 'a great multitude'; how much greater, then, must be the full complement of Christian martyrs! **from every nation, tribe, people and language:** John certainly does not confine his vision to Jewish Christians. These martyrs, having already glorified God in death, have no need to be sealed against the eschatological judgment like the 'servants of our God' in the preceding episode; yet in either case we are reminded that the Israel of God knows no national frontiers. **standing before the throne and in front of the Lamb:** Now that their number is complete, they no longer remain 'under the altar' (6: 9) but stand in the presence of God; to the **white robes** of blessedness (cf. 6: 11) are now

added the **palm branches** of victory. But they ascribe their victory to God and to Christ (verse 10); the Lamb's conquest (5: 5) is also theirs. **10. Salvation** (Gk. *sōtēria*) has the fuller sense of 'victory'; cf. the synonymous parallelism of victory, salvation, righteousness in Ps. 98: 1–3; Isa. 59: 16 f. **11. they fell down on their faces before the throne and worshiped God:** The triumph of the martyrs elicits similar praise to that which hailed the triumph of the Lamb in 5: 8–14; rightly so, because their triumph is His, and won in the same way (cf. 12: 11). **13. one of the elders asked me:** Acting as interpreter, as in 5: 5. **14. These are they who have come out of the great tribulation:** Lit., 'these are the comers (Gk. *erchomenoi*) . . .'; the present participle may be timeless, or may have imperfect force here: 'these are they who came . . .' It is plain that they are not still in process of arriving; their number is complete. This **great tribulation** is different from that of 2: 22, from the 'hour of trial' of 3: 10, and from the wrath against which the elect were sealed in verses 3–8; in all these places it is divine judgment against the wicked that is in view. It must also be distinguished from the tribulation predicted in Mk 13: 19, which fell on Judaea and Jerusalem in A.D. 70. The tribulation of our present passage is the persecution of the followers of Christ which broke in such intense malignity in John's day and continues until the ultimate triumph of Christ. (We western Christians may forget too easily that the present day is one of intense and large-scale persecution of the church.) **they have washed their robes and made them white in the blood of the Lamb:** A vivid way of saying that their present blessedness and their fitness to appear in the presence of God have been won for them by the sacrifice of Christ. **15. serve him** (Gk. *latreuō*): Priestly service is implied (cf. 20: 6; 22: 3). **in his temple:** Since the heavenly dwelling-place of God described in 4: 2 ff. is itself His temple, this phrase is practically synonymous with 'before the throne of God'. **will spread his tent over them:** Lit. 'will tabernacle over them'; the verb is *skēnoō*, as in Jn 1: 14. There is probably an allusion here to the divine *shekinah*, God's presence in glory among His people (cf 21: 3). **16. Never again will they hunger . . . :** The blessedness of the glorified martyrs is elaborated in language derived from Isa. 49: 10, where Yahweh guides the liberated exiles home. **17. the Lamb at the center of the throne will be their shepherd:** In Isa. 49: 10 it is Yahweh who takes pity on His people and leads them (cf. Isa. 40: 11); here it is Christ who acts as shepherd (cf. Jn. 10: 11 ff.). Plainly 'the Lamb' is here used as an established title of Christ, with no stress on the original figure as there is in 5: 6. **he will lead them to springs**

of living water: Cf. Ps. 23: 2 as well as Isa. 49: 10. **God will wipe away every tear from their eyes:** In Isa. 25: 8 this promise refers to the new age when God *will swallow up death for ever* (cf. 1 C. 15: 54); it is repeated below in 21: 4.

vii. The Seventh Seal (8: 1–5)

The fearful expectation of the sixth seal (6: 15–17) is due to be realized with the breaking of the seventh. **1. there was silence in heaven for about half an hour:** 'Half an hour' is the duration of the silence as it appeared to John's consciousness in the vision. All heaven breathlessly awaits the final act of divine judgment. **2. the seven angels who stand before God:** Gabriel identifies himself as one of these (Lk. 1: 19); cf. Tob. 12: 15, where Raphael describes himself as 'one of the seven holy angels who present the prayers of the saints and stand before the presence of the glory of the Holy One'. The names of all seven appear in 1 Enoch 20: 2–8 as Uriel, Raphael, Raguel, Michael, Sariel, Gabriel and Remiel: 'the archangels' names are seven'. **and to them were given seven trumpets:** As the Jewish new year was inaugurated with the blowing of trumpets (Lev. 23: 24; Num. 29: 1), so the day of the LORD is heralded by the eschatological trumpet-blasts (cf. Isa. 27: 13; Jl 2: 1; Mt. 24: 31; 1 C. 15: 52; 1 Th. 4: 16). **3. Another angel . . . came and stood at the altar:** For the altar cf. 6: 9. **He was given much incense to offer, with the prayers of all the saints:** Better: 'he was given much incense to offer, consisting of the prayers of all the saints'. So in verse 4 **The smoke of the incense** consists of the **prayers of the saints**. The preposition 'with' represents the Greek dative case, which, however, is used in these two verses as the equivalent of the Heb. *le* of definition. In 5: 8 the incense is identified with 'the prayers of the saints', and so it is here. **5. the angel took the censer, filled it with fire from the altar, and hurled it on the earth:** So in Ezek. 10: 2 ff., after the sealing of the godly in Jerusalem, burning coals are taken from the chariot-throne of God (cf. Ezek. 1: 13) and scattered over the city. But here it is the prayers of the saints that fall in judgment on the earth: the cry 'How long?' of 6: 10 is answered at last. **peals of thunder, rumblings, flashes of lightning and an earthquake:** Such as marked the theophany on Sinai (Exod. 19: 16 ff.); see note on 4: 5.

V. THE BLOWING OF THE SEVEN TRUMPETS (8: 6–11: 19)

i–iv. The First Four Trumpets (8: 6–12)

The first four trumpets are blown in swift succession and each lets loose on mankind a plague paralleled in the Exodus narrative of the plagues of Egypt, but more deadly in its effect. The last three trumpets announce calamities more frightful still, the three 'Woes' of verse 13. The fifth and sixth involve not merely natural disasters, like the first four, but demonic assaults on the human race. The seventh trumpet, like the seventh seal, is preceded by an interlude. The **hail and fire, mixed with blood** (7) which follows the first trumpet, may be compared with the seventh plague of Egypt (Exod. 9: 22 ff.); the admixture of blood may have been suggested by a climatic phenomenon of Mediterranean lands (H. B. Swete), but is more probably a purely apocalyptic portent (cf. Jl 2: 30, *blood and fire . . .*). The **huge mountain, all ablaze,** which **was thrown into the sea** when the second trumpet sounded (8), so that **a third of the sea turned into blood** (8) recalls the first plague of Egypt (Exod. 7: 17 ff.), but the undrinkable character of the fresh water, which is a feature of the first Egyptian plague (Exod. 7: 24), is paralleled in the effect of the **great star** called **Wormwood** (Gk. *apsinthos*), which fell on **a third of the rivers and springs of** (fresh) **water** after the third trumpet-blast (10 f.). The darkness which follows the fourth trumpet-blast is reminiscent of the ninth Egyptian plague (Exod. 10: 21 ff.); it is caused, however, by no mere passing sandstorm like Egypt's *darkness that can be felt,* but by a disturbance of the heavenly luminaries (cf. Lk. 21: 25 f.). These four plagues destroy one-third respectively of earth, sea, fresh water and natural light.

These four judgments remind us that the sin of man can and does adversely affect the rest of creation in a way that reacts disastrously upon his own life. John would have agreed with all that Paul says about the creation's bondage to frustration and decay (Rom. 8: 20 f.), and he later expresses the same hope as Paul's for that 'revealing of the sons of God' which will liberate creation from this bondage, when he envisages the manifestation of the new Jerusalem, the glorified community of the people of God, accompanied by the appearance of 'a new heaven and a new earth' (Rev. 21: 1 f.). But first judgment must work itself out to the bitter end.

The Three 'Woes' (8: 13)

It is not only in man's natural environment that the repercussions of his sin are felt; that same sin unleashes demonic forces, uncontrollable by man, which bring woe after woe upon him. This is what is symbolized in the judgments which follow the next trumpet-blasts, preceded as they are by the **Woe! Woe! Woe** proclaimed against **the inhabitants of the earth** (see note on 3: 10) by the **eagle . . . that was flying in mid-air** (13). **Eagle** and not 'angel' is the best-attested reading here; an eagle as heavenly messenger, although not found elsewhere in canonical scripture, appears in other apocalyptic writings (cf. 2 Esd. 11: 1) and in Christian apocrypha. That each of the three 'woes' announced by the eagle refers to one of the three remaining trumpets is made clear by 9: 12 and 11: 14.

v. The Fifth Trumpet (9: 1–12)

As in the sequence of the seals, so in the trumpets the fifth and sixth are described at greater length than the first four. **1. a star fallen from the sky to the earth:** Probably a fallen angel (cf. 12: 4), possibly identical with Abaddon-Apollyon, the angel of the abyss (verse 11). In 1 Enoch 86: 1 'a star fell from heaven' refers to the first fallen angel, who was followed by other 'stars' (see notes on 12: 4, 9; 20: 1–3). **The star was given the key to the shaft of the Abyss:** The abyss is the abode of demons, as in Lk. 8: 31; it is pictured here as a hollow place in the heart of the earth, communicating with the upper air by means of a shaft or well (Gk. *phrear*), the cover of which is locked. **3. out of the smoke locusts came down upon the earth:** We recall the Egyptian plague of locusts, so dense a swarm *that the ground was black* (Exod. 10: 15), and the plague of locusts foretold by Joel, bringing *a day of darkness and gloom, a day of clouds and blackness* (Jl 2: 2). But the locusts now seen by John are no ordinary locusts, but demon-locusts from the abyss; unlike ordinary locusts they leave the vegetation alone but with the sting of their scorpion-tails they torment those men who did not receive the seal of God in their foreheads (cf. 7: 3). The repeated mention of **five months** (5, 10) as the term of their activity has been explained by the five-months' life cycle of certain species of natural locust. **6. men will seek death, but will not find it:** Bodily death would afford an escape from physical pain, but not from the torment of an evil conscience. **7. The locusts looked like horses prepared for battle:** Cf. Jl 2: 4, *They have the appearance of horses:* but what is a bold simile in the description of Joel's locusts takes shape in John's vision, and is further elaborated in verses 7–10. **9. like the thundering of . . . many chariots:** Cf. Jl 2: 5, *With a noise like that of chariots.* **11. They had as king over them the angel of the Abyss:** This 'angel of the Abyss' is possibly the fallen 'star' of verse 1. **whose name in Hebrew is Abaddon:** Abaddon (lit. 'destruction') occurs 6 times in the Hebrew Bible (Job 26: 6; 28: 22; 31: 12; Ps. 88: 11; Prov. 15: 11; 27: 20) as a poetical synonym for Sheol, death, or the grave; here it is given personal force ('the destroyer') and glossed by Gk. *Apollyon*, the present participle of the verb *apollymi* ('destroy') —perhaps with a side-glance at the god Apollo, who in certain phases of his activity symbolized destructive forces.

vi. The Sixth Trumpet (9: 13–21)

13. a voice . . . from the horns of the golden altar: Perhaps the voice of the angel who was seen offering incense there in 8: 3. The heavenly incense-altar is equipped with horns like its earthly copy (Exod. 30: 2 f.). **14. Release the four angels who are bound at the great river Euphrates:** The Euphrates (cf. 16: 12) is significant as the eastern frontier of the Roman Empire, beyond which lay the Parthian menace (see note on 6: 2). These demon-horsemen with their mounts, hitherto held in leash, are now let loose like avenging furies upon the Roman provinces at the **hour and day and month and year** appointed (15). **15. to kill a third of mankind:** The demon-locusts were prohibited from killing men, but the demon-cavalry are more lethal: the first four trumpet-plagues blasted one-third of nature, and now **a third of mankind** is massacred. **16. two hundred million:** (lit. 'two myriads of myriads'; cf. 5: 11): To express the product of these numbers prosaically is to lose their evocative overtones. **17. The horses and riders . . . looked like this:** The colours of the riders' breastplates, **fiery red, dark blue** (lit. 'hyacinth') **and yellow as sulfur**, correspond respectively to the **fire, smoke and sulfur** which issue from the horses' mouths, thus denoting their demonic nature (cf. 14: 10 f., 19: 20, etc.), and destroy **a third of mankind** (18). The horses' lion-like heads (17) and serpent-like tails (19) further emphasize their destructive power. However symbolically they may be portrayed, there is no doubting the reality of those demonic forces which thrive on men's unbelief and are bent on their ruin; but those who are allied to their Conqueror are immune against their malignity. **20. The rest of mankind . . . did not repent:** Plague and similar disasters, which bring out the best qualities in some people bring out the worst in many others. Samuel Pepys speaks of the Plague of London (1665) as 'making us more cruel to one another than if we are dogs'; Thucydides made a similar observation in the Plague of Athens over 2000 years earlier. God has pledged His ready pardon wherever a glimmer of repentance is shown, but what if men persist in impenitence?

Interlude before the Seventh Trumpet (10: 1–11: 14)

(a) The Angel with the Little Scroll (10: 1–11)

Although the **mighty angel** whom John now sees **coming down from heaven** has features which recall the vision of Christ in 1: 13 ff., especially **his face . . . like the sun** (1), he is not to be identified with Christ. Holding a **little scroll . . . open in his hand** (2)—for its character and contents see notes on verses 8–11—he bestrides the narrow world like a colossus, and his voice, **like the roar of a lion**, awakens **the seven thunders** (3). The **seven thunders** (cf. the sevenfold *voice of the* Lord in Ps. 29) are a further heptad of divine visitations, like the seals, trumpets and bowls, but the revelation which they convey (unlike that contained in the **little scroll**) is not ready to be revealed yet, so John is commanded to **seal up** their utterance and **not write it down** (4; cf. Dan. 12: 4 and contrast Rev. 22: 10). (S. H. Hooke has suggested that what John was forbidden to write down on this occasion was later divulged in Jn 12: 31 f.) The colossal angel then swears by God that there will be **no more delay** (6; NIV gives the true sense of Gk. *chronos* here, whereas it is obscured by the AV rendering 'that there should be time no longer'); the purpose of God will now advance swiftly to its fulfilment, at the seventh trumpet-blast. **7. the mystery of God:** The secret purpose, 'hidden for long ages past' (cf. Rom. 16: 25), had been **announced to his servants the prophets** (cf. Am. 3: 7), but even so knowledge of the time when it would be accomplished had been withheld from them (cf. Mk 13: 32). **10. I took the little scroll from the angel's hand and ate it:** A similar visionary experience is recorded by Ezekiel (Ezek. 2: 8–3: 3). To eat the scroll is to assimilate its contents; the prophet digests the divine revelation himself before communicating it to others. Ezekiel's scroll was *as sweet as honey* in his mouth (Ezek. 3: 3), although *on . . . it were written words of lament and mourning and woe* (Ezek. 2: 10); John similarly records that he found the little scroll **sweet as honey in my mouth**, because it contained God's word (cf. Pss. 19: 10; 119: 103; Jer. 15: 16), but since that word was a word of judgment, he found it bitter to digest, just as Ezekiel, after eating his scroll, *went in bitterness* to communicate its contents to the exiles at Tel-abib (Ezek. 3: 14). The contents of John's little scroll are apparently represented by Rev. 11: 1–13, originally a separate and earlier apocalypse now incorporated in John's record and reinterpreted by him. **11. You must prophesy again:** Having digested the contents of the little scroll he must now make them known to others.

(b) The Two Witnesses (11: 1–14)
1. I was given a measuring rod like a staff: This fragmentary vision is reminiscent of Ezek. 40: 3 ff., where, however, it is the interpreting angel and not the prophet himself who measures the temple of the new commonwealth, as in the measuring of the new Jerusalem in Rev. 21: 15 ff. No details are preserved here of the dimensions of **the temple of God and the altar and . . . those who worship there. 2. But exclude the outer court; do not measure it, because it has been given to the Gentiles:** The apocalypse contained in the 'little scroll' probably referred to the literal city and temple of Jerusalem, and reflected the interval between July 24 and August 27, A.D. 70, when the Romans under Titus were in

occupation of the outer court of the temple but had not yet taken the holy house itself. A term of **forty-two months** is prescribed for their occupation of the city (cf. Lk. 21: 24); this is the traditional apocalyptic term of Gentile domination, derived from Dan. 9: 27; 12: 7 (where its primary reference is to the period of the defilement of the temple by the 'abomination of desolation' set up by Antiochus IV from 167 to 164 B.C.). It is identical with the **one thousand two hundred and sixty days** of v. 3 (cf. also 12: 6, 14; 13: 5), during which the **two witnesses** exercise their ministry, **clothed in sackcloth**, the rough garment of hair traditionally associated with prophets (cf. 2 Kg. 1: 8; Zech. 13: 4; Mk 1: 6). The original reference is to the ministry in Jerusalem of a latter-day Moses and Elijah (cf. Dt. 18: 15 ff.; Mal. 4: 5 f.; Mk 9: 4 f., 11 ff.), which is terminated by their martyrdom at the hands of the occupying Roman power. Their martyrdom brings relief to the people whose consciences had been disturbed by their call to repentance; but this relief is short-lived, for after **three and a half days**, during which their dead bodies are publicly exposed in the city, they are raised to life and taken up to heaven (9–12). Their translation is the signal for **a severe earthquake** (13), which causes havoc to the city and its inhabitants, so that the survivors are moved to confession and repentance.

But this little apocalypse is now to be reinterpreted in the light of the new context which it acquired by its incorporation in John's Apocalypse, especially in the light of ch. 13. The temple is now the people of God; the measuring of the worshippers (1) is analogous to the sealing of the servants of God in 7: 3–8. The external approaches to this spiritual temple may be assaulted and trodden down by pagan imperialism as some Christians yield to the temptation to compromise with idolatry and so deny Christ. But the true dwelling-place of God is immune from earthly invasion; the church's life is 'hidden with Christ in God' (Col. 3: 3) throughout the period of tribulation and loyal confession, symbolized by the three and a half years of verses 2 and 3. The two witnesses now become symbolic figures for the church in its royal and priestly functions, as is suggested by the two metaphors by which the witnesses are designated in v. 4, **the two olive trees and the two lampstands that stand before the Lord of the earth**. In Zech. 4: 2 f., 11–14, where they originally appear, these figures denote Zerubbabel the governor, prince of the house of David, and Joshua the high priest, *the two who are anointed*. **5. fire comes from their mouth and devours their enemies:** Cf. Elijah's power in 2 Kg. 1: 10, 12; the fire from heaven which consumed the men who came to take him came from his mouth in the sense that it fell upon them at his word (cf. Lk. 9: 54). **6. These men have power to shut up the sky, so that it will not rain:** A further point in common with Elijah (1 Kg. 17: 1); moreover, **the time they are prophesying** (cf. verse 3) lasts as long as Elijah's drought did (cf. Lk. 4: 25; Jas 5: 17). **they have power to turn the waters into blood:** As Moses had (Exod. 4: 9; 7: 17 ff.). **and to strike the earth with every . . . plague:** Perhaps a reference to the nine other plagues of Egypt (cf. 8: 7 ff.; 16: 2 ff.). **7. the beast that ascends from the Abyss:** Indicating demonic origin and character (cf. 9: 1 ff.). This beast from the abyss reappears in 13: 1 ff. and 17: 3 ff., where he is plainly the persecuting Roman Empire, or else the imperial antichrist of the end-time in whom the power and malignity of the persecuting empire are finally embodied and brought to a head; it is this latter sense that is uppermost here. The Gk. word for this **beast** is *thērion*, 'wild beast', as distinct from *zōon*, which is used for the 'living creatures' (AV, unfortunately, 'beasts') of 4: 6 ff. **will attack them, and overpower . . . them:** Similar language is used of the assault on the saints by the *little horn* of Dan. 7: 21 (cf. Rev. 13: 7). **8. Their dead bodies will lie in the street of the great city which is figuratively called Sodom and Egypt:** Jerusalem is called Sodom because of her unrighteousness in Isa. 1: 10; but why is she also called Egypt here? Perhaps because Egypt is an apt symbol for the oppression of the people of God. **where also their Lord was crucified:** This points to Jerusalem rather than Rome. Jesus was crucified by Roman law, but even in apocalyptic language this can scarcely be expressed by saying that He was crucified in Rome. Yet Rome has its advocates in this context—most recently J. Munck, who thinks of Peter and Paul as the two witnesses. It might be said that Jesus suffered in His followers when they were put to death in Rome, but **where also** distinguishes Him from His witnesses, and presents Him as being crucified personally in the city where they subsequently were martyred. However, we must distinguish our two levels of interpretation—the earlier one, in which **the great city** is Jerusalem: and the later one, in which it is, more generally, the world which has rejected first Christ and then His people. The **three and a half days** (9, 11) during which the witnesses' bodies lie exposed to public gaze, before their resurrection and ascension to heaven, may designedly correspond to the duration of their ministry in the ratio of a day to a year. **10. The inhabitants of the earth:** Cf. 3: 10. The phrase here is synonymous with **men from every people, tribe, language and nation** (9), and confirms the more general interpretation of **the great**

city as the whole earth. The **two prophets had tormented** them, because the witness of the godly is a condemnation to the ungodly (cf. 1 Kg. 18: 17). The language of v. 11 echoes Ezek. 37: 10. **12. Come up here:** This is the plural equivalent of the summons to John in 4: 1; but here the rapture of the resurrected martyrs to heaven is described, and described in language reminiscent of that in which Luke records the ascension of Christ (Ac. 1: 9); cf. 1 Th. 4: 17. **13. the survivors gave glory to the God of heaven:** Unlike the survivors of 9: 20 f., these turn to God as a result of their experience of His judgments.

14. The second woe has passed: This sentence marks the end of the interlude; it resumes the trumpet visions where they were broken off in 9: 21. The **third woe** is heralded by the blowing of the last trumpet.

vii. The Seventh Trumpet (11: 15–19)
The last trumpet is followed by the proclamation that **the kingdom of the world has become the kingdom of our Lord and of his Christ, and he will reign for ever and ever** (15). The sovereignty of God has never ceased, but now it is universally manifested and acknowledged; at last the time has come for the full realization of the divine purpose that in Jesus name 'every knee should bow, . . . and every tongue confess that Jesus Christ is Lord' (Phil. 2: 10 f.). **17. who is and who was,** but no longer 'who is to come' (as in 1: 4, 8; 4: 8); the Coming One has now come. **you have . . . begun to reign:** The proper rendering of the ingressive aorist *ebasileusas*. (The aorist of *basileuō* is used differently in 19: 6.) **18. The nations were angry:** Cf. Ps. 2: 1. **your wrath has come:** Divine judgment and reward (especially judgment) have been present in abundance in the previous stages of John's vision, but they reach their climax at the seventh trumpet. The climax of judgment is to be elaborated in the vision of the seven bowls (15: 5 ff.); the climax of reward in the vision of the new Jerusalem (21: 9 ff.). Preparation is made for the vision of the seven bowls by the opening of the heavenly sanctuary (Gk. *naos*)—implying the revelation of God's hidden counsel—with attendant thunder-peals and lightning-flashes (19) such as preceded the sounding of the seven trumpets (8: 5). **the ark of his covenant:** This is the first mention of the ark in Rev.; it is the archetype of the ark in the Mosaic tabernacle and Solomon's temple. Its exposure now is a token that God will fulfil to the last detail His covenant-promises to His people.

We are now carried back to the beginning of the story of salvation: a new series of visions or tableaux portrays significant figures and episodes from the course of events outlined in chapters 5–11.

Second Division: Tableaux of Conflict and Triumph (12: 1–22: 5)

I. THE WOMAN, THE CHILD AND THE DRAGON (12: 1–17)
i. The Birth of the Child (12: 1–6)
1. a great and wondrous sign appeared in heaven: Cf. 12: 3; 15: 1. **a woman clothed with the sun, with the moon under her feet:** Cf. Ca. 6: 10. The precise source of this imagery cannot be determined; various partial parallels from the ancient Near East are adduced by commentators. The woman is no individual human being, but the celestial counterpart of an earthly community; the fact that she wears **a crown of twelve stars on her head** (cf. Gen. 37: 9) marks her out as being the true Israel, from which the Messiah was born. One of the Qumran hymns similarly pictures the faithful community as a woman enduring birth-pangs until she brings to birth a man child, *a wonder of a counsellor* (quoting Isa. 9: 6, where this is one of the titles of the Davidic prince of the four names). John sees no discontinuity in the life of the true Israel before and after the birth and exaltation of Messiah; the faithful remnant of the old Israel was the nucleus of the new. **2. she was pregnant and cried out in pain:** Cf. Isa. 7: 14; Mic. 5: 3. **3. an enormous red dragon with seven heads and ten horns:** This is Leviathan, the primaeval dragon of chaos, whose overthrow by God in the beginning (Ps. 74: 14; Isa. 51: 9) and at the end-time (Isa. 27: 1) is declared in various OT writings. That his heads (Ps. 74: 14) were seven in number is attested in the Ugaritic texts, where he is called 'the accursed one of seven heads'. His **ten horns** are probably borrowed from the fourth beast of Dan. 7: 7 (cf. Rev. 13: 1; 17: 12). Here he is identified with the serpent of Eden and with Satan (verse 9).
4. His tail swept a third of the stars out of the sky: Cf. Dan. 8: 10, where the *little horn* (Antiochus Epiphanes) casts *some of the starry hosts* down to the ground and tramples upon them. This may refer to Antiochus's discouraging the worship of certain deities in favour of Olympian Zeus, whose manifestation on earth he claimed to be. But here (whatever the source of the imagery may have been) the reference is probably to the angels who were involved in Satan's fall (cf. 9: 1; also verse 9 below). For the third part of the stars cf. 8: 12. **5. She gave birth to a male child, who will rule all the nations with an iron scepter:** These words from Ps. 2: 9 identify the child with the Davidic Messiah (cf. 19: 15); in 2: 27 they have already been applied to the overcoming confessor, but they are applicable to him only by virtue of his association with the Messiah (cf. verse 11

below). **her child was snatched up to God and to his throne:** It is strange that the ascension of Christ is here presented as the immediate sequel to His birth, but it would not be less strange if the child represents the people of Christ, or Christ with His people. John is using ancient material, which he re-moulds so that its elements tell the gospel story, but its elements evidently included nothing that could be reinterpreted of the events between Christ's birth and ascension. There are admittedly exegetical problems here whose solution escapes us. **6. The woman fled into the desert:** A reference to the flight of the Palestinian church in A.D. 66, at the outbreak of the Jewish revolt; according to Eusebius, she found a refuge in the territory of Pella beyond Jordan—but did some members settle in the wilderness of Judaea? The true Israel of whom Christ was born lives on, according to the seer, in the Palestinian church; Christians elsewhere are **the rest of her offspring** (v. 17). **to a place prepared by . . . God:** Cf. Isa. 26: 20. **one thousand two hundred and sixty days:** Cf. v. 14; 11: 2 f.; 13: 5. During this period of Satanic wrath the woman is safe, while her children are persecuted; the Palestinian church escaped the most hostile attentions of the imperial power during the first-century campaign against the Christians of Rome and Asia Minor.
ii. The Downfall of the Dragon (12: 7–12)
7. And there was war in heaven: Satan's fall from heaven 'as lightning' (Lk. 10: 18) is here portrayed in pictorial terms. Jesus' ministry involved his overthrow, for his kingdom could not stand against the inbreaking kingdom of God, and he received his *coup de grâce* through the cross, the crown of Jesus' ministry (cf. Col. 2: 15). In the early Christian hymn-book curiously called the *Odes of Solomon* (Ode 22) Christ, speaking of His triumph over death, addresses God as the One 'that overthrew by my hands the dragon with seven heads: and thou hast set me over his roots that I might destroy his seed'. **9. that ancient serpent:** Cf. Gen. 3: 1 ff.; also Isa. 27: 1. **called the devil or Satan:** Gk. *diabolos* ('calumniator') is the equivalent of Heb. *satan* ('accuser'); in OT Satan appears as chief prosecutor in the heavenly court (Zech. 3: 1 f.; cf. Job 1: 6 ff.; 1 Chr. 21: 1), hence he is called in verse 10 **the accuser of our brothers**. Thanks to the victory of Christ, however, he is the principal target of the challenge: 'Who will bring any charge against those whom God has chosen? It is God who justifies. Who is he that condemns?' (Rom. 8: 33 f.). The victory of Christ and the downfall of Satan are celebrated in the triumphal shout of vv. 10–12. In Christ's victory the victory of His people is included (cf. Rom. 8: 37; 1 C. 15: 57; 2 C. 2: 14). As He conquered by His Passion (Rev. 5: 5 f.), so they

in turn conquer the dragon **by the blood of the Lamb and by the word of their testimony; they did not love their lives so much as to shrink from death** (11). But the dragon's downfall means an intensification of his malignant activity on earth, during the brief interval before he is put out of harm's way (cf. 20: 1 ff.).

iii. The Assault on the Woman and her other Children (12: 13-17)

14. The woman was given the two wings of a great eagle, so that she might fly to the desert: Cf. Exod. 19: 4, where God speaks thus of Israel's escape from Egypt into the wilderness: *I carried you on eagles' wings and brought you to myself* (cf. also Dt. 32: 10-12). **a time, times, and half a time:** This variant designation of the 1260 days of verse 6 is derived from Dan. 7: 25; 12: 7. **15. Then from his mouth the serpent spewed water like a river, to overtake the woman:** This may refer to some incident of the war of A.D. 66-73 no longer identifiable which threatened to cut off the church's escape. The reference is unlikely to be to a literal flood, like that which prevented the Jews of Gadara from escaping across the Jordan from the Romans in March, A.D. 68 (Josephus, *War* iv. 433-436); a literal flood would scarcely be spoken of as *'like a river'*. **16. the earth . . . opening its mouth and swallowing the river:** For the personification of earth cf. Gen. 4: 11; Num. 16: 30. **17. the dragon . . . went off to make war against the rest of her offspring:** Frustrated in his attack on the Palestinian church, the dragon stirs up fierce persecution against Christians in other parts of the empire. That Christians are meant is shown by the fact that they not only **obey God's commandments** but also **hold to the testimony of Jesus**—the very activity for which John was in exile (1: 9; cf. 19: 10). **And the dragon stood on the shore of the sea:** The bulk of later manuscripts read 'I stood' (Gk. *estathēn*), and link the clause to what follows in 13: 1 (so AV); but he **stood** (Gk. *estathē*) is right; the subject is the dragon, not the seer, who is still viewing the earthly scene from his heavenly vantage-point.

II. THE TWO BEASTS (13: 1-18)
i. The Beast from the Sea (13: 1-10)

1. I saw a beast coming out of the sea: This beast is the persecuting Roman Empire. We may think of it as rising in its home, the city of Rome, far west across the Mediterranean Sea from Patmos; but **sea** means more than this: 'the beast from the Abyss', as it is called in 11: 7, is thrown up, like other chaotic forces of evil, by the cosmic deep (cf. Dan. 7: 2 f.). **he had ten horns and seven heads:** The **ten horns** (cf. 12: 3) are derived from Dan. 7: 7, where the fourth beast in Daniel's vision of

judgment is so equipped. The horns of Daniel's fourth beast (Dan. 7: 24) are ten Hellenistic rulers, between Alexander the Great (332-323 B.C.) and Antiochus IV (175-163 B.C.); for their significance in Rev., cf. 17: 12-14. The **seven heads** are derived from the dragon (12: 3), signifying that the beast's authority is received from him (v. 2); but they are further explained in terms of the seven hills of Rome (17: 9) and seven Roman emperors (17: 10). **with ten crowns on his horns:** Indicating their royal character. **and a blasphemous name on each head:** Indicating the claims to divine honour made by or on behalf of the Roman emperors. **2. The beast I saw resembled a leopard:** Like the third beast of Dan. 7: 6. **but had feet like those of a bear:** The second beast of Dan. 7: 5 was *like a bear*. **a mouth like that of a lion:** The first beast of Dan. 7: 4 was *like a lion*. Thus John's beast, while it is mainly a representation of Daniel's fourth beast, has features drawn from Daniel's first three beasts. **3. One of the heads . . . seemed to have had a fatal wound:** A reference probably to Nero, who committed suicide on June 9, A.D. 68. **the fatal wound had been healed:** When Nero, deposed by the senate in A.D. 68, committed suicide to escape the ignominious death to which that body had condemned him, many of his eastern subjects (among whom he had enjoyed great popularity) refused to believe that he was really dead. For some twenty years after his death, therefore, the belief persisted that he had not really died but gone into hiding, probably beyond the Euphrates, and that he would return one day at the head of an army of Parthians to recover his dominions and rule once more as emperor. Several opportunists profited by this widespread belief to set themselves up as pretended Neros. After 88, the last year in which one of these pretenders is known to have arisen, the belief that Nero was still alive was generally given up; but it was replaced by the belief that one day Nero would return from the dead and regain his sovereignty. This later belief in a *Nero redivivus*, which can be traced right on almost to the end of the second century, was not only a subject of hope to pagans in the eastern empire, but also a subject of dread to Christians, who identified *Nero redivivus* with the last antichrist. The persecuting rage of the empire had already been experienced by John and his fellow-Christians, but when the imperial beast is embodied in the revived ruler who had previously received a **fatal wound**—an embodiment still future to the seer—that persecuting rage will reach an unprecedented intensity. **5. a mouth to utter proud words and blasphemies:** Cf. Dan. 7: 8; 11: 36, **forty-two months:** The duration of the *little horn's* authority in Dan. 7: 25. **7. He was given**

power to make war against the saints and to conquer them: An echo of Dan. 7: 21 (cf. Rev. 11: 7); this conquest consists in the infliction of bodily death on them, but the ultimate victory is theirs (15: 2). World-wide power is exercised by the beast, and world-wide worship paid to it. Cf. 2 Th. 2: 3 f., where the 'man of lawlessness . . . opposes and exalts himself over everything that is called God or is worshiped (cf. Dan. 11: 37), and even sets himself up in God's temple, proclaiming himself to be God'. **8. all inhabitants of the earth** (cf. 3: 10) are here identified as those **whose names have not been written in the book of life belonging to the Lamb that was slain from the creation of the world**. It is better to follow the marginal rendering, where **from the creation of the world** refers to **written**, not to **slain** (cf. 17: 8; also 3: 5; 20: 12, 15). **10. Patient endurance and faithfulness of the saints** are rooted in their recognition of the sovereignty of God over the world of mankind; His righteous retribution and reward will assuredly be manifested in due course (cf. Hab. 2: 3 f.; also Mt. 26: 52).

ii. The Beast from the Earth (13: 11–18)
11. I saw another beast: Thus the unholy trinity of dragon, beast and false prophet is completed. As the true Christ received His authority from the Father (Mt. 11: 27; 28: 18; Jn 13: 3), so Antichrist receives authority from the dragon (verse 4); as the Holy Spirit glorifies the true Christ (Jn 16: 14), so the false prophet glorifies Antichrist (verse 12). **coming out of the earth:** John on Patmos may have in view the neighbouring mainland of Asia Minor, where the cult of Rome and Augustus flourished (cf. 2: 13). The second beast is the embodiment of this cult, or its priesthood, in its final development. It looks as harmless as **a lamb**, but its real nature is revealed when it opens its mouth, for it speaks **like a dragon**. The imperial worship which was fostered already in provincial Asia would spread over the world, and the final intensification of imperial persecution would be accompanied by world-wide pressure of every form, psychological and economic, to worship the divinity of Caesar. The mighty works and 'counterfeit . . . signs and wonders' which, according to Paul, attend the parousia of Antichrist and seduce unbelievers (2 Th. 2: 9 f.) are manipulated by this second beast, who acts as Antichrist's Minister of Propaganda. The **image of the beast** (14 f.) recalls the 'abomination that causes desolation standing where he does not belong' (Mk 13: 14, mg.). The economic boycott of nonconformists (16 f.) is almost startling in its prophetic clarity. The **mark** stamped **on his right hand or his forehead**, where Jews wore their phylacteries (cf. Dt. 6: 8), is **the name of the beast** worshipped by those who receive it

—an unholy travesty of the seal stamped on the foreheads of the servants of God (7: 3; 14: 1; cf. 22: 4). **18. This calls for wisdom:** Similarly the prophecies of Daniel were conveyed in symbolical terms which required divine enlightenment for their elucidation: *None of the wicked will understand; but those who are wise (the maskilim) will understand* (Dan. 12: 10). **If anyone has insight, let him calculate the number of the beast:** The beast is embodied in the emperor, and it is one of the emperors whose 'number' is to be reckoned. **for it is man's number:** Lit., 'the number of a man', i.e. the total numerical value of the letters in some person's name, when spelt in the Greek, or possibly in the Hebrew, alphabet. This reckoning of the numerical value of words and names was a riddle-game among the Greeks and Romans (as in the frequently quoted Greek graffito from Pompeii, 'I love the girl whose number is 545'); among the Jews (who called it 'gematria') and some early Christians it was treated as a matter of mystical significance—as in the *Sibylline Oracles* (i. 328), where the appropriateness of 888 as the numerical value of the name of Jesus in Greek is pointed out. There is nothing mystical about the present passage; the seer's use of gematria could be a precaution against a charge of sedition if the name of the individual were spelt out in full. **His number is six hundred and sixty-six:** So successful was the seer's precaution that the solution of his riddle had been forgotten by the time of Irenaeus (A.D. 180) and remains uncertain to this day. One must hope that the original readers of Rev. understood his allusion. To complicate the matter there is a variant reading 616, but this may have been a deliberate change in order to identify the 'beast' with Gaius Caesar (spelt in Greek). Gaius's attempt to have his image erected in the Jerusalem temple in A.D. 40 marked him out as belonging to the authentic succession of Antichrist. A popular explanation of the true reading, 666, takes it as the sum of letters in 'Nero Caesar', as spelt in Hebrew or Aramaic (precisely the required spelling appears on an Aramaic document of Nero's reign from the Wadi Murabba'at, in Jordan). Another attractive suggestion is that John had in mind a type of coin circulating in the province of Asia, on which the abbreviated style of Domitian in Greek ('Emperor Caesar Domitian Augustus Germanicus') yields the total 666. But complete certainty is unattainable. George Salmon's 'three rules' for making any desired name yield the required total are still carried out in deadly seriousness by earnest Bible readers who imagine that John was really referring to the latest nine days' wonder in world politics of the 20th century. The three rules are: 'First, if the proper name by itself will not yield it, add a title;

secondly, if the sum cannot be found in Greek, try Hebrew, or even Latin; thirdly, do not be too particular about the spelling' (*Introduction to the NT*, 1889, p. 253).

III. FIRST FRUITS, HARVEST AND VINTAGE (14: 1–20)

The series of tableaux in ch. 14 may be summed up under the heads of first fruits (1–5), harvest (14–16) and vintage (17–20), the first fruits and harvest being separated by four angelic proclamations (6–13).

i. First Fruits (14: 1–5)

1. the Lamb, standing on Mount Zion: That is, on the heavenly Zion (cf. Heb. 12: 22), since He and His 'fair army' appear **before the throne and before the four living creatures and the elders** (3; cf. 4: 2 ff.; 7: 9 ff.). The fact that His 144,000 companions have **his name and his Father's name written on their foreheads** suggests their identity with the 144,000 servants of God who are sealed on their foreheads in 7: 3 ff.; while the fact that they **follow the Lamb wherever he goes** (4) links them also with the white-robed multitude of 7: 9 ff. (cf. especially 7: 17). The scene has a noteworthy parallel in 2 Esd. 2: 42 ff., 'I, Ezra, saw on Mount Zion a great multitude which I could not number, and they all were praising the Lord with songs'. Ezra goes on to describe how in their midst stood 'the Son of God, whom they confessed in the world'. **2. I heard a sound from heaven.** For **the sound of many waters** cf. 1: 15; 19: 6; for **the sound of loud thunder** cf. 19: 6, and for **the sound of harpers playing on their harps** cf. 5: 8; 15: 2. The sound which John hears is the **new song** (3) of redemption, accompanied by the music of heaven. It is not a different song from the 'new song' of 5: 9 f., except that now it is sung in the first person, as only those can sing it who have themselves been **redeemed from the earth. 4. they kept . . . pure:** Lit. 'they are virgins'—an exceptional use of Gk. *parthenos* in the masculine. The term has usually been interpreted here of celibacy, as though these men had, in Christ's words, 'made themselves eunuchs (NIVmg) because of the kingdom of heaven' (Mt. 19: 12). In that case we might compare Paul's injunction in view of the 'present crisis': 'those who have wives should live as if they had none' (1 C. 7: 26, 29). Cf. E. Stauffer: 'There is here no suggestion either of human impotence on the one side or of successful monkish achievement on the other. The reference is to the genuine heroism of those who are called for the sake of a unique situation and commission.' But this implies that married men have 'defiled themselves with women'— something so contrary to the uniform biblical teaching on marriage (cf. Heb. 13: 4) that it is unlikely to be introduced incidentally in so

thoroughly 'Hebraic' a book as this. More probably the reference is to people who have been, in the language of the Pastoral Letters, 'the husband of one wife'. **They were purchased from among men and offered as firstfruits to God and the Lamb:** The first fruits are the earnest of the much greater harvest to come (cf. verses 15 f.): as Paul speaks of his first converts in Asia and Achaia as the 'first fruits' (Gk. *aparchē*) of these provinces, so John thinks of these 144,000 as the first instalment of redeemed humanity, presented as a living sacrifice to God and to Christ. **5. No lie was found in their mouths:** The same testimony was borne to their Master (1 Pet. 2: 22; quoting Isa. 53: 9). **they are blameless:** Cf. the white robes of 7: 9, 13 f.

ii. Angel Proclamations (14: 6–13)

(a) An Eternal Gospel (14: 6–7)

6. another angel: This phrase appears six times in this chapter, but it would have been more consistent with English idiom to render it on its first appearance here by 'an angel' (Gk. *allos* in a sequence like this is used for both 'one' and 'another'). **flying in mid-air:** Cf. 8: 13. **with an eternal gospel to proclaim to those who live on the earth:** The earth-dwellers are here designated by a different verb from that used in 3: 10, etc.; for this use of Gk. *kathēmai* (lit. 'sit') cf. Lk. 21: 35. The gospel which is preached to them calls for submission to God as Creator and Judge rather than faith in Christ as Saviour and Lord. **7. Fear God and give him glory:** Cf. 11: 13. To give God glory may imply making confession to Him, as in Jos. 7: 19. **the sea and the springs of water:** Salt water and fresh water are here distinguished; the Creator has power over both, as the second and third trumpet judgments showed (8: 8 f., 10 f.).

(b) The Fall of Babylon (14: 8)

8. Fallen! Fallen is Babylon the Great: This proclamation echoes such OT passages as Isa. 21: 9; Jer. 51: 8; it is elaborated in the dirge over Babylon in ch. 18. **which made all the nations drink the maddening wine of her adulteries:** Cf. Jer. 51: 7; Rev. 17: 2, 4. For 'maddening' we should probably render 'intoxicating' here (as also in v. 10; 16: 19; 18: 3; 19: 15), Gk. *thymos* having here the sense borne by Heb. *chemah* in Isa. 51: 17, 22; Jer. 25: 15; Hab. 2: 15.

(c) The Doom of Apostates (14: 9–11)

The third angel follows with a loud warning of the divine judgment which will fall on anyone who **worships the beast and his image**, or receives 'the mark of the beast' **on the forehead or on the hand** (9: cf. 13: 15–17). The warning may be intended for all mankind, but it is especially directed at apostate Christians (cf. Heb. 6: 4–6). It may be a mitigation of the fierceness of their judgment that it is endured

in the presence of the holy angels and of the Lamb (10); to be judged in His presence is less intolerable than to be banished from His presence unjudged. Yet would their anguish not be rendered the more acute by the very presence of the one whom they have denied by their apostasy? **11. the smoke of their torment rises for ever and ever:** The language is drawn from the description of the overthrow of the cities of the plain under the rain of brimstone and fire; cf. Gen. 19: 24, 28; Isa. 34: 9 f.; Jude 7.

(*d*) **The Bliss of the Faithful Departed (14: 12–13)**
On the other hand, those who maintain their confession steadfastly and resist the blandishments and intimidation of the antichristian power, even at the cost of life (12; cf. 13: 10), are pronounced **blessed** in their death by a further **voice from heaven**, because they **die in the Lord** (13). The seer is commanded to write down this beatitude, for the encouragement of those who **from now on** suffer as martyrs of Christ. The heavenly voice is confirmed by the Spirit: for apostates and faithful confessors alike it is true that **their deeds will follow them**; but whereas this means tribulation for the former, it means rest after suffering for the blessed. The **labor** from which they rest represents the troubles they endured, not the works which they accomplished.

iii. Harvest (14: 14–16)
14. seated on the cloud was one 'like a son of man': The language is derived from Dan. 7: 13 (cf. Rev. 1: 13), where *one like a son of man* comes with the clouds of heaven to receive from the Ancient of Days universal and everlasting dominion; this is He to whom the Father has also given 'authority to judge, because he is the Son of Man' (Jn 5: 27). Once again (as in 11: 15 ff.) we are brought to the final judgment: as in Mt. 13: 39, 'the harvest is the end of the age'. In Mt. 13: 39 ff., however, 'the harvesters are angels', sent by the Son of man to 'weed out of his kingdom everything that causes sin and all who do evil'; here the Son of man is himself the reaper, and his angel-servants are absent from the picture. **15. Take your sickle:** Cf. Jl 3: 13a (to which the present passage ultimately goes back); Mk 4: 29.

iv. Vintage (14: 17–20)
At the grain-harvest the grain is gathered into barns, although the tares and chaff are burned. But this vintage-scene symbolizes unmitigated judgment: this is perhaps why the angel who gathers the vintage receives his orders from the **angel, who had charge of the fire** (18), fire being another judgment-symbol (cf. Mt. 3: 11 f.; 1 C. 3: 13 ff.). The use of the vintage as a judgment-symbol probably goes back to Joel 3: 13b; it also recalls Isa. 63: 1–6, where the conqueror over Edom has his garments all stained with the lifeblood of his enemies whom he has trampled underfoot as grapes are trodden in the wine press (cf. Rev. 19: 13, 15). So here the vintage **of the earth** is trodden so unrelentingly in **the great winepress of God's wrath** (19) that blood flows bridle-high for a distance of **one thousand six hundred stadia** or furlongs (20). We may rephrase this measurement as 200 miles, but if we do so we miss the symbolic completeness of 1600, which is the square of 40. Yet the remark that the vintage was trodden **outside the city** (20) may remind us of one who absorbed in His own person the judgment due to mankind, and did so outside the city (cf. Jn 19: 20; Heb. 13: 12).

IV. THE SEVEN LAST PLAGUES (15: 1–16: 21)
i. Introduction of the Seven Angels and Victory-Song of the Redeemed (15: 1–8)
1. another great and marvellous sign: Cf. 12: 1, 3. **seven angels with the seven last plagues:** Cf. verse 6, which is apparently anticipated by verse 1. But before more is said about the seven angels, John describes another vision of the beatified martyrs. **2. a sea of glass mixed with fire:** Cf. 4: 6; the fire which is added here may symbolize the judgment about to be consummated in the seven last plagues. **those who had been victorious over the beast:** This is the true sense; RV 'them that had come victorious from the beast' is more literal, but the Greek here imitates a Hebrew construction (literally 'to conquer from'), translated 'prevailed over' in 1 Sam. 17: 50. They had won the victory by refusing to worship the **beast and his image** or to be sealed with **the number of his name** (cf. 13: 15–17; 14: 9–11). **standing beside the sea:** Or perhaps 'on the sea of glass' (AV); the preposition *epi* is ambiguous. In either case, they stand before the heavenly throne (cf. 7: 9). **They held harps given them by God:** Cf. the harpers of 14: 2. This company recalls the 144,000 of 14: 1 ff.; but now their song is called **the song of Moses the servant of God and the song of the Lamb** (3). **The song of the Lamb** is probably 'Worthy is the Lamb' (5: 12); **the song of Moses** refers not only to the hymn of praise for redemption in Exod. 15: 1–18 but also to the judgment-song of Dt. 32, for in verses 3 f. we can discern clear echoes of Dt. 32: 4:

He is the Rock, his works are perfect;
and all his ways are just.
A faithful God who does no wrong,
upright and just is he.

But the song of verses 3 f. is a cento of passages from various places in OT. **Great and marvelous are your deeds:** Cf. Pss. 104: 24; 111: 2; 139: 14. **Lord God Almighty:** Cf. 4: 8 (echoing Isa. 6: 3). **Just and true are your ways:** Cf. Ps. 145: 17. **King of the ages:** Or 'Eternal

King'; cf. Jer. 10: 10. The strongly attested variant reading,'O King of the nations' is due to the influence of Jer. 10: 7, *Who would not revere you, O King of the nations?* A much more weakly attested variant is 'King of saints' (AV). **4. you alone are holy:** Cf. Pss. 86: 10; 99: 3, 5, 9. **All nations will come and worship . . . you:** Cf. Ps. 86: 9. **5. the temple, that is, the tabernacle of the Testimony, was opened:** The opening of the sanctuary, denoting the unfolding and fulfilment of God's purpose, recalls 11: 19, and may well be a resumption of it, after the 'signs' and other visions which have intervened. In that case, just as the breaking of the seventh seal was the cue for the blowing of the seven trumpets (8: 1 ff.), so the blowing of the seventh trumpet is the cue for the emptying of the seven bowls of wrath on earth. **6. dressed in clean, shining linen:** They are vested in priestly garments for their terrible liturgy. The remarkable variant 'stone' (Gk. *lithon*) for 'linen' (Gk. *linon*) is preferred by some on the principle that the more difficult reading is more likely to be original; it has been explained in terms of the stones in the high-priest's breastplate, or of the description of the king of Tyre in Ezek. 28: 13, *every precious stone adorned you.* But the weight of the evidence favours 'linen' here. **golden sashes around their chests:** Like the Son of man (1: 13). **7. seven golden bowls filled with the wrath of God:** A contrast to the golden bowls containing the prayers of the saints (5: 8), and yet the outpouring of wrath on the earth-dwellers is the response to those prayers (6: 10; 8: 3 ff.). **8. the temple was filled with smoke from the glory of God:** The cloud envelops the divine *shekinah* as in Exod. 40: 34 f.; 1 Kg. 8: 10 ff.; Isa. 6: 4. Long deferred though God's judgment may be, when once it is begun it proceeds with terrible swiftness. The seven receptacles of His wrath are not narrow-necked 'vials' (as in AV), from which the contents trickle slowly, but wide, shallow bowls, whose entire contents splash out immediately when they are upturned. But while the strange and swift work is going on, the sanctuary is inaccessible; the meaning may be that the time for intercession is past.

ii. The Outpouring of the Seven Plagues (16: 1–21)
There is a remarkable parallelism between most of the seven trumpet judgments of chapters 8–11 and the last plagues of chapter 16. In the first form of each series the earth, sea, fresh water and sun are respecively affected; but the present judgments are more severe than their 'trumpet' counterparts; where the former judgments affected one-third of the area in question, these affect the whole. The sixth plague in the present series, like the sixth trumpet-judgment, affects the Euphrates; and the emptying of the

seventh bowl, like the blowing of the last trumpet, is followed by a proclamation from heaven. We may also be struck by the resemblances between these 'last plagues' and the plagues of Egypt. Unpalatable as the work of judgment may be, it is inseparable from a moral universe. Is God 'unjust in bringing his wrath on us?' asks Paul. 'Certainly not!' is his reply. 'If that were so, how could God judge the world?' (Rom. 3: 5 f.). Symbolical as the details of these plagues are, they denote terrible realities. More terrible than the plagues themselves, however, is the way in which those on whom they fall are but hardened in their impenitence.

1. I heard a loud voice from the temple: The voice of God Himself. **pour out . . . on the earth:** Here 'earth' is used in a general sense, and is not restricted to the dry land, as it is in verse 2. **2. ugly and painful sores:** Like the Egyptian plague of boils (Exod. 9: 8 ff.). **3. the sea . . . turned into blood like that of a dead man, and every living thing in the sea died:** A more wholesale judgment than the similar one of 8: 8 f. **4. the rivers and springs of water . . . became blood:** As in the first plague of Egypt (Exod. 7: 17 ff.). **5. the angel in charge of waters:** The various natural elements and forces are all placed under the control of their appropriate angels in Jewish literature of this period; cf. the four angels who controlled the four winds in 7: 1, and the angel of fire in 14: 18. **You are just in these judgments:** The hymn of vv. 5 f. strikes the same note as that of 15: 3 f., and similarly echoes Moses' song of Dt. 32. **You who are and who were the Holy One:** Even in 1611 there was no justification for the AV reading 'which art, and wast, and shalt be'; all the earlier English versions read 'holy' and have no knowledge of 'shalt be' (which resulted from a misreading of Gk. *hosios*, 'holy', as the future participle *esomenos*). **6. as they deserve:** The same Gk. words as are rendered 'they are worthy' in 3: 4—'a terrible antithesis' (H. B. Swete). **7. I heard the altar respond:** The incense-altar responds with an Amen to the angel's affirmation of divine righteousness; why the altar? Perhaps because it was witness to the martyrs' prayer of 6: 10. **8. the sun . . . was given power to scorch people with fire:** Contrariwise, when the fourth trumpet sounded, one-third of the sunlight (and of the light of the other luminaries) was darkened. **9. they refused to repent and glorify him:** Unlike those who survived the earthquake of 11: 13; but cf. 9: 20 f. and the note there. **10. The fifth angel poured out his bowl on the throne of the beast:** Presumably on Rome; the centre of world-power is now attacked. **his kingdom was plunged into darkness:** Cf. the ninth plague of Egypt (Exod. 10: 21 ff.). **Men gnawed their tongues in agony:** Hardly on account of the darkness, but because of the continuing pain of the previous plague, which was aggravated by the darkness. **11. and cursed the God of heaven . . . but . . . refused to repent:** A repetition of verse 9. **12. the great river Euphrates . . . was dried up:** After the blowing of the sixth trumpet four demon-angels bound at the Euphrates frontier were released to invade the Roman Empire. Now, across the dry bed of the river, **the kings from the East** (a reference to the Parthians and their allies) may invade the Roman provinces unimpeded. But worse than this overrunning of ordered civilization by the incursion of alien armies is the perversion of the minds of those in authority by demonic powers, operating on a world-wide scale to engulf humanity in ultimate catastrophe. These demonic powers are here pictured as the **three evil spirits . . . like frogs** (13) from the mouths of the unholy trinity. The picture may be suggested by the second plague of Egypt (Exod. 8: 2 ff.); but this is a plague infinitely more destructive. The kings of the whole world— not only the invaders from the east but the rulers of the Roman Empire and the outer barbarians (cf. 17: 12 ff.)—are gathered **for battle on the great day of God Almighty** (14), the day when His cause is finally vindicated.

15. Behold, I come like a thief: This parenthetic announcement by Christ (cf. 3: 3) is no accidental displacement: 'the day of the Lord will come like a thief in the night' (1 Th. 5: 2; cf. Mt. 24: 43 f.). **Blessed is he who stays awake and keeps his clothes . . . :** The soldier who is alert and prepared for a sudden attack or call to action will not lose time by looking for his clothes or incur disgrace *by fleeing away naked in that day* (Am. 2: 16; cf. Mk 14: 52). Spiritual alertness is here enjoined, 'because you do not know the day or the hour' (Mt. 25: 13). **that he may not go naked and be shamefully exposed:** According to the Mishnah, the captain of the temple in Jerusalem went his rounds of the precincts by night, and if a member of the temple police was caught asleep at his post, his clothes were taken off and burned, and he was sent away naked in disgrace. Cf. 3: 18.

16. Then they gathered the kings: The subject ('they') is the three demonic spirits of verses 13 f.; AV 'he' is due to the singular verb *synēgagen*, but the verb is singular because the subject is neuter plural. **at the place that in Hebrew is called Armageddon:** Better: 'Har-Magedon', which could be interpreted in Hebrew as 'Mount Megiddo'—the spelling Megiddon appears in Zech. 12: 11 *MT* and *Magedōn* in the LXX of 2 Chr. 35: 22. Megiddo was the scene of many a decisive battle in antiquity, as in more recent times. The difficulty with this, however, is that there is no

'Mount Megiddo'; Megiddo was the name of a city which gave its name to the pass which it commanded. An alternative suggestion, which is not without difficulties of its own, is that the reference is to Heb. *har mo'ed, the mount of assembly* of Isa. 14: 13: the place of divine assembly has its demonic counterpart. In any case, it is on no ordinary battlefield that these kings and their armies are mustered for the eschatological conflict. The sequel to their mustering is described in 19: 19. **17. It is done:** The last plague has now been poured out: Cf. 21: 6. **18. flashes of lightning, rumblings, peals of thunder:** Such as followed the blowing of the seventh trumpet (11: 19). **a severe earthquake:** More disastrous than that of 11: 13. **19. The great city split into three parts:** Cf. 11: 8; perhaps it is the world-city rather than Jerusalem. It is not Rome, which receives separate mention as **Babylon the Great** (cf. 14: 8); what is said of her here is amplified in 17: 1–18: 24. **20. Every island fled away and the mountains could not be found:** Compare the result of the breaking of the sixth seal (6: 14); see also 20: 11. **21. From the sky huge hailstones . . . fell upon men:** Compare the Egyptian plague of hail (Exod. 9: 22 ff.); but these hailstones, **about a hundred pounds each,** are no ordinary ones; in the general convulsion of nature a rain of meteorites may be pictured. But it produces no repentance, even for the time being, as the hail in Egypt did.

V. BABYLON THE GREAT (17: 1–19: 5)

One of the angelic announcements of ch. 14 proclaimed the fall of 'Babylon the Great'; and later, when the seventh bowl of judgment was emptied, 'God remembered Babylon the Great and gave her the cup . . . of the fury of his wrath' (16:19). The judgment of great Babylon is now portrayed in a further vision.

i. The Scarlet Woman (17: 1–18)

1. One of the seven angels who had the seven bowls: Cf. 15: 7; 21: 9. **the great prostitute:** For similar descriptions of other cities cf. Nah. 3: 4 (Nineveh); Isa. 23: 15 f. (Tyre); Ezek. 23: 5 ff. (Samaria). Jerusalem herself is so portrayed in Ezek. 16: 15 ff.; 23: 11 ff. **who sits on many waters:** The language is borrowed from Jer. 51: 13, where the literal Babylon dwells 'by many waters'; for its present meaning cf. verse 15. **2. With her the kings of the earth committed adultery:** Have concluded political and economic treaties. **the inhabitants of the earth were intoxicated with the wine of her adultery:** Cf. 14: 8; the reference is to Rome's domination of the Mediterranean world. **3. the angel carried me away in the Spirit:** For this language of prophetic ecstasy cf. Ezek. 37: 1; 40: 1 f. **a woman**

sitting on a scarlet beast: The beast is patently the beast from the sea of 13: 1 ff.; the imperial city is maintained by the empire. The colour of the beast, like the woman's finery (4), bespeaks Rome's ostentatious splendour. **4. She held a golden cup in her hand:** Cf. Jer. 51: 7, where the literal *Babylon was a gold cup in the Lord's hand; she made the whole earth drunk.* **5. This title was written on her forehead: Mystery:** 'mystery' indicates that the name she bears (as Roman harlots wore their names on their foreheads) is not to be understood literally, but allegorically: **Babylon the Great** is read, but 'Rome' is meant (cf. verses 9, 18). **mother of prostitutes and of . . . abominations:** A reference to the concentration of idolatry, superstition and vice in the imperial city; cf. Tacitus's description of Rome as the place 'where all the horrible and shameful things in the world congregate and find a home' (although Tacitus, unlike John, includes Christianity among these things). **6. drunk with the blood of the saints, the blood of those who bore testimony to Jesus:** A reference to the persecution of Christians in Rome, beginning with Nero's assault on them after the great fire of A.D. 64. **7. I will explain to you the mystery of the woman:** In apocalyptic, revelations are made in symbols which remain mysteries until the appropriate interpretation is supplied; cf. Dan. 2: 18 ff.; 4: 9 ff.; 5: 5 ff.; 7: 15 ff. **8. The beast, which you saw:** The beast is described as in 11: 7; 13: 3, 8. While the beast is the empire, the interpretation oscillates between the empire and its personification in the persecuting emperor who after his mortal wound comes to life again as the last Antichrist (cf. v. 11). **once was, now is not, and yet will come:** A profane parody of the divine name of 1: 4, etc. **9. This calls for a mind with wisdom:** Cf. 13: 18. **The seven heads are seven hills on which the woman sits:** Even if the imperial police missed the reference to Rome elsewhere in the vision, the proverbial **seven hills**, the *septimontium*, could not be mistaken. Rome was at first a conurbation of seven hill-settlements on the left bank of the Tiber, the principal settlement being that on the Palatine hill. **They are also seven kings:** Seven Roman emperors (Gk. *basileus* is used in this sense in Jn 19: 15; Ac. 17: 7; 1 Pet. 2: 13, 17). **10. Five have fallen:** If we reckon from the first emperor, these would be Augustus (27 B.C.-A.D. 14), Tiberius (A.D. 14–37), Gaius (37–41), Claudius (41–54) and Nero (54–68). **one is:** Probably Vespasian (69–79); the three emperors Galba, Otho and Vitellius, who ruled in quick succession at Rome during the 18 months between Nero's death and the capture of Rome by Vespasian's troops on December 21, A.D. 69, hardly come into the reckoning from the viewpoint of the eastern provinces.

In them Vespasian's authority was undisputed after his proclamation at Alexandria on July 1, A.D. 69. (His accession to the imperial throne had been predicted two years previously by Josephus, who regarded Vespasian as destined to fulfil part of the messianic prophecies.) **the other has not yet come, . . . he must remain for a little while:** Titus, Vespasian's successor, reigned for only two years (A.D. 79–81). **11. The beast who was once, and now is not, it is an eighth king:** Here again we have the oscillation between the empire (the beast) and the emperor (one of the heads) who embodied its power at any one time (cf. 13: 3, 12). At the end the power of the persecuting empire will be embodied in the imperial Antichrist, who **belongs to the seven**, presumably in the sense that he is a reincarnation of one of them. It was natural for commentators from the second century onwards to identify him with Domitian (81–96), successor to his brother Titus, and to envisage him as a second Nero. But John is not thinking of Domitian (whose traditional reputation as a persecutor of the church rests on a very modest historical foundation), but of a demonic potentate, *Nero redivivus* (see note on 13: 3). **going to his destruction:** Cf. 19: 20. Antichrist is designated 'the man doomed to destruction' in 2 Th. 2: 3. **12. The ten horns** have a different significance from that of their prototypes on the nameless beast of Dan. 7: 7. They represent **ten kings** who are yet to arise as allied dependants of Rome in making **war against the Lamb** (13 f.), but who subsequently, in concert with the people of the empire itself, turn and rend her (16). They cannot be identified with known historical characters. The city of Rome was indeed sacked in 410 by the Goths, who had entered into alliance with the emperor; but it is doubtful if John would have regarded that event as a fulfilment of his vision. By that time Rome had long since capitulated to the sovereignty of Christ. Particular announcements of judgment in Scripture are regularly liable to be averted by timely repentance (cf. Jer. 18: 7 f.; Jon. 3: 10). Even so, John reminds us, with reference to the empire that he knew best, that imperial dominion does not endure, and that any power which sets itself *against the* LORD *and against his Anointed One* (Ps. 2: 2) signs its own death-warrant. **14. the Lamb will overcome them, because he is Lord of lords and King of kings:** Cf. 19: 11–21 for details of this eschatological victory, and 19: 16 for the Lamb's title. **with him will be his called, chosen and faithful followers:** In 19: 14 they are described as 'the armies of heaven, dressed in fine linen, white and clean.' **16. The beast and the ten horns . . . will hate the prostitute:** The imperial allies and provinces unite in this annihilating attack on **the great**

city that rules over the kings of the earth (18).

ii. Dirge over Babylon (18: 1–24)
The theme of great Babylon's downfall is continued, but it is now presented in terms of the destruction of a great mercantile city. In John's day Rome was the centre of world commerce —'Rome was the whole world, and all the world was Rome' (Spenser)—and what is here portrayed is not merely the doom of an ancient city, but the sure collapse of all human organization, commercial and otherwise, that leaves God out of its reckoning:

> *Lo, all our pomp of yesterday*
> *Is one with Nineveh and Tyre!*

First, a mighty and resplendent angel (v. 1) announces the fall of Babylon (v. 2) in language drawn from Isa. 21: 9 (cf. Rev. 14: 8); 13: 21 f., and Jer. 51: 8, where the desolation of Babylon on the Euphrates is vividly portrayed. For the language of verse 3 cf. 14: 8; 17: 2. It might seem unnecessary to mention that Babylon of ch. 18 is identical with Babylon of ch. 17, were it not that some commentators have tried to make a distinction between them. **3. her excessive luxuries:** Lit. 'the power of her luxuriance', 'power' (Gk. *dynamis*) being used here in the extended sense of Heb. *chayil* ('might', 'wealth'). Next, another voice from heaven calls upon the people of God to leave the doomed city, in language drawn from Jer. 50: 8; 51: 6, 45; Isa. 48: 20; 52: 11 f., lest they **share in her sins** and **receive . . . her plagues** (4). **5. for her sins are piled up to heaven:** Cf. Jer. 51: 9. **6. Give back to her as she has given:** A statement of the principle of retribution in human history which recurs throughout the Bible; cf. , with special reference to Babylon, Ps. 137: 8; Jer. 50: 15, 29. **7. I sit as queen; I am not a widow . . . :** These and the following phrases are quoted from Isa. 47: 7 ff., where the plight of captive Babylon is depicted. **8. in one day:** Cf. Isa. 47: 9, *in a moment, in a single day:* cf. also verses 10, 17, 19 below ('in one hour'). **for mighty is the Lord God who judges her:** Cf. , in similar contexts, Isa. 47: 4; Jer. 50: 34. John's transference of older prophecies to suit new conditions may encourage modern readers (although they can lay no claim to his prophetic gift) to apply the *principles* of John's prophecy to the present day, where they are applicable to it. But it is one of the oddities of the history of biblical interpretation that Christian communities have been so prone to identify one another with the apocalyptic Babylon; it is too easy and agreeable to apply the denunciations of Scripture to others and claim the blessings for oneself. **9. the kings of the earth . . . will weep and mourn over her:** The laments in verses 9–19 by rulers and merchants who grew prosperous by their commerce with the great city echo the dirges over

Tyre in Ezek. 26: 17–19; 27: 25–36. **10. Woe! Woe! O great city . . . city of power:** Cf. Ezek. 26: 17. **11. the merchants of the earth will weep and mourn over her:** Because the city's fall deprives them of so inexhaustible a market for their wares. **cargoes of gold, silver, precious stones and pearls . . . :** Cf. the catalogue of Tyrian merchandise in Ezek. 27: 12 ff. **13. bodies and souls of men:** There is a slight change in construction in the Greek which suggests that 'souls (lives) of men' is in apposition to 'bodies'. Cf. Ezek. 27: 13, where *the persons of men* (Heb. *nephesh 'adam*) is in LXX *psychai anthrōpōn*, the same expression as John uses here. There is good Hellenistic evidence for taking 'bodies' in the sense of 'slaves'. **17. Every sea captain, and all who travel by ship, the sailors, and all who earn their living from the sea, will stand far off:** Cf. Ezek. 27: 29, *the mariners and all the seamen will stand on the shore.* In Ezekiel the fall of Tyre is depicted as the foundering of a great merchantman, laden with goods from many lands, *in the heart of the sea* (Ezek. 27: 25); here the spectators come to witness and mourn over the disappearance of a great city in a gigantic conflagration, and they keep their distance because of the intense heat (verses 9 f., 15, 17 f.); cf. Abraham's view of the burning cities of Sodom and Gomorrah in Gen. 19: 27 f. **20. Rejoice over her, O heaven:** This is not the malignant delight which some take in the discomfiture of their enemies, but a call to rejoice in the judgments of God. There is unmistakable pathos in the dirge over Rome, just as there was in the dirge over Tyre which it echoes, and we need not suppose that either Ezekiel or John did not feel this pathos at heart. But *when your judgments come upon the earth, the people of the world learn righteousness* (Isa. 26: 9). In the judgments of God, rightly considered, the people of God can properly rejoice, but they will 'rejoice with trembling', remembering that His judgments begin with His own household (1 Pet. 4: 17; f. Ezek. 9: 6; Am. 3: 2). **21.** The angel's action in throwing **a boulder the size of a large millstone . . . into the sea** in token of Rome's annihilation recalls the acted prophecy which Jeremiah commanded Seraiah to carry out at Babylon in 593 B.C. (Jer. 51: 59–63). The angel now takes up the dirge with its heavy refrain **never . . . again** (cf. Ezek. 26: 21; 27: 36). The activities and recreations of city life will come to a full stop, and great Babylon will vanish as though she had never been. **22. the music of harpists . . . will never be heard in you again:** Cf. Ezek. 26: 13 (of Tyre). **23. The voice of bridegroom and bride will never be heard in you again:** Cf. Jeremiah's similar language with regard to Jerusalem (Jer. 7: 34; 16: 9; 25: 10). **24. In her was found the blood of prophets and of the**

saints, and of all who have been killed on the earth: Cf. our Lord's similar words about Jerusalem's impending expiation of 'the blood of all the prophets . . . shed since the beginning of the world' (Lk. 11: 50; Mt. 23: 35). It is not for her wealth and commercial enterprise that the great city is doomed. If prosperity is no proof of divine approval, neither does it arouse divine envy. But godlessness brings on its own nemesis, and where godlessness is conjoined with the unconscionable exploitation of the underprivileged and the persecution of the righteous, nothing but timely and whole-hearted repentance can avert the death-sentence. Where, however, the sins of civilization reach their utmost limit and there is no further room for repentance, the judgment falls with the decisiveness of the 'large millstone' of v. 21.

iii. Exultation over Babylon (19: 1–5)
1. I heard . . . the roar of a great multitude in heaven: The collapse of godless rebellion and oppression on earth gives rise to jubilation in heaven. For mortal men the vindication of God's righteousness is a sobering spectacle, even when it is most welcome, for there is none who is not liable to His judgment in some degree: 'If you, O LORD, kept a record of sins, O Lord, who could stand?' But saints and angels in heaven with purified vision see this lower world in the light of God's glory, and their praise need not be disturbed by uneasy reflections.

VI. THE MARRIAGE OF THE LAMB (19: 6–10)
6. Hallelujah! For our Lord God Almighty reigns: This is the keynote of the whole book. Though the enemies of God rage against His people like savage beasts and great Babylon exults in her insolence, He remains supreme, 'keeping watch above His own' and ready to call His foes to account when their rebellion has passed the point of no return. The present tense **reigns** represents the Gk. aorist *ebasileusen* (cf. 11: 17), which here follows the LXX of Ps. 93: 1, etc., where the aorist serves as the equivalent of the Hebrew perfect (NIV, *The LORD reigns*). **7. the wedding of the Lamb has come, and his bride has made herself ready:** The ancient motif of the sacred marriage is introduced towards the end of the apocalyptic drama. For the messianic bridal theme cf. Jn 3: 29 (the figure of speech appears more generally in Mt. 25: 1 ff.; Mk 2: 19 f.; 2 C. 11: 2; Eph. 5: 25 ff.). The Lamb is the Messiah: the bride is the messianic community (cf. 21: 2, 9 ff.). **8. Fine linen, bright and clean, was given her to wear:** Cf. the white garments of the multitude in 7: 9 ff. The **fine linen** represents 'the sum of the saintly acts of members of Christ, wrought in them by His

Spirit' (H. B. Swete). **9. the angel said to me:** The interpreting angel of 1: 1 (cf. 17: 1; 21: 9). **Blessed are those who are invited to the wedding supper of the Lamb:** While the beloved community is the bride, its individual members can be envisaged as wedding guests. Cf. the pious remark in Lk. 14: 15. **These are the true words of God:** This assurance is repeated in 21: 5; 22: 6. **10. Do not do it!:** Cf. 22: 9. Bearing Col. 2: 18 in mind, we may recognize a warning to the Asian churches against angel-worship. **I am a fellow servant:** 'angels, although they are stronger and more powerful' (2 Pet. 2: 11), do not share the divine nature but are 'ministering spirits sent to serve' (Heb. 1: 14). **Worship God!:** Cf. Mt. 4: 10, 11; Lk. 4: 8, quoting Dt. 6: 13. **the testimony of Jesus is the spirit of prophecy:** Here NT prophecy is meant; for a similar statement about OT prophecy see 1 Pet. 1: 10 f. (cf. Jn 5: 39; Ac. 10: 43).

VII. THE HOLY WAR (19: 11–21)
11. I saw heaven standing open: Cf. 4: 1; Ezek. 1: 1. **a white horse:** A symbol of victory, as in 6: 2. **. . . whose rider is called Faithful and True:** This horseman is different from the first horseman of ch. 6; he is the conquering Messiah, the 'faithful and true witness' of 3: 14. **With justice he judges and makes war:** Cf. Isa. 11: 4. The theme of the holy war of the end-time (already announced in 16: 14, 16; 17: 14) recurs frequently in apocalyptic; its features were well established, but John resolutely bends them, recalcitrant as they may be to his purpose, to serve as symbols of the victory of the Lion of the tribe of Judah who conquered by his death (5: 5 f.). **12. His eyes are like blazing fire:** Cf. 1: 14; 2: 18. **on his head are many crowns:** More than the dragon's seven (12: 3) or the imperial beast's ten (13: 1); they represent the universal allegiance which He receives (5: 11–13). **he has a name written on him that no one knows but he himself:** Cf. the secret name given to the overcomer in 2: 17. Here the mystery of the person of Christ is suggested (cf. Mt. 11: 27, 11; Lk. 10: 22); this name is apparently neither of the revealed names of verses 13, 16. **13. He is dressed in a robe dipped in blood:** For 'dipped' (Gk. *bebammenon*, from *baptō*) some early manuscripts and versions read 'sprinkled' (Gk. *rerantismenon*, from *rhantizō*). The picture is drawn from Isa. 63: 1–3, but there the conqueror's *crimsoned garments* are dyed with the blood of his Edomite foes. This is one of the recalcitrant features of the imagery which John re-shapes to portray the gospel of the Christ who triumphed by the shedding of His own blood. **and his name is the Word of God:** A notable point of contact with the Johannine Gospel (cf. Jn 1: 1–14). **14. The**

armies of heaven: The 'called, chosen and faithful' of 17: 14. **dressed in fine linen, white and clean:** Cf. verse 8. **on white horses:** Cf. verse 11; they share their Leader's victory (cf. 12: 11). **15. Out of his mouth comes a sharp sword with which to strike down the nations:** From Isa. 11: 4; cf. 1: 16; 2: 16. The sword symbolizes the irresistible power of His word of judgment and grace. **He will rule them with an iron scepter:** From Ps. 2: 9; cf. 12: 5 (also 2: 27). **He treads the winepress of the fury of the wrath of God Almighty:** From Isa. 63: 2 f., 6; cf. 14: 19 f. **16. on his thigh:** On the assumption that a Semitic original underlies John's Greek, it has been conjectured that Heb. or Aram. *regel* ('leg') has inadvertently replaced an original *degel* ('banner'). **King of kings and Lord of lords:** This name of universal dominion (cf. 17: 14) resembles the designation of Israel's God in Dt. 10: 17; to Christ is given 'the name that is above every name' (Phil. 2: 9), and world dominion is His. **17. an angel standing in the sun:** From which vantagepoint he can be heard by all the birds of the air. **Come, gather . . . for the great supper of God:** This ghastly picture is drawn from Ezek. 39: 17–20. The battle of Armageddon, once joined, is quickly won; the powers that militated against God and His people suffer final and irreparable destruction. Cf. the fate of Daniel's fourth beast, whose dead body was *thrown into the blazing fire* (Dan. 7: 11). But here the creatures which embody imperial force and emperor-worship are **thrown alive into the fiery lake of burning sulfur** (20)—John's symbol for 'the second death' (cf. 20: 14; 21: 8). With verse 21, these words emphasize the completeness of the overthrow of the enemies of God. From first to last Rev. is the book of the triumph of Christ. It was by no material weapons, but by the power of the gospel, that Christ conquered the pagan Roman Empire; by that same power He has continued to conquer in history, and will conquer to the end. The analogy of Scripture discourages the idea that Christ, having conquered thus throughout preceding ages, will change His weapons for the final struggle and have recourse to those which He rejected in the day of temptation in the wilderness.

VIII. THE BINDING OF SATAN AND REIGN OF THE MARTYRS (20: 1–6)

The subordinate powers of evil having been destroyed, only Satan remains to be dealt with. An angel from heaven—not the fallen angel of the abyss (9: 1, 11)—chains him and locks him in the abyss **for a thousand years** (1–3). Cf. 1 Enoch 88:1, where one of the principal archangels 'seized that first star which had fallen from heaven, and bound it hand and foot, and cast it into an abyss', into which the other fallen

stars were then thrown bound (see note on 9: 1). Satan's consignment to the abyss is clearly later than his expulsion from heaven (12: 9); that preceded the rise of the beast and false prophet, whereas this follows their destruction. The thousand years of Satan's imprisonment in the abyss are surely identical with the thousand years of verse 4, during which the risen martyrs reign with Christ.

In some phases of Jewish eschatology 'the days of the Messiah', introduced by the appearance of Messiah on earth, were expected to precede the age to come. The duration of these days was variously estimated (cf. the 400 years of 2 Esd. 7: 28 f.); the estimate of a thousand years was related to Ps. 90: 4 (cf. 2 Pet. 3: 8). But for Christians the Messiah had already come, and with His exaltation to God's right hand His reign had already begun (5: 6 ff.; cf. 1C. 15: 24–28). The millennial period of vv. 4–6, however, does not commence with the enthronement of Christ but at a later point, with the resurrection of the martyrs to share His throne (cf. 3: 21). **4. I saw thrones:** Cf. Dan. 7: 9, *thrones were set in place.* **on which were seated those who had been given authority to judge:** Cf. Dan. 7: 22 (RV), *judgment was given to the saints of the Most High* (cf. also 1 C. 6: 2 f.). In verse 4 **the souls of those who had been beheaded because of their testimony for Jesus and because of the word of God** (cf. 1: 9; 12: 11) are probably identical with all who **had not worshiped the beast or his image and had not received his mark** (cf. 13: 15 ff.). No longer 'under the altar' (6: 9), they are glorified with Christ (as we have already seen in 14: 1 ff.; 15: 2). **They came to life:** The correct translation of the Gk. aorist *ezēsan.* **and reigned with Christ a thousand years:** It is not said, and perhaps not even implied, that earth is the place where they reign with Him (see note on 5: 10), although earth certainly enjoys a blessed respite during this period of the binding of Satan (verse 3). **5. The rest of the dead did not come to life until the thousand years were ended:** Cf. verses 12 f. **This is the first resurrection:** That is, the resurrection of those who **came to life** again in verse 4. **6. The second death has no power over them:** See note on verse 14. **they will be priests of God and of Christ**, in addition to reigning with Christ; cf. 1: 6; 5: 10.

IX. GOG AND MAGOG (20: 7–10)

The binding of Satan is a restraint on evil, but does not extirpate it. A brief spell of renewed devilry intervenes between the thousand years and the last judgment. Satan, released from the abyss, resumes his deception of the nations, and finds obedient tools in **Gog and Magog:** Here, as in Ezek. 38: 1 ff., and in several other (but not all) places where Gog appears in Jewish literature, his attack comes between the messianic age and the establishment of the new Jerusalem. Whereas Ezekiel places *Gog, of the land of Magog* (Ezek. 38: 1) in his precise geographical setting (Asia Minor), together with his subject-allies (from north, east, and southwest of the Fertile Crescent), the geographical delimitation disappears here, and the reference comprises the marginal forces of evil from **the four corners of the earth** (8). (In the *Sibylline Oracles* iii. 319 f., the 'land of Gog and Magog' is located 'in the midst of the rivers of Ethiopia'.) Again, whereas in Ezek. 38: 1 Magog is the territory of which Gog is ruler, Gog and Magog here, as in Sibylline and rabbinic literature, are parallel names, used together as a symbol of the world-powers opposed to God. **In number they are like the sand on the seashore:** Cf. Gen. 22: 17; 1 Sam. 13: 5, etc. for the simile; Ezekiel describes Gog's army as *a cloud covering the land* (Ezek. 38: 16). **9. They marched across the breadth of the earth:** From Hab. 1: 6, where a Chaldaean invasion is similarly described. **surrounded the camp of God's people, the city he loves:** Cf. for the latter phrase Pss. 78: 68; 87: 2. Some have thought of a new foundation on the site of the old city 'which is figuratively called Sodom and Egypt' (11: 8); we need not think, however, of a walled and built-up city (cf. Ezek. 38: 11, 14), but rather of a community of the true Israel, encamped, as earlier Israel once was, in the wilderness. Not the resurrected confessors, but the mother-church of 12: 13 ff., which had been protected against her enemies in the persecution under the 'beast', should probably be identified as the target of this attack. **fire came down from heaven and devoured them:** Cf. Ezek. 38: 22 (and more generally Gen. 19: 24 ff.; 2 Kg. 1: 10, 12). **10. the devil, who deceived them, was thrown into the lake of burning sulfur:** This must be 'the eternal fire prepared for the devil and his angels' of Mt. 25: 41. The 'adamantine chains and penal fire' which Milton envisages as Satan's dungeon at his primaeval fall are assigned to him by John at the end of time. **where the beast and the false prophet had been thrown:** Cf. 19: 20. The two earlier prisoners are evidently still there, for, together with their new companion, **they will be tormented day and night for ever and ever.** Since the beast and the false prophet are figures for systems rather than individual persons, the permanent destruction of evil is evidently meant.

X. THE LAST ASSIZE (20: 11–15)
11. I saw a great white throne and him who was seated on it: In Dan. 7: 9 *and the Ancient of Days took his seat* as judge at the final assize.

But in Rev. 1: 13 ff. the one *like a son of man* shares the features of Daniel's Ancient of Days; and since, according to Jn 5: 27, the Father 'has given him authority to judge, because he is the Son of Man', we may think of the Son of Man as seated on this throne (cf. Mt. 19: 28; 25: 31). **Earth and sky fled from his presence:** Cf. Isa. 34: 4; Mk 13: 31; 2 Pet. 3: 10. But the language here serves chiefly to underline the awesome majesty of the Judge and the judgment. **12. I saw the dead, great and small, standing before the throne:** These are 'the rest of the dead' of verse 5; now they too have been raised. **books were opened:** As in Dan. 7: 10, these are the records of men's lives; cf. Wis. 4: 20 (of the wicked): 'They will come with dread when their sins are reckoned up, and their lawless deeds will convict them to their face'. **the book of life:** Cf. 3: 5; 13: 8; 17: 8. **the dead were judged by what was written in the books:** The last assize is conducted with scrupulous justice; if salvation is always by grace, divine judgment is always according to men's works (cf. 2: 23; 22: 12; Rom. 2: 6, etc.). **13. The sea gave up the dead . . . in it:** Death at sea, with no monument to mark the spot where one's body lay, was thought of as a terribly desolate fate. In some Jewish circles resurrection was thought of as possible only for those buried on dry land. **14. death and Hades were thrown into the lake of fire:** Death and Hades are personified as in 6: 8. The gospel proclaims Christ as the 'Death of death, and hell's destruction'; in 1 C. 15: 26 death is viewed as 'the last enemy to be destroyed' by Him, but in 2 Tim. 1: 10 faith sees Him as the One who, by His own death and resurrection, has already 'destroyed death and has brought life and immortality to light through the gospel'. **The lake of fire is the second death:** Perhaps because it befalls men who have been raised from the 'first' death (cf. Heb. 9: 27). **15. If any one's name was not found written in the book of life, he was thrown into the lake of fire:** It is curious exegesis that would infer from this that all who appear at the last assize are consigned to perdition. True, those who have committed apostasy and worshipped 'the image of the beast' have no place in the book of life (13: 8); but the dead who stand before the throne include all mankind from earliest days. The scene which John paints here, with its vivid and sombre hues, is unforgettably impressive; it is not intended to gratify curiosity about eschatological details but to challenge the reader with a reminder of the One to whom the final account must be rendered.

O may we stand before the Lamb,
When earth and seas are fled;
And hear the Judge pronounce our name
With blessings on our head!

XI. THE NEW CREATION (21: 1–8)

1. **I saw a new heaven and a new earth:** He sees the fulfilment and transcendence of the promise of Isa. 65: 17; 66: 22. The way has been cleared for the emergence of this new creation 'the home of righteousness' (2 Pet. 3: 13), by the abolition of evil and the passing of **the first heaven and the first earth** before the advent of the divine Judge (20: 11). **there was no longer any sea:** The sea was to the Jews a symbol of separation (not, as to the Greeks, a means of communication); moreover, throughout the Bible it symbolizes restless insubordination (cf. Job 38: 8–11; Ps. 89: 9; Isa. 57: 20), and in Rev. 13: 1 it casts up the system which incarnates hostility to God and His people. Naturally, then, there is no room for it in the new creation. **2. I saw the Holy City, the new Jerusalem:** The glorified community of the people of Christ (cf. Gal. 4: 26; Heb. 12: 22). **coming down out of heaven from God:** Cf. 3: 12. It is thus emphasized that the church is 'the city . . . whose architect and builder is God' (Heb. 11: 10), not a voluntary association of men. Hitherto the glorified saints have been seen in heaven with Christ (cf. 14: 1 ff.; 15: 2). **prepared as a bride beautifully dressed for her husband:** Cf. Isa. 62: 4. The beloved community is both city and bride (cf. verses 9 ff.; 19: 7 f.). **3. a loud voice from the throne:** Cf. 16: 17; 19: 5. Now the voice proclaims the eternal consummation of the blessings of the gospel. **the dwelling** (Gk. *skēnē*, 'tent') **of God is with men, and he will live** (Gk. *skēnoō*, as in Jn 1: 14) **with them:** Cf. Exod. 25: 8. So it was when the Word became flesh and pitched his tabernacle among men; so it is in the renewed earth because of the presence of the redeemed community, reflecting the glory of God (v. 23). **They will be his people, and God himself will be with them:** The covenant blessings promised in Jer. 31: 33; Ezek. 37: 27; Zech. 8: 8 are now extended world-wide. **4. He will wipe every tear from their eyes:** The consolation enjoyed by the martyrs in 7: 17 is now enjoyed by mankind, in fulfilment of Isa. 25: 8. **There will be no more death**, because it has been destroyed in the fiery lake (20: 14; cf. again Isa. 25: 8). **the old order of things has passed away:** Cf. Isa. 42: 9; 2 C. 5: 17; both these passages are also echoed in the divine proclamation of verse 5. **I am making everything new:** 'If anyone is in Christ', says Paul, 'he is (or 'there is') a new creation' (2 C. 5: 17); now, through those who are elect 'in Christ' God communicates His blessings to the world (cf. Rom. 8: 18–25). To the same effect James writes: 'He chose to give us birth through the word of truth, that we might be a kind of firstfruits of all he created' (Jas 1: 18). Cf. 14: 4. **5. Write this:** Cf. 19: 9 (also 22: 6) for the confirmation. **6.**

It is done: Cf. the utterance at the outpouring of the last bowl of wrath (16: 17). **I am the Alpha and the Omega:** Cf. 1: 8 (also 22: 13). **To him who is thirsty I will give to drink without cost from the spring of the water of life:** An application of Isa. 55: 1 in the light of Jesus' invitation in Jn 7: 37 f. Cf. 22: 1. The free offer of the gospel sounds clearly and repeatedly in the last two chapters of Rev. **7. He who overcomes . . . :** Here are summed up the blessings promised to the victorious confessors in the letters to the seven churches (2: 7, 11, 17, 26 ff.; 3: 5, 12, 21). The words of 2 Sam. 7: 14, applied to Christ in Heb. 1: 5, are here applied to Christ's loyal followers. **8. But the cowardly, the unbelieving . . . :** Characteristically, John's catalogue of those who are excluded from the blessings of the new creation begins with those who through fear have denied the faith in face of persecution. His universalism is eschatological, but not retrospectively effective.

XII. THE NEW JERUSALEM (21: 9–22: 5)

9. One of the seven angels: Cf. 17: 1. The holy Jerusalem is revealed to the seer either by the same angel, or by one of the colleagues of the angel, who previously showed him the spectacle of great Babylon. **the bride, the wife of the Lamb:** With a sovereign disregard of rules against mixing metaphors, the beloved community is portrayed as both bride (cf. 19: 7 f.) and city (21: 10 ff.). **he carried me away in the Spirit to a mountain great and high:** Cf. the *very high mountain* from which Ezekiel in vision saw *buildings that looked like a city* (Ezek. 40: 2). **11. It shone with the glory of God:** John ransacks the resources of language and metaphor—jewels, gold and pearls—to describe the indescribable glory which the holy city reflects (cf. Isa. 26: 1 f.; 54: 11 f.; 60: 18 ff.). **12. On the gates were written the names of the twelve tribes of Israel:** The beloved city is thus marked out as the true Israel or people of God; this is emphasized by the recurrence of the number twelve and its multiples throughout the description of the city. Cf. the number of the elect in 7: 4 ff.; 14: 1 ff. **14. twelve foundations, and on them were the names of the twelve apostles of the Lamb:** The true Israel is the *new* Israel, as indeed Jesus implied when 'he appointed twelve, that they might be with him, and that he might send them out . . .' (Mk 3: 14; cf. the implication of Mt. 19: 28; Lk. 22: 30); it comprises all the faithful of Old and New Testament times alike. **15. a measuring rod of gold:** Ezekiel's angelic mentor had *a linen cord and a measuring rod* for a similar purpose (Ezek. 40: 3; cf. also Zech. 2: 1 f.; Rev. 11: 1). **16. The city was laid out**

like a square: Like Ezekiel's city (Ezek. 48: 16) and the heavenly *ekklēsia* in Hermas, *Vision* iii. 2. 5; but John's city is a cube, like the holy of holies in Solomon's temple (1 Kg. 6: 20) and the heavenly Jerusalem in the Talmud tractate *Baba Bathra* 75b (we are scarcely intended to envisage it as a pyramid). **twelve thousand stadia:** The measurement is symbolic, and its significance would be lost if it were re-stated as 1500 miles. Ezekiel's foursquare city was built on a side of 4500 cubits, approximately a mile and a quarter. **17. a hundred and forty-four cubits** is probably the thickness of the wall; such a height would be disproportionately small for so high a city. But this might be irrelevant when such schematic numbers are in question. In any case, the **man** whose measurements are used as the scale of reference here is, like the 'man' of Ezek. 40: 3 ff., an angel. **19. The foundations of the city walls were decorated with every . . . precious stone:** The twelve precious stones mentioned in verses 19, 20 are reminiscent of those in the high-priestly breastplate, engraved with the names of the twelve sons of Israel (Exod. 28: 17–21); nine out of the twelve appear in both lists (though not in the same order), and perhaps John intends to reproduce all twelve of the earlier list, though we cannot be sure because of the possibility of choosing a variety of Greek equivalents for some of the Hebrew words. According to Philo and Josephus, the twelve jewels on the breastplate were believed by some Jews in the first century A.D. to represent the signs of the zodiac; R. H. Charles points out that, in this case, the sequence of the signs is reversed in John's list, as though to suggest that the divine purpose upsets the basis and findings of pagan astrology. **21. The twelve gates were twelve pearls:** The pearly gates, like the city foursquare itself, are applied in popular hymnody to heaven; but John uses this language to convey some idea of the splendour of the glorified people of God. **22. I did not see a temple in the city**—because God and the Lamb together constitute the city's holiness, and it is itself God's dwelling-place on earth (v. 3). **23. the city does not need the sun or the moon:** Cf. Isa. 60: 19 f.; there, as here, *the LORD will be your everlasting light, and your God will be your glory*; but here (as from ch. 5 onwards) the Lamb is seen in the closest association with God. **24. The nations will walk by its light:** Cf. Isa. 60: 1–3. In the Bible the election of some does not imply the damnation of others, but rather their blessing. The AV wording, 'the nations of them which are saved', represents an inferior reading, but is sound exegesis. **the kings of the earth will bring their splendor into it:** Cf. Isa. 60: 5 ff.; Ps. 72: 10 f. **25. On no day will its gates ever be shut:** Cf. Isa. 60: 11, where they stand

open day and night, but such language would be inappropriate in the present context, for **there will be no night there**—no intermission of the glory of God's presence. **26. The glory and the honor of the nations will be brought into it:** Cf. Isa. 60: 11 (*the wealth of the nations*); Hag. 2: 7 (*the desired things of all nations*). The glory of the church is incompatible with a dead-level uniformity; the variety of national contributions helps to make up her many-splendoured life. **Nothing impure will ever enter** the city; **the Lamb's book of life** is her burgess-roll.

The opening verses of ch. 22 depict the new creation as Paradise restored, with the serpent banished, the curse abolished, and access to the tree of life continually open to all. **1. the river of the water of life, as clear as crystal, flowing from the throne of God and of the Lamb:** Cf. the life-giving river of Ezek. 47: 1 ff. which rises beneath the eastern threshold of the temple and flows down the Kidron valley to sweeten the water of the Dead Sea (see also Zech. 14: 8, *living water will flow out from Jerusalem*). **2. down the middle of the great street of the city:** Cf. Ps. 46: 4, where the *river whose streams make glad the city of God* is God's own presence (see also the *place of broad rivers and streams* in Isa. 33: 21). **the tree of life:** Cf. Gen. 2: 9; 3: 22; Rev. 2: 7. The Paradise motif suggests that the river of water of life may have a further antecedent in the river which flowed out of Eden in Gen. 2: 10. The tree of life and the river of life are both symbols of the eternal life brought near in the gospel. **twelve crops of fruit:** Cf. Ezek. 47: 12, *Every month they will bear*. **the leaves of the tree are for the healing of the nations:** Cf. Ezek. 47: 12, *Their fruit will serve for food and their leaves for healing*. The saving benefits of the gospel promote the well-being of all aspects of personal and communal life. **3. No longer will there be any curse:** The sentence of Gen. 3: 17 is cancelled; the curse cannot survive in the presence of God. **his servants will serve him:** The verb is Gk. *latreuō*, as in 7: 15. **4. They will see his face, and his name will be on their foreheads:** In the words of 1 Jn 3: 2, they are 'like him', because they 'see him as he is'. Here and now the sanctification of believers consists in their being progressively conformed to the likeness of God by the power of the Spirit, as they reflect the divine glory revealed to them in the face of Christ (cf. 2 C. 3: 18–4: 6); John describes the climax of that process, for the beatific vision involves the perfect glorification of those who receive it. Cf. 3: 12, 'I will write on him the name of my God, . . . and my new name.' **5. they will reign for ever and ever**—sharing in the eternal 'kingdom of our Lord and of his Christ' (11: 15). Cf. Dan. 12: 3.

Epilogue (22: 6–21)

i. Attestation by the Angel (22: 6–7)

6. These words are trustworthy and true: Cf. 19: 9; 21: 5. **The Lord, the God of the spirits of the prophets, sent his angel to show his servants the things that must soon take place:** Cf. 1: 1; 22: 16. Here Jesus Himself seems to be identified with 'the God of the spirits of the prophets' (cf. the end of 19: 10).

7. I am coming soon: The angel apparently speaks in the Lord's name. Cf. verses 12, 20. **Blessed is he who keeps the words of the prophecy in this book:** A repetition of the beatitude of 1: 3. Keeping the words involves not only retaining them in memory but regulating one's life by them, especially maintaining one's Christian confession without compromise.

ii. Attestation by John (22: 8–11)

8. I, John, am the one who heard and saw these things: Cf. 1: 1, 9. He affirms that the visions of Revelation were his authentic experiences and not literary inventions. The angel's repudiation of the homage which John attempts to pay him (verses 8b, 9) follows 19: 10 closely. **10. Do not seal up the words of the prophecy of this book, because the time is near:** Daniel was commanded to seal up the record of his visions *until the time of the end* (Dan. 12: 4, 9), because centuries were to elapse between the third year of Cyrus (Dan. 10: 1) and the fulfilment of the visions which bear that date; but no such time-lag is envisaged here (contrast 10: 4). The problem of the postponement of the parousia (as commonly understood) is thus underlined. Because the time is short, there will be but little opportunity for repentance and change: the wicked are confirmed in their wickedness, the righteous in their righteousness (verse 11; cf. Dan. 12: 10).

In the Christian doctrine of the Last Things however, the imminence of the end is moral rather than chronological; each successive Christian generation, for aught that is known to the contrary, may be the last generation. In that sense the time is always near (1: 3); it is therefore the path of wisdom for believers to be ready to meet their Lord. When He comes and institutes the final judgment, the verdict will be that which men by their attitude to God and their way of life have already incurred for themselves (cf. Jn 3: 18). Till then the 'water of life' remains available to whosoever will, as verse 17 makes plain.

iii. Attestation by Jesus (22: 12–16)

The Lord announces His swift advent, to recompense **every one according to what he has done** (12). The principle has already been laid down in 2: 23; 20: 12; cf. also 1 C. 4: 5;

Eph. 6: 8; Col. 3: 23–25. **13. I am the Alpha and the Omega, the First and the Last, the Beginning and the End:** A combination of 1: 8, 17b; 21: 6. **14. Blessed are those who wash their robes:** Cf. 7: 14. An inferior, though well-attested, variant reads 'Blessed are those who keep his commandments' (this could have arisen in the copying of a rather faded Greek text). Those who are excluded from the city (v. 15) belong to the categories already indicated in 21: 8, 27 (cf. 1 C. 6: 9 f.; Gal. 5: 19–21). Verses 14 and 15 may be a parenthesis between the two parts of Jesus' attestation in verses 13 and 16; it has frequently been suspected that the closing paragraphs of Rev. have suffered some primitive dislocation. **16. I, Jesus, have sent my angel:** Cf. 1: 1; 22: 6. **the Root and the Offspring of David:** For the former title see 5: 5. His eternal being (verse 13) and His Davidic descent are set in paradoxical juxtaposition; cf. Mk 12: 35–37; Rom. 1: 3 f. **the bright Morning Star:** Cf. 2: 28. The *star . . . out of Jacob* or *scepter . . . out of Israel* foretold by Balaam (Num. 24: 17) was primarily a reference to David and his conquering career, and is therefore transferred, not inappropriately, to great David's greater Son. In the Qumran texts Num. 24: 17 is a recurring *testimonium* of the messianic warrior of the end-time. Another NT reference to Christ as the morning star may be detected in 2 Pet. 1: 19 (where the word is *phōsphoros*, 'light-bringer'; here *astēr . . . prōinos* is the expression used).

iv. Invocation, Invitation and Response (22: 17–20)

17. The Spirit and the bride say, 'Come!': This 'Come' (singular) is addressed to the Lord. We may regard the Spirit as indwelling the beloved community and inspiring it to respond thus to the Lord's promise of verse 12, or we may take the Spirit to be the Spirit of prophecy, in which case **the Spirit and the bride** 'is practically equivalent to "the prophets and the saints"' (H. B. Swete). **let him who hears say, 'Come!':** Every one who listens to the reading of the book (cf. 1: 3) must at this point break in with his personal response: 'Come!' The Aramaic form of the invocation, *Maranatha*, 'Come, O Lord!' (1 C. 16: 22) was retained even in Greek-speaking churches, especially at the celebration of the Eucharist. This we gather from the *Didache* (c. A.D. 100) where, strikingly enough, *Marana-tha* is immediately preceded by the call: 'If any man is holy, let him come; if any man is not, let him repent' (*Didache* 10: 6). So here the invocation to the Lord is closely associated with the invitation to the outsider, **Whoever is thirsty, let him come; and whoever wishes, let him take the free gift of the water of life**—take it, as 21: 6

declares, from the Alpha and Omega, to whom
all power is given. In a book so full of judgment, it is exhilarating to find the gospel invitation extended so plainly and freely at the end.
No assessment of the Christian quality of Rev.
is adequate which does not give full weight to
these words. If 'whoever wishes' (AV 'whosoever will') is felt by some to present a problem,
it is a problem imported from outside; it does
not arise from the context. The blindest idolater, the fiercest persecutor, were he Nero himself—and might we add the most abject apostate?—may come if he will and accept the full
and free benefits which the gospel provides.
18. I warn every one: The warning not to add
to or subtract from the words of the prophecy
(verses 18 f.) echoes Dt. 4: 2; 12: 32. It was not
intended for textual critics who prefer longer
or shorter readings in this or any other book
of the NT! **20. He who testifies to these
things**—Jesus Himself, 'the faithful witness' (1: 5). His repeated **'Yes, I am coming
soon'** is His reply to His people's invocation (v. 17), and evokes from them the further
call: **'Amen. Come, Lord Jesus.'** So, in
Didache 10: 6, *Marana-tha* is confirmed by
Amen.

v. Benediction (22: 21)
The final benediction has a form familiar in NT
letters; our early witnesses to the text oscillate
between the longer reading 'with all the saints'
and the shorter reading **with God's people**
(AV 'with you all' reproduces a later and inferior
reading).

BIBLIOGRAPHY

BEASLEY-MURRAY, G. R., *The Book of Revelation.* NCentB (London, 1974).

BECKWITH, I. T., *The Apocalypse of John* (London, 1919).

CAIRD, G. B., *The Revelation of St. John the Divine.* BNTC (London, 1966).

CHARLES, R. H., *A Critical and Exegetical Commentary on the Revelation of St. John* [on the Greek text]. ICC (2 vols. Edinburgh, 1920).

FARRER, A. M., *The Revelation of St. John the Divine* (Oxford, 1964).

HENDRIKSEN, W., *More than Conquerors* (London, 1962).

KELLY, W., *Lectures on the Book of Revelation* (London, 1874).

KIDDLE, M., *The Revelation of St. John.* MNT (London, 1940).

LADD, G. E., *A Commentary on the Revelation of John* (Grand Rapids, 1927).

LANG, G. H., *The Revelation of Jesus Christ* (London, 1945).

McDOWELL, E. A., *The Meaning and Message of the Book of Revelation* (Nashville, Tenn., 1951).

MOUNCE, R. H., *The Book of Revelation.* NICNT (Grand Rapids, 1977).

NEWTON, B. W., *Thoughts on the Apocalypse*[3] (London 1904).

PEAKE, A. S., *The Revelation of John* (London, 1919).

PRESTON, R. H., and HANSON, A. T., *The Revelation of Saint John the Divine.* Torch Commentaries (London, 1949).

RAMSAY, W. M., *The Letters to the Seven Churches of Asia* (London, 1909).

STAUFFER, E., *Christ and the Caesars,* E.T. (London, 1955).

SWETE, H. B., *The Apocalypse of St. John* [on the Greek text] (London, 1906).